DIRECTORY

Historical Agencies
in North America

Thirteenth Edition

Compiled and edited by **Betty Pease Smith**

American Association for State and Local History

Nashville, Tennessee

FRICK ART REFERENCE
LIBRARY
NEW YORK

Library of Congress Cataloging in Publication Data

Main entry under title:

Directory of historical agencies in North America.

Includes index.
1. United States—History—Societies, etc.—Directories. 2. Canada—History—Societies, etc.—Directories. I. Pease, Betty.
E172.D48   1986   971.'0025   85–30589
ISBN 0–910050–77–5

Contents

Preface   v

Historical Agencies in the United States   1

Suppliers' Section   Center Section

Historical Agencies in American Territories   509

Historical Agencies in Canada   510

Questionnaires Received after the Deadline   569

General Index   571

Special Interest Index   640
    Agriculture   640
    Archaeology   641
    Ethnic, Racial, Religious   642
    Genealogy   646
    Historic Person   651
    History of Era   654
    Industry   661
    Maritime   662
    Military   663
    Pioneer   665
    Preservation, Restoration   668
    Transportation   677

Historical and Archaeological Areas Administered by
  the National Park Service   680

National Archives and Records Administration:
  National Archives Field Branches   686

Preface

In 1936, the Conference of Historical Societies published the first directory, *Historical Societies in the United States and Canada: A Handbook.* The first edition was true to its name: with 583 listings, it fit easily into the palm of one hand. The American Association for State and Local History succeeded the Conference in 1940 and published the second handbook in 1944. Despite difficulties caused by World War II, the second edition listed 904 societies.

By contrast, the thirteenth edition of the *Directory of Historical Agencies in North America* lists 9,375 agencies—3,510 listings more than 1982's twelfth edition, and 8,471 listings more than the number found by the second edition's editors during World War II.

The historical agency field has flung itself farther and wider in real growth rate, scope, and area saturation than at any previous point in its history. Our purpose in compiling, editing, and publishing the directory is as much to reflect that growth as to provide an easy, accessible reference. Thus, the thirteenth edition contains listings for genealogical groups, oral history centers, folklore societies, living history groups, libraries and archival depositories, and other groups that are at least natural "first cousins" to the history field. This edition also includes an expanded special index section, which lists groups and organizations by category of special interest or affiliation.

Compilation for this directory began in August, 1984, when we requested the most complete, up-to-date list of historical agencies from large, statewide societies in each state. (Such major state agencies are indicated in the directory by an open diamond ◇ to the left of the agency's name.) Some states' listings were more extensive than others, which is why our listings for California and New York, for example, are greater than listings for other states. Several agencies listed in the twelfth edition did not respond to our questionnaire; these agencies are included in the thirteenth edition as "Questionnaire not received," and are not included in the index.

We cross-referenced the state lists with our twelfth edition, the AASLH membership list, and other current directories to put together a mailing list of approximately 25,000 organizations. Then we mailed a questionnaire to each of them. This book is the result, and we believe that it is the most comprehensive directory of historical agencies compiled to date.

Several people must be thanked for their hard work, diligence, general helpfulness, and much-needed sense of humor. First on the list is Gillian Murrey, production manager and designer of the AASLH Press, who wrapped up the final details for the departing editor. Betty Elder, former director of the Press, and Martha Strayhorn, editor of the Press, are due heartfelt thanks for their leadership and endless patience, without which the book could not have been produced. To David J. Maurer, professor of history and historical administration at Eastern Illinois University, and AASLH's first scholar-in-residence, a most deserving laurel wreath for his enthusiasm (he actually volunteered to help)—his editorial assistance proved invaluable, as did his wonderful smile. Thanks to others who helped on the project—Ginny and Francis Hollo, who typeset the whole thing; Lucettia Birdsong, who helped with the vast mass mailings; my husband, Chester Smith; and AASLH staffers Ruth Kennedy, Maggie Martin, Doris Armstrong, Karen Lloyd, and Ernest Williamson, for their moral support.

If you find omissions in this directory, please help future editors by sending the missing organization's name and location to AASLH Directory, AASLH Press, 172 Second Avenue, North, Nashville, Tennessee 37201.

Betty Pease Smith
Editor

April 1986

Historical Agencies in the United States

ALABAMA

ABBEVILLE

Henry County Historical Society
106 W. Washington St.
Telephone: (205) 585-3020
Mail to: P.O. Box 222, 36310
Private agency
Founded in: 1968
William W. Nordan, President
Number of members: 200
Staff: volunteer 10
Major programs: library, archives, manuscripts, markers, tours/pilgrimages, oral history, school programs, book publishing, newsletters/pamphlets, historic preservation, audiovisual programs, photographic collections, genealogical services
Period of collections: 1783-present

ALBERTVILLE

Alabama Division, United Daughters of the Confederacy
403 Sunset Ave., 35950
Telephone: (205) 878-2920
Private agency
Founded in: 1896
Mrs. John H. Livingston, President
Number of members: 2,542
Staff: volunteer 9
Major programs: historic site(s), markers, junior history, oral history, historic preservation, genealogical services, scholarships to lineal descendants of Confederate Veterans
Period of collections: Civil War era

ALICEVILLE

Aliceville Historical Preservation, Inc.
103 4th Ave., NE, 35442
Telephone: (205) 373-6364
City agency
Founded in: 1979
Billy McKinzey, President
Number of members: 48
Staff: volunteer 1
Major programs: historic preservation

ANDALUSIA

Covington Historical Society
P.O. Box 1582, 36420
Private agency
Founded in: 1976
Mrs. C. B. Wiggins, President
Number of members: 125
Major programs: museum, audiovisual programs
Period of collections: 1884-1984

ANNISTON

Anniston Museum of Natural History
4301 McClellan Blvd.
Telephone: (205) 237-6766
Mail to: P.O. Box 1587, 36202
City agency, authorized by City Council
Founded in: 1930
Christopher J. Reich, Director
Number of members: 0
Staff: full time 16, part time 7, volunteer 200
Major programs: library, museum, school programs, newsletters/pamphlets, exhibits, natural history
Period of collections: pre-industrial

ARITON

Dale County Historical Society
Mail to: P.O. Box 196, 36311
Questionnaire not received

ATHENS

Athens-Limestone County Arts Council
P.O. Box 384, 35611
Telephone: (205) 232-1802
Private agency, authorized by State Arts Council
Founded in: 1979
Angie Nazaretian, President
Number of members: 100
Major programs: tours/pilgrimages, school programs, exhibits, audiovisual programs, photographic collections, fine arts

Department of Continuing Education and Community Services
Athens State College
Telephone: (205) 232-1802
Mail to: Beaty St., 35611
State agency
Founded in: 1822
Angeline Nazavetian, Director
Staff: full time 2
Major programs: oral history, school programs, newsletters/pamphlets, historic preservation, living history, audiovisual programs, genealogical services

Limestone County Archives
310 W. Washington St., 35611
Telephone: (205) 232-1320
County agency, authorized by Limestone County Commission
Eulalia Wellden, Archivist
Major programs: historic site(s), historic reservation, records management, research, genealogical services
Period of collections: 1818-1900

Limestone County Historical Society
P.O. Box 82, 35611
Private agency
Founded in: 1968
Angie Nazaretian, President
Number of members: 200
Staff: volunteer 25
Magazine: *Limestone Legacy*
Major programs: archives, museum, historic site(s), markers, tours/pilgrimages, book publishing, newsletters/pamphlets, historic preservation, research, archaeology programs, genealogical services, maps

AUBURN

Auburn Heritage Association
159 N. College St.
Mail to: P.O. Box 2248, 36830
Founded in: 1971
Questionnaire not received

BESSEMER

West Jefferson County Historical Society, Inc.
1740 Eastern Valley Rd., 35020
Telephone: (205) 426-6604
Mail to: P.O. Box 184, 25021
Private agency
Founded in: 1973
Mrs. W. B. Marsh, President
Number of members: 377
Staff: volunteer 20
Magazine: *A Journal of History*
Major programs: museum, historic site(s), tours/pilgrimages, school programs
Period of collections: 1817-1850

BIRMINGHAM

**Alabama Baptist Historical Society—
Special Collections, Samford University Library**
800 Lakeshore Dr., 35229
Telephone: (205) 870-2749
Founded in: 1936
F. Wilbur Helmbold, Curator
Staff: full time 2, part time 1
Magazine: *Alabama Baptist Historian*
Major programs: library, archives, manuscripts, markers, oral history, newsletters/pamphlets, microfilming
Period of collections: 1780s-present

◊**Alabama Historical Association**
3121 Carlisle Rd., 35213
Telephone: (205) 324-0998
Founded in: 1947
James F. Sulzby, Jr., Secretary
Number of members: 1,776
Magazine: *The Alabama Review*
Major programs: markers, tours/pilgrimages, educational programs

Arlington Antebellum Home and Gardens
331 Cotton Ave., SW, 35211
Telephone: (205) 780-5656
City agency
Founded in: 1953
E. Bryding Adams, Director
Number of members: 500
Staff: full time 7, part time 1, volunteer 30
Major programs: library, museum, historic site(s), school programs
Period of collections: 19th century

Arlington Historical Association
15 Woodhill Rd., 37213
Questionnaire not received

Birmingham Genealogical Society
Mail to: P.O. Box 2432, 35201
Questionnaire not received

Birmingham Historical Society
1421 22nd St., S, 35205
Telephone: (205) 254-2138
Private agency
Founded in: 1942
Madge D. Barefield, Executive Secretary
Number of members: 1,000
Staff: full time 1, volunteer 200
Magazine: *The Journal*
Major programs: library, archives, markers, tours/pilgrimages, school

programs, book publishing, newsletter/pamphlets, historic preservation, research, exhibits, audiovisual programs, photographic collections
Period of collections: 1871-1925

Birmingham-Jefferson Historical Association
2709 5th Ave., S, 35233
Telephone: (205) 323-2442
Founded in: 1978
Edward T. Douglass, Jr., Executive President
Number of members: 450
Staff: full time 1
Major programs: newsletters/pamphlets, historic preservation

Birmingham-Jefferson Historical Society
3084 Sterling Rd., 35213
Telephone: (205) 870-2784
Founded in: 1975
Ed Douglass, President
Number of members: 500
Staff: volunteer 20
Major programs: manuscripts, newsletters/pamphlets
Period of collections: 1820-present

Birmingham Public Library—Linn-Henley Research Library
2100 Park Place, 35203
Telephone: (205) 226-3665
City agency
Founded in: 1927
Mary Bess Kirksey Paluzzi, Coordinator
Staff: full time 12, part time 7
Major programs: library, archives, manuscripts, oral history, book publishing, records management, research, exhibits, audiovisual programs, photographic collections, genealogical services
Period of collections: 1600-present

Forney Historical Society
3084 Sterling Rd.
Telephone: (205) 870-2784
Mail to: Samford University, S-215, 35229
Private agency
Founded in: 1955
Margaret Sizemore Douglass, President
Number of members: 300
Major programs: library, museum, historic site(s), markers, book publishing
Period of collections: 19th century

Jefferson County Historical Development Commission
20 N. 21st St., 35203
Telephone: (205) 324-0988
County agency
Founded in: 1971
Margaret Sizemore Douglass, Chair
Staff: full time 1
Major programs: markers, book publishing, newsletters/pamphlets, historic preservation, research, photographic collections
Period of collections: 1870-present

Louisiana Collection Series of Books and Documents on Colonial Louisiana
520 S. 22nd Ave., 35205
Telephone: (205) 328-5367
Private agency
Founded in: 1965
Jack D. L. Holmes, Director
Staff: full time, 2
Major programs: library, archives, manuscripts, book publishing, research, audiovisual programs, photographic collections, genealogical services, maps, cartography
Period of collections: 1763-1821

Reynolds Library Associates
1700 University Blvd.
Mail to: Reynolds Historical Library, University Station, 35294
State agency, authorized by University of Alabama at Birmingham
Founded in: 1978
Mary Claire Britt, Curator
Number of members: 92
Staff: full time 2, part time 1
Major programs: library, archives, manuscripts, newsletters/pamphlets, research, exhibits, health science history
Period of collections: 13th century-early 1900s

Samford University
35229
Telephone: (205) 879-7237
Private agency, authorized by Alabama Baptist State Convention
Founded in: 1841
Thomas E. Corts, President
Staff: full time 475, part time 45
Magazine: *Seasons: The Magazine of Samford University*
Major programs: library, archives, manuscripts, oral history, school programs, records management, genealogical services
Period of collections: 20th century

Sloss Furnaces National Historic Landmark
3105 1st Ave., N
Telephone: (205) 254-2367
Mail to: P.O. Box 11781, 35202
Private agency, authorized by Sloss Furnace Association
Founded in: 1976
Jim H. Waters, Jr., President
Number of members: 200
Staff: full time 1, part time 1, volunteer 11
Major programs: archives, historic site(s), tours/pilgrimages, oral history, newsletters/pamphlets, historic preservation, records management, audiovisual programs, photographic collections

BREWTON

Escambia County Historical Society
P.O. Box 276, 36427
Telephone: (205) 867-4832, ext. 68
County agency
Founded in: 1973

Nettie T. Parker, President
Number of members: 300
Magazine: *Escambia Historical Quarterly*
Major programs: archives, museum, historic site(s), markers, tours/pilgrimages, newsletters/pamphlets, research, archaeology programs, photographic collections, genealogical services
Period of collections: 1813-1920

BRIDGEPORT

Russell Cave National Monument
Rt. 1, Box 175, 35740
Telephone: (205) 495-2672
Federal agency, authorized by National Park Service
Founded in: 1961
Dorothy H. Marsh, Unit Manager
Staff: full time 2, part time 4, volunteer 2
Major programs: museum, school programs, historic preservation, exhibits, living history, audiovisual programs, archaeology programs
Period of collections: 6000 B.C.-present

BRIERFIELD

Bibb County Heritage Association
Rt. 1, Box 147, 35035
Telephone: (205) 665-1856
Private agency
Founded in: 1978
Martin L. Everse, President
Number of members: 50
Staff: volunteer 20
Major programs: library, markers, genealogical services

Brierfield Ironworks Park
Rt 1, Box 147, 35035
Telephone: (205) 665-1856
Private agency, authorized by Brierfield Ironworks Park Foundation
Founded in: 1977
Martin Lee Everse, President
Staff: full time 2, part time 2, volunteer 15
Magazine: *Brierfield Puddler*
Major programs: historic site(s), oral history, newsletters/pamphlets, historic preservation, research, living history
Period of collections: 1865-1900

BUTLER

Choctaw County Historical Society
Rt. 1, Box 320, 36904
Telephone: (205) 459-3888
Private agency
Founded in: 1978
James E. Evans, President
Number of members: 100
Major programs: museum, historic site(s), tours/pilgrimages, oral history, book publishing, newsletters/pamphlets, historic preservation, research, archaeology programs, photographic collections

CENTRE

Coosa River Valley Historical and Genealogical Society
P.O. Box 295, 35960
Telephone: (205) 447-2939
Private agency
Founded in: 1976
Mrs. Frank Ross Stewart, President
Major programs: library, book publishing, genealogical services

Southern Society of Genealogies
P.O. Box 295, 35960
Telephone: (205) 447-2939
Private agency
Founded in: 1962
Mrs. Frank Ross Stewart, President
Number of members: 50
Major programs: library, archives, manuscripts, book publishing, research, genealogical services

CHATOM

Washington County Museum
Washington County Courthouse
Mail to: P.O. Box 52, 36518
County agency
Fritz E. Schell, Jr., Treasurer
Major programs: museum
Period of collections: early 20th century

CITRONELLE

Citronelle Historical Preservation Society
P.O. Box 384, 36522
Telephone: (205) 866-7868
Private agency
Founded in: 1976
Glenn L. Vernon, President
Major programs: museum
Period of collections: 1880-1930

CLANTON

Chilton County Historical Society and Archives, Inc.
P.O. Box 644, 35045
Founded in: 1981
Ben Roberts, President
Number of members: 65
Staff: volunteer 3
Major programs: newsletters/pamphlets, records management, architectural survey
Period of collections: 1870-1920

CLAYTON

Clayton Historical Preservation Authority
P.O. Box 385, 36016
Telephone: (202) 775-3542
Town agency
Founded in: 1983
William M. Fenn, Jr., President
Staff: volunteer 1
Major programs: historic site(s), historic preservation, photographic collections
Period of collections: 1920-1950

COLUMBIANA

Shelby County Historical Society— Shelby County Archives and Museum
1854 Courthouse, Main St.

Telephone: (205) 669-3488
Mail to: P.O. Box 457, 35051
Private agency
Founded in: 1974
Miriam Fowler, Museum Curator
Number of members: 350
Staff: full time 3
Magazine: *Shelby County Historical Quarterly*
Major programs: library, archives, museum, markers, junior history, oral history, school programs, historic preservation, genealogical services
Period of collections: 1814-early 20th century

CULLMAN

Cullman County Historical Society
Cullman Historical Museum
Telephone: (205) 739-1258
Mail to: 500 3rd St., SE, 35055
Founded in: 1968
Nancy Reichwein, President
Number of members: 41
Staff: volunteer 12
Major programs: museum, historic site, historical preservation, audiovisual programs, resource services, research

DADEVILLE

Horseshoe Bend National Military Park
Hwy. 49, N
Telephone: (205) 234-7111
Mail to: Rt. 1, Box 103, 36256
Federal agency, authorized by National Park Service
Founded in: 1959
Philip R. Brueck, Superintendent
Staff: full time, 7, part time 2, volunteer 2
Major programs: library, museum, historic site(s), tours/pilgrimages, school programs, historic preservation, research, exhibits, living history
Period of collections: Creek War 1813-1814

DECATUR

Morgan County Historic Preservation Society
Mail to: P.O. Box 214, 35602
Founded in: 1969
Questionnaire not received

North Alabama Historical Association
705 13th Ave., SE, 35601
Questionnaire not received

DEMOPOLIS

Marengo County Historical Society
Bluff Hall, 407 N. Commissioner's Ave.
Telephone: (205) 289-1666
Mail to: P.O. Box 159, 36732
Private agency
Founded in: 1962
Marks Abernathy, President
Number of members: 250
Staff: volunteer 2
Major programs: archives, museum, historic site(s), markers,

tours/pilgrimages, school
programs, book publishing,
newsletters/pamphlets, historic
preservation, records
management, exhibits,
photographic collections, 1832
house museum
Period of collections: 1830s-1920s

DORA

Alabama Mining Museum
Allbritton Ave.
Telephone: (205) 648-2442
Mail to: P.O. Box 457, 35062
Authorized by East Walker Chamber
of Commerce
Founded in: 1982
Harrison Gruman, Director
Number of members: 416
Staff: full time 1, part time 2,
volunteer 12
Major programs: museum,
tours/pilgrimages, oral history,
school programs,
newsletters/pamphlets, historic
preservation, exhibits, audiovisual
programs, photographic
collections
Period of collections: 1890-1940

DOTHAN

Landmark Park
Hwy. 431, N
Telephone: (205) 794-3452
Mail to: P.O. Box 6362, 36302
Private agency
Founded in: 1977
Sam W. Kates, Executive Director
Number of members: 1
Staff: full time 4, part time 2,
volunteer 20
Major programs: library, archives,
museum, historic site(s), markers,
tours/pilgrimages, junior history,
oral history, school programs,
newsletters/pamphlets, historic
preservation, exhibits, living
history, audiovisual programs,
photographic collections, field
services, natural history and
science
Period of collections: 1890-1920

DOUBLE SPRINGS

**Free State of Winston Historical
Society**
Mail to: P.O. Box 451, 35553-0451
Founded in: 1968
Mrs. Wynelle S. Dodd,
Secretary/Treasurer
Number of members: 50
Major programs: historic site(s),
markers, oral history, book
publishing, historic preservation
Period of collections: Antebellum and
Civil War era

ELBERTA

**Baldwin Heritage Museum
Association**
Rt. 98, Box 356, 36530
Telephone: (205) 943-1555
Mail to: P.O. Box 1117, Foley, 36536
Founded in: 1981
Francis H. Shimshock, Chair

Number of members: 279
Staff: volunteer 22
Major programs: museum
Period of collections: 1900-1950

ENTERPRISE

**Pea River Historical and
Genealogical Society**
P.O. Box 628, 36331
Telephone: (205) 347-6148
(president)
Private agency
Founded in: 1970
James B. Jolley, President
Number of members: 290
Staff: volunteer 10
Magazine: *Pea River Trails*
Major programs: library, museum,
historic site(s), markers, oral
history, historic preservation,
research, exhibits, genealogical
services

EUFAULA

Eufaula Heritage Association
340 N. Eufaula Ave.
Telephone: (205) 687-3793
Mail to: P.O. Box 486, 36027
Founded in: 1965
Hilda C. Sexton, manager
Number of members: 350
Staff: full time 1, part time 4,
volunteer 5
Major programs: museum, historic
site, tours/pilgrimages, book
publishing, historic preservation
Period of collections: 1800-1900

**Historic Chattahoochee
Commission**
630 E. Broad St.
Telephone: (205) 687-9755/687-6631
Mail to: P.O. Box 33, 36027
Founded in: 1970
Douglas Clare Purcell,
Executive Director
Staff: full time 2, part time 1,
volunteer 29
Magazine: *Chattahoochee Tracings*
Major programs: historic site(s),
markers, tours/pilgrimages, book
publishing, newsletters/pamphlets,
historic preservation, research,
genealogical services, tourism
promotion
Period of collections: 1830-1980

EUTAW

Greene County Historical Society
P.O. Box 746, 35462
Founded in: 1966
Ralph L. Liverman, President
Number of members: 110
Staff: volunteer 6
Major programs: library, manuscripts,
historic site, markers, tours/
pilgrimages, oral history, book
publishing, historic preservation
Period of collections: 1840-1860

FAYETTE

Fayette County Historical Society
c/o Holder and Moore, First National
Bank Bldg., 35555
Telephone: (205) 932-3255
Founded in: 1970

Louis P. Moore, President
Number of members: 20
Major programs: library, archives,
museum, historic site(s), oral
history, book publishing, historic
preservation, exhibits,
genealogical services
Period of collections: 1835-present

FLORENCE

Florence Historical Board
2207 Berry Ave., 35630
Telephone: (205) 386-2742
City agency
Founded in: 1968
William L. McDonald, Chair
Staff: full time 3
Major programs: library, archives,
manuscripts, museum, historic
site(s), markers, tours/pilgrimages,
school programs, historic
preservation, research
Period of collections: 1800-1900

Kennedy-Douglass
217 E. Tuscaloosa St., 35630
Telephone: (205) 764-7271
City agency
Founded in: 1976
Barbara Kimberlin, Director
Number of members: 240
Staff: full time 2, part time 2,
volunteer 240
Major programs: library, manuscripts,
museum, oral history, school
programs, exhibits

**Natchez Trace Genealogical
Society**
P.O. Box 420, 35631
Founded in: 1980
Number of members: 312
Magazine: *Natchez Trace Traveler*
Major programs: book publishing,
records management,
genealogical services

Walnut Street Historic District, Inc.
501 N. Walnut St., 35630
Telephone: (205) 766-4094
Founded in: 1977
Billy R. Warren, President
Number of members: 27
Staff: volunteer 15
Major programs: historic site(s),
markers, tours/pilgrimages, school
programs, newsletters/pamphlets,
historic preservation

FORT MCCLELLAN

Women's Army Corps Museum
USAMP and CS/TC and Ft. McClellan,
36205
Telephone: (205) 238-3512/238-5559
Founded in: 1954
Gabriele E. Torony, Curator
Number of members: 3,000
Staff: full time 3
Major programs: library, archives,
museum, oral history,
newsletters/pamphlets, research,
exhibits, audiovisual programs,
photographic collections
Period of collections: 1942-present

U.S. Army Chemical Corps Museum
Ft. McClellan, Bldg. 2299,
36205-5020
Telephone: (205) 238-4449
Federal agency, authorized by the
U.S. Army
Founded in: 1920
Thomas K. Miller, Curator
Staff: full time 3
Major programs: archives, museum,
historic site(s), markers,
tours/pilgrimages, oral history,
newsletters/pamphlets, historic
preservation, research, exhibits,
living history
Period of collections: 1915-present

**U.S. Army Military Police Corps
Museum**
U.S. Army Military Police School,
36205
Telephone: (205) 238-3522
Federal agency, authorized by the
U.S. Army
Founded in: 1960
Scott L. Norton, Director
Staff: full time 3
Major programs: archives,
manuscripts, museum,
tours/pilgrimages, oral history,
school programs, reserach,
exhibits, photographic collections
Period of collections: W.W. II-Vietnam
Conflict

FORT PAYNE

Landmarks of DeKalb County, Inc.
706 Alabama Ave., NW
Telephone: (205) 845-0419
Mail to: P.O. Box 518, 35967
Private agency
Founded in: 1969
James R. Kuykendall, Vice President
Number of members: 700
Staff: volunteer 40
Magazine: The Dekalb Legend,
Landmarks News
Major programs: markers,
tours/pilgrimages, oral history,
book publishing,
newsletters/pamphlets, historic
preservation, audiovisual
programs, photographic
collections, genealogical services,
opera house
Period of collections: 1889-present

FORT RUCKER

U.S. Army Aviation Museum
36362
Founded in: 1955
Thomas J. Sabiston, Curator
Staff: full time 5
Major programs: archives, museum,
tours/pilgrimages, historic
preservation, exhibits, photagphic
collections
Period of collections: W.W. II-present

GADSDEN

Etowah Historical Society
c/o President, Rt. 10, Box 88, 35901
Private agency
Founded in: 1954
Woodrow Dawson, President
Number of members: 40

Major programs: library, oral history,
historic preservation

**General John H. Forney Historical
Society, Inc.**
c/o Life of Alabama, P.O. Box 349,
35902
Telephone: (205) 543-2022, ext. 266
(secretary)
Founded in: 1955
Private agency, authorized by board
of directors
Margaret Dogulas, President
Number of members: 300
Staff: volunteer 20
Major programs: library, archives,
museum, markers, book
publishing, historic preservation,
awards program
Period of collections: 1860s-present

GREENVILLE

Butler County Historical Society
Telephone: (205) 382-6852
Mail to: P.O. Box 526, 36037
Founded in: 1965
Judith Taylor, President
Number of members: 264
Staff: volunteer 8
Major programs: historic sites
preservation, genealogy, markers,
tours/pilgrimages
Period of collections: 1783-1918

GULF SHORES

Ft. Morgan Museum
Hwy. 180, W
Telephone: (205) 540-7125
Mail to: Rt. 1, Box 3540, 36542
State agency, authorized by Alabama
Historical Commission
Staff: full time 2
Major programs: library, archives,
museum, historic site(s), markers,
tours/pilgrimages, school
programs, historic preservation,
records management, research,
exhibits, living history,
photographic collections,
genealogical services
Period of collections: 1519-W.W. II

HALESBURG

Halesburg Historical Society
Telephone: (205) 696-4655
Mail to: Rt. 1, Box 83, Columbia,
36319
Questionnaire not received

HELENA

Shelby County Historical Society
Mail to: P.O. Box 28, 35808
Questionnaire not received

HUNTSVILLE

Alabama Archaeological Society
1004 Appalachee Rd., 35801
Telephone: (205) 881-0527
State agency
Founded in: 1955
James W. Lee, President
Number of members: 500
Magazine: Journal of Alabama
Archaeology
Major programs: manuscripts, book

publishing, newsletters/pamphlets,
research, archaeology programs

Burritt Museum and Park
3101 Burritt Dr., 35801
Telephone: (205) 536-2882
City agency
Founded in: 1955
Melinda Herzog, Director
Number of members: 225
Staff: full time 7, volunteer 65
Major programs: library, archives,
museum, historic site(s), school
programs, book publishing,
newsletters/pamphlets, historic
preservation, records
management, research, exhibits,
living history, audiovisual
programs, photographic
collections
Period of collections: 1810-1900

Constitution Hall Park
301 Madison St., 35801
Telephone: (205) 532-7551
City agency
Founded in: 1982
Dana Lee Tatum, Director
Staff: full time, 4, part time 2,
volunteer 50
Major programs: library, museum,
tours/pilgrimages, junior history,
school programs,
newsletters/pamphlets, exhibits,
living history, audiovisual programs
Period of collections: Federal period

Historic Huntsville Foundation, Inc.
P.O. Box 786, 35804
Telephone: (205) 837-2925
Founded in: 1974
Freeda B. Darnell, Board Chair
Number of members: 1,000
Staff: volunteer 100
Magazine: Historic Huntsville
Foundation Quarterly
Major programs: museum, historic
site(s), tours/pilgrimages, junior
history, school programs, book
publishing, newsletters/pamphlets,
historic preservation, research,
exhibits, living history, audiovisual
programs, photographic
collections, genealogical services
Period of collections: 1800-present

The Huntsville Depot
320 Church St., 35801
Telephone: (205) 539-1860
Mail to: P.O. Box 951, 35804
Founded in: 1976
George Martin, Project Supervisor
Major programs: library, museum,
educational programs,
newsletters/pamphlets
Period of collections: 1865-present

JASPER

**Walker County Heritage
Association**
Rt. 1, Box 355, 35579
Telephone: (205) 387-1570
Founded in: 1973
Dianne Lollar, President
Number of members: 78
Major programs: library,
tours/pilgrimages, historic
preservation, records
management, genealogical
services

LANETT

Chattahoochee Valley Historical Society, Inc.
913 1st St., 36863
Telephone: (205) 644-4702
Founded in: 1953
Leonard L. Blanton, President
Number of members: 149
Magazine: *The Voice*
Major programs: library, archives, manuscripts, museum, historic site, markers, tours/pilgrimages, oral history, educational programs, book publishing, newsletters/pamphlets, historic preservation
Period of collections: 1830-present

Cobb Memorial Archives
Telephone: (205) 644-4702
Mail to: 913 1st St., 36863
Founded in: 1953
Leonard L. Blanton, President
Number of members: 157
Staff: part time 2, volunteer 4
Magazine: *The Voice*
Major programs: archives, markers, tours, oral history, book publishing, newsletters/pamphlets, historic preservation, exhibits, audiovisual programs, genealogical services, educational programs
Period of collections: 1850-present

LOACHAPOKA

Lee County Historical Society
P.O. Box 206, 36865
Private agency
Founded in: 1968
Forrest Shivers, President
Number of members: 270
Magazine: *Trails*
Major programs: library, archives, manuscripts, museum, historic site, markers, junior history, oral history, educational programs, book publishing, newsletters/pamphlets, historic preservation

McCALLA

Iron & Steel Museum of Alabama—Tannehill Historical State Park
Rt. 1, Box 124, 35111
Telephone: (205) 477-5761
State agency, authorized by Tannehill Furnace & Foundry Commission
Founded in: museum 1981, park 1969
Vicki Gentry, Director
Number of members: 1
Staff: full time 1, part time 6, volunteer 10
Magazine: *Tannehill Blast*
Major programs: library, museum, historic site(s), markers, school programs, newsletters/pamphlets, historic preservation, records management, exhibits, history of technology
Period of collections: 1800-1920

MOBILE

Alabama Society, Daughters of the American Colonists
433 W. Vista Court, 36609
Telephone: (205) 342-6350

Founded in: 1939
Mrs. G. Wade Cox, State Regent
Number of members: 400
Magazine: *Colonial Courier*
Major programs: library, archives, museum, historic site(s), markers, oral history, school programs, newsletters/pamphlets, historic preservation, research, audiovisual programs, genealogical services
Period of collections: Colonial

Historic Mobile Preservation Society
300 Oakleigh Place, 36604
Telephone: (205) 433-5119
Founded in: 1935
Joan M. Hartwell, Executive Director
Number of members: 1,500
Staff: full time 2, part time 15, volunteer 200
Magazine: *Landmark Letter*
Major programs: library, archives, historic site(s), markers, tours/pilgrimages, book publishing, newsletters/pamphlets, historic preservation, research, photographic collections
Period of collections: late 1700s-present

Mobile Historic Development Commission
City Hall, 111 S. Royal St., 36602
Telephone: (205) 438-7281
Mail to: P.O. Box 1827, 36633
City and county agency
Founded in: 1962
Michael S. Leventhal, Executive Director
Number of members: 40
Staff: full time 4, part time 2
Major programs: markers, historic preservation, research, photographic collections
Period of collections: 1840-1920

Museums of the City of Mobile
355 Government St., 36602
Telephone: (205) 438-7569
City agency, authorized by Mobile Museum Board, Inc.
Founded in: 1962

Caldwell Delaney, Museum Director
Staff: full time 4, part time 13, volunteer 8
Major programs: library, archives, manuscripts, museum, book publishing, exhibits
Period of collections: 1699-Civil War

MONTGOMERY

◊**Alabama Department of Archives and History**
624 Washington Ave., 36130
Telephone: (205) 261-4361
State agency
Founded in: 1901
Edwin C. Bridges, Director
Major programs: library, archives, manuscripts, museum, school programs, records management, research, exhibits, genealogical services
Period of collections: 1783-present

Alabama Historical Commission
725 Monroe St., 36130
Telephone: (205) 261-3184
State agency
Founded in: 1966
F. Lawrence Oaks, Executive Director
Staff: full time 67
Newsletter: *Preservation Report*
Major programs: historic site(s), markers, historic preservation
Period of collections: prehistoric-present

Alabama Pilgrimage Council
725 Monroe St., 36130
Telephone: (205) 261-3184
State agency, authorized by Alabama Historical Commission
Founded in: 1977
Jackson R. Stell, Historic Resources Coordinator
Staff: part time 4, volunteer 32
Magazine: *Doors*
Major programs: tours/pilgrimages

Black Heritage Council
c/o Alabama Historical Commission
Telephone: (205) 261-3184
Mail to: 725 Monroe St., Montgomery, 36130

Oakleigh House Museum, operated by the Historic Mobile Preservation Society.—Historic Mobile Preservation Society

State agency, authorized by Alabama
Historical Commission
Founded in: 1983
Shirley D. Qualls, Council Liaison
Staff: volunteer 3
Major programs: black churches
Period of collections: 1900s

**First White House of the
Confederacy**
644 Washington Ave., 36130
Telephone: (205) 261-4624
Mail to: P.O. Box 1861, 36103
State agency, authorized by White
House Association
Founded in: 1900
Mrs. John H. Napier, III, Regent,
White House Association
Number of members: 58
Staff: part time 4
Major programs: library, archives,
museum, historic site(s),
tours/pilgrimages, book publishing,
newsletters/pamphlets, historic
preservation, research,
photographic collections
Period of collections: 1861

**Governor Lurleen B. Wallace
Museum**
725 Monroe St., 36130
Telephone: (205) 261-3184
State agency, authorized by Alabama
Historical Commission
Founded in: 1976
Jackson R. Stell, Coordinator
Staff: full time 1, part time 3
Major programs: museum,
audiovisual programs
Period of collections: 1963-1978

**Landmarks Foundation—Old North
Hull Historic District**
Lucas Tavern, 310 N. Hull St., 36104
Telephone: (205) 263-4355
Founded in: 1967
Mary Ann Neeley, Director
Number of members: 1,300
Staff: full time 2, part time 2,
volunteer 20
Magazine: Landmarks Quarterly
Major programs: museum, historic
site, markers, tours/pilgrimages,
educational programs,
newsletters/pamphlets, historic
preservation, restoration
Period of collections: 1820s-1900

Live-In-A-Landmark Council
725 Monroe St., 36130
Telephone: (205) 261-3184
Founded in: 1973
Mary Lou Price, Coordinator
Number of members: 300
Staff: part time 1
Major programs: tours/pilgrimages,
historic preservation

Society of Pioneer of Montgomery
P.O. Box 413, 36101
Private agency
Founded in: 1955
J. Allen Reynolds, Jr., President
Number of members: 100
Major programs: archives, book
publishing, newsletters/pamphlets,
historic preservation, genealogical
services
Period of collections: 1855-present

**U.S. Air Force Historical Research
Center**
Maxwell Air Force Base, Bldg. 1405,
36112-6678
Telephone: (205) 293-5342
Federal agency, authorized by the
U.S. Air Force
Lloyd H. Cornett, Jr., Director
Staff: full time 76, part time 4
Major programs: archives,
manuscripts, oral history, book
publishing, research
Period of collections: 1942-1984

**White House Association of the
State of Alabama**
First White House of the Confederacy,
644 Washington St.
Telephone: (205) 261-4624
Mail to: P.O. Box 1861, 36103
Founded in: 1900
Mrs. John H. Napier III, Regent
Number of members: 58
Staff: full time 1, part time 3,
volunteer 3
Major programs: library, archives,
manuscripts, museum, historic site,
tours/pilgrimages, historic
preservation, photographic
collections
Period of collections: Spring of 1861

MONTROSE

**Baldwin County Historic
Development Commission**
Telephone: (205) 928-2313
Mail to: P.O. Box 86, 36559
County agency
Jack Thomas, Chair
Major programs: historic site(s),
markers, historic preservation

ONEONTA

Blount County Historical Society
204 2nd St., N
Telephone: (205) 625-6905
Mail to: P.O. Box 87, 35121
Founded in: 1959
Mrs. Carroll Y. Linder, Museum
Custodian
Number of members: 175
Staff: part time 2, volunteer 2
Major programs: archives, museum,
historic site(s) markers, oral history,
book publishing,
newsletters/pamphlets,
genealogical services
Period of collections: 1818-1900

PIEDMONT

**Piedmont Historical and
Genealogical Society**
R.F.D. 5, Box 109, 36272
Telephone: (205) 447-2939
Founded in: 1976
Mrs. Frank Ross Stewart, President
Number of members: 50
Staff: volunteer 50
Major programs: library, archives,
manuscripts, museum, historic site,
oral history, educational programs,
book publishing, historic
preservation
Period of collections: 1800-present

PRATTVILLE

**Autauga County Heritage
Association**
135 1st St.
Telephone: (205) 361-0961
Mail to: P.O. Box 178, 36067
Private agency
Founded in: 1976
Jeannie Johnson, President
Number of members: 250
Staff: volunteer 3
Major programs: tours/pilgrimages,
oral history, newsletters/pamphlets,
historic preservation
Period of collections: 1820-present

ROBERTSDALE

**John Pelham Historical
Association**
Rt. 1, Box 627, 36567
Telephone: (205) 946-3370
Private agency
Founded in: 1982
Charles H. Hooper, President
Number of members: 120
Staff: full time 1
Major programs: archives, markers,
tours/pilgrimages,
newsletters/pamphlets, historic
preservation, photographic
collections, genealogical services
Period of collections: 1861-1865

SCOTTSBORO

**Jackson County Historical
Association**
Rt. 1, Langston, 35755
Private agency
Founded in: 1976
David Campbell, President-elect
Number of members: part time 1
Major programs: library, museum,
historic site(s), tours/pilgrimages,
oral history, newsletters/pamphlets,
historic preservation, archaeology
programs, genealogical services
Period of collections: mid-late 1800s

**Scottsboro-Jackson Heritage
Center**
Peachtree and Houston Sts.
Telephone: (205) 259-2122
Mail to: P.O. Box 53, 35768
Privage agency, authorized by The
Heritage Center Association
Founded in: 1981
Mrs. Lee A. Langston, Director
Number of members: 250
Staff: full time 1, volunteer 10
Magazine: Archives
Major programs: archives,
manuscripts, museum, historic
site(s), tours/pilgrimages, junior
history, oral history, school
programs, newsletters/pamphlets,
historic preservation, records
management, research, exhibits,
living history, audiovisual
programs, archaeology programs,
photographic collections, field
services, visual and performing
arts lectures, classes, workshops
Period of collections: 1800s-present

SEALE

Russell County Historical Commission
801 Dillingham St., 36867
Telephone: (205) 298-9735
Founded in: 1968
Eloise Cumbaa, President
Number of members: 45
Major programs: historic sites preservation, markers, tours/pilgrimages, oral history, books, newsletters/pamphlets
Period of collections: 1830s-present

SELMA

Selma-Dallas County Historic and Preservation Society
719 Tremont St., 36701
Telephone: (205) 872-8265
Founded in: 1957
Mrs. Joe Sexton, President
Number of members: 487
Major programs: historic site(s), markers, tours/pilgrimages, school programs, newsletters/pamphlets, historic preservation
Period of collections: 1820-1920

SHAWMUT

Chattahoochee Valley Historical Society
Cobb Memorial Archives, Dalley
Telephone: (205) 768-2161
Mail to: Bradshaw Library, 36876
Founded in: 1948
Leonard Blanton, President
Number of members: 150
Staff: part time 1
Magazine: *The Voice*
Major programs: library, manuscripts, oral history, educational programs, book publishing, newsletters/pamphlets
Period of collections: 1850-present

SHEFFIELD

Tennessee Valley Historical Society
Mail to: P.O. Box 149, 35660
Founded in: 1923
Harry E. Wallace, President
Number of members: 250
Staff: volunteer 3
Magazine: *Journal of Muscle Shoals History*
Major programs: archives, manuscripts, museum, tours/pilgrimages, educational programs, newsletters/pamphlets
Period of collections: 1783-1950

SOMERVILLE

Somerville Preservation Commission
Broad St.
Telephone: (205) 778-8282
Mail to: P.O. Box 133, 35670
Town agency, authorized by Somerville Town Council
Founded in: 1975
J. D. Williams, Chair
Number of members: volunteer 15
Major programs: historic site(s), historic preservation
Period of collections: 1818-1930

SPRINGVILLE

St. Clair Historical Society
Rt. 1, Box 241, 35146
Founded in: 1972
Questionnaire not received

STOCKTON

Baldwin County Historical Society
P.O. Box 69, 36579
Telephone: (205) 937-9464
County agency
Founded in: 1923
Davida R. Hastie, Treasurer
Number of members: 100
Magazine: *Baldwin County Historical Quarterly*
Major programs: library, research, genealogical services

TALLADEGA

Talladega County Historical Association
106 Broome St., 35160
Telephone: (205) 362-2219
Founded in: 1970
James E. Burt, President
Number of members: 565
Major programs: newsletters/pamphlets, historic preservation, photographic collections, genealogical services
Period of collections: 1832-present

TROY

Pike County Historical and Genealogical Society
c/o Troy Public Library, 36081
Founded in: 1953
John P. Johnston, President
Number of members: 40
Major programs: library, records management, research
Period of collections: 1821-present

Pike Pioneer Museum
231 North, 36081
Telephone: (205) 566-3597
Mail to: Rt. 6, Box 241, 36081
Private agency
Founded in: 1969
Curren A. Farmer, Board Chair
Number of members: 300
Major programs: museum, exhibits, photographic collections
Period of collections: 19th century

TUSCALOOSA

Alabama Association of Historians
17 Pinemont Dr., 35401
Questionnaire not received

Heritage Commission of Tuscaloosa
Telephone: (205) 752-2575
Mail to: P.O. Box 1776, 35401
Founded in: 1980
Lewis E. McCay, Chair
Number of members: 11
Staff: full time 1
Major programs: archives, manuscripts, historic sites preservation, markers, junior history, educational programs, newsletters/pamphlets

Tuscaloosa County Preservation Society
2828 6th St., Strickland House, 35401
Telephone: (205) 758-2238
Mail to: P.O. Box 1665, 35403
Private agency
Founded in: 1965
Marvin L. Harper, Executive Director
Number of members: 1,200
Staff: part time 5
Magazine: *Preservationist*
Major programs: historic site(s), tours/pilgrimages, newsletters/pamphlets
Period of collections: 19th century

TUSCUMBIA

Colbert County Historical Landmarks Foundation, Inc.
1004 E. 3rd St., 35674
Telephone: (205) 383-8466
Private agency
Founded in: 1979
Eleanor Holder, Chair
Number of members: 35
Major programs: museum, historic site(s), tours/pilgrimages, historic preservation
Period of collections: 1800s

Helen Keller Property Board
300 W. North Commons, 35674
Telephone: (205) 381-0968
City agency
Founded in: 1952
Jeanie McNees, Executive Director
Staff: full time 3, part time 8, volunteer 9
Major programs: museum, historic site(s) tours/pilgrimages, historic preservation
Period of collections: 1820-1900

Tuscaloosa County Preservation Society
P.O. Box 1665, 35403
Telephone: (205) 758-2238
County agency
Founded in: 1964
Marvin Harper, Executive Director
Number of members: 1,200
Staff: part time 5, volunteer 50
Major programs: museum, markers, tours/pilgrimages, historic preservation

ALASKA

ANCHORAGE

Alaska Association for Historic Preservation
524 W. 4th Ave., Suite 203, 99501
Telephone: (907) 272-2119
Private agency
Founded in: 1981
Janet McCabe, Executive Director
Number of members: 150
Staff: volunteer 3
Major programs: newsletters/pamphlets, supports historic preservation legislation

◇**Alaska Historical Commission**
524 W. 4th Ave., Suite 207, 99501
Telephone: (907) 274-6222
Founded in: 1973

William S. Hanable, Executive
Director
Staff: full time 3
Magazine: *Alaska in Perspective*
Major programs: manuscripts, junior
history, oral history, book
publishing, newsletters/pamphlets,
research, archaeology programs,
photographic collections

Alaska Historical Society
Mail to: 524 W. 4th Ave., Suite 208,
99501
Founded in: 1967
Renee Blahuta, President
Number of members: 450
Major programs: historic sites
preservation, markers, oral history,
educational programs, books,
newsletters/pamphlets
Period of collections: 1783-present

Alaskana Collection and Archives
4101 University Dr., 99508
Telephone: (907) 561-1265
Private agency, authorized by Alaska
Pacific University
Founded in: 1961
Dale Stirling, Curator
Major programs: library, archives,
manuscripts, records
management, research,
photographic collections
Period of collections: 1900-present

**Anchorage Museum of History and
Art**
121 W. 7th Ave., 99501
Telephone: (907) 264-4326
City agency
Founded in: 1968
R. L. Shalkop, Director
Number of members: 1,500
Staff: full time 2, part time 3,
volunteer 50
Major programs: library, archives,
museum, exhibits, photographic
collections
Period of collections: 19th-20th
centuries

**Anchorage Historical and Fine Arts
Museum**
121 W. 7th Ave., 99501
Telephone: (907) 264-4326
Private agency
Founded in: 1955
Joan M. Antonson, President
Number of members: 259
Staff: volunteer 10
Major programs: library, archives,
manuscripts, museum, historic
site(s), book publishing, historic
preservation, audiovisual
programs, archaeology programs,
education programs
Period of collections: 1918-present

Historic Anchorage Inc.
524 W. 4th Ave., Suite 202, 99501
Telephone: (907) 562-6100 338
Private agency
Founded in: 1976
Dennis R. Campbell, President
Number of members: 300
Staff: full time 1, volunteer 11
Major programs: manuscripts,
museum, historic site(s),
tours/pilgrimages, junior history,

school programs,
newsletters/pamphlets, historic
preservation, records
management, research,
audiovisual programs

**National Park Service, State of
Alaska**
2525 Gambell St., Room 107, 99503
Telephone: (907) 271-4230
Federal agency, authorized by
Department of Interior
Leslie Starr Hart, Chief, Cultural
Resources
Major programs: museum, historic
site(s), historic preservation,
research, archaeology programs

◇**Office of History and
Archaeology,
Alaska Division of Parks and
Outdoor Recreation**
Pouch 7001, 99510
State agency
Founded in: 1970
Judith E. Bittner, Chief
Staff: full time 8
Magazine: *Heritage*
Major programs: historic site(s),
newsletters/pamphlets, historic
preservation, research, exhibits

BETHEL

Yugtarvik Regional Museum
P.O. Box 388, 99559
Telephone: (907) 543-2098
City agency
Founded in: 1967
Elizabeth A. Mayock, Curator
Number of members: 50
Staff: full time 2
Major programs: museum, school
programs, newsletters/pamphlets,
records management, exhibits,
living history, audiovisual
programs, photographic
collections, field services
Period of collections: 1850s-present

CENTRAL

**Circle District Museum—
Circle District Historical
Society, Inc.**
127 5 Mile-Steese Hwy.
Mail to: P.O. Box 1893, 99730
Private agency
Founded in: 1975
Patricia Oakes, Historian
Major programs: library, archives,
manuscripts, museum, oral history,
school programs,
newsletters/pamphlets, historic
preservation, research, exhibits,
photographic collections
Period of collections: 1890-present

CORDOVA

Cordova Historical Society, Inc.
1st St.
Telephone: (907) 424-7443
Mail to: P.O. Box 391, 99574
City agency
Founded in: 1966
Number of members: 100
Staff: part time 1, volunteer 12
Magazine: *Cordova Discoverer*

Major programs: archives, museum,
book publishing, historic
preservation, photographic
collections
Period of collections: 1906-1930

EAGLE CITY

Eagle Historical Society
99738
Founded in: 1961
John Borg, President
Number of members: 145
Staff: volunteer 20
Major programs: library, archives,
museum, historic site(s), junior
history, oral history, school
programs, newsletters/pamphlets,
historic preservation, research,
exhibits, photographic collections
Period of collections: 1898-present

FAIRBANKS

Tanana-Yukon Historical Society
Mail to: P.O. Box 1794, 99701
Private agency
Founded in: 1968
Jane G. Haigh, President
Number of members: 60
Major programs: museum, historic
site(s), newsletters/pamphlets,
research, photographic collections
Period of collections: 1902-1920

University of Alaska Museum
907 Yukon Dr., 99701
Telephone: (907) 474-7505
State agency, authorized by
University of Alaska
Basil C. Hedrick, Director
Number of members: 120
Staff: full time 33, part time 23,
volunteer 12
Major programs: museum, historic
preservation, research, exhibits,
archaeology programs,
photographic collections, natural
history
Period of collections: Upper
proterozoic-present

FORT YUKON

Dinjii Zhuu Enjit Museum
Telephone: (907) 662-2487
Mail to: P.O. Box 42, 99740
Founded in: 1976
Questionnaire not received

HAINES

Alaska Indian Arts, Inc.
Bldg. 13, Ft. Seward Dr.
Telephone: (907) 766-2160
Mail to: P.O. Box 271, 99827
Questionnaire not received

Chilkat Valley Historical Society
Sheldon Museum, Main St.
Telephone: (907) 766-2207
Mail to: P.O. Box 623, 99827
Founded in: 1975
Joan M. Snyder, President
Number of members: 160
Staff: volunteer 15
Major programs: museum
Period of collections: 1865-present

Sheldon Museum and Cultural Center
25 Main St.
Telephone: (907) 766-2366
Mail to: P.O. Box 623, 99817
Borough agency, authorized by
  Chilkat Valley Historical Society
Founded in: 1975
Elisabeth S. Hakkinen,
  Curator/Director
Number of members: 85
Staff: full time 1, part time 1
  volunteer 16
Major programs: archives, museum,
  photographic collections
Period of collections: 19th-20th
  centuries

HOMER

Homer Society of Natural History—Pratt Museum
Telephone: (907) 235-8635
Mail to: 3779 Bartlett St., 99603
Private agency
Founded in: 1955
Betsy Pitzman, Museum Director
Number of members: 350
Staff: full time 3, part time 7,
  volunteer 10
Major programs: library, museum,
  tours/pilgrimages, school
  programs, book publishing, natural
  history
Period of collections:
  prehistoric-present

JUNEAU

Alaska Historical Library
Telephone: (907) 465-2925
Mail to: Pouch G, 99811
State agency, authorized by Division
  of State Libraries and Museums
Founded in: 1900
Phyllis J. DeMuth, Librarian
Staff: full time 3

Major programs: library, manuscripts,
  oral history, newsletters/pamphlets,
  photographic collections
Period of collections: 1800s-present

Alaska State Archives
141 Willoughby Ave.
Telephone: (907) 465-2275
Mail to: Pouch C-0207, 99811
State agency
Founded in: 1972
John M. Kinney, State Archivist
Staff: full time 19
Major programs: archives, records
  management
Period of collections: 1882-present

◇Alaska State Museum
Telephone: (907) 465-2902
Mail to: Pouch FM, 99811
State agency
Founded in: 1900
Alan R. Munro, Director
Staff: full time 16, part time 6,
  volunteer 20
Magazine: *Northern Notebook*
Major programs: museum, school
  programs, book publishing,
  newsletters/pamphlets, research,
  exhibits, audiovisual programs,
  field services
Period of collections: 100
  B.C.-present

KENAI

Kenai Historical Society, Inc.
Telephone: (907) 283-7618
Mail to: P.O. Box 1348, 99611
Founded in: 1968
Roger Meeks, President
Number of members: 30
Major programs: archives, museum,
  historic sites preservation,
  educational programs,
  newsletters/pamphlets, book
  publishing
Period of collections: 1865-present

KETCHIKAN

Tongass Historical Society, Inc.
629 Dock St., 99901
Telephone: (907) 225-5600
Town agency
Founded in: 1961
Virginia McGillvray, Director
Number of members: 151
Staff: full time 5, part time 1,
  volunteer 28
Major programs: library, archives,
  manuscripts, museum, oral history,
  historic preservation, research,
  exhibits, photographic collections,
  native arts and crafts
Period of collections: 1850-present

Totem Heritage Center
(907) 225-5900
Mail to: 629 Dock St., 99901
City agency
Founded in: 1976
Elnore I. Corbett, Senior Curator of
  Programs
Number of members: full time 2, part
  time 6, volunteer 1
Major programs: library, archives,
  manuscripts, museum, historic
  preservation, exhibits,
  photographic collections, classes,
  workshops, native art and culture
Period of collections: 1850-1900

KODIAK

Kodiak Historical Society
101 Marine Way, 99615
Telephone: (907) 486-5920
Private agency
Founded in: 1954
Marian Johnson, Director
Number of members: 125
Staff: part time 5, volunteer 25
Major programs: archives, museum,
  historic site(s) tours/pilgrimages,
  oral history, school programs,
  historic preservation, photographic
  collections
Period of collections: 1700-present

KOTZEBUE

Kotzebue Museum, Inc.
Mail to: P.O. Box 73, 99752
Questionnaire not received

METLAKATLA

Duncan Cottage Museum
Duncan St.
Mail to: P.O. Box 282, 99926
Founded in: 1975
Questionnaire not received

NAKNEK

Bristol Bay Historical Society
Mail to: P.O. Box 43, 99633
Founded in: 1969
Questionnaire not received

NOME

Carrie M. McLain Memorial Museum
Front St.
Telephone: (907) 443-2566
Mail to: P.O. Box 53, 99762
City agency
Founded in: 1970
Mary McBurney, Museum Director

The Alaska State Museum in Juneau highlights native culture with a display of Klukwan Frog House Posts from Klukwan, Alaska.—The Alaska State Museum

Staff: full time 1, volunteer 2
Major programs: archives, museum, markers, oral history, school programs, newsletters/pamphlets, exhibits
Period of collections: 1898-present

PALMER

Alaska Historical and Transportation Museum, Inc.
Mile 40.2 Glenn Hwy.
Telephone: (907) 745-4493
Mail to: P.O. Box 920, 99645
Private agency
Founded in: 1976
John P. Cooper, Director
Number of members: 323
Staff: full time 6, part time 3, volunteer 20
Major programs: library, archives, museum, historic site(s), tours/pilgrimages, school programs, newsletters/pamphlets, historic preservation, records management, research, exhibits, living history, audiovisual programs, photographic collections, field services
Period of collections: 1900-1950

PETERSBURG

Clausen Memorial Museum
301 Fram St.
Telephone: (907) 772-3598
Mail to: P.O. Box 708, 99833
Private agency
Founded in: 1964
Michale Edgington, Director
Number of members: 134
Staff: full time 1, part time 4
Major programs: museum, oral history, school programs, newsletters/pamphlets, records management, exhibits, photographic collections
Period of collections: 1897-1950s

Museum Society of Petersburg
2nd and F St.
Telephone: (907) 772-3598
Mail to: P.O. Box 708, 99833
Questionnaire not received

SEWARD

Resurrection Bay Historical Society
5th and Adams Sts.
Mail to: P.O. Box 871, 99664
Private agency
Founded in: 1967
Lee E. Poleske, President
Number of members: 37
Staff: part time 1, volunteer 3
Major programs: museum, newsletters/pamphlets
Period of collections: 1900-present

SITKA

Sheldon Jackson Museum
104 College Dr.
Mail to: P.O. Box 479, 99835
State agency, authorized by Department of Education, Alaska State Museum
Founded in: 1888
Bette Hulbert, Director
Staff: full time 3, volunteer 5

Major programs: museum, historic site(s)
Period of collections: 1880-1900

Sitka Historical Society
Telephone: (907) 747-6455
Mail to: 330 Harbor Dr., 99835
Joe Ashby, President
Number of members: 44
Staff: part time 1, volunteer 15
Major programs: archives, museum, photographic collections
Period of collections: 1830-present

SKAGWAY

Trail of '98 Museum
Spring St.
Telephone: (907) 983-2420
Mail to: P.O. Box 415, 99840
City agency
Founded in: 1961
Allene Rohlf, Director
Staff: part time 4
Major programs: archives, museum, records management, exhibits, photographic collections
Period of collections: 1898 Gold Rush

TALKEETNA

Talkeetna Historical Society, Inc.
Mail to: P.O. Box 76, 99676
Founded in: 1972
Questionnaire not received

VALDEZ

Valdez Heritage Center
101 Chenga Ave.
Telephone: (907) 835-2764
Mail to: P.O. Box 307, 99686
City agency, authorized by Heritage Services Department
Founded in: 1976
M. Joseph Leahy, Museum/Archive Director
Staff: full time 3, part time 4, volunteer 25
Major programs: archives, museum
Period of collections: 1890-present

Valdez Historical Society, Inc.— "Archives Alive"
Royal Center on Egan Dr.
Telephone: (907) 835-4367
Mail to: P.O. Box 6, 99686
Founded in: 1959
Dorothy I. Clifton, Director
Number of members: 38
Staff: volunteer 5
Major programs: library, archives, manuscripts, museum, historic site, markers, oral history, educational programs, historic preservation, audiovisual programs

WASILLA

Wasilla-Knik-Willow-Creek Historical Society
214 Main St.
Telephone: (907) 376-2005
Mail to: P.O. Box 870874, 99687
Private agency
Founded in: 1967
James Ede, Agent
Number of members: 147
Staff: volunteer 5
Major programs: museum, historic preservation
Period of collections: 1918-present

WRANGELL

Wrangell Historical Society
126 2nd St.
Mail to: P.O. Box 1050, 99929
Founded in: 1967
Questionnaire not received

ARIZONA

APACHE JUNCTION

Superstition Mountain Historical Society
P.O. Box 1535, 85220
Private agency
Founded in: 1980
Ronald Lorenz, Secretary/Treasurer
Number of members: 130
Staff: volunteer 8
Magazine: *Superstition Mountain Journal*
Major programs: archives, newsletters/pamphlets

BENSON

San Pedro Valley Arts and Historical Society
142 S. San Pedro
Mail to: P.O. Box 1090, 85602
Private agency
Founded in: 1983
Elizabeth A. Brenner, President
Number of members: 79
Staff: volunteer 14
Major programs: museum, historic site(s), oral history, school programs, historic preservation, exhibits, photographic collections
Period of collections: 1870-1930

BISBEE

Bisbee Mining and Historical Museum
5 Copper Queen Plaza
Telephone: (602) 432-7071
Mail to: P.O. Box 451, 85603
Founded in: 1968
Nancy Davis, Chair
Number of members: 675
Staff: full time 1, part time 4, volunteer 35
Major programs: library, archives, museum, oral history, historic site(s), photographic collections
Period of collections: 1880-1925

CAMP VERDE

Ft. Verde State Historical Park
Lane St.
Telephone: (602) 567-3275
Mail to: P.O. Box 397, 86322
State agency, authorized by Arizona State Parks Board
Founded in: 1970
Duane Hinshaw, Park Manager
Staff: full time 3, part time 1
Major programs: museum, historic site(s), school programs, historic preservation, exhibits, photographic collections
Period of collections: 1880s

CASA GRANDE

Casa Grande Valley Historical Society
110 W. Florence Blvd., 85222
Telephone: (602) 836-2223
Private agency
Founded in: 1964
Alta Norville, President
Staff: part time 2, volunteer 50
Major programs: museum, historic
site(s), markers, tours, oral history,
school programs, book publishing,
newsletters/pamphlets, historic
preservation, exhibits,
photographic collections
Period of collections: 1865-present

CHANDLER

Chandler Historical Society
78 W. Chicago
Mail to: P.O. Box 926, 85224
Questionnaire not received

COOLIDGE

Casa Grande Ruins National Monument
(602) 723-3172
Mail to: P.O. Box 518, 85228
Federal agency, authorized by
National Park Service
Founded in: 1890
Staff: full time 7, part time 2,
volunteer 2
Major programs: library, museum,
historic site(s), tours/pilgrimages,
historic preservation, exhibits,
archaeology programs,
photographic collections
Period of collections: 300 B.C.-A.D.
1450

DOUGLAS

Cochise County Historical and Archaeological Society
1116 G Ave.
Telephone: (602) 364-5655
(president)
Mail to: P.O. Box 818, 85608-0818
Private agency
Founded in: 1966
Winifred G. Meskus, President
Number of members: 300
Staff: volunteer 20
Magazine: *The Cochise Quarterly*
Major programs: museum, markers,
newsletters/pamphlets,
archaeology programs, tour annual
journals

DRAGOON

Amerind Foundation, Inc.
Dragoon Rd.
Telephone: (602) 586-3003
Mail to: P.O. Box 248, 85609
Private agency
Founded in: 1937
Anne I. Woosley, Director
Staff: full time 10, part time 6,
volunteer 1
Magazine: *Amerind Publications*
Major programs: library, archives,
manuscripts, museum, historic
site(s), tours/pilgrimages, school
programs, book publishing, historic
preservation, research, exhibits,

audiovisual programs, archaeology
programs, photographic
collections, field services
Period of collections: prehistoric

FLAGSTAFF

Arizona Historical Society Pioneer Museum
N. Ft. Valley Rd.
Telephone: (602) 774-6272
Mail to: P.O. Box 1968, 86002
State agency, authorized by Arizona
Historical Society
Founded in: 1953
Joseph M. Meehan, Curator
Staff: full time 2, part time 2,
volunteer 8
Major programs: library, archives,
manuscripts, museum, historic
site(s), markers, tours/pilgrimages,
oral history, school programs, book
publishing, newsletters/pamphlets,
historic preservation, exhibits,
living history, audiovisual
programs, photographic
collections.
Period of collections: 1540-present

Center for Colorado Plateau Studies
Northern Arizona University
Telephone: (602) 523-2562
Mail to: P.O. Box 5613, 86011
State agency, authorized by the
university
Founded in: 1983
Valeen T. Avery, Director
Staff: full time 1, part time 4,
volunteer 2
Major programs: manuscripts,
newsletters/pamphlets, research

Museum of Northern Arizona
Ft. Valley Rd., Rt. 4, Box 720, 86001
Telephone: (602) 774-5211
Founded in: 1928
Philip M. Thompson, Director
Number of members: 403
Magazine: *Plateau*
Major programs: library, archives,
manuscripts, museum, historic
site(s), tours/pilgrimages, school
programs, book publishing,
newsletters/pamphlets, research,
exhibits
Period of collections:
prehistoric-present

Northern Arizona Pioneers' Historical Society, Inc.
Ft. Valley Rd., 86001
Telephone: (602) 774-6272
Mail to: P.O. Box 1968, 86002
State agency, authorized by Arizona
Historical Society
Founded in: 1953
Joseph M. Meehan, Director
Number of members: 350
Staff: full time 1, part time 2,
volunteer 7
Major programs: archives, museum,
historic site(s)

FLORENCE

Pinal County Historical Society, Inc.
2201 S. Main St.
Mail to: P.O. Box 851, 85232
Questionnaire not received

GANADO

Hubbell Trading Post National Historic Site
P.O. Box 150, 86505
Telephone: (602) 755-3475
Federal agency
Founded in: 1967
Elizabeth Bauer, Curator
Staff: full time 2
Major programs: museum, historic
site(s), tours/pilgrimages, historic
preservation
Period of collections: 1880-1930

GLENDALE

Arizona Pharmacy Historical Foundation
Telephone: (602) 937-6946
Mail to: P.O. Box 414, 85311
Founded in: 1977
A. J. Duncan, Secretary
Major programs: history of pharmacy
in Arizona

Glendale Arizona Historical Society
Mail to: P.O. Box 2544, 85301
Private agency
Founded in: 1973
Ruth Byrne, President
Number of members: 200
Staff: volunteer 10
Major programs: library, museum,
tours/pilgrimages
Period of collections: 1895-present

GLOBE

Gila County Historical Society
1330 N. Broad St.
Telephone: (602) 425-7385
Mail to: P.O. Box 2891, 85501
Private agency
Founded in: 1950
Rayna Barela, Curator
Number of members: 70
Staff: full time 1, volunteer 10
Major programs: museum,
newsletters/pamphlets,
tours/pilgrimages, school
programs
Period of collections: A.D. 1125-1930

GRAND CANYON

Grand Canyon Natural History Association
Telephone: (602) 638-2411, ext. 275
Mail to: P.O. Box 399, 86023
Private agency
Founded in: 1932
John C. O'Brien, Executive Secretary
Number of members: 550
Staff: full time 3, part time 12
Major programs: library, archives,
oral history, book publishing,
newsletters/pamphlets, research,
natural history

HEREFORD

Coronado National Memorial
R.R. 1, Box 126, 85615
Telephone: (602) 366-5515
Federal agency, authorized by
National Park Service
Founded in: 1952
Laurel W. Dale, Superintendent
Staff: full time 5

Major programs: museum, living
history, natural site
Period of collections: 16th century

HOLBROOK

Navajo County Historical Society
Navajo Blvd. and Arizona Sts.
Telephone: (602) 524-6529
Mail to: P.O. Box 563, 86025
County agency
Founded in: 1969
Garnette Franklin, Historian
Number of members: 75
Staff: volunteer 20
Major programs: museum, historic
site(s), historic preservation,
research, exhibits, photographic
collections
Period of collections:
prehistoric-present

JEROME

Jerome Historical Society
Main and Merome Sts.
Telephone: (602) 634-7349/634-5477
Mail to: P.O. Box 156, 86331
Private agency
Founded in: 1953
Nancy R. Smith, Assistant Curator
Number of members: 225
Staff: full time 2, part time 3,
volunteer 1
Magazine: *Jerome Chronicle*
Major programs: archives, museum,
markers, book publishing,
newsletters/pamphlets, historic
preservation, records
management, research,
photographic collections, copper
mining history
Period of collections: 1895-1960

KINGMAN

**Mohave Museum of History and
Arts—
Mohave County Historical Society**
400 W. Beale St., 86401
Telephone: (602) 753-3195
Private agency
Founded in: 1960
Norma Hughes, Director
Number of members: 350
Staff: full time 1, part time 2,
volunteer 110
Major programs: library, archives,
museum, oral history,
newsletters/pamphlets, historic
preservation, exhibits,
photographic collections,
genealogical services

MESA

Mesa Museum
53 N. Macdonald, 85201
Telephone: (602) 834-2230
Founded in: 1977
Tracy Mead, Museum Director
Staff: full time 6, part time 4,
volunteer 100
Major programs: museum, historic
site(s), markers, tours/pilgrimages,
oral history, exhibits, archaeology
programs
Period of collections: prehistoric-1900

MOCCASIN

Pipe Spring National Monument
86022
Telephone: (602) 643-7105
Federal agency, authorized by
National Park Service
Founded in: 1923
William M. Herr, Superintendent
Staff: full time 4
Major programs: library, archives,
museum, historic site(s), historic
preservation, records
management, research, exhibits,
living history, photographic
collections
Period of collections: 1870-1890

NOGALES

Pimeria Alta Historical Society
Old City Hall, 223 Grand Ave.
Telephone: (602) 287-5402
Mail to: P.O. Box 2281, 85628
Private agency
Founded in: 1948
Susan Clarke Spater, Director
Number of members: 850
Staff: full time 2, part time 3,
volunteer 75
Major programs: museum, markers,
tours, oral history, educational
programs, newsletters/pamphlets,
library, archives, exhibits
Period of collections: A.D.
1000-present

ORACLE

Oracle Historical Society, Inc.
Mt. Lemmon Hwy.
Telephone: (602) 896-9140
Mail to: P.O. Box A, 85623
Private agency
Commission
Founded in: 1977
Darrell Klesch, President
Number of members: 100
Staff: volunteer 10
Magazine: *Oracle Historian*
Major programs: library, museum,
historic site(s), historic
preservation, living history
Period of collections: 1880-1900s

PAGE

**John Wesley Powell Memorial
Museum**
6 Lake Powell Blvd.
Telephone: (602) 645-2741
Mail to: P.O. Box 547, 86040
Private agency
Founded in: 1967
Julia P. Betz, President
Number of members: 30
Staff: volunteer 10
Major programs: library, museum,
oral history, exhibits, audiovisual
programs, photographic
collections
Period of collections: 1869-present

PARKER

**Colorado River Indian Tribes
Museum and Library**
Rt. 1, Box 23-B, 85344
Telephone: (602) 669-9211, ext. 213
Founded in: 1956

Charles A. Lamb, Museum Director
Staff: full time 2, part time 3
Magazine: *Smoke Signals*
Major programs: library, archives,
manuscripts, museum, historic
sites preservation, markers,
tours/pilgrimages, oral history,
educational programs, books,
newsletters/pamphlets,
archaeological consultant program
Period of collections:
prehistoric-present

PAYSON

**Northern Gila County Historical
Society**
Star Rt., Box 35, 85541
Questionnaire not received

Logo for the Arizona Historical Society Museum in Phoenix. Founded by Arizona pioneers in 1884, the society operates four regional museums.—The Arizona Historical Society

PHOENIX

◇**Arizona Historical Society
Museum of History**
1242 N. Central Ave., 85004
Telephone: (602) 255-4470
State agency, authorized by Arizona
Historical Society
Founded in: 1971
Joyce Barrett, Acting Director
Staff: full time 6, part time 3,
volunteer 100
Major programs: library, archives,
manuscripts, museum, historic
site(s), markers, tours/pilgrimages,
oral history, school programs, book
publishing, newsletters/pamphlets,
historic preservation, research,
exhibits, audiovisual programs,
photographic collections,
commemorative events
Period of collections: 1875-present

◇**Arizona Humanities Council**
100 N. Washington, Suite 1290, 85003
Telephone: (602) 257-0335
Federal agency, authorized by
National Endowment for the
Humanities
Founded in: 1973
Lorraine W. Frank, Executive Director
Staff: full time 3, volunteer 2
Major programs: library, museum,
oral history, historic preservation,
exhibits, archaeology programs

Arizona Jewish Historical Society—
Phoenix Chapter
2928 N. 7th Ave., 85013
Telephone: (602) 234-3176
Private agency
Founded in: 1981
Pearl Newmark, Executive Director
Number of members: 150
Staff: part time 1, volunteer 2
Major programs: archives, oral history

The Arizona Museum
1001 W. Van Buren St., 85007
Telephone: (602) 253-2734
Mail to: P.O. Box 926, 85001
Private agency
Founded in: 1923
Elizabeth O. Garretson, Director
Number of members: 370
Staff: full time 1, part time 1,
volunteer 20
Major programs: museum
Period of collections:
prehistoric-W.W.I

◇**Arizona State Department of**
Library, Archives and Public
Records
State Capitol, 3rd Floor, 85007
Telephone: (602) 255-3701
State agency
Founded in: 1864
Sharon Turgeon, Director
Staff: full time 103
Major programs: library, archives,
manuscripts, museum, markers,
school programs, records
management, research,
audiovisual programs,
photographic collections,
genealogical services, field
services
Period of collections: 1864-present

Arizona State Parks Board
1688 W. Adams, 85007
Telephone: (602) 255-4174
Founded in: 1957
Michael Ramnes, Director
Staff: full time 115
Major programs: museum, historic
sites preservation,
newsletters/pamphlets
Period of collections: 1750-1950

Hall of Flame—National Historical
Fire Foundation
6101 E. Van Buren, 85008
Telephone: (602) 275-3473
Founded in: 1961
George F. Getz, Jr., President
Staff: full time 3, part time 1
Major programs: library, museum,
tours/pilgrimages, educational
programs, historic preservation
Period of collections: 1900s

Judaica Museum of Temple Beth
Israel
3310 N. 10th Ave., 85013
Telephone: (602) 264-4428
Founded in: 1965
Sylvia Plotkin, Director
Number of members: 1,500
Staff: volunteer 86
Major programs: library, archives,
museum, book publishing, exhibits,
audiovisual programs
Period of collections: 1850-1920

Pioneer's Cemetery
Association, Inc.
1002 W. Van Buren St., 85003
Telephone: (602) 253-2734
Mail to: P.O. Box 6252, 85005
Private agency
Founded in: 1982
Jose Villela, President
Number of members: 126
Staff: volunteer 7
Magazine: *Arizona Pioneer*
Major programs: archives,
manuscripts, historic site(s),
markers, tours/pilgrimages, oral
history, school programs,
newsletters/pamphlets, historic
preservation, research,
photographic collections,
genealogical services, field
services
Period of collections: 1800-1950

Pioneer Arizona Living-History
Museum
Interstate 17, Pioneer Rd. Exit
Mail to: P.O. Box 11242, 85061
Questionnaire not received

Pueblo Grande Museum
4619 E. Washington St., 85034
Telephone: (602) 275-3452
City agency, authorized by Parks,
Recreation and Library Department
Founded in: 1931
David E. Doyel, Museum Director
Number of members: 99
Staff: full time 6, part time 2,
volunteer 25
Major programs: museum, historic
site(s), exhibits
Period of collections: 600-A.D. 1450

State Capitol Museum
1700 W. Washington St., 85007
Telephone: (602) 255-4675
Authorized by Department of Library,
Archives and Public Records
Founded in: 1978
Michael D. Carman, Curator
Staff: full time 8, part time 5
Major programs: museum, historic
site(s), tours/pilgrimages, school
programs, exhibits, audiovisual
programs
Period of collections: 1890-1920

◇**State Historic Preservation Office**
1688 W. Adams, 85007
Telephone: (602) 255-4174
State agency, authorized by State
Parks Board
Donna J. Schober, State Historic
Preservation Officer
Staff: full time 9
Magazine: *Arizona Preservation*
News
Major programs: historic site(s),
historic preservation, archaeology
programs

PIMA

Eastern Arizona Museum and
Historical Society
2 N. Main St.
Mail to: P.O. Box 274, 85543
Private agency
Founded in: 1963
Reece Jarvis, President

Staff: part time 2
Major programs: museum, historic
preservation
Period of collections: 1885-present

PRESCOTT

Sharlot Hall Historical
Society—Prescott Historical
Society
415 W. Gurley St., 86301
Telephone: (602) 445-3122
Founded in: 1929
Kenneth R. Kimsey, Director
Number of members: 470
Staff: full time 15, part time 4,
volunteer 135
Magazine: *Sharlot Hall Gazette*
Major programs: library, archives,
manuscripts, museum, historic
site(s), tours/pilgrimages, school
programs, newsletters/pamphlets,
records management, research,
exhibits, photographic collections
Period of collections: 1860-1930

SAFFORD

Graham County Historical Society
808 8th Ave., 85546
Questionnaire not received

ST. MICHAELS

St. Michaels Historical Museum
P.O. Box D, 86511
Telephone: (602) 871-4172
Private agency, authorized by The
Franciscan Friars
Founded in: 1973
Michael J. Andrews, Project Director
Staff: volunteer 12
Major programs: library, archives,
manuscripts, museum, historic
preservation, research, exhibits,
photographic collections
Period of collections: 1898-1950

SCOTTSDALE

Scottsdale Historical Society
3720 N. Marshall Way
Mail to: P.O. Box 143, 85252
Private agency
Founded in: 1969
Jean Scott, President
Number of members: 105
Major programs: museum,
tours/pilgrimages, oral history,
newsletters/pamphlets, historic
preservation
Period of collections: 1900

SUN CITY

Sun City Historical Society
Sun City Library
Telephone: (602) 933-6919
Mail to: 16828 99th Ave., 85351
Private agency
Founded in: 1985
Jane Freeman, President
Staff: volunteer 10
Major programs: archives, oral
history, photographic collections
Period of collections: 1960-present

TEMPE

Arizona Historical Foundation—Hayden Library, Arizona State University
85287
Telephone: (602) 966-8331
Private agency
Founded in: 1959
Dean E. Smith, Executive Vice President
Staff: full time 1
Major programs: library, archives, manuscripts, book publishing, photographs, oral history, research, congressional papers
Period of collections: 1850-present

Heritage Foundation of Arizona
P.O. Box 25616, 85282
Private agency
Founded in: 1979
Robert C. Giebner, President
Number of members: 125
Staff: part time 2
Major programs: newsletters/pamphlets, historic preservation, technical workshops

Sons of Sherman's March to the Sea
1725 S. Farmer Ave., 85281
Telephone: (602) 967-5405
Founded in: 1966
Stan Schirmacher, National Director
Number of members: 404
Magazine: *Bulletin*
Major programs: newsletters/pamphlets, Civil War service records
Period of collections: 1860-1865

Tempe Historical Museum
3500 S. Rural Rd., 85282
Telephone: (602) 966-7253
Town agency
Founded in: 1972
Mary Ellen Conaway, Director
Number of members: 350
Staff: full time 3, part time 1, volunteer 40
Major programs: archives, museum, historic site(s), tours, historic preservation, research, exhibits, photographic collections
Period of collections: 1865-present

Tempe Historical Society
3500 S. Rural Rd.
Telephone: (602) 966-7902
Mail to: P.O. Box 27394, 85282
Private agency
Founded in: 1969
Larry Diehl, President
Number of members: 350
Magazine: *Tempe Historical Highlights*
Major programs: museum, historic site
Period of collections: 1865-present

TOMBSTONE

Tombstone Courthouse State Historic Park
3rd and Toughnut Sts.
Telephone: (602) 457-3311
Mail to: P.O. Box 216, 85638
Founded in: 1959
Hollis N. Cook, Park Manager

Staff: full time 4
Major programs: museum, historic site, historic preservation, exhibits

TSAILE

Ned A. Hatathli Center Museum
Navajo Community College, 86556
Telephone: (602) 724-3311
Federal agency
Founded in: 1968
Harry Walters, Director
Staff: full time 2, part time 2
Major programs: museum, historic site(s), tours/pilgrimages, junior history, oral history, school programs, historic preservation, research, exhibits, living history, field services
Period of collections: 1850-present

TUBAC

Tubac Historical Society
Telephone: (602) 398-2919
Mail to: P.O. Box 3261, 85646
Private agency, authorized by Arizona Corporation Commission
Founded in: 1965
Harry G. Richardon, President
Number of members: 300
Major programs: library, markers, tours/pilgrimages, oral history, book publishing, historic preservation, research
Period of collections: 1752-present

Tubac Presidio State Historic Museum
River Rd. and Broadway
Telephone: (602) 398-2252
Mail to: P.O. Box 1296, 85646
State agency, authorized by Arizona State Park
Founded in: 1959
Gary M. Kuhn, Park Manager
Staff: full time 3
Major programs: museum, school programs, historic preservation, exhibits, audiovisual programs
Period of collections: 1752-1865

TUCSON

American Division, Jesuit Historical Institute
Arizona State Museum, 85721
Telephone: (602) 621-6280
Private agency, authorized by Jesuit Conference of the U.S.
Founded in: 1975
Charles W. Polzer, Ethnohistorian
Staff: full time 1, part time 1
Major programs: library, archives, book publishing, research
Period of collections: 1570-1820

Arizona Archaeological and Historical Society
University of Arizona, 85721
Telephone: (602) 621-4011
Private agency
Founded in: 1916
Richard C. Lange, President
Number of members: 500
Staff: volunteer 20
Magazine: *The Kiva*
Major programs: museum, tours/pilgrimages, book publishing, newsletters/pamphlets, audiovisual programs

◇**Arizona Historical Society**
949 E. 2nd St., 85719
Telephone: (602) 628-5774
State agency
Founded in: 1884
James Moss, Executive Director
Number of members: 4,000
Staff: full time 35, part time 6
Magazine: *The Journal of Arizona History*
Major programs: library, archives, manuscripts, museum, historic site(s), markers, tours/pilgrimages, oral history, school programs, book publishing, newsletters/pamphlets, historic preservation, research, exhibits, living history, audiovisual programs, photographic collections, field services
Period of collections: 1770-1945

Arizona Historical Society Ft. Lowell Museum
2900 N. Craycroft, 85712
Telephone: (602) 885-3832
State agency, authorized by Arizona Historical Society
Founded in: 1963
Michael F. Weber, Director
Staff: full time 1, volunteer 5
Major programs: museum, historic site(s), school programs, commemorative events
Period of collections: 1875-1895

Arizona Historical Society Heritage Center
949 E. 2nd St., 85719
Telephone: (602) 628-5774
State agency, authorized by Arizona Historical Society
Founded in: 1953
Michael F. Weber, Director
Staff: full time 22, volunteer 100
Major programs: museum, library, archives, manuscripts, photographs, educational programs, commemorative events, tours, oral history, exhibits
Period of collections: 1770-present

Arizona Historical Society John C. Fremont House—Casa Del Governador
151 S. Granada, 85701
Telephone: (602) 622-0956
State agency, authorized by Arizona Historical Society
Founded in: 1973
Michael F. Weber, Director
Staff: full time 1, volunteer 30
Major programs: museum, historic site, educational programs, commemorative events, historic preservation, tours
Period of collections: 1850-1890

Arizona State Genealogical Society
Telephone: (602) 886-1261
Mail to: P.O. Box 42075, 85733
Founded in: 1965
Lant Haymore, President
Number of members: 290
Staff: volunteer 30
Magazine: *Copper State Bulletin*
Major programs: library, genealogy, educational programs, books, newsletters/pamphlets

◇**Arizona State Museum**
University of Arizona, 85721
Telephone: (602) 621-6281
State agency, authorized by Arizona
    Board of Regents
Founded in: 1893
Raymond H. Thompson, Director
Staff: full time 77, part time 61,
    volunteer 7
Major programs: library, museum,
    research, exhibits, archaeology
    programs, photographic
    collections

Pima Air Museum
6400 S. Wilmot Rd., 85706
Telephone: (602) 574-0462
Private agency, authorized by Tucson
    Air Museum Foundation of Pima
    County
Founded in: 1976
Ned S. Robinson, Director
Number of members: 715
Staff: full time 11, part time 5,
    volunteer 45
Major programs: museum, exhibits
Period of collections: W.W. II

**Southwestern Mission Research
    Center**
University of Arizona, 85721
Telephone: (602) 621-6278
Private agency
Founded in: 1965
Charles W. Polzer,
    Secretary/Treasurer
Number of members: 700
Major programs: archives, tours,
    book publishing,
    newsletters/pamphlets, research
Period of collections: 1600-1800

Tucson Festival Society
8 W. Paseo Redondo, 85705
Telephone: (602) 622-6911
Private agency
Founded in: 1950
Jarvis Harriman, Executive Director
Number of members: 800
Staff: full time 3
Magazine: *Tohono Talk*
Major programs: tours/pilgrimages,
    school programs, living history,
    Festival of Heritage

**Western Archeological and
    Conservation Center Library**
1415 N. 6th Ave., 85717
Telephone: (602) 629-6995
Federal agency, authorized by
    National Park Service
W. Richard Horn, Librarian
Staff: full time 2, part time 2,
    volunteer 1
Major programs: library, archives

Western Postal History Museum
920 N. 1st Ave.
Telephone: (602) 623-6652
Mail to: P.O. Box 40725, 85717
Private agency
Founded in: 1960
Arthur E. Springer, Director
Staff: volunteer 30
Magazine: *Overland Stage and
    Express*
Major programs: library, archives,
    manuscripts, museum,
    tours/pilgrimages, oral history,
    school programs,

newsletters/pamphlets, historic
    preservation, research, exhibits,
    postal history
Period of collections: 1863-present

Westerners International
Mail to: P.O. Box 2304, La Placita
    Station, 85702
Questionnaire not received

WICKENBURG

**Desert Caballeros Western
    Museum**
20 N. Frontier St.
Telephone: (602) 684-2272
Mail to: P.O. Box 1446, 85358
Private agency, authorized by
    Maricopa County Historical Society
Founded in: 1968
Veeva Fletcher, Curator
Number of members: 310
Staff: full time 4, volunteer 25
Major programs: museum,
    newsletters/pamphlets, exhibits
Period of collections: 1910

Maricopa County Historical Society
20 N. Frontier St.
Telephone: (602) 684-2272
Mail to: P.O. Box 1446, 85358
Private agency
Founded in: 1969
Veeva Fletcher, Curator
Number of members: 325
Staff: full time 4, volunteer 100
Major programs: museum, tours,
    newsletters/pamphlets, historic
    preservation, exhibits, audiovisual
    programs
Period of collections: 1864-present

WILLCOX

Chiricahua National Monument
Dos Cabezas Rt., Box 6500, 85643
Telephone: (602) 824-3560
Federal agency, authorized by
    National Park Service
Founded in: 1924
Charles C. Milliken, Chief
    Interpretation
Staff: full time 1, part time 1
Major programs: library, museum,
    tours/pilgrimages, oral history,
    school programs, exhibits,
    audiovisual programs,
    photographic collections, geology
Period of collections: pioneer

WINDOW ROCK

**Bureau of Indian Affairs—Navajo
    Area Office, Environmental
    Quality Services**
P.O. Box M, 86515
Telephone: (602) 871-5151, ext. 5108
Federal agency, authorized by
    Department of the Interior
Founded in: 1892
Mark Henderson, Area Archeologist
Staff: full time 7
library, archives, historic site(s), oral
    history, historic preservation,
    records management, research,
    archaeology programs,
    photographic collections, field
    services
Period of collections: 12,000
    B.C.-present

Navajo Tribal Museum
Hwy. 264
Telephone: (602) 871-6673
Mail to: P.O. Box 308, 86515
Authorized by Navajo Tribe
Founded in: 1961
Russell P. Hartman, Director
Staff: full time 2
Major programs: museum, exhibits,
    archaeology programs,
    photographic collections
Period of collections: Paleo
    Indian-20th century

YUMA

**Arizona Historical Society Century
    House Museum and Gardens**
240 Madison Ave., 85364
Telephone: (602) 783-8020
State agency, authorized by Arizona
    Historical Society
Founded in: 1963
Andrew Masich, Director
Staff: full time 4, volunteer 62
Major programs: library, archives,
    manuscripts, museum, historic
    site(s), markers, tours/pilgrimages,
    oral history, school programs, book
    publishing, newsletters/pamphlets,
    historic preservation, records
    management, research, exhibits,
    living history, audiovisual
    programs, archaeology programs,
    photographic collections
Period of collections: 1850-1945

Quechan Indian Museum
Ft. Yuma Indian Hill
Telephone: (714) 572-0661
Mail to: P.O. Box 1352, 85364
Private agency, authorized by
    Quechan Tribe
Founded in: 1850
Vincent Harvier, Tribal President
Staff: full time 1, part time 1
Major programs: museum, historic
    site

Yuma County Historical Society
240 S. Madison Ave., 85364
Telephone: (602) 783-8020
Private agency
Founded in: 1963
Irene Hendrickson, President
Number of members: 200
Major programs: book publishing

ARKANSAS

ARKADELPHIA

**Clark County Historical Associa-
    tion**
Ouachita Baptist University
Telephone: (501) 246-4531
Mail to: P.O. Box 3742, 71923
Private agency
Founded in: 1972
Ray Granade, President
Number of members: 255
Staff: part time 1, volunteer 4
Magazine: *Clark County Historical
    Association Journal*
Major programs: library, archives,
    manuscripts, historic preservation,
    research, photographic collections

ASH FLAT

Sharp County Historical Society
P.O. Box 185, 72513
Telephone: (501) 257-3098
Founded in: 1980
Questionnaire not received

BATESVILLE

Arkansas College Historic Preservation Program—Regional Studies Center
Arkansas College, 72501
Telephone: (501) 793-9813
Founded in: 1980
Daniel Fagg, Professor of History
Staff: full time 2, part time 2
Major programs: historic preservation
Period of collections: 19th-early 20th centuries

Independence County Historical Society
115 N. 4th St.
Telephone: (501) 793-2383
Mail to: P.O. Box 2036, 72501
Founded in: 1958
Wilson Powell, Secretary/Treasurer
Number of members: 560
Staff: volunteer 3
Magazine: *Independence County Chronicle*
Major programs: library, archives, manuscripts, museum, historic site(s), markers, historic preservation, genealogical services
Period of collections: 1783-present

BEAVER

Missouri and Arkansas Railroad Museum, Inc.
1 Railroad Ave.
Telephone: (501) 253-7329
Mail to: P.O. Box 44, 72613
Private agency
Founded in: 1978
Reat R. Younger, Executive Director
Number of members: 150
Staff: volunteer 9
Magazine: *Oakleaves*
Major programs: museum, book publishing, historic preservation, photographic collections
Period of collections: 1880-1950

BELLA VISTA

Bella Vista Historical Society
1 Abbey Circle, 72712
Founded in: 1976
Questionnaire not received

BENTON

Gann Museum of Saline County
S. Market St.
Telephone: (501) 776-1290 (board chair)
Mail to: c/o Gingles Furniture Store, 102 S. Main, 77015
Founded in: 1980
Mrs. Max Laird, Board Chair
Staff: volunteer 30
Major programs: manuscripts, museum, tours/pilgrimages, school programs, research, exhibits
Period of collections: Pioneer-W.W. II

BERRYVILLE

Carroll County Historical Society and Heritage Center
1880 Court House, 2nd and 3rd Floors, 72616
Telephone: (501) 423-6312
Founded in: 1955
Eunice Southard, Secretary
Number of members: 800
Staff: part time 3, volunteer 4
Magazine: *Carroll County Historical Society Quarterly*
Major programs: museum, historic site(s), markers, oral history
Period of collections: 1830-present

CLARKSVILLE

Johnson County Historical Society
P.O. Box 505, 72830
Telephone: (501) 754-2824
Founded in: 1974
Gene Riable, President
Number of members: 291
Staff: volunteer 7
Magazine: *Johnson County Historical Society Journal*
Major programs: library, tours/pilgrimages, school programs, newsletters/pamphlets, historic preservation
Period of collections: 1800-1900

CLINTON

Van Buren County Historical Society
P.O. Box 439, 72031
Telephone: (501) 884-3780
Founded in: 1976
Questionnaire not received

CONWAY

Faulkner County Historical Society
P.O. Box 731, 73032
Telephone: (501) 327-7788
Founded in: 1959
Guy W. Murphy, President
Number of members: 312
Magazine: *Faulkner Facts & Fiddlings*
Major programs: archives, manuscripts, historic site(s), markers, newsletters/pamphlets, historic preservation, audiovisual programs, photographic collections, genealogical services
Period of collections: 1880-present

DARDANELLE

Yell County Historical and Genealogical Society
Telephone: (501) 968-5760
Mail to: P.O. Box 356, Russellville, 72801
Founded in: 1976
Erma Lee Masters, President
Number of members: 398
Major programs: museum, book publishing, newsletters/pamphlets, research, county museum, genealogical services
Period of collections: 1860-present

DOLPH

Izard County Historical Society
P.O. Box 84, 72528
Telephone: (501) 297-3751

Founded in: 1969
Helen C. Lindley, Director
Number of members: 550
Staff: volunteer 3
Magazine: *Izard County Historian*
Major programs: archives, manuscripts, historic site(s), oral history, historic preservation, research
Period of collections: 1865-present

DUMAS

Desha County Museum Society
Hwy. 165, E
Telephone: (501) 382-4222
Mail to: P.O. Box 141, 71639
Private agency
Founded in: 1979
Mary Jo Tucker, Curator
Number of members: 125
Staff: part time 1, volunteer 10
Major programs: museum, historic preservation
Period of collections: early 20th century

EUREKA SPRINGS

Castle and Museum at Inspiration Point
Rt. 2, Box 375, 72632
Telephone: (501) 253-9462
Private agency
Founded in: 1973
Vernon R. Baker, Partner
Staff: part time 4
Major programs: museum
Period of collections: early 1900s

Gay 90 Button & Doll Museum
Rt. 1, Box 788, 72632
Telephone: (501) 253-9321
Private agency, authorized by Destiny of America Foundation, Inc.
Founded in: 1936
Muriel H. Schmidt, President
Staff: volunteer 5
Major programs: library, museum, exhibits, costume history
Period of collections: 1850-1950

Eureka Springs Preservation Society
172 Spring St.
Mail to: P.O. Box 404, 72632
Founded in: 1979
Harriett Mason, President
Number of members: 75
Major programs: library, tours/pilgrimages, newsletters/pamphlets, historic preservation

FAYETTEVILLE

◇**Arkansas Historical Association**
History Department, 12 Ozark Hall, University of Arkansas, 72701
Telephone: (501) 575-5884
Private agency
Founded in: 1942
Walter L. Brown, Editor/Secretary-Treasurer
Number of members: 1,800
Staff: full time 2
Magazine: *Arkansas Historical Quarterly*
Major programs: book publishing, newsletters

University Museum, University of Arkansas
338 Hotz Hall, 72701
Telephone: (501) 575-3555
State agency, authorized by the university
Founded in: 1873
Johnnie L. Gentry, Jr., Director
Number of members: 250
Staff: full time 6, part time 8, volunteer 10
Major programs: museum, tours/pilgrimages, school programs, newsletters/pamphlets, records management, research, exhibits, archaeology programs, photographic collections
Period of collections: 1870-present

Washington County Historical Society
30 S. College, 72701
Telephone: (501) 521-2970
Founded in: 1951
Magazine: *Flashback*
Questionnaire not received

FORDYCE

Dallas County Genealogical and Historical Society
P.O. Box 28, 71742
Telephone: (501) 352-7413
Founded in: 1980
Magazine: *The Heritage Hunter*
Questionnaire not received

FORT SMITH

Arkansas Museums Association
72901
Telephone: (501) 372-3601
Mail to: c/o Arkansas Museums Services, Department of Parks and Tourism, 1 Capitol Mall, Little Rock, 72201
Private agency
Sandra Robinson, President
Staff: volunteer 10
Major programs: museum association

Ft. Smith Historical Society, Inc.
61 S. 8th St., 72901
Telephone: (501) 783-0229
Founded in: 1977
C.B. "Pat" Porter, President
Number of members: 600
Staff: volunteer 24
Magazine: *The Journal*
Major programs: manuscripts, oral history, research, photographic collections
Period of collections: 1810-present

Ft. Smith National Historic Site
Corner of Rogers Ave. and 2nd St.
Telephone: (501) 783-3961
Mail to: P.O. Box 1406, 72902
Federal agency
Founded in: 1963
Jo Ann M. Kyral, Superintendent
Staff: full time 6, part time 3, volunteer 10
Major programs: library, archives, museum, historic site(s), tours/pilgrimages, educational programs, historic preservation, research
Period of collections: 1817-1896

Old Fort Museum
320 Rogers Ave., 72901
Telephone: (501) 783-7841
Private agency
Founded in: 1910
Sandra Robinson, Director
Number of members: 500
Staff: full time 2, part time 6, volunteer 20
Magazine: *Fort Smithsonian*
Major programs: museum, research, exhibits
Period of collections: 1870s-present

William D. Darby Ranger Memorial Foundation
301-11 N. 8th St., Bell Grove Historic District, 72901
Mail to: P.O. Box 1571, 72902
Questionnaire not received

GILLETT

Arkansas Post County Museum
P.O. Box 32, 72055
Telephone: (501) 548-2634
County agency
Founded in: 1964
Myrtle Bergschneider, Curator/Manager
Staff: full time 1, part time 2
Major programs: museum, tours/pilgrimages, oral history, school programs, records management, exhibits, living history, genealogical services
Period of collections: 1686-present

Grand Prairie Historical Society
P.O. Box 122, 72055
Telephone: (501) 548-2458
Founded in: 1953
Sibyl Hightower, Editor
Number of members: 199
Staff: volunteer 4
Magazine: *Grand Prairie Historical Bulletin*
Major programs: library, archives, markers, book publishing
Period of collections: pre-territorial

GREENWOOD

Old Jail Museum
P.O. Box 311, 72936
Telephone: (501) 996-2881
Town agency, authorized by South Sebastian County Historical Society
Founded in: 1966
Hubert Curry, Curator
Major programs: museum

South Sebastian County Historical Society
Rt. 3, Box 42, 72936
Telephone: (501) 996-2843
Town agency
Founded in: 1963
Hubert Curry, Curator/Editor
Number of members: 300
Staff: volunteer 2
Magazine: *The Key*
Major programs: museum, markers, book publishing

HARRISON

Boone County Historical and Genealogical Society
P.O. Box 1094, 72601

Telephone: (501) 741-9012
Town agency
Robert McCorkindale, President
Number of members: 140
Staff: volunteer 8
Magazine: *Boone County Historian*
Major programs: historic site(s), markers, newsletters/pamphlets

HAZEN

Prairie County Historical Society
P.O. Box 451, 72064
Telephone: (501) 255-4522
Private agency
Founded in: 1982
Sam A. Weems, President
Number of members: 78
Staff: volunteer 5
Major programs: historic site(s), markers, oral history, school programs, historic preservation, research, exhibits

HEBER SPRINGS

Greers Ferry Visitor Center
Hwy. 25, N
Telephone: (501) 362-2416
Mail to: P.O. Box 310, 72543
Federal agency, authorized by U.S. Army Corps of Engineers
Founded in: 1983
Tony Perrin, Administrator
Number of members: 1
Staff: full time 1, part time 6
Major programs: exhibits, audiovisual programs
Period of collections: prehistoric-present

HELENA

Phillips County Foundation For Historic Preservation, Inc.
The Almer Store, Columbia at Miller Sts. 72342
Questionnaire not received

Phillips County Historical Society
623 Pecan St., 72342
Telephone: (501) 338-3537
Founded in: 1962
Number of members: 275
Magazine: *Phillips County Historical Quarterly*

Phillips County Museum
623 Pecan St., 72342
Telephone: (501) 338-3537
City and county agency, authorized by Helena Public Library Association
Founded in: 1929
Dale P. Kirkman, President
Number of members: 250
Staff: part time 1, volunteer 5
Major programs: library, exhibits, photographic collections, costume history
Period of collections: 1850-1900

HOT SPRINGS

Garland County Historical Society
914 Summer St., 71913
Telephone: (501) 623-5875
Private agency
Founded in: 1960
Inez E. Cline, County Historian
Number of members: 300

Magazine: *The Record*
Major programs: library, oral history, book publishing, photographic collections, genealogical services
Period of collections: 1873-present

Melting Pot Genealogical Society
402 Winans, 71901
Mail to: P.O. Box 2186, 71901
Founded in: 1976
Questionnaire not received

JASPER

Newton County Historical and Genealogical Society
P.O. Box 65, 72683
Telephone: (501) 434-5931
County agency
Thomas Niswonger, Secretary
Number of members: 100
Staff: volunteer 4
Magazine: *Newton County Homestead*
Major programs: records management
Period of collections: 1850-1900

JONESBORO

Arkansas State University Museum
P.O. Box 490, 72467
Telephone: (501) 972-2074
State agency, authorized by the university
Founded in: 1936
Charlott Jones, Director
Staff: full time 3, part time 6, volunteer 2
Major programs: library, manuscripts, museum, school programs, newsletters/pamphlets, research, exhibits, photographic collections
Period of collections: 1850-1950

Craighead County Historical Society
P.O. Box 1011, 72401
Telephone: (501) 932-9451
Private agency
Founded in: 1962
Herschel Eaton, President
Number of members: 210
Staff: volunteer 4
Magazine: *The Craighead County Historical Quarterly*
Major programs: archives, manuscripts, tours/pilgrimages, junior history, book publishing, photographic collections
Period of collections: 1865-1918

LEPANTO

Museum Lepanto U.S.A.
Main St., 72354
Founded in: 1980
JaRue Bradford, President
Number of members: 220
Staff: volunteer 4
Major programs: museum, tours, school programs, historic preservation, research, exhibits, photographic collections

LEWISVILLE

Lafayette County Historical Society
Telephone: (501) 921-4785
Mail to: P.O. Box 91, 71845
Private agency

Tom Maryman, President
Number of members: 120
Staff: volunteer 4
Major programs: archives, historic site(s), markers, historic preservation, genealogical services

LITTLE ROCK

Arkansas Archivists and Records Managers
1025 McCullough, Camden, 71701
Private agency
Founded in: 1979
Beverly Watkins, President
Number of members: 45
Major programs: tours/pilgrimages, newsletters/pamphlets, records management, workshops, seminars

Arkansas Endowment for the Humanities
1010 W. 3rd St., 72201
Telephone: (501) 372-2672
Private agency, authorized by National Endowment for the Humanities
Founded in: 1974
Jane Browning, Executive Director
Staff: full time 7, part time 2, volunteer 1
Magazine: *Reflections*
Major programs: archives, oral history, book publishing, research, exhibits, audiovisual programs, photographic collections
Period of collections: late 19th-early 20th century

◇**Arkansas History Commission**
1 Capitol Mall, 72201
Telephone: (501) 371-2141
State agency
Founded in: 1909
John L. Ferguson, Director
Staff: full time 20
Major programs: archives, manuscripts, records management, genealogical services
Period of collections: 1750-present

Arkansas Museum of Science and History
MacArthur Park, 72202
Telephone: (501) 371-3521
City agency
Founded in: 1941
Alison Sanchez, Executive Director
Number of members: 660
Staff: full time 7, part time 3, volunteer 20
Major programs: manuscripts, museum, junior history, school programs, book publishing, newsletters/pamphlets, exhibits, living history, audiovisual programs, statewide outreach, television programs, science programs

◇**Arkansas Museum Services**
Department of Parks and Tourism, 1 Capitol Mall, 72201
Telephone: (501) 371-3603
State agency, authorized by Arkansas General Assembly
Founded in: 1979

Wesley S. Creel, Director
Staff: full time 10
Major programs: museum, field services, grants-in-aid, technical and professional publications
Period of collections: late 19th-mid 20th centuries

Arkansas Territorial Restoration
3rd and Scott, 72201
Telephone: (501) 371-2348
State agency, authorized by Arkansas General Assembly
Founded in: 1939
William B. Worthen, Director
Staff: full time 16, part time 4, volunteer 20
Magazine: *Territorial Times*
Major programs: museum, historic site(s), tours/pilgrimages, school programs newsletters/pamphlets, historic preservation, research, museum
Period of collections: 1820-1870

Civil War Round Table of Arkansas
P.O. Box 7281, 72217
Telephone: (501) 225-3996
Private agency
Founded in: 1964
Jerry L. Russell, President
Number of members: 52
Major programs: tours/pilgrimages, newsletters/pamphlets
Period of collections: 1861-1865

Civil War Round Table Associates
9 Lefever Lane, 72207
Telephone: (501) 225-3996
Mail to: P.O. Box 7388, 72217
Private agency
Founded in: 1968
Jerry L. Russell, National Chair
Number of members: 1,100
Staff: volunteer 1
Magazine: *Civil War Round Table Digest*
Major programs: newsletters/pamphlets, historic preservation, annual meeting

Confederate Historical Institute
9 Lefever Lane, 72207
Telephone: (501) 225-3996
Mail to: P.O. Box 7388, 72217
Private agency
Founded in: 1979
Jerry L. Russell, National Chair
Number of members: 500
Magazine: *CHI Journal, CHI Dispatch*
Major programs: newsletters/pamphlets, historic preservation, annual meeting

Department of Arkansas Natural and Cultural Heritage
225 E. Markham, The Heritage East Bldg., Suite 200, 72201
Telephone: (501) 371-1639
State agency, authorized by Arkansas General Assembly
Founded in: 1975
Tom W. Dillard, Department Director
Staff: full time 81, part time 13
Magazine: *DANCH Directions*
Major programs: museum, historic site(s), school programs, book publishing, newsletters/pamphlets, historic preservation, records management, exhibits, audiovisual

programs, photographic collections
Period of collections: 1970-present

Historic Preservation Alliance of Arkansas
16th and Main, Madison Square
Telephone: (501) 372-4756
Mail to: P.O. Box 305, 72202
Private agency
Founded in: 1981
Sandra Hanson, Executive Director
Number of members: 900
Staff: part time 1, volunteer 2
Magazine: *Arkansas Preservation*
Major programs: tours/pilgrimages, newsletters/pamphlets, historic preservation, workshops, conferences

Old State House—Arkansas Commemorative Commission
300 W. Markham, 72201
Telephone: (501) 371-1749
Founded in: 1947
Lucy Kelly Robinson, Director
Staff: full time 22, part time 12
Major programs: museum, historic site(s), tours/pilgrimages, school programs, book publishing, newsletters/pamphlets, research, exhibits
Period of collections: 1840-1930

Oral History Program
33rd and University Ave., 72204
Telephone: (501) 569-3235
State agency, authorized by University of Arkansas at Little Rock
Founded in: 1975
Frances M. Ross, Director
Major programs: oral history, women's history

Order of the Indian Wars
9 Lefever Lane, 72207
Telephone: (501) 225-3996
Mail to: P.O. Box 7401, 72217
Founded in: 1979
Jerry L. Russell, National Chair
Number of members: 450
Staff: full time 1
Magazine: *OIW Journal Communique*
Major programs: annual meeting, newsletters/pamphlets, historic preservation

Pulaski County Historical Society
Telephone: (501) 663-7161
Mail to: P.O. Box 653, 72203
County agency
Founded in: 1951
Martha Williamson Rimmer, Editor
Number of members: 400
Staff: volunteer 10
Magazine: *Pulaski County Historical Review*
Major programs: markers, school programs, books, newsletters/pamphlets, historical journal

Quapaw Quarter Association
1321 S. Scott
Telephone: (501) 371-0075
Mail to: P.O. Box 1104, 72203
Private agency
Founded in: 1968
Cheryl G. Nichols, Executive Director
Number of members: 800

Staff: full time 1, part time 5
Magazine: *Quapaw Quarter Chronicle*
Major programs: library, archives, historic site(s), markers, tours/pilgrimages, historic preservation
Period of collections: 1819-1930

Revolutionary War Studies Forum
9 Lefever Lane
Telephone: (501) 225-3996
Mail to: P.O. Box 7401, 72207
Founded in: 1979
Jerry L. Russell, Historical Chair
Number of members: 150
Staff: full time 1
Magazine: *RWSF Journal*
Major programs: book publishing, newsletters/pamphlets, historic preservation

Victorian Military History Institute
P.O. Box 7401, 72207
Telephone: (501) 225-3996
Private agency
Founded in: 1983
Jerry L. Russell, Colonial Chair
Number of members: 225
Magazine: *Blue Book*
Major programs: newsletters/pamphlets
Period of collections: 1830-1905

LONOKE

Lonoke County Historical Society
P.O. Box 14, 72086
Telephone: (501) 676-2467
County agency
Founded in: 1980
Wayne Bennett, President
Number of members: 220
Staff: full time 12
Major programs: oral history, newsletters/pamphlets, field services

MALVERN

Hot Spring County Historical Society
2705 Southgate Dr.
Telephone: (501) 337-7488
Mail to: P.O. Box 674, 72104
County agency
Founded in: 1968
Number of members: 200
Magazine: *The Heritage*
Major programs: library, markers, oral history, book publishing, research, genealogical services
Period of collections: 1825-1925

Hot Spring County Museum—The Boyle House
302 E. 3rd St.
Telephone: (501) 332-5442
Mail to: 1220 Brownwood St., 72104
County agency, authorized by Hot Spring County Museum Commission
Founded in: 1979
Dorothy M. Keith, Director
Number of members: 100
Staff: volunteer 75
Major programs: museum, school programs, historic preservation, records management, exhibits
Period of collections: 1900

MARIANNA

Marianna-Lee County Museum
67 W. Main, 72360
Telephone: (501) 295-2469
Private agency
Founded in: 1982
Mrs. Tom Gist, Sr., President
Number of members: 100
Staff: volunteer 5
Major programs: museum

MARSHALL

Searcy County Historical Society
Mail to: P.O. Box 233, 72650
Questionnaire not received

MONTICELLO

Drew County Historical Society and Museum
404 S. Main St., 71655
Telephone: (501) 367-7446
Private agency
Founded in: 1959
Mrs. Barnett Miles, Board Chair
Number of members: 150
Staff: part time 4, volunteer 5
Major programs: archives, museum, markers
Period of collections: 1819-present

MOUNTAIN HOME

Baxter County Historical Society
c/o Vice President, 1210 Heatherdown Trail, 72653
Telephone: (501) 425-4269
County agency
Founded in: 1974
Quinby Smith, Vice President
Number of members: 100
Staff: volunteer 8
Major programs: newsletters/pamphlets, historic preservation, research, photographic collections

MOUNTAIN VIEW

Ozark Folk Center
P.O. Box 500, 72560
Telephone: (501) 269-3851
State agency, authorized by Arkansas Department of Parks and Tourism
Founded in: 1973
C. R. von Kronemann, General Manager
Staff: full time 20, part time 300, volunteer 110
Major programs: library, archives, manuscripts, museum, oral history, school programs, research, exhibits
Period of collections: 1820-1940

NEWPORT

Jackson County Historical Society
Telephone: (501) 523-6751
Founded in: 1961
Wayne Boyce, President
Number of members: 450
Staff: volunteer 3
Magazine: *The Stream of History*
Major programs: library, archives, manuscripts, museum, historic preservation, markers, books, newsletters/pamphlets
Period of collections: 1865-1918

PARIS

Logan County Historical Society
P.O. Box B, 72855
Telephone: (501) 675-4680
Founded in: 1980
Emma Parker, Secretary
Number of members: 389
Staff: volunteer 18
Magazine: *Wagon Wheels*
Major programs: library, archives,
oral history, school programs,
newsletters/pamphlets,
genealogical collections
Period of collections: 1830-1900

PINE BLUFF

**Jefferson County Historical
Society**
610 W. 35th St., 71603
Telephone: (501) 534-8596
Founded in: 1969
Mrs. William D. Hercher, President
Number of members: 200
Staff: volunteer 27
Magazine: *Jefferson County
Historical Quarterly*
Major programs: manuscripts,
museum, historic site(s), markers,
oral history, historic preservation,
research, audiovisual programs,
archaeology programs,
genealogical services
Period of collections: 1830-1930

**Southeast Arkansas Arts and
Science Center**
200 E. 8th, 71601
Telephone: (501) 536-3375
City agency
Founded in: 1968
Nelson C. Britt, Executive Director
Number of members: 600
Staff: full time 8, part time 14,
volunteer 200
Major programs: museum,
tours/pilgrimages, junior history,
school programs,
newsletters/pamphlets, records
management, research, exhibits,
audiovisual programs,
photographic collections, fine arts,
science programs

PINE RIDGE

Lum and Abner Museum
Hwy. 88
Telephone: (501) 326-4442
Mail to: P.O. Box 38, 71966
Private agency
Founded in: 1971
Kathryn Stucker, Manager
Staff: full time 2
Major programs: museum, historic
site(s), historic preservation,
exhibits, photographic collections
Period of collections: 1920-1940s

POCAHONTAS

**Good Earth
Association, Inc.—Living Farm
Museum of the Ozarks**
202 E. Church St., 72455-2899
Telephone: (501) 892-9545
Private agency
Founded in: 1984
Donald L. Waterworth, Sr., Board
Chair

Number of members: 54
Magazine: *Family Farm Fact Finder*
Major programs: living history,
preservation of historical farm
equipment
Period of collections: 1850-1950

POWHATAN

**Lawrence County Historical
Society**
Powhatan Courthouse, 72458
Telephone: (501) 878-6794
Founded in: 1973
Mrs. Bobby Flippo, President
Number of members: 150
Staff: full time 1
Major programs: archives, museum,
historic site(s), tours/pilgrimages,
historic preservation, research,
exhibits, photographic collections,
genealogical services

PRAIRIE GROVE

**Prairie Grove Battlefield Historic
State Park**
Hwy. 62, E
Telephone: (501) 846-2990
Mail to: P.O. Box 306, 72753
State agency, authorized by
Department of Parks and Tourism
Founded in: 1911
Ed Smith, Superintendent
Staff: full time 6
Major programs: museum, historic
site(s), markers, tours/pilgrimages,
oral history, historic preservation,
living history
Period of collections: 1860-1865

ROGERS

Rogers Historical Museum
322 S. 2nd St., 72756
Telephone: (501) 636-0162
City agency
Founded in: 1975
Marianne Woods, Director
Number of members: 365
Staff: full time 1, part time 1
Magazine: *The Friendly Note*
Major programs: museum,
tours/pilgrimages, junior history,
oral history, school programs,
newsletters/pamphlets, exhibits,
audiovisual programs,
photographic collections
Period of collections: 1880-present

RUSSELLVILLE

Pope County Historical Foundation
2206 Red Hill Lane, 72801
Telephone: (501) 968-1147
County agency
Founded in: 1970
Marjorie W. Crabaugh, President
Staff: part time 2, volunteer 2
Major programs: museum,
tours/pilgrimages,
newsletters/pamphlets, historic
preservation
Period of collections: 1850-1970

**Yell County Arkansas Historical
and Genealogical Association**
108 W. 18th
Telephone: (501) 968-5760
Mail to: P.O. Box 356, 72801

County agency
Founded in: 1975
Mary V. Humphrey, Corresponding
Secretary/Editor
Number of members: 400
Major programs:
newsletters/pamphlets, historic
preservation, genealogical
services
Period of collections: 1840-present

SCOTT

Toltec Mounds State Park
1 Toltec Mounds Rd.
Telephone: (501) 961-9442
State agency, authorized by
Arkansas Department of Parks and
Tourism
Founded in: 1975
James E. Mullins, Superintendent
Staff: full time 6, part time 2
Major programs: manuscripts,
museum, historic site(s), markers,
tours/pilgrimages, oral history,
school programs, book publishing,
newsletters/pamphlets, historic
preservation, records
management, research, exhibits,
audiovisual programs, archaeology
programs, photographic
collections, field services
Period of collections: 600-900

SHERIDAN

Grant County Museum
409 W. Center St., Hwy. 270, W,
72150
Telephone: (501) 942-4496
County agency
Founded in: 1970
Elwin L. Goolsby, Museum Director
Staff: full time 1, part time 3,
volunteer 10
Major programs: museum, oral
history, school programs, book
publishing, newsletters/pamphlets,
historic preservation, records
management, research, exhibits,
audiovisual programs,
photographic collections,
genealogical services
Period of collections: to present

Grant County Museum Guild
409 W. Center St., 72150
Telephone: (501) 942-4496
County agency
Founded in: 1981
Elwin L. Goolsby, Museum Director
Number of members: 275
Staff: full time 1, part time 1,
volunteer 1
Magazine: *Grassroots*
Major programs: museum, historic
preservation

SILOAM SPRINGS

Benton County Historical Society
Telephone: (501) 524-3217
Mail to: P.O. Box 355, 72761
Founded in: 1954
Questionnaire not received

**Benton County Sesquicentennial
Committee**
P.O. Box 411, 72761
Telephone: (501) 524-3591

County agency
Founded in: 1982
Maggie Smith, Sesquicentennial
  Coordinator
Magazine: *Sessie Facts*
Major programs: library, archives,
  museum, historic site(s), markers,
  tours/pilgrimages, oral history,
  school programs,
  newsletters/pamphlets, living
  history
Period of collections: 1836-present

Siloam Springs Museum
112 N. Maxwell
Telephone: (501) 524-4011
Mail to: P.O. Box 1164, 72761
Private agency, authorized by Siloam
  Springs Museum Society
Founded in: 1969
Gaye Keller Bland, Director
Number of members: 110
Staff: full time 1, part time 1,
  volunteer 4
Magazine: *The Hummer*
Major programs: archives, museum,
  newsletters/pamphlets, research,
  exhibits, photographic collections
Period of collections: 1850-1920

SMACKOVER

Arkansas Oil and Brine Museum
P.O. Box 77, 71762
Telephone: (501) 725-2877
State agency, authorized by
  Department of Parks and Tourism
Founded in: 1980
Don Lambert, Director
Staff: full time 6, part time 3,
  volunteer 6
Major programs: library, archives,
  manuscripts, museum, oral history,
  school programs,
  newsletters/pamphlets, research,
  exhibits, living history, audiovisual
  programs, photographic
  collections
Period of collections: 1920s-present

SPRINGDALE

Shiloh Museum
118 W. Johnson, 72764
Telephone: (501) 751-8411
City agency
Founded in: 1965
Robert D. Besom, Director
Number of members: 400
Staff: full time 3, part time 3,
  volunteer 18
Major programs: library, archives,
  manuscripts, museum, historic
  site(s), tours/pilgrimages, junior
  history, school programs,
  newsletters/pamphlets, historic
  preservation, research, exhibits,
  audiovisual programs,
  photographic collections
Period of collections: prehistoric-1930

STUTTGART

Stuttgart Agricultural Museum
921 E. 4th, 72160
Telephone: (501) 673-7001
Founded in: 1973
Helen L. Boyd, Director
Staff: full time 3, part time 3,
  volunteer 20

Major programs: museum,
  tours/pilgrimages, oral history,
  school programs,
  newsletters/pamphlets, historic
  preservation, records
  management, exhibits, audiovisual
  programs, photographic
  collections
Period of collections: 1887-1930

VAN BUREN

Crawford County Historical Society
P.O. Box 1317, 72956
Private agency
Founded in: 1957
Mrs. James E. West, Editor
Number of members: 150
Staff: volunteer 8
Magazine: *The Heritage*
Major programs: library, museum,
  markers, tours/pilgrimages, oral
  history, school programs, book
  publishing, historic preservation,
  research, exhibits, photographic
  collections, genealogical services

WASHINGTON

Old Washington Historic State Park
Telephone: (501) 983-2684
Mail to: P.O. Box 98, 71862
State agency, authorized by
  Department of Parks and Tourism
Founded in: 1973
Staff: full time 17, part time 10
Major programs: library, archives,
  manuscripts, museum, historic
  site(s), markers, tours/pilgrimages,
  oral history, school programs,
  newsletters/pamphlets, historic
  preservation, research, exhibits,
  living history, audiovisual
  programs, archaeology programs
Period of collections: 1824-1874

**SARA (Southwest Arkansas
  Regional Archives)**
P.O. Box 134, 71862
Telephone: (501) 983-2633
Private agency, authorized by Old
  Washington Historic State Park
Founded in: 1978
Mary Medearis, Director
Staff: full time 1, volunteer 5
Major programs: library, archives,
  manuscripts, research,
  photographic collections,
  genealogical services,
  cosponsorship of college credit
  course "Folkways Of Arkansas Red
  River Valley"
Period of collections: 1810-present

WEST FORK

Devil's Den State Park
72774
Telephone: (501) 761-3325
State agency, authorized by
  Department of Parks and Tourism
Founded in: 1925
Wally Scherrey, Park Superintendent
Staff: full time 6, part time 1
Major programs: oral history, school
  programs, exhibits, living history,
  audiovisual programs, archaeology
  programs
Period of collections: 1933-1942

WEST MEMPHIS

**Crittenden County Historical
  Society, Inc.**
401 Gibson, 72301
Telephone: (501) 735-1659
Private agency
Founded in: 1974
Mrs. Thomas J. Sims, President
Number of members: 25
Major programs: library, museum,
  slide program, photographic
  collections
Period of collections: 20th century

WYNNE

Cross County Genealogical Society
313 E. Merriman
Telephone: (501) 238-9219
Mail to: P.O. Box 1274, 72396
County agency
Founded in: 1982
Johnnie R. Swan, President
Number of members: 12
Staff: volunteer 5
Major programs: genealogical
  services

**Cross County Historical
  Society, Inc.**
Cross County Courthouse, 705 E.
  Union
Mail to: P.O. Box 943, 72396
Founded in: 1972
Mrs. Jimmie S. James,
  Secretary/Treasurer
Number of members: 45
Staff: full time 1
Major programs: archives,
  manuscripts, book publishing,
  historic preservation, research,
  photographic collections,
  genealogical services
Period of collections: from 1862

CALIFORNIA

AGOURA

Las Virgenes Historical Society
30473-50 Mulholland Hwy.
Telephone: (818) 889-0836
Mail to: P.O. Box 124, 91301
Private agency
Founded in: 1977
A.J. "Sandy" Sandoval, President
Number of members: 103
Staff: volunteer 15
Major programs: library, historic
  site(s), oral history,
  newsletters/pamphlets, historic
  preservation, records
  management, research, living
  history, photographic collections
Period of collections: 1900-present

ALAMEDA

Alameda Historical Society
2264 Santa Clara Ave., 94501
Questionnaire not received

ALTURAS

Modoc County Historical Society and Museum
600 S. Main St., 96101
Telephone: (916) 233-2944
County agency
Founded in: 1967
Add Odgers, Museum Curator
Number of members: 700
Staff: full time 1, part time 2, volunteer 5
Major programs: archives, museum, tours/pilgrimages, oral history, book publishing, newsletters/pamphlets, research, exhibits, photographic collections
Period of collections: 1850-1930

ANAHEIM

Mother Colony Household
685 N. Helena, 92805
Telephone: (714) 854-1115
Mail to: P.O. Box 3246, 92803

ARCADIA

Los Angeles State and County Arboretum
301 N. Baldwin Ave., 91006
Telephone: (818) 446-8251
County agency
Founded in: 1948
Sandra Snider, Curator Associate
Staff: full time 1, volunteer 25
Magazine: *Garden*
Major programs: library, archives, museum, historic site(s), oral history, school programs, newsletters/pamphlets, photographic collections
Period of collections: 1840-1909

ATASCADERO

Atascadero Historical Society
6500 Palma Ave.
Telephone: (805) 466-0506
Mail to: P.O. Box 1047, 93423
Private agency
Founded in: 1965
Clark Herman, President
Number of members: 125
Staff: volunteer 25
Major programs: archives, museum, tours/pilgrimages, oral history, book publishing, exhibits, photographic collections
Period of collections: 1900-1930

ATWATER

Atwater Historical Society, Inc.
1020 Cedar Ave.
Telephone: (209) 358-6955
Mail to: P.O. Box 111, 95301
Founded in: 1971
Questionnaire not received

Castle Air Museum
Sante Fe Hwy.
Telephone: (209) 723-2178
Mail to: P.O. Box 488, 95301
Private agency, authorized by U.S. Air Force Museum
Russell J. Morrison, Executive Director
Number of members: 401

Staff: full time 3, part time 4, volunteer 800
Major programs: library, museum, tours/pilgrimages, oral history, school programs, newsletters/pamphlets, historic preservation, exhibits, photographic collections
Period of collections: 1903-present

AUBURN

Placer County Historical Society
1273 High St.
Telephone: (916) 885-9570
Mail to: P.O. Box 643, 95603
Private agency
Founded in: 1955
Howard A. Fleming, Jr., President pro tem
Number of members: 250
Staff: volunteer 10
Magazine: *Newsletter*
Major programs: historic preservation
Period of collections: late 19th-early 20th centuries

Placer County Museum
1273 High St.
Telephone: (916) 885-9570
Mail to: 175 Fulweiler Ave., 95603
Founded in: 1948
David Tucker, Director
Number of members: 400
Staff: full time 3, part time 3 volunteer 40
Major programs: archives, museum, historic site(s), research, exhibits, photographic collections
Period of collections: 1850s-1940s

Placer County Parks and Historical Restoration Commission
175 Fulweiler Ave., Room 501, 95603
Questionnaire not received

AVALON

Catalina Island Museum Society, Inc.
Casino Bldg.
Mail to: P.O. Box 366, 90704
Private agency
Founded in: 1953
Patricia Anne Moore, Director/Curator
Number of members: 400
Staff: part time 2, volunteer 4
Major programs: archives, museum, oral history, school programs, book publishing, photographic collections
Period of collections: prehistoric-present

AZUSA

Azusa Historical Society, Inc.
City Hall Complex, 213 E. Foothill Blvd., 91702
Private agency
Founded in: 1960
Jack E. Williams, President
Number of members: 60
Staff: volunteer 10
Major programs: archives, museum, educational programs, photographic collections, Azusa history and memorabilia
Period of collections: 1865-present

BAKERSFIELD

Kern County Historical Society
P.O. Box 141, 93302
Telephone: (805) 325-4558
Founded in: 1931
W. Harland Voyd, Historian
Number of members: 350
Staff: volunteer 15
Magazine: *Historic Kern*
Major programs: markers, tours/pilgrimages, oral history, school programs book publishing, newsletters/pamphlets, historic sites preservation
Period of collections: 1850-present

Kern County Museum
3801 Chester Ave., 93301
Telephone: (805) 861-2132
County agency
Founded in: 1941
Staff: full time 9, part time 7
Major programs: museum, historic site(s), school programs, exhibits, photographic collections
Period of collections: 1860-1930s

BARSTOW

Mojave River Valley Museum Association
Virginia Way and Barstow Rd.
Telephone: (619) 256-5452
Mail to: P.O. Box 1282, 92311
Private agency
Founded in: 1964
Mrs. William Peterson, President
Number of members: 100
Staff: volunteer 10
Period of collections: 1776-present

BELVEDERE-TIBURON

Belvedere-Tiburon Landmarks Society
Esperanza St.
Telephone: (415) 435-1853
Mail to: P.O. Box 134, 94920
Founded in: 1959
Thomas Brown, President
Number of members: 600
Staff: part time 2, volunteer 30
Magazine: *The Landmark*
Major programs: library, archives, museum, historic preservation, markers, tours/pilgrimages, school programs, books, newsletters/pamphlets
Period of collections: 1865-present

BENICIA

Benicia Capitol State Historic Park
Telephone: (707) 745-3385
Mail to: P.O. Box 5, 94510
State agency, authorized by Department f Parks and Recreation
Founded in: 1956
Mary Angle, State Park Ranger
Staff: full time 4, part time 2, volunteer 25
Major programs: museum, tours/pilgrimages, school programs, historic preservation, living history
Period of collections: 1853-1854

Fischer-Hanlon House
131 G St.
Telephone: (707) 745-3385
Mail to: P.O. Box 5, 94510
State agency
Founded in: 1976
Mary Angle, State Park Ranger
Number of members: 50
Staff: full time 3, part time 1,
    volunteer 10
Magazine: *The Strait Facts*
Major programs: tours/pilgrimages
Period of collections: 1870-1890

BERKELEY

The Bancroft Library
University of California, Berkeley,
    94720
Telephone: (415) 642-6481
Authorized by Regents, University of
    California, Berkeley
Founded in: 1905
James D. Hart, Director
Magazine: *Bancroftiana*
Major programs: library, archives,
    manuscripts, oral history, exhibits,
    photographic collections

Berkeley Historical Society
2318-D McKinley St.
Telephone: (415) 540-0809
Mail to: P.O. Box 1190, 94701
Private agency
Founded in: 1978
T. Robert Yamada, President
Number of members: 250
Staff: volunteer 22
Major programs: library, archives,
    oral history, school programs, book
    publishing, newsletters/pamphlets,
    records management, research,
    exhibits, photographic collections

Council for Museum Anthropology
Lowie Museum of Anthropology,
    University of California, Berkeley,
    94720
Telephone: (415) 642-3681
Private agency
Founded in: 1975
Frank A. Norick, President
Number of members: 275
Staff: volunteer 12
Major programs: museum, book
    publishing, research, exhibits,
    archaeology programs,
    photographic collections

**R.H. Lowie Museum of
    Anthropology**
103 Kroeber Hall, University of
    California, Berkeley, 94720
Telephone: (415) 642-3681
State agency, authorized by Regents,
    University of California, Berkeley
Founded in: 1901
James Deetz, Director
Staff: full time 14, part time 31,
    volunteer 15
Major programs: museum, book
    publishing, research, exhibits,
    archaeology programs,
    photographic collections
Period of collections:
    Palaeolithic-present

**Western Jewish History
    Center—Judah L. Magnes
    Memorial Museum**
2911 Russell St., 94705
Telephone: (415) 849-2710
Private agency
Magnes Museum
Founded in: 1967
Ruth Rafael, Archivist
Number of members: 600
Staff: part time 2, volunteer 7
Major programs: library, archives,
    manuscripts, museum, historic
    site(s), markers, oral history, book
    publishing, historic preservation,
    research, exhibits, photographic
    collections, genealogical services,
    public outreach
Period of collections: 1840s-present

BIG BEAR CITY

Big Bear Valley Historical Society
P.O. Box 513, 92314
Telephone: (714) 585-8100/585-2371
Private agency
Founded in: 1967
Beverly Abbott, President
Number of members: 200
Staff: volunteer 40
Magazine: *Tall Pines Monthly*
Major programs: museum,
    tours/pilgrimages, school
    programs, book publishing, historic
    preservation, research,
    photographic collections,
Period of collections: 1850-1920

BISHOP

**Bishop Museum and Historical
    Society**
Laws Railroad Museum
Telephone: (619) 873-5950
Mail to: P.O. Box 363, 93514
Private agency
Founded in: 1966
Alice J. Boothe, Administrator
Number of members: 600
Staff: full time 4, volunteer 6
Major programs: library, museum,
    historic site(s), newsletters,
    pamphlets, historic preservation
Period of collections: 1883-present

BOLINAS

Bolinas Historical Society
P.O. Box 1007, 94924
Telephone: (415) 868-1729
Founded in: 1982
Ray Moritz, President
Number of members: 100
Staff: volunteer 80
Magazine: *Bolinas Historical
    Quarterly*
Major programs: oral history,
    photographic collections
Period of collections: 1830-present

BOONVILLE

**Anderson Valley Historical
    Museum**
Hwy. 128, N
Telephone: (707) 895-3207
Mail to: P.O. Box 676, 95415
Private agency

Founded in: 1978
Mrs. Walter L. Tuttle, Secretary
Number of members: 400
Staff: volunteer 10
Major programs: manuscripts,
    museum, historic site(s), junior
    history, school programs, book
    publishing, newsletters/pamphlets,
    historic preservation, records
    management, research, exhibits,
    photographic collections
Period of collections: late 1900s

BRENTWOOD

**East Contra Costa Historical
    Society**
2nd and Dainty, 94513
Questionnaire not received

BUENA PARK

Buena Park Historical Society
7842 Whitaker St., 90621
Founded in: 1968
Questionnaire not received

BURBANK

Walt Disney Archives
500 S. Buena Vista, 91521
Telephone: (818) 840-5424
Private agency, authorized by Walt
    Disney Productions
Founded in: 1970
David R. Smith, Archivist
Staff: full time 3
Major programs: library, archives,
    manuscripts, museum, oral history,
    photographic collections,
    entertainment
Period of collections: 1918-present

CALISTOGA

Bale Grist Mill State Historic Park
3801 St. Helena Hwy., N
Telephone: (707) 942-4575
Mail to: Bothe-Napa Valley State Park,
    94515
State agency, authorized by
    Department of Parks and
    Recreation
Founded in: 1846
Paula J. Peterson, District
    Superintendent
Major programs: historic sites
    preservation
Period of collections: 1860s

Sharpsteen Museum Association
1311 Washington St.
Telephone: (707) 942-5911
Mail to: P.O. Box 573, 94515
Founded in: 1978
Barbara Wurz, President
Number of members: 325
Staff: volunteer 65
Major programs: museum,
    tours/pilgrimages, junior history,
    exhibits
Period of collections: 1840-1912

CAMPBELL

Campbell Historical Museum
1st St. and Civic Center Dr.
Telephone: (408) 866-2119
Mail to: 51 N. Central Ave., 95008
City agency
Founded in: 1964

Peggy Coats, Historical Resources
  Coordinator
Number of members: 275
Staff: full time 1, part time 1,
  volunteer 43
Magazine: *Campbell Historical Visitor*
Major programs: museum, historic
  site(s), oral history, school
  programs, records management,
  research, exhibits, photographic
  collections
Period of collections: 1840-present

CARPINTERIA

**Carpinteria Valley Historical
Society and Museum**
956 Maple Ave., 93013
Telephone: (805) 684-3112
Private agency
Founded in: 1959
Kerry Candaete, Director
Number of members: 375
Staff: full time 1, volunteer 82
Magazine: *The Grapevine*
Major programs: library, museum,
  historic site(s), markers,
  tours/pilgrimages, junior history,
  oral history, school programs, book
  publishing, newsletters/pamphlets,
  historic preservation, research,
  exhibits, audiovisual programs,
  photographic collections,
  genealogical services
Period of collections: 10,000
  B.C.-1915

CHATSWORTH

Chatsworth Historical Society
Chatsworth Museum, 10385 Shadow
  Oak Dr.
Mail to: P.O. Box 413, 91311
Founded in: 1963
Questionnaire not received

CHEROKEE

**Cherokee Heritage and Museum
Association**
Rt. 7, Box 297, 95965
Telephone: (916) 533-1849
Private agency
Founded in: 1980
James W. Lenkoff, President
Number of members: 38
Staff: full time 4
Major programs: archives, museum,
  markers
Period of collections: 1850-1890

CHICO

**Association for Northern California
Records and Research**
1st and Hazel Sts.
Telephone: (916) 895-5710
Mail to: P.O. Box 3024, 95927
Private agency, authorized by
  Northern California University
  Foundation
Founded in: 1971
Margaret Trussell, Project Director
Number of members: 260
Staff: volunteer
Major programs: library, archives,
  manuscripts, oral history, school
  programs book publishing,
  newsletters/pamphlets,

photographic collections,
  genealogical services
Period of collections: 1850-1960

Bidwell Mansion Association
525 Esplanade, 95926
Telephone: (916) 895-6144
State agency, authorized by
  Department of Parks and
  Recreation
Founded in: 1958
Steve Feazel, State Park Ranger
Number of members: 250
Staff: volunteer 50
Major programs: library, archives,
  historic site(s), tours/pilgrimages,
  living history
Period of collections: 1840-1918

CHINA LAKE

**Maturango Museum of Indian Wells
Valley**
Halsey Ave.
Mail to: P.O. Box 1776, 93555
Founded in: 1962
Questionnaire not received

CHINO

Chino Valley Historical Society
5493 B St.
Telephone: (714) 628-1950
Mail to: P.O. Box 972, 91708
Private agency
Founded in: 1971
Charles Reher, President
Number of members: 180
Staff: volunteer 15
Major programs: library, manuscripts,
  museum, markers, school
  programs, newsletters/pamphlets,
  historic preservation, records
  management, exhibits,
  photographic collections
Period of collections: 1890-present

CITY OF INDUSTRY

**Workman and Temple
Homestead—Historical
Perspectives, Inc.**
15415 E. Don Julian Rd., 91744
Telephone: (818) 968-8492
City agency
Founded in: 1981
Carolyn Wagner, President
Staff: full time 6, part time 2,
  volunteer 20
Magazine: *Homestead Quarterly*
Major programs: museum, historic
  site(s), school programs, historic
  preservation, records
  management, research, exhibits
Period of collections: 1840-1930

CLAREMONT

Claremont Heritage
590 W. Bonita Ave.
Telephone: (714) 621-0848
Mail to: P.O. Box 742, 91711
Private agency
Founded in: 1977
Ginger Elliott, Executive Director
Number of members: 310
Staff: part time 1, volunteer 19
Magazine: *Heritage News*

Major programs: library,
  tours/pilgrimages, oral history,
  historic preservation
Period of collections: 1890-present

CLOVERDALE

Cloverdale Historical Society
215 N. Cloverdale Blvd.
Mail to: P.O. Box 433, 95425
Telephone: (707) 894-2246/894-2067
Private agency
Founded in: 1968
Jack D. Howell, President
Number of members: 40
Major programs: museum, historic
  site(s), oral history, book
  publishing, historic preservation,
  oral history, book publishing,
  historic preservation, exhibits,
  photographic collections
Period of collections: 1850-present

COALINGA

R.C. Baker Memorial Museum, Inc.
297 W. Elm, 93210
Telephone: (209) 935-1914
Private agency
Founded in: 1956
Audrey B. Acebedo,
  Curator/Secretary-Treasurer
Number of members: 200
Staff: full time 1, part time 1
Major programs: museum
Period of collections: 1890-1930

COLOMA

**Marshall Gold Discovery State
Historic Park**
P.O. Box 135, 95613
Telephone: (916) 622-3470
State agency, authorized by
  Department of Parks and
  Recreation
Founded in: 1937
Greg Picard, District Superintendent
Number of members: 80
Staff: full time 8, volunteer 12
Major programs: library, museum,
  historic site(s), markers, oral
  history, school programs, book
  publishing, historic preservation,
  research, exhibits, living history,
  audiovisual programs,
  photographic collections
Period of collections: 1848-1948

COLUMBIA

Columbia State Historic Park
Jackson St.
Telephone: (209) 532-0150
Mail to: P.O. Box 151, 95310
State agency, authorized by
  Department of Parks and
  Recreation
Founded in: 1945
John Hillerman, District Supervisor
Staff: full time 11, part time 2,
  volunteer 50
Major programs: archives, museum,
  historic site(s), tours, school
  programs, historic preservation,
  exhibits, living history,
  photographic collections
Period of collections: 1850-1900

COLUSA

Colusa County Historical Society
P.O. Box 448, 95932
Mail to: Rt. 1, Box 510, Glenn, 95943
Founded in: 1950
Questionnaire not received

CONCORD

Contra Costa County Historical Society
1700 Oak Park Blvd., Room C-5,
Pleasant Hill, 94523
Telephone: (415) 939-9180
Mail to: P.O. Box 821, 94522
Private agency
Andrew H. Young, President
Number of members: 200
Staff: volunteer 8
Major programs: archives,
photographic collections
Period of collections: 1850-present

CORONA DEL MAR

Sherman Library and Gardens
2647 E. Coast Hwy.
Telephone: (714) 673-1880
Mail to: 614 Dahlia Ave., 92625
W.O. Hendricks, Director of the
Library
Number of members: 2,400
Staff: full time 12, volunteer 66
Major programs: library, archives,
manuscripts, museum, school
programs newsletters/pamphlets
Period of collections: 1860s-present

CORONADO

Coronado Historical Association, Inc.
718 Orange Ave.
Mail to: P.O. Box 393, 92118
Private agency
Founded in: 1969
Gerry MacCartee, President
Major programs: museum, historic
preservation, markers, junior
history, oral history, school
programs newsletters/pamphlets
Period of collections: 1880s-1940

COSTA MESA

Costa Mesa Historical Society
595 Plumer St.
Mail to: P.O. Box 1764, 92628
Private agency
Founded in: 1966
Charles Ropp, President
Number of members: 211
Staff: volunteer 15
Major programs: library, archives,
historic site(s), oral history, school
programs, newsletters/pamphlets,
exhibits, photographic collections,
children's history
Period of collections: 1827-present

Pacific Coast Archaeological Society, Inc.
Telephone: (714) 848-3998
Mail to: P.O. Box 10926, 92627
Founded in: 1961
Pat Hammon, President
Number of members: 300
Staff: volunteer 40

Major programs: historic
preservation, school programs,
books, newsletters/pamphlets,
historic sites, archaeology
programs
Period of collections: prehistoric

COVINA

Covina Valley Historical Society, Inc.
125 E. College St., 91723
Founded in: 1969
Questionnaire not received

CUPERTINO

Cupertino Historical Society
Mail to: P.O. Box 88, 95015
Private agency
Founded in: 1965
Nancy Hertert, President
Number of members: 130
Staff: volunteer 15
Major programs: manuscripts,
museum, markers, school
programs, newsletters/pamphlets,
historic preservation, photographic
collections
Period of collections: 1850-1950

De Anza Trek Lancers Society
20739 Sunrise Dr., 95014
Telephone: (408) 252-6065
Private agency
Founded in: 1976
Joseph Adamo, Presiding Officer
Number of members: 10
Staff: volunteer 1
Major programs: historic site(s),
markers, oral history, historic
preservation, living history
Period of collections: 1776

CYPRESS

Cypress College Local History Association
90630
Telephone: (714) 826-2220, ext. 294
Authorized by N. Orange County
Community College District
Founded in: 1972
Thomas V. Reeve II, Executive
Secretary
Major programs: oral history, historic
preservation, archaeology
programs
Period of collections: 1865-present

DANVILLE

San Ramon Valley Historical Society
Telephone: (415) 837-4849/837-7593
Mail to: P.O. Box 521, 94526
Founded in: 1970
Ann Kaplan, President
Number of members: 175
Staff: volunteer 9
Major programs: library, archives,
historic preservation, markers,
school programs
newsletters/pamphlets
Period of collections: 1783-present

DEATH VALLEY

Death Valley National Monument
Death Valley, 92328
Telephone: (619) 786-2331
Federal agency, authorized by
National Park Service
Founded in: 1933
Virgil J. Olson, Chief Naturalist
Staff: full time 2, part time 3,
volunteer 6
Major programs: library, archives,
manuscripts, museum, historic
site(s), markers, junior history, book
publishing, historic preservation,
records management, research,
exhibits, audiovisual programs,
photographic collections
Period of collections: 1849-1960

DESERT HOT SPRINGS

Desert Hot Springs Historical Society
67616 E. Desert View Ave.
Telephone: (619) 329-7610
Mail to: P.O. Box 1267, 92240
Private agency, authorized by
Landmark Conservators
Founded in: 1969
Colbert H. Eyraud, President/Curator
Number of members: 35
Staff: volunteer 15
Major programs: library, archives,
museum, historic site(s), school
programs historic preservation,
exhibits
Period of collections: 1600-1936

DOWNEY

Downey Historical Society
12540 Rives Ave., 90242
Telephone: (213) 927-5255/869-7367
Mail to: P.O. Box 554, 90241
Private agency
Founded in: 1965
Joyce L. Lawrence, President
Number of members: 325
Major programs: library, archives,
manuscripts, museum, historic
site(s), markers, school programs,
newsletters/pamphlets, historic
preservation, research, audiovisual
programs, photographic
collections, genealogical services
Period of collections: 1781-present

DUARTE

Duarte Historical Museum Society—Friends of the Duarte Library, Inc.
1414 Buena Vista Ave.
Telephone: (818) 357-9419
Mail to: P.O. Box 263, 91010
City agency
Founded in: 1962
R. Aloysia Moore, Director
Number of members: 30
Staff: part time 1, volunteer 6
Magazine: *Branding Iron*
Major programs: library, archives,
museum, oral history, school
programs, book publishing,
newsletters/pamphlets, research,
exhibits, photographic collections
Period of collections: 1841-1925

Scotty's Castle in northern Death Valley, the ostentatious home of American adventurer Walter Scott.—National Park Service photograph

EAGLE ROCK

Eagle Rock Valley Historical Society
2035 Colorado Blvd., 90041
Walter Dickey, President
Number of members: 140
Major programs: archives, museum, oral history, exhibits, photographic collections, newsletters/pamphlets
Period of collections: 1890-present

EL CAJON

El Cajon Historical Society
Park and Magnolia Ave.
Telephone: (619) 444-3800
Mail to: P.O. Box 1973, 92020
Private agency
Founded in: 1973
Russ Stockwell, President
Number of members: 300
Staff: volunteer 40
Major programs: library, archives, museum, school programs, historic preservation, audiovisual programs, photographic collections
Period of collections: 1900-1980

EL MONTE

El Monte Historical Society
3150 Tyler Ave., 91731
Questionnaire not received

EL TORO

Saddleback Area Historical Society
P.O. Box 156, 92630
Telephone: (714) 586-8488
Private agency
Founded in: 1974
Nancy L. Thatcher, President
Number of members: 230
Staff: volunteer 75
Major programs: tours/pilgrimages, oral history, school programs, newsletters/pamphlets, historic preservation, research, exhibits, photographic collections
Period of collections: 1889-1930

ENCINO

Encino Historical Society
16756 Moorpark St., 91436
Founded in: 1945
Questionnaire not received

ESCONDIDO

Escondido Historical Society
321 N. Broadway
Telephone: (714) 743-8207
Mail to: P.O. Box 263, 92025
Private agency, authorized by Department of Community Services
Founded in: 1956
Harriett Church, President
Number of members: 450

Staff: volunteer 25
Major programs: library, archives, museum, historic site(s), junior history, school programs, newsletters/pamphlets, historic preservation, exhibits, photographic collections
Period of collections: 1880-1930

EUREKA

Clarke Memorial Museum
240 E St., 95501
Telephone: (707) 443-1947
Private agency
Founded in: 1960
Coleen J. Kelley, Curator
Number of members: 230
Staff: full time 2, part time 2, volunteer 18
Major programs: library, museum, historic site(s), tours, oral history, school programs, newsletters/pamphlets, historic preservation, research, exhibits, living history, photographic collections
Period of collections: 1850-1930

Humboldt County Historical Society
636 F St.
Telephone: (707) 443-3515
Mail to: P.O. Box 882, 95501
Private agency

Founded in: 1947
Arlene A. Hartin, President
Number of members: 4,500
Staff: volunteer 15
Magazine: *The Humboldt Historian*
Major programs:
   newsletters/pamphlets,
   photographic collections
Period of collections: late 1800s-early
   1900s

FALLBROOK

Fallbrook Historical Society
Mail to: P.O. Box 1375, 92028
Private agency
Founded in: 1976
Number of members: 348
Major programs: library, manuscripts,
   museum, exhibits
Period of collections: 1875-present

FALL RIVER MILLS

Ft. Crook Historical Society
Ft. Crook Ave.
Telephone: (916) 336-5110
Mail to: P.O. Box 397, 96028
Private agency
Founded in: 1963
Lindsay Jewett, President
Number of members: 90
Staff: full time 1, volunteer 2
Major programs: archives, museum,
   historic site(s), markers, school
   programs, research, exhibits,
   photographic collections,
   genealogical services
Period of collections: 1860-1940

FERNDALE

The Ferndale Museum
Shaw and 3rd Sts.
Telephone: (707) 786-4466
Mail to: P.O. Box 431, 95536
Private agency
Founded in: 1979
Jerry Lesandro, Museum Director
Number of members: 450
Staff: part time 2, volunteer 75
Major programs: archives, museum,
   oral history, school programs,
   newsletters/pamphlets, research,
   exhibits, photographic collections,
   genealogical services
Period of collections: 1860-1920

FILLMORE

Fillmore Historical Society
447 Main St.
Telephone: (805) 524-0948
Mail to: P.O. Box 314, 93015
Private agency, authorized by
   Fillmore Historical Museum, Inc.
Founded in: 1980
Dorothy Haase, Museum Curator
Number of members: 135
Staff: part time 2, volunteer 7
Major programs: museum
Period of collections: 1890-1930

FOLSOM

**Folsom Historical Society—Wells
   Fargo Building Museum**
823 Sutter St., 95630
Telephone: (916) 985-2707
Private agency

Founded in: 1960
Mary Otis, Recording Secretary
Number of members: 200
Staff: part time 2, volunteer 26
Major programs: archives, museum,
   historic site(s), oral history, book
   publishing, newsletters/pamphlets,
   historic preservation, audiovisual
   programs, photographic
   collections
Period of collections: 1800s-1900s

FONTANA

**Fonana Historical Society
   Corporation**
8863 Pepper St.
Telephone: (714) 823-1733
Mail to: P.O. Box 426, 92335
Founded in: 1974
Charles Dall, President
Number of members: 170
Staff: volunteer 10
Major programs: archives, museum,
   historic site(s), book publishing,
   newsletters/pamphlets, historic
   preservation, research, exhibits
Period of collections: 1890-1940

FORESTHILL

Foresthill Divide Historical Society
Telephone: (916) 367-2804
Mail to: P.O. Box 246, 95631
Founded in: 1977
Questionnaire not received

FORTUNA

Fortuna Historical Commission
621 11th St., 95540
Questionnaire not received

Fortuna Depot Museum
Park St., 95540
Telephone: (707) 725-2495
City agency
Founded in: 1976
Major programs: museum, school
   programs, historic preservation,
   exhibits, photographic collections
Period of collections: 1890

FREMONT

**Washington Township Historical
   Society**
43263 Mission Blvd., 94538
Telephone: (415) 656-3761
Mail to: P.O. Box 3045, 94539
Founded in: 1949
Cecelia Weed, Vice President
Number of members: 200
Staff: volunteer 25
Major programs: archives, museum,
   markers, historic site(s), markers,
   tours/pilgrimages, oral history,
   school programs,
   newsletters/pamphlets, historic
   preservation
Period of collections: 1809-present

FRESNO

**Fresno City and County Historical
   Society**
7160 W. Kearney Blvd., 93706
Questionnaire not received

Meux Home Museum Corporation
1007 R St.
Telephone: (209) 233-8007
Mail to: P.O. Box 70, 93707
Founded in: 1979
Number of members: 99
Staff: part time 3, volunteer 66
Magazine: *Meux Home News*
Major programs: museum, school
   programs newsletters/pamphlets,
   historic preservation
Period of collections: 1880-1920

FRIANT

**California Department of Parks and
   Recreation**
San Joaquin Valley District
Telephone: (209) 822-2332
Mail to: P.O. Box 205, 93626
State agency
Bruce Kranz, District Superintendent
Staff: full time 25, part time 20,
   volunteer 700
Major programs: museum, historic
   site(s), tours/pilgrimages, exhibits
Period of collections: early 1900

FULLERTON

**Fullerton Arboretum—Heritage
   House**
History Department, California State
   University, Fullerton
Telephone: (714) 773-3579
Mail to: 800 N. State College Blvd.,
   92634
City agency, authorized by
   joint-powers agreement between
   city and state
Founded in: 1976
Kathy Frazee, Educational
   Coordinator
Staff: part time 1, volunteer 50
Major programs: library, museum,
   historic site(s), tours/pilgrimages,
   school programs, historic
   preservation, exhibits,
   photographic collections
Period of collections: 1850-1900

Oral History Program
History Department, California State
   University, Fullerton
Telephone: (714) 773-3580
Mail to: 800 N. State College Blvd.,
   92634
State agency
Founded in: 1968
Shirley E. Stephenson, Associate
   Director/Archivist
Major programs: archives, oral history
Period of collections: 20th century

GARDEN GROVE

Garden Grove Historical Society
12174 Euclid St., 92640
Telephone: (714) 530-8871
Private agency
Founded in: 1966
Fred Coles, President
Number of members: 200
Staff: volunteer 25
Major programs: library, museum,
   historic site(s), markers, oral
   history, historic preservation
Period of collections: 1875-present

GILROY

Gilroy Historical Museum
195 5th St., 95020
Telephone: (408) 847-2685
City agency
Founded in: 1963
Mary A. Prien, Museum Director
Staff: full time 1, part time 1,
   volunteer 1
Major programs: archives, museum,
   tours/pilgrimages, school
   programs, research, exhibits,
   audiovisual programs,
   photographic collections,
   genealogical services
Period of collections: 1800-present

Gilroy Historical Society
P.O. Box 2190, 95021
Private agency
Founded in: 1963
James C. Williams, President
Number of members: 85
Major programs: tours/pilgrimages,
   school programs book publishing,
   newsletters/pamphlets, historic
   preservation, oral history
Period of collections: early 1850-1950

GLENDALE

**Southern California Genealogical
   Society, Inc.**
600 S. Central Ave., 91204
Questionnaire not received

GLENDORA

Glendora Historical Society
P.O. Box 532, 91740
Telephone: (818) 914-8228

Jack London State Historic Park
End of London Ranch Rd.
Mail to: P.O. Box 358, 95442
Founded in: 1959
Questionnaire not received

HALF MOON BAY

Johnston House Foundation
Higgins-Purissima Rd.
Telephone: (415) 641-9102
Mail to: P.O. Box 789, 94019
Founded in: 1972
Alanna Zuppann, President
Number of members: 150
Staff: volunteer 30
Major programs: historic sites
   preservation
Period of collections: 1783-1865

Spanishtown Historical Society
Telephone: (415) 728-5027
Mail to: P.O. Box 62, 94019
Private agency
Founded in: 1970
Kathryn Murdock, President
Number of members: 162
Staff: volunteer 30
Major programs: archives, markers,
   junior history, oral history, school
   programs, newsletters/pamphlets,
   research, exhibits, audiovisual
   programs, photographic
   collections, documentary research
Period of collections: 1855-1930

HAYWARD

Hayward Area Historical Society
22701 Main St., 94541
Telephone: (415) 581-0223
Founded in: 1956
Eugene G. Hirtle, Jr., Curator
Number of members: 790
Staff: part time 2, volunteer 35
Magazine: *Adobe Trails*
Major programs: library, archives,
   manuscripts, museum, historic
   preservation, markers,
   tours/pilgrimage, junior history, oral
   history, school programs books,
   newsletters/pamphlets
Period of collections: 1856-1930

Surveyors' Historical Society
31457 Hugh Way, 94544
Telephone: (415) 471-3905
Authorized by Worldwide Historical
   Society for Land Surveyors
Founded in: 1977
Myron A. Lewis, Secretary
Number of members: 198
Staff: volunteer 7
Magazine: *Backsights*
Major programs: archives, exhibits
Period of collections: 1790s-present

HEALDSBURG

**Edwin Langhart
   Museum—Healdsburg Historical
   Society**
133 Matheson St., 95448
Telephone: (707) 433-4717
City agency
Founded in: 1976
Hannah M. Clayborn,
   Director/Curator
Number of members: 400
Staff: full time 1, part time 2,
   volunteer 35
Major programs: library, archives,
   manuscripts, museum, book
   publishing, newsletters/pamphlets,
   historic preservation, records
   management, research, exhibits,
   audiovisual programs,
   photographic collections,
   genealogical services
Period of collections: 1850-1940

HOLLISTER

**San Benito County Historical
   Society**
Mail to: P.O. Box 357, 95023
Private agency
Founded in: 1956
Janet Brians, President
Number of members: 110
Staff: part time 1, volunteer 20
school programs, museum, oral
   history
Period of collections: 1870-present

INDEPENDENCE

Eastern California Museum
155 Grant St.
Mail to: P.O. Box 206, 93526
Founded in: 1928
Questionnaire not received

IRVINE

**Irvine Historical Society and
   Museum**
5 Rancho San Joaquin, 92715
Telephone: (714) 786-4112
Private agency
Founded in: 1976
Clifford D. Bodamer, Museum
   Director
Number of members: 150
Staff: full time 2, part time 1,
   volunteer 1
Major programs: archives, museum,
   historic site(s), tours, school
   programs, newsletters/pamphlets,
   historic preservation, exhibits,
   archaeology programs,
   photographic collections
Period of collections: 1890-1950

JACKSON

Amador County Historical Society
18708 Clinton Rd.
Mail to: P.O. Box 761, 95642
Private agency
Founded in: 1944
Frank Aliberti, Researcher/Publicity
   chair
Number of members: 160
Staff: volunteer 16
Magazine: *Past Times of Amador*
Major programs: historic site(s),
   markers, tours/pilgrimages, oral
   history, newsletters/pamphlets,
   historic preservation, research,
   genealogical services
Period of collections: late
   1800s-present

JENNER

Ft. Ross State Historic Site
19005 Coast Hwy., 95450
Questionnaire not received

JOLON

Old Mission San Antonio de Padua
P.O. Box 803, 93928
Telephone: (408) 385-4478
Founded in: 1771
Timothy Arthur, Executive Director
Staff: volunteer 3
Major programs: archives, historic
   site
Period of collections: 1700-1800s

JULIAN

Julian Historical Society
Mail to: P.O. Box 513, 92036
Founded in: 1961
Questionnaire not received

KERNVILLE

Kern River Valley Historical Society
P.O. Box 651, 93238
Founded in: 1968
Magazine: *The Saddlebag*
Questionnaire not received

KING CITY

**San Antonio Valley Historical
   Association**
216 Grove Place, 93930
Telephone: (408) 385-3587

Mail to: P.O. Box 184, Lockwood,
93932
Private agency
Founded in: 1968
Sue Watson, President
Number of members: 150
Staff: volunteer 6
Major programs: library, historic
site(s), oral history, historic
preservation
Period of collections: 1850-present

LAFAYETTE

Lafayette Historical Society
Mail to: P.O. Box 133, 94549
Private agency
Founded in: 1970
Ray Peters, President
Number of members: 250
Major programs: library, archives,
historic site(s), markers,
tours/pilgrimages, oral history,
school programs, book publishing,
newsletters/pamphlets, historic
preservation, records
management, research, exhibits,
audiovisual programs,
photographic collections
Period of collections: 1865-present

LAGUNA BEACH

Laguna Beach Historical Society
790 S. Coast Hwy.
Mail to: P.O. Box 1301, 92652
Founded in: 1970
Questionnaire not received

LAGUNA HILLS

**Leisure World Historical Society of
Laguna Hills, Inc.**
23522 Paseo de Valencia
Telephone: (714) 951-2330
Mail to: P.O. Box 2220, 92653
Private agency
Founded in: 1977
Isabella V. Leland, President
Number of members: 397
Staff: part time 1, volunteer 15
Magazine: *Historical Hi-lites*
Major programs: archives, historic
preservation, photographic
collections

LA HABRA

**La Habra Old Settlers Historical
Society**
2310 Vista Rd., 90631
Questionnaire not received

LA JOLLA

La Jolla Historical Society
7846 Eads Ave.
Telephone: (714) 459-5335
Mail to: P.O. Box 2085, 92038
Town agency
Founded in: 1964
Robert Barrymore, President
Number of members: 400
Major programs: library, archives,
museum, historic preservation,
school programs
newsletters/pamphlets, audiovisual
programs
Period of collections: 1865-present

LAKEPORT

Lake County Historical Society
Telephone: (707) 279-4466
Mail to: P.O. Box 1011, 95453
County agency
Founded in: 1955
Norma Wright, President
Number of members: 800
Staff: volunteer 11
Magazine: *Pomo Bulletin*
Major programs: archives, museum,
historic preservation, markers,
tours/pilgrimages, oral history,
school programs books,
newsletters/pamphlets, research,
photographic collections
Period of collections: 1800-present

LA MESA

La Mesa Historical Society, Inc.
8369 University Ave.
Telephone: (619) 463-0197
Mail to: P.O. Box 882, 92041
Private agency
Founded in: 1975
Patricia M. Kettler, President
Number of members: 400
Staff: volunteer 35
Magazine: *Lookout Avenue*
Major programs: archives, museum,
historic site(s), tours/pilgrimages,
oral history, school programs,
newsletters/pamphlets, historic
preservation, research, exhibits,
audiovisual programs,
photographic collections
Period of collections: 1890-present

LA MIRADA

Governor Pico Mansion Society
14216 Neargrove Rd., 90638
Questionnaire not received

LANCASTER

Kern-Antelope Historical Society
Mail to: P.O. Box 325, Rosamond,
93560
State agency
Founded in: 1959
Mildred Brackett, President
Number of members: 117
Staff: volunteer 9
Major programs: historic site(s),
school programs, book publishing,
historic preservation

LA PUENTE

**La Puente Valley Historical
Society, Inc.**
Mail to: P.O. Box 522, 91744
Founded in: 1960
Number of members: 135
Major programs: library, archives,
manuscripts, museum, historic
preservation, markers, junior
history, oral history, school
programs newsletters/pamphlets
Period of collections: 1865-present

LEADVILLE

Leadville Assembly, Inc.
414 W. 7th St., 80461
Telephone: (303) 486-0371
Founded in: 1952
Questionnaire not received

LIVERMORE

Livermore Heritage Guild
3rd and K Sts.
Telephone: (415) 443-3272
Mail to: P.O. Box 961, 94550
Private agency
Founded in: 1973
Carolyn Parrish, Chair
Number of members: 320
Staff: volunteer
Major programs: archives, museum,
historic site(s), oral history,
newsletters/pamphlets, historic
preservation, records
management, research, exhibits
Period of collections: 1860-1920s

LOCKWOOD

**San Antonio Valley Historical
Association**
93932
Telephone: (408) 385-5757
Mail to: P.O. Box 157
Questionnaire not received

LODI

**San Joaquin County Historical
Society and Museum**
11793 N. Micke Grove Rd., 95240
Telephone: (209) 368-9154/463-4119
Mail to: P.O. Box 21, 95241
County agency
Founded in: 1954
Michael W. Bennett, Museum Director
Number of members: 400
Staff: full time 6, volunteer 50
Magazine: *San Joaquin Historian*
Major programs: library, archives,
museum, markers, junior history,
oral history, school programs,
newsletters/pamphlets, historic
preservation, records
management, research, exhibits,
living history, audiovisual
programs, photographic
collections
Period of collections: 1846-1960

LOMITA

Lomita Historical Society
City Hall, 24300 Narbonne Ave.
Mail to: 24016 Benhill Ave., 90717
Questionnaire not received

LOMPOC

**Lompoc Valley Historical
Society, Inc.**
207 N. L St.
Telephone: (805) 735-4626
Mail to: P.O. Box 88, 93436
Private agency
Founded in: 1964
Dennis Headrick, President
Number of members: 530
Staff: volunteer 4
Magazine: *Lompoc Legacy*
Major programs: library, manuscripts,
museum, historic site(s), book
publishing, newsletters/pamphlets,
historic preservation, research,
photographic collections,
genealogical services
Period of collections: 1787-present

LONG BEACH

Historical Society of Long Beach
1150 E. 4th St.
Mail to: P.O. Box 1869, 90801
Private agency
Founded in: 1962
Number of members: 300
Staff: volunteer 12
Major programs: archives, oral
history, book publishing,
newsletters/pamphlets, historic
preservation, audiovisual
programs, photographic
collections
Period of collections: 1890-present

Los Pobladores 200
Telephone: (213) 633-6179
Mail to: 2830 E. 56th Way, 90805
Private agency
Founded in: 1982
Lillian Robles, President
Number of members: 80
Staff: volunteer 14
Magazine: *El Mensaje*
Major programs: historic site(s),
markers, historic preservation,
exhibits, photographic collections,
genealogical services
Period of collections: 1776

Rancho Los Alamitos Associates
6400 Bixby Hill Rd., 90815
Telephone: (213) 431-2511
City agency, authorized by Long
Beach Public Library
Founded in: 1969
Ellen Calomiris, Historical Curator
Number of members: 300
Staff: full time 3, part time 1,
volunteer 75
Major programs: museum, historic
site(s), historic preservation
Period of collections: 1878-1961

LOS ALTOS HILLS

**Foothill Electronics
Museum—DeForest Memorial
Library**
12345 El Monte Rd., 94022
Telephone: (415) 948-8590, ext. 383
Private agency
Founded in: 1966
Leonard M. Lansdowne, Curator
Staff: full time 1, volunteer 8
Major programs: library, archives,
manuscripts, museum, tours,
research, exhibits, audiovisual
programs
Period of collections: 1890-1960

Los Altos Hills Historical Society
26379 Fremont Rd.
Telephone: (415) 948-2487
Mail to: 27330 Elena Rd., 94022
Private agency
Founded in: 1972
Irma C. Goldsmith, President
Number of members: 45
Major programs: library, museum,
tours/pilgrimages,
newsletters/pamphlets, historic
preservation, photographic
collections

Los Altos Historical Commission
1 N. San Antonio Rd., 94022
Telephone: (415) 948-1491

City agency
Founded in: 1975
Sherry Lambach, Commission Liaison
Staff: part time 2, volunteer 7
Major programs: museum, historic
site(s), tours/pilgrimages, exhibits
Period of collections: 1900-present

LOS ANGELES

**American Historical Association,
Pacific Coast Branch**
c/o Secretary/Treasurer, Department
of History, University of Southern
California, 90007
Founded in: 1903
John A. Schutz, Secretary/Treasurer
Number of members: 2,100
Staff: full time 1, part time 1
Questionnaire not received

**American Society of Military
History**
1816 S. Figueroa St., Suite 200, 90015
Telephone: (213) 746-1776
Private agency
Founded in: 1962
Donald S. Michelson, Executive
Director
Number of members: 432
Staff: full time 4, volunteer 6
Major programs: library, manuscripts,
museum, newsletters/pamphlets,
historic preservation, research,
exhibits
Period of collections: 1914-present

**Barlow Society for the History of
Medicine**
634 S. Westlake Ave., 90057
Telephone: (213) 483-4555
Private agency, authorized by Library
of the Los Angeles County Medical
Association
Founded in: 1938
Elizabeth S. Crahan, Director of
Library Services
Major programs: library, museum,
lectures

**Cultural Heritage Foundation of
Southern California, Inc.**
Heritage Square, 3800 Homer St.,
90031
Telephone: (213) 222-3150
Private agency
Founded in: 1969
Sharon L. Shaw, Executive Director
Number of members: 580
Staff: full time 1, part time 1
Magazine: *On the Square*
Major programs: museum, historic
site(s), newsletters/pamphlets,
historic preservation, photographic
collections
Period of collections: Victorian era

**Eagle Rock Valley Historical
Society**
2035 Colorado Blvd., 90041
Founded in: 1961
Number of members: 110
Staff: volunteer 10
Questionnaire not received

**Electric Railway Historical
Association of Southern
California**
Mail to: P.O. Box 24315, 90024-0315
Private agency
Founded in: 1950

David G. Cameron, President
Number of members: 300
Staff: volunteer 8
Magazine: *Timepoints*
Major programs: tours/pilgrimages,
school programs
newsletters/pamphlets, audiovisual
programs
Period of collections: 1890-present

**El Pueblo de Los Angeles State
Historic Park**
845 N. Alameda, 90012
Telephone: (213) 628-1274
City agency, authorized by
Department of Recreation and
Parks
Founded in: 1953
Sheldon Jensen, General Manager
Staff: full time 37, part time 41,
volunteer 50
Major programs: manuscripts,
museum, historic site(s), markers,
tours, newsletters/pamphlets,
historic preservation, research,
exhibits, audiovisual programs,
archaeology programs,
photographic collections
Period of collections: 1875-1975

**Historical Society of Centinela
Valley**
7634 Midfield Ave., 90045
Telephone: (213) 649-6272
Founded in: 1965
Number of members: 322
Questionnaire not received

◇**Historical Society of Southern
California**
200 East Ave., 90031
Telephone: (213) 222-0546
Private agency
Founded in: 1883
Jacquelyn F. Wilson, Executive
Director
Number of members: 1,000
Staff: full time 1
Magazine: *Southern California
Quarterly*
Major programs: historic site(s),
tours/pilgrimages, junior history,
book publishing,
newsletters/pamphlets,
photographic collections
Period of collections: 1880-present

Los Angeles City Historical Society
10801 La Grange Ave., 90025
Mail to: P.O. Box 41046, 90041
Founded in: 1977
Number of members: 200
Staff: volunteer 6
Questionnaire not received

Los Angeles Corral of Westerners
1506 Linda Rosa Ave., 90041
Questionnaire not received

Museum of Cultural History
University of California, Los Angeles
Telephone: (213) 825-4361
Mail to: 405 Hilgard Ave., 90024
State agency
Founded in: 1963
Christopher B. Donnan, Director
Staff: full time 14, part time 20,
volunteer 60
Major programs: library, manuscripts,
museum, tours, school programs,
book publishing,

newsletters/pamphlets, research,
exhibits, archaeology programs,
museum studies
Period of collections:
prehistoric-present

**National Archives—Los Angeles
Branch**
24000 Avila Rd.
Telephone: (714) 831-4220
Mail to: P.O. Box 6719, Laguna
Niguel, 92677-6719
Founded in: 1969
Diane Nixon, Director
Staff: full time 6
Major programs: archives,
educational program, teachers'
workshops, genealogical
workshops, film series, open
houses and tours
Period of collections: 1851-1982

National Hispanic Museum
421 N. Ave. 19, 4th Floor, 90031
Telephone: (213) 222-1349
Mail to: P.O. Box 875377, 90087
Private agency, authorized by
Caminos Corporation
Founded in: 1979
Kirk Whisler, Publisher
Number of members: 24,000
Staff: full time 11, part time 4,
volunteer 5
Magazine: *Caminos Magazine*
Major programs: library, museum,
research, exhibits
Period of collections: 19th-20th
centuries

**Natural History Museum of Los
Angeles County**
900 Exposition Blvd., 90007
Telephone: (213) 744-3301
County agency
Founded in: 1910
Craig C. Black, Director
Number of members: 10,000
Staff: full time 250, volunteer 300
Magazine: *Terra*
Major programs: library, archives,
manuscripts, museum, historic
site(s), book publishing,
newsletters/pamphlets, historic
preservation, research, exhibits,
archaeology programs,
photographic collections, natural
history
Period of collections:
prehistoric-present

Pacific Railroad Society, Inc.
P.O. Box 80726, San Marino,
91108-8726
Telephone: (213) 283-0087
Private agency
Founded in: 1936
Marti Ann Draper, President
Staff: volunteer 50
Magazine: *Wheel Clicks*
Major programs: library, archives,
museum, tours/pilgrimages,
newsletters/pamphlets, historic
preservation, exhibits,
photographic collections, historic
railroad passenger car operation
Period of collections: 1930-1959

**Ramona Museum of California
History**
4580 N. Figueroa St., 90065
Telephone: (213) 222-0012
Private agency, authorized by
Ramona Parlor, N.S.G.W.
Founded in: 1887
Richard Byard, Director
Number of members: 280
Staff: full time 1, part time 1,
volunteer 2
Major programs: archives, museum,
markers, historic preservation
Period of collections: 1790-1900

**Seaver Center for Western History
Research, Natural
History Museum of Los Angeles
County**
900 Exposition Blvd., 90007
Telephone: (213) 744-3359
County agency
Founded in: 1910
Errol Stevens, Curator
Number of members: 10,000
Staff: 256
Magazine: *Terra*
Major programs: library, archives,
manuscripts, museum, historic
site(s), book publishing,
newsletters/pamphlets, historic
preservation, research, exhibits,
archaeology programs,
photographic collections, natural
history
Period of collections: 18th-19th
centuries

◊**Southern California Branch,
California Historical Society**
6300 Wilshire Blvd., 90048
Telephone: (213) 651-5655
Private agency, authorized by
California Historical Society, San
Francisco
Founded in: 1871
Louise Braunschweiger, Director
Number of members: 10,000
Staff: full time 2, part time 3,
volunteer 1
Magazine: *California
History/California Historical Courier*
Major programs: library, archives,
manuscripts, historic site(s),
tours/pilgrimages,
newsletters/pamphlets, exhibits,
photographic collections
Period of collections: 1880-1940

**Southern California Jewish
Historical Society**
850 Venice Blvd., 90015
Questionnaire not received

**SPACES (Saving and Preserving
Arts and Cultural Environments)**
1804 N. Van Ness, 90028
Telephone: (213) 463-1629
Private agency
Founded in: 1978
Seymour Rosen, Director
Number of members: 300
Staff: part time 3, volunteer 20
Major programs: library, archives,
historic site(s), markers, oral
history, newsletters/pamphlets,
historic preservation, research,
exhibits, photographic collections,

field services, folk arts,
documentation
Period of collections: 1820s-1980s

**Windsor Square-Hancock Park
Historical Society**
542½ N. Larchmont Blvd., 90004
Questionnaire not received

LOS BONOS

Ralph L. Milliken Museum
Mail to: 615 Pocheco Blvd., 93635
Questionnaire not received

MADERA

Madera County Historical Society
210 W. Yosemite, 93637
Telephone: (209) 673-0291
Mail to: P.O. Box 478, 93639
Private agency
Founded in: 1955
Lonnie Doshier, President
Number of members: 575
Staff: volunteer 65
Magazine: *Madera County Historian*
Major programs: library, archives,
manuscripts, museum, historic
site(s), school programs,
newsletters/pamphlets, historic
preservation, research, exhibits,
photographic collections,
genealogical services
Period of collections: 1865-present

MARIPOSA

Mariposa County Historical Society
5119 Jesse St.
Telephone: (209) 966-2924
Mail to: P.O. Box 606, 95338
Private agency
Founded in: 1957
Scott Pinkerton, President
Number of members: 550
Staff: part time 1, volunteer 75
Magazine: *The Sentinel*
Major programs: library, museum,
oral history, book publishing,
newsletters/pamphlets, historic
preservation, exhibits,
photographic collections
Period of collections: 1849-1900

MARKLEEVILLE

Historical Society of Alpine County
School St.
Mail to: P.O. Box 24., 96120
Private agency
Founded in: 1963
Number of members: 135
Major programs: museum,
photographic collections
Period of collections: 1860-1960

MARTINEZ

John Muir National Historic Site
4202 Alhambra Ave., 94553
Telephone: (415) 228-8860
Federal agency, authorized by
Department of the Interior
Founded in: 1964
Phyllis Shaw, Park Superintendent
Major programs: museum, historic
site(s), tours/pilgrimages, school
programs newsletters/pamphlets,

historic preservation, records
management, exhibits
Period of collections: 1880-1914

MARYSVILLE

**Mary M. Arron Memorial Museum
Association**
704 D St., 95901
Telephone: (916) 743-1004
Founded in: 1960
Danae M. Stewart, Curator
Number of members: 125
Staff: full time 1, volunteer 30
Magazine: *Memos From Mary*
Major programs: library, archives,
museum, historic site(s), school
programs historic preservation
Period of collections: 1850-1900

MENDOCINO

**Mendocino Historical
Research, Inc.**
45007 Albion St.
Telephone: (707) 937-5791
Mail to: P.O. Box 922, 95460
Founded in: 1973
Daniel Taylor, Administrative Director
Number of members: 550
Staff: full time 1, volunteer 40
Magazine: *Mendocino Historical
Review*
Major programs: library, archives,
manuscripts, museum, historic
site(s), tours/pilgrimages, book
publishing, newsletters/pamphlets,
historic preservation, records
management, research, exhibits,
photographic collections,
genealogical services
Period of collections: 1850-present

MERCED

Merced County Historical Society
Old County Courthouse, 21st and N
Sts., 95340
Telephone: (209) 385-7426
Private agency
Founded in: 1962
Thomas Olaeta, President
Number of members: 500
Staff: volunteer 50
Magazine: *For The Record*
Major programs: library, archives,
manuscripts, museum, historic
site(s), tours/pilgrimages, school
programs, newsletters/pamphlets,
historic preservation, research,
exhibits, audiovisual programs,
photographic collections
Period of collections: 1875-present

MILLBRAE

Millbrae Historical Society
P.O. Box 511, 94030
Founded in: 1970
Number of members: 115
Questionnaire not received

MILL VALLEY

Mill Valley Public Library
375 Throckmorton Ave., 94941
Telephone: (415) 388-2190
City agency
Founded in: 1908
Thelma Percy, City Librarian

Staff: full time 8, part time 2,
volunteer 25
Major programs: library,
photographic collections, local
history collection
Period of collections: 1900-present

MISSION HILLS

Archival Center
15151 San Fernando Mission Blvd.,
91345
Telephone: (818) 365-1501
Private agency, authorized by Roman
Catholic Archbishop of Los
Angeles
Founded in: 1962
Francis J. Weber, Archivist
Number of members: 150
Staff: full time 3, volunteer 35
Major programs: library, archives,
manuscripts, museum, historic
site(s), tours/pilgrimages, book
publishing, records management,
research, exhibits
Period of collections: from 1840

**San Fernando Valley Historical
Society, Inc.**
10940 Sepulveda Blvd., 91345
Telephone: (818) 365-7810
Private agency
Founded in: 1943
William A. Roberts, President
Number of members: 200
Staff: full time 1, volunteer 25
Major programs: library, archives,
museum, tours/pilgrimages, oral
history, school programs, book
publishing, newsletters/pamphlets,
historic preservation, research,
exhibits, photographic collections
Period of collections: 1834-present

MODESTO

McHenry Museum
1402 I St., 95354
Telephone: (209) 577-5366
City agency
Founded in: 1967
Heidi L. Warner, Curator
Number of members: 825
Staff: full time 1, part time 3,
volunteer 80
Major programs: archives, museum,
historic site(s), tours/pilgrimages,
oral history, school programs, book
publishing, newsletters/pamphlets,
historic preservation, records
management, research, exhibits,
photographic collections,
genealogical services, field
services
Period of collections: 1849-1929

**Stanislaus County Historical
Society**
Telephone: (209) 526-4412
Mail to: P.O. Box 4363, 95352
Founded in: 1966
Number of members: 750
Questionnaire not received

MONTECITO

Montecito History Committee
1469 E. Valley Rd., 93108
Telephone: (805) 969-1597

Private agency, authorized by
Montecito Association
Founded in: 1975
David F. Myrick, Volunteer
Number of members: 25
Staff: volunteer 10
Major programs: archives, oral
history, research, photographic
collections, architectural history
Period of collections: 1870-present

MONTEREY

**Colton Hall Museum of the City of
Monterey**
City Hall, 93940
Telephone: (408) 646-3851/375-9944
City agency
Founded in: 1939
Donna Penwell, Museum Manager
Staff: full time 1, part time 6
Major programs: archives, museum,
historic site(s), oral history, book
publishing, records management,
research, exhibits, photographic
collections, genealogical services
Period of collections: 1783-present

**Monterey History and Art
Association, Ltd.**
550 Calle Principal
Telephone: (408) 372-2608
Mail to: P.O. Box 805, 93940
Private agency
Founded in: 1931
David Hudson, President
Number of members: 2,000
Staff: part time 3
Major programs: library, archives,
manuscripts, museum, historic
site(s), markers, tours/pilgrimages,
oral history, newsletters/pamphlets,
exhibits, photographic collections
Period of collections: 1825-1945

Old Monterey Jail
Dutra St., City Hall, 93940
Telephone: (408) 375-9944
City agency
Founded in: 1956
Donna Penwell, Museum Manager
Staff: full time 1, part time 6,
volunteer 10
Major programs: historic site(s),
exhibits
Period of collections: 1854-1956

Old Monterey Preservation Society
210 Olivier, 93940
Telephone: (408) 649-2836
Founded in: 1975
Questionnaire not received

Presidio of Monterey Museum
Bldg. 113, Ewing Rd., 93940
Telephone: (408) 242-8547
Federal agency, authorized by the
U.S. Army
Founded in: 1965
Margaret B. Adams, Curator/Historian
Staff: full time 3
Major programs: library, archives,
museum, historic site(s),
pamphlets
Period of collections:
prehistoric-present

MONTEREY PARK

Historical Society of Monterey Park
P.O. Box 272, 91754
Telephone: (818) 281-9994
Private agency
Founded in: 1968
H. Russell Paine, President
Number of members: 55
Major programs: archives, museum, oral history, newsletters/pamphlets, historic preservation, exhibits, photographic collections
Period of collections: 1900-present

MOUNTAIN VIEW

Mountain View Pioneer and Historical Association
Telephone: (415) 968-6595
Mail to: P.O. Box 252, 94041
Founded in: 1954
Questionnaire not received

NAPA

Napa County Historical Society
1219 1st St., 94558
Telephone: (707) 224-1739
Founded in: 1948
Jess Doud, Executive Director
Number of members: 700
Staff: volunteer 15
Magazine: *Gleanings, Tidings*
Major programs: library, archives, museum, tours/pilgrimages, oral history, books, newsletters/pamphlets
Period of collections: 1847-present

NEVADA CITY

American Victorian Museum
325 Spring St. 95959
Telephone: (916) 265-5804
Mail to: P.O. Box 328
Founded in: 1972
Davis S. Osborn, President
Number of members: 300
Staff: full time 2, volunteer 4
Major programs: museum, historic site(s), school programs, historic preservation, educational, community radio
Period of collections: 1820-1900

Nevada County Historical Society
Telephone: (916) 265-4739
Mail to: P. O. Box 1300, 95959
Founded in: 1944
Bruce Bolinger, President
Number of members: 675
Staff: volunteer 30
Major programs: library, archives, manuscripts, museum, historic site(s), tours/pilgrimages, junior history, school programs, book publishing, newsletters/pamphlets, historic preservation, research, exhibits, photographic collections, genealogical services
Period of collections: 1849-1942

Searls Historical Library
214 Church St., 95959
Telephone: (916) 265-5910
Private agency, authorized by Nevada County Historical Society
Founded in: 1972
Edwin L. Tyson, Librarian

Staff: part time 3
Major programs: archives, photographic collections, genealogical services
Period of collections: 1849-1942

NEWHALL

Santa Clarita Valley Historical Society
24107 San Fernando Rd., 91321
Telephone: (805) 259-4669
Mail to: P.O. Box 875, 91322
Founded in: 1975
Number of members: 450
Staff: volunteer 21
Major programs: library, archives, museum, historic site(s), markers, tours/pilgrimages, oral history, school programs, newsletters/pamphlets, historic preservation, exhibits, audiovisual programs, photographic collections
Period of collections: 1880-present

OAKHURST

Sierra Historic Sites Association
Telephone: (209) 683-6570
Mail to: P. O. Box 451, 93644
Private agency
Founded in: 1968
Dwight H. Barnes, President
Number of members: 700
Staff: volunteer 40
Magazine: *Fresno Flats Gazette*
Major programs: library, museum, oral history, historic preservation, research, exhibits, photographic collections
Period of collections: 1890-1920

OAKLAND

Alameda County Historical Society
1066 Ardmore Ave., 94610
Telephone: (415) 451-1101
Founded in: 1966
Peter T. Conmy, Executive Secretary
Number of members: 400
Magazine: *Alameda County Historical Society Quarterly*
Major programs: historic preservation, markers, tours/pilgrimages, books, lectures

Camron-Stanford House Preservation Association
1418 Lakeside Dr., 94612
Telephone: (415) 836-1976
Private agency
Founded in: 1971
Elaine Oldham, President of Board
Number of members: 200
Staff: part time 1, volunteer 50
Major programs: museum, historic site(s), tours/pilgrimages, oral history, newsletters/pamphlets, historic preservation, exhibits, audiovisual programs, photographic collections
Period of collections: 1875-1890

East Bay Negro Historical Society, Inc.
5606 San Pablo Ave., 94608
Telephone: (415) 658-3158
Founded in: 1965
Eugene P. Lasartemay, President

Number of members: 230
Staff: volunteer 10
Major programs: library, museum, exhibits
Period of collections: 1492-present

Oakland Museum History Department
1000 Oak St., 94607
Telephone: (415) 273-3842
L. Thomas Frye, Chief Curator of History
Staff: full time 8, part time 3, volunteer 30
Magazine: *The Museum of California*
Major programs: archives, museum, junior history, educational programs, historic preservation, research, exhibits, audiovisual programs
Period of collections: 1850-1950

Pardee Home Foundation
672 11th St., 94607
Telephone: (415) 444-2187
Private agency
Founded in: 1981
David Casebolt, Historic Site Administrator
Staff: full time 1, part time 2, volunteer 15
Major programs: archives, museum, historic site(s), exhibits, photographic collections
Period of collections: 1850-1950

OJAI

Ojai Valley Historical Society and Museum
109 S. Montgomery St.
Telephone: (805) 646-2290
Mail to: P.O. Box 204, 93023
Private agency
Founded in: 1966
Number of members: 400
Staff: volunteer 30
Major programs: library, archives, museum, tours, newsletters/pamphlets, historic preservation, research, exhibits
Period of collections: prehistoric-pioneer

ONTARIO

Museum of History and Art, Ontario
225 S. Euclid St., 91761
Telephone: (714) 983-3198
City agency
Founded in: 1979
Louise Ann Svenson, Director
Number of members: 300
Staff: full time 2, volunteer 10
Magazine: *Master Key*
Major programs: museum, tours/pilgrimages, oral history, school programs, newsletters/pamphlets, historic preservation, records management, research, exhibits, audiovisual programs, fine arts
Period of collections: 1800-present

Ontario Historic Landmarks Society, Inc.
P.O. Box 1493, 91762
Founded in: 1975
Questionnaire not received

OROVILLE

Butte County Historical Society
P. O. Box 2195, 95965

OXNARD

Carnegie Cultural Arts Center
424 S. C St., 93030
Telephone: (805) 984-4649
City agency
Founded in: 1980
Andrew C. Voth, Director
Staff: full time 3, part time 1,
volunteer 25
Major programs: museum, historic
site(s), oral history, school
programs, historic preservation,
exhibits
Period of collections: 1903-present

PACIFIC GROVE

Pacific Grove Heritage Society
Laurel Ave. at 17th St.
Telephone: (408) 372-2898
Mail to: P.O. Box 1007, 93950
Private agency
Adam W. Weiland, President
Number of members: 340
Staff: volunteer 15
Major programs: historic site(s),
markers, oral history,
newsletters/pamphlets, historic
preservation, exhibits,
photographic collections
Period of collections: 1875-present

**William Penn Mott, Jr., Training
Center**
837 Asilomar Blvd., 93950
Telephone: (408) 649-2954
Mail to: P.O. Box 699, 93950
State agency, authorized by
Department of Parks and
Recreation
Founded in: 1973
Broc Stenman, Manager
Staff: full time 5, part time 2
Major programs: historic preservation
training, interpretive training

PACIFIC PALISADES

Pacific Palisades Historical Society
P.O. Box 1299, 90272
Telephone: (213) 454-1974
Private agency
Founded in: 1972
June G. Blum, President-elect
Number of members: 192
Staff: volunteer 30
Major programs: library, archives,
manuscripts, historic site(s),
markers, tours/pilgrimages, junior
history, oral history, school
programs, book publishing,
newsletters/pamphlets, historic
preservation, records
management, research, living
history, audiovisual programs,
archaeology programs,
photographic collections
Period of collections: 1868-present

PALM SPRINGS

Palm Springs Historical Society
221 S. Palm Canyon Dr., 92262
Telephone: (714) 323-8297
Mail to: P.O. Box 1498, 92263

Founded in: 1955
Elizabeth Kieley, President
Number of members: 250
Staff: full time 1, volunteer 35
Magazine: *Whispering Palms*
Major programs: museum, historic
site(s), junior history, oral history,
school programs,
newsletters/pamphlets, historic
preservation
Period of collections: 1884-present

PALO ALTO

Palo Alto Historical Association
P.O. Box 193, 94302
Private agency
Founded in: 1948
John M. Bracken, President
Number of members: 400
Staff: part time 1
Major programs: archives, markers,
oral history, newsletters/pamphlets,
historic preservation, photographic
collections
Period of collections: 1890-present

PARADISE

Paradise Fact and Folklore, Inc.
P. O. Box 1696, 95969
Telephone: (916) 877-3906
Founded in: 1960
James Johnson, President
Number of members: 250
Staff: volunteer 20
Magazine: *Tales of the Paradise
Ridge*
Major programs: tours/pilgrimages,
books
Period of collections: 1865-1918

PASADENA

Pasadena Historical Society
470 W. Walnut, 91103
Telephone: (818) 577-1660
Private agency
Founded in: 1924
Sue Schechter, Executive Director
Staff: full time 1, part time 4,
volunteer 90
Major programs: library, archives,
museum, historic site(s),
newsletters/pamphlets, exhibits,
audiovisual programs,
photographic collections
Period of collections: 1865-1918

PATTERSON

**Patterson Township Historical
Society**
Telephone: (209) 892-6882
Mail to: P.O. Box 15, 95363
Town agency
Founded in: 1972
Barbara Torrison, President
Number of members: 230
Staff: volunteer 15
Magazine: *Gateway*
Major programs: museum, oral
history, school programs,
newsletters/pamphlets, exhibits,
photographic collections
Period of collections: from early 1900

PERRIS

Orange Empire Railway Museum
2201 S. A St.
Telephone: (714) 657-2605
Mail to: P.O. Box 548, 92370
Founded in: 1956
James W. Walker, Jr., President
Number of members: 1,100
Staff: volunteer 80
Magazine: *Orange Empire Railway
Museum Gazette*
Major programs: library, museum,
school programs
newsletters/pamphlets
Period of collections: 1895-present

PETALUMA

**Petaluma Adobe State Historic
Park**
3325 Adobe Rd., 94952
Telephone: (707) 762-4871
State agency, authorized by
Department of Parks and
Recreation
Founded in: 1947
Fred Welcome, Ranger I
Staff: full time 1, part time 1,
volunteer 1
Major programs: historic site(s),
tours/pilgrimages, school
programs, historic preservation,
exhibits, living history
Period of collections: 1822-1846

**Petaluma Museum and Historical
Library**
20 4th St., 94952
Telephone: (707) 778-4398
City agency
Founded in: 1977
Evangeline M. Ruiz, President
Number of members: 145
Staff: volunteer 8

PIEDMONT

Piedmont Historical Society
358 Hillside Ave., 94611
Telephone: (415) 654-3314
Mail to: 95 Nova Dr., 94610
Founded in: 1972
June M. Rutledge, President
Number of members: 200
Staff: volunteer 3
Major programs: archives,
newsletters/pamphlets, historic
preservation
Period of collections: 1852-present

PINE GROVE

Amador County Historical Society
235 Church St., Jackson, 95642
Telephone: (209) 296-4662
Mail to: P.O. Box 147, 95665
Founded in: 1945
Sedrick Clute, Curator
Number of members: 170
Staff: volunteer 14
Major programs: library, archives,
museum, historic preservation,
markes, tours/pilgrimages, junior
history, oral history, school
programs newsletters/pamphlets
Period of collections: 1783-present

PLACERVILLE

El Dorado County Historical Society—County Museum
524 Main St., 95667
Telephone: (916) 626-2250
Founded in: 1939
Irene Barton, President
Number of members: 301
Staff: volunteer 301
Major programs: library, archives, manuscripts, museum, historic site(s), markers, tours/pilgrimages, oral history, book publishing, newsletters/pamphlets
Period of collections: 1849-present

Heritage Association of El Dorado County, Inc.
P.O. Box 62, 95667
Telephone: (916) 622-8388
Private agency
Founded in: 1972
Betty J. Harvey, President
Number of members: 25
Major programs: archives, historic site(s), markers, tours/pilgrimages, junior history, school programs, book publishing, newsletters/pamphlets, historic preservation, research, exhibits
Period of collections: 1850

PLEASANTON

Amador-Livermore Valley Historical Society
603 Main St.
Telephone: (415) 462-2766
Mail to: P.O. Box 573, 94566
Private agency
Founded in: 1963
Ann P. Doss, Museum Curator
Number of members: 300
Staff: part time 1, volunteer 20
Major programs: library, archives, manuscripts, museum, historic site(s), tours/pilgrimages, oral history, school programs, books, newsletters/pamphlets, historic preservation, research, exhibits, archaeology programs, photographic collections, genealogical services
Period of collections: 1880-1960

POMONA

Historical Society of Pomona Valley
1569 N. Park Ave., 91768
Telephone: (714) 623-2198
City agency
Founded in: 1916
Beth Page, President
Number of members: 260
Major programs: museum, historic site(s), markers, school programs, newsletters/pamphlets, historic preservation, research

PORTERVILLE

Porterville Museum
D St.
Mail to: 36 W. Cleveland, 93257
Private agency, authorized by Porterville Chamber of Commerce
Founded in: 1965
Number of members: 250

Staff: volunteer 5
Magazine: *Porterville Historical Museum*
Major programs: museum, school programs, newsletters/pamphlets, exhibits
Period of collections: 1850-1950

PORT HUENEME

CEC-Seabee Museum
Code 2232, Naval Construction Battalion Center, 93043
Telephone: (805) 982-5163
Federal agency, authorized by the U.S. Navy
Founded in: 1946
Y.H. Ketels, Director
Staff: full time 5, part time 1
Major programs: museum, tours/pilgrimages, oral history, exhibits
Period of collections: 1941-present

POTRERO

Potrero-East County Museum Society
P.O. Box 70, 92063
Telephone: (619) 478-5306
Private agency
Founded in: 1979
Etta V. Czech, President
Number of members: 39
Staff: volunteer 5
Major programs: manuscripts, museum, historic site(s), tours/pilgrimages, school programs, newsletters/pamphlets, historic preservation, records management, research, exhibits, audiovisual programs, archaeology programs, photographic collections, genealogical services, field services
Period of collections: 1868-present

POWAY

Poway Historical and Memorial Society
17105 Tam O'Shanter Dr.
Telephone: (714) 487-7199
Mail to: P.O. Box 19, 92064
Private agency
Founded in: 1966
Robert R. Dalley, President
Number of members: 93
Major programs: library, archives, manuscripts, museum, school programs newsletters/pamphlets, historic preservation, oral history, photographic collections

QUINCY

Plumas County Historical Society
P.O. Box 695, 95971
Founded in: 1961
Questionnaire not received

Plumas County Museum
500 Jackson St.
Telephone: (916) 283-1750
Mail to: P. O. Box 776, 95971
County agency
Founded in: 1968
Robert G. Moon, Curator
Number of members: 300

Staff: full time 2, part time 2, volunteer 10
Major programs: museum, historic preservation, exhibits, photographic collections
Period of collections: 1850-present

Plumas County Museum Association, Inc.
500 Jackson
Telephone: (916) 283-1750
Mail to: P.O. Box 776, 95971
Founded in: 1964
Florence Dedmon, President
Number of members: 300
Staff: full time 2, volunteer 16
Magazine: *Plumas County Museum Association Newsletter*
Major programs: library, archives, museum, newsletters/pamphlets
Period of collections: 1850-1930

RAMONA

Ramona Pioneer Historical Society, Inc.—Guy B. Woodward Museum
729 Main St.
Telephone: (619) 789-1062
Mail to: P.O. Box 625, 92065
Town agency
Founded in: 1962
Geneva Woodward, President
Number of members: 500
Major programs: library, museum, historic site(s), markers, tours/pilgrimages, junior history, oral history, school programs, book publishing, historic preservation, records management, research, exhibits, living history, audiovisual programs, photographic collections
Period of collections: 1850-1920

RANCHO CORDOVA

Surveyors' Historical Society
10324 Newton Way, 95670
Mail to: P.O. Box 160502, Sacramento, 95816
Private agency
Founded in: 1978
Myron Lewis, Board Member
Number of members: 228
Staff: volunteer, 228
Magazine: *Backsights*
Major programs: library, historic preservation, exhibits, photographic collections, history of surveying equipment
Period of collections: 1750-present

RANCHO PALOS VERDES

Salvation Army Western Territorial Museum
30840 Hawthorne Blvd., 90274
Telephone: (213) 541-4721
Private agency, authorized by the Salvation Army
Founded in: 1865
Frances C. Dingman, Museum Director
Magazine: *War Cry*
Major programs: archives, museum, oral history, historic preservation, records management, research, exhibits, photographic collections, genealogical services
Period of collections: 1865-present

RED BLUFF

**Kelly-Griggs House Museum
Association**
311 Washington St.
Mail to: P.O. Box 929, 96080
Questionnaire not received

REDDING

Redding Museum and Art Center
1911 Rio Dr.
Telephone: (916) 225-4155
Mail to: P. O. Box 427, 96099
City agency
Founded in: 1963
Cheri Gandy, President
Number of members: 915
Staff: full time 3, part time 9,
volunteer 75
Magazine: *The Covered Wagon*
Major programs: library, museum,
tours/pilgrimages, school
programs, exhibits, genealogical
services, contemporary fine arts
Period of collections:
prehistoric-present

**Shasta College Museum and
Research Center**
1065 N. Old Oregon Trail, 96001
Telephone: (916) 241-3523, ext. 354
Mail to: P.O. Box 6006, 96099
Founded in: 1968
Staff: part time 2, volunteer 3
Magazine: *Shasta College Newsletter*
Major programs: archives, museum,
newsletters/pamphlets
Period of collections: 1850-present

Shasta Historical Society
Telephone: (916) 225-4155
Mail to: P.O. Box 277, 96099
Founded in: 1930
Ann Hunt, President
Number of members: 380
Staff: volunteer 18
Magazine: *Covered Wagon*
Major programs: library, museum,
tours/pilgrimages, books,
newsletters/pamphlets
Period of collections: 1783-present

REDLANDS

**Archaeological Survey Association
of Southern California, Inc.**
Telephone: (714) 848-3998
Mail to: University of Redlands, 92374
Private agency
Founded in: 1951
Thomas J. Crum, President
Number of members: 300
Staff: volunteer, 27
Magazine: *ASA Journal*
Major programs: library, archives,
manuscripts, historic site(s),
markers, book publishing,
newsletters/pamphlets, historic
preservation, records
management, research, exhibits,
audiovisual programs, archaeology
programs, genealogical services,
field services, symposia
Period of collections: prehistoric

Lincoln Memorial Shrine
120 4th St., 92373
Telephone: (714) 793-6622
City agency, authorized by A. K.
Smiley Public Library

Founded in: 1932
Larry E. Burgess, Head of Special
Collections
Number of members: 200
Staff: full time 1, part time 1,
volunteer 18
Major programs: library, archives,
manuscripts, museum,
tours/pilgrimages,
newsletters/pamphlets
Period of collections: Civil War era

Redlands Area Historical Society
Mail to: P.O. Box 1024, 92373
Founded in: 1971
Staff: volunteer 9
Questionnaire not received

**San Bernardino County Museum
Association**
2022 Orange Tree Lane, 92373
Telephone: (714) 793-6345
Founded in: 1952
Gerald A. Smith, Director
Number of members: 1,600
Staff: full time 3, volunteer 20
Magazine: *San Bernardino County
Museum Association Quarterly*
Major programs: museum, historic
preservation, markers, school
programs books,
newsletters/pamphlets
Period of collections:
prehistoric-present

REEDLEY

Reedley Historical Society
1752 10th St.
Telephone: (209) 638-1913
Mail to: P.O. Box 877, 93654
Private agency
Founded in: 1976
Donald C. Fillmore, President
Number of members: 300
Staff: volunteer 30
Magazine: *Reedley Historian*
Major programs: archives, museum,
historic site(s), markers, tours,
school programs,
newsletters/pamphlets, historic
preservation, records
management, research, exhibits,
audiovisual programs,
photographic collections
Period of collections: from 1850

RIALTO

Rialto Historical Society
205 N. Riverside Ave.
Telephone: (714) 875-1750, 875-0141
Mail to: P.O. Box 413, 92376
Private agency
Founded in: 1971
Greta J. Hodges, President
Number of members: 248
Staff: volunteer 30
Major programs: manuscripts,
museum, historic preservation,
books, newsletters/pamphlets,
photographic collections
Period of collections: 1865-present

RICHMOND

**Richmond Museum
Association, Inc.**
400 Nevin Ave.
Telephone: (415) 235-7387

Mail to: P.O. Box 1267, 94802
Private agency
Founded in: 1954
Louis H. Boyle, President
Number of members: 250
Staff: part time 3, volunteer 50
Major programs: library, archives,
museum, oral history, research,
exhibits, photographic collections
Period of collections: late
1800s-present

RIDGECREST

**Maturango Museum of the Indian
Wells Valley**
Corner, Halsey and Knox, China Lake
Telephone: (619) 446-6900
Mail to: P.O. Box 1776, 93555
Private agency
Founded in: 1962
Patricia Brown-Berry, Director
Number of members: 2,000
Staff: full time 1, part time 4,
volunteer 100
Major programs: museum, tours,
school programs, book publishing,
newsletters/pamphlets, exhibits,
archaeology programs, natural
history
Period of collections: 19th-20th
centuries

RIO VISTA

Rio Vista Museum Association, Inc.
16 N. Front St., 94571
Telephone: (707) 374-5169
Private agency
Founded in: 1976
W.H.K. Dunbar, Curator
Number of members: 112
Staff: volunteer 16
Major programs: museum, exhibits
Period of collections: 1865-present

RIVERSIDE

California Museum of Photography
University of California, Riverside,
93921
Telephone: (714) 787-4787
State agency, authorized by the
university
Founded in: 1973
Charles Desmarais, Director
Number of members: 600
Staff: full time 6, part time 4,
volunteer 3
Magazine: *CMP Bulletin*
Major programs: library, museum,
book publishing,
newsletters/pamphlets, research,
exhibits, photographic collections
Period of collections: 1839-present

**Historic Resources Management,
History Department**
University of California, Riverside
Telephone: (714) 787-5403
Mail to: 4110 Library, S, 92521
State agency
Founded in: 1973
Ronald C. Tobey, Professor/Director
Staff: full time 17, part time 4
Major programs: archival
management, museum
curatorship, school programs
(Master's level), historic
preservation

Jensen-Alvarado Ranch Historic Park
P.O. Box 3507, 92519
Telephone: (714) 787-1285
County agency, authorized by
Riverside County Parks
Department
Founded in: 1984
Stephen A. Becker, Executive
Director
Number of members: 200
Staff: full time 1, volunteer 30
Magazine: *Los Compañeros*
Major programs: library, archives,
manuscripts, museum, historic
site(s), tours/pilgrimages, junior
history, newsletters/pamphlets,
historic preservation, exhibits,
living history
Period of collections: 1850-1930

Jurnpa Mountains Cultural Center
7621 Granite Hill Dr., 92509
Telephone: (714) 685-5818
Private agency
Founded in: 1964
Ruth A. Kirkby, Executive Director
Number of members: 1,000
Staff: full time 4, part time 4,
volunteer 72
Magazine: *Smoke Signal*
Major programs: library, museum,
historic site(s), school programs,
book publishing, photographic
collections
Period of collections: 3000 B.C.-1850

Mission Inn Foundation
3649 7th St., 92501
Telephone: (714) 781-8241
Private agency
Founded in: 1976
Katie Grigsby, Administrative
Director
Staff: full time 3, volunteer 50
Major programs: museum, historic
site(s), historic preservation
Period of collections: 1900-1935

Pioneer Historical Society of Riverside
4593 Rubidoux Ave., 92506
Telephone: (714) 683-5462
City agency
Founded in: 1903
R.L. Haglund, President
Number of members: 95
Major programs: oral history,
educational programs
Period of collections: 1870-present

Riverside County Historical Commission
4600 Crestmore Rd.
Mail to: P.O. Box 3507, 92519
County agency
Founded in: 1968
Stephen A. Becker, Director, History
Division
Staff: full time 2, part time 1,
volunteer 100
Major programs: library, museum,
historic site(s), markers,
tours/pilgrimages, oral history,
book publishing,
newsletters/pamphlets, historic
preservation, records
management, research, exhibits,
living history
Period of collections: 1850-present

Riverside Municipal Museum
3720 Orange St., 92501
Telephone: (714) 787-7273
City agency
Founded in: 1925
William G. Dougall, Director
Number of members: 500
Staff: full time 11 part time 2,
volunteer 150
Major programs: library, archives,
manuscripts, museum, historic
site(s), tours/pilgrimages, school
programs, book publishing,
newsletters/pamphlets, historic
preservation, exhibits, archaeology
programs, photographic
collections, natural history
Period of collections: 19th-20th
centuries

ROSEMEAD

Rosemead Library
8800 Valley Blvd., 91770
Telephone: (818) 573-5220
County agency, authorized by Los
Angeles County Public Library
Founded in: 1927
Sally Colby, Californiana Librarian
Staff: full time 1
Major programs: library
Period of collections: 1800s-present

SACRAMENTO

California Committee for the Promotion of History
6000 J St., 95819
Private agency
Founded in: 1976
James C. Williams, Chair
Number of members: 180
Staff: volunteer 4
Magazine: *California History Action*
Major programs: history advocacy

◇California State Archives
1020 O St., 95834
Telephone: (916) 445-4293
State agency
Founded in: 1850
John F. Burns, Chief of Archives
Staff: full time 17, part time 2,
volunteer 1
Magazine: *California Originals*
Major programs: archives,
newsletters/pamphlets, exhibits
Period of collections: 1850-present

California State Capitol Museum
State Capitol, Room 124, 95814
Telephone: (916) 324-0312
State agency, authorized by
Department of Parks and
Recreation
Founded in: 1981
David Vincent, Director
Number of members: 160
Staff: full time 16, part time 23,
volunteer 160
Major programs: museum, historic
site(s), tours, oral history, book
publishing, newsletters/pamphlets,
research, exhibits, living history,
audiovisual programs,
photographic collections
Period of collections: 1900-1910

◇California State Department of Parks and Recreation
Telephone: (916) 445-2358
Mail to: P.O. Box 2390, 95811
Founded in: 1928
William S. Briner, Director
Staff: full time 221, part time 297,
volunteer 225
Magazine: *News and Views*
Major programs: museum, historic
site(s), markers, tours/pilgrimages,
book publishing,
newsletters/pamphlets, historic
preservation, exhibits, living
history, audiovisual programs,
archaeology programs
Period of collections:
prehistoric-present

California State Indian Museum
2618 K St., 95816
Telephone: (916) 324-0971
State agency, authorized by
Department of Parks and
Recreation
Shana Watkins, Ranger I
Staff: full time 1, part time 2,
volunteer 30
Major programs: museum,
tours/pilgrimages, school
programs, exhibits, living history
Period of collections: 1870-1940

California State Library
Library and Courts Bldg., 9th St. and
Capitol Mall, 95814
Telephone: (916) 445-4027
Mail to: P.O. Box 2037, 95809
Founded in: 1850
Gary E. Strong, State Librarian
Major programs: library, archives,
manuscripts
Period of collections:
prehistoric-present

California State Railroad Museum
111 I St., 95814
Telephone: (916) 445-7373
State agency, authorized by
Department of Parks and
Recreation
Founded in: 1976
Stephen E. Drew, Curator
Number of members: 650
Staff: full time 50, part time 35,
volunteer 300
Major programs: library, archives,
manuscripts, museum, historic
site(s), school programs, historic
preservation, records
management, research, exhibits,
living history, audiovisual
programs, photographic
collections, operational steam train
Period of collections: 1830s-present

Californians for Preservation Action
Mail to: P.O. Box 2169, 95810
Founded in: 1975
Questionnaire not received

Friends of Sacramento City and County Museum
1009 7th St., 95814
Mail to: P.O. Box 1826, 95809
Questionnaire not received

Inter-Tribal Council of California, Inc.
2969 Fulton Ave., 95821
Questionnaire not received

Office of Historic Preservation, Department of Parks and Recreation
830 S St., 95814
Telephone: (916) 445-8006
Mail to: P.O. Box 2390, 95811
State agency
Marion Mitchell-Wilson, Deputy State Historic Preservation Officer
Staff: full time 17, part time 4
Major programs: markers, historic preservation, records management

Portuguese Historical and Cultural Society
Telephone: (916) 454-4414
Mail to: P.O. Box 161990, 95816
Private agency
Founded in: 1979
Joe D'Alessandro, Executive Director
Number of members: 1,000
Staff: volunteer 30
Magazine: *O Progresso*
Major programs: library, archives, manuscripts, museum, historic site(s), tours/pilgrimages, oral history, school programs, newsletters/pamphlets, historic preservation, research, exhibits, audiovisual programs, photographic ollections, genealogical services
Period of collections: 1849-present

Sacramento County Historical Society
Mail to: P.O. Box 1175, 95806
Telephone: (916) 443-6265
Private agency
Founded in: 1953
Walter Gray, President
Magazine: *Golden Notes*
Major programs: book publishing, newsletters/pamphlets

Sacramento Museum and History Commission
1930 J St., 95814
Telephone: (916) 447-2958
City and county agency
Founded in: 1973
James E. Henley, Executive Director
Staff: full time 7, part time 3, volunteer 160
Major programs: archives, museum, oral history, historic preservation, records management, research, exhibits, living history, archaeology programs, photographic collections, genealogical services
Period of collections: 1850-1950

Sacramento Trust for Historic Preservation
710 Coronado Blvd., 95825
Questionnaire not received

Sutter's Fort State Historic Park
2701 L St., 94816
Telephone: (916) 445-4422
State agency, authorized by Department of Parks and Recreation
Founded in: 1927
John D. Harbison, State Park Ranger I
Staff: full time 2, part time 2, volunteer 100
Major programs: museum, historic site(s), markers, tours/pilgrimages, school programs, living history
Period of collections: 1839-1849

ST. HELENA

Silverado Museum
1490 Library Lane
Mail to: P.O. Box 409, 94574
Founded in: 1969
Questionnaire not received

Vintage Hall, Inc.
473 Main St.
(707) 963-7411
Founded in: 1974
Questionnaire not received

SALINAS

Monterey County Agricultural and Rural Life Museum
c/o Monterey County Parks
Telephone: (408) 424-1971
Mail to: P.O. Box 367, 93902
County agency, authorized by Monterey County Parks
Founded in: 1981
Meg Welden, Historical Coordinator
Staff: full time 1, part time 1, volunteer 30
Major programs: museum, school programs, exhibits
Period of collections: 1860-1930

Monterey County Historical Society
333 Boronda Rd. 93907
Telephone: (408) 757-8085
Mail to: P.O. Box 3576, 93912
Founded in: 1933
Number of members: 500
Staff: full time 4, part time 1, volunteer 20
Major programs: archives, museum, historic site(s), tours/pilgrimages, school programs, newsletters/pamphlets
Period of collections: 1840-present

SAN ANDREAS

Calaveras County Historical Society
30 Main St.
Mail to: P.O. Box 721, 95249
Founded in: 1952
Questionnaire not received

Calaveras County Museum and Archives
30 N. Main St.
Telephone: (209) 754-4203
Mail to: Government Center, 95249
County agency
Founded in: 1936
Judith Cunningham, Director
Staff: full time 2, part time 1, volunteer 1
Major programs: library, archives, museum, historic site(s), oral history, research, exhibits, photographic collections, genealogical services
Period of collections: 1850-1930

Calaveras Heritage Council
Calaveras County Museum and Archives,
Old Courthouse, Main St.
Telephone: (209) 754-4203
Mail to: P.O. Box 1281, 95249
Judith Cunningham, Director/Curator
Number of members: 75
Staff: full time 2, part time 4, volunteer 3

Major programs: library, archives, museum, historic site(s), oral history, school programs, newsletters/pamphlets, historic preservation, research, exhibits, archaeology programs, photographic collections, genealogical services, field services
Period of collections: 1850-1930

SAN BERNARDINO

City of San Bernardino Historical and Pioneer Society
796 N. D St.
Telephone: (714) 888-5291
Mail to: P.O. Box 875, 92402
Town agency
Founded in: 1977
Fred Holladay, President
Number of members: 300
Staff: volunteer 25
Magazine: *Odyssey/Heritage Tales*
Major programs: library, archives, museum, historic site(s), markers, book publishing, newsletters/pamphlets, historic preservation, research, photographic collections
Period of collections: 1850-present

SAN CLEMENTE

San Clemente Historical Society
2600 Del Presidente
Telephone: (714) 492-3142
Mail to: P.O. Box 283, 92672
Private agency
Founded in: 1973
Charles E. Ashbaugh, Jr., President
Number of members: 150
Staff: volunteer 8
Major programs: archives, manuscripts, museum, historic site(s), markers, tours/pilgrimages, oral history, book publishing, newsletters/pamphlets, historic preservation, audiovisual programs
Period of collections: 1925-1981

SAN DIEGO

Cabrillo Historical Association
Telephone: (619) 293-5450
Mail to: P.O. Box 6670, 92106
Private agency
Founded in: 1956
Shirley Rees, Business Manager
Staff: full time 3, part time 3
Major programs: library, oral history, book publishing, audiovisual programs
Period of collections: 1918-present

Cabrillo National Monument
Catalina Blvd., Point Loma
Telephone: (714) 293-5450
Mail to: P.O. Box 6670, 92106
Federal agency
Founded in: 1913
Doris I. Omundson, Park Superintendent
Staff: full time 13, part time 5
Major programs: historic site(s), historic preservation, exhibits, audiovisual programs
Period of collections: 1850-1890

Historical Shrine Foundation
2482 San Diego Ave., 92110
Questionnaire not received

Maritime Research Society of San Diego
2427 Howard Ave., 92104
Telephone: (619) 295-0297
Private agency
Founded in: 1936
Robert LaFono, Secretary/Treasurer
Number of members: 48
Staff: volunteer 1
Major programs: library, archives, museum, historic site(s), historic preservation, research
Period of collections: 1930s-1960s

San Diego Maritime Museum
1306 N. Harbor Dr., 92101
Telephone: (714) 234-9153
Founded in: 1948
Questionnaire not received

San Diego Historical Society
2727 Presidio Dr.
Telephone: (619) 297-3258
Mail to: P.O. Box 81825, 92138
Founded in: 1928
Richard R. Esparza, Executive Director
Number of members: 2,900
Staff: full time 24, part time 4, volunteer 300
Magazine: Journal of San Diego History/San Diego History News
Major programs: library, archives, manuscripts, museum, historic preservation, markers, tours, oral history, school programs, books, newsletters/pamphlets
Period of collections: 1492-present

Save Our Heritage Organization
450 Heritage Park Row, Senlis Cottage, Heritage Park
Telephone: (619) 297-9327
Mail to: P.O. Box 3571, 92103
Private agency
Founded in: 1969
Mary Joralmon, President
Number of members: 700
Staff: volunteer 60
Magazine: Reflections
Major programs: library, historic site(s), tours/pilgrimages, school programs newsletters/pamphlets, historic preservation
Period of collections: 1870-1930

The Westerners—San Diego Corral
Mail to: P.O. Box 7174, 92107
Founded in: 1968
Questionnaire not received

SAN FRANCISCO

California Council for the Humanities
312 Sutter St., Suite 601, 94108
Telephone: (415) 391-1474
Private agency, authorized by National Endowment for the Humanities
Founded in: 1978
James D. Quay, Executive Director
Staff: full time 4, part time 4
Magazine: Humanities Network
Major programs: exhibits, audiovisual programs, conferences, symposia, workshops

California Genealogical Society
870 Market St., Flood Bldg., Room 1124, 94102
Telephone: (415) 989-5441
Private agency
Founded in: 1898
David M. Adams, President
Number of members: 350
Staff: part time 1, volunteer 11
Major programs: library, archives, manuscripts, school programs, book publishing, newsletters/pamphlets, research, genealogical services
Period of collections: 1492-1918

◇California Heritage Council—California Trust for Historic Preservation,
680 Beach St., Room 351, 94109
Telephone: (415) 776-6488
Founded in: 1959
Mary S. Rhodes, Executive Director
Number of members: 200
Staff: full time 1, volunteer 20
Magazine: The Report
Major programs: library, tours, historic preservation

◇California Historical Society
2090 Jackson St., 94109
Telephone: (415) 567-1848
Private agency
Founded in: 1871
Joseph Giovinco, Executive Director
Number of members: 9,800
Staff: full time 18, part time 11, volunteer 57
Magazine: California History
Major programs: library, archives, manuscripts, historic site(s), oral history, book publishing, newsletters/pamphlets, exhibits, photographic collections
Period of collections: 1576-present

Center for Museum Studies, John F. Kennedy University
1717 17th St., 94103
Telephone: (415) 626-1787
Private agency
Diane B. Frankel, Director
Staff: full time 1, part time 5
Magazine: Museum Studies Journal
Major programs: museum, field services, museum training

Chinese Historical Society of America
17 Adler Place, 94133
Telephone: (415) 391-1188
Founded in: 1963
Annie Soo, Editor
Number of members: 630
Staff: volunteer 48
Major programs: museum, books, newsletters/pamphlets
Period of collections: 1865-present

Ft. Point and Army Museum Association
Funston Ave. at Lincoln Blvd.
Telephone: (415) 921-8193
Mail to: P.O. Box 29163, 94129
Private agency
Founded in: 1959
Linda Wickart, Executive Director
Number of members: 700
Staff: full time 1, part time 1, volunteer 17
Magazine: Fort Point Salvo
Major programs: library, museum, historic site(s), oral history, school programs, newsletters/pamphlets, historic preservation, exhibits, outreach
Period of collections: 1865-present

Ft. Point National Historic Site
P.O. Box 29333, 94129
Telephone: (415) 556-1693

The Lenchner family camps in Golden Gate Park, San Francisco, in 1906.—Lenchner Collection, the Western Jewish History Center of the Judah L. Magnes Memorial Museum

Federal agency, authorized by
National Park Service
Founded in: 1970
Charles S. Hawkins, Site Manager
Staff: full time 9
Major programs: historic site(s),
tours/pilgrimages, school
programs, historic preservation,
exhibits, audiovisual programs,
photographic collections
Period of collections: 1850-1890

**Foundation for San Francisco's
Architectural Heritage**
2007 Franklin St., 94109
Telephone: (415) 441-3000
Private agency
Founded in: 1971
H. Grant Dehart, Executive Director
Number of members: 1,300
Staff: full time 9, part time 3
Magazine: *Heritage Newsletter*
Major programs: museum,
tours/pilgrimages, school
programs, newsletters/pamphlets,
historic preservation, research,
photographic collections, field
services, technical advice on
rehabilitation and restoration
Period of collections: to 1940

**Grand Parlor, Native Sons of the
Golden West**
414 Mason St., Room 304, 94102
Questionnaire not received

**Labor Archives and Research
Center**
San Francisco State University, 480
Winston Dr., 94132
Telephone: (415) 469-2011
Founded in: 1984
Lynn A. Bonfield, Archivist
Staff: full time 1, part time 2
Major programs: archives of labor
organizations and papers of
working women and men from the
six-county area, educational
programs
Period of collections: 1853-present

**National Archives—San Francisco
Branch**
1000 Commodore Dr., San Bruno,
94066
Telephone: (415) 876-9009
Founded in: 1969
Michael Anderson, Director
Staff: full time 6
Major programs: archives,
educational programs, teachers'
workshops, genealogical
workshops, film series, open
houses and tours
Period of collections: 1848-1976

**National Maritime Museum, San
Francisco—National
Maritime Museum Association**
Golden Gate National Recreation
Area, Ft. Mason, 94109
Telephone: (415) 556-3002
Federal agency
Founded in: 1951
Glennie Wall, Maritime Unit Manager
Number of members: 700
Staff: full time 45
Magazine: *Sea Letter*

Major programs: library, archives,
manuscripts, museum, historic
site(s), oral history, school
programs, historic preservation,
research, exhibits, photographic
collections, fine arts, fleet of
historic ships and small boats,
maritime artifacts
Period of collections: 1790s-1970s

Northern California Railroad Club
Mail to: P.O. Box 668, 94401
Founded in: 1937
Number of members: 300
Magazine: *NorCal Railfan/The
Western Railroader*
Questionnaire not received

Old Mint Museum
5th and Mission Sts., 94103
Telephone: (415) 974-0788
Federal agency
Founded in: 1874
Olga K. Widness, Public Area
Administrator
Staff: full time 9
Major programs: library, museum,
exhibits, audiovisual programs
Period of collections: 1874-present

**Pacific Coast Chapter, Railway and
Locomotive Historical
Society, Inc.**
Mail to: c/o Stuart A. Forsyth, 100
Cedro Ave., 94127
Private agency
Major programs: library, archives,
museum, tours/pilgrimages, book
publishing, newsletters/pamphlets,
historic preservation, research,
exhibits, photographic collections

Presidio Army Museum
Corner of Lincoln and Funston,
94129-5502
Telephone: (415) 561-3319
Federal agency, authorized by the
U.S. Army
Founded in: 1973
Eric J. Saul, Director/Curator
Staff: full time 4
Major programs: library, archives,
manuscripts, museum, historic
site(s), markers, tours/pilgrimages,
oral history, school programs,
newsletters/pamphlets, historic
preservation, records
management, research, exhibits,
photographic collections
Period of collections: 19th century

**San Francisco African American
Historical and Cultural Society**
680 McAllister St., 94102
Founded in: 1955
Questionnaire not received

**San Francisco Corral, Westerners
International**
201 Homer Ave., Palo Alto, 94301
Telephone: (415) 327-2717
Founded in: 1959
Number of members: 100
Staff: volunteer 10
Magazine: *Argonaut*
Major programs: tours/pilgrimages,
school programs
newsletters/pamphlets

**San Francisco Fire Department
Museum,
St. Francis Hook and Ladder
Society**
260 Golden Gate Ave., 94102
Telephone: (415) 826-6989
Founded in: 1964
Bill Koenig, Director
Number of members: 357
Staff: volunteer 50
Major programs: library, archives,
museum, historic site(s), markers,
tours/pilgrimages,
newsletters/pamphlets, historic
preservation, records
management, exhibits, living
history, photographic collections,
firefighting equipment and artifacts
Period of collections: 1849-present

**San Francisco Landmarks
Preservation Advisory Board**
100 Larkin St., 94114
Telephone: (415) 558-3055
Founded in: 1967
Questionnaire not received

**San Francisco Lesbian and Gay
History Project**
P.O. Box 42332, 94101
Private agency
Founded in: 1979
Eric Garber, Secretary
Number of members: 18
Major programs: archives, oral
history, research, exhibits
Period of collections: 1930-present

Society of California Pioneers
456 McAllister St., 94102
Telephone: (415) 861-5278
Founded in: 1850
J. Roger Jobson, Executive Director
Number of members: 1,200
Staff: full time 4
Magazine: *The Pioneer*
Major programs: library, archives,
museum
Period of collections: 1783-1918

Telephone Museum
1145 Larkin St., 94109
Telephone: (415) 441-3918
Private agency, authorized by
George S. Ladd Chapter,
Telephone Pioneers of America
Don T. Thrall, Director/Archivist
Staff: volunteer 5
Magazine: *Information Desk*
Major programs: library, archives,
museum

Treasure Island Museum
Bldg. 1, 94130
Telephone: (415) 765-6182
Federal agency, authorized by
Department of Transportation, U.S.
Navy
Founded in: 1975
Lisa Brandes, Director
Number of members: 190
Staff: full time 4, part time 2,
volunteer 35
Major programs: library, archives,
museum, newsletters/pamphlets,
records management, research,
exhibits, photographic collections
Period of collections: 1813-present

CALIFORNIA

Wells Fargo Bank History Department
475 Sansome St., 94111
Telephone: (415) 396-4157
Private agency, authorized by Wells Fargo Bank
Harold P. Anderson, Vice President/Corporate Archivist
Major programs: library, archives, museum, oral history, newsletters/pamphlets, research, exhibits, photographic collections
Period of collections: 1852-early 1900s

Western Regional Office, National Trust for Historic Preservation
802 Montgomery St., 94133
Questionnaire not received

Wine Museum of San Francisco
633 Beach St., 94109
Founded in: 1974
Questionnaire not received

"Young Ideas" Explorer Post 400
203 Clayton St., 94117
Telephone: (415) 386-1936
Private agency, authorized by The Public Eye, Inc.
Founded in: 1978
Keith O. St. Clare, Producer
Number of members: 108
Staff: full time 12, part time 2, volunteer 10
Major programs: junior history, oral history, living history, audiovisual programs
Period of collections: 1940-present

SAN GABRIEL

San Gabriel Historical Association
318 S. Mission Dr., 91776
Telephone: (818) 308-3223
Private agency
Founded in: 1959
Number of members: 200
Staff: volunteer 30
Major programs: museum, historic preservation, exhibits, photographic collections, genealogical services
Period of collections: 1771-present

San Gabriel Historical Society, Los Compadrinos Museum
807 Montecito Dr., 91776
Telephone: (213) 284-0255
Founded in: 1978
Questionnaire not received

SAN JACINTO

San Jacinto Valley Museum Association, Inc.
181 E. Main St.
Telephone: (714) 654-4952
Mail to: P.O. Box 922, 92383
City agency, authorized by San Jacinto City Council (Municipal Museum)
Founded in: 1939
William "Bill" Dugan, Director/Curator
Number of members: 150
Staff: full time 1, volunteer 4
Major programs: museum, oral history, book publishing, newsletters/pamphlets
Period of collections: 1800-present

SAN JOSE

California Pioneers of Santa Clara County
Mail to: P.O. Box 8208, 95155
Questionnaire not received

San Jose Historical Museum
635 Phelan Ave., 95112
Telephone: (408) 287-2290
City agency, authorized by Parks and Recreation Department
Founded in: 1951
Mignon Gibson, Director
Number of members: 1,300
Staff: full time 2, part time 6, volunteer 200
Magazine: San Jose Historical Museum Association Newsletter
Major programs: archives, museum, historic preservation, school programs, books, newsletters/pamphlets
Period of collections: 1792-1950s

San Jose Historic Landmarks Commission
14 S. 1st St., 95113
Telephone: (408) 277-5548
City agency
Leon S. Kimura, Development Officer
Staff: part time 2
Major programs: markers, school programs book publishing, historic preservation

Santa Clara County Historical Heritage Commission
County Government Center, E. Wing, 70 W. Hedding St., 95110
Telephone: (408) 299-4321
County agency
Founded in: 1973
Beth Wyman, Chair
Staff: part time 1, volunteer 1
Major programs: library, archives, historic site(s), markers, tours/pilgrimages, school programs, book publishing, historic preservation, records management, research, exhibits, photographic collections, historic American building survey, architectural drawings
Period of collections: 1850-present

Sourisseau Academy for California State and Local History
Telephone: (415) 324-0161
Mail to: History Department, San Jose State University, 95192
Private agency
Founded in: 1971
Glory Anne Caffey, Executive Secretary
Staff: part time 2
Major programs: library, archives, manuscripts, educational programs
Period of collections: 1769-present

SAN JUAN BAUTISTA

San Juan Bautista Historical Society
308 3rd St.
Telephone: (408) 623-4542
Mail to: P.O. Box 1, 95045
Founded in: 1964
Number of members: 82
Staff: volunteer 14

Major programs: library, museum, historic preservation, markers, books, newsletters/pamphlets
Period of collections: 1783-1918

SAN JUAN CAPISTRANO

San Juan Capistrano Historical Society
31831 Los Rios St.
Telephone: (714) 493-8444
Mail to: P.O. Box 81, 92675
Number of members: 400
Staff: part time 1, volunteer 25
Major programs: library, manuscripts, museum, historic site(s), markers, tours/pilgrimages, oral history, school programs book publishing, newsletters/pamphlets, historic preservation
Period of collections: 1880-present

SAN LEANDRO

San Leandro Library-Historical Commission
300 Estudillo Ave., 94577
Telephone: (415) 577-3480
City agency, authorized by San Leandro City Council
Founded in: 1973
Stephen D. Ewing, Secretary
Staff: full time 1
Major programs: library, museum, historic site(s), markers, tours/pilgrimages, oral history, newsletters/pamphlets, photographic collections
Period of collections: 1918-present

SAN LUIS OBISPO

Old Mission San Luis Obispo de Tolosa
782 Monterey, 93401
Telephone: (805) 543-1034
Mail to: P.O. Box 1483, 93406
Private agency, authorized by the Roman Catholic Church
Founded in: 1772
Jim Nisbet, Pastor
Staff: full time 5, part time 3
Major programs: archives, museum, historic site(s)

San Luis Obispo County Historical Society
696 Monterey St.
Telephone: (805) 696-0138
Mail to: P.O. Box 1391, 93406
Private agency
Founded in: 1953
Lura B. Rawson, Director of Museum
Number of members: 500
Staff: full time 2, part time 4, volunteer 40
Magazine: La Vista
Major programs: museum, historic site(s), tours/pilgrimages, oral history, school programs, newsletters/pamphlets, exhibits, audiovisual programs, photographic collections, genealogical services

SAN MARCOS

San Marcos Historical Society
149 E. San Marcos Blvd.
Telephone: (714) 744-9025

Mail to: P.O. Box 84, 92069
Founded in: 1967
Number of members: 275
Major programs: library, archives,
museum, tours/pilgrimages, oral
history, newsletters/pamphlets,
historic preservation, work with
schools
Period of collections: 1875-1920s

SAN MARINO

California Historical Society
1120 Old Mill Rd., 91108
Founded in: 1871
Questionnaire not received

**Huntington Corral of Westerners
International**
Telephone: (818) 284-2130
Mail to: P.O. Box 80241, 91108
Founded in: 1979
Jack Sherwood, Sheriff
Number of members: 125
Magazine: *Iron Horse Express*
Major programs: book publishing,
newsletters/pamphlets, exhibits
Period of collections: frontier
history-1900

San Marino Historical Society
Telephone: (818) 284-2130
Mail to: P.O. Box 80222, 91108
Private agency
Founded in: 1973
Midge Sherwood, Founder/Archivist
Number of members: 350
Major programs: archives,
manuscripts, museum, historic
site(s), tours, oral history, school
programs, book publishing, historic
preservation, photographic
collections, microfilm file of local
newspaper
Period of collections: from 1850

SAN MATEO

Portola Expedition Foundation
1700 W. Hillsdale Blvd.
Telephone: (415) 583-0424
Mail to: 355 Erica Dr., S. San
Francisco, 94080
Private agency
Founded in: 1965
F. Jose DeLarios, President
Number of members: 150
Major programs: historic site(s),
markers, junior history, historic
preservation

**San Mateo County Historical
Association and Museum**
1700 W. Hillsdale Blvd., 94402
Telephone: (415) 574-6441
Private agency
Founded in: 1935
Mitchell P. Postel, Executive Director
Number of members: 1,400
Staff: full time 5, part time 1,
volunteer 80
Magazine: *La Peninsula*
Major programs: library, archives,
manuscripts, museum, historic
site(s), school programs,
newsletters/pamphlets, exhibits,
photographic collections,
genealogical services
Period of collections: 1769-present

SAN MIGUEL

Friends of the Adobes, Inc.
Old Hwy. 101, Mission St., S
Telephone: (805) 467-3357
Mail to: P.O. Box 326, 93451
Private agency, authorized by County
of San Luis Obispo
Founded in: 1968
Joyce A. Herman, President
Number of members: 496
Staff: volunteer 20
Major programs: museum, historic
site(s), markers, tours/pilgrimages,
book publishing, historic
preservation, exhibits
Period of collections: 1880-1920

Mission San Miguel
801 Mission St.
Telephone: (805) 467-3256
Mail to: P.O. Box 69, 93451
Private agency, authorized by
Franciscan Friars
Founded in: 1797
Reginald McDonough, Superior
Staff: volunteer 8
Major programs: museum, historic
site(s), tours/pilgrimages, historic
preservation, exhibits
Period of collections: 1797-present

SAN PABLO

**San Pablo Historical and Museum
Society**
1 Alvarado Square, 94806
Telephone: (415) 236-7373
Private agency
Founded in: 1969
Ann Roberts, Curator
Number of members: 65
Staff: volunteer 12
Major programs: library, museum,
historic site(s),
newsletters/pamphlets, exhibits,
audiovisual programs,
photographic collections
Period of collections: 1825-1925

SAN RAFAEL

**Falkirk Community Cultural
Center—Robert Dollar Estate**
1408 Mission St.
Telephone: (415) 485-3328
Mail to: P.O. Box 60, 94915
City agency
Founded in: 1974
D.B. Finnigan, Director
Staff: full time 3, part time 4,
volunteer 6
Major programs: historic
preservation, exhibits,
contemporary visual and literary
arts program
Period of collections: Victorian era

Marin County Historical Society
1125 B St., 94901
Founded in: 1935
Questionnaire not received

Marin Heritage
Telephone: (415) 457-9280
Mail to: P.O. Box 1432, 94902
Founded in: 1973
Fred Dekker, Information Officer
Number of members: 100

Major programs: historic preservation,
education, restoration of
greenhouse

SANTA ANA

**Charles W. Bowers Memorial
Museum**
2002 N. Main St., 92706
Telephone: (714) 972-1900
City agency
Founded in: 1932
William B. Lee, Museum Director
Number of members: 1,700
Staff: full time 15, part time 6,
volunteer 100
Major programs: museum,
tours/pilgrimages, oral history,
school programs, book publishing,
newsletters/pamphlets, historic
preservation, exhibits, archaeology
programs
Period of collections: 19th-20th
centuries

**Orange County Historical
Commission**
Telephone: (714) 834-4741
Mail to: c/o Environmental
Management Agency, P.O. Box
4048, 92702
Robert R. Selway, Executive Officer
Staff: full time 1, part time 2
Major programs: archives, historic
site(s), markers, oral history,
newsletters, historic preservation,
research, archaeology programs
Period of collections: late 19th
century-present

Orange County Historical Society
2002 N. Main St., 92706
Founded in: 1919
Number of members: 250
Staff: volunteer 13
Magazine: *Courier*
Major programs: archives, book
publishing
Period of collections: 1796-present

SANTA BARBARA

**Public History Program, University
of California**
Telephone: (805) 961-2991
Mail to: 93106
State agency, authorized by the
university
Founded in: 1868
Carroll Pursell, Director
Magazine: *The Public Historian*
Major programs: education, graduate
program

**Reina del Mar Parlor 126, Native
Daughters of the Golden West**
P.O. Box 404, 93102
Telephone: (805) 687-2957
Private agency
Founded in: 1901
Anita Joyal, President
Number of members: 120
Major programs: markers,
cooperating with other local
historical organizations
Period of collections: 1901-present

Santa Barbara Historical Society
136 E. De la Guerra, 93101
Telephone: (805) 966-1601
Mail to: P.O. Box 578, 93102

Private agency
Founded in: 1932
Mrs. Henry Griffiths, Museum Director
Number of members: 1,350
Staff: full time 4, part time 6,
    volunteer 16
Major programs: library, archives,
    manuscripts, museum, historic
    site(s), school programs,
    photographic collections
Period of collections: 1783-1925

**Santa Barbara Trust for Historic
    Preservation**
123 E. Canon Perdido St.
Telephone: (805) 966-9719
Mail to: P.O. Box 388, 93102
Private agency
Founded in: 1963
John Hass, President
Number of members: 200
Staff: full time 5, part time 5,
    volunteer 10
Magazine: *La Campana*
Major programs: library, archives,
    museum, historic site(s), school
    programs newsletters/pamphlets,
    historic preservation, research,
    exhibits, audiovisual programs,
    archaeology programs,
    photographic collections
Period of collections: 1850-1900

**Society for the History of
    Technology**
University of California, 93106
Founded in: 1958
Number of members: 2,200
Magazine: *Technology and Culture*
Questionnaire not received

SANTA CLARA

**Santa Clara County Historical and
    Genealogical Society**
2635 Homestead Rd., 95051
Telephone: (408) 998-5596
Private agency
Founded in: 1957
Richard Ferman, President
Number of members: 228
Staff: volunteer 25
Major programs: library, archives,
    manuscripts, oral history,
    newsletters/pamphlets, records
    management, research,
    photographic collections,
    genealogical services
Period of collections: 1783-present

SANTA CRUZ

Forest History Society, Inc.
109 Coral St., 95060
Founded in: 1946
Number of members: 1,922
Staff: full time 9, part time 4
Magazine: *Journal of Forest History*
Major programs: library, archives,
    manuscripts, oral history, books
Period of collections: 1865-present

Julia Morgan Association
130 Getchell St., 95060
Telephone: (408) 427-0708
Private agency
Founded in: 1975
Sara Holmes Boutelle, Director
Staff: part time 1, volunteer 2

Major programs: archives,
    manuscripts, historic site(s),
    markers, tours/pilgrimages, oral
    history, historic preservation,
    research, exhibits, photographic
    collections
Period of collections: 1900-1950

**Santa Cruz County Society for
    Historic Preservation, Inc.**
118 Cooper St., 95060
Telephone: (408) 425-2540
County agency
Founded in: 1968
Harriet Deck, President
Major programs: museum, historic
    site(s), historic preservation,
    exhibits, photographic collections
library, 1860s-1960s

Santa Cruz Historical Society
Mail to: P.O. Box 246, 95061
Private agency
Founded in: 1954
Cynthia Mathews, President
Number of members: 250
Staff: volunteer 15
Major programs: book publishing,
    newsletters/pamphlets, historic
    preservation, research, exhibits,
    audiovisual programs
eriod of collections: 1783-present

SANTA FE SPRINGS

**Santa Fe Springs Historical
    Committee**
11710 Telegraph Rd.
Telephone: (213) 864-4538
Mail to: c/o President, 10146 Gridley
    Rd., 90670
City agency
Founded in: 1957
Ann Bartunek, President
Number of members: 24
Major programs: library, archives,
    manuscripts, historic site(s),
    markers, tours/pilgrimages, oral
    history, historic preservation,
    exhibits, archaeology programs,
    photographic collections
Period of collections: 1784-present

SANTA MARIA

**Santa Maria Valley Historical
    Society**
616 S. Broadway
Telephone: (805) 922-3130
Mail to: P.O. Box 584, 93454
Founded in: 1955
Luann Davis Powell, Director
Number of members: 300
Staff: full time 1, volunteer 26
Major programs: library, museum,
    tours/pilgrimages, oral history,
    school programs, books,
    newsletters/pamphlets
Period of collections:
    prehistoric-present

SANTA MONICA

**Santa Monica Heritage Square
    Museum**
2612 Main St., 90405
Telephone: (213) 392-8537
Private agency
Founded in: 1976

Cynthia Schubert, Museum
    Administrator
Number of members: 600
Staff: full time 1, part time 2,
    volunteer 60
Magazine: *Heritage*
Major programs: library, archives,
    museum, oral history, school
    programs, research, exhibits,
    photographic collections,
    decorative arts
Period of collections: 1890s-1930s

Santa Monica Historical Society
P.O. Box 3059, Will Rogers Station,
    90403
Telephone: (213) 828-2170
Private agency
Founded in: 1975
Louise B. Gabriel, President
Number of members: 850
Staff: volunteer 20
Major programs: archives, historic
    site(s), tours/pilgrimages, oral
    history, school programs,
    newsletters/pamphlets, historic
    preservation, research, exhibits,
    living history, photographic
    collections
Period of collections: 1769-1875

SANTA PAULA

California Oil Museum
1003 E. Main St., 93060
Telephone: (805) 525-6672
Private agency, authorized by Union
    Oil Company of California
Founded in: 1950
Jack Elliott, Special Clerk
Staff: full time 1
Major programs: manuscripts,
    museum, historic site(s), historic
    preservation, exhibits,
    photographic collections
Period of collections: 1865-1940

SANTA ROSA

**Sonoma County Genealogical
    Society**
P.O. Box 2273, 95405
Founded in: 1965
Questionnaire not received

Sonoma County Historical Society
509 4th St., S., 95401
Telephone: (707) 525-1155
Mail to: P.O. Box 1373, 95402
Private agency
Founded in: 1962
Emily Doll, President
Number of members: 500
Staff: volunteer 15
Magazine: *The Journal*
Major programs: tours/pilgrimages,
    book publishing,
    newsletters/pamphlets, research,
    photographic collections
Period of collections: 1890-1920

Sonoma County Museum
425 7th St., 95401
Telephone: (707) 579-1500
Mail to: P.O. Box 3424, 95402
Private agency, authorized by
    Historical Museum Foundation of
    Sonoma County, Inc.
Founded in: 1976
Dayton Lummis, Jr., Museum Director

Number of members: 1,750
Staff: full time 3, volunteer 50
Magazine: *Recollections*
Major programs: museum,
tours/pilgrimages, school
programs, historic preservation,
exhibits, photographic collections
Period of collections: 19th century

SANTA YNEZ

**Santa Ynez Valley Historical
Society and Museum**
3596 Sagunto St.
Telephone: (805) 688-5400
Mail to: P.O. Box 181, 93460
Founded in: 1961
R. J. Grigsby, President
Number of members: 352
Staff: volunteer 44
Major programs: library, archives,
museum, oral history,
newsletters/pamphlets, historic
preservation, research, exhibits,
photographic collections
Period of collections: 1880-present

SARATOGA

Saratoga Historical Foundation
20450 Saratoga Los Gratos Rd.
Mail to: P.O. Box 172, 95070
Founded in: 1960
Number of members: 115
Staff: volunteer 35
Major programs: archives, museum,
newsletters/pamphlets, historic
preservation
Period of collections: 1850-present

**Villa Montalvo Center for the Arts
and Arboretum**
15400 Montalvo Rd., 95070
Telephone: (408) 867-3421
Mail to: P.O. Box 158, 95071
Private agency
Founded in: 1952
Gardiner R. McCauley, Executive
Director
Number of members: 1,000
Staff: full time 6, part time 5,
volunteer 300
Magazine: *Montalvo News*
Major programs: historic site(s),
historic preservation, exhibits, fine
arts

SAUSALITO

Sausalito Historical Society
420 Litho St., 94965
Mail to: P.O. Box 352, 94966
Founded in: 1975
Number of members: 450
Staff: volunteer 10
Magazine: *Sausalito Historical*
Major programs: archives, museum,
historic site(s),
newsletters/pamphlets, historic
preservation
Period of collections: 1868-present

SEBASTOPOL

**Western Sonoma County Historical
Society**
P.O. Box 816, 95472
John McGrew, President
Number of members: 111

Magazine: *The Apple Press*
Major programs: archives, historic
site(s), newsletters/pamphlets,
historic preservation

SHAFTER

Shafter Historical Society, Inc.
150 Central Valley Hwy.
Telephone: (805) 746-4423
Mail to: P.O. Box 1088, 93263
Private agency
Founded in: 1979
Stan Wilson, Curator
Number of members: 200
Staff: part time 1, volunteer 5
Major programs: museum, historic
preservation, exhibits
Period of collections: 1915-1940

SHINGLETOWN

Mt. Lassen Historical Society
Telephone: (916) 474-3061
Mail to: P.O. Box 291, 96088
Number of members: 60
Questionnaire not received

SIERRA CITY

Sierra County Historical Society
Telephone: (916) 862-1310
Mail to: P.O. Box 260, 96125
Staff: full time 1, part time 1,
volunteer 20
Magazine: *Sierran*
Major programs: museum, historic
site(s), newsletters/pamphlets
Period of collections: Gold Rush era

SIERRA MADRE

Sierra Madre Historical Society
Mail to: P.O. Box 202, 91024
Founded in: 1931
Questionnaire not received

SIMI VALLEY

Simi Valley Historical Society
Telephone: (805) 526-6453
Mail to: P.O. Box 351, 93062
Authorized by Rancho Simi
Recreation and Park District
Founded in: 1964
Patricia Havens, Museum Director
Number of members: 425
Staff: part time 2, volunteer 50
Major programs: archives,
manuscripts, museum, historic
site(s), oral history, school
programs, newsletters/pamphlets,
historic preservation, research,
exhibits, living history, audiovisual
programs, archaeology programs,
photographic collections,
agriculture
Period of collections:
prehistoric-present

SONOMA

Depot Park Museum
270 1st St., W
Telephone: (707) 938-9765
Mail to: P.O. Box 861, 95476
Private agency, authorized by
Sonoma Valley Historical Society
Founded in: 1937

James C. Vanderbilt, Museum
Director
Number of members: 320
Staff: volunteer 8
Magazine: *Valley Notes*
Major programs: library, museum,
tours/pilgrimages, exhibits,
audiovisual programs,
photographic collections

**Sonoma League for Historic
Preservation**
129 E. Spain St.
Mail to: P.O. Box 766, 95476
Founded in: 1969
Richard Foorman, President
Number of members: 375
Staff: volunteer 150
Major programs: library, archives,
historic site(s), tours, book
publishing, newsletters/pamphlets,
historic preservation, research,
exhibits, photographic collections,
awards for building restorations
Period of collections: 1850-1900

Sonoma State Historic Park
20 E. Spain St., 95476
Telephone: (707) 938-1519
Mail to: P.O. Box 167
Founded in: 1943
Staff: full time 8, part time 3,
volunteer 8
Major programs: museum, historic
site(s), tours
Period of collections: 1783-1920

Sonoma Valley Historical Society
Mail to: P.O. Box 861, 95476
Founded in: 1937
Number of members: 340
Magazine: *Notes*
Major programs: archives, museum,
historic preservation, markers,
junior history, books
Period of collections: 1840-1945

**Tuolumne County Historical
Society**
158 W. Bradford Ave.
Telephone: (209) 532-1733
Mail to: P.O. Box 695, 95370
Founded in: 1956
Number of members: 56
Magazine: *Chispa*
Major programs: museum, historic
preservation, markers, books,
newsletters/pamphlets
Period of collections: 1848-present

SOUTH LAKE TAHOE

Lake Tahoe Historical Society
P.O. Box 404, 95705
Founded in: 1965
Number of members: 160
Staff: part time 2, volunteer 15
Major programs: library, museum,
markes, oral history, historical
photograph collection
Period of collections: 1880-present

SOUTH SAN FRANCISCO

South San Francisco History Room
Grand Avenue Library, 306 Walnut
Ave., 94080
Telephone: (415) 877-8533/877-8530
City agency
Founded in: 1967

Kathleen Kay, City Historian
Staff: part time 1, volunteer 3
Major programs: archives, museum,
  oral history, records management,
  exhibits
Period of collections: 1850-present

STOCKTON

◇Conference of California Historical Societies
University of the Pacific, 95211
Telephone: (209) 946-2169
Founded in: 1954
Ronald H. Limbaugh, Executive
  Secretary
Number of members: 676
Staff: part time 4
Magazine: *Californian Historian*
Major programs:
  newsletters/pamphlets
Period of collections: 1954-present

Haggin Museum
Victory Park, 1201 N. Pershing Ave.,
  95203
Telephone: (209) 462-4116
Private agency
Founded in: 1928
Keith E. Dennison, Director
Number of members: 1,350
Staff: full time 9, part time 6,
  volunteer 110
Major programs: library, archives,
  museum, tours/pilgrimages, oral
  history, school programs,
  newsletters/pamphlets, records
  management, research, exhibits,
  audiovisual programs,
  photographic collections
Period of collections: 1840s-1950s

Holt-Atherton Pacific Center for Western Studies
University of the Pacific, 95211
Telephone: (209) 946-2404
Private agency, authorized by the
  university
Founded in: 1947
Ronald H. Limbaugh, Director
Staff: full time 2, part time 6
Magazine: *The Pacific Historian*
Major programs: library, archives,
  manuscripts, tours/pilgrimages,
  book publishing,
  newsletters/pamphlets,
  photographic collections
Period of collections: 1849-1970

Jedediah Smith Society
University of the Pacific, 95211
Telephone: (209) 946-2405
Founded in: 1957
Robert W. Bussman, President
Number of members: 200
Staff: part time 1, volunteer 3
Major programs: school programs
  books, newsletters/pamphlets
Period of collections: 1783-1865

Methodist Historical Society
J.A.B. Fry Library, University of the
  Pacific, 95211
Telephone: (209) 946-2269
Staff: part time 1, volunteer 4
Major programs: library, archives
Period of collections: 1865-present

San Joaquin Pioneer and Historical Society
Haggin Museum, 1201 N. Pershing
  Ave., 95203
Telephone: (209) 462-4116
Private agency
Founded in: 1928
Keith E. Dennison, Museum Director
Number of members: 1,450
Staff: full time 9, part time 7,
  volunteer 90
Major programs: library, archives,
  manuscripts, museum, school
  programs, newsletters/pamphlets,
  exhibits, photographic collections
Period of collections: 1865-1945

Stockton Corral of Westerners
University of Pacific 95211
Founded in: (209) 946-2169
Founded in: 1959
Robert Bussman, Sheriff
Number of members: 50
Magazine: *Far Westerner*
Major programs: school programs
  newsletters/pamphlets,
Period of collections: 19th century

STRAFFORD

Strafford Historical Society
05072
Private agency
Founded in: 1955
E. Gwenda Smith, President
Number of members: 200
Staff: volunteer 5
Major programs: archives,
  manuscripts, historic site(s), school
  programs, historic preservation,
  photographic collections,
  genealogical services
Period of collections: 1761-present

SUISUN CITY

Bay Area Electric Railroad Association, Inc.—Western Railway Museum
5848 Hwy. 12, 94585
Telephone: (707) 374-2978
Mail to: P.O. Box 3694, San
  Francisco, 94119-3694
Private agency
Founded in: 1945
Harre W. Demoro, Chair
Number of members: 725
Staff: volunteer 100
Magazine: *The Review*
Major programs: library, archives,
  museum, tours/pilgrimages,
  exhibits
Period of collections: 1888-1948

SUNNYVALE

Sunnyvale Historical Society and Museum Association
Sunnyvale Ave. and California St.,
  Murphy Park
Telephone: (408) 749-0220
Mail to: P.O. Box 61301, 94088
Founded in: 1956
Linda Dahlberg, President
Number of members: 200
Staff: volunteer 15

Major programs: archives, museum,
  oral history, school programs,
  newsletters/pamphlets
Period of collections: 1865-present

SUSANVILLE

Lassen County Historical Society
105 N. Weatherlow St.
Mail to: P.O. Box 321, 96130
Private agency
Founded in: 1958
Tim I. Purdy, President
Number of members: 410
Magazine: *Lassen Ledger*
Major programs: library, museum,
  book publishing,
  newsletters/pamphlets, exhibits,
  photographic collections
Period of collections: 1854-present

TEHAMA

Tehama County Museum Foundation, Inc.
275 C St.
Telephone: (916) 384-2420
Mail to: P.O. Box 275, 96090
Private agency
Founded in: 1979
Margaret C. Bauer, Secretary
Staff: volunteer 15
Magazine: *Museum Tidings*
Major programs: museum, historic
  preservation, exhibits,
  photographic collections
Period of collections: 1850-1925

THOUSAND OAKS

Conejo Valley Historical Society
51 S. Vento Park Rd., Newbury Park,
  91320
Telephone: (805) 498-9441
Mail to: P.O. Box 1692, 91360
Founded in: 1964
Norma Stafford, President
Number of members: 600
Staff: volunteer 100
Major programs: library, museum,
  historic site(s), tours/pilgrimages,
  oral history, school programs,
  newsletters/pamphlets, historic
  preservation
Period of collections: 1850-1920

TOMALES

Tomales Elementary Local History Center
27955 Hwy. 1
Telephone: (707) 878-2398
Mail to: P.O. Box 6, 94971
Private agency
Founded in: 1978
Lois Parks, President
Number of members: 95
Major programs: library, archives,
  manuscripts, oral history,
  newsletters/pamphlets
Period of collections: 1850-1920

TORRANCE

Augustan Society, Inc.
1510 Cravens Ave., 90501
Telephone: (213) 320-7766
Private agency
Founded in: 1957
J. C. Bennett, President
Number of members: 3,812
Staff: part time 2, volunteer 5
Magazine: *The Augustan; Be-Ne-Lux Genealogist; The Colonial Genealogist; Eastern & Central European Genealogist; English Genealogist; French Genealogist; Genealogical Library Quarterly; Germanic Genealogist; Irish-American Genealogist; Italian Genealogist; Scottish-American Genealogist; Spanish-American Genealogist; Heraldry; Chivalry; Royalty & Monarchy*
Major programs: library, archives, manuscripts, books, lectures/seminars, genealogy, educational programs
Period of collections: prehistoric-present

Torrance Historical Society
1345 Post Ave., 90501
Telephone: (213) 328-5392
Private agency
Grace Elgin, Museum Coordinator
Number of members: 250
Staff: full time 1, part time 1, volunteer 5
Major programs: museum, historic site(s), markers, tours/pilgrimages, oral history, book publishing, newsletters/pamphlets, research, exhibits, audiovisual programs, photographic collections
Period of collections: 1920s

TRUCKEE

Truckee-Donner Historical Society, Inc.
Telephone: (916) 587-2876
Mail to: P.O. Box 893, 95734
Private agency
Founded in: 1967
John W. Curtis, President
Number of members: 228Staff: volunteer 24
Major programs: museum, historic site(s), markers, tours, junior history, newsletters/pamphlets, historic preservation, exhibits, photographic collections
Period of collections: 1865-1960

TUJUNGA

Little Landers Historical Society
10110 Commerce Ave., 91042
Telephone: (213) 352-3420
Private agency
Founded in: 1953
John A. Houk, President
Number of members: 50

Staff: volunteer 10
Major programs: library, archives, museum, oral history, records management, photographic collections
Period of collections: 1870-present

TULELAKE

Lava Beds National Monument
P.O. Box 867, 96134
Telephone: (916) 667-2282
Federal agency, authorized by Department of the Interior
Founded in: 1925
James Sleznick, Jr., Superintendent
Staff: full time 16, part time 30
Major programs: library, archives, manuscripts, museum, historic site(s), markers, tours/pilgrimages, historic preservation, research, exhibits, audiovisual programs, photographic collections
Period of collections: 1872-1873

TWENTY-NINE PALMS

29 Palms Historical Society
Mail to: P.O. Box 1926, 92277
Private agency
Founded in: 1982
Les Krushat, President
Number of members: 200
Staff: volunteer 24
Major programs: museum, tours/pilgrimages, oral history, historic preservation, exhibits, photographic collections
Period of collections: 1855-present

UKIAH

Mendocino County Historical Society, Inc.
603 W. Perkins St., 95482
Founded in: 1956
Number of members: 450
Staff: volunteer 30
Major programs: library, newsletters/pamphlets, historic preservation
Period of collections: early 1900s

The Sun House
431 S. Main
Telephone: (707) 462-3370
Mail to: P.O. Box 865, 95482
City agency
Founded in: 1978
Rosalie A. Prosser, Director
Number of members: 400
Staff: full time 1, volunteer 40
Major programs: archives, manuscripts, museum, historic site(s), markers, tours/pilgrimages, oral history, school programs, newsletters/pamphlets, historic preservation, research, exhibits, photographic collections
Period of collections: 1870-1940

Westerners: Redwood Coast Outpost
P.O. Box 175, 95482
Questionnaire not received

UPLAND

Chaffey Communities Cultural Center and Museum
525 W. 18th St.
Telephone: (714) 982-8010
Mail to: P.O. Box 772, 91786
Founded in: 1966
Number of members: 300
Major programs: archives, museum, historic site(s), school programs, historic preservation
Period of collections: 1865-present

VACAVILLE

Vacaville Heritage Council
P.O. Box 477, 95696
Private agency
Bob Allen, President
Number of members: 20

VALLEJO

Solano County Historical Society
P.O. Box 922, 94590
Founded in: 1956
Number of members: 450
Staff: volunteer 10
Magazine: *The Monthly Note Book*
Major programs: archives, museum, historic site(s), tours/pilgrimages, historic preservation, public programs
Period of collections: 1860-present

Vallejo Naval and Historical Museum
734 Martin St., 94590
Telephone: (707) 643-0077
Private agency
Founded in: 1974
John K. Nunneley, Director/Curator
Number of members: 685
Staff: full time 1, part time 2, volunteer 56
Magazine: *Chronicles*
Major programs: library, archives, museum, historic site(s), tours/pilgrimages, research, exhibits, audiovisual programs, photographic collections, genealogical services
Period of collections: 1848-present

VENTURA

City of San Buenaventura
P.O. Box 99, 93002
Telephone: (805) 654-7837
City agency, authorized by Department of Parks and Recreation
David R. Stuart, Recreation Supervisor
Staff: full time 3, part time 12, volunteer 40
Major programs: museum, historic site(s), school programs, historic preservation, exhibits, archaeology programs
Period of collections: 1860-1900

Ventura County Historical Society and Museum
100 E. Main St., 93001
Telephone: (803) 653-0323
Private agency
Founded in: 1913
Keith Foster, Executive Director
Number of members: 1,500
Staff: full time 6, part time 3, volunteer 90
Magazine: *Heritage and History*
Major programs: library, archives, manuscripts, museum, tours/pilgrimages, oral history, school programs, book publishing, newsletters/pamphlets, research, exhibits, audiovisual programs, archaeology programs, photographic collections
Period of collections: 1450-1930

VICTORVILLE

Mohahve Historical Society
Mail to: P.O. Box 68, 92392
Founded in: 1963
Number of members: 82
Staff: volunteer 8
Major programs: museum, tours/pilgrimages, school programs books

VILLA PARK

Villa Park Historical Society
City Hall of Villa Park
Mail to: 18551 Via Bravo, 92667
Founded in: 1973
Number of members: 25
Major programs: museum, book publishing
Period of collections: 1890-present

VISALIA

Tulare County Historical Society
Telephone: (209) 732-0773
Mail to: P.O. Box 295, 93279
County agency
Founded in: 1944
J. H. Hatakeda, President
Number of members: 1,193
Magazine: *Los Tulares*
Major programs: museum, historic site(s), markers, tours/pilgrimages, book publishing, newsletters/pamphlets, historic preservation
Period of collections: 1852-present

VISTA

Southwestern Antique Gas and Steam Engine Museum
2040 N. Santa Fe Dr., 92083
Telephone: (619) 941-1791
Private agency, authorized by California Early Day Gas Engine and Tractor Association
Founded in: 1976
Heather Johnson, Assistant Administrator
Number of members: 1,000
Staff: full time 1, volunteer 100
Magazine: *Ignitor*
Major programs: museum, school programs, newsletters/pamphlets, semi-annual threshing bees and antique engine show
Period of collections: 1890-1950

WALNUT CREEK

Walnut Creek Historical Society
2660 Ygnacio Valley Rd., 94598
Telephone: (415) 935-7871
Mail to: P.O. Box 4562, 94596
Private agency
Founded in: 1968
Barbara Lundy, Director
Number of members: 405
Staff: part time 3, volunteer 50
Magazine: *Shadelands News*
Major programs: archives, manuscripts, museum, oral history, school programs, historic preservation, research, exhibits, photographic collections
Period of collections: 1865-1918

WALNUT GROVE

Sacramento River Delta Historical Society
Mail to: P.O. Box 293, 95690
Founded in: 1976
Questionnaire not received

WATSONVILLE

Pajaro Valley Historical Association
261 E. Beach St., 95076
Telephone: (408) 722-0305
Founded in: 1956
Marilyn McLachlan, President
Number of members: 271
Staff: part time 1, volunteer 15
Major programs: archives, museum, historic site(s), markers, tours/pilgrimages, oral history, school programs, book publishing, newsletters/pamphlets, historic preservation, research, exhibits, photographic collections, genealogical services
Period of collections: 1783-present

WEAVERVILLE

Trinity County Historical Society
508 Main St.
Mail to: P.O. Box 333, 96093
Founded in: 1953
Number of members: 350
Staff: full time 2, part time 1, volunteer 10
Magazine: *Trinity*
Major programs: museum, book publishing, newsletters/pamphlets, historic preservation
Period of collections: 1854-1940

WHITTIER

Society of World War I Aero Historians
10443 S. Memphis Ave., 90604
Founded in: 1959
Number of members: 2,500
Staff: volunteer 9
Magazine: *Cross and Cockade Quarterly*
Major programs: books
Period of collections: 1914-1918

Whittier Historical Society
6755 Newlin Ave., 90601
Telephone: (213) 945-3871
Private agency
Founded in: 1970

Joe Da Rold, Executive Director
Number of members: 800
Staff: full time 1, part time 2, volunteer 100
Magazine: *Whittier Gazette*
Major programs: library, archives, museum, historic site(s), markers, tours/pilgrimages, oral history, book publishing, newsletters/pamphlets, historic preservation, exhibits, archaeology programs, photographic collections
Period of collections: 1860-present

WILLIAMS

Sacramento Valley Museum Association, Inc.
1491 Williams Ave.
Mail to: P.O. Box 53, 95987
Founded in: 1963
Number of members: 200
Staff: full time 1, part time 1
Major programs: museum
Period of collections: 1865-1918

WILLITS

Mendocino County Museum
400 E. Commercial St., 95490
Telephone: (707) 459-2736
Founded in: 1972
Mark H. Rawitsch, Director
Staff: full time 2, part time 1, volunteer 10
Major programs: archives, museum, oral history, research, exhibits, living history, photographic collections
Period of collections: prehistoric-present

WILMINGTON

Banning Residence Museum
401 E. M St.
Telephone: (213) 548-7777
Mail to: P.O. Box 397, 90748
City agency, authorized by Department of Parks and Recreation and Friends of Banning Park
Founded in: 1974
Marian Winter, Director
Number of members: 500
Staff: full time 3, part time 2, volunteer 150
Major programs: museum, historic site(s)
Period of collections: 1830-1900

WOODLAND

Yolo County Historical Society
123 Midway Dr.
Mail to: P.O. Box 1447, 95695
Founded in: 1965
Questionnaire not received

WOODSIDE

Filoli Center
Canada Rd., 94062
Telephone: (415) 364-8300
Private agency
Founded in: 1976
Hadley Osborn, Executive Director
Number of members: 4,000

Staff: full time 15, part time 6,
volunteer 500
Major programs: historic site(s),
historic preservation, horticulture
Period of collections: 1917-present

YOSEMITE NATIONAL PARK

**Yosemite National Park Research
Library**
P.O. Box 577, 95389
Telephone: (209) 372-4461, ext. 280
Federal agency, authorized by
National Park Service
Founded in: 1922
Mary Vocelka, Research Librarian
Staff: full time 1, part time 1
Major programs: library, archives,
manuscripts, museum, oral history,
records management, research,
photographic collections
Period of collections: 1851-present

**Yosemite Natural History
Association**
Mail to: P.O. Box 545, 95389
Questionnaire not received

YOUNTVILLE

California Veterans Museum
P.O. Box 258, 94599
Telephone: (707) 944-4398
Founded in: 1974
Janet M. Knudsen, Director/Curator
Staff: full time 2, part time 2,
volunteer 10
Major programs: museum, oral
history, historic preservation
Period of collections: 1860-present

YREKA

Klamath National Forest
1312 Fairlane Rd., 96097
Telephone: (916) 842-6131
Federal agency
Founded in: 1905
Gilbert W. Davies
Major programs: library, archives,
museum, oral history, exhibits,
photographic collections
Period of collections: 1900-present

**Siskiyou County Historical Society
and Museum**
910 S. Main St., 96097
Telephone: (916) 842-3836
Private agency
Founded in: 1945
Eleanor Brown, Director/Curator
Number of members: 1,300
Staff: full time 2, part time 1
Magazine: *The Siskiyou Pioneer*
Major programs: library, museum,
markers, tours/pilgrimages, school
programs, book publishing,
newsletters/pamphlets, historic
preservation, research, exhibits,
living history, photographic
collections, interpretive services,
field services
Period of collections:
prehistoric-present

Society of California Pioneers
456 McAllister St., 94102
Founded in: 1850
Number of members: 1,200
Staff: full time 4

Magazine: *The Pioneer*
Major programs: library, archives,
museum
Period of collections: 1783-1918

YUBA CITY

**Community Memorial Museum of
Sutter County**
1333 Butte House Rd., 95991
Telephone: (916) 674-0461
Mail to: P.O. Box 1555, 95992
County agency
Founded in: 1975
Mary R. Allman, Director/Curator
Number of members: 250
Staff: full time 2, part time 2,
volunteer 25
Major programs: library, museum,
exhibits, audiovisual programs,
genealogical services
Period of collections: 1880-1930

Sutter County Historical Society
P.O. Box 1004, 95992
Telephone: (916) 674-0461
Private agency
Founded in: 1954
Dewey Gruening, President
Number of members: 175
Staff: volunteer 10
Major programs: museum
Period of collections: 1850-present

YUCCA VALLEY

**Hi-Desert Nature Museum and
Association**
57117 Twenty-nine Palms Hwy.,
92284
Telephone: (619) 365-9814
County agency, authorized by Parks
and Recreation District
Founded in: 1964
Evelyn G. Conklin, Museum
Director/Curator
Number of members: 750
Staff: full time 1, part time 2,
volunteer 10
Major programs: museum, school
programs, newsletters/pamphlets,
historic preservation, exhibits,
audiovisual programs,
photographic collections,
genealogical services, natural
history
Period of collections:
prehistoric-present

COLORADO

ALAMOSA

San Luis Valley Historical Society
Mail to: P.O. Box 982, 81101
Questionnaire not received

ALMA

Alma Fire Department Museum
1 N. Main St.
Telephone: (303) 836-3117
Mail to: P.O. Box 1066, 80420
Private agency
Founded in: 1976
Joe E. Burton, Fire Chief
Staff: volunteer 8

Major programs: museum,
tours/pilgrimages, oral history,
newsletters/pamphlets, exhibits,
photographic collections
Period of collections: 1870-1960

ARVADA

**Arvada Center for the Arts and
Humanities Museum**
6901 Wadsworth Blvd., 80003
Telephone: (303) 431-3080
City agency
Founded in: 1976
Michael Crane, Director
Number of members: 1,000
Staff: full time 4
Magazine: *Center Magazine*
Major programs: museum, junior
history, oral history, school
programs, research, exhibits,
photographic collections
Period of collections: 1865-1950

Arvada Historical Society
Telephone: (303) 431-1261
Mail to: P.O. Box 419, 80001
Private agency
Founded in: 1972
Edna McCormack, President
Number of members: 400
Staff: part time 1, volunteer 21
Magazine: *Historian*
Major programs: archives, museum,
historic site(s), tours/pilgrimages,
oral history, school programs, book
publishing, newsletters/pamphlets,
historic preservation, research,
audiovisual programs
Period of collections: 1850-present

ASPEN

Aspen Historical Society
620 W. Bleeker St., 81611
Telephone: (303) 925-3721
Private agency
Founded in: 1963
Carol Blomquist, President
Number of members: 500
Staff: part time 2, volunteer 45
Magazine: *Aspen Historical Society
Newsletter*
Major programs: archives,
newsletters/ pamphlets,
audiovisual programs,
photographic collections
Period of collections: 1880-present

AURORA

Aurora Historical Society
13101 E. Florida Ave., 80012
Telephone: (303) 751-1544
Founded in: 1975
Dorothy Elwell, President
Number of members: 250
Staff: volunteer 25
Major programs: oral history, historic
preservation, educational
programs, newsletters/pamphlets

Aurora History Center
1633 Florence St., 80010
Telephone: (303) 340-8093
Founded in: 1979
Virginia Roberts Steele, Museum
Coordinator
Staff: full time 3, volunteer 10

Major programs: library, archives, manuscripts, museum, historic site, educational programs, historic preservation, exhibits
Period of collections: 1920-1950

Cherry Creek Valley Historical Society, Inc.
4950 S. Laredo St., 80015
Telephone: (303) 690-5005
Private agency
Founded in: 1975
Charles Dolezal, President
Number of members: 137
Staff: volunteer 12
Magazine: *The Quill*
Major programs: library, museum, historic site(s), oral history, school programs, historic preservation, research, exhibits, audiovisual programs, photographic collections
Period of collections: 1880-1950

BAILEY

Park County Historical Society
Mail to: P.O. Box 43, 80421
Telephone: (303) 838-7253 (president)
County agency
Founded in: 1971
C. Douglas Frost, President
Number of members: 100
Staff: volunteer 7
Major programs: museum, historic site(s), markers, tours/pilgrimages, historic preservation, photographic collections
Period of collections: 1875-1940s

BAYFIELD

Gem Village Museum
Rt. 1, 81122
Telephone: (303) 884-2811
Founded in: 1947
Elizabeth X. Gilbert, Secretary/Treasurer
Staff: volunteer 3
Major programs: library, museum
Period of collections: prehistoric

BERTHOUD

Berthoud Historical Society
224 Mountain Ave.
Telephone: (303) 532-2167
Mail to: P.O. Box 426, 80513
Private agency
Founded in: 1976
R. B. Fickel, President
Staff: volunteer 21
Major programs: museum, historic preservation, photographic collections

BOULDER

Boulder Historical Society and Museum
1206 Euclid, 80302
Telephone: (303) 449-3464
Private agency
Founded in: 1944
Tom Meier, President
Number of members: 450
Staff: full time 2, volunteer 4

Major programs: museum, tours/pilgrimages, school programs, newsletters/pamphlets, historic preservation, records management, research, exhibits, audiovisual programs, archaeology programs, undergraduate and traduate museum training
Period of collections: 1850s-present

Carnegie Branch Library for Local History
1125 Pine St.
Telephone: (303) 441-3110
Mail to: P.O. Drawer H, 80306
City agency, authorized by Boulder Public Library
Founded in: 1983
Lois Anderton, Librarian/Archivist
Staff: full time 1, part time 5, volunteer 26
Major programs: library, archives, manuscripts, historic site(s), oral history, school programs, research, photographic collections, genealogical services
Period of collections: 1859-present

Historic Boulder, Inc.
1733 Canyon Blvd., 80302
Telephone: (303) 444-5192
Private agency
Founded in: 1972
Judith Trent, Executive Director
Number of members: 450
Staff: part time 1, volunteer 8
Major programs: historic preservation
Period of collections: 1850s-1890s

University of Colorado Museum, Boulder
Telephone: (303) 492-6165
Mail to: Campus Box 218, 80309
Founded in: 1902
William W. Hay, Director
Staff: full time 11, part time 10
Major programs: museum, research, exhibits, archaeology programs
Period of collections: 1700-present

BRIGHTON

Adams County Historical Society
9755 Henderson Rd., 80601
Telephone: (303) 659-4150
Founded in: 1974
Number of members: 80
Staff: volunteer 9
Major programs: museum, historic sites preservation, oral history
Period of collections: 1918-present

BUENA VISTA

St. Elmo Historic Preservation
Home Comfort Hotel, St. Elmo
Mail to: P.O. Box 1884, 81211
Private agency
Founded in: 1979
Melanie I. Milam, Executive Director
Number of members: 50
Staff: full time 1, part time 1, volunteer 25
Major programs: historic site(s), tours/pilgrimages, historic preservation, research, living history
Period of collections: 1880-1900

CANON CITY

Fremont-Custer Historical Society, Inc.
Mail to: P.O. Box 965, 81212
Questionnaire not received

CASCADE

Ute Pass Historical Society—Ute Pass Trail Museum
8025 W. Hwy. 24
Mail to: P.O. Box 2, 80809
Founded in: 1976
Jan Pettit, Executive Director
Number of members: 300
Staff: volunteer 80
Major programs: archives, museum, historic site(s), oral history, school programs, newsletters/pamphlets, research, exhibits, audiovisual programs, photographic collections
Period of collections: 1865-present

CENTRAL CITY

Central City Opera House Association
1615 California St., Suite 614
Telephone: (303) 623-7167
Mail to: P.O. Box 218, 80427
Private agency
Founded in: 1932
Daniel Rule, General Manager
Staff: full time 8, part time 130, volunteer 3
Major programs: historic site(s), historic preservation, opera production
Period of collections: early 20th century

Gilpin County Historical Society
228 E. High
Mail to: P.O. Box 244, 80427
Founded in: 1969
Questionnaire not received

COLORADO SPRINGS

Colorado Midland Chapter, National Railroad Historical Society
P.O. Box 824, 80901
Telephone: (303) 597-0073
Private agency, authorized by national headquarters in Philadelphia, PA
Founded in: 1968
Wally Smith, President
Number of members: 92
Staff: volunteer 10
Magazine: *Colorado Midland Rails*
Major programs: tours/pilgrimages, oral history, newsletters/pamphlets, historic preservation, research, audiovisual programs
Period of collections: early-mid 20th century

Ft. Carson Museum
Ft. Carson, 80913-5000
Telephone: (303) 579-2908
Federal agency, authorized by the Chief of Military History
Founded in: 1957
James J. Bush, Jr., Director
Staff: full time 7

Major programs: library, museum,
school programs, research,
exhibits
Period of collections: W.W. I-present

Museum of the American Numismatic Association
818 N. Cascade Ave., 80903
Telephone: (303) 632-2646
Mail to: P.O. Box 2366, 80901
Private agency
Founded in: 1891
Edward C. Rochette, Executive Vice
President
Number of members: 37,500
Staff: full time 43, part time 2
Magazine: The Numismatist
Major programs: library, museum,
research, exhibits, audiovisual
programs, photographic
collections, certification service
Period of collections: 5000
B.C.-present

National Society of the Colonial Dames, Colorado
McAllister House Museum, 423 N.
Cascade Ave., 80903
Telephone: (303) 635-7925
Private agency
Founded in: 1961
Jane Busch Mouri, Head Curator
Number of members: 100
Staff: part time 2, volunteer 15
Major programs: museum, historic
site, historic preservation
Period of collections: 1880

Pioneers' Museum
215 S. Tejon, 80903
Telephone: (303) 578-6650
City agency
Founded in: 1937
William C. Holmes, Director
Number of members: 1,100
Staff: full time 10, volunteer 50
Major programs: library, archives,
manuscripts, museum, school
programs, newsletters/pamphlets,
research, exhibits, photographic
collections, genealogical services
Period of collections: 1871-1920

Western Museum of Mining and Industry
1025 N. Gate Rd., 80908
Telephone: (303) 495-2182
Private agency
Founded in: 1970
Peter M. Molloy, Director
Number of members: 330
Staff: full time 5, part time 3,
volunteer 5
Major programs: library, museum,
tours/pilgrimages, school
programs, newsletters/pamphlets,
research, exhibits, audiovisual
programs
Period of collections: 1890-1930

White House Ranch Historic Site
3202 Chambers Way, 80904
Telephone: (303) 578-6777
City agency, authorized by Parks and
Recreation Department
Founded in: 1978
Bruce Gillespie, Ranch Manager
Number of members: 400
Staff: full time 2, part time 2,
volunteer 300

Magazine: White House Ranch Living
History Association
Major programs: historic site(s),
tours/pilgrimages, school
programs, historic preservation,
research, living history
Period of collections: 1868, 1895,
1907

CRAIG

Moffat County Museum
Courthouse, 81625
Telephone: (303) 824-6360
County agency
Founded in: 1964
Louise Miller, Director of Volunteers
Staff: part time 2
Major programs: museum, exhibits
Period of collections:
prehistoric-present

CRIPPLE CREEK

Cripple Creek District Museum, Inc.
5th and Bennett Ave.
Mail to: P.O. Box 475, 80813
Questionnaire not received

DEL NORTE

Rio Grande County Museum
Courthouse, 7th and Cherry Sts.
Mail to: P.O. Box 160, 81132
County agency
Founded in: 1961
Carolyn Jones, Director/Curator
Staff: part time 4, volunteer 2
Major programs: archives, museum,
school programs, exhibits,
photographic collections
Period of collections: 1870-1920

DELTA

Delta County Historical Society
Delta County Courthouse Annex
Telephone: (303) 874-9350
Mail to: P.O. Box 681, 81416
Private agency
Founded in: 1964
Gordon Hodgin, President
Number of members: 149
Staff: volunteer 40
Major programs: archives,
manuscripts, museum, historic
site(s), oral history, historic
preservation, research,
photographic collections

DENVER

Archives Branch, Denver Federal Archives and Records Center
Bldg. 48, Denver Federal Center
Telephone: (303) 236-0817
Mail to: P.O. Box 25307, 80225
Federal agency, authorized by
National Archives and Records
Administration
Founded in: 1969
Joel Barker, Chief, Archives Branch
Staff: full time 4, part time 1,
volunteer 20
Major programs: archives, research,
exhibits, photographic collections,
genealogical services
Period of collections: 1875-1950

Buffalo Bill Memorial Museum
987 Lookout Mountain Rd., 80401
Telephone: (303) 526-0747
City agency, authorized by Parks and
Recreation Department
Founded in: 1921
Stanley W. Zamonski, Curator
Staff: full time 4
Major programs: archives,
manuscripts, museum, historic
site(s), junior history, oral history,
school programs, historic
preservation, research, exhibits,
archaeology programs,
photographic collections
Period of collections: 1876-1921

Central City Opera House Association
1615 California St., Suite 636, 80202
Founded in: 1932
Number of members: 650
Staff: full time 12, part time 30,
volunteer 400
Major programs: museum, historic
sites preservation, markers,
tours/pilgrimages
Period of collections: 1865-1918

◇Colorado Division of State Archives and Public Records
1313 Sherman St., 80203
Telephone: (303) 866-2055
State agency
Founded in: 1943
George E. Warren, State Archivist
Staff: full time 12
Major programs: archives, records
management
Period of collections: 1859-present

Colorado Genealogical Society
P.O. Box 9671, 80209
Private agency
Founded in: 1924
James Kroll, President
Magazine: Colorado Genealogist
Major programs: library, book
publishing, newsletters/pamphlets,
research, genealogical services

Denver Art Museum
100 W. 14th Ave. Parkway, 80204
Telephone: (303) 575-2793
City agency
Founded in: 1893
Lewis Story, Interim Director
Number of members: 16,500
Staff: full time 88, part time 13,
volunteer 660
Major programs: museum, exhibits,
fine arts
Period of collections:
pre-Columbian-contemporary

Denver Landmark Preservation Commission
1445 Cleveland Place, Room 400,
80202
Questionnaire not received

Denver Museum of Natural History
2001 Colorado Blvd., 80205
Telephone: (303) 370-6357
City agency
Founded in: 1900
Charles T. Crockett, Director
Number of members: 15,026
Staff: full time 97, part time 34,
volunteer 306

COLORADO

Magazine: *Bear Pause*
Major programs: library, archives, manuscripts, museum, tours/pilgrimages, oral history, school programs, newsletters/pamphlets, records management, research, exhibits, audiovisual programs, photographic collections, natural history
Period of collections: late 1800s-present

Denver Posse of Westerners
Mail to: c/o Johnson Publishing Co., P.O. Box 990, Boulder
Founded in: 1945
Mel Griffiths, Sheriff
Magazine: *The Denver Westerners Roundup*
Major programs: historic sites preservation, tours/pilgrimages, educational programs, books, newsletters/pamphlets

Forney Transportation Museum
1416 Platte St., 80202
Telephone: (303) 433-3643
Private agency
Founded in: 1960
J. D. Forney, President
Staff: full time 2, part time 2
Major programs: museum, historic site(s)
Period of collections: 1800-present

Four Mile Historic Park
715 S. Forest St., 80222
Telephone: (303) 399-1859
Private agency
Founded in: 1977
Charles H. Woolley, Director
Number of members: 800
Staff: full time 5, part time 3, volunteer 120
Magazine: *Four Mile Express*
Major programs: museum, historic site(s), school programs, newsletters/pamphlets, research, living history, folklife festival, building reconstruction using traditional methods
Period of collections: 1859-1883

Historic Denver, Inc.
1701 Wynkoop St., Suite 200, 80202
Telephone: (303) 534-1858
Private agency
Founded in: 1970
Lane Ittleson, President
Number of members: 2,500
Staff: full time 6, part time 4, volunteer 100
Magazine: *Historic Denver News*
Major programs: museum, tours/pilgrimages, book publishing, newsletters/pamphlets, historic preservation
Period of collections: 1858-1940

Ira M. Beck Memorial Collection of Rocky Mountain Jewish History
Center for Judaic Studies, University of Denver, 80208
Questionnaire not received

Molly Brown House Museum
1340 Pennsylvania St., 80203
Telephone: (303) 832-4092
Private agency, authorized by Historic Denver, Inc.

Founded in: 1971
Marcia L. Sky, Director
Staff: full time 1, part time 3, volunteer 125
Major programs: museum, historic site(s), tours/pilgrimages, school programs, book publishing, newsletters/pamphlets, historic preservation, exhibits
Period of collections: 1889-1932

Mountains-Plains Regional Office, National Trust for Historic Preservation
1407 Larimer St., Suite 200, 80202
Telephone: (303) 844-2245
Private agency
Founded in: 1949
Clark J. Strickland, Director
Staff: full time 6
Magazine: *Historic Preservation*
Major programs: historic site(s), book publishing, historic preservation

National Archives—Denver Branch
Bldg. 48, Denver Federal Center, 80225
Telephone: (303) 236-0818
Founded in: 1969
Joel Barker, Director
Staff: full time 4
Major programs: archives, educational programs, teachers' workshops, genealogical workshops, film series, open houses and tours
Period of collections: 1862-1978

Office of Archaeology and Historic Preservation, Colorado Historical Society
1300 Broadway, 80203
Telephone: (303) 866-3395
State agency
Founded in: 1970
Barbara Sudler, State Historic Preservation Officer
Staff: full time 16
Magazine: *Preservation On-Line*
Major programs: library, archives, newsletters/pamphlets, historic preservation, records management, archaeology programs, photographic collections
Period of collections: prehistoric-1930

Rocky Mountain Jewish Historical Society
Telephone: (303) 753-2068
Mail to: Center for Judaic Studies, University of Denver, 80208
Private agency, authorized by the university
Founded in: 1977
Jeanne Abrams, Director
Number of members: 425
Staff: full time 1, part time 2, volunteer 8
Magazine: *Rocky Mountain Jewish Historical Notes*
Major programs: archives, manuscripts, tours, oral history, book publishing, newsletters/pamphlets, research,

The Molly Brown House Museum, home of the "Unsinkable Molly Brown," heroine of the 1912 Titanic disaster.—Historic Denver, Inc.

52

audiovisual programs,
photographic collections
Period of collections: 1859-present

Society of Biblical Literature
2201 S. University Blvd., 80210
Telephone: (303) 744-1287
Private agency
Founded in: 1880
Kent Harold Richards, Executive
Secretary/Treasurer
Number of members: 5,000
Staff: full time 4, volunteer 80
Magazine: *Journal of Biblical
Literature*
Period of collections: 1880-present

◇**State Historical Society of
Colorado**
1300 Broadway, 80203
Telephone: (303) 866-3682
State agency
Founded in: 1879
Barbara Sudler, Executive Director
Number of members: 4,583
Staff: full time 68, part time 14,
volunteer 335
Magazine: *Colorado Heritage*
Major programs: library, manuscripts,
museum, historic site(s),junior
history, school programs, book
publishing, newsletters/pamphlets,
historic preservation, research,
exhibits, archaeology programs,
photographic collections,
genealogical services, field
services
Period of collections:
prehistoric-present

**Western History Department,
Denver Public Library**
1357 Broadway, 80203
Telephone: (303) 571-2009
City and county agency
Founded in: 1935
Eleanor M. Gehres, Manager
Staff: full time 8, part time 5,
volunteer 19
Major programs: library, archives,
manuscripts, oral history, book
publishing, research, exhibits,
photographic collections
Period of collections:
prehistoric-present

DILLON

Summit Historical Society
403 La Bonte
Telephone: (303) 468-6079
Mail to: P.O. Box 747, 80435
Private agency
Founded in: 1967
Rebecca Waugh, Museum
Administrator
Number of members: 1,000
Staff: full time 1, part time 3,
volunteer 32
Major programs: library, archives,
manuscripts, museum, historic
site(s), markers, tours/pilgrimages,
oral history, school programs, book
publishing, newsletters/pamphlets,
historic preservation, records
management, research, exhibits,
photographic collections,
genealogical services
Period of collections: 1880-1950

DURANGO

Animas School Museum
31st St. and W. 2nd Ave.
Telephone: (303) 249-2402
Mail to: P.O. Box 3384, 81301
Private agency, authorized by La
Plata County Historical Society
Founded in: 1974
Robert McDaniel, Director
Number of members: 40
Staff: part time 1, volunteer 10
Major programs: museum, historic
site(s), school programs,
newsletters/pamphlets, historic
preservation, exhibits, audiovisual
programs, archaeology programs,
photographic collections
Period of collections: 1880-1935

**Four Corners Museum
Association, Inc.**
2303 N. Main Ave. 81301
Questionnaire not received

EAGLE

**Eagle County Historical
Society, Inc.**
601 Capitol St.
Telephone: (303) 328-7311, ext. 256
Mail to: P.O. Box 240, 81631
Private agency
Founded in: 1980
Ross Bolt, President
Number of members: 100
Staff: volunteer 3
Major programs: archives, museum,
historic preservation, exhibits,
photographic collections,
genealogical services
Period of collections: 1880-1940

ENGLEWOOD

**Cherry Creek Schoolhouse
Museum**
9300 E. Union Ave., 80111
Telephone: (303) 773-8920
County agency, authorized by Cherry
Creek School District
Gwen Dennis, Director
Staff: part time 1
Major programs: museum, historic
site(s), tours/pilgrimages, junior
history, oral history, school
programs, historic preservation,
exhibits, photographic collections,
genealogical services
Period of collections: 1880s-1940s

ESTES PARK

Estes Park Area Historical Museum
200 4th St.
Telephone: (303) 586-6256
Mail to: P.O. Box 1691, 80517
Founded in: 1962
Melvin E. Busch, Director
Number of members: 300
Staff: full time 1, part time 1,
volunteer 20
Major programs: museum, oral
history, school programs,
newsletters/pamphlets,
photographic collections
Period of collections: late 19th-early
20th centuries

Lula W. Dorsey Museum
2515 Tunnel Rd., 80517
Telephone: (303) 586-3341, ext. 1137
Mail to: P.O. Box 597, 80511
Private agency, authorized by YMCA
of the Rockies
Founded in: 1979
Lulabeth Melton, Curator
Number of members: 195
Staff: full time 2, part time 2
Major programs: archives,
manuscripts, museum, historic
site(s), markers, tours/pilgrimages,
junior history, oral history, school
programs, book publishing,
newsletters/pamphlets, historic
preservation, research, exhibits,
audiovisual programs,
photographic collections
Period of collections: 1900-present

Rocky Mountain National Park
80517
Telephone: (303) 586-2371
Federal agency
Founded in: 1915
Glen Kaye, Chief Park Naturalist
Staff: full time 51, part time 33
Period of collections: 1970s-present

**Rocky Mountain Nature
Association, Inc.**
Rocky Mountain National Park, 80517
Telephone: (303) 586-2371
Private agency
Founded in: 1932
Glen Kaye, Association Coordinator
Number of members: 250
Staff: full time 1, part time 10
Major programs: library, museum,
book publishing,
newsletters/pamphlets, historic
preservation, research, exhibits,
living history, audiovisual
programs, photographic
collections, educational seminars,
natural history

EVERGREEN

**Jefferson County Historical
Society, Inc.**
Timbervale Dr.
Mail to: P.O. Box 703, 80439
Founded in: 1973
Number of members: 300
Staff: volunteer 100
Magazine: *Jefferson County
Historical Society Quarterly*
Major programs: library, museum,
historic sites preservation, oral
history, educational programs,
newsletters/pamphlets
Period of collections: 1865-1918

FAIRPLAY

South Park City Museum
100 4th St.
Telephone: (303) 836-2387
Mail to: P.O. Box 634, 80440
Private agency, authorized by South
Park Historical Foundation, Inc.
Founded in: 1957
Carol Davis, Director
Number of members: 125
Staff: full time 3
Major programs: museum, historic
site(s), school programs, book

publishing, historic preservation, research, exhibits, audiovisual programs
Period of collections: 1860-1900

South Park Historical Foundation, Inc.
4th and Front Sts.
Telephone: (303) 836-2387
Mail to: P.O. Box 634, 80440
Founded in: 1957
Carol A. Davis, General Manager
Number of members: 125
Staff: full time 3, part time 10
Major programs: museum, historic sites preservation, educational programs
Period of collections: 1865-1918

FLORENCE

Florence Pioneer Museum and Historical Society
Pikes Peak at Front St.
Telephone: (303) 784-3157
Mail to: 1099 County Rd., 81226
City agency, authorized by Pioneer Day Associations
Founded in: 1964
Charles E. Price, President
Number of members: 100
Staff: part time 1, volunteer 2
Major programs: museum, tours/pilgrimages, historic preservation
Period of collections: 1865-present

FLORISSANT

Florissant Fossil Beds
Telephone: (303) 748-3253
Mail to: P.O. Box 185, 80816
Federal agency, authorized by National Park Service
Founded in: 1969
Duncan G. Rollo, Chief, Visitors Services
Staff: full time 5, part time 5, volunteer 2
Major programs: museum, historic site(s), tours/pilgrimages, school programs, newsletters/pamphlets, historic preservation, research, exhibits, living history, audiovisual programs, paleontology

FORT COLLINS

Colorado-Wyoming Association of Museums
200 Mathews St., 80524
Telephone: (303) 221-6738
State agency
Founded in: 1972
Brian Moroney, Chair
Number of members: 200
Magazine: *Highlights*
Major programs: museum educational programs

Ft. Collins Historical Society
Ft. Collins Public Library, 201 Peterson St., 80524
Telephone: (303) 221-6740, ext. 7517
City agency
Founded in: 1974
Charlene Tresner, Local History Coordinator
Staff: full time 1, volunteer 5

Major programs: library, manuscripts, museum, historic site(s), tours/pilgrimages, oral history, school programs, newsletters/pamphlets, historic preservation, research, exhibits, photographic collections
Period of collections: 1860-present

Ft. Collins Museum
200 Mathews St., 80524
Telephone: (303) 221-6738
City agency
Founded in: 1941
Brian Moroney, Director
Staff: full time 3, part time 2, volunteer 30
Major programs: museum, tours, school programs, historic preservation, exhibits
Period of collections: prehistoric-1960

Poudre Landmarks Foundation
328 W. Mountain Ave., 80521
Telephone: (303) 221-4448
City agency
Founded in: 1972
Margareth C. Merrill, President
Staff: volunteer 35
Major programs: historic site(s), tours/pilgrimages, oral history, historic preservation, exhibits
Period of collections: 1879-1910

FORT MORGAN

Ft. Morgan Heritage Foundation and Museum
Telephone: (303) 867-6331
Mail to: P.O. Box 184, 80701
Marne Jurgemeyer, Director
Staff: full time 3, part time 1, volunteer 45
Major programs: museum, tours/pilgrimages, school programs, book publishing, research, exhibits, audiovisual programs, archaeology programs, photographic collections, microfilm
Period of collections: 1865-present

GEORGETOWN

Georgetown Society, Inc.
305 Argentine St.
Telephone: (303) 569-2840
Mail to: P.O. Box 667, 80444
Private agency
Founded in: 1970
Ronald J. Neely, Executive Director
Number of members: 555
Staff: full time 3, part time 5, volunteer 50
Magazine: *Silver Queen Preservation News, Georgetown Magazine*
Major programs: museum, historic site(s), markers, tours/pilgrimages, newsletters/pamphlets, historic preservation
Period of collections: 1865-1920

GLENWOOD SPRINGS

Frontier Historical Society and Museum
1001 Colorado Ave., 81601
Telephone: (303) 945-4448
Private agency
Founded in: 1964
Janet Riley, Director

Number of members: 130
Staff: part time 1, volunteer 35
Major programs: archives, museum, junior history, oral history, school programs, book publishing, newsletters/pamphlets, historic preservation, photographic collections
Period of collections: 1883-1940

GOLDEN

Buffalo Bill Memorial Museum
Rt. 5, Box 950, 80401
Telephone: (303) 526-0744
City and county agency
Founded in: 1921
Stanley W. Zamonski, Curator
Staff: full time 3
Major programs: library, manuscripts, museum
Period of collections: 1865-1918

Colorado Railroad Historical Foundation, Inc.
17155 W. 44th Ave.
Telephone: (303) 279-4591
Mail to: P.O. Box 10, 80402
Private agency
Founded in: 1958
Robert W. Richardson, Executive Director
Number of members: 1,110
Staff: full time 3, part time 4, volunteer 21
Magazine: *Iron Horse News*
Major programs: library, archives, museum, book publishing, newsletters/pamphlets, historic preservation, research, exhibits, photographic collections
Period of collections: 1865-present

The Geology Museum
16th and Maple, 80401
Telephone: (303) 273-3823
State agency, authorized by Colorado School of Mines
Founded in: 1880
John M. Shannon, Museum Director
Staff: full time 2, volunteer 3
Major programs: museum
Period of collections: 1859-1900

GRAND JUNCTION

Museum of Western Colorado
248 S. 4th St., 81501
Telephone: (303) 242-0971
County agency
Founded in: 1965
Michael L. Perry, Director
Number of members: 650
Staff: full time 8, volunteer 125
Magazine: *Dinotracks/Museum Journal*
Major programs: library, archives, manuscripts, museum, historic site(s), tours/pilgrimages, oral history, school programs, book publishing, newsletters/pamphlets, historic preservation, records management, research, exhibits, living history, audiovisual programs, archaeology programs, photographic collections, genealogical services, field services, natural history, paleontology
Period of collections: prehistoric-present

GRAND LAKE

Grand Lake Area Historical Society
Pitkin and Lake Ave.
Mail to: P.O. Box 656, 80447
Town agency
Founded in: 1973
Patience Kemp, President
Number of members: 260
Staff: volunteer 10
Major programs: archives,
 manuscripts, museum, historic site,
 markers, oral history, educational
 programs, newsletters/pamphlets,
 historic preservation
Period of collections: 1881-present

GRANITE

**Clear Creek Canyon Historical
 Society of Chaffee County, Inc.**
Telephone: (303) 486-2942
Mail to: P.O. Box 2181, 81228
Private agency
ounded in: 1971
James P. Rowe, Director
Number of members: 117
Staff: volunteer 7
Major programs: archives,
 manuscripts, museum, historic
 sites preservation, markers, oral
 history, educational programs,
 newsletters/pamphlets
Period of collections: 1865-1918

GREELEY

Centennial Village
N. 14th Ave., 80631
Founded in: 1976
Staff: full time 1, part time 4,
 volunteer 50
Period of collections: 1860-1910

City of Greeley Museums
919 7th St., 80631
Telephone: (303) 353-6123, ext. 391
Town agency
Founded in: 1968
Robert E. Monaghan, Superintendent
 of Museums
Staff: full time 4, part time 3,
 volunteer 50
Major programs: archives, museum,
 historic site(s), tours/pilgrimages,
 school programs,
 newsletters/pamphlets, historic
 preservation, research, exhibits,
 photographic collections,
 genealogical services
Period of collections: 1870-1920

Meeker Home Museum
1324 9th Ave., 80631
Founded in: 1927
Staff: full time 1, part time 2,
 volunteer 2
Major programs: museum, historic
 site, tours/pilgrimages
Period of collections: 1870-1890

GUNNISON

Gunnison County Pioneer Museum
S. Adams St., Hwy. 50
Mail to: 315 W. Ohio Ave. 81230
Founded in: 1936
Number of members: 350
Staff: volunteer 30
Major programs: museum, historic
 site, historic preservation
Period of collections: 1850-1920

HOT SULPHUR SPRINGS

**Grand County Historical
 Association**
Mail to: P.O. Box 168, 80451
Private agency
Founded in: 1974
Regina Black, President
Number of members: 480
Staff: volunteer 40
Magazine: *Grand County Journal*
Major programs: manuscripts,
 museum, historic site(s), markers,
 tours/pilgrimages, oral history,
 school programs, book publishing,
 newsletters/pamphlets, historic
 preservation, records
 management, research, exhibits,
 photographic collections
Period of collections: 1875-present

HUGO

**Lincoln County Historical
 Society—Lincoln County
 Museum**
615 3rd Ave.
Telephone: (303) 743-2209
Mail to: P.O. Box 626, 80821
City agency
Founded in: 1972
Mrs. J. R. Owen, Coordinator
Number of members: 50
Staff: volunteer 5
Major programs: museum, book
 publishing, local research
Period of collections: late 1800s-mid
 1900s

LA JUNTA

Koshare Indian Museum, Inc.
115 W. 18th St., 81050
Telephone: (303) 384-4801
Founded in: 1949
J.F. Burshears, Executive Director
Staff: part time 2
Major programs: library, museum
Period of collections:
 prehistoric-present

LAKE CITY

Hinsdale County Historical Society
2nd and Silver Sts.
Mail to: P.O. Box 353, 81235
Questionnaire not received

LAKEWOOD

Belmar Museum
797 S. Wadsworth Blvd., 80226
Telephone: (303) 987-7850
City agency
Founded in: 1976
Sheila A. Smyth, Curator
Staff: full time 1, part time 5,
 volunteer 83
Major programs: museum, junior
 history, oral history, school
 programs, exhibits, photographic
 collections
Period of collections: 1860-1960

Lakewood Historical Society
797 S. Wadsworth Blvd., 80226
Telephone: (303) 987-7850
Private agency
Founded in: 1976
Robert B. Wright, President
Number of members: 120

Staff: full time 2, volunteer 20
Major programs: library, archives,
 museum, oral history, educational
 programs, historic preservation
Period of collections: 1850-1950

LAMAR

Prowers County Historical Society
N. Santa Fe Trail
Telephone: (303) 336-2472
Mail to: P.O. Box 362, 81052
County agency
Founded in: 1966
Edith Birchier, Curator
Number of members: 200
Staff: part time 1, volunteer 1
Major programs: museum, historic
 site(s), markers, exhibits,
 photographic collections
Period of collections: 1865-present

LAS ANIMAS

**Kit Carson Museum and Historical
 Society**
Bent and 9th Sts.
Telephone: (303) 456-0829
Mail to: 425 Carson, 81054
County agency, authorized by
 Pioneer Historical Society
Founded in: 1959
W. T. Setchfield, Curator/Vice
 President
Number of members: 175
Staff: full time 1, volunteer 10
Major programs: library, manuscripts,
 museum, historic site(s),
 tours/pilgrimages, oral history,
 school programs, historic
 preservation, records
 management, research, exhibits,
 archaeology programs,
 photographic collections,
 genealogical services, field
 services
Period of collections: 1880-present

LA VETA

Huerfano County Historical Society
Mail to: P.O. Box 3, 81089
Founded in: 1958
Questionnaire not received

LEADVILLE

Healy House—Dexter Cabin
912 Harrison Ave., 80461
State agency, authorized by
 Colorado Historical Society
Founded in: 1936
Staff: full time 1, part time 12
Major programs: museum,
 tours/pilgrimages, historic
 preservation, living history
Period of collections: 1865-1918

**Lake County Civic Center
 Association, Inc.**
100-102 E. 9th St.
Telephone: (303) 486-1878
Mail to: P.O. Box 962, 80461
Founded in: 1971
Sherrill Warford, Secretary
Number of members: 300
Staff: full time 1, part time 4
Magazine: *Mountain Diggings*
Major programs: museum, historic
 sites preservation, educational

programs, newsletters/pamphlets, research materials, genealogical services
Period of collections: 1865-present

Leadville Historical Association
123 W. 4th St.
Telephone: (303) 486-0860
Mail to: P.O. Box 911, 80461
Private agency
Founded in: 1942
Mary B. Cassidy, President
Number of members: 96
Staff: volunteer 6
Major programs: oral history
Period of collections: late 1800-early 1900

Tabor Opera House
308 Harrison Ave.
Telephone: (303) 486-1147
Mail to: 815 Harrison Ave., 80461
Private agency
Founded in: 1955
Evelyn E. Furman, Owner
Major programs: library, museum, historic site(s), tours/pilgrimages, exhibits, historic preservation
Period of collections: 1879-1900s

LITTLETON

Littleton Historical Museum
6028 S. Gallup, 80120
Telephone: (303) 795-3850
City agency
Founded in: 1969
Robert McQuarie, Director
Staff: full time 10, part time 5, volunteer 300
Major programs: library, museum, historic site(s), historic preservation, exhibits, living history, photographic collections
Period of collections: 1865-present

LONGMONT

Longmont Museum
375 Kimbark St., 80501
Telephone: (303) 776-6050, ext. 374
City agency, authorized by Department of Human Services
Founded in: 1940
Kent C. Brown, Director
Number of members: 200
Staff: full time 4, part time 2
Major programs: museum, school programs, exhibits, photographic collections
Period of collections: 8000 B.C.-present

St. Vrain Historical Society
P.O. Box 705, 80501
Private agency
Joanne Amorosa, Administrative Assistant
Number of members: 500
Staff: part time 1
Major programs: historic site(s), tours/pilgrimages, historic preservation
Period of collections: 1800-1900

LOVELAND

Loveland Museum and Gallery
503 Lincoln Ave., 80537
Telephone: (303) 667-6070

City agency
Founded in: 1956
Susan Ison, Director
Staff: full time 2, part time 2, volunteer 15
Major programs: museum, school programs, exhibits, photographic collections, fine arts gallery
Period of collections: 1885-1930

LYONS

Lyons Historical Society
340 High St.
Telephone: (303) 823-6692
Mail to: P.O. Box 9, 80540
Founded in: 1973
LaVern M. Johnson, President
Number of members: 40
Staff: full time 1, part time 1, volunteer 10
Major programs: museum, historic site(s), markers, oral history, school programs, book publishing, newsletters/pamphlets, historic preservation, records management, research, exhibits, photographic collections
Period of collections: 1859-present

MANITOU SPRINGS

Manitou Springs Historical Society, Inc.
9 Capitol Hill Ave., 80829
Telephone: (303) 685-1011
Private agency
Founded in: 1971
William H. Copp, President
Number of members: 344
Staff: part time 6, volunteer 50
Major programs: library, archives, manuscripts, museum, historic site(s), markers, oral history, school programs, newsletters/pamphlets, historic preservation, records management, research, exhibits, audiovisual programs, photographic collections, historical trolley tour services
Period of collections: 1880-1920

Miramont Castle Museum and Conference Center
9 Capitol Hill Ave., 80829
Telephone: (303) 685-1011
Private agency, authorized by the Manitou Springs Historical Society, Inc.
Founded in: 1972
William H. Copp, President
Number of members: 344
Staff: full time 1, part time 3, volunteer 20
Major programs: library, archives, museum, historic site(s), markers, tours/pilgrimages, oral history, school programs, newsletters/pamphlets, historic preservation, records management, research, exhibits, audiovisual programs, photographic collections, 1895 children's museum, model railroad museum
Period of collections: 1895-1920

MARBLE

Marble Historical Society
415 W. Main St., 81623
Telephone: (303) 963-2143
Private agency
Founded in: 1977
Oscar D. McCollum, Board Chair
Number of members: 236
Staff: volunteer 12
Magazine: *Marble Chips*
Major programs: archives, museum, educational programs, newsletters/pamphlets
Period of collections: 1880-1942

MONTROSE

Black Canyon of the Gunnison National Monument
2233 E. Main
Telephone: (303) 240-6522
Mail to: P.O. Box 1648, 81402
Federal agency, authorized by National Park Service
Founded in: 1933
Joseph A. Kastellic, Superintendent

PALMER LAKE

Palmer Lake Historical Society
Mail to: P.O. Box 662, 80133
Questionnaire not received

PAONIA

North Fork Historical Society
P.O. Box 1239, 80915
Telephone: (303) 527-4348
Private agency
Founded in: 1970
Wallace D. Eubanks, President
Number of members: 200
Major programs: library, manuscripts, museum, markers, photographic collections
Period of collections: 1900-present

PUEBLO

El Pueblo Museum
905 S. Prairie, 81005
Telephone: (303) 564-5274
State agency, authorized by Colorado Historical Society
Founded in: 1891
Kerry Kramer, Regional Property Administrator
Number of members: 1
Staff: full time 1, part time 4, volunteer 8
Major programs: museum
Period of collections: 1850-1900

Rosemount Victorian House Museum
419 W. 14th St.
Telephone: (303) 545-5290
Mail to: P.O. Box 5259, 81002
Private agency
Founded in: 1967
Lockett Ford Ballard, Jr., Executive Director
Number of members: 750
Staff: full time 5, part time 3, volunteer 75
Magazine: *Rosemount News*
Major programs: museum, historic site(s), tours/pilgrimages, junior history, school programs,

newsletters/pamphlets, historic
preservation
Period of collections: 1890s

**Sangre de Cristo Arts and
Conference Center**
210 N. Santa Fe, 81003
Telephone: (303) 543-0130
City and county agency
Founded in: 1972
Donn Young, Executive Director
Staff: full time 24, part time 22,
volunteer 50
Magazine: *Town and Center Mosaic*
Major programs: library, museum,
tours/pilgrimages, school
programs, historic preservation,
exhibits, photographic collections
Period of collections: 1900

**Western Research Room, Pueblo
Library District**
100 E. Abriendo Ave., 81004
Telephone: (303) 542-4636
State agency
Raymonde Jones, Reference
Services Librarian
Staff: full time ½, volunteer 1
Major programs: library, archives,
manuscripts, oral history
Period of collections: 1870-present

SILVERTON

San Juan County Historical Society
Courthouse Square
Mail to: P.O. Box 154, 81433
Private agency
Founded in: 1964
Beverly Rich, Chair
Number of members: 149
Staff: part time 2, volunteer 10
Major programs: archives, museum,
historic site(s), oral history, school
programs, book publishing, historic
preservation, research, exhibits,
photographic collections,
genealogical services
Period of collections: 1870-present

STERLING

**Logan County Historical
Society, Inc.**
518 N. 4th St., 80751
Questionnaire not received

Overland Trail Museum
Hwy. 6 and 76
Telephone: (303) 522-3895
Mail to: Centennial Square, 80751
County agency, authorized by Logan
County Historical Society
Founded in: 1936
Anna Mae Hagemeier, Curator
Number of members: 30
Staff: part time 5
Major programs: archives, historic
preservation, photographic
collections
Period of collections: late 1880s-early
1900s

STRASBURG

**Comanche Crossing Historical
Society**
Rt. 1, Box 75, 80136
Telephone: (303) 622-4668
Private agency

Founded in: 1969
Emma Michell, Vice
President/Museum Director
Number of members: 170
Staff: volunteer 27
Major programs: museum, historic
site(s), tours/pilgrimages, oral
history, school programs, book
publishing
Period of collections: 1865-1918

TELLURIDE

**San Miguel County Historical
Society**
Mail to: P.O. Box 476, 81435
Questionnaire not received

**Telluride Historic and Architectural
Review Commission**
P.O. Box 397, 81435
Founded in: 1972
Wayne Iverson, Chair
Staff: part time 1
Major programs: architectural review
in national historic district

TRINIDAD

**Baca and Bloom Houses, Pioneer
Museum**
300 E. Main St.
Telephone: (303) 846-7217
Mail to: P.O. Box 472, 81082
State agency, authorized by
Colorado Historical Society
Founded in: 1955
Joy Poole, Regional Property
Administrator
Staff: full time 2, part time 8,
volunteer 100
Magazine: *Colorado Heritage*
Major programs: historic site(s),
tours/pilgrimages, historic
preservation, research, living
history

Trinidad Historical Society
1102 Corant Ave.
Mail to: P.O. Box 176, 81082
Olga Azar, President
Number of members: 345
Major programs: museum, historic
sites preservation,
tours/pilgrimages, oral history,
books
Period of collections: 1865-1918

VAIL

**Colorado Ski Museum—Ski Hall of
Fame**
15 Vail Rd.
Telephone: (303) 476-1876
Mail to: P.O. Box 1976, 81658
Private agency
Founded in: 1976
Pamela Horan-Kates, Executive
Director
Number of members: 200
Staff: full time 1, part time 1,
volunteer 40
Major programs: library, museum,
school programs,
newsletters/pamphlets, audiovisual
programs, photographic
collections
Period of collections: 1880-present

WRAY

**East Yuma County Historical
Society**
140 W. 4th St.
Telephone: (303) 332-5063
County agency
Founded in: 1967
Lettie B. Zion, President
Number of members: 25
Staff: volunteer 6
Major programs: library, museum,
historic site(s), oral history, book
publishing, historic preservation
Period of collections: 1858-1947

CONNECTICUT

ANDOVER

Andover Historical Society
Bunker Hill Rd., 06232
Telephone: (203) 742-6796
Private agency
Founded in: 1975
Alice Y. Moe, President
Number of members: 25
Staff: volunteer 4
Major programs: archives, historic
site(s), markers, tours/pilgrimages,
oral history, school programs,
newsletters/pamphlets, research,
audiovisual programs,
photographic collections,
genealogical services
Period of collections: 1730-1900

BALTIC

Sprague Historical Society
1 Main St., 06330
Founded in: 1970
Number of members: 35
Major programs: markers,
educational programs, junior
history
Period of collections: 1783-present

BANTAM

Bantam Historical Society, Inc.
Main St.
Mail to: P.O. Box 476, 06750
Private agency
Founded in: 1975
George Dudley, Chair
Number of members: 100
Major programs: archives
Period of collections: 1725-present

BARKHAMSTED

**Barkhamsted Historical
Society, Inc.**
Pleasant Valley, 06063
Private agency
Founded in: 1967
Steven Peter Blackburn, President
Number of members: 91
Staff: volunteer 6
Major programs: oral history, school
programs, book publishing
Period of collections: 1830s-present

CONNECTICUT

BETHEL

Bethel Historical Society
169 Greenwood Ave.
Mail to: 8 Blackman Ave., 06801
Questionnaire not received

BETHLEHEM

Old Bethlem Historical Society, Inc.
The Green
Telephone: (203) 266-7330
Mail to: P.O. Box 132, 06751
Private agency
Founded in: 1968
Doris B. Nicholls, President
Number of members: 169
Staff: volunteer 28
Major programs: museum, historic
preservation, exhibits
Period of collections: 1780-1860

BLOOMFIELD

Wintonbury Historical Society, Inc.
Mail to: 21 Westbrook Rd., 06002
Founded in: 1964
Number of members: 230
Major programs: archives,
manuscripts, historic sites
preservation, markers,
tours/pilgrimages, oral history,
educational programs
Period of collections: 1783-1865

BRANFORD

Branford Historical Society
124 Main St.
Telephone: (203) 488-4828/488-8835
Mail to: P.O. Box 504, 06405
Private agency
Founded in: 1960
Janet Gaines, President
Number of members: 450
Staff: volunteer 20
Major programs: archives,
manuscripts, museum, markers,
oral history, school programs,
newsletters/pamphlets, exhibits,
photographic collections
Period of collections: 1700-1800

BRIDGEPORT

Barnum Museum
820 Main St., 06604
Telephone: (203) 576-7320
City agency
Founded in: 1893
Robert S. Pelton, Curator
Staff: full time 3, part time 1,
volunteer 1
Major programs: museum
Period of collections: 1840-1910

**Historical Collections, Bridgeport
Public Library**
925 Broad St., 06604
Telephone: (203) 576-7417
Founded in: 1935
David W. Palmquist, Head, Historical
Collections
Staff: full time 4, part time 2
Major programs: library, archives,
manuscripts, oral history,
genealogical services
Period of collections: 1700-present

**Museum of Art, Science, and
Industry**
4450 Park Ave., 06604
Telephone: (203) 372-3521
Private agency
Founded in: 1958
Frederick S. Bayersdorfer, Jr.,
Director
Number of members: 983
Staff: full time 6, part time 9,
volunteer 30
Major programs: library, museum,
historic site(s), school programs,
newsletters/pamphlets, exhibits
Period of collections: 18th-20th
centuries

BRIDGEWATER

Bridgewater Historical Society
Main St., 06750
Town agency
Harold B. Schramm, President
Number of members: 200
Staff: volunteer 12
Major programs: museum, junior
history, oral history, school
programs, book publishing
Period of collections: Victorian era

BRISTOL

**American Clock and Watch
Museum, Inc.**
100 Maple St., 06010
Telephone: (203) 583-6070
Private agency
Founded in: 1952
Chris H. Bailey, Director
Number of members: 525
Staff: full time 1, part time 1,
volunteer 30
Magazine: *The Timepiece Journal*
Major programs: library, archives,
manuscripts, book publishing,
newsletters/pamphlets, research,
photographic collections
Period of collections: 1680-1940

BROOKFIELD

Brookfield Historical Society, Inc.
Whisconier Rd.
Mail to: P.O. Box 231, 06805
Founded in: 1968
Number of members: 200
Staff: volunteer 75
Major programs: library, archives,
museum, historic site, educational
programs

BROOKLYN

Brooklyn Historical Society
P.O. Box 90, 06234
Telephone: (203) 774-1423
Private agency
Founded in: 1950
M. B. Leonard, President
Number of members: 60
Major programs: library, museum,
historic site(s), markers

CANTERBURY

Prudence Crandall Museum
Rts. 14 and 169
Telephone: (203) 546-9916
Mail to: P.O. Box 47, 06331

State agency, authorized by The
Connecticut Historical Commission
Founded in: 1984
Kazimiera Kozlowski-Oparowski,
Curator
Staff: full time 2
Major programs: library, historic
site(s), historic preservation,
exhibits
Period of collections: 1800-early
1830s

CANTON CENTER

**Canton Historic District
Commission**
Town Hall, Collinsville, 06022
Founded in: 1975
Staff: volunteer 8
Major programs: historic site, historic
preservation
Period of collections: Colonial

COLCHESTER

Colchester Historical Society
Mail to: P.O. Box 13, 06415
Private agency
Founded in: 1964
Helen Piekarz, President
Number of members: 57
Major programs: archives,
manuscripts, historic site(s),
markers, records management,
living history, audiovisual
programs, photographic
collections, genealogical services
Period of collections: 1698-1950

COLEBROOK

Colebrook Historical Society, Inc.
Mail to: P.O. Box 85, 06021
Private agency
Mrs. William Betts, President
Number of members: 200
Major programs: library, museum,
historic site(s), book publishing,
exhibits
Period of collections: 1779-1945

COLLINSVILLE

Canton Historical Society
11 Front St., 06022
Founded in: 1969
Number of members: 390
Questionnaire not received

COLUMBIA

Columbia Historical Society
Mail to: c/o Mrs. Albert B. Gray, Rt.
87, 06237
Questionnaire not received

CORNWALL

Cornwall Historical Society
Pine St.
Mail to: P.O. Box 115, 06753
Founded in: 1964
Michael R. Gannett, President
Number of members: 100
Staff: volunteer 10
Major programs: manuscripts,
museum
Period of collections: 19th century

COS COB

Historical Society of the Town of Greenwich, Inc.
39 Strickland Rd., 06807
Telephone: (203) 869-6899
Private agency
Founded in: 1931
Lauren Kaminsky, Curator
Number of members: 700
Staff: full time 1, part time 2, volunteer 72
Major programs: library, archives, museum, historic site(s), tours/pilgrimages, school programs, newsletters/pamphlets, historic preservation, photographic collections, genealogical services
Period of collections: 1640-present

Postal History Society of Connecticut, Inc.
Mail to: P.O. Box 292, 06807
Questionnaire not received

COVENTRY

Coventry Historical Society, Inc.
South St.
Mail to: P.O. Box 307, 06238
Founded in: 1963
Number of members: 85
Major programs: archives, museum, historic site
Period of collections: 1760-1900

DANBURY

Danbury Scott-Fanton Museum and Historical Society, Inc.
43 Main St., 06810
Telephone: (203) 743-5200
Private agency
Founded in: 1941
Julie B. Barrows, Director
Number of members: 300
Staff: full time 2, part time 3, volunteer 10
Major programs: library, archives, museum, historic site(s), school programs, research, exhibits, photographic collections
Period of collections: 1684-present

DARIEN

Connecticut League of Historical Societies, Inc.
Mail to: P.O. Box 906, 06820
Founded in: 1949
Questionnaire not received

Darien Historical Society, Inc.
45 Old King's Hwy., N, 06820
Telephone: (203) 655-9233
Private agency
Founded in: 1953
Patricia Q. Wall, Executive Director
Number of members: 1,000
Staff: full time 1, part time 1, volunteer 50
Major programs: library, archives, museum, markers, oral history, school programs, newsletters/pamphlets, records management, photographic collections
Period of collections: 1700-present

DEEP RIVER

Deep River Historical Society, Inc.
66 Main St., 06426
Private agency
Founded in: 1939
Mrs. Donald Moore, Curator
Number of members: 210
Staff: part time 1
Major programs: museum, exhibits, audiovisual programs
Period of collections: 1840-present

DERBY

Derby Historical Society, Inc.
37 Elm St., Ansonia, 06401
Telephone: (203) 735-1908
Mail to: P.O. Box 331, 06418
Private agency
Founded in: 1947
Dorothy A. Larson, Executive Director
Number of members: 223
Staff: full time 1, part time 9, volunteer 5
Major programs: museum, historic site(s), school programs, historic preservation, living history
Period of collections: 18th century

DURHAM

Durham Historical Society
Main St.
Mail to: P.O. Box 345, 06422
Private agency
Founded in: 1949
Anne Mae Spooner, President
Number of members: 126
Staff: volunteer 4
Major programs: museum, newsletters/pamphlets, exhibits

EAST HADDAM

East Haddam Historical Society
Mail to: P.O. Box 27, 06423
Founded in: 1963
Number of members: 220
Major programs: archives, historic sites preservation, museum markers, tours/pilgrimages, educational programs
Period of collections: 1783-present

EAST HARTFORD

East Hartford Historical Society
52 Pitkin St., 06108
Questionnaire not received

EAST HARTLAND

Hartland Historical Society, Inc.
06027
Telephone: (203) 653-3055 (president)
Private agency
Founded in: 1954
Joan E. Stoltze, President
Number of members: 100
Staff: volunteer 25
Major programs: museum, historic site(s), oral history
Period of collections: 1800-1900

EAST HAVEN

Branford Electric Railway Association
17 River St., 06512

Telephone: (203) 467-6927
Private agency
Founded in: 1945
John R. Stevens, President
Number of members: 900
Staff: full time 1, part time 1, volunteer 130
Magazine: *Branford Electric Railway Journal*
Major programs: library, archives, museum, historic site(s), tours, newsletters/pamphlets, historic preservation, exhibits, living history, photographic collections, operating electric railway
Period of collections: 1878-present

EAST LYME

Smith-Harris House
33 Society Rd., Niantic, 06357
Telephone: (203) 739-0761
Mail to: P.O. Box 112, 06333
Town agency, authorized by Smith-Harris Commission
Founded in: 1978
Sandra Kozlowski, Curator
Major programs: school programs, living history
Period of collections: mid 19th century

EASTON

Historical Society of Easton, Inc.
P.O. Box 121, 06612
Telephone: (203) 268-4255
Private agency
Founded in: 1968
Janice Burroughs, President
Number of members: 375
Major programs: markers, oral history, photographic collections, historic house
Period of collections: 1800s

EAST WINDSOR

Connecticut Electric Railway Association, Inc.
58 N. Rd., Warehouse Point
Mail to: P.O. Box 436, 06088
Founded in: 1940
Number of members: 305
Staff: full time 1, volunteer 35
Major programs: museum, educational programs, books, newsletters/pamphlets
Period of collections: 1865-present

East Windsor Historical Society, Inc.
Scantic Rd.
Mail to: P.O. Box 232, 06088
Founded in: 1965
Nancy Masters, President
Number of members: 150
Staff: volunteer 4
Major programs: museum, markers, books
Period of collections: 1800-1918

ENFIELD

Enfield Historical Society, Inc.
1294 Enfield St., 06082
Private agency
Founded in: 1960
Michael K. Miller, President

Number of members: 264
Staff: volunteer 25
Major programs: museum, historic
site(s), school programs,
newsletters/pamphlets, historic
preservation
Period of collections: 1800-1930

ESSEX

Connecticut River Foundation
Steamboat Dock
Telephone: (203) 767-8269
Mail to: P.O. Box 261, 06426
Private agency
Founded in: 1974
Brenda Milkofsky, Director
Staff: full time 2, volunteer 50
Magazine: *Steamboat Log*
Major programs: library, archives,
manuscripts, museum, historic
site(s), oral history, book
publishing, newsletters/pamphlets,
historic preservation, exhibits,
photographic collections
Period of collections: 19th century

**Connecticut Valley Railroad
Museum, Inc.**
Railroad Ave.
Telephone: (203) 767-2021
Mail to: P.O. Box 97, 06426
Private agency
Founded in: 1968
William D. Sample, President
Number of members: 225
Staff: volunteer 35
Magazine: *Along the Valley Line*
Major programs: archives, museum,
newsletters/pamphlets, historic
preservation, exhibits, living
history, photographic collections,
volunteer operational support of
The Valley Railroad Co.
Period of collections: 1868-present

Essex Historical Society, Inc.
Hills Academy, Prospect St.
Telephone: (203) 767-8987
Mail to: P.O. Box 123, 06426
Private agency
Founded in: 1955
W. Campbell Hudson III, President
Number of members: 550
Staff: full time 1, volunteer 50
Major programs: archives, museum,
historic site(s), school programs,
research, exhibits
Period of collections: 1650-1850

FAIRFIELD

**Connecticut Firemen's Historical
Society, Inc.**
366 Wormwood Rd., 06430
Mail to: P.O. Box 738, Avon, 06001
Founded in: 1971
Number of members: 250
Staff: volunteer 15
Magazine: *The Trumpet*
Major programs: museum,
educational programs, historic
preservation
Period of collections: 1880s-1910

Fairfield Historical Society
636 Old Post Rd., 06430
Telephone: (203) 259-1598
Private agency
Founded in: 1903

L. Corwin Sharp, Director
Staff: full time 4, part time 4,
volunteer 3
Magazine: *FHS Chronicle*
Major programs: library, archives,
manuscripts, museum, historic
site(s), tours/pilgrimages, school
programs, newsletters/pamphlets,
historic preservation, records
management, research, exhibits,
living history, audiovisual
programs, photographic
collections, genealogical services
Period of collections: 1700-1950

Old Post Road Association
P.O. Box 581, 06430
Founded in: 1956
Questionnaire not received

FALLS VILLAGE

**Falls Village-Canaan Historical
Society**
Main St., 06031
Founded in: 1953
Randi Lemmon, President
Number of members: 180
Staff: volunteer 1
Major programs: museum,
newsletters/pamphlets, historic
preservation
Period of collections: 1840-present

FARMINGTON

Farmington Historical Society
P.O. Box 1645, 06034
Private agency
Founded in: 1954
Betty D. Coykendall, President
Number of members: 250
Major programs: library, book
publishing, historic preservation
Period of collections: 1800-1920

Farmington Museum
37 High St., 06032
Questionnaire not received

Hill-Stead Museum
671 Farmington Ave., 06032
Telephone: (203) 677-4787
Mail to: P.O. Box 353, 06034
Private agency
Founded in: 1946
Philip C. Wright, Director
Number of members: 1,000
Staff: full time 3, part time 18,
volunteer 2
Major programs: library, archives,
museum, historic preservation,
research, conservation, fine arts
Period of collections: 18th-19th
centuries

Stanley-Whitman House
37 High St., 06032
Telephone: (203) 677-9222
Private agency, authorized by
Farmington Village Green and
Library Association
Founded in: 1935
Dorothy Lunde, Director
Number of members: 250
Staff: full time 1, volunteer 60
Major programs: historic site(s),
school programs,
newsletters/pamphlets, historic
preservation, exhibits
Period of collections: 17th-19th
centuries

GLASTONBURY

**Connecticut Society of
Genealogists, Inc.**
2906 Main St.
Telephone: (203) 633-4203
Mail to: P. O. Box 435, 06033
Private agency
Founded in: 1968
Jacquelyn L. Ricker, Office Manager
Number of members: 4,200
Staff: full time 1, part time 2
Magazine: *Connecticut Nutmegger*
Major programs: book publishing,
newsletters/pamphlets, research,
genealogical services

Historical Society of Glastonbury
1944 Main St.
Telephone: (203) 633-6890
Mail to: P.O. Box 46, 06033
Private agency
Founded in: 1937
Lisa L. Broberg, Director
Number of members: 270
Staff: part time 1, volunteer 6
Magazine: *The PublicK Post*
Major programs: library, archives,
manuscripts, museum,
tours/pilgrimages, junior history,
book publishing,
newsletters/pamphlets, research,
exhibits, photographic collections
Period of collections:
prehistoric-1970s

GOSHEN

Goshen Historical Society
Old Middle Rd., 06756
Telephone: (203) 491-2665
Private agency
Founded in: 1955
Mrs. Ellsworth D. Wood, President
Number of members: 220
Staff: volunteer 8
Major programs: junior history, oral
history
Period of collections: 1800-1900

GRANBY

Salmon Brook Historical Society
208 Salmon Brook St.
Telephone: (203) 653-3965
Mail to: 16 Hummingbird Lane, 06035
Private agency
Founded in: 1959
Carol Laun, Curator
Number of members: 200
Staff: volunteer 15
Magazine: *Collections*
Major programs: library, archives,
museum, manuscripts, school
programs, historic preservation,
research, photographic collections
Period of collections: 1790-1890

GREENWICH

**Architectural Conservancy of
Greenwich**
P.O. Box 793, 06830
Private agency
Founded in: 1978
Richard Holleran, Chair
Major programs: historic
preservation, exhibits,
photographic collections
Period of collections: 1978-present

U S. Tobacco Museum
100 W. Putnam Ave., 06830
Telephone: (203) 869-5531
Private agency, authorized by U.S.
Tobacco Company
Founded in: 1977
Jacqueline M. Key, Curator
Staff: full time 2, part time 3
Major programs: library, archives,
museum, tours/pilgrimages,
research, exhibits, photographic
collections
Period of collections: 18th-19th
centuries

GRISWOLD

Griswold Historical Society
Mail to: P.O. Box 261, Jewett City,
06351
Founded in: 1974
Number of members: 48
Staff: volunteer 15
Major programs: historic sites
preservation, markers,
tours/pilgrimages
Period of collections: 1865-present

GROTON

Groton Bank Historical Association
Mail to: P.O. Box 4, Borough Station,
06340
Questionnaire not received

GUILFORD

**Dorothy Whitfield Historic
Society, Inc.**
84 Boston St.
Mail to: P.O. Box 229, 06437
Founded in: 1918
Number of members: 500
Staff: full time 2
Major programs: museum
Period of collections: 1660-1800

Guilford Keeping Society, Inc.
171 Boston St.
Mail to: P.O. Box 363, 06437
Founded in: 1947
Number of members: 190
Staff: part time 1
Major programs: archives, museum,
books
Period of collections: 1783-present

**Henry Whitfield State Historical
Museum**
Old Whitfield St.
Telephone: (203) 453-2457
Mail to: P.O. Box 210, 06437
State agency, authorized by
Connecticut Historical Commission
Founded in: 1899
Dorothy Y. Armistead, Curator
Staff: full time 1, part time 2
Major programs: library, museum
Period of collections: 17th-18th
centuries

HADDAM

Haddam Historical Society, Inc.
Hayden Hill and Walkley Hill Rd.,
06432
Mail to: P.O. Box 261, Higganum
06441
Founded in: 1956
Number of members: 160

Staff: volunteer 15
Major programs: library, archives,
museum, historic site
Period of collections: 1780-1810

HAMDEN

Eli Whitney Museum
Whitney Ave. at Armory St.
Telephone: (203) 777-1833
Mail to: P.O. Box 6099, 06517
Private agency
Founded in: 1976
Karyl Lee Hall, Director
Number of members: 165
Staff: part time 4
Major programs: museum, historic
site(s), historic preservation,
exhibits
Period of collections: 19th century

Hamden Historical Society
P.O. Box 5512, 06518
Founded in: 1928
Number of members: 200
Staff: volunteer 20
Major programs: library, markers,
historic preservation

HAMPTON

**Hampton Antiquarian and
Historical Society**
Main St.
Mail to: P.O. Box 12, 06247
Private agency
Founded in: 1967
Mrs. Sidney P. Marland, Jr., President
Number of members: 150
Major programs: archives, museum,
historic site(s), living history
Period of collections: 1830-1900

HARTFORD

**Antiquarian and Landmarks
Society, Inc.**
394 Main St.
Telephone: (203) 247-8996
Private agency
Founded in: 1936
Arthur W. Leibundguth, Director
Number of members: 2,000
Staff: full time 3, part time 35,
volunteer 30
Magazine: *The Connecticut
Antiquarian*
Major programs: manuscripts,
historic site(s), tours/pilgrimages,
school programs,
newsletters/pamphlets, historic
preservation
Period of collections: late 17th-mid
19th centuries

**Connecticut Historical
Commission**
59 S. Prospect St., 06106
Telephone: (203) 566-3005
State agency
Founded in: 1955
John W. Shannahan, Director
Staff: full time 20, part time 10
Major programs: historic site(s),
historic preservation
Period of collections: 1630s-1980s

◇**Connecticut Historical Society**
1 Elizabeth St., 06105
Telephone: (203) 236-5621

Founded in: 1825
Christopher P. Bickford, Director
Number of members: 2,150
Staff: full time 15, part time 15
Magazine: *Bulletin*
Major programs: library, archives,
manuscripts, museum, school
programs, book publishing,
newsletters/pamphlets, research,
exhibits, audiovisual programs,
photographic collections,
genealogical services
Period of collections: 1600-present

Connecticut State Library
231 Capitol Ave., 06115
Founded in: 1854
Staff: full time 5, part time 2
Major programs: library, archives,
manuscripts
Period of collections: 1635-present

Mark Twain Memorial
351 Farmington Ave., 06105
Telephone: (203) 247-0998
Private agency
Founded in: 1929
Wynn Lee, Director
Number of members: 1,000
Staff: full time 9, part time 27,
volunteer 1
Major programs: library, archives,
manuscripts, museum, historic
sites preservation,
tours/pilgrimages,
newsletters/pamphlets
Period of collections: 1874-1900

Old State House Association
800 Main St., 06103
Founded in: 1975
Number of members: 1,300
Staff: full time 5, part time 3,
volunteer 50
Major programs: historic site
Period of collections: 1796-present

**Society of the Descendants of the
Founders of Hartford**
c/o Connecticut Historical Society, 1
Elizabeth St., 06105
Founded in: 1931
Questionnaire not received

**Society of Mayflower Descendants
in Connecticutt**
81 Lawn Ave., 06457
Founded in: 1896
Number of members: 945
Staff: volunteer 20
Major programs: library, archives,
historic sites preservation, markers,
junior history, educational
programs

Stowe-Day Foundation
77 Forest St., 06105
Telephone: (203) 522-9258
Private agency
Founded in: 1941
Joseph S. Van Why, Director
Staff: full time 9
Major programs: library, manuscripts,
historic site(s), book publishing,
newsletters/pamphlets, research,
exhibits, photographic collections
Period of collections: 19th century

CONNECTICUT

HARWINTON

Harwinton Historical Society, Inc.
P.O. Box 84, 06791
Private agency
Founded in: 1971
Number of members: 200
Major programs: museum, living
  history
Period of collections: 1600s-present

HUNTINGTON

Huntington Historical Society, Inc.
Ripton Rd.
Mail to: P.O. Box 2155, 06484
Private agency
Robert Farnsworth, President
Number of members: 175
Staff: volunteer 10
Magazine: *Huntington Hills*
Major programs: tours/pilgrimages,
  school programs,
  newsletters/pamphlets
Period of collections: early 19th
  century

KILLINGWORTH

Killingworth Historical Society, Inc.
R.F.D. 3, Rt. 80, 06417
Questionnaire not received

LAKESIDE

Morris Historical Society, Inc.
South St., 06763
Founded in: 1959
Staff: volunteer 10
Major programs: archives, museum,
  historic preservation
Period of collections: 19th century

LEBANON

Lebanon Historical Society
P.O. Box 93, 06249
Founded in: 1962
Questionnaire not received

LITCHFIELD

Litchfield Historical Society
South and East Sts.
Founded in: (203) 567-5862
Mail to: P.O. Box 385, 06759
Private agency
Founded in: 1856
Robert G. Carroon, Director
Number of members: 900
Staff: full time 2, part time 2,
  volunteer 30
Major programs: library, archives,
  manuscripts, museum, historic
  site(s), exhibits, genealogical
  services
Period of collections: 1719-1900

MADISON

Allis-Bushnell House
853 Boston Post Rd.
Telephone: (203) 245-4567
Mail to: P.O. Box 17, 06443
Private agency, authorized by
  Madison Historical Society
Founded in: 1917
William T. Mills, President
Number of members: 450
Staff: volunteer 20

Major programs: library, museum,
  historic site(s)
Period of collections: 18th-19th
  centuries

Madison Historical Society
853 Boston Post Rd.
Telephone: (203) 245-4567
Mail to: P.O. Box 17, 06443
Founded in: 1917
Period of collections: 600
Staff: full time 1, volunteer 21
Major programs: library, museum,
  markers, junior history, educational
  programs, books,
  newsletters/pamphlets
Period of collections: 1783-present

MANCHESTER

**Connecticut Firemen's Historical
  Society, Inc.**
230 Pine St., 06040
Telephone: (203) 649-9436
Mail to: 366 Wormword Rd., Fairfield,
  06430
Private agency
Founded in: 1971
Arthur H. Selleck, President
Number of members: 325
Staff: volunteer 24
Magazine: *The Trumpet*
Major programs: museum, historic
  preservation, fire service history
Period of collections: 19th
  century-1925

**Institute of Local History,
  Manchester Community College**
60 Bidwell St., 06040
Telephone: (203) 647-6101
State agency, authorized by board of
  trustees for regional community
  colleges
Founded in: 1969
John F. Sutherland, Director
Staff: part time 1
Major programs: historic sites
  preservation, oral history,
  educational programs
Period of collections: late 19th-early
  20th centuries

Lutz Children's Museum
247 S. Main St., 06040
Telephone: (203) 643-0949
Private agency
Founded in: 1953
Steven Ling, Director
Number of members: 650
Staff: full time 4, part time 3,
  volunteer 80
Major programs: museum, junior
  history, school programs,
  newsletters/pamphlets, exhibits,
  audiovisual programs

Manchester Historical Society, Inc.
106 Hartford Rd., 06040
Telephone: (203) 643-5588
Private agency
Founded in: 1965
Edward W. Kloehn, President
Number of members: 525
Major programs: museum, historic
  site(s), markers, tours/pilgrimages
Period of collections: 1823-present

MANSFIELD

Mansfield Historical Society
Mail to: P.O. Box 145, Storrs, 06268
Founded in: 1957
Questionnaire not received

MARLBOROUGH

Marlborough Historical Society
P.O. Box 93, 06447
Founded in: 1967
Frances MacNaught, Chair
Number of members: 40
Period of collections: 1630-1930

MIDDLEBURY

Middlebury Historical Society
26 Wheeler Rd., 06762
Founded in: 1974
Number of members: 194
Questionnaire not received

MIDDLETOWN

**Conference of Connecticut River
  Historical Societies in
  Connecticut, Inc.**
151 Main St., 06457
Mail to: 460 Old Main St., Rocky Hill,
  06067
Questionnaire not received

◇**Connecticut Humanities Council**
41 Lawn Ave., Wesleyan Station,
  06457
Telephone: (203) 347-6888
Private agency
Founded in: 1973
Bruce Fraser, Executive Director
Staff: full time 4, part time 2,
  volunteer 25
Magazine: *The Connecticut Scholar:
  Occasional Papers of the
  Connecticut Humanities Council*
Major programs: library, museum,
  oral history, school programs,
  exhibits, archaeology programs

**Greater Middletown Preservation
  Trust, Inc.**
27 Washington St., 06457
Telephone: (203) 346-1646
Private agency
Founded in: 1972
Janice P. Cunningham, Executive
  Director
Number of members: 525
Staff: full time 2, part time 1,
  volunteer 3
Magazine: *Preservation Profile*
Major programs: book publishing,
  historic preservation, research,
  audiovisual programs

**Middlesex County Historical
  Society**
151 Main St., 06457
Telephone: (203) 346-0746
Private agency
Founded in: 1901
Lisa L. Broberg, Director
Number of members: 150
Staff: part time 1, volunteer 10
Magazine: *Historical Observer*
Major programs: archives, museum,
  newsletters/pamphlets, records
  management, research, exhibits,
  photographic collections,

genealogical services, decorative arts
Period of collections: 17th century-1870

MILFORD

Milford Historical Society, Inc.
34 High St.
Mail to: P.O. Box 337, 06460
Founded in: 1930
Number of members: 350
Magazine: *Wharf Lane Newsletter*
Major programs: museum, historic sites preservation, educational programs, books
Period of collections: prehistoric-present

MONROE

Monroe Historical Society, Inc.
Wheeler and Old Tannery Rds., 06468
Mail to: Georges Lane
Questionnaire not received

MOOSUP

Plainfield Historical Society
Mail to: P.O. Box 852, 06354
Questionnaire not received

MORRIS

Morris Historical Society
South St., 06763
Private agency
Founded in: 1959
Barbara Strong, Secretary
Number of members: 100
Staff: volunteer 10
Major programs: archives, museum, school programs
Period of collections: from 1700-present

MYSTIC

Denison Society, Inc.
Pequotsepos Rd.
Mail to: P.O. Box 42, 06355
Founded in: 1930
Questionnaire not received

Mystic Seaport Museum
Rt. 27, 06355
Telephone: (203) 572-0711
Private agency
Founded in: 1929
J. Revell Carr, Director
Number of members: 18,000
Staff: full time 200, part time 100, volunteer 300
Magazine: *The Log/The Wind-Rose*
Major programs: library, archives, manuscripts, museum, school programs, book publishing, newsletters/pamphlets, historic preservation, research, exhibits, living history, audiovisual programs, photographic collections
Period of collections: 1817-1917

NAUGATUCK

Naugatuck Historical Society
144 Meadow St.
Mail to: P.O. Box 317, 06770
Questionnaire not received

NEW BRITAIN

New Britain Youth Museum
30 High St., 06051
Telephone: (203) 225-3020
Private agency, authorized by New Britain Institute
Founded in: 1956
Alan J. Krauss, Director
Number of members: 200
Staff: full time 7, part time 3, volunteer 30
Major programs: museum, junior history, school programs, exhibits, natural history
Period of collections: 1850-1920

NEW CANAAN

New Canaan Historical Society
13 Oenoke Ridge, 06840
Telephone: (203) 966-1776
Private agency
Founded in: 1889
Carolyn M. Hummer, Administrative Director
Number of members: 950
Staff: full time 1, part time 2, volunteer 130
Major programs: library, archives, manuscripts, museum, historic site(s), tours/pilgrimages, junior history, oral history, school programs, newsletters/pamphlets, research, genealogical services
Period of collections: Colonial era-present

NEW FAIRFIELD

New Fairfield Historical Society, Inc.
Mail to: P.O. Box 8156, 06810
Questionnaire not received

NEW HAVEN

Connecticut Trust for Historic Preservation
152 Temple St., 06510
Telephone: (203) 561-6312
Founded in: 1975
Charles Granquist, Executive Director
Number of members: 600
Staff: full time 5, volunteer 2
Magazine: *Connecticut Preservation News*
Major programs: library, educational programs, newsletters/pamphlets, historic preservation, technical assistance conferences, field services

Knights of Columbus Charities, Inc.
1 Columbus Plaza, 06507
Telephone: (203) 772-2130
Private agency
Founded in: 1882
Kim S. Perry, Archivist
Staff: full time 2
Major programs: library, archives, manuscripts, museum, tours/pilgrimages, book publishing, records management, genealogical services

Knights of Columbus Headquarters Museum
1 Columbus Plaza, 06507
Telephone: (203) 772-2130
Private agency, authorized by Knights of Columbus Charities, Inc.
Founded in: 1982
Mary Lou Cummings, Curator
Staff: full time 1
Major programs: museum, research, exhibits, photographic collections
Period of collections: 1882-present

Sails from the 1841 whaleship Charles W. Morgan *tower above the 1908 steamboat* Sabino *along Mystic Seaport's waterfront. At right is the ship* Joseph Conrad, *built in 1882.—Claire White Peterson photo, Mystic Seaport, Mystic, Connecticut*

New Haven Colony Historical Society
114 Whitney Ave., 06510
Telephone: (203) 562-4183
Private agency
Founded in: 1862
David L. Parke, Jr., Executive Director
Number of members: 1,100
Staff: full time 5, part time 11, volunteer 38
Major programs: library, archives, manuscripts, museum, historic site(s), school programs, book publishing, newsletters/pamphlets, exhibits, photographic collections, genealogical services
Period of collections: 1638-present

New Haven Preservation Trust
254 College St., 06510
Telephone: (203) 562-5919
Mail to: P.O. Box 1671, 06507
Private agency
Founded in: 1962
Preston Maynard, Executive Director
Number of members: 569
Staff: full time 6, part time 1, volunteer 4
Major programs: historic preservation, research

Yale University Collection of Musical Instruments
15 Hillhouse Ave.
Telephone: (203) 436-4935
Mail to: P.O. Box 2117, 06520
Private agency, authorized by the university
Founded in: 1900
Richard Rephann, Director
Number of members: 123
Staff: full time 2, part time 1
Major programs: museum, newsletters/pamphlets, historic preservation, research, restoration and conservation of musical instruments
Period of collections: 1550-1900

NEW LONDON

New London County Historical Society
11 Blinman St., 06320
Telephone: (203) 443-1209
Private agency
Founded in: 1870
Elizabeth B. Knox, Curator
Number of members: 320
Staff: part time 2
Major programs: library, archives, manuscripts, museum, book publishing, newsletters/pamphlets
Period of collections: 18th-19th centuries

New London Landmarks—Union Railroad Station Trust, Inc.
309 Captain's Walk, Room 216
Telephone: (203) 442-0003
Mail to: P.O. Box 1134, 06320
Private agency
Founded in: 1976
Sharon Churchill, Executive Director
Number of members: 350
Staff: part time 3
Major programs: tours, school programs, newsletters/pamphlets, historic preservation, research, audiovisual programs, field services

Tale of The Whale
Three Whale Oil Row, 06320
Founded in: 1974
Questionnaire not received

NEWINGTON

American Radio Relay League Museum
225 Main St., 06111
Telephone: (203) 666-1541
Private agency
Founded in: 1914
David Sumner, Executive Vice President
Number of members: 135,000
Staff: full time 10, part time 5
Major programs: museum, history of amateur (ham) radio
Period of collections: post W.W. I-present

Newington Historical Society and Trust, Inc.
679 Willard Ave., 06111
Telephone: (203) 667-0545
Private agency
Founded in: 1971
Florence Urbanowicz, President
Major programs: museum, historic site(s), school programs, newsletters/pamphlets, historic preservation, research, exhibits, photographic collections
Period of collections: 19th century

NEW MILFORD

New Milford Historical Society, Inc.
6 Aspetuck Ave.
Mail to: P.O. Box 566, 06776
Questionnaire not received

NEWTOWN

Newtown Historical Society
44 Main St.
Mail to: P.O. Box 189, 06470
Questionnaire not received

NIANTIC

East Lyme Historical Society
Shore Rd., 06357
Mail to: 28 Damon Hts. Rd.
Questionnaire not received

NOANK

Noank Historical Society, Inc.
17 Sylvan St.
Telephone: (203) 536-3021
Mail to: P.O. Box 454, 06340
Private agency
Founded in: 1966
Mrs. Robert P. Anderson, Jr., President
Number of members: 300
Staff: volunteer 30
Major programs: museum, school programs, newsletters/pamphlets, research, exhibits, photographic collections, genealogical services
Period of collections: late 19th-early 20th centuries

NORFOLK

Norfolk Historical Society, Inc.
Village Green, 06058
Telephone: (203) 542-5761
Private agency

Founded in: 1960
Mrs. William Walcott, President
Number of members: 150
Staff: part time 1
Major programs: museum, exhibits, photographic collections
Period of collections: 1775-present

NORTH BRANFORD

Totoket Historical Society, Inc.
1605 Foxon Rd.
Telephone: (203) 488-0423
Mail to: P.O. Box 563, 06471
Founded in: 1958
Janet S. Gregan, President
Number of members: 150
Major programs: archives, museum, school programs, exhibits, newsletters/pamphlets, research, audiovisual programs, archaeology programs, photographic collections
Period of collections: 1700-present

NORTH FRANKLIN

Franklin Historical Society
Rt. 32, 06254
Questionnaire not received

NORTH HAVEN

North Haven Historical Society
27 Broadway 06473
Founded in: 1959
Nancy Pfeiffer, President
Number of members: 130
Staff: volunteer 24
Major programs: archives, manuscripts, museum, markers, tours/pilgrimages, educational programs
Period of collections: prehistoric-1950

NORTH STONINGTON

North Stonington Historical Society, Inc.
Main St.
Mail to: P.O. Box 134, 06359
Questionnaire not received

NORWALK

Lockwood-Mathews Mansion Museum
295 West Ave., 06850
Telephone: (203) 838-1434
Private agency
Founded in: 1966
David J. Byrnes, Executive Director
Number of members: 750
Staff: full time 1, part time 2, volunteer 50
Major programs: museum, historic site(s), school programs, newsletters/pamphlets, historic preservation, exhibits
Period of collections: 1865-1890

Norwalk Historical Commission
141 East Ave., 06851
Telephone: (203) 866-0202
City agency
Founded in: 1975
Ralph C. Bloom, Curator
Staff: full time 1, part time 1, volunteer 25

Major programs: library, archives, museum, historic site(s), historic preservation, photographic collections
Period of collections: 1750-1850

Norwalk Historical Society
P.O. Box 335, 06852
Number of members: 354
Major programs: historic site, educational programs
Questionnaire not received

NORWICH

Slater Memorial Museum and Converse Art Gallery
108 Crescent St., 06360
Telephone: (203) 887-2506
Private agency, authorized by the Norwich Free Academy
Founded in: 1888
Joseph P. Gualtieri, Director
Number of members: 500
Staff: full time 2, part time 2
Major programs: museum, school programs, exhibits, fine arts
Period of collections: 17th-20th centuries

Society of the Founders of Norwich, Connecticut, Inc.
348 Washington St., 06360
Mail to: P.O. Box 13, 06030
Founded in: 1901
Number of members: 800
Staff: full time 1, part time 1, volunteer 25
Magazine: *Annual Report*
Major programs: library, archives, museum, historic site, tours, junior history, educational programs, book publishing, newsletters/pamphlets, historic preservation
Period of collections: 18th century

OLD LYME

Lyme Historical Society—Florence Griswold Museum
96 Lyme St., 06371
Telephone: (203) 434-5542
Private agency
Founded in: 1936
Jeffrey W. Andersen, Director
Number of members: 1,270
Staff: full time 3, part time 5, volunteer 40
Magazine: *Lyme Ledger*
Major programs: library, archives, museum, historic site(s), oral history, school programs, book publishing, newsletters/pamphlets, records management, research, exhibits, photographic collections
Period of collections: 19th-early 20th centuries

OLD MYSTIC

Indian and Colonial Research Center
Main St., 06372
Telephone: (203) 536-9771
Private agency
Founded in: 1965
Mary V. Goodman, President
Number of members: 185
Staff: volunteer 10

Major programs: library, manuscripts, museum, oral history, school programs, book publishing, historic preservation, research, exhibits, audiovisual programs, photographic collections, genealogical services
Period of collections: 1600-1850

OLD SAYBROOK

Old Saybrook Historical Society
350 Main St.
Telephone: (203) 388-2622
Mail to: P.O. Box 4, 06475
Private agency
Founded in: 1959
James B. Platt, President
Number of members: 400
Staff: volunteer 45
Major programs: archives, museum, oral history, school programs, exhibits, genealogical services
Period of collections: 1790-1840

ORANGE

Orange Historical Society
615 Orange Center Rd.
Mail to: P.O. Box 784, 06477
Private agency
Founded in: 1964
Harry W. Jones, President
Number of members: 230
Staff: volunteer 13
Major programs: archives, manuscripts, museum, tours/pilgrimages, school programs, newsletters/pamphlets, historic preservation, exhibits, photographic collections
Period of collections: 1800s

OXFORD

Oxford Historical Society, Inc.
154 Bowers Hill Rd., 06483
Telephone: (203) 888-0363
Private agency
Founded in: 1974
Jane Fertig, President
Number of members: 60
Major programs: markers, oral history
Period of collections: 1800-present

PLAINVILLE

Farmington Canal Corridor Association
Telephone: (203) 747-0081
Mail to: P.O. Box 24, 06062
Founded in: 1972
Ruth Hummel, Secretary
Major programs: historic sites preservation, educational programs
Period of collections: 1821-1849

Plainville Historical Society, Inc.
29 Pierce St.
Telephone: (203) 747-6577
Mail to: P.O. Box 464, 06062
Private agency
Founded in: 1968
Mrs. Robert Hummel, President
Number of members: 100
Staff: volunteer 35
Major programs: archives, museum, school programs, historic preservation, exhibits, photographic collections
Period of collections: 1820-present

PLYMOUTH

Town of Plymouth Historical Society
7 W. Main, 06782
Founded in: 1967
Staff: volunteer 6
Major programs: archives, museum, historic site, markers, tours/pilgrimages, junior history, oral history, historic preservation
Period of collections: 1795-1900

PORTLAND

Portland Historical Society, Inc.
Mail to: P.O. Box 98, 06480
Founded in: 1972
Number of members: 230
Major programs: historic sites preservation, oral history, newsletters/pamphlets

PROSPECT

Prospect Historical Society
Center St.
Mail to: 31 Summit Rd., 06712
Questionnaire not received

REDDING

Redding Historical Society, Inc.
Redding Center, 06875
Founded in: 1963
Number of members: 274
Staff: volunteer 20
Major programs: oral history, historic preservation
Period of collections: late 18th-19th centuries

RIDGEFIELD

Keeler Tavern Preservation Society
132 Main St.
Telephone: (203) 438-5485
Mail to: P.O. Box 204, 06877
Private agency
Founded in: 1966
William J. Raftery, President
Number of members: 300
Staff: volunteer 100
Major programs: museum, historic site(s), tours/pilgrimages, historic preservation, living history
Period of collections: 1772-1865

Ridgefield Library and Historical Association
472 Main St., 06877
Founded in: 1901
Mrs. A. Daubenspeck, Director
Staff: full time 6, part time 4, volunteer 12
Major programs: library, archives

ROCKY HILL

Conference of Connecticut River Historical Societies in Connecticut, Inc.
460 Old Main St., 06067
Founded in: 1970
Peter J. Revill, President
Number of members: 10
Staff: volunteer 4
Magazine: *The Rangelight*
Major programs: history of the Connecticut River

French-Canadian Genealogical Society of Connecticut
P.O. Box 262, 06067
Telephone: (203) 529-1438
Private agency
Founded in: 1979
Roderick A. Wilscam, President
Number of members: 300
Staff: volunteer 14
Magazine: *Connecticut Maple Leaf*
Major programs: library, newsletters/pamphlets, research, genealogical services
Period of collections: 1600-1900

Rocky Hill Historical Society, Inc.
785 Old Main St.
Telephone: (203) 563-8710
Mail to: P.O. Box 185, 06067
Private agency
Founded in: 1962
Peter J. Revill, President
Number of members: 150
Staff: volunteer 20
Major programs: library, museum, exhibits
Period of collections: 1865-1945

ROWAYTON

Rowayton Historical Society
177 Rowayton Ave.
Mail to: P.O. Box 106, 06853
Founded in: 1960
Number of members: 200
Staff: volunteer 5
Major programs: library, archives, manuscripts, museum
Period of collections: 1865-present

ROXBURY

Roxbury Historical Society
Blue Stone Ridge, 06783
Telephone: (203) 354-7612
Founded in: 1965
Questionnaire not received

SALISBURY

Salisbury Association, Inc.
c/o Holley-Williams House, Lakeville, 06039
Telephone: (203) 435-2878
Mail to: P.O. Box 1681, Lakeville, 06039
Private agency
Founded in: 1902
Mrs. Henry W. Burgess, Chair
Number of members: 375
Staff: part time 1, volunteer 50
Major programs: archives, museum, oral history, newsletters/pamphlets, historic preservation, exhibits, photographic collections, genealogical services, land trust, lake study
Period of collections: 1740-1930

SEYMOUR

Seymour Historical Society, Inc.
c/o 69 Church St., 06483
Telephone: (203) 888-0037
Private agency
Founded in: 1975
David N. Kummer, President
Number of members: 47
Staff: volunteer 10

Major programs: museum, school programs, book publishing, historic preservation, research, photographic collections
Period of collections: 1855-present

SHELTON

Huntington Historical Society
70 Ripton Rd.
Mail to: P.O. Box 2155, 06484
Founded in: 1970
Number of members: 100
Staff: volunteer 20
Major programs: museum, educational programs, historic preservation
Period of collections: 1800-1850

Tree Farm Archives
272 Israel Hill Rd., 06484
Telephone: (203) 929-0126
Private agency
Founded in: 1960
Philip H. Jones, Director/Curator
Major programs: library, archives, manuscripts
Period of collections: 1830-1880

SHERMAN

Sherman Historical Society
Sherman Center
Mail to: P.O. Box 293, 06784
Private agency
Founded in: 1975
Mrs. M. T. Gloger, Co-president
Number of members: 200
Staff: volunteer 12
Major programs: archives, school programs, newsletters, exhibits
Period of collections: 1880s-present

SIMSBURY

Massacoh Plantation
800 Hopmeadow St.
Telephone: (203) 658-2500
Mail to: P.O. Box 2, 06070
Private agency, authorized by Simsbury Historical Society
Founded in: 1911
James B. Tanner, President
Number of members: 578
Staff: part time 3, volunteer 50
Magazine: *Signpost*
Major programs: library, museum, newsletters/pamphlets, records management, research, exhibits, living history, genealogical services
Period of collections: 1830-1850s

Simsbury Historical Society
800 Hopmeadow St., 06070
Founded in: 1911
Number of members: 534
Staff: full time 1, part time 2, volunteer 50
Magazine: *Sign Post*
Major programs: library, archives, museum, historic sites preservation, tours, educational programs, newsletters/pamphlets
Period of collections: 18th-20th centuries

SOMERS

Somers Historical Society
407 Main St.
Telephone: (203) 745-8540
Mail to: 103 Hall Hill Rd., 06071
Private agency
Founded in: 1968
William Jones, President
Number of members: 30
Staff: volunteer 10
Major programs: archives, manuscripts, museum, oral history, book publishing, historic preservation, exhibits, living history, photographic collections, genealogical services
Period of collections: 1860-1930

SOUTHBURY

Southbury Historical Society, Inc.
Mail to: P.O. Box 124, 06488
Private agency
Founded in: 1966
Richard C. Perry, President
Number of members: 200
Staff: volunteer 12
Major programs: library, archives, museum, historic site(s), tours/pilgrimages, oral history, historic preservation, research, photographic collections, genealogical services
Period of collections: 1700s-present

SOUTHINGTON

Southington Historical Society
239 Main St., 06489
Telephone: (203) 621-4811
Private agency
Founded in: 1963
Jim Filiaro, President
Number of members: 205
Staff: volunteer 2
Major programs: library, museum, school programs, historic preservation, exhibits, photographic collections
Period of collections: 19th century

SOUTH NORWALK

New England Old Graveyard Association
85 Soundview Ave., 06854
Questionnaire not received

SOUTH WINDSOR

South Windsor Historical Society, Inc.
Mail to: P.O. Box 216, 06074
Founded in: 1947
E. Woolam, Co-president
Number of members: 125
Staff: volunteer 20
Major programs: historic sites preservation, oral history, educational programs, books

STAFFORD SPRINGS

Stafford Historical Society, Inc.
Haymarket Square
Telephone: (203) 684-7244 (secretary)
Mail to: 11 Murphy Rd., 06076
Private agency

Founded in: 1962
Geoffrey T. Alson, President
Number of members: 44
Staff: volunteer 21Major programs:
museum, historic site(s), markers,
oral history, school programs,
exhibits, audiovisual programs,
photographic collections,
genealogical services

STAMFORD

Ft. Stamford Restoration, Inc.
900 Westover Rd., 06902
Questionnaire not received

**Stamford Genealogical
Society, Inc.**
Mail to: P.O. Box 249, 06904
Founded in: 1954
Mrs. Clifford P. Wicks, Jr., President
Number of members: 300
Staff: volunteer 10
Magazine: *Connecticut Ancestry*
Major programs: library, archives,
manuscripts, book publishing,
newsletters/pamphlets, research,
genealogical services, educational
programs
Period of collections: 1635-present

Stamford Historical Society
1508 High Ridge Rd., 06903
Telephone: (203) 329-1183
Private agency
Founded in: 1901
Ann M. Hermann, Director
Number of members: 500
Staff: full time 2, part time 1,
volunteer 50
Major programs: library, archives,
museum, tours/pilgrimages, school
programs, book publishing,
newsletters/pamphlets, research,
exhibits, photographic collections,
genealogical services
Period of collections: 1700-1940

STONINGTON

Mystic River Historical Society
P.O. Box 245, 06355
Private agency
Founded in: 1973
Forrest Mitchell, President
Number of members: 385
Major programs: archives,
newsletters/pamphlets, historic
preservation

Stonington Historical Society
Whitehall Ave., 06355
Mail to: P.O. Box 103, 06378
Founded in: 1895
Number of members: 600
Staff: full time 2, part time 4,
volunteer 22
Magazine: *Historical Footnotes*
Major programs: library, archives,
manuscripts, museum, historic
sites preservation, markers,
educational programs, books,
genealogy

STRATFORD

Boothe Memorial Park Museum
Main St. and Putney
Mail to: 165 Chapel St., 06497

Town agency, authorized by Boothe
Memorial Park Commission
Founded in: 1982
Bessie Burton, Commission Chair
Staff: volunteer 20
Major programs: archives, museum,
historic site(s)
Period of collections: 1850-1950

Stratford Historical Society
967 Academy Hill
Telephone: (203) 378-0630
Mail to: P.O. Box 382, 06497
Private agency
Founded in: 1925
Hiram Tindall, Curator
Number of members: 500
Staff: part time 5, volunteer 40
Major programs: archives,
manuscripts, museum,
tours/pilgrimages,
newsletters/pamphlets, exhibits,
photographic collections,
genealogical services
Period of collections: 1725-1900

SUFFIELD

Suffield Historical Society, Inc.
232 S. Main St., 06078
Telephone: (203) 668-5256
Mail to: P.O. Box 361, W. Suffield,
06093
Private agency
Founded in: 1940
Roger C. Loomis, President
Number of members: 240
Staff: volunteer 5
Major programs: museum, historic
site(s), historic preservation
Period of collections: 1750-1850

TERRYVILLE

Lock Museum of America, Inc.
130 Main St.
Telephone: (203) 589-6359
Mail to: P.O. Box 104, 06786
Private agency
Founded in: 1972
Thomas F. Hennessy, Curator
Number of members: 800
Staff: part time 1, volunteer 4
Major programs: library, archives,
exhibits
Period of collections: 1830-1930

THOMASTON

**Thomaston Historical
Society, Inc.**
Main St., 06787
Founded in: 1970
Number of members: 75
Major programs: archives,
manuscripts, museum, historic
sites preservation, educational
programs
Period of collections: 1783-present

THOMPSON

Thompson Historical Society, Inc.
Mail to: P.O. Box 47, 06277
Questionnaire not received

TOLLAND

Tolland Historical Society, Inc.
P.O. Box 107, 06084
Founded in: 1965
Number of members: 125
Staff: volunteer 125
Major programs: museum, historic
site, markers, tours/pilgrimages,
junior history, oral history,
educational programs, book
publishing, newsletters/pamphlets,
historic preservation
Period of collections: 1720

TORRINGTON

Torrington Historical Society, Inc.
192 Main St., 06790
Telephone: (203) 482-8260
Private agency
Founded in: 1946
Catherine Calhoun, Executive
Director
Number of members: 290
Staff: full time 2, volunteer 10
Major programs: library, archives,
museum, historic site(s),
tours/pilgrimages, school
programs, research, exhibits,
photographic collections
Period of collections: late 19th-early
20th centuries

TRUMBULL

Trumbull Historical Society
P.O. Box 312, 06611
Telephone: (203) 268-7091
Town agency
Founded in: 1964
Lois Levine, President
Number of members: 350
Staff: volunteer 20
Magazine: *The Gristmill*
Major programs: library, archives,
manuscripts, museum, historic
site(s), markers, oral history, book
publishing, newsletters/pamphlets,
historic preservation, research,
exhibits, photographic collections,
genealogical services
Period of collections: 19th century

UNION

Union Historical Society, Inc.
655 Buckley Hwy., 06076
Telephone: (203) 684-7078
Private agency
Founded in: 1974
Jeannine M. Upson, President
Number of members: 20
Staff: volunteer 10Major programs:
archives, museum, book
publishing, historic preservation,
records management, research,
exhibits, audiovisual programs,
photographic collections
Period of collections: late 19th-early
20th centuries

VOLUNTOWN

Voluntown Historical Society, Inc.
R.F.D., Box 514, N. Shore Dr., 06384
Founded in: 1970
Questionnaire not received

WALLINGFORD

Wallingford Historical Society, Inc.
180 S. Main St.
Mail to: P.O. Box 73, 06492
Private agency
Founded in: 1916
Mary I. Annis, President
Number of members: 300
Staff: volunteer 20

WARREN

Warren Historical Society
Rt. 45, 06754
Founded in: 1968
Questionnaire not received

WASHINGTON

American Indian Archaeological Institute
Rt. 199
Telephone: (203) 868-0518
Mail to: P.O. Box 260, 06793
Founded in: 1971
Susan F. Payne, President
Number of members: 1,500
Staff: full time 9, part time 11, volunteer 5
Magazine: *Artifacts*
Major programs: museum, educational programs, newsletters/pamphlets, book publications
Period of collections: prehistoric

Gunn Historical Museum
Wykeham Rd., 06793
Telephone: (203) 868-7756
Private agency, authorized by trustees of Gunn Memorial Library
Founded in: 1899
Gillian Edwards, Curator
Staff: full time 1, volunteer 2
Major programs: museum, exhibits
Period of collections: 18th-20th centuries

WATERBURY

Mattatuck Historical Society
119 W. Main St., 06702
Telephone: (203) 753-0381
Private agency
Ann Y. Smith, Director
Number of members: 800
Staff: full time 2, part time 5, volunteer 200
Major programs: school programs, exhibits
Period of collections: 1800s

WATERFORD

Waterford Historical Society, Inc.
Jordan Green, Rope Ferry Rd.
Mail to: P.O. Box 117, 06385
Questionnaire not received

WATERTOWN

Watertown Historical Society, Inc.
22 DeForest St., 06795
Questionnaire not received

WESTBROOK

Company of Military Historians
N. Main St., 06498
Telephone: (203) 399-9460
Private agency
Founded in: 1951
William R. Reid, Administrator
Number of members: 2,000
Staff: full time 1
Magazine: *Military Collector & Historian*
Period of collections: 20th century

WEST HARTFORD

Jewish Historical Society of Greater Hartford
335 Bloomfield Ave., 06117
Founded in: 1971
Number of members: 350
Staff: part time 1, volunteer 18
Major programs: archives, tours/pilgrimages, oral history, educational programs, newsletters/pamphlets
Period of collections: 1865-present

Noah Webster Foundation—Historical Society of West Hartford
227 S. Main St., 06107
Telephone: (203) 561-3479
Private agency
Founded in: 1965
Sally Williams, Director
Number of members: 450
Staff: full time 2, part time 3, volunteer 45
Major programs: archives, museum, historic site(s), school programs, historic preservation, exhibits, living history
Period of collections: 1750-present

WESTON

Weston Historical Society
104 Weston Rd.
Mail to: P.O. Box 1092, 06883
Private agency
Founded in: 1962
Louis F. Bregy, Chair
Number of members: 400
Major programs: museum, oral history, school programs, book publishing
Period of collections: 1850-1900

WESTPORT

Westport Historical Society
25 Avery Place, 06880
Telephone: (203) 222-1424
Private agency
Founded in: 1957
Joan Dickinson, President
Number of members: 588
Staff: volunteer 60
Major programs: library, archives, museum, historic site(s), markers, tours/pilgrimages, school programs, newsletters/pamphlets, exhibits, photographic collections, genealogical services
Period of collections: 1835-present

WETHERSFIELD

Webb-Deane-Stevens Museum
211 Main St., 06109
Telephone: (203) 529-0612
Private agency, authorized by National Society of the Colonial Dames of America
Founded in: 1919
Number of members: 550
Staff: full time 3, part time 12, volunteer 20
Major programs: library, archives, manuscripts, museum, historic site(s), school programs, newsletters/pamphlets, historic preservation, records management, research, exhibits
Period of collections: 1700-1840

Wethersfield Historical Society
150 Main St., 06109
Telephone: (203) 529-7656
Private agency
Founded in: 1932
C. Douglass Alves, Jr., Director
Number of members: 690
Staff: full time 2, part time 30, volunteer 30
Major programs: library, archives, museum, historic site(s), tours/pilgrimages, school programs, book publishing, newsletters/pamphlets, historic preservation, research, exhibits, archaeology programs, photographic collections, genealogical services
Period of collections: 1793-1918

WILLIMANTIC

Center for Connecticut Studies—J. Eugene Smith Library
Eastern Connecticut State University, 06226
Telephone: (203) 456-2231, ext. 443
Authorized by the university
Founded in: 1970
David M. Roth, Director
Staff: full time 1, part time 1
Major programs: library, archives, museum, oral history, school programs, book publishing, newsletters/pamphlets, research, audiovisual programs, photographic collections
Period of collections: 17th century-present

Joshua's Tract Conservation and Historic Trust
c/o Independent Bank and Trust, 06226
Private agency
Founded in: 1966
J. David Hankins, Chair
Number of members: 230
Major programs: museum, historic site(s), historic preservation
Period of collections: 1830

Windham Historical Society
Telephone: (203) 423-2968
Mail to: 215 Church St., 06226
Questionnaire not received

WILLINGTON

Willington Historical Society
Mirtl Rd., 06279
Telephone: (203) 429-3451
Founded in: 1969
Elizabeth Robertson, President
Number of members: 60
Staff: volunteer 7
Magazine: *Hourglass*

Major programs: educational
programs, book publishing,
newsletters/pamphlets
Period of collections: 1727-1890

WILTON

**Wilton Historical Society, Inc. and
Heritage Museum**
249 Danbury Rd., 06897
Telephone: (203) 762-7257
Private agency
Founded in: 1938
Marilyn Gould, Director
Number of members: 500
Staff: part time 3, volunteer 75
Major programs: archives,
tours/pilgrimages, school
programs, newsletters/pamphlets,
historic preservation, research,
exhibits, archaeology programs,
genealogical services, historic
house museum, costume collection
Period of collections: mid 18th-mid
19th centuries

WINDSOR

**Connecticut League of Historical
Societies, Inc.**
1207 Poquonock Ave., 06095
Founded in: 1949
Number of members: 180
Staff: part time 1, volunteer 18
Magazine: *League Bulletin*
Major programs:
newsletters/pamphlets

Windsor Historical Society
96 Palisado Ave., 06095
Telephone: (203) 688-3813
Private agency
Founded in: 1922
Robert T. Silliman, Director
Number of members: 360
Staff: full time 1, volunteer 20
Major programs: library, archives,
manuscripts, museum, historic
site(s), oral history,
newsletters/pamphlets, historic
preservation, records
management, exhibits, audiovisual
programs, photographic
collections, genealogical services
Period of collections: 17th-19th
centuries

WINDSOR LOCKS

**Connecticut Aeronautical
Historical Association, Inc.**
Bradley International Airport, 06096
Telephone: (203) 623-3305
Founded in: 1960
Philip C. O'Keefe, Museum Director
Number of members: 1,000
Staff: full time 5, part time 3,
volunteer 40
Major programs: library, archives,
museum, oral history, educational
programs, newsletters/pamphlets,
historic preservation

New England Air Museum
Bradley International Airport, 06096
Telephone: (203) 623-3305
Private agency, authorized by
Connecticut Aeronautical Historical
Association, Inc.
Founded in: 1960

Philip O'Keefe, Museum Director
Number of members: 1,100
Staff: full time 5, part time 2,
volunteer 40
Major programs: library, archives,
museum, oral history, school
programs, newsletters/pamphlets,
historic preservation, research,
exhibits, photographic collections

**Windsor Locks Historical
Society, Inc.**
58 West St., 06096
Telephone: (203) 623-7153
Private agency
Founded in: 1971
Howard J. White, President
Number of members: 97
Staff: volunteer 8
Major programs: museum, exhibits,
photographic collections
Period of collections: 19th century

WINSTED

Winchester Historical Society
Telephone: (203) 379-8433
Mail to: 35 Strong Terrace, 06098
Private agency
Founded in: 1905
Pauline E. Fancher, Curator
Number of members: 101
Staff: full time 2, volunteer 10
Major programs: archives, museum,
historic site(s),
newsletters/pamphlets, historic
preservation, research, exhibits,
photographic collections,
genealogical services
Period of collections: 1800s-present

WOODBRIDGE

**Amity and Woodbridge Historical
Society**
Thomas Darling House, Litchfield
Turnpike, 06525
Questionnaire not received

WOODBURY

Glebe House Museum
Hollow Rd.
Telephone: (203) 263-2855
Mail to: P.O. Box 245, 06798
Private agency, authorized by
Seabury Society for the
Preservation of Glebe House
Founded in: 1923
Mary E. Baker, Curator
Number of members: 500
Staff: part time 1
Major programs: library, manuscripts,
museum, historic site(s),
tours/pilgrimages, school
programs, research, audiovisual
programs, archaeology programs
Period of collections: 1750-1800

Old Woodbury Historical Society
222 Flanders Rd.
Mail to: P.O. Box 548, 06798
Questionnaire not received

**Seabury Society for the
Preservation of the Glebe House**
Hollow Rd.
Telephone: (203) 263-2855
Mail to: P.O. Box 125, 06798
Founded in: 1922

Number of members: 500
Staff: full time 1, volunteer 30
Major programs: historic sites
preservation, museum
Period of collections: Colonial

WOODSTOCK

Woodstock Historical Society
Mail to: P.O. Box 65, 06281
Private agency
Founded in: 1967
William Darr, President
Number of members: 100
Staff: volunteer 11
Major programs: historic site(s),
photographic collections
Period of collections: 1865-1940

DELAWARE

DOVER

Delaware Agricultural Museum
866 N. DuPont Hwy., 19901
Telephone: (302) 734-1618
Private agency
Founded in: 1974
Paula D. Schwartz, Acting
Director/Curator
Staff: full time 1, part time 2,
volunteer 10
Magazine: *Museum Gazette*
Major programs: library, museum,
oral history, educational programs,
newsletters/pamphlets, historic
preservation
Period of collections: 1700-1945

◇**Delaware Division of Historical
and Cultural Affairs**
Hall of Records, 19901
Telephone: (302) 736-5314
State agency
Founded in: 1905
John R. Kern, Director
Staff: full time 75, part time 25
Major programs: archives,
manuscripts, museum, historic
site(s), school programs,
newsletters/pamphlets, historic
preservation, research, exhibits,
archaeology programs,
photographic collections,
genealogical services, arts council,
public records management
Period of collections:
prehistoric-present

FREDERICA

**Commission on Archives and
History, Peninsula Annual
Conference**
Barratt's Chapel Museum, 19946
Telephone: (302) 335-5544
Private agency, authorized by United
Methodist Church
Allen B. Clark, Curator
Major programs: library, archives,
museum, historic site(s), markers,
book publishing,
newsletters/pamphlets, historic
preservation, research, center for
United Methodist Church history
Period of collections: 1784-1900

DELAWARE

MILFORD

Milford Historical Society
501 N.W. Front St.
Mail to: P.O. Box 352, 19963
Founded in: 1961
Number of members: 350
Staff: volunteer 25
Major programs: museum, historic
site, book publishing,
newsletters/pamphlets, historic
preservation
Period of collections: 1750-1850

MILLSBORO

Nanticoke Indian Association
Rt. 4, Box 107-A, 19966
Telephone: (302) 945-3400
Private agency, authorized by
Nanticoke Indian Tribe
Founded in: 1922
Kenneth S. Clark, Chief
Major programs: library, museum,
oral history, historic preservation,
living history, living history,
photographic collections
Period of collections: 1680s-present

NEWARK

**Mid-Atlantic Association of
Museums**
305 Old College, Main St.
Telephone: (302) 451-8420
Mail to: P.O. Box 817, 19715-0817
Private agency
Hope L. Schladen, Executive Director
Number of members: 1,200
Staff: full time 1, part time 1
Magazine: *The Museologist*
Major programs: services to
museums and museum
professionals

NEW CASTLE

New Castle Historical Society
40 E. 3rd St., 19720
Telephone: (302) 328-8215
Private agency
Founded in: 1934
Daniel F. Wolcott, President
Number of members: 200
Staff: full time 1, part time 6,
volunteer 20
Major programs: historic site(s),
school programs, historic
preservation
Period of collections: 1700-1850

ODESSA

Winterthur in Odessa
P.O. Box 507, Main St., 19730
Telephone: (302) 378-2681
Private agency, authorized by
Winterthur Museums and Gardens
Founded in: 1959
Steven M. Pulinka, Acting Curator
Staff: full time 2, part time 12
Major programs: historic site(s),
research, exhibits, decorative arts
Period of collections: 1760-1829

PORT PENN

**Port Penn Museum—Port Penn
Area Historical Society**
P.O. Box 120, 19731
Telephone: (302) 834-7519/834-7525

Town agency
Founded in: 1974
William S. Sidwell, President
Number of members: 38
Staff: volunteer 15
Major programs: museum,
newsletters/pamphlets, exhibits,
audiovisual programs,
photographic collections, field
services
Period of collections: from early 1800

REHOBOTH BEACH

**Rehoboth Beach Historical
Society, Inc.**
P.O. Box 42, 19971
Founded in: 1973
Marjorie H. Wellborn, President
Number of members: 235
Major programs: museum, oral
history, newsletters/pamphlets
Period of collections: 1872-1930

SEAFORD

Seaford Historical Society, Inc.
c/o Ross Mansion
Telephone: (302) 337-7660
Mail to: Rt. 1, Box 393, 19933
Private agency
Founded in: 1977
Dottie Faye Johnson, President
Number of members: 100
Staff: volunteer 20
Major programs: historic site(s),
historic preservation, annual
county fair
Period of collections: 1860-present

SMYRNA

Duck Creek Historical Society
118 S. Delaware St., 19977
Telephone: (302) 653-8844
Founded in: 1960
George L. Caley, President
Number of members: 120
Major programs: historic site,
tours/pilgrimages

WILMINGTON

**Delaware Society for the
Preservation of Antiquities**
606 Stanton-Christiana Rd., Newark,
19713
Telephone: (302) 998-3792
Private agency, authorized by
Delaware Division of Historical and
Cultural Affairs
Founded in: 1951
S.D.F. Miller, Vice President
Number of members: 70
Major programs: archives, historic
site(s), tours, historic preservation,
sponsorship of Hale-Byrnes House
Period of collections: late
1600s-1700s

**Eleutherian Mills-Hagley
Foundation, Inc.**
Greenville, 19807
Telephone: (302) 658-2400
Founded in: 1953
Staff: full time 94, part time 70
Major programs: library, archives,
manuscripts, museum, historic
sites preservation, educational
programs, books,
newsletters/pamphlets
Period of collections: 1783-present

Ft. Delaware Society
P.O. Box 1251, 19803
Telephone: (302) 478-1594
Private agency, authorized by
Delaware Division of Parks
Founded in: 1950
Carl E. W. Hauger, Jr., President
Number of members: 365
Staff: volunteer 25
Magazine: *Fort Delaware Notes*
Major programs: museum, historic
site(s), historic preservation,
audiovisual programs

Grand Opera House
818 Market St. Mall, 19801
Telephone: (302) 658-7897
Private agency
David W. Fleming, Executive Director
Number of members: 1,700
Staff: full time 20, part time 2,
volunteer 300
Major programs: educational
programs, performing arts
presentations
Period of collections: present

◇**Historical Society of Delaware**
505 Market St., 19801
Telephone: (302) 655-7161
Private agency
Founded in: 1864
Charles T. Lyle, Executive Director
Number of members: 1,300
Staff: full time 14, part time 42,
volunteer 10
Magazine: *Delaware History*
Major programs: library, archives,
manuscripts, museum, historic
site(s), school programs,
newsletters/pamphlets, research,
exhibits, photographic collections,
genealogical services
Period of collections: 17th-19th
centuries

Hagley Museum and Library
P.O. Box 3630, Greenville, 19807
Telephone: (302) 658-2400
Private agency, authorized by
Eleutherian Mills-Hagley
Foundation, Inc.
Founded in: 1952
Glenn Porter, Director
Number of members: 7
Staff: full time 98, part time 91,
volunteer 150
Major programs: library, archives,
manuscripts, museum, historic
site(s), oral history, school
programs, book publishing,
newsletters/pamphlets, historic
preservation, records
management, research, exhibits,
audiovisual programs, archaeology
programs, photographic
collections
Period of collections: 19th-early 20th
centuries

Historic Red Clay Valley, Inc.
P.O. Box 1374, 19899
Telephone: (302) 998-1930
Private agency
Founded in: 1959
Donald W. Callender, Jr., Executive
Director
Number of members: 400
Staff: full time 4, volunteer 50
Magazine: *The Lantern*

Major programs: historic site(s), markers, tours/pilgrimages, school programs, newsletters/pamphlets, historic preservation, research, living history, audiovisual programs, photographic collections, steam tourist railroad
Period of collections: late 19th-early 20th centuries

Holy Trinity (Old Swedes) Church Foundation, Inc.
606 Church St., 19801
Telephone: (302) 652-5629
Private agency
Founded in: 1947
Lisa A. Nichols, Curator
Number of members: 120
Staff: full time 1, part time 1, volunteer 10
Major programs: library, archives, manuscripts, museum, historic site(s), tours/pilgrimages, historic preservation, research, genealogical services
Period of collections: 18th century

Lombardy Hall Foundation
1611 Concord Park, 19803
Telephone: (302) 655-5254
Founded in: 1968
Harold J. Littleton, President
Staff: volunteer 9
Major programs: library, archives, museum, historic sites preservation
Period of collections: 1783-1865

Nemours Mansion and Gardens
Rockland Rd.
Telephone: (302) 651-6912
Mail to: P.O. Box 109, 19899
Private agency, authorized by Alfred I. duPont Institute of the Nemours Foundation
Founded in: 1977
Mrs. B. J. Whiting, Tour Supervisor
Major programs: historic site(s), tours, historic house and gardens, decorative arts
Period of collections: 1909-1910

Rockwood Museum
610 Shipley Rd., 19809
Telephone: (302) 571-7776
Founded in: 1976
John H. Braunlein, Director
Staff: full time 3, part time 5, volunteer 40
Major programs: museum, historic site(s), newsletters/pamphlets, historic preservation, research, educational and interpretive programming, decorative arts
Period of collections: 1850-1920

WINTERTHUR

Winterthur Museum and Gardens
19735
Telephone: (302) 656-8591/654-1548
Authorized by the Winterthur Corporation
Founded in: 1951
Wesley A. Adams, Acting Director
Number of members: 11,974
Staff: full time 259, part time 190, volunteer 120
Magazine: *Winterthur Newsletter/Winterthur Portfolio*

Major programs: library, archives, manuscripts, museum, school programs, book publishing, newsletters/pamphlets, historic preservation, research, photographic collections
Period of collections: 1650-1850

DISTRICT OF COLUMBIA

WASHINGTON

Advisory Council on Historic Preservation
1100 Pennsylvania Ave., NW, Suite 809, 20004
Founded in: 1966
Staff: full time 35
Major programs: historic preservation, educational programs, technical reports

Afro-American Communities Project
Constitution Ave., between 12th and 14th Sts.
Telephone: (202) 357-3182
Mail to: Room C-340, National Museum of American History, Smithsonian Institution, 20560
Private agency, sponsored by the Smithsonian and George Washington University
Founded in: 1981
James Oliver Horton, Director
Staff: part time 6, volunteer 2
Major programs: research
Period of collections: Antebellum period

Agricultural History Society
Economics Research Service, U.S.Department of Agriculture, 20250
Telephone: (202) 447-8183
Founded in: 1919
Wayne D. Rasmussen, Executive Secretary/Treasurer
Number of members: 800
Staff: volunteer 4
Magazine: *Agricultural History*
Major programs: books

American Association for the Advancement of Science
1333 H St., NW, 20005
Telephone: (202) 467-4400
Private agency
Founded in: 1848
William D. Cary, Executive Officer
Number of members: 150,000
Staff: full time 250
Magazine: *Science*
Major programs: archives, school programs, book publishing, history of science sessions at annual meeting
Period of collections: 20th century

American Association of Museums
1055 Thomas Jefferson St., NW, 20007
Telephone: (202) 338-5300
Founded in: 1906
Lawrence L. Reger, Director
Number of members: 9,000
Staff: full time 35

Magazine: *Museum News/Adviso*
Major programs: educational programs, books, newsletters/pamphlets, field services, accreditation, museum assessment, representation and advocacy, annual meeting

American Catholic Historical Association
Catholic University of America, Mullen Library Suite 318, 20064
Telephone: (202) 635-5079
Private agency
Founded in: 1919
Robert Trisco, Secretary/Treasurer
Number of members: 1,100
Staff: part-time 1, volunteer 1
Major programs: quarterly journal, annual meetings, book awards
Period of collections: 1st century A.D.-present

American Historical Association
400 A St., SE, 20003
Telephone: (202) 544-2422
Founded in: 1884
Samuel R. Gammon, Executive Director
Number of members: 15,000
Staff: full time 20
Magazine: *American Historical Review*

American Institute of Architects Foundation—The Octagon Museum
1799 New York Ave. NW, 20006
Telephone: (202) 638-3105
Private agency
Founded in: 1942
Susan R. Stein, Director
Staff: full time 4, part-time 22, volunteer 2
Major programs: archives, museum, exhibits, photographic collections, architecture
Period of collections: 1783-1828

American Institute for Conservation of Historic and Artistic Works
Klingle Mansion, 3545 Williamsburg Lane, NW, 20008
Telephone: (202) 364-1036
Private agency
Founded in: 1959
Elisabeth West FitzHugh, President, AIC Board
Number of members: 2,000
Staff: full time 3, part time 3, volunteer 52
Magazine: *AIC Newsletter*
Major programs: book publishing, newsletters/pamphlets

American Military Institute
23309 Chestnut St., NW, 20015
Private agency
Founded in: 1933
B. Franklin Cooling, Executive Director
Number of members: 1,200
Staff: part time 5
Magazine: *Military Affairs*
Period of collections: 18th century-present

Anderson House Museum of the Society of the Cincinnati
2118 Massachusetts Ave., NW, 20008
Telephone: (202) 785-2040
Private agency
Founded in: 1783
John D. Kilbourne, Director
Number of members: 2,700
Staff: full time 11, part-time 2, volunteer 15
Magazine: *Cincinnati Fourteen*
Major programs: library, archives, manuscripts, museum
Period of collections: 1492-1865

Archives of American Art
8th and G Sts., NW
Telephone: (202) 357-2781
Mail to: NPG 331, Smithsonian Institution, 20560
Federal agency, authorized by the Smithsonian Institution
Founded in: 1954
Richard Murray, Director
Number of members: 1,720
Staff: full time 32, part time 9, volunteer 3
Magazine: *Archives of American Art Journal*
Major programs: archives, manuscripts, oral history, newsletters/pamphlets, research, photographic collections, art history
Period of collections: 1850-present

Armed Forces Medical Museum
Armed Forces Institute of Pathology, 20306-6000
Telephone: (202) 576-2341
Federal agency, authorized by the Department of Defense
Founded in: 1862
Ann Elizabeth Zibrat, Chief, Professional Services
Staff: full time 10, part time 6
Major programs: archives, museum, medical history
Period of collections: Civil War-present

Armenian Assembly of America
1420 N St., NW, Suite 101, 20005
Telephone: (202) 332-3434
Private agency
Founded in: 1972
Ross Vartian, Administrative Director
Staff: full time 7
Major programs: oral history, school programs, newsletter/pamphlets, research
Period of collections: early 20th century

Association of Living History Farms and Museums
Museum of American History, Smithsonian Institution, Room 5053, 20560
Telephone: (202) 357-2095
Private agency
Founded in: 1969
John Schlebecker, Secretary/Treasurer
Number of members: 620
Magazine: *The Living Historical Farms Bulletin/Proceedings*
Major programs: newsletters/pamphlets, living history coordination

Bethune Museum-Archives, Inc.
1318 Vermont Ave., NW, 20005
Telephone: (202) 322-1233
Private agency
Founded in: 1977
Bettye Collier-Thomas, Executive Director
Number of members: 72
Staff: full time 3, part time 1, volunteer 25
Major programs: archives, museum, historic site(s), tours/pilgrimages, school programs, book publishing, living history, field services
Period of collections: 20th century

Black Catholic History Project, Office of Black Catholics
5001 Eastern Ave.
Telephone: (301) 853-4579
Mail to: P.O. Box 29260, 20017
Private agency, authorized by Catholic Archdiocese of Washington
Founded in: 1974
Jacqueline E. Wilson, Executive Director
Staff: full time 3, part time 1, volunteer 2
Magazine: *Black Catholic News*
Major programs: archives, manuscripts, oral history, school programs, newsletters/pamphlets, records management, research, exhibits, audiovisual programs, photographic collections, field services, advocacy, awards
Period of collections: 1700s-present

B'nai B'rith Kluznick Museum
1640 Rhode Island Ave., NW, 20036
Telephone: (202) 857-6583
Private agency, authorized by B'nai B'rith International
Founded in: 1956
Linda Altshuler, Director
Number of members: 450
Staff: full time 3, part time 1, volunteer 60
Major programs: archives, museum, tours, school programs, newsletters/pamphelts, exhibits, audiovisual programs
Period of collections: 16th-20th centuries

Capital Children's Museum
2800 3rd St., NE, 20002
Telephone: (202) 543-8600
Private agency
Founded in: 1974
Ann W. Levin, President/Executive Director
Major programs: tours/pilgrimages, school programs, exhibits, hands-on learning

Center for Museum Education
George Washington University, 20052
Questionnaire not received

◇**Columbia Historical Society**
1307 New Hampshire Ave., NW, 20036
Telephone: (202) 785-2068
Private agency
Founded in: 1894
Number of members: 950
Staff: full time 35, part-time 2, volunteer 5

Major programs: library, archives, manuscripts, museum, historic site(s), tours/pilgrimages, school programs, book publishing, newsletters/pamphlets, historic preservation, research, exhibits, photographic collections
Period of collections: 1783-present

COMMA (Committee on Military Museums in America)
c/o Marine Corps Museum, Bldg. 58, Navy Yard, 20374
Telephone: (202) 433-3839
Private agency
Founded in: 1980
F. B. Nihart, Chair
Number of members: 100
Staff: volunteer 4
Major programs: luncheons, meetings, professional sessions

Curatorial Services Branch, National Park Service
1100 L St., NW, 20240
Telephone: (202) 343-8142
Federal agency, authorized by Department of the Interior
Founded in: 1916
Ann Hitchcock, Chief Curator
Major programs: library, archives, manuscripts, museum, historic site(s), markers, tours/pilgrimages, oral history, school programs, book publishing, newsletters/pamphlets, historic preservation, records management, research, exhibits, living history, audiovisual programs, archaeology programs, photographic collections, field services
Period of collections: prehistoric

Daughters of the American Revolution Library
1776 D St., NW, 20006-5392
Telephone: (202) 879-3228
Private agency
Founded in: 1896
Eric G. Grundset, Library Director
Number of members: 212,000
Staff: full time 11, volunteer 3
Major programs: library, manuscripts, book publishing, genealogical services
Period of collections: 1750-1900

Daughters of the American Revolution Museum
1776 D St., NW, 20006
Telephone: (202) 879-3242
Private agency
Founded in: 1890
Christine Minter-Dowd, Curator
Number of members: 210,000
Staff: full time 11, volunteer 90
Major programs: museum, tours/pilgrimages, school programs, exhibits, decorativearts
Period of collections: 1700-1850

◇**D.C. Preservation League**
930 F St., NW, Suite 612, 20004
Telephone: (202) 737-1519
Private agency
Vicki A. Sherman, Executive Director
Number of members: 1,200
Staff: full time 1, volunteer 100
Major programs: tours, newsletters/pamphlets, historic preservation, research, education, lectures

Decatur House Museum
748 Jackson Place, NW, 20006
Telephone: (202) 673-4273
Private agency, authorized by
National Trust for Historic
Preservation
Founded in: 1949
Vicki E. Sopher, Director
Staff: full time 4, part time 18,
volunteer 12
Major programs: museum, historic
site(s), tours/pilgrimages, school
programs
Period of collections: 1819-1872

Department of the Interior Museum
Office of the Secretary, 20240
Telephone: (202) 343-2743
Federal agency, authorized by the
Office of the Secretary of the
Interior
Founded in: 1935
Stanley Olsen, Curator
Staff: full time 3
Major programs: museum, school
programs, research, exhibits,
history of the Department
of the Interior
Period cf collections: 1849-present

Dumbarton House
22715 Que St., 20007
Telephone: (202) 337-2288
Private agency, authorized by the
National Society of the Colonial
Dames of America
Founded in: late 1800
Jane Young, Chair
Staff: full time 6
Major programs: museum
Period of collections: 1780-1815

Folger Shakespeare Library
201 E. Capitol St., SE, 20003
Telephone: (202) 544-4600
Private agency
Founded in: 1932
Werner Gundersheimer, Director
Staff: full time 60
Major programs: library, manuscripts,
book publishing, research, exhibits
Period of collections: 16th-17th
centuries

Historical Division Office
Chief of Engineers, Department of the
Army, 20 Massachusetts Ave., NW
Mail to: DAEN-ASH, 20314
Founded in: 1942
Staff: full time 10, part time 2,
volunteer 1
Major programs: library, archives,
manuscripts, oral history, book
publishing, newsletters/pamphlets
Period of collections: 20th century

Historical Office, Federal Bureau of Investigation
9th St. and Pennslvania Ave., NW,
20535
Telephone: (202) 324-3000
Federal agency, authorized by the
U.S. Government
Founded in: 1984
Susan R. Falb, Historian
Staff: full time 1
Major programs: records
management, research, exhibits,
federal history
Period of collections: 20th century

History Section, U.S. Forest Service
S. Agriculture Bldg., Room 325
Telephone: (202) 447-2418
Mail to: P.O. Box 2417, 20013
Federal agency, authorized by U.S.
Department of Agriculture
Founded in: 1976
Dennis M. Roth, Chief Historian
Staff: full time 3
Magazine: *History Line*
Major programs: library, archives,
oral history, book publishing,
newsletters/pamphlets, historic
preservation, research
Period of collections: 1876-present

ICOM (International Council of Museums Committee of the AAM)
1055 Thomas Jefferson St., NW,
20007
Telephone: (202) 338-5300
Private agency, authorized by
American Association of Museums
Founded in: 1977
Ellen Herscher, Program Coordinator
Number of members: 1,000
Staff: part time 1
Major programs: tours/pilgrimages,
newsletters/pamphlets,
international exchange of museum
personnel

Jewish Historical Society of Greater Washington
701 3rd St., NW, 20001
Telephone: (202) 789-0900/(301)
881-0100
Founded in: 1965
Mrs. Hadassah Thursz, Museum
Directcr
Number of members: 350
Staff: part time 1, volunteer 12
Magazine: *The Record*
1Major programs: museum, historic
site, oral history, historic
preservation, exhibits
Period of collections: 1870-present

The L'Enfant Trust
1425 21st St., NW, 20036
Telephone: (202) 347-1814
Private agency
Founded in: 1978
Margaret S. Dean, Executive Director
Number of members: 220
Staff: part time 4
Major programs: histcric
preservation, exhibits
Period of collections: to 1920s

Marine Corps Historical Foundation
Washington Navy Yard, Bldg. 58,
20374
Telephone: (202) 433-3914
Private agency
Founded in: 1979
Donn J. Robertson, President
Number of members: 825
Staff: part time 1
Major programs: museum, school
programs, research, exhibits,
dissertation fellowship, college
internships
Period of collections: 1775-present

Moorland-Spingarn Research Center
500 Howard Place, NW, Howard
University, 20059

Telephone: (202) 636-7239
Founded in: 1914
Clifford L. Muse, Jr., Director
Staff: full time 43, part time 4
Major programs: library, archives,
manuscripts, museum, oral history,
records management, research,
exhibits, photographic collecticns
Period of collections: 1850-present

Museum of the City of Washington
5th and K Sts., NE, 20002
Telephone: (202) 842-2176
Private agency
Founded in: 1982
Charlotte Chapman, Board President
Number of members: 300
Major programs: museum, school
programs, exhibits
Period of collections: 1790-present

National Alliance of Preservation Commissions
Hall of States, Suite 332
Telephone: (301) 663-6820
Mail to: 444 N. Capital St., 20001
Private agency
Founded in: 1982
Cherilyn Widell, Executive Director
Number of members: 800
Staff: part time 1
Magazine: *NAPC News*
Major programs: historic preservation

The National Archives
8th and Constitution Ave., 20408
Telephone: (202) 523-3134
Federal agency, authorized by the
U.S. Government
Founded in: 1935
Robert M. Warner, Archivist of the
U.S.
Magazine: *Prologue: The Journal of
the Naticnal Archives*
Major programs: library, archives,
museum, tours/pilgrimages, school
programs, book publishing,
newsletters/pamphlets, records
management, research, exhibits,
audiovisual programs,
photographic collections,
genealogical services, field
services
Period of collections: 1726-present

National Endowment for the Humanities
Public Affairs Office, Room 409, 1100
Pennsylvania Ave., NW, 20506
Telephone: (202) 786-0438
Federal agency
Founded in: 1965
Staff: full time 260, part time 30
Magazine: *Humanities/Overview of
Endowment Programs*
Major programs: library, archives,
museum, school programs, book
publishinq, research, audiovisual
programs, archaeology programs

National Genealogical Society
1921 Sunderland Place, NW, 20036
Telephone: (202) 785-2123
Founded in: 1903
Margaret M. Redmond, Executive
Director
Number of members: 7,000
Staff: full time 3, part time 3,
volunteer 5

Magazine: *National Genealogical Society Quarterly*
Major programs: home study course
Period of collections: 1492-present

National Humanities Alliance
1055 Thomas Jefferson St., NW, Suite 428, 20007
Telephone: (202) 338-9194
Private agency
Founded in: 1981
Lisa Phillips, Executive Director
Number of members: 53
Staff: full time 2
Major programs: newsletters/pamphlets, research, advocate activities

National Institute for the Conservation of Cultural Property, Inc.
Smithsonian Institution, Arts and Industries Bldg., Room 2225, 20560
Telephone: (202) 357-2295
Private agency
Founded in: 1982
David A. Shute, Executive Director
Number of members: 70
Staff: full time 4
Major programs: library, archives, museum, architectural conservation, education, publications, historic preservation, research, conservation science, ethnography
Period of collections: 1976-present

National Inventors Hall of Fame Foundation, Inc.
Crystal Plaza Bldg., 2021 Jefferson Davis Hwy., 22301
Telephone: (703) 557-3341
Founded in: 1973
Thomas Fisher, President
Major programs: museum
Period of collections: 1790-present

National Museum of African Art
318 A St., NE, Smithsonian Institution, 20002
Telephone: (202) 287-3490
Founded in: 1964
Sylvia Williams, Director
Staff: full time 45, volunteer 60
Major programs: museum, educational programs, collection and exhibition of African art, research, tours, lectures, publications

National Park Service
18th and C Sts., NW, 20240
Telephone: (202) 345-4021
Founded in: 1916
Russell E. Dickenson, Director
Staff: full time 7,990, part time 5,190
Major programs: museum, historic site(s), markers, book publishing, newsletters/pamphlets, historic preservation, research, exhibits, living history, audiovisual programs, archaeology programs
Period of collections: 1600-1970

National Portrait Gallery
8th and F Sts., NW, 20560
Telephone: (202) 357-2700.
Federal agency, authorized by the Smithsonian Institution

Founded in: 1962
Alan M. Fern, Director
Staff: full time 60, part time 15, volunteer 59
Magazine: *Smithsonian Magazine*
Major programs: library, museum, school programs, exhibits, photographic collections, portraiture
Period of collections: 19th century

National Press Foundation
National Press Bldg., Room 5, 20045
Founded in: 1975
Magazine: *The Record*
Questionnaire not received

National Register of Historic Places
1100 L St., NW
Telephone: (202) 343-9536
Mail to: 18th and C Sts., NW, 20240
Federal agency, authorized by National Park Service, U.S. Department of the Interior
Founded in: 1966
Jerry L. Rogers, Keeper, National Register
Staff: full time 13, part time 2
Major programs: archives, historic preservation, records management, publication of technical information and guidance
Period of collections: prehistoric-1935

National Society, Children of the American Revolution
1776 D St., NW, 20006
Telephone: (202) 638-3153
Private agency
Founded in: 1895
Mrs. David D. Porter, National Executive Secretary
Number of members: 12,000
Staff: full time 7, part time 2, volunteer 12
Magazine: *C.A.R. Magazine*

Major programs: archives, museum, historic site(s), markers, tours/pilgrimages, historic preservation, records management, research, genealogical services
Period of collections: American Revolution-present

National Society, Colonial Dames XVII Century
1300 New Hampshire Ave., NW, 20036
Telephone: (202) 293-1700
Founded in: 1915
Barbara Dolan, Headquarters Secretary
Number of members: 13,000
Staff: full time 2, part time 1
Magazine: *Seventeenth Century Review*
Major programs: library, archives, museum, historic site, markers, historic preservation, scholarships
Period of collections: 17th century

National Society, Daughters of the American Revolution
1776 D St., NW, 20006-5392
Telephone: (202) 628-1776
Founded in: 1890
Mrs. Walter Hughey King, President General
Number of members: 211,342
Magazine: *Daughters of the American Revolution Magazine*
Major programs: library, archives, manuscripts, museum, historic sites preservation, markers, educational programs

National Society, Sons of the American Revolution
2412 Massachusetts Ave., NW, 20008
Questionnaire not received

Headquarters of the National Trust for Historic Preservation, this former luxury apartment building once housed Andrew Mellon, Perle Mesta, and Sumner Welles.—National Trust for Historic Preservation

National Society, United States Daughters of 1812
1461 Rhode Island Ave., NW, 20005
Telephone: (703) 751-0539
Mail to: 4705 Surry Place, Alexandria, VA, 22304
Private agency
Founded in: 1892
Mrs. Foley White Harris, National President
Number of members: 4,400
Major programs: library, markers
Period of collections: War of 1812

National Trust for Historic Preservation
1785 Massachusetts Ave., NW, 20036
Telephone: (202) 673-4000
Private agency
Founded in: 1949
J. Jackson Walter, President
Number of members: 140,000
Staff: full time 250, part time 56, volunteer 30
Magazine: *Historic Preservation*
Major programs: library, museum, historic site(s), tours/pilgrimages, book publishing, newsletters/pamphlets, historic preservation, research, audiovisual programs, photographic collections, field services, educational programs, conferences, workshops, technical advice and assistance, financial assistance, maritime preservation
Period of collections: 19th-20th centuries

Naval Historical Foundation
Bldg. 57, Washington Navy Yard, 20374
Telephone: (202) 433-2005
Founded in: 1926
J.L. Holloway III, President
Number of members: 983
Staff: full time 2, part time 6, volunteer 5
Major programs: library, archives, manuscripts, museum, books, newsletters/pamphlets, awards
Period of collections: 1783-present

Navy Memorial Museum
Washington Navy Yard, Bldg. 76, 20374
Telephone: (202) 433-2651
Federal agency, authorized by the U.S. Navy
Founded in: 1961
Oscar P. Fitzgerald, Director
Staff: full time 13, volunteer 1
Magazine: *Pull Together*
Major programs: library, archives, manuscripts, museum, historic site(s), markers, oral history, book publishing, newsletters/pamphlets, records management, research, exhibits, photographic collections
Period of collections: 19th-20th centuries

Office of the Curator, The White House
1600 Pennsylvania Ave., 20500
Telephone: (202) 456-1414
Federal agency, authorized by the U.S. Government
Clement E. Conger, Curator

Staff: full time 5
Major programs: museum, historic site(s), tours/pilgrimages, historic preservation, research, exhibits, photographic collections, presidential history
Period of collections: late 18th-20th centuries

Old Stone House
3051 M St., NW, 20007
Telephone: (202) 426-6851
Federal agency, authorized by Department of the Interior
Founded in: 1960
Rae Koch, Supervisor/Park Technician
Staff: full time 3
Major programs: tours/pilgrimages, school programs, living history

Preservation Action
2101 L St., NW, 20037
Telephone: (202) 466-8960
Founded in: 1975
Nellie L. Longworth, President
Questionnaire not received

Preservation Technology Reference Center
1100 L St., NW, Room 6320, 20240
Telephone: (202) 343-9573
Federal agency, authorized by Preservation Assistance Division National Park Service
Founded in: 1981
Charles Fisher, Director
Major programs: library, archives, historic preservation
Period of collections: 1700-present

Save the Tivoli, Inc.
3325 Holmead Place, NW, 20018
Telephone: (202) 462-2792
Private agency
Founded in: 1980
Patricia A. Meyer, Executive Director
Number of members: 70
Staff: full time 1, volunteer 25
Major programs: historic site(s), newsletters/pamphlets, historic preservation, litigation, public information
Period of collections: 1922-present

Sewall-Belmont House
Woman's Party Corporation Headquarters, 144 Constitution Ave., NE, 20002
Telephone: (202) 546-1210
Elizabeth L. Chittick, President
Major programs: museum, women's history

Smithsonian Institution
2000 Jefferson Dr., 20560
Telephone: (202) 357-1300
Founded in: 1846
Robert McCormick Adams, Secretary
Magazine: *Smithsonian*
Major programs: library, archives, manuscripts, museum, tours/pilgrimages, oral history, educational programs, books, newsletters/pamphlets
Period of collections: prehistoric-present

Society for Industrial Archaeology
National Museum of American History, Smithsonian Institution, 20560

Telephone: (202) 357-2225
Founded in: 1971
Helena E. Wright, President
Number of members: 1,200
Staff: volunteer 3
Major programs: tours/pilgrimages, educational programs, books, newsletters/pamphlets

Society of Systematic Zoology—Museum of Natural History
Smithsonian Institution, 20560
Telephone: (202) 357-2964
Private agency
Founded in: 1955
Austin B. Williams, Secretary
Number of members: 1,600
Staff: part time 1
Magazine: *Systematic Zoology*
Major programs: museum, exhibits, archaeology programs, zoology

U.S. Army Center of Military History
20 Massachusetts Ave., NW, 20314-0200
Telephone: (202) 272-0291
Federal agency, authorized by the U.S. Army
Founded in: 1945
C. Anderson, Librarian
Staff: full time 115
Magazine: *Army Historian*
Major programs: library, archives, manuscripts, museum, book publishing, newsletters/pamphlets, records management, research, exhibits
Period of collections: Colonial-present

U.S. Capitol Historical Society
200 Maryland Ave., NE, 20002
Telephone: (202) 543-8919
Private agency
Founded in: 1962
Fred Schwengel, President
Staff: full time 18, part time 22
Magazine: *Congressional Studies*
Major programs: historic sites preservation, oral history, educational programs, books, newsletters/pamphlets
Period of collections: 1780-present

U.S. Marine Corps Historical Center and Museum
Washington Navy Yard, Bldg. 58, 20374
Telephone: (202) 433-3839
Federal agency, authorized by the U.S. Marine Corps
Founded in: 1977
J. C. Owens, Administrative Officer
Staff: full time 48, volunteer 12
Magazine: *Fortitudine*
Major programs: library, archives, manuscripts, museum, historic site(s), oral history, book publishing, newsletters/pamphlets, research, exhibits, audiovisual programs, photographic collections, research grants, intern programs
Period of collections: 1775-present

U.S. Senate Commission on Art and Antiques
U.S. Capitol Bldg., Room S-411, 20510
Telephone: (202) 224-2955

Federal agency
Founded in: 1968
James R. Ketchum, Curator
Staff: full time 4, part time 8
Major programs: library, archives,
manuscripts, museum, historic
site(s), tours/pilgrimages, school
programs, newsletters/pamphlets,
historic preservation, records
management, research, exhibits,
photographic collections
Period of collections: 19th century

White House Historical Association
740 Jackson Place, NW, 20506
Telephone: (202) 737-8292
Founded in: 1961
Bernard R. Meyer, Executive Vice
President
Staff: full time 5, part time 9
Magazine: *White House History*
Major programs: books

Woodrow Wilson House Museum
2340 South St., NW, 20008
Telephone: (202) 673-4034
Private agency, authorized by
National Trust for Historic
Preservation
Founded in: 1961
Earl James, Director
Number of members: 400
Staff: full time 3, part time 2,
volunteer 15
Major programs: museum, historic
site(s), historic preservation,
exhibits
Period of collections: 1913-1924

FLORIDA

APALACHICOLA

Apalachicola Area Historical Society
P.O. Box 75, 32320
Telephone: (904) 653-9524
Private agency
Founded in: 1957
George L. Chapel, President
Number of members: 85
Staff: volunteer 7
Major programs: museum, markers,
tours/pilgrimages, oral history,
newsletters/pamphlets, living
history, audiovisual programs,
photographic collections
Period of collections: 1835-1870

APOPKA

Apopka Historical Society
9 W. Nightingale, 32703
Telephone: (305) 886-2383
Private agency
Julian Roberts, President
Number of members: 38
Staff: volunteer 3
Major programs: museum, school
programs, book publishing
Period of collections: 1865-1918

ARCADIA

Peace River Valley Historical Society, Inc.
P.O. Drawer 1379, 33821
Telephone: (813) 494-4601
Private agency

Founded in: 1964
R. H. Wod, Secretary
Number of members: 72
Major programs: museum, historic
site(s), markers, tours/pilgrimages,
book publishing
Period of collections: from 1840

ARCHER

Archer Historical Society, Inc.
Mail to: P.O. Drawer 1850, 32618
Founded in: 1977
Questionnaire not received

AVON PARK

Historical Society and Avon Park Museum
P.O. Box 483, 33825
Telephone: (813) 453-3938
City agency
Founded in: 1947
Leoma B. Maxwell, Director
Number of members: 100
Staff: part time 1
Major programs: archives,
manuscripts, museum,
photographic collections,
genealogical services
Period of collections: from 1885

BARTOW

Polk County Historical Association
2495 N. Hendry
Telephone: (813) 533-5146
Mail to: P.O. Box 1719, 33830
Founded in: 1974
Glenn Hooker, President
Number of members: 900
Staff: volunteer 50
Magazine: *Polk County Historical Quarterly*
Major programs: library, archives,
historic sites preservation, markers,
oral history, newsletters/pamphlets
Period of collections: 1865-present

Polk County Historical and Genealogical Library
495 N. Hendry Ave., 33830
Telephone: (813) 533-5146
Mail to: P.O. Box 1719, 33830
County agency, authorized by Polk
County Historical Commission
Founded in: 1937
LaCona Raines-Padgett, Head
Librarian
Number of members: 500
Staff: full time 2
Major programs: library, archives,
historic site(s), tours/pilgrimages,
oral history, newsletters/pamphlets,
historic preservation, research,
photographic collections,
genealogical services, public
quarterly
Period of collections: 1600-1900

BELLE GLADE

Glades Historical Society
530 S. Main St., 33430
Founded in: 1976
Number of members: 110
Staff: volunteer 10
Major programs: oral history,
educational programs, books,
newsletters/pamphlets
Period of collections: 1918-present

BRADENTON

Eaton Room, Manatee County Public Library System
1301 Barcarrota Blvd., W, 33505
Telephone: (813) 748-5555
County agency
Founded in: 1972
Philip A. Place, Director, Library
System
Staff: full time 2
Major programs: library, archives,
oral history, research, exhibits,
audiovisual programs,
photographic collections
Period of collections: 1840-1930

Manasota Genealogical Society, Inc.
Mail to: P.O. Box 9433, 33506
Founded in: 1974
Staff: volunteer 50
Major programs: library, archives,
newsletters/pamphlets, historic
preservation

Manatee County Historical Commission, Inc.
604 15th St. E
Mail to: P.O. Box 2197, 33508
Founded in: 1974
Staff: full time 2, volunteer 42
Major programs: historic site,
markers, slide shows
Period of collections: 1842-present

Manatee County Historical Society
8012 1st Ave., W, 33529
Founded in: 1946
Questionnaire not received

South Florida Museum and Bishop Planetarium
201 10th St., W, 33505
Telephone: (813) 746-4132
Private agency
Founded in: 1946
John Hare, Director
Number of members: 500
Staff: full time 7, part time 7,
volunteer 15
Major programs: museum, school
programs, exhibits, audiovisual
programs
Period of collections:
pre-Columbian--early 20th century

BUSHNELL

Dade Battlefield State Historic Site
P.O. Box 938, 33513
Telephone: (904) 793-4781
Founded in: 1921
L. W. Edwards, Manager
Staff: full time 1, part time 1
Major programs: museum, historic
site, markers, tours/pilgrimages
Period of collections: 1835-1837

CAPE CORAL

Cape Coral Historical Society, Inc.
c/o President, 4707 S.E. 5th Ave.,
Apt. 203, 33904
Telephone: (813) 542-4230
Private agency
Founded in: 1978
Betsy Zeiss, President
Number of members: 118
Magazine: *The Chronicler*
Major programs: museum
Period of collections: 1920s-present

CEDAR KEY

Cedar Key Historical Society
Hwy. 24 and 2nd St.
Mail to: P.O. Box 222, 32625
Founded in: 1979
Neda Ford, Director
Number of members: 200
Staff: volunteer 5
Magazine: *The Beacon*
Major programs: museum, oral
history
Period of collections: 1800-1920

CLEWISTON

Calusa Valley Historical Society
439 Hickpochee, LaBelle
Telephone: (813) 675-1616
Mail to: c/o President, P.O. Box 818,
LaBelle, 33935
Private agency
Richard T. Pfluge, President
Number of members: 84
Major programs: markers
Period of collections: 1900s

COCOA

**Brevard Museum of History and
Natural Science**
2201 Michigan Ave., 32926
Telephone: (305) 632-1830
Private agency
Founded in: 1969
Vera Zimmerman, President
Number of members: 300
Staff: full time 1, part time 1,
volunteer 30
Magazine: *The Armidillo's Tale*
Major programs: museum, school
programs, exhibits, audiovisual
programs, photographic
collections, natural science,
ecology, nature trails
Period of collections: 1865-1920

CORAL GABLES

**Planning Department, Coral Gables
Historic Preservation Division**
405 Biltmore Way, 33134
Telephone: (305) 442-6443
Mail to: P.O. Drawer 141549, 33114
City agency
Founded in: 1973
Robin Lang Krchak, Administrator
Staff: full time 2
Major programs: library, archives,
museum, historic site(s), markers,
tours/pilgrimages, junior history,
school programs,
newsletters/pamphlets, histcric
preservation, records
management, research, exhibits,
audiovisual programs,
photographic collections, field
services
Period of collections: 1900-present

CRYSTAL RIVER

**Crystal River State Archaeological
Site**
3400 N. Museum Point, 32629
Telephone: (904) 795-3817
State Agency, authorized by
Department of Natural Resources,
Division of Recreation and Parks
Founded in: 1965

James P. Mielock, Resident Park
Manager I
Staff: full time 3
Major programs: museum, school
programs, exhibits
Period of collections: 200 B.C.-A.D.
1400

DAYTONA BEACH

Halifax Historical Society, Inc.
128 Orange Ave.
Mail to: P.O. Box 5051, 32018
Founded in: 1949
Susan A. Lofaro, President
Number of members: 600
Staff: full time 2, volunteer 6
Magazine: *Halifax Historical Herald*
Major programs: library, archives,
museum, newsletters/pamphlets
Period of collections: 1870-present

DELAND

Florida Baptist Historical Society
Stetson University, P.O. Box 8353,
32720
Telephone: (904) 734-4121
Private agency, authorized by the
university and the Florida Baptist
Convention
Founded in: 1950
E. Earl Joiner, Curator
Number of members: 52
Staff: part time 1
Major programs: archives,
manuscripts, oral history, books,
newsletters/pamphlets, research
Period of collections: 1492-present

DELRAY BEACH

Delray Beach Historical Society
64 S.E. 5th Ave., 33444
Private agency
Founded in: 1964
Buster Musgrave, Vice President
Number of members: 200
Staff: volunteer 5
Major programs: archives, markers,
historic preservation, exhibits
Period of collections: late
1800s-present

**Morikami Museum of Japanese
Culture**
4000 Morikami Park Rd., 33446
Telephone: (305) 499-0631/495-0233
County agency, authorized by
Department of Parks and
Recreation
Fcunded in: 1976
Larry Rosenweig, Curator
Staff: full time 5, volunteer 80
Major programs: library, museum,
school programs,
newsletters/pamphlets, exhibits,
photographic collections,
Japanese garden
Period of collections: 1868-present

DUNEDIN

Dunedin Historical Society, Inc.
94 Diane Dr., 33528
Telephone: (813) 733-1291
Private agency
Founded in: 1969
Edward L. French, President
Number of members: 375

Staff: volunteer 30
Magazine: *Lest We Forget*
Major programs: library, archives,
museum, historic site, markers, oral
history, educational programs,
book publishing,
newsletters/pamphlets, historic
preservation
Period of collections: late 19th
century-present

E. NAPLES

**Collier County Museum and
Archives**
Collier County Government Center,
3301 E. Tamiami Trail, 33942
Telephone: (813) 774-8477
Founded in: 1976
Mary E. Manion, Director
Staff: full time 2
Major programs: library, archives,
museum, tours/pilgrimages,
educational programs
Period of collections:
prehistoric-present

FERNANDINA BEACH

**Duncan Lamont Clinch Historical
Society**
Mail to: P.O. Box 7, 32034
Questionnaire not received

FORT LAUDERDALE

**Broward County Historical
Commission**
100-B S.E. New River Dr., 33301
Telephone: (305) 765-5872
Founded in: 1973
Staff: full time 2, volunteer 23
Major programs: library, archives,
museum, historic site, markers,
tours/pilgrimages, oral history,
educational programs,
newsletters/pamphlets, historic
preservation
Period of collections: early
1900s-present

**Ft. Lauderdale Historical
Society, Inc.**
219 S.W. 2nd. Ave., 33066
Telephone: (305) 463-4431
Pirvate agency
Founded in: 1962
Daniel T. Hobby, Executive Director
Number of members: 800
Staff: full time 3, part time 7
Magazine: *New River News*
Major programs: library, archives,
manuscripts, museum, historic
site(s), oral history, school
programs, book publishing,
newsletters/pamphlets, historic
preservation, research, exhibits,
photographic collections
Period of collections: 1830s-present

**Ft. Lauderdale Historic
Preservation Board**
100 N. Andrews Ave.
Telephone: (305) 761-2661
Mail to: P.O. Box 14250, 33302
City agency
Founded in: 1975
Laura Ward, Board Liaison
Staff: volunteer 9

Major programs: historic site,
markers, historic preservation
Period of collections: 1900-1928

**Genealogical Society of Broward
County, Inc.**
P.O. Box 485, 33302
Private agency
Founded in: 1967
Harry L. Young, Jr., President
Number of members: 150
Staff: volunteer 16
Magazine: Imprints
Major programs: library, research,
genealogical services
Period of collections: 1600s-1800s

University School Library
7500 S.W. 36th St., 33066
S. Solomon, Director of
Administration
Major programs: library, school
programs, book publishing,
newsletters/pamphlets

FORT MYERS

Ft. Myers Historical Museum
2300 Peck St.
Telephone: (813) 332-5955
Mail to: P.O. Drawer 2217, 33902
City agency
Founded in: 1982
Patricia Bartlett, Museum Director
Staff: full time 3, part time 1,
volunteer 6
Major programs: museum, school
programs, exhibits, audiovisual
programs, photographic
collections
Period of collections: 1850-1950

**Southwest Florida Historical
Society, Inc.**
5111 Macgregor Blvd.
Mail to: P.O. Box 1362, 33902
Private agency
Founded in: 1960
Stanley H. Mulford, President
Number of members: 60
Major programs: archives,
manuscripts, oral history, book
publishing, records management,
research, living history,
photographic collections,
genealogical services
Period of collections: 1839-1865

**Thomas Edison Winter Home and
Museum**
2350 McGregor Blvd., 33901
Telephone: (813) 334-3614
City agency
Founded in: 1885
Robert Halgrim, Manager
Staff: full time 28, part time 12
Major programs: museum,
tours/pilgrimages, exhibits,
photographic collections
Period of collections: 1880-1930

FORT PIERCE

St. Lucie Historical Commission
414 Seaway Dr., 33449
Telephone: (305) 464-6635
County agency
Founded in: 1965
Edward T. McCarron, Jr., Director
Staff: full time 1, part time 2,
volunteer 30

Major programs: library, museum,
historic site(s), school programs,
historic preservation, research,
exhibits, audiovisual programs,
photographic collections,
genealogical services
Period of collections: 1560-1930

St. Lucie Historical Society
414 Seaway Dr., 33450
Telephone: (305) 464-6635
Private agency
Marjorie Smither, President
Number of members: 350
Major programs: manuscripts,
markers, publishing, newsletters,
research

FORT WALTON BEACH

**AFAM (Air Force Armament
Museum)**
Rt. 85, N
Telephone: (904) 882-4062
Mail to: Eglin Air Force Base, 32542
Federal agency, authorized by U.S.
Air Force
Founded in: 1971
Arnold Williams, Director
Staff: full time 10, part time 6
Major programs: library, archives,
museum, tours/pilgrimages, school
programs, historic preservation,
research, exhibits
Period of collections: from W.W. I

**Genealogical Society of Okaloosa
County, Inc.**
P.O. Box, 1175, 32549
Telephone: (904) 862-8388
Private agency
Founded in: 1976
Martha W. Rogers, President
Number of members: 80
Staff: volunteer 10
Major programs: library,
newsletters/pamphlets, research,
genealogical services

Temple Mound Museum
139 Miraclestrip Parkway
Telephone: (904) 243-6521
Mail to: P.O. Box 4009, 32548
City agency
Founded in: 1962
Yules W. Lazarus, Curator
Staff: full time 3, part time 2,
volunteer 4
Major programs: museum, historic
site(s), markers, tours/pilgrimages,
school programs, historic
preservation, research, exhibits,
audiovisual programs
Period of collections:
prehistoric-present

GAINESVILLE

**Alachua County Historical
Commission**
918 S.W. 8th Lane, 32601
Telephone: (904) 372-4031
County agency
Founded in: 1940
Helen Cubberly Ellerbe, Chair
Major programs: historic site(s),
markers, tours, book publishing,
exhibits, photographic collections
Period of cllections: 19th-20th
centuries

**Byelorussian Charitable
Educational Fund, Inc.**
1716 N.E. 7th Terrace, 32601
Founded in: 1976
Questionnaire not received

◇**Florida State Museum**
Museum Dr., 32611
Telephone: (904) 392-1721
State agency
Founded in: 1917
F. Wayne King, Director
Number of members: 400
Staff: full time 50, part time 90,
volunteer 45
Magazine: Florida State Museum
News Notes
Major programs: museum, school
programs, historic preservation,
records management, research,
exhibits, audiovisual programs,
photographic collections, field
services, natural history

**P. K. Yonge Library of Florida
History**
University of Florida Libraries
Telephone: (904) 392-0319
Mail to: 404 Library, W, 32611
State agency
Founded in: 1944
Elizabeth Alexander, Librarian/Chair
Staff: full time 3
Major programs: library, archives,
manuscripts, microfilms of
newspapers and Spanish
dccuments
Period of collections: 1492-present

HIALEAH

Hialeah John F. Kennedy Library
190 W. 49th St., 33012
Telephone: (305) 821-2700
City agency
Founded in: 1965
Rema Comras, Library Director
Staff: full time 28
Major programs: library

HOLIDAY

**Peninsular Archaeological
Society, Inc.**
1412 6th Ave., 33590
Telephone: (813) 397-3901
Private agency
Founded in: 1966
Henry G. Pilcher, President
Number of members: 48
Staff: volunteer 5
Magazine: Early Man
Major programs: museum, oral
history, book publishing, exhibits,
archaeology programs
Period of collections: prehistoric

HOLLYWOOD

**Broward County Archaeological
Society, Inc.**
5430 S.W. 36th St., 33023
Questionnaire not received

INDIAN

Florida Aviation Historical Society
P.O. Box 127, 33535
Telephone: (813) 595-6256
Private agency

Founded in: 1979
Edward C. Hoffman, President
Number of members: 496
Staff: volunteer 12
Magazine: *Florida Aviation*
Major programs: library, archives, museum, historic site(s), markers, oral history, book publishing, historic preservation, audiovisual programs, photographic collections
Period of collections: 1900-present

JACKSONVILLE

Ft. Caroline National Memorial
12713 Ft. Caroline Rd., 32225
Federal agency, authorized by National Park Service
Founded in: 1950
Number of members: 9
Major programs: museum, historic site(s), school programs, historic preservation, exhibits
Period of ccllections: late 1500s

Jacksonville Historic Landmarks Commission
Mayor's Office, City Hall, 220 E. Bay St., 32202
Telephone: (904) 633-3812
Founded in: 1971
Jake M. Godbold, Mayor
Staff: full time 1, part time 1, volunteer 15
Major programs: archives, museum, book publishing, historic preservation, research, photographic collections
Period of collections: 1890-1930

Jacksonville Museum of Arts and Sciences
1025 Gulf Life Dr., 32207
Telephone: (904) 396-7062
Founded in: 1938
Joseph L. Cartwright, Executive Director
Number of members: 800
Staff: full time 21, part time 12, volunteer 35
Major programs: museum, planetarium, historic site, educational programs, newsletters/pamphlets, exhibits, audiovisual programs
Period of collections: 19th century-present

Northeast Florida Anthropological Society
Telephone: (904) 771-6648
Mail to: P.O. Box 2925, 32203
Donald Thompson, President
Number of members: 30
Major programs: school programs, newsletters/pamphlets, historic preservation, archaeology programs, field services
Period of collections: 2600 B.C. - A.D. 1500

Riverside Avondale Preservation, Inc.
2624 Riverside Ave., 32204
Telephone: (904) 389-2449
Private agency
Founded in: 1974
Leslee F. Keyes, Executive Director
Number of members: 2,000

Staff: full time 2, volunteer 60
Major programs: library, archives, tours/pilgrimages, book publishing, newsletters/phamphlets, historic preservation, research, photographic collections, field services
Period of collections: 1870-1935

Southern Genealogist's Exchange Society, Inc.
1580 Blanding Blvd., 32210
Telephone: (904) 387-9142
Mail t0 PO. Box 2801, 32203
Private agency
Founded in: 1964
Mildred Tomlinson, President
Number of members: 200
Staff: volunteer 25
Magazine: *The Exchange*
Major programs: library, archives, newsletters/pamphlets, research, genealogical services
Period of collections: 1600s-present

JACKSONVILLE BEACH

Beaches Area Historical Society
P.O. Box 50646, 32250
Founded in: 1978
Number of members: 250
Staff: volunteer 50
Major programs: library, archives, museum, historic site, markers, oral history, newsletters/pamphlets, historic preservation
Period of collections: 1886-present

JASPER

Hamilton County Historical Society
505 Central Ave., 32052
Telephone: (904) 792-2726
Founded in: 1978
Loraine Kiefer, President
Staff: volunteer 4
Major programs: museum, historic site, markers, historic preservation

JUPITER

Loxahatchee Historical Society, Inc.
Lighthouse Park, Hwy. 1
Telephone: (305) 747-6639
Mail to: P.O. Box 1506, 33458
Founded in: 1971
Dorothy B. Kaster, President
Number of members: 300
Staff: volunteer 60
Major programs: library, archives, museum, historic site(s), markers, tours/pilgrimages, oral history, school programs, book publishing, newsletters/pamphlets, historic preservation, research, exhibits, living history, audiovisual programs, photographic collections
Period of collections: 500 B.C.-present

KEY WEST

Ernest Hemingway Museum
907 Whitehead
Telephone: (305) 294-1575
Mail to: P.O. Box 1519, 33040
Private agency
Founded in: 1964

Bernice Dickson, Owner
Staff: full time 0
Major programs: museum, historic preservation
Period of collections: 1928-1961

Ft. Jefferson National Monument
c/o U.S. Coast Guard Base, Dry Tortugas, 33040
Federal agency, authorized by National Park Service
Founded in: 1935
Dick Newgren, Superintendent
Staff: full time 7, part time 1, volunteer 15
Major programs: historic site(s), historic preservation, exhibits, audiovisual programs
Period of collections: 1846-present

Historic Key West Preservation Board
Monroe County Courthouse, 33040
Telephone: (305) 294-7511
State agency
Founded in: 1969
Wright Langley, Director
Staff: full time 2
Major programs: historic sites preservation, book publishing, research

Key West Art and Historical Society
S. Roosevelt Blvd., 33040
Telephone: (305) 296-3913
Founded in: 1949
Lee Dodez, Executive Director
Number of members: 1,400
Staff: full time 5, part time 3, volunteer 50
Major programs: museum, newsletters/pamphlets
Period of collections: 1865-present

Old Island Restoration Foundation, Inc.
Mail to: P.O. Box 689, 33040
Founded in: 1960
Questionnaire not received

KISSIMMEE

Historical Association of Osceola—Osceola County Art and Culture Center
E. U.S. Hwy. 441
Telephone: (305) 846-6257/847-7464
Mail to: P.O. Box 552, 32741
Founded in: 1949
Number of members: 54
Staff: volunteer 15
Magazine: *The Osceola Journal*
Major programs: library, archives, museum, tours/pilgrimages, oral history, newsletters/phamphlets, genealogy
Period of collections: 1880-1930

LAKE CITY

Columbia County Historical Society
Chamber of Commerce, 15 E. Orange St. 32052
Private agency
Founded in: 1973
Gerald Witt, Chair
Number of members: 30
Major programs: museum, book publishing
Period of collections: 1900-1950

LAKE WALES

Depot Museum
325 S. Scenic Hwy., 33853
Telephone: (813) 676-5443
City agency
Founded in: 1976
Mimi Reid Hardman, Director
Staff: full time 2, part time 1,
  volunteer 1
Magazine: *The Semaphore*
Major programs: museum, school
  programs, exhibits, photographic
  collections
Period of collections: 1911-1940

**Lake Wales Museum and Cultural
Center**
325 S. Scenic Hwy., 33853
Telephone: (813) 676-5443
City agency
Founded in: 1976
Julie Adams Scofield, Curator
Number of members: 200
Staff: full time 2, part time 1,
  volunteer 3
Major programs: archives, museum,
  school programs, photographic
  collections
Period of collections: 1910-1945

LARGO

**Heritage Park/Pinellas County
Historical Museum**
11909 125th St., N, 33544
Telephone: (813) 462-3474
County agency
Founded in: 1961
Kendrick T. Ford, Museum Director
Staff: full time 9
Major programs: library, archives,
  museum, tours/pilgrimages, oral
  history, school programs, historic
  preservation, exhibits, living
  history, audiovisual programs,
  photographic collections
Period of collections: late 19th-early
  20th centuries

Largo Area Historical Society
805 S. Palm Dr., 33541
Telephone: (813) 584-3480
Private agency
Founded in: 1973
Danny Howard, President
Number of members: 150
Major programs: library, museum,
  historic site, educational programs,
  historic preservation

Pinellas County Historical Society
11909 125th St., N
Telephone: (813) 462-3474
Private agency
Founded in: 1976
Marion Sabatini, President
Number of members: 680
Staff: volunteer 3
Magazine: *Punta Pinal*
Major programs: library, archives,
  museum, tours, junior history, oral
  history, school programs, book
  publishing, newsletters/pamphlets,
  living history, audiovisual
  programs, photographic
  collections
Period of collections: 1865-1945

LUTZ

**Florida Historical Research
Foundation**
2301 E. 148th Ave., 33549
Telephone: (813) 971-2968
Founded in: 1969
James Gray, Director
Staff: volunteer 14
Major programs: library, archives,
  manuscripts, historic site, historic
  preservation, displays
Period of collections: to 1865

MACCLENNY

Baker County Historical Society
McIver St.
Mail to: P.O. Box 856, 32063
Private agency
Founded in: 1978
Beulah Wilford, President
Number of members: 125
Major programs: library, historic
  site(s), newsletters/pamphlets,
  historic preservation, research,
  genealogical services
Period of collections: 1890-1930

MARIANNA

Florida Caverns State Park
2701 Caverns Rd., 32446
Telephone: (904) 482-3632
State agency, authorized by
  Department of Natural Resources,
  Division of Recreation and Parks
Founded in: 1935
A. W. Smith, Jr., Park Manager
Staff: full time 11, part time 6
Major programs: historic site(s),
  tours, historic preservation,
  exhibits

MIAMI

Dade Heritage Trust, Inc.
190 S.E. 12th Terrace, 33131
Telephone: (305) 358-9572
Private agency
Founded in: 1972
Paul E. Thompson, Executive Director
Number of members: 200
Staff: full time 3, volunteer 100
Magazine: *Preservation Today*
Major programs: library, museum,
  historic site, tours/pilgrimages,
  newsletters/phamphlets, historic
  preservation, research
Period of collections: 20th century

◇**Historical Association of
Southern Florida**
101 W. Flagler St., 33130
Telephone: (305) 375-1492
Private agency
Founded in: 1940
Randy F. Nimnicht, Director
Number of members: 3,000
Staff: full time 21, part time 18
Magazine:
  Tequesta/Update/Currents
Major programs: library, archives,
  manuscripts, museum, markers,
  tours/pilgrimages, oral history,
  school programs, book publishing,
  newsletters/pamphlets, research
  exhibits, audiovisual programs,
  archaeology programs,
  photographic collection

Period of collections:
  prehistoric-present

Miami Beach Public Library
2100 Collins Ave., 33139
Telephone: (305) 673-7535
City agency
Founded in: 1927
Phyllis A. Gray, Director
Number of members: 1
Staff: full time 28, part time 4,
  volunteer 2
Major programs: library, archives,
  records management

The Villagers, Inc.
P.O. Box 14, 1843 Coral Gables,
  33114
Private agency
Founded in: 1966
Patricia B. Godard, President
Number of members: 140
Staff: volunteer 80
Major programs: archives, historic
  site(s), tours/pilgrimages, school
  programs, book publishing, historic
  preservation, research, exhibits
Period of ccllections: 1965-present

Vizcaya Museum and Gardens
3251 S. Miami Ave., 33129
Telephone: (305) 579-2708
County agency
Founded in: 1952
Richard N. Gregg, Director
Number of members: 1,800
Staff: full time 40, part time 17,
  volunteer 200
Magazine: *Vizcayans Newsletter*
Major programs: museum,
  tours/pilgrimages, educational
  programs, historic preservation,
  exhibits, European decorative art
Period of collections: 15th-19th
  cénturies

MONTICELLO

**Jefferson County Historical
Association**
Telephone: (904) 997-2565
Mail to: P.O. Box 496, 32344
Private agency
Founded in: 1962
Mrs. Frederick W. Connolly, President
Number of members: 100
Staff: volunteer 20
Major programs: historic site(s),
  tours/pilgrimages, historic
  preservation, photographic
  collections
Period of collections: 1840-1880

MOUNT DORA

Mt. Dora Historical Society
1 Royellou Lane
Telephone: (904) 383-3519
Mail to: c/o Museum Supervisor, 111
  S. Grandview St., 32757
Private agency
Founded in: 1953
Helen L. Whittington, Museum
  Supervisor
Number of members: 240
Staff: volunteer 30
Major programs: museum
Period of collections: 1856-present

NAPLES

Collier County Museum
Collier County Government Center
3301 Tamiami Trail, 33962
Telephone: (813) 774-8476
County agency
Founded in: 1976
Ron D. Jamro, Director
Staff: full time 2, volunteer 8
Major programs: library, archives,
manuscripts, museum, historic
preservation, research, exhibits,
photographic collections
Period of collections:
prehistoric-present

NEW PORT RICHEY

West Pasco Historical Society, Inc.
100 Circle Blvd., Telephone: (813)
847-0680
Mail to: P.O. Box 1855, 34291-1855
Private agency
Founded in: 1973
Alex Acey, President
Number of members: 350
Staff: volunteer 15
Major programs: library, museum
Period of collections: late 1800s-early
1930s

OAKLAND PARK

Oakland Park Historical Society
3876 N.E. 6th Ave., 33334
Questionnaire not received

OCALA

Kingdom of the Sun
4911 N.E. 7th St., 32671
Telephone: (904) 236-4740
Founded in: 1979
Questionnaire not received

OCALA

Marion County Historical Society
P.O. Box 3215, 32678
Telephone: (904) 629-1929
Mail to: P.O. Box 165, Anthony, 32617
Private agency
Founded in: 1980
Alyce F. Tincher, President
Number of members: 100
Staff: volunteer 11
Major programs: manuscripts,
historic site(s), markers,
tours/pilgrimages, oral history,
school programs, book publishing,
newsletters/pamphlets, historic
preservation, audiovisual
programs, archaeology programs,
photographic collections,
genealogical services, field
services
Period of collections: 1860-present

ORLANDO

**Central Florida Genealogical and
Historical Society, Inc.**
P.O. Box 177, 32802
Private agency
Founded in: 1969
Betty Brinsfield Hughson, President
Number of members: 230
Staff: volunteer 20
Magazine: *Buried
Treasures/Treasure Chest News*

Major programs: library, archives,
school programs, book publishing,
newsletters/pamphlets,
genealogical services
Period of collections: 1800-1900

**Orange County Historical
Society, Inc. and Museum**
812 E. Rollins Ave., 32803
Telephone: (305) 898-8320
County agency, authorized by
Orange County Parks Department
Founded in: 1957
Jean Yothers, Director/Curator
Number of members: 1,228
Staff: full time 3, part time 2,
volunteer 40
Magazine: *Orange County Historical
Quarterly*
Major programs: library, archives,
manuscripts, museum,
tours/pilgrimages, school
programs, book publishing,
newsletters/pamphlets, historic
preservation, research, exhibits,
photographic collections
Period of collections: 1795-present

PALATKA

Palatka Public Library
216 Reid St., 32077
Telephone: (904) 328-5682
City agency
Gary F. Frizzell, Director
Staff: full time 4, part time 4,
volunteer 1
Major programs: library, genealogical
services

**Putnam County Archives and
History Commission**
515 Reid St., 32077
Telephone: (904) 328-5181
Mail to: P.O. Box 1976 32078
County agency, authorized by Clerk
of Courts
Founded in: 1976
Janice S. Mahaffey, Archivist
Staff: full time 2, volunteer 5
Major programs: archives, museum,
school programs, records
management, photographic
collections, genealogical services
Period of collections: 1849-present

PALM BEACH

**Henry Morrison Flagler
Museum/Whitehall Historic
House Museum**
Cocoanut Row
Telephone: (305) 655-2833
Mail to: P.O. Box 969, 33480
Private agency
Founded in: 1959
Charles B. Simmons, Executive
Director
Number of members: 1,400
Staff: full time 13, part time 15,
volunteer 180
Major programs: archives, museum,
historic site(s), tours/pilgrimages,
school programs,
newsletters/pamphlets, historic
preservation, exhibits, audiovisual
programs, photographic
collections
Period of collections: 1865-1918

**Historical Society of Palm Beach
County**
1 Whitehall Way
Telephone: (305) 655-1492
Mail to: P.O. Box 1147, 33480
Private agency
Founded in: 1937
Nan Dennison, Director
Number of members: 400
Staff: volunteer 20
Magazine: *The Sunlit Road*
Major programs: library, archives,
manuscripts, museum, research,
exhibits, photographic
collections
Period of collections: 1850-20th
century

**Palm Beach Landmarks
Preservation Commission**
360 S. County Rd.
Telephone: (305) 655-5341, ext. 248
Mail to: P.O. Box 2029, 33480
Town agency
Founded in: 1979
Stephen J. Tool, Jr., Coordinator
Staff: full time 2, volunteer 10
Major programs: library, archives,
markers, newsletters/pamphlets,
historic preservation, records
management, research,

*Whitehall, a mansion built in 1901 by Standard Oil Company co-founder Henry Morrison
Flagler, was restored by the Henry Morrison Flagler Museum.*—The Henry Morrison
Flagler Museum, Palm Beach, Florida

photographic collections, field
services
Period of collections: late 19th-20th
centuries

PANAMA CITY

**Northwest Florida Chapter, Florida
Anthropological Society**
4702 W. 19th Court
Mail to: P.O. Box 4641, 32405
Founded in: 1969
Questionnaire not received

PENSACOLA

**Environmental Studies Center and
Museum**
207 E. Main St., 32501
Questionnaire not received

Gulf Islands National Seashore
P.O. Box 100, Gulf Breeze, 32561
Telephone: (904) 932-5302
Federal agency, authorized by the
National Park Service
Founded in: 1971
Jerry Eubanks, Superintendent
Staff: full time 80
Major programs: library, museum,
historic site(s), tours/pilgrimages,
oral history, school programs,
newsletters/pamphlets, historic
preservation, exhibits, audiovisual
programs, archaeology programs,
photographic collections
Period of collections:
prehistoric-W.W. II

**Historic Pensacola Preservation
Board of Trustees**
205 E. Zaragoza St., 32501
Telephone: (904) 434-1042
State agency
Founded in: 1967
James M. Moody, Jr., Director
Major programs: archives, museum,
historic site(s), school programs,
historic preservation, exhibits, field
services
Period of collections:
prehistoric-present

Naval Aviation Museum
U.S. Naval Air Station, 32508
Telephone: (904) 452-3604
Federal agency, authorized by the
U.S. Navy
Founded in: 1963
Grover Walker, Director
Staff: full time 15
Major programs: library, archives,
museum, exhibits
Period of collections: 1918-present

**Pensacola Historic Preservation
Society**
204 S. Alcaniz St.
Mail to: P.O. Box 12404, 32582
Founded in: 1960
Number of members: 63
Staff: volunteer 25
Major programs: historic sites
preservation, tours/pilgrimages
Period of collections: 1783-1865

Pensacola Historical Society
405 S. Adams St., 32501
Telephone: (904) 433-1559
Private agency
Founded in: 1933

Gordon N. Simons, Curator
Number of members: 810
Staff: full time 3, part time 2
Magazine: *Pensacola History
Illustrated*
Major programs: library, archives,
manuscripts, museum, historic
site(s), book publishing,
newsletters/pamphlets, research,
exhibits, photographic collections,
genealogical services
Period of collections:
prehistoric-W.W. II

**Special Collections Department,
Library of the University of West
Florida**
32514
Telephone: (904) 474-2213
State agency, authorized by the
university
Founded in: 1966
Dean DeBolt, Head, Special
Collections
Staff: full time
Major programs: library, archives,
manuscripts, research, exhibits,
photographic collections,
genealogical services
Period of collections: 1559-present

T. T. Wentworth, Jr., Museum
8382 N. Palafox Hwy., 32504
Telephone: (904) 476-3443
Mail to: P.O. Box 806, 32594
Founded in: 1957
T.T. Wentworth, Jr., President
Number of members: 1,000
Staff: volunteer 26
Magazine: *Pensacola Picture Books*
Major programs: museum
Period of collections:
prehistoric-present

PLANT CITY

**East Hillsborough Historical
Sciety**
507 N. Collins St.
Mail to: P.O. Box 1418, 33566
Founded in: 1975
Questionnaire not received

SAFETY HARBOR

**Safety Harbor Museum of History
and Fine Arts**
329 S. Bayshore Blvd., 33572
Private agency
Founded in: 1977
John Michael, President
Number of members: 38
Staff: volunteer 15
Major programs: museum, historic
site(s), markers, tours/pilgrimages,
school programs, historic
preservation, exhibits, archaeology
programs, photographic
collections
Period of collections: A.D.
600-present

ST. AUGUSTINE

**Castillo de San Marcos/Ft.
Matanzas National Monument**
Castillo Dr., 32084
Telephone: (904) 829-6506
Federal agency, authorized by
National Park Service

Founded in: 1933
B. J. Griffin, Superintendent
Staff: full time 26, part time 3,
volunteer 7
Major programs: library, museum,
historic preservation, living history,
photographic collections
Period of collections: 1670-1821

Historic Florida Militia
42 Spanish St. 32084
Telephone: (904) 829-9792
Private agency
Founded in: 1974
Robert Hall, Adjutant
Number of members: 65
Staff: volunteer 5
Major programs: tours/pilgrimages,
school programs,
newsletters/pamphlets, research,
living history
Period of collections: 1565-1865

**Historic St. Augustine Preservation
Board**
48 King St.
Telephone: (904) 824-3355
Mail to: P.O. Box 1987, 32084
Founded in: 1959
William R. Adams, Director
Staff: full time 30, part time 21,
volunteer 100
Major programs: library, museum,
historic site(s), tours/pilgrimages,
oral history, school programs,
newsletters/pamphlets, historic
preservation, records
management, research, exhibits,
living history, audiovisual
programs, archaeology programs,
photographic collections, field
services
Period of collections: 18th-20th
centuries

Lightner Museum
75 King St., 32084
Telephone: (904) 824-2874
Mail to: P.O. Box 334, 32085-0334
City agency
Founded in: 1948
Robert W. Harper III, Director
Staff: full time 6, part time 7,
volunteer 50
Major programs: library, museum,
historic site(s), school programs,
research, exhibits
Period of collections: 19th century

Oldest House and Tovar House
14 St. Francis St.
Telephone: (904) 824-2872
Mail to: 271 Charlotte St., 32084
Private agency, authorized by St.
Augustine Historical Society
Founded in: 1883
Page Edwards, Jr., Director
Number of members: 530
Staff: full time 4, part time 14,
volunteer 50
Magazine: *East-Florida Gazette*
Major programs: library, archives,
manuscripts, museum, historic
site(s), markers, tours/pilgrimages,
junior history, oral history, school
programs, book publishing,
newsletters/pamphlets, historic
preservation, records
management, research, exhibits,

archaeology programs,
photographic collections,
genealogical services
Period of collections:
prehistoric-present

St. Augustine Historical Society
271 Charlotte St., 32084
Telephone: (904) 824-2872
Founded in: 1883
Page Edwards, Director
Number of members: 550
Staff: full time 5, part time 12
Magazine: *El Escribano*
Major programs: library, archives,
manuscripts, museum, markers,
books, newsletters/phamphlets
Period of collections: 1492-present

**St. Photios Greek Orthodox
National Shrine**
41 St. George St., 32084
Telephone: (504) 829-8205
Mail to: Drawer AF, 32085
Private agency, authorized by St.
Photios Foundation, Inc.
Founded in: 1981
Dimitrios G. Couchell, Executive
Director
Staff: full time 3, part time 3,
volunteer 10
Major programs: historic site(s),
exhibits, audiovisual programs
Period of collections: 1749-present

ST. PETERSBURG

**Florida Society for Genealogical
Research**
8461 54th St., N, Pinellas Park, 33565
Telephone: (813) 391-2914
Private agency
Founded in: 1972
Dorothy M. Boyer, President
Number of members: 110
Staff: volunteer 5
Major programs: library, genealogical
services
Period of collections: 1780-present

St. Petersburg Historical Society
335 2nd Ave., NE, 33701
Telephone: (813) 894-1052
Private agency
Founded in: 1920
Dorothy K. White, Curator
Number of members: 400
Staff: full time 2, part time 4,
volunteer 50
Magazine: *Sea Breeze*
Major programs: museum, school
programs, exhibits
Period of collections:
prehistoric-1950s

SAN JUAN BAUTISTA

**San Juan Bautista Historical
Society**
308 3rd St.
Telephone: (408) 623-4542
Mail to: P.O. Box 1, 95045
Founded in: 1964
Richard A. Gularte, President
Number of members: 82
Staff: volunteer 14
Major programs: library, museum,
historic site(s), markers,
books,newsletters/pamphlets
Period of collections: 1783-1918

SARASOTA

**Historical Society of Sarasota
County**
900 S. Euclid Ave., 33577
Founded in: 1959
Number of members: 291
Staff: part time 1, volunteer 6
Major programs: museum,
tours/pilgrimages, educational
programs, newsletters/pamphlets,
historic preservation
Period of collections: 1890-1910

STARKE

**Bradford County Historical Board
of Trustees**
W. Call and Court Sts.
Telephone: (904) 964-6305
Mail to: P.O. Drawer A, 32091
County agency
Founded in: 1973
Eugene L. Matthews, President
Staff: part time 1
Major programs: historic site(s),
historic preservation, photographic
collections
Period of collections: 1880s-1950

STUART

Historical Society of Martin County
825 N.E. Ocean Blvd., 33494
Telephone: (305) 225-1961
Private agency
Founded in: 1955
Janet Hutchinson, Director
Staff: full time 3, part time 5,
volunteer 55
Major programs: museum, historic
sites preservation, books
Period of collections: 1865-present

TALLAHASSEE

**Black Archives Research Center
and Museum**
P.O. Box 809, Florida A&M University,
32307
Telephone: (904) 599-3020
State agency
Founded in: 1975
James N. Eaton, Sr.,
Historian/Archivist-Curator
Staff: full time 2, part time 2
Magazine: *Voice of the Archivist*
Major programs: archives, museum,
oral history, historic preservation,
research, photographic
collections, field services
Period of collections: 1619-1985

Bureau of Historic Preservation
500 S. Bronough St.
Telephone: (904) 487-2333
Mail to: State Capitol Bldg., 32301
State agency
Founded in: 1983
George Percy, Chief
Staff: full time 24, volunteer 2
Major programs: historic site(s),
markers, newsletters/pamphlets,
historic preservation, field services

**Florida Collection, State Library of
Florida**
R. A. Gray Bldg., 32301-8021
Telephone: (904) 487-2651
State agency

Founded in: 1925
Linda Gail Brown, Librarian, Florida
Collection
Staff: full time 2
Major programs: library, research
Period of collections: 1500-present

◇**Florida Division of Archives,
History and Records
Management**
R.A. Gray Bldg., Pensacola and
Bronough Sts., 32301
Telephone: (904) 488-1480
Founded in: 1969
Randall Kelley, Director
Staff: full time 143
Major programs: archives, museum,
historic preservaticn, markers,
junior history, educational
programs, records management,
folklife program
Period of collections:
prehistoric-present

Florida Heritage Foundation, Inc.
2227 Ruadh Ride, 32303
Questionnaire not received

**Florida State Genealogical
Society, Inc.**
P.O. Box 10249, 32302-2249
Private agency
Founded in: 1977
Elizabeth McCall, President
Number of members: 428
Staff: volunteer 14
Magazine: *The Florida Genealogist*
Major programs: library, archives,
newsletters/pamphlets,
genealogical services
Period of collections: Territorial
era-present

**Historic Tallahassee Preservation
Board**
329 N. Meridian St., 32301
Telephone: (904) 488-3901
State agency
Founded in: 1970
Linda V. Ellsworth, Director
Staff: full time 4, parttime 4
Major programs: library, historic
site(s), oral history, book
publishing, historic preservation,
research, photographic collections
Period of collections: 1821-1930

Museum of Florida History
500 S. Bronough St., 32301
Telephone: (904) 488-1484
State agency, authorized by Division
of Archives, History and Records
Management, Florida Department
of State
Founded in: 1967
Lee H. Warner, Director
Staff: full time 29, part time 6,
volunteer 75
Major programs: museum, historic
site(s), research, exhibits,
archaeology programs
Period of collections: 17th-19th
centuries

Tallahassee Historical Society
Mail to: History Department, Florida
State University, 32306
Founded in: 1933
Magazine: *Apalachee*
Questionnaire not received

Tallahassee Junior Museum
3945 Museum Dr., 32304
Telephone: (904) 576-1636
Founded in: 1957
Lane Green, Director
Number of members: 3,000
Staff: full time l6, part time 1
Major programs: museum,
  educational programs
Period of collections: 1880-1920

TAMPA

◇**Florida Historical
  Society/University of South
  Florida Library**
4202 Fowler Ave., 33620
Telephone: (813) 974-2731
Private agency
Founded in: 1856
Gary R. Mormino, Executive Director
Number of members: 1,500
Staff: full time 1
Major programs: library, archives,
  manuscripts, junior history, school
  programs, newsletters/pamphlets,
  photographic collections
Period of collections: 1512-present

**Florida Trust for Historic
  Preservation, Inc.**
Mail to: P.O. Box 10368, 33679
Founded in: 1978
Questionnaire not received

Henry B. Plant Museum
401 W. Kennedy Blvd., 33606
Telephone: (813) 253-3333
City and private agency, authorized
  by University of Tampa
Founded in: 1933
Susan V. Carter, Acting Director
Number of members: 275
Staff: full time 2, part time 3,
  volunteer 70
Major programs: tours/pilgrimages,
  school programs, exhibits
Period of collections: 1890s

**Hillsborough County Historical
  Commission**
Ccurthouse, 2nd Floor, 33602
Telephone: (813) 272-5919
County agency
Founded in: 1949
Staff: full time 1
Major programs: library, manuscripts,
  museum, research, genealogical
  services
Period of collections: 1800s

Oral History Center
4202 Fowler Ave., 33620
Questionnaire not received

**Special Collections Department,
  Tampa-Hillsborough County
  Public Library System**
900 N. Ashley St., 33602
Telephone: (813) 223-8865
County agency
Founded in: 1917
Joseph L. Hipp, Department Head
Number of members: full time 6
Major programs: library,
  photographic collections,
  genealogical services
Period of collections:
  Colonial-present

Tampa Historical Society
University of Tampa, Kennedy Blvd.
Mail to: P.O. Box 18672, 33679
Questionnaire not received

TAVARES

Lake County Historical Society
315 N. New Hampshire Ave., 32778
Private agency
Founded in: 1954
Miriam Johnson, President
Number of members: 85
Staff: part time 1, volunteer 1
Major programs: library, manuscripts,
  museum, historic site(s), oral
  history, historic preservation,
  genealogical services
Period of collections: 1880-present

VALPARAISO

Historical Society Museum
115 Westview Ave.
Telephone: (904) 678-2615
Mail to: P.O. Box 488, 32580
Founded in: 1971
Christian S. LaRoche, Director
Number of members: 150
Staff: full time 1, volunteer 25
Magazine: *New Growth*
Major programs: library, manuscripts,
  museum, junior history, oral history,
  educational programs,
  newsletters/pamphlets, research,
  exhibits
Period of collections: 1800-1950

WEST PALM BEACH

**Palm Beach County Genealogical
  Society, Inc.**
West Palm Beach Public Library, 100
  Clematis St.
Telephone: (305) 832-3279
Mail to: P.O. Box 1746, 33402
Private agency
Founded in: 1964
Number of members: 260
Staff: volunteer 50
Magazine: *Ancestry Quarterly*
Major programs: library, manuscripts,
  junior history, school programs,
  book publishing,
  newsletters/pamphlets, records
  management, research,
  audiovisual programs,
  genealogical services,
  genealogical seminars
Period of collections: 1620-present

WHITE SPRINGS

Florida Folklife Programs
Stephen Foster State Folk Culture
  Center, U.S. Hwy. 41 and State Rd.
  136
Telephone: (904) 397-2192
Mail to: P.O. Box 265, 32096
State agency, authorized by Division
  of Archives, History and Records
  Management
Founded in: 1979
Ormond H. Loomis, Director
Staff: full time 13, part time 1
Major programs: archives, museum,
  oral history, school programs,
  newsletters/pamphlets, research,
  exhibits, audiovisual programs,

photographic collections, field
  services, festivals, teacher
  programs, folklife documentaries
Period of collections: living memory

**Stephen Foster State Folk Culture
  Center**
U.S. Hwy. 41, N
Telephone: (904) 397-2733
Mail to: P.O. Drawer G, 32906
State agency, authorized by Division
  of Recreation and Parks
Founded in: 1950
R. W. Miller, Park Manager
Staff: full time 18
Major programs: museum, school
  programs, exhibits

GEORGIA

ALBANY

Thronateeska Heritage Foundation
100 Roosevelt Ave., 31701
Telephone: (912) 432-6955
Private agency
Founded in: 1964
James A. Macbeth, Executive
  Director
Staff: full time 5, part time 2,
  volunteer 8
Magazine: *The Heritage
  Express/Currents*
Major programs: archives, museum,
  historic site(s), book publishing,
  newsletters/pamphlets, historic
  preservation, research, exhibits,
  photographic collections,
  planetarium, natural history
Period of collections: 20th century

ALMA

**Historical Society of Alma-Bacon
  County**
Telephone: (912) 632-8450
Mail to: P.O. Box 2026, 31510
Founded in: 1974
Bonnie T. Baker, Director
Staff: part time 1
Major programs: library, archives,
  book publishing, research,
  photographic collections,
  genealogical services
Period of collections: 1783-present

ALPHARETTA

**Old Milton County Historical and
  Genealogical Society, Inc.**
Alpharetta City Bldg., 10 S. Main St.
Mail to: 367 Karen Dr., 30201
Founded in: 1979
Questionnaire not received

ANDERSONVILLE

Andersonville Guild
Church St., 31711
Founded in: 1973
Number of members: 100
Staff: full time 1, part time 2,
  volunteer 25
Magazine: *Andersonville Guild
  Chatter*

Major programs: museum, historic
site, tours/pilgrimages, historic
preservation
Period of collections: 1860-1865

**Andersonville National Historic
Site**
Hwy. 49, 31711
Federal agency, authorized by
National Park Service
Founded in: 1970
John N. Tucker, Superintendent
Staff: full time 15, part time 1
Major programs: library, archives,
museum, historic site(s), markers,
tours/pilgrimages, school
programs, historic preservation,
records management, research,
exhibits, living history, audiovisual
programs, archaeology programs,
photographic collections,
genealogical services, prisoner of
war history
Period of collections: 1860-1865

National Society of Andersonville
305 Ellaville St., 31711
Telephone: (912) 924-7228
Private agency
Helen H. Harden, Secretary General
Number of members: 137
Staff: volunteer 10

ATHENS

Athens-Clarke Heritage Foundation
Fire Hall 2, 489 Prince Ave., 30601
Telephone: (404) 353-1801
Private agency
Founded in: 1967
Shelia Hackney, Administrative
Director
Number of members: 400
Staff: full time 1, part time 1,
volunteer 100
Major programs: museum, historic
site, tours/pilgrimages, oral history,
educational programs,
newsletters/pamphlets, historic
preservation, exhibits,
photographic collections
Period of collections: 1820-1900

Garden Club of Georgia, Inc.
325 S. Lumpkin St., 30602
Telephone: (404) 542-3631
State agency, authorized by state
board
Founded in: 1928
Janiece L. Brannen, Executive
Secretary
Number of members: 19,704
Staff: full time 1, volunteer 91
Magazine: *Garden Gateways*
Major programs: archives, museum,
historic site(s), markers,
tours/pilgrimages, school
programs, book publishing,
newsletters/pamphlets, historic
preservation, audiovisual
programs, field services,
scholarships, botanical garden

Historic Cobbham, Inc.
Mail to: P.O. Box 534, 30603
Founded in: 1971
Number of members: 100
Staff: volunteer 25

Major programs: tours/pilgrimages,
oral history, newsletters/pamphlets,
historic preservation, photo
exhibits

**Northeast Georgia Area Planning
and Development Commission**
305 Research Dr., 30605
Telephone: (404) 548-3141
Founded in: 1961
Clinton Lane, Executive Director
Staff: full time 28, part time 1
Major programs: historic site(s),
newsletters/pamphlets, historic
preservation, records
management, research, exhibits,
audiovisual programs, field
services

Southern Historical Association
Department of History, University of
Georgia, 30602
Telephone: (404) 542-8848
Founded in: 1934
Bennett H. Wall, Secretary/Treasurer
Number of members: 3,500
Staff: full time 1, part time 1
Magazine: *Journal of Southern
History*

ATLANTA

American Society for Legal History
Telephone: (404) 658-2048
Mail to: Georgia State University
College of Law, 30303
Private agency
Founded in: 1956
L. Lynn Hogue, Secretary
Number of members: 1,000
Magazine: *Law and History Review*
Major programs: books,
newsletters/pamphlets

**Atlanta Chapter, Victorian Society
in America**
Mail to: P.O. Box 54382, Civic Center
Station 30308
Questionnaire not received

Atlanta Historical Society, Inc.
3101 Andrews Dr., NW, 30305
Telephone: (404) 261-1837
Private agency
Founded in: 1926
John H. Ott, Executive Director
Number of members: 3,550
Staff: full time 33, part time 29,
volunteer 300
Magazine: *The Atlanta Historical
Journal*
Major programs: library, archives,
manuscripts, museum, historic
site(s), school programs,
newsletters/pamphlets, records
management, research, exhibits,
photographic collections
Period of collections: 1840-1940

Atlanta Preservation Center
401 Flatiron Bldg., 84 Peachtree St.,
NW, 30303
Telephone: (404) 522-4345
Private agency
Founded in: 1980
Eileen Segrest, Executive Director
Number of members: 2,000
Staff: full time 2, part time 1,
volunteer 150
Magazine: *The Preservation Times*

Major programs: tours/pilgrimages,
junior history, school programs,
newsletters/pamphlets, historic
preservation, exhibits, audiovisual
programs
Period of collections: 1840s-present

Atlanta Urban Design Commission
10 Pryor St., Suite 200, 30303
Founded in: 1975
Questionnaire not received

**Carter Presidential Materials
Project**
77 Forsyth St., SW, 30303
Telephone: (404) 221-3942
Federal agency, authorized by
National Archives and Records
Administration
Founded in: 1981
Robert Bohanan, Archivist/Librarian
Staff: full time 13, part time 1,
volunteer 2
Major programs: library, archives,
museum, research, photographic
collections
Period of collections: 1976-1981

Cyclorama of the Battle of Atlanta
Cherokee and Park Ave., SE, 30315
Questionnaire not received

◇**Georgia Department of Archives
and History**
330 Capitol Ave., SE, 30334
Telephone: (404) 656-2393/656-2358
State agency
Founded in: 1918
Edward Weldon, Director
Staff: full time 84
Major programs: library, archives,
manuscripts, records
management, research,
micrographics, conservation
laboratory, reference service,
information management services
Period of collections: 1730-present

**Georgia Endowment for the
Humanities**
1589 Clifton Rd., NE, Emory
University, 30322
Telephone: (404) 329-7500
Private agency, authorized by
National Endowment for the
Humanities
Founded in: 1970
Ronald E. Benson, Executive Director
Staff: full time 3, part time 3, volunter
21
Magazine: *Georgia Humanities*
Major programs: library, museum,
oral history, historic preservation,
exhibits, audiovisual programs,
humanities disciplines, grants to
non-profit organizations

**Georgia Trust for Historic
Preservation, Inc.**
1516 Peachtree St., NW, 30309
Telephone: (404) 881-9980
Private agency
Founded in: 1973
Gregory Paxton, Executive Director
Number of members: 5,000
Staff: full time 9, part time 3,
volunteer 100
Major programs: museum, historic
site(s), tours/pilgrimages, school

programs, newsletters/pamphlets, historic preservation, records management, research, exhibits, audiovisual programs, field services
Period of collections: 1850-1910

Hart County, Georgia Historial Society
2073 McLendon Ave., NE, 30307
Telephone: (404) 377-5612
Private agency
Travis Parker, President
Number of members: 100
Staff: volunteer 5
Magazine: *Pioneers of Hart County, Georgia*
Major programs: archives, historic site(s), book publishing, historic preservation, research, photographic collections, genealogical services
Period of collections: 1780-1950

Historic Oakland Cemetery, Inc.
248 Oakland Ave., SE, 30312
Founded in: 1976
Number of members: 225
Staff: full time 2, volunteer 5
Magazine: *Historic Oakland News*
Major programs: historic sites preservation, tours/pilgrimages, educational programs, newsletters/pamphlets
Period of collections: 1850-present

Historic Preservation Section, Department of Natural Resources
270 Washington St., Room 704, 30334
Telephone: (404) 656-2840
State agency, authorized by State Historic Preservation Office
Founded in: 1973
Elizabeth A. Lyon, Chief, Historic Preservation
Staff: full time 20, part time 2
Major programs: newsletters/pamphlets, historic preservation, research, archaeology programs, field services
Period of collections: prehistoric-present

Inman Park Restoration, Inc.
Telephone: (404) 588-9745 (secretary)
Mail to: P.O. Box 5234, 30307
Private agency
Founded in: 1971
Jerry Thomas, President
Number of members: 300
Staff: volunteer 6
Major programs: historic preservation

Martin Luther King, Jr., Center for Nonviolent Social Change
449 Auburn Ave., NE, 30312
Telephone: (404) 524-1956
Private agency
Founded in: 1968
Coretta Scott King, President
Staff: 45
Major programs: library, archives, manuscripts, museum, historic site(s), tours/pilgrimages, oral history, research, exhibits, audiovisual programs
Period of collections: 1955-1970

Martin Luther King, Jr., National Historic Site
522 Auburn Ave., NE, 30312
Telephone: (404) 221-5190
Federal agency, authorized by National Park Service
Founded in: 1980
Floretta P. Daniel, Administrative Officer

National Archives—Atlanta Branch
1557 St. Joseph Ave., 30344
Telephone: (404) 763-7477
Founded in: 1969
Gayle P. Peters, Director
Staff: full time 4
Major programs: archives, educational programs, teachers' workshops, genealogical workshops, film series, open houses and tours
Period of collections: 1716-1982

Society of Georgia Archivists
Telephone: (404) 658-2476/656-2379
Mail to: P.O. Box 261, Georgia State University, 30303
Founded in: 1969
Nancy Bryant, President
Number of members: 200
Magazine: *Provenance*
Major programs: educational programs, newsletters/pamphlets

AUGUSTA

Augusta Genealogical Society, Inc.
598 Telfair St., East Room, 3rd Floor, 30902
Telephone: (404) 722-4073/738-2241
Mail to: P.O. Box 3743, 30904
Private agency
Founded in: 1979
Russell R. Moores, President
Number of members: 804
Staff: volunteer 200
Magazine: *Ancestoring/Southern Echoes*
Major programs: library, archives, manuscripts, tours, school programs, book publishing, newsletters/pamphlets, research, genealogical services
Period of collections: 1780-present

Augusta Richmond County Museum
540 Telfair St., 30901
Telephone: (404) 722-8454
Private agency
Founded in: 1937
Richard Wescott, Director
Number of members: 500
Staff: full time 3, part time 3, volunteer 50
Major programs: museum, educational programs, historic preservation
Period of collections: prehistoric-W.W. II

Historic Augusta, Inc.
1840 Broad St., 30904
Telephone: (404) 733-6768
Private agency
Founded in: 1964
P. D. Baxter, Executive Director
Number of members: 350
Staff: full time 1, part time 2, volunteer 10

Major programs: historic site(s), tours/pilgrimages, school programs, historic preservation
Period of collections: 1800-1850

Richmond County Historical Society
Reese Library, Augusta College, 2500 Walton Way, 30910
Telephone: (404) 737-1745
Private agency
Founded in: 1946
A. Ray Rowland, Curator
Number of members: 707
Staff: volunteer 2
Magazine: *Richmond County History*
Major programs: library, archives, manuscripts, book publishing, newsletters/pamphlets, research, genealogical services
Period of collections: 1786-present

BARNESVILLE

Barnesville-Lamar County Historical Society
888 Thomaston St., 30204
Telephone: (404) 358-1289
Founded in: 1973
Sid Cheatham, President
Number of members: 25
Major programs: book publishing
Period of collections: 1850-present

BAXLEY

Appling County Historical Society, Inc.
Appling County Community Education Center
Telephone: (912) 367-2431
Mail to: P.O. Box 1063, 31513-7063
Private agency
Founded in: 1984
Carlos F. Crosby, Jr., President/Director of Community Education
Number of members: 110
Staff: volunteer 7
Major programs: library, archives, historic site(s), oral history, newsletters/pamphlets, historic preservation, records management, exhibits, living history, audiovisual programs, archaeology programs, photographic collections, community education

BLAKELEY

Early County Historical Society, Inc.
255 N. Main, 31723
Founded in: 1968
Number of members: 85
Staff: volunteer 2
Period of collections: 1865-present

BRUNSWICK

Coastal APDC Advisory Council on Historic Preservation
Bay and F Sts.
Telephone: (912) 264-7363
Mail to: P.O. Box 1917, 31521
Authorized by Coastal Area Planning and Development Commission
Founded in: 1978

Ty Potterfield, Historic Preservation
 Planner
Number of members: 30
Staff: full time 1, part time 1
Major programs: tours/pilgrimages,
 school programs, historic
 preservation, research
Period of collections: 1733-1920

BUCHANAN

**Haralson County Historical
 Society, Inc.**
Courthouse Square, 30113
Private agency
Founded in: 1973
Mrs. H.D. Lasseter, Treasurer
Number of members: 100
Staff: volunteer 15
Major programs: library, museum,
 historic site(s), oral history, historic
 preservation, living history
Period of collections: 1891-present

BUFORD

Lanier Museum of Natural History
2601 Buford Dam Rd., 30518
Telephone: (404) 945-3543
County agency
Founded in: 1976
Elfrieda Phillips, Director
Staff: full time 1
Major programs: museum, historic
 site(s), tours/pilgrimages, school
 programs, newsletters/pamphlets,
 historic preservation, wildlife
 exhibits, natural history
Period of collections: 1818s

CALHOUN

**Gordon County Historical
 Society, Inc.**
102 Court St.
Mail to: P.O. Box 342, 30701
Founded in: 1974
Number of members: 225
Staff: full time 1, volunteer 10
Major programs: museum, historic
 sites preservation, markers, books,
 newsletters/pamphlets
Period of collections: 1918-present

CARROLLTON

**Carroll County Historical
 Society, Inc.**
c/o West Georgia Regional Library,
 P.O. Box 160, 30117
Founded in: 1975
Mrs. Frances Long, President
Number of members: 31
Major programs: tours, educational
 programs

CARTERSVILLE

Etowah Valley Historical Society
Rt. 1, 30120
Mail to: Rt. 2, Kingston, 30145
Questionnaire not received

CEDARTOWN

Polk County Historical Society
College St.
Mail to: P.O. Box 7, 30125
Private agency
Founded in: 1974
Mary Clyde Rentz, President

Number of members: 200
Staff: volunteer 15
Major programs: museum, historic
 preservation, exhibits
Period of collections: 1850-present

CLEVELAND

White County Historical Society
Town Square
Mail to: Box 281, 30528
Founded in: 1965
Number of members: 200
Staff: volunteer 4
Major programs: library, manuscripts,
 historic sites preservation,
 tours/pilgrimages,
 newsletters/pamphlets
Period of collections: 1865-present

CLINTON

Old Clinton Historical Society, Inc.
31032
Telephone: (912) 986-3384
Private agency
Founded in: 1974
Mrs. Earl H. Hamilton, President
Number of members: 128
Staff: volunteer 26
Major programs: tours/pilgrimages,
 school programs,
 newsletters/pamphlets, historic
 preservation, research, living
 history, audiovisual programs
Period of collections: 1783-1865

COCHRAN

Bleckley County Historical Society
Middle Georgia College, 31014
Telephone: (912) 934-6221
Private agency
Founded in: 1976
Louis C. Alderman, Jr., President
Major programs: library, museum,
 historic site(s), markers,
 tours/pilgrimages, oral history,
 exhibits

COLLEGE PARK

**College Park Historical
 Society, Inc.**
3336 E. Main St.
Mail to: P.O. Box F, 30337
Private agency
Founded in: 1978
Ralph L. Presley, President
Number of members: 92
Major programs: library, archives,
 oral history, audiovisual programs,
 photographic collections,
 genealogical services
Period of collections: 1896-present

COLUMBUS

**Historic Columbus
 Foundation, Inc.**
700 Broadway, 31901
Telephone: (404) 322-0756
Mail to: P.O. Box 5312, 31906
Private agency
Founded in: 1966
Mrs. James J.W. Biggers, Jr.,
 Executive Director
Number of members: 1,300
Staff: full time 3, volunteer 600
Major programs: archives, museum,
 historic site(s), markers,

tours/pilgrimages, school
 programs, newsletters/pamphlets,
 historic preservation, research,
 audiovisual programs,
 photographic collections
Period of collections: 1828-present

**Historic District Preservation
 Society, Inc.**
545 Broadway, 31901
Telephone: (404) 571-2245
Mail to: P.O. Box 263, 31902
Founded in: 1975
Staff: volunteer 12
Magazine: *The District Voice*
Major programs: library, markers,
 tours/pilgrimages, educational
 programs, newsletters/pamphlets,
 historic preservation, tree planting
 program, public grounds
 maintenance and beautification

**William Henry Spencer Golden
 Owlettes, Inc.**
P.O. Box 1516, 31902
Telephone: (404) 322-1014
Founded in: 1973
Charlotte H. Frazier, Program Director
Number of members: 31
Staff: full time 1, volunteer 31
Major programs: archives, museum,
 historic site, markers,
 tours/pilgrimages, oral history,
 educational programs,
 newsletters/pamphlets, historic
 preservation, neighborhood rehab
 in the minority community
Period of collections: 1800-present

CONYERS

Rockdale County Historical Society
Mail to: P.O. Box 351, 30207
Founded in: 1973
Harriet B. Gattis, President
Number of members: 175
Major programs: archives, museum,
 historic site(s), junior history, oral
 history, newsletters/pamphlets,
 historic preservation, research
Period of collections: 1865-1918

CRAWFORDVILLE

**Taliaferro County Historical
 Society, Inc.**
Broad St.
Telephone: (404) 456-2140
Mail to: P.O. Box 32, 30631
Founded in: 1979
A. Mell Lunceford, Jr., President
Number of members: 150
Staff: volunteer 4
Magazine: *Historical Highlights*
Major programs: library, archives,
 manuscripts, historic site(s),
 tours/pilgrimages, oral history,
 book publishing,
 newsletters/pamphlets, historic
 preservation, exhibits,
 photographic collections,
 genealogical services
Period of collections: 1900

CUTHBERT

Randolph Historical Society, Inc.
Mail to: P.O. Box 456, 31740
Founded in: 1973
Questionnaire not received

DAHLONEGA

Dahlonega Courthouse Gold Museum
Public Square
Telephone: (404) 864-2257
Mail to: P.O. Box 2042, 30533
State agency, authorized by Georgia
Department of Natural Resources
Founded in: 1966
Sharon Johnson, Superintendent
Staff: full time 2, part time 2
Major programs: library, archives, museum, historic site(s), markers, tours/pilgrimages, junior history, oral history, school programs, book publishing, newsletters/pamphlets, historic preservation, records management, research, exhibits, audiovisual programs, photographic collections, genealogical services, field services
Period of collections: 1830-1930

DALTON

Whitfield-Murray Historical Society, Inc.
715 Chattanooga Ave., 30720
Telephone: (404) 278-0217
Private agency
Founded in: 1976
Polly Boggess, Executive Director
Number of members: 525
Staff: full time 1, volunteer 6
Major programs: library, archives, manuscripts, museum, historic site, tours/pilgrimages, oral history, educational programs, book publishing, newsletters/pamphlets, historic preservation, research, genealogical services
Period of collections: 1832-present

DARIEN

Ft. King George Historic Site
Ft. King George Dr.
Telephone: (912) 437-4770
Mail to: P.O. Box 711, 31305
State agency, authorized by Department of Natural Resources, Parks, Recreation and Historic Sites Division
Founded in: 1968
Staff: full time 3, part time 4
Major programs: museum, historic site(s), markers, school programs, historic preservation, research, exhibits, living history, audiovisual programs, photographic collections
Period of collections: prehistoric-1925

DECATUR

DeKalb Historical Society
Old Courthouse on the Square, 30030
Telephone: (404) 373-1088
Founded in: 1947
Dorothy Nix, Executive Director
Number of members: 1,264
Staff: full time 2, part time 1, volunteer 20
Major programs: library, archives, museum, historic site(s), tours/pilgrimages, oral history, newsletters/pamphlets, genealogical services
Period of collections: 1822-1922

DUBLIN

Dublin-Laurens Museum
Bellevue at Church St.
Telephone: (912) 272-9242
Mail to: P.O. Box 1461, 31040
Private agency, authorized by Laurens County Historical Society, Inc.
Founded in: 1967
John N. Ross, Director
Number of members: 850
Staff: full time 1, volunteer 40
Major programs: manuscripts, museum, historic site(s), markers, tours/pilgrimages, oral history, school programs, newsletters/pamphlets, exhibits, audiovisual programs, photographic collections
Period of collections: late 19th-early 20th centuries

Laurens County Historical Society, Inc.
Bellevue and Academy Ave.
Telephone: (912) 272-9242
Mail to: P.O. Box 1461, 31021
Private agency
Founded in: 1967
John N. Ross, Director
Number of members: 800
Staff: volunteer 50
Major programs: museum, newsletters/pamphlets, exhibits, photographic collections
Period of collections: late 19th-early 20th centuries

DULUTH

Southeastern Railway Museum
3966 Buford Hwy., 30136
Telephone: (404) 476-2013
Private agency
Founded in: 1968
Michael E. Cosgrove, President
Number of members: 275
Staff: volunteer 30
Magazine: *Hot Box*
Major programs: library, museum, historic preservation, exhibits
Period of collections: 1890-present

EAST POINT

East Point Historical Society, Inc.
City Hall Annex, 2847 Main St., 30344
Telephone: (404) 767-4656
City agency
Founded in: 1979
Douglas H. Purdie, President
Staff: volunteer 10
Major programs: archives, book publishing, records management
Period of collections: 1895-present

EATONTON

Eatonton-Putnam County Historical Society, Inc.
Mail to: P.O. Box 331, 31024
Telephone: (404) 485-7701
Private agency
Founded in: 1974
James P. Marshall, Jr., President
Number of members: 225
Staff: volunteer 25
Major programs: archives, museum, historic site(s), markers,

tours/pilgrimages, newsletters/pamphlets, historic preservation, exhibits, living history, photographic collections, genealogical services
Period of collections: 1810-present

ELBERTON

Elbert County Historical Society, Inc.
Mail to: P.O. Box 1033, 30635
Questionnaire not received

FAIRBURN

Old Campbell County Historical Society, Inc.
Courthouse, E. Broad St.
Mail to: P.O. Box 153, 30213
Questionnaire not received

FAYETTEVILLE

Fayette County Historical Society, Inc.
Telephone: (404) 461-7152
Mail to: P.O. Box 421, 30214
Private agency
Founded in: 1972
Carolyn J. Cary, President
Number of members: 50
Staff: volunteer 10
Major programs: archives, historic site(s), tours/pilgrimages, oral history, books, historic preservation, records management, photographic collections
Period of collections: 1821-present

FOLKSTON

Charlton County Historical Society
Rt. 3, Box 142-C, 31537
Telephone: (912) 496-7401
Private agency
Founded in: 1977
Lois B. Mays, President
Number of members: 30
Staff: part time 1, volunteer 5
Major programs: archives, book publishing
Period of collections: 1900-1950

FORT BENNING

National Infantry Museum
Baltzell Ave., 31905.
Questionnaire not received

FORT GAINES

Ft. Gaines Historical Society, Inc.
308 E. Jefferson St.
Mail to: P.O. Box 6, 31751
Founded in: 1969
Questionnaire not received

FORT GORDON

Ft. Gordon Museum, U.S. Army Signal Center
36th St. and 4th Ave., Bldg. 36301, 30905
Telephone: (404) 791-2818
Federal agency, authorized by Center of Military History
Founded in: 1965
Theodore F. Wise, Director/Curator
Number of members: 2

Staff: full time 6
Major programs: archives, museum, historic site(s), tours/pilgrimages, school programs, historic preservation, records management, research, exhibits, audiovisual programs, archaeology programs
Period of collections: 1860-present

FORT OGLETHORPE

Chickamauga and Chattanooga National Military Park
P.O. Box 2128, 30742
Telephone: (404) 866-9241
Federal agency, authorized by National Park Service
Founded in: 1890
M. Ann Belkov, Superintendent
Staff: full time 12, part time 10, volunteer 20
Major programs: library, museum, historic site(s), markers, tours/pilgrimages, historic preservation, research, exhibits, living history, audiovisual programs
Period of collections: Civil War era

Ft. Oglethorpe Preservation Society
Mail to: P.O. Box 5321, 37042
Founded in: 1974
Number of members: 48
Questionnaire not received

FT. STEWART

Ft. Stewart Museum, 24th Infantry Division
Bldg. T-814, Wilson Ave. at Utility St.
Telephone: (912) 767-7885
Mail to: ATTN: AFZP-PTO-PM, 31314-5082
Federal agency, authorized by the U.S. Army
Founded in: 1977
Ray J. Kinder, Museum Curator
Staff: full time 2
Major programs: library, archives, museum, tours
Period of collections: Civil War-Vietnam Conflict

GAINESVILLE

Gainesville Heritage Group
Mail to: Brenau College, 30501
Questionnaire not received

GREENSBORO

Greene County Historical Society
County agency, authorized by Greene County Commission
Founded in: 1976
E. H. Armor, County Historian
Number of members: 300
Staff: volunteer 12
Major programs: museum, historic site(s), tours/pilgrimages, research, exhibits, archaeology programs, photographic collections, genealogical services, cemetery cataloguing

GRIFFIN

Griffin Historical and Preservation Society
406 N. Hill St., 30223
Mail to: P.O. Box 196, 30224

Founded in: 1969
N. Crouch, Secretary
Staff: part time 1
Magazine: *The Artifact*
Major programs: archives, historic site, markers, newsletters/pamphlets, historic preservation
Period of collections: 1840-present

GUYTON

Guyton Historical Society
Central Blvd.
Telephone: (912) 772-3344
Mail to: P.O. Box 15, 31312
Private agency
Founded in: 1976
Herman Alsobrook, President
Number of members: 200
Major programs: markers, tours/pilgrimages, oral history, historic preservation, research
Period of collections: 1838-1920

HAWKINSVILLE

Pulaski Historical Commission, Inc.
Telephone: (912) 783-1717
Mail to: P.O. Box 447, 31036
Private agency
Founded in: 1972
Frances T. Kimberly, President
Number of members: 50
Staff: volunteer 15
Major programs: museum, historic preservation of opera house
Period of collections: 1907

HINESVILLE

Liberty County Historical Society
Mail to: P.O. Box 797, 31313
Founded in: 1967
Questionnaire not received

HOMERVILLE

Huxford Genealogical Society, Inc.
Old High School Bldg.
Telephone: (912) 487-2310
Mail to: P.O. Box 595, 31634
Private agency
Founded in: 1972
Michele S. Beach, Secretary
Number of members: 430
Staff: full time 1, part time 1
Magazine: *Huxford Genealogical Society Quarterly*
Major programs: library
Period of collections: 1492-present

JEFFERSON

Jackson County Historical Society
Mail to: c/o President, Rt. 2, Box 222, Commerce, 30529
Founded in: 1974
Mrs. W. H. Booth, President
Number of members: 40
Major programs: school programs

JEKYLL ISLAND

Jekyll Island Museum
375 Riverview Dr., 31520
Telephone: (912) 635-2236
State agency, authorized by Jekyll Island Authority
Founded in: 1947

Thomas A. Rhodes, Museums and Historic Preservation Director
Staff: full time 11, part time 13, volunteer 3
Major programs: archives, museum, historic site(s), tours/pilgrimages, school programs, historic preservation, research, exhibits, photographic collections
Period of collections: 1885-1930

JONESBORO

Historical Jonesboro, Inc.
Mail to: P.O. Box 922, 30236
Private agency
Founded in: 1968
Mrs. Robert Woodward, Chair
Number of members: 285
Staff: volunteer 18
Major programs: museum, historic site(s), tours/pilgrimages, school programs, newsletters/pamphlets, historic preservation, research, exhibits, audiovisual programs
Period of collections: Civil War era

JULIETTE

Jarrell Plantation Historic Site
Rt. 1, Box 40, 31046
Telephone: (912) 986-5172
State agency, authorized by Department of Natural Resources
Founded in: 1974
Edwill R. Holcomb, Superintendent
Staff: full time 2, part time 2
Major programs: historic site(s), school programs, historic preservation, living history
Period of collections: 1890-1930

KENNESAW

Big Shanty Museum
2829 Cherokee St.
Mail to: P.O. Box 418, 30144
Founded in: 1972
Questionnaire not received

LAFAYETTE

Walker County Historical Society
305 S. Duke St.
Mail to: P.O. Box 707, 30728
Founded in: 1976
Questionnaire not received

LA GRANGE

Ocfuskee Historical Society, Inc.
Mail to: P.O. Box 1051, 30241
Questionnaire not received

Troup County Historical Society, Inc.—Archives
136 Main St.
Telephone: (404) 884-1828
Mail to: P.O. Box 1051, 30241
Private agency
Founded in: 1972 (society); 1982 (archives)
Kaye Lanning, Director
Number of members: 300
Staff: full time 2, part time 2, volunteer 5
Major programs: library, archives, manuscripts, junior history, newsletters/pamphlets, historic preservation, records management, research, exhibits,

photographic collections,
genealogical services
Period of collections: 1828-present

LAWRENCEVILLE

**Gwinnett County Historical
Society, Inc.**
221 N. Clayton St.
Telephone: (404) 963-9584
Mail to: P.O. Box 261, 30246
Private agency
Founded in: 1966
Alice Smythe McCabe, President
Number of members: 400
Staff: volunteer 5
Major programs: book publishing,
newsletters/pamphlets, historic
preservation
Period of collections: 1818-present

LITHIA SPRINGS

Bartram Trail Society
6688 Marsh Ave., 30057
Founded in: 1970
Questionnaire not received

LUMPKIN

**Stewart County Historical
Commission**
Corner, Broad and Cotton Sts.
Telephone: (912) 838-4201
Mail to: P.O. Box 817, 31815
Private agency
Founded in: 1965
Mrs. W.E. Cannington, Chair
Staff: volunteer 25
Major programs: museum, historic
site, tours/pilgrimages, book
publishing, historic preservation
Period of collections: 1836-1846

Westville Historic Handicrafts, Inc.
Troutman Rd.
Telephone: (912) 838-6310
Mail to: P.O. Box 1850, 31815
Private agency
Founded in: 1966
Matthew Moye, Executive Director
Number of members: 507
Staff: full time 12, part time 15,
volunteer 100
Magazine: *Westville Mirror*
Major programs: library, museum,
oral history, school programs,
newsletters/pamphlets, historic
preservation, research, living
history
Period of collections: 1827-1860

MACON

Georgia Baptist Historical Society
Mercer University Library, Colman
Ave., 31207
Telephone: (912) 745-6811
Founded in: 1964
Mary Overby, Curator
Number of members: 135
Staff: full time 1
Magazine: *Viewpoints in Georgia
History*
Major programs: library, archives,
manuscripts, historic preservation

Hay House
934 Georgia Ave., 31201
Telephone: (912) 742-8155

Private agency, authorized by
Georgia Trust for Historic
Preservation
Founded in: 1977
Bruce T. Sherwood, Director
Staff: full time 1, part time 4,
volunteer 27
Major programs: museum, historic
site(s), tours/pilgrimages, school
programs, historic preservation,
architecture
Period of collections: 1820-1920

Macon Heritage Foundation, Inc.
652 Mulberry St., 31201
Telephone: (912) 742-5084
Mail to: P.O. Box 6092, 31208
Private agency
Founded in: 1975
Maryel Battin, Executive Director
Number of members: 800
Magazine: *Preservation Gazette*
Major programs: historic preservation

**Middle Georgia Historical
Society, Inc.**
935 High St., 31201
Telephone: (912) 743-3851
Private agency
Founded in: 1964
Katherine C. Oliver, Executive
Director
Number of members: 1,000
Staff: full time 2, part time 8,
volunteer 150
Major programs: archives, historic
site, educational programs,
newsletters/pamphlets, research
Period of collections: 1780s-present

Ocmulgee National Monument
1207 Emery Hwy., 31201
Telephone: (912) 742-0447
Federal agency, authorized by
National Park Service
Founded in: 1936
Sibbald Smith, Superintendent
Staff: full time 11, part time 3,
volunteer 1
Major programs: library, museum,
markers, tours/pilgrimages, historic
preservation, records
management, research, exhibits,
audiovisual programs, archaeology
programs, photographic
collections
Period of collections: Ice Age-Creek
Indian era

MADISON

**Madison-Morgan Cultural Center,
Morgan County Foundation, Inc.**
434 S. Main St., 30650
Telephone: (404) 342-4743
Private agency
Founded in: 1957 (foundation); 1976
(cultural center)
Elizabeth P. Reynolds, Executive
Director
Number of members: 1,500
Staff: full time 4, part time 1,
volunteer 50
Major programs: museum, school
programs, newsletters/pamphlets,
exhibits
Period of collections: 1830-1920

**Morgan County Landmarks
Society, Inc.**
373 W. Central Ave., 30650
Founded in: 1970
Questionnaire not received

MARIETTA

Cobb County Genealogical Society
P.O. Box 1413, 30062
Telephone: (404) 233-7328
Private agency
Douglas R. Davis, President
Number of members: 90
Staff: volunteer 15
Magazine: *Family Tree*
Major programs: book publishing,
newsletters/pamphlets, cemetery
cataloguing

**Kennesaw Mountain National
Battlefield Park**
Stilesboro Rd.
Telephone: (404) 427-4686
Mail to: P.O. Box 1167, 30061
Federal agency, authorized by
National Park Service
Founded in: 1929
Ralph Bullard, Superintendent
Staff: full time 18, part time 4,
volunteer 10
Major programs: library, museum,
historic site(s), markers, historic
preservation, exhibits, living history
Period of collections: 1864

METTER

Candler County Historical Society
Telephone: (912) 685-2771
Mail to: P.O. Box 235, 30439
Private agency
Founded in: 1981
Willette Watson, President
Number of members: 20
Staff: volunteer 15
Major programs: markers, records
management, research

MIDWAY

Midway Museum, Inc.
U.S. Hwy. 17
Mail to: P.O. Box 195, 31320
Joann Clark, Curator
Number of members: 125
Staff: volunteer 24
Major programs: museum,
tours/pilgrimages, junior history,
oral history, newsletters/pamphlets,
research, exhibits, audiovisual
programs, genealogical services

MILLEDGEVILLE

**Museum and Archives of Georgia
Education**
131 Clark St.
Telephone: (912) 453-4391
Mail to: Georgia College, P.O. Box
702, 31061
State agency, authorized by the state
university system
Founded in: 1975

Louiseann Richter, Director
Staff: part time 3
Major programs: library, archives,
manuscripts, tours/pilgrimages,
oral history, school programs, book
publishing, records management,
research, exhibits, audiovisual
programs, archaeology programs,
photographic collections,
education history
Period of collections: to 1950

Old Capital Historical Society
Mail to: P.O. Box 4, 31061
Founded in: 1954
Questionnaire not received

MONROE

**Historical Society of Walton
County, Inc.**
238 N. Broad St., 30655
Questionnaire not received

MONTICELLO

**Jasper County Historical
Foundation, Inc.**
College St.
Telephone: (404) 468-6637
Mail to: 128 Robert Dr., 31064
Private agency
Founded in: 1975
Marcia Carnes
Number of members: 55
Staff: volunteer 10
Major programs: archives, book
publishing, historic preservation,
research, genealogical services
Period of collections: mid 1800s-early
1900s

MORROW

**Clayton County Heritage
Association**
P.O. Box 305, 30260
Telephone: (404) 961-3460
Private agency
Founded in: 1983
Carl Rhodenizer, President
Number of members: 40
Major programs: museum, historic
site(s), school programs, historic
preservation

MOULTRIE

Colquitt County Historical Society
31768
Mail to: Norman Park, Rt. 1, 31771
Founded in: 1976
Number of members: 50
Staff: volunteer 3
Major programs: museum,
tours/pilgrimages, historic
preservation

NEWNAN

Newnan-Coweta Historical Society
30 Temple Ave., 30263
Telephone: (404) 251-0207
Mail to: P.O. Box 1001, 30264
Founded in: 1972
Elizabeth A. Beers, President
Number of members: 200
Staff: volunteer 12
Major programs: museum, historic
site, markers, tours/pilgrimages,

junior history, educational
programs, book publishing, historic
preservation
Period of collections: 19th-early 20th
centuries

OXFORD

Oxford Historical Shrine Society
Mail to: P.O. Box 243, 30267
Founded in: 1974
Questionnaire not received

PELHAM

**Arts and Heritage Council of
Pelham**
415 W. Railroad St.
Mail to: P.O. Box 389, 31779
Founded in: 1978
Questionnaire not received

PORTAL

Portal Heritage Society
c/o Denver Hollingsworth, 301
College Blvd., Statesboro, 30458
Telephone: (912) 764-3047
Private agency
Founded in: 1982
Denver Hollingsworth, President
Number of members: 100
Staff: volunteer 40
Major programs: historic site(s),
historic preservation, exhibits,
living history, annual festival
Period of collections: 1900-1939

REIDSVILLE

**Tattnall County Historic
Preservation, Inc.**
Telephone: (912) 557-4802
Mail to: P.O. Box 392, 30453
Private agency
Founded in: 1980
Jack Hill, President
Number of members: 75
Staff: volunteer 20
Major programs: historic site(s),
newsletters/pamphlets, historic
preservation

Tattnall County Historical Society
30453
Founded in: 1973
Questionnaire not received

ROME

**Northwest Georgia Historical and
Genealogical Society**
Mail to: P.O. Box 2484, 30161
Founded in: 1965
Questionnaire not received

ROOPVILLE

**Roopville Historical Society and
Archives**
Hwy. 27, S.
Telephone: (404) 854-4170
Mail to: 124 Old Franklin St., 30171
City agency
Founded in: 1983
Rebecca Merrell, President
Number of members: 15
Major programs: archives, historic
preservation, photographic
collections
Period of collections: 1983-present

ROSSVILLE

Chief John Ross House
212 Andrews St.
Telephone: (404) 861-0342
Mail to: P.O. Box 863, 30741
Private agency, authorized by John
Ross House Association
Founded in: 1963
Frances W. Jackson, President
Number of members: 135
Staff: part time 1, volunteer 9
Major programs: historic site(s),
tours/pilgrimages, oral history,
school programs, historic
preservation, living history,
photographic collections
Period of collections: 1798-1820

**Whistles in the Woods Museum
Services**
Hwy. 341, Rt. 1, Box 265-A, 30741
Founded in: 1954
Questionnaire not received

ROSWELL

Roswell Historical Society
P.O. Box 274, 30075
Telephone: (404) 992-1665
Founded in: 1973
Gloria Conrad, President
Number of members: 800
Staff: volunteer 200
Major programs: library, archives,
manuscripts, museum, historic
site(s), markers, tours/pilgrimages,
junior history, oral history, school
programs, book publishing,
newsletters/pamphlets, historic
preservation, audiovisual
programs, photographic
collections
Period of collections: 1840-1860

Roswell Historical Society
Bulloch Ave., 30075
Mail to: P.O. Box 274, 30077
Founded in: 1971
Number of members: 549
Staff: volunteer 38
Major programs: archives, museum,
historic site, markers,
tours/pilgrimages, oral history,
book publishing,
newsletters/pamphlets, historic
preservation
Period of collections: 1836-1900s

ST. MARYS

Guale Historical Society, Inc.
P.O. Box 398, 31558
Founded in: 1979
Number of members: 31
Magazine: *Guale News*
Major programs: historic
preservation, cemetery surveys

**St. Marys Historic Preservation
Commission**
414 Osborne St., 31558
Telephone: (912) 882-4667
Town agency
Founded in: 1984
Wiley King
Staff: full time 1, part time 1

Major programs: historic site(s),
historic preservation
Period of collections: 1788-1920

ST. SIMONS ISLAND

Arthur J. Moore Methodist Museum
Arthur Moore Dr., P.O. Box 407,
31522
Telephone: (912) 638-4050
Private agency, authorized by S.
Georgia Conference Center
Founded in: 1965
Betty Bryde, Director/Curator
Staff: full time 1, part time 1,
volunteer 6
Magazine: *Historical Highlights*
Major programs: library, archives,
manuscripts, museum, records
management, research, exhibits,
audiovisual programs,
genealogical services
Period of collections: 1850-present

**Coastal Georgia Historical
Society—Museum of Coastal
History**
610 Beachview
Telephone: (912) 638-4666
Mail to: P.O. Box 1136, 31522
Private agency
Founded in: 1965
Anne Shelander, Director/Curator
Number of members: 510
Staff: full time 2, volunteer 70
Major programs: archives,
manuscripts, museum, historic
site(s), tours,
newsletters/pamphlets, research,
exhibits, photographic collections
Period of collections: 1788-present

Ft. Frederica National Monument
Rt. 4, Box 286-C, 31522
Telephone: (912) 638-3630
Federal agency, authorized by
National Park Service
Founded in: 1936
Ellen Britton, Superintendent
Staff: full time 9, part time 8,
volunteer 5
Major programs: museum, historic
site(s), tours/pilgrimages, book
publishing, historic preservation,
living history, archaeology
programs
Period of collections: 1736-1760s

**Historical Society of the South
Georgia Conference, United
Methodist Church**
P.O. Box 407, 31522
Telephone: (912) 638-4050
Private agency
Founded in: 1915
Mrs. Alvis Waite, President
Number of members: 200
Staff: full time 1, part time 1,
volunteer 12
Magazine: *Historical Highlights*
Major programs: archives, museum,
historic preservation, exhibits,
audiovisual programs, Methodism
Period of collections: 19th century

SAVANNAH

Coastal Heritage Society
1 Ft. Jackson Rd., 31402
Telephone: (912) 232-3945

Private agency
Founded in: 1975
Scott W. Smith, Director
Number of members: 500
Staff: full time 2, part time 3,
volunteer 100
Major programs: museum, historic
site(s), school programs, book
publishing, newsletters/pamphlets,
historic preservation, research,
exhibits, living history, audiovisual
programs
Period of collections: 1808-1876

◇**Georgia Historical Society**
501 Whitaker St., 31499
Telephone: (912) 944-2128
Private agency
Founded in: 1839
Harold B. Gill, Jr., Director
Number of members: 2,300
Staff: full time 4, part time 2,
volunteer 5
Magazine: *Georgia Historical
Quarterly*
Major programs: library, archives,
manuscripts,
newsletters/pamphlets, research,
photographic collections,
genealogical services
Period of collections: 18th-19th
centuries

Georgia Salzburger Society
9375 Whitfield Ave., 31406
Telephone: (912) 355-1825
Private agency
Founded in: 1925
Mrs. Charles A. LeBey, Curator
Number of members: 1,700
Staff: volunteer 15
Major programs: museum, historic
site, book publishing,
newsletters/pamphlets, historic
preservation, genealogical
services
Period of collections: 1734-1900

Historic Savannah Foundation, Inc.
41 W. Broad St., 31401
Mail to: P.O. Box 1733, 31402
Founded in: 1955
Number of members: 1,000
Staff: full time 13, part time 3,
volunteer 250
Major programs: museum, historic
sites preservation, tours, books,
newsletters/pamphlets
Period of collections: 1790-1850

**Juliette Gordon Low Girl Scout
National Center**
142 Bull St., 31401
Telephone: (912) 233-4501
Private agency, authorized by Girl
Scouts of the U.S.A.
Founded in: 1956
Fran W. Powell, Director
Staff: full time 9, part time 20,
volunteer 30
Major programs: archives, museum,
educational programs, historic
sites
Period of collections: 1820-1927

Old Ft. Jackson
1 Old Ft. Jackson Rd., 31401
Telephone: (912) 232-3945
Private agency, authorized by
Coastal Heritage Society
Founded in: 1976

Scott W. Smith, Director
Number of members: 300
Staff: full time 3, part time 6,
volunteer 24
Major programs: museum, historic
site(s), school programs, book
publishing, newsletters/pamphlets,
historic preservation, research,
living history
Period of collections: Civil War era

Owens-Thomas House Museum
124 Abercorn St., 31401
Telephone: (912) 233-9743
Private agency, authorized by Telfair
Academy of Arts and Sciences
Founded in: 1951
Agnes M. Tison, Curator
Staff: full time 4, part time 5,
volunteer 3
Major programs: library,
newsletters/pamphlets, historic
preservation
Period of collections: 1780-1870

**Savannah-Yamacraw Branch,
Association for the Study of
Afro-American Life and History**
King-Tisdell Cottage, 514 E.
Huntingdon St., 31401
Telephone: (912) 234-8000
Private agency
Founded in: 1977
W. W. Law, President
Number of members: 500
Staff: full time 1, volunteer 25
Major programs: library, archives,
museum, markers,
tours/pilgrimages, oral history,
school programs, historic
preservation, research, exhibits,
audiovisual programs,
photographic collections
Period of collections: 1800-1950

Ships of the Sea Museum
503 River St., 31401
Telephone: (912) 232-1511
Founded in: 1966
David T. Guernsey, Jr., Executive
Director
Staff: full time 7
Major programs: library, archives,
museum, historic sites
preservation, tours/pilgrimages
Period of collections: 1492-present

**Telfair Academy of Arts and
Sciences, Inc.**
121 Barnard St.
Telephone: (912) 232-1177
Mail to: P.O. Box 10081, 31412
Private agency
Founded in: 1875
David M. Robb, Jr., Executive
Director
Number of members: 1,100
Staff: full time 11, part time 3
Major programs: library, museum,
historic site(s), tours/pilgrimages,
historic preservation, research,
exhibits
Period of collections: 18th-early 20th
centuries

SOCIAL CIRCLE

**Historic Preservation Society of
Social Circle, Inc.**
P.O. Box 832, 30279
Telephone: (404) 464-2345

Private agency
Founded in: 1980
R. A. Hathaway, President
Number of members: 50
Staff: volunteer 12
Major programs: library, archives, historic site(s), markers, tours/pilgrimages, historic preservation, photographic collections
Period of collections: 1840-1910

SOPERTON

Treutlen County Historical Society
Treutlen County Courthouse, 30457
Telephone: (912) 529-6711
Private agency
Founded in: 1977
J. Clayton Stephens, Jr., President
Number of members: 100
Major programs: library, historic sites, genealogy
Period of collections: 1900-present

STATESBORO

Georgia Southern Museum
Georgia Southern College
Mail to: P.O. Box 8061, 30460
State agency, authorized by the college
Founded in: 1981
Delma E. Presley, Director
Number of members: 62
Staff: full time 1, part time 9, volunteer 6
Magazine: *Through the Rotunda*
Major programs: museum, school programs, exhibits, natural history
Period of collections: prehistoric

SWAINSBORO

Emanuel Historic Preservation Society
P.O. Box 1101, 30401
Founded in: 1977
Number of members: 175
Staff: volunteer 10
Magazine: *Pinelog Echoes*
Major programs: archives, manuscripts, museum, markers, book publishing, newsletters/pamphlets, historic preservation
Period of collections: 1890

THOMASVILLE

Thomas County Historical Society, Inc.
725 N. Dawson St., 31792
Telephone: (912) 226-7664
Mail to: P.O. Box 1922, 31799
Private agency
Founded in: 1952
Charles T. Hill, Director
Number of members: 832
Staff: full time 1, part time 2, volunteer 30
Major programs: archives, manuscripts, museum, tours/pilgrimages, oral history, school programs, book publishing, newsletters/pamphlets, research, exhibits, audiovisual programs, photographic collections
Period of collections: 1880s-present

Lapham-Patterson House
626 N. Dawson St., 31792
Telephone: (912) 226-0405
State agency, Department of Natural Resources, Parks, Recreation and Historic Sites
Founded in: 1970
Beth A. Poulk, Historic Site Superintendent
Staff: full time 2, part time 1, volunteer 11
Magazine: *The Star*
Major programs: historic site(s), markers, tours/pilgrimages, school programs, newsletters/pamphlets, historic preservation, research, exhibits, audiovisual programs, lectures, historic celebrations, educational programs
Period of collections: 1884-1900

Thomasville Landmarks, Inc.
312 N. Broad St., 31792
Telephone: (912) 226-6016
Mail to: P.O. Box 1285, 31799
Private agency
Founded in: 1964
Erick D. Montgomery, Executive Secretary
Number of members: 800
Staff: full time 1, part time 25, volunteer 25
Magazine: *Oak Leaves*
Major programs: historic site(s), markers, tours/pilgrimages, book publishing, newsletters/pamphlets, historic preservation, research, photographic collections

THOMSON

Wrightsboro Quaker Community Foundation, Inc.
633 Hemlock Dr., 30824
Telephone: (404) 595-5584
Private agency
Founded in: 1965
Dorothy M. Jones, Administrator
Number of members: 100
Staff: volunteer 1
Major programs: library, museum, historic site(s), tours/pilgrimages, school programs, book publishing, historic preservation, research, exhibits, audiovisual programs, archaeology programs, genealogical services
Period of collections: 18th century

TIFTON

Georgia Agrirama Development Authority—State Museum of Agriculture
8h St. at Hwy. I-75
Telephone: (912) 386-3344
Mail to: P.O. Box Q, 31794
State agency
Founded in: 1972
Wilmon H. Droze, Executive Director
Number of members: 400
Staff: full time 27, part time 47, volunteer 100
Magazine: *Georgia Recorder, Agri Ramblins*
Major programs: museum, historic preservation, research, living history, photographic collections
Period of collections: 1870-1900

Quilting, an important pastime in 1890s rural Georgia, is kept alive at Georgia Agrirama.—Georgia Agrirama, Tifton, Georgia

TYBEE ISLAND

Ft. Pulaski National Monument
U.S. Hwy. 80
Telephone: (912) 786-5787
Mail to: P.O. Box 98, 31328
Federal agency, authorized by
National Park Service
Founded in: 1924
Daniel W. Brown, Superintendent
Staff: full time 12, part time 18,
volunteer 25
Major programs: archives, museum,
historic site(s), tours, school
programs, historic preservation,
exhibits, living history,
photographic collections
Period of collections: 1825-1875

Tybee Museum Association
Ft. Screven
Telephone: (912) 786-4077
Mail to: P.O. Box 97, 31328
Founded in: 1960
T.A. Bradley, Jr., President
Number of members: 120
Staff: part time 2, volunteer 32
Major programs: museum
Period of collections: 1700-1960

VALDOSTA

The Garden Center
Patterson at Gordon Ave., 31601
Mail to: P.O. Box 2423, 31602
Private agency
Margaret Fowler, President
Number of members: 175
Staff: volunteer 2
Major programs: library, historic
preservation, gardening, flower
shows, antique shows, historic
restoration
Period of collections: Victorian era

Lowndes County Historical Society
305 W. Central Ave.
Telephone: (912) 247-4780
Mail to: P.O. Box 434, 31601
Founded in: 1967
Joe Tomberlin, President
Number of members: 250
Staff: volunteer 25
Major programs: museum,
tours/pilgrimages,
newsletters/pamphlets
Period of collections: 1865-1918

Southern Jewish Historical Society
History Department, Valdosta State
College
Mail to: P.O. Box 179, 31698
Telephone: (912) 333-5947
Private agency
Founded in: 1978
Janice R. Blumberg, President
Number of members: 350
Major programs: book publishing,
newsletters/pamphlets,
genealogical services, field
services

WARM SPRINGS

**Roosevelt's Little White House and
Museum**
31580
Telephone: (404) 655-3511
State agency, authorized by
Department of Natural Resources
Founded in: 1946
Norman Edwards, Superintendent

Staff: full time 14, part time 12
Major programs: museum, historic
site(s), tours/pilgrimages, historic
preservation, research, exhibits,
audiovisual programs,
photographic collections
Period of collections: 1880s-1945

WASHINGTON

Robert Toombs House
216 E. Robert Toombs Ave.
Telephone: (404) 678-2226
Mail to: P.O. Box 605, 30673
State agency, authorized by
Department of Natural Resources
Founded in: 1982
Jane Garner, Superintendent
Staff: full time 2
Major programs: museum, historic
site(s), historic preservation,
exhibits, living history, audiovisual
programs
Period of collections: Civil War era

**Washington-Wilkes Historical
Foundation, Inc.**
308 E. Robert Toombs Ave., 30673
Telephone: (404) 678-2105
Founded in: 1968
Number of members: 100
Staff: full time 1
Major programs: museum, historic
site, tours/pilgrimages, historic
preservation
Period of collections: to 1860

WATKINSVILLE

Watkinsville Historical Society
Main St., 30177
Private agency
Founded in: 1982
Anthony F. Gergely, President
Major programs: tours/pilgrimages,
historic preservation, exhibits

WAYCROSS

Okefenokee Heritage Center, Inc.
N. Augusta Ave.
Telephone: (912) 285-4260
Mail to: Rt. 5, Box 406-A, 31501
Private agency
Founded in: 1975
William J. Martin, Executive Director
Number of members: 350
Staff: full time 2, part time 1,
volunteer 15
Major programs: museum,
educational programs, historic
preservation
Period of collections: 1870-1935

Southern Forest World, Inc.
N. Augusta Ave.
Telephone: (912) 285-4056
Mail to: Rt. 5, Box 406-B, 31501
Private agency
Founded in: 1980
William J. Martin, Executive Director
Staff: full time 1, part time 2,
volunteer 21
Period of collections: 1700-present

WAYNESBORO

**Burke County Historical
Association**
Mail to: c/o Mrs. Alden Dye, Quaker
Rd., 30830
Questionnaire not received

WINDER

Barrow County Historical Society
Porter St.
Telephone: (404) 867-9003
Mail to: 409 Candler St., 30680
County agency
Founded in: 1973
C. Fred Ingram, President
Number of members: 135
Staff: volunteer 10
Major programs: museum, historic
site(s), markers,
newsletters/pamphlets, audiovisual
programs
Period of collections: 1850-present

WOODBINE

Bryan Lang Historical Libray
Mail to: P.O. Box 725, 31569
Founded in: 1984
Major programs: library, archives,
books, records management,
photographic collections,
genealogical services

WRIGHTSVILLE

**Johnson County Historical
Society, Inc.**
P.O. Box 86, 31096
Founded in: 1977
Questionnaire not received

HAWAII

HAWAII

HILO

Lyman House Memorial Museum
276 Haili St., 96720
Telephone: (808) 935-5021
Private agency
Founded in: 1932
Leon H. Bruno, Director
Number of members: 550
Staff: full time 7, part time 6,
volunteer 35
Major programs: library, archives,
manuscripts, museum,
tours/pilgrimages, oral history,
school programs, book publishing,
newsletters/pamphlets, historic
preservation, research, exhibits,
photographic collections,
genealogical services
Period of collections: 1783-present

Wailoa Center Advisory Committee
75 Aipuni St.
Telephone: (808) 961-7360
Mail to: P.O. Box 936, 96720
State agency, authorized by
Department of Land and Natural
Resources
Founded in: 1970
Mabel Meyer, Manager
Staff: full time 2, volunteer 11
Major prorams: oral history,
educational programs,
newsletters/pamphlets, cultural
and civic programs, art exhibits
Period of collections: 1492-present

KAILUA

KONA

Huilihee Palace
Telephone: (808) 329-1877
Mail to: P.O. Box 1838, 96740
Private agency, authorized by
    Daughters of Hawaii
Founded in: 1903
Number of members: 1,300
Staff: full time 16, part time 5,
    volunteer 100
Major programs: museum, historic
    site(s), school programs, historic
    preservation

Kona Historical Society
Captain Cook
Telephone: (808) 323-3188
Mail to: P.O. Box 398, 96704
Private agency
Founded in: 1976
Sherwood R.H. Greenwell, President
Number of members: 275
Staff: volunteer 10
Period of collections: 1865-present

KAUAI

HANALEI

Hanalei Museum
P.O. Box 91, 96714
Telephone: (808) 826-7387
Private agency, authorized by
    Hanalei Hawaiian Civic Club
Founded in: 1967
Nickols C. Beck, Director
Staff: volunteer 20
Major programs: museum, historic
    site(s)
Period of collections: 1880-1950s

LIHUE

Kauai Museum Association, Ltd.
4428 Rice St.
Telephone: (808) 245-6931
Mail to: P.O. Box 248, 96766
Private agency
Founded in: 1960
David P. Penhallow, Director
Number of members: 500
Staff: full time 4, part time 9,
    volunteer 12
Major programs: library, manuscripts,
    museum, oral history, exhibits,
    photographic collections,
    genealogical services
Period of collections: A.D. 300-1960

MAUI

LAHAINA

Lahaina Restoration Foundation
Front and Dickenson
Telephone: (808) 661-3262
Mail to: P.O. Box 338, 96761
Founded in: 1962
James C. Luckey, Vice
    President/General Manager
Number of members: 800
Staff: full time 4, part time 8,
    volunteer 5
Major programs: library, archives,
    manuscripts, museum, historic
    site(s), markers, tours/pilgrimages,
    newsletters/pamphlets, historic
    preservation, research, exhibits,
    audiovisual programs,
    photographic collections,
    genealogical services
Period of collections: 1823-1860

PUUNENE

**Alexander and Baldwin Sugar
    Museum**
3957 Hansen Rd.
Telephone: (808) 871-8058
Mail to: P.O. Box 125, 9674
Private agency
Founded in: 1980
Gaylord C. Kubota, Director
Major programs: museum, exhibits,
    photographic collections
Period of collections: 1850-1950

WAILUKU

**Maui Historical Society and
    Museum**
2375-A Main St.
Telephone: (808) 244-3326
Mail to: P.O. Box 1018, 96793
Private agency
Founded in: 1956
Merie-Ellen Fong Mitchell, Museum
    Director
Staff: full time 2, part time 2,
    volunteer 10
Major programs: museum, school
    programs, book publishing,
    newsletters/pamphlets, research,
    photographic collections
Period of collections: prehistoric-1900

OAHU

HONOLULU

Bernice P. Bishop Museum
1525 Bernice St.
Telephone: (808) 847-3511
Mail to: P.O. Box 19000-A, 96817
Private agency
Founded in: 1889
W. Donald Duckworth, Director
Number of members: 2,500
Staff: full time 100, part time 200,
    volunteer 49
Magazine: *Ka Elele*
Major programs: library, archives,
    manuscripts, museum, oral history,
    book publishing, historic
    preservation, research, exhibits,
    archaeology programs,
    photographic collections
Period of collections: 1783-present

**Daughters of Hawaii/Queen Emma
    Summer Palace**
2913 Pali Hwy., 96817
Telephone: (808) 595-6291
Private agency
Founded in: 1903
Catherine Thoene, Regent
Number of members: 1,300
Staff: full time 10, volunteer 50
Major programs: museum, historic
    sites preservation
Period of collections: 1850-1885

Friends of 'Iolani Palace
King and Richards Sts.
Telephone: (808) 536-3552
Mail to: P.O. Box 2259, 96804

State agency, authorized by
    Department of Land and Natural
    Resources
Founded in: 1965
James R. Pavelle, Museum Director
Number of members: 1,400
Staff: full time 14, part time 10,
    volunteer 46
Major programs: museum, historic
    site(s), tours, school programs,
    newsletters/pamphlets, historic
    preservation, audiovisual programs
Period of collections: 1882-1893

Hawaii Bottle Museum
P.O. Box 25153, 96825
Telephone: (808) 395-4671
Private agency
Founded in: 1976
Sue Loewenhardt, Director
Number of members: 112
Staff: full time 4, volunteer 20
Magazine: *Hawaii Bottle Museum
    News*
Major programs: library, museum,
    newsletters/pamphlets, research,
    exhibits
Period of collections: 1776-1900

Hawaii Chinese History Center
111 N. King St., Room 410, 96817
Telephone: (808) 521-5948
Private agency
Founded in: 1970
Puanani Kini, President
Number of members: 600
Staff: part time 1, volunteer 10
Major programs: library, historic
    site(s), oral history, book
    publishing, newsletters/pamphlets,
    research, genealogical services
Period of collections: 1850-present

◇**Hawaiian Historical Society**
560 Kawaiahao St., 96813
Private agency
Founded in: 1892
Barbara E. Dunn, Executive
    Secretary/Librarian
Number of members: 1,000
Staff: full time 1, part time 1
Magazine: *The Hawaiian Journal of
    History*
Major programs: library, manuscripts,
    book publishing,
    newsletters/pamphlets,
    photographic collections, lecture
    series
Period of collections: 1783-1918

**Hawaiian Mission Children's
    Society**
553 S. King St., 96813
Telephone: (808) 531-0481
Private agency
Founded in: 1852
Gerard Berg, Director
Number of members: 720
Staff: full time 8, part time 3,
    volunteer 11
Major programs: library, museum,
    school programs,
    newsletters/pamphlets, historic
    preservation, research, exhibits,
    genealogical services
Period of collections: 1820-1900

Hawaii State Archives
Iolani Palace Grounds, 96813
Telephone: (808) 548-2355
Ruth S. Itamura, State Archivist

Staff: full time 23
Major programs: archives,
manuscripts, records
management, photographic
collections
Period cf collections: 1783-present

Hawaii State Historic Preservation Office
P.O. Box 621, 06809
Telephone: (808) 548-7460
State agency
Founded in: 1967
Susumu Ono, State Historic
Preservation Officer
Staff: full time 7
Major programs: historic site(s),
historic preservation, records
management, archaeology
programs, photographic
collections
Period of collections:
prehistoric-present

◊Historic Hawaii Foundation
119 Merchant St., 96813
Telephone: (808) 537-9564
Mail to: P.O. Box 1658, 96806
Private agency
Founded in: 1974
Phyllis G. Fox, Executive Director
Number of members: 2,300
Staff: full time 3, part time 1,
volunteer 250
Magazine: *Historic Hawaii News*
Major programs:
newsletters/pamphlets, field
services, historic preservation
Period of collections: 1918-present

Moanalua Gardens Foundation, Inc.
1352 Pineapple Place, 96819
Telephone: (808) 839-5334
Private agency
Founded in: 1970
Mary Ann Lentz, Executive Director
Number of members: 300
Staff: full time 7, volunteer 23
Magazine: *Na Makani O Moanalua*
Major programs: historic site(s),
tours/pilgrimages, school
programs, archaeology programs,
environmental studies, special
events

Oral History Project, Social Science Research Institute
2424 Maile Way, Porteus 724, 96822
Telephone: (808) 948-6259
State agency, authorized by
University of Hawaii
Founded in: 1976
Warren S. Nishimoto, Project Director
Staff: full time 4
Magazine: *Oral History Recorder*
Major programs: archives, oral
history, newsletters/pamphlets,
audiovisual programs,
photographic collections
Period of collections: 1900-present

State Foundation on Culture and the Arts
335 Merchant St., Room 202, 96813
Telephone: (808) 548-4145
State agency, authorized by
Department of Accounting and
General Services
Founded in: 1965

Sarah M. Richards, Executive
Director
Staff: full time 12, part time 3
Major programs: oral history, historic
preservation, field services

PEARL HARBOR

Pacific Submarine Museum
Naval Submarine Base, 96860
Telephone: (808) 471-0632
Federal agency, authorized by the
· U.S. Navy
Founded in: 1970
Ray W. de Yarmin, Museum Curator
Staff: full time 2, volunteer 3
Major programs: library, archives,
museum, historic site(s), markers,
tours/pilgrimages, oral history,
book publishing, historic
preservation, research
Period of collections: W.W. I-present

USS Arizona Memorial
1 Arizona Memorial Dr., Honolulu,
96818
Telephone: (808) 422-2771
Federal agency, authorized by
National Park Service
Founded in: 1980
Mark Tanaka-Sanders, Curator
Staff: full time 1, part time 2,
volunteer 2
Major programs: library, archives,
museum, historic site(s), markers,
tours/pilgrimages, oral history,
book publishing, historic
preservation, research, exhibits,
audiovisual programs, archaeology
programs
Period of collections: 1940-1942

IDAHO

BOISE

◊Idaho State Historical Society
610 N. Julia Davis Dr., 83702
Telephone: (208) 334-2120
Founded in: 1907
Arthur A. Hart, Director
Number of members: 1,100
Staff: full time 24, part time 11,
volunteer 105
Magazine: *Idaho Yesterdays*
Major programs: library, archives,
manuscripts, museum, historic
sites preservation, markers,
tours/pilgrimages, junior history,
oral history, educational programs,
books, newsletters/pamphlets
Period of collections:
prehistoric-present

Old Idaho Penitentiary
2445 Old Penitentiary Rd., 83706
Telephone: (208) 334-2844
State agency, authorized by Idaho
State Historical Society
Jerry L. Ostermiller, Administrator
Staff: full time 3, part time 2,
volunteer 25
Major programs: museum, historic
site(s), tours/pilgrimages, historic
preservation, research, exhibits,
audiovisual programs
Period of collections: 1889-1973

BURLEY

Cassia County Historical Society, Inc.
Highland and Main Sts.
Telephone: (208) 678-7172
Mail to: P.O. Box 331, 83318
County agency
Founded in: 1971
Zatelle Pace, Curator

The Old Idaho Penitentiary, an office of the Idaho State Historical Society in Boise, houses displays on the prison's history and the Idaho Transportation Museum.—The Idaho State Historical Society

Number of members: 80
Staff: part time 3, volunteer 30
Magazine: *Cassia Diary*
Major programs: museum, historic site(s), markers, tours/pilgrimages, oral history, newsletters/pamphlets, research
Period of collections: 1840s-present

CALDWELL

Orma J. Smith Museum of Natural History
College of Idaho, 83605
Telephone: (208) 459-5331
Private agency, authorized by the college
Founded in: 1976
Eric Yensen, Director
Staff: part time 4, volunteer 12
Major programs: library, museum, school programs, research, archaeology programs, natural history collections
Period of collections: 19th-20th centuries

CAMBRIDGE

Cambridge Museum
Telephone: (208) 257-3485
Mail to: HC69, Box 3380, 83610
Town agency
S. Hansen, Director of Collections
Staff: volunteer 13
Major programs: library, museum, junior history, oral history, school programs, research, exhibits, living history, photographic collections, genealogical services
Period of collections: 1890-1930

CATALDO

Old Mission State Park
P.O. Box 135, 83810
Telephone: (208) 682-3814
State agency, authorized by Department of Parks and Recreation
Founded in: 1976

COEUR D'ALENE

Ft. Sherman Museum
North Idaho College Campus
Telephone: (208) 664-3448
Mail to: P.O. Box 812, 83814
Private agency
Founded in: 1968
Dorothy Dahlgren, Curator
Staff: part time 1, volunteer 50
Major programs: museum, historic site(s), newsletters/pamphlets, exhibits, photographic collections
Period of collections: 1878-1900

Museum of North Idaho, Inc.
Mail to: P.O. Box 812, 83814
Private agency
Founded in: 1973
Doug Cranston, President
Number of members: 200
Staff: volunteer 50
Major programs: museum, newsletters/pamphlets, exhibits, photographic collections
Period of collections: 1900

CLAYTON

Custer Museum
Yankee Fork Ranger District, 83227
Telephone: (208) 838-2201
Founded in: 1970
Staff: part-time 4, volunteer 2
Major programs: museum, historic site, markers, historic preservation
Period of collections: late 1800s-early 1900s

COTTONWOOD

St. Gertrude's Museum
P.O. Box 107, 83522
Telephone: (208) 962-3224
Private agency, authorized by Priory of St. Gertrude
Founded in: 1931
M. Catherine Manderfeld, Director
Staff: volunteer 4
Major programs: museum
Period of collections: 1850-present

DONNELLY

Long Valley Preservation Society
P.O. Box 444, 83615
Founded in: 1971
Number of members: 40
Major programs: museum, historic site, historic preservation
Period of collections: 1890-1920

DUBOIS

Heritage Hall Museum
83423
City agency
Founded in: 1969
Anne Leonardson, Secretary/Treasurer
Staff: volunteer 5
Major programs: museum, historic preservation, exhibits, photographic collections
Period of collections: 1880-1920

FILER

Twin Falls County Historical Society
Rt. 2, 83328
Telephone: (208) 733-0341
Questionnaire not received

GLENNS FERRY

Three Island Crossing State Park
P.O. Box 609, 83623
Telephone: (208) 366-2394
State agency, authorized by Department of Parks and Recreation
Founded in: 1971
Brian Miller, Park Manager
Staff: full time 3, part time 3
Major programs: historic site(s), exhibits
Period of collections: 1836-1880

HAGERMAN

Hagerman Valley Historical Society
P.O. Box 86, 83332
Founded in: 1982
Fern Pothier, President
Number of members: 75
Staff: volunteer 4

Major programs: manuscripts, oral history, newsletters/pamphlets, research, exhibits, living history, archaeology programs, photographic collections
Period of collections: 7,000 B.C.-present

IDAHO FALLS

Bonneville County Historical Society
Mail to: P.O. Box 1784, 83403
County agency, authorized by Upper Snake River Historical Society
Founded in: 1975
John E. Weida, President
Number of members: 70
Staff: volunteer 14
Major programs: museum, oral history, historic preservation, exhibits, living history, audiovisual programs, photographic collections, genealogical services, field services
Period of collections: 1850-present

JEROME

Jerome County Historical Society
Pioneer Hall
Telephone: (208) 324-2017
Mail to: Rt. 4, Box 4542, 83338
Founded in: 1981
Lloyd McCord, President
Number of members: 93

JULIAETTA

Castle Museum
1st and Main Sts.
Telephone: (208) 276-3081
Mail to: P.O. Box 454, 83535
Private agency
Founded in: 1970
Donna Cope, Owner
Staff: part time 2, volunteer 2
Major programs: museum, tours/pilgrimages, school programs, historic preservation, research, exhibits, audiovisual programs, photographic collections
Period of collections: 1800-1945

KETCHUM

Regional History Department, Community Library
619 4th St., E
Telephone: (208) 726-5544
Mail to: P.O. Box 2168, 83340
Private agency, authorized by Community Library Association, Inc.
Founded in: 1982
Ginger Piotter, Librarian
Staff: full time 1, volunteer 2
Major programs: library, archives, manuscripts, oral history, school programs, historic preservation, research, photographic collections, genealogical services
Period of collections: 1860-present

LAVA HOT SPRINGS

South Bannock County Historical Center
8 E. Main St.

Telephone: (208) 776-5254
Mail to: P.O. Box 387, 83246
Private agency
Founded in: 1980
Ruth Ann Olson, Administrator
Number of members: 145
Staff: part time 3, volunteer 10
Major programs: museum,
newsletters/pamphlets, historic
preservation, research, exhibits,
photographic collections
Period of collections: 1920-present

LEWISTON

**Nez Perce County Historical
Society, Inc.**
3rd and C Sts., 83501
Telephone: (208) 743-2535
Private agency
Founded in: 1961
Pamela Green, Museum Director
Number of members: 300
Staff: part time 4
Major programs: archives, museum,
historic site(s), school programs,
photographic collections
Period of collections: 1880-1930

MONTPELIER

**Daughters of Utah Pioneers Relic
Hall**
420 Clay St.
Telephone: (208) 847-1069
Mail to: Old Mill Rd., 83254
Private agency
Founded in: 1947
Allene K. Daines, Director
Number of members: 200
Major programs: library, archives,
manuscripts, museum, historic
site(s), markers, oral history, book
publishing, newsletters/pamphlets,
historic preservation, records
management, research, exhibits,
living history, photographic
collections, genealogical services
Period of collections: 1847-1869

MOSCOW

Latah County Historical Society
110 S. Adams St., 83843
Telephone: (208) 882-1004
Private agency
Founded in: 1968
Mary E. Reed, Director
Number of members: 525
Staff: part time 3, volunteer 8
Magazine: *Latah Legacy*
Major programs: library, archives,
museum, book publishing,
newsletters/pamphlets, research,
exhibits, audiovisual programs,
photographic collections,
genealogical services
Period of collections: 1860-present

MOUNTAIN HOME

**Elmore County Historical
Foundation, Inc.**
180 S. 3rd, E
Telephone: (208) 587-8271
Mail to: P.O. Box 204, 83647
Private agency
Founded in: 1961
Alma Bartlett, President
Number of members: 173
Staff: part time 4

Magazine: *Our Heritage*
Major programs: archives, museum,
historic site(s), markers,
tours/pilgrimages, historic
preservation, research, exhibits,
audiovisual programs,
photographic collections,
genealogical services
Period of collections: 1800-present

MURPHY

**Owyhee County Historical Society
and Museum**
83650
Telephone: (208) 495-2319
County agency
Founded in: 1960
Linda Morton, Director
Number of members: 300
Staff: full time 1, volunteer 4
Magazine: *Owyhee Outpost*
Major programs: library, archives,
manuscripts, museum,
tours/pilgrimages, oral history,
book publishing,
newsletters/pamphlets, research,
exhibits
Period of collections: 1865-present

NAMPA

Canyon County Historical Society
1200 Front St.
Telephone: (208) 467-7611
Mail to: P.O. Box 595, 83651
Founded in: 1974
Katherine L. Hamlett,
Director/Curator
Number of members: 275
Staff: full time 1, part time 1,
volunteer 3
Major programs: library, archives,
museum, historic site(s), markers,
oral history, school programs,
newsletters/pamphlets, research,
exhibits, photographic collections,
genealogical services
Period of collections: 1770-1950

POCATELLO

Ft. Hall Replica Commission
4th and Fredrigill, Ross Park
Telephone: (208) 232-4311, ext. 121
Mail to: P.O. Box 4169, 83205
City agency, authorized by
Department of Parks and
Recreation
Founded in: 1834
Leonard H. Carlson, Parks
Superintendent
Major programs: museum,
newsletters/pamphlets, exhibits
Period of collections: 1834-1860

REXBURG

**Upper Snake River Valley Historical
Society**
Telephone: (208) 356-9101
Mail to: P.O. Box 244, 83440
County agency
Founded in: 1965
Louis J. Clements, Director
Number of members: 150
Magazine: *Snake River Echoes*
Major programs: library, museum,
oral history, photographic
collections, genealogical services
Period of collections: 1880-present

RIGBY

**Jefferson County Historical
Society**
Mail to: P.O. Box 284, 83442
Founded in: 1974
Thelma McMurtrey, President
Number of members: 75
Staff: volunteer 6
Major programs: tours/pilgrimages,
junior history, oral history
Period of collections: 1918-present

RUPERT

**Minidoka County Historical
Society, Inc.**
100 E. Baseline
Telephone: (208) 436-0336
Mail to: P.O. Box 21, 83350
County agency
Founded in: 1970
Paul B. Courtright, President
Number of members: 64
Staff: full time 1, part time 1,
volunteer 5
Major programs: museum, historic
site(s), markers, oral history, school
programs, book publishing, historic
preservation, research, exhibits

SALMON

Lemhi County Historical Society
Mail to: P.O. Box 645, 83467
Questionnaire not received

SANDPOINT

**Bonner County Historical
Society, Inc.**
Ontario and Ella Sts.
Telephone: (208) 263-2344
Mail to: P.O. Box 1063, 83864
Private agency
Founded in: 1972
Number of members: 125
Staff: full time 1, volunteer 10
Major programs: library, museum,
school programs
Period of collections: 1909-present

SODA SPRINGS

Caribou Historical Society, Inc.
290 W. 3rd, S, 83276
Telephone: (208) 547-3506
Private agency
Founded in: 1978
Elaine S. Johnson, Chair
Number of members: 30
Major programs: markers,
tours/pilgrimages, oral history,
research, exhibits, photographic
collections

SPALDING

Nez Perce National Historical Park
U.S. Hwy. 95, S
Telephone: (208) 843-2261
Mail to: P.O. Box 93, 83551
Federal agency, authorized by
National Park Service
Founded in: 1965
Fahy C. Whitaker, Superintendent
Major programs: library, museum,
markers, historic preservation,
exhibits, audiovisual programs,
archaeology programs
Period of collections: 1880-1910

STANLEY

Sawtooth Interpretive Association
P.O. Box 75, 83278
Telephone: (208) 774-3321
Private agency
Founded in: 1973
Laurii Gadwa, Executive Secretary
Number of members: 100
Staff: part time 1, volunteer 3
Major programs: museum, historic
preservation, exhibits,
photographic collections
Period of collections: 1800s-present

SUN VALLEY

**Sun Valley Center for the Arts and
Humanities—Institute of the
American West**
Dollar Rd.
Telephone: (208) 622-9371
Mail to: P.O. Box 656, 83353
Private agency
Founded in: 1971
Chris Montague, Director of
Programs
Number of members: 500
Staff: full time 8, volunteer 10
Magazine: *Idaho Arts Journal*
Major programs: oral history, school
programs, book publishing,
newsletters/pamphlets, exhibits,
living history, audiovisual programs

TWIN FALLS

The Herrett Museum
315 Falls Ave., W
Telephone: (208) 733-9554
Mail to: P.O. Box 1238, 83303-1238
State agency, authorized by the
College of Southern Idaho
Founded in: 1958
James C. Woods, Director
Number of members: full time 6,
volunteer 50
Major programs: museum, school
programs, research, exhibits,
archaeology programs
Period of collections: prehistoric

**South Central Idaho Historical
Council**
315 Falls Ave., W
Telephone: (208) 733-9554
Mail to: P.O. Box 1238, 83303-1238
Private agency, authorized by the
College of Southern Idaho
Founded in: 1982
James R. Gentry, Chair
Major programs: research
Period of collections: 1900-present

WALLACE

**Coeur d'Alene Mining District
Museum**
509 Bank St.
Telephone: (208) 753-7151
Mail to: P.O. Box 1167, 83873
Private agency
Founded in: 1955
Wava Beehner, Director
Staff: full time 1, part time 1
Major programs: museum, historic
site(s), historic preservation,
photographic collections
Period of collections: 1880-1920

WEISER

**Intermountain Cultural Center and
Museum**
840 W. Butterfield, 83672
Telephone: (208) 549-1994
Founded in: 1962
Blake Coats, Executive Director
Number of members: 300
Staff: full time 3, part-time 6,
volunteer 20
Major programs: archives, museum,
historic site, oral history, book
publishing, newsletters/pamphlets,
historic preservation
Period of collections: 1860-1930

WINCHESTER

Winchester Museum
Telephone: (208) 924-7772
Mail to: Rt. 2, Box 28, 83524
Private agency
Founded in: 1966
Lois Tiede, President
Staff: volunteer 10
Major programs: museum,
photographic collections
Period of collections: 1906-present

ILLINOIS

ADDISON

**Addison Historical Society—
Historical Museum of Addison**
131 W. Lake St., 60101
Telephone: (312) 628-1433
City agency, authorized by Addison
Historical Commission
Founded in: 1974 (society); 1976
(museum)
Gloria Thew, President/Museum
Curator
Number of members: 50
Staff: full time 6
Magazine: *Salt Creek Tattler*
Major programs: archives,
manuscripts, museum, historic
site(s), markers, tours/pilgrimages,
junior history, oral history, school
programs, book publishing,
newsletters/pamphlets, historic
preservation, records
management, research, exhibits,
audiovisual programs,
photographic collections,
genealogical services
Period of collections: late 1800s-early
1900s

ALBION

Edwards County Historical Society
P.O. Box 205, 62806
Telephone: (618) 445-343
Private agency
Founded in: 1939
Terry L. Harper, Vice President
Number of members: 205
Staff: volunteer 4
Major programs: library, archives,
museum, book publishing,
newsletters/pamphlets, genealogy,
historic site
Period of collections: 1800-1930

ALEDO

Essley-Noble Museum
1400 S.E. 2nd Ave., 61231
Private agency, authorized by Mercer
County Historical Society
Founded in: 1959
Ruth Giffin, Curator
Number of members: 400
Staff: part time 1, volunteer 15
Major programs: museum,
genealogical services
Period of collections: 1850-1900

ALTON

**Alton Area Historical Society and
Research Library**
301 E. Broadway
Telephone: (618) 462-0343
(president)
Mail to: P.O. Box 971, 62002
Private agency
Founded in: 1948
Mary Lou Mann, President
Number of members: 100
Staff: volunteer 12
Major programs: library,
tours/pilgrimages, oral history,
book publishing,
newsletters/pamphlets, historic
preservation, research, living
history, genealogical services
Period of collections: 1840-present

**Alton Area Landmarks
Association, Inc.**
212 State St.
Telephone: (618) 465-0782
Mail to: P.O. Box 232, 62002
Founded in: 1970
Robert E. St. Peters, President
Number of members: 150
Staff: volunteer 50
Major programs: archives, historic
site, markers, tours/pilgrimages,
book publising,
newsletters/pamphlets, historic
preservation, operates the
Landmarks Visitors Center
Period of collections: 1970-present

**Alton Museum of History and
Art, Inc.**
121-123 E. Broadway, 62002
Telephone: (618) 462-2763
Private agency
Founded in: 1971
Charlene Gill, President
Number of members: 300
Staff: part time 1, volunteer 20
Major programs: museum, school
programs, book publishing,
newsletters/pamphlets, historic
preservation, exhibits,
photographic collections

ANDOVER

Andover Historical Society
61233
Founded in: 1970
Number of members: 200
Major programs: museum, historic
preservation
Period of collections: early 1900s

ARLINGTON HEIGHTS

Historical Society and Museum of Arlington Heights
500 N. Vail Ave., 60004
Telephone: (312) 255-1225
Founded in: 1957
Virgil K. Horath, Executive Director
Number of members: 500
Staff: volunteer 20
Magazine: *The Dunton Post*
Major programs: library, museum, tours/pilgrimages, oral history, photographic collections
Period of collections: 1836-1920

AURORA

Aurora Historical Museum
305 Cedar St., 60506
Telephone: (312) 897-9029
Mail to: P.O. Box 905, 60507
Private agency, authorized by Aurora Historical Society
Founded in: 1906
John R. Jaros, Curator
Number of members: 700
Staff: full time 1, volunteer 20
Magazine: *McCarty-Mills Gazette*
Major programs: archives, manuscripts, museum, newsletters/pamphlets, exhibits, photographic collections, genealogical services
Period of collections: 1820-1920

Aurora Preservation Commission
44 E. Downer, 60507
Founded in: 1980
Questionnaire not received

Blackberry Historical Farm-Village
R.R. 3, Box 591, 60504
Telephone: (312) 892-1550
Authorized by Fox Valley Park District
Founded in: 1969
LuAnn Bombard, Curator
Staff: full time 3, part time 45
Major programs: museum, school programs, exhibits, living history, period craft demonstrations
Period of collections: 1840-1910

BARRINGTON

Barrington Area Historical Society
218 W. Main St., 60010
Telephone: (312) 381-1730
Private agency
Founded in: 1968
Barbara Benson, Director
Number of members: 450
Staff: full time 1, part time 1
Major programs: archives, museum, tours/pilgrimages, school programs, newsletters/pamphlets, historic preservation
Period of collections: 1835-present

BARTLETT

Bartlett Historical Society
240 S. Main St.
Telephone: (312) 837-2501
Mail to: P.O. Box 8257, 60103
Private agency
Founded in: 1973
Dorothy V. Heinberg, President
Number of members: 40
Staff: volunteer 3

Major programs: museum, historic site(s), photographic collections
Period of collections: 1900-present

BATAVIA

Batavia Depot Museum
155 Houston St., 60510
Telephone: (312) 879-1800
City agency, authorized by Batavia Park District
Carla L. Hill, Curator
Staff: full time 1, volunteer 60
Major programs: archives, museum, school programs, exhibits, photographic collections
Period of collections: 1850s-present

Batavia Township Historical Society
Mail to: P.O. Box 15, 60510
Questionnaire not received

BELLEVILLE

St. Clair County Genealogical Society
Mail to: P.O. Box 431, 62221
Private agency
Founded in: 1977
Judith Ullrich Wallin, President
Number of members: 445
Major programs: library, newsletters/pamphlets, genealogical services, copying of tombstone inscriptions and records
Period of collections: 1790-present

St. Clair County Historical Society
701 E. Washington St., 62221
Telephone: (618) 234-0600
Private agency
Founded in: 1905
Mark A. Westhoff, President
Number of members: 500
Staff: part time 1, volunteer 100
Major programs: library, museum, historic site(s), markers, tours/pilgrimages, school programs, book publishing, newsletters/pamphlets, historic preservation, exhibits, photographic collections
Period of collections: 1800-1900

BELLFLOWER

Bellflower Historical Society
Latcha St., 61724
Founded in: 1976
Phyllis J. Kumler, President
Number of members: 15
Staff: volunteer 10
Major programs: museum, historic preservation
Period of collections: 1871-present

BEMENT

Bryant Cottage State Historic Site
146 E. Wilson, 61813
Telephone: (217) 678-8184
State agency, authorized by Department of Conservation
Founded in: 1925
Keith Herron, Site Superintendent
Staff: full time 1, part time 1, volunteer 4
Major programs: museum, historic site, oral history, educational programs, historic preservation
Period of collections: 1850-1870

BENTON

Franklin County Historical Society
Benton Public Library
Telephone: (618) 435-4853
Mail to: P.O. Box 19, 62812
Private agency
Founded in: 1960
Betty Cunningham, President
Number of members: 40
Staff: volunteer 40
Major programs: archives, manuscripts, museum, historic sites preservation, markers, tours/pilgrimages, educational programs, books
Period of collections: 1783-1865

BISHOP HILL

Bishop Hill Heritage Association
P.O. Box 1853, 61419
Telephone: (309) 927-3899
Private agency
Founded in: 1964
Bernadine C. Nelson, Coordinator
Staff: full time 2, part time 6, volunteer 15
Major programs: library, archives, manuscripts, museum, historic site, tours, oral history, educational programs, newsletters/pamphlets, historic preservation
Period of collections: 1846-1920

Bishop Hill State Historic Site
Telephone: (309) 927-3345
Mail to: P.O. Box D, 61419
State agency, authorized by Historic Sites Division, Department of Conservation
Founded in: 1846
Martha Jane Downey, Site Superintendent
Staff: full time 5
Major programs: museum, historic site(s), school programs, historic preservation, exhibits
Period of collections: 1846-1861

BLOOMINGDALE

Bloomingdale Historical Society
P.O. Box 322, 60108
Telephone: (312) 529-0787
Founded in: 1972
Dolores Howe, President
Number of members: 10
Major programs: museum

BLOOMINGTON

Bloomington-Normal Genealogical Society
201 E. Grove, McBarnes Bldg., 61701
Mail to: P.O. Box 488, 61761
Private agency
Founded in: 1968
Mrs. Charles Waugh, President
Number of members: 350
Staff: volunteer 30
Magazine: *Gleanings From the Heart of the Cornbelt*
Major programs: library, book publishing, genealogical services
Period of collections: 1830-1900

Commission on Archives and History, Central Illinois Conference, United Methodist Church
1211 N. Park St.

Telephone: (309) 828-5092
Mail to: P.O. Box 2050, 61702-2050
Private agency
Founded in: 1887
Richard A. Chrisman, Historian
Number of members: 300
Staff: part time 2
Magazine: *The Historical Messenger*
Major programs: library, archives, manuscripts, museum, historic site(s), markers, oral history, research, photographic collections, genealogical services
Period of collections: 1783-present

McLean County Historical Society
201 E. Grove St., 61701
Telephone: (309) 827-0428
Private agency
Founded in: 1892
Barbara Dunbar, Director
Number of members: 1,200
Staff: full time 3, part time 4, volunteer 82
Major programs: library, archives, manuscripts, museum, historic site(s), book publishing, newsletters/pamphlets, historic preservation, research, exhibits, photographic collections
Period of collections: 1840-1920

BLUE ISLAND

Blue Island Historical Society
c/o Blue Island Public Library, 2433 York St., 60406
Telephone: (312) 388-1078
Private agency
Founded in: 1971
Phyllis J. Bell, Chair
Number of members: 300
Staff: volunteer 5
Major programs: museum, markers, tours/pilgrimages, newsletters/pamphlets, historic preservation, exhibits, audiovisual programs, photographic collections, genealogical services
Period of collections: 1835-present

BOLINGBROOK

Bolingbrook Historical Society
529 Concord Lane
Telephone: (312) 759-3189
Mail to: P.O. Box 1025, 60439
Founded in: 1975
Number of members: 40
Magazine: *The Melting Pot*
Major programs: library, historic site, markers, tours/pilgrimages, oral history, educational programs, newsletters/pamphlets, historic preservation

BUSHNELL

Bushnell Area Historical Society
Bushnell Recreation and Cultural Center
Telephone: (309) 772-3467
Mail to: 196 W. Hail St., 61422
Private agency
Founded in: 1975
Dorothy B. Williams, President
Number of members: 100
Staff: volunteer 4
Major programs: archives, museum, school programs, exhibits
Period of collections: 1880-1960

CAHOKIA

Cahokia Courthouse State Historic Site
108 W. 1st and Elm Sts., 62206
Telephone: (618) 332-1782
State agency, authorized by Department of Conservation
Founded in: 1940
Molly McKenzie, Site Superintendent
Staff: full time 2, volunteer 2
Major programs: historic site(s), tours/pilgrimages, historic preservation, exhibits, audiovisual programs
Period of collections: 1790-1820

CALUMET CITY

Calumet City Historical Society, Inc.
Mail to: P.O. Box 1917, 60409
Private agency
Founded in: 1974
Wayne Scrivner, President
Number of members: 30
Staff: volunteer 15
Major programs: archives, historic preservation
Period of collections: 1830s-present

CAMBRIDGE

Henry County Historical Society
P.O. Box 161, 61238
Telephone: (309) 937-5840
Private agency
Founded in: 1963
Eugene M. Gray, Museum Chair
Number of members: 180
Staff: full time 1, part time 1, volunteer 10
Major programs: museum, historic sites preservation, library
Period of collections: late 19th century

CANTON

Fulton County Historical and Genealogical Society
45 N. Park Dr., 61520
Telephone: (309) 647-0771
Founded in: 1967
Marjorie R. Bordner, President
Number of members: 350
Staff: volunteer 12
Magazine: *Fulton County Historical and Genealogical Society Newsletter*
Major programs: library, archives, manuscripts, museum, historic sites preservation, markers, oral history, educational programs, books, newsletters/pamphlets, genealogy
Period of collections: prehistoric-present

CARBONDALE

Morris Library
Southern Illinois University, 62901
Telephone: (618) 453-2683
State agency, authorized by the university
Founded in: 1969
Kenneth G. Peterson, Dean of Library Affairs
Staff: full time 120
Magazine: *ICarbS*

Major programs: library, archives, manuscripts, historic preservation, records management, research, photographic collections, genealogical services
Period of collections: 1900-present

University Museum
Southern Illinois University, 62901
Telephone: (618) 453-5388
State agency, authorized by the Museum and Art Galleries Associations
Founded in: 1869
John J. Whitlock, Director
Staff: full time 10, part time 22, volunteer 23
Major programs: library, archives, museum, tours/pilgrimages, school programs, newsletters/pamphlets, historic preservation, research, exhibits, photographic collections, field services, fine arts, science, ethnography
Period of collections: 19th and 20th centuries

CARLINVILLE

Macoupin County Historical Society
Breckenridge St., 62626
Telephone: (217) 854-2850
Private agency
Founded in: 1970
Mrs. Stanley Klaus, President
Number of members: 350
Staff: volunteer 50
Major programs: museum, junior history, book publishing, newsletters/pamphlets, historic preservation, exhibits
Period of collections: 1850-1920

CARMI

White County Historical Society
62821
Private agency
E.T. Baldwin, President
Number of members: 325
Major programs: museum, historic site, markers, historic preservation
Period of collections: 19th century

CAROL STREAM

Carol Stream Historical Society
391 Illini Dr., 60187
Telephone: (312) 665-2311
Founded in: 1976
Questionnaire not received

CARROLLTON

Greene County Historical and Genealogical Society
221 N. 5th St., 62016
Helen Richards Widdowson, Secretary
Number of members: 100
Staff: volunteer 16
Major programs: library, museum, historic site(s), book publishing, newsletters/pamphlets, historic preservation, records management, research, exhibits, genealogical services
Period of collections: 1818-present

CARTERVILLE

Genealogy Society of Southern Illinois
Rt. 2, c/o John A. Logan College, 62918
Founded in: 1973
Number of members: 900
Staff: volunteer 40
Magazine: *Saga of Southern Illinois*
Major programs: library, archives, manuscripts, historic site, oral history, educational programs, book publishing, newsletters/pamphlets, historic preservation, genealogy
Period of collections: 1700-1900

CARTHAGE

Hancock County Historical Society
P. O. Box 68, 62321
Telephone: (217) 842-5472
Private agency
Founded in: 1968
Donald Parker, President
Number of members: 220
Staff: full time 1, volunteer 8
Major programs: archives, manuscripts, museum, historic sites preservation, markes, tours/pilgrimages, oral history, educational programs, books, newsletters/pamphlets, genealogy
Period of collections: 1783-present

CHAMPAIGN

Champaign County Historical Museum, Inc.
709 W. University Ave., 61820
Telephone: (217) 356-1010
Private agency
Founded in: 1972
Laurie McCarthy, Director
Number of members: 1,200
Staff: full time 1, part time 5, volunteer 150
Major programs: museum, historic site(s), junior history, school programs, book publishing, newsletters/pamphlets, historic preservation, exhibits
Period of collections: 19th-20th centuries

Illinois Heritage Association
602 E. Green St.
Telephone: (217) 359-5600
Mail to: Station A, Box C, 61820
Private agency
Founded in: 1981
Patricia L. Miller, Executive Director
Staff: part time 1
Major programs: library, newsletters/pamphlets, field services

World Heritage Museum
484 Lincoln Hall, 702 S. Wright St., 61820
Telephone: (217) 333-2360
State agency, authorized by the University of Illinois
Founded in: 1911
Barbara Bohen, Director
Number of members: 200
Staff: full time 4, part time 4, volunteer 5
Magazine: *Heritage*

Major programs: library, archives, manuscripts, museum, tours/pilgrimages, school programs, book publishing, newsletters/pamphlets, records management, research, exhibits, audiovisual programs, archaeology programs, photographic collections
Period of collections: prehistoric-present

CHARLESTON

Coles County Historical Society
800 Hayes Ave., 61920
Telephone: (217) 581-3310
Private agency
Founded in: 1963
E. Duane Elbert, Curator
Number of members: 258
Staff: volunteer 75
Major programs: manuscripts, museum, school programs, newsletters/pamphlets, historic preservation, exhibits, audiovisual programs, photographic collections
Period of collections: 1830-present

Coles County, Illinois, Genealogical Society
Mail to: P.O. 225, 61920
Founded in: 1975
Thomas F. Ryan, President
Number of members: 200
Staff: volunteer 12
Magazine: *Among the Coles*
Major programs: library, archives, oral history, educational programs, book publishing, genealogy
Period of collections: 1820-1900

CHICAGO

American Police Center and Museum
1130 S. Wabash, 60605
Telephone: (312) 431-0005
Private agency
Founded in: 1975
Joseph Saccomonto, Curator
Staff: volunteer 4
Magazine: *The American Police Center Safety Book*
Major programs: museum, oral history, school programs, exhibits
Period of collections: 1865-present

Archives of the Lutheran Church in America
1100 E. 55th St., 60615-5199
Telephone: (312) 753-0766
Private agency, authorized by the Lutheran Church in America
Founded in: 1962
Elisabeth Wittman, Associate Archivist
Staff: full time 1, part time 2, volunteer 2
Magazine: *News of the LCA Archives*
Major programs: archives
Period of collections: 1860s-present

Balzekas Museum of Lithuanian Culture
4012 Archer Ave., 60632
Telephone: (312) 847-2441
Private agency

Founded in: 1966
Stanley Balzekas, Jr., President
Number of members: 925
Staff: full time 3, part time 10, volunteer 15
Magazine: *Lithuanian Museum Review*
Major programs: library, archives, museum, junior history, book publishing, newsletters/pamphlets, research, exhibits, photographic collections, genealogical services
Period of collections: 1875-present

Chicago Architecture Foundation
1800 S. Prairie, 60616
Telephone: (312) 326-1393
Founded in: 1966
Morton Weisman, Executive Director
Staff: full time 9, volunteer 250
Major programs: museum, tours/pilgrimages, educational programs, newsletters/pamphlets, historic preservation, exhibits
Period of collections: 1800-1900

Chicago Genealogical Society
P.O. Box 1160, 60690
Private agency
Founded in: 1967
Sheila Weber Aszling, President
Number of members: 800
Staff: volunteer 24
Magazine: *Chicago Genealogist*
Major programs: genealogical services

Chicago Historical Society
Clark St. at North Ave., 60614
Telephone: (312) 642-4600
Private agency
Founded in: 1856
Ellsworth H. Brown, President/Director
Number of members: 5,000
Staff: full time 85, part time 20, volunteer 300
Magazine: *Chicago History*
Major programs: library, archives, manuscripts, museum, school programs, book publishing, newsletters/pamphlets, research, exhibits, photographic collections, genealogical services, architectural records
Period of collections: 1865-present

Chicago Jewish Historical Society
618 S. Michigan Ave., 60605
Telephone: (312) 663-5634
Private agency
Founded in: 1977
Norman D. Schwartz, President
Number of members: 350
Major programs: archives, tours/pilgrimages, oral history, newsletters/pamphlets

Chicago Maritime Society
c/o Truitt, Brown and Truitt, 1642 E. 56th St., 60637
Telephone: (312) 643-2600
Mail to: 60 W. Walton St., 60610
Private agency
Founded in: 1982
Philip R. Elmes, President
Number of members: 100
Staff: part time 1, volunteer 15
Magazine: *Chicago Maritime News*

Major programs: museum, newsletters/pamphlets, research, exhibits
Period of collections: 19th century

Chicago and North Western Historical Society
1812 Hood Ave., 60660
Founded in: 1973
Questionnaire not received

Commission on Chicago Historical and Architectural Landmarks
320 N. Clark St., Room 516, 60610
Telephone: (312) 744-3200
City agency
Founded in: 1968
William M. McLenahan, Director
Staff: full time 12Major programs: library, markers, historic preservation, research
Period of collections: 1870-present

Croatian Ethnic Institute, Inc.
4851 S. Drexel Blvd., 60615
Founded in: 1975
Questionnaire not received

DuSable Museum of African-American History
740 E. 56th Place, 60637
Telephone: (312) 947-0600
Private agency
Founded in: 1961
Amina Dickerson, President
Number of members: 1,500
Staff: full time 20, part time 4, volunteer 50
Major programs: archives, manuscripts, museum, tours/pilgrimages, junior history, book publishing, newsletters/pamphlets, historic preservation, records management, research, exhibits, living history, audiovisual programs, photographic collections, field services

Field Museum of Natural History
Roosevelt Rd. at Lake Shore Dr., 60605
Telephone: (312) 922-9410
Private agency
Founded in: 1893
Lorin I. Nevling, Jr., Director
Staff: full time 330, part time 41, volunteer 309
Magazine: *Fieldiana*
Major programs: library, archives, manuscripts, museum, tours/pilgrimages, school programs, book publishing, research, exhibits, audiovisual programs, archaeology programs, photographic collections, field services, natural history
Period of collections: 1850-present

Garfield Park Conservatory
300 N. Central Park Blvd., 60624
Telephone: (312) 533-1281
City agency, authorized by Chicago Park District
Founded in: 1934
Frank A. Horath, Chief Horticulturist
Staff: full time 68, part time 12
Major programs: exhibits, horticulture

Grand Army of the Republic Memorial Hall
Chicago Public Library Special Collections, 78 E. Washington St., 60602
Questionnaire not received

Great Lakes Naval and Maritime Museum
600 E. Grand Ave., 60611
Telephone: (312) 884-6312
Mail to: P.O. Box A-3785, 60690
Private agency
Founded in: 1972
Wayne W. Schmidt, President
Number of members: 200
Staff: full time 2, part time 5, volunteer 30
Magazine: *Notes and Knots*
Major programs: library, archives, museum, historic site(s), school programs, historic preservation, research, exhibits, audiovisual programs
Period of collections: 20th century

Historic Pullman Foundation, Inc.
11111 S. Forrestville Ave., 60628
Telephone: (312) 785-8181
Founded in: 1973
Number of members: 400
Staff: full time 2, part time 4, volunteer 50
Major programs: archives, historic sites preservation, tours/pilgrimages, educational programs, newsletters/pamphlets
Period of collections: 1865-1918

Holiday Cruises, Inc.—S.S. CLIPPER
600 E. Grand Ave.
Telephone: (312) 329-1800
Mail to: 600 N. Lake Shore Dr., 60611
Private agency
Founded in: 1980
James W. Gillon, General Manager
Number of members: 100
Staff: full time 3, part time 75, volunteer 5
Magazine: *Clipper Lines*
Major programs: manuscripts, museum, historic site(s), oral history, newsletters/pamphlets, historic preservation, living history, photographic collections, retired passenger steamer
Period of collections: 1905-present

Hyde Park Historical Society
5437 S. Lake Park Ave., 60637
Founded in: 1977
Staff: volunteer 30
Questionnaire not received

Illinois Labor History Society
28 E. Jackson Blvd., 60604
Telephone: (312) 663-4107
Private agency
Founded in: 1969
Leslie F. Orear, President
Number of members: 236
Staff: volunteer 1
Magazine: *ILHS Reporter*
Major programs: book publishing, photographic collections, history advocacy, state labor history
Period of collections: 1940-1976

International Museum of Surgery and Hall of Fame
1524 N. Lake Shore Dr., 60610
Telephone: (312) 642-3555
Private agency
Founded in: 1954
F.C. Ottati, International Secretary General
Number of members: 70
Staff: full time 2, part time 2, volunteer 4
Major programs: museum, historic site(s)
Period of collections: prehistoric-present

Jane Addams' Hull-House
800 S. Halsted St.
Telephone: (312) 996-2793
Mail to: P.O. Box 4348, University of Illinois, 60680
State agency, authorized by the university
Founded in: 1889
Mary Ann Johnson, Director
Staff: full time 3, part time 3
Major programs: museum, historic site(s), tours/pilgrimages, oral history, school programs, historic preservation, exhibits, audiovisual programs
Period of collections: 1890-1935

John Brown Historical Association of Illinois, Inc.
5933 S. Aberdeen St., 60621
Telephone: (312) 434-1946
Private agency
Founded in: 1982
A. Sherwood Nelson, Curator
Number of members: 59
Staff: volunteer 19
Magazine: *The John Brown Forte*
Major programs: library, archives, book publishing, newsletters/pamphlets, research, audiovisual programs, seminars, workshops
Period of collections: 1800-1860

K.A.M. Isaiah Israel Congregation
1100 Hyde Park Blvd., 60615
Telephone: (312) 924-1234
Private agency
Founded in: 1847
Ilene Herst, Administrator
Number of members: 650
Major programs: library, archives, museum, tours/pilgrimages

Landmarks Preservation Council of Illinois
407 S. Dearborn St., 60605
Telephone: (312) 922-1742
Private agency
Founded in: 1971
Amy R. Hecker, Executive Director
Number of members: 1,500
Staff: full time 5, part time 2, volunteer 125
Magazine: *Landmarks Preservation Council of Illinois Newsletter*
Major programs: library, book publishing, newsletters/pamphlets, historic preservation, technical publications, advocacy
Period of collections: 1850-1935

Lincoln Park Conservatory
Stockton Dr. at Fullerton Parkway
Telephone: (312) 294-4770
Mail to: 2400 N. Stockton Dr., 60614
City agency, authorized by Chicago
 Park District
Founded in: 1892
Frank Horath, Chief Horticulturist
Staff: full time 40, part time 6,
 volunteer 3
Major programs: tours/pilgrimages,
 pamphlets, exhibits, horticulture

**Midwest Regional Office, National
 Trust for Historic Preservation**
407 S. Dearborn, Suite 710, 60605
Telephone: (312) 353-3419
Private agency
Founded in: 1949
Tim Turner, Regional Director
Number of members: 140,000
Staff: full time 9, part time 1
Magazine: *Historic Preservation*
Major programs: library, historic
 site(s), historic preservation, field
 services, financial assistance

Museum of Science and Industry
57th St. and Lake Shore Dr., 60611
Telephone: (312) 684-1414
Private agency
Founded in: 1926
Victor J. Danilov, President/Director
Number of members: 8,000
Staff: full time 325, part time 200,
 volunteer 100
Magazine: *Progress*
Major programs: library, museum,
 school programs,
 newsletters/pamphlets, exhibits,
 audiovisual programs, science and
 technology
Period of collections: present

**National Archives—Chicago
 Branch**
7358 S. Pulaski Rd., 60629
Telephone: (312) 581-7816
Founded in: 1969
Peter Bunce, Director
Staff: full time 5
Major programs: archives,
 educational programs, teachers'
 workshops, genealogical
 workshops, film series, open
 houses and tours
Period of collections: 1800-1972

The Newberry Library
60 W. Walton St., 60610
Telephone: (312) 943-9090
Private agency
Founded in: 1887
Lawrence W. Towner,
 President/Librarian
Number of members: 1,800
Staff: full time 112, part time 34,
 volunteer 38
Magazine: *A Newberry Newsletter*
Major programs: library, archives,
 manuscripts, tours/pilgrimages,
 oral history, newsletters/pamphlets,
 historic preservation, research,
 exhibits, genealogical services
Period of collections: before 1900

**Northwestern Memorial Hospital
 Archives**
516 W. 36th St., 60609
Telephone: (312) 649-3090

Mail to: Superior St. and Fairbanks
 Court, 60611
Private agency
Founded in: 1849
Ira Berlin, Hospital Archivist
Staff: full time 4
Major programs: library, archives,
 manuscripts, museum, book
 publishing, records management,
 research, exhibits, photographic
 collections, genealogical services,
 appraisal services, health care
 history
Period of collections: 1849-present

Open Lands Project
53 W. Jackson, 60604
Telephone: (312) 427-4256
Private agency
Founded in: 1963
Judith M. Stockdale, Executive
 Director
Number of members: 900
Staff: full time 7, part time 1
Major programs: historic site(s),
 newsletters/pamphlets, historic
 preservation, photographic
 collections
Period of collections: 1963-present

Oriental Institute Museum
1155 E. 58th St., 60637
Telephone: (312) 962-9520
Private agency, authorized by the
 University of Chicago
Founded in: 1894
Janet H. Johnson, Director
Number of members: 2,500
Staff: full time 12, part time 1,
 volunteer 150
Magazine: *Oriental Institute News
 and Notes*
Major programs: library, archives,
 manuscripts, museum,
 tours/pilgrimages, school
 programs, book publishing,
 newsletters/pamphlets, research,
 exhibits, audiovisual programs,
 photographic collections
Period of collections: 8000 B.C.-300
 B.C.

**Polish American Historical
 Association**
984 N. Milwaukee Ave., 60622
Telephone: (312) 384-3352
Founded in: 1942
Thaddeus V. Gromada, President
Number of members: 650
Staff: volunteer 5
Magazine: *Polish American Studies*
Major programs: books,
 newsletters/pamphlets

Polish Genealogical Society, Inc.
984 N. Milwaukee Ave., 60611
Telephone: (312) 586-4242
Private agency
Founded in: 1978
Edward A. Peckwas, President
Number of members: 500
Staff: volunteer 500
Major programs: library, archives,
 historic site, educational programs,
 book publishing,
 newsletters/pamphlets, ancestor
 index file
Period of collections: A.D.
 966-present

Polish Museum of America
984 Milwaukee Ave., 60622
Telephone: (312) 384-3352
Private agency, authorized by Polish
 Roman Catholic Union of America
Founded in: 1937
Ted Swigon, President
Staff: part time 5, volunteer 1
Major programs: library, archives,
 manuscripts, museum,
 tours/pilgrimages, historic
 preservation, records
 management, research, exhibits,
 living history, archaeology
 programs, photographic
 collections, genealogical services
Period of collections: 1890

Printers Row Printing Museum
715 S. Dearborn, 60605
Founded in: 1980
Questionnaire not received

Public Works Historical Society
1313 E. 60th St., 60637
Telephone: (312) 667-2200
Private agency
Founded in: 1975
Number of members: 1,320
Staff: full time 3
Magazine: *Essays in Public Works
 History*
Major programs: oral history,
 educational programs, books,
 newsletters/pamphlets

**Ravenswood—Lake View Historical
 Association**
4544 N. Lincoln Ave., 60625
Telephone: (312) 728-8652
Private agency
Founded in: 1936
Leah L. Steele, Secretary/Treasurer
Number of members: 200
Staff: full time 1, volunteer 2
Major programs: manuscripts,
 exhibits, photographic collections
Period of collections: late 1800s-1920

Ridge Historical Society
10621 S. Seeley Ave., 60643
Telephone: (312) 881-1675
Private agency
Founded in: 1971
Doris Moulton, President
Number of members: 400
Staff: volunteer 20
Major programs: library, archives,
 museum, oral history, educational
 programs, newsletters/pamphlets
Period of collections: 1865-present

Society of American Archivists
600 S. Federal, Suite 504, 60605
Telephone: (312) 922-0140
Private agency
Founded in: 1936
Ann Morgan Campbell, Executive
 Director
Number of members: 3,000
Staff: full time 7, part time 2
Magazine: *American Archivist*
Major programs: archives,
 manuscripts, book publishing,
 newsletters/pamphlets,
 photographic collections

South Shore Historical Society
7651 S. Shore Dr., 60649
Founded in: 1976
Mikkel R. Hansen, President

Number of members: 250
Staff: full time 1, part-time 1,
volunteer 1
Major programs: library, archives,
manuscripts, historic site, markers,
tours/pilgrimages, oral history,
book publishing,
newsletters/pamphlets, historic
preservation
Period of collections: 1850-present

Spertus Museum of Judaica
618 S. Michigan Ave., 60605
Telephone: (312) 922-9012
Private agency, authorized by
Spertus College of Judaica
Founded in: 1967
Arthur M. Feldman, Director
Number of members: 700
Staff: full time 4, part time 10,
volunteer 10
Major programs: museum, school
programs, historic preservation,
research, exhibits
Period of collections: early 18th
century-present

**Swedish-American Historical
Society**
5125 N. Spaulding, 60625
Telephone: (312) 583-5722
Private agency
Founded in: 1948
James U. Erickson, Executive
Director
Number of members: 1,900
Staff: full time 3, part time 7
Major programs: library, archives,
manuscripts, tours/pilgrimages,
oral history, school programs, book
publishing, newsletters/pamphlets,
historic preservation, records
management, research, exhibits,
audiovisual programs,
photographic collections,
genealogical services
Period of collections: 1800s-1900s

**Theatre Historical Society of
America**
2215 W. North Ave., 60647
Telephone: (312) 252-7200
Private agency
Founded in: 1969
Robert K. Headley, Jr., Editor
Number of members: 900
Staff: part time 3, volunteer 20
Magazine: *Marquee*
Major programs: library, archives,
architecture clipping file
Period of collections: 1900-present

Ukrainian National Museum
2453 W. Chicago Ave., 60622
Telephone: (312) 276-6565
Private agency
Founded in: 1952
Emilian Basiuk, President
Number of members: 282
Staff: part time 1, volunteer 10
Major programs: library, archives,
manuscripts, museum
Period of collections: 1933

CHICAGO HEIGHTS

Chicago Heights Historical Society
Telephone: (312) 672-5543
Mail to: 3893 Merioneth Dr., Crete,
60417

Founded in: 1961
Questionnaire not received

CLINTON

**DeWitt County Museum
Association**
219 E. Woodlawn St., 61727
Founded in: 1967
Number of members: 400
Staff: full time 1, volunteer 25
Major programs: archives, museum,
tours/pilgrimages, junior history,
oral history, educational programs
Period of collections: 1850-1918

COBDEN

Cobden Museum
206 Front St.
Telephone: (618) 893-2067
Mail to: c/o Owner, R.R. 2, Box 1,
62920
Private agency
Founded in: 1961
Patrick Brumleve, Owner
Major programs: museum, historic
preservation, photographic
collections
Period of collections: prehistoric

COLLINSVILLE

Cahokia Mounds Museum Society
7850 Collinsville Rd., E. St. Louis,
62201
Telephone: (618) 344-9221
Mail to: P.O. Box 382, 62234
State agency, authorized by
Department of Conservation
Founded in: 1976
Ettus Hiatt, President
Number of members: 560
Staff: full time 1, part time 4,
volunteer 2
Major programs: library, archives,
manuscripts, museum,
tours/pilgrimages, school
programs, book publishing,
newsletters/pamphlets, historic
preservation, records
management, research, exhibits,
audiovisual programs, archaeology
programs, photographic
collections, field services
Period of collections: A.D. 800-A.D.
1550

**SIMAPC (Southwestern Illinois
Metropolitan and Regional
Planning Commission)**
203 W. Main St., 62234
Telephone: (618) 344-4250
Founded in: 1963
Edward R. Crow, Senior Planner
Staff: full time 24, part time 7
Magazine: *Southwest Advisor*
Major programs: library, educational
programs, newsletters/pamphlets,
economic development,
information and technical
assistance, graphic and computer
services
Period of collections: 1950-present

DANVILLE

**Illiana Genealogical and Historical
Society**
P.O. Box 207, 61832

Private agency
Founded in: 1965
Joan Griffis, President
Number of members: 345
Staff: volunteer 5
Magazine: *Illiana Genealogist*
Major programs: library, book
publishing, research, genealogical
services
Period of collections: 1826-present

Vermilion County Museum Society
116 N. Gilbert St., 61832
Telephone: (217) 442-2922
Founded in: 1964
Ann Bauer, Director/Curator
Number of members: 1,200
Staff: full time 1, part time 2,
volunteer 12
Magazine: *The Heritage of Vermilion
County*
Major programs: library, museum,
historic site(s), tours/pilgrimages,
historic preservation, exhibits
Period of collections: 1870-1900

DARIEN

Darien Historical Society
7422 Cass Ave., 60559
Telephone: (312) 323-8926
Private agency
Founded in: 1976
Patricia A. Rodgers, President
Number of members: 54
Staff: volunteer 20
Major programs: museum, historic
site(s), tours/pilgrimages, oral
history, exhibits
Period of collections: 1835-present

DECATUR

Governor Oglesby Mansion, Inc.
421 W. William St., 62521
Telephone: (217) 429-9422
County agency, authorized by Macon
County Conservation District
Founded in: 1976
Martha A. Montgomery, President
Number of members: 330
Staff: volunteer 50
Major programs: historic site(s),
historic preservation, house
restoration
Period of collections: 19th century

James Millikin Homestead, Inc.
125 N. Pine St., 62522
Telephone: (217) 422-9003
Mail to: P.O. Box 1501, 62525
Private agency, authorized by Millikin
University
Founded in: 1975
Barbara Hackel, President
Number of members: 300
Staff: volunteer 35
Magazine: *The Homestead Family
Gazette*
Major programs: museum, historic
site(s), tours/pilgrimages, school
programs, newsletters/pamphlets,
historic preservation
Period of collections: 1875-1909

**Macon County Historical
Society—Macon County Museum
Complex**
5580 N. Fork Rd., 62521
Telephone: (217) 422-4919

Private agency
Founded in: 1916
Catherine Bruck, Director
Number of members: 850
Staff: full time 4, part time 1,
    volunteer 60
Major programs: museum, school
    programs, book publishing,
    newsletters/pamphlets, exhibits,
    open-air pioneer village
Period of collections: 1850-1945

DEKALB

The Anthropology Museum
Stevens Bldg., Northern Illinois
    University, 60115
Telephone: (815) 753-0246
State agency, authorized by the
    university
Founded in: 1964
Milton Deemer, Director
Staff: full time 1, part time 8,
    volunteer 15
Major programs: library, museum,
    research, exhibits, archaeology
    programs, educational programs,
    ethnography

**City of Dekalb Landmark
    Commission**
200 S. 4th St., 60115
Telephone: (815) 756-4881
City agency
Founded in: 1978
Jerry Brauer, Chair
Major programs: historic site(s),
    tours/pilgrimages, historic
    preservation, research, exhibits
Period of collections: 1856-present

DeKalb County Historical Society
Telephone: (815) 758-0853
Mail to: P.O. Box 472, 60115
Private agency
Founded in: 1972
Stephen J. Bigolin, President
Major programs: markers,
    tours/pilgrimages, oral history,
    book publishing,
    newsletters/pamphlets, historic
    preservation

Ellwood House Museum
509 N. 1st St., 60115
Telephone: (815) 756-4645
Private agency, authorized by
    Ellwood House Association
Founded in: 1964
Gerald J. Brauer, Museum Director
Number of members: 500
Staff: full time 1, part time 5,
    volunteer 100
Major programs: museum, historic
    site(s), school programs, docent
    program
Period of collections: 1860-1920

Regional History Center
Swen Parson Hall, Room 155,
    Northern Illinois University, 60115
Telephone: (815) 753-1779
State agency, authorized by the
    university
Founded in: 1965
Glen A. Gildermeister, Director
Staff: full time 5, part time 4
Major programs: archives,
    manuscripts, research,
    photographic collections,

genealogical services, field
    services
Period of collections: 1850-1970

DELAVAN

**DeLavan Community Historical
    Society**
Locust St., 61734
Private agency
Founded in: 1973
Edna K. Sampen, Secretary
Number of members: 250
Staff: volunteer 20
Major programs: museum,
    tours/pilgrimages,
    newsletters/pamphlets, exhibits,
    photographic collections,
    genealogical services
Period of collections: 1820-present

Wings and Things Museum, Inc.
R.R. 2, Box 19, 61734
Telephone: (309) 244-7389
Private agency
Founded in: 1978
David H. Shipton, President
Major programs: archives, museum
Period of collections: 1938-present

DES PLAINES

Des Plaines Historical Society
789 Pearson St.
Telephone: (312) 391-5399
Mail to: P.O. Box 225, 60017
Private agency
Founded in: 1967
James R. Williams, Director
Number of members: 500
Staff: part time 3
Magazine: *Cobweb*
Major programs: library, archives,
    manuscripts, museum, markers,
    oral history, school programs,
    newsletters/pamphlets, historic
    preservation, exhibits, living
    history, audiovisual programs,
    photographic collections,
    genealogical services
Period of collections: 1783-present

DOWNERS GROVE

Downers Grove Historical Society
831 Maple Ave., 60515
Telephone: (312) 963-1309
Private agency
Founded in: 1968
Pauline Wandschneider, Curator
Number of members: 300
Staff: part time 2, volunteer 50
Major programs: library, archives,
    museum, historic site(s), markers,
    tours/pilgrimages, junior history,
    oral history, school programs, book
    publishing, newsletters/pamphlets,
    research, exhibits, audiovisual
    programs, photographic
    collections
Period of collections: 1832-present

DUNDEE

**Dundee Township Historical
    Society, Inc.**
426 Highland Ave., 60118
Telephone: (312) 428-6996
Private agency
Founded in: 1964

John Wendt, Museum Committee
    Co-chair
Staff: volunteer 20
Magazine: *The Informer*
Major programs: library, archives,
    manuscripts, museum, historic
    site(s), markers, tours/pilgrimages,
    newsletters/pamphlets
Period of collections: 1850-1930

EAST PEORIA

**Illinois Terminal Railroad Historical
    Society**
c/o A. Gill Siepert, Illinois Central
    College, 61635
Telephone: (309) 694-5501
Private agency
Founded in: 1976
A. Gill Siepert, Manager, History and
    Research
Number of members: 250
Staff: volunteer 10
Magazine: *Current Lines*
Major programs: archives,
    manuscripts, oral history,
    newsletters/pamphlets, historic
    preservation, research, audiovisual
    programs, photographic
    collections
Period of collections: 1900-1982

EDWARDSVILLE

**Madison County Historical
    Society, Inc.**
715 N. Main, 62025
Telephone: (618) 656-7562
Private agency
Founded in: 1921
Anna Symanski, Superintendent
Staff: full time 1, part time 3,
    volunteer 25
Major programs: library, archives,
    manuscripts, museum, school
    programs, book publishing,
    newsletters/pamphlets, historic
    preservation, records
    management, research, exhibits,
    photographic collections,
    genealogical services
Period of collections: 1750-present

EFFINGHAM

**Effingham County Genealogical
    Society**
P.O. Box 1166, 62401
Private agency
Founded in: 1980
Eleanor Bounds, President
Number of members: 180
Magazine: *Crossroad Trails*
Major programs: library, book
    publishing, newsletters/pamphlets,
    genealogical services

ELGIN

Elgin Area Historical Society
1196 Nottingham Lane, 60120
Telephone: (312) 742-8373
Mail to: P.O. Box 1027, 60121
Private agency
Founded in: 1961
Mrs. R. A. Huddleston, President
Number of members: 439
Magazine: *Crackerbarrel*

Major programs: historic site(s), markers, tours/pilgrimages, newsletters/pamphlets, historic preservation, exhibits, genealogical services
Period of collections: 1835-present

Elgin Genealogical Society
P.O. Box 1418, 60121-0818
Private agency
Founded in: 1972
Margaret Hetzel, President
Number of members: 140
Staff: volunteer 15
Major programs: library, newsletters/pamphlets, research, genealogical services

ELMHURST

Elmhurst Historical Museum
120 Park Ave., 60126
Telephone: (312) 832-8651
City agency
Founded in: 1957
Virginia R. Stewart, Director
Number of members: 325
Staff: full time 2, part time 3, volunteer 50
Magazine: *Heritage News*
Major programs: library, archives, manuscripts, museum, school programs, records management, research, exhibits, photographic collections, genealogical services
Period of collections: 1870-present

ELMWOOD

Elmwood Historical Society—Lorado Taft Museum
302 N. Magnolia
Telephone: (309) 742-2431
Mail to: c/o President, R.R. 2, 61529
Founded in: 1962
Alice Roffey, President
Number of members: 60
Staff: volunteer 12
Major programs: tours/pilgrimages
Period of collections: 19th century

ELSAH

Historic Elsah Foundation
Telephone: (618) 374-1242
Mail to: P.O. Box 117, 62028
Private agency
Founded in: 1971
Ingeborg Mack, Executive Director
Number of members: 300
Staff: full time 1
Magazine: *Elsah History*
Major programs: historic site(s), tours/pilgrimages, oral history, newsletters/pamphlets
Period of collections: 1865-1930

EVANSTON

Evanston Historical Society
225 Greenwood, 60201
Telephone: (312) 475-3410
Founded in: 1898
Mikell C. Darling, Director
Number of members: 2,300
Staff: full time 4, volunteer 90
Major programs: library, archives, museum, markers, tours/pilgrimages, newsletters/pamphlets
Period of collections: 1865-present

FT. SHERIDAN

Ft. Sheridan Museum
Bldg. 33, 60037-5000
Telephone: (312) 926-5519
Federal agency, authorized by the U.S. Army
Founded in: 1957
Thomas G. Kocher, Curator
Staff: full time 2
Major programs: museum, oral history, school programs, historic preservation, photographic collections
Period of collections: 1887-present

FREEPORT

Stephenson County Historical Society
1440 S. Carroll, 61032
Telephone: (815) 232-8419
County agency, authorized by Freeport Park District
Founded in: 1945
Ann Lathrop, Curator
Number of members: 325
Staff: full time 2, volunteer 8
Major programs: museum, tours/pilgrimages, school programs, book publishing, historic preservation, exhibits, photographic collections
Period of collections: 1850-present

GALENA

Galena-Jo Daviess County Historical Society
211 S. Bench St., 61036
Telephone: (815) 777-9129
Private agency
Founded in: 1938
Tacie N. Campbell, Director
Number of members: 500
Staff: full time 5, part time 8
Major programs: museum, tours, oral history, school programs, book publishing, newsletters/pamphlets, research, exhibits, audiovisual programs, archaeology programs, genealogical services
Period of collections: 1820-1918

Old Market House State Historic Site
Market Square, 61036
Telephone: (815) 777-2570/777-3310
Mail to: 908 3rd St., 61036
State agency, authorized by Department of Conservation
Founded in: 1947
Thomas A. Campbell, Jr., Site Superintendent
Staff: full time 7
Major programs: museum, historic site(s)
Period of collections: 1820-1900

U.S. Grant's Home State Historic Site
509 Bouthillier St.
Telephone: (815) 777-0248/777-3310
mail to: 908 3rd St., 61036
State agency, authorized by Department of Conservation
Founded in: 1932
Thomas A. Campbell, Jr., Site Superintendent
Staff: full time 7

Major programs: archives, museum, historic site(s), school programs, historic preservation, research, exhibits, audiovisual programs, photographic collections
Period of collections: 1820-1900

GALESBURG

Carl Sandburg Birthplace
331 E. 3rd St., 61401
Telephone: (309) 342-2361
State agency, authorized by Illinois State Historical Library
Founded in: 1945
Carol Nelson, Curator
Staff: full time 1, part time 2
Major programs: museum, historic site(s)
Period of collections: 1875-1905

Galesburg Historical Society, Inc.
218 Weinberg Arcade, 61401
Telephone: (309) 342-6155
City agency
Founded in: 1975
Frank A. Ward II, President
Number of members: 650
Staff: volunteer 10
Major programs: newsletters/pamphlets, historic preservation
Period of collections: 1880-1890

GENEVA

Geneva Historical Society
Telephone: (312) 232-4951
Mail to: P.O. Box 345, 60134
Private agency
Founded in: 1943
Helen Jane Hamlin, President
Number of members: 368
Staff: volunteer 50
Major programs: library, museum, historic site(s), markers, newsletters/pamphlets, historic preservation, research, exhibits, photographic collections, genealogical services
Period of collections: 1865-present

GENOA

Kishwaukee Valley Heritage Society
Mail to: P.O. Box 59, 60135
Private agency
Founded in: 1977
Robin Brown, President
Number of members: 100
Major programs: museum
Period of collections: 1900-present

GLENCOE

Glencoe Historical Society
999 Green Bay Rd., 60022
Private agency, authorized by Glencoe Park Recreation District
Founded in: 1935
Ellen Shubart, President
Number of members: 100
Staff: volunteer 20
Major programs: archives, historic preservation, exhibits, photographic collections
Period of collections: 1869-present

GLEN ELLYN

Glen Ellyn Historical Society
557 Geneva Rd., 60137
Telephone: (312) 858-8696
Mail to: P.O. Box 283, 60138
Founded in: 1968
Mary Jane Woods, President
Number of members: 204
Staff: volunteer 60
Major programs: library, archives, manuscripts, museum, historic site(s), markers, oral history, school programs, newsletters/pamphlets, historic preservation, records management, exhibits, photographic collections, genealogical services
Period of collections: to 1850

GLENVIEW

Glenview Area Historical Society
1121 Waukegan Rd., 60025
Telephone: (312) 724-2235
Private agency
Founded in: 1965
Edward G. Dierks, President
Number of members: 435
Magazine: *Heritage to Horizons*
Major programs: library, archives, manuscripts, museum, oral history, school programs, newsletters, records management, audiovisual programs, photographic collections
Period of collections: 1930-present

Grove National Historic Landmark
Glenview Park District, 1421 Milwaukee Ave., 60025
Telephone: (312) 299-6096
Authorized by Glenview Park District
Founded in: 1972
Stephan Swanson, Director of Interpretive Services
Number of members: 425
Staff: full time 2, part time 10, volunteer 120
Magazine: *Rustlings From The Grove*
Major programs: library, museum, historic site(s), tours/pilgrimages, school programs, newsletters/pamphlets, historic preservation, research, exhibits, living history, photographic collections
Period of collections: 1850s

Hartung's Automotive Museum
3623 W. Lake St., 60025
Telephone: (312) 724-4354
Private agency
Founded in: 1971
Lee Hartung, Owner
Major programs: museum, license plate history from all states and Canada, antique cars and motorcycles
Period of collections: 1900-present

GRAYSLAKE

Northern Illinois Historical Society
P.O. Box 50, 60030
Private agency
Founded in: 1971
Richard F. Johnson, President
Number of members: 38
Magazine: *Northern Illinois Record*

Major programs: manuscripts, historic site(s), markers, junior history, school programs, newsletters/pamphlets

GREENUP

Cumberland County Historical Society
R.R. 1, Box 15, 62428
Telephone: (217) 923-5425
Private agency
Founded in: 1964
Ellen B. Decker, President
Number of members: 12
Major programs: museum, tours/pilgrimages, historic preservation
Period of collections: 1834-present

GREENVILLE

Bond County Historical Society, Inc.
R.R. 2, Box 44, 62246
Telephone: (618) 664-0819
Founded in: 1955
Mrs. Frank V. Davis, President
Number of members: 75
Staff: volunteer 15
Major programs: library, manuscripts, museum, historic site(s), markers, school programs, book publishing
Period of collections: 1818-1918

HAMPTON

Hampton Historical Society
431 2nd Ave., 61256
Telephone: (309) 755-0362
Private agency
Founded in: 1974
Merlin A. Nelson, President
Number of members: 200
Staff: volunteer 10
Major programs: library, museum, historic site(s), markers, tours/pilgrimages, junior history, oral history, school programs, newsletters/pamphlets, historic preservation, exhibits, living history
Period of collections: 1849-1900

HARDIN

Calhoun County Historical Society
62047
County agency, authorized by county commissioners
Founded in: 1975
Tina Pluester, President
Number of members: 150
Staff: part time 1
Major programs: museum, school programs, book publishing, newsletters/pamphlets, records management, research, exhibits, genealogical services

HARVARD

Great Harvard Area Historical Society
Mail to: P.O. Box 505, 60033
Town agency
Founded in: 1978
Edward O'Brien, President
Staff: part time 1
Major programs: museum, oral history, school programs
Period of collections: 1840-1930

HAVANA

Mason County Genealogical and Historical Society
P.O. Box 246, 62644
Private agency
Founded in: 1980
Leah C. DeVore, Correspondence Secretary
Number of members: 200
Staff: volunteer 15
Major programs: library, book publishing, newsletters/pamphlets, historic preservation, genealogical services
Period of collections: 1841-present

HENNEPIN

Putnam County Historical Society
High St., 61327
Private agency
Founded in: 1963
Julia Edgerley, President
Number of members: 246
Staff: part time 2
Magazine: *Putnam Past Times*
Major programs: library, archives, museum, newsletters/pamphlets, historic preservation, audiovisual programs, genealogical services
Period of collections: early 19th century

HIGHLAND PARK

Highland Park Historical Society
326 Central Ave.
Telephone: (312) 432-7090
Mail to: P.O. Box 56, 60035
Private agency
Founded in: 1966
Robert Kohn, President
Number of members: 2,050
Staff: part time 2, volunteer 45
Major programs: library, museum, junior history, newsletters/pamphlets, exhibits, photographic collections
Period of collections: 1865-present

HILLSBORO

Historical Society of Montgomery County
Solomon Harkey House, S. Broad St.
Mail to: 904 S. Main, 62049
Private agency
Founded in: 1964
Idabel Evans, President
Number of members: 80
Major programs: library, archives, museum, book publishing, newsletters/pamphlets, historic preservation, research, exhibits, photographic collections
Period of collections: 1800-1918

HINSDALE

Hinsdale Historical Society
1 S. Clay
Telephone: (312) 325-7485
Mail to: P.O. Box 336, 60521
Private agency
Founded in: 1973
Sandra L. Williams, President
Number of members: 250
Staff: volunteer 25
Major programs: archives, museum, historic site(s), book publishing,

newsletters/pamphlets, historic
preservation
Period of collections: to 1890

HOMER

Homer Historical Society
105 N. Main St., 61849
Founded in: 1977
A. Williams, Secretary
Number of members: 45
Staff: volunteer 20
Major programs: archives, museum,
oral history, photographic
collections
Period of collections: 1880s-1920s

JACKSONVILLE

**Jacksonville Area Genealogical
and Historical Society**
Telephone: (217) 243-2502
Mail to: P.O. Box 21, 62651
Private agency
Founded in: 1972
Florence Hutchison, President
Number of members: 625
Staff: volunteer 9
Magazine: *Jacksonville Genealogy
Journal*
Major programs: library, research,
genealogical services
Period of collections: 1818-1916

Morgan County Historical Society
234 N. Webster Ave., 62650
Telephone: (217) 245-5390
Private agency
Founded in: 1904
James E. Davis, President
Number of members: 90
Major programs: historic preservation

KAMPSVILLE

**Center for American
Archeology—Kampsville
Archeological Center**
Telephone: (618) 653-4316
Mail to: P.O. Box 365, 62053
Private agency
Founded in: 1959
Marvin D. Jefer, Director, KAC
Staff: full time 40, part time 45
Major programs: oral history, book
publishing, research, living history
Period of collections: prehistoric

KANKAKEE

**Kankakee County Historical
Society Museum**
8th Ave. and Water St., 60901
Telephone: (815) 932-5279
Town agency
Founded in: 1948
Thomas M. Cuttie, Director/Curator
Number of members: 525
Staff: full time 1, part time 1,
volunteer 7
Major programs: library, archives,
manuscripts, museum, historic
site(s), junior history, oral history,
school programs,
newsletters/pamphlets, historic
preservation, records
management, research, exhibits,
genealogical services
Period of collections: 19th
century-present

KENILWORTH

Kenilworth Historical Society
415 Kenilworth Ave., 60043
Telephone: (312) 251-2565
Mail to: P.O. Box 81
Town agency
Founded in: 1922
Mrs. Willard T. Grimm, President
Number of members: 345
Staff: volunteer 13
Major programs: library, archives,
manuscripts, museum, school
programs, books
Period of collections: 1890-present

KEWANEE

Kewanee Historical Society, Inc.
211 N. Chestnut St., 61443
Telephone: (309) 894-9701
Founded in: 1976
Robert C. Richards, Sr., President
Number of members: 291
Major programs: library, historic
site(s), oral history
Period of collections: 1836-present

LACON

Marshall County Historical Society
314 5th St., 61540
Telephone: (309) 246-2349
Private agency
Founded in: 1956
Eleanor M. Bussell, Museum Curator
Number of members: 135
Staff: full time 1
Major programs: library, museum,
school programs, exhibits,
archaeology programs,
photographic collections,
genealogical services
Period of collections: 1830-present

LA FOX

Garfield Farm and Tavern Museum
P.O. Box 403, 60147
Telephone: (312) 584-8485/584-4034
Private agency, authorized by
Garfield Heritage Society, Inc. and
Campton Historic Agricultural
Lands, Inc.
Founded in: 1977
Jerome M. Johnson,
Curator/Development Officer
Number of members: 300
Number of members: full time 1, part
time 2, volunteer 200
Magazine: *The Fairfield-Campton
Crier*
Major programs: library, archives,
manuscripts, museum, historic
site(s), historic preservation, living
history, archaeology programs,
photographic collections,
genealogical services, agricultural
land preservation
Period of collections: 19th century

LA GRANGE

La Grange Area Historical Society
53 S. La Grange Rd., 60525
Telephone: (312) 354-7889
Town agency
Founded in: 1972
E. E. Marita Kingman, President
Number of members: 510

Staff: volunteer 15
Major programs: archives,
manuscripts, museum, oral history,
book publishing,
newsletters/pamphlets,
photographic collections
Period of collections: 1783-present

LANSING

Lansing Historical Society
2750 Indiana Ave.
Telephone: (618) 474-6160
Mail to: P.O. Box 1776, 60438
Private agency
Founded in: 1976
Julie Gavet, Museum Curator
Major programs: manuscripts,
museum, historic site(s),
tours/pilgrimages, junior history,
oral history, school programs,
newsletters/pamphlets, historic
preservation, exhibits,
photographic collections,
genealogical services
Period of collections: 1820-present

LAWRENCEVILLE

**Lawrence County Historical
Society**
1106 Ash St., 62439
Telephone: (618) 943-2769
Private agency
Founded in: 1961
June Dollahan, President
Major programs: library, historic
site(s), markers, book publishing
Period of collections: 1818-present

LEBANON

Lebanon Historical Society
309 W. St. Louis St., 62254
Telephone: (618) 537-4498
Private agency
Founded in: 1964
H. L. Church, Spokesperson
Number of members: 200
Staff: volunteer 8
Major programs: historic site(s),
historic preservation

LERNA

**Lincoln Log Cabin State Historic
Site**
R.R. 1, Box 175, 62440
Telephone: (217) 345-6489
State agency, authorized by
Department of Conservation
Founded in: 1936
Thomas Vance, Site Superintendent
Number of members: 75
Staff: full time 3, part time 1,
volunteer 75
Magazine: *Goosenest Prairie Gazette*
Major programs: historic site(s),
school programs, historic
preservation, research, living
history
Period of collections: 1840-1870

LEWISTOWN

Dickson Mounds Museum
Illinois State Museum, R.R. 1, 61542
Telephone: (309) 547-3721
State agency
Founded in: 1927

Judith A. Franke, Deputy Director
Staff: full time 20, volunteer 5
Major programs: museum, historic
site(s), newsletters/pamphlets,
research, exhibits, audiovisual
programs, archaeology programs
Period of collections: 3000 B.C.-A.D.
900

LIBERTYVILLE

Lake County Genealogical Society
Cook Memorial Library, 413 N.
Milwaukee Ave., 60048
Telephone: (312) 362-2330
Founded in: 1978
Number of members: 100
Magazine: *Quarterly*
Major programs: educational
programs

**Libertyville-Mundelein Historical
Society, Inc.**
413 N. Milwaukee Ave., 60048
Telephone: (312) 362-3130
Private agency
Founded in: 1955
Robert O. Dunn, President
Number of members: 186
Staff: volunteer 17
Major programs: library, archives,
Victorian home museum, oral
history, newsletters/pamphlets
Period of collections: 1830-present

LINCOLN

Illinois State Genealogical Society
P.O. Box 157, 62656
Telephone: (217) 732-3988
Private agency
Founded in: 1968
Lester L. Wickline, Executive
Secretary
Number of members: 2,300
Staff: part time 2
Magazine: *Genealogical Society
Quarterly*
Major programs: book publishing,
newsletters/pamphlets, research,
exhibits, genealogical services

**Logan County Genealogical
Society**
P.O. Box 283, 62656
Telephone: (217) 732-4698
Private agency
Founded in: 1978
Number of members: 120
Magazine: *Logan County
Genealogical Quarterly*
Major programs: library, research,
exhibits, genealogical services

**Postville Courthouse State Historic
Site**
914 5th St.
Telephone: (217) 732-8930
Mail to: P.O. Box 355, 62656
State agency
Founded in: 1953
Richard Schachtsiek, Site
Superintendent
Staff: full time 4
Major programs: museum, historic
site(s), tours/pilgrimages,
educational programs
Period of collections: 1839-1855

LISLE

Jurica Nature Museum
5700 College Rd., 60532
Telephone: (312) 960-1500
Private agency, authorized by Illinois
Benedictine College
Founded in: 1970
Theodore D. Suchy, Curator
Staff: part time 1
Major programs: museum,
tours/pilgrimages, exhibits, natural
history

LITCHFIELD

**Montgomery County Genealogical
Society**
P.O. Box 212, 62056
Private agency
Founded in: 1978
Marcella White, Corresponding
Secretary
Number of members: 210
Magazine: *Montgomery County
Genealogical Society Quarterly*
Major programs: library, book
publishing, genealogical services
Period of collections: to 1900

LOCKPORT

Illinois Canal Society
1109 Garfield St., 60441
Telephone: (815) 838-7316
Private agency
Founded in: 1976
John Lamb, President
Number of members: 60
Staff: volunteer 2
Major programs: library, archives,
tours/pilgrimages,
newsletters/pamphlets, research,
exhibits, photographic collections
Period of collections: 1830-present

Will County Historical Society
803 S. State St., 60441
Private agency
Rose V. Bucciferro, Curator
Number of members: 650
Staff: full time 1, volunteer 35
Magazine: *W.C.H.S. Quarterly*
Major programs: library, archives,
museum, historic site(s), school
programs, newsletters/pamphlets
Period of collections: 1837-1938

LOMBARD

Lombard Historical Society, Inc.
23 W. Maple, 60148
Telephone: (312) 629-1885
Founded in: 1969
David A. Gorak, President
Number of members: 400
Staff: volunteer 100
Major programs: library, museum,
markers, tours/pilgrimages, junior
history, oral history, school
programs, books,
newsletters/pamphlets
Period of collections: 1850-1920

LONG GROVE

Long Grove Historical Society
Telephone: (312) 634-9440
Mail to: P.O. Box 3110, 60047
Founded in: 1974

Virginia L. Park, President
Number of members: 155
Staff: volunteer 20
Major programs: library, archives,
historic site(s), markers,
tours/pilgrimages, junior history,
oral history, school programs, book
publishing, newsletters/pamphlets,
historic preservation, records
management, research, exhibits,
living history, audiovisual
programs, photographic
collections
Period of collections: 1850-1900

MACOMB

Western Museum
900 W. Adams St., 61455
Telephone: (309) 298-1727
Town agency, authorized by
Auxilliary Services, Western Illinois
University
Founded in: 1974
Paul Jensen, Curator
Number of members: 150
Staff: full time 1, part time 1,
volunteer 2
Major programs: museum,
tours/pilgrimages,
newsletters/pamphlets, historic
preservation, exhibits
Period of collections: 1840-1930

MAHOMET

**Early American Museum and
Gardens**
P.O. Box 336, 61853
Telephone: (217) 586-2612
County agency, authorized by
Champaign County Forest
Preserve
Founded in: 1968
Raylene Scholtens, Director
Staff: full time 4, part time 5,
volunteer 80
Major programs: museum, school
programs, research, exhibits,
weekend events
Period of collections: 18th-19th
centuries

MANITO

Manito Historical Society
61546
Private agency
Founded in: 1978
Alice E. Talbott, President
Number of members: 80
Staff: volunteer 10
Magazine: *The Jailhouse Key*
Major programs: book publishing,
newsletters/pamphlets, historic
preservation
Period of collections: late 19th-early
20th centuries

MARION

**Williamson County Historical
Society**
105 S. Van Buren, 62959
County agency
Founded in: 1935
Helen Davis, President
Number of members: 110

Major programs: library, museum, historic site(s), markers, school programs, book publishing, newsletters/pamphlets, exhibits, photographic collections, genealogical services
Period of collections: 1814-present

MARISSA

Marissa Historical and Genealogical Society
S. Main
Mail to: P.O. Box 27, 62257
Founded in:
Dorothy Elrod, President
Number of members: 175
Staff: volunteer 10
Magazine: *Branching Out From St. Clair County Illinois*
Major programs: library, museum, historic site(s), book publishing

MARSHALL

Clark County Genealogical Society
309 Maple
Telephone: (217) 826-2864
Mail to: P.O. Box 153, 62441
Private agency
Founded in: 1970
Lawrence Goekler, President
Number of members: 60
Staff: volunteer 5
Major programs: library, research, genealogical services
Period of collections: 1818-present

MATTESON

Matteson Historical Society
813 School Ave., 60443
Telephone: (312) 748-3033
Private agency
Founded in: 1975
Shirley Smith, Society Office Aide
Number of members: 120
Staff: part time 1
Major programs: museum, markers, oral history
Period of collections: 1895-1915

MELROSE PARK

Melrose Park Historical Society
1000 N. 25th Ave., 60160
Mail to: P.O. Box 1453, 60161
Private agency

Founded in: 1974
J. Lorne Essery, President
Number of members: 128
Staff: full time 10, volunteer 10
Major programs: archives, markers, oral history, newsletters/pamphlets, exhibits, photographic collections

MENDOTA

Time Was Village Museum
Rt. 51
Telephone: (815) 539-6042
Mail to: 1325 Burlington St., 61342
Private agency
Founded in: 1970
Kenneth B. Butler, Director
Staff: full time 5, part time 3
Major programs: museum, historic preservation, exhibits, photographic collections
Period of collections: 1865-1960

METAMORA

Mennonite Heritage Center
Rt. 116
Telephone: (309) 266-6974
Mail to: 140 N. Missouri Ave., 61550
Private agency, authorized by Illinois Mennonite Historical and Genealogical Society
Founded in: 1969
George Unger, President
Number of members: 450
Staff: volunteer 20
Magazine: *Mennonite Heritage*
Major programs: library, archives, museum, genealogical services
Period of collections: 1830-present

METROPOLIS

Ft. Massac Historic Site
P.O. Box 708, 62960
Telephone: (618) 524-9321
State agency
Ernest Mohr, Site Superintendent
Staff: full time 1, part time 1, volunteer 2
Major programs: museum, historic site(s), research, exhibits

Massac County Historical Society
405 Market St., 62960
Private agency
Founded in: 1975
Gary Stevens, President

Major programs: library, museum, historic site(s), historic preservation, exhibits
Period of collections: 1870-1900

MOLINE

Rock Island County Historical Society
822 11th Ave.
Telephone: (309) 764-8590
Mail to: P.O. Box 632, 61265
Private agency
Founded in: 1905
James R. Sampson, President
Number of members: 260
Founded in: volunteer 8
Major programs: library, archives, manuscripts, museum, markers, newsletters/pamphlets, research, photographic collections, genealogical services
Period of collections: 1860-present

MONTICELLO

Illinois Pioneer Heritage Center, Inc.
315 W. Main, P.O. Box 12, 61856
Telephone: (217) 762-4731
Private agency
Founded in: 1965
Ralph McInnes, President
Number of members: 50
Staff: volunteer 10
Major programs: museum
Period of collections: 1860-present

Piatt County Historical and Genealogical Society
Courthouse, Room 106, 61856
Private agency
Founded in: 1980
Hugh Finson, President
Magazine: *The Piatt County Historical and Genealogical Society Quarterly*
Major programs: library, book publishing, newsletters/pamphlets, research, genealogical services
Period of collections: 1841-1968

MORRISON

Morrison Historical Society
Mail to: 16959 Tanglewild Dr., 61270
Private agency
Founded in: 1976
Loyal Hammer, President
Number of members: 25
Major programs: library, manuscripts, museum, tours/pilgrimages, newsletters/pamphlets
Period of collections: 1830-present

MOUNT CARROLL

Campbell Center for Historic Preservation Studies
203 E. Seminary
Telephone: (815) 244-1173
Mail to: P.O. Box 66, 61053
Private agency, authorized by the Restoration College Association, Inc.
Founded in: 1979
Number of members: 120
Staff: full time 5
Major programs: preservation education workshops

The Early American Museum and Botanical Garden in Mahomet displays over 3000 items depicting 19th-century rural life.—Early American Museum and Gardens

Carroll County Historical Society
P.O. Box 65, 61053
Private agency
Founded in: 1964
Mary E. Boyd, President
Number of members: 59
Staff: volunteer 5
Major programs: museum, markers, books, historic preservation
Period of collections: 1860-1920

MOUNT PROSPECT

Mt. Prospect Historical Society of Elk Grove and Wheeling Townships
1100 S. Linneman Rd.
Telephone: (312) 956-6777
Mail to: P.O. Box 81, 60056
Private agency
Founded in: 1968
Gertrude Francek, Museum Director
Number of members: 220
Staff: part time 1, volunteer 20
Magazine: State Board
Major programs: library, museum, tours/pilgrimages, school programs, newsletters/pamphlets
Period of collections: 1832-present

Northwest Suburban Council of Genealogists
P.O. Box AC, 60056
Private agency
Founded in: 1977
Brian Scott Donovan, President
Number of members: 84
Major programs: library, genealogical services

MT. VERNON

Jefferson County Historical Society
1703 Oakland, 62864
Telephone: (618) 242-0732
Founded in: 1946
Oren Drew, President
Number of members: 221
Staff: volunteer 20
Major programs: library, museum, historic site(s), tours/pilgrimages, oral history, school programs, book publishing, newsletters/pamphlets, historic preservation
Period of collections: 1819-present

Mitchell Museum
Richview Rd.
Telephone: (618) 242-1236
Mail to: P.O. Box 923, 62864
Private agency
Founded in: 1973
David Prince, Acting Director/Curator
Staff: full time 5, volunteer 210
Major programs: museum, exhibits, natural history, ethnobotany
Period of collections: 19th-20th centuries

MUNDELEIN

Historical Society of the Ft. Hill Country
Mail to: P.O. Box 582, 60060
Town agency
Founded in: 1956
Leonard J. Schmitt, President
Number of members: 58

Major programs: archives, manuscripts, historic site(s), markers, tours/pilgrimages, oral history, newsletters/pamphlets, historic preservation, research, exhibits, living history, audiovisual programs, archaeology programs, photographic collections
Period of collections: 1880-present

MURPHYSBORO

Jackson County Historical Society
1401 Walnut St.
Mail to: P.O. Box 7, 62966
Private agency
Founded in: 1969
Clifton Swafford, President
Number of members: 362
Staff: volunteer 8
Magazine: The Jacksonian Ventilator
Major programs: library, museum, book publishing, newsletters/pamphlets, photographic collections, genealogical services
Period of collections: 1880-1920

NAPERVILLE

Naperville Heritage Society—Naper Settlement
201 W. Porter Ave., 60540
Telephone: (312) 420-6010
Private agency
Founded in: 1969
Margaret Lynn Frank, Executive Director
Number of members: 1,070
Staff: full time 4, part time 13, volunteer 210
Magazine: Plough Shares
Major programs: museum, historic site(s), markers, tours/pilgrimages, school programs, newsletters/pamphlets, historic preservation, living history, genealogical services
Period of collections: 1831-1900

May Watts House and Garden Society
227 E. Jefferson
Telephone: (312) 355-1988
Mail to: P.O. Box D, 60540
Questionnaire not received

NASHVILLE

Washington County Historical Society
302 S. Kaskaskia, 62263
Private agency
Founded in: 1965
Number of members: 200
Major programs: museum, historic site(s), newsletters/pamphlets, historic preservation

NAUVOO

Joseph Smith Historic Center
P.O. Box 338, Water St., 62354
Telephone: (217) 453-2246
Private agency, authorized by Reorganized Church of Jesus Christ of Latter Day Saints
Founded in: 1918
Kenneth E. Stobaugh, Director

Staff: full time 3, part time 1, volunteer 8
Major programs: historic site, tours/pilgrimages, summer intern program
Period of collections: 1840

Nauvoo Historical Society
62354
Founded in: 1952
Questionnaire not received

Nauvoo Restoration, Inc.
Young and Partridge Sts., 62354
Telephone: (217) 453-2237
Private agency
Founded in: 1962
J. LeRoy Kimball, President
Number of members: full time 10, part time 6, volunteer 75
Major programs: museum, historic site, historic preservation
Period of collections: 1839-1846

NEWMAN

Douglas County Historical Society
61942
Founded in: 1967
Questionnaire not received

NILES

Jewish Genealogical Society of Illinois
P.O. Box 481022, 60648
Telephone: (312) 965-8277
Private agency
Founded in: 1980
Freya B. Maslov, President
Number of members: 100
Staff: volunteer 20
Magazine: Search
Major programs: oral history, newsletters/pamphlets, historic preservation, research, genealogical services

NORMAL

The University Museums
Illinois State University, 61761
Telephone: (309) 438-8800
State agency, authorized by board of regents
Gordon A. Davis, Director
Staff: full time 7, part time 1, volunteer 5
Major programs: museum, tours/pilgrimages, school programs, newsletters/pamphlets, exhibits
Period of collections: 1830-present

NORTHBROOK

Northbrook Historical Society
1776 Walter's Ave., 60062
Telephone: (312) 498-3404
Questionnaire not received

NORTH CHICAGO

Lake County Museum Association
Mail to: P.O. Box 205, 60064
Founded in: 1971
Questionnaire not received

OAK BROOK

Graue Mill and Museum
York and Spring Rds.

Telephone: (312) 655-2090
Mail to: P.O. Box 293, 60521
Private agency, authorized by
    DuPage Graue Mill Corporation
Founded in: 1950
Chris Meier, Administrator
Number of members: 350
Staff: part time 13, volunteer 100
Major programs: museum
Period of collections: 1840-1880

Oak Brook Historical Society
Telephone: (312) 833-8154
Mail to: P.O. Box 1106, 60521
Private agency
Founded in: 1975
Arlene Birkhahn, President
Number of members: 209
Major programs: library, historic
    site(s), school programs, historic
    preservation, research
Period of collections:
    prehistoric-present

OAK LAWN

Moraine Valley Oral History Association
9427 S. Raymond Ave., 60453
Telephone: (312) 422-4990
Private agency
Founded in: 1976
Gerald R. Anderson, President
Number of members: 25
Staff: volunteer 10
Major programs: library, oral history
Period of collections: 1890-present

Oak Lawn Historical Society
9526 S. Cook Ave.
Telephone: (312) 425-3424
Mail to: 4332 W. 109th St., 06453
Private agency
Founded in: 1976
William J. Sullivan, Director
Number of members: 125
Staff: full time 1, volunteer 10
Magazine: Oak Lawn Acorns
Major programs: archives, museum,
    historic sites preservation, markers,
    educational programs,
    newsletters/pamphlets
Period of collections: 1865-present

Oak Lawn Public Library
9427 S. Raymond Ave., 60453
Telephone: (312) 422-4990
Town agency
Founded in: 1943
James M. O'Brien, Head Librarian
Staff: full time 24, part time 30
Major programs: library, manuscripts,
    oral history, photographic
    collections, news indexing
Period of collections: 1870-present

OAK PARK

Frank Lloyd Wright Home and Studio Foundation
951 Chicago Ave., 60302
Telephone: (312) 848-1976
Private agency, authorized by
    National Trust for Historic
    Preservation
Founded in: 1974
Carla Lind, Executive Director
Number of members: 1,000
Staff: full time 6, part time 6,
    volunteer 350
Magazine: Wright Angles

Major programs: library, museum,
    historic site(s), tours/pilgrimages,
    junior history, school programs,
    book publishing,
    newsletters/pamphlets, research,
    photographic collections
Period of collections: 1880-1925

Historical Society of Oak Park and River Forest
Farson-Mills House
Telephone: (312) 386-2300
Mail to: P.O. Box 771, 60302
Private agency
Founded in: 1967
Warren D. Stevens, President
Number of members: 496
Staff: part time 1, volunteer 25
Magazine: Village Yesterdays
Major programs: museum, markers,
    tours/pilgrimages, oral history,
    book publishing,
    newsletters/pamphlets, exhibits,
    photographic collections
Period of collections: 1835-present

ODELL

Odell Prairie Trails Historical and Genealogical Society
P.O. Box 82, 60460
Telephone: (815) 998-2324
Private agency
Founded in: 1978
Lorraine Hare, Secretary
Number of members: 35
Staff: volunteer 7
Magazine: Prairie Trails
Major programs: library, archives,
    museum, book publishing,
    newsletters/pamphlets, research,
    genealogical services
Period of collections: 1860s-1920s

OGLESBY

Oglesby Historical Society
128 W. Walnut St.
Mail to: 100 Oak St., 61348
Founded in: 1919
Questionnaire not received

OLNEY

Embarras Regional Planning and Development Commission
P.O. Box 362, Richland County
    Courthouse 3rd Floor 62450
Telephone: (618) 395-2151
Founded in: 1971
Staff: full time 7
Magazine: Historic Preservation:
    Opportunities for the Embarras
    Region
Major programs: planning material

Richland County Genealogical and Historical Society
P.O. Box 202, 62450
Mail to: Rt. 1, Claremont, 62421
Private agency
Founded in: 1977
Jan Doan, Editor
Number of members: 300
Staff: volunteer 15
Magazine: Footprints Past and
    Present
Major programs: library, museum,
    historic site(s), book publishing,
    newsletters/pamphlets,
    genealogical services

ORLAND PARK

Orland Historical Society
P.O. Box 324, 60462
Private agency
Founded in: 1975
Mona L. Creer, President
Number of members: 50
Major programs: museum, oral
    history, newsletters/pamphlets,
    historic preservation, photographic
    collections
Period of collections: 1850-1900

OTTAWA

La Salle County Historical Society
Mail to: P.O. Box 577, 61350
Founded in: 1952
Number of members: 650
Staff: part time 2
Major programs: library, archives,
    museum, educational programs,
    newsletters/pamphlets
Period of collections: 1865-1918

PALATINE

Palatine Historical Society
224 E. Palatine Rd.
Mail to: P.O. Box 134, 60067
Private agency
Founded in: 1955
Donna Dwyer, President
Number of members: 300
Staff: volunteer 25
Magazine: Palatine Palaver
Major programs: library, museum,
    oral history, school programs, book
    publishing, newsletters/pamphlets,
    historic preservation,
    photographic collections,
    genealogical services
Period of collections: 1860-1920

PALOS PARK

Palos Historical Society
12021 S. 93rd Ave., 60464
Founded in: 1957
Major programs: library, markers,
    tours/pilgrimages, oral history,
    historic preservation
Period of collections: 1832-present
Questionnaire not received

PARIS

Edgar County Historical Society
414 N. Main, 61944
Telephone: (217) 463-5305
Private agency
Founded in: 1969
Walter Kimble, Historian
Number of members: 250
Staff: volunteer 20
Major programs: manuscripts,
    museum, tours/pilgrimages, oral
    history, school programs, book
    publishing, newsletters/pamphlets,
    historic preservation, exhibits,
    living history, photographic
    collections, genealogical services,
    field services
Period of collections: 1824-present

PARK FOREST

Park Forest Historical Society
c/o Park Forest Public Library
Telephone: (312) 748-3731

Mail to: 400 Lakewood Blvd., 60466
Private agency
Founded in: 1985
Jane Nicoll, Reference Librarian
Number of members: 30
Staff: full time 2
Major programs: archives, oral
history, photographic collections
Period of collections: from 1949

PARK RIDGE

Park Ridge Historical Society
41 Prairie, 60068
Telephone: (312) 696-1973
Private agency
Founded in: 1973
Peter Malone, President
Number of members: 280
Staff: part time 18
Major programs: museum,
tours/pilgrimages,
newsletters/pamphlets, records
management, research, exhibits
Period of collections: 1870-present

**Wood Library—Museum of
Anesthesiology**
515 Busse Hwy., 60068
Telephone: (312) 825-5586
Private agency, authorized by the
American Society of
Anesthesiologists
Founded in: 1951
Patrick Sim, Librarian
Major programs: library, archives,
museum, living history, history of
medicine and anesthesia
Period of collections: 19th
century-present

PAXTON

Ford County Historical Society
145 W. Center St. 60957
Telephone: (217) 379-3121
Founded in: 1967
James Anderson, President
Founded in: 120
Staff: volunteer 3
Major programs: archives, museum,
junior history, oral history
Period of collections: prehistoric-1920

PEKIN

**Everett McKinley Dirksen
Congressional Leadership
Research Center**
Broadway and 4th Sts., 61554
Telephone: (309) 347-7113
Private agency, authorized by Everett
McKinley Dirksen Endowment Fund
Founded in: 1963
Frank H. Mackaman, Executive
Director
Staff: full time 3, part time 3,
volunteer 130
Major programs: manuscripts,
museum, school programs,
newsletters/pamphlets, research,
exhibits
Period of collections: 1900-present

**Tazewell County Historical
Association**
Mail to: P.O. Box 636, 61554
Questionnaire not received

PEORIA

Peoria Historical Society
942 N.E. Glen Oak, 61603
Telephone: (309) 674-1921
Private agency
Founded in: 1934
Robert A. Jones, President
Number of members: 750
Staff: part time 4
Major programs: library, archives,
manuscripts, museum,
newsletters/pamphlets, historic
preservation, research,
photographic collections
Period of collections: 1783-present

PEOTONE

**Historical Society of Greater
Peotone**
213 W. North St., 60468
Telephone: (312) 258-3436
Private agency
Founded in: 1977
Michael R. Morrison, President
Number of members: 35
Major programs: library, historic
site(s), historic preservation,
archaeology programs
Period of collections: 1870-1940

PETERSBURG

Lincoln's New Salem State Park
R.R. 1, 62675
Telephone: (217) 632-7953
State agency, authorized by
Department of Conservation
Founded in: 1919
David Hedrick, Superintendent
Staff: full time 25, part time 5,
volunteer 120
Major programs: museum, historic
site(s), exhibits, living history
Period of collections: 1830-1840

PITTSFIELD

Pike County Historical Society
Mail to: P.O. Box 44, 62363
County agency
Founded in: 1960
Elizabeth L. Lacy, President
Number of members: 80
Staff: volunteer 10
Major programs: archives,
manuscripts, museum, historic
site(s), tours/pilgrimages, oral
history, book publishing,
newsletters/pamphlets, historic
preservation, records
management, research, exhibits,
living history, archaeology
programs, photographic
collections, genealogical services

PLEASANT PLAINS

Clayville Folk Arts Guild
Clayville Rural Life Center, 62611
Founded in: 1967
Number of members: 400
Magazine: Whig
Major programs: museum,
educational programs
Period of collections: 1783-1865

Clayville Rural Life Center
62677
Founded in: 1961
Questionnaire not received

PRINCETON

Bureau County Historical Society
109 Park Ave., W, 61356
Telephone: (815) 875-2184
Private agency
Founded in: 1911
Mrs. Field Williams, Curator
Number of members: 400
Staff: part time 2, volunteer 4
Major programs: library, manuscripts,
museum, tours/pilgrimages, junior
history, school programs, historic
preservation, records
management, research, exhibits,
photographic collections,
genealogical services
Period of collections: 1830-present

QUINCY

**Gardner Museum of Architecture
and Design**
4th and Maine Sts., 62301
Telephone: (217) 224-6873
Private agency, authorized by
Gardner Quincy Adams County
Museum
Founded in: 1974
J. Willis Gardner III, President
Number of members: 50
Staff: full time 3
Major programs: museum, exhibits,
history of architecture and design
Period of collections: 1860s-1970s

**Historical Society of Quincy and
Adams County**
425 S. 12th, 62301
Telephone: (217) 222-1835
Private agency
Philip Germann, Executive Director
Major programs: library, archives,
manuscripts, historic site(s), school
programs, historic preservation,
exhibits, photographic collections
Period of collections: 1830-1900

RIDGWAY

Gallatin County Historical Society
R.R. I, 62979
Telephone: (618) 272-7092
Private agency
Founded in: 1966
Mrs. James T. Lawler, President
Number of members: 210
Staff: part time 1, volunteer 10
Major programs: archives,
manuscripts, museum, historic
site(s), markers, tours/pilgrimages,
junior history, school programs,
newsletters/pamphlets, exhibits,
audiovisual programs,
photographic collections,
genealogical services
Period of collections: 1810-1880

RIVER GROVE

**Cernan Earth and Space Center—
Triton College**
2000 N. 5th Ave., 60656
Telephone: (312) 456-5815
State agency, authorized by the
college
Founded in: 1974
Steve Bishop, Director
Staff: full time 4, part time 8,
volunteer 3

Major programs: museum, school programs, exhibits, audiovisual programs, planetarium programs

ROBINSON

Crawford County Historical Society, Inc.
R.R. 3
Telephone: (618) 544-2300
Mail to: P.O. Box 554, 62454
Bill Bachelor, President
Number of members: 145
Major programs: museum, markers, junior history, book publishing, newsletters/pamphlets, historic preservation, research, exhibits, genealogical services
Period of collections: 1810-1940

ROCHELLE

Flagg Township Historical Society
921 6th St., 61068
Telephone: (815) 562-7345
Questionnaire not received

ROCKFORD

Burpee Museum of Natural History
813 N. Main St., 61103
Telephone: (815) 965-3132
Private agency, authorized by Burpee Gallery Association
Founded in: 1942
Milton W. Mahlburg, Director
Staff: full time 2, part time 1
Major programs: museum, exhibits, natural history

North Central Illinois Genealogical Society
P.O. Box 1071, 61105
Founded in: 1979
Number of members: 196
Staff: volunteer 6
Magazine: News of the North Central Illinois Genealogical Society
Major programs: library, educational programs, book publishing, newsletters/pamphlets
Period of collections: 1835-1900

North Western Illinois Chapter, National Railway Historical Society
P.O. Box 5632, 61125
Private agency
Founded in: 1967
Lloyd Rinehart, President
Number of members: 108
Staff: volunteer 10
Magazine: North Western Limited
Major programs: tours/pilgrimages, oral history, book publishing, newsletters/pamphlets, audiovisual programs, photographic collections
Period of collections: 1940-present

Rockford Historical Society
Mail to: 1518 Comanche Dr., 61107
Founded in: 1961
Hazel M. Hyde, Corresponding Secretary
Number of members: 250
Magazine: Nuggets of History
Major programs: archives, historic sites preservation, markers, tours/pilgrimages, oral history, educational programs, books
Period of collections: 1783-present

Rockford Museum Center and Midway Village
6799 Guilford Rd., 61107
Telephone: (815) 397-9112
City agency, authorized by Rockford Museum Association
Founded in: 1973
Tara C. Busser, Director
Number of members: 835
Staff: full time 4, part time 1, volunteer 150
Magazine: ArtiFacts
Major programs: museum, historic preservation, exhibits
Period of collections: early 1900s

Swedish Historical Society of Rockford
404 S. 3rd St., 61108
Telephone: (815) 963-5559/965-7972
Private agency
Founded in: 1938
Armer Severin, President
Number of members: 200
Staff: volunteer 20
Major programs: archives, museum, historic site(s), book publishing, historic preservation
Period of collections: 1850-1900

The Time Museum
7801 E. State St.
Telephone: (815) 398-6000, ext. 2941
Mail to: P.O. Box 5285, 61125-0285
Private agency
Founded in: 1970
William Andrewes, Curator
Major programs: museum
Period of collections: 3000 B.C.-present

Tinker Swiss Cottage, Inc.
411 Kent St., 61103
Founded in: 1942
Number of members: 500
Magazine: Tinker Topics
Major programs: museum, historic site, tours/pilgrimages, historic sites preservation
Period of collections: 1860-1920

ROCK ISLAND

Augustana Historical Society
639 38th St., 61201
Telephone: (309) 794-7000
Private agency, authorized by Augustana College
Founded in: 1930
Ann Boaden, President
Number of members: 230
Staff: volunteer 10
Major programs: library, archives, book publishing, historic preservation, research
Period of collections: 1860-present

Hauberg Indian Museum, Black Hawk State Park
1510 46th Ave., 61201
Telephone: (309) 788-9536
State agency, authorized by Department of Conservation
Founded in: 1927
Neil Rangen, Site Superintendent
Staff: full time 4
Major programs: museum, historic site(s), markers, tours/pilgrimages, school programs, book publishing, research, exhibits, audiovisual programs, archaeology programs
Period of collections: 1880-1920

John M. Browning Memorial Museum
SMCRI-AOW-B, Rock Island Arsenal, 61299-5000
Telephone: (309) 794-5021
Federal agency, authorized by the U.S. Army
Founded in: 1905
Daniel T. Whiteman, Museum Director
Staff: full time 4, part time 1, volunteer 5
Major programs: archives, museum, tours/pilgrimages, research, exhibits, photographic collections
Period of collections: 1800-1950

Modern Woodmen of America
Mississippi River at 17th St., 61201
Telephone: (309) 786-6481
Private agency
Founded in: 1883
Gail Ann Levis, Historian
Number of members: 1
Staff: full time 1
Magazine: The Modern Woodmen
Major programs: archives, historic site(s), markers, oral history, records management, research, exhibits, genealogical services
Period of collections: 1883-1957

Rock Island Arsenal Historical Society
SMCRI-ADW-B, Rock Island Arsenal, 61299
Telephone: (309) 794-5021
Private agency
Founded in: 1972
Jerry W. Bates, Treasurer
Number of members: 70
Staff: volunteer 4
Major programs: museum, historic site(s)

ROMEOVILLE

Isle a la Cache Museum
501 Romeo Rd., 60441
Telephone: (815) 886-1467
County agency, authorized by the Forest Preserve of Will County
Founded in: 1983
Jack MacRae, Museum Coordinator
Staff: full time 2, part time 2
Major programs: museum, school programs, exhibits, living history
Period of collections: 1673-1850

ROSELLE

Roselle Historical Society
Roselle Village Hall, 31 S. Prospect, 60172
Telephone: (312) 980-2000
Town agency, authorized by Village of Roselle
Founded in: 1978
Joan Beauprez, Mayor/Chair
Staff: volunteer 11
Major programs: book publishing, historic preservation, exhibits
Period of collections: 1843-present

RUSHVILLE

Schuyler-Brown Historical Society
200 S. Congress, 62681
Founded in: 1968
Vernon Lickey, President
Number of members: 300
Staff: volunteer 6
Magazine: The Schuylerite

Major programs: book publishing,
genealogical services
Period of collections: late 1800s-early
1900s

ST. CHARLES

Restorations of Kane County
P.O. Box 903, 60174
Telephone: (312) 232-2044
Private agency
Founded in: 1974
Nancy M. Polivka, President
Number of members: 169
Magazine: *Restoration Advocate*
Major programs: museum
Period of collections: 19th century

SALEM

Marion County Genealogical and Historical Society
Mail to: P.O. Box 342, 62881
Private agency
Founded in: 1976
Harold Boyles, President
Number of members: 430
Staff: volunteer 12
Magazine: *Footprints in Marion County*
Major programs: archives, historic
site(s), markers, oral history, book
publishing, historic preservation,
genealogical services
Period of collections: 1783-1918

SHAWNEETOWN

Gallatin County Historical Society
62984
Founded in: 1966
Number of members: 220
Staff: part time 1, volunteer 10
Major programs: archives,
manuscripts, museum, historic site,
markers, tours, pilgrimages,
historic preservation
Period of collections: 1800-1840

SHELBYVILLE

Shelby County Historical and Genealogical Society
303 N. Morgan St., 62565
Founded in: 1963
Number of members: 275
Staff: full time 2
Major programs: library, museum,
historic site, markers,
tours/pilgrimages, junior history,
oral history, educational programs,
book publishing, newsletters/
pamphlets, historic preservation
Period of collections: 1800-1900

SKOKIE

Skokie Historical Society
8031 Floral Ave., 60077
Telephone: (312) 673-1888
Private agency
Founded in: 1978
Rosemary Schmitt, President
Number of members: 150
Staff: volunteer 6
Major programs: archives, museum,
historic site(s),
newsletters/pamphlets, historic
preservation, research,
photographic collections
Period of collections: 1840-present

SOUTH HOLLAND

South Holland Historical Society
16250 Wausau Ave., 60473
Founded in: 1969
Number of members: 80
Staff: volunteer 20
Major programs: library, manuscripts,
museum, markers,
tours/pilgrimages, oral history,
educational programs
Period of collections: 1865-1918

South Suburban Genealogical and Historical Society
Roosevelt Community Center, 320 E.
161st Place, 60473
Founded in: 1969
Questionnaire not received

SPRINGFIELD

Abraham Lincoln Association
Old State Capitol
Telephone: (217) 782-4836
Private agency
Founded in: 1908
Harlington Wood, Jr., President
Number of members: 360
Staff: volunteer 2
Magazine: *Papers of the Abraham Lincoln Association*
Major programs: book publishing,
symposium

AIRCHIVE Association
326 S. MacArthur Blvd., 62704
Telephone: (217) 789-9754
Private agency
Founded in: 1977
Job C. Conger IV, Founder/Executive
Director
Number of members: 300
Magazine: *AIRChatter*
Major programs: library, archives,
museum, newsletters/pamphlets,
research, exhibits, audiovisual
programs, photographic
collections
Period of collections: 20th century

Division of Historic Sites, Illinois Department of Conservation
405 E. Washington, 62706
Telephone: (217) 525-6302
Founded in: 1928
Michael Witte, Director
Magazine: *Historic Illinois*
Major programs: museum, historic
site(s), markers, tours/pilgrimages,
junior history, school programs,
newsletters/pamphlets, historic
preservation, research, exhibits,
living history, audiovisual
programs, archaeology programs
Period of collections: 1783-present

Illinois Bell's Oliver P. Parks Telephone Museum
529 S. 7th St., 62721
Telephone: (217) 753-8436
Private agency, authorized by Illinois
Bell Telephone Company
Founded in: 1976
Geri Braun, Administrator
Staff: full time 2, parr time 1
Major programs: museum, school
programs, audiovisual programs
Period of collections: 1876-present

Illinois Historic Preservation Agency
Old State Capitol, 62701
Telephone: (217) 782-4836
State agency
Founded in: 1985
Michael J. Devine, Director
Staff: 225
Magazine: *Historic Illinois*
Major programs: library, manuscripts,
historic site(s), markers, oral
history, school programs, historic
preservation, research, exhibits,
living history, photographic
collections, genealogical services,
national and state registration of
historic places
Period of collections: 19th century

Illinois State Archives
Archives Bldg., 62756
Telephone: (217) 782-4682
State agency
Founded in: 1921
John Daly, Director
Staff: full time 45
Major programs: archives, records
management, genealogical
services
Period of collections: 19th-20th
centuries

Illinois State Historical Library
Old State Capitol, 62701
Telephone: (217) 782-4836
State agency
Founded in: 1889
Michael J. Devine, State Historian
Staff: full time 70
Magazine: *Illinois Historical Journal/Illinois History Magazine*
Major programs: library, archives,
manuscripts, oral history, school
programs, records management,
research, photographic
collections, genealogical services
Period of collections: 19th century

◊Illinois State Historical Society
Old State Capitol, 62701
Telephone: (217) 782-4836
Private agency
Founded in: 1899
Michael J. Devine, Executive Director
Number of members: 3,000
Staff: part time 3
Magazine: *Dispatch*
Major programs: markers,
tours/pilgrimages, junior history,
educational programs,
newsletters/pamphlets, field
services
Period of collections: 19th century

◊Illinois State Museum
Spring and Edwards Sts., 62706
Telephone: (217) 782-7386
State agency, authorized by
Department of Energy and Natural
Resources
Founded in: 1877
Jean Lerche, Public Information
Coordinator
Staff: full time 96, part time 32
Magazine: *The Living Museum*
Major programs: library, museum,
tours/pilgrimages, school
programs, research, exhibits,

archaeology programs, scientific and fine arts
Period of collections: 19th-20th centuries

Lincoln Tomb State Historic Site
Oak Ridge Cemetery, 62702
Telephone: (217) 782-2717
State agency, authorized by Department of Conservation
Founded in: 1874
Carol A. Andrews, Site Superintendent
Staff: full time 6, part time 2, volunteer 3
Major programs: historic site(s), tours/pilgrimages, school programs, historic preservation, research
Period of collections: 1861-1931

Oral History Office, Sangamon State University
Shepherd Rd., 62708
Telephone: (217) 786-6521
State agency, authorized by the university
Founded in: 1971
Cullom Davis, Director/Professor of History
Staff: full time 6, part time 3, volunteer 3
Major programs: archives, oral history, book publishing, exhibits
Period of collections: 20th century

The Pearson Museum
801 N. Rutledge
Telephone: (217) 785-2128
Mail to: P.O. Box 3926, 62702
State agency, authorized by School of Medicine, Southern Illinois University
Founded in: 1974
Glen W. Davidson, Department Chair
Staff: full time 1
Major programs: library, manuscripts, museum, school programs, historic preservation, records management, research, exhibits, audiovisual programs, history of medicine
Period of collections: 19th-20th centuries

Sangamon County Genealogical Society
P.O. Box 1829, 62705
Telephone: (217) 789-0788
Private agency
Founded in: 1967
Betsy Keefe, Corresponding Secretary
Number of members: 400
Magazine: *Circuit Rider*
Major programs: book publishing

Sangamon County Historical Society
308 E. Adams, 62701
Telephone: (217) 522-2500
Private agency
Founded in: 1961
Jacqueline Wright, President
Number of members: 550
Magazine: *Historico*
Major programs: library, tours/pilgrimages, newsletters/pamphlets
Period of collections: 1820-present

Sangamon Valley Collection, Lincoln Library
326 S. 7th St., 62701
Telephone: (217) 753-4910
City agency
Founded in: 1970
Edward J. Russo, Head
Staff: full time 4, part time 1, volunteer 4
Major programs: library, photographic collections, genealogical services
Period of collections: 1830-present

Vachel Lindsay Association, Inc.
603 S. 5th St., 62704
Telephone: (217) 528-9254
Private agency
Founded in: 1946
Janel E. Lundgren, President
Number of members: 475
Staff: full time 1, volunteer 50
Major programs: library, archives, manuscripts, museum, historic site(s), historic preservation, fine arts
Period of collections: 1879-1931

STEELEVILLE

Randolph County Historical Society
Founded in: 1954
Questionnaire not received

STERLING

Whiteside County Genealogists
P.O. Box 145, 61081
Telephone: (815) 625-3977
Private agency
Founded in: 1973
Mary Lou Jackson, President
Number of members: 71
Staff: volunteer 5
Major programs: library, book publishing, newsletters/pamphlets, research, genealogical services
Period of collections: before 1900

STONE PARK

Italian Cultural Center
1621 N. 39th Ave., 60163
Telephone: (312) 345-3842
Private agency, authorized by Fathers of St. Charles
Founded in: 1971
Peter Gandolfi, Director
Number of members: 300
Staff: full time 2, part time 3, volunteer 8
Major programs: library, museum, oral history, school programs, newsletters/pamphlets, exhibits, photographic collections

Stone Park Historical Society
1629 N. Mannhiem Rd., 60165
Telephone: (312) 343-5550
Town agency
Founded in: 1963
George Danda, Chair
Staff: volunteer 5
Major programs: archives, records management, photographic collections
Period of collections: 1939-present

STREATOR

Streatorland Historical Society, Inc.
401 E. Main, Room 317, 61364
Telephone: (815) 673-7671
Private agency
Founded in: 1976
James Reynolds, Board Chair
Number of members: 270
Staff: volunteer 15
Magazine: *Unionville Dispatch*
Major programs: book publishing, newsletters/pamphlets, exhibits, audiovisual programs, photographic collections
Period of collections: 1870-1983

SULLIVAN

Moultrie County Historical and Genealogical Society
117 E. Harrison St.
Telephone: (217) 728-4085
Mail to: P.O. Box MM, 61951
Founded in: 1972
Ina Roney, President
Number of members: 375
Staff: volunteer 14
Magazine: *Moultrie County Heritage*
Major programs: library, archives, manuscripts, museum, historic site(s), junior history, oral history, book publishing, newsletters/pamphlets, records management, research, genealogical services
Period of collections: 1783-present

TAYLORVILLE

Christian County Historical Society
E. Rt. 29
Telephone: (217) 824-6922
Mail to: P.O. Box 254, 62568
Private agency
Founded in: 1965
Bill Estes, President
Number of members: 200
Staff: part time 1, volunteer 10
Major programs: library, museum, historic site, tours/pilgrimages, educational programs, exhibits
Period of collections: 1900

TEUTOPOLIS

Teutopolis Monastery Museum Committee
110 S. Garrett St.
Telephone: (217) 857-3328
Mail to: 210 N. John St., P.O. Box 341, 62467
Private agency, authorized by St. Francis Church
Founded in: 1975
Sophia Hartke, President
Number of members: 30
Staff: volunteer 30
Major programs: museum, tours/pilgrimages, school programs, historic preservation, exhibits, photographic collections, genealogical services
Period of collections: 1839-1939

THORNTON

Thornton Historical Society
208 Schwab St.

Mail to: P.O. Box 34, 60476-0034
Private agency
Founded in: 1975
Oscar M. Claus, President
Number of members: 49
Staff: volunteer 17
Major programs: museum, markers, exhibits
Period of collections: 1870-present

TINLEY PARK

Bremen Historical Society of Tinley Park
6727 W. 174th St.
Telephone: (312) 429-4210
Mail to: P.O. Box 325, 60477
Town agency, authorized by Village of Tinley Park
Founded in: 1976
Robert Kovarik, Museum Director
Number of members: 100
Staff: volunteer 11
Major programs: library, museum, tours, oral history, exhibits
Period of collections: 1850-present

UNION

Illinois Railway Museum
Olson Rd., P.O. Box 431, 60180
Telephone: (815) 923-4391
Private agency
Founded in: 1953
Nick Kallas, General Manager
Number of members: 1,100
Magazine: *Rail and Wire*
Major programs: library, archives, museum, educational programs, book publishing, newsletters/pamphlets, historic preservation, exhibits
Period of collections: 1890-1960

McHenry County Historical Society
6422 Main St., 60180
Private agency
Founded in: 1963
Irene Borre, President
Number of members: 1,000
Staff: full time 1, volunteer 160
Major programs: archives, manuscripts, museum, oral history, books, newsletters/pamphlets, school programs, markers, audiovisual programs
Period of collections: late 19th-early 20th centuries

URBANA

Illinois Historical Survey
Library 346, Univeristy of Illinois
Telephone: (217) 333-1777
Mail to: 1408 W. Gregory Dr., 61801
Founded in: 1910
Staff: full time 2, part time 1
Major programs: library, archives, manuscripts
Period of collections: 18th-20th centuries

UTICA

La Salle County Historical Society
Mill and Canal Sts.
Telephone: (815) 667-4861
Mail to: P.O. Box 278, 61373
Private agency
Founded in: 1952

Sara E. Smith, Museum Director
Number of members: 550
Staff: full time 1, part time 4, volunteer 6
Magazine: *Society Story*
Major programs: library, archives, museum, tours/pilgrimages, school programs, newsletters/pamphlets, exhibits, genealogical services
Period of collections: 1865-1945

VANDALIA

Historical Vandalia, Inc.
Founded in: 1969
Questionnaire not received

Vandalia Historical Society
307 N. 6th St., 62471
Telephone: (618) 283-0024
Private agency
Founded in: 1954
Josephine Burtschi, President
Number of members: 25
Staff: volunteer 2
Major programs: library, archives, manuscripts, museum, historic site(s), markers, tours/pilgrimages, oral history, school programs, book publishing, pamphlets, historic preservation, research, exhibits, audiovisual programs, photographic collections
Period of collections: 1819-1839

Vandalia Statehouse State Historic Site
315 W. Gallatin, 62471
Telephone: (618) 283-1161
State agency, authorized by Department of Conservation
Founded in: 1940
Nan L. Wynn, Site Superintendent
Staff: full time 4, part time 1, volunteer 5
Magazine: *Historic Illinois*
Major programs: historic site(s), markers, tours/pilgrimages, school programs, newsletters/pamphlets
Period of collections: 1819-1839

VILLA PARK

Villa Park Historical Society, Inc.
220 S. Villa Ave., 60181
Telephone: (312) 941-0223
Private agency
Founded in: 1976
Charlotte Burgess, President
Number of members: 170
Staff: volunteer 15
Magazine: *The Whistlestop*
Major programs: archives, museum, newsletters/pamphlets, exhibits, audiovisual programs, photographic collections
Period of collections: 1915-present

VIRGINIA

Cass County Historical Society
282 S. Cass, 62691
Telephone: (217) 452-3360
Founded in: 1963
Marjorie Taylor, President
Number of members: 124
Staff: volunteer 7
Major programs: museum, oral history, newsletters/pamphlets
Period of collections: 1865-1918

WADSWORTH

Newport Township Historical Society
P.O. Box 98, 60083
Telephone: (312) 623-0939
Private agency
Founded in: 1976
G.V. Shields, President
Number of members: 25
Staff: volunteer 4
Major programs: manuscripts, historic site(s), oral history, historic preservation, exhibits
Period of collections: 1870s

WARSAW

Warsaw Historical Society
401 Main St.
Telephone: (217) 256-3382
Mail to: 411 Main St., 62379
Private agency
Founded in: 1960
Richard O. Prior, President
Number of members: 120
Staff: volunteer 10
Major programs: library, museum, historic site(s), tours/pilgrimages, oral history, research, photographic collections, genealogical services
Period of collections: 1812-1950

WATERLOO

Peterstown Heritage Society
Founded in: 1973
Questionnaire not received

WATSEKA

Iroquois County Genealogical Society
Old Courthouse Museum, 103 W. Cherry, 60970
Telephone: (815) 432-2215
Private agency
Founded in: 1969
Louise Clifton, President
Number of members: 265
Staff: part time 4, volunteer 6
Magazine: *The Iroquois County Stalker*
Major programs: library, archives, manuscripts, oral history, educational programs, book publishing, newsletter/pamphlets, research, genealogical services
Period of collection: 1850-present

Iroquois County Historical Society
2nd and Cherry Sts., 60970
Telephone: (815) 432-2215
Private agency
Founded in: 1967
Wayne Rosenberger, President
Number of members: 780
Staff: full time 2, part time 1, volunteer 2
Major programs: library, archives, museum, tours, newsletters/pamphlets, historic preservation, exhibits, photographic collections, genealogical services
Period of collections: 1890-1920

WAUCONDA

Lake County Museum—Lake County Museum Association
Lakewood Forest Preserve, 60084
Telephone: (312) 526-7878
County agency
Founded in: 1957
Rebecca Goldberg, Director
Number of members: 300
Staff: full time 2, part time 2, volunteer 25
Major programs: museum
Period of collections: 1830-present

WAUKEGAN

Waukegan Historical Society
1917 N. Sheridan Rd., 60085
Telephone: (312) 336-1859
Founded in: 1968
Walter Griffin, President
Number of members: 500
Staff: part time 1, volunteer 20
Magazine: *Historically Speaking*
Major programs: library, museum, tours/pilgrimages, educational programs, books, newsletters/pamphlets
Period of collections: 1865-present

WEST CHICAGO

West Chicago Historical Museum
132 Main St., 60185
Telephone: (312) 231-3376
City agency
Founded in: 1976
Jerry Musich, Curator
Staff: full time 2, part time 2, volunteer 6
Major programs: archives, museum, tours, school programs, book publishing, research, exhibits, audiovisual programs, photographic collections, genealogical services, field services, railroad park
Period of collections: 1849-1918

West Chicago Historical Society—Kruse House Museum
527 Main St.
Telephone: (312) 231-0564/231-3376
Mail to: P.O. Box 246, 60185
Private agency
Founded in: 1975
Alice Minaga, President
Number of members: 300
Staff: volunteer 15
Major programs: museum, markers, school programs, newsletters, exhibits
Period of collections: 1910-1929

WEST FRANKFORT

Frankfort Area Historical Society and Museum
2000 E. St. Louis St., 62896
Telephone: (618) 932-6159
Private agency
Founded in: 1974
Mavis L. Wright, Director
Number of members: 550
Staff: volunteer 50
Magazine: *The Messenger*
Major programs: library, archives, manuscripts, museum, historic site(s), markers, tours/pilgrimages, oral history, school programs, book publishing, newsletters/pamphlets, historic preservation, records management, research, exhibits, living history, photographic collections, genealogical services, field services
Period of collections: 1800s-1900s

WESTERN SPRINGS

Western Springs Historical Society
740 Hillgrove Ave., 60558
Private agency
Founded in: 1968
John Gilbert, President
Number of members: 475
Staff: volunteer 12
Major programs: archives, museum, tours/pilgrimages, oral history, newsletters/pamphlets, historic preservation, exhibits, genealogical services
Period of collections: 1865-present

WESTMONT

Westmont Historical Society
Founded in: 1976
Questionnaire not received

WHEATON

Billy Graham Center at Wheaton College
500 E. Seminary, 60187
Telephone: (312) 260-5910
Private agency, authorized by the college
Founded in: 1974
James Kraakevik, Director
Staff: full time 30, part time 16
Magazine: *Centerline/From the Archives of the Billy Graham Center/Bulletin of the Institute for the Study of American Evangelicals*
Major programs: library, archives, manuscripts, museum, oral history, newsletters/pamphlets, records management, research, exhibits, audiovisual programs, photographic collections, educational programs
Period of collections: 1850s-present

Billy Graham Center Museum
500 E. Seminary, 60187
Telephone: (312) 260-5909
Private agency, authorized by Wheaton College
Founded in: 1974
James D. Stambaugh, Director
Number of members: 180
Staff: full time 3, part time 4, volunteer 6
Major programs: library, archives, museum, tours/pilgrimages, newsletters/pamphlets, exhibits
Period of collections: late 18th-early 20th centuries

DuPage County Historical Society and Museum
102 E. Wesley St., 60187
Telephone: (312) 682-7343
County agency
Founded in: 1965
Patricia A. Wallace, Director
Number of members: 400

Staff: full time 3, part time 3, volunteer 50
Major programs: library, archives, museum, tours/pilgrimages, school programs, book publishing, newsletters/pamphlets, records management, research, exhibits, audiovisual programs, photographic collections
Period of collections: 1860-1915

WILMETTE

Wilmette Historical Museum and Society
565 Hunter Rd., 60091
Telephone: (312) 256-5838
Founded in: 1950
Eileen S. Ramm, Director
Number of members: 150
Staff: part time 3, volunteer 12
Magazine: *Ouilmette Heritage*
Major programs: library, archives, museum, school programs, exhibits, photographic collections
Period of collections: 1872-present

WILMINGTON

Wilmington Area Historical Society
Founded in: 1976
Questionnaire not received

WINFIELD

Winfield Historical Society
P.O. Box 315, 60190
Telephone: (312) 653-1489
Private agency
Founded in: 1978
Adrienne K. Rose, President
Number of members: 52
Staff: volunteer 12
Major programs: historic preservation
Period of collections: mid-late 1800s

WINNETKA

North Suburban Genealogical Society
c/o Winnetka Public Library, 768 Oak St., 60093
Telephone: (312) 446-7220
Private agency
Founded in: 1975
Frank A. Randall, Jr., President
Number of members: 200
Major programs: library, newsletters/pamphlets, research, exhibits, genealogical services
Period of collections: 1800-present

WYANET

Wyanet Historical Society
Main St.
Mail to: P.O. Box 169, 61379
Private agency
Founded in: 1977
Maxine Trotter, President
Number of members: 45
Staff: volunteer 7
Major programs: archives, manuscripts, museum, historic site(s), tours/pilgrimages, school programs, historic preservation, research, photographic collections, genealogical services
Period of collections: 1865-1976

YORKVILLE

Kendall County Historical Society
Rt. 71
Mail to: P.O. Box 123, 60560
Private agency
Founded in: 1970
John Shaddle, President
Number of members: 491
Staff: volunteer 40
Major programs: library, archives,
museum, historic site(s),
tours/pilgrimages,
newsletters/pamphlets, exhibits,
photographic collections,
genealogical services
Period of collections: 1900

ZION

Zion Historical Society
1300 Shiloh Blvd.
Telephone: (312) 746-2427
Mail to: P.O. Box 333, 60099
Private agency
Founded in: 1967
H. Lee Deming, President
Number of members: 275
Staff: volunteer 15
Major programs: library, archives,
museum, historic site,
newsletters/pamphlets, historic
preservation
Period of collections: 1900-1910

INDIANA

ALBION

Noble County Genealogical Society
109 N. York St., 46701
Telephone: (219) 636-7197
County agency
Founded in: 1981
Linda J. Shultz, Executive Secretary
Number of members: 35
Major programs: library, book
publishing, newsletters/pamphlets,
genealogical services
Period of collections: 1850-1930

Noble County Historical Society
210 E. Main St.
Mail to: P.O. Box 152, 46701
Private agency
Founded in: 1965
Geneva Zink, Secretary/Director
Number of members: 165
Staff: volunteer 7
Magazine: *Pioneer Echoes*
Major programs: museum, markers,
newsletters/pamphlets, exhibits
Period of collections: early
1800s-present

ALTON

Crawford County Indiana Museum
Rt. 1, Leavenworth, 47137
Mail to: 704 Bradford Circle,
Indianapolis, 46224
Founded in: 1980
Staff: full time 7, part time 9,
volunteer 8
Magazine: *Events—Crawford County
Indian Museum*

Major programs: library, museum,
tours/pilgrimages, educational
programs, newsletters/pamphlets,
historic preservation
Period of collections: prehistoric

ANDERSON

**Madison County Historical
Society, Inc.**
Mail to: P.O. Box 523, 46015
Private agency
Founded in: 1965
Elwood H. Phillips, President
Number of members: 325
Staff: volunteer 3
Magazine: *Madison County Historical
Society Gazette*
Major programs: library, archives,
museum, markers,
tours/pilgrimages, oral history,
newsletters/pamphlets,
genealogical services

Madison County Historic Home
626 Main St.
Telephone: (317) 646-5771/646-5753
Mail to: 120 E. 8th St., P.O. Box 2100,
46018
City agency
Founded in: 1974
Jack B. Nicholson, Commission
President
Number of members: 50
Staff: volunteer 25
Major programs: museum, historic
site(s), historic preservation, living
history
Period of collections: late 19th
century

AUBURN

**Auburn Automotive
Heritage, Inc.—Auburn-Cord-Duesenl
Museum**
1600 S. Wayne St.
Telephone: (219) 925-1444
Mail to: P.O. Box 271, 46706
Private agency
Founded in: 1973
Skip Marketti, Executive Director
Number of members: 2,000
Staff: full time 7, part time 5
Magazine: *The Accelerator*
Major programs: library, archives,
manuscripts, museum, historic
site(s), oral history, school
programs, historic preservation,
research, exhibits, audiovisual
programs, photographic
collections
Period of collections: 1900-1937

Dekalb County Historical Society
Telephone: (219) 925-4560
Mail to: P.O. Box 686, 46706-0686
Founded in: 1966
Kathleen Vose, President
Number of members: 50
Major programs: oral history,
educational programs

AURORA

**Hillforest Historical
Foundation, Inc.**
213 5th St.
Telephone: (812) 926-0087
Mail to: P.O. Box 127, 47001

Private agency
Founded in: 1956
Edward L. Kerr, Executive Secretary
Number of members: 490
Staff: part time 2, volunteer 120
Major programs: library, archives,
manuscripts, museum, junior
history, school programs,
newsletters/pamphlets, historic
preservation, records
management, research, exhibits,
photographic collections,
genealogical services
Period of collections: 1852-1884

BATTLE GROUND

Tippecanoe Battlefield Museum
Tippecanoe and Railroad Sts.
Telephone: (317) 567-2147
Mail to: P.O. Box 225, 47920
Founded in: 1972
Number of members: 700
Staff: full time 2, part time 4,
volunteer 150
Magazine: *Battlefield Banner*
Major programs: library, museum,
tours/pilgrimages, school
programs, newsletters/pamphlets,
historic preservation, exhibits,
living history, archaeology
programs, sponsorship of fairs
Period of collections: 1720-1780

BEDFORD

**Lawrence County Historical
Society**
Courthouse, 47421
Telephone: (812) 297-9946
Questionnaire not received

BLOOMINGTON

**Elizabeth Sage Historical Costume
Collection and Gallery**
Wylie Hall 203, Indiana University,
47401
Telephone: (812) 335-4627
Authorized by the Department of
Home Economics, Indiana
University
Founded in: 1936 (collection); 1984
(gallery)
Nelda M. Christ, Curator
Staff: volunteer 5
Major programs: museum,
newsletters/pamphlets, research,
exhibits, audiovisual programs,
historic costumes
Period of collections: 19th-20th
centuries

Indiana University Museum
209 Student Bldg., Indiana University,
47405
Telephone: (812) 337-7224
Founded in: 1963
Staff: full time 4, part time 20,
volunteer 3
Major programs: library, museum,
educational programs, book
publishing, newsletters/pamphlets
Period of collections: 1800-present

**Monroe County Historical Society
and Museum**
202 E. 6th St., 47401
Telephone: (812) 332-2517
Private agency

Founded in: 1905 (society); 1980 (museum)
Pamela Service, Museum Curator
Number of members: 300
Staff: part time 5, volunteer 70
Major programs: museum, book publishing, newsletters/pamphlets, exhibits, genealogical services
Period of collections: 19th-20th centuries

Organization of American Historians
112 N. Bryan, 47401
Telephone: (812) 337-7311
Private agency
Founded in: 1907
Joan Hoff Wilson, Executive Secretary
Number of members: 11,900
Staff: full time 6, part time 1
Magazine: *Journal of American History*
Major programs: manuscripts, tours/pilgrimages, junior history, oral history, school programs, book publishing, newsletters/pamphlets, research, exhibits, field services

Stone Hills Area Library Services Authority
911 E. 2nd St., 47401
Telephone: (812) 334-8347
State agency
Founded in: 1974
Sara Laughlin, Coordinator
Number of members: 55
Staff: full time 3, part time 8
Magazine: *SHALSA Speaks*
Major programs: library, consulting, program planning

William Hammond Mathers Museum
601 E. 8th St., 47405
Telephone: (812) 335-6873
State agency, authorized by Indiana University
Founded in: 1963
Geoffrey W. Conrad, Director
Staff: full time 9, part time 12, volunteer 10
Major programs: museum, school programs, book publishing, newsletters/pamphlets, records management, research, exhibits, photographic collections, ethnography
Period of collections: 19th-20th centuries

BLUFFTON

Wells County Historical Society
420 W. Market St.
Mail to: P.O. Box 143, 46714
Private agency
Founded in: 1935
Fred Park, President
Number of members: 425
Staff: volunteer 11
Major programs: library, archives, museum, historic site(s), markers, tours/pilgrimages, newsletters/pamphlets, historic preservation, exhibits, photographic collections, genealogical services
Period of collections: 1875-present

BOONVILLE

Warrick County Museum
S. 1st St., Ella Williams School Bldg., 2nd Floor
Mail to: P.O. Box 581, 47601
County agency
Founded in: 1977
Valada Simpson, Board President
Number of members: 200
Staff: volunteer 8
Period of collections: early 20th century

BRAZIL

Clay County Genealogical Society, Inc.
R.R. 17, Box 190
Telephone: (812) 448-8481
Mail to: P.O. Box 211, 47834
Private agency
Founded in: 1980
Carl Zukumft, President
Number of members: 170
Staff: volunteer 7
Magazine: *Clay County Researcher*
Major programs: genealogical services

BRISTOL

Elkhart County Historical Society, Inc.
204 W. Vistula St.
Telephone: (219) 848-4322
Mail to: P.O. Box 434, 46507
Founded in: 1896
Carol Buckley, Curator
Number of members: 150
Staff: part time 7
Major programs: archives, museum, tours, newsletters/pamphlets, records management, exhibits, genealogical services
Period of collections: 1880-1940s

BROWNSTOWN

Jackson County Historical Society
115 N. Sugar St., 47220
Founded in: 1916
Questionnaire not received

CAMBRIDGE CITY

Upper Whitewater Historical Association
302 E. Main, 47327
Founded in: 1962
Questionnaire not received

CHESTERTON

Duneland Historical Society, Inc.
411 Bowser Ave., 46304
Telephone: (219) 926-2264
Founded in: 1948
Norris D. Coambs, President
Staff: volunteer 3
Magazine: *Duneland Notes*
Major programs: historic site(s), tours/pilgrimages
Period of collections: 1830-present

COLUMBIA CITY

Whitley County Historical Museum and Society
108 W. Jefferson St., 46725
Telephone: (219) 244-6372

Private agency
Founded in: 1958
Lannie Maloney, Curator
Number of members: 780
Staff: part time 3
Magazine: *The Bulletin*
Major programs: archives, museum, markers, tours/pilgrimages, school programs, newsletters/pamphlets, historic preservation, records management, research, exhibits, living history, archaeology programs, photographic collections, genealogical services, educational programming, special events
Period of collections: 1830-1930

COLUMBUS

Bartholomew County Historical Society
524 3rd St., 47201
Telephone: (812) 372-3541
Private agency
Founded in: 1921
Renée Dancu Henry, Director
Number of members: 550
Staff: full time 1, part time 1, volunteer 30
Magazine: *Quarterly Connections*
Major programs: library, museum, historic site(s), tours/pilgrimages, junior history, oral history, school programs, book publishing, newsletters/pamphlets, exhibits, photographic collections, genealogical services
Period of collections: 1860-present

CONNERSVILLE

Henry Blommel Historic Automotive Data Collection
Rt. 5, 47331
Telephone: (317) 825-9259
Private agency
Founded in: 1928
Henry H. Blommel, Curator
Major programs: library, archives, museum, historic site(s), markers, tours/pilgrimages, junior history, school programs, book publishing, historic preservation, research
Period of collections: 1891-present

Historic Connersville, Inc.
111 E. 4th St.
Mail to: P.O. Box 197, 47331
Founded in: 1965
Questionnaire not received

CORYDON

Corydon Capital State Memorial—Division of Historic Preservation, Department of Natural Resources
202 E. Walnut St., 47112
Telephone: (812) 738-4890
State agency
Founded in: 1930
Staff: full time 2
Major programs: historic site, oral history, historic preservation
Period of collections: 1816-1840

Harrison County Historical Society
117 W. Beaver St., 47112
Questionnaire not received

COVINGTON

Fountain County Historical Society
Mail to: P.O. Box 148, Kingman,
47952
Founded in: 1962
Questionnaire not received

CRAWFORDSVILLE

Henry S. Lane Place
212 S. Water St., 47933
Telephone: (317) 362-3416
Private agency, authorized by
Montgomery County Historical
Society
Robert F. Wernle, President
Number of members: 350
Staff: volunteer 20
Major programs: museum, historic
site(s), tours, school programs,
historic preservation, photographic
collections
Period of collections: 1844-1914

**Montgomery County Historical
Society**
212 S. Water St., 47933
Telephone: (317) 362-3416
Founded in: 1918
Number of members: 300
Staff: full time 1
Major programs: museum
Period of collections: 1783-1865

CROWN POINT

**Lake County Parks and Recreation
Department**
2293 N. Main St., 46307
Telephone: (219) 738-2020, ext. 391
County agency
Founded in: 1967
Robert Nickovich, Superintendent
Staff: full time 40, volunteer 100
Major programs: historic site(s),
school programs, historic
preservation, living history
Period of collections: 1850s-1950s

CUTLER

Adams Mill Historic Site
R.R. 1, Box 131-A, 46920
Telephone: (317) 268-2174
Questionnaire not received

DANVILLE

**Hendricks County Historical
Society**
249 S. Wayne St., 46122
Telephone: (317) 745-2573
Questionnaire not received

Hendricks County Museum
170 S. Washington St., 46122
County agency, authorized by
Hendricks County Historical
Society
Founded in: 1975
Dorothy Kelley, Museum Board
President
Staff: volunteer 20
Major programs: historic site(s),
junior history, school programs,
exhibits, genealogical services
Period of collections: 1865-1930

DECATUR

**Adams County Historical
Society, Inc.**
420 W. Monroe St.
Telephone: (219) 724-2121
Mail to: 141 S. 2nd St., 46733
Private agency
Founded in: 1957
Claren J. Neuenschwander,
President
Staff: volunteer 24
Major programs: library, museum,
school programs, book publishing,
genealogical services
Period of collections: 19th century

DUGGER

Dugger Coal Museum Society, Inc.
Main St., 47848
Founded in: 1980
Number of members: 266
Major programs: museum,
tours/pilgrimages, oral history,
educational programs,
newsletters/pamphlets, historic
preservation
Period of collections: 1900-present

DUNKIRK

The Glass Museum
309 S. Franklin St., 47336
Telephone: (317) 768-9950
Authorized by the Dunkirk Public
Library
Founded in: 1979
Kennet C. Lyon, President, Library
Board
Staff: volunteer 10
Major programs: museum, historic
preservation, history of glass
Period of collections: 1890-1910

EAST CHICAGO

East Chicago Historical Society
c/o E. Chicago Public Library
Telephone: (219) 397-2453
Mail to: 2401 E. Columbus Dr., 46312
City agency
Founded in: 1966
Charles Dahlin, President
Number of members: 200
Staff: volunteer 20
Major programs: archives,
manuscripts, oral history, books,
newsletters/pamphlets, genealogy,
educational programs
Period of collections: 1840-present

EVANSVILLE

Angel Mounds State Memorial
8215 Pollack Ave., 47715
Telephone: (812) 853-3956
State agency, authorized by Indiana
State Museum and Memorials
Founded in: 1938
Cary A. Floyd, Historic Site Curator
Staff: full time 4
Major programs: museum, historic
site, educational programs, historic
preservation
Period of collections: prehistoric

**Evansville Museum of Arts and
Science**
411 S.E. Riverside Dr., 47713
Telephone: (812) 425-2406

Private agency
Founded in: 1927
John W. Streetman III, Director
Staff: full time 9, part time 6,
volunteer 10
Major programs: museum, school
programs, newsletters/pamphlets,
exhibits
Period of collections: 1890-1915

**Reitz Home Preservation
Society, Inc.**
224 S.E. 1st St., 47713
Telephone: (812) 476-4218
Mail to: P.O. Box 2478, 47714
Private agency
Founded in: 1974
Mrs. Edmund L. Hafer, President
Number of members: 250
Staff: full time 1, volunteer 35
Major programs: museum,
newsletters/pamphlets, historic
preservation, school programs,
exhibits
Period of collections: late Victorian
era

**Southwestern Indiana Historical
Society**
713 S. Rotherwood, 47714
Telephone: (219) 477-2023
Private agency
Founded in: 1881
James E. Morlock, Director
Number of members: 304
Staff: volunteer 8
Major programs: historic site(s),
markers, book publishing,
newsletters/pamphlets, historic
preservation, research, audiovisual
programs, archaeology programs,
photographic collections,
genealogical services
Period of collections: 1920-present

Tri-State Genealogical Society
c/o Willard Library, 21 1st Ave., 47710
Founded in: 1977
Number of members: 300
Staff: volunteer 12
Magazine: *Tri-State Packett*
Major programs: library, educational
programs, book publishing,
genealogy
Period of collections:
prehistoric-present

FORT MADISON

**North Lee County Historical
Society**
Ave. H and 9th Sts.
Telephone: (319) 372-7661
Mail to: P.O. Box 385, 52627
Founded in: 1962
Dorothy I. Adams, President
Number of members: 225
Major programs: museum
Period of collections: 1865-1925

FORT WAYNE

**Allen County-Ft. Wayne Historical
Society**
302 E. Berry St., 46802
Telephone: (219) 426-2882
Private agency
Founded in: 1921
Michael C. Hawfield, Executive
Director

Number of members: 1,600
Staff: full time 5, part time 4
Magazine: *Old Fort News*
Major programs: library, archives,
manuscripts, museum, markers,
tours/pilgrimages, school
programs, book publishing,
newsletters/pamphlets, records
management, research, exhibits,
photographic collections
Period of collections: 1820-1945

Arch, Inc.
124 W. Washington, 46802
Telephone: (219) 743-5117
Mail to: P.O. Box 11383, 46857
Private agency
Founded in: 1975
Mrs. Lee Bailey, Executive Director
Number of members: 350
Staff: full time 1, volunteer 50
Major programs: historic site(s),
tours/pilgrimages, school
programs, newsletters/pamphlets,
historic preservation, audiovisual
programs

Canal Society of Indiana
302 E. Berry St., 46816
Telephone: (219) 426-5556
Private agency
Founded in: 1981
Clarence Hudson, President
Number of members: 180
Staff: volunteer 9
Magazine: *Indiana Waterways*
Major programs: markers,
tours/pilgrimages,
newsletters/pamphlets
Period of collections: 1832-1880

Historic Ft. Wayne, Inc.
107 S. Clinton St., 46802
Telephone: (219) 424-3476
Private agency
Founded in: 1971
Gregory L. Manifold, Managing
Director
Staff: full time 4, part time 20,
volunteer 120
Major programs: museum, historic
sites preservation,
newsletters/pamphlets, living
history
Period of collections: 1783-1819

Indiana Jewish Historical Society
215 E. Berry St., Room 303, 46802
Telephone: (219) 422-3862
Founded in: 1972
Joseph Levine, Executive Secretary
Number of members: 655
Staff: full time 1, part time 2
Major programs: archives,
manuscripts, oral history, book
publishing, newsletters/pamphlets,
records management, research,
living history, photographic
collections, genealogical services
Period of collections: 1783-present

**Louis A. Warren Lincoln Library
and Museum**
1300 S. Clinton St.
Mail to: P.O. Box 1110, 46801
Private agency, authorized by Lincoln
National Life Insurance Company
Founded in: 1928
Mark E. Neely, Jr., Director
Staff: full time 4, part time 2

Magazine: *Lincoln Lore*
Major programs: library, manuscripts,
museum, book publishing,
newsletters/pamphlets,
photographic collections
Period of collections: 1809-1865

FOUNTAIN CITY

Levi Coffin House Association
P.O. Box 77, U.S. Hwy. 27, 47341
Telephone: (317) 847-2885
Founded in: 1967
Robert McGuire, President
Number of members: 82
Staff: part time 2, volunteer 66
Major programs: historic site,
tours/pilgrimages, junior history,
oral history, historic preservation
Period of collections: before 1847

FOWLER

**Benton County, Indiana Historical
Society, Inc.**
602 E. 7th St., 47944
Telephone: (317) 844-1848
Private agency
Number of members: 11
Major programs: museum, historic
preservation, genealogical
services

FRANKFORT

Clinton County Historical Society
301 E. Clinton St., 46041
Telephone: (317) 659-4911
Founded in: 1936
Questionnaire not received

FRANKLIN

**Johnson County Historical
Museum and Society**
150 W. Madison St., 46131
Telephone: (317) 736-4655
County agency
Founded in: 1923
Rachel Henry, Curator
Number of members: 619
Staff: part time 2, volunteer 5
Magazine: *Nostalgia News*
Major programs: archives,
manuscripts, museum, markers,
school programs, book publishing,
newsletters/pamphlets, historic
preservation, research,
photographic collections,
genealogical services
Period of collections: 1888-present

GARRETT

Garrett Historical Society
Quincy and Franklin Sts.
Telephone: (219) 357-5575/357-5582
Mail to: P.O. Box 225, 46738
Private agency
Founded in: 1971
Merritt Scheurich, President
Number of members: 121
Staff: volunteer 20
Major programs: library, museum,
historic site(s), audiovisual
programs
Period of collections: 1875-1950

GARY

Calumet Regional Archives
3400 Broadway, 46408
Telephone: (219) 980-6628
State agency, authorized by
Northwest Library, Indiana
University
Founded in: 1973
Stephen McShane, Archivist/Curator
Staff: full time 1
Major programs: archives,
manuscripts,
newsletters/pamphlets, research,
exhibits, photographic collections,
urban history
Period of collections: 1900-present

**Gary Historical and Cultural
Society**
300 W. 21st Ave., 46407
Founded in: 1977
Number of members: 150
Staff: volunteer 6
Magazine: *Gary History In Review*
Major programs: archives,
manuscripts, historic site, junior
history, oral history, educational
programs, book publishing,
newsletters/pamphlets, historic
preservation, choral and
instrumental music society
Period of collections: 1906-present

Le Cercle de La Fleur de Lis
P.O. Box 2756, 46403
Telephone: (219) 938-7403/882-2655
Private agency
Founded in: 1983
Yvette Hoppe, President
Number of members: 160
Staff: volunteer 12
Magazine: *Le Cercle*
Major programs: museum, school
programs, newsletters/pamphlets,
archaeology programs,
genealogical services, French
language programs

GENEVA

Limberlost State Historic Site
200 N. 6th St.
Telephone: (219) 368-7428
Mail to: P.O. Box 356, 46740
State agency, authorized by Division
of Museums and Memorials,
Department of Natural Resources
Founded in: 1947
James McFaul, Historic Site Curator
Number of members: 1
Staff: full time 1, part time 2,
volunteer 2
Major programs: historic site(s),
tours/pilgrimages, school
programs, adult outreach
Period of collections: 1895-1913

GENTRYVILLE

Colonel William Jones House
Old Boonville—Corydon Rd.
Telephone: (812) 336-3961
Mail to: 1208 E. Wylie St.,
Bloomington, 47401
Private agency
Founded in: 1976
William Cook, Co-owner
Staff: part time 1, volunteer 40

Major programs: museum, historic
site(s), tours/pilgrimages, festivals
Period of collections: 1834-1864

GOSHEN

Goshen Historical Society, Inc.
P.O. Box 701, 46526
Telephone: (219) 533-5485
Private agency
Founded in: 1981
Tom Marquis, President
Number of members: 254
Major programs: tours/pilgrimages,
book publishing,
newsletters/pamphlets, historic
preservation

GREENCASTLE

**Archives of DePauw University and
Indiana United Methodism**
Roy O. West Library, DePauw
University, 46135
Telephone: (317) 658-4501
Private agency, authorized by the
university and the United Methodist
Church
Founded in: 1951
Wesley W. Wilson, Archives and
Special Services Coordinator
Staff: full time 3, part time 1
Major programs: library, archives,
manuscripts, research, field
services
Founded in: 1830-1980

Putnam County Historical Society
Roy O. West Library, DePauw
University, 46135
Telephone: (317) 658-4501
Private agency
Founded in: 1949
Number of members: 60
Staff: volunteer 3
Major programs: library, manuscripts
Period of collections: 1783-present

GREENFIELD

Hancock County Historical Society
Main and Apple Sts.
Telephone: (317) 462-2835
(president)
Mail to: P.O. Box 375, 46140
Private agency
Founded in: 1964
Larry L. Fox, President
Number of members: 300
Staff: part time 2, volunteer 5
Magazine: Log Chain
Major programs: museum, markers,
newsletters/pamphlets, historic
preservation
Period of collections: 1840s-1950s

GREENSBURG

Decatur County Historical Society
Telephone: (812) 663-2605
c/o D. Swegman, 435 E. Main St.,
47240
Founded in: 1959
Questionnaire not received

**Historical Society of Decatur
County, Inc.**
222 N. Franklin St.
Telephone: (812) 663-2478
(president)
Mail to: P.O. Box 163, 42740

County agency
Founded in: 1959
Diana E. Swegman, Corresponding
and Membership Secretary
Number of members: 655
Staff: volunteer 60
Major programs: museum,
tours/pilgrimages, oral history,
school programs, book publishing,
newsletters/pamphlets, historic
preservation, genealogical
services
Period of collections: 1850s-1950s

HAMMOND

Hammond Historical Society
Telephone: (219) 932-0400
Mail to: 260 165th St., 46324
Roger K. Reeder, President
Number of members: 300
Staff: volunteer 6
Major programs: library, archives,
manuscripts, museum, historic
sites preservation, markers, oral
history, educational programs,
books, newsletters/pamphlets
Period of collections: 1864-present

HARTFORD CITY

**Blackford County Historical
Society**
321 N. High
Telephone: (317) 348-1905
Mail to: P.O. Box 264, 47348
Questionnaire not received

HIGHLAND

Highland Historical Society, Inc.
2611 Highway Ave., 46322
Founded in: 1976
Questionnaire not received

HOBART

Hobart Historical Society, Inc.
706 E. 4th St.
Telephone: (219) 942-2724
Mail to: P.O. Box 24, 46342
Private agency
Founded in: 1965
Elin Christianson, President
Number of members: 300
Staff: volunteer 24
Major programs: library, archives,
manuscripts, museum, historic
site(s), markers, tours/pilgrimages,
oral history, school programs, book
publishing, newsletters/pamphlets,
historic preservation, records
management, research, exhibits,
photographic collections,
genealogical services
Period of collections: 1840-present

HUNTINGTON

**Huntington County Historical
Society**
1041 S. Jefferson St.
Telephone: (219) 356-5874
Mail to: Auditor's Office, County
Courthouse, 46750
County agency
Founded in: 1951
Paul Schock, Curator
Number of members: 39
Staff: part time 1

Major programs: museum, book
publishing
Period of collections: 1860-1950

INDIANAPOLIS

The Children's Museum
3000 N. Meridian St., 46208
Telephone: (317) 924-5431
Mail to: P.O. Box 3000, 46206
Private agency
Founded in: 1925
Peter V. Sterling, Executive Director
Staff: full time 97, part time 70,
volunteer 500
Major programs: library, archives,
museum, tours/pilgrimages, junior
history, school programs,
newsletters/pamphlets, records
management, exhibits, audiovisual
programs, archaeology programs
Period of collections: 1800-present

**Historic Landmarks Foundation of
Indiana**
3402 Boulevard Place, 46208
Telephone: (317) 926-2301
Private agency
Founded in: 1960
J. Reid Williamson, Jr., President
Number of members: 3,000
Staff: full time 18, part time 9,
volunteer 40
Magazine: The Indiana
Preservationist
Major programs: library, museum,
historic site(s), tours,
newsletters/pamphlets, historic
preservation, photographic
collections, information center
Period of collections: 1840-1918

Indiana Arts Commission
105 E. Market St., 46204
Telephone: (317) 232-1268
Founded in: 1969
Number of members: 1
Staff: full time 18, volunteer 1
Magazine: IAC News
Major programs: museum, oral
history, educational programs,
historic preservation, arts funding
including most museum functions

**Indiana Committee for the
Humanities**
3135 N. Meridian St., 46208
Telephone: (317) 925-5316
Private agency, authorized by
independent board of directors and
the National Endowment for the
Humanities
Founded in: 1971
Kenneth L. Gladish, Executive
Director
Staff: full time 6, part time 3
Major programs: library, museum,
oral history, school programs,
newsletters/pamphlets, exhibits,
audiovisual programs, grants for
public history programs

**Indiana Division, Historic
Preservation and Archaeology**
202 N. Alabama St., 46204
Telephone: (317) 232-1646
Founded in: 1977
Richard A. Gantz, Director
Number of members: full time 6

Major programs: historic
preservation, records
management, archaeology
programs

Indiana Historical Bureau
140 N. Senate Ave., Room 408, 46204
Telephone: (317) 232-2537
State agency
Founded in: 1915
Pamela J. Bennett, Director
Staff: full time 10
Magazine: *Indiana History Bulletin*
Major programs: junior history,
educational programs, books,
newsletters/pamphlets

◇**Indiana Historical Society**
315 W. Ohio St., 46202
Telephone: (317) 232-1882
Private agency
Founded in: 1830
Peter T. Harstad, Executive Secretary
Number of members: 5,800
Staff: full time 46, part time 4
Magazine: *Indiana Magazine of
History*
Major programs: library, archives,
manuscripts, junior history, book
publishing, newsletters/pamphlets,
exhibits, archaeology programs,
photographic collections,
genealogical services, field
services
Period of collections:
prehistoric-present

Indiana Junior Historical Society
140 N. Senate, 46204
Telephone: (317) 232-2536
Founded in: 1938
Robert W. Kirby, State Director
Number of members: 8,000
Staff: full time 3, part time 4,
volunteer 25
Major programs: junior history, oral
history, educational programs,
newsletters/pamphlets, field
services, summer camps,
workshops
Period of collections: 1816-present

Indiana State Library
140 N. Senate Ave., 46204
Telephone: (317) 232-3675
Stage agency
Founded in: 1825
Charles Ray Ewick, Director
Staff: full time 95
Magazine: *Indiana Libraries/Focus on
Indiana Libraries*
Major programs: library, manuscripts,
oral history

◇**Indiana State Museum and
Memorials**
202 N. Alabama St., 46204
Telephone: (317) 232-1637
State agency
Founded in: 1869
Lee Scott Theisen, Executive Director
Number of members: 2,000
Staff: full time 51, volunteer 200
Major programs: museum, historic
sites preservation, oral history,
educational programs
Period of collections: A.D. 1000-1980

**Indiana War Memorials
Commission**
431 N. Meridian St. 46204

Telephone: (317) 635-1964
Questionnaire not received

**Indianapolis Historic Preservation
Commission**
1821 City-County Bldg., 46204
Telephone: (317) 236-4406
City agency
Founded in: 1975
Vicki Jo Sandstead, Administrator
Staff: full time 6, part time 2
Major programs: historic
preservation, research
Period of collections: late 19th-early
20th centuries

**Indianapolis Motor Speedway Hall
of Fame Museum**
4790 W. 16th St., 46222
Telephone: (317) 241-2501
Private agency
Founded in: 1956
Jack L. Martin, Museum Director
Number of members: full time 2
Major programs: library, archives,
museum, historic site(s), historic
preservation, records
management, exhibits, audiovisual
programs, photographic
collections, race-related and
vintage passenger cars
Period of collections: 1896-1980s

Indianapolis Museum of Art
1200 W. 38th St., 46208
Telephone: (317) 923-1331
Private agency
Founded in: 1883
Robert A. Yassin, Museum Director
Number of members: 11,000
Staff: full time 90, part time 54,
volunteer 1,300
Major programs: library, archives,
museum, school programs, book
publishing, newsletters/pamphlets,
research, exhibits, fine arts
Period of collections:
prehistoric-present

**Marion County-Indianapolis
Historical Society**
140 N. Senate, Room 408, 46208
Telephone: (317) 232-2581
Private agency
Founded in: 1961
Thomas Hendrickson, President
Number of members: 250
Magazine: *MCHS Circular*
Major programs: tours/pilgrimages,
book publishing,
newsletters/pamphlets, research,
curriculum materials, speaker's
bureau
Period of collections: 20th century

Museum of Indian Heritage
6040 DeLong Rd., Eagle Creek Park,
46254
Telephone: (317) 293-4488
Private agency
Founded in: 1967
Vicki Cummings, Executive Director
Number of members: 130
Staff: full time 2, volunteer 15
Major programs: library, museum,
school programs, exhibits
Period of collections:
pre-Columbian-present

**President Benjamin Harrison
Memorial Home**
1230 N. Delaware St., 46202
Telephone: (317) 631-1898
Founded in: 1937
Dorothy C. Sallee, Director
Number of members: full time 3, part
time 3, volunteer 50
Major programs: museum, historic
site(s), tours/pilgrimages, school
programs, book publishing,
newsletters/pamphlets, records
management, exhibits, audiovisual
programs, photographic
collections
Period of collections: 1865-1918

Society of Indiana Archivists
140 N. Senate Ave., 46204
Telephone: (317) 232-2537
Founded in: 1972
Thomas Krasean, Secretary
Number of members: 115
Staff: volunteer 7
Major programs: educational
programs, newsletters/pamphlets

Society of Indiana Pioneers
315 W. Ohio St., 46202
Private agency
Founded in: 1916
Caroline Dunn, Secretary
Number of members: 1,500
Staff: part time 2
Magazine: *Year Book*
Major programs: genealogical
services, record of early settlers

U.S. Army Finance Corps Museum
Ft. Benjamin Harrison, 46249
Telephone: (317) 542-2169
Federal agency, authorized by the
U.S. Army
Founded in: 1953
William H. Carnes, Jr., Museum
Curator
Staff: full time 2
Period of collections: American
Revolution-present

JASPER

Dubois County Historical Society
737 W. 8th St., 47546
Founded in: 1925
Number of members: 50
Staff: volunteer 30
Major programs: archives,
manuscripts, historic sites
preservation, markes,
tours/pilgrimages, books,
newsletters/pamphlets
Period of collections: 1865-1918

Historic Jasper, Inc.
Telephone: (812) 482-3848
Mail to: P.O. Box 525, 47546
Founded in: 1976
Mrs. C.H. Klamer, President
Number of members: 140
Staff: volunteer 15
Major programs: museum, historic
site, markers, historic preservation,
local historic research and
education
Period of collections: 1849

JEFFERSONVILLE

Clark County Historical Society—Howard Steamboat Museum
1101 E. Market St.
Telephone: (812) 283-3728
Mail to: P.O. Box 606, 47130
Private agency
Founded in: 1958
Louise M. Schildroth, President
Number of members: 230
Staff: volunteer 1
Major programs: museum, historic site(s), tours, newsletters/pamphlets, exhibits
Period of collections: 1834-1958

KENTLAND

Newton County Historical Society, Inc.
Telephone: (219) 474-6364
Mail to: P.O. Box 103, 47951
Founded in: 1966
Questionnaire not received

KINGMAN

Fountain County Historical Society
Courthouse, 47932
Telephone: (317) 397-3127
Mail to: P.O. Box 148, 47952
Founded in: 1962
Davey Puckett, Membership
Number of members: 254
Staff: volunteer 6
Major programs: manuscripts, museum, markers, junior history
Period of collections: 1918-present

KNOX

Starke County Historical Museum
401 S. Main St., 46534
Telephone: (219) 772-5393
County agency, authorized by Starke County Historical Society
Founded in: 1976
Mrs. Herbert Golding, President
Number of members: 150
Staff: part time 1
Major programs: museum, historic site(s), markers, junior history, oral history, school programs, newsletters/pamphlets, historic preservation, exhibits
Period of collections: 1865-present

KOKOMO

Howard County Historical Society, Inc.
1200 W. Sycamore St., 46901
Telephone: (317) 452-4314
Founded in: 1916
Richard A. Kastl, Director
Number of members: 300
Staff: full time 1, part time 2, volunteer 50
Magazine: *Museum Hi-Lites*
Major programs: museum, newsletters/pamphlets, historic preservation, research, archaeology programs
Period of collections: 1840-present

LAFAYETTE

Tippecanoe County Historical Association
909 South St., 47901
Telephone: (317) 742-8411
Private agency
Founded in: 1925
John M. Harris, Director
Number of members: 1,000
Staff: full time 6, part time 10
Magazine: *Weatenotes*
Major programs: library, archives, museum, historic site(s), markers, newsletters/pamphlets, archaeology programs, photographic collections, genealogical services
Period of collections: 19th century

LA GRANGE

La Grange County Historical Society, Inc.
Rt. 1, 46761
Telephone: (219) 463-2632
Founded in: 1966
J. Scott McKibben, Director
Number of members: 65
Staff: volunteer 20
Major programs: historic site(s), markers, book publishing, historic preservation, exhibits, audiovisual programs, photographic collections, genealogical services, cemetery survey
Period of collections: 1832-1982

LA PORTE

La Porte County Historical Society
La Porte County Complex, 46350
Telephone: (219) 326-6808
Founded in: 1903
Devere Thompson, Director
Number of members: 542
Staff: full time 1, part time 2, volunteer 150
Magazine: *The Old Letter*
Major programs: library, archives, manuscripts, museum, markers, tours/pilgrimages, junior history, oral history, educational programs, book publishing, newsletters/pamphlets
Period of collections: 1832-present

LIGONIER

Stone's Trace Historical Society
State Rds. 5 and 33, 46767
Private agency
Founded in: 1964
Dick Hursey, President
Number of members: 100
Staff: volunteer 30
Major programs: museum, historic site(s), school programs, historic preservation
Period of collections: 1840

LINCOLN CITY

Lincoln Boyhood National Memorial
Telephone: (812) 937-4757
Federal agency, authorized by National Park Service
Founded in: 1962
Norman D. Hellmers, Superintendent

Major programs: museum, historic site(s), tours/pilgrimages, historic preservation, living history
Period of collections: 1816-1830

LOGANSPORT

Cass County Historical Society
1004 E. Market St., 46947
Telephone: (219) 753-3866
County agency
Founded in: 1907
Samuel M. Upton, Curator
Number of members: 275
Staff: full time 1, volunteer 20
Major programs: library, archives, manuscripts, museum, historic site(s), markers, tours, junior history, oral history, school programs, book publishing, newsletters/pamphlets, historic preservation, research, exhibits, photographic collections, genealogical services

L'Anguille Valley Historical Association
502 Front St., 46947
Private agency
Founded in: 1937
Robert B. Whitsett, Co-founder/Acting President
Number of members: 52
Staff: full time 1
Major programs: historic site(s), markers, newsletters/pamphlets, historic preservation, research, exhibits, genealogical services, field services
Period of collections: 1700-1850

LOWELL

Three Creeks Historical Association
160 S. Viant, 46356
Telephone: (219) 696-9336
Private agency
Founded in: 1976
Kay Harness, President
Number of members: 90
Staff: volunteer 15
Major programs: tours, oral history, historic preservation, exhibits, genealogical services
Period of collections: 1880-1920

MADISON

Historic Madison, Inc.
500 West St., 47250
Telephone: (812) 265-2967
Private agency
Founded in: 1960
Major programs: museum, historic site(s), tours/pilgrimages, historic preservation, photographic collections
Period of collections: 1817-early 20th century

Jefferson County Historical Society, Inc.
410 N. Elm St., 47250
Telephone: (812) 265-2335
Private agency
Founded in: 1922
John Trout, President
Number of members: 120

Staff: volunteer 20
Major programs:
    museum, school programs,
    audiovisual programs
Period of collections: 1850-1899

J.F.D. Lanier State Memorial
511 W. 1st St., 47250
Telephone: (812) 265-3526
State agency, Division of Museums
and Memorials, Department of
Natural ResourcesRuth N. Bartlett,
Curator
Staff: full time 2, part time 5,
    volunteer 20
Major programs: historic site(s),
    markers, school programs,
    exhibits, audiovisual programs
Period of collections: 1840-1895

MARION

**Grant County Historical
    Society, Inc.**
2400 S. Washington St.
Telephone: (317) 662-9133
Founded in: 1964
Emily Morio, Secretary
Number of members: 200
Staff: volunteer 12
Major programs: library, museum,
    historic sites preservation, markers
Period of collections: 1865-1918

**Wesleyan Church Archives and
Historical Library**
50th St. and State Rd. 37
Mail to: P.O. Box 2000, 46952
Private agency
Founded in: 1968
Paul W. Thomas, Director of Archives
Staff: full time 1, part time 2
Magazine: *The Wesleyan Advocate*
Major programs: library, archives,
    manuscripts
Period of collections: 1843-present

MARTINSVILLE

**Archives of the American Camping
Association**
5000 State Hwy. 67, N., 56151
Telephone: (317) 342-8456
Private agency, authorized by the
    American Camping Association
Founded in: 1910
Armand B. Ball, Jr., Executive Vice
President
Number of members: 5,400
Staff: full time 27
Magazine: *Camping Magazine*
Major programs: library, archives,
    book publishing
Period of collections: 1920-present

**Drake's Midwest Phonograph
Museum**
2245 State Rd. 252, 46151
Telephone: (317) 342-7666
Private agency
Founded in: 1973
Kathleen M. Drake, Co-owner
Staff: volunteer 2
Major programs: museum,
    educational programs, historic
    preservation, research
Period of collections: 1858-1927

MICHIGAN CITY

**Michigan City Historical
    Society, Inc.**
Heisman Harbor Rd., Washington
Park
Telephone: (219) 872-6133
Mail to: P.O. Box 512, 46360
Private agency
Founded in: 1927
Patricia A. Harris, Curator/Director
Number of members: 500
Staff: part time 1, volunteer 50
Magazine: *Old Lighthouse Museum
News*
Major programs: library, archives,
    manuscripts, museum, historic
    site(s), markers,
    newsletters/pamphlets, historic
    preservation, research, exhibits,
    photographic collections,
    genealogical services
Period of collections: 1832-present

Old Lighthouse Museum
Heisman Harbor Rd., Washington
Park
Telephone: (219) 872-6133
Mail to: P.O. Box 512, 46360
Private agency, authorized by
    Michigan City Historical
    Society, Inc.
Founded in: 1973
Patricia A. Harris, Curator/Director
Number of members: 500
Staff: part time 1, volunteer 40
Magazine: *Old Lighthouse Museum
News*
Major programs: library, archives,
    museum, historic site(s), markers,
    book publishing,
    newsletters/pamphlets, historic
    preservation, exhibits,
    photographic collections,
    genealogical services
Period of collections: 1832-present

MISHAWAKA

Beiger Heritage Corporation
317 Lincoln Way, E., 46544
Telephone: (219) 256-0365
Private agency
Founded in: 1973
Mrs. G.F. Speiser, Coordinator
Number of members: 500
Staff: part time 5, volunteer 125
Magazine: *Beiger Heritage Gazette*
Major programs: library, museum,
    historic site(s), tours/pilgrimages,
    oral history, book publishing,
    newsletters/pamphlets, historic
    preservation, culture center
Period of collections: 1857-present

**Hannah Lindahl Children's
    Museum**
1402 S. Main St., 46544
Telephone: (219) 258-3056
Authorized by Mishawaka City School
Founded in: 1946
Betty Hans, Curator
Staff: full time 1
Major programs: museum, oral
    history, exhibits
Period of collections: 1835-1935

**Society for the Preservation of Old
    Mills**
123 N. Wenger, 46544

Telephone: (219) 259-4483
Private agency
Founded in: 1972
Fred Beals, President
Number of members: 1,350
Staff: volunteer 10
Magazine: *Old Mill News*
Major programs: archives, historic
    preservation
Period of collections: 1600s-present

MONTICELLO

**White County Historical Society
    and Museum**
P.O. Box 884, 47960
Telephone: (219) 583-7281
Founded in: 1911
Number of members: 53
Staff: part time 1, volunteer 3
Magazine: *The Hamill Heritage
    Newsletter*
Major programs: library, archives,
    manuscripts, museum,
    tours/pilgrimages, oral history,
    newsletters/pamphlets, historic
    preservation
Period of collections: 1834-present

MT. VERNON

Posey County Historical Society
Mail to: P.O. Box 171, 47620
Private agency
Founded in: 1974
Mildred Blake, President
Number of members: 44
Staff: volunteer 12
Major programs: historic site(s),
    markers, oral history, book
    publishing, genealogical services

MUNCIE

Delaware County Historical Society
P.O. Box 1262, 47304
Telephone: (317) 282-4890
Private agency
Oliver C. Bumb, President
Number of members: 200
Major programs: archives, museum,
    markers, historic preservation,
    genealogical services
Period of collections: 1850-1900

NASHVILLE

**Brown County Historical
    Society, Inc.**
State Rd. 135, N.
Telephone: (812) 988-6089
Mail to: P.O. Box 668, 47448
Private agency
Founded in: 1957
Herman E. Weidner, President
Number of members: 330
Staff: volunteer 105
Major programs: archives, museum,
    historic sites preservation, oral
    history, educational programs,
    books, newsletters/pamphlets,
    genealogical services
Period of collections: 1850-1900

NEW ALBANY

**Culbertson Mansion State
    Memorial**
914 E. Main St., 47150
Telephone: (812) 944-9600

State agency
Founded in: 1976
William R. Krueger, Property Manager
Staff: full time 3
Major programs: manuscripts,
  museum, historic site,
  tours/pilgrimages, oral history,
  educational programs, historic
  preservation
Period of collections: 1870s

Floyd County Historical Society
Mail to: P.O. Box 455, 47150
Lola K. Sloan, President
Number of members: 65
Major programs: museum, markers,
  oral history, historic preservation,
  genealogical services
Period of collections: 1865-present

Floyd County Museum
201 E. Spring St., 47150
Telephone: (812) 944-7336
Private agency
Founded in: 1972
Peggy Roberson, Executive
  Secretary
Number of members: 175
Staff: full time 1, part time 2,
  volunteer 5
Major programs: museum, junior
  history, exhibits
Period of collections: late 1800s

NEWCASTLE
Henry County Historical Society
606 S. 14th St., 47362
Telephone: (317) 529-4028
County agency
Founded in: 1887
Evelyn S. Clift, Curator
Number of members: 1,100
Staff: part time 4
Magazine: *Historicalog*
Major programs: library, archives,
  manuscripts, museum, historic
  site(s), junior history, oral history,
  newsletters/pamphlets,
  genealogical services
Period of collections: Victorian era

NEW HARMONY
Historic New Harmony, Inc.
344 W. Church St., 47631
Telephone: (812) 682-4488
State agency, authorized by Indiana
  State University, Evansville
Founded in: 1974
James Sanders, Director
Staff: full time 9, part time 9
Major programs: archives, museum,
  historic site(s), tours/pilgrimages,
  historic preservation, exhibits
Period of collections: 1800-1850

**New Harmony Workingmen's
  Institute**
407 Tavern St.
Telephone: (812) 682-4806
Mail to: P.O. Box 368, 47631
Founded in: 1838
Mary Aline Cook, Librarian
Staff: full time 2
Major programs: library, archives,
  manuscripts, museum, historic
  site(s), research, photographic
  collections
Period of collections: 1812-present

NOBLESVILLE
Conner Prairie Pioneer Settlement
13400 Allisonville Rd., 46060
Telephone: (317) 776-6000
Private agency, authorized by
  Earlham College
Founded in: 1964
Polly Jontz, Director
Number of members: 1,000
Staff: full time 49, part time 73,
  volunteer 110
Magazine: *The Peddler*
Major programs: library, manuscripts,
  museum, historic site(s), oral
  history, school programs, historic
  preservation, research, living
  history
Period of collections: 1820-1840

Hamilton County Historical Society
Mail to: P.O. Box 397, 46060
Private agency
Founded in: 1962
Kent Ward, President
Number of members: 225
Staff: volunteer 25
Major programs: museum,
  newsletters/pamphlets, historic
  preservation, genealogical
  services
Period of collections: 1820-present

Indiana Transportation Museum
325 Cicero Rd.
Telephone: (317) 773-0300
Mail to: P.O. Box 83, 46060
Private agency
Founded in: 1960
John S. Johnson, President
Number of members: 450
Staff: full time 4, part time 1,
  volunteer 80
Major programs: library, museum,
  school programs,
  newsletters/pamphlets, historic
  preservation, research
Period of collections: 1900-1950

NORTH MANCHESTER
**North Manchester Historical
  Society, Inc.**
P.O. Box 361, 46962
Telephone: (219) 982-4732
Private agency
Founded in: 1972
Keith E. Ross, President
Number of members: 160
Staff: volunteer 15
Major programs: manuscripts,
  museum, markers,
  tours/pilgrimages, oral history,
  newsletters/pamphlets, historic
  preservation, genealogical
  services
Period of collections: from 1800

NOTRE DAME
**Theatre Historical Society of
  America**
P.O. Box 101, 46556
Founded in: 1969
Number of members: 900
Staff: part time 1, volunteer 20
Magazine: *Marquee*

Major programs: library, archives,
  newsletters/pamphlets,
  architecture
Number of members: 1900-present

University of Notre Dame Archives
607 Memorial Library, 46556
Telephone: (219) 239-6447
Private agency, authorized by the
  university
Founded in: 1871
Wendy Clauson Schlereth, University
  Archivist
Staff: full time 8, part time 15
Major programs: archives,
  manuscripts, oral history, records
  management, research,
  photographic collections
Period of collections: 19th-20th
  centuries

PERU
Circus City Festival, Inc.
154 N. Broadway, 46970
Telephone: (317) 472-3918
Private agency
Founded in: 1959
Joyce Ferguson, Vice President
Number of members: 450
Staff: volunteer 1
Magazine: *Circus City Festival,
  Museum*
Major programs: archives, tours,
  newsletters/pamphlets,
  photographic collections
Period of collections: 1900-present

**Miami County Historical
  Society, Inc.**
Courthouse, Room 102, 46970
Telephone: (317) 472-1570
Private agency
Founded in: 1916
Bill Nichols, President
Number of members: 350
Staff: volunteer 20
Magazine: *Historically Speaking*
Major programs: educational
  programs, books,
  newsletters/pamphlets
Period of collections: 1850-1940

PLAINFIELD
**Guilford Township Historical
  Collection, Plainfield Public
  Library**
1120 Stafford Rd., 46168
Telephone: (317) 839-6602
Authorized by library board of
  trustees
Founded in: 1967 (collection); 1901
  (library)
Susan Miller Carter, Historical
  Librarian
Staff: full time 1, part time 1,
  volunteer 2
Major programs: library, archives,
  manuscripts, research,
  genealogical services, field
  services
Period of collections: 1816-present

PLYMOUTH
**Marshall County Historical
  Society, Inc.**
317 W. Monroe St., 46563
Telephone: (219) 936-2306

County agency
Founded in: 1957
Mary Hawkins Durnan,
Director/Curator
Number of members: 416
Staff: full time 2, part time 1,
volunteer 1
Major programs: library, archives,
museum, oral history, educational
programs, genealogy
Period of collections: 1836-1920

PORTER

Indiana Dunes National Lakeshore
1100 N. Mineral Springs Rd., 46304
Telephone: (219) 926-7561
Federal agency, authorized by
National Park Service
Dale B. Engquist, Superintendent
Major programs: library, archives,
historic site(s), tours/pilgrimages,
oral history, school programs,
newsletters/pamphlets, historic
preservation, records
management, research, exhibits,
living history, audiovisual
programs, photographic
collections

RENSSELAER

Jasper County Historical Society
Augusta St., 47978
Founded in: 1966
Questionnaire not received

RICHMOND

Wayne County Historical Society
1150 N. A St., 47374
Founded in: 1882
Number of members: 650
Staff: full time 2, part time 1,
volunteer 27
Major programs: library, archives,
manuscripts, museum, historic
sites preservation,
tours/pilgrimages, oral history,
educational programs, books,
newsletters/pamphlets
Period of collections:
prehistoric-present

RISING SUN

**Ohio County Historical
Society, Inc.**
218 S. Walnut St., 47040
Telephone: (812) 438-2056
Private agency
Founded in: 1966
Dillon Dorrell, Sr., President
Number of members: 115
Staff: volunteer 10
Major programs: museum,
tours/pilgrimages, historic
preservation, educational
programs
Period of collections: 1900-present

ROCHESTER

**Fulton County Historical
Society, Inc.**
Civic Center, 7th and Pontiac, 46975
Telephone: (219) 223-4436
County agency
Founded in: 1963

Shirley Willard, Museum
Director/Society President
Number of members: 700
Staff: full time 1, part time 1,
volunteer 8
Major programs: library, museum,
markers, oral history, book
publishing, living history,
photographic collections,
genealogical services
Period of collections: 1840-present

ROCKVILLE

Parke County Historical Society
503 W. Ohio
Mail to: 503 E. Oak Dr., 47872
Founded in: 1917
Kathryn Malone, Museum Chair
Number of members: 150
Staff: volunteer 12
Major programs: museum, historic
sites preservation, markers
Period of collections: 1850-present

ROME

Perry County Historical Society
Mail to: P.O. Box 220, 47574
Founded in: 1929
Questionnaire not received

ROME CITY

**Gene Stratton Porter Historic
Site—Gene Stratton Porter
Society**
Rt. 1, Box 364, 46784
Telephone: (219) 854-3790
State agency, authorized by Division
of Museums and Memorials,
Department of Natural Resources
Founded in: 1947
Margie Sweeney, Curator
Number of members: 204
Staff: full time 2, volunteer 1
Major programs: historic site(s)
Period of collections: 1880-1925

SALEM

Stevens Museum
307 E. Market St., 47167
Telephone: (812) 883-6495
Private agency, authorized by
Washington County Historical
Society
Founded in: 1915
Willie Harlen, President
Number of members: 950
Staff: full time 2, volunteer 12
Major programs: museum, research
Period of collections: 1900-present

**Washington County Historical
Society**
307 E. Market St., 47167
Telephone: (812) 833-6495
Private agency
Founded in: 1897
Willie Harlen, President
Number of members: 950
Staff: full time 2, volunteer 15
Major programs: library, archives,
manuscripts, museum,
tours/pilgrimages
Period of collections: 1783-present

SCOTTSBURG

Scott County Historical Society
1221 Lakeview Dr., 47170
Questionnaire not received

SHELBYVILLE

Shelby County Historical Society
52 W. Broadway
Telephone: (317) 392-4634
Mail to: P.O. Box 74, 46176
Private agency
Founded in: 1922
Gary Henry, Director
Number of members: 500
Staff: full time 1
Magazine: *Echoes of Old Shelby*
Major programs: museum, historic
site(s), tours/pilgrimages, oral
history, newsletters/pamphlets,
historic preservation, records
management, research, exhibits,
photographic collections
Period of collections: 19th-early 20th
centuries

SHOALS

**Martin County Historical
Society, Inc.**
Telephone: (812) 247-2351
Mail to: P.O. Box 84, 47581
Private agency
Founded in: 1963
Jessie V. Stiles, Resident Agent
Number of members: 131
Major programs: museum
Period of collections: 1830-1945

SOUTH BEND

Discovery Hall Museum
120 S. St. Joseph, 46601
Telephone: (219) 284-9714
City agency
Founded in: 1966
Gust A. Saros, Jr., Director
Staff: full time 8, part time 4
Major programs: library, archives,
museum, school programs,
newsletters/pamphlets, exhibits,
audiovisual programs,
photographic collections
Period of collections: 1860-present

Northern Indiana Historical Society
112 S. LaFayette Blvd., 46601
Telephone: (219) 284-9664
Private agency
Founded in: 1895
Kathleen S. Stiso, Executive Director
Number of members: 800
Staff: full time 2, part time 5,
volunteer 20
Magazine: *Old Courthouse News*
Major programs: library, archives,
manuscripts, museum, historic
site(s), tours, junior history, oral
history, school programs, book
publishing, newsletters/pamphlets,
research, exhibits, living history,
audiovisual programs,
photographic collections,
genealogical services, museum
theatre, artifact kits
Period of collections: 19th-20th
centuries

STAR CITY

Pulaski County Genealogy Society
Rt. 2, Box 130, 46985
Telephone: (219) 595-7203
Founded in: 1969
Mildred Weaver, President
Number of members: 60
Major programs: library, archives,
book publishing,
newsletters/pamphlets,
genealogical services
Period of collections: 1830-present

TELL CITY

Tell City Historical Society, Inc.
P.O. Box 205, 47586
Telephone: (812) 547-2797/547-2424
Private agency
Founded in: 1923
Doris Leistner, Archivist/Genealogy
Chair
Number of members: 72
Staff: volunteer 8
Major programs: archives,
manuscripts, oral history, book
publishing, research, exhibits,
living history, photographic
collections, genealogical services,
microfilming of local newspapers
and church records
Period of collections: 1814-present

TERRE HAUTE

Eugene V. Debs Foundation
451 N. 8th St., 47802
Mail to: P.O. Box 843, 47808
Founded in: 1962
Number of members: 400
Staff: volunteer 2
Major programs: library, archives,
museum, historic sites

preservation, markers,
tours/pilgrimages, oral history,
educational programs,
newsletters/pamphlets
Period of collections: 1855-present

Vigo County Historical Society
1411 S. 6th St., 47802
Telephone: (812) 235-9717
County agency
Founded in: 1923
Georgia Jones, Executive Director
Number of members: 900
Staff: part time 3
Magazine: *Leaves of Thyme*
Major programs: museum, school
programs, newsletters/pamphlets,
exhibits, photographic collections
Period of collections: Victorian era

VALPARAISO

**Historical Society of Porter
County, Inc.—Old Jail Museum**
153 Franklin St., 46383
Telephone: (219) 464-8661, ext. 229
Founded in: 1912
Bertha Stalbaum, Curator
Number of members: 93
Staff: full time 2, part time 2,
volunteer 1
Major programs: museum,
newsletters/pamphlets,
educational programs, tours
Period of collections:
prehistoric-present

VERNON

Our Heritage, Inc.
Brown and Pike Sts.
Mail to: P.O. Box 245, 47282
Founded in: 1961
Questionnaire not received

VERSAILLES

**Ripley County Indiana Historical
Society, Inc.**
Telephone: (812) 689-5019
Mail to: P.O. Box 224, 47042
Founded in: 1924
Number of members: 180
Staff: volunteer 15
Magazine: *Ripley History News Letter*
Major programs: museum, historic
sites preservation, educational
programs, newsletters/pamphlets
Period of collections: 1783-1918

VINCENNES

Byron R. Lewis Historical Library
Vincennes University, 1002 N. 1st St.,
47591
Telephone: (812) 885-4330
Founded in: 1967
Robert R. Stevens, Director
Staff: full time 3
Major programs: library, archives,
manuscripts, oral history, books
Period of collections: 1732-present

**Francis Vigo Chapter, Daughters of
the American Revolution**
3 W. Scott St.
Telephone: (812) 882-2096
Mail to: 427 N. 2nd St., 47591
Private agency, authorized by the
national society
Founded in: 1908
Lorethea Hamke, Curator
Number of members: 443
Staff: part time 3, volunteer 20
Major programs: library, museum,
historic site(s), markers,
tours/pilgrimages, junior history,
school programs, book publishing,
historic preservation, research,
exhibits, archaeology programs,
genealogical services
Period of collections: 1783-1865

Old Northwest Corporation
P.O. Box 1979, 47591
Telephone: (812) 885-4173
Private agency
Founded in: 1973
Robert R. Stevens, Board Chair
Number of members: 250
Staff: part time 1, volunteer 45
Major programs: museum, historic
site(s), tours/pilgrimages,
newsletters/pamphlets, historic
preservation
Period of collections: prehistoric-1806

**Vincennes Historical and
Antiquarian Society—Lewis
Historical Collections Library**
Vincennes University, Library Room
22, 47591
Telephone: (812) 882-3265
Private agency
Founded in: 1808
Dennis Latta, President
Number of members: 250
Major programs: archives, historic
site(s), markers, tours/pilgrimages,
book publishing,
newsletters/pamphlets, historic
preservation
Period of collections: 1793-present

*Workers place finishing touches on a buggy in the Studebaker Brothers Manufacturing
Company. The photograph is from the Studebaker Corporate Archives Collection, housed
at the Studebaker Museum, which is operated by Discovery Hall.—Discovery Hall Archival
Collections, South Bend, Indiana*

WABASH

Wabash County Historical Society
Memorial Hall, 46992
Founded in: 1926
Questionnaire not received

WARSAW

**Kosciusko County Historical
Society**
P.O. Box 214, 46580
Telephone: (219) 267-4271/453-3609
Founded in: 1965
Number of members: 319
Staff: volunteer 20
Magazine: *Our Missing Links*
Major programs: library, manuscripts,
museum, historic site, markers,
tours/pilgrimages, educational
programs, newsletters/pamphlets,
historic preservation
Period of collections: 1830s-present

WASHINGTON

Daviess County Historical Society
P.O. Box 2341, 47501
Founded in: 1966
Questionnaire not received

WEST LAFAYETTE

**American Poultry Historical
Society**
Poultry Science Bldg., Purdue
University, 47907
Founded in: 1952
Questionnaire not received

WHITING

**Whiting-Robertsdale Historical
Society**
City Hall, 1443 119th St., 46394
Telephone: (219) 659-6316
Founded in: 1976
Betty Gehrke, Librarian
Number of members: 130
Staff: volunteer 2
Major programs: library, archives,
manuscripts, museum, markers,
oral history, school programs, book
publishing, newsletters, historic
preservation, photographic
collections
Period of collections: 1890-present

WINAMAC

**Pulaski County Historical
Society, Inc.**
400 S. Market St., 46996
Founded in: 1956
Questionnaire not received

WINCHESTER

**Randolph County Historical
Society**
416 S. Meridian, 47394
Mail to: 424 S. Meridian
Questionnaire not received

ZIONSVILLE

Zionsville Historical Society, Inc.
900 E. State Rd. 32, 46052
Telephone: (317) 482-1848
Founded in: 1962

Mrs. John A. Lyons, Correspondence
Secretary
Number of members: 100
Major programs: markers, historic
preservation, exhibits,
genealogical services

IOWA

ADEL

Adel Historical Society
1129 Main
Telephone: (515) 993-4124
Mail to: 1307 Hy Vue, 50003
Founded in: 1972
Juanita Lewis, President
Number of members: 60
Staff: volunteer 20
Major programs: museum, historic
site, oral history
Period of collections: 1900s

AGENCY

Chief Wapello's Memorial Park
R.R. 1, Box 25, 52530
Telephone: (515) 937-5720
State agency
Donald Harryman, President
Number of members: 210
Staff: volunteer 11
Major programs: historic site(s),
newsletters/pamphlets, historic
preservation
Period of collections: 1783-1865

ALBERT CITY

**Albert City Historical
Association, Inc.**
212 N. 2nd St.
Telephone: (712) 843-5404
Mail to: R.R. 1, Box 30, 50510
Town agency
Founded in: 1975
Gladys Anderson, President
Number of members: 50
Staff: volunteer 20
Major programs: museum, historic
sites preservation, exhibits
Period of collections: 1865-1918

ALBIA

Monroe County Historical Society
114-116 A Ave., E, 52531
Telephone: (515) 932-7046
Private agency
Founded in: 1969
E. St. Clair Gantz, President
Staff: volunteer 10
Major programs: museum

ALLISON

Butler County Historical Society
303 6th and Maple St., 50602
Questionnaire not received

AMANA

**Amana Heritage Society and
Museum of Amana History**
52203
Telephone: (319) 622-3567
Private agency

Founded in: 1968
Lanny Haldy, Director
Number of members: 400
Staff: full time 1, part time 16
Major programs: library, archives,
museum, oral history, school
programs, historic preservation,
research, exhibits, photographic
collections, genealogical services
Period of collections: 1700-present

AMES

**Brunnier Gallery—Farm House
Museum**
Scheman Bldg., Iowa State Center,
Lincoln Way, 50011
Telephone: (515) 294-3342
State agency
Founded in: 1975
Lynette Pohlman, Director
Staff: full time 4, part time 1,
volunteer 25
Major programs: museum, historic
site(s), tours, school programs,
newsletters/pamphlets, historic
preservation, exhibits
Period of collections: 18th-19th
centuries

**Iowa Genealogical Society, Story
County**
Telephone: (515) 292-3283
Mail to: c/o Chamber of Commerce,
50010
Founded in: 1967
Number of members: 40
Major programs: genealogy
Period of collections: 1865-present

AUDUBON

Audubon County Historical Society
Rt. 2, 50025
Telephone: (712) 563-3984
County agency
Founded in: 1960
Fred Sievers, President
Staff: part time 2, volunteer 24
Major programs: museum, festivals
Period of collections: 1880-1930

BEDFORD

Taylor County Historical society
Telephone: (712) 537-2475
Mail to: P.O. Box 8, Gravity, 50848
Questionnaire not received

BETTENDORF

Bettendorf Museum
533 16th St.
Telephone: (319) 355-8687
Mail to: P.O. Box 430, 52722
City agency, authorized by city
council
Founded in: 1974
Miriam Ingram, Director
Staff: part time 1, volunteer 10
Major programs: museum,
newsletters/pamphlets, exhibits
Period of collections: 1830-1940

BLAKESBURG

Airpower Museum, Inc.
R.R. 2 Ottumwa, 52501
Questionnaire not received

BLOCKTON

Barbed Wire Hall of Fame
58036
Questionnaire not received

BLOOMFIELD

Davis County Historical Society
302 E. Franklin St.
Telephone: (515) 664-2408
Mail to: Rt. 6, 52537
Founded in: 1961
Questionnaire not received

BOONE

**Boone County Genealogical
Society**
423 Benton, 50036
Telephone: (515) 432-5647
Private agency
Founded in: 1974
Bertha Harten, President
Number of members: 65
Major programs: newsletters,
genealogical services, cemetery
records, marriage index
Period of collections: 1850-present

Boone County Historical Society
P.O. Box 1, 50036
Telephone: (515) 432-1931/232-1449
Private agency
Founded in: 1966
Jack Shelley, President
Number of members: 1,150
Staff: volunteer 20
Magazine: *Trail Tales*
Major programs: library, museum,
historic site(s), tours/pilgrimages,
junior history, school programs,
book publishing,
newsletters/pamphlets, historic
preservation, research, exhibits,
audiovisual programs,
photographic collections
Period of collections: 1850s-present

Boone Railroad Historical Society
P.O. Box 603, 50036
Telephone: (515) 432-4249
Private agency
Founded in: 1982
Dean Briley, President/General
Manager
Number of members: 2,375
Staff: full time 4, volunteer 200
Major programs: museum,
tours/pilgrimages,
newsletters/pamphlets, historic
preservation
Period of collections: 1890s-present

**Mamie Doud Eisenhower
Birthplace Foundation, Inc.**
709 Carroll St.
Telephone: (515) 432-1896
Mail to: P.O. Box 55, 50036
Private agency
Founded in: 1970
Larry Adams, Curator
Number of members: 30
Staff: full time 1, volunteer 75
Major programs: library, archives,
manuscripts, museum, historic
site(s), markers, tours/pilgrimages,
junior history,
newsletters/pamphlets, historic
preservation, records

management, research, exhibits,
audiovisual programs,
photographic collections,
genealogical services
Period of collections: 1880s-present

BRIGHTON

**Polishville Cemetery and Grotto
Association**
R.R. 2, 52540
Telephone: (319) 694-3495
Private agency
Founded in: 1977
William E. Peck, President
Staff: volunteer 23
Major programs: markers, book
publishing, newsletters/pamphlets,
historic preservation, genealogical
services
Period of collections: 1900-present

BURLINGTON

**Des Moines County Historical
Society**
1616 Dill St., 52601
Telephone: (319) 753-2449
Private agency
Founded in: 1968
Betty Beck, Executive Secretary
Staff: part time 1
Major programs: museum,
tours/pilgrimages, oral history,
newsletters/pamphlets,
photographic collections
Period of collections: 1833-1900

BURR OAK

**Laura Ingalls Wilder Park and
Museum**
P.O. Box 354, 52101
Telephone: (319) 735-5916
Private agency
Founded in: 1973
Lorraine Houck, President
Staff: part time 4, volunteer 6

Major programs: museum, historic
site(s), junior history, school
programs, newsletters/pamphlets,
historic preservation, exhibits
Period of collections: late 19th
century

CAMANCHE

Camanche Historical Society
12th Ave. and 2nd St.
Telephone: (319) 259-1268
Mail to: c/o City Hall, 2nd St., 52730
Private agency
Founded in: 1984
R. Jaye Nash, President
Number of members: 25
Staff: volunteer 12
Major programs: museum, exhibits,
photographic collections
Period of collections: 1860-present

CARROLL

Carroll County Historical Society
126 E. 6th
Mail to: c/o President, 514 W. 9th St.,
51401
Founded in: 1967
Dean Bruhn, Curator
Number of members: 40
Staff: volunteer 15
Major programs: museum,
tours/pilgrimages, oral history,
educational programs, historic
preservation
Period of collections: 1840-present

CASTALIA

Bloomfield Historical Society
52133
Founded in: 1963
Number of members: 45
Staff: volunteer 4
Major programs: museum, historic
site(s), markers, book publishing,
historic preservation, research,
field services

*The George Wyth House, located in Cedar Falls, was built in 1907 and was acquired by
the Cedar Falls Historical Society in 1979.*—Cedar Falls Historical Society

CEDAR FALLS

Cedar Falls Historical Society
303 Franklin St., 50613
Telephone: (319) 277-8817
Founded in: 1964
David Correll, President
Number of members: 1,000
Staff: full time 1, part time 1, volunteer 20
Major programs: library, archives, museum, historic site(s), tours/pilgrimages, oral history, school programs, book publishing, newsletters/pamphlets, historic preservation, research, exhibits, audiovisual programs, photographic collections, genealogical services
Period of collections: 1850s-1940s

George Wyth House Museum
303 Franklin St., 50613
Telephone: (319) 277-8817
Authorized by Cedar Falls Historical Society
Founded in: 1983
Rosemary Beach, Executive Director
Staff: full time 1
Major programs: museum, historic preservation, Art Deco
Period of collections: 1925

Ice House Museum
303 Franklin St., 56013
Telephone: (319) 277-8817
Rosemary Beach, Executive Director
Staff: volunteer 30
Major programs: museum, historic preservation, agricultural programs
Period of collections: 1860-1940

University of Northern Iowa Museum
31st St.
Telephone: (319) 273-2188
Mail to: University of Northern Iowa, 50614
State agency, authorized by the university
Founded in: 1890
Ronald C. Wilson, Director
Staff: full time 1, part time 4
Major programs: museum, school programs, exhibits, natural history
Period of collections: 1820-present

Victorian House Museum
303 Clay St., 50613
Telephone: (319) 266-5149
City agency, authorized by Cedar Falls Historical Society
Founded in: 1964
Rosemary Beach, Executive Director
Staff: full time 1
Major programs: museum, historic preservation
Period of collections: Victorian era

CEDAR RAPIDS

Iowa Postal History Society
1298 29th St., NE, 52402
Telephone: (319) 363-8087
Founded in: 1951
Steven Bahnsen, President
Number of members: 105
Staff: volunteer 5
Major programs: manuscripts, newsletters/pamphlets, research, exhibits
Period of collections: 1830-present

Linn County Heritage Society
Cedar Rapids Public Library
Mail to: P.O. Box 175, 52406
Founded in: 1965
Number of members: 140
Major programs: library, books

Pioneer Village Commission
City Hall, 52401
Telephone: (319) 398-5104
City agency
Founded in: 1974
Richard L. Pankey, Director
Staff: part time 6, volunteer 5
Major programs: museum, historic site(s), school programs, historic preservation, exhibits
Period of collections: 1900

Seminole Valley Farm, Inc.
Seminole Valley Park
Mail to: P.O. Box 605, 52406
Founded in: 1969
Phyllis Hall, President
Staff: volunteer 30
Major programs: tours, school programs, historic preservation, exhibits, audiovisual programs
Period of collections: 1880-1900

CHARITON

Lucas County Museum
17th St. and Braden Ave.
Telephone: (515) 774-4464
Mail to: c/o Curator, P.O. Box 64, Lucas, 50151
County agency, authorized by Lucas County Historical Society
Founded in: 1965
Jean Hager, Curator
Number of members: 460
Staff: volunteer 9
Major programs: library, museum, tours/pilgrimages, oral history, school programs, historic preservation, exhibits, living history, photographic collections
Period of collections: late 19th-early 20th centuries

CHARLES CITY

Floyd County Historical Society Museum
500 Gilbert St.
Telephone: (515) 228-1099/228-2547
Mail to: 405 4th Ave., 50616
County agency
Founded in: 1954
Vera M. Brenton, President
Number of members: 600
Staff: part time 1, volunteer 40
Major programs: library, manuscripts, museum, historic site(s), markers, tours, school programs, newsletters/pamphlets, research, exhibits, genealogical services
Period of collections: 1850-1980

CHEROKEE

Cherokee Area Archives, Inc.
1308 Greta St.
Telephone: (712) 225-2963
Mail to: P.O. Box 255, 51012
Private agency
Founded in: 1980
Marguerite S. Whiting, Archivist/Administrator

Number of members: 40
Staff: full time 1, volunteer 1
Major programs: archives, genealogical services
Period of collections: 1856-1925

Cherokee County Historical Society
Mail to: P.O. Box 1067, 51012
Questionnaire not received

Joseph A. Tallman Museum
1200 W. Cedar St., 51012
Telephone: (712) 225-2594
State agency
Founded in: 1961
Jeanette E. Ludwig, Assistant Business Manager
Major programs: museum, historic preservation
Period of collections: 1896-present

Northwest Chapter, Iowa Archaeological Society
Sanford Museum, 117 E. Willow, 51012
Telephone: (712) 225-3922
Founded in: 1952
Mike Hosbein, President
Number of members: 80
Major programs: museum, educational programs, newsletters/pamphlets, field trips, excavations
Period of collections: prehistoric-present

Sanford Museum and Planetarium
117 E. Willow St., 51012
Telephone: (712) 225-3922
Private agency, authorized by Trustees, Tiel Sanford Memorial Fund
Founded in: 1951
J. Jerry Walker, Director
Number of members: 130
Staff: full time 1, part time 4
Major programs: library, archives, museum, school programs, newsletters/pamphlets, exhibits, archaeology programs, natural history
Period of collections: prehistoric-20th century

CLARION

Wright County Genealogical Searchers
P.O. Box 225, 50525
Founded in: 1973
Number of members: 32
Major programs: library, genealogy
Period of collections: 1865-present

Wright County Historical Society
615 5th Ave., 50525
Telephone: (515) 532-3669
Private agency
Founded in: 1976
William I. Mock, President
Number of members: 125
Period of collections: 1854-present

CLERMONT

Montauk
Hwy. 18, E.
Telephone: (319) 423-7173
Mail to: P.O. Box 372, 52135
State agency, authorized by Iowa State Historical Department

Founded in: 1968
Henry A. Follett, Director
Staff: full time 1, part time 7
Major programs: manuscripts,
  museum, historic site(s), school
  programs
Period of collections: 1874-1912

CLINTON

Clinton County Historical Society
Root Park
Telephone: (319) 242-9552/242-4450
Mail to: P.O. Box 3135, 52732
Founded in: 1965
Major programs: historic preservation

CORALVILLE

Johnson County Historical Society
310 5th St.
Telephone: (319) 351-5738
Mail to: P.O. Box 5081, 52241
Private agency
Founded in: 1973
Dick Myers, President
Number of members: 98
Staff: full time 1, volunteer 30
Magazine: *Johnson County Historian*
Major programs: museum, book
  publishing, newsletters/pamphlets,
  historic preservation, exhibits
Period of collections: 19th century

CORYDON

**Wayne County Genealogical
Society**
302 N. Franklin, 50060
Telephone: (515) 872-1393
Founded in: 1975
Number of members: 85
Staff: volunteer 5
Magazine: *Wayne County Genie
News*
Major programs: library, educational
  programs, genealogy
Period of collections: 1850-1900

Wayne County Historical Society
Hwy. 2, 50060
Private agency
Founded in: 1942
Amy Robertson, President
Number of members: 1,100
Major programs: library, museum,
  historic sites preservation,
  genealogy
Period of collections: 1865-present

COUNCIL BLUFFS

**Historical Society of Pottawattamie
County**
P.O. Box 2, 51501
Private agency
Founded in: 1960
Number of members: 150
Major programs: archives, museum,
  historic site(s), markers,
  tours/pilgrimages, book publishing,
  newsletters/pamphlets, historic
  preservation, records
  management, research, exhibits,
  living history, photographic
  collections, genealogical services,
  preservation and restoration
Period of collections: 1850-present

Historic General Dodge House
605 3rd St., 51501
Telephone: (712) 322-2406
City agency
Founded in: 1964
Number of members: 500
Staff: full time 2, part time 15,
  volunteer 7
Major programs: museum, historic
  site(s), tours/pilgrimages,
  newsletters/pamphlets, exhibits,
  photographic collections, historic
  costume
Period of collections: 1865-1916

CRESCO

Howard County Historical Society
114 4th Ave., W, 52136
Founded in: 1924
Questionnaire not received

CRESTON

Union County Historical Society
1101 N. Vine, 50801
Telephone: (515) 782-4247
Private agency
Founded in: 1966
Marcella M. Howe,
  Secretary/Treasurer
Number of members: 74
Staff: volunteer 16
Major programs: library, markers,
  book publishing, records
  management, exhibits,
  genealogical services

DAVENPORT

Putnam Museum
1717 W. 12th St., 52804
Telephone: (319) 324-1933
Private agency
Founded in: 1867
Michael J. Smith, Director
Number of members: 2,500
Staff: full time 12, part time 3,
  volunteer 120
Major programs: manuscripts,
  museum, school programs,
  research, exhibits, photographic
  collections
Period of collections:
  prehistoric-present

**Scott County Iowa Genealogical
Society**
Mail to: P.O. Box 3132, 52808
Telephone: 1973
Questionnaire not received

**16th Iowa Veteran
Volunteer Infantry, Reactivated**
1906 E. 12th St., 52803
Telephone: (309) 786-3504
Founded in: 1980
Questionnaire not received

**Village of East Davenport
Association, Inc.**
2200 E. 11th St., 52803
Telephone: (319) 323-2735
Founded in: 1973
Len Mock, President
Number of members: 51
Staff: volunteer 9
Major programs: historic site(s),
  tours/pilgrimages, historic
  preservation, living history

DE WITT

**Central Community Historical
Society of Clinton County**
724 12th St., 52742
Telephone: (319) 659-3472
Founded in: 1977
Questionnaire not received

DECORAH

Elsworth-Porter House Museum
401 W. Broadway, 52101
Founded in: 1968
Questionnaire not received

Luther College Preus Library
Luther College, 52101
Telephone: (319) 387-1166
Private agency, authorized by
  American Lutheran Church
Founded in: 1861
Leigh Jordahl, Head Librarian
Staff: full time 6
Major programs: library, archives,
  manuscripts, photographic
  collections, genealogical services
Period of collections: 1861-present

**Vesterheim-Norwegian-American
Museum**
502 W. Water St., 52101
Telephone: (319) 382-9681
Private agency, authorized by
  Norwegian-American Museum
  Corporation
Founded in: 1877
Marion John Nelson, Director
Number of members: 6,800
Staff: full time 8, part time 5,
  volunteer 40
Major programs: museum, historic
  site(s), newsletters/pamphlets,
  historic preservation, research,
  exhibits, photographic collections,
  ethnic craft education
Period of collections: 1650-1925

**Winneshiek County Historical
Society**
c/o President, 907 Pine Ridge Court,
  52101
Telephone: (319) 382-5347
Private agency
Founded in: 1962
E. J. Weighe, President
Major programs: archives,
  manuscripts, historic site(s),
  markers, photographic collections,
  genealogical services
Period of collections: 1875-present

DENISON

Crawford County Historical Society
1428 1st Ave., N, 51442
Founded in: 1967
Questionnaire not received

Little Red Schoolhouse Museum
Rt. 3, 51442
Telephone: (712) 263-5329
Private agency
Founded in: 1976
Ramona Laubscher, Owner/Operator
Staff: full time 2
Major programs: library, museum,
  historic site(s), tours, school
  programs, historic preservation,
  records management, exhibits,
  living history, field services
Period of collections: 1890-1940

DES MOINES

Foundation for Historic Conservation
216 Davidson Bldg., 50309
Telephone: (515) 244-0319
Founded in: 1976
Questionnaire not received

Hoyt Sherman Place
1501 Woodland Ave., 50309
Telephone: (515) 243-0913
Private agency, authorized by Des Moines Women's Club
Founded in: 1907
Anna Belle Wonders, Executive Director
Number of members: 750
Staff: full time 4, part time 7, volunteer 175
Major programs: museum, fine arts
Period of collections: 19th century

Iowa Society for the Preservation of Historic Landmarks
E. 12th St. and Grand Ave., 50319
Telephone: (515) 281-5111
Private agency
Founded in: 1956
Barbara Liesman, President
Number of members: 225
Staff: volunteer 6
Major programs: tours/pilgrimages, book publishing, newsletters/pamphlets, historic preservation
Period of collections: 1950s-present

Iowa State Historical Department
E. 12th and Grand Ave., 50319
Telephone: (515) 281-5113
State agency
Founded in: 1898
David Crosson, Director
Staff: full time 66, part time 11, volunteer 60
Major programs: library, archives, manuscripts, museum, historic site(s), historic preservation, genealogical services, field services
Period of collections: 19th century

Latvian Society of Iowa
1372 E. 12th, 50319
Telephone: (515) 262-9932
Questionnaire not received

Living History Farms
2600 N.W. 111th St., 50322
Telephone: (515) 278-8256
Private agency, authorized by Living History Farms Foundation, Inc.
Steve Green, Executive Director
Magazine: *Almanac*
Major programs: museum, historic site(s), school programs, historic preservation, research, living history
Period of collections: 1840-1900

Polk County Historical Society
317 S.W. 42nd St., 50312
Telephone: (515) 255-6657
Private agency
Founded in: 1938
LeRoy G. Pratt, Editor
Number of members: 150
Major programs: historic site(s), markers, book publishing, newsletters/pamphlets, historic preservation
Period of collections: 1870s-present

Salisbury House, Iowa State Education Association
4025 Tonawanda Dr., 50312
Telephone: (515) 279-9711
Private agency, authorized by state education association
Founded in: 1954
William Pritchard, Associate Executive Director, Administration
Number of members: 24,000
Staff: full time 5, part time 15
Magazine: *ISEA Communiqué*
Major programs: library, archives, manuscripts, museum, historic site(s), school programs
Period of collections: 16th-17th centuries

Scottish Heritage Society of Iowa
P.O. Box 155, 50311
Telephone: (515) 276-3922
Founded in: 1974
Number of members: 280
Major programs: library, tours/Scottish, educational programs, historic preservation

Sherman Hill Association
705 19th St., 50314
Telephone: (515) 284-5717
Private agency
Founded in: 1977
Sheila R. Navis, Executive Director
Number of members: 176
Staff: full time 1, volunteer 3
Major programs: tours/pilgrimages, newsletters/pamphlets, historic preservation, funding resources, architectural salvage, political action

Iowa Chapter, Victorian Society in America
2940 Cottage Grove, 50311
Telephone: (515) 274-4996
Patrice K. Beam, Executive Director
Founded in: 1979
Number of members: 150
Staff: part time 1, volunteer 20
Magazine: *Victorian News*
Major programs: tours, school programs, book publishing, newsletters/pamphlets, historic preservation, decorative arts, special events
Period of collections: 1846-1918

DE WITT

Central Community Historical Society of Clinton County
R.R. 2, Box 96, 52742
Telephone: (319) 659-3686
County agency
Founded in: 1977
Mrs. Floyd Soenksen, President
Number of members: 75
Staff: volunteer 9
Major programs: museum, historic site(s), tours/pilgrimages, oral history, book publishing, historic preservation, photographic collections, genealogical services
Period of collections: 1865-present

DEXTER

Dexter Historical Museum
50070
City agency, authorized by Dexter Park Board

Founded in: 1971
Mrs. Robert Weesner, Curator
Staff: volunteer 6
Major programs: archives, manuscripts, museum, photographic collections, genealogical services
Period of collections: 1865-present

DUBUQUE

Dubuque County Historical Society—Mathias Ham House
2nd St. Harbor
Telephone: (319) 557-9545
Mail to: P.O. Box 305, 52001
Private agency
Founded in: 1950
Number of members: 500
Jerome A. Enzler, Director
Staff: full time 6, part time 16, volunteer 40
Major programs: archives, manuscripts, museum, historic site(s), tours/pilgrimages, oral history, school programs, newsletters/pamphlets, historic preservation, research, exhibits, audiovisual programs, photographic collections
Period of collections: 1700-present

Key City Genealogical Society
P.O. Box 13, 52001
Founded in: 1976
Linda L. Gomall, Corresponding Secretary
Number of members: 55
Staff: volunteer 20
Major programs: library, archives, newsletters/pamphlets, research, genealogical services
Period of collections: 1830-present

Research Center for Dubuque Area History
Wahlert Library, Loras College, 52001
Telephone: (319) 588-7125
Mail to: P.O. Box 178, 52004-0178
Private agency, authorized by the college
Founded in: 1976
Michael D. Gibson, Archivist
Staff: part time 3
Major programs: library, archives, manuscripts, research, photographic collections
Period of collections: 1830-present

DYERSVILLE

Dyersville Historical Society
340 1st Ave., E, 52040
Telephone: (319) 875-8912
Founded in: 1962
Questionnaire not received

EAGLE GROVE

Eagle Grove Chapter, Wright County Historical Society
Broadway and N. Iowa Sts.
Telephone: (515) 448-4220
Mail to: 917 W. Broadway, 50533
City agency
Founded in: 1976
Mrs. Orin N. Emerson, President
Number of members: 75
Major programs: museum, historic site(s), historic preservation, photographic collections
Period of collections: 1881-present

ELDORA

Hardin County Historical Society
1603 S. Washington St.
Telephone: (515) 858-3616 (curator)
Mail to: 1101 16th Ave., 50627
County agency
Founded in: 1971
Kermith S. Huehn, Curator
Number of members: 400
Magazine: *Hitching Post*
Major programs: library, archives,
    manuscripts,
    newsletters/pamphlets, research,
    photographic collections,
    genealogical services
Period of collections: 1854-present

ELDRIDGE

**Scott County Historical
    Society, Inc.**
52748
Telephone: (319) 285-4288
Mail to: c/o President, Rt. 3, 52804
Founded in: 1969
Lucille Pollock, President
Number of members: 57
Staff: volunteer 12
Major programs: manuscripts,
    historic sites preservation, markes,
    tours/pilgrimages, oral history,
    educational programs, books
Period of collections:
    prehistoric-present

ELKADER

Elkader Historical Society
52043
Telephone: (319) 245-2622
Private agency
Founded in: 1970
Arlene Fischer, President
Number of members: 179
Staff: volunteer 12
Major programs: museum, markers
Period of collections: 1840s-1920s

ESTHERVILLE

**Emmet County Historical
    Society, Inc.**
1720 3rd Ave., S
Mail to: P.O. Box 101, 51334
County agency
Founded in: 1964
Ivadell Ross, Treasurer
Number of members: 253
Staff: volunteer 5
Major programs: museum, historic
    sites preservation, markers, books
Period of collections: 1900-present

EXIRA

Audobon County Historical Society
50076
Founded in: 1966
Questionnaire not received

FAIRFIELD

**Jefferson County Historical
    Society**
304 S. Main St., 52556
Telephone: (515) 472-3221
Founded in: 1963
Number of members: 25
Major programs: volunteer, historic
    site, book publishing, markers

FARMINGTON

Pioneer Historical Society, Inc.
203 S. 4th St., 52626
Private agency
Founded in: 1964
Robert M. Satterly, President
Number of members: 125
Staff: volunteer 15
Major programs: museum, exhibits,
    photographic collections
Period of collections: 1900-1950

FOREST CITY

Winnebago Historical Society
336 N. Clark St., 50436
Number of members: 145
Staff: volunteer 30
Major programs: library, archives,
    manuscripts, museum, historic site,
    markers, tours/pilgrimages, oral
    history, educational programs,
    pamphlets, historic preservation
Period of collections: 1895-present

FORT DODGE

**Ft. Dodge Chapter, Iowa Society for
    Preservation of Historic
    Landmarks**
1226 N. 24th Place, 50501
Telephone: (515) 573-2919
State agency
Founded in: 1956
Elizabeth B. Craw, President
Number of members: 300
Staff: volunteer 6
Major programs: tours/pilgrimages,
    newsletters/pamphlets, historic
    preservation, education

**Ft. Dodge Historical
    Foundation—Fort Museum**
U.S. Hwy. 20 and Museum Rd.
Telephone: (515) 573-4231
Mail to: P.O. Box 1798, 50501
Private agency
Founded in: 1964
David Parker, Executive Director
Number of members: 400
Staff: full time 1, part time 7,
    volunteer 10
Major programs: museum,
    tours/pilgrimages, exhibits, living
    history
Period of collections: 1850-1900

FORT MADISON

**North Lee County Historical
    Society**
Avenue H and 9th Sts., 52627
Telephone: (319) 372-7661
Founded in: 1962
Questionnaire not received

GARNAVILLO

Garnavillo Historical Society
52049
Founded in: 1965
Arnold D. Roggman, Director
Staff: volunteer 6
Major programs: library, archives,
    manuscripts, museum, historic site,
    tours/pilgrimages, educational
    programs, book publishing
Period of collections: prehistoric-1876

GLENWOOD

Mills County Genealogical Society
109 N. Vine, 51534
Telephone: (712) 527-5252
Private agency
Founded in: 1977
Beverly Boileau, Corresponding
    Secretary
Number of members: 45
Staff: volunteer 10
Major programs:
    newsletters/pamphlets, research,
    genealogical services
Period of collections: 1850-1900

Mills County Historical Society
Telephone: (712) 527-9339
Mail to: c/o 406 3rd St. 51534
Questionnaire not received

GOLDFIELD

Wright County Historical Society
Rt. 2, Box 106, 50542
Telephone: (515) 825-3641
Founded in: 1976
Number of members: 125
Period of collections: 1854-present

GOWRIE

Gowrie Historical Society
P.O. Box 175, 50543
Town agency
Founded in: 1970
Lucile Swenson, President
Number of members: 55
Staff: volunteer 11
Major programs: museum, historic
    site(s), oral history, historic
    preservation, exhibits
Period of collections: 1870-present

GRAFTON

Grafton Heritage Depot
Main St., 50440
Telephone: (515) 748-2727
Founded in: 1976
Questionnaire not received

GREENFIELD

Adair County Anquestors
Greenfield Public Library, 215 S. 1st
    St.
Mail to: P.O. Box 8, 50849
Private agency
Founded in: 1973
Amelia Brockman, President
Number of members: 80
Staff: volunteer 4
Major programs: library, manuscripts,
    research, exhibits, genealogical
    services
Period of collections: 1856-1915

Adair County Historical Society
c/o Board President, 410 N. 1st St.,
    50849
Telephone: (515) 743-2022
Private agency
Founded in: 1967
R. L. Mayes, President
Number of members: 203
Staff: volunteer 5
Major programs: museum, historic
    site(s), markers, book publishing,
    newsletters
Period of collections: 1900-1925

GRINNELL

Grinnell Historical Museum
1125 Broad St.
Telephone: (515) 236-7827
Mail to: 631 Park St., A-104, 50112
Private agency
Founded in: 1956
Elizabeth H. Ernst
Number of members: 273
Staff: volunteer 30
Period of collections: 1854-present

GRISWOLD

Hillcrest Farm Museum and Library
605 N. Park, 51535
Founded in: 1924
Questionnaire not received

GRUNDY CENTER

Grundy County Historical Society
R.F.D. 1, 50638
Telephone: (319) 824-3585
Private agency
Founded in: 1975
Leland Bentley, President
Number of members: 40

GUTHRIE

Guthrie County Historical Society
901 Grand, 56115
Telephone: (515) 747-3403
Private agency
Founded in: 1952
Frank Bancroft, President
Number of members: 21
Staff: volunteer 14
Major programs: library, museum,
    historic site(s), markers,
    tours/pilgrimages, school
    programs, book publishing,
    newsletters/pamphlets, historic
    preservation, exhibits, audiovisual
    programs, genealogical services
Period of collections: 1800-1900

HAMPTON

Franklin County Historical Society
50475
Telephone: (515) 456-3052
Private agency
Founded in: 1969
James Jorgensen, President
Number of members: 200
Staff: volunteer 25
Major programs: library, archives,
    museum, school programs, historic
    preservation, research, exhibits,
    photographic collections,
    genealogical services
Period of collections: 1850-1940

HARLAN

Shelby County Historical Society
Morse and Pine Sts.
Telephone: (712) 744-3662
Mail to: c/o Publicity Director, R.F.D.
    4, 51537
Founded in: 1965
Mrs. G.R. Heflin, Publicity Director
Number of members: 150
Staff: volunteer 25
Major programs: library, museum,
    oral history, educational programs,
    book publishing, historic
    preservation
Period of collections: 1885-1930

HAWARDEN

**Big Sioux River Valley Historical
    Society**
c/o Charter President, 1115 15th St.,
    51023
Telephone: (712) 552-2797
Town and county agency
Founded in: 1979
Mrs. Lyle Ver Hoef, Charter President
Number of members: 200
Staff: volunteer 20
Major programs: historic site(s),
    junior history, oral history, historic
    preservation, exhibits,
    photographic collections,
    genealogical services
Period of collections: late 1800s-early
    1900s

HOPKINTON

Delaware County Historical Society
52237
Telephone: (319) 926-2575
Private agency
Founded in: 1959
Kenneth M. Bacon, President
Number of members: 727
Staff: volunteer 150
Major programs: museum, historic
    site(s), school programs, historic
    preservation, exhibits, audiovisual
    programs, photographic
    collections
Period of collections: 1865-present

HUMBOLDT

**Humboldt County Historical
    Association**
P.O. Box 162, 50548
Telephone: (515) 332-5280
Private agency
Founded in: 1962
Jean Hinkle, President
Number of members: 250
Staff: part time 2, volunteer 100
Major programs: library, archives,
    manuscripts, museum, historic
    site(s), tours, junior history, oral
    history, school programs,
    newsletters/pamphlets, historic
    preservation, records
    management, research, exhibits,
    living history, archaeology
    programs, genealogical services,
    field services
Period of collections: 1880s-1920s

IDA GROVE

Ida County Historical Society
Grant Center School, Moorehead
    Pioneer Park, 51445
Telephone: (712) 364-3605
Mail to: R.R. Box 38, Galva, 51020
County agency
Founded in: 1973
Walter Voge, President
Number of members: 325
Staff: volunteer 21
Major programs: museum, historic
    site(s), tours/pilgrimages, oral
    history, newsletters/pamphlets,
    exhibits, genealogical services
Period of collections: 1880-1900

INDEPENDENCE

**Buchanan County Genealogical
    Society**
City Hall, 331 1st, E
Mail to: 408 3rd NE, 50644
Founded in: 1976
Questionnaire not received

**Buchanan County Iowa Historical
    Society**
514 5th Ave., SW, 50644
Telephone: (319) 334-4506
Questionnaire not received

IOWA CITY

Iowa Archaeological Society
University of Iowa, Eastlawn Bldg.,
    52242
Telephone: (319) 353-5177
State agency
Founded in: 1951
Deb Zieglowsky, Secretary
Number of members: 500
Staff: volunteer 15
Magazine: *Journal of the Iowa
    Archaeological Society*
Major programs: historic site(s),
    newsletters/pamphlets, research,
    audiovisual programs, archaeology
    programs, photographic
    collections, field services
Period of collections: prehistoric

Iowa City Genealogical Society
Mail to: P.O. Box 822, 52244
Founded in: 1967
Questionnaire not received

Iowa Humanities Board
Oakdale Campus, 52242
Telephone: (319) 353-6754
Private agency, authorized by
    National Endowment for the
    Humanities
Founded in: 1969
Thomas H. Hartig, Executive Director
Staff: full time 5, part time 1
Magazine: *Muses*
Major programs: grants-in-aid
    program

◊**Iowa State Historical Department,
    Iowa City Research Center**
402 Iowa Ave., 52240
Telephone: (319) 338-5471
State agency
Founded in: 1857
Carol L. Ulch, Deputy Director
Number of members: 7,500
Staff: full time 15, part time 2
Magazine: *Annals of Iowa/The
    Palimpsest/The Goldfinch*
Major programs: library, manuscripts,
    markers, school programs, book
    publishing, newsletters/pamphlets,
    historic preservation, research,
    genealogical services, field
    services
Period of collections: 1800-present

Old Capitol
c/o University of Iowa, 52242
Telephone: (319) 353-7293
State agency, authorized by the
    university
Founded in: 1970
Margaret N. Keyes, Director
Staff: part time 6, volunteer 70

Major programs: library, museum,
   historic site(s), tours/pilgrimages,
   historic preservation, exhibits
Period of collections: 1783-1865

JAMAICA

**Guthrie County Genealogical
Society**
P.O. Box 96, 50128
Telephone: (515) 429-3362
Private agency
Founded in: 1978
Dana Lowery, Librarian
Number of members: 130
Staff: volunteer 1
Major programs: library,
   newsletters/pamphlets, research,
   genealogical services
Period of collections: 1850-present

JEFFERSON

Greene County Historical Society
106 E. State St.
Telephone: (515) 386-4937
Mail to: 406 S. Cedar, 50129
Private agency
Founded in: 1967
Bessie Ann McClelland, Curator
Number of members: 120
Staff: full time 1, volunteer 15
Major programs: library, museum,
   historic site(s), tours/pilgrimages,
   oral history, school programs,
   historic preservation, research,
   exhibits, audiovisual programs,
   photographic collections,
   genealogical services
Period of collections: 19th century

KALONA

**Mennonite Historical Society of
Iowa, Inc.**
Telephone: (319) 656-3271
Mail to: P.O. Box 576, 52247
Founded in: 1948
Clarence Bender, President
Number of members: 80
Staff: part time 3, volunteer 7
Major programs: archives, museum,
   tours/pilgrimages, educational
   programs, books
Period of collections: 1865-present

KEOKUK

Keokuk Museum Commission
Johnson St.
Telephone: (319) 524-4765
Mail to: 226 High St., 52632
Founded in: 1964
William L. Talbot, Chair
Staff: part time 3, volunteer 3
Major programs: museum
Period of collections: 1865-present

Lee County Historical Society
318 N. 5th St.
Telephone: (319) 524-9378
Mail to: P.O. Box 125, 52632
Private agency
Founded in: 1956
Robert J. Wustrow, President
Number of members: 200
Staff: volunteer 50
Magazine: *Prologue*
Major programs: archives, museum,
   historic site, tours/pilgrimages
Period of collections: 1900s

Midwest Riverboat Buffs
P.O. Box 1225, 52632
Telephone: (319) 524-3286
Private agency
Founded in: 1972
William L. Talbot, President
Number of members: 175
Staff: volunteer 3
Magazine: *River Ripples*
Major programs: manuscripts,
   tours/pilgrimages,
   newsletters/pamphlets, research,
   photographic collections
Period of collections: 19th century

KINGSLEY

Kingsley Historical Society
51028
Telephone: (712) 378-6291
Founded in: 1973
Douglas L. Baker, President
Number of members: 12
Staff: volunteer 8
Major programs: historic sites
   preservation, markers,
   tours/pilgrimages
Period of collections: 1865-1918

KNOXVILLE

Marion County Historical Society
Marion County Park
Mail to: R.R. 3, 50138
Founded in: 1969
Questionnaire not received

LAMONI

**John Whitmer Historical
Association**
Graceland College, 50140
Telephone: (515) 784-5350
Private agency
Founded in: 1972
Betty Winholtz, Executive Secretary
Number of members: 400
Staff: volunteer 11
Magazine: *John Whitman Historical
   Association Journal*
Major programs: archives, book
   publishing, newsletters/pamphlets,
   lecture series, annual meeting
Period of collections: 1820-present

Liberty Hall Historic Center
W. Main St., 50140
Telephone: (515) 784-6133
Private agency, authorized by
   Reorganized Church of Jesus
   Christ of Latter Day Saints
Founded in: 1974
Norma Derry Hiles, Director/Curator
Staff: full time 3, part time 1,
   volunteer 10
Major programs: museum, historic
   site(s), junior history, oral history,
   historic preservation, records
   management, research, exhibits,
   living history, audiovisual
   programs, archaeology programs
Period of collections: 1881-1906

LA PORTE CITY

**La Porte City FFA Agricultural
Museum**
413 Chestnut, 50651
Founded in: 1969
Questionnaire not received

LE CLAIRE

**Buffalo Bill Museum of Le
Claire, Inc.**
Jones St.
Telephone: (319) 289-5580
Mail to: P.O. Box 284, 52753
Founded in: 1957
Harold Kennedy, Curator
Number of members: 500
Staff: part time 3, volunteer 30
Major programs: museum, historic
   site(s), oral history, book
   publishing, historic preservation,
   research, exhibits, photographic
   collections, steamboats
Period of collections: 1830-1980

LE MARS

**Plymouth County Historical
Museum**
335 1st Ave., SW
Telephone: (712) 546-7002
Mail to: P.O. Box 444, 51031
Private agency
Founded in: 1965
Michael S. Wright, Head Supervisor
Number of members: 120
Staff: part time 3, volunteer 8
Major programs: museum, historic
   preservation, exhibits
Period of collections: 1870-1940

LEON

Decatur County Historical Society
Main St., 50144
Telephone: (515) 446-4186
Questionnaire not received

LOGAN

Harrison County Historical Society
109 E. 6th St., 51546
Telephone: (712) 644-2519
Founded in: 1968
Questionnaire not received

LOVILIA

**Monroe County Genealogical
Society**
Mail to: Rt. 3, Albia, 52531
Founded in: 1976
Questionnaire not received

LOWDEN

Lowden Historical Society
52255
Private agency
Founded in: 1973
Raymond Kroener, President
Number of members: 55
Major programs: manuscripts,
   museum, oral history, historic
   preservation, exhibits
Period of collections: 1865-present

MAQUOKETA

Jackson County Historical Museum
Pearson Memorial Center, Fair
   Grounds
Telephone: (319) 652-5020
Mail to: P.O. Box 1245, 52060
Questionnaire not received

MARBLE ROCK

Marble Rock Historical Society Museum
313 Bradford St., 50653
Telephone: (515) 397-2216 (president)
Private agency
Founded in: 1972
Arnold Staudt, President
Number of members: 100
Staff: volunteer 26
Major programs: museum
Period of collections: 1860s-present

MARENGO

Iowa County Historical Society
790 W. Hilton St., 52301
Telephone: (319) 642-5615
Founded in: 1964
Number of members: 85
Staff: volunteer 12
Magazine: *Vignette*
Major programs: museum, tours/pilgrimages, educational programs, newsletters/pamphlets
Period of collections: 1861

MARSHALLTOWN

Historical Society of Marshall County
201 E. State St., 50158
Telephone: (515) 752-2697
Founded in: 1908
Number of members: 125
Staff: part time 5, volunteer 3
Major programs: museum, historic sites preservation, markers, educational programs
Period of collections: prehistoric-present

MASON CITY

Pioneer Museum and Historical Society of North Iowa
P.O. Box 421, 50401
Telephone: (515) 423-1258
County agency, authorized by North Iowa Historical Society
Founded in: 1965
Ralph Peterson, Director
Number of members: 400
Staff: volunteer 40
Major programs: museum, exhibits
Period of collections: 1850-1950

MAXWELL

Community Historical Society
50161
Telephone: (515) 387-1380
Private agency
Founded in: 1965
L. Lenfred Link, President
Number of members: 125
Staff: volunteer 20
Major programs: museum, tours/pilgrimages, school programs, exhibits
Period of collections: 1865-1945

MCGREGOR

Effigy Mounds National Monument
P.O. Box K, 52157
Telephone: (319) 873-2356
Federal agency, authorized by National Park Service
Founded in: 1949
Thomas A. Munson, Superintendent
Staff: full time 6, part time 10, volunteer 8
Major programs: library, archives, manuscripts, museum, historic site(s), tours, school programs, historic preservation, exhibits, audiovisual programs, archaeology programs
Period of collections: prehistoric

McGregor Historical Society
120 Main St., 52157
Telephone: (319) 873-2207
Private agency
Founded in: 1941
Dorothy Huebsch, Secretary
Number of members: 28
Major programs: museum, historic site(s), markers, historic preservation, photographic collections
Period of collections: from 1837

MISSOURI VALLEY

Bertrand Collection and Laboratory, DeSoto National Wildlife Refuge Visitor Center
R.R. 1, Box 114, 51555
Telephone: (712) 642-2772
Federal agency, authorized by Department of the Interior
Founded in: 1969
Allan L. Montgomery, Collection Manager
Staff: part time 2, full time 4
Major programs: library, museum, historic site(s), pamphlets, historic preservation, records management, research, exhibits
Period of collections: 1865

MONONA

Monona Historical Society
302 S. Egbert St.
Telephone: (319) 539-2689
Mail to: P.O. Box 15, 52159
Private agency
Founded in: 1968
Willa Helwig, Curator
Number of members: 40
Major programs: museum, oral history, school programs, historic preservation, exhibits, genealogical services
Period of collections: 1865-present

MONTEZUMA

Poweshiek County Historical and Genealogical Society
114 S. 3rd St., 50171
Telephone: (515) 623-5188
Private agency
Founded in: 1978
Velma R. James, President
Number of members: 77
Staff: volunteer 10
Major programs: library, archives, junior history, school programs, book publishing, newsletters/pamphlets, historic preservation, research, genealogical services
Period of collections: 1800s

MONTICELLO

Jones County Iowa Historical Society, Inc.
Telephone: (319) 465-3564
Mail to: c/o President, P.O. Box 124, 52310
Private agency
Founded in: 1973
C.L. Norlin, President
Number of members: 600
Staff: volunteer 30
Magazine: *Jones County Iowa Historical Review*
Major programs: library, archives, manuscripts, museum, historic site(s), markers, school programs, book publishing, newsletters/pamphlets, historic preservation, exhibits, audiovisual programs
Period of collections: 1835-present

MT. AYR

Ringgold County Historical Society, Inc.
50854
Telephone: (515) 464-2615
Founded in: 1939
Number of members: 200
Staff: volunteer 50
Major programs: library, archives, manuscripts, museum, historic sites preservation, markers, junior history, educational programs, newsletters/pamphlets
Period of collections: 1865-present

MT. PLEASANT

Henry County Historical Society
Telephone: (319) 367-5157
Mail to: President, Rt. 1, Box 224, New London, 52645
Number of members: 25
Major programs: library, markers, genealogical services
Period of collections: 1850-present

Midwest Old Settlers and Threshers Association, Inc.
R.R. 1, 52641
Telephone: (319) 385-8937
Private agency
Founded in: 1950
Lennis Moore, Administrator
Number of members: 65,000
Staff: full time 9, part time 2, volunteer 4,000
Magazine: *Threshers Chaff*
Major programs: library, archives, manuscripts, museum, school programs, book publishing, newsletters/pamphlets, research, exhibits, living history, photographic collections
Period of collections: 1880-1920

MUSCATINE

Muscatine Art Center
1314 Mulberry Ave., 52761
Telephone: (319) 263-8282
City agency
Founded in: 1965
William A. McGonagle, Director
Number of members: 800
Staff: full time 3, part time 4, volunteer 50

Major programs: museum, exhibits,
  visual arts
Period of collections: 19th-20th
  centuries

NASHUA

**Chickasaw County Historical
  Society**
R.R. 50658
Telephone: (515) 435-4701
Questionnaire not received

NEMAHA

Sac County Historical Society
50567
Telephone: (712) 636-4513
Private agency
Founded in: 1974
Gale W. Davis, President
Number of members: 300
Major programs: museum, school
  programs, historic preservation,
  exhibits, photographic collections
Period of collections: 1865-present

NEW HAMPTON

**Chickasaw County Genealogical
  Society**
P.O. Box 434, 50659
Telephone: (515) 394-4343
Private agency
Founded in: 1979
Mrs. Kenneth Koolas, Secretary
Number of members: 20
Staff: volunteer 4
Major programs. genealogical
  services
Period of collections: 1860-present

NEW PROVIDENCE

Honey Creek Preservation Group
Telephone: (515) 497-5458
Founded in: 1852
Mabel C. Reece, Secretary
Staff: volunteer 15
Major programs: manuscripts,
  historic site,
  newsletters/pamphlets, historic
  preservation
Period of collections: 1852-present

NEWTON

**Jasper County Genealogical
  Society**
Jasper County Courthouse
Telephone: (515) 792-1522
Mail to: P.O. Box 163, 50208
Private agency
Founded in: 1977
Elmer Van Arkel, President
Number of members: 300
Staff: volunteer 9
Major programs: library, archives,
  newsletters/pamphlets, historic
  preservation, research,
  genealogical services
Period of collections: 1850-present

Jasper County Historical Society
1700 S. 15th Ave., W
Telephone: (515) 792-9118
Mail to: P.O. Box 834, 50208
Private agency
Founded in: 1973
Herb Rucker, Museum Director
Number of members: 1,160

Staff: full time 1, part time 2,
  volunteer 200
Major programs: museum, historic
  preservation, exhibits
Period of collections: 1850-1920

OAKLAND

Oakland Historical Society
117 N. Main, 51560
Telephone: (712) 482-6802
Private agency
Founded in: 1969
Merle Davis, Curator
Number of members: 30
Staff: volunteer 12
Major programs: museum,
  tours/pilgrimages, school
  programs, book publishing,
  newsletters/pamphlets, historic
  preservation, research, exhibits,
  living history, photographic
  collections
Period of collections: 1880-1900

OSAGE

Mitchell County Historical Society
50461
Telephone: (515) 732-3059
County agency
Founded in: 1960
Anita Suchy, Curator
Number of members: 250
Staff: part time 2, volunteer 2
Major programs: library, manuscripts,
  museum, historic site(s), markers,
  junior history, school programs,
  historic preservation, research,
  exhibits
Period of collections: 1865-present

OSCEOLA

Clarke County Historical Society
Hwy. 69, S
Telephone: (515) 342-4246
Mail to: 139 N. Main St., 50213
Private agency
Founded in: 1970
Mrs. Gerald Cottrell, Director
Number of members: 615
Staff: volunteer 16
Major programs: archives, museum,
  junior history, oral history,
  educational programs, books,
  genealogical services, history of
  machinery
Period of collections: 1865-present

OSKALOOSA

Mahasha County Historical Society
R.R. 1, Glendale Rd.
Telephone: (515) 672-2989
Mail to: P.O. Box 578, 52577
Private agency
Founded in: 1942
Agnes Ahrens, Curator
Staff: full time 1, part time 2,
  volunteer 1
Major programs: library, museum,
  school programs,
  newsletters/pamphlets,
  genealogical services
Period of collections: 1844-1900

OTTUMWA

Wapello County Historical Society
402 Chester Ave., 52501

Founded in: 1959
Number of members: 340
Staff: volunteer 16
Major programs: library, museum
Period of collections: 1865-present

PELLA

Pella Historical Society
507 Franklin, 50219
Telephone: (515) 628-2409
Private agency
Founded in: 1935
Harry Vermeer, President
Number of members: 1,000
Staff: volunteer 30
Major programs: museum, historic
  site(s), newsletters/pamphlets,
  historic preservation
Period of collections: 1865-1918

PETERSON

Peterson Heritage, Inc.
Telephone: (712) 295-6551
Mail to: P.O. Box 67, 51047
Founded in 1971
Art Johnson, President
Number of members: 130
Staff: volunteer 20
Major programs: archives, museum,
  historic site(s), tours/pilgrimages,
  book publishing, historic
  preservation, exhibits
Period of collections: 1865-1918

POSTVILLE

Postville Historical Society
205 W. Williams
Telephone: (319) 864-3818
Mail to: P.O. Box 396, 52162
Founded in: 1975
Edward W. Kozelka, Contact Person
Number of members: 97

PRIMGHAR

O'Brien County Historical Society
540 15th St.
Telephone: (712) 757-8915
Mail to: P.O. Box 385, 51245
Private agency
Founded in: 1941
William Schwartz, President
Number of members: 240
Staff: volunteer 6
Major programs: museum,
  newsletters/pamphlets, exhibits
Period of collections: 1865-present

RED OAK

**Montgomery County Historical
  Society**
P.O. Box 289, 51566
Private agency
Founded in: 1946
W. Lee Honeyman, President
Number of members: 172
Major programs: archives, historic
  site(s), tours/pilgrimages, exhibits

ROCK RAPIDS

Lyon County Historical Society
51246
Private agency
Founded in: 1972
Lucy Jo Colby, President
Number of members: 150

Major programs: museum, historic
preservation, exhibits
Period of collections: 1880-1940

ROCKWELL CITY

Calhoun County Genies
c/o President, R.R. 2, 50579
Private agency
Founded in: 1976
Judy Webb, President
Number of members: 27
Staff: volunteer 8
Major programs: library, museum,
genealogical services, microfilm of
local newspaper
Period of collections: 1854-1920

Calhoun County Historical Society
868 8th St. 50579
Mail to: c/o Judy Webb, Rt. 2
Founded in: 1957
Eunice Merrill, President
Number of members: 340
Staff: volunteer 30
Major programs: manuscripts,
museum, oral history, educational
programs
Period of collections: 1865-present

ROLFE

**Pocahontas County Historical
Society**
R.R. 2, Box 12, 50581
Private agency
Founded in: 1960
Florence MacVey, President
Number of members: 125
Staff: volunteer 50
Major programs: archives, museum,
historic site(s), markers,
tours/pilgrimages, school
programs, book publishing,
newsletters/pamphlets, historic
preservation, exhibits, living
history, genealogical services
Period of collections: 1800-present

SHELDON

**Sheldon Historical Society—Prairie
Museum**
51201
Founded in: 1972
Richard E. Bauer, Chair
Number of members: 500
Staff: volunteer 15
Major programs: museum
Period of collections: 1865-present

SIBLEY

Osceola County Historical Society
603 7th Ave., 51249
Questionnaire not received

SIGOURNEY

Keokuk County Historical Society
Telephone: (515) 622-3300
Mail to: P.O. Box 67, 52591
Questionnaire not received

SIOUX CITY

**Lewis and Clark Historical
Association of Sioux City, Iowa**
101 Pierce St., 51101
Telephone: (712) 255-0107
Mail to: P.O. Box 1804, 51102

Founded in: 1956
Questionnaire not received

**Sioux City Public Museum and
Historical Association**
2901 Jackson St., 51104
Telephone: (712) 279-6174
Private agency
Founded in: 1961
B.R. Diamond, Museum Director
Number of members: 443
Staff: part time 1
Major programs: archives,
manuscripts, museum, oral history,
school programs, book publishing,
newsletters/pamphlets, exhibits,
audiovisual programs
Period of collections: 1865-present

SLOAN

Sloan Historical Society
51055
Founded in: 1968
Number of members: 75
Staff: volunteer 20
Major programs: museum
Period of collections: 1865-present

SPENCER

**Parker Historical Society of Clay
County**
300 E. 3rd St., 51301
Telephone: (712) 262-9800
Founded in: 1960
Helen Groenwold, President
Staff: volunteer 70
Major programs: museum,
tours/pilgrimages
Period of collections: 1783-present

SPILLVILLE

**Spillville Historic Action
Group, Inc.**
P.O. Box 157, 51268
Telephone: (319) 562-3655
Private agency
Founded in: 1978
Fran Osborn, Secretary
Number of members: 49
Staff: volunteer 6
Magazine: *Spillville Harbinger*
Major programs: archives, museum,
newsletters/pamphlets, historic
preservation, photographic
collections
Period of collections: 1849-present

SPIRIT LAKE

**Dickinson County Museum and
Historical Society**
1708 Keokuk Ave., 51360
Telephone: (712) 338-2138
Mail to: 507 11th, Milford, 51351
Number of members: 100
Staff: part time 1, volunteer 1
Major programs: museum, historic
sites preservation, oral history,
educational programs,
newsletters/pamphlets
Period of collections: 1857-present

STORM LAKE

**Buena Vista County Historical
Society**
5th and Erie Sts., 50588
Telephone: (712) 732-4955

Mail to: P.O. Box 882, Storm Lake,
50581
Private agency
Founded in: 1962
James Bauer, President
Number of members: 150
Staff: volunteer 12
Major programs: museum, historic
site(s), book publishing, historic
preservation, photographic
collections,
Period of collections: 1870-1940

STRAWBERRY POINT

Clayton County Historical Society
52076
Telephone: (319) 933-4461
Private agency
Founded in: 1977
Marcey F. Alderson, President
Number of members: 8
Major programs: historic sites
preservation, markers,
genealogical services
Period of collections: 1783-1918

Strawberry Point Historical Society
52076
Telephone: (319) 933-4461
Founded in: 1967
Number of members: 100
Staff: full time 2, part time 2,
volunteer 1
Major programs: museum,
manuscripts, historic sites
preservation, markers
Period of collections: 1783-1918

TIPTON

Cedar County Historical Society
607 Orange St., 52772
Telephone: (319) 886-2740
Founded in: 1957
Number of members: 566
Staff: volunteer 10
Magazine: *Cedar County Historical
Review*
Major programs: historic sites
preservation, markers, books
Period of collections: 1865-present

TOLEDO

Tama County Historical Society
200 N. Broadway, 52342
Telephone: (515) 484-6767
County agency
Founded in: 1942
Shirley Eriksen, President
Number of members: 100
Staff: part time 5
Major programs: library, archives,
manuscripts, museum, historic
site(s), tours/pilgrimages, historic
preservation, research, exhibits,
photographic collections,
genealogical services
Period of collections: 1850-present

WASHINGTON

Alexander Young Log House
Sunset Park
Mail to: c/o DAR Member, Rt. 3,
52353
Private agency, authorized by
Washington Chapter, Daughters of
the American Revolution

Founded in: 1912
Major programs: museum, historic
site(s), tours/pilgrimages, junior
history, school programs, exhibits
Period of collections: 1840-1875

Jonathan Clark Conger House, Inc.
903 E. Washington St., 52353
Telephone: (319) 653-4728
Founded in: 1972
Number of members: 350
Staff: volunteer 43
Major programs: museum, historic
sites preservation,
tours/pilgrimages, educational
programs, books,
newsletters/pamphlets
Period of collections: 1865-present

**Washington County Historical
Society**
727 N. Marion Ave.
Telephone: (319) 653-2281
Founded in: 1959
Mike Zahs, President
Number of members: 100
Staff: volunteer 5
Major programs: library, manuscripts,
museum, historic site(s),
tours/pilgrimages, junior history,
oral history, school programs,
historic preservation, records
management, research, exhibits,
photographic collections,
genealogical services
Period of collections: 1836-present

WASHTA

Grand Meadow Heritage Center
R.R. 1, Box 45, 51061
Telephone: (712) 375-5117
Private agency
Founded in: 1975
Elma Klingensmith, Secretary
Number of members: 60
Staff: volunteer 15
Major programs: museum,
tours/pilgrimages, school
programs, festival, memorials
Period of collections: 1900

WATERLOO

**Association for the Preservation of
the Rensselaer Russell House**
520 W. 3rd St., 50701
Telephone: (319) 233-8431
Mail to: P.O. Box 1024, 50704
Founded in: 1964
Number of members: 250
Staff: volunteer 30
Major programs: museum
Period of collections: 1865-1918

**Grout Museum of History and
Science**
503 South St., 50701
Telephone: (319) 234-6357
Private agency, authorized by H.W.
Grout Trust
Founded in: 1956
Margo Dundon, Director
Staff: full time 5, part time 3,
volunteer 90
Major programs: library, archives,
museum, tours, school programs,
newsletters/pamphlets, exhibits,
photographic collections,
genealogical services
Period of collections: 1875-1930

WAUKON

**Allamakee County Historical
Society**
N. Allamakee St.
Telephone: (319) 568-4680
Mail to: 400 4th Ave., SW, 52172
Founded in: 1964
Jim W. Magner, President
Number of members: 50
Staff: volunteer 20
Major programs: museum, historic
site, book publishing, historic
preservation
Period of collections: early 1900s

WAVERLY

Bremer County Historical Society
402 W. Bremer Ave., 50677
Telephone: (319) 276-4674
Mail to: P.O. Box 218, Plainfield,
50666-0218
Private agency
Founded in: 1958
J. W. Lynes, President
Number of members: 200
Staff: volunteer 6
Major programs: museum, historic
preservation, exhibits,
photographic collections
Period of collections: 1840-1940

WEST BEND

West Bend Historical Society
P.O. Box 379, 50597
Telephone: (515) 887-3241 (treasurer)
Town agency
Mrs. C. Munson, Treasurer
Number of members: 65
Staff: volunteer 30
Major programs: museum, historic
preservation
Period of collections: 1890-1970

WEST BRANCH

**Herbert Hoover National Historic
Site**
Parkside Dr. and Main St.
Telephone: (319) 643-2541
Mail to: P.O. Box 607, 52358
Federal agency, authorized by
National Park Service
Founded in: 1964
Malcolm J. Berg, Superintendent
Staff: full time 15, part time 4,
volunteer 10
Major programs: historic site(s),
tours/pilgrimages, school
programs, historic preservation,
research, exhibits
Period of collections: 1870-1880

**Herbert Hoover Presidential
Library**
52358
Telephone: (319) 643-5301
Federal agency, authorized by
National Archives and Records
Administration
Founded in: 1962
Robert S. Wood, Director
Staff: full time 15, part time 3
Major programs: library, archives,
manuscripts, museum, oral history
Period of collections: 1865-1973

WEST DES MOINES

West Des Moines Historical Society
Historic Jordan House, 2001 Fuller
Rd.
Telephone: (515) 223-0566
Mail to: 1110 16th St., 50265
Private agency
Founded in: 1970
Vicki D. Baker, President
Number of members: 220
Staff: volunteer 12
Major programs: historic site(s), oral
history, historic preservation,
restoration
Period of collections: 1850-1895

WEST UNION

**Fayette County Helpers Club and
Historical Society**
Fayette County Historical Center, 100
N. Walnut, 52175
Telephone: (319) 422-9213
Private agency
Founded in: 1975
Mona Ladwig, Coordinator
Number of members: 132
Staff: part time 2, volunteer 4
Major programs: library, manuscripts,
museum, book publishing,
newsletters/pamphlets, historic
preservation, records
management, research, exhibits,
photographic collections,
genealogical research
Period of collections: 1846-present

WILLIAMSBURG

Iowa County Historical Society
P.O. Box 237, 52361
Telephone: (319) 668-1597
Questionnaire not received

WINTERSET

Madison County Historical Society
812 S. 2nd Ave., 50273
Telephone: (515) 462-2134
Private agency
Founded in: 1911
Wayne Breeding, President
Number of members: 200
Staff: volunteer 25
Major programs: library, museum,
historic site(s), historic
preservation, exhibits
Period of collections: 1850-1925

KANSAS

ABILENE

**Dickinson County Historical Soci-
ety**
412 S. Campbell
Telephone: (913) 263-2681
Mail to: P.O. Box 506, 67410
Private agency
Founded in: 1928
Lynda Millner, Director
Number of members: 375
Staff: part time 2, volunteer 86
Magazine: *Gazette*

Major programs: library, archives, manuscripts, museum, tours/pilgrimages, school programs, newsletters/pamphlets, historic preservation, research, exhibits, living history, audiovisual programs, photographic collections, genealogical services
Period of collections: 1870-1900

Dwight D. Eisenhower Library
67410
Telephone: (913) 263-4751
Founded in: 1962
John E. Wickman, Director
Staff: full time 30, part time 10
Major programs: library, archives, manuscripts, museum, oral history, historic preservation, research, exhibits, photographic collections
Period of collections: 1916-1969

Museum of Independent Telephony
412 S. Campbell, 67410
Telephone: (913) 263-2681
County agency, authorized by Dickinson County Historical Society
Founded in: 1973
Peg Chronister, Curator
Major programs: library, archives, museum, research, exhibits, telephone history
Period of collections: 1880s-1960s

ALMA

Wabaunsee County Historical Society Museum
3rd and Missouri, 66401
Telephone: (913) 765-2200
Private agency
Founded in: 1968
Betty Roberts, Curator
Number of members: 200
Staff: part time 2, volunteer 25
Major programs: library, museum, tours

ARGONIA

Argonia and West Sumner County Historical Society and Museum
67004
Telephone: (316) 435-6733
Town agency
Founded in: 1961
Ruth Harper, President
Number of members: 30
Staff: volunteer 10
Major programs: museum, historic site(s), historic preservation, photographic collections

ARKANSAS CITY

Cherokee Strip Living Museum
S. Summit Street Rd., 67005
Telephone: (316) 442-6750
Founded in: 1966
Questionnaire not received

ASHLAND

Clark County Historical Society—The Pioneer Museum
430 W. 4th St.
Telephone: (316) 635-2227
Mail to: P.O. Box 862, 67831
Founded in: 1939
Rosa Lee McGee, Curator

Number of members: 366
Staff: full time 1, volunteer 60
Major programs: archives, manuscripts, museum, books
Period of collections: 1865-1918

ATWOOD

Rawlins County Historical Society
308 State St.
Mail to: 203 S. 6th St., 67730
Private agency
Founded in: 1961
Inez Walters, Treasurer/Director of Museum
Number of members: 60
Major programs: archives, museum, historic site(s), tours/pilgrimages, pamphlets, exhibits, photographic collections
Period of collections: 1865-present

AUGUSTA

Augusta Historical Museum
303 State St.
Telephone: (316) 775-9917
Mail to: P.O. Box 545, 67010
County agency
Founded in: 1938
Burl Allison, Jr., Treasurer
Number of members: 267
Staff: full time 4, volunteer 10
Major programs: library, archives, museum, historic site(s), exhibits, genealogical services
Period of collections: 1850-present

BALDWIN CITY

Old Castle Museum Complex
515 5th St.
Telephone: (913) 594-6809
Mail to: P.O. Box 296, 66006
Private agency, authorized by Baker University
Founded in: 1858
Miles H. Stotts, Curator
Staff: part time 2, volunteer 6
Major programs: library, archives, museum, historic site(s), markers, tours/pilgrimages, junior history, oral history, school programs, newsletters/pamphlets, historic preservation, research, exhibits, living history, genealogical services
Period of collections: 1800-1950

Santa Fe Trail Historical Society, Inc.
1599 High St.
Telephone: (913) 594-6862 (president)
Mail to: 1115 10th St., Box 668, 66006
County agency
Founded in: 1969
P. Philip Barnthouse, President
Number of members: 126
Staff: volunteer 12
Major programs: historic site(s), markers, historic preservation, exhibits
Period of collections: 1855-1920

United Methodist Historical Library
Baker University, 66006
Telephone: (913) 594-6451, ext. 380
Questionnaire not received

BAXTER SPRINGS

Baxter Springs Historical Society
8th and East Ave., 66713
Telephone: (316) 856-9860
Mail to: R.R. 2, Box 314, 66713
Founded in: 1881
Questionnaire not received

BELLEVILLE

Republic County Historical Society
Courthouse, 66935
County agency
Founded in: 1960
Henry Strnad, President
Number of members: 100
Staff: part time 2
Major programs: library, archives, newsletters/pamphlets, historic preservation, genealogical services
Period of collections: 1870-present

BONNER SPRINGS

Agricultural Hall of Fame
630 N. 126th St., 66012
Telephone: (913) 721-1075
Private agency
Founded in: 1960
Harold L. Adkins, Executive Director
Number of members: 1,200
Staff: full time 3, part time 3, volunteer 16
Major programs: museum, living history
Period of collections: 1830-present

Wyandotte County Historical Society and Museum
631 N. 126th St., 66012
Telephone: (913) 721-1078
County agency
Founded in: 1889
Jean Curl, President
Number of members: 330
Staff: full time 3
Magazine: *History News*
Major programs: library, archives, manuscripts, museum, exhibits, audiovisual programs, photographic collections
Period of collections: early 1800s-1950s

BURLINGTON

Coffey County Historical Society—County Museum
1101 Neosho, 66839
Telephone: (316) 364-2653
County agency
Founded in: 1967
Mayree E. White, President
Number of members: 65
Staff: part time 1
Major programs: library, archives, museum, historic site(s), oral history, historic preservation, records management, research, exhibits, photographic collections, genealogical services
Period of collections: 19th-20th centuries

Coffey County Genealogical Society, Inc.
Rt. 3, Box 11, 66839
Telephone: (316) 364-2548

Mail to: c/o President, New Strawn, 66838
Private agency
Founded in: 1983
Helen Bahr, President
Number of members: 50
Magazine: *Coffey County Footprints*
Major programs: library, book publishing, newsletters/pamphlets, historic preservation, records management, research, genealogical services
Period of collections: 1854-present

CANEY

Caney Valley Historical Society
Telephone: (316) 879-2935
Mail to: R.R. 1, 67333
Founded in: 1984
Ivan L. Pfalser, President
Number of members: 220
Major programs: museum, oral history, book publishing, research, genealogical services

CAWKEE CITY

North Central Kansas Genealogical Society and Library, Inc.
802 Locust St.
Mail to: P.O. Box 251, 67430
Private agency
Founded in: 1977
F. Lee Nichols, President
Number of members: 116
Staff: volunteer 5
Magazine: *Waconda Roots and Branches*
Major programs: library, oral history, historic preservation, research, living history, genealogical services

CEDAR VALE

Cedar Vale Historical Society
600 Cedar St., 67024
Questionnaire not received

CHANUTE

Martin and Osa Johnson Safari Museum, Inc.
16 S. Grant St., 66720
Telephone: (316) 431-2730
Founded in: 1961
Sondra Alden, Director
Number of members: 200
Staff: full time 1, part time 4
Major programs: museum, exhibits, library, photographic collections, research
Period of collections: 18th century-present

Neosho Valley Historical Society
201 E. Main 66720
Telephone: (316) 431-4339
Mail to: P.O. 828, 66720
Founded in: 1975
Nancy Huffman, Vice-President
Number of members: 200
Major programs: historic site, historic preservation

CLAY CENTER

Clay County Historical Society
2121 7th St., 67432
Telephone: (913) 632-3786

Mail to: c/o President, Idana, 67453
County agency
Founded in: 1972
Pauline Palmer Meek, President
Number of members: 250
Staff: part time 1, volunteer 15
Major programs: archives, museum, historic site(s), exhibits, photographic collections, educational programs
Period of collections: 1885-1920

COFFEYVILLE

Coffeyville Historical Society, Inc.
113 E. 8th St.
Telephone: (316) 251-3529
Mail to: P.O. Box 656, 67337
Founded in: 1954
Charles Clough, President
Staff: full time 6, volunteer 25
Major programs: museum, historic sites preservation
Period of collections: 1865-1918

Montgomery County Genealogical Society
P.O. Box 444, 67337
Founded in: 1965
Herman Guy, President
Number of members: 65
Magazine: *Descender*
Major programs: library, genealogical services, cemetery records
Period of collections: before 1900

COLBY

Thomas County Historical Society and Museum
75 W. 4th St., 67701
Telephone: (913) 462-6301
County agency
Founded in: 1959
Helen L. Smith, Director
Number of members: 1,165
Staff: full time 3, part time 4, volunteer 22
Major programs: library, archives, manuscripts, museum, junior history, oral history, school programs, book publishing, newsletters/pamphlets, historic preservation, research, exhibits, living history, audiovisual programs, photographic collections, genealogical services
Period of collections: 1885-present

CONCORDIA

Cloud County Historical Museum
635 Broadway, 66901
Telephone: (913) 243-2866
County agency
Founded in: 1959
Thelma Schroth, Curator
Number of members: 185
Staff: full time 1, part time 2, volunteer 2
Magazine: *Cloud Comments*
Major programs: museum, historic preservation, research, exhibits, photographic collections, genealogical services
Period of collections: 1860-1950

Cloud County Historical Society
635 Broadway, 66901
County agency

Founded in: 1959
Charles Everitt, President
Number of members: 300
staff: full time 1, part time 4, volunteer 4
Major programs: manuscripts, museum, research, exhibits, photographic collections, genealogical services
Period of collections: 1793-present

COTTONWOOD FALLS

Chase County Historical Society, Inc.
301 Broadway, 66845
Mail to: R.R. 1, Box 11, Elmdale, 66850
Private agency
Founded in: 1934
Whitt E. Laughridge, President
Number of members: 622
Major programs: library, archives, manuscripts, museum, tours/pilgrimages, junior history, oral history, educational programs, book publishing, historic preservation, photographs, genealogical services
Period of collections: late 1800s-early 1900s

DIGHTON

Lane County Historical Museum
Main St.
Telephone: (316) 397-5652
Mail to: P.O. Box 821, 67839
Founded in: 1954
Questionnaire not received

Lane County Historical Society
333 N. Main
Telephone: (316) 397-5652
Mail to: P.O. Box 821, 67839
Founded in: 1954
Questionnaire not received

DODGE CITY

Boot Hill Museum
Front St., 67801
Telephone: (316) 227-8188
Private agency
Founded in: 1947
Number of members: 500
Staff: full time 5, part time 60, volunteer 10
Magazine: *Front Street Times*
Major programs: library, museum, historic site(s), school programs, newsletters/pamphlets, historic preservation, exhibits, living history, audiovisual programs, photographic collections
Period of collections: 1870-1900

Ford County Historical Society, Inc.
Telephone: (316) 227-6791
Mail to: P.O. Box 131, 67801
Number of members: 400
Staff: part time 2, volunteer 50
Major programs: museum, historic sites preservation, markers, newsletters/pamphlets
Period of collections: 1865-1918

Kansas Genealogical Society
700 Ave. G and Vine St.
Mail to: P.O. Box 103, 67801

State agency
Founded in: 1959
Staff: volunteer 40
Magazine: *The Treesearcher*
Major programs: library, research, genealogical services, seminars, workshops
Period of collections: from 1850

DOUGLASS

Douglass Historical Museum
314-316 S. Forest
Mail to: P.O. Box 35, 67039
Founded in: 1950
Jean Valentine, Curator
Number of members: full time 1, part time 1, volunteer 6
Major programs: library, archives, museum
Period of collections: 1865-1918

EDGERTON

Lanesfield School Historical Society
R.R. 1, 66021
Telephone: (913) 882-6645
Mail to: R.R. 1, Box 156, Gadner, 66030
Founded in: 1966
Questionnaire not received

EL DORADO

Butler County Historical Society
383 E. Central
Telephone: (316) 321-9333
Mail to: P.O. Box 696, 67042
Private agency
Founded in: 1955
William Galvani, Director
Number of members: 200
Major programs: library, museum, book publishing, nature trail
Period of collections: 1870-1930

ELLSWORTH

Ellsworth County Historical Society
104 W. S. Main St., 67439
Telephone: (913) 472-3059
County agency
Founded in: 1962
Francis L. Wilson, Board President
Number of members: 225
Staff: part time 1
Major programs: historic site(s), markers, tours/pilgrimages, historic preservation, exhibits
Period of collections: 1860-early 1900s

EMPORIA

Flint Hills Genealogical Society
Mail to: P.O. Box 555, 66801
Private agency
Founded in: 1977
William E. Ikerd, President
Number of members: 50
Major programs: museum, genealogical services

Lyon County Historical Society and Museum
118 E. 6th Ave., 66801
Telephone: (316) 342-0933
Founded in: 1938
Thomas Haskett, President

Number of members: 300
Staff: full time 3, part time 4, volunteer 20
Major programs: library, archives, manuscripts, museum, oral history, school programs, book publishing, newsletters/pamphlets, historic preservation, records management, exhibits, photographic collections, genealogical services
Period of collections: 1857-present

EUDORA

Eudora Area Historical Society
c/o President, R.R. 2, 66025
Telephone: (913) 542-2502
Tri-county and town agency
Founded in: 1980
Pennie von Achen, President
Staff: volunteer 5
Major programs: library, tours/pilgrimages, school programs, newsletters/pamphlets, research, audiovisual programs, photographic collections, genealogical services
Period of collections: 1900-1960

EUREKA

Bluestem Genealogical Society
c/o Greenwood County Historical Museum
Mail to: P.O. Box 582, 67045
Private agency
Founded in: 1976
Doris Blankley, President
Major programs: library, archives, records management, research, genealogical services

Greenwood County Historical Society
117 N. Main, 67045
County agency
Founded in: 1973
Alfred Ferguson, President
Number of members: part time 3, volunteer 2
Major programs: museum, research, genealogical services
Period of collections: 1900

EVEREST

Everest Community Historical Society
7th and Chestnut Sts., 66424
Telephone: (913) 548-7496
Founded in: 1973
Lenore F. Munsey, Secretary
Number of members: 211
Major programs: library, museum, photographic collections, genealogical services
Period of collections: 1882-present

FLORENCE

Florence Historical Society
204 W. 3rd St.
Telephone: (316) 878-4474
Mail to: 408 W. 7th St., 66851
Private agency
Founded in: 1969
Bessie Suffield, President
Number of members: 35
Staff: volunteer 4

Major programs: museum, oral history, newsletters/pamphlets, historic preservation, exhibits, photographic collections
Period of collections: 1870-1940s

FORT LEAVENWORTH

Ft. Leavenworth Historical Society
Post Museum, Bldg. 801, 66027
Telephone: (913) 651-7440
Private agency, authorized by the U.S. Army
Founded in: 1955
John Hardaway, President
Number of members: 115
Staff: full time 1, part time 2
Major programs: historic site, markers, tours, educational programs

Ft. Leavenworth Museum
Reynolds and Gibbon, 66027
Telephone: (913) 684-3191
Federal agency, authorized by the U.S. Army
Founded in: 1956
N. Jean Lenahan, Director
Staff: full time 5, volunteer 40
Major programs: library, museum, tours/pilgrimages, school programs, audiovisual programs
Period of collections: 1827-1900

Leavenworth Afro-American Historical Society
Telephone: (913) 651-4584
Mail to: P.O. Box 3151, 66027
Private agency
Founded in: 1984
Joseph A. Walkes, Jr., President
Number of members: 55
Staff: volunteer 55
Magazine: *Eureka*
Major programs: historic site(s), tours/pilgrimages, research, genealogical services

FORT RILEY

U.S. Cavalry Museum
66442
Telephone: (913) 239-2737
Federal agency, authorized by the U.S. Army
Founded in: 1957
Terry Van Meter, Director
Staff: full time 6
Major programs: library, archives, manuscripts, museum, research, exhibits, photographic collections
Period of collections: 1812-1950

FORT SCOTT

Ft. Scott National Historic Site
Old Fort Blvd., 66701
Telephone: (316) 223-0310
Federal agency
Founded in: 1978
Sheridan Steele, Superintendent
Number of members: 1
Staff:volunteer 4
Major programs: museum, historic site, markers, educational programs, historic preservation, tours, research, exhibits, living history, audiovisual programs
Period of collections: 1842-1873

Historic Preservation Association of Bourbon County, Inc.
502 S. National Ave., 66701
Telephone: (316) 223-3300
Founded in: 1972
Donald D. Bannart, President
Number of members: 500
Staff: volunteer 16
Major programs: library, museum, markers, book publishing, historic preservation

FREDONIA

Wilson County Historical Society
420 N. 7th St., 66736
Telephone: (316) 378-3965
County agency
Founded in: 1940
Number of members: 240
Staff: part time 4
Major programs: library, museum, markers, junior history, school programs, genealogical services
Period of collections: 1865-present

GALENA

Galena Mining and Historical Museum Association, Inc.
P.O. Box 367, 66739
Telephone: (316) 783-1371
Private agency
Founded in: 1983
Jerry L. Derfelt, President
Number of members: 100
Staff: volunteer 10
Major programs: museum, history of mining
Period of collections: from 1890

GARDEN CITY

Finney County Historical Society
Finnup Park
Telephone: (316) 275-6664
Mail to: P.O. Box 59, 67846
County agency
Founded in: 1948
Nancy Harness, Director
Number of members: 398
Staff: full time 1, part time 4
Magazine: *Sequoyan*
Major programs: library, museum, school programs, newsletters/pamphlets, research, exhibits, photographic collections
Period of collections: 1870-1950

GARDNER

Lanesfield School Historical Society
Telephone: (913) 884-8458
Mail to: R.R. 1, Box 156, 66030
Founded in: 1966
Questionnaire not received

GARNETT

Anderson County Historical Society
5th and Main Sts.
Telephone: (913) 448-5881
Mail to: 745 W. 1st. Ave., 66032
Questionnaire not received

GOESSEL

Mennonite Immigrant Historical Foundation
403 E. Marion
Telephone: (316) 367-8200
Mail to: P.O. Box 231, 67053
Private agency
Founded in: 1974
Otto D. Unruh, Manager
Number of members: 250
Staff: part time 2
Major programs: museum, historic preservation
Period of collections: 1875-1925

GOODLAND

Sherman County Historical Society
P.O. Box 684, 67735
Telephone: (913) 899-2983
Founded in: 1975
Betty Walker, Secretary/Treasurer
Number of members: 219
Major programs: oral history, book publishing
Period of collections: 1886-1890

GOVE

Gove County Historical Association
67736
Founded in: 1968
Number of members: 50
Staff: volunteer 10
Major programs: museum, tours/pilgrimages
Period of collections: 1865-present

GREAT BEND

Barton County Genealogical Society
P.O. Box 425, 67530
Private agency
Clara Mae Brown, President
Number of members: 59
Magazine: *B.C. Quarterly*
Major programs: genealogical services
Period of collections: 1700-1800

Barton County Historical Society
P.O. Box 1091, 67530
Telephone: (316) 793-9831
County agency
Founded in: 1960
R. E. Gunn, President
Number of members: 150
Staff: volunteer 50
Major programs: museum, tours, historic preservation, exhibits, photographic collections
Period of collections: 1875-1950

HALSTEAD

Kansas Health Museum
309 Main St., 67056
Telephone: (316) 835-2662
Private agency, authorized by Hertzler Research Foundation
Founded in: 1965
Maxwell E. Sloop, Education Director
Number of members: 200
Staff: full time 2, part time 2
Major programs: library, museum, school programs, research, exhibits, history of health and medical practice

HARPER

Harper County Genealogical Society
1524 Ash St.
Telephone: (316) 896-7571
Mail to: Rt. 2, Box 46, 67058
Private agency
Founded in: 1974
Ruth Hershberger, Librarian
Number of members: 25
Major programs: research, genealogical services
Period of collections: 1800s-1900s

HAVEN

Reno County Historical Society, Inc.
108 W. Main
Telephone: (316) 662-2029
Mail to: 126 W. 12th, 67501
Founded in: 1960
Number of members: 140
Staff: volunteer 10
Major programs: museum

HAYS

Ellis County Historical Society
100 W. 7th St., 67601
Telephone: (913) 628-2624
Founded in: 1973
Leonard Day, Director
Number of members: 875
Staff: full time 1, part time 2, volunteer 30
Magazine: *The Homesteader*
Major programs: archives, museum, historic sites preservation, markers, newsletters/pamphlets, tours/pilgrimages
Period of collections: 1918-present

Frontier Historical Park
Rt. 2, Box 338, 67601
Telephone: (913) 625-6812
State agency, authorized by Kansas State Historical Society
Founded in: 1965
Ronald Parks, Curator
Staff: full time 3, part time 2, volunteer 2
Major programs: museum, historic site(s), tours/pilgrimages, historic preservation, research, exhibits, living history
Period of collections: 1867-1889

HERINGTON

Tri-County Historical Society
Herington Fairgrounds
Telephone: (913) 258-2842
Mail to: P.O. Box 9, 67449
Private agency
George Kohls, President
Number of members: 163
Staff: volunteer 17
Major programs: museum, historic preservation, photographic collections, genealogical services

HILL CITY

Graham County Historical Sociey
414 N. West St., 67642
Founded in: 1971
Questionnaire not received

HILLSBORO

Pioneer Adobe House Museum
Ash and D Sts., 67063
Telephone: (316) 947-3775
Town agency
Founded in: 1958
David F. Wiebe, Curator
Staff: full time 1, volunteer 2
Major programs: museum, exhibits,
photographic collections, pioneer
Mennonite house
Period of collections: 1874-1890

**Center for Mennonite Brethren
Studies, Tabor College**
400 S. Jefferson, 67063
Telephone: (316) 947-3121, ext. 55
Questionnaire not received

Hillsboro Historical Society
P.O. Box 1, 67063
Founded in: 1977
Eileen Butler, President
Number of members: 50
Major programs: archives, oral
history, educational programs,
newsletters/pamphlets

HOLTON

Jackson County Historical Society
4th and New York Sts.
Mail to: P.O. Box 104, 66436
Private agency
Founded in: 1984
Lloyd J. Copeland, President
Number of members: 165
Staff: volunteer 8
Major programs: museum, historic
site(s), markers, historic
preservation, genealogical
services

HOWARD

Elk County Historical Society
251 S. Wabash, 67349
Telephone: (316) 374-2266
Founded in: 1970
Questionnaire not received

HOXIE

**Sheridan County Historical
Society, Inc.**
Courthouse Square, between 9th and
8th Sts.
Telephone: (913) 675-3501
Mail to: P.O. Box 274, 67740
County agency, authorized by
Society board and county
commissioners
Founded in: 1975
Mrs. Ross Carder, Recording Clerk
Number of members: 161
Staff: part time 1, volunteer 26
Major programs: tours/pilgrimages,
oral history, book publishing,
research, photographic
collections, genealogical services
Period of collections: 1880-1920

HUGOTON

**Stevens County Gas and Historical
Museum**
905 S. Adams St., 67951
Telephone: (316) 544-8751
Founded in: 1961
Esther Horner, Curator

Staff: full time 2, part time 1
Major programs: museum, tours,
pamphlets
Period of collections: 1886-1927

HUTCHINSON

Reno County Genealogical Society
P.O. Box 5, 67504-0005
Private agency
Winnie Hendershot, Corresponding
Secretary
Number of members: 175
Staff: volunteer 19
Magazine: *Sunflower*
Major programs: oral history, school
programs, book publishing,
newsletters/pamphlets, records
management, research,
genealogical services, marriages
and cemetery records
Period of collections: 1865-1978

Reno County Historical Society
Telephone: (316) 663-2238
Mail to: P.O. Box 664, 67501
County agency
Founded in: 1961
Jeanette Mull, President
Number of members: 250
Staff: volunteer 25
Period of collections: 1880s-present

**Swiss Mennonite Cultural and
Historical Society**
315 E. 15th St., 67561
Telephone: (316) 665-8500
Private agency
Arthur C. Waltner, President
Number of members: 200
Major programs: historic site(s),
markers, historic preservation
Period of collections: 1874

IOLA

**Allen County Historical
Society, Inc.**
207 N. Jefferson, 66749
Telephone: (316) 365-3051
Founded in: 1956
Helen Henderson, Executive Director
Number of members: 270
Magazine: *Al Co Gaslight*
Staff: part time 1, volunteer 15
Major programs: museum, historic
site, historic preservation
Period of collections: 1855-1965

JETMORE

Haun Museum
67854
Telephone: (316) 357-6181
Founded in: 1957
Number of members: 88
Staff: part time 1, volunteer 5
Major programs: historic sites
preservation, books,
newsletters/pamphlets
Period of collections: 1865-1918

JOHNSON

Stanton County Historical Society
Courthouse Block, 67855
Telephone: (316) 492-2324
Questionnaire not received

KANSAS CITY

Grinter House Museum
1420 S. 78th St., 66111
Telephone: (913) 299-0373
State agency, authorized by Kansas
State Historical Society
Founded in: 1971
Jefferson M. Brown, Historic Property
Curator I
Major programs: historic site(s),
tours/pilgrimages, historic
preservation
Period of collections: 1857

KINGMAN

**Kingman County Historical
Museum**
400 N. Main
Telephone: (316) 532-9950
Mail to: P.O. Box 281, 67068
Byron Walker, President
Number of members: 175
Major programs: museum, historic
site(s), book publishing, exhibits,
photographic collections
Period of collections: 1870-present

LACROSSE

Barbed Wire Museum
614 Main St.
Telephone: (913) 222-3116
Mail to: P.O. Box 716, 67548
Private agency, authorized by
Kansas Barbed Wire Collectors
Association
Founded in: 1971
Barbara R. Grass,
Secretary/Treasurer
Number of members: 123
Staff: part time 1
Major programs: museum, history of
fencing wires and tools
Period of collections: 1853-present

LAKIN

Kearny County Historical Society
101-111 S. Buffalo St., 67860
Telephone: (316) 355-7448
Private agency
Founded in: 1958
Lucile Dieast, Executive Director
Number of members: 400
Major programs: library, museum,
historic site(s), school programs,
book publishing,
newsletters/pamphlets,
photographic collections,
genealogical services
Period of collections: 1873-present

LARNED

Ft. Larned National Historic Site
Rt. 3, 67550
Telephone: (316) 285-6911
Federal agency, authorized by
National Park Service
Founded in: 1964
John B. Arnold, Superintendent
Staff: full time 8, part time 7,
volunteer 25
Major programs: library, museum,
historic site(s), historic
preservation, living history,
archaeology programs
Period of collections: 1859-1878

Santa Fe Trail Center
Rt. 3, 67550
Telephone: (316) 285-2054
Private agency, authorized by Ft.
Larned Historical Society
Founded in: 1923
Ruth Olson, Director/Curator
Number of members: 300
Staff: full time 4, part time 5,
volunteer 15
Major programs: library, museum,
archives
Period of collections: 1865-1918

LAWRENCE

Douglas County Historical Society
1047 Massachusetts St., 66044
Telephone: (913) 841-4109
Private agency
Founded in: 1933
Steven Jansen, Museum Director
Number of members: 400
Staff: full time 1, part time 4,
volunteer 30
Major programs: library, archives,
manuscripts, museum,
newsletters/pamphlets, research,
exhibits, audiovisual programs,
photographic collections
Period of collections: 1854-present

Elizabeth M. Watkins Community Museum
1047 Massachusetts St., 66044
Telephone: (913) 841-4109
Private agency, authorized by
Douglas County Historical Society
Founded in: 1935
Steven Jansen, Director
Number of members: 250
Staff: full time 1, part time 6,
volunteer 10
Major programs: library, manuscripts,
museum, school programs,
newsletters/pamphlets, research,
exhibits, audiovisual programs,
photographic collections
Period of collections: 1854-present

Kansas All-Sports Hall of Fame
1047 Massachusetts St., 66044
Telephone: (913) 841-4109
State agency
Founded in: 1961
Steven Jansen, Executive Secretary
Staff: part time 1
Major programs: archives, exhibits,
history of sports
Period of collections: 1890-1974

Kansas Collection, University of Kansas Libraries
Telephone: (913) 864-4274
Sheryl Williams, Curator
Staff: full time 6, part time 3,
volunteer 1
Major programs: library, archives,
manuscripts, tours, oral history,
research, exhibits, photographic
collections
Period of collections: 1850-present

LEAVENWORTH

Leavenworth County Genealogical Society
P.O. Box 362, 66048
Telephone: (913) 727-1505
Private agency

Founded in: 1979
Carolyn Dossey, President
Number of members: 175
Staff: volunteer 5
Magazine: *Rooting Around*
Major programs: library, archives,
oral history, newsletters/pamphlets,
research, genealogical services
Period of collections: 1850-present

Leavenworth County Historical Society
334 5th Ave. 66048
Questionnaire not received

LIBERAL

Seward County Historical Society, Inc.
567 E. Cedar, 67901
Telephone: (316) 624-7624
County agency, authorized by county
commissioners
Founded in: 1961
Robert Larrabee, President
Number of members: 75
Staff: full time 1, part time 1,
volunteer 21
Major programs: historic site(s),
markers, tours/pilgrimages, historic
preservation, exhibits, living history
Period of collections: 1865-1977

LINCOLN

Lincoln County Historical Society
214 W. Lincoln
Mail to: 913 N. 4th St., 67455
Private agency
Founded in: 1978
Penny Andreson, President
Number of members: 100
Staff: full time 7
Major programs: museum
Period of collections: 1860-1950

LINDSBORG

McPherson County Old Mill Museum and Park
120 Mill St.
Telephone: (913) 227-3595
Mail to: P.O. Box 94, 67456
County agency
Founded in: 1962
Jeanne Mogenson, Director
Staff: full time 2, part time 5
Major programs: museum, historic
site(s), historic preservation,
exhibits
Period of collections: 1880s-1930s

LYNDON

Osage County Genealogical Society
c/o Lyndon Carnegie Library, 127 E-6
Telephone: (913) 828-4520
Mail to: P.O. Box 277, 66451
Private agency
Founded in: 1981
Sarah Walker-Hitt, President
Number of members: 40
Staff: volunteer 10
Magazine: *The Tracer*
Major programs: library, oral history,
historic preservation, research,
exhibits, living history,
genealogical services

Period of collections: late 19th-early
20th centuries

Osage County Historical Society
Mail to: P.O. Box 361, 66451
Founded in: 1964
Number of members: 220
Staff: volunteer 10
Magazine: *Hedgepast*
Major programs: archives, museum
Period of collections: 1865-1918

LYONS

Rice County Historical Society
105 W. Lyon, 67554
Telephone: (316) 257-3941
County agency
Founded in: 1927
Florence Monroe, Interim Curator
Number of members: 325
Staff: full time 1, volunteer 1
Major programs: library, archives,
museum, educational programs
Period of collections: 1541-present

MANHATTAN

Goodnow Museum and Historical Site
2224 Stone Post Rd., 66502
Telephone: (913) 539-3731
State agency, authorized by Kansas
State Historical Society
Founded in: 1875
Glen F. Lojka, Curator
Staff: full time 1, part time 2,
volunteer 4
Major programs: school programs,
exhibits, living history
Period of collections: 1800s

Riley County Historical Society
2309 Claflin, 66502
Telephone: (913) 537-2210
Private agency
Founded in: 1914
Jean Caskey Dallas, Director
Number of members: 1,057
Major programs: library, archives,
museum, historic site(s),
tours/pilgrimages, junior history,
oral history, school programs,
newsletters/pamphlets, historic
preservation, records
management, research, exhibits,
audiovisual programs,
photographic collections,
genealogical services
Period of collections: 1855-1955

MARYSVILLE

Marshall County Historical Society
66508
Founded in: 1971
John Sanderson, President
Number of members: 1,000
Major programs: library, historic site,
newsletters/pamphlets, historic
preservation

Pony Express Museum
c/o Curator, 605 N. 11th St., 66508
Private agency
Founded in: 1984
Howard C. Funk, Curator
Major programs: museum,
tours/pilgrimages, historic
preservation, exhibits, living history

MCPHERSON

**McPherson County Historical
Society**
1130 E. Euclid, 67460
Telephone: (316) 241-5977
County agency
Founded in: 1962
S.M. Dell, President
Number of members: 65
Major programs: markers,
tours/pilgrimages, historic
preservation
Period of collections: 1865-1940

MEADE

Meade County Historical Society
200 E. Carthage, 67864
Telephone: (316) 873-2359
Founded in: 1969
Number of members: 261
Staff: full time 1, volunteer 25
Magazine: *Meade County Historian*
Major programs: library, manuscripts,
museum, tours/pilgrimages,
newsletters/pamphlets
Period of collections: 1865-1918

MERRIAM

Historic Merriam
9516 Hocker Dr.
Telephone: (913) 831-9339
City agency
Founded in: 1981
Roger Werner, President
Number of members: 30
Staff: volunteer 20
Major programs: library, archives,
historic site(s), oral history, school
programs, historic preservation,
research, living history,
photographic collections, publicity
Period of collections: 1865-present

MILAN

Milan Historical Association
Monroe and Market Sts.
Telephone: (316) 435-6423
Mail to: P.O. Box 144, 67105
Private agency
Founded in: 1979
Richard Larson, President
Staff: volunteer 8
Period of collections: 1800-present

MULVANE

Mulvane Historical Society
224 W. Main St.
Telephone: (316) 777-1766/777-0506
Mail to: P.O. Box 117, 67110
Authorized by city and school district
museum commission
Founded in: 1972
Madeline K. Farber, Board Chair
Number of members: 98
Staff: volunteer 12
Major programs: museum,
tours/pilgrimages, junior history,
oral history, school programs, book
publishing, historic preservation,
records management, research,
exhibits, audiovisual programs,
photographic collections,
genealogical services
Period of collections: 1860-present

NEODESHA

Heritage Genealogical Society
P.O. Box 73, 66757
Private agency
Founded in: 1969
Clyde Lovett, President
Number of members: 60
Major programs: genealogical
services

NESS CITY

Ness County Historical Society
67560
County agency
Founded in: 1930
Mary Lou Hall, President
Number of members: 70
Staff: volunteer 10
Period of collections: 1878-present

NEWTON

Harvey County Historical Society
203 N. Main
Telephone: (316) 283-2221
Mail to: P.O. Box 4, 67114
County agency
Number of members: 1960
Mike Smurr, Director
Number of members: 250
Staff: part time 3, volunteer 10
Magazine: *Historical Notes*
Major programs: library, museum,
markers
Period of collections: late 1800s-early
1900s

NORTH NEWTON

Kauffman Museum
Bethel College, 67117
Telephone: (316) 283-1612
Private agency, authorized by
Kauffman Museum Association
Founded in: 1941
John M. Janzen, Director
Staff: part time 4, volunteer 25
Major programs: museum, research,
exhibits
Period of collections: late 19th-early
20th centuries

Mennonite Library and Archives
67117
Telephone: (316) 283-2500
Private agency, authorized by Bethel
College and General Conference,
Mennonite Church
Founded in: 1936
David A. Haury, Director/Archivist
Staff: full time 5, part time 2,
volunteer 1
Magazine: *Mennonite Life / Gleanings
from the Threshing Floor*
Major programs: library, archives,
manuscripts, oral history, research,
exhibits, audiovisual programs,
photographic collections,
genealogical services
Period of collections: 1870s-present

NORTON

Norton County Historical Society
307 W. Warsaw, 67654
Telephone: (913) 877-2475
County agency
Founded in: 1974

Clarence Collins, President
Number of members: 53
Major programs: manuscripts, oral
history, research, audiovisual
programs, photographic
collections, genealogical services
Period of collections: late 19th-early
20th centuries

OBERLIN

**Decatur County Historical
Society—Last Indian Raid in
Kansas Museum**
258 S. Penn Ave., 67749
Telephone: (913) 475-2712
Founded in: 1981
Questionnaire not received

OLATHE

**Mahaffie Farmstead and
Stagecoach Stop**
1100 Kansas City Rd.
Telephone: (913) 782-6972
Mail to: P.O. Box 768, 66061
City agency, authorized by Parks and
Recreation Department
Founded in: 1979
Michael E. Duncan, Historic Site
Manager
Number of members: 250
Staff: full time 2, part time 2,
volunteer 60
Major programs: historic site(s),
school programs, research
Period of collections: 1860-1880

ONAGA

Onaga Historical Society
Mail to: c/o Merrie Pinick, Havensville,
66432
Questionnaire not received

OSAWATOMIE

Friends of Adair Cabin, Inc.
Rt. 2, Box 119, 66064
Telephone: (913) 755-4976
Private agency, authorized by Adair
Cabin, John Brown Museum, and
Kansas State Historical Society
Founded in: 1984
Helen Stafford, President
Number of members: 12
Staff: volunteer 12
Major programs: historic site(s),
exhibits, living history
Period of collections: 1854-1910

Osawatomie Historical Society
194 14th St., 66064
Telephone: (913) 755-3496/755-4452
Founded in: 1948
Number of members: 40
Staff: volunteer 5
Major programs: historic sites
preservation
Period of collections: 1783-present

OSBORNE

**Osborne County Genealogical and
Historical Society, Inc.**
307 W. Main, 67413
Private agency
Founded in: 1975
Lillian Zvolanek, President
Number of members: 30

Magazine: *Leaves of Lineage*
Major programs: library, museum,
 historic preservation, photographic
 collections, genealogical services,
 educational programs

OSKALOOSA

**Jefferson County Genealogical
 Society, Inc.**
Hwy. 59
Mail to: P.O. Box 174, 66066
Private agency
Founded in: 1978
Ruth Clark, President
Number of members: 230
Staff: volunteer 12
Magazine: *Yesteryears*
Major programs: library,
 newsletters/pamphlets,
 genealogical services
Period of collections: 1850-present

**Jefferson County Historical
 Society**
Mail to: P.O. Box 146, 66066
Founded in: 1960
Charles Hauck, President
Number of members: 125
Staff: volunteer 25
Major programs: historic preservation
Period of collections: late 1800s

OTTAWA

**Franklin County Historical
 Society, Inc.**
Telephone: (913) 242-5383
Mail to: P.O. Box 145, 66067
Private agency
Founded in: 1937
John Mark Lambertson, Director
Number of members: 100
Staff: volunteer 50
Major programs: museum, historic
 sites preservation, markers
Period of collections: 1850-present

OVERBROOK

**Clinton Lake Historical
 Society, Inc.**
R.R. 2, 66524
Telephone: (913) 748-9836
Founded in: 1977
Missy Rosson, President
Number of members: 130
Major programs: archives,
 manuscripts, museum, exhibits,
 genealogical services
Period of collections: 1854-present

OZAWKIE

**RevMex (Revolutionary Mexican
 Historical Society)**
Sunset Ridge Rd., 66070
Telephone: (913) 945-3800
Private agency
Founded in: 1976
Verne R. Walrafen, Founder
Number of members: 160
Staff: volunteer 1
Magazine: *The Mexican Revolution
 Reporter*
Major programs:
 newsletters/pamphlets
Period of collections: 1910-1920

PLEASANTON

Linn County Historical Society
Park St.
Telephone: (913) 352-8739
Mail to: P.O. Box 137, 66075
Founded in: 1968
Ola May Earnest, President
Number of members: 450
Staff: part time 4, volunteer 12
Magazine: *The Heritage*
1Major programs: library, archives,
 manuscripts, museum, markers,
 tours/pilgrimages, book publishing,
 newsletters/pamphlets, genealogy
Period of collections: 1850-1950

PRATT

Pratt County Historical Society
212 S. Ninnescah, 67124
Telephone: (316) 672-7874
Private agency
Founded in: 1968
Quenten Hannawald, President
Number of members: 320
Staff: volunteer 4
Major programs: library, museum,
 historic preservation, photographic
 collections, genealogical services
Period of collections: 1880-1920

RUSSELL

Russell County Historical Society
331 Kansas St.
Telephone: (913) 483-3637
Mail to: P.O. Box 245, 67665
County agency
Founded in: 1950
Jill A. Holt, Secretary/Treasurer
Number of members: 185
staff: volunteer 4
Major programs: library, archives,
 museum, historic site(s), exhibits,
 genealogical services
Period of collections: 1871-1940

RUSSELL SPRINGS

**Butterfield Trail
 Association—Logan County
 Historical Society**
Hwy. 25 and Museum Dr.
Telephone: (913) 751-4242
Mail to: P.O. Box 336, 67755
Private agency
Founded in: 1964
Michael L. Baughn, President
Number of members: full time 1, part
 time 1, volunteer 50
Major programs: archives, museum,
 historic sites preservation, markers,
 educational programs, exhibits
Period of collections: 1865-1945

SABETHA

Albany Historical Society
Rt. 1, Albany Rd., 66534
Telephone: (913) 284-2587
Founded in: 1965
Questionnaire not received

ST. FRANCIS

**Cheyenne County Historical
 Society**
212 E. Washington
Mail to: P.O. Box 611, 67756

County agency
Marilyn Holzwarth, Archivist
Number of members: 125
Staff: part time 1, volunteer 1
Major programs: archives, historic
 site(s), markers, tours/pilgrimages,
 oral history, book publishing,
 newsletters/pamphlets, research,
 genealogical services
Period of collections: 1885-1940s

SALINA

**Saline County Historical
 Society, Inc.**
P.O. Box 32, 67401
Private agency
Founded in: 1975
Mary A. Schwartz, President
Number of members: 90

Smoky Hill Historical Museum
Oakdale Park
Telephone: (913) 827-3958
Mail to: P.O. Box 119, 67401
Questionnaire not received

**Smoky Valley Genealogical Society
 and Library, Inc.**
615 S. 11th St., 67401
Telephone: (913) 825-7573
Private agency
Founded in: 1970
Mrs. Lewis C. Crawford, President
Number of members: 199
Staff: volunteer 50-75
Magazine: *Tree Climber*
Major programs: library, archives,
 book publishing,
 newsletters/pamphlets, historic
 preservation, research,
 genealogical services
Period of collections: 1600s-present

SCOTT CITY

Scott County Historical Society
211 College St., 67871
Telephone: (316) 872-3708
Private agency
M.H. Rector, President
Number of members: 98
Staff: volunteer 6
Major programs: historic site,
 markers, tours, book publishing
Period of collections: 1900-present

SENECA

**Nemaha County Historical
 Society, Inc.**
c/o Treasurer, 505 Walnut, 66538
Telephone: (913) 336-2494
Private agency
Founded in: 1976
Earl Volz, President
Number of members: 269
Major programs: library, museum,
 historic site, markers
Period of collections: 1879-present

SHAWNEE

**Johnson County Historical
 Museum**
6305 Lackman Rd., 66217
Telephone: (913) 631-6709
County agency
Founded in: 1964
Stephanie Norby, Curator

Staff: full time 1, part time 1
Major programs: museum, exhibits
Period of collections: 1860s-present

Shawnee Historical Society, Inc.—Old Shawnee Town
11501 W. 57th St.
Telephone: (913) 268-6663
Mail to: P.O. Box 3042, 66203
Private agency
Founded in: 1966
Judy Owens, Co-manager
Number of members: 250
Staff: full time 4, part time 6, volunteer 6
Major programs: museum, tours/pilgrimages, historic preservation, exhibits, handcrafts
Period of collections: before 1900

SHAWNEE MISSION

Native Sons of Kansas City
4200 W. 54th St., 66205
Telephone: (913) 432-9231
Mail to: P.O. Box 1111, 66222
Questionnaire not received

Shawnee Mission Indian Historical Society
Telephone: (913) 631-9990
Mail to: 4833 Black Swan, 66202
Founded in: 1930
Number of members: 142
Major programs: historic sites preservation, markes, tours/pilgrimages, junior history, educational programs
Period of collections: 1825-present

Smoky Hill Railway and Historical Society, Inc.
P.O. Box 124, 66201
Private agency
Founded in: 1964
Alan A. Kamp, President
Number of members: 150
Staff: volunteer 12
Magazine: *The Flyer*
Major programs: archives, museum, school programs, newsletters/pamphlets, historic preservation, exhibits, photographic collections, railroad equipment restoration
Period of collections: 1890s-present

STAFFORD

Stafford County Historical and Genealogical Society
100 S. Main, 67578
Telephone: (316) 234-5664
Private agency
Founded in: 1978
Ruth Henry, Executive Secretary
Number of members: 175
Staff: full time 1, volunteer 20
Major programs: museum, tours/pilgrimages, oral history, school programs, newsletters/pamphlets, historic preservation, records management, exhibits, photographic collections, genealogical services
Period of collections: 1862

STOCKTON

Rooks County Historical Society
Fairgrounds
Telephone: (913) 425-6669
Mail to: 517 S. 2nd St., 67669
County agency
Founded in: 1975
Vada H. Hazen, President
Number of members: 45
Staff: full time 1, part time 1, volunteer 6
Major programs: library, archives, museum, historic preservation, records management, photographic collections
Period of collections: from 1860

SUBLETTE

Haskell County Historical Society
Fairgrounds, NE
Telephone: (316) 675-8344
Mail to: P.O. Box 639, 67877
County agency
Founded in: 1982
Duane Murphy, President
Number of members: 80
Staff: part time 1
Major programs: museum, markers, historic preservation, exhibits, photographic collections
Period of collections: from 1886

TONGANOXIE

Tonganoxie Community Historical Society
515 E. 4th
Telephone: (913) 845-2102
Town agency
Founded in: 1981
John C. Lenahan, Sr., President
Number of members: 110

TOPEKA

Historic Topeka, Inc.
P.O. Box 903, 66601
Private agency
Founded in: 1975
Marjorie Schnacke, President
Major programs: museum, historic site(s), tours/pilgrimages, book publishing, newsletters/pamphlets, historic preservation
Period of collections: 1855-present

Kansas Museum of History
6425 W. 6th St., 66615
Telephone: (913) 272-8681
State agency, authorized by Kansas State Historical Society

Kansas Museums Association
6425 S.W. 6th St., 66615
Private agency
Founded in: 1969
Dennis H.J. Medina, President
Number of members: 175
Magazine: *Exchange*
Major programs: newsletters/pamphlets, audiovisual programs, annual meeting, workshops, awards

◇Kansas State Historical Society—Center for Historical Research
120 W. 10th St., 66612
Telephone: (913) 296-3251
State agency
Founded in: 1875
Joseph W. Snell, Executive Director
Number of members: 5,000
Staff: full time 144, part time 9, volunteer 95
Magazine: *Kansas History: A Journal of the Central Plains*
Major programs: library, archives, manuscripts, museum, historic site(s), markers, school programs, book publishing, newsletters/pamphlets, historic preservation, research, exhibits, audiovisual programs, archaeology programs, photographic collections, genealogical services, field services, folklore
Period of collections: 1854-present

Menninger Foundation Museum and Archives
5800 W. 6th St.
Telephone: (913) 273-7500
Mail to: P.O. Box 829, 66601
Private agency
Founded in: 1925
Robert G. Menninger, Director
Anne Marvin, Curator
Staff: full time 2, part time 2
Major programs: archives, museum, records management, exhibits, photographic collections, history of psychiatry
Period of collections: 1918-present

The Kansas Museum of History, operated by the Kansas State Historical Society.—Earl Kintner, photographer, The Kansas State Historical Society, Topeka, Kansas

Shawnee County Historical Society
Mail to: P.O. Box 56, 66601
Founded in: 1946
John W. Ripley, Director Publications
Number of members: 1,150
Staff: part time 1, volunteer 2
Magazine: *The Bulletin*
Major programs: oral history, books
Period of collections: 1855-1945

TRADING POST

Trading Post Historical Museum
Rt. 2, Box 145-A, 66075
Telephone: (913) 352-6441
Authorized by Trading Post Historical
Society
Founded in: 1974
Alice Widner, Curator/Secretary
Number of members: 70
Staff: full time 1, volunteer 16
Major programs: archives, museum,
research, living history,
photographic collections,
genealogical services
Period of collections: 1825-1950

TRIBUNE

Greeley County Historical Society
E. Harper, 67879
Telephone: (316) 376-4996
Private agency
Founded in: 1973
Dorothy Higgins, President
Number of members: 86
Staff: volunteer 15
Major programs: museum, book
publishing, historic preservation
Period of collections: from 1885

ULYSSES

**Grant County Historical
Society, Inc.**
300 E. Oklahoma
Telephone: (316) 356-3009
Mail to: P.O. Box 906, 67880
Founded in: 1966
Fern Bessire, Administrator
Number of members: 102
Staff: full time 1, part time 2,
volunteer 10
Major programs: museum,
educational programs, book
publishing, newsletters/pamphlets
Period of collections: 1890-1930

Grant County Museum
300 E. Oklahoma
Telephone: (316) 356-3009
Mail to: P.O. Box 906, 67880
County agency, authorized by Grant
County Historical Society
Founded in: 1965
Fern Bessire, Administrator
Number of members: 120
Staff: full time 2
Major programs: museum, tours, oral
history, book publishing, historic
preservation, records
management, research, exhibits,
audiovisual programs,
photographic collections,
genealogical services
Period of collections: late 1800s-early
1900s

VALLEY CENTER

**Valley Center Historical and
Cultural Society**
112 N. Meridian
Telephone: (316) 755-0275
Mail to: P.O. Box 173, 67147
Private agency
Founded in: 1976
Lois Riley, President
Number of members: 80
Staff: volunteer 6
Major programs: museum, books
Period of collections: 1865-present

WAKEENEY

Trego County Historical County
Trego County Fairgrounds, 67672
Telephone: (913) 743-2964
Mail to: c/o Sadie Simmons, Ogallah,
67656
Questionnaire not received

WASHINGTON

**Washington County Historical
Society**
208 Ballard St.
Telephone: (913) 325-2198
Mail to: P.O. Box 31, 66968
Private agency
Founded in: 1978
Richard Pannbacker, President
Number of members: 650
Staff: volunteer 15
Major programs: library, museum,
tours/pilgrimages, oral history,
newsletters/pamphlets,
genealogical services
Period of collections: 1860-1940

WELLINGTON

**Chisholm Trail Museum
Corporation**
502 N. Washington, 67152
Telephone: (316) 326-2174
Founded in: 1964
Dorothea W. Miller, Director
Number of members: 210
Staff: volunteer 8
Major programs: library, archives,
museum, genealogical services
Period of collections: 1865-present

WESTMORELAND

**Rock Creek Valley Historical
Society and Museum**
66549
Telephone: (913) 457-3578
Mail to: c/o President, R.R., Wheaton,
66551
Private agency
Founded in: 1977
Rose Wahl, President
Number of members: 100
Staff: volunteer 7
Major programs: library, museum,
historic site(s), markers,
tours/pilgrimages, oral history,
newsletters/pamphlets, historic
preservation, exhibits,
photographic collections

WICHITA

**Fellow-Reeve Museum of History
and Science**
2100 University, 67213

Telephone: (316) 261-5800, ext. 794
Private agency, authorized by
Friends University
Founded in: 1898
Philip Nagley, Director
Staff: part time 3, volunteer 14
Major programs: museum
Period of collections: 1880-1930

**Historic Wichita—Sedgwick
County, Inc.**
1871 Sim Park Dr., 67203
Telephone: (316) 264-0671
Private agency
Founded in: 1950
Elizabeth D. Kennedy, Interim
Managing Director
Number of members: 200
Staff: full time 14, part time 2,
volunteer 200
Major programs: museum, school
programs, newsletters/pamphlets,
historic preservation, research,
exhibits, living history
Period of collections: 1865-1880

**Midwest Historical and
Genealogical Society, Inc.**
1871 Sim Park Dr.
Mail to: P.O. Box 1121, 67201
Private agency
Founded in 1966
Donna Woods, President
Number of members: 625
Staff: volunteer 50
Magazine: *The Midwest Historical
and Genealogical Register*
Major programs: library, archives,
manuscripts, tours/pilgrimages,
school programs, book publishing,
newsletters/pamphlets, historic
preservation, genealogical
services
Period of collections: 1770-present

**Office of Museum Programs,
Wichita Public Schools**
640 N. Emporia, 67214
Telephone: (316) 268-7752
Authorized by Board of Education
Founded in: 1975
Paul Chancy Obero, Supervisor
Staff: full time 4
Magazine: *Wichita Museum News*
Major programs: archives, museum,
school programs,
newsletters/pamphlets
Period of collections: 1870-present

Old Cowtown Museum
1871 Sim Park Dr., 67203
Telephone: (316) 264-0671
Private agency, authorized by
Historic Wichita—Sedgwick
County, Inc.
Founded in: 1950
Elizabeth D. Kennedy, Interim
Managing Director
Staff: full time 16, part time 4,
volunteer 700
Major programs: museum, school
programs, newsletters/pamphlets,
historic preservation, living history
Period of collections: 1865-1880

**Wichita-Sedgwick County
Historical Museum**
204 S. Main, 67202
Telephone: (316) 265-9314
Private agency

Founded in: 1939
Robert A. Puckett, Director
Number of members: 1,400
Staff: full time 2, part time 7,
  volunteer 20
Magazine: *Heritage*
Major programs: archives, library,
  museum, historic sites
  preservation, educational
  programs
Period of collections: 1865-1920

WINFIELD

Cowley County Historical Society and Museum
1011 Mansfield
Telephone: (316) 221-4141
Mail to: 1714 E. 11th, 67156
Questionnaire not received

KENTUCKY

ALBANY

Clinton County Historical Society
Telephone: (606) 387-5519
  (president)
Private agency
Founded in: 1980
Martha Brummett, President
Major programs: library, archives,
  manuscripts, markers, oral history,
  research

ASHLAND

Boyd County Historical Society and Public Library
1740 Central Ave., 41101
Telephone: (606) 329-0090
Founded in: 1956
John W. Newman, President
Number of members: 149
Major programs: library, archives,
  junior history, school programs,
  book publishing, research,
  educational programs
Period of collections: 1865-1918

AUGUSTA

Mary Ingles Heritage Foundation
4th St.
Telephone: (606) 756-2101
Mail to: 305 Elizabeth St., 41002
Founded in: 1969
Questionnaire not received

BARBOURVILLE

Knox County Historical Society
P.O. Box 528, 40906
Private agency
Founded in: 1974
Susan Arthur, President
Number of members: 50
Staff: volunteer 8
Magazine: *Mountain Heritage*
Major programs: markers, oral
  history, book publishing,
  newsletters/pamphlets, historic
  preservation, research,
  photographic collections
Period of collections: 1800-1920

BARDSTOWN

Oscar Getz Museum of Whiskey History
5th St. at Xavier Dr., 40004
Telephone: (502) 348-2999
City agency
Founded in: 1984
Flaget M. Nally, Curator
Staff: full time 1, part time 2,
  volunteer 1
Major programs: archives,
  manuscripts, historic site(s),
  tours/pilgrimages, historic
  preservation, exhibits
Period of collections:
  1759-post-Prohibition

BEDFORD

Trimble County Historical Society
P.O. Box 187, 40006
Private agency
Founded in: 1977
Greg Black, President
Number of members: 40

BENTON

Jackson Purchase Historical Society
1202 Joe Creason Dr., 42025
Telephone: (502) 527-3705
Questionnaire not received

BEREA

Berea College Appalachian Museum
Jackson St.
Telephone: (606) 986-9341, ext. 560
Mail to: P.O. Box 2298, 40404
Private agency, authorized by the
  college
Founded in: 1969
John S. Lewis, Director
Staff: full time 1, part time 14
Major programs: museum, oral
  history, exhibits, audiovisual
  programs
Period of collections: 1800-present

BOWLING GREEN

Hobson House Association, Inc.
Riverview, Historic Hobson House,
  1100 W. Main St., 42101
Telephone: (502) 842-6932/842-8957
Founded in: 1854
Questionnaire not received

Kentucky Museum and Library
Western Kentucky University, 42101
Telephone: (502) 745-2592
State agency, authorized by the
  university
Founded in: 1931
Riley Handy, Head, Department of
  Special Collections
Staff: full time 10, part time 3,
  volunteer 10
Major programs: library, archives,
  manuscripts, museum, oral history,
  school programs,
  newsletters/pamphlets, exhibits,
  photographic collections,
  genealogical services
Period of collections: 19th-20th
  centuries

Landmark Association of Bowling Green and Warren County, Inc.
914½ State St.
Telephone: (502) 781-8106
Mail to: P.O. Box 1812, 42102-1812
Private agency
Founded in: 1976
Richard M. Pfefferkorn, Executive
  Vice President
Number of members: 470
Staff: full time 2, part time 1
Magazine: *Landmark Report*
Major programs:
  newsletters/pamphlets, historic
  preservation, Main St. project
Period of collections: 1800-1940

Riverview, the Historic Hobson House
1100 W. Main, 42101
Telephone: (502) 842-6932
City agency
Founded in: 1972
Margaret S. Bush, Director
Staff: full time 3
Magazine: *Riverview*
Major programs: archives,
  manuscripts, museum, historic
  site(s), junior history, oral history,
  book publishing,
  newsletters/pamphlets, historic
  preservation, research, exhibits,
  living history, photographic
  collections
Period of collections: Civil War
  era—Restoration period

Southern Kentucky Genealogical Society
1717-B Canton Dr., 42101
Telephone: (502) 843-1477
Founded in: 1977
Questionnaire not received

Wood County Historical Society
301 Sand Ridge Rd., 43402
Telephone: (419) 353-1475
Founded in: 1955
Clark Duncan, President
Number of members: 350
Staff: full time 1, part time 1,
  volunteer 5
Magazine: *The Black Swamp Chanticleer*
Major programs: library, museum,
  historic site(s), markers,
  tours/pilgrimages,
  newsletters/pamphlets, exhibits
Period of collections: 1860-1910

BROWNSVILLE

Edmonson County Historical Society
42210
Founded in: 1978
Verbil Gipson, President
Number of members: 35
Major programs: historic site,
  markers, oral history, book
  publishing, historic sites
  preservation

CAMPBELLSVILLE

Taylor County Historical Society
P.O. Box 14, 42718
Founded in: 1969
Margaret Rogers, President
Number of members: 70

Staff: volunteer 1
Magazine: *Central Kentucky Researcher*
Major programs: library, archives, manuscripts, museum, markers, newsletters/pamphlets
Period of collections: 1800-1900

CENTRAL CITY

Otto Rothert Historical Society
Broad St., 42330
Mail to: c/o Alexander Cather, Rt. 1, Box 198-A, Drakesboro, 42337
Questionnaire not received

CLAY CITY

Red River Historical Society
Main St., P.O. Box 195, 40312
Telephone: (606) 663-2555
Founded in: 1966
Questionnaire not received

CLINTON

Hickman County Historical Society
P.O. Box 213, 42031
Telephone: (502) 653-4190
Private agency
Founded in: 1982
LaDonna H. Latham, President
Number of members: 30
Major programs: book publishing, newsletters/pamphlets, genealogical services

COVINGTON

Acadian Genealogy Exchange
863 Wayman Branch Rd., 41015
Telephone: (606) 356-9825
Private agency
Founded in: 1972
Janet B. Jehn, Publisher/Editor
Number of members: 565
Staff: full time 1
Magazine: *Acadian Genealogy Exchange*
Major programs: book publishing, newsletters/pamphlets, research, genealogical services
Period of collections: 1600s-present

Behringer-Crawford Museum
1600 Montague Rd., Devou Park
Telephone: (606) 491-4003
Mail to: P.O. Box 67, 41012
Private agency
Founded in: 1950
Gregory F. Harper, Executive Director
Number of members: 259
Staff: full time 1, part time 2, volunteer 17
Major programs: library, archives, museum, school programs, newsletters/pamphlets, research, exhibits, archaeology programs, photographic collections, teacher in-service program
Period of collections: prehistoric-present

Kenton County Historical Society
5th and Scott Sts., 41011
Telephone: (606) 491-7610
Mail to: P.O. Box 641, 41012
County agency
Founded in: 1977
Joseph F. Gastright, Member, Board of Directors

Number of members: 180
Staff: volunteer 10
Major programs: markers, tours/pilgrimages, oral history, educational programs, book publishing, newsletters/pamphlets, genealogy

Kenton County Public Library
5th and Scott Sts., 41011
Telephone: (606) 491-7610
Founded in: 1968
Mary Ann Mongan, Director
Number of members: 40,000
Staff: full time 50
Major programs: library, photographic collections, genealogical services, newspaper index
Period of collections: 1790-1910

Kentucky Association of Museums
c/o Behringer-Crawford Museum
Telephone: (606) 491-4003
Mail to: P.O. Box 67, Devou Park, 41012
Founded in: 1974
Greg Harper, President
Number of members: 65
Major programs: newsletters/pamphlets

CRAB ORCHARD

Lincoln County Historical Society
40419
Telephone: (606) 355-2204
Founded in: 1951
Questionnaire not received

DANVILLE

McDowell House and Apothecary Shop
125-127 S. 2nd St., 40422
Telephone: (606) 236-2804
Private agency, authorized by Kentucky Medical Association
Founded in: 1939
Susan Nimocks, House Manager
Staff: full time 1, part time 7, volunteer 20
Major programs: museum, historic site(s), tours/pilgrimages, oral history, school programs, newsletters/pamphlets, historic preservation, exhibits, audiovisual programs, restoration
Period of collections: 1795-1830

DIXON

Webster County Historical and Genealogical Society
300 E. Leiper St., 42409
Telephone: (502) 639-9171
Private agency
Founded in: 1980
Lowell G. Childress, President
Number of members: 95
Magazine: *Webster's Wagon Wheel*
Major programs: library, book publishing, genealogical services
Period of collections: 1800-present

EDDYVILLE

Lyon County Historical Society, Inc.
Shelby and Water Sts.
Telephone: (502) 388-2717

Mail to: P.O. Box 811, 42038
Private agency
Founded in: 1982
Bill Cunningham, President
Number of members: 175
Staff: volunteer 25
Major programs: archives, museum, historic site(s), markers, oral history, book publishing, newsletters/pamphlets, historic preservation, genealogical services
Period of collections: 1800-1976

ELIZABETHTOWN

Hardin County Historical Society
128 N. Main St.
Telephone: (502) 769-2301
Mail to: c/o Secretary, Box C, 42701
Founded in: 1931
J. R. Pritchard, President
Number of members: 176
Major programs: library, manuscripts, historic sites preservation, markers, books, newsletter, research
Period of collections: 1783-present

Memorabilia Museum, Inc., Coca-Cola Bottling Company of Elizabethtown
1201 N. Dixie Hwy.
Telephone: (502) 737-4000
Mail to: P.O. Box 647, 42701
Private agency, authorized by Coca-Cola Bottling Company
Founded in: 1978
William B. Schmidt, President
Major programs: museum
Period of collections: 1897-1964

FAIRVIEW

Jefferson Davis Monument Shrine
422211
Telephone: (502) 886-1765
State agency
Founded in: 1924
Lucy H. Birkhead, Manager
Staff: full time 2, part time 3
Major programs: museum, audiovisual programs
Period of collections: 1808-1898

FT. CAMPBELL

Don F. Pratt Memorial Museum
Wickam Hall, 42223-5000
Telephone: (502) 798-3215
Federal agency
Founded in: 1956
Charles H. Cureton, Curator
Staff: full time 4
Major programs: library, archives, manuscripts, museum, oral history, research, exhibits, photographic collections
Period of collections: 1942-present

FORT KNOX

Patton Museum of Cavalry and Armor
4554 Fayette Ave.
Telephone: (502) 624-3812
Mail to: P.O. Box 208, 40121
Federal agency, authorized by the U.S. Army
Founded in: 1949
John A. Campbell, Director
Staff: full time 9, volunteer 35

Major programs: library, museum,
markers, living history,
photographic collections
Period of collections: 1918-present

FORT MITCHELL

Northern Kentucky Heritage League
Mail to: P.O. Box 104, 41017
Questionnaire not received

FORT THOMAS

Kentucky Covered Bridge Association
62 Miami Parkway, 41075
Telephone: (606) 441-7000
Private agency
Founded in: 1969
L. K. Patton, Executive Director
Number of members: 170
Staff: volunteer 3
Magazine: *Timbered Tunnel Talk*
Major programs: library, museum,
markers, historic preservation
Period of collections: 1850-present

Northern Kentucky Historical Society, Inc.
P.O. Box 151, 41075
Telephone: (606) 441-7000
Private agency
Founded in: 1963
L.K. Patton, Executive Director
Number of members: 300
Staff: volunteer 10
Major programs: library, archives,
manuscripts,
newsletters/pamphlets
Period of collections: 1792-present

FRANKFORT

Historic Frankfort, Inc.
P.O. Box 775, 40602
Telephone: (502) 223-7793
Founded in: 1968
Robert M. Polsgrove, President
Number of members: 105
Major programs: historic preservation

◇Historical Confederation of Kentucky
P.O. Box H, 40601
Telephone: (502) 564-2662
State agency, authorized by
Kentucky Historical Society
Founded in: 1980
William B. Chescheir, Secretary
Number of members: 117
Staff: part time 3
Magazine: *The Circuit Rider*
Major programs: book publishing,
newsletters/pamphlets, field
services, regional workshops,
annual meeting

Kentucky Department of Parks
Capital Plaza Tower, 10th Floor,
40601
Telephone: (502) 564-3811
Founded in: 1924
Major programs: library, archives,
manuscripts, museum, historic
sites preservation, markers,
tours/pilgrimages, junior history,
oral history, educational programs,
books, newsletters/pamphlets
Period of collections:
prehistoric-present

Kentucky Genealogical Society
Telephone: (502) 223-0492
Mail to: P.O. Box 153, 40602
Private agency
Founded in: 1973
Mary Jane N. Rodgers, President
Number of members: 1,200
Staff: volunteer 21
Magazine: *Blue Grass Roots*
Major programs: library, research,
genealogical services, annual
sminar
Period of collections: 1776-present

Kentucky Heritage Council
Capital Plaza Tower, 12th Floor,
40601
Telephone: (502) 564-7005
State agency
Founded in: 1966
David L. Morgan, Executive Director
Number of members: full time 18
Major programs: historic site(s),
newsletters/pamphlets, historic
preservation, research,
archaeology programs

◇Kentucky Historical Society
300 W. Broadway, 40601
Telephone: (502) 564-3016
Mail to: P.O. Box H, 40602-2108
State agency
Founded in: 1836
Robert B. Kinnaird, Director
Number of members: 9,500
Staff: full time 61, part time 20,
volunteer 1,600
Magazine: *Register/Kentucky
Ancestors/Kentucky
Heritage/Bulletin*
Major programs: library, archives,
manuscripts, museum, markers,
tours/pilgrimages, junior history,
oral history, school programs, book
publishing, newsletters/pamphlets,
research, exhibits, living history,
audiovisual programs, archaeology
programs, photographic
collections, genealogical services,
field services, Historymobile,
micrographics
Period of collections: 1783-present

Kentucky Oral History Commission
Telephone: (502) 564-7644
Mail to: P.O. Box H, 40602-2108
State agency, authorized by
Education and Humanities Cabinet
Founded in: 1976
Kimberly Lady, Director
Staff: full time 2
Major programs: oral history
Period of collections: 20th century

Kentucky Military History Museum
Old State Arsenal, E. Main St.
Telephone: (502) 564-3265
Mail to: c/o Kentucky Historical
Society, P.O. Box H, 40602-2108
State agency, authorized by
Kentucky Historical Society and
Kentucky National Guard
Founded in: 1973
Nicky Hughes, Curator
Staff: full time 3, part time 2
Major programs: library, manuscripts,
museum, school programs,
research, exhibits, living history,
photographic collections
Period of collections: 1774-present

Library and Archives Department, Kentucky Public Records Division
Telephone: (502) 875-7000
Mail to: P.O. Box 537, 40602
State agency
Founded in: 1958
Lewis J. Bellardo, State Archivist
Number of members: 2
Staff: full time 43, part time 8,
volunteer 10
Major programs: archives, records
management, genealogical
services
Period of collections: 1792-1980

Liberty Hall—Orlando Brown House
218 Wilkinson St., 40601
Telephone: (502) 227-2560
Private agency, authorized by the
National Society of the Colonial
Dames of America
Founded in: 1956
Julia Rome, Director of Public
Relations
Number of members: part time 4
Major programs: library, museum,
historic site(s), tours/pilgrimages,
school programs, pamphlets,
historic preservation, exhibits,
archaeology programs,
genealogical services, historic
houses
Period of collections: 1796-1900s

Luscher's Farm Relics of Yesterday
Rt. 9, Manly-Leestown Rd., 40601
Telephone: (502) 227-7936
Private agency
Founded in: 1978
Virginia C. Luscher, Part Owner
Major programs: museum, tours,
historic preservation, exhibits

Office of Historic Properties
Berry Hill, 40601
Telephone: (502) 564-3000
Jolene Greenwell, Executive Director
State agency
Major programs: museum, historic
site(s), tours/pilgrimages, school
programs, book publishing,
newsletters/pamphlets, historic
preservation, records
management, research, exhibits,
photographic collections, field
services
Period of collections:
prehistoric-present

Office of Vital Statistics
275 E. Main St., 40621
Telephone: (502) 564-4212
State agency
Founded in: 1911
Omar L. Greeman, Registrar
Staff: full time 61, part time 4
Major programs: records
management, genealogical
services, legal records of births
and deaths
Period of collections: 1911-present

FRANKLIN

Simpson County Historical Society
Goodnight Library, 42134
Telephone: (502) 586-8397
Private agency

Founded in: 1959
Sarah Richardson, Librarian
Number of members: 50
Staff: volunteer 5
Major programs: library, archives,
    markers, book publishing, records
    management, research,
    photographic collections,
    genealogical services
Period of collections: 1800s

FRENCHBURG

Menifee County Roots
c/o Owner, P.O. Box 114, 40322
Telephone: (606) 768-3323
Private agency
Founded in: 1984
Barbara W. Ingram,
    Owner/Researcher
Major programs: records
    management, research,
    genealogical services
Period of collections: 1869-present

FULTON

Fulton Genealogical Society
Mail to: P.O. Box 31, 42041
Questionnaire not received

GEORGETOWN

**Kentucky Association of Teachers
of History**
c/o History Department, Georgetown
    College, 40324
Telephone: (502) 863-8076
Private agency
Founded in: 1975
James L. Heizer, President
Number of members: 100
Staff: volunteer 12
Major programs: school programs,
    newsletters/pamphlets,
    conferences, workshops

Scott County Genealogical Society
Scott County Public Library, E. Main,
    40324
Telephone: (502) 863-3566
Founded in: 1983
Earlene H. Arnett, Secretary
Number of members: 55
Major programs:
    newsletters/pamphlets,
    genealogical services

GLASGOW

**South Central Kentucky Historical
and Genealogical Society**
Telephone: (502) 651-5514
Mail to: P.O. Box 80, 42141
Founded in: 1973
Number of members: 300
Magazine: *Quarterly of the South
Central Kentucky Historical and
Genealogical Society*
Major programs: historic site,
    markers, oral history, educational
    programs, book publishing, historic
    preservation

GOLDEN POND

The Homeplace-1850
Land Between the Lakes, 42231
Telephone: (502) 924-5602
Federal agency, authorized by
    Tennessee Valley Authority

Founded in: 1976
Ron Westphal, Manager
Staff: full time 3, part time 8
Major programs: museum, school
    programs, historic preservation,
    living history
Period of collections: mid-19th
    century

GREENSBURG

**Green County Historical
Society, Inc.**
P.O. Box 276, 42743
Private agency
Wilma De Spain, President
Number of members: 335
Staff: volunteer 1
Magazine: *Green County Review*
Major programs: archives, historic
    site(s), markers, book publishing,
    newsletters/pamphlets, historic
    preservation, records
    management, research,
    genealogical services
Period of collections: 1793-present

HARLAN

Genealogical Society of Harlan
P.O. Box 1498, 40831
Private agency
Founded in: 1982
Holly Fee, President
Number of members: 215
Magazine: *Footprints*
Major programs:
    newsletters/pamphlets, research,
    genealogical services
Period of collections: 1800-1900

HARRODSBURG

Harrodsburg Historical Society
220 S. Chiles St.
Mail to: P.O. Box 316, 40330
Founded in: 1908
Howard Gregory, President
Number of members: 100
Staff: volunteer 16
Major programs: library, book
    publishing, historic preservation,
    research, genealogical services
Period of collections: 1785-present

Old Ft. Harrod State Park
S. College St.
Telephone: (606) 734-3314
Mail to: P.O. Box 156, 40330
State agency, authorized by State
    Parks Department
Susan T. Barrington, Park
    Superintendent
Staff: full time 1, part time 16
Major programs: museum, historic
    preservation, exhibits, living history
Period of collections: 1770s-1900

Shakertown at Pleasant Hill, Inc.
3500 Lexington Rd., 40330
Telephone: (606) 734-5411
Private agency
Founded in: 1961
James C. Thomas, President
Number of members: 2,000
Staff: full time 140, part time 40
Major programs: museum, historic
    site(s), historic preservation,
    research, exhibits
Period of collections: 1805-1910

HARTFORD

**Ohio County Historical
Society, Inc.**
415 Mulberry St.
Telephone: (502) 298-3177
Mail to: P.O. Box 44, 42347
Private agency
Founded in: 1971
Earl Russell, President
Number of members: 250
Staff: volunteer 20
Major programs: museum, historic
    site(s), markers, book publishing,
    newsletters/pamphlets, annual
    pageant
Period of collections: 1800-1900

Pennyroyal Area Museum
217 E. 9th St., 42240
Telephone: (502) 887-4270
Founded in: 1975
Questionnaire not received

HAWESVILLE

Hancock County Historical Society
County Administration Bldg., 42348
County agency
Founded in: 1974
Horace L. Temple, President
Number of members: 85
Major programs: archives, museum,
    historic site(s), markers, junior
    history, oral history,
    newsletters/pamphlets, historic
    preservation

HAZARD

**Perry County Genealogical and
Historical Society, Inc.**
301 Kentucky Blvd., 41701
Telephone: (606) 436-3864
Private agency
Founded in: 1979
Virginia Stephens, Vice President
Number of members: 152
Staff: volunteer 4
Major programs: library, junior
    history, book publishing,
    newsletters/pamphlets
Period of collections: 1700-1900

HENDERSON

**Henderson County Genealogical
and Historical Society**
City Bldg.
Telephone: (502) 826-7565
Mail to: P.O. Box 715, 42420
County agency
Founded in: 1922
Frieda Dannheiser, Director
Number of members: 52
Major programs: markers, book
    publishing, newsletters/pamphlets,
    historic preservation, research,
    photographic collections,
    genealogical services
Period of collections: 1700-present

**John J. Audubon Memorial
Museum**
U.S. Hwy. 41, N
Telephone: (502) 827-1893
Mail to: P.O. Box 576, 42420
State agency, authorized by
    Department of Parks
Founded in: 1938
Terry Sheckels, Curator

Staff: full time 1, part time 1
Major programs: museum, records
  management, exhibits,
  photographic collections
Period of collections: 1810-1865

HIGHLAND HEIGHTS

Museum of Anthropology
Landrum Academic Center, Northern
  Kentucky University, 41076
Telephone: (606) 572-5259
State agency, authorized by the
  university
Founded in: 1976
James F. Hopgood, Director
Staff: volunteer 2
Major programs: archives,
  manuscripts, museum, exhibits,
  archaeology programs, contract
  archaeology
Period of collections: prehistoric

HOPKINSVILLE

Christian County Historical Society
Mail to: P.O. Box 890, 42240
Founded in: 1963
William T. Turner, City-County
  Historian
Number of members: 250
Major programs: archives, museum,
  tours/pilgrimages, oral history,
  educational programs
Period of collections: 1784-present

**Hopkinsville-Christian County
  Pride, Inc.**
P.O. Box 4096, 42240
Telephone: (502) 887-4026
City and state agency
Founded in: 1982
Kit Garrett, Executive Director
Staff: full time 2, part time 1
Major programs: historic
  preservation, beautification and
  downtown revitalization project

Pennyroyal Area Museum
217 E. 9th St., 42240
Telephone: (502) 887-4270
City and county agency
Founded in: 1975
Anita J. Darnell, Director
Number of members: 235
Staff: full time 3, volunteer 4
Major programs: archives, museum,
  tours/pilgrimages, oral history,
  book publishing,
  newsletters/pamphlets, records
  management, research, exhibits
Period of collections: 1840s-1970s

HYDEN

Leslie County Historical Society
Telephone: (606) 672-2460
Mail to: P.O. Box 498, 41749
County agency, authorized by Leslie
  County Public Library
Founded in: 1976
Willa Hood, Society Advisor
Staff: volunteer 5
Major programs: library, archives,
  museum, historic site(s), school
  programs, records management,
  audiovisual programs,
  genealogical services
Period of collections: 1865-present

IRVINE

**Edwards and Rose Genealogical
  Heritage**
Telephone: (606) 723-7366/723-4759
Mail to: P.O. Box 217, 40336
Private agency
Founded in: 1980
Eva Dean Edwards, Co-administrator
Staff: volunteer 2
Major programs: library, manuscripts,
  book publishing, research,
  genealogical services
Period of collections: 1800-1900

IRVINGTON

**Frymire Weather Service and
  Museum**
314 N. Chestnut St.
Telephone: (502) 547-3951
Mail to: P.O. Box 33, 40146
Private agency
Founded in: 1966
L. H. Frymire, Treeologist/President
Staff: volunteer 5
Major programs: museum, historic
  site(s), oral history, school
  programs, newsletters/pamphlets,
  historic preservation, research,
  exhibits, folklore, history of cock
  fighting

JEFFERSONTOWN

**Jeffersontown and Southeast
  Jefferson County Historical
  Society**
2432 Merriwood Dr., 40299
Telephone: (502) 267-1715
Founded in: 1974
Questionnaire not received

LEITCHFIELD

Grayson County Historical Society
E. Main St., 42754
Telephone: (502) 879-8694
Mail to: Falls of Rough, 40119
County agency
Founded in: 1977
Burl St. Clair, President
Number of members: 200
Staff: volunteer 10
Magazine: The Graysonite
Major programs: museum, markers,
  historic preservation
Period of collections: 1810-1900

LEXINGTON

**Betty D. Eastin Historical Costume
  Collection, Department of Human
  Environment**
315 Erikson Hall, University of
  Kentucky, 40506
Telephone: (606) 257-4917
State agency, authorized by the
  university
Staff: volunteer 2
Major programs: museum, history of
  costumes and textiles
Period of collections: post-1890s

**Blue Grass Trust for Historic
  Preservation**
Hunt-Morgan House, 201 N. Mill St..
  40508
Telephone: (606) 253-0362
Private agency

Founded in: 1955
Kirby Turner, Executive Director
Number of members: 700
Staff: full time 3, part time 3,
  volunteer 50
Magazine: Preservation News
Major programs: library, museum,
  historic site(s), markers,
  tours/pilgrimages, school
  programs, newsletters/pamphlets,
  historic preservation, exhibits,
  audiovisual programs, revolving
  fund, lecture series
Period of collections: 1700-1945

Kentucky Heritage Quilt Society
P.O. Box 23392, 40503
Telephone: (502) 863-0939
  (president)
Private agency
Founded in: 1981
Lysa Scarborough, President
Number of members: 300
Staff: volunteer 14
Major programs: oral history, book
  publishing, newsletters/pamphlets,
  exhibits, seminars, workshops,
  documentation of quiltmaking and
  quilting instruction and contests

Kentucky Horse Park
4089 Iron Works Pike, 40511
Telephone: (606) 233-4303
State agency, authorized by Tourism
  Cabinet
Founded in: 1978
Bill Cooke, Museum Director
Staff: full time 6, part time 8
Major programs: library, museum,
  research, exhibits, equine history
Period of collections: 15th
  century-present

Kentucky Humanities Council
Ligon House, University of Kentucky,
  40506-0442
Telephone: (606) 257-5932
Authorized by the National
  Endowment for the Humanities
Founded in: 1973
Ramona Lumpkin, Executive Director
Staff: full time 3, part time 2
Magazine: THINK The Humanities IN
  Kentucky
Major programs: library, archives,
  museum, historic site(s), oral
  history, school programs, historic
  preservation, exhibits, living
  history, audiovisual programs,
  archaeology programs,
  photographic collections, public
  prgramming in the humanities

Lexington Cemetery Company, Inc.
833 W. Main St., 40508-2094
Telephone: (606) 255-5522
Private agency
Founded in: 1849
Robert F. Wachs, General Manager
Staff: full time 6
Major programs: archives, historic
  site(s), tours, genealogical services
Period of collections: 1849-present

**Lexington-Fayette County Historic
  Commission**
253 Market St., 40508
Telephone: (606) 255-8312
Founded in: 1973

Staff: full time 2, part time 1,
volunteer 15
Major programs: library, historic sites
preservation, markers, oral history,
educational programs, books,
newsletters/pamphlets
Period of collections: 1783-present

Photographic Archives
University of Kentucky Libraries,
40506
Telephone: (606) 258-8634
Founded in: 1977
Staff: full time 2, part time 2
Major programs: archives, museum,
educational programs
Period of collections: 1840-1920

**Special Collections and Archives,
M.I. King Libraries**
University of Kentucky, 40506
Telephone: (606) 257-8611
State agency, authorized by the
university
Major programs: library, archives,
manuscripts, oral history, exhibits,
audiovisual programs,
photographic collections,
genealogical services
Period of collections: 19th-20th
centuries

**University Museum of
Anthropology**
211 Lafferty Hall, University of
Kentucky, 40502
Telephone: (606) 257-8840
State agency, authorized by the
university
Founded in: 1931
George R. Milner, Director/Curator
Staff: full time 1, part time 3,
volunteer 3
Major programs: museum, school
programs, research, exhibits,
archaeology programs
Period of collections: prehistoric

Waveland State Shrine
Higbee Mill Rd., 40503
Telephone: (606) 272-3611
Questionnaire not received

LIBERTY

**Bicentennial Heritage Corporation
of Casey County, Inc.**
P.O. Box 356, 42539
Telephone: (606) 787-6194
County agency
Founded in: 1975
Gladys Cotham Thomas, President
Number of members: 100
Staff: volunteer 6
Magazine: *Casey County, Ky. Kinfolk*
Major programs: library, book
publishing, newsletters/pamphlets,
genealogy
Period of collections: 1700-present

LONDON

Laurel County Historical Society
P.O. Box 816, 40741
State agency, authorized by
Kentucky Historical Society
Founded in: 1961
Larry Gray, President
Number of members: 59
Staff: volunteer 5

Major programs: archives, book
publishing, genealogical services
Period of collections: 1920-present

LOUISA

Big Sandy Valley Historical Society
407 Madison St., 41230
Telephone: (606) 638-4889
State agency, authorized by
Kentucky Historical Society
Founded in: 1970
James F. Moore, Treasurer
Number of members: 205
Staff: volunteer 9
Magazine: *Sandy Valley Heritage*
Major programs: historic site(s),
junior history, book publishing,
historic preservation, genealogical
services
Period of collections: 1700s-present

LOUISVILLE

American Saddle Horse Museum
730 W. Main St., 40202
Telephone: (502) 585-1342
Founded in: 1962
Questionnaire not received

The Brennan House
631 S. 5th St., 40202
Telephone: (502) 584-7425
Private agency, authorized by the
Filson Club and the Kentucky
Opera
Founded in: 1982
Anita Streeter, Manager
Staff: full time 1, part time 1,
volunteer 12
Major programs: museum,
tours/pilgrimages, exhibits,
audiovisual programs
Period of collections: 1880-1910

The Filson Club
118 W. Breckinridge St., 40203
Telephone: (502) 582-3727
Private agency
Founded in: 1884
James R. Bentley, Director

Number of members: 3,000
Staff: full time 11, part time 4
Magazine: *The Filson Club History
Quarterly*
Major programs: library, manuscripts,
museum, historic site(s), book
publishing, newsletters/pamphlets,
photographic collections,
genealogical services, lectures,
educational programs
Period of collections: 1750-1950

Historic Homes Foundation, Inc.
3033 Bardstown Rd., 40205
Telephone: (502) 458-5386
Private agency
Founded in: 1956
Gladys Horvath, Executive Director
Number of members: 1,500
Staff: full time 7, part time 16,
volunteer 100
Major programs: museum, historic
site(s), newsletters/pamphlets,
historic preservation, audiovisual
programs
Period of collections: 1790-1830

**Historic Landmarks and
Preservation Districts
Commission**
727 W. Main St., 40202
Telephone: (505) 587-3501
City agency
Founded in: 1973
Ann S. Hassett, Executive
Administrator
Staff: full time 7
Major programs: historic
preservation, research,
photographic collections, design
and technical assistance,
investment consultation
Period of collections: 1860-1920

**Jefferson County Office of Historic
Preservation and Archives**
100 Fiscal Court Bldg., 40202
Telephone: (502) 581-5761
County agency, authorized by
Jefferson Fiscal Court

Farmington, owned by Historic Homes Foundation, Inc., in Louisville.—Photograph by
Charles W. Hill

Founded in: 1978
Douglas Stern, Administrator
Staff: full time 4, part time 2
Major programs: archives, historic
site(s), historic preservation,
records management,
scenic-historic preservation
easements
Period of collections: late 1700s-early
1900s

Kentucky Derby Museum Corporation
704 Central Ave., 40208
Telephone: (502) 637-1111
Mail to: P.O. Box 3513, 40201
Private agency
Founded in: 1981
William W. Ray, Executive Director
Staff: full time 6
Magazine: *Inside Track*
Major programs: library, archives,
museum, tours/pilgrimages, school
programs, newsletters/pamphlets,
research, exhibits, audiovisual
programs, photographic
collections, sports history
Period of collections: 1875-present

Kentucky Railway Museum
Ormsby Station, Dorsey Lane at
LaGrange Rd., 40223
Telephone: (502) 245-6035
Mail to: P.O. Box 295, 40201
Private agency
Founded in: 1957
Edward Hawkins, President
Number of members: 182
Staff: volunteer 75
Magazine: *Kentucky Railway
Museum News*
Major programs: archives, museum,
markers, tours, excursions, school
programs, newsletters/pamphlets,
historic preservation, exhibits, main
line railway operations
Period of collections: 1900-1960

Locust Grove Historic Home
561 Blankenbaker Lane, 40207
Telephone: (502) 897-9845
County agency, authorized by
Historic Homes Foundation
Founded in: 1961
Nancy Jacoby, Director
Number of members: 900
Staff: full time 3, part time 3,
volunteer 88
Major programs: museum, historic
site(s), tours/pilgrimages, oral
history, newsletters/pamphlets,
historic preservation, exhibits,
living history, audiovisual
programs, photographic
collections
Period of collections: Colonial era

Louisville Historical League
716 W. Main St., 40202
Telephone: (502) 581-9124
Private agency
Founded in: 1972
Debra C. Reynolds, President
Number of members: 500
Staff: volunteer 10
Major programs: markers,
tours/pilgrimages, oral history,
school programs,
newsletters/pamphlets, audiovisual
programs

Lou Tate Foundation, Inc.—The Little Loomhouse
328 Kenwood Hill Rd., 40214
Telephone: (502) 367-4792/239-7382
Private agency
Founded in: 1980
Debra C. Reynolds, Executive
Director
Number of members: 200
Staff: volunteer 15
Major programs: library, archives,
museum, historic site(s),
tours/pilgrimages, oral history,
school programs, book publishing,
newsletters/pamphlets, historic
preservation, research, exhibits,
living history, photographic
collections, hand-weaving and
spinning lessons
Period of collections: 1700s-present

Middle Ohio River Chapter, Sons and Daughters of Pioneer Rivermen, Inc.
4223 Cutliff Dr., 40218
Telephone: (502) 491-0009
Founded in: 1976
Jack E. Custer, President
Number of members: 200
Staff: volunteer 5
Magazine: *M.O.R. Riverview*
Major programs: living history,
steamboat operations
Period of collections: 1810-present

Museum of History and Science
727 W. Main St., 40202
Private agency
Founded in: 1975
William M. Sudduth, Executive
Director
Staff: full time 25, part time 4,
volunteer 120
Magazine: *Devonian Ledger*
Major programs: library, archives,
museum, book publishing,
newsletters/pamphlets, exhibits,
living history, archaeology
programs, science programs
Period of collections: 1871-present

Portland Museum
2308 Portland Ave., 40212
Telephone: (502) 776-7678
Private agency
Founded in: 1978
Nathalie Taft Andrews, Director
Staff: full time 2, volunteer 2
Major programs: archives, museum,
junior history, book publishing,
research, exhibits, audiovisual
programs, photographic
collections, field services
Period of collections: 19th century

Preservation Alliance of Louisville and Jefferson County, Inc.
716 W. Main St., 40202
Telephone: (502) 583-8622
Private agency
Founded in: 1972
Richard Jett, Executive Director
Number of members: 900
Staff: full time 4, volunteer 200
Magazine: *Preservation Press*
Major programs: historic site(s),
tours/pilgrimages, school
programs, book publishing,
newsletters/pamphlets, historic
preservation, research, audiovisual

programs, photographic
collections, architecture, historic
property development and
planning, special events,
preservation consultation
Period of collections: 1779-present

Sons of the American Revolution Museum
1000 4th St., 40203
Private agency, authorized by
American Association, Sons of the
American Revolution
Founded in: 1896
James A. Williams, Jr., Director
Number of members: 23,000
Major programs: library, archives,
manuscripts, museum, historic
site(s), markers, tours/pilgrimages,
junior history, oral history, school
programs, newsletters/pamphlets,
historic preservation, records
management, research, exhibits,
living history, audiovisual
programs, photographic
collections, genealogical service
Period of collections: 1763-1815

Jacques Timothé Boucher Sieur De Montbrun French Heritage Society
Telephone: (502) 895-5682
Mail to: 3004 Beals Dr., 40206
Founded in: 1976
T. Weldon DeMunbrun, President
Number of members: 500
Staff: volunteer 25
Major programs: historic sites
preservation, junior history, books,
newsletters/pamphlets
Period of collections: 1770-1820

University Photographic Archives
University of Louisville, 40292
Telephone: (502) 588-6752
State agency
Founded in: 1967
James C. Anderson, Curator
Staff: full time 4, part time 1
Major programs: library, archives,
manuscripts, museum,
photographic collections
Period of collections: 1839-present

University Archives
University of Louisville, 40292
Telephone: (502) 588-6674
State agency
Founded in: 1973
William J. Morison, Director
Staff: full time 7, part time 2
Major programs: library, archives,
manuscripts, oral history, records
management
Period of collections: post-Civil
War-present

MADISONVILLE

Historical Society of Hopkins County, Inc.
107 Union St., 42431
Telephone: (502) 821-3986
Private agency, authorized by city
and county governments
Founded in: 1974
Donna F. Slaton, President
Number of members: 400
Staff: part time 1, volunteer 8

Major programs: library, museum, historic sites preservation, book publishing
Period of collections: 1783-present

Hopkins County Genealogical Society, Inc.
31 S. Main St., Hopkins County Public Library
Telephone: (502) 821-3736
Mail to: P.O. Box 51, 42431
Founded in: 1969
Debbie Hammonds, President
Number of members: 125
Staff: volunteer 8
Magazine: *Yesterdays Tuckaways*
Major programs: book publishing, genealogy
Period of collections: 1750-present

MARION

Crittenden County Historical Society, Inc.
W. Carlisle St.
Telephone: (502) 965-9257
Mail to: P.O. Box 25, 42064
Private agency
Founded in: 1962
Barney P. McNeely, Chair
Number of members: 130
Major programs: library, museum, junior history, oral history, historic preservation, exhibits
Period of collections: 1783-1900

MARTHA

Lawrence County Regional Historical Society
HC-80, Box 10, 41159
Telephone: (606) 652-3818
Founded in: 1982
Lucille Sparks-Smallwood, Board Chair
Number of members: 50
Magazine: *Lawrence County Regional Quarterly*
Major programs: newsletters/pamphlets, exhibits, genealogical services, folklore

MAYSVILLE

Mason County Museum—Maysville and Mason County Historical and Scientific Association
215 Sutton St., 41056
Telephone: (606) 564-5865
Private agency
Founded in: 1878
Louis N. Browning, Administrator
Number of members: 345
Staff: full time 2, part time 2, volunteer 10
Major programs: library, archives, manuscripts, museum, tours/pilgrimages, school programs, book publishing, newsletters/pamphlets, research, exhibits, photographic collections, genealogical services
Period of collections: 1783-1900

MIDDLESBORO

Bell County Historical Society, Inc.
P.O. Box 1344, 40965
Private agency
Founded in: 1982

Frances Hyde Gambrel, President
Number of members: 112
Staff: full time 6, volunteer 6
Magazine: *Gateway*
Major programs: junior history, oral history, book publishing, newsletters/pamphlets, historic preservation, exhibits, audiovisual programs, photographic collections, genealogical services
Period of collections: 1887-present

MIDDLETOWN

Historic Middletown, Inc.
Mail to: P.O. Box 43013, 40243
Founded in: 1966
Blaine A. Guthrie, Jr., President
Number of members: 200
Staff: volunteer 30
Major programs: historic sites preservation, markers, tours/pilgrimages, oral history, educational programs

Kentucky Baptist Historical Commission—Kentucky Baptist Historical Society
10701 Shelbyville Rd.
Telephone: (502) 245-4101
Mail to: P.O. Box 43433, 40243
Private agency, authorized by Kentucky Baptist Convention
Founded in: 1905 (society); 1966 (commission)
Doris Yeiser, Secretary
Number of members: 172
Magazine: *The Kentucky Baptist Heritage*
Major programs: manuscripts, historic site(s), markers, tours/pilgrimages, book publishing, newsletters/pamphlets, genealogical services
Period of collections: 1905-present

MONTICELLO

Wayne County Historical Society
Mail to: P.O. Box 320, 42633
Private agency
Founded in: 1977
Andrea M. Simpson, Secretary
Number of members: 60
Major programs: historic site(s), book publishing, newsletters/pamphlets, records management, genealogical services
Period of collections: 1800-1900

MOREHEAD

Dean and Creech Families of America
Rt. 6, Box 498, 40351
Telephone: (606) 784-9145
Private agency
Founded in: 1975
Lloyd Dean, Co-director
Staff: volunteer 20
Magazine: *Dean & Creech Family News*
Major programs: manuscripts, oral history, newsletters/pamphlets, historic preservation, living history, photographic collections, genealogical services
Period of collections: A.D. 1200-present

Rowan County Historical Society
Rowan Public Library, 1st St.
Telephone: (606) 784-9145
Mail to: Rt. 6, Box 498, 40351
Founded in: 1977
Questionnaire not received

MT. STERLING

Montgomery County Historical Society
Telephone: (606) 498-1154
Mail to: c/o Raymond Parker, 40353
Questionnaire not received

MT. WASHINGTON

Mt. Washington Historical Society
410 Flatlick Rd., 40047
Founded in: 1977
Charles Long, President
Number of members: 25
Major programs: museum, markers, tours/pilgrimages, oral history, school programs, book publishing, historic preservation, exhibits, audiovisual programs, photographic collections, genealogical services

MORGANTOWN

Butler County Historical and Genealogical Society, Inc.
Telephone: (502) 526-4328
Mail to: P.O. Box 435, 42261
Founded in: 1976
Ermie Lee Martin, President
Number of members: 50
Staff: volunteer 8
Magazine: *Kentucky Traces*
Major programs: museum, book publishing
Period of collections: 1810-1900

MUNFORDVILLE

Hart County Historical Society
Chapline Bldg., Main St.
Mail to: P.O. Box 606, 42765
County agency
Founded in: 1969
Jerry Ralston, President
Number of members: 397
Staff: full time 1, volunteer 7
Major programs: museum, historic preservation, genealogical services
Period of collections: early 1800s-present

MURRAY

National Museum of the Boy Scouts of America
Murray State University, 42071-3308
Telephone: (502) 762-3383
Private agency, authorized by national organization and the university
Founded in: 1959
Darwin P. Kelsey, Director
Staff: full time 11, part time 36, volunteer 90
Major programs: library, manuscripts, museum, oral history, school programs, research, exhibits, national and international scouting
Period of collections: 1900-present

Wrather West Kentucky Museum
Murray State University, 42071-3308
Telephone: (502) 762-4771
Authorized by the university
Founded in: 1982
Martha L. Guier, Director
Staff: full time 2
Major programs: museum
Period of collections: 19th-20th
  centuries

NEWPORT

Kentucky Covered Bridge
  Association
(606) 441-7000
Mail to: P.O. Box 100, 41076
Questionnaire not received

NICHOLASVILLE

Jessamine Historical Society
311 W. Maple St., 40356
Founded in: 1969
Mrs. Lyman Hager, President
Number of members: 45
Major programs: historic site(s),
  junior history, oral history, book
  publishing, historic preservation,
  genealogical services
Period of collections: 1783-1865

OLDTOWN

Greenup County Historical Society
41163
Questionnaire not received

OWENSBORO

Kentucky Room,
  Owensboro-Daviess County
  Public Library
450 Griffith Ave., 42301
Telephone: (502) 684-0211
City and county agency
Founded in: 1911
Shelia E. Heflin, Supervisor
Staff: full time 1, part time 1
Major programs: library, archives,
  oral history, research, genealogical
  services
Period of collections: 1792-present

Owensboro Area Museum
2829 S. Griffith Ave., 42301
Telephone: (502) 683-0296
Private agency
Founded in: 1966
Joe Ford, Director
Number of members: 450
Staff: full time 5, part time 3,
  volunteer 50
Major programs: archives, museum,
  oral history, school programs,
  records management, exhibits,
  archaeology programs, field
  services, planetarium
Period of collections: 1750-present

West-Central Kentucky Family
  Research Association
Telephone: (502) 684-4150
Mail to: P.O. Box 1932, 42301
Private agency
Founded in: 1968
Anna Midkiff, President
Number of members: 750
Magazine: The Bulletin/Kentucky
  Family Records

Major programs: library, archives,
  manuscripts, museum, oral history,
  book publishing,
  newsletters/pamphlets, historic
  preservation, living history,
  genealogical services, microfilming
  of historic records
Period of collections: 1700-present

OWENTON

Owen County Historical Society
304 Roland Ave., 40359
Telephone: (502) 484-3976
Questionnaire not received

PADUCAH

Paducah-McCracken County
  Growth, Inc.
500 Clark St.
Telephone: (502) 443-9284
Mail to: P.O. Box 2267, 42001
Private agency
Founded in: 1980
Richard Holland, Director
Staff: full time 2
Major programs:
  newsletters/pamphlets, historic
  preservation

William Clark Market House
  Museum
S. 2nd St.
Telephone: (502) 443-7759
Mail to: P.O. Box 12, 42001
Private agency
Founded in: 1968
Charles Manchester, Director
Number of members: 250
Staff: full time 1, volunteer 35
Major programs: museum
Period of collections: 1850-1950

PAINTSVILLE

Big Sandy Valley Genealogical
  Society
1215 Stafford Ave., 41240
Telephone: (606) 789-3416
Founded in: 1977
Questionnaire not received

Big Sandy Valley Historical Society
1215 Stafford Ave., 41240
Telephone: (606) 789-3416
Founded in: 1970
Questionnaire not received

Johnson County Historical Society
P.O. Box 788, 41240
Telephone: (606) 789-4355
County agency
Founded in: 1961
W. H. Pelphney, President
Number of members: 100
Staff: volunteer 10
Magazine: The Highland Echo
Major programs: library, archives,
  manuscripts, historic site(s),
  markers, book publishing,
  newsletters/pamphlets, historic
  preservation, research,
  genealogical services
Period of collections:
  prehistoric-present

Research Historians
Rts. 23 and 460, N, 41240
Telephone: (606) 789-4890
Founded in: 1969
Questionnaire not received

PARIS

Cane Ridge Meeting House
1655 Cane Ridge Rd., 40361
Telephone: (606) 987-5350
Private agency, authorized by Cane
  Ridge Preservation Project, Inc.
Founded in: 1791
Franklin R. McGuire, Curator
Staff: part time 5, volunteer 8
Magazine: Cane Ridge Bulletin
Major programs: archives, museum,
  historic site(s), tours/pilgrimages,
  oral history, book publishing,
  newsletters/pamphlets, historic
  preservation, exhibits, audiovisual
  programs, photographic
  collections

PIKEVILLE

Pike County Historical Society
256 Win Right Rd., 41501
Telephone: (606) 432-0400
County agency
Founded in: 1980
Eldon J. May, President
Number of members: 68
Staff: volunteer 6
Major programs: historic site(s), oral
  history, book publishing, historic
  preservation
Period of collections: 1800-present

PIPPA PASSES

Appalachian Oral History Project
Alice Lloyd College, 41844
Telephone: (606) 368-2101
Private agency, authorized by the
  college
Founded in: 1970
Katherine R. Martin, Director
Staff: part time 1
Magazine: Mountain Memories
Major programs: oral history,
  newsletters/pamphlets, research
Period of collections: 1930-1950

RICHMOND

Eastern Kentucky University
  Archives
Cammack Bldg., Eastern Kentucky
  University, 40475
Telephone: (606) 624-2760
State agency
Founded in: 1906
Charles Hay, Archivist
Number of members: 1
Staff: full time 2
Major programs: archives,
  manuscripts, oral history, records
  management, research, exhibits,
  audiovisual programs,
  photographic collections,
  university history
Period of collections: 20th century

John Wilson Townsend Room,
  University Library
Eastern Kentucky University, 40475
Telephone: (606) 622-1792
State agency, authorized by the
  university
Founded in: 1930
Sharon Brown McConnell, Curator
Staff: full time 2, part time 6
Major programs: library, manuscripts
Period of collections: 1790

Jonathan Truman Dorris Museum
Eastern Kentucky University, 40475
Telephone: (606) 622-5585
Founded in: 1926
Questionnaire not received

Madison County Historical Society
515 W. Main St., 40475
Telephone: (606) 623-1250
Private agency
Founded in: 1933
James J. Shannon, Jr., President
Number of members: 250
Staff: volunteer 16
Magazine: *Kentucky Pioneer*
Major programs: library, manuscripts,
   museum, historic site(s), markers,
   book publishing,
   newsletters/pamphlets
Period of collections: from 1775

Society of Boonesborough
515 W. Main St., 40475
Private agency
Founded in: 1975
James J. Shannon, Jr., President
Number of members: 500
Staff: volunteer 2
Magazine: *Boonesborough Post*
Major programs: library, museum,
   historic site(s), markers
Period of collections: 1775-1810

RINEYVILLE

Bewley Family Association
Telephone: (502) 877-2475
Mail to: P.O. Box 78, 40162
Private agency
Founded in: 1980
Jack Bewley, Editor
Number of members: 180
Magazine: *Bewley Roots*
Major programs: historic site(s), book
   publishing, newsletters/pamphlets,
   genealogical services, family
   reunions
Period of collections: 1720-present

Holbert Family Associaiton
Telephone: (502) 877-2475
Mail to: P.O. Box 78, 40162
Private agency
Founded in: 1980
S. Jack Bewley, Editor
Magazine: *Holbert Herald*
Major programs:
   newsletters/pamphlets, family
   reunions
Period of collections: 1700-present

RUSSELLVILLE

Hardy Memorial Museum
296 S. Main, 42276
Questionnaire not received

**Logan County Genealogical
Society, Inc.**
c/o Logan County Library, 201 W. 6th
   St., 42276
Private agency
Founded in: 1980
Mrs. Hershel Russell, President
Number of members: 20
Staff: volunteer 10
Major programs: library, oral history,
   book publishing, historic
   preservation, research,
   genealogical services
Period of collections: 1790-1800

SALYERSVILLE

Magoffin County Historical Society
Church St.
Telephone: (606) 349-2411 (library)
Mail to: P.O. Box 222, 41465
County agency
Founded in: 1978
Todd Preston, President
Number of members: 602
Staff: volunteer 30
Major programs: markers, school
   programs, book publishing,
   newsletters/pamphlets, historic
   preservation, research,
   photographic collections,
   genealogical services
Period of collections: 1800-present

SHELBYVILLE

Shelby County Historical Society
Telephone: (502) 633-2767
Mail to: P.O. Box 444, 40065
Founded in: 1963
Lewis D. Cottongim, President
Number of members: 187
Major programs: library, historic
   site(s), tours/pilgrimages, book
   publishing, newsletters/pamphlets,
   historic preservation, research
Period of collections: 1783-1918

SOMERSET

**Pulaski County Historical
Society, Inc.**
Library Bldg., N. Main St., 42501
Telephone: (606) 679-1734
Founded in: 1966
Mabel Pitts, President
Number of members: 236
Staff: volunteer 12
Major programs: library, book
   publishing, newsletters/pamphlets,
   historic preservation, photographic
   collections, genealogical services
Period of collections: 1799-1900

SOUTH UNION

Shakertown at South Union
Hwy. 73, 42283
Telephone: (502) 542-4167
Private agency, authorized by
   Shakertown Revisted, Inc.
Founded in: 1960
John Campbell, Director
Number of members: 150
Staff: full time 1, part time 6,
   volunteer 15
Magazine: *South Union Messenger*
Major programs: museum, historic
   sites preservation,
   tours/pilgrimages,
   newsletters/pamphlets, exhibits
Period of collections: 1807-1922

SPRINGFIELD

Lincoln Homestead State Park
Rt. 1, 40069
Telephone: (606) 336-7461
State agency, authorized by
   Commonwealth of Kentucky State
   Parks
Founded in: 1934
Bill Padgett, Superintendent
Staff: full time 6
Major programs: historic site(s)
Period of collections: 1777-1806

**Washington County Historical
Society**
Simmstown, 40069
Telephone: (606) 336-3290
Founded in: 1933
Questionnaire not received

SUMMER SHADE

Metcalfe County Historical Society
Rt. 1, Box 371, 42166
Telephone: (502) 428-3391
County agency
Founded in: 1979
Kay Harbison, President
Number of members: 55
Magazine: *History Speaks*

UNION

Big Bone Lick State Park
Rt. 2
Telephone: (606) 384-3522
Mail to: P.O. Box 92, 41091
Founded in: 1960
Staff: full time 8, part time 18
Major programs: museum
Period of collections: prehistoric-1783

VANCEBURG

Lewis County Historical Society
P.O. Box 212, 41179
Telephone: (606) 796-3778
Founded in: 1976
Number of members: 109
Magazine: *Shakin' and Diggin'*
Major programs: library, archives,
   oral history, newsletters/pamphlets,
   historic preservation
Period of collections: 1807-present

VINE GROVE

Ancestral Trails Historical Society
127 W. Main St.
Mail to: P.O. Box 573, 40175
Private agency
Founded in: 1967
Jack Bewley, President
Number of members: 445
Staff: volunteer 12
Major programs: book publishing,
   newsletters/pamphlets,
   genealogical services
Period of collections: 1790-1900

WARSAW

Gallatin County Historical Society
Gallatin County Courthouse Annex,
   W. Main, 41095
Telephone: (606) 567-2639
Founded in: 1972
Number of members: 55
Staff: volunteer 5
Major programs: archives,
   manuscripts, museum, historic
   sites preservation,
   tours/pilgrimages, junior history,
   oral history, educational programs,
   newsletters/pamphlets
Period of collections: 1783-present

WASHINGTON

**Limestone Chapter, Daughters of
   the American Revolution**
Washington, 41096
Mail to: c/o Regent, Maysville, 41056

Private agency, authorized by
National Society, Daughters of the
American Revolution
Founded in: 1923
Mrs. James D. Burrows, Regent
Number of members: 104
Major programs: museum, historic
site(s), junior history, historic
preservation
Period of collections: 1810-1860

WICKLIFFE

Wickliffe Mounds Research Center
Hwy. 51, W.
Telephone: (502) 335-3681
Mail to: P.O. Box 155, 42087
State agency, authorized by Murray
State University
Founded in: 1983
Kit W. Wesler, Director
Staff: full time 2
Major programs: museum, historic
site(s), junior history, school
programs, research, exhibits,
archaeology programs
Period of collections: prehistoric

WILLIAMSTOWN

Grant County Historical Society
41097
Telephone: (606) 824-389
County agency
Founded in: 1976
Blanche Klinglesmith, President
Major programs: book publishing,
newsletter, historic preservation
Period of collections: 1865-present

WINCHESTER

Clark County Historical Society
14 Fairwood Lane, 40391
Founded in: 1965
Jack K. Hodgkin, President
Number of members: 50
Major programs: historic site(s),
markers, book publishing, historic
preservation, photographic
collections

LOUISIANA

ALEXANDRIA

**Historical Association of Central
Louisiana**
Mail to: P.O. Box 843, 71301
Founded in: 1975
Questionnaire not received

Kent Plantation House, Inc.
3601 Bayou Rapides, 71303
Telephone: (318) 445-5611
Private agency
Florence Hall, President
Number of members: 200
Major programs: museum, historic
site(s), historic preservation
Period of collections: 1800-1850

BASTROP

**Snyder Memorial Museum and
Creative Arts Center**
1620 E. Madison, 71220
Telephone: (318) 281-8760

Parish agency
Founded in: 1974
Patricia Price,
Director/Scholar-in-Residence
Number of members: 300
Staff: full time 1, part time 1
Major programs: museum,
tours/pilgrimages, junior history,
oral history, school programs,
research, exhibits, living history,
archaeology programs,
photographic collections
Period of collections: 1860-1910

BATON ROUGE

**Arts and Humanities Council of
Greater Baton Rouge**
427 Laurel St., 70801
Telephone: (504) 344-8558
Private agency
Founded in: 1948
Joseph Kyle Walls, Executive Director
Number of members: 1,000
Staff: 14
Major programs: museum, historic
site(s), tours/pilgrimages, oral
history, school programs, book
publishing, newsletters/pamphlets,
historic preservation, grantmaking,
local arts and humanities
Period of collections: 1924

Baton Rouge Firefighters' Museum
427 Laurel St., 70801
Telephone: (504) 344-8558
Founded in: 1978
Kyle Walls, Executive Director
Number of members: 900
Staff: full time 7, part time 1,
volunteer 300
Magazine: *Discover*
Major programs: museum
Period of collections: 1850-1930

**Comité des Archives de la
Louisiane**
124 Main St., 70801
Telephone: (504) 346-8050
Mail to: P.O. Box 44370, 70804
Private agency
Founded in: 1979
Damon Veach, President
Number of members: 50
Staff: volunteer 6
Magazine: *Le Raconteur*
Major programs: archives, book
publishing, newsletters/pamphlets,
historic preservation, records
management, research, exhibits,
genealogical services
Period of collections: Colonial
Louisiana-1900

**Department of Archives and
Manuscripts**
Middleton Library, Room 202, LSU,
70803
Telephone: (504) 388-2240
State agency, authorized by
Louisiana State University
Founded in: 1936
M. Stone Miller, Jr., Head
Staff: full time 5, part time 2
Major programs: archives,
manuscripts, oral history,
photographic history
Period of collections: late 1700s-early
1960s

Division of Archaeology
666 N. Foster Dr., 70806
Telephone: (504) 922-0368
Mail to: P.O. Box 44247, 70804
State agency
Founded in: 1974
Kathleen Byrd, State Archaeologist
Staff: full time 5, part time 2
Major programs:
newsletters/pamphlets, records
management, exhibits, audiovisual
programs, archaeology programs

Division of Historic Preservation
666 N. Foster Dr., Bldg. A, 70806
Telephone: (504) 922-0358
Mail to: P.O. Box 44247, 70804-4247
State agency, authorized by National
Historic Preservation Act
Founded in: 1968
Robert B. DeBlieux, State Historic
Preservation Officer
Staff: full time 8
Major programs: historic site(s),
markers, historic preservation

**Foundation for Historical
Louisiana, Inc.**
900 North Blvd., 70802
Telephone: (504) 387-2464
Private agency
Founded in: 1963
Carolyn Grega Bennett, Executive
Director
Number of members: 1,500
Staff: full time 3, part time 20,
volunteer 125
Magazine: *Foundation Flashes*
Major programs: museum,
tours/pilgrimages, educational
programs, markers
Period of collections: early 19th
century-present

Louisiana Arts and Science Center
100 S. River Rd., 70802
Telephone: (504) 344-9463
Mail to: P.O. Box 3373, 70821
Private agency
Founded in: 1956
Carol Sommerfeldt Gikas, Executive
Director
Staff: full time 23, part time 9
Major programs: museum, historic
site(s), school programs, exhibits
Period of collections: 1930-1962

**Louisiana Genealogical and
Historical Society**
Mail to: P.O. Box 3454, 70821
Founded in: 1954
Questionnaire not received

**Louisiana State Archives and
Records Service**
1515 Choctaw Dr., 70805
Telephone: (504) 342-5440
Mail to: P.O. Box 94125, 70804
State agency
Founded in: 1956
Donald J. Lemieux, Director/State
Archivist
Staff: full time 41, part time 1
Magazine: *Legacy*
Major programs: library, archives,
manuscripts, oral history,
newsletters/pamphlets, records
management, research, exhibits,
photographic collections,
genealogical services
Period of collections: 1764-present

LSU Rural Life Museum
4560 Essen Lane
Telephone: (504) 766-8241
Mail to: 6200 Burden Lane, 70808
State agency, authorized by
  Louisiana State University
Founded in: 1970
John E. Dutton, Head Curator
Staff: full time 3, volunteer 60
Major programs: library, museum,
  tours/pilgrimages, historic
  preservation, research, artifact
  identification
Period of collections: 1800-1920

Magnolia Mound Plantation
2161 Nicholson Dr., 70802
Telephone: (504) 343-4955
County agency
Founded in: 1975
Timothy J. Mullin, Director
Staff: full time 2, part time 12,
  volunteer 80
Major programs: museum, historic
  site(s), school programs, living
  history
Period of collections: 1780-1830

19th Louisiana Volunteer Infantry
2519 June St., 70808
Telephone: (504) 387-4295
Private agency
Founded in: 1980
Richard H. Holloway, Commander
Number of members: 20
Staff: volunteer 3
Magazine: The Pelican Dispatch
Major programs: historic site(s),
  markers, tours/pilgrimages, oral
  history, school programs, book
  publishing, newsletters/pamphlets,
  historic preservation, records
  management, research, exhibits,
  living history, photographic
  collections, field services
Period of collections: 1861-1865

Office of Cultural Development, Division of Historic Preservation
Louisiana Department of Culture,
  Recreation and Tourism
666 N. Foster Dr., 70806
Telephone: (504) 922-0358
Mail to: P.O. Box 44247, 70804
State agency
Founded in: 1969
Staff: full time 8
Major programs: historic site(s),
  markers, tax programs,
  environmental reviews

Oregon Trail Museum Association
Telephone: (308) 436-4340
Mail to: P.O. Box 427, 69341
Private agency, authorized by
  National Park Cooperating
  Association
Founded in: 1956
Jolene Kaufman, Business Manager
Number of members: 75
Staff: part time 1
Major programs: library, museum,
  historic site(s), markers, junior
  history, oral history, school
  programs, newsletters/pamphlets,
  historic preservation, research,
  living history, audiovisual
  programs, field services

BENTON

Bossier Restoration Foundation
Telephone: (318) 965-2218
Mail to: P.O. Box 94, 71006
Questionnaire not received

BLANCHARD

First Baptist Church Archives
201 Attaway
Telephone: (318) 929-3594
Mail to: P.O. Box 112, 71009
Private agency
Founded in: 1979
Kevin W. Sandifer, Director
Staff: volunteer 5
Major programs: library, archives,
  oral history, book publishing,
  newsletters/pamphlets, historic
  preservation, research, exhibits,
  photographic collections
Period of collections: 1865-present

CLINTON

East Feliciana Historical Preservation Society, Inc.
Mail to: P.O. Box 121, 70722
Private agency
Founded in: 1976
Mildred P. Worrell, President
Number of members: 200
Major programs: markers, historic
  preservation

East Feliciana Pilgrimage and Garden Club
Bank St.
Telephone: (504) 683-8708
Mail to: P.O. Box 560, 70722
Private agency
Founded in: 1968
Carolyn P. Thompson, President
Number of members: 125
Major programs: tours/pilgrimages,
  historic preservation
Period of collections: 1840-early
  1900s

DESTREHAN

Destrehan Plantation
9999 River Rd.
Telephone: (504) 764-9315
Mail to: P.O. Box 5, 70047
Private agency, authorized by River
  Road Historical Society
Founded in: 1968
Joan J. Douville, Administrator
Number of members: 350
Staff: full time 6, part time 6,
  volunteer 60
Major programs: museum, historic
  site(s), tours/pilgrimages, historic
  preservation, exhibits
Period of collections: 1787-1960

River Road Historical Society
9999 River Rd.
Telephone: (504) 764-9315
Mail to: P.O. Box 5, 70047
Founded in: 1968
Joan Douville, Administrator
Number of members: 500
Staff: full time 6, part time 4,
  volunteer 200
Magazine: Le Communique
Major programs: museum, historic
  site, tours/pilgrimages, educational

  programs, historic preservation,
  archaeology programs
Period of collections: 1787-1910

FORT POLK

Ft. Polk Military Museum
S. Carolina Ave., Bldg. 917
Telephone: (318) 535-7905
Mail to: P.O. Drawer R, 71459
Federal agency
Founded in: 1973
George S. Hammerschmidt,
  Director/Curator
Staff: full time 5
Major programs: library, museum,
  exhibits, photographic collections
Period of collections: W.W. II-present

HAMBURG

Commission des Avoyelles, Inc.
Telephone: (318) 964-2675
Mail to: P.O. Box 26, 71339
County agency
Founded in: 1974
Carlos A. Mayeux, Jr., President
Staff: volunteer 8
Major programs: archives,
  manuscripts, museum, historic
  site(s), markers, tours/pilgrimages,
  oral history, school programs, book
  publishing, newsletters/pamphlets,
  historic preservation, records
  management, research, exhibits,
  living history, audiovisual
  programs, photographic
  collections, genealogical services
Period of collections: 1790-present

HAMMOND

Southeast Louisiana Historical Association
Mail to: P.O. Box 1088, SLU, 70402
Founded in: 1972
Questionnaire not received

HOUMA

Terrebonne Genealogical Society
Mail to: Station 2, P.O. Box 295,
  70360
Private agency
Founded in: 1981
Phil Chauvin, President
Number of members: 400
Magazine: Terrebonne Life Lines
Major programs: library, school
  programs, book publishing,
  newsletters/pamphlets,
  genealogical services
Period of collections: 1800-1900

Terrebonne Historical and Cultural Society, Inc.
Telephone: (504) 851-0154
Mail to: P.O. Box 2095, 70360
Private agency
Founded in: 1968
C. J. Olivier, Jr., President
Number of members: 1,000
Major programs: library, archives,
  manuscripts, museum,
  tours/pilgrimages, oral history,
  school programs,
  newsletters/pamphlets, exhibits,
  audiovisual programs,
  photographic collections,
  genealogical services
Period of collections: 1893-present

JACKSON

Jackson Assembly, Inc.
P.O. Box 494, 70748
Telephone: (504) 634-7155
Private agency
Founded in: 1964
Henry C. Howell IV, President
Number of members: 130
Major programs: historic site(s),
   markers
Period of collections: Antebellum
   period

LAFAYETTE

Lafayette Museum
1122 Lafayette St., 70501
Telephone: (318) 234-2208
Authorized by Lafayette Museum
   Association
Founded in: 1954
Mrs. Ernest Yongue, President
Number of members: 24
Staff: part time 2
Major programs: historic preservation
Period of collections: 1800-1900

**Lafayette Natural History Museum,
   Planetarium and Nature Station**
637 Girard Park Dr., 70503
Telephone: (318) 261-8350
City agency
Founded in: 1969
Beverly D. Latimer, Director
Number of members: 950
Staff: full time 8, part time 9,
   volunteer 15
Major programs: museum, school
   programs, exhibits, natural history
Period of collections: 20th century

Louisiana Historical Association
Center for Louisiana Studies,
   University of Southwestern
   Louisiana
Telephone: (318) 231-6029
Mail to: P.O. Box 40831, USL, 70504
Founded in: 1889
Lawrence D. Rice,
   Secretary/Treasurer
Number of members: 1,500
Staff: full time 1, part time 4,
   volunteer 2
Magazine: *Louisiana History*
Major programs: museum, books,
   newsletters/pamphlets

LAKE CHARLES

Imperial Calcasieu Museum, Inc.
204 W. Sallier St., 70601
Telephone: (318) 439-3797
Private agency
Founded in: 1963
Jane Gibson Barham, President
Number of members: 350
Staff: full time 1, part time 2
Major programs: museum, historic
   site(s), tours, school programs,
   newsletters/pamphlets, exhibits,
   photographic collections
Period of collections: 1492-present

**Southwest Lousiana Genealogical
   Society**
P.O. Box 5652, 70606
Founded in: 1973
Mrs. Pat Huffaker, Elected President
Number of members: 175
Staff: volunteer 7

Magazine: *Kinfolks*
Major programs:
   newsletters/pamphlets, research,
   genealogical services

LOREAUVILLE

**Loreauville Heritage Village
   Museum**
403 Main St. 70552
Telephone: (318) 229-4740
Mail to: P.O. Box 11
Founded in: 1966
Abby R. Kerne, Director
Number of members: 1
Major programs: museum, historic
   site, tours/pilgrimages, historic
   preservation
Period of collections: 18th
   century-present

MANSFIELD

De Soto Historical Society
Telephone: (318) 872-0302
Mail to: P.O. Box 523
Founded in: 1961
Raymond E. Powell, President
Number of members: 187
Staff: volunteer 3
Magazine: *De Soto Plume*
Major programs: library, museum,
   historic sites preservation, markers,
   tours/pilgrimages,
   newsletters/pamphlets
Period of collections: 1783-1918

MARKSVILLE

**Marksville State Commemorative
   Area**
700 Allen St., 71351
Telephone: (318) 253-9546
State agency, authorized by
   Louisiana Office of State Parks
Founded in: 1950
George H. McCluskey, Historic Site
   Manager
Staff: full time 4, part time 2
Major programs: archives,
   manuscripts, museum, historic
   site(s), markers, tours/pilgrimages,
   school programs, historic
   preservation, records
   management, research, exhibits,
   audiovisual programs, archaeology
   programs, photographic
   collections
Period of collections: A.D. 1-400

METAIRIE

Comité Louisiane Francaise
2717 Massachusetts Ave., 70003
Telephone: (504) 469-2555
Private agency
Founded in: 1975
Donald J. Landry, President
Magazine: *Tribune des Francophiles*
Major programs:
   newsletters/pamphlets

NATCHITOCHES

**Association for the Preservation of
   Historic Natchitoches**
316 Jefferson
Telephone: (318) 352-6472
Mail to: P.O. Box 2654, 71457
Private agency

Founded in: 1943
Ora Vesta Watson, President
Number of members: 400
Staff: volunteer 100
Major programs: tours/pilgrimages,
   historic preservation, living history
Period of collections: 1790-present

**Center for History of Louisiana
   Education**
Northwestern State University, 71497
Telephone: (318) 357-4396
State agency, authorized by the
   university
Founded in: 1979
Maxine Southerland, Director
Staff: full time 1, part time 5
Major programs: museum, oral
   history, school programs, historic
   preservation, archaeology
   programs
Period of collections: 1850-1940

Ft. Saint-Jean Baptiste
P.O. Box 1127, 71458-1127
Telephone: (318) 357-0001
State agency, authorized by Office of
   State Parks
Founded in: 1981
Reinaldo Webb Barnes, Manager
Major programs: museum, research,
   exhibits, living history, audiovisual
   programs
Period of collections: 1714-1738

Museum Contents, Inc.
424 Jefferson St.
Telephone: (318) 352-5342
Mail to: P.O. Box 37, 71457
Founded in: 1963
Questionnaire not received

NEW IBERIA

Shadows-on-the-Teche
117 E. Main St.
Telephone: (318) 369-6446
Mail to: P.O. Box 254, 70560
Private agency, authorized by
   National Trust for Historic
   Preservation
Founded in: 1958
Shereen Minvielle, Director
Number of members: 500
Staff: full time 4, part time 7,
   volunteer 100
Major programs: museum, historic
   site(s), school programs,
   newsletters/pamphlets, historic
   preservation, restoration of historic
   gardens
Period of collections: 1834-1870

NEW ORLEANS

Amistad Research Center
400 Esplanade Ave., 70116
Telephone: (504) 522-0432
Private agency
Founded in: 1966
Clifton H. Johnson, Executive Director
Number of members: 1
Staff: full time 8, part time 4,
   volunteer 2
Major programs: library, archives,
   manuscripts, oral history,
   newsletters/pamphlets, exhibits,
   photographic collections
Period of collections: 1826-present

Beauregard-Keyes House
1113 Chartres St., 70116
Telephone: (504) 523-7257
Private agency, authorized by Keyes
Foundation
Founded in: 1953
Alma H. Neal, Director
Staff: full time 2, part time 5,
volunteer 7
Major programs: historic preservation
Period of collections: mid-Victorian

Christian Woman's Exchange—Hermann-Grima Historic House
820 St. Louis St., 70112
Telephone: (504) 525-5661
Private agency
Founded in: 1881
Charles L. Mackie, Administrator
Number of members: 700
Staff: full time 5, part time 8,
volunteer 150
Major programs: library, museum,
historic site(s), tours/pilgrimages,
school programs
Period of collections: 1831-1859

City Lights, Inc.
632 Julia St., 70130
Telephone: (509) 524-5759
Private agency
Founded in: 1974
James Maumus, Administrator
Number of members: 29
Staff: volunteer 13
Major programs: archives,
tours/pilgrimages, oral history,
historic preservation, photographic
collections
Period of collections: 1900-1930

Friends of Cabildo
701 Charters, 70115
Telephone: (504) 523-3939
Private agency
Founded in: 1956
Stephen A. Moses, President
Number of members: 5,000
Staff: full time 3
Major programs: museum,
tours/pilgrimages, oral history,
book publishing,
newsletters/pamphlets, historic
preservation, exhibits
Period of collections: 1700-1950

Ft. Pike State Commemorative Area
Rt. 6, Box 194, 70129
Telephone: (504) 662-5703
State agency, authorized by
Louisiana Office of State Parks
Founded in: 1934
Charles F. Bendzans, Historic Site
Manager
Staff: full time 5
Major programs: historic site(s),
exhibits
Period of collections: 1820-1880

Gallier House Museum
1118-1132 Royal St., 70116
Telephone: (504) 523-6722
Private agency, authorized by Gallier
House Museum Foundation
Founded in: 1971
Ann M. Masson, Director
Number of members: 735
Staff: full time 9, part time 1,
volunteer 15

Magazine: *Gallier House*
Major programs: library, museum,
historic site(s), tours/pilgrimages,
school programs,
newsletters/pamphlets, exhibits,
audiovisual programs,
photographic collections
Period of collections: mid-19th
century

Genealogical Research Society of New Orleans
P.O. Box 51791, 70151
Private agency
Founded in: 1960
Jack Belsom, President
Number of members: 275
Staff: part time 1, volunteer 20
Magazine: *New Orleans Genesis*
Major programs: book publishing,
research, genealogical services
Period of collections: 1700-1900

Greater New Orleans Archivists
400 Esplanade Ave., 70116
Telephone: (504) 522-0432
Private agency
Founded in: 1982
Florence E. Borders, President
Number of members: 35
Staff: volunteer 3
Major programs: library, archives,
manuscripts, museum,
tours/pilgrimages, oral history,
school programs,
newsletters/pamphlets, records
management, research,
audiovisual programs,
photographic collections
Period of collections: 19th-20th
centuries

Historic New Orleans Collection
533 Royal St., 70130
Telephone: (504) 523-4662
Founded in: 1966
Stanton M. Frazar, Director
Staff: full time 47, part time 25,
volunteer 2
Major programs: library, archives,
manuscripts, museum, historic
site(s), book publishing,
newsletters/pamphlets, research,
exhibits, photographic collections
Period of collections: 19th century

Longue Vue House and Gardens
7 Bamboo Rd., 70124
Telephone: (504) 488-5488
Private agency, authorized by
Longue Vue Foundation
Founded in: 1968
Florence Coyle Treadway, Director
Number of members: 1,000
Staff: full time 17, part time 16,
volunteer 45
Major programs: museum,
tours/pilgrimages, school
programs, historic preservation,
exhibits
Period of collections: 19th-20th
centuries

Louisiana Committee for the Humanities
1001 Howard Ave., Suite 4407, 70113
Telephone: (504) 523-4352
Private agency, authorized by
National Endowment for the
Humanities

Founded in: 1972
Michael Sartisky, Executive Director
Number of members: 20
Staff: full time 5, part time 2
Magazine: *Chronicle*
Major programs: library, museum,
historic site(s), book
publishing, newsletters/pamphlets,
historic preservation, exhibits,
living history, audiovisual
programs, archaeology programs,
photographic collections

Louisiana Historical Association Confederate Museum
929 Camp St., 70130
Telephone: (504) 523-4522
Private agency, authorized by
Louisiana Historical Association
Founded in: 1891
Pat Eymard, Curator
Staff: full time 1, part time 2,
volunteer 35
Major programs: museum, school
programs
Period of collections: 1861-1865

◇Louisiana Historical Society
2727 Prytania St., 70130
Telephone: (504) 891-9061
State agency
Founded in: 1836
J. Raymond Samuel, President
Number of members: 1,500
Staff: volunteer 4
Major programs: tours/pilgrimages,
newsletters/pamphlets, historic
preservation, research, audiovisual
programs, lectures, annual
banquet, commemorative activities

◇Louisiana State Museum
751 Chartres St., 70116
Telephone: (504) 581-4321
State agency
Founded in: 1906
Staff: full time 144, part time 48
Major programs: library, archives,
manuscripts, museum, historic
sites preservation, educational
programs, books
Period of collections: 1492-1918

Preservation Resource Center of New Orleans
823 Perdido St., Suite 200, 70112
Telephone: (504) 581-7032
Questionnaire not received

St. Charles Avenue Association
5801 St. Charles Ave., 70115
Private agency
Founded in: 1972
Sally Evans Reeves, President
Number of members: 200
Magazine: *Streetcar Tracks*
Major programs: historic preservation

Save Our Cemeteries, Inc.
900 Amethyst St., 70124
Telephone: (504) 282-0215
State agency
Founded in: 1974
Mary Louise Christovich, Acting
Director
Number of members: 1,500
Staff: volunteer 20
Major programs: tours/pilgrimages,
newsletters/pamphlets, historic
preservation, research, audiovisual

programs, archaeology programs, photographic collections
Period of collections: late 18th-20th centuries

Southern Historical Association
Tulane University, 70118
Telephone: (504) 865-6201
Questionnaire not received

OIL CITY

Caddo-Pine Island Oil and Historical Society Museum
207 Land Ave.
Telephone: (318) 995-6845
Mail to: P.O. Box 897, 71061
Private agency
Founded in: 1981
Sara Buford, Director
Number of members: 450
Staff: full time 3, part time 3, volunteer 10
Magazine: *Museum Pipeline*
Major programs: library, archives, museum, oral history, school programs, newsletters/pamphlets, historic preservation, exhibits, audiovisual programs, photographic collections
Period of collections: early 20th century

PLAQUEMINE

Promotion and Preservation of Iberville Parish, Inc.
P.O. Box 146, 70764
Telephone: (504) 687-8496
County agency
Founded in: 1983
Sue G. Herbert, Secretary/Treasurer
Number of members: 76
Major programs: historic site(s), tours/pilgrimages, historic preservation

PORT ALLEN

West Baton Rouge Historical Association
845 N. Jefferson, 70767
Telephone: (504) 383-2392
County agency
Founded in: 1968
Number of members: 236
Staff: full time 2, part time 3, volunteer 3
Major programs: archives, museum, oral history, research, photographic collections, genealogical services
Period of collections: 1800-present

RUSTON

Lincoln Parish Museum and Historical Society
609 N. Vienna St.
Telephone: (318) 251-0018

Mail to: P.O. Drawer F, 71270
Private agency
Founded in: 1975
Rowland P. Gill, Curator
Number of members: 375
Staff: full time 1
Major programs: archives, manuscripts, museum, historic site(s), oral history, historic preservation, research, exhibits, photographic collections, genealogical services
Period of collections: 1865-present

North Louisiana Genealogical Society
P.O. Box 324, 71270
Private agency
Founded in: 1981
Major programs: library, genealogical services
Period of collections: 19th-early 20th centuries

North Louisiana Historical Association
Louisiana Tech University
Mail to: P.O. Box 8607, Tech Station, 71272
Founded in: 1950
Questionnaire not received

ST. FRANCISVILLE

Audubon State Commemorative Area—Oakley Plantation
Hwy. 965
Telephone: (504) 635-3739
Mail to: P.O. Box 546, 70775
Authorized by Office of State Parks
Founded in: 1947
David Floyd, Director
Major programs: manuscripts, museum, historic site(s), tours/pilgrimages, oral history, historic preservation, research, exhibits, archaeology programs, photographic collections
Period of collections: 1820-1829

West Feliciana Historical Society
Telephone: (504) 635-6330
Mail to: P.O. Box 338, 70775
Private agency
Founded in: 1969
Mary E. Young, Curator
Number of members: 400
Staff: full time 1, part time 1
Magazine: *Audubon Pilgrimage*
Major programs: museum, historic sites preservation, tours/pilgrimages, educational programs, newsletters/pamphlets, school programs, living history, photographic collections
Period of collections: 1783-1900

ST. MARTINVILLE

Longfellow Evangeline State Commemorative Area
Hwy. 31
Telephone: (318) 394-3754
Mail to: P.O. Box 497, 70582

The Old State House in Baton Rouge was designed by James H. Dakin in 1847 and was acquired by the Louisiana State Museum in 1983. The Gothic revival building will house a museum on Louisiana's political history and folk culture.—Courtesy the Louisiana State Museum

Founded in: 1931
Staff: full time 10, part time 5
Major programs: museum, historic site, tours/pilgrimages, oral history, historic preservation, day use recreation
Period of collections: 1780-1860

SHREVEPORT

Chapter 425, Children of the Confederacy
6318 E. Ridge Dr., 71106
Telephone: (318) 868-8214
Private agency
Founded in: 1920
E. L. Davidson, Director
Number of members: 100
Staff: volunteer 20
Major programs: library, archives, museum, historic site(s), markers, tours/pilgrimages, school programs, book publishing, newsletters/pamphlets, historic preservation, records management, research, exhibits, living history, audiovisual programs, archaeology programs, photographic collections, genealogical services, field services
Period of collections: 1861-1865

Grindstone Bluff Museum
501 Jenkins Rd.
Telephone: (318) 425-5646
Mail to: P.O. Box 7965, 71107
Private agency
Founded in: 1976
J. Ashley Sibley, Jr., Director
Major programs: library, museum, tours/pilgrimages, junior history, oral history, school programs, historic preservation, research, exhibits, archaeology programs
Period of collections: 10,000 B.C.-present

Historic Preservation of Shreveport
Mail to: P.O. Box 857, 71162
Telephone: (318) 221-3334
Private agency
Bill Wiener, Jr., President
Major programs: archives, historic site(s), oral history, newsletters/pamphlets, historic preservation, research, exhibits, living history

North Louisiana Historical Association
Louisiana State University
Mail to: P.O. Box 6701, 71106
Private agency
Founded in: 1950
LeRoy Musselman, Membership Secretary/Treasurer/Editor
Number of members: 720
Staff: volunteer 3
Magazine: *Journal*
Major programs: archives, manuscripts, junior history, school programs, historic preservation, research, living history, genealogical services
Period of collections: 1783-1918

Pioneer Heritage Center
8515 Youree Dr., 71115
Telephone: (318) 797-5332

State agency, authorized by Louisiana State University, Shreveport
Founded in: 1977
Marguerite R. Plummer, Executive Director
Staff: full time 1, part time 1, volunteer 52
Major programs: museum, school programs, historic preservation, research, living history, audiovisual programs
Period of collections: Antebellum period

SLIDELL

Slidell Museum
2020 1st St., 70458
Telephone: (504) 646-4380
Mail to: P.O. Box 1564, 70459
City agency
Founded in: 1976
Dale E. Tidrick, Director
Staff: volunteer 1
Major programs: manuscripts, museum, historic site(s), oral history, historic preservation, photographic collections
Period of collections: 1888-1988

SULPHUR

Brimstone Historical Society
800 Picard Rd., 70663
Telephone: (318) 527-7142
Mail to: P.O. Box 242, 70664
Private agency
Founded in: 1975
Genelle S. Pickens, Director
Number of members: 98
Staff: full time 2, part time 1, volunteer 12
Major programs: museum, markers, tours/pilgrimages, oral history, newsletters/pamphlets, exhibits, audiovisual programs, photographic collections
Period of collections: 1880s-1930s

TALLULAH

Madison Parish Historical Society
100 S. Chestnut St., 71282
Telephone: (318) 574-2450
Private agency
Founded in: 1969
C. Calvin Adams, Jr., Administrator

THIBODAUX

Fourche Heritage Society
Mail to: P.O. Box 913, 70302
County agency
Founded in: 1977
David D. Plater, President
Number of members: 150
Staff: volunteer 25
Major programs: tours/pilgrimages, oral history, book publishing, newsletters/pamphlets, historic preservation, genealogical services

TROUT

Lasalle Art-Historical Association
Rt. I, Box 234, 71371
Telephone: (318) 992-6210
County agency

Founded in: 1968
Louise Windham, President
Number of members: 25
Staff: volunteer 5
Major programs: library, archives, museum, historic site(s), markers, tours/pilgrimages, oral history, school programs, newsletters/pamphlets, historic preservation, research, exhibits, living history, archaeology programs, photographic collections, field services, crafts workshops
Period of collections: early 1900s

VILLE PLATTE

Evangeline Genealogical and Historical Society
P.O. Box 664, 70586
Private agency
Founded in: 1980
Barbara Braun West, Editor
Number of members: 130
Staff: volunteer 15
Magazine: *La Voix des Prairies*
Major programs: newsletters/pamphlets, historic preservation, genealogical services
Period of collections: 1780s-1980s

MAINE

ALEXANDER

Alexander-Crawford Historical Society
R.R. 1, Box 1616, 04694
Telephone: (207) 454-8472
Private agency
Founded in: 1980
Jane Gerow Dudley, President/Editor
Number of members: 500
Major programs: newsletters/pamphlets

The Maine (N.B.) Connection
R.R. 1, Box 1616, 04694
Telephone: (207) 454-8472
Private agency
Founded in: 1984
Jane Gerow Dudley, Editor/Publisher
Number of members: 73
Staff: full time 1
Magazine: *The Maine (N.B.) Connection*
Major programs: newsletter, research, genealogical services

ANDOVER

Andover Historical Society
Town agency
Founded in: 1977
Beverly Swan, President
Number of members: 14
Staff: volunteer 4
Major programs: historic site(s), newsletters/pamphlets, historic preservation, exhibits, photographic collections, genealogical services

AUBURN

Androscoggin Historical Society
Mail to: County Bldg., 2 Turner St., 04210
Founded in: 1923
Leon M. Norris, Curator/Executive Secretary
Number of members: 187
Staff: volunteer 4
Major programs: library, archives, manuscripts, museum, oral history, educational programs, books, exhibits, photographic collections
Period of collections: 1855-1920

AUBURN-LEWISTON

Father Leo E. Begin Chapter, American-Canadian Genealogical Society
P.O. Box 2125, Lewiston, 04240-2125
Private agency
Founded in: 1980
Eli Duguay, President
Number of members: 100
Staff: volunteer 10
Major programs: library, archives, manuscripts, tours/pilgrimages, oral history, school programs, newsletters/pamphlets, research, living history, audiovisual programs, genealogical services
Period of collections: 1600-present

Franco-American Heritage Center
P.O. Box 1251, Lewiston, 04240-1251
Private agency
Founded in: 1978
Jo Anne Lapointe, Archivist
Number of members: 200
Staff: part time 1, volunteer 5
Major programs: library, archives, manuscripts, museum, historic site(s), tours/pilgrimages, oral history, school programs, newsletters/pamphlets, historic preservation, records management, research, exhibits, living history, audiovisual programs, photographic collections, genealogical services
Period of collections: 1800-present

AUGUSTA

Ft. Western Museum
Bowman St., 04330
Telephone: (207) 622-1234
City agency
Founded in: 1922
Robert Hotelling, Chair
Number of members: 300
Staff: part time 12, volunteer 25
Major programs: museum, historic site(s), markers, school programs, newsletters/pamphlets, research, exhibits, archaeology programs
Period of collections: 1754-1830

Genealogical Section, Le Club Calumet
P.O. Box 110, 04330-0110
Private agency
Founded in: 1983
Gerard F. Samson, Director
Number of members: 200
Staff: volunteer 5
Major programs: library, archives, manuscripts, tours/pilgrimages,

oral history, school programs, newsletters/pamphlets, research, living history, audiovisual programs, genealogical services
Period of collections: 1600-present

Maine Department of Conservation, Bureau of Parks and Recreation
State House, Station 22, 04333
Telephone: (207) 289-3821
State agency
Founded in: 1972
Sheila McDonald, Interpretive Specialist
Staff: full time 1, part time 45
Major programs: historic site(s), markers, historic preservation, research

Maine State Archives
State Capitol, Station 84, 04333
Telephone: (207) 289-2451
Founded in: 1965
Staff: full time 18
Major programs: archives
Period of collections: 1635-present

Maine State Museum
State House, Station 83, 04333
Telephone: (207) 289-2301
State agency, authorized by Department of Educational and Cultural Services
Founded in: 1967
Paul E. Rivard, Director
Staff: full time 25, part time 4, volunteer 20
Magazine: *Broadside*
Major programs: museum, school programs, book publishing, newsletters/pamphlets, exhibits, archaeology programs, photographic collections
Period of collections: prehistoric-present

BANGOR

Bangor Historical Society
159 Union St., 04401
Telephone: (207) 942-5766
Private agency
Founded in: 1864
Marilyn A. Gass, Executive Director
Number of members: 400
Staff: volunteer 15
Major programs: archives, museum, educational programs, exhibits
Period of collections: late 18th-late 19th centuries

Penobscot Heritage Museum of Living History
159 Union St., 04401
Telephone: (207) 942-5766
Questionnaire not received

BAR HARBOR

Bar Harbor Historical Society
34 Mt. Desert St., 04609
Telephone: (207) 288-4245
Private agency
Founded in: 1946
Herman Woodworth, President
Number of members: 125
Staff: part time 1, volunteer 5
Major programs: archives, museum, research
Period of collections: 1870-present

BATH

Bath, Maine, Maritime Museum
963 Washington St., 04530
Telephone: (207) 443-6311
Private agency
Founded in: 1964
John S. Carter, Director
Number of members: 1,500
Staff: full time 10, part time 2, volunteer 200
Magazine: *The Long Reach Log*
Major programs: library, archives, museum, historic site(s), tours/pilgrimages, school programs, historic preservation, research, exhibits, photographic collections
Period of collections: 19th-20th centuries

Sagadahoc Preservation, Inc.
804 Washington St.
Mail to: P.O. Box 322, 04530
Private agency
Founded in: 1971
Mary Donnell Rogers, President
Number of members: 300
Staff: volunteer 25
Major programs: historic preservation
Period of collections: 19th century

BELFAST

Belfast Historical Society, Inc.
Ivy House, 7 Park St., 04915
Telephone: (207) 338-3403
Private agency
Founded in: 1953
Morris Slugg, President
Number of members: 50
Staff: volunteer 10
Major programs: museum, school programs, historic preservation, exhibits, photographic collections
Period of collections: 1770-present

Belfast Museum, Inc.
66 Church St., 04915
Private agency, authorized by Belfast Historical Society, Inc.
Founded in: 1975
Morris L. Slugg, President
Number of members: 50
Staff: volunteer 3
Major programs: museum, historic preservation
Period of collections: 1850-present

BERWICK

Berwick Historical Society, Inc.
P.O. Box 113, 03901
Private agency
Founded in: 1979
Brian D. Cincotta, President
Number of members: 45
Period of collections: 19th century

BETHEL

Bethel Historical Society, Inc.
15 Broad St.
Telephone: (207) 824-2908
Mail to: P.O. Box 12, 04217
Private agency
Founded in: 1966
Stanley Russell Howe, Director
Number of members: 600
Staff: full time 1, part time 2, volunteer 100

Magazine: *The Bethel Courier*
Major programs: library, archives,
manuscripts, museum, historic
site(s), oral history, school
programs, book publishing,
newsletters/pamphlets, research,
exhibits, audiovisual programs,
photographic collections,
genealogical services
Period of collections: 1800-1950

BIDDEFORD

Biddeford Historical Society
McArthur Library, Main St., 04005
Questionnaire not received

**Franco-American Genealogical
Society of York County**
P.O. Box 180, 04005-0180
Private agency
Founded in: 1983
Patricia Sansoucy, President
Number of members: 50
Staff: volunteer 10
Magazine: *Maine's Franco-American
Heritage*
Major programs: library, archives,
manuscripts, tours/pilgrimages,
oral history, school programs,
newsletters/pamphlets, research,
living history, genealogical
services
Period of collections: 1600-present

BINGHAM

Old Carratunk Historical Society
Mail to: P.O. Box 303, 04920
Private agency
Founded in: 1962
Irene Foster, Founder
Number of members: 20
Staff: volunteer 2
Major programs: genealogical
services
Period of collections: 1783-1865

BLUE HILL

Jonathan Fisher Memorial, Inc.
04614
Telephone: (207) 374-2780
Founded in: 1954
William Hinckley, President
Number of members: 250
Staff: part time 3
Major programs: museum, books
Period of collections: 1768-1847

BOOTHBAY

Boothbay Railway Village
Rt. 27
Telephone: (207) 633-4727
Mail to: P.O. Box 123, 04537
Private agency
Founded in: 1961
Robert Ryan, Director
Number of members: 25
Staff: full time 5, part time 20,
volunteer 5
Magazine: *Village Dispatch*
Major programs: museum, historic
preservation
Period of collections: 1880-1930

Boothbay Theatre Museum
Corey Lane, 04537
Telephone: (207) 633-4536

Founded in: 1957
Questionnaire not received

BOOTHBAY HARBOR

**Boothbay Region Historical
Society**
70 Oak St.
Mail to: P.O. Box 272, 04538
Private agency
Founded in: 1967
Beatrice Walker, President
Number of members: 130
Major programs: museum, book
publishing
Period of collections: early 20th
century

**Grand Banks Schooner Museum
Trust**
100 Commercial St., 04538
Telephone: (207) 633-2756
Mail to: P.O. Box 123, 04537
Private agency
Founded in: 1968
Robert Ryan, Director
Staff: part time 2
Major programs: museum, historic
preservation

BRADFORD

**Bradford Heritage Museum and
Historical Society**
Main Rd., Rt. 221
Mail to: P.O. Box 500, 04410
Private agency
Founded in: 1978
Robert E. Strout, President
Number of members: 20
Major programs: library, museum,
historic preservation
Period of collections: 1850-1950

BREWER

Brewer Historical Society
199 Wilson St., 04412
Telephone: (207) 989-7825
Town agency
Founded in: 1976
Hazen Danforth III, President
Number of members: 50
Staff: volunteer 5
Major programs: archives, museum,
historic site(s), markers, historic
preservation, exhibits, sports
history
Period of collections: 1900-present

BRIDGTON

Bridgton Historical Society
Gibbs Ave.
Telephone: (207) 647-3474
Mail to: P.O. Box 317, 04009
Private agency
Founded in: 1953
Henry A. Shorey, President
Staff: volunteer 2
Major programs: archives, museum,
markers
Period of collections: 1850-1925

BRUNSWICK

Peary-MacMillan Arctic Museum
Hubbard Hall, Bowdoin College,
04011
Telephone: (207) 725-8731

Private agency, authorized by the
college
Founded in: 1967
Richard G. Condon, Curator
Staff: full time 2, part time 1,
volunteer 15
Major programs: archives,
manuscripts, museum, research,
exhibits, photographic collections
Period of collections: 1908-1945

Pejepscot Historical Society
159 Maine St., 04011
Telephone: (207) 729-6606
Private agency
Founded in: 1888
Paul R. Copeland, Director
Number of members: 789
Staff: part time 5, volunteer 27
Major programs: archives, museum,
historic site(s), school programs,
historic preservation, exhibits,
photographic collections
Period of collections: 1700-present

BUCKSPORT

Bucksport Historical Society, Inc.
Main St., 04416
Telephone: (207) 469-2591
Private agency
Founded in: 1964
Charles T. Brown, President
Number of members: 60
Staff: volunteer 20
Major programs: museum
Period of collections: 1783-1865

BURLINGTON

**Stewart M. Lord Memorial
Historical Society**
Telephone: (207) 732-4121
Mail to: P.O. Box 307, Howland,
04448
Private agency
Founded in: 1968
Fern P. Cummings, Secretary
Number of members: 47
Staff: volunteer 10
Major programs: museum, historic
preservation
Period of collections: 1800-1900

BUSTINS ISLAND

**Bustins Island, Maine, Historical
Society**
04013
Mail to: P.O. Box 118, S. Freeport,
04078
Private agency
Founded in: 1977
W. A. Baker, Treasurer
Number of members: 109
Major programs: archives, museum,
oral history, newsletters/pamphlets,
historic preservation
Period of collections: 1890-present

CAMDEN

**Camden-Rockport Historical
Society**
Conway Rd., Rt. 1
Mail to: P.O. Box 897, 04843
Private agency
Founded in: 1960
James Perry, President
Number of members: 300

Staff: part time 6, volunteer 12
Major programs: museum, historic
  site(s), book publishing, historic
  preservation, exhibits,
  photographic collections
Period of collections: 1812-1920

CARIBOU

Caribou Historical Society
Mail to: c/o Dora Clark, 98-A High St.,
  04736
Founded in: 1974
Number of members: 50
Major programs: library, manuscripts,
  book publishing

Nylander Museum
393 Main St.
Telephone: (207) 493-4474/498-3098
Mail to: P.O. Box 1062, 04736
Constance Simon, Director
Staff: part time 2
Major programs: museum, tours,
  school programs,
  newsletters/pamphlets, historic
  preservation, exhibits, geological
  collections
Period of collections:
  prehistoric-present

CASCO

Raymond-Casco Historical Society
04015
Telephone: (207) 627-4220
Questionnaire not received

CASTINE

Castine Scientific Society
Perkins St., 04421
Private agency
Founded in: 1921
E.W. Doudiet, President
Staff: part time 7
Magazine: *Wilson Museum Bulletin*
Major programs: museum, historic
  sites preservation
Period of collections:
  prehistoric-present

**John Perkins House—Wilson
  Museum**
Perkins St.
Telephone: (207) 326-8753
Mail to: P.O. Box 196, 04421
Private agency, authorized by
  Castine Scientific Society
Founded in: 1921
E. W. Doudiet, President
Staff: full time 1, part time 3,
  volunteer 20
Major programs: manuscripts,
  museum, historic site(s), exhibits
Period of collections: 18th-19th
  centuries

CHERRYFIELD

**Cherryfield-Narraguagus Historical
  Society**
Main St.
Mail to: P.O. Box 96, 04622
Private agency
Founded in: 1974
Margery Brown, President
Number of members: 250
Staff: volunteer 4

Major programs: archives, museum,
  genealogical services
Period of collections: 1790-1900

CHINA

China Historical Society
Maine St., 04330
Mail to: P.O. Box 245, S. China, 04358
Private agency
Number of members: 75
Staff: volunteer 7
Major programs: museum, markers
Period of collections: 19th century

COLUMBIA FALLS

Ruggles House Society
04623
Telephone: (207) 288-3597
Mail to: Bar Harbor, 04609
Founded in: 1950
Questionnaire not received

CUMBERLAND CENTER

Cumberland Historical Society
Mail to: R.R. 2, Box 479-A, 04021
Founded in: 1939
Mrs. David Pomeroy, President
Number of members: 30
Period of collections: 1783-present

CUSHING

Cushing Historical Society
Hathorn Point Rd., 04563
Founded in: 1969
Questionnaire not received

DEER ISLE

**Deer Isle-Stonington Historical
  Society**
Founded in: 1960
Raymond L. Eaton, President
Number of members: 500
Staff: volunteer 50
Major programs: archives, museum,
  markers, newsletters/pamphlets,
  historic preservation, research,
  exhibits, genealogical services
Period of collections: 1800s

DEXTER

Dexter Historical Society
Main St., 04930
Founded in: 1965
Frank Spizuoco, President
Number of members: 46
Staff: volunteer 12
Major programs: archives, museum,
  educational programs
Period of collections: 1865-1918

DOVER-FOXCROFT

**Dover-Foxcroft Historical
  Society—Blacksmith Shop
  Museum**
Chandler Rd.
Telephone: (207) 564-2549
Mail to: 88 Lincoln St., 04426
Private agency
Founded in: 1963
George L. Dunham, Curator
Number of members: 30
Staff: volunteer 3

Major programs: museum, historic
  site(s), school programs, historic
  preservation, living history
Period of collections: 1863-1905

DRESDEN

Dresden Historical Society
04342
Telephone: (207) 737-8892
Founded in: 1968
Number of members: 40
Staff: volunteer 10
Major programs: museum, genealogy
Period of collections: 1700s-present

EAST MACHIAS

East Machias Historical Society
04630
Private agency
Nita Johnson, President
Number of members: 100
Major programs: museum, historic
  site(s), oral history, historic
  preservation
Period of collections: from 1826

EAST VASSALBORO

Vassalboro Historical Society
c/o Secretary, 04935
Telephone: (207) 923-3533
Private agency
Founded in: 1961
Betty Taylor, Secretary
Number of members: 75
Staff: volunteer 6
Major programs: museum
Period of collections: 1800-present

EASTPORT

Border Historical Society
74 Washington St., Barracks Museum
Mail to: 3 Green St., 04631
Telephone: 1959
Ruth McInnis, President
Number of members: 75
Staff: volunteer 10
Major programs: archives,
  manuscripts, museum
Period of collections: 1800-1920

ELIOT

Maine Old Cemetery Association
6 Sherwood Dr., 03903
Telephone: (207) 439-0655
Private agency
Founded in: 1969
Alan H. Hawkins, President
Number of members: 1,200
Staff: volunteer 10
Major programs: archives,
  newsletters/pamphlets, historic
  preservation, preservation of
  gravestone inscriptions throughout
  state
Period of collections: 1750-present

ELLSWORTH

Ellsworth Historical Society
State St., 04605
Founded in: 1978
Questionnaire not received

FALMOUTH

Falmouth Historical Society
5 Lunt Rd., 04105
Founded in: 1967
Sarah Connolly, President
Number of members: 25
Major programs: tours/pilgrimages,
  books
Period of collections: 1865-present

FARMINGTON

Little Red Schoolhouse Museum
Rts. 2 and 4
Telephone: (207) 778-2234
Mail to: P.O. Box 62, 04938
Private agency
Founded in: 1968
Harold Karkos, President
Staff: part time 3, volunteer 12
Major programs: library, museum,
  historic site, educational programs,
  historic preservation
Period of collections: 1840-1920

Nordica Memorial Association, Inc.
Rt. 3, 53 Holley Rd., 04938
Telephone: (207) 778-2042
Founded in: 1927
Questionnaire not received

FORT KENT

Ft. Kent Historical Society
P.O. Box 282, 04743
Telephone: (207) 834-3933
Town agency
Founded in: 1974
James Grandmaison, President
Number of members: 100
Staff: volunteer 5
Major programs: museum, historic
  site(s), historic preservation,
  exhibits, photographic collections
Period of collections: 1900-1920

FREEPORT

Freeport Historical Society
45 Main St.
Mail to: P.O. Box 358, 04032
Private agency
Founded in: 1969
Rocky Cianchette, President
Number of members: 450
Staff: part time 1, volunteer 40
Major programs: archives,
  manuscripts, historic site(s), school
  programs, book publishing,
  newsletters/pamphlets, historic
  preservation, research, exhibits,
  living history, archaeology
  programs, photographic
  collections
Period of collections: 1850-1920

FRENCHBORO

Frenchboro Historical Society
04635
Founded in: 1980
Vivian Lunt, President
Number of members: 45
Staff: volunteer 7
Major programs: museum, markers,
  newsletters/pamphlets, artifacts
Number of members: 1875-1930

FRIENDSHIP

Friendship Museum, Inc.
Rt. 220
Telephone: (207) 832-4221
Mail to: P.O. Box 321, 04547
Private agency
Founded in: 1968
Mary S. Carlson, Secretary
Number of members: 90
Staff: part time 1
Major programs: museum
Period of collections: before 1930

GARDINER

**The Cumberland and Oxford Canal
  Association**
R.F.D. 1-A, 04345
Telephone: (207) 582-4696
Questionnaire not received

GREENVILLE

Moosehead Historical Society
Pritham Ave.
Telephone: (207) 695-2716
Mail to: P.O. Box 1116, 04441
Private agency
Founded in: 1958
Linda Hubbard, Registrar
Number of members: 50
Major programs: historic site(s),
  exhibits
Period of collections: 1850-1950

HAMPDEN

Hampden Historical Society
Kinsley House, Main St.
Mail to: P.O. Box 456, 04444
Private agency
Founded in: 1970
Mrs. Richard Newcomb, President
Number of members: 85
Major programs: archives, museum,
  junior history, school programs,
  book publishing,
  newsletters/pamphlets, historic
  preservation, research, exhibits,
  photographic collections,
  genealogical services

HARPSWELL

Harpswell Historical Society
R.F.D. 1, S. Harpswell, 04079
Telephone: (207) 883-7798
Founded in: 1979
H. Franklin Williams, President
Number of members: 220
Major programs: historic site(s),
  markers, historic preservation,
  conservation, scenic preservation
Period of collections: 1783-1865

HINCKLEY

L. C. Bates Museum
Rt. 201, Campus of Hinckley School
Telephone: (207) 453-7335
Mail to: Hinckley Home-School-Farm,
  04944
Private agency, authorized by Good
  Will Home Association
Founded in: 1889
James W. Hennigar, Executive
  Director
Staff: full time 1
Major programs: museum, tours,
  school programs, exhibits

HOULTON

**Aroostook Historical and Art
  Museum**
109 Main St., 04730
Private agency
Elizabeth R. Blake, Curator
Staff: part time 1
Major programs: museum
Period of collections: from early 1800s

**Southern Aroostook Historical
  Society**
109 Main St., 04730
Private agency
Major programs: genealogical
  services

ISLESBORO

Islesboro Historical Society
Telephone: (207) 734-6719
Private agency
Founded in: 1964
Jean H. Hayden, President
Number of members: 380
Major programs: museum, book
  publishing, exhibits, genealogical
  services
Period of collections: 1780-1920

JAY

Jay Historical Society
Holmes-Crafts Homestead, Jay Hill
Telephone: (207) 645-2723
Mail to: c/o President, R.F.D. 1, Box
  3915, Wilton, 04294
Private agency
Founded in: 1972
Muriel G. David, President
Staff: volunteer 12
Major programs: archives,
  manuscripts, museum, school
  programs, historic preservation,
  records management, exhibits,
  photographic collections,
  genealogical services
Period of collections: 19th-early 20th
  centuries

KENNEBUNK

Brick Store Museum
117 Main St., 04043
Telephone: (207) 985-4802
Private agency
Founded in: 1936
Sandra Siver Hubka, Director
Number of members: 400
Staff: full time 4, part time 2,
  volunteer 10
Major programs: museum, library,
  manuscripts, educational
  programs
Period of collections: late 18th-early
  20th centuries

KENNEBUNKPORT

Kennebunkport Historical Society
North St.
Telephone: (207) 967-2751
Mail to: P.O. Box 405, 04046
Private agency
Founded in: 1952
Mary Z. Bryant, Curator
Number of members: 450
Staff: part time 1, volunteer 50
Magazine: *The Log*

Major programs: library, archives, museum, markers, genealogical services
Period of collections: 1750-present

New England Electric Railway Historical Society, Inc.—Seashore Trolley Museum
Log Cabin Rd.
Telephone: (207) 967-2712
Mail to: Drawer A, 04046
Founded in: 1939
Frederick J. Perry, General Manager
Number of members: 1,000
Staff: full time 4, part time 20, volunteer 200
Magazine: *The Trolley Museum Dispatch*
Major programs: museum, historic site(s), tours/pilgrimages, newsletters/pamphlets, historic preservation, exhibits, living history
Period of collections: late 1800s-early 1900s

KITTERY

Kittery Historical and Naval Museum
Rogers Rd.
Telephone: (207) 439-3080
Mail to: P.O. Box 453, 03904
Private agency
Founded in: 1976
Richard V. Palmer, Director
Number of members: 270
Staff: full time 1, part time 1, volunteer 4
Major programs: library, museum, exhibits, archaeology programs, photographic collections
Period of collections: 19th-20th centuries

LEBANON

Lebanon Historical Society
Academy Lane
Mail to: R.F.D. 1, Box 13, E. Lebanon, 04027
Private agency
Founded in: 1959
Arthur Wyman, President
Number of members: 25
Major programs: historic site(s), markers, tours/pilgrimages, oral history, newsletters/pamphlets, exhibits, photographic collections, genealogical services
Period of collections: 1800s

LEE

Partisan Prohibition Historical Society
Telephone: (207) 738-3321
Mail to: P.O. Box 283, 04455
Questionnaire not received

LEWISTON

Father Leo E. Begin Chapter (ACGS)
5 Beckett St., 04240
Telephone: (207) 784-2709
Mail to: 12 Tanglewood Dr., Apt. 4
Founded in: 1980
Questionnaire not received

Lewiston Historical Commission
36 Oak St., 04240
City agency
Founded in: 1969
Franklin Larrabee, Board Chair
Staff: volunteer 16
Major programs: tours/pilgrimages, book publishing, historic preservation, audiovisual programs
Period of collections: 1850-1920

Maine League of Historical Societies and Museums
10 Brann Ave., 04240
Founded in: 1961
Questionnaire not received

L'ILLE

Mt. Carmel Cultural and Historical Center
P.O. Box 155, 04749-0155
Private agency
Founded in: 1982
Donald Cyr, Director
Number of members: 50
Major programs: library, archives, manuscripts, museum, tours/pilgrimages, oral history, school programs, newsletters/pamphlets, historic preservation, exhibits, living history, audiovisual programs, photographic collections, genealogical services

LINCOLNVILLE

Lincolnville Historical Society and Mini-Museum
c/o President, Rt. 52, Lincolnville Center
Telephone: (207) 763-3447
Mail to: P.O. Box 154, 04850
Private agency
Founded in: 1975
Jacqueline Young Watts, President
Number of members: 100
Major programs: museum, book publishing, newsletters/pamphlets, photographic collections, genealogical services
Period of collections: early 1800s-mid-1900s

LIVERMORE

Norlands Living History Center
R.F.D. 2, 04254
Telephone: (207) 897-2236
Private agency
Founded in: 1974
Mrs. Alfred Q. Gammon, Administrator
Number of members: 313
Staff: full time 6, part time 7, volunteer 4
Major programs: library, archives, historic site(s), school programs, historic preservation, living history
Period of collections: 1850-1880

MACHIAS

Burnham Tavern Museum
Telephone: (207) 255-4432
Mail to: 60 Court St., 04654
Private agency, authorized by Hannah Weston Chapter, Daughters of the American Revolution

Founded in: 1910
Valdine C. Atwood, Director
Number of members: 130
Staff: volunteer 4
Major programs: museum, markers, oral history, historic preservation, research
Period of collections: 1763-1830

MACHIASPORT

Machiasport Historical Society
04655
Telephone: (207) 255-8461
Private agency
Founded in: 1964
Lyman L. Holmes, President
Number of members: 450
Major programs: library, museum, tours/pilgrimages, newsletters/pamphlets, historic preservation, research, exhibits, genealogical services
Period of collections: 1783-1918

MADAWASKA

Madawaska Historical Society
Library Bldg., Main St.
Telephone: (207) 738-4272
Private agency
Founded in: 1968
Claude Cyr, President
Number of members: 200
Staff: volunteer 25
Major programs: library, archives, museum, historic site(s), oral history, school programs, newsletters/pamphlets, historic preservation, living history
Period of collections: 1605-present

MORRILL

Morrill Historical Society
04952
Founded in: 1935
Dale Merrithew, President
Number of members: 33

NEWFIELD

Willowbrook at Newfield Restoration Village
P.O. Box 80, 04056
Telephone: (207) 793-2784
Founded in: 1970
Questionnaire not received

NEW GLOUCESTER

New Gloucester, Maine, Historical Society
c/o Historian, Cobb's Bridge Rd., 04260
Private agency
Founded in: 1934
Mrs. Malcolm Berry, Historian
Number of members: 20
Major programs: archives, manuscripts, historic site(s), markers, school programs, historic preservation, records management, research, exhibits, audiovisual programs, photographic collections, genealogical services
Period of collections: 1730s-present

**United Society of Shakers,
Sabbathday Lake**
Rt. 26, 04260
Telephone: (207) 926-4865
Mail to: Poland Spring, 04274
Founded in: 1782
Theodore E. Johnson, Director
Staff: full time 4
Magazine: *The Shaker Quarterly*
Major programs: library, archives,
manuscripts, museum, historic
sites preservation, oral history,
educational programs,
newsletters/pamphlets
Period of collections: 1782-present

NEW HARBOR

The Fishermen's Museum
Rt. 130, 04554
Telephone: (207) 677-2494
Town agency, authorized by Bristol
Park Commission
Founded in: 1972
Mary Norton Orrick, Director
Staff: full time 1, part time 1,
volunteer 20
Major programs: museum, historic
preservation, exhibits,
photographic collections
Period of collections: from late 19th
century

NEW SWEDEN

New Sweden Historical Society
Historical Museum, 04762
Telephone: (207) 896-3018
Founded in: 1925
Questionnaire not received

NOBLEBORO

Nobleboro Historical Society
P.O. Box 57, 04555
Telephone: (207) 563-5874
Founded in: 1978
George F. Dow, Curator
Number of members: 180
Staff: volunteer 50
Major programs: library, archives,
manuscripts, museum, historic old
school house, educational
programs, historic preservation
Period of collections: 1780-present

NORTH YARMOUTH

North Yarmouth Historical Society
P.O. Box 391, Cumberland Center,
04021
Telephone: (207) 846-9406
(treasurer)
Private agency
Founded in: 1977
Ursula Baier, President
Number of members: 70
Staff: volunteer 5
Major programs: manuscripts, oral
history, school programs, book
publishing, historic preservation,
records management, research,
photographic collections
Period of collections: 1800s-present

NORWAY

Norway Historical Society
232 Main St.
Telephone: (207) 743-7377
Mail to: R.F.D. 1, Box 2750, 04268
Town agency
Founded in: 1974

Herbert Marshall, President
Staff: volunteer 15
Major programs: library, exhibits,
genealogical services
Period of collections: 1800s-1900s

OLD TOWN

Old Town Museum
N. 4th St. Exit
Telephone: (207) 827-7256
Mail to: P.O. Box 375, 04468
Private agency
Founded in: 1976
Charles Buck, Chair
Number of members: 175
Staff: full time 1, part time 2,
volunteer 15
Major programs: museum, oral
history, school programs, historic
preservation, exhibits,
photographic collections
Period of collections: 1800-1930

**Penobscot National Historical
Society**
Center St.
Mail to: P.O. Box 313 04468
Founded in: 1978
Questionnaire not received

ORLAND

Orland Historical Society
Main St., 04472
Ruth Meigg, Secretary
Number of members: 30
Staff: volunteer 10
Major programs: library, museum
Period of collections: 1783-1918

ORONO

Maine Archaeological Society, Inc.
Department of Anthropology,
University of Maine at Orono, 04473
Mail to: O.S. Code, Rt. 2 Winthrop,
04364
Questionnaire not received

Northeast Folklore Society
S. Stevens Hall, University of Maine,
04469
Telephone: (207) 581-1891
Founded in: 1958
Edward D. Ives, President
Number of members: 500
Staff: part time 2
Magazine: *Northeast Folklore*
Major programs: archives, oral
history, folklore study
Period of collections: 1865-present

OWLS HEAD

Owls Head Transportation Museum
Rt. 73
Telephone: (207) 594-9219
Mail to: P.O. Box 277, 04468
Private agency, authorized by
foundation and board of trustees
Founded in: 1974
Charles Chiarchiaro, Director
Number of members: 1,500
Staff: full time 5, volunteer 150
Major programs: library, museum,
newsletters/pamphlets, research,
exhibits, historical meets and
events
Period of collections: 1890-1940

Meetinghouse was constructed in 1794 by master builder Moses Johnson.—United Society of Shakers, Sabbathday Lake, Maine

PATTEN

Lumberman's Museum
Shin Pond Rd., 04765
Telephone: (207) 528-2650/528-2547
Town agency
Founded in: 1962
Lenore D. Hanson, Curator
Staff: part time 8, volunteer 2
Major programs: museum, historic
  preservation, exhibits,
  photographic collections
Period of collections: 1820-early
  1900s

PEMAQUID

Pemaquid Historical Association
Old Harrington Rd., 04558
Telephone: (207) 677-2400
Founded in: 1965
Questionnaire not received

PHIPPSBURG

Phippsburg Historical Society, Inc.
Parker Head Rd.
Mail to: P.O. Box 21, 04562
Private agency
Founded in: 1961
Mrs. Peter A. Isaacson, President
Number of members: 160
Major programs: museum, book
  publishing, newsletters/pamphlets,
  photographic collections,
  genealogical services
Period of collections: to 1920

PITTSTON

**Arnold Expedition Historical
  Society**
Arnold Rd.
Telephone: (207) 582-7080
Mail to: P.O. Box 1775, Gardiner,
  04345
Founded in: 1968
Questionnaire not received

POLAND SPRING

The Shaker Museum
Rt. 26
Telephone: (207) 926-4597
Mail to: R.F.D. 1, 04274
Private agency, authorized by United
  Society of Shakers
Founded in: 1983
Theodore E. Johnson, Director
Staff: full time 5, part time 5,
  volunteer 1
Magazine: *The Shaker Quarterly*
Major programs: library, archives,
  manuscripts, museum, historic
  site(s), oral history, school
  programs, book publishing,
  newsletters/pamphlets, historic
  preservation, research, exhibits,
  living history, archaeology
  programs, photographic
  collections
Period of collections: from 1783

PORTLAND

**Cumberland and Oxford Canal
  Association**
36 Lester Dr., 04103
Telephone: (207) 797-2745
Private agency
Founded in: 1972

Joel W. Eastman, Secretary/Treasurer
Number of members: 71
Staff: volunteer 4
Major programs: tours/pilgrimages,
  newsletters/pamphlets, annual
  meeting
Period of collections: 1830-1870

George Tate House
1260 Westbrook St.
Telephone: (207) 772-2023
Mail to: 4 Walker St., 04102
Private agency, authorized by
  National Society of Colonial Dames
  of America, Maine
Founded in: 1896
Mrs. Phineas Sprague, Chair
Staff: part time 5, volunteer 50
Major programs: library, school
  programs, book publishing, historic
  preservation, archaeology
  programs
Period of collections: 1755-1803

Greater Portland Landmarks, Inc.
165 State St., 04101
Telephone: (207) 774-5561
Private agency
Founded in: 1964
Deborah G. Andrews, Executive
  Director
Number of members: 1,021
Staff: full time 3, part time 3,
  volunteer 70
Magazine: *Landmarks Observer*
Major programs: library, markers,
  tours/pilgrimages, school
  programs, book publishing,
  newsletters/pamphlets, historic
  preservation, research
Period of collections: 1865-1918

◊**Maine Historical Society**
485 Congress St., 04101
Telephone: (207) 774-1822
Private agency
Founded in: 1822
Neal W. Allen, Jr., Interim Director
Number of members: 1,800
Staff: full time 10, volunteer 5
Magazine: *Maine Historical Society
  Quarterly*
Major programs: library, manuscripts,
  historic site(s), tours/pilgrimages,
  school programs, book publishing,
  newsletters/pamphlets, research,
  photographic collections,
  genealogical services
Period of collections: 1492-present

Maine Humanities Council
24 Exchange St.
Telephone: (207) 773-5051
Mail to: P.O. Box 7202, 04112
Private agency, authorized by
  National Endowment for the
  Humanities
Founded in: 1975
Dorothy Schwartz, Executive Director
Staff: full time 3, part time 1
Magazine: *Polis*
Major programs: library, museum,
  oral history, school programs,
  newsletters/pamphlets, research,
  exhibits, audiovisual programs,
  archaeology programs

**National Society of Colonial Dames
  of America, Maine**
1270 Westbrook St.
Telephone: (207) 772-2023

Mail to: 4 Walker St., 04102
Private agency
Founded in: 1896
Mrs. Herbert Holmes, Jr., President
Number of members: 160
Staff: full time 1, part time 2
Major programs: museum, school
  programs, book publishing, historic
  preservation, exhibits, archaeology
  programs
Period of collections: 1750-1800

Neal Dow Memorial
714 Congress St., 04102
Telephone: (207) 773-7773
Private agency, authorized by Maine
  Women's Christian Temperance
  Union
Founded in: 1971
Vivian Russell, Curator/Historian
Staff: full time 1, volunteer 6
Major programs: library, manuscripts,
  tours, historic preservation, historic
  site, educational programs
Period of collections: 19th century

Portland Fire Museum
157 Spring St.
Mail to: P.O. Box 3161, 04104
City and private agency
Robert L. Sherwood, Sr., President
Number of members: 30
Major programs: museum, fire
  department history and lore
Period of collections: 1866-present

Tate House, (NSCDA) in Maine
4 Walker St., 04102
Telephone: (207) 772-2023
Founded in: 1755
Questionnaire not received

**Victoria Society of Maine—The
  Victoria Mansion**
109 Danforth St.
Telephone: (207) 772-4841
Private agency
Founded in: 1943
Mrs. A. H. Stockly, President
Number of members: 475
Staff: volunteer 32
Major programs: library, museum,
  historic sites preservation,
  educational programs,
  newsletters/pamphlets
Period of collections: 1859-1910

Wadsworth-Longfellow House
487 Congress St.
Telephone: (207) 772-1807
Mail to: 485 Congress St., 04101
Private agency, authorized by Maine
  Historical Society
Founded in: 1901
Elizabeth S. Hamill, Curator
Number of members: 1,800
Staff: part time 2, volunteer 3
Major programs: manuscripts,
  historic site(s), school programs,
  historic preservation
Period of collections: 1785-1900

PROSPECT

Ft. Knox
R.F.D. 1, Box 1316, 04981
Telephone: (207) 469-7719
State agency, authorized by Bureau
  of Parks and Recreation
Founded in: 1943
Michael K. Leighton, Manager

Staff: part time 7
Major programs: historic site(s),
   tours/pilgrimages
Period f collections: 1844-1900

RANGELEY

**Rangeley Lakes Region Historical
   Society**
P.O. Box 521, 04970
Founded in: 1955
Number of members: 100
Staff: volunteer 20
Major programs: library, archives,
   manuscripts, museum, historic site,
   oral history
Period of collections: 1900-present

RAYMOND

**Hawthorne Community
   Association**
Hawthorne Rd., 04077
Questionnaire not received

ROCKLAND

**William A. Farnsworth Library and
   Art Museum**
19 Elm St.
Telephone: (207) 596-6457
Mail to: P.O. Box 466, 04841
Founded in: 1935
Marius B. Peladeau, Director
Number of members: 1,000
Staff: full time 7, part time 6,
   volunteer 60
Major programs: library, archives,
   museum, historic site(s), tours,
   book publishing,
   newsletters/pamphlets, historic
   preservation, art collection,
   catalogues
Period of collections: 1700-present

RUMFORD

**Greater Rumford Area Historical
   Society**
04276
Founded in: 1970
Sarah Spencer, President
Number of members: 45
Major programs: library, archives,
   museum
Period of collections: early
   1800-present

RUMFORD-MEXICO
Acadian Heritage Society
6 Porter Bridge Rd.
Telephone: (207) 364-2702
Mail to: P.O. Box 239, 04247-0239
   Private agency
Founded in: 1980
Therese Martin, President
   Number of members: 200
Staff: volunteer 8
   Major programs: library, archives,
   oral history, school programs,
   newsletters/pamphlets, historic
   preservation, living history,
audiovisual programs

SACO

Dyer Library
371 Main St., 04072
Telephone: (207) 283-0754

Private agency
Founded in: 1881
Stephen J. Podgajny, Executive
   Director
Number of members: 400
Staff: full time 3, part time 6,
   volunteer 10
Major programs: library, archives,
   manuscripts, museum, book
   publishing, historic preservation,
   research, audiovisual programs,
   photographic collections
Period of collections: 19th century

**Saco Pump and Telephone
   Museum**
257 North St., 04072
Telephone: (207) 284-4928
Founded in: 1966
Questionnaire not received

York Institute Museum
375 Main St., 04072
Telephone: (207) 282-3031
Private agency
Founded in: 1867
Stephen Podgajny, Executive
   Director
Number of members: 300
Staff: part time 2
Major programs: library, archives,
   manuscripts, museum, tours,
   school programs, newsletters,
   exhibits, photographic collections,
   genealogical services, decorative
   arts, portraiture
Period of collections: 1700-1920

ST. AGATHA

St. Agatha Historical Society
P.O. Box 239, 04772-0237
Private agency
Founded in: 1980
Philippe Morin, President
Number of members: 200
Staff: volunteer 25
Major programs: library, archives,
   manuscripts, museum,
   tours/pilgrimages, oral history,
   school programs,
   newsletters/pamphlets, historic
   preservation, exhibits, living
   history, audiovisual programs,
   photographic collections,
   genealogical services

SANFORD

Sanford Historical Committee
1 Fogg's Court
Mail to: P.O. Box 747, 04073
Town agency
founded in: 1927
Russell J. Goodall, Chair
Major programs: archives,
   manuscripts, school programs,
   book publishing, historic
   preservation, research, exhibits,
   photographic collections

SCARBOROUGH

**Scarborough Historical
   Society, Inc.**
U.S. Rt. 1, 04074
Founded in: 1961
Number of members: 40
Staff: volunteer 12

Major programs: library, museum,
   historic sites preservation,
   tours/pilgrimages, educational
   programs
Period of collections: 1783-1865

SEARSPORT

Penobscot Marine Museum
Church St., 04974
Telephone: (207) 548-6634
Private agency
Founded in: 1936
C. Gardner Lane, Director
Number of members: 600
Staff: full time 5, part time 12,
   volunteer 8
Major programs: library, archives,
   museum, historic site(s), school
   programs, newsletters/pamphlets,
   historic preservation, exhibits,
   photographic collections,
   genealogical services
Period of collections: 1783-1920

SEBAGO

**Jones Gallery of Glass and
   Ceramics**
Douglas Hill, 04024
Telephone: (207) 787-3370
Founded in: 1978
Dorothy-Lee Jones, Director
Number of members: 300
Staff: full time 3, part time 1,
   volunteer 3
Major programs: library, museum,
   exhibits, audiovisual programs,
   photographic collections,
   decorative arts
Period of collections:
   prehistoric-present

SEDGWICK

**Sedgwick-Brooklin Historical
   Society**
04676
Private agency
Founded in: 1963
Brockway McMillan, President
Number of members: 175
Major programs: museum
Period of collections: 1850-1930

SKOWHEGAN

History House Association
Elm St.
Telephone: (207) 474-3140
Mail to: 75 Mt. Pleasant Ave., 04976
Private agency
Founded in: 1937
Marjorie Ensminger, Curator
Number of members: 20
Staff: part time 1, volunteer 20
Major programs: museum, historic
   site(s), tours/pilgrimages, school
   programs, historic preservation,
   research
Period of collections: to 1800s

SOMESVILLE

**Mount Desert Island Historical
   Society**
Main St. 04660
Founded in: 1929
Questionnaire not received

SOUTH BERWICK

Old Berwick Historical Society
Liberty St., 03908
Mail to: Old Mill Rd.
Questionnaire not received

SOUTH PORTLAND

South Portland-Cape Elizabeth Historical Society
245 High St.
Telephone: (207) 799-1977
Mail to: P.O. Box 2623, 04106
Founded in: 1963
Lenora K. Bangert, President
Number of members: 50
Major programs: archives, museum, markers, oral history, historic preservation
Period of collections: middle 1800s-early 1900s

SOUTH WINDHAM

Windham Historical Society, Inc.
Old Town House, Windham Center Rd.
Telephone: (207) 892-6589
Mail to: R.R. E. Montgomery Rd., 04082
Private agency
Founded in: 1967
Mrs. Malcolm H. Barto, Historian
Number of members: 200
Staff: volunteer 8
Major programs: museum, historic site(s), junior history, school programs, newsletters/pamphlets, genealogical services
Period of collections: 1783-present

SPRINGDALE

Sanford—Alfred Historical Society
P.O. Box 365, 04083
Telephone: (207) 324-8319
Founded in: 1954
Questionnaire not received

STANDISH

Standish Historical Society
Municipal Bldg., 04075
Private agency
Founded in: 1974
Jolene Webber, President
Number of members: 20
Staff: volunteer 8
Major programs: library, archives, manuscripts, museum, historic site(s), school programs, historic preservation, audiovisual programs, photographic collections
Period of collections: 1760s-present

STOCKHOLM

Stockholm Historical Society
Lake and S. Main Sts., 04783
Private agency
Founded in: 1976
Rosemary Hede, Secretary
Number of members: 100
Staff: part time 1, volunteer 100
Major programs: museum, oral history, newsletters, exhibits, photographic collections
Period of collections: 1881-present

SULLIVAN-SORRENTO

Sullivan-Sorrento Historical Society
P.O. Box 67, W. Sullivan, 04689
Telephone: (207) 422-6253 (curator)
Mail to: c/o Curator, R.F.D. 1, Box 104, E. Sullivan, 04607
Private agency
Founded in: 1972
Ruth H. Watson, Curator
Number of members: 49
Staff: volunteer 6
Major programs: archives, museum, oral history, newsletters, research, exhibits
Period of collections: 1789-present

THOMASTON

Knox Memorial Association
High St.
Mail to: c/o Mrs. L. French, 33 Knox St., 04861
Number of members: 1920
Questionnaire not received

VAN BUREN

Living Heritage Society
P.O. Box 165, 04785
Private agency
Founded in: 1980
Ann L. Roy, President
Staff: volunteer 10
Major programs: library, manuscripts, museum, historic site(s), tours/pilgrimages, junior history, oral history, school programs, newsletters/pamphlets, historic preservation, exhibits, living history, audiovisual programs, photographic collections
Period of collections: 1785-present

VASSALBORO

Vassalboro Historical Society
c/o Betty Taylor, Secretary, E. Vassalboro, 04935
Telephone: (207) 923-3533
Founded in: 1961
Questionnaire not received

VINALHAVEN

Vinalhaven Historical Society, Inc.
High St.
Telephone: (207) 863-4969
Mail to: P.O. Box 339, 04863
Private agency
Founded in: 1963
Roy Van. N. Heisler, President
Number of members: 100
Staff: volunteer 20
Major programs: museum, school programs, photographic collections
Period of collections: 1860-1914

WARREN

Georges River Canal Association
R.F.D. 1, 04864
Telephone: (207) 273-2622
Founded in: 1970
William Gross, President
Staff: volunteer 16
Major programs: markers, tours/pilgrimages, newsletters/pamphlets
Period of collections: 1783-1918

Maine Society for the History of Medicine
R.F.D. 1, 04864
Telephone: (207) 785-4547
Private agency
Founded in: 1979
Richard J. Kahn, Program Chair
Number of members: 50
Staff: volunteer 3
Major programs: museum, research, exhibits, lectures, medical history

Warren Historical Society
Mail to: P.O. Box 11, 04864
Private agency
Founded in: 1964
Number of members: 160
Major programs: library, oral history, book publishing, historic preservation, photographic collections
Period of collections: 1783-1930

WATERBORO

Waterborough Historical Society
Rt. 5, E. Waterboro, 04030
Telephone: (207) 247-5878
Founded in: 1969
Number of members: 120
Staff: volunteer 25
Magazine: *The Waterborough*
Major programs: museum, historic site, newsletters/pamphlets, historic preservation
Period of collections: 1787-present

WATERFORD

Waterford Historical Society—Mary Gage Rice Museum—Waterford Village
Rts. 35 and 37
Mail to: P.O. Box 2, 04088
Private agency
Founded in: 1965
James Tyler, President
Number of members: 80
Staff: volunteer 5
Magazine: *The Waterford Echoes*
Major programs: manuscripts, oral history, book publishing, newsletters/pamphlets, historic preservation, exhibits, special events
Period of collections: late 19th century-present

WATERVILLE

Colby College Museum of Art
Mayflower Hill, 04901
Telephone: (207) 873-1131
Founded in: 1959
Questionnaire not received

Waterville Historical Society
64 Silver St. 04901
Telephone: (207) 872-9439
Founded in: 1902
Agatha R. Fullam, Assistant Curator
Staff: full time 1
Major programs: museum, tours
Period of collections: 1814-1918

WELD

Weld Historical Society, Inc.
Wilton Rd., 04285
Telephone: (207) 585-2340
Private agency

Founded in: 1975
Kenneth P. Blake, President
Number of members: 187
Staff: volunteer 10
Major programs: archives,
manuscripts, museum, historic
site(s), newsletters/pamphlets,
exhibits, photographic collections,
genealogical services
Period of collections: 1800-present

WELLS

**Historical Society of Wells and
Ogunquit, Maine**
Post Rd., Box 801, 04090
Telephone: (207) 646-4775
Private agency
Founded in: 1954
Mary Jo Lee, President
Number of members: 150
Staff: volunteer 12
Major programs: library, manuscripts,
museum, tours/pilgrimages, school
programs, book publishing, historic
preservation, records
management, research, exhibits,
archaeology programs,
photographic collections,
genealogical services
Period of collections: 17th-18th
centuries

Wells Auto Museum
Rt. 1
Telephone: (207) 646-9064
Mail to: P.O. Box 496, 04090
Private agency
Founded in: 1954
Kenneth E. Creed III, Managing
Director
Staff: full time 1, volunteer 2
Major programs: museum, exhibits
Period of collections: 1900-1963

WICASETT

**Lincoln County Cultural and
Historical Association**
Federal St., 04578
Telephone: (207) 882-6817
Mail to: P.O. Box 61, 04544
Private agency
Founded in: 1954
Stanton Whitney, President
Number of members: 420
Staff: part time 1
Major programs: archives, museum,
historic site(s), tours/pilgrimages,
newsletters/pamphlets, historic
preservation, exhibits
Period of collections: 1750-1875

WILTON

**Wilton Historical Society—Farm
and Home Museum**
Kineowatha Park
Mail to: P.O. Box 33, 04294
Founded in: 1962
Lafayette Cochran, President
Number of members: 40
Staff: volunteer 40
Major programs: museum, historic
preservation, records
management, exhibits,
genealogical services
Period of collections: early
1800s-1960

WINDHAM

Windham Historical Society
The Bodge House, Chute Rd. 04082
Telephone: (207) 892-6589
Founded in: 1967
Malcolm H. Barto, President
Number of members: 215
Major programs:
newsletters/pamphlets
Period of collections: 1783-present

WINSLOW

Winslow Historical Society
Lithgow St. 04902
Mail to: 16 Benton Ave.
Mary L. Morrison, President
Number of members: 25
Major programs: museum,
educational programs
Period of collections: 1800-1925

WINTER HARBOR

Winter Harbor Historical Society
Main St.
Telephone: (207) 963-7461
Mail to: P.O. Box 400, 04693
Private agency
Founded in: 1976
Robert Coombs, President
Number of members: 28
Staff: volunteer 2
Major programs: archives,
manuscripts, museum, historic
site(s), oral history, historic
preservation, research, exhibits,
living history, audiovisual
programs, photographic
collections, genealogical services
Period of collections: 1850-1950

WINTERPORT

Winterport Historical Association
P.O. Box 172, 04496
Telephone: (207) 223-4887
Private agency
Gordon W. Wildes, Secretary
Major programs: historic site(s),
markers, historic preservation
Period of collections: 1779-present

WINTHROP

Winthrop Historical Society
Mail to: P.O. Box 111, E. Winthrop,
04343
Founded in: 1977
Period of collections: 1770-1920

WISCASSET

**Lincoln County Cultural and
Historical Association**
Federal St.
Telephone: (207) 882-6817
Mail to: P.O. Box 61, 04578
Founded in: 1954
Questionnaire not received

Musical Wonder House
18 High St., 04578
Telephone: (207) 882-7163
Private agency
Founded in: 1962
Danilo Konvalinka, President
Staff: full time 4
Major programs: museum, recorded
music collections
Period of collections: 1780-1955

**Society for the Preservation of Old
Mills**
Mail to: P.O. Box 435, 04578
Founded in: 1972
Questionnaire not received

YARMOUTH

**Yarmouth Historical
Society—Museum of Yarmouth
History**
Main St.
Telephone: (207) 846-5004
Mail to: P.O. Box 107, 04906
Founded in: 1960
Mrs. John W. Page, Director/Curator
Number of members: 300
Staff: part time 8, volunteer 12
Major programs: library, archives,
manuscripts, museum, oral history,
school programs, historic
preservation, records
management, research, exhibits,
living history, archaeology
programs, photographic
collections, genealogical services
Period of collections: 18th-19th
centuries

YORK

Old Gaol Museum Committee
Lindsay Rd.
Telephone: (207) 363-3872
Mail to: P.O. Box 188, 03909
Founded in: 1900
Questionnaire not received

Old York Historical Society
P.O. Box 312, 03909
Telephone: (207) 363-4974
Founded in: 1984
Number of members: 350
Staff: full time 5, part time 20
Major programs: museum,
newsletters/pamphlets, historic
preservation, genealogical
services, educational programs
Period of collections: 1680-1900

**Society for the Preservation of
Historic Landmarks in York
County, Inc.**
03909
Founded in: 1952
Number of members: 250
Staff: full time 1, part time 15
Major programs: historic sites
preservation, educational
programs, books
Period of collections: 1700-1900

MARYLAND

ABERDEEN

**Aberdeen Appearance and
Preservation Commission**
P.O. Box 331, 21001
Town agency
Founded in: 1977
Richard Morton, Co-chair
Number of members: 65
Major programs: historic site(s),
tours/pilgrimages, historic
preservation, exhibits
Period of collections: early 1900s

U.S. Army Ordnance Museum
Aberdeen Proving Ground, 21005
Telephone: (301) 278-3602
Federal agency, authorized by the
  U.S. Army
Daniel E. O'Brien, Director
Staff: full time 2, part time 3
Major programs: archives, museum,
  markers, tours/pilgrimages,
  educational programs
Period of collections: 1865-present

ACCOKEEK

National Colonial Farm of the Accokeek Foundation, Inc.
3400 Bryan Pt. Rd., 20607
Telephone: (301) 283-2113
Private agency
Founded in: 1957
David O. Percy, Executive Vice
  President
Number of members: 475
Staff: full time 9, part time 8
Major programs: museum,
  tours/pilgrimages, educational
  programs
Period of collections: 18th century

ANNAPOLIS

Banneker-Douglas Museum of Afro-American Life and History
84 Franklin St., 21401
Telephone: (301) 269-2894
State agency, authorized by
  Maryland Commission on
  Afro-American History and Culture
Founded in: 1969
Carroll Greene, Jr., Curator
Staff: full time 7, volunteer 9
Major programs: library, archives,
  manuscripts, museum, historic
  site(s), tours/pilgrimages,
  newsletters/pamphlets, historic
  preservation, research, exhibits,
  photographic collections
Period of collections: late 19th-early
  20th centuries

Cultural and Historical Resources, Maryland Forest, Park and Wildlife Service
580 Taylor Ave., 21401
Telephone: (301) 269-3771
State agency, authorized by
  Department of Natural Resources
Founded in: 1896
Ross M. Kimmel, Supervisor
Major programs: museum, historic
  site(s), markers, tours, oral history,
  school programs, pamphlets,
  historic preservation, research,
  exhibits, living history, audiovisual
  programs, archaeology programs,
  conservation history
Period of collections: Colonial
  period-1950s

Hammond-Harwood House Association
19 Maryland Ave., 21401
Telephone: (301) 269-1714
Private agency
Founded in: 1938
Barbara A. Brand, Administrator
Staff: full time 1, part time 7,
  volunteer 30
Major programs: museum, historic
  site
Period of collections: 1760-1800

Historic Annapolis, Inc.
194 Prince George St., 21401
Telephone: (301) 267-7619
Private agency
Founded in: 1952
Mrs. John Symonds, President
Number of members: 2,000
Staff: full time 16, part time 14,
  volunteer 80
Magazine: Mercury
Major programs: archives, museum,
  historic site(s), tours/pilgrimages,
  school programs,
  newsletters/pamphlets, historic
  preservation, research, exhibits,
  archaeology programs
Period of collections: 18th-19th
  centuries

Historic District Commission, City of Annapolis
160 Duke of Gloucester St., 21401
Telephone: (301) 263-7941
City agency
Founded in: 1969
Joseph Sachs, Chair
Staff: part time 2, volunteer 5
Major programs: historic preservation

Maryland Commission on Afro-American History and Culture
84 Franklin St., 21401
Telephone: (301) 269-2893
State agency, authorized by
  Department of Economic and
  Community Development
Founded in: 1969
Carroll Greene, Jr., Executive
  Director
Number of members: 22
Staff: full time 7, volunteer 42
Magazine: The Maryland Pendulum
Major programs: library, archives,
  manuscripts, museum, historic
  site(s), tours/pilgrimages,
  newsletters/pamphlets, historic
  preservation, research, exhibits,
  photographic collections
Period of collections: late 19th-early
  20th centuries

Maryland State Archives, Hall of Records
St. John's St. and College Ave.
Telephone: (301) 269-3915
Mail to: P.O. Box 828, 21404
State agency
Founded in: 1936
Edward C. Papenfuse, State Archivist
Number of members: 2
Staff: full time 22, part time 13
Major programs: library, archives,
  manuscripts, tours/pilgrimages,
  book publishing,
  newsletters/pamphlets, records
  management, research, exhibits,
  photographic collections,
  genealogical services
Period of collections: 1635-present

Maryland Historical Trust
21 State Circle, 21401
Telephone: (301) 269-2212
Founded in: 1961
Questionnaire not received

Maryland Park Service
580 Taylor Ave., 21401
Telephone: (301) 269-3771
Staff: full time 2, part time 7,
  volunteer 1
Major programs: historic sites
  preservation, markers, oral history,
  educational programs,
  newsletters/pamphlets
Period of collections: prehistoric-1865

U. S. Naval Academy Museum
U. S. Naval Academy, 21402
Telephone: (301) 267-2108
Federal agency
Founded in: 1845
William W. Jeffries, Director
Staff: full time 10
Major programs: library, manuscripts,
  museum, research, exhibits
Period of collections: 16th-20th
  centuries

Colonial kitchen at The National Colonial Farm in Accokeek.—The National Colonial Farm

BALTIMORE

Ballestone Preservation Society
Rocky Point Golf Course, Back River
   Neck Rd., 21221
Telephone: (301) 574-3630, 686-3406
Founded in: 1975
Susan Mairose, President
Number of members: 135
Staff: volunteer 50
Major programs: tours/pilgrimages,
   historic preservation
Period of collections: early 1800s

**Baltimore Center for Urban
   Archaeology, Municipal Museum
   of Baltimore**
c/o The Peale Museum, 225 N.
   Holliday St., 21202
Telephone: (301) 396-1866
City agency
Founded in: 1983
Elizabeth Anderson Comer, City
   Archaeologist/Director
Number of members: full time 3, part
   time 9, volunteer 200
Major programs: tours/pilgrimages,
   school programs,
   newsletters/pamphlets, records
   management, research, exhibits,
   archaeology programs
Period of collections: 1750-present

**Baltimore City Archives and
   Records Center**
211 E. Pleasant St., 21202
Telephone: (301) 396-4861
City agency, authorized by
   Department of Legislative
   Reference
Founded in: 1954
William G. LeFurgy, City
   Archivist/Records Management
   Officer
Staff: full time 6
Major programs: archives, records
   management, genealogical
   services
Period of collections: 1729-present

**Baltimore Conference, United
   Methodist Historical Society**
2200 St. Paul St., 21218
Telephone: (301) 889-4458
Founded in: 1855
Edwin Schell, Executive Secretary
Number of members: 625
Staff: part time 3, volunteer 12
Magazine: *Third Century Methodism*
Major programs: library, archives,
   manuscripts, museum, historic
   sites preservation, markers,
   tours/pilgrimages, educational
   programs, books,
   newsletters/pamphlets
Period of collections: 1640-present

Baltimore Heritage, Inc.
P.O. Box 4687, 21212
Telephone: (301) 669-2419
Private agency
Founded in: 1960
Licien King Harris, President
Number of members: 250
Staff: volunteer 9
Major programs: manuscripts,
   markers, junior history, school
   programs, newsletters/pamphlets,
   historic preservation, research,
   exhibits, historic interiors survey

Baltimore Museum of Industry
1415 Key Hwy., 21230
Telephone: (301) 727-4808
Private agency
Founded in: 1977
Dennis Zembala, Executive Director
Number of members: 300
Staff: full time 5, part time 2,
   volunteer 50
Major programs: archives, museum,
   historic site(s), tours/pilgrimages,
   oral history, school programs,
   newsletters/pamphlets, historic
   preservation, research, exhibits,
   living history, audiovisual
   programs, photographic
   collections, field services,
   machinery and craft
   demonstrations
Period of collections: 1750-1950

**Baltimore Public Works
   Museum, Inc.**
701 Eastern Ave., 21202
Telephone: (301) 396-5565
Private agency
Founded in: 1980
Nancy m. Andryszak, Curator
Staff: full time 3
Major programs: museum,
   newsletters/pamphlets, records
   management, exhibits, print
   collection, public works history
Period of collections: 1895-present

**Carroll Mansion, Municipal
   Museum of Baltimore**
800 E. Lombard St., 21202
Telephone: (301) 396-3523
Private agency
Founded in: 1967
Nancy Brennan, Director
Period of collections: 1800-present

Catonsville Historical Society, Inc.
1824 Frederick Rd.
Telephone: (301) 744-3034
Mail to: P.O. Box 9311, 21228
Town agency
Founded in: 1973
Nancy Miller, President
Number of members: 700
Staff: part time 1
Major programs: audiovisual
   programs, speaker program

**Cloisters Children's Museum of
   Baltimore City**
10440 Falls Rd., 21022
Telephone: (301) 823-2551
Founded in: 1977
Questionnaire not received

**Commission for Historical and
   Architectural Preservation**
601 City Hall, 100 N. Holliday St.,
   21202
Telephone: (301) 396-4866
City agency
Founded in: 1964
Kathleen Kotarba, Executive Director
Staff: volunteer 8
Major programs: library, museum,
   historic site(s), markers,
   tours/pilgrimages, school
   programs, historic preservation,
   research, exhibits, photographic
   collections
Period of collections: 19th century

**Essex-Middle River Heritage
   Society**
516 Eastern Ave., 21221
Telephone: (301) 574-6148
County agency
Founded in: 1968
Lyle A. Becker, President
Number of members: 164
Staff: volunteer 30
Major programs: library, museum,
   historic site, tours/pilgrimages,
   junior history, oral history,
   educational programs, historic
   preservation, audiovisual programs
Period of collections: 1900-1950

**Evergreen House
   Foundation—John Work Garrett
   Rare Book Library**
4545 N. Charles St., 21210
Telephone: (301) 338-7641
Private agency, authorized by Johns
   Hopkins University
Founded in: 1952
Meredith P. Millspaugh, Director
Number of members: 350
Staff: full time 8, part time 2
Major programs: library, manuscripts,
   museum, historic site(s),
   tours/pilgrimages, oral history,
   historic preservation, research,
   exhibits, photographic collections,
   concerts, theater
Period of collections: 1500-date

**Flickinger Foundation For
   American Studies, Inc.**
300 St. Dunstan's Rd., 21212
Telephone: (301) 323-6284
Private agency
Founded in: 1973
B. Floyd Flickinger, President
Staff: volunteer 4
Major programs: library, archives,
   manuscripts, tours/pilgrimages,
   oral history, school programs,
   newsletters/pamphlets, research,
   field services
Period of collections: 17th-19th
   centuries

**Ft. McHenry National Monument
   and Historic Shrine**
E. Fort Ave., 21230
Telephone: (301) 962-4290
Federal agency, authorized by
   National Park Service
Founded in: 1925
Juin A. Crosse-Barnes,
   Superintendent
Staff: full time 18, part time 11,
   volunteer 40
Major programs: library, museum,
   historic site(s), tours/pilgrimages,
   school programs, historic
   preservation, exhibits, living history
Period of collections: 1800-1920

Historic Flag House
844 E. Pratt St., 21202
Telephone: (301) 837-1793
Founded in: 1793
Verna Pearthree, Director
Questionnaire not received

**Jewish Historical Society of
   Maryland, Inc.—Jewish Heritage
   Center**
15 Lloyd St., 21202
Telephone: (301) 358-9417

Private agency, authorized by
Associated Jewish Charities of
Baltimore, Inc.
Founded in: 1960
Mrs. Allan T. Hirsh, Jr., President
Number of members: 1,200
Staff: full time 1, part time 3,
volunteer 50
Magazine: *Generations*
Major programs: archives, museum,
historic site(s), tours/pilgrimages,
oral history, newsletters/pamphlets
Period of collections: mid-19th
century-present

Lansdowne Historical Society, Inc.
3206 Hilltop Ave., 21227
Telephone: (301) 242-4284
Private agency
Founded in: 1977
Mrs. Frances C. Bannan, President
Staff: volunteer 3
Major programs: museum, historic
site(s), tours/pilgrimages, historic
preservation, exhibits, audiovisual
programs
Period of collections: Civil War era

Lovely Lane Museum
2200 St. Paul St., 21202
Telephone: (301) 889-4458
Private agency, authorized by
Baltimore Conference, United
Methodist Church
Founded in: 1855
Edwin Schell, Executive Secretary
Number of members: 542
Staff: part time 3, volunteer 10
Magazine: *Third Century Methodism*
Major programs: library, archives,
manuscripts, museum, historic
site(s), research, exhibits
Period of collections: from 1700

Maryland Environmental Trust
501 St. Paul Place, Suite 1310, 21202
Telephone: (301) 659-6440
State agency, authorized by
Department of Natural Resources
Founded in: 1967
Robert Beckett, Executive Director
Staff: full time 3
Major programs:
newsletters/pamphlets, historic
preservation, audiovisual
programs, field services,
conservation programs

◊**Maryland Historical Society**
201 W. Monument St., 21201
Telephone: (301) 685-3750
Private agency
Founded in: 1844
J. Jefferson Miller II, Director
Number of members: 6,900
Staff: full time 48, part time 21,
volunteer 463
Magazine: *Maryland Historical
Magazine, Maryland Magazine of
Genealogy*
Major programs: library, archives,
manuscripts, museum, markers,
oral history, school programs, book
publishing, newsletters/pamphlets,
research, exhibits, photographic
collections, genealogical services
Period of collections: 1634-present

Municipal Museum of Baltimore
800 E. Lombard St., 21202

Telephone: (301) 396-3523
City agency
Founded in: 1932
Nancy Brennan, Director
Number of members: 500
Staff: full time 14, volunteer 55
Magazine: *City Past-Times*
Major programs: library, archives,
manuscripts, museum, historic
site(s), tours/pilgrimages, school
programs, newsletters/pamphlets,
historic preservation, research,
exhibits, living history, archaeology
programs, photographic
collections
Period of collections: post-Civil War
era

**Museum of the Baltimore College
of Dental Surgery**
University of Maryland Dental School
Telephone: (301) 528-3388
Mail to: 666 W. Baltimore St., 21201
State agency, authorized by the
university
Founded in: 1840
James F. Craig, Director
Major programs: museum, exhibits,
dental history
Period of collections: 1800s

The Peale Museum
225 Holliday St., 21202
Telephone: (301) 396-3523
Founded in: 1931
Questionnaire not received

**Society for the Preservation of
Federal Hill and Fell's Point**
804 S. Broadway, 21231
Telephone: (301) 675-6750
Private agency
Founded in: 1967
Carolyn M. Donkervoet, Executive
Director
Number of members: 270
Staff: full time 1, part time 1
Magazine: *The Packet*
Major programs: museum, historic
site(s), tours/pilgrimages,
newsletters/pamphlets, historic
preservation, research, exhibits
Period of collections: 1730-1860

**Star-Spangled Banner Flag
House—1812 Museum**
844 E. Pratt St., 21202
Telephone: (301) 837-1793
Private agency, authorized by
Star-Spangled Banner Flag House
Association, inc.
Founded in: 1927
M. Linda Vahrenkamp, Director
Number of members: 465
Staff: full time 3, part time 7,
volunteer 25
Magazine: *The Star*
Major programs: museum, historic
site(s), tours/pilgrimages, school
programs, newsletters/pamphlets,
historic preservation, research,
exhibits, living history, audiovisual
programs, photographic
collections
Period of collections: 1800-1850

**Steamship Historical Society of
America, Inc.**
Library Collection, University of
Baltimore, 1420 Maryland Ave.,
21201

Telephone: (301) 625-3134
Mail to: 414 Pelton Ave., Staten
Island, N.Y., 10310
Private agency
Founded in: 1935
Alice S. Wilson, Secretary
Number of members: 3,500
Staff: part time 2, volunteer 4
Magazine: *Steamboat Bill*
Major programs: library, archives,
book publishing, photographic
collections
Period of collections: 1790-present

BEL AIR

**Historical Society of Harford
County, Inc.**
324 Kenmore Ave., 21014
Telephone: (301) 838-7691
Founded in: 1885
Andrew M. Bristow, President
Number of members: 305
Staff: volunteer 25
Magazine: *Harford Historical Bulletin*
Major programs: library, archives,
manuscripts, museum, book
publishing, newsletters/pamphlets,
records management
Period of collections: 1700-present

BOONSBORO

Boonsboro Museum of History
113 N. Main St., 21713
Telephone: (301) 432-6969/432-5151
Private agency
Founded in: 1974
Douglas G. Bast, Owner/Director
Staff: volunteer 2
Major programs: library, archives,
manuscripts, museum, educational
programs
Period of collections: 1776-1920

BOYDS

**Boyds-Clarksburg-Germantown
Historical Society, Inc.**
16112 Barnesville Rd., 20841
Telephone: (301) 972-3452
Private agency
Founded in: 1979
Margaret M. Coleman, President
Number of members: 65
Staff: volunteer 4
Major programs: manuscripts,
museum, markers,
newsletters/pamphlets, historic
preservation, living history,
photographic collections,
genealogical services
Period of collections: 1800-1960

BROOKLANDVILLE

**Cloisters Children's Museum of
Baltimore City**
10440 Falls Rd., 21022
Telephone: (301) 823-2551
Mail to: P.O. Box 66
City agency, authorized by Mayor's
Advisory Committee on Art and
Culture
Founded in: 1977
Jody Albright, Director of the Mayor's
Advisory Committee on Art and
Culture
Staff: full time 6, part time 2,
volunteer 30

Major programs: museum,
tours/pilgrimages, school
programs, research, conservation
Period of collections:
Renaissance-19th century

CAMBRIDGE

**Dorchester County Historical
Society, Inc.**
902 LaGrange St.
Telephone: (301) 228-7953
Mail to: P.O. Box 361, 21613
Founded in: 1953
Naomi L. Dickerson, President
Number of members: 700
Staff: volunteer 50
Major programs: library, museum,
tours/pilgrimages,
newsletters/pamphlets, exhibits,
genealogical services
Period of collections: 1865-1918

CATONSVILLE

Historical Old Salem, Inc.
P.O. Box 9347, Baltimore, 21228
Private agency
Founded in: 1976
Leo J. Ritter, President
Number of members: 200
Staff: volunteer 20
Major programs: historic site(s),
historic preservation
Period of collections: 1850-1900

CENTREVILLE

**Queen Anne's County Historical
Society**
P.O. Box 62, 21617
Founded in: 1960
Number of members: 800
Staff: volunteer 100
Major programs: library, archives,
museum, historic site, markes,
tours/pilgrimages, oral history,
educational programs, book
publishing, newsletters/pamphlets,
historic preservation
Period of collections: 18th century

CHARLESTOWN

Colonial Charlestown, Inc.
107 Market St.
Telephone: (301) 287-8793
Mail to: P.O. Box 11, 21914
Private agency
Founded in: 1973
Nelson H. McCall, President
Number of members: 80
Staff: volunteer 8
Magazine: Colonial Charlestown
Society
Major programs: archives, museum,
historic site(s), historic
preservation, research,
genealogical services
Period of collections: 1742-1842

CHESTERTOWN

**Historical Society of Kent
County, Inc.**
101 Church Alley
Telephone: (301) 778-3499
Mail to: P.O. Box 665, 21520
Private agency
Founded in: 1936

Katherine Myrick DeProspo, Curator
Number of members: 675
Staff: part time 1, volunteer 20
Major programs: museum, historic
site(s), tours/pilgrimages, oral
history, historic preservation,
genealogical services
Period of collections: mid-18th
century

Preservation, Inc.
P.O. Box 420, 21620
Private agency
Founded in: 1971
Christian Havenmeyer, President
Major programs: historic preservation

CLEAR SPRING

**Clear Spring District Historical
Association**
P.O. Box 211, 21722
Telephone: (301) 842-2342
Private agency
Founded in: 1981
David E. Wiles, President
Number of members: 50
Major programs: museum, historic
site(s), markers, tours/pilgrimages,
book publishing,
newsletters/pamphlets, historic
preservation, archaeology
programs, photographic
collections
Period of collections: 1807-present

CLINTON

The Surratt Society
Mary E. Surratt House and Tavern,
9110 Brandywine Rd.
Telephone: (301) 868-1121
Mail to: P.O. Box 427, 20735
Authorized by Maryland-National
Capital Park and Planning
Commission
Founded in: 1975
Nancy Griffith, President
Number of members: 700
Major programs: library, museum,
historic site(s), tours/pilgrimages,
school programs,
newsletters/pamphlets, research
Period of collections: 1800-1865

COCKEYSVILLE

**Baltimore County Historical
Society**
P.O. Box 81, 21030
Founded in: 1959
Number of members: 750
Staff: volunteer 20
Magazine: History Trails
Major programs: library, manuscripts,
museum, historic sites
preservation, markers, educational
programs, books,
newsletters/pamphlets
Period of collections: 1865-1918

COLLEGE PARK

Friends of the College Park Airport
6709 Cpl. Frank Scott Dr.
Telephone: (301) 927-1909
Mail to: P.O. Box Y, 20740
County agency, authorized by
Maryland-National Capital Park and
Planning Commission

Founded in: 1975
Walter Starling, Chair
Number of members: 1,400
Staff: volunteer 20
Major programs: archives, museum,
historic site(s), markers,
tours/pilgrimages,
newsletters/pamphlets, historic
preservation, exhibits, living
history, audiovisual programs,
photographic collections, historical
airport, early aviation history
Period of collections: 1909-present

CUMBERLAND

**Allegany County Historical
Society, Inc.**
218 Washington St., 21502
Telephone: (301) 777-8678
Private agency
Founded in: 1937
Rita L. Knox, Director
Number of members: 400
Staff: full time 1, volunteer 30
Major programs: museum, historic
site(s), tours, book publishing,
newsletters/pamphlets, exhibits,
photographic collections
Period of collections: Victorian era

**Preservation Society of Allegany
County, Inc.**
Bedford Rd., Maryland Motel, 21502
Telephone: (301) PA2-2836
Founded in: 1970
Questionnaire not received

DICKERSON

Sugarloaf Regional Trails, Inc.
23720 Mt. Ephraim Rd., 20842
Telephone: (301) 972-8375
Private agency
Founded in: 1973
Frederick Gutheim, Chair
Staff: volunteer 3
Major programs: historic site,
tours/pilgrimages, oral history,
book publishing, historic
preservation, research,
photographic collections, films,
environmental history, black and
ethnic history, planning,
preservation
Period of collections: 1865-1960

EASTON

**Historical Society of Talbot
County, Inc.**
25 S. Washington St.
Telephone: (301) 822-0773
Mail to: P.O. Box 964, 21601
Private agency
Founded in: 1954
Norman Harrington, Vice
President/Managing Director
Number of members: 1,300
Staff: full time 5, part time 7,
volunteer 130
Major programs: archives,
manuscripts, museum, historic
site(s), junior history, school
programs, book publishing,
newsletters/pamphlets, historic
preservation, records
management, research, exhibits,
audiovisual programs, archaeology

programs, photographic collections
Period of collections: Colonial period-present

EDGEWAGER

London Town Publik House and Gardens
839 Londontown Rd., 21037
Telephone: (301) 956-4900
County agency, authorized by Anne Arundel County Department of Recreation and Parks
Founded in: 1971
John T. Keene, Administrator
Number of members: 120
Staff: full time 5, volunteer 135
Major programs: library, historic site(s), school programs, research, living history
Period of collections: 1740-1770

ELKTON

Elk Creeks Preservation Society, Inc.
192 Booth Rd., 21921
Telephone: (301) 398-1843
Private agency
Founded in: 1977
Richard D. Mackie, Chair
Number of members: 75
Major programs: archives, historic site(s), tours/pilgrimages, school programs, historic preservation, research, exhibits, photographic collections, genealogical services
Period of collections: 1681-1910

Historical Society of Cecil County
135 E. Main St., 21921
Telephone: (301) 398-0914
Private agency
Founded in: 1931
Number of members: 450
Staff: volunteer 6
Major programs: library, archives, manuscripts, museum, historic site(s), markers, tours/pilgrimages, oral history, school programs, book publishing, newsletters/pamphlets, historic preservation, research, exhibits, audiovisual programs, photographic collections, genealogical services
Period of collections: 1740-1900

ELLICOTT CITY

Ellicott City Restoration Foundation, Inc.
8243 Main St.
Telephone: (301) 465-0980
Mail to: P.O. Box 92, 21043
Private agency
Founded in: 1980
Thomas F. Herbert, Board President
Staff: part time 1
major programs: historic preservation

Historic Ellicott City, Inc.
P.O. Box 244, 21043
Telephone: (301) 465-0980
Private agency
Founded in: 1972
Pat Francis, General Manager
Number of members: 600
Staff: part time 1
Magazine: *Heritage*

Major programs: library, museum, historic site(s), oral history, school programs, historic preservation, audiovisual programs
Period of collections: 1800s

Howard County Historical Society Inc.
8328 Court Ave.
Telephone: (301) 461-1050
Mail to: P.O. Box 109, 21043
Private agency
Founded in: 1957
Edward Walter, President
Number of members: 500
Staff: volunteer 10
Major programs: library, archives, manuscripts, museum, tours/pilgrimages, genealogical services
Period of collections: 1800-present

FORT MEADE

Ft. George G. Meade Museum
4674 Griffin Ave., 20755
Telephone: (301) 677-6966
Federal agency, authorized by the U.S. Army
Founded in: 1963
David C. Cole, Curator
Staff: full time 5
Major programs: library, archives, museum, school programs, research, exhibits
Period of collections: 1900-present

FREDERICK

Frederick City Historic District Commission
City Hall, 124 N. Market St., 21701
Telephone: (301) 662-5161
City agency
Founded in: 1968
G. Bernard Callan, Jr., Chair
Staff: part time 2
Major programs: educational programs, newsletters/pamphlets, historic preservation, historic district ordinance enforcement

Frederick County Landmarks Foundation
1110 Rosemont Ave., 21701
Telephone: (301) 663-6225
Private agency
Founded in: 1970
Richard Lebherz, Prsident
Number of members: 300
Staff: full time 1, volunteer 2
Major programs: library, museum, markers, book publishing, newsletters/pamphlets, historic preservation, exhibits, audiovisual programs, genealogical services
Period of collections: 1750-1800

Historical Society of Frederick County, Inc.
24 E. Church St., 21701
Telephone: (301) 663-1188
Private agency
Founded in: 1890
Elaine A. Heiberg, President
Number of members: 614
Major programs: library, museum, newsletters/pamphlets
Period of collections: 1783-1940

Maryland Association of Historic District Commissions
P.O. Box 783, 21701
Telephone: (301) 663-6820
Private agency,
Founded in: 1981
Cherilyn Widell, Executive Director
Number of members: 27
Staff: part time 1
Major programs: newsletters/pamphlets, historic preservation, audiovisual programs, field services

Rose Hill Manor—Children's Museum and Carriage Museum
1611 N. Market St., 21701
Telephone: (301) 694-1648
County agency, authorized by Frederick County Parks and Recreation Department
Founded in: 1972
Ain Colin Clevenger, Curator
Staff: full time 1
Major programs: museum, tours/pilgrimages, school programs, newsletters/pamphlets, living history
Period of collections: 1800-1890

GERMANTOWN

National Center for the Study of History
Drawer 730, 20874
Telephone: (301) 330-0442
Private agency, authorized by the District of Columbia
Founded in: 1984
Philip L. Cantelon, Vice President
Staff: volunteer 5
Major programs: field services

GREENSBORO

Caroline County Historical Society
Goldsborough Hall, Railroad Ave., 21639
Founded in: 1952
Questionnaire not received

HAGERSTOWN

Hager House
19 Key St., 21740
Telephone: (301) 739-8393
City agency
Founded in: 1962
Spring Ward, Curator
Staff: full time 1, part time 3, volunteer 10
Major programs: museum, historic site(s), exhibits
Period of collections: early 18th century

Washington County Historical Society
135 W. Washington St.
Telephone: (301) 797-8782
Mail to: P.O. Box 1281, 21740
Private agency
Founded in: 1911
Marjorie S. Peters, Executive Secretary
Number of members: 500
Staff: full time 1, volunteer 65
Major programs: library, museum, historic site(s), tours/pilgrimages,

newsletters/pamphlets, exhibits,
genealogical services
Period of collections: 1820-1870

HAVRE DE GRACE

**Steppingstone Museum
Association, Inc.,**
461 Quaker Bottom Rd., 21078
Telephone: (301) 939-2299
Private agency
Founded in: 1967
Lori D. Olsen, Coordinator
Number of members: 350
Staff: full time 1, part time 1,
volunteer 100
Magazine: *Steppingstone*
Major programs: museum, school
programs, newsletters/pamphlets,
exhibits, living history
Period of collections: 1880-1920

**Susquehanna Museum of Havre de
Grace, Inc.**
Conesteo St.
Telephone: (301) 939-3905
Mail to: P.O. Box 253, 21078
Private agency
Founded in: 1970
David H. Witt, Board Chair
Number of members: 135
Staff: volunteer 75
Major programs: museum, historic
preservation, photographic
collections

HOLLYWOOD

Sotherby Mansion Foundation, Inc.
Sotherby Rd.
Telephone: (301) 373-2280
Mail to: P.O. Box 67, 20636
Founded in: 1963
Staff: full time 4, part time 4,
volunteer 20
Major programs: historic site

HUNT VALLEY

**Unitarian and Universalist
Genealogical Society**
10605 Lakespring Way, 21030
Telephone: (301) 628-2490
Private agency
Founded in: 1971
Willis Clayton Tull, Jr., Executive
Director
Number of members: 301
Staff: part time 5, volunteer 5
Major programs: library, archives,
genealogical services
Period of collections: 1492-present

LEONARDTOWN

**St. Mary's County Historical
Society**
11 Courthouse Dr., 20650
Telephone: (301) 475-2467
Founded in: 1951
Joseph A. Dillow, President
Number of members: 825
Staff: full time 1
Magazine: *Chronicles of St. Mary's*
Major programs: library, archives,
museum, newsletters/pamphlets,
genealogical services
Period of collections: 1783-1865

MARRIOTTSVILLE

**Society for the Preservation of
Maryland Antiquities**
2335 Marriottsville Rd., 21104
Telephone: (301) 442-1772
Private agency
Founded in: 1931
Nancy Miller, Executive Director
Number of members: 1,300
Staff: full time 2, part time 1,
volunteer 4
Magazine: *The Phoenix*
Major programs: historic site(s),
tours/pilgrimages,
newsletters/pamphlets, historic
preservation

OAKLAND

**Garrett County Historical
Society, Inc.**
123 E. Center St., 21550
Telephone: (301) 334-3226
Founded in: 1941
Questionnaire not received

OCEAN CITY

Ocean City Museum Society
Boardwalk at Inlet Sts.
Telephone: (301) 289-4991
Mail to: P.O. Box 603, 21842
City agency
Founded in: 1977
Suzanne B. Hurley, Curator
Number of members: 286
Staff: full time 2, part time 3,
volunteer 15
Major programs: museum,
tours/pilgrimages, records
management, exhibits,
photographic collections
Period of collections: 1875-present

PERRYVILLE

Friends of Rodgers Tavern
Telephone: (301) 658-5399
Mail to: P.O. Box M, 21903
Private agency
Founded in: 1956
Charles Emery, President
Number of members: 150
Major programs: historic site,
tours/pilgrimages, junior history,
educational programs, historic
preservation, research
Period of collections: late 18th
century

POOLESVILLE

Historic Medley District, Inc.
19923 Fisher Ave.
Telephone: (301) 972-8588
Mail to: P.O. Box 232, 20837
Private agency
Founded in: 1974
Winsome Brown, President
Number of members: 50
Staff: volunteer 10
Major programs: museum, historic
site(s), historic preservation,
exhibits
Period of collections: 1695-present

PORT DEPOSIT

Port Deposit Heritage Corporation
P.O. Box 101, 21904

Telephone: (301) 378-3866
Private agency
Founded in: 1975
Grace C. Humphries, President
Number of members: 150
Staff: volunteer 12
Major programs: historic site(s)
Period of collections: 1813-1900

PORT TOBACCO

**Historical Society of Charles
County, Inc.**
20677
Telephone: (301) 934-3112
Mail to: P.O. Box 261
Number of members: 400
Staff: volunteer 60
Magazine: *The Record*
Major programs: library, historic sites
preservation, markers,
tours/pilgrimages
Period of collections: 1783-1865

PRINCE FREDERICK

**Calvert County Historical
Society, Inc.**
Telephone: (301) 535-2452
Mail to: P.O. Box 358, 20678
Private agency
Founded in: 1953
Edward C. Sledge, President
Number of members: 500
Staff: part time 1
Major programs: archives,
manuscripts, museum, markers,
oral history, book publishing,
newsletters/pamphlets, historic
preservation, research,
genealogical services, county
history education
Period of collections: 17th century

**Calvert County Historic District
Commission**
c/o Calvert County Planning and
Zoning Department, Courthouse
Annex, 20678
Telephone: (301) 535-1600, ext. 238
County agency
Founded in: 1974
William R. Pittman, Jr., Principal
Planner
Major programs: historic site(s),
historic preservation, records
management

RIVERDALE

**Prince George's County Historical
Society**
4811 Riverdale Rd.
Telephone: (301) 779-2313
Mail to: P.O. Box 14, 20737
Private agency
Founded in: 1952
John A. Giannetti, President
Number of members: 500
Staff: volunteer 6
Magazine: *News and Notes*
Major programs: library, archives,
manuscripts, tours/pilgrimages,
book publishing,
newsletters/pamphlets,
photographic collections
Period of collections: 1492-present

ROCKVILLE

Montgomery County Historical Society
103 W. Montgomery Ave., 20850
Telephone: (301) 762-1492
Private agency
Founded in: 1944
Nancy Hafer, President
Number of members: 850
Staff: part time 4, volunteer 14
Magazine: *Montgomery County Story*
Major programs: library, archives, museum, historic site(s), tours, oral history, school programs, newsletters/pamphlets, historic preservation, research, exhibits, living history, photographic collections, genealogical services
Period of collections: 19th century

Peerless Rockville Historic Preservation, Ltd.
103 S. Adams St.
Telephone: (301) 762-0096
Mail to: P.O. Box 4262, 20850
Private agency
Founded in: 1974
Eileen McGuckian, Executive Director
Number of members: 600
Staff: part time 1, volunteer 100
Magazine: *Walking Guide to Peerless Rockville*
Major programs: historic site(s), tours/pilgrimages, newsletters/pamphlets, historic preservation, research
Period of collections: late 19th century

ST. MARY'S CITY

St. Mary's City Commission
Telephone: (301) 994-0779
Mail to: P.O. Box 38, 20686
Founded in: 1966
Questionnaire not received

Friends of St. Mary's City
P.O. Box 39, 20686
Telephone: (301) 862-9882
Authorized by St. Mary's City Foundation
Founded in: 1979
William Carrico, President
Number of members: 425
Staff: part time 1
Major programs: museum, historic site, educational programs, newsletters/pamphlets, archaeology
Period of collections: 17th century

Historic St. Mary's City
Telephone: (301) 862-9880
Mail to: P.O. Box 39, 20686
State agency, authorized by Department of Economic and Community Development
Founded in: 1966
Daniel J. Reed, Director
Number of members: 300
Staff: full time 40, part time 50, volunteer 200
Major programs: library, museum, historic site(s), tours/pilgrimages, school programs, newsletters/pamphlets, historic preservation, research, exhibits, living history, audiovisual

programs, archaeology programs, field services, natural history
Period of collections: 17th-18th centuries

ST. MICHAELS

Chesapeake Bay Maritime Museum
21663
Telephone: (301) 745-2916
Private agency
Founded in: 1963
R.J. Holt, Director
Number of members: 3,640
Staff: full time 24, part time 20, volunteer 135
Magazine: *The Weather Gauge*
Major programs: museum, historic sites preservation
Period of collections: 1783-present

SALISBURY

City Hall Museum and Cultural Center
110 W. Church St.
Telephone: (301) 546-9007
Mail to: P.O. Box 884, 21801
Founded in: 1977
Questionnaire not received

Newtown Association, Inc.
P.O. Box 543, 21881
Telephone: (301) 543-2111
City agency
Founded in: 1975
Number of members: 150
Staff: volunteer 15
Major programs: historic site(s), markers, tours/pilgrimages, newsletters/pamphlets, historic preservation

North American Wildfowl Art Museum
Salisbury State College, 21801
Telephone: (301) 742-4988
Private agency, authorized by the Ward Foundation
Founded in: 1975
Kenneth A. Basile, Director
Number of members: 9,000
Staff: full time 1, part time 6, volunteer 300
Magazine: *Ward Foundation News*
Major programs: archives, manuscripts, museum, tours/pilgrimages, book publishing, newsletters/pamphlets, records management, research, exhibits, audiovisual programs
Period of collections: 1865-present

Pemberton Hall Foundation, Inc.
313 Lemmon Hill Lane, 21801
Telephone: (301) 749-0125
Private agency
Founded in: 1964
Robert L. McFarlin, President
Number of members: 200
Staff: volunteer 20
Magazine: *Pemberton News*
Major programs: historic site(s), tours/pilgrimages, school programs, historic preservation, records management, research, living history, archaeology programs, genealogical services
Period of collections: 18th century

Wicomico Historical Society, Inc.
Mail to: P.O. Box 573, 21801
Private agency
Founded in: 1935
Number of members: 400
Major programs: museum, historic site, book publishing, historic preservation
Period of collections: 1850-1950

SANDY SPRING

Sandy Spring Museum
18045 Georgia Ave., Olney, 20832
Telephone: (301) 774-0022
Mail to: P.O. Box 1484
Private agency
Founded in: 1980
Lesley Van der Lee, Director
Number of members: 435
Staff: full time 1, part time 1, volunteer 15
Magazine: *Sandy Spring Legacy*
Major programs: museum, newsletters/pamphlets, research, exhibits, photographic collections
Period of collections: late 19th-early 20th centuries

SEVERNA PARK

Ann Arrundell County Historical Society
Jones Station and Old Annapolis Rds.
Mail to: P.O. Box 836, 21146
Founded in: 1962
Mark N. Schatz, President
Number of members: 300
Staff: volunteer 10
Magazine: *Anne Arundel History Notes*
Major programs: library, archives, manuscripts, museum, historic site, markes, newsletters/pamphlets, historic preservation
Period of collections: 19th-20th centuries

SHARPSBURG

Antietam National Battlefield
P.O. Box 158, 21782
Telephone: (301) 432-5125
Federal agency, authorized by National Park Service
Founded in: 1890
Betty J. Otto, Librarian/Curator
Staff: full time 24, part time 2, volunteer 298
Major programs: library, museum, historic site(s), markers, historic preservation, records management, research, exhibits, living history, audiovisual programs, photographic collections, national cemetery
Period of collections: Civil War era

Barron's C & O Canal Museum
P.O. Box 356, 21782
Telephone: (301) 432-8726
Private agency
Founded in: 1970
Lee D. Barron, Owner
Staff: full time 2
Major programs: library, archives, manuscripts, museum, oral history, book publishing, research, exhibits, audiovisual programs, photographic collections
Period of collections: 1800-1925

SILVER SPRING

Archaeological Society of Maryland, Inc.
Telephone: (301) 426-0840
Mail to: c/o President, 3505 Gibbons Ave., 21214
Private agency
Founded in: 1964
Norma A. Wagner, President
Number of members: 500
Magazine: *Maryland Archaeology*
Major programs: historic site(s), book publishing, newsletters/pamphlets, exhibits, archaeology programs
Period of collections: prehistoric-Colonial period

National Capital Historical Museum of Transportation, Inc.
Bonifant Rd.
Telephone: (301) 384-9797
Mail to: P.O. Box 4007, Colesville Branch, 20904
Founded in: 1959
Questionnaire not received

SNOW HILL

Worcester County Historical Society
P.O. Box 111, 21863
Founded in: 1965
Number of members: 280
Major programs: archives, museum, historic sites preservation, markers, books
Period of collections: 1865-present

SOLOMONS

Calvert Marine Museum
P.O. Box 97, 20688
Telephone: (301) 326-2042
County agency, authorized by county commissioners
Founded in: 1970
Virginia M. Nickelson, Administrative Assistant
Number of members: 1,300
Staff: full time 13, part time 13, volunteer 20
Magazine: *Bugeye Times*
Major programs: library, archives, museum, oral history, school programs, newsletters/pamphlets, historic preservation, research, exhibits, audiovisual programs, photographic collections
Period of collections: 1870-present

TAKOMA PARK

Takoma Park Historical Society
c/o Municipal Bldg., 7500 Maple Ave., 20012
Telephone: (301) 585-3542
Founded in: 1912
Number of members: 65
Staff: volunteer 5
Major programs: archives, markers, oral history
Period of collections: 1865-present

THURMONT

Catoctin Furnace Historical Society, Inc.
Catoctin Furnace 21788
Telephone: (301) 271-2306
Questionnaire not received

TOWSON

Hampton National Historic Site
535 Hampton Lane, 21204
Telephone: (301) 823-7054
Federal agency, authorized by National Park Service
Founded in: 1948
Adam G. Karalius, Site Manager
Number of members: 1
Staff: full time 4, part time 8, volunteer 60
Major programs: manuscripts, historic site, educational programs, historic preservation, interpretation
Period of collections: 1785-1885

Historic Towson, Inc.
120 Allegheny Ave., 21204
Telephone: (301) 444-4413
Private agency
Founded in: 1977
Jay Ulrich, President
Number of members: 100
Staff: volunteer 10
Major programs: archives, historic site(s), historic preservation, exhibits

Landmarks Preservation Commission of Baltimore County
401 Bosley Ave., County Courts Bldg., 21204
Telephone: (301) 494-3521
County agency, authorized by Office of Planning and Zoning
Founded in: 1976
John McGrain, Executive Secretary
Number of members: 15
Staff: full time 1
Major programs: archives, historic site(s), historic preservation
Period of collections: 19th century

Maryland House and Garden Pilgrimage
600 W. Chesapeake, 21204
Telephone: (301) 821-6933
Founded in: 1939
Questionnaire not received

UNION BRIDGE

Western Maryland Railway Historical Society, Inc.
41 N. Main St.
Telephone: (301) 775-2206
Mail to: 6 S. Main St., 21791
Private agency
Founded in: 1968
James H. McDermott, President
Number of members: 170
Staff: volunteer 8
Magazine: *Blue Mountain Express*
Major programs: library, archives, manuscripts, museum, book publishing, newsletters/pamphlets, historic preservation, exhibits, living history, photographic collections
Period of collections: 1850-present

UPPER MARLBORO

Society of Mareen Duvall Descendants
c/o President, 12504 Croom Rd., 20772
Telephone: (301) 888-2168
Private agency
Founded in: 1926

David D. Duvall, President
Number of members: 385
Staff: volunteer 15
Major programs: archives, manuscripts, museum, historic site(s), markers, tours/pilgrimages, book publishing, newsletters/pamphlets, historic preservation, research, archaeology programs, genealogical services
Period of collections: 1657-present

WARWICK

Old Bohemia Historical Society, Inc.
P.O. Box 61, 21912
Telephone: (609) 299-0582
Founded in: 1953
Frank W. Krastel, President
Number of members: 350
Staff: volunteer 10
Major programs: library, museum, historic site, newsletters/pamphlets, historic preservation, religious services
Period of collections: 18th-19th centuries

WESTMINSTER

Carroll County Farm Museum
500 S. Center St., 21157
Telephone: (301) 848-7775
County agency, authorized by county commissioners
Founded in: 1966
JoAnn Hunter, Director
Number of members: 300
Staff: full time 5, part time 4, volunteer 300
Major programs: library, archives, museum, historic site(s), tours/pilgrimages, school programs, historic preservation, research, exhibits
Period of collections: 1800-1900

Historical Society of Carroll County, Inc.
210 E. Main St., 21157
Telephone: (301) 848-6494
Founded in: 1939
Harry O. Humbert, President
Number of members: 650
Staff: part time 3, volunteer 100
Major programs: library, archives, museum, tours/pilgrimages, books, newsletters/pamphlets
Period of collections: 1783-present

Springdale School
Springdale Rd., New Windsor, 21776
Telephone: (301) 848-8355
Mail to: 6 N. Court St., 21157
Private agency
Founded in: 1854
Marker J. Lovell, Owner
Major programs: historic preservation
Period of collections: late 1800s-early 1900s

Union Mills Homestead Foundation
3311 Littlestown Pike, 21157
Telephone: (301) 848-2288
Founded in: 1964
Questionnaire not received

WYE MILLS
Old Wye Mill Society
MD Rt. 662
Telephone: (301) 827-8009/827-6909
Mail to: P.O. Box 81, 21679
Founded in: 1957
Questionnaire not received

MASSACHUSETTS

ABINGTON
Abington Historical Commission
Town Hall, 33 Randolph St., 02351
Town agency
Founded in: 1980
George R. Horner, Chair
Major programs: library, historic
site(s), markers, school programs,
historic preservation, genealogical
services

Historical Society of Old Abington
P.O. Box 22, Dyer Memorial Library,
Centre Ave., 02351
Founded in: 1939
Questionnaire not received

ACTON
Acton Historical Society
300 Main St., Box 389, 01720
Founded in: 1960
Questionnaire not received

Iron Work Farm in Acton, Inc.
128 Main St., 01720
Mail to: P.O. Box 11, 01720
Private agency
Founded in: 1964
Wesley W. Mowry, President
Number of members: 120
Staff: volunteer 10
Major programs: museum, historic
site, historic preservation
Period of collections: early 18th
century-present

ADAMS
Adams Historical Society
McKinley Square, 01220
Founded in: 1973
Number of members: 250
Staff: volunteer 12
Major programs: library, museum,
oral history, educational programs,
newsletters/pamphlets, film
restoration
Period of collections: 1880-1920

AMHERST
Amherst Historical Society
67 Amity St., 01002
Mail to: P.O. Box 739, 01004
Founded in: 1899
Mary E. P. Commager, Administrator
Number of members: 240
Staff: part time 1, volunteer 30
Major programs: archives, museum,
oral history, educational programs,
book publishing,
newsletters/pamphlets, lectures,
symposia
Period of collections: 18th-19th
centuries

ANDOVER
Andover Historical Society
97 Main St., 01810
Telephone: (617) 475-2236
Private agency
Founded in: 1911
Marsha Rooney, Director/Curator
Number of members: 500
Staff: full time 2, volunteer 85
Magazine: *Andover Historical Society
Newsletter*
Major programs: library, manuscripts,
museum, oral history, school
programs, newsletters/pamphlets,
research, exhibits, audiovisual
programs, photographic
collections, adult educational
programs
Period of collections: 1800-1930

**Northeast Document Conservation
Center**
Abbot Hall, School St., 01810
Telephone: (617) 470-1010
Founded in: 1973
Ann Russell, Director
Staff: full time 26, part time 5
Major programs: educational
programs, conservation/
preservation services for books,
manuscripts, works of art on paper;
microfilming, photographic copy
work

ARLINGTON
Arlington Historical Society
7 Jason St., 02174
Telephone: (617) 648-4300
Private agency
Founded in: 1897
David W. Baldwin, Museums Director
Number of members: 450
Staff: part time 1, volunteer 14
Major programs: archives, museum,
historic site, tours/pilgrimages,
book publishing
Period of collections: 1740-1900

Old Schwamb Mill
17 Mill Lane, 02174
Telephone: (617) 643-0554
Founded in: 1969
Number of members: 250
Staff: full time 4, part time 11,
volunteer 1
Major programs: museum, historic
site, tours/pilgrimages, educational
programs, historic preservation,
framemaking, conservation framing
Period of collections: 1865-1918

ASHBURNHAM
**Ashburnham Historical
Society, Inc.**
Main St., 01430
Questionnaire not received

ASHFIELD
Ashfield Historical Society, Inc.
Main St.
Mail to: P.O. Box 277, 01330
Private agency
Founded in: 1961
Carrolle Markle, President
Number of members: 300
Staff: volunteer 20

Major programs: archives, museum,
markers, tours/pilgrimages, school
programs, book publishing,
newsletters/pamphlets, exhibits,
photographic collections
Period of collections: 18th
century-present

ASHLAND
Ashland Historical Society
Town Hall, Main St.
Telephone: (617) 881-3075
Mail to: P.O. Box 321, 01721
Founded in: 1905
Mrs. Robert P. Winterhalter, Curator
Number of members: 40
Staff: volunteer 2
Major programs: library, archives,
manuscripts, pamphlets
Period of collections: 1870-1945

ASHLEY FALLS
Colonel John Ashley House
Cooper Hill Rd.
Telephone: (413) 229-8600
Mail to: P.O. Box 128, 01222
Private agency, authorized by the
Trustees of Reservations
Founded in: 1891
Debra Cross, Head Host
Number of members: 3,800
Staff: full time 2
Major programs: museum, historic
site(s), tours/pilgrimages, exhibits
Period of collections: 1735-1950s

ATHOL
Athol Historical Society
1307 Main St.
Telephone: (617) 249-4115
Mail to: P.O. Box 21, 01331
Founded in: 1953
Questionnaire not received

ATTLEBORO
Attleboro Area Industrial Museum
42 Union St., 02703
Telephone: (617) 222-0801
Private agency
Founded in: 1975
Emilio Gautier, Jr., President
Staff: volunteer 5
Major programs: library, archives,
manuscripts, museum, junior
history, newsletters/pamphlets,
historic preservation, research,
exhibits, photographic collections
Period of collections: 1850-present

The Bronson Museum
8 N. Main St., 02703
Telephone: (617) 222-5470
Private agency
Founded in: 1946
T. E. Lux, Director
Staff: part time 1, volunteer 10
Major programs: museum, exhibits
Period of collections: 10,000
B.C.-A.D. 1700

**Massachusetts Archaeological
Society, Inc.**
8 N. Main St., 02703
Telephone: (617) 222-5470
Private agency
Founded in: 1939
Elizabeth A. Little, President

Number of members: 1,000
Staff: part time 1, volunteer 6
Magazine: *Bulletin of the
Massachusetts Archaeological
Society*
Major programs: library, archives,
museum, tours/pilgrimages,
newsletters/pamphlets,
archaeology programs
Period of collections: 10,000
B.C.-present

BARNSTABLE

**Historical Society of the Town of
Barnstable, Inc.**
3353 Main St., 02630
Telephone: (617) 362-2092
Mail to: General Delivery
Founded in: 1882
Questionnaire not received

Tales of Cape Cod, Inc.
Rendezvous Lane and Rt. 64
Mail to: P.O. Box 41, 02630
Private agency
Founded in: 1957
Marion Vuilleumier, President
Number of members: 65
Major programs: oral history, book
publishing, exhibits, lecture series
Period of collections: Colonial period

BARRE

Barre Historical Society, Inc.
Common St., 01005
Founded in: 1954
Mrs. Charles S. Connington, Curator
Number of members: 75
Staff: volunteer 5
Major programs: manuscripts,
museum, tours/pilgrimages, junior
history, educational programs,
books
Period of collections: 1763-1920s

BEDFORD

Bedford Historical Society
15 Great Rd., 01730
Founded in: 1893
Number of members: 200
Staff: volunteer 20
Magazine: *Bedford Historical Society
Banner*
Major programs: archives,
educational programs, book
publishing, historic preservation
Period of collections: 18th
century-present

BELCHERTOWN

Belchertown Historical Association
Maple St., 01007
Questionnaire not received

BELMONT

Becket Historical Commission
c/o Chair, Bancroft Rd., Chester,
01011
Telephone: (413) 623-5324
Town agency
Founded in: 1975
Esther Moulthrope, Chair
Staff: volunteer 7
Major programs: book publishing,
historic preservation
Period of collections: 1740-present

Belmont Historical Society
Belmont Memorial Library
Telephone: (617) 489-2000
Mail to: P.O. Box 125, 02178
Private agency
Founded in: 1965
Richard Van S. Lenk, President
Number of members: 600
Major programs: library, archives,
museum, tours/pilgrimages,
newsletters/pamphlets, exhibits,
audiovisual programs,
photographic collections
Period of collections: 1850-1950

BEVERLY

Beverly Historical Society
117 Cabot St., 01915
Telephone: (617) 922-1186
Founded in: 1891
Daniel J. Hoisington, Director
Number of members: 450
Staff: volunteer 25
Major programs: library, archives,
manuscripts, museum,
tours/pilgrimages
Period of collections: 1783-1918

**Essex County Historical
Association**
23 Bancroft Ave.
Telephone: (617) 927-0138
Founded in: 1945
Questionnaire not received

BILLERICA

Billerica Historical Society
36 Concord Rd.
Mail to: P.O. Box 381, 01821
Questionnaire not received

Middlesex Canal Association
P.O. Box 333, 01821
Telephone: (617) 729-2557
Private agency
Founded in: 1964
Nolan T. Jones, President
Number of members: 250
Staff: volunteer 13
Magazine: *Towpath Topics*
Major programs: archives,
manuscripts, museum, historic
site(s), tours/pilgrimages,
newsletters/pamphlets, exhibits
Period of collections: 1797-1853

BOLTON

Bolton Historical Society, Inc.
Great Rd., 01740
Questionnaire not received

BOSTON

American History Workshop
67 Pinckney St., 02114
Telephone: (617) 720-1532
Founded in: 1980
Questionnaire not received

**Ancient and Honorable Artillery
Company**
Quincy Marret
Telephone: (617) 227-1638
Mail to: Faneuil Hall, 02109
Private agency
Founded in: 1938
Sylveser A. Ray, Captain
Commanding
Number of members: 550

Staff: full time 2
Major programs: library, manuscripts,
museum, historic preservation,
photographic collections
Period of collections: 1638-present

Architectural Heritage Foundation
45 School St., 02108
Telephone: (617) 523-8678
Questionnaire not received

Bay State Historical League
Room 51, State House, 02133
Telephone: (617) 742-7989
Founded in: 1903
Questionnaire not received

Beacon Hill Civic Association
74 Joy St., 02114
Telephone: (617) 227-1922
Founded in: 1920
Major programs:
newsletters/pamphlets, historic
preservation

Boston Athenaeum
10½ Beacon St., 02108-3777
Telephone: (617) 227-0270
Private agency
Founded in: 1807
Rodney Armstrong, Director/Librarian
Number of members: 3,000
Staff: full time 37, part time 3,
volunteer 5
Magazine: *Athenaeum Items*
Major programs: library, archives,
manuscripts, museum, historic
site(s), tours/pilgrimages, book
publishing, newsletters/pamphlets,
research, exhibits, photographic
collections
Period of collections: 19th century

Boston Art Commission
Environment Department, Room 805,
Boston City Hall, 02201
Telephone: (617) 725-3850
City agency
Founded in: 1890
Mary O. Shannon, Executive
Secretary
Staff: full time 1
Major programs: archives,
newsletters/pamphlets, historic
preservation, photographic
collections, public art
Period of collections: from 1890

Boston Organ Club
33 Bowdoin St., 02114
Telephone: (603) 827-3055
Mail to: P.O. Box 104, Harrisville, NH,
03450
Founded in: 1965
Questionnaire not received

The Bostonian Society
Old State House, 206 Washington St.,
02109
Telephone: (617) 242-5655/242-5610
Private agency
Founded in: 1881
Thomas Wendell Parker, Director
Number of members: 1,150
Staff: full time 6, part time 8
Magazine: *Proceedings of the
Bostonian Society*
Major programs: library, museum,
historic site(s), school programs,
research, exhibits, photographic
collections
Period of collections: 1700-present

Boston Landmarks Commission
Boston City Hall, Room 805, 02201
Telephone: (617) 725-3850
City agency
Founded in: 1975
Marcia Myers, Executive Director
Staff: full time 4, part time 3
Major programs: historic
preservation, records
management, research,
archaeology programs, field
services, architectural resources
Period of collections: 1629-present

Boston Marine Society
National Historical Park, Bldg. 32,
Charlestown Navy Yard, 02129
Telephone: (617) 242-0522
Private agency
Founded in: 1742
Harold F. Lynch, Secretary/Treasurer
Staff: full time 2
Major programs: library, museum,
historic site(s), tours/pilgrimages,
historic preservation, exhibits

Boston National Historical Park
Bldg. 32, Charlestown Navy Yard,
02129
Telephone: (617) 242-5601
Federal agency, authorized by
National Park Service
Founded in: 1974
John J. Burchill, Superintendent
Staff: full time 82, part time 47
Major programs: library, archives,
manuscripts, museum, historic
site(s), markers, tours/pilgrimages,
oral history, school programs,
historic preservation, records
management, research, exhibits,
photographic collections
Period of collections: 19th-20th
centuries

Bunker Hill Monument
Boston National Historical Park,
Charlestown Navy Yard, 02129
Telephone: (617) 242-5641
Federal agency, authorized by
National Park Service
Founded in: 1976
John J. Burchill, Superintendent
Staff: full time 2, part time 3
Major programs: museum, historic
site(s), tours/pilgrimages, historic
preservation, exhibits
Period of collections: 19th century

Charlestown Navy Yard
Boston National Historical Park,
02129
Telephone: (617) 242-5601
Federal agency, authorized by
National Park Service
Founded in: 1974
John J. Burchill, Superintendent
Staff: full time 42, part time 20
Major programs: library, archives,
historic site(s), tours/pilgrimages,
oral history, school programs,
historic preservation, research,
exhibits, photographic collections
Period of collections: 20th century

Colonial Society of Massachusetts
87 Mt. Vernon St., 02108
Telephone: (617) 227-2782
Private agency
Founded in: 1892

Frederick S. Allis, Jr., Editor of
Publications
Number of members: 240
Major programs: book publishing
Period of collections: 1606-1820

The Commandant's House
Boston National Historical Park,
Charlestown Navy Yard, 02129
Telephone: (617) 242-5601
Federal agency, authorized by
National Park Service
Founded in: 1976
John J. Burchill, Superintendent
Staff: part time 4, volunteer 2
Major programs: museum, historic
site(s), tours/pilgrimages, historic
preservation, exhibits
Period of collections: 1850-1976

**Commission Archives and History,
Southern New England
Conference, United Methodist
Church**
745 Commonwealth Ave., 02215
Telephone: (617) 353-3034
Founded in: 1890
Staff: part time 3
Major programs: library, archives,
manuscripts
Period of collections: 1783-present

**Committee for a New England
Bibliography, Inc.**
233 Bay State Rd., 02215
Telephone: (617) 266-9706
Founded in: 1969
Questionnaire not received

**Congregational Christian Historical
Society**
14 Beacon St., 02108
Telephone: (617) 523-0470
Private agency
Founded in: 1952
Harold Field Worthley, Executive
Secretary/Archivist
Number of members: 700
Staff: part time 2
Magazine: *News from The
Congregational Christian Historical
Society*
Major programs: library, archives,
markers, tours/pilgrimages,
newsletters/pamphlets, research,
genealogical services
Period of collections: 1492-present

**Congregational Library of the
American Congregational
Association**
14 Beacon St., 02108
Telephone: (617) 523-0470
Private agency
Founded in: 1853
Harold Field Worthley, Librarian
Staff: full time 3, part time 5,
volunteer 1
Magazine: *Bulletin of the
Congregational Library*
Major programs: library, archives,
manuscripts, research
Period of collections: 1620-present

Dorchester Heights Monument
Boston National Historical Park,
Charlestown Navy Yard, 02129
Telephone: (617) 269-4212
Federal agency, authorized by
National Park Service

Founded in: 1980
John J. Burchill, Superintendent
Staff: full time 1
Period of collections: early 20th
century

French Library in Boston, Inc.
53 Marlborough St., 02116
Telephone: (617) 266-4351
Private agency
Founded in: 1945
Jane M. Stahl, Director/Librarian
Number of members: 1,800
Staff: full time 9, part time 2
Major programs: library, archives,
exhibits, audiovisual programs,
French cultural activities
Period of collections: 20th century

**Gibson House Museum—Gibson
Society, Inc.**
137 Beacon St., 02116
Telephone: (617) 267-6338
Private agency
Founded in: 1957
George Ursul, President
Major programs: museum,
tours/pilgrimages
Period of collections: 1860-1918

Historic Boston, Inc.
3 School St., 02108
Telephone: (617) 227-4679
Private agency
Founded in: 1960
Stanley M. Smith, Executive Director
Staff: full time 2, part time 1
Major programs: historic
preservation, field services

**Historic Neighborhoods
Foundation**
92 South St., 02111
Private agency
Founded in: 1977
Nina R. Meyer, Director
Number of members: 750
Staff: full time 3, part time 20,
volunteer 12
Major programs: tours, school
programs, newsletters/pamphlets,
historic preservation, research,
photographic collections,
neighborhood awareness
programs, urban architectural
history
Period of collections: 19th-20th
centuries

**John F. Kennedy Presidential
Library**
Columbia Point, 02125
Telephone: (617) 929-4500
Federal agency, authorized by
National Archives and Records
Service
Founded in: 1969
Dan H. Fenn, Jr., Director
Number of members: full time 30, part
time 26, volunteer 15
Major programs: library, archives,
manuscripts, museum, oral history,
school programs, records
management, research, exhibits,
audiovisual programs,
photographic collections
Period of collections: 1950s-1960s

Massachusetts Historical Commission
80 Boylston St., 02116
Telephone: (617) 727-8470
State agency
Founded in: 1963
Valerie A. Talmage, Executive Director/State Historic Preservation Officer
Staff: full time 20, part time 9, volunteer 2
Major programs: historic site(s), newsletters/pamphlets, historic preservation, archaeology programs

◇Massachusetts Historical Society
1154 Boylston, 02215
Telephone: (617) 536-1608
Private agency
Founded in: 1791
Louis L. Tucker, Director
Staff: full time 21, volunteer 1
Magazine: Proceedings
Major programs: library, manuscripts, book publishing
Period of collections: 1620-1980

Massachusetts Society of Mayflower Descendants
101 Newbury St., 02116
Telephone: (617) 266-1624
Private agency, authorized by the national society
Founded in: 1896
Alicia Williams, Editor
Number of members: 1,300
Staff: full time 1, part time 2, volunteer 8
Magazine: The Mayflower Descendant/The Compact
Major programs: library, school programs, book publishing, newsletters/pamphlets, research
Period of collections: 1620-1850

Massachusetts State Archives
State House, Room 55, 02133
Telephone: (617) 727-2816
State agency, authorized by the Secretary of State
Albert H. Whitaker, Jr., State Archivist
Staff: full time 15
Major programs: archives, museum, newsletters/pamphlets, records management, research, photographic collections, genealogical services
Period of collections: 17th century-present

Museum of Afro American History
8 Smith Court, 02114
Telephone: (617) 723-8863
Questionnaire not received

Museum of Transportation
300 Congress St., 02110
Telephone: (617) 426-6633
Questionnaire not received

New England Historic Genealogical Society
101 Newbury St., 02116
Telephone: (617) 536-5740
Private agency
Founded in: 1845
Ralph J. Crandall, Director
Number of members: 8,000
Staff: full time 14, part time 4, volunteer 15

Magazine: New England Historical and Genealogical Register
Major programs: library, archives, manuscripts, book publishing, newsletters/pamphlets, genealogical services
Period of collections: 1800-present

New England Museum Association
Boston National Historic Park, Charlestown Navy Yard, 02129
Telephone: (617) 720-1573
Private agency
Founded in: 1979
Pamela Brusic, Executive Director
Number of members: 680
Staff: full time 2
Magazine: NEMA News
Major programs: archives, newsletters/pamphlets, field services, workshops and annual conference for museum professionals

Nichols House Museum
55 Mt. Vernon St., 02108
Telephone: (617) 227-6993
Private agency
Founded in: 1961
William H. Pear, Curator
Number of members: 317
Staff: part time 1, volunteer 3
Major programs: museum, historic site(s), historic preservation
Period of collections: 1750-1850

North Atlantic Regional Office, National Park Service
15 State St., 02109
Telephone: (617) 223-3778
Federal agency
Founded in: 1916
Francis P. McManamon, Chief, Division of Cultural Resources
Staff: full time 18
Major programs: historic site(s), historic preservation, research

Old North Church
193 Salem St., 02113
Telephone: (617) 523-6676
Private agency, authorized by Episcopal Diocese of Massachusetts
Founded in: 1723
Robert W. Golledge, Vicar
Staff: full time 5, part time 2
Major programs: historic site(s), tours/pilgrimages, oral history, historic preservation, living history
Period of collections: 1723-present

Old South Meeting House
310 Washington St., 02108
Telephone: (617) 482-6439
Private agency, authorized by Old South Association in Boston
Founded in: 1877
Cynthia Stone, Director
Staff: full time 4
Major programs: museum, historic site(s), tours/pilgrimages, school programs, newsletters/pamphlets, historic preservation, exhibits
Period of collections: 18th-19th centuries

Paul Revere House
19 North Square, 02112
Telephone: (617) 523-2338

Private agency, authorized by Paul Revere Memorial Association
Founded in: 1908
Patricia Sullivan, Director
Staff: full time 6, part time 9, volunteer 4
Major programs: manuscripts, museum, historic site(s), tours, school programs, book publishing, newsletters/pamphlets, historic preservation, research, exhibits, living history, audiovisual programs, photographic collections, genealogical services
Period of collections: 18th century

Society for Commercial Archeology
c/o Museum of Transportation, 300 Congress St., 02210
Founded in: 1977
Questionnaire not received

Society for the Preservation of New England Antiquities
141 Cambridge St., 02114
Telephone: (617) 227-3956
Private agency
Founded in: 1910
Nancy R. Coolidge, Director
Number of members: 3,000
Staff: full time 37, part time 40
Major programs: library, archives, manuscripts, museum, book publishing, newsletters/pamphlets, historic preservation, research, exhibits, photographic collections, administration of 41 historic house museums
Period of collections: 1660-1860

Société Historique Franco-Américaine
Mail to: 1 Social St., Box F, Woonsocket, RI, 02895
Telephone: (401) 769-0520
Private agency
Founded in: 1899
Oda Beaulieu, President
Number of members: 217
Staff: volunteer 4
Major programs: archives, oral history, book publishing, historic preservation, exhibits, audiovisual programs, genealogical services
Period of collections: 1899-present

State Library of Massachusetts
341 State House, 02133
Telephone: (617) 727-2590
State agency
Founded in: 1826
Gasper Caso, State Librarian
Staff: full time 26
Major programs: library, archives, manuscripts, newsletters/pamphlets, exhibits, photographic collections
Period of collections: Colonial period-present

Unitarian Universalist Historical Society
c/o 25 Beacon St., 02108
Telephone: (617) 742-2100
Founded in: 1978
Number of members: 400
Magazine: Proceedings of the Unitarian Universalist Historical Society

Major programs: archives, manuscripts, educational programs
Period of collections: 19th-20th centuries

USS Cassin Young
Boston National Historical Park, Charlestown Navy Yard, 02129
Telephone: (617) 242-5604
Federal agency, authorized by National Park Service
Founded in: 1978
John J. Burchill, Superintendent
Staff: full time 2, part time 4, volunteer 6
Major programs: archives, historic site(s), tours/pilgrimages, oral history, historic preservation, exhibits, photographic collections
Period of collections: 1943-1960

USS Constitution Museum Foundation, Inc.
Charlestown Navy Yard
Telephone: (617) 426-1812
Mail to: P.O. Box 1812, 02129
Private agency
Founded in: 1972
Richard C. Wheeler, Director
Number of members: 1,500
Staff: full time 10, part time 5
Magazine: *Constitutional Chronicle*
Major programs: library, archives, museum, junior history, school programs, newsletters/pamphlets, historic preservation, records management, exhibits, living history, photographic collections, demonstrations
Period of collections: 1794-present

Veteran Association of the First Corps of Cadets
227 Commonwealth Ave. 02116
Telephone: (617) 267-1726
Founded in: 1726
Craig W.C. Brown, Museum Director
Number of members: 350
Staff: full time 2, part time 2
Magazine: *VAICC Newsletter*
Major programs: museum, newsletters/pamphlets, book publishing
Period of collections: 1726-present

BOURNE

Bourne Historical Society
24 Aptucxet Rd.
Telephone: (617) 759-9511
Mail to: P.O. Box 95, 02532
Private agency
Founded in: 1930
Warren G. Odom, President
Number of members: 223
Staff: part time 1, volunteer 40
Major programs: archives, museum, historic site(s), oral history, school programs, newsletters/pamphlets, historic preservation, exhibits
Period of collections: 18th-early 19th centuries

Bourne Town Archives
36 Sandwich Rd., 02532
Town agency
Founded in: 1979
Alice M. Gibbs, Archives Committee Chair

Staff: part time 1, volunteer 4
Major programs: archives, oral history, historic preservation, slide shows
Period of collections: 1884-present

BOYLSTON

Boylston Historical Society, Inc.
7 Central St.
Telephone: (617) 869-2720
Mail to: P.O. Box 459, 01505
Private agency
Founded in: 1971
Robert Goulet, President
Number of members: 223
Staff: volunteer 12
Magazine: *Potpourri/Strangers and Pilgrims*
Major programs: library, archives, manuscripts, museum, historic site(s), markers, oral history, school programs, book publishing, newsletters/pamphlets, historic preservation, records management, research, exhibits, living history, audiovisual programs, photographic collections, genealogical services
Period of collections: 1786-present

BRAINTREE

Braintree Historical Society, Inc.
786 Washington St., 02184
Telephone: (617) 848-1640
Private agency
Founded in: 1930
Number of members: 675
Staff: volunteer 40
Major programs: library, archives, museum, historic site(s), school programs, historic preservation
Period of collections: 1783-present

BREWSTER

Drummer Boy Museum
Rt. 6-A, 02631
Telephone: (617) 896-3823
Private agency
Founded in: 1961
Lewis A. McGowan, Jr., Owner
Major programs: museum, oral history, school programs
Period of collections: American Revolution

New England Fire and History Museum
1439 Main St., Rt. 6-A, 02631
Telephone: (617) 896-5711
Founded in: 1973
Questionnaire not received

BRIGHTON

Brighton Historical Society
68 N. Beacon St.
Telephone: (617) 254-6955
Mail to: P.O. Box 163, 02135
Founded in: 1968
Questionnaire not received

BROCKTON

Brockton Art Museum
Oak St., 02401
Telephone: (617) 588-6000
Private agency, authorized by trustees of the Fuller Memorial

Founded in: 1969
Joseph L. Kagle, Jr., Director
Number of members: 1,600
Staff: full time 6, part time 15, volunteer 150
Major programs: museum, school programs, photographic collections, American art collections
Period of collections: 19th-20th centuries

Little Red Schoolhouse Association, Inc.
Concord Ave., 02401
Mail to: P.O. Box 3036, 02403
Founded in: 1968
Questionnaire not received

Old Colony Planning Council
9 Belmont St., 02401
Telephone: (617) 583-1833
Founded in: 1967
Daniel M. Crane, Executive Director
Staff: full time 14
Major programs: library, newsletters/pamphlets, historic preservation, land use, housing, economic development, area agency on aging
Period of collections: present

BROOKLINE

Brookline Historical Commission
333 Washington St., Town Hall, 02146
Telephone: (617) 232-9000
Town agency, authorized by board-appointed commissioners
Founded in: 1974
Carla Benka, Co-consultant
Staff: part time 2
Major programs: tours/pilgrimages, newsletters/pamphlets, historic preservation, research
Period of collections: 19th-early 20th centuries

Brookline Historical Society
347 Harvard St., 02146
Telephone: (617) 566-5747
Private agency
Founded in: 1901
Mrs. James McIntosh, Curator
Number of members: 285
Major programs: historic site(s), markers, tours/pilgrimages, school programs
Period of collections: 1725-present

Frederick Law Olmsted National Historic Site
99 Warren St., 02146
Telephone: (617) 566-1689
Federal agency, authorized by National Park Service
Founded in: 1979
Shary Page Berg, Park Manager
Staff: full time 11, part time 7
Major programs: archives, museum, historic site(s), tours/pilgrimages, historic preservation, records management, research, exhibits, audiovisual programs, photographic collections
Period of collections: 1858-1960

John F. Kennedy National Historic Site
83 Beals St., 02146
Telephone: (617) 566-7937

Federal agency, authorized by
National Park Service
Founded in: 1969
Kevin M. Carroll, Site Manager
Staff: full time 2, part time 4
Major programs: historic site(s)
Period of collections: early 20th
century

Longyear Historical Society and Museum
120 Seaver St., 02146
Telephone: (617) 277-8943
Private agency
Founded in: 1926
Constance Johnson, Director
Number of members: 6,300
Staff: full time 19, part time 18
Major programs: library, archives,
museum, historic sites preservation
Period of collections: 1821-1910

BUCKLAND

Buckland Historical Society
Upper St., 01338
Founded in: 1958
Number of members: 100
Staff: volunteer 7
Major programs: library, archives,
museum, historic sites preservation
Period of collections: 1783-present

BURLINGTON

Burlington Historical Society, Inc.
Town Hall, 01803
Telephone: (617) 272-4840
Founded in: 1964
Questionnaire not received

CAMBRIDGE

Cambridge Historical Commission
City Hall Annex, 57 Inman St., 02139
Telephone: (617) 498-9040
City agency
Founded in: 1964
Charles M. Sullivan, Executive
Director
Staff: full time 3, part time 4
Major programs: archives, markers,
book publishing, historic
preservation, research,
photographic collections,
architectural history and
development programs
Period of collections: 19th century

Cambridge Historical Society
159 Brattle St., 02138
Telephone: (617) 547-4252
Private agency
Founded in: 1905
Bettina A. Norton, Director
Number of members: 420
Staff: part time 2
Magazine: *Proceedings*
Major programs: library, archives,
manuscripts, historic site(s),
tours/pilgrimages, junior history,
book publishing,
newsletters/pamphlets
Period of collections: from 1630

Longfellow National Historic Site
105 Brattle St., 02138
Telephone: (617) 876-4491
Federal agency, authorized by
National Park Service

Founded in: 1973
Stephen Whitesell, Superintendent
Staff: full time 5, part time 8,
volunteer 1
Major programs: library, archives,
manuscripts, museum, historic
site(s), oral history, historic
preservation, records
management, research,
photographic collections
Period of collections: Victorian era

MIT (Massachusetts Institute of Technology) Museum
265 Massachusetts Ave., 02138
Telephone: (617) 253-4444
Private agency, authorized by the
institute
Founded in: 1971
Warren A. Seamans, Director
Staff: full time 9, part time 1,
volunteer 1
Major programs: library, museum,
school programs,
newsletters/pamphlets, records
management, research, exhibits,
audiovisual programs,
photographic collections, history of
technology
Period of collections: 19th-20th
centuries

National Association for Armenian Studies and Research, Inc.
175 Mt. Auburn St., 02138
Telephone: (617) 876-7630
Founded in: 1955
Number of members: 1,000
Staff: full time 1, part time 3,
volunteer 6
Magazine: *Journal of Armenian Studies*
Major programs: library, archives,
tours/pilgrimages, educational
programs, book publishing,
newsletters/pamphlets, books
distribution
Period of collections: 900
B.C.-present

CANTON

Canton Historical Society
1400 Washington St., 02021
Telephone: (617) 828-4962
Questionnaire not received

CENTERVILLE

Centerville Historical Society, Inc.
513 Main St., 02632
Founded in: 1952
Number of members: 458
Staff: volunteer
Major programs: library, archives,
museum, newsletters/pamphlets
Period of collections: 1865-1918

CHATHAM

Chatham Historical Society, Inc.
347 Stage Harbor Rd.
Telephone: (617) 945-2493
Mail to: P.O. Box 381, 02633
Founded in: 1924
Edmond Meany, President
Number of members: 850
Staff: part time 2, volunteer 150

Major programs: museum, markers,
newsletters/pamphlets, genealogy
Period of collections: 1600-present

CHELMSFORD

Chelmsford Historical Society, Inc.
40 Byam Rd., 01824
Telephone: (617) 256-2311
Founded in: 1930
Helen R. Poland, Curator
Number of members: 280
Staff: volunteer 20
Major programs: archives, museum,
tours/pilgrimages, junior history,
educational programs
Period of collections: 1700-1900

CHELSEA

Chelsea Public Library
569 Broadway, 02150
Telephone: (617) 884-2335
City agency
Founded in: 1970
Nicholas J. Minadakis, Library
Director
Staff: full time 12
Major programs: library, archives,
school programs, exhibits,
photographic collections,
genealogical services
Period of collections: 1840-present

CHESTERFIELD

Chesterfield Historical Society
North Rd., 01012
Private agency
Founded in: 1951
Ruth Z. Temple, Curator
Number of members: 60
Staff: volunteer 3
Major programs: archives,
manuscripts, museum, oral history,
school programs, photographic
collections, genealogical services
Period of collections: 19th century

CLINTON

Clinton Historical Society
210 Church St., 01510
Telephone: (617) 368-0084/365-4877
Founded in: 1894
Number of members: 150
Staff: part time 1, volunteer 25
Major programs: library, archives,
museum, historic preservation
Period of collections: 1830-1920

COHASSET

Cohasset Historical Society
14 Summer St.
Telephone: (617) 383-6930
Mail to: P.O. Box 324, 02025
Private agency
Founded in: 1928
Constance W. Parker, President
Number of members: 500
Staff: full time 1, volunteer 30
Magazine: *Historical Highlights*
Major programs: library, museum,
book publishing,
newsletters/pamphlets, historic
preservation, exhibits,
genealogical services
Period of collections: late 18th-early
20th centuries

COLLEGE PARK

Old Town College Park Preservation Association
7400 Dartmouth Ave., 20740
Telephone: (301) 864-6709
Private agency
Founded in: 1979
Number of members: 100
Staff: volunteer 8
Major programs: historic site(s), historic preservation

CONCORD

Concord Antiquarian Museum
200 Lexington Rd.
Telephone: (617) 369-9609
Mail to: P.O. Box 146, 01742
Founded in: 1895
Dennis Fiori, Director
Number of members: 2,000
Staff: full time 4, part time 2, volunteer 85
Major programs: library, archives, museum, school programs, newsletters/pamphlets, historic preservation, research, exhibits, photographic collections, conservation
Period of collections: 1640-1885

Louisa May Alcott Memorial Association
Orchard House, 399 Lexington Rd.
Telephone: (617) 369-4118
Mail to: P.O. Box 343, 01742
Founded in: 1912
Jayne Gordon, Director
Number of members: 40
Staff: full time 2, part time 22
Major programs: museum, educational programs, books
Period of collections: 1840-1888

Minute Man National Historical Park
174 Liberty St., 01742
Telephone: (617) 369-6993
Mail to: P.O. Box 160, 01742
Federal agency
Founded in: 1968
Robert Nash, Superintendent
Staff: full time 20, part time 30, volunteer 50
Major programs: library, archives, museum, historic site(s), markers, tours/pilgrimages, school programs, historic preservation, research, exhibits, living history, audiovisual programs, archaeology programs
Period of collections: 1775

Orchard House, Home of the Alcotts
399 Lexington Rd.
Telephone: (617) 369-4118
Mail to: P.O. Box 343, 01742
Private agency, authorized by Louisa May Alcott Memorial Association
Founded in: 1911
Jayne K. Gordon, Director
Number of members: 300
Staff: full time 1, part time 23
Major programs: manuscripts, museum, historic site(s), tours, school programs, newsletters/pamphlets, historic preservation, research, living

history, audiovisual programs, photographic collections
Period of collections: 1840-1880

The Thoreau Lyceum
156 Belknap St., 01742
Telephone: (617) 369-5912
Founded in: 1966
Questionnaire not received

COTUIT

Santuit-Cotuit Historical Society
1148 Main St., 02635-1484
Telephone: (617) 428-3895
Private agency
Founded in: 1954
Beatrice K. Williams, President
Number of members: 317
Staff: volunteer 12
Major programs: archives, manuscripts, museum, markers, tours/pilgrimages, newsletters/pamphlets, exhibits, photographic collections
Period of collections: 1800-1925

CUMMINGTON

William Cullen Bryant Homestead
Luther Shaw Rd., 01026
Telephone: (413) 634-2244
Private agency, authorized by the Trustees of Reservations
Founded in: 1891
Mark DeMaranville, Warden
Number of members: 3,800
Staff: full time 3, part time 4
Major programs: museum, historic site(s), tours/pilgrimages, historic preservation
Period of collections: 1785-1900

CUTTYHUNK

Cuttyhunk Historical Society
Broadway
Mail to: P.O. Box 165, 02713
Private agency
Founded in: 1978
Mrs. Lloyd Bosworth, Curator/Vice President
Number of members: 150
Staff: volunteer 4
Major programs: archives, oral history, newsletters/pamphlets, historic preservation, research, exhibits, photographic collections, genealogical services
Period of collections: 1830-1930

DALTON

Dalton Historical Committee
Main St., 01226
Telephone: (617) 684-0032
Town agency, authorized by board of selectmen
Founded in: 1965
Mary Jane Caliento, Chair
Staff: volunteer 20
Major programs: research, exhibits, living history, photographic collections
Period of collections: 1890-present

DANVERS

Danvers Alarm List Company, Inc.
149 Pine St., 01923
Telephone: (617) 774-8799

Private agency
Founded in: 1974
George Meehan, Captain
Number of members: 547
Staff: part time 1, volunteer 30
Major programs: museum, historic site(s), tours/pilgrimages, school programs, newsletters/pamphlets, historic preservation, exhibits, living history
Period of collections: 1670s-1770s

Danvers Archival Center
15 Sylvan St., 01923
Telephone: (617) 774-0554
Town agency, authorized by Peabody Institute Library of Danvers
Founded in: 1972
Richard B. Trask, Town Archivist
Staff: full time 1, part time 1, volunteer 3
Major programs: library, archives, manuscripts, markers, school programs, records management, research, audiovisual programs, photographic collections, genealogical services
Period of collections: 1672-present

Danvers Historical Commission
c/o Town Hall, Sylvan St., 01923
Telephone: (617) 777-2821
Founded in: 1965
Questionnaire not received

Danvers Historical Society
13 Page St., 01923
Telephone: (617) 777-1666
Private agency
Founded in: 1889
Sarah E. Symmes, President
Number of members: 425
Staff: full time 1, volunteer 9
Major programs: museum, historic sites preservation, educational programs, books, newsletters/pamphlets, exhibits
Period of collections: 1630-1900

Salem Village Cotorie
c/o 35 Centre St., 01923
Telephone: (617) 774-5593
Founded in: 1971
Questionnaire not received

DARTMOUTH

Childrens Museum and Museum Outdoors
100 Old Westport Rd. N
Mail to: P.O. Box 98, 02714
Founded in: 1953
Robert O. Bailey, Director
Number of members: full time 2
Major programs: museum, educational programs, newsletters/pamphlets

DEDHAM

Dedham Historical Society
612 High St.
Telephone: (617) 326-1385
Mail to: P.O. Box 215, 02026
Founded in: 1858
Robert B. Hanson, President
Number of members: 460
Staff: part time 3, volunteer 20
Major programs: library, archives, manuscripts, museum, historic sites preservation, educational

programs, books,
newsletters/pamphlets
Period of collections: 1600-present

Fairbanks House
511 East St., 02026
Telephone: (617) 326-1170
Founded in: 1904
Questionnaire not received

DEERFIELD

Historic Deerfield, Inc.
The St.
Telephone: (413) 774-5581
Mail to: P.O. Box 321, 01342
Private agency
Founded in: 1952
Donald R. Friary, Executive Director
Number of members: 909
Staff: full time 57, part time 145,
volunteer 77
Magazine: *Historic Deerfield
Quarterly*
Major programs: library, archives,
manuscripts, museum, historic
site(s), tours/pilgrimages, oral
history, school programs,
newsletters/pamphlets, historic
preservation, research, exhibits,
audiovisual programs, archaeology
programs, photographic
collections, genealogical services,
forums, workshops, lectures,
college programs, decorative arts
Period of collections: 1650-1850

Indian House Memorial, Inc.
Main St., 01342
Telephone: (413) 772-0845
Questionnaire not received

**Pocumtuck Valley Memorial
Association—Memorial Hall
Museum**
Memorial St., 01342
Telephone: (413) 774-7476
Private agency
Founded in: 1870
Timothy C. Neumann, Director
Number of members: 750
Staff: full time 2, part time 2,
volunteer 10
Major programs: library, manuscripts,
museum, educational programs,
books, newsletters/pamphlets
Period of collections: 1670-present

DIGHTON

Dighton Historical Society
1217 Williams, 02715
Private agency
Founded in: 1962
Ann Eckman, President
Number of members: 50
Staff: volunteer 15
Major programs: archives, museum,
historic site(s), tours/pilgrimages,
junior history, oral history, school
programs, newsletters/pamphlets,
historic preservation, research,
exhibits, photographic collections,
genealogical services
Period of collections: 1712-present

DORCHESTER

Dorchester Historical Society
195 Boston St., 02125
Telephone: (617) 436-8367

Founded in: 1843
Anthony Sammarco, Jr., Director
Number of members: 300
Staff: volunteer 2
Major programs: library, manuscripts,
museum, historic sites
preservation,
newsletters/pamphlets
Period of collections: 1630-1920

DOVER

**Dover Historical Society—Sawin
Museum**
Dedham St., 02030
Telephone: (617) 785-1832
Private agency
Founded in: 1898
Robert Campbell, President
Number of members: 215
Staff: volunteer 3
Major programs: museum, historic
preservation
Period of collections: 1700-1900

**Dover Historical and Natural
History Society**
Dedham St., 02030
Founded in: 1903
Questionnaire not received

DUXBURY

Alden Kindred of America, Inc.
105 Alden St.
Telephone: (617) 934-6001
(secretary)
Mail to: 1 Abrams Hill, 02332
Private agency
Founded in: 1902
John Alden Keyser, President
Number of members: 1,000
Staff: part time 5
Major programs: historic site(s),
historic preservation, genealogical
services
Period of collections: 1700-1900

**Duxbury Rural and Historical
Society—Drew House**
Telephone: (617) 934-6106
Mail to: P.O. Box 176, Snug Harbor,
02331
Founded in: 1883
G. Lincoln Dow, Jr., President
Number of members: 700
Staff: part time 1, volunteer 100
Major programs: archives, museum,
historic sites preservation, markes,
tours/pilgrimages, junior history,
educational programs, books,
newsletters/pamphlets
Period of collections: 1492-1865

EAST BRIDGEWATER

**East Bridgewater Historical
Commission**
c/o Secretary, 418 Plymouth St.,
02333
Telephone: (617) 378-7775
Town agency, authorized by
Massachusetts Historical
Commission
Founded in: 1978
Thomas R. Turner, Chair
Major programs: archives, historic
site(s), markers, oral history, book
publishing, historic preservation,

research, exhibits, photographic
collections
Period of collections: 1800s

EAST DOUGLAS

Douglas Historical Society, Inc.
Main St.
Mail to: P.O. Box 176, 01516
Founded in: 1968
Number of members: 200
Major programs: museum
Period of collections: 1870-1920

EASTHAM

Eastham Historical Society, Inc.,
P.O. Box 8, 02642
Telephone: (617) 255-4968
Private agency
Founded in: 1963
James Owens, President
Number of members: 500
Staff: volunteer 100
Major programs: library, museum,
historic site(s), oral history,
newsletters/pamphlets
Period of collections: 18th-20th
centuries

EASTHAMPTON

**Easthampton Historical
Commission**
Town Hall, Main St., 01027
Town agency, authorized by board of
selectmen
Founded in: 1979
William F. Carroll, Chair
Staff: volunteer 7
Major programs: historic site(s),
historic preservation, records
management, research,
photographic collections, other
Period of collections:
17th-century-present

EAST LONGMEADOW

**East Longmeadow Historical
Commission**
Center Square, 01028
Telephone: (413) 525-3305
Town agency
Founded in: 1970
Barbara Forbes, Chair
Number of members: 105
Staff: volunteer 8
Major programs: archives, oral
history, book publishing, historic
preservation, research, exhibits
Period of collections: 1850

EAST SANDWICH

Wing Family of America, Inc.
69 Spring Hill, 02537
Telephone: (617) 888-3591
Founded in: 1902
Questionnaire not received

EDGARTOWN

Dukes County Historical Society
Cooke and School Sts.
Telephone: (617) 627-4441
Mail to: P.O. Box 827, 02539
Founded in: 1922
Thomas E. Norton, Director
Number of members: 1,000

Staff: full time 2, part time 8,
volunteer 5
Magazine: *The Dukes County
Intelligencer*
Major programs: library, archives,
museum, oral history, books,
newsletters/pamphlets
Period of collections: 1660-1918

ERVING

Erving Historical Society
Main St., 01344
Mail to: 9 Moore St., Millers Falls,
01349
Founded in: 1972
Number of members: 75
Period of collections: mid-1800s

ESSEX

**Essex Historical Society—Essex
Shipbuilding Museum**
Main St., 01929
Telephone: (617) 768-7541
Private agency
Founded in: 1937
Maria P. Burnham, President
Number of members: 200
Staff: part time 1, volunteer 10
Major programs: museum, junior
history, school programs, exhibits,
photographic collections
Period of collections: 1830-1947

FALL RIVER

Battleship Massachusetts
Battleship Cove, 02721
Telephone: (617) 678-1100
Founded in: 1964
Number of members: 750
Staff: full time 10, part time 9,
volunteer 10
Major programs: library, museum,
tours/pilgrimages, junior history,
oral history, educational programs,
newsletters/pamphlets, historic
preservation, restoration of historic
ships
Period of collections: W.W. II-Vietnam
era

Fall River Historical Society
451 Rock St., 02720
Telephone: (617) 679-1071
Private agency
Founded in: 1921
Florence C. Brigham, Curator
Number of members: 300
Staff: full time 2, volunteer 9
Major programs: library, museum,
educational programs, exhibits
Period of collections: 19th century

Marine Museum at Fall River
70 Water St.
Telephone: (617) 674-3533
Mail to: P.O. Box 1147, 02722
Founded in: 1968
Number of members: 550
Staff: full time 1, part time 5,
volunteer 20
Magazine: *Crosswinds*
Major programs: library, archives,
manuscripts, museum, educational
programs, book publishing,
newsletters/pamphlets, historic
preservation
Period of collections: 1840s-1850s

Office of Historic Preservation
1 Government Center, 02722
Telephone: (617) 675-6011
City agency, authorized by
community development agency
Founded in: 1979
William R. Hargraves, Jr., City
Preservation Officer
Staff: full time 2
Major programs: archives, historic
preservation, research

Preservation Society of Fall River
456 Rock St., 02720
Telephone: (617) 678-7276
Private agency
Founded in: 1976
Federico Santi, President
Number of members: 200
Staff: volunteer 5
Magazine: *Fall River Line*
Major programs: markers,
tours/pilgrimages, oral history,
school programs,
newsletters/pamphlets, historic
preservation,research, exhibits,
living history, audiovisual
programs, photographic
collections
Period of collections: 1830-1900

FALMOUTH

Falmouth Historical Society
Palmer Ave. at the Village Green
Telephone: (617) 548-4857
Mail to: P.O. Box 174, 02541
Private agency
Founded in: 1900
Dudley W. Hallett, President
Number of members: 1,200
Staff: volunteer 45
Major programs: archives,
manuscripts, museum, oral history,
school programs, book publishing,
historic preservation, photographic
collections, genealogical services
Period of collections: 1700-present

FITCHBURG

Fitchburg Historical Society
50 Grove St.
Telephone: (617) 345-1157
Mail to: P.O. Box 953, 01420
Private agency
Founded in: 1892
Eleanora F. West, Curator
Number of members: 330
Staff: full time 1, part time 1,
volunteer 8
Major programs: library, museum
Period of collections: 1764-present

FOXBOROUGH

**Foxborough Historical
Commission**
Memorial Hall, 02035
Telephone: (617) 543-5301
Questionnaire not received

FRAMINGHAM

**Framingham Historical and Natural
History Society**
Vernon and Grove Sts.
Mail to: P.O. Box 2032, 01701
Founded in: 1888
Questionnaire not received

FRANKLIN

Franklin Historical Commission
Washington St.
Mail to: P.O. Box 112, 02038
Town agency
Founded in: 1970
D. G. Arnold, Chair
Major programs: museum, historic
site(s), historic preservation,
exhibits, audiovisual programs,
photographic collections
Period of collections: from 1850

FREETOWN

Freetown Historical Society, Inc.
Slab Bridge Rd., Assonet, 02717
Questionnaire not received

GLOUCESTER

Cape Ann Historical Association
27 Pleasant St., 01930
Telephone: (617) 283-0455
Ellen Story, Administrator
Number of members: 880
Staff: full time 2, part time 3,
volunteer 20
Major programs: library, archives,
manuscripts, museum, historic
site(s), tours/pilgrimages, school
programs, newsletters/pamphlets,
historic preservation, exhibits,
photographic collections,
genealogical services
Period of collections: mid-1800s

Channel One Clearinghouse Corp.
26 River Rd.
Telephone: (617) 283-2503
Mail to: P.O. Box 8, Lanseville Station,
01930
Founded in: 1971
Questionnaire not received

Hammond Castle Museum, Inc.
80 Hesperus Ave., 01930
Telephone: (617) 283-2080
Private agency
Founded in: 1930
Ben DeLuca, Jr., Executive Director
Number of members: 200
Staff: full time 10, part time 8,
volunteer 10
Major programs: museum, historic
site(s), tours/pilgrimages, school
programs, exhibits
Period of collections: Medieval period

GRAFTON

**Willard House and Clock
Museum, Inc.**
11 Willard St., 01619
Telephone: (617) 839-3335
Private agency
Founded in: 1971
George Abbott, Jr., Curator
Staff: full time 1
Major programs: museum, historic
site(s), historic preservation,
exhibits
Period of collections: 1700-1850

GREENFIELD

Greenfield Historic Commission
Court Square, 01301
Telephone: (413) 774-5363
Town agency

Founded in: 1970
Peter S. Miller, Chair
Number of members: 7
Major programs: archives, book
publishing, historic preservation,
research
Period of collections: 1753-present

Historical Society of Greenfield
43 Church St.
Mail to: P.O. Box 415, 01301
Private agency
Founded in: 1907
Eugene H. Mason, Jr., President
Number of members: 167
Staff: volunteer 13
Major programs: library, archives,
museum, tours/pilgrimages, junior
history, historic preservation,
books, research
Period of collections: 1783-present

HADLEY

Hadley Farm Museum Association
147 Russell St., 01035
Telephone: (413) 584-8279
Founded in: 1934
Number of members: 130
Staff: part time 1, volunteer 15
Major programs: museum
Period of collections: 1750-1900

Hadley Historical Society, Inc.
Goodwin Memorial Library, Middle
St., 01035
Private agency
Founded in: 1973
Lee Parman, President
Number of members: 105
Major programs: museum, school
programs, newsletters/pamphlets
Period of collections: 1800-1920

**Porter-Phelps-Huntington
Foundation, Inc.**
130 River Dr., 01035
Telephone: (413) 584-4699
Private agency
Founded in: 1955
Number of members: 530
Staff: part time 4
Major programs: archives, museum,
historic site(s), tours/pilgrimages,
concert series, folk traditions
program, family history program
Period of collections: 1750-1860

HALIFAX

Halifax Historical Society, Inc.
69 Pratt St., 02338
Telephone: (617) 697-2179
Questionnaire not received

HAMILTON

Hamilton Historical Society
Town Hall
Telephone: (617) 468-3570
(president)
Mail to: P.O. Box 108, 01936
Private agency
Founded in: 1961
Mrs. Gordon W. McKey, President
Number of members: 215
Staff: volunteer 4
Major programs: library, archives,
manuscripts, tours/pilgrimages,
junior history, book publishing,

newsletters/pamphlets, records
management, exhibits,
photographic collections
Period of collections: 18th-19th
centuries

HAMPDEN

**Historical Society of the Town of
Hampden, Inc.**
616 Main St.
Mail to: P.O. Box 363, 01036
Private agency
Founded in: 1965
Mary C. Cesan, President
Number of members: 130
Major programs: archives, museum,
historic preservation, exhibits,
photographic collections, cemetery
registration
Period of collections: 1780-present

HANCOCK

Shaker Community, Inc.
U.S. Rt. 20, 01201
Telephone: (413) 443-0188
Mail to: P.O. Box 898, Pittsfield, 01202
Founded in: 1960
Questionnaire not received

HANOVER

Hanover Historical Commission
Town Hall
Telephone: (617) 826-6254 (chair)
Mail to: 429 Main St., 02339
Town agency
Founded in: 1982
Barbara U. Barker, Chair
Major programs: historic site(s)

Hanover Historical Society
1526 Hanover St.
Telephone: (617) 878-5667
(treasurer)
Private agency
Founded in: 1928
John Goldthwait, President
Number of members: 200
Major programs: archives, book
publishing, historic preservation,
genealogical services
Period of collections: 1727-present

HANSON

Hanson Historical Society Inc.
565 Main St.
Mail to: 819 Main St., 02341
Founded in: 1960
Questionnaire not received

HARDWICK

Hardwick Historical Society, Inc.
On the Common, 01037
Founded in: 1959
Questionnaire not received

HARVARD

Fruitlands Museums, Inc.
R.R. 2, Box 87, Prospect Hill Rd.,
01451
Telephone: (617) 456-3924
Private agency
Founded in: 1914
Richard S. Reed, Director
Staff: full time 4, part time 40

Major programs: library, manuscripts,
museum, historic site(s), school
programs, exhibits, audiovisual
programs
Period of collections: 19th century

Harvard Historical Society
Still River, 01467
Mail to: Depot Rd., 01467
Private agency
Founded in: 1897
Mrs. David F. Remington, President
Number of members: 200
Staff: volunteer 17
Major programs: school programs,
photographic collections,
genealogical services
Period of collections: 19th century

HARWICH

Harwich Historical Society
Mail to: Box 17, 02695
Founded in: 1953
Questionnaire not received

HAVERHILL

Haverhill Historical Society
240 Water St., 01830
Telephone: (617) 374-4626
Founded in: 1904
Number of members: 500
Staff: part time 2, volunteer 2
Major programs: museum,
tours/pilgrimages, educational
programs
Period of collections: 1640-1918

HINGHAM

Hingham Historical Society
21 Lincoln St., 02043
Telephone: (617) 749-0013
Founded in: 1914
Number of members: 450
Staff: volunteer 60
Magazine: *Notes Out of The Ordinary*
Major programs: tours/pilgrimages,
educational programs
Period of collections: 18th-early 19th
century

HOLDEN

Holden Historical Society
P.O. Box 421, 01520
Private agency
Founded in: 1967
Ross W. Beales, Jr., President
Number of members: 110
Major programs: educational
programs, oral history, library
Period of collections: 1800-present

HOLLISTON

Holliston Historical Society
547 Washington St.
Telephone: (617) 429-5795
Mail to: P.O. Box 17, 01746
Founded in: 1920
Number of members: 220
Major programs: library, archives,
manuscripts, junior history, historic
preservation
Period of collections: 1700-present

HOLYOKE

Wistariahurst Museum
Holyoke Historical Commission, 238
  Cabot St., 01040
Telephone: (413) 536-6771
City agency
Founded in: 1959
Elizabeth Ottes, Director
Number of members: 350
Staff: full time 4, part time 1
Major programs: museum, historic
  site(s), school programs, exhibits
Period of collections: 19th-20th
  centuries

HOPKINTON

Hopkinton Historical Society, Inc.
26 Spring St., 01748
Telephone: (617) 435-4170
Founded in: 1951
Questionnaire not received

HUBBARDSTON

Hubbardston Historical Society
Main St., 01452
Private agency
Founded in: 1964
Barry Heiniluome, President
Number of members: 40
Major programs: museum, markers,
  tours/pilgrimages, oral history,
  school programs, book publishing,
  newsletters/pamphlets, historic
  preservation, records
  management, research, exhibits,
  living history, audiovisual
  programs, archaeology programs,
  photographic collections,
  genealogical services
Period of collections: 1850-present

HUDSON

Hudson Historical Commission
102 Washington St., 01749
Telephone: (617) 562-3296
Town agency, authorized by board of
  selectmen
Founded in: 1974
Alfred M. Braga, Chair
Major programs: historic site(s),
  markers, historic preservation,
  research
Period of collections: 1825-present

Hudson Historical Society
Hudson Public Library, Wood Square,
  01749
Town agency
Founded in: 1916
Alice MacNeill, President
Number of members: 75
Major programs: archives, museum,
  school programs, historic
  preservation, research
Period of collections: 1860-present

HYDE PARK

Hyde Park Historical Society
Weld Hall, 35 Harvard Ave.
Telephone: (617) 361-4398
Mail to: 30 Ayles Rd., 02136
Private agency
Founded in: 1887
Nancy H. Hannan, President
Number of members: 100

Staff: volunteer 2
Major programs: library, archives,
  manuscripts, museum, historic
  preservation, records
  management, research,
  photographic collections,
  genealogical services
Period of collections: Civil War era

IPSWICH

**Ipswich Historical
  Society—Whipple House**
53 S. Main St., 01938
Telephone: (617) 356-2811
Private agency
Founded in: 1890
Elizabeth H. Newton, Curator
Number of members: 270
Staff: volunteer 7
Major programs: library, archives,
  manuscripts, historic site(s),
  research, photographic collections
Period of collections: 17th-early 19th
  centuries

LANCASTER

First Church of Christ
Town Green, 01523
Telephone: (617) 365-2427
Private agency
Founded in: 1653
Thomas D. Wintle, Minister
Number of members: 150
Staff: full time 1, part time 3
Major programs: archives,
  manuscripts, historic site(s),
  tours/pilgrimages,
  newsletters/pamphlets, historic
  preservation
Period of collections: 1708-present

Lancaster Historical Commission
Town Hall, 01523
Telephone: (617) 365-2762
Town agency
Founded in: 1964
Phyllis A. Farnsworth, Chair
Staff: volunteer 7
Major programs: archives,
  manuscripts, markers, historic
  preservation, photographic
  collections
Period of collections: 1653-present

LAWRENCE

Immigrant City Archives, Inc.
38 Lawrence St., 01840
Telephone: (617) 686-9230
Founded in: 1977
Questionnaire not received

LEOMINSTER

**Lancaster League of Historical
  Societies**
56 Manchester St., 01453
Telephone: (607) 537-3684
Private agency
Founded in: 1972
Evelyn B. Hachey, President
Major programs: oral history, school
  programs, exhibits

Leominster Historical Commission
City Hall, 25 West St., Room 13
Telephone: (617) 534-7519
City agency

Founded in: 1972
Evelyn B. Hachey, Chair
Major programs: markers, historic
  preservation, research, historic
  district
Period of collections: 1740-present

Leominster Historical Society
17 School St., 01453
Telephone: (617) 537-5424
Founded in: 1906
Questionnaire not received

LEXINGTON

Lexington Historical Society
Telephone: (617) 861-0928
Mail to: P.O. Box 514, 02173
Private agency
Founded in: 1886
Wilbur M. Jaquith, President
Number of members: 1,317
Staff: part time 25, volunteer 60
Major programs: archives,
  manuscripts, museum, historic
  sites preservation, markers
Period of collections: 1750-1950

Museum of Our National Heritage
33 Marrett Rd.
Telephone: (617) 861-6559
Mail to: P.O. Box 519, 02173
Private agency, authorized by
  Scottish Rite Masonic Museum and
  Library, Inc.
Founded in: 1971
Clement M. Silvestro, Director
Staff: full time 15, part time 11,
  volunteer 25
Major programs: library, museum,
  school programs, research,
  exhibits
Period of collections: 1700-present

LINCOLN

Lincoln Historical Society
01773
Telephone: (617) 259-8958
Questionnaire not received

LITTLETON

Littleton Historical Society
Telephone: (617) 486-4393
Mail to: P.O. Box 254, 324 Harwood
  Ave., 01460
Number of members: 80
Major programs: museum, markers,
  oral history, book publishing,
  historic preservation
Period of collections: 18th-19th
  centuries

LONGMEADOW

Longmeadow Historical Society
697 Longmeadow St.
Telephone: (413) 567-3600
Mail to: 693 Longmeadow St., 01106
Private agency
Founded in: 1899
Brewster Sturtevant, President
Number of members: 515
Staff: part time 1, volunteer 25
Major programs: archives,
  manuscripts, museum, book
  publishing, newsletters/pamphlets,
  historic preservation, records
  management, research,

MASSACHUSETTS

archaeology programs,
photographic collections
Period of collections: 1700-1865

LOWELL

Lowell Historical Society
P.O. Box 1826, 01853
Founded in: 1868
Number of members: 500
Staff: volunteer 12
Major programs: archives,
tours/pilgrimages, book publishing,
newsletters/pamphlets, lectures
Period of collections: 1820-1940

Lowell Museum
560 Suffolk St., 01854
Telephone: (617) 459-6782
Founded in: 1974
Questionnaire not received

**St. Anne's Episcopal Church
Historical Commission**
10 Kirk St., 01852
Telephone: (617) 452-2150
Private agency
Founded in: 1979
Louise Hunt, Parish
Historian/Commission Co-chair
Staff: volunteer 8
Major programs: library, archives,
manuscripts, historic site(s), tours,
historic preservation, records
management, research, exhibits,
photographic collections,
genealogical services
Period of collections: 1824-present

**Society for the Preservation of
Colonial Culture**
52 New Spring St., 01851
Telephone: (617) 459-9864
Questionnaire not received

LYNN

Lynn Historical Society
125 Green St., 01902
Telephone: (617) 592-2465
Private agency
Founded in: 1897
Faith Magoun, Director
Number of members: 400
Staff: full time 2, part time 3,
volunteer 30
Major programs: library, archives,
manuscripts, museum,
tours/pilgrimages, school
programs, newsletters/pamphlets,
historic preservation, research,
exhibits, photographic collections,
genealogical services
Period of collections: 1629-present

LYNNFIELD

Lynnfield Historical Commission
7 Smith Farm Trail, 01940
Telephone: (617) 334-3408
Founded in: 1967
Questionnaire not received

Lynnfield Historical Society, Inc.
Lynnfield Public Library, Summer St.,
01940
Telephone: (617) 334-5411
Private agency
Founded in: 1954
Warren Falls, Librarian
Number of members: 250

Magazine: *Historical Lynnfield*
Major programs: archives,
manuscripts, historic site(s), oral
history, historic preservation
Period of collections: 1714-present

MALDEN

Malden Historical Society
Public Library, Salem St., 02148
Mail to: 116 Conant Rd., Melrose,
02176
Private agency
Founded in: 1887
Robert W. Graham, Treasurer

MANCHESTER

Manchester Historical Society
10 Union St., 01944
Telephone: (617) 526-7230
Private agency
Founded in: 1886
Mrs. George G. Loring, Curator
Number of members: 458
Staff: part time 1, volunteer 25
Major programs: library, museum,
newsletters/pamphlets, exhibits,
photographic collections,
genealogical services
Period of collections: 1700-1950

MANSFIELD

Mansfield Historical Society, Inc.
71 Rumford Ave.
Telephone: (617) 339-7831
Mail to: 121 Rumford Ave., 02048
Questionnaire not received

MARBLEHEAD

Marblehead Historical Society
161 Washington St.
Telephone: (617) 631-1069
Mail to: P.O. Box 1048, 01945
Private agency
Founded in: 1898
Mrs. John P. Hunt, Executive
Secretary
Number of members: 740
Staff: full time 1, part time 2,
volunteer 120
Major programs: library, archives,
manuscripts, museum, historic
preservation
Period of collections: 1650-1920

MARION

Sippican Historical Society
Front St., 02738
Telephone: (617) 748-0088
Private agency
H. Edmund Tripp, President
Number of members: 165
Major programs: museum, historic
site, markers, educational
programs, book publishing, historic
preservation, exhibits
Period of collections: 1840-1950

MARLBOROUGH

Marlborough Historical Society
377 Elm St.
Mail to: P.O. Box 513, 01752
Founded in: 1962
Questionnaire not received

MARSHFIELD

Marshfield Historical Commission
Town Hall, 02050
Telephone: (617) 837-5141
Founded in: 1965
Staff: volunteer 7
Major programs: library, archives,
manuscripts, museum, historic
sites preservation, markers,
tours/pilgrimages, books,
newsletters/pamphlets
Period of collections: 1492-1865

Marshfield Historical Society
Webster and Careswell Sts.
Telephone: (617) 834-7236
Mail to: Box 1244, 02050
Questionnaire not received

MASHPEE

**Mashpee Wampanoag Indian Tribal
Council, Inc.**
Rt. 130
Telephone: (617) 477-0208
Mail to: P.O. Box 1048, 02649
Telephone: 1974
Number of members: 500
Staff: full time 6, volunteer 10
Magazine: *Mittark*
Major programs: historic site,
newsletters/pamphlets, historic
preservation
Period of collections:
prehistoric-present

MATTAPOISETT

**Mattapoisett Museum and Carriage
House and Historical Society**
5 Church St., 02739
Telephone: (617) 758-2844
Questionnaire not received

MAYNARD

Maynard Historical Society
Town Bldg., 01754
Telephone: (617) 897-8153
Private agency
Founded in: 1961
Henry T. Hanson, President
Number of members: 30
Major programs: archives, museum,
tours, historic preservation,
photographic collections
Period of collections: 1871-present

MEDFIELD

Medfield Historical Society
6 Pleasant St.
Mail to: P.O. Box 233, 02052
Private agency
Founded in: 1891
Paul A. Hurd, President
Number of members: 200
Staff: volunteer 15
Magazine: *Bulletin*
Major programs: historic site,
newsletters/pamphlets, historic
preservation
Period of collections: 18th-19th
centuries

MEDFORD

Medford Historical Society
10 Governor's Ave., 02155
Telephone: (617) 395-7863

Founded in: 1896
Questionnaire not received

Royall House Association
15 George St., 02155
Telephone: (617) 396-9032
Private agency
Founded in: 1908
William Slagle, Jr., President
Number of members: 285
Staff: full time 2, volunteer 4
Magazine: *Royall House Reporter*
Major programs: museum, historic
 preservation
Period of collections: 1690-1783

MELROSE

Melrose Historical Commission
76 Linden Rd., 02176
Telephone: (617) 665-5010
City agency
Founded in: 1972
Arnold W. Williams, Chair
Staff: volunteer 5
Major programs: historic
 preservation, inventory of old
 houses

Melrose Historical Society
131 W. Emerson St.
Telephone: (617) 665-5010
Mail to: P.O. Box 301, 02176
Private agency
Founded in: 1976
Arnold W. Williams, President
Number of members: 85
Staff: volunteer 15
Magazine: *Ell Pond Echoes*
Major programs: tours/pilgrimages,
 oral history, school programs,
 newsletters/pamphlets, historic
 preservation

MENDON

Mendon Historical Society
Main St., 01756
Founded in: 1896
Questionnaire not received

MIDDLEBORO

Eddy Homestead Association, Inc.
1 Cedar St. at Plympton, 02346
Mail to: 1441 Beech Lane, E. Meadow,
 NY, 11554
Founded in: 1962
Questionnaire not received

**Middleborough Historical
 Association, Inc.**
Jackson St., 02346
Telephone: (617) 947-1969
Questionnaire not received

MILFORD

Milford Historical Commission
Memorial Hall, School St.
Mail to: 2 Nicholas Rd., 01757
Town agency, authorized by board of
 selectmen
Founded in: 1971
Robert M. Andreda, Chair
Staff: volunteer 10
Major programs: library, archives,
 manuscripts, museum, historic
 site(s), book publishing,
 pamphlets, records management,
 research, exhibits, audiovisual

programs, photographic
 collections
Period of collections: 19th century

MILTON

Friends of the Blue Hills Trust
1894 Canton Ave., 02186
Telephone: (617) 326-0079
Private agency
Founded in: 1976
David P. Hodgdon, President
Number of members: 300
Staff: volunteer 20
Magazine: *Friends of the Blue Hills*
Major programs: manuscripts,
 historic site(s), tours/pilgrimages,
 oral history, school programs, book
 publishing, newsletters/pamphlets,
 historic preservation, research,
 exhibits, audiovisual programs,
 archaeology programs,
 photographic collections, field
 services, three national
 environment study areas
Period of collections: 7,000-present

Milton Historical Society
Suffolk Resolves House, 1370 Canton
 Ave., 02186
Telephone: (617) 333-0644
Founded in: 1904
Questionnaire not received

**Museum of the American China
 Trade**
215 Adams St., 02186
Telephone: (617) 696-1815
Founded in: 1965
Number of members: 1,200
Staff: full time 8, part time 8,
 volunteer 100
Magazine: *China Trade Register*
Major programs: library, archives,
 manuscripts, museum
Period of collections: 18th-19th
 centuries

Trustees of Reservations
224 Adams St., 02186
Telephone: (617) 698-2066
Private agency
Founded in: 1891
Frederic Winthrop, Jr., Director
Number of members: 4,000
Staff: full time 41, part time 130,
 volunteer 200
Magazine: *The Trustees*
Major programs: historic
 preservation, property
 management of natural and cultural
 historic and esthetic sites
Period of collections: 1735-1921

MONSON

Monson Historical Society, Inc.
94 Main St.
Telephone: (413) 283-8143
Mail to: P.O. Box 93, 01057
Founded in: 1958
Questionnaire not received

MONTAGUE

Montague Historical Society, Inc.
Telephone: (413) 367-2216
Mail to: 34 Central St., 01351
Founded in: 1968
Questionnaire not received

MONTEREY

Monterey Historical Society
Main St., 11563
Founded in: 1962
Mrs. John Fijux, President
Number of members: 55
Staff: volunteer 5
Major programs: museum, markers,
 tours/pilgrimages
Period of collections: 19th century

NANTUCKET

Nantucket Historical Association
Old Town Bldg.
Telephone: (617) 228-1894
Mail to: P.O. Box 1016, 02554
Founded in: 1894
John N. Welch, Administrator
Number of members: 2,500
Staff: full time 10, part time 50,
 volunteer 25
Magazine: *Historic Nantucket*
Major programs: library, archives,
 manuscripts, museum, historic
 sites preservation, markers, oral
 history, educational programs,
 books, newsletters/pamphlets
Period of collections: 1659-present

NATICK

Natick Historical Society
58 Eliot St., S. Natick, 01760
Telephone: (617) 235-6015
Private agency
Founded in: 1870
Anne K. Schaller, Museum Director
Number of members: 127
Staff: part time 1, volunteer 6
Magazine: *The Arrow*
Major programs: library, archives,
 manuscripts, museum, oral history,
 research, exhibits, photographic
 collections, genealogical services
Period of collections: 1650-present

NEEDHAM

**Association for Gravestone
 Studies**
46 Plymouth Rd., 02192
Telephone: (617) 444-6263
Private agency
Founded in: 1977
Rosalee F. Oakley, Executive
 Secretary
Number of members: 500
Staff: part time 1, volunteer 15
Major programs: archives, markers,
 book publishing,
 newsletters/pamphlets, historic
 preservation, exhibits, lectures,
 annual conference
Period of collections: Colonial New
 England period

Needham Historical Society, Inc.
53 Glendoon Rd., 02192
Telephone: (617) 444-3181
Private agency
Founded in: 1915
Henry Hicks, President
Number of members: 380
Staff: volunteer 15
Major programs: archives, museum,
 historic sites preservation, markers,
 newsletters/pamphlets
Period of collections:
 prehistoric-present

NEW BEDFORD

New Bedford Glass Society
50 N. 2nd St., 02740
Telephone: (617) 994-0115
Private agency
Founded in: 1974
Janie Chester Young, Director
Number of members: 950
Staff: full time 2, part time 3,
volunteer 40
Major programs: library, archives,
museum, historic site(s), school
programs, book publishing,
newsletters/pamphlets, historic
preservation, research, exhibits,
audiovisual programs, history of
glass
Period of collections: 1867-1956

New Bedford Whaling Museum
18 Johnny Cake Hill, 02740
Telephone: (617) 997-0046
Private agency, authorized by Old
Dartmouth Historical Society
Founded in: 1903
Richard C. Kugler, Director
Number of members: 2,200
Staff: full time 20, part time 3,
volunteer 80
Major programs: library, manuscripts,
museum, school programs, book
publishing, newsletters/pamphlets,
research, exhibits, photographic
collections
Period of collections: 19th century

New England Preservation
Institute, Inc.
345 Union St., 02740
Telephone: (617) 996-3383
Private agency
Founded in: 1980
Maximilian L. Ferro, President
Major programs: historic preservation

Old Dartmouth Historical Society
18 Johnny Cake Hill, 02740
Telephone: (617) 997-0046
Questionnaire not received

Rotch-Jones-Duff House and
Garden Museum
396 County St., 02740
Telephone: (617) 997-1401
Founded in: 1834
Susan L. Cline, Executive Director
Number of members: 200
Staff: full time 1, part time 3,
volunteer 300
Major programs: concert series,
children's programs, garden
activities, historic preservation and
restoration, furniture and family
exhibits
Period of collections: 1800-1981

WHALE (Waterfront Historic
Area League)
13 Centre St., 02740
Telephone: (617) 996-6912
Founded in: 1962
John K. Bullard, Agent
Number of members: 1,145
Staff: full time 3, part time 1,
volunteer 250
Magazine: *Soundings*
Major programs: library, historic site,
tours, educational programs,
newsletters, historic preservation
Period of collections: 1790-1923

NEWBURYPORT

Historical Society of Old
Newbury—Cushing House
Museum
98 High St., 01950
Telephone: (617) 462-6643
Private agency
Founded in: 1877
Wilhelmina V. Lunt, Curator
Number of members: 800
Staff: full time 2, part time 11,
volunteer 3
Major programs: museum, historic
preservation, research, exhibits
Period of collections:
Colonial-Federal periods

NEW SALEM

Swift River Valley Historical
Society, Inc.
Elm St., 01355
Telephone: (617) 544-6807
Private agency
Founded in: 1936
Althea B. Daniels, President
Number of members: 643
Staff: volunteer 7
Major programs: tours/pilgrimages,
oral history, school programs,
historic preservation, genealogical
services
Period of collections: 1700-1938

NEWTON

Boston College
140 Commonwealth Ave.
Telephone: (617) 552-3248
Mail to: Chestnut Hill, 02167

Gravestone carved in the 1700s by William Young, a stonecarver from Worcester.—Association for Gravestone Studies, photo by Daniel Farber

Private agency, authorized by the
college
Founded in: 1863
Paul A. FitzGerald, University
Archivist
Staff: full time 3, part time 2
Major programs: archives, historic
preservation, records
management, photographic
collections
Period of collections: 1900-present

Jackson Homestead
527 Washington St., 02158
Telephone: (617) 552-7238
City agency
Founded in: 1950
Duscha S. Scott, Director
Number of members: 700
Staff: full time 3, volunteer 50
Magazine: *The Jackson Homestead
News*
Major programs: archives,
manuscripts, museum, historic
site(s), book publishing, research,
exhibits, photographic collections
Period of collections: 19th century

NORTH ABINGTON

Mayflower Society
4 Winslow, 02360
Telephone: (617) 746-2590
Private agency, authorized by
General Society of Mayflower
Descendants
Founded in: 1897
William Davis, Governor General
Number of members: 20,000
Staff: full time 9, part time 10
Major programs: library,
tours/pilgrimages, historic
preservation, genealogical
services
Period of collections: 1800-1914

NORTHAMPTON

Northampton Historical Society
46 Bridge St., 01060
Telephone: (413) 584-6011
Private agency
Founded in: 1905
Ruth E. Wilbur, Director
Number of members: 500
Staff: full time 3, part time 5,
volunteer 25
Major programs: library, archives,
manuscripts, museum, historic
site(s), tours/pilgrimages, oral
history, school programs, book
publishing, newsletters/pamphlets,
records management, exhibits,
photographic collections
Period of collections: 1783-present

NORTH ANDOVER

**Museum of American Textile
History**
800 Massachusetts Ave., 01845
Telephone: (617) 686-0191
Founded in: 1960
Thomas W. Leavitt, Director
Staff: full time 15, part time 22,
volunteer 16
Major programs: library, manuscripts,
museum, educational programs,
books
Period of collections: 1700-1960

**New England Document
Conservation Center**
Abbott Hall, School St. 01810
Telephone: (617) 470-1010
Founded in: 1973
Ann Russell, Director
Staff: full time 20, part time 5
Major programs: educational
programs

North Andover Historical Society
153 Academy Rd., 01845
Telephone: (617) 686-4035
Private agency
Founded in: 1913
Martha D. Hamilton, Director/Curator
Number of members: 570
Staff: part time 2, volunteer 45
Major programs: archives, museum,
tours/pilgrimages, school
programs, book publishing,
newsletters/pamphlets, historic
preservation, exhibits
Period of collections: 1670-1840

**Stevens Coolidge Place, Trustees
of Reservations**
137 Andover St.
Telephone: (617) 682-3580
Mail to: 5 Wood Lane, 01845
Private agency
Founded in: 1963
Robert Murray, Superintendent
Staff: full time 2, part time 4,
volunteer 4
Major programs: museum, historic
preservation
Period of collections: 1918-1940s

NORTHBOROUGH

**Northborough Historical
Society, Inc.**
52 Main St., 01532
Private agency
Founded in: 1906
Christine L. Fipphen, Curator
Staff: part time 1, volunteer 4
Magazine: *The Hourglass*
Major programs: library, archives,
manuscripts, museum,
tours/pilgrimages, school
programs, newsletters/pamphlets,
research, exhibits, photographic
collections, genealogical services
Period of collections: 1783-present

NORTH EASTON

Easton Historical Society
P.O. Box 3, 02356
Founded in: 1948
Number of members: 200
Staff: volunteer 25
Major programs: historic site, book
publishing, newsletters/pamphlets,
historic preservation

NORTH READING

**North Reading Historical and
Antiquarian Society, Inc.**
Bow St.
Telephone: (617) 664-3086
Mail to: 318 Haverhill St., 01864
Founded in: 1952
Number of members: 92
Staff: volunteer 15
Major programs: library, museum
Period of collections: 1713-present

NORWOOD

Norwood Historical Society
93 Day St., 02062
Founded in: 1907
Number of members: 200
Staff: full time 2, volunteer 20
Major programs: educational
programs
Period of collections: 1865-present

ORANGE

Orange Historical Society
N. Main St.
Telephone: (617) 544-6286
Mail to: 80 Fountain St., 01364
Founded in: 1960
Mrs. Grover Ballou, President
Number of members: 81
Major programs: historic preservation
Period of collections: 1850-1930

ORLEANS

**Orleans Historical
Society—Margaret Stranger
House**
River Rd. and Main St.
Telephone: (617) 255-2658
Mail to: P.O. Box 353, 02653
Private agency
Founded in: 1958
Charles H. Thomsen, President
Number of members: 450
Staff: volunteer 15
Major programs: archives, museum,
historic site(s), markers, book
publishing, historic preservation,
photographic collections,
genealogical services, public
information programs
Period of collections: 1812-present

OSTERVILLE

Osterville Historical Society
W. Bay and Parker Rds., 02655
Telephone: (617) 428-5861
Mail to: P.O. Box 3, 02655
Private agency
Founded in: 1931
John M. Groff, Curator
Number of members: 300
Staff: part time 1, volunteer 100
Major programs: museum, historic
site(s), oral history, exhibits
Period of collections: 19th century

OXFORD

**Huguenot Memorial Society of
Oxford**
Ft. Hill Rd.
Telephone: (617) 987-2010
Mail to: 2 Maple Rd., 01540
Founded in: 1881
Questionnaire not received

PALMER

Palmer Historical Commission
Town Administration Bldg., Main St.,
01069
Telephone: (413) 283-5061
Town agency
Founded in: 1976
Marion F. Lis, Treasurer
Staff: volunteer 7
Major programs: archives,
manuscripts, historic site(s),

markers, newsletters/pamphlets, historic preservation, records management, research, genealogical services
Period of collections: 1700s-present

Urbain Baudreall Graveline Genealogical Association, Inc.
P.O. Box 191, 01069
Telephone: (413) 283-3418
Private agency
Founded in: 1978
Robert Graveline, President
Number of members: 364
Staff: volunteer 5
Magazine: *The Descendants*
Major programs: markers, tours/pilgrimages, book publishing, newsletters/pamphlets, historic preservation, research
Period of collections: late 17th-18th centuries

PEABODY

Peabody Historical Society
35 Washington St., 01960
Telephone: (617) 531-0805
Founded in: 1896
Number of members: 120
Staff: volunteer 15
Major programs: library, museum, historic site, historic preservation
Period of collections: Colonial-present

PETERSHAM

Petersham Historical Society, Inc.
N. Main St., 01366
Telephone: (617) 724-3380
Private agency
Founded in: 1912
Mrs. Donald B. Haines, Curator
Major programs: library, museum, research, exhibits, photographic collections, genealogical services
Period of collections: 1770-present

PITTSFIELD

Berkshire Athenaeum, Local History and Literature Services
1 Wendell Ave., 01201
Telephone: (413) 442-1559
City agency
Founded in: 1876
Ruth T. Degenhardt, Department Head
Staff: full time 1, part time 1
Major programs: library, manuscripts, genealogical materials
Period of collections: 1620-present

Berkshire County Historical Society
780 Holmes Rd., 01201-7199
Telephone: (413) 442-1793
Private agency
Founded in: 1962
Susan C. S. Edwards, Executive Director
Number of members: 833
Staff: full time 2, part time 5, volunteer 100
Magazine: *Berkshire History, News and Notes*
Major programs: library, archives, museum, historic site(s), tours/pilgrimages, school

programs, newsletters/pamphlets, research, exhibits, photographic collections, field services
Period of collections: 1820-1900

The Berkshire Museum
39 South St., 01201
Telephone: (413) 443-7171
Private agency
Founded in: 1903
Gary Burger, Director
Number of members: 1,150
Staff: full time 13, volunteer 1
Major programs: museum
Period of collections: 19th century

Hancock Shaker Village, Inc.
U.S. Rt. 20
Telephone: (413) 443-0188/447-7284
Mail to: P.O. Box 898, 01202
Private agency
Founded in: 1960
Beverly Hamilton, Acting Director
Number of members: 1,000
Staff: full time 20, part time 40, volunteer 85
Major programs: library, manuscripts, museum, historic site(s), tours/pilgrimages, school programs, book publishing, newsletters/pamphlets, historic preservation, records management, research, exhibits, living history, audiovisual programs, craft program
Period of collections: 19th century

Local History and Literature Services of the Berkshire Athenaeum
1 Wendell Ave., 01201
Telephone: (413) 442-1559
Founded in: 1876
Questionnaire not received

PLAINFIELD

Plainfield Historical Society, Inc.
Main St., 01070
Private agency
Founded in: 1960
Arvilla L. Dyer, President
Number of members: 190
Staff: volunteer 1
Major programs: museum, genealogical services
Period of collections: 1785-present

PLYMOUTH

Cranberry World Visitors Center
Ocean Spray Cranberries, Inc., Water St., 02360
Telephone: (617) 747-1000
Private agency
Founded in: 1977
Herbert N. Colcord, Manager
Staff: full time 2, part time 15
Major programs: museum, educational programs
Period of collections: 19th-20th centuries

General Society of Mayflower Descendants
4 Winslow St., 02360
Telephone: (617) 746-3188
Mail to: P.O. Box 3297, 02361
Private agency
Founded in: 1897

Mrs. Clayton M. Merrick, Jr., Historian General
Staff: full time 1, part time 4, volunteer 12
Magazine: *Mayflower Quarterly*
Major programs: library, archives, museum, tours/pilgrimages, book publishing, newsletters/pamphlets, historic preservation, research, genealogical services
Period of collections: 1620-present

Mayflower Society
4 Winslow, 02360
Telephone: (617) 746-2590
Founded in: 1897
Questionnaire not received

Parting Ways—The Museum of Afro-American Ethnohistory, Inc.
130 Court St.
Telephone: (617) 746-6028
Mail to: P.O. Box 1976, 02360
Founded in: 1974
Number of members: 200
Staff: volunteer 25
Major programs: museum, historic sites preservation, markers, tours/pilgrimages, oral history, educational programs, newsletters/pamphlets
Period of collections: 1750-1860

Pilgrim John Howland Society—Howland House
33 Sandwich St., 02360
Telephone: (617) 746-9590
Mail to: c/o Secretary, 73 Pound Hill Rd., N. Smithfield, RI, 02895
Private agency
Founded in: 1897
Mrs. W. Russell Greenwood, Secretary
Number of members: 870
Staff: part time 7
Magazine: *The Howland Quarterly*
Major programs: historic site(s), archaeology programs
Period of collections: 1638-1705

Pilgrim Society
75 Court St., 02360
Telephone: (617) 746-1620
Private agency
Founded in: 1820
Laurence R. Pizer, Director
Number of members: 900
Staff: full time 5, part time 7, volunteer 8
Magazine: *Pilgrim Society Notes*
Major programs: library, archives, manuscripts, museum, historic site(s), book publishing, newsletters/pamphlets, research, exhibits, photographic collections
Period of collections: 1600-present

Plimoth Plantation, Inc.
Warren Ave.
Telephone: (617) 746-1622
Mail to: P.O. Box 1620, 02360
Private agency
Founded in: 1947
David K. Case, Director
Number of members: 2,250
Staff: full time 50, part time 100, volunteer 5
Magazine: *Plimoth Plantation Newsletter*

Major programs: library, museum, school programs, newsletters/pamphlets, research, exhibits, living history, photographic collections
Period of collections: Colonial New England

Plymouth Antiquarian Society
Telephone: (617) 746-9697
Mail to: P.O. Box 1137, 02360
Private agency
Founded in: 1919
Mrs. Eliot Sargent, President
Number of members: 500
Staff: full time 1, part time 20, volunteer 50
Major programs: museum, historic site(s), newsletters/pamphlets, historic preservation, exhibits
Period of collections: 1677-1850

Plymouth Historical Commission
Plymouth Historic District Commission, c/o Pilgrim Hall, 75 Court St. 02360
Telephone: (617) 746-1620
Founded in: 1972
Questionnaire not received

Richard Sparrow House, Inc.
42 Summer St., 02360
Telephone: (617) 746-6735
Founded in: 1962
Questionnaire not received

PRINCETON

Princeton Historical Society
Goodnow Rd., 01541
Founded in: 1939
Number of members: 150
Period of collections: 18th-19th centuries

PROVINCETOWN

Cape Cod Pilgrim Memorial Association
Town Hill
Telephone: (617) 487-1310
Mail to: Provincetown Monument and Museum, P.O. Box 1125, 02657
Founded in: 1892
Questionnaire not received

QUINCY

Adams National Historic Site
135 Adams St.
Telephone: (617) 773-1177
Mail to: P.O. Box 531, 02269
Federal agency, authorized by National Park Service
Founded in: 1946
Wilhelmina S. Harris, Superintendent
Staff: full time 9, part time 9
Major programs: library, historic site(s), tours/pilgrimages, school programs, newsletters/pamphlets, historic preservation, research, lecture series
Period of collections: 1764-1927

Quincy Historical Society
Adams Academy Bldg., 8 Adams St., 02169
Telephone: (617) 773-1144
Founded in: 1893
Lawrence J. Yerdon, Director/Curator
Number of members: 1,300

Staff: full time 1, part time 4, volunteer 25
Major programs: library, archives, manuscripts, museum, historic site(s), school programs, newsletters/pamphlets, research, exhibits, photographic collections, genealogical services
Period of collections: 1625-present

RANDOLPH

Randolph Historical Commission
Town Hall
Telephone: (617) 963-4385
Mail to: 54 South St., 02368
Town agency
Founded in: 1960
Raymond P. MacGerrigle, Chair
Number of members: 5
Major programs: library, archives, manuscripts, museum, historic site(s), markers, tours/pilgrimages, junior history, oral history, school programs, book publishing, newsletters/pamphlets, historic preservation, records management, research, exhibits
Period of collections: 1700-present

Randolph Historical Society
360 N. Main St., 02368
Founded in: 1976
Questionnaire not received

READING

Reading Antiquarian Society
103 Washington St.
Mail to: 26 Vine St., 01867
Private agency
Founded in: 1916
Mrs. Robert M. Barclay, Secretary
Number of members: 175
Staff: volunteer 10
Major programs: museum, tours/pilgrimages, school programs, historic preservation, exhibits
Period of collections: 1750-present

Reading Historical Commission
Town Hall, 01867
Telephone: (617) 942-0500
Town agency, authorized by board of selectmen
Founded in: 1977
Virginia M. Adams, Chair
Major programs: archives, historic site(s), historic preservation, records management

REHOBOTH

Annawan Historical Society of Rehoboth
P.O. Box 71, 02769
Telephone: (617) 669-6464
Founded in: 1966
Number of members: manuscripts, museum, historic site, markers, oral history, historic preservation
Questionnaire not received

Rehoboth Antiquarian Society
Bay State Rd.
Mail to: P.O. Box 2, 02769
Founded in: 1885
Charles Evans, President
Number of members: 150

Staff: volunteer 15
Major programs: library, museum
Period of collections: 1783-1865

ROCKPORT

Sandy Bay Historical Society
40 King St.
Mail to: P.O. Box 63, 01966
Private agency
Harry L. Walen, President
Number of members: 300
Major programs: library, archives, museum, exhibits
Period of collections: from 1770

ROWE

Rowe Historical Society
Zoar Rd.
Telephone: (413) 339-5598
Mail to: Potter Rd., 01367
Private agency
Founded in: 1958
Nancy Williams, Secretary
Number of members: 200
Staff: volunteer 20
Magazine: *Bulletin*
Major programs: museum, historic site, historic preservation
Period of collections: 1800-early 1900s

ROWLEY

Rowley Historical Society
Main St., 01969
Telephone: (617) 948-3381
Questionnaire not received

ROXBURY

Roxbury Historical Society
183 Roxbury St.
Telephone: (617) 445-7400
Mail to: Dudley Station, P.O. Box 5, 02119
Founded in: 1901
Questionnaire not received

ROYALSTON

Royalston Historical Society
The Common, 01368
Telephone: (617) 249-4964
Mail to: Fernald Rd., S. Royalston, 01331
Private agency
Founded in: 1941
Waino J. Kirkman, President
Number of members: 30
Staff: volunteer 20
Major programs: museum, historic preservation

SALEM

Essex County Historical Association
c/o Essex Institute, 132 Essex St., 01970
Private agency
Founded in: 1936
Number of members: 35
Staff: volunteer 5
Major programs: federation of 35 historical societies in the county

Essex Institute
132 Essex St., 01970
Telephone: (617) 744-3390

MASSACHUSETTS

Private agency
Founded in: 1848
Anne Farnam, Director
Number of members: 1,600
Staff: full time 26, part time 20, volunteer 64
Magazine: *Essex Institute Historical Collections*
Major programs: library, archives, manuscripts, museum, historic site(s), junior history, oral history, school programs, book publishing, newsletters/pamphlets, historic preservation, research, exhibits, genealogical services, field services
Period of collections: early 17th century-present

Historic Salem, Inc.
Old Town Hall, Derby Square
Telephone: (617) 745-6470
Mail to: P.O. Box 865, 01970
Private agency
Founded in: 1944
Janet A. Porter, Executive Director
Number of members: 375
Staff: part time 1, volunteer 5
Major programs: historic site(s), markers, tours/pilgrimages, school programs, book publishing, newsletters/pamphlets, historic preservation, research

House of Seven Gables
54 Turner St., 01970
Telephone: (617) 744-0991
Private agency
Founded in: 1910
Edward M. Stevenson, Executive Director
Number of members: 700
Staff: full time 5, part time 50
Major programs: historic site(s), historic preservation
Period of collections: 1660-1850

Peabody Museum of Salem
E. India Square, 01970
Telephone: (617) 745-1876
Private agency
Founded in: 1799
Peter J. Fetchko, Director
Number of members: 2,700
Staff: full time 39, part time 15, volunteer 210
Magazine: *The American Neptune*
Major programs: library, archives, museum, tours/pilgrimages, school programs, book publishing, newsletters/pamphlets, historic preservation, research, exhibits, audiovisual programs, archaeology programs, photographic collections, field services
Period of collections: 1783-present

Ropes Memorial
318 Essex St., 01970
Telephone: (617) 744-0718
Founded in: 1912
Questionnaire not received

Salem Maritime National Historic Site
Custom House, Derby St., 01970
Telephone: (617) 744-4323
Federal agency, authorized by National Park Service
Founded in: 1937

Cynthia Pollack, Superintendent
Staff: full time 10, volunteer 4
Major programs: library, historic site(s), school programs, historic preservation, research, exhibits
Period of collections: 1760-1937

SANDWICH

Heritage Plantation of Sandwich
Pine and Grove Sts.
Telephone: (617) 888-3300
Mail to: P.O. Box 566, 02563
Private agency
Founded in: 1969
Gene A. Schott, Director
Number of members: 2,500
Staff: full time 30, part time 30, volunteer 48
Magazine: *View From the Cupola*
Major programs: museum, school programs, newsletters/pamphlets, historic preservation, exhibits, archaeology programs, horticulture
Period of collections: 19th century

Sandwich Archives and Historical Center
145 Main St., 02563
Telephone: (617) 888-0340
Town agency
Founded in: 1977
Russell A. Lovell, Jr., Archivist/Historian
Staff: part time 3
Major programs: archives, book publishing, research, genealogical services
Period of collections: 1651-present

Sandwich Historical Commission
145 Main St., 02563
Telephone: (617) 888-0340
Town agency
Founded in: 1971
Barbara L. Gill, Chair
Staff: volunteer 7
Major programs: research, photographic collections, survey of buildings and historic assets
Period of collections: 18th-19th centuries

Sandwich Historical Society and Glass Museum
129 Main St.
Mail to: P.O. Box 103. 02563
Private agency
Founded in: 1907
Blanche E. Robinson, President
Number of members: 1,333
Staff: full time 5, part time 5, volunteer 58
Magazine: *The Acorn*
Major programs: manuscripts, museum, school programs, book publishing, newsletters/pamphlets, research, exhibits
Period of collections: early 18th-20th centuries

Thornton W. Burgess Museum
4 Water St.
Telephone: (617) 888-4668
Mail to: P.O. Box 972, 02563
Private agency
Founded in: 1976
Nancy E. Titcomb, Director
Number of members: 2,500
Staff: full time 4, part time 2, volunteer 60

Major programs: museum, school programs, exhibits, living history, natural history
Period of collections: 1910-present

Yesteryears Museum Association, Inc.
Main and River Sts.
Telephone: (617) 888-1711
Mail to: P.O. Box 609, 02563
Founded in: 1960
Questionnaire not received

SAUGUS

Saugus Historical Society
59 Water St., 01906
Telephone: (617) 233-1191
Mail to: 21 Lovell Rd., Lynnfield, 01940
Number of members: 150
Magazine: *Saugus Historical Society Times*
Major programs: library, archives, tours/pilgrimages, oral history, educational programs, book publishing, newsletters/pamphlets, historic preservation
Period of collections: 1639-present

SCITUATE

Scituate Historical Society
First Parish Rd.
Telephone: (617) 545-0474
Mail to: 121 Maple St., 02066
Private agency
Founded in: 1916
Mrs. Elliot C. Laidlaw, President
Number of members: 725

SHARON

Kendall Whaling Museum
27 Everett St.
Telephone: (617) 784-5642
Mail to: P.O. Box 297, 02067
Private agency
Founded in: 1956
Stuart M. Frank, Director
Number of members: 500
Staff: full time 4, part time 8, volunteer 10
Major programs: library, archives, manuscripts, museum, tours/pilgrimages, oral history, school programs, book publishing, newsletters/pamphlets, historic preservation, records management, research, exhibits, audiovisual programs, archaeology programs, photographic collections, field services, musical programs, teaching training, consultation
Period of collections: 16th century-present

SHEFFIELD

Sheffield Historical Society
Main St., 01257
Telephone: (413) 229-8668
Private agency
Founded in: 1972
Christopher J. Coenen, President
Number of members: 160
Major programs: library, archives, historic site(s), tours/pilgrimages, school programs,

204

newsletters/pamphlets, historic
preservation, exhibits,
photographic collections
Period of collections: 1733-present

SHELBURNE FALLS

Shelburne Historical Society
N. Maple St.
Mail to: P.O. Box 86, 01370
Founded in: 1963
Questionnaire not received

SHIRLEY

Shirley Historical Society
Telephone: (617) 425-9328/425-4513
Mail to: P.O. Box 295, 01464
Private agency
Founded in: 1972
Meredith Marcinkewicz, Secretary
Number of members: 80
Staff: volunteer 6
Major programs: archives, historic
sites preservation, educational
programs
Period of collections: 1865-present

SHREWSBURY

Shrewsbury Historical Society
Church St., 01545
Number of members: 150
Major programs: historic preservation
Period of collections: 19th century

SOMERVILLE

Somerville Historical Society
1 Westwood Rd., 02143
Founded in: 1897
Major programs: archives, historic
site

Somerville Historical Museum
1 Westwood Rd., 02143
Telephone: (617) 666-9810
Private agency, authorized by
Somerville Historical Society
Founded in: 1897
Thomas Grillo, Program Director
Number of members: 250
Staff: full time 3
Major programs: library, archives,
manuscripts, museum,
tours/pilgrimages, school
programs, exhibits, audiovisual
programs, photographic
collections
Period of collections: late 18th-early
19th centuries

SOUTH CARVER

Edaville Railroad
Rt. 58
Telephone: (617) 866-4526
Mail to: P.O. Box 7, 02366
Private agency
Founded in: 1946
George E. Bartholomew, President
Staff: full time 7, part time 40
Major programs: museum
Period of collections: 1800s-early
1900s

SOUTH CHELMSFORD

**"Old Chelmsford" Garrison House
Association**
105 Garrison Rd.

Telephone: (617) 256-8832
Mail to: P.O. Box 161, 01824
Founded in: 1959
Questionnaire not received

SOUTH DARTMOUTH

Childrens Museum
276 Gulf Rd., 02748
Private agency
Founded in: 1953
Robert O. Bailey, Director of
Education
Number of members: 1,000
Major programs: museum, school
programs, exhibits, natural
science, hands-on education

SOUTH HADLEY

Skinner Museum
Woodbridge St., Rt. 116
Telephone: (413) 538-2085
Mail to: Mt. Holyoke College, 01075
Private agency, authorized by the
college
Founded in: 1946
Teri J. Edelstein, Director
Number of members: part time 5
Major programs: museum
Period of collections: 19th century

SOUTH HAMILTON

Hamilton Historical Society
23 Walnut Rd., 01982
Telephone: (617) 468-2779
Questionnaire not received

SPRINGFIELD

**Connecticut Valley Historical
Museum**
194 State St., 01103
Telephone: (413) 732-3080
Private agency, authorized by
Springfield Library and Museums
Association
Founded in: 1876
Arthur C. Townsend, Director
Number of members: full time 3, part
time 3, volunteer 35
Major programs: manuscripts,
museum, school programs,
exhibits
Period of collections: early 19th
century

**Springfield Armory National
Historic Site**
1 Armory Square, 01105
Telephone: (413) 734-6477
Federal agency, authorized by
National Park Service
Founded in: 1978
W. Douglas Lindsay, Jr.,
Superintendent
Staff: full time 9, part time 5
Major programs: library, museum,
historic site(s), oral history, exhibits
Period of collections: 1794-1968

STERLING

Sterling Historical Society, Inc.
7 Pine St., 01564
Telephone: (617) 422-6139
Private agency
Founded in: 1963
Barbara R. Dudley, President
Number of members: 330

Staff: volunteer 3
Major programs: archives, museum,
book publishing,
newsletters/pamphlets, historic
preservation, photographic
collections
Period of collections: 1770-1850

STOCKBRIDGE

Chesterwood
Off Rt. 183, Glendale Section
Telephone: (413) 298-3579
Mail to: P.O. Box 248, 01262
Private agency, authorized by
National Trust for Historic
Preservation
Founded in: 1969
Paul W. Ivory, Director
Staff: full time 5, part time 16,
volunteer 9
Magazine: *The Pedestal*
Major programs: archives,
manuscripts, museum, historic
site(s), tours/pilgrimages, oral
history, school programs,
newsletters/pamphlets, historic
preservation, research, exhibits,
photographic collections, field
services
Period of collections: 1900-1931

**Historical Room of Stockbridge
Library**
Main St., 01262
Telephone: (413) 298-5501
Private agency, authorized by
Stockbridge Library Association
Founded in: 1862
Pauline D. Pierce, Curator
Staff: full time 1
Major programs: library, archives,
manuscripts, museum, oral history,
research, exhibits, photographic
collections, genealogical services
Period of collections: 1735-present

The Mission House
Sergeant and Main Sts.
Telephone: (413) 298-3239
Mail to: P.O. Box 115, 01262
Private agency, authorized by the
Trustees of Reservations
Founded in: 1891
Delphine Williams, Administrator
Number of members: 3,800
Staff: full time 5, part time 2,
volunteer 1
Major programs: museum, historic
site(s), tours/pilgrimages, historic
preservation, exhibits
Period of collections: 1739-1920s

Naumkeag
Prospect Hill
Telephone: (413) 298-3239
Mail to: P.O. Box 115, 01262
Private agency, authorized by the
Trustees of Reservations
Founded in: 1891
Delphine Williams, Administrator
Number of members: 3,800
Staff: full time 5, part time 10,
volunteer 3
Major programs: museum,
tours/pilgrimages, historic
preservation, research, exhibits
Period of collections: 1886-1958

Norman Rockwell Museum at the Old Corner House
Main St., 01262
Telephone: (413) 298-3822
Private agency
Founded in: 1969
David H. Wood, Director
Number of members: 1,100
Staff: full time 6, part time 20
Magazine: *Portfolio*
Major programs: archives, museum, book publishing, newsletters/pamphlets, historic preservation, records management, research, exhibits, photographic collections
Period of collections: 20th century

STONEHAM

Stoneham Historical Society, Inc.
36 William St., 02180
Private agency
Founded in: 1922
Lloyd Ekholm, President
Number of members: 70
Major programs: museum, markers, oral history, educational programs
Period of collections: 1725-1975

STOUGHTON

Stoughton Historical Society
6 Park St.
Telephone: (617) 344-5456
Mail to: P.O. Box 542, 02072
Private agency
Founded in: 1895
William McDonald, President
Number of members: 200
Staff: volunteer 10
Magazine: *Old and New*
Major programs: archives, museum, markers, tours/pilgrimages, oral history, book publishing, historic preservation, research, exhibits
Period of collections: 1690s-present

STOW

Stow Historical Commission
Harvard Rd., 01775
Telephone: (617) 897-7417
Town agency, authorized by Massachusetts Historical Commission
Founded in: 1976
C. Schwarzkopf, Chair
Major programs: markers, historic preservation
Period of collections: 1680-1900

Stow Historical Society
Telephone: (617) 897-7908
Mail to: 40 Samuel Prescott Dr., 01775
Private agency
Founded in: 1961
Ralph E. Crowell, Jr., President
Staff: volunteer 6
Major programs: archives, manuscripts, markers, oral history, book publishing, newsletters/pamphlets, historic preservation, research, exhibits, photographic collections
Period of collections: 1669-present

Stow West School Society, Inc.
Harvard Rd., 01775
Telephone: (617) 897-7417

Private agency
Founded in: 1974
C. Schwarzkopf, Executive Secretary
Staff: volunteer 3
Major programs: museum, exhibits, living history
Period of collections: 1825-1900

STURBRIDGE

Old Sturbridge Village
Rt. 20, 01566
Telephone: (617) 347-3362
Private agency
Founded in: 1946
Crawford Lincoln, President
Number of members: 11,000
Staff: full time 360, part time 240, volunteer 100
Magazine: *Old Sturbridge Visitor*
Major programs: library, archives, manuscripts, museum, school programs, book publishing, newsletters/pamphlets, historic preservation, research, exhibits, living history, archaeology programs, photographic collections
Period of collections: late 18th-early 19th centuries

Sturbridge Historical Commission
Town Hall, 01566
Telephone: (617) 347-3000
Questionnaire not received

SUDBURY

Longfellow's Wayside Inn
Wayside Inn Rd., 01776
Telephone: (617) 443-8846
Number of members: 130
Major programs: historic site, historic preservation
Period of collections: 1700-present

Sudbury Historical Society
Loring Parsonage, Old Sudbury Rd.
Mail to: P.O. Box 233, 01776
Founded in: 1956
Questionnaire not received

SUTTON

Sutton Historical Society, Inc.
Mail to: P.O. Box 127 Manchaug 01526
Questionnaire not received

SWAMPSCOTT

Swampscott Historical Society
99 Paradise Rd. 01907
Telephone: (617) 592-6250
Founded in: 1921
Davis W. Callahan, President
Number of members: 210
Period of collections: 1783-1918

SWANSEA

Swansea Historical Society, Inc.
Old Warren Rd.
Mail to: P.O. Box 67, 02777
Private agency
Founded in: 1941
Ruth Doodson, President
Number of members: 150
Staff: volunteer 50
Major programs: library, archives, manuscripts, museum, historic

site(s), markers, tours/pilgrimages, junior history, oral history, book publishing, newsletters/pamphlets, exhibits, audiovisual programs, photographic collections
Period of collections: 18th-19th centuries

TAUNTON

Old Colony Historical Society
66 Church Green, 02780
Telephone: (617) 822-1622
Private agency
Founded in: 1853
Lisa A. Compton, Director
Number of members: 575
Staff: full time 3, part time 5
Major programs: library, archives, manuscripts, museum, school programs, newsletters/pamphlets, research, exhibits, photographic collections, genealogical services, lecture series
Period of collections: 1637-1900

TOPSFIELD

Topsfield Historical Society
1 Howell St.
Telephone: (617) 887-5625
Mail to: 29 Perkins Row, 01983
Founded in: 1894
Gordon Brandes, President
Number of members: 450
Staff: volunteer 25
Major programs: library, museum, educational programs, historic preservation
Period of collections: 1900-1930

TRURO

Truro Historical Society, Inc.
Highland Rd., N. Truro, 02652
Telephone: (617) 487-3397
Mail to: P.O. Box 486, 02666
Private agency
Founded in: 1965
Elizabeth J. Allen, Curator
Number of members: 350
Staff: full time 1, volunteer 25
Major programs: library, archives, museum, historic site(s), exhibits, photographic collections
Period of collections: 1850-present

TYRINGHAM

Tyringham Historical Commission
c/o Chair, Geo Canon Rd., 01264
Telephone: (413) 243-0416
Town agency
Founded in: 1975
C. Elliott, Chair
Number of members: 10
Major programs: library, archives, manuscripts, markers, oral history, book publishing, research, genealogical services
Period of collections: 1739-present

VINEYARD HAVEN

Tisbury Museum
Beach Rd.
Telephone: (617) 693-5353
Mail to: P.O. Box 2153, 02568
Private agency
Founded in: 1980

Anthony K. Van Riper, President
Number of members: 231
Staff: part time 1, volunteer 10
Major programs: museum, exhibits
Period of collections: 19th-20th
centuries

WALTHAM

American Jewish Historical Society
2 Thornton Rd., 02154
Telephone: (617) 891-8110
Private agency
Founded in: 1892
Bernard Wax, Director
Number of members: 3,750
Staff: full time 6, part time 1
Magazine: *American Jewish History*
Major programs: library, archives,
manuscripts, book publishing,
newsletters/pamphlets, records
management, research, exhibits,
audiovisual programs,
photographic collections,
genealogical services
Period of collections: 1592-present

Gore Place Society
52 Gore St., 02154
Telephone: (617) 894-2798
Founded in: 1935
Number of members: 1
Staff: full time 1, part time 5,
volunteer 1
Major programs: museum, historic
site
Period of collections: 1780-1830

National Archives—Boston Branch
380 Trapelo Rd., 02154
Telephone: (617) 647-8100
Founded in: 1969
James K. Owens, Director
Staff: full time 5
Major programs: archives,
educational programs, teachers'
workshops, genealogical
workshops, film series, open
houses and tours
Period of collections: 1789-1981

Waltham Museum Inc.
7 Viles Court
Telephone: (617) 893-8017/894-2609
Mail to: 15 Noonan St., 02154
Private agency
Founded in: 1971
Albert A. Arena, Director
Number of members: 38
Staff: volunteer 7
Major programs: library, museum,
newsletters/pamphlets, historic
preservation, exhibits, audiovisual
programs
Period of collections: 1850-1950

WATERTOWN

Historical Society of Watertown
63 Mt. Auburn St., 02172
Telephone: (617) 924-7229
Founded in: 1900
Number of members: 50
Staff: volunteer 12
Major programs: archives, junior
history, educational programs,
newsletters/pamphlets
Period of collections: 1630-1865

WAYLAND

**Wayland Historic District
Commission**
Wayland Town Bldg., 01778
Telephone: (617) 358-7701
Founded in: 1965
George I. Emery, Chair
Major programs: historic preservation

Wayland Historical Society, Inc.
12 Cochituate Rd.
Telephone: (617) 358-7959
Mail to: P.O. Box 56, 01778
Founded in: 1954
Questionnaire not received

WEBSTER

**Webster Dudley Historical
Society, Inc.**
School St., P.O. Box 64, 01570
Number of members: 100
Questionnaire not received

WELLESLEY

Wellesley Historical Society, Inc.
229 Washington St.
Mail to: P.O. Box 142, 02181
Private agency
Barbara G. Teller, Director/Curator
Number of members: 375
Major programs: library, archives,
museum, tours, oral history,
research, exhibits, audiovisual
programs
Period of collections: 1783-present

WELLFLEET

**Wellfleet Historical Society—Rider
House**
Main St.
Telephone: (617) 349-9215
(president)
Mail to: P.O. Box 58, 02667
Private agency, authorized by
Wellfleet Historical Society, Inc.
Founded in: 1952
Rebecca Eikonberry, President
Number of members: 300
Staff: part time 1
Magazine: *Beacon*
Major programs: museum, historic
site(s), markers, junior history, oral
history, school programs,
newsletters/pamphlets, historic
preservation, research, exhibits,
living history, audiovisual
programs, photographic
collections, genealogical services
Period of collections: late
1600s-present

WENHAM

**Wenham Historical Association
and Museum, Inc.**
132 Main St., 01984
Telephone: (617) 468-2377
Private agency
Founded in: 1921
Eleanor E. Thompson, Director
Number of members: 700
Staff: full time 1, part time 3,
volunteer 70
Major programs: library, archives,
museum, historic site(s), school
programs, newsletters/pamphlets,

historic preservation, research,
exhibits, photographic collections
Period of collections: 1650-1930

**Wenham Historic District
Commission**
Wenham Town Hall, 01984
Telephone: (617) 468-4468
Town agency
Founded in: 1972
H.W. Boothroyd, Chair
Staff: volunteer 7
Major programs: library, historic site,
markers, tours, pamphlets, historic
preservation, photographic
collections, dwelling and site
survey
Period of collections: 1970-1972

WESTBOROUGH

**Westborough Historical
Commission**
Public Library, 55 W. Main St., 01581
Telephone: (617) 366-0725
Town agency, authorized by board of
selectmen
Founded in: 1977
Jackqueline C. Tidman, Chair
Staff: volunteer 6
Major programs: archives, museum,
historic site(s), markers, oral
history, historic preservation,
research, audiovisual programs,
archaeology programs,
photographic collections,
genealogical services, historic
mapping
Period of collections: 2600 B.C.-1930

Westborough Historical Society
7 Parkman St.
Mail to: P.O. Box 149, 01581
Number of members: 100
Major programs: museum,
tours/pilgrimages, educational
programs
Period of collections: late
Colonial-Victorian eras

WEST BOYLSTON

**West Boylston Historical
Society, Inc.**
P.O. Box 201, 01583
Telephone: (617) 853-1947
Founded in: 1971
Questionnaire not received

WEST BRIDGEWATER

Old Bridgewater Historical Society
162 Howard St.
Mail to: P.O. Box 17, 02379
Founded in: 1895
Francis J. Beary, President
Number of members: 649
Staff: volunteer 9
Major programs: manuscripts,
museum, newsletters/pamphlets,
historic preservation, research,
genealogical services
Period of collections: 1642-present

WEST FALMOUTH

**Saconesset Homestead
Museum—Ship's Bottom Roof
House**
Rt. 28-A
Telephone: (617) 548-5850

Mail to: P.O. Box 366, 02574
Founded in: 1678
Questionnaire not received

WESTFIELD

**Edwin Smith Historical Museum,
Westfield Athenaeum**
6 Elm St., 01085
Telephone: (413) 568-7833
Private agency
Founded in: 1928
Harold F. Maschin, Curator
Staff: full time 28, part time 2
Major programs: archives,
manuscripts, museum
Period of collections: Colonial period

**Western Hampden Historical
Society—Dewey House**
P.O. Box 256, 01086
Telephone: (413) 562-3657
Private agency
Founded in: 1901
Barbara Bush, Board Chair
Number of members: 326
Major programs: museum, school
programs, historic preservation,
public and adult educational
programs

WESTFORD

Westford Historical Society, Inc.
2 Boston Rd.
Mail to: P.O. Box 411, 01886
Town agency
Founded in: 1963
Alexander Belida, President
Number of members: 39
Staff: volunteer 4
Major programs: archives,
manuscripts, museum, historic
site(s), markers, historic
preservation, records
management, research, exhibits,
living history, photographic
collections, genealogical services
Period of collections: 1850-1945

WESTMINSTER

Westminster Historical Society
P.O. Box 177, 10473
Private agency
Founded in: 1921
Claudia Ballard, Presient
Number of members: 74
Major programs: museum, junior
history, oral history, school
programs, book publishing,
newsletters/pamphlets, historic
preservation, research, exhibits,
living history, audiovisual
programs, photographic
collections
Period of collections: Colonial
period-19th century

WESTON

**Cardinal Spellman Philatelic
Museum**
235 Wellesley St., 02193
Telephone: (617) 894-6735
Private agency
Founded in: 1960
Russell Dillaway, Director
Number of members: 550
Staff: full time 6, part time 3

Magazine: *Museum Post Rider*
Major programs: library, museum,
school programs, book publishing,
research, exhibits, stamps and
postal history
Period of collections: 1840-present

Golden Ball Tavern Trust
662 Boston Post Rd.
Telephone: (617) 894-1751
Mail to: P.O. Box 223, 02193
Private agency
Founded in: 1964
William A. Whittemore, Acting Chair
Number of members: 425
Staff: volunteer 92
Magazine: *Golden Ball Tavern
Grapevine*
Major programs: library, archives,
museum, school programs, historic
preservation, research, exhibits,
audiovisual programs, archaeology
programs, photographic
collections
Period of collections: 1768-1864

WESTPORT

Westport Historical Society, Inc.
25 Drift Rd.
Telephone: (617) 636-6011
Mail to: P.O. Box C-31, 02790
Private agency
Founded in: 1965
Lincoln S. Tripp, President
Number of members: 300
Staff: volunteer 10
Major programs: museum, historic
site(s), newsletters/pamphlets
Period of collections: 1800-present

WEST ROXBURY

West Roxbury Historical Society
West Roxbury Library
Telephone: (617) 325-2615
Mail to: 63 Vermont St., 02132
Questionnaire not received

WEST SPRINGFIELD

**Pioneer Valley Planning
Commission**
26 Central St., 01089
Telephone: (413) 781-6045
Regional agency
Founded in: 1962
Timothy W. Brennan, Executive
Director
Staff: full time 18
Major programs: historic site(s),
historic preservation, public
education

**Ramapogue Historical
Society—The Day House**
70 Park St., 01089
Telephone: (413) 734-8322
Private agency
Founded in: 1903
William C. Girotti, President
Number of members: 300
Staff: volunteer 15
Major programs: museum
Period of collections: 1754-1904

Storrowton Village Museum
1305 Memorial Ave., 01089
Founded in: (413) 787-0137
Private agency, authorized by
Eastern States Exposition

Founded in: 1931
June H. Cook, Director
Number of members: 186
Staff: full time 3, part time 2,
volunteer 59
Major programs: tours, school
programs, historic preservation
Period of collections: 1760-1860

**West Springfield Historical
Commission**
203 Cayenne St., 01089
Telephone: (413) 732-8197
Town agency
Founded in: 1973
Collette L. Wright, Chair
Staff: volunteer 7
Major programs: archives, historic
site(s), oral history, historic
preservation, research, exhibits,
photographic collections,
genealogical services, inventory of
local dwellings
Period of collections: 1740s-20th
century

WEYMOUTH

Weymouth Historical Society
158 Pleasant St.
Telephone: (617) 335-4310
Mail to: P.O. Box 56, South
Weymouth, 02190
Founded in: 1879
Questionnaire not received

WILBRAHAM

Atheneum Society of Wilbraham
450 Main St.
Telephone: (413) 596-4097
Mail to: P.O. Box 294, 01095
Founded in: 1963
James B. McGuire, Co-president
Number of members: 135
Staff: volunteer 16
Major programs: archives, museum,
historic preservation, public
meetings, lectures
Period of collections: 1790-1850

WILLIAMSTOWN

**Center for Environmental Study,
Williams College**
271 N.W. Hill Rd., 01267
Telephone: (413) 597-2346
Private agency, authorized by the
college
Founded in: 1970
Henry Art, Director
Staff: full time 2, part time 4
Major programs: library, museum,
oral history, historic preservation,
research, exhibits

Hopkins Forest Farm Museum
271 N.W. Hill Rd.
Telephone: (413) 597-2346
Mail to: Center for Environmental
Study, Williams College, 01267
Private agency, authorized by the
college
Founded in: 1976
Nan Jenks-Jay, Assistant Director,
CES
Staff: full time 2, part time 2
Major programs: museum
Period of collections: late 1700s-early
1900s

House of Local History
762 Main St. 01267
Founded in: 1941
Murray D. Smith, President
Number of members: 100
Staff: volunteer 12
Major programs: library, archives, museum
Period of collections: late 18th-20th century

WILMINGTON

Wilmington Historical Commission
Town Hall, 01887
Questionnaire not received

WINCHENDON

Winchendon Historical Society
50 Pleasant St., 01475
Telephone: (617) 297-0300
Founded in: 1930
Lois S. Greenwood, Curator
Number of members: 150
Staff: volunteer 12
Major programs: museum
Period of collections: 1800-1920

WINCHESTER

Henry E. Simonds Memorial Archival Center
15 High St., 01890
Telephone: (617) 721-7146
Town agency
Founded in: 1975
Evelyn Marie Hinde, Historical Services Coordinator
Staff: part time 2, volunteer 10
Major programs: library, archives, manuscripts, oral history, school programs, exhibits, photographic collections, genealogical services
Period of collections: 1700-present

Winchester Historical Commission
15 High St., 01890
Telephone: (617) 721-7146
Town agency
Founded in: 1967
Michael Lovine, Chair
Staff: volunteer 7
Major programs: archives, markers, historic preservation

Winchester Historical Society
15 High St., 01890
Telephone: (617) 729-3063
Founded in: 1884
Marcia B. Wood, President
Number of members: 200
Staff: volunteer 25
Magazine: *Black Horse Bulletin*
Major programs: tours/pilgrimages, educational programs, newsletters/pamphlets

WINTHROP

Winthrop Improvement and Historical Association
40 Shirley St., 02152
Telephone: (617) 846-7341
Founded in: 1903
Questionnaire not received

WOODS HOLE

Woods Hole Library's Historical Collection—Bradley House Museum
Telephone: (617) 548-7270
Mail to: P.O. Box 185, 02543
Founded in: 1976
Questionnaire not received

WORCESTER

American Antiquarian Society
185 Salisbury St., 01609
Telephone: (617) 755-5221
Founded in: 1812
Marcus A. McCorison, Diretor/Librarian
Number of members: 375
Staff: full time 40, part time 11 volunteer 2
Magazine: *Proceedings of the American Antiquarian Society*
Major programs: library, publications, educational programs, fellowships
Period of collections: 1600-1876

Higgins Armory Museum
100 Barber Ave., 01606-2434
Telephone: (617) 853-6015
Founded in: 1928
Warren M. Little, Director
Number of members: 475
Staff: full time 9, part time 11, volunteer 6
Magazine: *The Ventail Voice*
Major programs: library, museum, school programs, newsletters/pamphlets, research, exhibits, audiovisual programs, outreach programs
Period of collections: Medieval-Renaissance periods

Worcester Art Museum
55 Salisbury St., 01608
Telephone: (617) 799-4406
Private agency
Founded in: 1896
Tom L. Freudenheim, Director
Major programs: museum
Period of collections: prehistoric-present

Worcester Historical Museum
39 Salisbury St., 01608
Telephone: (617) 753-8278
Private agency
Founded in: 1875
William D. Wallace, Executive Director
Number of members: 800
Staff: full time 8, part time 2, volunteer 30
Major programs: library, archives, manuscripts, museum, tours/pilgrimages, newsletters/pamphlets, educational programs
Period of collections: 1680-present

Worcester Heritage Society, Inc.
71 Pleasant St., 01609
Telephone: (617) 754-8760
Founded in: 1969
Questionnaire not received

WRENTHAM

Wrentham Historical Commission
677 South St.

Mail to: P.O. Box 841, 02093
Town agency
Founded in: 1967
Earle T. Stewart, Chair
Staff: volunteer 7
Major programs: archives, markers, photographic collections
Period of collections: 19th-early 20th centuries

YARMOUTH PORT

Historical Society of Old Yarmouth
2 Strawberry Lane
Telephone: (617) 362-3021
Mail to: P.O. Box 11, 02675
Founded in: 1953
Questionnaire not received

MICHIGAN

ADRIAN

Lenawee County Historical Society, Inc.
110 E. Church
Telephone: (517) 265-6071
Mail to: P.O. Box 511, 49221
Founded in: 1928
Charles Lindquist, Curator
Number of members: 700
Staff: full time 1, part time 3, volunteer 24
Major programs: archives, museum, educational programs, newsletters/phamphlets, books, tours
Period of collections: 1825-1970

ALBION

Albion Historical Society
509 S. Superior St.
Mail to: 606 Linden Lane, 49224
Private agency
Founded in: 1955
John Hart, President
Number of members: 750
Major programs: archives, museum, historic sites preservation, newsletters/pamphlets, historic preservation
Period of collections: Victorian era

ALLEGAN

Allegan County Historical Society
13 Walnut St.
Mail to: 2142 30th St., 49010
County agency
Founded in: 1952
Marguerite Miller, Museum Director
Number of members: 130
Staff: volunteer 4
Major programs: museum, tours/pilgrimages, book publishing, exhibits, photographic collections
Period of collections: 1800s

ALPENA

Jesse Besser Museum
491 Johnson St., 49707
Telephone: (517) 356-2202
Private agency

Founded in: 1966
Dennis R. Bodem, Director
Number of members: 400
Staff: full time 3, part time 4,
  volunteer 300
Major programs: library, archives,
  museum, historic site(s),
  tours/pilgrimages, junior history,
  school programs,
  newsletters/pamphlets, historic
  preservation, research, living
  history, audiovisual programs,
  audiovisual programs, archaeology
  programs, photographic
  collections, genealogical services
Period of collections:
  prehistoric-present

**Northeastern Michigan
Genealogical Society**
c/o Jesse Besser Museum, 491
  Johnson St., 49707
Telephone: (517) 354-8728
Founded in: 1976
Questionnaire not received

ANN ARBOR

**Ann Arbor Historic District
Commission**
312 S. Division, 48104
Telephone: (313) 996-3008
City agency
Founded in: 1963
Louisa Pieper, Staff Director
Staff: full time 1, part time 6,
  volunteer 50
Major programs: library, historic
  site(s), markers, historic
  preservation, research
Period of collections: 1850-1940

Ann Arbor Hands-On Museum
219 E. Huron St.
Telephone: (313) 995-5439
Private agency
Founded in: 1979
Cynthia C. Yao, Director
Number of members: 400
Staff: full time 1, part time 5
  volunteer 50
Major programs: museum,
  tours/pilgrimages, school
  programs, newsletters/pamphlets,
  historic preservation, records
  management, exhibits, audiovisual
  programs, science and art
  programs

**Bentley Historical Library,
University of Michigan**
1150 Beal Ave., 48109
Telephone: (313) 764-3482
State agency
Authorized by the university
Founded in: 1935
Francis X. Blouin, Jr. Director
Staff: full time 12, part time 5,
  volunteer 5
Major programs: library, archives,
  manuscripts, records
  management, research
Period of collections: 1880-1970

Cobblestone Farm Association
2781 Packard Rd.

Telephone: (313) 994-2928
Mail to: P.O. Box 7362, 48107
Private agency
Founded in: 1974
Emilie Polens, Supervisor
Number of members: 300
Staff: part time 1, volunteer 20
Magazine: Cobblestone Farm News
Major programs: historic site(s),
  tours/pilgrimages, school
  programs, newsletters/pamphlets,
  historic preservation, living history
Period of collections: 1850s-1900

Gerald R. Ford Library
1000 Beal Ave., 48109
Telephone: (313) 668-2218
Federal agency, authorized by
  National Archives and Records
  Service
Founded in: 1977
Don W. Wilson, Director
Staff: full time 11, part time 3
Major programs: library, archives,
  manuscripts,
  newsletters/pamphlets, exhibits,
  photographic collections
Period of collections: 1948-present

Historical Society of Michigan
2117 Washtenaw Ave., 48104
Telephone: (313) 769-1828
Founded in: 1828
Thomas L. Jones, Director

Number of members: 5,000
Staff: full time 1, part time 3
Magazine: Chronicle
Major programs: markers,
  tours/pilgrimages, school
  programs, book publishing,
  newsletters/pamphlets, historic
  preservation, annual meeting,
  conferences, program for teachers
  of state history

**Kempf House Center for Local
History**
312 S. Division, 48104
Telephone: (313) 996-3008
City agency, authorized by Ann Arbor
  Historic District Commission
Founded in: 1970
Louisa Pieper, Staff Director
Staff: full time 1, part time 7,
  volunteer 30
Major programs: library, museum,
  markers, historic preservation,
  research
Period of collections: 1824-1940

**Michigan Historical Collections,
Bentley Historical Library**
1150 Beal Ave., 48109
Telephone: (313) 764-3482
Founded in: 1935
Staff: full time 10, part time 11,
  volunteer 4
Magazine: Michigan Gazette

Drawing of historic Tuomy House, headquarters of the Historical Society of Michigan in Ann Arbor.—Historical Society of Michigan

Major programs: library, archives, manuscripts, educational programs, newsletters/pamphlets
Period of collections: 1783-present

Washtenaw County History District Commission
Main and Huron Sts.
Telephone: (313)
Mail to: P.O. Box 8645, 48107
County agency
Founded in: 1975
Jay Snyder, Staff Person
Staff: part time 1
Major programs: historic site(s), markers, oral history, historic preservation

Washtenaw County Historical Society
312 S. Division, 48104
Telephone: (313) 996-3008
County agency
Founded in: 1857
Number of members: 500
Magazine: *Washtenaw Impressions*
Major programs: tours, educational programs, newsletters, markers
Period of collections: 1823-present

AU GRES

Arenac County Historical Society
Michigan Ave.
Telephone: (517) 846-9967
Mail to: P.O. Box 272, 48703
County agency
Founded in: 1970
Mrs. Jeannette Wubbena, President
Number of members: 132
Staff: volunteer 15
Major programs: archives, museum, historic preservation, exhibits, educational programs
Period of collections: 1865-1940

BAD AXE

Bad Axe Historical Society (Chapter of Huron County Historical Society)
223 Willis St., 48413
Telephone: (517) 269-8165
Founded in: 1968
Thomas Lenehan, President
Number of members: 108
Major programs: museum, historic preservation, exhibits, pioneer log village home, chapel, blacksmith shop, general store
Period of collections: 1875-1930

BATTLE CREEK

Historical Society of Battle Creek/Kimball House Museum
196 Capital Ave., NE, 49017
Private agency
Telephone: (616) 965-2613
Founded in: 1967
Carol M. Kime, Secretary
Number of members: 475
Staff: part time 1
Magazine: *Up-to-Date*
Major programs: archives, museum, school programs, historic preservation, living history
Period of collections: 1886-1910

Kingman Museum of Natural History--Leila Arboretum
W. Michigan Ave. at 20th St., 49017
elephone: (616) 965-5117
Founded in: 1869
Robert Learner, Director
Number of members: 1,700
Staff: full time 8, part time 2, volunteer 20
Magazine: *Explorer*
Major programs: library, museum, educational programs, newsletters/pamphlets
Period of collections: 1865-1918

BAY CITY

Bay County Historical Society/Historical Museum of Bay County
1700 Center Ave. 48706
Telephone: (517) 893-5733
Private agency
Founded in: 1919
Gay McIrney, Executive Director
Number of members: 300
Staff: full time 2
Major programs: library, archives, manuscripts, museum, tours/pilgrimages, school programs, bookpublishing, newsletters/pamphlets, historic preservation, exhibits, photographic collections
Period of collections: 1850-present

BELLAIRE

Bellaire Area Historical Society
S. Bridge
Mail to: P.O. Box 1016, 49615
Founded in: 1976
Questionnaire not received

BELLEVUE

Bellevue Area Historical Society
212 N. Main St., 49021
Telephone: (616) 763-3369
Founded in: 1975
Number of members: 250
Major programs: museum, historic preservation, genealogy
Period of collections: late 1800s-present

BELLE ISLE

Dossin Great Lakes Museum
Strand Dr., 48207
Telephone: (313) 267-6440
Founded in: 1949
John Polacsek, Curator
Staff: full time 6, part time 1, volunteer 5
Major programs: library, archives, museum, education programs
Period of collections: 1701-present

Great Lakes Maritime Institute
c/o Dossin Museum, 48207
Telephone: (313) 267-6440
Founded in: 1950
Kathleen McGraw, Coordinating Director
Number of members: 1,600
Staff: volunteer 25
Magazine: *Telescope*

Major programs: educational programs, books, newsletters/pamphlets
Period of collections: 1865-present

BERRIEN SPRINGS

Berrien County Historical Association, Inc./1839 Courthouse Museum
313 N. Case St.
Telephone: (616) 471-1202
Mail to: P.O. Box 261, 49103
Private agency
Founded in: 1967
Jan House, Director
Number of members: 250
Staff: full time 2
Magazine: *The Docket*
Major programs: museum, historic sites preservation, newsletters/pamphlets
Period of collections: 1775-1950

BEULAH

Benzie Area Historical Society
Telephone: (616) 780-3860
Mail to: 1396 Norton Ave., Apt. Q-4 , Muskegon, 49441
Questionnaire not received

BIG RAPIDS

Mecosta County Historical Society
401 Elm St.
Telephone: (616) 796-5238
Mail to: 129 Ives Ave., 49307
Questionnaire not received

BLISSFIELD

Blissfield Historical Society/Victorsville School House
424 Adrian St., 49228
Telephone: (517) 456-2141
Private agency
Founded in: 1978
Michael Weeber, President
Number of members: 30
Staff: volunteer 12
Major programs: historic preservation
Period of collections: 1830s-1900s

BRIDGEPORT

Historical Society of Bridgeport
3804 State St.
Telephone: (517) 777-3328
Mail to: P.O. Box 117, 48722
Town agency
Founded in: 1969
W. W. Schomaker, Curator
Number of members: 60
Staff: volunteer 9
Major programs: museum, historic site(s), markers, oral history, book publishing, historic preservation
Period of collections: 1840-present

BRIGHTON

Green Oak Township Historical Society—Gage Museum
6440 Kensington Rd.
Mail to: P.O. Box 84, 48116
Private agency
Founded in: 1975
Mona Wenzel, President

Number of members: 150
Staff: volunteer 30
Major programs: manuscripts,
museum, tours/pilgrimages, oral
history, book publishing,
newsletters/pamphlets, historic
preservation, research,
exhibits,photographic collections,
genealogical services
Period of collections: 1550-1950

CADILLAC

Wexford County Historical Society
127 Beech St.
Telephone: (616) 775-1717
Mail to: P.O. Box 124, 49601
Private agency
Founded in: 1956
Joseph B. Lockwood, Board
President
Number of members: 100
Staff: volunteer 10
Major programs: museum, markers,
markers, tours/pilgrimages, school
programs, book publishing,
newsletters/pamphlets, historic
preservation, exhibits,
photographic collections
Period of collections: 1870-1930

CALUMET

Coppertown USA
Red Jacket Rd.
Telephone: (906) 337-4579
Mail to: 1197 Calumet Ave., 49913
Private agency
Founded in: 1973
John Vertin, President
Number of members: 67
Staff: part time 2, volunteer 20
Major programs: museum, exhibits,
mining history
Period of collections: 1585-1915

CANTON

Canton Historical Commission
c/o 46870 Cherry Hill, 48187
Telephone: (313) 981-0087
Town agency
Founded in: 1979
Staff: voluneer 7
Major programs: historic site(s),
historic preservation

Canton Historical Society Museum
Canton Center and Proctor Rd.
Telephone: (313) 495-0811/397-1000
Mail to: 48630 Michigan Ave., 48188
Town and private agency
Founded in: 1975
Bart Berg, President
Number of members: 115
Staff: volunteer 6
Major programs: museum, historic
preservation, exhibits
Period of collections: 1825-1950

CARO

**Watrousville-Caro Area Historical
Society**
102 Joy St., 48723
Telephone: (517) 673-6073
Founded in: 1972
Marie G. Cole, President
Number of members: 100
Staff: volunteer 20

Major programs: library, museum,
markers, historic preservation
Period of collections: 1880-present

CASPIAN

**Iron County Historical and Museum
Society**
Rt. 424, Museum St., 49915
Telephone: (906) 265-3942/265-2617
Mail to: 233 Bernhardt Rd., Iron River,
49935
Founded in: 1962
Harold O. Berhnardt, President
Number of members: 195
Staff: part time 6, volunteer 18
Magazine: *Past-Present Prints*
Major programs: archives, museum,
historic sites preservation, markers,
junior history, oral history,
educational programs, books,
newsletters/pamphlets
Period of collections: 1878-present

CEDARVILLE

**Les Cheneaux Historical
Association**
Meridian Rd.
Telephone: (906) 484-2521
Mail to: P.O. Box 301, 49719
Private agency
Founded in: 1967
Howard R. Williams, President
Number of members: 175
Major programs: archives,
manuscripts, museum, markers,
photographic collections,
genealogical services
Period of collections: 1880-1950

CHEBOYGAN

**Cheboygan County Genealogical
Society**
P.O. Box 51, 49721
County agency
Founded in: 1979
Number of members: 42
Major programs: library, newsletters,
research, genealogical services
Period of collections: 1850-present

**Historical Society of Cheboygan
County, Inc.**
Huron and Court Sts.
Mail to: P.O. Box 500, 49721
Private agency
Founded in: 1969
Quincy Leslie, President
Number of members: 150
Staff: part time 1, volunteer 10
Major programs: museum, historic
preservation

CLAWSON

Clawson Historical Museum
41 Fisher Ct.
Telephone: (313) 588-9169
Mail to: 425 N. Main, 48017
City agency
Founded in: 1973
Delorise Kumler, Curator
Staff: part time 1, volunteer 12
Major programs: museum,
photographic collections
Period of collections: 1920s

COLDWATER

**Branch County Genealogical
Society**
P.O. Box 443, 49036
Private agency
Founded in: 1978
Number of members: 20
Major programs: publication of
cemetery records
Period of collections: 1830-1980

COLOMA

North Berrien Historical Society
Telephone: (616) 468-4228
Mail to: P.O Box 417, 49038
Questionnaire not received

COLON

Community Historical Society
217 N. Blackstone Ave.
Telephone: (616) 432-2462
(treasurer)
Mail to: P.O. Box 130, 49040
Private agency
Founded in: 1974
David Tomlinson, President
Number of members: 50
Staff: volunteer 15
Major programs: library, archives,
museum, exhibits, genealogical
services
Period of collections: 1832-1920

DEARBORN

Dearborn Historical Museum
Commandant's Quarters, 21950
Michigan Ave.
Telephone: (313) 565-3000
Mail to: 915 Brady St., 48124
Founded in: 1950
Winfield H. Arneson, Chief Curator
Staff: full time 7, part time 8,
volunteer 40
Magazine: *The Dearborn Historian*
Major programs: library, archives,
manuscripts, museum, historic
sites preservation, markers,
tours/pilgrimages, junior history,
oral history, educational
programs, books,
newsletters/pamphlets
Period of collections: 1780-present

**Dearborn Historical
Society/McFadden-Ross House**
915 Brady, 48124
Telephone: (313) 565-3000
Mail to: 234 Highview St., 48128
City agency
Founded in: 1940
Winfield H. Arneson, Chief Curator
Staff: full time 6, part time 7,
volunteer 125
Major programs: library, archives,
manuscripts, museum, historic
site(s), markers, tours/pilgrimages,
junior history, oral history, school
programs, book publishing,
newsletters/pamphlets, historic
preservation, records
management, research, exhibits,
living history, audiovisual
programs, photographic
collections, genealogical services
Period of collections: 1830s-present

The Edison Institute—Henry Ford Museum, Greenfield Village
Oakwood Blvd., 48121
Telephone: (313) 271-1620
Private agency
Founded in: 1929
Harold K. Skramstad, Jr., President
Staff: full time 275, part time 600
Magazine: *The Herald*
Major programs: library, archives, manuscripts, museum, historic sites preservation, tours/pilgrimages, junior history, oral history, educational programs, books, newsletters/pamphlets
Period of collections: 1600-present

Henry Ford Estate/Fair Lane
4901 Evergreen Rd., 48128
Telephone: (313) 593-5590
State agency, authorized by Board of Regents, University of Michigan
Founded in: 1915
Donn Weeling, Director
Staff: full time 5, part time 1, volunteer 50
Major programs: museum, historic site(s), tours/pilgrimages, historic preservation
Period of collections: 1914-1950

DECATUR

Historic Newton Home
Marcellus Hwy., 49054
County agency
Founded in: 1974
M. S. Federowski, Secretary
Major programs: historic site(s)

DELTON

Bernard Historical Society and Museum
7135 W. Delton Rd. 49046
Telephone: (616) 623-5451
Founded in: 1962
E. Bernard, Agent
Number of members: 75
Staff: part time 2, volunteer 10
Major programs: museum, historic sites preservation, markers, books
Period of collections: 1812-present

DETROIT

Archives of the Archdiocese of Detroit
1234 Washington Blvd., 48226
Telephone: (313) 237-5846
Elizabeth Yakel, Archivist
Staff: full time 2
Major programs: library, archives, genealogical services, school programs
Period of collections: 1704-present

Archives of Labor and Urban Affairs
Walter P. Reuther Library, Wayne State University, 48202
Telephone: (313) 577-4024
Founded in: 1960
Philip P. Mason, Director
Staff: full time 14, part time 15
Major programs: library, archives, manuscripts, oral history, newsletters/pamphlets, records management, exhibits, audiovisual

programs, photographic collections
Period of collections: 1930s-present

Burton Historical Collection, Detroit Public Library
5201 Woodward, 48202
Telephone: (313) 833-1480
City agency, authorized by Detroit Library Commission
Founded in: 1914
Alice C. Dalligan, Chief
Staff: full time 11, part time 4, volunteer 8
Major programs: library, archives, manuscripts, genealogical services

Detroit Chapter, FCHSM (French-Canadian Heritage Society of Michigan)
c/o President, 1056 Balfour Rd., Grosse Point, 48230
Private agency
Founded on: 1982
Jerry Ricard, President
Number of members: 100
Staff: volunteer 5
Major programs: library, archives, manuscripts, oral history, school programs, historic preservation, research, living history, audiovisual programs, genealogical services
Period of collections: 1600-present

Detroit Historical Museum
5401 Woodward, 48202
Telephone: (313) 833-1805
Founded in: 1928
Betty J. Allen , Deputy Director
Staff: full time 61, part time 8, volunteer 50
Major programs: museum, markers, tours, educational programs, historic preservation, exhibits
Period of collections: 1701-present

Detroit Historical Society
5401 Woodward, 48202
Telephone: (313) 833-7934
Private agency
Founded in: 1921
John W. Buckbee, Executive Director
Number of 2,300
Staff: full time 5, volunteer 4
Magzine: Detroit in Perspective: A Journal of Regional History
Major programs: tours/pilgrimages, educational programs, newsletters/pamphlets, exhibits

Fred Hart Williams Genealogical Society
Detroit Public Library, 5201 Woodward Ave., 48202
Telephone: (313) 833-1480
Private agency, authorized by Independent agency in cooperation with public library
Founded in: 1979
De Witt G. Dykes, Jr., President
Number of members: 110
Staff: volunteer 50
Major programs: speakers and programs on black family history
Period of collections: 19th-20th centuries

Historic Ft. Wayne
6325 W. Jefferson, 48209
Telephone: (313) 297-9360

Founded in: 1949
William P. Phenix, Curator
Number of members: 10
Staff: full time 21, part time 13, volunteer 150
Major programs: library, museum, historic sites preservation, educational programs, living history
Period of collections: 1701-present

Indian Village Association
2177 Burns, 48214
Telephone: (313) 821-9165
Founded in: 1937
Number of members: 290
Staff: part time 1, volunteer 25
Magazine: *Smoke Signals*
Major programs: archives, historic sites preservation, tours, newsletters/pamphlets, historic preservation
Period of collections: 1895-present

Jewish Historical Society of Michigan
163 Madison Ave., 48226
Telephone: (313) 548-9176
Mail to: 24680 Rensselaer, Oak Park 48237
Founded in: 1959
Phillip Applebaum, President
Number of members: 325
Magazine: *Michigan Jewish History*
Major programs: archives, manuscripts, historic sites preservation, markers, oral history, newsletters/pamphlets
Period of collections: 1840-present

Moross House, Home of the Detroit Garden Center
1460 E. Jefferson, 48208
Telephone: (313) 259-6363
Private agency
Founded in: 1939 center; 1845 house
Barbara Hayes, Secretary
Number of members: 500
Staff: full time 1, part time 1, volunteer 50
Magazine: *Detroit Garden Center Bulletin*
Major programs: library, historic site(s), markers, tours/pilgrimages, school programs, newsletters/pamphlets, audiovisual programs, mental health and craft workshops, horticulture
Period of collections: 1850s-Federal period

Museum of African American History
1553 W. Grand Blvd., 48208
Telephone: (313) 899-2500
Private agency
Founded in: 1965
K. Audley Smith, Executive Director
Number of members: 5,000
Staff: full time 3, part time 2, volunteer 5
Magazine: *The Gallery*
Major programs: museum, tours/pilgrimages, oral history, book publishing, historic preservation, research, exhibits, living history, audiovisual programs, genealogical services
Period of collections: 1900-1980

Polish Genealogical Society of Michigan
Detroit Public Library, 5201
 Woodward Ave., 48202
Telephone: (313) 533-1450
Private agency
Founded in: 1979
Pamela Lazar, President
Number of members: 225
Staff: volunteer 12
Magazine: *The Eaglet*
Major programs:
 newsletters/pamphlets,
 genealogical services

Preservation Wayne—David Mckenzie House
4735 Call Ave.,48202
Telephone: (131) 577-3559
Mail to: P.O. Box 100, S.C.B. Wayne
 State University
Founded in: 1975
Questionnaire not received

DEXTER

Dexter Area Historical Society
3443 Inverness St., 48130
Private agency
Founded in: 1971
Number of members: 140
Major programs: archives,
 manuscripts, museum, school
 programs, newsletters/pamphlets,
 historic preservation, research,
 exhibits, photographic collections,
 genealogical services
Period of collections: 19th-20th
 centuries

DOUGLAS

Peterson Steamship Company—SS Keewatin
Union St. at Red Dock
Telephone: (616) 857-2151, ext. 26 or
 28/857-2107
Mail to: P.O. Box 511, 49406
Private agency
Founded in: 1967
Diane Peterson, Manager/Owner
Staff: full time 1, part time 6,
 volunteer 1
Major programs: library, museum,
 historic site(s), tours, historic
 preservation, exhibits, living
 history, photographic collections
Period of collections: early 1900s

DRUMMOND ISLAND

Drummond Island Historical Society
49726
Telephone: (906) 493-5245
Founded in: 1938
Kathryne B. Lowe, President
Number of members: 154
Staff: part time 1
Major programs: archives,
 manuscripts, museum, markers,
 historic preservation
Period of collections: 1865-present

DURAND

Shiawassee County Historical Society
Telephone: (517) 288-3058
Mail to: P.O. Box 2, 48429
Questionnaire not received

EAGLE HARBOR

Keweenaw County Historical Society
Star Rt. 1, 49951
Telephone: (313) 289-4440
Private agency
Founded in: 1981
E. C. "Ned" Humphreys, Jr.,
 President
Number of members: 250
Staff: volunteer 10
Magazine: *The Superior Signal*
Major programs: library. archives,
 manuscripts, museum, historic
 site(s), historic preservation,
 photographic collections,
 schoolhous restoration
Period of collections: mid-late 1800s

EAST JORDAN

East Jordan Portside Art and Historical Museum Society
Rt. 2, Box 569, N, M-66 Hwy., 49727
Telephone: (616) 536-2393
Town agency
Founded in: 1976
Cygred Riley, Trustee
Number of members: 100
Staff: volunteer 12
Major programs: archives
Period of collections: 1890-1900s

EAST LANSING

Michigan Council for the Humanities
1407 S. Harrison Rd., Suite 30 48824
Telephone: (517) 355-0160
Private agency, authorized by
 National Endowment for the
 Humanities
Founded in: 1974
Ronald D. Means, Executive Director
Staff: full time 4, part time 2,
 volunteer 25
Magazine: *Michigan
 Connection/Michigan Humanities
 Update*
Major programs: grant funds for
 public humanities programs

Michigan State University Museum
W. Circle Dr., 48824
Telephone: (517) 355-2370
State agency
Founded in: 1860
C. Kurt Dewhurst, Director
Staff: full time 13, part time 4
Major programs: archives, museum,
 junior history, oral history, school
 programs, newsletters/pamphlets,
 research, exhibits, archaeology
 programs, photographic
 collections
Period of collections:
 prehistoric-present

University Archives and Historical Collections
Michigan State University, Main
 Library Building
Telephone: (517) 355-2330
Authorized by the university
Founded in: 1969
Frederick L. Honhart, Director
Staff: full time 3, part time 2.5
Major programs: archives,
 manuscripts, oral history, records

management, research,
 photographic collections,
 university records
Period of collections: 19th
 century-present

EAST TAWAS

Iosco County Historical Museum
405 W. Bay, P.O. Box 135, 48730
Telephone: (517) 362-8911
County agency, authorized by Iosco
 County Historical Society
Founded in: 1976
Harris Barkman, President
Number of members: 45
Staff: volunteer 7
Major programs: library, manuscripts,
 museum, markers, book
 publishing, historic preservation,
 exhibits, photographic collections
Period of collections: 1860-present

ELK RAPIDS

Elk Rapids Area Historical Society
509 River St., 49629
Telephone: (616) 264-8886
Founded in: 1972
Questionnaire not received

ELSIE

Elsie Historical Society
15l W. Main St.
C/o President, 9540 Meade Rd.,
 48831
Town agency, authorized by Elsie
 Public Library
Founded in: 1974
Betty J. Lewis, President
Number of members: 20
Staff: volunteer 5
manuscripts, historic site(s), oral
 history, schcol programs, records
 management, photographic
 collections, genealogical services
Period of collections: 1880-1980

FARMINGTON

Farmington Historical Commission
23600 Liberty St., 48024
Telephone: (313) 474-4608
Private agency
Founded in: 1973
Margaret Walker, Chair
Major programs: archives,
 manuscripts, museum, markers,
 historic preservation
Period of collections: 1824-present

Farmington Historical Society
22998 Warner, 48024
Telephone: (313) 474-5460.
Founded in: 1959
Number of members: 90
Magazine: *Farmington Heritage*
Major programs: archives,
 manuscripts, markers, oral history,
 newsletters/
pamphlets
Period of collections: 1825-present
Questionnaire not received

Farmington Genealogical Society
21615 Liberty St 48024
Telephone: (313) 477-3956
Private agency
Founded in: 1973
Rebecca S. Davis, President

Number of members: 68
Staff: volunteer 20
Major programs: library, museum, newsletters/phamphlets, genealogical services

FARMINGTON HILLS

Farmington Hills Historical Commission
31555 Eleven Mile Rd., 48018
Telephone: (313) 474-6115
City agency
Founded in: 1976
Kathryn Briggs, Chair
Major programs: archives, manuscripts, markers, educational programs, books, historic preservation
Period of collections: 1824-present

FLAT ROCK

Flat Rock Historical Society
P.O. Box 386, 48134
Private agency
Founded in: 1974
James C. Bobcean, President
Number of members: 40
Staff: volunteer 10
Major programs: museum, newsletters/pamphlets

FLINT

Alfred P. Sloan Museum
1221 E. Kearsley St., 48503
Telephone: (313) 762-1169
Private agency, authorized by board of education
Founded in: 1966
Phillip C. Kwiatkowski , Director
Number of members: 300
Staff: full time 10, part time 3, volunteer 35
Magazine: *Sloan News*
Major programs: archives, museum, tours/pilgrimages, school programs, newsletters/pamphlets, records management, research, exhibits, photographic collections, genealogical services
Period of collections: 1860-1940

Flint Genealogical Society
P.O. Box 1217, 48501
Founded in: 1956
Number of members: 425
Staff: volunteer 9
Magazine: *Flint Genealogical Quarterly*
Major programs: genealogy

Flint Historic Commission
1101 S. Saginaw St., 45506
Telephone: (313) 766-7426
City agency
Founded in: 1979
Ronald Campbell, Commissioner
Staff: volunteer 8
Major programs: historic preservation
Period of collections: 1850s-1930s

Genesee County Historical and Museum Society
Mail to: P.O. Box 453, 48501
Private agency
Founded in: 1945
David C. White, President
Number of members: 250
Magazine: *Citizen*

Major programs: markers, book publishing, newsletters/pamphlets, historic preservation

Historical Crossroads Village/Huckleberry Railroad
G-5055 Branch Rd., 48506
Telephone: (313) 736-7100
County agency
Founded in: 1966
Kenneth J. Smithee, Director
Staff: full time 3, part time 35, volunteer 25
Major programs: library, archives, historic preservation, records management, library, living history, accessions and restoration
Period of collections: 1960-1890

Whaley Historical House
624 E. Kearsley St., 48503
Telephone: (313) 235-6841
Private agency, authorized by Whaley Historical House Association
Founded in: 1975
Ava Norman, President
Number of members: 175
Staff: volunteer 12
Major programs: museum, tours/pilgrimages, oral history, school programs, newsletters/pamphlets, historic preservation, research, exhibits
Period of collections: 1884-1900

FLUSHING

Flushing Area Historical Society
Mail to: P.O. Box 87, 48433
Founded in: 1975
Paul W. Wightman, President
Number of members: 223
Staff: volunteer 1
Major programs: library, archives, museum, manuscripts, historic sites preservation, oral history, book publishing, newsletters/pamphlets, historic preservation
Period of collections: 19th-early 20th centuries

FRANKENMUTH

Frankenmuth Historical Museum
613 S. Main, 48734
Telephone: (517) 652-9701
Private agency, authorized by Frankenmuth Historical Association
Founded in: 1963
Carl R. Hansen, Director
Number of members: 425
Staff: full time 3, part time 2, volunteer 75
Major programs: archives, manuscripts, museum, historic site(s), newsletters/pamphlets, records management, research, exhibits, photographic collections, genealogical services
Period of collections: 1783-1918

Michigan Museums Association
613 S. Main St., 48734
Private agency
Founded in: 1971
Carl R. Hansen, President
Number of members: 450
Major programs: educational programs,

newsletters/phamphlets, workshops, statewide museum service agency

FRANKLIN VILLAGE

Franklin Historical Society
Telephone: (313) 626-5160
Mail to: P.O. Box 7, 48025
Founded in: 1969
Virginia Debenham Rodgers, President
Number of members: 300
Staff: volunteer 15
Magazine: *Kite & Key*
Major programs: historic sites preservaticn, markers, tours/pilgrimages, books, Period of collections: 1865-present

FREMONT

Windmill Gardens Museum Village
4634 S. Luce, 49412
Telephone: (616) 924-0318
Private agency
Founded in: 1960
Harley Stroven, Owner
Staff: volunteer 2
Major programs: museum, historic site(s), historic preservation, research
Period of collections: 1890-1910

GARDEN

Fayette State Historic Park
Garden Rt. 1, 49835
Telephone: (906) 644-2603
William R. Manning, Park Manager
Staff: full time 3, part time 9
Major programs: museum, historic site(s), markers, historic preservation, research, exhibits, photographic collections, genealogical services
Period of collections: 1870-1890

GARDEN CITY

Garden City Historical Commission
6000 Middlebelt, 48135
Telephone: (313) 421-1262
City agency
Founded in: 1961
Marshal Henry, Chair
Major programs: museum, historic site(s), markers, historic preservation, exhibits, photographic collections
Period of collections: 1820s-1970s

GRAND BLANC

Grand Blanc Heritage Association
203 E. Grand Blanc Rd., 48439
Telephone: (313) 694-1111
Town agency
Founded in: 1972
Clare Ann Hatten, President
Number of members: 200
Staff: volunteer 12
Major programs: library, archives, museum, historic site(s), oral history, school programs, book publishing, newsletters/pamphlets, historic preservation, research, exhibits, photographic collections, genealogical services
Period of collections: 1820s-present

GRAND HAVEN

Tri-Cities Historical Society
1 N. Harbor Ave.
Telephone: (616) 842-0700
Mail to: P.O. Box 234 49417
Private agency
Founded in: 1959
Gertrude V. Kloepfer, Acting Director
Number of members: 500
Staff: part time 1, volunteer 8
Major programs: museum, historic
site(s), school programs,
newsletters/pamphlets, research,
exhibits, audiovisual programs,
photographic collections,
genealogical services
Period of collections: 1834-present

GRAND LEDGE

**Grand Ledge Area Historical
Society**
Telephone: (517) 627-6717
Mail to: P.O. Box 203, 48837
City agency
Fuunded in: 1976
Lucille Robinson, President
Number of members: 100
Major programs: archives, museum,
oral history, book publishing,
newsletters/pamphlets, research,
exhibits
Period of collections: 1965-present

GRAND RAPIDS

**Association for the Advancement
of Dutch-American Studies**
Calvin Library, 3207 Burton, SE,
49506
Telephone: (616) 957-6310
Private agency
Founded in: 1979
Conrad Bult, Secretary/Treasurer
Number of members: 200
Staff: volunteer 5
Major programs: tours/pilgrimages,
newsletters/pamphlets, research,
conferences

Gerald R. Ford Museum
303 Pearl St., NW, 49504
Telephone: (616) 456-2674
Federal agency
Founded in: 1977
William K. Jones, Curator
Staff: full time 9
Major programs: museum, school
programs, exhibits, audiovisual
programs, American political
history
Period of collections: 1948-present

Grand Rapids Historical Society
C/o Grand Rapids Public Library, 60
Library Plaza, NE, 49503
Private agency
Founded in: 1894
Henry Ippel, President
Number of members: 475
Staff: volunteer 25
Magazine: *Grand River Valley Review*
Major programs:
newsletters/pamphlets, book
publishing, reprints, lecture series
Period of collections: 1880-1925

Grand Rapids Public Museum
54 Jefferson Ave., SE, 49503
Telephone: (616) 456-3977

City agency
Founded in: 1854
W. D. Frankforter, Director
Staff: full time 26, part time 25,
volunteer 950
Major programs: museum, historic
site(s), school programs,
newsletters/pamphlets, historic
preservation, exhibits, living
history, photographic collections,
Period of collections: 1850-1950

Heritage Hill Association
126 College, SE, 49503
Telephone: (616) 459-8950
Private agency
Founded in: 1969
Number of members: 700
Staff: full time 3, part time 1,
volunteer 30
Magazine: *Heritage Herald*
Major programs: library,
tours/pilgrimages, educational
programs, books,
newsletters/pamphlets, historic
preservation, photographic
collections
Period of collections: 1850-1925

**Kent County Council for Historic
Preservation**
115 College Ave., SE, 49503
Telephone: (616) 458-2422
County agency, authorized by Grand
Rapids Public Museum
Founded in: 1971
Barbara Raelofs, President
Major programs: museum, histcric
site(s), markers
Period of collections: 1895-1930

Voight House
115 College Ave., SE, 49503
City agency, authorized by Kent
County Council for Historic
Preservation
Founded in: 1971
Bette Battaglia, Manager
Staff: full time 2, volunteer 125
Period of collections: Victorian era

GRANDVILLE

**Grandville Historical Association
and Museum**
3195 Wilson, SW
Telephone: (616) 531-3030
Mail to: P.O. Box 14, 49418
Founded in: 1970
Staff: volunteer 16
Major programs: library, archives,
manuscripts, museum, markers,
tours/pilgrimages, junior history,
oral history, educational programs,
books
Period of collections: 1865-present

GREENVILLE

**Flat River Historical Society and
Museum**
213 N. Franklin St.
Telephone: (616) 754-5296
Mail to: P.O. Box 188, 48838
Founded in: 1967
Thomas C. Blinn, President
Number of 250
Staff: volunteer 8
Magazine: *Log Mark*

Major prcgrams: library, archives,
manuscripts, museum, historic
site(s), tours/pilgrimages, oral
history, newsletters/pamphlets,
historic preservation, research,
exhibits, audiovisual programs,
photographic collections,
genealogical services
Period of collections: 1844-present

GROSSE ILE

Grosse Ile Historical Society
E. River Rd. at Parkway
Mail to: P.O. Box 131, 48138
Founded in: 1959
Mrs. Howard Grostick, President
Number of members: 400
Staff: volunteer 21
Major programs: archives, museum,
historic site(s), markers,
tours/pilgrimages, junior history,
oral history, school programs,
newsletters/pamphlets, historic
preservation, research, exhibits,
photographic collections
Period of collections: 1776-present

HANCOCK

**Quincy Mine Hoist
Association, Inc.**
P.O. Box 265, 40993
Telephone: (906) 482-3101
Private agency
Founded in: 1961
Burton H. Boyum, President
Staff: volunteer 16
Major programs: museum, historic
preservation, exhibits, buildings
and machinary
related to native copper mining
Pericd of collections: 1848-1945

HARTFORD

**Van Buren County Historical
Society**
6215 E. Red Arrow Hwy., E
Telephone: (616) 621-2188
Mail to: General Delivery, 49057
Founded in: 1956
Questionnaire not received

HASTINGS

Barry County Historical Society
2545 S. Charlton Park Rd.
Telephone: (616) 945-2256
Mail to: 543 Indian Hills Dr., 49058
Founded in: 1964
Questionnaire not received

Charlton Park Village and Museum
2545 S. Charlton Park Rd., 49058
Telephone: (616) 945-3775
Founded in: 1936
Questionnaire not received

**Historic Charlton Park Village and
Museum**
2545 S. Charlton Park Rd., 49508
Telephone: (616) 945-3775
County agency, authorized by Barry
County Parks and Recreation
Comission
Founded in: 1936
Kevin Woods, Chair
Staff: full time 3, part time 30,
volunteer 50

Major programs: museum, school
programs, exhibits, living history
Period of collections: 1850-1920

HILLSDALE

Hillsdale County Historical Society
101 W. Hallett Rd., 49242
Telephone: (517) 437-4112
Founded in: 1965
Vernon Stevens, President
Number of members: 214
Major programs: museum, historic
site(s), markers, school programs,
historic preservation, awards for
restoration and for history
proficiency at the high school level

HINCKLEY

Hinckley Fire Museum
Old Hwy. 61, 55037
Telephone: (612) 384-7338
Private agency, authorized by Pine
County Historical Society
Founded in: 1976
Jeanne Coffey, Curator
Staff: full time 2, part time 2,
volunteer 10
Magazine: *Telegraph*
Major programs: museum, bock
publishing, historic preservation,
exhibits, audiovisual programs,
photographic collections
Period of collections: 1865-1918

HOLLAND

Baker Furniture Museum
6th and Columbia Ave.
Telephone: (616) 392-8761
Mail to: P.O. Box 3014-D, 49423
Private agency
Founded in: 1941
James S. Symons, Curator
Staff: part time 5
Major programs: museum, research,
exhibits, furniture
Period of collections: 2345
B.C.-present

Netherlands Museum
8 E. 12th St., 49423
Telephone: (616) 392-9084
Private agency
Founded in: 1937
Willard C. Wichers, President of the
Board
Staff: part time 6
Major programs: library, archives,
museum, exhibits, audiovisual
programs, genealogical services
Period of collections: 1847-present

Poll Museum of Transportation
U.S. Hwy. 31 and New Holland St.
Telephone: (616) 399-1955
Mail to: 353 E. 6th St., 49423
Private agency
Founded in: 1954
Henry Poll, Owner
Period of collections: 1902-1949

HOLLY

**Northwest Oakland County
Historical Society**
500 Maple St.
Telephone: (313) 634-4673
Mail to: 4053 Elliot Rd., 48442
Questionnaire not received

HOMER

Homer Historical Society
505 Grandview, 49245
Telephone: (517) 568-3116
Private agency
Founded in: 1974
Mrs. Clem Camp, President
Number of members: 96
Staff: volunteer 18
Major programs: museum, school
programs, newsletters/pamphlets,
historic preservation, exhibits
Period of collections: 1890-1910

HOUGHTON

**Houghton County Historical
Museum Society**
Hwy. M-26, Lake Linden, 49945
Telephone: (906) 296-4121
Mail to: Lock Box D
Founded in: 1961
William Barkell, President
Number of members: 265
Staff: part time 7, volunteer 25
Major programs: museum, historic
sites preservation, educational
programs
Period of collections: 1865-present

Isle Royale National Park
87 N. Ripley St., 49931
Telephone: (906) 482-3310
Federal agency
Founded in: 1931
Don Brown, Superintendent
Staff: full time 19, part time 16,
volunteer 15
Major programs: library, archives,
museum, historic site(s), markers,
tours/pilgrimages, oral history,
school programs, book publishing,
newsletters/pamphlets, historic
preservation, research, exhibits,
living history, audiovisual
programs, archaeology programs,
photographic collections
Period of collections:
prehistoric-present

HOUGHTON LAKE HEIGHTS

**Houghton Lake Area Historical
Society**
1625 W. Houghton Lake Dr., 48651
Telephone: (517) 422-5074
Mail to: c/c R. W. Carman, P.O. Box
146, 48630
Founded in: 1972
Questionnaire not received

HOWELL

**Livingston County Historical
Society**
Foot of Walnut, 48843
Founded in: 1969
Questionnaire not received

IONIA

Ionia County Historical Society
359 E. Main St.
Mail to: P.O. Box 1776, 48846
County agency
Founded in: 1974
Ralph Bartelt, President
Staff: volunteer 20

Major programs: historic site(s),
newsletters/pamphlets, historic
preservation
Period of collections: 1880-1910

IRONWOOD

Ironwood Area Historical Society
226 E. McLeod Ave., 49938
Founded in: 1971
Questionnaire not received

ISHPEMING

National Ski Hall of Fame
Mather Ave. and Poplar St.
Telephone: (906) 486-9281
Mail to: P.O. Box 191, 36205
Private agency, authorized by the
U.S. Ski Association
Founded in: 1954
Raymond A. Leverton,
Curator/Manager
Staff: full time 1, part time 4,
volunteer 1
Major programs: library, archives,
museum, oral history, book
publishing,
newsletters/phamplets, historic
preservation, history of skiing
Period of collections: 1904-present

ITHACA

Gratiot County Historical Society
P.O. Box 73, 48847
Telephone: (517) 875-4290
County agency
Founded in: 1978
Thomas Austin, President
Number of members: 90
Major programs: library, archives,
museum, historic site(s), markers,
tours/pilgrimages, book publishing,
historic preservation, research,
genealogical services
Period of collections: 1850-present

JACKSON

**Ella Sharp Museum Association of
Jackson**
3225 4th St., 49203
Telephone: (517) 787-2320
Founded in: 1964
Mildred I. Hadwin, Museum Director
Number of members: 1,295
Staff: full time 12, part time 2,
volunteer 110
Major programs: museum, historic
sites preservation, educational
programs, newsletters/pamphlets
Period of collections: 1830-1912

**Jackson County Genealogical
Society**
c/o Jackson District Library, 244 W.
Michigan Ave., 49201
Telephone: (515) 758-4316
Private agency
Founded in: 1977
Robert A. Hoffman, President
Number of members: 65
Staff: volunteer 20
Magazine: *Lexicon*
Major programs: library,
newsletters/pamphlets, research,
genealogical services

JENISON

Jenison Historical Association
Port Sheldon and Main St.
Telephone: (616) 457-2340
Mail to: P.O. Box 164, 49428
Founded in: 1971
Questionnaire not received

KALAMAZOO

Archives and Regional History Collections
Western Michigan University, 49008
Telephone: (616) 383-1826
State agency, authorized by the University
Founded in: 1956
Wayne C. Mann, Director
Staff: full time 6, part time 2, volunteer 4
Major programs: library, archives, manuscripts, oral history, records management, research, photographic collections, genealogical services
Period of collections: 1830-present

Kalamazoo Ccunty Historical Society
315 S. Rose St. 49007
Telephone: (616) 345-7092
Private agency
Founded in: 1948
Number of members: 50
Major programs: histcric sites preservation, markers, tours/pilgrimages, books

Kalamazoo Public Museum
315 S. Rose St., 49007
Telephone: (616) 345-7092
Founded in, 1927
Staff: full time 8, part time 8
Major programs: library, archives, manuscripts, museum, historic site preservation, markers, tours/pilgrimages, educational programs, books, newsletters/pamphlets, exhibits
Period of collections: prehistoric-present

Kalamazoo Valley Genealogical Society
315 S. Rose, 49007
Private agency, authorized by Kalamazoo Public Museum
Founded in: 1959
Mrs. Robert Jackson, President
Number of members: 205
Major programs: library, book publishing, newsletters/pamphlets, genealogical services
Period of collections: 1800-present

KALKASKA

Kalkaska County Historical Society
Cedar St.
Mail to: Rt. 3, Box 10, Kalkaska Rd., 49646
County agency
Founded in: 1967
Hazel Butler, President
Number of members: 325
Staff: volunteer 115
Major programs: library, manuscripts, museum, historic sites preservation, markers,

tours/pilgrimages, oral history, educational programs
Period of collections: 1865-1918

LAKE LINDEN

Houghton County Historical Society
M-26, 49945
Telephone: (906) 296-4121
Mail to: Lock Box D, 49945
County agency
Founded in: 1960
Helen Harris, Treasurer
Number of members: 300
Staff: part time 1, volunteer 20
Major programs: museum, historic site(s), school programs, book publishing, newsletters/pamphlets, historic preservation, exhibits, audiovisual programs, photographic collections
Period of collections: 1880-1930

LAKE ODESSA

Lake Odessa Area Historical Society
Page Bldg., 839 4th Ave., 48849
Telephone: (616) 374-8698
Private agency
Founded in: 1968
Mrs. Merton Garlock, Director/Editor
Number of members: 118
Staff: volunteer 4
Magazine: *The Bonanza Bugle*
Major programs: newsletters/pamphlets
Period of collections: 1880-present

L'ANSE

Baraga County Historical Society, Inc.
Rt. 1, Box 97, 49946
Telephone: (906) 524-6052
County agency
Founded in: 1958
Alvin Lydman, President
Number of members: 25
Staff: volunteer 5
Major programs: library, museum, oral history, book publishing, historic preservation, Indian cemetary
Period of collections: 1900-present

LANSING

Aviation Museum Foundation
Telephone: (517) 321-1746
Mail to: c/o 5580 W. State Rd., R-4, 48906
Founded in: 1976
Wes Van Malsen, Chair
Questionnaire not received

◊**Bureau of History, Michigan Department of State**
208 N. Capital, 48918
Telephone: (517) 373-6362/373-0510
State agency, authorized by the Secretary of State
Founded in: 1913
Martha M. Bigelow, Director
Staff: full time 39, part time 25
Magazine: *Michigan History*
Major programs: archives, manuscripts, museum, historic site(s), historic preservation
Period of collections: 1795-present

Clinton County Historical Commission
5580 W. State Rd., 48906
Telephone: (51) 321-1746
Founded in: 1977
Geneva K. Wiskemann, Chair
Staff: volunteer 5
Major programs: historic site(s), markers, oral history, school programs, historic preservation, research, photographic collections

French-Canadian Heritage Society of Michigan
Library of Michigan, 48913
Private agency
Founded in: 1980
Carol Hamp, President
Number of members: 300
Staff: volunteer 20
Magazine: *Michigan's Habitant Heritage*
Major programs: library, archives, manuscripts, tours/pilgrimages, oral history, school programs, books, newsletters/pamphlets, research, living history, audiovisual programs, genealogical services
Period of collections: 1600-present

Friends of Turner-Dodge House
100 E. North St., 48906
Telephone: (517) 487-1079
Sard Basso, President
Major programs: historic site, historic presentation, tours/pilgrimages
Questionnaire not received

Historical Society of Greater Lansing
Telephone: (617) 321-1746
Mail to: P.O. Box 12095, 48901
Founded in: 1955
Number of members: 150
Major programs: tours/pilgrimages, educational programs, newsletters/pamphlets

Library of Michigan
735 E. Michigan Ave.
Telephone: (517) 373-1593
Mail to: P.O. Box 30007, 48909
State agency, authorized by legislative council
Founded in: 1828
James W. Fry, State Librarian
Staff: full time 101
Magazine: *Family Trails/Michigan in Books*
Major programs: library, archives, newsletters/pamphlets, genealogical services
Period of collections: 1700-present

◊**Michigan Historical Museum**
208 N. Capitol, 48918
Telephone: (517) 373-0515
Founded in: 1879
Questionnaire not received

R. E. Olds Museum
240 Museum Dr., 48933
Telephone: (517) 372-0422
Private agency
Founded in: 1977
Sue Neller, Executive Director
Number of members: 454
Staff: full time 2, part time 3, volunteer 230
Major programs: library, archives, museum, historic site(s), markers, tours/pilgrimages, junior history,

oral history, newsletters/pamphlets,
historic preservation, research,
exhibits, living history, audiovisual
programs, photographic
collections
Period of collections: 1900-present

LAPEER

Lapeer County Historical Museum
637 W. Nepessing St.
Mail to: 3034 W. Oregon Rd., 48446
Questionnaire not received

Lapeer County Historical Society
Old Courthouse
Mail to: P.O. Box 72, 48446
Founded in: 1969
Number of members: 120
Staff: volunteer 19
Major programs: archives, museum,
historic sites preservation, markers,
historic preservation
Period of collections: 1834-1930

LELAND

Leelanau Historical Society Inc.
Telephone: (616) 256-9285
Mail to: P.O. Box 246, 49654
Private agency
Founded in: 1957
Joseph H. Sutton, President
Number of members: 300
Major programs: museum, markers,
educational programs, historic
preservation
Period of collections: 1865-1918

LINCOLN PARK

Lincoln Park Hisotorical Society
1832 Coleophus
Telephone: (313) 381-0374
Mail to: P.O. Box 1776, 48146
Founded in: 1972
Questionnaire not received

LINDEN

Linden Mills Historical Society
P. O. Box 551, 48451
Private agency
Founded in: 1975
M.R. Costello, Secretary
Number of members: 30
Staff: volunteer 20
Major programs: museum,
tours/pilgrimages
Period of collections: late 1800s-early
1900s

LIVONIA

**Livonia Historical
Commission—Greenmead
Historic Site**
38125 Eight Mile Rd., 48152
Telephone: (313) 499-7373
City agency
Founded in: 1958
Suzanne Daniel, President
Staff: part time 1, volunteer 30
Major programs: library, museum,
historic preservation, photographic
collections
Period of collections: 1824-present

**Livonia Historic Preservation
Commission**
33000 Civic Center Dr., 48154

Telephone: (313) 421-2000
Charles Chandler, President
Major programs: historic preservaion

LUDINGTON

Mason County Historical Society
1687 S. Lakeshore Dr., 49431
Telephone: (616) 843-4808/843-2001
Private agency
Founed in: 1937
Thomas A. Hawley, Executive
Director
Number of members: 500
Staff: full time 3, part time 3,
volunteer 125
Magazine: *Mason Memories*
Major programs: library, archives,
manuscripts, museum,
tours/pilgrimages, oral history,
school programs, book publishing,
newsletteps/pamphlets, historic
preservation, records
management, research, exhibits,
living history, audiovisual
programs, photographic
collections, genealogical services
Period of collecticns: 1850-present

MACKINAC ISLAND

Mackinac Associates
P.O. Box 370, 49757
Telephone: (906) 847-3328
Mail to: P.O. Box 30028, 48909
Private agency
Founded in: 1980
Victor H. Hogg, Clerk
Number of members: 350
Magazine: *Curiosities*
Major programs: historic site(s),
newsletters/pamphlets, historic
preservation
Period of collections: 1715-1898

**Mackinac Island State Park
Commission**
P.O. Box 370, 49747
Telephone: (906) 847-3328
State agency
Founded in: 1895
Eugene T. Petersen, Superintendent
Staff: full time 11, part time 45
Major programs: library, archives,
museum, historic site(s),
tours/pilgrimages, book publishing,
historic preservation, research,
exhibits, living history, audiovisual
programs, archaeology programs,
photographic collections
Period of collections: 1715-1898

Stuart House Museum
Market St.
Telephone: (906) 847-3808
(secretary)
Mail to: P.O. Box 1194, 49757
City agency
Founded in: 1817
Sheldon B. Roots, Curator
Staff: full time 1, part time 1,
volunteer 1
Major programs: library, museum,
historic site(s), markers, historic
preservation, exhibits,
photographic collections
Period of collections: 1810-1834

MACKINAW CITY

**Teysen's Woodland Indian
Museum**
416 S. Huron Ave.
Telephone: (616) 436-7011
Mail to: P.O. Box 399, 49701
Private agency
Founded in: 1950
Kenneth Teyson, Owner
Staff: full time 1
Major programs: museum
Period of collections: 8000 B.C.-1900

MANISTEE

**Manistee County Historical
Museum**
425 River St., 4966-
Telephone: (616) 723-5531
Questionnaire not received

MARQUETTE

Bishop Baraga Association
239 Baraga Ave., 49855
Telephone: (906) 226-7372
Questionnaire not received

**Marquette County Historical
Society**
213 N. Front St., 49855
Telephone: (906) 226-3571
Founded in: 1918
Frank O. Paull, Jr., Director
Number of members: 870
Staff: full time 3, part time 6
Magazine: *Harlow's Wooden Man*
Major programs: library, archives,
manuscripts, museum, school
programs, book publishing,
newsletters/pamphlets, exhibits,
living history, photographic
collections
Period of collections: 1849-present

MARSHALL

Marshall Historical Society, Inc.
Mail to: P.O. Box 68, 49068
Private agency
Founded in: 1974
Number of members: 300
Staff: part time 2, volunteer 30
Major programs: archives, museum,
historic site)s), markers,
tours/pilgrimages, book publishing,
historic preservation, exhibits,
photographic collections,
genealogical services
Period of collections: 1840-1940

MASON

Mason Historical Society
City Hall, 48854
Telephone: (517) 676-4643
Questionnaire not received

MAYVILLE

Mayville Historical Society
22 Turner
Telephone: (517) 843-6429
Mail to: P.O. Box 242, 48744
Private agency
Founded in: 1972
Mrs. Willard Phelps, Curator
Major programs: museum, book
publishing, historic preservation,

exhibits, photographic collections,
genealogical services
Period of collections: 1855-present

MENOMINEE

**Menominee County Historical
Societ, Inc.**
904 11th Ave.
Telephone: (906) 863-2679
Mail to: P.O. Box 151, 49858
Founded in: 1967
Questionnaire not received

MIDLAND

Midland County Historical Society
1801 W. St. Andrews Dr., 48640
Telephone: (517) 835-7401
County agency, authorized by
Midland Center for the Arts
Founded in: 1952
Kathryn Cummins, Director
Number of members: 400
Staff: full time 2, volunteer 20
Magazine: *Midland Log*
Major programs: museum, archives,
manuscripts, historic site(s),
markers, tours/pilgrimages, oral
history, school programs,
newsletters/pamphlets, historic
preservation, research, exhibits,
audiovisual programs,
photrgraphic collections,
genealogical services
Period of collections: 1860-1920

Midland Genealogical Society
Grace A. Dow Library, 1710 W. St.
Andrews Dr., 48640
Telephone: (517) 835-7151
Founded in: 1972
Number of members: 100
Magazine: *Pioneer Record*
Major programs: library, book
publishing, historic preservation,
research, genealogical services
Period of collections: 1600s-present

Midland Historic District
202 Ashman St., 48640
Telephone: (517) 835-7711
City agency, authorized by Historic
Advisory Commission
Founded in: 1979
E. William Day, City Planner
Staff: volunteer 7
Major programs: historic site(s),
markers

MILFORD

Milford Historical Society
124 E. Commerce St., 48042
Telephone: (313) 685-7308
Private agency
Founded in: 1973
Mary Lou Gharrity, Director of
Museum
Major programs: museum,
tours/pilgrimages, oral history,
newsletters/pamphlets,
photographic collections
Period of collecticns: mid
1800s-present

MIO

**Au-Sable River Valley Historical
Society**
Mail to: P.O. Box 304, 48647

Founded in: 1967
Number of members: 35
Staff: volunteer 5
Major programs: library, archives,
markers, oral history
Period of collections: 1865-present

MONROE

**Monroe County Historical
Commission and Museum**
126 S. Monroe St., 48161
Telephone: (313) 243-7137
County agency
Founded in: 1939
Matthew C. Switlik, Director
Staff: full time 3, part time 4,
volunteer 60
Major programs: archives,
manuscripts, museum, historic
site(s), markers, school programs,
exhibits
Period of collections:
prehistoric-present

MONTAGUE

**Montague Museum and Historical
Association**
Church and Meade Sts., 49437
Telephone: (616) 894-6972
Mail to: 8636 Old Channel Trail
City agency
Founded in: 1964
Henry E. Roesler, Jr., President
Staff: volunteer 31
Major programs: archives, museum,
markers
Period of collections: 1865-1918

MORRICE

Morrice Farm Museum
691 Purdy Lane, 48857
Telephone: (517) 625-3143
Private agency
Founded in: 1976
David A. Fahrenbach,
Teacher/Director
Number of members: 150
Major programs: museum, historic
site(s), junior history, oral history,
school programs, book publishing,
newsletters/pamphlets, historic
preservation, research, exhibits,
living history

MOUNT CLEMENS

Macomb County Historical Society
15 Union St., 48043
Telephone: (313) 465-2488
Founded in: 1964
Jean MacArthur, President
Number of members: 225
Staff: full time 5, volunteer 50
Major programs: museum,
newsletters/pamphlets, historic
preservation, exhibits
Period of collections: 1850-1920

MT. PLEASANT

**Center for Cultural and Natural
History**
124 Rowe Hall, Central Michigan
University, 48859
Telephone: (517) 774-3829,
authorized by the University
Founded in: 1970

Lynn N. Fauver, Director
Staff: full time 2, part time 15,
volunteer 15
Major programs: museum, research,
exhibits, natural history
Period of collections: 1865-1918

Clarke Historical Library
Central Michigan University, 48859
Telephone: (517) 774-3352
State agency
Founded in: 1955
William H. Mulligan, Jr., Director
Staff: full time 6, part time 4
Major programs: library, archives,
manuscripts, book publishing,
newsletters/pamphlets, research,
exhibits, photographic collections,
genealogical services, field
services
Period of collections: 1700-present

MUNISING

Alger County Historical Society
203 W. Onota St.
Telephone: (906) 387-4186
Mail to: P.O. Box 201, 49862
Founded in: 1966
Isabella K. Sullivan, Executive
Secretary
Number of members: 800
Staff: volunteer 20
Magazine: *Alger Footprints*
Major programs: library, museum,
historic site(s), markers, oral
history, book publishing,
newsletters/phamphlets, historic
preservation, exhibits,
photographic collections
Period of collections: 1918-present

MUSKEGON

Hackley Heritage Association, Inc.
484 W. Webster Ave., 49440
Telephone: (616) 722-7578/759-2505
Mail to: P.O. Box 32, 49443-0032
Private agency
Founded in: 1966
Josephine Bartscht, President
Number of members: 525
Staff: volunteer 125
Major programs: museum, historic
site(s), book publishing, historic
preservation, genealogical
services
Period of collections: 1865-1918

Historic District Commission
933 Terrace St., 49443
Telephone: (616) 724-6702
City agency
Founded in: 1974
Rick Chapla. Director, Department of
Planning and Community
Development
Major programs: regulates
construction and improvements in
historic districts

**Muskegon County Genealogical
Society**
Hackley Library, 316 W. Webster
Ave., 49444
Private agency
Founded in: 1972
Sharon Miller, President
Number of members: 56
Magazine: *Family Tree Talks*

Major programs: library, book
publishing, historic preservation,
research, genealogical services
Period of collections: 1800s-present

Muskegon County Museum
430 W. Clay Ave., 49440
Telephone: (616) 728-4119
County agency
Founded in: 1937
Frank E. Walsh, Director
Number of members: 400
Staff: full time 7, part time 3,
volunteer 6
Magazine: *Explorer*
Major programs: library, archives,
museum, tours/pilgrimages, school
programs, newsletters/pamphlets,
research, exhibits, audiovisual
programs, photographic
collections
Period of collections: 1880-1940

NEW BALTIMORE
New Baltimore Historical Society
P.O. Box 387, 48047
Telephone: (313) 725-9406
Private agency
Founded in: 1975
John P. McPartlin, Treasurer
Number of members: 118
Staff: volunteer 5
Major programs: archives, museum,
historic site(s), markers, oral
history, school programs,
newsletters/pamphlets, historic
preservation, research, exhibits,
living history, photographic
collections, genealogical services,
field services, annual festival of
Colonial crafts
Period of collections: 1776-1876

NEWBERRY
**Newberry Historical Restoration
Association, Inc.**
515 Newberry Ave., 49868
Telephone: (906) 293-8808
Private agency
Founded in: 1980
Billie Hermanson, President
Staff: part time 3, volunteer 12
Major programs: museum, historic
site(s), school programs, historic
preservation, photographic
collections
Period of collections: 1890-present

NILES
**Fernwood Botanic Garden, Nature
Center/Arts and Crafts Center**
1720 Rangeline Rd., 49120
Telephone: (616) 695-6491
Private agency
Founded in: 1964
Stan Beikmann, Director
Number of members: 1,100
Staff: full time 7, part time 18,
volunteer 125
Magazine: *The Fernwood Notes*
Major programs: tours/ilgrimages,
oral history, school programs,
newsletters/pamphlets, records
management, exhibits, living
history, audiovisual prcgrams,
photographic collections,
conservation studies
Period of collections: present

**Ft. St. Joseph Historical
Association**
508 E. Main St., 49120
Telephone: (616) 683-4702
City agency
Founded in: 1932
Wayne Stiles, Director
Number of members: 130
Staff: full time 1, part time 2
Major programs: museum, historic
site(s), markers, school programs,
newsletters/pamphlets, historic
preservation, research, exhibit,
living history, photographic
collections, reconstruction as living
history site
Period of collections: 1700-present

NORTHVILLE
Northville Historical Society
Griswold Ave.
Telephone: (313) 349-2659
Mail to: P.O. Box 71, 48167
Private agency
Founded in: 1964
John Brugeman, President
Number of members: 400
Magazine: *Mill Race Quarterly*
Major programs: library, manuscripts,
historic site(s), school programs,
book publishing,
newsletters/pamphlets, historic
preservation, research, exhibits,
living history
Period of collections: 1865-1918

OKEMOS
Friends of Historic Meridian
Telephone: (517) 349-1993
Mail to: P.O. Box 155, 48864
Private agency
Founded in: 1973
Elaine Davis, President
Number of members: 70
Staff: volunteer 20
Magazine: *The Gate-Keeper*
Major programs: museum,
newsletters/pamphlets, archives,
building restoration
Period of collections: 1865-1918

ONTONAGON
**Ontonagon County Historical
Scciety**
233 River St., 49953
Telephone: (906) 884-2342
Mail to: P.O. Box 7
Founded in: 1957
Charles Willman, Secretary/Treasurer
Number of members: 150
Staff: volunteer 1
Major programs: museum, oral
history
Period of collections: 1865-present

ORCHARD LAKE
**Greater West Bloomfield Historical
Society**
Mail to: P.O. Box 5024 48033
Private agency
Founded in: 1974
Ed Sullivan, President
Number of members: 90
Staff: volunteer 15
Major programs: archives,
tours/pilgrimages, oral history,

newsletters/pamphlets, exhibits,
photographic collections
Period of collections: 1830-present

OSCODA
AuSable-Oscoda Historical Society
P.O. Box 173, 48750
Telephone: (517) 739-5356
Private agency, authorized by
Oscoda Township
Founded in: 1977
Mrs. John Hennigar, Chair
Major programs: historic site(s), oral
history, book publishing,
newsletters/pamphlets, research,
photographic collections,
genealogical services
Period of collections: 1880-1930

OWOSSO
**Shiawassee County Genealogical
Society**
P.O. Box 145, 48867
Founded in: 1968
Patricia L. Yott, President
Number of members: 107
Magazine: *The Shiawassee Stepping
Stones*
Major programs: library,
photographic collections,
genealogical services
Period of collections: 1836-present

PETOSKEY
**Little Traverse Regional Historical
Society**
Water Front Park
Telephone: (616) 347-2620
Mail to: P.O. Box 162, 49770
Founded in: 1968
Questionnaire not received

PINCKNEY
Pinckney Area Historical Scciety
P.O. Box 606, 48169
Private agency
Founded in: 1979
Tony Tadeo, President
Number of members:
Staff: full time 2
Major programs: museum, historic
site(s)
Period of collections: 1835-1935

PLYMOUTH
Plymouth Historical Society
155 S. Main St., 48170
Telephone: (313) 455-8940
Founded in: 1948
Margaret Kidston, President
Number of members: 340
Staff: full time 1, part time 3,
volunteer 65
Major programs: archives, museum,
tours/pilgrimages, oral history,
school programs, exhibits,
photographic collections,
genealogical services
Period of collections: 1827-1900

PONTIAC
**Oakland County Pioneer and
Historical Society**
405 Oakland Ave., 48058
Telephone: (313) 338-6732

Private agency
Founded in: 1874
Mary Ann Treais, Administrative
Coordinator
Number of members: 600
Staff: full time 1, part time 1,
volunteer 70
Magazine: *The Oakland Gazette*
Major programs: library, archives,
manuscripts, museum, historic
site(s), markers, tours/pilgrimages,
junior history, oral history, school
programs, newsletters/pamphlets,
historic preservation, records
management, research, exhibits,
living history, audiovisual
programs, archaeology programs,
photographic collections,
genealogical services, field
services
Period of collections: 1873-present

**Pine Grove Historical
Museum/Governor Moses Wisner
Historic House**
405 Oakland Ave., 48508
Telephone: (313) 338-6732
Private agency, authorized by
Oakland County Pioneer and
Historical Society
Major programs: library, archives,
manuscripts, museum, historic
site(s), markers, tours/pilgrimages,
junior history, oral history, school
programs, newsletters/pamphlets,
historic preservation, records
management, research, exhibits,
living history, audiovisual
programs, archaeology programs,
photographic collections,
genealogical services, field
services
Period of collections: Civil War
era-1900

**Pontiac Area Historical and
Genealogical Society**
35 E. Huron St., 48058
Private agency
Founded in: 1980
Ruth Keith, Vice President
Number of members: Staff:
volunteer 8
Magazine: *Connections*
Major programs: library,
newsletters/pamphlets,
genealogical services
Period of collections: 1600-present

PORT AUSTIN

Huron City Museum
7930 Huron City Rd., 48467
Telephone: (517) 428-4123
Private agency
Founded in: 1953
Charles Scheffner, Director
Staff: full time 2, part time 15
Major programs: library, museum,
historic sites preservation, historic
preservation, exhibits
Period of collections: 1881-1930s

PORT HURON

Museum of Arts and History
1115 6th St., 48060
Telephone: (313) 982-0891

Private Agency
Founded in: 1967
Stephen R. Williams, Director
Number of members: 600
Staff: full time 2, part time 4,
volunteer 50
Major programs: archives,
manuscripts, museum, oral history,
educational programs,
newsletters/pamphlets, traditional
music and dance, archeology
Period of collections: 1783-1930

PORT SANILAC

Sanilac County Historical Society
228 S. Ridge St. and State Hwy. M-25
Telephone: (313) 622-9946
Mail to: P.O. Box 156, 48469
Private agency
Founded in: 1964
Jane A. Miller, Administrator
Number of members: 140
Major programs: museum, historic
preservation
Period of collections: 19th century

ROCHESTER

**City of Rochester Hills Museum at
Van Hoosen Farm**
1005 Van Hoosen Rd.
Telephone: (313) 656-4663
Mail to: 1275 W. Avon Rd., 48063
City agency
Founded in: 1979
Elizabeth A. Black, Museum
Coordinator
Staff: full time 1
Major programs: museum, historic
site(s), tours/pilgrimages,
pamphlets, historic preservation
Period of collections: 1824-1950

**Oakland Township Historical
Society**
4393 Collins Rd.
Telephone: (313) 651-6332
Mail to: 1801 Silverbell Rd., 48064
Private agency
Founded in: 1975
Doris Barkham, President
Number of members: 64
Major programs: historic site(s),
markers, oral history, book
publishing, historic preservation,
audiovisual programs,
photographic collections

**Rochester Hills Historic District
Commission**
1275 W. Avon Rd., 48063
Telephone: (313) 656-4663
City agency
Founded in: 1978
Earl E. Borden, Mayor
Staff: full time 1
Major programs: museum, historic
site(s), historic preservation
Period of collections: 1830-1930

ROCKFORD

Rockford Area Historical Society
Mail to: 140 E. Bridge St., 49341
Number of members: 25
Major programs: museum, book
publishing
Period of collections: 1840-1940

ROGERS CITY

**Presque Isle County Historical
Museum**
176 W. Michigan Ave.
Telepone: (517) 734-4121
Mail to: P.O. Box 175, 49779
Private agency
Founded in 1973
Mary Ann Morley, Curator
Staff: part time 1
Major programs: archives,
manuscripts, museum, tours,
pilgrimages, oral history, school
programs, historic preservation,
exhibits, photographic collections
Period of collections: 1890-1930

ROMEO

Romeo Historical Society
132 Church St.
Telephone: (313) 752-4111
Mail to: P.O. Box 412, 48065
Private agency
Founded in: 1961
Peggy Grandstaff, Museum Director
Number of members: 95
Staff: part time 1, volunteer 15
Major programs: archives, museum,
newsletters/pamphlets, research,
exhibits, photographic collections,
genealogical services
Period of collections: 1800-1910

ROMULUS

Romulus Historical Society
11121 Wayne Rd., 48174
Telephone: (313) 941-0775
City agency
Founded in: 1979
Pearl Varner, President
Staff: volunteer 4
Major programs: library, archives,
historic site(s), markers, oral
history, historic preservation,
records management, research,
exhibits photographic collections,
genealogical services

ROSE CITY

**Rose City Area Historical
Society, Inc.**
Ogemaw District Library, 107 W. Main
Mail to: P.O. Box 427, 48654
Town agency
Founded in: 1983
James A. Hendricks, President
Number of members: 78
Staff: volunteer 1
Major programs: library, oral history,
school programs, historic
preservation, research, exhibits,
photographic collections,
genealogical services
Period of collections: 1871-present

SAGINAW

**Historical Society of Saginaw
County**
500 Federal Ave., 48607
Telephone: (517) 752-2861
Mail to: P.O. Box 390, 48606
Private agency
Founded in: 1946
Charles F. Hoover, Executive Director

Number of members: 685
Staff: full time 7, part time 1,
  volunteer 133
Magazine: *Saginaw Historian*
Major programs: archives, museum,
  markers, oral history, school
  programs, book publishing,
  newsletters/pamphlets, historic
  preservation, exhibits, living
  history, archaeology programs,
  photographic collections
Period of collections: 1815-present

Michigan Archaeological Society
P.O. Box 359, 48606
Telephone: (517) 790-3836
Private agency
Founded in: 1952
Mark C. Branstner, President
Number of members: 400
Magazine: *The Michigan
  Archaeologist*
Major programs: historic
  preservation, research,
  archaeology programs

**Saginaw Archaeological
Commission**
County Castle Bldg., 500 Federal
  Ave.
Telephone: (517) 753-3537
Mail to: P.O. Box 359, 48606
Founded in: 1975
Questionnaire not received

Saginaw County Historical Society
County Castle Bldg., 500 Federal
  Ave.
Telephone: (517) 752-2861
Mail to: P.O. Box 390, 48606
Private agency
Founded in: 1964
Charles F. Hoover, Director
Number of members: 857
Staff: full time 7, part time 8,
  volunteer 137
Major programs: archives, museum,
  historic site(s), markers, oral
  history, school programs, book
  publishing, newsletters/pamphlets,
  research, exhibits, living history,
  archaeology programs,
  photographic collections
Period of collections: 1815-present

Saginaw Genealogical Society
Saginaw Public Library, 505 Janes,
  48605
Telephone: (517) 755-0904
Private agency
Founded in: 1971
Alice Schlesswohl, President
Number of members: 259
Staff: volunteer 1
Major programs: library, manuscripts,
  book publishing,
  newsletters/pamphlets, research,
  genealogical services
Period of collections: 19th century

ST. CLAIR SHORES

**St. Clair Shores Historical
Commission**
22500 Eleven Mile Rd., 48081
Telephone: (313) 771-9020
City agency
Founded in: 1976
Mary Karshner, Museum
  Curator/Archivist

Number of members: 175
Staff: full time 1
Magazine: *Muskrat Tales*
Major programs: archives, museum,
  school programs, book publishing,
  newsletters/pamphlets, historic
  preservation, photographic
  collections, genealogical services
Period of collections: late 19th-20th
  centuries

ST. IGNACE

Michilimackinac Historical Society
Mail to: P.O. Box 451, 49781
Founded in: 1936
Questionnaire not received

ST. JAMES

Beaver Island Historical Society
Main and Forest Sts., 49782
Telephone: (616) 448-2254/445-2486
Private agency
Founded in: 1957
Gwin Langford, President
Number of members: 254
Staff: part time 1
Major programs: museum, historic
  site(s), markers, book publishing,
  newsletters/pamphlets, exhibits,
  photographic collections
Period of collections: 1783-1918

ST. JOHNS

Clinton County Historical Society
Mail to: P.O. Box 174, 48879
Founded in: 1972
Ford Caesar, President
Number of members: 170
Staff: volunteer 12
Major programs: archives, museum,
  markers, tours/pilgrimages, oral
  history, book publishing,
  photographic collections,
  genealogical services
Period of collections: 1840-present

ST. JOSEPH

**Genealogical Association of
Southwestern Michigan**
P.O. Box 573, 49085
Telephone: (616) 429-7914
Private agency
Founded in: 1971
Lois Wier, President
Number of members: 150
Magazine: *The Pastfinder*
Major programs: genealogical
  services, cemetery records
Period of collections: 1850-present

SANFORD

Sanford Historical Society
N. Saginaw at Smith St.
Telephone: (517) 687-2771
Mail to: P.O. Box 243, 48657
Private agency
Founded in: 1970
Don Marquardt, President
Number of members: 127
Staff: full time 1, volunteer 12
Major programs: library, museum,
  newsletters/pamphlets,
  genealogical services
Period of collections: 1890

SAULT SAINTE MARIE

**Chippewa County Historical
Society, Inc.**
Telephone: (906) 632-6255
County agency
Founded in: 1919
Reeta V. Freeborn, Secretary
Major programs: museum, junior
  history, historic preservation,
  research, exhibits, genealogical
  services
Period of collections: from 1792

**Sault de Ste. Marie Historical
Sites, Inc.**
Johnston and Water Sts.
Telephone: (906) 632-3658
Mail to: P.O. Box 1668, 49783
Private agency
Founded in: 1967
Thomas J. Marse, Chief Administrator
  /Curator
Number of members: 200
Staff: fu:l time 20, part time 5,
  volunteer 15
Major programs: archives,
  manuscripts, museum, historic
  site(s), school programs,
  newsletters/pamphlets, historic
  preservation, research, exhibits,
  audiovisual programs,
  photographic collections
Period of collections: 1880-present

SHEPHERD

Shepherd Area Historical Society
3426 E. Blanchard Rd., 48883
Private agency
Founded in: 1978
Major programs: museum, historic
  site(s), oral history, school
  programs, genealogical services
Period of collections: 1920-1980

SKANEE

Arvon Township Historical Society
Telephone: (906) 524-6934
Mail to: P.O. Box 151, 49962
Founded in: 1972
Questionnaire not received

SOUTHFIELD

**Finnish American Historical
Society of Michigan, Inc.**
19885 Melrose, 48075
Questionnaire not received

SOUTH HAVEN

Lake Michigan Maritime Museum
Dyckman Ave.
Telephone: (616) 637-8078
Mail to: P.O. Box 534, 49090
Private agency
Founded in: 1976
Dorris Akers, Director
Number of members: 500 Staff: full
  time 2, part time 1
Major programs: library, archives,
  museum, tours/pilgrimages, oral
  history, school programs,
  newsletters/pamphlets, historic
  preservation, research, exhibits,
  audiovisual programs, archaeology
  programs, photographic
  collections, boat-building school

Period of collections: 19th & early
20th centuries

SOUTH LYON

**South Lyon Area Historical
Society, Inc.**
300 Dorothy St.
Telephone: (513) 437-9929
Mail to: P.O. Box 263, 48178
Private agency
Founded in: 1975
Greta D. McMahon, President
Number of members: 140
Staff: volunteer 25
Magazine: *Witch's Chatter*
Major programs: museum, markers,
tours/pilgrimages, oral history,
newsletters/pamphlets, historic
preservation, exhibits,
photographic collections
Period of collections: 1890-1950

South Lyon Historical Commission
214 W. Lake St.
Telephone: (313) 437-1735
Mail to: P.O. Box 263, 48178
City agency
Founded in: 1975
Gail Smolarz, Commission Member
Staff: volunteer 7
Major programs: museum, markers,
tours/pilgrimages, oral history,
newsletters/pamphlets, historic
preservation, exhibits,
photographic collections
Period of collections: 1890-1950

STOCKBRIDGE

Dewey Schoolhouse
11501 Territorial Rd.
Telephone: (517) 851-8247
Mail to: 14155 M-52, 49285
Private agency, authorized by
Waterloo Area Historical Society
Founded in: 1963
Helen Hannewald, Director Guide
Staff: volunteer 8
Major programs: museum, historic
site(s), oral history, historic
preservation
Period of collections: 1850-1890

Waterloo Area Historical Society
Telephone: (517) 851-7636
Mail to: P.O. Box 37, 49285
Private agency
Founded in: 1962
Betty A. Turner, Treasurer
Number of members: 255
Staff: part time 3, volunteer 100
Major programs: museum, historic
site(s), tours/pilgrimages, junior
history, oral history, school
programs, historic preservation
Period of collections: 1850s

TRAVERSE CITY

Con Foster Museum
Grandview Parkway
Telephone: (616) 941-2332
Mail to: 400 Boardman Ave., P.O. Box
592, 49685-0592
City agency, authorized by
Department of Public Services
Founded in: 1954
Caroline M. deMauriac, Curator

Staff: full time 1, part time 1,
volunteer 50
Major programs: museum,
newsletters/pamphlets, records
management, exhibits,
photographic collections
Period of collections:
prehistoric-present

Pioneer Study Center
Telephone: (616) 946-3151
Mail to: P.O. Box 1032, 49684
Founded in: 1975
Questionnaire not received

TRENTON

Trenton Historical Commission
St. Joseph at 3rd St.
Telephone: (313) 675-2130
Mail to: 2800 3rd St., 48183
Founded in: 1962
Barbara Walsh, Chair
Staff: volunteer 26
Major programs: museum,
tours/pilgrimages, oral history
Period of collections: 1865-present

TROY

Troy Historical Museum
60 W. Wattles, 48098
Telephone: (313) 524-3570
City agency
Founded in: 1967
Steven J. Mrozek, Museum Curator
Number of members: 300
Staff: full time 1, part time 4,
volunteer 21
Major programs: library, archives,
manuscripts, museum, historic
site(s), oral history, school
programs, book publishing,
newsletters/pamphlets, historic
preservation, research, exhibits,
living history, audiovisual
programs, photographic
collections, genealogical services
Period of collections: 1820-present

Troy Historical Society
60 W. Wattles Rd., 48098
Telephone: (313) 689-9178
Founded in: 1966
Questionnaire not received

VANDALIA

**Cass County Historical
Commission**
P.O. Box 98, 49095
County agency, authorized by board
of commissioners
Founded in: 1973
Marjorie S. Federowski, Secretary
Major programs: library, historic
site(s), markers, tours/pilgrimages,
oral history, school programs,
historic preservation, research,
exhibits, genealogical services
Period of collections: 1800-present

VERMONTVILLE

**Kalamo Township Historical
Society**
8889 Spore Hwy., 49096
Telephone: (517) 726-0408
Questionnaire not received

VICKSBURG

Vicksburg Historical Society
Rt. 1, Box 22-DD, 49097
Telephone: (616) 649-0349
Questionnaire not received

WALLED LAKE

**CTAHS (Commerce Township Area
Historical Society)**
207 Liberty St.
Telephone: (313) 624-2554/624-2309
Mail to: P.O. Box 264, 48088
Private agency
Founded in: 1972
Ruth Tuttle, President
Number of members: 85
Major programs: archives, museum,
historic site(s), markers,
tours/pilgrimages, oral history,
school programs, book publishing,
newsletters/pamphlets, historic
preservation, research, exhibits,
audiovisual programs, archaeology
programs, photographic
collections, genealogical services
Period of collections: 1825-present

WAYLAND

**Wayland Area Tree Tracers
Genealogical Society**
129 Cedar St., 49348
Private agency
Founded in: 1975
Donna L. Benedict, Corresponding
Secretary
Number of members: 16
Staff: volunteer 3
Major programs: library, manuscripts,
research, photographic
collections, genealogical services
Period of collections: 1857-present

WAYNE

Wayne Historical Commission
1 Town Square, 48184
Telephone: (313) 722-0113
Founded in: 1963
Staff: part time 2, volunteer 1
Major programs: archives, museum
Period of collections: 1820-present

Wayne Historical Society
1 Town Square, 48184
Telephone: (313) 722-0113
Founded in: 1956
Number of members: 45
Major programs: educational
programs

WEST BRANCH

**Ogemaw Genealogical and
Historical Society**
West Branch Public Library, 119 N.
4th St., 48611
Founded in: 1978
Mary Ellen Good, President
Number of members: 20
Major programs: research,
photographic collections,
genealogical services
Period of collections: 1870s-present

WESTLAND

Marine Historical Society of Detroit
29825 Joy Rd., 48185

Telephone: (313) 421-6130
Private agency
Founded in: 1945
Wayne Garrett, President
Number of members: 1,000
Staff: volunteer 12
Magazine: *The Marine Historian*
Major programs: archives,
  manuscripts, museum, book
  publishing, newsletters/pamphlets,
  research, photographic collections
Period of collections: 1860-present

WHITE CLOUD

**Newaygo County Society of History
and Genealogy**
1038 W. Wilcox
Telephone: (616) 689-6631
Mail to: P.O. Box 68, 49349
Private agency
Founded in: 1968
Barbara J. Billerbeck, President
Number of members: 300
Staff: volunteer 6
Major programs: library, archives,
  manuscripts, museum, school
  programs, book publishing,
  newsletters/pamphlets, records
  management, research,
  audiovisual programs,
  photographic collections,
  genealogical services
Period of collections: 1870-1940

WYANDOTTE

Wyandotte Museum
2610 Biddle Ave., 48192
Telephone: (313) 283-0818
City agency
Founded in: 1958, authorized by
  Wyandotte Cultural and Historical
  Commission
Chey L. Hunt, Director
Number of members: 600
Staff: full time 1, part time 2,
  volunteer 20
Major programs: archives, museum,
  historic site(s), tours/pilgrimages,
  oral history, school programs, book
  publishing, newsletters/pamphlets,
  historic preservation, records
  management, research, exhibits,
  photographic collections,
  genealogical services
Period of collections: 19th century

WYOMING

**Grand Valley Cap "M" Ballers
Muzzleloading Gun Club**
559 Oakcrest, SW, 49509
Telephone: (616) 538-5394
Private agency
Founded in: 1956
Jum Galiger, President
Number of members: 105
Magazine: *Smoke Pole*
Major programs: oral history, schcol
  programs, newsletters/pamphlets,
  exhibits, living history
Period of collections: early 1700s-late
  1800s

**Wyoming Historical and Cultural
Commission**
1155-28th St., SW, 49509
Telephone: (616) 534-7671

Founded in: 1964
Questionnaire not received

YPSILANTI

Ypsilanti Historical Society
220 N. Huron St., 48197
Telephone: (313) 482-4990
City agency
Founded in: 1960
Foster Fletcher, Archivist
Number of members: 325
Staff: part time 2, volunteer 64
Magazine: *Ypsilanti Gleanings-Past
  Scenes and Old Times*
Major programs: arhives, museum,
  newsletters/pamphlets
Period of collections: 1809-present

ZEELAND

Zeeland Historical Society
37 E. Main Ave.
Telephone: (616) 772-4079
Mail to: P.O. Box 165, 49464
Private agency
Founded in: 1974
Al Johnson, President
Number of members: 343
Staff: volunteer 12
Major programs: museum, oral
  history, educational programs,
  historic preservation
Period of collections: 1870-1920

MINNESOTA

ADA

Norman County Historical Area
404 W. 5th Ave., 56510
Telephone: (218) 784-4911
County agency
Founded in: 1949
Lenora I. Johnson, Museum Director
Number of members: 300
Staff: part time 2, volunteer 20
Major programs: library, museum,
  oral history, historic preservation,
  records management, exhibits,
  photographic collections
Period of collections: 1865-1978

ALBERT LEA

**Freeborn County Genealogical
Society**
Mail to: P.O. Box 403, 56007
Private agency
Founded in: 1979
Love Cruikshank, President
Number of members: 50
Magazine: *Freeborn County Tracer*
Major programs: library, historic
  preservation, research,
  genealogical services
Period of collections: 1856-present

Freeborn County Historical Society
County Fairgrounds, N. Bridge Ave.
Telephone: (507) 373-8003
Mail to: P.O. Box 105, 56007
Founded in: 1948
Questionnaire not received

ALDEN

Community Historical Society
117 N. Broadway, 56009
Private agency
Founded in: 1972
Ruben F. Schmidt, President
Number of members: 100
Staff: volunteer 15
Major programs: museum
Period of collections: 1880s-present

ALEXANDRIA

**Douglas County Genealogical
Society**
P.O. Box 505, 56308
Telephone: (612) 763-3896
Private agency
Founded in: 1981
Ginny Swartz, Editor
number of members: 25
Staff: volunteer 6
Major programs: library,
  newsletters/pamphlets,
  genealogical services
Period of collections: 1700-1850

Douglas County Historical Society
206 N. Broadway
Telephone: (612) 762-0305
Mail to: P.O. Box 805, 56308
County agency
Founded in: 1976
Kerry T. Nelson, Director
Number of members: 300
Staff: full time 3, part time 2
Major programs: oral history, school
  programs, book publishing,
  newsletters/pamphlets, research,
  living history, audiovisual
  programs, photographic
  collections, field services
Period of collections: 1890-present

Kensington Runestone Museum
206 Broadway
Telephone: (612) 763-3161
Mail to: P.O. Box 517, 56308
Private agency
Founded in: 1960
James R. Clayton, Executive
  Secretary
Staff: full time 2, part time 2
Major programs: archives, museum,
  tours/pilgrimages, school
  programs, research, exhibits,
  photographic collections
Period of collections: 1800s-present

ANNANDALE

Minnesota Pioneer Park
Hwy. 55, P.O. Box 219, 55302
Telephone: (612) 274-8489
Private agency
Founded in: 1972
Nobel Shadduck, Director
Number of members: 125
Staff: full time 3, volunteer 30
Major programs: library, museum,
  historic site(s), tours/pilgrimages,
  school programs, exhibits,
  audiovisual programs, archaeology
  programs
Period of collections: 1800s

ANOKA

Anoka County Genealogical Society
1900 3rd Ave., S, 55303
County agency, authorized by Anoka County Historical Society
Lucille Elrite, President
Number of members: 60
Major programs: library, newsletters/pamphlets, research
Period of collections: 1850s-present

Anoka County Historical Society
1900 3rd Ave., S, 55303
Telephone: (612) 421-0600
County agency, authorized by Anoka County Commissioners
Founded in: 1934
Pat Schwappach, Museum Director
Number of members: 180
Staff: full time 1, part time 3, volunteer 1
Magazine: *Colonial Hall Crier Newsletter*
Major programs: archives, museum, historic site(s), tours/pilgrimages, oral history, historic preservation, research, exhibits, photographic collections, genealogical services
Period of collections: 1850s-present

ASKOU

Pine County Historical Society
55704
County agency, authorized by board of commissioners
Founded in: 1948
Ronald L. Nelson, President
Number of members: 220
Staff: part time 2, volunteer 10
Magazine: *Pine Aire News*
Major programs: archives, museum, historic sites preservation, markers, tours/pilgrimages, newsletters/pamphlets
Period of collections: 1880-1930

AUSTIN

Mower County Historical Society
Fairgrounds, 12th St. SW
Telephone: (507) 433-1868
Mail to: P.O. Box 426, 55912
Founded in: 1947
Questionnaire not received

BAGLEY

Clearwater County Historical Society
112 2nd Ave., 56621
Telephone: (218) 694-6574
Founded in: 1969
Arnold Higdem, President
Number of members: 115
Staff: part time 4
Major programs: library, archives, museum, historic sites preservation, markers, book publishing
Period of collections: 1865-present

BAUDETTE

Lake of the Woods Historical Society
County Museum, 56623
Telephone: (218) 634-1200

Private agency
Founded in: 1965
Everett Helmstetter, President
Number of members: 84
Staff: full time 1, volunteer 4
Major programs: museum, oral history, school programs, book publishing, cemetery documentation
Period of collections: 1900-1950

BECKER

Sherburne County Historical Society
Telephone: (612) 261-4550
Founded in: 1970
Questionnaire not received

BEMIDJI

Beltrami County Historical Society
3rd St. and Bemidji Ave.
Mail to: P.O. Box 683, 56601
Private agency
Founded in: 1949
Betty Rossi, President
Number of members: 150
Staff: volunteer 1
Major programs: manuscripts, museum, historic site(s), oral history, school programs, book publishing, newsletters/pamphlets, historic preservation, records management, exhibits, photographic collections
Period of collections: early 1900s

BENSON

Swift County Historical Society
W. Hwy. 12
Mail to: Rt. 2, Box 4D1, 56215
Founded in: 1929
Mildred Torgerson, Curator
Number of members: 200
Staff: full time 1
Major programs: museum
Period of collections: 1865-present

BERTHA

Bertha Historical Society
Telephone: (218) 924-4095
Mail to: P.O. Box 307, 56437
Founded in: 1970
Mrs. Ray Foster, President
Number of members: 50
Staff: volunteer 8
Major programs: museum
Period of collections: 1865-1918

BLUE EARTH

Faribault County Historical Society
405 E. 6th, 56013
Telephone: (507) 526-5421
Private agency
Founded in: 1948
Herbert Hansen, President
Number of members: 300
Staff: volunteer 12
Major programs: museum, newsletters/pamphlets, historic preservation, photographic collections
Period of collections: 1865-1945

BRAINERD

Crow Wing County Historical Society
Crow Wing County Courthouse, 320 Laurel St., 56401
Telephone: (218) 829-3268
Mail to: P.O. Box 722, 56401
Gail M. Christensen, Museum Director
Number of members: 600
Staff: full time 1, volunteer 8
Major programs: archives, museum, newsletters/pamphlets, exhibits
Period of collections: 1865-1950

Historic Heartland Association Inc.
P.O. Box 1, 56401
Telephone: (218) 963-2218/377-7294
Founded in: 1970
Questionnaire not received

BRECKENRIDGE

Wilkin County Historical Society
704 Nebraska Ave. 56520
Telephone: (218) 630-5841
Mail to: Box 212
Founded in: 1965
Oscar J. Karlgaard, President
Number of members: 500
Staff: volunteer 6
Major programs: museum, books
Period of collections: 1865-present

BROOKLYN CENTER

Brooklyn Historical Society
3824 58th Ave., N, 55429
Telephone: (612) 537-2118
Private agency
Founded in: 1970
Barbara Sexton, Secretary
Number of members: 50
Staff: volunteer 10
Major programs: museum, historic sites preservation, oral history, book publishing, newsletters/pamphlets
Period of collections: 1865-present

BROWNS VALLEY

Browns Valley Historical Society
P.O. Box 334, 56219
Telephone: (612) 695-2110
Founded in: 1964
Staff: part time 2
Major programs: archives, museum, historic site, markers, book publishing, historic preservation
Period of collections: 1870-1940

BUFFALO

Wright County Historical Society
101 Lake Blvd., NW, 55313
Telephone: (612) 682-3900, ext. 191/291
Private agency
Founded in: 1946
Marion K. Jameson, Historian
Number of members: 524
Staff: full time 2, part time 4
Major programs: library, archives, museum, historic site, markers, tours, oral history, educational programs, book publishing, newsletters/pamphlets, historic

preservation, photograph
collections
Period of collections: 1855-present

BUFFALO LAKE

Renville County Historical Society
55314
Founded in: 1942
Questionnaire not received

BUHL

Range Genealogical Society, Inc.
P.O. Box 726, 55713
Telephone: (218) 258-3676
Private agency
Founded in: 1968
Gary Plombon, President
Number of members: 30
Staff: volunteer 15
Major programs: library,
newsletters/pamphlets, cemetery
records
Period of collections: early
1700s-early 1900s

BUTTERFIELD

**Butterfield Threshermen's
Association**
Telephone: (507) 956-2241
Private agency
Founded in: 1966
Art Peek, President
Major programs: museum
Period of collections: 1900-present

CAMBRIDGE

Isanti County Historical Society
P.O. Box 525, 55008
Telephone: (612) 396-3957
County agency, authorized by Isanti
County Board of Commissioners
Founded in: 1965
Marilyn McGriff, Director
Number of members: 400
Staff: part time 1, volunteer 2
Major programs: school programs,
newsletters/pamphlets, records
management, living history,
audiovisual programs,
photographic collections
Period of collections: 1860-1930

CARLTON

Carlton County Historical Society
Telephone: (218) 384-3271
Mail to: P.O. Box 245, 55718
Founded in: 1949
Henry E. Walter, President
Number of members: 30
Staff: part time 1
Major programs: educational
programs
Period of collections: 1865-present

CARVER

Carver-on-the-Minnesota, Inc.
Telephone: (612) 448-3436
Mail to: P.O. Box 135, 55315
Founded in: 1969
Questionnaire not received

CASS LAKE

Old Logging Artifacts Museum
222 Cedar Ave.

Telephone: (218) 335-6778
Mail to: P.O. Box 85, 56633
Founded in: 1973
Lyle W. Chisholm, Chair
Staff: volunteer 10
Major programs: museum
Period of collections: 1918-present

CENTER CITY

Center City Historical Society
55012
Telephone: (612) 257-6818
Founded in: 1981
Lloyd Hackl, President
Number of members: 46
Staff: volunteer 10
Major programs: library, archives,
historic site(s), markers,
tours/pilgrimages, oral history,
school programs,
newsletters/pamphlets, historic
preservation, research, exhibits,
photographic collections,
genealogical services
Period of collections: from 1851

Chisago County Historical Society
P.O. Box 366, 55012
County agency
Founded in: 1951
Judith Dupree, Executive Coordinator
Number of members: 130
Staff: full time 1
Major programs: library, museum,
markers, tours/pilgrimages,
newsletters/pamphlets,
genealogical services
Period of collections: 1850-present

CHATFIELD

Chatfield Historical Society
314 S. Main St., 55923
Founded in: 1978
Questionnaire not received

CHISHOLM

**Iron Range Interpretative
Center—Iron Range Research
Center**
P.O. Box 392, 55719
State agency, authorized by Iron
Range Resources and
Rehabilitation Board
Founded in: 1971
Robert T. Scott, Director
Number of members: 1,200
Staff: full time 22, part time 10,
volunteer 72
Major programs: library, archives,
manuscripts, museum, historic
site(s), oral history, school
programs, newsletters/pamphlets,
records management, research,
exhibits, audiovisual programs,
photographic collections,
genealogical services

CLOQUET

Carlton County Historical Society
Garfield Community Center, 14th St.
and Carlton Ave.
Telephone: (218) 879-1938
Private agency
Founded in: 1949
Barbara Sommer, Director
Number of members: 125

Staff: part time 3, volunteer 10
Magazine: *Society News*
Major programs: library, archives,
museum, oral history, school
programs, newsletters/pamphlets,
exhibits, photographic collections
Period of collections: 1880s-present

COKATO

Cokato Historical Society
95 W. 4th St., 55321
Telephone: (612) 286-2427
City agency
Founded in: 1974
C.E. Mitchell, President
Number of members: 105
Staff: part time 1, volunteer 45
Major programs: museum, oral
history, educational programs,
tours/pilgrimages
Period of collections: 1865-present

COLUMBIA

Boone County Historical Society
802 S. Edgewood Ave.
Telephone: (314) 449-5876
Private agency
Founded in: 1965
Bill Thomas Crawford, President
Number of members: 250
Staff: volunteer 15
Major programs: museum, historic
site(s), markers, tours/pilgrimages,
book publishing,
newsletters/pamphlets, historic
preservation, genealogical
services
Period of collections: 1835-present

COON RAPIDS

**Coon Rapids Historical
Commission**
1313 Coon Rapids Blvd., 55433
Telephone: (612) 755-2880
Founded in: 1974
Gaylord Aldinger, Staff Liaison
Major programs: oral history, book
publishing
Period of collections: 1850-present

CROOKSTON

Polk County Historical Society
E. Robert St. and U.S. Hwy. 2
Telephone: (218) 281-1038
Mail to: P.O. Box 214, 56716
Private agency
Founded in: 1922
Henry Greduig, President
Number of members: 500
Staff: full time 1, part time 2
Major programs: museum,
newsletters/pamphlets, historic
preservation, exhibits
Period of collections: 1880-1920

CROSBY

Cuyuna Range Historical Society
101 1st St., NW
Telephone: (218) 546-5345
Mail to: P.O. Box 128, 56441
Private agency
Founded in: 1968
Elsie Mooers, President
Number of members: 125
Staff: part time 2, volunteer 2

Major programs: museum, historic
site(s), historic preservation,
photographic collections
Period of collections: 1890-1960

DETROIT LAKES

Becker County Historical Society
Courthouse, 915 Lake Ave., 56501
Telephone: (218) 847-2938
Private agency
Founded in: 1885
Nash Perrine, President
Staff: full time 2, part time 1
Major programs: library, archives,
museum, tours/pilgrimages, junior
history, oral history, school
programs, newsletters/pamphlets,
exhibits, living history,
photographic collections,
genealogical services
Period of collections: 1865-present

DULUTH

A.M. Chisholm Museum
506 W. Michigan St., 55802
Telephone: (218) 722-8563
Private agency
Founded in: 1930
Bonnie A. Cusick, Executive Director
Number of members: 420
Staff: full time 3, part time 1,
volunteer 15
Major programs: museum, school
programs, exhibits
Period of collections: 1850-present

Canal Park Marine Museum
Canal Park, 55802
Telephone: (218) 727-2497
Federal agency, authorized by U.S.
Army Corps of Engineers
Founded in: 1973
C. Patrick Labadie, Curator
Staff: full time 3, part time 3
Magazine: *Nor'Easter*
Major programs: library, museum,
school programs,
newsletters/pamphlets, exhibits,
audiovisual programs,
photographic collections
Period of collections: 1870-present

Glensheen
3300 London Rd., 55804
Telephone: (218) 724-8864
State agency, authorized by
University of Minnesota
Founded in: 1979
Michael J. Lane, Director
Number of members: 4
Staff: full time 6, part time 15,
volunteer 250
Magazine: *Glensheen Gleanings*
Major programs: museum, historic
site(s), tours/pilgrimages, school
programs, newsletters/pamphlets,
historic preservation, research,
exhibits, audiovisual programs
Period of collections: 1900-1920

Lake Superior Museum of
Transportation
506 W. Michigan St., 55802
Telephone: (218) 727-0687/722-8011
Private agency
Founded in: 1973
Lawrence Sommer, Director
Staff: full time 1, part time 6

Major programs: library, archives,
museum, historic site(s), tours,
school programs,
newsletters/pamphlets, historic
preservation, exhibits,
photographic collections
Period of collections: 1861-present

Northeast Minnesota Historical
Center
Library 375, University of Minnesota,
55812
Telephone: (218) 726-8526
Founded in: 1976
Pat Maus, Administrator/Curator of
Manuscripts
Staff: full time 1
Major programs: library, archives,
manuscripts, oral history
Period of collections: 20th century

Nordic Heritage Association, Inc.
Room 5, Duluth National Bank Bldg.,
55806
Telephone: (218) 722-4079
Founded in: 1974
Questionnaire not received

St. Louis County Historical Society
506 W. Michigan St., 55802
Telephone: (218) 722-8011
County agency
Founded in: 1922
Lawrence J. Sommer, Director
Number of members: 800
Staff: full time 7, part time 2
Period of collections: 19th
century-present

EDINA

Edina Heritage Preservation Board
4801 W. 50th St., 55424
Telephone: (612) 927-8861
City agency
Founded in: 1976
Harold Sand, Planner
Staff: part time 1

Major programs: historic site(s),
markers, tours/pilgrimages, book
publishing, historic preservation

Edina Historical Society
4801 W. 50th St., 55424
Telephone: (612) 927-8861
Founded in: 1969
Donna Skagerberg, President
Number of members: 150
Staff: volunteer 25
Major programs: library, archives,
manuscripts, museum, historic site,
tours/pilgrimages, oral history,
educational programs,
newsletters/pamphlets, historic
preservation
Period of collections: 1890-1940

ELBOW LAKE

Grant County Historical Society
56531
Telephone: (218) 685-4864
Founded in: 1944
George M. Shervey, President
Number of members: 386
Staff: full time 1, part time 5,
volunteer 4
Major programs: museum, historic
sites preservation, markers, oral
history, educational programs
Period of collections: 1918-present

ELY

Ely-Winton Historical Society
417 E. Chapman St., 55731
Telephone: (218) 365-4537
Founded in: 1962
Number of members: 30
Major programs: archives, museum
Period of collections: 1900

Vermilion Interpretive Center
1900 E. Camp, 55731
Telephone: (218) 365-3256
Town agency, authorized by
Ely-Winton Historical Society

The St. Louis County Heritage and Arts Center, home of the St. Louis County Historical Society in Duluth.—Photograph by Bruce Ojard

Founded in: 1982
Kathy Kainz, Director
Number of members: 25
Staff: full time 1
Major programs: archives,
manuscripts, museum, oral history,
research, exhibits, audiovisual
programs
Period of collections: 1900s

ELYSIAN

**LeSueur County Historical Society
and Museum**
4th and Frank Sts., 56028
Telephone: (507) 362-8350/267-4620
County agency
Founded in: 1962
James E. Hruska, Director
Number of members: 475
Staff: part time 6
Magazine: *History Abounds*
Major programs: museum,
newsletters/pamphlets, exhibits,
genealogical services
Period of collections: 1885-present

ESKO

Esko Historical Society
Hwy. 61, W
Telephone: (218) 879-4400
Mail to: c/o Correspondent, 5
Elizabeth Ave., 55733
Private agency
Founded in: 1953
Ray Mattinen, Correspondent
Number of members: 36
Staff: volunteer 15
Major programs: museum, historic
preservation, exhibits
Period of collections: 1878-1900

EXCELSIOR

**Excelsior-Lake Minnetonka
Historical Society**
Village Hall, 3rd St.
Telephone: (612) 474-5880
Mail to: P.O. Box 305, 55331
Founded in: 1972
Maggie Cassidy, President
Number of members: 200
Staff: volunteer 21
Magazine: *ELMHS News*
Major programs: library, archives,
manuscripts, museum, historic
sites preservation, oral history,
educational programs, books,
newsletters/pamphlets
Period of collections: 1850s-present

FAIRMONT

**Martin County Historical
Society, Inc.**
304 E. Blue Earth Ave., 56031
Telephone: (507) 235-5178
Private agency
Founded in: 1929
Marwin Zenk, President
Number of members: 991
Staff: part time 1
Major programs: library, museum,
historic site(s), historic
preservation, records
management, exhibits,
photographic collections,
genealogical services
Period of collections: 1850-present

FARIBAULT

**Rice County Historical Society and
Museum**
1814 2nd Ave., NW, 55021
Founded in: 1926
Susan McKenna, Director
Number of members: 700
Staff: full time 1, volunteer 100
Magazine: *Rice County Historian*
Major programs: library, manuscripts,
museum, historic site(s),
tours/pilgrimages, junior history,
oral history, book publishing,
newsletters/pamphlets, historic
preservation, research, exhibits,
audiovisual programs, archaeology
programs, photographic
collections, genealogical services
Period of collections: 1870-1940

FALCON HEIGHTS

Gibbs Farm Museum
2097 W. Larpenteur Ave., 55113
Telephone: (612) 646-8629
Authorized by Ramsey County
Historical Society
Founded in: 1949
Major programs: museum, historic
site(s), tours, exhibits, living history
Period of collections: 1870s-1910

FERGUS FALLS

Heritage Preservation Commission
1110 W. Lincoln
Telephone: (218) 739-3117
Mail to: 317 N. Cascade, 56537
City agency
Founded in: 1970
Marjorie Barton, Chair
Staff: volunteer 7
Major programs: library, historic
site(s), tours/pilgrimages, school
programs, book publishing, historic
preservation, research, audiovisual
programs, photographic
collections
Period of collections: 1870-1950

**Minnesota Finnish-American
Historical Society**
Rt. 2, Box 305, 56537
Telephone: (218) 739-9013
Private agency
Founded in: 1942
Lester C. Ristinen, President
Number of members: 880
Staff: volunteer 5
Magazine: *Seuranlehti*
Major programs: archives, museum,
historic site(s), markers, oral
history, book publishing, historic
preservation
Period of collections: 1900-present

Otter Tail County Historical Society
1110 Lincoln Ave., W, 56537
Telephone: (218) 736-6038
Private agency
Founded in: 1927
Number of members: 1,480
Staff: full time 3, part time 3,
volunteer 125
Magazine: *Otter Tail Record*
Major programs: library, archives,
manuscripts, museum, markers,
oral history, school programs, book
publishing, newsletters/pamphlets,

records management, research,
exhibits, photographic collections,
genealogical services
Period of collections: 1865-present

FULDA

Fulda Heritage Society
Telephone: (507) 425-2583
Mail to: P.O. Box 275, 56131
Private agency
Founded in: 1975
Howard Anderson, President
Number of members: 70
Staff: volunteer 20
Major programs: museum, historic
site(s), exhibits
Period of collections: 1900-present

GILBERT

Iron Range Historical Society
P.O. Box 786, 55741
Founded in: 1973
Jean Stimac, Administrator
Number of members: 375
Staff: full time 1, part time 1,
volunteer 3
Magazine: *Range History*
Major programs: library, archives,
manuscripts, historic site(s), oral
history, school programs, book
publishing, newsletters/pamphlets,
historic preservation, records
management, research, exhibits,
audiovisual programs,
photographic collections,
genealogical services, field
services
Period of collections: late
1800s-present

GLENWOOD

**Pope County Historical Society and
Museum**
Hwy. 104, Rt. 2, 56334
Telephone: (612) 634-3293
County agency
Founded in: 1930
Judy Anderson, Treasurer
Staff: full time 2, part time 2
Major programs: museum,
newsletters/pamphlets, historic
preservation, photographic
collections, genealogical services
Period of collections: 1800-present

GOODRIDGE

**Goodridge Area Historical
Society, Inc.**
R.R. 1, 56725
Telephone: (218) 378-4380
Private agency
Founded in: 1977
Norma Hanson, President
Number of members: 55
Staff: volunteer 12
Major programs: archives,
manuscripts, museum, historic
site(s), tours/pilgrimages, oral
history, school programs,
newsletters/pamphlets, historic
preservation, records
management, research, exhibits,
living history, photographic
collections
Period of collections: 1900-present

GRAND MARAIS

Cook County Historical Society
12 S. Broadway
Telephone: (218) 387-1678
Mail to: P.O. Box 681, 55604
Founded in: 1931
Number of members: 500
Staff: full time 1, part time 1,
  volunteer 5
Major programs: library, museum,
  historic site, markers, oral history,
  book publishing,
  newsletters/pamphlets
Period of collections: 1870-1940

GRAND RAPIDS

Itasca County Historical Society
Telephone: (218) 326-6431
Mail to: P.O. Box 664, 55744
Private agency
Founded in: 1942
Dorman Lehman, Executive Director
Number of members: 400
Staff: full time 2, part time 12
Major programs: library, museum,
  markers, junior history, oral history,
  book publishing,
  newsletters/pamphlets, historic
  preservation, exhibits,
  photographic collections
Period of collections: 1880-present

GRANITE FALLS

**City of Granite Falls—Andrew
  Volstead House**
885 Prentice, 56241
Telephone: (612) 564-3011
City agency
Founded in: 1879
Richard Voller, City Manager
Staff: full time 30, part time 20,
  volunteer 10
Major programs: library, museum
Period of collections: 1910-1925

**Hardanger Fiddle Association of
  America**
Rt. 3, Box 86, 56241
Telephone: (612) 564-3408
Private agency
Founded in: 1983
Thorwald O. Quale, President
Number of members: 170
Staff: volunteer 6
Magazine: *Sound Post*
Major programs: archives, book
  publishing, newsletters/pamphlets,
  historic preservation, research,
  exhibits, audiovisual programs,
  photographic collections
Period of collections: 1850-present

Valdres Samband
Rt. 3, Box 86, 56241
Telephone: (612) 564-3408
Private agency
Founded in: 1899
Carl T. Narvestad, Editor
Number of members: 1,400
Magazine: *Budstikken*
Major programs: archives,
  tours/pilgrimages, book publishing,
  newsletters/pamphlets, research,
  exhibits, genealogical services,
  ethnic crafts
Period of collections: 1900s

**Yellow Medicine County Historical
  Society Museum**
Rt. 2
Telephone: (612) 564-4479
Mail to: R.R. 1, Box 98-D, 56241
Private agency
Founded in: 1952
Zula D. Aakre, Museum Curator
Number of members: 113
Staff: full time 3, part time 1,
  volunteer 15
Major programs: library, museum,
  markers, junior history, oral history,
  book publishing,
  newsletters/pamphlets, historic
  preservation, exhibits, living
  history, genealogical services
Period of collections: 1865-present

HAWLEY

**Western Minnesota Steam
  Threshers Reunion, Inc.**
Telephone: (218) 937-5316
Mail to: P.O. Box 632, 56549
Private agency
Founded in: 1954
Lyle K. Nelson, Treasurer
Number of members: 600
Staff: volunteer 200
Major programs: historic
  preservation, exhibits, steam
  power history
Period of collections: early 1900s

HENDERSON

**Sibley County Historical
  Society, Inc.**
700 Main St., 56044
Founded in: 1940
Questionnaire not received

HENDRICKS

Lincoln County Historical Society
610 W. Elm, 56136
Telephone: (507) 275-3537
Founded in: 1969
Questionnaire not received

HIBBING

Hibbing Historical Society
21st St. and 4th Ave., E, 55746
Telephone: (218) 262-3486
Private agency, authorized by St.
  Louis County Historical Society
Founded in: 1975
Patricia Mestek, Director/Curator
Number of members: 370
Staff: part time 3, volunteer 12
Major programs: archives,
  manuscripts, museum, historic
  site(s), markers, tours, oral history,
  book publishing,
  newsletters/pamphlets, historic
  preservation, exhibits, audiovisual
  programs, photographic
  collections
Period of collections: 1893-present

HINCKLEY

Hinckley Fire Museum
Old Hwy. 61, 55037
Telephone: (612) 384-7338
Founded in: 1976
Staff: full time 2, part time 2,
  volunteer 10

Magazine: *Telegraph*
Major programs: museum, historic
  sites preservation
Period of collections: 1865-1918

HOPKINS

Hopkins Historical Society
33 14th Ave., N
Telephone: (612) 935-8474
Mail to: 1010 1st St., S, 55343
Private agency
Founded in: 1972
Alfred G. Larson, President
Number of members: 135
Staff: volunteer 1
Major programs: library, manuscripts,
  oral history, school programs,
  exhibits, photographic collections,
  genealogical services
Period of collections: 1852-present

HUTCHINSON

McLeod County Historical Society
Telephone: (612) 587-2109
Mail to: P.O. Box 399, 55350
Private agency
Founded in: 1940
Patsy Prieve, Administrator
Number of members: 475
Staff: full time 1, part time 1,
  volunteer 15
Major programs: museum,
  tours/pilgrimages, oral history,
  newsletters/pamphlets
Period of collections: 1900s

INTERNATIONAL FALLS

**Koochiching County Historical
  Society**
216 6th Ave., Smoky Bear Park
Telephone: (218) 283-4316
Mail to: P.O. Box 1147, 56649
Private agency
Founded in: 1958
Mary Hilke, Curator
Number of members: 636
Staff: part time 4
Major programs: archives,
  manuscripts, museum,
  tours/pilgrimages, oral history,
  school programs, book publishing,
  newsletters/pamphlets, historic
  preservation, research, exhibits,
  audiovisual programs,
  photographic collections,
  genealogical services
Period of collections: 1890-present

ISABELLA

**Historical Committee of the
  Isabella Community Council**
P.O. Box 500, 55607
Telephone: (218) 323-7738
Founded in: 1976
Questionnaire not received

ISLE

Mille Lacs Lake Historical Society
Main St.
Mail to: P.O. Box 42, 56342
Private agency
Founded in: 1983
Questionnaire not received

LAKE BRONSON

Kittson County Historical Society
Telephone: (218) 754-4100
Mail to: P.O. Box 98, 56734
Founded in: 1971
Darlene Perry, Director
Number of members: 200
Staff: full time 1, part time 1
Major programs: library, manuscripts, museum, book publishing, exhibits, audiovisual programs
Period of collections: 1880-present

LAKE CITY

Wabasha County Historical Society
Rt. 3, Box 25, 55041
Telephone: (612) 345-2647
Private agency
Founded in: 1965
Lester A. Howatt, President
Staff: part time 1, volunteer 60
Major programs: museum
Period of collections: 1860-1950

LAKEFIELD

Jackson County Historical Society
307 Hwy. 86, 56150
Telephone: (507) 662-5505
Mail to: P.O. Box 132, Jackson, 56143
Founded in: 1931
Number of members: 270
Staff: part time 1, volunteer 15
Magazine: *Historical Society Notes*
Major programs: library, manuscripts, museum
Period of collections: 1865-present

LANESBORO

Lanesboro Historical Preservation Association
105 Parkway, S
Mail to: P.O. Box 345, 55949
City agency
Founded in: 1981
Ted Bell, Secretary
Number of members: 432
Staff: volunteer 12
Major programs: museum, historic site(s), tours/pilgrimages, historic preservation, exhibits, photographic collections, interpretive center
Period of collections: 1856-1956

LESUEUR

LeSueur Historians
N. 2nd St., 56057
Private agency
Founded in: 1972
Helen Meyer, Chair
Number of members: 16
Staff: part time 1
Major programs: museum
Period of collections: 1890-present

LITCHFIELD

GAR (Grand Army of the Republic) Hall—Meeker County Museum
308 N. Marshall, 55355
Telephone: (612) 693-8911
Private agency
Founded in: 1948
Velda P. Yordi, Curator
Number of members: 400

Staff: part time 1
Major programs: museum, historic site(s), newsletters/pamphlets, genealogical services
Period of collections: 1860-present

LITTLE CANADA

Historical Society of Little Canada
2443 Morrison Ave., St. Paul, 55117
Telephone: (612) 484-9739
Town agency
Johanna Gallagher, Liaison
Number of members: 54
Staff: volunteer 4
Major programs: historic site(s), markers, school programs, research, living history, photographic collections
Period of collections: 1848-1930

LITTLE FALLS

Lindbergh Historic Site—Lindbergh State Park
Rt. 3, Box 245, Lindbergh Dr., 56345
Telephone: (612) 632-3154
State agency, authorized by Minnesota Historical Society
Founded in: 1930
Charles A. Stone, Manager
Staff: full time 1, part time 9
Major programs: library, museum, historic site(s), tours/pilgrimages, oral history, school programs, historic preservation, research, exhibits, audiovisual programs, photographic collections
Period of collections: 1859-present

Morrison County Historical Society
Lindbergh Dr.
Telephone: (612) 632-4007
Mail to: P.O. Box 239, 56345
Private agency
Founded in: 1936
Jan Warner, Museum Director
Number of members: 170
Staff: volunteer 16
Major programs: archives, museum, newsletters/pamphlets, historic preservation, exhibits, archaeology programs
Period of collections: 1900s-present

LONG LAKE

Western Hennepin County Pioneer Association
Hwy. 12
Mail to: 235 N. Lakeview, 55356
Telephone: (612) 473-6557
Founded in: 1907
Roger Avery Stubbs, Curator
Number of members: 500
Staff: part time 20, volunteer 20
Major programs: library, archives, manuscripts, museum, newsletters/pamphlets
Period of collections: 1850-present

LONG PRAIRIE

Todd County Historical Society, Inc.
215 1st Ave., S, 56347
Telephone: (612) 732-6181, ext. 269
Private agency
Founded in: 1928
Morrie A. Olson, Curator

Number of members: 414
Staff: part time 1, volunteer 20
Major programs: museum, historic preservation, research, exhibits, photographic collections
Period of collections: 1783-present

MADELIA

Watonwan County Historical Society
423 Dill Ave., SW
Telephone: (507) 642-3247
Mail to: P.O. Box 126, 56062
County agency
Founded in: 1935
Mrs. Alton Anderson, Executive Secretary
Number of members: 900
Staff: full time 1, part time 1, volunteer 30
Major programs: library, archives, manuscripts, museum, markers, tours/pilgrimages, exhibits
Period of collections: 1865-1918

MADISON

Lac qui Parle County Historical Society
S. Hwy. 75
Telephone: (612) 598-7678
Mail to: President, P.O. Box 124, 56256
Private agency
Founded in: 1948
Jeanette Breberg, Curator
Number of members: 98
Staff: full time 1, part time 1, volunteer 20
Major programs: library, museum, exhibits, field services
Period of collections: 1880-1920

MAHNOMEN

Mahnomen County Historical Society
Courthouse, 56557
Telephone: (218) 935-2175
County agency
Founded in: 1981
Joseph Vold, President
Number of members: 80
Staff: full time 1
Major programs: museum, oral history, historic preservation, living history
Period of collections: 1920-1940

MANKATO

Bethany Lutheran Theological Seminary
447 N. Division, 56001
Telephone: (507) 625-2977
Private agency, authorized under Evangelical Lutheran Synod
Founded in: 1946
Wilhelm W. Petersen, President
Staff: full time 3, part time 5
Magazine: *Lutheran Synod Quarterly*
Major programs: library, archives, historic preservation, theological programs
Period of collections: 1500-present

Blue Earth County Historical Society
606 S. Broad St., 56001

Telephone: (507) 345-4154
Private agency
Founded in: 1916
Denise A. Hudson, Executive Director
Number of members: 350
Staff: full time 3, part time 7,
volunteer 6
Major programs: archives, museum,
junior history, school programs,
newsletters/pamphlets, exhibits,
photographic collections,
genealogical services
Period of collections:
prehistoric-present

**Department of Archives and
History, Evangelical Lutheran
Synod**
Bethany Lutheran College
Telephone: (507) 625-2977
Mail to: 734 Marsh St., 56001
Private agency
Walter C. Gullixson, Secretary
Staff: part time 1
Major programs: archives,
manuscripts
Period of collections: 1880s-present

**Southern Minnesota Historical
Center**
Memorial Library, Mankato State
University, 56001
Telephone: (507) 389-1029
State agency
Founded in: 1969
William E. Lass, Director
Staff: part time 6
Major programs: library, archives,
manuscripts, oral history, records
management
Period of collections: 1870-1950

MANTORVILLE

Dodge County Historical Society
Hilltop Church
Mail to: P.O. Box 433, 55955
Founded in: 1949
Questionnaire not received

**Mantorville Restoration
Association**
55955
Founded in: 1963
Gene Lushinsky, President
Number of members: 50
Staff: part time 3, volunteer 15
Major programs: archives, historic
sites preservation
Period of collections: 1854-present

MARINE ON ST. CROIX

**Marine Historical Society—Stone
House Museum**
c/o Volunteer Director, P.O. Box 84,
55047
Town agency
Founded in: 1963
Mrs. Loren Ecklund,
Volunteer Director
Number of members: 30
Staff: volunteer 2
Major programs: museum
Period of collections: from 1840s

MARSHALL

Lyon County Historical Society
Courthouse, 607 W. Main, 56258
Telephone: (507) 532-4694

County agency
Founded in: 1935
Ralph Larson, President
Number of members: 80
Staff: part time 1
Major programs: archives, museum,
tours/pilgrimages, oral history,
photographic collections
Period of collections: late 1800-1935

Prairieland Genealogical Society
703 N. 6th St., 56258
Telephone: (507) 532-6544
Founded in: 1976
Questionnaire not received

**Southwest Minnesota Historical
Center**
Southwest State University, 56258
Telephone: (507) 537-7373
State agency, authorized by Social
Science Department of the
university
Founded in: 1972
David L. Nass, Director
Staff: part time 6
Major programs: manuscripts, oral
history, educational programs
Period of collections: 1865-present

MENDOTA

**Mendota-West St. Paul Chapter,
Dakota County Historical Society**
c/o City Jail, 55118
City agency
Founded in: 1981
John Schwartz, President
Number of members: 30
Magazine: *Little Historian*
Major programs: historic site(s),
markers, newsletters/pamphlets,
historic preservation, photographic
collections
Period of collections: 1850-present

**Sibley House Association of the
Minnesota Society, Daughters of
the American Revolution**
55150
Telephone: (612) 452-1596
Founded in: 1910
Questionnaire not received

MILACA

Milaca Museum
City Hall, 145 Central Ave., S
Telephone: (612) 983-6666
(committee chair)
Mail to: 440 2nd Ave., NW, 56353
Private agency, authorized by Milaca
Civic Club
Founded in: 1920
Karen Reincke, Historical Committee
Chair
Number of members: 50
Major programs: museum, historic
preservation
Period of collections: late 19th
century-Depression era

MINNEAPOLIS

**African American Museum of Art
and History**
2429 S. 8th St., 55454
Telephone: (612) 332-3506
Private agency
Founded in: 1959

LeClair Grier Lambert, Director
Number of members: 320
Staff: full time 2, part time 2,
volunteer 2
Magazine: *Visions*
Major programs: library, archives,
museum, school programs, book
publishing, newsletters/pamphlets,
historic preservation, records
management, research, exhibits,
living history, audiovisual
programs, photographic
collections, reference and referral
Period of collections: 1800-present

American Swedish Institue
2600 Park Ave., 55407
Telephone: (612) 871-4907
Founded in: 1929
John Z. Lofgren, Executive Director
Number of members: 7,000
Staff: full time 8, part time 3,
volunteer 200
Magazine: *A.S.I. Posten*
Major programs: archives, museum,
historic sites preservation, tours,
educational programs,
newsletters/pamphlets
Period of collections: 1845-1927

Ard Godfrey House
Chute Square, 28 University Ave., SE,
55414
Telephone: (612) 379-9707
Mail to: 410 Oak Grove St., 55403
Founded in: 1976
Questionnaire not received

Bakken Library of Electricity in Life
3537 Zenith Ave., S, 55416
Telephone: (612) 927-6508
Private agency, authorized by
Bakken Foundation
Founded in: 1975
John E. Senior, Director
Staff: full time 5, part time 5,
volunteer 2
Magazine: *Electric Quarterly*
Major programs: library, archives,
manuscripts, museum,
tours/pilgrimages,
newsletters/pamphlets, records
management, research, exhibits,
audiovisual programs, history of
science and technology
Period of collections: 18th-19th
centuries

**Commission on Archives and
History, Minnesota Annual
Conference, United Methodist
Church**
122 W. Franklin Ave., Room 400,
55404
Telephone: (612) 870-3657
Founded in: 1856
Thelma Boeder, Executive
Secretary/Archivist
Number of members: 30
Staff: part time 1
Major programs: library, archives
Period of collections: 1856-present

Danish American Fellowship
4200 Cedar Ave., S, 55407
Telephone: (612) 729-3800
Shelly Madson, President
Number of members: 600
Staff: part time 2

Hennepin County Historical Society Museum
2303 3rd Ave., S, 55404
Telephone: (612) 870-1329
Private agency
Founded in: 1938
Donna Lind, Executive Director
Number of members: 825
Staff: full time 5, part time 5, volunteer 15
Magazine: *Hennepin County History*
Major programs: archives, museum, tours, exhibits, audiovisual programs, photographic collections, genealogical services, membership program
Period of collections: 1850-1910

Historical Research, Inc.
5525 Richmond Curve, 55410
Telephone: (612) 929-2921
Private agency
Founded in: 1979
Norene A. Roberts, President
Staff: full time 2, part time 3
Major programs: historic site(s), historic preservation, research, exhibits, field services
Period of collections: 1820-1950

Minneapolis Heritage Preservation Commission
City Hall, 55415
Telephone: (612) 348-6538
Founded in: 1972
Staff: full time 1
Major programs: historic preservation

Minneapolis History Collection, Minneapolis Public Library and Information Center
300 Nicollet Mall, 55401
Telephone: (612) 372-6648
City agency
Founded in: 1940
Joseph Kimbrough, Director
Staff: full time 2
Major programs: library, archives, manuscripts, oral history, research, exhibits, photographic collections, genealogical services, architectural history
Period of collections: 1860-present

Minnesota Society American Institute of Architects
314 Clifton Ave., 55403
Telephone: (612) 874-8711
Founded in: 1935
Peter Rand, Executive Director
Number of members: 1,100
Staff: full time 10
Magazine: *Architecture Minnesota*
Major programs: library, tours, educational programs, book publishing, newsletters/pamphlets, historic preservation, architecture

Minnesota Transportation Museum, Inc.
4832 York Ave., S
Telephone: (612) 922-4706
Mail to: P.O. Box 1300, 55343
Private agency
Founded in: 1961
Number of members: 752
Magazine: *Minnegazette*
Major programs: museum, historic site(s), newsletters, historic

preservation, living history, audiovisual programs, photographic collections
Period of collections: from 1893

Sons of Norway
1455 W. Lake St., 55408
Telephone: (612) 827-3611
Private agency
Founded in: 1895
Ralph Durand, Chief Executive Officer
Number of members: 110,000
Staff: full time 70
Magazine: *Viking*
Major programs: library, tours, school programs, newsletters/pamphlets, records management, research, exhibits, living history, audiovisual programs, genealogical services
Period of collections: 1830-present

MINNEOTA

Society for the Preservation of Minneota's Heritage
Jefferson St.
Mail to: P.O. Box 176, 56264
Private agency
Founded in: 1978
John H. Geiwitz, Secretary
Number of members: 80
Staff: volunteer 9
Major programs: historic site(s), historic preservation, plays
Period of collections: 1900

MINNETONKA

City of Minnetonka Historical Society
13209 McGinty Rd., E, 55343
Telephone: (612) 933-1611
Founded in: 1970
Doris Rasche, Board member
Number of members: 146
Staff: volunteer 25
Major programs: museum, historic site, historic preservation
Period of collections: 1853-1920

MONTEVIDEO

Chippewa County Historical Society
Hwys. 7 and 59
Telephone: (612) 269-7636
Mail to: P.O. Box 303, 56222
County agency
Founded in: 1938
Jana Groothuis, Curator
Number of members: 200
Staff: full time 1, volunteer 25
Major programs: library, archives, manuscripts, museum, historic site(s), tours/pilgrimages, oral history, school programs, newsletters/pamphlets, historic preservation, research, exhibits, audiovisual programs, photographic collections, genealogical services
Period of collections: 1890-present

MOORHEAD

Bergquist Pioneer Cabin Society
8th St., N, at 11th Ave., 56560
Telephone: (701) 232-8080

Mail to: 1541 S. 10th St., Fargo, ND, 58103
Private agency
Founded in: 1967
Dewey Bergquist, President
Major programs: museum, historic site(s), historic preservation, photographic collections, 1870 cabin restoration project
Period of collections: 1870

Clay County Historical Society and Museum
22 N. 8th St.
Telephone: (218) 233-4604
Mail to: P.O. Box 501, 56560
Private agency
Founded in: 1932
John Schermeister, Executive Director
Number of members: 400
Staff: full time 2
Major programs: library, archives, manuscripts, museum, newsletters/pamphlets, records management, research, exhibits, photographic collections, genealogical services
Period of collections: 1865-present

Comstock Historic House Society
506 8th St., S, 56560
Telephone: (218) 233-0848/233-1772
State agency
Founded in: 1974
Robert J. Loeffler, President
Number of members: 200
Staff: part time 4, volunteer 6
Major programs: archives, manuscripts, historic site(s), tours/pilgrimages, oral history, school programs, newsletters/pamphlets, historic preservation, living history, audiovisual programs, photographic collections
Period of collections: 1871-1951

Red River Valley Heritage Society
P.O. Box 733, 56560
Telephone: (218) 236-9140
Founded in: 1964
Gary L. Phillips, Executive Director
Number of members: 1,500
Staff: full time 3
Magazine: *Heritage Press*
Major programs: tours/pilgrimages, book publishing, newsletters/pamphlets, research, exhibits, field services

MORA

Kanabec County Historical Society and Museum
W. Forest Ave.
Telephone: (612) 679-1665
Mail to: P.O. Box 113, 55051
Edna Cole, Executive Director
Number of members: 436
Staff: full time 2, part time 5, volunteer 12
Magazine: *Kanabec Quarterly*
Major programs: manuscripts, museum, school programs, newsletters/pamphlets, exhibits, photographic collections, genealogical services
Period of collections: 1880-1920

MORRIS

Stevens County Historical Society
W. 6th and Nevada Sts., 56267
Founded in: 1922
Carol M. Day, Director
Number of members: 125
Staff: full time 1, part time 3,
volunteer 8
Major programs: archives,
manuscripts, museum,
newsletters/pamphlets,
photographic collections
Period of collections: W.W. I

**West Central Minnesota Historical
Center**
4th and College Sts., 56267
Telephone: (612) 589-2211, ext. 6170
State agency, authorized by
University of Minnesota
Founded in: 1973
Wilbert N. Ahern, Director
Staff: part time 3
Major programs: archives,
manuscripts, oral history
Period of collections: 1880-1975

NEW BRIGHTON

**New Brighton Area Historical
Society**
1203 12th Ave. N.W. 55112
Telephone: (612) 633-4281
Founded in: 1979
Julie C. Beisswenger, President
Number of members: 75
Staff: volunteer 12
Major programs: library,
tours/pilgrimages, oral history,
educational programs, book
publishing, historic preservation
Period of collections: 1850-present

NEW LONDON

Monongalia Historical Society
56273
Telephone: (612) 354-2557
Founded in: 1972
Erwin Kalevik, President
Number of members: 50
Staff: part time 1, volunteer 12
Major programs: library, museum,
historic sites preservation, markers
Period of collections: 1865-present

NEW PRAGUE

New Prague Historical Society
Telephone: (612) 758-2201
Mail to: Rt. 3, Box 37, 56071
City agency
Founded in: 1983
Dennis F. Dvorak, President
Number of members: 85
Staff: volunteer 12
Major programs: oral history,
research, exhibits, audiovisual
programs, photographic
collections, genealogical services

NEW ULM

Brown County Historical Society
2 N. Broadway, 56073
Telephone: (507) 354-2016
County agency
Founded in: 1930
Kathleen Juni, Director

Number of members: 675
Staff: full time 4
Major programs: library, archives,
manuscripts, museum, historic site,
markers, educational programs,
newsletters/pamphlets, historic
preservation
Period of collections: 1850-present

NEW YORK MILLS

Finn Creek Museum
P.O. Box 316, 56567
Telephone: (218) 385-3481
Private agency
Founded in: 1975
Einar Saarela, President
Number of members: 143
Staff: volunteer 14
Major programs: museum, historic
preservation
Period of collections: 1900-1910

NORTHFIELD

Northfield Historical Society
408 Division St.
Telephone: (507) 645-9268
Mail to: P.O. Box 372, 55057
Authorized by Rice County Historical
Society
Founded in: 1975
Beverly Voldseth Allers, Director
Number of members: 270
Staff: full time 1, part time 1,
volunteer 50
Magazine: *Scriver Scribbler*
Major programs: museum, historic
site(s), tours, oral history, school
programs, newsletters/pamphlets,
historic preservation, audiovisual
programs, photographic
collections
Period of collections: 1865-present

**Norwegian-American Historical
Association**
St. Olaf College Library, 55057
Telephone: (507) 663-3221
Founded in: 1925
Lawrence O. Hauge, President
Number of members: 1,300
Staff: part time 3, volunteer 2
Major programs: library, archives,
manuscripts, books,
newsletters/pamphlets
Period of collections: 1865-present

NORTH ST. PAUL

North St. Paul Historical Society
2526 E. 7th Ave., 55109
Founded in: 1977
Barbara Larson, Museum Director
Number of members: 167
Staff: volunteer 4
Major programs: archives, museum,
tours/pilgrimages, junior history,
oral history, newsletters, historic
preservation
Period of collections: 1887-present

OLIVIA

**Olivia Historic Preservation
Corporation**
907 W. Park
Telephone: (612) 523-1322
Mail to: P.O. Box 148, 56277
City agency

Founded in: 1981
Donald H. Walser, President
Major programs: museum, historic
preservation
Period of collections: 1878-1910

OWATONNA

Steele County Historical Society
Steele County Fairgrounds
Mail to: P.O. Box 204, 55060
County agency
Founded in: 1949
Robert Hollinger, President
Number of members: 236
Staff: volunteer 15
Major programs: archives, museum,
historic preservation, exhibits,
photographic collections
Period of collections: 1850-1930

PAYNESVILLE

Paynesville Historical Society
543 River St.
Telephone: (612) 243-4433
Mail to: 635 Hudson St., 56362
Town agency
Founded in: 1969
Bertha Zniewski, President
Number of members: 70
Staff: full time 2, volunteer 23
Major programs: library, museum,
tours/pilgrimages, oral history,
school programs, book publishing,
exhibits, audiovisual programs,
photographic collections,
genealogical services
Period of collections: 1865-1980

PETERSON

1877 Peterson Station Museum
Mill and Centennial Sts.
Telephone: (507) 895-2551
Mail to: P.O. Box 233, 55962
City agency
Founded in: 1973
John Erickson, Curator
Staff: volunteer 1
Major programs: library, oral history,
book publishing, research, living
history, audiovisual programs,
photographic collections,
genealogical services
Period of collections: 1856-present

PICKWICK

Pickwick Mill, Inc.
Telephone: (507) 454-3820
(evenings)
Mail to: P.O. Box 645, 55987
Private agency
Founded in: 1981
Margaret Shaw Johnson, President
Number of members: 150
Staff: volunteer 50
Major programs: historic site(s),
historic preservation, living history,
restoration of state's oldest mill
Period of collections: 1854-1900

PIPESTONE

Historic Pipestone, Inc.
P.O. Box 470, 56164
Telephone: (507) 825-3333
City agency
Founded in: 1976

Chuck Draper, Chair
Number of members: 50
Staff: volunteer 12
Major programs: markers, historic
preservation
Period of collections: 1880-1940

**Pipestone County Historical
Society**
113 S. Hiawatha
Telephone: (507) 825-2563
Mail to: P.O. Box 175, 56164
Founded in: 1880
Jeffery E. Allen, Museum Director
Number of members: 500
Staff: full time 1, part time 4,
volunteer 5
Major programs: library, museum,
historic site, educational programs,
newsletters/pamphlets, historic
preservation
Period of collections: prehistoric-1930

PRESTON

Fillmore County Historical Center
Courthouse Square
Telephone: (507) 765-2368
Mail to: P.O. Box 373, 55965
County agency, authorized by
Fillmore County Historical Society
Founded in: 1934
Marlyn L. Cox, Executive Director
Number of members: 240
Staff: full time 2, part time 3,
volunteer 3
Magazine: *Rural Roots*
Major programs: library, museum,
book publishing, living history,
genealogical services
Period of collections: 1860-1900

Fillmore County Historical Society
P.O. Box 373, 55965
Telephone: (507) 765-2368
Private agency
Founded in: 1934
Marlon L. Cox, Executive Director
Number of members: 250
Staff: full time 1, part time 3,
volunteer 6
Magazine: *Fillmore History*
Major programs: library, archives,
manuscripts, museum, historic
site(s), book publishing,
newsletters/pamphlets, historic
preservation, research, exhibits,
photographic collections,
genealogical services
Period of collections: 1850-1915

Ravine House, Inc.
Telephone: (507) 765-3309
Mail to: P.O. Box 522, Harmony,
55939
Founded in: 1975
Questionnaire not received

READS LANDING

Wabasha County Historical Society
Mail to: Minneiska, 55958
Founded in: 1854
Questionnaire not received

RED WING

Goodhue County Historical Society
166 Oak St., 55066
Telephone: (612) 388-6024

County agency
Founded in: 1869
Orville Olson, Curator
Number of members: 600
Staff: part time 7, volunteer 70
Magazine: *Goodhue County
Historical News*
Major programs: library, archives,
museum, tours/pilgrimages, oral
history, educational programs,
newsletters/pamphlets
Period of collections:
prehistoric-present

Heritage Preservation Commission
City Hall, 55066
Telephone: (612) 388-6734
City agency
Founded in: 1976
G. J. Kunau, Chair
Staff: volunteer 7
Major programs: historic site,
markers, tours/pilgrimages, historic
preservation

RENVILLE

**Historic Renville Preservation
Commission**
Main St.
Telephone: (612) 329-3541
Mail to: 813 N. Main St., 56284
City agency
Founded in: 1976
Anna Van Zee, President
Number of members: 85
Period of collections: 1870-1930

RICHFIELD

Richfield Historical Society
6901 Lyndale Ave., S
Telephone: (612) 869-4761
Mail to: P.O. Box 23304, 55423
City agency, authorized by Richfield
Schools
Founded in: 1967
Richard A. Lindquist, President
Number of members: 100
Major programs: museum,
tours/pilgrimages, educational
programs
Period of collections: 1865-1918

ROCHESTER

**First District Historical Assembly
of Minnesota**
400 S. Broadway, 55901
Telephone: (507) 288-5555
Questionnaire not received

Mayo Historical Unit, Mayo Clinic
200 1st St., SW, 55905
Telephone: (507) 284-4054
Private agency, authorized by Mayo
Foundation
Founded in: 1960
Clark W. Nelson, Archivist/Historian
Staff: part time 2
Major programs: archives,
manuscripts, historic site(s),
tours/pilgrimages, oral history,
historic preservation, research,
exhibits, photographic collections,
medical history
Period of collections: from 1900

**Olmsted County Genealogical
Society**
Telephone: (507) 282-9447

Mail to: P.O. Box 6411, 55903
Private agency, authorized by
Olmsted County Historical Society
Founded in: 1977
Kathleen McMullin, President
Number of members: 70
Staff: volunteer 6
Major programs: library, archives,
genealogical services
Period of collections: 1859-present

Olmsted County Historical Society
Telephone: (507) 282-9447
Mail to: P.O. Box 6411, 55901
Founded in: 1926
George V. Tyrrell, Director
Number of members: 400
Staff: full time 4, part time 20,
volunteer 4
Major programs: library, archives,
manuscripts, museum, historic
sites preservation, markers, junior
history, educational programs,
newsletters/pamphlets
Period of collections: 1850-present

ROSEAU

Pioneer Farm and Village
800 2nd St., SE, 56751
Telephone: (218) 463-1820
County agency
Founded in: 1985
Millard A. Jenson, President
Number of members: 302
Staff: part time 1, volunteer 10
Major programs: museum,
newsletters/pamphlets, historic
preservation, exhibits,
photographic collections,
agricultural museum
Period of collections: 1880-1950

**Roseau County Historical Society
Museum**
2nd Ave., 56751
Telephone: (218) 463-1918
County agency, authorized by
Roseau County Historical Society
Founded in: 1927
Ardyce Stein, Curator
Number of members: 150
Staff: full time 1, volunteer 5
Major programs: museum, historic
site(s), markers, tours/pilgrimages,
oral history, school programs,
newsletters/pamphlets, historic
preservation, research, exhibits,
genealogical services
Period of collections: 1850-present

ROSEVILLE

**Old Rose Township Historical
Society**
2407 Irene St., 55113
Telephone: (612) 483-4487
Private agency
Founded in: 1976
Daniel J. Simundson, President
Number of members: 60
Major programs: historic site(s),
markers, tours/pilgrimages, junior
history, oral history,
newsletters/pamphlets, records
management, photographic
collections
Period of collections: 1900-1940

ROYALTON

Royalton Historical Society
Center St., 56373
Telephone: (612) 584-5641/ 584-5417
Founded in: 1955
Questionnaire not received

ST. CLOUD

Central Minnesota Historical Center
Room 14-B, Centennial Hall, St. Cloud State University, 56301
Telephone: (612) 255-3254
State agency, authorized by the university
Founded in: 1968
Calvin W. Gower, Professor of History
Staff: part time 3
Major programs: archives, manuscripts, oral history, research
Period of collections: 1837-present

St. Cloud Area Genealogists, Inc.
P.O. Box 213, 56301
Telephone: (612) 252-6673
Founded in: 1973
Questionnaire not received

Stearns County Historical Society
33rd Ave. and 2nd St., S
Telephone: (612) 253-8424
Mail to: P.O. Box 702, 56302
County agency
Founded in: 1930
David Ebnet, Executive Director
Number of members: 800
Staff: full time 8, volunteer 100
Magazine: *Crossings*
Major programs: library, archives, manuscripts, museum, markers, tours/pilgrimages, oral history, school programs, newsletters/pamphlets, records management, research, exhibits, audiovisual programs, photographic collections, genealogical services, explorer post
Period of collections: 1858-present

ST. LOUIS PARK

Northwest Territory French and Canadian Heritage Institute
P.O. Box 26372, 55426
Private agency
Founded in: 1978
Kevin R. LeVoir, President
Number of members: 600
Staff: volunteer 12
Magazine: *Cousins et Cousines*
Major programs: library, archives, manuscripts, book publishing, newsletters/pamphlets, historic preservation, research, genealogical services
Period of collections: 1600-present

St. Louis Park Historical Society
6210 W. 37th St., 55426
Telephone: (612) 929-9486
City agency
Founded in: 1971
Marie Hartmann, Board Chair
Number of members: 42
Staff: volunteer 5
Major programs: historic site(s), oral history, school programs, historic preservation
Period of collections: 1886-present

ST. PAUL

Alexander Ramsey House
265 S. Exchange St., 55102
Telephone: (612) 296-8719
State agency, authorized by Minnesota Historical Society
Founded in: 1849
Vera Stanton, Site Manager
Staff: full time 3, part time 24
Major programs: historic site(s), tours/pilgrimages, school programs, exhibits, living history, audiovisual programs
Period of collections: 1860-1900

Catholic Historical Society of St. Paul
2260 Summit Ave., 55105
Telephone: (612) 690-4355
Private agency, authorized by Archdiocese of St. Paul and Minneapolis
Founded in: 1912
Leo J. Tibesar, Librarian
Staff: part time 1
Major programs: library, archives, manuscripts, museum
Period of collections: 1783-present

IHRC (Immigration History Research Center)
826 Berry St., 55114
Telephone: (612) 373-5581
State agency, authorized by University of Minnesota
Founded in: 1965
Rudulph J. Vecoli, Professor/Director
Staff: full time 6, part time 6, volunteer 10
Magazine: *Spectrum*
Major programs: library, archives, manuscripts, oral history, book publishing, newsletters/pamphlets, historic preservation, research, exhibits
Period of collections: 1880-present

Irish American Cultural Institute
683 Osceola, 55105
Telephone: (612) 647-5678
Founded in: 1962
Number of members: 8,900
Eoin McKiernan, President
Staff: full time 7, part time 4, volunteer 10
Magazine: *Eire-Ireland*
Major programs: tours, educational programs, newsletters/pamphlets, school programs

Landmark Center
75 W. 5th St., 55102
Private agency
Founded in: 1978
Sandy Hedeen, Executive Director
Staff: full time 3, part time 1, volunteer 150
Major programs: archives, museum, historic site, tours, newsletters, weekly concerts, ethnic festivals, community events

Minnesota Brigade
1438 Mechanic Ave., 55106
Telephone: (612) 771-7493
Questionnaire not received

Minnesota Genealogical Society
P.O. Box 16069, 55116
Founded in: 1969
Marvin Lyddon, President
Number of members: 1,100
Staff: volunteer 20
Magazine: *Minnesota Genealogist*
Major programs: library, book publishing, newsletters/pamphlets, research, exhibits, genealogical services

◇**Minnesota Historical Society**
690 Cedar St. 55101
Telephone: (612) 296-2747
Private agency
Founded in: 1849
Russell W. Fridley, Director
Number of members: 6,700
Staff: full time 205, part time 105, volunteer 100
Magazine: *Minnesota History/Roots*
Major programs: library, archives, manuscripts, museum, historic site(s), markers, tours, oral history, school programs, book publishing, newsletters/pamphlets, historic preservation, research, exhibits, living history, audiovisual programs, archaeology programs, photographic collections, genealogical services, field services
Period of collections: 19th-20th centuries

New Brighton Area Historical Society
1786 Glenview Ave., 55112
Telephone: (612) 633-6991
City agency
Founded in: 1979
Janet R. Newham, President
Number of members: 75
Staff: volunteer 12
Major programs: library, museum, oral history, book publishing, newsletters/pamphlets, exhibits
Period of collections: 1850-present

Old Town Restorations, Inc.
411 Selby Ave., 55104
Telephone: (612) 224-3857
Founded in: 1966
Questionnaire not received

Ramsey County Historical Society
323 Landmark Center, 75 W. 5th St., 55102
Telephone: (612) 222-0701
Private agency
Founded in: 1949
Virginia B. Kunz, Executive Director
Number of members: 1,200
Staff: full time 5, part time 13, volunteer 110
Magazine: *Ramsey County History*
Major programs: museum, historic site(s), tours, book publishing, newsletters/pamphlets, historic preservation, exhibits, living history, audiovisual programs, photographic collections
Period of collections: 1870s-1910

WHOM (Women Historians of the Midwest)
Mail to: P.O. Box 8021, Como Station, 55108
Telephone: (612) 925-3632

Private agency
Founded in: 1973
Susan Gross, President
Number of members: 200
Staff: volunteer 16
Major programs:
newsletters/pamphlets,
conventions, public educational
programs, women's history
programs

ST. PETER

**Nicollet County Historical Society
and Museum**
300 S. 5th
Telephone: (507) 931-2160
Mail to: P.O. Box 153, 56082
County agency
Founded in: 1928
Karen Mesrobian, Curator
Number of members: 150
Staff: part time 1, volunteer 10
Major programs: library, archives,
manuscripts, museum, historic
site(s), markers, tours/pilgrimages,
school programs, exhibits,
photographic collections,
genealogical services
Period of collections: 1850-1920

SAUK CENTRE

Sinclair Lewis Foundation, Inc.
Hwys. I-94 and 71
Telephone: (612) 352-5202
Mail to: P.O. Box 162, 56378
Founded in: 1960
Questionnaire not received

SAUM

Saum Community Club, Inc.
Telephone: (218) 647-8673
(president)
Private agency
Founded in: 1962
Arnold Wolden, President
Number of members: 100
Staff: volunteer 6
Major programs: historic site(s),
community center for local
activities
Period of collections: 1907-1960

SEBEKA

**Chapter 38, Minnesota Finnish
American Historical Society**
Rt. 1, Box 223, 56477
Questionnaire not received

SHAKOPEE

Murphy's Landing
Telephone: (612) 445-6900
Mail to: P.O. Box 275, 55379
Private agency
Founded in: 1968
Janis Obst, Director
Number of members: 850
Staff: full time 5, volunteer 80
Major programs: historic site(s),
school programs, historic
preservation, research, living
history
Period of collections: 1840-1890

Scott County Historical Society
Telephone: (612) 445-6900
Mail to: P.O. Box 275, 55379

Founded in: 1968
Questionnaire not received

SLAYTON

Murray County Historical Society
Murray County Fairgrounds, 56172
County agency
Orville E. Klasse, Vice President
Staff: full time 3, part time 2,
volunteer 13
Major programs: museum, school
programs, historic preservation,
records management, living
history, photographic collections

SOUTH ST. PAUL

Dakota County Historical Society
130 3rd Ave., N, 55075
Telephone: (612) 451-6260
County agency
Founded in: 1939
R. L. Zostrow, Director
Number of members: 350
Staff: full time 3, part time 1
Magazine: *Over the Years*
Major programs: library, archives,
manuscripts, museum, markers,
newsletters/pamphlets, historic
preservation, research, exhibits,
audiovisual programs,
genealogical services
Period of collections: 1860s-present

SPRING VALLEY

**Spring Valley Community
Historical Society, Inc.**
Main and Washington Sts.
Mail to: 909 S. Broadway, 55975
Private agency
Founded in: 1955
Mrs. Gordon Dathe, Secretary
Number of members: 125
Staff: volunteer 12
Major programs: museum, historic
sites preservation, exhibits
Period of collections: 1865-1918

STILLWATER

**Washington County Historical
Society**
602 N. Main St.
Telephone: (612) 439-5956
Mail to: P.O. Box 167, 55082
County agency
Founded in: 1934
Yvette Bergeron Handy, Curator
Number of members: 600
Staff: full time 1, part time 4,
volunteer 10
Magazine: *Historical Whisperings*
Major programs: library, archives,
museum, historic site(s), markers,
tours, book publishing,
newsletters/pamphlets, historic
preservation, research,
photographic collections
Period of collections: 1865-1945

TAYLORS FALLS

**Taylors Falls Chapter, Chicago
County Historical Society**
55084
Telephone: (612) 465-3125
Town agency
Founded in: 1978

Herbert V. Caneday, President
Number of members: 42
Staff: full time 2, volunteer 30
Major programs: historic site
Period of collections: 1850-early
1900s

TWO HARBORS

**Lake County Historical Society and
Railroad Museum**
Depot Bldg., 55616
Telephone: (218) 834-4898
Founded in: 1925
Peter Naysmith, President
Number of members: 170
Major programs: manuscripts,
museum, historic site(s), markers,
oral history, historic preservation,
research, exhibits, photographic
collections
Period of collections: 1854-present

TWIN CITIES

**Société Canadienne Française du
Minnesota**
3146 Kentucky Ave., N, 55111
Telephone: (612) 593-1175
Private agency
Founded in: 1979
Louis Ritchet, President
Number of members: 200
Magazine: *Chez Nous*
Major programs: archives,
tours/pilgrimages, oral history,
school programs,
newsletters/pamphlets, historic
preservation, exhibits, audiovisual
programs, photographic
collections, genealogical services

ULEN

**Ulen Historical Recreation and
Conservation Association, Inc.**
Northern Pacific Ave., W, 56585
Telephone: (218) 596-8548
Private agency
Founded in: 1963
Harold Dinsmore, President
Number of members: 25
Staff: part time 2
Major programs: museum

UPSALA

Upsala Area Historical Society
56384
Telephone: (612) 573-2294
Private agency
Founded in: 1979
Wanda Erickson, President
Number of members: 100
Major programs: museum, tours,
school programs
Period of collections: 1900-1920

VERNDALE

Verndale Historical Society
N. Farwell St., 56481
Private agency
Founded in: 1975
Marylu McClure, President
Number of members: 100
Staff: volunteer 15
Major programs: museum, book
publishing, genealogical services
Period of collections: late 19th
century-present

VIRGINIA

Virginia Area Historical Society—Heritage Center Museum
3rd St., N, and 76th Ave.
Telephone: (218) 741-1136/741-2249
Mail to: P.O. Box 736, 55792
Founded in: 1983 (museum); 1978 (society)
Virginia C. Kirby, President
Number of members: 161
Major programs: museum, historic preservation, research, exhibits, audiovisual programs, photographic collections, genealogical services
Period of collections: 1890s-present

WACONIA

Carver County Historical Society, Inc.
119 Cherry St., 55387
Telephone: (612) 442-4234
Private agency
Founded in: 1940
Francis H. Klein, President
Number of members: 350
Staff: part time 3, volunteer 15
Major programs: museum, research, exhibits, photographic collections, genealogical services
Period of collections: 1850-present

WALKER

Cass County Historical Society
56484
Founded in: 1969
Don Vollman, President
Number of members: 89
Major programs: library, archives, museum, tours/pilgrimages, oral history, educational programs
Period of collections: prehistoric-present

WALNUT GROVE

Laura Ingalls Wilder Museum and Tourist Information Center
P.O. Box 248, 56180
Telephone: (507) 859-2368
Private agency, authorized by Wilder Museum, Inc.
Founded in: 1975
Shirley Knakmuhs, Museum Director
Staff: volunteer 12
Major programs: museum, historic site(s), historic preservation, exhibits, photographic collections
Period of collections: 1840-1950

WARREN

Marshall County Historical Society
P.O. Box 103, 56762
County agency
Founded in: 1930
Phyllis L. Haynes, Curator
Staff: full time 3, part time 2
Major programs: museum, historic site, educational programs, book publishing, historic preservation, exhibits, cataloguing of artifacts
Period of collections: 1880-1930s

WARROAD

Warroad Area Historical Society
56763
Questionnaire not received

WASECA

Farmamerica-Minnesota Agricultural Interpretive Center
P.O. Box 111, 56093
Telephone: (507) 835-2052
Private agency
Founded in: 1979
George G. Brophy, Executive Director
Staff: full time 8, part time 1, volunteer 20
Magazine: *Over the Fencepost*
Major programs: museum, school programs, newsletters/pamphlets, research, exhibits, living history
Period of collections: 1850s-present

Waseca County Historical Society
315 2nd Ave., NE
Telephone: (507) 835-7700
Mail to: P.O. Box 314, 56093
Peggy Korsmo-Kennon, Director
Number of members: 400
Staff: full time 2, part time 6, volunteer 20
Major programs: library, museum, oral history, school programs, newsletters/pamphlets, research, exhibits, genealogical services
Period of collections: 1880-1915

WHEATON

Traverse County Historical Society
Broadway, 56296
Founded in: 1977
Donald Neumann, Board Chair
Number of members: 50

WHITE BEAR LAKE

White Bear Lake Area Historical Society
2350 Joy Ave., 55110
Telephone: (612) 429-5014
Questionnaire not received

WILLMAR

Heritage Searchers Genealogical Society
610 Hwy. 71, NE, 56201
Private agency, authorized by Kandiyoshi County Historical Society
Leeann Nelson, President
Number of members: 50
Major programs: library, records management, research, genealogical services

Kandiyohi County Historical Society
610 Hwy. 71, NE, 56201
Telephone: (612) 235-1881
Private agency
Founded in: 1898
D. E. Miller, President
Number of members: 1,600
Staff: full time 2, part time 4
Major programs: library, archives, manuscripts, museum, historic site(s), markers, oral history, school programs, newsletters/pamphlets,

historic preservation, research, exhibits, living history, audiovisual programs, photographic collections, genealogical services
Period of collections: prehistoric-present

WINDOM

Cottonwood County Historical Society
841 4th Ave., 56101
Telephone: (507) 831-1134
Questionnaire not received

WINNEBAGO

Winnebago Area Museum
36 N. Main St., 56098
Telephone: (507) 893-3196
City agency
Founded in: 1976
Marion Muir, President
Number of members: 32
Staff: volunteer 20
Major programs: archives, museum, historic site(s), oral history, school programs, exhibits, audiovisual programs, archaeology programs, photographic collections, genealogical services
Period of collections: 5000 B.C.-A.D. 1600

WINONA

Southeast Minnesota Historical Center
Fitzgerald Library, St. Mary's College, 55987
Telephone: (507) 452-4430
Private agency
Paul J. Ostendorf, Director
Major programs: archives, manuscripts

Winona County Historical Society Inc.
160 Johnson, 55987
telephone: (507) 454-2723
Private agency
Founded in: 1935
Mark F. Peterson, Executive Director
Number of members: 1,625
Staff: full time 4, part time 6, volunteer 150
Magazine: *Chronicles*
Major programs: library, archives, manuscripts, museum, historic site(s), tours/pilgrimages, school programs, book publishing, newsletters/pamphlets, historic preservation, exhibits, photographic collections, genealogical services
Period of collections: 1850-present

WORTHINGTON

Nobles County Historical Society
56187
Telephone: (507) 376-4431
Founded in: 1933
Number of members: 200
Staff: part time 2, volunteer 50
Major programs: museum, historic sites preservation, oral history, books, newsletters/pamphlets
Period of collections: 1865-1918

MISSISSIPPI

ABERDEEN

Evans Memorial Library
105 S. Long St. 39730
Telephone: (601) 369-4601
Founded in: 1939
Tommy G. Rye, Librarian
Major programs: library, archives, manuscripts, museum, historic preservation
Period of collections: 1800s

Monroe County Historical Society
410 S. Meridian St., 39730
Telephone: (601) 369-8120
County agency
Founded in: 1974
Mrs. Charles G. Hamilton, President
Number of members: 154
Staff: volunteer 154
Magazine: *The Journal of Monroe County Historical*
Major programs: manuscripts, markers, oral history, book publishing, historic preservation, living history
Period of collections: 19th century

BALDWYN

Brice's Crossroads Museum
P.O. Box 100, 38824
Telephone: (601) 365-9371
Founded in: 1961
Claude Gentry, Owner-Director
Period of collections: 20th century

BAY ST. LOUIS

Hancock County Historical Society
P.O. Box 1340, 113 Citizen St. 39520
Telephone: (601) 467-3907
Founded in: 1974
Margaret M. Gibbens, President
Major programs: library, manuscripts, historic site, markers, junior history, educational programs, historic preservation, genealogy

BILOXI

Beauvoir, Jefferson Davis Shrine
W. Beach Blvd.
Telephone: (601) 388-1313
Mail to: P.O. Box 200, W. Beach Blvd., 39531
Private agency, authorized by Mississippi Division, United Sons of Confederate Veterans, Inc.
Founded in: 1896
Newton W. Carr, Jr., Superintendent
Staff: full time 6, part time 19
Major programs: library, archives, museum, historic site(s), school programs, research, living history
Period of collections: 1861-1865/1877-1889

Mississippi Coast Historical and Genealogical Society
Telephone: (601) 388-5576
Mail to: Box 513, 39533
Founded in: 1968
L. H. Richard, President
Number of members: 124
Staff: volunteer 20
Magazine: *Mississippi Coast Historical and Genealogical Society Tri-annual*
Major programs: library, museum, historic sites preservation, markers, oral history
Period of collections: 1783-1865

Seafood Industry Museum of Biloxi
P.O. Box 775, 39533
Telephone: (601) 374-8600, ext. 320
City agency
Founded in: 1984
F. Val Husley, Director
Number of members: 30
Staff: full time 1, part time 2, volunteer 10
Major programs: museum, historic preservation, exhibits
Period of collections: 1880-1930

BRANDON

Rankin County Historical Society, Inc.
P.O. Box 841, 39042
County agency
Founded in: 1978
Sara Richardson, President
Number of members: 110
Staff: volunteer 20
Major programs: museum, markers, book publishing, newsletters/pamphlets, historic preservation, exhibits, photographic collections, genealogical services
Period of collections: 1820-present

CARROLLTON

Carroll Society for the Preservation of Antiques
Mail to: P.O. Box 354, 38917
Telephone: (601) 237-4737
County agency
Founded in: 1961
Sarah W. Grantham, President
Major programs: historic preservation

CLARKSDALE

Delta Blues Museum, Carnegie Public Library
114 Delta Ave.
Telephone: (601) 624-4461
Mail to: P.O. Box 280, 38614
Authorized by Carnegie Public Library of Clarksdale and Coahoma County
Founded in: 1914 (library); 1979 (museum)
Sid F. Graves, Jr., Director
Staff: full time 11, part time 2
Major programs: library, museum, book publishing, exhibits, archaeology programs, photographic collections, genealogical services
Period of collections: 1800-present

CLEVELAND

Bolivar County Historical Society
1615 Terrace Rd., 38732
Telephone: (601) 843-8204
Private agency
Founded in: 1971
Margaret Gunn, President
Number of members: 125
Staff: volunteer 12
Magazine: *Journal of Bolivar County Historical Society*
Major programs: historic site(s)

CLINTON

Mississippi Baptist Historical Commission
Mississippi College Library, College St.
Telephone: (601) 924-6172
Mail to: P.O. Box 51, 39056
Private agency
Founded in: 1956
Alice G. Cox, Librarian
Staff: full time 1, part time 1
Major programs: library, archives, manuscripts, historic sites preservation, oral history, books
Period of collections: 1800-present

COLUMBIA

Marion County Historical Society
John Ford Home, Sandy Hook Community
Telephone: (601) 736-5378
Mail to: P.O. Box 430, 39429
County agency
Founded in: 1962
Forest M. Dantin, President
Number of members: 80
Staff: part time 1, volunteer 6
Major programs: museum, historic site(s), tours/pilgrimages, historic preservation
Period of collections: 19th century

COLUMBUS

The Columbus and Lowndes County Historical Society
316 7th St. 39701
Telephone: (601) 328-5437
Mail to: 916 College St.
Founded in: 1959
Mrs. George S. Hazard, Museum Director
Number of members: 215
Staff: part-time 1, volunteer 20
Major programs: archives, manuscripts, museum, tours/pilgrimages, oral history
Period of collections: 1833-1908

Archives and Museum, Mississippi University for Women
W Box 369, 39701
Telephone: (601) 329-4750, ext. 325
State agency
Founded in: 1884
Gloria Jean Atkinson, Director
Staff: full time 1, part time 2, volunteer 2
Major programs: archives, manuscripts, museum, historic site(s), markers, tours/pilgrimages, oral history, research, exhibits, photographic collections, genealogical services
Period of collections: 1890s-present

CORINTH

Jacinto Foundation, Inc.
P.O. Box 1048, 38834
Telephone: (601) 287-4296
Private agency
Founded in: 1966

Betsy Whitehurst, Executive Director
Staff: part time 6, volunteer 9
Major programs: museum, historic
site(s), tours/pilgrimages, historic
preservation, exhibits
Period of collections: 1832-1870

CROSBY

Homochitto Valley Historical Society
Telephone: (601) 639-4435
Mail to: P.O. Box 337, 39633
Questionnaire not received

ELEPORA

Webster County Historical Society
Rt. 3, 39744
Telephone: (601) 258-6898
Mail to: Box 14
Founded in: 1974
Albert Latham, President
Number of members: 15
Major programs: archives,
manuscripts, museum, historic site,
oral history, historic preservation

GREENWOOD

Cottonlandia Museum
Hwy. 82, E
Telephone: (601) 493-0925
Mail to: P.O. Box 1635, 38930
Private agency
Founded in: 1969
William R. Hony, Executive Director
Number of members: 1,000
Staff: full time 3, part time 1,
volunteer 30
Major programs: library, archives,
manuscripts, museum, historic
site(s), tours/pilgrimages, school
programs, book publishing,
newsletters/pamphlets, historic
preservation, records
management, research, exhibits,
archaeology programs,
photographic collections,
genealogical services, field
services, annual research
conference
Period of collections: A.D. 1000

HATTIESBURG

Bay Landmark Foundation
500 Bay St. 39401
Telephone: (601) 582-1771
Founded in: 1966
J. H. Turner, Jr., Chairman
Number of members: 140
Major programs: library, archives,
manuscripts, museum, historic site,
markers, tours/pilgrimages, book
publishing, historic preservation
Period of collections: 1900-1910

Mississippi Junior Historical Society
William Carey College 39401
Telephone: (601) 582-5051
Founded in: 1961
E. M. Wheeler, Chairman
Number of members: 704
Magazine: The Junior Historian
Major programs: manuscripts,
tours/pilgrimages, junior history,
oral history, educational programs,

newsletters/pamphlets, historic
preservation
Period of collections: 19th-20th
centuries

Sons of Confederate Veterans
Southern Station, P.O. Box 5164,
39406
Private agency
Founded in: 1896
William D. McCain, Adjutant-in-Chief
Number of members: 7,000
Staff: volunteer 3
Magazine: Confederate Veteran
Major programs: archives, museum,
historic site(s),
newsletters/pamphlets, historic
preservation
Period of collections: mid-1800s

HOLLY SPRINGS

Marshall County Historical Society, Inc.
220 E. College Ave.
Telephone: (601) 252-4437
Mail to: P.O. Box 806, 38635
Private agency
Founded in: 1970
Mrs. R. L. Wyatt, President
Number of members: 85
Staff: volunteer 10
Major programs: museum,
tours/pilgrimages, book publishing,
newsletters/pamphlets, historic
preservation, photographic
collections, genealogical services
Period of collections: 1836-1980

INDIANOLA

Sunflower County Historical Society, Inc.
200 2nd. St.
Telephone: (601) 887-3312
Mail to: P.O. Box 229, 38751
Founded in: 1974
Howard Q. Davis, Jr., President
Number of members: 100
Staff: volunteer 3
Major programs: book publishing
Period of collections: 1844-present

JACKSON

Historical and Genealogical Association of Mississippi
618 Avalon Rd., 39206
Telephone: (601) 362-3079
State agency
Founded in: 1977
Jackie Ratcliffe,
Secretary-Treasurer/Editor
Number of members: 175
Staff: volunteer 5
Magazine: Family Trails
Major programs: library, book
publishing, records management,
research, genealogical services,
preservation of state records
Period of collections: from 1800

Jackson Civil War Roundtable, Inc.
809 N. State, Apt. 8-16, 39201
Telephone: (601) 355-4796
Private agency
Founded in: 1962
Mrs. A. P. Andrews, Treasurer/Editor
Magazine: Rebel Yell

Major programs: book publishing,
newsletters/pamphlets
Period of collections: Civil War era

J. B. Cain Archives of Mississippi Methodism
Millsaps-Wilson Library, Millsaps
College, 39210
Telephone: (601) 354-5201
Private agency, authorized by
Millsaps College and the United
Methodist Church
Founded in: 1982
Mrs. Gerry Reiff, College Archivist
Staff: part time 2
Major programs: archives,
manuscripts
Period of collections: 1830-present

Manship House
420 E. Fortification St., 39202
Telephone: (601) 961-4724
State agency, authorized by
Department of Archives and History
Founded in: 1980
V. A. Patterson, Curator
Staff: full time 4, part time 3,
volunteer 5
Major programs: museum, historic
site(s), tours/pilgrimages, school
programs, historic preservation,
living history
Period of collections: 1836-1888

Mississippi Agriculture and Forestry Museum—National Agricultural and Aviation Museum
1150 Lakeland Dr., 39516
Telephone: (601) 354-6142
Mail to: P.O. Box 1609, 39215
State agency, authorized by
Department of Agriculture and
Commerce
Fred Gill, Director
Staff: full time 25, volunteer 5
Major programs: museum, historic
site(s), historic preservation,
exhibits, living history, audiovisual
programs
Period of collections: 1850-1980

Mississippi Committee for the Humanities
3825 Ridgewood Rd., Room 111,
39211
Telephone: (601) 982-6752
Private agency
Founded in: 1972
Cora Norman, Executive Director
Number of members: 22
Staff: full time 4, part time 2
Major programs: public humanities
program
Period of collections: 1972-present

◊Mississippi Department of Archives and History
100 S. State St., 39201
Telephone: (601) 359-1424
Mail to: P.O. Box 571, 39205-0571
Founded in: 1902
Elbert R. Hilliard, Director
Staff: full time 93, part time 18
Magazine: Journal of Mississippi
History
Major programs: library, archives,
manuscripts, museum, historic
site(s), markers, oral history, book
publishing, newsletters/pamphlets,

historic preservation, records management, exhibits, archaeology programs, photographic collections, genealogical services
Period of collections: prehistoric-present

Mississippi Governor's Mansion
300 E. Capitol St., 39201
Telephone: (601) 359-3175
State agency, authorized by Department of Archives and History
Founded in: 1976
Margaret Brown, Curator
Staff: full time 1, volunteer 35
Major programs: museum, tours/pilgrimages, exhibits
Period of collections: 1842-1865

◇**Mississippi Historical Society**
100 S. State St., 39201
Telephone: (601) 359-1424
Mail to: P.O. Box 571, 39205-0571
Private agency
Founded in: 1858
Elbert R. Hilliard, Secretary/Treasurer
Number of members: 1,518
Magazine: *Journal of Mississippi History*
Major programs: junior history, oral history, publications

Mississippi Military Museum
120 N. State
Mail to: P.O. Box 627, 39205
Private agency, authorized by War Veterans Memorial Commission
Founded in: 1976
John Tipten Lewis, Executive Director
Staff: volunteer 2
Period of collections: Spanish American War-Vietnam eras

Mississippi Museums Association
111 N. Jefferson St., 39202
Telephone: (601) 354-7303
Private agency
Founded in: 1975
Amanda Johnson, President
Number of members: 60
Staff: volunteer 7
Magazine: *Artifacts*
Major programs: museum, educational programs, newsletters/pamphlets, historic preservation
Period of collections: prehistoric-present

◇**Mississippi Museums Council**
803 Arlington St., 39202
Telephone: (601) 355-3221
State agency
Founded in: 1980
Betty B. Mitchell, State Museums Coordinator
Number of members: 250
Staff: full time 1, part time 1, volunteer 2
Magazine: *Artifacts*
Major programs: technical assistance for museums

Mississippi Park Commission
717 Robert E. Lee Bldg., Lamar St. 39201
Telephone: (601) 354-6322
Questionnaire not received

LIBERTY

Amite County Foundation For Historic Preservation
Rt. 4, Box 110, 39645
Telephone: (601) 684-1281
Questionnaire not received

MACON

Noxubee County Historical Society
201 E. Pearl St.
Telephone: (601) 726-4814
Mail to: P.O. Box 386, 39341
Founded in: 1966
Number of members: 100
Staff: volunteer 2
Major programs: archives, manuscripts, museum
Period of collections: 1865-present

MANTACHIE

Itawamba Historical Society, Inc.
N. Church St.
Mail to: P.O. Box 7, 38855
Private agency
Founded in: 1982
Bob Franks, President
Number of members: 242
Staff: volunteer 26
Magazine: *Itawamba Settlers*
Major programs: library, archives, museum, markers, newsletters/pamphlets, historic preservation, research, living history, audiovisual programs, genealogical services
Period of collections: 1830-1920

MERIDIAN

Jimmie Rodgers Memorial Festival, Inc.
P.O. Box 1928, 38301
Telephone: (601) 693-2686
Private agency
Founded in: 1972
James A. Skelton, President
Number of members: 800
Staff: full time 1, part time 2
Major programs: museum, annual festival week

Meridian Restorations Foundation, Inc.
905 31st Ave., 39301
Telephone: (601) 483-8439
Private agency
Founded in: 1978
Mrs. Earl Fortenberry, President
Number of members: 210
Staff: part time 2
Major programs: museum, historic preservation
Period of collections: Antebellum-Victorian eras

NATCHEZ

Grand Village of the Natchez Indians
400 Jefferson Davis Blvd., 39120
Telephone: (601) 446-6502
State agency, authorized by Department of Archives and History
Jim Barnett, Director, Division of Historic Properties
Staff: full time 6, part time 6

Major programs: museum, historic site(s), markers, school programs, research, exhibits
Period of collections: A.D. 1200-1730

Historic Natchez Foundation
Telephone: (601) 442-6495
Mail to: P.O. Box 1761, 39120
Private agency
Founded in: 1974
Charles H. Petkovsek, Jr., President
Number of members: 650
Major programs: newsletters/pamphlets, historic preservation, audiovisual programs, field services, Main Street Project
Period of collections: 19th century

Natchez Historical Society
307 S. Wall St.
Mail to: P.O. Box 49, 39120
Questionnaire not received

Natchez Pilgrimage Tours
410 N. Commerce St., 39120
Telephone: (601) 446-6631
Authorized by Pilgrimage Garden Club
Founded in: 1937
Hattie C. Stacy, Director of Marketing
Number of members: 823
Staff: full time 8, part time 2, volunteer 50
Major programs: historic site(s), tours/pilgrimages, newsletters/pamphlets, historic preservation, antique forum

Rosalie Daughters of the American Revolution
100 Orleans St., 39120
Telephone: (601) 445-4555
Private agency, authorized by National Society, Daughters of the American Revolution
Founded in: 1897
Carolyn C. Nugent, President
Number of members: 7,000
Staff: part time 12
Major programs: library, historic site(s), markers, tours/pilgrimages, oral history, newsletters/pamphlets, historic preservation
Period of collections: 1820-1895

OCEAN SPRINGS

1699 Historical Committee
810 Iberville, 39564
Telephone: (601) 875-5853
Private agency
Founded in: 1974
Mrs. Billie Brown, President
Number of members: 223
Major programs: historic site(s), tours/pilgrimages, historic preservation, living history

PASCAGOULA

Jackson County Historical Society
4602 Fort Dr., 39567
Telephone: (601) 769-1505
Founded in: 1949
Staff: volunteer 3
Major programs: archives, museum
Period of collections: 1783-1865

PASS CHRISTIAN

Pass Christian Historical Society
P.O. Box 58, 39571
Questionnaire not received

PORT GIBSON

Grand Gulf Military Monument Commission
Rt. 2, Box 389, 39150
Telephone: (601) 437-5911
Founded in: 1958
Glyn S. Slay, Park Manager
Staff: full time 3, part time 1,
volunteer 5
Major programs: museum, historic
site(s), markers, tours/pilgrimages,
newsletters/pamphlets, historic
preservation, exhibits
Period of collections: Civil War era

Port Gibson-Clairborne County Historical Society
39150
Telephone: (601) 437-4865
Founded in: 1957
Number of members: 95
Staff: volunteer 3
Major programs: archives,
manuscripts, historic sites
preservation, tours/pilgrimages,
books
Period of collections: 1783-1918

STARKVILLE

Oktibbeha County Heritage Museum
Fellowship St., 39759
Telephone: (601) 323-0211
County agency
Founded in: 1975
Mrs. A. G. Bennett, Sr., Board Chair
Staff: volunteer 25
Major programs: museum

TUPELO

Northeast Mississippi Historical and Genealogical Society
Mail to: P.O. Box 434, 38801
Founded in: 1976
Number of members: 400
Magazine: *Northeast Mississippi
Historical & Genealogical Quarterly*
Major programs: library, markers, oral
history, educational programs,
book publishing, historic
preservation, genealogy
Period of collections: 1800s

VICKSBURG

Vicksburg and Warren County Historical Society
1008 Cherry St., 39180
Telephone: (601) 636-0741
Private agency
Founded in: 1946
Gordon A. Cotton, Director/Curator
Number of members: 800
Staff: full time 5, part time 3
Major programs: library, archives,
museum, research, photographic
collections, genealogical services
Period of collections: 19th century

Vicksburg Foundation for Historic Preservation
P.O. Box 254, 39180

Private agency
Founded in: 1958
Ed Hinman, President
Number of members: 400
Staff: full time 2, part time 4
Major programs: museum, historic
site(s), tours/pilgrimages, oral
history, book publishing,
newsletters/pamphlets, historic
preservation, research, field
services

Vicksburg National Military Park
3201 Clay St., 39180
Telephone: (601) 636-0583
Federal agency, authorized by
National Park Service
Founded in: 1899
Paul F. McCrary, Superintendent
Staff: full time 35, part time 4,
volunteer 10
Major programs: museum, historic
site, markers, tours/pilgrimages,
historic preservation
Period of collections: 1861-1865

WASHINGTON

Historic Jefferson College
P.O. Box 100, 39190
Telephone: (601) 442-2901
State agency, authorized by
Department of Archives and History
Founded in: 1971
Jim Barnett, Director
Number of members: full time 10,
part-time 2
Major programs: library, museum,
historic site(s), markers, oral
history, school programs, historic
preservation, research, exhibits,
living history
Period of collections: 1802-1964

WOODVILLE

Davis Family Association
Hwy. 24, E
Telephone: (601) 888-6809
Mail to: P.O. Box 814, 39669
Private agency
Founded in: 1976
Ernesto Caldeira, Executive Director
Number of members: 200
Staff: volunteer 24
Major programs: archives, museum,
historic site(s),
newsletters/pamphlets, historic
preservation, research,
genealogical services, scholarship
program, studies of Jefferson Davis
lineage

YAZOO CITY

Yazoo Historical Society
332 N. Main St.
Telephone: (601) 746-2273
Mail to: P.O. Box 575, 39194
Private agency
Founded in: 1976
Linda R. Crawford, Director
Number of members: 565
Staff: full time 2
Major programs: museum, oral
history, educational programs,
books, newsletters/pamphlets
Period of collections:
prehistoric-present

MISSOURI

ALLENDALE

Worth County Historical Society
64420
Telephone: (816) 786-2318
County agency
Vanita R. Clark, President
Number of members: 47
Major programs: manuscripts,
markers, oral history, historic
preservation, exhibits, living
history, photographic collections

ALTENBURG

Perry County Lutheran Historical Society
63732
Telephone: (314) 824-5542
Private agency
Founded in: 1912
Leonard A. Kuehnert, President
Number of members: 30
Staff: volunteer 4
Major programs: archives, museum,
historic sites preservation, markers,
oral history, books
Period of collections: 1783-1865

ANABEL

Macon County Historical Society
R.R. 1, 63431
Telephone: (816) 699-3548
Founded in: 1955
Number of members: 115
Staff: volunteer 4
Major programs: markers, book
publishing
Period of collections: 1865-1918

ARROW ROCK

Arrow Rock State Historic Site
Department of Natural Resources,
65320
Telephone: (816) 837-3300
State agency
Authorized by: Division of Parks and
Historic Preservation
Founded in: 1829
Richard R. Forry, Historic Site
Administrator
Staff: full time 4, part time 1
Major programs: historic site,
tours/pilgrimages, educational
programs, historic preservation,
living history
Period of collections: 1820-1900

Friends of Arrow Rock
Main St., 65320
Private agency
Founded in: 1959
Day Kerr, President
Number of members: 250
Staff: full time 1, part time 2,
volunteer 16
Major programs: museum,
tours/pilgrimages, school
programs, book publishing,
newsletters/pamphlets, historic
preservation
Period of collections: 1840-1870

AVA

Douglas County Historical and Genealogical Society
Telephone: (417) 683-5113

Mail to: P.O. Box 873, 65608
Founded in: 1973
Number of members: 46
Major programs: historic sites
preservation, oral history,
newsletters/pamphlets
Period of collections: 1865-present

BELTON

Belton Historical Society
512 Main St.
Mail to: P.O. Box 1144, 64012
City agency
Authorized by: Belton Community
Projects, Inc.
Founded in: 1977
A. L. Dodson, President
Number of members: 178
Staff: volunteer 20
Major programs: museum, markers,
tours/pilgrimages, oral history,
historic preservation, exhibits,
living history, photographic
collections

BETHANY

Harrison County Historical Society
1604 Fuller St.
Telephone: (816) 425-8360
Mail to: P.O. Box 65, 64424
County agency
Founded in: 1965
Orville A. Kelim, President
Number of members: 75
Major programs: museum, oral
history, newsletters/pamphlets,
historic preservation, records
management, exhibits,
photographic collections,
genealogical services
Period of collections: 19th-20th
centuries

BETHEL

**Bethel German Communal
Colony, Inc.**
P.O. Box 127, 63434
Telephone: (816) 284-6493
Private agency
Founded in: 1972
Jeanne Adams, Executive Director
Number of members: 75
Staff: full time 4, part time 4
Major programs: museum, historic
site(s), markers, tours/pilgrimages,
newsletters/pamphlets, historic
preservation, audiovisual
programs, photographic
collections
Period of collections: 1844-1879

BLUE SPRINGS

Friends of Missouri Town 1855
22807 Woods Chapel Rd., 64015
Telephone: (816) 795-8200
County Agency
Authorized by: Jackson County Parks
and Recreation
Founded in: 1976
Richard L. Hart, President
Number of members: 230
Staff: volunteer 12
Magazine: *Missouri Messenger*
Major programs: tours/pilgrimages,
oral history, school programs,
newsletters/pamphlets, research,
living history, audiovisual

programs, photographic
collections
Period of collections: 1840-1860

**Jackson County Parks and
Recreation Department**
22807 Woods Chapel Rd.
Telephone: (816) 795-8200
Questionnaire not received

Missouri Town 1855
22807 Woods Chapel Rd., 64015
Telephone: (816) 524-8770
County agency
Authorized by: Jackson County Parks
and Recreation
Founded in: 1962
Leonard G. Bates, Lead Historic Site
Interpretor
Staff: full time 4, part time 5,
volunteer 75
Major programs: museum, school
programs, research, exhibits, living
history
Period of collections: 1820-1860

BOLIVAR

Polk County Historical Society
516 N. Water Ave.
Telephone: (417) 326-7698
Mail to: P.O. Box 298, 65613
Founded in: 1971
Questionnaire not received

BOONVILLE

Boonslick Historical Society
Telephone: (816) 882-5621
Mail to: P.O. Box 324, 65233
Founded in: 1937
Adolph E. Hilden
Number of members: 198
Staff: volunteer 4
Major programs: historic site(s),
markers, newsletters/pamphlets,
historic preservation, genealogical
services
Period of collections: from 1800

Friends of Historic Boonville, Inc.
612-614 Morgan St.
Telephone: (816) 7977
Mail to: P.O. Box 1776, 65233
Private agency
Founded in: 1971
Sharon Korte, President
Number of members: 200
Staff: full time 2
Major programs: archives, historic
site(s), tours/pilgrimages, school
programs, historic preservation,
genealogical services, annual
performing arts festival
Period of collections: 1810-1930s

BUFFALO

Dallas County Historical Society
Telephone: (417) 345-7297
Mail to: P.O. Box 594, 65622
Private agency
Founded in: 1966
Leni Howe, Secretary
Number of members: 180
Staff: volunteer 5
Major programs: museum, markers,
book publishing,
newsletters/pamphlets, historic
preservation, genealogical
services
Period of collections: 1867-1900

BURFORDVILLE

Bollinger Mill State Historic Site
P.O. Box 248, 63739
Telephone: (314) 243-4591
State agency
Authorized by: Department of Natural
Resources, Division of Parks and
Historic Preservation
Founded in: 1967
Jack Smoot, Historic Site
Administrator III
Staff: full time 2, part time 1
Major programs: historic site(s),
historic preservation, exhibits
Period of collections: mid-late 1800s

BUTLER

Bates County Historical Society
10 W. Ohio, 64730
Founded in: 1962
Questionnaire not received

CABOOL

Cabool History Society
City Hall, 65689
Telephone: (417) 962-4775
Private agency
Number of members: 10
Staff: volunteers 4
Major programs: archives, oral
history, genealogical services

CALEDONIA

Bellevue Valley Historical Society
Telephone: (314) 779-3757
Mail to: R.R. 1, Box 4098, Potosi,
63664
Private agency
Authorized by: Missouri Historical
Society
Founded in: 1975
Eula Eye, Secretary
Number of members: 81
Staff: volunteers 11
Major programs: manuscripts,
historic site(s), markers,
tours/pilgrimages, book publishing,
historic preservation, genealogical
services
Period of collections: 1763-1981

CALIFORNIA

Moniteau County Historical Society
Mail to: P.O. Box 263, 65018
Private agency
Founded in: 1966
David Jungmeyer, President
Number of members: 130
Staff: volunteer 10
Major programs: museum, historic
sites preservation,
tours/pilgrimages, books,
genealogy, records management
Period of collections: 1865-1918

CAMERON

Caldwell County Historical Society
Rt. 4, Box 150, 64429
Telephone: (816) 632-2320
Private agency
Founded in: 1980
David Reed, President
Number of members: 45
Major programs: book publishing,
newsletters/pamphlets, historic
preservation

CANTON

Lewis County Historical Society
614 Clark St., 63435
Telephone: (314) 288-3861
County agency
Founded in: 1968
S. H. Purvines, President
Number of members: 71
Staff: volunteers 2
Major programs: historic
preservation, records
management, research,
genealogical services
Period of collections: 1830-present

CAPE GIRARDEAU

**Historical Association of Greater
Cape Girardeau, Inc.**
325 S. Spanish St., 63701
Telephone: (314) 334-1177
Founded in: 1967
Shirley Palen, President
Number of members: 400
Staff: part time 1, volunteer 30
Magazine: *The Bulletin*
Major programs: library, archives,
manuscripts, museum, historic
site(s), tours/pilgrimages, junior
history, oral history, school
programs, newsletters/pamphlets,
historic preservation, research,
exhibits, photographic collections,
genealogical services
Period of collections: 1850-present

CARTHAGE

Powers Museum
Telephone: (417) 358-2667
Mail to: P.O. Box 593, 64836
City agency
Founded in: 1982
Michele Newton, Curator
Staff: full time 1, part time 3
Major programs: library, archives,
museum, research, exhibits,
photographic collections
Period of collections: 1870-1950

CARUTHERSVILLE

Pemiscot County Historical Society
7th and Carleton Sts.
Mail to: 600 Carleton Ave., 63830
County agency
Founded in: 1970
Rachel Dawson, President
Number of members: 60
Staff: volunteer 3
Magazine: *Pemiscot County Missouri
Quarterly*

CASSVILLE

Barry County Historical Society
Mail to: 204 West St., 65625
County agency
Founded in: 1960
Charles A. Vaughan, President
Number of members: 10
Staff: volunteers 1
Major programs: museum, exhibits,
Period of collections: prehistoric

CENTRALIA

Centralia Historical Society
319 E. Sneed, 65240

Telephone: (314) 682-5711
Founded in: 1975
Questionnaire not received

CHARLESTON

**Mississippi County Historical
Society**
500 N. Green, 63834
Telephone: (314) 683-4348
Questionnaire not received

CHILLICOTHE

**Grand River Historical Society and
Museum**
818 Sunset
Telephone: (816) 646-4323/646-4433
Mail to: P.O. Box 154, 64601
Founded in: 1959
Frank E. Stark, President
Number of members: 350
Magazine: *The Herald*
Major programs: museum, school
programs, book publishing,
newsletters/pamphlets, historic
preservation, records
management, research, exhibits,
audiovisual programs,
photographic collections
Period of collections: 1900-present

Livingston County Library
450 Locust, 64601
Telephone: (816) 646-0547
County agency
Founded in: 1921
Karen L. Hicklin, Director
Staff: full time 6, part time 4,
volunteers 4
Major programs: library
Period of collections: 1900-present

CLAYTON

Concordia Historical Institute
801 DeMun Ave., 63105
Telephone: (314) 721-5934, ext. 320
Founded in: 1927
Questionnaire not received

**St. Louis County Department of
Parks and Recreation**
41 S. Central Ave., 63105
Telephone: (314) 889-3357
County agency
Founded in: 1957
Virginia Stith, Director, Historic Sites
and Preservation
Staff: full time 10, part time 3,
volunteers 10
Major programs: historic site(s),
school programs, historic
preservation
Period of collections: 1800-1945

CLINTON

Henry County Historical Society
205 E. Franklin, 64735
Telephone: (816) 885-8414
Questionnaire not received

COLE CAMP

Cole Camp Area Historcial Society
c/o President, 65325
Telephone: (816) 668-4813
Private agency
Founded in: 1977
Roy Donnell, President

Number of members: 90
Major programs: library, archives,
manuscripts, historic site(s),
markers, oral history, school
programs, historic preservation,
research, photographic
collections, genealogical services
Period of collections: 1840-present

COLUMBIA

**Joint Collection, University of
Missouri Western Historical
Manuscript Collection—Columbia
and State Historical Society of
Missouri Manuscripts**
23 Ellis Library, University of Missouri,
Columbia, 65201
Telephone: (314) 882-6028
State agency
Authorized by: the university and
Missouri State Historical Society of
Missouri
Founded in: 1943
Nancy Lankford, Associate Director
Staff: full time 15, part time 3
Major programs: manuscripts,
exhibits, photographic collections
Period of collections: 1800-present

◊**Missouri Cultural Heritage Center**
400 Hitt St., 201 S, 65211
Telephone: (314) 882-6296
State agency
Authorized by: University of Missouri,
Columbia
Founded in: 1982
Howard W. Marshall, Director
Staff: full time 5, part time 2,
volunteer 4
Major programs: oral history,
newsletters/pamphlets, historic
preservation, research, exhibits,
living history, field services,
consultation services, folklife and
folklore programs

**Museum of Anthropology,
University of Missouri**
100 Swallow Hall 65211
Telephone: (314) 882-3764
Founded in: 1949
Lawrence H. Feldman, Curator
Staff: full time 1, part time 1,
volunteer 10
Major programs: museum
Period of collections: prehistoric

◊**State Historical Society of
Missouri**
1020 Lowry St., 65201
Telephone: (314) 882-7083
Founded in: 1898
Richard S. Brownlee,
Director/Secretary
Number of members: 10,000
Staff: full time 19, part time 4
Magazine: *Missouri Historical Review*
Major programs: library, manuscripts,
research, exhibits, photographic
collections, genealogical services,
field services
Period of collections: 1783-present

University of Missouri Archives
701 Lewis Hall, 65201
Telephone: (314) 882-7567
Founded in: 1839
Staff: full time 5, part time 5

Major programs: archives,
manuscripts, educational
programs
Period of collections: 1918-present

CRESTWOOD

Sappington House Foundation
1015 Sappington Rd.
Telephone: (314) 966-4700, ext. 271
Private Agency
Founded in: 1969
Ruth B. Jones, President
Number of members: 150
Staff: volunteer 125
Major programs: library, museum,
tours/pilgrimages, school
programs, audiovisual programs

CREVE COEUR

**Creve Coeur-Chesterfield
Historical Society**
11631 Olive Blvd.
Telephone: (314) 434-5163
Mail to: 1222 Prinster, St. Louis, 63141
Founded in: 1968
Questionnaire not received

CRYSTAL CITY

Crystal City Historical Society
130 Mississippi, 63019
Private agency
Founded in: 1979
Questionnaire not received

CUBA

**Crawford County Historical
Society, Inc.**
Recklein Hall
Telephone: (314) 885-7912
Mail to: Rt. 2, Box 213-B, 65453
Founded in: 1967
Questionnaire not received

DEFIANCE

Daniel Boone Home
Hwy. F, 63341
Telephone: (314) 987-2221
Private agency
Authorized by: Rolla P. Andrae Family
Trust
Founded in: 1959
Rolla P. Andrae, President/Curator
Major programs: museum, historic
site(s), tours/pilgrimages, school
programs, historic preservation

DILLARD

Dillard Mill State Historic Site
Rt. 286, Box 65, 65458
Telephone: (314) 244-3120
State agency
Authorized by: Department of Natural
Resources
Founded in: 1975
George A. Czech, Site Administrator
Staff: full time 2, part time 2
Major programs: archives, historic
site(s), school programs, historic
preservation, research, exhibits
Period of collections: 1904-1960

DONIPHAN

Ripley County Historical Society
805 Elm St.
Telephone: (314) 996-3376

Mail to: P.O. Box 385, 63935
Questionnaire not received

EDINA

Knox County Historical Society
Courthouse, 63537
County agency
Founded in: 1966
Brenton Karhoff, President
Number of members: 100
Staff: volunteer 20
Major programs: library, manuscripts,
museum, historic preservation,
photographic collections,
genealogical services
Period of collections: 1865-present

EXCELSIOR SPRINGS

**Excelsior Springs Historical
Museum**
101 E. Broadway, 64024
Telephone: (816) 637-3712
City agency
Founded in: 1967
Virginia Dykes, President
Number of members: 500
Staff: volunteer 10
Magazine: *The Phunn*
Major programs: museum, school
programs, book publishing,
newsletters/pamphlets, research,
exhibits, audiovisual programs,
photographic collections,
genealogical services
Period of collections: 1880-present

FAYETTE

**Stephens Museum of Natural
History—United Methodist
Historical Collection**
Central Methodist College, 65248
Telephone: (816) 248-3391
Private agency
Authorized by: the college
Founded in: 1879
Maryellen H. McVicker, Director
Staff: part time 4, volunteer 20
Major programs: museum,
tours/pilgrimages, school
programs, historic preservation,
exhibits
Period of collections: 1800-1880

FERGUSON

Ferguson Historical Society
315 Darst Rd., 63135
Telephone: (314) 521-0977
Private agency
Founded in: 1972
Lawrence Nienabor, President
Number of members: 150
Staff: volunteer 13
Major programs: manuscripts, book
publishing, newsletters/pamphlets,
research, exhibits, photographic
collections
Period of collections: 1880-1920

FLORIDA

Friends of Florida
Telephone: (314) 565-3353
Mail to: Rt. 1, Stoutsville, 65283
Private agency
Founded in: 1965
Orland Yates, Chair

Number of members: 37
Major programs: town restoration
Period of collections: 1835-1840

**Mark Twain Birthplace State
Historic Site**
P.O. Box 54, Stoutsville, 65283
Telephone: (314) 565-3449
State agency
Authorized by: Department of Natural
Resources
Founded in: 1960
Stanley Fast, Site Administrator
Staff: full time 3, part time 3
Major programs: library, museum,
historic site(s)
Period of collections: 1835-1910

FLORISSANT

Florissant Valley Historical Society
No. 1, Traille de Noyer, 63031
Telephone: (314) 524-1100
Mail to: P.O. Box 298, 63032
Founded in: 1958
Questionnaire not received

Historic Florissant, Inc.
180 Dunn Rd., 63031
Telephone: (314) 831-0305
Private agency
Founded in: 1969
Rosemary Davison, President
Staff: volunteer 12
Major programs: historic site(s),
historic preservation

FORT LEONARD WOOD

Ft. Leonard Wood Museum
Nebraska and S. Dakota Sts.,
ATZT-PTS-OM, 65473
Telephone: (314) 368-4249
Federal agency
Authorized by: the U. S. Army
Founded in: 1971
Robert K. Combs, Director
Staff: full time 2
Major programs: archives, museum,
historic site(s), school programs,
historic preservation, archaeology
programs, photographic
collections
Period of collections: 1940s-present

FULTON

**Kingdom of Callaway Historical
Society**
7th and Westminister Ave., 65251
Questionnaire not received

**Winston Churchill Memorial and
Library**
7th and Westminster
Telephone: (314) 642-3361/624-6648
Mail to: Westminster College,
65251-1299
Founded in: 1965
Warren Hollrah, Museum
Manager/Archivist
Staff: full time 3, part time 6,
volunteer 25
Magazine: *Churchill Memorial Memo*
Major programs: library, archives,
museum, historic sites
preservation, tours/pilgrimages,
newsletters/pamphlets
Period of collections: 1935-1945

MISSOURI

GALLATIN

Daviess County Historical Society
c/o Treasurer, 64640
Telephone: (816) 663-3384
Private agency
Founded in: 1973
Mrs. Robert W. Dale, Treasurer
Number of members: 100
Major programs: historic site(s), book
publishing, records management

GERALD

**Oregon-California Trails
Association**
P.O. Box 42, 63037
Telephone: (314) 764-2801
Private agency
Founded in: 1982
Gregory M. Franzwa, President
Number of members: 700
Staff: full time 1, volunteer 5
Major programs: historic site(s),
markers, tours/pilgrimages,
newsletters/pamphlets, historic
preservation, research
Period of collections: 1840-1870

GLADSTONE

Clay County Historical Society
202 N.W. 65th, 64118
Telephone: (816) 436-0156
Questionnaire not received

GRAHAM

Graham Historical Society, Inc.
Telephone: (816) 939-2275
Mail to: P.O. Box 72, 64455
Founded in: 1965
Letha Marie Mowry, Files Secretary
Number of members: 19
Staff: volunteer 9
Major programs: archives, museum,
historic sites preservation, books,
genealogy
Period of collections: 1783-present

GREENFIELD

**Dade County Missouri Historical
Society**
207 McPherson, 65661
Telephone: (417) 637-2744
Z. Hazel Yates,
Publications-Genealogy Chair
Number of members: 35
Staff: volunteer 6
Major programs: library, archives,
manuscripts, museum, historic
site(s), tours/pilgrimages, oral
history, book publishing,
newsletters/pamphlets, historic
preservation, records
management, research, exhibits,
living history, audiovisual
programs, archaeology programs,
photographic collections,
genealogical services, field
services
Period of collections: 1865-1918

HANNIBAL

Marion County Historical Society
5021 College, 63401
Telephone: (314) 248-1884
Founded in: 1956

Richard Schwartz, President
Number of members: 35
Major programs: historic sites
preservation, markers
Period of collections: 1819-present

Mark Twain Home Board
208 Hill St., 63401
Telephone: (314) 221-9010
City agency
Founded in: 1936
Henry H. Sweets III, Curator
Staff: full time 1, part time 4
Major programs: library, museum,
historic site(s), school programs,
historic preservation, exhibits,
photographic collections
Period of collections: 1840-present

HARRISONVILLE

**Cass County Historical
Society, Inc.**
400 E. Mechanic, 64701
Telephone: (816) 884-5352
County agency
Founded in: 1965
Mrs. Oren S. Webster, Treasurer
Number of members: 210
Staff: volunteer 12
Magazine: *Cass County Historical
Society Newsletter*
Major programs: archives, museum,
school programs,
newsletters/pamphlets,
genealogical services
Period of collections: 1835-present

HAZELWOOD

Hazelwood Historical Society
450 Brookes Lane
Telephone: (314) 731-1589
Mail to: P.O. Box 64, 63042
Private agency
Founded in: 1961
M. V. Faatz, President
Number of members: 20
Staff: volunteer 4
Major programs: archives, museum,
historic site(s), historic
preservation, genealogical
services
Period of collections: 1865-present

HERMANN

Brush and Palette Club, Inc.
Telephone: (314) 486-2537
Mail to: c/o Lois Hoerstkamp,
President, 114 W. 9th, 65041
Questionnaire not received

Deutschheim State Historic Site
109 W. 2nd St., 65041
Telephone: (314) 486-2200
State agency
Authorized by: Department of Parks
and Historic Preservation
Founded in: 1978
Erin McCawley Renn, Site
Administrator
Staff: full time 2
Major programs: museum, historic
site(s), tours/pilgrimages,
research, exhibits
Period of collections: 1830-1880

**Gasconade County Historical
Society**
114 W. 9th St., 65041

Telephone: (314) 486-3464
County agency
Founded in: 1969
Patrick Steele, Sr., President
Number of members: 75
Staff: volunteer 15
Major programs: museum, historic
sites preservation, markers,
tours/pilgrimages, books
Period of collections: 1821-present

Historic Hermann, Inc.
German School Bldg., 4th and
Schiller Sts.
Telephone: (314) 486-2017/486-2781
Mail to: P.O. Box 88, 65041
Private agency
Founded in: 1952
Gennie Tesson, President
Number of members: 123
Staff: part time 5, volunteer 12
Major programs: museum, historic
site(s), tours/pilgrimages, school
programs, book publishing,
newsletters/pamphlets, historic
preservation
Period of collections: 1838-present

HIGGINSVILLE

**Confederate Memorial State
Historic Site**
R.R. 1, Box 221-A, 64037
Telephone: (816) 584-2853
State agency
Authorized by: Department of Natural
Resources
Founded in: 1978
Janae Fuller, Administrator
Staff: full time 2
Major programs: library, archives,
historic site(s), tours/pilgrimages,
oral history, photographic
collections, genealogical services
Period of collections: Civil War era

HILLSBORO

**Sandy Creek Covered Bridge State
Historic Site**
Old LeMay Ferry Rd., 63050
Telephone: (314) 937-3697
Mail to: 2901 Hwy. 61, Festus, 63028
State agency
Authorized by: Department of Natural
Resources
Founded in: 1967
Gary Walrath, Assistant Regional
Supervisor
Major programs: historic site(s)
Period of collections: 1872-1886

INDEPENDENCE

**Harry S. Truman Courtroom and
Office**
Independence Square Courthouse,
Suite 109, 64050
Telephone: (816) 881-4467/881-4431
County agency
Authorized by: Jackson County Parks
and Recreation
Founded in: 1973
Gary R. Toms, Historic Curator
Staff: full time 1, part time 1
Major programs: museum, historic
site(s)
Period of collections: 1922-1934

Harry S. Truman Library
64050
Telephone: (816) 833-1400
Federal agency
Authorized by: National Archives and
Records Administration
Founded in: 1957
Benedict K. Zobrist, Director
Number of members: 3
Staff: full time 30, part time 1
Magazine: *Whistle Stop*
Major programs: library, archives,
manuscripts, museum, oral history,
research, exhibits, photographic
collections
Period of collections: 1945-1953

Independence Heritage Commission
103 N. Main, 64050
Telephone: (816) 836-8300
Founded in: 1973
Questionnaire not received

Jackson County Historical Society
Independence Square Courthouse,
Room 103, 64050
Telephone: (816) 836-1827
Founded in: 1958
Sarah F. Schwenk, Director
Number of members: 2,500
Staff: full time 4, part time 4,
volunteer 250
Magazine: *Jackson County Historical
Society Journal*
Major programs: library, archives,
manuscripts, museum, historic
sites tours/pilgrimages, oral
history, school programs, book
publishing, newsletters/pamphlets,
historic preservation, records
management, research, exhibits,
photographic collections,
genealogical services
Period of collections: 1783-present

**Reorganized Church of Jesus
Christ of Latter Day Saints
History Commission**
Auditorium, River and Walnut
Telephone: (816) 833-1000
Mail to: P.O. Box 1059, 64051
Questionnaire not received

Restoration Trail Foundation
1235 W. Lexington, 64050
Telephone: (816) 836-4671
Founded in: 1970
Number of members: 1,250
Staff: part time 1, volunteer 4
Magazine: *Restoration Trail Forum*
Major programs: historic sites
preservation, historic preservation
Period of collections: 1830-1890

IRONTON

Iron County Historical Society
Telephone: (314) 546-3714
Mail to: 318 Edison Ct., 63650
Founded in: 1974
Number of members: 191

JEFFERSON CITY

Cole County Historical Society
109 Madison, 65101
Telephone: (314) 635-1850
County agency
Founded in: 1941
Barb Tyler, Curator
Number of members: 1,000

Staff: part time 1, volunteer 35
Major programs: library, manuscripts,
museum, historic site(s),
tours/pilgrimages, school
programs, newsletters/pamphlets,
historic preservation, research,
living history, photographic
collections, genealogical services
Period of collections: 1850-present

**Mid-Missouri Civil War Round
Table**
P.O. Box 562, 65102
Private agency
Founded in: 1982
Steve Yoakum, Secretary/Treasurer
Number of members: 43
Major programs:
newsletters/pamphlets
Period of collections: 1861-1865

**Missouri Department of Natural
Resources**
Telephone: (314) 751-2479
Mail to: P.O. Box 176, 65101
Founded in: 1924
Questionnaire not received

Missouri Heritage Trust, Inc.
Telephone: (314) 635-6877
Mail to: P.O. Box 895, 65102
Founded in: 1976
Number of members: 500
Staff: part time 2
Magazine: *Missouri Preservation
News*
Major programs: historic sites
preservation, educational
programs, newsletters/pamphlets

Missouri State Library
301 W. High St.
Telephone: (314) 751-3615
Mail to: P.O. Box 387, 65102
State agency
Founded in: 1907
Charles O'Halloran, State Librarian
Staff: full time 30, part time 1
Magazine: *Show-Me Libraries*
Major programs: library

◇**Missouri State
Museum—Jefferson Landing
State Historic Site**
Capitol Bldg., Room B-2, 65101
Telephone: (314) 751-2854
State agency
Authorized by: Department of Natural
Resources
Number of members: 1970
Martin E. Shay, Site Administrator
Staff: full time 10, part time 10,
volunteer 5
Major programs: museum,
tours/pilgrimages, book publishing,
newsletters/pamphlets, historic
preservation, records
management, research, exhibits,
audiovisual programs
Period of collections: 19th-20th
centuries

JOPLIN

Joplin Historical Society
Schifferdecker Park
Telephone: (417) 623-1180
Mail to: P.O. Box 555, 64801
Private agency
Founded in: 1966
Barbara Hicklin, President

Number of members: 497
Staff: full time 1, volunteer 52
Major programs: archives, museum,
markers, tours/pilgrimages, oral
history, historic preservation,
exhibits, photographic collections
Period of collections: 1865-1920

KAHOKA

Clark County Historical Society
R.R. 3, Box 164-D, 63445
Telephone: (816) 727-3029
County agency
Steve Murphy, President
Number of members: 80
Staff: volunteer 7
Major programs: museum, historic
site(s), tours/pilgrimages, historic
preservation, photographic
collections, genealogical services
Period of collections: 1840s

KANSAS CITY

**American Family Records
Association**
311 E. 12th St., 64106
Telephone: (816) 453-1294
Private agency
Founded in: 1978
Kermit B. Karns, President
Number of members: 400
Staff: volunteer 5
Magazine: *TODAY, The Journal of
American Family Records*
Major programs: library, book
publishing, records management,
genealogical services
Period of collections: 1750-present

**Archives of the Episcopal Diocese
of West Missouri**
415 W. 13th St., 64111
Telephone: (816) 471-6161
Questionnaire not received

**Archives of St. Luke's Hospital of
Kansas City**
Wornall Rd. at 44th St., 64111
Telephone: (816) 932-2517
Private agency
Authorized by: the Protestant
Episcopal Church
Founded in: 1882
Ferne Malcolm Welles, Archivist
Staff: full time 1, part time 1,
volunteer 3
Major programs: library, archives,
manuscripts, oral history, records
management, research, exhibits,
audiovisual programs,
photographic collections,
medical/hospital history
Period of collections: 1865-present

Black Archives of Mid-America
2033 Vine, 64108
Telephone: (816) 483-1300
Mail to: 2033 Vine
Founded in: 1974
Horace M. Peterson III, Director
Number of members: 50
Staff: full time 9, part time 4,
volunteer 3
Magazine: *The Archival Gri öt*
Major programs: archives, museum
Period of collections: 1863-present

Daughters of Old Westport
937 W. 42nd, 64111
Telephone: (816) 931-5260
Founded in: 1912
Mrs. Richard W. Graff, President
Number of members: 35
Period of collections: 1865-present

Grace and Holy Trinity Cathedral
415 W. 13th St.
Telephone: (816) 474-8260
Mail to: P.O. Box 23218, 64141
Private agency
Authorized by: Episcopal Diocese of
W. Missouri
Founded in: 1981
Nancy J. Hulston, Archivist
Staff: part time 2
Major programs: archives, historic
site(s), tours/pilgrimages, oral
history, records management,
research, audiovisual programs
Period of collections: 1870-present

**Heritage League of Greater Kansas
City**
Library Bldg. 212, University of
Missouri
Telephone: (816) 276-1543
Mail to: 5100 Rockhill Rd., 64110
Private agency
Founded in: 1980
Janet Bruce, President
Number of members: 100
Major programs:
newsletters/pamphlets, workshops

Heritage Village
7000 N.E. Barry Rd.
Telephone: (816) 444-4363
Mail to: 5600 E. Gregory, 64130
Founded in: 1975
Questionnaire not received

Historic Kansas City Foundation
20 W. 9th St., Suite 450, 64105
Telephone: (816) 471-3391
Private agency
Founded in: 1974
Mark D. Shapiro, Executive Director
Number of members: 1,100
Staff: full time 6, part time 1,
volunteer 42
Magazine: *Historic Kansas City
Foundation Gazette, Possum
Trotter*
Major programs: library, historic sites
preservation, tours/pilgrimages,
educational programs,
newsletters/pamphlets, historic
preservation
Period of collections: 1865-present

**International Headquarters, Church
of the Nazarene Archives**
6401 The Paseo, 64131
Telephone: (816) 333-7000
Founded in: 1944
Questionnaire not received

**Kansas City Branch, National
Archives**
2312 E. Bannister Rd., 64131
Telephone: (816) 926-7271
Federal agency
Authorized by: National Archives and
Records Administration
Founded in: 1968
R. Reed Whitaker, Director
Staff: full time 8, part time 4,
volunteers 46

Major programs: archives
Period of collections: 1880-1960

Kansas City Museum
3218 Gladstone Blvd., 64123
Telephone: (816) 483-8300
Private agency
Authorized by: the Kansas City
Museum Association
Founded in: 1939
Baryy H. Rosen, Executive Director
Number of members: 1,300
Staff: full time 25, part time 15,
volunteer 255
Magazine: *Museum Piece*
Major programs: archives,
manuscripts, museum, historic
site(s), tours/pilgrimages, school
programs, newsletters/pamphlets,
historic preservation, records
management, research, exhibits,
living history, audiovisual
programs, photographic
collections, field services,
planetarium programs
Period of collections:
prehistoric-1900s

**Kansas City Posse—The
Westerners**
1250 W. Gregory Blvd., 64114
Telephone: (816) 363-8174
Private agency
Authorized by: The Westerners, Int.
Founded in: 1951
Lawrence H. Larsen, Sheriff
Number of members: 50
Magazine: *Trail Guide*
Major programs: monthly meeting

**Landmarks Commission of Kansas
City**
City Hall, 26th Floor, 414 E. 12th St.,
64106
Telephone: (816) 274-2555
City agency
Founded in: 1970
Jane F. Flynn, Administrator
Staff: full time 4
Major programs: book publishing,
newsletters/pamphlets, historic
preservation, research
Period of collections: 1890-1980

**Liberty Memorial Association and
Museum**
100 W. 26th St., 64108
Telephone: (816) 221-1918
Private agency
Founded in: 1919
Mark Beveridge, Museum Curator
Staff: full time 2, part time 3,
volunteers 3
Major programs: library, archives,
manuscripts, museum,
newsletters/pamphlets, research,
exhibits, photographic collections,
artifact restoration
Period of collections: World War I

**Missouri Valley Room, Kansas City
Public Library**
311 E. 12th St., 64106
Telephone: (816) 221-2685
Founded in: 1960
Daniel J. Bradbury, Library Director
Staff: full time 5, volunteers 3
Major programs: library, archives,
manuscripts
Period of collections: 1855-present

**National Archives—Kansas City
Branch**
2312 E. Bannister Rd., 64131
Telephone: (816) 926-7271
Founded in: 1969
R. Reed Whitaker, Director
Staff: full time 7
Major programs: archives,
educational programs, teachers'
workshops, genealogical
workshops, film series, open
houses and tours
Period of collections: 1822-1978

Native Sons of Kansas City
11 E. Gregory
Telephone: (816) 523-0901
Mail to: P.O. Box 8576, 64114
Founded in: 1932
Questionnaire not received

Peter Willcocks Society
815 W. 39th Terrace, 64111
Telephone: (816) 931-7040
Mail to: P.O. Box 1832, 64141
Founded in: 1971
Questionnaire not received

**The Smoky Hill Railway and
Historical Society—The Kansas
City Railroad Museum**
Mail to: P.O. Box 124, Shawnee
Mission, 66201
Founded in: 1964
Questionnaire not received

**Thomas Hart Benton Home and
Studio**
3616 Belleview, 64111
Telephone: (816) 931-5722
State agency
Authorized by: Department of Natural
Resources
Founded in: 1977
Dudley J. McGovern, Site
Administrator
Staff: full time 2, part time 3,
volunteer 5
Major programs: historic site(s), tours
Period of collections: 1939-1975

**Union Cemetery Historical
Society, Inc.**
2727 Main St., Room 300, 64108
City agency
Authorized by: Parks and Recreation
Department
Founded in: 1984
Susan Wickern, President
Number of members: 47
Staff: volunteer 15
Magazine: *The Epitaph*
Major programs: historic site(s),
tours/pilgrimages,
newsletters/pamphlets, historic
preservation, research,
genealogical services
Period of collections: 1889-1953

**University of Missouri—Kansas
City Archives**
5100 Rockhill Rd., 64110
Telephone: (816) 276-1539
Founded in: 1978
Sharron G. Uhler, Associate Archivist
Staff: full time 2, part time 1
Major programs: archives
Period of collections: 1881-present

Western Historical Manuscript Collection—Kansas City
5100 Rockhill Rd., 64110
Telephone: (816) 276-1543
Mail to: Library Bldg., University of Missouri, Kansas City
State agency
Authorized by: the university
Founded in: 1968
Gordon O. Hendrickson, Associate Director
Staff: full time 2, part time 2
Major programs: archives, manuscripts, research
Period of collections: 20th century

Westport Historical Society
c/o Harris Kearney House, 4000 Baltimore
Telephone: (816) 561-1821
Mail to: P.O. Box 10076, Westport Station, 64111
Founded in: 1950
Clair Schroeder, President
Number of members: 400
Major programs: library, archives, manuscripts, historic site(s), markers, tours/pilgrimages, book publishing, newsletters/pamphlets, historic preservation, research
Period of collections: 1825-1890

Wornall House Museum
146 W. 61 Terrace, 64113
Telephone: (816) 444-1858
Private agency
Authorized by: Jackson County Historical Society
Founded in: 1972
Janet Bruce, Director
Number of members: 400
Staff: full time 1, part time 1, volunteer 150
Major programs: historic site(s), school programs, historic preservation, research
Period of collections: 1830-1865

KEARNEY

Clay County Division of Historic Sites
Jesse James Farm Dr.
Telephone: (816) 635-6065
Mail to: Rt. 2, Box 236, 64060
County agency
Founded in: 1978
Milton F. Perry, Superintendent
Staff: full time 5, part time 7
Major programs: museum, historic site(s), markers, oral history, historic preservation, research, exhibits, archaeology programs, photographic collections, genealogical services
Period of collections: 19th century

Friends of Jesse James Farm
Jesse James Farm Dr.Telephone: (816) 635-6065
Mail to: Rt. 2, Box 236, 64060
Founded in: 1980
Martin McGrane, President
Number of members: 300
Magazine: *James Farm Journal*
Major programs: book publishing, newsletters/pamphlets, genealogical services
Period of collections: 19th century

KENNETT

Dunklin County Museum
122 College, 63857
Private agency
Founded in: 1976
Sandra Brown, Director
Staff: volunteer 15
Major programs: museum, exhibits, photographic collections

KEYTESVILLE

Friends of Keytesville, Inc.
304 Bridge St., 65261
Private agency
Founded in: 1964
Sue Ann Hughes, President
Number of members: 150
Staff: volunteer 10
Major programs: museum, historic sites preservation, markers, historic preservation
Period of collections: 1800s-1900s

KING CITY

Tri-County Historical and Museum Society of King City, Inc.
508 N. Grand Ave. and Jct. Hwy. 169, 64463
Founded in: 1975
Carroll B. Simmons, President
Number of members: 130
Staff: volunteer 40
Major programs: manuscripts, museum, historic site(s), book publishing, newsletters/pamphlets, historic preservation, records management, research, exhibits, living history, genealogical services
Period of collections: 1865-present

KIRKSVILLE

Northeast Missouri State University Division of Libraries and Museums: University Archives, Missouriana Library and Violette Museum
63501
Telephone: (816) 785-4537
Founded in: 1867
Questionnaire not received

Still National Osteopathic Museum
311 S. 4th St., 63501
Telephone: (816) 626-2359
Private agency
Founded in: 1978
Mrs. James R. Stookey, Board President
Number of members: 255
Staff: part time 2, volunteer 3
Major programs: archives, manuscripts, museum, historic preservation, exhibits, photographic collections
Period of collections: 1875-1917

LACLEDE

General John J. Pershing Boyhood Home State Historic Site
1000 Pershing Dr., 64651
Telephone: (816) 963-2525
State agency
Authorized by: Department of Natural Resources
Founded in: 1960
Moses W. Harrison, Administrator
Staff: full time 1, part time 3
Major programs: historic site(s), school programs, historic preservation, exhibits, living history, photographic collections, site interpretation
Period of collections: 1860-1890

Locust Creek Covered Bridge
Telephone: (816) 963-2525
Mail to: P.O. Box 141, 64651
State agency
Authorized by: Department of Natural Resources
Founded in: 1868
Moses W. Harrison, AdministratorStaff: full time 1
Major programs: historic site(s), historic preservation
Period of collections: 1868

Pershing Park Memorial Association, Inc.
Telephone: (816) 963-2587, 963-2312
Mail to: P.O. Box 177, 64651
Founded in: 1932
Number of members: 175
Major programs: museum, historic sites preservation
Period of collections: 1860-1948

LAMAR

Barton County Historical Society
Barton County Courthouse
Telephone: (417) 682-3297
Mail to: P.O. Box 416, 64759
Private agency
Founded in: 1969
Robert E. Douglas, President
Number of members: 85
Staff: volunteer 6
Major programs: library, museum, markers, cemetery inventories
Period of collections: 1870-1970

Harry S. Truman Birthplace
1109 Truman Ave., 64759
State agency
Authorized by: Department of Natural Resources
Founded in: 1959
Rita L. Embry, Administrator
Staff: full time 2, part time 1, volunteer 3
Major programs: archives, historic site(s), tours/pilgrimages, oral history, newsletters/pamphlets, Period of collections: research, living history, audiovisual programs, photographic collections
Period of collections: 1884-1972

LAWSON

Watkins Mill Association
Rt. 2, Box 270-M, 64062
Telephone: (816) 296-3357
Mail to: 4016 Blue Ridge Blvd., Independence, 64052
Private agency
Founded in: 1958
L.E. Oberholtz, Secretary
Number of members: 15
Major programs: archives, historic site(s), research
Period of collections: 1830-1940

Watkins Woolen Mill State Historic Site
Rt. 2, Box 270-M, 64062
Telephone: (816) 296-3357
State agency
Authorized by: Department of Natural Resources
Founded in: 1964
Ann M. Matthews, Site Administrator
Staff: full time 5, part time 4
Major programs: archives, historic site(s), tours/pilgrimages, school programs, historic preservation, exhibits, living history
Period of collections: 1860-1890

LEBANON

Laclede County Historical Society
N. Adams
Mail to: P.O. Box 1100, 65536
Founded in: 1976
Number of members: 200
Staff: part time 2
Major programs: archives, museum, genealogy
Period of collections: 1918-present

LEWISTOWN

Lewis County Historical Society
Box 72, Rt. 1, 63452
Telephone: (314) 497-2279
Questionnaire not received

LEXINGTON

Battle of Lexington Historic Site
64067
Telephone: (816) 259-2112
State agency
Authorized by: Department of Natural Resources
Founded in: 1959
Bob Schweitzer, Site Administrator
Staff: full time 3, part time 2
Major programs: historic site(s), historic preservation, living history, archaeology programs
Period of collections: 1850-1900

Lafayette County Historical Society
2215 Aullis Lane, 64067
Telephone: (816) 259-3742
Founded in: 1960
Questionnaire not received

Lexington Library and Historical Association
104 S. 13th
Telephone: (816) 259-2023
Mail to: 1905 South St., 64067
Questionnaire not received

LIBERTY

Clay County Historical Society
Mail to: P.O. Box 99, 100F Administration Bldg., 64068
Founded in: 1935
Questionnaire not received

Clay County Museum Association
14 N. Main, 64068
Telephone: (816) 781-8062
Private agency
Founded in: 1961
Ron Fuenfhasusen, Curator
Number of members: 275
Staff: volunteer 10

Major programs: archives, museum
Period of collections: 1840-1930

Historic Liberty Jail Visitor's Center
216 N. Main
Telephone: (816) 781-3188
Mail to: P.O. Box 313, 64068
Private agency
Authorized by: Church of Jesus Christ of Latter Day Saints
Founded in: 1963
Staff: volunteer 8
Major programs: historic site(s), tours/pilgrimages, historic preservation, exhibits
Period of collections: 1830-1840

Jesse James Bank Museum
104 E. Franklin, 64068
Telephone: (816) 781-4458
Private agency
Founded in: 1966
Jack B. Wymore, Owner
Staff: volunteer 1
Major programs: museum, historic site(s), historic preservation, exhibits, photographic collections
Period of collections: 1860-1882

LIBERTYVILLE

Cook Settlement Historical Society
Rt. 5
Mail to: Rt. 5, Box 179-C, Farmington, 63640
Founded in: 1975
Staff: volunteer 5
Major programs: historic sites preservation
Period of collections: 1783-1865

LINN CREEK

Camden County Historical Society
Telephone: (314) 346-7191
Mail to: P.O. Box 19, 65052
Founded in: 1962
Questionnaire not received

LONE JACK

Lone Jack Civil War Museum
Bynum Rd., 64078
Telephone: (816) 566-2272/881-4431
County agency
Authorized by: Jackson County Parks and Recreation
Founded in: 1963
Gary R. Toms, Historic Curator
Staff: part time 3
Major programs: museum, historic site(s), school programs, book publishing, research, exhibits
Period of collections: 1858-1865

MANCHESTER

Old Trails Historical Society
P.O. Box 852, 63011
Telephone: (314) 227-5772
Private agency
Founded in: 1967
Til Keil, President
Number of members: 60
Staff: volunteer 10
Major programs: museum, historic site(s), tours/pilgrimages, junior history, oral history, school programs, book publishing,

newsletters/pamphlets, historic preservation
Period of collections: 1850-1920

MANSFIELD

Laura Ingalls Wilder-Rose Wilder Lane Home Association
Rocky Ridge Farm, 65704
Telephone: (417) 924-3626
Founded in: 1957
Questionnaire not received

MARBLE HILL

Bollinger County Historical Society
P.O. Box 183, 63764
Telephone: (314) 238-2802
Founded in: 1977
Number of members: 145
Staff: volunteer 25
Major programs: manuscripts, markers, tours, books, historic preservation
Period of collections: 1800-present

MARSHFIELD

Webster County Historical Society
Telephone: (417) 468-2284
Founded in: 1954
Number of members: 100
Staff: volunteer 4
Magazine: Webster County Historical Society Journal
Major programs: educational programs
Period of collections: 1865-1918

MARYLAND HEIGHTS

Missouri Committee for the Humanities, Inc.
11425 Dorsett Rd., 63043
Telephone: (314) 739-7368
Private agency
Authorized by: National Endowment for the Humanities
Founded in: 1971 Robert G. Walrond, Executive Director
Staff: full time 3, part time 1
Magazine: Humanities News
Major programs: junior history, oral history, school programs, exhibits, audiovisual programs, archaeology programs, adult educational programs

MARYVILLE

Nodaway County Historical Society
422 W. 2nd St., 64468
Telephone: (816) 582-4955
County agency
Founded in: 1945
Jennie Newby, President
Number of members: 180
Staff: volunteer 4
Major programs: museum, markers, tours/pilgrimages, school programs, book publishing, historic preservation

MAYSVILLE

DeKalb County Historical Society
Rt. 3, Box 100, 64469
Telephone: (816) 449-2480
Founded in: 1969
Questionnaire not received

MEMPHIS

Scotland County Historical Society
112 S. Market, 63555
Mail to: c/o Scotland County Museum
Questionnaire not received

MEXICO

Audrain County Historical Society
501 S. Muldrow
Telephone: (314) 581-3910
Mail to: P.O. Box 3, 65265
Private agency
Founded in: 1939
Leta Hodge, Executive Director
Number of members: 920
Staff: part time 3, volunteer 50
Major programs: library, archives,
    museum, books,
    newsletters/pamphlets, genealogy
Period of collections: 1830-1950

MILAN

Sullivan County Historical Society
63556
Founded in: 1974
Questionnaire not received

MOBERLY

Moberly Historical and Railroad Museum
100 N. Sturgeon St., 65270
Founded in: 1976
Questionnaire not received

Randolph County Historical Society
P.O. Box 116, 65270
Telephone: (816) 263-7576
Private agency
Founded in: 1966
Karl C. Rice, President
Number of members: 285
Staff: volunteer 3
Major programs: library, museum,
    newsletters/pamphlets,
    photographic collections,
    genealogical services
Period of collections: 1880-1945

MONTGOMERY CITY

Montgomery County Historical Society
112 W. 2nd. St., 63361
County agency
Founded in: 1976
W. J. Auchly, President
Number of members: 245
Staff: volunteer 4
Major programs: archives, museum,
    historic site(s), tours/pilgrimages,
    school programs, historic
    preservation, records
    management, research, exhibits,
    photographic collections,
    genealogical services
Period of collections: 1860-1920

MOUND CITY

Mound City Museum Association
104 E. 7th, 64470
Telephone: (816) 442-5635
Private agency
Founded in: 1973
Mrs. Frances Scott, Secretary
Number of members: 300

Staff: volunteer 7
Major programs: museum, historic
    sites preservation
Period of collections: early 1900s

MOUNT VERNON

Lawrence County Historical Society
P.O. Box 406, 65712
Telephone: (417) 466-3446
Founded in: 1960
Questionnaire not received

NEVADA

Vernon County Historical Society
231 N. Main, 64772
Telephone: (417) 667-5841
Founded in: 1939
Number of members: 300
Staff: part time 2, volunteer 18
Major programs: museum, books,
    newsletters/pamphlets
Period of collections: 1783-present

NEW LONDON

Ralls County Historical Society
c/o President, 413 Depot St.
Mail to: P.O. Box 375, 63459
Private agency
Founded in: 1970
Oliver N. Howard, President
Number of members: 20
Major programs: school programs,
    exhibits, discussion group

NEW MADRID

Hunter-Dawson Home State Historic Site
Dawson Rd.
Telephone: (314) 748-5340
Mail to: Rt. 1, Box 4-A, 63869
State agency
Authorized by: Division of Parks and
    Historical Preservation
Founded in: 1967
Delecia B. Huitt, Site Administrator
Staff: full time 2, part time 2,
    volunteer 15
Major programs: archives,
    manuscripts, historic site(s),
    tours/pilgrimages, oral history,
    school programs, historic
    preservation, research, exhibits,
    living history, photographic
    collections, genealogical services
Period of collections: 1860-1880

OLD MINES

Old Mines Area Historical Society
Rt. 1, Box 300-Z, Cadet, 63630
Telephone: (316) 586-5121
Private agency
Founded in: 1980
Alice Widemer, President
Number of members: 100
Staff: volunteer 3
Major programs: library, archives,
    manuscripts, museum, historic
    site(s), tours/pilgrimages, oral
    history, school programs,
    newsletters/pamphlets, historic
    preservation, exhibits, living
    history, audiovisual programs,
    genealogical services
Period of collections: 1700-present

OVERLAND

Overland Historical Society
Telephone: (314) 427-2064
Mail to: P.O. Box 2303, 63114
City agency
Founded in: 1976
Shirley Needy, President
Number of members: 150
Major programs: museum, historic
    site(s), markers,
    newsletters/pamphlets, Period of
    collections: research, exhibits,
    audiovisual programs,
    photographic collections, log
    house reconstruction
Period of collections: 1865-1918

OZARK

Christian County Museum and Historical Society
401 N. 2nd Ave.
Telephone: (417) 485-2929
Mail to: P.O. Box 12, Nixa, 65714
Private agency
Founded in: 1977
Paul W. Johns, Director
Major programs: museum, oral
    history, school programs, research,
    exhibits, audiovisual programs
Period of collections: 1850-1950

PALMYRA

Heritage Seekers
S. Spring St., 63461
Questionnaire not received

PARIS

Union Covered Bridge State Historic Site
65275
Telephone: (314) 565-3449
Mail to: Stoutsville, 65283
State agency
Authorized by: Department of Natural
    Resources
Founded in: 1968
Stanley Fast, Site Administrator
Major programs: historic site(s)
Period of collections: 1871

PARKVILLE

Park College Historical Society
64152
Telephone: (816) 741-2000
Private agency
Authorized by: the college
Founded in: 1985
Harold F. Smith, Librarian
Number of members: 15
Staff: part time 1, volunteer 1
Major programs: library, archives,
    museum, historic site(s), oral
    history, newsletters/pamphlets,
    records management, audiovisual
    programs, photographic
    collections
Period of collections: 1875-present

PLATTE CITY

Platte County Historical Society
Telephone: (816) 431-5121
Mail to: P.O. Box 103, 64079
County agency
Founded in: 1945
Betty Soper, Executive Secretary

Number of members: 500
Staff: part time 1, volunteer 10
Magazine: *Platte County Historical Bulletin*
Major programs: library, archives, museum, historic site(s), newsletters/pamphlets, historic preservation, genealogical services
Period of collections: 1840-present

PLATTSBURG

Clinton County Historical Society and Museum
304 Birch St.
Mail to: c/o President, 503 Missouri Ave., 64477
County agency
Founded in: 1968
Kelsay Scearce, President
Number of members: 80
Major programs: museum

PLEASANT HILL

Pleasant Hill Historical Society
125 Wyoming St.
Mail to: P.O. Box 4, 64080
Questionnaire not received

POINT LOOKOUT

Ralph Foster Museum
School of the Ozarks, 65726
Telephone: (417) 334-6411
Private agency
Authorized by: the school
Founded in: 1930
Robert S. Esworthy, Director
Number of members: 28
Staff: full time 5, part time 20
Major programs: museum, exhibits
Period of collections: 20th century

White River Valley Historical Society
Telephone: (417) 334-4807
Mail to: P.O. Box 565, 65726
Founded in: 1961
Ionamae Rebenstorf, Secretary/Treasurer
Number of members: 300
Staff: volunteer 13
Magazine: *White River Valley Historical Quarterly*
Major programs: historic sites preservation, books, genealogical services
Period of collections: to 1960

POPLAR BLUFF

Butler County Historical Society
414 Poplar, 63901
Telephone: (314) 785-1374
Private agency
Founded in: 1962
Robert W. Manns, President
Number of members: 45
Staff: volunteer 6
Major programs: archives, museum, tours/pilgrimages, tours/pilgrimages, historic preservation, exhibits, audiovisual programs
Period of collections: 1849-present

Genealogical Society of Butler County, Inc.
316 N. Main

Mail to: P.O. Box 426, 63901
Founded in: 1973
Number of members: 55
Staff: volunteer 12
Magazine: *Area Footprints*
Major programs: genealogy

POTOSI

Mine Au Breton Historical Society
204 E. Jefferson St., 63664
Telephone: (314) 438-3198
Private agency
Founded in: 1963
George W. Showalter, President
Number of members: 140
Staff: volunteer 30
Major programs: library, archives, museum, historic site(s), markers, tours/pilgrimages, historic preservation, research, photographic collections, genealogical services
Period of collections: 1804-1940

PRINCETON

Mercer County Historical Society Inc.
902 E. Oak St., 64673
Telephone: (816) 748-3905
Questionnaire not received

REPUBLIC

Wilson's Creek National Battlefield
Missouri Hwy. 22 and Farm Rd. 182
Telephone: (417) 732-2662
Mail to: Drawer C, 65619
Federal agency
Authorized by: National Park Service
Founded in: 1960
David L. Lane, Superintendent
Staff: full time 3, part time 2
Major programs: library, museum, historic preservation, research, exhibits, living history
Period of collections: Civil War era

RICHMOND

Ray County Historical Society and Museum Inc.
W. Royle St.
Telephone: (816) 776-2305
Mail to: P.O. Box 2, 64085
Founded in: 1960
Number of members: 300
Staff: full time 1, volunteer 15
Magazine: *The Ray County Mirror*
Major programs: exhibits, photographic collections
Period of collections: 1865-present

ROCHEPORT

Friends of Rocheport
Moniteau St.
Mail to: 406 2nd St., 65279
Private agency
Founded in: 1967
Dorothy Caldwell, Curator
Number of members: 250
Staff: volunteer 15
Major programs: archives, manuscripts, museum, historic site(s), markers, historic preservation, exhibits, photographic collections
Period of collections: 1865-1918

ROLLA

Joint Collection, University of Missouri Western Historical Manuscript Collection—State Historical Society of Missouri Manuscripts
Library, Room G-3, University of Missouri, Rolla, 65401
Telephone: (314) 341-4874
State agency
Authorized by: the university and State Historical Society of Missouri
Founded in: 1980
Mark C. Stauter, Associate Director
Staff: full time 2, part time 1
Major programs: manuscripts
Period of collections: 1800-present

Phelps County Genealogical Society
P.O. Box 417, 65401
Telephone: (314) 341-4874
Private agency
Founded in: 1982
Mark C. Stauter, President
Number of members: 72
Staff: volunteer 5
Magazine: *Phelps County Genealogical Society Quarterly*
Major programs: library, newsletters/pamphlets, county cemetery records

Phelps County Historical Society
4th St.
Telephone: (314) 364-2372
Mail to: 654 Salem Ave., 65401
Private agency
Founded in: 1940
Earl Strebeck, President
Number of members: 40
Staff: volunteer 6
Major programs: manuscripts, museum, historic site(s), markers, tours/pilgrimages, school programs, newsletters/pamphlets
Period of collections: 1870-1930

ST. CHARLES

First Missouri State Capitol
208-214 S. Main, 63301
Telephone: (314) 723-3256
Mail to: P.O. Box 721, 63302
State agency
Authorized by: Department of Natural Resources
Founded in: 1971
Nancy B. Honerkamp, Site Administrator
Staff: full time 4, part time 2
Major programs: historic site(s), historic preservation
Period of collections: 1820

St. Charles County Historical Society and Archives
101 S. Main St., 63301
Telephone: (314) 723-2939
County agency
Founded in: 1956Dana King, Director
Number of members: 1,100
Staff: volunteers 10
Major programs: archives, museum, historic preservation, research, exhibits, genealogical services
Period of collections: 1800-1920

ST. CLAIR

Phoebe Apperson Hearst Historical Society, Inc.
Telephone: (314) 629-3186
Mail to: P.O. Box 1842, 63077
Founded in: 1961
Ralph Gregory, President
Number of members: 90
Staff: volunteer 7
Major programs: library, archives, museum, historic site(s), oral history, school programs, newsletters/pamphlets
Period of collections: 1865-present

STE. GENEVIEVE

Felix Valle State Historic Site
198 Merchant St.
Telephone: (314) 883-7102
Mail to: P.O. Box 89, 63670
State agency
Authorized by: Department of Natural Resources
Founded in: 1970
James Baker, Administrator
Staff: full time 3
Major programs: historic site(s)
Period of collections: 1830s

Foundation for Restoration of Ste. Genevieve
70 S. 3rd St., 63670
Telephone: (314) 883-2839
Private agency
Founded in: 1967
Gerald Fallert, President
Number of members: 250
Major programs: archives, historic site(s), newsletters/pamphlets, historic preservation, research, living history
Period of collections: French Colonial era

ST. JOSEPH

Buchanan County Historical Society
10th and Edmons Sts., 64501
Telephone: (816) 364-1485
Questionnaire not received

Jesse James Home—Pony Express Historical Association, Inc.
1202 Penn St.
Telephone: (816) 232-8206
Mail to: P.O. Box 1022, 64502
Private agency
Founded in: 1964
Gary Chilcote, President
Number of members: 392
Staff: part time 6, volunteer 60
Magazine: *Pony Express Mail*
Major programs: library, museum, historic site(s), tours/pilgrimages, school programs, newsletters/pamphlets, exhibits
Period of collections: 1860-1920

Patee House Museum
1202 Penn St.
Telephone: (816) 232-8206
Mail to: P.O. Box 1022, 64502
Private agency
Authorized by: Pony Express Historical Association
Founded in: 1963
Gary Chilcote, Museum Director
Number of members: 350
Staff: part time 6, volunteer 50
Major programs: library, museum, historic site(s), newsletters/pamphlets, historic preservation, exhibits
Period of collections: 1860-1910

St. Joseph Museum
11th and Charles Sts., 64501
Telephone: (816) 232-8471

City agency
Founded in: 1926
Richard A. Nolf, Director
Number of members: 204
Staff: full time 6, part time 6, volunteer 20
Magazine: *Happenings*
Major programs: museum, historic site(s), records management, exhibits, photographic collections
Period of collections: prehistoric-1941

St. Joseph State Hospital Psychiatric Museum
3400 Frederick Ave., 64506
Telephone: (816) 232-8431
P.O. Box 263, 64502
State agency
Authorized by: Department of Mental Health
Founded in: 1967
George Glore, Museum Curator
Staff: part time 2
Major programs: museum, psychiatric and hospital history
Period of collections: 18th-20th centuries

ST. LOUIS

Affton Historical Society
7801 Genesta
Telephone: (314) 352-5654
Mail to: P.O. Box 28855, 63123
Private agency
Founded in: 1974
Jeannine Cook, President
Number of members: 750
Staff: volunteer 35
Major programs: archives, historic site(s), junior history, oral history, school programs, historic preservation, audiovisual programs, photographic collections
Period of collections: 1850-1900

Archives-Records-Corporate Library, Anheuser-Busch Companies, Inc.
721 Pestalozzi St. 63118
Telephone: (314) 577-2179
Founded in: 1971
Major programs: library, archives
Period of collections: 1865-present

Campbell House Museum
1508 Locust St., 63103
Telephone: (314) 421-0325
Private agency
Founded in: 1943
Theron R. Ware, Curator
Number of members: 400
Staff: full time 1, part time 5, volunteer 35
Major programs: archives, manuscripts, museum, tours/pilgrimages, school programs, newsletters/pamphlets, historic preservation, exhibits, photographic collections
Period of collections: 1840-1880

Carondelet Historical Society
6517 Minnesota, 63111
Telephone: (314) 832-3598
Founded in: 1967
Questionnaire not received

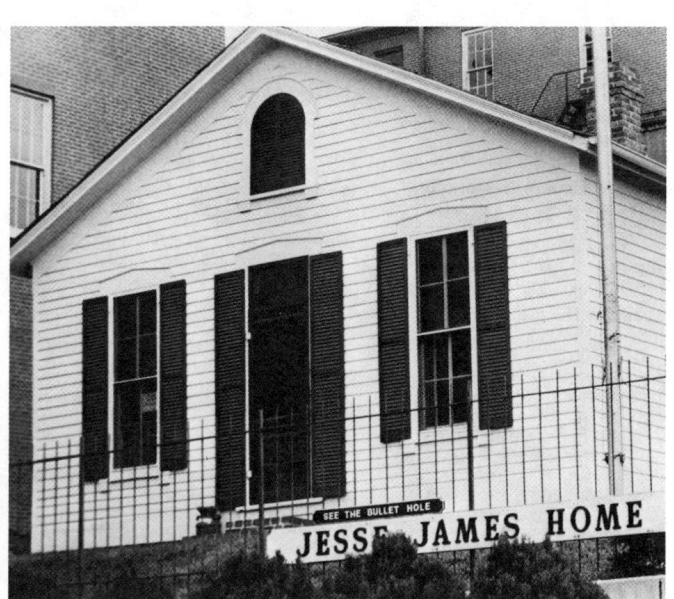

The Jesse James Home, where outlaw Jesse James was shot and killed on April 3, 1882. Listed on the National Register, the James home is operated by the Pony Express Historical Association.–Pony Express Historical Association

Civil War Round Table of St. Louis
8726 Glenwood Dr., 63126
Telephone: (314) 231-0333
Questionnaire not received

Concordia Historical Institute
801 De Mun Ave., 63105
Telephone: (314) 721-5934
Private agency, authorized by the
Lutheran Church, Missouri Synod
A. R. Suelflow, Director
Number of members: 1,650
Staff: full time 8, part time 17,
volunteer 50
Magazine: *Concordia Historical
Institute Quarterly*
Major programs: library, archives,
manuscripts, museum, historic
site(s), newsletters/pamphlets,
historic preservation, research,
exhibits, genealogical services
Period of collections: 1830-present

**Creve Coeur-Chesterfield
Historical Society**
11631 Olive Blvd.
Telephone: (314) 434-5163
Mail to: 1222 Prinster, 63141
Private agency
Founded in: 1968
Gloria Dalton, President
Number of members: 30
Staff: volunteer 15
Major programs: archives,
manuscripts, museum, historic
site(s), tours/pilgrimages, school
programs, book publishing,
newsletters/pamphlets, historic
preservation, photographic
collections
Period of collections: 1865-present

**Eugene Field House and Toy
Museum**
634 S. Broadway, 63102
Telephone: (314) 421-4689
Private agency, authorized by
Eugene Field House
Foundation, Inc.
Founded in: 1936
John Scholz, Director
Staff: full time 1, volunteer 25
Period of collections: 1750-present

General Daniel Bissell House
10225 Bellefontaine, 63105
Telephone: (314) 889-3196
Founded in: 1962
Questionnaire not received

Golden Eagle River Museum
Bee Tree Park
Telephone: (314) 846-9073
Mail to: 7408 Weil Ave., 63119
Founded in: 1975
Questionnaire not received

**Historical Association of Greater
St. Louis**
3601 Lindell Blvd., 63108
Telephone: (314) 658-2588
Private agency
Founded in: 1922
William Barnaby Faherty, President
Number of members: 40
Staff: volunteer 3

Historical Society of University City
6701 Delmar, University City, 63130
Telephone: (314) 727-3150
Private agency

Founded in: 1979
Marilyn H. Lindsley, President
Number of members: 350
Magazine: *Collectors Page*
Major programs: archives, historic
site(s), newsletters/pamphlets,
historic preservation, photographic
collections
Period of collections: 1904-1945

**International Library, Archives and
Museum of Optometry**
243 N. Lindbergh Blvd., 63141
Telephone: (314) 991-0324
Founded in: 1902
Maria Dablemont, Librarian/Archivist
Staff: full time 5
Major programs: library, archives,
museum, oral history
Period of collections: 1865-present

**Jefferson National Expansion
Memorial**
11 N. 4th St., 63102
Telephone: (314) 425-4465
Federal agency, authorized by
National Park Service
Founded in: 1935
Jerry L. Schober, Superintendent
Staff: full time 40, part time 23,
volunteer 30
Major programs: library, archives,
manuscripts, museum, historic
site(s), tours/pilgrimages, school
programs, exhibits, audiovisual
programs
Period of collections: 1803-1890

**Joint Collection, Western Historical
Manuscript Collection—State
Historical Society of Missouri
Manuscripts**
University of Missouri, St. Louis, 8001
Natural Bridge, 63121
Telephone: (314) 553-5143
State agency, authorized by the
university and State Historical
Society of Missouri
Anne R. Kenney, Associate Director
Staff: full time 3, part time 3
Major programs: archives,
manuscripts, oral history, exhibits,
photographic collections
Period of collections: 20th century

**Lafayette Square Restoration
Committee**
2023 Lafayette Ave., 63104
Telephone: (314) 772-5724
Founded in: 1970
Questionnaire not received

◊**Missouri Historical Society**
Jefferson Memorial Bldg, Forest Park,
63112-1099
Telephone: (314) 361-1424
Private agency
Founded in: 1866
Raymond F. Pisney, Director
Number of members: 3,100
Staff: full time 40, part time 10,
volunteer 680
Magazine: *Gateway Heritage*
Major programs: library, archives,
manuscripts, museum,
tours/pilgrimages, book publishing,
newsletters/pamphlets, research,
exhibits, audiovisual programs,
photographic collections,
genealogical services
Period of collections: 1763-present

National Museum of Transport
3015 Barrett Station Rd., 63122-3398
Telephone: (314) 965-6885
Private agency
Founded in: 1944
William Streckfus, Director
Number of members: 1,100
Staff: full time 20
Major programs: library, archives,
manuscripts, museum, historic
site(s), newsletters/pamphlets,
exhibits
Period of collections: 19th-20th
centuries

**St. Louis County Department of
Parks and Recreation**
7900 Forsyth, 63105
Telephone: (314) 889-3196
Questionnaire not received

St. Louis Genealogical Society
1695 S. Brentwood Blvd., Suite 203,
63144
Telephone: (314) 968-2763
Founded in: 1966
Questionnaire not received

**Soldiers' Memorial Military
Museum**
1315 Chestnut St., 63103
Telephone: (314) 622-4550
City agency
Founded in: 1938
Alfred J. Giuffrida, Superintendent
Staff: full time 10
Major programs: museum

Transport Museum Association
3015 Barrett Station Rd., 63122-3398
Telephone: (314) 965-6885
Private agency, authorized by
National Museum of Transportation
Founded in: 1944
John Payne Roberts, Secretary
Number of members: 1,000
Staff: volunteer 2
Magazine: *Transport Museum*
Major programs: library, museum
Period of collections: 1800-present

**Western Historical Manuscript
Collection**
Thomas Jefferson Library, 8001
Natural Bridge, 63121
Telephone: (314) 553-5143
Founded in: 1968
Staff: full time 3, part time 3
Major programs: archives,
manuscripts, oral history
Period of collections: 20th century

SALEM

Dent County Historical Society
1210 Gertrude St., 65560
Telephone: (314) 729-5707
Questionnaire not received

SALISBURY

Chariton County Historical Society
115 E. 2nd St., 65281
Telephone: (816) 388-5338
(president)
County agency
Martha Fellows, President
Number of members: 250
Major programs: museum,
newsletters/pamphlets, exhibits
Period of collections: 1850-1950

SARCOXIE

Eastern Jasper County Historical Society
c/o President, R.R. 1, 64862
Telephone: (417) 548-3970
Paul Palmer, President
Number of members: 25
Staff: volunteer 4
Major programs: historic site(s), markers, historic preservation
Period of collections: to Civil War era

SAVANNAH

Andrew County Historical Society
Clasbey Center
Mail to: P.O. Box 12, 64485
County agency
Founded in: 1972
Frank W. Shores, President
Number of members: 100
Staff: volunteer 30
Magazine: *Diggin' History*
Major programs: library, museum, oral history, school programs, book publishing, newsletters/pamphlets, exhibits, photographic collections, genealogical services
Period of collections: 1870s-1920s

SAVERTON

Ralls County Historical Society
63467
Founded in: 1976
Questionnaire not received

SEDALIA

Pettis County Historical Society
Pettis County Courthouse
Telephone: (816) 826-1314
Mail to: c/o Sedalia Public Library, 3rd and Kentucky, 65301
Founded in: 1946
Questionnaire not received

SHELBINA

Shelby County Historical Society
63468
Founded in: 1963
Number of members: 75
Major programs: museum, historic sites preservation, markers, tours/pilgrimages, books
Period of collections: 1865-1918

SIBLEY

Ft. Osage Historic Site and Museum
Rt. 1, Box 122, 64088
Telephone: (816) 249-5737
County agency, authorized by Jackson County Parks and Recreation
Founded in: 1948
Edward J. Ady, Lead Historic Site Coordinator
Staff: full time 2, part time 2, volunteer 7
Major programs: museum, historic site(s), school programs, living history
Period of collections: 8000 B.C.-1827

SPRINGFIELD

Greene County Historical Society
2214 E. Cherryvale, 65804
Telephone: (417) 883-8396
Founded in: 1954
Questionnaire not received

Museum of Evangel College of Arts and Sciences
Social Science Bldg. Lobby, 1111 N. Glenstone, 65802
Telephone: (417) 865-2811
Founded in: 1955
Staff: part time 2, volunteer 7
Major programs: archives, museum, educational programs
Period of collections: 2000 B.C.-1900

Museum of the Ozarks
603 E. Calhoun, 65802
Telephone: (417) 869-1976
Private agency
Founded in: 1975
Julie March, Director
Number of members: 650
Staff: full time 1, part time 2, volunteer 50
Magazine: *Bentley House Beacon*
Major programs: library, archives, manuscripts, museum, historic site(s), tours/pilgrimages, school programs, newsletters/pamphlets, historic preservation, exhibits, audiovisual programs, photographic collections
Period of collections: 1850-1900

STOCKTON

Cedar County Historical Society
P.O. Box 424, 65785
Telephone: (417) 276-4974
Founded in: 1970
Questionnaire not received

STOUTSVILLE

Mark Twain Birthplace Memorial
Mark Twain State Park, 65283
Telephone: (314) 565-3449
State agency, authorized by Division of Parks and Historic Preservation
Founded in: 1960
Stanley Fast, Administrator
Staff: full time 3
Major programs: library, archives, manuscripts, museum, historic site(s), tours, historic preservation, research, exhibits, audiovisual programs
Period of collections: 1835-1924

SULLIVAN

William S. Harney Historical Society
P.O. Box 36, 63080
Private agency
Founded in: 1980
Bernard M. Brown, Historian/Secretary
Number of members: 58
Staff: volunteer 15
Major programs: library, museum, newsletters/pamphlets, historic preservation, research, exhibits, living history
Period of collections: 1860-1890

TARKIO

Atchison County Historical Society
64491
Founded in: 1966
Questionnaire not received

TRENTON

Grundy County Historical Society
1100 Mabel Dr.
Telephone: (816) 359-9297
Mail to: c/o Secretary, 140 E. 5th St., 64683
County agency
Founded in: 1976
Leola Harris, Secretary
Staff: volunteer 200
Major programs: manuscripts, museum, historic site(s), tours/pilgrimages, school programs, book publishing, newsletters/pamphlets, historic preservation, records management, research, exhibits, living history, audiovisual programs, archaeology programs, photographic collections, genealogical services
Period of collections: late 1800s

UNION

Franklin County Historical Society
Telephone: (314) 583-5193
Mail to: P.O. Box 556, 63084
Questionnaire not received

VERSAILLES

Morgan County Historical Society
120 N. Monroe St., 65084
Founded in: 1966
Questionnaire not received

WARRENSBURG

Central Missouri State University Museum
104 Clark St., 64093
Telephone: (816) 429-4649
State agency, authorized by the university
Founded in: 1968
John Sheets, Museum Director
Staff: part time 2, volunteer 1
Major programs: museum, historic preservation, research, exhibits, anthropology, natural history
Period of collections: 19th-20th centuries

Johnson County Historical Society
410 Grover, 64093
Telephone: (816) 747-3717
Founded in: 1920
Questionnaire not received

WARRENTON

Warren County Historical Society
308 E. Boone's Lick Rd.
Telephone: (314) 456-2414
Mail to: P.O. Box 57, 63383
County agency
Founded in: 1970
William Q. Frick, President
Number of members: 165
Major programs: library, museum, historic site(s), book publishing, newsletters/pamphlets, historic

preservation, research, exhibits, photographic collections, genealogical services
Period of collections: 1833-1980

WARSAW

Benton County Historical Society
65355
Founded in: 1969
Questionnaire not received

WEBB CITY

Webb City Preservation Committee
108 W. Broadway, 64870
Telephone: (417) 673-5154
Town agency
Founded in: 1984
Bud Corner, President
Number of members: 50
Staff: volunteer 3
Major programs: tours/pilgrimages, promotion and preservation of downtown
Period of collections: 1900s

WEBSTER GROVES

Webster Groves Historical Society
4 E. Lockwood Ave., 63119
Telephone: (314) 961-4100
Private agency
Founded in: 1965
Charles F. Rehkopf, Secretary
Number of members: 300
Staff: part time 1, volunteer 25
Major programs: archives, museum, historic sites preservation, markers, junior history, oral history, books, newsletters/pamphlets, historic preservation
Period of collections: 1865-present

WELLSVILLE

Montgomery County Historical Society
Telephone: (314) 684-2828
Mail to: c/o Mrs. Frederick Bohl, Sr., RFD 1, 63384
Questionnaire not received

WESTPHALIA

Westphalia Historical Society, Inc.
65085
Telephone: (314) 455-2337
Questionnaire not received

WEST PLAINS

Howell County Historical Society
Telephone: (417) 256-8509
Mail to: P.O. Box 771, 65775
Questionnaire not received

WHEATLAND

Hickory County Historical Society
Telephone: (417) 282-5996
Mail to: Hermitage, 65668
Founded in: 1950
Questionnaire not received

MONTANA

ANACONDA

Cooper Village Museum and Arts Center
110 E. 8th St.
Telephone: (406) 563-8421, ext. 242
Mail to: Courthouse, 59711
County agency
Founded in: 1971
Mary Blaskovich, Director
Number of members: 190
Staff: full time 2, part time 1, volunteer 15
Major programs: manuscripts, museum, tours/pilgrimages, oral history, historic preservation, exhibits, photographic collections, genealogical services
Period of collections: 1865-1918

Tri-County Historical Society
800 S. Main
Telephone: (406) 563-8421, ext. 203
Mail to: P.O. Box 33, 59711
County agency
Founded in: 1976
Alice Finnegan, Director
Number of members: 150
Staff: volunteer 10
major programs: archives, museum, oral history, school programs, historic preservation, records management, research, photographic collections, genealogical services
Period of collections: 1865-1950

BILLINGS

Western Heritage Center
29th and Montana Ave., 59101
Telephone: (406) 256-6809
Founded in: 1971
Brian Bergheger, Director
Number of members: 450
Staff: full time 5, part time 3, volunteer 22
Major programs: museum, exhibits, educational programs, annual folklife festival
Period of collections: 1865-present

BOZEMAN

Gallatin County Historical Society—Pioneer Museum
317 W. Main, 59741
Telephone: (406) 586-0805/282-7220
Founded in: 1977
Grace Bates, Vice President
Number of members: 700
Staff: volunteer 20
Major programs: library, archives, manuscripts, museum, historic site(s), tours/pilgrimages, oral history, school programs, book publishing, newsletters/pamphlets, historic preservation, records management, research, exhibits, audiovisual programs, genealogical services
Period of collections: 1864-present

Museum of the Rockies
S. 7th and Kagy Blvd.
Telephone: (406) 994-2251
Mail to: Montana State University, 59717

State agency, authorized by the university
Founded in: 1958
Michael W. Hager, Director
Number of members: 925
Staff: full time 12, part time 1, volunteer 60
Magazine: News & Views
Major programs: archives, museum, historic preservation, research, exhibits, archaeology programs, photographic collections
Period of collections: 1865-present

BUTTE

Butte-Silver Bow Public Archives
17 W. Quartz St.
Telephone: (406) 723-8262, ext. 306
Mail to: c/o Butte Public Library, 106 W. Broadway, 59701
City agency, authorized by Butte-Silver Bow County Commission
Founded in: 1980
John W. Hughes, Archivist
Staff: part time 1, volunteer 3
Major programs: library, archives, manuscripts, oral history, historic preservation, records management, research, photographic collections, genealogical services, newspaper indexing
Period of collections: 1879-present

Butte Historical Society
P.O. Box 3913, 59702
Telephone: (406) 723-4577
Private agency
Founded in: 1976
Alice Smith, President
Number of members: 250
Staff: part time 11, volunteer 12
Magazine: The Speculator
Major programs: archives, oral history, book publishing, historic preservation, research
Period of collections: 1890-1930

Copper King Mansion
219 W. Granite
Telephone: (406) 782-7580
Private agency
Founded in: 1967
Ann Cote Smith, Owner
Staff: full time 2, part time 10
Major programs: museum, historic site(s)
Period of collections: 1880-1900

World Museum of Mining
Telephone: (406) 723-7211
Mail to: P.O. Box 3333, 59702
Private agency
Founded in: 1963
David Johns, President
Number of members: 176
Staff: full time 2, part time 3, volunteer 10
Major programs: museum, historic preservation, photographic collections
Period of collections: 1865-1918

CHESTER

Liberty County Museum Association
210 2nd St., E, 59522
Telephone: (406) 759-5256

County agency
Founded in: 1969
Troy Lakey, President
Staff: part time 3
Major programs: exhibits,
photographic collections
Period of collections: 1910-present

CHINOOK

Blaine County Historical Society
501 Indiana
Telephone: (406) 357-2590
Mail to: P.O. Box 927, 59523
County agency
Founded in: 1950
James Blevins, President
Number of members: 40
Major programs: museum
Period of collections: early 1900s

Blaine County Museum
501 Indiana
Telephone: (406) 357-2590
Mail to: P.O. Box 927, 59523
County agency
Founded in: 1977
Madeleine M. Marsonette, Manager
Staff: part time 1
Major programs: museum, historic
site(s), oral history, historic
preservation, records management
Period of collections: 1900-1950

CIRCLE

McCone County Museum
59215-0334
Telephone: (406) 485-2414
County agency, authorized by
McCone County Commission
Founded in: 1953
Orville M. Quick, Curator
Number of members: 28
Major programs: museum
Period of collections: 1900-1930

CROW AGENCY

Custer Battlefield Historical and Museum Association
Custer Battlefield National Monument
Telephone: (406) 638-2382
Mail to: P.O. Box 39, 59022
Founded in: 1952
Authorized by National Park Service
Neil C. Mangum, Executive Secretary
Number of members: 1,500
Staff: full time 2, part time 2
Major programs: library, archives,
manuscripts, museum, historic
site(s), markers, tours/pilgrimages,
oral history, book publishing, living
history, newsletters/pamphlets,
historic preservation
Period of collections: 1876

Custer Battlefield National Monument
P.O. Box 39, 59022
Telephone: (406) 638-2622
Federal agency, authorized by
National Park Service
Founded in: 1940
James V. Court, Superintendent
Staff: 9
Major programs: library, archives,
manuscripts, museum, historic
site(s), markers, tours/pilgrimages,

newsletters/pamphlets, exhibits,
living history, audiovisual
programs, archaeology programs,
photographic collections
Period of collections: 1876

DARBY

Pioneer Memorial Museum
Hwy. 93, Council Park
Mail to: R.R., 59829
Private agency, authorized by Darby
Federated Woman's Club and
Friends of Pioneer Memorial
Museum
Founded in: 1980
Mrs. Glenn Wright,
Secretary/Treasurer
Number of members: 25
Staff: part time 1, volunteer 10
Major programs: oral history,
photographic collections
Period of collections: 1880s-1930s

DEER LODGE

Grant-Kohrs Ranch National Historic Site
North of Deer Lodge
Telephone: (406) 846-2070
Mail to: P.O. Box 790, 59722
Federal agency, authorized by
National Park Service
Founded in: 1971
Jimmy D. Taylor, Superintendent
Staff: full time 15, part time 8,
volunteer 7
Major programs: historic site(s),
tours/pilgrimages, historic
preservation, living history
Period of collections: 1860-1930

Old Montana Prison
1106 Main St., 59722
Telephone: (406) 846-3111

Private agency, authorized by Powell
County Museum and Arts
Foundation
Founded in: 1980
Ernest Hartley, Museum Director
Staff: full time 5, part time 5,
volunteer 86
Major programs: museum, historic
site(s), tours, historic preservation
Period of collections: 1890-1979

Powell County Museum
308 Cottonwood St., 59722
Private agency, authorized by Powell
County Museum and Arts
Foundation
Founded in: 1975
Steve Owens, president
Number of members: 160
Staff: volunteer 30
Major programs: museum, historic
preservation, photographic
collections
Period of collections: 1871-1950

Towe Antique Ford Museum
1106 Main St., 59722
Telephone: (406) 846-3111
Private agency, authorized by Powell
County Museum and Arts
Foundation
Founded in: 1978
Ernest Hartley, Museum Director
Staff: full time 5, part time 5
Major programs: museum, historic
preservation, exhibits
Period of collections: 1903-1952

DILLON

Beaverhead County Museum
15 S. Montana
Telephone: (406) 683-5511
Mail to: P.O. Box 830, 59725
County agency

Rancher Pete Cartwright stops Belgian draft horses to chat with visitors at Grant-Kohrs Ranch.—Grant-Kohrs Ranch NHS, Deer Lodge, Montana

Founded in: 1947
Helen B. Andrus, Board President
Staff: full time 2, volunteer 5
Major programs: museum,
pamphlets, historic preservation,
exhibits, photographic collections
Period of collections: 1880-present

FORT BENTON

Ft. Benton Museum
1800 Front St.
Mail to: c/o Joel F. Overholser, P.O.
Box 69, 59442
Private agency, authorized by Ft.
Benton Community Improvement
Association
Founded in: 1957
Jack Lepley, Chair
Staff: part time 2, volunteer 6
Major programs: museum, historic
preservation
Period of collections: 1805-1918

GREAT FALLS

Cascade County Historical Society
1400 1st Ave., N, 59401
Telephone: (406) 452-3462
Private agency
Founded in: 1976
Janet W. Postler, Director/Curator
Number of members: 400
Staff: full time 1, part time 2,
volunteer 30
Major programs: library, archives,
museum, oral history,
newsletters/pamphlets, historic
preservation, research, exhibits,
photographic collections
Period of collections: 1900-1945

Charles M. Russell Log Cabin Studio
1215 4th Ave., N
Telephone: (406) 727-8787
Mail to: 1201 4th Ave., N, 59401
City agency, authorized by
Trigg-Russell Foundation, Inc.
Founded in: 1945
Jerry Goroski, Assistant Museum
Director
Number of members: 900
Staff: full time 9, part time 6,
volunteer 30
Major programs: library, archives,
museum, historic site(s),
newsletters, exhibits
Period of collections: 1880s-1930

C. M. Russell Museum
1201 4th Ave., N, 59401
Telephone: (406) 452-7369
Founded in: 1953
Ray W. Steele, Director
Number of members: 800
Staff: full time 4, part time 3,
volunteer 50
Major programs: library, museum,
tours/pilgrimages, school
programs, newsletters/pamphlets
Period of collections: 1880-present

HAMILTON

Bitter Root Valley Historical Society
Old Courthouse, Ravalli County
Museum, 59840
Telephone: (406) 363-3338

County agency
Founded in: 1979
Erma L. Owings, Director
Number of members: 160
Staff: full time 1
Major programs: library, archives,
museum, historic site(s),
tours/pilgrimages, book publishing,
historic preservation
Period of collections: 1890-1970s

Ravalli County Museum
205 Bedford, Old Courthouse, 59840
Telephone: (406) 363-3338
County agency, authorized by Ravalli
County and Bitter Root Valley
Historical Society
Founded in: 1979
Erma L. Owings, Director
Number of members: 150
Major programs: library, museum,
school programs, book publishing,
research, xhibits, audiovisual
programs, photographic
collections, genealogical services
Period of collections: 1880-1930s

Ricketts Memorial Museum
205 Bedford, Old Courthouse, 59840
Telephone: (406) 363-3338
County agency, authorized by Ravalli
County Museum and Bitter Root
Valley Historical Society
Founded in: 1979
William Jellison, Co-director
Major programs: library, archives,
museum
Period of collections: 1910-1960s

HARDIN

Big Horn County Historical Society—Museum and Visitor Center
Rt. 1, Box 1206-A, 59034
Telephone: (406) 665-1671
County agency
Founded in: 1963
Gary W. Zowada, Museum Director
Number of members: 510
Staff: full time 1, part time 3,
volunteer 80
Major programs: museum, oral
history, newsletters/pamphlets,
historic preservation, exhibits,
living history
Period of collections: 1850-present

HAVRE

H. Earl Clack Memorial Museum
Fairgrounds
Telephone: (406) 265-9913
Mail to: P.O. Box 1675 or 1484, 59501
County agency
Founded in: 1964
Duane Nabor, Business Manager
Staff: part time 5, volunteer 37
Major programs: museum,
tours/pilgrimages, exhibits,
audiovisual programs, archaeology
programs, preservation of
prehistoric bison kill site
Period of collections:
prehistoric-present

Northern Montana College Collections
Northern Montana College, 59501
Telephone: (406) 265-7821, ext. 3285

State agency
Founded in: 1949
L. W. Hagener, Curator/Chair,
Science Department
Staff: volunteer 8
Period of collections: 1850-present

HELENA

Department of Fish, Wildlife and Parks
1420 E. 6th Ave., 59601
Telephone: (406) 444-3750
State agency
Founded in: 1965
Don Hyyppa, Parks Division
Administrator
Major programs: historic site(s),
historic preservation, audiovisual
programs
Period of collections: 1862-1940

Montana Historical Society
225 N. Roberts, 59601
Telephone: (406) 444-2694
State agency
Founded in: 1865
Robert Archibald, Director
Number of members: 10,000
Staff: full time 39, part time 5,
volunteer 75
Magazine: *Montana, The Magazine of
Western History*
Major programs: library, archives,
manuscripts, museum, historic
site(s), tours/pilgrimages, oral
history, book publishing,
newsletters/pamphlets, historic
preservation, records
management, exhibits,
photographic collections,
genealogical services
Period of collections: 1864-present

Montana Oral History Association
P.O. Box 1282, 59624
Private agency
Founded in: 1981
Diane Sands, President
Number of members: 50
Major programs: oral history,
newsletters/pamphlets, public
education, technical assistance
and training

JORDAN

Garfield County Museum
P.O. Box 145, 59337
Telephone: (406) 557-2589
County agency
Founded in: 1976
Ruth Coulter, Chair
Number of members: 51
Staff: volunteer 9
Major programs: historic
preservation, archaeology
programs, photographic
collections
Period of collections: 1880s-present

KALISPELL

Conrad Mansion Historic Site Museum—Conrad Mansion Directors, Inc.
Woodland Ave. and 3rd St., E
Telephone: (406) 755-6558
Mail to: P.O. Box 1195, 59901
City agency

Founded in: 1975
Louis A. Bibler, President
Staff: part time 6
Major programs: museum, historic
site(s), tours/pilgrimages, exhibits
Period of collections: 1895

LIVINGSTON

Park County Historical Society
118 W. Chinook, 59047
Telephone: (406) 222-3506
County agency
Founded in: 1964
Doris Whithorn, Museum Curator
Number of members: 50
Staff: volunteer 75
Major programs: library, archives,
manuscripts, museum, historic
site(s), oral history, historic
preservation, photographic
collections, genealogical services
Period of collections: 1883-present

Park County Museum Association
118 W. Chinook, 59047
Telephone: (406) 222-3506
County agency
Founded in: 1964
Doris Whithorn, Caretaker/Curator
Number of members: 50
Staff: volunteer 75
Major programs: library, archives,
manuscripts, museum, historic
site(s), oral history, research,
exhibits, living history,
photographic collections,
genealogical services
Period of collections: 1883-present

LOLO

Lolo Pass Visitor Center
c/o Powell Ranger Station, 59847
Telephone: (208) 942-3113
Federal agency, authorized by Forest
Service, U.S. Department of
Agriculture
Richard W. Farrar, District Ranger
Major programs: historic
preservation, exhibits
Period of collections: 1805-present

MISSOULA

Historical Museum at Ft. Missoula
Bldg. 322, Ft. Missoula, 59801
Telephone: (406) 728-3476
County agency, authorized by
Missoula County Board of Trustees
for Museums
Founded in: 1974
Wes Hardin, Director
Staff: full time 3, part time 1,
volunteer 75
Major programs: library, museum,
historic site(s), school programs,
newsletters/pamphlets, records
management, exhibits, living
history
Period of collections: 1860-1950

Montana Women's History Project
315 S. 4th St., E, 59801
Telephone: (406) 728-3041
Private agency
Founded in: 1975
Diane Sands, Director
Major programs: oral history,
newsletters/pamphlets, research,
women's history, public education,
technical assistance and training
Period of collections: 1900-1970

OSBORN

**Huntley Project Museum of
Irrigated Agriculture**
U.S. Hwy. 10, East of Huntley
Founded in: (406) 967-3464
Mail to: P.O. Box 86, Ballantine,
59006
Private agency, authorized by the
Cooperative Association's Act
Founded in: 1972
Charles A. Banderob, Coordinator
Number of members: 185
Staff: part time 5, volunteer 21
Major programs: museum, historic
preservation, records
management, exhibits, living
history, preserving early
agricultural machinery and family
stories
Period of collections: 1890-1960

POLSON

Polson-Flathead Historic Museum
Main St. at 8th and 9th Ave.
Telephone: (406) 883-5969
Mail to: c/o Secretary, S. Shore,
59860
Private agency
Founded in: 1968
Lorin Jacobson, Secretary
Staff: part time 5, volunteer 12
Major programs: museum
Period of collections: 1910-1930

PRYOR

**Chief Plenty Coups State
Monument**
Telephone: (406) 252-1289
Mail to: P.O. Box 35, 59066
Founded in: 1932
Harley Sorrells, Curator
Staff: full time 1, part time 1
Major programs: archives, museum,
historic site(s) preservation
Period of collections: prehistoric-1918

RAVALLI

**Ravalli Schoolhouse Restoration
Society**
Buffalo St.
Telephone: (406) 745-4556
Mail to: P.O. Box 49, 59863
Private agency
Founded in: 1975
Richard H. Taylor, President
Number of members: 25
Staff: volunteer 2
Major programs: historic preservation
Period of collections: 1910-1920

RICHEY

Richey Historical Society
59259
Private agency
Founded in: 1970
Betty Whiteman, Secretary/Treasurer
Number of members: 24
Staff: full time 1
Major programs: museum
Period of collections: 1918-present

RONAN

**Mission Valley Heritage—Garden of
the Rockies Museum**
600 Round Butte Rd., W
Telephone: (406) 676-4220
Mail to: 128 Main St., SW, 59864
City agency, authorized by Mission
Valley Heritage Association
Founded in: 1975
Calvin Lindburg, President
Number of members: 100
Staff: full time 10, volunteer 10
Major programs: museum
Period of collections: 1900-1950

ROUNDUP

**Musselshell Valley Historical
Museum**
524 1st St., W, 59072
Telephone: (406) 323-1403
Private agency
Founded in: 1972
Bobbye Wise, President
Staff: volunteer 20
Major programs: museum, school
programs, book publishing, historic
preservation, exhibits,
photographic collections
Period of collections: 1920

ST. IGNATIUS

**Flathead Culture Committee,
Confederated Salish and
Kootenai Tribes**
P.O. Box 418, 59865
Telephone: (406) 745-4572
Private agency, authorized by
Confederated Salish and Kootenai
Tribal Council
Founded in: 1976
Clarence Woodcock, Director
Staff: full time 6, part time 20
Major programs: historic site(s), book
publishing, historic preservation,
research, exhibits, living history,
photographic collections,
genealogical services

SHELBY

Marias Museum of History and Art
206 12th Ave., N, 59474
Telephone: (406) 434-2551
County agency
Major programs: museum, historic
site(s), markers, oral history, school
programs, exhibits
Period of collections: 1880-1950

SHERIDAN

**Madison County History
Association**
207 Mill St., 59749
Telephone: (406) 842-5410
Private agency
Founded in: 1973
Marguerita Odden, President
Number of members: 22
Major programs: manuscripts, oral
history, photographic collections,
genealogical services
Period of collections: 1864-1950

SIDNEY

MonDak Historical and Arts Society—MonDak Heritage Center
Telephone: (406) 482-3500
Mail to: P.O. Box 50, 59270
County agency, authorized by Richland County Museum and Society
Founded in: 1967
Don Rees, President
Number of members: 300
Staff: full time 2, volunteer 30
Major programs: library, archives, museum, historic site(s), oral history, newsletters/pamphlets, research, exhibits, photographic collections, genealogical services
Period of collections: 1890-1930

STANFORD

Sod Buster Museum
Judith Basin, 59479
Telephone: (406) 423-5358
Private agency
Founded in: 1964
Ivan Zimmer, Owner
Major programs: museum, exhibits
Period of collections: 1890-1925

SUN RIVER

Sun River Valley Historical Society
59483
Telephone: (406) 264-5572
Valley agency
Founded in: 1977
Emma Toman, Agent
Number of members: 81
Staff: volunteer 20
Major programs: historic site(s), newsletters, historic preservation, research, photographic collections
Period of collections: 1855-1928

SUPERIOR

Mineral County Historical Society and Museum
301 2nd Ave., E, 59872
Telephone: (406) 822-4078
County agency
Founded in: 1975
Deborah J. Davis, Board Member
Number of members: 40
Major programs: library, archives, manuscripts, museum, oral history, school programs, photographic collections, genealogical services
Period of collections: 1890-1927

Mineral County Museum and Historical Society
Mail to: P.O. Box 533, 59872
County agency
Founded in: 1977
Francis Nelson, President
Number of members: 25
Magazine: *Mineral County Pioneer*
Major programs: library, museum, oral history, records management, research, photographic collections, genealogical services
Period of collections: 1870-1930

THREE FORKS

Headwater's Heritage Museum
104 Main St.

Telephone: (406) 285-3495
Mail to: P.O. Box 116, 59752
Private agency, authorized by Three Forks Area Historical Society
Founded in: 1978
Ruth Myers, Curator
Number of members: 180
Staff: part time 1, volunteer 50
Major programs: museum, book publishing, exhibits
Period of collections: 1900-1940

TOWNSEND

Broadwater County Museum and Library
133 N. Walnut
Telephone: (406) 266-5252
Mail to: c/o Museum Director, Rt. 1, Box 32, 59644
County agency
Founded in: 1975
Rose S. Flynn, Museum Director
Number of members: 300
Staff: full time 1, part time 1
Major programs: archives, museum, oral history, book publishing, historic preservation, records management, exhibits, photographic collections, genealogical services
Period of collections: from 1869

UTICA

Utica Historical and Museum Society
59452
Telephone: (406) 423-5208
Private agency
Founded in: 1967
Barbara Twiford, Secretary/Treasurer
Number of members: 20
Staff: volunteer 20
Major programs: archives, museum, exhibits
Period of collections: 1910-1940

VALIER

Paul and Olive Bruner Museum
P.O. Box 833, 59486
Telephone: (406) 279-3469
Private agency
Founded in: 1969
Paul E. Bruner, Owner
Staff: volunteer 2
Major programs: museum, tours, exhibits

VIRGINIA CITY

Vigilance Club
P.O. Box 295, 59755
Town agency
Founded in: 1932
Joseph Williams, Secretary/Treasurer
Number of members: 12
Staff: full time 1, part time 3
Major programs: museum, historic site(s)
Period of collections: 1859-1875

WEST GLACIER

George C. Ruhle Library
Glacier National Park, 59936
Telephone: (406) 888-5441
Federal agency, authorized by Glacier National Park

Founded in: 1967
Clyde M. Lockwood, Chief of Interpretation
Staff: full time 1, part time 1, volunteer 2
Major programs: library, archives, manuscripts, oral history
Period of collections: 1880s-present

WEST YELLOWSTONE

Museum of the Yellowstone
146 Yellowstone Ave.
Telephone: (406) 646-7814
Mail to: P.O. Box 411, 59758
Private agency
Founded in: 1972
Joel C. Janetski, Director
Staff: full time 1, part time 4
Major programs: tours/pilgrimages, exhibits, audiovisual programs
Period of collections: A.D. 1700-A.D. 1800

WHITE SULPHUR SPRINGS

Meagher County Historical Association
310 2nd Ave., NE
Telephone: (406) 547-3965
Mail to: P.O. Box 47, 59645
Sarah Foster, Treasurer
Number of members: 125
Staff: full time 3, part time 2, volunteer 5
Major programs: museum
Period of collections: 1890-1940

WOLF POINT

Wolf Point Area Historical Society
120 Fallon St., 59201
Telephone: (406) 653-2605/653-1912
Authorized by Roosevelt County
Founded in: 1970
Edna Bilyeu, Curator
Number of members: 150
Staff: full time 2, part time 2
Major programs: library, museum, markers, historic preservation
Period of collections: 1875-1925

NEBRASKA

AINSWORTH

Brown County Historical Society
122 E. 4 St., 69210
Telephone: (402) 387-1689
Founded in: 1973
Questionnaire not received

ALLEN

Dixon County Historical Society
68710
Founded in: 1964
Questionnaire not received

ALLIANCE

Alliance Knight Museum
908 Yellowstone, 69301
Telephone: (308) 762-2384
Founded in: 1965
Debra J. Dopheide, Director

Staff: full time 1, part time 1,
  volunteer 9
Major programs: library, museum
Period of collections: 1890-1940

**Box Butte County Historical
Society**
207 E. 9th, 69301
Telephone: (308) 762-5159
Questionnaire not received

ARTHUR

Arthur County Historical Society
69121
Telephone: (308) 764-2203
Founded in: 1934
Questionnaire not received

AURORA

Hamilton County Historical Society
210 16th St., 68818
Telephone: (402) 694-6531
Number of members: 137
Staff: part time 1, volunteer 8
Major programs: museum
Period of collections: 1861-1935

Plainsman Museum
210 16th St., 68818
Telephone: (402) 694-6531
Founded in: 1976
Wesley Huenefeld, President
Number of members: 300
Staff: full time 1, volunteer 15
Major programs: museum, historic
  preservation

BANCROFT

John G. Neihardt Center
Telephone: (402) 648-3388
Mail to: P.O. Box 344, 68004
State agency
Founded in: 1976
John Lindahl, Curator
Staff: full time 3, part time 1,
  volunteer 13
Major programs: library, archives,
  museum, historic site(s),
  tours/pilgrimages, exhibits
Period of collections: 1865-present

BASSETT

Rock County Historical Society
68714
Telephone: (402) 684-3774
Mail to: P.O. Box 116
Founded in: 1975
Leona Allen, Curator
Number of members: 67
Staff: volunteer 20
Major programs: museum, historic
  preservation
Period of collections: 1880-present

BEATRICE

Gage County Historical Society
2nd
Telephone: (402) 228-1679
Mail to: P.O. Box 793, 68310
Founded in: 1971
Rachel Southwick, Curator
Number of members: 400
Staff: full time 2
Major programs: museum, historic
  site(s), book publishing,
  newsletters/pamphletsPeriod of
  collections: 1850s-present

Homestead National Monument
Rt. 3, Box 47, 68310
Telephone: (402) 223-3514
Federal agency
Founded in: 1936
Randall K. Baynes, Superintendent
Staff: full time 6, part time 9
Major programs: museum, historic
  site(s)
Period of collections: 1860-1890

**Southeast Nebraska Genealogical
Society**
Mail to: P.O. Box 562, 68310
Private agency
Founded in: 1978
Betty Sorenson, President
Number of members: 100
Magazine: The Homesteader
Major programs: library,
  newsletters/pamphlets, historic
  preservation, research,
  genealogical services

BELLEVUE

Sac Museum Memorial Society
2510 Clay St., 68005
Telephone: (402) 292-2001
State agency
Founded in: 1981
Jack L. Allen, Museum Director
Number of members: 25
Major programs: museum, historic
  preservation, exhibits
Period of collections: 1937-present

Sarpy County Historical Museum
2402 Clay St., 68005
Telephone: (402) 292-1880
Private agency
Founded in: 1970
Francis s. LaRock, Director/Curator
Number of members: 225
Staff: full time 1, part time 3,
  volunteer 6
Major programs: library, museum,
  historic site(s), markers,
  newsletters/pamphlets, historic
  preservation, exhibits
Period of collections:
  prehistoric-1920s

BELVIDERE

Thayer County Historical Society
68315
Telephone: (402) 768-2147
Founded in: 1967
Jacqueline Williamson, Co-curator
Number of members: 100
Staff: part time 2, volunteer 3
Magazine: The Museum Muse
Major programs: library, museum,
  newsletters/pamphlets, research,
  exhibits, photographic collections,
  genealogical services
Period of collections: 1865-present

BOYS TOWN

Phila Matic Center
Visitor's Center, Father Flanagan's
  Boys' Home
Telephone: (402) 498-1360
Mail to: P.O. Box 1, 68010
Private agency, authorized by Father
  Flanagan's Boys' Home
Founded in: 1951
Ivan E. Sawyer, Curator

Staff: full time 4
Major programs: museum, collections
  of coins, stamps, and paper money
Period of collections: 1850-present

BREWSTER

Blaine County Historical Society
68821
County agency
Founded in: 1976
Elsie B. Pickering, Secretary

BROKEN BOW

**Custer County Historical
Society, Inc.**
255 S. 10th Ave., 68822
Telephone: (308) 872-2203
Founded in: 1965
Number of members: 252
Staff: part time 1, volunteer 3
Major programs: library, archives,
  manuscripts, museum, markers,
  tours/pilgrimages, books
Period of collections: 1783-present

BROWNVILLE

Brownville Historical Society, Inc.
68321
Telephone: (402) 825-6001
Private agency
Founded in: 1956
Homer J. Anville, President
Number of members: 300
Staff: volunteer 20
Major programs: museum, historic
  site(s), tours/pilgrimages, oral
  history, newsletters/pamphlets,
  historic preservation, photographic
  collections, festivals
Period of collections: 1850s-1860s

Museum of Missouri River History
Brownville State Recreation Area
Telephone: (402) 825-3341
Mail to: P.O. Box 124, 68321
State agency, authorized by
  Nebraska State Historical Society
Founded in: 1977
Carl Hugh Jones, Curator
Staff: full time 3, part time 2,
  volunteer 1
Major programs: museum, research,
  exhibits, living history
Period of collections: 1900s

BURWELL

Ft. Hartsuff State Historical Park
R.R., 68823
Telephone: (308) 346-4715
State agency, authorized by Game
  and Parks Commission
Founded in: 1961
Roye D. Lindsay, Superintendent
Staff: full time 1, part time 6,
  volunteer 1
Major programs: historic site(s),
  historic preservation, living history
Period of collections: 1874-1881

Garfield County Historical Society
737 H St.
Telephone: (308) 346-5070
Mail to: P.O. Box 517, 68823
County agency
Founded in: 1965
Mrs. Wilbur Bristol, President

Number of members: 35
Staff: volunteer 10
Major programs: museum, markers, tours, books, historic preservation
Period of collections: 1872-1950

CALLAWAY

Seven Valleys Historical Society
68825
Telephone: (308) 836-2728
Founded in: 1970
Questionnaire not received

CENTRAL CITY

Merrick County Historical Museum
215 East St. 68826
Telephone: (308) 946-3309
Mail to: c/o President, 1415 15th St., 68826
County agency
Founded in: 1969
Stanley B. Bice, President
Number of members: 75
Staff: volunteer 12
Major programs: library, archives, museum, historic sites preservation, markers, tours/pilgrimages, junior history, oral history, educational programs
Period of collections: 1865-present

CHADRON

Dawes County Historical Society
Hwy. 385
Telephone: (308) 432-4999
Mail to: P.O. Box 1319, 69337
Private agency
Founded in: 1959
Lucille Redfern, Curator
Number of members: 290
Staff: full time 2, volunteer 25
Major programs: library, manuscripts, museum, historic site(s), newsletters/pamphlets, historic preservation, exhibits, living history, genealogical services
Period of collections: 1884-present

Mari Sandoz Heritage Society
Chadron State College, 69337
Telephone: (308) 432-6271
Founded in: 1971
Magazine: *Mari Sandoz Heritage*
Major programs: historic sites preservation, tours/pilgrimages, oral history, educational programs
Period of collections: 1884-present

Museum Association of the American Frontier
HC-74, Box 18, 69337
Telephone: (308) 432-3843
Founded in: 1949
Charles E. Hanson, Jr., Director
Number of members: 1,400
Staff: full time 3, part time 5, volunteer 4
Magazine: *Museum of the Fur Trade Quarterly*
Major programs: library, museum, historic sites preservation, educational programs, newsletters/pamphlets, research
Period of collections: 1600-1900

Museum of the Fur Trade
HC-74, Box 18, 69337
Telephone: (308) 432-3843
Private agency
Founded in: 1949
Charles E. Hanson, Jr., Director
Number of members: 1,500
Staff: full time 3, part time 1, volunterr 6
Magazine: *Museum of the Fur Trade Quarterly*
Major programs: library, museum, historic site(s), markers, school programs, newsletters/pamphlets, research
Period of collections: 1600-1900

CLAY CENTER

Clay County Historical Society
Glenvil and Martin Sts.
Telephone: (402) 762-3644, 762-3563
Mail to: P.O. Box 205, 68933
Founded in: 1972
Questionnaire not received

COZAD

Cozad Historical Society
Telephone: (308) 537-7217
Mail to: 503 Lake Ave., Gothenburg, 69138
Questionnaire not received

CRAWFORD

Ft. Robinson Museum
Telephone: (308) 665-2852
Mail to: P.O. Box 304, 69339
Founded in: 1956
Staff: full time 4, part time 10
Magazine: *Nebraska History*
Major programs: library, museum, historic sites preservation, markers, tours/pilgrimages, oral history, educational programs
Period of collections: 1865-1948

CRETE

Railroad Station Historical Society
430 Ivy Ave., 68333
Telephone: (402) 826-3356
Founded in: 1968
William F. Rapp, Editor
Number of members: 480
Staff: volunteer 5
Magazine: *The Bulletin*
Major programs: library, archives, tours/pilgrimages, newsletters/pamphlets, photographic collections
Period of collections: 1865-present

DAKOTA CITY

Dakota County Historical Society
R.R., 68731
Telephone: (402) 698-2288/987-3503
County agency
Founded in: 1963
Maurice Crofoot, President
Number of members: 85
Staff: part time 2, volunteer 8
Major programs: museum, historic site(s), school programs, book publishing, historic preservation

DAVID CITY

Butler County Historical Society
200 D St., 68632
Telephone: (402) 367-3855
County agency
Founded in: 1968
Gerald Hayhurst, President
Number of members: members: 35
Staff: volunteer 16
Major programs: museum, historic preservation
Period of collections: 1870s-1930

DORCHESTER

Saline County Historical Society, Inc.
68343
Telephone: (402) 946-2391
Founded in: 1956
Questionnaire not received

FAIRBURY

Jefferson County Historical Society, Inc.
709 5th St., 68352
Telephone: (402) 720-3191
Founded in: 1956
Number of members: 150
Staff: volunteer 25
Major programs: museum, historic sites preservation, markers, educational programs
Period of collections: 1865-1918

Rock Creek Station State Historical Park
Rt. 4, Box 36, 68352
Telephone: (402) 729-5777
State agency, authorized by Game and Parks Commission
Founded in: 1980
Wayne Brandt, Superintendent
Staff: full time 2, part time 8
Major programs: museum, historic site(s), living history
Period of collections: 1860

FORT CALHOUN

Washington County Historical Association
14th and Monroe Sts., 68023
Telephone: (402) 468-5740
County agency
Founded in: 1926
Edward H. Lorenzen, President
Number of members: 180
Staff: part time 1, volunteer 4
Major programs: manuscripts, museum, historic site(s), newsletters/pamphlets, historic preservation, photographic collections, genealogical services
Period of collections: 1783-present

FRANKLIN

Franklin County Historical Society
P.O. Box 36, 68939
Telephone: (308) 425-3603
County agency
Founded in: 1949
Veda Clements, Senior Advisor
Number of members: 60
Staff: volunteer 20
Major programs: museum, tours/pilgrimages, book publishing,

historic preservation, photographic
collections, genealogical services
Period of collections: early 1870s

FREMONT

Dodge County Historical Society
1643 N. Nye Ave.
Telephone: (402) 721-4515
Mail to: P.O. Box 766, 68025
Founded in: 1955
Loell R. Jorgensen, Director
Number of members: members: 500
Staff: full time 2, part time 3,
volunteer 125
Major programs: library, archives,
museum, historic sites
preservation, markers,
tours/pilgrimages, oral history,
educational programs, books,
newsletters/pamphlets
Period of collections: 1865-1918

FULLERTON

Nance County Historical Society
501 Broadway, 68638
County agency
Founded in: 1971
E. James Kula, President
Number of members: 200
Staff: volunteer 9
Major programs: manuscripts,
museum, historic preservation,
exhibits, photographic collections

GERING

**North Platte Valley Historical
Association, Inc.**
11th and J St.
Telephone: (308) 436-5411
Mail to: P.O. Box 495, 69341
Founded in: 1969
Jan Spencer, Manager
Number of members: 510
Staff: full time 1, part time 4,
volunteer 3
Major programs: museum, markers,
tours/pilgrimages, educational
programs, books,
newsletters/pamphlets, historic
preservation, exhibits
Period of collections: 1918-present

Oregon Trail Museum Association
Telephone: (308) 436-4340
Mail to: P.O. Box 427, 69341
Founded in: 1956
Questionnaire not received

Scotts Bluff National Monument
P.O. Box 427, 69341
Telephone: (308) 436-4340
Federal agency, authorized by
Department of the Interior
Founded in: 1919
Alford J. Banta, Superintendent
Staff: full time 6, part time 3,
volunteer 36
Major programs: library, museum,
historic site(s), exhibits, living
history, audiovisual programs
Period of collections: 1850-1860s

GIBBON

Gibbon Heritage Center
2nd and Court Sts.
Mail to: P.O. Box 116, 68840

City agency, authorized by Gibbon
City Council
Founded in: 1976
Leroy A. Walker, Board Chair
Number of members: 38
Staff: volunteer 5
Major programs: archives, museum,
exhibits, photographic collections
Period of collections: 1871-present

GOTHENBURG

Gothenburg Historical Society
503 Lake Ave., 69138
Private agency
Kieth Buss, President
Number of members: 35
Major programs: museum, oral
history, book publishing, research
Period of collections: 1882-present

Old Brown House Doll Museum
1421 Ave. F, 69138
Telephone: (308) 537-7596
Private agency
Founded in: 1975
LaVon Pape, Owner
Major programs: museum
Period of collections: 1880-present

GRAND ISLAND

Hall County Historical Society, Inc.
1720 M Kruse St., 68801
Telephone: (308) 382-0968
County agency
Founded in: 1922
Eldon P. Cunningham, President
Number of members: 125
Major programs: historic site(s),
markers, tours/pilgrimages, junior
history, oral history,
newsletters/pamphlets, living
history
Period of collections: 1783-present

**Stuhr Museum of the Prairie
Pioneer**
3133 W. Hwy. 34, 68801
Telephone: (308) 384-1380
County agency
Founded in: 1961
Jack A. Learned, Executive Director
Number of members: 2,685
Staff: full time 17, part time 7,
volunteer 175
Major programs: archives, museum,
junior history, oral history,
educational programs,
newsletters/pamphlets, research,
exhibits
Period of collections: 1865-1918

GRANT

Perkins County Historical Society
Central Ave. at 6th, 69140
Founded in: 1964
Questionnaire not received

HARRISBURG

Banner County Historical Society
69345
Questionnaire not received

HARRISON

**Sioux County Historical
Society, Inc.**
Telephone: (308) 668-2379

Mail to: P.O. Box 336, 69346
Founded in: 1974
Questionnaire not received

HASTINGS

Adams County Historical Society
1330 N. Burlington Ave.
Telephone: (402) 463-5838
Mail to: P.O. Box 102, 68901
Founded in: 1965
Wayne Youngblood, Acting Director
Number of members: 1,000
Staff: full time 5, volunteer 5
Magazine: *Historical News*
Major programs: library, archives,
manuscripts, markers,
tours/pilgrimages, junior history,
oral history, educational programs,
books, newsletters/pamphlets,
genealogical services
Period of collections: 1871-present

Hastings Museum
1330 N. Burlington, Hwy. 281 at 14th
St., 68901
Telephone: (402) 463-7126
City agency
Founded in: 1926
Ed Bisaillon, Director
Number of members: 1,500
Staff: full time 11, part time 2
Magazine: *Yester News*
Major programs: museum,
educational programs,
newsletters/pamphlets
Period of collections: 1550-present

HAYES CENTER

Hayes County Historical Society
Telephone: (308) 286-3235
Mail to: R.R. 2, 69032
Questionnaire not received

HOLDREGE

Phelps County Historical Society
Hwy. 183
Telephone: (308) 995-5015
Mail to: P.O. Box 215, 68949
Founded in: 1966
Don Lindgren, President
Number of members: 400
Staff: volunteer 30
Major programs: library, archives,
museum, historic sites
preservation, markers, oral history,
educational programs, books,
historic preservation
Period of collections: 1873-present

HYANNIS

Grant County Historical Society
Grant County Courthouse, 69350
Telephone: (308) 458-2226
Founded in: 1961
Mrs. R. R. Bilstein, Secretary
Number of members: 50
Staff: volunteer 1
Major programs: museum
Period of collections: 1890-present

IMPERIAL

Chase County Historical Society
69033
Telephone: (308) 882-5525
Founded in: 1963
Questionnaire not received

KEARNEY

Buffalo County Historical Society
710 W. 11th St.
Telephone: (308) 234-3041/237-7858
Mail to: P.O. Box 523, 68847
Private agency
Founded in: 1960
Marian Johnson, President
Number of members: 450
Staff: full time 1, volunteer 20
Magazine: *Buffalo Tales*
Major programs: archives, museum,
tours/pilgrimages, school
programs, newsletters/pamphlets,
historic preservation, research
Period of collections: 1872-1925

The Frank House
W. Hwy. 30, 68847
Telephone: (308) 237-3446/234-8284
State agency, authorized by Kearney
State College
Founded in: 1974
Marian Johnson, Curator
Staff: full time 1, part time 1
Major programs: museum, historic
site(s), historic preservation
Period of collections: 1888-1890s

Nebraska Museums Coalition
1915 W. 24th, 68847
Telephone: (308) 234-4525
Founded in: 1958
Questionnaire not received

LEXINGTON

Dawson County Historical Society
805 N. Taft
Telephone: (308) 324-5340
Mail to: P.O. Box 369, 68850
County agency
Founded in: 1958
Steve Holen, Director
Number of members: 185
Staff: full time 2, part time 2,
volunteer 2
Major programs: library, archives,
museum, newsletters/pamphlets,
research, exhibits, photographic
collections
Period of collections: 1870-1930

LINCOLN

**American Historical Society of
Germans from Russia**
631 D St., 68502
Telephone: (402) 474-3363
Ruth M. Amen, Executive Director
Number of members: 6,000
Staff: full time 5, part time 3,
volunteer 150
Magazine: *Clues*
Major programs: library, archives,
museum, oral history, book
publishing, newsletters/pamphlets,
historic preservation, research,
genealogical services
Period of collections: 1763-present

**Capitol Restoration and Promotion,
State Building Division,
Nebraska State Capitol**
1445 K St., 68509
Telephone: (402) 471-3191
State agency, authorized by State
Executive Branch
Founded in: 1974

Robert C. Ripley, Manager
Staff: full time 3
Major programs: archives, historic
site(s), historic preservation,
photographic collections
Period of collections: 1919-present

**Department of History and
Archives, Nebraska Conference,
United Church of Christ**
2055 E St., 68510
Telephone: (402) 477-4131
Authorized by United Church of
Christ
Founded in: 1958
Doris Chatfield, Historian
Staff: volunteer 3
Magazine: *The Historian*
Major programs: library, archives
Period of collections: 1855-present

Friends of Fairview
4900 Sumner, 68506
Telephone: (402) 489-4900
Qquestionnaire not received

**Historical Center, Nebraska
Wesleyan University**
68504
Telephone: (402) 465-2175
State agency, authorized by
Nebraska Conference, United
Methodist Church
Founded in: 1942
Bernice M. Boilesen, Curator
Staff: part time 1, volunteer 3
Major programs: library, archives,
museum
Period of collections: 1798-present

January 12th 1888 Blizzard Club
1201 Lincoln Mall, Suite 611
Telephone: (402) 477-2779
Founded in: 1940
Doris Jenkins, Historian
Number of members: 43
Major programs: markers, book
publishing, newsletters/pamphlets,
research
Period of collections: 1888

National Museum of Roller Skating
7700 A St., 68510
Telephone: (402) 489-8811
Private agency
Founded in: 1981
Michael W. Brooslin, Director
Staff: full time 1, part time 1,
volunteer 3
Magazine: *Historical Roller Skating
Overview*
Major programs: library, archives,
manuscripts, museum, book
publishing, newsletters/pamphlets,
research, exhibits, photographic
collections, sports history
Period of collections: 1860-1980

**Nebraka Committee for the
Humanities**
211 N. 12th St., Suite 405, 68508
Telephone: (402) 474-2131
Private agency, authorized by
National Endowment for the
Humanities
Founded in: 1973
Sarah Z. Rosenberg, Executive
Director
Staff: full time 5
Magazine: *The Nebraska Humanist*

Major programs:
newsletters/pamphlets, exhibits,
audiovisual programs, regrants to
non-profit organizations, public
programs in the humanities

**Nebraska Game and Parks
Commission**
2200 N. 33rd St.
Telephone: (402) 464-0641
Mail to: P.O. Box 30370, 68503
State agency
Dale R. Bree, Assistant Director
Staff: full time 12, part time 20
Major programs: museum, historic
site(s), historic preservation,
records management, research,
exhibits, living history, audiovisual
programs, archaeology programs
Period of collections: 1820-present

◇**Nebraska State Historical Society**
150 R St.
Mail to: P.O. Box 82554, 68501
Telephone: (402) 471-3270
State agency
Founded in: 1878
James A. Hanson, Director
Number of members: 4,800
Staff: full time 100, part time 40,
volunteer 30
Magazine: *Nebraska History*
Major programs: library, archives,
manuscripts, museum, historic
site(s), markers, junior history, book
publishing, newsletters/pamphlets,
historic preservation, records
management, research, exhibits,
audiovisual programs, archaeology
programs, photographic
collections, genealogical services
Period of collections: 1870-1920

Webster County Historical Society
471 4th Ave., Red Cloud
Telephone: (402) 746-2444
Mail to: P.O. Box 427, 68970
Number of members: 23
Staff: part time 4
Major programs: museum
Period of collections: 1840-present

LOUP CITY

Sherman County Historical Society
Telephone: (308) 452-3051
Founded in: 1976
Questionnaire not received

McCOOK

High Plains Historical Society
423 Norris Ave., 69001
Telephone: (308) 345-3661
Private agency
Founded in: 1963
Marilyn Hawkins, Director
Number of members: 135
Staff: part time 2
Major programs: museum, book
publishing, exhibits
Period of collections: 1880s-1930s

MINDEN

**Harold Warp Pioneer Village
Foundaton**
(308) 832-1181
Harold Warp, Foundation President
Period of collections: from 1830

The Nebraska State Historical Society's State Museum of History in Lincoln interprets the experience of prehistoric and historic peoples of Nebraska.—The Nebraska State Historical Society.

South Central Nebraska Genealogical Society
Mail to: Rt. 2, Box 57, 68959
Founded in: 1980
Questionnaire not received

NEBRASKA CITY

Arbor Lodge State Historical Park
R.F.D. 2, 68410
Telephone: (402) 873-3221
State agency, authorized by Game and Parks Commission
Founded in: 1923
Randall Fox, Superindendent
Staff: full time 2, part time 15
Major programs: museum, historic site(s), school programs, historic preservation, exhibits
Period of collections: 1860-1920

Otoe County Historical Society
711 3rd Corso, 68410
Telephone: (402) 873-7198
Questionnaire not received

NIOBRARA

Niobrara Historical Society
P.O. Box 334, 68760
Private agency
Founded in: 1974
Arlene Kee, Board Chair
Number of members: 75
Major programs: museum, historic preservation
Period of collections: 1925-1975

NORTH PLATTE

Buffalo Bill's Ranch—State Historical Park
Rt. 1, Box 229, 69101
Telephone: (308) 532-4795

Thomas B. Morrison, Superintendent
Staff: full time 3, part time 8
Major programs: museum, historic sites preservation, newsletters/pamphlets, historic preservation, exhibits, photographic collections
Period of collections: 1860s-1917

Lincoln County Historical Society Western Heritage Center
2403 N. Buffalo
Telephone: (308) 534-5640
Mail to: 201 Circle Dr., 69101
Founded in: 1861
Grace Mae Rasmussen Egle, President
Number of members: 300
Staff: full time 2, volunteer 100
Major programs: library, archives, manuscripts, museum, historic sites preservation, markers, junior history, oral history, educational programs
Period of collections: 1783-1865

OGALLALA

Keith County Historical Society
1004 Spruce, 69153
Telephone: (308) 284-2306
Founded in: 1958
Questionnaire not received

OMAHA

Douglas County Historical Society—General Crook House
30th and Fort, Ft. Omaha
Telephone: (402) 455-9990
Mail to: P.O. Box 11398, 68111
Private agency
Founded in: 1956
Patricia Pixley, Executive Secretary

Number of members: 674
Staff: full time 2, part time 14, volunteer 60
Major programs: library, museum, markers, educational programs
Period of collections: 1865-1918

Landmarks Heritage Preservation Commission
1819 Farnam St., Suite 1110, 68183
Telephone: (402) 444-5208
Founded in: 1977
Major programs: archives, educational programs, books, historic preservation
Period of collections: 1870-1940

Union Pacific Museum
1416 Dodge, 68179
Telephone: (402) 271-3530
Private agency, authorized by Union Pacific Railroad
Founded in: 1922
Donald D. Snoddy, Director
Staff: full time 1
Major programs: archives, museum, photographic collections
Period of collections: 1862-present

University Archives, University Library
University of Nebraska, Omaha, 68182
Telephone: (402) 554-2362
Authorized by the university
Founded in: 1976
Carol Speicher, University Archivist
Staff: full time 2, part time 3
Major programs: archives, oral history, historic preservation, records management, research, exhibits, photographic collections
Period of collections: 1908-present

Western Heritage Society, Inc.
801 S. 10th St., 68108
Telephone: (402) 444-5071
Founded in: 1973
Number of members: 950
Staff: full time 11, part time 5, volunteer 25
Magazine: *The Western Heritage Bee*
Major programs: library, museum, markers, educational programs, newsletters/pamphlets
Period of collections: 1850-present

O'NEILL

Holt County Historical Society
68763
Telephone: (402) 394-5486
Mail to: R.R. 1, Box 45, Inman, 48742
County agency
Founded in: 1971
Harvey A. Tompkins, Vice President

ORLEANS

Harlan County Historical Society
68966
Telephone: (308) 473-3725
Founded in: 1971
Questionnaire not received

OSCEOLA

Polk County Historical Society
S. State St., 68666
Founded in: 1960
Questionnaire not received

OSHKOSH

Historical Society of Garden County
W. 1st and Ave E
Telephone: (308) 772-4333
Mail to: P.O. Box 41, 69154
Founded in: 1969
Questionnaire not received

PARKS

Dundy County Historical Society
69041
Telephone: (308) 423-2578
Questionnaire not received

PAWNEE CITY

Pawnee City Historical Society and Museum
68420
Questionnaire not received

PIERCE

Pierce County Historical Society
Gilman Park
Telephone: (402) 329-6345
Mail to: 104 E. Willow, 68767
County agency
Founded in: 1934
Greg Hoffman, President
Number of members: 200
Staff: volunteer 50
Major programs: museum, historic site(s), exhibits
Period of collections: 1871-present

PILGER

Historical Society of Stanton County
N. Main St., 68768
County agency
Founded in: 1965
Mrs. Emil Christiansen, President
Number of members: 60
Staff: volunteer 2
Major programs: museum, historic site(s), markers, oral history, book publishing, historic preservation
Period of collections: 1880-1950

PLATTSMOUTH

Cass County Historical Society
646 Main St., 68048
Telephone: (402) 296-4770
County agency
Founded in: 1935
Donald Hill, Curator
Staff: full time 1, part time 3
Major programs: library, archives, manuscripts, museum, historic site(s), school programs, newsletters/pamphlets, research, exhibits, photographic collections, genealogical services
Period of collections: 1850-1950

RED CLOUD

Webster County Historical Museum
721 W. 4th St., 68970
Telephone: (402) 746-2444
County agency
Founded in: 1961
Dorothy Johnson, Assistant Secretary
Staff: full time 1, part time 3, volunteer 7

Major programs: museum, genealogical services
Period of collections: 1800s

Willa Cather Pioneer Memorial and Educational Foundation
326 N. Webster, 68970
Telephone: (402) 746-2653
Questionnaire not received

RUSHVILLE

Sheridan County Historical Society, Inc.
P.O. Box 274, E. Hwy. 20, 69360
Telephone: (308) 327-2961
County agency
Founded in: 1933
Gertrude Bare, Secretary
Number of members: 110
Staff: part time 1, volunteer 1
Major programs: library, archives, manuscripts, museum, historic sites preservation, markers, books, newsletters/pamphlets
Period of collections: prehistoric-present

SCHUYLER

Schuyler Historical Society
10th and B Sts.
Telephone: (402) 352-3781
Mail to: Rt. 1, Box 76, 68661
City agency
Founded in: 1976
Harold H. Griepentrog, President
Number of members: 140
Staff: volunteer 15
Major programs: museum, tours/pilgrimages, oral history, photographic collections
Period of collections: 1860-1920

SEWARD

Seward County Historical Society
Rt. 2, Box 165A, 68405
Telephone: (402) 761-3181
Founded in: 1966
Questionnaire not received

SIDNEY

Cheyenne County Historicl Associaton
6th and Jackson
Mail to: P.O. Box 596, 69162
County agency
Founded in: 1964
Lawrence Marrin, President
Staff: part time 1, volunteer 3
Major programs: museum, historic site(s), markers, historic preservation, exhibits
Period of collections: 1864-present

SPRINGVIEW

Keya Paha County Historical Society
68778
Founded in: 1968
Questionnaire not received

STANTON

Historical Society of Stanton County
68779
Founded in: 1965
Questionnaire not received

STUART

North Central Nebraska Historical Society
68780
Questionnaire not received

TABLE ROCK

Table Rock Historical Society
68447
Telephone: (402) 839-6485
Questionnaire not received

TECUMSEH

Johnson County Historical Society, Inc.
3rd and Lincoln, 68450
Telephone: (402) 335-2671
Founded in: 1962
Number of members: 50
Staff: part time 1, volunteer 6
Major programs: library, archives, manuscripts, museum, historic sites preservation, tours/pilgrimages, junior history, oral history, educational programs
Period of collections: 1783-1918

TEKAMAH

Burt County Museum
Telephone: (402) 374-1505
Mail to: P.O. Box 125, 68061
County agency
Founded in: 1967
Lois Backer, President
Number of members: 175
Staff: 1 part time 1
Major programs: library, archives, museum, photographic collections, genealogical services

TOBIAS

Tobias Community Historical Society
68453
Telephone: (402) 243-2228
Town agency
Founded in: 1968
Helen R. Kottas, President-Curator
Number of members: 20
Staff: volunteer 12
Major programs: museum, markers, historic preservation
Period of collections: 1865-present

TRENTON

Hitchcock County Historical Society
311 E. 1st St.
Mail to: P.O. Box 174, 69044
County agency
Founded in: 1938
Lillian Phelps, Secretary/Treasurer
Number of members: 216
Staff: volunteer 14
Major programs: archives, museum, historic site(s), markers, tours/pilgrimages, school programs, book publishing, newsletters/pamphlets, historic preservation, research, exhibits, living history, photographic collections, genealogical services
Period of collections: 1850-present

VALENTINE

Cherry County Historical Society
Hwy. 20 and Main
Telephone: (402) 376-2015
Mail to: P.O. Box 284, 69201
County agency
Founded in: 1928
Ruth E. Harms, Secretary/Treasurer
Number of members: 200
Staff: full time 1
Major programs: library, archives, museum, historic site(s), markers, school programs, book publishing, historic preservation, research, exhibits, photographic collections, genealogical services
Period of collections: 1883-1940s

VALLEY

Valley Community Historical Society
214 W. Alexander St.
Mail to: P.O. Box 685, 68064
Founded in: 1967
Questionnaire not received

VERDIGRE

Verdigre Heritage Museum
68783
Private agency
Founded in: 1979
Max Randa, President
Number of members: 10
Staff: volunteer 12
Major programs: archives, museum
Period of collections: 1900-present

WAHOO

Saunders County Historical Society
P.O. Box 255, 68066
Telephone: (402) 443-3090
Founded in: 1963
Kenneth Schoen, President
Number of members: 250
Staff: full time 1, part time 1, volunteer 15
Major programs: archives, museum, newsletters/pamphlets, exhibits, genealogical services
Period of collections: 1865-present

WAYNE

Wayne County Historical Society
Telephone: (402) 375-1513
Mail to: 420 Douglas St., 68787
Private agency
Founded in: 1938
Loreta Tomkins, President
Number of members: 114
Major programs: museum

WEEPING WATER

Weeping Water Valley Historical Society
68463
Telephone: (402) 267-5447
Founded in: 1965
John F. Boomer, President
Number of members: 329
Staff: volunteer 8
Major programs: museum, historic sites preservation, markers
Period of collections: early 20th century

WEST POINT

Cuming County Historical Society
940 N. Main, 68788
Telephone: (402) 372-3690
Questionnaire not received

WILBER

Wilber Czech Museum
102 W. 3rd St.
Telephone: (402) 821-2183
Mail to: P.O. Box 253, 68465
Irma Ourecky, President
1Staff: part time 1, volunteer 10
Major programs: museum, markers
Period of collections: 1865-1918

YORK

Anna Palmer Museum
211 E. 7th St.
Telephone: (402) 362-5549
Mail to: P.O. Box 507, 68467
Founded in: 1967
Questionnaire not received

York County Historical Association
Mail to: Rt. 1, 68467
Founded in: 1968
Questionnaire not received

NEVADA

CARSON CITY

Nevada Division of State Parks
1060 Mallory Way
Telephone: (702) 885-4379
Mail to: Mormon Historic State Station M, 89701
State agency

Founded in: 1850
Gary J. Downs, District Ranger
Staff: part time 2
Major programs: museum, historic site(s), school programs
Period of collections: 1850-1910

◇Nevada State Museum
Capital Complex, 89710
Telephone: (702) 885-4810
Founded in: 1941
Scott Miller, Director
Number of members: 370
Staff: full time 21, part time 4, volunteer 30
Major programs: museum, exhibits, natural history, anthropology programs
Period of collections: late 1800s-early 1900s

State Division of Archives and Records
101 S. Fall St.
Telephone: (702) 885-5210
Mail to: Capitol Complex, 89710
State agency, authorized by Nevada State Library
Founded in: 1965
Guy Louis Rocha, State Archivist
Staff: full time 2, part time 1, volunteer 1
Major programs: archives, records management, research, genealogical services,
Period of collections: 1855-present

State Division of Historic Preservation and Archaeology
201 S. Fall St., Room 106, 89710
Telephone: (702) 885-5138
State agency
Founded in: 1978
Ronald James, Supervisor
Staff: full time 5

The Nevada State Museum in Carson City.—Photograph by Daun Bohall

Major programs: historic site(s), markers, historic preservation, archaeology
Period of collections: 1859-1940

Virginia and Truckee Railroad Museum
S. Carson St. at Fairview Dr.
Telephone: (702) 885-4810
Mail to: Capitol Complex, 89710
State agency, authorized by Nevada State Museum
Founded in: 1980
Scott Miller, Administrator
Number of members: 47
Staff: full time 2, part time 1, volunteer 2
Magazine: *The Sagebrush Headlight*
Major programs: library, archives, manuscripts, museum, historic preservation, research, exhibits, living history, photographic collections
Period of collections: 1875-1950

ELKO

Northeastern Nevada Genealogical Society
Willow and College Parkway
Mail to: P.O. Box 1903, 89801
Private agency
Founded in: 1978
Don Lemons, President
Number of members: 23
Staff: volunteer 10
Magazine: *Chart and Quill*
Major programs: library, newsletters/pamphlets, research, genealogical services
Period of collections: 1869-present

Northeastern Nevada Museum
1515 Idaho St.
Telephone: (702) 738-3418
Mail to: P.O. Box 2550, 89801
Private agency, authorized by Northeastern Nevada Historical Society
Founded in: 1968
Howard Hickson, Director
Number of members: 1,807
Staff: full time 4, part time 5
Magazine: *Northeastern Nevada Historical Society Quarterly*
Major programs: library, archives, museum, oral history, school programs, exhibits, audiovisual programs, photographic collections
Period of collections: 1870-present

ELY

White Pine County Historical Society
237 Fay Ave., 89301
Founded in: 1975
Questionnaire not received

EXCHANGE

Braxton Historical Society
Rt. 1, Box 14, 26619
Telephone: (304) 765-2415
Founded in: 1973
Helen Traugh, President
Number of members: 300

Staff: volunteer 4
Major programs: museum, oral history, newsletters/pamphlets
Period of collections: 1863-present

FALLON

Churchill County Museum Association—Churchill County Museum and Archives
1050 S. Maine St., 89406
Telephone: (702) 423-3677
County agency
Founded in: 1968
Sharon Lee Taylorc, Museum Director/Association Advisor
Number of members: 350
Staff: full time 1, part time 5, volunteer 10
Major programs: library, archives, manuscripts, museum, tours/pilgrimages, oral history, school programs, research, exhibits, archaeology programs, genealogical services
Period of collections: 1855-present

GENOA

Carson Valley Historical Society
Telephone: (702) 782-2476
Mail to: P.O. Box 193, 89411
Founded in: 1961
Major programs: archives, museum, markers, books
Period of collections: 1865-present

HAWTHORNE

Mineral County Museum
400 D St.
Telephone: (702) 945-5142
Mail to: P.O. Box 1561, 89419
County agency
Founded in: 1972
Frances Hawkins, Board Chair
Number of members: 17
Staff: volunteer 9
Major programs: museum, exhibits, audiovisual programs
Period of collections: 1900-1940

HAZEN

Hazen Preservation Society
550 Reno Hwy.
Telephone: (702) 867-3066
Mail to: P.O. Box 609, Fallon, 89406
State agency
Founded in: 1982
Alva L. Emberlin, President
Major programs: library, museum, historic preservation, exhibits
Period of collections: 1867-1940

HENDERSON

Southern Nevada Museum and Cultural Center
240 Water St., 89015
Telephone: (702) 564-5336
Questionnaire not received

LAS VEGAS

Association for the Preservation of the Las Vegas Mormon Fort, Inc.
3149 Hebard Dr., 89121
Telephone: (702) 457-2127
Questionnaire not received

Museum of Natural History
University of Nevada, Las Vegas, 4505 S. Maryland Parkway, 89154
Telephone: (702) 739-3381
Founded in: 1967
Staff: full time 5, part time 8
Major programs: museum, educational programs, archaeology
Period of collections: prehistoric-1930

◇**Nevada State Museum and Historical Society**
700 Twin Lakes Dr., 89107
Telephone: (702) 385-0115
State agency
Founded in: 1982
Scott Miller, Administrator
Number of members: 125
Staff: full time 9, part time 2, volunteer 40
Major programs: library, museum, tours/pilgrimages, school programs, newsletters/pamphlets, research, exhibits
Period of collections: 20th century

OVERTON

Lost City Museum of Archaeology
721 S. Hwy. 169
Telephone: (702) 397-2193
Mail to: P.O. Box 807, 89040
State agency
Founded in: 1935
Kathryne Olson, Curator
Staff: full time 4, part time 1
Major programs: museum, historic site(s), exhibits, archaeology programs
Period of collections: 6000 B.C.-A.D. 1150

RENO

Desert Research Institute—Social Science Center
7010 Dandini Blvd.
Telephone: (702) 673-7303
Mail to: P.O. Box 60220, 89506
State agency, authorized by University of Nevada System
Founded in: 1959
Cynthia Irwin-Williams, Executive Director
Major programs: library, archives, manuscripts, book publishing, research, archaeology programs
Period of collections: 5000 B.C.-A.D. 400

◇**Nevada Historical Society**
1650 N. Virginia St., 89503
Telephone: (702) 789-0190
Founded in: 1904
Peter L. Bandurraga, Director
Number of members: 1,000
Staff: full time 7, part time 4, volunteer 50
Magazine: *Nevada Historical Society Quarterly*
Major programs: library, archives, manuscripts, museum, historic site(s), markers, tours/pilgrimages, book publishing, newsletters/pamphlets, research, exhibits, audiovisual programs, photographic collections
Period of collections: 1840-present

Oral History Program
University of Nevada, Reno, 89557
Telephone: (702) 784-6932
State agency, authorized by the
university
Founded in: 1969
R. T. King, Director
Number of members: 1
Staff: full time 2
Major programs: library, oral history,
research, audiovisual programs,
photographic collections, field
services

Washoe County Historical Society
629 Jones St., 89503
Private agency
Founded in: 1977
Kathryn Totton, President
Number of members: 100
Staff: volunteer 5
Magazine: *Washoe Rambler*
Major programs: markers,
newsletters/pamphlets

Washoe Heritage Council
1795 Stardust
Telephone: (702) 747-6642
Mail to: P.O. Box 10271, 89510
Private agency
Founded in: 1981
Grahame A. Ross, Director
Number of members: 170
Staff: full time 1
Magazine: *Washoe News*
Major programs: historic site(s),
historic preservation

Western History Association
Department of History, University of
Nevada, Reno, 89557
Telephone: (702) 322-7645
Private agency, authorized by the
university
Founded in: 1961
William D. Rowley, Executive
Secretary
Number of members: 2,000
Staff: part time 2
Magazine: *Western Historical
Quarterly*
Major programs: historic
preservation, research

SILVER SPRINGS

**Ft. Churchill Historic State
Monument**
89429
Telephone: (702) 577-2345
State agency, authorized by Nevada
Division of State Parks
Jim Prida, Park Ranger 2
Staff: full time 1, part time 2,
volunteer 3
Major programs: library, archives,
museum, historic site(s), markers,
school programs, historic
preservation, records
management, research, exhibits,
living history, audiovisual
programs, photographic
collections
Period of collections: 1860s

TONOPAH

Central Nevada Historical Society
P.O. Box 326, 89049
Telephone: (702) 482-3454

Founded in: 1978
Number of members: 400
Major programs: library, archives,
museum, markers,
tours/pilgrimages,
newsletters/pamphlets, historic
preservation
Period of collections: 1850-present

WINNEMUCCA

**North Central Nevada Historical
Society**
Maple Ave. and Jungo Rd.
Telephone: (702) 623-2912
Mail to: P.O. Box 819, 89445
Private agency
Founded in: 1974
Pansilee Larson, Curator
Number of members: 506
Staff: full time 1, part time 1,
volunteer 16
Magazine: *The Humboldt Historian*
Major programs: archives, museum,
books, historic preservation
Period of collections: 1906-1967

NEW HAMPSHIRE

ACWORTH

Acworth Silsby Library
03601
Town agency
Founded in: 1891
Staff: part time 2, volunteer 15
Major programs: library,
newsletters/pamphlets, historic
preservation, archaeology
programs, photographic
collections
Period of collections: late 19th-20th
centuries

ALEXANDRIA

Haynes Memorial Library
Washburn Rd.
Telephone: (603) 744-8987
Mail to: R.F.D. 1, Box 883, 03222
Private agency
Founded in: 1887
Francis Butler, Librarian

AMHERST

Historical Society of Amherst
P.O. Box 717, 03031
Founded in: 1958
William A. Bean, Sr., President
Number of members: 468
Staff: volunteer 25
Major programs: archives, museum,
historic site(s), markers, oral
history, book publishing,
newsletters/pamphlets, audiovisual
programs, photographic
collections
Period of collections: 1783-1865

ASHLAND

**Ashland Historical Society—
Whipple House Museum**
Pleasant St., 03217
Founded in: 1968
Mary Ruell, President

Number of members: 110
Staff: volunteer 10
Major programs: museum, historic
preservation, research, exhibits,
photographic collections
Period of collections: 1840-1940

ATKINSON

Atkinson Historical Society
Academy Ave.
Mail to: P.O. Box 116 03811
Founded in: 1954
Frederick G. Helmuth, President
Number of members: 30
Major programs: archives, museum,
historic sites preservation
Period of collections: 1492-present

BERLIN

**Library, New Hampshire Votech
College**
2020 Riverside Dr., 03570
Telephone: (603) 752-1113
State agency
Authorized by: Department of
Education
Virginia L. Heard, Librarian
Staff: full time 1, part time 1
Major programs: library, technical
material
Period of collections: 1970 and 1980s

BOSCAWEN

Boscawen Historical Society, Inc.
Mail to: P.O. Box 3067, 03303
Private agency
Founded in: 1967
Elmer Wiggin, President
Number of members: 75
Staff: volunteer 9
Major programs: library, museum,
school programs, book publishing,
exhibits, genealogical services
Period of collections: 1732-present

BRENTWOOD

Brentwood Historical Society
Middle Rd., 03833
Telephone: (603) 772-9010
Mail to: R.F.D. 1, Exeter
Questionnaire not received

BROOKLINE

**Brookline New Hampshire
Historical Society**
10 Main St., 03033
Telephone: (603) 673-0543
Private agency
Founded in: 1980
Peter A. Cook, President
Number of members: 45
Staff: volunteer 15
Major programs: archives,
manuscripts, oral history, historic
preservation, living history,
photographic collections
Period of collections: 19th-20th
centuries

CANAAN

**Canaan Historical Society and
Museum**
Canaan St., 03741
Telephone: (603) 523-4202
Questionnaire not received

CANTERBURY

Canterbury Historical Society
Old Tilton Rd.
Telephone: (603) 783-9831
Mail to: P.O. Box 400, 03224
Founded in: 1969
Questionnaire not received

Shaker Village, Inc.
Shaker Rd., 03204
Telephone: (603) 783-9977
Private agency
Founded in: 1969
Richard Kathmann, Director
Number of members: 500
Staff: full time 4, part time 5
Magazine: *The Canterbury Shakers*
Major programs: archives, museum,
  historic site(s), tours/pilgrimages,
  newsletters/pamphlets, historic
  preservation, exhibits,
  photographic collections
Period of collections: 1790-1930

CENTER SANDWICH

Sandwich Historical Society
Maple St., 03227
Telephone: (603) 284-6269
Founded in: 1917
Questionnaire not received

CENTRE HARBOR

Centre Harbor Historical Society
Mail to: P.O. Box 74, 03226
Founded in: 1971
Questionnaire not received

CHARLESTOWN

Old Fort Number Four Associates
Telephone: (603) 826-5700
Mail to: P.O. Box 336, 03603
Founded in: 1948
John P. C. Moon, Executive Director
Number of members: 210
Staff: part time 15, volunteer 25
Major programs: museum, school
  programs, newsletters/pamphlets,
  historic preservation, records
  management, research, exhibits,
  living history, audiovisual
  programs, archaeology programs
Period of collections: 1735-1789

CHESTER

Chester Historical Society
115 Hanson Rd., 03036
Telephone: (603) 895-4418
Private agency
Founded in: 1978
Joan R. Watts, Secretary
Number of members: 70
Staff: volunteer 5
Major programs: library, archives,
  manuscripts, historic site(s),
  markers, tours/pilgrimages, junior
  history, oral history, school
  programs, historic preservation,
  records management, research,
  exhibits, living history, audiovisual
  programs, photographic
  collections, genealogical services,
  field services
Period of collections: 1720-1920

CHESTERFIELD

Chesterfield Historical Society, Inc.
03443
Founded in: 1974
Mrs. Peter Jenness III, President
Number of members: 100
Staff: volunteer 200
Major programs: archives, junior
  history, oral history, educational
  programs, books, newsletters,
  historic preservation
Period of collections: 1761-present

CLAREMONT

Claremont Historical Society, Inc.
26 Mulberry St., 03743
Founded in: 1963
Questionnaire not received

CONCORD

Concord Public Library
45 Green St., 03301
Telephone: (603) 225-2743
City agency
Founded in: 1857
Louis Ungarelli, Director
Staff: full time 19, part time 19
Major programs: library
Period of collections: 1830-present

**New Hampshire Division of
  Records Management and
  Archives**
71 S. Fruit St., 03301
Telephone: (603) 271-2236
State agency
Founded in: 1961
Frank C. Mevers, Director/State
  Archivist
Staff: full time 5, part time 2
Major programs: archives,
  manuscripts, records
  management, research
Period of collections: 1679-present

◊**New Hampshire Historical Society**
30 Park St., 03301
Telephone: (603) 225-3381
Founded in: 1823
R. Stuart Wallace, Director
Number of members: 2,100
Staff: full time 14, part time 1,
Major programs: library, manuscripts,
  museum, school programs,
  newsletters/pamphlets, historic
  preservation, research, exhibits,
  archaeology programs,
  photographic collections
Period of collections: 1675-1900

**New Hampshire State Historic
  Preservation Office, Department
  of Resources and Economic
  Development**
Prescott Park, 105 Loudon Rd.
Telephone: (603) 271-3483
Mail to: P.O. Box 856, 03301
State agency
Founded in: 1974
Ralph E. Brickett, Commissioner,
  DRED/State Historic Preservation
  Officer
Staff: full time 5
Major programs: markers, historic
  preservation, audiovisual
  programs, archaeology programs,
  conservation of cultural resources
Period of collections:
  prehistoric-present

**New Hampshire State Historical
  Commission**
71 S. Fruit St., 03301
Telephone: (603) 271-2236
Staff: part time 1
Major programs: markers,
  newsletters/pamphlets

The Pierce Brigade
14 Penacook St.
Mail to: P.O. Box 425, 03301
Private agency
Founded in: 1966
Mrs. William Avery, President
Number of members: 238
Staff: volunteer 25
Major programs: museum, historic
  sites preservation
Period of collections: 1840s

CONWAY

Conway Public Library
Main St.
Telephone: (603) 447-5552
Mail to: P.O. Box 2100, 03818
Town agency
Founded in: 1900
Margaret Marschner, Librarian
Major programs: library
Period of collections: 1760-present

CORNISH

Cornish Historical Society
Saint-Gaudens Rd., 05089
Telephone: (603) 675-2209
Mail to: R.F.D. 2, 03745
Private agency
Founded in: 1973
Virginia Colby, President
Number of members: 44
Staff: volunteer 6
Major programs:
  newsletters/pamphlets, indexing
  gravestones and vital records of
  Cornish
Period of collections: 1825-1925

**Saint-Gaudens National Historic
  Site**
Off N. Hwy., Rt. 12-A
Telephone: (603) 675-2175
Mail to: R.R. 2, Box 73, 03745
Federal agency, authorized by
  National Park Service
John H. Dryfhout, Superintendent
Number of members: full time 6, part
  time 10, volunteer 10
Major programs: museum, historic
  site(s), school programs, book
  publishing, historic preservation,
  exhibits, living history, audiovisual
  programs, photographic
  collections
Period of collections: late 19th-early
  20th centuries

DANBURY

George Gamble Library
Rt. 104
Mail to: R.F.D., 03230
Town agency
Founded in: 1911
Ruth B. Ford, Librarian
Major programs: library
Period of collections: 1700s-1930s

DANVILLE

Hawke Historical Society
03819
Questionnaire not received

DERRY

Derry Historical Society and Museum
Fire Station, E. Broadway
Mail to: c/o Program Director, 75 Birch St., 03038
Town agency, authorized by Bicentennial Town Committee
Ralph Bonner, Program Director
Number of members: 25
Staff: volunteer 6
Major programs: museum, historic site(s), tours/pilgrimages, school programs, research, exhibits, photographic collections, genealogical services
Period of collections: 1880

DOVER

Northam Colonists Historical Society of Dover N.H.
R.F.D. 1, Box 449, 03820
Telephone: (603) 742-4674
Founded in: 1900
Questionnaire not received

Woodman Institute
182 Central Ave., 03820
Telephone: (603) 742-1038
Staff: full time 2, volunteer 1
Major programs: museum
Period of collections: 1783-1918

DUBLIN

Dublin Seminar for New England Folklife
P.O. Box 386, 03444
Telephone: (617) 369-7382
Founded in: 1976
Questionnaire not received

DURHAM

Durham Historic Association, Inc.
Dover and Newmarket Rd.
Telephone: (603) 868-5560
Mail to: Town Office Bldg., or P.O. Box 305, 03824
Private agency
Founded in: 1851
Maryanna Hatch, Curator
Number of members: 250
Staff: part time 1
Major programs: museum, historic sites preservation, markers, educational programs, newsletters/pamphlets
Period of collections: 1723-present

Lee Historical Society
R.F.D. 1, Toon Lane, 03824
Private agency
Founded in: 1970
Marjorie T. Keeler, President
Number of members: 80
Major programs: library, museum, exhibits
Period of collections: 1800s

EFFINGHAM

Effingham Historical Society
Rt. 153
Mail to: P.O. Box 33, S. Effingham, 03882
Private agency
Founded in: 1953
Stephen H. Schofield, President
Number of members: 100
Staff: volunteer 30
Major programs: museum, historic site(s), historic preservation
Period of collections: 1783-1918

ENFIELD

Enfield Historical Society
Rt. 4-A
Telephone: (603) 632-7486
Mail to: R.R. 2, Box 397, 03748
Private agency
Founded in: 1976
Richard M. Henderson, President
Number of members: 164
Staff: volunteer 10
Major programs: archives, manuscripts, museum, historic site(s), markers, oral history, historic preservation, research, photographic collections, genealogical services
Period of collections: 1761-present

EPPING

Epping Historical Society
Water St.. 03042
Questionnaire not received

EXETER

Exeter Historical Society
27 Front St., 03833
Private agency
Founded in: 1928
Edward S. Chose, President
Number of members: 200
Staff: part time 1, volunteer 40
Major programs: archives, manuscripts, book publishing

FITZWILLIAM

Fitzwilliam Historical Society
c/o Amos J. Blake House, 03447
Private agency
Founded in: 1962
J. Mark Ansart, President
Number of members: 200
Staff: volunteer 80
Major programs: library, archives, manuscripts, museum, historic site(s), markers, tours/pilgrimages, oral history, school programs, pamphlets, historic preservation, research, exhibits, photographic collections, genealogical services
Period of collections: 1800-1900

FRANCESTOWN

Francestown Improvement and Historical Society
03043
Telephone: (603) 547-6610/547-2036
Private agency
Founded in: 1907
Brooks Rice, President
Number of members: 60
Staff: volunteer 8
Major programs: archives, museum, historic site(s), oral history, historic preservation, exhibits, photographic collections, village improvements
Period of collections: late 1800s-early 1900s

FRANCONIA

New England Ski Museum
Rt. 3, Franconia Notch
Telephone: (603) 823-7177
Mail to: P.O. Box 267, 03580
Private agency
Founded in: 1977
Arthur F. March, Jr., Executive Director
Number of members: 700
Staff: part time 3, volunteer 6
Major programs: library, museum, oral history, historic preservation, exhibits, audiovisual programs, photographic collections
Period of collections: 1900-1960

FREMONT

Fremont Historical Society
R.F.D. 1, Box 453, 03044
Telephone: (603) 895-4032
Private agency
Founded in: 1966
Matthew E. Thomas, President
Number of members: 64
Staff: volunteer 4
Major programs: archives, manuscripts, museum, markers, tours/pilgrimages, audiovisual programs, photographic collections
Period of collections: 1764-present

GILMANTON

Gilmanton Historical Society
Gilmanton 03237
Telephone: (603) 267-6565
Founded in: 1966
Number of members: 105
Staff: volunteer 8
Major programs: archives, museum, historic sites preservation, markers, books, historic preservation
period of collections1820-1890

GILSUM

Gilsum Historical Society
P.O. Box, 03448
Telephone: (603) 352-8542
State agency
Founded in: 1979
Gretchen Law Imperiale, President
Number of members: 30
Staff: volunteer 40
Major programs: oral history, living history
Period of collections: 19th century

GOFFSTOWN

Goffstown Historical Society
Parker Station
Telephone: (603) 497-2889
Mail to: 14-A Main St., 03045
Private agency
Founded in: 1969
Mary Carroll Hillis, Curator
Number of members: 150
Staff: volunteer 15
Major programs: museum
Period of collections: 1865-1918

GOSHEN

Goshen Historical Society, Inc.
03752
Telephone: (603) 863-1509
Questionnaire not received

GREENLAND

Greenland Historical Society
132 Breakfast Hill Rd., 03840
Telephone: (603) 436-2784
Town agency
Founded in: 1967
Paul C. Hughes, Historian
Number of members: 180
Major programs: library, historic
  site(s), oral history,
  newsletters/pamphlets, historic
  preservation
Period of collections: 1635-1950

HAMPTON

Hampton Historians, Inc.
c/o 3 Thomsen Rd., 03842
Telephone: (603) 926-2111
Founded in: 1974
Questionnaire not received

**Meeting House Green Memorial
  and Historical Association, Inc.**
Tuck Memorial Museum, Hampton
  Historical Society, 40 Park Ave.,
  03842
Telephone: (603) 926-3287/926-2654
Founded in: 1925
Questionnaire not received

HAMPTON FALLS

New Hampshire Farm Museum, Inc.
Sanborn Rd., 03834
Telephone: (603) 772-4964
Questionnaire not received

HANCOCK

Hancock Historical Society
Main St., 03449
Questionnaire not received

Webster Cottage
32 N. Main St., 03755
Telephone: (603) 646-3371
Questionnaire not received

HANOVER

Dartmouth College Archives
Baker Library, Dartmouth College,
  03755
Telephone: (603) 646-2037
Private agency, authorized by the
  college
Founded in: 1929
Kenneth C. Cramer, College Archivist
Staff: full time 3, part time 3
Major programs: library, archives,
  manuscripts, oral history, records
  management, exhibits,
  photographic collections
Period of collections: 18th-20th
  centuries

The Hanover Historical Society
N. Main St., 03755
Telephone: (603) 646-3371
Founded in: 1950
Questionnaire not received

HENNIKER

Henniker Historical Society
Tucker Free Library
Private agency
Founded in: 1970
Richard A. Martin, President
Number of members: 30
Major programs: archives,
  manuscripts, tours/pilgrimages,
  historic preservation, photographic
  collections, genealogical services
Period of collections: 19th-20th
  century

HILLSBORO

Deering Historical Society
03244
Telephone: (603) 464-3017
Private agency
Founded in: 1980
Mrs. Daniel K. Poling, President
Number of members: 82
Major programs: museum, historic
  site(s), book publishing, historic
  preservation, records
  management, research, cemetery
  records
Period of collections: 1774-present

Hillsborough Historical Society
P.O. Box 318, E. Washington Rd.,
  03244
Telephone: (603) 478-5721
Joseph Copper, President
Number of members: 62
Staff: volunteer 20
Major programs: historic sites
  preservation, historic preservation
period of collections1852-1858

**Hillsborough Historical
  Society, Inc.—Franklin Pierce
  Homestead**
P.O. Box 896, 03244
Telephone: (603) 498-3204
Private agency
Founded in: 1954
Mrs. Herbert S. Judd, Jr., President
Number of members: 111
Major programs: library, archives,
  manuscripts, museum,
  tours/pilgrimages, school
  programs, newsletters/pamphlets,
  historic preservation, records
  management, exhibits
Period of collections: 1804-1869

HINSDALE

Hinsdale Historical Society
Town Hall, Main St.
Telephone: (603) 336-7408
Mail to: P.O. Box 122, 03451
Founded in: 1971
Questionnaire not received

HOLLIS

Hollis Historical Society
Ruth E. Wheeler House, 03049
Private agency
Founded in: 1958
Ruth Greenaway, President
Number of members: 65
Staff: volunteer 30
Major programs: museum, exhibits,
  audiovisual programs
Period of collections: 1800s

HOPKINTON

**New Hampshire Antiquarian
  Society**
Main St.
Mail to: c/o President, Putney Hill Rd.,
  03301
Private agency
Founded in: 1889
Rosalind P. Hanson, President
Number of members: 388
Staff: part time 1, volunteer 50
Major programs: library, archives,
  manuscripts, museum, historic
  site(s), markers, tours/pilgrimages,
  junior history, oral history, school
  programs, newsletters/pamphlets,
  historic preservation, exhibits,
  living history, photographic
  collections, genealogical services
Period of collections: 1765-1930

HUDSON

Hudson Historical Society, Inc.
Derry Rd.
Telephone: (603) 882-7474
Mail to: c/o Arlene Mac Intyre, 18
  Ledge Rd., 03051
Private agency
Founded in: 1966
Number of members: 100
Staff: full time 1
Major programs: museum, historic
  site(s), markers, school programs,
  book publishing, historic
  preservation, exhibits,
  genealogical services
Period of collections: 1775-present

JAFFREY

Jaffrey Historical Society, Inc.
123 Main St., Jaffrey Civic Center,
  03452
Telephone: (603) 532-6527
Questionnaire not received

JEFFERSON

Jefferson Historical Society
Rt. 2, Jefferson Hill
Telephone: (603) 586-4488
Mail to: P.O. Box 124, 03583
Private agency
Founded in: 1977
Helen Marshal Merrill, President
Number of members: 44
Staff: volunteer 6
Major programs: archives, museum,
  historic sites preservation
Period of collections: late 19th
  century

KEENE

**Historical Society of Cheshire
  County**
246 Main St.
Telephone: (603) 352-1895
Mail to: P.O. Box 803, 03457
Private agency
Founded in: 1927
Alan F. Rumrill, Director
Number of members: 450
Staff: full time 1, part time 1,
  volunteer 3
Major programs: library, archives,
  manuscripts, museum, school

programs, exhibits, audiovisual
programs, photographic
collections, genealogical services
Period of collections: 1770-1900

Horatio Colony House Museum
199 Main St.
Telephone: (603) 352-0460
Mail to: P.O. Box 722, 03431
Private agency, authorized by Horatio
Colony Memorial Trust
Founded in: 1977
Richard Peloquin, Administrator
Staff: full time 1, part time 2
Major programs: library, museum,
school programs, book publishing
Period of collections: 1800s

KENSINGTON

Kensington Historical Society
c/o President, Osgood Rd., R.F.D. 2,
Exeter, 03833
Telephone: (603) 772-2460
Town agency
Founded in: 1970
Allan H. Boudreau, President
Number of members: 72
Staff: volunteer 7
Major programs: historic site(s),
historic preservation
Period of collections: 1720-1944

KINGSTON

**Kingston Improvement and
Historical Society, Inc.**
Main St.
Mail to: P.O. Box 54, 03848
Private agency
Founded in: 1956
Marion L. Clark, President
Number of members: 84
Major programs: museum, historic
sites preservation, markers,
educational programs
Period of collections: 1783-1918

LACONIA

Belknap Mill Society
Mill Plaza, 03246
Telephone: (603) 524-8813
Private agency
Founded in: 1970
Judith Buswell, Executive Director
Number of members: 500
Staff: full time 1, part time 5,
volunteer 15
Major programs: historic sites
preservation, historic preservation,
community arts center
Period of collections: 19th-20th
centuries

Laconia Historical Society
P.O. Box 1126, 03247
Private agency
Founded in: 1980
Warren D. Huse, President
Number of members: 130
Major programs: historic
preservation, exhibits, audiovisual
programs, photographic
collections
Period of collections: 1885-present

LEBANON

Lebanon Historical Society, Inc.
1 Campbell St.
Telephone: (603) 448-3118
Mail to: 40 Mascoma St., 03766
Founded in: 1958
Questionnaire not received

LEE

Lee Historical Society
Mast Rd.
Mail to: R.F.D. Durham, 03824
Founded in: 1970
Questionnaire not received

LITTLETON

Farm and Forest Museum
R.F.D. 1, 03561
Telephone: (603) 444-2236
Mark E. Finnegan, Curator
Number of members: 130
Staff: full time 3, part time 3,
volunteer 5
Major programs: museum
period of collectionslate 1800s-early
1900s

Littleton Area Historical Society
109 Main St.
Telephone: (603) 444-5741
Mail to: 4 Merrill St., 03561
Founded in: 1967

LONDONDERRY

Londonderry Historical Society
03053
Private agency
Founded in: 1960
Betsy McKinney, President
Number of members: 42
Major programs: books

MADBURY

Madbury Historical Society
c/o President, Freshet Rd., 03820
Telephone: (603) 742-7713
Private agency
Founded in: 1978
Diane C. Hodgson, President
Number of members: 80
Staff: volunteer 10
Major programs: archives,
tours/pilgrimages,
newsletters/pamphlets, historic
preservation, records
management, photographic
collections
Period of collections: 1800-present

MADISON

Madison Historical Society
Main St., 03849
Private agency
Founded in: 1956
Jack Alexander, President
Number of members: 40
Major programs: archives, historic
site(s), book publishing
Period of collections: 1850-1945

MANCHESTER

**Acadian Genealogical and
Historical Association of New
Hampshire**
52 Concord St., 03101

Mail to: P.O. Box 668, 03105
Founded in: 1980
Lillian G. Leger, President
Number of members: 750
Staff: volunteer 5
Magazine: *L'Etoile D'Acadie*
Major programs: library, archives,
tours/pilgrimages, educational
programs, newsletters/pamphlets
Period of collections: 1600-present

**American-Canadian Genealogical
Society**
P.O. Box 668, 03105-0668
Telephone: (603) 622-2883
Private agency
Founded in: 1973
Richard J. Gagnon, President
Number of members: 2,200
Staff: volunteer 40
Magazine: *The Genealogist*
Major programs: library, archives,
manuscripts, tours/pilgrimages,
oral history, school programs,
newsletters/pamphlets, research,
living history, audiovisual
programs, genealogical services
Period of collections: 1600-present

Association Canado-Americaine
52 Concord St., 03101
Telephone: (603) 625-8577
Private agency
Founded in: 1896
Eugene A. Lemieux, President
General
Number of members: 31,000
Staff: part time 1
Magazine: *Le Canado-Americain*
Major programs: library, archives,
manuscripts, museum, tours,
historic preservation, research,
exhibits, photographic collections,
genealogical services
Period of collections: 17th
century-present

**Association
Nouvelle-Angleterre/Acadie**
P.O. Box 3558, 03105-3558
Telephone: (603) 356-3009
Private agency
Founded in: 1984
Richard L. Fortin, President
Number of members: 25
Staff: volunteer 5
Major programs: tours/pilgrimages,
oral history, school programs,
newsletters/pamphlets, historic
preservation, living history,
audiovisual programs, cultural
programs

**Franco-American Heritage Center
of New Hampshire**
P.O. Box 3558, 03105-3558
Telephone: (603) 669-3264
Private agency
Founded in: 1979
Jean L. Pellerin, Secretary
Number of members: 50
Staff: volunteer 2
Major programs: tours/pilgrimages,
oral history, historic preservation,
living history

Institut Canado-Americaine
52 Concord St., 03101
Telephone: (603) 625-8577
Mail to: P.O. Box 989, 03105-0989

Private agency, authorized by
Association Canado-Americaine
Founded in: 1896
Robert A. Beaudoin, Chair, Archival
Commission
Number of members: 26,000
Staff: full time 1, volunteer 2
Magazine: *Le Canado Americain*
Major programs: library, archives,
manuscripts, museum, historic
site(s), markers, tours/pilgrimages,
junior history, oral history, school
programs, book publishing,
newsletters/pamphlets, historic
preservation, records
management, research, exhibits,
living history, audiovisual
programs, photographic
collections, genealogical services
Period of collections: 1600-present

Manchester Historic Association
129 Amherst St., 03104
Telephone: (603) 622-7531
Private agency
Founded in: 1896
George S. Comtois, Director
Number of members: 500
Staff: full time 3, part time 2,
volunteer 10
Magazine: *Reflections*
Major programs: library, archives,
manuscripts, museum,
tours/pilgrimages, school
programs, newsletters/pamphlets,
research, exhibits, photographic
collections, genealogical services
Period of collections:
pre-Columbian-1946

**National Federation of
Franco-American Genealogical
and Historical Societies**
P.O. Box 3558, 03105-3558
Telephone: (603) 356-3009
Private agency
Founded in: 1980
Richard L. Fortin, President
Number of members: 20
Staff: volunteer 3
Major programs: tours/pilgrimages,
oral history, school programs,
newsletters/pamphlets, research,
living history, audiovisual
programs, genealogical services
Period of collections: 1600-present

MASON

Mason Historical Society
717 Greenville Rd., 03048
Telephone: (603) 878-2918
Town agency
Founded in: 1968
Susan Youngblood, President
Number of members: 30
Staff: volunteer 6
Major programs: library, archives,
manuscripts, museum, markers

MELVIN VILLAGE

Tuftonboro Historical Society
Main St., 03850
Canon Gordon E. Gillett, President
Private agency
Number of members: 181
Major programs: museum
Period of collections: 1865-present

MEREDITH

Meredith Historical Society
Telephone: (603) 279-6136
Mail to: P.O. Box 920, 03253
Private agency
Founded in: 1949
Esther C. Wyatt, President
Magazine: *Early Meredith*
Major programs: museum, historic
preservation, exhibits,
photographic collections,
genealogical services
Period of collections: 1865-present

MILFORD

Milford Historical Society
6 Union St., 03055
Founded in: 1895
Questionnaire not received

MILTON

New Hampshire Farm Museum, Inc.
Rt. 16, Plummer's Ridge
Telephone: (603) 652-7840
Mail to: P.O. Box 644, 03851
Private agency
Founded in: 1969
Melissa Walker, Coordinator
Staff: full time 1, part time 1,
volunteer 125
Major programs: museum,
tours/pilgrimages, oral history,
school programs,
newsletters/pamphlets, historic
preservation, records
management, exhibits, living
history, archaeology programs
Period of collections: mid 1800s-early
1900s

MOULTONBORO

Moultonboro Public Library
Main St., 03254
Telephone: (603) 476-8828
Town agency
Founded in: 1900
Adele V. Taylor, Librarian
Staff: part time 2
Major programs: library
Period of collections: 1930-present

NASHUA

Daniel Webster College
University Dr., 03063
Telephone: (603) 883-3556
Private agency
Founded in: 1965
Hannah M. McCarthy, President
Staff: full time 60, part time 50,
volunteer 25
Magazine: *Omnibus*
Major programs: library,
newsletters/pamphlets, records
management, audiovisual
programs

Nashua Historical Society
5 Abbott St., 03060
Founded in: 1872
Questionnaire not received

Nashua Public Library
2 Court St., 03060
Telephone: (603) 883-4141
City agency
Founded in: 1867
Clarke S. Davis, Director
Staff: full time 25, part time 10
Major programs: library, book
publishing, research, genealogical
services

NELSON

Olivia Rodham Memorial Library
Telephone: (603) 847-3214
Mail to: R.F.D. Nelson, Marlborough,
03457
Town agency
Founded in: 1925
Patricia W. Packard, Librarian
Staff: part time 1, volunteer 1
Major programs: library
Period of collections: 1900-present

NEW CASTLE

**Town of New Castle Archives and
Records Committee**
03854
Telephone: (603) 431-6854
Founded in: 1974
Questionnaire not received

NEW DURHAM

**New Durham Archives and
Historical Collections**
Town Hall, Main St., 03885
Telephone: (603) 859-6881
Town agency, authorized by New
Durham Library
Founded in: 1975
Eloise Bickford, Town Historian
Major programs: library, archives,
oral history, historic preservation,
records management, research,
photographic collections,
genealogical services
Period of collections: 1750-present

NEW LONDON

New London Historical Society
Little Sunapee Rd., 03257
Private agency
Debbie Stanley, President
Major programs: archives, museum,
newsletters/pamphlets, historic
preservation, exhibits,
photographic collections
Period of collections: 1820-1860

NEWMARKET

New Market Historical Society
Zion's Hill
Telephone: (603) 659-3652
Mail to: 51 N. Main St., 03857
Founded in: 1966
Questionnaire not received

NEWPORT

Newport Historical Society Inc.
Courthouse Square
Telephone: (603) 863-2079

Mail to: P.O. Box 492, 03773
Founded in: 1975
Questionnaire not received

NORTH HAMPTON

North Hampton Historical Society
03862
Town agency
Founded in: 1969
Mrs. Earl H. Coffey, President
Number of members: 21
Staff: volunteer 21
Major programs: library, educational
programs, audiovisual programs

North Hampton Public Library
Atlantic Ave., 03862
Telephone: (603) 964-6326
Town agency
Founded in: 1898
Robin LeBlanc, Librarian
Staff: part time 3, volunteer 5
Major programs: library
Period of collections: 19th-20th
centuries

NOTTINGHAM

Nottingham Historical Society
Star Rt., Box 4, 03290
Telephone: (603) 679-8741
Founded in: 1971
Julia C. Case, President
Number of members: 57
Staff: volunteer 6
Major programs: library, museum
Period of collections: 1783-1865

OSSIPEE

Ossipee Historical Society
Old Rt. 16, Center Ossipee
Mail to: Maple Ridge Farm, 03864
Founded in: 1920
Edward M. Cook, President
Number of members: 40
Staff: part time 2, volunteer 9
Major programs: archives, museum,
historic sites preservation, books,
historic preservation
Period of collections: 1775-present

PELHAM

Pelham Historical Society
President, Currier Rd., 03076
Telephone: (603) 635-2368
Founded in: 1963
Herbert S. Currier, President
Number of members: 14
Staff: volunteer 7
Major programs: historic site(s), oral
history, school programs, historic
preservation
Period of collections: 1850-1950

PETERBOROUGH

Peterborough Historical Society
Grove St.
Telephone: (603) 924-3235
Mail to: P.O. Box 58, 03458
Private agency
Founded in: 1902
Esther A. Fitts, President
Number of members: 480
Staff: part time 3, volunteer 15
Major programs: library, museum,
school programs, photographic
collections, genealogical services
Period of collections: 1800-present

PIERMONT

Piermont Historical Society
High St., 03779
Private agency
Founded in: 1974
George Isae, President
Number of members: 25
Staff: volunteer 10
Major programs: library, historic
site(s), tours/pilgrimages, oral
history, school programs, historic
preservation, exhibits, audiovisual
programs, photographic
collections, genealogical services

PLAINFIELD

Philip Read Memorial Library
Telephone: (603) 675-6866
Town agency
Founded in: 1922
Nancy Norwalk, Librarian
Number of members: full time 1, part
time 1, volunteer 12
Major programs: library, oral history,
genealogical services
Period of collections: 1761-present

Plainfield Historical Society
Mail to: P.O. Box 506, 03781
Private agency
Founded in: 1977
Dorothy McNamara, President
Number of members: 90
Staff: volunteer 50
Major programs: archives, museum,
oral history, school programs
Period of collections: 1761-present

PLYMOUTH

**Department of History, Plymouth
State College**
Rounds Hall, 03264
Telephone: (603) 536-1550
State agency, authorized by the
college
Founded in: 1871
Major programs: library, oral history,
archaeology programs,
photographic collections

PORTSMOUTH

Portsmouth Athenaeum, Inc.
9 Market Square
Telephone: (603) 431-2538
Mail to: P.O. Box 848, 03801
Private agency
Founded in: 1817
Joseph Sawtelle, President
Number of members: 225
Staff: part time 1, volunteer 12
Major programs: library, archives,
manuscripts, museum, historic
site(s), book publishing, historic
preservation, photographic
collections, genealogical services
Period of collections: 18th-19th
centuries

**Portsmouth Historical
Society—John Paul Jones House**
State and Middle Sts.
Telephone: (603) 436-8924
Mail to: 54 Court St., 03801
Private agency
Founded in: 1921
Albert W. Aykroyd, President
Number of members: 200

Major programs: archives, museum,
tours
Period of collections: Colonial
era-early 19th century

Strawbery Banke
454 Court St.
Telephone: (603) 436-8010
Mail to: P.O. Box 300, 03801
Private agency
Founded in: 1958
David A. Donath, Director
Staff: full time 24, part time 15
Major programs: library, historic
site(s), school programs,
newsletters/pamphlets, historic
preservation, research, exhibits,
archaeology programs
Period of collections: 18th-19th
centuries

RAYMOND

Raymond Historical Society, Inc.
Main St.
Mail to: P.O. Box 1764, 03077
Founded in: 1970
Questionnaire not received

ROCHESTER

Rochester Historical Society
Telephone: (603) 335-1605
Mail to: P.O. Box 3211, 03867
Founded in: 1950
Lester Hurd, President
Staff: volunteer 7
Major programs:
newsletters/pamphlets, historic
preservation, records
management, photographic
collections, genealogical services
Period of collections: 1850s-present

SALEM

Salem Historical Society
79 Brady Ave., 03079
Telephone: (603) 898-2047
Founded in: 1956
Questionnaire not received

SALISBURY

Salisbury Historical Society
Salisbury Hts.
Telephone: (603) 648-2526
Mail to: P.O. Box 10, 03268
Founded in: 1968
Questionnaire not received

SANBORNTON

Sanbornton Historical Society
03269
Founded in: 1952
Elizabeth A. Weiant, President
Number of members: 210
Major programs: educational
programs
period of collections 1783-1865

SEABROOK

Historical Society of Seabrook
P.O. Box 500, 03874
Telephone: (603) 474-2232
Private agency
Founded in: 1964
Eric N. Small, President
Number of members: 150

Staff: volunteer 4
Major programs: museum, historic
preservation, photographic
collections
Period of collections: to 1900

SOMERSWORTH

Summersworth Historical Society
P.O. Box 733, 03878
Private agency
George Gould, President
Number of members: 60
Major programs:
newsletters/pamphlets, audiovisual
programs
Period of collections: late 19th-early
20th centuries

SPRINGFIELD

Springfield Historical Society Inc.
Four Corners Rd., Box 63, 03284
Telephone: (603) 763-2292
Private agency
Founded in: 1983
Robert E. Moore, President
Number of members: 50
Major programs: manuscripts,
markers, oral history,
newsletters/pamphlets, audiovisual
programs, photographic
collections, genealogical services

SUGAR HILL

Sugar Hill Historical Museum
Village Green, 03585
Telephone: (603) 823-8142
Founded in: 1976
Mitchell C. Vincent, Director
Number of members: 152
Staff: volunteer 9
Major programs: library, archives,
museum, oral history, school
programs, historic preservation,
records management, research,
exhibits, audiovisual programs,
photographic collections,
genealogical services
Period of collections: 1850-1950

Sugar Hill Historical Society
03585
Founded in: 1976
Questionnaire not received

TAMWORTH

Cook Memorial Library
Main St., 03886
Telephone: (603) 323-8510
Town agency
Founded in: 1895
Jean Ulitz, Librarian
Staff: volunteer 3
Major programs: library, oral history,
photographic collections,
genealogical services
Period of collections: late 19th-early
20th centuries

Tamworth Historical Society
Center of Village, 03886
Questionnaire not received

TEMPLE

Mansfield Public Library
Main St.
Telephone: (603) 878-3100

Mail to: P.O. Box L-95, 03084
Town agency
Founded in: 1890
Priscilla A. Weston, Librarian
Staff: part time 1
Major programs: library, genealogical
services

TROY

Gay-Kimball Public Library
Main St., 03465
Telephone: (603) 242-7743
Town agency
Founded in: 1882
Shirley M. Lang, Librarian
Staff: full time 1, part time 1
Major programs: library

TUFTONBORO

Tuftonboro Historical Society
Main St., Melvin Village
Mail to: P.O. Box 112, Melvin Village,
03850
Private agency
Founded in: 1958
Mary H. Antonucci, Secretary
Number of members: 100
Staff: volunteer 18
Major programs: museum
Period of collections: 1800-1920

WAKEFIELD

**Wakefield-Brookfield Historical
Society**
Mt. Laural Rd., Rt. 153
Telephone: (603) 522-3739
Mail to: R.F.D. 1, Brookfield, 03872
Private agency
Founded in: 1938
Peter Lamb, President
Number of members: 220
Staff: volunteer 12
Major programs: museum, historic
site(s), oral history, exhibits,
genealogical services
Period of collections: 1780-1930

WALPOLE

Bridge Memorial Library
Main St., 03608
Telephone: (603) 756-3308
Town agency
Founded in: 1795
Virginia Putnam, Librarian
Staff: full time 1, part time 1
Major programs: library, research,
genealogical services
Period of collections: late
1700s-present

Walpole Historical Society
Main St., 03608
Telephone: (603) 756-3602
Private agency
James E. Yanizyn, President
Major programs: museum,
tours/pilgrimages, school
programs, exhibits
Period of collections: 1800-1930

WARNER

Warner Historical Society
c/o President, Iron Kettle Rd., 03278
Telephone: (603) 456-3997
Private agency

Founded in: 1969
Rebecca Courser, President
Number of members: 140
Staff: part time 25
Major programs: archives, museum,
oral history, exhibits, archaeology
programs, photographic
collections, genealogical services
Period of collections: 1974-present

WHITEFIELD

Whitefield Historical Society
Mail to: P.O. Box 21, 03598
Private agency
Founded in: 1980
Louise Miller, President
Number of members: 85
Staff: volunteer 8
Major programs: archives,
photographic collections
Period of collections: 1850-1925

WILMOT

Wilmot Historical Society, Inc.
03287
Private agency
Founded in: 1976
Frances B. Wilcox, President
Number of members: 72
Major programs: markers, junior
history, oral history, exhibits
Period of collections: 1890-1920

WILTON

Wilton Historical Society
Highland St., 03086
Telephone: (603) 654-2581
Private agency
Helen Ring, Administrator
Major programs: library, archives,
photographic collections,
genealogical services
Period of collections: 1800s

WINCHESTER

Conant Public Library
Telephone: (603) 239-4331
Mail to: P.O. Box 6, 03470
Town agency
Founded in: 1876
Edith W. Atkins, Librarian
Staff: part time 4
Major programs: library, museum,
historic preservation, genealogical
services
Period of collections: 1733-present

WOLFEBORO

**New Hampshire Old Graveyard
Association**
Star Rt. 1
Founded in: 1976
Questionnaire not received

Wolfeboro Historical Society
S. Main St., 03894
Mail to: P.O. Box 443, Wolfeboro
Falls, 03895
Founded in: 1925
Questionnaire not received

NEW JERSEY

ALLAIRE

Deserted Village at Allaire, Inc.
Allaire State Park, Rt. 524, 07727
Telephone: (201) 938-2253
Private agency
Founded in: 1957
Craig D. Maibius, Executive Director
Number of members: 375
Staff: full time 1, part time 7,
  volunteer 75
Major programs: museum, historic
  sites, educational programs,
  newsletters/pamphlets, historic
  preservation, research, exhibits
Period of collections: 1800-1860

ALLENDALE

Allendale Historical Society, Inc.
Mail to: P.O. Box 294, 07401
Founded in: 1974
Questionnaire not received

ALLENTOWN

**Allentown-Upper Freehold
  Historical Society**
Mail to: P.O. Box 328, 08501
Elizabeth S. Poinsett, President
Number of members: 140
Major programs: library, historic sites
  preservation, tours/pilgrimages,
  educational programs,
  newsletters/pamphlets
Period of collections: 1918-present

ATLANTIC CITY

**Atlantic County Office of Cultural
  Affairs**
1125 Atlantic Ave., Room 625, 08401
Telephone: (609) 345-6700, ext. 2243
Founded in: 1971
Jeffrey Pergament, Administrator,
  Cultural and Heritage Affairs
Staff: full time 1, volunteer 1
Magazine: *Art, Culture and Heritage*
Major programs: historic site(s),
  markers, tours/pilgrimages, oral
  history, school programs,
  newsletters/pamphlets, historic
  preservation, research, exhibits,
  audiovisual programs, archaeology
  programs, photographic
  collections, field services
Period of collections: 1837-present

**Down Jersey Marine Historical
  Society**
Historic Gardner's Basin, 08075
Telephone: (609) 461-1698
Founded in: 1974
Questionnaire not received

**Historic Gardner's Basin Maritime
  Park and Museum**
N. Hampshire Ave. at the Bay, 08401
Telephone: (609) 348-2880
Founded in: 1976
Staff: full time 30, volunteer 12
Magazine: *Sea Letter*
Major programs: museum, historic
  sites preservation, educational
  programs, historic preservation,
  marine mammal rescue
Period of collections: 1800-1900

ATLANTIC HIGHLANDS

**Atlantic Highlands Historical
  Society**
Telephone: (201) 291-2718
Mail to: P.O. Box 108, 07716
Private agency
Michael E. Scherfen, President
Number of members: 670
Major programs: library, museum,
  historic sites preservation, markers,
  tours/pilgrimages, book publishing,
  newsletters/pamphlets, exhibits
Period of collections: 1865-1918

BARNEGAT

Barnegat Historical Society
E. Bay Ave.
Telephone: (609) 698-8340
Mail to: 402 N. Main St., 08005
Founded in: 1965
Questionnaire not received

BARNEGAT LIGHT

Barnegat Light Historical Society
5th and Central
Telephone: (609) 494-9196
Mail to: P.O. Box 386, 08006
Private agency
Founded in: 1950
A. Jerome Walnut, President
Number of members: 100
Staff: volunteer 12
Major programs: museum, historic
  sites preservation,
  newsletters/pamphlets
Period of collections: 1865-present

BASKING RIDGE

Basking Ridge Historical Society
107 Dyckman Place, 07920
Telephone: (201) 766-3786
Questionnaire not received

BATSTO

Batsto Citizens Committee
Visitor Center, R.D. 4, 08037
Telephone: (609) 561-0024
Founded in: 1956
Questionnaire not received

BAYONNE

Bayonne Firefighters' Museum
10 W. 47th St., 07002
Telephone: (201) 858-6005
Founded in: 1979
Questionnaire not received

**National Archives—New York
  Branch**
Military Ocean Terminal, Bldg. 22,
  07002-5388
Telephone: (201) 823-7545
Founded in: 1969
Joel Buckwald, Director
Staff: full time 3
Major programs: archives,
  educational programs, teachers'
  workshops, film series, open
  houses, and tours, genealogical
  services
Period of collections: 1789-1978

BEACH HAVEN

**Long Beach Island Historical
  Association**
Engleside and Beach Ave.
Telephone: (609) 492-0700
Mail to: P.O. Box 222, 08008
Town agency
Founded in: 1975
Rebecca Tarditi, President
Number of members: 385
Staff: volunteer 35
Major programs: museum, oral
  history, newsletters/pamphlets,
  historic preservation, exhibits,
  audiovisual programs,
  photographic collections
Period of collections: 1865-1918

BELLE MEAD

**Van Harlingen Historical Society of
  Montgomery, Inc.**
P.O. Box 23, 08502
Telephone: (201) 874-3582
Private agency
Founded in: 1967
Jean M. Balcom, President
Number of members: 259
Staff: volunteer 20
Magazine: *The Van Harlingen
  Historian*
Major programs: historic preservation
Period of collections: 18th-19th
  centuries

BELLEVILLE

Belleville Historical Society
155 Main St., 07109
Private agency
Edward W. O'Neil, President
Number of members: 75
Staff: volunteer 4
Major programs: library, manuscripts,
  museum, historic site(s), markers,
  tours/pilgrimages, junior history,
  school programs, historic
  preservation, exhibits, living
  history, photographic collections
Period of collections: 1700-present

BELVIDERE

Belvidere Historic Committee
300 Greenwich St., 07823
Telephone: (201) 475-2512
Town agency
Founded in: 1979
Irene M. Smith, Permanent
  Member/Organizer
Number of members: 10
Major programs: historic site(s),
  markers, oral history, historic
  preservation

**Warren County Cultural and
  Heritage Commission**
Courthouse, 2nd St.
Telephone: (201) 852-2394
Mail to: P.O. Box 53, Hackettstown,
  07840
County agency
Founded in: 1975
Howard J. Niper, Chair
Staff: volunteer 9
Major programs: historic site(s),
  markers
Period of collections: Colonial era

Warren County Historical and Genealogical Society
313 Mansfield St.
Telephone: (201) 475-2512/475-4298
Mail to: P.O. Box 313, 07823
Private agency
Founded in: 1931
Mrs. John K. Wieghorst, President
Number of members: 180
Major programs: library, museum, tours/pilgrimages, junior history, book publishing, historic preservation, research, exhibits, genealogical services
Period of collections: 19th century

White Township Historical Society
R.D. 1 Box 231, 07823
Telephone: (201) 475-2265
Founded in: 1969
Betty Jo King, President
Number of members: 50
Staff: volunteer 12
Major programs: museum
Period of collections: 1800-present

BERGENFIELD

Bergenfield Museum Society
91 Highgate Terrace, 07621
Telephone: (201) 385-4599
Private agency
Founded in: 1976
Elizabeth Schmelz, President
Number of members: 175
Staff: volunteer 25
Major programs: museum, educational programs
Period of collections: 1895-1940

BLOOMFIELD

Historical Society of Bloomfield
c/o Bloomfield Public Library, 90 Broad St., 07003
Telephone: (201) 429-9292
Private agency
Founded in: 1966
Mildred F. Stone, President
Number of members: 175
Major programs: museum, markers, research, exhibits
Period of collections: 19th-20th centuries

BOONTON

Boonton Historical Society
Telephone: (201) 627-6205
Mail to: P.O. Box 32, 07005
Founded in: 1959
Questionnaire not received

BORDENTOWN

Bordentown Historical Society
13 Crosswicks St.
Telephone: (609) 298-1740
Mail to: P.O. Box 182, 08505
Founded in: 1930
Mrs. Walter Varlgy, President
Number of members: 225
Staff: volunteer 18
Major programs: historic sites preservation, markers, tours/pilgrimages, newsletters/pamphlets
Period of collections: 1865-present

BRICK TOWNSHIP

Brick Township Historical Society, Inc.
Mail to: P.O. Box 160, 08723
Questionnaire not received

BRIDGETON

George J. Woodruff Collection of Indian Artifacts, Bridgeton Free Public Library
150 E. Commerce St., 08302
Telephone: (609) 451-2620
Founded in: 1811
Staff: full time 10, volunteer 4
Major programs: library, museum
Period of collections: 1600-present

BRIDGEWATER

Somerset County Historical Society
Van Veghten House, Rustic Industrial Mall, Finderne
Telephone: (201) 722-0018
Mail to: P.O. Box 632, 08807
Founded in: 1882
Questionnaire not received

BRIELLE

Union Landing Historical Society
Telephone: (201) 528-5867 (president)
Mail to: P.O. Box 473, 08730
Private agency
Founded in: 1973
John E. Belding, President
Number of members: 59
Major programs: historic site(s), markers, oral history, research
Period of collections: 1830s-present

BURLINGTON

Burlington County Historical Society
457 High St., 08016
Telephone: (609) 386-4773
Founded in: 1915
Susan B. G. Bradman, President
Number of members: 475
Staff: full time 2, part time 3, volunteer 50
Major programs: library, archives, manuscripts, museum, historic site(s), school programs, newsletters/pamphlets, exhibits, genealogical services
Period of collections: 1700-1865

City of Burlington Historical Society
City Hall
Telephone: (609) 386-3993
Mail to: 432 High St., 08016
City agency
Founded in: 1975
Sandra Fabi, President
Number of members: 104
Staff: volunteer 104
Major programs: historic site(s), markers, tours/pilgrimages, school programs, newsletters/pamphlets, historic preservation, research, exhibits, photographic collections
Period of collections: 1700-1800

CALDWELL

Grover Cleveland Birthplace
207 Bloomfield Ave., 07006
Telephone: (201) 226-1810
State agency
Sharon Farrell, Caretaker
Staff: full time 1
Major programs: museum, historic site(s), tours/pilgrimages, oral history, historic preservation
Period of collections: 1837-1897

CALIFON

Califon Historical Society
P.O. Box 424, 07830
Telephone: (201) 832-7138
Private agency
Founded in: 1971
Madeline A. Morris, Founder
Magazine: Califon Story
Major programs: manuscripts, historic sites preservation, markers, oral history, books, historic preservation

CAMDEN

Camden County Historical Society
Park Blvd. and Euclid Ave., 08103
Telephone: (609) 964-3333
Founded in: 1899
Number of members: 600
Staff: full time 2, part time 5, volunteer 15
Magazine: The Bulletin of the Camden County Historical Society
Major programs: library, archives, manuscripts, museum, historic sites preservation, tours/pilgrimages, oral history, educational programs, books, newsletters/pamphlets, genealogy
Period of collections: 1780-present

Campbell Museum
Campbell Place
Telephone: (609) 342-6440
Private agency, authorized by Campbell Soup Company
Founded in: 1966
Ralph Collier, President
Magazine: Selections from the Campbell Museum Collection
Major programs: newsletters/pamphlets, exhibits, decorative arts
Period of collections: 18th-19th centuries

Walt Whitman Association
330 Mickle St., 08103
Telephone: (609) 964-5383
Mail to: P.O. Box 1221, Haddonfield, 08033
Private agency
Founded in: 1946
Geoffrey M. Sill, President
Number of members: 100
Staff: part time 1, volunteer 6
Magazine: Mickle Street Review
Major programs: library, museum, historic site(s), newsletters/pamphlets
Period of collections: 1819-1892

CAPE MAY

Greater Cape May Historical Society
P.O. Box 495, 08204
Founded in: 1974
Questionnaire not received

Historic District Commission
643 Washington St., 08204
Telephone: (609) 884-8411
City agency
Founded in: 1970
Staff: part time 1
Major programs: historic preservation

Mid-Atlantic Center for the Arts
1048 Washington St.
Telephone: (609) 884-5404
Mail to: P.O. Box 164, 08204
Private agency
Founded in: 1970
B. Michael Zuckerman, Director
Number of members: 600
Staff: full time 4, part time 50, volunteer 300
Major programs: historic site(s), tours/pilgrimages, newsletters/pamphlets, repertory theater
Period of collections: 1870-1900

CAPE MAY COURT HOUSE

Cape May County Historical and Genealogical Society
DN-707, Rt. 9, 08210
Telephone: (609) 465-3535
Private agency
Founded in: 1927
Somers Corson, Acting Curator
Number of members: 1,000
Staff: full time 2, part time 3, volunteer 125
Magazine: *The Cape May County Magazine of History and Genealogy*
Major programs: library, museum, school programs, book publishing, newsletters/pamphlets, exhibits, audiovisual programs, genealogical services
Period of collections: 1750-1900

CEDAR GROVE

Cedar Grove Historical Society
96 Westland Rd.
Telephone: (201) 239-5264
Mail to: c/o Public Library, 07009
Town agency
Founded in: 1968
Henry Stoeckert, President
Number of members: 60
Staff: volunteer 9
Major programs: library, archives, manuscripts, historic sites preservation, educational programs, books, photographic collections
Period of collections: 1783-present

CHATHAM

Chatham Historical Society
Mail to: P.O. Box 682, 07928
Founded in: 1923
Linda Winterberg, President
Number of members: 300
Staff: volunteer 35

Major programs: library, tours/pilgrimages, educational programs, books
Period of collections: 1865-present

CHERRY HILL

Friends of Barclay Farmstead
Barclay Lane
Telephone: (609) 795-6225
Mail to: P.O. Box 3042, 08034
Private agency, authorized by Cherry Hill Township
Founded in: 1974
Bonnie Cocchiaraley, Director
Number of members: 345
Staff: full time 1, volunteer 50
Major programs: library, museum, historic site(s), tours/pilgrimages, junior history, oral history, school programs, newsletters/pamphlets, historic preservation, exhibits, living history, archaeology programs
Period of collections: 1800-1880

CHESTER

Chester Historical Society
Telephone: (201) 879-7740
Mail to: P.O. Box 376, 07930
Private agency
Founded in: 1969
Carmen Smith, President
Number of members: 70
Staff: volunteer 10
Major programs: archives, oral history, book publishing, newsletters/pamphlets, photographic collections
Period of collections: 19th century

CLARK

Clark Historical Society
Clark Public Library, 303 Westfield Ave., 07066
Private agency
Founded in: 1970
Lucia Pascale, President
Number of members: 100
Major programs: museum
Period of collections: 1690-early 1700s

CLEMENTON

New Jersey Postal History Society
26 Windmill Dr., 08021
Private agency
Founded in: 1972
Joyce Groot, Secretary
Number of members: 150
Magazine: *NJPH: The Journal of the New Jersey Postal History Society*
Major programs: library, books, newsletters/pamphlets, postal and communications history
Period of collections: 1730-present

CLIFTON

Hamilton House Museum
971 Valley Rd., 07013
Telephone: (201) 744-5707
Private agency
Founded in: 1974
Elvira Hessler, Director
Number of members: 517

Staff: full time 1, volunteer 20
Period of collections: 19th century

CLINTON

Clinton Historical Museum Village
56 Main St., Box 5005, 08809
Telephone: (201) 735-4101
Private agency
Founded in: 1960
Catherine Callan West, Director
Number of members: 515
Staff: full time 3, part time 2, volunteer 65
Major programs: museum, historic site(s), exhibits
Period of collections: 1860s-1918

CLOSTER

Abram Demaree Homestead
110 Schraalenburgh Rd., 07624
Telephone: (201) 385-7309
Mail to: 252 Schraalenburgh Rd., Haworth, 07641
Private agency
Founded in: 1979
Mary Crain, President
Staff: volunteer 10
Major programs: historic site(s), tours/pilgrimages, junior history, school programs
Period of collections: 1800

COLLINGSWOOD

Collingswood-Newton Colony Historical Society
Haddon and Frazer Ave., 08108
Telephone: (609) 858-0649
Private agency
Founded in: 1971
Glen A. Koster, President
Number of members: 78
Major programs: library, historic site(s), historic preservation
Period of collections: Colonial era-1900

COLTS NECK

Colts Neck Historical Society
16 Crusius Place
Telephone: (201) 462-1378 Mail to: P.O. Box 101, 07722
Private agency
Founded in: 1964
Louise Whitney, President
Number of members: 85
Staff: volunteer 6
Major programs: library, historic site(s), markers, book publishing, newsletters/pamphlets, historic preservation, genealogical services

COLUMBUS

Mansfield Township Historical Society
Telephone: (609) 499-9583
Mail to: P.O. Box 150, 08022
Founded in: 1973

Mary Ellen Lister, President
Number of members: 60
Staff: volunteer 10
Major programs: museum, historic
sites, markers, tours/pilgrimages,
oral history, educational programs,
newsletters/pamphlets, historic
preservation
Period of collections: 1688-present

CRANBURY

**Cranbury Historical and
Preservation Society**
4 Park Place, 08512
Founded in: 1967
Betty Wagner, President
Number of members: 292
Major programs: library, museum,
markers, oral history, educational
programs, newsletters/pamphlets
Period of collections: 19th century

CRANFORD

Cranford Historical Society
124 Union Ave., N, 07016
Telephone: (201) 276-0082
Town agency
Founded in: 1927
Loretta Widdows, Curator
Number of members: 325
Staff: part time 1, volunteer 50
Magazine: *Mill Wheel*
Major programs: library, archives,
manuscripts, museum, historic
site(s), markers, tours/pilgrimages,
junior history, oral history, school
programs, newsletters/pamphlets,
historic preservation, records
management, research, exhibits,
living history, archaeology
programs, photographic
collections, genealogical services
Period of collections: 19th century

DOVER

Dover Area Historical Society
Telephone: (201) 366-0786
Mail to: P.O. Box 609, 07801
Founded in: 1966
Questionnaire not received

EAST BRUNSWICK

East Brunswick Historical Society
Telephone: (201) 254-4343
Mail to: P.O. Box 12, 08816
Founded in: 1971
Questionnaire not received

**East Brunswick Museum
Corporation**
16 Maple St., 08816
Telephone: (201) 257-1508
Founded in: 1978
Questionnaire not received

EASTAMPTON

**Burlington County Cultural and
Heritage Commission**
Smithville-Jacksonville Rd.
Telephone: (609) 201-5068
Mail to: 49 Rancoras Rd., Mt. Holly,
08060
Founded in: 1970
Questionnaire not received

EDISON

**Edison Township Historical
Society**
328 Plainfield Ave., 08817
Telephone: (201) 287-0900
Private agency
Founded in: 1983
David C. Sheehan, President
Number of members: 40
Staff: volunteer 10
Major programs: historic site(s),
tours/pilgrimages, oral history,
school programs, historic
preservation, research, exhibits,
audiovisual programs,
photographic collections
Period of collections: 1870s

EGG HARBOR TOWNSHIP

**Greater Egg Harbour Township
Historical Society**
Township Hall, Rd. 1, 08221
Founded in: 1979
Questionnaire not received

ELIZABETH

Boxwood Hall, State Historic Site
1073 E. Jersey St., 07201
Telephone: (201) 648-4540
Founded in: 1943
Questionnaire not received

Elizabethtown Heritage Society
500 N. Broad St., 07207
Telephone: (201) 558-3044
Private agency
Founded in: 1983
Charles L. Aquilina, President
Number of members: 28
Staff: volunteer 3
Major programs: museum, historic
site(s), markers, oral history, school
programs, historic preservation,
exhibits, living history,
photographic collections
Period of collections: Colonial
era-present

◇**League of Historical Societies of
New Jersey**
Mail to: P.O. Box 531, 07207
Founded in: 1966
Questionnaire not received

**New Jersey Society, Sons of the
American Revolution**
1045 E. Jersey St., 07201
Telephone: (201) 355-1776
Private agency
Founded in: 1889
Howard W. Wiseman, Executive
Secretary/Librarian
Number of members: 750
Staff: part time 1, volunteer 1
Magazine: *Sons of the American
Revolution Magazine/The Patriot*
Major programs: library, archives,
museum, historic site(s), markers,
tours/pilgrimages,
newsletters/pamphlets, historic
preservation, research,
genealogical services
Period of collections: 1775-1783

**Society of Colonial Wars in the
State of New Jersey**
1045 E. Jersey St., 07201
Telephone: (201) 355-1776

Founded in: 1893
Howard W. Wiseman, Registrar
Number of members: 200
Staff: volunteer 1
Major programs: library, museum,
markers, book publishing,
research, genealogical services
Period of collections: to 1776

**Society of the War of 1812 in the
State of New Jersey**
1045. East Jersey St., 07201
Telephone: (201) 355-1776
Founded in: 1898
Howard W. Wiseman, President
Number of members: 30
Staff: volunteer 1
Magazine: *The War Cry*
Major programs: archives,
tours/pilgrimages,
newsletters/pamphlets
Period of collections: 1800-1825

Union County Historical Society
633 Pearl St., 07202
Telephone: (201) 245-9386
Private agency
Founded in: 1869
Charles Louis Aquilina, President
Number of members: 58
Staff: volunteer 6
Major programs: historic site(s),
markers, tours/pilgrimages, historic
preservation, research
Period of collections: early Colonial
era-19th century

ENGLEWOOD

Englewood Historical Society
500 Liberty Rd.
Telephone: (201) 568-0678
Private agency
Founded in: 1976
Eleanor S. Harvey, President
Number of members: 70
Major programs: historic
preservation, records
management, audiovisual
programs
Period of collections: from 1870s

ENGLISHTOWN

Costume Society of America
15 Little John Rd.
Telephone: (201) 536-4123
Mail to: P.O. Box 761, 07726
Private agency
Founded in: 1973
Elizabeth Jachimowicz, President
Number of members: 1,083
Staff: full time 1
Magazine: *The Journal of the
Costume Society of America*
Major programs:
newsletters/pamphlets, costume
symposium

FAIR HAVEN

Fair Haven Historical Society
142 Lexington Ave.
Telephone: (201) 842-4453
Mail to: P.O. Box 72, 07701
Private agency
Founded in: 1972
Timothy J. McMahon, President
Number of members: 25

Staff: volunteer 10
Major programs: archives, historic
site(s), tours/pilgrimages, oral
history, historic preservation,
research, exhibits, genealogical
services
Period of collections: late 19th
century-present

FARMINGDALE

Deserted Village at Allaire, Inc.
Allaire State Park, 07727
Telephone: (201) 938-2253
questionnaire not received

Farmingdale Historical Society
Asbury Ave.
Mail to: 106 Main St., 07727
Private agency
Founded in: 1974
S. Allan Grove, President
Number of members: 15
Major programs: library, archives,
manuscripts, museum, markers,
oral history, school programs,
research, living history
Period of collections: 1900-present

**New Jersey Museum of
Transportation, Inc.**
Rt. 524, Allaire State Park
Telephone: (201) 938-5524
Mail to: P.O. Box 622, 07727
Founded in: 1963
Donald E. Newman, Board Chair
Number of members: 150
Staff: volunteer 20
Magazine: *The Order Board*
Major programs: historic
preservation, railroad operations
Period of collections: 1900-1945

FLEMINGTON

**Hunterdon County Cultural and
Heritage Commission**
65 Main St., c/o Administration Bldg.,
08822
Telephone: (201) 788-1256
Staff: part time 1
Major programs: museum, oral
history, historic preservation

**Hunterdon County Historical
Society**
114 Main St., 08822
Telephone: (201) 782-1091
Founded in: 1885
Mrs. George E. Carkhuff,
Corresponding Secretary
Number of members: 525
Staff: volunteer 12
Major programs: library, archives,
manuscripts, museum, books,
newsletters/pamphlets
Period of collections: 1750-1920

Liberty Village Foundation
2 Church St., 08822
Telephone: (201) 782-8550
Questionnaire not received

FLORHAM PARK

Historical Society of Florham Park
P.O. Box 193, 07932
Private agency
Founded in: 1935
Mrs. Peter J. Metsopulos, President
Number of members: 105

Magazine: *Report Card*
Major programs: museum, book
publishing, exhibits
Period of collections: 1850

FORKED RIVER

Lacey Township Historical Society
Rt. 9
Mail to: P.O. Box 412, 08731
Founded in: 1962
Ralph K. Turp, President
Number of members: 74
Staff: volunteer 13
Major programs: museum
Period of collections: 1865-1918

FT. MONMOUTH

U.S. Army Chaplain Museum
Walters Hall, Bldg. 1207, USACHCS,
Ft. Monmouth, 07703-5511
Telephone: (201) 532-3487
Federal agency, authorized by the
U.S. Army Chaplain School
Founded in: 1950
Michael A. Rusnock, Curator
Number of members: 500
Staff: full time 3, part time 2,
volunteer 4
Major programs: museum,
tours/pilgrimages, school
programs, newsletters/pamphlets
Period of collections: Colonial
era-present

FRANKLIN PARK

**Franklin Township Historical
Society**
84 Hillview Ave., 08823
Telephone: (201) 297-2641
Questionnaire not received

FREEHOLD

Battleground Historical Society
P.O. Box 1776, Tennent, 07763
Telephone: (201) 431-0649
Private agency
Founded in: 1969
Mary T. Evans, President
Number of members: 175
Staff: volunteer 30
Major programs: historic site(s),
historic preservation
Period of collections: Colonial era

**Monmouth County Historical
Association**
70 Court St., 07728
Telephone: (201) 462-1466
Founded in: 1898
Wilson E. O'Donnell, Director
Number of members: 850
Staff: full time 5, part time 19,
volunteer 60
Major programs: library, archives,
manuscripts, museum, historic
site(s), school programs,
newsletters/pamphlets, historic
preservation, records
management, research, exhibits,
audiovisual programs,
photographic collections,
genealogical services
Period of collections: 1700-1830

National Broadcasters Hall of Fame
22 Throckmorton St., 07728
Telephone: (201) 431-4656

Private agency
Founded in: 1978
Arthur S. Schreiber,
Founder/President
Staff: volunteer 3
Major programs: archives, museum,
audiovisual programs
Period of collections: 1910-present

**World War II Glider Pilots
Association**
136 W. Main St., 07728
Telephone: (201) 462-1838
Founded in: 1971
S. Tipton Randolph,
Secretary/Executive Counsel
Number of members: 1,500
Staff: volunteer 60
Magazine: *Silent Wings*
Major programs: museum,
audiovisual programs
Period of collections: W.W. II

FRENCHTOWN

**Oak Summit School Historical
Society**
R.D. 1, 08822
Telephone: (201) 996-2255
State agency
Founded in: 1979
Carl F. Kettler, President
Number of members: 50
Major programs: archives, historic
site(s), historic preservation, living
history
Period of collections: mid 1800s

GLEN RIDGE

Glen Ridge Historical Society
c/o Glen Ridge Congregational
Church
Telephone: (201) 743-6409
Mail to: P.O. Box 164, 07028
Private agency
Founded in: 1977
Dorothy Sachs, President
Number of members: 295
Major programs: museum,
tours/pilgrimages,
newsletters/pamphlets, historic
preservation, research, exhibits
Period of collections: 1895-present

GREENWICH

**Cumberland County Historical
Society**
Ye Greate St.
Telephone: (609) 455-4055
Mail to: P.O. Box 16, 08323
Private agency
Sara C. Watson, President
Number of members: 1,000
Staff: full time 1
Major programs: library, archives,
manuscripts, museum, historic
site(s), markers, junior history,
newsletters/pamphlets, historic
preservation, genealogical
services
Period of collections: 1650-1899

GRIGGSTOWN

Griggstown Historical Society
R.D. 1, Canal Rd., 08540
Telephone: (201) 359-6288
Town agency

Founded in: 1978
Sue Rightmire, President
Number of members: 56
Staff: volunteer 9
Major programs: museum, historic
site(s), oral history, historic
preservation, schoolhouse
restoration
Period of collections: 1830-1932

HACKENSACK

**Bergen County Office of Cultural
and Historic Affairs**
355 Main St., Room 101, 07601
Telephone: (201) 646-2882
County agency
Founded in: 1979
Ruth Van Wagoner, Administrator
Staff: full time 6
Major programs: library, archives,
historic sites management,
educational programs,
newsletters/pamphlets, historic
preservation, coordinate all artistic
and historic activities in county,
research
Period of collections: 17th
century-present

Historic Sites Advisory Board
355 Main St., Room 101, 07601
Telephone: (201) 646-2882
County agency
Founded in: 1968
Ruth Van Wagoner, Administrator,
Bergen County Office of Cultural
and Historic Affairs
Staff: full time 6
Major programs: library, historic
site(s), historic preservation,
research
Period of collections: 1780s-present

**Submarine Memorial
Association—USS Ling 297**
Court and River Sts.
Telephone: (201) 487-9493
Mail to: P.O. Box 395, 07601
Private agency, authorized by the
U.S. Navy
Founded in: 1972
Herbert J. Georgius, Director of
Operations
Number of members: 45
Staff: full time 1, part time 4,
volunteer 5
Major programs: library, museum,
historic site(s), tours/pilgrimages,
historic preservation, exhibits,
living history, photographic
collections
Period of collections: W.W. II

HACKETTSTOWN

Hackettstown Historical Society
106 Church St., 07840
Telephone: (201) 852-8797
Founded in: 1975
Ruth E. Scarborough, President
Number of members: 110
Staff: volunteer 2
Major programs: library, archives,
museum, historic site(s),
tours/pilgrimages, oral history,
historic preservation, exhibits,
genealogical services
Period of collections: 19th-20th
centuries

HADDONFIELD

**Historic District Advisory
Committee of Haddonfield
Planning**
483 Loucroft Rd., 08033
Telephone: (609) 429-4204
Founded in: 1971
Questionnaire not received

Historical Society of Haddonfield
343 King's Hwy., E, 08033
Telephone: (609) 429-7375
Founded in: 1914
Questionnaire not received

HADDON HEIGHTS

Haddon Heights Historical Society
08035
Telephone: (609) 547-7132
Founded in: 1972
Questionnaire not received

HADDON TOWNSHIP

**Camden County Cultural and
Heritage Commission**
Hopkins House, 250 S. Park Dr.,
08057
Telephone: (609) 858-0040
County agency
Founded in: 1972
Gail Greenberg, Executive Director
Staff: full time 3
Major programs: school programs,
book publishing, newsletters,
audiovisual programs, field
services
Period of collections: 18th-19th
centuries

**Haddon Township—Newton
Colony Historical Society**
Telephone: (609) 854-0589
Mail to: 224 Hazel Terrace,
Westmont, 08108
Founded in: 1975
Questionnaire not received

HALEDON

**American Labor Museum—Botto
House National Landmark**
83 Norwood St., 07508
Telephone: (201) 595-7953
Private agency
Founded in: 1980
John A. Herbst, Executive Director
Number of members: 1,000
Staff: full time 5, part time 6,
volunteer 40
Major programs: museum, historic
site(s), school programs,
newsletters/pamphlets, historic
preservation, exhibits, living
history, audiovisual programs,
photographic collections, labor
history
Period of collections: from 1850

HAMBURG

**Hardyston Heritage Society—Old
Monroe Schoolhouse Museum**
R.D. 1, Box 599, 07419
Telephone: (201) 827-4459
Private agency
Founded in: 1977
Carrie Papa, Museum Director
Number of members: 65

Staff: part time 1, volunteer 12
Major programs: archives, museum,
historic site(s), markers,
tours/pilgrimages, oral history,
school programs,
newsletters/pamphlets, historic
preservation, living history,
audiovisual programs,
photographic collections
Period of collections: 1890-1926

HAMMONTON

Hammonton Historical Society
Central and Vine
Telephone: (609) 564-0888
Mail to: 643 Bellevue Ave., 08037
Private agency
Founded in: 1956
Mamie Vaughn, President
Number of members: 100
Staff: volunteer 10
Major programs: archives, museum,
markers, oral history, book
publishing, newsletters/pamphlets,
research, photographic
collections, genealogical services
Period of collections: 1854-present

HARRINGTON PARK

Harrington Park Historical Society
10 Herring St., 07640
Telephone: (201) 768-5675
Private agency
Founded in: 1975
Fred H. Quantmeyer, Sr., President
Number of members: 10
Staff: volunteer 4
Major programs: library, manuscripts,
historic site(s), markers, historic
preservation, research,
archaeology programs,
photographic collections,
genealogical services

HIGHLANDS

Sandy Hook Museum
Gateway N.R.A., Sandy Hook Unit
Telephone: (201) 872-0115
Mail to: P.O. Box 437, 07732
Federal agency, authorized by
National Park Service
Founded in: 1968
John Krisko II, Chief/Interpretation
Staff: full time 2, part time 1
Major programs: library, archives,
manuscripts, museum, historic
site(s), oral history, school
programs, historic preservation,
research, exhibits, living history,
audiovisual programs, archaeology
programs, photographic
collections
Period of collections: 1764-present

HIGHTSTOWN

Aaron Burr Association
R.D. 1, Rt. 33, Box 429, 08520
Telephone: (609) 448-2218
Private agency
Founded in: 1946
Samuel Engle Burr, Jr., President
General
Number of members: 100
Magazine: *The Chronicle of ABA*
Major programs: library, archives,
markers, tours/pilgrimages
Period of collections: 1756-1836

Hightstown East Windsor Historical Society
164 N. Main St., 08520
Private agency
Founded in: 1971
David G. Martin, President
Number of members: 230
Staff: volunteer 20
Major programs: library, archives, manuscripts, museum, historic site(s), markers, tours/pilgrimages, oral history, newsletters/pamphlets, historic preservation, records management, research, exhibits, living history, archaeology programs, photographic collections, genealogical services, field services
Period of collections: 17th century-present

HILLSIDE

Hillside Historical Society
111 Conant St., 07205
Telephone: (201) 352-9270
Private agency
Founded in: 1973
Arnold H. McClow, President
Number of members: 160
Staff: volunteer 10
Major programs: museum, historic site(s), junior history, school programs, newsletters/pamphlets, historic preservation
Period of collections: 1790-1920

HO-HO-KUS

Friends of the Hermitage, Inc.
335 N. Franklin Turnpike, 07423
Telephone: (201) 445-8311
Founded in: 1972
Florence Leon, Director
Number of members: 300
Staff: volunteer 25
Major programs: archives, historic sites preservation, oral history, educational programs, historic preservation, research, exhibits, living history, photographic collections, clothing textiles
Period of collections: 19th century

The Hermitage
07423
Telephone: (201) 445-8311/444-8558
Founded in: 1972
Nancy B. Gay, President
Number of members: 600
Staff: volunteer 75
Major programs: archives, historic site(s), tours/pilgrimages, oral history, school programs, newsletters/pamphlets, historic preservation, research, exhibits, living history, audiovisual programs, photographic collections, field services
Period of collections: 1850-1900

HOLMDEL

Holmdel Historical Society
Stilwell Rd.
Telephone: (201) 946-8618
Mail to: P.O. Box 282, 07733
Founded in: 1973
Staff: volunteer 15
Questionnaire not received

Longstreet Farm
Longstreet Rd.
Telephone: (201) 842-4000
Mail to: Monmouth County Park System, Newman Springs Rd., Lincroft, 07738
County agency, authorized by Monmouth County Board of Recreation Commissioners
Founded in: 1967
Howard E. Wikoff, Senior County Park Manager
Staff: full time 8, part time 10, volunteer 25
Major programs: historic site(s), tours/pilgrimages, oral history, school programs, historic preservation, living history
Period of collections: 1865-1918

Pleasant Valley Preservation Society
P.O. Box 102, 07733
Telephone: (201) 946-4174
Private agency
Founded in: 1965
Number of members: 10
Major programs: historic preservation, research, audiovisual programs, environmental programs

HOPE

Hope Historical Society
High St.
Telephone: (201) 459-4609
Mail to: P.O. Box 52, 07844
Private agency
Founded in: 1954
Mrs. Richard E. Harris, President
Number of members: 80
Major programs: museum, markers, tours/pilgrimages, school programs, newsletters/pamphlets, exhibits
Period of collections: 1769-early 1900s

HOPEWELL

Hopewell Museum
28 E. Broad St., 08525
Telephone: (609) 466-0103
Founded in: 1922
Questionnaire not received

HOPEWELL TOWNSHIP

Howell Living Historical Farm
Valley Rd.
Telephone: (609) 397-0449
Mail to: R.R. 2, Box 187, Hunter Rd., Titusville, 08560
County agency, authorized by Mercer County Park Commission
Founded in: 1974
Peter Watson, Farm Administrator
Staff: full time 4, part time 6, volunteer 20
Magazine: *Howell Farm Journal*
Major programs: historic site(s), school programs, newsletters/pamphlets, historic preservation, research, living history, audiovisual programs
Period of collections: 1880-1910

INDIAN MILLS

Indian Mills Historical Society
Telephone: (609) 268-0439

Mail to: R.D. 5, Box 252, Atsion Rd., Vincentown, 08088
Questionnaire not received

IRVINGTON

Irvington Historical Society
P.O. Box 256, 08834
Telephone: (201) 996-3170
Founded in: 1965
George Sobin, President
Number of members: 70
Major programs: library, archives, books, newsletters/pamphlets, genealogy
Period of collections: 1800-present

ISLAND HEIGHTS

Island Heights Cultural and Heritage Association
Telephone: (201) 929-0695
Mail to: P.O. Box 670, 08732
Founded in: 1978
Questionnaire not received

JACKSON

Jackson Heritage Preservation Society
R.D. 5, Box 70-D, Cooks Bridge Rd., 08527
Telephone: (201) 364-7448
Founded in: 1978
Alexander S. Platt, President
Number of members: 42
Staff: volunteer 8
Major programs: museum, historic sites preservation, markers, educational programs, historic preservation
Period of collections: 1700s-1940s

JAMESBURG

Jamesburg Historical Association
203 Buckelew Ave., 08831
Telephone: (201) 521-2040
Private agency
Founded in: 1977
Marcia R. Kirkpatrick, President
Number of members: 30
Staff: volunteer 25
Major programs: historic site(s), tours/pilgrimages, historic preservation, exhibits, photographic collections
Period of collections: 1690-1900

JERSEY CITY

Historic Paulus Hook Association, Inc.
108 Grand St. 07302
Telephone: (201) 333-6048
City agency
Founded in: 1974
Joseph R. Duffy, President
Number of members: 89
Staff: volunteer 33
Major programs: historic sites, markers, tours/pilgrimages, historic preservation

Jersey City Free Public Library
472 Jersey Ave., 07302
Telephone: (201) 547-4517
Questionnaire not received

KEARNY

Kearny Museum
318 Kearny Ave., 07032
Telephone: (201) 997-6911
Town agency
Founded in: 1978
Jessie M. Hipp, Chair
Staff: volunteer 40
Major programs: archives,
manuscripts, museum, historic
site(s), school programs,
pamphlets, historic preservation,
research, exhibits, fine arts

KEYPORT

Keyport Historical Society
2 Broad St.
Mail to: P.O. Box 312, 07735
Private agency
Founded in: 1972
Lester Horner, President
Number of members: 225
Staff: volunteer 40
Major programs: archives, historic
site(s), markers, oral history,
historic preservation, exhibits,
audiovisual programs,
photographic collections
Period of collections: 1793-1918

KINNELON

Kinnelon Historical Commission
Municipal Bldg., Kinnelon Rd., 07405
Founded in: 1976
Questionnaire not received

LAMBERTVILLE

**Delaware Valley Old Time Power
and Equipment Association**
New Rd., Box 221, 08530
Telephone: (609) 466-1949
Private agency
Founded in: 1977
Nancy Brokaw, Treasurer
Number of members: 150
Major programs: historic preservation

Lambertville Historical Society
52 Bridge St.
Mail to: P.O. Box 2, 08530
Questionnaire not received

LAUREL SPRINGS

Whitman Stafford Committee
315 Maple, 08021
Telephone: (609) 784-1105
Founded in: 1978
Fred Lynch, Site Director
Number of members: 200
Staff: volunteer 15
Magazine: *Laurel Springs Courier*
Major programs: historic sites
preservation, markers, educational
programs
Period of collections: 1785-1890

LAWRENCEVILLE

**Holocaust Council of New Jersey
Professors**
Rider College, P.O. Box 6400, 08648
Telephone: (609) 896-5353
Private agency
Founded in: 1980
Albert Nissman, President
Number of members: 40

Major programs: newsletters,
audiovisual programs, lectures and
convention presentations

Lawrence Historical Society
P.O. Box 6025, 08648
Private agency
Founded in: 1975
Frances G. McCarthy, President
Number of members: 200
Major programs: museum, historic
site(s), newsletters/pamphlets,
historic preservation, exhibits,
photographic collections
Period of collections: 1840-1900

**Medical History Society of New
Jersey**
Academy of Medicine of New Jersey,
2 Princess Rd., 08648
Telephone: (609) 896-1717
Private agency
Founded in: 1980
Charles J. Heitzmann, Executive
Director
Number of members: 100
Major programs: oral history,
newsletters/pamphlets, symposia

LINCROFT

Monmouth County Park System
P.O. Box 326, Newman Springs Rd.,
07738
Telephone: (201) 842-4000
Founded in: 1961
Questionnaire not received

LITTLE FALLS

**Little Falls Township Historical
Society**
Little Falls Library, Warren St.
Telephone: (201) 256-5334
Mail to: c/o President, 95 Jacobus
Ave., 07424
Founded in: 1968
Mrs. John J. Curreri, President
Number of members: 24
Major programs: library, historic sites
preservation, markers,
tours/pilgrimages, oral history,
educational programs, books,
microfilming out-of-print borough
newspaper
Period of collections: 1918-present

LITTLE SILVER

Little Silver Historical Society
480 Prospect Ave., 07739
Telephone: (201) 842-2400
Private agency
Founded in: 1973
Gloria Hill, President
Number of members: 100
Staff: volunteer 12
Major programs: museum, oral
history, school programs,
newsletters/pamphlets, historic
preservation, exhibits
Period of collections: 1800s-present

LIVINGSTON

Livingston Historical Society
S. Livingston Ave.
Mail to: P.O. Box 220, 07039
Town agency, authorized by
Recreation Department of
Livingston

Founded in: 1962
Mrs. Charles Neff, President
Number of members: 190
Staff: volunteer 35
Major programs: historic site(s),
tours/pilgrimages, book publishing,
newsletters/pamphlets, historic
preservation
Period of collections: to 1830

Railroadians of America, Inc.
18 Okner Parkway, 07039
Telephone: (201) 992-1060
Private agency
Founded in: 1939
John Markoe, President
Number of members: 400
Staff: volunteer 6
Magazine: *The Train Sheet*
Major programs: tours/pilgrimages,
book publishing, historic
preservation
Period of collections: 1910-present

LONG BRANCH

Long Branch Historical Museum
1260 Ocean Ave., 07740
Telephone: (212) 229-0600
Founded in: 1953
Edgar N. Dinkelspiel, President
Staff: volunteer 1
Major programs: museum,
tours/pilgrimages, art festival
Period of collections: 1865-present

LONG VALLEY

**Washington Township Historical
Society**
Telephone: (201) 876-3395
Mail to: R.D. 3, W. Mill Rd., 07853
Founded in: 1960
Questionnaire not received

LUMBERTON

Lumberton Historical Society
Mail to: P.O. Box 22, 08048
Founded in: 1975
Questionnaire not received

MADISON

**Commission on Archives and
History, United Methodist Church**
36 Madison Ave.
Telephone: (201) 822-2787/822-2826
Mail to: P.O. Box 127, 07940
Private agency, authorized by the
United Methodist Church
Founded in: 1885
Charles Yrigoyen, Jr., General
Secretary
Staff: full time 7, part time 3
Magazine: *Methodist History*
Major programs: library, archives,
museum, historic site(s),
tours/pilgrimages, oral history,
newsletters/pamphlets, records
management, research, exhibits,
photographic collections,
genealogical services
Period of collections: 1783-present

**Loantaka Chapter, Daughters of the
American Revolution**
Telephone: (201) 539-6852
Mail to: 19 Edwin Rd., Morris Plains,
07950

Private agency, authorized by
National Society, Daughters of the
American Revolution
Founded in: 1927
Mrs. Peter J. Taburro, Jr., President
Number of members: 37
Staff: volunteer 10
Major programs: library, museum,
junior history, school programs,
book publishing, historic
preservation, genealogical
services
Period of collections: Revolutionary
War period

MAHWAH

Mahwah Historical Society
1871 Old Station Lane, 07430
Telephone: (201) 529-2897
Founded in: 1965
Questionnaire not received

MAPLE SHADE

Maple Shade Historical Society
415 W. Main St.
Telephone: (609) 779-7022
Mail to: 27 E. Linwood Ave., 08052
Questionnaire not received

MAPLEWOOD

**Durand-Hedden House and Garden
Association**
523 Ridgewood Rd., 07040
Telephone: (201) 763-7712
Town agency·
Founded in: 1979
Gus Hinkele, Board President
Number of members: 260
Staff: volunteer 30
Major programs: historic site(s),
school programs, living history
Period of collections: 1800

MARGATE

Save Lucy Committee, Inc.
9200 Atlantic Ave.
Telephone: (609) 822-6519
Mail to: P.O. Box 3000, 08402
Founded in: 1970
Josephine L. Harron, President
Staff: volunteer 40
Major programs: museum, historic
site(s), tours, oral history, historic
preservation

MATAWAN

Matawan Historical Society
P.O. Box 41, 07747
Telephone: (201) 566-2036
Private agency
Founded in: 1969
Stevenson M. Enterline, President
Number of members: 100
Major programs: museum, historic
sites preservation,
newsletters/pamphlets
Period of collections: 18th-19th
centuries

**Madison Township Historical
Society—Thomas Warne
Historical Museum and Library**
Rt. 516, Old Bridge Township
Telephone: (201) 566-0348
Mail to: R.D. 1, Box 150, 07747

Private agency
Founded in: 1964
Lorna Kerr, President
Number of members: 75
Staff: volunteer 23
Major programs: library, archives,
manuscripts, museum, historic
site(s), markers, tours, school
programs, book publishing,
newsletters/pamphlets, research,
exhibits, photographic collections,
genealogical services
Period of collections: 1865-present

MAURICETOWN

Maurice River Historical Society
P.O. Box 161, 08329
Founded in: 1971
Questionnaire not received

MEDFORD

Medford Historical Society
P.O. Box 362, 08055
Telephone: (609) 654-7767
Founded in: 1968
Questionnaire not received

MERCHANTVILLE

Merchantville Historical Society
Greenleigh Court, Community Center
Mail to: P.O. Box 1093, 08109
Founded in: 1976
Edith Silberstein, Chair
Number of members: 35
Staff: volunteer 10
Major programs: archives, markers,
historic preservation, oral history
Period of collections: 1900

MIDDLETOWN

**Battleship New Jersey Historical
Museum Society**
Telephone: (201) 291-0825
Mail to: P.O. Box BB-62, 07748
Private agency
Founded in: 1975
Thomas J. Gorman, President
Number of members: 650
Staff: volunteer 10
Major programs: museum,
newsletters/pamphlets, historic
preservation
Period of collections: W.W. II-present

**Middletown Landmarks
Commission**
Town Hall, 1 King's Hwy., 07748
Telephone: (201) 671-3100
town agency
Founded in: 1976
Donnie E. Snedeker, Chair
Staff: volunteer 7
Major programs: library, archives,
historic site(s), historic
preservation, research, audiovisual
programs
Period of collections: 1700s-1800s

Poricy Park Citizens Committee
Oak Hill Rd.
Telephone: (201) 842-5966
Mail to: P.O. Box 36, 07748
Private agency
Founded in: 1969
Patricia Contreras, Director
Number of members: 800

Staff: full time 4, part time 3,
volunteer 100
Major programs: museum, historic
site(s), school programs, historic
preservation
Period of collections: 18th century

MILLBURN TOWNSHIP

**Millburn-Short Hills Historical
Society**
Telephone: (201) 376-1568
Mail to: P.O. Box 243, Short Hills,
07078
Founded in: 1975
Questionnaire not received

MILLTOWN

Milltown Historical Society
116 S. Main St.
Telephone: (201) 828-0458
Mail to: P.O. Box 96, 08850
Founded in: 1967
Grace Riha, President
Number of members: 22
Staff: volunteer 22
Major programs: museum, historic
sites preservation,
tours/pilgrimages, educational
programs, exhibits
Period of collections: 1865-1918

MILLVILLE

Wheaton Historical Association
Wheaton Village, 08332
Telephone: (609) 825-6800
Private agency
Founded in: 1968
Berry Taylor, Managing Director
Number of members: 856
Staff: full time 21, part time 18,
volunteer 36
Major programs: library, archives,
museum, research, exhibits, living
history
Period of collections: 19th-20th
centuries

**Wheaton Museum of American
Glass**
Wheaton Village, 08332
Telephone: (609) 825-6800
Founded in: 1968
Questionnaire not received

MONTAGUE

**MARCH (Montague Association for
the Restoration of Community
History)**
R.D. 5, Box 246, U.S. Rt. 206, 07827
Telephone: (201) 293-3577/293-3296
Founded in: 1979
Michele Cantelmo, President
Number of members: 121
Staff: volunteer 2
Major programs: museum, historic
sites preservation, educational
programs, newsletters/pamphlets
Period of collections: 1850-early 20th
century

MONTCLAIR

Israel Crane House Museum
110 Orange Rd.
Telephone: (201) 744-1796
Mail to: P.O. Box 322, 07042

Private agency
Founded in: 1965
Amy M. Hatrak, Administrator
Number of members: 800
Staff: part time 3, volunteer 150
Major programs: library, manuscripts, museum, historic site(s), tours/pilgrimages, junior history, oral history, school programs, book publishing, newsletters/pamphlets, historic preservation, research, exhibits, living history, genealogical services
Period of collections: 1796-1840

Montclair Historical Society
110 Orange Rd.
Telephone: (201) 744-1796
Mail to: P.O. Box 322, 07042
Questionnaire not received

Northern New Jersey Chapter, Victorian Society
Telephone: (201) 744-8267
Mail to: P.O. Box 717, 07042
Founded in: 1975
Questionnaire not received

MONTVILLE

Montville Historical Society
Taylortown Rd., 07045
Telephone: (201) 334-0304
Questionnaire not received

MOORESTOWN

Historical Society of Moorestown
12 High St., 08057
Telephone: (609) 428-9000 (president)
Private agency
Founded in: 1970
Donald G. Rypka, President
Number of members: 360
Staff: volunteer 25
Major programs: library, historic site(s), oral history
Period of collections: 18th century-present

MORRISTOWN

Canal Society of New Jersey
Macculloch Hall
Telephone: (201) 233-9752
Mail to: P.O. Box 737, 07960
Private agency
Founded in: 1969
Edward J. Barry, President
Number of members: 600
Staff: volunteer 25
Magazine: *The Towpath Post*
Major programs: museum, historic site(s), markers, tours/pilgrimages, newsletters/pamphlets, historic preservation, audiovisual programs, photographic collections
Period of collections: 1820-1931

Fosterfields Living Historic Farm—Morris County Park Commission
E. Hanover Ave.
Telephone: (201) 829-0474
Mail to: P.O. Box 1295-R, 07960
County agency
Major programs: historic site(s), school programs, historic

preservation, living history, audiovisual programs,
Period of collections: 1880-1910

Historic Speedwell
333 Speedwell Ave., 07960
Telephone: (201) 540-0211
Private agency
Founded in: 1967
Michaela M. McCausland, Administrator
Number of members: 400
Staff: full time 1, part time 1
Magazine: *News From Historic Speedwell*
Major programs: school programs, book publishing, exhibits
Period of collections: 1807-1864

Local History Department, Joint Free Public Library of Morristown and Morris Township
1 Miller Rd., 07960
Telephone: (201) 538-6161
Town agency
Diane Solomon, Head, Local History Department
Staff: full time 3, part time 5, volunteer 3
Major programs: library

Macculloch Hall Historical Museum
45 Macculloch Ave., 07960
Telephone: (201) 538-2404
Founded in: 1954
Alice Caulkins, Conservator
Staff: part time 3, volunteer 20
Major programs: archives, museum, tours/pilgrimages
Period of collections: 19th century

Morris County Heritage Commission
Courthouse Administration Wing, 07960
Telephone: (201) 285-6198
Founded in: 1970
Questionnaire not received

Morris County Historical Society
68 Morris Ave. 07960
Telephone: (201) 267-3465
Mail to: P.O. Box 170-M
Founded in: 1946
Jeanne H. Watson, Director
Number of members: 400
Staff: part time 1, volunteer 50
Magazine: *The Morris Gazette*
Major programs: library, museum, historic sites preservation, tours/pilgrimages, educational programs, books, newsletters/pamphlets
Period of collections: 1783-1918

Morris County Park Commission
E. Hanover Ave.
Telephone: (201) 285-6166
Mail to: P.O. Box 1295-R, 07960
Questionnaire not received

Morristown National Historical Park
Washington Place, 07960
Telephone: (201) 539-2016
Federal agency
Founded in: 1933
Janet Wolf, Superintendent
Staff: full time 24, part time 8

Major programs: museum, historic site(s), historic preservation, living history
Period of collections: Colonial-Revolutionary War eras

Tri-State Railway Historical Society, Inc.
P.O. Box 2243, Clifton, 07015
Telephone: (201) 857- 2987
Private agency
Founded in: 1960
Vincent Stagnitto, President
Number of members: 300
Staff: volunteer 100
Magazine: *Block Line*
Major programs: library, archives, museum, historic site(s), tours/pilgrimages, books, newsletters/pamphlets, historic preservation, records management, research, exhibits, audiovisual programs, photographic collections, restores and owns historical railroad cars
Period of collections: 1880-present

Washington Association of New Jersey
Park Square Bldg., 10 Park Place, 07960
Telephone: (201) 538-4456
Founded in: 1874
Ralph H. Cutler, Jr., President
Number of members: 350
Staff: volunteer 12
Major programs: library, museum, books, newsletters/pamphlets, research
Period of collections: 1492-1783

MOUNTAIN LAKES

Landmarks Committee
Borough Hall, 400 Blvd., 07046
Telephone: (201) 334-3131
Town agency
Founded in: 1978
John Steen, Chair
Staff: volunteer 6
Major programs: archives, books, exhibits, photographic collections
Period of collections: 1911-1923

Mountain Lakes Historical Society
P.O. Box 153, 07046
Private agency
Founded in: 1931
Carol Steen, President
Number of members: 25
Major programs: historical site(s), school programs
Period of collections: 20th century

MOUNT HOLLY

Burlington County Cultural and Heritage Commission
Smithville-Jacksonville Rd.
Telephone: (609) 261-5068
Mail to: 49 Rancocas Rd., 08060
County agency
Founded in: 1970
Carter R. Jones, Administrator
Staff: full time 4
Magazine: *The County Bell*
Major programs: museum, historic sites preservation, educational programs, books,

newsletters/pamphlets, audiovisual
programs
Period of collections: 1860-1890

Burlington County Genealogy Club
Burlington County Library, Woodlane
Rd., 08060
Telephone: (609) 267-9660
Founded in: 1975
Number of members: 43
Major programs: library, archives,
genealogy, cemetery
transcriptions, indexing newspaper
vital statistics
Period of collections: 1790-present

**Friends of the Mansion of
Smithville**
c/o 49 Rancocas Rd., 08060
Telephone: (609) 261-3780
Founded in: 1977
Henry W. Metzger, President
Number of members: 340
Staff: volunteer 60
Major programs: museum, historic
sites preservation,
tours/pilgrimages, educational
programs
Period of collections: 1860-1880

**Historic Burlington County Prison
Museum Association**
128 High St., 08060
Telephone: (609) 261-5068
Private agency, authorized by
Burlington County Cultural and
Heritage Commission
Founded in: 1966
Rosann Hickey, Program Coordinator
Number of members: 67
Staff: part time 1, volunteer 12
Major programs: historic site(s),
penology
Period of collections: 1830-1960

**National Society, Colonial Dames
of America in the State of New
Jersey**
Buris Rd., 08060
Telephone: (609) 267-1054
Private agency, authorized by
National Society, Colonial Dames of
America
Founded in: 1892
Mrs. A.V.S. Olcot, President
Number of members: 301
Staff: part time 1, volunteer 45
Major programs: manuscripts,
museum, historic site(s), book
publishing, historic preservation,
genealogical services
Period of collections: 18th-19th
centuries

MT. LAUREL

Mt. Laurel Historical Society
P.O. Box 1866, 08054
Telephone: (609) 234-2108
Founded in: 1975
Number of members: 60
Staff: volunteer 20
Period of collections: 1783-1918

MULLICA HILL

**Harrison Township Historical
Society**
Rts. 77 and 45
Telephone: (609) 478-4949
Mail to: P.O. Box 4, 08062

Private agency
Founded in: 1971
Kathryn S. Dodson, President
Number of members: 200
Staff: volunteer 50
Magazine: *Milestones*
Major programs: library, archives,
manuscripts, museum, historic
site(s), oral history, school
programs, newsletters/pamphlets,
exhibits, audiovisual programs,
photographic collections
Period of collections: 19th-early 20th
centuries

NEPTUNE

Neptune Historical Museum
25 Neptune Blvd.. 07753
Telephone: (201) 775-8241
Town agency, authorized by Neptune
Historical Society
Founded in: 1971
Margaret Goodrich, Curator/Historian
Staff: part time 1
Major programs: library, museum,
tours, oral history, historic
preservation, research, exhibits,
photographic collections,
genealogical services
Period of collections: 1879-present

Neptune Historical Society
25 Neptune Blvd., 07753
Telephone: (201) 775-8241
Town agency
Founded in: 1968
Margaret Goodrich, Curator/Historian
Number of members: 50
Staff: full time 1
Major programs: library, archives,
museum, oral history, school
programs, research, exhibits,
genealogical services
Period of collections: 1869-present

NESHANIC

**Hillsborough Township Historic
Commission**
Planning Board Office, Municipal
Annex
Telephone: (201) 369-4313
Mail to: Municipal Bldg., Amwell Rd.,
08853
Town agency
Founded in: 1974
Robert Moevs, Chair
Staff: volunteer 5
Major programs: archives, historic
site(s), markers, book publishing
Period of collections:
Colonial-Federal eras

NEWARK

**Newark Fire Department Historical
Association**
49 Washington St., 07101
Telephone: (201) 733-6647
Founded in: 1967
Number of members: 650
Staff: volunteer 15
Major programs: museum,
educational programs
Period of collections: 1783-present

The Newark Museum
49 Washington St., 07101
Telephone: (201) 733-6600
Founded in: 1909

Samuel C. Miller, Director
Number of members: 4,900
Staff: full time 87, part time 66,
volunteer 85
Magazine: *The Newark Museum
Quarterly*
Major programs: library, archives,
museum, historic sites
preservation, educational
programs, books,
newsletters/pamphlets, exhibits,
photographic collections
Period of collections: late 17th
century-present

**Newark Preservation and
Landmarks Committee**
868 Broad St., 07102
Telephone: (201) 622-4910
Private agency
Founded in: 1974
Elizabeth Deltufo, President
Number of members: 350
Major programs: historic site(s),
markers, newsletters/pamphlets,
historic preservation
Period of collections: Victorian era

◇**New Jersey Historical Society**
230 Broadway, 07104
Telephone: (201) 483-3939
Private agency
Founded in: 1845
Robert B. O'Brien, Jr., Chair
Number of members: 3,268
Staff: full time 20, part time 9,
volunteer 18
Magazine: *New Jersey History*
Major programs: library, archives,
manuscripts, museum,
tours/pilgrimages, junior history,
school programs, book publishing,
newsletters/pamphlets, research,
exhibits, living history,
photographic collections,
genealogical services, field
services
Period of collections: 1660-present

NEW BRUNSWICK

Buccleuch Mansion Museum
Buccleuch Parks, Easton Ave. and
George St.
Telephone: (201) 745-5094
Mail to: 25 Shelly Dr., Somerset,
08873
City agency
Founded in: 1915
Louise G. Miller, Curator
Number of members: 130
Staff: volunteer 50
Major programs: museum, historic
sites preservation, historic
preservation, genealogical
services
Period of collections: 1740-1915

**Historical Society of the Reformed
Church in America**
21 Seminary Place, 08901
Telephone: (201) 246-1779
Private agency, authorized by
Commission on History, Reformed
Church in America
Founded in: 1980
Russell L. Gasero, Manager
Number of members: 300
Staff: full time 1, part time 1,
volunteer 10

Magazine: *Historical Highlights, Dutch-American Genealogist*
Major programs: archives, oral history, book publishing, newsletters/pamphlets, records management, photographic collections, genealogical services
Period of collections: 1630-present

Historic Hiram Market Preservation Association
9 Bayard St., 08901
Telephone: (201) 545-1005
Private agency
Founded in: 1978
J. David Muyskens, Secretary
Number of members: 20
Major programs: historic site(s)
Period of collections: 19th century

Jewish Historical Society of Central Jersey
1050 George St., Box 1-L, 08901
Telephone: (201) 247-0288
Private agency, authorized by the American Jewish Historical Society
Founded in: 1977
Ruth M. Patt, President
Number of members: 150
Major programs: archives, oral history, newsletters/pamphlets, research
Period of collections: 1850-present

New Brunswick Historical Club
278 George St., 08901
Telephone: (201) 247-1695
Founded in: 1870
Questionnaire not received

New Jersey Committee for the Humanities
73 Easton Ave., 08903
Telephone: (201) 932-7726
Federal agency, authorized by National Endowment for the Humanities
Miriam Murphy, Executive Director
Staff: part time 4
Major programs: library, archives, historic site(s), school programs, newsletters/pamphlets, historic preservation, exhibits, audiovisual programs, archaeology programs, photographic collections

New Jersey Folk Festival Association
American Studies Department, Douglas College-Rutgers University, 08903
Telephone: (201) 932-9179
Founded in: 1975
Angus K. Gillespie, Director
Number of members: 52
Staff: full time 52
Magazine: *New Jersey Folklore-A Statewide Journal*
Major programs: archives, exhibits, concerts, craft demonstrations, folklore

Van Voorhees Association
151 George St., 08901
Telephone: (201) 246-1278
Founded in: 1932
Questionnaire not received

NEWFOUNDLAND

North Jersey Highlands Historical Society
Telephone: (201) 835-5634
Mail to: P.O. Box 1, 07435
Founded in: 1954
Number of members: 160
Staff: volunteer 10
Magazine: *North Jersey Highlander*
Major programs: library, archives, historic sites preservation, educational programs, newsletters/pamphlets
Period of collections: 1740-1880

NEW PROVIDENCE

New Providence Historical Society
1350 Springfield Ave., 07974
Founded in: 1966
Number of members: 150
Staff: volunteer 15
Magazine: *Turkey Tracks*
Major programs: library, manuscripts, newsletters/pamphlets, historic preservation
Period of collections: 1755-present

NEW VERNON

Harding Township Historical Society
P.O. Box 1777, 07976
Founded in: 1977
Questionnaire not received

NORTH BRUNSWICK

Johnston National Scouting Museumprehistoric
Rt. 130, 08902
Telephone: (201) 249-6000, ext. 428
Questionnaire not received

Middlesex County Cultural and Heritage Commission
841 Georges Rd., 08902
Telephone: (201) 745-2788
County agency, authorized by County of Middlesex Board of Chosen Freeholders
Founded in: 1971
Anna M. Aschkenes, Director
Staff: full time 13, part time 5, volunteer 1
Magazine: *Signal Fire*
Major programs: library, archives, museum, historic sites tours, educational programs, newsletters/pamphlets, historic preservation, exhibits, support of local art groups

NUTLEY

Historic Restoration Trust of Nutley
3 Kingsland St., 07110
Telephone: (201) 667-2800
Private agency, authorized by Nutley Parks and Public Properties
Founded in: 1973
Eleanor Storer, President
Number of members: 130
Staff: volunteer 48
Major programs: manuscripts, newsletters/pamphlets, historic preservation, research, exhibits, audiovisual programs, archaeology programs, genealogical services
Period of collections: 1790s-present

Nutley Historical Society
65 Church St., 07110
Telephone: (201) 667-1528
Private agency
Founded in: 1945
John K. Tiene, President
Number of members: 300
Magazine: *Courier*
Major programs: museum, oral history
Period of collections: 1800s

OAKLAND

Oakland Historical Society
1 Franklin Ave.
Telephone: (201) 337-0924
Mail to: P.O. Box 296, 07436
Private agency
Founded in: 1966
Christopher Curran, IV, President
Number of members: 50
Staff: volunteer 8
Major programs: archives, museum, historic site(s), oral history, school programs, historic preservation, genealogical services
Period of collections: 1783-1918

OAK RIDGE

Jefferson Township Historical Society
P.O. Box 1776, 07438
Telephone: (201) 697-6840
Town agency
Founded in: 1961
Walter Harlacher, President
Number of members: 25
Staff: volunteer 20
Major programs: archives, museum, historic sites preservation, tours/pilgrimages, oral history, school programs, newsletters/pamphlets, photographic copywork, slide programs
Period of collections: 1850-present

OCEAN CITY

Ocean City Historical Museum
409 Wesley Ave., 08226
Telephone: (609) 399-1801
Founded in: 1964
Helen R. Kroesser, President
Number of members: 455
Staff: full time 1, volunteer 87
Major programs: library, archives, manuscripts, museum, historic site(s), markers, tours/pilgrimages, junior history, newsletters/pamphlets, exhibits, photographic collections
Period of collections: 1690-1940

OCEAN GROVE

Historical Society of Ocean Grove
Telephone: (201) 774-0042
Mail to: P.O. Box 446, 07756
Founded in: 1970
Questionnaire not received

OLD BRIDGE TOWNSHIP

Madison Township Historical Society
Thomas Warne Historical Museum and Library, Rt. 516, 07747

Telephone: (201) 566-0348
Founded in: 1964
Questionnaire not received

Old Bridge Historical Commission
1Old Bridge Plaza, 08857
Telephone: (201) 721-5600
Town agency, authorized by township
council
Founded in: 1978
Hank Bignell, Planner
Staff: full time 1, volunteer 9
Major programs: historic site(s),
markers, tours/pilgrimages, historic
preservation, research
Period of collections: 1700-1900

**Thomas Warne Historical Museum
and Library**
Rt. 516
Telephone: (201) 566-0348
Mail to: Rd. 1, Box 150, Matawan,
07747
Private agency, authorized by
Madison Township Historical
Society
Founded in: 1964
Alvia D. Martin, Curator
Number of members: 100
Staff: volunteer 7
Major programs: library, archives,
manuscripts, museum, historic
site(s), markers, tours/pilgrimages,
school programs, book publishing,
newsletters/pamphlets, historic
preservation, research, exhibits,
photographic collections,
genealogical services
Period of collections: 1880s

PARAMUS

Bergen Museum of Art and Science
Ridgewood and Farview Ave., 07652
Telephone: (201) 265-1248
Founded in: 1966
Judith Harris, Director
Number of members: 800
Staff: full time 3, part time 2,
volunteer 56
Major programs: museum, tours,
school programs, art classes,
lectures, exhibition environments,
science exhibits, art exhibits
Period of collections: 20th century

**David Ackerman
Descendants—1662**
N. Reformed Church
Telephone: (201) 257-5927
Mail to: 13 Frost Ave., E. Brunswick,
08816
Founded in: 1961
Questionnaire not received

PARK RIDGE

Pascack Historical Society
19 Ridge Ave.
Mail to: P.O. Box 285, 07656
Questionnaire not received

PATERSON

**Great Falls Development
Corporation**
176 Maple St., 07522
Telephone: (201) 881-3848
Founded in: 1971
Questionnaire not received

Passaic County Historical Society
Lambert Castle, Garret Mt.
Reservation, 07503
Telephone: (201) 881-2761
Founded in: 1926
Catherine A. Keene, Director
Number of members: 350
Staff: full time 2, part time 5,
volunteer 12
Magazine: *Castle Lite*
Major programs: library, archives,
museum, school programs,
newsletters/pamphlets, exhibits,
photographic collections,
genealogical services
Period of collections: 1783-present

Paterson Museum
2 Market St., 07501
Telephone: (201) 881-3874
Founded in: 1926
Thomas A. Peters, Director
Staff: full time 2, part time 2
Major programs: museum, school
programs, exhibits, audiovisual
programs, photographic
collections
Period of collections: prehistoric-1918

PENNINGTON

Hopewell Valley Historical Society
P.O. Box 371, 08534
Telephone: (609) 737-0465
Founded in: 1975
Betty Hirschmann, President
Number of members: 140
Staff: volunteer 13
Magazine: *Hopewell Valley Historical
Society's Newsletter*
Major programs: historic site(s),
markers, newsletters/pamphlets,
photographic collections

PERTH AMBOY

Kearny Cottage
63 Catalpa Ave., 08861
Telephone: (201) 826-1826
Authorized by: Kearny Cottage
Historical Association
Founded in: 1924
Marian Stone, President
Number of members: 55
Staff: volunteer 24
Major programs: museum, historic
site(s)
Period of collections: 1840-1860

**Kearny Cottege Historical
Association**
63 Catalpa Ave., 08861
Telephone: (201) 826-1826
Private agency
Founded in: 1923
Marian Stone, President
Number of members: 60
Staff: volunteer 20
Major programs: museum, historic
site(s), school programs,
newsletters/pamphlets, historic
preservation, exhibits
Period of collections: 1820-1870

PISCATAWAY

East Jersey Olde Towne, Inc.
P.O. Box 661, 08854
Telephone: (201) 463-9077
Private agency

Founded in: 1971
Marjorie V. Kler, President
Number of members: 1,200
Staff: volunteer 10
Major programs: library, archives,
museum, tours/pilgrimages, school
programs, newsletters/pamphlets
Period of collections: 18th century

Fellowship for Metlar House
1281 River Rd., 08854
Telephone: (201) 463-8363
State agency
Founded in: 1979
Marion Serna, Board President
Number of members: 50
Staff: part time 1, volunteer 5
Major programs: museum,
tours/pilgrimages, historic
preservation, exhibits, living history
Period of collections: 18th-19th
centuries

**Piscataway Cultural Arts
Commission**
455 Hoes Lane, 08854
Telephone: (201) 463-0273
Town agency
Founded in: 1973
E. J. Coleman, Chair
Staff: volunteer 13
Major programs: historic site(s),
newsletters/pamphlets, exhibits,
audiovisual programs,
photographic collections
Period of collections: 1633-1745

PLAINFIELD

**Historical Society of Plainfield and
North Plainfield**
602 W. Front St., 07060
Telephone: (201) 755-5831
Founded in: 1921
Number of members: 150
Staff: full time 2, part time 1,
volunteer 35
Magazine: *Communique*
Major programs: museum,
educational programs
Period of collections: 1746-1900

**Seventh Day Baptist Historical
Society**
510 Watchung Ave.
Telephone: (201) 561-8700
Mail to: P.O. Box 868, 07061
Founded in: 1916
Magazine: *The Sabbath Recorder*
Major programs: library, archives,
manuscripts, museum, books,
newsletters/pamphlets, historic
preservation, genealogy
Period of collections: 1664-present

PLAINSBORO

Plainsboro Historical Society
Municipal Bldg., P.O. Box 278, 08536
Telephone: (609) 799-0909
Town agency
Founded in: 1975
Clifford E. Sohl, President
Number of members: 25
Staff: volunteer 5
Major programs: library, manuscripts,
historic site(s), oral history, historic
preservation, exhibits,
photographic collections
Period of collections: mid 1800s-early
1900s

PLEASANTVILLE

Firefighters Museum of Southern New Jersey
E. Ryon Ave., 08232
Telephone: (609) 641-9300
Private agency
Founded in: 1968
Harold J. Swartz, Sr., Owner
Major programs: library, archives, museum, tours/pilgrimages, oral history, school programs, historic preservation, photographic collections
Period of collections: 1780-present

PORT REPUBLIC

Port Republic Historical Society
56 Main St., 08241
Telephone: (609) 652-9186
Founded in: 1977
Questionnaire not received

PRINCETON

Central Jersey Chapter, American Italian Historical Association
120 John St., 08540
Private agency, authorized by National American Italian Historical Association
Founded in: 1966
Robert B. Immordino, President
Number of members: 52
Staff: volunteer 2
Major programs: book publishing, newsletters/pamphlets, exhibits, conferences, public programs
Period of collections: since 1900s

Historical Society of Princeton
Bainbridge House, 158 Nassau St., 08540
Telephone: (609) 921-6748
Private agency
Founded in: 1938
Nancy R. Clark, Director
Number of members: 850
Staff: full time 1, part time 4
Magazine: *Princeton History*
Major programs: library, archives, manuscripts, museum, historic site(s), markers, tours/pilgrimages, school programs, books, newsletters/pamphlets
Period of collections: 18th-20th centuries

Preservation New Jersey, Inc.
P.O. Box 864, Mapleton Rd., 08540
Telephone: (609) 452-0446
Private agency
Founded in: 1981
Diane Jones Sliney, Editor
Number of members: 550
Staff: part time 1
Magazine: *Preservation Perspective*
Major programs: newsletters/pamphlets, historic preservation, exhibits, conferences and seminars

Princeton Battlefield Area Preservation Society
Mail to: P.O. Box 1777, 08540
Founded in: 1970
Questionnaire not received

Princeton History Project
158 Nassau St., 08540

Telephone: (609) 921-8330
Founded in: 1975
Elric J. Endersby, Director
Number of members: 1,400
Staff: volunteer 10
Magazine: *The Princeton Recollector*
Major programs: archives, oral history, educational programs, newsletters/pamphlets, historic preservation, research, photographic collections
Period of collections: 1880-present

RAHWAY

North Jersey Electic Railway Historical Society
756 Bryant St., 07065
Telephone: (201) 388-0369
Private agency
Founded in: 1984
Tony Hall, Director
Major programs: historic preservation, research, exhibits, photographic collections
Period of collections: 1910-1953

Rahway Historical Society, Inc.
1632 St. Georges Ave., 07065
Mail to: 1670 Irving St.
Founded in: 1969
Questionnaire not received

RAMSEY

Ramsey Historical Association
538 Island Rd,. 07446
Telephone: (201) 825-1126
Founded in: 1956
Diane L. McNicholas, President
Number of members: 200
Staff: volunteer 22
Major programs: library, museum, historic site(s), tours/pilgrimages, junior history, school programs, historic preservation, exhibits
Period of collections: 1700s

RANDOLPH

Historical Society of Old Randolph
P.O. Box 1776, Ironia, 07845
Telephone: (201) 895-4155
Private agency
Founded in: 1977
Linda Pawchak, President
Number of members: 55
Staff: volunteer 5
Major programs: archives, oral history, educational programs, historic preservation
Period of collections: 1760-present

Township of Randolph Landmarks Committee
Millbrook Ave., 07869
Telephone: (201) 361-8200
Town agency
Founded in: 1973
Linda Pawchak, Chair
Staff: volunteer 8
Major programs: historic site(s), markers, tours/pilgrimages, oral history, school programs, historic preservationaudiovisual programs, photographic collections
Period of collections: 1760-present

RED BANK

Red Bank Historical Society, Inc.
P.O. Box 52, 07701
Telephone: (201) 741-1019
Private agency
Founded in: 1974
Mary H. Kirby, President
Number of members: 59
Major programs: markers, tours/pilgrimages, audiovisual programs
Period of collections: early 1900s

RINGWOOD

North Jersey Highlands Historical Society
P.O. Box 248, 07456
Telephone: (201) 839-2389
Private agency
Founded in: 1954
Ralph Colfax, President
Number of members: 160
Magazine: *The North Jersey Highlander*
Major programs: library, archives, historic sites preservation, newsletters/pamphlets
Period of collections: 19th century

Ringwood Manor House
Ringwood State Park, 1304 Sloatsburg Rd.
Telephone: (201) 962-7031
Mail to: P.O. Box 1304, 07456
Founded in: 1936
Elbertus Prol, Curator
Staff: full time 8, volunteer 1
Major programs: archives, manuscripts, museum, historic sites preservation, educational programs, historic preservation, art
Period of collections: 18th-19th centuries

RIVER EDGE

Bergen County Historical Society
1201 Main St.
Telephone: (201) 487-1739
Mail to: P.O. Box 55, 07661
Founded in: 1902
John E. Spring, President
Number of members: 600
Staff: volunteer 10
Magazine: *In Bergen's Attic*
Major programs: library, manuscripts, museum, markers, tours/pilgrimages, educational programs, newsletters/pamphlets, historic preservation
Period of collections: 18th-19th centuries

RIVERSIDE

Riverside Township Historical Society
Town Hall
Telephone: (609) 461-7850
Mail to: 532 Polk St., 08075
Questionnaire not received

RIVERTON

Historical Society of Riverton
08077
Private agency
Founded in: 1970

Number of members: 133
Major programs: archives, markers, tours/pilgrimages, oral history, newsletters/pamphlets, historic preservation, photographic collections
Period of collections: 1851-present

ROEBLING

Roebling Historical Society
140 3rd Ave., 08554
Town agency
Founded in: 1980
Louis Borbi, President
Number of members: 340
Staff: volunteer 8
Major programs: archives, manuscripts, historic site(s), tours/pilgrimages, junior history, oral history, school programs, historic preservation, records management, research, exhibits, audiovisual programs, archaeology programs, photographic collections, genealogical services
Period of collections: 1905-present

ROSELLE

Roselle Historical Society
116 E. 4th Ave., 07203
Telephone: (201) 245-9010
Private agency
Founded in: 1972
William Frolich, President
Number of members: 22
Staff: volunteer 22
Major programs: library, markers, oral history, school programs, book publishing, exhibits, audiovisual programs, photographic collections
Period of collections: 1865-present

ROSELLE PARK

Roselle Park Historical Society
P.O. Box 135, 07204
Telephone: (201) 245-9260
Private agency
Founded in: 1972
Robert A. Lehr, President
Major programs: library, archives, manuscripts, oral history, school programs, newsletters/pamphlets, historic preservation, records management, research, exhibits, photographic collections

RUTHERFORD

Meadowlands Museum
91 Crane Ave.
Telephone: (201) 935-1175
Mail to: P.O. Box 3, 07070
Private agency
Founded in: 1961
Marjorie Reenstra, President, Board of Governors
Number of members: 650
Staff: part time 2, volunteer 25
Major programs: museum, historic site(s), newsletters/pamphlets, records management, exhibits, graphic arts and crafts
Period of collections: 1865-present

SALEM

Salem County Historical Society
79 Market St., 08079
Telephone: (609) 935-5004
Private agency
Founded in: 1884
Number of members: 1,300
Staff: part time 2
Major programs: library, museum, newsletters/pamphlets, genealogical services

SCOTCH PLAINS

Historical Society of Scotch Plains and Fanwood
1840 Front St.
Mail to: P.O. Box 261, 07076
Town agency, authorized by Scotch Plains Town Council
Founded in: 1972
Martha Dimmick, President
Number of members: 89
Staff: volunteer 50
Major programs: museum, historic site(s), tours/pilgrimages, school programs, historic preservation, exhibits, photographic collections
Period of collections: from 1684

SHREWSBURY

Shrewsbury Historical Society
Mail to: P.O. Box 333, 07701
Town agency
Founded in: 1972
Louise Jost, President
Number of members: 200
Staff: volunteer 20
Major programs: library, archives, manuscripts, museum, junior history, school programs, newsletters/pamphlets, exhibits, photographic collections, genealogical services
Period of collections: 1660-present

SOMERS POINT

Atlantic County Historical Society
907 Shore Rd.
Telephone: (609) 927-5218
Mail to: P.O. Box 301, 08244
Private agency
Founded in: 1913
John Braniff, President
Number of members: 600
Staff: volunteer 30
Magazine: *Atlantic County Historical Society Yearbook*
Major programs: library, manuscripts, museum, oral history, school programs, newsletters/pamphlets, research, exhibits, photographic collections, genealogical services
Period of collections: 1750-1900

SOMERVILLE

Wallace House—Old Dutch Parsonage
38 Washington Place, 08876
Telephone: (201) 725-1015
State agency, authorized by Department of Environmental Protection
Founded in: 1897
Susan L. Taylor, Curator

Staff: full time 1, part time 1, volunteer 25
Major programs: museum, historic site(s), tours/pilgrimages, school programs, newsletters/pamphlets, historic preservation, research, exhibits, living history
Period of collections: late 17th-19th centuries

SOUTH AMBOY

South Amboy Historical Society
2nd St. and Stevens Ave., 08879
Telephone: (201) 721-6060
Founded in: 1972
Questionnaire not received

SOUTH ORANGE

Archaeological Society of New Jersey
Seton Hall University, 07079
Telephone: (201) 762-6680
Questionnaire not received

SOUTH PLAINFIELD

South Plainfield Historical Society
P.O. Box 11, 07080
Town agency
Founded in: 1975
Mrs. Edward Mazepa, President
Number of members: 37
Major programs: markers, oral history, historic preservation, research, exhibits, audiovisual programs, photographic collections
Period of collections: from 1926

SPRINGFIELD

Springfield Historical Society
126 Morris Ave.
Telephone: (201) 467-3580
Mail to: c/o M. Lancaster, 23 Alvin Terrace, 07081
Founded in: 1954
Questionnaire not received

SPRING LAKE

Spring Lake Historical Society, Inc.
Municipal Bldg.
Telephone: (201) 449-0772
Mail to: P.O. Box 703, 07762
Private agency
Founded in: 1977
Gale D'Luhy, President
Staff: volunteer 50
Major programs: library, archives, museum, markers, tours/pilgrimages, educational programs, books, newsletters/pamphlets, photographic collections
Period of collections: 1880s-1930s

STOCKTON

Sand Brook Historical Society
R.D. 1, 08559
Telephone: (201) 782-2942
Founded in: 1962
Questionnaire not received

SUCCASUNNA

Ferro Monte Chapter, Daughters of the American Revolution
Telephone: (201) 697-4236
Mail to: Milton Rd., Oak Ridge, 07438
Private agency, authorized by
National Society, Daughters of the American Revolution
Founded in: 1973
Mrs. Joseph Riggs, Regent
Number of members: 60
Staff: volunteer 30
Major programs: library, archives, manuscripts, museum, historic site(s), markers, school programs, historic preservation, research, genealogical services
Period of collections: Revolutionary War era

SUMMIT

Summit Historical Society, Inc.
Mail to: P.O. Box 464, 07901
Founded in: 1963
Questionnaire not received

TABERNACLE

Tabernacle Historical Society
Telephone: (609) 268-0473
Mail to: 162 Carranza Rd., Vincentown, 08088
Founded in: 1975
Number of members: 89
Major programs: markers, tours/pilgrimages, oral history, educational programs
Period of collections: 1865-1918

TETERBORO

Aviation Hall of Fame of New Jersey
Teterboro Airport, 07608
Telephone: (201) 288-6344
State agency
Founded in: 1972
H. V. Pat Reilly, Executive Director
Number of members: 800
Staff: full time 1, part time 2, volunteer 32
Magazine: *Propwash*
Major programs: museum, historic preservation
Period of collections: 1793-present

TITUSVILLE

Hopewell Township Historic Sites Committee
Municipal Bldg., 08560
Telephone: (609) 737-0638
Town agency, authorized by
Hopewell Township Committee
Founded in: 1973
Karl J. Niederer, Chair
Staff: volunteer 8
Major programs: library, archives, historic site(s), historic preservation, research
Period of collections: late 1700s-early 1900s

Washington Crossing Association of New Jersey
P.O. Box 1776, 08500
Telephone: (609) 883-3054
Mail to: 104 Bull Run Rd., 08638
Questionnaire not received

TOMS RIVER

Ocean County Historical Society
26 Hadley Ave., 08753
Telephone: (201) 341-1880
Founded in: 1950
Carolyn Campbell, President
Number of members: 300
Staff: volunteer 30
Major programs: museum, books
Period of collections: 1850-1918

Toms River Seaport Society
Hooper Ave. and E. Water St.
Mail to: P.O. Box 1111, 08754
Private agency
Founded in: 1976
Joseph Lappin, President
Number of members: 150
Staff: volunteer 20
Major programs: museum, historic site(s), historic preservation
Period of collections: mid 1800s-present

TRENTON

Landmarks Commission for Historic Preservation
City Hall Annex, 08608
Telephone: (609) 989-3604
City agency
Founded in: 1972
Major programs: historic site(s), markers, historic preservation, review of restoration proposals

Mercer County Cultural and Heritage Commission
640 S. Broad St., 08607
Telephone: (609) 989-6701
County agency
Founded in: 1970
Linda Osborne, Division Director
Staff: full time 1, volunteer 9
Major programs: school programs, newsletters/pamphlets, historic preservation, exhibits, photographic collections, performing and visual arts programs

◊**Museums Council of New Jersey**
c/o New Jersey State Museum, CN-530, 08625
Telephone: (609) 292-6300
Private agency
Founded in: 1950
Cynthia M. Koch, Chair
Number of members: 94
Major programs: museum, historic site(s), professional museum organization

New Jersey Bureau of Law and Reference Services
New Jersey State Library, 185 W. State St., 08625-0520
Telephone: (609) 292-6274
Robert Lupp, Supervisor
Staff: full time 29
Major programs: library, genealogical services, official state documents depository
Period of collections: 19th-20th centuries

New Jersey Department of Environmental Protection, Office of Cultural and Environmental Services
109 W. State St., 08625

Telephone: (609) 292-2023
Lawrence C. Schmidt, Chief
Staff: full time 13
Major programs: historic sites preservation

◊**New Jersey Historical Commission**
113 W. State St., CN-520, 08625
Telephone: (609) 292-6062
State agency
Founded in: 1966
Bernard Bush, Executive Director
Staff: full time 16
Major programs: oral history, book publishing, newsletters/pamphlets, research, Afro-American history, ethnic custom, folklife

New Jersey State House, Department of State
08625
Telephone: (609) 633-7083
State agency
Founded in: 1776
Jane Burgio, Secretary of State
Number of members: 4
Magazine: *Arts New Jersey*
Major programs: archives, museum, oral history, school programs, book publishing, newsletters/pamphlets, historic preservation, records management, research, exhibits, living history, audiovisual programs, archaeology programs, photographic collections, genealogical services, field services
Period of collections: Colonial era-present

◊**New Jersey State Museum**
205 W. State St., 08625-0530
Telephone: (609) 292-5421
State agency
Founded in: 1836
Suzanne Corlette Crilley, Curator of Cultural History
Staff: full time 60, part time 16, volunteer 60
Major programs: museum, school programs, newsletters/pamphlets, research, exhibits, audiovisual programs, archaeology programs
Period of collections: 19th century

Old Barracks Association and Museum
Barrack St., 08608
Telephone: (609) 396-1776
Founded in: 1902
Cynthia Koch, Director
Number of members: 455
Staff: full time 8, part time 8
Major programs: museum, historic site(s), tours/pilgrimages, school programs, newsletters/pamphlets, historic preservation, living history
Period of collections: 1750-1830

Trenton Historical Society
Mail to: P.O. Box 1112, 08606
Founded in: 1919
Number of members: 200
Major programs: historic sites preservation, educational programs

Trenton Museum Society
Trenton City Museum, Cadwalder Park, 08606

Telephone: (609) 989-3632
Founded in: 1973
Questionnaire not received

Trent House Association
15 Market St., 08611
Founded in: 1939
Questionnaire not received

UNION

Union Township Historical Society
909 Caldwell Ave., 07083
Founded in: 1957
Questionnaire not received

VERNON

Vernon Township Historical Society
Mail to: P.O. Box 762, Highland Lakes, 07422
Town agency
Founded in: 1971
Ronald J. Dupont, Jr., President
Number of members: 45
Staff: volunteer 5
Major programs: historic site(s), newsletters/pamphlets, exhibits, audiovisual programs, photographic collections
Period of collections: 1860-1920

VINCENTOWN

Southampton Historical Society
Mill St.
Telephone: (609) 859-9503
Mail to: P.O. Box 2086, 08088
Founded in: 1974
Dorothy J. Best, President
Number of members: 130
Staff: volunteer 10
Magazine: *Hello, Central*
Major programs: library, museum, historic sites preservation, oral history, newsletters/pamphlets
Period of collections: 1800-present

VINELAND

Cumberland County Cultural and Heritage Commission
511 W. Walnut Rd., 08360
Telephone: (609) 691-8572
County agency, authorized by Cumberland County Chosen Board of Freeholders
Founded in: 1969
Evelyn E. Pilla, Executive Secretary
Staff: part time 1
Major programs: library, school programs, newsletters/pamphlets, historic preservation, audiovisual programs, archaeology programs, performing arts programs

Vineland Historical and Antiquarian Society
108 S. 7th St.
Telephone: (609) 691-1111
Mail to: P.O. Box 35, 08360
Private agency
Founded in: 1864
Nancy S. Snyder, President
Number of members: 296
Staff: full time 1, volunteer 8
Magazine: *The Vineland Historical Magazine*

Major programs: library, archives, manuscripts, museum, historic sites, tours/pilgrimages, educational programs, books, newsletters/pamphlets, historic preservation
Period of collections: 1800s-present

WALL

Old Wall Historical Society
1701 New Bedford Rd.
Telephone: (201) 681-6959
Mail to: P.O. Box 1203, 07719
Private agency
Founded in: 1972
Beryl Mount, President
Number of members: 49
Staff: volunteer 28
Major programs: museum, historic site(s), markers, tours, school programs, newsletters, genealogical services
Period of collections: 1841-1900

WAYNE

The Dey
199 Totowa Rd., 07470
Telephone: (201) 696-1776
Questionnaire not received

Wayne Township Historical Commission
533 Berdan Ave., 07470
Telephone: (201) 694-7192
Lydia Hall, Chair
Staff: full time 1, part time 3
Major programs: library, archives, manuscripts, museum, historic site(s), oral history, school programs, book publishing, research, exhibits, archaeology programs
Period of collections: 1783-1865

WEEHAWKEN

Weehawken Historical Society Inc.
212 Dodd St., 07087
Telephone: (201) 867-2050
Founded in: 1969
Questionnaire not received

WEST CALDWELL

Historical Society of West Caldwell
278 Westville Ave.
Telephone: (201) 226-7845
Mail to: P.O. Box 1701, 07006
Founded in: 1976
Ruth C. Shepard, President
Number of members: 180
Staff: volunteer 30
Major programs: historic sites preservation, markers, tours/pilgrimages, educational programs, newsletters/pamphlets, historic preservation
Period of collections: 1800-1900

WESTFIELD

Miller-Cory House Museum
614 Mountain Ave., 07090
Telephone: (201) 232-1776
Mail to: P.O. Box 455, 07091
Founded in: 1971
Irene W. Hekeler, Corresponding Secretary, Board of Governors

Number of members: 253
Staff: part time 1, volunteer 100
Magazine: *The Bee Line/The Broadside*
Major programs: archives, manuscripts, museum, historic site(s), tours, junior history, school programs, historic preservation, living history
Period of collections: 1740-1820

Union County Office of Cultural and Heritage Affairs
300 North Ave., E, 07090
Telephone: (201) 233-7906
County agency
Founded in: 1970
William J. Higginson, Administrator
Staff: full time 3, part time 1, volunteer 20
Magazine: *The Beacon*
Major programs: library, archives, historic site(s), markers, school programs, book publishing, newsletters/pamphlets, historic preservation, audiovisual programs
Period of collections: 1783-present

Westfield Historical Society
614 Mountain Ave.
Telephone: (201) 232-1776
Mail to: P.O. Box 613, 07091
Private agency
Founded in: 1969
Ralph H. Jones, President
Number of members: 688
Staff: part time 1, volunteer 100
Major programs: library, archives, museum, istoric site(s), markers, tours/pilgrimages, oral history, school programs, book publishing, newsletters/pamphlets, historic preservation, research, exhibits, living history, audiovisual programs, photographic collections
Period of collections: 1850-1980

WEST LONG BRANCH

West Long Branch Historical Society
P.O. Box 151, 07764
Town agency
Founded in: 1977
Thomas D. Bazley, President
Number of members: 29
Staff: volunteer 5
Major programs: markers, books, historic preservation, photographic collections
Period of collections: 1850-present

WEST ORANGE

Edison National Historic Site
Main St. and Lakeside Ave., 07052
Telephone: (201) 736-0550
Founded in: 1956
Edward Jay Pershey, Museum Curator
Staff: full time 26, part time 19, volunteer 6
Major programs: manuscripts, museum, historic sites preservation, historic preservation
Period of collections: 1887-1931

Union County Cultural and Heritage Programs Advisory Board
300 North Ave., E, 07090
Telephone: (201) 233-7906
Founded in: 1970
Questionnaire not received

WEST TRENTON

Motor Bus Society, Inc.
Mail to: P.O. Box 7058, 08628
Private agency
Founded in: 1948
Number of members: 1,200
Staff: volunteer 4
Magazine: *Motor Coach Age*
Major programs: library, book publishing, newsletters/pamphlets, historic preservation, research
Period of collections: 1910-present

WHIPPANY

Landmark Commission, Township of Hanover
1000 State Hwy. 10
Mail to: P.O. Box 250, 07981
Town agency
Founded in: 1978
Mrs. Donald Kitchell, Chair
Staff: volunteer 7
Major programs: historic site(s), markers, historic preservation, living history, audiovisual programs
Period of collections: early 1700s-mid 1800s

Yesteryear Museum
20 Harriet Dr., 07981-1906
Telephone: (201) 386-1920
Private agency
Founded in: 1970
Lee R. Munsick, Executive Director
Staff: volunteer 20
Magazine: *Yesteryear*
Major programs: library, archives, historic preservation
Period of collections: 1850-1950

WHITEHOUSE STATION

Clinton Music Hall Preservation Society
P.O. Box 554, 08889
Telephone: (204) 534-2371
Founded in: 1978
Questionnaire not received

WILDWOOD

Wildwood Historical Commission
4400 New Jersey Ave., 08260
Telephone: (609) 522-2444, ext. 35
Founded in: 1962
Questionnaire not received

WILLIAMSTOWN

Munroe Township Historical Society
Main and Library Sts.
Mail to: P.O. Box 474, 08094
Town agency
Founded in: 1974
Ruth White, President
Number of members: 80
Staff: volunteer 3
Major programs: archives, manuscripts, museum, tours, oral history, school programs, book publishing, newsletters/pamphlets, historic preservation, records management, exhibits, living history, photographic collections
Period of collections: late 1800s-present

WOODBURY

Gloucester County Cultural and Heritage Commission
P.O. Box 598, 08096
Telephone: (609) 848-8900
County agency
Founded in: 1977
Paul Oland, Freeholder
Staff: part time 1
Magazine: *The Legend*
Major programs: historic site(s), markers, school programs, book publishing, newsletters/pamphlets, historic preservation, audiovisual programs, field services

Gloucester County Historical Society
17 Hunter St.
Telephone: (609) 845-4771
Mail to: P.O. Box 409, 08096
Private agency
Founded in: 1903
Edith Hoelle, Librarian
Number of members: 1,139
Staff: volunteer 14
Major programs: library, archives, manuscripts, books, newsletters/pamphlets, restoration
Period of collections: 1686-present

NEW MEXICO

ABIQUIU

Ghost Ranch Living Museum
Rt. 84, 87510
Telephone: (505) 685-4312
Federal agency, authorized by U.S. Department of Agriculture
Founded in: 1959
Albert Martinez, Director
Staff: full time 5
Major programs: library, museum, school programs, exhibits, conservation

ACOMA

Acoma Tourist and Visitation Center
Hwy. 23 and 38
Telephone: (505) 552-6606
Mail to: P.O. Box 309, 87034
Private agency, authorized by Acoma Tribal Council
Matthew J. Cerno, Director
Staff: full time 20
Major programs: museum, historic site(s), tours/pilgrimages, oral history
Period of collections: A.D. 600-present

ALAMOGORDO

Space Center/International Space Hall of Fame and Tombaugh Space Theater
Hwy. 2001
Telephone: (505) 437-2840
Mail to: P.O. Box 533, 88311-0533
State agency, authorized by Office of Cultural Affairs
Founded in: 1976
Bob Content, Executive Director
Staff: full time 23, part time 7, volunteer 60
Magazine: *Space Log*
Major programs: museum, school programs, newsletters/pamphlets, exhibits, living history, audiovisual programs, space history and science
Period of collections: 1940s-present

Tularosa Basin Historical Society
P.O. Box 518, 88311
Private agency
Founded in: 1965
Mel Wall, President
Number of members: 93
Staff: volunteer 30
Major programs: museum, book publishing
Period of collections: from 1890

ALBUQUERQUE

Albuquerque Archaeological Society
Mail to: P.O. Box 4029, 87196
Founded in: 1966
Betty Garrett, President
Magazine: *Pottery Southwest*
Major programs: archaeology
Period of collections: prehistoric

Albuquerque Conservation Association
709 Central Ave., NW, 87102
Telephone: (505) 242-4843
Mail to: P.O. Box 946, 87103
Private agency
Founded in: 1980
Berent Groth, Chair
Number of members: 400
Staff: full time 1, volunteer 20
Major programs: tours/pilgrimages, educational programs, newsletters/pamphlets, historic preservation, grants and award programs

Albuquerque Historical Society
1611 Bayita Lane, NW, 87107
Telephone: (505) 344-2590
Founded in: 1940
Questionnaire not received

Albuquerque Museum
2000 Mountain Rd., W
Telephone: (505) 766-7878
Mail to: P.O. Box 1293, 87104
Founded in: 1968
Questionnaire not received

Center for Anthropological Studies
11728 Linn, NE
Telephone: (505) 296-4836
Mail to: P.O. Box 14576, 87191
Private agency
Founded in: 1975
Albert E. Ward, Director
Number of members: 322

Staff: full time 3, part time 4,
volunteer 3
Major programs: historic site(s),
tours, book publishing, research,
archaeology programs,
photographic collections, artifact
analysis and reporting

**Colonial Infantry Albuquerque
(Infanteria Colonial Albuquerque)**
2215 Lead, SE, 87106
Telephone: (505) 268-7805
Mail to: P.O. Box 25531, 87125-0531
Private agency
Founded in: 1971
Elmer Martinez, Director/Founder
Staff: volunteer 2
Major programs: museum, book
publishing, research, exhibits,
living history, color heraldic
escutcheons and reports
Period of collections: 1492-1821

**Department of Geology, University
of New Mexico**
87131
Telephone: (505) 277-1646
State agency, authorized by the
university
Founded in: 1888
Spencer G. Lucas, Curator
Staff: full time 1, part time 2,
volunteer 10
Major programs: museum, records
management, research, exhibits,
natural history

Ernie Pyle Public Library
900 Girard, SE, 87106
Telephone: (505) 766-7921
City agency
Founded in: 1947
Susan A. Sultemeier, Branch
Manager
Staff: full time 3, part time 3
Major programs: library, manuscripts,
historic site(s), tours/pilgrimages,
photographic collections
Period of collections: 1940-1948

**Genealogy Club of the
Albuquerque Public Library**
423 Central Ave., NE, 87102
Elaine Jones, President
Number of members: 212
Staff: volunteer 5
Major programs:
newsletters/pamphlets, audiovisual
programs, library acquisitions

**Historic Landmarks Survey of
Albuquerque**
Plaza Del Sol 710, 600 2nd St., NW,
87102
Telephone: (505) 766-4720
Mail to: Redevelopment Planning,
P.O. Box 1293, 87103
Questionnaire not received

Indian Pueblo Cultural Center
2401 12th St., NW, 87102
Telephone: (505) 843-7270
Authorized by All-Indian Pueblo
Council
Clyde W. Caudill, Museum Technical
Administrator
Staff: full time 17, volunteer 50
Magazine: *Pueblo Horizons*
Major programs: museum, oral
history, exhibits, living history,

audiovisual programs, archaeology
programs, photographic
collections
Period of collections:
prehistoric-present

Maxwell Museum of Anthropology
University of New Mexico, 87131
Telephone: (505) 277-4404
State agency, authorized by Maxwell
Museum Association
Founded in: 1932
Lewis R. Binford, Acting Director
Staff: full time 15 part time 6,
volunteer 75
Major programs: school programs,
book publishing, research,
exhibits, photographic collections
Period of collections:
prehistoric-present

Menaul Historical Library
301 Menaul Blvd., NE, 87107
Telephone: (505) 345-7727
Private agency, authorized by
Presbyterian Church and Menaul
School
Founded in: 1974
Carolyn Atkins, Founder
Number of members: 500
Staff: volunteer 7
Magazine: *Menaul Historical Review*
Major programs: library, archives,
manuscrips, historic site(s), oral
history, book publishing,
newsletter, historic preservation,
records management, research,
exhibits, photographic collections
Period of collections: 1865-present

National Atomic Museum
Telephone: (505) 844-8443
Mail to: P.O. Box 5400, DOE/ALO,
87115
Federal agency, authorized by U.S.
Department of Energy
Founded in: 1969
Joni Hezlep, Director
Staff: full time 6, part time 5
Major programs: library, museum,
oral history, educational programs
Period of collections: 1943-present

New Mexico Genealogical Society
P.O. Box 8330, 87198
Private agency
Founded in: 1960
Ralph L. Hayes, President
Number of members: 220
Staff: volunteer 36
Magazine: *New Mexico Genealogist*
Major programs: library, archives,
book publishing,
newsletters/pamphlets, historic
preservation, genealogical
services

New Mexico Historical Review
1013 Mesa Vista Hall, University of
New Mexico, 87131
Telephone: (505) 277-5839
State agency, authorized by the
university
Founded in: 1926
Nancy M. Brown, Office Manager
Number of members: 1,300
Staff: full time 1, part time 3
Magazine: *New Mexico Historical
Review*

Major programs:
newsletters/pamphlets
Period of collections: to late 19th
century

**New Mexico Medical History
Program**
Medical Center Library, University of
New Mexico, 87131
Telephone: (505) 277-0656
State agency, authorized by the
university
Founded in: 1982
Janet H. Johnson, Archives Manager
Major programs: library, archives,
manuscripts, oral history,
photographic collections, history of
medicine and medical practice
Period of collections: 1880s-present

**New Mexico Sons of Confederate
Veterans**
3021 Espanola, NE
Private agency
C. W. Buck, Commander
Number of members: 24
Major programs: historic site(s),
markers

**Preservation Planning, City of
Albuquerque**
600 2nd St., NW, 87102
Telephone: (505) 766-4720
City agency
Founded in: 1975
Mary P. Davis, Preservation Planner
Major programs: historic
preservation, audiovisual programs
Period of collections: 1880-1945

Presidio Lancers
715 Morningside, NE, 87110
Telephone: (505) 268-2896
Private agency
Founded in: 1977
Andrew L. Garcia, President/Founder
Staff: full time 1, part time 6,
volunteer 6
Major programs: museum, historic
site(s), living history
Period of collections: Spanish
Colonial-late 18th century

Quivira Research Center
3017 Commercial, NE, 87107
Telephone: (505) 344-2755
Private agency
Founded in: 1978
Carol J. Condie, President
Staff: full time 1, part time 8
Major programs: oral history, exhibits,
archaeology programs, field
services

Society for Historical Archaeology
c/o National Park Service, 5000
Marble, NE, Room 211, 87110
Telephone: (505) 766-5944
Founded in: 1967
Questionnaire not received

**Special Collections Branch,
Albuquerque Public Library**
423 Central, NE, 87102
Telephone: (505) 766-5009
City agency
Founded in: 1978
Laurel E. Drew, Librarian
Staff: full time 2, part time 1,
volunteer 2

Major programs: library, genealogical
services
Period of collections: 1540-present
**Special Collections Department,
University of New Mexico**
87131
Telephone: (505) 277-6451
State agency, authorized by the
university
Founded in: 1889
William E. Tydeman, Department
Head
Staff: full time 8
Major programs: library, archives,
manuscripts, oral history, records
management, research,
photographic collections
Period of collections: 1846-present
Telephone Pioneers of America
1209 Mountain Rd., NE, 87110
Telephone: (505) 256-2105
Private agency, authorized by
Mountain Bell Telephone Company
Founded in: 1911
Lela Marks, Administrator
Number of members: 2,300
Staff: full time 2, volunteer 1
Magazine: *Pioneer Trails*
Major programs: museum
Period of collections: 1875-present

ARTESIA

**Artesia Historical Museum and Art
Center**
505 W. Richardson Ave., 88210
Telephone: (505) 748-2390
City agency
Founded in: 1970
Terry R. Koenig, Director
Staff: full time 1, part time 2
Major programs: archives, museum,
oral history, research,
photographic collections
Period of collections: 1900-1930
Artesia Historical Society
319 W. Grand, 88210
Telephone: (505) 746-2948
Founded in: 1969
Questionnaire not received

AZTEC

Aztec Museum Association
125 N. Main, 87410
Telephone: (505) 334-9829
Private agency
Founded in: 1964
Mary K. Atwood, Curator
Number of members: 297
Staff: part time 2, volunteer 2
Major programs: archives,
manuscripts, museum,
tours/pilgrimages, oral history,
school programs,
newsletters/pamphlets, historic
preservation, exhibits, archaeology
programs, photographic
collections, genealogical services.
Period of collections:
prehistoric-present

BERNALILLO

Sandoval County Historical Society
P.O. Box 638, 87004
Telephone: (505) 867-2309
Private agency

Founded in: 1979
Martha Liebert, President
Number of members: 30
Major programs: library, archives,
manuscripts, tours/pilgrimages,
oral history, research, exhibits,
photographic collections,
genealogical services

CARLSBAD

**Southeastern New Mexico
Historical Society**
101 S. Halagueno, 88220
Telephone: (505) 885-6776
Founded in: 1970
Questionnaire not received

CHURCH ROCK

Gallup Museum of Indian Art
Red Rock State Park
Telephone: (505) 722-6196
Mail to: P.O. Box 328, 87311
Founded in: 1951

CIMARRON

Philmont Museums
Philmont Scout Ranch 87714
Telephone: (505) 376-2281
Mail to: Box 38-A
Founded in 1951
Stephen Zimmer, Director
Staff: full time 2, part time 11
Major programs: library, archives,
manuscripts, museum, educational
programs Period of collections:
prehistoric-present

CLOUDCROFT

**Sacramento Mountains Historical
Society, Inc.**
U.S. Hwy. 82
Telephone: (505) 682-2958
Mail to: P.O. Box 435, 88317
Founded in: 1977
T. Karl H. Wuersching, President
Number of members: 110
Staff: volunteer 6
Major programs: library, museum,
historic sites preservation, oral
history, educational programs,
historic preservation, pioneer
village.
Period of collections: 1880-1920

CLOVIS

**High Plains Historical
Foundation, Inc.**
411 Main St., 88101
Telephone: (505) 763-6361
County agency
H.A. Kilmer, President
Founded in: 1972

COLUMBUS

Columbus Historical Society, Inc.
P.O. Box 562, 88029
Founded in: 1973
Nikki English, President
Number of members: 286
Staff: volunteer 10
Major programs: library, archives,
museum, historic sites
preservation, historic preservation,
exhibits
Period of collections: 1902-1924

DEMING

**Luna County Historical
Society, Inc.**
301 S. Silver St.
Telephone: (505) 546-2382
Mail to: P.O. Box 1617, 88031
County agency
Founded in: 1955
Richard W. Gilmore, President
Staff: volunteer 50
Major programs: historic
preservation, exhibits,
photographic collections
Period of collections: from 1880

ESPANOLA

San Gabriel Historical Society
Telephone: (505) 852-2112
Mail to: P.O. Box 1528, Santa Cruz,
87567
Questionnaire not received

FARMINGTON

Farmington Museum
302 N. Orchard Ave.
Telephone: (505) 327-7701
Mail to: P.O. Box 900, 87413
City agency
Founded in: 1964
Diana Ohlson, Curator
Staff: full time 1, part time 2,
volunteer 11
Major programs: archives,
manuscripts, museum,
tours/pilgrimages, oral history,
newsletters/pamphlets, historic
preservation, records
management, research, exhibits,
photographic collections
Period of collections: 1890-1920

**San Juan County Archaeological
Research Center and Library**
975 U.S. Hwy. 64, 87401
Telephone: (505) 632-2013
Private agency, authorized by San
Juan County Museum Association
Founded in: 1964
Jo Davenport Smith, Director
Number of members: 150
Staff: full time 13, part time 7,
volunteer 18
Major programs: library, archives,
museum, historic site(s), oral
history, book publishing,
newsletters/pamphlets, historic
preservation, records
management, research, exhibits,
audiovisual programs, archaeology
programs, photographic
collections, genealogical services
Period of collections: 1877-1950

**San Juan County Museum
Association**
Rt. 3, Box 858, 87401
Telephone: (505) 632-2013
Founded in: 1962
Questionnaire not received

Southwestern Oral History Institute
512 E. 18th St.
Telephone: (505) 325-5411
Mail to: P.O. Box 3411, 87499
Private agency
Founded in: 1982
Diana Lynn Ohlson, Director

Staff: full time 1
Major programs: oral history
Period of collections: 1910-1980

FT. SUMNER

Billy the Kid Museum
1601 E. Sumner Ave.
Telephone: (505) 355-2380
Mail to: Rt. 1, Box 36, 88119
Private agency
Founded in: 1952
Donald E. Sweet, Owner
Major programs: museum
Period of collections: 1850-1950

GALLUP

Plateau Sciences Society
P.O. Box 2433, 87301
Private agency
Founded in: 1960
Martin Link, President
Number of members: 75
Staff: full time 2, volunteer 9
Magazine: *Call of the Plateau*
Major programs: library, museum,
educational programs,
newsletters/pamphlets
Period of collections: A.D.
1000-present

Red Rock Museum
P.O. Box 328, Church Rock, 87311
Telephone: (505) 722-6196
City agency
Founded in: 1951
Belinda Casto-Landolt, Curator
Staff: full time 2, part time 3
Major programs: museum, exhibits
Period of collections: A.D. 1000

HOBBS

Lea County Cowboy Hall of Fame
New Mexico Junior College,
Lovington Hwy., 88240
Telephone (505) 392-4510
Private agency, authorized by the
junior college
Founded in: 1978
Sylvia Benge, Director
Number of members: 600
Staff: full time 1, part time 1
Major programs: museum,
tours/pilgrimages, school
programs, newsletters/pamphlets,
exhibits, audiovisual programs,
photographic collections,
genealogical services
Period of collections: 1890-1920

Llano Estacado Heritage, Inc.
925 W. Copper Ave.
Telephone: (505) 392-6394
Mail to: P.O. Box 2446, 88240
Questionnaire not received

LAS CRUCES

Rio Grande Historical Collections
P.O. Box 3475, University Library,
88003
Telephone: (505) 646-4727
Founded in: 1972
Number of members: 300
Staff: full time 4, part time 2
Magazine: *Rio Grande History*
Major programs: archives,
manuscripts, oral history
Period of collections: 1850-present

The University Museum
Kent Hall, University Ave. at Solano
Dr.
Telephone: (505) 646-3739
Mail to: P.O. Box 3564, 88003
State agency, authorized by New
Mexico State University
Founded in: 1959
Fred Plog, Acting Director
Number of members: 150
Staff: full time 3, part time 6,
volunteer 10
Magazine: *El Eco de la Garza*
Major programs: museum,
tours/pilgrimages, school
programs, book publishing,
newsletters/pamphlets, exhibits,
lectures
Period of collections: A.D. 600-1920s

LAS VEGAS

**Citizens' Committee for Historic
Preservation**
P.O. Box 707, 87701
Telephone: (505) 454-1401, ext. 77
City agency
Founded in: 1977
Anita Ehl Vernon, Director
Number of members: 25
Staff: volunteer 1
Magazine: *Preservation Bulletin*
Major programs: museum,
newsletters/pamphlets, historic
preservation, photographic
collections
Period of collections: 1870-present

Galeria de los Artesanos
220 N. Plaza
Telephone: (505) 425-8331
Mail to: P.O. Box 1657, 87701
Private agency
Founded in: 1949
Joseph W. Stein, Co-owner
Major programs: archives,
manuscripts, historic site(s),
tours/pilgrimages, oral history,
newsletters/pamphlets, historic
preservation, research, exhibits,

**Las Vegas Rough Rider and City
Museum**
731 Grand Ave.
Telephone: (505) 425-8156
Mail to: P.O. Box 179, 87701
City agency
Founded in: 1958
Harold F. Thatcher, Director/Curator
Staff: part time 2
Major programs: museum
Period of collections: 18th-19th
centuries

**Las Vegas-San Miguel Chamber of
Commerce**
727 Grand Ave.
Telephone: (505) 425-8631
Mail to: P.O. Box 148,87701
Private agency
Founded in: 1928
Patricia L. Halverson, Executive
Director
Number of members: 240
Staff: full time 2
Magazine: *Roadrunner*
Major programs: tours/pilgrimages,
newsletters/pamphlets
Period of collections: 1879-1930

**Rough Rider Memorial and City
Museum**
727 Grand Ave.
Telephone: (505) 425-8156
Mail to: P.O. Box 148, 87701
City agency
Founded in: 1958
H. F. Thatcher, Director/Curator
Staff: full time 2
Major programs: museum, T.
Roosevelt and the Spanish
American War, local history and
heritage
Period of collections:
pre-Columbian-Spanish frontier
eras

LINCOLN

Lincoln County Heritage Trust
P.O. Box 98, 88338
Telephone: (505) 653-4025
Private agency
Founded in: 1976
Gary Miller, Director
Staff: full time 2, part time 6
Major programs: museum, historic
site(s), tours/pilgrimages, school
programs, historic preservation,
exhibits, audiovisual programs
Period of collectins: 1870-1880

**Old Lincoln County Memorial
Commission**
Telephone: (505) 653-4381
Mail to: P.O. Box 98, 88338
Questionnaire not received

LOS ALAMOS

**Los Alamos County Historical
Museum and Society**
1921 Juniper
Telephone: (505)
662-6272/6620-4493
Mail to: P.O. Box 43, 87544
Private agency
Founded in: 1968
Hedy M. Dunn, Director
Number of members: 450
Staff: part time 2, volunteer 50
Major programs: archives, museum,
historic sites preservation, tours,
oral history, educational programs,
books, newsletters/pamphlets,
publishing, lecture series
Period of collections: 1915-1950

**Los Alamos National Laboratory
Archives**
MS-C322, 87545
Telephone: (505) 667-3809
Federal agency, authorized by U.S.
Department of Energy and the
University of California
Founded in: 1981
Tony A. Rivera, Group Leader
Staff: full time 18
Major programs: archives, oral
history, records management,
history of nuclear technology
Period of collections: 1942-present

LOS OJOS

**Sociedad Historica de la Tierra
Amarilla**
c/o General Delivery, 87551
Telephone: (505) 345-5147
Private agency

Founded in: 1982
Robert J. Torrez, Director
Staff: volunteer 3
Major programs: oral history, historic
preservation, research
Period of collections: 19th century

MADRID

Old Coal Mine Museum/Madrid Opera House
Turquoise Trail, Madrid Star Rt., 87010
Telephone: (505) 473-0743
Private agency
Founded in: 1963
H. D. Salkeld, Director
Staff: volunteer 9
Major programs: museum, historic
site(s), historic preservation,
research
Period of collections: 1882-1956

MAGDALENA

Bandar Log, Inc.
Main St.
Telephone: (505) 854-2715
Mail to: P.O. Box 86, 87825
Private agency
Founded D: 1979
Ms. Jacky Barrington, Editor
Staff: volunteer 2
Magazine: *Magdalena Mountain Mail*
Major programs: book publishing,
newsletters/pamphlets
Period of collections: from 1888

MORIARTY

Moriarty Historical Society and Museum
777 Central Ave., SW
Telephone: (505) 832-4764
Mail to: P.O. Box 133, 87035
Founded in: 1974
Teddie Cannon, President
Number of members: 58
Staff: volunteer 6
Major programs: museum, historic
preservation, exhibits, living
history, local history
Period of collections: late 1800-early
1900

MOUNTAINAIR

Salinas National Monument
P.O. Box 496, 87036
Telephone: (505) 847-2585
Federal agency, authorized by
National Park Service.
Founded M: 1980
Glenn M. Fulfer, Supervisory Park
Ranger
Major programs: historic site(s),
tours/pilgrimages, historic
preservation, records
management, research, exhibits,
archaeology programs,
photographic collections
Period of collections: A.D. 1300-A.D.
1670

NORE

Chaco Culture National Historical Park
Telephone: (505) 786-5384

Mail to: Star Rt. 4, Box 6500,
Bloomfield; 87413
Federal agency, authorized by
National Park Service
Founded in: 1906
Major programs: library, museum,
historic site(s), tours/pilgrimages,
historic preservation, research,
exhibits, archaeology programs,
photographic collections
Period of collections: A.D. 800-A.D.
1300

PECOS

Pecos National Monument
P.O. Drawer 11, 87552
Telephone: (505) 757-6414
Federal agency, authorized by
National Park Service
Founded in: 1965
John Bezy, Superintendent
Number of members: full time 5, part
time 4
Major programs: museum, historic
site(s), tours/pilgrimages, school
programs, historic preservation,
exhibits, living history,
photographic collections
Period of collections: 1100-1850

PORTALES

Roosevelt County Genealogical and Historical Society
1505 S. Abilene, 12157
Telephone: (505) 356-5054
Private agency
Founded in: 1972
Number of members: 20

RADIUM SPRINGS

Ft. Selden State Monument
P.O. Box 58, 88054
Telephone: (505) 526-8911
State agency
Founded in: 1909
Rudy Saucedo, Monument Director
Staff: full time 1, part time 1
Magazine: *Ft. Selden*
Major programs: library, museum,
tours/pilgrimages, historic
preservation, living history
Period of collections: 1800s

RAMAH

El Morro National Monument
87321
Telephone: (505) 783-4226
Federal agency, authorized by
National Park Service
Founded in: 1906
Douglas E. Eury, Superintendent
Staff: full time 6, part time 5,
volunteer 3
Major programs: museum, historic
preseration, exhibits, audiovisual
programs
Period of collections: A.D. 1200 - A.D.
1900

RATON

Raton Museum
216 S. 1st St., 87740
Telephone: (505) 445-8979
City agency, authorized by Raton City
Commission

Founded in: 1939
Thomas W. Burch, Curator
Staff: volunteer 20
Major programs: school programs,
historic preservation, research,
exhibits, photographic collections,
genealogical services
Period of collections: 1850-present

ROSWELL

Chaves County Historical Society
200 N. Lea Ave., 88201
Telephone: (505) 622-8333
Private agency
Founded in 1935
Lillian McDonald, Executive
Secretary
Number of members: 670
Staff: full time 1, part time 1
Magaine: *Facts and Traditions*
Major programs: library, archives,
manuscripts, museum, historic
sitre(s), tours/pilgrimages, oral
history, school programs, book
publishing, newsletters/pamphlets,
historic preservation, research,
exhibits, photographic collections
Period of collections: 1865-present

General D. L. McBridge Museum
NMMI Campus, 88201
Telephone: (505) 622-3155
State Agency
Founded in: 1984
Keith E. Gibson, Director
Major programs: Museum, oral
history, school programs, records
management, exhibits, audiovisual
programs
Period of collections: 1891-present

SANTA FE

Colonial New Mexico Historical Foundation
135 Camino Escondido, 87501
Telephone: (505) 982-5644
Founded in: 1971
Questionnaire not received

Guadalupe Historic Foundation
100 Guadalupe St., 87503
Telephone: (505) 988-2027
Private agency
Founded in: 1974
Virginia Castellano, Executive
Director
Number of members: 150
Staff: full time 1, part time 1,
volunteer 6
Major programs: museum, historic
site(s), tours/pilgrimages,
newsletters/pamphlets, historic
preservation, exhibits, living
history, photographic collections,
performing arts
Period of collections: 1700s

Historical Society of New Mexico
Mail to: P.O. Box 5819, 87502
Private agency
Founded in: 1859
John P. Conron, President
Number of members: 500
Staff: part time 1
Magazine: *La Cronica de Nuevo
Mexico*
Major programs: markers, book
publishing, newsletters/pamphlets

Historic Preservation Division, Office of Cultural Affairs
228 E. Palace Ave., 87504
Telephone: (505) 827-8320
State agency
Founded in: 1969
Thomas W. Merlan, State Historic Preservation Officer
Staff: full time 12
Magazine: *Preservation New Mexico*
Major programs: historic site(s), book publishing, newsletters/pamphlets, historic preservation, records management, research, archaeology programs

Historic Santa Fe Foundation
136 Griffin
Telephone: (505) 983-2567
Mail to: P.O. Box 2535, 87501
Founded in: 1961
Questionnaire not received

Institute of American Indian Arts Museum
1369 Cerrillos Rd., 87501
Telephone: (505) 988-6281
Federal agency, authorized by Bureau of Indian Affairs
Founded in: 1962
Charles Dailey, Museum Director
Staff: full time 4, volunteer 6
Major programs: library, archives, museum, oral history, records management, research, exhibits, audiovisual programs, photographic collections, field services, nation-wide museum consultations
Period of collections: 1960-present

◇**Museum of New Mexico**
113 Lincoln Ave.
Telephone: (505) 827-6451
Mail to: P.O. Box 2087, 87503
State agency
Founded in: 1909
George Ewing, Interim Director
Staff: full time 133, part time 3, volunteer 250
Magazine: *El Palacio/El Portal*
Major programs: library, archives, manuscripts, museum, historic site(s), tours/pilgrimages, school programs, book publishing, newsletters/pamphlets, historic preservation, records management, research, exhibits, living history, audiovisual programs, archaeology programs, photographic collections, contract archaeology, folk and fine arts
Period of collections: prehistoric-present

◇**New Mexico Association of Museums**
Telephone: (505) 662-6272
Mail to: P. O. Box 5746, 87502
Private agency
Founded in: 1959
Hedy M. Dunn, President
Number of members: 200
Major programs: museum, school programs, newsletters/pamphlets,

research, exhibits, archaeology programs, photographic collections, field services, fine arts, adult education, cultural resources

New Mexico Records Center and Archives
404 Montezuma St., 87503
Telephone: (505) 827-8860
State agency, authorized by Commission of Public Records
Founded in: 1959
Dixie Lee Bradley, State Records Administrator
Number of members: 1
Staff: full time 26, part time 1
Major programs: archives, manuscripts, markers, oral history, school programs, historic preservation, records management, research, photographic collections, genealogical services
Period of collections: 1621-present

Old Cienega Village Museum
Rt. 2, Box 214, 87505
Telephone: (505) 471-2261
Private agency, authorized by El Rancho de las Golondrinas Charitable Trust
Founded in: 1971
George B. Paloheimo, Curator
Staff: full time 6, part time 2, volunteer 12
Major programs: museum, historic site(s), tours/pilgrimages, junior history, school programs, newsletters/pamphlets, exhibits, living history
Period of collections: 1700-1885

Palace of the Governors
Palace Ave.
Telephone: (505) 827-6473
Mail to: P.O. Box 2087, 87504
State agency, authorized by Museum of New Mexico
Founded in: 1909
Thomas E. Chavez, Director
Staff: full time 17, part time 7, volunteer 20
magazine: *El Palacio*
Major programs: library, archives, manuscripts, museum, historic site(s), tours/pilgrimages, research, exhibits, living history, photographic collections, genealogical services
Period of collections: 1500-present

Santa Fe Historical Society
Mail to: P.O. Box 4904, 87502
Private agency
Founded in: 1967
Sherry Smith-Gonzales, President
Number of members: 178
Major programs: oral history, newsletters/pamphlets, fund raising for local historical and archaeogical projects

Wheelwright Museum of the American Indian
704 Camino Lejo
Telephone: (505) 982-4636
Mail to: P.O. Box 5153, 87502
Private agency
Founded in: 1937
Richard W. Lang, Director

Number of members: 1,600
Staff: full time 10, part time 3, volunteer 150
Magazine: *Transitions*
Major programas: archives, manuscripts, museum, school programs, research, exhibits
Period of collections: late 19th century-20th centuries

SILVER CITY

Grant County Archaeological Society
627 B St., 88061
Telephone: (505) 538-3444
Private agency
Founded in: 1938
Mary Margaret Soule, Secretary
Number of members: 75
Staff: volunteer 5
Major programs: library, museum, tours/pilgrimages, school programs, research, archaeology programs
Period of collections: A.D. 800-A.D. 1300

Historical Society of Southwestern New Mexico
WNMU Museum, 88061
Telephone: (505) 538-6386
Founded in: 1976
Questionnaire not received

Silver City Museum
312 W. Broadway, 88061
Telephone: (505) 538-5921
Founded in: 1967
Susan Berry, Director
Staff: full time 3, part time 1, volunteer 1
Major programs: archives, museum, historic sites preservation, tours/pilgrimages, oral history, newsletters/pamphlets, historic preservation
Period of collections: 1870-1920

Western New Mexico University Museum
Telephone: (505) 538-6386
Mail to: College of Arts and Letters, 88062
State agency, authorized by the university
Founded in: 1974
Douglas M. Dinwiddle, Museum Director
Staff: full time 1, part time 4, volunteer 4
Major programs: archives, museum, educational programs
Period of collections: prehistoric-present

SOCORRO

Socorro County Historical Society, Inc.
Telephone: (505) 835-5242
Mail to: P. O. Box 923, 87801
Private agency
Founded in: 1963
Sherry Krukowski, President
Number of members: 87
Staff: volunteer 10
Major programs: library, archives, manuscripts, historic site(s)
Period of collections: 1880s-1950s

TAOS

Governor Bent Museum and Gallery
18 Bent
Telephone (505) 758-2376
Mail to: P.O. Box 153, 87571
Private agency
Founded in: 1958
Otto Noeding, Co-owner
Staff: full time 2
Major programs: museum, historic site(s), historic preservation, exhibits
Period of collections: 1847-1941

The Harwood Foundation
25 Ledoux St.
Telephone; (505) 758-3063
Mail to: P.O. Box 766, 87571
Town agency, authorized by University of New Mexico
Founded in: 1923
David L. Caffey, Director
Number of members: 350
Staff: full time 6, part time 5, volunteer 21
Major programs: library, archives, museum, historic site(s), oral history, newsletters/pamphlets, exhibits, photographic collections, fine arts
Period of collections: 1898-present

Kit Carson Memorial Foundation, Inc.
Old Kit Carson Rd.
Telephone: (505) 758-4741
Mail to: P.O. Drawer B, 87571
Founded in: 1949
Jack K. Boyer, Executive Director
Number of members: 239
Staff: full time 7, part time 12, volunteer 5
Magazine: La Noticias Alegre de Casa Kit Carson
Major programs: library, archives, manuscripts, museum, historic site(s), oral history, school programs, newsletters/pamphlets, historic preservation, research, exhibits, archaeology programs, photographic collections, field services
Period of collections: A.D. 900-present

Millicent Rogers Museum
Museum Rd.
Telephone: (505) 758-2462
Mail to: P.O. Box A, 87571
Private agency
Founded in: 1953
Arthur H. Wolf, Director
Number of members: 600
Staff: full time 6, part time 2, volunteer 10
Magazine:Las Palabras
Major programs: library, museum, tours/pilgrimages, school programs, newsletters/pamphlets, records management, research, exhibits, archaeology programs, photographic collections, ethnology, fine arts

Taos County Historical Society
Mail to: P. O. Box 2447, 87571
Private agency
Founded in: 1960

David L. Caffey, President
Number of members: 107
Major programs: markers, tours/pilgrimages, newsletters/pamphlets, research, audiovisual programs, photographic collections
Period of collections: 1880-present

TOME

Tome Parish Museum
State Hwy. 47
Telephone: (505) 865-7497
Mail to: P. O. Box 397, 87060
Founded in: 1969
Robert M. Beach, Pastor
Staff: volunteer 2
Major programs: museum
Period of collections: 1783-1918

TRUTH OR CONSEQUENCES

Sierra County Historical Society
325 Main St.
Telephone: (505) 894-6600
Mail to: P.O. Box 1029, 87901
Founded in: 1970
Number of members: 400
Staff: full time 1, part time 2, volunteer 35
Major programs: museum
Period of collections: A.D. 1000-1960

TUCUMCARI

Tucumcari Historical Research Institute
416 S. Adams St., 88401
Telephone: (505) 461-4201
Founded in: 1965
Lalla Landess, Board Director
Number of members: 135
Staff: part time 3, volunteer 10
Major programs: museum, tour/pilgrimages, historic preservation, exhibits, photographic collections
Period of collections: 1900-1945

TULAROSA

Tularosa Village Historical Society
Mail to: Star Rt. 2, Box 1750, 88352
Private agency
Founded in: 1975
Norma E. Cincert, Secretary
Number of members: 25
Period of collection: 1850-1940

VADITO

Lauriano Cordova Memorial Museum
Rt. Box 14, Rockwall, 87579
Telephone: (505) 587-2328
Mail to: P.O. Box 28, Llano, 87543
Private agency
Founded in: 1978
Rafael Lobato, Founder/Director
Staff: volunteer 6
Major programs: museum, historic site(s), tours/pilgrimages, oral history, school programs, historic preservation, exhibits, living history, flour mill site
Period of collections: 1800s-early 1900s

WATROUS

Ft. Union National Monument
87753
Telephone: (505) 425-8025
Federal agency, authorized by National Park Service
Founded in: 1956
Clark Crane, Superintendent
Number of members: full time 5, part time 10, volunteer 4
Major programs: library, historic site(s), markers, tours/pilgrimages, historic preservation, exhibits
Period of collections: 1851-1891

WHITE'S CITY

Million Dollar Museum
Carlsbad Caverns Hwy., 88268
Telephone: (505) 785-2291
Private agency, authorized by White's City, Inc.
Founded in: 1927
Jack White, Jr., Vice President
Staff: full time 1, part time 1
Major programs: museum, exhibits
Period of collections: mid-19th century-present

NEW YORK

ADAMS

Historical Association of South Jefferson
9 E. Church St., 13605
Telephone: (315) 232-2616
Founded in: 1973
Questionnaire not received

AFTON

Jericho Historical Society
169 Main St., 13730
Telephone: (607) 639-2720
Questionnaire not received

AKRON

Newstead Historical Society
Telephone: (716) 542-9672
Mail to: P.O. Box 222, 14001
David N. Wakeman, President
Staff: volunteer 6
Major programs: archives, manuscripts
Period of collections: 1802-present

ALBANY

Albany County Hall of Records
27 Western Ave., 12203
Telephone: (518) 434-3527
County agency
Founded in: 1980
Robert W. Arnold III, Executive Director
Number of members: full time 17, part time 8, volunteer 3
Magazine: 8 Miles High
Major programs: archives, manuscripts, junior history, oral history, school programs, newsletters/pamphlets, records

management, research,
photographic collections,
genealogical services, field
services, micrographics
Period of collections: 1650-present

**Albany County Historical
Association**
9 Ten Broeck Place, 12210
Telephone: (518) 436-9826
Private agency
Founded in: 1942
David Veeder, Executive Director
Number of members: 350
Staff: full time 1, part time 1,
volunteer 15
Major programs: museum, historic
site(s), school programs, exhibits,
living history
Period of collections: 19th century

Albany Institute of History and Art
125 Washington Ave., 12210
Telephone: (518) 463-4478
Private agency
Founded in: 1791
Norman S. Rice, Director
Number of members: 2,300
Staff: full time 16, part time 6,
volunteer 300
Major programs: library, archives,
manuscripts, museum, school
programs, historic preservation,
research, exhibits
Period of collections: 17th-20th
centuries

Bureau for Historical Services
27 Western Ave., 12203
Telephone: (518) 438-5168
Founded in: 1971
Questionnaire not received

**Capital District Genealogical
Society**
P.O. Box 2175, Empire State Plaza
Station, 12220
Private agency
Founded in: 1981
Florence Christoph, President
Number of members: 160
Staff: volunteer 10
Major programs: newsletters

**Division for Historic Preservation,
New York State Parks and
Recreation**
Agency Bldg. One, Empire State
Plaza, 12238
Telephone: (518) 474-0468
Questionnaire not received

◇**Division of History and
Anthropology, New York State
Museum**
3099 Cultural Center, Empire State
Plaza, 12230
Telephone: (518) 473-1299
Founded in: 1895
Questionnaire not received

Dutch Settlers Society of Albany
6 DeLucia Terrace, 12211
Telephone: (518) 462-3011
Questionnaire not received

**Early American Industries
Association, Inc.**
c/o John Watson, P.O. Box 2128,
Empire State Plaza Station, 12220
Telephone: (518) 473-1746

Private agency
Founded in: 1933
Douglas Hough, President
Number of members: 2,800
Staff: part time 4
Magazine:*Chronicle*
Major programs: library, book
publishing, newsletters/pamphlets,
research, exhibits, grants-in-aid
program to assist research and
publication, history of technology
and tools

**Franco-American Genealogical
Association**
Telephone: (518) 861-6205
Mail to: c/o Chair, R.F.D. 2,
Voorheesville, 12186
Private agency
Founded in: 1984
Jacqueline C. Imai, Chair,
Organizational Committee
Major programs: library, archives,
manuscripts, oral history, school
programs, newsletters/pamphlets,
historic preservation, research,
living history, audiovisual
programs, genealogical services

Historic Albany Foundation, Inc.
44 Central Ave., 12206
Telephone: (518) 463-0622
Founded in: 1974
Miriam Trementozzi, Executive
Director
Staff: full time 7, part time 1
Major programs: markers, tours,
books, newsletters/pamphlets,
historic preservation, design and
technical services, advocacy,
special events

Historic Cherry Hill
523½ S. Pearl St., 12202
Telephone: (518) 434-4791
Private agency
Founded in: 1964
Anne W. Ackerson, Director
Number of members: 160
Staff: full time 3, part time 4,
volunteer 125
Magazine: *New Gleanings*
Major programs: library, archives,
historic site(s), tours, oral history,
school programs, book publishing,
newsletters/pamphlets, research
Period of collections: 1760-1963

**Historical Society of Early
American Decoration, Inc.**
2/19 Dove St., 12210
Private agency
Founded in: 1946
Mrs. J. August Duval, President
Number of members: 850
Staff: volunteer 75
Magazine: *The Decorator*
Major programs: library, museum,
book publishing,
newsletters/pamphlets, exhibits,
educational programs, decorative
arts
Period of collections: 1783-1865

New York State Archives
Cultural Education Center, Empire
State Plaza, 12230
Telephone: (518) 474-1195
Founded in: 1971
Larry Hackman, State Archivist

Staff: full time 31
Major programs: archives, school
programs, records management,
research, genealogical services,
field services
Period of collections: 17th
century-present

**Preservation League of New York
State**
307 Hamilton St., 12210
Telephone: (518) 462-5658
Founded in: 1974
Questionnaire not received

**Schuyler Mansion State Historic
Site**
32 Catherine St., 12202
State agency, authorized by Office of
Parks, Recreation and Historic
Preservation
Susan May Haswell, Historic Site
Manager II
Staff: full time 9
Major programs: historic sites,
tours/pilgrimages, educational
programs, historic preservation
Period of collections: late 18th
century

Shaker Heritage Society
Albany-Shaker Rd., 12211
Telephone: (518) 456-7890
Private agency
Founded in: 1977
Phoebe Bender, President
Number of members: 175
Staff: part time 1, volunteer 4
Major programs: school programs
Period of collections: 19th century

**Temporary State Commission of
the Restoration of the Capitol**
P.O. Box 7016, Alfred E. Smith Office
Bldg., 12225
Telephone: (518) 473-0341
State agency
Founded in: 1979
Dennis McFadden,Director
Staff: full time 3, part time 1
Magazine: *Capitol Preservation News*
Major programs: historic site(s),
newsletters/pamphlets, historic
preservation, research, exhibits
Period of collections: late 19th
century

ALBION

Cobblestone Society Museum
14393 Ridge Rd., 14411
Telephone: (716) 589-9013/589-9510
Private agency, authorized by
Cobblestone Society
Founded in: 1964
C. W. Lattin, Museum Director
Number of members: 634
Staff: full time 1, volunteer 5
Magazine: *Cobblestoner*
Major programs: library, archives,
museum, markers,
tours/pilgrimages, junior history,
school programs, book publishing,
newsletters/pamphlets, historic
preservation, research, exhibits,
field services
Period of collections: 1800-1918

Orleans County Historical Association
13979 Allen Rd., 14411
Telephone: (716) 589-4690
County agency
Founded in: 1976
Woodrow A. Baker, President
Number of members: 104
Staff: volunteer 70
Major programs: historic site(s), oral history, book publishing, newsletters/pamphlets, exhibits, archaeology programs, genealogical services
Period of collections: from 1825

ALDEN

Alden Historical Society
13213 Broadway, 14004
Telephone: (716) 937-7606
Private agency, authorized by State Education Department
Founded in: 1965
Sally A. Wood, President
Number of members: 30
Staff: volunteer 5
Major programs: museum, markers, educational programs
Period of collections: 1865-present

ALEXANDRIA BAY

Alexandria Township Historical Society
Market St. 13607
Telephone: (315) 482-4586
Private agency, authorized by State Education Department
Founded in: 1974
Doris Langlois, President
Number of members: 225
Staff: part time 2, volunteer 15
Major programs: museum, historic site(s), oral history, newsletters/pamphlets, historic preservation, exhibits, living history
Period of collections: 1866-1929

ALFRED

Alfred Historical Society
Mail to: P.O. Box 1137, 14802
Telephone: (607) 587-8886
Questionnaire not received

ALLEGANY

Allegany Area Historical Association
25 N. 2nd St.
Mail to: P.O. Box 162, 14706
Private agency, authorized by State Education Department
Founded in: 1982
Mrs. Robert G. Potter, President
Number of members: 175
Staff: volunteer 25
Major programs: museum, newsletters/pamphlets, photographic collections, genealogical services
Period of collections: 1900-1940

ALMOND

Almond Historical Society, Inc.
1830 Magadorn House, 11 N. Main St., 14804
Telephone: (607) 276-6166

Private agency
Founded in: 1965
Linn L. Phelan, President
Number of members: 735
Staff: volunteer 30
Major programs: library, archives, museum, historic site(s), school programs, newsletters/pamphlets, exhibits, living history, photographic collections, genealogical services, renovation program, local costumes and maps
Period of collections: 1800-present

AMITYVILLE

Amityville Historical Society
170 Broadway
Telephone: (516) 598-1486
Mail to: P.O. Box 764, 11701
Founded in: 1969
Ethel Macgill, President
Number of members: 1,015
Staff: part time 1, volunteer 125
Major programs: library, archives, museum, historic sites preservation, tours/pilgrimages, educational programs, newsletters/pamphlets
Period of collections: 1865-present

AMSTERDAM

Walter Elwood Museum
300 Guy Park Ave., 12010
Telephone: (518) 843-3180, ext. 445
Authorized by Greater Amsterdam School District and Mohawk Valley Heritage Association
Founded in: 1940
Mary Margaret Gage, Curator
Number of members: 350
Staff: volunteer 6
Major programs: library, archives, museum, tours/pilgrimages, school programs, newsletters/pamphlets, research, exhibits, audiovisual programs, photographic collections, art gallery
Period of collections: 1600-1900s

ANDES

Andes Society for History and Culture
Main St., 13731
Private agency
Founded in: 1975
James Andrews, President
Number of members: 246
Staff: volunteer 7
Magazine: *Hunting House News*
Major programs: museum, historic site(s), school programs, newsletters/pamphlets, historic preservation, photographic collections
Period of collections: 1840-1920

ANGOLA

Town of Evans Historical Society
Rt. 5, 14006
Town agency
Founded in: 1965
Jack Ehmhe, President
Number of members: 80
Staff: volunteer 10
Major programs: museum
Period of collections: 1865-1940

ANNANDALE-ON-HUDSON

Hudson Valley Studies
Bard College, 12504
Telephone: (914) 758-6971
Private agency, authorized by Bard College Center
Founded in: 1976
Richard C. Wiles, Director/Professor of Economics
Magazine: *Hudson Valley Regional Review*
Major programs: newsletters/pamphlets, research, exhibits

ARCADE

Arcade Historical Society
365 W. Main St., 14009
Telephone: (716) 492-4542
Founded in: 1970
Questionnaire not received

ARKVILLE

Catskill Regional Folklife Program/Erpf Catskill Cultural Center, Inc.
Rt. 28, 12406
Telephone: (914) 586-3326
Private agency
Founded in: 1974
Whitty Sanford, Executive Director
Number of members: 380
Staff: full time 1, part time 2, volunteer 15
Major programs: archives, oral history, newsletters/pamphlets, historic preservation, exhibits, living history, photographic collections, field services, folklife programs, visual and performing arts programs
Period of collections: 19th-20th centuries

ARMONK

North Castle Historical Society
440 Bedford Rd., 10504
Telephone: (914) 273-9773
Private agency
Founded in: 1971
Guy H. Papale, President
Number of members: 500
Staff: volunteer 50
Magazine: *North Castle History*
Major programs: library, museum, school programs, newsletters/pamphlets, historic preservation, exhibits, photographic collections
Period of collections: 19th century

AUBURN

Cayuga County Agricultural Museum
R.D. 1, Box 309, 13021
Telephone: (315) 252-7994
Founded in: 1974
Questionnaire not received

Cayuga County Historian
County Office Bldg., Genesee St., 13021
Telephone: (315) 253-1300
County agency
Founded in: 1969
Thomas G. Eldred, County Historian

Staff: full time 2, part time 2, volunteer 3
Major programs: library, markers, junior history, school programs, newsletters/pamphlets, research, exhibits, photographic collections, genealogical services
Period of collections: 1830-present

Cayuga County Historical Society
203 Genesee St., 13021
Telephone: (315) 253-8051
Founded in: 1876
Walter K. Long, President
Major programs: museum, historic sites preservation, markers, historic preservation

Cayuga Museum of History and Art
203 Genesee St., 13021
Telephone: (315) 253-8051
Founded in: 1936
Walter K. Long, Director
Number of members: 1,000
Staff: full time 4, part time 1, volunteer 4
Major programs: museum, markers, tours, educational programs
Period of collections: 1865-1918

Foundation Historical Association, Inc.
33 South St., 13021
Telephone: (315) 252-1283
Founded in: 1951
Betty Mae Lewis, Curator
Staff: full time 4, part time 2
Major programs: library, archives, museum, historic site(s), junior history, school programs, historic preservation, exhibits, photographic collections, genealogical services
Period of collections: 1860s

Owasco Stockaded Indian Village
Emerson Park
Telephone: (315) 252-9635
Mail to: 203 Genesee St., 13021
Quustionnaire not received

Schweinfurth Art Center
205 Genesee St.
Telephone: (315) 255-1553
Mail to: P.O. Box 916, 13021
Private agency
Founded in: 1976
H. Tunis, Director
Number of members: 250
Staff: full time 3, part time 2, volunteer 24
Major programs: museum, newsletters/pamphlets, historic preservation, exhibits, outreach education, arts and architecture
Period of collections: 1900-present

AVERILL PARK

Sand Lake Historical Society
Telephone: (518) 674-3127
Mail to: P.O. Box 492, W. Sand Lake, 12196
Founded in: 1974
L. Ross French, President
Number of members: 150
Staff: volunteer 12
Magazine: *Historical Highlights*
Major programs: library, historic site(s), tours/pilgrimages, junior history, oral history, school

programs, book publishing, newsletters/pamphlets, historic preservation, audiovisual programs
Period of collections: early 1700s-present

BABYLON

Long Island-Sunrise Trail Chapter, National Railway Historical Society
75 Parkwood Rd., 11795
Telephone: (516) 587-9841
Founded in: 1965
Questionnaire not received

BALDWIN

Baldwin Historical Society Inc. and Museum
1980 Grand Ave., 11510
Telephone: (516) 223-6900
Private agency
Founded in: 1972
Glenn F. Sitterly, Curator
Number of members: 250
Staff: volunteer 25
Major programs: archives, museum, oral history, school programs, book publishing, newsletters/pamphlets, research, exhibits, photographic collections
Period of collections: late 19th-early 20th centuries

BALLSTON SPA

National Bottle Museum
20 Church Ave., Rt. 50 and 67
Telephone: (518) 885-7589
Mail to: P.O. Box 621, 12020
Private agency
Founded in: 1979
Marilyn Stephenson, President
Major programs: library, museum, educational programs
Period of collections: 1783-1918

Saratoga County Historical Society
Brookside, 12020
Telephone: (518) 885-4000
Private agency
Founded in: 1962
Field Horne, Executive Director
Number of members: 562
Staff: full time 2, part time 2
Magazine: *The Grist Mill*
Major programs: library, manuscripts, museum, oral history, school programs, book publishing, research, living history, audiovisual programs, photographic collections
Period of collections: 1860-1940

BATAVIA

Holland Purchase Historical Society
131 W. Main St., 14020
Telephone: (716) 343-4727
County agency
Founded in: 1894
Rosalind Hayes, Curator
Number of members: 500
Staff: part time 2, volunteer 15
Major programs: library, archives, manuscripts, museum, tours/pilgrimages, school programs, genealogical services
Period of collections: 1865-1918

BATH

Bath Historic Committee
Cameron St.
Mail to: 5 Ellis Ave., 14810
Town agency
Founded in: 1960
Nancy V. Sprague, Chair
Staff: volunteer 7
Major programs: manuscripts, museum, historic site(s), oral history, school programs, historic preservation, research, exhibits, living history, audiovisual programs
Period of collections: 1850-present

Steuben County Historical Society
Telephone: (607) 583-4439
Mail to: P.O. Box 349, 14810
Founded in: 1958
John A. Roy, President
Number of members: 65
Staff: volunteer 12
Magazine: *Steuben Echoes*
Major programs: library, tours/pilgrimages, books
Period of collections: 1865-1918

BAYPORT

Bayport Heritage Association
P.O. Box 4, 11705
Telephone: (516) 472-4625
Private agency, authorized by State Department of Education
Founded in: 1983
Donald H. Weinhardt, President
Number of members: 231
Staff: volunteer 50
Magazine: *Heritage*
Major programs: library, museum, historic site(s), newsletters/pamphlets, research, exhibits, audiovisual programs, photographic collections
Period of collections: 1850-present

BAY SHORE

Sagtikos Manor Historical Society
Montauk Hwy.
Telephone: (516) 665-0093
Mail to: P.O. Box 344, 11706
Founded in: 1961
Questionnaire not received

BAYSIDE, L.I.

Bayside Historical Society
Telephone: (212) 224-5707
Mail to: P.O. Box 133, 11361
Founded in: 1964
Number of members: 300
Staff: volunteer 40
Major programs: archives, historic sites preservation, oral history, educational programs
Period of collections: 1635-present

BAYVILLE

Bayville Historical Museum
34 School St., 11709
Telephone: (516) 628-1720, 628-8975
Founded in: 1971
Questionnaire not received

BEACON

Beacon Historical Society
P.O. Box 89, 12508
Founded in: 1976
Questionnaire not received

Howland Center for Cultural Exchange
471 Main St.
Telephone: (914) 831-4988
Mail to: P.O. Box 606, 12508-0606
Private agency
Founded in: 1977
Nilufer Ozizmir, Program Director
Number of members: 75
Staff: volunteer 20
Major programs: museum, historic site(s), historic preservation, exhibits, Hispanic art and culture, performing arts and education

Madam Brett Homestead
50 Van Nydeck Ave., 12508
Telephone: (914) 831-6533
Private agency, authorized by Melzingah Chapter, Daughters of the American Revolution
Founded in: 1954
Mrs. Frank Ward, Regent
Number of members: 107
Staff: volunteer 30
Major programs: museum, historic site(s), tours/pilgrimages, historic preservation
Period of collections: pre-Revolutionary War-Victorian era

Mt. Gulian Society
145 Sterling St., 12508
Telephone: (914) 831-8172
Founded in: 1966
Barbara Peters, Director
Number of members: 152
Staff: full time 1, volunteer 8
Major programs: museum, educational programs, newsletters/pamphlets
Period of collections: 1730-1830

BEDFORD

Bedford Historical Society
Village Green
Telephone: (914) 234-9328
Mail to: P.O. Box 491, 10506
Private agency
Founded in: 1916
Molly C. Long, Director of Development
Number of members: 430
Staff: full time 1, part time 2, volunteer 8
Major programs: museum, historic site(s), historic preservation
Period of collections: early 1700s-1915

BELLMORE

Historical Society of the Bellmores
2717 Grand Ave., 11710
Telephone: (516) 826-0333
Private agency
Founded in: 1974
Trudi Cowan, President
Number of members: 100
Staff: volunteer 10
Major programs: archives, school programs, research, exhibits, photographic collections
Period of collections: 1890-present

BELLPORT

Bellport-Brookhaven Historical Society
31 Bellport Lane, 11713
Telephone: (516) 286-8773
Founded in: 1960
Robert H. Pelletreau, President
Number of members: 438
Staff: volunteer 25
Major programs: archives, manuscripts, museum, historic site(s), tours/pilgrimages, historic preservation, photographic collections
Period of collections: 1783-1918

BELMONT

Allegany County Department of History
Courthouse, Court St., 14813
Telephone: (716) 268-7612
Founded in: 1894
Questionnaire not received

Allegany County Historical Society
20 Willets Ave., 14813
Telephone: (716) 268-7428
Private agency
Founded in: 1970
William Greene, Director
Number of members: 20
Magazine: Ye Olde Alleganian
Major programs: historic site(s), markers, tours/pilgrimages, oral history, book publishing, newsletters/pamphlets, historic preservation, research, exhibits, archaeology programs, genealogical services
Period of collections: 1800-1900

American Manse, Whitney-Halsey Home
39 South St., 14813
Telephone: (716) 268-5130
Private agency
Founded in: 1964
Ruth L. Gankus, Director
Major programs: museum, historic site(s), book publishing, historic preservation, research, exhibits, living history, archaeology programs, genealogical services
Period of collections: Victorian era

BERGEN

Bergen Historical Society
7547 S. Lake Rd., 14416
Telephone: (716) 494-1511
Mail to: 6833 Pocock Rd.
Private agency
Founded in: 1979
Sharon Pocock, President
Number of members: 30
Staff: volunteer 12
Major programs: museum, educational programs
Period of collections: 1865-1940

BERNE

Town of Berne Historical Society
Historical Center, Main St.
Mail to: P.O. Box 22, 12023
Founded in: 1970
Questionnaire not received

BIG FLATS

Big Flats Historical Society
Main St.
Telephone: (607) 562-3101
Mail to: P.O. Box 106, 14814
Founded in: 1970
Questionnaire not received

BINGHAMTON

Broome County Historical Society
Roberson Center, 30 Front St., 13905
Telephone: (607) 772-0660
County agency
Founded in: 1919
Ross McGuire, Curator of History
Number of members: 225
Staff: full time 1, part time 3, volunteer 8
Magazine: Broome County Historical Society Bulletin
Major programs: library, archives, manuscripts, museum, newsletters/pamphlets, photographic collections
Period of collections: 19th-20th century

SUNY-Binghamton, University Art Gallery
c/o Fine Arts Bldg., Vestal Parkway, 13901
Telephone: (607) 798-2634
State agency
Founded in: 1968
Josephine Gear, Director
Staff: full time 2, part time 2, volunteer 6
Major programs: archives, museum, book publishing, newsletters/pamphlets, historic preservation, records management, research, exhibits, photographic collections, fine arts
Period of collections: 20th century

BLUE MOUNTAIN LAKE

Adirondack Museum/Adirondack Historical Association
12812
Telephone: (518) 352-7311
Private agency
Founded in: 1952
Craig Gilborn, Director
Staff: full time 15, part time 40
Major programs: library, archives, manuscripts, museum, historic site(s), school programs, book publishing, research, exhibits, audiovisual programs, photographic collections
Period of collections: 1820-1950

BRASIE CORNERS

Macomb Historical Association
Rt. 3, Hammond, 13646
Telephone: (315) 578-2349
Founded in: 1964
Questionnaire not received

BREWERTON

Ft. Brewerton Historical Society
13029
Telephone: (315) 676-7804
Questionnaire not received

BREWSTER

Landmarks Preservation Society of Southeast
Oak St., 10509
Telephone: (914) 279-6576
Private agency
Founded in: 1969
Eleanor B. Fitchen, President
Number of members: 284
Major programs: library, archives, historic site(s), markers, tours/pilgrimages, school programs, book publishing, newsletters/pamphlets, historic preservation, photographic collections
Period of collections: 18th-19th centuries

Southeast Museum Association, Inc.
Main St.
Telephone: (914) 279-7500
Mail to: P.O. Box 88, 10509
Founded in: 1962
Patricia A. Baker, Administrative Manager
Number of members: 205
Staff: part time 3, volunteer 45
Major programs: museum, research, exhibits, genealogical services
Period of collections: 1870-1910

BRIDGEHAMPTON

Bridgehampton Historical Society
Montauk Hwy., 11932
Telephone: (516) 537-1088
Founded in: 1956
Questionnaire not received

BROCKPORT

Western Monroe Historical Society
151 S. Main St., 14420
Telephone: (716) 637-3645
Private agency
Founded in: 1965
Eunice Chesnut, Historian/Program Director
Number of members: 413
Staff: part time 2, volunteer 63
Major programs: museum, junior history, oral history, educational programs, newsletters/pamphlets, historic preservation
Period of collections: 1850-1900

BRONX

Bronx County Historical Society
3309 Bainbridge Ave., 10467
Telephone: (212) 881-8900
Private agency
Founded in: 1955
Gary D. Hermalyn, Executive Director
Number of members: 900
Staff: full time 9, part time 12, volunteer 10
Magazine: *The Bronx Historian/The Bronx County Historical Society Journal*
Major programs: library, archives, manuscripts, museum, historic site(s), markers, tours/pilgrimages, junior history, oral history, school programs, book publishing, newsletters/pamphlets, historic preservation, records

management, research, exhibits, audiovisual programs, photographic collections, genealogical services, field services
Period of collections: late 17th century

City History Club of New York
2516 Poplar St., 10461
Private agency
Founded in: 1897
Edith McGinnis, President
Number of members: 28
Staff: full time 1, volunteer 18
Major programs: library, junior history, oral history, educational programs, exhibits

Huntington Free Library and Reading Room
Museum of the American Indian, 9 Westchester Square 10461
Telephone: (212) 829-7770
Founded in: 1892
Questionnaire not received

BROOKLYN

Antique Phonograph and Record Society
650 Ocean Ave., 11226
Telephone: (212) 941-6835
Founded in: 1968
Questionnaire not received

Brooklyn Historic Railway Association
599 E. 7th St., 11218
Telephone: (718) 941-3160
Private agency
Founded in: 1982
Robert Diamond, President
Number of members: 56
Staff: part time 1, volunteer 15
Magazine: *Historic Railway News*
Major programs: museum, historic site(s), newsletters/pamphlets, historic preservation, research, exhibits, audiovisual programs, archaeology programs, photographic collections, field services
Period of collections: 1830-1880

Flatbush Historical Society
P.O. Box N-314, 2255 Church Ave., 11226
Telephone: (718) 856-3700
Private agency
Founded in: 1976
Irving Choban, President
Number of members: 120
Staff: volunteer 6
Major programs: library, historic site(s), tours/pilgrimages, school programs, historic preservation, exhibits, photographic collections
Period of collections: 1776-present

Ft. Hamilton Historical Society
Ft. Hamilton, 11252
Telephone: (718) 630-4349
Private agency
Founded in: 1979
Joseph Tedeschi, President
Number of members: 400
Staff: volunteer 5
Magazine: *The Caponier*
Major programs: museum, markers, tours, school programs,

newsletters/pamphlets, historic preservation, research
Period of collections: 1800-1970

James A. Kelly Institute for Local Historical Studies
St. Francis College, 180 Remsen St., 11201
Telephone: (212) 522-2300
Founded in: 1956
Questionnaire not received

Kingsborough Historical Society
2001 Oriental Blvd., 11235
Telephone: (212) 934-3122
Founded in: 1972
Questionnaire not received

Long Island Historical Society
128 Pierrepont St., 11201
Telephone: (718) 624-0890
Founded in: 1863
David M. Kahn, Executive Director
Number of members: 1,100
Staff: full time 10, part time 8, volunteer 15
Major programs: library, archives, oral history, school programs, newsletters, research, exhibits, photographic collections, genealogical services, newspapers, maps, prints, paintings
Period of collections: 17th century-present

Museum of the Borough of Brooklyn at Brooklyn College
Bedford Ave. and Ave. H, 11210
Telephone: (718) 780-5152
City agency, authorized by City University of New York
Founded in: 1981
Shelly Mehlman Dinhofer, Director
Staff: full time 2, part time 7, volunteer 2
Major programs: museum, school programs, newsletters/pamphlets, exhibits, audiovisual programs, visual and cultural history

National Maritime Historical Society
2 Fulton St., 11201
Telephone: (212) 858-1348
Founded in: 1963
Questionnaire not received

Prospect Park South Association
c/o Board Director, 196 Marlborough Rd., 11226
Telephone: (718) 282-3141
Private agency
Founded in: 1900
Mary Kay Gallagher, Board Director
Number of members: 165
Staff: volunteer 10
Major programs: historic site(s), markers, tours/pilgrimages, junior history, oral history, newsletters/pamphlets, historic preservation, photographic collections
Period of collections: 1900

Society for the Preservation of Weeksville and Bedford-Stuyvestant History/The Weeksville Society
1698 Bergen St.
Telephone: (718) 756-5250

Mail to: P.O. Box 120, St. Johns
Station, 11213
Private agency, authorized by State
Education Department
Founded in: 1971
Joan Maynard, Executive Director
Number of members: 450
Staff: full time 5, part time 2
Major programs: historic site(s),
historic preservation
Period of collections: 1830-1900

BROOKTONDALE

**Historical Association of Caroline
Township, Inc.**
76 Boad, 14817
Telephone: (607) 539-6129
Founded in: 1973
Questionnaire not received

BROWNVILLE

**General Jacob Brown Historical
Society**
Bronn Mansion, 216 Brown Blvd.,
13615
Founded in: 1978
Questionnaire not received

BUFFALO

**Buffalo and Erie County Historical
Society**
25 Nottingham Court, 14216
Telephone: (716) 873-9644
Private agency
Founded in: 1862
G. Rollie Adams, Executive Director
Number of members: 1,200
Staff: full time 15, part time 3,
volunteer 30
Major programs: library, archives,
manuscripts, museum, school
programs, newsletters/pamphlets,
historic preservation, research,
exhibits, audiovisual programs,
photographic collections
Period of collections: 1800

**Landmark Society of the Niagara
Frontier**
25 Nottingham Court, 14216
Telephone: (716) 873-9644
Founded in: 1968
Questionnaire not received

**Theodore Roosevelt Inaugural
National Historic Site**
641 Delaware Ave., 14202
Telephone: (716) 884-0095
Federal agency, authorized by
Theodore Roosevelt Inaugural Site
Foundation and National Park
Service
Founded in: 1968
Barbara B. Brandt, Site
Superintendent
Number of members: 234
Staff: full time 4, part time 6,
volunteer 200
Magazine: *Columns*
Major programs: historic site(s),
tours/pilgrimages, junior history,
school programs,
newsletters/pamphlets, historic
preservation, research, exhibits,
audiovisual programs
Period of collections: 1900

BYRON

Byron Historical Society
14422
Founded in: 1967
Questionnaire not received

CALEDONIA

Big Springs Historical Society
Main St., 14423
Telephone: (716) 538-4473
Mail to: 1067 Main St., Mumford,
14511
Founded in: 1936
Questionnaire not received

CALLICOON

Upper Delaware Heritage Alliance
P.O. Box 143, 12723 (secretary)
Telephone: (717) 685-4871
Mail to: R.D. 1, Box 480, Honesdale,
PA, 18431 (editor)
Private agency
Founded in: 1981
Bert Feldman, President
Number of members: 62
Magazine: *Upper Delaware Heritage
Alliance*
Major programs: historic preservation

CAMBRIDGE

Cambridge Historical Society, Inc.
12 Broad St., 12816
Founded in: 1929
Questionnaire not received

CAMDEN

**Queen Village Historical
Society/Carriage House Museum**
2 N. Park St.
Mail to: P.O. Box 38, 13316
Questionnaire not received

CAMILLUS

Camillus Historical Society
5420 W. Genesee St., 13031
Questionnaire not received

CAMPBELL HALL

Hill-Hold
Telephone: (914) 294-7661
Mail to: Rt. 416, Box 299, 10916
ounty agency, authorized by
Department of Parks, Recreation
and Conservation
Robert C. Eurich, Museum Curator
Staff: full time 2, part time 2,
volunteer 10
Major programs: museum, historic
sites preservation, educational
programs
Period of collections: 1830s

CANAJOHARIC

Canajoharic Library and Art Gallery
Eric Blvd., 13317
Telephone: (518) 673-2314
Private agency
Founded in: 1915
Marie Moore, Director
Staff: full time 1, part time 7
Major programs: library, archives,
exhibits, genealogical services, art
gallery
Period of collections: late
1800s-present

CANANDAIGUA

Granger Homestead Society
295 N. Main St., 14424
Telephone: (716) 394-1472
Private agency
Founded in: 1946
Mrs. John E. Miller, Board President
Number of members: 525
Staff: full time 3, part time 4,
volunteer 53
Major programs: museum, historic
site(s), tours/pilgrimages, oral
history, school programs,
newsletters/pamphlets, historic
preservation, records
management, research, exhibits,
audiovisual programs
Period of collections: 1816-1930

Ontario County Historical Society
55 N. Main St., 14424
Telephone: (716) 394-4975
Private agency
Founded in: 1902
Donald Muller, Director
Number of members: 600
Staff: full time 3, part time 2,
volunteer 50
Major programs: library, manuscripts,
museum, school programs, book
publishing, newsletters/pamphlets,
historic preservation, exhibits,
audiovisual programs,
photographic collections
Period of collections: 1700-present

Sonnenberg Gardens and Mansion
151 Charlotte St.
Telephone: (716) 394-4922
Mail to: P.O. Box 663, 14424
Private agency
Founded in: 1973
Mary Ann Bell, Director
Number of members: 700
Staff: full time 8, part time 45,
volunteer 200
Major programs: museum, historic
site(s), markers, exhibits,
arboretum, botanical gardens
Period of collections: 1887-1923

CANASTOTA

**Canastota Canal Town
Corporation/Canal Town
Museum**
N. Canal St., 13032
Telephone: (315) 697-3451
Private agency
Founded in: 1968
Stephen Cimino, President
Number of members: 125
Staff: volunteer 12
Major programs: museum, historic
sites preservation, educational
programs, books, exhibits
Period of collections: 1783-1865

CANTON

**North Country Reference and
Research Resources Council**
P.O. Box 568, 13617
Telephone: (315) 386-4560
Founded in: 1965
Questionnaire not received

**St. Lawrence County Historical
Association**
3 E. Main

Telephone: (315) 386-2780
Mail to: P.O. Box 8, 13617
Private agency
Founded in: 1947
John A. Baule, Director
Number of members: 1,200
Staff: full time 2
Major programs: library, archives, manuscripts, museum, historic sites preservation, tours/pilgrimages, educational programs, books, newsletters/pamphlets
Period of collections: 1783-1918

St. Lawrence County History Center
3 E. Main St.
Telephone: (315) 386-8118
Mail to: P.O. Box 43, 13617
Questionnaire not received

CAPE VINCENT

Cape Vincent Historical Museum
Market St.
Telephone: (315) 654-3126
Mail to: P.O. Box 223, James St., 13618
Authorized by Cape Vincent Village Board
Founded in: 1969
Dorothy B. Allen, President
Staff: volunteer 10
Major programs: archives, museum, historic preservation, records management, exhibits, photographic collections, genealogical services
Period of collections: late 19th-early 20th centuries

CARMEL

Kent Historical Society
P.O. Box 123, 10512
Telephone: (9l4) 878-6218
Founded in: 1977
Questionnaire not received

CARTHAGE

4 River Valleys Historical Society
P.O. Box 504, 13619
Telephone: (315) 773-5133
Private agency
Founded in: 1977
Nelson Eddy, President
Number of members: 400
Staff: volunteer 45
Magazine: *4 Rivers Journal*
Major programs: markers, tours/pilgrimages, junior history, oral history, book publishing, newsletters/pamphlets, historic preservation, research, exhibits, photographic collections, genealogical services, heritage room of library
Period of collections: from 1800

CASTILE

Castile Historical Society
17 E. Park Rd., 14427
Telephone: (716) 493-5370
Town agency
Founded in: 1953
Lucy Breslin, President
Number of members: 200

Staff: full time 1, part time 1
Major programs: manuscripts, museum, school programs, research, exhibits, genealogical services
Period of collections: 1850-1975

Letchworth State Park Pioneer and Indian Museum
14427
Telephone: (716) 493-2611
State agency
Founded in: 1913
Thomas A. Breslin, Park Manager
Staff: part time 2
Major programs: library, archives, museum, historic site(s), tours/pilgrimages, historic preservation, exhibits, audiovisual programs, photographic collections
Period of collections: 1820-1937

CASTLETON-ON-HUDSON

Historical Society of Esquatak
12033
Telephone: (518) 732-2626
Founded in: 1971
Questionnaire not received

CATSKILL

Thomas Cole Foundation
218 Spring St., 12414
Telephone: (518) 943-6533
Private agency
Founded in: 1982
Donelson Hoopes, Director
Staff: full time 1
Major programs: historic site(s), historic preservation, exhibits, photographic collections
Period of collections: early 19th century

CATTARAUGUS

Cattaraugus Area Historical Society
23 Main St.
Telephone: (716) 257-9012
Mail to: Lover's Lane Rd., 14719
Town and city agency
Founded in: 1955
Kenneth Kysor, President
Number of members: 50
Staff: volunteer 2
Major programs: archives, manuscripts, museum, exhibits, photographic collections, genealogical services
Period of collections: 19th-20th centuries

CAZENOVIA

Lorenzo State Historic Site
Ledyard Ave., 13035
Telephone: (315) 655-3200
State agency, authorized by Office of Parks, Recreation and Historic Preservation
Founded in: 1969
Russell A. Grills, Historic Site Manager
Staff: full time 6, part time 5, volunteer 35
Major programs: archives, manuscripts, historic site(s), book

publishing, newsletters/pamphlets, photographic collections
Period of collections: 1800-1875

CEDAR SWAMP

Cedar Swamp Historical Society
11545
Telephone: (516) 671-6156
State agency, authorized by State Department of Education
Founded in: 1976
John G. Peterkin, Founder/President
Number of members: 200
Staff: volunteer 12
Major programs: archives, historic site(s), markers, tours/pilgrimages, junior history, oral history, school programs, newsletters/pamphlets, historic preservation, research, exhibits, living history, audiovisual programs, archaeology programs, photographic collections, genealogical services, field services
Period of collections: 1609-1790

CENTER MORICHES

Moriches Bay Historical Society
Montauk Hwy.
Telephone: (516) 878-1776
Mail to: P.O. Box 31, 11934
L. Reeve, President
Number of members: 250
Staff: volunteer 50
Magazine: *Moriches Bay Historical Society News Letter*
Major programs: library, museum, oral history, historic preservation
Period of collections: 1900-1950

CHAPPAQUA

New Castle Historical Society
200 S. Greeley Ave.
Telephone: (914) 238-4771, ext. 53
Mail to: P.O. Box 55, 10514
Founded in: 1966
Richard R. Reynolds, President
Number of members: 460
Staff: full time 1, volunteer 30
Major programs: museum, historic sites preservation, markers, tours/pilgrimages, oral history, educational programs, books
Period of collections: 1783-present

CHARLESTON

Charleston Historical Society
R.D. 1, Box 713, Esperance, 12066
Telephone: (518) 875-6533
Private agency
Founded in: 1978
Edythe J. Meserand, Board Chair
Number of members: 201
Staff: volunteer 10
Period of collections: 1700s-1800s

CHEEKTOWAGA

Erie County Historical Federation
11 Danforth St., 14227
Telephone: (716) 683-2269
Founded in: 1952
Julia Boyer Reinstein, President
Number of members: 150
Staff: volunteer 4
Magazine: *Federation Newsletter*

Major programs: tours/pilgrimages, educational programs, newsletters/pamphlets

CHERRY VALLEY

Cherry Valley Historical Association
Main St., 13320
Telephone: (607) 264-3303/264-3318
Private agency
Founded in: 1957
James Johnson, President
Number of members: 200
Staff: volunteer 50
Major programs: museum, historic site(s), exhibits, genealogical services
Period of collections: 1783-1900

CHESTERTOWN

Historical Society of the Town of Chester, Inc.
S. Canada Dr., 12817
Telephone: (518) 494-2711
Questionnaire not received

CHURCHVILLE

Chili Historical Society
1365 Paul Rd., 14428
Telephone: (716) 889-2823
Private agency
Founded in: 1964
Edward G. Cornwell, Jr., President
Number of members: 110
Staff: volunteer 10
Major programs: archives, manuscripts, newsletters/pamphlets, historic preservation, exhibits, photographic collections, genealogical services
Period of collections: 19th-early 20th centuries

CINCINNATUS

Cincinnatus Area Heritage Society
Telephone: (607) 863-4334
Mail to: P.O. Box 373, 13040
Private agency, authorized by State Education Department
Founded in: 1978
Larry McFarland, President
Number of members: 110
Major programs: archives, historic site(s), school programs, newsletters/pamphlets, exhibits, photographic collections, education and cultural programs
Period of collections: 1900-present

CLAY

Clay Historical Association
4591 Ver Plank Rd., 13041
Telephone: (315) 652-3288
Founded in: 1974
Questionnaire not received

CLAYTON

Clayton Thousand Islands Area Historical Society
403 Riverside Dr., 13624
Telephone: (315) 686-5794
Questionnaire not received

Thousand Islands Craft School and Textile Museum
314 John St., 13624
Telephone: (315) 686-4123
Private agency
Founded in: 1966
Jane Gillett, Director
Number of members: 210
Staff: full time 2, part time 25, volunteer 20
Major programs: library, archives, museum, exhibits, folk arts
Period of collections: 19th-20th centuries

Thousand Islands Shipyard Museum
750 Mary St., 13624
Telephone: (315) 686-4104
Private agency, authorized by University of the State of New York
Founded in: 1964
F. I. Collins, Jr., Director
Number of members: 900
Staff: full time 8, part time 2, volunteer 4
Magazine: *The Gazette*
Major programs: library, museum, tours/pilgrimages, educational programs, newsletters/pamphlets, historic preservation
Period of collections: 1800s-present

CLINTON

Clinton Historical Society, Inc.
2nd Floor, Kirkland Town Library
Mail to: P.O. Box 42, 13323
Founded in: 1962
Clarence E. Aldridge, President
Number of members: 410
Staff: volunteer 10
Major programs: archives, historic sites preservation, markers, tours/pilgrimages, newsletters/pamphlets, historic preservation
Period of collections: 1783-present

CLYDE

Galen Historical Society
P.O. Box 43, 14433
Private agency
Founded in: 1975
Arthur Benning, President
Major programs: museum, newsletters/pamphlets, exhibits
Period of collections: 1850-1950

CLYMER

French Creek Historical Society, Inc.
R.D. 2, French Creek, 14724
Telephone: (716) 355-4101
Founded in: 1976
Questionnaire not received

COBLESKILL

Town of Cobleskill Historical Society
Union St. Public Library, 12043
Founded in: 1974
Questionnaire not received

COHOCTON

Cohocton Historical Society
6 Maple Ave.

Telephone: (716) 384-5572/384-5188
Mail to: P.O. Box 177, 14826
Town agency
Founded in: 1973
Ruth Sprague, President
Number of members: 200
Staff: volunteer 30
Magazine: *The Cohocton Journal*
Major programs: archives, newsletters/pamphlets, exhibits, photographic collections, genealogical services
Period of collections: 1800-present

COLD SPRING

Historical Preservation Projects, Inc.
77 Main St.
Telephone: (914) 265-3060
Mail to: P.O. Box 114, 10516
Founded in: 1976
Questionnaire not received

Putnam County Historical Society
63 Chestnut St., 10516
Telephone: (914) 265-4010
Private agency
Founded in: 1906
Stephen G. Tomann, Curator
Number of members: 300
Staff: volunteer 20
Major programs: library, archives, manuscripts, museum, markers, junior history, oral history, educational programs, newsletters/pamphlets, photographic collections, genealogical services
Period of collections: 1783-present

CONKLIN

Conklin Historical Society
R.D. 2, Box 55, Ketchum Rd., 13748
Founded in: 1979
Questionnaire not received

CONSTABLEVILLE

Constable Hall Association
John St., 13325
Telephone: (315) 397-2323
Private agency
Founded in: 1949
Avis Graves, President
Number of members: 1,000
Staff: full time 1, part time 5, volunteer 50
Major programs: historic site(s), school programs, newsletters/pamphlets, exhibits
Period of collections: 19th century

COOPERSTOWN

Art Conservation Department, State University College at Buffalo
Lake Rd.
Telephone: (607) 547-8768
Mail to: P.O. Box 71, 13326
State agency, authorized by the university
Founded in: 1970
F. Christopher Tahk, Director
Staff: full time 6
Major programs: art conservation training

Farmers Museum, Inc.
P.O. Box 800, Lake Rd., 13326
Telephone: (607) 547-2593
Private agency
Founded in: 1943
Daniel R. Porter III, Director
Staff: full time 14, part time 23
Major programs: museum, school
programs, exhibits, living history
Period of collections: 19th century

**National Baseball Hall of Fame and
Museum, Inc.**
Main St., 13326
Telephone: (607) 547-9988
Founded in: 1936
Howard C. Talbot, Jr., Director
Staff: full time 20, part time 30
Magazine: *National Baseball Hall of
Fame and Museum Yearbook*
Major programs: library, museum,
tours/pilgrimages,
newsletters/pamphlets
Period of collections: late
1800s-present

◇**New York State Historical
Association**
Lake Rd. Rt. 80, 13326
Telephone: (607) 547-2533
Mail to: P.O. Box 800, 13326
Private agency
Founded in: 1899
Daniel R. Porter, Director
Number of members: 5,194
Staff: full time 45, part time 75,
volunteer 19
Magazine: *New York History and
Heritage*
Major programs: library, manuscripts,
museum, junior history, school
programs, book publishing,
newsletters/pamphlets, research,
exhibits, audiovisual programs,
photographic collections,
genealogical services
Period of collections: 19th century

**Town of Middlefield Historical
Association**
Mail to: P.O. Box 348, 13326
Private agency
Founded in: 1959
R. Wesley Graham, President
Number of members: 210
Staff: volunteer 30
Major programs: archives,
manuscripts, museum, school
programs, newsletters/pamphlets,
research, exhibits, photographic
collections, genealogical services
Period of collections: 1875-present

CORNING

Corning Museum of Glass
Corning Glass Center, 14831
Telephone: (607) 937-5371
Private agency
Founded in: 1951
Dwight P. Lanmon, Director
Staff: full time 31, part time 2
Magazine: *Journal of Glass Studies*
Major programs: library, archives,
manuscripts, museum,
tours/pilgrimages, junior history,
oral history, school programs, book
publishing, newsletters/pamphlets,
historic preservation, records

management, research, exhibits,
audiovisual programs, archaeology
programs, photographic
collections
Period of collections:
prehistoric-present

**Corning-Painted Post Historical
Society**
59 W. Pulteney St., 14830
Telephone: (607) 937-5281
Founded in: 1946
Phyllis Martin, Museum Director
Number of members: 286
Staff: full time 1, volunteer 10
Magazine: *Andaste Inquirer*
Major programs: museum, historic
site(s), school programs,
newsletters/pamphlets, historic
preservation, records
management, photographic
collections
Period of collections: 1796-1850

Market Street Restoration Agency
2 W. Market St., 14830
Telephone: (607) 937-5427
Founded in: 1974
Questionnaire not received

The Rockwell Museum
Baron Steuben Place, 14830
Telephone: (607) 937-5386
Founded in: 1976
Questionnaire not received

CORTLAND

Cortland County Historical Society
25 Homer Ave., 13045
Telephone: (607) 756-6071
Private agency
Founded in: 1925
Leslie O'Malley, Director
Number of members: 756
Staff: full time 2, part time 4,
volunteer 104
Magazine: *Roots and Branches*
Major programs: library, archives,
manuscripts, museum, school
programs, book publishing,
newsletters/pamphlets, research,
exhibits, photographic collections,
genealogical services, Period of
collections: 1798-present

The 1890 House
37 Tompkins St., 13045
Telephone: (607) 756-7551
Private agency
Founded in: 1975
Cathy Rosa Klimaszewski, Interim
Director
Number of members: 500
Staff: full time 4, part time 2,
volunteer 50
Magazine: *Whispers Near the
Inglenook*
Major programs: library, museum,
historic site(s), tours/pilgrimages,
school programs,
newsletters/pamphlets, historic
preservation, research, exhibits,
photographic collections
Period of collections: 1890-1910

COXACKIE

Greene County Historical Society
R.D. 12051
Telephone: (518) 731-6822

Founded in: 1929
Shelby Kriele, Curator
Number of members: 1,050
Staff: part time 4, volunteer 35
Magazine: *The Quarterly Journal*
Major programs: library, museum,
historic site(s),
newsletters/pamphlets,
genealogical services
Period of collections: 19th century

CROTON-ON-HUDSON

**Croton-on-Hudson Historical
Society**
171 Cleveland Dr.
Telephone: (914) 271-3663
Mail to: P.O. Box 215, 10520
Founded in: 1972
William A. Ryder, President
Number of members: 107
Staff: volunteer 4
Major programs: archives,
tours/pilgrimages, oral history,
book publishing,
newsletters/pamphlets, exhibits,
audiovisual programs, archaeology
programs, photographic
collections, genealogical services
Period of collections: 1783-present

CUDDEBACKVILLE

Neversink Valley Area Museum
Telephone: (914) 754-8870
Mail to: P.O. Box 263, 12729
Founded in: 1967
Charles R. Thomas,
Curator/Coordination
Number of members: 380
Staff: full time 1, part time 3
Major programs: museum, historic
site(s), oral history, historic
preservation, living history
Period of collections: 1800-1900

CUTCHOGUE

**Cutchogue-New Suffolk Historical
Council**
11935
Telephone: (516) 734-5900
Questionnaire not received

DANSVILLE

Dansville Area Historical Society
Church and W. Liberty Sts., 14437
Founded in: 1961
Questionnaire not received

DAVENPORT

Davenport Historical Society
Town Hall, Davenport Center, 13751
Town agency
Founded in: 1971
Mary S. Briggs, President
Number of members: 50
Major programs: school programs,
book publishing, research, exhibits
Period of collections: 1806-1900

DEANSBORO

The Musical Museum
13328
Telephone: (315) 841-8774
Private agency
Founded in: 1948
Arthur H. Sanders, Curator

Staff: full time 4, part time 1
Major programs: library, archives, manuscripts, museum, oral history, school prgrams, book publishing, newsletters/pamphlets, historic preservation, research, exhibits, audiovisual programs
Period of collections: 1840-1920

DELHI

Delaware County Historical Association
R.D. 2, 13753
Telephone: (607) 746-3849
Private agency
Founded in: 1945
Linda Norris, Director
Number of members: 550
Major programs: library, archives, manuscripts, museum, historic site(s), newsletters/pamphlets, records management, research, exhibits
Period of collections: 1800-1950

DEWITT

Canal Center/Erie Canal Museum
Cedar Bay Park, Kinne Rd., 13214
Telephone: (315) 471-0593
Mail to: 318 Erie Blvd., E, 13202
Private agency
Founded in: 1976
Vicki B. Ford, Director
Staff: part time 2
Major programs: historic site(s), historic preservation, exhibits
Period of collections: 20th century

DOBBS FERRY

Dobbs Ferry Historical Society
Library Bldg., 153 Main St., 10522
Telephone: (914) 693-7766
Private agency, authorized by State Education Department
Founded in: 1976
Tema G. Harnik, Director
Number of members: 380
Magazine: *The Ferryman*
Major programs: archives, tours/pilgrimages, junior history, oral history, school programs, newsletters/pamphlets, research, audiovisual programs, photographic collections, storefront history theater
Period of collections: 1880-present

DOLGEVILLE

Salisbury Historical Society
c/o Dorothea S. Ives, R.D. 1, 13329
Telephone: (315) 429-3330
Founded in: 1963
Number of members: 30
Staff: volunteer 6
Major programs: archives, manuscripts, historic site(s), markers, tours/pilgrimages, junior history, oral history, newsletters/pamphlets, historic preservation, exhibits, audiovisual programs, photographic collections, genealogical services
Period of collections: 1800-1960

EAST AURORA

Aurora Historical Society, Inc.
5 S. Grove St., 14052
Telephone: (716) 652-3280
Private agency
Founded in: 1951
Virginia Vidler, Town Historian
Number of members: 250
Staff: volunteer 8
Major programs: library, archives, manuscripts, museum, historic sites preservation, markers, tours/pilgrimages, oral history, educational programs, books, newsletters/pamphlets
Period of collections: 1865-present

EAST BLOOMFIELD

Historical Society of the Town of East Bloomfield, Inc.
South Ave., 14443
Founded in: 1969
Questionnaire not received

EASTCHESTER

Eastchester Historical Society
388 California Rd., Bronxville, 10708
Telephone: (914) 793-1900
Mail to: P.O. Box 37, 10709
Private agency
Founded in: 1958
Madeline Schaeffer, President
Number of members: 500
Major programs: library, archives, museum, junior history, school programs, research, photographic collections, genealogical services
Period of collections: 19th century

EAST DURHAM

Durham Center Museum, Inc.
Rt. 1457, 12423
Telephone: (518) 239-8461
Founded in: 1940
Questionnaire not received

EAST HAMPTON

East Hampton Historical Society
101 Main St., 11937
Telephone: (516) 324-6850
Private agency
Founded in: 1921
David A. Swickard, Director
Number of members: 675
Staff: full time 8, part time 1, volunteer 60
Major programs: museum, historic site(s), tours/pilgrimages, oral history, school programs, historic preservation, records management, research, exhibits, audiovisual programs, lectures, dramatic presentations
Period of collections: 1670-1940

Home Sweet Home Museum/John Howard Payne Boyhood Home
14 James Lane, 11937
Telephone: (516) 324-0713
Village agency
Founded in: 1928
Margaret H. Tarr, Historic Site Manager
Staff: part time 1

Major programs: museum, historic site(s), tours/pilgrimages, historic preservation, exhibits
Period of collections: 1750-1850

EAST MEREDITH

Hanford Mills Museum
13757
Telephone: (607) 278-5744
Private agency
Founded in: 1973
Jim Williams, Director
Number of members: 100
Staff: full time 5, part time 9
Major programs: archives, museum, historic site(s), historic preservation, living history, archaeology programs, industrial history and archaeology
Period of collections: 1870-1930

EAST SETAUKET

Three Village Historical Society
Telephone: (516) 928-9534
Mail to: P.O. Box 1776, 11733-0076
Private agency, authorized by State Education Department
Founded in: 1964
Ruth Regan, President
Number of members: 325
Staff: full time 1, volunteer 100
Magazine: *Three Village Historian*
Major programs: archives, manuscripts, historic site(s), markers, tours/pilgrimages, oral history, school programs, book publishing, newsletters/pamphlets, archaeology programs, photographic collections
Period of collections: 19th century

EDEN

Eden Historical Society
8837 S. Main St., 14057
Telephone: (716) 992-9141 (town historian)
Private agency, authorized by State Education Department
Founded in: 1966
William J. Morris, Jr., President
Number of members: 227
Staff: volunteer 20
Major programs: archives, historic site(s), genealogical services
Period of collections: 19th century

ELIZABETHTOWN

Essex County Historical Society
Court St., 12932
Telephone: (518) 873-6466
Private agency
Founded in: 1954
Miriam Wilson Richard, Director
Number of members: 300
Staff: full time 1, part time 4
Major programs: library, archives, manuscripts, museum, oral history, school programs, historic preservation, exhibits, audiovisual programs, photographic collections, genealogical services
Period of collections: 19th-20th centuries

ELLENVILLE

Ellenville Public Library and Museum
40 Center St., 12428
Telephone: (914) 647-5530
Authorized by University of the State of New York
Founded in: 1893
Marion M. Dumond, Library Director
Staff: part time 1
Major programs: library, museum, research, exhibits
Period of collections: 19th century-present

ELMA

Marilla Historical Society
1351 Jamison Rd., 14059
Telephone: (716) 652-5529
Private agency
Founded in: 1960
Warren H. Bleekman, President
Number of members: 35
Staff: volunteer 10
Major programs: museum
Period of collections: early 1900s-present

ELMIRA

Chemung County Historical Society, Inc.
415 E. Water St., 14091
Private agency
Founded in: 1923
Constance B. Barone, Director
Number of members: 1,300
Staff: full time 4, part time 4, volunteer 30
Magazine: *Chemung County Historical Journal*
Major programs: library, archives, manuscripts, museum, tours/pilgrimages, school programs, book publishing. newsletters/pamphlets, exhibits, photographic collections, genealogical services
Period of collections: 1870-1920

National Soaring Museum
Harris Hill, R.D. 3, 14903
Telephone: (607) 754-3128
Private agency
Founded in: 1972
Shirley Sliwa, Director
Number of members: 2,500
Staff: full time 4, part time 3, volunteer 10
Major programs: library, archives, manuscripts, museum, markers, oral history, school programs, newsletters/pamphlets, historic preservation, records management, research, exhibits, audiovisual programs, photographic collections, sailplane and glider collection
Period of collections: 1920-present

Underwater Archaeology Association
Gillett Hall, Elmira College, 14901
Telephone: (607) 733-2440
Mail to: 153 Oakwood Ave., Elmira Hts., 14903
Private agency
Founded in: 1970

Ronald W. Hynes, President
Number of members: 10
Staff: volunteer 10
Magazine: *Grid Marker*
Major programs: oral history, school programs, historic preservation, research, archaeology programs, field services, documentation of boats and steamers
Period of collections: 19th century

ELMIRA HEIGHTS

Elmira Heights Historical Society, Inc.
266 E. 14th St.
Telephone: (607) 734-7156
Mail to: 215 Elmwood Ave., 14903
Founded in: 1979
Ernest T. Gibbs, President
Number of members: 150
Magazine: *ECHO*
Major programs: library, archives, manuscripts, museum, historic sites, newsletters/pamphlets, historic preservation, exhibits
Period of collections: 1890s-1950s

ELMSFORD

◇**Lower Hudson Conference: Historical Agencies and Museums**
2199 Saw Mill River Rd., 10523
Telephone: (914) 592-6726
Authorized by State Education Department
Founded in: 1979
Ann Kiewel, Director
Number of members: 275
Staff: full time 1, part time 1, volunteer 1
Magazine: *Directory: Historical Agencies, Museums and Local Historians*
Major programs: newsletters/pamphlets, technical assistance workshops and consultants

ENDICOTT

Endicott Historical and Preservation Society
P.O. Box 52, 13760
Telephone: (607) 783-8373
Private agency
Founded in: 1968
James V. Fiori, President
Number of members: 31
Major programs: oral history, school programs
Period of collections: 1906-present

ESPERANCE

Esperance Historical Society and Museum
Church St.
Telephone: (518) 875-6417
Mail to: P.O. Box 99, 12066
Town agency
Founded in: 1970
Kenneth M. Jones, President
Number of members: 150
Staff: volunteer 17
Major programs: museum, tours/pilgrimages, exhibits, genealogical services,

newsletters/pamphlets, audiovisual programs, photographic collections
Period of collections: 1780-present

ESSEX

ECHO (Essex Community Heritage Organization, Inc.)
Main St., 12936
Telephone: (518) 963-7088
Private agency
Founded in: 1969
Robert J. Hammerslag, Executive Director
Number of members: 200
Staff: full time 2, part time 1, volunteer 12
Major programs: newsletters/pamphlets, historic preservation
Period of collections: 1765-present

FAIR HAVEN

Sterling Historical Society
Rt. 104-A, Sterling Center, 13064
Telephone: (716) 947-5257
Questionnaire not received

FAIRPORT

Perinton Historical Society
18 Perrin St., 14450
Founded in: 1935
Questionnaire not received

FARMINGDALE

Farmingdale-Bethpage Historical Society
P.O. Box 500, 11735
Founded in: 1964
Questionnaire not received

FISHERS

Victor Historical Society/Valentown Museum
Valentown Square, 14453
Telephone: (716) 924-2645
Private agency
Founded in: 1948
J. Sheldon Fisher, President
Number of members: 30
Period of collections: 1600-1864

FISHKILL

Fishkill Historical Society Inc.—Van Wyck Museum
Rt. 9 and I-84, 12524
Telephone: (914) 896-9560
Questionnaire not received

FLUSHING

Bowne House Historical Society
37-01 Bowne St., 11354
Telephone: (718) 359-0528
Private agency
Founded in: 1945
Audrey Braver, Director
Number of members: 610
Staff: volunteer 70
Major programs: historic sites preservation, educational programs
Period of collections: 1750-1850

Flushing Historical Society
Telephone: (212) 961-7236
Mail to: 153-10 60th Ave., 11355
Questionnaire not received

Queens Historical Society
143-35 37th Ave.
Telephone: (718) 939-0647
Private agency
Founded in: 1967
Mary Anne Mrozinski, Executive
 Director
Number of members: 250
Staff: full time 1, volunteer 30
Major programs: library, archives,
 museum, tours/pilgrimages, school
 programs, newsletters/pamphlets,
 historic preservation, exhibits,
 photographic collections
Period of collections: 1774-present

The Queens Museum
Flushing Meadow, Corona Park,
 11368
Telephone: (718) 592-2405
City agency
Founded in: 1972
Janet Schneider, Executive Director
Number of members: 600
Staff: full time 25, part time 4,
 volunteer 70
Major programs: museum, exhibits

FONDA

Heritage and Genealogical Society of Montgomery County
Old Courthouse, 12068
Telephone: (518) 853-3431, ext. 293
Authorized by Montgomery County
 Department of History and Archives
Founded in: 1976
Dorothea N. Cooper, President
Number of members: 60

Montgomery County Department of History and Archives
Old Courthouse, 12068
Telephone: (518) 853-3431
County agency
Founded in: 1934
Violet D. Fallone, County Historian
Staff: full time 2
Major programs: library, archives,
 manuscripts, historic site(s),
 historic preservation, research,
 exhibits, photographic collections,
 genealogical services
Period of collections: 1800-1900

Preserve It Now
P.O. Box 325, 12068
Telephone: (518) 922-7051
Private agency, authorized by State
 Department of Education
Founded in: 1980
Ronald J. Burch, President
Number of members: 20
Major programs: historic
 preservation, research, audiovisual
 programs

FORT EDWARD

Ft. Edward Historical Association
22 Broadway
Telephone: (518) 747-9600
Mail to: P.O. Box 106, 12828
Founded in: 1925
Paul McCarty, President

Number of members: 448
Staff: part time 4, volunteer 12
Major programs: library, archives,
 manuscripts, museum, historic
 preservation, markers,
 tours/pilgrimages, educational
 programs, historic preservation
Period of collections: 19th century

Washington County Historical Society
167 Broadway
Mail to: P.O. Box 106, 12828
Private agency, authorized by State
 Department of Education
Founded in: 1940
Dorothy Offensend, President
Number of members: 337
Staff: volunteer 8
Major programs: archives, historic
 site(s), markers, book publishing,
 newsletters/pamphlets, historic
 preservation, exhibits,
 photographic collections
Period of collections: 1760s-present

FORT HUNTER

Schoharie Crossing State Historic Site
P.O. Box 77, Main St., 12069
Telephone: (518) 829-7516
State agency, authorized by Office of
 Parks, Recreation and Historic
 Preservation
Founded in: 1966
Donnarae Gordon, Historic Site
 Manager
Staff: full time 2, part time 7,
 volunteer 5
Major programs: historic site(s),
 markers, tours, school programs,
 historic preservation
Period of collections: 1817-present

FORT JOHNSON

Montgomery County Historical Society
Old Ft. Johnson, Rt. 5, 12070
Telephone: (518) 842-0683
Founded in: 1904
Number of members: 300
Staff: full time 1, part time 1,
 volunteer 20
Major programs: museum, historic
 sites preservation
Period of collections: prehistoric-1918

FORT PLAIN

Ft. Plain Museum
Canal St.
Telephone: (518) 993-2527
Mail to: P.O. Box 324, 13339
Private agency
Founded in: 1963
Number of members: 150
Staff: full time 1, volunteer 12
Major programs: museum, historic
 site(s), tours/pilgrimages, school
 programs, historic preservation,
 records management, research,
 exhibits, archaeology programs
Period of collections: 1600-1920

FORT TICONDEROGA

Ft. Ticonderoga
12883
Telephone: (518) 585-2821

Private agency
Jane M. Lape, Curator/General
 Manager
Staff: full time 7
Magazine: Bulletin of the Fort
 Ticonderoga Museum
Major programs: library, manuscripts,
 museum, school programs, historic
 preservation, research, exhibits,
 audiovisual programs, archaeology
 programs
Period of collections: 1492-1783

FRANKLIN SQUARE

Franklin Square Historical Society
Museum at John Street School,
 Nassau Blvd.
Mail to: P.O. Box 45, 11010
Founded in: 1979
William F. Weidner, President
Number of members: 95
Major programs: archives, museum,
 exhibits
Period of collections: 1900s

FRANKLINVILLE

Ischua Valley Historical Society
40 Maple Ave., 14737
Telephone: (716) 676-5704
Private agency
Founded in: 1965
Kaye E. Hall, President
Number of members: 240
Staff: volunteer 15
Major programs: library, archives,
 museum, historic site(s),
 newsletters/pamphlets, historic
 preservation, photographic
 collections, genealogical services
Period of collections: 1865-present

FREDONIA

Historical Museum of the Darwin R. Barker Library
20 E. Main St.
Telephone: (716) 672-2114
Mail to: 7 Day St., 14063
Founded in: 1884
Ann M. Fahnestock, Curator
Staff: part time 3, volunteer 25
Major programs: library, archives,
 museum, research, exhibits,
 audiovisual programs,
 photographic collections,
 genealogical services
Period of collections: 1800-present

FULTON

Friends of History in Fulton, NY, Inc.
177 S. 1st St., 13069
Telephone: (315) 598-4616
Private agency
Founded in: 1979
Michele Anne Bazley, Coordinator
Staff: full time 1, volunteer 6
Major programs: museum, school
 programs, newsletters/pamphlets,
 research, exhibits, photographic
 collections
Period of collections late 19th-early
 20th centuries

GARDEN CITY

Nassau County Historical Society, Inc.
Mail to: P.O. Box 207, 11530
Founded in: 1915
Samuel U. Mitchell, President
Number of members: 540
Staff: volunteer 30
Major programs: tours/pilgrimages, educational programs, books
Period of collections: 1700-present

GARRISON

Mid-Atlantic Regional Archives Conference
c/o Archives, Graymoor, 10524
Telephone: (914) 424-3671
Founded in: 1972
Bruce Ambacher, Chair
Magazine: *Mid-Atlantic Archivist*
Major programs: library, archives, manuscripts

GARRISON-ON-HUDSON

Boscobel Restoration, Inc.
Rt. 9-D, 10524
Telephone: (914) 265-3638
Private agency
Founded in: 1955
Frederick W. Stanyer, Executive Director
Staff: full time 7, part time 25
Major programs: museum, historic sites preservation, tours/pilgrimages
Period of collections: 1810-1825

GENEVA

Geneva Historical Society and Museum
543 S. Main St., 14456
Telephone: (315) 789-5151
Private agency
Founded in: 1883
Helen P. Maney, Executive Director
Number of members: 750
Staff: full time 5, part time 2, volunteer 30
Major programs: library, archives, manuscripts, museum, historic sites preservation, markers, tours, oral history, educational programs, newsletters/pamphlets
Period of collections: 1783-1930

Rose Hill Mansion
Rt. 96-A, Box 464, 14456
Telephone: (315) 789-3848
Private agency, authorized by Geneva Historical Society
Founded in: 1967
H. Merrill Roenke, Jr., Administrator/Curator
Number of members: 694
Staff: full time 6, part time 4, volunteer 10
Major programs: school programs, book publishing, historic preservation, living history, audiovisual programs
Period of collections: 1840-1890

GERMANTOWN

Clermont State Historic Park
P.O. Box 215, 12526

Telephone: (518) 537-4240
State agency, authorized by Office of Parks, Recreation and Historic Preservation
Founded in: 1962
Bruce E. Naramore, Historic Site Manager
Number of members: 340
Staff: full time 8, part time 10, volunteer 12
Magazine: Views From Clermont
Major programs: library, archives, historic site(s), markers, tours/pilgrimages, school programs, book publishing, newsletters/pamphlets, historic preservation, research, audiovisual programs, archaeology programs, special events
Period of collections: 1730-1930

Friends of Clermont, Inc.
P.O. Box 217, 12526
Telephone: (518) 537-4240
Private agency
Founded in: 1977
Clare Brandt, President
Number of members: 340
Magazine: Views from Clermont
Major programs: book publishing, newsletters/pamphlets, exhibits, financial support of museum program at Clermont State Historic Park

GILBERTSVILLE

Gilbertsville Library Historical Committee
Gilbertsville Library, 13776
Telephone: (607) 783-2405
Founded in: 1969
Major programs: archives
Period of collections: 1797-present

GLEN COVE

Glen Cove Historical Society
P.O. Box 248, 11542
Telephone: (516) 759-0527 (director)
Private agency
Founded in: 1973
Mary Anne Mrozinski, Director
Number of members: 150
Staff: volunteer 20
Major programs: tours/pilgrimages, newsletters/pamphlets, research, lecture and presentation programs

GLENS FALLS

Chapman Historical Museum of the Glens Falls-Queensbury Historical Association, Inc.
348 Glen St., 12801
Telephone: (518) 793-2826
Private agency
Founded in: 1963
Joseph A. Cutshall King, Director
Number of members: 550
Staff: full time 3, part time 1, volunteer 45
Magazine: Echo
Major programs: library, museum, educational programs, newsletters/pamphlets
Period of collections: 1763-present

GORHAM

Marcus Whitman Historical Society
P.O. Box 204, 14461
Private agency
Robert E. Dicker, President
Number of members: 120
Major programs: archives, manuscripts, museum, historic site(s), historic preservation, records management, exhibits, living history
Period of collections: late 19th-early 20th centuries

GOSHEN

Goshen Library and Historical Society
203 Main St., 10924
Telephone: (914) 294-6606
Founded in: 1894
Number of members: 2,500
Major programs: library
Period of collections: 1750-1870

Hall of Fame of the Trotter
240 Main St., 10924
Telephone: (914) 294-6330
Founded in: 1949
Number of members: 1,000
Staff: full time 4, part time 5
Major programs: library, museum, junior history, educational programs, newsletters/pamphlets
Period of collections: 1783-present

GOWANDA

Gowanda Area Historical Society
Persia Town Hall, W. Main St.
Mail to: P.O. Box 372, 14070
Founded in: 1969
Lorraine T. Marvin, Curator/Director
Number of members: 100
Staff: volunteer 6
Major programs: library, archives, manuscripts, museum, school programs, records management, research, exhibits, photographic collections, genealogical services
Period of collections: 1810-present

GRAND ISLAND

Grand Island Historical Society
Beaver Island State Park
Mail to: P.O. Box 135, 14072
Questionnaire not received

GRANVILLE

Granville Slate Museum
Church St.
Telephone: (518) 642-2640
Mail to: 5 North St., 12832
Village agency
Wayne D. Williams, Mayor
Staff: volunteer 10
Major programs: museum, school programs, exhibits, audiovisual programs, photographic collections
Period of collections: late 1800s-present

Pember Library and Museum
33 W. Main St., 12832
Telephone: (518) 642-1515
Town agency
Founded in: 1909

Delight Gartlein, Museum Director
Number of members: 200
Staff: full time 2, part time 4,
volunteer 15
Major programs: library, museum,
school programs, historic
preservation, exhibits,
photographic collections, natural
history
Period of collections: 1800-present

GRAVESEND

Gravesend Historical Society
Telephone: (212) 339-9089
Mail to: P.O. Box 1643, Gravesend
Station, 11223
Private agency, authorized by State
Department of Education
Founded in: 1972
Eric J. Ierardi, President
Number of members: 110
Staff: volunteer 5
Major programs: museum, historic
site(s), markers, tours/pilgrimages,
oral history, school programs,
newsletters/pamphlets, historic
preservation, exhibits,
photographic collections
Period of collections: 1865-1918

GREAT NECK

**American Merchant Marine
Museum**
U.S. Merchant Marine Academy,
King's Point, 11024
Telephone: (516) 482-8200
Private agency
Founded in: 1978
Charles Renick, Liaison
Number of members: 200
Staff: part time 2, volunteer 6
Magazine: *The Manifest*
Major programs: museum, school
programs, book publishing
Period of collections: W.W. II-present

GREECE

**Historical Society of Greece, New
York**
Telephone: (716) 865-0387
Mail to: P.O. Box 7429, Rochester,
14616
Founded in: 1969
Questionnaire not received

GREENLAWN

**Greenlawn-Centerport Historical
Assccation and Museum**
31 Broadway
Telephone: (516) 754-1180
Mail to: P.O. Box 354, 11740
State agency
Founded in: 1973
Carol Bloomgarden, President
Number of members: 150
Staff: volunteer 40
Major programs: museum,
newsletters/pamphlets, research,
exhibits, photographic collections
Period of collections: 1870-1930

GREENPORT

Stirling Historical Society, Inc.
Main St.
Telephone: (516) 477-0099

Mail to: P.O. Box 500, 11944
Founded in: 1946
Frank S. Coyle, President
Number of members: 325
Staff: volunteer 25
Magazine: *Stirling Historical Society
Newsletter*
Major programs: museum
Period of collections: 1830-present

GROTON

**Town of Groton Historical
Association**
Main St.
Telephone: (607) 898-3979
Mail to: 114 Williams St., 13073
Founded in: 1971
Barbara Ingraham, President
Number of members: 100
Staff: volunteer 20
Major programs: museum, junior
history, oral history, educational
programs
Period of collections: 1783-present

GUILDERLAND

Guilderland Historical Society
P.O. Box 76, Guilderland Center,
12085
Founded in: 1971
Questionnaire not received

HAINES FALLS

**Mountain Top Historical Society of
Greene County, Inc.**
Twilight Park, 12436
Telephone: (518) 589-5357
Questionnaire not received

HAMBURG

Hamburg Historical Society
P.O. Box 400, 14075
Private agency, authorized by State
Department of Education
Founded in: 1954
Lester Burgwardt, President
Number of members: 425
Staff: volunteer 25
Magazine: The Ethnographer
Major programs: museum, historic
preservation
Period of collections: 1800s-present

HAMLIN

Hamlin Historical Society
731 Walker Lake, Ontario Rd., Hilton,
14468
Telephone: (716) 964-2101
Private agency
Founded in: 1971
Mary E. Smith, President
Number of members: 30
Major programs: library, archives,
manuscripts, museum, oral history,
exhibits, photographic collections,
genealogical services
Period of collections: 1880-1950

HAMMONDSPORT

**Glenn H. Curtiss Museum of Local
History**
Lake and Main Sts., 14840
Telephone: (607) 569-2160
Private agency, authorized by State
Department of Education

Founded in: 1963
Merrill Stickler, Director
Staff: full time 1, part time 5,
volunteer 6
Major programs: library, museum,
photographic collections, early
aviation
Period of collections: 1865-1920

Greyton H. Taylor Wine Museum
Greyton H. Taylor Memorial Dr.,
14840
Telephone: (607) 868-4814
Founded in: 1967
Questionnaire not received

HARPURSVILLE

Old Onaquaga Historical Society
St. Luke's Museum, 13787
Telephone: (607) 693-1298
Mail to: P.O. Box 24, Onaquaga,
13826
Questionnaire not received

HARRISON

Harrison Historical Society
Mail to: P.O. Box 1696, 10528
Founded in: 1972
Questionnaire not received

HASTINGS-ON-HUDSON

Hastings Historical Society
41 Washington Ave., 10706
Telephone: (914) 478-2249
Private agency, authorized by State
Department of Education
Founded in: 1970
Sue Smith, President
Number of members: 750
Staff: volunteer 20
Major programs: library, archives,
oral history, newsletters/pamphlets,
exhibits, photographic collections
Period of collections: 1870-present

HEBRON

Hebron Preservation Society
Telephone: (518) 854-3102
Mail to: R.D. 2, Salem, 12865
Private agency
Founded in: 1974
Arch Craig, Co-president
Number of members: 170
Staff: volunteer 11
Major programs: museum,
tours/pilgrimages, oral history,
school programs, historic
preservation, research, exhibits,
audiovisual programs,
photographic collections,
genealogical services
Period of collections: late 19th-early
20th centuries

HERKIMER

Herkimer County Historical Society
400 N. Main St., 13350
Telephone: (315) 866-6413
Private agency
Founded in: 1896
Jane S. Spellman, Director
Number of members: 750
Staff: full time 2, part time 4,
volunteer 30
Magazine: *Herkimer County
Historical Crier*

Major programs: library, archives,
manuscripts, museum, historic
site(s), tours/pilgrimages, school
programs, book publishing,
newsletters/pamphlets, historic
preservation, research, exhibits,
audiovisual programs,
photographic collections,
genealogical services, field
services
Period of collections: 19th-early 20th
centuries

HIGH FALLS

**Delaware and Hudson Canal
Historical Society**
Mohonk Rd., 12440
Telephone: (914) 687-9311
Founded in: 1788
Questionnaire not received

HIGHLAND

Lloyd Historical Society
38-A Bellevue Rd., 12528
Telephone: (914) 691-2145
Founded in: 1969
Questionnaire not received

**New York State Association of
European Historians**
27 Maple Ave., 12528
Telephone: (914) 691-8062
Founded in: 1951
Questionnaire not received

HILTON

Parma Meetinghouse Museum
460 Parma Center Rd.
Mail to: 1300 Hilton, Parma Rd., 14468
Town agency
Founded in: 1977
Shirley Cox Husted, Curator
Staff: full time 1, part time 1,
volunteer 15
Major programs: library, archives,
museum, book publishing,
research, exhibits, photographic
collections, genealogical services
Period of collections: 1808-present

HOGANSBURG

**Akwesasne Museum/Akwesasne
Library and Culture Center, Inc.**
Rt. 37, 13655
Telephone: (518) 358-2272, ext.
269/358-2240
Private agency
Founded in: 1972
Salli Benedict, Director
Number of members: 120
Staff: full time 6, part time 20,
volunteer 20
Major programs: library, museum,
tours/pilgrimages, junior history,
oral history, school programs, book
publishing, exhibits, living history,
photographic collections, field
services, native arts classes, films
Period of collections: 1450-present

HOLCOMB

Antique Wireless Association, Inc.
Main St., 14469
Telephone: (716) 657-7489
Founded in: 1952
Bruce Kelley, Secretary

Number of members: 2,500
Staff: volunteer 24
Magazine: *Journal: Old Timers
Bulletin*
Major programs: library, museum,
educational programs
Period of collections: 1850-present

HOLTSVILLE

Sachem Historical Society, Inc.
1057 Waverly Ave., 11747
Mail to: 288 Gillette Ave., Bayport,
11705
Questionnaire not received

HOMER

Glen Haven Historical Society
7331 E. Lake Rd., R.D. 1, 13077
Founded in: 1975
Marilyn G. Mowry, President
Number of members: 85
Staff: volunteer 25
Major programs: library, historic sites
preservation, educational
programs, books, historic
preservation
Period of collections: early
1900s-present

Homeville Museum
49 Clinton St., 13077
Telephone: (607) 749-3105
Private agency
Founded in: 1973
Kenneth M. Eaton, Owner
Major programs: museum, historic
preservation, exhibits
Period of collections: Civil
War-Vietnam

**Landmark Society of Cortland
County, Inc.**
Town Hall, 13077
Telephone: (607) 749-3322
Questionnaire not received

HONEOYE FALLS

**Village of Honeoye Falls/Town of
Mendon Historical Society**
1 Allen Park Dr.
Telephone: (716) 624-3810
Mail to: 50 East St., 14472
Private agency
Founded in: 1969
Robert R. Borsching, Sr., President
Number of members: 69
Staff: volunteer 41
Major programs: library, museum,
tours/pilgrimages, school
programs, newsletters/pamphlets,
research, exhibits, audiovisual
programs, archaeology programs,
photographic collections,
genealogical services
Period of collections: 1840s

HOOSICK FALLS

**Hoosick Township Historical
Society—Louis Miller Museum**
166 Main St.
Telephone: (518) 686-4682/686-4503
Mail to: P.O. Box 366, 12090
Town agency
Founded in: 1974
Edith Beaumont, President
Number of members: 75
Staff: volunteer 10

Major programs: library, museum,
historic preservation, exhibits,
audiovisual programs,
photographic collections,
genealogical services
Period of collections: 1860-present

HORICON

**Horicon Historical Society's
Museum**
Brant Lake, 12815
Telephone: (518) 494-2804
Founded in: 1976
Questionnaire not received

HORSEHEADS

**Chemung Valley Old Timers
Association, Inc.**
624 W. Broad St., 14845
Telephone: (607) 739-1526
Mail to: 220 Sunnyfield Dr., 14845
Private agency, authorized by State
Department of Education
Founded in: 1978
William Jaynes, President
Number of members: 225
Staff: volunteer 11
Magazine: *Gasup/Gossip*
Major programs:
newsletters/pamphlets, historic
preservation
Period of collections: late 19th-early
20th centuries

**Horseheads Cultural Center and
Historical Society, Inc.**
Zim Center
Telephone: (607) 739-3938
Private agency
Founded in: 1972
Dorothy Charwat, Corresponding
Secretary
Number of members: 450
Staff: part time 1, volunteer 50
Major programs: museum,
newsletters/pamphlets, historic
preservation, exhibits,
photographic collections
Period of collections: 1860-present

HUDSON

Friends of Olana
(518) 828-0135
Mail to: P.O. Box 199, 12534
Private agency
Founded in: 1971
Mrs. Craig Thorn III, President
Number of members: 275
Staff: volunteer 22
Magazine: *The Crayon*
Major programs: manuscripts,
historic site(s),
newsletters/pamphlets, historic
preservation
Period of collections: late 19th
century

**Hudson Athens Lighthouse
Preservation Committee, Inc.**
725 Warren St., 12534
Telephone: (518) 823-4612
Private agency
Founded in: 1983
Ruth Moser, Executive Secretary
Number of members: 150
Staff: volunteer 18

Major programs: museum, historic
site(s), junior history, school
programs, historic preservation,
research, exhibits, living history,
audiovisual programs,
photographic collections

Olana State Historic Site
R.D. 2, Rt. 9-G, 12534
Telephone: (5l8) 828-0135
State agency, authorized by Office of
Parks, Recreation and Historic
Preservation
Founded in: 1966
James Ryan, Historic Site Manager
Staff: full time 4, part time 4,
volunteer 10
Magazine: *The Crayon*
Major programs: archives, historic
site(s), school programs, historic
preservation, research,
photographic collections
Period of collections: 1826-1900

HUNTINGTON

Huntington Historical Society
209 Main St., 11743
Telephone: (516) 427-7045
Private agency
Founded in: 1903
Gay Wagner, Director
Number of members: 1,400
Staff: full time 6, part time 6,
volunteer 200
Major programs: library, archives,
manuscripts, museum, historic
site(s), junior history, oral history,
school programs, book publishing,
newsletters/pamphlets, historic
preservation, records
management, research, exhibits,
living history, audiovisual
programs, photographic
collections, genealogical services
Period of collections: 1650-present

HUNTINGTON STATION

**Walt Whitman Birthplace
Association**
246 Walt Whitman Rd., 11746
Telephone: (516) 427-5240
Private agency
Founded in: 1949
William Walter, President
Number of members: 100
Staff: part time 3
Magazine: *West Hills Review*
Major programs: library, museum,
historic site(s), school programs,
newsletters/pamphlets, exhibits,
poetry programs
Period of collections: early 19th
century

HURLEYVILLE

Sullivan County Historical Society
Telephone: (914) 434-8044
Mail to: P.O. Box 247, 12747
Founded in: 1929
Questionnaire not received

HYDE PARK

**Eleanor Roosevelt Center at
Val-Kill**
Rt. 9-G
Telephone: (914) 229-5302

Mail to: P.O. Box 255, 12538
Private agency
Founded in: 1976
Margaret R. Zamierowski, Director
Number of members: 600
Staff: full time 1, part time 2,
volunteer 5
Major programs: historic site(s),
junior history, oral history, school
programs, book publishing,
newsletters/pamphlets, historic
preservation, research, exhibits,
audiovisual programs,
conferences, panels, lectures
Period of collections: 1925-1935

Franklin D. Roosevelt Library
259 Albany Post Rd., 12538
Telephone: (914) 229-8114
Federal agency
Founded in: 1939
William R. Emerson, Director
Staff: full time 21, part time 4
Major programs: library, archives,
manuscripts, museum, books
Period of collections: 1930s-1940s

Hyde Park Historical Association
Telephone: (914) 229-9115
Mail to: P.O. Box 235, 12538
Questionnaire not received

Hyde Park Historical Society
P.O. Box 182, 12538
Founded in: 1970
Leon Froats, President
Number of members: 200
Staff: volunteer 30
Major programs: archives, museum,
historic site(s), tours/pilgrimages,
oral history, school programs,
historic preservation, records
management, exhibits,
photographic collections
Period of collections: 1800-1900

ILION

Remington Gun Museum
Catharine St., 13357
Telephone: (315) 894-9961
Private agency, authorized by
Remington Arms Company, Inc.
Founded in: 1816
L.K. Goodstal, Museum Curator
Staff: full time 1
Major programs: museum
Period of collections: 1860s-present

INTERLAKEN

Interlaken Historical Society
Main St., 14847
Founded in: 1953
Maurice L. Patterson, President
Number of members: 140
Staff: volunteer 8
Magazine: *Between the Lakes
Newsletter*
Major programs: library, archives,
manuscripts, museum,
newsletters/pamphlets
Period of collections: 1783-present

IRVINGTON-ON-HUDSON

Irvington Historical Society
Telephone: (914) 591-7221
Mail to: P.O. Box 1, 10533
Questionnaire not received

ITHACA

Cornell Plantations
1 Plantations Rd., 14850
Telephone: (607) 256-3020
State agency, authorized by Cornell
University
Founded in: 1933
Robert E. Cook, Director
Number of members: 2,500
Staff: full time 20, part time 15,
volunteer 35
Magazine: *The Cornell Plantations*
Major programs: library,
tours/pilgrimages, book publishing,
newsletters/pamphlets, records
management, exhibits, living
history, audiovisual programs,
photographic collections,
arboretum, botanical gardens

**DeWitt Historical Society of
Tompkins County, Inc.**
Clinton House, 116 N. Cayuga St.,
14850
Telephone: (607) 273-8284
Private agency
Founded in: 1863
Margaret Hobbie, Director
Number of members: 725
Staff: full time 1, part time 6,
volunteer 60
Major programs: library, archives,
manuscripts, museum, school
programs, book publishing,
newsletters/pamphlets, research,
exhibits, photographic collections,
genealogical services
Period of collections: 1790-1970

The Hinckley Foundation
410 E. Seneca St., 14850
Telephone: (607) 273-7053
Private agency
Founded in: 1970
Kevin McMahon, President
Number of members: 120
Staff: part time 3, volunteert 2
Major programs: museum, school
programs, exhibits
Period of collections: 1760-1930

**Historic Ithaca and Tomkins
County, Inc.**
120 N. Cayuga St., 14850
Telephone: (607) 273-6633
Private agency
Founded in: 1966
Geoffrey M. Gyrisco, Executive
Director
Number of members: 600
Staff: full time 3, part time 2,
volunteer 20
Magazine: *Historic Ithaca Newsletter*
Major programs: library, historic
preservation, educational
programs, newsletters/pamphlets,
exhibits, field services, research
Period of collections: 1783-present

**Ithaca Landmarks Preservation
Commission**
City Hall, 108 E. Green St., 14850
Telephone: (607) 272-1713
Founded in: 1970
Questionnaire not received

◇**New York Historical Resources
Center**
Olin Library, Cornell University, 14853

Telephone: (607) 256-4614
Private agency
Founded in: 1977
G. David Brumberg, Director
Number of members: full time 10, part time 4
Major programs: archives, manuscripts, research, accessibility of information on state archival holdings

JAMESTOWN

Fenton Historical Society
67 Washington St., 14701
Telephone: (716) 661-2296
Private agency
Founded in: 1964
Cancy Larson, Director
Number of members: 900
Staff: full time 2, part time 8, volunteer 10
Major programs: library, archives, museum, school programs, research, exhibits, genealogical services
Period of collections: 1865-1920

JOHNSTOWN

Johnson Hall State Historic Site
Hall Ave., 12095
Telephone: (518) 762-8712
State agency, authorized by Office of Parks, Recreation and Historic Preservation
Founded in: 1763
Wanda Burch, Historic Site Manager
Staff: full time 3, part time 1
Major programs: historic site(s), tours/pilgrimages, school programs, historic preservation, research, exhibits, living history
Period of collections: 1763-1774

Johnstown Historical Society
17 N. William St., 12095
Telephone: (518) 762-7076
Founded in: 1892
Questionnaire not received

JORDANVILLE

Holy Trinity Orthodox Seminary Museum
Holy Trinity Monastery, 13381-0036
Telephone: (315) 858-0940
Private agency
Founded in: 1980
Paul Loukianoff, Curator
Major programs: museum

Town of Warren Historical Society
Main St.
Telephone: (315) 858-1089
Mail to: R.D. 2, Richfield Springs, 13439
Town agency
Founded in: 1965
Louise Armstrong, President
Staff: volunteer 5
Major programs: library, archives, newsletters/pamphlets, research
Period of collections: 19th century

KATONAH

Caramoor Center for Music and the Arts, Inc.
Girdle Ridge Rd.
Telephone: (914) 232-5035

Mail to: P.O. Box R, 10536
Private agency
Founded in: 1946
Michael Sweeley, President
Number of members: 1,500
Staff: full time 9, part time 4, volunteer 55
Major programs: museum, tours/pilgrimages, school programs, music festival
Period of collections: 1450-1800

Friends of John Jay Homestead State Historic Site
Rt. 22, Jay St.
Telephone: (914) 232-5651
Mail to: P.O. Box A-H, 10536
State agency
Founded in: 1959
Linda McLean Connelly, Historic Site Manager/Director
Number of members: 450
Staff: full time 6, part time 10, volunteer 20
Major programs: museum, historic sites preservation, tours/pilgrimages, historic preservation
Period of collections: 1790s-1950s

MALFA (Material Archives and Laboratory for Archaeology)
Muscoot Farm Park, 10536
Private agency, authorized by State Department of Education
Founded in: 1961
Allen Vegotsky, President
Number of members: 100
Staff: volunteer 100
Major programs: library, museum, historic site(s), newsletters/pamphlets, research, exhibits, archaeology programs
Period of collections: prehistoric-1900

Muscoot Farm Park
Rt. 100, 10536
Telephone: (914) 232-7118
County agency, authorized by Westchester County Departmet of Parks, Recreation and Conservation
Founded in: 1975
Carl H. Specht, Farm Manager
Staff: full time 2, part time 5, volunteer 5
Major programs: living history
Period of collections: 1890-1930

KEESEVILLE

Northern New York American-Canadian Genealogical Society
P.O. Box 1256, Plattsburg, 12901-1256
Telephone: (515) 561-2791
Private agency
Founded in: 1983
William H. Marquis, President
Number of members: 200
Staff: volunteer 10
Magazine: *Lifelines*
Major programs: library, archives, manuscripts, tours/pilgrimages, oral history, school programs, newsletters/pamphlets, research, living history, audiovisual programs, genealogical services
Period of collections: 1600-present

KINDERHOOK

Columbia County Historical Society
12106
Telephone: (518) 758-9265
Private agency
Founded in: 1916
Sally A. Bottiggi, Executive Director
Number of members: 900
Staff: full time 1, part time 3, volunteer 65
Major programs: library, archives, manuscripts, museum, historic site(s), school programs, newsletters/pamphlets, historic preservation, research, exhibits, photographic collections, genealogical services
Period of collections: 18th-19th centuries

Martin Van Buren National Historic Site
Rt. 9-H
Telephone: (518) 758-9689
Mail to: P.O. Box 545, 12106
Federal agency, authorized by National Park Service
Founded in: 1974
Bruce W. Stewart, Superintendent
Staff: full time 7, part time 3
Major programs: historic sites preservation, educational programs
Period of collections: 1800-1862

KINGSTON

Senate House State Historic Site
Palisades Region, 296 Fair St., 12401
Telephone: (914) 338-2786
State agency, authorized by Office of Parks, Recreation and Historic Preservation
Founded in: 1887
Shelley B. Weinreb, Historic Site Manager
Staff: full time 8, part time 3, volunteer 8
Major programs: library, archives, manuscripts, museum, historic site(s), tours/pilgrimages, school programs, historic preservation, research, exhibits, photographic collections
Period of collections: 18th-19th centuries

Ulster County Historical Society
P.O. Box 3752, 12401
Telephone: (914) 338-5614
Founded in: 1859
Questionnaire not received

LAFARGERVILLE

Northern New York Agricultural Historical Society
Agricultural Museum, Stone Mills, Rt. 180, 13656
Private agency, authorized by State Education Department
Telephone: (315) 658-2582
Founded in: 1968
Rose P. Cullen, Curator
Number of members 189
Staff: volunteer 30

Major programs: museum, oral history, school programs, historic preservation, exhibits
Period of collections: 1800-1940

LAKE GEORGE

Lake George Historical Association
Canada St.
Telephone: (518) 668-5044
Mail to: P.O. Box 472, 12845
Founded in: 1963
Questionnaire not received

LAKE PLACID

Lake Placid-North Elba Historical Society
Mail to: c/o Secretary, 30 Lakeview St., 12946
Questionnaire not received

LANCASTER

Lancaster Historical Society
39 Glendale Dr., 14086
Telephone: (716) 653-0576
Town agency
Founded in: 1976
Jan Pecqueur, President
Number of members: 220
Staff: volunteer 20
Major programs: historic site(s), tours/pilgrimages, historic preservation
Period of collections: 1850

LARCHMONT

Larchmont Historical Society
46 Magnolia Ave.
Telephone: (914) 834-6143
Mail to: P.O. Box 742, 10538
Private agency, authorized by State Education Department
Founded in: 1980
June Freeman Allen, President
Number of members: 189
Staff: volunteer 20
Major programs: tours/pilgrimages, junior history, educational programs, newsletters/pamphlets, historic preservation, preservation, restoration & microfilming of old local newspapers
Period of collections: 1870-present

LE ROY

Le Roy Historical Society
23 E. Main St., 14482
Telephone: (716) 768-7433
Private agency
Founded in: 1940
Edward G. Cornwell, Curator
Number of members: 400
Major programs: library, archives, manuscripts, oral history, school programs, exhibits
Period of collections: 1783-present

LEWISTON

Historical Association and Society of Lewiston
Corner of Plain and Niagara Sts.
Telephone: (716) 754-4214
Mail to: P.O. Box 43, 14092
Private agency
Founded in: 1973

Judith Serbacki, Board President
Number of members: 125
Staff: volunteer 5
Major programs: museum, newsletters/pamphlets, historic preservation, exhibits, lecture series
Period of collections: early 1800s-1900

LIMA

Lima Historical Society
1850 Rochester St., 14485
Mail to: P.O. Box 532, 14485
Town agency
Founded in: 1972
Kathleen Reynolds, President
Number of members: 90
Staff: volunteer 20
Major programs: museum, tours, educational programs, historic preservation
Period of collections: 1790s-present

LINDENHURST

Lindenhurst Historical Society
Old Village Hall Museum, 215 S. Wellwood Ave.
Mail to: P.O. Box 296, 11757
Founded in: 1948
Lane S. Ellis, President
Number of members: 557
Staff: part time 6, volunteer 55
Major programs: archives, museum, oral history, educational programs, historic preservation
Period of collections: 1865-present

Old Village Hall Museum
215 S. Wellwood Ave.
Telephone: (516) 957-4385
Mail to P.O. Box 296, 11757
Private agency, authorized by Lindenhurst Historical Society
Founded in: 1958
Lorraine S. Ryan, Director
Staff: part time 6, volunteer 25
Major programs: archives, oral history, research, exhibits, photographic collections
Period of collections: 1865-present

LITTLE FALLS

Herkimer Home State Historic Site
Rt. 169
Telephone: (315) 823-0398
Mail to: P.O. Box 631, 13365
State agency, authorized by Office of Parks, Recreation and Historic Preservation
Founded in: 1914
William H. Watkins, Historic Site Manager
Staff: full time 3, part time 6, volunteer 30
Major programs: museum, historic site(s), school programs, historic preservation, exhibits, living history, audiovisual programs
Period of collections: 1750-1814

Little Falls Historical Society
Telephone: (315) 823-3786
Mail to: 42 Petrie St., 13365
Private agency
Founded in: 1901
Margaret M. Nolan, President

Number of members: 100
Staff: volunteer 40
Major programs: library, archives, manuscripts, museum, educational programs
Period of collections: 1723-present

LITTLE VALLEY

Cattaraugus County Historical Museum
Court St., 14755
Telephone: (716) 938-9111, ext. 440
Founded in: 1914
Questionnaire not received

LIVERPOOL

Office of Museums and Historic Sites, Onondaga County
106 Lake Dr.
Telephone: (315) 457-2990
Mail to: P.O. Box 146, 13088
County agency, authorized by Onondaga County, Department of Parks and Recreation
Founded in: 1974
Dennis J. Connors, Curator
Number of members: 135
Staff: full time 4, part time 10, volunteer 10
Magazine: *Insights*
Major programs: library, manuscripts, museum, historic site(s), markers, tours/pilgrimages, school programs, research, exhibits, living history, archaeology programs, photographic collections
Period of collections: 19th century

Ste. Marie De Gannentaha
Telephone: (315) 457-2990
Mail to: P.O. Box 146, 13088
Founded in: 1933
Questionnaire not received

LLOYD HARBOR

Lloyd Harbor Historical Society
P.O. Box 582, Huntington, 11743
Private agency
Founded in: 1974
Mary Ryan, President
Number of members: 740
Major programs: library, historic site(s), book publishing, historic preservation, archaeology programs
Period of collections: 1710-1750

LOCKPORT

Cambria Historical Society
4159 Lower Mountain Rd., 14094
Telephone: (716) 434-8937
Town agency
Founded in: 1971
Vernette A. Genter, President
Number of members: 150
Major programs: museum, tours/pilgrimages, oral history, newsletters/pamphlets, research, exhibits, photographic collections
Period of collections: 1808-1900s

Niagara County Historical Society, Inc.
215 Niagara St., 14094
Telephone: (716) 434-7433
Private agency
Founded in: 1947

Jan J. Losi, Curator/Director
Number of members: 350
Staff: full time 1, part time 3,
  volunteer 12
Major programs: museum, historic
  site(s), school programs,
  newsletters/pamphlet, exhibits
Period of collections: 1820-present

LOCUST VALLEY

Locust Valley Historical Society
170 Buckram Rd., 11560
Telephone: (516) 671-1837
Private agency
Founded in: 1982
Charles D. W. Thompson, President
Number of members: 38
Staff: volunteer 7
Major programs: library, archives,
  manuscripts, oral history, historic
  preservation, genealogical
  services
Period of collections: 1830-present

LODI

Lodi Historical Society
Main St., 14860
Authorized by State Education
  Department
Founded in: 1973
Noel Clawson, President
Number of members: 93
Staff: volunteer 50
Major programs: historic sites
  preservation, markers,
  tours/pilgrimages, oral history
Period of collections: 1865-present

LONG EDDY

**Basket Historical Society of the
Upper Delaware Valley**
R.D. 11, 12760
Telephone: (914) 887-5417
Private agency, authorized by State
  Education Department
Founded in: 1980
John B. Niflot, President
Number of members: 165
Staff: volunteer 18
Magazine: *Echo*
Major programs:
  newsletters/pamphlets, research,
  photographic collections
Period of collections: 1850-present

LONG ISLAND CITY

**LaGuardia Archives, LaGuardia
Community College**
31-10 Thomson Ave., 11101
Telephone: (718) 626-5078
City agency, authorized by the City
  University of New York
Founded in: 1982
Richard K. Lieberman, Director
Staff: full time 10, part time 3
Major programs: archives,
  manuscripts, exhibits,
  photographic collections
Period of collections: 20th century

LYONS

Wayne County Historical Society
21 Butternut St., 14489
Telephone: (3l5) 946-4943
Private agency

Founded in: 1957
Fred H. Rollins, Director
Number of members: 802
Staff: full time 1, part time 4,
  volunteer 6
Major programs: library, archives,
  museum, tours/pilgrimages, oral
  history, school programs, book
  publishing, newsletters/pamphlets,
  historic preservation, records
  management, research, exhibits
Period of collections: 1830-1950

LYONS FALLS

Lewis County Historical Society
High St.
Telephone: (315) 348-8089
Mail to: P.O. Box 306, 13368
Private agency
Founded in: 1926
Arlene S. Hall, Director
Number of members: 600
Staff: full time 1, part time 3,
  volunteer 50
Magazine: *Journal of the Lewis
  County Historical Society*
Major programs: museum, school
  programs, exhibits
Period of collections: 19th-early 20th
  centuries

MACEDON

Macedon Historical Society, Inc.
1185 Macedon Center Rd.
Telephone: (315) 986-2300
Mail to: 103 Quaker Rd., 14502
Founded in: 1962
Questionnaire not received

MAHOPAC

Town of Carmel Historical Society
Town Hall, McAlpin Ave., 10541
Telephone: (914) 628-1500
Town agency
Founded in: 1979
Dorothy G. Jewell, Liaison Officer
Number of members: 141
Major programs: oral history, school
  programs, newsletters/pamphlets,
  historic preservation, audiovisual
  programs, photographic
  collections, genealogical services,
  field services

MAINE

Nanticoke Valley Historical Society
Mail to: Nanticoke Rd., P.O. Box 23,
  13802
Private agency
Founded in: 1969
Janet Bothwell, Curator
Number of members: 150
Major programs: museum, oral
  history, historic preservation,
  research, exhibits, photographic
  collections
Period of collections: 1850-1930

MALONE

**Franklin County Historical and
Museum Society**
51 Milwaukee St., 12953
Telephone: (518) 483-2750
Private agency, authorized by
  University of State of New York

Founded in: 1969
Ethel Belknap, Assistant to President
Staff: part time 1, volunteer 50
Magazine: *Franklin Historical Review*
Major programs: museum,
  tours/pilgrimages, school
  programs, newsletters/pamphlets,
  exhibits, audiovisual programs,
  genealogical services
Period of collections: 1805-1950

MAMARONECK

Mamaroneck Free Library
Library Lane, 10543
Telephone: (914) 698-1250
Founded in: 1922
Sally Poundstone, Director
Number of members: 600
Staff: full time 15, part time 10,
  volunteer 30
Major programs: library,
  photographic collections
Period of collections: late 19th-early
  20th centuries

Mamaroneck Historical Society
P.O. Box 776, 10543
Telephone: (914) 698-1250
Founded in: 1937
Gloria Poccia Pritts, President
Number of members: 430
Staff: volunteer 430
Major programs: historic site(s),
  markers, oral history, school
  programs, newsletters/pamphlets

MANHASSET

**Historical Society of the Town of
North Hempstead**
220 Plandome Rd., 11030
Telephone: (516) 627-0590
Founded in: 1962
Questionnaire not received

MANHATTAN

General Grant National Memorial
122nd St. and Riverside Dr., 10027
Telephone: (212) 666-1640
Founded in: 1897
Staff: full time 3, part time 3,
  volunteer 5
Major programs: museum, historic
  sites preservation,
  tours/pilgrimages, oral history,
  educational programs, historic
  preservation
Period of collections: 1822-1897

**Hamilton Grange National
Memorial**
287 Convent Ave., 10031
Telephone: (212) 283-5154
Founded in: 1962
Staff: full time 3, part time 3,
  volunteer 5
Major programs: museum, historic
  sites preservation,
  tours/pilgrimages, oral history,
  educational programs, historic
  preservation

Society of American Historians
610 Fayerweather Hall, Columbia
  University, 10027
Telephone: (212) 280-2555/(914)
  666-5721
Founded in: 1939

Kenneth T. Jackson,
Secretary/Treasurer
Number of members: 250
Staff: part time 2
Major programs: educational
programs, awards for distinguished
writing

MANLIUS

Manlius Historical Society
101 Scoville Ave.
Telephone: (315) 682-6660
Mail to: P.O. Box 173, 13104
Private agency
Founded in: 1975
Number of members: 300
Staff: volunteer 60
Major programs: library, archives,
manuscripts, museum, educational
programs, newsletters/pamphlets
Period of collections: late 18th-early
20th centuries

MARCELLUS

**Central New York Chapter National
Railway Historical Society**
P.O. Box 10, 13108
Founded in: 1965
Questionnaire not received

Marcellus Historical Society
Main St.
Mail to: 1 Park St., 13108
Founded in: 1960
Questionnaire not received

MARILLA

Marilla Historical Society
Bullis Rd., 14102
Telephone: (716) 652-5529
Mail to: 1351 Jamison Rd., Elma,
14059
Founded in: 1960
Questionnaire not received

MASSENA

**Town of Massena Museum and
Historian's Office**
200 E. Orvis St., 13662
Telephone: (315) 769-8571
Town agency
Founded in: 1960
Eleanor L. Dumas, Curator and
Historian
Staff: volunteer 3
Period of collections: 1800-present

MASTIC BEACH

**William Floyd Estate, Fire Island
National Seashore**
20 Washington Ave., 11951
Telephone: (516) 399-2030
Mail to: 120 Laurel St., Patchogue,
11772
Federal agency, authorized by
National Park Service
Founded in: 1982
Jack Hauptmann, Superintendent
Staff: full time 4, part time 4,
volunteer 30

Major programs: manuscripts,
historic site(s), school programs,
newsletters/pamphlets, historic
preservation

MATTITUCK

Mattituck Historical Society
P.O. Box 766, 11952
Founded in: 1966
Questionnaire not received

MAYFIELD

Mayfield Historical Society
33 W. Main St., 12117
Telephone: (518) 661-5085
Town agency
Founded in: 1980
Betty Tabor, Treasurer
Number of members: 30
Major programs: historic site(s),
school programs,
newsletters/pamphlets, historic
preservation, records
management, research, exhibits
Period of collections: early 20th
century

MAYVILLE

Peacock Land Mark Society
Morris Rd., 14757
Questionnaire not received

MEDINA

Medina Historical Society
406 West Ave., 14103
County agency
Founded in: 1972
John Wasnock, President
Number of members: 70
Major programs: museum, junior
history, exhibits

MERRICK

Historical Society of the Merricks
2279 S. Merrick Ave., 11566
Private agency
Founded in: 1975
Mildred M. Donnelly, President
Number of members: 180
Staff: volunteer 15
Major programs: markers, oral
history, educational programs,
books
Period of collections: 19th-20th
century

MIDDLETOWN

**Historical Society of Middletown
and the Wallkill Precinct, Inc.**
25 East Ave. 10940
Telephone: (914) 342-0941
Founded in: 1923
Charles L. Radzinsky, Curator
Number of members: 270
Staff: part time 2, volunteer 5
Magazine: Yearbook
Major programs: library, archives,
manuscripts, museum, historic
preservation

MILFORD

**Greater Milford Historical
Association**
13807
Private agency

Founded in: 1971
Niles Eggleston, President
Number of members: 70
Staff: volunteer 15
Major programs: historic sites
preservation, historic preservation
Period of collections: 1810-1840

MINERVA

Minerva Historical Society
12851
Telephone: (518) 251-2382
Founded in: 1955
Number of members: 104
Staff: volunteer 6
Magazine: Minerva Historical
Quarterly
Major programs: museum,
educational programs, historic
preservation

MOHAWK

**Mohawk Valley Historic
Association**
22 Columbia St., 12068
Telephone: (315) 866-3575/(518)
853-3358
Private agency
Founded in: 1920
Clarke Blair, President
Number of members: 40
Major programs: library, oral history,
historic preservation, living history

MONROE

**Monroe Historical Preservation
Society**
P.O. Box 625, 10950
Town agency
Founded in: 1974
Paul M. Simon, President
Number of members: 6
Staff: volunteer 10
Major programs: archives,
tours/pilgrimages, oral history,
photographic collections
Period of collections: 1850-1940

Museum Village in Orange County
Museum Village Rd., 10950
Telephone: (914) 782-8247
Private agency
Founded in: 1950
Bradford Beers, Director
Number of members: 350
Staff: full time 7, part time 35
Major programs: museum,
educational programs,
newsletters/pamphlets
Period of collections: 1840-1900

MONTAUK

Montauk Historical Society
Montauk Hwy., 11954
Founded in: 1960
Peggy Joyce, President
Number of members: 169
Staff: full time 1, volunteer 20
Major programs: museum, historic
sites preservation,
tours/pilgrimages, educational
programs, historic preservation
Period of collections: early 1900s

MONTGOMERY

Brick House
Rt. 17-K, 12549

Telephone: (914) 457-5951
Questionnaire not received

MONTOUR FALLS

Schuyler County Historical Society
108 N. Catherine St.
Telephone: (607) 535-9741
Mail to: P.O. Box 651, 14865
Founded in: 1960
Questionnaire not received

MORAVIA

Cayuga-Owasco Lakes Historical Society
History House, Main St.
Telephone: (315) 784-5505
Mail to: P.O. Box 247, 13118
Private agency
Founded in: 1966
Hurley Stevens, President
Number of members: 90
Major programs: archives, museum, historic site(s), historic preservation, exhibits, photographic collections, genealogical services
Period of collections: early 1800s-present

MOUNT UPTON

Unadilla Valley Historical Society
7-AA Main St., 13809
Telephone: (607) 764-8492
Private agency, authorized by State Education Department
Founded in: 1976
Jewell Hayes, President
Number of members: 66
Major programs: library, junior history, oral history, school programs, book publishing, records management, exhibits, photographic collections, genealogical services
Period of collections: 1850-1930

MOUNT VERNON

Landmark and Historical Society of Mt. Vernon
Local History Room, Mt. Vernon Library, 28 S. 1st Ave., 10550
Telephone: (914) 668-1840
Founded in: 1964
Number of members: 70
Major programs: library, archives, museum, tours/pilgrimages, oral history, educational programs, newsletters/pamphlets
Period of collections: 1851-present

St. Pauls National Historic Site
897 S. Columbus Ave. 10550
Telephone: (914) 667-4116
Private agency, authorized by Society of the National Shrine of the Bill of Rights, St. Paul's Church, Eastchester, Inc.
Founded in: 1945
Connie M. Cullen, Administrator
Staff: full time 3, part time 1, volunteer 45
Magazine: *Zenger's Journal*
Major programs: library, archives, museum, historic site(s), tours/pilgrimages, oral history,

book publishing, historic preservation, research, exhibits, audiovisual programs, archaeology programs, photographic collections, genealogical services
Period of collections: 18th-early 19th centuries

MUNNSVILLE

Fryer Memorial Museum
Peterboro St.
Telephone: (315) 495-5395
Mail to: P.O. Box 177, 13409
Town agency, authorized by Town of Stockbridge
Founded in: 1977
Olive S. Boylan, Museum Director
Number of members: 100
Staff: volunteer 5
Major programs: manuscripts, museum, school programs, records management, research, exhibits, photographic collections, genealogical services
Period of collections: 1836-present

NAPLES

Naples Historical Society
P.O. Box 115, 14512
Telephone: (716) 374-2560
Founded in: 1976
Questionnaire not received

NARROWSBURG

Ft. Delaware Museum of Colonial History
12764
Telephone: (914) 252-6660/252-3279
County agency, authorized by Sullivan County Department of Public Works
Founded in: 1957
Ethel M. Poley, Director
Staff: full time 1, part time 12
Major programs: museum, tours/pilgrimages, oral history, school programs, historic preservation, exhibits, living history, audiovisual programs, genealogical services, field services
Period of collections: 1750-1800s

NEWARK VALLEY

Newark Valley Historical Society
Mail to: P.O. Box 222, 13811
Telephone: (607) 642-8075
Founded in: 1976
Edward Nizalowski, Secretary/Treasurer
Number of members: 150
Staff: part time 2
Major programs: museum, historic site(s), school programs, historic preservation
Period of collections: 1790-1850

NEWBURGH

Historical Society of Newburgh Bay and the Highlands
189 Montgomery St., 12550
Telephone: (914) 561-2585
Private agency
Founded in: 1883
Regina Angelo, President

Number of members: 350
Major programs: library, archives, museum, historic sites preservation, newsletters/pamphlets, musical events, exhibitions, historic house, research
Period of collections: early 19th century

Washington's Headquarters State Historic Site
84 Liberty St., 12550-5603
Telephone: (914) 562-1195
State agency, authorized by Office of Parks, Recreation and Historic Preservation
Founded in: 1850
Thomas A. Hughes, Historic Site Manager
Major programs: library, archives, manuscripts, museum, historic site(s), school programs, historic preservation, research, exhibits, archaeology programs
Period of collections: Revolutionary War period

NEW CITY

Historical Society of Rockland County
20 Zukor Rd., 10956
Telephone: (914) 634-9629
Private agency
Founded in: 1965
Ralph Sessions, Director
Number of members: 2,000
Staff: full time 1, part time 2, volunteer 150
Magazine: *South of the Mountains*
Major programs: library, archives, manuscripts, museum, historic site(s), markers, school programs, book publishing, newsletters/pamphlets, research, exhibits, photographic collections, genealogical services
Period of collections: late 18th-20th centuries

NEW HARTFORD

New Hartford Historical Society
48 Genesee St.
Telephone: (315) 735-2332
Mail to: P.O. Box 238, 13413
Town agency, authorized by State Education Department
Founded in: 1976
Arthur G. Baker, President
Number of members: 166
Staff: volunteer 12
Major programs: library, oral history, books, newsletters/pamphlets
Period of collections: 1890-present

NEW PALTZ

Huguenot Historical Society
Telephone: (914) 255-1660
Mail to: P.O. Box 339, 12561
Founded in: 1894
Kenneth E. Hasbrouck, President
Number of members: 4,150
Staff: full time 8, part time 20, volunteer 20
Magazine: *Huguenot Historical Society*

Major programs: library, archives, museum, historic sites preservation, tours/pilgrimages, educational programs, books, newsletters/pamphlets
Period of collections: 1660-1950

NEW ROCHELLE

Huguenot-Thomas Paine National Historical Association
983 North Ave., 10804
Telephone: (914) 632-5376
Founded in: 1886
Questionnaire not received

NEW SCOTLAND

Town of New Scotland Historical Association
Telephone: (518) 765-4419
Mail to: P.O. Box 72, 12127
Founded in: 1971
Questionnaire not received

NEW WOODSTOCK

New Woodstock Historical Society
13122
Mail to: 14 Mill St., Cazenovia, 13035
Founded in: 1968
Questionnaire not received

NEW YORK CITY

Abigail Adams Smith Museum
421 E. 61st St., 10021
Telephone: (212) 838-6878
Private agency, authorized by Colonial Dames of America
Founded in: 1939
David L. Reese, Director
Staff: full time 3, part time 2, volunteer 50
Major programs: library, museum, historic site(s), school programs, newsletters/pamphlets, historic preservation, research, decorative arts
Period of collections: 1800-1830

Alley Pond Environmental Center
228-06 Northern Blvd., Douglaston, 11363
Telephone: (718) 229-4000
Private agency
Founded in: 1972
George O. Pratt, Jr., Executive Director
Number of members: 850
Staff: full time 9, part time 4, volunteer 4
Major programs: museum, tours/pilgrimages, newsletters/pamphlets, exhibits, photographic collections, field services, ecology programs
Period of collections: 20th century

American Craft Museum of the American Craft Council
77 W. 53rd St.
Telephone: (212) 391-8770
Mail to: 45 W. 45th St., 10036

American Museum—Hayden Planetarium
81st St. at Central Park, W
Telephone: (212) 873-1300
Private agency, authorized by Hayden Planetarium Authority

Founded in: 1935
William Gutsch, Jr., Chair
Staff: full time 16, part time 1, volunteer 2
Major programs: library, school programs, exhibits, audiovisual programs, educational astronomy and space science shows

American Museum of Immigration
Statue of Liberty National Monument, Liberty Island, 10004
Telephone: (212) 732-1236
Federal agency, authorized by National Park Service
Founded in: 1972
Paul J. Kinney, Museum Curator
Staff: full time 6, volunteer 2
Major programs: library, archives, museum, tours/pilgrimages, oral history, exhibits, photographic collections
Period of collections: 1850-present

American Museum of the Moving Image
34-12 36th St., Astoria, 11106
Telephone: (718) 784-4520
Private agency
Founded in: 1977
Rochelle Slovin, Executive Director
Staff: full time 8, part time 8, volunteer 4
Major programs: archives, museum, historic site(s), oral history, school programs, research, exhibits, audiovisual programs, photographic collections
Period of collections: 1910-present

American Numismatic Society Museum
Broadway at 155th St., 10032
Telephone: (212) 234-3130
Private agency
Founded in: 1858
Leslie A. Elam, Director
Number of members: 2219
Staff: full time 29, part time 3, volunteer 2
Magazine: *American Numismatic Society Museum Notes*
Major programs: library, museum, book publishing, newsletters/pamphlets, historic preservation, records management, research, exhibits, archaeology programs, photographic collections, numismatic education, lectures and conferences
Period of collections: 650 B.C.-present

Anthropology Museum of the People of New York
3801 23rd Ave., Astoria, 11105
Telephone: (718) 626-0307
Private agency, authorized by the University of the State of New York and Cultural Center, Albany
Founded in: 1978
Margaret C. Tellalian Kyrkostas, Director
Number of members: 140
Staff: volunteer 15
Major programs: museum, tours/pilgrimages, oral history, school programs,

newsletters/pamphlets, research, exhibits, audiovisual programs, archaeology programs, photographic collections, anthropology

Archives of American Art
Smithsonian Institution, 41 E. 65th St., 10021
Telephone: (212) 826-5722
Founded in: 1954
Questionnaire not received

The Asia Society
725 Park Ave., 10021
Telephone: (212) 288-6400
Private agency
Founded in: 1956
Jan Arnet, Vice President, Finance and Administration
Number of members: 4,000
Staff: full time 84, part time 3, volunteer 200
Magazine: *Focus*
Major programs: museum, tours/pilgrimages, school programs, newsletters/pamphlets, records management, exhibits, audiovisual programs, performing arts
Period of collections: A.D. 1-19th century

Biblical Garden of the Cathedral of St. John the Divine
1047 Amsterdam Ave., 10025
Telephone: (212) 678-6888
Private agency
Founded in: 1974
Joan Evanish, Vice President
Number of members: 308
Staff: volunteer 4
Major programs: tours/pilgrimages, newsletters/pamphlets, botanical garden

Bronx County Historical Society
3266 Bainbridge Ave., 10467
Telephone: (212) 881-8900
Founded in: 1955
Questionnaire not received

Bund Archives of the Jewish Labor Movement
25 E. 78th St.
Founded in: (212) 535-1209
Founded in: 1899
Benjamin Nadel, Executive Director
Staff: full time 9, volunteer 2
Magazine: *Bulletin of the Bund Archives of the Jewish Labor Movement*
Major programs: library, archives
Period of collections: 1880-1939

Castle Clinton National Monumemt
Battery Park
Telephone: (212) 344-7220
Mail to: 26 Wall St., 10005
Federal agency, authorized by National Park Service
Founded in: 1946
Walter Tegge, Supervisory Park Ranger
Staff: full time 4
Major programs: museum, historic sites preservation, tours/pilgrimages, educational programs, cultural events
Period of collections: 1812-1941

Center for Arts Information
625 Broadway, 10012
Telephone: (212) 677-7548
Private agency, authorized by Arts
Information, Inc.
Founded in: 1977
Rita K. Roosevelt, Executive Director
Staff: full time 5, part time 2
Magazine: *For Your Information*
Major programs: library, book
publishing, newsletters/pamphlets,
information on visual and
performing arts
Period of collections: 1960

Church of St. Andrew
40 Old Mill Rd., Staten Island, 10306
Telephone: (212) 351-0900
Founded in: 1708
Questionnaire not received

City Island Historical Society and Museum
190 Fordham St., 10464
Telephone: (212) 885-1616
Private agency, authorized by State
Education Department
Founded in: 1964
Number of members: 125
Staff: part time 4, volunteer 10
Major programs: library, archives,
manuscripts, museum, historic
site(s), oral history, historic
preservation, research, exhibits,
living history, audiovisual
programs, photographic
collections, genealogical services
Period of collections: 1800-1930

Colonial Farmhouse Restoration Society of Bellerose, Inc.
Queens County Farm Museum,
Adriance Farm, 73-50 Little Neck
Parkway, Floral Park, 11004
Telephone: (212) 468-4355
Founded in: 1975
Questionnaire not received

Cooper-Hewitt Museum, the Smithsonian Institution's National Museum of Design
2 E. 91st St., 10128
Telephone: (212) 860-6868
Federal agency, authorized by the
Smithsonian Board of Regents
Founded in: 1897
Lisa Taylor, Director
Number of members: 6,000
Staff: full time 80, part time 40,
volunteer 60
Major programs: library, archives,
museum, historic site(s), book
publishing, newsletters/pamphlets,
research, exhibits, history of design
Period of collections:
prehistoric-present

Federal Hall National Memorial
26 Wall St., 10005
Telephone: (212) 264-8711
Federal agency, authorized by
National Park Service
Founded in: 1939
Walt Tegge, Supervisory Park Ranger
Staff: full time 8, volunteer 1

Major programs: historic site(s),
tours/pilgrimages, school
programs, newsletters/pamphlets,
historic preservation, exhibits,
audiovisual programs
Period of collections: Colonial era

Fraunces Tavern Museum
54 Pearl St., 10004
Telephone: (212) 425-1778
Private agency, authorized by Sons of
the American Revolution
Founded in: 1907
Christine Miles Director
Staff: full time 8, part time 3,
volunteer 40
Major programs: library, museum,
historic sites preservation,
educational programs, historic
preservation
Period of collections: 18th-19th
centuries

The Frick Collection
1 E. 70th St., 10021
Telephone: (212) 258-0700
Private agency
Founded in: 1920
Everett Fahy, Director
Number of members: 300
Staff: full time 71, part time 8
Major programs: library, museum,
fine art
Period of collections: 15th-19th
centuries

Greater Astoria Historical Society
34-31 35th St., Astoria, 10006
Telephone: (718) 786-3335
Private agency
Founded in: 1978
Madeleine Gillis, President
Number of members: 275
Staff: volunteer 9
Major programs: archives,
tours/pilgrimages,
newsletters/pamphlets, historic
preservation, exhibits, audiovisual
programs, photographic
collections
Period of collections: 1750-1940

Greenwich Village Society for Historic Preservation
47 5th Ave.. 10003
Telephone: (212) 924-3895
Private agency
Founded in: 1980
Regina Kellerman, Executive Director
Number of members: 400
Staff: part time 3
Magazine: *Anthemion*
Major programs: historic preservation
Period of collections: 19th century

Hall of Fame for Great Americans
Bronx Community College, University
Avenue and W. 181st St., Bronx,
10453
Telephone: (212) 220-6187
Founded in: 1900
Questionnaire not received

Hamilton Grange National Memorial
287 Convent Ave., 10031
Telephone: (212) 283-5154
Federal agency, authorized by
National Park Service
Diane Dayson, Site Supervisor
Staff: full time 3, part time 1,
volunteer 5
Major programs: historic site(s), oral
history, historic preservation,
research, exhibits, audiovisual
programs
Period of collections:
Colonial-Federal periods

Hampden-Booth Theatre Library
16 Gramercy Park, 10003
Telephone: (212) 228-7610
Private agency
Founded in: 1957
Louis A. Rachow, Curator/Librarian
Number of members: 1,000
Staff: full time 2, volunteer 2
Major programs: library, archives,
manuscripts, museum, research,
exhibits, photographic collections
Period of collections: 19th-early 20th
centuries

Headquarters Museum and Library, National Society of Colonial Dames
215 E. 71st St., 10021
Private agency, authorized by the
national society
Mrs. Charles Fleming, President
Major programs: books,
newsletters/pamphlets, historic
preservation, records
management, genealogical
services

Holland Society of New York
122 E. 58th St., 10022
Telephone: (212) PL8-1675
Private agency
Founded in: 1885
Barbara W. Stankowski, Executive
Officer
Number of members: 939
Staff: full time 2, part time 1
Magazine: *De Halve Maen*
Major programs: library, books,
genealogical services
Period of collections: early 17th
century-Dutch Colonial

Huguenot Society of America
122 E. 58th St., 10022
Telephone: (212) 755-0592
Private agency
Founded in: 1883
Mrs. Hans A. French, President
Number of members: 439
Staff: part time 1
Major programs: library, manuscripts,
research, scholarship program
Period of collections: Huguenot
history to 1787

J. Walter Thompson Company Archives
466 Lexington Ave., 10017
Telephone: (212) 210-7124
Founded in: 1979

Cynthia G. Swank, Archives
Staff: full time 3
Major programs: archives,
manuscripts, records
management, research, exhibits,
photographic collections,
advertisement collection
Period of collections: 1900-present

**Jewish Historical Society of New
York, Inc.**
8 W. 70th St., 10023
Telephone: (212) 813-0300
Private agency
Founded in: 1973
Number of members: 450
Major programs: educational
programs, newsletters, lecture
program

The Jewish Museum
1109 5th Ave., 10028
Telephone: (212) 860-1888
Founded in: 1904
Questionnaire not received

Masonic Library and Museum
71 W. 23rd St., 10010
Telephone: (212) 741-4500
Private agency, authorized by Grand
Lodge of Free and Accepted
Masons
Founded in: 1781
Allan Boudreau, Director
Number of members: 150,000
Staff: full time 20, part time 10
Magazine: *The Empire State
Mason/Transactions of the
American Lodge of Research*
Major programs: library, archives,
manuscripts, museum, historic
site(s), markers, tours/pilgrimages,
newsletters/pamphlets, research,
exhibits
Period of collections: 1781-present

**Metropolitan Historic Structures
Association**
3 W. 51st St. 604, 10019
Telephone: (212) 247-5340
Founded in: 1976
Questionnaire not received

Museum of American Folk Art
125 W. 55th St., 10019
Telephone: (212) 581-2474
Private agency, authorized by State
Education Department
Founded in: 1961
Robert Bishop, Director
Number of members: 4,500
Staff: full time 23, part time 13,
volunteer 25
Magazine: *The Clarion*
Major programs: library, archives,
museum, school programs,
newsletters/pamphlets, research,
exhibits, folk and decorative arts
Period of collections: 17th-20th
centuries

Museum of the American Indian
Broadway at 155th St., 10032
Telephone: (212) 283-2420
Private agency
Founded in: 1916
Roland W. Force, Director
Number of members: 1,500
Staff: full time 40, part time 6,
volunteer 5

Major programs: archives, museum,
school programs, book publishing,
research, exhibits, audiovisual
programs, photographic
collections
Period of collections:
prehistoric-present

Museum of Broadcasting
1 E. 53rd St., 10022
Telephone: (212) 752-4690
Founded in: 1976
Number of members: 2,000
Staff: full time 25, part time 10,
volunteer 15
Magazine: *MB News*
Major programs: library, archives,
museum, educational programs,
exhibitions, seminars
Period of collections: 1920-present

Museum of the City of New York
5th Ave. at 103rd St., 10029
Telephone: (212) 534-1672
Private agency
Founded in: 1923
Robert R. Macdonald, Director
Number of members: 3,000
Staff: full time 70, part time 7,
volunteer 30
Magazine: *Bulletin*
Major programs: library, archives,
museum, junior history, school
programs, newsletters/pamphlets,
research, exhibits, audiovisual
programs, photographic
collections
Period of collections: 1609-present

Museum of Holography
11 Mercer St., 10013
Telephone: (212) 925-0581
State agency
Founded in: 1976
David H. Katzive, Director
Number of members: 500
Staff: full time 10, part time 1,
volunteer 3
Magazine: *Holosphere*
Major programs: library, archives,
museum, school programs,
newsletters/pamphlets, historic
preservation, research, exhibits,
living history, audiovisual
programs, photographic
collections, history of holography
and technology
Period of collections: 1940s-present

Museums Collaborative, Inc.
15 Gramercy Park, 10003
Telephone: (212) 674-0030
Private agency
Founded in: 1972
Pamela J. Johnson, Executive
Director
Staff: full time 5, part time 1
Major programs: school programs,
research, field services

**National Maritime Historical
Society**
Fulton Ferry Museum
Telephone: (212) 858-1348
Founded in: 1963
Questionnaire not received

**Native New Yorkers Historical
Association**
503 W. 22nd St., 10011
Telephone: (212) 847-9869
Founded in: 1961

Felix J. Cuervo, President
Staff: volunteer 6
Major programs: markers, tours

New York Archival Society
31 Chambers St., 10007
Telephone: (212) 566-5292
Private agency
Founded in: 1976
Catha Grace Rambusch, Executive
Director
Number of members: 180
Staff: part time 1, volunteer 3
Major programs: archives,
newsletters/pamphlets, field
services

**New York City Fire Department
Museum**
104 Duane St., 10007
Telephone: (212) 570-4230
Founded in: 1932
Questionnaire not received

◊**New York Council for the
Humanities**
33 W. 42 St., 10036
Telephone: (212) 354-3040
Private agency
Founded in: 1975
Jay L. Kaplan, Executive Director
Staff: full time 8, part time 4
Magazine: *Humanities News*
Major programs: public programs in
the humanities

**New York Genealogical and
Biographical Society**
122 E. 58th St., 10022-1939
Telephone: (212) 755-8532
Private agency
Founded in: 1869
Carolyn G. Stifel, Executive Secretary
Number of members: 1,290
Staff: full time 5, part time 7,
volunteer 1
Magazine: *The New York
Genealogical and Biographical
Record*
Major programs: library, manuscripts,
educational programs, research,
genealogy
Period of collections: 1600s-present

New-York Historical Society
170 Central Park, W, 10024
Telephone: (212) 873-3400
Private agency
Founded in: 1804
James B. Bell, Director
Number of members: 2,300
Major programs: library, archives,
manuscripts, museum
Period of collections: 1783-1918

**New York Landmarks
Conservancy, Inc.**
17 Battery Place, 10004
Telephone: (212) 425-4085
Questionnaire not received

**New York Public Library,
Schomburg Center for Research
in Black Culture**
515 Lenox Ave., 10037
Telephone: (212) 862-4000
Founded in: 1925
Howard Dodson, Chief
Staff: full time 46, part time 8
Major programs: library, archives,
manuscripts, tours/pilgrimages,

oral history, newsletters/pamphlets, research, exhibits, audiovisual programs, photographic collections, genealogical services
Period of collections: 16th century-present

Old Merchants House of New York, Inc.
29 E. 4th St., 10003
Telephone: (212) 777-1089
Private agency
Founded in: 1935
Carolyn Roberto, Director
Number of members: 400
Staff: full time 1, part time 1, volunteer 16
Major programs: museum, historic site(s), tours
Period of collections: 1815-1880

Pilsudski Institute of America
381 Park Ave., S, Suite 701, 10016
Telephone: (212) 683-4342
Founded in: 1943
Questionnaire not received

Queens County Farm Museum
73-50 Little Neck Parkway, Floral Park, 11004
Telephone: (718) 468-4355
Private agency, authorized by Colonial Farm House Restoration Society of Bellerose, Inc.
Founded in: 1975
Lillian Naar, Executive Director
Number of members: 550
Staff: part time 7, volunteer 25
Magazine: *Broadsides*
Major programs: museum, historic site(s), historic preservation, living history
Period of collections: 1772-1930

Records and Information Center, Lutheran Council/Archives of Cooperative Lutheranism
360 Park Ave., S, 10010
Telephone: (212) 532-6350
Private agency, authorized by Lutheran Council in the U.S.
Founded in: 1967
Alice M. Kendrick, Director
Staff: full time 4, part time 1
Major programs: library, archives, oral history, records management, research
Period of collections: 17th-20th centuries

Salvation Army Archives and Research Center
145 W. 15th St., 10011
Telephone: (212) 620-4392
Private agency, authorized by the Salvation Army
Founded in: 1974
Thomas Wilsted, Archivist/Administrator
Staff: full time 7, volunteer 1
Magazine: *Historical News-View*
Major programs: library, archives, manuscripts, newsletters/pamphlets, records management, research, exhibits, archaeology programs, photographic collections
Period of collections: 1865-present

Society of Illustrators
128 E. 63 St., 10021
Telephone: (212) 838-2560
Private agency
Founded in: 1901
Terrence Brown, Director
Number of members: 900
Staff: part time 1, volunteer 25
Magazine: *The Annual of American Illustration*
Major programs: library, archives, museum, book publishing, newsletters/pamphlets, exhibits, photographic collections, illustration art
Period of collections: 1920-1950

Sons of the Revolution in the State of New York
54 Pearl St., 10004
Telephone: (212) 425-1776
Founded in: 1876
Questionnaire not received

Theodore Roosevelt Birthplace National Historic Site
28 E. 20th St., 10003
Telephone: (212) 260-1616
Federal agency, authorized by National Park Service
Founded in: 1923
John R. Lancos, Site Manager
Staff: full time 4, part time 2
Major programs: museum, historic site(s), tours/pilgrimages, school programs, historic preservation, exhibits, audiovisual programs
Period of collections: 1870-1915

Trinity Museum
Broadway and Wall Sts.
Telephone: (212) 602-0848
Mail to: 74 Trinity Place, 10006
Private agency, authorized by Parish of Trinity Church
Founded in: 1697
Phyllis Barr, Curator/Archivist
Staff: full time 2, part time 2, volunteer 15
Major programs: archives, museum, historic site(s), tours/pilgrimages, oral history, school programs, newsletters/pamphlets, historic preservation, records management, exhibits, audiovisual programs, archaeology programs, photographic collections, genealogical services
Period of collections: 1697-present

The Ukrainian Museum
203 2nd Ave., 10021
Telephone: (212) 228-0110
Private agency
Founded in: 1976
Maria Shust, Director
Number of members: 1,800
Staff: full time 3, part time 5, volunteer 20
Major programs: archives, museum, catalogue publishing, research, exhibits, photographic collections

Period of collections: late 19th-early 20th centuries

U.S. Army Chaplain Museum
Ft. Hamilton, 11252
Telephone: (212) 836-4100, ext. 4282
Questionnaire not received

Washington Headquarters Association
W. 160th St. and Edgecomb Ave., 10032
Tlephone: (212) 923-8008
Founded in: 1904
Questionnaire not received

Yeshiva University Museum
2520 Amsterdam Ave., 10003
Telephone: (212) 960-5390
Private agency
Founded in: 1973
Sylvia A. Herskowitz, Director
Number of members: 200
Staff: full time 6, part time 5, volunteer 27
Major programs: library, museum, tours/pilgrimages, school programs, catalogue publishing, research, exhibits, audiovisual programs, photographic collections

NIAGARA FALLS

Niagara Falls Historical Society, Inc.
Telephone: (716) 278-8229
Mail to: c/o President, Public Library, 1425 Main St., 14305
Founded in: 1926
Donald E. Loker, President
Number of members: 25
Staff: volunteer 3
Magazine: *Out of the Mist*
Major programs: library, archives, manuscripts, newspapers, photographs
Period of collections: prehistoric-present

NORFOLK

Town of Norfolk Historical Museum
39 Main St.
Telephone: (315) 384-3223
Mail to: P.O. Box 645, 13667
Town agency
Founded in: 1985
Jean A. Young, Acting Curator
Staff: part time 1, volunteer 4
Major programs: museum, historic preservation
Period of collections: early 1800s-present

NORTH COLLINS

North Collins Historical Society
14111
Telephone: (716) 337-2215
Questionnaire not received

NORTHPORT

Northport Historical Society and Museum
215 Main St.
Telephone: (516) 757-9859
Mail to: P.O. Box 545, 11768
Private agency
Founded in: 1962

Marguerite Mudge, Museum Director
Number of members: 625
Staff: full time 1, part time 3,
volunteer 100
Major programs: archives, museum,
tours, junior history, oral history,
educational programs,
newsletters/pamphlets, exhibits
Period of collections: 19th-early 20th
centuries

NORTH TONAWANDA

**Carousel Society of the Niagara
Frontier, Inc.**
180 Thompson St.
Telephone: (716) 694-2859
Mail to: P.O. Box 672, 14120
Private agency
Founded in: 1980
Douglas A. Bathke, President
Number of members: 640
Staff: volunteer 21
Major programs: archives,
manuscripts, museum, historic
site(s), markers, tours/pilgrimages,
oral history, school programs,
newsletters/pamphlets, historic
preservation, records
management, research, exhibits,
audiovisual programs, restoration
of carousels
Period of collections: 1883-present

NORTH WHITE PLAINS

**Washington's Headquarters/Elijah
Miller Farmhouse**
Virginia Rd., 10803
Telephone: (914) 949-1236
County agency, authorized by
Department of Parks, Recreation,
Conservation and Historic
Preservation
Founded in: 1917
Teren Duffin, Curator
Staff: volunteer 2
Major programs: museum, historic
site(s), school programs, living
history
Period of collections: 18th century

NORWICH

**Chenango County Historical
Society**
45 Rexford St., 13815
Telephone: (607) 334-9227
Private agency
Founded in: 1936
E. J. Frink, President
Number of members: 300
Staff: volunteer 15
Major programs: museum
Period of collections: 1850-1900

NORWOOD

**Norwood Historical Association
and Museum**
39 N. Main St., 13668
Founded in: 1962
Questionnaire not received

NYACK

**Edward Hopper Landmark
Preservation Foundation/Hopper
House**
82 N. Broadway, 10960

Telephone: (914) 358-0774
Private agency
Founded in: 1971
Eleanor Hall Gibson, President
Number of members: 400
Staff: volunteer 25
Major programs: historic site(s),
historic preservation, exhibits
Period of collections: 1890-1900

Friends of the Nyacks, Inc.
P.O. Box 384, 10960
Telephone: (914) 358-2113
Private agency
Founded in: 1974
Ken Benjamin, Chair
Number of members: 274
Staff: part time 2, volunteer 20
Major programs: manuscripts,
historic site(s), oral history,
newsletters/pamphlets, historic
preservation, living history,
audiovisual programs,
photographic collections
Period of collections: 1974-present

OAKDALE

**William K. Vanderbilt Historical
Society**
P.O. Box 433, Idle Hour, 11769
Telephone: (516) 567-2277
Private agency
Founded in: 1965
Elizabeth Kuss, Chair
Number of members: 150
Staff: volunteer 10
Major programs: library, museum,
newsletters/pamphlets, historic
preservation
Period of collections: 1850-present

OHIO

Ohio Historical Society
R.D. Cold Brook, 13324
Telephone: (315) 826-3160
Founded in: 1974
Questionnaire not received

OLD CHATHAM

Federation of Historical Services
Shaker Museum Rd., 12136
Telephone: (518) 794-7400
Founded in: 1978
Questionnaire not received

Shaker Museum
149 Shaker Museum Rd., 12136
Telephone: (518) 794-9100
Founded in: 1950
Questionnaire not received

OLD WESTBURY

Old Westbury Gardens
P.O. Box 430, 11568
Telephone: (516) 333-0048
Private agency
Founded in: 1959
Carl A. Totemeier, Director
Number of members: 1,200
Staff: full time 29, part time 20,
volunteer 150
Major programs: museum, historic
site(s), school programs,
newsletters/pamphlets, historic
preservation, exhibits, living
history, horticultural garden
Period of collections: 1906-1959

ONEIDA

Madison County Historical Society
435 Main St., 13421
Telephone: (315) 363-4136
Private agency
Founded in: 1899
Barbara J. Giambastiani, Director
Number of members: 1,035
Staff: full time 2, part time 3,
volunteer 25
Magazine: *Madison County Heritage
Studies in Traditional American
Crafts*
Major programs: library, archives,
manuscripts, museum, oral history,
school programs, book publishing,
newsletters/pamphlets, historic
preservation, research, exhibits,
audiovisual programs,
photographic collections
Period of collections: Victorian era

ONEONTA

Museums at Hartwick
13820
Telephone: (607) 432-4200
Private agency, authorized by
Hartwick College
Founded in: 1960
Jane desGrange, Director
Staff: full time 2, part time 5
Major programs: archives, museum,
exhibits
Period of collections: 9000 B.C.-A.D.
1600

National Soccer Hall of Fame
58 Market St., 13820
Telephone: (607) 432-3351
Private agency, authorized by State
Education Department and U.S.
Soccer Federation
Founded in: 1981
Albert Colone, Director
Number of members: 200
Staff: full time 5, part time 3,
volunteer 9
Major programs: archives,
newsletters/pamphlets, exhibits,
photographic collections
Period of collections: 1920-mid 1950s

**Upper Susquehanna Historical
Society and Museum**
11 Ford Ave.
Telephone: (607) 432-5143/432-2888
Mail to: 203 River St., 13820
Founded in: 1939
Otto Sohder, Jr., President
Number of members: 78
Major programs: library, museum,
historic sites preservation,
tours/pilgrimages, books, historic
preservation

Yager Museum
Hartwick College, 13820
Telephone: (607) 432-4200
Founded in: 1967
Questionnaire not received

ONTARIO

Ontario Historical Society
P.O. Box 462, 14519
Telephone: (315) 524-3441
Private agency
Founded in: 1968
Number of members: 125

Major programs: museum, historic
site(s), school programs,
newsletters/pamphlets, historic
preservation, records
management, exhibits, audiovisual
programs, photographic
collections
Period of collections: 1860-1920

**Town of Ontario Historical and
Landmark Preservation Society**
7155 Ontario Center Rd.
Telephone: (315) 524-3441
Mail to: P.O. Box 462, 14519
Founded in: 1969
Questionnaire not received

ORCHARD PARK

Orchard Park Historical Society
E. Quaker St.
Mail to: 5800 Armor Rd., 14127
Founded in: 1950
John N. Printy, President
Number of members: 60
Staff: volunteer 2
Major programs: historic site(s),
markers, school programs,
photographic collections
Period of collections: late 1900s

ORIENT

**Oysterponds Historical
Society, Inc.**
Village Lane, 11957
Telephone: (516) 323-2480
Private agency
Founded in: 1944
E. Richard Keogh, Managing Director
Number of members: 450
Magazine: *Oysterponds Historical
Society Museum News*
Major programs: library, archives,
manuscripts, museum, historic
site(s), markers, tours/pilgrimages,
oral history, school programs, book
publishing, newsletters/pamphlets,
historic preservation, records
management, research, exhibits,
living history, audiovisual
programs, photographic
collections, genealogical services
Period of collections: mid 18th-19th
centuries

ORISKANY

**Battle of Oriskany Historical
Society**
Utica St.
Telephone: (315) 768-7224
Mail to: P.O. Box 517, 13424
Founded in: 1967
Questionnaire not received

OSSINING

**Ossining Historical Society and
Museum**
196 Croton Ave., 10562
Telephone: (914) 941-0001
Private agency
Founded in: 1931
Virginia Cavanaugh, President
Number of members: 300
Staff: volunteer 25

Major programs: library, archives,
museum, historic site(s), markers,
oral history, school programs, book
publishing, newsletters/pamphlets,
historic preservation, research,
exhibits, genealogical services
Period of collections:
prehistoric-present

Westchester Preservation League
36 S. Highland Ave., 10562
Telephone: (914) 941-2750
Private agency
Founded in: 1979
Robin Moroz Imhoff, President
Number of members: 175
Magazine: *Columns*
Major programs: library, archives,
historic site(s), tours/pilgrimages,
historic preservation

OSWEGO

Ft. Ontario State Historic Site
E. 7th St.
Telephone: (315) 343-4711
Mail to: P.O. Box 102, 13126
State agency, authorized by Office of
Parks, Recreation and Historic
Preservation
Founded in: 1949
Donald I. Laird, Jr., Interpretive
Programs Assistant
Staff: full time 6, part time 17,
volunteer 20
Major programs: library, museum,
historic site(s), school programs,
historic preservation, exhibits,
living history, archaeology
programs, photographic
collections
Period of collections: 1840-1880

**Heritage Foundation of Oswego
County**
161 W. 1st St., 13126
Telephone: (315) 342-3354
Private agency
Founded in: 1962
Susan Rapaport, President
Number of members: 192
Staff: full time 1, part time 1
Major programs: library, tours,
newsletters/pamphlets, historic
preservation, research, audiovisual
programs

Oswego County Historical Society
135 E. 3rd St., 13126
Telephone: (315) 343-1342
Private agency
Founded in: 1896
Ann L. Koski, Director
Number of members: 350
Staff: full time 4, part time 1
Magazine: *Oswego County Historical
Society Journal*
Major programs: archives, museum,
school programs, research,
exhibits, photographic collections
Period of collections: 1830-1930

OWEGO

Susquhanna Valley Flintlocks, Inc.
Telephone: (607) 687-5788
Mail to: R.D. 2, Box 188, 13827
Founded in: 1975
Questionnaire not received

Tioga County Historical Society
110-112 Front St., 13827
Telephone: (607) 687-2460
Private agency
Founded in: 1914
William Lay, Jr., Curator
Number of members: 900
Staff: full time 1, part time 4,
volunteer 30
Major programs: library, archives,
museum, book publishing,
newsletters/pamphlets, exhibits,
genealogical services
Period of collections: 1790-1960

OYSTER BAY

**Coe Hall at Planting Fields
Arboretum**
Planting Fields Rd.
Telephone: (516) 922-0479
Mail to: P.O. Box 58, 11771
Private agency, authorized by
Planting Fields Foundation
Founded in: 1978
Lorraine Gilligan, Curator
Staff: full time 2, part time 1,
volunteer 50
Major programs: museum, historic
site(s), tours/pilgrimages, school
programs, historic preservation,
photographic collections
Period of collections: 1920s

Oyster Bay Historical Society
20 Summit St.
Telephone: (516) 922-5092
Mail to: P.O. Box 297, 11771
Private agency
Founded in: 1966
Peter R. Fisher, President
Number of members: 198
Staff: part time 2, volunteer 5
Major programs: library, archives,
manuscripts, museum, school
programs, book publishing, historic
preservation, research, exhibits,
photographic collections,
genealogical services
Period of collections: 1700-1915

Raynham Hall Museum
20 W. Main St., 11771
Telephone: (516) 922-6808
Private agency
Founded in: 1953
Stuart A. Chase, Director
Number of members: 300
Staff: full time 1, part time 2,
volunteer 30
Major programs: library, archives,
museum, historic site(s),
tours/pilgrimages, school
programs, newsletters/pamphlets,
research, exhibits, audiovisual
programs, photographic
collections
Period of collections: 1750-1875

**Scipio Society of Naval and Military
History, Inc.**
143 Cove Rd., 11771
Telephone: (516) 922-3918
Private agency, authorized by the
University of the State of New York
Founded in: 1979
Robert S. Robe, Jr., President
Number of members: 40
Staff: part time 3, volunteer 1

Magazine: *The Grenade*
Major programs: library, museum, oral history, school programs, historic preservation, living history, audiovisual programs, field services
Period of collections: 1850-1950

Townsend Society of America, Inc.
107 E. Main St., 11771
Mail to: P.O. Box 40, Greenport, 11944
Founded in: 1962
Questionnaire not received

PAINTED POST

Erwin-Painted Post Museum
115 Water St.
Telephone: (607) 962-1382
Mail to: 108 Hamilton Circle, 14870
Town agency
Founded in: 1945
Joseph J. Kane, Curator
Staff: part time 2
Major programs: library, archives, museum, school programs, records management, living history
Period of collections: 1775-present

PALMYRA

Historic Palmyra, Inc.
122 William St., 14522
Private agency
Founded in: 1967
Robert Leopard, President
Number of members: 280
Staff: volunteer 60
Magazine: *Historic Palmyra News*
Major programs: museum, historic site(s), markers, tours/pilgrimages, school programs, book publishing, newsletters/pamphlets, historic preservation, research, exhibits, living history, audiovisual programs, photographic collections, genealogical services
Period of collections: 1800-1900

PARISHVILLE

Parishville Historical Association
Main St.
Telephone: (315) 265-7619
Mail to: P.O. Box 534, 13672
Founded in: 1950
Questionnaire not received

PATCHOGUE

Museum-Manor of St. George
William Floyd Parkway, Smith's Point, Near Mastic Beach
Telephone: (516) 281-5034
Mail to: P.O. Box 349, 11772
Founded in: 1955
Questionnaire not received

PAVILION

Covington Historical Society
La Grange Rd., 14525
Telephone: (716) 584-3254 (historian)
Private agency
Herbert Toal, President
Number of members: 40
Staff: volunteer 10

Major programs: museum, living history, photographic collections
Period of collections: 1875-present

PAWLING

Historical Society of Quaker Hill and Pawling, Inc.
P.O. Box 99, 12564
Telephone: (914) 855-5891
Private agency
Founded in: 1910
Charline H. Daniels, President
Number of members: 200
Staff: volunteer 40
Major programs: archives, museum, markers, tours/pilgrimages, oral history, genealogical services
Period of collections: 1764-present

PEEKSKILL

The Peekskill Museum
124 Union Ave.
Telephone: (914) 737-1885
Mail to: P.O. Box 84, 10566
Private agency
Founded in: 1946
John Leslie, President
Number of members: 150
Staff: volunteer 20
Major programs: museum, educational programs
Period of collections: 1776-1920

Van Cortlandtville Historical Society
297 Locust Ave., 10566
Founded in: 1922
Charles Perry, President
Number of members: 80
Staff: volunteer 20
Major programs: historic site(s), school programs

PENN YAN

Yates County Genealogical and Historical Society, Inc.
200 Main St., 14527
Telephone: (315) 536-7318
Founded in: 1860
Virginia H. Gibbs, Director
Number of members: 300
Staff: full time 1, part time 4, volunteer 40
Major programs: archives, museum, tours/pilgrimages, school programs, newsletters/pamphlets, historic preservation, research, exhibits, audiovisual programs, photographic collections, genealogical services
Period of collections: 19th century

PERRY

Wyoming Pioneer Historical Association
14 Covington St., 14530
Telephone: (716) 237-3458
Founded in: 1872
Questionnaire not received

PERTH

Town of Perth Historical Society
R.D. 6, Amsterdam, 12010
Telephone: (518) 842-9497
Town agency, authorized by State Education Department

Sylvia Zierak, Research Historian
Major programs: book publishing, records management, research
Period of collections: 1700s-present

PINE PLAINS

Little Nine Partners Historical Society
P.O. Box 243, 12567
Private agency
Founded in: 1962
Mrs. E. Matthew Netter, President
Number of members: 98
Major programs: library, books, historic preservation, oral history, genealogical services
Period of collections: 19th century

PITTSFORD

Historic Pittsford
18 Monroe Ave.
Telephone: (716) 381-3799
Mail to: P.O. Box 38, 14534
Private agency
Founded in: 1966
Mrs. Douglas Menzie, President
Number of members: 300
Staff: part time 1, volunteer 20
Major programs: museum, historic site(s), markers, book publishing, newsletters/pamphlets, historic preservation
Period of collections: from 1830s

PLATTSBURGH

Benjamin F. Feinberg Library, State University College
12901
Telephone: (518) 564-3180
State agency
Founded in: 1962
Joseph G. Swinyer, Special Collections Librarian
Staff: full time 1, part time 2
Major programs: library, manuscripts
Period of collections: 1783-present

Clinton County Historical Association
City Hall
Telephone: (518) 561-0340
Mail to: P.O. Box 332, 12901
Private agency
Founded in: 1945
Helen W. Allan, Museum Director
Number of members: 400
Staff: full time 1, part time 2, volunteer 12
Magazine: *North Country Notes/The Antiquarian*
Major programs: museum, school programs, book publishing, newsletters/pamphlets, historic preservation, exhibits, audiovisual programs, photographic collections
Period of collections: 1784-1940

Crown Point Foundation
P.O. Box A-140, New York, 10163
Founded in: 1960
Questionnaire not received

Kent-Delord House Museum
17 Cumberland Ave., 12901
Telephone: (518) 561-1035

Private agency, authorized by
Kent-Delord House Museum
Corporation
Founded in: 1928
Roger G. Nyce, Director
Number of members: 385
Staff: full time 2, part time 2,
volunteer 45
Major programs: library, archives,
manuscripts, museum, historic
site(s), school programs,
newsletters/pamphlets, research,
exhibits, photographic collections
Period of collections: 1800-1913

**Northern New York
American-Canadian
Genealogical Society**
P.O. Box 1256, 12901
Telephone: (518) 561-2791
(president)
Private agency
Founded in: 1983
William H. Marquis, President
Number of members: 176
Magazine: *Lifelines*
Major programs: library, genealogical
services
Period of collections: 1660-1980

PORT JEFFERSON

**Historical Society of Greater Port
Jefferson**
115 Prospect St.
Telephone: (516) 473-2665
Mail to: P.O. Box 586, 11777
Founded in: 1967
Barry Warren, President
Number of members: 105
Staff: volunteer 25
Major programs: library, archives,
museum, historic sites
preservation, markers,
tours/pilgrimages, oral history,
books, newsletters/pamphlets,
craft classes, harbor diorama
Period of collections: early 1900s

PORT JERVIS

Minisink Valley Historical Society
138 Pike St.
Telephone: (914) 856-2375
Mail to: P.O. Box 659, 12771
Private agency
Founded in: 1889
Peter Osborne, Executive Director
Number of members: 350
Staff: full time 1, volunteer 10
Major programs: library, manuscripts,
museum, historic site(s), historic
preservation, research, exhibits,
photographic collections,
genealogical services
Period of collections: 1870-1930

PORT WASHINGTON

**Cow Neck Peninsula Historical
Society**
336 Port Washington Blvd., 11050
Telephone: (516) 365-9074
Founded in: 1962
Questionnaire not received

POTSDAM

Potsdam Public Museum
Civic Center, P. O. Box 191, 13676
Telephone: (315) 265-6910
City agency
Founded in: 1940
Katharine F. Wyant, Director
Staff: full time 1, part time 6,
volunteer 6
Major programs: archives, museum,
school programs,
newsletters/pamphlets, exhibits
Period of collections: 19th century

POUGHKEEPSIE

Brick House
Rt. 17-K, 12549
Telephone: (914) 457-5951
County agency
Robert C. Eurich, Museum Curator
Staff: full time 3, volunteer 3
Major programs: museum, historic
site(s), historic preservation
Period of collections: 18th-20th
centuries

**Dutchess County Genealogical
Society**
P.O. Box 708, 12602
Founded in: 1971
Stanley Newman, President
Number of members: 250
Magazine: *The Dutchess*
Major programs: library, book
publishing, newsletters/pamphlets

Dutchess County Historical Society
Mail to: P.O. Box 88, 12602
Private agency
Founded in: 1914
Eileen Mylod Hayden, President
Number of members: 700
Staff: part time 2
Magazine: *Yearbook*
Major programs: library, archives,
historic site(s), tours/pilgrimages,
book publishing,
newsletters/pamphlets, historic
preservation
Period of collections: 18th
century-present

**Dutchess County Landmarks
Association, Inc.**
Clinton House, 549 Main St., 12601
Telephone: (914) 471-8777
Mail to: P.O. Box 944, 12602
Founded in: 1969
Magazine: *Landmarks Newsletter*
Major programs: historic
preservation, consultation services

**Hudson River Sloop
Clearwater, Inc.**
112 Market St., 10601
Telephone: (914) 454-7673
Private agency
Founded in: 1966
John Mylod, Executive Director
Number of members: 7,000
Staff: full time 25, part time 5,
volunteer 3
Magazine: *Clearwater Navigator*
Major programs: library, school
programs, newsletters/pamphlets,
historic preservation, exhibits,
living history

Poughkeepsie Historical Society
Telephone: (914) 454-0744
Mail to: P.O. Box 92, 12602
Private agency
Founded in: 1980
Timothy Allred, President
Major programs: audiovisual
programs

**Regional History Programs, Marist
College**
North Rd., 1260l
Telephone: (914) 471-3240
Private agency, authorized by the
college
Founded in: 1980
Wilma J. Burke, Director
Staff: full time 2, part time 1
Major programs: library, archives,
manuscripts, museum, oral history,
school programs,
newsletters/pamphlets, records
management, research, exhibits,
audiovisual programs,
photographic collections, student
internships
Period of collections: Colonial
era-present

POUGHQUAG

Beekman Historical Society
P.O. Box 165, 12533
Private agency
John G. Williams, President
Number of members: 25
8taff: volunteer 15
Major programs: tours/pilgrimages,
newsletters/pamphlets, research,
genealogical services
Period of collections: 1800-present

POUND RIDGE

Pound Ridge Historical Society
P.O. Box 1718, 10576
Telephone: (914) 764-5106
Private agency
Nancy Wasserman, President
Number of members: 300
Staff: part time 1, volunteer 25
Major programs: museum,
newsletters/pamphlets, records
management, exhibits
Period of collections: 18th-20th
centuries

PRATTSBURG

**Committee to Preserve the
Narcissa Prentiss House, Inc.**
Mill Pond Rd.
Telephone: (607) 522-3753
Mail to: P.O. Box 205, 14873
Private agency, authorized by
University of the State of New York
Founded in: 1979
Valentine B. Pratt, Chair
Major programs: historic preservation

PRATTSVILLE

Zadock Pratt Museum, Inc.
Main St., 12468
Telephone: (518) 299-3395
Founded in: 1963
Charles E. Proper, Curator
Number of members: 127
Staff: full time 1, volunteer 10

Major programs: manuscripts, museum, markers, tours, school programs, newsletters/pamphlets, research, exhibits, photographic collections
Period of collections: 1824-1871

PULTNEYVILLE

Pultneyville Historical Society
14538
Questionnaire not received

PUTNAM VALLEY

Putnam Valley Historical Society
Peeksill Hollow Rd.
Telephone: (914) 528-8842
Mail to: P.O. Box 297, 10579
Founded in: 1968
Questionnaire not received

REMSEN

Remsen-Steuben Historical Society
Didymus Thomas Library, Main St.
Telephone: (315) 831-8781
Mail to: P.O. Box 116, 13438
Private agency, authorized by State Department of Education
Founded in: 1975
Lorena S. Jersen, President
Number of members: 50
Major programs: historic site(s), tours/pilgrimages, oral history, book publishing, genealogical services, rehabilitation of neglected cemeteries
Period of collections: 1790s-early 1900s

RENSSELAER

Friends of Ft. Crailo
Ft. Crailo State Historic Site
9 Riverside Ave., 12144
Telephone: (518) 463-8738
Founded in: 1924
Questionnaire not received

RENSSELAERVILLE

Rensselaerville Historical Society
Telephone: (518) 797-5154
Mail to: P.O. Box 8, 12147
Private agency
Founded in: 1964
Robert Scardamalia, President
Number of members: 425
Staff: volunteer 35
Magazine: *Rural Folio*
Major programs: archives, museum, newsletters/pamphlets
Period of collections: 1783-1918

REXFORD

Vischer Ferry Association
P.O. Box 179, Sugar Hill Rd., 12148
Telephone: (518) 371-5702
Founded in: 1972
Questionnaire not received

RHINEBECK

Hudson River Heritage, Inc.
Telephone: (914) 876-7775
Mail to: P.O. Box 287, 12572
Founded in: 1974
Number of members: 150
Staff: volunteer 15

Major programs: archives, historic sites preservation, tours/pilgrimages, newsletters/pamphlets, historic preservation
Period of collections: 19th century

Old Rhinebeck Aerodrome, Inc.
Stone Church Rd.
Telephone: (914) 758-8610
Mail to: R.D. 1, Box 89, 12572
Private agency
Founded in: 1958
Cole Palen, General Manager
Staff: full time 6, part time 30
Major programs: museum, living history
Period of collections: 1908-1940

RICHLAND

Half-Shire Historical Society
P.O. Box 73, Main St., 13144
Telephone: (315) 298-2986 (secretary)
State agency, authorized by State Department of Education
Founded in: 1972
George O. Widrig, Secretary
Staff: volunteer 15
Major programs: archives, museum, genealogical services
Period of collections: 1800-present

RICHVILLE

Richville Historical Association
Mail to: Gimlet St., 13681
Questionnaire not received

RIVERHEAD

Suffolk County Historical Society
300 W. Main St., 11901
Telephone: (516) 727-2881
Private agency
Founded in: 1886
Wallace W. Broege, Director
Number of members: 950
Staff: full time 5, part time 12, volunteer 25
Magazine: *Register*
Major programs: library, archives, manuscripts, museum, school programs, book publishing, newsletters/pamphlets, research, exhibits, photographic collections, genealogical services
Period of collections: 19th century

ROCHESTER

American Baptist Historical Society
1106 S. Goodman St., 14620
Telephone: (716) 473-1740
Private agency, authorized by American Baptist Churches
Founded in: 1853
William H. Brackney, Executive Director/Archivist
Staff: full time 2, part time 4
Magazine: *American Baptist Quarterly*
Major programs: library, archives, manuscripts
Period of collections: 1800-present

Baker-Cederberg Archives of the Rochester General Hospital
1425 Portland Ave., 14621
Telephone: (716) 338-4000
Founded in: 1947
Philip G. Maples, Archivist
Staff: part time 1, volunteer 5
Major programs: library, exhibits, oral history
Period of collections: 1847-present

Brighton Historical Society
52 Kimbark Rd., 14610
Telephone: (716) 381-6802
Private agency
Founded in: 1928
Roberta La Chiusa, President
Number of members: 40
Staff: volunteer 5
Major programs: archives, historic site(s), oral history
Period of collections: 1817-present

Charlotte-Genesee Lighthouse Historical Society
70 Lighthouse St., 14612
Telephone: (716) 621-6179
Private agency
Founded in: 1983
Felipe de Chateauvieux, President
Number of members: 132
Staff: volunteer 100
Magazine: *The Beach*
Major programs: museum, tours/pilgrimages, book publishing, newsletters/pamphlets, historic preservation, audiovisual programs, photographic collections

Genesee Country Museum
Flint Hill Rd., Mumford, 14511
Telephone: (716) 325-1776
Mail to: P.O. Box 1819, 14603
Private agency
Founded in: 1976
Stuart B. Bolger, Director
Number of members: 1,275
Staff: full time 12, part time 120
Major programs: archives, historic site(s), school programs, historic preservation, living history
Period of collections: 19th century

Historical Society of Greece
1077 English Rd.
Telephone: (716) 225-0293
Mail to: P.O. Box 16249, 14616
Private agency
Founded in: 1969
Number of members: 145
Major programs: book publishing, audiovisual programs
Period of collections: 1890-1920

International Museum of Photography/George Eastman House
900 East Ave., 14607
Telephone: (716) 271-3361
Private agency
Founded in: 1947
Robert A. Mayer, Director
Number of members: 2,500
Staff: full time 61, part time 8, volunteer 30
Magazine: *Image*
Major programs: library, archives, museum, educational programs, newsletters/pamphlets, exhibition
Period of collections: 1830-present

Irondequoit Historical Society
1280 Titus Ave., 14617
Telephone: (716) 467-8840
Founded in: 1963
Questionnaire not received

Landmark Society of Western New York, Inc.
130 Spring St., 14608
Telephone: (716) 546-7029
Private agency
Founded in: 1937
Henry McCartney, Executive Director
Number of members: 2,300
Staff: full time 14, part time 5, volunteer 300
Major programs: museum, historic sites preservation
Period of collections: 1783-1865

Margaret Woodbury Strong Museum
1 Manhattan Square, 14607
Telephone: (716) 263-2700
Private agency
Founded in: 1968
William T. Alderson, Director
Number of members: 750
Staff: full time 84, part time 4, volunteer 176
Magazine: *The Inkwell*
Major programs: library, archives, museum, school programs, book publishing, newsletters/pamphlets, research, exhibits, audiovisual programs, photographic collections
Period of collections: 1820-1940

New York Museum of Transportation
E. River Rd.
Telephone: (716) 533-1113
Mail to: P.O. Box 136, W. Henrietta, 14686
Questionnaire not received

New York State Archaeological Association
657 East Ave.
Telephone: (716) 271-4320
Mail to: P.O. Box 1480, 14603
Private agency
Founded in: 1916
Gordon C. DeAngelo, President
Number of members: 1,000
Staff: volunteer 80
Major programs: library, archives, manuscripts, educational programs, books, newsletters/pamphlets
Period of collections: prehistoric-1865

Office of the City Historian
115 South Ave., 14604
Telephone: (716) 428-7340
Founded in: 1921
Questionnaire not received

Rochester Historical Society
485 East Ave., 14607
Telephone: (716) 271-2705
Private agency
Founded in: 1861
Elizabeth G. Holahan, President
Number of members: 800
Staff: part time 3, volunteer 17
Major programs: library, archives, manuscripts, museum, historic site(s), newsletters/pamphlets,

research, exhibits, photographic collections, genealogical services
Period of collections: 1820-present

Rochester Museum and Science Center
657 East Ave.
Telephone: (716) 271-4320
Mail to: P.O. Box 1480, 14603
Private agency
Founded in: 1912
Richard C. Shultz, President
Number of members: 7,400
Staff: full time 93, part time 50, volunteer 240
Major programs: library, archives, museum, school programs, newsletters/pamphlets, research, exhibits, audiovisual programs, archaeology programs, photographic collections
Period of collections: prehistoric-present

Stone-Tolan House
2370 East Ave., 14610
Telephone: (716) 546-7028
Mail to: 130 Spring St., 14608
Private agency, authorized by Landmark Society of Western New York
Founded in: 1937
Ann C. Salter, Director of Museums
Number of members: 2,400
Staff: full time 13, part time 3, volunteer 45
Major programs: library, museum, historic preservation
Period of collections: late 18th-early 19th centuries

Susan B. Anthony Memorial, Inc.
17 Madison St.
Telephone: (716) 381-6202
Mail to: 52 Kimbark Rd., 14610
Founded in: 1946
Roberta LaChiusa, President
Number of members: 400
Major programs: museum, historic sites preservation
Period of collections: 1865-present

Visual Studies Workshop Research Center
4 Elton St., 14607
Telephone: (716) 442-8676
Questionnaire not received

ROCKVILLE CENTRE

Phillips House Museum
28 Hempstead Ave.
Mail to: P.O. Box 605, 11571
Private agency
Founded in: 1977
Carol Cole, Board President
Number of members: 200
Staff: part time 1
Major programs: archives, museum, tours, exhibits
Period of collections: early 1800s-present

ROME

Afro-American Heritage Association
P.O. Box 451, 13440
Telephone: (315) 337-5018
Private agency
Founded in: 1978

Jessie Thorpe, President
Number of members: 20
Major programs: historic preservation, research, exhibits, audiovisual programs
Period of collections: to present

Erie Canal Village
5789 New London Rd., 13440
Telephone: (315) 336-6000, ext. 249
City agency
Founded in: 1972
Mary Reynolds, Assistant Curator
Staff: full time 3, part time 4, volunteer 50
Major programs: library, museum, historic site(s), school programs, research, exhibits, living history
Period of collections: 1825-1870

Ft. Stanwix National Monument
112 E. Park St., 13440
Telephone: (315) 336-2090
Federal agency, authorized by National Park Service
William N. Jackson, Superintendent
Staff: full time 8, part time 8
Major programs: living history
Period of collections: 1777-1778

Historic Rome Development Authority
5789 New London Rd., 13440
Telephone: (315) 337-0021
Questionnaire not received

Rome Historical Society
200 Church St., 13440
Telephone: (315) 336-5870
Founded in: 1936
Number of members: 950
Staff: full time 4, part time 3
Magazine: *Annals and Recollections*
Major programs: library, manuscripts, museum, historic sites preservation, tours
Period of collections: to present

ROSCOE

Catskill Fly Fishing Center
Broad St.
Mail to: P.O. Box 473, 12776
Private agency
Founded in: 1983
Alan Fried, President
Number of members: 2,300
Staff: part time 1, volunteer 20
Magazine: *Catskill Angler*
Major programs: library, archives, manuscripts, museum, newsletters/pamphlets, historic preservation, research, exhibits, living history, photographic collections, history of fly fishing
Period of collections: 1890-present

ROSLYN

Roslyn Landmark Society
Paper Mill Rd., 11576
Telephone: (516) 621-3040
Private agency
Founded in: 1961
Roger G. Gerry, President
Number of members: 500
Staff: volunteer 75
Major programs: archives, manuscripts, museum, historic site(s), markers, tours, historic

preservation, research, exhibits, archaeology programs, photographic collections
Period of collections: 1680-1900

ROXBURY

Roxbury Burrough's Club
Main St., 12474
Private agency
Founded in: 1952
Wheldon Farleigh, President
Number of members: 52
Major programs: historic site(s), school programs, photographic collections
Period of collections: 1890-1920

RYE

Lower Hudson Conference
c/o Rye Historical Society, 1 Purchase St., 10580
Telephone: (914) 967-7595
Founded in: 1978
Questionnaire not received

Rye Historical Society
1 Purchase St., 10580
Telephone: (914) 967-7588
Founded in: 1964
Susan A. Morison, Director
Number of members: 850
Staff: full time 2, part time 2, volunteer 75
Major programs: library, manuscripts, museum, oral history, educational programs, newsletters/pamphlets
Period of collections: mid 18th century-present

SACKET HARBOR

Pickering-Beach Historical Museum
W. Main St., 13685
Telephone: (315) 646-2052/646-3868
Founded in: 1927
Questionnaire not received

Sacket Harbor Battlefield State Historic Site
505 W. Washington St.
Telephone: (315) 646-36334
Mail to: P.O. Box 27, 13683
State agency
Founded in: 1933
Gary G. Ernest, Historic Site Manager II
Staff: full time 5, part time 13, volunteer 1
Major programs: museum, historic site(s), markers, school programs, historic preservation, research, exhibits, audiovisual programs, archaeology programs
Period of collections: 1811-1815

Sacket Harbor Historical Society
Main St., 13685
Telephone: (315) 646-3525
Questionnaire not received

SAG HARBOR

Sag Harbor Whaling and Historical Museum
Main and Garden Sts.
Telephone: (516) 725-0770
Mail to: P.O. Box 1327, 11963
Founded in: 1936

George A. Finckenor, Sr., Curator/Village Historian
Number of members: 102
Staff: full time 4
Major programs: library, manuscripts, museum, tours, oral history, school programs, book publishing, research, exhibits, photographic collections
Period of collections: 1700-present

ST. JOHNSVILLE

Ft. Klock Historic Restoration
Rt. 5, R.D. 3, 13452
Telephone: (518) 568-7779
Private agency
Founded in: 1963
Dan Nellis, President
Number of members: 50
Staff: part time 2, volunteer 25
Major programs: museum, historic site(s), school programs, historic preservation, audiovisual programs
Period of collections: 1750-1850

Palatine Settlement Society
78 W. Main St., 13452
Telephone: (518) 568-7582
Private agency
Founded in: 1983
Milford A. Decker, President
Number of members: 115
Major programs: historic site(s), historic preservation, living history
Period of collections: 1725-1840

SALAMANCA

Salamanca Rail Museum
170 Main St., 14779
Telephone: (716) 945-3589
City agency
Founded in: 1984
William J. Fries, President
Number of members: 200
Staff: full time 15
Major programs: museum, historic site(s), tours/pilgrimages, exhibits
Period of collections: 1850-present

Seneca-Iroquois National Museum
Alleghany Indian Reservation, Broad St. Extension
Telephone: (716) 945-1738
Mail to: P.O. Box 442, 14779
Founded in: 1976
George H. Abrams, Director
Staff: full time 15, part time 2, volunteer 2
Major programs: museum, school programs, records management, research, exhibits, archaeology programs, photographic collections

SALEM

Hebron Preservation Society
R.D. 1 12865
Founded in: (518) 854-7610
Founded in: 1973
Gertrude Getty, President
Number of members: 120
Staff: volunteer 50
Major programs: museum, historic sites preservation, tours/pilgrimages, oral history, educational programs, historic preservation
Period of collections: 1876-present

SALT SPRINGVILLE

Salt Springville Community Restoration
Clinton Rd.
Telephone: (607) 264-3684
Mail to: P.O. Box 124, Cherry Valley, 13320
Private agency
Founded in: 1975
Roberta Miller, Board Chair
Staff: part time 1, volunteer 20
Major programs: historic site(s), markers, exhibits

SARANAC LAKE

Historic Saranac Lake
N. Elba Town House, 132 River St.
Telephone: (518) 891-0971
Mail to: P.O. Box 1030, 12983
Private agency
Founded in: 1980
Mary B. Hotaling, Executive Director
Staff: full time 1, part time 3
Major programs: book publishing, newsletters/pamphlets, historic preservation
Period of collections: 1884-1954

SARATOGA

Saratoga Historical Foundation
20450 Saratoga Los Gratos Rd.
Mail to: P.O. Box 172, 95071
Private agency
Founded in: 1960
Louise Cooper, President
Number of members: 125
Staff: volunteer 35
Major programs: library, museum, book publishing, newsletters/pamphlets, historic preservation, photographic collections
Period of collections: 1850-present

SARATOGA SPRINGS

Historical Society of Saratoga Springs
Casino Congress Park
Telephone: (518) 584-6920
Mail to: P.O. Box 216, 12866
Private agency
Founded in: 1883
Heidi A. Fuge, Museum Director
Number of members: 500
Staff: full time 2, volunteer 32
Magazine: *Saratoga Chips*
Major programs: museum, school programs, newsletters/pamphlets, research, exhibits
Period of collections: 19th century

National Museum of Racing, Inc.
Union Ave., 12866
Telephone: (518) 584-0400
Founded in: 1950
Elaine E. Mann, Director
Staff: full time 5, part time 6
Major programs: museum
Period of collections: 1865-present

Saratoga Springs Preservation Foundation
P.O. Box 442, 12866
Telephone: (518) 587-5030
Private agency
Founded in: 1977
Theodore Corbett, Director

Number of members: 300
Staff: full time 3, part time 1,
     volunteer 3
Major programs: library, historic
     site(s), markers, tours/pilgrimages,
     junior history, school programs,
     newsletters/pamphlets, historic
     preservation, living history, field
     services
Period of collections: 19th century

SARDINIA

Sardinia Historical Society
Savage Rd., 14134
Telephone: (716) 496-8847
Mail to: 3829 Creek Rd., Chaffee,
     14030
Founded in: 1973
Questionnaire not received

SAYVILLE

Sayville Historical Society
P.O. Box 658, 11782
Founded in: 1947
Magazine: Homestead Happenings
Major programs: library, museum,
     historic sites preservation,
     tours/pilgrimages,
     newsletters/pamphlets, historic
     preservation, photo collection
Period of collections: 1900

Suffolk Marine Museum
P.O. Box 44, Montauk Hwy., 11796
Telephone: (516) 567-1733
County agency, authorized by State
     Education Department
Founded in: 1966
Rober B. Dunkerley, Director
Number of members: 2,000
Staff: full time 2, part time 9,
     volunteer 20
Magazine: Dolphin
Major programs: library, museum,
     oral history, school programs,
     newsletters/pamphlets, historic
     preservation, research, exhibits,
     photographic collections
Period of collections: 1850-present

SCARSDALE

**Early American Industries
     Association**
2 Winding Lane, 10583
Telephone: (914) 472-4897
Founded in: 1933
Questionnaire not received

Scarsdale Historical Society
937 Post Rd.
Telephone: (914) 723-1744
Mail to: P.O. Box 431, 10583
Private agency
Founded in: 1972
Eda L. Newhouse, President
Staff: full time 2, part time 2
Magazine: What's Happening
Major programs: archives, museum,
     historic site(s), school programs,
     newsletters/pamphlets, historic
     preservation, records
     management, research, exhibits,
     living history
Period of collections: late 18th-early
     19th centuries

SCHAGHTICOKE

**Knickerbocker Historical
     Society, Inc.**
Knickerbocker Rd.
Mail to: P.O. Box 1363, 12154
Questionnaire not received

SCHENECTADY

City History Center Library
City Hall Top Floor, 12305
Telephone: (518) 377-7061
Founded in: 1946
Questionnaire not received

Princetown Historical Society
R.D. 5, S. Kelly Rd., 12306
Town agency
Founded in: 1976
Alice A. Miron, President
Major programs: markers

**Schenectady County Historical
     Society**
32 Washington Ave., 12305
Telephone: (518) 374-0263
Founded in: 1905
Wayne Harvey, President
Number of members: 750
Staff: part time 3
Major programs: library, archives,
     manuscripts, museum, historic
     site(s), markers, oral history, school
     programs, book publishing,
     newsletters/pamphlets, research,
     exhibits, genealogical services
Period of collections: 1750-1920

Schenectady Museum
Nott Terrace Hts., 12308
Telephone: (518) 382-7890
Private agency
Founded in: 1934
Michael Brockbank, Board President
Number of members: 2,000
Staff: full time 8, part time 12,
     volunteer 75
Magazine: Museum Notes
Major programs: museum, tours,
     educational programs, exhibits

SCHENEVUS

**Town of Maryland Historical
     Association**
R.D. 2, Box 410, 12155
Telephone: (607) 638-9708
Private agency
Founded in: 1979
Dorothy Scott Fielder, President
Number of members: 30
Staff: volunteer 3
Major programs: tours/pilgrimages,
     newsletters/pamphlets, exhibits,
     audiovisual programs, public
     educational programs
Period of collections: late 18th-20th
     centuries

SCHOHARIE

**Schoharie Colonial Heritage
     Association**
Telephone: (518) 295-8617
Mail to: R.D. 2, 12157
Founded in: 1961
Questionnaire not received

**Schoharie County Historical
     Society/Old Stone Fort Museum
     Complex**
Telephone: (518) 295-7192
Mail to: P.O. Box 69, 12157
Private agency
Founded in: 1888
Helene S. Farrell, Director
Number of members: 800
Staff: full time 2, part time 20,
     volunteer 20
Magazine: Schoharie County
     Historical Review
Major programs: library, archives,
     manuscripts, museum, historic
     site(s), tours/pilgrimages, oral
     history, school programs,
     newsletters/pamphlets, historic
     preservation, records
     management, research, exhibits,
     living history, audiovisual
     programs, pnotographic
     collections, genealogical services
Period of collections: 1711-1890

**Schoharie Museum of the Iroquois
     Indian**
N. Main St.
Telephone: (518) 295-8553/234-2276
Mail to: P.O. Box 158, 12157
Founded in: 1980
Christina B. Johannsen, Director
Number of members: 300
Staff: full time 1, part time 1,
     volunteer 20
Magazine: Museum Notes
Major programs: museum, school
     programs, newsletters/pamphlets,
     research, exhibits, archaeology
     programs, photographic
     collections
Period of collections:
     prehistoric-present

SCHROON LAKE

**Schroon-North Hudson Historical
     Society, Inc.**
Main St., 12870
Telephone: (518) 532-7854
Private agency
Founded in: 1972
Charles W. Millard, President
Staff: volunteer 10
Major programs: archives,
     manuscripts, museum, historic
     site(s), oral history, school
     programs, newsletters/pamphlets,
     historic preservation, exhibits,
     photographic collections,
     genealogical services
Period of collections: 1880s-present

SCOTIA

Scotia History Center
4 N. 10 Broeck St., 12302
Telephone: (518) 374-1071
Founded in: 1936
Questionnaire not received

SCOTTSVILLE

**Scottsville Area Historical
     Association**
2416 North Rd., 14546
Telephone: (716) 538-6958
Questionnaire not received

SEA CLIFF

Sea Cliff Landmarks, Inc.
P.O. Box 69, 11579
Telephone: (516) 671-1447
Private agency
Founded in: 1972
James W. Foote, President
Number of members: 100
Major programs: archives, markers, tours/pilgrimages, school programs, historic preservation
Period of collections: 1880s-1900s

Sea Cliff Village Museum
95 10th Ave., 11579
Telephone: (516) 671-0090
Town agency
Founded in: 1979
Charles L. Hurley, Board Chair
Staff: volunteer 25
Major programs: archives, museum, exhibits, photographic collections
Period of collections: 1880-present

SEAFORD

Seaford Historical Society
Waverly Ave.
Telephone: (516) 781-5217
Mail to: 2234 Jackson Ave., 11783
Founded in: 1969
Number of members: 270
Staff: volunteer 15
Magazine: *Seaford Historical Quarterly*
Major programs: museum, educational programs, books
Period of collections: 1865-1918

SELKIRK

Town of Bethlehem Historical Association
Old Cedar Hill Schoolhouse, 12158
Telephone: (518) 767-9432
Private agency
Founded in: 1965
M. A. Terrell, Corresponding Secretary
Major programs: museum, historic site(s), oral history, book publishing, photographic collections, genealogical services
Period of collections: mid 1800s-present

SENECA FALLS

Seneca Falls Historical Society
55 Cayuga St., 13148
Telephone: (315) 568-8412
Founded in: 1896
Geralyn T. Heisser, Executive Director
Number of members: 325
Staff: full time 1, part time 3, volunteer 99
Major programs: library, archives, museum, oral history, school programs, book publishing, newsletters/pamphlets, records management, research, exhibits, photographic collections, genealogical services
Period of collections: 1865-1918

Women's Rights National Historical Park
116 Fall St.
Telephone: (315) 568-2991
Federal agency, authorized by National Park Service
Founded in: 1980
Judy Hart, Superintendent
Staff: full time 5, part time 6, volunteer 1
Major programs: historic site(s), tours/pilgrimages, school programs, historic preservation, exhibits, audiovisual programs, history of women's rights

SETAUKET

Society for the Preservation of Long Island Antiquities
93 N. Country Rd., 11733
Telephone: (516) 941-9444
Private agency
Founded in: 1948
Robert B. MacKay, Director
Number of members: 1,400
Staff: full time 8, part time 15, volunteer 30
Major programs: historic site(s), book publishing, historic preservation, field services
Period of collections: 1640-1840/

Three Village Historical Society
N. Country Rd.
Telephone: (516) 928-9534
Mail to: P.O. Box 1776, E. Setauket, 11733
Founded in: 1964
Questionnaire not received

SHARON SPRINGS

Sharon Historical Society
Main St., 13459
Telephone: (518) 284-2177
Founded in: 1971
James Bowmaker, President
Number of members: 54
Major programs: library, museum, tours, school programs, exhibits, photographic collections
Period of collections: 1800s

SILVER CREEK

Silver Creek Historical Society
172 Central Ave., 14136
Telephone: (716) 934-3240
Founded in: 1984
Louis F. Pelletter, President
Number of members: 34
Staff: volunteer 5
Major programs: historic site(s), markers, exhibits

SINCLAIRVILLE

Valley Historical Society
Main St., 14782
Telephone: (716) 595-3526
Town agency, authorized by State Education Department
Founded in: 1977
Wilma Gilbert, President
Number of members: 85
Staff: volunteer 12
Major programs: archives, museum, historic site(s), tours/pilgrimages, school programs, archaeology programs, photographic collections
Period of collections: 1800s

SMITHTOWN

Smithtown Branch Preservation Association
211 E. Main St., 11787
Founded in: 1967
Questionnaire not received

Smithtown Historical Society
N. Country Rd.
Telephone: (516) 265-6768
Mail to: P.O. Box 69, 11787
Private agency, authorized by State University of New York
Founded in: 1955
Louise P. Hall, Director
Number of members: 350
Staff: full time 1, part time 8, volunteer 20
Major programs: library, archives, museum, historic site(s), school programs, historic preservation, research, exhibits, photographic collections, genealogical services
Period of collections: 18th-19th centuries

SOMERS

Somers Historical Society
Elephant Hotel, 10589
Telephone: (914) 277-4977
Private agency
Founded in: 1956
Elizabeth O. Macaulay, President
Number of members: 200
Major programs: library, archives, museum, school programs, book publishing, newsletters/pamphlets, historic preservation, exhibits, genealogical services

SOUTHAMPTON

Southampton Historical Museum/Old Halsey Homestead
17 Meeting House Lane
Telephone: (516) 283-1612/283-0605
Mail to: P.O. Box 303, 11968
Private agency
Founded in: 1898
Robert Keene, President
Number of members: 500
Major programs: library, archives, museum, historic site(s), historic preservation, exhibits
Period of collections: 1640-1900

SOUTHOLD

Southold Historical Society and Museum
Main Rd. and Maple Lane
Telephone: (516) 765-5500
Mail to: P.O. Box 1, 11971
Founded in: 1960
George D. Wagoner, Director
Number of members: 547
Staff: full time 2, volunteer 80
Major programs: museum, historic sites preservation, markers, tours/pilgrimages, educational programs, newsletters/pamphlets
Period of collections: 1640-1900

SOUTH OTSELIC

Gladding International Sport Fishing Museum
Maple Ave., 13155
Telephone: (3l5) 653-7211

Founded in: 1971
J. G. Mayer, Chair
Number of members: 12
Staff: part time 3
Major programs: library, museum,
exhibits
Period of collections: 1700-present

SOUTH SALEM

**Textile Conservation
Workshop, Inc.**
Main St., 10590
Telephone: (914) 763-5805
Private agency
Founded in: 1977
Patsy Orlofsky, Executive Director
Staff: full time 6, part time 2,
volunteer 2
Major programs: field services, texile
conservation laboratory

SPENCER

Spencer Historical Society
Center St.
Mail to: P.O. Box 71, 14883
Private agency
Founded in: 1973
Neil Riker, Treasurer
Number of members: 150
Staff: part time 1, volunteer 10
Major programs: museum
Period of collections: 1850-present

SPENCERPORT

Ogden Historical Society, Inc.
568 Colby St., 14559
Founded in: 1967
Questionnaire not received

SPRINGVILLE

Concord Historical Society
98 E. Main St.
Telephone: (716) 592-2342
Mail to: 13153 Mortons Corners Rd.,
14141
Town agency
Founded in: 1941
Janet Engel, President
Number of members: 22
Staff: volunteer 8
Major programs: manuscripts,
museum, markers, photographic
collections
Period of collections: 1900s

STAATSBURG

Mills Mansion State Historic Site
Old Post Rd., 12580
Telephone: (914) 889-4100
Founded in: 1938
John J. Feeney, Historic Site Manager
Staff: full time 5, part time 6
Major programs: historic sites
preservation, tours, concerts,
workshops, lectures
Period of collections: 1890s-1920s

STANFORD

Stanford Historical Society
12581
Private agency
Founded in: 1969
Number of members: 35
Major programs: archives, records
management
Period of collections: from 1790

STATEN ISLAND

**American Italian Historical
Association**
209 Flagg Place, 10304
Telephone: (212) 351-8800
Questionnaire not received

**Archaeology Society of Staten
Island**
Museum of Archaeology at Staten
Island, 631 Howard Ave., 10301
Telephone: (212) 273-3300
Founded in: 1962
Jacques Noel Jacobsen, Jr.,
President/Director
Number of members: 300
Staff: full time 2, part time 3,
volunteer 10
Magazine: *Archaeological Report*
Major programs: library, museum,
tours/pilgrimages, educational
programs, lectures
Period of collections: 4000 B.C.-A.D.
1800

**Berkshire Conference of Women
Historians**
c/o College of Staten Island (Cony),
10301
Telephone: (212) 390-7988
Mail to: c/o Jochens History,
Baltimore, MD., 21204
Founded in: 1928
Questionnaire not received

Garibaldi-Meucci Museum
420 Tompkins Ave.
Mail to: 98 Cutter Mill Rd., Suite
321-N, Great Neck, 11021
Private agency, authorized by Grand
Lodge of the State of New York
Founded in: 1905
Teresa G. Piropato, Executive
Director
Number of members: 17,000
Staff: full time 2, part time 1,
volunteer 35
Magazine: *The Golden Lion*
Major programs: archives,
tours/pilgrimages, school
programs
Period of collections: 1850-present

Snug Harbor Cultural Center
914 Richmond Terrace, 10301
Telephone: (212) 448-2500
Founded in: 1976
Questionnaire not received

Staten Island Children's Museum
15 Beach St., 10304
Telephone: (718) 273-2060
Private agency
Kate Bennett-Mendez, Director
Number of members: 232
Staff: full time 15, part time 18,
volunteer 5
Major programs: manuscripts,
museum, tours/pilgrimages, school
programs, newsletters/pamphlets,
exhibits

**Staten Island Historical
Society—Richmondtown
Restoration**
441 Clarke Ave., 10301
Telephone: (718) 351-1617
Private agency
Founded in: 1856
Barnett Shepherd, Executive Director

Number of members: 1,000
Staff: full time 35, part time 35,
volunteer 200
Magazine: *The Staten Island
Historian*
Major programs: library, archives,
manuscripts, museum, historic
site(s), school programs, book
publishing, newsletters/pamphlets,
historic preservation, research,
exhibits, living history, audiovisual
programs, archaeology programs,
photographic collections,
genealogical services
Period of collections: 17th
century-present

**Staten Island Institute of Arts and
Sciences**
75 Stuyvesant Place, 10301
Telephone: (718) 727-1135
Private agency
Founded in: 1881
Patricia G. Michael, Executive
Director
Staff: full time 26, part time 26,
volunteer 12
Magazine: *Proceedings*
Major programs: library, archives,
museum, school programs,
newsletters/pamphlets, exhibits,
photographic collections, field
services, natural history collections
Period of collections: 1800-1945

**Steamship Historical Society of
America, Inc.**
414 Pelton Ave., 10310
Telephone: (718) 727-9583
Private agency
Founded in: 1935
Alice S. Wilson, Secretary
number of members: 3,500
Staff: full time 1, volunteer 5
Magazine: *Steamboat Bill*
Major programs: library, archives,
book publishing, research,
photographic collections
Period of collections: 1790-present

STEPHENTOWN

Stephentown Historical Society
P.O. Box 313, West Rd., 12168
Telephone: (518) 733-5716
Town agency
Founded in: 1974
Sylvia Leibensperger, President
Number of members: 48
Major programs: museum, historic
preservation, genealogical
services
Period of collections: 1825-1925

STILLWATER

Saratoga National Historical Park
R.D. 2, Box 33, 12170
Telephone: (518) 664-9821
Founded in: 1938
W. Glen Gray, Superintendent
Staff: full time 12, part time 12,
volunteer 24
Major programs: museum, historic
site(s), school programs, historic
preservation, living history,
audiovisual programs
Period of collections: 1777

STONY BROOK

Long Island Archives Conference
Department of Special Collections,
 SUNY Library, 11794-3323
Telephone: (516) 246-3615
Private agency
Founded in: 1974
Number of members: 115
Major programs: archives, historic
 preservation, meetings on archival
 preservation, cataloguing, and
 collecting

Long Island Studies Council
P.O. Box 555, 11790
Telephone: (516) 246-3615
Private agency
Founded in: 1980
Number of members: 22
Major programs: meetings with
 presentations on Long Island

Museum Computer Network, Inc.
ECC, Bldg. 26, SUNY, 11794-4400
Telephone: (516) 246-6077
Private agency
Founded in: 1967
David Vance, President
Number of members: 102
Staff: full time 1
Magazine: SPECTRA
Major programs: library, archives,
 records management, research,
 consultations on computers in
 museums
Period of collections: 1964-present

Museums at Stony Brook
1208 Rt. 25-A, 11790
Telephone: (516) 751-0066
Private agency
Founded in: 1942
Susan Stitt, Director
Number of members: 550
Staff: full time 35, part time 15,
 volunteer 150
Major programs: archives,
 manuscripts, museum, historic
 site(s), school programs, book
 publishing, newsletters/pamphlets,
 research, exhibits
Period of collections: 1783-1918

**Suffolk County Archaeological
 Association**
Telephone: (516) 929-8725
Mail to: P.O. Drawer AR, 11790
Private agency
Founded in: 1975
Donna Ohusch-Kianka, President
Staff: volunteer 15
Major programs: archives, school
 programs, book publishing,
 newsletters/pamphlets, historic
 preservation, research, exhibits,
 audiovisual programs, archaeology
 programs, photographic
 collections

STONY CREEK

Stony Creek Historical Association
Lanfear Rd., 12878
Telephone: (518) 696-3488
Questionnaire not received

STONY POINT

**Stony Point Battlefield State
 Historic Site**
Park Rd., Off Rt. 9-W

Telephone: (914) 786-2521
Mail to: P.O. Box 182, 10965
Founded in: 1898
Questionnaire not received

SUFFERN

Suffern Village Museum
61 Washington Ave., 10901
Telephone: (914) 357-2600
Town agency
Founded in: 1982
Robert Goetschius, Board President
Number of members: 75
Staff: volunteer 12
Major programs: archives, museum,
 oral history, school programs,
 newsletters/pamphlets, audiovisual
 programs, photographic
 collections
Period of collections: 1896-1946

SYOSSET

**Nassau County Museum, Division
 of Museum Services**
1864 Muttontown Rd., 11791
Telephone: (516) 364-1050
County agency, authorized by
 Department of Recreation and
 Parks
Founded in: 1956
Edward J. Smits, Director
Staff: full time 170, part time 120,
 volunteer 350
Major programs: library, archives,
 museum, historic sites, school
 programs, historic preservation,
 research, exhibits, living history,
 archaeology programs,
 photographic collections, natural
 history
Period of collections: 1750-1950

SYRACUSE

Canal Society of New York State
311 Montgomery St., 13202
Telephone: (315) 428-1862
Founded in: 1956
Richard N. Wright, Secretary
Number of members: 400
Major programs: library, archives

**Daniel Parrish Witter Agricultural
 Museum**
New York State Fairgrounds, 13209
State agency, authorized by Division
 of Agriculture and Markets
Gretchen Sorin, Director
Staff: part time 6
Major programs: museum
Period of collections: 1800-present

Erie Canal Museum
Weighlock Bldg.
Telephone: (315) 471-0593
Mail to: 318 Erie Blvd., E, 13202
Private agency
Founded in: 1962
Vicki B. Ford, Director
Staff: full time 6, part time 4,
 volunteer 50
Major programs: library, archives,
 manuscripts, museum, historic
 site(s), markers, school programs,
 book publishing,
 newsletters/pamphlets, historic
 preservation, research, exhibits,
 audiovisual programs, archaeology

programs, photographic
 collections
Period of collections: mid-late 1800s

Onondaga Historical Association
311 Montgomery St., 13202
Telephone: (315) 428-1862
Founded in: 1862
Richard N. Wright, President
Number of members: 500
Staff: full time 5, part time 1,
 volunteer 5
Major programs: library, archives,
 manuscripts

**Regional Conference of Historical
 Agencies**
1509 Park St., 13208
Telephone: (315) 475-1525
Private agency
Founded in: 1971
Michael P. O'Lear, Executive Director
Number of members: 425
Staff: full time 4
Major programs: library, oral history,
 school programs,
 newsletters/pamphlets, historic
 preservation, records
 management, research, exhibits,
 living history, audiovisual
 programs, genealogical services,
 field services

**Society for the Preservation and
 Appreciation of Antique Motor
 Fire Apparatus in America**
Mail to: P.O. Box 450, Eastwood
 Station, 13206
Telephone: (914) 343-4219
 (secretary)
Private agency, authorized by State
 Education Department
Founded in: 1956
Marvin H. Cohen, Secretary
Number of members: 3,200
Staff: volunteer 12
Magazine: Enjine!-Enjine!
Major programs: archives,
 tours/pilgrimages,
 newsletters/pamphlets, historic
 preservation, research
Period of collections: 1840-1960

Syracuse Area Landmark Theatre
362 S. Salina St., 13202
Telephone: (315) 475-7979
Founded in: 1928
Questionnaire not received

**Syracuse Landmark Preservation
 Board**
1100 Civic Center, 421 Montgomery
 St., 13202
Telephone: (315) 425-2611
Founded in: 1975
Questionnaire not received

TAPPAN

Tappantown Historical Society
Mail to: P.O. Box 71, 10983
Telephone: (914) 359-5490
Founded in: 1965
Sally Dewey, President
Number of members: 500
Magazine: The Drummer Boy
Major programs: school programs,
 historic preservation, research,
 genealogical services
Period of collections: 1704-present

TARRYTOWN

Historical Society of the Tarrytowns
1 Grove St., 10591
Telephone: (914) 631-8374
Founded in: 1889
Mrs. J. Floyd Smith, Curator
Number of members: 400
Staff: full time 1, part time 1, volunteer 12
Major programs: library, archives, manuscripts, museum, historic site(s), markers, school programs, genealogical services
Period of collections: 18th-19th centuries

Lyndhurst
635 S. Broadway, 10591
Telephone: (914) 631-0046
Authorized by the National Trust for Historic Preservation
Founded in: 1964
John L. Frisbee, Director
Staff: full time 7, part time 24, volunteer 5
Major programs: museum, historic site(s), newsletters/pamphlets, historic preservation, research, archaeology programs
Period of collections: 1838-1960

Sleepy Hollow Restorations, Inc.
150 White Plains Rd., 10591
Telephone: (914) 631-8200
Private agency
Founded in: 1951
John W. Harbour, Jr., Executive Director
Staff: full time 56, part time 84
Major programs: library, historic site(s), junior history, school programs, books, historic preservation, research, living history
Period of collections: 1720-1859

TICONDEROGA

Ticonderoga Historical Society
Hancock House, Moses Circle, 12883
Telephone: (518) 585-7868
Founded in: 1909
Elizabeth E. McCaughin, Curator
Number of members: 97
Staff: full time 1, part time 1, volunteer 10
Major programs: library, archives, manuscrlpts, museum, historic site(s), markers, junior history, book publishing, research, exhibits, photographic collections, genealogical services
Period of collections: 1750s-present

TONAWANDA

Historical Society of the Tonawandas, Inc.
113 Main St., 14150
Telephone: (716) 694-7406

Founded in: 1961
Willard B. Dittmar, Executive Director
Number of members: 385
Staff: full time 1, volunteer 75
Magazine: *The Lumber Shover*
Major programs: library, archives, manuscripts, museum, historic site(s), markers, junior history, school programs, book publishing, newsletters/pamphlets, historic preservation, research, exhibits, audiovisual programs, photographic collections, genealogical services, Period of collections: 1830s-present

Tonawanda-Kenmore Historical Society
100 Knoche Rd., 14150
Telephone: (716) 873-5774
Town agency
Founded in: 1929
John W. Percy, Town Historian
Number of members: 236
Staff: volunteer 30
Major programs: library, archives, museum, historic site(s), markers, school programs, newsletters/pamphlets, historic preservation, exhibits
Period of collections: 1865-present

TOWN OF COLONIE

Historical Society of the Town of Colonie, Inc.
Memorial Town Hall, Newtonville, 12128
Telephone: (518) 783-2713
Founded in: 1971
Questionnaire not received

TOWN OF NORTH HEMPSTEAD

Historical Society of the Town of North Hempstead
220 Plandome Rd., Manhasset, 11030
Telephone: (516) 627-0590
Founded in: 1962
Questionnaire not received

TROY

Federation of Historical Services
189 2nd St., 12180
Telephone: (518) 273-3400
Private agency
Founded in: 1978
Molly Lowell, Director
Number of members: 300
Staff: full time 2, part time 2, volunteer 2
Major programs: newsletters/pamphlets, field services, workshops

Hudson-Mohawk Industrial Gateway
457 Broadway, 12180
Telephone: (518) 274-5267
Private agency
Caroline A. King, Executive Director
Number of members: 360
Staff: part time 2, volunteer 1
Major programs: tours/pilgrimages, newsletters/pamphlets, research
Period of collections: 19th-early 20th centuries

Lansingburgh Historical Society
2 114th St.

Mail to: P.O. Box 219, Lansingburgh, 12182
Founded in: 1965
Questionnaire not received

Rensselaer County Historical Society
59 2nd St., 12180
Telephone: (518) 272-7232
Private agency
Founded in: 1927
Breffny A. Walsh, Director
Number of members: 500
Staff: full time 3, part time 3, volunteer 20
Major programs: library, archives, manuscripts, museum, tours/pilgrimages, school programs, newsletters/pamphlets, historic preservation, exhibits, photographic collections, field services
Period of collections: 1783-1918

TRUMANSBURG

Ulysses Historical Society
Main St., 14886
Telephone: (607) 387-7833
Founded in: 1975
Mrs. Robert Wolverton, President
Number of members: 350
Staff: volunteer 30
Major programs: archives, manuscripts, museum, educational programs
Period of collections: 1865-1918

TUCKAHOE

Westchester County Historical Society
43 Read Ave., 10707
Telephone: (914) 337-1753
Founded in: 1874
Anita Inman Comstock, President
Number of members: 850
Staff: full time 2, volunteer 10
Magazine: *Westchester Historian*
Major programs: library, archives, manuscripts, historic sites preservation tours/pilgrimages, oral history, educational programs
Period of collections: 1492-1865

TULLY

Tully Area Historical Society
24 State St.
Telephone: (315) 696-5219
Mail to: P.O. Box 22, 13159-0022
Private agency, authorized by State Department of Education
Founded in: 1978
John C. Van Buskirk, President
Number of members: 300
Major programs: library, museum, historic site(s), exhibits, living history
Period of collections: 1850s-present

TUXEDO

Tuxedo Historical Society
P.O. Box 188, Rt. 17, 10987
Telephone: (914) 351-5611
Private agency
Founded in: 1982
Albert J. Winslow, Director

Number of members: 254
Major programs: museum, historic
site(s), tours/pilgrimages, junior
history, oral history, school
programs, research, exhibits, living
history, photographic collections,
field services
Period of collections: 1886-present

UNION SPRINGS

Frontenac Historical Society
1 Foundry St., 13160
Telephone: (315) 889-7767
Founded in: 1975
Questionnaire not received

UTICA

**Children's Museum of History,
Natural History and Science**
311 Main St., 13501
Telephone: (315) 724-6128
Founded in: 1963
Deborah L. Goodwin, Director
Number of members: 400
Staff: full time 4, part time 3,
volunteer 7
Magazine: *Fingerprints*
Major programs: museum,
educational programs
Period of collections: 1800s-1900s

**Fountain Elms/Munson-
Williams-Proctor Institute
Museum of Art**
310 Genesee St., 13502
Telephone: (3l5) 797-0000
Private agency
Founded in: 1919
Christopher Bensch, Assistant
Curator of Decorative Arts
Number of members: 3,000
Staff: full time 1, part time 8
Major programs: library, museum,
school programs, exhibits
Period of collections: 19th century

Landmarks Society of Greater Utica
261 Genesee St., 13501
Telephone: (315) 732-9376
Founded in: 1974
Questionnaire not received

Mohawk Valley Museum
620 Memorial Parkway, 13501
Telephone: (315) 724-2075
Questionnaire not received

Oneida Historical Society
3l8 Genesee St., 13502
Telephone: (315) 735-3642
Founded in: 1876
Douglas M. Preston, Director
Number of members: 450
Staff: full time 2, part tie 1, volunteer 4
Magazine: *Oniota*
Major programs: library, manuscripts,
museum, tours/pilgrimages,
educational programs,
newsletters/pamphlets,
photographic collections
Period of collections: 1750-present

VAILS GATE

National Temple Hill Association
P.O. Box 315, 12584
Telephone: (914) 562-6397
Private agency
Founded in: 1933

Donald C. Gordon, President
Number of members: 200
Major programs: historic sites, book
publishing, historic preservation
Period of collections: 1750-1800

VALHALLA

**Westchester County Historical
Society**
Hartford House, 75 Grasslands Rd.,
10595
Telephone: (914) 592-4323
County agency
Founded in: 1874
Christine Stiassni, Executive Director
Number of members: 850
Staff: part time 3, volunteer 5
Magazine: *Westchester Historian*
Major programs: library, archives,
manuscripts, museum, school
programs, book publishing, historic
preservation, research,
photographic collections,
genealogical services
Period of collections: 1719-1810

VERNON

Vernon Historical Society
5 Peterboro St.
Telephone: (315) 829-2022
Mail to: P.O. Box 786, 13476
Founded in: 1972
Catherine Cresswell, President
Number of members: 18
Major programs: museum,
educational programs, historic
preservation
Period of collections: 1800-present

VIRGIL

Virgil Historical Society
E. State Rd., Rt. 90
Telephone: (607) 835-3764
Mail to: R.D. 2 Cortland, 13045
Founded in: 1978
Questionnaire not received

WALDEN

**Historical Society of Walden and
Wallkill Valley**
P.O. Box 48, 12586
Telephone: (914) 778-5862
Founded in: 1959
Doris Borland, President
Number of members: 85
Staff: volunteer 15
Major programs: historic site(s),
newsletters/pamphlets,
photographic collections
Period of collections: 1855-present

WANTAGH

Wantagh Preservation Society
Telephone: (516) 781-4328
Mail to: P.O. Box 132, 11793
Founded in: 1966
Questionnaire not received

WAPPINGERS FALLS

**Bowdoin Park Historical and
Archaeological Association**
Bowdoin Park, Sheafe Rd., 12590
Telephone: (914) 297-1224
Private agency
Founded in: 1978

E. J. Buchanan, Jr., President
Number of members: 31
Staff: volunteer 6
Major programs: school programs,
exhibits, archaeology programs
Period of collections:
prehistoric-present

WARSAW

Warsaw Historical Society
15 Perry Ave.
Telephone: (716) 796-3422
Mail to: P.O. Box 245, 14569
Questionnaire not received

WATERFORD

**Council for Northeast Historical
Archaeology**
Peebles Island, 12188
Founded in: 1966
Sherene Baugher, Chair
Number of members: 300
Staff: volunteer 15
Magazine: *Northeast Historical
Archaeology*
Major programs: annual meeting

**Waterford Historical Museum and
Cultural Center**
2 Museum Lane, 12188
Questionnaire not received

WATERLOO

Terwilliger Museum
31 E. Williams St., 13165
Telephone: (315) 539-3313
Private agency, authorized by
Waterloo Library and Historical
Society
Founded in: 1960
Ruth A. Semtner, Director
Staff: full time 1
Major programs: museum, tours,
school programs, research,
exhibits, photographic collections,
genealogical services,
Period of collections: 1876-present

Waterloo Memorial Day Museum
35 E. Main St., 13165
Telephone: (315) 539-9611/539-2474
Private agency, authorized by
Waterloo Library and Historical
Society
Founded in: 1966
Ruth A. Semtner, Director
Staff: full time 1, volunteer 6
Major programs: museum, tours,
school programs, historic
preservation, research, exhibits,
genealogical services
Period of collections: Civil
War-Vietnam

WATER MILL

Water Mill Museum
Old Mill Rd., 11976
Telephone: (516) 726-9685
Private agency
Number of members: 500
Staff: full time 7
Major programs: archives, museum,
historic site(s), oral history, school
programs, exhibits

WATERTOWN

Jefferson County Historical Society
228 Washington St., 13601
Telephone: (315) 782-3491
Private agency
Founded in: 1886
Margaret W. M. Shaeffer, Director
Staff: full time 5, part time 3
Magazine: *Jefferson County Historical Society Bulletin*
Major programs: archives, museum, historic site(s), tours/pilgrimages, school programs, newsletters/pamphlets, historic preservation, exhibits, archaeology programs
Period of collections: 19th century

WATERVLIET

Watervliet Arsenal Museum
Watervliet Arsenal, SMCWV-1NM, 12189
Federal Agency, authorized by the U.S. Army
Founded in: 1973
William Bradford, Director/Curator
Staff: full time 2
Major programs: museum

Watervliet Historical Society
P.O. Box 123, 12189
Founded in: 1975
Marion Fotache, President
Number of members: 92
Major programs: historic sites preservation, markers, newsletters/pamphlets

WATKINS GLEN

American Life Foundation and Study Institute
101 S. Monroe St.
Telephone: (607) 535-4737
Mail to: P.O. Box 349, 14891
Questionnaire not received

WEBSTER

Rochester Association of Performing Arts
97 South Ave., 14580
Telephone: (716) 265-9855
Private agency
Founded in: 1981
Judi Andreano, Executive Director
Staff: full time 1, part time 15, volunteer 40
Major programs: historic site(s), historic preservation
Period of collections: 1876-1925

Webster Museum and Historical Society
1000 Ridge Rd., 14580
Telephone: (716) 872-1000
Town, Private agency
Founded in: 1976
Richard J. Batzing, Museum Director
Number of members: 300
Staff: volunteer 60
Major programs: archives, museum, tours/pilgrimages, junior history, school programs, research, exhibits, genealogical services
Period of collections: 1840-1940

WEEDSPORT

Old Brutus Historical Society, Inc.
8943 N. Seneca St., 13166
Telephone: (315) 834-6779
Private agency
Founded in: 1967
Howard J. Finley, Director
Number of members: 75
Staff: volunteer 15
Major programs: museum, photographic collections, genealogical services
Period of collections: 1800-present

WESTBURY

Historical Society of the Westburys
454 Rockland St., 11590
Telephone: (516) 333-0176
Founded in: 1976
Robert Ernst, President
Number of members: 85
Staff: part time 1
Major programs: library, archives, manuscripts, tours/pilgrimages, oral history, school programs
Period of collections: 1800s-1930s

WEST EDMESTON

Brookfield Township Historical Society
13314
Telephone: (315) 899-3348
Questionnaire not received

WESTFIELD

Patterson Library
40 S. Portage St., 14787
Telephone: (716) 326-2154
Founded in: 1896
Questionnaire not received

WEST POINT

Constitution Island Association
179 Main St., Highland Falls, 10928
Telephone: (914) 446-8676
Mail to: P.O. Box 41, 10996
Private agency
Founded in: 1916
Elliott C. Cutler, Jr., Chair
Number of members: 250
Staff: part time 1, volunteer 25
Major programs: tours/pilgrimages, school programs, exhibits
Period of collections: 1856-1915

West Point Museum
U.S. Military Academy, 10996-5000
Telephone: (914) 938-2203
Federal Agency, authorized by the U.S. Army
Founded in: 1854
Richard E. Kuehne, Director
Staff: full time 14, part time 4
Major programs: museum, historic sites
Period of collections: 19th-20th centuries

WESTPORT

Westport Historical Society
Barksdale Rd., 12993
Telephone: (518) 962-4809
Questionnaire not received

WEST SAYVILLE

Suffolk County Historic Trust/Suffolk County Division of Cultural and Historic Services
Hard Estate, Montauk Hwy.
Telephone: (516) 567-1487
Mail to: P.O. Box 144, 11796
County agency
Founded in: 1975
J. Lance Mallamo, Director of Historic Services
Staff: full time 4, part time 30, volunteer 40
Magazine: *The Suffolk Historian*
Major programs: historic site(s), markers, newsletters/pamphlets, historic preservation, research, exhibits, audiovisual programs, archaeology programs, field services
Period of collections: 19th century

Suffolk Marine Museum
Montauk Hwy., 11796
Telephone: (516) 567-1733
Founded in: 1966
Questionnaire not received

WEST SENECA

West Seneca Historical Society and Museum
919 Mill Rd.
Telephone: (716) 674-9878
Mail to: P.O. Box 2, 14224
Town agency
Founded in: 1957
Willeam Doering, President
Number of members: 150
Staff: part time 1, volunteer 10
Major programs: library, archives, museum, junior history, exhibits
Period of collections: 1860-1960

WHITEHALL

Skemesborough Museum
Skenesborough Dr.
Telephone: (518) 499-0225/499-0754
Mail to: P.O. Box 131, 12887
Founded in: 1959
Questionnaire not received

WHITE PLAINS

Charles Dawson History Center of Harrison, New York
2 E. Madison St., 10604
Telephone: (914) 948-2550
Mail to: P.O. Box 1696, Harrison, 10528
Town agency
Founded in: 1981
Michael R. Casarella, Historian
Number of members: 75
Staff: part time 2, volunteer 20
Major programs: library, archives, historic site(s), markers, tours/pilgrimages, oral history, newsletters/pamphlets, historic preservation, records management, research, exhibits, genealogical services, Period of collections: 1662-present

Westchester County Genealogical Society
P.O. Box 518, 10603
Private agency

Founded in: 1982
William E. Newell, President
Number of members: 95
Major programs: library, archives,
newsletters/pamphlets, research,
audiovisual programs,
genealogical services

WILSON

Wilson Historical Society
Lake St., 14172
Telephone: (716) 751-9827
Town agency
Founded in: 1972
Mildred E. Croop, Treasurer
Number of members: 630
Staff: volunteer 150
Major programs: museum, historic
site(s), markers, school programs,
newsletters/pamphlets, exhibits,
genealogical services
Period of collections: 1800-present

WILTON

Grant Cottage
Mt. McGregor Wilton, 12866
Telephone: (518) 587-8277
State agency, authorized by State
Parks Commission
Founded in: 1889
Cheryl Gold, Chief of Historic Sites
Staff: full time 1, part time 50,
volunteer 10
Major programs: library, archives,
manuscripts, museum, historic
site(s), markers, tours/pilgrimages,
oral history, newsletters/pamphlets,
historic preservation, records
management, exhibits,
photographic collections
Period of collections: 1885

Wilton Heritage Society
Woodard Rd., 12866
Lorraine Westcott, President
Questionnaire not received

WORCESTER

Worcester Historical Society
72 Main St., 12197
Founded in: 1970
Questionnaire not received

WYOMING

Middlebury Historical Society
24 S. Academy St.
Telephone: (716) 495-6495
Mail to: 6174 Lamb Rd., 14591
Questionnaire not received

YONKERS

Hudson River Museum
511 Warburton Ave., 10701
Telephone: (914) 963-4550
Private agency
Found in: 1924
Peter G. Langlykke, Director
Number of members: 900
Staff: full time 33, part time 5,
volunteer 130
Major programs: museum, historic
sites preservation, educational
programs, catalogues, book
publishing
Period of collections: 1876-1910

**Philipse Manor Hall State Historic
Site**
29 Warburton Ave.
Telephone: (914) 965-4027
Mail to: P.O. Box 496, 10702
State agency, authorized by
Department of Parks, Recreation
and Historic Preservation
Yvonne Smith, Historic Site Manager
Staff: full time 4, part time 6,
volunteer 1
Major programs: museum, historic
site(s), school programs, exhibits
Period of collections: 18th century

U. S. Catholic Historical Society
P.O. Box 498, 10702
Telephone: (914) 476-9115
Private agency
Founded in: 1884
James J. Mahoney, Executive
Director
Number of members: 750
Staff: full time 1, part time 2
Magazine: *U.S. Catholic Historian*
Major programs: book publishing,
newsletters/pamphlets, exhibits
Period of collections: 1790-1955

Yonkers Historical Society
511 Wharburton Ave., 10701
Telephone: (914) 963-4550
Founded in: 1952
Questionnaire not received

YORKTOWN HEIGHTS

Town of Yorktown Museum
1974 Commerce St., 10598
Telephone: (914) 962-2970
Town agency
Founded in: 1966
Doris E. Auser, Director
Number of members: 300
Staff: full time 3, volunteer 68
Major programs: library, archives,
manuscripts, museum,
tours/pilgrimages, history, school
programs, newsletters/pamphlets,
research, exhibits, photographic
collections, genealogical services
Period of collections: 1865-present

YOUNGSTOWN

Old Ft. Niagara Association, Inc.
Telephone: (716) 745-7611
Mail to: P.O. Box 169, 14174
Private agency, authorized by Office
of Parks, Recreation and Historic
Preservation
Founded in: 1925
Brian Leigh Dunnigan, Executive
Director
Number of members: 450
Staff: full time 6, part time 62
Major programs: museum, historic
site(s), newsletters/pamphlets,
historic preservation, research,
exhibits, living history, archaeology
programs, photographic
collections
Period of collections: 1678-present

NORTH CAROLINA

ALBEMARLE

**Stanly County-Albemarle Historical
Museum Association, Inc.**
112 N. 3rd St., 28001
Telephone: (704) 983-1623
Private agency
Founded in: 1971
P. E. Suggs, President
Number of members: 61
Staff: volunteer 10
Major programs: museum, historic
site(s), school programs
Period of collections: 1865-1918

**Stanly County Historical
Society, Inc.**
813 W. Main St., 28001
Telephone: (704) 982-1825
Questionnaire not received

**Stanly County Historic Properties
Commission**
112 N. 3rd. St., 28001
Telephone: (704) 983-1623
County agency
Founded in: 1973
J. C. Holbrook, Chair
Staff: full time 1, volunteer 10
Major programs: archives, historic
site(s), tours/pilgrimages, book
publishing, research, archaeology
programs
Period of collections: 1841-present

ASHEBORO

**Randolph County Historical
Society**
201 Worth St., 27203
Telephone: (919) 629-3329
Private agency
Founded in: 1911
Charlesanna L. Fox, Secretary
Number of members: 200
Staff: part time 2, volunteer 5
Major programs: archives, museum,
historic site(s), junior history, oral
history, genealogical services
Period of collections: 1700-present

ASHEVILLE

Blue Ridge Parkway
700 Northwest Bank Bldg., 28801
Telephone: (704) 259-0779
Federal agency, authorized by
National Park Service
Founded in: 1935
Gary Everhardt, Superintendent
Major programs: historic site(s), oral
history, historic preservation,
exhibits, audiovisual programs,
photographic collections

**Historic Resources Commission of
Asheville and Buncombe County**
P.O. Box 7148, 28807
Telephone: (704) 255-5434
County agency
Founded in: 1981
Carolyn A. Humphries, Executive
Director
Staff: part time 1, volunteer 20
Major programs: historic site(s),
historic preservation, field services

Preservation Society of Asheville and Buncombe County
Telephone: (704) 254-2343
Mail to: P.O. Box 2806, 28802
Private agency
Founded in: 1977
Marge Turcot, President
Number of members: 185
Staff: volunteer 3
Major programs: tours/pilgrimages, newsletters/pamphlets, historic preservation, audiovisual programs, photographic collections

Southern Highland Handicraft Guild Museum and Library
Blue Ridge Parkway and Riceville Rd., 28805
Telephone: (704) 298-7928
Mail to: P.O. Box 9545, 28815
Private agency
Founded in: 1930
James Gentry, Director
Number of members: 642
Staff: full time 8, part time 1, volunteer 16
Major programs: library, archives, museum, newsletters/pamphlets, exhibits, photographic collections
Period of collections: early 1900s-present

Thomas Wolfe Memorial
P.O. Box 7143, 28807
Telephone: (704) 253-8304
State agency, authorized by Department of Cultural Resources
Steven A. Hill, Manager
Staff: full time 4
Major programs: historic site(s)
Period of collections: early 20th century

Western North Carolina Historical Association, Inc.
283 Victoria Rd., 28801
Telephone: (704) 253-9231
Private agency
Founded in: 1952
William Highsmith, President
Number of members: 300
Staff: full time 1, part time 1, volunteer 12
Major programs: museum, school programs, historic preservation
Period of collections: 1840-1900

Western Office, Division of Archives and History
13 Veterans Dr., 28805
Telephone: (704) 298-5024
State agency
J. Ron Holland, Manager
Staff: full time 7
Major programs: school programs, historic preservation, records management, exhibits, archaeology programs, photographic collections, field services

BAILEY

Country Doctor Museum
Vance St.
Telephone: (919) 235-4165
Mail to: P.O. Box 34, 27807
Private agency, authorized by Country Doctor Museum Foundation

Founded in: 1968
Joyce R. Cooper, Executive Secretary
Staff: full time 1, part time 2
Major programs: library, museum
Period of collections: 1865-early 20th century

BATH

Historic Bath State Historic Site
Hwy. 92
Telephone: (919) 923-3971
Mail to: P.O. Box 148, 27808
State agency, authorized by Department of Cultural Resources
Founded in: 1962
Gerald W. Butler, Manager
Staff: full time 5, part time 5
Major programs: historic sites preservation
Period of collections: 1725-1850

BEAUFORT

Beaufort Historical Association
138 Turner St.
Telephone: (919) 728-5225/728-7647
Mail to: P.O. Box 1709, 28516
Private agency
Founded in: 1962
Kathryn Cloud, President
Number of members: 600
Staff: full time 1, part time 2, volunteer 100
Major programs: historic site(s), tours, newsletters/pamphlets, historic preservation
Period of collections: 1767-1936

Carteret Historical Research Association
Telephone: (919) 354-3215
Mail to: P.O. Box 1722, 28516
Founded in: 1971
Doris L. Thompson, President
Number of members: 100
Staff: volunteer 100
Major programs: markers, junior history, educational programs, books, newsletters/pamphlets, historic preservation
Period of collections: 1663-1981

Hampton Mariners Museum
315 Front St., 28516
Telephone: (919) 728-7317
State agency
Founded in: 1975
Charles R. McNeill, Curator
Staff: full time 6, part time 3
Major programs: library, museum, school programs, book publishing, newsletters/pamphlets, historic preservation, research, exhibits
Period of collections: late 19th-early 20th centuries

BELHAVEN

Belhaven Memorial Museum, Inc.
Main St.
Telephone: (919) 943-2241
Mail to: P.O. Box 220, 27810
Private agency
Founded in: 1965
Mrs. Stanley McKnight, President
Staff: part time 2, volunteer 4
Major programs: museum
Period of collections: late 19th-early 20th centuries

BOONE

North Carolina Folklore Society
Department of English, Appalachian State University, 28608
Telephone: (704) 262-3098
Founded in: 1913
Thomas McGowan, Secretary/Treasurer
Number of members: 600
Staff: volunteer 1
Magazine: *North Carolina Folklore Journal*
Major programs: educational programs, books, newsletters/pamphlets

Southern Appalachian Historical Association, Inc.
Horn in the West Dr.
Telephone: (704) 264-2120
Mail to: P.O. Box 295, 28607
Private agency
Founded in: 1951
James W. Jackson, Executive Vice President
Number of members: 132
Staff: full time 2, part time 2
Major programs: museum, tours/pilgrimages, newsletters/pamphlets, historic preservation, exhibits, living history, historical drama
Period of collections: late 1700s

BOONVILLE

Historic Richmond Hill Law School Commission
Telephone: (919) 367-7251
Mail to: P.O. Box 309, 27011
County agency, authorized by Yadkin County Board of Commissioners
Founded in: 1971
Jimmie R. Hutchens, Chair
Staff: part time 1, volunteer 15
Major programs: historic sites preservation

BURLINGTON

Alamance Battleground
Rt. 1, Box 108, 27215
Telephone: (919) 227-4785
Bryan Dalton, Manager
State agency, authorized by Historic Sites Section, Department of Cultural Resources
Major programs: historic site(s), tours/pilgrimages, oral history, school programs, research, living history
Period of collections: 1760-1825

Alamance County Historical Museum
Rt. 1, Box 71, 27215
Telephone: (919) 226-8254
Private agency
Founded in: 1976
Peggy Boswell, Director
Number of members: 200
Staff: full time 1, part time 2, volunteer 25
Major programs: museum, book publishing, exhibits
Period of collections: 1870-1890

CAMDEN

Camden County Historical Society
Telephone: (919) 336-2747
County agency
Founded in: 1953
W. W. Forehand, Secretary
Number of members: 24
Major programs: historic site(s),
historic preservation, research,
exhibits, photographic collections,
genealogical services
Period of collections: 1840-1900

CARY

Cary Historical Society
Mail to: P.O. Box 134, 27511
Private agency
Founded in: 1976
Anne Kratzer, President
Number of members: 30
Major programs: historic preservation

CHAPEL HILL

**Archaeological Society of North
Carolina**
P.O. Box 561, 27514

Telephone: (919) 933-6574
Founded in: 1934
Questionnaire not received

Chapel Hill Historical Society
Mail to: P.O. Box 503, 27514
Founded in: 1966
Questionnaire not received

**Manuscript Department and
Southern Historical Collection**
Wilson Library 024-A, University of
North Carolina at Chapel Hill, 27514
Telephone: (919) 933-1345
Authorized by the university
Founded in: 1930
Carolyn A. Wallace, Director
Staff: full time 7, part time 1
Major programs: archives,
manuscripts, photographic
collections
Period of collections: 19th-20th
centuries

North Carolina Collection
University of North Carolina Library,
27514
Telephone: (919) 962-1172

State agency, authorized by the
university
Founded in: 1917
H. G. Jones, Curator of North
Caroliniana
Staff: full time 7, part time 12
Magazine: *North Caroliniana Society
Imprints*
Major programs: library, research,
exhibits
Period of collections: 16th
century-present

CHARLOTTE

Hezekiah Alexander Homesite
3500 Shamrock Dr., 28215
Telephone: (704) 568-1774
City agency, authorized by Mint
Museum
Founded in: 1976
Stuart C. Schwartz, Curator
Staff: full time 4, part time 2,
volunteer 130
Major programs: museum, historic
site(s), school programs, historic
preservation, research, living
history
Period of collections: late 18th
century

History Department, Mint Museum
2700 Randolph Rd., 27601
City agency
Founded in: 1975
Stuart C. Schwartz, Curator
Staff: full time 4, part time 2,
volunteer 130
Major programs: museum, historic
site(s), school programs, historic
preservation, research, exhibits,
living history, photographic
collections
Period of collections: 1750-1950

**Mecklenburg Historical
Association**
Mail to: P.O. Box 35032, 28235
Private agency
Founded in: 1954
Stewart Lillard, President
Number of members: 550
Major programs: historic site(s),
tours/pilgrimages, book publishing,
newsletters/pamphlets, historic
preservation
Period of collections: 1740s-present

North Carolina Museums Council
Charlotte Nature Museum, 1658
Sterling Rd., 28209
Telephone: (704) 333-0506
Founded in: 1963
Questionnaire not received

CHARLESTON

Charles Towne Landing
1500 Old Towne Rd., 29407
Telephone: (803) 556-4450
State agency, authorized by
Department of Parks, Recreation
and Tourism
Founded in: 1969
Janson L. Cox, Director
Number of members: 2,500
Staff: full time 35, part time 15,
volunteer 11
Magazine: *Instruc'ns*

Volunteers in front of the 1774 Hezekiah Alexander Homesite.—Mint Museum, Charlotte,
North Carolina.

Major programs: historic site(s), school programs, newsletters/pamphlets, historic preservation, exhibits, living history, audiovisual programs, archaeology programs, natural history
Period of collections: 1600s

CHEROKEE

Cherokee Historical Association
P.O. Box 398, U.S. Hwy. 441, N, 28719
Telephone: (704) 497-2111
Founded in: 1948
Carol E. White, General Manager
Staff: full time 25, part time 200
Magazine: *Unto These Hills*
Major programs: museum, living history, historical drama

CLIMAX

Old Time Historical Association
Hwy. 22
Telephone: (919) 685-4407
Mail to: P.O. Box 70, 27233
Private agency
Founded in: 1974
James S. Ferree, Jr., President
Number of members: 400
Staff: volunteer 25
Major programs: archives, museum
Period of collections: 1875-1940

CLINTON

Sampson County Historical Society
P.O. Box 422, 28328
Founded in: 1979
Questionnaire not received

CRESWELL

Somerset Place
P.O. Box 215, 27928
Telephone: (919) 797-4560
State agency, authorized by Department of Cultural Resources
William B. Edwards, Jr., Manager
Staff: full time 2
Period of collections: 1800-1860

CULLOWHEE

Mountain Heritage Center
Western Carolina University, University Dr., 28723
Telephone: (704) 227-7129
Founded in: 1975
Aaron Hyatt, Director
Staff: full time 3, part time 2, volunteer 10
Magazine: *Broadside*
Major programs: museum, oral history, school programs, exhibits, audiovisual programs
Period of collections: 1870s-1920s

CURRIE

Moores Creek National Battlefield
P.O. Box 69, 28435
Telephone: (919) 283-5591
Federal agency, authorized by National Park Service
Founded in: 1926
Staff: full time 6, part time 2

Major programs: historic site(s), school programs
Period of collections: Revolutionary War-1776

DALLAS

Gaston County Museum of Art and History
131 W. Main St.
Telephone: (704) 866-3437
Mail to: P.O. Box 429, 28034
County agency
Founded in: 1976
Alan D. Waufle, Director
Number of members: 600
Staff: full time 3, part time 2, volunteer 10
Major programs: museum, historic sites preservation, tours/pilgrimages, oral history, educational programs
Period of collections: 1865-1918

DURHAM

Bennett Place State Historic Site
4409 Bennett Memorial Rd., 27705
Telephone: (919) 383-4345
State agency
Founded in: 1923
Harold G. Mozingo, Historic Site Manager
Staff: full time 4, part time 5
Major programs: historic site(s), markers, tours, school programs, historic preservation, exhibits, living history, audiovisual programs
Period of collections: 1860-1865

Duke Homestead State Historic Site and Tobacco Museum
2828 Duke Homestead Rd., 27705
Telephone: (919) 477-5498
State agency, Department of Cultural Resources
Founded in: 1974
A. Dale Coats, Historic Site Manager
Number of members: 1
Staff: full time 4, part time 8, volunteer 15
Major programs: museum, historic site(s), oral history, school programs, newsletters/pamphlets, research, living history
Period of collections: 1830-present

Forest History Society
701 Vickers Ave., 27701
Telephone: (919) 682-9319
Private agency
Founded in: 1946
Harold K. Steen, Executive Director
Number of members: 2,000
Staff: full time 6
Magazine: *Journal of Forest History*
Major programs: library, archives, manuscripts, oral history, book publishing, newsletters/pamphlets, research, photographic collections, conservation
Period of collections: 1800-present

Friends of West Point
5101 N. Roxboro Rd., 27704
Telephone: (919) 471-1623
Private agency
Founded in: 1975
Beth O'Neill, Assistant Park Manager
Number of members: 200

Staff: full time 2, part time 2, volunteer 25
Major programs: museum, historic site(s), school programs, historic preservation, exhibits, audiovisual programs, photographic collections
Period of collections: late 19th-early 20th centuries

Historic Preservation Society of Durham
3008 Ithaca St., 27707
Telephone: (919) 489-7810
Questionnaire not received

◊**North Carolina Humanities Committee**
112 Foust Bldg., University of North Carolina at Greensboro, 27412
Telephone: (919) 379-5325
Private agency, authorized by National Endowment for the Humanities
Founded in: 1972
Brent D. Glass, Executive Director
Staff: full time 4
Major programs: public humanities programs

St. Joseph's Historic Foundation, Inc.
804 Fayetteville St., 27701
Telephone: (919) 682-3453
Founded in: 1976
Questionnaire not received

Society for the History of Technology
Department of History, Duke University, 27706
Telephone: (919) 684-2758
Founded in: 1958
Alex Roland, Secretary
Number of members: 2,200
Magazine: *Technology and Culture*
Major programs: museum, newsletters/pamphlets, conferences

Stagville Center
Old Oxford Hwy.
Telephone: (919) 477-9835
Mail to: P.O. Box 15628, 27704
State agency, authorized by Department of Cultural Resources
Founded in: 1977
Kenneth McFarland, Site Manager
Number of members: 56
Staff: full time 3, volunteer 37
Magazine: *Stagville Update*
Major programs: historic site(s), historic preservation
Period of collections: 1787-1925

EDEN

Eden Historic Properties Commission
350 W. Stadium Dr., 27288
Telephone: (919) 623-9707
Town agency
Founded in: 1979
Mrs. Thomas S. Harrington, Chair
Number of members: 11
Major programs: inventory of historic properties

EDENTON

Cupola House Association
S. Broad St., 27932
Telephone: (919) 482-3663
Questionnaire not received

Edenton Historical Commission
S. Broad St.
Telephone: (919) 482-3663
Mail to: P.O. Box 474, 27932
Private agency, authorized by
Department of Cultural Resources
Founded in: 1969
Linda Jordan Eure, Site Manager
Staff: full time 1, part time 10,
volunteer 80
Major programs: historic site(s),
markers, tours/pilgrimages, historic
preservation, audiovisual programs

Historic Edenton
Telephone: (919) 482-2637
Mail to: P.O. Box 474, 27932
State agency, authorized by
Department of Cultural Resources
Linda Jordan Eure, Site Manager
Staff: full time 4, part time 8,
volunteer 100
Major programs: museum, historic
site(s), markers, tours/pilgrimages,
school programs, historic
preservation, exhibits, living
history, audiovisual programs,
photographic collections
Period of collections: 1725-1815

**James Iredell House State Historic
Site**
105 E. Church St.
Telephone: (919) 482-2637
Mail to: P.O. Box 474, 27932
State agency, authorized by
Department of Cultural Resources
Founded in: 1955
Linda Jordan Eure, Site Manager
Staff: full time 3, volunteer 20
Major programs: historic site(s),
tours/pilgrimages, school
programs, audiovisual programs
Period of collections: 18th century

ELIZABETH CITY

Museum of the Albemarle
Rt. 6, Hwy. 17, S, 27909
Telephone: (919) 335-1453/335-2987
State agency, authorized by
Department of Cultural Resources
Founded in: 1967
Barbara E. Taylor, Director
Number of members: 325
Staff: full time 6, part time 2
Major programs: museum, school
programs, historic preservation,
records management, exhibits
Period of collections: late 1800s-early
20th century

**Pasquotank Historical and
Genealogical Society**
P.O. Box 523, 27909
Telephone: (919) 335-2041 (historian)
County agency
Founded in: 1953
Fred P. Markham III, President
Number of members: 45
Staff: volunteer 6
Major programs: museum, markers,
book publishing, historic

preservation, research,
genealogical services
Period of collections: from 17th
century

Society of Mayflower Descendants
1904 Rivershore Rd., 27909
Private agency, authorized by
General Society, Mayflower
Descendants
Founded in: 1924
Shirley Spaeth, Governor
Number of members: 502
Magazine: *The Mayflower News*

ENFIELD

**Halifax County Historical
Association**
301 W. Burnette Ave.
Telephone: (919) 445-5210
Mail to: 126 N. Church St., 27823
Questionnaire not received

ENGLEHARD

Hyde County Historical Society
President, P.O. Box 159, Main St.,
27824
Telephone: (919) 925-4591
Founded in: 1962
R. S. Spencer, Jr., President
Number of members: 150
Magazine: *High Tides*
Major programs: library, book
publishing, newsletters/pamphlets,
archaeology programs
Period of collections: 19th century

FAYETTEVILLE

**Cumberland County Historical
Society**
312 DeVane St., 28305
Telephone: (919) 484-5217
Questionnaire not received

**Historic Fayetteville
Foundation, Inc.**
Telephone: (919) 483-2101
Mail to: P.O. Box 1507, 28302
Founded in: 1978
Charles Speegle, President
Number of members: 175
Staff: volunteer 40
Major programs: museum,
tours/pilgrimages, junior history,
oral history, book publishing,
newsletters/pamphlets, historic
preservation

FLAT ROCK

**Carl Sandburg Home National
Historic Site**
Little River Rd.
Telephone: (704) 693-4178
Mail to: P.O. Box 395, 28731
Federal agency, authorized by
National Park Service
Founded in: 1969
Benjamin Davis, Superintendent
Staff: full time 5, part time 5,
volunteer 2
Major programs: museum, historic
sites preservation, historic
preservation
Period of collections: 1900-1960

Historic Flat Rock, Inc.
P.O. Box 295, 28731
Telephone: (704) 693-1638
Private agency
Founded in: 1973
J. W. MacDonald, President
Number of members: 200
Staff: volunteer 28
Major programs: historic site(s),
tours, historic preservation,
audiovisual programs
Period of collections: 1850-1900

FOREST CITY

**Genealogical Society of Old Tryon
County, Inc.**
U.S. Hwy. 74, Isothermal Community
College Library Bldg.
Mail to: P.O. Box 938, 28043
Private agency
Founded in: 1972
Harold A. Cannon, President
Number of members: 750
Staff: volunteer 8
Major programs: library, historic
preservation, research,
genealogical services
Period of collections: 1700-1900

FORT BRAGG

JFK Special Warfare Museum
Bldg. D, 2502 Ardennes and Marion
Sts.
Telephone: (919) 396-4272/396-1533
Mail to: P.O. Box 70060, 28307-5000
Federal agency, authorized by the
U.S. Army
Founded in: 1963
Roxanne M. Merritt, Curator
Number of members: 1
Staff: full time 3, part time 1
Major programs: museum, markers,
newsletters/pamphlets, research,
exhibits, photographic collections
Period of collections: 1945-present

FRANKLIN

Macon County Historical Society
Macon County Public Library
Mail to: P.O. Box 822, 28734
Private agency
Founded in: 1946
Barbara S. McRae, President
Number of members: 110
Staff: volunteer 5
Major programs: archives, exhibits,
audiovisual programs,
photographic collections
Period of collections: 1850-1925

FREMONT

Charles B. Aycock Birthplace
P.O. Box 207, 27830
Telephone: (919) 242-5581
Questionnaire not received

GASTONIA

**Schiele Museum of Natural
History/Living History Farm and
Catawba Indian Village**
1500 E. Garrison Blvd.
Telephone: (704) 865-6131
Mail to: P.O. Box 953, 28053-0953
City agency
Founded in: 1960

Richard Alan Stout, Executive
Director
Number of members: 500
Staff: full time 23, part time 4,
volunteer 200
Magazine: *Keeping Track*
Major programs: museum, historic
site(s), tours/pilgrimages, school
programs, book publishing,
newsletters/pamphlets, historic
preservation, research, exhibits,
living history, audiovisual
programs, archaeology programs
Period of collections: 1565-1900

GATESVILLE

Gates County Historical Society
c/o President, 27937
Telephone: (919) 357-1733
County agency
Founded in: 1975
Edith F. Seiling, President
Number of members: 150
Staff: volunteer 6
Major programs: library, manuscripts,
tours/pilgrimages,
newsletters/pamphlets, historic
preservation
Period of collections: 1800-1950

GERMANTON

Stokes County Historical Society
(919) 591-7969
Mail to: P.O. Box 250, 27019
Private agency
Jerry Rutledge, President

GRAHAM

**Alamance County Historic
Properties Commission**
124 W. Elm St., 27253
Telephone: (919) 228-1312
County agency
Founded in: 1977
M. M. Way, Technical Advisor
Major programs: museum, historic
site(s), book publishing, historic
preservation, records
management, audiovisual
programs, historic site inventory
Period of collections: 1800-present

GREENSBORO

African Heritage Center
North Carolina Agricultural and
Technical State University, 27401
Telephone: (919) 379-7874
Questionnaire not received

Blandwood Mansion
447 W. Washington, 27401
Telephone: (919) 272-5003
Mail to: P.O. Box 13136, 27405
Private agency, authorized by
Greensboro Preservation Society
Founded in: 1966
James C. Jordan, Executive Director
Number of members: 1,100
Staff: full time 1, part time 2,
volunteer 30
Magazine: *Landmarks*
Major programs: library, historic
site(s), research
Period of collections: 1820-1860

**Greensboro Historical
Museum, Inc.**
130 Summit Ave., 27401
Telephone: (919) 373-2043
Founded in: 1924
William J. Moore, Director
Staff: full time 6, part time 14
Magazine: *The Greensboro Historical
Museum Journal*
Major programs: archives, museum,
tours/pilgrimages, junior history,
school programs,
newsletters/pamphlets, records
management, research, exhibits,
audiovisual programs,
photographic collections
Period of collections: 19th century

**Guilford Courthouse National
Military Park**
P.O. Box 9806, 27429-0806
Telephone: (919) 288-1776
Federal agency, authorized by
National Park Service
Founded in: 1887
W. W. Danielson, Superintendent
Staff: full time 10, part time 4,
volunteer 150
Major programs: library, museum,
historic site(s), markers,
tours/pilgrimages,
newsletters/pamphlets, historic
preservation, exhibits, living
history, audiovisual programs,
genealogical services
Period of collections: 1780-1781

Heritage Center
North Carolina Conference, 27411
Telephone: (919) 379-7874
Questionnaire not received

**Mattye Reed African Heritage
Center**
2711 McConnell Rd., 27401
Telephone: (919) 379-7874
State agency
Founded in: 1968
Mattye Reed, Director
Staff: full time 1, part time 10,
volunteer 3
Major programs: library, museum,
tours/pilgrimages, school
programs, exhibits, audiovisual
programs, photographic
collections

**Old Greensborough Preservation
Society**
447 Arlington St., 27406
Telephone: (919) 272-6617
Mail to: P.O. Box 1047, 27402
Private agency
Founded in: 1977
Liz Hampton, Director
Number of members: 250
Staff: part time 1
Major programs: archives,
tours/pilgrimages, oral history,
newsletters/pamphlets, historic
preservation, audiovisual
programs, photographic
collections, community
involvement
Period of collections: 1870-present

GREENVILLE

Pitt County Historical Society
P.O. Box 5063, 27834
Telephone: (919) 752-3129
Founded in: 1950
Questionnaire not received

HALIFAX

Historic Halifax State Historic Site
St. David St.
Telephone: (919) 583-7191
Mail to: P.O. Box 406, 27839
State agency, authorized by
Department of Cultural Resources
Founded in: 1965
Margaret R. Phillips, Historic Site
Manager
Staff: full time 6, part time 8
Major programs: museum, historic
site(s), tours/pilgrimages, historic
preservation, exhibits, archaeology
programs
Period of collections: 1750-1840

HAMILTON

Historic Hamilton Commission, Inc.
Front St., 27840
Telephone: (919) 442-7941
Mail to: 508 Glenn Ave., Rocky Mount,
27801
Private agency
Founded in: 1967
Samuel W. Johnson, President
Number of members: 30
Major programs: historic site(s),
historic preservation
Period of collections: 1850-1920

HERTFORD

**Perquimans County Historical
Society**
P.O. Box 652, 27944
Private agency
Founded in: 1958
Raymond A. Winslow, Jr., President
Number of members: 5
Magazine: *Perquimans County
Historical Society Year Book*
Major programs: educational
programs, newsletters/pamphlets

HICKORY

**American Furniture Academy and
Hall of Fame**
Telephone: (704) 328-3827
Mail to: P.O. Box 2644, 28601
Questionnaire not received

HIGH POINT

High Point Historical Society, Inc.
1805 E. Lexington Ave., 27262
Telephone: (919) 885-6859
Private agency
Founded in: 1966
Dennis T. Lawson, Executive Director
Number of members: 320
Staff: full time 5, part time 6,
volunteer 10
Major programs: museum, historic
site(s), tours/pilgrimages, school
programs, newsletters/pamphlets,
exhibits, living history
Period of collections: 1750-present

High Point Museum
1805 E. Lexington Ave., 27262
Telephone: (919) 885-6859
Private agency
Founded in: 1969
Dennis T. Lawson, Director
Number of members: 500
Staff: full time 5, part time 4,
    volunteer 25
Major programs: museum,
    newsletters/pamphlets, exhibits,
    living history
Period of collections: 1859-present

HILLSBOROUGH

Hillsborough Historical Society
Corbin St.
Telephone: (919) 732-8648
Mail to: P.O. Box 871, 27278
Founded in: 1962
Chester Andrews President
Number of members: 500
Staff: volunteer 25
Major programs: historic site(s),
    markers, tours/pilgrimages,
    newsletters/pamphlets, historic
    preservation, photographic
    collections
Period of collections: 1754-1900

JACKSONVILLE

Onslow County Historical Society
Telephone: (919) 347-5287
Mail to: P.O. Box 5203, 28540
Founded in: 1957
JoAnn Becker, President
Number of members: 80
Staff: volunteer 80
Major programs: museum, historic
    site(s), oral history, school
    programs, book publishing, historic
    preservation, genealogical
    services, recording of county
    cemeteries

JAMESTOWN

Historic Jamestown Society, Inc.
Telephone: (919) 454-3819
Mail to: P.O. Box 512, 27282
Questionnaire not received

JAMESVILLE

**Historic Burras House
Foundation, Inc.**
U.S. 64, E
Telephone: (919) 792-3001
Mail to: P.O. Box 220, 27846
Private agency
D. Phelps, Co-chair
Number of members: 50
Staff: volunteer 6
Major programs: historic site(s),
    school programs, historic
    preservation
Period of collections: 1700s

KINSTON

**Richard Caswell Memorial/CSS
Neuse**
P.O. Box 3043, 28501
Telephone: (919) 522-2091
G. Eugene Brown, Manager
Staff: full time 4
State agency, authorized by
    Department of Cultural Resources

Major programs: historic site(s),
    school programs, historic
    preservation, research, exhibits,
    living history, audiovisual programs
Period of collections: 1861-1865

KURE BEACH

Ft. Fisher State Historic Site
P.O. Box 68, 28449
Telephone: (919) 458-5538
State agency, authorized by
    Department of Cultural Resources
E. Gehrig Spencer, Manager
Staff: full time 4
Major programs: museum, historic
    site(s), tours/pilgrimages, oral
    history, school programs, historic
    preservation, research, exhibits,
    living history, audiovisual
    programs, archaeology programs
Period of collections: 1861-1865

LAKE JUNALUSKA

**Commission on Archives and
History of The United Methodist
Church**
39 Lake Shore Dr.
Telephone: (704) 456-9433
Mail to: P.O. Box 488, 28745
Founded in: 1885
Questionnaire not received

LEXINGTON

**Davidson County Historical
Association**
1 S. Main
Telephone: (919) 476-7213
Mail to: P.O. Box 404, 27292
Founded in: 1955
Questionnaire not received

Davidson County Museum
Old Courthouse on the Square, 27292
Telephone: (704) 249-7011
County agency
Founded in: 1976
Catherine M. Hoffmann, Curator
Staff: full time 1, part time 1
Major programs: museum, exhibits
Period of collections: 1800-1930

MANTEO

**Cape Hatteras National Seashore
Library**
Rt. 1, Box 675, 27954
Telephone: (919) 473-2111
Major programs: library, historic sites
    preservation, educational
    programs, historic preservation

Elizabeth II State Historic Site
Ice Plant Island
Telephone: (919) 473-1144
Mail to: P.O. Box 155, 27954
State agency, authorized by
    Department of Cultural Resources
Horace Whitfield, Site Manager
Staff: full time 6, part time 14,
    volunteer 48
Major programs: historic site(s),
    school programs, exhibits, living
    history, audiovisual programs
Period of collections: 1580s

Ft. Raleigh National Historic Site
Rt. 1, Box 675, 27954
Telephone: (919) 473-5772

Federal agency, authorized by
    National Park Service
Founded in: 1941
Thomas L. Hartman, Superintendent
Staff: full time 2, part time 4
Major programs: museum, historic
    site(s), markers, school programs,
    exhibits, living history, audiovisual
    programs, archaeology programs
Period of collections: 1585-1590

**Roanoke Island Historical
Association, Inc.**
Ft. Raleigh
Telephone: (919) 473-2127
Mail to: P.O. Box 40, 27954
Private agency
Founded in: 1932
Robert Knowles, General Manager
Number of members: 947
Staff: full time 7, part time 150,
    volunteer 30
Major programs: outdoor drama
Period of collections: 1584-1587

Wright Brothers National Memorial
Telephone: (919) 441-7430
Mail to: Rt. 1, Box 675, 27954
Federal agency, authorized by
    National Park Service
Robert Woody, Chief of Interpretation
    and Visitor Services
Staff: full time 7, part time 2,
    volunteer 9
Major programs: museum, historic
    site(s), markers, photographic
    collections
Period of collections: 1900-1908

MARSHALL

Madison County Historical Society
Telephone: (704) 689-1153
Mail to: P.O. Box 236, 28753
Questionnaire not received

MONTREAT

**Historical Foundation of the
Presbyterian and Reformed
Churches**
Telephone: (704) 669-7061
Mail to: Box 847, 28757
Private agency
Founded in: 1927
Jerrold Lee Brooks, Executive
    Director
Number of members: 1,000
Staff: full time 10
Magazine: *The Historical Foundation
News*
Major programs: library, archives,
    manuscripts, museum,
    newsletters/pamphlets, historic
    preservation, records management
    research, exhibits, photographic
    collections
Period of collections: 1800-present

MORGANTON

Burke County Historical Society
204 S. King St.
Mail to: P.O. Box 151, 28655
Private agency
Founded in: 1959
Millie M. Barbee, President
Number of members: 150

Major programs: library, archives,
manuscripts, school programs,
book publishing, historic
preservation
Period of collections: mid 18th
century-present

Historic Burke Foundation, Inc.
102 E. Union St.
Telephone: (704) 437-4104
Mail to: P.O. Box 915, 28655
Private agency
Founded in: 1982
Millie M. Barbee, Executive Director
Number of members: 325
Staff: part time 1
Major programs: museum, historic
site(s), tours/pilgrimages, oral
history, school programs, book
publishing, newsletters/pamphlets,
historic preservation, research,
exhibits, audiovisual programs,
photographic collections
Period of collections: 1700-present

**North Carolina School for the Deaf
Historical Museum**
Hwy. 64, 28655
Telephone: (704) 433-2951
Founded in: 1977
Questionnaire not received

MT. GILEAD

**Town Creek Indian Mound State
Historical Site**
Rt. 3, Box 50, 27306
Telephone: (919) 439-6802
State agency, authorized by
Department of Cultural Resources
Founded in: 1936
Archie C. Smith, Jr., Site Manager
Staff: full time 4, part time 4
Major programs: museum, historic
site(s), school programs, exhibits,
audiovisual programs, archaeology
programs
Period of collections: 15th century

MT. PLEASANT

**Eastern Cabarrus Historical
Society Museum**
N. Main St.
Telephone: (704) 436-6570
(president)
Mail to: P.O. Box 484, 28124
Private agency
Founded in: 1973
Billie McAllister, President
Number of members: 265
Staff: volunteer 15
Major programs: library, museum,
school programs, historic
preservation, exhibits, living
history, photographic collections
Period of collections: late 1800s-early
1900s

MT. ULLA

**Rowan County Historic Properties
Commission**
Rt. 1, Box 22, Sloan Rd., 28125
Telephone: (704) 633-6498
County agency, authorized by Rowan
County Commissioners
Founded in: 1972
Beulah Davis, Secretary
Major programs: historic site(s)

MURFREESBORO

**Murfreesboro Historical
Association**
116 E. Main St.
Telephone: (919) 398-4886
Mail to: P.O. Box 3, 27855
Private agency
Founded in: 1967
Kay P. Ditt, Executive Director
Number of members: 900
Staff: part time 1
Major programs: museum,
tours/pilgrimages,
newsletters/pamphlets,
photographic collections
Period of collections: 1790-1900

**Murfreesboro Historic Properties
Commission**
207 N. Wynn St., 27855
Telephone: (919) 398-5659
Town agency
Founded in: 1981
Ed Burchins, Town Administrator
Staff: full time 1
Major programs: historic site(s), oral
history, historic preservation,
research, exhibits, archaeology
programs
Period of collections: 18th-20th
centuries

MURPHY

**Cherokee County Historical
Museum**
Peachtree St., 28906
Telephone: (704) 837-6792
Private agency
Founded in: 1977
Alice D. White, Director
Number of members: 18
Staff: full time 1
Major programs: museum, oral
history, exhibits

NEW BERN

**New Bern Historical Society
Foundation, Inc.**
511 Broad St.
Telephone: (919) 638-8558
Mail to: P.O. Box 119, 28560
Private agency
Founded in: 1923
Newsom Williams, President
Number of members: 440
Staff: volunteer 4
Major programs: museum,
tours/pilgrimages,
newsletters/pamphlets, historic
preservation
Period of collections: late 18th-19th
centuries

**New Bern Preservation
Foundation, Inc.**
510 Pollock St., 28560
Telephone: (919) 633-6445
Private agency
Founded in: 1972
Susan Moffat, Executive Director
Number of members: 250
Major programs: tours/pilgrimages,
newsletters/pamphlets, historic
preservation, archaeology
programs

Tryon Palace Restoration Complex
610 Pollock St.
Telephone: (919) 638-5109/638-1560

Mail to: P.O. Box 1007, 28560
State agency, authorized by Tryon
Palace Commission
Founded in: 1945
Kay P. Williams, Administrator
Staff: full time 25, part time 70
Major programs: library, archives,
manuscripts, museum, historic
site(s), junior history, school
programs, book publishing,
records management, research,
exhibits, living history, audiovisual
programs
Period of collections: 1770-1840

NEWTON GROVE

**Bentonville Battleground State
Historic Site**
Rt. 1, Four Oaks, 27524
Telephone: (919) 594-0789
Mail to: P.O. Box 27, 28366
State agency, authorized by
Department of Cultural Resources
Jack M. Rose, Site Manager
Staff: full time 3, part time 6,
volunteer 25
Major programs: historic site(s),
markers, school programs,
exhibits, living history,
photographic collections
Period of collections: 19th century

**Catawba County Historical
Association, Inc.**
1716 S. College Dr.
Telephone: (704) 465-0383
Mail to: P.O. Box 73, 28658
Private agency
Founded in: 1936
Sidney Halma, Director
Number of members: 1,170
Staff: full time 14, part time 6,
volunteer 96
Major programs: archives,
manuscripts, museum, historic
site(s), markers, oral history, school
programs, book publishing,
newsletters/pamphlets, historic
preservation, records
management, research, exhibits,
living history, audiovisual
programs, photographic
collections, genealogical services
Period of collections: 1745-present

OLD FORT

Mountain Gateway Museum
106 Water St.
Telephone: (704) 668-4137
Mail to: P.O. Box 477, 28762
Founded in: 1970
Questionnaire not received

PEMBROKE

Native American Resource Center
Pembroke State University, 28372
Telephone: (919) 521-4214
State agency, authorized by the
university
Founded in: 1980
Linda E. Oxendine, Director
Staff: full time 2
Major programs: museum, exhibits,
audiovisual programs
Period of collections: 19th-20th
centuries

PINEVILLE

James K. Polk Memorial
P.O. Box 475, 28134
Telephone: (704) 889-7145
State agency
Joyce M. White, Manager
Staff: full time 4
Major programs: museum, historic
site(s), tours/pilgrimages, oral
history, school programs,
newsletters/pamphlets, exhibits,
living history, audiovisual
programs, field services
Period of collections: 1795-1849

RALEIGH

◇Federation of North Carolina Historical Societies
109 E. Jones St., 27611
Telephone: (919) 733-7305
Authorized by North Carolina Division
of Archives and History
Founded in: 1976
Elizabeth F. Buford,
Secretary/Treasurer
Number of members: 117
Staff: part time 2
Magazine: *Federation Bulletin*

Friends of the Archives, Inc.
109 E. Jones St., 27611
Telephone: (919) 733-3952
Private agency, authorized by North
Carolina State Archives
Founded in: 1978
David J. Olson, Secretary/Treasurer
Number of members: 370

Friends of North Carolina Archaeology, Inc.
109 E. Jones St., 27611
Telephone: (919) 733-7342
Private agency
Founded in: 1984
J. Michael Smith, President
Number of members: 90
Staff: volunteer 6
Major programs: school programs,
newsletters/pamphlets, historic
preservation, archaeology
programs

Historic Preservation Foundation of North Carolina, Inc.
P.O. Box 27644, 27611
Telephone: (919) 832-3652
Private agency
Founded in: 1939
J. Myrick Howard, Executive Director
Number of members: 2,000
Staff: full time 5, volunteer 15
Magazine: *North Carolina
Preservation*
Major programs: historic sites
preservation,
newsletters/pamphlets, awards,
tours

◇Historical Society of North Carolina
109 E. Jones St., 27611
Telephone: (919) 733-9375
Private agency
Founded in: 1845
Jerry C. Cashion, Secretary
Number of members: 75
Major programs: educational
programs, research

Mordecai Square Historical Society, Inc.
1 Mimosa St., 27604
Telephone: (919) 834-4844
Private agency, authorized by
Raleigh Parks and Recreation
Founded in: 1968
Daniel M. Ellison, Executive Director
Number of members: 700
Staff: full time 2, volunteer 180
Magazine: *Square Notes*
Major programs: museum, historic
site(s), school programs,
newsletters/pamphlets, historic
preservation, linen conservation
Period of collections: 19th century

North Carolina Chapter, Victorian Society in America
400 Polk Dr., 27604
Founded in: 1978
Oakley L. Herring, President
Number of members: 350
Magazine: *Victoria's Parrot*
Major programs: Victorian art and
literature

◇North Carolina Division of Archives and History
109 E. Jones St., 27611
Telephone: (919) 733-7305
State agency
Founded in: 1903
William S. Price, Director
Staff: full time 340, volunteer 85
Magazine: *North Carolina Historical
Review/Carolina Comments/Tar
Heel Junior Historian*
Major programs: archives,
manuscripts, museum, historic
site(s), markers, junior history,
school programs, book publishing,
newsletters/pamphlets, historic
preservation, records
management, research, exhibits,
living history, audiovisual
programs, archaeology programs,
photographic collections,
genealogical services, field
services
Period of collections: 16th
century-present

North Carolina Genealogical Society
Mail to: P.O. Box 1492, 27511
Private agency
Founded in: 1974
J. Marshall Daniel, President
Number of members: 1,900
Staff: full time 1, part time 2
Magazine: *The North Carolina
Genealogical Society Journal*
Major programs: library, book
publishing, newsletters/pamphlets,
genealogical services
Period of collections: to 1850

North Carolina Literary and Historical Association
109 E. Jones St., 27611
Telephone: (919) 733-7305
Private agency
Founded in: 1900
John L. Bell, Jr., President
Number of members: 1,200
Staff: part time 1
Major programs: book publishing,
newsletters/pamphlets, state
literature and history

Raleigh Historic Properties Commission, Inc.
1 Mimosa St., 27604
Telephone: (919) 832-7238
City agency
Founded in: 1961
Linda H. Edmisten, Executive
Director
Number of members: 32
Staff: full time 2
Major programs: historic site(s),
markers, tours/pilgrimages, junior
history, book publishing, historic
preservation, research, audiovisual
programs, photographic
collections

Society of North Carolina Archivists
(919) 787-6313 (secretary/treasurer)
Mail to: P.O. Box 20448, 27619
Private agency
Founded in: 1984
Richard Shrader, President
Number of members: 125
Major programs: archives,
manuscripts, records
management, preservation and
conservation of archival materials

State Capitol
109 E. Jones St., 27611
Telephone: (919) 733-4994
State agency
Samuel P. Townsend, Administrator
Staff: full time 6
Major programs: tours/pilgrimages,
school programs, historic
preservation, audiovisual
programs, traditional celebrations
and official state ceremonies
Period of collections: 1840-1865

ROCKY MOUNT

Nash County Historical Association, Inc.
4009 Lochinvar Lane, 27801
Telephone: (919) 443-6708
Private agency
Founded in: 1970
T. E. Ricks, President
Number of members: 100
Staff: volunteer 10
Major programs: museum,
tours/pilgrimages, historic
preservation, exhibits

ROSE HILL

Duplin County Historical Society—Leora H. McEachern Library of Local History
306 E. Main St.
Telephone: (919) 289-2654/289-2430
Mail to: P.O. Box 130, 28458
Private agency
Founded in: 1963
W. D. Herring, Chair, Research
Committee
Number of members: 65
Staff: volunteer 6
Magazine: *Footnotes*
Major programs: library, oral history,
book publishing,
newsletters/pamphlets, research,
photographic collections,
genealogical services
Period of collections: Colonial
era-19th century

ROXBORO

Person County Historical Society, Inc.
Mail to: P.O. Box 887, 27573
Founded in: 1959
Herman A. Gentry, Jr., President
Number of members: 50
Major programs: markers, books, newsletters/pamphlets, historic preservation

SALISBURY

Historic Salisbury Foundation, Inc.
Wallace Bldg.
Telephone: (704) 636-0103
Mail to: P.O. Box 4221, 28144
Founded in: 1972
Anne R. Williams, Executive Director
Number of members: 700
Staff: part time 2, volunteer 30
Magazine: *Salisbury Watchman*
Major programs: museum, historic sites preservation, tours/pilgrimages, educational programs, newsletters/pamphlets, historic preservation, restoration; revolving fund
Period of collections: late 1800s-present

North Carolina Synod, Lutheran Church in America
P.O. Box 2049, 28145
Telephone: (704) 366-4861
Private agency
Founded in: 1803
James A. Chesky, Secretary/Archivist
Staff: part time 1
Major programs: library, archives, tours, records management, exhibits
Period of collections: 1803-present

Rowan Museum, Inc.
114 S. Jackson St.
Telephone: (704) 633-5946
Mail to: 202 S. Fulton St., 28144
Founded in: 1953
Questionnaire not received

Salisbury Historic District Commission
c/o City of Salisbury, 132 N. Main St., 28144
Telephone: (704) 637-2200
City agency, authorized by City Economic Development Department
Founded in: 1975
Ronald Buffaloe, Chair
Staff: part time 2, volunteer 9
Major programs: historic preservation
Period of collections: 1799-present

SANFORD

House in the Horseshoe
Rt. 3, Box 924, 27330
Telephone: (919) 947-2051
State agency, authorized by Department of Cultural Resources
Founded in: 1955
Royal Windley, Site Manager
Number of members: 1
Staff: full time 3, part time 6
Major programs: historic site(s), oral history, school programs, newsletters/pamphlets, records management
Period of collections: 1770-1850

SHALLOTTE

Brunswick County Historical Society
Mail to: P.O. Box 874, 28459
Founded in: 1954
J. M. Holden, President
Number of members: 28
Major programs: historic site(s), book publishing, research, living history, archaeology programs

SHELBY

Broad River Genealogical Society, Inc.
316 Dale St.
Telephone: (704) 482-3016
Mail to: P.O. Box 2261, 28151-2261
Private agency
Founded in: 1979
Virginia Greene DePriest, President
Number of members: 275
Staff: volunteer 50
Magazine: *Eswau Huppeday*
Major programs: archives, book publishing, newsletters/pamphlets, audiovisual programs, genealogical services
Period of collections: 1800s

Cleveland County Historical Association and Museum
Telephone: (704) 482-8186
Mail to: P.O. Box 1335, Court Square, 28150
Private agency
Founded in: 1965
Dean Whisnant, President
Number of members: 1,013
Staff: full time 3, volunteer 40
Major programs: library, archives, museum, historic site(s), tours/pilgrimages, junior history, oral history, school programs, book publishing, exhibits, archaeology programs, photographic collections, genealogical services, field services
Period of collections: to 1950s

SMITHFIELD

Johnston County Genealogical Society
305 Market St., 27577
Telephone: (919) 934-8146
Founded in: 1973
Luby F. Royall, Jr., President
Number of members: 250
Staff: volunteer 12
Magazine: *Johnston County Genealogical Society*
Major programs: library, books, newsletters/pamphlets, genealogy, cemetery records
Period of collections: 1759-1910

SOUTHERN PINES

Moore County Historical Association
P.O. Box 324, 28387
Telephone: (919) 949-3274
Founded in: 1946
Sherman W. Betts, President
Number of members: 350
Staff: volunteer 70
Major programs: library, museum, historic sites preservation, books, historic preservation
Period of collections: 1760-1970

SOUTHPORT

Brunswick Town
P.O. Box 356, 28461
Telephone: (919) 371-6613
Questionnaire not received

Southport Historical Society
Telephone: (919) 457-6940
Mail to: 501 N. Atlantic Ave., 28461
Founded in: 1976
Susan S. Carson, Archivist
Number of members: 60
Staff: volunteer 4
Magazine: *Whittlers' Bench*
Major programs: library, archives, historic sites preservation, markers, oral history, newsletters/pamphlets
Period of collections: 1725-present

SPARTA

Alleghany Historical-Genealogical Society Inc./Floyd Crouse House
Telephone: (919) 372-8864
Mail to: P.O. Box 817, 28675
Private agency
Founded in: 1978
Wilma R. Foster, President
Number of members: 135
Staff: volunteer 11
Major programs: museum, book publishing, newsletters/pamphlets, historic preservation, genealogical services

SPENCER

Spencer Shops
P.O. Box 165, 28159
Telephone: (704) 636-2889
State agency, authorized by Department of Cultural Resources
Michael C. Wells, Manager
Staff: full time 3
Major programs: museum, historic site(s), tours/pilgrimages, oral history, school programs, newsletters/pamphlets, historic preservation, research, exhibits, audiovisual programs
Period of collections: 1600-present

STANFIELD

Reed Gold Mine
Rt. 2, Box 101, 28163
Telephone: (704) 786-8337
State agency, authorized by Division of Archives and History, Historic Sites Section
John Dysart, Manager
Staff: full time 6
Major programs: historic site(s), school programs, exhibits
Period of collections: late 1800s

STATESVILLE

Ft. Dobbs
Rt. 9, Box 415-A, 28677
Telephone: (704) 873-5866
Louise N. Huston, Manager
Staff: full time 1

Genealogical Society of Iredell County
Corner of Court and S. Center Sts.
Telephone: (704) 873-6100
Mail to: P.O. Box 946, 28677
Founded in: 1977

Edith R. Walker, President
Staff: volunteer 4
Major programs: library, book
  publishing, newsletters/pamphlets,
  research, genealogical services
Period of collections: from 1760

SWANSBORO

**Swansboro Historical
  Association, Inc.**
telephone: (919) 726-1421, 326-5361
Mail to: P.O. Box 21, 28584
Founded in: 1961
H. J. Dudley, President
Number of members: 40
Staff: volunteer 12
Major programs: manuscripts,
  museum, markers, educational
  programs, newsletters/pamphlets,
  historic preservation
Period of collections: 1750-1950

**Swansboro's 200th Anniversary
  Celebration Committee**
P.O. Box 21, 28584
Telephone: (919) 326-5361
Founded in: 1980
Tucker R. Littleton, Chairman
Staff: volunteer 50
Major programs: tours/pilgrimages,
  educational programs,
  newsletters/pamphlets
Period of collections: 1750-1950

TARBORO

**Edgecombe County Historical
  Society**
130 Bridgers St.
Telephone: (919) 823-4159
Mail to: P.O. Box 1258, 27886
Private agency
Founded in: 1964
Earl L. Roberson, President
Number of members: 400
Staff: part time 1, volunteer 12
Magazine: *Non Nulla*
Major programs: archives, museum,
  historic site(s), markers,
  tours/pilgrimages,
  newsletters/pamphlets, historic
  preservation, photographic
  collections
Period of collections: 1760-present

**Historic Preservation Fund of
  Edgecombe County, Inc.**
112 W. Church St.
Telephone: (919) 823-3080
Mail to: P.O. Box 1595, 26886
Private agency
Founded in: 1982
Louise W. Boney, Executive Director
Staff: full time 1, volunteer 11
Major programs: historic site(s),
  tours/pilgrimages, historic
  preservation, research,
  photographic collections, field
  services
Period of collections: 1742-present

**Tarboro Historic District
  Commission**
112 W. Church St.
Telephone: (919) 823-8121
Mail to: P.O. Box 220, 27886
Town agency

E. Watson Brown, Director of
  Planning
Staff: part time 2, volunteer 7
Major programs: library, museum,
  historic site(s), markers,
  tours/pilgrimages, historic
  preservation, research,
  photographic collections
Period of collections: 1760-present

TRENTON

Jones County Historical Society
Mail to: P.O. Box 219, 28585
Telephone: (919) 448-3911
Founded in: 1971
Questionnaire not received

VALDESE

Museum of Waldensian Heritage
Rodoret St., 28690
Telephone: (704) 874-2531
Authorized by Waldensian
  Presbyterian Church
Founded in: 1893
Hilda Jones, Chair
Major programs: library, museum,
  oral history, school programs, book
  publishing, historic preservation,
  photographic collections
Period of collections: late 19th
  century

WADESBORO

Anson County Historical Society
210 E. Wade St.
Telephone: (704) 694-6694
Mail to: P.O. Box 732, 28170
Private agency
Founded in: 1963
Linn Garibaldi, President
Number of members: 250
Staff: volunteer 50
Major programs: archives, museum,
  historic sites preservation, markers,
  tours/pilgrimages, educational
  programs, books,
  newsletters/pamphlets
Period of collections: 1790-1880

WAGRAM

**Richmond Temperance and
  Literary Society**
Laurel Hill Rd., 28396
Questionnaire not received

WAKE FOREST

**Wake Forest College Birthplace
  Society, Inc.**
N. Main St.
Mail to: P.O. Box 494, 27587
Founded in: 1956
Mrs. I. Beverly Lake, Sr., President
Number of members: 275
Staff: volunteer 12
Major programs: historic sites
  preservation, museum
Period of collections: 1834-1956

WALLACE

Duplin County Historical Society
416 E. Main St., 28466
Telephone: (919) 285-2432
Questionnaire not received

WEAVERVILLE

Zebulon B. Vance Birthplace
911 Reems Creek Rd., 28787
Telephone: (704) 645-6706
Sudie Wheeler, Manager
Staff: full time 3
Major programs: historic site(s),
  tours/pilgrimages, school
  programs, historic preservation,
  research, living history
Period of collections: 1830

WENTWORTH

**Rockingham County History
  Society**
P.O. Box 84, 27375
Founded in: 1967
Number of members: 232
Major programs: manuscripts,
  historic site(s), junior history,
  newsletters/pamphlets, historic
  preservation, genealogical
  services, restoration

WILMINGTON

**Historic Wilmington
  Foundation, Inc.**
400 S. Front St., 28401
Telephone: (919) 762-2511
Private agency
Founded in: 1966
Angela K. Barnett, Executive Director
Number of members: 900
Staff: full time 2, part time 5,
  volunteer 300
Magazine: *Foundation Highlights*
Major programs: historic site(s),
  historic preservation, field services
Period of collections: 1840-1900

**Lower Cape Fear Historical
  Society, Inc.**
126 S. 3rd St., 28401
Telephone: (919) 762-0492
Mail to: P.O. Box 813, 28402
Founded in: 1956
Frank S. Conlon, President
Number of members: 400
Staff: part time 1
Magazine: *Lower Cape Fear
  Historical Society Bulletin*
Major programs: library, archives,
  manuscripts, museum, historic
  site(s), tours/pilgrimages, book
  publishing, newsletters/pamphlets,
  historic preservation, records
  management, research, exhibits,
  photographic collections,
  genealogical services
Period of collections: 1700-1900

**New Hanover County Museum of
  the Lower Cape Fear**
814 Market St., 28401
Telephone: (919) 763-0852
County agency
Janet K. Seapker, Director
Staff: full time 8, part time 2,
  volunteer 40
Major programs: museum, school
  programs, newsletters/pamphlets,
  research, exhibits, audiovisual
  programs, photographic
  collections
Period of collections: 1860-1960

North Carolina Museums Council
814 Market St., 28401

Telephone: (919) 763-0852
Private agency
Founded in: 1964
Janet K. Seapker, President
Number of members: 149
Staff: volunteer 15
Major programs: museology training
and workshops

**USS North Carolina Battleship
Memorial**
Eagles Island, 28401
Telephone: (919) 762-1829
Mail to: P.O. Box 417, 284023
State agency, authorized by USS
North Carolina Battleship
Commission
Founded in: 1962
F. S. Conlon, Director
Staff: full time 18
Major programs: museum, historic
site(s), historic preservation, War
Memorial
Period of collections: 1937-1947

WILSON

**City of Wilson Historic Properties
Commission**
112 N. Goldsboro St.
Telephone: (919) 291-8111
Mail to: P.O. Box 10, 27893
City agency
Founded in: 1976
Harry V. Hamilton, Jr., City Planner
Staff: part time 2
Major programs: archives, historic
site(s), markers, book publishing,
historic preservation, audiovisual
programs, photographic
collections
Period of collections: 1840-1940

WINDSOR

Historic Hope Foundation, Inc.
Telephone: (919) 794-3140
Mail to: P.O. Box 601, 27983
Private agency
Founded in: 1965
Number of members: 1,000
Staff: part time 5, volunteer 50
Major programs: library,
newsletters/pamphlets, historic
preservation, audiovisual programs
Period of collections: 1750-1825

WINSTON-SALEM

**Archives of The Moravian Church
in America, Southern Province**
4 E. Bank St., 27101
Telephone: (919) 722-1742
Mail to: Drawer M, Salem Station,
27108
Private agency, authorized by
Provincial Elder's Conference,
Moravian Church in America
Founded in: 1763
Thomas J. Haupert, Archivist
Staff: full time 1, part time 2,
volunteer 1
Major programs: library, archives,
manuscripts, records
management, photographic
collections, genealogical services
Period of collections: 1753-present

Historic Bethabara Park
2147 Bethabara Rd., 27106
Telephone: (919) 924-8191
Private agency
Founded in: 1966
William Hinman Director
Staff: full time 2, part time 16
Magazine: *Das Wachau Diarium*
Major programs: library, museum,
historic site(s), markers, tours,
newsletters/pamphlets, historic
preservation, research, exhibits,
audiovisual programs,
archaeology, programs,
interpretive programs
Period of collections: 1752-1830

Moravian Music Foundation, Inc.
20 Cascade Ave., 27107
Telephone: (919) 725-0551
Private agency
Founded in: 1956
Staff: full time 6, part time 1
Magazine: *Moravian Music
Foundation Journal*
Major programs: library, archives,
manuscripts
Period of collections: 1760-1900

**Museum of Early Southern
Decorative Arts**
924 S. Main St.
Telephone: (919) 722-6148
Mail to: P.O. Box 10310, 27108
Founded in: 1965
Questionnaire not received

**North Carolina Baptist Historical
Collection**
P.O. Box 77777, Reynolda Station,
27109
Private agency, authorized by Wake
Forest University
Founded in: 1871
John R. Woodard Jr., Director
Staff: full time 2, part time 6
Magazine: *Tar Heel Baptist Footprints*
Major programs: library, archives,
manuscripts,
newsletters/pamphlets, exhibits
Period of collections: 1770-present

Old Salem, Inc.
600 S. Main St., 27101
Telephone: (919) 723-3688
Mail to: Drawer F, Salem Station,
27108
Founded in: 1950
R. Arthur Spaugh, Jr., President
Staff: full time 37, part time 133
Major programs: library, museum,
historic sites preservation,
educational programs, books,
newsletters/pamphlets
Period of collections: 1760-1830

Reynolda House, Inc.
Reynolda Rd.
Telephone: (919) 725-5325
Mail to: P.O. Box 11765, 27106
Founded in: 1964
Questionnaire not received

YADKINVILLE

Yadkin County Historical Society
E. Main St.
Telephone: (919) 679-2795
Mail to: P.O. Box 1250, 27055
Founded in: 1972
Questionnaire not received

YANCEYVILLE

**Caswell County Historical
Association, Inc.**
Mail to: P.O. Box 278, 27379
Founded in: 1956
Anne Daniel, President
Number of members: 125
Staff: part time 5
Major programs: manuscripts,
museum, historic sites
preservation, tours/pilgrimages,
oral history, educational programs,
books
Period of collections: 1783-1865

NORTH DAKOTA

ALEXANDER

Lewis and Clark Trail Museum
58331
Telephone: (701) 828-3595
Founded in: 1968
Questionnaire not received

ASHLEY

McIntosh County Historical Society
101 3rd Ave., NE
Telephone: (701) 288-3605
Mail to: P.O. Box 10, 521 1st Ave., NE,
58413
County agency
Founded in: 1967
William E. Meidinger, President
Major programs: museum, historic
preservation, exhibits
Period of collections: from 1884

BEACH

**Golden Valley County Historical
Society**
1st Ave., S, 58621
Telephone: (701) 872-3631
County agency
Founded in: 1970
Jim Johnstone, President
Number of members: 100
Staff: volunteer 7
Major programs: library, archives,
manuscripts, museum, historic
site(s), historic preservation,
records management, exhibits,
living history, photographic
collections, genealogical services,
county fair and special events
Period of collections: late
1800s-present

BEULAH

Mercer County Historical Society
c/o President, P.O. Box 168, 58523
Founded in: 1976
Leland Erickson, President
Number of members: 100
Staff: volunteer 100
Major programs: library, archives,
museum, tours/pilgrimages, oral
history, educational programs,
newsletters/pamphlets, historic
preservation
Period of collections: early 1920s

BISMARCK

Bismarck-Mandan Historical and Genealogical Society
2708 N. 4 St., 58501
Telephone: (701) 223-2929
Private agency
Founded in: 1971
David Enyant, President
Number of members: 98
Staff: volunteer 7
Major programs: newsletters/pamphlets

Germans from Russia Heritage Society
1008 E. Central, 58501
Telephone: (701) 223-6167
Founded in: 1971
Beata Mertz, President
Number of members: 1,970
Staff: part time 2
Magazine: *Heritage Review*
Major programs: library, archives, newsletters/pamphlets, historic preservation, research, exhibits, genealogical services
Period of collections: 1800s-early 1900s

◇**State Historical Society of North Dakota/North Dakota Heritage Center**
58505
Telephone: (701) 224-2666
Founded in: 1895
James E. Sperry, Superintendent
Staff: full time 51, part time 20, volunteer 80
Magazine: *North Dakota History: Journal of the Northern Plains*
Major programs: library, archives, manuscripts, museum, historic sites preservation, educational programs, newsletters/pamphlets, historic preservation, archeology, photographic collections
Period of collections: 19th-20th centuries

BOTTINEAU

Bottineau Historical Society
N. Main St.
Mail to: 321 Alexander St., 58318
Founded in: 1972
Kenneth E. Johnson, President
Number of members: 150
Staff: volunteer 15
Major programs: museum, historic preservation
Period of collections: early 1900s

CARRINGTON

Foster County Historical Society
16 Ave., S
Mail to: c/o President, 311 5th Ave., N, 58421
County agency
Founded in: 1967
Alan Trullinger, President
Number of members: 20
Period of collections: 1900

CARSON

Grant County Historical Society
Telephone: (701) 622-3541
Mail to: P.O. Box 135, 58551

County agency
Founded in: 1972
Muron Thearer, President
Number of members: 80
Staff: part time 5, volunteer 15
Major programs: museum, historic site(s), book publishing, historic preservation, exhibits, photographic collections

CENTER

Oliver County Historical Society
Telephone: (701) 794-3116
Mail to: New Salem, 58563
County agency
Laurence Porsborg, President
Staff: volunteer 6
Major programs: archives, museum, historic site(s), markers, newsletters/pamphlets, historic preservation, exhibits, living history, photographic collections, Period of collections: 1885-1940

COLEHARBOR

◇**North Dakota Historical Society, Inc.**
58531
Telephone: (701) 442-5335
Private agency
Founded in: 1895
Mrs. Dave Robinson, Secretary
Number of members: 636
Staff: volunteer 3
Major programs: newsletters/pamphlets, genealogical services

COOPERSTOWN

Griggs County Historical Society
Telephone: (701) 797-2267
Mail to: Rt. 2, Box 95, 58425
Founded in: 1960
Number of members: 50
Staff: volunteer 6
Major programs: museum, historic sites preservation
Period of collections: 1881-present

DUNN CENTER

Dunn County Historical Society
Telephone: (701) 548-5412
County agency
Founded in: 1975
Ella Guenther, President
Number of members: 200
Staff: volunteer 10
Magazine: *Tales and Trails*
Major programs: manuscripts, museum, historic site(s), markers, oral history, book publishing, newsletters/pamphlets, historic preservation, living history, photographic collections
Period of collections: 1900-present

EPPING

Buffalo Trails Museum
P.O. Box 22, 58843
Telephone: (701) 859-4361
Private agency
Founded in: 1966
Elmer H. Halvorson, Curator
Number of members: 200
Staff: part time 1, volunteer 4

Major programs: library, museum, oral history, newsletters/pamphlets, historic preservation, records management, research, exhibits, photographic collections, Period of collections: early 1900s

FARGO

Fargo Heritage Society, Inc.
Telephone: (70l) 235-1240
Mail to: 905 S. 8th St., 58102
Founded in: 1975
Nancy Henning, President
Number of members: 125
Major programs: historical sites and districts preservation, tours, educational programs

North Dakota Institute for Regional Studies
North Dakota State University, 58105
Telephone: (701) 237-8914
Founded in: 1950
John E. Bye, Archivist
Staff: full time 1, part time 2
Major programs: library, archives, manuscripts, book publishing, photographic collections
Period of collections: 1865-present

Plains Architecture
620 Main Ave., 58102
Telephone: (701) 237-8614
Mail to: Box 5412, State University Station, 58105
Founded in: 1972
Ronald L. M. Ramsey, Director
Number of members: 75
Staff: part time 3
Major programs: archives, educational programs, books
Period of collections: 1870-present

FESSENDEN

Wells County Historical Society
Telephone: (701) 547-3467
Mail to: P.O. Box 554, 58438
County agency, authorized by Wells County Commission
Founded in: 1965
William Geier, President
Number of members: 300
Staff: volunteer 10
Major programs: library, museum, historic site(s), markers, oral history, newsletters/pamphlets, historic preservation, records management, exhibits, photographic collections
Period of collections: 1970-present

FLASHER

Flasher Historical Society
58535
City agency
Founded in: 1978
Peter Deichert, President
Number of members: 69
Major programs: archives, manuscripts, museum, historic preservation, exhibits
Period of collections: early 1900s

FORBES

Coteau Hills Historical Center
58439
Telephone: (701) 357-7011

Founded in: 1976
Questionnaire not received

FORT RANSOM

Ransom County Historical Society
58033
Telephone: (701) 973-2211
Founded in: 1972
Major programs: museum, historic
sites preservation, markers, historic
preservation

GLEN LILLIN

Glen Lillin Historical Society
c/o President, 58631
Telephone: (701) 348-3149
Private agency
Founded in: 1979
Alois E. Feser, President
Number of members: 15
Staff: volunteer 9
Major programs: library, museum,
school programs, book publishing,
photographic collections,
genealogical services, Period of
collections: 1883-present

GRAND FORKS

**Grand Forks County Historical
Society**
2405 Belmont Rd., 58201
Telephone: (701) 775-2216
Private agency
Founded in: 1970
Jay A. Hillier, Director/Curator
Number of members: 400
Staff: full time 1, part time 2,
volunteer 30
Major programs: museum, historic
site(s), newsletters/pamphlets,
historic preservation, exhibits,
photographic collections, special
events
Period of collections: 1850-1950

HATTON

Hatton-Eielson Museum
58240
Telephone: (701) 543-3726
Town agency, authorized by
Historical Association
Founded in: 1973
Eieleen Mork, President
Number of members: 200
Staff: volunteer 15
Major programs: museum, historic
site(s), historic preservation,
exhibits, photographic collections
Period of collections: 1874-present

HEBRON

Hebron Historical and Arts Society
58638
City agency
Founded in: 1978
Paul Schlenvogt, President
Staff: volunteer 8
Major programs: museum, historic
site(s), oral history, historic
preservation, photographic
collections

HOPE

Steele County Historical Society
P.O. Box 144

Founded in: 1957
Mail to: R.R. 1, Box 94, 58230
County agency
Founded in: 1958
Edith Sampson, President
Number of members: 100
Staff: volunteer 12
Major programs: archives, museum,
historic sites preservation,
tours/pilgrimages, oral history,
educational programs
Period of collections: 1883-present

LANGDON

Cavalier County Historical Society
Rural Langdon
Telephone: (701) 283-5284
Mail to: c/o President, Wales, 58281
County agency
Founded in: 1970
Fannie Valentine, President
Number of members: 489
Major programs: archives, museum,
historic preservation
Period of collections: 1884

LANSFORD

**Lansford Threshers and Historical
Association, Inc.**
58750
Telephone: (701) 784-5422
Founded in: 1970
Questionnaire not received

MANDAN

Ft. Abraham Lincoln State Park
R.R. 2, Box 139, 58554
Telephone: (701) 663-9571
State agency, authorized by Parks
and Recreation Department
Founded in: 1908
Chuck Erickson, Superintendent
Staff: full time 3, part time 20,
volunteer 12
Major programs: museum, historic
site(s), markers, tours/pilgrimages,
school programs, living history,
audiovisual programs
Period of collections: 1700s-1870s

MARMARTH

Marmarth Historical Society
59313
Founded in: 1975
Questionnaire not received

MEDORA

**Theodore Roosevelt Nature and
History Association**
P.O. Box 167, 58645
Telephone: (701) 623-4466
Private agency, authorized by
National Park Service
Founded in: 1951
Marilyn Sahlstrom, Business Manager
Number of members: 153
Staff: full time 1, part time 1
Major programs: library, historic
site(s), school programs, book
publishing, research, exhibits,
audiovisual programs,
photographic collections, support
of NPS interpretation programs

MINTO

Walsh County Historical Society
58261
County agency
Founded in: 1967
Number of members: 750
Major programs: museum, historic
site(s), markers,
newsletters/pamphlets
Period of collections: 1880-present

NECHE

**Pembina County Chapter of
Pioneer Daughters**
58265
Telephone: (701) 886-7619
Founded in: 1939
Questionnaire not received

NIAGARA

**Niagara Community Historical
Society**
58266
Telephone: (701) 397-5774
Questionnaire not received

NOME

**Nome Community Historical
Association, Inc.**
P.O. Box 51, 58062
Telephone: (701) 924-8831
City agency
Founded in: 1983
Randy Peterson, President
Number of members: 100
Staff: volunteer 6
Major programs: book publishing,
historic preservation

PEMBINA

Ft. Pembina Historical Society
c/o President, Rt. 1, Box 68, 58271
Private agency
Founded in: 1978
Peter Kostiuk, President
Number of members: 32
Staff: volunteer 4
Major programs: historic preservation
Period of collections: 1797-present

POWERS LAKE

**Burke County and White Earth
Valley Historical Society**
58773
Telephone: (701) 464-5566
Mail to: Rt. 2, Flaxton, 58737
Founded in: 1971
Questionnaire not received

REGENT

Hettinger County Historical Society
Main St., 58650
Telephone: (701) 563-4547
Founded in: 1962
Questionnaire not received

REYNOLDS

Reynolds Community Museum
Mail to: P.O. Box 14, 58275
Town agency
Founded in: 1980
Joe Scholand, President
Number of members: 55

Staff: volunteer 10
Major programs: archives, museum

RUGBY

Geographical Center Historical Society
Telephone: (701) 776-6414
Mail to: P.O. Box 135, 38368
County agency
Founded in: 1959
Richard Blessum, President
Number of members: 255
Staff: full time 3, part time 6, volunteer 10
Major programs: museum, oral history, newsletters/pamphlets
Period of collections: 1800s-1960s

STANTON

Knife River Indian Villages National Historic Site
R.R. 1, 58571
Telephone: (701) 745-3309
Federal agency, authorized by National Park Service
Founded in: 1976
Area Manager, Area Manager
Staff: full time 4, part time 1, volunteer 10
Major programs: museum, historic site(s), historic preservation, research, exhibits, audiovisual programs, archaeology programs
Period of collections: prehistoric-1845

TAYLOR

Stark County Historical Society
58656
Telephone: (701) 974-3605
Founded in: 1974
Questionnaire not received

TOKIO

Brenorsome Historical Society
P.O. Box 232, 58379
Telephone: (701) 294-3351
Private agency, authorized by State Historical Society of North Dakota
Founded in: 1976
Louis Garcia, President
Number of members: 10
Staff: volunteer 10
Major programs: library, archives, manuscripts, museum, markers, tours/pilgrimages, oral history, school programs, research, photographic collections
Period of collections: 1800-present

Historical Society of York County
250 E. Market St., 17403
Telephone: (717) 848-1587
Private agency
Founded in: 1895
Mrs. Charles H. Brimfield, President
Number of members: 1,800
Staff: full time 10, part time 4, volunteer 250
Major programs: library, archives, manuscripts, museum, historic site(s), school programs, newsletters/pamphlets, exhibits, photographic collections, genealogical services
Period of collections: 1700-present

VALLEY CITY

Barnes County Historical Society, Inc.
Telephone: (701) 845-0966
Mail to: P.O. Box 188, 58072
Private agency
Founded in: 1975
Thomas P. Elliott, President
Number of members: 30
Staff: volunteer 6
Major programs: museum, historic preservation, research
Period of collections: 1865-present

WAHPETON

Richland County Historical Society
2nd St. and 7th Ave., 58075
Telephone: (701) 642-3075
Founded in: 1946
R. M. Johnson, President
Staff: full time 1
Major programs: manuscripts, museum, markers, tours, oral history
Period of collections: 1865-present

WASHBURN

McLean County Historical Society
610 Main Ave., 58577
Telephone: (701) 462-3526 (president)
County agency
Mrs. Lyle Luttrell, President
Number of members: 180
Staff: volunteer 20
Major programs: museum, historic site(s), markers, book publishing, newsletters/pamphlets, historic preservation, photographic collections
Period of collections: 1880-1940s

WATFORD CITY

McKenzie County Museum and Historical Society, Inc.
P.O. Box 602, 58854
Telephone: (701) 842-5286
County agency, authorized by North Dakota State Historical Society
Founded in: 1966
Clyde Holman, President
Number of members: 70
Staff: full time 4, volunteer 12
Major programs: museum, historic site(s)
Period of collections: 1905

WEST FARGO

Cass County Historical Society/Bonanzaville U.S.A.
U.S. Hwy. 10
Telephone: (701) 282-2822
Mail to: P.O. Box 719, 58078
County agency, authorized by North Dakota Historical Society
Founded in: 1954
Alice M. Carlson, Curator
Number of members: 638
Staff: full time 2, part time 4, volunteer 10
Major programs: museum, historic site(s), tours/pilgrimages, school programs, newsletters/pamphlets, historic preservation, exhibits, living history

Period of collections: 1870-Depression era

WILLISTON

Ft. Union Trading Post National Historic Site
Buford Rt., 58801
Telephone: (701) 572-9083
Federal agency, authorized by National Park Service
Founded in: 1966
Paul L. Hedren, Superintendent
Staff: full time 3, part time 4, volunteer 50
Major programs: library, archives, museum, historic site(s), tours/pilgrimages, research, living history
Period of collections: 1820-1860s

Frontier Museum
R.R. 2, Box 9, 58801
Telephone: (701) 572-5009
Founded in: 1958
Olive Beard, President
Staff: volunteer 4
Period of collections: late 1800s-present

OHIO

AKRON

Archival Services, University of Akron
The Bierce Library, 44325
Telephone: (216) 375-7670
Authorized by the university
Founded in: 1965
John V. Miller, Director
Staff: full time 5, part time 3
Major programs: library, archives, manuscripts, oral history, records management, photographic collections, genealogical services
Period of collections: 1900-present

Department of History, University of Akron
244325
Telephone: (216) 375-7006
State agency, authorized by the university
Founded in: 1876
Robert H. Jones, Head
Staff: full time 20
Major programs: library, archives, manuscripts, research, adult education

Goodyear World of Rubber Museum
1201 E. Market St., 44316
Telephone: (216) 796-2044
Private agency, authorized by Goodyear Tire and Rubber Company
Founded in: 1898
Richard J. Willett, Curator
Staff: full time 1, part time 4
Major programs: museum, exhibits
Period of collections: 1898-present

Supplier's Section

Is There a Fine Current History of Your Community?

¶ Windsor Publications offers North America's most comprehensive series of city and regional histories – nearly 200 distinguished titles published or in progress. These handsome showcases of fine contemporary scholarship include superb illustrations – contemporary and modern photographs, paintings, and other graphics. Each subject community's past comes imaginatively alive to satisfy scholar and general reader alike.

¶ From a two-volume study of the Windy City or a fresh glimpse of Duluth to a scholarly re-examination of the Granite State, Windsor's titles do very well indeed in the marketplace. Many are bestsellers. And a *Windsor* book invariably renews and invigorates public interest in civic, county, and state heritage.

¶ Behind every Windsor book is a strong creative team: local writers of proven ability (scholars, career historians, journalists) and seasoned editors, artists, and production professionals. Adding vital resources to each project are historical societies, colleges and universities, museums, and commercial and cultural organizations.

¶ To learn how your community may benefit from this tradition of exemplary history books, please contact us. Windsor Publications, Inc., 8910 Quartz Avenue, Post Office Box 9071, Northridge, California 91328 • Telephone (800) 423-5761, In California, (818) 700-0200

Some things you just can't put in a museum...

The experiences of our forefathers deserve to be preserved as much as do the objects they created and cherished. For almost half a century, Taylor Publishing Company has committed itself to helping historical groups record forever the memories of their ancestors in beautiful, limited edition volumes destined to become heirlooms and collector pieces.

Let Taylor help your organization create such a book for *your* area — because there are some things you just can't put in a museum.

For information on Taylor's complete historical publishing program, please call or write to Taylor Publishing Company, Fine Books Division, 1550 W. Mockingbird, Dallas, Texas 75235, (214) 637-2800.

TAYLOR PUBLISHING COMPANY
Preserving America's Heritage

So much more...

Did you know that the American Association for State and Local History is so much more than the leading publisher of books and educational materials for museum and historical agency personnel and local historians? AASLH is a service organization dedicated to providing you with information on the work you do.

If you are involved as a professional at work in the history field, a student preparing for such work, a scholar seeking new avenues of investigation, or a citizen with a solid commitment to understanding and preserving the unique history of your family or community, you need to be a member of AASLH. You'll then receive the benefits from a series of programs and publications AASLH has developed over the years specifically for the individual workers in the field.

History News, AASLH's award-winning magazine, puts you on the cutting edge of the museum and historical agency profession. Reporting on significant developments in the field, *History News* will keep you on top through lively written, informative feature articles. And for fast breaking, up-to-the-minute news, AASLH provides a monthly newsletter — *History News Dispatch* — that covers what's going on in the field, current information on the Association itself, and the latest job listings for historical agency and museum professionals.

Both publications are sent to you with your paid subscription.

But wait, there's more.

AASLH also holds seminars and a national meeting every year where history professionals, volunteers, scholars, and students meet to discuss topics and receive the best instruction for their work.

The Consultant Service provides the practical and technical assistance your organization needs by sending nationally known experts to you for an "on site" evaluation and a recommendation for filling your needs.

The National Information Center for Local Government Records provides local governments with the beginning steps to starting a successful records management program.

To fund research and other projects in local, state, and regional history, the Grants-in-Aid program is available to help you. The Awards Program provides national recognition for the best achievements in state and local history. AASLH also secures a voice in Congress to transmit your concerns about the well-being of historical initiatives.

There's an AASLH representative in every state and throughout Canada that would welcome the opportunity to tell you more about the AASLH. For the name of your representative, contact the membership manager at AASLH.

Become a member of AASLH today! You can do so by requesting a membership form from: Membership Manager, AASLH, 172 Second Avenue North, Suite 102, Nashville, Tennessee 37201 (615) 255-2971.

By joining AASLH, you'll get *History News*, *History News Dispatch*, valuable discounts on AASLH Press publications, and the AASLH Advantage: technical expertise, practical advice, philosophical guidance, and professional recognition.

Explore your heritage
with AASLH Press books!

Whether you work in an historical agency or museum, teach history in the classroom, or research your family and community history, the AASLH Press has the books you need.

The American Association for State and Local History Press has established itself as the leading publisher of books for museum and historical agency professionals and volunteers, and has also become a valuable resource for local historians, historic house owners, and living history enthusiasts.

We publish books about identifying American architecture and furniture, recreating historic house interiors and gardens, historical interpretation and living history programs, taking oral histories, tracing your genealogical roots, museum management and public relations, collections care and conservation, exhibit ideas and methods, and photographing architecture and works of art.

For a free mail-order catalog listing all of our books, technical leaflets, and educational materials, write to the AASLH Marketing Manager, 172 Second Avenue North, Suite 102, Nashville, Tennessee 37201 (615) 255-2971.

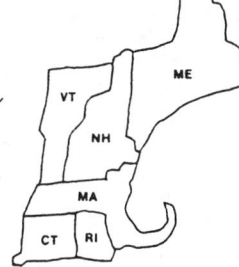

Factual
Readable
Up-to-date

Today's advances in technology and continuing developments in the historical agency and museum field demand high levels of expertise among professionals and volunteers alike.

For this reason, AASLH offers the Technical Information Service, a broad-based program designed to seek out late breaking developments in a wide spectrum of technical subjects and then to prepare and disseminate reports to subscribers on a regular basis.

AASLH's Technical Information Service provides the latest word in an easy-to-read format on a wide range of topics for historical agencies and museums. Libraries will find the Technical Reports to be an inexpensive way to keep their patrons informed with up-to-date information on the everyday problems faced by museum and historical agency personnel.

TIS issues six Technical Reports a year, dealing with such subjects as:
- Producing professional quality slide shows
- Managing photograph collections
- Controlling environmental conditions in museums
- Organizing teacher workshops
- Interpreting artifacts of associative value
- Managing traveling exhibitions
- Developing collection manuals
- Job descriptions in state and local history

The opportunity to subscribe to the TIS is a special benefit of an AASLH membership. If you are not an AASLH member, you can receive a year's subscription to *Technical Reports*, *History News*, and *History News Dispatch*, and valuable discounts on AASLH Press publications all for a special price.

For information and subscription prices, contact the AASLH Marketing Department, 172 Second Avenue North, Suite 102, Nashville, Tennessee 37201 (615) 255-2971.

The AASLH Technical Information Service: THE source for the latest technical information in the museum and historical agency field.

Pioneer America Society, Inc.
Department of Geography, University
of Akron, 44325
Telephone: (216) 375-7620
Private agency
Founded in: 1967
Allen G. Noble, Director
Number of members: 540
Magazine: *Material
Culture/PAST/Pioneer America
Society Transactions*
Major programs: historic sites
preservation, educational
programs, newsletters/pamphlets,
research, vernacular architecture

Stan Hywet Hall and Gardens
714 N. Portage Path, 44303
Telephone: (216) 836-5533
Private agency, authorized by Stan
Hywet Hall Foundation, Inc.
Founded in: 1957
John Franklin Miller, Executive
Director
Number of members: 2,800
Staff: full time 22, part time 14,
volunteer 600
Major programs: museum, historic
site(s), tours/pilgrimages, book
publishing, newsletters/pamphlets,
historic preservation, exhibits
Period of collections: 1400-1915

Stan Hywet Hall Foundation, Inc.
714 N. Portage Path, 44303
Telephone: (216) 836-5533
Private agency
Founded in: 1957
John Franklin Miller, Executive
Director
Number of members: 2,950
Staff: full time 20, part time 10,
volunteer 400
Magazine: *Stan Hywet Newsletter*
Major programs: museum, historic
site(s), tours/pilgrimages,
newsletters/pamphlets, historic
preservation
Period of collections: 1400-1915

Summit County Historical Society
550 Copley Rd., 44320
Telephone: (216) 535-1120
Private agency
Founded in: 1925
Jeffrey E. Smith, Director
Number of members: 1,000
Staff: full time 2, part time 5,
volunteer 100
Magazine: *Old Portage Trail Review*
Major programs: museum, historic
site(s), newsletters/pamphlets,
historic preservation, research,
exhibits
Period of collections: 1825-1900

ALLIANCE

**Marlboro Township Historical
Society**
12205 Marlboro Ave., NE, 44601
Telephone: (216) 935-2229
Private agency
Founded in: 1977
Mrs. Harold Devies, President
Number of members: 10
Major programs: book publishing,
audiovisual programs
Period of collections: 1850-1950

AMHERST

Amherst Historical Society
P.O. Box 272, 44001
Telephone: (216) 988-4234
Private agency
Founded in: 1973
Vivienne Bickley, President
Number of members: 100
Staff: volunteer 9
Major programs: archives, museum,
historic site(s), markers,
tours/pilgrimages,
newsletters/pamphlets, historic
preservation, research, exhibits
Period of collections: 1890s

ANTWERP

**Otto E. Ehrhart-Paulding County
Historical Society**
City Hall, 45813
Telephone: (419) 258-8161
Founded in: 1962
Questionnaire not received

ARCHBOLD

Sauder Farm and Craft Village
Rt. 2
Telephone: (419) 446-2541
Mail to: P.O. Box 332, 43502
Private agency
Founded in: 1971
Cecily Rohrs, Public Relations
Number of members: 1,300
Staff: full time 3, part time 155,
volunteer 125
Major programs: museum, school
programs, newsletters/pamphlets,
exhibits, living history
Period of collections: 1830-1900

ASHLAND

Ashland County Historical Society
414 Center St.
Telephone: (419) 289-3111
Mail to: P.O. Box 484, 44805
Private agency
Founded in: 1976
Mrs. Everett R. DeVaul, Jr., President
Number of members: 532
Staff: volunteer 50
Magazine: *The Town Crier*
Major programs: library, archives,
museum, tours/pilgrimages, school
programs, book publishing,
newsletters/pamphlets, historic
preservation, records
management, research, exhibits,
audiovisual programs,
photographic collections,
genealogical services
Period of collections: Victorian era

ASHVILLE

Ashville Area Heritage Society
150 W. Main St.
Telephone: (614) 983-3166
Mail to: 34 Long St., 43103

Town agency
Founded in: 1978
Charles W. Morrison, Director
Number of members: 250
Staff: volunteer 25
Major programs: museum, oral
history, school programs,
newsletters/pamphlets, historic
preservation, exhibits, audiovisual
programs, photographic
collections
Period of collections: 1875-1975

ATHENS

**Athens County Historical Society
and Museum**
65 N. Court St., 45701
Telephone: (614) 593-6216
Private agency
Founded in: 1980
Joanne Dove Prisley, Acting Director
Number of members: 385
Staff: part time 1, volunteer 13
Major programs: museum,
tours/pilgrimages, school
programs, book publishing,
newsletters/pamphlets, exhibits,
genealogical services
Period of collections: 1860-present

**Department of Archives and
Special Collections, Ohio
University Libraries**
45701
Telephone: (614) 594-5755
State agency
Founded in: 1804
Gary A. Hunt, Head
Staff: full time 3
Major programs: library, archives,
manuscripts, records
management, exhibits,
photographic collections,
genealogical services
Period of collections: 19th-20th
centuries

AURORA

Aurora Historical Society
Aurora Rd.
Mail to: P.O. Box 241, 44202
Private agency
Founded in: 1968
Richard Fetzer, President
Number of members: 200
Staff: volunteer 20
Major programs: archives, museum,
junior history, oral history, book
publishing, newsletters/pamphlets,
historic preservation, exhibits,
audiovisual programs,
photographic collections,
genealogical services

AVON

Avon Historical Society
2940 Stoney Ridge Rd., 44011
Telephone: (216) 934-6106
Private agency
Founded in: 1964
Delbert L. Fischer, President

Number of members: 120
Major programs: historic sites
  preservation, markers, educational
  programs, newsletters/pamphlets,
  audiovisual programs
Period of collections: from 1814

BARBERTON

Barberton Historical Society
P.O. Box 666, 44203
Telephone: (216) 745-9383
Private agency
Foundd in: 1974
Stephen Kelleher, President
Number of members: 600
Staff: volunteer 25
Major programs: archives, historic
  site(s), historic preservation,
  photographic collections
Period of collections: 1900-1920

BARNESVILLE

Belmont County Historical Society
Mail to: P.O. Box 434, 43713
Founded in: 1964
W. L. Brigg, President
Number of members: 500
Staff: volunteer 25
Major programs: museum
Period of collections: 1865-1918

BATAVIA

Clermont County Historical Society
P.O. Box 14, 45103
Telephone: (513) 724-2923
Private agency
Founded in: 1958
Frank Parker, President
Number of members: 100
Staff: volunteer 25
Magazine: *Clermont Historian*
Major programs: tours/pilgrimages,
  newsletters/pamphlets, records
  management
Period of collections: 1800-present

BATH

Hale Farm and Village
2686 Oakhill Rd.
Telehone: (216) 666-3711
Mail to: P.O. Box 256, 44210
Private agency, authorized by
  Western Reserve Historical Society
Founded in: 1958
Siegfried F. Buerling, Director
Number of members: 400
Staff: full time 20, part time 50
Major programs: museum, historic
  site(s), school programs, historic
  preservation, living history
Period of collections: 1800-1850

BEDFORD

Bedford Historical Society
30 S. Park St.
Telephone: (216) 232-0796
Mail to: P.O. Box 46282, 44146
Private agency
Founded in: 1955
Richard J. Squire, Director
Number of members: 400
Staff: part time 1, volunteer 16
Magazine: *Bedford Bee*
Major programs: library, archives,
  manuscripts, museum, historic

site(s), school programs, book
  publishing, newsletters/pamphlets,
  historic preservation, research,
  exhibits, photographic collections,
  genealogical services
Period of collections: 1820-present

BELLEFONTAINE

**Logan County Archeological and
  Historical Society**
Chillicothe and Seymour Sts.
Telephone: (513) 593-1428
Mail to: P.O. Box 296, 43311
County agency
Founded in: 1946
Daniel E. Gilbert, President
Number of members: 60
Staff: volunteer 10
Major programs: library, museum,
  markers, oral history,
  newsletters/pamphlets,
  photographic collections,
  genealogical services

**Logan County Genealogical
  Society**
Chillicothe and Seymore Sts.
Mail to: P.O. Box 296, 43311
County agency
Founded in: 1979
Ralph K. Henman, President
Number of members: 90
Staff: volunteer 10
Magazine: *Branches and Twigs*
Major programs: library, research,
  genealogical services

Logan County Historical Society
Chillicothe Ave. and Seymour Sts.
Mail to: P.O. Box 296, 43311
Founded in: 1946
J. E. and Martha Gilbert, Curators
Number of members: 66
Staff: volunteer 4
Major programs: museum, historic
  sites preservation, markers,
  tours/pilgrimages
Period of collections: 1776-present

BELLEVUE

Historic Lyme Village Association
R.R.1, State Rt. 113, E, 44811
Telephone: (419) 483-6052
Private agency
Founded in: 1971
Alvina L. Schaeffer, Village Curator
Number of members: 230
Major programs: library, museum,
  historic sites preservation,
  tours/pilgrimages, educational
  programs, books,
  newsletters/pamphlets
Period of collections: 1800-present

BEXLEY

Bexley Historical Society
2242 E. Main St., 43209
Telephone: (614) 239-0558
Private agency
Founded in: 1974
Eleanore Eckert, Secretary
Number of members: 450
Staff: part time 1, volunteer 2
Magazine: *Historical Herald*
Major programs: library, archives,
  manuscripts, museum, junior
  history, oral history, school

programs, book publishing,
  newsletters/pamphlets, research,
  exhibits, living history,
  photographic collections
Period of collections: 1850-present

BLUFFTON

**Swiss Community Historical
  Society**
Bixel Rd., Pandora, 45877
Mail to: P.O. Box 5, 45817
Private agency
Founded in: 1959
Keith Sommer, President
Major programs: museum, historic
  sites preservation, oral history,
  educational programs
Period of collections: 1825-present

BOWLING GREEN

Center for Archival Collections
Jerome Library, 5th Floor,
  43403-0175
Telephone: (419) 372-2411
State agency, authorized by Bowling
  Green State University
Founded in: 1969
Paul D. Yon, Director
Staff: full time 6, part time 1
Major programs: library, archives,
  manuscripts,
  newsletters/pamphlets, historic
  preservation, records
  management, research,
  photographic collections,
  genealogical services
Period of collections: late 19th-early
  20th centuries

**Northwest Ohio Historic
  Preservation Office**
Jerome Library, Bowling Green State
  University, 43403-0175
Telephone: (419) 372-2411
State agency, authorized by Ohio
  Historical Society
Founded in: 1981
Gloria Scott, Regional Coordinator
Staff: full time 1, part time 1
Major programs: historic
  preservation, field services
Period of collections: 1800-1935

Wood County Historical Society
13660 County Home Rd., 43402
Telephone: (419) 352-0967
Private agency
Founded in: 1955
Diane Macias, Curator
Number of members: 300
Staff: full time 1, volunteer 10
Magazine: *Black Swamp Chanticleer*
Major programs: museum, markers,
  book publishing,
  newsletters/pamphlets
Period of collections: 1860-1920

BREWSTER

**Brewster-Sugar Creek Township
  Historical Society**
45 S. Wabash Ave.
Telephone: (216) 767-4575
Mail to: c/o President, 426 Mohican,
  NE, 44613
Private agency
Founded in: 1976
Wayne Lutes, President

Number of members: 75
Staff: full time 1
Major programs: historic site(s),
school programs, historic
preservation, exhibits,
photographic collections
Period of collections: 1906-present

BROOKLYN

Brooklyn Historical Society
4442 Ridge Rd., 44144
Telephone: (216) 749-2804
Private agency
Founded in: 1970
Barbara Stedic, President
Number of members: 175
Staff: volunteer 50
Major programs: museum, oral
history, exhibits, living history
Period of collections: 1860-1930

BROOKVILLE

Brookville Historical Society
14 Market St.
Telephone: (513) 833-3470
Mail to: P.O. Box 82, 45309
Private agency
Founded in: 1973
Dottie Watkins, President
Number of members: 195
Staff: volunteer 35
Major programs: library, museum,
newsletters/pamphlets, research,
exhibits, photographic collections,
genealogical services
Period of collections: 1870-1910

BUCYRUS

Bucyrus Historical Society
202 S. Walnut St.
Mail to: P.O. Box 493, 44820
Private agency
Founded in: 1969
John K. Kurtz, President
Number of members: 250
Staff: volunteer 15
Major programs: museum,
tours/pilgrimages
Period of collections: 1800-1899

BURTON

Geauga County Historical Society
14653 E. Park St.
Telephone: (216) 834-4012
Mail to: P.O. Box 153, 44021
Private agency, authorized by
Century Village
Founded in: 1938
Marlene F. Collins, Office Manager
Number of members: 475
Staff: full time 2, 3part time 8,
volunteer 10
Major programs: library, museum,
tours/pilgrimages, school
programs, newsletters/pamphlets,
exhibits
Period of collections: 19th century

CADIZ

Harrison County Historical Society
435 Park Ave., 43907
Questionnaire not received

CALDWELL

**Noble County Chapter, Ohio
Genealogical Society**
Noble County Courthouse, 300
Cumberland St.
Telephone: (614) 263-3608
Mail to: P.O. Box 444, 43724
Private agency
Founded in: 1983
Mary Evelyn Archer Scott, President
Number of members: 100
Staff: volunteer 10
Major programs: library, archives,
oral history, book publishing,
newsletters/pamphlets,
genealogical services
Period of collections: 1850-present

CAMBRIDGE

**Degenhart Paperweight and Glass
Museum, Inc.**
State Rt. 22 and Hwy. 77
Telephone: (614) 432-2626
Mail to: P.O. Box 186, 43725
Private agency
Founded in: 1980
Carol M. Chamberlain, Director
Number of members: 450
Staff: full time 3
Magazine: *The Heartbeat*
Major programs: library, archives,
museum, school programs, book
publishing, newsletters/pamphlets,
research, exhibits, audiovisual
programs
Period of collections: 1850-20th
century

**Guernsey County Historical
Society**
218 N. 8th St.
Telephone: (216) 439-4686
Mail to: P.O. Box 741, 43725
Private agency
Founded in: 1960
John T. Lanning, President
Number of members: 200
Major programs: museum, historic
site(s), markers,
newsletters/pamphlets, historic
preservation, exhibits,
photographic collections

CANAL FULTON

Canal Fulton Heritage Society
103 Tuscarawas St.
Telephone: (216) 854-3808
Mail to: P.O. Box 584, 44614
Private agency
Founded in: 1968
Ann McLaughlin, President
Number of members: 155
Major programs: archives, museum,
historic site(s), markers, junior
history, oral history, school
programs, newsletters/pamphlets,
historic preservation, records
management, research, exhibits,
living history, audiovisual
programs, photographic
collections, genealogical services,
field services
Period of collections: 1827-1913

CANFIELD

**Mahoning County Agricultural
Society**
Rt. 46
Telephone: (216) 533-4107
Mail to: P.O. Box 27, 44406
Questionnaire not received

CANTON

Canton Palace Theatre Association
605 Market Ave., 044702
Telephone: (216) 454-8172
Private agency
Founded in: 1926
Bea W. Constantino, Executive
Director
Number of members: 396
Staff: full time 1, part time 1,
volunteer 40
Magazine: *The Annunciator*
Major programs: historic site(s),
tours/pilgrimages, school
programs, historic preservation
Period of collections: 1926

Canton Preservation Society
331 Market Ave., S, 44702
Telephone: (216) 452-5184
Mail to: P.O. Box 174, 44701
Private agency
Founded in: 1977
Nancy Holwick, President
Number of members: 450
Staff: volunteer 5
Magazine: *The Preservationist*
Major programs:
newsletters/pamphlets, historic
preservation, research

**McKinley Museum of History,
Science and Industry**
749 Hazlett Ave., NW, 44708
Telephone: (216) 455-7043
Mail to: P.O. Box 483, 44701
Private agency, authorized by Stark
County Historical Society
Founded in: 1946
Richard E. Werstler, Executive
Director
Number of members: 1,100
Staff: full time 5, part time 5,
volunteer 2
Major programs: library, archives,
museum, historic site(s), tours,
school programs,
newsletters/pamphlets, exhibits,
audiovisual programs,
genealogical services
Period of collections: 19th-20th
centuries

Pro Football Hall of Fame
2121 Harrison Ave., NW, 44708
Telephone: (216) 456-8207
Private agency
Founded in: 1963
Joseph A. Horrigan, Curator
Staff: full time 14, part time 3
Major programs: library, archives,
museum, school programs, book
publishing, newsletters/pamphlets,
historic preservation, records
management, research, exhibits,
audiovisual programs,
photographic collections
Period of collections: 1892-present

OHIO

Ridgewood Preservation Inc.
256 21st St., NW, 44709
Telephone: (216) 454-8471
Private agency
Founded in: 1978
Harley M. Miller, President
Number of members: 200
Major programs: historic preservation

Stark County Historical Society
749 Hazlett Ave., NW
Telephone: (216) 455-7043
Mail to: P.O. Box 483, 44708
Number of members: 1,600
Staff: full time 4, part time 6,
volunteer 52
Major programs: library, archives,
museum, tours, school programs,
newsletters/pamphlets, historic
preservation, research, exhibits,
genealogical services, history of
science and industry, planetarium
Period of collections: 1783-present

Stark Preservation Alliance
511 County Office Bldg., 44702
Telephone: (216) 438-0400
Private agency
Founded in: 1983
Nancy Welch, President
Number of members: 50
Staff: volunteer 15
Magazine: *Preservation Pact*
Major programs:
newsletters/pamphlets, historic
preservation, exhibits

CARLISLE

Carlisle Area Historical Society
453 Park Dr.
Mail to: 441 Park Dr., 45005
Private agency
Founded in: 1984
Mary Jane Enterman, President
Number of members: 50
Staff: volunteer 10
Major programs: museum
Period of collections: early
1800s-present

CARROLLON

Carroll County Historical Society
Telephone: (216) 735-2839
Mail to: P.O. Box 174, 44615
County agency
Founded in: 1963
Carl A. Saltsman, President
Number of members: 657
Major programs: archives, museum,
markers, educational programs,
newsletters/pamphlets
Period of collections: 1865-1918

CELINA

**Mercer County Chapter, Ohio
Genealogical Society**
P.O. Box 437, 45822
State agency
Founded in: 1980
Carolyn Brandon, President
Number of members: 77
Staff: volunteer 12
Magazine: *The Monitor*
Major programs: research

**Mercer County Historical
Society, Inc. and Museum**
130 E. Market, 45822

Telephone: (419) 586-6065
Private agency
Founded in: 1959
Joyce L. Alig, Director
Number of members: 450
Staff: full time 1, part time 3,
volunteer 250
Major programs: archives,
manuscripts, museum, historic
site(s), junior history, oral history,
school programs, book publishing,
newsletters/pamphlets, historic
preservation, records
management, research, exhibits,
living history, audiovisual
programs, archaeology programs,
photographic collections,
genealogical services, field
services, special displays, grants
programs
Period of collections: 19th century

CENTERVILLE

Centerville Historical Society
89 W. Franklin St., 45459
Telephone: (513) 433-0123
Private agency
Founded in: 1967
Mary C. Aldridge, Administrator
Number of members: 214
Staff: part time 2
Magazine: *Curator Newsletter*
Major programs: library, archives,
museum, markers,
tours/pilgrimages, oral history,
school programs, book publishing,
newsletters/pamphlets, historic
preservation, research, exhibits,
photographic collections,
genealogical services
Period of collections: 1830-1930

CHAGRIN FALLS

Chagrin Falls Historical Society
21 Walnut St.
Telephone. (215) 247-6306
Mail to: P.O. Box 15, 44022
Founded in: 1946
Questionnaire not received

CHILLICOTHE

Adena State Memorial
Adena Rd.
Telephone: (614) 772-1500
Mail to: P.O. Box 831-A, 45601
Authorized by Ohio Historical Society
Founded in: 1953
Mary Anne Brown, Curator
Staff: full time 3, part time 4,
volunteer 2
Major programs: historic site(s),
restoration
Period of collections: 1773-1827

**Mound City Group National
Monument**
16062 State Rt. 104, 45601
Telephone: (614) 744-1125
Federal agency, authorized by
National Park Service
Founded in: 1923
Kenneth E. Apschnikat,
Superintendent
Staff: full time 8, part time 4,
volunteer 2

Major programs: museum, historic
site(s), tours/pilgrimages, historic
preservation, research, exhibits
Period of collections: 200 B.C.-A.D.
500

Ross County Historical Society
45 W. 5th St., 45601
Telephone: (614) 772-1936
Founded in: 1896
William H. Nolan, Director
Number of members: 682
Staff: full time 1, part time 2,
volunteer 10
Major programs: library, archives,
manuscripts, museum,
tours/pilgrimages,
newsletters/pamphlets, historic
preservation
Period of collections: 1790-1917

Scioto Society, Inc.
215 W. 2nd St.
Telephone: (614) 775-4100
Mailto: P.O. Bcx 73, 45601
Founded in: 1970
W. L. Mundell, President
Staff: full time 5
Major programs: museum, school
programs, living history, outdoor
drama production
Period of collections: 1785-1812

**SCOPS (All Southern Ohio
Preservation Society)**
178 Church St., 45601
Telephone: (614) 774-3510
Founded in: 1966
Mrs. Joseph Vanmeter, Coordinator
Major programs: library, archives,
manuscripts, museum, historic
site(s), markers, tours/pilgrimages,
junior history, oral history, school
programs, newsletters/pamphlets,
historic preservation, exhibits,
living history, audiovisual
programs, archaeology programs,
genealogical services, natural and
cultural history

CINCINNATI

American Jewish Archives
3101 Clifton Ave., 45220-2488
Telephone: (513) 221-1875
Private agency, authorized by
Hebrew Union College, Jewish
Institute of Religion
Founded in: 1947
Jacob R. Marcus, Director
Staff: full time 8, part time 6
Magazine: *American Jewish Archives*
Major programs: archives, book
publishing, newsletters/pamphlets,
research, exhibits, photographic
collections, genealogical services

**Anderson Township Historical
Society, Inc.**
6540 Clough Rd.
Telephone: (513) 231-2114
Mail to: P.O. Box 30174, 45230
Founded in: 1968
Questionnaire not received

Cary Cottage
7000 Hamilton Ave., 45231
Telephone: (513) 522-3860
Mail to: c/o President, 727 Daphne
Court, 45240

Private agency, authorized by
Clovernook Home and School for
the Blind
Sonya Kirkland, President.
Staff: volunteer 18
Major programs: historic site(s),
tours/pilgrimages, historic
preservation, exhibits

Cincinnati Art Museum
Eden Park, 45202
Telephone: (513) 721-5204
Private agency, authorized by
Cincinnati Museum Association
Founded in: 1881
Millard F. Rogers, Jr., Director
Number of members: 5,800
Staff: full time 70, part time 39,
volunteer 500
Magazine: *Cincinnati Art Museum
Bulletin*
Major programs: museum, visual arts
Period of collections:
prehistoric-present

Cincinnati Fire Museum
315 W. Court St., 45202
Telephone: (513) 621-5553
Private agency, authorized by
Cincinnati Fire Museum
Association
Founded in: 1853
Geoffrey J. Giglierano, Acting
Director
Number of members: 330
Staff: full time 2, part time 2,
volunteer 40
Magazine: *Outtap*
Major programs: museum, school
programs, newsletters/pamphlets,
exhibits
Period of collections: 1808-1980

Cincinnati Historical Society
Eden Park, 45202
Telephone: (513) 241-4622
Private agency
Founded in: 1831
Gale E. Peterson, Director
Number of members: 3,100
Staff: full time 16, part time 11,
volunteer 20
Magazine: *Queen City Heritage*
Major programs: library, archives,
manuscripts, tours/pilgrimages,
oral history, school programs, book
publishing, newsletters/pamphlets,
research, exhibits, audiovisual
programs, photographic
collections
Period of collections: 1783-present

College Hill Historical Society
5907 Belmont Ave., 45229
Telephone: (513) 681-2470
City agency
Founded in: 1979
Doug Trimmel, President
Number of members: 200
Staff: volunteer 8
Major programs: tours/pilgrimages,
oral history, newsletters/pamphlets,
audiovisual programs,
photographic collections
Period of collections: from 1840

Delhi Historical Society
4702 Shadylawn Terrace, 45238
Telephone: (513) 251-1390
Town agency

Founded in: 1977
Shirley Atthoff, Curator
Number of members: 88
Major programs: archives,
tours/pilgrimages, junior history,
school programs, book publishing,
newsletters/pamphlets, historic
preservation, records
management, research, exhibits,
audiovisual programs, fashion
shows
Period of collections: 1880

**Hamilton County Chapter, Ohio
Genealogical Society**
Mail to: P.O. Box 15851, 45215
Founded in: 1973
Number of members: 380
Staff: volunteer 5
Magazine: *The Tracer*
Major programs:
newsletters/pamphlets,
genealogical services
Period of collections: 1790-1880

Historic Southwest Ohio, Inc.
812 Dayton St., 45214
Telephone: (513) 721-4506
Private agency
Founded in: 1984
Mariana Kirk, Executive Secretary
Number of members: 1,200
Staff: full time 1, part time 4,
volunteer 250
Major programs: library, museum,
historic site(s), tours/pilgrimages,
school programs,
newsletters/pamphlets, records
management, research, exhibits,
audiovisual programs
Period of collections: 1800-1900

**Indian Hill Historical Museum
Association**
8100 Given Rd., 45243
Telephone: (513) 891-1873
Founded in: 1974
Mrs. Alfred K. White, Jr., President
Number of members: 450
Staff: volunteer 10
Magazine: The Sampler
Major programs: historic sites
preservation, educational
programs, historic preservation,
book publishing, photographic
collections
Period of collections: 1850

**Miami Purchase Association for
Historic Preservation**
812 Dayton St., 45214
Telephone: (513) 721-4506
Private agency
Founded in: 1964
John C. Meunier, President
Number of members: 1,200
Staff: full time 3, part time 7,
volunteer 2
Major programs: library,
newsletters/pamphlets, historic
preservation, research,
archaeology programs,
photographic collections

Ohio Academy of History
Department of History, University of
Cincinnati, 45221
Telephone: (513) 475-4784
Founded in: 1932
Questionnaire not received

Ohio Covered Bridge Committee
18 Elm Ave., 45215
Telephone: (513) 761-1789
Founded in: 1940
Questionnaire not received

**Old St. Mary's Historic Community
Center**
123 E. 13th St., 45210
Telephone: (513) 721-2298
Private agency, authorized by
Archdiocese of Cincinnati
Founded in: 1840
Mary A. Heller, Director of
Development
Number of members: 210
Major programs: historic site(s)
Period of collections: 1842-1900

Princeton Museum of Education
515 Greenwood Ave., 45246
Telephone: (513) 771-3824
Founded in: 1974
Questionnaire not received

The Taft Museum
316 Pike St., 45202
Telephone: (513) 241-0343
Private agency, authorized by
Cincinnati Institute of Fine Arts
Founded in: 1927
Ruth K. Meyer, Director
Staff: full time 15, part time 7,
volunteer 110
Major programs: museum, exhibits,
fine arts
Period of collections: 19th century

**William Howard Taft National
Historic Site**
2038 Auburn Ave., 45219
Telephone: (513) 684-3262
Federal agency, authorized by
National Park Service
Founded in: 1969
Mary Maxine Boyd, Superintendent
Staff: full time 5, part time 3
Major programs: museum, historic
site(s), tours/pilgrimages, school
programs, research, audiovisual
programs
Period of collections: 1900-1930

CIRCLEVILLE

Pickaway County Historical Society
Mail to: P.O. Box 85, 43113
Founded in: 1959
Questionnaire not received

CLEVELAND

**Afro-American Cultural and
Historical Society Museum**
Richard Allen Bldg., 1839 E. 81st St.,
44103
Telephone: (216) 231-2131
Founded in: 1953
Questionnaire not received

Cleveland Landmarks Commission
City Hall, Room 28, 44114
Telephone: (216) 664-2531
City agency
Founded in: 1971
John D. Cimperman, Director
Staff: full time 4, part time 1,
volunteer 2
Major programs: historic site(s),
newsletters/pamphlets, historic

preservation, photographic collections
Period of collections: 1870-present

Cleveland Police Historical Society, Inc./Cleveland Police Museum
1300 Ontario St., 44113
Telephone: (216) 623-5055
Private agency, authorized by Cleveland Police Department
Founded in: 1983
Florence E. Schwein, Museum Director
Number of members: 400
Staff: full time 1, volunteer 10
Major programs: museum, school programs, newsletters/pamphlets, research, exhibits, photographic collections
Period of collections: 1900-present

Cleveland Restoration Society
423 Statler Office Tower, E. 12th and Euclid Ave., 44115
Telephone: (216) 621-1498
Founded in: 1972
Questionnaire not received

Dunham Tavern Museum/Society of Collectors' Inc.
6709 Euclid Ave., 44107
Telephone: (216) 431-1060
Private agency
William F. Ruper, President
Number of members: 120
Major programs: library, museum, historic site(s), tours/pilgrimages, historic preservation, exhibits
Period of collections: mid-19th century

Howard Dittrick Museum of Historical Medicine
11000 Euclid Ave., 44106
Telephone: (216) 368-3648
Private agency, authorized by Cleveland Medical Library Association
Founded in: 1894
James M. Edmonson, Curator
Staff: full time 4, part time 2, volunteer 2
Major programs: library, archives, manuscripts, museum, newsletters/pamphlets, research, exhibits, photographic collections, lectures
Period of collections: 1870-1940

Lewis Research Center/National Aeronautics and Space Administration
21000 Brookpark Rd.
Telephone: (216) 267-1187
Mail to: Center 8-1, 44135
Federal agency
Founded in: 1976
Richard C. Athey, Visitor Center Contract Manager
Staff: full time 11, part time 3, volunteer 25
Major programs: museum, tours/pilgrimages, school programs, newsletters/pamphlets, exhibits, audiovisual programs, photographic collections, field services, aerospace science
Period of collections: from 1960

National History Day
11201 Euclid Ave., 44106
Telephone: (216) 421-8803
Private agency
Founded in: 1974
Lois Scharf, Executive Director
Staff: full time 2, part time 1, volunteer 275
Major programs: school programs

Society of Collectors, Inc.
Dunham Tavern Museum
6709 Euclid Ave., 44103
Telephone: (216) 431-1060
Founded in: 1936
Questionnaire not received

Ukrainian Museum-Archives, Inc.
1202 Kenilworth Ave., 44113
Telephone: (216) 741-4537
Private agency
Founded in: 1952
Stepan Kikta, President
Number of members: 110
Staff: volunteer 4
Major programs: library, archives, museum, newsletters/pamphlets, exhibits, photographic collections
Period of collections: from 1952

Upper Prospect Area Association, Inc.
3206 Prospect Ave., 44115
Telephone: (216) 881-3194
Founded in: 1975
Questionnaire not received

Western Reserve Historical Society
10825 East Blvd., 44106
Telephone: (216) 721-5722
Private agency
Founded in: 1867
Theodore Anton Sande, Executive Director
Number of members: 3,046
Staff: full time 70, part time 35, volunteer 100
Magazine: *Western Reserve Historical Society News*
Major programs: library, archives, manuscripts, museum, historic site(s), oral history, school programs, newsletters/pamphlets, historic preservation, records management, research, exhibits,

photographic collections, genealogical services
Period of collections: 1783-present

CLEVELAND HEIGHTS

Western Reserve Architectural Historians
1095 Brandon Rd., 44112
Telephone: (216) 371-3081
Private agency
Founded in: 1965
Elizabeth Breckenridge, President
Number of members: 105
Staff: volunteer 4
Major programs: tours/pilgrimages, newsletters/pamphlets, audiovisual programs, architectural history
Period of collections: 19th-20th centuries

CLEVES

Three Rivers Historical Society
112 S. Miami Ave., 45002
Telephone: (513) 941-33664
Founded in: 1967
Questionnaire not received

CLYDE

Clyde Heritage League, Inc.
131 S. Main St.
Mail to: P.O. Box 97, 43410
Private agency
Founded in: 1975
John D. Maines, President
Number of members: 138
Staff: volunteer 10
Major programs: archives, manuscripts, museum, historic site(s), markers, historic preservation, photographic collections, genealogical services
Period of collections: 1840-1900

COLUMBIANA

Columbiana-Fairfield Township Historical Society
Mail to: P.O. Box 63, 44408
Private agency
Founded in: 1953
Ray G. Spiker, President

The Hay Mansion and Garden, located in Cleveland, houses the Western Reserve Historical Society's History Museum.—Courtesy of The Western Reserve Historical Society

Number of members: 110
Major programs: manuscripts,
museum, markers,
newsletters/pamphlets, historic
preservation, records
management, archaeology
programs, genealogical services
Period of collections: 1860-1950

COLUMBUS

Bureau of Environmental Services, Ohio Department of Transportation
25 S. Front St., Room 608, 43215
Telephone: (614) 466-6981
State agency
Founded in: 1905
Byrd Finley, Jr., Administrator
Number of members: 2
Staff: full time 7, part time 4
Major programs: book publishing,
historic preservation, records
management, archaeology
programs, photographic
collections, field services
Period of collections: 1700-1860

Center of Science and Industry
Franklin County Historical Society,
280 E. Broad St., 43215
Telephone: (614) 228-6362
Founded in: 1964
Questionnaire not received

Central Ohio Alliance of Historical Societies
1742 Franklin Ave., 43205
Telephone: (614) 253-4459
Private agency
Founded in: 1980
Thomas T. Smith, Director
Staff: volunteer 1

Columbus Landmarks Foundation
22 N. Front St., 43215
Telephone: (614) 221-0227
Private agency
Founded in: 1977
Edward R. Lentz, Executive Director
Number of members: 500
Staff: full time 1, part time 1,
volunteer 20
Major programs: tours/pilgrimages,
junior history, school programs,
newsletters/pamphlets, historic
preservation, research, audiovisual
programs, field services
Period of collections: 1800-present

Franklin County Genealogical Society
1725 Alum Creek Dr., 43207
Telephone: (614) 444-5583
Mail to: P.O. Box 2503, 43216
Authorized by Columbus Chapter,
Ohio Genealogical Society
Founded in: 1970
Emily S. Garner, Executive Secretary
Number of members: 581
Staff: volunteer 25
Magazine: The Franklintonian
Major programs: library, archives,
tours, book publishing,
newsletters/pamphlets, historic
preservation, research,
genealogical services, seminars
Period of collections: 1800s-1900s

Franklin County Historical Society
280 E. Broad St., 43215
Telephone: (614) 228-5613
Founded in: 1948
Daniel F. Prugh, Director
Number of members: 12,800
Staff: full time 38, part time 40,
volunteer 117
Magazine: Sights and Sounds of CSOI
Major programs: library, museum,
historic sites preservation, markers,
oral history, educational programs,
newsletters/pamphlets,
photographic collections
Period of collections: 1783-present

German Village Society
624 S. 3rd St., 43206
Private agency
Founded in: 1960
Fred J. Holdridge, President
Staff: full time 1
Major programs: library, historic
site(s), newsletters/pamphlets,
historic preservaton, audiovisual
programs
Period of collections: early
1800s-present

Heritage Museum of Kappa Kappa Gamma
530 E. Town St.
Telephone: (614) 228-6515
Mail to: P.O. Box 2079, 43216
Private agency, authorized by Kappa
Kappa Gamma Fraternity
Founded in: 1980
Nancy S. Pennell, Acting Director
Staff: full time 1, part time 1,
volunteer 20
Magazine: The Key
Major programs: library, archives,
manuscripts, museum, historic
site(s), tours/pilgrimages,
newsletters/pamphlets, historic
preservation, research, exhibits,
audiovisual programs,
photographic collections
Period of collections: Victorian era

Institute of Lithuanian Studies, Inc.
4082 Ruxton Lane, 43220
Telephone: (614) 451-0576
Founded in: 1950
Questionnaire not received

Kelton House
586 E. Town St., 43215
Telephone: (614) 464-2022
Private agency, authorized by Junior
League of Columbus
Founded in: 1976
Pat O'Dell, House Manager
Staff: full time 1
Major programs: museum,
tours/pilgrimages, school
programs, historic preservation,
research, special events
Period of collections: 1850-1900

National Afro-American Museum and Cultural Center
1985 Velma Ave., 43211
Telephone: (614) 466-1500
Private agency
Founded in: 1972
John E. Fleming, Project Director
Staff: full time 8, part time 1,
volunteer 3

Major programs: library, manuscripts,
museum, school programs,
exhibits, photographic collections,
public programs
Period of collections: 19th-20th
centuries

◇Ohio Association of Historical Societies and Museums
Local History Department, Ohio
Historical Society
Telephone: (614) 466-1500
Mail to: 1985 Velma Ave., 43211
Private agency
Founded in: 1960
James D. Strider, Head, Local History
Department
Number of members: 150
Staff: volunteer 25
Magazine: The Local Historian
Major programs:
newsletters/pamphlets, field
services, awards program

Ohio Camera Collector's Society
Telephone: (614) 488-7444
Mail to: P.O. Box 282, 43216
Founded in: 1969
Questionnaire not received

Ohio Historic Preservation Office, Ohio Historical Society
1985 Velma Ave., 43211
Telephone: (614) 466-1500
Staff: full time 14
Major programs: educational
programs, newsletters/pamphlets,
historic preservation

◇Ohio Historical Society
1985 Velma Ave., 43211
Telephone: (614) 466-1500
Private agency
Founded in: 1885
Gary C. Ness, Director
Number of members: 8,000
Staff: full time 350
Magazine: Timeline/Ohio
History/Echoes
Major programs: library, archives,
manuscripts, museum, historic
site(s), markers, tours/pilgrimages,
junior history, oral history, school
programs, newsletters/pamphlets,
historic preservation, records
management, research, exhibits,
living history, audiovisual
programs, archaeology programs,
photographic collections,
genealogical services, field
services

Ohioana Library
65 S. Front St., Room 1105, 43215
Telephone: (614) 466-3831
Private agency
Founded in: 1929
Kathy Babeaux, Librarian
Staff: full time 3, part time 1
Major programs: library, archives,
genealogical services
Period of collections: 1900s

Society of Ohio Archivists
2121 Tuttle Park Place, 43210-1169
Telephone: (614) 422-2409
Private agency
Founded in: 1968
Raimund E. Goerler, President
Number of members: 150

Staff: volunteer 7
Magazine: *The Ohio Archivist*
Major programs: archives,
manuscripts, museum,
photographic collections

CONNEAUT

Conneaut Railroad Museum
342 Depot St., 44030
Telephone: (216) 599-7878
Private agency
Founded in: 1964
Vincent A. Gildone, President
Number of members: 175
Magazine: *Semaphore*
Major programs: library, museum,
photographic collections
Period of collections: 1829-present

COSHOCTON

**Coshocton County Archaeological
and Historical Society**
1956 Melbourne Rd., 43812
Telephone: (614) 622-1632
Questionnaire not received

**Coshocton County Genealogical
Society**
Telephone: (614) 622-1711
Mail to: 186 Park Ave., 43812
Questionnaire not received

**Coshocton County Restoration
Society**
Telephone: (614) 622-8107
Mail to: 301 Main St., 43812
Questionnaire not received

Roscoe Village Foundation
381 Hill St., 43812
Telephone: (614) 622-9315
Founded in: 1968
Joel L. Hampton, Executive Director
Staff: full time 50, part time 50,
volunteer 20
Magazine: *Roscoe Village News*
Major programs: library, museum,
historic site(s), junior history, oral
history, school programs,
newsletters/pamphlets, historic
preservation, exhibits, living
history, audiovisual programs,
photographic collections
Period of collections: 1783-1918

CRESTLINE

Crestline Historical Society
211 Thoman St.
Telephone: (419) 683-3301
Mail to: 440 North St., 44827
Founded in: 1947
Questionnaire not received

DAYTON

Carillon Park
2001 S. Patterson Blvd., 45409
Telephone: (513) 293-3412
Private agency, authorized by
Educational and Musical Arts, Inc.
Founded in: 1942
Mary Mathews, Executive Director
Staff: full time 4, part time 26,
volunteer 3
Major programs: museum, markers,
tours/pilgrimages, historic
preservation, records

management, exhibits, audiovisual
programs
Period of collections: 1796-1930

**Dayton-Montgomery County Park
District**
Carriage Hill Farm, 7860 Shull Rd.,
45424
Telephone: (513) 879-0461
Founded in: 1968
Donald P. Schmidt, Director
Staff: full time 5, part time 4,
volunteer 400
Major programs: museum,
tours/pilgrimages, school
programs, historic preservation,
living history
Period of collections: 1880s

Gallery at the Old Post Office
120 W. 3rd St., 45402
Telephone: (513) 223-6500
Private agency
Founded in: 1980
Marilyn K. Shannon, Gallery Director
Staff: full time 1
Major programs: tours, exhibits,
architecture

**Miami Valley Council on Genealogy
and History**
4290 Honeybrook Ave., 45415
Telephone: (513) 290-2811
Private agency
Founded in: 1983
Vicki Frazer Arnold, President
Number of members: 49
Major programs:
newsletters/pamphlets,
genealogical services, yearly
educational conferences, speakers
bureau

Miami Valley Genealogical Society
Mail to: P.O. Box 1364, 45401
Private agency
Founded in: 1970
Eric C. Nagle, President
Number of members: 220
Staff: volunteer 17
Magazine: *Genealogical Aids Bulletin*
Major programs: library, archives,
newsletters/pamphlets,
genealogical services
Period of collections: 1800-1900

**Montgomery County Chapter, Ohio
Genealogical Society**
Mail to: P.O. Box 1584, 45401-1584
Founded in: 1974
Janet Adkins President
Magazine: *The Family Tree*
Major programs: library, archives,
book publishing,
newsletters/pamphlets, records
management, research,
genealogical services
Period of collections: 1974-present

**Montgomery County Historical
Society**
7 N. Main St., 45402
Telephone: (513) 228-6271
County agency
Founded in: 1897
Patrick A. Foltz, Executive Director
Number of members: 600
Staff: full time 6, part time 5,
volunteer 60
Magazine: *Ionic Columns*

Major programs: library, archives,
museum, tours/pilgrimages, school
programs, newsletters/pamphlets,
exhibits, photographic collections
Period of collections: 1865-1918

Ohio Museums Association
405 W. Riverview Ave., Dayton Art
Institute
Telephone: (513) 223-5277
Mail to: P.O. Box 941, 45401-0941
Private agency
Founded in: 1976
Jane A. Dunwoodie, Director
Number of members: 251
Staff: full time 1
Major programs:
newsletters/pamphlets, field
services, workshops, seminars,
conferences, directories

Patterson Homestead
1815 Brown St., 45409
Telephone: (513) 222-9724
City agency
Founded in: 1953
Anne Digan, Director
Staff: full time 1, part time 3,
volunteer 4
Major programs: historic sites
preservation, educational
programs
Period of collections: 1800-1865

**Richard Montgomery Chapter,
National Society, Sons of the
American Revolution**
540 Monteray Ave., 45419
Telephone: (513) 293-2539
Private agency
Founded in: 1912
Robert W. Mayne, President
Number of members: 85
Staff: volunteer 7
Major programs: library, markers,
school programs,
newsletters/pamphlets,
genealogical services
Period of collections: 1775-present

**Wright State University Archives
and Special Collections**
University Library, 45435
Telephone: (513) 873-2092
State agency, authorized by the
university
Founded in: 1964
Patrick B. Nolan, Head of Archives
Staff: full time 5, part time 14,
volunteer 1
Major programs: library, archives,
manuscripts, oral history, records
management, photographic
collections, genealogical services

DEFIANCE

**Defiance County Chapter, Ohio
Genealogy Society**
P.O. Box 675, 43512
County agency, authorized by Ohio
Genealogy Society
Founded in: 1977
Janice L. Sharp, President
Number of members: 80
Magazine: *Yesteryear's Trails*
Major programs: library,
newsletters/pamphlets,
genealogical services

Defiance County Historical Society
Krouse Rd.
Telephone: (419) 784-0107
Mail to: P.O. Box 801, 43512
Founded in: 1953
Jim Lehman, President
Number of members: 950
Staff: full time 1, part time 4,
    volunteer 30
Major programs: museum,
    educational programs
Period of collections: 1865-1918

DELAWARE

United Methodist Archives
Beeghly Library, 43 University St.,
    43015
Telephone: (614) 369-4431, ext. 214
Private agency, authorized by the
    Methodist Church
Fran Harter, Archivist
Major programs: archives,
    manuscripts, research,
    genealogical services

DOVER

**Dover Historical Society/J. E.
Reeves Home and Museum**
325 E. Iron Ave., 44622
Telephone: (216) 343-7040
Private agency
Founded in: 1958
Thomas H. Conwell, Director
Number of members: 475
Staff: full time 1, part time 12,
    volunteer 7
Major programs: museum, historic
    site(s), book publishing,
    newsletters/pamphlets, exhibits
Period of collections: 1865-present

DOYLESTOWN

Rogues' Hollow Historical Society
17500 Galehouse Rd., 44230
Telephone: (216) 658-4561
Founded in: 1960
Questionnaire not received

DUBLIN

Dublin Historical Society, Inc.
6669 Coffman Rd.
Telephone: (614) 764-9906
Mail to: P.O. Box 164, 43017
State agency
Founded in: 1974
Bruce Graham, President
Number of members: 200
Staff: Volunteer 25
Major programs: archives,
    manuscripts,
    newsletters/pamphlets, historic
    preservation, research,
    photographic collections,
    genealogical services
Period of collections: 1860-1920

EAST CANTON

Osnaburg Historical Society
P.O. Box 1664, 44730
Private agency

Founded in: 1976
Laurie D. Soliday, President
Number of members: 60
Staff: volunteer 12
Major programs: museum,
    audiovisual programs

EAST LIVERPOOL

East Liverpool Historical Society
305 Walnut St.
Telephone: (216) 385-2550/385-7853
Mail to: P.O. Box 476, 43920
Private agency
Founded in: 1907
Charles R. Thomas, Jr., President
Number of members: 100
Staff: volunteer 35
Major programs: museum, historic
    site(s), markers, book publishing,
    newsletters/pamphlets, historic
    preservation, exhibits,
    photographic collections, public
    programs
Period of collections: mid 19th
    century-present

Museum of Ceramics
400 E. 5th St., 43920
Telephone: (216) 386-6001
State agency, authorized by Ohio
    Historical Society
Founded in: 1980
Bill Gates, Curator
Staff: full time 4, part time 2,
    volunteer 2
Major programs: archives,
    manuscripts, museum, school
    programs, research, exhibits,
    photographic collections
Period of collections: 1840-1920

EATON

Preble County Historical Society
7693 Swartsel Rd., 45320
Telephone: (513) 787-4256
Private agency
Founded in: 1972
Kay Reeves, Executive Director
Number of members: 350
Staff: part time 1, volunteer 25
Magazine: *Tell-Tale*
Major programs: library, archives,
    museum, historic site(s), school
    programs, book publishing,
    newsletters/pamphlets, historic
    preservation, exhibits
Period of collections: 1830-1930

ELYRIA

**Lorain County Historical
Scciety, Inc.**
509 Washington Ave., 44035
Telephone: (216) 322-3341
Private agency
Founded in: 1889
Phyllis Strayer, Director
Number of members: 625
Staff: full time 3, part time 1,
    volunteer 75
Major programs: library, archives,
    manuscripts, museum, historic
    sites

preservation, markers,
    tours/pilgrimages, junior history,
    educational programs, books,
    newsletters/pamphlets
Period of collections: 1800-1950

ENON

**Enon Community Historical
Society**
Indian Dr.
Telephone: (513) 864-7756
Mail to: P.O. Box 442, 45323
Private agency
Founded in: 1977
Robert L. Fowble, President
Number of members: 200
Staff: volunteer 25
Magazine: *Images*
Major programs: library, archives,
    museum, oral history, school
    programs, historic preservaticn,
    exhibits, audiovisual programs,
    photographic collections,
    genealogical services
Period of collections: late
    1800s-present

EUCLID

Euclid Historical Society
21129 North St., 44117
Telephone: (216) 383-8299
Private agency
Founded in: 1959
Roy R. Larick, Jr., President
Number of members: 80
Staff: volunteer 6
Major programs: library, archives,
    oral history, exhibits
Period of collections: from 1890

FAIRPORT HARBOR

Fairport Harbor Historical Society
129 2nd St., 44077
Telephone: (216) 354-4825
Town agency
Founded in: 1945
John L. Killinen, President
Number of members: 150
Staff: volunteer 20
Major programs: library, museum,
    historic site(s), tours, newsletters,
    historic preservation, exhibits,
    photographic collections,
    restoration of lighthouse
Period of collections: early
    1800s-present

FAIRVIEW PARK

Fairview Park Historical Society
21779 Seabury, 44126
Telephone: (216) 734-2067
Questionnaire not received

FARMERSVILLE

**Farmersville Historical
Society, Inc.**
P.O. Box 198, 45325
Town agency
Founded in: 1980
Number of members: 311
Staff: volunteer 7

Major programs: oral history,
newsletters/pamphlets, historic
preservation, research, exhibits,
photographic collections
Period of collections: 1890-1930

FINDLAY

**Hancock Historical Museum
Association**
422 W. Sandusky St., 45840
Telephone: (419) 423-4433
Founded in: 1970
Betty Dunlap, Director
Number of members: 1,500
Staff: part time 2, volunteer 23
Major programs: library, museum,
historic sites preservation,
educational programs,
newsletters/pamphlets
Period of collections: 1865-1918

**Preservation Guild of Hancock
County**
P.O. Box 621, 45839
Private agency
Founded in: 1962
Richard H. Deerhale, President
Number of members: 200
Major programs: markers, historic
preservation
Period of collections: Victorian era

FT. LORAMIE

Ft. Loramie Historical Association
Main and Elm St.
Telephone: (513) 295-3071
Mail to: P.O. Box 276, 45845
Founded in: 1971
Questionnaire not received

FOSTORIA

**Fostoria Area Historical Society
and Museum**
121-123 W. North St.
Mail to: P.O. Box 142, 44830
City agency
Founded in: 1972
George A. Gray, President
Number of members: 210
Staff: volunteer 8
Major programs: museum,
tours/pilgrimages, school
programs, newsletters/pamphlets
Period of collections: 1870-1930

Fostoria Mausoleum Association
762 Van Buren St., 44830
Telephone: (419) 435-4416
Private agency
Founded in: 1917
Robert Gocdyear, Statutory Agent
Staff: volunteer 5
Major programs: historic preservation

FRANKLIN

Franklin Area Historical Society
302 Park Ave.
Telephone: (513) 423-7977
Mail to: P.O. Box 345, 45005
Private agency
Founded in: 1965
Harriet Foley, President
Number of members: 225
Staff: full time 1, volunteer 10
Major programs: museum,
newsletters/pamphlets
Period of collections: 1800-1965

FREMONT

Ft. Stephenson Museum
Birchard Public Library, 423 Croghan
St., 43420
Telephone: (419) 334-7101
Mary Anne Culbertson, Director
Major programs: library, museum,
school programs

**Rutherford B. Hayes Presidential
Center**
Spiegel Grove, 43420
Telephone: (419) 332-2081
Private agency, authorized by Ohio
Historical Society
Founded in: 1916
Leslie H. Fishel, Jr., Director
Staff: full time 18, part time 16,
volunteer 12
Magazine: *Hayes Historical Journal:
A Journal of the Gilded Age*
Major programs: library, archives,
manuscripts, museum, historic
site(s), school programs, book
publishing, newsletters/pamphlets,
historic preservation, research,
exhibits, photographic collections,
genealogical services, outdoor
programs, nature preserve
Period of collections: Civil War-W.W.I

**Sandusky County Historical
Society**
514 Birchard Ave.
Mail to: 1337 Hayes Ave., 43420
Private agency
Founded in: 1874
Phillip A. Schwochow, President
Number of members: 425
Staff: volunteer 12
Major programs: museum, markers,
tours, school programs,
newsletters/pamphlets, historic
preservation, exhibits, archaeology
programs
Period of collections: 1850-1830

GAHANNA

Gahanna Historical Society
101 S. High St.
Telephone: (614) 471-6108
Mail to: P.O. Box 30602, 43230
Private agency
Founded in: 1965
Jama L. Cumbo, President
Number of members: 65
Staff: volunteer 20
Major programs: historic site(s),
school programs, book publishing,
historic preservation, photographic
collections, genealogical services
Period of collections: 1825-1900

GALION

Galion Historical Society, Inc.
955 Bucyrus Rd., 44833
Telephone: (419) 468-1026
Private agency
Founded in: 1955
Bernard M. Mansfield, President
Number of members: 125
Staff: volunteer 50
Major programs: library, manuscripts,
museum, tours/pilgrimages, oral
history, newsletters/pamphlets,
exhibits, living history,
photographic collections
Period of collections: 1850-present

GEORGETOWN

**Brown County Chapter, Ohio
Genealogical Society**
Cherry and Apple Sts.
Telephone: (513) 378-4541
(president)
Mail to: P.O. Box 83, 45121
Private agency
Founded in: 1977
Patricia R. Donaldson, President
Number of members: 300
Staff: volunteer 10
Magazine: *On the Trail*
Major programs: library,
newsletters/pamphlets,
genealogical services
Period of collections: 1800-1900

Brown County Historical Society
Telephone: (513) 379-1847
Mail to: P.O. Box 238, 45121
Questionnaire not received

GERMANTOWN

Historical Society of Germantown
33 W. Center St., 45327
Founded in: 1973
Questionnaire not received

GIRARD

Girard Historical Society
c/o Secretary, 143 E. Wilson Ave.,
44420
Telephone: (216) 545-3861
Private agency
Founded in: 1975
Elizabeth DeChant, Secretary
Number of members: 125
Major programs: museum, historic
site(s), historic preservation,
renovation

GRADENHUTTEN

Gradenhutten Historical Society
P.O. Box 38, 44629
Telephone: (614) 254-4522
Town agency
Founded in: 1843
R. M. Virtue, Curator
Number of members: 100
Staff: volunteer 3
Major programs: museum, historic
site(s), tours/pilgrimages, oral
history

GRAFTON

Main Street Preservation Society
P.O. Box 101, 44044
Telephone: (216) 926-3488
Private agency
Founded in: 1978
David L. Bescan, Chair
Number of members: 12
Staff: volunteer 12
Major programs: markers,
newsletters/pamphlets, historic
preservation, exhibits, audiovisual
programs, photographic
collections

GRAND RAPIDS

Historical Society of Grand Rapids
P.O. Box 124, 43522
Telephone: (419) 832-5931
(president)
Founded in: 1975

Robert Marlow, President
Number of members: 75
Staff: volunteer 200
Major programs: markers, book publishing, newsletters/pamphlets, historical activities and special events
Period of collections: 1835-present

GRANVILLE

Granville Ohio Historical Museum, Inc.
117 E. Broadway
Mail to: 420 E. Broadway, 43023
Founded in: 1885
Richard H. Howe, Curator
Number of members: 100
Staff: full time 3
Major programs: museum, books
Period of collections: 1805-1920

H. P. Robinson Life-Style Museum
121 S. Main St.
Telephone: (614) 587-3350 (director)
Mail to: P.O. Box 134, 43023
Private agency, authorized by Hubert and Oese Robinson Foundation
Founded in: 1983
Gloria Hoover, Development Director
Staff: full time 1, volunteer 16
Major programs: museum, historic preservation, exhibits, photographic collections
Period of collections: 1840-1981

Robbins Hunter Museum
221 E. Broadway
Telephone: (614) 587-0430
Mail to: P.O. Box 183, 43023
Private agency, authorized by Licking County Historical Society
Founded in: 1981
Paul A. Goudy, Executive Director
Staff: full time 1, part time 1, volunteer 39
Magazine: Avery-Downer House Notes
Major programs: library, archives, manuscripts, museum, historic site(s), tours/pilgrimages, historic preservation, research, photographic collections, field services
Period of collections: 1750-1900

GREENVILLE

Darke County Historical Society
205 N. Broadway, 45331
Telephone: (513) 548-5250
Founded in: 1903
Toni Seiler, Director
Number of members: 300
Staff: full time 2, volunteer 2
Major programs: museum
Period of collections: 1795-present

Garst Museum
205 N. Broadway, 45331
Telephone: (513) 548-5250
Private agency, authorized by Darke County Historical Society
Founded in: 1903
Mrs. Toni Seiler, Director
Number of members: 400
Staff: full time 2, volunteer 4
Major programs: museum, exhibits, genealogical services
Period of collections: 1791-1900

GROVE CITY

Southwest Franklin County Historical Society
P.O. Box 38, 43123
Private agency
Founded in: 1982
William L. Howison, President
Number of members: 70
Staff: volunteer 3
Major programs: library, historic site(s), oral history, school programs, newsletters/pamphlets, research, exhibits, archaeology programs, photographic collections, genealogical services
Period of collections: 1900

HAMILTON

Butler County Historical Society
327 N. 2nd St., 45011
Telephone: (513) 893-7111
County agency
Founded in: 1934
Helen L. Miller, Curator
Number of members: 275
Staff: full time 1, part time 3
Major programs: library, archives, manuscripts, museum, school programs, book publishing, newsletters/pamphlets, historic preservation, research, exhibits, photographic collections, genealogical services
Period of collections: 1800

Butler County Historic Restoration Commission
Telephone: (513) 867-6120
Mail to: P.O. Box 387, 45012
Founded in: 1966
Questionnaire not received

HARRISON

Village Historical Society, Inc.
6590 Kilby Rd., 45030
Private agency
Founded in: 1962
Eugene B. Woelfel, President
Number of members: 72
Period of collections: 1804-1805

HILLIARD

Northwest Franklin County Historical Society and Museum
Mail to: P.O. Box 413, 43026
Founded in: 1966
Questionnaire not received

HILLSBORO

Highland County Historical Society
E. Main St., 45133
Telephone: (513) 393-3392
County agency
Founded in: 1969
Charles Harsha, President
Number of members: 300
Staff: volunteer 20
Major programs: library, museum, tours/pilgrimages, historic preservation, research
Period of collections: 19th-20th centuries

HIRAM

Hiram Township Historical Society, Inc.
Mail to: P.O. Box 444, 44234
Founded in: 1951
Mrs. Jamie Barrow, President
Number of members: 163
Staff: volunteer 12
Major programs: historic sites preservation

HOMEWORTH

Western Columbiana County Historical Society
Homeworth-Alliance Rd.
Mail to: P.O. Box 162, 44634
Founded in: 1964
Questionnaire not received

HUDSON

CHIPS (Council of Historic Institutions and Preservation Societies in Summit and Portage Counties)
c/o Hudson Library, 22 Aurora St., 44236
Telephone: (216) 653-6658
Private agency
Founded in: 1980
James F. Caccamo, Coordinator
Staff: volunteer 1

Hudson Heritage Association
Brewster Mansion, 9 Aurora St.
Telephone: (216) 653-9817
Mail to: P.O. Box 2218, 44236
Private agency
Founded in: 1962
George Hoy, Co-president
Number of members: 300
Staff: volunteer 12
Major programs: historic site(s), markers, tours/pilgrimages, newsletters/pamphlets, historic preservation, research, photographic collections
Period of collections: 19th century

Hudson Library and Historical Society
22 Aurora St., 44236
Telephone: (216) 653-6658
Founded in: 1910
Thomas L. Vince, Curator
Number of members: 285
Staff: full time 4, part time 9, volunteer 4
Major programs: library, archives, manuscripts, museum, markers, tours/pilgrimages, junior history, school programs, newsletters/pamphlets, research, exhibits, audiovisual programs, photographic collections, genealogical services
Period of collections: 1800-1910

IRONTON

Lawrence County Historical Society
Telephone: (614) 532-0478
Mail to: c/o President, 1513 Charlotte St., 45638
County agency
Founded in: 1925
Mrs. M. B. Edmundson, President

OHIO

Number of members: 24
Staff: part time 1
Major programs: museum
Period of collections: 1865-present

JEFFERSON

Ashtabula County Historical Society
P.O. Box 206, 44047-0206
Telephone: (216) 466-7337
County agency
Founded in: 1938
Arland L. Gibbs, President
Number of members: 339
Magazine: *Ashtabula County Covered Bridges*
Major programs: historic site(s), historic preservation

Lenox Historical Society, Inc.
c/o President, 3424 Lenox and New Lyme Rd., 44047
Telephone: (216) 294-2640
Town agency
Founded in: 1984
Harry Smith, President
Number of members: 46
Major programs: museum, oral history, school programs
Period of collections: 19th century

JUNCTION CITY

Perry County Chapter, Ohio Genealogical Society
P.O. Box 275, 43748
County agency
Founded in: 1981
Rita Wooten, President
Number of members: 239
Magazine: *Perry County Heirlines*
Major programs: library, book publishing, newsletters/pamphlets

KALIDA

Putnam County Historical Society
201 E. Main St.
Telephone: (419) 532-9008
Mail to: P.O. Box 260, 45853
County agency
Founded in: 1873
Rita Turnwald, President
Number of members: 320
Staff: part time 1, volunteer 25
Magazine: *Putnam County Heritage*
Major programs: library, archives, museum, historic site(s), markers, oral history, book publishing, newsletters/pamphlets, historic preservation, records management, research, exhibits, photographic collections, genealogical services
Period of collections: 1800-present

KENT

Brimfield Memorial House Association, Inc.
4158 State Rt. 43, 44240
Telephone: (216) 673-1058
Private agency
Founded in: 1963
Edgar L. McCormick, Director
Number of members: 285
Staff: volunteer 6
Magazine: *The Kelso Courier*

Major programs: archives, museum, newsletters/pamphlets, exhibits
Period of collections: 19th century

Kent State University Archives
1115 University Library, 44242
Telephone: (216) 672-2411
State agency, authorized by the university
Founded in: 1970
Stephen C. Morton, University Archivist
Staff: full time 2, part time 4, volunteer 2
Major programs: library, archives, manuscripts
Period of collections: 1910-present

KENTON

Hardin County Chapter, Ohio Genealogy Society
P.O. Box 520, 43326
Telephone: (419) 675-1839
State agency, authorized by Ohio Genealogy Society
Founded in: 1980
Mrs. Calvin Kraft, President
Magazine: *Track and Trace*
Period of collections: 1800s

Sullivan-Johnson Museum of Hardin County
223 N. Main St., 43326
Telephone: (419) 673-7147
County agency
Founded in: 1983
Elizabeth Mackey, Board President
Staff: full time 1, volunteer 12
Major programs: tours/pilgrimages, records management, research, exhibits, audiovisual programs, photographic collections
Period of collections: 1820-1940

KIRTLAND

Kirtland Temple Historic Center
9020 Chillicothe Rd., 44094
Telephone: (216) 256-3318
Private agency, authorized by Reorganized Church of Jesus Christ of Latter Day Saints
Founded in: 1836
Kenneth E. Stobaugh, Director
Staff: full time 3, part time 3, volunteer 6
Major programs: historic sites preservation
Period of collections: 1833-1838

LAKESIDE

Lakeside Heritage Club, Inc.
238 Maple Ave.
Mail to: 416 Walnut Ave., 43440
Private agency
Founded in: 1968
Neil L. Allen, President
Number of members: 150
Staff: part time 1, volunteer 24
Major programs: museum
Period of collections: 1890s

LAKEWOOD

Lakewood Historical Society
14710 Lake Ave., 44107
Telephone: (216) 221-7343
Private agency
Founded in: 1952

Sandra Koozer, Curator
Number of members: 500
Staff: part time 2, volunteer 75
Magazine: *Lakewood Historical Society News*
Major programs: museum, oral history, school programs, historic preservation, exhibits, living history, photographic collections
Period of collections: 1840-1870

LANCASTER

Fairfield Heritage Association Inc.
105 E. Wheeling St., 43130
Telephone: (614) 654-9923
Founded in: 1963
Questionnaire not received

Sherman House
137 E. Main St., 43130
Telephone: (614) 687-5891
Authorized by Fairfield Heritage Association
Mrs. Phillip Leitnaker, Director
Major programs: museum, artifacts and mementos of historic persons
Period of collections: 1811-1860s

LEBANON

Warren County Historical Society
105 S. Broadway, 45036
Telephone: (513) 932-1817
Founded in: 1941
Victoria Van Harlingen, Museum Director
Number of members: 800
Staff: full time 1, part time 3, volunteer 40
Magazine: *Historicalog*
Major programs: library, archives, manuscripts, museum, historic sites preservation, tours, oral history, educational programs, newsletters/pamphlets
Period of collections: prehistoric-1865

LeROY TOWNSHIP

LeRoy Heritage Association
13668 Painesville-Warren Rd.
Telephone: (216) 254-4955
Mail to: 12941 Girdled Rd., 44077
Private agency
Founded in: 1975
Phil Hausch, President
Number of members: 125
Staff: volunteer 15
Major programs: archives, museum, historic site(s), markers, school programs, newsletters/pamphlets, historic preservation, exhibits, photographic collections
Period of collections: early 1800-present

LEXINGTON

Richland County Genealogical Society
Mail to: P.O. Box 3154, 44904
Founded in: 1965
Questionnaire not received

LIMA

Allen County Historical Society and Museum
620 W. Market St., 45801
Telephone: (419) 222-9426

Private agency
Founded in: 1908
Raymond F. Schuck, Curator
Number of members: 605
Staff: full time 6, part time 8,
volunteer 55
Magazine: *Allen County Reporter*
Major programs: library, archives,
manuscripts, museum, historic
site(s), markers, junior history,
school programs, book publishing,
newsletters/pamphlets, historic
preservation, research, exhibits,
archaeology programs,
photographic collections,
genealogical services, field
services
Period of collections: 1830-present

LIMAVILLE

Limaville Historical Society, Inc.
P.O. Box 13, 44640
Town agency
Founded in: 1970
Jean Pfeifer, President
Major programs: historic preservation

LISBON

Lisbon Historical Society
100 E. Washington St., 44432
Founded in: 1938
Questionnaire not received

LOUISVILLE

**Louisville Area
Historical-Preservation Society**
523 E. Main St., 44641
Telephone: (216) 875-4180
Private agency
Founded in: 1982
Candace L. Bishop, President
Number of members: 50
Staff: volunteer 10
Major programs: museum, historic
site(s), newsletters/pamphlets,
historic preservation
Period of collections: 1850-1950

Louisville Historical Society, Inc.
908 W. Main St., 44641
Telephone: (216) 875-2349
Questionnaire not received

LOVELAND

Loveland Historical Museum
Riverside and Park Ave., 45140
Telephone: (513) 683-5692
Private agency, authorized by
Greater Loveland Historical Society
Founded in: 1984
John Steinle, Director
Number of members: 230
Staff: full time 1, volunteer 50
Major programs: library, archives,
manuscripts, museum,
tours/pilgrimages, oral history,
school programs, exhibits,
photographic collections
Period of collections: 1850-1950

LUCAS

Malabar Farm State Park
Bormfield Rd., P.O. Box 469, 44843
Telephone: (419) 892-2784
State agency, authorized by
Department of Natural Resources

Founded in: 1939
James M. Berry, Park Manager
Staff: full time 11, part time 6,
volunteer 6
Major programs: historic site(s),
tours/pilgrimages, school
programs, historic preservation,
exhibits, living history, working farm
Period of collections: 1930s-1950s

LYNDHURST

**Johannes Schwalm Historical
Association, Inc.**
4983 S. Sedgewick Rd., 44124
Telephone: (216) 382-5711
Private agency
Founded in: 1979
Richard C. Barth, President
Number of members: 280
Staff: volunteer 10
Magazine: *Journal of the Johannes
Schwalm Historical
Association, Inc.*
Major programs: archives,
newsletters/pamphlets, research
Period of collections: Revolutionary
War

MADISON

Madison Historical Society
13 W. Main St.
Telephone: (216) 428-6107
Mail to: P.O. Box 91, 44057
Private agency
Founded in: 1978
Louanna Billington, President
Number of members: 125
Major programs: library, museum,
historic site(s), tours/pilgrimages,
oral history, research
Period of collections: 1840-present

MANSFIELD

Ohio Genealogical Society
419 W. 3rd St.
Telephone: (419) 522-9077
Mail to: P.O. Box 2625, 44906
Private agency
Founded in: 1960
Julie Overton, President
Number of members: 5,900
Staff: full time 1, volunteer 15
Magazine: *Ohio Records and Pioneer
Families*
Major programs: library, manuscripts,
tours/pilgrimages,
newsletters/pamphlets, research,
genealogical services
Period of collections: 1620-1900

Richland County Historical Society
3 N. Main St., 44902
Telephone: (419) 522-1752
County agency
Founded in: 1913
Richard R. Stander, President
Number of members: 200
Staff: volunteer 24
Major programs: museum, historic
site(s), historic preservation
Period of collections: 1847-1885

MARCY

Slate Run Living Historical Farm
9094 Marcy Rd., 43154
Telephone: (614) 833-1880

County agency, authorized by Metro
Parks of Franklin County
Founded in: 1981
Carole L. Cunningham, Director
Number of members: 250
Staff: full time 2, part time 4,
volunteer 100
Major programs: historic site(s),
school programs, living history
Period of collections: 1880-1900

MARIETTA

Campus Martius Museum
602 2nd St., 45750
Telephone: (614) 373-3750
Private agency, authorized by Ohio
Historical Society
Founded in: 1927
John B. Briley, Manager
Staff: full time 3, part time 1,
volunteer 25
Major programs: museum, historic
site(s), school programs,
genealogical services
Period of collections: 1790-1900

Ohio River Museum
601 Front St., 45750
Telephone: (614) 373-3750
Private agency, authorized by Ohio
Historical Society
Founded in: 1941
John B. Briley, Manager
Staff: part time 2, volunteer 10
Major programs: museum, school
programs
Period of collections: mid 19th
century

**Washington County Chapter, Ohio
Genealogical Society**
c/o President, P.O. Box 133, Little
Hocking, 45742
Founded in: 1983
Catherine J. Sams, President
Number of members: 150
Magazine: *Washington*
Major programs: genealogical
services
Period of collections: 1798-present

**Washington County Historical
Society, Inc.**
401 Aurora St., 45750
Founded in: 1961
Major programs: library, archives,
museum, historic sites
preservation, books
Period of collections: 1783-1918

MARION

Marion County Historical Society
Telephone: (614) 382-3829
mail to: P.O. Box 169, 43302
County agency
Founded in: 1969
Norman W. Fogt, President
Number of members: 325
Staff: volunteer 25
Major programs: archives, markers,
tours/pilgrimages, school
programs, book publishing,
newsletters/pamphlets, historic
preservation
Period of collections: 1822-1950

Ohio Academy of History
Marion Campus, Ohio State
University, 43302

Telephone: (614) 389-2361
Founded in: 1932
Vladimir Steffel, Secretary/Treasurer
Number of members: 600
Magazine: *Ohio Academy of History Newsletter*
Major programs: educational programs

President Harding's Home
380 Mt. Vernon Ave., 43302
Telephone: (614) 387-9630
State agency
Founded in: 1925
Herbert S. Gary, Museum Manager
Major programs: museum, historic site(s), tours/pilgrimages, oral history, school programs, audiovisual programs
Period of collections: 1890-1923

MARYSVILLE

Union County Historical Society
246 W. 6th St., 43040
Questionnaire not received

MASSILLON

Jackson Township Historical Society
44646
Mail to: P.O. Box 35171, Canton, 44735
Founded in: 1979
Bonnie Sprankle, Executive Director
Number of members: 54
Major programs: exhibits, audiovisual programs, photographic collections
Period of collections: 1890-1930

The Massillon Museum
212 Lincoln Way, E, 44646
Telephone: (216) 833-4061
County agency, authorized by Massillon Public Library
Founded in: 1933
John P. Klassen, Director
Number of members: 1,200
Staff: full time 3, part time 2, volunteer 35
Major programs: archives, manuscripts, museum, school programs, newsletters/pamphlets, exhibits, photographic collections, genealogical services
Period of collections: 1800-present

MAUMEE

Maumee Valley Historical Society
1031 River Rd., 43537
Telephone: (419) 893-9602
Private agency
Founded in: 1864
Ronald L. Burdick, Director
Number of members: 460
Staff: full time 3, part time 4, volunteer 100
Magazine: *Northwest Ohio Quarterly; Ohio Cues*
Major programs: library, archives, museum, historic site(s), markers, tours/pilgrimages, oral history, school programs, book publishing, newsletters/pamphlets, historic preservation, research, exhibits
Period of collections: 1800-1918

Ohio Baseball Hall of Fame and Museum
2901 Key St., 43537
Mail to: c/o President, 2729 Shelley Rd., Shaker Heights, 44122
County agency, authorized by Lucas County Recreation Department
Founded in: 1976
Thomas C. Eakin, Founder/President
Major programs: museum
Period of collections: 1880s-present

MAYFIELD VILLAGE

Mayfield Township Historical Society
6688 Metro Park Dr., 44143
Telephone: (216) 442-4960
Founded in: 1976
Questionnaire not received

MCARTHUR

Vinton County Historical Society
County Courthouse
Telephone: (614) 596-5401
Mail to: P.O. Box 474, 45651
Private agency
Founded in: 1950
Deanne Tribe, Executive Director
Number of members: 20
Staff: volunteer 6
Major programs: archives, historic site(s), tours/pilgrimages, research, genealogical services
Period of collections: 19th-20th centuries

MCCONNELSVILLE

Morgan County Historical Society
142 E. Main, 43756
Telephone: (614) 962-4785
Private agency
Founded in: 1950s
Si Jones, President
Number of members: 620
Staff: part time 1, volunteer 50
Magazine: *The Elk Eye*
Major programs: library, archives, manuscripts, museum, historic site(s), newsletters/pamphlets, research, exhibits, photographic collections, genealogical services
Period of collections: 19th-20th centuries

MEDINA

Medina Community Design Committee
30 Public Square, 44256
Telephone: (216) 725-7516
Private agency, authorized by Letha House Foundation
Founded in: 1967
Janet Senkar, Project Coordinator
Number of members: 15
Staff: part time 1, volunteer 20
Magazine: *Medina Journal*
Major programs: library, archives, tours/pilgrimages, junior history, oral history, school programs, newsletters/pamphlets, historic preservation, research, exhibits, audiovisual programs, photographic collections
Period of collections: 1870-present

Medina County Historical Society
206 N. Elmwood St.
Telephone: (216) 722-1341
Mail to: P.O. Box 306, 44258
Private agency
Joann G. King, Curator
Number of members: 125
Staff: part time 2, volunteer 10
Major programs: museum, markers, oral history, historic preservation, exhibits, genealogical services
Period of collections: 1818-1920

MENTOR

Lake County Historical Society
8610 King Memorial Rd., 44060
Telephone: (216) 255-8979
Private agency
Founded in: 1938
Eric J. Cardinal, Executive Director
Number of members: 525
Staff: part time 3, volunteer 28
Magazine: *Lake County Historical Quarterly*
Major programs: library, museum, markers, school programs, newsletters/pamphlets, historic preservation, audiovisual programs, genealogical services
Period of collections: 1800-1930s

New York Central System Historical Society, Inc.
P.O. Box 745, 44060
Telephone: (215) 687-1207 (president)
Mail to: P.O. Box 58994, Philadelphia, PA, 19102
Private agency
Founded in: 1970
Charles M. Smith, President
Number of members: 1,300
Staff: volunteer 6
Magazine: *Central Headlight*
Major programs: archives, book publishing, research, photographic collections
Period of collections: 1880-1968

MIAMISBURG

Miamisburg Preservation and Restoration, Inc.
P.O. Box 455, 45342
Telephone: (513) 866-4879
Founded in: 1980
Questionnaire not received

MIDDLETOWN

Middletown Historical Society
1605 Verity Parkway
Telephone: (513) 539-7798
Mail to: P.O. Box 1802, 45042
Private agency
Founded in: 1966
George Crout, Curator
Number of members: 335
Staff: volunteer 3
Major programs: museum, historic site(s), tours/pilgrimages, oral history, newsletters/pamphlets, audiovisual programs
Period of collections: 1825-1929

MILAN

Edison Birthplace Association, Inc.
9 Edison Dr., 44846

Telephone: (419) 499-2135
Founded in: 1951
John Edison Sloane, Director
Staff: part time 6
Major programs: museum,
educational programs, books
Period of collections: 1783-1865

Milan Historical Museum, Inc.
10 Edison Dr., 44846
Telephone: (419) 499-2968
Founded in: 1954
M. B. Stauffer, President
Staff: full time 4, part time 10,
volunteer 40
Major programs: manuscripts,
museum, tours/pilgrimages, school
programs, exhibits
Period of collections: 1783-1918

MILFORD

Milford Area Historical Society
906 Main St., 45150
Telephone: (513) 831-0815
Private agency
Founded in: 1967
Raymond H. Schumacher, President
Number of members: 125
Major programs: museum
Period of collections: 1788-present

MILLERSBURG

**Holmes County Chapter, Ohio
Genealogical Society**
P.O. Box 136, 44654
County agency
Founded in: 1983
Robert E. Strock, President
Number of members: 150
Staff: volunteer 25
Magazine: *Holmes County Heirs*
Major programs: genealogical
services

Holmes County Historical Society
233 N. Washington St.
Mail to: P.O. Box 126, 44654
Private agency
David L. Weiss, President
Major programs: tours, historic
preservation
Period of collections: Victorian era

MINERVA

Minerva Area Historical Society
128 N. Market
Telephone: (216) 868-4287
Mail to: 103 Murray Ave., 44657
Founded in: 1967
Questionnaire not received

MONROEVILLE

Monroeville Historical Society
2 N. Main St.
Telephone: (419) 465-2411
Mail to: P.O. Box 217, 44847
Private agency
Founded in: 1973
Richard F. Betschman, President
Number of members: 18
Staff: volunteer 6
Major programs: library, archives,
museum, school programs, historic
preservation, exhibits
Period of collections: 1880s

MONTPELIER

Williams County Historical Society
1222 Linden St., 43543
Telephone: (419) 485-5071
County agency
Founded in: 1956
Martin Sosto, President
Number of members: 523
Staff: volunteer 50
Major programs: museum, historic
site(s), markers, tours/pilgrimages,
book publishing,
newsletters/pamphlets, historic
preservation, audiovisual
programs, photographic
collections, genealogical services
Period of collections: 1800-present

MORELAND HILLS

Moreland Hills Historical Society
Telephone: (216) 248-8437
Mail to: 200 Sterncrest Dr., 44022
Town agency
Founded in: 1982
Caroline G. Dingle, President
Number of members: 45
Major programs: archives, historic
site(s), historic preservation
Period of collections: from 1830

MT. GILEAD

Morrow County Historical Society
Mail to: P.O. Box 21, 43338
County agency
Founded in: 1970
Daniel L. Rhodebeck, President
Number of members: 125
Staff: volunteer 10
Major programs: museum,
newsletters/pamphlets, historic
preservation, exhibits
Period of collections: 1880-present

MT. PLEASANT

Mt. Pleasant Historical Society, Inc.
Union and Concord, 43939
Telephone: (614) 769-7637
(president)
Private agency
Founded in: 1946
Earl F. Coleman, President
Number of members: 200
Major programs: manuscripts,
museum, historic site(s),
tours/pilgrimages,
newsletters/pamphlets, exhibits
Period of collections: 1800-1900

MUNROE FALLS

Munroe Falls Historical Society
P.O. Box 4, 44262
Telephone: (216) 920-1976
Private agency
Founded in: 1976
Briana L. Caccamo, President
Number of members: 25
Major programs: historic
preservation, audiovisual programs

NAVARRE

**Navarre-Bethlehem Township
Historical Society**
123 High St.
Mail to: P.O. Box 491, 44662
Private agency

Founded in: 1972
June Lynn, President
Staff: volunteer 20
Major programs: library, archives,
manuscripts, museum, historic
site(s), markers, tours/pilgrimages,
oral history, school programs, book
publishing, newsletters/pamphlets,
historic preservation, research,
exhibits, audiovisual programs,
archaeology programs,
photographic collections,
genealogical services, field
services, lectures
Period of collections: 1806-1819

NEW ALBANY

**New Albany-Plain Township
Historical Society**
4659 Reynoldsburg-New Albany Rd.,
43054
Telephone: (614) 855-1759
Private agency
David E. Curtis, President
Number of members: 35
Staff: volunteer 35
Major programs: tours/pilgrimages,
junior history, school programs,
exhibits, living history,
photographic collections,
genealogical services
Period of collections: early
1900-present

NEWARK

Dawes Aboretum Museum
7770 Jacksontown Rd., SE, 43055
Telephone: (614) 323-2990
Private agency
Founded in: 1929
Donald R. Hendricks, Director
Number of members: 1,250
Staff: full time 25
Major programs: library, museum,
historic site(s), markers,
tours/pilgrimages, school
programs, newsletters/pamphlets,
records management, audiovisual
programs, photographic
collections, horticulture
Period of collections: 1800-present

**Licking County Genealogical
Society**
743 E. Main St.
Telephone: (614) 345-3571
Mail to: P.O. Box 4037, 43055
State agency
Founded in: 1972
Delcie Pound, President
Number of members: 450
Staff: volunteer 12
Magazine: *Licking Lantern*
Major programs: library, genealogical
services
Period of collections: 1700-1900

Licking County Historical Society
6th St. Park
Telephone: (614) 345-4898
Mail to: P.O. Box 785, 43055
Founded in: 1947
Questionnaire not received

NEW BREMEN

New Bremen Historic Association
120 N. Main St.
Mail to: P.O. Box 73, 45869

Private agency
Founded in: 1973
Janet I. Fledderjohn, Curator
Number of members: 70
Staff: volunteer 12
Magazine: *Towpath*
Major programs: library, archives,
museum, newsletters/pamphlets,
genealogical services
Period of collections: 1835-1900

NEWCOMERSTOWN

**Newcomerstown Historical
Society—Old Temperance House
Tavern Museum**
221 W. Canal St.
Mail to: 414 Cross St., 43832
Founded in: 1940
Questionnaire not received

NEW PHILADELPHIA

**Schoenbrunn Village State
Memorial**
E. High Ave.
Telephone: (216) 339-3636
Mail to: P.O. Box 129, 44663
State agency, authorized by Ohio
Historical Society
Founded in: 1923
Persijs Kolberg, Sites Manager
Staff: full time 2, part time 3,
volunteer 30
Major programs: museum, historic
site(s), school programs, living
history
Period of collections: 1770s

**Tuscarawas County Historical
Society**
629 Wabash Ave., NW
Telephone: (216) 364-5577
Mail to: P.O. Box 462, 44663
Founded in: 1921
Questionnaire not received

NEW RICHMOND

Historic New Richmond
125 George St., 45157
Telephone: (513) 553-4101
Private agency
Founded in: 1971
Carroll Hinson, President
Number of members: 35
Major programs: museum, historic
preservation, photographic
collections

NORTH CANTON

Hoover Historical Center
2225 Easton St., NW, 44720
Telephone: (226) 499-0287
Private agency
Founded in: 1978
Stacy Krammes, Director
Staff: full time 2, part time 8
Major programs: museum, oral
history, school programs, historic
preservation, research, audiovisual
programs, photographic
collections
Period of collections: 1850-present

**Jackson Township Historical
Society**
P.O. Box 2535, 44720
Telephone: (216) 833-5862
Founded in: 1980
Questionnaire not received

NORWALK

**Firelands Historical Society
Museum**
4 Case Ave., 44857
Telephone: (419) 668-6038
Private agency, authorized by
Firelands Historical Society
Founded in: 1857
James M. Overhuls, Museum Director
Number of members: 350
Staff: part time 4, volunteer 4
Magazine: *Firelands Pioneer*
Major programs: library, archives,
museum, school programs, historic
preservation, exhibits
Period of collections: 1800-1900

NORWICH

National Road/Zane Grey Museum
8850 E. Pike, 43767
Telephone: (614) 872-3143
Private agency, authorized by Ohio
Historical Society
Founded in: 1885
Elizabeth A. Reeb, Museum Manager
Staff: full time 4, part time 1,
volunteer 3
Major programs: museum
Period of collections: 1800-1940

OREGON

**Oregon Jerusalem Historical
Society of Ohio, Inc.**
3320 Starr Ave.
Telephone: (419) 691-7193
Mail to: 3464 Starr Ave., 43616
Founded in: 1963
Questionnaire not received

OXFORD

Pioneer Farm and House Museum
Brown Rd.
Mail to: 6295 Timothy Lane, 45056
Private agency, authorized by Oxford
Museum Association
Founded in: 1959
Richard McSollmann, Association
President
Number of members: 110
Staff: volunteer 25
Major programs: museum,
tours/pilgrimages, exhibits
Period of collections: 1830-1880

**William E. and Ophia D. Smith
Library of Regional History**
15 S. College Ave., 45056
Telephone: (513) 523-3035
County agency, authorized by Lane
Public Library, Hamilton
Founded in: 1981
Irene M. Lindsey, Acting Director
Staff: part time 2, volunteer 6
Major programs: library, archives,
manuscripts, historic site(s),
markers, book publishing,
research, exhibits, audiovisual
programs, photographic
collections, genealogical services
Period of collections: 1820-1900.

**William Holmes McGuffey House
Museum**
Oak and Spring, 45056
Telephone: (513) 529-4917/529-2232
Founded in: 1961
Questionnaire not received

PAINESVILLE

Lake County Genealogical Society
184 Phelps St., 44077
Telephone: (216) 352-3383
Private agency
Founded in: 1968
Ruth Rhinehart, President
Number of members: 110
Staff: volunteer 3
Major programs: library,
newsletters/pamphlets,
genealogical services
Period of collections: 1820-present

PARMA

Parma Area Historical Society
6975 Ridge Rd.
Telephone: (216) 845-9770
Mail to: P.O. Box 29002, 44129
Private agency, authorized by Parma
Area Historical Society
Founded in: 1972
Harvey A. Day, President
Number of members: 800
Staff: part time 1, volunteer 20
Major programs: library, archives,
museum, historic site(s), oral
history, newsletters/pamphlets,
historic preservation, research
Period of collections: 1880-1935

PENINSULA

**Peninsula Library and Historical
Society**
6105 Riverview Rd.
Telephone: (216) 657-2291
Mail to: P.O. Box 236, 44264
Edith M. Minns, Librarian/Director
Staff: full time 3, part time 4
Magazine: *Current Events &
Information*
Major programs: library
Period of collections: 1813-present

PERRYSBURG

Ft. Meigs State Memorial
Telephone: (419) 874-4121
Mail to: P.O. Box 3, 43551
Private agency, authorized by Ohio
Historical Society
Founded in: 1975
Larry L. Nelson, Site Manager
Staff: full time 3, part time 5,
volunteer 90
Major programs: museum, historic
site(s), research, living history,
archaeology programs
Period of collections: War of 1812

Historic Perrysburg, Inc.
420 E. Front St.
Telephone: (419) 874-2815
Mail to: P.O. Box 703, 43551
Private agency
Founded in: 1976
Peggy Orser, President
Number of members: 250
Staff: volunteer 40
Magazine: *The Broadside*
Major programs: junior history, oral
history, school programs, historic
preservation, research

PIKETON

South Central Ohio Preservation Society, Inc.
P.O. Box 6, 45661
Telephone: (614) 289-2147
Mail to: 122 S. Paint St., Chillicothe, 45601
Questionnaire not received

PIQUA

Piqua Historical Society
223 W. North St., 45356
Telephone: (513) 773-7098
Town agency
Founded in: 1976
James C. Oda, President
Number of members: 120
Staff: volunteer 4
Major programs: school programs, newsletters/pamphlets, historic preservation
Period of collections: 19th century

POMEROY

Meigs County Genealogical Society
34465 Crew Rd., 45769
Telephone: (614) 992-7874
Private agency
Founded in: 1979
Karen Werry, President
Number of members: 165
Magazine: *Megaphone*
Major programs: library, book publishing, newsletters/pamphlets, historic preservation, genealogical services
Period of collections: 1800-1910

Meigs County Pioneer and Historical Society, Inc.
144 Butternut Ave.
Telephone: (614) 992-3810
Mail to: P.O. Box 145, 45769
County agency
Founded in: 1876
Margaret Parker, President
Number of members: 100
Staff: part time 2, volunteer 3
Magazine: *The Meigs Historian*
Major programs: library, archives, museum, school programs, book publishing, newsletters/pamphlets, research, exhibits, genealogical services
Period of collections: mid 19th-early 20th centuries

PORT CLINTON

Ottawa County Historical Society
P.O. Box 385, 43452
Founded in: 1963
Questionnaire not received

PORTSMOUTH

Boneyfiddle Association
Rt. 6, Box 350, 45662
Telephone: (614) 456-4746
Town agency
Founded in: 1975
Major programs: historic preservation, arts and crafts fair

Southern Ohio Museum and Cultural Center
825 Gallia St.
Telephone: (614) 354-5629

Mail to: P.O. Box 990, 45662
Authorized by Southern Ohio Museum Corporation
Founded in: 1977
R. Matthew Neiburger, Director
Number of members: 700
Staff: full time 3, part time 2, volunteer 75
Major programs: museum, school programs, newsletters/pamphlets, exhibits

PUT-IN-BAY

Perry's Victory and International Peace Memorial
P.O. Box 549, 43456
Telephone: (419) 285-2184
Federal agency, authorized by National Park Service
Founded in: 1936
Harry C. Myers, Superintendent
Staff: full time 5, part time 2
Major programs: tours, oral history, historic preservation, research, living history
Period of collections: War of 1812

RAVENNA

Portage County Chapter, Ohio Genealogical Society
6252 N. Spring St., 44266
Telephone: (216) 296-9873
Founded in: 1972
Patti Harjung, President
Number of members: 50
Magazine: *Portage Path to Genealogy*
Major programs: markers, newsletters/pamphlets, research, genealogical services, indexing of county birth and death records
Period of collections: 19th-20th centuries

Portage County Historical Society, Inc.
6549 N. Chestnut St., 44266
Telephone: (216) 296-3523
Private agency
Founded in: 1951
Thomas Cadwallader, President
Number of members: 400
Staff: volunteer 16
Major programs: library, archives, museum, historic site(s), tours/pilgrimages, book publishing, newsletters/pamphlets, research, exhibits, archaeology programs, photographic collections, genealogical services
Period of collections: 19th century

Ravenna Heritage
223 North Ave., 44266
Telephone: (216) 296-3753
Private agency
Founded in: 1983
Mrs. E. A. Kyle, President
Number of members: 33
Staff: volunteer 4
Major programs: historic preservation

RITTMAN

Rittman Historical Society
133 Pinewood, 44270
Telephone: (216) 925-4656
Founded in: 1959
Questionnaire not received

ROCKY RIVER

Rocky River Historical Society
1600 Hampton Rd., 44116
Telephone: (216) 333-7610
Founded in: 1968
Charles S. Greanoff, President
Number of members: 230
Staff: volunteer 15
Major programs: markers, tours/pilgrimages, oral history, educational programs, newsletters/pamphlets
Period of collections: 1865-present

SALEM

Columbiana County Chapter, Ohio Genealogical Society
P.O. Box 681, 44460
County agency
Founded in: 1975
Linda McElroy, President
Number of members: 150
Magazine: *Columbiana County Connections*
Major programs: library, book publishing, genealogical services

Salem Historical Society & Museum
204 S. Broadway
Mail to: 836 S. Lincoln Ave., 44460
Private agency
Founded in: 1947
Richard Wooten, President
Number of members: 200
Staff: volunteer 50
Major programs: library, arhives, manuscripts, museum, historic site(s), markers, oral history, school programs, book publishing, newsletters, historic preservation, records management, research, exhibits, audiovisual programs, photographic collections, genealogical services, field services
Period of collections: 1806-present

SANDUSKY

Erie County Historical Society
c/o Sandusky Library, Adams St. at Columbus Ave., 44870
Private agency
Founded in: 1953
Janet A. Senne, President
Number of members: 95

Follett House Museum
404 Wayne St., 44870
Telephone: (419) 627-9608
Authorized by Sandusky Library
Founded in: 1976
Mrs. Tom Steinemann, House Chair
Staff: part time 5
Major programs: museum, school programs, newsletters/pamphlets, research, photographic collections, genealogical services
Period of collections: to 1900

Old House Guild of Sandusky
429 Lawrence St.
Telephone: (419) 625-9331
Mail to: P.O. Box 1464, 44870
Private agency
Founded in: 1979
Ellie Damm, President
Number of members: 100
Staff: volunteer 1

Major programs: markers,
tours/pilgrimages, school
programs, newsletters/pamphlets,
historic preservation, research,
photographic collections
Period of collections: 1827-1927

SHAKER HEIGHTS

**Shaker Historical Society and
Museum**
16740 S. Park Blvd., 44120
Telephone: (216) 921-1201
Private agency
Founded in: 1945
V. M. Atkinson, Curator
Number of members: 300
Staff: part time 1
Major programs: library, museum,
historic site(s)
Period of collections: 1810-1930

SHARON CENTER

Sharon Township Heritage Society
Telephone: (216) 336-3832
Mail to: P.O. Box 154, 44274
Private agency
Founded in: 1969
Robert J. Remark, President
Number of members: 35
Staff: volunteer 17
Major programs: historic sites
preservation
Period of collections: 1865-present

SHEFFIELD LAKE

**103rd Ohio Volunteer Infantry
Memorial Foundation**
5505 E. Lake Rd., 44054
Telephone: (216) 333-0656
Founded in: 1972
Questionnaire not received

SOLON

Solon Historical Society
33975 Bainbridge Rd., 44139
Telephone: (216) 248-5933
(president)
Private agency
Founded in: 1968
Elsie H. Kluter, President
Number of members: 155
Staff: volunteer 15
Major programs: museum, historic
site(s), oral history, school
programs, exhibits, audiovisual
programs, photographic
collections
Period of collections: 1850-1920

SOMERSET

Perry County Historical Society
104 S. Columbus, 43783
Telephone: (614) 743-2285
Founded in: 1968
Questionnaire not received

SOUTH CHARLESTON

Heritage Commission Corporation
112 Church St., 45368
Telephone: (513) 462-7236
Founded in: 1980
Questionnaire not received

SOUTH EUCLID

South Euclid Historical Society
7399 Tattersall Rd., 44026
Telephone: (216) 729-0161
Private agency
Founded in: 1966
Anthony Palermo, President
Number of members: 125
Staff: volunteer 20
Major programs: library, archives,
manuscripts, museum, historic
site(s), book publishing,
newsletters/pamphlets, historic
preservation, records
management, research, exhibits,
photographic collections
Period of collections: 1850-present

SPRINGFIELD

Clark County Historical Society
300 W. Main St., 45504
Telephone: (513) 324-0657
Founded in: 1897
Questionnaire not received

STEUBENVILLE

**Jefferson County Historical
Association and Genealogical
Library**
426 Franklin Ave., 43952
Telephone: (614) 283-1133
County agency
Founded in: 1973
Vivian Snyder, Museum Director
Number of members: 350
Staff: full time 2, part time 1,
volunteer 21
Major programs: library, archives,
manuscripts, museum, markers,
tours/pilgrimages, school
programs, book publishing,
newsletters/pamphlets, historic
preservation, research,
genealogical services
Period of collections: 1800-present

STRONGSVILLE

Strongsville Historical Society, Inc.
13305 Pearl Rd., 44136
Telephone: (216) 238-6769
Private agency
Founded in: 1962
Ray Dellner, President
Number of members: 160
Staff: volunteer 15
Major programs: museum, markers,
tours/pilgrimages, junior history,
newsletters/pamphlets, exhibits,
audiovisual programs

STOW

Stow Historical Society
Young Rd.
Telephone: (216) 688-1708
Mail to: P.O. Box 1425, 44224
City agency
Founded in: 1949
Dean Martin, President
Number of members: 268
Staff: volunteer 20
Major programs: museum, tours,
junior history, school programs,
newsletters/pamphlets, historic
preservation, genealogical
services
Period of collections: 1804-present

SUGARCREEK

Alpine Hills Historical Museum
106 W. Main St.
Telephone: (216) 852-2223/852-4113
Mail to: P.O. Box 1776, 44681
Private agency, authorized by Alpine
Hills Historical Society
Founded in: 1976
Leslie A. Kaser, Curator
Number of members: 131
Staff: full time 1, volunteer 75
Major programs: museum, book
publishing, newsletters/pamphlets,
historic preservation, records
management, exhibits, audiovisual
programs
Period of collections: 1880-1920

Ragersville Historical Society, Inc.
Telephone: (216) 343-4072
Mail to: 1924 Dover Ave., Dover,
44622
Founded in: 1979
Questionnaire not received

TIFFIN

Seneca County Historical Society
Telephone: (419) 447-5955
Mail to: P.O. Box 253, 44883
Questionnaire not received

Seneca County Museum
28 Clay St., 44883
Telephone: (419) 447-5955
County agency
Founded in: 1938
Rosalie Adams, Director
Staff: full time 1, part time 1,
volunteer 18
Major programs: tours/pilgrimages,
junior history, oral history, school
programs, book publishing, historic
preservation, photographic
collections, genealogical services
Period of collections: 18th century

Tiffin Historic Trust
Mail to: P.O. Box 333, 44883
Private agency
Jane Hossler, President
Number of members: 125
Staff: volunteer 15
Magazine: *Preservation Post*
Major programs: library, archives,
markers, tours/pilgrimages, school
programs, newsletters/pamphlets,
historic preservation, exhibits,
audiovisual programs,
photographic collections
Period of collections: 1870-1910

TIPP CITY

Miami County Historical Society
P.O. Box 407, 45371
Telephone: (513) 667-4936/667-6102
County agency
Founded in: 1950
Harold Baker, Sr., President
Number of members: 100
Staff: volunteer 5
Major programs: tours/pilgrimages,
oral history, book publishing,
newsletters/pamphlets

**Studebaker Family National
Association**
6555 S. State Rt. 202, 45371
Private agency

Founded in: 1964
D. Emmert Studebaker, President
Number of members: 1,600
Staff: full time 1, volunteer 20
Magazine: *The Studebaker Family*
Major programs: library, archives, manuscripts, museum, markers, books, newsletters/pamphlets, genealogy
Period of collections: 1492-1600

TOLEDO

American Society for Legal History
Telephone: (419) 537-4177
Mail to: Toledo College of Law, 43606
Founded in: 1956
Questionnaire not received

Local History and Genealogy Department, Toledo-Lucas County Public Library
325 Michigan St., 43624
Telephone: (419) 255-7055
County agency
Founded in: 1941
James C. Marshall, Department Head
Staff: full time 5, part time 5
Major programs: library, archives, manuscripts, oral history, research, audiovisual programs, photographic collections, genealogical services

Toledo Firefighter Museum, Inc.
918 Sylvania, 43616
Telephone: (419) 478-3473
Private agency
Founded in: 1976
Robert J. Wuest, President
Number of members: 100
Staff: volunteer 50
Major programs: library, archives, museum, tours/pilgrimages, school programs, historic preservation, records management, exhibits, audiovisual programs, photographic collections
Period of collections: 1850-1950

Ward M. Canaday Center
University of Toledo, 43606
Telephone: (419) 537-2443
State agency
Founded in: 1979
Joel F. Wurl, Archivist
Staff: full time 3, part time 9
Major programs: library, archives, manuscripts, oral history, records management, exhibits, photographic collections
Period of collections: 1900-present

TROY

Brukner Nature Center
5995 Horseshoe Bend Rd., 45373
Telephone: (513) 698-6493
Private agency
Founded in: 1967
Robert F. Heidelberg, Operations Director
Staff: full time 7, part time 4, volunteer 75
Magazine: *Grey Fox Gazette*
Major programs: historic site(s), tours/pilgrimages, school programs, living history, natural history
Period of collections: 1825

Great Miami River Corridor Committee of Miami and Shelby Counties, Inc.
Great Miami Corridor Safety Bldg., 45373
Telephone: (513) 335-8341
County agency
Founded in: 1975
Deb Millhouse, Director
Staff: full time 3
Magazine: *The Cry of the Crane*
Major programs: library, archives, museum, historic site(s), markers, tours, oral history, school programs, book publishing, newsletters/pamphlets, historic preservation, research

Troy Historical Society
301 W. Main St., 45373
Telephone: (513) 339-0457
Founded in: 1965
Questionnaire not received

TWINSBURG

Twinsburg Historical Society
Darrow Rd.
Telephone: (216) 425-2571
Mail to: P.O. Box 7, 44087
Private agency
Founded in: 1963
Lea M. Bissell, President
Number of members: 100
Staff: volunteer 6
Major programs: museum, school programs, book publishing, newsletters/pamphlets, photographic collections
Period of collections: 1800-1900

URBANA

Champaign County Historical Society
809 E. Lawn Ave., 43078
Telephone: (513) 653-6721
Founded in: 1934
Questionnaire not received

VALLEY CITY

Liverpool Township Historical Society
Center Rd.
Telephone: (216) 483-3994
Mail to: P.O. Box 399, 44280
Town agency
Founded in: 1976
La Verne Tolsma, President
Number of members: 60
Staff: volunteer 7
Major programs: museum, historic preservation
Period of collections: 1870s

VAN WERT

Van Wert County Historical Society
602 N. Washington St.
Mail to: P.O. Box 621, 45891
County agency
Jeanne Dineen, President
Number of members: 164
Staff: volunteer 18
Major programs: museum, newsletters/pamphlets, historic preservation, exhibits, genealogical services
Period of collections: 1800s-1900s

VERMILION

Great Lakes Historical Society
480 Main St., 44089
Telephone: (216) 967-3467
Private agency
Founded in: 1944
Alexander C. Meakin, President
Number of members: 3,000
Staff: full time 4, part time 4, volunteer 25
Magazine: *Inland Seas*
Major programs: library, archives, museum, oral history, book publishing, newsletters/pamphlets, records management, exhibits, living history, audiovisual programs, photographic collections
Period of collections: 1750-present

Lorain County Chapter, Ohio Genealogy Society
Telephone: (216) 967-7158
Mail to: P.O. Box 39, 44089
Founded in: 1982
Mary Mulligan Konik, Secretary
Number of members: 82
Staff: volunteer 4
Magazine: *Lorain County Researcher*
Major programs: genealogical services

WARREN

Trumbull County Chapter, Ohio Genealogy Society
P.O. Box 309, 44482
County agency
Founded in: 1969

Trumbull County Historical Society
309 South St., SE, 44483
Telephone: (216) 394-4653
Founded in: 1938
Questionnaire not received

WASHINGTON COURT HOUSE

Fayette County Genealogical Society
c/o Executive Secretary, 144½ S. Fayette St.
Telephone: (614) 335-0266
Mail to: P.O. Box 342, 43160
Founded in: 1981
Sandy Fackler, Executive Secretary
Number of members: 285
Staff: volunteer 9
Magazine: *The Fayette Connection*
Major programs: library, book publishing, newsletters/pamphlets, genealogical services

Fayette County Historical Society
517 Columbus Ave., 43160
Telephone: (614) 335-0788
Private agency
Founded in: 1947
Carol A. Witherspoon, Curator
Number of members: 520
Staff: part time 1, volunteer 35
Major programs: museum, school programs, audiovisual programs
Period of collections: 1880-1920

WAUSEON

Fulton County Historical Society
229 Monroe St., 43567
Telephone: (419) 335-7489
Questionnaire not received

WAVERLY

Pike Heritage Museum
211 W. North St.
Telephone: (614) 947-5281
Mail to: P.O. Box 663, 45690
Private agency, authorized by Pike
Heritage Foundation
Founded in: 1983
Luticia A. Minter, Director
Number of members: 400
Staff: full time 1, volunteer 35
Major programs: museum, school
programs, historic preservation,
exhibits, archaeology programs,
photographic collections
Period of collections: 1796-present

WELLINGTON

**Southern Lorain County Historical
Society**
201 N. Main St.
Telephone: (216) 647-4531/647-4367
Mail to: 292 Grand Ave., 44090
Founded in: 1968
Ernst L. Henes, Director
Number of members: 266
Staff: volunteer 12
Major programs: manuscripts,
museum, markers, educational
programs, books
Period of collections: 1818-present

WELLSVILLE

Wellsville Historical Society
1003 Riverside
Mail to: P.O. Box 13, 43968
Founded in: 1952
Questionnaire not received

WESTERVILLE

Amalthea Historical Society
c/o President, 3791 Dempsey Rd.,
43081
Telephone: (614) 891-6363
Private agency
Founded in: 1977
Fred J. Milligan, Jr., President
Number of members: 75
Major programs: library, archives,
manuscripts, markers,
tours/pilgrimages
Period of collections: 1810-1900

Westerville Historical Society
c/o President, 111 W. Park, 48081
Telephone: (614) 882-3856
Private agency
Founded in: 1946
Number of members: 204
Staff: volunteer 30
Major programs: archives, museum,
historic site(s), markers,
tours/pilgrimages, oral history,
school programs, book publishing,
newsletters/pamphlets, historic
preservation, audiovisual programs

WEST LIBERTY

**Castle Piatt
Mac-A-Cheek/Mac-Ochee Castle**
Telephone: (513) 465-2821
Mail to: 10052 Rt. 47, 43357
Private agency, authorized by Piatt
Castles Corporation
Founded in: 1947

William Piatt II, Director
Major programs: archives, museum,
tours, school programs, historic
preservation, exhibits,
photographic collections,
genealogical services
Period of collections: 1828-1895

WEST UNION

**Adams County Genealogical
Society, Inc.**
P.O. Box 213, 45693
Telephone: (513) 444-3521
Founded in: 1979
Betty Lathrop, President
Number of members: 345
Staff: volunteer 8
Magazine: *Our Heritage*
Major programs: library, archives,
junior history, book publishing,
newsletters/pamphlets, research,
exhibits, audiovisual programs,
genealogical services
Period of collections: 1796-present

WICKLIFFE

Wickliffe Historical Society, Inc.
900 Worden Rd., Room 107
Telephone: (216) 943-1134
Mail to: P.O. Box 134, 44092-0134
Private agency
Founded in: 1980
Richard Pochervina, President
Number of members: 125
Staff: volunteer 20
Magazine: *The Wick Leaf*
Major programs: library, archives,
manuscripts, historic site(s), oral
history, newsletters/pamphlets,
historic preservation, research,
exhibits, audiovisual programs,
photographic collections
Period of collections: 1817-present

WILLARD

Willard Area Historical Society
818 S. Main St., 44890
Telephone: (419) 935-0600
Private agency
Founded in: 1975
John Leitz, President
Number of members: 118
Staff: volunteer 2
Major programs: archives, museum,
oral history, newsletters/pamphlets,
historic preservation, research,
exhibits, archaeology programs,
photographic collections,
genealogical services
Period of collections: 1875-present

WILMINGTON

Clinton County Historical Society
149 E. Locust St.
Telephone: (513) 382-4684
Mail to: P.O. Box 529, 45177
Private agency
Founded in: 1949
Karen Gano, Curator
Number of members: 425
Staff: part time 2, volunteer 60
Major programs: library, archives,
museum, markers, junior history,
school programs, book publishing,
newsletters/pamphlets, historic

preservation, research, exhibits,
photographic collections,
genealogical services
Period of collections: 19th-20th
centuries

Organ Historical Society, Inc.
Telephone: (617) 791-2169
Mail to: P.O. Box 209, 45177
Founded in: 1956
Questionnaire not received

WILMOT

**Wilmot Area Historical, Research
and Restoration Association, Inc.**
Massillon St., 44689
Private agency
Founded in: 1975
Hubert Bair, President
Number of members: 10-30
Major programs: museum
Period of collections: 1830-1930

WOODSFIELD

Monroe County Historical Society
Telephone: (614) 472-1933
Mail to: P.O. Box 538, 43793
Private agency
Founded in: 1974
Carolyn Zogg Wolf, President
Number of members: 400
Staff: volunteer 20
Major programs: library, archives,
manuscripts, museum, historic
site(s), markers, tours/pilgrimages,
school programs, book publishing,
newsletters/pamphlets,
photographic collections,
genealogical services
Period of collections: 1798-present

WOOSTER

**Archaeological Committee, Wayne
County Historical Society**
3546 E. Bowman St.
Telephone: (216) 264-8856/262-0112
Mail to: 755 Western Dr., 44691
Private agency
Founded in: 1973
Roger Rowe, Chair
Number of members: 6
Staff: volunteer 6
Major programs: records
management, research,
archaeology programs, field
services
Period of collections: prehistoric

Wayne County Historical Society
546 E. Bowman St.
Telephone: (216) 264-8856
Private agency
Founded in: 1954
Patricia R. Crook, Executive
Secretary
Number of members: 650
Staff: part time 2, volunteer 60
Major programs: museum, school
programs, historic preservation
Period of collections: 1803-1903

WORTHINGTON

Ohio Railway Museum
990 Proprietors Rd.
Telephone: (614) 885-7345
Mail to: P.O. Box 171, 43085
Private agency

Founded in: 1947
Douglas R. Kruest, President
Number of members: 189
Staff: volunteer 15
Magazine: *East Bound-West Bound*
Major programs: operating railway
and trolley demonstration
Period of collections: 1895-1948

Worthington Historical Society
965 N. High St.
Telephone: (614) 885-1247
Mail to: P.O. Box 355, 43085
Founded in: 1955
Questionnaire not received

WRIGHT-PATTERSON AIR FORCE
BASE

U.S. Air Force Museum
45433-6518
Telephone: (513) 255-3284
Federal agency, authorized by the
U.S. Air Force
Founded in: 1923
Richard L. Uppstrom, Director
Staff: full time 65, volunteer 175
Major programs: archives, museum,
school programs
Period of collections: 1903-present

WYOMING

Ohio Covered Bridge Committee
18 Elm Ave., 45215
Telephone: (513) 761-1789
State agency
Founded in: 1940
John A. Diehl, Chair
Staff: volunteer 34
Major programs: library, archives,
historic site(s), historic
preservation, photographic
collections
Period of collections: 1800-1920

XENIA

**Greene County Chapter, Ohio
Genealogical Society**
P.O. Box 706, 45385
Telephone: (513) 376-2995
Private agency
Founded in: 1980
Sharon Compton, President
Number of members: 170
Staff: volunteer 170
Magazine: *Leaves of Greene*
Major programs: library, archives,
manuscripts, oral history, book
publishing, newsletters/pamphlets,
research, living history,
photographic collections,
genealogical services
Period of collections: 19th-20th
centuries

Greene County Historical Society
74 W. Church St., 45385
Telephone: (513) 372-8644
Founded in: 1931
Edwin A. Wolf, President
Number of members: 450
Staff: full time 1, part time 1
Magazine: *Our Heritage*
Major programs: museum, historic
sites preservation,
tours/pilgrimages, books, historic
preservation
Period of collections: 1797

YELLOW SPRINGS

Yellow Springs Historical Society
405 Corry St.
Telephone: (513) 767-7375
Mail to: P.O. Box 501, 45387
Private agency
Founded in: 1985
Mary Morgan, Statutory Agent
Major programs: markers,
tours/pilgrimages, oral history,
newsletters/pamphlets,
photographic collections

YOUNGSTOWN

Mahoning Valley Historical Society
648 Wick Ave., 44502-1289
Telephone: (216) 743-2589
Private agency
Founded in: 1875
Patricia W. Cummins, Director
Number of members: 630
Staff: full time 6, part time 35,
volunteer 6
Magazine: *Historical Happenings in
the Mahoning Valley*
Major programs: library, archives,
manuscripts, museum, school
programs, newsletters/pamphlets,
records management, exhibits,
photographic collections
Period of collections: 1796-present

St. Ephrem Educational Center
1555 Meridian Rd., 44511
Telephone: (216) 792-2371
Private agency
Founded in: 1977
Dominic Ashkar, Pastor
Major programs: library, manuscripts,
oral history, educational programs,
newsletters/pamphlets, Maronite
history
Period of collections: 1910-present

ZANESVILLE

**Muskingum County Genealogical
Society**
Ohio University Library
Mail to: P.O. Box 3066, 43701
Private agency
Founded in: 1975
Franklin Rich, President
Number of members: 450
Magazine: *Muskingum*
Major programs: library, archives,
manuscripts,
newsletters/pamphlets, research,
genealogical services
Period of collections: 19th-20th
centuries

**Pioneer and Historical Society of
Muskingum County**
304 Woodlawn Ave., 43701
Private agency
James Jordan, President
Number of members: 500
Staff: part time 1
Major programs: museum, historic
site(s), tours/pilgrimages,
newsletters/pamphlets, exhibits,
audiovisual programs

ZOAR

Zoar Village State Memorial
Main St.
Telephone: (216) 874-3011

Mail to: P.O. Box 404, 44697
State agency, authorized by Ohio
Historical Society
Founded in: 1933
Persijs Kolberg, Sites Manager
Staff: full time 4, part time 12
Major programs: museum,
tours/pilgrimages, school
programs, historic preservation,
research, audiovisual programs
Period of collections: 1817-1898

OKLAHOMA

ADA

**Pontotoc County Historical and
Genealogical Society**
221 W. 16th St., 74820
Founded in: 1967
Questionnaire not received

ALINE

Sod House
Rt. 1, 73716
Telephone: (405) 463-2441
State agency, authorized by
Oklahoma Historical Society
Founded in: 1968
Erma Hunter, Site Attendant
Staff: full time 1
Major programs: historic site(s),
exhibits
Period of collections: 1889-1910

ALTUS

Museum of the Western Prairie
1100 N. Hightower
Telephone: (405) 482-1044
Mail to: P.O. Box 574, 73521
State agency, authorized by
Oklahoma Historical Society
Founded in: 1970
Loweta Chesser, Supervisor
Number of members: 300
Staff: full time 3, part time 1,
volunteer 5
Major programs: library, archives,
museum, oral history, school
programs, exhibits, audiovisual
programs, photographic
collections
Period of collections: 1850-1930

**Western Trail Historical and
Genealogical Society**
1100 N. Hightower
Telephone: (405) 482-1044
Mail to: P.O. Box 574, 73521
Private agency
Founded in: 1966
Octava Felty, President
Number of members: 350
Staff: volunteer 14
Major programs: library, archives,
museum, oral history, photographic
collections
Period of collections: 1870-1940

ALVA

Cherokee Strip Museum of Alva
901 14th St., 73717
Telephone: (405) 327-2030

Private agency
Founded in: 1961
Mrs. N. J. Strasbaugh, President
Number of members: 174
Staff: full time 1, part time 2,
  volunteer 72
Major programs: museum, historic
  preservation, exhibits,
  photographic collections
Period of collections: early 1900s

ANADARKO

Anardarko Philomathic Museum
311 E. Main St., 73005
Telephone: (405) 247-3240
City agency
Founded in: 1936
Laveta Cash, Curator
Number of members: 40
Staff: part time 1, volunteer 10
Major programs: museum, historic
  preservation, records
  management, photographic
  collections
Period of collections: pioneer-early
  1900s

Indian City U.S.A., Inc.
P.O. Box 695, 73005
Telephone: (405) 247-5661
Private agency
Founded in: 1955
John P. Buzbee, President
Staff: full time 15, part time 35
Major programs: museum, historic
  site(s), tours/pilgrimages, oral
  history, newsletters/pamphlets,
  exhibits

ARDMORE

Ardmore Public Library
Grand at East St., NW, 73401
Telephone: (405) 223-8290
City agency
Founded in: 1906
Carolyn J. Franks, Director
Staff: full time 12
Major programs: library

ATOKA

Atoka County Historical Society
306 W. 3rd St., 74525
Telephone: (405) 889-2470
Founded in: 1969
Questionnaire not received

BARTLESVILLE

Frank Phillips Home
1107 S. Cherokee, 74003
Telephone: (918) 336-2491
State agency, authorized by
  Oklahoma Historical Society
Founded in: 1973
Norma F. Hettick, Curator
Staff: full time 2
Major programs: historic sites
  preservation
Period of collections: 1930-1931

**Washington County Historical
Society, Inc.**
Telephone: (918) 333-0073
Mail to: P.O. Box 255, 74003
Private agency
Founded in: 1964
Robert Finney, President

Number of members: 300
Staff: volunteer 10
Major programs: museum, markers,
  tours/pilgrimages, oral history,
  newsletters/pamphlets
Period of collections: 1880-present

Woolaroc
Rt. 3, 74003
Telephone: (918) 336-6747
Founded in: 1929
Questionnaire not received

BEAVER

**Beaver County Historical
Society, Inc.**
Beaver County Courthouse, 73932
Telephone: (405) 625-4726
Questionnaire not received

BLACKWELL

**Top of Oklahoma Historical
Society—Cherokee Outlet
Museum**
300 S. Main St.
Telephone: (405) 363-0209
Mail to: P.O. Box 108, 74631
Founded in: 1972
Ocie Anderson, Director
Number of members: 500
Staff: volunteer 20
Major programs: museum, historic
  site(s), markers, historic
  preservation, exhibits,
Period of collections: 1890-1925

CADDO

**Caddo Indian Territory Museum
and Library**
110 Buffalo
Telephone: (405) 367-2580
Mail to: P.O. Box 274, 74729
Founded in: 1976
Mrs. T. M. Markham, Curator
Number of members: 52
Staff: volunteer 18
Major programs: library, archives,
  manuscripts, museum, historic
  sites preservation, markers,
  educational programs, historic
  preservation
Period of collections: 1850-present

CAMARGO

Dewey County Historical Society
Rt. 1, Box 53, 73835
Telephone: (405) 328-5623
County agency
Founded in: 1973
Woodrow Gore, Past President
Major programs: oral history, book
  publishing
Period of collections: 1892-1900s

CHEROKEE

Alfalfa County Historical Society
300 W. Main St.
Mail to: P.O. Box 201, 73728
Founded in: 1974
Mildred Fisher, President
Number of members: 79
Staff: volunteer 10
Major programs: museum
Period of collections: 1893-1950

CHICKASHA

Grady County Historical Society
Mail to: P.O. Box 495, 73023
Private agency
Major programs: museum
Period of collections: late
  1890s-present

CLAREMORE

Will Rogers Memorial
W. Will Rogers Blvd.
Telephone: (918) 341-0719
Mail to: P.O. Box 157, 74018
State agency
Founded in: 1938
Reba Collins, Director
Number of members: 3
Staff: full time 12, part time 2
Major programs: library, archives,
  manuscripts, museum, research,
  photographic collections
Period of collections: 1900-1935

CLINTON

Western Trails Museum
2229 Gray Freeway
Telephone: (405) 323-1020
Mail to: P.O. Box 145, 73601
Founded in:. 1967
Questionnaire not received

CORDELL

Washita County Historical Society
105 E. 1st St.
Telephone: 405) 343-2554
Mail to: P.O. Box 440, 73632
Founded in: 1973
Questionnaire not received

DAVIS

Arbuckle Historical Society
12 W. Main St.
Telephone: (405) 369-3721
Mail to: P.O. Box 834, 73030
Private agency
Founded in: 1976
Gary Schilling, President
Number of members: 35
Staff: volunteer 35
Major programs: library, archives,
  manuscripts, museum, book
  publishing, newsletters/pamphlets,
  research, exhibits, photographic
  collections, genealogical services
Period of collections: 1889-present

DEWEY

Tom Mix Museum
721 N. Delaware, 74029
Telephone: (918) 534-1555
State agency, authorized by
  Oklahoma Historical Society
Founded in: 1973
Mary McHargue, Site Attendant
Staff: full time 1
Major programs: museum,
  tours/pilgrmages, exhibits,
  audiovisual programs,
  photographic collections
Period of collections: 1900-1930

DRUMRIGHT

Drumright Community Historical Society, Inc.
Broadway and Harley Sts.
Telephone: (918) 352-2898
Mail to: 118 S. Creek, 74030
Founded in: 1965
Questionnaire not received

DUNCAN

Stephens County Historical Museum
Fuqua Park, Box 1294, 73533
Telephone: (405) 252-0717
Founded in: 1970
Questionnaire not recieved

DURANT

Ft. Washita
Star Rt. 213, 7470
Telephone: (405) 924-6502
State agency, authorized by
Oklahoma Historical Society
Founded in: 1962
James Fricke, Field Museum
Supervisor
Staff: full time 3
Major programs: museum
Period of collections: 1840-1870

Red River Valley Historical Association
Southeastern Oklahoma State
University, 74701
Telephone: (405) 924-0121, ext. 203
Founded in: 1973
Questionnaire not received

EL RENO

Canadian County Historical Society
600 W. Wade, 73036
Telephone: (405) 262-5121
Founded in: 1968
Questionnaire not received

ENID

Museum of the Cherokee Strip
507 S. 4th St., 73701
Telephone: (405) 237-1907
State agency, authorized by
Oklahoma Historical Society
Founded in: 1976
Fran Nulph, Curator I
Staff: full time 2
Major programs: museum, exhibits,
audiovisual programs,
photographic collections
Period of collections: 1865-1940

FORT GIBSON

Ft. Gibson Military Park
110 E. Ash Ave.
Telephone: (918) 478-2669
Mail to: P.O. Box 457, 74434
State agency, authorized by
Oklahoma Historical Society
Founded in: 1936
Donald H. Westfall, Curator
Staff: full time 3, volunteer 1
Major programs: museum, historic
site(s), markers, tours/pilgrimages,
historic preservation, research,
exhibits, living history, audiovisual
programs
Period of collections: 1824-1890

FORT SILL

U.S. Army Field Artillery and Ft. Sill Museum
437 Quanah Rd., 73503-5000
Telephone: (405) 351-5123
Founded in: 1934
Ronald L. Stewart, Director
Staff: full time 9, volunteer 47
Major programs: library, museum,
historic preservation, exhibits,
audiovisual programs,
photographic collections
Period of collections: 1870-present

FT. TOWSON

Ft. Towson Historic Site
HC-65, Box 5, 74735
Telephone: (405) 873-2634
State agency, authorized by
Oklahoma Historical Society
Founded in: 1968
William Vandever, Historic Property
Manager I
Staff: full time 3
Major programs: historic site(s)
Period of collections: 1824-1865

GAGE

Ellis County Historical Society
R.R. 2, Box 14, 73843
Telephone: (405) 938-2151
County agency
Bonnie Brown, President
Major programs: historic site(s),
markers, book publishing, historic
preservation

GATE

GATEway to the Panhandle
Main St.
Mail to: P.O. Box 27, 73844
Founded in: 1975
L. E. Maphet, President
Staff: volunteer 1
Major programs: library, manuscripts,
museum, historic site(s),
tours/pilgrimages, historic
preservation, exhibits, living history
Period of collections: Civil War-early
1900s

GEARY

Canadian Rivers Historical Society
R.P. 1, Box 135, 73040
Private agency
Carla S. Burns, President
Number of members: 25
Staff: volunteer 2
Major programs: museum, historic
site(s), markers, historic
preservation, photographic
collections
Period of collections: 1900-1940

GOODWELL

No Man's Land Historical Society and Museum
Sewell St.
Mail to: P.O. Box 278, 73939
Telephone: (405) 349-2670
State agency, authorized by
Oklahoma Historical Society
Founded in: 1934
Barbara Joan Kachel, Curator

Number of members: 140
Staff: full time 1, part time 1,
volunteer 1
Major programs: library, archives,
manuscripts, museum, oral history,
exhibits
Period of collections: 1880-1970

GUTHRIE

Logan County Historical Society
107 E. Oklahoma
Telephone: (405) 282-3706
Mail to: P.O. Box 1280, 73044
Private agency
Founded in: 1974
Susan Guthrie, Executive Director
Number of members: 155
Staff: full time 1, part time 1
Major programs: markers, historic
preservation, audiovisual programs
Period of collections: 1889-1910

Oklahoma Territorial Museum
402 E. Oklahoma Ave., 73044
Telephone: (405) 282-1889
State agency, authorized by
Oklahoma Historical Society
Founded in: 1968
Clifton Chappell, Curator II
Staff: full time 3
Major programs: museum,
tours/pilgrimages, school
programs, research, exhibits,
audiovisual programs,
photographic collections
Period of collections: 1866-1907

State Capital Publishing Museum
301 W. Harrison, 73044
Telephone: (405) 282-4123
State agency, authorized by
Oklahoma Historical Society
Founded in: 1975
Keith Tolman, Curator I
Staff: full time 2
Major programs: historic site(s),
tours/pilgrimages, exhibits,
photographic collections
Period of collections: 1889-1911

HEALDTON

Healdton Oil Museum
315 W. Main St., 73438
Telephone: (405) 229-0317
State agency, authorized by
Oklahoma Historical Society
Founded in: 1980
Jim Phelan, Historic Property
Manager I
Staff: full time 1
Major programs: museum, exhibits
Period of collections: 1900-1970

HEAVENER

Heavener Runestone Recreation Area
Rt. 1, Box 74-G, 74937
Telephone: (918) 653-2241
State agency, authorized by Tourism
and Recreation Department
Founded in: 1967
Eddie Hurst, Park Supervisor
Staff: full time 3, part time 1
Major programs: historic site(s)
Period of collections: Viking
exploration era

Peter Conser House
Star Rt., Box 101, 74937
Telephone:(918) 653-2493
State agency, authorized by
  Oklahoma Historical Society
Founded in: 1967
R. L. Crawford, Historic Property
  Manager I
Staff: full time 1
Major programs: historic site(s),
  tours/pilgrimages

HOMINY

Drummond Home
305 N. Price, 74035
Telephone: (918) 385-2374
State agency, authorized by
  Oklahoma Historical Society
Founded in: 1981
Shirley Pettengill, Curator II
Staff: full time 1
Major programs: historic site(s),
  historic preservation
Period of collections: 1913-1919

IDABEL

Museum of the Red River
812 E. Lincoln, 74745
Telephone: (405) 286-3616
Town agency, authorized by Herron
  Research Foundation, Inc.
Founded in: 1974
Mary Herron, Director
Staff: full time 2, part time 1
Major programs: museum, research,
  archaeology programs
Period of collections: prehistoric

KINGFISHER

**Chisholm Trail Museum &
  Governor Seay Mansion**
605 Zellars Ave., 73750
Telephone: (405) 375-5176
Questionnaire not received

LAWTON

Lawton Heritage Association
1006 S.W. 5th St.
Mail to: P.O. Box 311, 73502
Private agency
Founded in: 1971
Paul Fisher, President
Number of members: 200
Staff: volunteer 50
Magazine: *Newsletter of the Lawton
  Heritage Association*
Major programs: museum, historic
  site(s), school programs, historic
  preservation
Period of collections: 1901-1935

Lawton Public Library
110 S.W. 4th St., 73501
Telephone: (405) 248-6287
City agency
Founded in: 1904
Marion F. Donaldson, Library Director
Staff: full time 15, part time 7,
  volunteer 14
Major programs: library, genealogical
  services

Museum of the Great Plains
601 Ferris
Telephone: (405) 353-5675
Mail to: P.O. Box 68, 73502

City agency, authorized by Institute of
  the Great Plains
Founded in: 1960
Steve Wilson, Director
Number of members: 750
Staff: full time 10, part time 2,
  volunteer 10
Magazine: *Great Plains Journal*
Major programs: library, archives,
  manuscripts, museum, oral history,
  school programs, book publishing,
  newsletters/pamphlets, research,
  exhibits, living history,
  photographic collections
Period of collections:
  prehistoric-1930s

**Southwest Oklahoma Genealogical
  Society**
P.O. Box 2882, 73502
Telephone: (405) 248-6287
Private agency
Founded in: 1976
Donna Irwin, President

LINDSAY

Murray Lindsay Mansion
R.R. 3, Box 119, 73052
Telephone: (405) 756-3826
State agency, authorized by
  Oklahoma Historical Society
Founded in: 1970
Paul Niblett, Historic Property Site
  Attendant
Staff: full time 1
Major programs: historic site(s)

MANGUM

**Old Greer County Museum and Hall
  of Fame, Inc.**
222 W. Jefferson, 73554
Telephone: (405) 782-2851
Founded in: 1973
Questionnaire not received

MEDFORD

Grant County Historical Society
124 N. Main, 73759
Questionnaire not received

MOUNTAIN PARK

Kiowa County Historical Society
Hobart Public Library, 73651
Telephone: (405) 726-2535
Mail to: P.O. Box 331, 73559
Questionnaire not received

MUSKOGEE

Bacone College Museum
E. Shawnee, 74401
Telephone: (918) 683-4581
Founded in: 1932
Questionnaire not received

Five Civilized Tribes Museum
Agency Hill, Honor Heights Dr.,
  74401
Telephone: (918) 683-1701
Private agency
Founded in: 1966
Mrs. Spencer Denton, Director
Number of members: 1,200
Staff: full time 6, part time 4,
  volunteer 150

Major programs: library, archives,
  manuscripts, museum, educational
  programs, newsletters/pamphlets,
  genealogical services
Period of collections: 1820-present

Muskogee War Memorial Park
2 Port Place, 74403
Telephone: (918) 682-6294
Mail to: P.O. Box 253, 74402
City agency
Newton C. Baker, Board Chair
Staff: full time 1, volunteer 20
Major programs: museum, historic
  site(s), markers
Period of collections: W.W. II-Vietnam

NEWKIRK

**Newkirk Community Historical
  Society**
101 S. Maple St.
Telephone: (405) 362-3330
Mail to: 500 W. 8th, 74647
Private agency
Founded in: 1968
Karen Dye, Board Member
Staff: part time 1, volunteer 12
Major programs: museum, historic
  site(s), school programs, exhibits,
  photographic collections
Period of collections: 1893-1945

NORMAN

**Cleveland County Historical
  Society**
508 N. Peters, 73069
Telephone: (405) 321-0156
Mail to: P.O. Box 260, 73070
Founded in: 1967
Questionnaire not received

**Norman and Cleveland County
  Historical Museum**
508 N. Peters
Telephone: (405) 321-0156
Mail to: P.O. Box 260, 73070
City and private agency
Founded in: 1973
Michael R. Sellon, Museum Director
Number of members: 300
Staff: full time 1, part time 6
Magazine: *The Round Tower*
Major programs: archives, museum,
  school programs,
  newsletters/pamphlets,
  photographic collections
Period of collections: to 1907

**Stovall Museum of Science and
  History**
University of Oklahoma, 1335 Asp
  Ave., 73019
Telephone: (405) 325-4712
State agency
Founded in: 1899
Michael A. Mares, Director
Number of members: 200
Staff: full time 11, part time 2
Major programs: museum, school
  programs, book publishing,
  newsletters/pamphlets, research,
  exhibits, audiovisual programs,
  archaeology programs, field
  services
Period of collections:
  prehistoric-present

OKLAHOMA CITY

Amateur Softball Association Museum
2801 N.E. 50th St., 73111
Telephone: (405) 424-5266
Private agency
Founded in: 1934
Don Porter, Executive Director
Staff: full time 20
Magazine: *Balls and Strikes*
Major programs: library, museum, tours/pilgrimages, newsletters/pamphlets, historic preservation, research, exhibits, audiovisual programs, photographic collections
Period of collections: from 1887

45th Infantry Division Museum
2145 N.E. 36th St., 73111
Telephone: (405) 424-5313
State agency
Founded in: 1976
Scott Wells, Curator
Staff: full time 1, part time 7, volunteer 45
Major programs: library, archives, manuscripts, museum, tours/pilgrimages, oral history, newsletters/pamphlets, historic preservation, records management, research, exhibits, audiovisual programs, photographic collections, theater
Period of collections: 1850-present

Heritage Hills Historical Preservation, Inc.
300 N.W. 17th St., 73103
Telephone: (405) 528-6866
Founded in: 1969
Questionnaire not received

National Cowboy Hall of Fame and Western Heritage Center
1700 N.E. 63rd St., 73111
Telephone: (405) 278-2250
Founded in: 1954
Questionnaire not received

National Softball Hall of Fame
2801 N.E. 50th
Telephone: (405) 424-5266
Mail to: P.O. Box 11437, 73111
Founded in: 1957
Questionnaire not received

Oklahoma City Historical Preservation and Landmark Commission
200 N. Walker Ave., 73102
Telephone: (405) 231-2417
Founded in: 1969
Questionnaire not received

Oklahoma County Historical Society
4300 N. Sewell, 73118
Telephone: (405) 521-1889
Private agency
Founded in: 1978
William D. Welge, President
Number of members: 324
Staff: volunteer 4
Major programs: library, archives, manuscripts, museum, historic site(s), markers, school programs, book publishing, newsletters/pamphlets, historic preservation, exhibits, audiovisual programs, photographic collections
Period of collections: 1830s-present

◇Oklahoma Heritage Association
201 N.W. 14th St., 73103
Telephone: (405) 235-4458
Founded in: 1927
Paul F. Lambert, Executive Director
Number of members: 2,600
Staff: full time 6, part time 3, volunteer 300
Magazine: *Oklahoma Heritage*
Major programs: library, archives, museum, markers, tours/pilgrimages, educational programs, books, newsletters/pamphlets
Period of collections: 1918-present

◇Oklahoma Historical Society
2100 N. Lincoln Blvd., 73105
Telephone: (405) 521-2491
Mail to: Wiley Post Historical Bldg., State Capitol Complex
State agency
Founded in: 1893
C. E. Metcalf, Executive Director
Number of members: 3,975
Staff: full time 107, part time 3, volunteer 35
Magazine: *The Chronicles of Oklahoma/Mistletoe Leaves*
Major programs: library, archives, manuscripts, museum, historic sites preservation, markers, oral history, educational programs, books, newsletters/pamphlets
Period of collections: 1800-present

Oklahoma Museums Association
Kirkpatrick Center, 2100 N.E. 52, 73111
Telephone: (405) 424-7757
Carolyn Pool, Director
Number of members: 80
Magazine: *Musenews*
Major programs: professional development services, administration of traveling exhibitions

◇Oklahoma State Museum
2100 N. Lincoln
Telephone: (405) 521-2491
Mail to: Historical Bldg., 73105
State agency, authorized by Oklahoma Historical Society
Founded in: 1893
Bill Pitts, Director/Curator
Number of members: 3,550
Staff: full time 3, part time 4, volunteer 4
Major programs: museum, school programs, newsletters/pamphlets, records management, research, exhibits, audiovisual programs
Period of collections: 1830-1970

Overholser Mansion
405 N.W. 15th St., 73103
Telephone: (405) 528-8485
State agency, authorized by Oklahoma Historical Society
Founded in: 1972
R. W. Jones, Curator II
Staff: full time 1
Major programs: historic site(s), tours/pilgrimages, exhibits
Period of collections: 1889-1910

PAWHUSKA

Osage County Historical Society
700 N. Lynn Ave., 74056
Telephone: (918) 287-9924
County agency
Founded in: 1964
Betty Smith, Director
Number of members: 100
Staff: full time 1, volunteer 3
Major programs: museum, book publishing
Period of collections: 1890-1930

PAWNEE

Oklahoma Steam Thresher Association
74058
Telephone: (918) 762-9911/762-2716
Private agency
Number of members: 110
Staff: volunteer 6
Major programs: museum, historic preservation, living history

Pawnee County Historical Society
P.O. Box 472, 74058
Telephone: (918) 762-2053
Private agency
Founded in: 1977
Dana Hicks, President
Number of members: 25
Major programs: markers, oral history, exhibits, photographic collections

PERRY

Cherokee Strip Museum
W. Fir Ave., 73077
Telephone: (405) 336-2405
State agency, authorized by Oklahoma Historical Society
Founded in: 1968
Ceilia M. Stratton, Curator
Staff: full time 2, part time 1, volunteer 15
Major programs: museum, school programs, research, exhibits, photographic collections
Period of collections: 1890-1920

PONCA CITY

Marland Mansion and Estate
901 Monument Rd., 74601
Telephone: (405) 765-2421
Founded in: 1975
Questionnaire not received

Pioneer Historical Society
P.O. Box 2577, 74601
Private agency
Founded in: 1972
Art Meibuhr, President
Number of members: 70
Major programs: library, markers, book publishing

Pioneer Woman Museum
701 Monument, 74604
Telephone: (405) 765-6108
State agency
Founded in: 1958
Jan Prough, Acting Curator
Staff: full time 3
Period of collections: 1893-1920s

Ponca City Cultural Center and Museums
1000 E. Grand, 74601
Telephone: (405) 765-5268
City agency
Founded in: 1967
La Wanda French, Supervisor
Staff: full time 2, part time 2
Period of collections: 1800-early 1900s

POTEAU

Eastern Oklahoma Historical Society
Kerr Museum, P.O. Box 387, 74953
Telephone: (918) 647-2756
Founded in: 1968
Questionnaire not received

PRYOR

Mayes County Historical Society, Inc./Coo-Y-Yah Country Museum
8th St. and S. 69 Hwy.
Telephone: (918) 476-5493/825-0789
Mail to: P.O. Box 969, 74362
County agency
Founded in: 1973
Cornelia Sifferman
Number of members: 200
Staff: volunteer 40
Major programs: library, museum, historic site(s), tours/pilgrimages, oral history book publishing, newsletters/pamphlets, historic preservation, exhibits, photographic collections
Period of collections: prehistoric-present

PURCELL

McClain County Historical Society and Museum
203 Washington St., 73080
Private agency
Founded in: 1973
Wesley Cavnar, President
Number of members: 58
Staff: part time 1, volunteer 10
Major programs: museum, newsletters/pamphlets, research, exhibits, genealogical services, publish county death records

RALSTON

White Hair Memorial
P.O. Box 185, 74650
Telephone: (918) 538-2417
State agency, authorized by Oklahoma Historical Society
Founded in: 1984
Dan Swan, Director
Staff: full time 1
Major programs: library, archives, manuscripts, research, photographic collections

SALLISAW

Sequoyah Home Site
Rt. 1, Box 141, 74955
Telephone: (918) 775-2413
State agency, authorized by Oklahoma Historical Society
Founded in: 1969

Dillard Jordan, Historic Property Site Attendant
Staff: full time 2
Major programs: historic site(s), tours/pilgrimages, historic preservation, research, exhibits, audiovisual programs
Period of collections: 1820

SAPULPA

Sapulpa Historical Society, Inc.
100 E. Lee
Telephone: (918) 224-4871
Mail to: P.O. Box 278, 74066
Private agency
Founded in: 1968
Houston Shirley, President
Number of members: 537
Staff: part time 1, volunteer 10
Major programs: library, archives, museum, tours/pilgrimages, oral history, newsletters/pamphlets, historic preservation, exhibits, photographic collections
Period of collections: 1865-1918

SHAWNEE

Historical Society of Pottawatomie County
1301 E. Farrall, 74801
Telephone: (405) 273-5062
Founded in: 1926
Questionnaire not received

Mabee-Gerrer Museum of Art
1900 W. MacArthur Dr., 74801
Telephone: (405) 273-9999
Private agency, authorized by St. Gregory Abbey and College
Founded in: 1904
John L. Walch, Director
Staff: full time 2, part time 3, volunteer 92
Major programs: museum, exhibits, fine art
Period of collections: 322 B.C.-present

Oklahoma Baptist Historical Society
1141 N. Robinson, Oklahoma City, 73103
Telephone: (405) 236-4341
Founded in: 1956
J. M. Gaskin, Archivist
Questionnaire not received

STILLWATER

Museum of Natural and Cultural History, Oklahoma State University
103 USDA Bldg., 74078
Telephone: (405) 624-6531
State agency
Founded in: 1966
Bryan P. Glass, Director
Staff: full time 2, part time 2
Major programs: manuscripts, museum, records management, exhibits, audiovisual programs, archaeology programs
Period of collections: 1900-present

Old Central Museum of Higher Education
Oklahoma State University, 74078
Telephone: (405) 624-3220

State agency, authorized by Oklahoma Historical Society
Founded in: 1982
James Showalter, Curator
Staff: full time 2, part time 2, volunteer 7
Major programs: museum, historic site(s), historic preservation, photographic collections
Period of collections: 1890-1920

Payne County Historical Society
P.O. Box 194, 74076
County agency
Founded in: 1980
Carol Borman, President
Number of members: 200
Magazine: *Payne County Historical Society*
Major programs: archives manuscripts historic site(s) markers, historic preservation
Period of collections: 1880-present

STILWELL

Adair County Cherokee Historical Society
Telephone: (918) 774-2159
Mail to: P.O. Box 226, 74960
Questionnaire not received

SWINK

Old Choctaw Chief's House
P.O. Box 165, 74761
Telephone: (405) 873-2492
State agency, authorized by Oklahoma Historical Society
Founded in: 1960
Gale Carter, Site Attendant
Staff: full time 1
Major programs: historic site(s), tours/pilgrimages
Period of collections: 1830

TAHLEQUAH

Cherokee National Historical Society, Inc.
Telephone: (918) 456-6007
Mail to: P.O. Box 515, Tsa-la-gi, 74465
Private agency
Founded in: 1963
Duane H. King, Executive Director
Number of members: 1,600
Staff: full time 10, part time 2
Magazine: *The Columns*
Major programs: library, archives, museum, historic sites preservation, educational programs
Period of collections: 1492-present

Murrell Home
Rt. 5, Box 212, 74464
Telephone: (918) 456-2751
State agency, authorized by Department of Tourism and Recreation
Founded in: 1948
Bruce Ross, Curator
Staff: full time 2, part time 4, volunteer 10
Major programs: historic preservation
Period of collections: 1830-1880

TISHOMINGO

**Chickasaw Council House Historic
Site**
Courthouse Square
Telephone: (405) 371-3351
Mail to: P.O. Box 717, 73460
State agency, authorized by
Oklahoma Historical Society
Founded in: 1969
Beverly J. Wyatt, Site Director/Curator
Staff: full time 2, volunteer 4
Magazine: *Oklahoma Chronicles*
Major programs: library, museum,
historic site(s), junior history, oral
history, school programs, historic
preservation, exhibits, living
history, photographic collections,
genealogical services
Period of collections: 1540-1920

**Johnston County Genealogical and
Historical Society**
308 E. 21st St., 73460
Telephone: (405) 371-3351
Private agency
Founded in: 1970
Mary Ann Park, President
Number of members: 150
Major programs: historic preservation
Period of collections: 1838-present

TONKAWA

Tonkawa Historical Society
P.O. Box 336, 74653
Telephone: (405) 628-2702
Founded in: 1972
Questionnaire not received

TULSA

**Thomas Gilcrease Institute of
American History and Art**
1400 Gilcrease Museum Rd.
Telephone: (918) 582-3122
City agency
Founded in: 1942
Fred A. Myers, Director
Number of members, 3,000
Staff: full time 21, part time 2,
volunteer 150
Magazine: *Gilcrease Magazine*
Major programs: library, archives,
manuscripts, museum, school
programs, newsletters/pamphlets,
research, genealogical services
Period of collections:
prehistoric-present

Tulsa County Historical Society
400 Civic Center, 74103
Telephone: (918) 592-7941/592-2595
City agency
Founded in: 1962
Nina Dunn, President
Number of members: 690
Staff: part time 2, volunteer 15
Major programs: library, archives,
manuscripts, museum, historic
sites preservation, markers, oral
history, newsletters/pamphlets,
photographic collections
Period of collections: 1865-present

**Tulsa County Historical Society
Museum**
2401 W. Newton, 74127
Telephone: (918) 592-2595
Mail to: P.O. Box 27303, 74149
Private agency, authorized by Tulsa
County Historical Society

Founded in: 1962
Robert N. Powers, Curator
Staff: full time 1, part time 1
Magazine: *Tulsa Journal*
Major programs: library, archives,
museum, historic site(s), markers,
tours/pilgrimages, oral history,
school programs,
newsletters/pamphlets, records
management, research, exhibits,
audiovisual programs,
photographic collections
Period of collections: early 20th
century

VINITA

Eastern Trails Museum, Inc.
215 W. Illinois
Mail to: P.O. Box 437, 74301
Founded in: 1969
O. B. Campbell, President
Staff: volunteer 9
Major programs: library, archives,
museum, historic site(s),
tours/pilgrimages, book publishing,
audiovisual programs,
photographic collections,
genealogical services
Period of collections: 1860-1940s

WAGONER

Oklahoma Historic Fashions, Inc.
810 N. State St.
Telephone: (918) 485-9111
Mail to: 802 N. Parkinson Ave., 74467
Private agency
Founded in: 1976
Nellie F. Harris, President
Staff: volunteer 10
Major programs: library, museum,
tours/pilgrimages, school
programs, newsletters/pamphlets,
historic preservation, records
management, research, exhibits,
photographic collections, large
fashion shows
Period of collections: 1851-1980

WATONGA

**Blaine County People and Place
History, Inc.**
104 E. Main, 73772
Telephone: (405) 623-4922
County agency
Founded in: 1979
Merle Rinehart, President
Number of members: 56
Major programs: photographic
collections
Period of collections: 1892-present

WAURIKA

**Chisholm Trail Historical Museum
Association**
Rt. 2, Box 124, 73573
Telephone: (405) 228-2166
State agency, authorized by
Oklahoma Historical Society
Founded in: 1974
Marjory Phelan, Historic Property Site
Attendant
Staff: full time 1
Major programs: museum,
tours/pilgrimages, exhibits
Period of collections: 1860-1920

WESTVILLE

**Goingsnake District Heritage
Association**
Westville John Henderson Library
Telephone: (918) 723-5002
Mail to: P.O. Box 180, 74965
Private agency
Founded in: 1979
Jack D. Baker, President
Number of members: 220
Staff: volunteer 6
Magazine: *The Goingsnake
Messenger*
Major programs: library, archives,
historic site(s), markers, oral
history, book publishing,
newsletters/pamphlets,
photographic collections,
genealogical services
Period of collections: 1835-1920

WEWOKA

Seminole Nation Historical Society
3524 S. Wewoka
Telephone: (405) 257-5580
Mail to: P.O. Box 1532, 74884
Private agency
Founded in: 1973
T. B. Miller, Director
Number of members: 300
Staff: full time 2, volunteer 30
Major programs: museum, exhibits,
genealogical services
Period of collections: 1832-1932

WILBURTON

Lutie Coal Miner's Museum
P.O. Box 456, 74578
Telephone: (918) 465-2216
Private agency
Founded in: 1983
Thomas L. Pate, Board Chair
Staff: volunteer 3
Major programs: museum, historic
site(s), historic preservation,
research, photographic collections
Period of collections: 1890-1930

WOODWARD

Pioneer Museum and Art Center
2009 Williams Ave., 73801
Telephone: (405) 256-6136
Mail to: P.O. Box 1167, 73802
Private agency, authorized by Plains
Indians and Pioneers Historical
Foundation
Founded in: 1966
Sarah Taylor, Director
Number of members: 400
Staff: full time 2, part time 1,
volunteer 42
Major programs: museum, school
programs, book publishing,
newsletters/pamphlets, exhibits,
photographic collections
Period of collections: 1805-1950s

**Plains Indians and Pioneer
Historical Foundation**
2009 Williams Ave.
Telephone: (405) 256-6136
Mail to: P.O. Box 1167, 73801
Founded in: 1954
Questionnaire not received

WYNNEWOOD

Wynnewood Historical Society
73098
Private agency
Gay Whitaker, Vice President
Number of members: 48
Major programs: museum, historic
preservation, photographic
collections

YALE

Jim Thorpe Home
706 E. Boston, 74085
Telephone: (918) 387-2815
State agency, authorized by
Oklahoma Historical Society
Founded in: 1973
Meredith Prough, Historic Property
Manager II
Staff: full time 1
Major programs: historic site(s)
Period of collections: 1920s

OREGON

ASHLAND

Ashland Historic Commission
20 E. Main St., 97520
Telephone: (503) 482-3211
Questionnaire not received

ASTORIA

Clatsop County Historical Society
1618 Exchange St., 97103
Telephone: (503) 325-2203
Private agency
Founded in: 1950
Stephen L. Recken, Director
Number of members: 750
Staff: full time 3, part time 2,
volunteer 60
Magazine: *Cumtux*
Major programs: museum, historic
site(s), tours/pilgrimages,
newsletters/pamphlets, historic
preservation, genealogical
services
Period of collections: 1810-1930

Columbia River Maritime Museum
1792 Marine Dr., 97103
Telephone: (503) 325-2323
Private agency
Founded in: 1962
Michael Naab, Director
Number of members: 2,000
Staff: full time 12, part time 6,
volunteer 30
Magazine: *Quarterdeck Review*
Major programs: library, archives,
museum, school programs, book
publishing, newsletters/pamphlets,
exhibits, photographic collections,
historic ship preservation
Period of collections: 19th-20th
centuries

Ft. Clatsop National Museum
Rt. 3, Box 604-FC, 97103
Telephone: (503) 861-2471
Founded in: 1958
Questionnaire not received

AURORA

Aurora Colony Historical Society
2nd and Liberty Sts.
Telephone: (503) 678-5754
Mail to: P.O. Box 202, 97002
Private agency
Founded in: 1963
Patrick J. Harris, Museum Director
Number of members: 180
Staff: full time 2, volunteer 30
Major programs: manuscripts,
museum, historic site(s), markers,
tours/pilgrimages, school
programs, newsletters/pamphlets,
historic preservation, research,
exhibits, audiovisual programs,
photographic collections,
genealogical services
Period of collections: 1856-1883

BEND

**Deschutes County Historical
Society**
129 N.W. Idaho St.
Telephone: (503) 389-1813
Mail to: P.O. Box 5252, 97708
County agency, authorized by
Deschutes Pioneer Association
Founded in: 1975
Perry C. Herford, President
Number of members: 400
Major programs: library, archives,
manuscripts, museum, historic
site(s), markers, tours/pilgrimages,
junior history, oral history, book
publishing, newsletters/pamphlets,
historic preservation, research,
exhibits, audiovisual programs,
photographic collections,
genealogical services
Period of collections: 1900-present

Deschutes Pioneers' Association
454 N.E. Burnside, 97701
Telephone: (503) 389-1945
Mail to: P.O. Box 508, 97709
Founded in: 1948
Questionnaire not received

BROWNSVILLE

Linn County Museum
101 Park Ave.
Telephone: (503) 466-3390
Mail to: P.O. Box 600, 97327
County agency, authorized by Linn
County Parks Department
Founded in: 1962
Oscar Hult, Museum Coordinator
Staff: full time 1, volunteer 40
Major programs: museum, historic
site(s), exhibits
Period of collections: 1880-1920

BURNS

Harney County Historical Society
18 W. D St.
Telephone: (503) 573-2636
Mail to: P.O. Box 388, 97720
Founded in: 1950
Questionnaire not received

CANBY

Barlow House
24670 S. Hwy. 99-E, 97013
Telephone: (503) 266-4375

Private agency
Virginia L. Miller, Owner
Major programs: museum, tours,
historic preservation
Period of collections: 1870-1905

CANYON CITY

**Herman and Eliza Oliver Historical
Museum**
101 S. Canyon City Blvd., Hwy. 395
Telephone: (503) 575-0362
Mail to: P.O. Box 464, 97820
Questionnaire not received

CLACKAMAS

Oregon Military Museum
Camp Withycombe, 97015
Telephone: (503) 657-6806
State agency, authorized by Military
Department, State of Oregon
Founded in: 1973
Terrill M. Aitken, Curator
Staff: full time 1, part time 3,
volunteer 8
Major programs: library, archives,
museum, restoration of major
military artifacts
Period of collections: 1900-present

COOS BAY

**Native American Research Center
and Museum**
Telephone: (503) 269-1611
Mail to: Box 3506, 97420
Founded in: 1975
Esther M. Stutzman, Director
Staff: volunteer 6
Major programs: archives,
manuscripts, museum, markers,
junior history, oral history,
educational programs, books,
historic preservation
Period of collections: 1010
B.C.-present

CORVALLIS

Horner Museum
Oregon State University, 97331
Telephone: (503) 754-2951
State agency, authorized by the
university
Founded in: 1925
Lucy S. Skjelstad, Director
Number of members: 400
Staff: full time 3, part time 5,
volunteer 20
Major programs: museum, tours, oral
history, research, exhibits,
photographic collections
Period of collections: 18th-20th
centuries

DALLAS

Polk County Museum Commission
Telephone: (503) 364-4250
Mail to: P.O. Box 200, 97338
Founded in: 1975
Questionnaire not received

EUGENE

Eugene Historic Review Board
Housing and Community
Conservation Dept., 777 Pearl St.,
Room 106, 97401

Telephone: (503) 687-5443
Founded in: 1975
Questionnaire not received

Lane County Historical Society
89239 Old Coburg Rd., 97401
Telephone: (503) 686-1835
Founded in: 1853
Questionnaire not received

Lane County Museum
740 W. 13th Ave., 97402
Telephone: (503) 687-4239
Founded in: 1935
Questionnaire not received

Museum of Natural History
University of Oregon, 97403
Telephone: (503) 686-3024
State agency, authorized by the
university
Founded in: 1936
Patty Krier, Assistant Director
Staff: part time 5, volunteer 15
Major programs: museum, exhibits,
archaeology programs

**Oregon Museum Park/Lane County
Historical Museum**
740 W. 13th St., 97402
Telephone: (503) 687-4239
County agency
Founded in: 1951
Carole Daly
Number of members: 200
Staff: full time 3, part time 3,
volunteer 35
Major programs: library, archives,
museum, photographic collections
Period of collections: to 1900

FLORENCE

Siuslaw Pioneer Museum
07959 Siuslaw Rd., 97439
Telephone: (503) 997-3037
Private agency, authorized by
Siuslaw Pioneer Museum
Association, Inc.
Founded in: 1973
Eileen Huntington, Director
Number of members: 300
Staff: full time 2, volunteer 4
Magazine: *Siuslaw Sampler*
Major programs: museum, markers,
junior history, oral history, historic
preservation, exhibits,
genealogical services
Period of collections: 1800-1936

FOREST GROVE

**Pacific University Museum, Old
College Hall**
2043 College Way, 97116
Telephone: (503) 357-6151
Private agency, authorized by the
university
Founded in: 1949
Karen L. Shield, Curator
Staff: part time 1, volunteer 10
Major programs: library, archives,
museum, historic site(s), tours,
school programs, photographic
collections
Period of collections: 1800s-early
1900s

**Oregon Electric Railway Historical
Society, Inc.**
HCR-71, Box 1318, 97116
Telephone: (503) 357-3574

Private agency
Founded in: 1959
Charles M. Statton, President
Number of members: 165
Staff: full time 1, part time 3,
volunteer 75
Magazine: *Trolley Park News*
Major programs: museum,
newsletters/pamphlets, historic
preservation, exhibits, living history
Period of collections: 1895-1945

Tualatin Plains Historical Society
Old College Hall, Pacific University,
97116
Telephone: (503) 557-2805
Founded in: 1952
Questionnaire not received

GLENWOOD

**Oregon Electric Railway Historical
Society, Inc.**
Telephone: (503) 357-3574
Mail to: Star Rt., Box 1318, 97120
Founded in: 1957
Questionnaire not received

GOLD BEACH

Curry County Historical Society
920 S. Ellensburg, 97444
Telephone: (503) 247-6113
Private agency
Founded in: 1974
Walt Schroeder, President
Number of members: 350
Staff: part time 1, volunteer 10
Magazine: *Curry County Echoes*
Major programs: museum, markers,
tours/pilgrimages, oral history,
book publishing,
newsletters/pamphlets, historic
preservation, research, exhibits,
audiovisual programs,
photographic collections,
genealogical services
Period of collections: mid 1800s-early
1900s

GRANTS PASS

**Josephine County Historical
Society**
716 N.W. A St.
Telephone: (503) 479-7827
Mail to: P.O. Box 742, 97526
Questionnaire not received

GRESHAM

Gresham Historical Society
P.O. Box 65, 97030
Telephone: (503) 665-5579
Private agency, authorized by Board
of Directors
Founded in: 1976
Karl Hayes, President
Number of members: 185
Major programs: museum, historic
site(s), oral history, school
programs, newsletters/pamphlets,
historic preservation, photographic
collections
Period of collections, 1800-1930

HAINES

Eastern Oregon Museum
School and 3rd Sts.
Telephone: (503) 856-3568

Mail to: Rt. 1, Box 109, 97833
Founded in: 1959
Bertha Boesch, Secretary
Number of members: 25
Staff: volunteer 14
Major programs: museum
Period of collections: 1865-present

HALSEY

Linn County Historical Society
32865 Lake Creek Dr., 97348
Private agency
Founded in: 1958
Margaret Carey, President
Number of members: 60
Major programs: historic preservation

HAMMOND

Friends of Old Ft. Stevens
Ft. Stevens State Park
Telephone: (503) 861-2000
Mail to: P.O. Box 138, 97121
Private agency, authorized by Parks
and Recreation Division
Founded in: 1978
Gale Visavatanaphongse, Historian of
Park
Number of members: 100
Staff: full time 1, volunteer 4
Magazine: *In Battery*
Major programs: museum, historic
site(s), newsletters/pamphlets,
historic preservation, exhibits,
audiovisual programs,
photographic collections
Period of collections: W.W. I-W.W. II

HEPPNER

Morrow County Historical Society
Main St., 97856
Mail to: c/o Ruth McCabe, Secretary,
Ione, 97843
Founded in: 1974
Questionnaire not received

HILLSBORO

Washington County Museum
641 E. Main St., 97123
Telephone: (503) 648-8601
Founded in: 1939
Questionnaire not received

JACKSONVILLE

Southern Oregon Historical Society
375 E. California at 6th St.
Telephone: (503) 899-1847
Mail to: P.O. Box 480, 97530
Private agency
Founded in: 1949
Nicholas L. Clark, Executive Director
Number of members: 2,173
Staff: full time 20, part time 13
volunteer150
Magazine: *Table Rock Sentinel*
Major programs: library, archives,
manuscripts, museum, historic
site(s), markers, tours/pilgrimages,
junior history, oral history, school
programs, book publishing,
newsletters/pamphlets, historic
preservation, records
management, research, exhibits,
living history, photographic
collections, genealogical services
Period of collections: 1852-present

JOSEPH

Wallowa County Museum
Main St., 97846
County agency
Founded in: 1976
Grace Bartlett, General Director
Staff: full time 3
Major programs: archives, museum,
exhibits

JUNCTION CITY

Junction City Historical Society
615 Holly St., 97448
Private agency
Founded in: 1971
Jo Brown, Board President
Number of members: 175
Staff: volunteer 2
Major programs: museum

KLAMATH FALLS

**Favell Museum of Western Art and
Indian Artifacts**
125 W. Main
Telephone: (503) 882-9996
Mail to: P.O. Box 165, 97601
Private agency
Founded in: 1972
Beverly Jackson, Manager
Number of members: 15
Staff: full time 2, part time 1
Major programs: museum, school
programs
Period of collections: 1800s

Klamath County Museum Complex
1451 Main St., 97601
Telephone: (503) 882-2501, ext. 208
County agency
Founded in: 1953
Patsy H. McMillan, Director
Staff: full time 1, part time 1,
volunteer 60
Major programs: library, archives,
museum, oral history, school
programs, historic preservation,
research, exhibits, photographic
collections
Period of collections: 1850s-present

LAFAYETTE

Yamhill County Historical Society
6th and Market St.
Mail to: P.O. Box 484, 97127
Founded in: 1969
Questionnaire not received

LAKEVIEW

**Schminck Memorial
Museum/Daughters of the
American Revolution, Oregon**
128 S. E. St., 97630
Telephone: (503) 947-3134
Founded in: 1936
Charlotte Pendleton, Curator
Staff: part time 3
Major programs: museum, school
programs, exhibits, genealogical
services
Period of collections: 1840-1940

LINCOLN

545 S. W. 9th St., 97365
County agency
Gail B. Carey, Co-director

Number of members: 210
Staff: part time 6, volunteer 3
Major programs: library, museum,
markers, book publishing, exhibits,
genealogical services

MARYLHURST

**Sisters of the Holy Names of Jesus
and Mary, Oregon Province**
Convent of the Holy Names, 97036
Telephone: (503) 636-8105
Founded in: 1859
Caroline Ann Gimpl, Archivist
Number of members: 1
Staff: full time 1
Major programs: archives,
manuscripts, museum, historic
preservation
Period of collections: 1859-present

MONMOUTH

Polk County Historical Society
Mail to: P.O. Box 67, 97361
Founded in: 1959
Questionnaire not received

MORO

Sherman County Historical Society
2nd and Dewey Sts., 97039
Telephone: (503) 565-3232
County agency
Founded in: 1945
Patricia R. Moore,
Secretary/Treasurer
Number of members: 71
Staff: volunteer 55
Magazine: *Sherman County: For the
Record*
Major programs: archives,
manuscripts, museum,
tours/pilgrimages,
newsletters/pamphlets, living
history, audiovisual programs,
photographic collections
Period of collections: 1880-1930

NEWBERG

Hoover-Minthorn House Museum
115 S. River St., 97132
Telephone: (503) 538-6629
Private agency, authorized by
National Society, Colonial Dames in
America
Founded in: 1955
Barbara Curington, Curator
Number of members: 100
Staff: full time 1, part time 2,
volunteer 5
Major programs: museum, historic
site(s), historic preservation
Period of collections: 1880s

NEWPORT

Lincoln County Historical Society
Burroughs House Museum, 545 S.W.
9th, 97365
Telephone: (503) 265-7509
Founded in: 1948
Questionnaire not received

NORTH BEND

**Coos-County Historical Society
Museum**
Simpson Park, 97459
Telephone: (513) 756-6320

Private agency
Founded in: 1891
Sarah Heigho, Director
Number of members: 300
Staff: full time 1, volunteer 6
Major programs: library, museum,
tours/pilgrimages, books,
newsletters/pamphlets
Period of collections: 1865-1950

OAKLAND

**Oakland Museum Historical
Society**
130 Locust St.
Mail to: Kellogg Star Rt., Box 11,
97462
Private agency
Founded in: 1969
Louise J. Stearns, Director
Major programs: museum
Period of collections: 1840s-1960s

ONTARIO

Malheur Country Historical Society
589 S.W. 2nd St., 97914
Telephone: (503) 889-5443
Founded in: 1972
Ross E. Butler, President
Staff: volunteer 7
Magazine: *Malheur Country Review*
Major programs: markers,
tours/pilgrimages, oral history

OREGON CITY

McLoughlin Memorial Association
713 Center St., 97045
Telephone: (503) 656-5146
Private agency
Founded in: 1909
Nancy E. Wilson, Curator
Number of members: 186
Staff: full time 2, part time 3
Major programs: museums, school
programs, newsletters/pamphlets,
audiovisual programs
Period of collections: 1800s

PENDLETON

Umatilla County Historical Society
Telephone: (503) 276-0012
Mail to: P.O. Box 253, 97801
Founded in: 1964
C. William Burk, Executive Director
Number of members: 550
Staff: full time 1, volunteer 23
Magazine: *Pioneer Trails*
Major programs: library, archives,
book publishing,
newsletters/pamphlets, research,
photographic collections,
genealogical services
Period of collections: 1880s-1920s

PHILOMATH

Benton County Historical Society
1101 Main St.
Telephone: (503) 929-6230
Mail to: P.O. Box 47, 97370-0047
Private agency
Founded in: 1951
William R. Lewis, Director
Number of members: 500
Staff: full time 5, volunteer 50
Major programs: library, archives,
museum, historic site(s), historic
preservation
Period of collections: 1840s-present

PORTLAND

Architectural Preservation Gallery
26 N.W. 2nd, 97209
Telephone: (503) 243-1923
Founded in: 1977
Questionnaire not received

Finnish-American Historical Society of the West
Mail to: P.O. Box 5522, 97208
Founded in: 1962
Questionnaire not received

Genealogical Forum of Portland
425 N.E. 66th Ave., 97205
Telephone: (503) 227-2398
Private agency
Founded in: 1946
Lois L. Lehl, President
Number of members: 841
Staff: volunteer 100
Major programs: library, book publishing, newsletters/pamphlets, historic preservation, research, genealogical services

Georgia-Pacific Historical Museum
900 S.W. 5th, 97204
Telephone: (503) 248-7500/248-7529
Founded in: 1973
Questionnaire not received

Historic Preservation League of Oregon
P.O. Box 40053, 97240
Private agency
Catherine Galbraith, President
Magazine: *Historic Preservation League of Oregon*
Major programs: library, newsletters/pamphlets, historic preservation, exhibits, audiovisual programs, legislation

History Resources
1665 N.W. 131st Ave., 97229
Telephone: (503) 644-8921
Private agency, authorized by Department of Commerce
Founded in: 1983
Linda S. Dodds, Proprietor
Major programs: oral history, historic preservation, research

Jewish Historical Society of Oregon, Inc.
6651 S.W. Capitol Hwy., 97219
Founded in: 1977
Questionnaire not received

National Railway Historical Society, Pacific Northwest Chapter
Room 1, Union Station, 97209
Founded in: 1955
Questionnaire not received

Old Church Society, Inc.
1422 S.W. 11th Ave., 97201
Telephone: (503) 222-2031
Founded in: 1968
Questionnaire not received

◇**Oregon Historical Society**
1230 S.W. Park Ave., 97205
Telephone: (503) 222-1741
Private agency
Founded in: 1873
Thomas Vaughan, Executive Director
Number of members: 8,600
Staff: full time 55, part time 3, volunteer 200

Magazine: *Oregon Historical Quarterly*
Major programs: library, archives, manuscripts, museum, historic site(s), tours/pilgrimages, oral history, school programs, book publishing, newsletters/pamphlets, historic preservation, research, exhibits, audiovisual programs, photographic collections, genealogical services, field services
Period of collections: prehistoric-present

Oregon Lewis & Clark Heritage Foundation
1230 S.W. Park Ave., 97205
Telephone: (503) 429-3713
Mail to: 511 E. Bridge St., Vernonia, 97064
State agency, authorized by Oregon Historical Society
Founded in: 1973
John H. Stofiel, Secretary/Treasurer
Number of members: 43
Staff: volunteer 14
Major programs: tours/pilgrimages, research
Period of collections: 1803-1806

Pacific Northwest Chapter, National Railway Historical Society
Union Station, Room 1, 97209
Telephone: (503) 226-6747
Richard Carlson, President
Number of members: 502
Staff: volunteer 1
Magazine: *The Trainmaster*
Major programs: library, archives, museum, tours/pilgrimages, newsletters/pamphlets, historic preservation
Period of collections: 1883-present

Pittock Mansion
3229 N.W. Pittock Dr., 97210
Telephone: (503) 248-4469
City agency, authorized by Bureau of Parks and Recreation
Founded in: 1964
Daniel Crandall, Director
Number of members: 800
Staff: full time 4, part time 5, volunteer 120
Magazine: *Pittock Papers*
Major programs: museum, historic site(s), oral history, book publishing, newsletters/pamphlets, historic preservation, research, exhibits
Period of collections: 1650-1919

Portland Friends of Cast Iron Architecture
1030 S.W. 2nd Ave., 97204
Telephone: (503) 228-5154
Questionnaire not received

Portland Historical Landmarks Commission
424 S.W. Main St., 97204
Telephone: (503) 248-4468
Questionnaire not received

Records Division, City of Portland
9360 N. Columbia Blvd., 97202
Telephone: (503) 248-4631
City agency
Founded in: 1851
Stanley T. Parr, Records Management Officer
Staff: full time 6
Major programs: archives, records management
Period of collections: 1851-present

Records Management Office, Portland Public Schools
531 S.E. 14th Ave., 97214
Telephone: (503) 232-2458, ext. 82
Founded in: 1979
Chris Blackburn, Records Manager
Staff: full time 2, part time 1
Major programs: archives, school programs, records management
Period of collections: 1856-present

Tigard Area Historical and Preservation Association
32042 S.W. Custer, 97219
Telephone: (503) 244-1547
Private agency
Founded in: 1978
LaVerne B. Sharp, Corporate Secretary
Number of members: 30
Major programs: library, archives, manuscripts, museum, historic site(s), markers, tours/pilgrimages, junior history, oral history, school programs, newsletters/pamphlets, historic preservation, research, exhibits, living history, audiovisual programs, photographic collections
Period of collections: 1880s-early 1900s

PRINEVILLE

Crook County Historical Society/A. R. Bowman Museum
246 N. Main St., 97754
Telephone: (503) 447-3715
Founded in: 1971
Irene H. Helms, Librarian/Attendant
Number of members: 400
1Staff: full time 2, part time 1, volunteer 15
Major programs: library, museum, historic sites preservation, tours/pilgrimages, educational programs, newsletters/pamphlets
Period of collections: 1890-present

ROSEBURG

Douglas County Museum of History and Natural History
1299 S.W. Medford
Telephone: (503) 440-4507
Mail to: P.O. Box 1550, 97470
County agency
Founded in: 1969
Daniel C. Robertson, Director
Staff: full time 6, part time 1, volunteer 52
Major programs: library, manuscripts, museum, historic site(s), tours/pilgrimages, oral history, school programs, historic preservation, research, exhibits, audiovisual programs,

photographic collections,
genealogical services, field
services
Period of collections: 1870-1920

ST. HELENS

**St. Helens Branch, Columbia
County Historical Society**
Old County Courthouse, 97051
County agency
Founded in: 1946
Billie S. Ivey, Curator
Number of members: 45
Staff: full time 1
Magazine: *Columbia County History*
Major programs: library, museum,
historic site(s),
newsletters/pamphlets, historic
preservation, photographic
collections
Period of collections: 1800s-1940s

ST. PAUL

**Champoeg State Park/Friends of
Champoeg**
8239 Champoeg Rd., NE, 97437
Telephone: (503) 678-1251
State agency, authorized by
Department of Parks and
Recreation
Founded in: 1901
Sallie Jacobsen, Park Historian
Number of members: 25
Staff: full time 13, part time 10,
volunteer 20
Magazine: *Champoeg Gazette*
Major programs: library, archives,
museum, historic site(s), school
programs, newsletters/pamphlets,
historic preservation, exhibits,
living history, audiovisual
programs, archaeology programs
Period of collections: 1840-1860

SALEM

Bush House/Salem Art Association
600 Mission St., SE, 97302
Telephone: (503) 363-4714
Private agency
Founded in: 1953
Jennifer Hagloch, Curator
Staff: full time 1, part time 4,
volunteer 60
Major programs: archives, museum,
oral history, school programs,
research, exhibits, living history,
photographic collections
Period of collections: 1870-1900

Friends of Deepwood
1116 Mission St., SE, 97302
Telephone: (503) 363-1825
Private agency
Founded in: 1974
Nancy Burke, President
Number of members: 200
Staff: part time 2, volunteer 10
Magazine: *Deepwood Stories*
Major programs: museum, historic
site(s), tours, newsletters, historic
preservation, exhibits, historic
gardens
Period of collections: 1894-1924

**Marion County Historical
Society/Marion Museum of
History**
260 12th St., SE, 97301
Telephone: (503) 364-2128
Private agency
Founded in: 1950
Daniel E. McElhinny, Curator
Number of members: 300
Staff: full time 1, part time 3,
volunteer 20
Magazine: *Marion County History*
Major programs: library, archives,
museum, oral history, book
publishing, newsletters/pamphlets,
research, exhibits, photographic
collections
Period of collections: 1890-1950

Mission Mill Museum Association
260 12th St., SE, 97301
Telephone: (503) 585-7012
Founded in: 1964
Questionnaire not received

Oregon State Library
State Library Bldg., 97310
Telephone: (503) 378-4277
State agency
Founded in: 1905
Wes Doak, State Librarian
Staff: full time 53, volunteer 3
Major programs: library, records
management, genealogical
services, distribution of official
state publications
Period of collections: 1859-present

SCOTTS MILLS

Scotts Mills Area Historical Society
2nd and Grandview
Mail to: P.O. Box 80, 97375
Founded in: 1974
Questionnaire not received

SPRINGFIELD

Springfield Historical Commission
225 N. 5th St., 97477
Telephone: (503) 726-3759
City agency
Founded in: 1977
Jacqueline Murdoch, Assistant
Planner
Staff: part time 1, volunteer 75
Major programs: archives, museum,
historic site(s), markers,
tours/pilgrimages, oral history,
school programs,
newsletters/pamphlets, historic
preservation, exhibits, audiovisual
programs, photographic
collections
Period of collections: from 1850s

THE DALLES

**St. Peter's Landmark
Preservation, Inc.**
405 Lincoln
Telephone: (504) 296-5686
Mail to: P.O. Box 882, 97058
Founded in: 1970
Questionnaire not received

**Wasco County, City of the Dalles
Museum Commission**
15th and Garrison Sts. 97058
Telephone: (503) 296-4547

Mail to: Box 806
Gladys Seufert, Corresponding
Secretary
Staff: full time 1
Major programs: museum
Period of collections: 1865-present

TILLAMOOK

Tillamook County Pioneer Museum
2106 2nd St., 97141
Telephone: (503) 842-4553
County agency
Founded in: 1935
M. Wayne Jensen, Jr., Director
Staff: full time 2, volunteer 20
Major programs: library, archives,
museum, oral history, exhibits,
photographic collections,
genealogical services
Period of collections: 1850-present

UNION

Union County Museum Society
311 S. Main St.
Telephone: (503) 562-6163
Mail to: P.O. Box 190, 97883
Founded in: 1968
Questionnaire not received

WEDDERBURN

**Curry County Historical
Society, Inc.**
Telephone: (503) 247-6113
Mail to: P.O. Box 1856, 97491
Founded in: 1966
Questionnaire not received

WOODWARD

**Plains Indians and Pioneer
Historical Foundation**
2009 Williams Ave.
Telephone: (405) 256-6136
Mail to: P.O. Box 1167, 73801
Private agency
Founded in: 1954
Sarah Taylor, Museum Curator
Number of members: 450
Staff: full time 2, part time 1,
volunteer 40
Major programs: museum,
tours/pilgrimages, school
programs, book publishing,
exhibits, photographic collections
Period of collections: 1865-1960s

PENNSYLVANIA

AARONSBURG

Aaronsburg Historical Museum
Plum St., 16820
Telephone: (814) 349-5328
Founded in: 1968
Questionnaire not received

ALLENTOWN

Lehigh County Historical Society
Old Courthouse, Hamilton at 5th St.,
18101
Telephone: (215) 435-1074

Private agency
Founded in: 1904
Mrs. William C. Wickkiser, Executive
Director
Number of members: 1,500
Staff: part time 8, volunteer 10
Magazine: *Proceedings*
Major programs: library, archives,
manuscripts, museum, historic
site(s), tours/pilgrimages, oral
history, school programs, book
publishing, newsletters/pamphlets,
historic preservation, records
management, research, exhibits,
audiovisual programs,
photographic collections,
genealogical services
Period of collections: 1750-1950

Liberty Bell Shrine of Allentown, Inc.
622 Hamilton Mall, 18101
Telephone: (215) 435-4232
Private agency
Founded in: 1962
Carl Fatzinger, Curator
Number of members: 300
Staff: part time 8, volunteer 23
Major programs: museum, historic
site(s), tours/pilgrimages, school
programs, newsletters/pamphlets,
exhibits, audiovisual programs
Period of collections: Revolutionary
War

Phi Alpha Theta International Honor Society in History
2333 Liberty St., 18104
Telephone: (215) 433-4140
Founded in: 1921
Donald B. Hoffman, Executive
Secretary/Treasurer
Number of members: 130,000
Staff: full time 3, part time 3
Magazine: *The Historian*

ALLISON PARK

Depreciation Lands Association
4743 S. Pioneer Rd.
Telephone: (412) 486-0563
Mail to: P.O. Box 174, 15101
Town agency
Founded in: 1974
Fred Hunt, Chair
Number of members: 125
Staff: part time 1, volunteer 20
Magazine: *The Newyth*
Major programs: museum, school
programs, newsletters/pamphlets,
exhibits, genealogical services
Period of collections: to 1865

Hampton Historical Commission
4743 S. Pioneer Rd., 15101
Telephone: (412) 486-0563
Mail to: 3101 McCully Rd.
Questionnaire not received

ALTOONA

Blair County Historical Society
3501 Oak Lane, 1602
Telephone: (814) 942-3916
Mail to: P.O. Box 1083, 16603
Private agency
Founded in: 1906
Michael E. Ward, President
Number of members: 602

Staff: part time 1, volunteer 7
Magazine: *The Mansion*
Major programs: library, archives,
museum, historic site(s), school
programs, newsletters/pamphlets,
historic preservation, exhibits,
genealogical services
Period of collections: 1840-present

Ft. Roberdeau
Sinking Spring Valley, R.D.
Mail to: Courthouse, Ft. Roberdeau
Office, Highland Mall,
Hollidaysburg
Questionnaire not received

Railroader's Memorial Museum
1300 9th Ave., 16602
Telephone: (814) 946-0834
Private agency
Founded in: 1980
Theodore J. Holland, Jr., Executive
Director
Number of members: 200
Staff: full time 1, part time 2,
volunteer 10
Major programs: archives, museum,
tours/pilgrimages, school
programs, exhibits
Period of collections: 1920-1955

AMBRIDGE

Harmonie Associates, Inc.
Old Economy, 14th and Church Sts.,
15003
Telephone: (412) 266-1803
Private agency
Founded in: 1956
Ann T. Nickerson, Executive Director
Number of members: 350
Staff: full time 4, part time 30,
volunteer 200
Magazine: *On Common Ground*
Major programs: museum, school
programs, newsletters/pamphlets,
historic preservation, living history
Period of collections: 1783-1865

Old Economy Village
14th and Church Sts., 15003
Telephone: (412) 266-4500
State agency, authorized by
Pennsylvania Historical and
Museum Commission
Founded in: 1919
Raymond V. Shepherd, Jr., Director
Staff: full time 19, part time 18,
volunteer 50
Major programs: archives, museum,
historic site(s), school programs,
historic preservation, research,
exhibits, living history, audiovisual
programs
Period of collections: 1824-1850

ARDMORE

Lower Merion Historical Society
Ashbridge House, Rosemont
Telephone: (215) 525-5831
Mail to: P.O. Box 51, 19003
Town agency
Mary G. Kane, President
Number of members: 175
Major programs: library, manuscripts,
museum, oral history, exhibits
Period of collections: 1700-present

Scottish Historic and Research Society of the Delaware Valley, Inc.
102 St. Pauls Rd., 19003
Telephone: (215) 649-4144
Private agency
Founded in: 1964
Blair C. Stonier, President
Number of members: 500
Staff: volunteer 25
Magazine: *The Rampant Lion*
Major programs: library, school
programs, newsletters/pamphlets,
exhibits
Period of collections: A.D. 500-20th
century

ASHLAND

Ashland Anthracite Museum
17th and Dine Sts., 17911
Telephone: (717) 875-4708
State agency, authorized by
Anthracite Museum Complex
Founded in: 1971
David L. Salay, Director
Staff: full time 2, part time 1,
volunteer 3
Major programs: library, museum,
school programs, research,
exhibits, photographic collections
Period of collections: 1830-1950

AVELLA

Meadowcroft Village
Meadowcroft Foundation, R.D. 2,
15312
Telephone: (412) 587-3412
Founded in: 1969
Questionnaire not received

BADEN

Anthony Wayne History Society of Beaver County
Telephone: (412) 869-9672
Mail to: P.O. Box 124, 15005
Questionnaire not received

BEAVER

Beaver Area Heritage Foundation
Mail to: P.O. Box 147, 15009
Private agency
Founded in: 1967
Robert Smith, President
Number of members: 200
Major programs: historic sites
preservation, markers, books,
living history
Period of collections: 1778-1865

Historical Research and Landmarks Foundation
699 5th St., 15009
Telephone: (412) 728-5708
Founded in: 1971
Questionnaire not received

Richmond Little Red School House Association
Dutch Ridge Rd., 15009
Telephone: (412) 412-7073
Mail to: R.D. 1, Fombell, 16123
Questionnaire not received

BEAVER FALLS

Beaver Falls Historical Society and Museum
1301 7th Ave., 15010
Telephone: (412) 843-6930
City agency
Founded in: 1944
Robert Bonnage, President/Curator
Number of members: 32
Staff: volunteer 30
Major programs: museum
Period of collections: 1795-present

Resource and Research Center for Beaver County Local History
1301 7th Ave., 15010
Telephone: (412) 846-4340, ext. 8
County agency
Founded in: 1971
Vivian L. McLaughlin, Director
Staff: part time 1
Magazine: *Milestones and Gleanings*
Major programs: library, archives, historic site(s), markers, book publishing, newsletters/pamphlets, research, photographic collections, genealogical services
Period of collections: 1800-present

BEDFORD

Bedford County Heritage Commission Inc.
137 E. Pitt St.
Telephone: (814) 623-1771
Mail to: P.O. Box 1771, 15522
Founded in: 1965
Questionnaire not received

Old Bedford Village
Exit 11, south of PA Turnpike
Telephone: (814) 623-1156
Mail to: P.O. Box 1976, 15522
County agency, authorized by Bedford County Redevelopment Authority
Founded in: 1975
Robert K. Sweet, President
Staff: full time 22, part time 76, volunteer 27
Major programs: historic site(s), tours/pilgrimages, oral history, school programs, book publishing, historic preservation, research, exhibits, living history, audiovisual programs, archaeology programs
Period of Collections: 1750-1850

BELLEFONTE

Centre County Library and Historical Museum
203 N. Allegheny St., 16823
Telephone: (814) 355-1516
Private agency
Founded in: 1938
Gary D. Wolf, Administrator
Staff: full time 16, part time 5, volunteer 7
Major programs: library, archives, manuscripts, museum, research, audiovisual programs, genealogical services
Period of collections: 1795-present

BERWYN

Tredyffrin Easttown History Club
Telephone: (215) 644-7093
Mail to: Rumrill, P.O. Box 111, 19312

Private agency
Founded in: 1936
R. Leighton Haney, President
Number of members: 56
Magazine: *Tredyfftin Easttown History Club Quarterly*
Major programs: educational programs, newsletters/pamphlets, historic preservation, photographic collections

BETHLEHEM

Annie S. Kemerer Museum
427 N. New St., 18018
Telephone: (215) 868-6868
Private agency
Founded in: 1954
Deborah L. Evans, Director
Number of members: 300
Staff: full time 2, part time 1, volunteer 50
Major programs: museum, newsletters/pamphlets, research, exhibits
Period of collections: 18th-20th centuries

Historic Bethlehem Inc.
501 Main St., 18018
Telephone: (215) 691-5300
Private agency
Founded in: 1957
Joan Lardner Ward, Executive Director
Number of members: 1,200
Staff: full time 6, part time 3, volunteer 350
Major programs: library, museum, historic site(s), markers, school programs, newsletters/pamphlets, historic preservation, exhibits, living history
Period of collections: 18th century

The Moravian Archives
41 W. Locust St., 18018
Telephone: (215) 865-3255
Private agency
Vernon H. Nelson, Archivist
Staff: full time 2, part time 3
Major programs: library, archives, manuscripts, research, exhibits, photographic collections
Period of collections: 1740-present

Moravian Museums and Tours
Gemein Haus, 66 W. Church St., 18018
Telephone: (215) 867-0173
Founded in: 1938
Mrs. Robert Pharo, President
Staff: volunteer 80
Major programs, museum, historic site(s), tours/pilgrimages, historic preservation
Period of collections: 1740-present

Sun Inn Preservation Association, Inc.
564 Main St., 18018
Telephone: (215) 866-1758
Founded in: 1971
Mrs. Leon J. McGeady, Executive Director
Number of members: 1,600
archivesfull time 3, part time 3, volunteer 200
Magazine: *Sonnen Schein*

Major programs: historic site(s), school programs, newsletters/pamphlets, historic preservation, research, audiovisual programs, public lectures
Period of collections: 1758-mid 19th century

BIRDSBORO

Daniel Boone Homestead
Daniel Boone Rd., Baumstown
Telephone: (215) 582-4900
Mail to: R.D. 2, Box 162, 19508
State agency, authorized by Pennsylvania Historical and Museum Commission
Founded in: 1938
James A. Lewars, Administrator
Staff: full time 5
Major programs: museum, historic site(s), exhibits
Period of collections: 1730-1790

Pennsylvania German Society
P.O. Box 397, 19508
Telephone: (215) 582-1441
Private agency
Founded in: 1891
Richard Druckenbrod, President
Number of members: 1,850
Staff: part time 2
Major programs: tours/pilgrimages, school programs, book publishing
Period of collections: 1683-present

BLOOMSBURG

Columbia County Historical Society
Telephone: (717) 683-6011
Mail to: P.O. Box 197, Orangeville, 17859
Founded in: 1914
Questionnaire not received

North Central Pennsylvania Historical Association
Telephone: (717) 784-5177
Mail to: c/o Columbia County Historical Society, 17815
Questionnaire not received

BLUE BELL

Wissahickon Valley Historic Society
1400 Blue Bell Rd., 14422
Telephone: (215) 643-1442
Founded in: 1975
Questionnaire not received

BOALSBURG

Columbus Chapel—Boal Mansion and Museum
Telephone: (814) 466-6210
Mail to: P.O. Box 116, 16827
Private agency
Founded in: 1952
Christopher Lee, Director
Staff: full time 4
Major programs: museum, historic site(s), tours/pilgrimages, historic preservation
Period of collections: 1789-present

Pennsylvania Military Museum
28th Division Shrine, P.O. Box 148, 16827
Telephone: (814) 466-6263

Founded in: 1919
Donald J. Morrison, Museum-Historic
Site Administrator
Staff: full time 5
Major programs: museum, historic
sites preservation
Period of collections: 1914-1945

BOYERTOWN

**Boyertown Museum of Historic
Vehicles**
28 Warwick St., 19512
Telephone: (215) 367-2090
Private agency, authorized by Hafer
Foundation
Founded in: 1965
Kenneth D. Wells II, Executive
Director
Staff: full time 1, part time 1
Major programs: museum, exhibits
Period of collections: 17th-19th
centuries

BRADDOCK

**Braddock's Field Historical
Society, Inc.**
P.O. Box 149, 15104
Telephone: (412) 661-5535
Private agency
Founded in: 1978
Colleen M. Collins, President
Number of members: 200
Staff: volunteer 15
Major programs: library, historic
site(s), tours/pilgrimages,
newsletters/pamphlets, historic
preservation
Period of collections: 1889

BRADFORD

Bradford Landmark Society
45 E. Corydon St., 16701
Telephone: (814) 362-3906
City agency
Founded in: 1970
Harry E. Taylor, President
Number of members: 300
Staff: volunteer 10
Major programs: museum, historic
site(s), oral history, school

programs, historic preservation,
genealogical services
Period of collections: 1870-1930

BROOKVILLE

**Jefferson County Historical and
Genealogical Society**
232 Jefferson St.
Telephone: (814) 849-8696
Mail to: P.O. Box 51, 15825
Founded in: 1967
Questionnaire not received

BROOMALL

1696 Thomas Massey House
467 Lawrence Rd.
Telephone: (215) 353-3644
Mail to: P.O. Box 18, 19008
Town agency
Founded in: 1964
Susan L. Lucas, Curator/Director
Staff: part time 1, volunteer 30
Major programs: historic site(s),
junior history, school programs,
historic preservation, living history
Period of collections: late 17th-early
19th centuries

**Scottish Historic and Research
Society of the Delaware
Valley, Inc.**
2137 MacLarie Lane, 19008
Telephone: (215) 566-1253
Mail to: P.O. Box 1008, Bryn Mawr,
19010
Founded in: 1964
Questionnaire not received

BRYN MAWR

Harriton House
500 Harriton Rd.
Telephone: (215) LA5-0201
Mail to: P.O. Box 1364, 19010
Private agency
Founded in: 1962
B. Gill, Curator/Director
Number of members: 1,000
Major programs: museum, historic
site(s)
Period of collections: 1750-1810

BURGETTSTOWN

Ft. Vance Historical Society
2 Kerr St., 15021
Questionnaire not received

BUSHKILL

**Delaware Water Gap National
Recreation Area**
18324
Telephone: (717) 588-6637
Federal agency, authorized by
National Park Service
Founded in: 1965
Albert Amos Hawkins,
Superintendent
Staff: full time 85, part time 15,
volunteer 12
Major programs: museum, historic
site(s), school programs, historic
preservation, research, exhibits,
living history, audiovisual
programs, recreation, natural
history
Period of collections: 1870-1920

BUTLER

Butler County Historical Society
P.O. Box 414, 16003-0414
Telephone: (412) 287-1105/283-8116
Founded in: 1960
Thomas Hannon, President
Number of members: 415
Staff: volunteer 16
Major programs: museum, historic
site(s), book publishing,
newsletters/pamphlets
Period of collections: early 1800s

CARLISLE

**Cumberland County Historical
Society/The Hamilton Library
Association**
21 N. Pitt St.
Telephone: (717) 249-7610
Mail to: P.O. Box 626, 17013
Private agency
Founded in: 1874
Kathryn E. Kresge, Executive Director
Number of members: 1,000
Staff: full time 3, part time 4,
volunteer 65
Major programs: library, archives,
manuscripts, museum, school
programs, newsletters/pamphlets,
historic preservation, research,
exhibits, audiovisual programs,
photographic collections,
genealogical services
Period of collections: 1750-1950

**Mid Atlantic Regional Archives
Conference**
Telephone: (717) 245-1399
Mail to: c/o Martha Slotten, Dickinson
College Library, 17013
Founded in: 1972
Questionnaire not received

CARLISLE BARRACKS

U.S. Army Military History Institute
17013-5008
Telephone: (717) 245-3152
Federal agency, authorized by the
U.S. Army
Founded in: 1967

1912 S.G.V. Roadster from the Boyertown Museum of Historic Vehicles, operated by the Hafer Foundation in Boyertown.—Boyertown Museum of Historic Vehicles

Colonel Rod Paschall, Director
Staff: full time 44
Major programs: library, archives,
  manuscripts, museum, oral history,
  newsletters/pamphlets, exhibits,
  photographic collections
Period of collections: 15th
  Century-present

CHADDS FORD

Brandywine Battlefield Park
Baltimore Pike, U.S. Hwy. 1
Telephone: (215) 459-3342
Mail to: P.O. Box 202, 19317
State Agency, authorized by
  Pennsylvania Historical and
  Museum Commission
Founded in: 1948
Number of members: 100
Staff: volunteer 10
Major programs: library, museum,
  historic site(s), tours/pilgrimages,
  junior history, school programs,
  newsletters/pamphlets, research,
  living history, audiovisual programs
Period of collections: 1690-1840

Brandywine Conservatory
P.O. Box 141, Rt. 1 19317
Telephone: (215) 459-1900
Private agency
Founded in: 1967
James H. Duff, Executive Director
Number of members: 3,000
Staff: full time 33, part time 16,
  volunteer 100
Magazine: *The Brandywine Catalyst*
Major programs: library, museum,
  historic site(s),
  newsletters/pamphlets, historic
  preservation, research, exhibits,
  field services
Period of collections: 1840-present

Brandywine River Museum
Rt. 1
Telephone: (215) 388-7601
Mail to: P.O. Box 141, 19317
Questionnaire not received

Chadds Ford Historical Society
P.O. Box 27, 19317
Telephone: (215) 388-7376
Private agency
Founded in: 1968
Mrs. W. L. Ellis, Administrator
Number of members: 641
Staff: part time 1
Major programs: living history
Period of collections: early 18th
  century

Christian C. Sanderson Museum
Rt. 100, north of Rt. 1
Telephone: (215) 388-6545
Mail to: P.O. Box 153 19317
Private agency
Founded in: 1967
Thomas R. Thompson, President
Number of members: 300
Staff: volunteer 6
Major programs: museum
Period of collections: 1777-1966

CHAMBERSBURG

Franklin County Heritage
E. King at N. 2nd St., 17201
Telephone: (717) 264-6364

Private agency
Founded in: 1968
Raymond H. Depuy, President
Number of members: 425
Staff: full time 2, volunteer 10
Major programs: museum, historic
  sites preservation, markers,
  tours/pilgrimages, school
  programs
Period of collections: 1783-present

Kittochtinny Historical Society
175 E. King St., 17201
Private agency
Founded in: 1898
Roger C. Mowrey, President
Number of members: 275
Staff: volunteer 35
Magazine: *Franklin County Footnotes*
Major programs: library, museum,
  markers, tours/pilgrimages, book
  publishing, photographic
  collections, genealogical services
Period of collections: Colonial
  era-present

CHESTER

Delaware County Historical Society
Wolfgram Memorial Library, Widener
  University, 19013
Telephone: (215) 874-6444
Founded in: 1895
Judy Buck, Curator
Staff: part time 5, volunteer 5
Magazine: *The Bulletin*
Major programs: library, archives,
  manuscripts, school programs,
  newsletters/pamphlets,
  photographic collections,
  genealogical services
Period of collections: 1683-present

CHESTER SPRINGS

Historic Yellow Springs, Inc.
Art School Rd., 19425
Telephone: (215) 827-7911
Founded in: 1974
Questionnaire not received

CHESTNUT HILL, PHILADELPHIA

The Ely Association, Inc.
11 W. Chestnut Hill Ave., 19118
Telephone: (215) 248-4491
Questionnaire not received

CLARION

Clarion County Historical Society
18 Grant St., 16214
Telephone: (814) 226-4450
Private agency
Founded in: 1955
Timothy L. Decker, Director/Curator
Number of members: 870
Staff: full time 1, part time 2
Major programs: library, museum,
  historic sites preservation,
  educational programs,
  newsletters/pamphlets
Period of collections: 1865-1918

CLEARFIELD

**Clearfield County Historical
  Society**
104 E. Pine St., 16830
Telephone: (814) 765-6125

Founded in: 1955
George A. Scott, President
Number of members: 550
Staff: volunteer 50
Magazine: *The Bulletin*
Major programs: library, archives,
  manuscripts museum, books
Period of collections: 1850-1950

COATESVILLE

Fallowfield Historical Society
R.D. 3, Box 209, 19320
Telephone: (215) 383-1591
State agency, authorized by
  Pennsylvania Federation of
  Historical Societies
Founded in: 1980
Margaret S. Young, President
Number of members: 53
Staff: volunteer 4
Magazine: *Pennsylvania Heritage*
Major programs: oral history, historic
  preservation, research, exhibits,
  photographic collections,
  genealogical services
Period of collections: 1737

COLUMBIA

**Louise Steinman von Hess
  Foundation**
2nd and Cherry Sts.
Telephone: (717) 684-4325
Mail to: P.O. Box 68, 17512
Private agency
Founded in: 1974
Elizabeth Meg Schaefer, Curator
Staff: full time 2, part time 3,
  volunteer 1
Major programs: archives,
  manuscripts, museum, historic
  site(s), historic preservation,
  research, decorative arts collection
Period of collections: 1700-1750

**National Association of Watch and
  Clock Collectors, Inc.**
514 Poplar St.
Telephone: (717) 684-8261
Mail to: P.O. Box 33, 17512
Founded in: 1943
Stacy B. C. Wood, Jr.,
  Administrator/Museum Director
Number of members: 32,500
Staff: full time 12, part time 1
Magazine: *Bulletin; Mart*
Major programs: library, archives,
  manuscripts, museum, educational
  programs
Period of collections:
  prehistoric-present

CONNELLSVILLE

**Connellsville Area Historical
  Society, Inc.**
410 E. Cedar Ave., 15425
Telephone: (412) 628-6609
Questionnaire not received

CORRY

Corry Area Historical Society
935 Mead Ave.
Mail to: P.O. Box 107, 16407
Founded in: 1967
Robert L. Lindsey, President
Staff: volunteer 12

Major programs: museum, oral
history
Period of collections: 1865-present

COUDERSPORT

Potter County Historical Society
308 N. Main St., 16915
Telephone: (814) 274-8124
Founded in: 1919
Robert K. Currin, President
Number of members: 330
Staff: part time 2, volunteer 4
Magazine: *Potter County Historical
Society Bulletin*
Major programs: library, archives,
manuscripts, museum
Period of collections: 1850-present

CRESSON

**Allegheny Portage Railroad
National Historic Site**
Rt. 22
Telephone: (814) 886-8176
Mail to: P.O. Box 247, 16630
Federal agency, authorized by
National Park Service
Founded in: 1964
Larry Trombello, Chief of
Interpretation
Staff: full time 3, part time 5,
volunteer 50
Major programs: historic sites
preservation, educational
programs
Period of collections: 1830-1860

DARLINGTON

**Little Beaver Historical
Society, Inc.**
P.O. Box 304, 16115
Telephone: (412) 843-5688
Private agency, authorized by
Executive Board of L.B.H.S.
Founded in: 1962
Ray O. Hill, President
Number of members: 218
Staff: volunteer 25
Major programs: museum,
newsletters/pamphlets, historic
preservation
Period of collections: 19th century

Little Beaver Museum
Plum St., Rt. 168, 16115
Telephone: (412) 336-4671
Founded in: 1971
Lois McKean, Corresponding
Secretary
Number of members: 250
Staff: volunteer 25
Major programs: museum, historic
site(s), markers, junior history,
newsletters/pamphlets, historic
preservation, exhibits
Period of collections: 19th century

DELMONT

**Salem-Crossroads Historical
Restoration Society**
26 E. Pittsburgh St., 15626
Telephone: (412) 468-4876
Founded in: 1971
Dale W. Hanks, Executive Director
Number of members: 450
Staff: full time 7, volunteer 50

Major programs: library, archives,
museum, historic sites
preservation, tours/pilgrimages,
newsletters/pamphlets, historic
preservation
Period of collections: 1830-1870

DONORA

Donora Historical Society
7th St. and McKean Ave.
Telephone: (412) 379-7854
Mail to: 778 Thompson Ave., 15033
Founded in: 1946
Questionnaire not received

DOWNINGTOWN

**Downington Historical
Commission**
Borough of Townington, 4 W.
Lancaster Ave., 19335
Telephone: (215) 269-0344
Town agency
Founded in: 1974
Major programs: historic site(s),
markers, tours/pilgrimages, oral
history, book publishing, historic
preservation, records
management, photographic
collections, genealogical services
Period of collections: 1680-present

Downington Historical Society
P.O. Box 9, 19335
Private agency
Founded in: 1978
Alice D. Ezrah, President
Number of members: 125
Major programs: archives, museum,
historic site(s), markers,
tours/pilgrimages, oral history,
book publishing,
newsletters/pamphlets, historic
preservation, exhibits

DOYLESTOWN

**Bucks County Genealogical
Society**
Spruance Library, Mercer Museum,
Pine and Ashland Sts.
Telephone: (215) 345-0210, ext. 37
Mail to: P.O. Box 1092, 18901
Private agency
Founded in: 1981
J. Fletcher Walls, President
Number of members: 550
Staff: volunteer 5
Major programs: library, book
publishing, newsletters/pamphlets,
genealogical services
Period of collections: 1682-present

Bucks County Historical Society
Mercer Museum, Pine St., and Fonthill
Museum, E. Court St., 18901
Telephone: (215) 345-0210, 348-9461
Founded in: 1880
Questionnaire not received

Division of Historic Properties
Swamp Rd., 18901
Telephone: (215) 348-6098
County agency, authorized by Paris
and Recreation Department
Charles J. Yeske, Manager
Staff: full time 14, part time 1
Major programs: historic site(s),
historic preservation, living history
Period of collections: 1800-1930

**Mercer Museum of the Bucks
County Historical Society**
Pine St., 18901
Telephone: (215) 345-0210
Private agency
Founded in: 1880
Douglas C. Dolan, Executive Director
Number of members: 1,600
Staff: full time 12, part time 10,
volunteer 250
Magazine: *Mercer Mosaic*
Major programs: library, archives,
museum, historic site(s),
tours/pilgrimages, school
programs, book publishing,
newsletters/pamphlets, research,
exhibits, photographic collections,
genealogical services, crafts
Period of collections: to 1850

Museum Store Association, Inc.
61 S. Pine St., 18901
Telephone: (215) 348-7144
Private agency
Founded in: 1955
Sydney Boisbrun, Administrative
Secretary
Number of members: 1,390
Staff: full time 2
Magazine: *Must*
Major programs: museum,
newsletters/pamphlets

EASTON

**Canal Museum and Hugh Moore
Historical Park**
200 S. Delaware Dr.
Telephone: (215) 258-7155
Mail to: P.O. Box 877, 18044-0877
Private agency
Founded in: 1969
J. Steven Humphrey, Executive
Director
Staff: full time 3, part time 8,
volunteer 3
Major programs: archives,
manuscripts, museum, historic
site(s), tours/pilgrimages, school
programs, book publishing,
audiovisual programs,
photographic collections, field
services
Period of collections: 1783-present

**Northampton County Historical and
Genealogical Society**
101 S. 4th St., 18042
(Telephone: (215) 253-1222
Private agency
Founded in: 1905
Charles A. Waltman, President
Number of members: 375
Staff: volunteer 6
Major programs: library, archives,
museum, genealogical services
Period of collections: 19th century

EBENSBURG

Cambria County Historical Society
521 W. High, 15931
Telephone: (814) 472-6674
Founded in: 1924
Questionnaire not received

ELVERSON

Hopewell Village National Historic Site
R.D. 1, Box 345, 195203
Telephone: (215) 582-8773
Federal agency, authorized by National Park Service
Founded in: 1938
Elizabeth E. Disrude, Superintendent
Staff: full time 12, part time 4, volunteer 123
Major programs: library, archives, manuscripts, museum, historic sites preservation, historic preservation
Period of collections: 1771-1883

EMPORIUM

Cameron County Historical Society, Inc.
Rt. 2, Box 54, 15834
Telephone: (814) 483-3636
Founded in: 1921
Questionnaire not received

EPHRATA

Ephrata Cloister Associates, Inc.
632 W. Main St.
Telephone: (717) 733-4811
Mail to: P.O. Box 155, 17522
Private agency, authorized by Pennsylvania Historical and Museum Commission
Founded in: 1957
Shirley A. Bischoff, Coordinator
Number of members: 465
Staff: full time 1, part time 8, volunteer 75
Major programs: historic site(s), tours/pilgrimages, junior history, school programs, living history, crafts, drama, music
Period of collections: 1750-1850

Historical Society of the Cocalico Valley
249 W. Main St.
Telephone: (717) 733-1616
Mail to: P.O. Box 193, 17522
Private agency
Founded in: 1957
Clarence E. Spohn, Curator
Number of members: 600
Staff: volunteer 12
Magazine: *Journal of the Historical Society of the Cocalico Valley*
Major programs: library, archives, manuscripts, museum, books
Period of collections: 1750-1900

Student Historians of Pennsylvania, Inc.
Telephone: (717) 733-4811
Mail to: c/o Ephrata Cloister Association, P.O. Box 155, 17522
Founded in: 1941
Questionnaire not received

ERIE

Erie County Historical Society
417 State St., 16501
Telephone: (814) 454-1813
Private agency
Founded in: 1903
John R. Claridge, Executive Director
Number of members: 575
Staff: full time 1, part time 2, volunteer 10
Magazine: *Journal of Erie Studies*
Major programs: library, archives, museum, tours/pilgrimages, books, newsletters/pamphlets, historic preservation
Period of collections: 1753-1913

Erie Historical Museum and Planetarium
356 W. 6th St., 16507
Telephone: (814) 453-5811
City agency, authorized by Erie School District
Founded in: 1899
Eugene A. Jenneman, Executive Director
Staff: full time 5, part time 6, volunteer 10
Major programs: archives, museum, exhibits, planetarium
Period of collections: 1750-1950

EXTON

Newcomen Society of the United States
412 Newcomen Rd., 19341
Telephone: (215) 363-6600
Private agency
Founded in: 1923
Charles Penrose, Jr., President
Number of members: 15,000
Staff: full time 10, part time 1
Major programs: library, manuscripts, museum, photographic collections, steam technology
Period of collections: 1650-1920

West Whiteland Historical Commission
The Zook House, Exton Square Mall
Telephone: (215) 363-8091
Mail to: 222 N. Pottstown Pike, 19341
Town agency
Founded in: 1971
Diane S. Snyder, Chair
Staff: volunteer 11
Major programs: library, oral history, educational programs, historic preservation, research
Period of collections: 1765-1930

FALLSINGTON

Historic Fallsington, Inc.
4 Yardley Ave., 19054
Telephone: (215) 295-6567
Private agency
Founded in: 1953
Lu Ann De Cunzo, Executive Director
Number of members: 500
Staff: full time 2, part time 3, volunteer 20
Major programs: archives, manuscripts, museum, historic site(s), school programs, historic preservation, research, exhibits, archaeology programs, photographic collections
Period of collections: 1700-1900

FARMINGTON

Ft. Necessity National Battlefield
National Pike, 15437
Telephone: (412) 329-5512
Founded in: 1932
Robert L. Warren, Superintendent
Staff: full time 8, part time 15
Major programs: museum, historic sites preservation, tours/pilgrimages
Period of collections: 1750-1763/1825-1855

FINLEYVILLE

Peters Creek Historical Society
c/o President, P.O. Box 53, 1533
Telephone: (412) 833-5543
Town agency
Founded in: 1967
Raymond H. Matthews, President
Number of members: 100
Major programs: library, archives, museum, historic site(s), markers, tours/pilgrimages, newsletters/pamphlets, historic preservation, photographic collections

FORT LOUDON

Ft. Loudon Historical Society
P.O. Box 181, 17224
Telephone: (717) 369-3473
Private agency
Founded in: 1975
Anna O. Rotz, President
Number of members: 100
Major programs: historic site(s), living history, archaeology programs
Period of collections: 1756-1800

FORT WASHINGTON

Highlands Historical Society
7001 Sheaff Lane, 19034
Telephone: (215) 641-2687
State agency, authorized by Pennsylvania Historical and Museum Commission
Founded in: 1975
Mrs. P. Canby Dushane, Director
Number of members: 400
Staff: fuul time 1, volunteer 50
Major programs: historic site(s), tours/pilgrimages, newsletters/pamphlets, historic preservation
Period of collections: 1796-1900

Historical Society of Ft. Washington
473 Bethlehem Pike, 19034
Telephone: (215) 646-6065
Private agency
Founded in: 1935
John W. Jackson, President
Number of members: 320
Staff: volunteer 30
Major programs: library, museum, book publishing, newsletters/pamphlets, genealogical services
Period of collections: Colonial era

Hope Lodge/Mather Mill
553 Bethlehem Pike, 19034
Telephone: (215) 646-1959
State agency, authorized by Pennsylvania Historical and Museum Commission
Founded in: 1957
LaVerne E. Pokorski, Acting Historic Site Manager
Staff: full time 2
Major programs: historic site(s), decorative arts
Period of collections: 1700-1880s

FOUNTAINVILLE

Fountainville Historical Farm Association of Bucks County, Inc.
Chapman Rd.
Telephone: (215) 348-5306
Mail to: P.O. Box 223, 18923
Founded in: 1972
Questionnaire not received

FRANKLIN

Venango County Historical Society
301 S. Park St.
Telephone: (814) 437-2275
Mail to: P.O. Box 101, 16323
Private agency
Founded in: 1950
John Egan, President
Number of members: 300
Magazine: *The Intelligence*
Major programs: library, archives, museum, tours/pilgrimages, school programs, book publishing, newsletters/pamphlets, historic preservation, records management, research, exhibits, photographic collections, genealogical services
Period of collections: 1870-1920

GALETON

Pennsylvania Lumber Museum
P.O. Box K, 16922
Telephone: (814) 435-2652
State agency
Founded in: 1972
Dolores M. Buchsen, Curator
Number of members: 362
Staff: full time 3, part time 1, volunteer 14
Major programs: museum, exhibits, living history, photographic collections
Period of collections: 1880-1910

GEIGERTOWN

Hay Creek Valley Historical Association
Furnace Rd.
Telephone: (215) 582-4938/469-9530
Mail to: P.O. Box 36, 19523
Private agency
Founded in: 1975
Shirley Fleming, President
Number of members: 1,126
Staff: volunteer 50
Magazine: *Joanna Furnace Journal*
Major programs: archives, historic site(s), oral history, newsletters/pamphlets, historic preservation, exhibits, living history, archaeology programs
Period of collections: 1790s-1940s

GETTYSBURG

Adams County Historical Society
Samuel Simon Schmucker Hall, Lutheran Theological Seminary Campus
Telephone: (717) 334-4723
Mail to: Drawer A, 17325
Private agency
Founded in: 1939
Charles H. Glatfelter, Director
Number of members: 375

Staff: volunteer 2
Major programs: library, archives, manuscripts, museum
Period of collections: 1492-present

Eisenhower National Historic Site
17325
Telephone: (717) 334-1124
Federal agency, authorized by National Park Service
Founded in: 1967
John Earnst, Superintendent
Staff: full time 20, part time 14, volunteer 15
Major programs: library, archives, museum, historic site(s), tours/pilgrimages, school programs, historic preservation, research, audiovisual programs, photographic collections
Period of collections: 1950s-1960s

Gettysburg National Military Park
17325
Telephone: (7l7) 334-1124
Federal agency, authorized by National Park Service
Founded in: 1895
Kathleen R. Georg, Historian
Staff: full time 50, volunteer 33
Major programs: library, archives, museum, historic site(s), markers, tours/pilgrimages, school programs, historic preservation, research, living history, audiovisual programs, photographic collections, genealogical services
Period of collections: Civil War era

Historic Gettysburg/Adams County, Inc.
12 Lincoln Square, 17325
Telephone: (717) 334-8188
Private agency
Founded in: 1979
Chester S. Byers, Administrator
Number of members: 223
Staff: full time 2, part time 3
Magazine: *Preserve*
Major programs: archives, museum, markers, historic preservation, photographic collections

GLENWILLARD

Crescent-Shousetown Area Historical Association
P.O. Box 253, 15046
Town agency
Paul W. Frey, President
Number of members: 40
Major programs: archives, markers, newsletters/pamphlets, exhibits
Period of collections: 1800-1850

GORDON

Mahanoy Valley Historical Society
312 Hobart St., 17936
Telephone: (717) 875-3347
Private agency
Founded in: 1982
Virginia Yarnell, President
Number of members: 30
Major programs: tours/pilgrimages, oral history, research, living history, photographic collections, genealogical services

GRANTHAM

Brethren in Christ Historical Society
Messiah College, 17027
Telephone: (717) 766-2511
Private agency
Founded in: 1978
Arthur Climenghaga, President
Number of members: 400
Staff: volunteer 2
Period of collections: 1780-present

GREEN LANE

Goschenhoppen Historians, Inc.
Rt. 29, Box 476, 18054
Telephone: (215) 234-8953
Private agency
Founded in: 1965
Richard L. Hate, President
Number of members: 700
Staff: volunteer 21
Major programs: library, manuscripts, museum, oral history, school programs, book publishing, newsletters/pamphlets, historic preservation, living history, Period of collections: 1750-1860

GREENOCK

Elizabeth Township Historical Society
546 Moray Lane, 15047
Telephone: (412) 751-8367
Founded in: 1976
Ronald F. Morgenstern, President
Number of members: 154
Staff: volunteer 8
Magazine: *Two Rivers Bulletin*
Major Programs: library, archives, museum, oral history, historic sites preservation, newsletters/pamphlets, genealogy
Period of collections: 1700s-present

GREENSBURG

Westmoreland County Historical Society
102 N. Main St., Suite 250, 15601
Telephone: (412) 836-1800
Private agency
Founded in: 1908
Edward F. Nowlin, President
Number of members: 500
Staff: full time 2, part time 1, volunteer 45
Major programs: library, archives, manuscripts, historic site(s), tours, school programs, newsletters/pamphlets, research, living history, archaeology programs, genealogical services
Period of collections: 1770-present

GREENVILLE

Greenville Area Historical Society
P.O. Box 25, 16125
Telephone: (412) 588-2133
Founded in: 1978
Questionnaire not received

HANOVER

Hanover Area Historical Society
113 W. Chestnut St., 17331
Telephone: (717) 632-3207

Private agency
Founded in: 1965
Jane S. Schott, Administrator
Number of members: 500
Staff: part time 2, volunteer 25
Major programs: archives,
newsletters/pamphlets, historic
preservation, exhibits,
genealogical services
Period of collections: early 1800s

HARMONY

Harmonist Historic and Memorial Association
On the Diamond
Telephone: (412) 452-7341
Mail to: P.O. Box 524, 16037
Number of members: 200
Staff: part time 1, volunteer 40
Major programs: library, museum,
historic sites preservation,
newsletters/pamphlets
Period of collections: 1783-1865

HARRISBURG

Bureau of History and Archives, Roman Catholic Diocese of Harrisburg
4800 Union Deposit Rd., Box 2153,
17105
Telephone: (717) 657-4804, ext. 214
Private agency
Founded in: 1977
Robert J. Maher, Archivist
Staff: part time 1
Major programs: library, archives,
historic preservation, research,
photographic collections,
genealogical services
Period of collections: mid
1800s-present

Dauphin County Historical Society
219 S. Front St., 17104
Telephone: (717) 233-3462
Private agency
Founded in: 1869
Mr. Dawson Flinchbaugh, President
Number of members: 425
Staff: full time 5, part time 6,
volunteer 10
Magazine: The Oracle
Major programs: archives, museum,
historic site(s), tours/pilgrimages,
oral history, school programs, book
publishing, newsletters/pamphlets,
historic preservation, exhibits,
audiovisual programs,
genealogical services
Period of collections: 1760s-present

Early American Society
Cameron and Kelker Sts.
Telephone: (717) 255-7710
Mail to: P.O. Box 1831, 17105
Founded in: 1970
Questionnaire not received

Ft. Hunter Mansion and Park
5300 N. Front St., 17110
Telephone: (717) 590-5751
County agency, authorized by
Dauphin County Parks and
Recreation
Founded in: 1933
Carl A. Dickson, Director
Number of members: 150

Staff: full time 3, part time 4,
volunteer 15
Magazine: Fort Hunter Chronicler
Major programs: museum, historic
site(s), historic preservation
Period of collections: 19th century

Historical Society of Dauphin County
219 S. Front St., 17104
Telephone: (717) 235-3462
Founded in: 1869
Questionnaire not received

National Historical Society
P.O. Box 8200, 17105
Telephone: (717) 657-9555
Private agency
Founded in: 1970
Number of members: 140,000
Staff: full time 10
Magazine: American History
Illustrated
Major programs: tours/pilgrimages,
books

◇Pennsylvania Historical and Museum Commission/William Penn Memorial Museum
3rd and North St.
Telephone: (717) 787-2891
Mail to: P.O. Box 1026, 17120
State agency
Founded in: 1913
Larry E. Tise, Executive Director
Staff: full time 300, part time 100,
volunteer 5,000
Magazine: Pennsylvania Heritage
Major programs: library, archives,
manuscripts, museum, historic
site(s), markers, tours/pilgrimages,
junior history, oral history, school
programs, book publishing,
newsletters/pamphlets, historic
preservation, records
management, research, exhibits,
audiovisual programs, archaeology
programs, photographic
collections, genealogical services,
field services, natural history, fine
arts
Period of collections:
prehistoric-present

◇State Museum of Pennsylvania
William Penn Memorial Bldg., 3rd and
North Sts., 17120
Telephone: (717) 787-4980
Mail to: P.O. Box 1026, 17108-1026
State agency, authorized by
Pennsylvania Historical and
Museum Commission
Founded in: 1905
Carl R. Nold, Director
Number of members: 350
Staff: full time 47, part time 4,
volunteer 95
Major programs: library, museum,
school programs, research,
exhibits, audiovisual programs,
archaeology programs
Period of collections: 18th-20th
centuries

HATBORO

Amy B. Yerkes Museum of Hatboro Baptist Church
32 N. York Rd., 19040
Telephone: (215) 675-0119

Private agency
Founded in: 1978
David T. Shannon, Jr.,
Historian/Curator of Museum
Staff: volunteer 3
Major programs: archives, museum,
oral history, school programs,
exhibits, audiovisual programs,
photographic collections
Period of collections: 1840-present

The Millbrook Society
42 Harding Ave., 19040
Telephone: (215) 675-0119
Private agency
Founded in: 1984
David T. Shannon, Jr., President
Staff: volunteer 20
Major programs: museum, historic
site(s), school programs, historic
preservation, research, exhibits,
living history, archaeology
programs
Period of collections: 1734-1930

HAVERFORD

Friends Historical Association
Haverford College Library, 19041
Telephone: (215) 896-1161
Private agency, authorized by Society
of Friends
Founded in: 1873
John M. Moore, President
Number of members: 825
Staff: part time 1
Magazine: Quaker History
Major programs: tours/pilgrimages,
book publishing,
newsletters/pamphlets, research

Quaker Collection, Haverford College
19041
Telephone: (215) 896-1161
Private agency, authorized by
Haverford College Library
Founded in: 1833
Edwin B. Bronner, Curator
Staff: full time 1, part time 4
Major programs: library, archives,
manuscripts, exhibits

HAVERTOWN

Friends of The Grange
141 Myrtle Ave.
Telephone: (215) 446-4958
Mail to: P.O. Box 853, 19083
Town agency
Founded in: 1974
William K. Penn, President
Major programs: museum, historic
site(s), tours/pilgrimages,
newsletters/pamphlets, historic
preservation, living history
Period of collections: 1700s

Haverford Township Historical Society
Karokung Dr., Powder Mill Valley Park
Telephone: (215) 446-1026
Mail to: P.O. Box 825, 19083
Founded in: 1939
Margaret Johnston, Curator
Staff: volunteer 12
Major programs: library, archives,
manuscripts, museum, historic
sites preservation,

tours/pilgrimages, educational
programs
Period of collections: 1783-1918

HAZELTON

Eckley Miners' Village
R.D. 2, Box 236, Weatherly, 18255
Telephone: (717) 636-2070
State agency, authorized by
Anthracite Museum Complex
Founded in: 1971
David L. Salay, Director
Number of members: 90
Staff: full time 7, part time 4,
volunteer 70
Magazine: *Patchwork*
Major programs: library, archives,
manuscripts, museum, historic
site(s), tours/pilgrimages, oral
history, school programs,
newsletters/pamphlets, historic
preservaton, research, exhibits,
living history, audiovisual
programs, archaeology programs,
photographic collections, field
services
Period of collections: 1850-1950

**Pennsylvania Historical and
Museum Commission: Eckley
Miners' Village**
R.D. 2, Box 236, Weatherly 18255
Telephone: (717) 636-2070
Founded in: 1969
David L. Slay, Director, Anthracite
Museum Complex
Number of members: 50
Staff: full time 6, part time 1,
volunteer20
Major programs: library, museum,
historic sites preservation,
tours/pilgrimages, oral history,
educational programs,
newsletters/pamphlets, historic
preservation
Period of collections: 1830-1930

HELLERTOWN

Gilman Museum
E. Durham St.
Telephone: (215) 838-8767
Mail to: P.O. Box 103, 18055
Beverly Gilman, Director
Staff: full time 4
Major programs: museum, natural
history, weaponry
Period of collections: 1500-present

HERSHEY

Hershey Museum of American Life
Hersheypark Arena
Telephone: (717) 534-3439
Mail to: P.O. Box 170, 17033
Private agency, authorized by M.S.
Hershey Foundation
Founded in: 1938
Eliza Cope Harrison, Director
Number of members: 700
Staff: full time 7, part time 15,
volunteer 100
Major programs: museum
Period of collections: 19th century

HOLLIDAYSBURG

**Armstrong-Kittanning Trail Society
of Pennsylvania**
514 Penn St. 16648
Telephone: (814) 495-0777
Founded in: 1956
Mrs. Arnold C. Emerson,
Secretary-Treasurer
Number of members: 50
Staff: volunteer 4
Major programs: tours/pilgrimages,
historic preservation
Period of collections: 1754-present

Ft. Roberdeau
Sinking Valley, R.D.
Mail to: Courthouse, Ft. Roberdeau
Office, Highland Mall, 16648
County agency
Fred E. Long, Director
Staff: volunteer 12
Major programs: museum, historic
site(s), tours/pilgrimages, school
programs, research, living history
Period of collections: 1776-1781

HONESDALE

Wayne County Historical Society
810 Main St.
Telephone: (717) 253-3240
Mail to: P.O. Box 446, 18431
Private agency
Founded in: 1917
Alma E. Hames, Secretary
Number of members: 600
Staff: part time 3
Major programs: library, archives,
manuscripts, museum, historic
site(s), school programs, book
publishing, historic preservation,
research, exhibits, photographic
collections, geneological services
Period of collections: 19th century

HORSHAM

Graeme Park
859 County Line Rd., 19044
Telephone: (215) 343-0965
State agency, authorized by
Pennsylvania Historical and
Museum Commission
Founded in: 1958
Marian Ann J. Matwiejczyk, Historic
Site Manager
Number of members: 60
Staff: full time 1, volunteer 30
Magazine: *Pennsylvania Heritage*
Major programs: historic site(s),
school programs, research, living
history
Period of collections: 1760-1780

HULMEVILLE

Hulmeville Historical Society, Inc.
114 Trenton Ave.
Telephone: (215) 757-6886
Mail to: P.O. Box 2, Penndel, 19047
Town agency
Founded in: 1974
Howard A. Martin, President
Number of members: 187
Staff: volunteer 187
Magazine: *Town Crier*
Major programs: library, manuscripts,
historic sites preservation, markers,
historic preservation

HUMMELSTOWN

**Hummelstown Area Historical
Society**
Main and Rosana Sts.
Telephone: (717) 566-6314
Mail to: P.O. Box 252, 17036
Private agency
Founded in: 1972
William A. Yottey, President
Number of members: 234
Staff: volunteer 15
Major programs: library, archives,
museum, school programs,
newsletters/pamphlets, records
management, research,
photographic collections,
genealogical services
Period of collections: late 19th
century-present

HUNTINGDON

**Huntingdon County Historical
Society**
106 4th St.
Telephone: (814) 643-5449
Mail to: P.O. Box 305, 16652
Private agency
Founded in: 1937
Nancy S. Shedd, President
Number of members: 450
Staff: volunteer 12
Major programs: library, archives,
museum, historic sites
preservation, educational
programs, books
Period of collections: 1783-present

Swigart Museum
P.O. Box 214, Museum Park, 16652
Telephone: (814) 643-0885
Private agency
Founded in: 1927
William E. Swigart, Jr., Chief
Executive Officer
Staff: part time 5
Magazine: *Museum Gazette*
Major programs: library, archives,
museum, historic preservation,
research
Period of collections: 1898-1950

INDIANA

**Historical and Genealogical
Society of Indiana County**
6th St. and Wayne Ave., 15701
Telephone: (412) 463-9600
Private agency
Founded in: 1937
Number of members: 450
Staff: full time 1, part time 1,
volunteer 20
Magazine: *Indiana County Heritage*
Major programs: library, archives,
manuscripts, historic sites
preservation, educational
programs, books
Period of collections: 1860-1918

**Special Collections, Library,
Indiana University of
Pennsylvania**
15705
Telephone: (412) 357-3039
State agency, authorized by the
university
Founded in: 1981

Phillip J. Zorich, Special Collections
Librarian
Staff: full time 1, volunteer 1
Major programs: library, archives,
manuscripts
Period of collections: 20th century

JEANNETTE

Bushy Run Battlefield
Bushy Run Rd., 15644
Telephone: (412) 527-5584
State agency, authorized by
Pennsylvania Historical and
Museum Commission
Founded in: 1918
John C. Leighow, Jr., Historical Site
Manager
Number of members: 84
Staff: full time 3, part time 5,
volunteer 10
Major programs: historic site(s),
tours/pilgrimages, junior history,
school programs, exhibits, living
history, audiovisual programs
Period of collections: 1750-1780

JENKINTOWN

Old York Road Historical Society
c/o Jenkintown Library, York and
Vista Rd., 19046
Telephone: (215) 884-0593
Private agency
Founded in: 1936
Elaine W. Rothschild, President
Number of members: 260
Staff: part time 4
Major programs: archives,
photographic collections
Period of collections: from 1683

JERSEY SHORE

Jersey Shore Historical Society
200 S. Main St.
Telephone: (717) 398-1973
Town agency, authorized by
Lycoming County Court
Founded in: 1963
Ruth Weiler, President
Number of members: 165
Staff: volunteer 15
Major programs: library, archives,
museum, historic site(s),
tours/pilgrimages, junior history,
historic preservation, research,
exhibits, photographic collections,
genealogical services
Period of collections: 1860-1920

JOHNSTOWN

**Johnstown Flood Museum
Association**
304 Washington St., 15901
Telephone: (814) 539-1889
Private agency
Founded in: 1971
Richard A. Burkert, Executive
Director
Number of members: 775
Staff: full time 3, part time 7,
volunteer 9
Major programs: library, archives,
manuscripts, museum, book
publishing, newsletters/pamphlets,
research, exhibits, photographic
collections
Period of collections: 1800-present

KANE

Thomas L. Kane Memorial Chapel
30 E. Chestnut St., 16735
Telephone: (814) 837-9729
Authorized by Church of Jesus Christ
of Latter-Day Saints
Staff: volunteer 2
Major programs: museum, historic
site(s), tours/pilgrimages,
audiovisual programs

KENNETT SQUARE

Bayard Taylor Memorial Library
216 E. State St., 19348
Telephone: (215) 444-2988
Private agency
Founded in: 1895
Joseph A. Lordi, Director
Staff: full time 7
Major programs: library, museum,
oral history, research
Period of collections: 19th century

KINZERS

**Rough and Tumble Engineers'
Historical Association, Inc.**
P.O. Box 9, 17535
Telephone: (717) 442-4249
Private agency
Founded in: 1950
Otis Astle, President
Number of members: 1,400
Staff: volunteer 30
Magazine: *The Whistle*
Major programs:
newsletters/pamphlets, historic
preservation, exhibits
Period of collections: 1835-1935

KITTANNING

**Armstrong County Historical and
Museum Society, Inc.**
300 N. McKean St.
Telephone: (412) 548-5707
Mail to: P.O. Box 735, 16201
Private agency
Founded in: 1924
Lee J. Calarie, President
Number of members: 200
Staff: volunteer 10
Major programs: library, museum,
genealogical services
Period of collections: 1850-1950

KUTZTOWN

Kutztown Area Historical Society
P.O. Box 307, 19530
Private agency
Founded in: 1975
Luther Moyer, Board Chair
Number of members: 238
Staff: volunteer 5
Magazine: *Along the Saucony*
Major programs: library, archives,
museum, tours/pilgrimages,
historic preservation
Period of collections: 19th-early 20th
centuries

LACEYVILLE

**Tuscarora Township Historical
Society**
R.D. 2, Box 105-C
Town agency
Founded in: 1982

Hedwig Chaffee, Presiding Director
Number of members: 140
Staff: volunteer 3
Magazine: *Once Upon a Time*
Major programs:
newsletters/pamphlets, historic
preservation, research,
photographic collections,
genealogical services
Period of collections: 1790-present

LANCASTER

**Evangelical and Reformed
Historical Society**
555 W. James St., 17603
Telephone: (717) 393-0654
Authorized by United Church of
Christ
Founded in: 1863
Herbert B. Anstaett, Executive
Secretary
Number of members: 1,400
Staff: volunteer 6
Major programs: library, archives
Period of collections: 1783-present

Fairfield Heritage Association, Inc.
105 E. Wheeling St., 43130
Telephone: (614) 654-9923
Founded in: 1963
Mrs. George R. Utley, Georgian
Museum Director
Number of members: 1,006
Staff: volunteer 40
Major programs: library, archives,
manuscripts, museum, historic
site(s), tours/pilgrimages, oral
history, school programs, book
publishing, newsletters/pamphlets
Period of collections: 1800-1977

**Heritage Center of Lancaster
County, Inc.**
Center Square
Telephone: (717) 299-6440
Mail to: P.O. Box 997, 17603
Private agency
Founded in: 1974
Patricia J. Keller-Conner, Curator
Number of members: 550
Staff: full time 3, part time 3,
volunteer 40
Major programs: museum, exhibits
Period of collections: 1735-1850

**Historic Preservation Trust of
Lancaster County**
123 N. Prince St., 17603
Telephone: (717) 291-5861
Private agency
Founded in: 1966
Jane E. Higinbotham, Executive
Director
Number of members: 1,303
Staff: full time 3, part time 1,
volunteer 75
Magazine: *Preservation*
Major programs: library,
tours/pilgrimages,
newsletters/pamphlets, historic
preservation, research, audiovisual
programs, field services

**James Buchanan Foundation for
the Preservation of Wheatland**
1120 Marietta Ave., R.R. 23, 17603
Telephone: (717) 392-8721
Founded in: 1936
Sally S. Cahalan, Director

Number of members: 600
Staff: full time 1, part time 6,
  volunteer 65
Period of collections: 1828-1868

**Lancaster County Historical
Society**
230 N. President Ave., 17603
Telephone: (717) 392-4633
Private agency
Founded in: 1886
John W. Aungst, Jr., Administrator
Number of members: 1,520
Staff: full time 2, part time 2,
  volunteer 15
Magazine: *Journal of the Lancaster
County Historical Society*
Major programs: library, archives,
  manuscripts, museum, junior
  history, newsletters/pamphlets
Period of collections: 1729-present

**Lancaster Mennonite Historical
Society**
2215 Millstream Rd., 17602-1499
Telephone: (717) 393-9745
Private agency, authorized by
  Lancaster Conference, Mennonite
  Church
Founded in: 1958
Carolyn C. Wenger, Director
Number of members: 2,000
Staff: full time 8, part time 2,
  volunteer 7
Magazine: *Pennsylvania Mennonite
Heritage*
Major programs: library, archives,
  manuscripts, museum, historic
  site(s), tours/pilgrimages, book
  publishing, newsletters/pamphlets,
  research, audiovisual programs,
  photographic collections,
  genealogical services
Period of collections: 1522-present

**Pennsylvania Farm Museum of
Landis Valley**
2451 Kissel Hill Rd., 17601
Telephone: (717) 569-0401
State agency, authorized by
  Pennsylvania Historical and
  Museum Commission
Founded in: 1953
John L. Kraft, Director
Number of members: 3
Major programs: museum,
  tours/pilgrimages,
  newsletters/pamphlets, exhibits,
  living history
Period of collections: 19th century

Rock Ford Plantation
881 Rock Ford Rd., 17602
Telephone: (717) 392-7223
Mail to: P.O. Box 264, 17603
Private agency, authorized by Rock
  Ford Foundation
Founded in: 1957
Ann L. Taylor, Manager
Number of members: 450
Staff: full time 2, part time 8,
  volunteer 20
Major programs: historic site(s),
  school programs,
  newsletters/pamphlets
Period of collections: 18th century

**Student Historians of
Pennsylvania, Inc.**
230 N. President Ave., 17603
Telephone: (701) 392-4633

Founded in: 1943
Questionnaire not received

LANGHORNE

Historic Langhorne Association
160 W. Maple Ave., 19047
Telephone: (215) 757-1888
Founded in: 1968
Christopher J. Blaydon, President
Questionnaire not received

LAPORTE

Sullivan County Historical Society
Courthouse Square, 18626
Telephone: (717) 482-2311
Founded in: 1953
Questionnaire not received

LATROBE

Greater Latrobe Historical Society
1714 Lincoln Ave., 15650
Telephone: (412) 539-1291
Private agency
Major programs: library, archives,
  manuscripts, historic preservation,
  photographic collections
Period of collections: from 1850

LEBANON

**Historic Preservation Trust of
Lebanon County**
Mail to: P.O. Box 844, 17042
Founded in: 1967
Robert A. Heilman, President
Major programs: historic sites
  preservation

Lebanon County Historical Society
924 Cumberland St., 17042
Telephone: (717) 272-1473
Private agency
Founded in: 1898
Earl Leiby, President
Number of members: 1,361
Staff: full time 2, volunteer 60
Magazine: *Seeds of History*
Major programs: library, museum,
  newsletters/pamphlets, exhibits,
  genealogical services
Period of collections: 1820-1920

LENHARTSVILLE

**Pennsylvania Dutch Folk Culture
Society, Inc.**
Bauer Memorial Library, 19534
Telephone: (215) 562-4803
Private agency, authorized by
  Pennsylvania Dutch Folk Culture
  Society, Inc.
Founded in: 1966
Florence Baver, President
Number of members: 300
Staff: volunteer 5
Magazine: *Pennsylvania Dutch News
and Views*
Major programs: library, museum,
  historic site(s), school programs,
  newsletters/pamphlets, historic
  preservation, audiovisual
  programs, photographic
  collections, genealogical services
Period of collections: 1865-present

LEWISBURG

Packwood House Museum
10 Market St.

Telephone: (717) 524-0323
Mail to: 15 N. Water St., 17837
Private agency
Founded in: 1972
David W. Dunn, Curator/Director
Number of members: 325
Staff: full time 3, part time 3,
  volunteer 110
Magazine: *Chanticleer*
Major programs: museum, school
  programs, newsletters/pamphlets,
  research, exhibits, audiovisual
  programs, photographic
  collections, decorative arts
Period of collections: 1790-1930

Union County Historical Society
St. Louis St., 17837
Telephone: (717) 524-4461, ext. 56
County agency
Founded in: 1963
Gary W. Slear, President
Number of members: 286
Staff: volunteer 15
Magazine: *Union County Heritage*
Major programs: archives,
  manuscripts, museum, historic
  site(s), tours/pilgrimages, oral
  history, school programs, book
  publishing, newsletters/pamphlets,
  historic preservation, research,
  exhibits, audiovisual programs,
  photographic collections,
  genealogical services
Period of collections: 1800-present

LEWISTOWN

**Mifflin County Historical
Society/McCoy House**
17 N. Main St., 17044
Telephone: (717) 242-1022
Questionnaire not received

LIGONIER

Ft. Ligonier Memorial Foundation
S. Market St., 15658
Telephone: (412) 238-9701
Private agency
Founded in: 1946
J. Martin West, Director
Number of members: 850
Staff: full time 5, part time 15
Major programs: archives, museum,
  historic site(s), school programs,
  newsletters/pamphlets, research,
  exhibits, living history, archaeology
  programs
Period of collections: 18th century

**Ligonier Valley Historical
Society/Compass Inn Museum**
Rt. 30 E., 15655
Telephone: (412) 238-6818
Mail to: Star Rt. E., Box 115, 15658
Founded in: 1964
Patricia Wolford, Secretary
Number of members: 700
Staff: full time 2, part time 2,
  volunteer 75
Major programs: museum, exhibits,
  living history
Period of collections: 1799-1840

LITITZ

Lititz Historical Foundation, Inc.
137-139 E. Main St.
Telephone: (717) 626-7958

Mail to: P.O. Box 65, 17543
George Roosen, President
Number of members: 450
Staff: part time 3
Major programs: archives,
manuscripts, museum, historic
sites preservation,
newsletters/pamphlets, historic
preservation
Period of collections: 18th-19th
centuries

LOCK HAVEN

Clinton County Historical Society
362 E. Water, 17745
Telephone: (717) 748-7254
Founded in: 1921
Questionnaire not received

MARIETTA

**Marietta Restoration
Associates, Inc.**
Mail to: P.O. Box 3, 17547
Founded in: 1965
Vivian M. Carroll, President
Number of members: 125
Staff: volunteer 15
Major programs: tours/pilgrimages,
oral history, educational programs,
newsletters/pamphlets, historic
preservation
Period of collections: 1812-present

MCCONNELLSBURG

**Fulton County Historical
Society, Inc.**
P.O. Box 115, 17233
Telephone: (717) 485-3529
Private agency
Founded in: 1973
John H. Nelson, President
Number of members: 400
Staff: volunteer 5
Major programs: library
Period of collections: 1790-present

MEADVILLE

Crawford County Historical Society
848 N. Main St., 16335
Telephone: (814) 724-6080
Founded in: 1880
L. Richard Pierson, President
Number of members: 640
Staff: part time 6, volunteer 20
Major programs: library, archives,
manuscripts, museum, historic
site(s), markers, tours/pilgrimages,
oral history, school programs, book
publishing, newsletters/pamphlets,
historic preservation, records
management, research, exhibits,
audiovisual programs, archaeology
programs, photographic
collections, genealogical services,
field services
Period of collections: 1788-1900

MECHANICSBURG

**Mechanicsburg Museum
Association**
P.O. Box 182, 17055
Private agency
Founded in: 1975
Foster M. Berkheimer, President
Number of members: 350

Staff: volunteer 23
Major programs: museum, historic
site(s), school programs,
newsletters/pamphlets
Period of collections: 1830-1870

MENDENHALL

Hillendale Museum
Hillendale and Hickory Hill Rds.,
19357
Telephone: (215) 388-7393
Founded in: 1961
Questionnaire not received

MERCER

Mercer County Historical Society
119 S. Pitt St., 16137
Telephone: (412) 662-3490
County agency
Orvis Anderson, Curator
Number of members: 650
Staff: part time
Magazine: *Mercer County History*
Major programs: library, museum,
tours/pilgrimages,
newsletters/pamphlets

MIDDLEBURG

**Snyder County Historical
Society, Inc.**
30 E. Market St.
Telephone: (717) 837-6191
Mail to: P.O. Box 276, 17842
Founded in: 1898
Questionnaire not received

MIDDLETOWN

Middletown Historical Association
Telephone: (215) 968-5119
Mail to: P.O. Box 279, Langhorne,
R.D. 1, 19047
Questionnaire not received

Slovak Museum and Archives
Jednota Estates, Box 150, 17057
Telephone: (717) 944-2403/546-1000
Mail to: 826 S. Main St., Old Forge,
18518
Private agency, authorized by First
Catholic Slovak Union, Cleveland,
OH
Founded in: 1890
Cyril M. Bosak, Chair
Staff: full time 2
Magazine: *Jednota*
Major programs: archives, museum
Period of collections: 19th-20th
centuries

MIFFLIN

Juniata County Historical Society
Telephone: (717) 436-2896
Mail to: P.O. Box 263, 17058
Founded in: 1931
Questionnaire not received

MIFFLINBURG

**Mifflinburg Buggy Museum
Association**
P.O. Box 86, 17844
Telephone: (717) 966-0233
Private agency
Founded in: 1978
Kathleen Ranney, President
Number of members: 326

Staff: volunteer 15
Major programs: museum, historic
site(s), newsletters/pamphlets,
historic preservation
Period of collections: 1870-1920

MILFORD

**Grey Towers National Historic
Landmark**
P.O. Box 188, 18337
Telephone: (717) 296-6401
Federal agency, authorized by Forest
Service, Department of Agriculture
Founded in: 1963
Edmund J. Vandermillen, Director
Staff: full time 10, part time 7,
volunteer 5
Major programs: historic site(s),
tours/pilgrimages,
newsletters/pamphlets, historic
preservation, records
management, exhibits,
photographic collections
Period of collections: 1855-1935

MILLERSBURG

**Historical Society of Millersburg
and Upper Paxton Township**
Telephone: (717) 692-3511
Mail to: P.O. Box 171, 17061
Town agency
Founded in: 1980
William Schreffler, President
Number of members: 300
Major programs: museum,
newsletters/pamphlets, historic
preservation, genealogical
services
Period of collections: 1870-1935

MILTON

**North-Central Pennsylvania Histor-
ical Association**
311 N. Front St., 17847
Telephone: (717) 742-9323
Founded in: 1975
Thomas R. Deans, President
Number of members: 29
Staff: part time 1, volunteer 5
Major programs:
newsletters/pamphlets, historic
preservation, conferences

MONACA

Great Arrow Historical Association
968 Chapel Rd., 15061
Telephone: (412) 744-8129
Questionnaire not received

**Mill Creek Valley Historical
Association**
Baker-Dungan Museum,
Pennsylvania State University,
Beaver Campus Monaca, 15061
Telephone: (412) 643-8969
Mail to: c/o Clude Piquet, 1334
Midland Beaver Rd., Industry,
15052
Founded in: 1965
Questionnaire not received

MONTROSE

**Susquehanna County Historical
Society and Free Library
Association**
Monument Square, 18801

Telephone: (717) 278-1881
County agency
Founded in: 1907
Betty Smith, Curator
Number of members: 800
Staff: full time 1, part time 2
Major programs: archives,
manuscripts, museum, educational
programs
Period of collections: 1783-present

MORRISVILLE

Pennsbury Manor
400 Pennsbury Memorial Rd., 19067
Telephone: (215) 946-0400
State agency, authorized by
Pennsylvania Historical and
Museum Commission
Founded in: 1939
Alice Hemenway, Director
Number of members: 250
Staff: full time 13, part time 6,
volunteer 100
Major programs: library, historic
site(s), school programs,
newsletters/pamphlets, historic
preservation, research, living
history, programs for adults and
families
Period of collections: 1680-1720

MT. BETHEL

Slate Bett Historical Society
Rt. 611
Telephone: (717) 897-6181
Mail to: P.O. Box 58, 18343
Private agency
Founded in: 1977
Walter C. Emery, President
Number of members: 20
Staff: volunteer 20
Major programs: museum
Period of collections: 1850-1950

MT. PLEASANT

**Commission on Archives and
History-Western Pennsylvania
Conference of the United
Methodist Church**
714 Walnut St., 15666
Telephone: (412) 547-2288
Questionnaire not received

MUNCY

**Muncy Historical Society and
Museum of History**
44 N. Main St.
Telephone: (717) 546-3431
Mail to: 131 S. Main St., 17756
Founded in: 1936
Questionnaire not received

NATRONA HEIGHTS

Burtner House Restoration, Inc.
P.O. Box 292, 15065
Telephone: (412) 224-7537
Private agency, authorized by
Pennsylvania Historical and
Museum Commission
Founded in: 1970
Vera B. Ferree, President
Number of members: 427
Major programs: museum, historic
site(s), newsletters/pamphlets,
historic preservation
Period of collections: 1800-1850

NAZARETH

Jacobsburg Historical Society
P.O. Box 345, 18064
Private agency
Founded in: 1972
John J. Schlamp, President
Number of members: 425
Staff: volunteer 35
Magazine: *The Jacobsburg Record*
Major programs: historic site(s), book
publishing, historic preservation,
archaeology programs,
genealogical services
Period of collections: early 18th-mid
19th centuries

Moravian Historical Society
214 E. Center St., 18064
Telephone: (215) 759-0292
Founded in: 1856
Beth Pearce, Curator
Number of members: 401
Staff: full time 1, volunteer 2
Magazine: *Transactions of Moravian
Historical Society*
Major programs: museum, historic
sites preservation
Period of collections: 1740-present

NEW BERLIN

New Berlin Heritage Association
Market and Vine St., 17855
Telephone: (717) 966-0065
Private agency
Founded in: 1970
Margaret Strome, President
Number of members: 31
Staff: volunteer 31
Magazine: *Heritage*
Major programs: library, archives,
manuscripts, museum, historic
sites preservation,
tours/pilgrimages, junior history,
oral history, educational programs,
books, historic preservation
Period of collections: 1800-1900

NEW BLOOMFIELD

**Historical Society of Perry
County, Pa.**
30 W. Main St., 17068
Telephone: (717) 582-4216
Founded in: 1924
Questionnaire not received

NEW GENEVA

Friendship Hill Association
Telephone: (412) 725-9190
Mail to: P.O. Box 24, 15467
Private agency, authorized by
National Park Service
Founded in: 1982
Brenda S. Quertinmont, President
Number of members: 275
Staff: volunteer 25
Magazine: *Friendship Hill Echoes*
Major programs: historic site(s),
tours, newsletters/pamphlets,
historic preservation, research

NEW HOPE

New Hope Historical Society
P.O. Box 41, 18938
Telephone: (215) 862-5652, 794-8143
Founded in: 1958
Questionnaire not received

NEW MILFORD

Old Mill Village Museum
Telephone: (717) 465-3448
Mail to: P.O. Box 434, 18834
Founded in: 1960
Robert S. Pease, Secretary/Associate
Member
Number of members: 400
Staff: part time 8, volunteer 200
Magazine: *Old Mill Village Gazette*
Major programs: museum,
educational programs
Period of collections: 1865-1918

NEWPORT

Historical Society of Perry County
P.O. Box 81, 17074
Telephone: (717) 567-3079
County agency
Founded in: 1924
Resta M. Tressler, President
Number of members: 398
Staff: volunteer 11
Major programs: library, historic
site(s), newsletters/pamphlets,
exhibits, genealogical services

The Perry Historians
Telephone: (717) 566-0990
Mail to: P.O. Box 73, 17074
Founded in: 1976
Harry A. Focht, Chair, Research
Committee
Number of members: 755
Staff: volunteer 10
Major programs: library, archives,
tours/pilgrimages, oral history,
book publishing,
newsletters/pamphlets, historic
preservation, research,
photographic collections,
genealogical services
Period of collections: 1755-present

NEWTOWN

Newtown Historic Association
Centre Ave. and Court St.
Telephone: (215) 968-4004
Mail to: P.O. Box 303, 18940
Founded in: 1962
Major programs: archives, historic
sites preservation, educational
programs, newsletters/pamphlets,
historic preservation
Period of collections: to 1850

NEWTON SQUARE

Marple Newtown Historical Society
Box 355, Broomall, 19008
Telephone: (215) 356-3644
Founded in: 1965
Questionnaire not received

NEWVILLE

Newville Historical Society
Mail to: 69 S. High St., 17241
Private agency
Founded in: 1960
Dorothy C. Marquart, Director
Number of members: 100
Staff: volunteer 10
Major programs: library, museum,
historic site(s), tours/pilgrimages,
historic preservation, genealogical
services
Period of collections: 1800s-1900s

NORRISTOWN

Historical Society of Montgomery County
1654 Dekalb St., 19401
Telephone: (215) 272-0297
Private agency
Founded in: 1881
William H. Smith, Director
Number of members: 1,090
Staff: full time 2, volunteer 6
Major programs: library, archives, museum, genealogical services
Period of collections: 1784-1900

NORTH EAST

Lake Shore Railway Historical Society, Inc.
Wall St. at Robinson St.
Mail to: P.O. Box 571, 16428
Private agency
Founded in: 1956
Bert E. Page, President
Number of members: 150
Staff: volunteer 30
Magazine: *The Lake Shore Timetable*
Major programs: library, archives, museum, historic site(s), tours/pilgrimages, newsletters/pamphlets, historic preservation, exhibits, audiovisual programs, photographic collections
Period of collections: 1850-present

NORTH WALES

Plymouth Meeting Historical Society
Mail to: P.O. Box 167, 19462
Private agency
Founded in: 1952
Sonya Driscoll, President
Number of members: 200
Magazine: *Plymouth Meeting Historical Society Newsletter*
Major programs: archives, historic site(s), markers, tours/pilgrimages, junior history, historic preservation, archaeology programs
Period of collections: 1820-1910

PAOLI

Wharton Esherick Museum
P.O. Box 595, 19301
Telephone: (215) 644-5822
Private agency
Founded in: 1971
Ruth E. Bascom, President
Number of members: 300
Staff: part time 3, volunteer 10
Major programs: museum, historic site(s), newsletters/pamphlets, historic preservation, fine art
Period of collections: 1920-1970

PARKESBURG

Octorara Area Historical Society
Telephone: (215) 857-4326
Mail to: 512 W. 2nd Ave., 19365
Questionnaire not received

Octorara Valley Historical Society
Telephone: (215) 857-5478
Mail to: P.O. Box 98, 19365
Private agency
Founded in: 1968

Kerry D. Glenn, President
Staff: volunteer 6
Major programs: tours/pilgrimages, junior history, oral history, historic preservation, living history, photographic collections, genealogical services
Period of collections: to 1960

PAUPACK

Pennsylvania Postal History Society
Telephone: (717) 857-0518/226-4524
Founded in: 1974
Joseph von Hake, President
Number of members: 210
Staff: volunteer 20
Magazine: *Historian*
Major programs: manuscripts, research, exhibits, audiovisual programs, postal history
Period of collections: Colonial era-1940

PENNSBURG

Schwenkfelder Library
1 Seminary St., 18073
Telephone: (215) 679-3103
Private agency
Founded in: 1946
Dennis K. Moyer, Director
Staff: volunteer 2
Major programs: library, archives, manuscripts, museum, book publishing, research, exhibits, photographic collections, genealogical services
Period of collections: 17th-19th centuries

PERKASIE

Perkasie Anniversary and Historical Society
Borough Hall, 18944
Telephone: (215) 257-4483
Founded in: 1957
Questionnaire not received

PERRYOPOLIS

Perryopolis Area Historical Society, Inc.
104 N. Liberty St.
Telephone: (412) 736-4542
Mail to: P.O. Box 238, 15473
Questionnaire not received

PHILADELPHIA

Afro-American Historical and Cultural Museum
7th and Arch Sts., 19106
Telephone: (215) 574-0380
Founded in: 1976
Rowena Stewart, Director
Number of members: 3,500
Staff: full time 20, part time 4, volunteer 50
Major programs: museum, exhibits
Period of collections: late 19th-early 20th centuries

American Catholic Historical Society
263 S. 4th St.
Telephone: (215) 925-5752
Mail to: P.O. Box 84, 19105

Private agency
Founded in: 1884
James P. McCoy, President
Number of members: 950
Staff: volunteer 10
Major programs: library, archives, manuscripts, museum, newsletters/pamphlets, research, exhibits
Period of collections: 1600-present

American Historical Museum
1900 Pattison Ave., 19145
Telephone: (215) 389-1776
Founded in: 1926
Questionnaire not received

American Studies Association
307 College Hall, University of Pennsylvania, 19104
Telephone: (215) 243-5408
Private agency
Founded in: 1951
John F. Stephens, Executive Director
Number of members: 2,300
Staff: full time 1, part time 2, volunteer 60
Magazine: *American Quarterly/ASA Newsletter*
Major programs: school programs, book publishing, newsletters/pamphlet, research, curriculum development, American studies, conferences and meetings

American Swedish Historical Museum
1900 Pattison Ave., 19145
Telephone: (315) 389-1776
Private agency
Founded in: 1928
Lynn C. Malmgren, President
Number of members: 800
Staff: full time 5, part time 2, volunteer 100
Major programs: museum, school programs, newsletters/pamphlets, exhibits, audiovisual programs, genealogical services
Period of collections: from 1638

Athenaeum of Philadelphia
219 S. 6th St., 19106
Telephone: (215) 925-2688
Private agency
Founded in: 1814
Roger W. Moss, Jr., Executive Director
Number of members: 1,000
Staff: full time 6, part time 3
Magazine: *Athenaeum Annotations/Athenaeum Bookshelf*
Major programs: library, archives, manuscripts, museum, historic site(s), historic preservation, research, exhibits
Period of collections: 1814-1914

Atwater Kent Museum
15 S. 7th St., 19106
Telephone: (215) 922-3031
City agency
Founded in: 1938
John V. Alviti, Executive Director
Staff: full time 8, part time 7
Major programs: library, museum, oral history, school programs, newsletters/pamphlets, research, exhibits, audiovisual programs, photographic collections
Period of collections: 19th-20th centuries

Balch Institute for Ethnic Studies
18 S. 7th St., 19106
Telephone: (215) 925-8090
Private agency
Founded in: 1971
M. Mark Stolarik, President
Number of members: 530
Staff: full time 21, part time 2, volunteer 18
Major programs: library, archives, manuscripts, museum, educational programs, books, newsletters/pamphlets
Period of collections: 19th-20th centuries

Chestnut Hill Historical Society
8419 Germantown Ave., 19118
Telephone: (215) 247-0417
Private agency
Founded in: 1966
Kathryn G. Shaifer, Executive Director
Number of members: 600
Staff: part time 1
Major programs: historic site(s), oral history, newsletters/pamphlets, historic preservation
Period of collections: 1800-present

CIGNA Corporation Museum
1600 Arch St., 19101
Telephone: (215) 241-4894
Mail to: P.O. Box 7728
Private agency
Founded in: 1926
Melissa E. Hough, Curator/Director
Staff: full time 3, part time 2
Major programs: library, manuscripts, museum, tours/pilgrimages, oral history, newsletters/pamphlets, research
Period of collections: mid 18th-early 20th centuries

Cliveden
6401 Germantown Ave., 19144
Telephone: (215) 848-1777
Private agency, authorized by Cliveden, Inc. and National Trust for Historic Preservation
Founded in: 1972
Jennifer Esler, Executive Director
Number of members: 255
Staff: full time 2, part time 22, volunteer 10
Major programs: historic site(s), school programs, newsletters/pamphlets, historic preservation, exhibits

Colonial Philadelphia Historical Society
292 St. James Place, 19106
Telephone: (215) 923-5662
Private agency
Founded in: 1925
Harold S. Gilbert, Chair
Number of members: 120
Major programs: historic site(s), tours/pilgrimages, school programs, historic preservation

Conservation Center for Art and Historic Artifacts
264 S. 23rd St., 19102
Telephone: (215) 545-0613
Founded in: 1977
Abby A. Shaw, Executive Director
Number of members: 103
Staff: full time 9, part time 3

Major programs: library, archives, manuscripts, museum, newsletters/pamphlets, photographic collections, conservation treatment, consultation and long-range preservation planning

Eastern Pennsylvania Conference of the United Methodist Church Historical Society
326 New St., 19106
Telephone: (215) 925-7788
Questionnaire not received

Ebenezer Maxwell Mansion, Inc.
200 W. Tulpehocken St., 19144
Telephone: (215) 438-1861
Private agency
Founded in: 1965
Beth A. Twiss-Garrity, Director
Number of members: 250
Staff: full time 1, part time 1, volunteer 50
Magazine: Quarterly Intelligencer
Major programs: museum, historic sites preservation, newsletters/pamphlets
Period of collections: 1850-1880

Edgar Allan Poe National Historic Site
532 N. 7th St., 19123
Telephone: (215) 597-8780
Federal agency, authorized by National Park Service
Founded in: 1936
Mary O. Reinhart, Supervisory Park Ranger
Staff: full time 3
Major programs: historic site(s), tours, school programs, exhibits

Free Library of Philadelphia
Logan Square, 19103
Telephone: (215) 686-5322
City agency
Founded in: 1891
Keith Doms, Director
Staff: 912
Major programs: library

Friends of Independence National Historical Park
313 Walnut St., 19106
Telephone: (215) 597-7919
Private agency
Founded in: 1972
Carolyn Hubbard, Executive Director
Number of members: 1,500
Staff: full time 2, part time 2, volunteer 15
Major programs: historic site(s), tours/pilgrimages, book publishing, newsletters/pamphlets, historic preservation, exhibits
Period of collections: 1730-1830

Genealogical Society of Pennsylvania
1300 Locust St., 19107
Telephone: (215) 545-0391
Founded in: 1892
Margaret M. Fox, Executive Secretary
Number of members: 2,000
Staff: full time 2, volunteer 35
Magazine: The Pennsylvania Genealogical Magazine
Major programs: library, educational programs, newsletters/pamphlets,

microfilming of church and civil records
Period of collections: 1700s-early 1900s

German Society of Pennsylvania
611 Spring Garden St., 19123
Telephone: (215) 627-4365
Founded in: 1764

Germantown Historical Society
5214 Germantown Ave., 19144
Telephone: (215) 844-0514
Private agency
Founded in: 1900
Sharon Ann Burnston, Director
Number of members: 502
Staff: full time 2, part time 3, volunteer 15
Magazine: Germantown Crier
Major programs: library, archives, museum, historic sites preservation, tours/pilgrimages, educational programs, newsletters/pamphlets, historic preservation, genealogical services
Period of collections: 1680-1980

Germantown Mennonite Corporation
6117 Germantown Ave., 19144
Telephone: (215) 843-0943
Private agency, authorized by Eastern Pennsylvania Area Mennonite Churches
Founded in: 1952
Marcus Miller, Administrator
Number of members: 250
Staff: full time 1, part time 2
Magazine: Friends of Germantown
Major programs: library, historic site(s), tours/pilgrimages, newsletters/pamphlets
Period of collections: 18th-19th centuries

Goldie Paley Design Center
4200 Henry Ave., 19144
Telephone: (215) 951-2861
Private agency, authorized by Philadelphia College of Textiles and Science
Founded in: 1978
Patricia C. O'Donnell, Director
Staff: full time 2, part time 11
Major programs: museum, historic preservation, records management, research, exhibits, audiovisual programs, textile display and restoration
Period of collections: 1st century A.D.-present

Historical Dental Museum, Temple University
3223 N. Broad St., 19140
Telephone: (215) 221-2889
State agency
Founded in: 1938
Pauline B. Mucha, Curator
Staff: full time 1
Major programs: museum
Period of collections: 1860

◇Historical Society of Pennsylvania
1300 Locust St., 19107
Telephone: (215) 732-6200
Private agency
Founded in: 1824

Peter J. Parker, Acting Director
Number of members: 3,414
Staff: full time 34, part time 4,
volunteer 8
Magazine: *Pennsylvania Magazine of
History and Biography*
Major programs: library, archives,
manuscripts, museum, oral history,
book publishing, research,
exhibits, photographic collections,
genealogical services, field
services
Period of collections: 17th
century-present

**Independence National Historical
Park**
3rd and Chestnut Sts.
Telephone: (215) 597-8974
Mail to: 313 Walnut St., 19106
Federal agency
Founded in: 1948
Hobart G. Cawood, Superintendent
Staff: full time 180, part time 20,
volunteer 125
Major programs: museum, historic
site(s), tours/pilgrimages, school
programs, historic preservation,
research, exhibits, living history,
audiovisual programs,
photographic collections
Period of collections: 1775-1800

**John Bartram
Association/Bartram's Garden**
54th St. and Lindbergh Blvd., 19143
Telephone: (215) 729-5281
Private agency
Founded in: 1893
Roger Mower, Administrator
Number of members: 550
Staff: full time 2, part time 3,
volunteer 5
Magazine: *The Bartram Broadside*
Major programs: museum, historic
site(s), tours/pilgrimages, school
programs, historic preservation,
research, genealogical services
Period of collections: 1728-1823

Library Company of Philadelphia
1314 Locust St., 19107
Telephone: (215) 546-3181
Private agency
Founded in: 1731
John C. Van Horne, Librarian
Number of members: 930
Staff: full time 13, part time 1,
volunteer 3
Major programs: library, exhibits,
photographic collections
Period of collections: to 1880

**Lutheran Historical Society of
Eastern Pennsylvania**
7301 Germantown Ave., 19119
Mail to: P.O. Box 272, Pottstown,
19464
Questionnaire not received

**Mutter Museum, College of
Physicians of Philadelphia**
19 S. 22nd St., 19103
Telephone: (215) 561-6059
Private agency
Founded in: 1863
Gretchen Worden, Curator
Staf: full time 2, part time 3,
volunteer 2

Major programs: museum, medical
history
Period of collections: 19th century

**National Archives—Philadelphia
Branch**
9th and Market St., 19107
Telephone: (215) 597-3000
Founded in: 1969
Robert Plowman, Director
Staff: full time 6
Major programs: archives,
educational programs, teachers'
workshops, genealogical
workshops, film series, open
houses and tours
Period of collections: 1789-1978

**National Museum of American
Jewish History**
55 N. 5th St., 19106
Telephone: (215) 923-3811
Private agency
Founded in: 1976
Alice M. Greenwald, Executive
Director
Staff: full time 10, part time 5,
volunteer 100
Major programs: library, archives,
museum, tours/pilgrimages, school
programs, newsletters/pamphlets,
research, exhibits, audiovisual
programs, photographic
collections
Period of collections: 1654-present

**New Year's Shooters and Mummers
Museum**
2nd St. at Washington Ave., 19147
Telephone: (215) 336-3050
Private agency
Founded in: 1975
Joseph F. Dinella, Executive Director
Number of members: 400
Staff: full time 6, part time 1,
volunteer 13
Magazine: *Mummers Museum News*
Major programs: library, archives,
museum, oral history, school
programs, newsletters/pamphlets,
research, exhibits, audiovisual
programs, photographic
collections, field services
Period of collections: 1900-present

Pennsylvania Folklore Society
Room 415, Logan Hall/CN, University
of Pennsylvania, 19104
Telephone: (215) 243-7352
Founded in: 1958

◇**Pennsylvania Humanities Council**
401 N. Broad St., 19108
Telephone: (215) 925-1005
State agency
Founded in: 1973
Craig R. Eisendrath, Executive
Director
Staff: full time 9, part time 3,
volunteer 32
Magazine: *Public News*
Major programs: library, museum,
historic site(s), tours/pilgrimages,
junior history, oral history, school
programs, historic preservation,
exhibits, living history, audiovisual
programs, archaeology programs,
photographic collections

**Pennsylvania Labor History
Society**
1816 Chestnut St., 19103
Telephone: (215) 587-6738
State agency
Founded in: 1971
Ted Kirsch, President
Number of members: 500
Major programs: historic site(s),
markers, tours/pilgrimages,
newsletters/pamphlets

**Philadelphia Branch, National
Archives**
9th and Market Sts., 19107
Telephone: (215) 597-3000
Federal agency, authorized by
National Archives and Records
Administration
Founded in: 1969
Robert J. Plowman, Director
Staff: full time 6, part time 2,
volunteer 15
Major programs: archives, school
programs, newsletters/pamphlets,
research, exhibits
Period of collections: 1790-1960

◇**Philadelphia Historical
Commission**
1313 City Hall Annex, 19107
Telephone: (2l5) 686-4543
City agency
Founded in: 1955
Richard Tyler, Historian
Staff: full time 5
Major programs: historic preservation
Period of collections: 1680-present

**Philadelphia Jewish Archives
Center**
625 Walnut St., 19106
Telephone: (215) 923-2729
Founded in: 1972
Questionnaire not received

Philadelphia Maritime Museum
321 Chestnut St., 19106
Telephone: (215) 925-5439
Private agency
Founded in: 1961
Theodore T. Newbold, President
Staff: full time 13
Magazine: *Spindrift*
Major programs: library, museum,
school programs, book publishing,
newsletters/pamphlets, exhibits
Period of collections: 17th
century-present

Philadelphia Mummers Museum
2nd St. and Washington Ave., 19147
Telephone: (215) 336-3050
Private agency
Founded in: 1976
Joseph F. Dinella, Executive
Secretary
Staff: full time 5, part time 5, volunteer
20
Magazine: *Mummers Souvenir
Yearbook*
Major programs: library, museum,
oral history, school programs,
records management, research,
exhibits, audiovisual programs,
photographic collections
Period of collections: late
1800s-present

Philadelphia Society for the Preservation of Landmarks
321 S. 4th St., 19106
Founded in: 1931
Maria M. Thompson, Director
Number of members: 1,000
Staff: part time 2, volunteer 100
Major programs: museum, historic preservation
Period of collections: 1725-1840

Presbyterian Historical Society
425 Lombard St., 19147
Telephone: (215) 627-1852
Private agency, authorized by the Presbyterian Church
Founded in: 1852
William B. Miller, Director
Number of members: 900
Staff: full time 14, part time 1, volunteer 1
Magazine: *Journal of Presbyterian History*
Major programs: library, archives, manuscripts, museum, historic site(s), oral history, book publishing, newsletters/pamphlets, records management
Period of collections: 1706-present

Rosenbach Museum and Library
2010 Delancey Place, 19103
Telephone: (215) 732-1600
Private agency
Founded in: 1953
Ellen S. Dunlap, Director
Number of members: 750
Staff: full time 7, part time 7, volunteer 50
Major programs: library, archives, manuscripts, museum, books, newsletters, tours/pilgrimages, exhibits
Period of collections: 8th century B.C.-present

Roxborough-Manayunk-Wissahickon Historical Society
3612 Earlham St., 19129
Telephone: (215) 438-1368
Private agency
Founded in: 1965
James A. Poupard, President
Number of members: 85
Staff: volunteer 12
Major programs: archives, historic site(s), markers, school programs, exhibits
Period of collections: 19th-early 20th centuries

Shackamaxon Society, Inc.
315 S. 12th St.
Telephone: (215) 923-8299
Mail to: P.O. Box 1777, 19107
Questionnaire not received

Society of Architectural Historians
1700 Walnut St., 19103
Telephone: (215) 735-0224
Founded in: 1940
Questionnaire not received

Society of Mayflower Descendants in the Commonwealth of Pennsylvania
1300 Locust St., 19107
Telephone: (215) 732-6200
Questionnaire not received

Stenton/Home of James Logan
18th St. and Windrim Ave., 19140
Telephone: (215) DA9-7312
Mail to: 1630 Latimer St., 19103
Private agency, authorized by National Society, Colonial Dames of America
Founded in: 1891
Mary Costello, Secretary
Number of members: 800
Staff: full time 3, part time 1, volunteer 20
Major programs: archives, museum, historic site(s), tours/pilgrimages, school programs, historic preservation, research
Period of collections: 1730-1830

Swedish Colonial Society
1300 Locust St., 19107
Founded in: 1909
Number of members: 425
Major programs: historic sites preservation, markers, tours/pilgrimages, oral history, books, historic preservation
Period of collections: 1638-date

Victorian Society in America
E. Washington Square, 219 S. 6th St., 19106
Telephone: (215) 627-4252
Founded in: 1966
Judith Snyder, Executive Director
Number of members: 4,000
Staff: full time 1, part time 2
Magazine: *The Victorian, Nineteenth Century*
Major programs: archives, historic sites preservation, educational programs, newsletters/pamphlets, tours
Period of collections: 1865-1918

War Library and Museum, Military Order of the Loyal Legion of the United States
1805 Pine St., 19103
Telephone: (215) 735-8196
Founded in: 1888
Russ A. Pritchard, Director
Staff: full time 2
Major programs: library, archives, manuscripts, museum
Period of collections: Civil War era

The Welsh Society
450 Broadway, Camden, NJ, 08103
Telephone: (609) 964-0891
Mail to: P.O. Box 190, Darby, 19023
Founded in: 1729
Questionnaire not received

Woodford Mansion
E. Fairmont Park, 33rd Ave., 19132
Telephone: (215) 229-6115
Private agency
Martin P. Snyder, Trustee
Staff: volunteer 50
Major programs: museum, historic site(s)

PITTSBURGH

Ft. Pitt Museum Associates
Point State Park, 15222
Telephone: (412) 281-9284
Founded in: 1969
Questionnaire not received

Greene County Historical Society
R.D. 2, 15370
Telephone: (412) 627-3204
Private agency
Founded in: 1926
Farley Toothman, President
Number of members: 675
Staff: full time 2, part time 2, volunteer 8
Magazine: *Greene Hills Echo*
Major programs: library, museum, school programs, book publishing, historic preservation, research, living history, photographic collections, genealogical services
Period of collections: 1880

Historical Society of Western Pennsylvania
4338 Bigelow Blvd., 15213
Telephone: (412) 681-5533
Founded in: 1879
John G. Labanish, Director/Curator
Number of members: 1,000
Staff: full time 9, volunteer 10
Magazine: *Western Pennsylvania Historical Magazine*
Major programs: library, archives, manuscripts, museum, tours/pilgrimages, educational programs, books, newsletters/pamphlets
Period of collections: 19th-century

History and Heritage Committee, American Society of Civil Engineers
60 Magee Rd., 15143
Telephone: (412) 741-2707
Mail to: 221 Fawcett Church Rd., Bridgeville, 15017
Private agency
Founded in: 1918
James Barrick, Committee Chair
Number of members: 1,400
Major programs: historic site(s), markers, book publishing, research

Oral History Program, Plum Senior High School
900 Elicker Rd., 15339
Telephone: (412) 795-4880
Town agency
Founded in: 1976
Richard Allen Williams, Teacher
Major programs: library, junior history, oral history, school programs, exhibits, audiovisual programs, genealogical services
Period of collections: 20th century

Pittsburgh Children's Museum
1 Landmarks Square, 15212
Telephone: (412) 322-5059
Private agency
Founded in: 1980
David Crosson, Executive Director
Number of members: 700
Staff: full time 8, part time 12, volunteer 40
Major programs: manuscripts, museum, school programs, exhibits, educational program, puppetry
Period of collections: B.C.-present

Pittsburgh History and Landmarks Foundation
450 Landmarks Bldg., Station Square, 15219

Telephone: (412) 471-5808
Private agency
Founded in: 1964
Louise King Ferguson, Executive
Director
Number of members: 2,400
Staff: full time 20, part time 6,
volunteer 40
Major programs: historic site(s),
markers, tours/pilgrimages, school
programs, book publishing,
newsletters/pamphlets, historic
preservation, audiovisual programs
Period of collections: Victorian era

**Polish Historical Commission,
Central Council of Polish
Organizations**
4291 Stanton Ave., 15201
Telephone: (412) 782-2166
County agency
Founded in: 1946
Joseph A. Borkowski, Director
Number of members: 80
Staff: full time 1, volunteer 14
Magazine: *Polish Day*
Major programs: library, archives,
historic preservation, research,
exhibits, genealogical services
Period of collections: 1870-present

Ross Township Historical Society
102 Evergreen Hamlet, 15209
Telephone: (412) 821-8888
Founded in: 1979
Susan Grieve, Founder/President
Number of members: 150
Staff: volunteer 25
Magazine: *Ross Township Historical
Newsletter*
Major programs: library, historic
site(s), markers, tours/pilgrimages,
junior history, oral history, school
programs, newsletters/pamphlets,
historic preservation, audiovisual
programs, photographic
collections, field services
Period of collections: 1800s

Stephen Foster Memorial
University of Pittsburgh, 15260
Telephone: (412) 624-4100
Private agency
Founded in: 1937
Deane L. Root, Curator
Staff: full time 3, part time 2
Major programs: library, archives,
manuscripts, museum, pamphlets,
historic preservation, research,
exhibits, music programs
Period of collections: 1840-1940

PLYMOUTH MEETING
**Plymouth Meeting Historical
Society**
Mail to: P.O. Box 167, 19462
Questionnaire not received

POINT MARION
**Friendship Hill National Historic
Site**
Rt. 166
Telephone: (412) 725-9190
Mail to: R.D. 1, Box 149-A, 15474
Federal agency, authorized by
National Park Service
Founded in: 1978
William O. Fink, Site Manager

Staff: full time 3, part time 3,
volunteer 25
Major programs: historic site(s),
historic preservation, research,
exhibits, audiovisual
programs
Period of collections: 1785-1840

POTTSTOWN
**French and Pickering Creek
Conservation Trust, Inc.**
R.D. 2, Box 360, 19464
Telephone: (215) 469-0150
Founded in: 1967
Questionnaire not received

POTTSVILLE
**Historical Society of Schuylkill
County**
14 N. 3rd St., 17901
Telephone: (717) 622-7540
County agency
Founded in: 1904
John S. Joy, Jr., Curator
Number of members: 286
Staff: full time 1
Major programs: library, archives,
manuscripts, museum, historic
site(s), book publishing,
photographic collections,
genealogical services
Period of collections: Colonial
era-1930s

PUNXSUTAWNEY
**Punxsutawney Area Historical and
Genealogical Society**
401 W. Mahoning St.
Telephone: (814) 938-2555
Mail to: P.O. Box 286, 15767
Private agency
Founded in: 1977
S. Thomas Curry, President
Number of members: 360
Staff: volunteer 8
Major programs: museum,
tours/pilgrimages,
newsletters/pamphlets,
photographic collections,
genealogical services
Period of collections: 1870-1930

QUAKERTOWN
**Pennsylvania Society, Sons of the
American Revolution**
312 Edgemont Ave., 18951
Telephone: (215) 536-2239
Private agency, authorized by
National Society, Sons of the
American Revolution
Founded in: 1889
Earnest K. Bossert, Secretary
Number of members: 2,000
Staff: part time 3
Magazine: *The Pennsylvania
Minuteman*
Major programs: historic site(s),
markers, historic preservation,
genealogical services
Period of collections: 1775-1790
Quakertown Historical Society, Inc.
26 N. Main St., 18951
Telephone: (215) 536-3499
Questionnaire not received

READING
**Historic Preservation Trust of
Berks County**
Telephone: (215) 775-1710
Mail to: P.O. Box 1681, 19603
Questionnaire not received

◇**Historical Society of Berks County**
940 Centre Ave., 19601
Telephone: (215) 375-4375
Private agency
Founded in: 1869
Harold E. Yoder, Jr., Executive
Director
Number of members: 2,100
Staff: full time 3, part time 6
Magazine: *Historical Review of Berks
County*
Major programs: library, archives,
museum, tours/pilgrimages, school
programs, book publishing,
exhibits, genealogical services
Period of collections: 1700-1950

**Reading Public Museum and Art
Gallery**
500 Museum Rd., 19611
Telephone: (215) 371-5850
City agency, authorized by Reading
School District
Founded in: 1904
Bruce L. Dietrich, Director
Staff: full time 23, volunteer 40
Major programs: library, archives,
museum, educational programs,
books, exhibits
Period of collections:
prehistoric-present

RED LION
Red Lion Area Historical Society
P.O. Box 94, 17356
Telephone: (717) 244-2032
Private agency
Founded in: 1981
Edward Grissinger, President
Number of members: 115
Major programs: oral history,
newsletters/pamphlets
Period of collections: 1860-1930

RICHFIELD
**Historical Center, Mennonite
Churches**
HCR 63, 17086
Telephone: (717) 694-3211
Private agency, authorized by Juniata
District, Mennonite Churches
Founded in: 1978
Noah L. Zimmerman, Director
Number of members: 50
Staff: part time 1, volunteer 3
Major programs: library, archives,
manuscripts, genealogical
services
Period of collections: 1700-present

RIDGWAY
Elk County Historical Society
Elk County Courthouse, Main St.
Telephone: (814) 776-1161
Mail to: P.O. Box 361, 15853
County agency
Founded in: 1964
C. William Reed, President
Number of members: 450
Staff: volunteer 1

Magazine: *The Elk Horn*
Major programs: library, archives, museum, book publishing, newsletters/pamphlets, photographic collections
Period of collections: 1850-present

ST. MARY'S

Historical Society of St. Mary's and Benzinger Township
319 Erie Ave., Room 13
Telephone: (814) 834-6525
Mail to: P.O. Box 584, 15857
Founded in: 1960
Questionnaire not received

SCHWENKSVILLE

Pennypacker Mills
5 Haldeman Rd., 19473
Telephone: (215) 287-9349
County agency, authorized by County of Montgomery
Founded in: 1981
Margaretta B. Sander, Administrator/Curator
Staff: full time 4, part time 3, volunteer 10
Major programs: archives, historic site(s), school programs, historic preservation, research, audiovisual programs, archaeology programs, landscape history, restoration program
Period of collections: 1901-1916

SCOTTDALE

Westmoreland-Fayette Historical Society
Telephone: (412) 887-7910
Mail to: W. Overton, 15683
Private agency
Founded in: 1928
Susan U. Endersbe, Executive Director
Number of members: 170
Staff: full time 1, part time 2, volunteer 35
Major programs: library, manuscripts, museum, tours, oral history, school programs, newsletters/pamphlets, research, exhibits, audiovisual programs, photographic collections, heritage play
Period of collections: late 19th-early 20th centuries

SCRANTON

Lackawanna Historical Society
232 Monroe Ave., 18510
Telephone: (717) 344-3841
Private agency
Founded in: 1886
Dorothy Allen, Executive Director
Number of members: 500
Staff: full time 1, part time 1, volunteer 10
Magazine: *Lackawanna Historical Society Bulletin*
Major programs: library, archives, manuscripts, museum, historic site(s), tours/pilgrimages, newsletters/pamphlets, photographic collections
Period of collections: 1840-1920

Scranton Anthracite Museum
R.D. 1, Bald Mt. Rd., 18504
Telephone: (717) 961-4804
State agency, authorized by Anthracite Museum Complex
Founded in: 1971
David L. Salay, Director, AMC
Number of members: 200
Staff: full time 5, part time 3, volunteer 90
Major programs: library, archives, manuscripts, museum, historic site(s), tours/pilgrimages, oral history, school programs, book publishing, newsletters/pamphlets, historic preservation, research, exhibits, audiovisual programs, photographic collections, field services
Period of collections: 1850-1950

SEWICKLEY

Dixmont State Hospital Historical Committee
Huntington Rd., 15143
Telephone: (412) 761-1780
Founded in: 1971
Questionnaire not received

SHIPPENSBURG

Shippensburg Historical Society
73 W. King St., 17257
Telephone: (717) 532-4508
Founded in: 1945
Questionnaire not received

SKIPPACK

Skippack Historical Society
Mail to: Box F, Eagleville, 19408
Founded in: 1960
Questionnaire not received

SMETHPORT

McKean County Historical Society
Courthouse, 16749
Telephone: (814) 887-5142
Private agency
Founded in: 1902
George Berkwater, President
Number of members: 200
Staff: volunteer 14
Major programs: library, archives, manuscripts, museum, school programs, newsletters/pamphlets, exhibits, photographic collections, genealogical services
Period of collections: 1850-1956

SOLEBURY

Solebury Township Historical Society
P.O. Box 223, 18963
Telephone: (215) 297-8771
Private agency
Founded in: 1980
Gwen R. Davis, Executive Director
Number of members: 200
Staff: full time 1, volunteer 6
Major programs: historic site(s), school programs, newsletters/pamphlets, research
Period of collections: 1700-1935

SOMERSET

Historical and Genealogical Society of Somerset County
Telephone: (814) 445-6077
Mail to: P.O. Box 533, 15501
James A. Bochy, President
Number of members: 1,000
Magazine: *Laurel Messenger*
Major programs: tours/pilgrimages, educational programs, books, genealogy, newsletters/pamphlets
Period of collections: 1783-1865

Somerset Historical Center
R.D. 2, Box 238, 15501
Telephone: (814) 445-6077
State agency, authorized by Pennsylvania Historical and Museum Commission
John C. Leighow, Jr., Director
Staff: full time 3, part time 2, volunteer 18
Major programs: library, museum, junior history, school programs, exhibits
Period of collections: 1750-1850

SOUDERTON

Mennonite Historians of Eastern Pennsylvania
Mennonite Heritage Center, 24 S. Main St., 18964
Telephone: (215) 723-1700, 287-8888
Mail to: 1171 Old Sumneytown Pike Harleysville, 19438
Founded in: 1974
Questionnaire not received

SPRINGS

Springs Historical Society of the Casselman Valley
15562
Telephone: (814) 662-2106/662-2625
Founded in: 1957
Ray V. Haning, Treasurer
Number of members: 250
Staff: full time 1, part time 1, volunteer 3
Magazine: *Casselman Chronicle*
Major programs: museum, newsletters/pamphlets, historic preservation
Period of collections: 1825-1975

STATE COLLEGE

Centre County Historical Society—Centre Furnace Mansion
1001 E. College Ave., 16801
Private agency
Founded in: 1904
Jacqueline J. Melander, President
Number of members: 550
Magazine: *Centre County Heritage*
Major programs: tours/pilgrimages, newsletters/pamphlets, historic preservation
Period of collections: 1800s

STRASBURG

Railroad Museum of Pennsylvania
Rt. 741
Telephone: (717) 687-8628
Mail to: P.O. Box 15, 17579
State agency, authorized by Pennsylvania Historical and Museum Commission

PENNSYLVANIA

Founded in: 1974
Robert L. Emerson, Director
Number of members: 375
Staff: full time 7, part time 5,
    volunteer 30
Major programs: library, archives,
    museum, newsletters/pamphlets,
    records management, exhibits,
    living history, photographic
    collections, railroad operations
Period of collections: 1826-present

Train Collectors Association
Telephone: (717) 687-8976
Mail to: P.O. Box 248, 17579
Founded in: 1954
Questionnaire not received

STRONGSTOWN

Strongstown Historical Society
Rt. 422, 15957
Telephone: (814) 749-9106
Questionnaire not received

STROUDSBURG

**Historical Farm Association—Quiet
    Valley Living Historical Farm**
R.D. 2, Box 2495, 18360
Telephone: (717) 992-6161
Private agency
Founded in: 1963
Sue W. Oiler, Co-manager
Number of members: 525
Staff: part time 25, volunteer 25
Major programs: museum, school
    programs, living history
Period of collections: 1765-1900

Monroe County Historical Society
900 Main St.
Telephone: (717) 421-7703
Mail to: P.O. Box 488, 18360-0488
Private agency
Founded in: 1921
Vertie Knapp, Curator
Number of members: 550
Magazine: *The Fan Light*
Major programs: library, archives,
    manuscripts, museum, historic
    site(s), tours/pilgrimages, school
    programs, newsletters/pamphlets,
    records management, research,
    exhibits, archaeology programs,
    photographic collections,
    genealogical services
Period of collections: 1800-1950

**Monroe County Museum
    Association**
537 Ann St., 18360
Telephone: (717) 424-1776
Private agency
Founded in: 1976
Carol H. Kern, President
Number of members: 280
Staff: part time 1, volunteer 10
Major programs: museum, school
    programs, newsletters/pamphlets,
    historic preservation, exhibits
Period of collections: 1850-1935

SWARTHMORE

**American Association of Botanical
    Gardens and Arboreta, Inc.**
515 College Ave.
Telephone: (215) 328-9145

Mail to: P.O. Box 206, 19081
Private agency
Founded in: 1940
Susan H. Lathrop, Executive Director
Number of members: 900
Staff: full time 2, volunteer 30

**Friends Historical Library of
    Swarthmore College**
Swarthmore College, 19081
Telephone: (215) 447-7496
Founded in: 1871
J. William Frost, Director
Staff: full time 3, part time 4
Major programs: library, archives,
    manuscripts
Period of collections: 1650-present

**Swarthmore College Peace
    Collection**
19081
Telephone: (215) 447-7557
Private agency, authorized by the
    college
Founded in: 1930
Jean R. Soderlund, Curator
Staff: full time 1, part time 4,
    volunteer 2
Major programs: library, archives,
    manuscripts, research,
    photographic collections, history of
    peace and reform movements
Period of collections: 1880-present

TARENTUM

**Allegheny-Kiski Valley Historical
    Society, Inc.**
224 E. 7th Ave., 15084
Telephone: (412) 224-7666
Private agency
Founded in: 1967
Howard L. Jester, President
Staff: volunteer 20
Magazine: *Historia*
Major programs: library, archives,
    museum, tours/pilgrimages, oral
    history, exhibits, audiovisual
    programs, photographic
    collections
Period of collections: 1800-present

TITUSVILLE

Drake Well Museum
R.D. 3, 16354
Telephone: (814) 827-2797
State agency, authorized by
    Pennsylvania Historical and
    Museum Commission
Founded in: 1934
Vance Packard, Director
Staff: full time 10, part time 10,
    volunteer 8
Period of collections: 1850-1930

Titusville Historical Society
c/o Benson Memorial Library, 213 N.
    Franklin St., 16354
Private agency
Founded in: 1977
Richard Fox, President
Number of members: 75
Major programs: historic
    preservation, audiovisual
    programs, photographic
    collections
Period of collections: 1870-1920

TOWANDA

Bradford County Historical Society
21 Main St., 18848
Telephone: (717) 265-2240
County agency, authorized by
    Bradford County Commissioners
Founded in: 1870
Richard M. Robinon, President
Number of members: 900
Staff: full time 1, volunteer 16
Magazine: *The Settle*
Major programs: library, junior
    history, book publishing,
    newsletters/pamphlets, exhibits,
    genealogical services
Period of collections: 18th
    century-20th centuries

French Azilum Inc.
R.D. 2, Box 266, 18848
Telephone: (717) 265-3376
Founded in: 1954
Questionnaire not received

TUNKHANNOCK

Wyoming County Historical Society
Corner, Bridge and Harrison Sts.
Telephone: (717) 836-5303
Mail to: P.O. Box 309, 18657
County agency
Founded in: 1977
Jean M. Brewer, Curator
Magazine: *Lest-We-Forget-Wyoming
    County Pioneers*
Major programs: library, museum,
    newsletters/pamphlets, research,
    genealogical services
Period of collections: 1842-present

TURBOTVILLE

**Warrior Run Fort Freeland Heritage
    Society**
P.O. Box 26, 17772
Telephone: (717) 538-1417
Private agency
Founded in: 1978
June Shuman, President
Number of members: 305
Staff: volunteer 22
Major programs: historic site(s),
    newsletters/pamphlets, historic
    preservation, genealogical
    services

UNIVERSITY PARK

**North American Society for Sport
    History**
101 White Bldg., Penn State
    University, 16802
Telephone: (814) 865-7591
Private agency
Founded in: 1972
Ronald A. Smith, Secretary/Treasurer
Number of members: 600
Staff: part time 1, volunteer 20
Magazine: *Journal of Sport History*
Major programs: archives,
    newsletters/pamphlets, research,
    exhibits
Period of collections: 1970-present

◇**Pennsylvania Historical
    Association**
704 New Liberal Arts Tower,
    Department of History,
    Pennsylvania State

University, 16802
Telephone: (814) 863-0105/865-1367
Private agency
Founded in: 1933
Neil A. McNall, Business Secretary
Number of members: 775
Staff: part time 2
Magazine: *Pennsylvania History*
Major programs:
   newsletters/pamphlets

UPLAND

Friends of Caleb Pusey House, Inc.
15 Race St., 19015
Telephone: (215) 874-0900
Questionnaire not received

VALLEY FORGE

**American Motley
   Association—Valley Forge Office
   Colony**
Telephone: (215) 933-1775
Mail to: P.O. Box 708, 19481
Founded in: 1976
Thomas Motley-Freeman, Director
Number of members: 300
Staff: full time 2, volunteer 4
Magazine: *Motley Ancestral
   Gleanings*
Major programs: library, archives,
   manuscripts,
   newsletters/pamphlets
Period of collections: 1635-present

Valley Forge Historical Society
P.O. Box 122, 19481
Telephone: (215) 783-0535
Private agency
Founded in: 1918
Mrs. L. Davis Jones, President
Number of members: 1,000
Staff: full time 2, part time 2,
   volunteer 50
Magazine: *The Valley Forge Journal*
Major programs: library, museum,
   exhibits
Period of collections: Revolutionary
   War era

**Valley Forge National Historical
   Park**
19481
Telephone: (215) 783-1000
Federal agency, authorized by
   Department of the Interior
Founded in: 1977
Wallace B. Elms, Superintendent
Staff: full time 61, part time 50,
   volunteer 125
Major programs: library, archives,
   museum, historic site(s),
   tours/pilgrimages, school
   programs, newsletters/pamphlets,
   historic preservation, exhibits,
   living history, audiovisual
   programs, genealogical services
Period of collections: Revolutionary
   War

WALLINGFORD

**Friends of the Thomas Leiper
   House**
521 Avondale Rd., 19086
Telephone: (215) 566-6365
Private agency
Founded in: 1977
Mrs. Thomas Hewett, President

Number of members: 100
Staff: volunteer 10
Major programs: historic site(s),
   historic preservation
Period of collections: 1780s-1830

WARREN

Warren County Historical Society
210 4th Ave.
Telephone: (814) 723-1795
Mail to: P.O. Box 427, 16365
County agency
Founded in: 1900
Chase Putnam, Executive Director
Staff: full time 3, part time 1,
   volunteer 35
Magazine: *Stepping Stones*
Major programs: library, archives,
   museum, book publishing,
   newsletters/pamphlets,
   genealogical services
Period of collections: 1790-1920

WASHINGTON

David Bradford House
175 S. Main
Telephone: (412) 222-3604
Mail to: P.O. Box 537, 15301
State agency, authorized by Bradford
   House Historical Association
Founded in: 1982
Roberta Wilkinson, Director/Curator
Number of members: 50
Staff: full time 1, volunteer 8
Major programs: historic site(s), oral
   history, historic preservation, living
   history
Period of collections: 18th century

**Pennsylvania Railway Museum
   Association, Inc./Arden Trolley
   Museum**
N. Main St., 15301
Telephone: (412) 734-5780
Mail to: P.O. Box 832, Pittsburgh,
   15230
Private agency
Founded in: 1953
Oliver Miller, President
Number of members: 350
Staff: volunteer 36
Magazine: *Trolley Fare*
Major programs: library, museum,
   tours/pilgrimages, book publishing,
   newsletters/pamphlets, historic
   preservation, exhibits
Period of collections: 1896-1945

**Washington County Historical
   Society**
LeMoyne House, 49 E. Maiden St.,
   15301
Telephone: (412) 225-6740
Founded in: 1900
Edna B. Miller, Director
Number of members: 300
Staff: full time 1
Major programs: library, museum
Period of collections: 1776-present

WASHINGTON CROSSING

Washington Crossing Historic Park
P.O. Box 103, 18977
Telephone: (2l5) 493-4076
State agency, authorized by
   Pennsylvania Historical and
   Museum Commission

Founded in: 1917
Thomas A. Lainhoff, Administrator
Number of members: 2,755
Staff: full time 17, part time 1,
   volunteer 50
Major programs: library, museum,
   historic site(s)
Period of collections: 1750-1830

Washington Crossing Foundation
General DeFermoy Rd.
Telephone: (215) 493-6755
Mail to: P.O. Box 1976, 18977
Private agency
Founded in: 1964
Ann Hawkes Hutton, Chair and Chief
   Executive Officer
Number of members: 1,265
Staff: full time 1, part time 3,
   volunteer 25
Magazine: *Spirit of '76 Sentinel*
Major programs: library, manuscripts,
   historic site(s),
   newsletters/pamphlets, historic
   preservation
Period of collections: American
   Revolution

WAYNE

Radnor Historical Society
113 W. Beechtree Lane, 19087
Telephone: (215) 688-2668
Founded in: 1948
Questionnaire not received

WAYNESBORO

Renfrew Museum and Park
1010 E. Main St., 17268
Telephone: (717) 762-4723
Founded in: 1973
Questionnaire not received

Waynesboro Historical Society
323 E. Main St., 17268
Telephone: (717) 762-7123
Founded in: 1963
Frances H. Miller, Secretary
Number of members: 150
Major programs: museum, historic
   site(s), book publishing, historic
   preservation

WAYNESBURG

Cornerstone Genealogical Society
519 4th Ave.
Telephone: (412) 627-5255
Mail to: P.O. Box 547, 15370
Founded in: 1975
Questionnaire not received

Greene County Historical Society
R.D. 2, 15370
Telephone: (412) 627-3204
Founded in: 1926
Questionnaire not received

Warrior Trail Association, Inc.
312 County Office Bldg., 15370
Telephone: (412) 627-5030
Private agency
Founded in: 1965
W. B. Waychoff, President
Number of members: 150
Staff: volunteer 20
Period of collections: prehistoric

WEATHERLY

Eckley Miners' Village
R.D. 2, Box 236, 18255
Telephone: (717) 636-2070
Authorized by Pennsylvania Historical
and Museum Commission
Founded in: 1969
David L. Salay, Director, Anthracite
Museum Complex
Number of members: 200
Staff: full time 7, part time 3,
volunteer 50
Major programs: library, museum,
historic site(s), tours, oral history,
school programs,
newsletters/pamphlets, historic
preservation, research, exhibits,
photographic collections
Period of collections: 1850-1950

WELLSBORO

Tioga County Historical Society
The Robinson House, 120 Main St.
Telephone: (717) 724-6116
Mail to: P.O. Box 724, 16901
Private agency
Founded in: 1906
A. William Ladd, President
Number of members: 400
Major programs: library, archives,
manuscripts, museum, historic
site(s), oral history, book
publishing, newsletters/pamphlets,
historic preservation, records
management, research, exhibits,
photographic collections,
genealogical services
Period of collections: 1804-present

WEST CHESTER

Chester County Historical Society
225 N. High St., 19380
Telephone: (215) 692-4800
Founded in: 1893
Roland H. Woodward, Executive
Director
Number of members: 1,300
Staff: full time 16, part time 4
Major programs: library, archives,
manuscripts, museum, historic
site(s), newsletters/pamphlets,
records management, exhibits,
photographic collections,
genealogical services
Period of collections: 17th
century-present

WILKES-BARRE

**Wyoming Historical and Geological
Society**
49 S. Franklin St., 18701
Telephone: (717) 823-6244
Private agency
Founded in: 1858
Burt Logan, Executive Director
Number of members: 750
Staff: full time 4, part time 4,
volunteer 25
Magazine: *Forecast*
Major programs: library, archives,
manuscripts, museum, historic
site(s), schoolprograms, book
publishing, newsletters/pamphlets,
historic preservation, research,

exhibits, photographic collections,
genealogical services
Period of collections: 1700-present

WILLIAMSPORT

**Lycoming County Historical
Museum**
858 W. 4th St., 17701
Telephone: (717) 326-3326
Private agency, authorized by
Lycoming County Historical Society
Founded in: 1907
Joseph J. Zebrowski, Director
Number of members: 1,100
Staff: full time 1, part time 3,
volunteer 25
Magazine: *The Journal of the
Lycoming County Historical Society*
Major programs: library, archives,
manuscripts, museum,
tours/pilgrimages, junior history,
oral history, school
programs,newsletters/pamphlets,
research, exhibits, audiovisual
programs, archaeology programs,
photographic collections,
genealogical services
Period of collections: 1769-present

WORCESTER

Peter Wentz Farmstead
Schultz Rd.
Telephone: (215) 584-5104
Mail to: P.O. Box 240, 19490
County agency, authorized by
Commissioners of Montgomery
County
Founded in: 1976
Albert T. Gamon,
Director/Administrator
Number of members: 230
Staff: full time 3, volunteer 70
Magazine: *Wentz Post*
Major programs: library, museum,
historic site(s), school programs,
newsletters/pamphlets, historic
preservation, audiovisual programs
Period of collections: 1777

WYNNEWOOD

**Pennsylvania Society, Order of
Founders & Patriots of America**
1034 Nicholson Rd., 19096
Telephone: (215) 642-4501
Founded in: 1896
Questionnaire not received

YARDLEY

Yardley Historical Association, Inc.
46 W. Afton Ave.
Telephone: (215) 493-9883
Mail to: P.O. Box 212, 19067
Private agency
Founded in: 1964
Annamae D. Bakun, President
Number of members: 200
Staff: volunteer 3
Major programs: library, archives,
manuscripts, oral history,
newsletters/pamphlets, exhibits,
photographic collections
Period of collections: mid
1800s-present

YORK

American Canal Society, Inc.
809 Rathton Rd., 17403
Telephone: (717) 843-4035
Founded in: 1972
William H. Shank, President
Number of members: 750
Staff: volunteer 8
Magazine: *American Canals*
Major programs: markers,
newsletters/pamphlets, field trips
Period of collections: 1783-present

Historic York, Inc.
Telephone: (717) 843-0320
Mail to: P.O. Box 2312, 17405
County agency
Founded in: 1975
Lynn S. Rosental, Executive Director
Number of members: 500
Staff: full time 4, part time 1,
volunteer 30
Major programs: library,
tours/pilgrimages, book publishing,
newsletters/pamphlets, historic
preservation, field services
Period of collections: 1760s-present

Historical Society of York County
250 E. Market St., 17403
Telephone: (717) 848-1587
Private agency
Founded in: 1895
Philip D. Zimmerman, Executive
Director
Number of members: 2
Staff: full time 10, part time 4,
volunteer 100
Magazine: *York Gazette and Public
Advertiser*
Major programs: library, archives,
manuscripts, museum, historic
site(s), school programs,
newsletters/pamphlets, exhibits,
photographic collections,
genealogical services
Period of collections: 1750-present

ZELIENOPLE

Zelienople Historical Society
243 S. Main St., 16063
Telephone: (412) 452-9457
Private agency
Founded in: 1975
Margaretta Foyle, Executive Director
Number of members: 650
Staff: part time 3, volunteer 35
Major programs: library, archives,
manuscripts, museum, historic
site(s), tours/pilgrimages, oral
history, school programs, book
publishing, newsletters/pamphlets,
historic preservation, records
management, research, exhibits,
living history, audiovisual
programs, photographic
collections, genealogical services,
field services, speaking
engagements
Period of collections: 19th-century

RHODE ISLAND

BARRINGTON

Barrington Preservation Society
P.O. Box 178, 02806
Private agency
Founded in: 1965
Jean Buffum, President
Number of members: 118
Staff: volunteer 20
Major programs: museum, exhibits, photographic collections, historic house research

BLOCK ISLAND

Block Island Historical Society
P.O. Box 79, 02807
Telephone: (401) 466-2481
Mail to: c/o Executive Director, 25 Salisbury Rd., Darien, CT., 06820
Private agency
Founded in: 1942
Bernice M. Gill, Executive Director
Number of members: 992
Staff: part time 3, volunteer 10
Major programs: museum, markers, historic preservation, exhibits, archaeology programs, photographic collections, genealogical services, architectural survey
Period of collections: 19th-20th centuries

BRISTOL

Blithewold Gardens and Arboretum
101 Ferry Rd., 02809
Telephone: (401) 253-8714
Private agency, authorized by Heritage Foundation of Rhode Island
Mark Zelonis, Director
Number of members: 425
Staff: full time 1, part time 24
Magazine: *Blithewold News Letter*
Major programs: library, museum, historic site(s), markers, tours/pilgrimages, newsletters/pamphlets, historic preservation
Period of collections: 1895-1930

Bristol Historical and Preservation Society
48 Court St., 02809
Telephone: (401) 253-5705/253-8825
Founded in: 1936
Questionnaire not received

Coggeshall Farm Museum
Colt State Park
Telephone: (401) 253-9062
Mail to: P.O. Box 562, 02809
Private agency
Founded in: 1973
Richard Sullivan, Director
Number of members: 200
Staff: part time 1, volunteer 10
Major programs: museum
Period of collections: late 18th-mid 19th centuries

CHEPACHET

Company of Light Infantry of the Town of Gloucester
P.O. Box 1774, Dorr Dr., 02814

Telephone: (401) 568-6691
Founded in: 1774
Questionnaire not received

Glocester Heritage Society
Main St.
Mail to: P.O. Box 269, 02814
Private agency
Founded in: 1967
Clinton Gustafson, President
Number of members: 102
Staff: volunteer 40
Major programs: archives, book publishing, newsletters/pamphlets, historic preservation, photographic collections
Period of collections: 1870-1930

COVENTRY

Coventry Historical Society
Rt. 117
Mail to: P.O. Box 401, 02816
Questionnaire not received

Western Rhode Island Civic Historical Society
1 Station St., 02816
Telephone: (401) 231-9492
Founded in: 1945
Questionnaire not received

CRANSTON

Cranston Historic District Commission
869 Park Ave., 02910
Telephone: (401) 781-6729
City agency
Arthur W. Butler, Jr., Associate Planner/Staff Assistant
Major programs: historic site(s), markers, school programs, pamphlets

Cranston Historical Society
Governor Sprague Mansion, 1351 Cranston St., 02920
Telephone: (401) 944-9226
Founded in: 1947
Questionnaire not received

EAST GREENWICH

Continental Ladies
57 Pierce St.
Telephone: (401) 884-4110
Mail to: P.O. Box 14, 02818
Questionnaire not received

General James Mitchell Varnum House
57 Pierce St.
Mail to: 36 Bayview Ave., 02818
Founded in: 1773
Questionnaire not received

Varnum Continentals
6 Main St.
Telephone: (401) 884-4110
Mail to: P.O. Box 14, 02818
Founded in: 1907
Questionnaire not received

FOSTER

Foster Preservation Society
P.O. Box 51, 02825
Private agency
Founded in: 1969
Mrs. Thomas J. Matthews, President
Number of members: 75

HOPE VALLEY

Historical Archives, Langworthy Public Library
Spring St., 02832
Telephone: (401) 539-2851
Private agency
Founded in: 1888
Hope Greene Andrews, Archivist
Staff: volunteer
Major programs: library, archives, research, photographic collections, genealogical services
Period of collections: 1636-present

Lincoln Group of Boston
R.F.D. Hope Valley Rd., 02832
Telephone: (401) 331-2222
Private agency
Founded in: 1938
Frank J. Williams, President
Number of members: 79
Staff: volunteer 4
Major programs: library, archives, museum, newsletters/pamphlets
Period of collections: 1809-1865

HOPKINTON

Hopkinton Historical Association
Town House Rd.
Telephone: (401) 337-2219
Mail to: Egypt St., P.O. Box 475, Ashaway, 02804
Private agency
Founded in: 1957
Marge Candal, President
Number of members: 52
Staff: volunteer 12
Major programs: archives, markers, school programs, historic preservation, exhibits

JAMESTOWN

Jamestown Historical Society
92 Narragansett Ave., 02835
Telephone: (401) 423-0784
Private agency
Founded in: 1912
Wilbur T. Holmes, President
Number of members: 200
Major programs: archives, museum, historic site(s), markers, exhibits, photographic collections, genealogical services
Period of collections: early 19th century-present

KINGSTON

Pettaguamscatt Historical Society
1348 Kingstown Rd., 02881
Telephone: (401) 783-1328
Founded in: 1958
Elizabeth R. Albro, President
Number of members: 258
Staff: part time 1, volunteer 3
Magazine: *Volunteer Pettaguamscutt Reporter*
Major programs: library, museum, research, genealogical services
Period of collections: 1783-present

LIME ROCK

Blackstone Valley Historical Society
Old Louisquisett Pike, 02865
Private agency
Founded in: 1958

Edward B. McDermott, President
Number of members: 220
Staff: volunteer 50
Major programs: library, junior
  history, oral history, book
  publishing
Period of collections: 1700-1900

LITTLE COMPTON

Little Compton Historical Society
West Rd., 02837
Telephone: (401) 635-4559
Private agency
Founded in: 1937
Carlton C. Brownell, Director
Number of members: 510
Staff: part time 3, volunteer16
Major programs: library, archives,
  museum, historic site(s), book
  publishing, historic preservation,
  research, exhibits, photographic
  collections
Period of collections: 18th-19th
  centuries

MIDDLETOWN

**International Tennis Hall of
  Fame—Tennis Museum**
194 Bellvue Ave., 02840
Telephone: (401) 849-3990
Founded in: 1954
Private agency
Jane G. Brown, Executive Director
Staff: full time 7, part time 2
Major programs: library, archives,
  museum, historic site(s), historic
  preservation, exhibits, sports
  history
Period of collections: 1880-present

Middletown Historic Society, Inc.
Telephone: ((401) 846-2186
Mail to: P.O. Box 196, 02840
Founded in: 1976
Questionnaire not received

**Whitehall, Home of Bishop
  Berkeley**
Berkeley Ave., 02840
Telephone: (401) 846-3116
Private agency, authorized by
  National Society Colonial Dames of
  America
Founded in: 1893
Mrs. Pickett M. Greig, Chair, Whitehall
  Committee
Major programs: museum
Period of collections: 1729-1731

NARRAGANSETT

South County Museum
Canonchet Farm
Telephone: (401) 783-5400
Mail to: P.O. Box 709, 02882
Private agency
Founded in: 1934
William D. Metz, President
Number of members: 150
Staff: part time 1, volunteer 10
Major programs: museum, exhibits
Period of collections: 19th century

NEWPORT

Artillery Company of Newport
23 Clarke St.
Telephone: (401) 846-8488

Mail to: P.O. Box 14, 02840
Founded in: 1741
Questionnaire not received

**International Tennis Hall of Fame
  and Tennis Museum**
194 Bellevue Ave., 02840
Telephone: (401) 846-4567
Founded in: 1954
Questionnaire not received

Naval War College Museum
Coasters Harbor Island, 02840
Telephone: (401) 841-4052
Federal agency, authorized by the
  U.S. Navy
Founded in: 1978
Anthony S. Nicolosi, Director
Staff: full time 3, part time 3
Major programs: museum, historic
  sites preservation,
  newsletters/pamphlets
Period of collections: 1865-present

Newport Historical Society
82 Touro St., 02840
Telephone: (401) 846-0813
Founded in: 1853
Daniel Snydacker, Executive Director
Number of members: 1,150
Staff: full time 6, part time 1,
  volunteer 6
Magazine: *Newport History*
Major programs: library, archives,
  manuscripts, museum, historic
  site(s), oral history, school
  programs, newsletters/pamphlets,
  historic preservation, research,
  exhibits, photographic collections,
  genealogical services, educational
  outreach
Period of collections: mid 17th
  century-present

Newport Historical Society, Inc.
Courthouse Square
Telephone: (603) 863-2079
Mail to: P.O. Box 492, 03773
Founded in: 1975
Mrs. Myron Tenney, Vice President

Major programs: museum, historic
  preservation, tours/pilgrimages,
  oral history, school programs

**Preservation Society of Newport
  County**
118 Mill St. 02840
Telephone: (401) 847-1000
Private agency
Founded in: 1945
John A. Cherol, Executive Director
Number of members: 2,300
Staff: full time 47, part time 200,
  volunteer 75
Magazine: *Newport Gazette*
Major programs: historic sites
  preservation, books,
  newsletters/pamphlets
Period of collections: 1748-1902

Redwood Library and Athenaeum
50 Bellevue Ave., 02840
Telephone: (401) 847-0292
Founded in: 1747
Questionnaire not received

**Royal Arts Foundation, Belcourt
  Castle**
Bellevue Ave., 02840
Telephone: (401) 846-0669
Private agency
Founded in: 1969
Mrs. Harold B. Tinney,
  President/Treasurer
Staff: full time 6, part time 6,
  volunteer 4
Major programs: museum, historic
  sites preservation, historic
  preservation
Period of collections: 17th-19th
  centuries

Seaport 76 Foundation Limited
Telephone: (401) 846-1776
Mail to: P.O. Box 76, 02840
Founded in: 1974
Questionnaire not received

NORTH KINGSTOWN

South County Museum, Inc.
Quaker Lane, Rt. 2

Coronation coach from Belcourt Castle in Newport. The four-ton coach was crafted by the Harold B. Tinney family with delicate oil paintings and decorations in 23-carat gold.—
Photograph by John T. Hopf

Telephone (401) 295-0498
Mail to: P.O. Box 182, 02852
Founded in: 1933
Questionnaire not received

NORTH SCITUSTE

Western Rhode Island Civic Historical Society
1 Station St.
Telephone: (401) 231-9492/647-3119
William F. Sedgley, President
Number of members: 225
Staff: volunteer 10
Magazine: *The Hinterlander*
Major programs: museum, historic preservation, exhibits
Period of collections: 1750-1850

NORTH SMITHFIELD

North Smithfield Heritage Association
Main St. Forestdale, 02895
Mail to: P.O. Box 413, Slatersville, 02876
Founded in: 1970
Questionnaire not received

PASCOAG

Burrillville Historical and Preservation Society
Mail to: P.O. Box 93, 02859
Telephone: (401) 569-5451
Founded in: 1971
Joyce G. Knibb, Executive Committee Chair
Staff: full time 1, volunteer 10
Major programs: library, historic site(s), oral history, school programs, newsletters/pamphlets, research, exhibits, audiovisual programs, photographic collections
Period of collections: 1806-present

PAWTUCKET

American-French Genealogical Society
P.O. Box 2113, 02861-2113
Telephone: (401) 769-8079
Private agency
Founded in: 1978
Lucille F. Rock, President
Number of members: 500
Staff: volunteer 25
Magazine: *Je Me Souviens*
Major programs: library, archives, manuscripts, oral history, school programs, newsletters/pamphlets, research, living history, audiovisual programs, genealogical services
Period of collections: 1600-present

2nd Rhode Island Regiment of the Continental Line
141 Lafayette St., 02860
Telephone: (401) 723-0063
Private agency
Founded in: 1977
Carl Becker, Captain
Number of members: 30
Staff: volunteer 5
Major programs: school programs, newsletters/pamphlets, research, living history, audiovisual programs
Period of collections: 1700-1800

Slater Mill Historic Site
Telephone: (401) 725-8638
Mail to: P.O. Box 727, 02862
Founded in: 1952
Patrick M. Malone, Director
Number of members: 700
Staff: full time 4, part time 5
Magazine: *The Flyer*
Major programs: library, museum, historic site(s), school programs, newsletters/pamphlets, historic preservation, research, exhibits
Period of collections: 1783-1936

PROVIDENCE

First Baptist Church in America
75 N. Main St., 02903
Telephone: (401) 751-2266
Private agency
Founded in: 1638
Camille C. Bedard, Chair, Meeting House Guides Committee
Staff: volunteer 20
Major programs: archives, museum, tours/pilgrimages, oral history, school programs, newsletters/pamphlets, historic preservation
Period of collections: 1775

Governor Stephen Hopkins House
Hopkins, Corner of Benefit St., 02903
Private agency, authorized by National Society of Colonial Dames
Founded in: 1929
Viki Ott, Chair
Number of members: 200
Staff: part time 2, volunteer 30
Major programs: museum, historic site(s), tours/pilgrimages, historic preservation
Period of collections: 1730-1785

Heritage Foundation of Rhode Island
Telephone: (401) 278-8353
Mail to: R. I. Hospital Trust National Bank, 1 Hospital Trust Plaza, 02903
Questionnaire not received

League of Rhode Island Historical Societies
52 Power St., 02906
Telephone: (401) 331-8575
Founded in: 1965
Questionnaire not received

Museum of Art, Rhode Island School of Design
224 Benefit St., 02903
Telephone: (401) 331-3511
Private agency
Founded in: 1877
Franklin W. Robinson, Director
Number of members: 3,300
Staff: full time 37, part time 12, volunteer 75
Major programs: museum, tours/pilgrimages, educational programs, books, newsletters/pamphlets
Period of collections: 3,000 B.C.-present

The Providence Athenaeum
251 Benefit St., 02903
Telephone: (401) 421-6970
Private agency
Founded in: 1753
Sally Duplaix, Executive Director

Number of members: 1,300
Staff: full time 10, part time 8, volunteer 10
Magazine: *The Athenaeum Bulletin*
Major programs: library, museum, tours/pilgrimages, educational programs, newsletters/pamphlets, conservation
Period of collections: 1783-1895

Providence City Archives
Dorrance St., 02903
Telephone: (401) 421-7740, ext. 290
Mail to: Providence City Hall
Linda J. McElroy, City Archivist
Staff: full time 1, volunteer 3
Major programs: archives
Period of collections: 1636-present

Providence Preservation Society
24 Meeting St., 02903
Telephone: (401) 831-7440
Founded in: 1956
Wendy Nicholas, Executive Director
Number of members: 1,500
Staff: full time 4, part time 1, volunteer 100
Magazine: *PPS News*
Major programs: markers, tours/pilgrimages, educational programs, newsletters/pamphlets
Period of collections: 1750-present

Rhode Island Black Heritage Society
1 Hilton St., 02905
Telephone: (401) 751-3490
Private agency
Founded in: 1975
Rowena Stewart, Director
Number of members: 600
Staff: full time 3, part time 2, volunteer 5
Magazine: *Black in R. I.*
Major programs: library, archives, museum, markers, tours/pilgrimages, oral history, newsletters/pamphlets, records management, research, exhibits, photographic collections, field services
Period of collections: 1652-present

Rhode Island Cemeteries
Office of Veterans Affairs, 46 Aborn St., 02903
Telephone: (401) 277-2488
Questionnaire not received

◇Rhode Island Committee for the Humanities
463 Broadway
Telephone: (401) 273-2250
Authorized by: National Endowment for the Humanities
Founded in: 1972
Tomas H. Roberts, Executive Director
Staff: full time 3, part time 3, volunteer 23
Major programs: library, archives, museum, oral history, school programs, newsletters/pamphlets, historic preservation, research, exhibits, photographic collections

Rhode Island Heritage Month, Inc.
Telephone: (401) 277-2601
Mail to: c/o R. I. Dept. of Economic Development, 7 Jackson Walkway, 02903
Leonard J. Panaggio, Director

Rhode Island Historical Preservation Commission
150 Benefit St., 02903
Telephone: (401) 277-2678
Founded in: 1968
Edward F. Sanderson, Executive Director
Staff: full time 8, part time 5, volunteer 1
Major programs: historic site(s), newsletters/pamphlets, historic preservation, research, archaeology programs, field services
Period of collections: prehistoric-present

◊Rhode Island Historical Society
110 Benevolent St., 02906
Telephone: (401) 331-8575
Founded in: 1822
Albert T. Klyberg, Director
Number of members: 3,000
Staff: full time 35, part time 5, volunteer 150
Magazine: *Rhode Island History*
Major programs: library, archives, manuscripts, museum, historic site(s), tours/pilgrimages, junior history, oral history, school programs, book publishing, newsletters/pamphlets, historic preservation, records management, research, exhibits, photographic collections, genealogical services, field services
Period of collections: to 1900s

Rhode Island Jewish Historical Association
130 Sessions St., 02906
Telephone: (401) 331-1360
Private agency
Founded in: 1951
Seebert J. Goldowsky, President
Number of members: 500
Staff: part time 3, volunteer 5
Major programs: library, archives, book publishing
Period of collections: 1650s-present

Rhode Island State Archives
State House, Room 43, 02903
Telephone: (401) 277-2353
State agency
Phyllis C. Silva, Assistant-in-Charge
Major programs: archives, museum, historic preservation, research, genealogical services
Period of collections: 1636-1800

Roger Williams Park Museum of Natural History
Roger Williams Park, 02905
Telephone: (401) 875-9450
City agency, authorized by Department of Parks
Staff: full time 4, part time 3, volunteer 10
Major programs: library, archives, museum, historic site(s), tours/pilgrimages, school programs, exhibits
Period of collections: prehistoric-present

RICHMOND

Richmond Historical Society
02898
Telephone: (401) 539-7683/539-7676
Private agency
Founded in: 1968
Eleanor H. Smith, Archivist
Number of members: 54
Major programs: archives, museum, newsletters/pamphlets, photographic collections, genealogical services
Period of collections: late 1800s-early 1900s

ROCKVILE

Anthro/Arts
Canonchet Rd., Box 56, 02873
Telephone: (401) 539-2793
Private agency
Founded in: 1983
David Marshall, Director
Staff: full time 1
Major programs: oral history, research, field services
Period of collections: 1900-1940

SAUNDERSTOWN

Gilbert Stuart Memorial, Inc.
Gilbert Stuart Rd., 02874
Telephone: (401) 294-3001
Founded in: 1930
Mrs. Kenneth Pettigrew, Curator
Number of members: 200
Staff: full time 1, part time 2, volunteer 2
Major programs: museum, historic sites preservation, tours/pilgrimages, educational programs
Period of collections: 1750-1783

SCITUATE

Preservation and Heritage Society of Scituate
P.O. Box 551, 02857
Private agency
Founded in: 1975
Barbara Sarkesian, President
Number of members: 100
Major programs: archives, junior history, oral history, school programs, newsletters/pamphlets, research, exhibits, photographic collections, genealogical services
Period of collections: 1800-1920

WARREN

Massasoit Historical Association
Mail to: P.O. Box 203, 02885
Private agency
Founded in: 1907
Ray Medley, President
Number of members: 150
Major programs: museum, historic site(s), tours, school programs, book publishing, historic preservation, exhibits, living history, photographic collections, genealogical services
Period of collections: 1750-1850

WARWICK

Gaspee Day Committee
Telephone: (401) 781-1772
Mail to: P.O. Box 1772, Pilgrim Station, 02888
Founded in: 1966
Questionnaire not received

Warwick Historical Society
25 Roger Williams Circle, 02888
Telephone: (401) 467-7647
Private agency
Founded in: 1932
Eileen Naughton, President
Number of members: 300
Staff: part time 1, volunteer 15
Major programs: library, archives, museum, historic site(s), tours/pilgrimages, oral history, school programs, newsletters/pamphlets, exhibits, audiovisual programs
Period of collections: 1642-present

Warwick Museum
334 Knight St., 02886
Telephone: (401) 737-0010
Questionnaire not received

WESTERLY

Westerly Historical Society
124 Granite St.
Telephone: (401) 596-4424
Mail to: P.O. Box 19, 02891
Private agency
Founded in: 1913
Number of members: 276
Staff: volunteer 40
Major programs: manuscripts, museum, historic site(s), tours/pilgrimages, oral history, school programs, newsletters/pamphlets, historic preservation, records management, research, exhibits, audiovisual programs, photographic collections, genealogical services
Period of collections: 1734-present

Westerly Public Library Granite Collection
Broad St., 02891
Telephone: (401) 596-2877
Private agency
Founded in: 1892
David Panciers, Executive Director
Staff: full time 20, part time 13, volunteer 14
Major programs: library, archives, oral history, research, photographic collections, genealogical services
Period of collections: 1880-1940

WICKFORD

Main Street Association of Wickford
68 Main St., 02852
Telephone: (401) 294-6479
Private agency
Founded in: 1934
Violet R. Daniel, Secretary
Number of members: 384
Major programs: historic site(s), markers, tours/pilgrimages, historic preservation
Period of collections: 17th-18th centuries

Smith's Castle at Cocumscussoc
Rt. 1, 02852
Telephone: (401) 294-3521
Private agency
Founded in: 1678
Number of members: 250
Staff: full time 2, volunteer 40
Major programs: museum, historic
site(s), tours/pilgrimages, junior
history, school programs, historic
preservation, exhibits, living history
Period of collections: 1780-1840

WOONSOCKET

**La Societe Historique
Franco-Americaine**
P.O. Box F, 02895
Private agency
Founded in: 1899
Oda Beaulieu, President
Number of members: 200
Staff: volunteer 3
Major programs: historic site(s),
markers, oral history,
newsletters/pamphlets, historic
preservation, living history
Period of collections: 1899-present

Woonsocket Historical Society
563 S. Main St., 02895
Telephone: (401) 769-9846
Founded in: 1915
Phyllis H. Thomas, President
Number of members: 65
Major programs: historic sites
preservation, markers,
tours/pilgrimages, educational
programs, books
Period of collections: 1777-present

SOUTH CAROLINA

ABBEVILLE

Abbeville County Historical Society
202 Church St., 29620
Telephone: (803) 459-2466
County agency
Founded in: 1957
Mrs. Rufus W. Hutchinson, President
Number of members: 88
Staff: volunteer 6
Major programs: tours/pilgrimages,
historic preservation, photographic
collections
Period of collections: early 20th
century

**Abbeville Historic Preservation
Commission**
313 Greenville, 29620
Telephone: (803) 459-4297
Private agency
Founded in: 1971
Margaret Flynn Bowie, Chair
Staff: volunteer 7
Major programs: tours/pilgrimages,
historic preservation, living history

AIKEN

**Aiken County Historical
Commission**
433 Newberry St., SW, 29801

Telephone: (803) 649-4658
County agency
Founded in: 1970
Joyce P. Ross, Museum Director
Major programs: museum

Aiken County Historical Museum
433 Newberry St., SW, 29801
Telephone: (803) 649-4658
County agency, authorized by Aiken
County Historical Commission
Founded in: 1970
Joyce P. Ross, Director
Number of members:338
Staff: full time 2, part time 2,
volunteer 85
Major programs: library, archives,
museum, historic site(s), school
programs, newsletters/pamphlets,
exhibits, archaeology programs,
photographic collections
Period of collection: 1800s-present

Aiken County Historical Society
P.O. Box 1775, 29801
Private agency
Founded in: 1960
Robert Laird, President
Number of members: 100
Mail to: archives, manuscripts,
museum, markers, school
programs, research, genealogical
services
Period of collection: 1835-present

**South Carolina Society, Colonial
Dames XVII Century**
124 Dunbarton Circle, 29801
Telephone: (803) 648-8516
Private agency, authorized by
National Society, Colonial Dames
SVII Century
Founded in: 1955
Mrs. Herbert B. Fincher, State
President
Number of members: 635
Major programs: library, historic
site(s), markers, historic
preservation, genealogical
services
Period of collection: Colonial era

ALLENDALE

Allendale County Historical Society
University of South Carolina,
Salkehatchie, 29810
Telephone: (803) 584-3446
Private agency
Founded in: 1978
Arthur Mitchell, President
Number of members: 20
Major programs: museum, exhibits

ANDERSON

**Anderson County Historical
Society**
Telephone: (803) 296-1283
Mail to: P.O. Box 479, 29622
Questionnaire not received

Anderson Heritage, Inc.
P.O. Box 58, 29622
Telephone: (803) 226-7700
City agency
Founded in: 1973
Albert E. Smith, Director
Number of members: 100
Staff: part time 1

Major programs: historic site(s),
tours/pilgrimages,
newsletters/pamphlets, historic
preservation, audiovisual programs

BAMBERG

**Bamberg County Historical and
Genealogical Society**
County Courthouse
Telephone: (803) 245-2901
Mail to: P.O. Box 338, 29003
Private agency
Founded in: 1974
James Lewis Stoller, President
Number of members: 15
Major programs: historic site
preservation, markers,
genealogical services
Period of collection: 1783-1865

BEAUFORT

Historic Beaufort Foundation
801 Bay St.
Telephone: (803) 524-6334
Mail to: P.O. Box 11, 29901
Founded in: 1967
Mrs. W. Brantley Harvey, Jr.,
President
Number of members: 700
Staff: full time 1, volunteer 100
Major programs: museum, book
publishing, newsletters/pamphlets,
historic preservation
Period of collection: 1785-1825

John Mark Verdier House Museum
801 Bay St.
Telephone: (803) 524-6334
Mail to: P.O. Box 11, 29901
Private agency, authorized by
Historic Beaufort Foundation
Founded in: 1967
Henrietta B. Smith, Administrative
Assistant
Number of members: 800
Staff: full time 1, volunteer 100
Major programs: museum, book
publishing, newsletters/pamphlets,
historic preservation
Period of collection: 1790-1825

Parris Island Museum
29905
Telephone: (803) 525-2951
Federal agency, authorized by the
U.S. Marine Corps.
Founded in: 1975
Stephen R. Wise, Director
Staff: full time 3
Major programs: library, archives,
manuscripts, museum, historic
site(s), marker, oral history
research, exhibits
Period of collection: 1520-present

BENNETTSVILLE

**General Francis Marion Chapter,
Sons of the American Revolution**
106 S. Marlboro St.
Telephone: (803) 479-7194
Mail to: P.O. Box 29512
Private agency, authorized by
National Society, Sons of the
American Revolution
Founded in: 1979
Greg Ohanesian, President

Number of members: 34
Staff: volunteer 3
Major programs: markers,
newsletters/pamphlets
Period of collection: Revolutionary
War

**Marlborough County Historical
Preservation Commission**
Mail to: 116 S. Everett St., 29512
County agency
Founded in: 1970
Walter M. Newton, President
Major programs: museum

Marlboro County Museums
Mail to: 117 S. Marlboro St., 29512
Doris Moore, Host
Major programs: museum

Marlborough Historical Society
119 S. Marlboro St., 29512
Telephone: (803) 479-7748
Founded in: 1967
Suzanne Linder, President
Number of members: 400
Staff: full time 1, volunteer 50
Major programs: museum, historic
site preservation, markers,
tours/pilgrimages, oral history,
educational programs, books,
newsletters/pamphlets
Period of collection: 1865-1918

BETHUNE

Lynches River Historical Society
College St.
Mail to: P.O. Box 26, 29009
Questionnaire not received

BLACKSBURG

**Kings Mountain National Military
Park**
Rt. 2, Box 334, 29702
Telephone: (803) 936-7921
Mail to: P.O. Box 31, 28086
Federal agency, authorized by
National Park Service
Founded in: 1931
Andrew M. Lovelass, Superintendent
Staff: full time 3, part time 3
Major programs: library, museum,
historic site(s), markers, school
programs, historic preservation,
research, exhibits, living history,
photographic collections
Period of collection: Revolutionary
War

BLUFFTON

**Bluffton Historical Preservation
Society, Inc.**
Telephone: (803) 757-3650
(president)
Mail to: P.O. Box 742, 29910
Private agency
Founded in: 1981
W. Hunter Saussy, President
Number of members: 280
Major programs: historic site(s), book
publishing, historic preservation,
research, photographic
collections, genealogical services
Period of collection: to 1850s

CAMDEN

Camden Archives
1314 Broad St., 29020
Telephone: (803) 432-3242
City agency, authorized by Camden
Archives Commission
Founded in: 1973
Risher R. Fairey, Director/Archivist
Staff: full time 1, part time 2,
volunteer 1
Major programs: library, archives,
manuscripts, museum, records
management, research, exhibits,
genealogical services

**Camden District Heritage
Foundation**
U.S. Hwy. 521, S. Broad St.
Telephone: (803) 432-9841
Mail to: P.O. Box 710, 29020
Private agency
Founded in: 1967
Mrs. M. L. DuVal, Chair
Number of members: 450
Staff: full time , part time 2,
volunteer 15
Major programs: museum, historic
site(s), historic preservation,
research, exhibits audiovisual
programs, archaeology programs
Period of collection: 1732-1781

Camden Historical Commission
S. Broad St., 29020
Telephone: (803) 432-9841
City agency, authorized by Camden
District Heritage Foundation
Staff: full time 1, part time 1,
volunteer 12
Major programs: museum, historic
site(s), tours/pilgrimages, school
programs, newsletters/pamphlets,
historic preservation, exhibits,
living history, audiovisual
programs, archaeology programs
Period of collection: Revolutionary
War

Kershaw County Historical Society
Telephone: (803) 432-9841
Mail to: P.O. Box 501, 29020
Private agency
Founded in: 1954
Kathleen Stahl, Executive Secretary
Number of members: 200
Staff: part time 1, volunteer 20
Major programs: historic site
preservation, markers,
tours/pilgrimages, books
Period of collection: 1783-1865

CAYCE

**Granby Society for Historic
Preservation**
Mail to: P.O. Box 1062, 29033
Founded in: 1975
Questionnaire not received

CHARLESTON

Archives-Museum, The Citadel
29409
Telephone: (803) 577-6900, ext. 2119
Questionnaire not received

**Avery Institute of Afro-American
History and Culture**
College of Charleston, 58 George St.,
29424

Telephone: (803) 792-5742
Mail to: P.O. Box 2262, 29403
Private agency
Founded in: 1978
Lucille S. Whipper, President
Number of members: 350
Staff: volunteer 15
Magazine: *The Bulletin*
Major programs: archives, historic
site(s), oral history,
newsletters/pamphlets, exhibits
Period of collection: 1870-1957

Charles Towne Landing/1670
1500 Old Towne Rd., 29407-6099
Telephone: (803) 556-4450
State agency, authorized by
Department of Parks, Recreation
and Tourism
Founded in: 1970
Janson L. Cox, Manager
Number of members: 1,941
Staff: full time 25, part time 25,
volunteer 15
Major programs: museum, historic
site(s), school programs, exhibits,
living history, audiovisual programs
Period of collections: 1670

**Charleston Chapter, South
Carolina Genealogical Society**
315 King St., Suite 201, 29401
Telephone: (803) 577-5898
Mail to: P.O. Box 2266, 29403
Private agency
Founded in: 1971
W. Donald Kay, President
Number of members: 110
Magazine: *The Low Country Courier*
Major programs: library, archives,
newsletters/pamphlets, research,
genealogical services

Charleston Library Society
164 King St., 29401
Telephone: (803) 723-9912
Founded in: 1748
Catherine E. Sadler, Librarian
Number of members: 1,100
Staff: full time 3, part time 5
Major programs: library, research,
genealogical services
Period of collection: 1492-present

Charleston Museum
360 Meeting St., 29403
Telephone: (803) 722-2996
Private agency
Founded in: 1773
John R. Brumgardt, Director
Number of members: 2,960
Staff: full time 33, part time 6,
volunteer 100
Major programs: library, archives,
museu m, historic site(s), junior
history, school programs,
newsletters/pamphlets, historic
preservation, research exhibits,
archaeology programs,
photographic collections, natural
history
Period of collection: 1770-1940

Church Street Historic Foundation
59 Church St., 29401
Telephone: (803) 723-5424
Founded in: 1962
Questionnaire not received

The Citadel Museum & Archives
The Citadel
Telephone: (803) 792-6846
State agency, authorized by The
Military College of South Carolina
Founded in: 1961
CDR Mal J. Collet, Director
Staff: full time 3, part time 5, volunteer
35
Major programs: archives, museum,
exhibits

**Dalcho Historical Society of the
Protestant Episcopal Church in
South Carolina**
1020 King St.
Telephone: (803) 722-4075
Mail to: P.O. Box 2127, 29403
Founded in: 1945
George W. Williams, President
Major programs: books,
newsletters/pamphlets
Period of collection: 1865-1918

**Division of Archives and Records,
City of Charleston**
100 Broad St., Suite 300, 29401
Telephone: (803) 724-7301/724-7302
Mail to: P.O. Drawer C., 29402
City agency
Founded in: 1977
Gail McCoy, Supervisor
Staff: full time 2
Major programs: archives, records
management, research,
micrographics
Period of collection: 19th-20th
centuries

Drayton Hall
Rt. 4, Box 276, 29401
Telephone: (803) 766-0188
Private agency, authorized by
National Trust for Historic
Preservation
Founded in: 1949
Letitia Galbraith, Director
Number of members: 1,000
Staff: full time 6, part time 10,
volunteer 8
Major programs: historic site(s),
school programs,
newsletters/pamphlets, historic
preservation, research,
genealogical services
Period of collection: 1738-present

Gulluh Gyap
1243 Sunset Dr., 29407
Telephone: (803) 556-4701
Private agency
Founded in: 1979
Virginia Mixson Geraty
Staff: volunteer 3
Major programs: archives, oral
history, Gullah language,
linguistics
Period of collection: pre Civil War

Historic Charleston Foundation
51 Meeting St., 29401
Telephone: (803) 723-1623
Private agency
Founded in: 1947
Frances R. Edmunds, Director
Staff: full time 5, part time 6,
volunteer 350
Major programs: museum,
tours/pilgrimages, historic
preservation, research
Period of collection: 1700-present

**Macaulay Museum of Dental
History**
171 Ashley Ave, 29425
Telephone: (803) 792-2288
State agency, authorized by Medical
University of South Carolina
Founded in: 1975
Anne K. Donato, Curator
Staff: full time 1
Major programs: manuscripts,
museum, research, exhibits, dental
history
Period of collection: 19th-early 20th
centuries

Middleton Place Foundation
Ashley River Rd., 29407
Telephone: (803) 556-6025
Founded in: 1974
Sarah A. Lytle, Director
Number of members: 600
Staff: full time 35, part time 15,
volunteer 70
Magazine: *Middleton Place Notebook*
Major programs: archives,
manuscripts, museum, historic
site(s), school programs, historic
preservation, research, landscape
architecture, garden history
Period of collection: 1741-1900

**Miriam B. Wilson Foundation/Old
Slave Mart Museum and Library**
6 Chalmers St., 29401
Telephone: (803) 883-3797
Mail to: P.O. Box 446, Sullivans
Island, 29482
Private agency, authorized by the
foundation
Founded in: 1962
Judith W. Chase, Board
Secretary/Treasurer
Staff: full time 2, part time 4,
volunteer 2
Major programs: library, archives,
manuscripts, museum, historic
site(s), historic preservation,
research, exhibits, audiovisual
programs, photographic
collections, maps, documents,
scholarly publications
Period of collection: 1670-1865

**National Society of the Colonial
Dames of America in the State of
South Carolina**
79 Cumberland St., 29401
Telephone: (803) 722-3767
Private agency
Founded in: 1893
Mrs. Richard Champion Davis,
President
Numbers of members: 700
Staff: full time 2
Major programs: library, museum,
historic site(s), markers, oral
history, exhibits
Period of collection: Colonial era

**Old Exchange Building and Provost
Dungeon**
122 Bay St., 29401
Telephone: (803) 792-5020
State agency
Founded in: 1976
Shirley V. McGinnis, Executive
Director
Staff: full time 4

Major programs: museum, historic
site(s), school programs, exhibits,
living history
Period of collection: 1767-1976

**Orangeburgh German Swiss
Genealogical Society**
315 King St., Suite 201
Telephone: (803) (803) 577-6455
Mail to: P.O. Box 2266, 29403
Private agency
Founded in: 1980
Harold W. Syfrett, President
Number of members: 110
Staff: volunteer 1
Major programs: library, archives,
newsletters/pamphlets, research,
genealogical services

Preservation Society of Charleston
147 King St.
Telephone: (803) 722-4630
Mail to: P.O. Box 521, 29402
Private agency
Founded in: 1920
Henry F. Cauthen, Jr.,.Executive
Director
Number of members: 1,800
Staff: full time 4, part time 3,
volunteer 8
Magazine: *Preservation Progress*
Major programs: markers,
tours/pilgrimages, book publishing,
newsletters/pamphlets, historic
preservation

**Society of First Families of South
Carolina, 1670-1700**
P.O. Box 31681, 29407
Telephone: (803) 766-2564
State agency
Founded in: 1976
Edward H. Boinest, Jr., President
Number of members: 346
Major programs: library, archives,
historic site(s), markers,
newsletters/pamphlets, historic
preservation, records
management, photographic
collections, genealogical services
Period of collection: 1670-1700

South Carolina Historical Society
100 Meeting St.
Telephone: (803) 723-3225
Mail to: Fireproof Bldg., 29401
Private agency
Founded in: 1855
David Molteke-Hansen, Director
Number of members: 5,000
Staff: full time 5, part time 4,
volunteer 20
Magazine: *South Carolina Historical
Magazine*
Major programs: library, manuscripts,
tours/pilgrimages, book
publishings,
newsletters/pamphlets, records
management, research,
genealogical services, field
services
Period of collection: 1670-present

Waring Library Society
171 Ashley Ave., 29425
Telephone: (803) 792-2288
State agency, authorized by Medical
University of South Carolina
Founded in: 1966
W. Curtis Worthington, Jr., Director

Number of members: 250
Staff: full time 2
Major programs: library, archives,
manuscripts, museum, historic
site(s), tours/pilgrimages, oral
history, newsletters/pamphlets,
historic preservation, research,
exhibits, photographic collections,
genealogical services, medical
history
Period of collection: 18th-early 20th
centuries

WCSC Broadcast Museum
80 Alexander St.
Telephone: (803) 723-8371
Mail to: P.O. Box 186, 29402
Founded in: 1976
Questionnaire not received

CHERAW

**Chesterfield County Historic
Preservation Commission**
230 3rd St., 29520
Telephone: (803) 537-3387
County agency
Founded in: 1974
Sarah C. Spruill, Chair
Staff: volunteer 7
Major programs: historic site(s),
tours/pilgrimages, historic
preservation
Period of collection: 1760-1860

CHESTER

Chester County Historical Society
McAlily St.
Mail to: P.O. Box 326, 29706
Founded in: 1960
Questionnaire not received

CLEMSON

Ft. Hill: John C. Calhoun Mansion
Ft. Hill St., Clemson University, 29631
Telephone: (803) 656-2475
State agency, authorized by the
university
Mary Paige Wylie, Public Information
Specialist
Staff: full time 1, part time 2
Major programs: historic site(s),
tours/pilgrimages, oral history,
historic preservation, audiovisual
programs
Period of collection: early-mid 1800s

**Pendleton Chapter, South Carolina
Genealogical Society**
101 Cherokee Rd., 29631
Private agency
William C. Whitten, Jr., President
Number of members: 60
Major programs: library, archives,
manuscripts, book publishing,
newsletters/pamphlets
Period of collection: 1800-present

COLUMBIA

**Archeological Society of South
Carolina**
South Carolina Institute of Archeology
and Anthropology, 29208
Telephone: (803) 777-8170
Private agency, authorized by
University South Carolina,
Columbia

Founded in: 1968
Robert A. Parler, President
Number of members: 250
Staff: volunteer 14
Magazine: *South Carolina
Antiquities/Features & Profiles*
Major programs: manuscripts, school
programs, newsletters/pamphlets,
research, exhibits, archaeology
programs
Period of collection: prehistoric

**Columbia Chapter, South Carolina
Genealogical Society**
P.O. Box 11353, 29211
Telephone: (803) 787-4918
(treasurer)
Private agency
Founded in: 1976
Ralph H. Baer, Jr., Treasurer
Number of members: 193
Magazine: *Columbia Journal*
Major programs: archives,
genealogical services

Columbia Museum
1112 Bull St., 29201
Telephone: (803) 799-2810
City agency
Founded in: 1950
Walter M. Hathaway, Director
Number of members: 2,000
Staff: full time 19, part time 10,
volunteer 200
Major programs: library, museum,
historic site(s), tours/pilgrimages,
school programs,
newsletters/pamphlets, records
management, research, exhibits,
fine art

◊**Confederation of South Carolina
Local Historical Societies**
Telephone: (803) 758-5816
Mail to: P.O. Box 11669, 29211
Private agency
Founded in: 1965
A. Jack Blanton, President
Number of members: 81
Staff: volunteer 14

Historic Columbia Foundation
1616 Blanding St., 29201
Telephone: (803) 252-7742
Founded in: 1961
Cynthia E. Grant, Director
Number of members: 1,200
Staff: full time 5, part time 3,
volunteer 150
Major programs: museum, historic
site(s), school programs,
newsletters/pamphlets, historic
preservation, research
Period of collections: 1820-1875

Institute for Southern Studies
University of South Carolina, 29208
Telephone: (803) 777-2340
State agency, authorized by the
university
Founded in: 1980
Walter B. Edgar, Director
Number of members: full time 3

Magazine: *South by Southeast*
Major programs: library, book
publishing, newsletters/pamphlets,
research, exhibits, audiovisual
programs, photographic
collections
Period of collections: 19th century

**Mann-Simons Cottage: Museum of
African-American Culture**
1403 Richland St., 29201
Private agency, authorized by
Richland County Historic
Preservation Commission
Founded in: 1978
CeCe Byers, Director
Staff: full time 1, volunteer 15
Major programs: historic site(s),
tours/pilgrimages, school
programs, historic preservation
Period of collections: 1900

McKissick Museum
University of South Carolina, 29208
Telephone: (803) 777-7251
State agency, authorized by the
university
Founded in: 1976
George D. Terry, Director
Staff: full time 10, part time 40
Major programs: library, archives,
museum, school programs,
research, exhibits, state and
regional folk arts and material
culture
Period of collections: 19th century

**Richland County Historic
Preservation Commission**
1616 Blanding St., 29201
Telephone: (803) 252-7742
State agency
Founded in: 1963
Cynthia E. Grant, Director
Staff: full time 1
Major programs: historic site(s),
historic preservation
Period of collections: 19th century

2nd South Carolina Regiment
3418 Keenan Dr., 29201
Telephone: (803) 252-8499
Private agency
Founded in: 1975
Jim Prater, President
Number of members: 60
Staff: volunteer 60
Major programs: school programs,
living history
Period of collections: Revolutionary
War

◊**South Carolina Committee for the
Humanities**
6-C Monckton Blvd.
Telephone: (803) 738-1850
Mail to: P.O. Box 6925, 29260
Private agency, authorized by
National Endowment for the
Humanities
Founded in: 1970
Leland H. Cox, Jr., Executive Director
Staff: full time 3, part time 2
Magazine: *Humanities Newsletter*

Major programs: museum, junior history, oral history, school programs, exhibits, audiovisual programs, archaeology programs, photographic collections
Period of collections: 18th-19th centuries

South Carolina Confederate Relic Room and Museum
World War Memorial Bldg., 920 Sumter St., 29201
Telephone: (803) 758-2144
State agency
Founded in: 1896
LaVerne H. Watson, Director
Staff: full time 5
Major programs: museum, tours, research, exhibits
Period of collections: Colonial-present

South Carolina Criminal Justice Hall of Fame
5400 Broad River Rd., 29210
Telephone: (803) 758-6101
State agency
Jami A. Bennett, Directress
Number of members: 1
Staff: full time 2
Major programs: museum
Period of collections: early 1900s

◇South Carolina Department of Archives and History
1430 Senate St., 29201
Telephone: (803) 758-5816
Mail to: P.O. Box 11669, 29211
Founded in: 1905
Charles E. Lee, Director
Staff: full time 118, part time 2, volunteer 1
Magazine: *The New South Carolina State Gazette*
Major programs: archives, historic site(s), markers, book publishing, newsletters/pamphlets, historic preservation, records management, archaeology programs, photographic collections, genealogical services, field services
Period of collections: 1671-present

South Carolina Department of Parks, Recreation and Tourism
Edgar A. Brown Bldg., 1205 Pendleton St., 29201
Telephone: (803) 758-3622
State agency
Founded in: 1967
Mike Foley, Chief Historian
Period of collections: mid-19th century

South Carolina Genealogical Society
Telephone: (803) 766-1476
Mail to: 11 Beverly Rd., 29407
Founded in: 1970
Questionnaire not received

South Carolina Heritage Trust Program
1000 Assembly St., 29201
Telephone: (803) 758-0014
Mail to: P.O. Box 167, 29202
State agency
Founded in: 1976
Tom Kohlsaat, Supervisor

Staff: full time 12, part time 2
Major programs: historic site(s)

South Carolina Institute of Archaeology and Anthropology
University of South Carolina, 29208
Telephone: (803) 777-8170
State agency
Founded in: 1962
Bruce E. Rippeteau, Director/State Archaeologist
Staff: full time 65, volunteer 12
Major programs: newsletters/pamphlets, records management, research, archaeology programs, photographic collections, field services
Period of collections: 12,000 B.C.-present

South Carolina Society, Sons of the American Revolution
230 White Falls Dr., 29210
Telephone: (803) 781-2544
State agency
Founded in: 1906
G. F. Oliver, Secretary/Treasurer
Number of members: 511
Staff: full time 1, part time 1, volunteer 509
Magazine: *Palmetto Patriot*
Major programs: library, manuscripts, historic site(s), markers, tours/pilgrimages, school programs, newsletters/pamphlets, historic preservation, research, archaeology programs, genealogical services
Period of collections: 1906-present

◇South Carolina State Museum
2221 Devine St., Suite 312, 29205
Telephone: (803) 758-8197
Mail to: P.O. Box 11296, 29211
Founded in: 1973
David C. Sennema, Director
Staff: full time 23
Magazine: *Images*

Major programs: museum, educational programs, newsletters/pamphlets
Period of collections: prehistoric-present

South Carolina State Society, National Society Daughters of the American Colonists
235 Shareditch Rd., 29210
Telephone: (803) 798-1994
Authorized by National Society, Daughters of the American Colonists
Founded in: 1930
Mrs. C. Howard Reinhard, State Regent
Number of members: 245
Major programs: historic site(s), markers
Period of collections: to 1776

University South Caroliniana Society
South Caroliniana Library, University of South Carolina, 29208
Telephone: (803) 777-3131
Founded in: 1937
Allen Stokes, Secretary/Treasurer
Number of members: 2,100
Major programs: library, manuscripts, research, exhibits, photographic collections, genealogical services, sheet music and records, maps, newspapers
Period of collections: 17th century-present

CONWAY

Horry County Historical Society
1008 5th Ave., 29526
Telephone: (803) 248-4898
Private agency
Founded in: 1966
Number of members: 430
Magazine: *The Independent Republic Quarterly*
Major programs: tours/pilgrimages, books

Artist's rendering of the new South Carolina State Museum, which is scheduled to open in the summer of 1988.—South Carolina State Museum.

Period of collections: 18th
century-present

CROSS

**Berkeley County Historic
Preservation Commission**
Rt. 1, Box 1-E, 29436
Telephone: (803) 753-2336
County agency
Founded in: 1967
J. Russell Cross, Chair
Major programs: museum, historic
site(s), markers, tours/pilgrimages,
school programs, book publishing,
newsletters/pamphlets, research,
exhibits, audiovisual programs,
photographic collections,
genealogical services
Period of collections: 1680-present

Berkeley County Historical Society
Rt. 1, Box 1-E, 29436
Telephone: (803) 753-2336
Questionnaire not received

DARLINGTON

**Darlington County Historical
Commission**
104 Hewitt St., 29532
Telephone: (803) 393-8106
County agency, authorized by
Darlington County Council
Founded in: 1968
Horace F. Rudisill, Secretary
Staff: full time 1, volunteer 3
Major programs: archives, historic
site(s), markers, historic
preservation, records
management, photographic
collections, genealogical services
Period of collections: 1738-1950

**Darlington County Historical
Society**
418 Cashua St., 29532
Telephone: (803) 393-0231
Private agency
Founded in: 1938
Kevin P. Kennedy, President
Number of members: 210
Major programs: markers,
tours/pilgrimages, oral history,
historic preservation, genealogical
services
Period of collections: 1738-1950

DILLON

Dillon County Historical Society
Telephone: (803) 759-2773
Mail to: P.O. Box 187, Lake View,
29563
Questionnaire not received

EDGEFIELD

Red Shirt Shrine, Oakley Park
300 Columbia Rd., 29824
Telephone: (803) 637-6576
Town agency
Founded in: 1891
Mrs. George Covar, Host
Number of members: 45

Magazine: *United Daughters of the
Confederacy*
Major programs: historic site(s),
historic preservation
Period of collections: 1876

FLORENCE

Florence Heritage Foundation, Inc.
1159 Brunwood, 29501
Telephone: (803) 662-3258
Mail to: P.O. Box 1909, 29503
Founded in: 1978
Questionnaire not received

Florence Museum
558 Spruce St., 29501
Telephone: (803) 662-3351
Questionnaire not received

**South Carolina Historical
Association**
Francis Marion College, 29501
Private agency
Founded in: 1932
Joseph T. Stukes, President
Number of members: 100
Magazine: *Proceeding*
Major programs: manuscripts,
research

FORT JACKSON

Ft. Jackson Museum
29207
Telephone: (803) 751-7419
Federal agency, authorized by U.S.
Army Center of Military History
Founded in 1974
Clayton B. Kleckley, Museum
Director/Curator
Staff: full time 4
Major programs: library, museum,
markers, tours/pilgrimages, oral
history, school programs, historic
preservation, research, exhibits,
living history, audiovisual
programs, photographic
collections
Period of collections: 1775-present

GAFFNEY

**Cherokee Historic and
Preservation Society, Inc.**
Winnie Davis Hall of History,
Limestone College
Telephone: (803) 489-4172
Mail to: P.O. Box 998, 29340
Founded in: 1969
Questionnaire not received

GEORGETOWN

**Georgetown County Historical
Commission**
Telephone: (803) 546-7423
Mail to: P.O. Box 902, 29440
Questionnaire not received

**Georgetown County Historical
Society**
2 Cypress Court
Telephone: (803) 546-5604
Mail to: P.O. Box 1278, 29440
Private agency
Founded in: 1950

Thomas P. Davis, President
Number of members: 250
Major programs: archives,
manuscripts, historic sites
preservation, markers, oral history,
educational programs,
newsletters/pamphlets
Period of collections: 1865-1918

Hopsewee Plantation
Rt. 2, Box 205, 29440
Telephone: (803) 546-7891
Private agency
Helen B. Maynard, Owner
Major programs: historic site(s),
tours/pilgrimages, historic
preservation
Period of collections: 18th century

Rice Museum
Front and Screven Sts.
Telephone: (803) 546-7423
Mail to: P.O. Box 902, 29440
Questionnaire not received

GREENVILLE

**Andrew Pickens Chapter, Sons of
the American Revolution**
158 Ingleoak Lane, 29615
Telephone: (803) 235-5647
Private agency, authorized by
National Society, Sons of the
American Revolution
Morris D. van Patten, President
Number of members: 54
Major programs: historic site(s),
markers, school programs,
newsletters/pamphlets, historic
preservation, genealogical
services

**Greenville Chapter, South Carolina
Genealogical Society**
P.O. Box 16236, 29606
Telephone: (803) 246-4519
County agency
Founded in: 1974
Katherine Hester, President
Number of members: 171
Staff: volunteer 22
Magazine: *The Carolina Herald*
Major programs: library, archives,
book publishing,
newsletters/pamphlets, research,
genealogical services
Period of collections: 1750-present

**Greenville County Historical
Society**
Telephone: (803) 233-4351
Mail to: P.O. Box 10167, 29603
County agency
Founded in: 1962
Vance B. Drawdy, President
Number of members: 325
Staff: volunteer 10
Major programs: library, archives,
manuscripts, museum, historic
site(s), markers, book publishing,
newsletter/pamphlets, historic
preservation, research
Period of collections: 1886-present

**Greenville County Historic
Preservation Commission**
Furman University, 29613

Telephone: (803) 294-2182
County agency
A. V. Huff, Jr., Chair
Major programs: historic site(s),
historic preservation

**Greenville County Historical
Society**
Mail to: P.O. Box 2048, 29602
Founded in: 1962
Sam R. Zimmerman, President
Number of members: 200
Magazine: *The New Greenville
Mountaineer*
Major programs: markers,
educational programs, books
Period of collections: 1783-present

**South Carolina Appalachian
Council of Governments**
Century Plaza, Century Dr.
Mail to: Drawer 6668, 29606
Questionnaire not received

**South Carolina Baptist Historical
Society**
Special Collections Department,
Furman University Library, 29613
Telephone: (803) 294-2194
Founded in: 1948
J. Glenwood Clayton, Curator
Number of members: 200
Staff: full time 2, part time 1
Magazine: *Journal of the South
Carolina Baptist Historical
Society*
Major programs: library, archives,
manuscripts, markers, oral history
Period of collections: 1730-present

**South Carolina Historical
Association**
Furman University, 29613
Telephone: (803) 294-2182
Private agency
Founded in: 1931
A. V. Huff, Jr., President
Number of members: 100
major programs: meeting and
periodical

**South Carolina Historical Room for
History and Genealogy**
300 College St., 29601
Telephone: (803) 242-5000
County agency, authorized by
Greenville County Public Library
Founded in: 1888
Steve Richardson, Archivist
Staff: full time 3, part time 2,
volunteer 1
Period of collections: 1790-1900

**South Carolina State Society,
Daughters of the American
Revolution**
701 S. Main St., Mullins 29574
Telephone: (803) 464-9528
Private agency, authorized by
National Society, Daughters of the
American Revolution
Founded in: 1890
Mrs. Langdon B. Dunn, State Regent
Number of members: 4,300
Major programs: library, museum,
historic site(s), markers,
tours/pilgrimages, school
programs, newsletters/pamphlets,
historic preservation, genealogical
services, children's home

GREENWOOD

**Greenwood County Historical
Society**
No. Main St., Greenwood Public
Library, 29646
Founded in: 1958
Questionnaire not received

**Historic Preservation Office, Upper
Savannah Council of
Governments**
Professional Bldgs., Oak and Main
Sts.
Telephone: (803) 229-6627
Mail to: P. O. Box 1366, 29648-1366
Private agency
Founded in: 1967
John C. Blythe, Jr., Historic
Preservation Planner
Staff: full time 1
Magazine: *Update*
Major programs: historic preservation
Period of collections: 1750-1940

**Old Abbeville District Historical
Commission**
410 Jenning Ave.
Telephone (803) 223-4824
Mail to: P. O. Box 1102, 29646
Founded in: 1976
Arthur L. Murray, Chair
Major programs: historic preservation

The Museum
106 Main St., 29646
Telephone: (803) 229-7093
Mail to: P. O. Box 3131, 29648
Private agency
Founded in: 1967
Number of members: 409
Staff: full time 3, volunteer 23
Major programs: museum
Period of collections: 19th-early 20th
centuries

HAMPTON

Hampton County Historical Society
P.O. Box 2021, 29924
Telephone: (803) 943-3908
Founded in: 1970
Betty Ruth Crews, President
Number of members: 56
Major programs: library, museum,
historic site(s), oral history, historic
preservation, exhibits, living
history, archaeology programs,
genealogical services

HARTSVILLE

Hartsville Museum
P.O. Box 431, 29550
Telephone: (803) 383-5991
City agency, authorized by Hartsville
Museum Commission
Founded in: 1980
Pat Wilmot, Curator
Major programs: museum, historic
site(s), tours/pilgrimages, school
programs, exhibits, photographic
collections
Period of collections: 1850-present

Pee Dee Heritage Center
Coker College, 29550
Telephone: (803) 332-1381
Private agency, authorized by Coker
College and Francis Marion
College

Founded in 1980
Robert R. Simpson, Director
Magazine: *The Pee Dee Recorder*
Major programs: oral history, book
publishing, newsletter/pamphlets,
public programs

HEMINGWAY

Three Rivers Historical Society
P.O. Box 811, 29554
Telephone: (803) 558-2355
Private agency
Founded in: 1976
Mrs. LeGrande Hanna, President
Number of members: 100
Staff: volunteer 6
Magazine: *Three Rivers Chronicle*
Major programs: museum, historic
site(s), markers, book publishing,
newsletters/pamphlets, historic
preservation, records
management, research,
genealogical services
Period of collections: 1732-1900

HILTON HEAD ISLAND

**Hilton Head Island Historical
Society**
8 Moon Shell Rd.
Telephone: (803) 785-3967
Private agency
Founded in: 1961
Robert E. H. Peeples, President
Number of members: 220
Major programs: historic site(s),
markers, book publishing, historic
preservation, research, lecture
series
Period of collections: 1861-1865

KINGSTREE

**Williamsburg County Historical
Society**
124 S. Academy St.
Telephone: (803) 354-7124
Mail to: P.O. Box 24, 29556
Private agency
Founded in: 1971
Samuel E. McIntosh, President
Number of members: 200
Staff: volunteer 20
Major programs: museum,
tours/pilgrimages, historic
preservation
Period of collections: 1971-present

LANCASTER

**Lancaster County Historical
Commission**
117 Williams St., 29720
Telephone (803) 283-4069
County agency
Ben F. Emanuel, Chair
Major programs: library, archives,
manuscripts, historic site(s),
markers, school programs, book
publishing, newsletters/pamphlets,
historic preservation, research,
genealogical services

**Lancaster County Society for
Historic Preservation, Inc.**
Mail to: P.O. Box 1132, 29720
Telephone: (803) 285-9455
Founded in: 1976
D. Lindsay Pettus, President

419

Number of members: 125
Major programs: historic site(s),
    historic preservation, photographic
    collections

LAURENS

Laurens County Historical Society
Telephone (803) 984-3648
Mail to: P.O. Box 292, 29360
Private agency
John R. Ferguson, President

LEXINGTON

**Lexington County Historical
Society**
P.O. Box 637, 29072
Telephone: (803) 359-8369
Private agency
Founded in: 1958
Horace E. Harmon, Director
Number of members: 130
Staff: full time 1, part time 4
Major programs: museum, markers,
    school programs, living history
Period of collections: 1865-1870

Lexington County Museum
P. O. Box 637, 29072
Telephone: (803) 359-8369
County agency
Founded in: 1969
Horace Harmon, Director
Number of members: 109
Staff: full time 1, part time 5
Major programs: museum, historic
    site(s), historic preservation,
    exhibits, living history
Period of collections: 1800-1900

Marion County Museum
101 Willcox Ave.
Telephone: (803) 423-7909
Mail to: P.O. Box 220, 29571
County agency
Founded in: 1981
Maggi Hall, Director
Number of members: 250
Staff: full time 1, volunteer 30
Major programs: Marion County
    Museum News
Major programs: museum, historic
    site(s), school programs, book
    publishing, newsletters/pamphlets,
    historic preservation, records
    management, exhibits, audiovisual
    programs, photographic
    collections, genealogical services,
    concert series and art programs
Period of collections: 1800-1950

MANNING

**Clarendon County Historical
Society**
Telephone: (803) 485-4245
Mail to: P.O. Box 266, Summerton,
    29148
Questionnaire not received

McCLELLANVILLE

Hampton Plantation State Park
1950 Rutledge Rd., 29458
Telephone: (803) 546-9361
State agency, authorized by
    Department of Parks, Recreation
    and Tourism

Founded in: 1971
Robert A. Mitchell, Park
    Superintendent
Staff: full time 2
Major programs: museum, historic
    site(s), oral history, school
    programs, historic preservation,
    research, exhibits, living history,
    audiovisual programs, field
    services
Period of collections: 1750

McCONNELLS

**York County Historical
Commission**
Rt. 1, Brattonsville Rd., 29726
Telephone: (803) 684-2327
County agency
Founded in: 1959
Wade B. Fairey, Executive Director
Number of members: 200
Staff: full time 1, part time 1,
    volunteer 25
Major programs: historic site(s),
    markers, school programs, historic
    preservation, living history
Period of collections: 1800-1860

McCORMICK

**Abbeville District Historical
Association**
Telephone: (803) 465-2347
Mail to: P.O. Box 578, 29835
Questionnaire not received

**Dorn Historical Restoration
Association**
Telephone: (803) 465-2433
Mail to: P.O. Box 927, 29835
Questionnaire not received

**McCormick County Historical
Commission**
Telephone: (803) 465-2347
Mail to: P.O. Box 578, 29835
Questionnaire not received

**McCormick County Historical
Society**
29835
Telephone: (803) 465-2754
County agency, authorized by
    Confederation of South Carolina
    Historical Societies
Founded in: 1970
Wilton M. Browne, Co-president
Number of members: 100
Staff: volunteer 12
Major programs: markers, book
    publishing, historic preservation
Period of collections: 1770s-1870s

MONCKS CORNER

Berkeley County Historical Society
P.O. Box 65, 29461
Telephone: (803) 899-3220
Private agency
Founded in: 1973
Oliver Buckles, President
Number of members: 300
Staff: volunteer 30
Major programs: tours/pilgrimages,
    book publishing, exhibits

MT. PLEASANT

**Patriots Point Development
Authority**
P.O. Box 986, 29464
Telephone: (803) 884-2727
State agency
Founded in: 1973
J. E. Guerry, Jr., Executive Director
Staff: full time 35, part time 5
Magazine: Deck Log
Major programs: museum, historic
    preservation
Period of collections: 1941-1970

MURRELLS INLET

Brookgreen Gardens
29576
Telephone: (803) 237-4218
Founded in: 1931
Questionnaire not received

NEWBERRY

**Newberry County Historical
Society**
Telephone: (803) 276-8522
Mail to: P.O. Box 364, 29108
Private agency
Founded in: 1970
M. Foster Farley, Editor
Number of members: 200
Staff: volunteer 14
Magazine: Bulletin of the Newberry
    County Historical Society
Major programs: manuscripts,
    markers, tours/pilgrimages, historic
    preservation, genealogical
    services
Period of collections: 1783-1865

NORTH MYRTLE BEACH

**Horry County Historic Preservation
Commission**
706 15th Ave., S, 29582
Telephone: (803) 272-6303
County agency
Founded in: 1966
C. B. Berry, Chair
Staff: volunteer 5
Major programs: museum, markers,
    school programs, historic
    preservation, archaeology
    programs

ORANGEBURG

**Orangeburg County Historical
Commission**
Courthouse
Telephone: (803) 534-5176
Mail to: P.O. Box 219, 29115
Questionnaire not received

**Orangeburg County Historical
Society, Inc.**
P.O. Box 1881, 29115
Private agency
Number of members: 230
Staff: volunteer 1
Major programs: archives,
    manuscripts, museum,
    genealogical services
Period of collections: from 1735

**Orangeburg Genealogical
 Society, Inc.**
467 Palmetto Parkway, NE, 29115
Telephone: (803) 536-1305
Founded in: 1968
Questionnaire not received

PENDLETON

**Foundation for Historic
 Restoration in Pendleton Area**
Mail to P.O. Box 444, 29670
Private agency
Founded in: 1960
Mrs. John T. Meehan, President
Number of members: 200
Staff: volunteer 50
Major programs: historic site(s),
 tours/pilgrimages, book publishing,
 historic preservation, research

**Pendleton District Historical and
 Recreational Commission**
125 E. Queen St.
Telephone: (803) 646-3782
Mail to: P.O. Box 565, 29670
County agency
Founded in: 1966
Hurley E. Badders, Executive Director
Staff: full time 4, volunteer 1
Major programs: library, archives,
 museum, historic site(s),
 tours/pilgrimages, historic
 preservation, exhibits,
 photographic collections,
 genealogical services
Period of collections: 1790-1880

**Pendleton Foundation for Black
 History and Culture**
305 Morse, 29670
Telephone: (803) 646-3792
Founded in 1976
Questionnaire not received

PICKENS

Pickens County Historical Society
Pendleton and Johnson Sts.
Telephone: (803) 878-4965/878-7818
Mail to: P.O. Box 621, 29671
Founded in: 1958
Dorothy H. Blase, Museum Host
Number of members: 200
Staff: part time 1, volunteer 1
Major programs: prehistoric-present

ST. MATTHEWS

Calhoun County Museum
303 Butler St., 29135
Telephone: (803) 874-3964
Founded in: 1954
Questionnaire not received

SALUDA

**Saluda County Historical
 Commission**
100 E. Butler Ave.
Telephone: (803) 445-8961
Mail to: P.O. Box 644, 29138
Questionnaire not received

SPARTANBURG

**Spartanburg County Historical
 Association**
501 Otis Blvd., 29302
Telephone: (803) 596-3501
Founded in: 1957
Questionnaire not received

**Spartanburg County Natural Park,
 Recreation and Historic
 Preservation Commission**
205 Magnolia St.
Telephone: (803) 582-5630
Mail to: P.O. Box 451, 29304
Founded in: 1968
Questionnaire not received

SULLIVAN'S ISLAND

Ft. Sumter National Monument
1214 Middle St., 29482
Telephone: (803) 883-3123
Federal agency, authorized by
 National Park Service
R. Brien Varnado, Superintendent
Staff: full time 15, part time 1,
 volunteer 20
Major programs: library, archives,
 museum, markers, historic
 preservation, research, exhibits,
 living history, audiovisual programs
Period of collections: 1776-1947

SUMMERVILLE

Summerville Preservation Society
Telephone: (803) 873-1006
Mail to: P.O. Box 511, 29483
Private agency
Founded in: 1972
Randall L. Charpia, President
Number of members: 150
Major programs: library,
 tours/pilgrimages

SUMTER

**South Carolina Society, Colonial
 Dames XVII Century**
221 Hasell St., 29150
Telephone: (803) 775-0243
Founded in: 1955
Questionnaire not received

**Sumter Chapter, S.C. Genealogical
 Society**
Mail to: P.O. Box 2543, 29150
Founded in: 1974
Questionnaire not received

**Sumter County Historical
 Commission**
Courthouse, 29150
County agency
Founded in: 1950
William Robert Ferrell, Chair
Major programs: archives,
 manuscripts, historic site(s),
 markers, tours/pilgrimages, junior
 history, oral history, school
 programs, book publishing, historic
 preservation, research, exhibits,
 photographic collections,
 genealogical services

**Sumter County Historical
 Society, Inc.**
122 N. Washington St., 29150
Telephone: (803) 775-0908
Founded in: 1950
Questionnaire not received

**Sumter County Museum and
 Archives**
122 N. Washington St.
Telephone: (803) 775-0908
Mail to: P.O. Box 1456, 29150
Private agency, authorized by Sumter
 County Historical Society, Inc.

Founded in: 1950
Sherman F. Smith, Director
Staff: part time 2, volunteer 2
Magazine: *Chanticleer*
Major programs: archives, museum,
 oral history, newsletters/pamphlets,
 exhibits, photographic collections,
 genealogical services

UNION

**Union County Historical
 Foundation**
1st Federal S & L Bldg.
Mail to: P.O. Drawer 280, 29379
Founded in: 1960
Questionnaire not received

WALHALLA

**Oconee County Historical and
 Recreational Society, Inc.**
680 Catherine St., 29691
Telephone: (803) 638-9202
Founded in: 1958
Questionnaire not received

WALTERBORO

Walterboro Preservation Society
203 Witsell St., 29488
Telephone: (803) 549-1639
Questionnaire not received

WINNSBORO

**Fairfield County Historical
 Commission**
Fairfield County Museum, 231 S.
 Congress St., 29180
Telephone: (803) 635-9811
County agency
Mrs. H. G. Phillips, Jr., Chair
Staff: full time 3, volunteer 1
Major programs: museum
Period of collections: late 18th-early
 19th centuries

Fairfield County Museum
231 S. Congress St., 29180
Telephone: (803) 635-9811
County agency, authorized by
 Fairfield County Historical
 Commission
Founded in: 1976
Kathlynn Ann Fritz, Curator
Staff: full time 1, part time 3,
 volunteer 1
Major programs: museum, research,
 exhibits, genealogical services
Period of collections: 19th-early 20th
 centuries

**South Carolina Railroad
 Museum, Inc.**
1603 Valley Rd., 29204
Telephone: (803) 782-6242
Mail to: P.O. Box 7246, 29202-7246
Private agency
Founded in: 1973
H. Carter Siegling, Director/Secretary
Number of members: 120
Staff: volunteer 20
Major programs: library, museum,
 historic site(s),
 newsletters/pamphlets, historic
 preservation, living history,
 audiovisual programs
Period of collections: 1880-present

SOUTH DAKOTA

YORK

Colonel William Bratton Chapter, Sons of American Revolution
P.O. Box 295, 29745
Telephone: (803) 684-4650
Private agency, authorized by National Society, Sons of American Revolution
Founded in: 1930
William Floyd Allison, President
Number of members: 34
Major programs: school programs, genealogical services

SOUTH DAKOTA

ABERDEEN

Aberdeen Area Genealogical Society
Mail to: P.O. Box 493, 57401
Founded in: 1975
Questionnaire not received

Brown County Museum and Historical Society
21 S. Main
Telephone: (605) 229-1608
Mail to: P.O. Box 395, 57401
Questionnaire not received

Brown County Territorial Pioneers
4202 N.W. 24th Ave., 57401
Telephone: (605) 225-6643
County agency
Founded in: 1948
Helen J. Borgh, President
Number of members: 45
Major programs: museum, markers, book publishing
Period of collections: 1879-1910

Dacotah Prairie Museum
21 S. Main St.
Telephone: (605) 229-1608
Mail to: P.O. Box 395, 57401
County agency
Founded in: 1963
Kevin Gramer, Director
Staff: full time 3, part time 3, volunteer 13
Magazine: *Dacotah Prairie Times*
Major programs: library, archives, museum, tours/pilgrimages, school programs, newsletters/pamphlets, records management, exhibits, photographic collections
Period of collections: 1865-1930

ARMOUR

Douglas County Historical Society
Courthouse Grounds, 57313
Telephone: (605) 724-2129
County agency
Founded in: 1956
Sharon A. Wiese, President
Major programs: museum, historic site(s), markers, school programs, book publishing, historic preservation, exhibits, photographic collections
Period of collections: 1884-present

BELLE FOURCHE

Butte County Historical Society
57717
Questionnaire not received

BISON

Perkins County Historical Society
HCR 2, Box 417-C, 57620
Telephone: (605) 244-5416
County agency
Dorothy Haugen, Secretary
Number of members: 32
Staff: volunteer 9
Major programs: historic site(s), markers, historic preservation
Period of collections: early 19th century

BLUNT

Mentor Graham House
103 N. Commercial Ave.
Telephone: (605) 962-6445
Mail to: P.O. Box 136, 57522
State agency
Founded in: 1950
Junius R. Fishburne, Director
Period of collections: 1880

BRANDT

Deuel County Historical Society
57218
Founded in: 1970
Questionnaire not received

BRITTON

Prayer Rock Museum
Main St., 57430
Questionnaire not received

BROOKINGS

Agricultural Heritage Museum
925 11th St.
Telephone: (605) 688-6226
Mail to: South Dakota State University, Box 2207, 57007
State agency, authorized by South Dakota Office of History
Founded in: 1967
John C. Awald, Director
Number of members: 400
Staff: full time 3, part time 4, volunteer 1
Magazine: *News from the Agricultural Heritage Museum*
Major programs: library, archives, manuscripts, museum, tours/pilgrimages, oral history, school programs, newsletters/pamphlets, historic preservation, records management, research, exhibits, audiovisual programs, photographic collections, consulting services
Period of collections: 1860-1950

Brookings Area Genealogical Society
524 4th St., 57007
Founded in: 1977
Bonnie Marquardt, President
Number of members: 73
Magazine: *Dakota Frontier Days*
Major programs: library, newsletters/pamphlets, research, genealogical services

BURKE

Gregory County Historical Society, Inc.
P.O. Box 376, 57523
Telephone: (605) 775-2641
Private agency
Founded in: 1972
L. L. Lillibridge, Secretary
Number of members: 350
Staff: volunteer 10
Major programs: book publishing
Period of collections: 1866-present

Case 65-horsepower steam traction engine, manufactured in 1915 by J.I. Case. The engine was restored by the State Agricultural Heritage Museum's staff in 1983.—State Agricultural Heritage Museum, a program of the South Dakota Historical Society Board of Trustees

CHAMBERLAIN

Old West Museum
P.O. Box 275, 57325
Telephone: (605) 734-6157
Private agency
Founded in: 1969
Gene Olson, Co-owner
Staff: part time 9
Period of collections: late
1800s-present

CLARK

Clark County Historical Society
100 S. Cloud, 57236
Telephone: (605) 532-3722
County agency
Founded in: 1975
Ailene Luckhurst, President
Number of members: 80
Major programs: archives, museum,
historic site(s), markers,
newsletters/pamphlets, historic
preservation, photographic
collections, genealogical services
Period of collections: 1890-1910

CLEAR LAKE

**Deuel County Historical
Society, Inc.**
57226
Telephone: (605) 874-2397
Questionnaire not received

CROOKS

**Crooks Council of the Minnekaka
County Historical Society**
Rt. 11, Box 339, 57020
Telephone: (605) 543-5232
County agency
Founded in: 1984
Janet Johnson, President
Number of members: 63
Major programs: oral history, book
publishing, historic preservation
Period of collections: 1870-present

CUSTER

Custer County Historical Society
Mt. Rushmore Rd., 57730
Founded in: 1969
Betty Painter, President
Number of members: 50
Staff: part time 1, volunteer 40
Major programs: museum, historic
sites preservation, markers,
educational programs
Period of collections: 1874-present

DEADWOOD

Adams Memorial Museum
54 Sherman
Telephone: (605) 578-1714
Mail to: P.O. Box 583, 57732
Founded in: 1930
Questionnaire not received

**House of Roses/Senator Wilson
Home**
15 Forest Ave., 57732
Telephone: (605) 578-1879
Private agency
Founded in: 1976
Harry Lehman, Owner
Major programs: library, archives,
manuscripts, museum, historic

site(s), tours/pilgrimages, oral
history, historic preservation,
records management, research,
exhibits, living history,
photographic collections
Period of collections: 1800s

**Lawrence County Historical
Society**
435 Williams St., 57732
Telephone: (605) 578-2821
County agency
Founded in: 1969
Linfred Schutler, President
Staff: volunteer 8
Major programs: archives, historic
site(s), markers, tours/pilgrimages,
oral history, photographic
collections, Period of collections:
1875-1940s

Society of Black Hills Pioneers
700 Main St., 57732
Telephone: (605) 578-3400
Founded in: 1888
Questionnaire not received

DE SMET

De Smet Depot Museum
P.O. Box 454, 47231
Telephone: (605) 854-3731
City agency, authorized by Finance
Office, City of De Smet
Founded in: 1984
Alyce Klinkel, Board Chair
Staff: volunteer 25
Major programs: museum, historic
site(s), tours/pilgrimages
Period of collections: 1860-1915

**Laura Ingalls Wilder Memorial
Society**
Telephone: (605) 854-3383
Mail to: P.O. Box 344, 57231
Founded in: 1957
Vivian Glover, Secretary
Staff: full time 3, part time 5,
volunteer 10
Magazine: *Laura Ingalls Wilder Lore*
Major programs: historic site(s),
markers, tours/pilgrimages,
newsletters/pamphlets, exhibits
Period of collections: 1878-1936

DUPREE

**Ziebach County Historical
Committee**
P.O. Box 1, 57623
Telephone: (605) 365-5319
County agency
Founded in: 1980
Thelma Frame, President
Staff: volunteer 10
Major programs: book publishing,
research, photographic collections
Period of collections: 1900-1982

EUREKA

**Eureka Pioneer Museum of
McPherson County, Inc.**
Eureka, 57437
Telephone: (605) 284-2711
Founded in: 1978
Questionnaire not received

FAULKTON

Faulk County Historical Society
P.O. Box 584, 57438

County agency
Founded in: 1971
Shirley Pritchard, President
Number of members: 130
Staff: volunteer 14
Major programs: museum, book
publishing, historic preservation
Period of collections: 1900

FLANDREAU

Moody County Historical Society
E. Park Rd., 57028
Telephone: (605) 997-2198
Questionnaire not received

FORT MEADE

State Archaeological Center
P.O. Box 152, 57741
Telephone: (605) 347-3652
State agency, authorized by South
Dakota Office of History
Founded in: 1973
Robert Alex, Director
Staff: full time 2, part time 15
Major programs: library, school
programs, research, archaeology
programs, field services
Period of collections: late prehistoric

FORT PIERRE

**Old Stanley County Historical
Society**
410 W. Main, 57532
Telephone: (605) 223-2757
Questionnaire not received

**South Dakota Cowboy and Western
Heritage Hall of Fame**
10 E. Main
Telephone: (605) 223-2574
Mail to: P.O. Box 568, 57532
Founded in: 1974
Dale Lewis, Executive Director
Number of members: 1,700
Staff: full time 1, part time 2,
volunteer 2
Magazine: *Dakota West*
Major programs: archives, exhibits,
audiovisual programs

Verendrye Museum
Deadwood St., 57532
City agency
Founded in: 1967
C. M. Bendewald, President
Staff: volunteer 30
Major programs: museum

GARY

Gary Historical Association
57237
Telephone: (605) 272-5553
Questionnaire not received

GEDDES

**Charles Mix County Historical
Restoration Society**
Telephone: (605) 337-2501
Mail to: P.O. Box 297, 57342
Founded in: 1972
Ron Dufek, Secretary
Number of members: 20
Staff: volunteer 15
Major programs: museum, historic
sites preservation, historic
preservation
Period of collections: 1857-present

GETTYSBURG

Potter County Historical Association
Telephone: (605) 765-5691
Mail to: P.O. Box 1, 57442
Questionnaire not received

HIGHMORE

Hyde County Historical and Genealogical Society
Telephone: (605) 852-2376
Mail to: Rt. 2, Box 112, 57345
Founded in: 1973
Questionnaire not received

HILL CITY

Hill City Historical Society
57745
Questionnaire not received

HOT SPRINGS

Fall River County Historical Society
Telephone: (605) 745-4815 (president)
Mail to: P.O. Box 597, 57747
Private agency
Founded in: 1961
Marshall J. Truax, President
Number of members: 100
Staff: volunteer 25
Major programs: museum, historic site(s), markers, book publishing, historic preservation, living history, audiovisual programs
Period of collections: 1889-1980s

Mammoth Site of Hot Springs, South Dakota
19th and Evanston
Telephone: (605) 745-4140
Mail to: P.O. Box 606, 57747
Founded in: 1976
Questionnaire not received

HURLEY

Hurley Historical Society
P.O. Box 302, 57036
Telephone: (605) 238-5725
Private agency
Founded in: 1975
Marie P. Anderson, President
Number of members: 15

HURON

East River Genealogical Forum
17 5th St., SW, 57350
Telephone: (605) 883-4117
Mail to: R.R. 2 Box 148, Wolsey, 57384
Founded in: 1970
Questionnaire not received

James Valley Historical Society
Rt. 4, Box 137, 57350
Telephone: (605) 352-2139
Questionnaire not received

State Fair Pioneer Museum
State Fairgrounds
Mail to: 479 Montana, SW, 57350
Questionnaire not received

KADOKA

Jackson-Washabough County Historical Society
57543
Telephone: (605) 837-2671
County agency
Founded in: 1961
Lois J. Prokop, President
Staff: volunteer 4
Major programs: museum, book publishing, historic preservation
Period of collections: from early 1900s

KEYSTONE

Big Thunder Gold Mine
P.O. Box 706, 57751
Telephone: (605) 666-4847
Founded in: 1958
James Hersrud, President
Staff: full time 6
Major programs: museum, historic site(s), tours/pilgrimages, oral history, historic preservation, exhibits, audiovisual programs, photographic collections
Period of collections: 1880-1910

Keystone Area Historical Society
P.O. Box 658, 57751
Telephone: (605) 666-4667
Private agency
Founded in: 1983
Beverly Pechan, President
Number of members: 70
Staff: volunteer 10
Magazine: Holy Terror Tattler
Major programs: museum, markers, newsletters/pamphlets, research
Period of collections: 1890-present

LENNOX

Lennox Area Historical Society
Main St.
Telephone: (605) 647-2287
Mail to: P.O. Box 337, 57039
Private agency
Founded in: 1979
Mrs. Carl Renz, Corresponding Secretary
Number of members: 35
Magazine: National Preservation Registry of Historic Places
Major programs: archives, museum, oral history, historic preservation, living history, photographic collections
Period of collections: 1860-present

MADISON

Lake County Historical Society
Dakota State College, 57042
Telephone: (605) 256-3551, ext. 218
Founded in: 1952
Questionnaire not received

Prairie Historical Society, Inc.
P.O. Box 256, 57042
Telephone: (605) 256-3644
Private agency
Founded in: 1966
Byron F. Henry, President
Number of members: 410
Staff: part time 5, volunteer 31

Major programs: historic site(s), markers, historic preservation, photographic collections
Period of collections: 19th century

Smith-Zimmermann State Museum
Dakota State College, 57042
Telephone: (605) 256-5308
Founded in: 1952
Deborah Strahan Rosenthal, Director
Staff: full time 1, part time 2
Major programs: museum
Period of collections: 1880-1940

MARVIN

American Indian Culture Research Center
Telephone: (605) 432-5528
Founded in: 1967
Questionnaire not received

MILBANK

Grant County Historical Society, Inc.
302 E. 4th Ave.
Mail to: P.O. Box 201, 57252
Founded in: 1970
Questionnaire not received

MITCHELL

Friends of the Middle Border Museum
1131 S. Duff St.
Telephone: (605) 996-2122
Mail to: P.O. Box 1071, 57301
Private agency
Founded in: 1939
Hazel Jordan, Office Manager
Number of members: 565
Staff: part time 1, volunteer 125
Magazine: Middle Border Bulletin
Major programs: museum, oral history, school programs, historic preservation, photographic collections, fine art collection
Period of collections: 1880-1935

Mitchell Prehistoric Indian Village Preservation Society
Telephone: (605) 996-5473
Mail to: P.O. Box 621, 57301
Private agency
Founded in: 1978
Darrell W. Fulmer, Archaeologist
Number of members: 100
Staff: full time 1, part time 6, volunteer 25
Magazine: Mitchell Prehistoric Indian Village Newsletter
Major programs: museum, historic preservation
Period of collections: 11th century

Mitchell Site National Historic Landmark
Indian Village Rd.
Telephone: (605) 996-5473
Mail to: P.O. Box 621, 57301
Private agency, authorized by Mitchell Prehistoric Indian Village Preservation Society
Founded in: 1978
Darrell W. Fulmer, Director/Curator
Number of members: 100
Staff: full time 1, part time 10

Major programs: museum, historic
site(s), school programs, historic
preservation, research, exhibits,
archaeology programs
Period of collections: 11th century

MOBRIDGE

Klein Foundation Inc.
W. Hwy 12, 57601
Telephone: (605) 845-7243
Private agency
Founded in: 1975
Delores S. Rice, Director
Number of members: 250
Staff: full time 1, part time 1,
volunteer 10
Major programs: museum
Period of collections: early 1900s

Northern Oake Historical Society
12th Ave. and 2nd St., E
Mail to: P.O. Box 953, 57601
Questionnaire not received

MURDO

**Pioneer Auto Museum and Antique
Town**
P.O. Box 76, 57559
Telephone: (605) 669-2393/669-2641
Private agency
Founded in: 1954
Dave Getsler, President/Owner
Staff: full time 12, part time 3,
volunteer 9
Major programs: museum, historic
site(s)
Period of collections: from 1900

OLDHAM

**Oldham Library and Historical
Association**
Telephone: (605) 482-8659
Mail to: Secretary, 57051
Founded in: 1976
Questionnaire not received

PHILIP

Prairie Homestead
Telephone: (605) 386-4523
Mail to: Rt. 1, Box 51, 57567
Pivate agency
Founded in: 1963
Dorothy Crew, Owner
Staff: full time 2
Major programs: oral history,
audiovisual programs
Period of collections: 1862-1932

PIERRE

**Association of South Dakota
Museums**
Robinson State Museum, 500 E.
Capitol
Telephone: (605) 773-3797
Mail to: 200 W. 6th St., Sioux Falls,
57102
Private agency
Rebecca Hunt, President
Number of members: 25
Staff: volunteer 6
Major programs:
newsletters/pamphlets, annual
meeting and workshops

Office of Cultural Preservation
State Library, 57501

Telephone: (605) 773-3458
Founded in: 1973
Questionnaire not received

◇**Office of History, South Dakota
State Historical Society**
800 N. Illinois, State Library Bldg,
57501
Telephone: (605) 773-3458
State agency
Founded in: 1901
J. R. Fishburne, Director
Staff: full time 2
Major programs: archives,
manuscripts, museum, historic
site(s), markers, oral history, school
programs, newsletters/pamphlets,
historic preservation, research,
exhibits, archaeology programs,
photographic collections,
genealogical services
Period of collections:
prehistoric-present

Robinson State Museum
Memorial Bldg., 500 E. Capitol 57501
Telephone: (605) 773-3797
State agency, authorized by South
Dakota Office of History
Founded in: 1901
David B. Hartley, Director
Staff: full time 3, part time 3,
volunteer 1
Major programs: museum, research,
exhibits
Period of collections: 1865-present

South Dakota State Archives
Office of History
Telephone: (605) 224-3173
Mail to: State Library 57501
State agency
Founded in: 1974
Staff: full time 1
Major programs: archives, records
management, research,
photographic collections,
genealogical services
Period of collections: 1900-present

**South Dakota Division of Parks and
Recreation**
445 E. Capitol Ave., 57501
Telephone: (605) 773-3391
State agency
Founded in: 1945
Edward Raventon, Interpretive
Services Coordinator
Major programs: historic site(s),
tours/pilgrimages, school
programs, historic preservation,
living history, audiovisual
programs, Period of collections:
1870s

◇**South Dakota Office of History**
Soldiers' & Sailors' Memorial Bldg., E.
Capitol Ave., 57501
Telephone: (605) 773-3615
Founded in: 1901
Dayton W. Canaday, Director
Number of members: 1,963
Staff: full time 7
Magazine: *South Dakota History*
Major programs: library, manuscripts,
markers, oral history, book
publishing, research, photographic
collections, genealogical services
Period of collections: 1743-present

PINE RIDGE

Heritage Center, Inc.
Red Cloud Indian School
Telephone: (605) 867-5491
Mail to: P.O. Box 100, 57770
Private agency
Founded in: 1974
C. M. Simon, Director
Staff: part time 1, volunteer 1
Major programs: library, archives,
museum, research, photographic
collections, native american art
Period of collections: 1880-present

PUKWANA

Brule County Historical Society
R.R. 1 Box 175, 57370
Telephone: (605) 894-4337
County agency
Founded in: 1974
Evelyn Sharping, Secretary
Number of members: 200
Staff: volunteer 12
Major programs: historic site(s), book
publishing, restored church
Period of collections: 1880-present

RAPID CITY

**Rapid City Society for Genealogical
Research, Inc.**
Mail to: P.O. Box 1495, 57701
Founded in: 1966
Questionnaire not received

REDFIELD

Spink County Historical Society
Telephone: (605) 472-0758
Mail to: Frankfort, 57440
Questionnaire not received

ST. FRANCIS

Buechel Memorial Lakota Museum
P.O. Box 146, 57572
Telephone: (605) 747-2745/747-9997
Private agency, authorized by St.
Francis Indian Mission
Founded in: 1947
Emil Her Many Horses, Director
Staff: full time 1, part time 2
Major programs: archives, museum
Period of collections: 1865-present

SALEM

McCook County Historical Society
Telephone: (605) 247-3367
Mail to: c/o Vice President, Rt. 1,
57058
County agency
Founded in: 1978
Amy Behrendt, Vice President
Number of members: 10
Staff: volunteer 10
Major programs: tours/pilgrimages,
oral history, research, living history,
audiovisual programs,
photographic collections,
genealogical services, Period of
collections: 1889-present

SCOTLAND

Scotland Historical Society
531 4th St., 57059
Telephone: (605) 583-4531
Founded in: 1976

Ivan Downer, President
Number of members: 70
Staff: volunteer 6
Major programs: museum, historic
   sites preservation
Period of collections: 1865-present

SIOUX FALLS

Archaeological Society of South Dakota
521 E. 21st, 57105
Telephone: (605) 338-3172
Questionnaire not received

Archives of the North American Baptist Conference
1605 S. Euclid Ave., 57105
Telephone: (605) 336-6805
Private agency
Founded in: 1850
George A. Dunger, Archivist
Staff: part time 1
Major programs: archives,
   manuscripts, historic preservation,
   research, photographic
   collections, genealogical services,
   field services
Period of collections: 1850-present

Center for Western Studies
29th and Summit Sts.
Telephone: (605) 336-4007
Mail to: Augustana College, P.O. Box
   727, 57197
Founded in: 1964
Sven G. Froiland, Executive Director
Number of members: 250
Staff: full time 3, part time 1,
   volunteer 9
Magazine: *Buffalo Chips*
Major programs: library, archives,
   manuscripts, museum, oral history,
   school programs, book publishing,
   newsletters/pamphlets, research,
   exhibits, archaeology programs,
   photographic collections,
   genealogical services
Period of collections: 1750-present

Dakotah Corral, Westerners International
1905 S. 6th Ave., 57105
Telephone: (605) 332-4188
Private agency
Dorand C. Young, Sheriff
Number of members: 35

Great Plains Zoo and Museum
15th and Kiwanis Sts.
Telephone: (605) 339-7059
Mail to: 600 E. 7th St., 57102
City agency, authorized by Parks and
   Recreation Department
Founded in: 1963 (zoo); 1984
   (museum)
Roger A. Shepherd, Manager
Staff: full time 9, part time 6,
   volunteer 2
Major programs: zoological gardens,
   natural history museum

Minnehaha County Historical Society
200 W. 6th St. 57102
Telephone: (605) 338-7090
County agency
Founded in: 1926
Robert Kolbe, President
Number of members: 325
Staff: volunteer 12

Major programs: historic site(s),
   markers, tours/pilgrimages, school
   programs, book publishing,
   newsletters/pamphlets, historic
   preservation
Period of collections: 1857-1927

North American Baptists Archives
1605 S. Euclid Ave., 57105
Telephone: (605) 336-6588
Questionnaire not received

Sioux Empire Medical Museum
1200 S. Euclid St., 57105
Telephone: (605) 333-1000, ext. 6397
Private agency, authorized by Alumni
   Association of Sioux Valley Hospital
   School of Nursing
Founded in: 1975
Staff: volunteer 59

Siouxland Heritage Museums
200 W. Sixth St., 57102
Telephone: (605) 335-4210
Founded in: 1930
Geoffrey R. Hunt, Director
Number of members: 540
Staff: full time 13, part time 4,
   volunteer 89
Magazine: *Prairie People*
Major programs: library, archives,
   manuscripts, museum, historic
   sites preservation, junior history,
   oral history, educational programs,
   newsletters/pamphlets, historic
   preservation, exhibits
Period of collections: 1850-1930

Sioux Valley Genealogical Society
Old Courthouse Museum, 200 W. 6th
   St., 57102
Mail to: P.O. Box 655, 57101
Founded in: 1972
Number of members: 250
Staff: full time 1, volunteer 12
Magazine: *Pioneer Pathfinder*
Major programs: library,
   newsletters/pamphlets, research,
   genealogical services
Period of collections: 1865-present

South Dakota Archaeological Society
Archeology Lab, 2032 S. Grange
   Ave., 57105
Telephone: (605) 366-5493
Founded in: 1970
L. Adrien Hannus, Editor
Number of members: 200
Staff: volunteer 2
Magazine: *South Dakota Archaeology*
Major programs: book publishing,
   newsletters/pamphlets, historic
   preservation
Period of collections:
   paleolithic-present

SPEARFISH

High Plains Heritage Society
135 S. Main St.
Telephone: (605) 642-4700
Mail to: P.O. Box 542, 57783
Private agency
Founded in: 1974
Kay Jorgensen, Executive Director
Number of members: 800
Staff: full time 3
Magazine: *High Plains News*

Major programs: archives, museum,
   oral history, historic preservation
Period of collections: 1870s-1900s

Leland Case Library
Black Hills State College, 57702
Telephone: (605) 642-6446
State agency, authorized by Black
   Hills State College Library
Founded in: 1974
Charles Schaid, College Relations
Number of members: 70
Major programs: library, archives,
   manuscripts, school programs,
   historic preservation, research,
   photographic collections, field
   services

SPRINGFIELD

Springfield Historical Society
P.O. Box 333, 57062
Telephone: (605) 369-2498
City agency
Founded in: 1970
Julius O. Sandvick, President
Number of members: 50
Staff: volunteer 7
Major programs: museum, historic
   preservation

TIMBER LAKE

Timber Lake and Area Historical Society
P.O. Box 181, 57656
Telephone: (605) 865-3141
Private agency
Founded in: 1982
Martin A. Biegler, President
Number of members: 200
Staff: volunteer 35
Major programs: archives, oral
   history, book publishing,
   newsletters/pamphlets,
   photographic collections, annual
   calendar
Major programs: 1908-present

VERMILLION

Shrine to Music Museum
414 E. Clark St., 57069
Telephone: (605) 677-5306
State agency, authorized by
   University of South Dakota
Founded in: 1973
Andre P. Larson, Director
Number of members: 500
Staff: full time 4, part time 1,
   volunteer 4
Major programs: library, archives,
   museum, school programs, book
   publishing, newsletters/pamphlets,
   research, exhibits, photographic
   collections, history of music and
   musical instruments
Period of collections: 16th
   century-present

State Historical Preservation Center
P.O. Box 417, 57969
Telephone: (605) 677-5314
State agency, authorized by South
   Dakota Office of History
Founded in: 1973
Paul Putz, Director
Staff: full time 7

Major programs: library, historic
site(s), book publishing, historic
preservation, research, audiovisual
programs, archaeology programs,
photographic collections, field
services
Period of collections: 1866-1945

**South Dakota Archaeological
Society**
Archaeology Lab., University of South
Dakota, 57069
Telephone: (605) 677-5401
Founded in: 1970
Questionnaire not received

W. H. Over Museum
University of South Dakota, 57069
Telephone: (605) 677-5228
Founded in: 1883
Julia R. Vodicka, Director
Number of members: 250
Staff: full time 5, volunteer 20
Major programs: exhibits,
photographic collections
Period of collections: 1865-present

VOLGA

**Brookings County Historical
Society**
Telephone: (605) 627-9493
Questionnaire not received

WAGNER

**Charles Mix County Historical
Society**
57380
Telephone: (605) 384-5642
Founded in: 1970
Harry Crisman, President
Number of members: 60
Staff: volunteer 30
Major programs: museum, oral
history, historic preservation
Period of collections: 1900-present

WATERTOWN

**Codington County Historical
Society, Inc./Kampeska Heritage
Museum**
Telephone: (605) 886-7335
Mail to: 27 1st Ave., SE, 57201
Private agency
Founded in: 1973
Joanita Kant Fisher, Director
Number of members: 250
Staff: full time 1, part time 8,
volunteer 12
Major programs: library, archives,
manuscripts, museum, oral history,
school programs, book publishing,
newsletters/pamphlets, research,
exhibits, archaeology programs,
photographic collections
Period of collections: 1880-1910

WESSINGTON SPRINGS

Dunham Historical Society
57382
Telephone: (605) 539-5002
Questionnaire not received

WHITE RIVER

Mellette County Historical Society
Telephone: (605) 259-3429
County agency

Founded in: 1980
Laura E. Kirsch, President
Number of members: 40
Staff: volunteer 9
Major programs: museum, oral
history, exhibits
Period of collections: 1911-present

WINNER

Tripp County Historical Society
E. Hwy. 18, 57580
Questionnaire not received

YANKTON

Cramer-Yankton Heritage Home
509 Pine St., 57078
Telephone: (605) 665-7470
Founded in: 1886
Questionnaire not received

Dakota Territorial Museum
Westside Park, 610 Summit
Telephone: (605) 665-3898
Mail to: P.O. Box 1033, 57078
Private agency, authorized by
Yankton County Historical Society
Founded in: 1936
Donald J. Binder, Director/Curator
Number of members: 200
Staff: full time 1, part time 1,
volunteer 20
Major programs: archives, museum,
newsletters/pamphlets, exhibits,
photographic collections
Period of collections: 1861-present

Yankton County Historical Society
Westside Park, 610 Summit St.
Telephone: (605) 665-3898
Mail to: P.O. Box 1033, 57078
Founded in: 1961
Donald J. Binder, Director/Curator
Number of members: 150
Staff: full time 1, part time 2,
volunteer 25
Major programs: museum
Period of collections: 1880-1920

TENNESSEE

ATHENS

**McMinn County Living Heritage
Museum**
Old College Bldg., Tennessee
Wesleyan College
Telephone: (615) 745-0329
Mail to: P.O. Box 889, 37303
Private agency, authorized by the
college
Founded in: 1982
Jan Wilkins, Director
Number of members: 529
Staff: full time 1, part time 2,
volunteer 5
Major programs: museum, historic
site(s), school programs,
newsletters/pamphlets, records
management, exhibits
Period of collections: 1820-1940

BEECH GROVE

**Beech Grove Confederate
Cemetery**
Rt. 1, 37018
Telephone: (615) 394-2157
County agency, authorized by
Tennessee Historical Commission
Founded in: 1954
David L. Jacobs,
Chair/Superintendent
Staff: volunteer 4
Major programs: historic site(s),
school programs
Period of collections: 1861-1865

BENTON

**Polk County Chapter, East
Tennessee Historical Society**
Mail to: 2800 Wesdell Lane,
Cleveland, 37311
Founded in: 1957
Questionnaire not received

BRENTWOOD

**Tennessee Baptist Historical
Society**
P.O. Box 347, 37027
Telephone: (615) 373-2255
Private agency, authorized by
Tennessee Baptist Convention
Jerry Self, Consultant
Staff: full time 1
Major programs: archives, markers,
historic preservation
Period of collections: 1850-present

CASTILIAN SPRINGS

Wynnewood
Rt. 1, Box 5, 37031
Telephone: (615) 452-5463
Founded in: 1971
Questionnaire not received

CHATTANOOGA

**Chattanooga Area Historical
Association**
Mail to: P.O. Box 1663, 37401
Founded in: 1948
Questionnaire not received

**Chattanooga Museum of Regional
History**
176 S. Crest Rd., 37404
Telephone: (615) 698-1084
Founded in: 1978
Questionnaire not received

Chattanooga Nature Center
Rt. 4, Garden Rd., 37409
Telephone: (615) 821-1160
Private agency
Founded in: 1979
Sandra L. Kurtz, Director
Number of members: 1,200
Staff: full time 5, part time 6,
volunteer 100
Major programs: museum,
tours/pilgrimages, school
programs, newsletters/pamphlets,
exhibits, natural history, wildlife
rehabilitation laboratory

**Chicamauga and Chattanooga
National Military Park**
Point Park, Lookout Mountain, 37350
Telephone: (615) 821-7786

Federal agency, authorized by
National Park Service
Founded in: 1890
Larry S. Steeler, Unit Manager
Staff: full time 5, part time 3,
volunteer 15
Major programs: historic site(s), living
history
Period of collections: Civil War

Houston Antique Museum
201 High St., 37403
Telephone: (615) 267-7176
Founded in: 1961
Thomas G. Garner, Director
Number of members: 600
Staff: full time 2, part time 1,
volunteer 50
Magazine: *Sugar Chest*
Major programs: museum,
educational programs, antique
show, decorative arts
Period of collections: 19th century

Hunter Museum of Art
10 Bluff View, 37403
Telephone: (615) 267-0968
Private agency
Founded in: 1951
Cleve K. Scarbrough, Director
Staff: full time 17, part time 4,
volunteer 200
Major programs: library, museum,
school programs,
newsletters/pamphlets, exhibits,
audiovisual programs, fine art
Period of collections: 19th-20th
centuries

**Mary Walker Historical and
Educational Foundation**
3031 Wilcox Blvd., 37411
Telephone: (615) 622-3217
Founded in: 1970
J. Loyd Edwards, Founder/President
Number of members: 75
Major programs: library, museum,
historic sites preservation, markers,
tours/pilgrimages, junior history,
oral history, educational programs,
books, newsletters/pamphlets

**Tennessee Valley Railroad
Museum, Inc.**
4119 Cromwell Rd., 37421
Telephone: (615) 894-8028
Mail to: P.O. Box 5263, 37406
Founded in: 1961
Questionnaire not received

CLARKSVILLE

**Clarksville-Montgomery County
Historical Museum**
200 S. 2nd St.
Telephone: (615) 645-2507
Mail to: P.O. Box 383, 37040
City agency
Founded in: 1982
Robert Patterson, Director
Staff: full time 3, part time 1,
volunteer 100
Major programs: archives, museum,
school programs, research,
exhibits, photographic collections,
field services
Period of collections: Victorian era

**Montgomery County Historical
Society**
Public Library, 329 Main St., 37040

Telephone: (615) 647-6817
Mail to: c/o President, 1650 Simpson
Dr., 37043
County agency
Founded in: 1960
Jessie V. Robinette, President
Number of members: 85
Magazine: *Montgomery County
Genealogical Journal*
Major programs: library, archives,
historic sites preservation
Period of collections: 1783-present

CLEVELAND

Bradley County Historical Society
Lee College
Mail to: P.O. Box 2424, 37311
Telephone: (615) 476-8431
Private agency
Ruth Hynes, President
Number of members: 100
Major programs: library, manuscripts,
tours/pilgrimages
Period of collections: 1865-1918

Cherokee-Red Clay Association
1995 Keith St., NW, 37311
Telephone: (615) 472-6511
Private agency
Founded in: 1962
Tom Rowland, President
Major programs: library, museum,
historic site(s)

**Polk County Chapter, East
Tennessee Historical Society**
Telephone: (615) 479-4652
Mail to: 2800 Wesdell Lane, NE,
37311
Private agency
Founded in: 1957
Roy G. Lillard, President
Number of members: 50
Major programs: historic sites
preservation, educational
programs

Red Clay State Historical Area
Rt. 6, Box 734, 37311
Telephone: (615) 472-2627
State agency, authorized by
Department of Conservation,
Division of Parks and Recreation
Founded in: 1979
Lois Osborne, Park Manager
Staff: full time 3, part time 4,
volunteer 6
Major programs: museum, historic
site(s), school programs, exhibits
Period of collections: 19th century

COLUMBIA

**James K. Polk Memorial
Association**
W. 7th and High Sts.
Telephone: (615) 388-2354
Mail to: P.O. Box 741, 38402
Private agency
Founded in: 1929
John C. Holtzapple, Coordinator
Number of members: 350
Staff: full time 1, part time 4,
volunteer 7
Major programs: museum, historic
site(s), tours/pilgrimages, school
programs, historic preservation,
genealogical services
Period of collections: 1820-1850

COOKEVILLE

**Cookeville Committee to Preserve
the Depot**
Telephone: (615) 528-3616
Mail to: P.O. Box 1135, 38503
City agency
Founded in: 1984
Mary Jean DeLozier, Chair
Staff: volunteer 8
Major programs: historic site(s),
newsletters/pamphlets, exhibits,
photographic collections
Period of collections: 1880-1950

**Upper Cumberland Humanities and
Social Sciences Institute**
Tennessee Technical University, P.O.
Box 5183, 38505
Telephone: (615) 528-3338
State agency, authorized by the
university
Founded in: 1983
Homer D. Kemp, Director
Staff: full time 1
Major programs: archives, oral
history, school programs, historic
preservation, research
Period of collections: 19th-20th
centuries

DANDRIDGE

Restore Our County, Inc.
Telephone: (615) 397-9392/397-2373
Mail to: P.O. Box 329, 37725
Private agency
Founded in: 1978
George A. Bauman, Managing
Director
Number of members: 200
Staff: volunteer 5
Major programs: archives,
manuscripts, museum, historic
site(s), tours/pilgrimages, oral
history, school programs, book
publishing, newsletters/pamphlets,
historic preservation, records
management, research,
audiovisual programs,
photographic collections,
genealogical services, annual
festival
Period of collections: 1792-present

DEER LODGE

**Deer Lodge Abner Ross Memorial
Center**
Harker St.
Telephone: (615) 965-3704/965-3472
Mail to: Star Rt., Box 90, 37726
Town agency
Founded in: 1983
Conrad Strand, Chair
Major programs: library, historic
site(s), markers, school programs,
book publishing, research,
exhibits, photographic collections,
genealogical services

DOVER

Ft. Donelson National Military Park
U.S. Hwy. 79, 37058
Telephone: (615) 232-5348
Mail to: P.O. Box F, 37058
Founded in: 1928
Questionnaire not received

FAYETTEVILLE

Lincoln County Historical Society
202 E. Washington St., 37334
Telephone: (615) 433-5767
County agency
Founded in: 1971
Don Wyett, Agent
Number of members: 82
Staff: volunteer 4
Magazine: *The Volunteer*
Major programs:
newsletters/pamphlets, research,
exhibits, photographic collections

FRANKLIN

Carnton Association, Inc.
Carnton Lane Rt. 2, 37064
Telephone: (615) 794-0903
Private agency
Founded in: 1978
Bernice Seiberling, Executive
Secretary
Number of members: 535
Staff: full time 2, part time 1,
volunteer 8
Major programs: historic site(s),
tours/pilgrimages, oral history,
book publishing,
newsletters/pamphlets, historic
preservation, records
management, audiovisual
programs
Period of collections: 1826-1861

Carnton Mansion
Rt. 2, Carnton Lane, 37064
Private agency, authorized by
Carnton Association, Inc.
Founded in: 1978
Bernice Seiberling, Executive
Secretary
Number of members: 565
Staff: full time 2
Major programs: markers,
tours/pilgrimages, oral history,
school programs,
newsletters/pamphlets, historic
preservation, research, audiovisual
programs
Period of collections: 1826-1861

Carter House, A.P.T.A.
1140 Columbia Ave.
Telephone: (615) 791-1861
Mail to: P.O. Box 555, 37064
Founded in: 1951
Dolores Kestner, Curator
Number of members: 300
Staff: full time 1, part time 5
Major programs: museum, historic
sites preservation,
tours/pilgrimages, oral history
Period of collections: 1865-1918

**Heritage Foundation of Franklin
and Williamson County**
209 E. Main St.
Telephone: (615) 790-0378
Mail to: P.O. Box 723, 37064
Private agency
Founded in: 1968
Mary Evins, Executive Director
Number of members: 1,500
Staff: full time 2, volunteer 12
Magazine: *Sentinel*
Major programs: historic site(s),
markers, tours/pilgrimages, school
programs, newsletters/pamphlets,
historic preservation

GALLATIN

**Sumner County Chapter,
Association for the Preservation
of Tennessee Antiquities**
Rt. 1, Box 42, Castalian Springs,
37031
Telephone: (615) 452-7070
Founded in: 1952
Questionnaire not received

Sumner County Historical Society
Belvedere Dr., 37066
Telephone: (615) 452-6700
Questionnaire not received

**Sumner County Museum
Association**
183 W. Smith St.
Mail to: P.O. Box 1064, 37066
Founded in: 1976
Questionnaire not received

GATLINBURG

**Great Smoky Mountains National
Park**
U.S. Hwy. 441, 37738
Telephone: (615) 436-5615
Federal agency
Founded in: 1934
Edward Trout, Park Historian
Major programs: library, archives,
manuscripts, museum, historic
site(s), markers, tours/pilgrimages,
oral history, newsletters/pamphlets,
historic preservation, audiovisual
programs, photographic
collections, genealogical services,
natural science
Period of collections: 1830-1980

GOODLETTSVILLE

**Bowen-Campbell House
Association, Inc.**
Caldwell Rd.
Telephone: (615) 859-3214
Mail to: P.O. Box 781, 37072
Private agency
Founded in: 1976
David Carver, President
Number of members: 75
Staff: volunteer 12
Major programs: historic site(s),
tours/pilgrimages, school
programs, historic preservation,
exhibits, photographic collections
Period of collections: 1787

GREENEVILLE

**Andrew Johnson National Historic
Site**
College and Depot Sts.
Telephone: (615) 638-3551/638-1326
Mail to: P.O. Box 1088, 37744-1088
Federal agency, authorized by
National Park Service
Founded in: 1942
Grady C. Webb, Superintendent
Staff: full time 5, part time 6
Major programs: library, museum,
historic site(s), historic
preservation, exhibits,
photographic collections
Period of collections: 1808-present

Greene County Heritage Trust
Telephone: (615) 638-6303
Mail to: P.O. Box 108, 37743
Questionnaire not received

HARROGATE

**Abraham Lincoln Library and
Museum**
Lincoln Memorial University, 37752
Telephone: (615) 869-3611
Founded in: 1897
Questionnaire not received

HENDERSONVILLE

Rock Castle Historic Home
139 Rock Castle Lane, 37075
Telephone: (615) 824-0502
State agency, authorized by Friends
of Rock Castle
Founded in: 1796
Roy K. Pace, Resident Director
Number of members: 300
Staff: part time 2, volunteer 26
Period of collections: 1784-1831

HERMITAGE

**Hermitage: Plantation Home of
President Andrew Jackson**
4580 Rachel's Lane, 37076
Telephone: (615) 889-2941
Founded in: 1889
George M. Anderjack, Resident
Director
Number of members: 2,500
Staff: full time 35, part time 35,
volunteer 20
Major programs: manuscripts,
museum, historic sites
preservation, educational
programs, books
Period of collections: 1837-1845

HOHENWALD

Meriwether Lewis Monument
Natchez Trace Parkway and Hwy. 20
Telephone: (615) 796-2921
Mail to: Rt. 2, Box 368, 38462
Federal agency, authorized by
National Park Service
Founded in: 1925
M. Eugene Phillips, Jr.,
Supervisor/Park Ranger
Staff: full time 3
Major programs: historic site(s),
markers, exhibits

HUNTSVILLE

Scott County Historical Society
P.O. Box 7, 37756
Telephone: (615) 663-2316
County agency
Founded in: 1965
Irene B. Baker, President
Number of members: 120
Staff: volunteer 6
Major programs: archives,
manuscripts, oral history, book
publishing, newsletters/pamphlets,
records management, research,
photographic collections,
genealogical services
Period of collections: 1849-1935

JACKSON

**Home of Casey Jones and Railroad
Museum**
211 W. Chester
Telephone: (901) 427-8382
Mail to: P.O. Box 682, 38301
Questionnaire not received

JAMESTOWN

Fentress County Historical Society
Telephone: (615) 879-7575
Mail to: P.O. Box 324, 38556
Questionnaire not received

JOHNSON CITY

**Appalachian History of Medicine
Society**
Box 23296-A, East Tennessee State
University, 37614
Telephone: (615) 928-6426, ext. 252
Authorized by Quillen-Dishner
College of Medicine Library
Founded in: 1978
Martha Whaley, History of Medicine
Librarian
Number of members: 31
Staff: volunteer 4
Major programs: library, archives,
museum, oral history, exhibits,
published proceedings
Period of collections: 19th-20th
centuries

Carroll Reece Museum
East Tennessee State University
Telephone: (615) 929-4392
Mail to: P.O. Box 22300-A, 37614
State agency, authorized by the
university
Founded in: 1931
Helen K. Roseberry, Director
Number of members: 200
Staff: full time 4, part time 7,
volunteer 10
Major programs: museum,
tours/pilgrimages, school
programs, newsletters/pamphlets,
historic preservation, research,
exhibits, audiovisual programs,
photographic collections
Period of collections: late 18th-20th
centuries

**Tipton-Haynes Historical
Association**
J. C. Erwin Hwy. and Buffalo Rd.,
37601
Telephone: (615) 926-3631
Questionnaire not received

JONESBOROUGH

Jonesborough Civic Trust
Telephone: (615) 753-5281
Mail to: P.O. Box 451, 37659
Private agency
Founded in: 1970
Daniel J. Bell, Curator
Number of members: 200
Staff: full time 1, part time 1
Major programs: library, museum,
tours/pilgrimages, historic
preservation
Period of collections: prehistoric-19th
century

KINGSPORT

Netherland Inn Association
1638 Crescent Dr.
Telephone: (615) 247-3211
Mail to: P.O. Box 293, 37662
Private agency
Founded in: 1968
Mrs. Hal T. Spoden, Chair
Number of members: 360

Staff: full time 1, part time 4,
volunteer 52
Major programs: manuscripts,
museum, historic site(s), markers,
tours/pilgrimages, junior history,
oral history, school programs,
newsletters/pamphlets, historic
preservation, records
management, research, exhibits,
audiovisual programs, costume
collection
Period of collections: 1770s-1800s

Sullivan County Historical Society
Telephone: (615) 288-2752
Mail to: P.O. Box 153, 37662
Founded in: 1977
Questionnaire not received

KNOXVILLE

**Beck Cultural Exchange
Center, Inc.**
1927 Dandridge Ave., 37915
Telephone: (615) 524-8461
Founded in: 1975
Questionnaire not received

Blount Mansion
200 W. Hill Ave., 37901
Telephone: (615) 525-2375
Private agency, authorized by Blount
Mansion Association
Founded in: 1926
Mark Brown, Executive Director
Number of members: 900
Staff: full time 1, part time 7,
volunteer 30
Major programs: historic site(s) 3
Period of collections: late 18th
century

**Crescent Bend: Armstrong-Lockett
House and Gardens**
2728 Kingston Pike, 37919
Private agency, authorized by the
Toms Foundation
Founded in: 1938
William P. Beall, Curator
Staff: full time 3, part time 2
Major programs: library, historic
site(s), historic preservation
Period of collections: 1640-1820

East Tennessee Historical Society
500 W. Church Ave., 37902
Telephone: (615) 523-0781
Founded in: 1925
Charles F. Bryan, Jr., Executive
Director
Number of members: 1,500
Staff: full time 2, part time 2,
volunteer 4
Major programs: community history
education, exhibits, historical and
genealogical conferences, books,
newsletters/pamphlets,
educational programs

Frank H. McClung Museum
1027 Circle Park Dr., University of
Tennessee, 37916
Telephone: (615) 974-2144
State agency, authorized by the
university
Founded in: 1961
Paul W. Parmalee, Director
Staff: full time 6, part time 3,
volunteer 4

Major programs: research, exhibits,
archaeology programs,
photographic collections
Period of collections: 8000 B.C.-A.D.
1500

Knoxville Heritage, Inc.
Telephone: (615) 522-0832
Mail to: P.O. Box 11501, 37919
Questionnaire not received

Knoxville-Knox County Archives
500 W. Church Ave., 37902-2505
Telephone: (615) 523-0781, ext. 139
County agency, authorized by Knox
County Public Library System
Founded in: 1975
Robert W. Harvey, Archivist
Staff: full time 5, part time 1
Major programs: library, archives,
records management,
photographic collections,
genealogical services
Period of collections: from 1900

Speedwell Manor
2112 Manor Rd., 37920
Telephone: (615) 577-2757
Founded in: 1973
Questionnaire not received

Tennessee Valley Authority
400 W. Summit Hill Dr., 37902
Telephone: (615) 632-3466
Federal agency
Founded in: 1933
Jesse C. Mills, Chief Librarian
Staff: full time 40
Major programs: library, archives,
oral history, newsletters/pamphlets,
historic preservation, archaeology
programs, photographic
collections
Period of collections: 1933-present

LAFAYETTE

Macon County Historical Society
Key Park, 37083
County agency
Founded in: 1983
Randy Gene East, President
Number of members: 24
Staff: volunteer 4
Magazine: *History Happenings*
Major programs: library, archives,
manuscripts, oral history, book
publishing, newsletters/pamphlets,
historic preservation, research,
photographic collections,
genealogical services
Period of collections: 1842-present

LAWRENCEBURG

**Lawrence County Historical
Society**
Mail to: P.O. Box 431, 38464
Founded in: 1954
Questionnaire not received

LEBANON

**History Associates of Wilson
County**
Telephone: (615) 444-2562
Mail to: Simms Home Entertainment
Center, 111 S. College, 37087
Founded in: 1961
Questionnaire not received

Stockton Archives, Cumberland University
37087
Telephone: (615) 444-2562
Private agency, authorized by the university
Founded in: 1984
Sue Lynn Stone, University Archivist
Staff: full time 1, part time 1
Major programs: archives, manuscripts, records management, photographic collections, institutional history
Period of collections: 1842-present

LEXINGTON

Henderson County Historical Society
P.O. Box 128, Wildersville, 38388
Private agency
Founded in: 1976
John Graves, President
Number of members: 35
Period of collections: 1818-present

LIVINGSTON

Overton County Historical Society
P.O. Box 172, 38570
Questionnaire not received

MANCHESTER

Coffee County Historical Society
304 S. Irwin St.
Telephone: (615) 728-0764
Mail to: P.O. Box 524, 37355
Private agency
Founded in: 1970
Mrs. John R. Bridgewater, President
Number of members: 225
Staff: volunteer 4
Magazine: *Coffee County Historical Quarterly*
Major programs: library, archives, book publishing, newsletters/pamphlets, historic preservation, research, genealogical services
Period of collections: 1836-present

MANCHESTER

Old Stone Fort State Archaeological Park
Rt. 7, Box 7400, 37355
Telephone: (615) 728-0751
State agency, authorized by Department of Conservation
Founded in: 1970
C. Ward Weems, Historic Area Manager
Staff: full time 8, part time 6, volunteer 1
Major programs: museum, historic site(s), school programs, research, exhibits, audiovisual programs, archaeology programs

MARTIN

Weakley County Genealogical Society
P.O. Box 92, 38237
Private agency
Founded in: 1978
Pansy N. Baker, President
Number of members: 200

Staff: volunteer 9
Major programs: library, book publishing, newsletters/pamphlets, genealogical services
Period of collections: 1800s

MARYVILLE

Blount County Historic Trust, Inc.
P.O. Box 161, 37803-0161
Private agency
Founded in: 1977
Sarah B. McNiell, President
Number of members: 250
Major programs: historic site(s), book publishing, historic preservation, audiovisual programs, photographic collections
Period of collections: 19th-20th centuries

Sam Houston Memorial Association
Rt. 8, Sam Houston School House Rd., 37801
Telephone: (615) 983-1550
Founded in: 1943
Questionnaire not received

McKENZIE

Carroll County Historical Society—Governor Gordon Browning Museum
141 N. Broadway, 38201
Telephone: (901) 352-5741
Private agency
Founded in: 1971
Mary Ruth Devault, Executive Secretary
Number of members: 50
Staff: full time 1
Major programs: museum, markers, genealogical services
Period of collections: 1821-present

MEMPHIS

Center for Southern Folklore
1216 Peabody Ave.
Telephone: (901) 726-4205
Mail to: P.O. Box 40105, 38174
Private agency
Founded in: 1972
Judy Peiser, Executive Director
Staff: full time 6, part time 9, volunteer 30
Major programs: archives, historic site(s), oral history, school programs, book publishing, newsletters/pamphlets, research, exhibits, audiovisual programs, photographic collections, interpretive center, folk and ethnic studies
Period of collections: early 1900s-present

Center for Voluntary Action Research
103 Clement Bldg., Memphis State University, 38152
Telephone: (901) 454-2751
State agency, authorized by the university
Founded in: 1981
Stanley E. Hyland, Co-director
Staff: full time 1, part time 1, volunteer 5

Major programs: oral history, research, audiovisual programs, photographic collections, neighborhood studies

C. H. Nash Museum at Chucalissa
1987 Indian Village Dr., 38109
State agency, authorized by Memphis State University
Founded in: 1955
Gerald P. Smith, Curator
Staff: full time 10
Major programs: museum, school programs, research, exhibits, archaeology programs
Period of collections: prehistoric

Fontaine House
680 Adams, 38105
Telephone: (901) 526-1469
Private agency, authorized by Association for Preservation of Tennessee Antiquities
Founded in: 1952
Jeanne Crawford, Director
Number of members: 250
Staff: full time 1, part time 3, volunteer 70
Major programs: historic site(s), historic preservation, exhibits
Period of collections: 1870-1890

Historical Foundation of the Cumberland Presbyterian Church
168 E. Parkway, S, 38104
Telephone: (901) 323-8795
Private agency
Founded in: 1980
Jane K. Williamson, Director/Archivist
Number of members: 90
Staff: full time 1
Magazine: *Cumberland Presbyterian Quill*
Major programs: library, archives, research
Period of collections: 1810-present

Magevney House
198 Adams Ave., 38103
Telephone: (901) 785-3160
City agency, authorized by Memphis Museum System
Founded in: 1941
Marjorie Holmes, Curator
Staff: part time 1, volunteer 10
Magazine: *MuseumScope*
Major programs: tours/pilgrimages, school programs, audiovisual programs
Period of collections: 1850

Mallory-Neely Home
652 Adams Ave., 38105
Telephone: (901) 523-1484
Founded in: 1973
Questionnaire not received

Memphis Heritage, Inc.
8 N. 3rd St., Suite 615
Telephone: (901) 529-9828
Mail to: P.O. Box 3143, 38103
Private agency
Founded in: 1975
Kay B. Newman, Board President
Number of members: 500
Staff: part time 2
Magazine: *The Keystone*
Major programs: historic site(s), tours/pilgrimages, school

programs, newsletters/pamphlets, historic preservation, research, audiovisual programs, technical services

Memphis Landmarks Commission
22 N. Front St., 38103
Telephone: (901) 528-2834
Founded in: 1975
Questionnaire not received

Memphis Pink Palace Museum
3050 Central Ave., 38111
Telephone: (901) 454-5600
City agency
Founded in: 1930
Douglas R. Noble, Director
Number of members: 2,750
Staff: full time 37, part time 21, volunteer 175
Major programs: library, archives, manuscripts, museum, historic site(s), school programs, newsletters/pamphlets, historic preservation, exhibits, archaeology programs
Period of collections: prehistoric-present

Mississippi River Museum
Mud Island
Telephone: (901) 528-3570
Mail to: City Hall, 125 N. Main, 38103
City agency
Founded in: 1978
Steve Masler, Director
Staff: full time 5, part time 20
Major programs: museum, tours, school programs, newsletters/pamphlets, exhibits, audiovisual programs
Period of collections: prehistoric-present

Mississippi Valley Collection, Special Collections Department, Memphis State University Libraries
Brister Library, 38152
Telephone: (901) 454-2210
State agency
Founded in: 1964
Delanie Ross, Curator
Staff: full time 3, part time 4, volunteer 2
Major programs: library, archives, manuscripts, oral history, pamphlets, historic preservation, audiovisual programs, photographic collections, sheet music
Period of collections: 1600-present

P.T. Boats, Inc.
663 S. Cooper, Suite 4, 38104
Telephone: (901) 272-9980
Mail to: P.O. Box 109, 38101
Founded in: 1967
J. M. Newberry, Founder/Director
Number of members: 8,000
Staff: full time 3, volunteer 15
Major programs: library, archives, manuscripts, museum, markers, book publishing, newsletters/pamphlets, historic preservation, exhibits, photographic collections
Period of collections: W. W. II

West Tennessee Historical Society
P.O. Box 111046, 38111
Telephone: (901) 458-3384
Private agency
Founded in: 1957
Charles W. Crawford, President
Number of members: 792
Major programs: archives, markers, tours/pilgrimages, book publishing, newsletters/pamphlets
Period of collections: 1819-present

MORRISTOWN

Morristown-Hamblen Historical and Bicentennial Commission
Rose Center, 432 W. 2nd St., N
Telephone: (615) 581-4330
Mail to: P.O. Box 1976, 37814
Founded in: 1976
Bill Kornrich, Executive Director
Number of members: 300
Staff: full time 1, part time 1, volunteer 150
Major programs: historic site(s), tours, school programs, exhibits, photographic collections
Period of collections: 1783-present

MT. JULIET

Mt. Juliet-West Wilson County Historical Society
3125 Cloverwood Dr., Nashville, 37214
Telephone: (615) 883-1398
Private agency
Founded in: 1976
Mrs. Jack Hailey, President
Number of members: 100
Staff: volunteer 20
Major programs: library, archives, manuscripts, historic site(s), tours/pilgrimages, oral history, book publishing, newsletters/pamphlets, research, exhibits, photographic collections, genealogical services
Period of collections: 1790-present

MURFREESBORO

Cannonsburgh: A Living Museum Village of Early Southern Life
N. Front St.
Telephone: (615) 893-5432
Mail to: 507 E. Northfield Blvd., 37130
Founded in: 1974
Questionnaire not received

Center for Historic Preservation
1421 E. Main St.
Telephone: (615) 898-2300, ext. 2947
Mail to: P.O. Box 80, Middle Tennessee State University, 37132
State agency
Founded in: 1973
James K. Huhta, Director
Number of members: full time 4, part time 2
Major programs: museum, oral history, school programs, historic preservation, audiovisual programs, field services

Oaklands Association, Inc.
900 N. Maney Ave.
Telephone: (615) 890-7953
Mail to: P.O. Box 432, 37130
Private agency

Founded in: 1959
Mary Hoffschwelle, Executive Director
Number of members: 700
Staff: full time 2, part time 1, volunteer 90
Major programs: historic site(s), historic preservation, exhibits
Period of collections: 1840-1865

Rutherford County Historical Society, Inc.
Mail to: Box 906, 37133-0906
Private agency
Founded in: 1970
Number of members: 309
Staff: volunteer 50
Major programs: manuscripts, book publishing, newsletters/pamphlets, research

NASHVILLE

African-American Cultural Alliance
2814 Buena Vista Pike, 37218
Telephone: (615) 254-0970
Private agency
Founded in: 1983
Leo Lillard, President
Number of members: 17
Major programs: oral history, research, exhibits

American Association for State and Local History
172 2nd Ave., N, Suite 102, 37201
Telephone: (615) 255-2971
Founded in: 1940
Gerald George, Director
Number of members: 7,500
Staff: full time 30, part time 3
Magazine: *History News*
Major programs: school programs, book publishing, newsletters/pamphlets, audiovisual programs, representation for the field, awards

APTA (Association for the Preservation of Tennessee Antiquities)
110 Leake Ave., 37205
Telephone: (615) 352-8247
Private agency
Founded in: 1951
Sara A. Bond, Executive Secretary
Number of members: 2,700
Staff: full time 1, part time 1
Magazine: *Inter-Com*
Major programs: historic site(s), historic preservation
Period of collections: 1700-1900

Bellevue-Harpeth Historical Society
c/o Verla Hodges, Rt. 2, Box 59-A, Old Charlotte Rd., 37209
Telephone: (615) 352-9365
Founded in: 1970
Ilene J. Cornwell, Founder
Number of members: 40
Magazine: *Harpeth Gleanings*
Major programs: library, archives, manuscripts, oral history, newsletters/pamphlets, cemetery transcriptions
Period of collections: 1780-1900

Belle Meade Mansion
110 Leake Ave., 37205
Telephone: (615) 352-7350

Private agency, authorized by APTA
Founded in: 1954
Susan Olsen, Director
Number of members: 350
Staff: full time 1, part time 10
Major programs: historic site(s), tours/pilgrimages, school programs, historic preservation, research
Period of collections: 19th century

Black Civil War Tribute Committee
2814 Buena Vista Pike, 37218
Telephone: (615) 254-0970
Private agency
Founded in: 1979
Leo Lillard, Coordinator
Staff: volunteer 8
Major programs: historic site(s), tours/pilgrimages, oral history, research, exhibits, living history
Period of collections: Civil War

Calumet Center
1101 Kermit Dr., 37217
Telephone: (615) 361-8700
Private agency, authorized by United South and Eastern Tribes
Founded in: 1969
Charles L. Baker, Director
Number of members: 4,300
Staff: full time 13
Magazine: *Calumet*
Major programs: archives, museum, oral history, newsletters/pamphlets, historic preservation, exhibits, living history, field services, artifact recovery for member tribes
Period of collections: 1300s-present

Country Music Foundation
4 Music Square, E, 37203
Telephone: (615) 256-1630
Private agency
Founded in: 1964
William Ivey, Executive Director
Staff: full time 30, part time 35
Magazine: *Journal of Country Music*
Major programs: library, archives, museum, historic site(s), oral history, school programs, book publishing, newsletters/pamphlets, historic preservation, research, exhibits, photographic collections
Period of collections: 20th century

Cumberland Museum and Science Center
800 Ridley Blvd., 37203
Telephone: (615) 259-6099
Private agency
Founded in: 1944
William C. Bradshaw, Director
Number of members: 3,500
Staff: full time 22, part time 7, volunteer 125
Magazine: *Cumberland Notes*
Major programs: museum, school programs, newsletters/pamphlets, exhibits, audiovisual programs

Disciples of Christ Historical Society
1101 19th Ave., S, 37212
Telephone: (615) 327-1444
Founded in: 1941
James M. Seale, President
Staff: full time 4, part time 4, volunteer 1
Magazine: *Discipliana*

Major programs: library, archives, manuscripts, museum, oral history, newsletters/pamphlets, historic preservation
Period of collections: 1783-present

Fine Arts Center, Cheekwood
Forrest Park Dr., 37205
Telephone: (615) 352-8632
Private agency, authorized by Tennessee Botanical Gardens and Fine Arts Center, Inc.
Founded in: 1960
Kevin Grogan, Director
Staff: full time 5, part time 2
Major programs: museum, exhibits, fine arts
Period of collections: 19th-20th centuries

Ft. Nashborough
170 1st Ave., N, 37201
Telephone: (615) 255-8192
Mail to: Metro Postal Service, Centennial Park Office, 37201
Founded in: 1930
Naomi C. Levia, Director
Staff: full time 1, part time 1
Major programs: educational programs, museum, living history

Historic Belmont Association
Belmont College, Box A-39, 37203
Telephone: (615) 269-9537
Founded in: 1972
Lola Newman, President
Number of members: 700
Staff: volunteer 5
Period of collections: 1850-1885

Historic Landmarks Association
Old Hickory Blvd., 37221
Telephone: (615) 832-4068
Mail to: P.O. Box 15312, 37215
Founded in: 1967
Questionnaire not received

Historic Nashville, Inc.
214 2nd Ave., N, 37201
Telephone: (615) 248-9120
Private agency
Founded in: 1969
Debby Dale Mason, Executive Director
Number of members: 1,000
Staff: full time 2, volunteer 100
Magazine: *Historic Register*
Major programs: oral history, school programs, newsletters/pamphlets, historic preservation, audiovisual programs, field services

Historical Commission of Metropolitan Nashville-Davidson County
701 Broadway, B-20, 37203
Telephone: (615) 259-5027
Founded in: 1966
Ann Reynolds, Executive Director
Staff: full time 6, part time 1
Major programs: markers, tours, newsletters/pamphlets, historic preservation

Historical Commission of the Southern Baptist Convention
127 9th Ave. N. 37234
Telephone: (615) 251-2660
Founded in: 1951
Lynn E. May, Jr., Executive Director-Treasurer

Staff: full time 7, part time 2
Major programs: library, archives, oral history, educational programs, newsletters/pamphlets
Period of collections: 1600-present

Metropolitan Historical Commission
2nd Ave., N., 37201
Telephone: (615) 259-5027
Founded in: 1966
Questionnaire not received

Middle Tennessee Conference of Afro-American Culture
Tennessee State University
Telephone: (615 320-3220
Mail to: P.O. Box 130, Department of History and Geography, 37203
Founded in: 1970
Questionnaire not received

Middle Tennessee Conference, Afro-American Scholars
1721 14th Ave. S., 37212
Telephone: (615) 297-3416
Private agency
Founded in: 1966
A. T. Stephens, Professor of History
Major programs: historic preservation, research, clearing house for preservation and research, seminars

Museum of Tobacco Art and History
800 Harrison St., 37203
Telephone: (615) 242-9218
Private agency, authorized by U.S. Tobacco Company
Founded in: 1982
David Wright, Museum Manager
Staff: full time 1, part time 4
Major programs: museum, research
Period of collections: A.D. 800-present

Nashville Room, Nashville Public Library
222 8th Ave., N and Union St., 37203
Telephone: (615) 244-4700
City agency
Founded in: 1904
David Marshall Stewart, Director
Staff: full time 4, part time 1
Major programs: library, archives, manuscripts, museum, oral history, photographic collections, genealogical services
Period of collections: 19th-20th centuries

National Society, Colonial Dames of America in Tennessee
Travellers' Rest Historic House, Farrell Parkway, 37220
Telephone: (615) 832-2962
Founded in: 1896
Questionnaire not received

NICLOG (National Information Center for Local Government Records)
172 2nd Ave., N, Suite 102, 37201
Telephone: (615) 255-2971
Private agency, authorized by American Association for State and Local History
Founded in: 1984
James Summerville, Resources Coordinator

Bristol glass pipe, early tobacco jars, Staffordshire puzzle pipe, and Dutch brass tobacco box from the Museum of Tobacco Art and History's collection.—Museum of Tobacco Art and History, Nashville, Tennessee

Staff: full time 3
Major programs: book publishing, newsletters/pamphlets, records management, research, audiovisual programs

Oscar Farris Agricultural Museum
Ellington Agricultural Center, Hogan Rd.
Telephone: (615) 360-0197
Mail to: P.O. Box 40627, Melrose Station, 37204
State agency, authorized by Department of Agriculture
Founded in: 1957
Dorothy Curtis, Curator
Staff: full time 1, volunteer 3
Major programs: museum, tours/pilgrimages, school programs, living history
Period of collections: 1800-1930

Richland West End Neighborhood Association, Inc.
3708 Richland Ave., 37205
Telephone: (615) 297-1818
Private agency
Founded in: 1974
Betsy Woods, Chair
Major programs: historic preservation

Southern Baptist Historical Library and Archives
901 Commerce, Suite 400, 27203
Telephone: (615) 244-0344
Authorized by Southern Baptist Historical Commission
Lynn E. May, Executive Director
Number of members: 4
Staff: full time 13
Magazine: *Baptist History and Heritage*
Major programs: library, archives, oral history, book publishing, historic preservation, research, exhibits, photographic collections, field services
Period of collections: 1845-present

Southern Resources Unlimited
P.O. Box 29, 37221
Telephone: (615) 646-0199
Private agency
Founded in: 1980
Ilene J. Cornwell, President
Staff: part time 4
Major programs: manuscripts, oral history, book publishing, research, audiovisual programs
Period of collections: 1600-present

Tennessee Association of Museums
4 Music Square, E, 37203
Telephone: (615) 256-1639
Private agency
Founded in: 1960
Angelia Gacesa, President
Number of members: 150
Major programs: newsletters/pamphlets, conferences, workshops

◇**Tennessee Historical Commission**
701 Broadway, 37203
Telephone: (615) 742-6716
State agency
Founded in: 1919
Herbert L. Harper, Executive Director
Staff: full time 14
Magazine: *The Courier*
Major programs: historic site(s), markers, book publishing, newsletters/pamphlets, historic preservation

◇**Tennessee Historical Society**
War Memorial Bldg., 37219
Telephone: (615) 741-2660
Private agency
Founded in: 1849
James A. Hoobler, Executive Director
Number of members: 3,000
Staff: full time 1, part time 2
Magazine: *Tennessee Historical Quarterly*
Period of collections: prehistoric-present

Tennessee Humanities Council, Inc.
1001 18th Ave., S, 37212
Telephone: (615) 320-7001
Mail to: P.O. Box 24767, 37202
Private agency, authorized by National Endowment for the Humanities
Founded in: 1973
Robert Cheatham, Executive Director
Staff: full time 5, part time 1
Magazine: *Touchstone*
Major programs: library, museum, historic site(s), oral history, exhibits, audiovisual programs, archaeology programs, photographic collections, public education in the humanities

Tennessee State Library and Archives
403 7th Ave., N, 37219
Telephone: (615) 741-2764
State agency
Founded in: 1854
Robert B. Croneberger, State Librarian and Archivist
Staff: full time 80
Major programs: library, archives, manuscripts, genealogical services
Period of collections: prehistoric-present

◇**Tennessee State Museum**
Polk Center, 505 Deaderick St., 37219
Telephone: (615) 741-2692
State agency
Founded in: 1937
Lois Riggins, Director
Number of members: 700
Staff: full time 32, volunteer 85
Major programs: library, museum, oral history, school programs, newsletters/pamphlets, historic preservation, records management, research, exhibits, audiovisual programs, photographic collections, field services
Period of collections: 1780-1955

Travellers' Rest Museum House 1799
Farrell Parkway, 37205
Private agency, authorized by National Society of the Colonial Dames of America
Founded in: 1964
Mrs. Alex Pirtle, Jr., Chair
Number of members: 660
Staff: full time 1, part time 4, volunteer 40
Major programs: manuscripts, museum, historic site(s), tours/pilgrimages, school programs, newsletters/pamphlets, historic preservation, research, exhibits, living history, audiovisual programs
Period of collections: 1799-1832

United Methodist Publishing House Library
201 8th Ave., S, 37202
Telephone: (615) 749-6437
Private agency, authorized by United Methodist Church
Rosalyn Lewis, Librarian

Staff: full time 5
Major programs: library, archives
Period of collections: 18th
century-present

Vanderbilt Television News Archive
312 Vanderbilt University Library,
37203
Telephone: (615) 322-2927
Founded in: 1968
Questionnaire not received

NORRIS

**Lenoir Museum—Norris Dam State
Park**
Hwy. 441
Telephone: (615) 494-9688/494-0488
Mail to: P.O. Box 53, 37828
State agency
Founded in: 1975
W. G. Lenoir, Curator
Staff: full time 2, part time 1
Period of collections: early
1800s-1930s

Museum of Appalachia
Hwy. 61
Telephone: (615) 494-7680
Mail to: P.O. Box 359, 37828
Private agency
Founded in: 1968
John Rice Irwin, Owner/Operator
Staff: full time 5, part time 4
Major programs: manuscripts,
museum, historic site(s),
tours/pilgrimages, book publishing,
newsletters/pamphlets, historic
preservation, research, exhibits,
living history, audiovisual programs
Period of collections: 1780-1800

OAK RIDGE

Children's Museum of Oak Ridge
461 W. Outer Dr.
Telephone: (615) 482-1074
Mail to: P.O. Box 3066, 37830
Private agency
Founded in: 1973
Selma Shapiro, Executive Director
Number of members: 1,100
Staff: full time 5, part time 5,
volunteer 27
Major programs: library, archives,
museum, junior history, oral history,
school programs, book publishing,
newsletters/pamphlets, historic
preservation, records
management, research, exhibits,
living history, audiovisual
programs, photographic
collections, field services
Period of collections: 1880-present

PINEY FLATS

**Rocky Mount Historical
Association**
Rt. 11-E
Telephone: (615) 538-7396
Mail to: Rt. 2, Box 70, 37686
Founded in: 1958
E. Alvin Gerhardt, Jr., Executive
Director
Number of members: 600
Staff: full time 6, part time 6,
volunteer 55
Major programs: museum, historic
sites preservation, educational
programs, newsletters/pamphlets
Period of collections: 1760-present

PINSON

**Pinson Mounds State
Archaeological Area**
Rt. 1, Box 316, 38366
Telephone: (901) 988-5614
State agency, authorized by
Department of Conservation
Founded in: 1980
Mary L. Kwas, Historical Area
Supervisor
Number of members: full time 6, part
time 5
Major programs: library, archives,
museum, historic site(s), school
programs, research, exhibits,
audiovisual programs, archaeology
programs
Period of collections: prehistoric-A.D.
500

PLEASANT HILL

**Pleasant Hill Historical Society of
the Cumberlands, Inc.**
Main St.
Telephone: (615) 277-3193
Mail to: P.O. Box 264, 38578
Founded in: 1976
Questionnaire not received

PULASKI

Giles County Historical Society
122 S. 3rd St.
Telephone: (615) 363-2720
Mail to: P.O. Box 693, 38478
County agency
Founded in: 1974
A. Frank Tate, President
Number of members: 900
Staff: volunteer 25
Major programs: library, archives,
manuscripts, museum, historic
site(s), markers, tours/pilgrimages,
book publishing,
newsletters/pamphlets, historic
preservation, exhibits, archaeology
programs, genealogical services
Period of collections: 1809-present

ROGERSVILLE

Hale Springs Hotel
110 W. Main St., 37857
Telephone: (615) 272-9967
Private agency
Founded in: 1824
Marlena W. Livesay, Vice President
Staff: full time 2
Major programs: historic sites
preservation, historic preservation

RUGBY

Historic Rugby, Inc.
Hwy. 52, P.O. Box 8, 37733
Telephone: (615) 628-2441
Private agency
Founded in: 1966
Barbara Stagg, Executive Director
Number of members: 700
Staff: full time 6, part time 2,
volunteer 1
Magazine: The Rugbeian
Major programs: library, archives,
manuscripts, museum, historic
site(s), tours/pilgrimages,
newsletters/pamphlets, historic
preservation, exhibits,

photographic collections
Period of collections: 1870-1900

Rugby Restoration Association
Hwy. 52
Telephone: (615) 628-2441
Mail to: P.O. Box 8, 37733
Founded in: 1966
Questionnaire not received

SAVANNAH

Hardin County Historical Society
P.O. Box 630, 38372
Telephone: (901) 925-3106
Private agency
Founded in: 1970
Henry E. Williams, Jr.,
Secretary/Treasurer
Number of members: 150
Staff: volunteer 4
Magazine: Hardin County Historical
Quarterly
Major programs: oral history, book
publishing, audiovisual programs,
archaeology programs,
photographic collections,
genealogical services, field
services
Period of collections: 1820-1945

SEWANEE

**University of the South Archives,
Jessie Ball duPont Library**
University of the South, 37375-4005
Telephone: (615) 598-1387
Private agency, authorized by the
university
Founded in: 1941
David Kearley, Librarian
Staff: full time 1, part time 1
Major programs: library, archives,
manuscripts
Period of collections: 1857-present

SHELBYVILLE

Bedford County Historical Society
37160
Gilley Stephens, President
Number of members: 225
Questionnaire not received

SHILOH

Shiloh National Military Park
38376
Founded in: 1894
Zeb V. McKinney, Superintendent
Staff: full time 13, part time 8,
volunteer 5
Major programs: museum, historic
site(s), markers, tours/pilgrimages,
school programs, historic
preservation, living history,
audiovisual programs, archaeology
programs
Period of collections: Civil War

SMITHVILLE

**Caney Fork River Historical
Association, Inc.**
Luttrell Ave.
Telephone: (615) 597-4646
Mail to: P.O. Box 153, 37166
Private agency
Founded in: 1984
J. G. Driver, President

Number of members: 10
Staff: volunteer 1
Major programs: historic site(s), markers, oral history, historic preservation, research, exhibits, photographic collections
Period of collections: 1800-1950

SMYRNA

Sam Davis Memorial Association
Sam Davis Rd., 37167
Telephone: (615) 459-2341
State agency, authorized by Sam Davis Memorial Association
Founded in: 1931
Mrs. Richard E. McClary, Sr., Regent
Number of members: 500
Staff: full time 2, part time 2, volunteer 20
Major programs: museum, historic site(s), markers, tours/pilgrimages, junior history, oral history, school programs, newsletters/pamphlets, historic preservation, living history
Period of collections: to 1860

SPARTA

White County Retired Teachers' Association
411 Gaines St., 38583
Telephone: (615) 836-3760
Private agency, authorized by state and national associations
Founded in: 1964
Anna Grace Bandy, Publications Chair
Major programs: library, manuscripts, tours/pilgrimages, oral history, school programs, book publishing, newsletters/pamphlets, historic preservation, research, living history, photographic collections, history of county schools, sponsorship of county history study and publication
Period of collections: 1815-present

SPENCER

Van Buren County Historical Society
P.O. Box 126, 38585
Telephone: (615) 946-2121
Private agency
Founded in: 1980
Landon Medley, President
Number of members: 125
Staff: volunteer 5
Magazine: *Van Buren County Historical Journal*
Major programs: library, manuscripts, book publishing, newsletters/pamphlets, research, photographic collections, genealogical services
Period of collections: 1840-present

SPRINGFIELD

Robertson County Historical Society
500 N. Pawnee Dr., 37172
Telephone: (615) 384-7353
Founded in: 1970
Questionnaire not received

UNION CITY

Obion County Historical Society
P.O. Box 1, 38261
Private agency
Founded in: 1957
M. H. Stubblefield, President
Number of members: 40
Major programs: library, museum, markers, oral history, book publishing

WAVERLY

Humphreys County Historical Society
Court Square
Telephone: (615) 296-3445
Mail to: 105 Carroll Ave., 37185
Founded in: 1970
Questionnaire not received

WAYNESBORO

Wayne County Historical Society
P.O. Box 451, 38485
County agency
Founded in: 1970
Charles D. Gallaher, President
Number of members: 50
Staff: volunteer 7
Major programs: historic site(s), markers, records management, research, genealogical services
Period of collections: 1817-present

WINCHESTER

Franklin County Historical Society
105 S. Porter
Telephone: (615) 967-3706
Mail to: P.O. Box 130, 37398
Founded in: 1969
Nelle Hudson, Local History Librarian
Number of members: 700
Staff: part time 1, volunteer 20
Magazine: *Franklin County Historical Review*
Major programs: library archives manuscripts museum, books genealogy, newsletters/pamphlets
Period of collections: 1800-present

Hundred Oaks Castle
100 Oaks Place, 37398
Telephone: (615) 967-0100
Private agency, authorized by Franklin County Adult Activity Center, Inc.
Founded in: 1979
George E. O'Connor, Executive Director
Staff: full time 10, volunteer 25
Major programs: library, archives, museum, historic site(s), markers, tours/pilgrimages, oral history, school programs, historic preservation, exhibits, living history

Old Jail Museum
400 1st Ave., NE, 37398
Telephone: (615) 967-0524
County agency, authorized by Franklin County Old Jail Museum Commission
Founded in: 1973
Mrs. John Fandrich, Sr., Treasurer
Staff: full time 1
Major programs: museum, historic site(s), junior history, school programs, exhibits, photographic collections, genealogical services

ABILENE

West Texas Historical Association
Hardin Simmons University, P.O. Box 152, 79698
Telephone: (915) 677-7281, ext. 278
Founded in: 1924
B.W. Aston, Secretary/Treasurer
Number of members: 300
Staff: part time 2, volunteer 3
Magazine: *West Texas Historical Association Year Book*
Period of collections: 1865-present

ALBANY

Old Jail Art Center
Hwy. 6, S
Telephone: (915) 762-2269
Mail to: Rt. 1, Box 1, 76430
Private agency
Founded in: 1977
W. Reilly Nail, Jr., Director
Number of members: 700
Staff: full time 2, part time 2, volunteer 70
Major programs: library, archives, museum, tours/pilgrimages, junior history, school programs, historic preservation, exhibits, photographic collections, performing arts
Period of collections: 1850-present

ALICE

South Texas Museum
66 S. Wright St.
Telephone: (512) 668-8891
Mail to: P.O. Box 3232, 78332
Private agency
Founded in: 1973
Teresa W. Baker, Curator
Number of members: 100
Staff: part time 1
Major programs: museum, historic site(s), oral history, photographic collections
Period of collections: early 1900s

ALPINE

Museum and Archives of the Big Bend
Sul Ross State University, P.O. Box C-210, 79832
Telephone: (915) 837-8143
State agency, authorized by the university
Founded in: 1968
Kenneth D. Perry, Director
Staff: full time 4, part time 5, volunteer 30
Major programs: library, archives, manuscripts, museum, junior history, oral history, school programs, newsletters/pamphlets, research, exhibits, photographic collections, genealogical services
Period of collections: 1850-1940

AMARILLO

Catholic Historical Society of the Diocese of Amarillo
1800 N. Spring, 79107
Telephone: (806) 383-2243

Private agency
Founded in: 1974
Nellie Rooney, President
Number of members: 45
Staff: volunteer 5
Major programs: library, archives, manuscripts, oral history, newsletters/pamphlets, living history
Period of collections: 1875-present

ANDERSON

Historic Anderson, Inc.
229 Main St.
Telephone: (409) 873-2943
Mail to: P.O. Box 1836, 77830
Town agency
Founded in: 1973
Trinston Harris, President
Number of members: 93
Staff: volunteer 11
Major programs: historic site(s), tours/pilgrimages, historic preservation
Period of collections: early 1800s

ANGLETON

Brazoria County Historical Museum
100 E. Cedar St., 77515
Telephone: (409) 849-5711, ext. 1208
County agency, authorized by Texas Historical Commission
Founded in: 1983
Margaret A. Kelly, Director
Number of members: 350
Staff: full time 3
Major programs: library, museum, oral history, school programs, newsletters/pamphets, exhibits
Period of collections: 1845-present

ARCADIA

Santa Fe Area Historical Foundation, Inc.
P.O. Box 275, 77517
Telephone: (713) 925-3009
Private agency
Founded in: 1973
Charles C. Meek, President
Number of members: 105
Staff: volunteer 3
Major programs: museum, historic sites preservation, educational programs
Period of collections: 1865-1918

ARCHER CITY

Archer County Historical Commission
Rt. 1, Windthurst, 76389
Telephone: (817) 423-6426
County agency, authorized by Archer County Court
Founded in: 1962
Jack Loftin, Chair
Staff: volunteer 20
Major programs: library, archives manuscripts, museum, historic site(s), markers, tours/pilgrimages, junior history, oral history, school programs, book publishing, newsletters/pamphlets, historic preservation, research, exhibits, living history, archaeology programs, photographic

collections, genealogical services, field services
Period of collections: 250,000,000 B.C.

ARLINGTON

Arlington Historical Society
P.O. Box 13025, 76013
Telephone: (817) 274-7601
Private agency, authorized by Texas Historical Commission
Founded in: 1976
Dorothy Rencurrel, Director
Number of members: 200
Staff: volunteer 50
Major programs: historic site(s), tours/pilgrimages, oral history, school programs
Period of collections: 1854-present

Fielder Museum
1616 W. Abrams St., 76013
Telephone: (817) 460-4001
Private agency, authorized by Fielder House Foundation, Inc.
Founded in: 1978
Jerrie L. Crabb, Director
Number of members: 600
Staff: full time 1, part time 2, volunteer 45
Major programs: museum, historic site(s), school programs, newsletters/pamphlets, historic preservation, exhibits, photographic collections
Period of collections: 1890-1930

Society of Southwest Archivists
3501 Quail Lane, 76016
Telephone: (817) 429-2674
Questionnaire not received

AUSTIN

Archives and Records Division, Texas General Land Office
1700 N. Congress, 78701
Telephone: (512) 475-6501
State agency
Founded in: 1837
Michael Q. Hooks, Director/Archivist
Number of members: 1
Staff: full time 23, part time 8
Major programs: archives, records management, genealogical services
Period of collections: 19th century

Archives of the Episcopal Church
606 Rathervue Place, 78705
Telephone: (512) 472-6816
Mail to: P.O. Box 2247, 78768
Authorized by General Convention of the Episcopal Church
Founded in: 1910
V. Nelle Bellamy, Archivist
Staff: full time 4
Major programs: library, archives, manuscripts, records management
Period of collections: 1783-present

Austin History Center, City of Austin Library Department
810 Guadalupe St., 78701
Telephone: (512) 472-5433
Mail to: P.O. Box 2287, 78768
Founded in: 1955
Audray Bateman, Curator
Staff: full time 5, part time 9, volunteer 50

Major programs: library, archives, manuscripts, oral history, book publishing, newsletters/pamphlets, research, exhibits, audiovisual programs, photographic collections
Period of collections: 1839-present

Catholic Archives of Texas
16th and Congress
Telephone: (512) 476-4888
Mail to: Capitol Station, P.O. Box 13327, 78711
Private agency, authorized by Catholic Bishops of Texas
Founded in: 1923
Dolores Kasner, Archivist
Staff: part time 1
Major programs: archives, genealogical services
Period of collections: 1690-present

Daughters of the Republic of Texas
112 E. 11th, 78701
Telephone: (512) 477-1822
Founded in: 1891
Questionnaire not received

Elisabet Ney Museum
304 E. 44th St., 78751
Telephone: (512) 458-2255
City agency, authorized by Parks and Recreation Department
Founded in: 1907
James D. Fisher, Supervisor
Number of members: 200
Staff: full time 6, part time 3, volunteer 20
Major programs: museum, historic site(s)
Period of collections: 1850-1910

Eugene C. Barker Texas History Center, University of Texas at Austin
Sid Richardson Hall, 78713
Telephone: (512) 471-1741
State agency, authorized by the university
Founded in: 1945
Don E. Carleton, Director
Staff: full time 16, part time 19, volunteer 1
Major programs: library, archives, manuscripts, exhibits, photographic collections, genealogical services
Period of collections: 1717-present

French Legation Museum
802 San Marcos, 78702
Telephone: (512) 472-8180
Founded in: 1956
John J. Cleary, Director
Staff: full time 2, part time 2
Major programs: museum, historic site(s), historic preservation
Period of collections: 1836-1845

Friends of the Governor's Mansion
305 W. 9th St.
Telephone: (512) 474-9960
Mail to: P.O. Box 13022, 76711
Private agency
Founded in: 1979
Dorothy Anne Alcorn, Administrator/Curator
Staff: full time 1, volunteer 140
Major programs: museum, book publishing, newsletters/pamphlets,

historic preservation, research,
audiovisual programs
Period of collections: early-mid 19th
century

Heritage Society of Austin, Inc.
Driskill Hotel 78701
Telephone: (512) 474-5198
Mail to: Box 2113, 78768
Founded in: 1953
Elaine U. Mayo, Executive Secretary
Number of members: 2,200
Staff: full time 1
Major programs: tours/pilgrimages,
educational programs, books,
newsletters/pamphlets, historic
preservation
Period of collections: 1840-1930

**Interpretation and Exhibits Branch,
Texas Parks and Wildlife
Department**
4200 Smith School Rd., 78744
Telephone: (512) 479-4880
Founded in: 1962
Wilson E. Dolman, Director of
Programs
Staff: full time 16
Magazine: *Texas Parks and Wildlife*
Major programs: museum, historic
site(s), historic preservation
Period of collections: 1840-1900

**Jollyville-Pond Springs Historical
Association**
7203 S. Ute Terrace, 78729
Telephone: (512) 258-5688
Private agency
Founded in: 1977
Karen R. Thompson, President
Number of members: 40
Major programs: markers, cemetery
transcriptions
Period of collections: 1880s-date

Jourdan Bachman Pioneer Farm
11418 Sprinkle Cut-Off, 78754
Telephone: (314) 837-1215
City agency, authorized by Parks and
Recreation Department
Founded in: 1975
John Hirsch, Director
Number of members: full time 6, part
time 5, volunteer 30
Major programs: historic site(s),
school programs,
newsletters/pamphlets, historic
preservation, exhibits, living history
Period of collections: 1880s

Lyndon Baines Johnson Library
2313 Red River, 78703
Telephone: (512) 397-5137
Founded in: 1971
Questionnaire not received

Neill Cochran Museum House
2310 San Gabriel, 78705
Telephone: (512) 478-2335
Private agency, authorized by
National Society, Colonial Dames of
America
Founded in: 1960
James H. Lupton, Jr., Conservator
Staff: full time 2, part time 2
Major programs: museum, historic
site(s), tours/pilgrimages, historic
preservation
Period of collections: 1850-1900

O. Henry Museum
409 E. 5th St., 78701
Telephone: (512) 472-1903
City agency, authorized by Parks and
Recreation Department
Founded in: 1934
M. Martha George, Curator
Staff: full time 1, part time 2
Major programs: museum, school
programs
Period of collections: 1890s

Texas Association of Museums
1108 W. Ave.
Telephone: (512) 472-0641
Mail to: P.O. Box 13353, 78711
Private agency
Amanda Stover, Executive Director
Number of members: 650
Staff: full time 2, part time 1,
volunteer 150
Magazine: *Texas Association of
Museums' Quarterly*
Major programs: book publishing,
newsletters/pamphlets, field
services, clearing house of
information and advocacy

**Texas Barbed Wire Collectors
Association**
c/o 3845 Honeysuckle, San Angelo,
76904
Telephone: (915) 949-9614
Private agency
Founded in: 1966
Number of members: 181
Magazine: *The Barbed Wire Collector*
Major programs: historic site(s),
markers, newsletters/pamphlets,
historic preservation, research
Period of collections: 1853-1900

**Texas Catholic Historical
Society, Inc.**
16th Congress
Telephone: (512) 476-4888
Mail to: Capital Station, P.O. Box
13327, 78711
Private agency, authorized by
Catholic Bishops of Texas
Founded in: 1947
Sister M. Dolores Kasner, Director
Number of members: 370
Staff: full time 1, volunteer 3
Major programs: archives,
manuscripts,
newsletters/pamphlets
Period of collections: 1690-present

◊**Texas Historical Commission**
15l1 Colorado, 78701
Telephone: (512) 475-3092
Mail to: Capitol Station, P.O. Box
12276, 78701
State agency
Founded in: 1953
Curtis Tunnell, Executive Director
Staff: full time 45, part time 2
Magazine: *Medallion*
Major programs: archives, museum,
historic site(s), markers, oral
history, book publishing,
newsletters/pamphlets, historic
preservation, records
management, research, exhibits,
audiovisual programs, archaeology
programs, photographic
collections, field services,
underwater archeology

Period of collections:
prehistoric-present

Texas Historical Foundation
305 W. 9th St.
Mail to: Capitol Station, P.O. Box
12243, 78711
Private agency
Founded in: 1954
Leon M. Lurie, Executive Director
Number of members: 6,500
Staff: full time 3, part time 1
Major programs: library, archives,
historic site(s), tours/pilgrimages,
school programs, book publishing,
newsletters/pamphlets, historic
preservation, exhibits, archaeology
programs, photographic
collections, field services
Period of collections: 1850-present

**Interpretation and Exhibits Branch,
Texas Parks and Wildlife
Department**
4200 Smith School Rd., 78744
Telephone: (512) 475-4941
Founded in: 1962
Questionnaire not received

◊**Texas Library and Historical
Commission**
Telephone: (512) 471-1525
Mail to: SRH 2-306, University Station,
78712
Founded in: 1897
Questionnaire not received

**Texas State Library and Archives
Commission**
1201 Brazos, 78701
Telephone: (512) 475-2166
Mail to: Capitol Station, Box 12927,
78711
State agency
Founded in: 1909
Dorman H. Winfrey, Director/Librarian
Staff: full time 22, part time 190
Magazine: *Texas Libraries*
Major programs: library, archives,
manuscripts, records
management, genealogical
services
Period of collections: 1783-present

BANDERA

**Bandera County Historical
Commission**
Off Hwy. 16, E
Telephone: (592) 796-4420
Mail to: P.O. Box 578, 78003
County agency, authorized by Texas
Historical Commission
Founded in: 1966
Peggy Tobin, Chair
Number of members: 40
Magazine: *Bandera County Historian*
Major programs: library, archives,
markers, newsletters/pamphlets,
historic preservation, research
Period of collections: 1856-present

Frontier Times Museum
506 13th St.
Telephone: (512) 796-3864
Mail to: P.O. Box 563, 78003
Town agency
Founded in: 1933
Mrs. John V. Saul, Assistant
Curator/Board Vice President

Staff: full time 1, part time 1,
volunteer 1
Major programs: museum, historic
preservation, exhibits
Period of collections: 1850-1950

BAY CITY

**Matagorda County Historical
Museum**
1824 6th St.
Telephone: (409) 245-7502
Mail to: P.O. Box 851, 77414
Founded in: 1963
A. B. Pierce, Jr., Board President
Number of members: 30
Staff: volunteer 7
Major programs: genealogical
services

BAYTOWN

Bay Area Heritage Society
3530 Market St.
Telephone: (713) 427-8768
Mail to: P.O. Box 4161, 77520
W. C. Smith III, President

Baytown Historical Museum
3530 Market St.
Telephone: (713) 427-8768
Mail to: P.O. Box 4161, 77520
City agency
Founded in: 1974
Jean Shepherd, Director
Number of members: 250
Staff: full time 1, part time 1,
volunteer 20
Major programs: archives,
manuscripts, museum, historic
site(s), markers, tours/pilgrimages,
junior history, oral history, school
programs, book publishing,
newsletters/pamphlets, historic
preservation, research, exhibits,
living history, archaeology
programs, photographic
collections
Period of collections: 1800s-present

BEAUMONT

Beaumont Heritage Society
2985 French Rd., 77706
Telephone: (409) 898-0348
Founded in: 1967
Lin Owen, Executive Director
Number of members: 1,400
Staff: full time 2, part time 8,
volunteer 300
Magazine: *Trading Post Times*
Major programs: museum, historic
site(s), markers, tours/pilgrimages,
junior history, oral history, school
programs, book publishing,
newsletters/pamphlets, historic
preservation, research, exhibits,
living history
Period of collections: 1840-1860

McFaddin-Ward House
1906 McFaddin Ave., 77701
Telephone: (409) 832-1906
Private agency, authorized by
McFaddin-Ward House, Inc.
Founded in: 1982
Dennis K. McDaniel, Director
Number of members: full time 13, part
time 3, volunteer 1

Major programs: manuscripts,
historic site(s), historic
preservation, research
Period of collections: 1890-1940

**Southeast Texas Genealogical and
Historical Society**
c/o Tyrrell Historical Library, 895
Pearl St.
Mail to: P.O. Box 3827, 77704
Private agency
Founded in: 1970
Mrs. J. W. Montana, President
Number of members: 300
Magazine: *Yellowed Pages*
Major programs: library, research

Spindletop Museum
Telephone: (409) 880-8896
Mail to: P.O. Box 10082, Lamar
University, 77710
State agency, authorized by the
university
Founded in: 1970
David L. Hartman, Operations
Director
Staff: full time 2, part time 5,
volunteer 35
Major programs: museum,
tours/pilgrimages, oral history,
exhibits
Period of collections: 1901-1906

Texas Gulf Historical Society
Goodhue Bldg.
Telephone: (409) 833-5684
Mail to: P.O. Box 1621, 77704
Private agency
Founded in: 1964
Gilbert T. Adams, Jr., President
Number of members: 20
Staff: volunteer 21
Magazine: *The Texas Gulf Historical
and Biographical Record*
Major programs: library, archives,
manuscripts, oral history, book
publishing

BIG FOOT

Bigfoot Wallace Museum
78005
Town agency
Founded in: 1957
W. W. Harvey, Vice President
Staff: volunteer 3
Period of collections: 1800

BIG LAKE

Hickman Library and Museum
609 Main St.
Telephone: (915) 884-2793
Mail to: P.O. Box 66, 76932
Private agency
Founded in: 1984
Doris Way, President
Number of members: 56
Staff: volunteer 10
Major programs: library, museum,
historic site(s), historic
preservation
Period of collections: 1900-present

BONHAM

Fannin County Historical Museum
Courthouse, 3rd Floor
Telephone: (214) 583-8042
Mail to: P.O. Drawer 338, 75418

County agency, authorized by Fannin
County Commissioner's Court
Founded in: 1965
Sam Morgan, Chair
Staff: part time 2
Major programs: library, archives,
museum, historic site(s), markers,
tours/pilgrimages, oral history,
book publishing, historic
preservation, exhibits,
photographic collections,
genealogical services
Period of collections: 19th-early 20th
centuries

Sam Rayburn House
Rt. 3, Box 308, 75418
Telephone: (214) 583-5558
State agency, authorized by Texas
Historical Commission
Founded in: 1975
Roger Durham, Director
Staff: full time 4, part time 3,
volunteer 40
Major programs:
newsletters/pamphlets, field
services
Period of collections: 1916-1961

Sam Rayburn Library
800 W. Sam Rayburn Dr.
Telephone: (214) 583-2455
Mail to: P.O. Box 309, 75418
Private agency, authorized by Sam
Rayburn Foundation
Founded in: 1957
H. G. Dulaney, Director
Staff: full time 5, part time 2
Major programs: library, museum,
oral history, newsletters/pamphlets
Period of collections: 1913-1961

BORGER

**Hutchinson County Museum/Boom
Town Revisited**
618 N. Main
Telephone: (806) 273-6121
Mail to: P.O. Box 325, 79007
County agency, authorized by
Hutchinson County
Founded in: 1977
Lewis E. Benz, Museum Director
Staff: full time 1, part time 3,
volunteer 30
Magazine: *Boom Town Revisited*
Major programs: museum, book
publishing, exhibits, living history
Period of collections: 1920s

BRECKENRIDGE

J. D. Sandefer Oil Annex
113 N. Breckenridge
Telephone: (817) 559-8471
Mail to: P.O. Box 350, 76024
Private agency, authorized by
Swenson Memorial Museum of
Stephens County
Founded in: 1983
Mrs. Russell B. Flournoy, Director
Staff: full time 1, part time 2,
volunteer 1
Major programs: museum, historic
preservation, research
Period of collections: 1916-1923

Swenson Memorial Museum of Stephens County
116-118 W. Walker
Telephone: (817) 559-8471
Mail to: P.O. Box 350, 76024
Founded in: 1976
Kathleen D. Upham, Director
Staff: full time 1, part time 4
Major programs: archives, museum
Period of collections: 1850-1945

BRENHAM

Texas Baptist Historical Center-Museum
Corner, FM-50 and FM-390
Telephone: (409) 836-5117
Mail to: Rt. 5, Box 222, 77833
Private agency, authorized by Baptist General Convention of Texas
Founded in: 1965
Jesse E. Bigbee, Director
Staff: full time 1, part time 1, volunteer 2
Major programs: museum, historic site(s), tours/pilgrimages, historic preservation, exhibits, audiovisual programs, photographic collections
Period of collections: 1836-1900

BROOKSHIRE

Waller County Historical Museum
4026 5th St.
Telephone: (713) 934-2826
Mail to: P.O. Box 235, 77423
County agency, authorized by County Commissioners' Court
Founded in: 1977
Minnie S. Bains, Administrator
Staff: part time 1, volunteer 1
Major programs: library, markers, junior history, book publishing, research, exhibits, photographic collections
Period of collections: 1900-present

Waller County Historical Society, Inc.
P.O. Box 336, 77423
Founded in: 1972
Oliver Kitzman, President
Number of members: 40
Staff: volunteer 5
Major programs: library, archives, manuscripts, museum, historic site(s), markers, tours/pilgrimages, junior history, oral history, school programs, book publishing, historic preservation, research, photographic collections

BROWNSVILLE

Brownsville Historical Association
1300 E. Washington
Telephone: (512) 542-3929
Mail to: P.O. Box 846, 78520
Private agency
Founded in: 1950
Robert B. Vezzetti, President
Number of members: 175
Staff: full time 1, volunteer 19
Major programs: archives, museum, historic site(s), markers, tours/pilgrimages, school programs, book publishing, newsletters/pamphlets, historic

preservation research, exhibits, photographic collections
Period of collections: 1850-1940

BROWNWOOD

Brown County Historical Society
Mail to: P.O. Box 146, 76804
Private agency
Founded in: 1978
Number of members: 150
Staff: volunteer 11
Major programs: museum, markers, book publishing, exhibits
Period of collections: 1856-present

BRYAN (COLLEGE STATION)

Brazos Valley Museum
111 University Dr., 77843
Private agency, authorized by Arts Council of Brazos Valley
Founded in: 1970
Bonnie Yarbrough, Executive Director, Arts Council
Number of members: 300
Staff: full time 1, part time 2, volunteer 50
Magazine: Community Arts Calendar
Major programs: school programs, newsletters/pamphlets, records management, exhibits

Lawrence Sullivan Ross, United Daughters of Confederacy
103 Fairview, College Station, 77840
Telephone: (409) 696-4557
Founded in: 1897
Mrs. David W. Fleming, President
Number of members: 62
Staff: volunteer 14
Major programs: library, archives, manuscripts, historic site(s), markers, book publishing, historic preservation, research, genealogical services

BURKEVILLE

Newton County Historical Commission
P.O. Box 56, 75932
Telephone: (409) 565-4215
County agency
Founded in: 1960
Pauline Hines, Chair
Staff: volunteer 25
Major programs: library, manuscripts, historic site(s), markers, tours/pilgrimages, junior history, oral history, school programs, book publishing, newsletters/pamphlets, historic preservation, research, exhibits, audiovisual programs, photographic collections
Period of collections: 1846-present

BURNET

Burnet County Historical Society Survey Commission
Mail to: P.O. Box 74, 78611
Questionnaire not received

Ft. Croghan Museum/Burnet County Heritage Society
Telephone: (512) 756-8281
Mail to: P.O. Box 74, 78611
County agency, authorized by Burnet County Historical Commission

Founded in: 1957
Staff: part time 2, volunteer 6
Major programs: manuscripts, museum, historic site(s), markers, school programs, newsletters/pamphlets
Period of collections: 1850s-1900

CAMERON

Milam County Historical Museum
Main and Fannin
Telephone: (817) 697-9223
Mail to: P.O. Box 966, 76520
Founded in: 1977
Questionnaire not received

CANYON

Panhandle Plains Historical Society and Museum
2401 4th Ave.
Telephone: (806) 655-7191
Mail to: P.O. Box 967, W. T. Station, 79016
State agency
Founded in: 1923
B. Byron Price, Jr., Executive Director
Number of members: 950
Staff: full time 20, part time 30, volunteer 50
Magazine: Panhandle Plains Historical Review
Major programs: library, archives, manuscripts, museum, oral history, educational programs
Period of collections: prehistoric-present

Texas Panhandle Heritage Foundation, Inc.
2010 4th Ave.
Telephone: (806) 655-2181
Mail to: P.O. Box 268, 79015
Private agency
Founded in: 1961
Raymond Raillard, Executive Vice President
Number of members: 985
Staff: full time 3, part time 3, volunteer 140
Major programs: performing arts, presentation of historical musical drama
Period of collections: 1880-1900

CHAPPELL HILL

Chappell Hill Historical Society
Telephone: (713) 836-5981
Founded in: 1964
Questionnaire not received

CHILDRESS

Childress County Heritage Museum
210 3rd St., NW, 79201
Telephone: (817) 937-2261
Private agency
Founded in: 1976
A. V. McFarland, Director
Number of members: 300
Staff: full time 1, part time 1, volunteer 25
Major programs: museum, school programs, exhibits, archaeology programs, photographic collections
Period of collections: 1887-present

CLEBURNE

Layland Museum
201 N. Caddo St., 76031
Telephone: (817) 641-3321, ext. 375
City agency
Founded in: 1962
Mildred Padon, Curator
Staff: full time 1, part time 2,
volunteer 10
Major programs: library, archives,
museum, markers,
tours/pilgrimages, junior history,
oral history, school programs, book
publishing, newsletters/pamphlets,
historic preservation, research,
exhibits, audiovisual programs,
archaeology programs,
photographic collections,
genealogical services
Period of collections: prehistoric-Civil
War

CLIFTON

Bosque Memorial Museum
S. Ave. Q, 76634
Telephone: (817) 675-8733
Private agency
Founded in: 1925
Mary C. Orbeck, President
Number of members: 200
Staff: part time 2, volunteer 22
Major programs: library, museum,
historic site(s), markers,
newsletters/pamphlets, historic
preservation, exhibits,
photographic collections,
genealogical services
Period of collections: 1854-1945

COLDSPRING

**San Jacinto County Historical
Commission and Heritage
Society**
P.O. Box 505, 77331
Telephone: (409) 653-2009
County agency
Founded in: 1967 (commission); 1984
(society)
Hilde Faulkner, Historical
Commission
Number of members: 400
Staff: volunteer 20
Major programs: museum, historic
site(s), markers, tours, junior
history, oral history, school
programs, book publishing,
exhibits
Period of collections: 1840-present

COLORADO CITY

Colorado City Historical Museum
183 W. 3rd. St., 79512
Telephone: (915) 728-8285
City agency
Founded in: 1960
Ruby Cawthron, Director
Major programs: museum, tours,
historic preservation, genealogical
services
Period of collections: 1890-present

COLUMBUS

**Fabulous Koliba Home Museum,
Columbus First Home Museum
and Complex**
1124 Front St., 78934

Telephone: (409) 732-2913
Private agency
Major programs: museum

Magnolia Homes Tour Inc.
435 Spring St.
Telephone: (713) 732-5881
Mail to: P.O. Box 817, 78934
Founded in: 1961
Questionnaire not received

COMANCHE

**Comanche County Historical and
Museum**
100 Moorman Dr.
Mail to: P.O. Box 22, 76442
County agency
Founded in: 1964
Ben Evridge, President
Number of members: 100
Staff: volunteer 12
Major programs: museum
Period of collections: from 1856

COMFORT

Comfort Historical Society
8th and High Sts.
Telephone: (512) 995-3807
Mail to: P.O. Box 244, 78013
Private agency
Founded in: 1933
Roy Perkins, Director
Number of members: 27
Staff: volunteer 6
Major programs: museum, historic
preservation, exhibits
Period of collections: 1854-present

COMSTOCK

**Seminole Canyon State Historical
Park**
P.O. Box 806, 78837
Telephone: (915) 292-4464
State agency, authorized by Texas
Parks and Wildlife Department
Founded in: 1980
Emmitt Brotherton III, Park
Superintendent
Staff: full time 4, part time 3
Major programs: historic site(s),
tours/pilgrimages, historic
preservation, exhibits
Period of collections: 6000 B.C.-A.D.
600

CONROE

**Montgomery County Genealogical
Society, Inc.**
Telephone: (713) 756-8625
Mail to: P.O. Box 751, 77301
Founded in: 1976
Questionnaire not received

CORPUS CHRISTI

Coastal Bend Genealogical Society
P.O. Box 606, 78362
Telephone: (512) 776-7376
Questionnaire not received

Corpus Christi Museum
1900 N. Chaparral, 78401
Telephone: (512) 853-2862
City agency
Founded in: 1957
Staff: full time 17, part time 5,
volunteer 40
Magazine: *Museum Notes*

Major programs: museum, oral
history, educational programs,
newsletters/pamphlets
Period of collections:
prehistoric-present

**Local History Collection, Corpus
Christi Public Libraries**
505 N. Mesquite, 78401
Telephone: (512) 882-1937
Questionnaire not received

Museum of Oriental Cultures
426 S. Staples, 78401
Telephone: (512) 883-1303
Private agency
Founded in: 1973
Richard L. Bowers, Board Chair
Number of members: 200
Staff: part time 5, volunteer 2
Major programs: library, archives,
manuscripts, museum,
tours/pilgrimages, school
programs, newsletters/pamphlets,
exhibits
Period of collections: mid 19th
century-present

CORSICANA

**Navarro County Genealogical
Society**
Mail to: P.O. Box 821, 75110
Founded in: 1978
Ailsa Flynn Anderson, President
Number of members: 180
Staff: volunteer 6
Magazine: *Leaves and Branches*
Major programs: library, educational
programs, books
Period of collections: 1836-present

CROCKETT

**Historical Projects of Houston
County, Texas, Inc.**
629 N. 4th St., 75835
Telephone: (409) 544-3269
Private agency
Founded in: 1975
Eliza H. Bishop, Board President
Number of members: 40
Staff: volunteer 10
Major programs: museum,
tours/pilgrimages, exhibits,
photographic collections
Period of collections: 1880-1940

**Houston County Historical
Commission**
3rd Floor, Houston County
Courthouse
Telephone: (409) 544-5304
Mail to: 629 N. 4th, 75835
County agency, authorized by Texas
Historical Commission
Founded in: 1961
Eliza H. Bishop, Chair
Number of members: 60
Staff: volunteer 3
Magazine: *The Discovery*
Major programs: archives, museum,
historic site(s), markers,
tours/pilgrimages, junior history,
oral history, school programs, book
publishing, newsletters/pamphlets,
historic preservation, research,
exhibits, living history, audiovisual
programs, photographic
collections, genealogical services
Period of collections: 1900-1960

Houston County Museum
303 S. 1st St.
Telephone: (409) 544-5304/544-3269
Mail to: 629 N. 4th St., 75835
County agency, authorized by
Historical Projects of Houston
County, Texas, Inc.
Founded in: 1984
Eliza H. Bishop, Executive
Director/Agent
Number of members: 15
Staff: volunteer 10
Major programs: museum, historic
site(s), tours/pilgrimages, junior
history, oral history, school
programs, research, exhibits, living
history, photographic collections
Period of collections: 1830-present

**Houston County Sesquicentennial
Committee**
629 N. 4th Crockett, 75835
Telephone: (409) 544-3269
County agency
Founded in: 1982
Eliza H. Bishop, Coordinator
Number of members: 275
Staff: volunteer 3
Magazine: *Texas Dispatch*
Major programs: museum, historic
site(s), markers, tours/pilgrimages,
junior history, oral history, school
programs, book publishing,
newsletters/pamphlets, historic
preservation, research, exhibits,
audiovisual programs, archaeology
programs, photographic
collections, genealogical services
Period of collections: 1890-1960

CROSBYTON

**Crosby County Pioneer Memorial
Museum**
101 Main
Telephone: (806) 675-2331
Mail to: P.O. Box 386, 79322
City agency
Founded in: 1957
Verna Anne Wheeler, Executive
Director
Number of members: 24,605
Staff: full time 3, part time 3,
volunteer 15
Major programs: archives, museum,
tours/pilgrimages, school
programs, book publishing,
newsletters/pamphlets, exhibits,
photographic collections
Period of collections: 1870-1930

**West Texas Pioneers and Old
Settlers**
101 Main, 79322
Telephone: (806) 675-2331
Private agency, authorized by Crosby
County Pioneer Memorial
Founded in: 1926
Verna Anne Wheeler,
Secretary/Treasurer
Number of members: 100
Staff: volunteer 25
Major programs: living history, field
services
Period of collections: 1926-present

CROWELL

**Foard County Museum/McAdams
Ranch**
P.O. Box 609, 79227
Telephone: (817) 655-3395
Private agency
Founded in: 1965
Period of collections: from 1930

CUERO

DeWitt County Historical Museum
312 E. Broadway
Telephone: (512) 275-6322
Mail to: P.O. Box 745, 77954
County agency
Founded in: 1958
Mrs. A. W. Schaffner, Curator
Number of members: 200
Staff: full time 6, part time 5,
volunteer 25
Major programs: archives, museum,
historic site(s), oral history,
exhibits, genealogical services
Period of collections: mid
1800s-present

DALHART

**Dallam-Hartley Counties XIT
Museum**
108 E. 5th St.
Telephone: (806) 249-5390
Mail to: P.O. Box 664, 79022
Private agency, authorized by
Dallam-Hartley Counties Historical
Association, Inc.
Founded in: 1975
Dessie M. Hanbury, President
Number of members: 326
Staff: volunteer 16
Major programs: museum
tours/pilgrimages school
programs, historic preservation,
records management, exhibits,
audiovisual programs
Period of collections: 1900-1950

DALLAS

**African American Cultural Heritage
Center/Children's Cultural
Heritage Center and Museum**
3434 S. R.L. Thornton Fwy., 75224
Telephone: (214) 375-7530
City agency, authorized by Dallas
Independent School District
Founded in: 1978
Laura J. Lacy, Curator
Major programs: archives, museum,
junior history, oral history, school
programs, research, exhibits,
photographic collections
Period of collections: 1800-present

**Age of Steam Railroad Museum,
Southwest Railroad Historical
Society**
Fair Park
Telephone: (214) 361-6936
Mail to: 7226 Wentwood Dr., 25225
Private agency
Founded in: 1963
Roland B. Peterson, General
Manager
Number of members: 300
Staff: volunteer 20
Major programs: museum, markers,
tours/pilgrimages, school

programs, newsletters/pamphlets,
historic preservation, research,
exhibits
Period of collections: late 19th
century-present

**Dallas County Heritage
Society, Inc.**
Old City Park, 1717 Gano St., 75215
Telephone: (214) 421-5141
Founded in: 1966
Thomas H. Smith, Executive Director
Number of members: 1,800
Staff: full time 18, part time 3,
volunteer 610
Magazine: *Heritage News*
Major programs: library, museum,
tours/pilgrimages, school
programs, newsletters/pamphlets,
historic preservation, research,
exhibits, audiovisual programs
Period of collections: 1840-1910

**Dallas County Historical
Commission**
100 S. Houston St., Suite 116,
75202-3509
Telephone: (214) 749-6238
County agency
Sharion Moore, Administrative
Secretary
Staff: full time 1, volunteer 35
Magazine: *The County Chronicle*
Major programs: historic site(s),
markers, tours/pilgrimages, junior
history, oral history, school
programs, newsletters/pamphlets,
historic preservation, research,
exhibits, audiovisual programs
Period of collections: 1841-present

Dallas Genealogical Society
Mail to: Box 12648, 75225
Founded in: 1955
Number of members: 525
Magazine: *The Quarterly*
Major programs: library, educational
programs, books,
newsletters/pamphlets

Dallas Historical Society
Hall of State, Fair Park
Telephone: (214) 421-5136
Mail to: P.O. Box 20038, 75226
Private agency
Founded in: 1922
John W. Crain, Director
Number of members: 1,500
Staff: full time 15, part time 7,
volunteer 15
Major programs: library, archives,
manuscripts, museum, educational
programs, newsletters/pamphlets
Period of collections: 1770-present

Dallas Landmark Committee
Dallas City Hall, 75201
Telephone: (214) 670-4120
City agency
Founded in: 1973
Tom Niederauer, Manager
Number of members: 15
Staff: full time 4, part time 4,
volunteer 50
Major programs: historic site(s),
markers, historic preservation,
research, preservation incentives,
city planning
Period of collections: 1850-1950

Fikes Hall of Special Collections, DeGolyer Library
Southern Methodist University, 75275
Telephone: (214) 692-3231
Private agency, authorized by the university
Founded in: 1956
Clifton H. Jones, Director
Staff: full time 5, part time 2, volunteer 1
Major programs: library, archives, manuscripts, book publishing, newsletters/pamphlets, research, exhibits, photographic collections
Period of collections: 1490-present

Greater Metroplex Council for Genealogical Research
2515 Sweetbriar Dr., 75228
Telephone: (214) 327-7101
Founded in: 1980
Questionnaire not received

Historic Preservation League, Inc.
2013 Kidwell St.
Telephone: (214) 827-5800
Mail to: P.O. Box 140460, 75214
Questionnaire not received

International Museum of Cultures
7500 W. Camp Wisdom Rd., 75236
Telephone: (214) 298-9446
Private agency, authorized by Summer Institute of Linguistics
Founded in: 1978
Ted Engel, Director
Number of members: 60
Staff: full time 1, part time 5, volunteer 15
Magazine: *Ethnogram*
Major programs: museum book publishing newsletters/pamphlets, historic preservation, exhibits, ethnography

Mexican American Cultural Heritage Center
2940 Singleton Blvd., 75212
Telephone: (214) 630-1680
City agency authorized by Dallas Independent School District
Founded in: 1976
Dennis Zamora, Curator of Education
Staff: full time 2, volunteer 2
Major programs: library, school programs, newsletters/pamphlets, historic preservation research, exhibits, audiovisual programs, archaeology programs, field services
Period of collections: to 1836

Southwest Railroad Historical Society
13560 Flagstone Lane, 75240
Telephone: (214) 239-1676
Private agency
Founded in: 1961
J. Gilson Wildhagen, Board Chair
Number of members: 150
Staff: volunteer 25
Major programs: museum, historic site(s), markers, tours/pilgrimages, school programs, book publishing, newsletters/pamphlets, historic preservation, research, exhibits, living history, photographic collections
Period of collections: 1900-1940

Texas-Dallas History and Archives Division, Dallas Public Library
1515 Young St., 75201
Telephone: (214) 749-4150
City agency
Founded in: 1901
Wayne Gray, Division Manager
Number of members: 2
Staff: full time 12, part time 2, volunteer 5
Major programs: library, archives, oral history, book publishing, exhibits, photographic collections, genealogical services
Period of collections: 1850-1950

Vineyard Neighborhood Association
2800 Rt. 221, 75201
Telephone: (214) 651-0129
Founded in: 1975
Questionnaire not received

DECATUR

Old Stone Prison
103 E. Pecan
Telephone: (817) 627-3732
Mail to: P.O. Box 427, 76234
County agency, authorized by Wise County Historical Society, Inc.
Rosalie Gregg, Executive Director
Number of members: 300
Staff: volunteer 1
Major programs: markers, historic preservation
Perod of collections: 1859-1889

Wise County Historical Society, Inc.
1602 S. Trinity
Telephone: (817) 627-5586
Mail to: P.O. Box 427, 76234
Founded in: 1966
Questionnaire not received

DEER PARK

Deer Park Independent School District Historical Museum
204 Ivy, 77536
Telephone: (713) 479-2831
Authorized by Deer Park Independent School District
Founded in: 1980
Mrs. Frankie Stephens, Chair
Staff: volunteer 19
Major programs: museum, historic site(s), junior history, oral history, historic preservation, exhibits, living history, audiovisual programs, photographic collections, history of school district
Period of collections: 1931-present

DENISON

Denison Historical Society
530 W. Hanna St., 75020
Telephone: (214) 465-1075
Questionnaire not received

Eisenhower Birthplace State Historic Site
208 E. Day, 75020
Telephone: (214) 465-8908
State agency, authorized by Texas Parks and Wildlife Department
Staff: full time 2, part time 1

Major programs: museum, historic site(s)
Period of collections: 1890s

Grayson County Frontier Village, Inc.
Loy Park, 72273
Telephone: (214) 463-2487
Mail to: 4200 Ansley Lane, 75020
County agency
Founded in: 1965
Kathryn Summers, Executive Director
Number of members: 50
Staff: part time 2, volunteer 25
Major programs: markers, tours/pilgrimages, oral history, school programs, book publishing, newsletters/pamphlets, historic preservation, research, exhibits, audiovisual programs, photographic collections, field services
Period of collections: 1800s

DENTON

Courthouse-on-the-Square Museum
Courthouse-on-the-Square, 76201
Telephone: (817) 566-1487
County agency, authorized by Denton County Historical Commission
Founded in: 1978
Peggy Hoffer, Director
Staff: part time 4
Major programs: library, archives, manuscripts, museum, historic site(s), markers, tours/pilgrimages, oral history, school programs, historic preservation, records management, research, exhibits, photographic collections, genealogical services
Period of collections: Victorian era

Historical Collection, North Texas State University
P.O. Box 13377 76203
Telephone: (817) 565-2386
State agency: authorized by the university
Founded in: 1930
Kathy A. Cyr, Director
Staff: full time 1, part time 4, volunteer 5
Major programs: archives, manuscripts, museum, historic site(s), school programs, research, exhibits, photographic collections
Period of collections: 1850-1930

New Mexico Studies Association
NTSU Station, P.O. Box 8021, 76203
Telephone: (817) 565-3399
Private agency
Founded in: 1975
G. L. Seligmanr, Jr., Executive Secretary
Major programs: manuscripts, junior history, oral history, research, essays
Period of collections: 1821-present

DENVER CITY

Denver City Museum
Drawer K, 79323
Telephone: (806) 592-3096
City agency
Mrs. Hazel M. Akin

DONNA

Donna Hooks Fletcher Historical Museum
331 S. Main St.
Telephone: (512) 464-3285
Mail to: P.O. Box 411, 78537
Private agency
Founded in: 1981
Larry McLain, Curator
Number of members: 35
Staff: volunteer 10
Major programs: museum, school programs, historic preservation, photographic collections
Period of collections: 1900-1930

DUMAS

Moore County Historical Museum
Dumas Ave. and W. 8th St.
Telephone: (806) 935-3113
Mail to: P.O. Box 851, 79029
Private agency
Founded in: 1976
Bert Clifton, Assistant Director
Number of members: 75
Staff: volunteer 60
Major programs: archives, museum, book publishing, exhibits, photographic collections, genealogical services
Period of collections: 1892-present

DUNCANVILLE

Duncanville Historical Commission, Inc.
100 E. Center
Telephone: (214) 296-1401
Mail to: P.O. Box 280, 75116
Founded in: 1973
Questionnaire not received

EDINBURG

Hidalgo County Historical Museum
121 E. McIntyre
Telephone: (512) 383-6911
Mail to: P.O. Box 482, 78540
Private agency
Founded in: 1967
Fran Alger, Director
Number of members: 300
Staff: full time 5, part time 3, volunteer 40
Major programs: library, archives, museum, exhibits
Period of collections: 1500-present

Hidalgo County Historical Society
Mail to: P.O. Box 81, 78540-0081
County agency
Founded in: 1967
Number of members: 175
Staff: volunteer 12

Special Collections, Pan American University Library
78539
Telephone: (512) 381-2799
State agency, authorized by the university
Founded in: 1978
George R. Gause, Jr., Special Collections Librarian
Staff: full time 1, part time 8
Major programs: library, archives, manuscripts, oral history, records management, photographic

collections, archival preservation, microfilming, county records depository
Period of collections: from 1900

EDNA

Texana Heritage Society
510 Apollo Dr.
Telephone: (512) 782-3400
Mail to: P.O. Box 746, 77957
Private agency
Founded in: 1978
Mrs. Thomas Mozisek, President
Number of members: 385
Staff: volunteer 16
Major programs: tours/pilgrimages, historic preservation, living history
Period of collections: 1859-1884

EL DORADO

Schleicher County Museum
Telephone: (915) 853-2709
Mail to: P.O. Box 473, 76936
Private agency
Founded in: 1976
Margaret B. Frost, Director
Number of members: 50
Staff: volunteer 3
Major programs: museum, historic preservation

EL PASO

El Paso Centennial Museum
University of Texas at El Paso, 79968
Telephone: (915) 747-5565
State agency
Founded in: 1936
James M. Day, Director
Staff: full time 2, part time 5, volunteer 15
Major programs: museum, school programs, exhibits, archaeology programs
Period of collections: 1680-1920

El Paso County Historical Commission
P.O. Box 2040, 79976
Telephone: (915) 544-6300, ext. 206
County agency
Founded in: 1970
Ann M. Enriquez, Chair
Number of members: 35
Staff: volunteer 45
Magazine: *El Paso Historical Alliance*
Major programs: historic site(s), markers, junior history, oral history, school programs, newsletters/pamphlets, historic preservation

El Paso County Historical Society
2331 Wyoming St.
Telephone: (915) 540-3090
Mail to: P.O. Box 28, 79940
Founded in: 1954
George Ross O. Borrett, President
Number of members: 815
Magazine: *The Password*
Major programs: archives, manuscripts, tours/pilgrimages, oral history, newsletters/pamphlets
Period of collections: 1681-present

El Paso Jewish Historical Society
Temple Mt. Sinai, 4408 N. Stanton, 79902
Telephone: (915) 532-5959

Authorized by El Paso Jewish Federation
Founded in: 1982
Floyd S. Fierman Director
Number of members: 200
Magazine: *El Paso Jewish Historical Review*
Period of collections: 1982-present

Ft. Bliss Replica Museum
Ft. Bliss, 79916
Telephone: (915) 568-2804
Founded in: 1955
Questionnaire not received

Historical Archives and Museum, Catholic Diocese of El Paso
124 Festival Dr., 79912
Telephone: (915) 581-6621
Private agency
Founded in: 1982
Okla M. McKee, Historical Archivist
Staff: full time 2, part time 1, volunteer 1
Major programs: library, archives, museum, historic site(s), markers, historic preservation, research, photographic collections
Period of collections: 1680-1914

Mission Trail—Los Pueblos Association
453 W. Burt, 79927
Telephone: (915) 859-6956
Private agency
Founded in: 1979
Dale Jones, President
Number of members: 25
Staff: volunteer 25
Major programs: historic site(s), school programs, historic preservation

U.S. Army Air Defense Artillery Association
P.O. Box 6101, Ft. Bliss, 79906
Telephone: (915) 568-5412
Founded in: 1979
Questionnaire not received

ENNIS

Ennis Heritage Society
Mail to: P.O. Box 189, 75119
Founded in: 1981
Questionnaire not received

FAIRFIELD

Freestone County Historical Museum
302 E. Main St.
Telephone: (214) 389-3738
Mail to: P.O. Box 524, 75840
County agency
Founded in: 1967
Sylvia B. Childs, Curator
Number of members: 100
Staff: full time 1
Major programs: museum, markers, tours/pilgrimages, historic preservation, research, exhibits, genealogical services
Period of collections: 1845-1850

FARMERS BRANCH

Farmers Branch Historical Park
Ford Rd. and Farmers Branch Lane
Telephone: (214) 247-3131
Mail to: P.O. Box 340435, 75234

City agency
John Burke, Director
Number of members: full time 1
Major programs: museum, historic
  site(s), markers, historic
  preservation, research
Period of collections: 1820s-1940s

FLOYDADA

Floyd County Historical Museum
105 E. Missouri St.
Telephone: (806) 983-2415
Mail to: P.O. Box 304, 79235
County agency
Founded in: 1971
Nancy Marble, President
Number of members: 150
Staff: part time 2, volunteer 4
Major programs: museum
Period of collections: early 1900s

FORT BLISS

Ft. Bliss Replica Museum
ATZC-DPT-PR, 79916
Telephone: (915) 568-4518
Federal agency, authorized by the
  U.S. Army
Founded in: 1954
Sam P. Hoyle, Director
Staff: full time 2
Major programs: archives, museum,
  school programs, research,
  exhibits, living history, audiovisual
  programs
Period of collections: 1846-present

**Museum of the Noncommissioned
  Officer**
ATSS-S-M, USASMA, Ft. Bliss, 79936
Telephone: (915) 568-8646
Federal agency, authorized by the
  U.S. Army
Founded in: 1979
Lawrence R. Arms, Director
Number of members: full time 3
Major programs: museum, oral
  history, exhibits
Period of collections: 1776-present

3rd Armored Cavalry Museum
Ft. Bliss, Bldg. 2407, 79916-6300
Telephone: (915) 568-1922
Federal agency, authorized by the
  U.S. Army
Founded in: 1972
Richard L. Fritz, Curator
Major programs: archives, museum,
  research, exhibits, audiovisual
  programs, photographic
  collections
Period of collections: 1846-present

**U.S. Army Air Defense Artillery
  Association**
P.O. Box 6101, Ft. Bliss, 79906
Telephone: (915) 568-5412
Private agency, authorized by the
  U.S. Army
Founded in: 1980
Marion Foote, Manager
Number of members: 278
Staff: full time 1, volunteer 30
Magazine: *Skysweeper*
Major programs: museum, oral
  history, school programs,
  newsletters/pamphlets, living
  history, audiovisual programs
Period of collections: 1846-present

**U.S. Army Air Defense Artillery
  Museum**
Pleasanton Rd., Bldg. 5000
Telephone: (915) 568-5412
Mail to: ATZC-DPT-PA, 79916
Federal agency, authorized by the
  U.S. Army
Founded in: 1975
Sam P. Hoyle, Director
Number of members: full time 4,
  volunteer 2
Major programs: library, archives,
  museum, school programs,
  research, exhibits, audiovisual
  programs, photograpic collections
Period of collections: 1917-present

FORT DAVIS

Ft. Davis Historical Society
Telephone: (915) 426-3565
Mail to: P.O. Box 233, 79734
Founded in: 1953
Questionnaire not received

Ft. Davis National Historic Site
P.O. Box 1456, 79734
Telephone: (915) 426-3225
Federal agency, authorized by
  National Park Service
Founded in: 1963
Douglas C. McChristian,
  Superintendent
Staff: full time 9
Major programs: museum, historic
  site(s), historic preservation,
  research, exhibits, living history,
  audiovisual programs
Period of collections: 1854-1891

FORT HOOD

1st Cavalry Division Museum
Headquarters Ave., Bldg. 2218
Telephone: (817) 287-3626
Mail to: P.O. Box 2187, 76544
Federal agency, authorized by the
  U.S. Army
Founded in: 1971
Rudeford M. Norman, Curator
Staff: full time 8
Major programs: archives, museum,
  tours/pilgrimages, research,
  exhibits, photographic collections
Period of collections: 1921-present

2nd Armored Division Museum
418 Battalion Ave.
Telephone: (817) 287-8812
Mail to: P.O. Box 5009, 76546
Federal agency, authorized by
  Department of the Army Center for
  Military History
Founded in: 1963
Leslie D. Jensen, Curator
Staff: full time 5
Major programs: library, archives,
  manuscripts, museum, research,
  exhibits, photographic collections
Period of collections: 1940-present

FORT McKAVETT

Ft. McKavett State Historic Site
P.O. Box 867 76841
Telephone: (915) 396-2358
State agency, authorized by Texas
  Parks and Wildlife Department
Founded in: 1967
David Bischofhauser, Park
  Superintendent I

Staff: full time 3
Major programs: museum, historic
  site(s), tours/pilgrimages, historic
  preservation, research, exhibits,
  living history
Period of collections: 1852-1883

FT. STOCKTON

Annie Riggs Museum
301 S. Main, 79735
Telephone: (915) 336-2167
Private agency, authorized by Ft.
  Stockton Historical Society
Founded in: 1899
Major programs: museum, historic
  site(s), tours/pilgrimages, oral
  history, school programs, historic
  preservation
Period of collections: 1900-1920s

Ft. Stockton Historical Society
301 S. Main St., 79735
Telepnone: (915) 336-2167
Private agency
Mary Kay Shannon, Director
Number of members: 200
Staff: full time 1, part time 2,
  volunteer 30
Major programs: museum, historic
  site(s), tours, oral history, school
  programs, historic preservation
Period of collections: early 1900s

FORT WORTH

**Amon Carter Museum of Western
  Art**
3501 Camp Bowie Blvd., 76107
Telephone: (817) 738-1933
Mail to: P.O. Box 2365, 76113
Founded in: 1961
Jan K. Muhlert, Director
Staff: full time 62, part time 12,
  volunteer 59
Major programs: library, educational
  programs, books, exhibits
Period of collections: 1783-present

Civil War Round Table of Texas
Telephone: (817) 732-5220
Mail to: P.O. Box 16382, 76133
Questionnaire not received

**Ft. Worth Museum of Science and
  History**
1501 Montgomery St., 76107
Telephone: (817) 732-1631
Founded in: 1939
Donald R. Otto, Executive Director
Staff: full time 67, part time 72,
  volunteer 85
Major programs: museum, school
  programs, newsletters/pamphlets,
  research, exhibits, audiovisual
  programs, theater, planetarium
Period of collections:
  prehistoric-present

**Historic Preservation Council for
  Tarrant County, Texas, Inc.**
1110 Penn St., 76102
Telephone: (817) 338-0267
Private agency
Founded in: 1980
Marty Craddock, Executive Director
Staff: full time 1, part time 1,
  volunteer 50
Major programs: historic
  preservation, research
Period of collections: 1900-1945

National Archives—Ft. Worth Branch
501 W. Felix St.
Telephone: (817) 334-5525
Mail to: P.O. Box 6216, 76115
Founded in: 1969
Kent Carter, Director
Staff: full time 6
Major programs: archives, educational programs, teachers' workshops, genealogical workshops, film series, open houses and tours
Period of collections: 1865-1973

North Ft. Worth Historical Society
131 E. Exchange Ave., Suite 115, 76106
Telephone: (817) 625-5082
Private agency
Founded in: 1976
Sue McCafferty, President
Number of members: 250
Staff: full time 1
Magazine: *Cowtown Dispatch*
Major programs: historic site(s), markers, tours/pilgrimages, historic preservation, research, exhibits, photographic collections
Period of collections: 1849-present

Pate Museum of Transportation
U.S. Hwy. 3775, Cresson
Telephone: (817) 332-1161
Mail to: P.O. Box 711, 76101
Private agency, authorized by Pate Foundation, Inc.
Founded in: 1969
Jim Peel, Curator
Staff: full time 5, part time 3
Major programs: library, museum
Period of collections: 1903-present

Tarrant County Black Historical and Genealogical Society, Inc.
1150 E. Rosedale St., 76104
Telephone: (817) 332-6049
Private agency
Founded in: 1977
Lenora Rolla, Director
Number of members: 200
Staff: part time 2, volunteer 5
Major programs: library, archives, museum, photographic collections, genealogical services
Period of collections: 1884-present

Tarrant County Historical Society
Telephone: (817) 625-1881
Mail to: 3724 Cresthaven Terrace, 76107
Questionnaire not received

Texas Heritage, Inc./Thistle Hill
1509 Pennsylvania, 76104
Telephone: (817) 336-1212
Private agency
Founded in: 1976
Deborah Philan, Executive Director
Number of members: 400
Staff: full time 2, part time 4, volunteer 30
Major programs: museum, school programs, newsletters/pamphlets, historic preservation
Period of collections: 1903-1912

Texas-New Mexico Field Office
500 Main St., Suite 606, 76102

Telephone: (817) 334-2061
Private agency, authorized by National Trust for Historic Preservation
Founded in: 1949
Major programs: historic preservation, audiovisual programs, field services, conferences, workshops, technical advice and assistance

Western Company Museum
600 Western Place, 76107
Telephone: (817) 731-5751
Private agency, authorized by Western Company of North America
Founded in: 1979
Francis J. Munch, Museum Director
Staff: full time 3
Major programs: archives, museum, tours/pilgrimages, oral history, school programs, newsletters/pamphlets, research, exhibits, audiovisual programs, photographic collections
Period of collections: 1789-present

FRANKSTON

Frankston Depot Library and Museum, Inc.
Town Square, S
Telephone: (214) 876-4463
Mail to: P.O. Box 213, 75763
Town agency
Founded in: 1981
Kathleen C. Fitzgerald, President
Staff: part time 2, volunteer 15
Major programs: library, museum, markers, historic preservation
Period of collections: 1800-1930

FREDERICKSBURG

Admiral Nimitz State Historical Park
340 E. Main St.
Telephone: (512) 997-4379
Mail to: P.O. Box 777, 78624
State agency
Founded in: 1966
Douglass H. Hubbard, Superintendent
Staff: full time 8, part time 6
Major programs: museum, exhibits
Period of collections: 1941-1945

Gillespie County Historical Society and Commission
309 W. Main St.
Telephone: (512) 997-2835
Mail to: P.O. Box 765, 78624
Founded in: 1936
Questionnaire not received

FRISCO

Old Post Office Museum/Collin County Historical Society, Inc.
Chestnut and Virginia Sts., 75069
Telephone: (214) 542-9457
Private agency
Founded in: 1976
Elisabeth R. Pink, President
Staff: volunteer 4

Major programs: library, archives, museum, historic site(s), markers, tours/pilgrimages, oral history, book publishing
Period of collections: 1850-1920

FULTON

Fulton Mansion State Historic Structure
Fulton Beach Rd. and Henderson St., 78358
Telephone: (512) 729-0386
Mail to: P.O. Box 1859, 78358
State agency, authorized by Texas Parks and Wildlife Department
Founded in: 1983
Staff: full time 6, volunteer 54
Major programs: historic site(s), tours
Period of collections: 1877-1887

GAINESVILLE

Cooke County Heritage Society, Inc.
Dixon and Pecan Sts. 76240
Telephone: (817) 668-8900
Mail to: P.O. Box 150, 76240
Private agency
Founded in: 1966
Richard A. Kastl, Director
Number of members: 244
Staff: full time 3, part time 2, volunteer 10
Magazine: *Heritage Highlights*
Major programs: archives, museum, historic site(s), junior history
Period of collections: 1880-1940

GALVESTON

Ashton Villa
2328 Broadway, 77550
Telephone: (409) 762-3933
Mail to: P.O. Box 1616, 77553
Private agency
Founded in: 1974
Judy Schiebel, Director
Staff: full time 4, part time 25, volunteer 50
Major programs: museum, historic site(s), tours, school programs, historic preservation, records management, exhibits, audiovisual programs, archaeology programs, photographic collections
Period of collections: 1850-1925

Center for Transportation and Commerce
123 Rosenberg, 77550
Telephone: (409) 765-5700
Private agency
Founded in: 1981
W. Phil Hewitt, Executive Director
Number of members: 346
Staff: full time 13, part time 3, volunteer 10
Magazine: *The Center Dispatch*
Major programs: library, museum, historic site(s), tours, junior history, school programs, newsletters/pamphlets, historic preservation, records management, exhibits, audiovisual programs
Period of collections: 1890-1950

1839 Williams Home
3601 Bernardo de Galvez, 77550
Telephone: (409) 765-1839
Mail to: P.O. Drawer 539, 77553
Private agency, authorized by
Galveston Historical Foundation
Founded in: 1984
Margaret Doran, Acting Director
Staff: full time 1, part time 5,
volunteer 15
Major programs: museum, historic
site(s), tours/pilgrimages, junior
history, school programs, historic
preservation, research, audiovisual
programs
Period of collections: 1825-1855

Galveston County Historical Museum
2219 Market St.
Telephone: (713) 766-2340
Mail to: P.O. Box 1047, 77553
Private agency, authorized by
Galveston Historical Foundation
Founded in: 1972
Betty A. Massey, Director
Staff: full time 3, part time 5,
volunteer 50
Major programs: museum, oral
history, school programs, historic
preservation, exhibits, living
history, audiovisual programs
Period of collections: 1830-present

Galveston Historical Foundation
The Strand
Telephone: (713) 765-7834
Mail to: Drawer 539, 77553
Founded in: 1871
Questionnaire not received

Texas Navy
202 Port Holiday Mall
Telephone: (713) 763-2408
Mail to: P.O. Box 125, 77553
Founded in: 1958
Questionnaire not received

Truman G. Blocker, Jr., History of Medicine Collections, Moody Medical Library
9th and Market Sts., 77550-2782
Telephone: (409) 761-2397
State agency, authorized by
University of Texas Medical Branch
Founded in: 1891
Emil F. Frey, Director
Staff: full time 2
Major programs: library, archives,
manuscripts, exhibits, medical
history
Period of collections: 16th
century-present

GATESVILLE

Coryell County Museum Foundation, Inc.
110 8th St.
Telephone: (817) 865-5421
Mail to: Drawer 119, 76528
County agency
Founded in: 1981
Staff: volunteer 10
Major programs: archives, museum,
book publishing, historic

preservation, audiovisual
programs, photographic
collections
Period of collections: 1850-present

GEORGE WEST

Cactus Park and Museum
Drawer F, 78022
Telephone: (512) 449-1556
City agency
Founded in: 1983
Brad Arvin, City Manager
Staff: volunteer 2
Major programs: museum, oral
history
Period of collections: 1850s-1920s

GIDDINGS

Texas Wendish Heritage Society
P.O. Box 311, 78942
Founded in: 1971
Questionnaire not received

GLEN ROSE

Somervell County Historical Society
Corner Vernon and Elm 76043
Telephone: (817) 897-2739, 897-4529
Mail to: Box 669, 76043
Founded in: 1966
Robert A. Mack, President
Number of members: 68
Staff: volunteer 3
Major programs: museum, oral
history, historic preservation
Period of collections: late 1800s-early
1900s

GOLIAD

Mission Nuestra Senora del Espiritu Santo de Zuniga/Goliad State Historical Park
U.S. Hwy. 183 and 77-A
Telephone: (512) 645-3405
Mail to: P.O. Box 727, 77963
State agency, authorized by Texas
Parks and Wildlife Department
Founded in: 1749
Jane von Dohlen, Exhibit Technician
Staff: full time 2, part time 1,
volunteer 4
Major programs: museum, historic
site(s), tours/pilgrimages, school
programs, historic preservation,
research, exhibits, living history,
audiovisual programs,
photographic collections
Period of collections: 1749-1830

Presidio La Bahia
U.S. Hwy. 183 and 77-A
Telephone: (512) 645-3752
Mail to: P.O. Box 57, 77963
Private agency, authorized by
Diocese of Victoria, Roman
Catholic Church
Founded in: 1966
John H. Collins, Director
Number of members: 90
Staff: full time 4, part time 2
Magazine: Friends of the Fort
Major programs: library, archives,
manuscripts, museum, historic

site(s), oral history, school
programs, newsletters/pamphlets,
historic preservation, research,
exhibits, living history, archaeology
programs, photographic
collections
Period of collections: 1749-1836

GRANBURY

Texas American Indian Museum
4002/8 S. Morgan St.
Telephone: (817) 573-2589
Mail to: P.O. Box 911, 76048
Private agency
Founded in: 1983
C. E. Chuck Blythe, Curator
Staff: volunteer 3
Major programs: museum, historic
site(s), school programs, research,
archaeology programs

GRAND PRAIRIE

Grand Prairie Historical Commission
P.O. Box 11, 75051
Telephone: (214) 264-2234/264-1571
City agency
Founded in: 1976
Mrs. Vernon Jackson, Chair
Staff: part time 1, volunteer 1
Major programs: archives, museum,
historic sites preservation, markers,
tours/pilgrimages, oral history,
educational programs, historic
preservation
Period of collections: 1845-present

Grand Prairie Historical Organization
c/o 214 Moore St., 75050
Telephone: (214) 264-5121
Founded in: 1975
Questionnaire not received

Wax Museum of the Southwest
601 E. Safari Parkway, 75051
Telephone: (214) 263-2391
Private agency, authorized by
Southwestern Historical Wax
Museum Corporation
Founded in: 1963
Bill Phillips, General Manager
Number of members: full time 7,
volunteer 25
Major programs: museum, historic
preservation
Period of collections: 1700s-present

GRAND SALINE

Grand Saline Public Library
201 E. Pacific Ave., 75140
Telephone: (214) 962-5516
City agency
Founded in: 1966
Catherine Jarvis, Director
Staff: full time 1, volunteer 10
Major programs: library, historic
site(s), historic preservation,
audiovisual programs
Period of collections: 1900-present

GREENVILLE

Audie Murphy Room, W. Walworth Harrison Public Library
3716 Lee St., 75401

Telephone: (214) 455-2205
City agency
Founded in: 1973
Dawn Lowell, Librarian
Staff: full time 3, part time 7
Major programs: library
Period of collections: 1940s-1970s

Greenville Revitalization Organization
2815 Lee St., 75407
Mail to: P.O. Box 1201, 75401
Founded in: 1976
Questionnaire not received

GROESBECK

Old Ft. Parker State Historic Site
Rt. 3, Box 220, 76642
Telephone: (817) 729-5253
State agency, authorized by Texas
Parks and Wildlife Department
Founded in: 1936
Thomas M. Fisher, Park
Superintendent
Staff: full time 2, part time 2
Major programs: historic site(s),
school programs, exhibits
Period of collections: 1834-1836

HARLINGEN

Confederate Air Force
Rebel Field, 78550
Telephone: (512) 425-1057
Mail to: P.O. Box C.A.F., 78551
Private agency
Founded in: 1956
Mack Sterling, Executive Director
Number of members: 7,300
Staff: full time 49, part time 1
Magazine: *C.A.F. Dispatch*
Major programs: library, archives,
museum, tours, school programs,
newsletters/pamphlets, historic
preservation, research, exhibits,
living history, audiovisual
programs, photographic
collections, air shows
Period of collections: 1939-1945

Harlingen Hospital Museum/Rio Grande Valley Museum
Boxwood St., Industrial Air Park,
78550
Telephone: (512) 428-6974
City agency
Founded in: 1923
Eleanor Galt, Director
Staff: part time 1
Major programs: museum
Period of collections: 1923-1925

Lon C. Hill Home Museum
Fair Park Blvd.
Telephone: (512) 423-3979
Mail to: c/o Rio Grande Valley
Museum, Boxwood St., Industrial
Air Park, 78550
City agency
Founded in: 1905
Eleanor Galt, Director
Staff: part time 1
Period of collections: early 1900s

Paso Real Stagecoach Inn Museum
Boxwood St., Industrial Air Park,
78550
Telephone: (512) 423-3979
City agency
Founded in: 1976

Eleanor Galt, Director
Staff: part time 1
Major programs: museum
Period of collections: 1890-1904

Rio Grande Valley Museum
Boxwood St., Industrial Air Park,
78550
Telephone: (512) 423-3979
Founded in: 1967
Questionnaire not received

HASKELL

J.U. and Florence B. Fields Museum
401 N. Ave. E
Telephone: (817) 864-3898
Mail to: P.O. Box 694, 79521
Private agency
Founded in: 1978
Peggy Vaughter, Trustee/Treasurer
Staff: part time 1, volunteer 3
Major programs: museum, school
programs
Period of collections: 1910-1960

HEARNE

Hearne Heritage League
402 Cedar St., 77859
Telephone: (409) 279-3655
Town agency, authorized by Texas
Historical Commission
Founded in: 1980
Mrs. Jack Holloway, President
Number of members: 104
Staff: volunteer 12
Major programs: library, historic
site(s), markers, tours/pilgrimages,
newsletters/pamphlets

HEMPSTEAD

Waller County Historical Commission
935 14th St., 77445
County agency
Patti Meyers, Chair
Major programs: library, archives,
manuscripts, museum, historic
site(s), markers, tours/pilgrimages,
junior history, oral history, school
programs, book publishing, historic
preservation, research,
photographic collections

HENDERSON

Depot Museum: History Museum and Children's Discovery Center
514 N. High St. 75652
Telephone: (214) 657-8557
County agency
Founded in: 1979
Susan Weaver, Supervisor
Staff: full time 1, part time 1
Major programs: museum, historic
preservation, exhibits, living history
Period of collections: 1830-1950

Rusk County Historical Foundation
509 E. Main
Telephone: (214) 657-2261
Mail to: P.O. Box 1773, 75653
Private agency
Founded in: 1984
Virginia Knapp, President
Number of members: 36
Staff: volunteer 36

Major programs: archives, museum,
historic site(s), tours/pilgrimages,
historic preservation, genealogical
services
Period of collections: 1843-present

HEREFORD

Deaf Smith County Museum
400 Sampson
Telephone: (806) 364-4338
Mail to: P.O. Box 1007, 79045
County agency
Founded in: 1967
Lois M. Gilliland, Executive Director
Number of members: 450
Staff: volunteer 15
Period of collections: 1880-1930

E. B. Black Historic House
508 W. 3rd St.
Telephone: (806) 364-4338
Mail to: P.O. Box 1007, 79045
County agency
Founded in: 1978
Lois M. Gilliland, Executive Director
Number of members: 450
Staff: full time 2, volunteer 5
Major programs: museum
Period of collections: 1909-1930

National Cowgirl Hall of Fame
515 Ave. B
Telephone: (806) 364-5252
Mail to: P.O. Box 1742, 79045
Founded in: 1975
Jackie Hammett, Administrator
Staff: full time 1, part time 2,
volunteer 25
Magazine: *Sidesaddle*
Major programs: library, archives,
newsletters/pamphlets, records
management, research, exhibits,
photographic collections
Period of collections: 1881-present

HILLSBORO

Confederate Research Center and Museum
Hill Junior College, Lamar St.
Telephone: (817) 582-2555
Mail to: P.O. Box 619, 76645
State agency
Founded in: 1923
W. R. Auvershine, President
Staff: full time 120, part time 40
Major programs: library, archives,
manuscripts, museum, historic
site(s), markers, school programs,
educational programs, book
publishing, newsletters/pamphlets,
historic preservation, research,
audiovisual programs,
photographic collections,
genealogical services, field
services
Period of collections: Civil War

Hood's Texas Brigade Association
P.O. Box 619
Telephone: (817) 582-2555
Founded in: 1969
Harold B. Simpson,
Secretary/Treasurer
Number of members: 565
Staff: part time 2 volunteer 1
Major programs: library, museum,
books, newsletters/pamphlets,
historic preservation
Period of collections: 1850-1865

HOUSTON

Archives of American Art, Texas Project
1001 Bissonnet
Telephone: (713) 526-1361
Mail to: P.O. Box 6826, 77265
Federal agency, authorized by Smithsonian Institution
Founded in: 1979
Sandra J. Levy, Area Director
Staff: full time 1, part time 3
Major programs: archives, fine art history
Period of collections: 1900-present

Armand Bayou Nature Center
8600 Bay Area Blvd.
Telephone: (713) 474-2551
Mail to: P.O. Box 58828, 77258
Private agency
Founded in: 1970
Laura J. Lehtonen, Educational Coordinator
Mail to: 5,000
Staff: full time 10, part time 5, volunteer 150
Major programs: museum, historic site(s), tours/pilgrimages, oral history, school programs, newsletters/pamphlets, historic preservation, research, exhibits, living history, audiovisual programs, archaeology programs, photographic collections
Period of collections: 1880-1915

Bayou Bend Collection, Museum of Fine Arts
1 Westcott St.
Telephone: (713) 529-8773
Mail to: P.O. Box 13157, 77219
Founded in: 1929
David B. Warren, Curator
Staff: full time 20
Major programs: museum, historic site(s), school programs, historic preservation
Period of collections: 17th-19th centuries

Gulf Coast Chapter, National Railway Historical Society, Inc.
7390 Mesa Rd., 77028
Telephone: (713) 635-3255
Mail to: P.O. Box 457, 77001
Founded in: 1961
Paul DeVerter, Director
Number of members: 130
Staff: volunteer 10
Magazine: *Gulf Coast Railroading*
Major programs: manuscripts, museum, tours/pilgrimages, newsletters/pamphlets, historic preservation

Harris County Heritage Society
1100 Bagby, 77002
Telephone: (713) 223-8367
Private agency
Founded in: 1954
William C. Griggs, Executive Director
Number of members: 2,500
Staff: full time 16, part time 4, volunteer 700
Major programs: museum, tours/pilgrimages, school programs, historic preservation, records management, exhibits, photographic collections
Period of collections: 19th century

Harris County Historical Society
Mail to: P.O. Box 27143, 77027
Questionnaire not received

Historical Research Center, Houston Academy of Medicine, Texas Medical Center Library
1133 M. D. Anderson Blvd., 77030
Telephone: (713) 797-1230
Private agency
Founded in: 1977
Elizabeth White, Director
Staff: full time 3
Major programs: library, archives, manuscripts, photographic collections, medical history and history of health care in county
Period of collections: 1920-1980

Houston Metropolitan Research Center, Houston Public Library
500 McKinney St., 77025
Telephone: (713) 222-4900
City agency
Founded in: 1974
Louis J. Marchiafava, Archivist
Magazine: *The Houson Review: History and Culture of the Gulf Coast*
Major programs: archives, manuscripts, oral history, research, photographic collections, architectural collections
Period of collections: 1836-present

Houston Museum of Natural Science
1 Hermann Circle Dr., 77030
Telephone: (713) 526-4273
Private agency
Founded in: 1909
Carl H. Aiken, Executive Director
Number of members: 3,000
Staff: full time 24, part time 25, volunteer 150
Major programs: library, museum, tours/pilgrimages, school programs, newsletters/pamphlets, exhibits
Period of collections: prehistoric-present

Jefferson Davis Association
419 Fondren Library, 6100 Main St., 77005
Telephone: (713) 527-4990
Mail to: P.O. Box 1892, 77251-1892
Private agency, authorized by Rice University
Founded in: 1963
Lynda L. Crist, Editor
Staff: full time 2, part time 1, volunteer 1
Major programs: research, historical editing project
Period of collections: 1820-1890

Museum of American Architecture and Decorative Arts
7502 Fondren, 77074
Telephone: (713) 774-7661
Private agency, authorized by Houston Baptist University
Founded in: 1965
Doris E. Anderson, Director
Number of members: 85
Staff: full time 6, volunteer 15
Major programs: library, archives, manuscripts, museum, tours/pilgrimages, oral history, school programs, book publishing, audiovisual programs, photographic collections
Period of collections: 1770-1950

NASA/Johnson Space Center
77058
Telephone: (713) 483-4321
Federal agency
Founded in: 1960
Harold Stall, Public Affairs Officer
Major programs: library, museum, tours/pilgrimages, school programs, exhibits

San Jacinto Descendants
5556 Cranbrook, 77027
Telephone: (713) 871-8099
Founded in: 1965
D. E. Anderson, President
Number of members: 200
Staff: volunteer 8
Major programs: archives, manuscripts, museum, historic sites preservation, markers, junior history, oral history, educational programs, newsletters/pamphlets
Period of collections: 1783-1865

San Jacinto Museum of History Association
San Jacinto Battleground State Park, 77536
Telephone: (713) 479-2421
Mail to: P.O. Box 755, Deer Park
Questionnaire not received

Texas Gulf Coast Historical Association
Department of History University of Houston, 77004
Telephone: (713) 749-4680
Founded in: 1956
James A. Tinsley, Executive Director
Number of members: 150
Staff: part time 2
Major programs: archives, manuscripts, oral history, books
Period of collections: 1900-present

Texas State Genealogical Society
2507 Tannehill, 77008-3052
Telephone: (713) 864-6862
Founded in: 1960
Trevia W. Beverly, President
Number of members: 1,000
Magazine: *Stirpes*
Major programs: genealogical services

HUNTSVILLE

Sam Houston Memorial Museum
1804 Sam Houston Ave., 77340
Telephone: (409) 295-7824
Mail to: P.O. Box 2024, 77341
State agency, authorized by Sam Houston State University
Founded in: 1936
Ann Fears Crawford, Director/Curator
Staff: full time 10, part time 2
Major programs: library, archives, museum, historic site(s), markers, tours/pilgrimages, school programs, historic preservation, exhibits, living history, audiovisual programs
Period of collections: 1820-1880

HURST

Northeast Historical Society
c/o President, (828) 281-7860
County agency
Founded in: 1976
J. Paul Davidson, President
Number of members: 25
Staff: volunteer 4
Major programs: archives,
newsletters/pamphlets, historic
preservation, photographic
collections, Period of collections:
1850-1900

INGLESIDE

Ingleside Historical Society
P.O. Box 514, 78362
Telephone: (512) 776-2405
Founded in: 1982
Lillie Dawson, President
Number of members: 30
Staff: volunteer 6
Major programs: museum, markers,
tours/pilgrimages, historic
preservation
Period of collections: from prehistoric

JACKSBORO

**Fort Richardson State Park
Museum**
Mail to: P.O. Box 4, 76056
Telephone: (817) 567-3506
Founded in: 1867
Bruce R. Bunn, Park Superintendent
Staff: full time 4, part time 3
Major programs: museum, historic
sites preservation, markers,
tours/pilgrimages, historic
preservation
Period of collections: 1867-1878

JAYTON

**Kent County Genealogical And
Historical Society**
P.O. Box 6, 79528
County agency
Founded in: 1978
Mark A. Geeslin, County Judge
Number of members: 15
Staff: full time 2, part time 1,
volunteer 15
Major programs: library, markers,
genealogical services

JEFFERSON

Excelsior House
211 W. Austin St., 75657
Telephone: (214) 665-2513
Private agency, authorized by
Jefferson Historical Restoration
and Preservation Corporation
Mary Ann Rhodes, Manager
Number of members: 35
Major programs: historic site(s),
tours/pilgrimages, historic
preservation
Period of collections: 1850-1900

**Jefferson Historical Restoration
and Preservation Corporation**
W. Austin St., 75657
Telephone: (214) 665-2513
Private agency
Number of members: Mary Ann
Rhodes, Manager

Number of members: 35
Major programs: historic site(s),
markers, tours/pilgrimages
Period of collections: 1850-1900

**Jefferson Historical Society and
Museum**
223 Austin St., 75657
Private agency
Founded in: 1948
A. M. Bower, Manager
Number of members: 175
Staff: full time 2, part time 2
Major programs: archives, museum,
tours/pilgrimages, exhibits,
photographic collections,
genealogical services
Period of collections: 1875-1925

JOHNSON CITY

**Lyndon B. Johnson National
Historical Park**
P.O. Box 329, 78636
Telephone: (512) 868-7128
Staff: full time 34, part time 40,
volunteer 2
Major programs: library, archives,
historic sites preservation,
tours/pilgrimages, oral history,
educational programs, historic
preservation
Period of collections: 1860-present

JOLLYVILLE

**Jollyville/Pond Springs Historical
Association**
7203 S. Ute Trail, Round Rock, 78664
Telephone: (512) 258-5688
Founded in: 1977
Karen Thompson, President
Number of members: 10
Major programs: markers, oral
history, educational programs
Period of collections: 1850s-present

JOSHUA

Joshua Historical Society
402 S. Main, 76058
Mail to: P.O. Box 256
Founded in: 1978
Opal O. Seals, President
Number of members: 128
Staff: volunteer 19
Magazine: Joshua Historical Herald
Major programs: library, archives,
manuscripts, museum, historic
sites preservation, markers,
tours/pilgrimages, junior history,
oral history, educational programs,
books, newsletters/pamphlets,
historic preservation
Period of collections: 1898-1920

KERMIT

**Medallion Home/Pioneer Park
Association**
School St.
Telephone: (915) 586-3620
(president)
Mail to: 1112 S. Poplar St., 79745
County agency
Founded in: 1964
Fean Adams., President
Number of members: 44
Period of collections: 1910-1930

KERRVILLE

**Cowboy Artists of America
Museum**
1550 Bandera Hwy.
Telephone: (512) 896-2553
Mail to: P.O. Box 1716, 78029
Private agency
Founded in: 1980
Griffiths C. Carnes, Director
Number of members: 700
Staff: full time 3, volunteer 75
Major programs: library, archives,
museum, newsletters/pamphlets,
records management, exhibits
Period of collections: 1860s-present

KILGORE

East Texas Oil Museum
Hwy. 259 at Ross St., 75662
Telephone: (214) 983-8295
Authorized by: Kilgore College
Founded in: 1980
Joe L. White, Director
Staff: full time 5, part time 5,
volunteer 30
Major programs: museum, oral
history, exhibits, living history,
audiovisual programs,
photographic collections
Period of collections: 1930-1935

KINGSVILLE

John E. Conner Museum
Santa Gertrudis
Telephone: (512) 595-2819
Mail to: Station 1, Box 2172, 78363
State agency, authorized by Texas A
& I University
Founded in: 1925
Mrs. Jimmie R. Picquet, Director
Number of members: 270
Staff: full time 9, part time 14,
volunteer 30
Magazine: Conner Corner
Major programs: archives,
manuscripts, museum, oral history,
school programs,
newsletters/pamphlets, records
management, research, exhibits,
photographic collections
Period of collections: 1850-1950

LAKE JACKSON

**Lake Jackson Historical
Association**
122 S. Parking Place
Telephone: (409) 297-2850
Mail to: P.O. Box 242, 77566
Private agency
Founded in: 1982
William M. Weddell, President
Number of members: 206
Staff: volunteer 20
Major programs: museum, oral
history, school programs,
newsletters/pamphlets, historic
preservation, research, exhibits,
photographic collections
Period of collections: from 1940

LAMESA

Lamesa-Dawson County Museum
S. 2nd St. and Ave. M
Mail to: 404 21st Place, 79331
City/County agency

Founded in: 1965
Wayne C. Smith, Board President
Staff: part time 2, volunteer 12
Major programs: exhibits
Period of collections: early 1900s

LANGTRY

Judge Roy Bean Visitor Center
Loop 25
Telephone: (915) 291-3340
Mail to: P.O. Box 160, 78871
State agency, authorized by Texas
Department of Highways and
Public Transportation
Founded in: 1968
Jack R. Skiles, Manager
Staff: full time 4
Major programs: museum, historic
preservation, exhibits
Period of collections: 1882-1903

LA PORTE

**Battleship Texas State Historic
Park**
3527 Battleground Rd., 77571
Telephone: (713) 479-2411
State agency, authorized by Texas
Parks and Wildlife Department
Founded in: 1948
Dan Harrison, Superintendent
Staff: 22
Major programs: archives, museum,
historic site(s), tours/pilgrimages,
oral history, historic preservation,
records management, research,
exhibits, photographic collections
Period of collections: 1912-1949

**San Jacinto Museum of History
Association**
3800 Park Rd. 1836, 77571
Telephone: (713) 479-2421
Founded in: 1938
James C. Martin, Director
Staff: full time 6, part time 7
Magazine: *The Advance*
Major programs: library, manuscripts,
museum, school programs, book
publishing, newsletters/pamphlets,
research, exhibits, audiovisual
programs, photographic
collections
Period of collections: 1800-1900

LAREDO

**Nuevo Santander Museum
Complex**
West End, Washington St., 78040
Telephone: (512) 722-0521, ext. 321
Authorized by: Laredo Junior College
Founded in: 1975
Denneth A. Wolfe, Executive Director
Number of members: 550
Staff: full time 4, part time 7,
volunteer 20
Major programs: library, museum,
historic site(s), oral history, historic
preservation, research, exhibits,
archaeology programs,
photographic collections
Period of collections: 1755-1946

**Webb County Heritage
Foundation, Inc.**
P.O. Box 29, 78042
Telephone: (512) 727-0977
Private agency

Founded in: 1980
S. Carol Gunter, Executive Director
Number of members: 450
Staff: full time 3, part time 1,
volunteer 2
Major programs: tours/pilgrimages,
newsletters/pamphlets, historic
preservation, research, exhibits

LEVELLAND

South Plains Museum Association
608 Ave. H
Telephone: (806) 894-7547
Mail to: P.O. Box 1304, 79336
Founded in: 1968
Pat Grappe, Curator
Number of members: 100
Staff: full time 1
Major programs: museum
Period of collections: 1900-present

LIBERTY

Atascosito Historical Society
P.O. Box 688, 77575
Telephone: (409) 336-7542
Founded in: 1973
Charles W. Fisher, Jr., President
Number of members: 500
Staff: volunteer 3
Major programs: archives, historic
preservation

**Sam Houston Regional Library and
Research Center**
Telephone: (409) 336-7097
Mail to: P.O. Box 989, 77575
State agency
Founded in: 1977
Robert L. Schaadt, Director/Archivist
Major programs: library, archives,
manuscripts, museum, historic
site(s), oral history, records
management, research, exhibits,
photographic collections,
genealogical services, field
services
Period of collections: 1820s-present

LIVINGSTON

Polk County Heritage Society
207 N. Beaty, 77351
Telephone: (409) 327-5945
Private agency
Founded in: 1979
Helen Malone, President
Number of members: 75
Staff: volunteer 30
Major programs: museum, historic
site(s), tours/pilgrimages, oral
history, newsletters/pamphlets,
historic preservation, living history,
photographic collections, field
services

**Polk County Historical
Commission**
601 W. Church St.
Telephone: (409) 327-8192
Mail to: P.O. Box 51177351
County agency
Founded in: 1963
Robert Doolittle, Chair
Staff: full time 1. part time 1,
volunteer 6
Major programs: library, archives,
manuscripts, museum, historic
site(s), markers, oral history, school

programs, historic preservation,
exhibits, audiovisual programs,
photographic collections
Period of collections: 1700s-present

LONGVIEW

**Gregg County Historical and
Genealogical Society**
214 N. Fredonia
Telephone: (214) 753-5840
Mail to: P.O. Box 542, 75606
County agency
Founded in: 1963
Mark Johnston, President
Number of members: 90
Staff: volunteer 4
Major programs: museum, junior
history, school programs, historic
preservation, exhibits, audiovisual
programs, photographic
collections, genealogical services
Period of collections: 1860-1945

Gregg County Historical Museum
214 N. Fredonia, 75601
Telephone: (214) 753-5840
Mail to: P.O. Box 3342, 75606
Private agency
Founded in: 1967 (foundation); 1983
(museum)
Ellie Caston, Museum Director
Number of members: 318
Staff: full time 1, part time 1,
volunteer 30
Major programs: library, archives,
museum, tours/pilgrimages,
historic preservation, records
management, research, exhibits,
audiovisual programs,
photographic collections
Period of collections: 1860-1945

Longview Museum and Arts Center
102 W. College, 75601
Telephone: (214) 753-8103
Mail to: P.O. Box 562, 75606
Private agency
Founded in: 1970
Donald P. Zuris, Executive Director
Number of members: 147
Staff: full time 2, volunteer 100
Major programs: museum, school
programs, newsletters/pamphlets,
exhibits, fine arts
Period of collections: Contemporary

Private Caddo Indian Museum
701 Hardy St., 75604
Telephone: (214) 759-5739
Private agency
Founded in: 1957
Mrs. James L. Jones, Director
Staff: full time 1
Major programs: museum,
tours/pilgrimages, historic
preservation, archaeology
programs

LUBBOCK

**The Museum, Texas Tech
University**
4th and Indiana Ave.
Telephone: (806) 742-2442
Mail to: P.O. Box 4499, 79409
State agency, authorized by the
university
Founded in: 1929
Clyde Jones, Director

Number of members: 3,000
Staff: full time 45 volunteer 400
Major programs: museum, research,
 exhibits, archaeology programs
Period of collections:
 prehistoric-present

Ranching Heritage Association
4th and Indiana Ave.
Telephone: (806) 742-2498
Mail to: P.O. Box 4040, 79409
Private agency
Founded in: 1969
Alvin G. Davis, Executive Vice
 President/General Manager
Number of members: 1,000
Staff: full time 7, part time 2,
 volunteer 111
Magazine: *Ranch Record*
Major programs: museum, historic
 site(s), markers, tours/pilgrimages,
 book publishing,
 newsletters/pamphlets, historic
 preservation, exhibits, living
 history, audiovisual programs,
 photographic collections
Period of collections: 1830s-1920s

Society of Southwest Archivists
Texas Tech University
Mail to: P.O. Box 4090, 79409
Private agency
Founded in: 1972
Number of members: 300
Staff: volunteer 10
Major programs: library, archives,
 manuscripts, museum,
 newsletters/pamphlets

LUFKIN

Texas Forestry Museum
1905 Alkinson Dr.
Telephone: (409) 632-8733
Mail to: P.O. Box 1488, 75901
Private agency
Founded in: 1972
Ed Wagoner, Trustee
Staff: part time 1, volunteer 30
Major programs: museum, history of
 forestry
Period of collections: 1850-1950

MARSHALL

Harrison County Historical Society
Old Courthouse, Peter Whetstone
 Square, 75670
Telephone: (214) 938-2680
Questionnaire not received

MCALLEN

**Hidalgo County Historical
 Commission**
313 Vermont St., 78501
Telephone: (512) 687-4736
County agency, authorized by Texas
 Historical Commission
Founded in: 1963
Number of members: volunteer 53
Major programs: historic site(s),
 markers, tours/pilgrimages, oral
 history, school programs, historic
 preservation, research,
 photographic collections
Period of collections: 1852-present

MCCAMEY

McCamey Junior Historians
McCamey High School
Telephone: (915) 652-8603
Mail to: P.O. Box 1069, 75752
County agency
James L. Collett, Sponsor
Major programs: museum, junior
 history, school programs

MCKINNEY

**Collin County Historical
 Society—Old Post Office**
Chestnut at Virginia Sts., 75069
Telephone: (214) 542-9457
Private agency
Founded in: 1973
Elisabeth R. Pink, President
Staff: volunteer 4
Major programs: library, museum,
 tours/pilgrimages, oral history,
 book publishing, exhibits
Period of collections: 1880-1925

**Heard Natural Science Museum
 and Wildlife Sanctuary, Inc.**
Rt. 6, Box 22, 75069
Telephone: (214) 542-5566
Private agency
Founded in: 1967
Harold E. Laughlin, Administrative
 Director
Number of members: 1,000
Staff: full time 7, part time 20,
 volunteer 125
Major programs: library, museum,
 school programs,
 newsletters/pamphlets, records
 management, research, exhibits,
 audiovisual programs, archaeology
 programs, photographic
 collections, field services
Period of collections: 1850-present

MIDLAND

**Alexander Daugherty Chapter,
 United States Daughters of 1812**
901 Storey, 79701
Telephone: (915) 683-2015
Mrs. Warren L. Faller, President
Major programs: library, genealogical
 services
Period of collections: 1812-1815

Midland County Historical Museum
301 W. Missouri, 79701
Telephone: (915) 683-2708
Founded in: 1932
Rosemary Rankin, Director
Staff: full time 1, part time 1

Midland County Historical Society
301 West Missouri, 79701
Telephone: (915) 682-2931
Mail to: 2102 Community Lane
Founded in: 1957
Mrs. John P. McKinley, President
Number of members: 75
Staff: part time 2, volunteer 10
Major programs: archives, museum,
 historic sites preservation, markers,
 tours/pilgrimages, oral history,
 educational programs, historic
 preservation
Period of collections: 1885-1925

Midland Regional Airport Museum
P.O. Box 6305, 79711
Telephone: (915) 563-1460

City agency
Founded in: 1970
Victor D. White, Director of Aviation
Major programs: museum, historic
 site(s)
Period of collections: 1905-1945

Museum of the Southwest
1705 W. Missouri, 79701
Telephone: (915) 683-2882
Founded in: 1965
Joan E. Hellen, Director
Staff: full time 9, part time 2
Magazine: *Muse-Letter*
Major programs: museum,
 educational programs,
 newsletters/pamphlets
Period of collections:
 prehistoric-present

**Nita Stewart Haley Memorial
 Library**
1805 W. Indiana, 79701
Telephone: (915) 682-5785
Private agency
Founded in: 1976
Beth E. Schneider, Librarian
Staff: full time 1, part time 2
Major programs: library, archives,
 manuscripts, research,
 photographic collections, history of
 cattle industry in Southwestern U.S.
Period of collections: late 19th-early
 20th centuries

**Permian Basin Petroleum Museum,
 Library, and Hall of Fame**
1500 Hwy. I-20, W, 79701
Telephone: (915) 683-4403
Founded in: 1969
Edward C. Rowland, Executive Vice
 President/Director
Number of members: 350
Staff: full time 9, part time 4,
 volunteer 200
Magazine: *Museum Memo*
Major programs: library, archives,
 museum, oral history, school
 programs, book publishing,
 newsletters/pamphlets, historic
 preservation, records
 management, research, exhibits,
 audiovisual programs,
 photographic collections
Period of collections: 1920-1940

MOBEETIE

**Old Mobeetie
 Association—Mobeetie Jail
 Museum**
P.O. Box 189, Wheeler, 79096
Telephone: (806) 826-8289
Town agency
Founded in: 1978
Sallei B. Harris, President
Major programs: oral history, historic
 preservation, exhibits, living history
Period of collections: 1870-1900

MONT BELVIEU

Chambers County Heritage Society
P.O. Box 870, 77580
Telephone: (713) 576-2594
Founded in: 1976
Harry G. Daves., Jr. President
Number of members: 100
Staff: volunteer 10

Major programs: historic site(s), markers, tours/pilgrimages, junior history, oral history, school programs, newsletters/pamphlets, exhibits, archaeology programs, photographic collections, genealogical services, field services
Period of collections: 1800-1900

NACOGDOCHES

East Texas Historical Association
Telephone: (409) 569-2407
Mail to: SFA Station, P.O. Box 6223, 75962
Private agency
Founded in: 1962
Archie P. McDonald, Editor
Number of members: 500
Staff: part time 2
Magazine: *East Texas Historical Journal*
Period of collections: 1865-present

Sterne-Hoya Home
211 S. LaNana, 75961
Telephone: (409) 564-4693
City agency
Founded in: 1958
Melva Hines, Librarian and Curator
Staff: full time 1, part time 3
Major programs: library, museum, historic sites preservation, oral history, historic preservation
Period of collections: 1828-Victorian era

Texas Folklore Society
115 Rusk Bldg., Stephen F. Austin
Telephone: (713) 569-4407
Mail to: SFA Station, P.O. Box 13007, 75962
State agency
Founded in: 1909
F. E. Abernathy, Secretary/Editor
Number of members: 800
Staff: volunteer 15
Major programs: book publishing
Period of collections: early 1800s-present

NEW BRAUNFELS

New Braunfels Conservation Society
Telephone: (512) 625-5593
Mail to: P.O. Box 933, 78130
Founded in: 1964
Edward R. Dedeke, President
Number of members: 300
Major programs: museum, newsletters/pamphlets, historic preservation
Period of collections: 1850-1890

Sophienburg Memorial Association, Inc.
401 W. Coll St., 78130
Telephone: (512) 629-1572
Private agency
Founded in: 1926
Margaret Fields, Director
Number of members: 600
Staff: full time 2, part time 5, volunteer 97
Major programs: archives, museum, tours/pilgrimages, oral history, newsletters/pamphlets
Period of collections: 1840-1930

NORDHEIM

Nordheim Historical Museum
Telephone: (512) 938-5886
Mail to: P.O. Box 104, 78141
Town agency, authorized by Nordheim Historical Museum Association
Founded in: 1976
Lula B. Kolodziejezk, Director
Number of members: 75
Staff: volunteer 75
Major programs: museum

ODESSA

Ector County Historical Commission
1705 W. 46th St., 79762
Telephone: (362) 362-3654
County agency, authorized by Texas Historical Commission
Founded in: 1959
Bobbie Jean Klepper, Chair
Major programs: historic site(s), markers, junior history, oral history, newsletters/pamphlets, historic preservation, photographic collections
Period of collections: 1880-present

Permian Historical Society
University of Texas of the Permian Basin, 4901 W. University, 7976-8301
Telephone: (915) 347-2128
Founded in: 1959
Bobbie Jean Klepper, Secretary/Archivist
Number of members: 283
Staff: volunteer 5
Magazine: *The Permian Historical Annual*
Major programs: archives, markers, tours/pilgrimages, oral history, newsletters/pamphlets
Period of collections: 1875-1930

The Presidential Museum
622 N. Lee St., 79761
Telephone: (915) 332-7123
Founded in: 1964
Lettie England, Administrator
Number of members: 152
Staff: full time 6, part time 2, volunteer 25
Major programs: library, museum, school programs, newsletters/pamphlets, exhibits
Period of collections: 1789-present

ORANGE

Heritage House Museum
905 W. Division
Telephone: (409) 886-5385
Mail to: P.O. Box F, 77630
Private agency, authorized by Heritage House Association of Orange County, Inc.
Founded in: 1977
Nell Truman, Director
Number of members: 320
Staff: full time 1, volunteer 35
Magazine: *Nostalgia News*
Major programs: museum, historic site(s), book publishing, historic preservation, audiovisual programs, photographic collections
Period of collections: 1880-1980

Orange County Historical Commission
12 Bayou Bend, 77630
Telephone: (409) 886-1313
County agency
Founded in: 1972
Howard C. Williams, Chair
Number of members: 12
Staff: volunteer 3
Major programs: archives, museum, markers, newsletters/pamphlets, historic preservation, records management, research, photographic collections, genealogical services
Period of collections: 1870-present

OZONA

Crockett County Historical Society
Telephone: (915) 392-3041
Mail to: Drawer B, 76943
Founded in: 1931
Ted M. White, President
Number of members: 75
Staff: part time 1, volunteer 20
Major programs: archives, museum, oral history, books
Period of collections: 1865-present

Crockett County Museum
Courthouse Annex, 11th St.
Telephone: (915) 932-2837
Mail to: P.O. Box B., 76943
Private agency, authorized by Crockett County Historical Society
Founded in: 1939
Pleasant Childress, Director
Staff: full time 1, volunteer 1
Major programs: museum, oral history, exhibits, photographic collections
Period of collections: prehistoric-1881

PALACIOS

Palacios Area Historical Associaton
404 4th St.
Telephone: (512) 972-5241
Mail to: P.O. Box 1050, 77465
Private agency
Founded in: 1981
Colleen Claybourn, Chair
Number of members: 54
Staff: volunteer 5
Major programs: archives, oral history, book publishing, records management, research, audiovisual programs, photographic collections, genealogical services
Period of collections: 1900-present

PALO PINTO

Palo Pinto County Historical Association
(817) 659-3751
Mail to: P.O. Box 42, 76072
Private agency
Founded in: 1968
Anita Taylor Hall, President
Number of members: 140
Staff: volunteer 13
Major programs: museum, markers, tours/pilgrimages, school programs, historic preservation

PAMPA

White Deer Land Museum
116 S. Cuyler St.
Telephone: (806) 655-5521
Mail to: P.O. Box 1556, 79065
Founded in: 1970
Mrs. Fred Thompson, Curator
Staff: full time 2, volunteer 2
Major programs: museum, historic
 sites preservation, oral history,
 educational programs, historic
 preservation
Period of collections: late 1880s-early
 1900s

PANHANDLE

**Carson County Historical Survey
 Committee**
5th and Elsie, 79084
Telephone: (806) 537-3118
Mail to: P.O. Box 276, 79068
Founded in: 1965
P. J. Pronger III, Director
Staff: full time 3, part time 3,
 volunteer 145
Major programs: library, archives,
 manuscripts, museum, historic
 sites preservation, markers, oral
 history, educational programs,
 newsletters/pamphlets
Period of collections:
 prehistoric-present

**Carson County Square House
 Museum**
5th and Elsie, 79084
Telephone: (806) 537-3118
Mail to: P.O. Box 276, 79068
County agency
Founded in: 1965
P. J. Pronger III, Director
Staff: full time 3, part time 4,
 volunteer 45
Major programs: archives, museum,
 historic site(s), markers, oral
 history, school programs, book
 publishing, newsletters/pamphlets,
 historic preservation, research,
 exhibits, photographic collections
Period of collections: 19th century

PARIS

**A. M. and Welma Aikin, Jr.,
 Regional Archives**
Paris Junior College, 75460
Authorized by the college
Founded in: 1977
Daisy Harvill, Director/Archivist
Staff: full time 1, part time 1
Major programs: archives, museum,
 tours/pilgrimages, research,
 photographic collections
Period of collections: 18th century

**Sam Bell Maxey House State
 Historic Structure**
812 Church St., 75460
Telephone: (214) 785-5716
State agency, authorized by Texas
 Parks and Wildlife Department
Founded in: 1980
Robert A. Burns, Superintendent
Staff: full time 2, part time 2,
 volunteer 20
Major programs: library, archives,
 manuscripts, museum, historic
 site(s), markers, tours/pilgrimages,
 school programs, historic

preservation, research, exhibits,
 living history, photographic
 collections, genealogical services
Period of collections: 1861-1965

PASADENA

**Harris County Genealogical
 Society**
Mail to: P.O. Box 391, 77501
Founded in: 1973
Number of members: 134
Robert Zimmerer, President
Staff: volunteer 134
Magazine: *The Living Tree News*
Major programs: library, books,
 historic preservation, genealogy

PECOS

West of the Pecos Museum
1st and Cedar Sts. at Hwy. 285
Telephone: (915) 445-5076
Mail to: P.O. Box 1784, 79772
City agency
Founded in: 1962
Genora B. Prewit, Curator
Staff: full time 2, part time 2
Major programs: museum
Period of collections: 1880-1950

PHARR

Old Clock Museum
929 Preston St., 78577
Telephone: (512) 787-1923
Founded in: 1968
James P. Shawn, Owner
Staff: full time 2
Major programs: museum, old clocks
 and watches
Period of collections: 1690-1920

PLAINS

Toa Mo Ga Memorial Museum
P.O. Box 455, 79355
Telephone: (806) 456-4823
Private agency
Founded in: 1957
Staff: volunteer 4
Major programs: library, museum,
 historic site(s), markers,
 tours/pilgrimages, oral history,
 school programs, historic
 preservation, living history
Period of collections: 1897-present

PLAINVIEW

**Hale County Historical
 Commission**
8th and Quincy, 79072
Mail to: P.O. Box 1282
Founded in: 1971
Mrs. Harley Wells, Chairman
Number of members: 160
Magazine: *Hale County History*
Major programs: archives,
 manuscripts, museum, historic
 sites preservation, markers,
 tours/pilgrimages, junior history,
 oral history, educational programs,
 newsletters/pamphlets
Period of collections: 1865-1918

PLANO

**Heritage Farmstead/Plano Heritage
 Association**
1900 W. 15th St., 75075
Telephone: (214) 424-7874

Private agency
Founded in: 1975
Beth Francell, Executive Director
Number of members: 320
Staff: full time 1, part time 2,
 volunteer 50
Major programs: museum, historic
 site(s), research, audiovisual
 programs
Period of collections: 1891-1930

PLEASANTON

Longhorn Museum, Inc.
Hwy. 97, E.
Telephone: (512) 569-6313
Mail to: P.O. Box 601, 78064
City agency
Founded in: 1976
Ben L. Parker, Board President
Number of members: 30
Staff: full time 2, volunteer 4
Major programs: museum, oral
 history, exhibits, audiovisual
 programs
Period of collections: 1960-present

PORT LAVACA

**Calhoun County Historical
 Commission**
201 W. Austin
Telephone: (512) 552-6342
Mail to: P.O. Box 988, 77979
County agency
Founded in: 1965
Marion A. Rhodes, Museum Chair
Staff: part time 1
Major programs: museum, markers,
 historic preservation, photographic
 collections
Period of collections: 1854-present

POST

Garza Historical Museum
Mail to: 810 W. Main St., 79356
County agency
Founded in: 1959
Mrs. W. M. Kirkpatrick, President
Number of members: 75
Staff: part time 1
Major programs: oral history,
 newsletters/pamphlets, records
 management, exhibits,
 photographic collections
Period of collections: 1900-present

PYOTE

Rattlesnake Bomber Base Museum
11th and Ward Sts., 79777
Telephone: (915) 389-5548
Private agency
Founded in: 1976
Lenora Price, Curator
Staff: part time 1
Major programs: museum
Period of collections: 1907-present

QUITMAN

**Governor Hogg Shrine State
 Historical Park**
Rt. 3, Park Rd. 45, 75783
Telephone: (214) 763-2701
State agency, authorized by Texas
 Parks and Wildlife Department
Founded in: 1942
W. T. Phillips, Park Superintendent
Staff: full time 3, part time 5

Major programs: museum, historic
site(s), markers, tours/pilgrimages,
oral history, school programs,
pamphlets, historic preservation,
records management, research,
exhibits, audiovisual programs
Period of collections: 1869-1895

RANKIN

Rankin Museum Association
5th and Main Sts.
Mail to: P.O. Box 82, 79778
County agency
Founded in: 1974
Ann M. Clark, Trustee
Staff: part time 1, volunteer 4
Major programs: archives, museum,
oral history, exhibits, photographic
collections
Period of collections: 1910-present

REFUGIO

Refugio County Historical Society
102 W. West St., 78377
Telephone: (512) 526-5555
Private agency
Founded in: 1970
Joe Cavanaugh, Museum Curator
Number of members: 270
Staff: part time 1, volunteer 15
Major programs: museum, markers,
tours/pilgrimages, oral history,
school programs, research,
exhibits, audiovisual programs,
photographic collections
Period of collections: 19th-early 20th
centuries

RICHMOND

The Confederate Museum
602 Preston
Telephone: (409) 342-8787
Mail to: P.O. Box 179, 77469
Private agency
Founded in: 1978
Stewart Morris, President
Number of members: 131
Staff: part time 1, volunteer 15
Magazine: *The Confederate Museum*
Major programs: library, archives,
museum, historic site(s), school
programs, newsletters/pamphlets,
living history
Period of collections: Civil War

Ft. Bend County Museum
500 Houston St.
Telephone: (713) 342-6478
Mail to: P.O. Box 251, 77469
Private agency
Founded in: 1970
Michael Rugeley Moore, Director
Number of members: 692
Staff: full time 3, volunteer 130
Major programs: archives,
manuscripts, museum, historic
site(s), tours/pilgrimages, oral
history, school programs,
newsletters/pamphlets, exhibits,
living history, photographic
collections, genealogical services
Period of collections: 1822-1922

RIO GRANDE CITY

Starr County Historical Society
801 E. Main 78582
Questionnaire not received

RIVIERA

Riviera Historical Museum
7th and North Blvd., 78379
Telephone: (512) 296-3676
Founded in: 1983
Idella Strubhart, Chair
Number of members: 45
Staff: volunteer 3
Major programs: museum, historic
preservation, research, exhibits
Period of collections: from 1907

ROBERT LEE

**Coke County Historical
Commission**
13 E. 7th St.
Telephone: (915) 453-2922
Mail to: c/o Chair, P.O. Box 33,
Bronte, 76933
County agency
Brenda Hines, Chair
Major programs: museum, historic
preservation

ROSANKY

**Central Texas Museum of
Automotive History**
Hwy. 304, 78953
Telephone: (512) 237-2051
Private agency
Founded in: 1982
John F. Burdick, Curator
Staff: full time 1, volunteer 1
Major programs: museum,
automotive history
Period of collections: 1900-1970

ROSCOE

Roscoe Historical Society
79545
Founded in: 1980
Billy Joe Jay, Chair
Staff: volunteer 5
Major programs: archives, museum,
historic site(s), markers, school
programs, historic preservation,
exhibits, photographic collections,
genealogical services
Period of collections: 1890-1940

ROUND ROCK

**Williamson County Genealogical
Society**
3601 Arrowhead Circle
Telephone: (512) 255-7057
Mail to: P.O. Box 585, 78680
Private agency
Founded in: 1981
Hazel Talbot, President
Number of members: 150
Staff: volunteer 6
Magazine: *The Chisholm Trail*
Major programs: library, book
publishing
Period of collections: 1850-1910

ROUND TOP

Texas Pioneer Arts Association
P.O. Box 82, 77954
Telephone: (409) 249-3308
Private agency
Founded in: 1970
Barry A. Greenlaw, Curator of
Collections
Staff: full time 1, volunteer 4
Major programs: museum, historic

site(s), tours/pilgrimages, historic
preservation, research, exhibits,
photographic collections
Period of collections: 1840-1890

**University of Texas Winedale
Historical Center**
FM Rd. 2714
Mail to: P.O. Box 11, 78954
Founded in: 1967
Gloria Jaster, Administrator
Number of members: 275
Staff: full time 6, part time 13
Magazine: *The Quid Nunc*
Major programs: historic sites
preservation, educational
programs, historic preservation
Period of collections: 1850s

SAN ANGELO

Ft. Concho Museum
213 E. Ave. D, 76903
Telephone: (915) 655-9121, ext. 441
City agency
Founded in: 1928
John F. Vaughan, Director
Staff: full time 14, part time 6,
volunteer 125
Magazine: *Ft. Concho Report*
Major programs: library, museum,
historic site(s), tours/pilgrimages,
school programs, book publishing,
historic preservation, research,
exhibits, living history, archaeology
programs, photographic
collections
Period of collections: 1865-1900

**Tom Green County Historical
Society**
2401 Colorado, 76901
Telephone: (915) 949-2920
Founded in: 1944
Nonie Green, President
Number of members: 35
Staff: volunteer 7
Major programs: archives,
manuscripts, research,
photographic collections
Period of collections: 1870s-1920s

SAN ANTONIO

The Alamo
Alamo Plaza at Crockett, 78205
Telephone: (512) 225-1071
Mail to: P.O. Box 2599, 78299
Private agency, authorized by
Daughters of the Republic of Texas
Founded in: 1942
Sharon R. Crutchfield, Library
Director
Staff: full time 4, part time 3
Major programs: library, archives,
manuscripts
Period of collections: 1600-present

**Archives of the Mexican Baptist
Convention of Texas**
8019 Panama Expressway, S, 78224
Telephone: (512) 924-4338
Private agency
Founded in: 1968
Ernest E. Atkinson, Archivist
Major programs: archives,
manuscripts, oral history
Period of collections: from 1910

Ft. Sam Houston Military Museum
Bldg. 123, Fort Sam Houston, 78234
Telephone: (512) 221-6117

Federal agency, authorized by U.S.
Army
Founded in: 1967
John Manguso, Curator
Staff: full time 3
Major programs: museum, exhibits,
living history, audiovisual
programs, photographic
collections
Period of collections: 1845-present

History and Traditions Museum
Lackland Air Force Base,
AFMTC/LGHM, 78236
Telephone: (512) 671-3444
Federal agency, authorized by the
U.S. Air Force
Founded in: 1956
Gloria M. Livingston, Director/Curator
Staff: full time 2
Major programs: library, museum,
historic preservation, records
management, research, exhibits,
audiovisual programs,
photographic collections, aircraft
and aircraft components
Period of collections: World War II

Institute of Texan Cultures
Hemisfair Plaza
Telephone: (512) 226-7651
Mail to: P.O. Box 1226, 78294
State agency, authorized by the
University of Texas
Founded in: 1967
Jack R. Maguire, Executive Director
Staff: full time 95, part time 12,
volunteer 295
Magazine: *Texas People*
Major programs: library, archives,
museum, tours/pilgrimages, oral
history, school programs, book
publishing, newsletters/pamphlets,
research, exhibits, audiovisual
programs, photographic
collections, field services
Period of collections: 1715-present

**Jose Antonio Navarro State
Historic Site**
228 S. Laredo St., 78207
Telephone: (512) 226-4801
State agency, authorized by Texas
Parks and Wildlife Department
Founded in: 1962
David R. McDonald, Park
Superintendent
Staff: full time 2
Major programs: historic site(s),
historic preservation, research,
exhibits
Period of collections: 1850-1871

King William Association
222 King William, Suite 2, 78204
Telephone: (512) 227-8786
Private agency
Founded in: 1967
Jean Alexander-Williams, Office
Manager
Number of members: 475
Staff: part time 1, volunteer 16
Major programs: tours/pilgrimages,
newsletters/pamphlets, historic
preservation, photographic
collections

Monte Vista Historical Association
Laurel Hts. Substation
Telephone: (512) 735-5533

Mail to: P.O. Box 12386, 78212
Private agency
Founded in: 1973
Emily Thuss, President
Number of members: 500
Major programs: markers, historic
preservation
Period of collections: late 19th-early
20th centuries

**Old Trail Driver's Association and
Museum**
3805 Broadway
Telephone: (512) 822-9011
Founded in: 1915
Elton R. Cude, Director
Number of members: 2
Staff: part time 2
Major programs: historic preservation
Period of collections: 1800s-present

Pioneer Hall and Museum
3805 Broadway, 78209
Telephone: (512) 822-9011
Founded in: 1936
Ruby C. Probst, Curator/Custodian
Staff: part time 2
Major programs: museum, historic
preservation
Period of collections: 1800s-1900s

**Pioneers, Texas Trail Drivers, and
Former Texas Rangers**
3805 Broadway
Telephone: (512) 824-2537
Mail to: P.O. Box 6553, 78209
Private agency
Founded in: 1936
Glo Hensley Stuart, President
Number of members: 1,500
Staff: full time 2, volunteer 50
Major programs: museum, oral
history, newsletters/pamphlets,
historic preservation, exhibits,
photographic collections
Period of collections: 1823-present

San Antonio Conservation Society
107 King William St., 78204
Telephone: (512) 224-6163
Private agency
Founded in: 1924
Maria Watson-White, Administrative
Director
Number of members: 3,400
Staff: full time 13, part time 8,
volunteer 500
Magazine: *The San Antonio
Conservation Society Newsletter*
Major programs: library, archives,
museum, historic site(s), markers,
tours/pilgrimages, oral history,
school programs,
newsletters/pamphlets, historic
preservation, research, exhibits
Period of collections: Victorian
era-early Texas settlement

**San Antonio Missions National
Historical Park**
727 E. Durango, A-612, 78206
Telephone: (512) 229-6000
Federal agency, authorized by
National Park Service
Founded in: 1978
Jose A. Cisneros, Superintendent
Staff: full time 25, part time 8
Major programs: library, historic
site(s), oral history, historic
preservation,

San Antonio Museum Association
3801 Broadway, 78209
Telephone: (512) 226-5544
Mail to: P.O. Box 2601, 78299
Private agency
Founded in: 1926
Helmuth Naumer, Director
Number of members: 5,000
Staff: full time 81, part time 15
Major programs: library, archives,
manuscripts, museum, historic
site(s), tours/pilgrimages, school
programs, book publishing,
newsletters/pamphlets, historic
preservation, research, exhibits,
audiovisual programs, archaeology
programs, photographic
collections, science and natural
history
Period of collections:
prehistoric-present

Spanish Governor's Palace
105 Plaza De Armas, 78205
Telephone: (512) 224-0601
Founded in: 1749
Nora Ward, Museum Curator
Staff: full time 2, part time 1
Major programs: museum, historic
sites preservation, historic
preservation
Period of collections: 1749-1821

**State Association of Texas
Pioneers**
3805 Broadway
Telephone: (512) 822-9011
Mail to: 137 W. Mafield, 78221
State agency
Founded in: 1919
Erwin Marschall, President
Number of members: 200
Major programs: museum
Period of collections: early Texan
settlement

Texas Archeological Society
Center for Archaeological Research,
University of Texas, San Antonio,
78285
Telephone: (512) 691-4462
Private agency
Founded in: 1929
Shirley M. Van der Veer,
Administrative Secretary
Number of members: 1,200
Staff: part time 2
Magazine: *Bulletin of the Texas
Archeological Society*
Major programs: book publishing,
archaeology programs

Witte Museum
3801 Broadway, 78209
Telephone: (512) 226-5544
Mail to: P.O. Box 2601, 78299-2601
Private agency, authorized by San
Antonio Museum Association
Founded in: 1923
Helmuth J. Navmer, Executive
Director
Number of members: 5,000
Staff: full time 35, part time 1
Major programs: library, archives,
museum, tours/pilgrimages, school
programs, book publishing, historic
preservation, research, exhibits,
living history, audiovisual
programs, archaeology programs,

photographic collections
Period of collections:
   prehistoric-present

SAN MARCOS

The Heritage Association of San Marcos, Inc.
308 E. Hopkins St. 78666
Telephone: (512) 392-9997
Mail to: 20 Timbercrest
Founded in: 1975
Emmie Craddock, President
Number of members: 635
Staff: volunteer 400
Major programs: markers,
   tours/pilgrimages, books,
   newsletters/pamphlets, historic
   preservation

SANTA ANNA

Old Rock House
Hwy. 84
Telephone: (915) 348-3283
Mail to: P.O. Box 335, 76878
Private agency
Founded in: 1958
Mrs. C. D. Bruce, Curator
Staff: volunteer 1
Major programs: museum, historic
   preservation
Period of collections: 1880

SAN YGNACIO

La Paz Museum/Zapata County Historical Commission
A.L. Benavides Elementary School
Telephone: (512) 765-5611
Mail to: P.O. Box 219, 78067
County agency, authorized by Zapata
   County Historical Commission
Founded in: 1982
Victoria Uribe, Chair
Number of members: 32
Staff: volunteer 5
Major programs: library, museum
Period of collections: 1750-present

SARATOGA

Big Thicket Association
FM-770
Telephone: (409) 274-5000
Mail to: P.O. Box 198
Private agency
Founded in: 1964
L. M. Rodes, Chair
Number of members: 1,000
Staff: volunteer 20
Magazine: Big Thicket Bulletin
Major programs: library, museum,
   historic site(s), tours/pilgrimages,
   school programs, book publishing,
   newsletters/pamphlets, historic
   preservation, exhibits, field
   services
Period of collections: 1890-1940

SEABROOK

Bay Area Museum
Clear Lake Park, NASA Rd I
Telephone: (713) 538-1254
Mail to: P.O. Box 642, 77586
Private agency, authorized by Lunar
   Rendezvous Festival
Founded in: 1981
Lynn Miller, Director

Number of members: 200
Major programs: museum, school
   programs, exhibits

Clear Lake Area Heritage Society
P.O. Box 24, 77586
Telephone: (713) 486-2200
County agency
Founded in: 1982
Bill Odell, President
Number of members: 103
Staff: volunteer 14
Major programs: library, archives,
   manuscripts, museum, historic
   site(s), markers, tours/pilgrimages,
   oral history, school programs,
   newsletters/pamphlets, historic
   preservation, research,
   photographic collections
Period of collections: 1960s-present

SEGUIN

The Seguin Conservation Society
Live Oak and S. River Sts. 78155
Telephone: (512) 379-4277
Mail to: 425 N. River St.
Questionnaire not received

SEYMOUR

Baylor County Historical Museum
200 W. McLain St.
Mail to: Rt. 2, Box 48, 76380
County agency, authorized by Baylor
   County Historical Society
Founded in: 1977
Patsy S. Cooper, Chair
Staff: volunteer 5
Major programs: museum, historic
   site(s), markers
Period of collections: 1890-1970

SHERMAN

Grayson County Historical Society
Telephone: (214) 892-6337
Mail to: Box 2032, 75090
Founded in: 1966
Joseph Dornstadter, President
Number of members: 45

Sherman Historical Museum
301 S. Walnut St., 75090
Telephone: (214) 893-7623
Town agency
Founded in: 1976
Dorothy L. Harrington, Director
Number of members: 150
Staff: part time 1, volunteer 20
Major programs: archives, museum,
   tours/pilgrimages, school
   programs, newsletters/pamphlets,
   historic preservation, research,
   exhibits, audiovisual programs,
   archaeology programs,
   photographic collections,
   genealogical services
Period of collections: 1850s-1940s

SHEFFIELD

Ft. Lancaster State Historic Site
P.O. Box 306, 79781
Telephone: (915) 836-4391
State agency, authorized by Texas
   Parks and Wildlife Department
Founded in: 1968
William S. Armstrong, Park
   Superintendent
Staff: full time 2

Major programs: museum, historic
   site(s), historic preservation,
   exhibits
Period of collections: 1850s-1860s

SHINER

Edwin Wolters Museum
306 S. Avenue I
Telephone: (512) 594-3887
Mail to: P.O. Box 161, 77984
Town agency
Willie Hagendorf, Custodian
Number of members: part time 1
Major programs: museum, historic
   preservation, exhibits, living history

SLATON

Slaton Museum Association
155 N. 8th, 79364
Mail to: P.O. Box 555
Founded in: 1976
Almarine Childers, President
Number of members: 150
Staff: full time 1, volunteer 12
Major programs: museum
Period of collections: 1918-present

SNYDER

Scurry County Museum
Western Texas College Campus
Telephone: (915) 573-6107
Mail to: P.O. Box 696, 79549
County agency
Founded in: 1974
Shirley Leftwich, Museum Director
Number of members: 151
Staff: full time 1, part time 2,
   volunteer 22
Magazine: Scurry Spokesman
Major programs: archives, museum,
   markers, oral history, school
   programs, historic preservation,
   exhibits
Period of collections: 18th
   century-present

SPEARMAN

Stationmasters' House Museum
30 S. Townsend, 79081
Telephone: (806) 659-3008
Authorized by Hansford County
   Historical Commission
Founded in: 1974
Helen Boyd, President
Staff: volunteer 16
Major programs: museum, historic
   site(s), markers, tours/pilgrimages,
   oral history, book publishing,
   historic preservation, records
   management, exhibits, living
   history, archaeology programs,
   photographic collections, field
   services

STAMFORD

Cowboy Country Museum
113 Wetherbee
Telephone: (915) 773-2411
Mail to: P.O. Box 1206, 79553
City agency
Founded in: 1975
Ike Hudson, Curator
Staff: volunteer 2
Major programs: museum, exhibits
Period of collections: early 1900

STANTON

Martin County Historical Museum
207 Broadway
Mail to: P.O. Box 929, 79782
Ruby Payne, Director/Curator
Number of members: 500
Staff: full time 2, volunteer 3
Major programs: museum,
newsletters/pamphlets, exhibits

STEPHENVILLE

**Stephenville Historical House
Museum**
525 E. Washington, 76401
Telephone: (817) 965-5880
City agency
Founded in: 1967
C. Richard King, Board President
Staff: full time 2, volunteer 12
Major programs: museum, historic
site(s), historic preservation,
exhibits, photographic collections
Period of collections: 1854-1940

STRATFORD

Sherman County Historical Society
17 N. Main
Mail to: P.O. Box 1248, 79804
County agency
Founded in: 1972
Marillyn Albert, President
Staff: volunteer 4
Major programs: museum, exhibits
Period of collections: 1886-present

SUGAR LAND

Sugar Land Heritage Society
302 Oyster Creek
Telephone: (713) 494-3485
Mail to: P.O. Box 471, 77478
Private agency
Founded in: 1982
Jane McMeans, President
Number of members: 150
Staff: volunteer 5
Major programs: school programs,
book publishing,
newsletters/pamphlets, historic
preservation, research,
photographic collections
Period of collections: 1928-present

SULPHUR SPRINGS

**Hopkins County Museum and
Heritage Park**
416 N. Jackson St.
Telephone: (214) 885-2387/885-5424
Mail to: 1200 Carter, 75482
County agency, authorized by
Hopkins County Historical Society
Founded in: 1976
Jeff Campbell, President
Number of members: 20
Staff: volunteer 20
Major programs: manuscripts,
museum, historic site(s), markers,
tours/pilgrimages, school
programs, book publishing, historic
preservation, exhibits, living
history, photographic collections,
genealogical services
Period of collections: 1836-present

SWEETWATER

Pioneer City County Museum
610 E. 3rd St., 79556
County agency
Founded in: 1968
Elizabeth Pepper, Manager
Staff: part time 2, volunteer 20
Major programs: museum,
tours/pilgrimages, book publishing,
historic preservation
Period of collections: early 1900s

TAYLOR

Moody Museum
114 W. 9th St.
Mail to: P.O. Box 765, 76574
City agency
Founded in: 1975
Ruby Neubauer, Vice
President/Curator
Staff: volunteer 4
Major programs: museum, historic
site(s), exhibits
Period of collections: 1876-present

**Taylor Conservation and Heritage
Society**
Telephone: (512) 352-7230
Mail to: P.O. Box 385, 76574
Private agency
Founded in: 1979
Mrs. Keith Schulz, President
Number of members: 150
Staff: volunteer 25
Major programs: library, archives,
historic site(s), tours/pilgrimages,
school programs,
newsletters/pamphlets, historic
preservation
Period of collections: 1876-present

TEAGUE

**Burlington-Rock Island Railroad
Museum**
208 S. 3rd Ave.
Telephone: (817) 739-2645
Mail to: 108 S. 9th Ave., 75860
City agency, authorized by B-RI
Railroad Museum Association
Founded in: 1969
Dorothy McVey, Curator
Staff: volunteer 18
Major programs: museum, historic
site(s), tours/pilgrimages, historic
preservation, exhibits,
photographic collections,
genealogical services
Period of collections: 1906-present

TEMPLE

Railroad and Pioneer Museum, Inc.
710 Jack Baskin St.
Telephone: (817) 778-6873
Mail to: P.O. Box 5126, 76501
Private agency
Founded in: 1966
Mary Pat McLaughlin, Director
Number of members: 140
Staff: full time 2, part time 1,
volunteer 1
Major programs: museum,
educational programs
Period of collections: 1881-1920

TERRELL

Silent Wings Museum
Municipal Airport, 75160
Telephone: (214) 368-6097
Mail to: 7038 Northaurn Rd., Dallas,
75230
Private agency, authorized by Military
Glider Pilots Association, Inc.
Founded in: 1980
William K. Horn, Director
Number of members: 1,500
Staff: volunteer 20
Magazine: *Silent Wings*
Major programs: museum, oral
history, historic preservation,
exhibits
Period of collections: W.W. II

TERLINGUA/LAJITAS

Lajitas Museum and Desert Garden
Star Rt. 70, Box 375, 79852
Telephone: (915) 424-3267
Private agency, authorized by Lajitas
Foundation
Founded in: 1983
Ray H. Duncan, Director
Number of members: 875
Staff: full time 7, part time 1,
volunteer 3
Major programs: library, museum,
tours/pilgrimages, oral history,
exhibits, photographic collections,
botanical gardens
Period of collections: 1900-1940

TEXARKANA

**Texarkana Historical Society and
Museum**
219 State Line Ave.
Telephone: (214) 793-4831
Mail to: P.O. Box 2343, 75501
Private agency
Founded in: 1970
Katy Caver, Director/Curator
Number of members: 1,000
Staff: full time 2, part time 2,
volunteer 49
Major programs: library, museum,
oral history, educational programs,
newsletters/pamphlets
Period of collections: 1865-1918

TEXAS CITY

Texas City Heritage Association
Telephone: (713) 948-3411
Mail to: P.O. Box 2091, 77590
Founded in: 1972
Mary J. Cain, President
Number of members: 200
Staff: volunteer 25
Major programs: archives, historic
sites preservation, markers,
tours/pilgrimages, junior history,
newsletters/pamphlets
Period of collections: 1895-present

TOMBALL

Chaparral Genealogical Society
P.O. Box 606, 77375
Founded in: 1972
Audra Gray, President
Number of members: 150
Staff: volunteer 15
Magazine: *Roadrunner*

Major programs: library, educational
programs, books, genealogy
Period of collections: 1600-present

TYLER

Smith County Historical Society and Historical Commission
624 N. Broadway, 75702
Telephone: (214) 597-5304
Founded in: 1959
D. M. Edwards, President/Chair
Number of members: 350
Major programs: library, archives,
manuscripts, museum, markers,
book publishing,
newsletters/pamphlets, historic
preservation, research, exhibits,
photographic collections
Period of collections: 1846-present

UVALDE

Caddel-Smith Chapter, Daughters of the Republic of Texas
Mail to: Mrs. Roger Garrison, Box
206, 78884
Founded in: 1891
Wilma Russell, President
Number of members: 64
Staff: volunteer 7
Major programs: manuscripts, oral
history, historic preservation,
records management, research,
photographic collections
Period of collections: 1836-1846

John Nance Garner Home and Museum
333 N. Park
Telephone: (512) 278-5018
Mail to: P.O. Box 799, 78801
City agency
Founded in: 1951
James Thurmond, City Manager
Staff: full time 2, part time 1
Major programs: museum, historic
site(s), photographic collections
Period of collections: 1880-1950

Uvalde County Historical Commission
141 Bluebonnet, S. 78801
Telephone: (512) 278-2193
County agency
Nancy Horner Feely, Chair
Number of members: 40
Staff: volunteer 8
Major programs: library, archives,
museum, historic site(s), markers,
tours/pilgrimages, junior history,
oral history, historic preservation,
research, archaeology programs,
photographic collections,
genealogical services
Period of collections: 1856-1920

VALLEY MILLS

Valley Mills History Museum
5th St. and Ave. E
Telephone: (817) 932-5277
Mail to: P.O. Box 168, 76689
Private agency, authorized by
Bosque Valley Heritage Society
Founded in: 1968
Mrs. Howard W. Johnson, Treasurer
Number of members: 100
Major programs: archives, museum,
oral history, exhibits
Period of collections: 1850-1929

VAN ALSTYNE

Van Alstyne Historical Society
216 E. Jefferson, 75095
Telephone: (214) 482-5426
Mail to: P.O. Box 638
Founded in: 1973
Robert E. B. Fielder, President
Number of members: 47
Staff: volunteer 5
Major programs: library, museum,
markers, oral history, educational
programs, newsletters/pamphlets
Period of collections: early
1800s-present

VICTORIA

Victoria County Historical Commission
210 E. Forrest, 77901
Telephone: (512) 575-5210
County agency
Founded in: 1962
Number of members: 33
Major programs: library, archives,
museum, markers,
tours/pilgrimages, historic
preservation, research, exhibits,
genealogical services
Period of collections: 1824-1900

Victoria Regional Museum Association, Inc./McNamara House Museum
502 N. Liberty
Telephone: (512) 512-8227
Mail to: 306 W. Commercial, 77901
Private agency
Founded in: 1960
Jim Edwards, Executive Director
Number of members: 450
Staff: full time 3, part time 5,
volunteer 25
Major programs: museum, historic
site(s), school programs, exhibits
Period of collections: 1860-1910

VIOLET

Violet Museum
Hwy. 44
Telephone: (512) 387-2273
Mail to: Rt. 3, Box 152, 78380
Private agency, authorized by Violet
Historical Society
Founded in: 1973
David L. Kircher, Curator
Number of members: 110
Staff: volunteer 5
Major programs: archives, museum,
historic site(s), markers,
tours/pilgrimages, historic
preservation, research, audiovisual
programs, photographic
collections
Period of collections: early 1900s

WACO

Baylor University Institute for Oral History
B03 Tidwell Bldg.
Telephone: (817) 755-3437
Mail to: C5B Box 401, 76798
Private agency, authorized by Baylor
University
Founded in: 1970
Thomas L. Charlton, Director

Staff: full time 4, part time 9
Major programs: oral history,
newsletters/pamphlets
Period of collections: 20th century

Earle-Harrison House
1901 N. 5th St., 76708
Telephone: (817) 753-2032
Private agency, authorized by G. H.
Pape Foundation
Founded in: 1960
Foy DuBois, Executive
Director/Curator
Staff: full time 4
Major programs: museum, historic
site(s), tours/pilgrimages, book
publishing, historic preservation
Period of collections:
Antebellum-Victorian eras

Historic Waco Foundation
407 Columbus Ave. 76701
Telephone: (817) 753-5166
Mail to: P.O. Box 3222, 76707
Private agency
Founded in: 1967
Paul Easley, President
Number of members: 1,135
Staff: full time 1, part time 1,
volunteer 3
Magazine: *Waco Heritage and
History*
Major programs: museum,
tours/pilgrimages, book publishing,
newsletters/pamphlets, historic
preservation
Period of collections: 19th century

Strecker Museum
Baylor University, 76798
Telephone: (817) 755-1110
Private agency, authorized by the
university
Founded in: 1893
Calvin B. Smith, Director
Staff: full time 6, part time 1,
volunteer 20
Major programs: library, museum,
tours/pilgrimages, school
programs, newsletters/pamphlets,
historic preservation, records
management, research, exhibits,
audiovisual programs, archaeology
programs, photographic
collections, field services, science
classes for children
Period of collections: 19th century

Texas Old Missions and Forts Association
524 N. 22 St., 76707
Telephone: (817) 753-7503
Founded in: 1962
William Hicks, President
Number of members: 125
Staff: volunteer 10
Magazine: *El Campanaro*
Major programs: historic sites
preservation,
newsletters/pamphlets, historic
preservation

Texas Oral History Association
C5B Box 401, 76798
Telephone: (917) 755-3437
Private agency
Founded in: 1982
Rebecca S. Jiminez,
Secretary/Treasurer
Number of members: 118

Major programs: oral history,
newsletters/pamphlets, field
services

**Texas Tennis Museum and Hall of
Fame/Texas Sports Hall of
Champions**
1401 Jefferson
Telephone: (817) 756-2307
Mail to: P.O. Box 3495, 76707
Private agency, authorized by Texas
Tennis Association
Foundation, Inc.
Founded in: 1981
Charles R. McCleary, Director
Staff: part time 2
Major programs: museum,
preservation of state's sports
Period of collections: 1900-present

WALLISVILLE

Wallisville Heritage Park
Hwy. I-10
Telephone: (409) 389-2252
Mail to: P.O. Box 16, 77597
Private agency
Founded in: 1979
Kevin Ladd, Director
Number of members: 150
Staff: full time 2, volunteer 4
Magazine: *The Age*
Major programs: library, archives,
manuscripts, museum, historic
site(s), markers, tours/pilgrimages,
junior history, oral history, school
programs, book publishing,
newsletters/pamphlets, historic
preservation, research,
archaeology programs,
photographic collections,
genealogical services
Period of collections:
prehistoric-present

WASHINGTON

Star of the Republic Museum
Washington-on-the-Brazos State
Historical Park
Telephone: (713) 878-2461
Mail to: P.O. Box 317, 77880
State agency, authorized by Blinn
College
Founded in: 1970
D. Ryan Smith, Director
Staff: full time 6, part time 3
Major programs: library, museum,
educational programs
Period of collections: 1820-1850

**Washington-on-the-Brazos State
Historical Park**
P.O. Box 305, 77880
Telephone: (409) 878-2214
State agency, authorized by Texas
Parks and Wildlife Department
Founded in: 1917
Tom Scaggs, Park Superintendent
Staff: full time 4, part time 3
Major programs: historic site(s),
school programs, historic
preservation, audiovisual programs
Period of collections: 1830-1860

WAXAHACHIE

Ellis County Museum, Inc.
201 S. College St.
Telephone: (214) 937-9283

Mail to: P.O. Box 706, 75165
Founded in: 1968
Josephine Ruskin, Curator
Number of members: 468
Staff: full time 1, part time 5,
volunteer 1
Major programs: museum,
tours/pilgrimages
Period of collections: 1850-present

WEATHERFORD

**Parker County Genealogical
Society**
1214 Charles, 76086
Telephone: (817) 594-2767
Founded in: 1969
Evlyn Broumley, Editor/Librarian
Number of members: 225
Staff: part time 1
Magazine: *Trails West*
Major programs: library, archives
Period of collections: 1856-present

WELLINGTON

**Collingsworth County Historical
Commission**
1307 Bowie, 79095
Telephone: (806) 447-5496
Mail to: P.O. Box 169
Founded in: 1960
Mrs. Clyde Drake, Chairman
Staff: volunteer 12
Major programs: manuscripts,
museum, markers, oral history,
newsletters/pamphlets
Period of collections: 1865-present

WEST COLUMBIA

Varner-Nogg State Historical Park
1702 N. 17th St.
Telephone: (409) 345-4656
Mail to: P.O. Box 696, 77486
State agency, authorized by Texas
Parks and Wildlife Department
Founded in: 1958
Joe Cariker, Park Superintendent
Staff: full time 6, part time 5
Period of collections: 1835-1850

WHARTON

**Wharton County Historical
Museum and Association**
231 S. Fulton
Telephone: (713) 532-2600
Mail to: P.O. Box 349, 77488
Private agency
Founded in: 1976
Eve Bartlett, Museum Director
Number of members: 300
Staff: part time 1, volunteer 3
Major programs: archives, museum,
educational programs, photo
preservation
Period of collections: 1830-1930

WHEELER

Old Mageetie Association
700 Alan Bean
Telephone: (806) 826-3289
Mail to: P.O. Box 189, 79096
Sallie B. Harris, President
Major programs: oral history, school
programs, historic preservation,
exhibits

WHITEFACE

Whiteface Historical Society
210 2nd St., 79379
Telephone: (806) 287-1132
Town agency
Founded in: 1980
Mrs. Marvin Lasiter, President
Number of members: 21
Staff: volunteer 7
Major programs: museum, historic
preservation, exhibits
Period of collections: 1900-1960

WHITE SETTLEMENT

White Settlement Historical Society
214 Meadow Park Rd., 76108
Telephone: (817) 246-4971
Private agency
Founded in: 1975
Mrs. John M. Waggoman, President
Number of members: 58
Staff: volunteer 10
Major programs: archives, historic
site(s), markers, tours/pilgrimages,
historic preservation, research,
genealogical services

WICHITA FALLS

Wichita County Heritage Society
900 Bluff, 76301
Telephone: (817) 723-0623
Private agency
Founded in: 1974
Kerry Jelley, Administrator
Number of members: 300
Staff: volunteer 20
Magazine: *The Heritage Review*
Major programs: historic site(s), book
publishing, newsletters/pamphlets
Period of collections: 1909-1940

**Wichita Falls Museum and Art
Center**
2 Eureka Circle, 76308
Telephone: (817) 692-0923
Founded in: 1967
Peter S. Lapaglia, Director
Number of members: 1,100
Staff: full time 12, part time 4,
volunteer 50
Major programs: library, archives,
museum, tours/pilgrimages, school
programs, newsletters/pamphlets,
research, exhibits, photographic
collections
Period of collections: 19th-20th
centuries

WIMBERLEY

Pioneer Town
Rt. 1 Box 259, 78676
Telephone: (512) 847-2517
Founded in: 1956
Raymond L. Czichas, President
Staff: full time 2, part time 2
Magazine: *Pioneer Gazette*
Major programs: museum, historic
preservation
Period of collections: 1860-1900

WINTERS

Z. I. Hale Museum
242 W. Dole St.
Mail to: P.O. Box 42, 79567
Town agency
Founded in: 1979

Edna England, President
Number of members: 125
Staff: volunteer 25
Major programs: museum, school
programs, historic preservation,
records management, research,
exhibits, archaeology programs,
photographic collections
Period of collections: early 1900s

YOAKUM

Yoakum Heritage Museum
215 Nelson
Telephone: (512) 293-6473
Mail to: P.O. Box 2, 77995
City agency
Founded in: 1982
Shirley Blundell, President/Curator
Number of members: 128
Staff: volunteer 17
Major programs: museum, oral
history, school programs, exhibits
Period of collections: 1880-1940

YORKTOWN

Yorktown Historical Society
144 W. Main St., 78164
Telephone: (512) 564-2661
Mail to: P.O. Box 884
Founded in: 1965
Kurt Hartmann, President
Number of members: 51
Staff: part time 1, volunteer 7
Major programs: museum, historic
sites preservation
Period of collections: 1852-1920

UTAH

ALTA

Alta Historical Society
84070
Founded in: 1969
Dale K. Gilson, Historian
Number of members: 40
Staff: volunteer 3
Major programs: archives, historic
sites preservation, markers,
newsletters/pamphlets
Period of collections: 1865-1918

BEAVER

Old Court House Museum
190 E. Center St., 84713
State agency, authorized by
Daughters of Utah Pioneers
Beatrice Hurst, Chair
Major programs: museum, historic
preservation
Period of collections: 1856-1976

BLANDING

Edge of the Cedars State Park
660 W. 400, N
Telephone: (801) 678-2238
Mail to: P.O. Box 788, 84511
State agency, authorized by State
Parks and Recreation
Founded in: 1978
Stephen J. Olsen, Park Manager

Staff: full time 4, part time 1,
volunteer 2
Major programs: library, museum,
historic site(s), exhibits,
audiovisual programs, archaeology
programs
Period of collections: A.D. 1-A.D. 1300
Huck's Museum and Trading Post
1387 S. Hwy. 191 and 79-1, 84511
Telephone: (801) 678-2329
Private agency
Founded in: 1976
Hugh Acton, Partner
Staff: 2
Period of collections: A.D. 700-A.D.
1300

BOULDER

**Anasazi Indian Village State
Historical Monument**
P.O. Box 393, 84716
Telephone: (801) 335-7308
State agency, authorized by Division
of Parks and Recreation
Founded in: 1970
Larry D. Davis, Park Manager
Staff: full time 2, part time 2
Major programs: museum, historic
preservation, exhibits, archaeology
programs
Period of collections: A.D. 1050-A.D.
1200

BRIGHAM CITY

Golden Spike National Historic Site
P.O. Box W, Promontory Summit,
84302
Telephone: (801) 471-2209
Federal agency, authorized by
National Park Service
Founded in: 1965
Staff: full time 11, part time 8,
volunteer 15
Major programs: library, archives,
museum, historic site(s), markers,
tours/pilgrimages, junior history,
school programs, research,
exhibits, living history, audiovisual
programs, photographic
collections
Period of collections: 1860-1942

**South Box Elder Daughters of Utah
Pioneers**
566 N. 1st St., E, 84302
Telephone: (801) 723-3819
Private agency, authorized by
National Daughters of the Utah
Pioneers
Founded in: 1915
Elizabeth P. Tingey, President
Number of members: 375
Staff: full time 200
Major programs: manuscripts,
museum, historic site(s), markers,
historic preservation, exhibits
Period of collections: 1847

CASTLE DALE

Emery County Historical Society
P.O. Box 862, 84513
Telephone: (801) 381-2428
County agency
Founded in: 1978
Sylvia H. Nelson, Secretary/Treasurer
Number of members: 15
Staff: full time 4

Emery County Museum
Telephone: (801) 748-2444
Mail to: P.O. Box 357, 84513
Dixon Peacock, President
Number of members: 69
Staff: full time 2, volunteer 3
Major programs: museum
Period of collections: 1865-1918
Questionnaire not received

CEDAR CITY

Iron County Historical Society
Southern Utah State College, 84720
Telephone: (801) 586-4411, ext. 358
Private agency
Founded in: 1963
Steven H. Heath, President
Number of members: 45
Staff: volunteer 11
Major programs: historic site(s), oral
history, historic preservation,
research, audiovisual programs
Period of collections: 1851-present
**Iron Mission State Historical
Monument**
585 N. Main, 84720
Telephone: (801) 586-9290
Mail to: P.O. Box 1079
Founded in: 1973
Norman L. Forbush, Superintendent
Staff: full time 4
Period of collections: 1865-1918
**Special Collections Library,
Southern Utah State College**
351 W. Center St., 84720
Authorized by the college
Mary Jane Cedar Face, Special
Collections Coordinator
Staff: full time 1, part time 4
Major programs: library, archives,
manuscripts, museum, oral history,
newsletters/pamphlets, historic
preservation, records
management, research, exhibits,
photographic collections
Period of collections: 1850-present

CENTERVILLE

Centerville Historical Society
383 E. 300, S
Telephone: 295-2742
Mail to: P.O. Box 578, 84014
Town agency
Founded in: 1982
Alzina H. Barton, President
Number of members: 45
Staff: full time 10
Major programs: library, archives,
manuscripts, museum, historic
site(s), oral history, school
programs, book publishing,
newsletters/pamphlets, historic
preservation, living history,
photographic collections,
genealogical services

DRAPER

Draper Historical Society
12441 S. 900, E, 84020
Private agency
Founded in: 1981
Erva A. Smith, President
Number of members: 30
Staff: volunteer 15

Major programs: library, museum, historic site(s), tours/pilgrimages, historic preservation, photographic collections, public lectures
Period of collections: 1850-1950

DUTCH JOHN

Daggett County Historical Society
Mail to: P.O. Box 428, 84023
Founded in: 1970
Eleen T. Williams, Historian
Number of members: 10
Staff: volunteer 5
Major programs: library, historic sites preservation, markers, tours/pilgrimages, oral history, educational programs, books
Period of collections: 1865-present

FAIRVIEW

Fairview Museum of History and Art
85 N. 100, E, 84629
Telephone: (801) 427-3767
County agency
Founded in: 1966
G. G. Sanderson, Director
Staff: full time 1, part time 1, volunteer 2
Major programs: museum, historic site(s), tours/pilgrimages, oral history, school programs, historic preservation, exhibits
Period of collections: 1856-1950

FARMINGTON

Pioneer Village
375 N. Hwy. 91
Telephone: (801) 451-0101
Mail to: P.O. Box "N", 84025
Private agency
Founded in: 1976
Howard Freed, Curator
Staff: full time 2, part time 30

Major programs: museum, oral history, school programs, historic preservation, exhibits, living history
Period of collections: to 1860

FORT DOUGLAS

Ft. Douglas Military Museum
Potter St., Bldg. 32, 84113
Telephone: (801) 524-4154
Federal agency, authorized by the U.S. Army
Founded in: 1976
Don De Vere, Curator
Major programs: library, museum, exhibits
Period of collections: 1862-Vietnam

HELPER

Helper Mining Museum-Archives
P.O. Box 221, 84526
Telephone: (801) 472-8463
City agency, authorized by Helper City Municipal Corporation
Founded in: 1963
Frances Cunningham, Curator/County Historian
Staff: part time 1, volunteer 2
Major programs: library, archives, museum, historic site(s), tours/pilgrimages, junior history, oral history, school programs, newsletters/pamphlets, historic preservation, records management, research, exhibits, audiovisual programs, photographic collections, genealogical services
Period of collections: 1875-present

HYRUM

Hyrum City Museum
3 S. Center
Telephone: 245-6850
Mail to: 42 W. 3, S, 84319
City agency
Founded in: 1978

Willis McBride, Museum Director
Staff: volunteer 2
Major programs: museum, historic preservation, exhibits, photographic collections, geology
Period of collections: early 1900s

KAMAS

Rhoades Valley Camp, Daughters of Utah Pioneers
84036
Private agency, authorized by Daughter of Utah Pioneers
Number of members: 24
Staff: volunteer 7
Major programs: manuscripts, markers, tours/pilgrimages, oral history
Period of collections: 1800s

LOGAN

Cache Valley Historical Society
c/o President, 290 W. Center St., 84321
City/County agency
Ray Somers, President
Number of members: 25

Man and His Bread Museum
R. V. Jensen Living Historical Farm, Utah State University, 84321
Telephone: (801) 750-2697, 245-4064
Founded in: 1970
Robb Russon, Director
Staff: full time 3, part time 10
Major programs: museum, junior history, educational programs
Period of collections: 1840-1950

MOAB

Canyonlands Natural History Association
446 S. Main, 84532
Telephone: (801) 259-8161
Private agency
Founded in: 1967
Eleanor Inskip, Executive Director
Number of members: 100
Staff: full time 1, part time 3
Major programs: library, books, newsletters/pamphlets, historic preservation, geology, botany, biology
Period of collections: A.D. 1200-present

Moab Museum
118 E. Center St., 84532
Telephone: (801) 259-7430
County agency
Founded in: 1960
Lloyd Pierson, Curator
Number of members: 200
Staff: full time 1, volunteer 4
Major programs: museum
Period of collections: 1900-1950

OGDEN

Union Station Museums
2501 Wall Ave., 84401
Telephone: (801) 399-8582
City agency
Founded in: 1975
Teddy Griffith, Executive Director
Number of members: 300
Staff: full time 8, part time 2, volunteer 150

The Pioneer Village Carriage Hall exhibits horse-drawn carriages used in the late 1800s.—Lagoon Pioneer Village, Farmington, Utah

Magazine: *The Inside Track*
Major programs: archives, museum, historic site(s), tours/pilgrimages, junior history, oral history, school programs, newsletters/pamphlets, historic preservation, exhibits, audiovisual programs, photographic collections
Period of collections: 1850-1950

U.S. Air Force in Utah Historical Society
Directorate of Material Management, Hill Air Force Base, 84056
Telephone: (801) 777-5076
Federal agency, authorized by Hill Air Force Base
Founded in: 1983
John Barton, Director
Number of members: 1,000
Staff: volunteer 9
Magazine: *Top of the Hill*
Major programs: museum, newsletters/pamphlets, historic preservation, research, exhibits
Period of collections: 1930-present

U.S. Forest Service, Intermountain Region
324 25th St., 84401
Telephone: (801) 625-5167
Federal agency, authorized by U.S. Department of Agriculture
Founded in: 1908
Phil Johnson, Forest Service Regional History Coordinator
Staff: part time 1
Major programs: archives, historic sites preservation, markers, tours/pilgrimages, oral history
Period of collections: 1900-present

PARK CITY

Park City Historical Society
P.O. Box 668, 84060
Private agency
Raye C. Ringholz, President
Number of members: 120
Major programs: archives, museum, oral history, photographic collections
Period of collections: 1880-present

Park City Museum
528 Main St.
Telephone: (801) 649-9461
Mail to: P.O. Box 555, 84060
City agency, authorized by Park City Historical Society
Founded in: 1984
Lynn Anderson, Director
Number of members: 150
Staff: volunteer 5
Major programs: museum, oral history, school programs, historic preservation, research, exhibits, photographic collections
Period of collections: 1860-present

PRICE

Carbon County Historical Society
P.O. Box 804, E. Carbon City, 84520
Telephone: (801) 888-3355
Private agency
Founded in: 1978
Gordon Parker, President
Number of members: 50
Staff: part time 1, volunteer 6

Magazine: *Carbon City Journal*
Major programs: archives, manuscripts, museum, junior history, school programs, historic preservation, research, genealogical services
Period of collections: 1900-1980

PROVO

Harold B. Lee Library, Brigham Young University
84602
Telephone: (801) 378-6197
Private agency, authorized by Church of Jesus Christ of Latter-day Saints
Founded in: 1875
K. Haybron Adams, Local History Librarian
Staff: full time 150, part time 350
Major programs: library, archives, manuscripts, oral history, newsletters/pamphlets, research, photographic collections, genealogical services
Period of collections: 1500s-present

Mormon History Association
123 Joseph Smith Bldg., Brigham Young University
Mail to: University Station, Box 7010, 84602
Private agency
Founded in: 1965
Jessie L. Embry, Executive Secretary
Number of members: 900
Staff: volunteer 4
Magazine: *Journal of Mormon History*
Period of collections: 1820-present

Museum of Peoples and Cultures
710 N. 100, E
Telephone: (801) 378-6112
Mail to: Brigham Young University Room 700 SWKT, 84602
Private agency, authorized by the university
Founded in: 1875
Joel C. Janetski, Director
Staff: full time 1, part time 5
Major programs: records management, research, archaeology programs
Period of collections: prehistoric-A.D.

SALT LAKE CITY

Association of Utah Historians
300 Rio Grande, 84101
Telephone: (801) 533-5755
Private agency
Founded in: 1981
Craig Fuller, Executive Secretary
Number of members: 35
Staff: volunteer 8
Major programs: umbrella organization for lobbying and general improvement of historical interests

Fort Douglas Military Museum
Bldg. 32, Potter St., Fort Douglas, 84113
Telephone: (801) 524-4154
Founded in: 1976
Don De Vere, Curator
Staff: full time 1
Major programs: museum
Period of collections: 1862-present

Genealogical Library, Church of Jesus Christ of Latter-day Saints
50 E. North Temple St., 84150
Telephone: (801) 531-2331
Private agency
Founded in: 1894
David M. Mayfield, Director
Staff: full time 197, part time 26, volunteer 400
Major programs: library, archives, books, genealogical services
Period of collections: 1500-1900

Historical Department, Church of Jesus Christ of Latter-day Saints
50 E. North Temple St., 84150
Telephone: (801) 531-2786
Private agency, authorized by Church of Jesus Christ of Latter-day Saints
Founded in: 1830
Earl E. Olson, Assistant Managing Director
Staff: full time 86, part time 2, volunteer 209
Major programs: library, archives, manuscripts, museum, historic site(s), markers, oral history, historic preservation, research, exhibits, audiovisual programs, photographic collections
Period of collections: 1830-present

Museum of Church History and Art
45 N. West Temple St., 84150
Telephone: (801) 531-2299
Private agency, authorized by the Church of Jesus Christ of Latter-day Saints
Founded in: 1869
Glen M. Leonard, Director
Staff: full time 35, volunteer 250
Major programs: museum, historic site(s), markers, exhibits, audiovisual programs, exhibit catalogues and brochures
Period of collections: 1800-present

National Society, Daughters of Utah Pioneers
300 N. Main, 84103
Telephone: (801) 533-5759
Private agency
Founded in: 1901
Emma R. Olsen, President
Number of members: 20,000
Staff: volunteer 30
Magazine: *An Enduring Legacy*
Major programs: museum, markers, school programs, book publishing, newsletters/pamphlets, historic preservation, research, exhibits, audiovisual programs
Period of collections: 1849-1869

Peoples of Utah Institute
300 Rio Grande, 84101
Telephone: (801) 533-5755
Private agency
Founded in: 1977
Craig Fuller, Secretary
Number of members: 25
Staff: volunteer 8
Major programs: newsletters/pamphlets, research, exhibits

Utah Endowment for the Humanities
10 W. Broadway 900, 84101
Telephone: (801) 531-7868

Private agency, authorized by
National Endowment for the
Humanities
Founded in: 1974
Delmont R. Oswald, Executive
Director
Staff: full time 3, part time 2,
volunteer 22
Major programs: junior history, oral
history, school programs, exhibits,
living history, audiovisual
programs, archaeology programs

Utah Heritage Foundation
355 Quince St., 84103
Telephone: (801) 533-0858
Private agency
Founded in: 1966
Stephanie D. Churchill, Director
Number of members: 800
Staff: full time 3, part time 1,
volunteer 60
Major programs: historic site(s),
tours/pilgrimages, school
programs, newsletters/pamphlets,
historic preservation

◇**Utah State Historical Society**
300 Rio Grande, 84101
Telephone: (801) 533-5755
State agency
Founded in: 1897
Melvin T. Smith, Director
Number of members: 3,200
Staff: full time 33, part time 4,
volunteer 5
Magazine: *Utah Historical Quarterly*
Major programs: library, manuscripts,
museum, historic site(s), markers,
book publishing,
newsletters/pamphlets, historic
preservation, research, exhibits,
archaeology programs,
photographic collections, field
services
Period of collections: 1825-1950

Wheeler Historic Farm
6351 S. 900, E, 84121
Telephone: (801) 264-2212
Founded in: 1976
A. Glen Humphreys, Curator/Director
Staff: full time 4, part time 5,
volunteer 40
Major programs: museum, historic
sites preservation, historic
preservation
Period of collections: 1890-1914

TORREY

Capitol Reef National Park Museum
84775
Telephone: (801) 425-3871
Federal agency, authorized by
National Park Service
Founded in: 1976
George E. Davidson, Chief Interpreter
Staff: full time 2, part time 3,
volunteer 2
Major programs: library, archives,
museum, historic site(s), markers,
tours/pilgrimages, oral history,
book publishing,
newsletters/pamphlets, historic
preservation, records
management, research, exhibits,
living history, photographic
collections
Period of collections: 1880-1937

WILLARD

Historic Willard Society
156 N. 200, W, 84340
Private agency
Founded in: 1974
Gardner W. Barlow, President
Staff: full time 4, part time 12
Major programs: historic site(s),
markers, historic preservation
Period of collections: 1974-present

VERMONT

ADDISON

Chimney Point Tavern
Rts. 125 and 17, 05491
Telephone: (802) 828-3226
Mail to: Historic Preservation,
Montpelier, 05602
State agency
Founded in: 1968
John P. Dumville, Historic Operations
Chief
Staff: full time 3, part time 1
Major programs: museum, historic
site(s), historic preservation,
archaeology programs
Period of collections: 4,000 B.C.-1930

ARLINGTON

**Russell Vermontiana Collection,
Martha Canfield Library**
05250
Private agency
Founded in: 1956
Mary Henning, Librarian
Staff: volunteer 6
Major programs: library, archives,
manuscripts, oral history, research,
photographic collections,
genealogical services
Period of collections: 1760-present

BARNET

Barnet Historical Society
R.F.D. 1, 05821
Telephone: (802) 633-2542
Private agency
Founded in: 1967
Robert L. Warden, Curator
Number of members: 60
Staff: volunteer 10
Major programs: archives, museum,
historic site(s), tours/pilgrimages,
historic preservation, genealogical
services
Period of collections: 1800s

BARRE

Aldrich Public Library
6 Washington St.
Telephone: (802) 479-0450
Mail to: P.O. Box 453, 05641
Private agency
Founded in: 1907
Karen Lane, Archivist/Curator
Staff: part time 2, volunteer 3
Major programs: library, archives,
manuscripts, museum,
tours/pilgrimages, oral history,

school programs, book publishing,
newsletters/pamphlets, research,
exhibits, audiovisual programs,
photographic collections,
discussion programs
Period of collections: 1788-present

**Barre Museum—Archives of Barre
History**
Washington St.
Telephone: (802) 479-0450
Mail to: P.O. Box 453, 05641
Town and city agency, authorized by
Aldrich Public Library
Founded in: 1908
Karen Lane, Archivist/Curator
Staff: part time 2, volunteer 4
Major programs: library, archives,
manuscripts, museum, oral history,
research, audiovisual programs,
photographic collections
Period of collections: 1788-present

BENNINGTON

**Bennington Museum and Peter
Matteson Tavern**
W. Main St., 05201
Telephone: (802) 447-1571
Private agency
Founded in: 1876
David W. Dangremond, Director
Number of members: 700
Staff: full time 12, part time 8,
volunteer 70
Major programs: library, archives,
manuscripts, museum, historic
site(s), oral history, school
programs, newsletters/pamphlets,
research, exhibits, living history,
photographic collections,
genealogical services
Period of collections: 19th century

BETHEL

Bethel Historical Society, Inc.
05032
Telephone: (802) 234-9202
Founded in: 1970
Manuel Miller, President
Number of members: 50
Major programs: archives, museum,
historic sites preservation,
genealogy, junior history,
tours/pilgrimages
Period of collections: 1777-1930

BRADFORD

Bradford Historical Society
Old River Rd., Box 193, 05033
Telephone: (802) 222-9359
Private agency
Founded in: 1968
Bruce Stevens, President
Number of members: 68
Staff: volunteer 4
Major programs: historic site(s),
newsletters/pamphlets
Period of collections: 1790-1890

BRAINTREE

Braintree Historical Society, Inc.
Braintree Hill
Telephone: (802) 728-5782
(president)
Mail to: Randolph, 05060

Painted chest, circa 1840, attributed to Thomas Matteson of Shaftsbury. The chest is part of The Bennington Museum's extensive collection of furniture and decorative arts from Vermont and New England.—Photograph by Erik Borg

Private agency
Founded in: 1961
Kathryne S. Fetherolf, President
Number of members: 120
Major programs: library, archives, museum, historic preservation, exhibits
Period of collections: 1800-1920

BRATTLEBORO

Brattleboro Historical Society
Telephone: (802) 254-2345
Mail to: P.O. Box 801, 05301
Private agency
Founded in: 1982
John H. Carnahan, Secretary
Number of members: 55
Staff: volunteer 10
Major programs: library, museum, historic preservation, photographic collections
Period of collections: 1820-present

Brattleboro Museum and Art Center
Vernon St.
Telephone: (802) 257-0124
Mail to: P.O. Box 662, 05301
Private agency
Founded in: 1972
Allison Devine, Acting Director
Staff: full time 2, part time 3, volunteer 200
Major programs: museum, historic site(s), school programs, newsletters/pamphlets, research, exhibits, audiovisual programs, lecture series and performance programs

Guilford Historical Society
R.F.D. 3, 05301
Private agency
Founded in: 1972
James Agnew, President
Number of members: 350
Magazine: *The Guilford Slate*
Major programs: museum, historic site(s), tours/pilgrimages, school programs, newsletters/pamphlets, historic preservation, exhibits, photographic collections
Period of collections: 1850-present

BRISTOL

Bristol Historical Society, Inc.
Main St., 05443
Founded in: 1977
Helen M. Lathrop, President
Number of members: 125
Major programs: library, museum, historic site(s), school programs, book publishing, historic preservation, research, exhibits, audiovisual programs, photographic collections
Period of collections: 1800s-early 1900s

BROOKFIELD

Museum of the Americas
Rt. 14, E. Brookfield, 05036
Telephone: (802) 276-3386
Private agency
Founded in: 1971
Earle W. Newton, President

Major programs: library, museum, research, exhibits, audiovisual programs
Period of collections: 1600-1900

BROWNINGTON

Orleans County Historical Society, Inc.
P.O. Box 27, 05860
Telephone: (802) 754-2022
Private agency
Founded in: 1853
Reed Cherington, Administrator
Number of members: 700
Staff: full time 1, part time 1, volunteer 12
Major programs: library, archives, manuscripts, museum, historic site(s), school programs, book publishing, newsletters/pamphlets, exhibits, photographic collections
Period of collections: 1780-present

BURLINGTON

Champlain Maritime Society
14 S. Williams St., 2nd Floor
Telephone: (802) 862-8270
Mail to: P.O. Box 745, 05402
Private agency
Founded in: 1981
R. Montgomery Fischer, Chair
Number of members: 150
Staff: part time 25, volunteer 15
Magazine: *Soundings*
Major programs: book publishing, newsletters/pamphlets, historic preservation, research, exhibits, archaeology programs, photographic collections, field services
Period of collections: 1760-1890

Chittenden County Historical Society
Bailey Library, University of Vermont, 05405
Telephone: (802) 656-2138
Founded in: 1965
J. K. Graffagnino, Correspondent
Number of members: 275
Staff: volunteer 16
Major programs: tours/pilgrimages, educational programs, books

Robert Hull Fleming Museum
University of Vermont, 05405
Telephone: (802) 656-2090
Private agency, authorized by University of Vermont
Founded in: 1826 (museum); 1791 (university)
Ildiko Heffernan, Director
Number of members: 700
Staff: full time 7, part time 2, volunteer 30
Major programs: library, museum, school programs, newsletters/pamphlets, research, exhibits, photographic collections

Vermont Archaeological Society
P.O. Box 663, 05402
Founded in: 1968
William Noel, President
Number of members: 100
Major programs: educational programs, books,

newsletters/pamphlets,
archaeological excavations
Period of collections: prehistoric
Questionnaire not received

Vermont Old Cemetery Association
308 S. Prospect, 05401
Telephone: (802) 864-6753
Questionnaire not received

CABOT

Cabot Historical Society, Inc.
Main St., 05647
Telephone: (802) 563-2547
Mail to: c/o L. H. Spencer, R.F.D.
Lower Cabot, Marshfield, 05658
Founded in: 1901
L. H. Spencer, President
Number of members: 33
Staff: volunteer 5
Major programs: museum, historic
sites preservation, historic
preservation
Period of collections: 1850-1950
Questionnaire not received

CANAAN

Canaan Historical Society
P. O. Box 192, 05903
Founded in: 1980
Marian Paquette
Major programs: library, historic sites
preservation, oral history, historic
preservation
Period of collections: 1846-present
Questionnaire not received

CAVENDISH

Cavendish Historical Society
Telephone: (802) 484-7498
Mail to: c/o President, R. F. D.
Cavendish, 05142
Founded in: 1955
Carmine Guica, President
Number of members: 115
Major programs: historic site(s),
tours/pilgrimages, historic
preservation, genealogical
services
Period of collections: 1700-present

CHELSEA

Chelsea Historical Society, Inc.
Main St., 05038
Private agency, authorized by State
of Vermont
Founded in: 1960
W. S. Gilman, President
Number of members: 50
Major programs: museum, historic
site(s), markers, tours/pilgrimages,
oral history, school programs, book
publishing, exhibits, photographic
collections

CUTTINGSVILLE

Shrewsbury Historical Society
05738
Founded in: 1971
Elliott Hayes, President
Number of members: 60
Staff: volunteer 10
Major programs: archives, historic
sites preservation, oral history,
books

Period of collections: 19th century
Questionnaire not received

DERBY

Derby Historical Society, Inc.
Main St.
Telephone: (802) 766-8841
Mail to: c/o Allen Yale, P. O. Box 332,
05829
Private agency
Founded in: 1980
Allen Yale, President
Number of members: 120
Staff: volunteer 20
Major programs: library, archives,
educational programs
Period of collections: early 20th
century

DORSET

Dorset Historical Society
Main St., 05251
Telephone: (802) 867-4423
Founded in: 1963
Donald S. Kellogg, President
Number of members: 240
Staff: volunteer 14
Major programs: museum
Period of collections: 1865-1918

ESSEX JUNCTION

Discovery Museum
51 Park St., 05452
Telephone: (802) 878-8687
Private agency
Founded in: 1974
Pamela Kay, Director
Number of members: 300
Staff: full time 3, part time 3,
volunteer 100
Major programs: museum, school
programs, newsletters/pamphlets,
exhibits

FAIRFAX

Fairfax Historical Society
Main St., Rt. 104
Telephone: (802) 849-6638
Mail to: P. O. Box 105, 05454
Founded in: 1963
Gene L. Cain, Secretary
Number of members: 50
Staff: volunteer 5
Magazine: *Fairfax News*
Major programs: library, museum,
historic sites preservation, markers,
oral history, historic preservation
Period of collections: 1790-present

FAIRLEE

Fairlee Historical Society
05045
Mail to: c/o Secretary, P. O. Box 273
Founded in: 1976
John Larson, President
Number of members: 30
Staff: volunteer 30
Major programs: archives,
manuscripts, tours/pilgrimages,
oral history, educational programs,
genealogy
Period of collections: 1800-present
Questionnaire not received

FERRISBURGH

**Rowland E. Robinson Memorial
Association**
Telephone: (802) 877-3406
Founded in: 1962
Number of members: 350
Staff: volunteer 2
Magazine: *Rokeby Messenger*
Major programs: library, archives,
museum, historic sites
preservation, tours/pilgrimages,
educational programs,
newsletters/pamphlets, historic
preservation
Period of collections: late 18th-early
20th centuries

GEORGIA

Georgia Historical Society
Rt. 7
Mail to: c/o President, R. D. H. 3,
05478
Private agency
Founded in: 1975
Edmund Wilcox, President
Number of members: 34
Staff: volunteer 10
Major programs: museum, oral
history, school programs, book
publishing, photographic
collections
Period of collections: 1860-present

GRAFTON

**Grafton Historical Museum
Society, Inc.**
Main St., 05146
Telephone: (802) 843-2388
Founded in: 1962
Helen M. Pettengill, Secretary
Number of members: 450
Staff: volunteer 40
Major programs: museum, historic
site(s), school programs, historic
preservation, exhibits,
genealogical services
Period of collections: 1783-present

GREENSBORO

Greensboro Historical Society
05841
Private agency
Wilhelmina V.O. Smith, President
Number of members: 350
Staff: volunteer 5
Magazine: *Hazen Road Dispatch*
Major programs:
newsletters/pamphlets, research

GROTON

Groton Historical Society
05040
Founded in: 1930s
Major programs: manuscripts
Period of collections: 1789-present

HOLLAND

Holland Historical Society, Inc.
Rt. 1, Box 37, 05830
Town agency
Founded in: 1972
Isabel McInnis, President
Number of members: 50
Staff: volunteer 12

Major programs: archives, museum, historic site(s), historic preservation, exhibits, photographic collections, genealogical services
Period of collections: 1805-present

HUBBARDTON

Hubbardton Battlefield
Battlefield Rd., 05749
Telephone: (802) 828-3226
Mail to: Historic Preservation, Montpelier, 05602
State agency, authorized by Division for Historic Preservation
Founded in: 1859
John P. Dumville, Historic Sites Operations Chief
Staff: full time 3, part time 1
Major programs: museum, historic site(s), markers, newsletters/pamphlets, historic preservation
Period of collections: 1777

HYDE PARK

Vermont Council on the Humanities and Public Issues
Grant Bldg., Main St.
Telephone: (802) 888-3183
Mail to: P. O. Box 58, 05655
Private agency, authorized by State of Vermont, Non-Profit Corporation
Founded in: 1972
Victor R. Swenson, Executive Director
Staff: full time 5, part time 1
Major programs: library, museum

ISLAND POND

Island Pond Historical Society Inc.
05846
Founded in: 1967
Peter Joseph, President
Number of members: 450
Staff: volunteer 25
Major programs: oral history, newsletters/pamphlets
Period of collections: 1865-present
Questionnaire not received

JERICHO

Jericho Historical Society
The Chittenden Mills
Telephone: (802) 899-3225
Mail to: P. O. Box 35, 05465
Founded in: 1972
Wayne Ellis, President
Number of members: 104
Staff: part time 1, volunteer 40
Major programs: archives, museum, historic site(s), audiovisual programs, photographic collections
Period of collections: 1850-present

LONDONDERRY

Londonderry Historical Society
05148
Telephone: (802) 824-6362
Private agency
Founded in: 1971
Ruth Chaskel, President
Staff: volunteer 4
Major programs: archives, manuscripts, museum, historic site(s), oral history, historic preservation, exhibits, living history
Period of collections: 1783-present

LUDLOW

Black River Historical Society, Inc.
P. O. Box 73, 05149
Telephone: (802) 228-5050
Private agency
Founded in: 1972
Kenneth H. Allen, President
Number of members: 125
Staff: volunteer 5
Major programs: museum, school programs, photographic collections
Period of collections: 1885-1920

MANCHESTER

American Museum of Fly Fishing
05254
Telephone: (802) 362-3300
John Merwin, Executive Director
Number of members: 800
Staff: full time 2, part time 1, volunteer 1
Magazine: *The American Fly Fisher*
Major programs: library, manuscripts, museum, school programs, newsletters/pamphlets
Period ofcollections: 1820-present

Friends of Hildene, Inc.
Rt. 7-A, S
Telephone: (802) 362-1788
Mail to: P.O. Box 337, 05254
Private agency
Founded in: 1978
David C. Sheldon, Executive Director
Number of members: 1,500
Staff: full time 6, part time 5, volunteer 170
Magazine: *News from Historic Hildene*
Major programs: museum, historic site(s), tours/pilgrimages, newsletters/pamphlets, historic preservation, community programs
Periiod of collections: 1905-1926

MARLBORO

Historical Society of Marlboro
Main St., 05344
Founded in: 1966
Mrs. Robert Bartlett, President
Number of members: 135
Staff: volunteer 25
Major programs: museum, historic sites preservation, eduational programs
Period of collections: 1783-1918

MIDDLEBURY

The Sheldon Museum
1 Park St. 05753
Telephone: (802) 388-2117
Mail to: P. O. Box 126
Private agency
Founded in: 1882
Polly C. Darnell, Co-Director
Number of members: 450
Staff: full time 1, part time 5, volunteer 90
Major programs: library, manuscripts, museum, school programs, exhibits, photographic collections
Period of collections: 19th century

MIDDLETOWN SPRINGS

Middletown Springs Historical Society, Inc.
On the Green, 05757
Telephone: (802) 235-2127
Private agency
Founded in: 1970
Mrs. Edwin Roach, Jr., President
Number of members: 200
Staff: volunteer 4
Major programs: archives, manuscripts, oral history, newsletters/pamphlets, research, genealogical services
Period of collections: 1783-1950

MILTON

Milton Historical Society
Main St.
Mail to: R. F. D. 4, 05468
Private agency
Founded in: 1978
Robert Hooker, President
Number of members: 100
Staff: volunteer 15
Major programs: museum, markers, tours/pilgrimages, junior history, oral history, school programs, newsletters/pamphlets, exhibits, photographic ollections
Period of collections: 1765-present

MONTGOMERY

Montgomery History Society
c/o Clare Coy, R. F. D. Richford, 05470
Telephone: (802) 326-4471
Founded in: 1974
Clare Coy, President
Number of members: 100
Staff: volunteer 8
Major programs: educational programs, books, newsletters/pamphlets, historic preservation
Period of collections: 1900
Questionnaire not received

Montgomery Historical Society
05470
Private agency
Founded in: 1975
Tony Jones, President
Number of members: 150
Staff: volunteer 6
Major programs: book publishing, historic preservation
Period of collections: 1800-present

MONTPELIER

Montpelier Heritage Group, Inc.
05602
Mail to: P. O. Box 671
Founded in: 1973
David Orrick, President
Questionnaire not received

Vermont Historical Society
109 State St., 05602
Telephone: (802) 828-2291
Private agency
Founded in: 1838
Weston A. Cate, Jr., Director
Number of members: 2,500
Staff: full time 7, part time 4, volunteer 15

Magazine: *Vermont History/Vermont History News/The Green Mountaineer*
Major programs: library, archives, manuscripts, museum, junior history, book publishing, exhibits, photographic collections, local society outreach
Period of collections: 1760-1920

Vermont State Archives
26 Terrace St., 05602
Telephone: (802) 828-2369
State agency, authorized by Secretary of State
Founded in: 1777
D. Gregory Sanford, State Archivist
Staff: full time 1, part time 2
Major programs: archives, manuscripts
Period of collections: 1777-present

NEWFANE

Historical Society of Windham County
Rt. 30, 05345
County agency
Founded in: 1933
Mrs. William B. Mantel, President
Number of members: 200
Staff: part time 1, volunteer 10
Magazine: *Vermont Life*
Major programs: museum, markers, historic preservation, exhibits, photographic collections
Period of collections: 18th-20th centuries

NORTH BENNINGTON

Park-McCullough House Association
West St., 05257
Telephone: (802) 442-2747
Founded in: 1968
Muriel Cummings Palmer, Executive Director
Number of members: 450
Staff: full time 7, part time 4, volunteer 50
Major programs: archives, museum, historic site(s), tours/pilgrimages, school programs, newsletters/pamphlets, historic preservation, exhibits, photographic collections, concerts, special events
Period of collections: 1865-present

NORTHFIELD

Northfield Historical Society
c/o President, 3 Spring St., 05663
Telephone: (802) 485-7736
Private agency
Founded in: 1975
Kenneth M. Kidd, President
Number of members: 450
Staff: volunteer 12
Magazine: *The Dog River Crier*
Major programs: museum, book publishing, newsletters/pamphlets, exhibits, photographic collections
Period of collections: 1900-present

NORTH TROY

Missisquoi Valley Historical Society
Main St.

Mail to: P.O. Box 237, 05859
Founded in: 1976
Carole Fortier, Curator
Number of members: 65
Staff: volunteer 5
Major programs: museum, oral history
Period of collections: late 1800s-early 1900s

PAWLET

Pawlett Historical Society
05761
Private agency
Founded in: 1973
Hiram J. Evans, President
Number of members: 110
Staff: volunteer 2
Major programs: newsletters/pamphlets
Period of collections: to 1910

PEACHAM

Peacham Historical Association
Church St.
Telephone: (802) 592-3361
Private agency
Founded in: 1924
Edmund A. Brown, President
Number of members: 130
Staff: volunteer 12
Major programs: manuscripts, museum, book publishing, newsletters/pamphlets, records management, exhibits, genealogical services
Period of collections: 1870-1950

PLAINFIELD

Twinfield Historical Society
R.D. 2, Box 290, 05667
Telephone: (802) 454-8419
State agency
Founded in: 1983
Cora Copping, Vice President
Staff: volunteer 12
Period of collections: 1900-present

PLYMOUTH

Calvin Coolidge Memorial Foundation, Inc.
05056
Telephone: (802) 672-3389
Private agency
Founded in: 1960
Kathleen Donald, Executive Secretary
Number of members: 550
Staff: full time 1, part time 1
Magazine: *Plymouth Notch News*
Major programs: oral history, school programs, book publishing, newsletters/pamphlets, research, audiovisual programs, photographic collections, genealogical services
Period of collections: late 1800s-early 1900s

PUTNEY

Putney Historical Society
Main St.
Telephone: (802) 387-5862

Mail to: Town Hall, 05346
Private agency
Founded in: 1959
Laura Heller, Co-curator
Number of members: 80
Staff: volunteer 2
Major programs: library, archives, manuscripts, museum, historic site(s), markers, oral history, school programs, book publishing, newsletters/pamphlets, historic preservation, research, exhibits, living history, archaeology programs, photographic collections, genealogical services
Period of collections: Colonial-present

READSBORO

Readsboro Historical Society
Main St., 05350
Private agency
Founded in: 1972
Barbara L. Coe, President
Number of members: 30
Staff: volunteer 5
Major programs: museum, historic preservation, exhibits, photographic collections
Period of collections: late 1800-early 1900

RUTLAND

New England Maple Museum
Rt. 7, Pittsford
Mail to: P.O. Box 1615, 05701
Private agency
Founded in: 1977
Thomas H. Olson, President
Staff: full time 2, part time 3
Major programs: museum, school programs, exhibits
Period of collections: 1650-present

Rutland Historical Society
101 Center St., 05701
Founded in: 1969
Number of members: 500
Staff: volunteer 20
Major programs: library, archives, museum, educational programs, newsletters
Period of collections: 1761-present

SHAFTSBURY

Shaftsbury Historical Society
Mail to: R.R. 1, Box 125, 05262
Town agency
Founded in: 1967
Michael Coppinger, President
Number of members: 180
Major programs: library, museum, historic preservation, photographic collections, genealogical services
Period of collections: 1770-1900

SHREWSBURY

Shrewsbury Historical Society, Inc.
Telephone: (802) 492-3410
Mail to: Cuttingsville, 05738
Private agency
Patricia Michaud, Curator
Number of members: 50
Staff: volunteer 8
Major programs: museum, oral history, school programs, book

publishing, research, exhibits, photographic collections
Period of collections: 19th century-present

SPRINGFIELD

Eureka Schoolhouse
Rt. 11, 05156
Telephone: (802) 828-3226
Mail to: Historic Preservation, Montpelier, 05602
State agency, authorized by Division for Historic Preservation
Founded in: 1968
John P. Dumville, Historic Sites Operations Chief
Staff: full time 3, part time 3
Major programs: museum, historic site(s), school programs, newsletters/pamphlets, historic preservation
Period of collections: 1790-1890

Springfield Art and Historical Society
9 Elm Hill, 05156
Telephone: (802) 885-2415
Private agency
Founded in: 1956
Mrs. Fred R. Herrick, Director
Number of members: 150
Staff: full time 1, volunteer 6
Major programs: museum, educational programs, art exhibits
Period of collections: 1783-present

ST. ALBANS

St. Albans Historical Society
Church St.
Telephone: (802) 527-7933
Mail to: P.O. Box 722, 05478
Founded in: 1966
George W. Beebe, President
Number of members: 250
Staff: volunteer 25
Major programs: library, museum, photographic collections, genealogical services

STRAFFORD

Justin Smith Morrill Homestead
Main St., 05072
Telephone: (802) 828-3226
Mail to: Historic Preservation, Montpelier, 05602
State agency, authorized by Division for Historic Preservation
Founded in: 1968
John P. Dumville, Historic Sites Operations Chief
Staff: full time 3, part time 2
Major programs: library, archives, museum, historic site(s), newsletters/pamphlets, historic preservation
Period of collections: 1848-1890

VERNON

Vernon Historians, Inc.
Main Rd.
Telephone: (802) 257-1788
Mail to: R.D. 1, Silver Lane, 05354
Private agency
Founded in: 1968
Jerry W. Kirk, President
Number of members: 200

Staff: volunteer 20
Major programs: museum, markers, educational programs
Period of collections: late 1700s-present

WESTMINSTER

Westminster Historical Society
Telephone: (802) 387-5778
Mail to: c/o President, R.F.D. 3, Box 634, Putney, 05346
Founded in: 1962
Patricia Haas, President
Number of members: 60
Staff: volunteer 10
Major programs: museum
Period of collections: from 1776

WESTON

Weston Historical Society
05161
Telephone: (802) 824-3388
Private agency
Founded in: 1936
Laurence Walker, President
Number of members: 150
Staff: volunteer 30
Major programs: museum, historic site(s), historic preservation
Period of collections: 19th century

WILLISTON

Williston Historical Society
05495
Telephone: (802) 878-3742
Town agency, authorized by Secretary of State, Vermont
Founded in: 1974
Mrs. David Yandell, President
Number of members: 60
Staff: volunteer 10
Major programs: archives, historic site(s), newsletters/pamphlets
Period of collections: 1763-present

WINDSOR

Old Constitution House
Main St., 05089
Telephone: (802) 828-3226
Mail to: Historic Preservation, Montpelier, 05602
State agency, authorized by Division for Historic Preservation
Founded in: 1914
John P. Dumville, Historic Sites Operations Chief
Staff: full time 3, part time 3
Major programs: museum, historic site(s), historic preservation
Period of collections: 1776-1920

WOODSTOCK

Billings Farm and Museum
P.O. Box 627, 05091
Telephone: (802) 457-2355
Founded in: 1983
David A. Donath, Director
Staff: full time 8, part time 10
Major programs: museum, school programs, operating farm, library, archives
Period of collections: 1860-1900

Woodstock Historical Society
26 Elm St., 05091

Private agency
Major programs: museum, historic preservation, exhibits, photographic collections
Period of collections: 1800-1900

VIRGINIA

ABINGDON

Historical Society of Washington County, Virginia, Inc.
P.O. Box 484, 24210
Founded in: 1936
Walter H. Hendricks, President
Number of members: 325
Staff: volunteer 5
Magazine: *Bulletin*
Major programs: library, archives, tours/pilgrimages, newsletters/pamphlets
Period of collections: 1770-present

ALEXANDRIA

Alexandria Archaeology
105 Union St., 22314
Telephone: (703) 838-4399
City agency, authorized by Office of Historic Alexandria
Founded in: 1977
Pamela J. Cressey, Director
Staff: full time 3, part time 1, volunteer 75
Major programs: library, newsletters/pamphlets, historic preservation, research, exhibits, archaeology programs
Period of collections: late 18th-19th centuries

Alexandria Historical Society, Inc.
201 S. Washington St., 22314
Telephone: (703) 548-1776
Founded in: 1974
Mrs. James H. L. Jacob, President
Number of members: 200
Major programs: books

Alexandria Library
717 Queen St., 22314
Telephone: (703) 838-4555
City agency
Founded in: 1794
Jeanne G. Plitt, Director of Libraries
Staff: full time 38, part time 21, volunteer 25
Major programs: library, archives, manuscripts, research, audiovisual programs, genealogical services
Period of collections: 1749-present

Alexandria Urban Archaeology Program
City Hall, P.O. Box 178, 22314
Telephone: (703) 838-4399
City agency
Founded in: 1977
Pamela J. Cressey, Director
Staff: full time 3, part time 1, volunteer 75
Publications: *Alexandria Papers in Urban Archaeology*

Major programs: oral history, historic preservation, research, exhibits, archaeology programs
Period of collections: 18th-20th centuries

Boyhood Home of Robert E. Lee
607 Oronoco, 22314
Telephone: (703) 548-8454
Private agency, authorized by the Lee Jackson Foundation
Katherine J. Cooke, Director
Staff:part time 3, volunteer 45
Major programs: museum, historic sites preservation, tours/pilgrimages, educational programs, historic preservation
Period of collections: 1795-1825

Ft. Ward Museum and Park
4301 W. Braddock Rd., 22304
Telephone: (703) 838-4848
City agency, authorized by Historic Alexandria
Founded in: 1964
Wanda S. Dowell, Curator
Staff: full time 4, part time 3
Major programs: library, museum, historic site(s), markers, tours/pilgrimages, oral history, school programs, newsletters/pamphlets, historic preservation, exhibits, living history
Period of collections: 1860-1870

Future Farmers of America
5632 Mount Vernon Memorial Highway, 22309
Telephone: (703) 360-3600
Mail to: P.O. Box 15160
Founded in: 1928
Byron Rawls, National Advisor
Number of members: 481,676
Magazine: *The National Future Farmer*
Major programs: library, archives, educational programs, newsletters/pamphlets
Period of collections: 1928-present

Gadsby's Tavern Museum
134 N. Royal St., 22314
Telephone: (703) 838-4242
City agency
Founded in: 1976
Suzanne H. Derby, Director
Staff: full time 2, part time 9, volunteer 65
Major programs: library, museum, historic site(s), tours/pilgrimages, oral history, school programs, newsletters/pamphlets, historic preservation, research, exhibits
Period of collections: 1770-1810

George Washington Bicentennial Center
201 S. Washington St., 22314
Telephone: (703) 838-4994
Founded in: 1974
Dory Twitchell, Director
Staff: full time 4, part time 9, volunteer 3
Major programs: museum, historic sites preservation, educational programs, cultural programs
Period of collections: 18th century

George Washington Masonic National Memorial
King St. and Callahan Dr.

Telephone: (703) 683-2007
Mail to: P.O. Box 2098, 22301
Founded in: 1910
Private agency, authorized by Grand Lodges of the U.S.
Marvin E. Fowler, Secretary/Treasurer
Major programs: museum
Period of collections: Colonial era

Historic Alexandria Foundation
220 S. Fayette St., 22314
Telephone: (202) 548-2267
Private agency
Founded in: 1957
Morgan D. Delaney, President
Number of members: 500
Staff: volunteer 12
Magazine: *The Plaque*
Major programs: library, historic site(s), markers, tours/pilgrimages, historic preservation, research
Period of collections: 18th-19th centuries

Office of Historic Alexandria, City of Alexandria
City Hall
Telephone: (703) 838-4554
Mail to: P.O. Box 178, 22313
Founded in: 1976
Jean Taylor Federico, Director
Staff: full time 20, part time 30, volunteer 400
Major programs: museum, historic sites preservation, educational programs, historic preservation
Period of collections: 18th-19th centuries

Stabler-Leadbeater Apothecary Shop Museum and Antique Shop
105-107 S. Fairfax St., 22314
Telephone: (703) 836-3713
Private agency, authorized by Landmark Society of Alexandria
Founded in: 1933
Kay MacDonald, Director
Staff: part time 1, volunteer 2
Major programs: museum, historic site(s)
Period of collections: 1792-1933

Virginia Trust for Historic Preservation/Lee-Fendall House Museum
614 Oronoco St., 22314
Telephone: (703) 548-1789
Private agency
Founded in: 1972
Merrill M. Blevins, Administrator
Staff: full time 1, part time 4, volunteer 25
Major programs: archives, museum, historic site(s), tours/pilgrimages, school programs, historic preservation, exhibits
Period of collections: 1785-1900

AMELIA

Amelia Historical Society
Church St., 23002
Founded in: 1958
Questionnaire not received

AMHERST

Amherst County Historical Museum
P.O. Box 741, 24521
Telephone: (804) 946-2460

Founded in: 1975
Kathryn E. Kresge, Museum Director
Number of members: 140
Staff: full time 1, part time 2, volunteer 9
Magazine: *The Muse*
Major programs: library, archives, museum, tours/pilgrimages, educational programs, newsletters/pamphlets
Period of collections: late 19th-20th centuries

ANNANDALE

Division of Historic Preservation, Fairfax County Park Authority
4030 Hummer Rd. 22003
Telephone: (703) 378-2532
County agency
Founded in: 1973
Staff: full time 12, part time 20, volunteer 200
Major programs: historic site(s), school programs, newsletters/pamphlets, historic preservation, research, exhibits, living history, photographic collections, field services
Period of collections: 1780-1930

APPOMATTOX

Appomattox Courthouse National Historical Park
Rt. 24
Telephone: (804) 352-8987
Mail to: P.O. Box 218, 24522
Federal agency, authorized by National Park Service
Founded in: 1940
Jon Montgomery, Superintendent
Staff: full time 14, part time 8, volunteer 8
Major programs: library, museum, historic site(s), historic preservation, exhibits, audiovisual programs
Period of collections: 1865

ARLINGTON

Arlington Historical Society and Museums
1805 S. Arlington Ridge Rd.
Telephone: (703) 528-1548
Mail to: P.O. Box 402, 22210
Founded in: 1956
Kathryn Holt, Museum Director
Number of members: 475
Staff: part time 1, volunteer 75
Magazine: *The Arlington Historical Magazine*
Major programs: archives, manuscripts, museum, historic site(s), tours/pilgrimages, school programs, newsletters/pamphlets, historic preservation, research, exhibits, photographic collections
Period of collections: 1790s-present

Chain Bridge Productions
501 N. Kenmore St., 22201
Telephone: (703) 522-3382
Private agency, authorized by the County business licensing division
Founded in: 1984
Susan Gilpin, Partner
Staff: part time 2

Major programs: tours/pilgrimages, oral history, research, exhibits, audiovisual programs, maps, architecture
Period of collections: 1860-1900

Gulf Branch Nature Center
3608 N. Military Rd., 22207
Telephone: (703) 558-2340
County agency, authorized by Arlington County Park Division
Founded in: 1968
Scott Silsby, Center Director
Staff: full time 5, part time 3
Major programs: historic site(s), school programs, exhibits, archaeology programs
Period of collections: 19th century

National Inventors Hall of Fame Foundation, Inc.
Crystal Plaza Bldg. 3-1D01, 2021 Jefferson Davis Hwy., 22301
Telephone: (703) 557-3428
Founded in: 1973
Frederick B. Ziesenheim, President
Major programs: museum
Period of collections: 1790-present

ASHLAND

Hanover County Historical Society
P.O. Box 91, Hanover Courthouse, 23069
Telephone: (804) 537-5502
Mail to: Rt. 4, Box 182, 23005
Private agency
Founded in: 1967
Mrs. W. C. Wickham, Curator
Number of members: 475
Staff: volunteer 2
Major programs: archives, museum, markers, tours/pilgrimages, books, historic preservation
Period of collections: to 1865

BASSETT

Henry County Historical Society
Telephone: (703) 629-2426
Founded in: 1967
Questionnaire not received

BEAVERDAM

Scotchtown, Home of Patrick Henry
Rt. 2, Box 168, 23015
Telephone: (804) 227-3500
Founded in: 1958
Questionnaire not received

BEDFORD

Bedford Historical Society, Inc.
Mail to: P.O. Box 602, 24523
Founded in: 1969
Mrs. Bolling Lambeth, Executive Secretary
Number of members: 200
Major programs: historic sites preservation, educational programs

BERRYVILLE

Clarke County Historical Association
Telephone: (703) 837-1799/837-1556
Mail to: General Delivery, 22611
Private agency
Founded in: 1928
R. C. Plater, Jr., Vice President
Number of members: 280
Staff: full time 1, volunteer 20
Magazine: *Proceedings*
Major programs: archives, manuscripts, museum, historic site(s), tours/pilgrimages, oral history, historic preservation, genealogical services
Period of collections: 18th-20th centuries

BIG STONE GAP

Southwest Virginia Museum Historical State Park
10 W. 1st St. and Wood Ave.
Telephone: (703) 523-1322
Mail to: P.O. Box 742, 24219
State agency, authorized by Department of Conservation and Economic Development
Founded in: 1943
John Zawatsky, Chief Ranger
Staff: full time 2, part time 2, volunteer 2
Major programs: museum, historic site(s), tours/pilgrimages, pioneer crafts and skills, mountain lifestyles program
Period of collections: late 19th-mid 20th centuries

BLACKSBURG

Smithfield Plantation
24060
Telephone: (703) 951-2060
Private agency, authorized by Association for the Preservation of Virginia Antiquities
Founded in: 1958
Leslie McCombs, President, APVA Montgomery Branch
Number of members: 185
Staff: part time 2, volunteer 60
Major programs: museum, historic site(s), tours/pilgrimages, school programs, newsletters/pamphlets, historic preservation, research
Period of collections: 1770-1850

BLACKSTONE

Nottoway County Historical Association
100 Bird Rd., 23824
Telephone: (804) 292-3381
Questionnaire not received

BRIDGEWATER

Reuel B. Pritchett Museum of Bridgewater College
E. College St., 22812
Telephone: (703) 828-2501, ext. 147
Mail to: P.O. Box 77, Bridgewater

College
Founded in: 1954
Questionnaire not received

BROOKNEAL

Red Hill Shrine
Rt. 2, Box 27, 24528
Telephone: (804) 376-2044
Private agency, authorized by Patrick Henry Memorial Foundation
Founded in: 1944
Patrick T. Daily, Director
Staff: full time 1, part time 3
Major programs: library, museum, historic site(s), school programs, newsletters/pamphlets, exhibits, genealogical services
Period of collections: 1790s

Staunton River Historical Society—Willie Hodges Booth Museum
Main St.
Mail to: P.O. Box 270, 24528
Private agency
Founded in: 1975
Bob Jeans, President
Number of members: 60
Staff: part time 1, volunteer 2
Major programs: museum, school programs
Period of collections: 1860-1940

CHARLES CITY

Sherwood Forest Plantation
P.O. Box 8, 23030
Telephone: (804) 829-5377
Private agency, authorized by Historic Sherwood Forest Corporation
Founded in: 1975
Mrs. Harrison Tyler, President
Staff: full time 4, part time 2
Major programs: library, archives, manuscripts, museum, markers, tours/pilgrimages, historic preservation, research
Period of collections: 1845

Shirley Plantation
Rt. 2, Box 130, 23030
Telephone: (804) 795-2385
Private agency
Founded in: 1952
Hill Carter, Jr., Owner
Staff: full time 6
Major programs: historic site(s), tours
Period of collections: 18th century

CHARLOTTESVILLE

Albemarle County Historical Society
220 Court Square, 22901
Telephone: (804) 296-1492
Private agency
Founded in: 1940
O. Allan Gianniny, Jr., President
Number of members: 800
Staff: volunteer 35
Magazine: *Magazine of Albemarle County History*
Major programs: library, museum, historic site(s), markers, genealogical services
Period of collections: 18th-19th century

Ash Lawn, Home of James Monroe

C. R. 795 (Off I-64, 2mi. past
  Monticello) 22901
Telephone: (804) 293-9539
Founded in: 1799
Carolyn C. Holmes, Resident
  Manager/Curator
Staff: full time 4, part time 25,
  volunteer 20
Major programs: museum, historic
  sites preservation, educational
  programs, newsletters/pamphlets,
  historic preservation
Period of collections: late 18th-early
  19th centuries

The Lee-Jackson Foundation

405 Citizens Commonwealth Center,
  22901
Telephone: (804) 977-1861
Founded in: 1953
Questionnaire not received

Manuscripts Department, University of Virginia Library

22903-2498
Telephone: (804) 924-3025
State agency, authorized by the
  university
Founded in: 1930
Edmund Berkeley, Jr., Curator of
  Manuscripts/University Archivist
Staff: full time 13, part time 7,
  volunteer 14
Major programs: archives,
  manuscripts, photographic
  collections
Period of collections: 1750-present

Rare Book Department, Alderman Library

University of Virginia, 22901
Telephone: (804) 924-3366
State agency, authorized by the
  university
Founded in: 1819
Julius P. Barclay, Curator of Rare
  Books
Staff: full time 9, part time 5
Major programs: library, archives,
  manuscripts, exhibits
Period of collections: 17th-20th
  centuries

Thomas Jefferson Memorial Foundation

Monticello, P.O. Box 316, 22902
Telephone: (804) 295-2657
Private agency
Founded in: 1923
Daniel P. Jordan, Director
Staff: full time 90, part time 70
Major programs: library, archives,
  manuscripts, museum, historic
  site(s), tours/pilgrimages, school
  programs, book publishing,
  newsletters/pamphlets, historic
  preservation, exhibits, archaeology
  programs
Period of collections: 1769-1809

Virginia Folklore Society

115 Wilson Hall, University of Virginia,
  22903
Telephone: (804) 924-6823
Private agency, authorized by
  Virginia Corporation Commission
Founded in: 1913
Charles L. Perdue, Jr., Registered
  Agent-Archivist/Editor

Number of members: 73
Staff: volunteer 7
Magazine: *Folklore and Folklife in
  Virginia*
Major programs: folklore and folklife
  programs
Period of collections: 1913-early
  1970s

CHATHAM

Pittsylvania Historical Society

112 N. Main St., 24531
Telephone: (804) 432-8180
Mail to: P.O. Box 943
Founded in: 1974
Questionnaire not received

CHESAPEAKE

Norfolk County Historical Society of Chesapeake

Chesapeake Public Library, 300
  Cedar Rd., 23320
Telephone: (804) 547-6591
Private agency
Founded in: 1963
Charles B. Cross, Jr., President
Number of members: 100
Staff: part time 1, volunteer 10
Major programs: historic site(s), book
  publishing
Period of collections: Colonial era

CHESTERFIELD

Chesterfield County Historical Society

P.O. Box 40, 23832
Telephone: (804) 748-1026
Private agency
Founded in: 1981
Mrs. Edward A. Moseley, President
Number of members: 500
Major programs: library, archives,
  manuscripts, museum, historic
  site(s), school programs,
  newsletters/pamphlets, audiovisual
  programs, archaeology programs,
  photographic collections,
  genealogical services
Period of collections: 1749-1950

CLARKSVILLE

Roanoke River Museum, Prestwould Foundation

Rt. 15-N, R.F.D. 2
Telephone: (804) 374-8672
Mail to: P.O. Box 872, 23927
Founded in: 1959
Number of members: 300
Major programs: library, museum,
  historic site(s), school programs,
  historic preservation, exhibits,
  genealogical services
Period of collections: 1790-1915

COURTLAND

Walter Cecil Rawls Library and Museum

Main St.
Telephone: (804) 653-2821
Mail to: P.O. Box 318, 23837
Regional agency
Founded in: 1958
K. Paul Johnson, Director/Curator
Number of members: 165
Staff: full time 11, part time 12

Major programs: library, museum,
  exhibits
Period of collections: 19th-20th
  centuries

CRITZ

The Reynolds Homestead

P.O. Box 21, 24082
Telephone: (703) 694-7181
State agency, authorized by Virginia
  Polytechnic Institute and State
  University
Founded in: 1970
David D. Britt, Executive Director
Staff: full time 3, part time 7
Major programs: museum, historic
  site(s), tours/pilgrimages, oral
  history, school programs, historic
  preservation, exhibits, living
  history, audiovisual programs,
  continuing education center
Period of collections: 1850

DANVILLE

Danville Historical Society

Mail to: P.O. Box 2291, 24541
Founded in: 1971
Questionnaire not received

Danville Museum of Fine Arts and History

975 Main St.
Telephone: (804) 793-5644
Mail to: P.O. Box 3769, 24543
Private agency
Founded in: 1971
Eugene C. Stryker, Interim Director
Number of members: 800
Staff: full time 5, part time 4
Major programs: museum, historic
  preservation, exhibits
Period of collections: 1850-present

DUMFRIES

Historic Dumfries Virginia, Inc.

300 Duke St., 22026
Telephone: (703) 221-3346
Founded in: 1973
Anne Flory, President
Number of members: 123
Staff: part time 1, volunteer 10
Major programs: library, archives,
  museum, historic site(s), markers,
  tours/pilgrimages,
  newsletters/pamphlets, historic
  preservation, research,
  genealogical services
Period of collections: 1740-1900

FAIRFAX

Fairfax County History Commission

2855 Annandale Rd., 22042
Telephone: (703) 237-4881
County agency
Founded in: 1968
C.J.S. Durham, Chair
Major programs: library, archives,
  oral history, historic preservation,
  records management, research,
  exhibits, archaeology programs,
  photographic collections

George Mason University Oral History Program

4400 University Dr., 22030

Telephone: (703) 323-2242
Authorized by the university
Founded in: 1981
Roy Rosenzweig, Director
Staff: part time 2, volunteer 6
Major programs: archives, oral history
Period of collections: 1930s-present

Historical Society of Fairfax County
P.O. Box 415, 22030
Private agency
Founded in: 1950
Robert Alden, President
Number of members: 350
Magazine: *Yearbook*
Major programs: book publishing

Northern Virginia Association of Historians
c/o History Department, George
  Mason University, 22030
Telephone: (703) 323-2242
Founded in: 1979
Nan Netherton, Executive Director
Number of members: 400
Staff: part time 1, volunteer 14
Magazine: *The Courier of Historical
  Events*
Major programs: museum, historic
  site(s), tours/pilgrimages, junior
  history, oral history, school
  programs, newsletters/pamphlets,
  audiovisual programs, archaeology
  programs, regional history
  workshops
Period of collections: from prehistoric

Virginia Room, Fairfax City Regional Library/Fairfax County Public Library
3915 Chain Bridge Rd., 22030
Telephone: (703) 691-2123
Mail to: 5502 Port Royal Rd.,
  Springfield, 22151
County agency, authorized by Fairfax
  County Public Library Board
Founded in: 1963
Suzanne S. Levy, Virginia Room
  Librarian
Staff: full time 3, part time 1,
  volunteer 3
Major programs: library, manuscripts,
  photographic collections,
  genealogical services
Period of collections: 1584-present

FALLS CHURCH

Fairfax County History Commission
Telephone: (703) 237-4881
Mail to: 2855 Annandale Rd., 22042
County agency
Founded in: 1966
C.J.S. Durham, Chair
Major programs: archives, historic
  site(s), oral history, book
  publishing, newsletters/pamphlets,
  historic preservation, records
  management, research, exhibits,
  archaeology programs,
  photographic collections,
  genealogical services

Falls Church Historical Commission
120 N. Virginia Ave. 22046
Telephone: (703) 534-7237
Founded in: 1965
R. D. Netherton, Chairman

Staff: volunteer10
Major programs: archives,
  manuscripts, museum, historic
  sites preservation, markers, oral
  history, books,
  newsletters/pamphlets
Period of collections: 1783-1918

FERRUM

Blue Ridge Institute—Blue Ridge Farm Museum
Rt. 40, W
Telephone: (703) 365-2121
Mail to: Ferrum College, 24088
Private agency, authorized by Ferrum
  College
Founded in: 1972
J. Roderick Moore, Director
Major programs: library, archives,
  museum, oral history, educational
  programs
Period of collections: 1780-1920

FINCASTLE

Historic Fincastle, Inc.
P.O. Box 19, 24090
Telephone: (703) 473-2022
Private agency
Founded in: 1969
Harry W. Kessler, President
Number of members: 100
Staff: volunteer 20
Major programs: archives,
  tours/pilgrimages, historic
  preservation, photographic
  collections, genealogical services
Period of collections: from 1770

FORT BELVOIR

Historical Division, Chief of Engineers, Department of the Army
Kingman Bldg., 22060-5577
Mail to: DAEN-ASH, 20314
Federal agency
Founded in: 1942
John T. Greenwood, Chief Historian
Staff: full time 10, part time 4
Major programs: library, archives,
  manuscripts, museum, oral history,
  book publishing,
  newsletters/pamphlets, research,
  exhibits, photographic collections

U.S. Army Engineer Museum
Bldg. 1000, 16th and Belvoir Rd.
  22060
Telephone: (703) 664-3171
Federal agency
Founded in: 1953
James L. Kochan, Director
Staff: full time 4
Major programs: manuscripts,
  museum, historic site(s), research,
  exhibits, audiovisual programs
Period of collections: 1775-present

FORT EUSTIS

U.S. Army Transportation Museum
P.O. Drawer D, 23604-5260
Telephone: (804) 878-3603
Federal agency, authorized by the
  U.S. Army
Founded in: 1959
Dennis P. Mroczkowski, Director
Staff: full time 7

Major programs: library, museum,
  historic site(s), tours/pilgrimages,
  research, exhibits, photographic
  collections
Period of collections: 1918-present

FORT LEE

U.S. Army Quartermaster Museum
A Ave. and 22nd St., 23801
Telephone: (804) 734-4203
Federal agency
Founded in: 1957
Philip M. Cavanaugh, Director
Staff: full time 4
Major programs: museum, school
  programs, exhibits
Period of collections: 1783-present

FORT MONROE

The Casemate Museum
20 Bernard Rd.
Telephone: (804) 727-3973, 729-3391
Mail to: P.O. Box 341, 23651
Founded in: 1951
R. Cody Phillips, Museum Director
Staff: full time 5, part time 5,
  volunteer 35
Major programs: archives, museum,
  historic site(s), exhibits,
  audiovisual programs
Period of collections: 1819-present

FORT MYER

Council on America's Military Past
P.O. Box 1151, 22211
Telephone: (202) 429-2200
Private agency, authorized by State
  of Arizona
Founded in: 1966
Herbert M. Hart, National Secretary
Number of members: 1,300
Staff: volunteer 15
Magazine: *Heliogram*
Major programs: historic site(s),
  tours, newsletters/pamphlets,
  historic preservation

Old Guard Museum
Sheridan Ave., Bldg. 249, 22211
Telephone: (202) 692-9721
Federal agency, authorized by
  Center of Military History
Founded in: 1975
Scott H. Harrelson, Museum Curator
Staff: full time 3
Major programs: museum
Period of collections: Civil War-W.W.
  II

FREDERICKSBURG

Center for Historic Preservation
1301 College Ave., Mary Washington
  College, 22401-5358
Telephone: (703) 899-4037
State agency
Founded in: 1979
Carter L. Hudgins, Director
Staff: full time 3, part time 2
Major programs: library, historic
  preservation, archaeology
  programs

Fredericksburg and Spotsylvania County National Military Park
Telephone: (703) 373-4461
Mail to: P.O. Box 679, 22404

Founded in: 1927
Robert K. Krick, Chief Historian
Staff: full time 30, part time 30,
    volunteer 10
Major programs: library, museum,
    historic sites preservation, markers,
    tours/pilgrimages, educational
    programs, historic preservation
Period of collections: 1861-1865

**Historic Fredericksburg
Foundation, Inc.**
623 Caroline St.
Telephone: (703) 371-4504
Mail to: P.O. Box 162, 22401
Founded in: 1955
Susan Ford Johnson, Executive
    Director
Number of members: 900
Staff: full time 1, part time 1,
    volunteer 75
Magazine: *Preservation Notes*
Major programs: archives, historic
    site(s), tours, school programs,
    book publishing,
    newsletters/pamphlets, historic
    preservation, archaeology
    programs, photographic
    collections, field services
Period of collections: 1783-present

**James Monroe Law Office/Museum
and Memorial Library**
908 Charles St. 22401
Telephone: (703) 373-8426
State agency, authorized by Mary
    Washington College
Founded in: 1927
Rosalie Mercein Sullivan, Director
Staff: full time 2, part time 10
Major programs: museum, tours, oral
    history
Period of collections: 1758-1831

Kenmore Association, Inc.
1201 Washington Ave., 22401
Telephone: (703) 373-3381
Private agency
Founded in: 1922
W. Vernon Edenfield, Director
Major programs: museum, historic
    site(s), newsletters/pamphlets,
    research, exhibits
Period of collections: 1750-1800

**Mary Washington Branch,
Association for the Preservation
of Virginia Antiquities**
1200 Charles St., 22401
Telephone: (703) 373-1569
State agency
Founded in: 1890
Mrs. H. Harrison Braxton, Jr., Director
Number of members: 159
Staff: full time 1, part time 36,
    volunteer 100
Major programs: historic site(s),
    markers, oral history, school
    programs, historic preservation,
    living history
Period of collections: 1772-1800

GALAX

Jeff Matthews Memorial Museum
606 W. Stuart Dr., 24333
City agency
Founded in: 1974
A. G. Pless, Chair

Staff: full time 1, volunteer 4
Major programs: museum
Period of collections:
    prehistoric-present

GLEN ALLEN

**Museum in Memory of Virginia E.
Randolph**
2200 Mountain Rd., 23060
Telephone: (804) 262-3363
County agency, authorized by
    Henrico County Public Schools
Founded in: 1970
William D. Cosby, Sr., Curator
Major programs: historic site(s), oral
    history, school programs, exhibits,
    photographic collections
Period of collections: 1874-1976

GOOCHLAND

**Goochland County Museum and
Historical Center**
Courthouse Green, 23063
County agency, authorized by
    Goochland County Historical
    Society
Forrest D. Sheets, Curator
Magazine: *Goochland County
    Historical Society Magazine*
Major programs: photographic
    collections

GORDONSVILLE

Historic Gordonsville, Inc.
Mail to: P.O. Box 542, 22942
Founded in: 1970
Questionnaire not received

GREAT FALLS

Great Falls Historical Society
P.O. Box 56, 22066
Founded in: 1977
W. Chadwick, President
Number of members: 150
Major programs: oral history,
    newsletters, photographic
    collections

Seneca Road Historical Society
625 Seneca Rd., 22006
Telephone: (703) 430-1066
Mail to: P.O. Box 32
Questionnaire not received

HAMPTON

Aerospace Museum and Park
413 W. Mercury Blvd., 23666
Telephone: (804) 727-6108
City agency
Founded in: 1969
Norma L. Agee, Assistant Director
Staff: full time 3, part time 4
Major programs: museum,
    tours/pilgrimages, exhibits,
    photographic collections
Period of collections: W.W. II

**Hampton Center for the Arts and
Humanities**
22 Wine St., Hampton Recreation
    Department, 23669
City agency
Founded in: 1967
Staff: full time 5
Major programs: library, archives,
    manuscripts, museum, school

programs, records management,
    research, exhibits, living history,
    audiovisual programs, archaeology
    programs, photographic
    collections, genealogical services,
    classes in performing and visual
    arts, entertainment programs
Period of collections: prehistoric-Civil
    War

Hampton Heritage Foundation, Inc.
22 Wine St., 23669
Telephone: (804) 723-1776
Mail to: P.O. Box 536
Founded in: 1977
Questionnaire not received

Hampton Heritage Trust
Telephone: (804) 851-3292
Mail to: c/o 23 Discovery Rd., 23664
Questionnaire not received

Hampton University Museum
Hampton University, 23668
Telephone: (804) 727-5308
Private agency, authorized by the
    university
Founded in: 1868
Jeanne Zeidler, Director
Staff: full time 3, part time 9
Major programs: library, archives,
    museum, research, exhibits,
    photographic collections
Period of collections: 1868-present

Syms-Eaton Museum
418 W. Mercury Blvd. 23669
Telephone: (804) 727-6248
Questionnaire not received

HANOVER

Hanover County Historical Society
P.O. Box 91, 23069
Telephone: (804) 537-5502
Mail to: Rt. 4, Box 182, Ashland,
    23005
Questionnaire not received

HARDY

**Booker T. Washington National
Monument**
Rt. 1, Box 195, 24101
Telephone: (703) 721-2094
Federal agency, authorized by
    Department of the Interior
Founded in: 1956
Geri Bell, Superintendent
Staff: full time 9, part time 3,
    volunteer 1
Major programs: historic site(s),
    tours/pilgrimages, exhibits, living
    history, audiovisual programs
Period of collections: 1860-1865

HARRISONBURG

**Harrisonburg-Rockingham
Historical Society**
301 S. Main St., 22801
Telephone: (703) 434-4762
Private agency
Founded in: 1898
Mary Hilton Geisler, Administrator
Number of members: 1,100
Staff: full time 1, part time 2,
    volunteer 40
Magazine: *The Rockingham
    Recorder*

Booker T. Washington National Monument in Hardy. Washington's birthplace and early childhood home has been restored as a living historical farm.—National Park Service photograph by Richard Frear

Major programs: library, archives, museum, book publishing, newsletters/pamphlets, research, exhibits, genealogical services

Menno Simons Historical Library and Archives
Eastern Mennonite College, 22801-2462
Telephone: (703) 433-2771, ext. 178
Private agency, authorized by Eastern Mennonite College and Seminary, Inc.
Founded in: 1943
Grace I. Showalter, Librarian
Staff: part time 3
Major programs: library, archives, manuscripts, genealogical services
Period of collections: 1525-present

HOPEWELL

Flowerdew Hundred Foundation
Rt. 1, Box 354-D, 23860
Telephone: (804) 541-8897
Founded in: 1971
Questionnaire not received

Merchants Hope Church Foundation, Inc.
P.O. Box 518, 24860
Founded in: 1954
Questionnaire not received

IRVINGTON

Foundation for Historic Christ Church, Inc.
Rts. 646 and 709
Telephone: (804) 438-6855
Mail to: P.O. Box 24, 22480

Private agency
Founded in: 1958
Mrs. Carl B. Headland, Executive Secretary
Number of members: 1,300
Staff: full time 1, part time 1, volunteer 234
Major programs: library, manuscripts, museum, historic site(s), tours/pilgrimages, book publishing, newsletters/pamphlets, historic preservation, research, exhibits, living history, audiovisual programs
Period of collections: 18th century

JAMESTOWN

Jamestown-Yorktown Foundation
Glasshouse Point, 23081
Telephone: (804) 253-4838
Mail to: P.O. Box JF, Williamsburg, 23185
Founded in: 1957
Questionnaire not received

KING & QUEEN

King and Queen County Historical Society
P.O. Box 128, 23085
Private agency
Founded in: 1953
Julia T. Henley, President
Number of members: 600
Major programs: library, archives, manuscripts, historic site(s), markers, school programs, book publishing, newsletters/pamphlets, records management, research, exhibits, photographic collections
Period of collections: from 1700

LANCASTER

Mary Ball Washington Museum and Library, Inc.
Rt. 3, Lancaster Courthouse
Telephone: (804) 462-7280
Mail to: P.O. Box 97, 22503
Private agency
Founded in: 1958
Ann Lewis Burrows, Executive Director
Number of members: 875
Staff: full time 3, part time 1, volunteer 35
Major programs: library, archives, manuscripts, museum, historic site(s), tours/pilgrimages, book publishing, newsletters/pamphlets, historic preservation, research archaeology programs, photographic collections, genealogical services
Period of collections: 19th century

LAWRENCEVILLE

Brunswick County Historical Society, Inc.
P.O. Box 1776, 23868
Telephone: (804) 949-7596
Mail to: P.O. Box 56, Alberta, 23821
Questionnaire not received

LEESBURG

The Loudoun County Historical Society
P.O. Box 344, 22075
Founded in: 1950
Questionnaire not received

Loudoun Museum, Inc.
16 Loudoun St., SW, 22075
Telephone: (703) 777-7427
Private agency
Founded in: 1967
Laura Dutton, Executive Director
Staff: full time 1, part time 3, volunteer 6
Magazine: *Museum Muse*
Major programs: museum, school programs, exhibits, living history
Period of collections: Civil War-late 19th century

Oatlands Plantation
Rt. 2, Box 352, 22075
Telephone: (703) 777-3174
Founded in: 1965
Nicole Sours, Executive Director
Staff: full time 10, part time 18, volunteer 20
Major programs: historic sites preservation, tours, historic preservation, exhibits, newsletters, historic garden restoration, horticulture
Period of collections: 1803-1964

LEXINGTON

George C. Marshall Research Foundation
VMI Parade
Telephone: (703) 463-7103
Mail to: Drawer 1600, 24450
Private agency
Founded in: 1953
Royster Lyle, Jr., Curator of Collections

Staff: full time 14, part time 4
Magazine: *Topics*
Major programs: library, archives, manuscripts, museum, oral history, book publishing, newsletters/pamphlets
Period of collections: 1918-present

Historic Lexington Foundation, Inc.
Mail to: P.O. Box 808, 24450
Questionnaire not received

Lee Chapel
Washington and Lee University, 24450
Telephone: (703) 463-8768
Private agency
Founded in: 1867
Robert C. Peniston, Director
Staff: full time 1, part time 4
Major programs: museum, historic site
Period of collections: 1757-1918

Rockbridge Historical Society
P.O. Box 514
Founded in: 1939
Questionnaire not received

Stonewall Jackson House
8 E. Washington St., 24450
Telephone: (703) 463-2552
Private agency, authorized by Historic Lexington Foundation
Founded in: 1966
Michael Anne Lynn, Director
Staff: full time 3, part time 10, volunteer 40
Major programs: library, museum, school programs, book publishing, newsletters/pamphlets, historic preservation, research, exhibits
Period of collections: 1851-1861

Virginia History and Museums Federation
VMI Museum, Virginia Military Institute, 24450
Telephone: (703) 463-6232
Questionnaire not received

Virginia Military Institute Museum
Jackson Memorial Hall, 24450
Telephone: (703) 463-6232
State agency, authorized by Virginia Military Institute
Founded in: 1907
June F. Cunningham, Director
Staff: full time 3, part time 1
Major programs: museum
Period of collections: 1839-present

LORTON

Gunston Hall
10709 Gunston Rd., 22079
Telephone: (703) 550-9220
State agency
Founded in: 1932
Donald R. Taylor, Director
Staff: full time 11, part time 20
Major programs: library, archives, manuscripts, museum, historic site(s), tours/pilgrimages, school programs, historic preservation, research, exhibits, audiovisual programs
Period of collections: 1725-1792

Pohick Episcopal Church: Parish of Mt. Vernon and Gunston Hall
9301 Richmond Hwy., 22079
Telephone: (703) 339-6572
Private agency, authorized by Diocese of Virginia
William H. Brake, Jr., Rector
Number of members: 1,000
Staff: full time 4, part time 2, volunteer 100
Magazine: *Pohick Post*
Major programs: historic site(s), newsletters/pamphlets, historic preservation, active church
Period of collections: 1700-1800

LURAY

Shenandoah Natural History Association, Inc.
Rt. 4, Box 292, 22835
Telephone: (703) 999-2243
Private agency
Founded in: 1950
Greta F. Miller, Business Manager
Number of members: 400
Staff: full time 1, part time 3
Major programs: library, book publishing, newsletters/pamphlets, natural history information

LYNCHBURG

Anne Spencer Memorial Foundation
1313 Pierce St., 24501
Telephone: (804) 845-1313
Mail to: 1306 Pierce St., 24501
Private agency
Founded in: 1977
Chauncey E. Spencer, Chair
Number of members: 586
Staff: volunteer 14
Major programs: museum, historic site(s), tours/pilgrimages, school programs, historic preservation
Period of collections: 1809-1975

Bicentennial Restoration Committee for South River Meeting House
5810 Fort Ave.
Telephone: (804) 239-9756
Mail to: 1162 Timberlake Dr., 24502
Private agency
Founded in: 1983
Carolyn A. Eubank, Chair
Staff: volunteer 13
Major programs: museum, historic site(s), tours/pilgrimages, book publishing, historic preservation, research, restoration
Period of collections: 1757-1839

Lynchburg Historical Foundation, Inc.
Mail to: P.O. Box 3154, 24503
Founded in: 1972
Questionnaire not received

Lynchburg Museum System
901 Court St., 24504
Telephone: (804) 847-1459
Mail to: P.O. Box 60, 24505
City agency
Founded in: 1976
Thomas G. Ledford, Administrator
Staff: full time 3, part time 2, volunteer 50
Magazine: *The Signpost*

Major programs: museum, historic site(s), tours/pilgrimages, newsletters/pamphlets, historic preservation, research, exhibits, living history, photographic collections
Period of collections: 1750-present

Point of Honor
112 Cabell St., 24504
Telephone: (804) 847-1449
Mail to: P.O. Box 60, 24505
Private agency, authorized by Lynchburg Museum System
Founded in: 1976
Thomas G. Ledford, Administrator
Staff: full time 3, part time 2, volunteer 37
Major programs: museum, historic site(s), tours/pilgrimages, historic preservation, research, living history
Period of collections: 1815-1830

MANASSAS

Manassas City Museum
9406 Main St., 22110
Telephone: (703) 368-1873
City agency
Founded in: 1974
Douglas K. Harvey, Curator
Number of members: 400
Staff: full time 1, part time 2, volunteer 22
Magazine: *Manassas Museum News*
Major programs: museum, markers, oral history, book publishing, newsletters/pamphlets, historic preservation, exhibits, photographic collections
Period of collections: 19th century

MARION

Smyth County Historical and Museum Society, Inc.
Stadium Rd.
Mail to: P.O. Box 574, 24354
Founded in: 1961
Eugene Hoover, President
Number of members: 100
Staff: part time 6
Major programs: archives, museum, book publishing, historic preservation, research, exhibits, photographic collections, genealogical services
Period of collections: 1865-1918

MATHEWS

Mathews County Historical Society, Inc.
Mail to: P.O. Box 855, 23109
Private agency
Founded in: 1964
Number of members: 115
Major programs: museum, historic site(s), book publishing, newsletters/pamphlets, archaeology programs
Period of collections: 19th century

MIDDLETOWN

Belle Grove
P.O. Box 137, 22645
Telephone: (703) 869-2028
Founded in: 1964
Questionnaire not received

MILLWOOD

Clarke County Historical Association
Telephone: (703) 837-1799/837-1556
Mail to: General Delivery
Founded in: 1928
Questionnaire not received

MONTROSS

Northern Neck of Virginia Historical Society
P.O. Box 716, 22520
Telephone: (804) 493-8425
Private agency
Founded in: 1951
Suzanne H. Semsch, Executive
 Secretary/Treasurer
Number of members: 700
Staff: part time 1, volunteer 5
Magazine: *The Northern Neck of Virginia Historical Magazine*
Major programs: library,
 tours/pilgrimages, research
Period of collections: 1600s-1800s

MOUNT VERNON

Mt. Vernon Ladies' Association of the Union
22121
Telephone: (703) 780-2000
Private agency
Founded in: 1853
John E. Harbour, Resident Director
Staff: full time 90, part time 30
Major programs: library, archives,
 manuscripts, museum, historic
 site(s), markers, tours/pilgrimages,
 book publishing,
 newsletters/pamphlets, historic
 preservation, records
 management, research, exhibits,
 audiovisual programs, archaeology
 programs, photographic
 collections, genealogical services
Period of collections: 1754-1799

Pope-Leighey House
9000 Richmond Hwy., Alexandria
Telephone: (703) 557-7880
Mail to: P.O. Box 37, 22121
Private agency, authorized by
 National Trust for Historic
 Preservation
Founded in: 1948
Gordon Alt, Acting Director
Number of members: 480
Staff: full time 9, part time 14,
 volunteer 25
Major programs: school programs,
 historic preservation, architectural
 history
Period of collections: 1940s

Woodlawn Plantation
9000 Richmond Hwy., Alexandria
Telephone: (703) 557-7880
Mail to: P.O. Box 37, 22121
Private agency, authorized by
 National Trust for Historic
 Preservation
Founded in: 1948
Gordon Alt, Acting Director
Number of members: 480
Staff: full time 9, part time 14,
 volunteer 25
Major programs: museum, historic
 site(s), school programs, historic

preservation, programs in the area
 of needlework
Period of collections: 1800-1840

NEW MARKET

New Market Battlefield Park
Telephone: (703) 740-3101
Mail to: Box 1864, 22844
State agency, authorized by Virginia
 Military Institute
Founded in: 1967
Robert S. Myers, Acting Director
Staff: full time 7, part time 2
Major programs: library, museum,
 historic site(s), markers, school
 programs, book publishing,
 newsletters/pamphlets, historic
 preservation, exhibits, living
 history, audiovisual programs
Period of collections: 1861-1865

NEWPORT NEWS

Fort Eustis Historical and Archaeological Association
Telephone: (804) 878-3480
Mail to: Box 4408, Fort Eustis, 23604
Founded in: 1965
Questionnaire not received

The Mariners' Museum
Museum Dr., 23606
Telephone: (804) 595-0368
Private agency
Founded in: 1930
William D. Wilkinson, Director
Number of members: 1,750
Staff: full time 43, part time 20,
 volunteer 135
Magazine: *Mariners Museum Journal*
Major programs: library, archives,
 manuscripts, museum, school
 programs, book publishing,
 newsletters/pamphlets, records
 management, research, exhibits,
 photographic collections,
 genealogical services
Period of collections: 1400-present

Newport News Historical Committee
Public Information Office, City Hall,
 2400 Washington Ave., 23607
Telephone: (804) 247-8487
Founded in: 1967
Questionnaire not received

U.S. Army Transportation Museum
Bldg. 300, Fort Eustis, 23604
Telephone: (804) 878-3603
Mail to: Drawer D, Fort Eustis
Founded in: 1959
Questionnaire not received

War Memorial Museum of Virginia
9285 Warwick Blvd., Huntington Park,
 23607
Telephone: (804) 247-8523
City agency
Founded in: 1923
John V. Quarstein, Chief Curator
Staff: full time 5, part time 9,
 volunteer 20
Major programs: library, archives,
 manuscripts, museum, oral history,
 school programs, book publishing,
 research, exhibits, audiovisual
 programs, photographic
 collections
Period of collections: 1775-1980

NORFOLK

Hampton Roads Naval Museum
Commander Naval Base,
 Pennsylvania Bldg., 23511-6002
Telephone: (804) 444-2243
Federal agency, authorized by the
 U.S. Navy
Founded in: 1979
Michael E. Curtin, Curator
Staff: full time 2, part time 2
Major programs: museum, historic
 site(s), historic preservation,
 research, exhibits
Period of collections: Revolutionary
 War-present

MacArthur Memorial
MacArthur Square, 23510
Telephone: (804) 441-2965
City agency
Founded in: 1964
Lyman H. Hammond, Director
Staff: full time 9, part time 3
Major programs: library, archives,
 museum, book publishing, historic
 preservation, exhibits,
 photographic collections
Period of collections: 1880-1964

Norfolk Historical Society
Telephone: (804) 423-0989
Mail to: P.O. Box 9472, 23505
Founded in: 1965
Questionnaire not received

Sargeant Memorial Room, Norfolk Public Library
301 E. City Hall Ave., 23510
Telephone: (804) 441-2503
City agency
Founded in: 1927
Lucile Portlock, Curator
Staff: full time 2, part time 1,
 volunteer 1
Major programs: library, archives,
 manuscripts, photographic
 collections, genealogical services
Period of collections: 1860-present

Swiss American Historical Society
216 E. 39th St., 23504
Questionnaire not received

Willoughby-Baylor House—Chrysler Museum
601 E. Freemason St., 23510
Telephone: (804) 622-1211, ext. 55/57
City agency
Founded in: 1961
Dorothy W. Wilkins, Manager
Staff: full time 1, part time 12
Major programs: tours/pilgrimages
Period of collections: 1794-1835

NORTHERN VIRGINIA

Council on Abandoned Military Posts, USA, Inc.
Telephone: (703) 379-2006
Mail to: P.O. Box 171, 22210
Founded in: 1966
Herbert M. Hart, Secretary
Number of members: 1,400
Magazine: *Periodical*
Major programs: historic sites
 preservation, markers,
 tours/pilgrimages, school
 programs, book publishing,
 newsletters/pamphlets
Period of collections: 1783-1918

OCCOQUAN

Historic Occoquan, Inc.
413 Mill St.
Telephone: (703) 491-7525
Mail to: P.O. Box 65, 22125
Founded in: 1971
Betty Strawderman, President
Number of members: 30
Staff: full time 3
Major programs: museum, historic
  site(s), exhibits, audiovisual
  programs
Period of collections: 1760-present

ONANCOCK

**Eastern Shore of Virginia Historical
  Society**
21 Market St., Kerr Place
Telephone: (804) 787-3394
Mail to: P.O. Box 193, 23417
Private agency
Founded in: 1959
Susan H. Patterson, Curator
Number of members: 800
Staff: part time 1
Major programs: library, archives,
  manuscripts, museum, historic
  preservation
Period of collections:
  Colonial-present

ORANGE

James Madison Museum
129 Caroline St., 22960
Telephone: (703) 672-1776
Private agency, authorized by The
  James Madison Memorial
  Foundation
Founded in: 1976
Mavis B. Middlemas, Administrator
Staff: full time 1
Major programs: museum,
  newsletters/pamphlets, exhibits,
  audiovisual programs
Period of collections: Colonial

**Orange County Historical
  Society, Inc.**
130 Caroline St.
Telephone: (703) 672-5366
Mail to: P.O. Box 591, 22960
Private agency
Founded in: 1965
Ann Miller, Research Historian
Number of members: 290
Staff: part time 1, volunteer 2
Major programs: library, archives,
  historic site(s),
  newsletters/pamphlets, research,
  genealogical services
Period of collections: 1734-1930s

PAEONIAN SPRINGS

American Work Horse Museum
P.O. Box 88, 22129
Telephone: (703) 338-6290
Private agency
Founded in: 1971
Henry L. Buckardt, President
Number of members: 50
Staff: full time 2, part time 5
Major programs: museum
Period of collections: 1700-1940

PETERSBURG

Centre Hill Mansion Museum
Franklin at Adams St., 23803
Telephone: (804) 732-8081
Mail to: c/o Dept. of Tourism, 15 W.
  Bank St.
Founded in: 1972
Questionnaire not received

Farmers Bank
Bollingbrook and Cockade, 23803
Telephone: (804) 861-1590
Mail to: 15 W. Bank St.
Founded in: 1817
Questionnaire not received

Information Center
400 E. Washington St., 23803
Telephone: (804) 861-8080
Mail to: P.O. Box 2107
Founded in: 1972
Questionnaire not received

Old Blandford Church
319 S. Crater Rd., 23803
Telephone: (804) 732-2230
Mail to: 15 W. Bank St.
Founded in: 1735
Questionnaire not received

The Petersburg Museums
15 W. Bank St., 23803
Telephone: (804) 733-7690
City agency, authorized by City of
  Petersburg Department of Tourism
Founded in: 1972
R. Dulaney Ward, Jr., Director of
  Tourism
Staff: full time 11, part time 24
Major programs: library, archives,
  manuscripts, museum, historic
  site(s), tours/pilgrimages, historic
  preservation, exhibits, audiovisual
  programs, photographic
  collections
Period of collections: 1800-1870

Petersburg National Battlefield
Rt. 36, E, Box 549, 23830
Telephone: (804) 732-3531
Federal agency, authorized by
  National Park Service
Founded in: 1926
Christopher Calkins, Park Historian
Staff: part time 23
Major programs: library, archives,
  manuscripts, museum, historic
  site(s), markers, tours/pilgrimages,
  school programs,
  newsletters/pamphlets, research,
  exhibits, living history, audiovisual
  programs, archaeology programs,
  photographic collections
Period of collections: Civil War

Siege Museum
15 W. Bank St., 23803
Telephone: (804) 861-2904
Founded in: 1976
Questionnaire not received

Trapezium House
244 N. Market St., 23803
Telephone: (804) 861-0563
Mail to: 15 W. Bank St.
Founded in: 1816
Questionnaire not received

PORTSMOUTH

Childrens Museums
400 High St.

Telephone: (804) 393-8983
Mail to: P.O. Box 850, 23705
Authorized by The Portsmouth
  Museums
Founded in: 1963
Nancy J. Melton, Museum Director
Major programs: museum, historic
  site(s), junior history,
  newsletters/pamphlets, historic
  preservation, research
Period of collections:
  prehistoric-present

Community Arts Center
400 High St.
Telephone: (804) 393-8983
Mail to: P.O. Box 850, 23705
City agency, authorized by The
  Portsmouth Museums
Founded in: 1963
Nancy J. Melton, Museums Director
Major programs: museum,
  newsletters/pamphlets, historic
  preservation, research

Portsmouth Historical Association
221 North St., 23704
Telephone: (804) 393-0241
Founded in: 1956
Questionnaire not received

Portsmouth Lightship Museum
London Slip and Water St.
Telephone: (804) 393-8741
Mail to: P.O. Box 248, 23705
City agency
Founded in: 1967
Alice C. Hanes, Curator
Staff: full time 2
Period of collections: 1915-1965

The Portsmouth Museums
400 High St.
Telephone: (804) 393-8983
Mail to: P.O. Box 850, 23705
City agency
Founded in: 1963
Nancy J. Melton, Director
Number of members: 422
Staff: full time 13, part time 3,
  volunteer 100
Major programs: archives, museum,
  historic site(s),
  newsletters/pamphlets, historic
  preservation, research
Period of collections:
  prehistoric-present

**Portsmouth Naval Shipyard
  Museum**
2 High St., 23704
Telephone: (804) 393-8591
Mail to: P.O. Box 248, 23705
Founded in: 1949
Alice C. Hanes, Curator
Staff: full time 3, volunteer 150

QUANTICO

Marine Corps Aviation Museum
Telephone: (703) 640-2606
Mail to: c/o Marine Corps Museums
  Branch Activities, 22134
Questionnaire not received

**U.S. Marine Corps Air-Ground
  Museum and Museums Branch
  Activities**
Telephone: (703) 640-2606
Mail to: 22134-5001

Federal agency, authorized by
Marine Corps Museum and
Historical Center, Washington, D.C.
Rudy T. Schwanda, Director
Staff: full time 8
Magazine: *Fortitudine*
Major programs: archives, tours,
historic preservation, historic
aviation hangars and aircraft,
aviation-related collections

RADFORD

New River Historical Society
Mail to: P.O. Box 711, 24141
Telephone: (703) 639-5723
Founded in: 1967
W. Keith Roberts, President
Number of members: 350
Staff: volunteer 2
Magazine: *Benchmarks*
Major programs: archives, museum,
historic site(s), tours/pilgrimages,
newsletters/pamphlets, historic
preservation, exhibits, audiovisual
programs
Period of collections: 1810-1875

RESTON

Patowmack Company 1803
11224 Wiehle Ave. Apt 15, 22090
Telephone: (703) 437-4176
Questionnaire not received

RICHMOND

Archaeological Society of Virginia
4414 Park Ave., 23221
Telephone: (804) 359-0442
Private agency
Founded in: 1941
William H. Anderson, Treasurer
Number of members: 700
Staff: volunteer 1
Major programs: historic site(s),
archaeology programs
Period of collections: 11,000
B.C.-present

**Association for the Preservation of
Virginia Antiquities**
2705 Park Ave., 23220
Telephone: (804) 359-0239
Private agency
Founded in: 1889
R. Angus Murdoch, Executive
Director
Number of members: 6,500
Staff: full time 15, part time 16,
volunteer 56
Magazine: *Discovery*
Major programs: historic site(s),
markers, newsletters/pamphlets,
historic preservation, research,
exhibits, genealogical services
Period of collections: 18th century

**Confederate Memorial Literary
Society**
1201 E. Clay St., 23219
Telephone: (804) 649-1861
Founded in: 1896
Questionnaire not received

**Congregation Beth Ahabah
Museum and Archives Trust**
1109 W. Franklin St., 23235
Telephone: (804) 353-2668
Private agency, authorized by
Congregation Beth Ahabah

Founded in: 1977
Cynthia N. Krumbein, Director
Number of members: 710
Staff: part time 2, volunteer 31
Major programs: archives,
manuscripts, museum, research,
exhibits, photographic collections,
genealogical services
Period of collections: 1790-present

Historic Richmond Foundation
2407 E. Grace St., 23223
Telephone: (804) 643-7407
Private agency
Founded in: 1957
John G. Zehmer, Executive Director
Number of members: 1,020
Staff: full time 4, volunteer 100
Major programs: historic sites
preservation, educational
programs

Maymont Foundation
1700 Hampton St., 23235
Telephone: (804) 358-7166
Private agency
Founded in: 1975
J. Robert Hicks, Jr., Executive
Director
Number of members: 900
Staff: full time 20, part time 7,
volunteer 200
Major programs: museum, historic
site(s), school programs, historic
preservation, living history
Period of collections: late Victorian

Meadow Farm Museum
Courtney and Mountain Rd.
Telephone: (804) 649-0566
Mail to: P.O. Box 27032, 23273
County agency
Founded in: 1978
Susan Hanson, Curator
Staff: full time 4, part time 1
Major programs: library, archives,
manuscripts, historic site(s),
markers, tours/pilgrimages, school
programs, records management,
research, exhibits, living history,
audiovisual programs, archaeology
programs, photographic
collections
Period of collections: 1850

**Museum of the Confederacy,
Brockenbrough Library**
1201 E. Clay St. 23219
Telephone: (804) 649-1861
Private agency, authorized by
Confederate Memorial Literary
Society
Founded in: 1890
Elizabeth Scott McKemie, Director
Number of members: 2,000
Staff: full time 8, part time 6,
volunteer 40
Magazine: *Museum of the
Confederacy Newsletter*
Major programs: library, archives,
manuscripts, museum, historic
site(s), school programs,
newsletters/pamphlets, historic
preservation, exhibits, living
history, audiovisual programs,
photographic collections,
genealogical services
Period of collections: 1850-1900

Poe Museum of the Poe Foundation
1914-16 E. Main St., 23223
Telephone: (804) 648-5523
Founded in: 1921
Questionnaire not received

**Richmond Independence
Bicentennial Commission**
900 E. Broad St., Room 404, City Hall,
23219
Telephone: (804) 649-1775
Questionnaire not received

Richmond National Battlefield Park
3215 E. Broad St., 23223
Telephone: (804) 226-1981
Founded in: 1944
Sylvester Putnam, Superintendent
Staff: full time 13, part time 7,
volunteer 33
Major programs: library, museum,
historic site(s), markers,
tours/pilgrimages, school
programs, historic preservation,
exhibits, living history, audiovisual
programs
Period of collections: Civil War

Steamer Company Number 5
200 W. Marshal St., 23220
Telephone: (804) 644-1849
Private agency
Founded in: 1976
Stephen Hadley, Director
Number of members: 20
Staff: part time 2, volunteer 20
Major programs: museum, historic
site(s), school programs, historic
preservation, history of fire-fighting
services
Period of collections: 1898-1955

**United Daughters of the
Confederacy**
Memorial Bldg., 328 North Blvd.,
23220
Telephone: (804) 355-1636
Private agency
Founded in: 1894
Number of members: 28,000
Staff: full time 2, part time 2
Magazine: *United Daughters of the
Confederacy*
Major programs: library, historic
site(s), book publishing,
newsletters/pamphlets, historic
preservation, research, living
history, genealogical services
Period of collections: 1861-1865

The Valentine Museum
1015 E. Clay St., 23219
Telephone: (804) 649-0711
Private agency
Founded in: 1892
Frank Jewell, Director
Number of members: 2,000
Staff: full time 12, part time 4,
volunteer 150
Magazine: *The Visitor*
Major programs: library, archives,
manuscripts, museum, historic
site(s), tours/pilgrimages, junior
history, school programs, research,
photographic collections
Period of collections: 19th century

Virginia Association of Museums
2500 W. Broad St., 23220
Telephone: (804) 257-1079

Private agency
Founded in: 1968
Edith McRee Whiteman, Executive
Director
Number of members: 190
Staff: full time 1, part time 1
Magazine: *VAMgram*
Major programs: museum,
educational programs,
newsletters/pamphlets, annual
meeting, clearinghouse of
information, professional training
programs

Virginia Baptist Historical Society
Boatwright Memorial Library
Telephone: (704) 285-6324
Mail to: P.O. Box 34, University of
Richmond, 23173
Private agency
Founded in: 1876
Fred Anderson, Executive Director
Number of members: 800
Staff: full time 2, part time 3
Magazine: *Virginia Baptist Register*
Major programs: library, archives,
manuscripts, museum, markers,
tours/pilgrimages, oral history,
book publishing,
newsletters/pamphlets, records
management, research, exhibits,
living history, audiovisual
programs, photographic
collections, genealogical services,
field services
Period of collections: 1760s-present

◊**Virginia Division of Historic
Landmarks**
Morsons Row, 221 Governor St.,
23219
Telephone: (804) 786-3143
State agency, authorized by
Department of Conservation and
Historic Resources
Founded in: 1966
H. Bryan Mitchell, Director
Staff: full time 39, part time 1
Magazine: *Notes on Virginia*
Major programs: archives, markers,
school programs,
newsletters/pamphlets, historic
preservation, archaeology
programs, photographic
collections, technical services
Period of collections:
prehistoric-present

Virginia Genealogical Society
Telephone: (807) 770-2306
Mail to: P.O. Box 7469, 23221
Founded in: 1960
James Morris Bagby, President
Number of members: 1,100
Staff: volunteer 15
Magazine: *Magazine of Virginia
Genealogy*
Major programs: manuscripts,
educational programs, books,
newsletters/pamphlets

◊**Virginia Historical Society**
428 North Blvd.
Telephone: (804) 358-4901
Mail to: P.O. Box 7311, 23221
Private agency
Founded in: 1831
Paul C. Nagel, Director
Number of members: 2,800

Staff: full time 26
Magazine: *Virginia Magazine of
History and Biography*
Major programs: library, manuscripts,
museum, books,
newsletters/pamphlets, exhibits
Period of collections: 1492-present

Virginia State Library
11th St. at Capitol Square, 23219
Telephone: (804) 786-2305
State agency
Founded in: 1823
Donald Haynes, State Librarian
Staff: full time 132
Magazine: *Virginia Cavalcade*
Major programs: library, archives,
manuscripts, book publishing,
newsletters/pamphlets, records
management, research,
photographic collections,
genealogical services, field
services
Period of collections: 1492-present

Wilton House Museum
S. Wilton Rd.
Telephone: (804) 282-5936
Mail to: P.O. Box 8225, 23226
Private agency, authorized by
National Society of Colonial Dames
Founded in: 1892
Staff: full time 2, part time 3,
volunteer 40
Major programs: archives, museum,
historic site(s), living history,
decorative arts
Period of collections: 1725-1815

ROANOKE

Roanoke Museum of Fine Arts
1 Market Square, 24011
Telephone: (703) 342-5760
Private agency
Founded in: 1951
Peter Rippe, Executive Director
Number of members: 2,000
Staff: full time 7, part time 11,
volunteer 130
Magazine: *Focus*
Major programs: library, museum,
school programs, book publishing,
newsletters/pamphlets, records
management, exhibits, fine arts

Roanoke Transportation Museum
802 Wiley Dr., SW, 24015
Telephone: (703) 342-5670
Private agency
Founded in: 1963
Nancy M. McBride, Executive
Director
Number of members: 500
Staff: part time 4, volunteer 15
Major programs: museum, school
programs, exhibits
Period of collections: 1884-1959

Roanoke Valley Historical Society
1 Market Square,
Center-in-the-Square, 24011
Telephone: (703) 342-5770
Mail to: P.O. Box 1904, 24008
Private agency
Founded in: 1957
Nomeka B. Sours, Executive Director
Number of members: 850
Staff: full time 2, part time 2,
volunteer 125

Magazine: *Journal of the Roanoke
Valley Historical Society*
Major programs: library, archives,
museum, tours/pilgrimages, oral
history, school programs,
newsletters/pamphlets, historic
preservation, exhibits
Period of collections: mid
1800s-present

ROCKY MOUNT

Franklin County Historical Society
P.O. Box 86, 24151
County agency
Founded in: 1968
J. Francis Amos, President
Number of members: 100
Staff: volunteer 5
Major programs: archives,
newsletters/pamphlets, research,
photographic collections,
genealogical services

SPOTSYLVANIA

**Spotsylvania Historical
Association, Inc.**
Telephone: (703) 582-5672
Mail to: P.O. Box 64, 22553
Founded in: 1962
Frances L. N. Waller, Director
Number of members: 206
Staff: full time 2, part time 4,
volunteer 3
Major programs: library, manuscripts,
museum, historic sites
preservation, markers,
tours/pilgrimages, oral history,
educational programs, books,
newsletters/pamphlets, genealogy
Period of collections: 1600-present

STANLEY

**Blue Ridge Preservation
Association**
P.O. Box 465, 22851
Telephone: (703) 778-2520
Private agency
Founded in: 1982
Alan S. Brenner, Director
Number of members: 25
Staff: volunteer 10
Magazine: *Shenandoah Heritage*
Major programs: oral history, book
publishing, research, photographic
collections, genealogical services
Period of collections: 19th
century-present

STAUNTON

Augusta County Historical Society
Mail to: P.O. Box 686, 24401
Founded in: 1964
Mrs. John E. True, President
Number of members: 430
Major programs: archives, book
publishing, genealogical services
Period of collections: 1800s-present

Woodrow Wilson Birthplace
20 N. Coalter St.
Telephone: (703) 885-0897
Mail to: P.O. Box 24, 24401
Private agency, authorized by
Woodrow Wilson Birthplace
Foundation, Inc.
Founded in: 1938

Katharine L. Brown, Executive
Director
Number of members: 900
Staff: full time 4, part time 12,
volunteer 6
Major programs: library, archives,
manuscripts, museum, historic
site(s), tours/pilgrimages, school
programs, newsletters/pamphlets,
photographic collections
Period of collections: 1850s-1920

STRATFORD

**Robert E. Lee Memorial
Association, Inc.**
Telephone: (804) 493-8038
Mail to: Stratford Hall Plantation,
22558
Founded in: 1929
Thomas E. Bass III, Executive
Director
Staff: full time 33, part time 30
Major programs: archives,
manuscripts, museum, historic
sites preservation,
tours/pilgrimages, oral history,
educational programs,
newsletters/pamphlets
Period of collections: 1700-1799

Stratford Hall Plantation
22558
Telephone: (804) 493-8038
Thomas E. Bass, Executive Director
Major programs: archives, museum,
newsletters/pamphlets
Period of collections: 1600-1900

SUFFOLK

**Suffolk-Nansemond Historical
Society**
P.O. Box 1255, 23434
Telephone: (804) 539-0296
Private agency
Thomas J. O'Connor, President
Number of members: 280
Major programs: library, archives,
tours/pilgrimages, school
programs, newsletters/pamphlets,
historic preservation, audiovisual
programs, photographic
collections
Period of collections: 1790

TAZEWELL

**Historic Crab Orchard Museum and
Pioneer Park, Inc.**
Rt. 19-460
Telephone: (703) 988-6755
Mail to: P.O. Box 12, 24651
Private agency
Nellie W. Bundy, Director
Mail to: 175
Staff: full time 3, part time 1,
volunteer 15
Major programs: library, archives,
museum, historic site(s),
tours/pilgrimages,
newsletters/pamphlets, historic
preservation, research, exhibits,
photographic collections,
genealogical services
Period of collections: 1550-1900

VIENNA

Historic Vienna, Inc.
Telephone: (703) 938-5187
Mail to: P.O. Box 53, 22180
Founded in: 1976
Questionnaire not received

VIRGINIA BEACH

**Princess Anne County Historical
Society**
1526 McCullough Lane, 23454
Telephone: (804) 481-6656
Founded in: 1961
Questionnaire not received

WARM SPRINGS

**Bath County Historical
Society, Inc.**
24484
Telephone: (703) 839-2543
Founded in: 1969
Hugh S. Gwin, President
Number of members: 300
Staff: volunteer 15
Major programs: library, museum,
newsletters/pamphlets
Period of collections:
prehistoric-present

WARRENTON

Fauquier Historical Society, Inc.
Mail to: P.O. Box 675, 22186
Private agency
Founded in: 1966
J. Willard Lineweaver, President
Number of members: 400
Staff: volunteer 30
Major programs: museum, oral
history, newsletters/pamphlets,
historic preservation, research,
exhibits, genealogical services
Period of collections: 1800-1900

WATERFORD

Waterford Foundation, Inc.
2nd and Main Sts., 22190
Telephone: (703) 882-3018
Founded in: 1943
Constance K. Chamberlin, Executive
Director
Number of members: 400
Staff: full time 1, part time 1,
volunteer 20
Major programs: historic sites
preservation, educational
programs
Period of collections: 1865-present

WILLIAMSBURG

**Abby Aldrich Rockefeller Folk Art
Collection**
S. England St.
Telephone: (804) 229-1000, ext. 2424
Mail to: Drawer C, 23187
Private agency, authorized by
Colonial Williamsburg Foundation
Founded in: 1957
Carolyn J. Weekley, Director
Staff: full time 8
Major programs: library, archives,
research, exhibits, folk art
Period of collections: 1715-1970

Bassett Hall
Francis St.

Telephone: (804) 229-1000
Mail to: P.O. Box C, 23187
Private agency, authorized by
Colonial Williamsburg Foundation
Founded in: 1750
Patricia A. Hurdle, Associate
Director, Museums Division,
Colonial Williamsburg Foundation
Staff: full time 4, part time 5
Major programs: historic sites
preservation, folk and decorative
arts collections, historic house
museum
Period of collections: 18th-20th
centuries

Colonial Williamsburg Foundation
Henry St., Goodwin Bldg.
Telephone: (804) 229-1000
Mail to: P.O. Box C, 23187
Private agency
Founded in: 1928
Charles R. Longsworth,
President/Chief Executive Officer
Staff: full time 1,600
Magazine: *Colonial Williamsburg*
Major programs: library, archives,
museum, historic site(s), school
programs, book publishing, historic
preservation, research, exhibits,
living history, audiovisual
programs, archaeology programs,
photographic collections
Period of collections: 18th-19th
centuries

**DeWitt Wallace Decorative Arts
Gallery**
325 Francis St.
Telephone: (804) 229-1000
Mail to: P.O. Box C, 23187
Private agency, authorized by
Colonial Williamsburg Foundation
Founded in: 1979
Beatrix T. Rumford, Vice President,
Museums
Staff: full time 10
Major programs: museum, historic
site(s), research, exhibits,
audiovisual programs, decorative
arts
Period of collections: 1650-1850

**Institute of Early American History
and Culture**
P.O. Box 220, 23187
Telephone: (804) 229-2771
Private agency, authorized by
College of William and Mary and
the Colonial Williamsburg
Foundation
Founded in: 1943
Thad W. Tate, Director
Number of members: 700
Staff: full time 12, part time 1
Magazine: *The William and Mary
Quarterly*
Major programs: book publishing,
newsletters/pamphlets, research,
conferences
Period of collections: before 1815

**James Anderson House
Archaeological Exhibit**
Duke of Gloucester St.
Telephone: (804) 229-1000
Mail to: P.O. Box C, 23187
Private agency, authorized by
Colonial Williamsburg Foundation

Founded in: 1975
Patricia A. Hurdle, Associate
 Director, Museums Division
Major programs: museum,
 archaeology programs
Period of collections: 18th
 century-present

Jamestown-Yorktown Foundation
P.O. Drawer JF, 23187
Telephone: (804) 253-4838
State agency
Founded in: 1952
Ross L. Weeks, Jr., Executive
 Director
Staff: full time 59, part time 30
Major programs: library, museum,
 historic site(s), school programs,
 research, exhibits, living history
Period of collections: 17th-18th
 centuries

**Virginia Research Center for
 Archeology**
Wren Kitchen, The College of William
 and Mary, 23186
Telephone: (804) 253-4836
Founded in: 1966
Questionnaire not received

Williamsburg Area Historical Society
285 Neck-O-Land Rd.
Telephone: (804) 229-7728
Private agency
Founded in: 1982
Ed Belvin/ Charles Hunter,
 Co-chairmen
Number of members: 20
Staff: volunteer 3
Major programs: oral history,
 photographic collections
Period of collections: 1800-present

WINCHESTER

**Preservation of Historic
 Winchester, Inc.**
8 E. Cork St., 22601
Telephone: (703) 667-3577
Private agency
Founded in: 1965
Karen Czaikowski, Executive Director
Number of members: 500
Staff: full time 1, part time 1,
 volunteer 30
Major programs: library, markers,
 tours/pilgrimages, school
 programs, book publishing,
 newsletters/pamphlets, historic
 preservation, exhibits,
 photographic collections, field
 services
Period of collections: 1780-present

**Winchester-Frederick County
 Historical Society**
Piccadilly and N. Braddock Sts.
Telephone: (703) 662-6550
Mail to: P.O. Box 97, 22601
Private agency, authorized by
 Winchester-Frederick County
 Historical Society
Founded in: 1930
Elaine Walker Hall, Executive Director
Number of members: 665
Staff: full time 1, part time 1,
 volunteer 5
Major programs: archives,
 manuscripts, museum, historic
 site(s), markers, tours/pilgrimages,

junior history, book publishing,
 newsletters/pamphlets, historic
 preservation, living history,
 photographic collections,
 genealogical services
Period of collections: 1740-present

WOODSTOCK

**Woodstock Museum of
 Shenandoah County, Inc.**
147 N. Main St., 22664
Telephone: (703) 459-5316
Private agency
Founded in: 1969
Joseph B. Clower, Jr., Vice President
Number of members: 150
Staff: volunteer 30
Major programs: archives, museum,
 oral history, book publishing,
 educational programs
Period of collections: 18th-early 20th
 centuries

WYTHEVILLE

Wythe County Historical Society
Rock House Museum, Monroe and
 Tazewell, 24382
Telephone: (703) 228-3841
Mail to: 465 Church St.
Questionnaire not received

YORKTOWN

**Colonial National Historical Park:
 Jamestown Island and Yorktown
 Battlefield**
P.O. Box 210, 23690
Telephone: (804) 898-3400
Federal agency, authorized by
 National Park Service
Founded in: 1931
Richard H. Maeder, Superintendent
Staff: full time 90, part time 65,
 volunteer 15
Major programs: library, archives,
 manuscripts, museum, historic
 site(s), markers, tours/pilgrimages,
 school programs,
 newsletters/pamphlets, historic
 preservation, records
 management, research, exhibits,
 living history, audiovisual
 programs, archaeology programs,
 photographic collections
Period of collections: 1607-1781

**Virginia Historic Landmarks
 Commission, Research Center
 for Archaeology**
Rt. 238
Telephone: (804) 253-4836
Mail to: P.O. Box 368, 23690
State agency, authorized by
 Commonwealth of Virginia
Founded in: 1966
Alain C. Outlaw, State Archaeologist
Staff: full time 16, volunteer 7
Major programs: archives, historic
 site(s), historic preservation
Period of collections:
 prehistoric-present

Watermens Museum in Yorktown
45 Water St.
Telephone: (803) 898-3180/887-2641
Mail to: P.O. Box 531, 23690
Private agency, authorized by
 Yorktown Arts Foundation

Founded in: 1981
Marian H. Bowditch, Chair
Staff: part time 1, volunteer 35
Major programs: museum,
 tours/pilgrimages, junior history,
 oral history, school programs,
 newsletters/pamphlets, historic
 preservation, exhibits
Period of collections:
 Colonial-present

Yorktown Victory Center
P.O. Box 1976, Rt. 238, 23690
Telephone: (804) 887-1776
Founded in: 1976
Questionnaire not received

WASHINGTON

ANDERSON ISLAND

Anderson Island Historical Society
Johnson Farm, 98303
Telephone: (206) 884-2135
Founded in: 1975
Questionnaire not received

ASOTIN

Asotin County Historical Society
215 Filmore
Telephone: (509) 243-4659
Mail to: P.O. Box 367, 99402
County agency
Founded in: 1970
Alexander Swantz, President
Staff: volunteer 10
Major programs: library, museum,
 historic site(s), markers,
 tours/pilgrimages, oral history,
 school programs, book publishing,
 newsletters/pamphlets, historic
 preservation, photographic
 collections
Period of collections: 1878-present

AUBURN

**White River Valley Historical
 Society**
918 H St., SE, 98002
Telephone: (206) 833-7784
Founded in: 1958
Questionnaire not received

BELFAIR

Mason County Historical Society
P.O. Box 843, 98528
Telephone: (206) 275-2032 (librarian)
Private agency
Founded in: 1958
Annette Munson, President
Number of members: 275
Staff: volunteer 30
Major programs: museum, book
 publishing, historic preservation
Period of collections: 1890-present

BELLEVUE

Newcastle Historical Society
14553 S.E. 55th St., 98006
Telephone: (206) 746-2482

Private agency
Founded in: 1979
Milton Swanson, President
Number of members: 20
Major programs: historic site(s),
historic preservation, research
Period of collections: 1863-1963

BELLINGHAM

Whatcom County Historical Society
P.O. Box 2116, 98227
Telephone: (206) 676-0582
County agency
Founded in: 1964
James Langston, President
Number of members: 150
Major programs: book publishing,
historic preservation

Whatcom Museum of History and Art
121 Prospect St., 98225
Telephone: (206) 676-6981
Founded in: 1938
Questionnaire not received

BLACK DIAMOND

Black Diamond Historical Society
32627 Railroad and Baker Sts.
Telephone: 886-1168
Mail to: P.O. Box 232, 98010
Town agency
Founded in: 1975
Robert Eaton, President
Number of members: 275
Staff: volunteer 10
Major programs: library, archives,
manuscripts, museum, historic
site(s), tours/pilgrimages, junior
history, oral history, school
programs, newsletters/pamphlets,
historic preservation, records
management, research, exhibits,
living history, photographic
collections
Period of collections: 1882-present

CASHMERE

Chelan County Historical Society
P.O. Box 22, 98815
Telephone: (509) 782-3230
County agency
Founded in: 1957
Geri Inabnit, Coordinator
Number of members: 400
Staff: full time 3
Major programs: museum, historic
site(s), markers, historic
preservation, exhibits
Period of collections: prehistoric

CHEHALIS

Lewis County Historical Museum
599 N.W. Front St., 98532
Telephone: (206) 748-0831
Private agency
Founded in: 1965
Jill Kangas, Museum Director
Number of members: 498
Staff: full time 1, part time 1,
volunteer 147
Magazine: *Lewis County Log*
Major programs: library, archives,
museum, oral history, school
programs, newsletters/pamphlets,

research, exhibits, audiovisual
programs, photographic
collections, genealogical services
Period of collections: 1850-present

Lewis County Historical Society
599 N.W. Front St., 98532
Telephone: (206) 748-0831
Founded in: 1965
Jill Kangas, Director
Number of members: 500
Staff: full time 3, volunteer 147
Magazine: *Lewis County Log*
Major programs: archives, museum,
markers, oral history, historic
preservation, exhibits,
photographic collections,
genealogical services
Period of collections: 1890-1940

CHELAN

Lake Chelan Historical Society
204 E. Woodin Ave.
Mail to: P.O. Box 1948, 98816
Private agency
Founded in: 1970
James E. Lindston, President
Number of members: 150
Staff: volunteer 40
Magazine: *Lake Chelan History Notes*
Major programs: archives, museum,
oral history, photographic
collections
Period of collections: 1850-present

CLE ELUM

Cle Elum Historical Society
223 E. First St.
Mail to: 202 Reed St., 98922
Questionnaire not received

COLFAX

Whitman County Historical Society
P.O. Box 67, 99111
Founded in: 1972
Questionnaire not received

COLVILLE

Stevens County Historical Society
700 N. Wynne St.
Telephone: (509) 684-5968
Mail to: P.O. Box 25, 99114
Questionnaire not received

COUPEVILLE

Island County Historical Society
903 Alexander St.
Mail to: P.O. Box 305, 98239
Private agency
Founded in: 1949
Murrieal Short, President
Number of members: 200
Staff: volunteer 20
Major programs: manuscripts,
museum, historic sites
preservation, tours/pilgrimages,
books, historic preservation
Period of collections: 1850-present

DES MOINES

Greater Des Moines-Zenith Historical Society
Mail to: P.O. Box 98033, 98188
Founded in: 1979
Questionnaire not received

DU PONT

Du Pont Historical Museum
207 Brandywine Ave. 98327
Telephone: (206) 964-8895
City agency
Founded in: 1977
Ruth Iafrati, Chair
Staff: full time 1, part time 1
Major programs: historic site(s),
historic preservation, records
management, exhibits
Period of collections: 1800s

DUVALL

Duvall Historical and Old Stuff Society
98019
Telephone: (206) 788-1662
Mail to: P.O. Box 342
Founded in: 1976
Questionnaire not received

EATONVILLE

Eatonville Historical Society
R.R. 2 Box 444, 98328
Telephone: (206) 832-6096
Private agency
Founded in: 1973
Donald B. Baublits, President
Number of members: 30
Major programs: historic site(s), oral
history, book publishing, historic
preservation, research, living
history
Period of collections: 1889-present

Pioneer Farm Museum—The D.O.V.E. Center
7716 Ohop Valley Rd., 98328
Telephone: (206) 832-6300
Founded in: 1977
Meryl G. Pruitt, Administrative
Coordinator
Number of members: 150
Staff: full time 3, part time 4,
volunteer 6
Magazine: *DOVE Tales*
Major programs: museum, historic
site(s), tours/pilgrimages, school
programs, book publishing,
newsletters/pamphlets, historic
preservation, living history,
audiovisual programs
Period of collections: 1887

EDMONDS

Edmonds-South Snohomish County Historical Society, Inc.
118 5th Ave., N.
Telephone: (206) 774-0900
Mail to: P.O. Box 52, 98020
Founded in: 1973
Vivian K. Smith, Museum Director
Number of members: 135
Staff: volunteer 43
Major programs: museum, markers,
historic preservation
Period of collections: 1926-1952

ELLENSBURG

Kittitas County Museum
114 E. 3rd. Ave.
Telephone: (509) 925-3778
Mail to: P.O. Box 265, 98926

Private agency, authorized by Kittitas County Historical Society, Inc.
Founded in: 1961
Larry J. Nickel, Director
Number of members: 100
Staff: part time 1, volunteer 1
Major programs: archives, museum, tours/pilgrimages, historic preservation, exhibits, audiovisual programs, photographic collections, genealogical services
Period of collections: 1880-1910

EVERETT

Snohomish County Museum and Historical Association
Legion Park
Mail to: 2602 Rainier St., 98201
Founded in: 1954
Faye Irwin, President
Number of members: 150
Staff: volunteer 4
Major programs: museum, tours/pilgrimages, school programs, historic preservation, photographic collections
Period of collections: 1800s-present

FORT LEWIS

Ft. Lewis Military Museum
Bldg. 4320, Main St. 98433
Telephone: (206) 967-7206
Founded in: 1970
Questionnaire not received

Friends of the Ft. Lewis Military Museum—Fort Lewis Military Museum
98433-5000
Telephone: (206) 967-7206
Private agency
Founded in: 1973
Vasco J. Fenili, President
Number of members: 140
Magazine: Friends Newsletter
Major programs: museum, tours/pilgrimages, newsletters/pamphlets, exhibits
Period of collections: 1804-present

FOX ISLAND

Fox Island Historical Society
1017 9th Ave., 98333
Telephone: (206) 549-2461
Founded in: 1897
Marian Ray Reid, President
Number of members: 68
Staff: volunteer 14
Major programs: museum, historic preservation
Period of collections: 1846-present

FRIDAY HARBOR

San Juan Historical Society
405 Price St., 98250
Mail to: P.O. Box 441
Questionnaire not received

GIG HARBOR

Peninsula Historical Society
3510 Rosedale St., 98335
Telephone: (206) 858-6722
Mail to: P.O. Box 744, 98335
Private agency
Founded in: 1963

Bob Lathrop, President
Number of members: 100
Major programs: archives, manuscripts, museum
Period of collections: 1865-present

GOLDENDALE

Goldendale Observatory State Park and Interpretation Center
Rt. 3, Box 68, 98620
Telephone: (509) 773-3141
State agency, authorized by Parks and Recreation Commission
Founded in: 1973
Steve R. Stout, Interpretive Specialist
Staff: full time 1, part time 1, volunteer 3
Major programs: library, archives, historic site(s), tours/pilgrimages, oral history, school programs, historic preservation, exhibits, audiovisual programs
Period of collections: 1973-present

Maryhill Museum of Art
Star Rt. 677, Box 23, 98620
Telephone: (509) 773-4792
Private agency
Founded in: 1926
Linda Brady Mountain, Director
Number of members: 1
Staff: full time 4, part time 4, volunteer 2
Major programs: library, archives, museum, historic site(s), newsletters/pamphlets, historic preservation, research, exhibits, photographic collections, fine arts
Period of collections: late 19th-early 20th centuries

GRANITE FALLS

Granite Falls Historical Society
Corner, Wabash and Indiana Sts.
Telephone: (206) 691-7640
Mail to: P.O. Box 135, 98252
Private agency
Founded in: 1969
Lillian Goodrich, President
Number of members: 50
Staff: volunteer 12
Major programs: museum, historic site(s), tours/pilgrimages, newsletters/pamphlets
Period of collections: 1918-present

HOQUIAM

Polson Park and Museum Historical Society
1607 Riverside Ave.
Telephone: (206) 533-5862
Mail to: P.O. Box 432, 98550
Founded in: 1976
Elsie Reynolds, President
Number of members: 600
Staff: volunteer 50
Major programs: library, museum, historic preservation, photographic collections, genealogical services
Period of collections: 1850-present

ILWACO

Ilwaco Heritage Foundation
117 S.E. Lake St.
Telephone: (503) 642-3446
Mail to: P.O. Box 153, 98624

Founded in: 1983
Noreen Robinson, Director
Number of members: 230
Staff: volunteer 12
Major programs: museum
Period of collections: 1792-present

Lewis and Clark Interpretive Center, Ft. Canby State Park
P.O. Box 488, 98624
Telephone: (206) 642-3029
State agency
Founded in: 1976
Jack W. Hartt, Ranger 2
Staff: full time 1, part time 3
Major programs: library, archives, historic site(s), markers, tours/pilgrimages, oral history, school programs, research, exhibits, audiovisual programs, photographic collections
Period of collections: 1804-1945

INDEX

Index Historical Society
P.O. Box 107, 98256
Telephone: (206) 793-1534
Private agency
Founded in: 1982
Louise Sumner, Secretary
Number of members: 55
Staff: volunteer 1
Major programs: archives, museum, oral history, newsletters/pamphlets
Period of collections: 1890-1940

ISSAQUAH

Issaquah Historical Society
165 S.E. Andrews St.
Telephone: (206) 392-3500
Mail to: P.O. Box 695, 98027
Private agency
Founded in: 1972
Greg Spranger, Chair
Number of members: 120
Staff: volunteer 10
Major programs: library, archives, manuscripts, museum, historic site(s), markers, tours/pilgrimages, junior history, school programs, book publishing, newsletters/pamphlets, historic preservation, records management, research, exhibits, photographic collections, field services
Period of collections: 1880s-1950s

KELSO

Cowlitz County Historical Society
405 Allen St., 98626
Telephone: (206) 577-3119
Founded in: 1949
Questionnaire not received

KENNEWICK

East Benton County Historical Society
P.O. Box 6710, 99336
Private agency
Founded in: 1977
Beryla Lande, President
Number of members: 700
Magazine: Courier of the East Benton County Historical Society

Major programs: archives, museum,
oral history, school programs,
newsletters/pamphlets, research,
exhibits, photographic collections
Period of collections: 1900-1930

KENT

**South King County Genealogical
Society**
Mail to: P.O. Box 3174, 98032
Founded in: 1984
Number of members: 150
Major programs: library, genealogical
services

KIRKLAND

Northwest Seaport
218B Kirkland Ave., 98033
Telephone: (206) 822-4410
Mail to: P.O. Box 395
Questionnaire not received

LACONNER

Skagit County Historical Society
Telephone: (206) 466-3365
Mail to: P.O. Box 8l8, 98257
Private agency
Founded in: 1958
Eunice W. Darvill, Director
Number of members: 700
Staff: part time 7, volunteer 6
Major programs: library, museum,
oral history, school programs, book
publishing, photographic
collections
Period of collections: late 1800s-early
1900s

LIND

**Adams County Historical Society
Museum**
Phillips Bldg., 99341
Telephone: (509) 677-3219
Founded in: 1963
Georgia Hays, Director
Number of members: 75
Major programs: library, archives,
museum, junior history, oral history,
educational programs
Period of collections: 1865-present

LONGMIRE

Longmire Museum
General Delivery, 98397
Telephone: (206) 569-2211
Federal agency, authorized by
National Park Service
Founded in: 1928
Bill Dengler, Chief Naturalist
Staff: full time 1, part time 8
Major programs: library, archives,
museum, oral history,
newsletters/pamphlets, historic
preservation, exhibits, audiovisual
programs, photographic
collections
Period of collections: 1890s-1930s

LOPEZ ISLAND

**Lopez Island Historical Society and
Museum**
P.O. Box 163, 98261
Telephone: (206) 468-2049
Private agency

Founded in: 1966
Nancy McCoy, Curator
Number of members: 100
Staff: part time 1, volunteer 6
Major programs: archives, museum,
oral history, school programs,
historic preservation, exhibits,
photographic collections,
genealogical services
Period of collections: 1850-present

MAPLE VALLEY

**Maple Valley Historical
Society, Inc., and Museum**
23015 S.E. 216
Telephone: (206) 255-7588
Mail to: P.O. Box 123, 98038
Private agency
Founded in: 1970
Marian Short, Chair
Number of members: 40
Staff: volunteer 5
Major programs: museum, book
publishing, records management,
exhibits, photographic collections
Period of collections: 1890-1950

MOLSON

**Old Molson Ghost Town and
Museum**
Molson Rt., Box 49
Telephone: (509) 485-3292
Mail to: Oroville, WA 98844
County agency, authorized by
Okanogan County Historical
Society and Molson Museum
Commission
Founded in: 1962
Mary Louise Loe, Museum Chair
Staff: volunteer 20
Major programs: museum, historic
site(s), historic preservation
Period of collections: 1900

MORTON

**Eastern Lewis County Historical
Society**
Gust. Backstrom Park
Telephone: (606) 496-5602
Mail to: P.O. Box 777, 98356
Founded in: 1973
Questionnaire not received

MOSES LAKE

Adam East Museum
5th and Balsam, 98837
Founded in: 1958
Questionnaire not received

NEAH BAY

**Makah Cultural and Research
Center**
P.O. Box 95, 98357
Telephone: (206) 645-2711
Founded in: 1979
Greig W. Arnold, Director
Staff: full time 6, part time 4
Major programs: museum, oral
history, newsletters/pamphlets,
research, exhibits, photographic
collections, language program

NORTH BEND

**Snoqualmie Valley Historical
Society**
320 N. Bend Blvd., S
Telephone: (206) 888-3200/888-0062
Mail to: P.O. Box 179, 98045
Founded in: 1960
Mary Ferrell, Curator
Number of members: 225
Staff: volunteer 12
Major programs: library, archives,
manuscripts, museum, markers,
tours, photographic collections,
audiovisual programs, research,
exhibits, oral history, educational
programs, books,
newsletters/pamphlets
Period of collections: 1865-1920s

OKANOGAN

**Okanogan County Historical
Society**
1410 2nd Ave., N
Telephone: (509) 422-4272
Mail to: P.O. Box 1129, 98840
Private agency
Founded in: 1950
Ada Lemaster, Registered Agent
Number or members: 1,150
Staff: part time 1, volunteer 30
Magazine: *Okanogan County
Heritage*
Major programs: archives,
manuscripts, museum, historic
site(s), markers, audiovisual
programs, photographic
collections
Period of collections: 1900-present

OLYMPIA

**State Capitol Historical
Association**
211 W. 21st Ave., 98501
Telephone: (206) 753-2580
Founded in: 1941
Derek R. Valley, Director
Number of members: 600
Staff: full time 6, volunteer 100
Magazine: *Musings*
Major programs: manuscripts,
museum, tours/pilgrimages, school
programs, newsletters/pamphlets,
research, exhibits, audiovisual
programs, photographic
collections, field services
Period of collections: 1800-1976

**Washington Commission for the
Humanities**
Evergreen State College, 98505
Telephone: (206) 866-6510
Private agency, authorized by
National Endowment for the
Humanities
Founded in: 1973
William H. Oliver, Executive Director
Number of members: 825
Staff: full time 7, part time 2,
volunteer 25
Major programs: museums,
tours/pilgrimages, school
programs, exhibits, living history,
audiovisual programs
Period of collections: 19th-20th
centuries

Washington State Heritage Council
111 W. 21st Ave., 98504
Telephone: (206) 753-4011
State agency
Founded in: 1983
David Hanser, Council Administrator

Washington State Parks and Recreation Commission
7150 Cleanwater Lane, KY 11
Telephone: (206) 753-2025
Mail to: P.O. Box 1128, 98504
Founded in: 1913
Questionnaire not received

Washington Trust for Historic Preservation
111 W. 21st Ave., 98501
Telephone: (206) 753-0099
Private agency
Founded in: 1975
Garry Schalliol, Executive Director
Number of members: 700
Staff: full time 2, volunteer 25
Major programs: tours/pilgrimages, newsletters/pamphlets, historic preservation, field services

OTHELLO

Othello Community Museum
3rd and Lurch
Telephone: (509) 488-2268
Mail to: P.O. Box 121, 99344
County agency
Founded in: 1972
Bill Morris, Director
Number of members: 100
Staff: volunteer 10
Major programs: archives, museum, educational programs, exhibits
Period of collections: 1918-present

PASCO

Franklin County Historical Society
305 N. 4th St.
Telephone: (509) 547-3714
Mail to: P.O. Box 1033, 99301
Private agency
Founded in: 1968
Sarah LeCompte, Curator/Director
Number of members: 900
Magazine: The Franklin Flyer
Major programs: museum, historic site(s), markers, school programs, book publishing, research, exhibits, photographic collections, mobile display/lecture program
Period of collections: 18th century-present

PORT ANGELES

Clallam County Historical Society
Clallam County Courthouse, 223 E. 4th St.
Mail to: P.O. Box 1024, 98362
Founded in: 1948
Questionnaire not received

Clallam County Museum
223 E. 4th St., 98362
Telephone: (206) 452-7831
Private agency, authorized by Clallam County Historical Society, Inc.
Foundn: 1948
Robert W. Keeler, Director
Number of members: 200

Staff: full time 1, part time 1, volunteer 80
Major programs: library, archives, manuscripts, museum, oral history, school programs, book publishing, newsletters/pamphlets, exhibits, photographic collections, genealogical services
Period of collections: 1860-present

PORT GAMMBLE

Of Sea and Shore, Inc.—Museum of Seashells and Marine Life
General Store Building
Telephone: (206) 297-2426
Mail to: P.O. Box 219, 98364
Private agency
Founded in: 1973
Thomas C. Rice, President
Staff: volunteer 3
Major programs: library, museum, tours/pilgrimages, newsletters/pamphlets, exhibits, audiovisual programs

PORT ORCHARD

Pacific Northwest Conservation Laboratory
1131 Mitchell Ave., 98366
Telephone: (206) 876-2343
Private agency
Founded in: 1977
Gerald H. Grosso, Director
Staff: full time 3
Major programs: historic preservation, research, research and application of conservation methods

Sidney Museum and Arts Association
202 Sidney Ave., 98366
Telephone: (206) 876-3693
Founded in: 1971
Questionnaire not received

PORT TOWNSEND

Coast Artillery Museum at Ft. Worden
Ft. Worden State Park, Administration Bldg., 98368
Telephone: (206) 491-2906
Mail to: 433 Ranger Dr., SE, Olympia, 98503
Private agency
Founded in: 1978
Stan Lilian, Director
Number of members: 135
Staff: part time 2
Major programs: library, museum, exhibits, audiovisual programs, photographic collections
Period of collections: 1898-1944

Jefferson County Historical Society
210 Madison St., 98368
Telephone: (206) 385-1003
County agency
Founded in: 1879
Dixie Romadka, Coordinator
Number of members: 287
Staff: full time 1, part time 1, volunteer 25
Major programs: museum, historic preservation, photographic collections
Period of collections: late 1800s

PROSSER

Benton County Museum & Historical Society, Inc.
7th St. and Paterson Rd.
Telephone: (509) 786-3842
Mail to: P.O. Box 591, 99350
Questionnaire not received

PULLMAN

Museum of Anthropology
110 College Hall
Telephone: (509) 335-3441
Mail to: Washington State University, 99164-4910
State agency, authorized by the university
Founded in: 1952
Kevin Erickson, Senior Curator
Number of members: 20
Staff: full time 2, part time 10, volunteer 15
Major programs: museum, school programs, research, exhibits, archaeology programs
Period of collections: 15,000 B.P.-present

Washington Archaeological Research Center
Washington State University, 99164-3620
Telephone: (509) 335-8566
State agency, authorized by the university
Founded in: 1972
Dale R. Croes, Director
Staff: part time 10
Magazine: The Thunderbird: Archaeological News of the Northwest
Major programs: library, manuscripts, newsletters/pamphlets, records management, research, exhibits, archaeology programs, photographic collections, field services

Whitman County Genealogical Society
P.O. Box 393, 99163
Telephone: (509) 332-1181
Private agency
Founded in: 1984
Linda Scott Lilles, President
Number of members: 80
Staff: volunteer 30
Major programs: library, newsletters/pamphlets, genealogical services, educational programs

PUYALLUP

Ezra Meeker Historical Society, Inc.
321 E. Pioneer
Telephone: (206) 848-1770
Mail to: P.O. Box 103, 98371
Founded in: 1970
Ron Book, President
Number of members: 190
Staff: volunteer 20
Major programs: historic sites preservation, tours, historic preservation
Period of collections: 1890s

Western Frontier Museum
2301 19th, SE, 98372
Telephone: (206) 845-4402

Private agency
Founded in: 1967
Vint Greeley, Co-owner
Period of collections: 18th-19th
centuries

REDMOND

Marymoor Museum
6046 W. Lake, Sammamisk Parkway
Telephone: (206) 885-3684
Mail to: P.O. Box 162, 98073
Private agency
Founded in: 1966
Vivian P. Elvidge, Director
Number of members: 160
Staff: part time 1, volunteer 14
Major programs: museum, school
programs, book publishing,
exhibits, photographic collections
Period of collections: 1870-1940

RENTON

**Renton Historical Society and
Museum**
235 Mill Ave. S., 98055
Telephone: (206) 255-2330
Private agency, authorized by Renton
Historical Society
Founded in: 1966
William Collins, President
Number of members: 664
Staff: part time 2, volunteer 40
Major programs: library, archives,
museum, historic site(s), markers,
oral history, school programs, book
publishing, newsletters/pamphlets,
historic preservation, exhibits,
audiovisual programs,
photographic collections
Period of collections: 1850-present

RICHLAND

Hanford Science Center
825 Jadwin
Telephone: (509) 376-6374
Mail to: P.O. Box 800, 99352
Federal agency, authorized by U.S.
Department of Energy
Founded in: 1963
M. Jay Haney, Manager
Staff: full time 4, part time 8,
volunteer 2
Major programs: library
Period of collections: 1900-present

ROSLYN

Roslyn Historical Museum Society
98941
Founded in: 1970
Questionnaire not received

SEATTLE

**Association of King County
Historical Organizations**
P.O. Box 3257, 98114
Telephone: (206) 623-5124
Private agency
Founded in: 1977
Kit Freudenberg, President
Number of members: 75
Staff: volunteer 12
Major programs: museum, historic
preservation

**Black Heritage Society of
Washington State, Inc.**
P.O. Box 22565, 98122
Telephone: (206) 325-8205/723-0334
Private agency
Founded in: 1977
Joseph Warner, President
Number of members: 55
Staff: volunteer 5
Major programs: archives,
tours/pilgrimages, oral history,
newsletters/pamphlets, exhibits
Period of collections: 1890s-present

Center for Wooden Boats
1010 Valley, 98109
Telephone: (206) 382-BOAT
Private agency
Founded in: 1977
Dick Wagner, Director
Number of members: 1,200
Staff: full time 2, part time 2,
volunteer 40
Magazine: *Shavings*
Major programs: library, oral history,
newsletters/pamphlets, historic
preservation, research, living
history
Period of collections: 1900s

Coast Guard Museum/Northwest
1519 Alaskan Way, S, 98134
Telephone: (206) 442-5019
Private agency
Founded in: 1975
E. L. Davis, President/Director
Number of members: 220
Staff: volunteer 10
Major programs: library, archives,
manuscripts, museum,
tours/pilgrimages, oral history,
research, exhibits, photographic
collections
Period of collections: 1857-present

**Ethnic Heritage Council of the
Pacific Northwest**
1107 NE 45th St., Suite 315-A 98105
Telephone: (206) 633-3239
Private agency
Founded in: 1980
Burton E. Bard, Jr., Executive Director
Number of members: 175
Staff: part time 2
Magazine: *Northwest Ethnic News*
Major programs: school programs,
newsletters/pamphlets, field
services, assistance to member
organizations, ethnic festival,
seminars

**Highline School District Museum at
Sunnydale**
15631 8th Ave., S, 98148
Telephone: (206) 433-2307
Private agency
Founded in: 1976
Carla St. John, Curator
Number of members: 35
Staff: volunteer 2
Major programs: archives, museum,
tours/pilgrimages, oral history,
book publishing, photographic
collections
Period of collections: late 1800s-early
1900s

**Historical Society of Seattle and
King County**
2161 E. Hamlin St., 98112

Telephone: (206) 324-1125
Founded in: 1911
Questionnaire not received

**King County Office of Historic
Preservation**
618 2nd Ave., 805 Alaska Bldg.,
98104
Telephone: (206) 587-4858
County agency, authorized by
Department of Planning and
Community Development
Founded in: 1978
Kjris R. Lund, Historic Preservation
Officer
Staff: full time 3
Major programs: museum,
newsletters/pamphlets, historic
preservation, field services

Kingdome Sports Museum
201 S. King St., 98104
Founded in: 1976
Carol Keaton, Information Specialist
Staff: full time 1
Major programs: sports memorabilia
Period of collections: 1900s-present

**Klondike Gold Rush National
Historical Park**
117 S. Main St., 98104
Telephone: (206) 442-7220
Federal agency, authorized by
National Park Service
Founded in: 1979
Willie Russell, Superintendent
Staff: full time 3, part time 3
Major programs: museum, school
programs, exhibits, audiovisual
programs, photographic
collections
Period of collections: 1897-1899

Laird Norton Company Archives
801 2nd Ave., Suite 1401, 98104
Telephone: (206) 464-5214
Private agency
Founded in: 1981
Elizabeth W. Adkins, Archivist
Staff: full time 2, part time 1,
volunteer 1
Major programs: archives, oral
history, records management,
research, exhibits, photographic
collections
Period of collections: 1855-1965

Museum of History and Industry
2700 24th Ave., E, 98112
Telephone: (206) 324-1125
Private agency, authorized by
Historical Society of Seattle and
King County
Founded in: 1914
James R. Warren, Executive Director
Number of members: 2,260
Staff: full time 14, part time 8,
volunteer 235
Magazine: *Portage*
Major programs: library, archives,
manuscripts, museum, oral history,
school programs, book publishing,
newsletters/pamphlets, records
management, research, exhibits,
audiovisual programs,
photographic collections
Period of collections: 1850-1960s

Museum of Sea and Ships
Waterfront Park, Pier 59, 98101

Telephone: (206) 628-0860
Private agency
Founded in: 1982
Kenneth Zmuda, Director
Staff: full time 1, part time 1,
  volunteer 2
Major programs: library, museum,
  school programs, historic
  preservation, research, exhibits,
  audiovisual programs,
  photographic collections, ship
  model seminars
Period of collections: 1800-1940

National Archives—Seattle Branch
6125 Sand Point Way, 98115
Telephone: (206) 526-6507
Founded in: 1969
Phil Lothyan, Director
Staff: full time 7
Major programs: archives,
  educational programs, teachers'
  workshops, genealogical
  workshops, film series, open
  houses and tours
Period of collections: 1859-1974

Nordic Heritage News
3014 N.W. 67th St., 98117
Telephone: (206) 789-5707
Private agency, authorized by Nordic
  Heritage Museum Foundation
Founded in: 1979
Marianne Forssblad, Director
Number of members: 800
Staff: full time 3, volunteer 100
Major programs: library, museum,
  educational programs,
  newsletters/pamphlets, exhibits,
  language and folk art classes
Period of collections: 1850-present

**North Seattle Community College
Art Gallery**
9600 College Way, N, 98103
Telephone: (206) 634-4513
State agency
Founded in: 1977
Elroy Christenson, Art Instructor
Staff: part time 4, volunteer 8
Major programs: school programs,
  exhibits

Northwest Seaport
860 Terry
Telephone: (206) 447-9800
Mail to: P.O. Box 2865, 98111
Founded in: 1963
Questionnaire not received

Pacific Northwest Historians Guild
c/o Department of Biomedical
  History, SB-20, University of
  Washington, 98195
Telephone: (206) 543-9123
Private agency
Founded in: 1980
Jack W. Berryman, President
Number of members: 55
Staff: volunteer 10
Major programs:
  newsletters/pamphlets, research,
  exhibits, conferences

**Pacific Northwest Labor History
Association**
Northgate Station, P.O. Box 25048,
  98125
Telephone: (206) 441-9752
Private agency

Founded in: 1968
Ross K. Rieder, President
Number of members: 250
Major programs: archives,
  tours/pilgrimages, oral history,
  living history, annual conference
Period of collections: 1915-1980

**Puget Sound Maritime Historical
Society, Inc.**
2161 E. Hamlin St., 98112
Telephone: (206) 324-1125
Founded in: 1948
Questionnaire not received

Scouting Trail Museum
156th St., SW, and Des Moines Way
Telephone: (206) 767-6467
Mail to: 10021 26th St., SW, 98146
Private agency
Founded in: 1968
Caroline M. Payne, Executive Director
Staff: volunteer 4
Magazine: *Along the Scouting Trail*
Major programs: library, archives,
  manuscripts, oral history, historic
  preservation, research, exhibits,
  photographic collections, Boy
  Scout history memorabilia
Period of collections: 1907-present

Seattle Branch—National Archives
6125 Sand Point Way, NE, 98115
Telephone: (206) 526-6507
Federal agency, authorized by
  National Archives and Records
  Administration
Founded in: 1969
David M. Piff, Director
Number of members: full time 5,
  volunteer 13
Major programs: archives
Period of collections: 1855-1960

Shoreline Historical Museum, Inc.
N. 175th and Linden Ave., N
Telephone: (206) 542-7111
Mail to: P.O. Box 7171, 98133
Private agency
Founded in: 1975
Betty Robertson, President
Number of members: 375
Staff: part time 1, volunteer 5
Major programs: museum
Period of collections: late
  1800s-1940s

Telephone Pioneers of America
1600 7th Ave., Room 409, Bell Plaza,
  98191
Telephone: (206) 345-6949
Private agency
Founded in: 1924
Linda Bowman, Pioneer Administrator
Number of members: 2,848
Staff: full time 3, volunteer 3,640
Magazine: *Pioneer Herald & Pioneer
  News*
Major programs: museum,
  newsletters/pamphlets, historic
  preservation, exhibits,
  photographic collections, field
  services, helping handicapped and
  disadvantaged

**Thomas Burke Memorial
Washington State Museum**
University of Washington, 98195
Telephone: (206) 543-5590
State agency, authorized by the
  university

Founded in: 1885
Patrick V. Kirch, Director
Number of members: 200
Staff: full time 7, part time 42,
  volunteer 50
Major programs: museum, research,
  exhibits, natural history,
  anthropology
Period of collections: 20th century

**Washington Park Arboretum—The
Arboretum Foundation**
2300 Arboretum Dr., E
Telephone: (206) 543-8800
Mail to: University of Washington,
  XD-10, 98195
Authorized by the university's Center
  for Urban Horticulture and the City
  of Seattle Parks Department
Founded in: 1934
H. B. Tukey, Jr., Director
Number of members: 2,500
Staff: full time 8, part time 1,
  volunteer 150
Magazine: *Arboretum Bulletin*
Major programs: library,
  tours/pilgrimages, school
  programs, newsletters/pamphlets,
  records management, research,
  photographic collections, outdoor
  interpretation of horticulture and
  botany
Period of collections: present

**Washington State Archives
Regional Branch**
3Sunset Activity Center, 1809 S. 140th
  St., 98168
Telephone: (206) 764-4276
State agency
Founded in: 1979
Michael S. Saunders, Regional
  Archivist
Staff: full time 1
Major programs: archives, records
  management, photographic
  collections
Period of collections: 1853-1979

**Waterfront Awareness—Institute
for Marine Studies**
2342 34th Ave., S, 98144
Telephone: (206) 543-3106
Mail to: HF-05, 98195
Private agency
Founded in: 1979
Marc J. Hershman, President
Number of members: 200
Staff: part time 1, volunteer 15
Major programs: historic site(s),
  markers, tours/pilgrimages, book
  publishing, newsletters/pamphlets,
  exhibits, living history, audiovisual
  programs, photographic
  collections, waterfront interpretive
  center

Wing Luke Memorial Museum
414 8th Ave., S, 98104
Telephone: (206) 623-5124
Private agency
Founded in: 1966
Kit Freudenberg, Director
Number of members: 250
Staff: full time 1, part time 3,
  volunteer 15
Major programs: museum, school
  programs, research, exhibits,
  preservation and conservation of
  Asian folk art
Period of collections: 1860-1940

Woodland Park Zoo—Family Farm
5500 Phinney, N, 98103
Telephone: (206) 625-2244
City agency
Founded in: 1903
David Towne, Zoo Director
Staff: full time 100, part time 20,
volunteer 350
Major programs: living history
Period of collections: 1900-1930

SEQUIM

Sequim-Dungeness Museum
175 W. Cedar
Telephone: (206) 682-8110
Mail to: P.O. Box 1002, 98382
Lydia Neidinger, Manager
Number of members: 300
Staff: volunteer 10
Major programs: museum, historic
preservation
Period of collections: 1850-1930

SHAW ISLAND

**Shaw Island Library and Historical
Society**
98286
Founded in: 1966
Questionnaire not received

SILVERDALE

Kitsap County Historical Society
3343 N.W. Byron St., 98383
Telephone: (206) 692-1949
Private agency
Founded in: 1948
Don Serry, President
Number of members: 310
Staff: volunteer 15
Major programs: library, museum,
books, historic preservation,
exhibits
Period of collections: 1850-present

SNOHOMISH

Snohomish Historical Society
118 Avenue B
Mail to: P.O. Box 174, 98290
Questionnaire not received

SOUTH BEND

**Pacific County Historical Society
and Museum Foundation**
1008 Bush Dr.
Telephone: (206) 875-5224
Mail to: P.O. Box P, 98586
County agency, authorized by Pacific
County Historical Society
Virginia Bassett, Museum Director
Number of members: 497
Staff: volunteer 17
Magazine: *Sou'Wester*
Period of collections: from 1890

SPOKANE

**Eastern Washington State
Historical Society—Cheney
Cowles Memorial Museum**
W. 2316 1st Ave., 99204
Telephone: (509) 456-3931
Private agency
Founded in: 1916
Glenn Mason, Director
Staff: full time 9, part time 4,
volunteer 100

Major programs: library, archives,
manuscripts, museum, historic
site(s), markers, tours/pilgrimages,
oral history, school programs,
newsletters/pamphlets, historic
preservation, records
management, research, exhibits,
audiovisual programs, archaeology
programs, photographic
collections, genealogical services,
fine arts, cultural programs, lecture
series
Period of collections: 1800-present

Fire Department Museum
W-44 Riverside, 99201
Telephone: (509) 456-2672
Private agency, authorized by
Spokane City Fire Department
Founded in: 1980
T. W. Hecklen, Lt. Inspector
Staff: volunteer 1
Major programs: archives, museum,
historic preservation, exhibits,
photographic collections
Period of collections: 1884-present

**Ft. George Wright Historical
Museum**
W. 4000 Randolph Rd., 99204
Telephone: (509) 328-2970
Mail to: P.O. Box 7496, 99207
Founded in: 1963
Questionnaire not received

**Museum of Native American
Cultures**
E. 200 Cataldo
Telephone: (509) 326-4550
Mail to: P.O. Box 3044, 99220
Private agency
Founded in: 1965
Michael Warner, Executive Director
Number of members: 350
Staff: full time 7, part time 1,
volunteer 50
Major programs: archives,
manuscripts, museum, junior
history, school programs,
newsletters/pamphlets, research,
exhibits
Period of collections: 19th century

**Oregon Province Archives of the
Society of Jesus**
Gonzaga University, E502 Boone
Ave., 99258
Telephone: (509) 328-4220
Founded in: 1932
Clifford A. Carroll, S.J., Archivist
Staff: volunteer 1
Major programs: archives,
manuscripts, oral history
Period of collections: 1842-present

Spokane Valley Historical Society
E. 10303 Sprague Ave., 99206
Telephone: (509) 924-4994
Questionnaire not received

STEILACOOM

**Steilacoom Historical Museum
Association**
P.O. Box 16, 98388
Telephone: (206) 588-8115
Private agency
Founded in: 1970
Lynn D. Scholes, Director
Number of members: 500
Staff: volunteer 25

Magazine: *Steilacoom Historical
Museum Quarterly*
Major programs: library, archives,
museum, historic site(s),
tours/pilgrimages, oral history,
newsletters/pamphlets, historic
preservation
Period of collections: 1850-1890

STEVENSON

**Skamania County Historical
Society**
Vancouver Ave.
Telephone: (509) 427-5141, ext. 218
Mail to: P.O. Box 396, 98648
County agency
Founded in: 1959
Sharon Tiffany, Director
Number of members: 200
Staff: full time 1, part time 2,
volunteer 10
Magazine: *Skamania County Heritage*
Major programs: museum, historic
sites preservation, markers, oral
history, newsletters/pamphlets,
exhibits
Period of collections: 1850-1940

SUMNER

Sumner Historical Society
1228 Main St.
Telephone: (206) 863-8936
Mail to: P.O. Box 517, 98390
City agency
Founded in: 1972
Jean Kyle, President
Number of members: 95
Staff: volunteer 10
Major programs: museum, historic
preservation, exhibits,
photographic collections
Period of collections: 1875-1910

SUNNYSIDE

**Sunnyside Museum and Historical
Association**
4th and Grant St.
Telephone: (509) 837-6010
Mail to: P.O. Box 782, 98944
Founded in: 1970
Questionnaire not received

SUQUAMISH

**Suquamish Tribal Cultural Center
and Museum**
Sandy Hook Rd.
Telephone: (206) 598-3311
Mail to: P.O. Box 498, 98392
Authorized by Suquamish Tribal
Council
Founded in: 1977
Carey Caldwell, Director
Staff: full time 7, volunteer 1
Major programs: museum, archives,
oral history, educational programs,
photographic collections,
research, cultural resource center
Period of collections: 1850-present

TACOMA

Ft. Nisqually Museum
Point Defiance Park, 98407
Telephone: (206) 591-5339
City agency, authorized by
Metropolitan Park District

Founded in: 1937
Steve Anderson, Curator
Staff: full time 1, part time 1,
  volunteer 4
Magazine: *Occurrences*
Major programs: library, museum,
  historic site(s), oral history, school
  programs, newsletters/pamphlets,
  historic preservation, research,
  exhibits, photographic collections
Period of collections: 1830s-1870s

**Historical Office, Washington
  National Guard**
Camp Murray, 98430
Telephone: (206) 964-6201
State agency, authorized by Military
  Department, State of Washington
Founded in: 1980
George E. Coates, Adjutant General,
  Military Department
Staff: full time 1
Major programs: archives, museum,
  oral history, records management
Period of collections: 1880s-present

**Salmon Beach Historical
  Committee**
65 Salmon Beach
Telephone: (206) 752-4567
Mail to: P.O. Box 7002, 98407
Founded in: 1973
Questionnaire not received

◇**Washington State Historical
  Society**
315 N. Stadium Way, 98403
Telephone: (206) 593-2830
State agency
Founded in: 1891
Anthony G. King, Director
Number of members: 1,200
Staff: full time 12, part time 7,
  volunteer 20
Magazine: *Pacific Northwest
  Quarterly*
Major programs: library, archives,

manuscripts, museum, educational
  programs, books,
  newsletters/pamphlets, records
  management, research, exhibits,
  photographic collections,
  genealogical services, internships
Period of collections: 1783-present

**Western Forest Industries
  Museum, Inc.**
P.O. Box 705, 98401
Telephone: (206) 924-3214
Private agency
Founded in: 1964
Gilbert L. Oswald, President
Staff: full time 2
Major programs: museum, historic
  site(s), historic preservation,
  exhibits
Period of collections: 1910-1940

Weyerhaeuser Company Archives
98477
Telephone: (206) 924-5051
Private agency, authorized by
  Weyerhaeuser Company
Founded in: 1900
Donnie Crespo, Archivist
Number of members: 1
Staff: full time 3
Major programs: archives, oral
  history, exhibits, photographic
  collections
Period of collections: from 1900

TENINO

**South Thurston County Historical
  Society**
Park St.
Telephone: (206) 264-4321
Mail to: P.O. Box 339, 98589
Town agency
Founded in: 1974
Jacob Scott, President
Number of members: 55
Staff: volunteer 20

Major programs: museum, historic
  sites preservation, markers, historic
  preservation
Period of collections: 1895-present

TOPPENISH

Toppenish Museum
1 S. Elm, 98948
Telephone: (509) 865-4510
Founded in: 1976
Tish Cooper, Director
Number of members: 50
Staff: part time 2
Major programs: archives, museum,
  historic preservation
Period of collections: late 1800s-early
  1900s

Yakima Nation Museum
Hwy. 97
Telephone: (509) 865-2800
Mail to: P.O. Box 151, 98948
Authorized by Yakima Nation Tribal
  Council
Founded in: 1980
Vivian M. Adams, Curator
Staff: full time 4, volunteer 2
Major programs: museum, oral
  history, newsletters/pamphlets,
  records management, research,
  exhibits
Period of collections:
  prehistoric-1950s

TUMWATER

Tumwater Historical Association
602 Des Chutes Way, 98501
Telephone: (206) 753-8583
City agency
Founded in: 1982
Jan Talianis, Director
Number of members: 280
Staff: full time 2
Major programs: museum, historic
  site(s), tours/pilgrimages, school
  programs, newsletters/pamphlets,
  historic preservation, records
  management, research, exhibits,
  living history, audiovisual
  programs, photographic
  collections, genealogical services
Period of collections: 1845-present

VANCOUVER

Clark County Historical Museum
1511 Main St., 98660
Telephone: (206) 695-4681
Mail to: c/o P.O. Box 1834, 98668
Private agency, authorized by Ft.
  Vancouver Historical Society
Founded in: 1946
David Freece, Museum Director
Number of members: 500
Staff: full time 1, part time 5,
  volunteer 35
Magazine: *Clark County History
  Annual*
Major programs: library, museum,
  school programs, research,
  exhibits, history annual
Period of collections:
  prehistoric-present

**Ft. Vancouver Historical Society of
  Clark County**
Telephone: (206) 695-4681
Mail to: P.O. Box 1834, 98668

Bella Coola ceremonial dance masks and Haida raven rattle from the Washington State Historical Society's collection.—Washington State Historical Society, Tacoma, Washington

Private agency
Founded in: 1964
David Freece, Museum Director
Number of members: 600
Staff: part time 7, volunteer 30
Magazine: *Clark County History*
Major programs: library, museum,
  historic site(s), school programs,
  book publishing,
  newsletters/pamphlets, historic
  preservation, exhibits,
  photographic collections

**Ft. Vancouver National Historic
Site**
1501 E. Evergreen Blvd., 98661-3897
Telephone: (206) 696-7655
Federal agency, authorized by
  National Park Service
Founded in: 1948
James M. Thomson, Superintendent
Staff: full time 10, part time 13,
  volunteer 154
Major programs: library, museum,
  historic site(s), tours/pilgrimages,
  school programs, historic
  preservation, exhibits, living
  history, audiovisual programs,
  archaeology programs,
  photographic collections
Period of collections: 1829-1860

Grant House Museum
1106 E. Evergreen Blvd., 98661
Telephone: (206) 693-9743
Founded in: 1949
Questionnaire not received

VASHON

**Vashon Maury Island Heritage
Association**
Telephone: (206) 567-4663
Mail to: P.O. Box 723, 98070
Private agency
Founded in: 1976
Reed Fitzpatrick, Agent
Number of members: 151
Staff: volunteer 13
Major programs: archives,
  manuscripts, oral history,
  newsletters/pamphlets
Period of collections: 1877-present

WAITSBURG

Waitsburg Historical Society
4th and Main Sts.
Mail to: P.O. Box 277, 99361
Founded in: 1971
Questionnaire not received

WALLA WALLA

Ft. Walla Walla Museum Complex
Myra Rd.
Telephone: (509) 525-7703
Mail to: P.O. Box 1616, 99362
Private agency, authorized by Walla
  Walla Valley Pioneer and Historical
  Society, Inc.
Founded in: 1968
Gerwyn A. Jones, Executive Director
Number of members: 475
Staff: part time 3, volunteer 40
Major programs: museum, historic
  site(s), school programs,
  newsletters/pamphlets, historic
  preservation
Period of collections: 1800-1920

**Historical Architecture
Development**
214 N. Colville, 99362
Telephone: (509) 529-4373
Founded in: 1974
Jo Bergevin, Restoration Director
Number of members: 400
Staff: full time 2, part time 2,
  volunteer 4
Major programs: library, school
  programs, newsletters/pamphlets,
  historic preservation, exhibits,
  photographic collections
Period of collections: 1880s

**Walla Walla Valley Pioneer and
Historical Society**
Telephone: (509) 525-7703
Mail to: P.O. Box 1616, 99362
Founded in: 1966
Questionnaire not received

**Whitman Mission National Historic
Site**
Rt. 2, Box 247, 99362
Telephone: (509) 522-6360
Federal agency, authorized by
  National Park Service
Founded in: 1936
Robert C. Amdor, Superintendent
Staff: full time 7, part time 10,
  volunteer 40
Major programs: library, museum,
  historic site(s), school programs,
  living history, photographic
  collections
Period of collections: 1830-1847

WENATCHEE

**North Central Washington Museum
Association**
127 S. Mission, 98801
Telephone: (509) 662-4728
Private agency
Founded in: 1939
William E. Steward, Director
Number of members: 500
Staff: full time 4, part time 2,
  volunteer 150
Magazine: *The Confluence*
Major programs: archives, museum,
  school programs,
  newsletters/pamphlets, exhibits,
  genealogical services
Period of collections: 1800-1935

Rocky Reach Dam
Chelan Hwy. 97
Telephone: (509) 663-8121
Mail to: P.O. Box 1231, 98801
County agency, authorized by Chelan
  County Public Utility District No. 1
Founded in: 1963
Gerald Copp, Manager
Staff: full time 4, part time 5
Major programs: museum, exhibits,
  archaeology programs, electrical
  history museum
Period of collections: 1800-present

WINSLOW

**Bainbridge Island Historical
Society**
Strawberry Hill Park
Mail to: P.O. Box 10003, 98110
Private agency
Founded in: 1949
Elnora A. Parfitt, Curator

Number of members: 60
Staff: volunteer 6
Major programs: museum,
  photographic collections
Period of collections: 1850-present

WOODINVILLE

**Greater Woodinville Historical
Society**
P.O. Box 495, 98926
Telephone: (206) 483-2811
County agency
Founded in: 1976
Lois Sharpe, President
Major programs: historic site(s),
  markers, school programs,
  exhibits, audiovisual programs
Period of collections: 1860-present

YAKIMA

**Northwest Association of Nautical
Archaeology**
1310 S. 63rd St., 98901
Telephone: (509) 575-0930/653-2582
Founded in: 1980
Questionnaire not received

**Yakima Valley Museum and
Historical Association**
2105 Tieton Dr., 98902
Telephone: (509) 248-0747
Founded in: 1954
Versa K'ang, Director
Number of members: 1,050
Staff: full time 3, part time 4,
  volunteer 200
Major programs: museum,
  educational programs, books,
  newsletters/pamphlets
Period of collections: 1865-1930

WEST VIRGINIA

ALDERSON

**Chesapeake and Ohio Historical
Society, Inc.**
Mail to: P.O. Box 417, 24910
Telephone: (304) 445-7365
Private agency
Founded in: 1975
Thomas W. Dixon, Jr., President
Number of members: 1,700
Staff: volunteer 35
Major programs: archives,
  manuscripts, tours/pilgrimages,
  book publishing,
  newsletters/pamphlets, historic
  preservation, records
  management, research, exhibits,
  audiovisual programs,
  photographic collections
Period of collections: 1872-present

ANSTED

Fayette County Historical Society
25812
Telephone: (304) 469-9505
Questionnaire not received

Members of the Chesapeake and Ohio Historical Society pose in front of the A Cabin C&O telegraph office in Alleghany, Virginia.—Photograph by David L. Powell

ATHENS

Mercer County Historical Society, Inc.
101 Caldwell St., 24712
Telephone: (304) 384-9661
Founded in: 1974
Questionnaire not received

BELLE

Belle Historical Restoration Society, Inc.
310 Stubb Dr.
Telephone: (304) 949-2380
Mail to: 148 W. Reynolds Ave., 25015
Founded in: 1976
Questionnaire not received

BUCKHANNON

Methodist Historical Society
West Virginia Wesleyan College
  Library, 26201
Telephone: (304) 473-8059
Founded in: 1942
Questionnaire not received

CHARLESTON

Archives and History Division, West Virginia State Museum
25305
Telephone: (304) 348-0230
State agency, authorized by
  Department of Culture and History
Founded in: 1905
Rodney A. Pyles, Director
Number of members: 5
Staff: full time 16, part time 2
Magazine: *West Virginia History*
Major programs: library, archives,
  manuscripts, museum, markers,
  research, exhibits, photographic
  collections, genealogical services
Period of collections: 1760-present

Department of Culture and History, State of West Virginia
The Cultural Center, Capitol
  Complex, 25305
Telephone: (304) 348-0220
State agency

Norman L. Fagan, Commissioner
Major programs: library, archives,
  museum, historic site(s),
  tours/pilgrimages, junior history,
  oral history, school programs, book
  publishing, newsletters/pamphlets,
  historic preservation, records
  management, research, exhibits,
  audiovisual programs,
  photographic collections,
  genealogical services

Kanawha Valley Historical and Preservation Society
Mail to: P.O. Box 2283, 25328
County agency
Founded in: 1970
Steven J. Jubelirer, President
Number of members: 125
Staff: volunteer 12
Magazine: *Up and Down the Valley*
Major programs: historic sites
  preservation, markers,
  tours/pilgrimages, educational
  programs, newsletters/pamphlets,
  historic preservation, audiovisual
  programs, field services

Sunrise Museums
746 Myrtle Rd., 25314
Telephone: (304) 344-8035
Private agency
Founded in: 1966
J. Hornor Davis IV, Executive Director
Number of members: 1,200
Staff: full time 22
Major programs: museum, historic
  site(s), tours, school programs,
  newsletters/pamphlets, exhibits
Period of collections: 18th-20th
  centuries

West Virginia Historical Society
c/o Dept. of Culture and History,
  Capitol Complex, 25305
Telephone: (304) 348-0230
Founded in: 1941
Questionnaire not received

CLARKSBURG

Harrison County Historical Society
123 W. Main St., 26301

Telephone: (304) 842-3073
Mail to: 511 Stout St., Bridgeport,
  26330
Private agency
Founded in: 1967
E. B. Dakan, Jr., President
Number of members: 340
Major programs: archives,
  manuscripts, museum, school
  programs, newsletters/pamphlets,
  historic preservation, genealogical
  services
Period of collections: Pioneer-present

DUNBAR

Kanawha Valley Genealogical Society, Inc.
Library, 1330 Myers Ave., 25064
Telephone: (304) 562-6614
Mail to: P.O. Box 8765, So.
  Charleston, 25303
Founded in: 1977
Questionnaire not received

ELKINS

Randolph County Historical Society
Telephone: (304) 636-0841
Mail to: P.O. Box 1164, 26241
Founded in: 1924
Questionnaire not received

EXCHANGE

Braxton Historical Society
Rt. 1, Box 14, 26619
Telephone: (304) 765-2415
Founded in: 1973
Questionnaire not received

FRANKLIN

Pendleton County Historical Society, Inc.
Main St., 26807
Telephone: (304) 358-7366
Questionnaire not received

GRIFFITHSVILLE

Lincoln County Genealogical Society
Telephone: (304) 524-7326
Mail to: P.O. Box 92, 25521
Founded in: 1980
Questionnaire not received

HAMBLETON

Hambleton Historic Preservation Society, Inc.
P.O. Box 17, 26269
Telephone: (304) 478-2354/(703)
  243-5608
Founded in: 1976
Questionnaire not received

HARPERS FERRY

Harpers Ferry Historical Association
Harpers Ferry National Historic Park,
  P.O. Box 147, 25425
Telephone: (304) 535-6881
Founded in: 1971
Paula Degen, President
Number of members: 200
Staff: full time 1, part time 3
Major programs: educational
  programs, books, book sales, film

sales and rentals Priod of
collections: 19th century

Mather Training Center
P.O. Box 27, 25425
Telephone: (304) 535-6371
Federal agency, authorized by
National Park Service
Staff: full time 8, part time 1,
volunteer 2
Major programs: library, archives,
manuscripts, museum, historic
site(s), markers, tours/pilgrimages,
junior history, oral history, school
programs, book publishing,
newsletters/pamphlets, historic
preservation, records
management, research, exhibits,
living history, audiovisual
programs, archaeology programs,
photographic collections,
genealogical services, field
services, training for National Park
Service employees

National Park Service Archives
Harpers Ferry Center, 25425
Telephone: (304) 535-6371, ext. 6493
Founded in: 1973
Questionnaire not received

**National Park Service History
Collection, Office of Library and
Archival Services**
Harpers Ferry Center, 25425
Telephone: (304) 535-6371, ext. 6493
Federal agency, authorized by
National Park Service
Founded in: 1971
David Nathanson, Chief
Staff: full time 1, part time 1
Major programs: library, archives,
manuscripts, museum, oral history,
research, exhibits, field services
Period of collections: 1870-1970

HELVETIA

Historical Society of Helvetia
General Delivery, 26224
Founded in: 1977
Questionnaire not received

HILLSBORO

**Pearl S. Buck Birthplace
Foundation, Inc.**
Telephone: (304) 653-4430
Mail to: P.O. Box 126, 24946
Private agency
Founded in: 1966
David C. Hyer, Executive Director
Number of members: 438
Staff: full time 5, part time 2
Major programs: library, archives,
manuscripts, museum, historic
sites preservation, markers,
tours/pilgrimages, junior history,
oral history, educational programs
Period of collections: 1865-1918

HINTON

**New River Chapter/West Virginia
Archaeological Society**
P.O. Box 129, 25951
Telephone: (704) 466-3388
Founded in: 1979
Questionnaire not received

**Summers County Historical
Society**
107 Miller Ave., 25951
Telephone: (304) 466-0794
Questionnaire not received

HUNTINGTON

Cabell-Wayne Historical Society
11th St. and 2nd Ave.
Mail to: P.O. Box 123, 25701
Questionnaire not received

**Collis P. Huntington Railroad
Historical Society, Inc.**
14th St. W. and Memorial Blvd. 25704
Telephone: (304) 522-6140
Mail to: P.O. Box 271, 25707
Private agency
Founded in: 1959
John Bledsoe, President
Number of members: 117
Staff: volunteer 117
Magazine: The Gondola Gazette
Major programs: museum,
tours/pilgrimages, historic sites
preservation,
newsletters/pamphlets, exhibits
Period of collections: 1930s-present

INSTITUTE

Humanities Foundation
232 Hill Hall, West Virginia State
College
Telephone: (304) 768-8869
Mail to: P.O. Box 204, 25112
Private agency
Founded in: 1974
Charles Daugherty, Executive
Director
Staff: full time 3, part time 1
Major programs: museum,
tours/pilgrimages, oral history,
research, exhibits, living history,
audiovisual programs,
photographic collections, public
history programs for adults
Period of collections: 19th-20th
centuries

KERMIT

Mingo County Historical Society
10 Collier St., 25674
Telephone: (304) 393-3370
Founded in: 1951
Questionnaire not received

KINGWOOD

Preston County Historical Society
215 Jackson St., 26537
Telephone: (304) 329-1468
County agency
Founded in: 1958
Summers D. McCrum, Jr., President
Number of members: 115
Staff: volunteer 5
Major programs: archives, historic
sites preservation, oral history,
books, genealogical services
Period of collections: 1863-present

LEWISBURG

Fort Savannah Museum
204 N. Jefferson St., 24901
Telephone: (304) 645-3055
Founded in: 1962
Questionnaire not received

Greenbrier Historical Society
101 Church St.
Telephone: (304) 645-3398
Mail to: 309 S. Court St., 24901
Private agency
Founded in: 1963
Mrs. Theodore Woodward, President
Number of members: 490
Major programs: library, museum,
book publishing
Period of collections: 18th-19th
centuries

LOST CREEK

**Watters Smith Memorial State Park
and Museum**
P.O. Box 296, 26385
Telephone: (304) 745-3081
State agency, authorized by
Department of Natural Resources
Founded in: 1949 (park); 1963
(museum)
Herman H. Freeman, Superintendent
Staff: full time 3, part time 2
Major programs: historic site(s),
historic preservation, exhibits
Period of collections: 1800s

MARLINTON

**Pocahontas County Historical
Society, Inc.**
810 2nd Ave., 24954
Telephone: (304) 799-4973
Private agency
Founded in: 1961
Carl Chestnut, President
Number of members: 350
Staff: volunteer 5
Major programs: archives, museum,
photographic collections
Period of collections: 1890-present

MARTINSBURG

**The Berkeley County Historical
Society**
Mail to: P.O. Box 679, 25401
Questionnaire not received

**General Adam Stephen Memorial
Association, Inc.**
309 E. John St.
Telephone: (304) 267-4434
Mail to: P.O. Box 862, 25401
City agency
Founded in: 1959
Herbert J. York, Curator
Number of members: 50
Staff: full time 1
Major programs: archives, museum,
historic site(s), exhibits,
photographic collections
Period of collections: 1750-1820

MASON

Mason City Historical Society
6 Brown St.
Telephone: (304) 773-5557
Mail to: Curator, 5 Pomeroy St., 25260
Founded in: 1974
Evelyn Proffitt, Curator
Number of members: 50
Major programs: historic sites
preservation
Period of collections: 1875-1925

MORGANTOWN

Monongalia County Historical Society
Telephone: (304) 292-0655
Mail to: P.O. Box 127, 26505
Founded in: 1924
Questionnaire not received

National Council on Public History
Department of History, West Virginia University, 26506
Telephone: (304) 293-2421
Founded in: 1980
Barbara J. Howe, Executive Secretary
Number of members: 1,000
Staff: full time 1, part time 2
Magazine: *The Public Historian*
Major programs: newsletters/pamphlets, curriculum development in public history, publicity about public history and history careers

West Virginia Antiquities Commission
77 Beechurst Ave.
Telephone: (304) 296-1791
Mail to: P.O. Box 630, 26505
Questionnaire not received

NEW MARTINSVILLE

Wetzel County Genealogical Society
Mail to: P.O. Box 464, 26155
Founded in: 1979
Questionnaire not received

PARKERSBURG

West Virginia Baptist Historical Society, Inc.
1019 Juliana St.
Telephone: (304) 422-6449
Mail to: P.O. Box 1019, 26101
Founded in: 1940
Questionnaire not received

Wood County Historical and Preservation Society, Inc.
1829 7th St.
Telephone: (304) 428-5561
Mail to: P.O. Box 617, 26101
County agency
Founded in: 1980
James P. Vaughan, President
Number of members: 65
Staff: volunteer 5
Major programs: library, exhibits, audiovisual programs, photographic collections
Period of collections: early 1800s-present

PETERSBURG

Grant County Historical Society, Inc.
P.O. Box 665, 26847
Telephone: (304) 257-1444
County agency
Founded in: 1967
Harold D. Garber, President
Number of members: 50
Staff: volunteer 12
Major programs: archives, museum, historic site(s), markers, tours/pilgrimages, historic

preservation, genealogical services
Period of collections: 1750-present

PHILIPPI

Barbour County Historical Society
Telephone: (304) 457-2634
Mail to: Volga, 26238
Questionnaire not received

RAVENSWOOD

Washington's Lands Museum
Lock 22
Mail to: 200 Henrietta St., 26164
Private agency, authorized by Jackson County Historical Society
Founded in: 1969
Ed Rauh, Chair of Museum Committee
Staff: volunteer 23
Major programs: museum
Period of collections: 1820-1920

RIPLEY

Jackson County Historical Society
Telephone: (304) 372-6508
Mail to: P.O. Box 22, 25271
Founded in: 1969
A. Ford Winters, President
Number of members: 144
Staff: volunteer 5
Magazine: *Jackson County History*
Major programs: library, museum, books, newsletters/pamphlets, historic preservation
Period of collections: 1831-1900

SAINT ALBANS

Upper Vandalia Historical Society
2128 Harrison Ave., 25303
Telephone: (304) 727-5709
Founded in: 1960
Questionnaire not received

SECOND CREEK

Early American Industries Association, Inc.
Pageland Farm, 24974
Telephone: (304) 647-4509
Questionnaire not received

SHEPHERDSTOWN

Historic Shepherdstown Commission
German and Princess Sts.
Mail to: P.O. Box 1786, 25443
Private agency
Founded in: 1961
Ben Miller, President
Number of members: 250
Staff: volunteer 35
Major programs: museum, historic site(s), historic preservation
Period of collections: 19th century

TERRA ALTA

Americana Museum
401 Aurora Ave., 26764
Telephone: (304) 789-2361
Private agency
Founded in: 1967
Ruth Teets, Owner
Staff: part time 7
Major programs: museum

WEIRTON

Hancock County Historical Society of West Virginia, Inc.
Swaney Library, New Cumberland, 26047
Telephone: (304) 748-4829
Mail to: 3669 Main St., 26062
Founded in: 1966
Questionnaire not received

WESTON

Jackson's Mill State 4-H Camp
Rt. 1, 26452
Telephone: (304) 269-5100
State agency, authorized by West Virginia University
Founded in: 1921
Daniel H. Tabler, Camp Director
Staff: full time 40, part time 12, volunteer 4
Major programs: museum, historic site(s), historic preservation, living history
Period of collections: mid 1800s

Lewis County Historical Society
252 Main Ave., 26452
Telephone: (304) 269-4297
Founded in: 1935
Questionnaire not received

WHEELING

Friends of Wheeling
P.O. Box 889, 26003
Telephone: (304) 242-0341
Founded in: 1970
Questionnaire not received

Oglebay Institute—Mansion Museum
Oglebay Park, 26003
Telephone: (304) 242-7272
Private agency
Founded in: 1930
John A. Artzberger, Museum Director
Number of members: 1,500
Staff: full time 5, part time 7, volunteer 65
Major programs: library, archives, museum, junior history, school programs, newsletters/pamphlets, historic preservation, records management, research, exhibits, audiovisual programs, photographic collections, industrial arts
Period of collections: 1790-present

WISCONSIN

ANTIGO

Langlade County Historical Society
404 Superior St., 54409
Telephone: (715) 623-3631
Founded in: 1929
Questionnaire not received

APPLETON

Outagamie County Historical Society, Inc.
History Workshop, 320 N. Durkee St., 54911

Telephone: (414) 733-8445
Private agency
Founded in: 1872
Douglas A. Ogilvie, President
Number of members: 450
Staff: full time 6
Magazine: *History Today*
Major programs: library, archives,
museum, historic site(s), school
programs, newsletters/pamphlets,
historic preservation, records
management, research, exhibits,
audiovisual programs,
photographic collections
Period of collections: 1850-1950

ASHLAND

Ashland Historical Society
P.O. Box 433, 54806
Telephone: (715) 682-4029
Private agency
Founded in: 1980
Suzan McCue, President
Number of members: 76
Staff: part time 1, volunteer 25
Magazine: *Garland City Gazette*
Major programs: museum,
tours/pilgrimages, school
programs, historic preservation,
audiovisual programs
Period of collections: 1880-1930

BALSAM LAKE

Polk County Historical Society
54810
Telephone: (715) 485-3136
County agency
Founded in: 1937
Frank J. Werner, President
Number of members: 140
Staff: volunteer 40
Major programs: library, manuscripts,
museum, markers
Period of collections: 1865-1918

BARABOO

Sauk County Historical Society
531 4th Ave.
Mail to: 1725 Elizabeth, 53913
County agency
Founded in: 1901
N. Etzwiler, Curator
Number of members: 225
Staff: part time 1, volunteer 25
Major programs: library, archives,
museum, historic site(s), markers,
tours/pilgrimages, junior history,
oral history, school programs, book
publishing, newsletters/pamphlets,
historic preservation, photographic
collections
Period of collections: 1840-1930

BARRON

Barron County Historical Society
426 S. 5th St., 54812
Telephone: (715) 537-3623
Questionnaire not received

BEAVER DAM

Dodge County Historical Society
105 Park Ave., 53916
Private agency
Founded in: 1937
Richard F. Jacobs, President

Number of members: 45
Staff: full time 1, volunteer 12
Major programs: museum,
tours/pilgrimages, audiovisual
programs, genealogical services
Period of collections: 1865-present

BELOIT

Beloit Historical Society
2149 St. Lawrence Ave., 53511
Telephone: (608) 365-3811
Founded in: 1910
Questionnaire not received

**Hanchett-Bartlett Museum—Beloit
Historical Society**
2149 St. Lawrence Ave., 53511
Telephone: (608) 365-3811
Private agency
Founded in: 1910
Evelyn T. Wehrle, Director
Number of members: 720
Staff: full time 1, part time 1,
volunteer 30
Major programs: museum, historic
site(s), school programs
Period of collections: 1860-1930

BERLIN

Berlin Historical Society
288 Van Horn St.
Telephone: (414) 361-2396
Mail to: Rt. 3, Box 93, 54923
Private agency
Founded in: 1962
Mrs. Norbert Secora, President
Major programs: library, museum,
junior history, research,
genealogical services
Period of collections: 1860-present

BLACK RIVER FALLS

Jackson County Historical Society
S. 1st St.
Telephone: (715) 284-4659
Mail to: 223 N. 4th St., 54615
Questionnaire not received

BLUE MOUNDS

Little Norway, Inc.
3576 Hwy. JG-N, 53517
Telephone: (608) 437-8211
Private agency
Founded in: 1937
Marcelaine Winner, President
Staff: full time 17, part time 2
Major programs: museum
Period of collections: 1850-early
1900s

BRODHEAD

Brodhead Historical Society
c/o Secretary, 805 1st Center Ave.,
53520
Telephone: (608) 897-2635
Private agency, authorized by
Historical Society of Wisconsin
Founded in: 1975
F. S. Gombar, President
Number of members: 74
Major programs: archives, museum,
historic site(s), oral history, historic
preservation, research, exhibits,
photographic collections

BROOKFIELD

Elmbrook Historical Society
P.O. Box 292, 53005
Telephone: (414) 782-3821
Founded in: 1976
Questionnaire not received

BROWN DEER

Brown Deer Historical Society, Inc.
4800 W. Green Brook Dr., 53223
Telephone: (414) 355-5220
Mail to: 8248 N. 38th St., 53209
Founded in: 1972
Questionnaire not received

BRUCE

Rusk County Historical Society
Rt. 2, 54819
Telephone: (715) 868-4382
Period of collections: 1865-1918
Questionnaire not received

BURLINGTON

Burlington Historical Society
232 N. Perkins Blvd.
Mail to: 432 Rose Ann Dr., 53105
Founded in: 1928
Questionnaire not received

CEDARBURG

Ozaukee County Historical Society
Telephone: (414) 377-4510
Mail to: P.O. Box 206, 53012
Questionnaire not received

CLINTONVILLE

Clintonville Area Historical Society
32 11th St.
Telephone: (715) 823-4680
Mail to: c/o Margaret McCauley,
President, Pine Lake, Rt. 4, Box
312, 54929
Founded in: 1975
Questionnaire not received

CROSS PLAINS

**Cross Plains—Berry Historical
Society**
2305 Church St., 53528
Telephone: (608) 798-2509
Authorized by State Historical Society
of Wisconsin
Founded in: 1972
Ray Virnig, President
Number of members: 28
Staff: volunteer 4
Major programs: oral history, historic
preservation, photographic
collections
Period of collections: 1870-1940

CUDAHY

Cudahy Historical Society
P. O. Box 332, 53110
Private agency, authorized by State
Historical Society of Wisconsin
Founded in: 1971
Betty Chovanec, Vice President
Number of members: 100
Major programs: archives, museum,
historic site(s), oral history, school
programs, newsletters/pamphlets
Period of collections: 1930

DARINGTON

Lafayette County Historical Society
525 Main St., 53530
Telephone: (608) 776-4171
Authorized by State Historical Society
of Wisconsin
Founded in: 1981
Marion Howard, President
Number of members: 150
Staff: volunteer 20
Magazine: *Looking Backwards*
Major programs: museum,
newsletters/pamphlets, exhibits

DEFOREST

DeForest Area Historical Society
212 Reigstad St., 53532
Questionnaire not received

DELAFIELD

Hawks Inn Historical Society, Inc.
426 Wells St.
Mail to: P.O. Box 104, 53018
Private agency
Founded in: 1960
Leland Felber, President
Number of members: 300
Staff: volunteer 300
Major programs: archives,
manuscripts, museum, historic
site(s), junior history, oral history,
book publishing,
newsletters/pamphlets, historic
preservation, research, exhibits,
photographic collections,
genealogical services
Period of collections: 1846-1863

DODGEVILLE

Iowa County Historical Society
Mail to: P.O. Box 38, 53533
Questionnaire not received

DRUMMOND

Drummond Historical Society
54832
Town agency
Founded in: 1976
Lawrence Gagner, President
Number of members: 50
Staff: volunteer 1
Major programs: museum
Period of collections: 1882-present

EAGLE

Old World Wisconsin
Rt. 2, Box 18, 53119
Telephone: (414) 594-2116
State agency
Founded in: 1973
John W. Reilly, Administrator
Staff: full time 11, part time 45
Major programs: historic site(s),
school programs, historic
preservation, living history
Period of collections: mid-late 19th
century

EAST TROY

**Wisconsin Electric Railway
Historical Society, Inc.**
2002 Church St.
Telephone: (414) 642-3833
Mail to: P.O. Box 726, 53120
Questionnaire not received

EAU CLAIRE

Chippewa Valley Museum
Carson Park
Telephone: (715) 834-7871
Mail to: P.O. Box 1204, 54702
Private agency
Founded in: 1964
Susan McLeod, Director
Number of members: 1,280
Staff: full time 3, part time 6,
volunteer 448
Major programs: library, archives,
manuscripts, museum, historic
site(s), oral history, school
programs, historic preservation,
exhibits, photographic collections,
genealogical services
Period of collections: 1850-present

Eau Claire Landmarks Commission
City of Eau Claire, City Hall
Mail to: 2916 Nimitz St., 54701
City agency
Founded in: 1974
Ann Ohl, Chair
Major programs: historic sites
preservation, markers, historic
preservation
Period of collections: 1800s-present

Wisconsin Archaeological Survey
University of Wisconsin, Eau Claire,
54701
State agency
Founded in: 1948
Robert Barth, Chair, Department of
Sociology and Anthropology
Number of members: 50
Major programs: historic site(s),
historic preservation, archaeology
programs

ELKHORN

Walworth County Historical Society
9 E. Rockwell St., 53121
Telephone: (414) 723-4248
Founded in: 1904
Fred H. Young, Curator
Number of members: 80
Staff: full time 1, volunteer 6
Major programs: library, museum,
school programs,
newsletters/pamphlets
Period of collections: 1840-1918

ELM GROVE

Elmbrook Historical Society
1050 Legion Dr.
Telephone: (414) 782-7818
Mail to: 845 Morningside Lane, 53122
Questionnaire not received

EVANSVILLE

Evansville Grove Society
53536
City agency, authorized by Rock
County Historical Society
Founded in: 1978
Terry L. Straka, President
Number of members: 80
Major programs: library,
tours/pilgrimages, junior history,
oral history, school programs,
newsletters/pamphlets, records
management

FIFIELD

Price County Historical Society
c/o HCR-2, Box 717, Park Falls, 54552

Telephone: (715) 762-4571
Mail to: Fifield, 54524
County agency, authorized by State
Historical Society of Wisconsin
Founded in: 1959
Patricia Schroeder, Board President
Number of members: 90
Staff: volunteer 15
Major programs: museum,
newsletters/pamphlets
Period of collections: 1876-1930

FOND DU LAC

**Fond du Lac County Historical
Society**
336 Old Pioneer Rd.
Telephone: (414) 922-6390
Mail to: P.O. Box 131, 54935
Founded in: 1948
Questionnaire not received

FORT ATKINSON

**Fort Atkinson Historical
Society-Hoard Historical
Museum**
407 Merchant Ave., 53538
Telephone: (414) 563-4521
Founded in: 1939
Questionnaire not received

Hoard Historical Museum
407 S. Merchants Ave., 53538
Telephone: (414) 648-5458
Private agency, authorized by Ft.
Atkinson Historical Society
Founded in: 1934
Helmut Knies, Curator
Number of members: 661
Staff: full time 1, part time 2,
volunteer 3
Major programs: archives, museum,
historic site(s), book publishing,
historic preservation, research,
exhibits, photographic collections,
genealogical services
Period of collections: 1800-1900

FOX LAKE

Fox Lake Historical Society, Inc.
53933
Founded in: 1977
Questionnaire not received

FRANKLIN

Franklin Historical Society
9220 W. Drexel
Telephone: (414) 425-3295
Mail to: P.O. Box 245, 53132
Questionnaire not received

GAY MILLS

Crawford County Historical Society
Prairie du Chien, 54631
Steven Picus, President
Major programs: educational
programs, historic preservation
Period of collections: 1850-1900
Questionnaire not received

GENESEE DEPOT

Genesee Heritage Society
P.O. Box 52, 53127
Telephone: (414) 968-3166
Town agency, authorized by State
Historical Society of Wisconsin
Founded in: 1979

Sharon Leair, President
Number of members: 40
Staff: volunteer 9
Major programs: oral history,
newsletters/pamphlets, living
history, audiovisual programs,
photographic collections

GERMANTOWN

**Germantown Historical
Society, Inc.**
P.O. Box 31, 53022
Telephone: (414) 251-6378
City agency
Founded in: 1975
Irene Blau, President
Number of members: 150
Staff: volunteer 30
Major programs: museum, historic
site(s), newsletters/pamphlets,
exhibits, photographic collections,
genealogical services
Period of collections: 1850-1920

GREEN BAY

Brown County Historical Society
P.O. Box 1411, 54305
Telephone: (414) 435-4922
Town agency
Founded in: 1899
George Nau Burridge, President
Number of members: 758
Magazine: *Voyageur*
Major programs: school programs,
book publishing,
newsletters/pamphlets, historic
preservation, audiovisual programs

Green Bay Packer Hall of Fame
1901 S. Oneida, 54304
Telephone: (414) 499-4281
Mail to: P.O. Box 10567, 54307-0567
Private agency
Founded in: 1976
James A. Van Matre, General
Manager
Staff: full time 7, part time 12
Major programs: archives,
manuscripts, school programs,
historic preservation, exhibits,
audiovisual programs,
photographic collections, sports
history
Period of collections: 1919-present

Hazelwood Historic House
1008 S. Monroe Ave., 54301
Telephone: (414) 497-3768
Mail to: 210 Museum Place,
54303-2780
Town agency, authorized by Neville
Public Museum
Staff: full time 1, part time 1,
volunteer 50
Major programs: archives,
manuscripts, historic site(s),
markers, tours/pilgrimages, junior
history, school programs,
newsletters/pamphlets, historic
preservation, records
management, research, exhibits,
living history, audiovisual
programs, photographic collections,
special events
Period of collections: 1936-present

Heritage Hill Corporation
2640 S. Webster Ave., 54301

Telephone: (414) 497-4368
Founded in: 1976
Nicholas L. Clark, Director
Staff: full time 7, part time 40,
volunteer 350
Magazine: *Heritage Hill Intelligencer*
Major programs: museum, historic
sites preservation,
tours/pilgrimages, educational
programs, historic preservation
Period of collections: 1800-1875

Heritage Hill State Park
2640 S. Webster, 54301
Telephone: (414) 497-4368
Private agency, authorized by
Heritage Hill Corporation
Founded in: 1976
Ross Fullam, Director
Staff: full time 5, part time 17,
volunteer 330
Major programs: historic
preservation, living history
Period of collections: late 18th
century-1902

**Neville Public Museum of Brown
County**
210 Museum Place, 54303-2780
Telephone: (414) 497-3767
County agency
Founded in: 1927
James L. Quinn, Director
Number of members: 1,250
Staff: full time 13, part time 1,
volunteer 99
Major programs: library, museum,
historic site(s), school programs,
newsletters/pamphlets, historic
preservation, research, exhibits,
audiovisual programs, archaeology
programs, photographic
collections, field services

**Rail America, the National Railroad
Museum**
2285 S. Broadway, 54304
Telephone: (414) 499-4281
Mail to: P.O. Box 10567, 54307-0567
Private agency, authorized by Rail
America Inc.
Founded in: 1956
James A. Van Matre, General
Manager
Staff: full time 7, part time 12
Magazine: *National Railroad Museum
Highlight and Data Catalog*
Major programs: museum, oral
history, school programs, historic
preservation, living history,
audiovisual programs,
photographic collections
Period of collections: 1830-1900

Wisconsin Postal History Society
1641 Bruce Lane, 54303
Telephone: (414) 499-3877
Questionnaire not received

GREENBUSH

**Superior
Restorations, Inc.—Finnish
Pioneer Crafts Guild**
P.O. Box 31, 53026
Telephone: (414) 526-3433
Private agency
Founded in: 1981
Alan C. Pape, President
Staff: volunteer 10

Major programs: archives, museum,
book publishing
Period of collections: 1910-1920

GREENDALE

Greendale Historical Society
6500 Northway, 53129
Telephone: (414) 421-1300
Founded in: 1974
Questionnaire not received

GREENFIELD

Greenfield Historical Society
56th St. and Layton Ave.
Telephone: (414) 543-3324
Mail to: 4759 W. Howard Ave., 53220
Private agency, authorized by State
Historical Society of Wisconsin
Founded in: 1965
Frank Palma, President
Number of members: 77
Staff: volunteer 8
Major programs: manuscripts,
museum, historic site(s), markers,
tours, oral history, school
programs, book publishing,
newsletters/pamphlets, historic
preservation, records
management, exhibits,
photographic collections
Period of collections: 1850-1910

GREEN LAKE

Dartford Historical Society
550 Mill St.
Mail to: P.O. Box 138, 54941
Private agency
Founded in: 1956
Lawrence D. Behlen, President
Number of members: 40
Staff: part time 2, volunteer 10
Major programs: museum, school
programs, records management,
exhibits, photographic collections,
genealogical services
Period of collections: 1860-1910

HALES CORNERS

Hales Corners Historical Society
5621 S. Bonnie Lane, 53130
Telephone: (414) 425-3312
Town agency, authorized by State
Historical Society of Wisconsin
Founded in: 1974
P. W. Riebs, President
Number of members: 55
Staff: volunteer 15
Major programs: archives, markers,
oral history, historic preservation
Period of collections: 1837-present

HILLSBORO

**Hillsboro Area Historical
Society, Inc.**
532 Water Ave., 54634
Telephone: (608) 489-2579
Private agency
Founded in: 1957
Margaret M. Kelley, President
Number of members: 100
Staff: volunteer 30
Major programs: manuscripts,
museum, historic site(s), historic
preservation, exhibits,
photographic collections
Period of collections: late 1800s

HORICON

Horicon Historical Society
Winter St.
Mail to: P.O. Box 65, 53032
Founded in: 1972
Questionnaire not received

HUDSON

St. Croix County Historical Society
1004 3rd St., 54016
Telephone: (715) 386-2654
Private agency
Founded in: 1948
Donna Hunter, President
Number of members: 300
Staff: full time 1
Major programs: museum, book
publishing, newsletters/pamphlets,
historic preservation, research,
exhibits, genealogical services
Period of collections: 1850-1890

HURLEY

Iron County Historical Society
Iron St.
Telephone: (715) 561-2244
Mail to: P.O. Box 4, 54534
Private agency
Founded in: 1967
Mrs. Edward Kopacz, President
Number of members: 106
Staff: volunteer 2
Major programs: library, archives,
museum, historic site(s), oral
history, historic preservation,
exhibits, photographic collections
Period of collections: 1918-present

HUSTISFORD

Hustisford Historical Society
53034
Private agency
Founded in: 1971
Herbert E. Neuenschwander,
President
Number of members: 45
Staff: volunteer 7
Major programs: archives, museum,
historic sites preservation,
photographic collections
Period of collections: 1836-present

IOLA

Iola Historical Society
300 N. Main, 54945
Telephone: (715) 445-3184
Mail to: Rt. 1, Scandinavia, 54945
Founded in: 1958
Questionnaire not received

IRON RIVER

**Western Bayfield County Historical
Society**
Telephone: (715) 372-4359
Mail to: Rt. 1, Box 34, 54847
County agency
Founded in: 1973
Bertha Lehman, President
Number of members: 90
Major programs: museum, markers
Period of collections: 1900s

JACKSON

Jackson Historical Society
2860 Division Rd., 53037
Questionnaire not received

JANESVILLE

Rock County Historical Society
10 S. High St.
Telephone: (608) 756-4509
Mail to: P.O. Box 896, 53545
Founded in: 1948
Richard P. Hartung, Director
Number of members: 950
Staff: full time 5, part time 3,
volunteer 520
Magazine: *The Rock County
Recorder*
Major programs: library, archives,
manuscripts, museum, historic
site(s), tours/pilgrimages, school
programs, newsletters/pamphlets,
historic preservation, exhibits
Period of collections: 1820-present

**Seventh Day Baptist Historical
Society**
3120 Kennedy Rd.
Telephone: (608) 752-5055
Mail to: P.O. Box 1678, 53547
Private agency
Founded in: 1916
D. Scott Smith, Historian
Number of members: 60
Staff: full time 1, part time 1,
volunteer 10
Magazine: *The Sabbath Recorder*
Major programs: library, archives,
manuscripts, museum, records
management, genealogical
services
Period of collections: 1650-present

Tallman Restorations
440 N. Jackson St.
Telephone: (608) 752-4519
Mail to: P.O. Box 896, 53545
Private agency, authorized by Rock
County Historical Society
Founded in: 1951
Paul M. Tropp, Sites Administrator
Staff: full time 1, volunteer 50
Major programs: museum, historic
sites preservation, educational
programs
Period of collections: 1830-1870

JEFFERSON

Jefferson Historical Society
333 E. Ogden St.
Telephone: (414) 674-5306
Mail to: 1035 W. Racine Rd., 53549
Founded in: 1962
Questionnaire not received

KENOSHA

Kenosha County Historical Society
6300 3rd Ave., 53140
Telephone: (414) 654-5770
County agency
Founded in: 1878
Phil Sander, Director
Number of members: 640
Staff: part time 6, volunteer 21
Major programs: library, archives,
museum, school programs,
newsletters/pamphlets, exhibits,

archaeology programs,
photographic collections,
genealogical services
Period of collections: 1850-present

**University Archives and Area
Research Center, University of
Wisconsin, Parkside**
P.O. Box 2000, 53141
Telephone: (414) 553-2411
State agency, authorized by State
Historical Society of Wisconsin
Founded in: 1972
Nicholas C. Burckel, Director
Staff: full time 2
Major programs: library, archives,
manuscripts, school programs,
records management,
genealogical services
Period of collections: 1840-1970

KEWASKUM

Kewaskum Historical Society, Inc.
1202 Park View Dr., 53040
Founded in: 1975
Daniel S. Schmidt, President
Number of members: 75
Staff: volunteer 75
Major programs: museum, historic
site(s), historic preservation,
exhibits, living history
Period of collections: 1850-1930

KEWAUNEE

**Kewaunee County Historical
Society**
Courthouse Square 54216
Telephone: (414) 388-2244
Mail to: Rt. 2, Box 263, Luxemburg,
54217
Private agency, authorized by State
Historical Society of Wisconsin
Founded in: 1921
Gerald V. Abitz, President
Number of members: 400
Staff: part time 5, volunteer 5
Major programs: museum, oral
history, book publishing,
photographic collections
Period of collections: 1870-1910

KIEL

Kiel Historical Society
Mail to: 325 Indian Hill Rd. 53042
Founded in: 1973
Questionnaire not received

KING

Wisconsin Veterans Museums
Marden Center, 54946
State agency
Founded in: 1935
Richard H. Zeitlin, Director
Staff: full time 2, part time 1,
volunteer 5
Major programs: museum
Period of collections: W.W. I-W.W. II

LA CROSSE

**La Crosse County Historical
Society, Inc.**
Mail to: P.O. Box 1272, 54602-1272
Private agency
David L. Henke, Director
Number of members: 850
Staff: full time 2, part time 3

Major programs: museum,
tours/pilgrimages, school
programs, book publishing,
newsletters/pamphlets, historic
preservation, exhibits, living history
Period of collections: 1800-present

LAKE TOMAHAWK

Northland Historical Society
P.O. Box 325, 54539
Telephone: (715) 277-2788
Founded in: 1957
Questionnaire not received

LAONA

**Camp Five Museums
Foundation, Inc.**
54541
Telephone: (715) 674-3414
Mail to: 1011 8th St., Wausau, 54401
Founded in: 1969
Mrs. Gordon R. Connor,
Curator/Manager
Staff: part time 20, volunteer 1
Major programs: museum,
tours/pilgrimages, historic
preservation, exhibits, audiovisual
programs, photographic
collections, ecological and
environmental programs
Period of collections: 1870s-1940s

LOYAL

**Clark County Historical
Society, Inc.**
Rt. 2, 54446
Telephone: (715) 255-8968
Questionnaire not received

MADISON

**American Institute of the History of
Pharmacy**
Pharmacy Bldg., 425 N. Charter St.,
53706-1508
Telephone: (608) 262-5378
Founded in: 1941
Glenn Sonnedecker, Director
Number of members: 1,100
Staff: full time 3, part time 3,
volunteer 1
Magazine: *Pharmacy in History*
Major programs: archives,
manuscripts, markers, school
programs, book publishing,
newsletters/pamphlets, research,
photographic collections,
grants-in-aid, history of pharmacy
and medicine
Period of collections: 1865-present

Dane County Historical Society
P.O. Box 5003, 53705
County agency, authorized by State
Historical Society of Wisconsin
Founded in: 1961
Claire Mulvey, President
Number of members: 150
Staff: part time 1
Major programs: archives, markers,
newsletters/pamphlets, exhibits
Period of collections: 19th-20th
centuries

G.A.R. Memorial Hall Museum
Capitol 419, N, 53702
Telephone: (608) 266-1680

State agency, authorized by
Department of Veterans Affairs
Founded in: 1901
Richard H. Zeitlin, Director
Staff: full time 2, part time 2
Major programs: museum, records
management, photographic
collections, battle flag conservation
Period of collections: Civil War

**Historic Blooming Grove Historical
Society**
1000 Nichols Rd., Monona, 53716
Founded in: 1972
Patricia Johnson, President
Number of members: 120
Staff: volunteer 12
Major programs: tours/pilgrimages,
oral history, newsletters/pamphlets,
historic preservation, records
management, research, exhibits,
living history, audiovisual
programs, photographic
collections
Period of collections: 1850s

Historic Madison, Inc.
Telephone: (608) 256-5697
Mail to: P.O. Box 2031, 53701
Founded in: 1973
Questionnaire not received

The Lemery Heritage Society
222 W. Gorham, 53703
Telephone: (608) 258-8967
Mail to: c/o The Family Tree, Box 9581
53715
Founded in: 1974
Questionnaire not received

**State Historical Society of
Wisconsin**
816 State St., 53706
Telephone: (608) 262-3266
State agency
Founded in: 1846
H. Nicholas Muller, Director
Number of members: 5,113
Staff: full time 146, part time 11,
volunteer 240
Magazine: *Wisconsin Magazine of
History*
Major programs: library, archives,
manuscripts, museum, historic
site(s), markers, oral history, school
programs, book publishing,
newsletters/pamphlets, historic
preservation, research, exhibits,
archaeology programs,
photographic collections,
genealogical services, field
services

**Wisconsin Council for Local
History**
816 State St., 53706
Telephone: (608) 262-2316
Founded in: 1960
Questionnaire not received

Wisconsin Humanities Committee
716 Langdon St., 53706
Telephone: (608) 262-0706
Authorized by National Endowment
for the Humanities
Founded in: 1972
Patricia C. Anderson, Executive
Director
Staff: full time 2, part time 3,
volunteer 25

Major programs: library, museum,
historic site(s), oral history

**Wisconsin State Genealogical
Society**
Mail to: 2109 20th Ave., Monroe,
53566
Founded in: 1939
Questionnaire not received

**Wisconsin State Old Cemetery
Society**
617 Clemons Ave., 53704
Mail to: WSOCS-SW Region, Carolyn
Habelman, Rt. 3 Box 253, Black
River Falls, 54615
Founded in: 1971
Winston F. Luck, President
Number of members: 1,200
Staff: volunteer 250
Magazine: *Inscriptions*
Major programs: library, archives,
newsletters/pamphlets
Period of collections: 1835-present

**Wooden Canoe Heritage
Association, Ltd.**
P.O. Box 5634, 53705
Telephone: (608) 231-2355
Founded in: 1979
Jeff Dean, President
Number of members: 600
Staff: volunteer 2
Magazine: *Wooden Canoe*
Major programs: library, educational
programs, newsletters/pamphlets,
historic preservation

MANAWA

Waupaca County Historical Society
823 Depot St., 54949
Telephone: (414) 596-3467
County agency
Founded in: 1976
Mary A. Craig, President
Number of members: 25
Staff: volunteer 14
Major programs: historic site(s), oral
history, research, photographic
collections

MANITOWOC

**Manitowoc County Historical
Society**
P.O. Box 574, 54220
County agency
Founded in: 1906
Armond Kueter, President
Number of members: 800
Staff: volunteer 12
Magazine: *Manitowoc County
Historical Society Monographs*
Major programs: archives,
manuscripts, historic site(s),
markers, school programs, book
publishing, newsletters/pamphlets,
historic preservation, research,
exhibits, audiovisual programs,
photographic collections
Period of collections: 1875-1930

Manitowoc Maritime Museum
809 S. 8th St., 54220
Telephone: (414) 684-0218
Private agency
Founded in: 1969
David L. Pamperin, Director
Number of members: 2,500

Staff: full time 4, part time 3,
volunteer 100
Magazine: *Anchor News*
Major programs: library, archives,
manuscripts, museum, historic
site(s), school programs,
newsletters/pamphlets, records
management, research, exhibits,
photographic collections
Period of collections: 1880s-1950s

Rahr-West Museum
Park St. at N. 8th, 54220
Telephone: (414) 683-4501
City agency
Founded in: 1941
Richard Quick, Director
Major programs: museum, historic
site(s), tours,
newsletters/pamphlets, exhibits,
photographic collections
Period of collections:
prehistoric-present

MARINETTE

Marinette County Historical Society
Telephone: (715) 732-0831
Mail to: P.O. Box 262, 54143
County agency
Major programs: museum, historic
site(s), markers,
newsletters/pamphlets
Period of collections: 1850-1910

MARSHFIELD

**North Wood County Historical
Society, Inc.**
Praschak Wayside, 54449
Telephone: (715) 384-4026
Mail to: 1109 E. 15th St.
Questionnaire not received

MAUSTON

Juneau County Historical Society
211 N. Union, 53948
Mail to: c/o Delbert Dumes, R.F.D.
Questionnaire not received

MAYVILLE

Mayville Historical Society, Inc.
12 Bridge St.
Telephone: (414) 387-5530
Mail to: P.O. Box 82, 53050
Founded in: 1968
Questionnaire not received

MAZOMANIE

Mazomanie Historical Society
Brodhead St., 53560
Telephone: (608) 795-4914
Founded in: 1965
Questionnaire not received

McFARLAND

McFarland Historical Society
5814 Main St.
Telephone: (608) 838-4185
Mail to: P.O. Box 62, 53558
Founded in: 1964
Questionnaire not received

MEDFORD

Taylor County Historical Society
W. 9765 Perkins Town Ave., 54451

County agency, authorized by State
Historical Society of Wisconsin
Founded in: 1965
Evangeline Griesbach, President
Number of members: 28
Staff: volunteer 7
Major programs: archives, museum,
historic site(s), markers,
newsletters/pamphlets, historic
preservation, research, exhibits,
archaeology programs
Period of collections: 1875-1940

MELLEN

Mellen Area Historical Society
City Hall, 54546
Questionnaire not received

MENASHA

Menasha Historical Society
600 1st St., 54952
Telephone: (414) 722-9022
Questionnaire not received

MENOMONEE FALLS

**Menomonee Falls Historical
Society**
N-96-W-15791 County Line Rd.
Telephone: (414) 251-6427
Mail to: P.O. Box 91, 53051
Founded in: 1966
Questionnaire not received

MENOMONIE

Dunn County Historical Society
Telephone: (715) 643-2043/235-3862
Mail to: P.O. Box 437, 54751
Founded in: 1950
Joseph M. Petryk, President
Number of members: 280
Staff: volunteer 30
Major programs: archives, museum,
historic site(s), markers, school
programs, book publishing,
exhibits, photographic collections
Period of collections: 1783-present

MIDDLETON

Middleton Historical Society
7426 Hubbard Ave., 53562
Telephone: (608) 831-6949
Founded in: 1972
Nel Ferstl, President
Number of members: 102
Staff: volunteer 16
Major programs: library, archives,
manuscripts, museum, markers,
tours/pilgrimages, oral history,
book publishing,
newsletters/pamphlets, research,
exhibits
Period of collections: 1856-1965

MILTON

Milton Historical Society
18 S. Janesville St.
Telephone: (608) 868-7772
Mail to: P.O. Box 245, 53563
Private agency
Founded in: 1938
Juliette H. Lukas,
Curator/Administrator
Number of members: 240
Staff: full time 1, part time 16,
volunteer 8

Major programs: library, archives,
museum, school programs,
newsletters/pamphlets, records
management, research, exhibits,
photographic collections,
genealogical services
Period of collections: 1800-1945

MILWAUKEE

**Menominee Indian Historical
Foundation, Inc.**
7817 N. Club Circle, 53217
Telephone: (414) 352-7683
Mail to: c/o Jacque D. Vallier
Founded in: 1968
Questionnaire not received

**Milwaukee County Historical
Society**
910 N. 3rd St., 53203
Telephone: (414) 273-8288
Founded in: 1935
Harry H. Anderson, Executive
Director
Number of members: 1,150
Staff: full time 9, part time 2,
volunteer 40
Magazine: *Milwaukee History*
Major programs: library, archives,
manuscripts, museum, historic
sites preservation, markers,
educational programs, books,
newsletters/pamphlets
Period of collections: 1783-present

Milwaukee Public Museum
800 W. Wells St., 53233
Telephone: (414) 278-2700
County agency, authorized by
Milwaukee County Board
Committee on Parks, Recreation
and Culture
Founded in: 1882
Kenneth Starr, Museum Director
Number of members: 1
Staff: full time 150, part time 28
Magazine: *Lore*
Major programs: library, archives,
manuscripts, museum, school
programs, book publishing,
newsletters/pamphlets, research,
exhibits, audiovisual programs,
archaeology programs,
photographic collections,
international
Period of collections: late 4th
millenium

**WELS (Wisconsin Evangelical
Lutheran Synod) Historical
Institute**
2929 N. Mayfair Rd., 53222
Telephone: (414) 771-9357
Private agency
Founded in: 1981
Roland Cap Ehlke, President
Number of members: 950
Magazine: *WELS Historical Institute
Journal*
Major programs: archives, museum,
historic site(s),
newsletters/pamphlets
Period of collections: 1850-present

**Wisconsin Chapter, National
Railway Historical Society, Inc.**
6600 N. Birchhill Ct., 53217
Telephone: (414) 352-9512
Private agency, authorized by State
Historical Society of Wisconsin

Founded in: 1950
L. Btrovinger, President
Number of members: 143
Magazine: *Sparks and Cinders*
Major programs:
newsletters/pamphlets, research,
audiovisual programs

Wisconsin Labor History Society
1910 E. Jarvis St., 53211
Telephone: (414) 332-4963
Authorized by State Historical Society
of Wisconsin
Founded in: 1981
Joanne Ricca, President
Number of members: 125
Major programs:
newsletters/pamphlets, annual
conferences, labor history

The Wisconsin Map Society
Mail to: c/o Virginia Schwartz,
Secretary-Treasurer, Milwaukee
Public Library, 814 W. Wisconsin
Ave.
Founded in: 1976
Chris Reinhard, President
Number of members: 20
Staff: volunteer 4

**Wisconsin Marine Historical
Society—Local History and
Marine Room**
814 W. Wisconsin Ave., 53233
Telephone: (414) 278-3074
Private agency
Founded in: 1959
Donald R. Jackson, President
Number of members: 315
Magazine: *Soundings*
Major programs: library, archives,
manuscripts, book publishing,
newsletters/pamphlets, historic
preservation, research,
photographic collections
Period of collections: 1800s-present

**Wisconsin Slovak Historical
Society**
P.O. Box 164, Cudahy, 53110-0164
Telephone: (414) 422-0067
State agency
Founded in: 1980
Aug Jurishica, President
Number of members: 700
Staff: volunteer 50
Magazine: *Wisconsin Slovak*
Major programs: living history
Period of collections: from 1850

MINERAL POINT

Pendarvis Restoration
114 Shake Rag St.
Telephone: (608) 987-2122
Mail to: P.O. Box 270, 53565
Founded in: 1971
Questionnaire not received

MONONA

**Historic Blooming Grove Historical
Society**
1000 Nichols Rd., 53716
Telephone: (608) 222-6127
Questionnaire not received

MONROE

Green County Historical Society
1617 9th St.
Mail to: 2109 20th Ave., 53566

Private agency
Founded in: 1937
Dorothy Holmes, President
Number of members: 155
Staff: part time 2, volunteer 10
Major programs: museum
Period of collections: 1865-present

**Wisconsin State Genealogical
Society, Inc.**
2109 20th Ave., 53566
Telephone: (608) 325-2609
Private agency
Founded in: 1939
Mrs. Robert Habelman, Jr., President
Number of members: 1,500
Staff: volunteer 10
Major programs:
newsletters/pamphlets,
genealogical services

MONTELLO

**Marquette County Historical
Society**
Telephone: (414) 297-2251
Mail to: Rt. 2 Box 237, 53949
Questionnaire not received

MOUNT HOREB

**Mount Horeb Area Historical
Society**
138 E. Main St.
Mail to: 408 Lake St., 53572
Founded in: 1975
Questionnaire not received

NEENAH

Neenah Historical Society
301 E. Wisconsin Ave., 54956
Telephone: (414) 722-5415
Questionnaire not received

NEILLSVILLE

Clark County Historical Society
215 E. 5th St., 54456
Telephone: (715) 743-6112
(caretaker)
Private agency
Founded in: 1965
Number of members: 125

NEOSHO

**Neosho Historical Society and
Museum**
222 Schyler St. and Hwy. 67
Telephone: (414) 625-3632
Mail to: P.O. Box 105, 53059
Private agency, authorized by State
Historical Society of Wisconsin
Founded in: 1978
Michael A. Weynand, President
Number of members: 45
Staff: volunteer 15
Magazine: *Neosho Museum
Researcher*
Major programs: library, manuscripts,
museum, historic site(s), school
programs, book publishing,
newsletters/pamphlets, historic
preservation, records
management, research, exhibits,
genealogical services
Period of collections: 1850s-W.W. II

NEW BERLIN

New Berlin Historical Society
19765 W. National Ave.
Telephone: (414) 679-1783
Mail to: 5575 S. Maberry Lane, 53151
City agency, authorized by Parks and
Recreation Department
Founded in: 1965
Jackie Hermann, President
Number of members: 100
Staff: volunteer 10
Magazine: *New Berlin Almanack*
Major programs: museum,
tours/pilgrimages, school
programs, book publishing,
newsletters/pamphlets
Period of collections: 1890-1920

NEW GLARUS

Chalet of the Golden Fleece
618 2nd St., 53574
Telephone: (608) 527-2614
Town agency, authorized by Village
Board
Founded in: 1955
Virginia Henning, Curator
Staff: part time 6
Period of collections: B.C.-early 1900

**New Glarus Historical
Society—Swiss Historical Village**
612 7th Ave.
Telephone: (608) 527-2305
Mail to: P.O. Box 745, 53574-0745
Private agency
Founded in: 1938
Margaret Duerst, President
Number of members: 20
Staff: full time 20
Major programs: museum, exhibits
Period of collections: 1845-1900

NEW HOLSTEIN

New Holstein Historical Society
2025 Randolph Ave., 53061
Telephone: (414) 898-4377
Private agency
Founded in: 1961
Pearl Keach Muenster, President
Number of members: 170
Staff: volunteer 25
Major programs: library, archives,
manuscripts, museum, historic
site(s), markers, tours/pilgrimages,
newsletters/pamphlets, historic
preservation, photographic
collections
Period of collections: 1848-1950

NEW LONDON

**New London Heritage Historical
Society**
1206 Smith St., 54961
Telephone: (414) 982-4484
Private agency, authorized by State
Historical Society of Wisconsin
Founded in: 1978
Leona Mech, Treasurer
Staff: volunteer 20
Major programs: archives, museum,
historic site(s), tours/pilgrimages,
junior history, oral history, school
programs, historic preservation,
research, exhibits, living history,
photographic collections
Period of collections: 1800s

NORTH FREEDOM

**Mid-Continent Railway Historical
Society and Museum**
53951
Telephone: (608) 522-4261
Private agency
Founded in: 1959
Richard Goddard, Manager
Number of members: 500
Staff: full time 2, part time 1,
volunteer 14
Magazine: *Railway Gazette*
Major programs: library, archives,
museum, historic preservation,
living history, photographic
collections
Period of collections: 1885-1920

OAK CREEK

Oak Creek Historical Society
3201 E. Forest Hill Ave.
Mail to: 9472 S. 27th St., 53154
City agency, authorized by State
Historical Society of Wisconsin
Founded in: 1963
Leroy N. Meyer, President
Number of members: 81
Staff: volunteer 25
Major programs: archives, museum,
newsletters/pamphlets, historic
preservation, exhibits
Period of collections: 1836-1960

OCONOMOWOC

Wisconsin Postal History Society
Telephone: (414) 966-7096
(secretary)
Mail to: N. Hwy. 95, W and 32259
County Line Rd., Hartland, 53029
Private agency, authorized by State
Historical Society of Wisconsin
Founded in: 1942
Merwin A. Leet, President
Number of members: 175
Magazine: *Badger Postal History*
Major programs: library, book
publishing, research, postal history
Period of collections: 1821-present

OCONTO

Oconto County Historical Society
917 Park Ave., 54153
Founded in: 1940
Questionnaire not received

OMRO

Omro Area Historical Society
P.O. Box 183, 54963
Founded in: 1978
Questionnaire not received

ONEIDA

**Records Management Program,
Oneida Tribe of Indians of
Wisconsin**
Norbert Hill Center
Telephone: (414) 869-2130
Mail to: P.O. Box 3797, 54155
Authorized by Bureau of Indian
Affairs
Founded in: 1822
Charlene E. Cornelius, Records
Manager
Number of members: 1

Staff: full time 1, volunteer 2
Major programs: records
management
Period of collections: 1930-present

OSHKOSH

Experimental Aircraft Association
Wittman Airfield, 54903-2591
Telephone: (414) 426-4800
Private agency
Founded in: 1953
Number of members: 90,000
Staff: full time 120, part time 20,
volunteer 3,000
Magazine: *Sport Aviation, Light Plane
World, Vintage Airplane, Warbirds,
Sport Aerobatics*
Major programs: library, archives,
museum, tours/pilgrimages, school
programs, book publishing,
newsletters/pamphlets, historic
preservation, research, exhibits,
audiovisual programs,
photographic collections, field
services

Oshkosh Public Museum
1331 Algoma Blvd., 54901
Telephone: (414) 236-5150
City agency
Founded in: 1924
John Kuony, Director
Staff: full time 8, part time 2,
volunteer 2
Major programs: library, archives,
manuscripts, museum,
tours/pilgrimages, school
programs, newsletters/pamphlets,
research, exhibits, archaeology
programs, photographic
collections, genealogical services
Period of collections: late 19th-early
20th centuries

**The Winnebago County Historical
and Archeological Society**
P.O. Box 401, 54902
Founded in: 1919
Questionnaire not received

PALMYRA

Palmyra Historical Society
c/o Treasurer, 242 Northwest St.,
53156
Private agency
Founded in: 1974
Dorothy Johnson, Treasurer
Number of members: 1,000
Staff: volunteer 20
Major programs: library, archives,
manuscripts, book publishing,
audiovisual programs
Period of collections: 1880s-1980s

PARDEEVILLE

**Columbia County Historical
Society**
Main St., 53954
Telephone: (608) 429-2981
Mail to: R.R. 1, Cambria, 53923
Founded in: 1958
Questionnaire not received

PARK FALLS

Price County Historical Society
c/o HCR-2, Box 717, 54552
Telephone: (715) 762-4571

County agency, authorized by State
Historical Society of Wisconsin
Founded in: 1959
Patricia M. Schroeder, President
Number of members: 148
Staff: volunteer 15
Major programs: museum,
newsletters/pamphlets
Period of collections: 1880-1920

PEPIN

**Laura Ingalls Wilder Memorial
Society, Inc.**
54759
Private agency, authorized by State
Historical Society of Wisconsin
Founded in: 1974
Marie Lund, President
Number of members: 395
Staff: volunteer 12
Magazine: *Notes From Laura Ingalls
Wilder Memorial Society, Inc.*
Major programs: historic sites
preservation, markers,
newsletters/pamphlets, historic
preservation
Period of collections: 1863-1957

PESHTIGO

Peshtigo Historical Society
400 Oconto Ave., 54157
Founded in: 1961
William Hammes, President
Staff: volunteer 6
Major programs: museum, historic
site(s)

PLATTEVILLE

**Department of Museums, City of
Platteville**
405 E. Main
Telephone: (608) 348-3301
Mail to: P.O. Box 252, 53818
Founded in: 1965
Stephen J. Kleefisch, Museum
Manager
Number of members: 400
Staff: full time 1, part time 9,
volunteer 19
Major programs: museum, historic
site(s), tours/pilgrimages, school
programs, historic preservation,
records management, research,
exhibits
Period of collections: early 19th-mid
20th centuries

Grant County Historical Society
Telephone: (608) 348-6091
Mail to: Box 410, 53818
Questionnaire not received

The Mining Museum
385 E. Main
Telephone: (608) 348-3301
Mail to: P.O. Box 252, 53818
City agency
Founded in: 1965
Stephen J. Kleefisch, Museum
Manager
Staff: full time 1, part time 9,
volunteer 19
Major programs: museum, historic
site(s), tours/pilgrimages, school
programs, historic preservation,
records management, research,
exhibits
Period of collections: early 19th-mid
20th centuries

Rollo Jamison Museum
405 E. Main
Telephone: (608) 348-3301
Mail to: P.O. Box 252, 53818
City agency
Founded in: 1980
Stephen J. Kleefisch, Museum
    Manager
Number of members: 400
Staff: full time 1, part time 9,
    volunteer 19
Major programs: museum,
    tours/pilgrimages, school
    programs, historic preservation,
    records management, research,
    exhibits
Period of collections: mid 19th-20th
    centuries

PORTAGE

**Columbia County Historical
    Society**
Telephone: (608) 742-4368
Mail to: c/o Mrs. Robert Wright, 413
    Adams
Questionnaire not received

Portage Canal Society, Inc.
529 W. Cook St., 53901
Telephone: (608) 742-7587
Founded in: 1977
Henry C. Abraham, President
Number of members: 40
Staff: volunteer 15
Major programs: library, archives,
    historic site(s), tours/pilgrimages,
    oral history, school programs, book
    publishing, newsletters/pamphlets,
    historic preservation, research,
    photographic collections
Period of collections: 1834-present

PORT WASHINGTON

**Port Washington Sunken
    Treasures Maritime Museum**
118 S. Wisconsin St. 53074
Telephone: (414) 284-3857
Mail to: P.O. Box 64
Founded in: 1975
Richard D. Smith,
    Curator/Vice-President
Staff: part time 2, volunteer 10
Major programs: museum,
    tours/pilgrimages, educational
    programs, historic preservation
Period of collections: 1800-1930

POYNETTE

Poynette Area Historical Society
3106 S. Main St., 53955
Telephone: (608) 635-2122
Founded in: 1972
Questionnaire not received

PRAIRIE DU CHIEN

Crawford County Historical Society
505 S. State St., 53821
Telephone: (608) 326-6330
Questionnaire not received

Villa Louis Historic Site
521 N. Villa Louis Rd.
Telephone: (608) 326-2721
Mail to: P.O. Box 65, 53821
State agency, authorized by State
    Historical Society of Wisconsin
Founded in: 1936

Michael P. Douglass, Site Manager
Staff: full time 3, part time 25,
    volunteer 50
Major programs: museum, historic
    site(s), school programs, living
    history
Period of collections: 1870-1900

PRINCETON

Princeton Historical Society, Inc.
632 W. Water St.
Telephone: (414) 295-3620
    (president)
Mail to: 339 Canal St., 54968
Private agency, authorized by State
    Historical Society of Wisconsin
Founded in: 1982
LaVerne Marshall, President
Number of members: 50
Major programs: museum,
    newsletters/pamphlets, historic
    preservation, exhibits,
    photographic collections,
    genealogical services
Period of collections: 1850-present

RACINE

**Racine County Historical Society
    and Museum**
701 S. Main St. 53403
Telephone: (414) 637-8585
Mail to: P.O. Box 1527, 53401
Founded in: 1962 (museum); 1940
    (society)
James R. Fiene, President
Number of members: 450
Staff: full time 3, part time 4,
    volunteer 35
Magazine: Footnotes
Major programs: library, museum,
    newsletters/pamphlets, historic
    preservation, exhibits,
    photographic collections,
    genealogical services
Period of collections: 1834-present

**Reedsburg Area Historical
    Society, Inc.**
Telephone: (608) 524-2238
Mail to: P.O. Box 405, 53959
Founded in: 1966
Questionnaire not received

RIB LAKE

Taylor County Historical Society
Mail to: P.O. Box 6, 54470
Founded in: 1965
Questionnaire not received

RIPON

Ripon Historical Society
508 Watson St.
Telephone: (414) 748-5354
Mail to: P.O. Box 274, 54971
Founded in: 1899
George H. Miller, Curator
Number of members: 125
Staff: volunteer 25
Major programs: library, museum,
    educational programs, exhibits,
    genealogical services
Period of collections: 1850-present

RIVER FALLS

**Pierce County Historical
    Association**
936 W. Maple St., 54022

Telephone: (715) 425-5271
Founded in: 1941
Questionnaire not received

**St. Croix Valley Historical Research
    Center**
Chalmer Davee Library, University of
    Wisconsin, River Falls, 54022
Telephone: (715) 425-3567
State agency, authorized by the
    university and Area Research
    Center Network, State Historical
    Society of Wisconsin
Founded in: 1960
Susan D. Steinwall, Director
Staff: full time 1, volunteer 9
Major programs: library, archives,
    manuscripts, oral history, records
    management, research,
    photographic collections,
    genealogical services
Period of collections: 1880-1970

SAUK CITY

Sauk-Prairie Historical Society, Inc.
Telephone: (608) 643-3000
Mail to: P.O. Box 118, 53583
Questionnaire not received

SEYMOUR

**Seymour Community Historical
    Society**
Telephone: (414) 833-2063
Mail to: P.O. Box 305, 54165
Questionnaire not received

SHAWANO

**Shawano County Historical
    Society, Inc.**
N. Franklin St.
Telephone: (715) 524-4744
Mail to: 1003 S. Main St., 54166
County agency
Founded in: 1940
Mrs. William Bayer, President
Number of members: 147
Staff: volunteer 20
Major programs: museum, historic
    preservation, audiovisual programs
Period of collections: 1860-1900

SHEBOYGAN

**Sheboygan County Historical
    Society**
3110 Erie Ave., 53081
Telephone: (414) 458-1103
County agency
Founded in: 1923
Roland Schomberg, President
Number of members: 325
Staff: full time 2, part time 2,
    volunteer 100
Major programs: library, archives,
    manuscripts, museum, oral history,
    book publishing,
    newsletters/pamphlets, historic
    preservation, records
    management, research, exhibits,
    photographic collections,
    genealogical services
Period of collections: 1850-1950

SHELL LAKE

**Washburn County Historical
    Society and Museum**
54871
Telephone: (715) 468-2982/468-7615

County agency
Founded in: 1956
Lucille Miller, President
Number of members: 90
Staff: part time 1, volunteer 10
Major programs: library, archives, manuscripts, museum, historic site(s), markers, oral history, books,historic preservation, photographic collections, genealogical services
Period of collections: late 1800s-present

SHERWOOD

High Cliff Historical Society
P.O. Box 1, 54169
Telephone: (414) 989-1954
Private agency
Founded in: 1974
Russell J. Bishop, President
Number of members: 40
Staff: volunteer 12
Major programs: museum, historic preservation
Period of collections: early 1900s

SHULLSBURG

Badger Historical Society
c/o President, P.O. Box 186, 53586
Telephone: (608) 965-3474
City agency, authorized by State Historical Society of Wisconsin
Founded in: 1975
Arlene Summers, President
Number of members: 15
Staff: volunteer 10
Major programs: historic site(s), markers, tours/pilgrimages, junior history, oral history, historic preservation
Period of collections: 1850-present

Lafayette County Genealogy Workshop, Inc.
113 E. Church St.
Telephone: (608) 965-3481
Mail to: 212 W. Church St., 53586
County agency, authorized by Wisconsin State Genealogical Society and the State Historical Society of Wisconsin
Founded in: 1984
Jeanne Tregoning, Chair
Number of members: 40
Staff: volunteer 20
Major programs: newsletters/pamphlets, exhibits, genealogical services, educational discussion programs and workshops
Period of collections: 1840s-1910

SINSINAWA

Sinsinawa Dominican Archives, Dominican Sisters
53824
Telephone: (608) 748-4411
Private agency, authorized by Congregation of the Most Holy Rosary
Founded in: 1847
Sister Marie Laurence Kortendick, Archivist
Staff: full time 4, part time 3
Major programs: archives, manuscripts, museum, historic

site(s), oral history, newsletters/pamphlets, records management, research, exhibits, audiovisual programs, photographic collections, genealogical services
Period of collections: 1847-present

SOUTH MILWAUKEE

South Milwaukee Historical Society
717 Milwaukee Ave.
Mail to: 104 Brookdale Dr., 53172
City agency
Founded in: 1972
Lois Schreiter, President
Number of members: 175
Staff: volunteer 15
Major programs: archives, museum, historic preservation, records management, exhibits, audiovisual programs, photographic collections
Period of collections: 1840s-present

SPARTA

Gateway Area Genealogical Society
418 E. Main, 54656
Telephone: (608) 269-6205
Questionnaire not received

Heritage Writers Round Table
418 E. Main, 54656
Telephone: (608) 269-6205
Questionnaire not received

Junior Historian Chapter/Monroe County Historical Society
418 E. Main, 54656
Telephone: (608) 269-6205
Founded in: 1973
Questionnaire not received

Monroe County Historical Society, Inc.
Telephone: (608) 269-2020
Mail to: P.O. Box 422, 54656
Private agency
Founded in: 1972
Carolyn Habelman, President
Number of members: 190
Staff: volunteer 10
Magazine: *Portals of Time Historical Time Capsules of Monroe County, Wisconsin*
Major programs: museum, newsletters/pamphlets, genealogical services
Period of collections: 1492-present

Monroe County Local History Room
Rt. 2, Box 21, 54656
Telephone: (608) 269-8680
County agency
Founded in: 1977
Audrey Johnson, County Historian
Staff: full time 1
Major programs: library, archives, manuscripts, museum, tours/pilgrimages, oral history, records management, research, exhibits, photographic collections, genealogical services
Period of collections: 1850-present

Wilfred E. Beaver Museum
418 E. Main, 54656
Telephone: (608) 269-6205

Founded in: 1970
Questionnaire not received

STANLEY

Stanley Area Historical Society and Museum
Mail to: 995 N. Emery St.
Private agency
Founded in: 1975
David Jankoski, President
Number of members: 48
Major programs: library, archives, manuscripts, museum, markers, tours, oral history, school programs, newsletters, historic preservation, research, photographic collections, genealogical services
Period of collections: 1865-present

STEVENS POINT

Portage County Historical Society, Inc.
P.O. Box 672, 54481
County agency
Founded in: 1952
Tim Siebert, President
Number of members: 243
Staff: volunteer 17
Major programs: archives, museum
Period of collections: late 1800s-early 1900s

STOUGHTON

Stoughton Historical Society
101 S. 4th St., 53589
Telephone: (608) 873-6507
Private agency
Founded in: 1960
Owen W. Scheldrup, President
Number of members: 150
Staff: part time 1
Major programs: museum, historic sites preservation
Period of collections: 1800s-early 1900s

STURGEON BAY

Door County Historical Society
18 N. 4th Ave., 54235
Telephone: (414) 743-5809
Questionnaire not received

SUN PRAIRIE

Sun Prairie Historical Library and Museum, Inc.
115 E. Main St., 53590
Mail to: 240 Jones St.
Questionnaire not received

SUPERIOR

Douglas County Historical Society
906 E. 2nd St., 54880
Telephone: (715) 394-5712
Founded in: 1902
Questionnaire not received

Fairlawn Museum—Douglas County Historical Society
906 E. 2nd St., 54880
Telephone: (715) 394-5712
County agency
Founded in: 1902
Thomas C. Hendrickson, Jr., Director
Number of members: 230

Staff: full time 2, part time 2,
   volunteer 37
Magazine: *History Times*
Major programs: library, archives,
   manuscripts, museum, oral history,
   school programs,
   newsletters/pamphlets, historic
   preservation, records
   management, exhibits,
   photographic collections,
   genealogical services
Period of collections: 1880-1910

TOMAH

**Monroe, Juneau, Jackson Counties
   Genealogy Workshop**
Telephone: (608) 378-4388
Mail to: Rt. 3, Box 253, Black River
   Falls, 54615
Number of members: 54
Staff: volunteer 9
Period of collections: 1850-present

VALTON

**Historical Society of the Upper
   Baraboo Valley**
Rt. 1, Box 168-A, Wonewoc, 53968
Telephone: (608) 983-2352
Private agency
Founded in: 1980
Lillian V. Johnson, President
Number of members: 75
Staff: volunteer 8
Major programs: museum, historic
   site(s), oral history, school
   programs, book publishing
Period of collections: 1895-1930

VIROQUA

Vernon County Historical Society
341 Terrace Ave., 54665
Telephone: (608) 637-7185
County agency
Janet A. Roou, President
Number of members: 38
Staff: part time 1, volunteer 6
Major programs: museum,
   photographic collections,
   genealogical services

WATERLOO

Waterloo Area Historical Society
R.F.D. 2, Box 227, 53594-1297
Telephone: (414) 478-2718
City agency, authorized by State
   Historical Society of Wisconsin
Founded in: 1976
William Knowles, President
Number of members: 150
Magazine: *Timescape*
Major programs: library, archives,
   manuscripts, museum,
   tours/pilgrimages, junior history,
   oral history, school programs,
   newsletters/pamphlets, historic
   preservation, records
   management, exhibits, living
   history, audiovisual programs,
   photographic collections,
   genealogical services
Period of collections: 1850-1920

WATERTOWN

Watertown Historical Society
919 Charles St., 53094
Telephone: (414) 261-2796

Private agency
Founded in: 1939
Judy Quam, Manager
Number of members: 500
Staff: full time 1, part time 10,
   volunteer 100
Major programs: archives, museum,
   historic sites preservation,
   tours/pilgrimages, oral history,
   books, historic preservation

WAUKESHA

**Waukesha County Historical
   Society**
101 W. Main St.
Telephone: (414) 544-8430
Mail to: P.O. Box 833, 53186
Founded in: 1906
Questionnaire not received

**Waukesha County Historical
   Museum**
101 W. Main St., 53186
Telephone: (414) 548-7186
County agency
Founded in: 1914
Jean Penn Loerke, County
   Historian/Museum Director
Number of members: 400
Staff: full time 6, part time 1,
   volunteer 20
Magazine: *Landmark*
Major programs: library, archives,
   manuscripts, museum, book
   publishing, newsletters/pamphlets,
   research, exhibits, genealogical
   services
Period of collections:
   prehistoric-present

WAUPUN

Waupun Heritage Museum
Madison St.
Mail to: c/o Edna Stopleman, 121 N.
   Mill St., 53963
Questionnaire not received

Waupun Historical Society
22 S. Madison St.
Telephone: (414) 324-4447
Mail to: c/o Edna Stopleman, 121 N.
   Mill St., 53963
Questionnaire not received

WAUSAU

Marathon County Historical Society
403 McIndoe St., 54401
Telephone: (715) 848-6143
Founded in: 1954
Tom Schleif, Director
Staff: full time 1, part time 3,
   volunteer 2
Major programs: library, museum,
   tours/pilgrimages, educational
   programs, historic preservation
Period of collections: 1870-1930

Wisconsin Archaeological Survey
NW-Marathon Center, 518 S. 7th Ave.,
   54401
Telephone: (715) 845-9602
Founded in: 1948
Questionnaire not received

WAUTOMA

**Waushara County Historical
   Society**
Telephone: (414) 787-4125

Mail to: P.O. Box 129, 54982
Founded in: 1941
Questionnaire not received

WAUWATOSA

Wauwatosa Historical Society Inc.
7611 Harwood Ave., 53213
Authorized by State Historical Society
   of Wisconsin
Founded in: 1977
Charles Causier, President
Number of members: 200
Magazine: *Historic Wauwatosa*
Major programs: historic site(s),
   tours/pilgrimages,
   newsletters/pamphlets, historic
   preservation, audiovisual
   programs, archaeology programs

WEBSTER

Burnett County Historical Society
Fir and Cedar St.
Telephone: (715) 866-8263
Mail to: P.O. Box 108, 54893
Private agency
Founded in: 1945
Edgar S. Oerichbauer, Executive
   Director
Number of members: 150
Staff: full time 2, part time 8,
   volunteer 4
Major programs: library, archives,
   manuscripts, museum, historic
   site(s), oral history, school
   programs, newsletters/pamphlets,
   historic preservation, research,
   exhibits, living history, audiovisual
   programs, archaeology programs,
   photographic collections,
   genealogical services
Period of collections: 19th century

WEST ALLIS

West Allis Historical Society
8405 W. National Ave., 53227
Telephone: (414) 541-6970
Founded in: 1966
Questionnaire not received

WEST BEND

**Washington County Historical
   Library and Museum**
506 3rd Ave., 53095
Telephone: (414) 338-8287
County agency
Founded in: 1937
Evelyn Zarling, Curator
Number of members: 35
Staff: part time 2, volunteer 7
Major programs: manuscripts,
   museum, tours, historic
   preservation, research, exhibits,
   audiovisual programs,
   photographic collections,
   genealogical services
Period of collections: 1850-1920

**Washington County Historical
   Society**
348 5th Ave.
County agency, authorized by State
   Historical Society of Wisconsin
Founded in: late 1800s
Mrs. Arthur Zarling, Curator
Number of members: 42

Staff: full time 1, part time 1,
    volunteer 12
Major programs: library, archives,
    manuscripts, museum,
    genealogical services
Period of collections: 1848-present

WEST MILWAUKEE

West Milwaukee Historical Society
4826 W. Beloit Rd., 53214
Telephone: (414) 384-3522
Private agency
Founded in: 1982
Eleanor Benda, President
Number of members: 15
Major programs: archives,
    manuscripts, oral history,
    audiovisual programs
Period of collections: 1906-1981

WEST SALEM

West Salem Historical Society
357 W. Garland St., 54669
Telephone: (608) 786-1399
Founded in: 1974
Jean Nickerson, President
Number of members: 1,050
Staff: volunteer 25
Major programs: museum, historic
    site(s), newsletters/pamphlets,
    historic preservation
Period of collections: 1865-present

WESTFIELD

**Marquette County Historical
Society**
213 Lawrence St.
Mail to: c/o Mrs. M. L. Kerst, Rt. 1,
    53964
Founded in: 1962
Questionnaire not received

WILD ROSE

Wild Rose Historical Society
Main St., 54984
Telephone: (414) 622-3555
Private agency
Founded in: 1963
Olive M. Covill, President
Number of members: 90
Staff: volunteer 45
Major programs: museum,
    tours/pilgrimages, junior history,
    school programs, historic
    preservation, exhibits,
    photographic collections
Period of collections: 1850s-1900s

WILMOT

**Western Kenosha County
Historical Society**
Telephone: (414) 877-2698
Mail to: P.O. Box 31, 53192
Questionnaire not received

WINNECONNE

Winneconne Historical Society
611 W. Main St., 54986
Telephone: (414) 582-4132
Private agency, authorized by State
    Historical Society of Wisconsin
Founded in: 1962
Mrs. Loren J. Driscoll, President
Number of members: 55

Staff: volunteer 30
Major programs: archives, museum,
    photographic collections
Period of collections: 1865-1918

WISCONSIN DELLS

Dells Country Historical Society
700 Broadway, 53960
Mail to: P.O. Box 177, 53965
State agency, authorized by State
    Historical Society of Wisconsin
Founded in: 1981
B. E. Gussel, Jr., President
Number of members: 54
Major programs: historic site(s),
    newsletters/pamphlets, historic
    preservation, exhibits,
    photographic collections
Period of collections: 1847-1947

WISCONSIN RAPIDS

**South Wood County Historical
Corporation**
540 3rd St., S, 54494
Private agency
Founded in: 1955
Ellen Sabetta, Curator
Number of members: 250
Major programs: museum

WITTENBERG

Wittenberg Area Historical Society
Summit St., 54499
Telephone: (715) 253-2766
Founded in: 1969
Arthur O. Larson, President
Number of members: 45
Staff: part time 1, volunteer 10
Major programs: archives, museum,
    junior history, educational
    programs
Period of collections: 19th
    century-present

WYOMING

AFTON

Star Valley Historical Society
Mail to: P.O. Box 921, 83110
County agency, authorized by
    Wyoming State Historical Society
Founded in: 1982
Victor Bradfield, President
Number of members: 51
Staff: volunteer 6
Major programs: historic site(s),
    tours/pilgrimages, historic
    preservation, exhibits,
    photographic collections
Period of collections: 1875-1930s

BIG HORN

**Bradford Brinton Memorial
Museum**
P.O. Box 23, 82833
Telephone: (307) 672-3173
Founded in: 1961
James T. Forrest, Director
Staff: part time 10
Major programs: library, museum,
    historic sites preservation
Period of collections: late 1800s-early
    1900s

CASPER

Ft. Caspar Museum
4001 Fort Caspar Rd., 82604
Telephone: (307) 235-8462
City agency
Founded in: 1936
Michael J. Menard, Director
Number of members: 3
Staff: full time 4, volunteer 45
Magazine: *Telegraph*
Major programs: library, archives,
    manuscripts, museum, historic
    site(s), markers, tours/pilgrimages,
    junior history, oral history, school
    programs, newsletters/pamphlets,
    historic preservation, research,
    exhibits, living history, audiovisual
    programs, archaeology programs,
    photographic collections,
    genealogical services
Period of collections: 1865-present

CENTENNIAL

**Centennial Valley Historical
Association**
Hwy. 130
Telephone: (307) 742-7158
Mail to: P.O. Box 200, 82055
Private agency
Founded in: 1974
Jane H. Houston, Secretary
Number of members: 145
Staff: volunteer 35
Major programs: museum, historic
    sites preservation, historic
    preservation, exhibits,
    photographic collections
Period of collections: 1900-1940

CHEYENNE

**Cheyenne Frontier Days Old West
Museum**
North Carey Ave., Frontier Park
Telephone: (307) 634-8400/632-6033
Mail to: P.O. Box 2824, 82001
Founded in: 1978
Questionnaire not received

Historic Governors' Mansion
300 E. 21st St., 82001
Telephone: (307) 777-7878
Mail to: 24th and Central Sts., Barrett
    Bldg., 82002
State agency, authorized by
    Museums and Historical
    Department, Wyoming State
    Archives
Founded in: 1904
Mike Mayfield, Head, Museums
    Division
Major programs: museum, historic
    site(s), tours/pilgrimages, school
    programs, historic preservation,
    exhibits, living history

State Historic Preservation Office
c/o Wyoming State Archives,
    Museums and Historical
    Department
604 E. 25th St., 82002
Telephone: (307) 777-7695
State agency
Founded in: 1967
Alvin Bastron, Director
Staff: full time 16
Major programs: historic site(s),
    markers, historic preservation,
    archaeology programs,
    photographic collections
Period of collections: 1967-present

◇**Wyoming State Archives,
Museums and Historical
Department**
c/o State Historic Preservation Office
Barrett Bldg., 82002
Telephone: (307) 777-7013
State agency, authorized by
Wyoming State Historical Society
Founded in: 1951
Robert D. Bush, Director
Number of members: 2,000
Staff: full time 57, part time 13,
volunteer 100
Magazine: *Annals of Wyoming*
Major programs: library, archives,
manuscripts, museum, historic
site(s), tours/pilgrimages, junior
history, oral history, school
programs, book publishing,
newsletters/pamphlets, historic
preservation, records
management, research, exhibits,
living history, photographic
collections, genealogical services,
field services
Period of collections: 1858-present

**Wyoming State Museum and Art
Gallery**
Barrett Bldg., 24th and Central,
82002
Telephone: (307) 777-7510
State agency, authorized by
Wyoming State Archives, Museums
and Historical Department
Founded in: 1895
Mike Mayfield, Division Head
Number of members: 150
Staff: 20
Major programs: museum,
tours/pilgrimages, school
programs, newsletters/pamphlets,
exhibits, living history
Period of collections: 1858-present

CODY

Buffalo Bill Historical Center
720 Sheridan Ave.
Telephone: (307) 587-4771

Historic Governors' Mansion in Cheyenne.—Wyoming State Archives, Museums and Historical Department

Mail to: P.O. Box 1000, 82414
Peter H. Hassrick, Director
Staff: full time 22, part time 55,
volunteer 75
Major programs: library, archives,
manuscripts, museum, oral history,
educational programs
Period of collections: 19th-early 20th
century

DOUGLAS

Ft. Fetterman State Historic Site
Rt. 3, Box 6, 82633
Telephone: (307) 358-2864
State agency, authorized by
Wyoming State Archives, Museums
and Historical Department
Founded in: 1867
Roger Doherty, Head, Historic Sites
Division
Major programs: museum, historic
site(s), tours/pilgrimages, school
programs, historic preservation,
exhibits, living history

**Wyoming Pioneer Memorial
Museum**
Wyoming State Fair Grounds
Telephone: (307) 358-9288
Mail to: Drawer 10, 82633
State agency, authorized by
Department of Agriculture
Founded in: 1956
Arlene Ekland-Earnst, Curator
Staff: full time 2, part time 2
Major programs: museum, exhibits
Period of collections: 1880s-1920

DUBOIS

Dubois Museum Association
Ramshorn St., 82513
Mail to: P.O. Box 896
Founded in: 1976
Bob Baker, President
Number of members: 22
Staff: volunteer 10
Major programs: museum, historic
sites preservation,

tours/pilgrimages, educational
programs, historic preservation
Period of collections: 1910-present

ENCAMPMENT

Grant Encampment Museum
82325
Telephone: (307) 327-5310
Private agency
Founded in: 1964
Vera Oldman, President
Staff: part time 1, volunteer 4
Major programs: library, manuscripts,
museum, historic site(s), markers,
oral history, historic preservation,
research, exhibits, living history,
photographic collections
Period of collections: 1865-1918

FT. BRIDGER

Ft. Bridger State Historic Site
82933
Telephone: (307) 782-3842
State agency, authorized by
Wyoming State Archives, Museums
and Historical Department
Founded in: 1843
Roger Doherty, Head, Historic Sites
Division
Major programs: museum, historic
site(s), tours/pilgrimages, school
programs, historic preservation,
exhibits, living history

FORT LARAMIE

**Fort Laramie Historical
Association/Fort Laramie
National Historic Site**
82212
Telephone: (307) 837-2221
Private agency, authorized by
National Park Service
Founded in: 1956
John C. Burns, Associate Coordinator
Number of members: 143
Major programs: library, museum,
historic site(s), historic
preservation, research, living
history, audiovisual programs
Period of collections: 1849-1890

Ft. Laramie National Historic Site
82212
Telephone: (307) 837-2221
Federal agency, authorized by
National Park Service
Founded in: 1938
Gary K. Howe, Superintendent
Staff: full time 15, part time 25
Major programs: historic site(s),
historic preservation, living history
Period of collections: 1834-1890

GILLETTE

Rockpile Museum
P.O. Box 455, 82716
Telephone: (307) 682-3248
County agency
Founded in: 1970
Dorothy Van Buggenum, Board Chair
Major programs: manuscripts,
museum, historic site(s), historic
preservation, living history,
photographic collections
Period of collections: 1880-present

GREEN RIVER

Sweetwater County Historical Society
50 W. Flaming Gorge
Telephone: (307) 875-2611, ext. 263
Mail to: P.O. Box 25, 82935
State agency, authorized by
    Wyoming State Historical Society
Founded in: 1956
Donald L. Tompkins, President
Number of members: 160
Staff: volunteer 8
Magazine: *Annals of Wyoming*
Major programs: museum,
    tours/pilgrimages, oral history,
    book publishing,
    newsletters/pamphlets

Sweetwater County Museum
c/o Courthouse, P.O. Box 25, 82935

GUERNSEY

Guernsey State Park Museum
P.O. Box 750, 82214
Telephone: (307) 836-2900
State agency, authorized by
    Wyoming Recreation Commission
Founded in: 1936
Major programs: museum, historic
    site(s), tours/pilgrimages, school
    programs, historic preservation,
    exhibits

JACKSON

Jackson Hole Museum
105 N. Glenwood
Telephone: (307) 733-2414
Mail to: P.O. Box 1005, 83001
Private agency, authorized by
    Jackson Hole Museum Foundation
Founded in: 1958
Robert Rudd, Director
Number of members: 800
Staff: full time 1, part time 4,
    volunteer 10
Major programs: museum, exhibits
Period of collections:
    prehistoric-1940s

Teton County Historical Research Center
105 Mercill
Mail to: c/o County Clerk's Office,
    83001
County agency
Founded in: 1965
Irene Brown, Chair
Staff: volunteer 7
Major programs: library, archives,
    oral history, research,
    photographic collections
Period of collections: 1880-present

LANDER

Fremont County Museums System
630 Lincoln St., 82520
Telephone: (307) 332-4137
County agency
Founded in: 1964
Staff: full time 1
Magazine: *Wind River Mountaineer*
Major programs: museum,
    administration of three county
    museums

Fremont County Pioneer Museum
630 Lincoln St., 82520

Telephone: (307) 332-4137
County agency
Founded in: 1886
Henry R. Hudson, Director
Staff: full time 3, part time 3
Major programs: library, archives,
    manuscripts, museum, oral history,
    school programs, book publishing,
    newsletters/pamphlets, historic
    preservation, records
    management, research, exhibits,
    audiovisual programs,
    photographic collections
Period of collections: 1870-1915

LARAMIE

Albany County Historical Society
1409 Downey St., 82070
Telephone: (307) 742-5988
Private agency, authorized by
    Wyoming State Historical Society
Founded in: 1935
Murray L. Carroll, President
Number of members: 50
Major programs: museum, historic
    site(s), historic preservation

American Heritage Center
13th and Ivinson Sts.
Telephone: (307) 766-4114
Mail to: P.O. Box 3334, 82070
State agency, authorized by
    University of Wyoming
Founded in: 1945
Gene M. Gressley, Assistant to
    President
Number of members: 3
Staff: full time 18, part time 5
Major programs: library, archives,
    museum, records management,
    research, exhibits
Period of collections: 1890-present

Laramie Plains Museum Association
603 Ivinson Ave., 82070
Telephone: (307) 742-4448
Founded in: 1968
Eugene E. Dunn, Director
Number of members: 450
Staff: full time 2, volunteer 100
Major programs: museum,
    educational programs
Period of collections: 1865-1975

LUSK

Niobrara County Historical Society
342 S. Main St.
Telephone: (307) 334-3444
Mail to: P.O. Box 1396, 82225
Questionnaire not received

NEWCASTLE

Anna Miller Museum
P.O. Box 698, 82701
Telephone: (307) 746-4188
Town agency
Founded in: 1966
Helen M. Larsen, Director
Staff: full time 2
Major programs: museum,
    tours/pilgrimages, oral history,
    book publishing, research,
    exhibits, photographic collections,
    genealogical services
Period of collections: 1920-1930

Weston County Historical Society
P.O. Box 698, 82701
Telephone: (307) 746-4188
County agency
Founded in: 1966
Debbie Mosley, President
Number of members: 85
Major programs: museum, school
    programs, historic preservation,
    audiovisual programs
Period of collections: early 1900s

PINEDALE

Sublette County Historical Society, Inc.
7 W. Pine St.
Telephone: (307) 367-4367/367-4737
Mail to: P.O. Box 666, 82941
County agency
Founded in: 1935
Alice E. Harrower, Persident
Number of members: 300
Staff: part time 2
Magazine: *The Beaver Plew*
Major programs: archives,
    manuscripts, museum, historic
    site(s), tours/pilgrimages
Period of collections: from 1936

RALSTON

Wyoming State Historical Society, Park County Chapter
Telephone: (307) 754-3787
Mail to: P.O. Box 774, 82440
Questionnare not received

RIVERTON

Riverton Museum
700 E. Park, 82501
Telephone: (307) 856-2665
Founded in: 1969
Questionnaire not received

SARATOGA

Saratoga Museum Center
Locust St. and Hwy. 230
Telephone: (307) 326-9980
Mail to: P.O. Box 1131, 82331
Private agency, authorized by
    Saratoga Historical and Cultural
    Association
Founded in: 1978
Gertrude Herold, Association
    President
Number of members: 60
Staff: volunteer 12
Major programs: museum,
    tours/pilgrimages, school
    programs, book publishing, historic
    preservation, exhibits, archaeology
    programs, photographic
    collections
Period of collections: 1875-1950

SHERIDAN

Sheridan County Historical Society, Inc.
400 Clarenden Ave.

Telephone: (307) 674-4589
Mail to: P.O. Box 186, 82801
Founded in: 1960
Questionnaire not received

Trail End Historic Center
400 E. Clarendon, 82801
Telephone: (307) 674-4589
State agency, authorized by
 Wyoming State Archives, Museums
 and Historical Department
Founded in: 1913
Roger Doherty, Head, Historic Sites
 Division
Major programs: museum, historic
 site(s), tours/pilgrimages, school
 programs, historic preservation,
 exhibits, living history

SOUTH PASS CITY

South Pass City State Historic Site
Rt. 62, Box 164, 82520
Telephone: (307) 332-6182
State agency, authorized by
 Wyoming Recreation Commission
Founded in: 1867
Major programs: museum, historic
 site(s), tours/pilgrimages, school

programs, historic preservation,
 exhibits, living history

THERMOPOLIS

**Hot Springs County Museum and
 Cultural Center**
700 Broadway, 82443
Telephone: (307) 864-5183
County agency, authorized by Hot
 Springs County Museum Board
Founded in: 1938
Thomas A. Shaffer, Director
Staff: full time 4, part time 2
Major programs: archives, museum,
 historic preservation, records
 management, exhibits, audiovisual
 programs
Period of collections: 1880-1940

WORLAND

**Washakie County Historical
 Society**
Mail to: P.O. Box 1427, 82401
County agency, authorized by
 Wyoming State Historical Society
Founded in: 1954
Dorthea Heitz, President
Number of members: 47

Major programs: museum, historic
 site(s), tours/pilgrimages, oral
 history, historic preservation, living
 history, audiovisual programs,
 archaeology programs,
 photographic collections,
 genealogical services

YELLOWSTONE NATIONAL PARK

**Yellowstone National
 Park—Albright Visitor Center**
Mammoth Hot Springs, 82190
Telephone: (307) 344-7381
Federal agency, authorized by
 National Park Service
Founded in: 1872
George B. Robinson, Chief of
 Interpretation
Staff: full time 10, volunteer 10
Major programs: library, archives,
 manuscripts, museum, historic
 site(s), markers, tours/pilgrimages,
 school programs, historic
 preservation, records
 management, research, exhibits,
 living history, audiovisual programs
Period of collections: 1830-1935

Historical Agencies
in American Territories

AMERICAN SAMOA

PAGO PAGO

**Historic Preservation Office,
 Department of Parks and
 Recreation**
96799
Telephone: (684) 633-1191/633-1192
Territorial agency, authorized by
 National Park Service
Founded in: 1970
Stan Sorensen, Deputy HPO
Staff: full time 1
Major programs: historic site(s),
 markers, oral history, historic
 preservation, archaeology
 programs
Period of collections: late 19th
 century-present

GUAM

MANGILAO

**MARC Pacific Collection,
 University of Guam**
University Station, 96913
Telephone: (671) 734-4473
State agency, authorized by the
 university
Founded in: 1967
Albert L. Williams, Librarian
Staff: full time 5

Major programs: library, archives,
 manuscripts, records management
Period of collections: 16th-20th
 centuries

MARIANA ISLANDS

SAIPAN

**Commonwealth Council for Arts
 and Culture**
P.O. Box 553 CHRB, 96950
Commonwealth agency, authorized
 by Community and Cultural Affairs
 Office, Office of the Governor
Founded in: 1980
Ana S. Teregeyo, Executive Director
Staff: full time 8, part time 1
major programs: school programs,
 exhibits, festival promotions

PUERTO RICO

SAN JUAN

Conservation Trust of Puerto Rico
P.O. Box 4747, 00905
Telephone: (809) 722-5834
Founded in: 1970
Francisco Javier Blanco, Executive
 Director

Staff: full time 4, part time 2
Major programs: historic sites
 preservation, historic preservation,
 conservation

VIRGIN ISLANDS

ST CROIX

FREDRIKSTED

St. Croix Landmarks Society
Centerline Rd., 00840
Telephone: (809) 772-0598
Mail to: P.O. Box 2855, 00840
Private agency
Founded in: 1951
Barbara M. Hagan-Smith, Executive
 Director
Number of members: 400
Staff: full time 3, part time 11,
 volunteer 12
Magazine: *Landmarks*
Major programs: library, manuscripts,
 museum, historic site(s), historic
 preservation, exhibits,
 photographic collections
Period of collections: 1730s-1917

Historical Agencies
in Canada

ALBERTA

ALBERTA BEACH

Alberta Beach Museum
T0E 0A0
Private agency
Founded in: 1945
John Oselies, Director
Staff: part time 4
Major programs: museum, school
   programs, archaeology programs
Period of collections: from B.C.

ALIX

Alix-Clive Historical Club
Telephone: (403) 747-2708
Mail to: P.O. Box 384, T0C 0B0
Private agency
Founded in: 1973
Mrs. M.L. Ludvigsson, Secretary
Number of members: 11
Magazine: *Pioneers and Progress*
Major programs: book publishing
Period of collections: 1878-1950

Wagon Wheel Regional Museum
Main St.
Telephone: (403) 747-2462
Mail to: P.O. Box 157, T0C 0B0
Private agency
Alice Whitfield, Director
Major programs: museum
Period of collections: 1878-present

ANDREW

**Andrew and District Local History
   Museum**
Hwy. 45 at 815
Telephone: (403) 365-3687
Mail to: P.O. Box 180, T0B 0C0
Verna Topolnisky, Supervisor
Questionnaire not received

BANFF

Archives of the Canadian Rockies
111 Bear St., T0L 0C0
Telephone: (403) 762-2291
Mail to: Box 160
Founded in: 1967
Edward J. Hart, Head Archivist
Staff: full time 4, part time 1

Magazine: *The Cairn*
Major programs: library, archives,
   manuscripts, oral history,
   newsletters/pamphlets
Period of collections: 1887-present

**Banff Centre School of
   Management**
P.O. Box 1020, T0L 0C0
Telephone: (403) 762-6125
Provincial agency, authorized by
   Alberta Department of Advanced
   Education
Founded in: 1933
G. Peter Greene, Director
Staff: full time 3, part time 30
Major programs: arts management
   studies

**Banff National Park Natural History
   Museum**
Banff Ave. T0L 0C0
Telephone: (403) 762-3324
Mail to: Box 900
Founded in: 1904
R. G. Seale, Chief Park Naturalist
Staff: full time 1
Major programs: museum
Period of collections: 1865-1918

Luxton Museum
Telephone: (403) 764-8300
Mail to: 1 Birch Avenue, T0L 0C0
Duncan Cameron, Director
Questionnaire not received

**Whyte Museum of the Canadian
   Rockies**
111 Bear St.
Telephone: (403) 762-2291
Mail to: P.O. Box 160, T0L 0C0
Private agency, authorized by Peter
   and Catharine Whyte Foundation
Founded in: 1967
Edward J. Hart, Director
Staff: full time 14, volunteer 1
Magazine: *Cairn*
Major programs: library, archives,
   manuscripts, museum,
   tours/pilgrimages,
   newsletters/pamphlets,
   photographic collections,
   programs in mountaineering
Period of collections: 1880s-present

BARRHEAD

**Barrhead and District Historical
   Society**
Telephone: (403) 674-4481
Mail to: P.O. Box 1394, T0G 0E0
Founded in: 1967
Mable Gravel, Secretary/Treasurer
Number of members: 25
Staff: part time 8, volunteer 12
Major programs: archives, museum,
   historic sites preservation
Period of collections: 1890-present

BEAVERLODGE

South Peace Centennial Museum
Telephone: (403) 354-8869
Mail to: P.O. Box 493, T0H 0C0
Questionnaire not received

BOWDEN

**Bowden Historical
   Society—Bowden Pioneer
   Museum**
Telephone: (403) 244-3892
Mail to: P.O. Box 576, T0M 0K0
Dorothy Charlton, Director
Major programs: museum
Period of collections: 1890-1940

BROOKS

Brooks and District Museum
568 Sutherland Dr.
Telephone: (403) 362-5073
Mail to: P.O. Box 2078, T0J 0J0
Private agency
Major programs: museum, historic
   preservation
Period of collections: 1880-1930

CALGARY

**Alberta Historical Resources
   Foundation**
102 8th Ave., SE, T2G 0K6
Telephone: (403) 297-7320
Provincial agency
Founded in: 1976
Esther Brown, Programme Officer
Number of members: 3,000
Staff: full time 4, part time 1,
   volunteer 10
Magazine: *Cornerstone*

Major programs: library, historic site(s), oral history, historic preservation, exhibits

Alberta Museums Association
P.O. Box 4036, T2T 5M9
Telephone: (403) 264-8300
Joyce Gibson, President
Questionnaire not received

Glenbow Museum, Glenbow-Alberta Institute
130 9th Ave., SE, T2G OP3
Telephone: (403) 264-8300
Private agency
Founded in: 1966
Duncan F. Cameron, Director
Number of members: 6,615
Staff: full time 131, part time 28, volunteer 300
Magazine: *Glenbow*
Major programs: library, archives, manuscripts, museum, school programs, book publishing, exhibits, photographic collections
Period of collections: 19th-20th centuries

Heritage Park Society
1900 Heritage Dr., SW, T2V 2X3
Telephone: (403) 255-1182
City agency
Founded in: 1964
R.R. Smith, Manager
Number of members: 115
Staff: full time 50, part time 50
Magazine: *Heritage Post*
Major programs: historic site(s), school programs, historic preservation, exhibits, living history
Period of collections: 1860-1914

Historical Society of Alberta
95 Holmwood Ave., NW
Telephone: (403) 289-8149
Mail to: Station C, Box 4035, T2V 3H3
Founded in: 1907
Hugh A. Dempsey, Editor
Number of members:2,400
Staff: part time 1
Magazine: *Alberta History*
Major programs: tours/pilgrimages, books, newsletters/pamphlets

Princess Patricia's Canadian Light Infantry Regimental Museum
Currie Barracks, T3E 1T8
Telephone: (403) 240-7525
Federal agency
Founded in: 1953
Captain W. C. Cruscott, Curator
Number of members:3,000
Staff: full time 2, part time 1, volunteer 3
Magazine: *The Patrician*
Major programs: archives, museum, markers, newsletters/pamphlets, records management, photographic collections
Period of collections: 1914-present

Telecommunications Hall of Fame Museum, Alberta Government Telephones
411 1st St., SE, Floor A-F, T2G 4Y5
Telephone: (403) 231-7978
Authorized by Crown Corporation
Founded in: 1906
M. C. Malyj, Administration Supervisor, Public Relations
Staff: full time 1, part time 3
Major programs: museum, historic preservation, records management, exhibits

University of Calgary Archives
2500 University Dr., NW, T3B 3C9
Telephone: (403) 284-7271
Founded in: 1982
Jean F. Tener, University Archivist
Staff: full time 2
Major programs: archives, research
Period of collections: 1960-1980

CAMROSE

Camrose and District Museum Society
P.O. Box 1622, T4V 1X6
Telephone: (403) 672-3298
Private agency
Founded in: 1967
Clarence Skalin, President
Staff: part time 4, volunteer 15
Major programs: museum, historic preservation, exhibits

CARDSTON

C.O. Card Home and Museum Society
337 Main St.
Telephone: (403) 653-3366
Mail to: P.O. Box 280, T0K 0K0
Lila Cahoon, Secretary
Questionnaire not received

CASTOR

Castor and District Museum
5101-49th Avenue
Telephone: (403) 882-3941
Mail to: P.O. Box 533, T0C 0X0
Ingrid Jacoby, President
Questionnaire not received

Calgary—yesterday and today. Left, a 1920s, view of the Imperial Bank of Canada in Calgary. Right, today the Imperial Bank building is headquarters of the Alberta Historical Resources Foundation.—left photograph courtesy of the Glenbow Alberta Institute; right photograph courtesy of E.H. Brown

CEREAL

Cereal Prairie Pioneer Museum
Old Railway Station
Telephone: (403) 326-3899
Mail to: P.O. Box 131, T0J 0N0
Mrs. F. Adams, Director
Questionnaire not received

CLARESHOLM

Claresholm Museum
5126 1st St. (Highway No. 2)
Mail to: P.O. Box 1000, T0L 0T0
Stuart Park, Director
Questionnaire not received

COCHRANE

Cochrane Ranch
Hwy. 1-A
Mail to: P.O. Box 959, Blairmore, T0K
0E0
Provincial agency
Founded in: 1979
David McIntyre, Visitor Services
Officer
Staff: part time 3
Major programs: historic site(s),
markers, tours/pilgrimages, school
programs, newsletters/pamphlets,
research, exhibits, audiovisual
programs, archaeology programs,
photographic collections
Period of collections: to late 1800s

COLINTON

Kinnoull Historical Museum
Telephone: (403) 695-4535
Mail to: General Delivery, T0G 0K0
Mildred Hay, Manager
Questionnaire not received

COUTTS

Altamont Museum
Telephone: (403) 349-3888
Mail to: P.O. Box 176, T0K 0N0
Belmore Schults, Director
Questionnaire not received

CZAR

Prairie Panorama Museum
Shorncliffe Park
Telephone: (403) 857-2123
Mail to: P.O. Box 156, T0B 0Z0
Questionnaire not received

DEBOLT

**DeBolt and District Pioneer
Museum Society**
P.O. Box 386, T0H 1B0
Telephone: (403) 957-3980
Private agency
Founded in: 1975
Winnie Moore, President
Number of members: 45
Staff: volunteer 4
Major programs: museum, book
publishing
Period of collections: 1920s-1950s

DELBURNE

Anthony Henday Museum
Main St.
Telephone: (403) 749-3949
Mail to: P.O. Box 121, T0M 0V0
John Pengelly, President
Questionnaire not received

DONALDA

**Donalda and District Museum
Society**
Main St. and Railway Ave.
Telephone: (403) 883-2345
Mail to: P.O. Box 40, T0B 1H0
Authorized by Donalda & District
Museum Society
Founded in: 1979
Georgina V. A. Brown,
Secretary/Treasurer
Staff: full time 2, part time 1,
volunteer 30
Major programs: museum
Period of collections: 1800s-present

DRUMHELLER

**Drumheller and District Fossil
Museum**
335 1st St., E
Telephone: (403) 823-2593
Mail to: P.O. Box 2135, T0J 0Y0
Ellen Manning, Curator
Major programs: historic preservation
Period of collections: prehistoric

Homestead Antique Museum
Dinosaur Trail, T0J 0Y0
Telephone: (403) 823-2600
Mail to: P.O. Box 700
Founded in: 1965
James Gaschnitz, President
Staff: full time 2, volunteer 6
Major programs: museum
Period of collections: 1865-present

Newcastle Coalminers Museum
12th St. at 4th Ave. W
Mail to: P.O. Box 2097, T0J 0Y0
Robert Llewellyn, Director
Questionnaire not received

DUCHESS

Frontier Memorial Museum
Memorial Arena
Telephone: (403) 378-4671
Mail to: P.O. Box 186, T0J 0Z0
June Endersby, Contact person
Questionnaire not received

DUNVEGAN

Historic Dunvegan
Hwy. 2, N
Telephone: (403) 835-4889/743-7471
Mail to: 8820 112th St., Edmonton,
T6G 2P8
Provincial agency
Founded in: 1976
C. Stephens, Visitor Services Officer
Staff: full time 1, part time 3,
volunteer 2
Major programs: historic site(s),
markers, tours/pilgrimages, school
programs, newsletters/pamphlets,
historic preservation, records
management, research, exhibits,
living history, audiovisual
programs, archaeology programs,
photographic collections
Period of collections: 1805-1911

EDMONTON

Alberta Historic Sites Service
Old St. Stephen's College, 8820
Mail to: 8820 112th St., T5G 0H1
Telephone: (403) 427-2022

Provincial agency
Founded in: 1973
F. Pannekoek, Director
Staff: full time 58
Major programs: historic site(s),
markers, tours/pilgrimages, book
publishing, newsletters/pamphlets,
historic preservation, research,
exhibits, living history, field
services
Period of collections: 1783-present

Alberta Museums Association
9912 106th St., T5K 1C5
Telephone: (403) 424-2626
Private agency
Founded in: 1971
Wilma A. Wood, Executive Director
Number of members: 300
Staff: full time 2
Magazine: *Alberta Museums Review*
Major programs:
newsletters/pamphlets, research,
field services

**Alberta Pioneer Railway
Association**
24215 34th St.
Telephone: (403) 973-9075
Mail to: Station C, Box 6102, T5B 4K5
Private agency
Founded in: 1968
Don Scafe, Treasurer
Number of members: 250
Staff: volunteer 15
Magazine: *The Marker*
Major programs: museum,
newsletters/pamphlets, historic
preservation, exhibits
Period of collections: 1900-present

Artifacts Center
10542 Ft. Hill Rd.
Telephone: (403) 432-0644
Mail to: C. N. Tower, 9th Floor, 10004
104th Ave., T5J 0K1
City agency, authorized by Edmonton
Parks and Recreation
Founded in: 1971
John E. McIsaac, Curator
Staff: full time 4
Major programs: museum, historic
preservation
Period of collections: 1880-1930

Canada's Aviation Hall of Fame
9797 Jasper Ave., T5J 1N9
Telephone: (403) 424-2458
Founded in: 1973
J. W. Strath, Chief Executive Officer
Staff: full time 3, volunteer 6
Major programs: library, archives,
museum, oral history,
newsletters/pamphlets, historic
preservation, records
management, exhibits, living
history, audiovisual programs,
photographic collections
Period of collections: 1906-present

City of Edmonton Archives
10105 112th Ave., T5G 0H1
Telephone: (403) 479-2069
Mail to: Edmonton Parks and
Recreation, T5J 0K1
Founded in: 1971
Helen LaRose, Manager
Staff: full time 5, volunteer 4
Major programs: library, archives,
manuscripts, oral history,

photographic collections, genealogical services
Period of collections: 1865-present

Edmonton Space Sciences Foundation
11211 142nd St., T5M 4A1
Telephone: (403) 452-9100
J. Hault, Director
Number of members: 400
Staff: full time 25, part time 30, volunteer 25
Major programs: museum, school programs, exhibits, audiovisual programs

Ft. Edmonton Park
SW Quesnell Fwy.
Telephone: (403) 436-5565
Mail to: 10004 104th Ave., T5J 0K1
City agency, authorized by Edmonton Parks and Recreation Department
Founded in: 1969
Hobie Clark, Interim Director
Staff: full time 18, part time 88, volunteer 150
Major programs: museum, historic site(s), oral history, school programs, historic preservation, research, exhibits, living history
Period of collections: 1846-1920

Friends of Devonian Botanic Garden
University of Alberta, T6G 2E1
Telephone: (403) 987-3054
Private agency
Founded in: 1971
P. D. Seymour, Trustee
Staff: full time 13, part time 1, volunteer 100
Major programs: library, newsletters/pamphlets, historic preservation, records management, research, exhibits, living history, botanic gardens
Period of collections: 1959

Historic Sites Service
8820 112th St., T6G 2P8
Telephone: (403) 427-2023
Provincial agency
Founded in: 1975
Frits Pannekoek, Director
Staff: full time 58
Magazine: *Historic Alberta Preservation Update*
Major programs: historic site(s), markers, tours/pilgrimages, oral history, school programs, book publishing, newsletters/pamphlets, historic preservation, research, exhibits, living history, audiovisual programs, photographic collections, historic resource inventory

Historical Society of Alberta, Amisk Waskahegan Chapter
Mail to: P.O. Box 1013, T5J 2M1
Helen Larose, President
Number of members: 785
Staff: volunteer 7
Major programs: tours/pilgrimages, educational programs, newsletters/pamphlets

John Walter Historic Site
10627 93rd Ave.
Telephone: (403) 433-7853

Mail to: 10004 104th Ave., T5J 0K1
City agency, authorized by Parks and Recreation Department
Founded in: 1958
Hobie Clark, Interim Director
Major programs: museum, historic site(s), school programs, historic preservation, living history

Man and Telecommunications Museum, Alberta Government Telephones
10020 100th St., Floor 33, T5J 0N5
Telephone: (403) 425-3978
Authorized by Crown Corporation
Founded in: 1906
M. C. Malyj, Administration Supervisor, Public Relations
Staff: full time 1, part time 3
Major programs: library, museum, school programs, historic preservation, records management, exhibits, telecommunications

Museum Services, Old St. Stephen's College
8820 112th St., T6G 2P8
Telephone: (403) 427-3182
Provincial agency, authorized by Historical Resources Division
Founded in: 1983
John Lunn, Executive Director
Staff: full time 2, part time 2
Major programs: museum, records management, exhibits, audiovisual programs, field services, museology

Provincial Archives of Alberta, Provincial Government Department of Culture
12845 102nd Ave., T5N 0M6
Telephone: (403) 427-1750
Provincial agency
Founded in: 1963
W. Brian Speirs, Provincial Archivist
Staff: full time 21
Major programs: library, archives, manuscripts, newsletters/pamphlets, photographic collections, genealogical services
Period of collections: 1880-present

Provincial Museum of Alberta
12845 102nd Ave., T5N 0M6
Telephone: (403) 427-1730
Provincial agency
Founded in: 1967
John Fortier, Director
Staff: full time 90, part time 15
Major programs: museum, educational programs, books, newsletters/pamphlets
Period of collections: early-mid 20th century

Ring House Galery
University of Alberta, T6G 2E2
Telephone: (403) 432-5818
Authorized by the university
Helen Collinson, Director
Staff: full time 6
Major programs: museum, research, exhibits
Period of collections: prehistoric-present

Rutherford House Provincial Historic Site
11153 Saskatchewan Dr.
Telephone: (403) 427-5708
Mail to: 8820 112th St., T6G 2P8
Provincial agency
Founded in: 1970
Frank Milligan, Visitor Services Officer
Staff: full time 1, part time 4, volunteer 25
Major programs: historic site(s), tours/pilgrimages, junior history, school programs, newsletters/pamphlets, historic preservation, research, living history
Period of collections: 1910-1930

Strathcona Archaeological Centre
17th St.
Telephone: (403) 427-5708
Mail to: 8820 112th St., T6G 2P8
Provincial agency
Founded in: 1974
Frank Milligan, Visitor Services Officer
Staff: full time 1, part time 4
Major programs: historic site(s), school programs, newsletters/pamphlets, exhibits, archaeology programs
Period of collections: prehistoric

Ukrainian Cultural Heritage Village
Hwy. 16, E
Telephone: (403) 662-3640
Mail to: 8820 112th St., T6G 2P8
Provincial agency
Founded in: 1971
Andrew Turzansky, Facility Manager
Staff: full time 18, volunteer 115
Major programs: library, historic site(s), tours, school programs, newsletters/pamphlets, historic preservation, records management, research, exhibits, living history, audiovisual programs
Period of collections: 1890-1930

University of Alberta Archives
1-19 Rutherford, S, T6G 2J4
Telephone: (403) 432-5146
Private agency, authorized by the university
Founded in: 1967
James M. Parker, University Archivist
Staff: full time 4, part time 1, volunteer 2
Major programs: archives, manuscripts, oral history, records management, photographic collections
Period of collections: 1890-present

University of Alberta Dental Museum
T6G 2N8
Telephone: (403) 432-2189
State agency, authorized by the university
Founded in: 1956
G. H. Sperber, Curator
Staff: full time 2, volunteer 2
Major programs: archives, museum
Period of collections: 1920-present

ELK POINT

Fort George Museum
Telephone: (403) 724-3654
Mail to: P.O. Box 66, T0A 1A0
Steve Andrishak, Director
Questionnaire not received

EVANSBURG

Pembina Lobstick Historical Museum
Telephone: (403) 727-2211
Mail to: T0E 0T0
Mrs. A. Fausak, Director
Questionnaire not received

FAIRVIEW

R.C.M.P. Centennial Celebration Museum
Telephone: (403) 835-2402
Mail to: P.O. Box 232, T0H 1L0
Viola Evans, Curator

FORT MACLEOD

Ft. Museum
219 25 St.
Telephone: (403) 553-4703
Mail to: P.O. Box 776, T0L 0Z0
Town agency, authorized by Ft.
  Macleod Historical Association
Founded in: 1957
Catherine D. Luck, Manager/Curator
Number of members: 100
Staff: full time 1, part time 27,
  volunteer 10
Major programs: archives, museum,
  records management, exhibits,
  audiovisual programs,
  photographic collections, history of
  Royal Canadian Mounted Police
Period of collections: 1874-1924

Fort Macleod Historical Association
25th St. and 3rd Ave.
Telephone: (403) 553-4703
Mail to: P.O. Box 776, T0L 0Z0
Town agency
Founded in: 1957
Catherine D. Luck, Manager/Curator
Staff: full time 1, part time 27,
  volunteer 10
Major programs: archives, museum,
  records management, exhibits,
  audiovisual programs,
  photographic collections
Period of collections: 1874-1924

Head-Smashed-In Buffalo Jump Interpretive Centre
Hwy. 516, W
Telephone: (403) 427-2022
Mail to: 8820 112th St., T6G 2P8
Provincial agency
Founded in: 1979
M. E. "Stevi" Stephens, Facility
  Manager
Staff: full time 1, part time 5
Major programs: historic site(s),
  tours/pilgrimages, school
  programs, newsletters/pamphlets,
  exhibits, audiovisual programs,
  archaeology programs
Period of collections: prehistoric

FORT MCMURRAY

Ft. McMurray Oil Sands Interpretive Centre
515 McKenzie Blvd., T9H 4H9
Telephone: (403) 743-7471/743-7166
Provincial agency
Founded in: 1983
Chris Stephens, Visitor Services
  Officer
Staff: full time 3, part time 5,
  volunteer 1
Major programs: library, historic
  site(s), tours, oral history, school
  programs, book publishing,
  newsletters/pamphlets, historic
  preservation, research, exhibits,
  audiovisual programs
Period of collections: 1898-present

Heritage Park—Historical Society of Ft. McMurray
P.O. Box 8058, T9H 4H9
Telephone: (403) 791-7575
Paul Noake, President
Major programs: historic
  preservation, living history,
  photographic collections
Period of collections: 1860-1960

FORT SASKATCHEWAN

Ft. Saskatchewan Historical Society
10104 101st St., T8L 1V9
Telephone: (403) 998-3533
Founded in: 1958
Peter Ream, President
Number of members: 45
Staff: part time 1, volunteer 25
Major programs: archives, museum,
  historic sites preservation,
  tours/pilgrimages
Period of collections: 1865-present

FORT VERMILION

Rocky Lane School Museum
Rocky Lane School, 27 km southwest
  of Ft. Vermilion
Telephone: (403) 927-3297
Mail to: P.O. Bag 9000, T0H 1N0
M. Nugent, Director
Major programs: museum, school
  programs
Period of collections: mid 1800-mid
  1900

FRANK (CROW'S NEST PASS)

Frank Slide Interpretive Centre
Hwy. 3
Telephone: (403) 562-7331
Mail to: P.O. Box 959, Blairmore, T0K
  0E0
Provincial agency
Founded in: 1985
Catherine Nimmo, Facility Manager
Staff: full time 3, part time 4
Major programs: library, historic
  site(s), markers, tours, school
  programs, newsletters/pamphlets,
  historic preservation, research,
  exhibits, audiovisual programs,
  photographic collections
Period of collections: early
  1900s-1930s

Leitch Collieries
Hwy. 3
Telephone: (403) 562-7331
Mail to: P.O. Box 959, Blairmore, T0K
  0E0
Provincial agency
Founded in: 1982
Catherine Nimmo, Facility Manager
Staff: full time 1, part time 3
Major programs: historic site(s),
  markers, tours, oral history, school
  programs, newsletters/pamphlets,
  historic preservation, exhibits
Period of collections: 1907-1915

GIROUXVILLE

Musée Girouxville Museum
Telephone: (403) 323-4252
Mail to: P.O. Box 129, T0H 1S0
Founded in: 1969
Element Desrockers, Director
Questionnaire not received

GRANDE PRAIRIE

Grande Prairie Pioneer Museum
Bear Creek Centennial Park
Telephone: (403) 532-2758
Mail to: P.O. Box 687, T8V 3A8
Douglas Clarkson, President
Major programs: museum
Period of collections: early
  1900s-present

HANNA

Hanna Pioneer Museum
Telephone: (403) 854-4424/854-3498
Mail to: P.O. Box 1528, T0J 1P0
Clarence Dafoe, President
Questionnaire not received

HIGH PRAIRIE

High Prairie and District Centennial Museum
Telephone: (403) 523-3456; 523-4197
Mail to: P.O. Box 629, T0G 1E0
Fern Fevang, Secretary

HIGH RIVER

Museum of the Highwood
4th Ave. and 1st St., W
Telephone: (403) 652-7156
Mail to: P.O. Box 456, T0L 1B0
Town agency
Founded in: 1961
Donald R. King, Curator
Number of members: 30
Staff: full time 1, part time 2,
  volunteer 12
Major programs: library, archives,
  manuscripts, museum, oral history,
  book publishing, historic
  preservation, exhibits,
  photographic collections
Period of collections: district
  settlement-present

HINTON

Alberta Forest Service Museum
Telephone: (403) 865-8211
Mail to: 1176 Switzer Dr., T0E 1B0
Authorized by Department of Energy
  and Natural Resources
T. S. Smith, Head, Administrative
  Services
Major programs: museum
Period of collections: 1900-present

IDDESLEIGH

Rainy Hills Historical Society
General Delivery, T0J 1T0
Telephone: (403) 898-2163
Town agency
Founded in: 1965
Ed Stegen, President
Number of members: 30
Period of collections: from 1910

Rainy Hills Pioneer Exhibits
Telephone: (403) 898-2360
Mail to: T0J 1T0
Anne Liboiron, Secretary
Questionnaire not received

INNISFAIL

Historical Village
Telephone: (403) 227-9025/227-3807
Mail to: P.O. Box 642, T0M 1A0
M. Godkin, Director
Questionnaire not received

Innisfail and District Historical Society
42nd St., between 51st and 52nd Ave.
Telephone: (403) 227-2906
Mail to: P.O. Box 642, T0M 1A0
Private agency
Founded in: 1969
Kay Dempster, Curator
Number of members: 200
Staff: part time 5, volunteer 10
Major programs: historic site(s), exhibits
Perod of collections: to 1930

IRVINE

Prairie Memories Museum
Telephone: (403) 834-3782
Mail to: P.O. Box 240, T0J 1V0
Town agency
Charles H. Trenouth, Chair
Major programs: library, archives, museum, historic site(s), oral history, school programs, historic preservation, research, exhibits, photographic collections
Period of collections: 1900-1960

ISLAY

Morrison Museum Association
Private agency
Founded in: 1962
Shirley Ronaghan, President
Number of members: 12
Staff: volunteer 2
Major programs: museum
Period of collections: 1900-1940

LETHBRIDGE

Ft. Whoop-Up Interpretative Society
P.O. Box 1074, T1J 4A2
Telephone: (403) 329-6831
Founded in: 1967
Harvey Wiens, Manager
Staff: full time 7, part time 6, volunteer 10
Major programs: museum, historic site(s), tours/pilgrimages, newsletters/pamphlets, exhibits, living history, audiovisual programs
Period of collections: 1874-1879

Lethbridge and District Japanese Garden Society
Telephone: (403) 328-3511
Mail to: P.O. Box 751
Founded in: 1966
James R. Bate, Manager
Questionnaire not received

Sir Alexander Galt Museum and Archives
5th Ave., S
Telephone: (403) 328-6455
Mail to: Community Services, 910 4th Ave., S, T1J 0P6
City agency
Founded in: 1964
W. J. Elliott, Museum Supervisor
Staff: full time 4, part time 2
Major programs: archives, museum, historic site(s), historic preservation, exhibits, photographic collections
Period of collections: 1885-1950

Whoop-up Country Chapter, Historical Society of Alberta
Telephone: (403) 328-5808
Mail to: P.O. Box 974, T1J 4A2
Founded in: 1888
Alex Johnston, President
Number of members: 300
Staff: volunteer 6
Major programs: museum, newsletters/pamphlets
Period of collections: 1885-1960s

LOUGHEED

Iron Creek Museum
Sports Grounds
Telephone: (403) 386-2107
Mail to: P.O. Box 6, T0B 2V0
C. Ingraldson, Secretary

MARKERVILLE

Stephansson House Provincial Historic Site
Hwy. 592
Telephone: (403) 728-3929
Mail to: 8820 112th St., Edmonton, T6G 2P8
Provincial agency
Founded in: 1982
Frank Milligan, Visitor Services Officer
Staff: full time 1, part time 3
Major programs: historic site(s), school programs, book publishing, newsletters/pamphlets, historic preservation, research, living history
Period of collections: late 1920s

MEDICINE HAT

Medicine Hat Museum and Art Gallery
1302 Bomford Cres., T1A 5E6
Telephone: (403) 527-6266
Founded in: 1951
Tom Willock, Director
Questionnaire not received

MIRROR

Mirror and District Museum Association
P.O. Box 246, T0B 3C0
Telephone: (403) 788-3828

Town agency, authorized by Mirror and District Museum Association
G. W. Neis, President
Number of members: 35
Major programs: museum, historic site(s), historic preservation
Period of collections: 1890-1960

MUNDARE

Basilian Fathers Museum
Telephone: (403) 764-3860
Mail to: P.O. Box 379, T0B 3H0
Private agency
Major programs: archives, manuscripts

OLDS

Mountain View Museum
5038 50th St.
Telephone: (403) 556-8464
Mail to: P.O. Box 63, T0M 1P0
Private agency, authorized by Olds Historical Society
Founded in: 1973
Joseph Benedek, Director
Number of members: 126
Staff: part time 1, volunteer 23
Major programs: library, archives, museum, oral history, school programs, records management, exhibits, photographic collections
Period of collections: 1900-1970

PALMONDON

Palmondon and District Museum
Telephone: (403) 798-3883
Mail to: T0A 2T0
Mrs. Ilnicki, Contact person
Questionnaire not received

PATRICIA

Dinosaur Provincial Park
P.O. Box 60, T0J 2K0
Telephone: (403) 378-4587
Provincial agency, authorized by Alberta Recreation and Parks
Founded in: 1955
Roger Benoit, Park Ranger
Staff: full time 3, part time 16
Major programs: tours, school programs, living history, palaeontology, geology
Period of collections: prehistoric

PEACE RIVER

Peace River Centennial Museum
Telephone: (403) 624-4261
Mail to: P.O. Box 747, T0H 2X0
Town agency
Major programs: archives, museum, historic preservation, exhibits, audiovisual programs, photographic collections
Period of collections: early 1900s

PINCHER CREEK

Pincher Creek and District Historical Society—Pincher Creek Museum and Kootenzi Brown Historical Village
James Ave.
Telephone: (403) 627-3684
Mail to: P.O. Box 1226, T0K 1W0
Private agency

Founded in: 1966 (society); 1973
  (museum and historical village)
E. F. Tucker, President
Number of members: 65
Staff: part time 2, volunteer 40
Major programs: archives, museum,
  historic preservation, audiovisual
  programs
Period of collections: 1880-1960

PONOKA

Alberta Hospital Museum
T0C 2H0
Telephone: (403) 783-3351
Founded in: 1969
Major programs: archives, museum,
  tours/pilgrimages, educational
  programs
Period of collections: 1910-present

Fort Ostell Museum
Centennial Park
Telephone: (403) 783-3858
Mail to: P.O. Box 2192, T0C 2H0
Dorothy Berg, Director
Questionnaire not received

REDCLIFF

**Redcliff Museum and Historical
  Society**
1 3rd St., NE
Telephone: (403) 548-3524
Mail to: P.O. Box 76, T0J 2P0
Town agency
Founded in: 1981
Cliff Dacre, Secretary
Number of members: 85
Staff: part time 1, volunteer 18
Major programs: library, manuscripts,
  museum, oral history, school
  programs, newsletters/pamphlets,
  historic preservation, research,
  exhibits, archaeology programs,
  photographic collections
Period of collections: 1895-1945

RED DEER

**Red Deer and District Museum and
  Archives**
4550-47 A Ave.
Telephone: (403) 343-6844
Mail to: P.O. Box 800, T4N 5H2
City agency
Morris Flewwelling, Director
Major programs: library, archives,
  manuscripts, museum, school
  programs, research, exhibits,
  photographic collections,
  genealogical services
Period of collections: 1880-1950

REDWATER

Redwater and District Museum
Telephone: (403) 942-3552
Mail to: T0A 2W0
Provincial agency
Anne Key, Contact person
Major programs: archives, museum,
  historic preservation, audiovisual
  programs,
photographic collections
Period of collections: 1900-1940

RIMBEY

Pas-Ka-Poo Historical Park
Telephone: (403) 843-6482
Mail to: T0C 2J0
Joan Freeman, Secretary
Questionnaire not received

ROCKY MOUNTAIN HOUSE

**Rocky Mountain House National
  Historic Park**
P.O. Box 2130, T0M 1T0
Telephone: (403) 845-2412
Founded in: 1980
Ross Innes, Area Superintendent
Staff: full time 5, part time 7,
  volunteer 50
Major programs: museum, historic
  site(s), tours/pilgrimages, school
  programs, historic preservation,
  audiovisual programs
Period of collections: 1799-1875

ROSEBUD

Rosebud Centennial Museum
Mail to: P.O. Box 667, T0J 2J0
Authorized by Rosebud Lions Club
Rial Barr, Director
Major programs: museum, school
  programs, historic preservation,
  research
Period of collections: 1900-1920

ST. ALBERT

Oblate Archives
3 St. Vital Ave., T8N 1K1
Telephone: (403) 458-0152
Private agency, authorized by Oblate
  Fathers of the Northwest Territories
Founded in: 1921
E. O. Drouin, Archivist
Staff: full time 1, part time 1
Major programs: archives,
  manuscripts, research, living
  history, photographic collections,
  genealogical services
Period of collections: 1838-present

**St. Albert Historical Society/Father
  Lacombe Chapel**
7 St. Vital Ave.
Telephone: (403) 458-9199
Mail to: P.O. Box 98, T8N 1N2
Founded in: 1972
Arlene Borgstede, Heritage Officer
Questionnaire not received

SANGUDO

**Lac Ste. Anne and District Pioneer
  Museum**
Mail to: P.O. Box 525, T0E 2A0
Private agency, authorized by Lac
  Ste. Anne Historical Society
Founded in: 1959
Mrs. M. Dinwoodie, President
Number of members: 15
Staff: part time 2, volunteer 4
Major programs: archives, museum,
  exhibits
Period of collections: 1900-1950

SHANDRO

**Historical Living Village and
  Pioneer Museum**
Telephone: (403) 367-2489
Mail to: P.O. Box 147, T0B 4R0

Ted Prescott, President
Questionnaire not received

SMOKY LAKE

Victoria Settlement Provincial Site
Smoky Lake
Telephone: (403) 656-2333
Mail to: 8820 112th St., Edmonton,
  T6G 2P8
Provincial agency, authorized by
  Alberta Culture Historic Sites
  Service
Founded in: 1981
Frank Milligan, Visitor Services
  Officer
Staff: full time 1, part time 3
Major programs: historic site(s),
  tours/pilgrimages, school
  programs, book publishing,
  newsletters/pamphlets, historic
  preservation, research, living
  history
Period of collections: late 1800s-early
  1900s

STETTLER

Stettler Town and Country Museum
44th Ave., W. Stettler
Telephone: (403) 742-4534/742-4291
Mail to: P.O. Box 2118, T0C 2L0
Founded in: 1973
Catherine M. Anderson, Curator
Number of members: 425
Staff: part time 2, volunteer 20
Major programs: museum
Period of collections: 1800s-1950

STONY PLAIN

Multicultural Heritage Centre
Telephone: (403) 963-2777
Mail to: P.O. Box 908, T0E 2G0
Authorized by Heritage Agricultural
  Society
Founded in: 1974
Steve Beamont, Director
Staff: full time 10, part time 15,
  volunteer 40
Major programs: library, archives,
  museum, tours/pilgrimages, oral
  history, school programs, book
  publishing, newsletters/pamphlets,
  records management, exhibits,
  living history, photographic
  collections, art classes
Period of collections: 1900-1950

SUNDRE

**Sundre and District Historical
  Society**
Telephone: (403) 638-4186
Mail to: T0M 1X0
Jim Miller, Curator/Secretary
Questionnaire not received

THREE HILLS

**Kneehill Historical Society RCMP
  Museum**
Telephone: (403) 443-5150
Mail to: P.O. Box 281, T0M 2A0
Paulina Jasman, Contact person
Questionnaire not received

TOFIELD

Tofield Historical Museum
General Delivery, T0B 4J0
Nola Ferguson, Secretary/Treasurer
Number of members: 14
Major programs: museum
Period of collections: 1880-present

TROCHU

Trochu Valley Historical Society
T0M 2C0
Telephone: (403) 442-2334
Founded in: 1975
George O. Braham, President
Number of members: 44
Staff: part time 1, volunteer 12
Magazine: *Trochu Valley Historical Society*
Major programs: archives, museum
Period of collections: from early 1900

VIKING

Viking Historical Society Museum
5024 58th Ave.
Mail to: P.O. Box 232, T0B 4N0
Founded in: 1967
J. H. Roddick, President
Number of members: 30
Staff: volunteer 20
Period of collections: 1900-present

WAINWRIGHT

Wainwright Museum
926-3rd Ave.
Mail to: P.O. Box 99, T0B 4P0
D. White, President
Questionnaire not received

WANHAM

Grizzly Bear Prairie Museum
Telephone: (403) 694-3858
Mail to: P.O. Box 203, T0H 3P0
Anne Shaw, Curator
Questionnaire not received

WETASKIWIN

Reynolds Aviation Museum
4118 57th St., T9A 2B6
Telephone: (403) 352-5201
Private agency
Founded in: 1955
Stanley G. Reynolds, President
Staff: part time 1, volunteer 1
Major programs: museum, historic preservation, exhibits
Period of collections: 1870-1945

WILLINGDON

Historical Village and Pioneer Museum at Shandro
P.O. Box 102, T0B 4R0
Telephone: (403) 367-2445/367-2452
Founded in: 1959
Nick P. Hawrelak, President
Number of members: 316
Staff: full time 1, part time 8, volunteer 30
Major programs: museum, tours/pilgrimages, historic preservation, living history
Period of collections: 1898-1929

BRITISH COLUMBIA

ABBOTSFORD

Trethewey House—Matsqui-Sumas-Abbotsford Museum Society
2313 Ware St., V2S 3C6
Telephone: (604) 853-0313
Private agency
Founded in: 1969
Diane Kelly, Curator
Number of members: 177
Staff: full time 2, part time 2, volunteer 55
Major programs: library, archives, museum, oral history
Period of collections: 1900-present

ALERT

Alert Bay Museum
199 Fir St.
Telephone: (604) 974-5721
Mail to: P.O. Box 208, V0N 1A0
Questionnaire not received

ASHCROFT

Ashcroft Museum
Brink and 4th St.
Telephone: (604) 453-2456
Mail to: P.O. Box 129, V0K 1A0
Robert Harper, Clerk-Treasurer
Major programs: museum
Period of collections: 1880-1970

ATLIN

Atlin Historical Museum
3rd and Trainor Sts.
Telephone: (604) 651-7522
Mail to: P.O. Box 111, V0W 1A0
Town agency
Christine Dickinson, President
Major programs: archives, manuscripts, museum, historic site(s), markers, oral history
Period of collections: 1898-present

BALDONNEL

Peace Island Park Museum
Taylor, 18km south of Fort St. John
Telephone: (604) 789-3615
Mail to: c/o D. Prosser, V0C 1C0
Doug Prosser, President
Questionnaire not received

BARKERVILLE

Barkerville Historic Park
V0K 1B0
Telephone: (604) 994-3209
Provincial agency
Founded in: 1958
Ron Candy, Curator
Staff: full time 14, part time 20
Major programs: museum, historic sites preservation, educational programs
Period of collections: 1869-1900

BRITANNIA BEACH

British Columbia Museum of Mining
Telephone: (604) 688-8735/896-2233
Mail to: P.O. Box 155, V0N 1J0
Private agency, authorized by Britannia Beach Historical Society

Marilyn Mullan, Curator
Major programs: school programs, exhibits, audiovisual programs, photographic collections
Period of collections: 1900-present

BURNABY

Burnaby Historical Society
106 6630 Sussex Ave., V5H 3C6
Telephone: (604) 434-6828
Founded in: 1950
Fraser Wilson, President
Questionnaire not received

Burnaby Village Museum
Canada Way (near Gilpin St.)
Telephone: (604) 294-1231
Mail to: 4900 Deer Lake Ave., V5G 3T6
R. P. Schofield, Museum Director
Major programs: museum, school programs
Period of collections: 1890-1920

CAMPBELL RIVER

Campbell River and District Museum and Archives Society
Tyee Plaza
Telephone: (604) 287-3103
Mail to: 1235 Island Hwy., V9W 2C7
Mrs. Jay S. Stewart, Director
Number of members: 60
Staff: full time 5, volunteer 55
Major programs: library, archives, manuscripts, museum, oral history, school programs, newsletters/pamphlets, research, exhibits, photographic collections
Period of collections: 18th century-present

CASTLEGAR

Doukhobour Village Museum
E. Kinnaird Bridge
Telephone: (604) 365-6622
Mail to: P.O. Box 3081, V1N 3H4
Authorized by Kootenay Doukhobour Historical Society
Elmer Verigin, President
Major programs: museum, audiovisual programs
Period of collections: 1908-1930

Selkirk College Archives and Local History Collection
Telephone: (604) 365-5518
Mail to: P.O. Box 1200, V1N 3J1
John Mansbridge, Chief Librarian

CHILLIWACK

Chilliwack Museum and Historical Society
9291 Corbould St., V2P 4A6
Telephone: (604) 795-5210
Private agency
Founded in: 1958
Nora Layard, Director/Curator
Number of members: 1,184
Staff: full time 3
Major programs: archives, museum, oral history, exhibits, photographic collections
Period of collections: 1858-1940

CLINTON

South Cariboo Historical Museum
Hwy. 97
Telephone: (604) 459-2442
Mail to: P.O. Box 46, V0K 1K0
Albert Dibben, President
Questionnaire not received

COURTENAY

Courtenay and District Historical Society
Telephone: (604) 334-3881
Mail to: P.O. Box 3128, V9N-5N4
Private agency
Founded in: 1953
Judy Carswell, Secretary
Number of members: 50
Staff: volunteer 15
Major programs: museum
Period of collections: present

CRANBROOK

Cranbrook Archives, Museum and Landmark Foundation
1 Van Horne St., N
Telephone: (604) 489-3918
Mail to: P.O. Box 400, V1C 4H9
Founded in: 1976
Garry W. Anderson, Executive Director
Number of members: 313
Staff: full time 2, volunteer 4
Major programs: archives, museum, historic site(s), historic preservation, exhibits
Period of collections: 1880-1930

Crowsnest Route Railway Museum
1 Van Horne St. N.
Telephone: (604) 489-3918
Mail to: P.O. Box 400, V1C 4H9
Garry Anderson, Executive Director
Questionnaire not received

CRESTON

Creston and District Historical and Museum Society
219 Devon Rd.
Telephone: (604) 428-9262
Mail to: P.O. Box 2948, V0B 1G0
Private agency
Founded in: 1971 (society); 1982 (museum)
Cyril Colonel, President
Staff: full time 1, volunteer 20
Major programs: museum
Period of collections: 1900

CUMBERLAND

Cumberland Museum
2680 Dunsmuir Ave.
Telephone: (604) 336-2622
Mail to: P.O. Box 258, V0R 1S0
State agency, authorized by Cumberland and District Historical Society
Major programs: museum, audiovisual programs
Period of collections: 1890s-1950s

DAWSON CREEK

Dawson Creek Museum and Pioneer Village
Telephone: (604) 782-4868/782-3143
Mail to: 609 103rd St., V1G 4T9

Walter Wright, Chairman
Questionnaire not received

Dawson Creek Station Museum
900 Alaska Ave., V1G 4T6
Telephone: (604) 782-9595
Major programs: museum, book publishing, historic preservation, exhibits, photographic collections

South Peace Historical Society
P.O. Box 2033, V1G 4K8
Telephone: (604) 782-9595
Major programs: museum, book publishing, historic preservation, exhibits, photographic collections

Walter Wright Pioneer Village
P.O. Box 2033, V1G 4K8
Telephone: (604) 782-9595
Major programs: museum, book publishing, historic preservation, exhibits, photographic collections

DELTA

Delta Museum and Archives
Telephone: (604)946-9322
Mail to: 4858 Delta St., V4K 2T8
Daphne Savage, Curator
Major programs: archives, museum, school programs, historic preservation, records management, exhibits, photographic collections
Period of collections: 1900-1920

DUNCAN

British Columbia Forest Museum
Trans Canada Hwy. and Drinkwater Rd.
Telephone: (604) 748-9389
Mail to: R.R. 4, V9L 3W8
Founded in: 1964
Terry Malone, Manager
Questionnaire not received

FORT LANGLEY

British Columbia Farm Machinery and Agriculture Museum Association
9131 King St.
Telephone: (604) 534-5747
Mail to: P.O. Box 279, V0X 1J0
Private agency
Art Wise, Curator
Major programs: museum, historic preservation, records management, exhibits
Period of collections: late 19th-20th centuries

Ft. Langley National Historic Park
23433 Mavis Ave.
Telephone: (604) 888-4424
Mail to: P.O. Box 129, V0X 1J0
B. Jackson, Interpretive Officer
Staff: full time 19, part time 10
Major programs: historic site(s), school programs, exhibits, living history
Period of collections: 1850s

Langley Centennial Museum and National Exhibition Centre
Mavis and King St., V0X 1J0
Telephone: (604) 888-3922
Town agency
Founded in: 1958

Warren F. Sommer, Curator/Director
Staff: full time 2, part time 2, volunteer 45
Major programs: archives, manuscripts, museum, oral history, school programs, newsletters/pamphlets, research, exhibits, photographic collections
Period of collections: prehistoric-1925

FORT ST. JAMES

Ft. St. James National Historic Park
Kwah Rd.
Telephone: (604) 996-7191
Mail to: P.O. Box 1148, V0J 1P0
Federal agency, authorized by Department of Environment, Parks Canada
Major programs: library, manuscripts, museum, historic site(s), tours/pilgrimages, junior history, oral history, school programs, newsletters/pamphlets, historic preservation, records management, research, exhibits, living history, audiovisual programs, photographic collections, field services
Period of collections: 1880s-1890s

FORT STEELE

Ft. Steele Historic Park
General Delivery, V0B 1N0
Telephone: (604) 489-3351
Provincial agency, authorized by Ministry of Lands, Parks and Housing
Founded in: 1961
Struan Robertson, District Manager
Staff: full time 17, part time 10, volunteer 50
Major programs: library, archives, manuscripts, museum, historic site(s), oral history, school programs, historic preservation, exhibits, living history, audiovisual programs, photographic collections
Period of collections: 1865-1918

GARIBALDI HIGHLANDS

Squamish Valley Museum
2nd Ave.
Telephone: (604) 898-3273
Mail to: P.O. Box 166, V0N 1T0
Doug Fenton, President
Questionnaire not received

GOLDEN

Golden District Historical Society
P.O. Box 992
Telephone: (604) 344-5169
Private agency
Founded in: 1974
Ina A. Carr-Bechthold, Museum Curator
Number of members: 30
Staff: part time 1, volunteer 7
Major programs: museum
Period of collections: 1910-1930

GRAND FORKS

Boundary Museum Society
7370 5th St.
Telephone: (604) 442-3737

Mail to: P.O. Box 817, V0H 1H0
P. L. Morrison, Chair
Major programs: archives, museum,
  historic preservation
Period of collections: 1890-present

GREENWOOD

Greenwood Museum
Copper St.
Telephone: (604) 445-6355
Mail to: P. O. Drawer 399, V0H 1J0
Mrs. R. Santopinto, Curator
Major programs: archives, museum,
  photographic collections
Period of collections: 1895-1950

HARRISON MILLS

Kilby Provincial Historic Park
Kilby Rd.
Telephone: (604) 796-9576
Mail to: P.O. Box 48
Period of collections: 1914-1939

HAZELTON

Ksan Association
Mail to: P.O. Box 326
Telephone: (604) 842-5544
Ron Burleigh, Project Director
Questionnaire not received

HOPE

Hope Museum
Water St.
Telephone: (604) 869-5671/869-5094
Mail to: P.O. Box 26, V0X 1L0
Town agency, authorized by Hope
  District Historical Society
Major programs: museum
Period of collections: from 1850

HORSEFLY

Jack Lynn Memorial Museum
Telephone: (604) 620-3304
Mail to: P.O. Box 148, V0L 1L0
Private agency, authorized by
  Horsefly Historical Society
Mrs. H. Erickson, Curator
Major programs: archives, museum,
  oral history, newsletters/pamphlets,
  exhibits, photographic collections
Period of collections: 1850-1930

HUDSON'S HOPE

Hudson's Hope Historical Society
Hwy. 29 and Fredette Ave., V0C 1V0
Telephone: (604) 783-5735
Mail to: P.O. Box 98
Founded in: 1967
Debbie Joslin, President
Questionnaire not received

INVERMERE

**Windermere District Historical
  Society**
7th Ave.
Mail to: General Delivery, V0A 1K0
Founded in: 1962
Harold Yeo, President
Questionnaire not received

KAMLOOPS

Kamloops Museum and Archives
207 Seymour St., V2C 2E7
Founded in: 1936

Ken Favrholdt, Curator/Archivist
Number of members: 50
Staff: full time 3, part time 4
Major programs: library, archives,
  museum, school programs, book
  publishing, research, exhibits,
  photographic collections,
  genealogical services
Period of collections: 1860-present

Kamloops Museum Association
207 Seymour St., V2C 2E7
Telephone: (604) 372-9931
Founded in: 1936
Ken Favrholdt, Curator/Archivist
Number of members: 50
Staff: full time 3, part time 7,
  volunteer 6
Major programs: library, archives,
  museum, school programs, book
  publishing, research, exhibits,
  photographic collections,
  genealogical services
Period of collections: 1860-present

KELOWNA

**Kelowna Centennial Museum and
  National Exhibition Centre**
Telephone: (604) 763-2417
Mail to: 470 Queensway Ave., V1Y
  6S7
Ursula Surtees, Director
Questionnaire not received

KEREMEOS

Keremeos Museum
Corner 6th Ave. and 6th St.
Telephone: (604) 499-5802
Mail to: P.O. Box 27, V0X 1N0
Mrs. Advocat, Secretary
Questionnaire not received

KITIMAT

**Kitimat Centennial Museum
  Association**
293 City Center, V8C 1P9
Founded in: 1969
James Tirrul-Jones, Curator
Staff: full time 1, part time 2,
  volunteer 2
Major programs: archives, museum,
  book publishing, research,
  exhibits, archaeology programs,
  photographic collections
Period of collections: A.D.
  1000-present

LAC LA HACHE

Lac La Hache Museum
Telephone: (604) 396-7332
Mail to: V0K 1T0
Questionnaire not received

LADYSMITH

**Crown Zellerbach Arboretum and
  Museum**
Island Highway
Telephone: (604) 245-2211
Mail to: P.O. Box 609, V0R 2E0
M. Pelto, Division Manager
Questionnaire not received

LANCASTER PARK

Canadian Airborne Forces Museum
144th Ave. and 109th St.

Telephone: (403) 456-2450, local 458
Mail to: Canadian Forces Base,
  Edmonton, T0A 2H0
D. Manuel, Director

LILLOOET

Lillooet Museum
Main St.
Telephone: (604) 256-4308
Mail to: P.O. Box 441, V0K IV0
Town agency, authorized by Lillooet
  District Historical Society
Hilda Bryson, Curator
Major programs: museum

MASSET

Ed Jones Haida Museum
Telephone: (604) 626-5159/559-4643
Mail to: V0T 1M0
Isabel Adams, Curator

MAYNE ISLAND

Mayne Island Museum
Fernhill Rd.
Telephone: (604) 539-5510
Mail to: P.O. Box 150, V0N 2J0
Authorized by Mayne Island
  Agricultural Society
F. Dodds, Curator
Major programs: museum
Period of collections: from 1925

MISSION

Mission Museum and Archives
33201 2nd Ave., V2V 1J9
Telephone: (604) 826-1011
Private agency, authorized by
  Mission District Historical Society
Founded in: 1972
Dorothy Crosby, Curator
Number of members: 120
Staff: volunteer 15
Major programs: archives, museum,
  oral history, educational programs
Period of collections: 1865-present

NAKUSP

Nakusp Museum
Telephone: (604) 265-3626
Mail to: P.O. Box 86, V0G 1R0
Doreen Des Rochers, Custodian
Questionnaire not received

NANAIMO

The Bastion
Front St.
Telephone: (604) 753-6044
Mail to: 211-450 Stewart Ave., V9S
  5E9
W. Stannard, Director
Questionnaire not received

**Nanaimo and District Museum
  Society**
100 Cameron Rd., V9R 2X1
Telephone: (604) 753-1821
City agency, authorized by Nanaimo
  Centennial Museum
Founded in: 1967
Henry Ferre, Administrator
Number of members: 66
Staff: full time 3, volunteer 50
Major programs: archives, museum,
  oral history, school programs, book

publishing, exhibits, audiovisual
programs, photographic
collections
Period of collections: 1850-1950

NARAMATA

Naramata Museum
Telephone: (604) 496-5567
Mail to: Centennial Hall, V0H 1N0
Questionnaire not received

NELSON

**Kootenay Museum Association and
Historical Society—Nelson
Museum**
Mail to: 402 Anderson St., V1L 3Y3
Private agency
Alan Ramsden, President
Major programs: museum,
photographic collections
Period of collections: 1880-1920

NEW WESTMINSTER

Canadian Lacrosse Hall of Fame
65 E. 6th Ave.
Mail to: P.O. Box 308, V3L 1H7
Telephone: (604) 521-7656
Founded in: 1967
Archie W. Miller, Curator
Major programs: archives, museum,
oral history, research, exhibits,
photographic collections, history of
lacrosse

**Irving House Historic Centre—New
Westminster Museum**
302 Royal Ave., V3L 1H7
Telephone: (604) 521-7656
Founded in: 1950
Archie W. Miller, Curator
Staff: full time 2
Major programs: archives, museum,
historic site(s), tours/pilgrimages,
oral history, school programs,
historic preservation, research,
exhibits, audiovisual programs,
photographic collections
Period of collections: 1850-present

**The Museum of The Royal
Westminster Regiment and The
Royal Westminster Regiment
Association**
The Armoury, 530 Queens Ave., V3L
1K3
Telephone: (604) 526-5116
Founded in: 1973
M.H.H. Steede, CD, Chairman
Questionnaire not received

**New Westminster Historical
Society**
#406, 320 Royal Ave., V3L 1H7
Telephone: (604) 521-7656
Founded in: 1976
Valerie Francis, Secretary
Major programs: newsletter,
research, audiovisual programs

**Royal Westminster Regimental
Museum**
Telephone: (604) 526-5116
Mail to: The Armoury, 530 Queens
Ave., V3L 1K3
Michael Steede, Director
Questionnaire not received

Samson V. Maritime Museum
Fraser River

Telephone: (604) 521-7656
Mail to: 302 Royal Ave., V3L 1H7
Founded in: 1983
Archie W. Miller, Curator
Major programs: museum, historic
preservation, research, exhibits

NORTH VANCOUVER

North Shore Museum and Archives
209 W. 4th St.
Telephone: (604) 987-5618
Founded in: 1971
W. H. J. Baker, Director
Staff: full time 1, part time 5
Major programs: archives,
educational programs
Period of collections: 1865-present

OSOYOOS

Osoyoos Museum
Main St., Community Park
Telephone: (604) 495-6723
Mail to: P.O. Box 791, V0H 1V0
Kate Willson, Director
Questionnaire not received

PENTICTON

R. N. Atkinson Museum
Telephone: (604) 492-6025
Mail to: 785 Main St., V2A 5E3
City agency
Joe Harris, Curator
Major programs: archives, museum,
historic site(s), historic
preservation, research, exhibits,
photographic collections,
genealogical services
Period of collections: 1860-1939

PORT ALBERNI

Alberni District Historical Society
Echo 67 Centre
Telephone: (604) 724-1833
Mail to: P.O. Box 284, V9Y 7M7
Private agency
Founded in: 1965
Dorrit MacLeod, President
Number of members: 67
Staff: volunteer 14
Major programs: archives,
manuscripts, book publishing,
research
Period of collections: 1860-present

PORT MOODY

Burrard-Fraser Heritage Society
2734 Murray St., V3H 1X2
Telephone: (604) 939-1648
Private agency
Founded in: 1969
Diane Rogers, Curator
Number of members: 150
Staff: volunteer 60
Major programs: archives, museum,
oral history, school programs,
newsletters/pamphlets, historic
preservation, exhibits,
photographic collections
Period of collections: 1900-1930

POUCE COUPE

Pouce Coupe Museum
Railway Station
Telephone: (604) 786-5962

Mail to: P.O. Box 293, V0C 2C0
Wilma Harmis, Curator
Questionnaire not received

POWELL RIVER

**Powell River Historical Museum
Association**
Telephone: (604) 485-2222
Founded in: 1967
Laura Everett, Curator
Questionnaire not received

PRINCE GEORGE

Fort George Regional Museum
Telephone: (604) 562-1612
Mail to: P.O. Box 1779, V2L 4V7
C. W. Jones, Director
Questionnaire not received

PRINCE RUPERT

**Museum of Northern British
Columbia**
1st Ave. & McBride St., V8J 3SI
Telephone: (604) 624-3207
Mail to: P.O. Box 669
Founded in: 1924
Ron Denman, Administrator
Questionnaire not received

PRINCETON

**Princeton and District Pioneer
Museum**
167 Vermilion Ave.
Telephone: (604) 295-3362/295-7588
Mail to: P.O. Box 687, V0X 1W0
Margaret Stoneberg, Archivist
Town agency
Major programs: library, archives,
museum, oral history, school
programs, newsletters/pamphlets,
records management, exhibits,
photographic collections,
genealogical services

QUESNEL

Quesnel and District Museum
Telephone: (604) 992-9580
Mail to: 707 Carson Ave., V2J 2B6
Sheila Hill, Curator
Questionnaire not received

REVELSTOKE

Revelstoke Museum
315 1st St., W
Telephone: (604) 837-3067
Mail to: P.O. Box 1908, V0E 2S0
City agency, authorized by
Revelstoke Historical Association
Cathy English, Curator
Major programs: archives, museum,
oral history
Period of collections: 1880-1940

RIMBEY

Pas-Ka-Poo Historical Park
Telephone: (403) 843-6482
Mail to: T0C 2J0
Town agency, authorized by Rimbey
Historical Society
Charles Plank, Secretary
Major programs: museum, historic
site(s), historic preservation,
records management
Period of collections: from 1900

ROSSLAND

Rossland Historical Museum Association
British Columbia Ski Hall of Fame, Hwy. Junction, V0G 1Y0
Telephone: (604) 362-7722
Mail to: P.O. Box 26
Founded in: 1955
J. D. McDonald, President
Staff: part time 10, volunteer 8
Major programs: archives, museum, oral history
Period of collections: 1890-present

SAANICHTON

Saanich Pioneer Society
Mail to: P.O. Box 134, V0S 1M0
Founded in: 1870
M. J. Brethour, President
Questionnaire not received

SALMON ARM

Salmon Arm Museum and Heritage Association
Telephone: (604) 832-6527
Mail to: P.O. Box 1642, V0E 2T0
Town agency
Arvid Kendall, President
Major programs: museum, oral history, book publishing, exhibits, photographic collections
Period of collections: 1900-1925

SAYWARD

Link and Pine Logging and Pioneer Museum
Telephone:(604) 282-3444
Mail to: V0P 1R0
Frances Duncan, Director
Questionnaire not received

SIDNEY

Sidney Military Museum
9831 Fourth St.
Telephone: (604) 656-9004
Mail to: P.O. Box 2051, V8L 3S3
John McLaughlin, Director
Questionnaire not received

Sidney Museum
Old Customs House
Telephone: (604) 656-1322
Mail to: 2538 Beacon Ave., V8L 1Y2
May Utting, Volunteer
Questionnaire not received

SKIDEGATE

Queen Charlotte Islands Museum Society
2nd Beach, Skidegate, Queen Charlotte
Mail to: P.O. Box 1, V0T 1S0
Trisha Gessler, Co-director/Curator
Number of members: 200
Staff: full time 2, part time 4, volunteer 10
Magazine: *The Charlottes: A Journal of the Queen Charlotte Islands*
Major programs: library, archives, museum, school programs, book publishing, newsletters/pamphlets, historic preservation, records management, research, exhibits, archaeology programs, photographic collections
Period of collections: 1780-present

SMITHERS

Bulkley Valley Museum
Central Park Bldg.
Mail to: P.O. Box 2615, V0J 2N0
Private agency
Tom Leach, Curator
Major programs: museum, exhibits
Period of collections: 1910-1950

SOOKE

Sooke Region Museum
2070 Phillips Rd.
Telephone: (604) 642-3121
Mail to: P.O. Box 774, V0S 1N0
Elida Peers, Contact person
Major programs: library, archives, manuscripts, museum, historic site(s), tours/pilgrimages, oral history, school programs, book publishing, research, exhibits, living history, audiovisual programs, photographic collections, genealogical services
Period of collections: 1890-1950

STEWART

Stewart Historical Society
Telephone: (604) 636-2568
Mail to: P.O. Box 690, V0T 1W0
Founded in: 1976
Mary Schindel, President
Number of members: 60
Staff: full time 3, volunteer4
Major programs: museum, historic sites preservation
Period of collections: 1900-present
Questionnaire not received

SUMMERLAND

Summerland Museum and Arts Society
9521 Wharton St.
Telephone: (604) 494-9395/494-1424
Mail to: P.O. Box 1491, V0H 1Z0
Ursula Richardson, Curator
Major programs: archives, museum, school programs, book publishing, exhibits, photographic collections
Period of collections: early 1900s

SURREY

Surrey Museum
17679 60th Ave., V3S 4P5
Telephone: (604) 574-5744
Mail to: P.O. Box 1006, Station A, Cloverdale
Founded in: 1938
D. R. Hooser, Curator
Staff: full time 1, part time 6
Major programs: archives, museum, books, newsletters/pamphlets
Period of collections: 1865-present

TATLA LAKE

Tatla Lake Centennial Museum
Mail to: V0L 1V0
Joyce Graham, Chairman
Questionnaire not received

VANCOUVER

British Columbia Historical Federation
Mail to: P.O. Box 35326, Station E, V6M 4G5

Major programs: newsletters/pamphlets

British Columbia Museum of Medicine
Telephone: (604) 687-2688
Mail to: Academy of Medicine Building, 1807 West 10th Ave., V6J 2A9
C. McDonnel, Director
Questionnaire not received

British Columbia Sports Hall of Fame and Museum
B.C. Pavilion, Pacific National Exhibition
Telephone: (604) 253-5655
Mail to: P.O. Box 69020, Station K, V5K 4W3
Private agency
Founded in: 1966
Marshal L. A. Smith, Executive Director
Staff: full time 4
Magazine: *Newsreview*
Major programs: library, archives, museum, oral history, school programs
Period of collections: 1900-present

Old Hastings Mill Store Museum
Alma Rd. and Jericho Beach
Telephone: (604) 224-3052
Mail to: 1575 Alma Rd., V6R 3P3
Reita Duffy, Chief Factor
Questionnaire not received

Seaforth Highlanders Regimental Museum
Telephone: (604) 738-9510
Mail to: Seaforth Armoury, 1650 Burrard St., V6J 3G4
Fairweather, Curator
Questionnaire not received

Ukrainian Museum of Canada: British Columbia Branch
Telephone: (604) 734-5048
Mail to: 154 East 10th Ave., V5T 1Z4
Mary Polonich, President
Questionnaire not received

Vancouver Historical Society
Telephone: (604) 738-0953
Mail to: P.O. Box 3071, V6B 3X6
Private agency
Founded in: 1925
Peggy Imredy, President
Number of members: 184
Staff: volunteer 17
Magazine: *Vancouver Historical Society Newsletter*
Major programs: tours/pilgrimages, oral history, book publishing, newsletters/pamphlets
Period of collections: 1886-present

Vancouver Maritime Museum
1905 Ogden Ave., V6J 1A3
Telephone: (604) 736-4431
Founded in: 1958
Robin Inglis, Director
Number of members: 3500
Major programs: museum, school programs
Period of collections: 1700-present

Vancouver Museum
1100 Chestnut St., V6J 3J9
Telephone: (604) 736-4431

City agency, authorized by
Vancouver Museums and
Planetarium Association
Founded in: 1968
Robert Watt, Director
Number of members: 3,500
Major programs: museum, school
programs, exhibits
Period of collections: prehistoric-mid
1900s

**West Coast Chinese Canadian
Historical Society**
3184 E. 17th Ave., V5M 2N7
Susan Ann Tong, President
Questionnaire not received

VEDDER CROSSING

**Canadian Military Engineers
Museum**
M.P.O. 612 Canadian Forces Base
Chilliwack, V0X 2E0
Telephone: (604) 858-3311
Founded in: 1956
T. G. Higgins, Museum Liaison
Officer
Staff: volunteer 1
Major programs: library, archives,
museum, historic sites
preservation, tours/pilgrimages,
educational programs
Period of collections: 1783-present

VERNON

Vernon Museum
Telephone: (604) 542-3142
Mail to: 3009 32nd Ave., V1T 2L8
John Shephard, Curator
Questionnaire not received

VICTORIA

**British Columbia Museums
Association**
609 Superior St., V8V 1V1
Telephone: (604) 387-3315/387-3971
Private agency
Founded in: 1959

Rick Duckles, Executive Director
Number of members: 350
Staff: full time 3
Magazine: *Museum Round-Up*
Major programs: archives, museum,
historic site(s),
newsletters/pamphlets

**British Columbia Provincial
Museum**
675 Belleville St., V8V 1X4
Telephone: (604) 387-3701
Provincial agency
Founded in: 1886
William Barkley, Director
Staff: full time 120, volunteer 250
Major programs: library, museum,
school programs, book publishing,
newsletters/pamphlets, historic
preservation, research, exhibits,
audiovisual programs, archaeology
programs, photographic
collections, lectures
Period of collections: 1780s-1980s

Craigflower Heritage Site
110 Island Hwy., V9B 1E9
Telephone: (604) 387-3067
Provincial agency
Founded in: 1967
Staff: full time 2
Major programs: historic site(s),
tours, historic preservation

**Helmcken House Historical
Museum**
Heritage Court
Telephone: (604) 382-2374
Mail to: c/o Provincial Archives,
Parliament Buildings, V8V 1X4
Mrs. M. Pettigrew, Curator
Questionnaire not received

**Heritage Conservation Branch,
Ministry of Provincial Affairs**
Secretary and Government Services,
Parliament Bldgs., V8V 1X4
Telephone: (604) 387-1011
Provincial agency
Russell J. Irvine, Director

Staff: full time 40
Major programs: library, historic
site(s), markers, historic
preservation, research,
archaeology programs, field
services

**Maritime Museum of British
Columbia**
28 Bastion Square, V8W 1H9
Telephone: (604) 385-4222
Private agency
Founded in: 1955
C. H. Shaw, Director
Number of members: 3,000
Staff: full time 5, part time 2,
volunteer 30
Magazine: *The Resolution*
Major programs: library, archives,
museum, school programs,
newsletters/pamphlets, exhibits,
photographic collections
Period of collections: 1783-present

Metchosin School Museum
611 Happy Valley Rd., R.R. 1
Telephone: (604) 478-2627
Mail to: c/o K. L. Leeming, 505 Witty
Beach Rd., R.R. 1, V8X 3W9
Julian Rapps, Curator
Questionnaire not received

Point Ellice House Museum
Telephone: (604) 385-3837
Mail to: 2616 Pleasant St., V8T 4V3
Provincial agency, authorized by
Heritage Conservation Branch
Michael Zarb, Curator
Major programs: historic site(s),
historic preservation
Period of collections: 1860-1914

**Provincial Archives of British
Columbia**
655 Belleville St.
Telephone: (604) 387-5885
Mail to: Parliament Bldgs., V8V 1X4
Provincial agency, authorized by
Ministry of Provincial Secretary and
Government Services
Founded in: 1893
John A. Bovey, Provincial Archivist
Staff: full time 39, part time 1
Major programs: library, archives,
manuscripts, oral history, exhibits,
photographic collections
Period of collections: 18th-20th
centuries

WAGLISLA (BELLA BELLA)

Heiltsuk Cultural Education Centre
Kumanukla St.
Telephone: (604) 957-2626
Mail to: General Delivery, V0T 1Z0
County agency, authorized by
Heiltsuk Tribal Council
Founded in: 1974
Jennifer G. Carpenter, Coordinator
Staff: full time 4, part time 3,
volunteer 10
Major programs: library, archives,
manuscripts, museum, historic
site(s), markers, oral history, school
programs, newsletters/pamphlets,
historic preservation, records
management, research, exhibits,
audiovisual programs, archaeology
programs, photographic
collections, genealogical services,

Hairy mammoth, an exhibit at the British Columbia Provincial Museum in Victoria.—British
Columbia Provincial Museum

field services, native language research and studies
Period of collections: 10,000 B.P.-present

WELLS

Wells Museum and Sunset Theatre
Pooley St.
Telephone: (604) 994-3349
Mail to: P.O. Box 244, V0K 2R0
Private agency, authorized by Wells Historical Society
Major programs: museum, historic preservation
Period of collections: 1930-1967

WHITE ROCK

City of White Rock Museum and Archives
Former Post Office Bldg.
Telephone: (604) 531-5628
Mail to: 1010 Martin St., V4B 5E3
Lorraine Ellenwood, Curator
Major programs: museum
Period of collections: from 1880

WILLIAMS LAKE

Williams Lake Museum
Cariboo Hwy. S
Telephone: (604) 392-5573
Mail to: c/o Reg Beck, R.R. 2, Fox Mountain, V2G 2P2
Reg Beck, Director
Questionnaire not received

MANITOBA

ANOLA

Anola and District Community Museum
Telephone: (204) 866-2271
Mail to: c/o Mrs. W. Kruchak, R0E 0A0
Mrs. W. Kruchak, Secretary
Questionnaire not received

AUSTIN

Manitoba Agricultural Museum
Telephone: (204) 637-2354
Mail to: P.O. Box 10, R0H 0C0
William Moncur, Administrator
Questionnaire not received

BEAUSEJOUR

Broken-Beau Historical Society Museum Village Complex
Brokenhead Centennial Park
Telephone: (204) 268-1835/268-1045
Mail to: c/o Peter Kozyra, P.O. Box 310, R0E 0C0
Rose Zielke, Secretary-Treasurer
Questionnaire not received

BOISSEVAIN

Beckoning Hills Museum
Telephone: (204) 534-6544
Mail to: P.O. Box, 670 R0K 0E0
Town agency
Mrs. E. Brake, Contact person

BRANDON

Brandon Museum
Telephone: (204) 727-1722/ 727-4119
Mail to: 122 18th St., R7A 5A4
City agency
Glen Olmstead, President
Major programs: archives, museum, newsletters/pamphlets, exhibits, photographic collections
Period of collections: 1890-1920

CARBERRY

Carberry Plains Museum
520 4th Ave.
Telephone: (204) 834-2195/834-2797
Mail to: P.O. Box 130, R0K 0H0
Town agency
R. W. Hadley, Chair
Major programs: archives, museum, exhibits
Period of collections: 1880

CARMAN

Dufferin Historical Museum
Kings Park
Telephone: (204) 745-2742/ 745-3507
Mail to: P.O. Box 426, R0G 0J0
L. Shilson, Chairman
Questionnaire not received

CARTWRIGHT

Badger Creek Museum
Telephone: (204) 529-2339
Mail to: c/o A. E. Thompson, R0K 0L0
A. Thompson, Contact person
Questionnaire not received

Cartwright Museum
Centennial Park
Telephone: (204) 529-2363
Mail to: Municipality of Roblin, P.O. Box 9, R0K 0L0
H. Lamb, Contact person
Questionnaire not received

CHURCHILL

Eskimo Museum
LaVerendrye St., R0B 0E0
Telephone: (204) 675-2252
Mail to: P.O. Box 10
Founded in: 1944
Bishop Omer Robidoux, Director
Staff: full time 1, part time 1
Major programs: archives, museum
Period of collections: prehistoric-present

COOKS CREEK

Cook's Creek Heritage Museum
Hwy. 212, Cooks Creek
Telephone: (204) 444-2248
Mail to: R.R. 2, Dugald, R0E 0K0
Alois Krivanek, Director
Major programs: archives, museum, tours/pilgrimages
Period of collections: 1880-1930

CYPRESS RIVER

Cypress River Historical Museum
Telephone: (204) 743-2046
Mail to: P.O. Box 10, R0K 0P0
Louise Chriscie, Director
Questionnaire not received

DAUPHIN

Dauphin Historical Society
R.R. 1, Sifton, R0L 1X0
Telephone: (204) 655-3250
Mail to: c/o Arnold J. Zihrul
Questionnaire not received

DELORAINE

Deloraine Museum
North Railway St.
Telephone: (204) 747-2679/747-2626
Mail to: P.O. Box 342, R0M 0M0
Doris Combs, Staff
Questionnaire not received

DUFRESNE

Aunt Margaret's Museum of Childhood
Telephone: (204) 422-8426
Mail to: General Delivery, R0A 0J0
Margaret Emke-Chisholm, Director/Curator
Questionnaire not received

EDDYSTONE

Village Site Museum
Telephone: (204) 448-2188
Mail to: R0L 0S0
J. Johnson, Director
Questionnaire not received

ELKHORN

Manitoba Automobile Museum
Telephone: (204) 845-2559
Mail to: P.O. Box 235, R0M 0N0
W. Bartley, Chairman
Questionnaire not received

EMERSON

Gateway Stopping Place Museum
Telephone: (204) 373-2721
Mail to: c/o Jessie Johnston, R0A 0L0
Mrs. L. McClelland, Director
Questionnaire not received

ERIKSDALE

Eriksdale Museum
Railway Ave. S
Telephone: (204) 739-5408
Mail to: P.O. Box 13, R0C 0W0
Lucy Lindell, Chairperson
Questionnaire not received

FLIN FLON

Flin Flon Community Archives
58 Main St., R8A 1J8
Telephone: (204) 687-3397
City agency, authorized by the Flin Flon Public Library
Founded in: 1984
Tracy Nilsen, Archivist
Staff: full time 1, part time 2
Major programs: archives, manuscripts, photographic collections
Period of collections: 1915-1940

GILLAM

Gillam Community Museum
Gillam School
Telephone: (204) 652-2193
Mail to: c/o Mrs. B. Winner, P.O. Box 393, R0B 0L0

Mrs. B. Winner, Contact person
Questionnaire not received

GIMLI

Gimli Historical Museum
1st Ave.
Telephone: (204) 642-5317
Mail to: P.O. Box 1200, R0C 1B0
Stefen Stefanson, Contact person
Major programs: archives, museum
Period of collections: 1875-1900

GLADSTONE

Gladstone Museum
Telephone: (204) 385-2138/ 385-2020
Mail to: P.O. Box 81, R0J 0I0
Mrs. C. Boyd, Chair

GRANDVIEW

Watson Crossley Community Museum
Railway Ave. N
Telephone: (204) 546-2040,
546-2598
Mail to: c/o Vivian Grexton, P.O. Box
342, R0L 0Y0
Questionnaire not received

HAMIOTA

Hamiota Pioneer Club Museum
Centennial Park
Telephone: (204)
764-2108/764-2332/764-2038
Mail to: P.O. Box 44, R0M 0T0
James Routledge, President
Questionnaire not received

KILLARNEY

J. A. Victor David Museum
414 Williams Ave.
Mail to: P.O. Box 1047, R0K 1G0
Charles Baskerville, Director

LA BROQUERIE

Musée Saint Joachim
Telephone: (204) 424-5356
Mail to: R0A 0W0
Léonie Granger, Director
Period of collections: 1900-1950

MARRINGHURST PARK

Marringhurst Pioneer Park Museum
Marringhurst Park
Telephone: (204) 825-2571
Mail to: R.R. 2, Pilot Mound, R0G 1P0
Lloyd Nelson, Contact person

MELITA

Antler River Historical Society Museum
Telephone: (204) 522-3418
Mail to: c/o Antler River Historical
Society, R0M 1L0
K. Williams, President
Questionnaire not received

MIAMI

Miami Museum
3rd St.
Mail to: c/o Shirley Watchorn, P.O.
Box 54, R0G 1H0
Shirley Watchorn, President
Questionnaire not received

Miami Station Museum
3rd St.
Telehone: (204) 475-7725
Mail to: c/o Midwestern Rail
Association, Box 1855, Winnipeg,
R3C 3R1
Shirley Watchorn, Director
Questionnaire not received

MINIOTA

Miniota Municipal Museum, Inc.
Government Rd., Hwy. 83
Telephone: (204) 567-3675
Mail to: P.O. Box 189, R0M 1M0
Glen Cameron, Chair
Major programs: museum,
tours/pilgrimages, junior history,
oral history, school programs,
records management, exhibits,
archaeology programs,
photographic collections
Period of collections: 1850-1950

MINNEDOSA

**Minnedosa and District
Co-Operative Museum**
Telephone: (204) 867-3444
Mail to: P.O. Box 312, R0J 1E0
Mrs. Ericson, President

MOOSEHORN

Moosehorn Museum
1st Ave. E
Telephone: (204) 768-2542/768-2178
Mail to: P.O. Box 27, R0C 2E0
Myrtle Buechler, President
Questionnaire not received

MORDEN

Morden District Museum
Recreation Centre, 2nd St. N
Telephone: (204) 822-3406/822-3764
Mail to: P.O. Box 728, R0G 1J0
Henry Isaak, Director
Questionnaire not received

NEEPAWA

Beautiful Plains Museum
Viscount Cultural Centre
Telephone: (204) 476-2185/476-5165
Mail to: c/o Mrs. M. Ishenberg,
General Delivery
Mrs. M. Ishenberg, Secretary
Questionnaire not received

PILOT MOUND

Pilot Mound Centennial Museum
Telephone: (204) 825-2394
Mail to: Centennial Building,
Broadway St., R0G 1P0
William Ross, Curator

PORTAGE LA PRAIRIE

**Fort La Reine Museum and Pioneer
Village**
Hwy. 1A E. and Hwy. 26, R1N 3C4
Telephone: (204) 857-3259
Mail to: P.O. Box 744
Founded in: 1967
Victor C. H. Stuart, Manager
Questionnaire not received

RAPID CITY

Rapid City Museum
4th Ave.

Telephone: (204) 820-2630
Mail to: P.O. Box 211, R0K 1W0
Town agency
M. Stefaniuk, President

RESTON

**Reston and District Historical
Museum**
9th St.
Telephone: (204) 877-3933/
877-3320
Mail to: P.O. Box 304, R0M 1X0
County agency, authorized by
Museum Board of Directors
Founded in: 1967
David Braddell, Researcher
Number of members: 50
Staff: part time 2, volunteer 1
Major programs: museum,
photographic collections
Period of collections: 1890-1930

Archibald Historical Museum
Telephone: (204) 242-2825
Mail to: P.O. Box 97, R0G 1A0
W. Wallcraft, Director

ROBLIN

Keystone Pioneer Museum
Telephone: (204) 937-2935
Mail to: P.O. Box 10, R0L 1P0
Art McIntyre, President
Major programs: museum, junior
history

ST. ANDREWS

Red River House Museum
Telephone: (204) 489-8228/
338-7707
Mail to: c/o 1705 Corydon Ave.,
Winnipeg, R3N 0J9
Edward Shaw, Director

SAINT-BONIFACE

**La Société historique de
Saint-Boniface**
200 Ave. de la Cathédrale, R2H 0H7
Telephone: (204) 233-4888
Mail to: C. P. 125, R2H 3B4
Founded in: 1907
Gilles Lesage, Director
Number of members: 250
Staff: full time 1, part time 2,
volunteer 10
Major programs: library, archives,
manuscripts, museum, book
publishing, newsletters/
pamphlets, research, exhibits,
photographic collections,
genealogical services
Period of collections: 1700-present

ST. CLAUDE

St. Claude Museum
Telephone: (204) 379-2084
Mail to: St. Claude Historical Society,
P.O. Box 304, R0G 1Z0
Arthur Rey, President
Questionnaire not received

SAINT-GEORGES

Musée Saint-Georges
Telephone: (204) 367-2927
Mail to: a/s La Société historique, R0E
1V0
Jean Dupont, Conservateur
Questionnaire not received

SAINT-JOSEPH

Musée Saint-Joseph
Telephone: (204) 737-2241/737-2369
Mail to: a/s Jean-Louis Perron, C.P.
47, R0G 2C0
Jean-Louis Perron, President
Questionnaire not received

SAINTE-ANNE

Musée Pointe des Chênes
Telephone: (204) 422-5207
Mail to: R0A 1R0
Eugène Voyer, Director
Questionnaire not received

SELKIRK

Lower Ft. Garry National Historic Park
Telephone: (204) 482-6843
Mail to: P.O. Box 7, Group 342, R.R. 3,
R1A 2A8
National agency, authorized by Parks
Canada, Department of
Environment
Major programs: historic site(s),
tours/pilgrimages, school
programs, newsletters/pamphlets,
historic preservation, exhibits,
living history, audiovisual programs
Period of collections: 1850-1860

Marine Museum of Manitoba
Selkirk Park
Telephone: (204) 482-7761
Mail to: 6-305 Mercy Ave., R1A 2E3
Mrs. Pat Surtee, Chairperson

SHILO

Royal Canadian Artillery Museum
Bldgs. C-2 and C-4
Telephone: (204) 765-2282
Major programs: library, archives,
museum, tours/pilgrimages,
historic preservation, records
management, research, exhibits,
photographic collections
Period of collections: 1796-present

SHOAL LAKE

Spruce Haven Museum
Lakeside Park
Telephone: (204) 759-2270
Mail to: c/o Mrs. I. Smith, P.O. Box
118, R0J 1Z0
Questionnaire not received

SNOWFLAKE

Star Mound School Museum
Telephone: (204) 876-4749
Mail to: R0G 2K0
County agency
Harry Goerz, President
Major programs: archives, museum,
historic site(s), historic
preservation, living history

SOURIS

Hillcrest Museum
266 Crescent E
Telephone: (204) 483-2008/483-3087
Mail to: P.O. Box 430, R0K 2C0
William Thompson, Contact person
Questionnaire not received

STEINBACH

Mennonite Village Museum, Inc.
Telephone: (204) 326-9661
Mail to: P.O. Box 1136, R0A 2A0
Founded in: 1962
Peter Goertzen, Manager/Curator
Number of members: 150
Staff: full time 1, part time 30,
volunteer 100
Major programs: school programs,
living history
Period of collections: 1865-1918

STRATHCLAIR

Strathclair Museum
Main St.
Telephone: (204) 365-2558
Mail to: P.O. Box 160, R0J 2C0
K. Rapley, Secretary-Treasurer
Questionnaire not received

SWAN RIVER

Swan River Valley Historical Society and Museum
P.O. Box 397, R0L 1Z0
Telephone: (204) 734-3585
County agency, authorized by Swan
River Valley Historical Society, Inc.
Founded in: 1970
Number of members: 100
Major programs: library, archives,
museum, markers,
tours/pilgrimages, oral history,
school programs, book publishing,
newsletters/pamphlets, historic
preservation, records
management, research, exhibits,
living history, photographic
collections

Swan Valley Museum
Telephone: (204) 734-2504
Mail to: P.O. Box 806, R0L 1Z0
Private agency
J. A. Dubreuil, President
Major programs: museum, historic
site(s), markers
Period of collections: 1895-present

TEULON

Teulon and District Museum
Owen Acres Park
Mail to: c/o Mary Revel, P.O. Box 197,
R0C 3B0
Kay Madill, President
Questionnaire not received

THE PAS

Pas Historical and Heritage Society, Inc.
15 Trager Dr.
Telephone: (204) 623-2337
Mail to: P.O. Box 547, R9A 1R6
Founded in: 1977
Sydney J. Allen, President
Number of members: 20
Staff: volunteer 20
Major programs: archives, historic
site(s), junior history, oral history,
book publishing, research, living
history, photographic collections
Period of collections: 1691-1950

Sam Waller Little Northern Museum
1359 Gordon Ave.
Telephone: (204) 623-3802

Mail to: P.O. Box 185, R9A 1K4
Town agency
Paul C. Thistle, Curator
Major programs: museum, school
programs, newsletters/pamphlets,
exhibits, photographic collections
Period of collections: 1930-1978

TREHERNE

Treherne Museum
Vanzile St.
Telephone: (204) 723-2621/723-2044
Mail to: P.O. Box 30, R0G 2V0
Phyllis Lee, Custodian
Questionnaire not received

VIRDEN

Pioneer Home Museum of Virden and District
390 King St., W
Telephone: (204) 748-1659/ 748-2740
Mail to: P.O. Box 2001, R0M 2C0
Town agency
Ruth Craik, Chair
Period of collections: 1884-1915

WASKADA

Waskada Museum
Railway Ave.
Telephone: (204) 673-2450
Mail to: c/o Mrs. H. Lowe, P.O. Box
59, R0M 2E0

WHITEMOUTH

Whitemouth Municipal Museum
Whitemouth Community Grounds
Telephone: (204) 348-2576
Mail to: P.O. Box 187, R0E 2G0
C. MacKenzie, Chairman

WINKLER

Pembina Thresherman's Museum
Telephone: (204) 325-8208
Mail to: P.O. Box 1103, R0G 2X0
George Rempel, President

WINNIPEG

Aquatic Hall of Fame and Museum of Canada
Pan-Am Pool, 25 Poseidon Bay
Telephone: (204) 947-0131
Mail to: 436 Main St., R3B 1B2
Vaughan Baird, Chair

Association of Manitoba Museums
c/o 190 Rupert St., R3B 0N2
Telephone (204) 943-3844
Timothy Worth, President
Questionnaire not received

Center for Mennonite Brethren Studies in Canada
77 Henderson Hwy., R2L 1L1
Telephone: (204) 667-9560
Founded in: 1976
Kenneth W. Reddig, Archivist
Questionnaire not received

Dalnavert (Macdonald House Museum)
Telephone: (204) 943-2835
Mail to: 61 Carlton St., R3C 1N7
Private agency
Tim Worth, Curator
Major programs: museum, school
programs, historic preservation
Period of collections: late Victorian

Fire Fighters Historical Society of Winnipeg, Inc.
151 Princess St., 5th Floor, R3B 1L1
Telephone: (204) 985-6369
Private agency
Founded in: 1982
J. T. Coulter, President
Number of members: 300
Staff: volunteer 11
Major programs: archives, manuscripts, museum, historic preservation, exhibits, photographic collections, preservation of fire apparatus and equipment

Ft. Garry Historical Society
650 Riverwood Ave., R3T 1K4
Telephone: (204) 452-6889
Private agency
W.O.S. Meredith, President
Major programs: library, archives, oral history, historic preservation, research
Period of collections: 1850-1912

Fort Garry Horse Regimental Museum
Telephone: (204) 582-5003
Mail to: McGregor Armoury, R2W 1A8
Brian McKinley, Commanding Officer

Grant's Old Mill
Corner Portage Ave. and Booth Dr., Sturgeon Creek Park
Telephone: (204) 885-6397
Mail to: c/o Inspector Dick Moore, 384 Lyle St., R3J 2C5
Inspector Dick Moore, Chairman of the Board
Questionnaire not received

German-Canadian Historical Association, Inc.
193 Wildwood Park, R3T 0E2
Founded in: 1973
D. Roger, Director
Number of members: 100
Staff: volunteer 10
Magazine: *Canadiana Germanica*
Major programs: library, archives, manuscripts, tours/pilgrimages, educational programs, books, newsletters/pamphlets
Period of collections: 1600-present

Heritage Winnipeg, Inc.
131 Letinsky Place, R3B 1G6
Telephone: (204) 942-2663
Private agency
Founded in: 1979
George Siamandas, Special Projects Director
Number of members: 24
Staff: full time 2, volunteer 5
Major programs: tours/pilgrimages, school programs, newsletters/pamphlets, historic preservation, exhibits, audiovisual programs, advocacy for supportive public policy
Period of collections: 1880-1920

Historic Resources Branch
177 Lombard Ave., 3rd Floor, R3B 0W5
Telephone: (204) 945-3844
Provincial agency
Founded in: 1974
Staff: full time 25, part time 7

Major programs: library, historic site(s), markers, tours/pilgrimages, book publishing, newsletters/pamphlets, historic preservation, records management, research, archaeology programs, photographic collections, field services, heritage resource management
Period of collections: prehistoric-present

Historical Museum of St. James-Assiniboia
Telephone: (204) 888-8706
Mail to: 3180 Portage Ave., R3K 0Y5
Walter Bannister, Curator

Ivan Franko Museum
200 McGregor St., R2W 5L6
Telephone: (204) 586-3594
Private agency
Anthony Bilecki, Director
Major programs: library, museum, exhibits
Period of collections: 1800-present

Jewish Historical Society of Western Canada, Inc.
404-365 Hargrave St., R3B 2K3
Telephone: (204) 942-4822
Founded in: 1968
Dorothy Hershfield, Executive Director
Staff: full time 2
Magazine: *Jewish Life and Times*
Major programs: archives, manuscripts, oral history, book publishing, newsletters/pamphlets, research, exhibits, photographic collections
Period of collections: early 1900s-present

Legislative Library
200 Vaughan St., R3C 1T5
Telephone: (204) 945-4330
Staff: full time 18
Major programs: library, historic preservation
Period of collections: 1870-present

Living Prairie Museum Park
Telephone: (204) 832-0167
Mail to: 2795 Ness Ave., R3J 3S4
City agency
Doug Ross, Chief Naturalist
Major programs: school programs, newsletters/pamphlets, exhibits, audiovisual programs, nature preserve of unique vegetation

Lord Selkirk Association of Rupert's Land
401-333 Wellington Crescent, R3M 0A1
Telephone: (204) 453-3742
Private agency
Founded in: 1908
Number of members: 230
Major programs: genealogical services
Period of collections: from 1812

Manitoba Historical Society
R3B 0N2
Telephone: (204) 947-0559
Founded in: 1879
Moira Jones, Executive Director
Number of members: 800

Staff: full time 3, part time 2, volunteer 56
Magazine: *Manitoba History*
Major programs: museum, historic site(s), tours, junior history, oral history, school programs, book publishing, newsletters/pamphlets

Manitoba Museum of Man and Nature
190 Rupert, R3B 0N2
Telephone: (204) 956-2830
Provincial agency
Founded in: 1965
H. D. Hemphill, Executive Director
Number of members: 450
Staff: full time 69, part time 40, volunteer 136
Magazine: *Locus*
Major programs: library, museum, tours/pilgrimages, school programs, book publishing, newsletters/pamphlets, research, exhibits
Period of collections: prehistoric-present

Mennonite Heritage Centre
600 Shaftesbury Blvd., R3P 0M4
Telephone: (204) 888-6781
Private agency, authorized by Conference of Mennonites in Canada
Founded in: 1933
Dennis Stoesz, Archivist
Staff: full time 2
Magazine: *Mennonite Historian*
Major programs: library, archives, manuscripts, newsletters/pamphlets, records management, exhibits, photographic collections, genealogical services
Period of collections: 1750-present

Provincial Archives of Manitoba
200 Vaughan St., R3C 1T5
Telephone: (204) 945-4233
Provincial agency
Founded in: 1885
Peter Bower, Provincial Archivist
Staff: full time 36, part time 1, volunteer 12
Major programs: archives, manuscripts, oral history, records management, research, exhibits, photographic collections, genealogical services, field service, conservation
Period of collections: from 1670

Queen's Own Cameron Highlanders Museum
Telephone: (204) 783-4610
Mail to: Room 219, Minto Armoury, 969 St. Matthew's St., R3G 0J7
Ian McGregor, Contact person
Questionnaire not received

Ross House Museum
Meade St., Point Douglas
Telephone: (204) 947-0559
Mail to: 190 Rupert Blvd., R3B 0N2
Authorized by Manitoba Historical Society
Founded in: 1879
Moira Jones, Executive Director
Number of members: 800
Staff: volunteer 6
Major programs: museum
Period of collections: 1854-1890

Seven Oaks-House Museum
Rupertsland Ave., West Kildonan
Telephone: (204) 339-7429
Mail to: 1760 Main St., R2V 1Z7
M. Johnson, Contact person
Questionnaire not received

Transcona Regional History Museum
141 Regent Ave. W
Telephone: (204) 222-0423
Mail to: c/o 131 St. Claire Blvd., R2C 0V5
Founded in: 1968
Mrs. L. T. Patterson, Curator
Questionnaire not received

Ukrainian Cultural and Educational Centre
184 Alexander Avenue, E, R3B 0L6
Telephone: (204) 942-0218
Founded in: 1944
Mrs. Motria Kydon, Administrator
Questionnaire not received

Ukrainian Free Academy of Sciences Historical Museum
Telephone: (204) 942-5861
Mail to: 202-456 Main St., R3B 0N2
Jaroslav Rozumnyi, Director

Western Canada Aviation Museum
11 Lily St.
Telephone: (204) 943-9053
Mail to: P.O. Box 99, Station C, R3M 3S6
G. Emberley, Executive Director

WINDSOR

Essex County Historical Association
University of Windsor, N9B 3P4
Telephone: (519) 253-4232
L.L. Kulisek, Head, Department of History
Questionnaire not received

Hiram Walker Historical Museum
254 Pitt St. W, N9A 5L5
Telephone: (519) 253-1812
Founded in: 1958
R. Alan Douglas, Curator
Questionnaire not received

WOODLANDS

Woodlands Pioneer Museum
Telephone: (204) 383-5522
Mail to: c/o Hazel Procter, R0C 3H0
Lloyd Procter, Director

WOODSTOCK

Oxford Museum
City Square, N4S 1C4
Telephone: (519) 537-8411
Founded in: 1947
Don Milton, Curator
Questionnaire not received

NEW BRUNSWICK

AULAC

Ft. Beausejour National Historic Park
E0A 3C0
Telephone: (506) 536-0720
National agency
Founded in: 1926
Steven C. Ridlington, Officer-In-Charge
Staff: full time 7
Major programs: visitor center, historic sites preservation, historic preservation
Period of collections: 1750-1900

BARTIBOG

MacDonald Farm Historic Park
Telephone: (506) 453-2324
Mail to: P.O. Box 6000, Fredericton, E3B 5H1
Provincial agency, authorized by Department of Historical and Cultural Resources
Major programs: historic site(s), living history
Period of collections: 1820-1850

BERTRAND

Société Historique Nicolas Denys
Site 19, C.P.6, E0B 1J0
Telephone: (506) 727-2059
County agency
Founded in: 1969
Laura Pinet, Secretary
Number of members: 380
Magazine: La Revue d'Histoire
Major programs: archives, historic site(s), newsletters/pamphlets
Period of collections: 1850-1950

BOIESTOWN

Central New Brunswick Woodmen's Museum
Rt. 8
Telephone: (506) 369-7214
Mail to: P.O. Box 7, E0H 1A0
Private agency
Francis Smith, Board President
Major programs: museum
Period of collections: late 1800s-early 1900s

CAMPOBELLO ISLAND

Roosevelt Campobello International Park Commission
Welshpool, E0G 3H0
Telephone: (506) 752-2922
Mail to: P.O. Box 97, Lubec, Maine, 04652
Federal agency
Founded in: 1964
Henry W. Stevens, Executive Secretary
Staff: full time 22, part time 22
Major programs: museum, historic site(s), oral history, newsletters/pamphlets, historic preservation, research, exhibits, audiovisual programs
Period of collections: 1883-1945

CARAQUET

Acadian Historical Village
CP 820, E0B 1K0
Telephone: (506) 727-3467
Founded in: 1974
Clarence LeBreton, Chief Curator
Staff: full time 28, part time 80
Major programs: educational programs, historic preservation
Period of collections: 1780-1880

Association des Familles Landry d'Amérique
C.P. 942, E0B 1K0
Telephone: (506) 727-2340
Private agency
Founded in: 1974
Gertrude Landry, President
Number of members: 200
Staff: volunteer 5
Major programs: archives, historic site(s), book publishing, newsletters/pamphlets, research, archaeology programs, photographic collections, genealogical services
Period of collections: 1755

Musée Acadien
15 Blvd. St. Pierre, E
Telephone: (506) 727-3189
Mail to: C.P. 420, E0B 1K0
Town agency
Founded in: 1967
Mrs. Graham LeBlanc, Town Clerk
Staff: part time 2
Major programs: museum

CHATHAM

Miramichi Natural History Association Museum
149 Wellington St.
Telephone: (506) 778-8006
Mail to: 75 McIntosh St., EIN 2B5
Town agency
Founded in: 1898
G. W. LeBlanc, Curator
Number of members: 20
Staff: volunteer 1
Period of collections: 1782

St. Michael's Museum Association, Inc.
10 Howard St., E1N 3A7
Telephone: (506) 773-4497
Private agency: authorized by St. Michael's Church
Founded in: 1974
B. M. Broderick, President
Number of members: 30
Staff: part time 1
Major programs: archives, manuscripts, museum, historic site(s), records management, research, photographic collections, genealogical services
Period of collections: 1800-present

CLIFTON ROYAL

Peninsula Heritage, Inc.
R.R. 1, E0G 1N0
Telephone: (506) 763-2970
Founded in: 1973
Mrs. George D. Hamilton, Secretary
Questionnaire not received

COLLEGE BRIDGE

Keillor House Museum
Telephone: (506) 379-6633
Mail to: R.R. 1, E0A 1L0
County agency, authorized by
  Westmorland Historical Society
Wayne Gillcash, President
Major programs: museum, tours,
  newsletters, historic preservation
Period of collections: 1813-1850

DALHOUSIE

Chalaeur Area Historical Research Society
Adelaide and George Sts., E0K 1B0
Telephone: (506) 684-4685
Mail to: P.O. Box 1717
Founded in: 1967
Mrs. Gary Archibald, President
Questionnaire not received

Restigouche Regional Museum
437 George St.
Telephone: (506) 684-4685
Mail to: P.O. Box 1717, E0K 1B0
Town agency, authorized by Chaleur
  Area Historical Society, Inc.
Founded in: 1962
Michelle Guitard, President
Staff: part time 1, volunteer 3
Major programs: museum, school
  programs, exhibits, genealogical
  services

DOAKTOWN

Central Miramichi Historical Society
E0C 1G0
Telephone: (506) 365-4677
Founded in: 1973
Joyce Charters, President
Number of members: 20
Major programs: manuscripts,
  museum, historic sites
  preservation, oral history
Period of collections: 1865-1918

Doak Historic Park
P.O. Box 38, E0C 1G0
Telephone: (506) 365-7919
Provincial agency, authorized by

Central Miramichi Historical
  Society, Inc.
Founded in: 1982
Wendy Robb, Curator
Staff: part time 4
Major programs: archives, historic
  site(s), tours/pilgrimages, living
  history
Period of collections: 1820-1900

DORCHESTER

Westmorland Historical Society—Keillor House Museum
E0A 1M0
Telephone: (506) 379-2205
County agency
Founded in: 1960
Mrs. M. Yeoman, Museum Chair
Number of members: 75
Staff: volunteer 2
Major programs: museum, historic
  site(s), newsletters/pamphlets,
  historic preservation, genealogical
  services
Period of collections: 1774-1900

EDMUNDSTON

Musée historique du Madawaska
195, boulevard Hébert
Telephone: (506) 453-2636/739-7254
Mail to: c/o Department of Historical
  Resources, P.O. Box 6000,
  Fredericton, E3V 5H1
Jean Pelletier, Conservateur

Société Historique du Madawaska, Inc.
C.P. 474, E3V 3L1
Private agency
Founded in: 1970
Jacques Albert, President
Number of members: 500
Staff: volunteer 8
Major programs: archives, museum,
  historic site(s), markers,
  photographic collections
Period of collections: from 1900

FREDERICTON

Archives and Special Collections, Harriet Irving Library
University of New Brunswick

Telephone: (506) 453-4748
Mail to: P.O. Box 7500, E3B 5H5
Provincial agency, authorized by the
  university
Founded in: 1931
Mary Flagg, Manager/Research
  Officer
Staff: full time 5, part time 1
Major programs: archives,
  manuscripts, oral history, research
Period of collections: 19th century

Diocese of Fredericton Archives
808 Brunswick St., E3B 1J1
Telephone: (506) 454-1006
Private agency
Alec Craig, Registrar
Major programs: library, archives,
  manuscripts, historic preservation
Period of collections: late
  1700s-present

Fredericton National Exhibition Centre
503 Queen St., E3B 1B8
Telephone: (506) 453-3747
Mail to: P.O. Box 6000, E3B 5H1
Provincial agency
Founded in: 1976
Linda Kelly-Quinlan, Acting Curator
Staff: full time 3, part time 3
Major programs: school programs,
  research, exhibits

Guard House and Barrack Room
Queen and Carleton Sts.
Telephone: (506) 453-3747
Mail to: P.O. Box 6000, E3B 5H1
Provincial agency
Founded in: 1971 (Guard House);
  1978 (Barrack Room)
Linda Kelly-Quinlan, Acting Curator
Staff: full time 3, part time 3
Major programs: museum, historic
  site(s)
Period of collections: 1860s

Kings Landing Corporation—Kings Landing Historical Settlement, Prince William
Telephone: (506) 363-3081
Mail to: P.O. Box 522
Provincial agency
Founded in: 1974
Paul Chalifour, General Manager
Staff: full time 35, part time 140
Major programs: museum, historic
  sites preservation, educational
  programs, newsletters/pamphlets
Period of collections: 1783-1890

New Brunswick Genealogical Society
P.O. Box 3235, Station B, E3A 5G9
Private agency
Founded in: 1978
Janice Dexter, President
Number of members: 600
Staff: volunteer 8
Magazine: *Generations*
Major programs: library, book
  publishing, genealogical services

New Brunswick Sports Hall of Fame
503 Queen St., E3B 1B8
Telephone: (506) 453-3747
Mail to: P.O. Box 6000, E3B 5H1
Provincial agency
Founded in: 1970

Musée historique du Madawaska in Edmunston.—Musée Madawaska Museum

Linda Kelly-Quinlan, Acting Curator
Staff: full time 3, part time 3
Major programs: library, archives,
    museum, local sports history
Period of collections: from 1900

**Provincial Archives of New
Brunswick**
University of New Brunswick
Telephone: (506) 453-2122
Mail to: P.O. Box 6000, E3B 5H1
Provincial agency
Founded in: 1968
Mrs. Marion Beyea, Provincial
    Archivist
Number of members: 1
Staff: full time 26, volunteer 4
Major programs: archives,
    manuscripts, records management
Period of collections: 1784-present

**Société d'histoire de la rivière
Saint-Jean de
Fredericton**
715 Priestman St., E3B 5W7
Private agency
Founded in: 1981
Bernard Poirier, President
Number of members: 70
Staff: volunteer 10
Magazine: Le Petit Courrier
Major programs: archives,
    manuscripts,
    newsletters/pamphlets, research
Period of collections: 1630-1770

York-Sunbury Historical Society
Officer's Square, Queen St.
Telephone: (506) 455-6041
Mail to: P.O. Box 1312, E3B 5C8
Private agency
Founded in: 1932
Lori Pauli, Museum Curator
Number of members: 150
Staff: full time 1, part time 3,
    volunteer 3
Major programs: museum,
    tours/pilgrimages, educational
    programs, books
Period of collections: 1784-1900

GAGETOWN

Queens County Museum
Rt. 102
Telephone: (506) 488-2966/488-2400
Mail to: E0G 1V0
Patricia Jenkins, Director
Questionnaire not received

GRAND FALLS

**Grand Falls Historical
Society, Inc.—Société Historique
de Grand Sault, Inc.**
209 Sheriff St.
Telephone: (506) 473-3705
Mail to: P.O. Box 1572, E0J 1M0
Private agency
Founded in: 1958
John H. Hughes, President/Museum
    Director
Number of members: 20
Major programs: archives, museum,
    oral history, research, exhibits,
    photographic collections,
    genealogical services
Period of collections: 1800s

GRAND MANAN

**Grand Manan Museum and Walter
B. McLaughlan Marine Gallery**
Telephone: (506) 662-8216
Mail to: P.O. Box 66, Grand Harbour,
    E0G 1X0
Eric Allaby, Curator
Questionnaire not received

HAMPTON

**Kings County Historical and
Archival Society, Inc.**
Centennial Bldg., E0G 1Z0
Telephone: (506) 433-3244
Mail to: Sussex Corner, E0E 1R0
Private agency, authorized by Kings
    County Historical Society
Founded in: 1968
W. Harvey Dalling, Curator
Number of members: 250
Staff: full time 1, part time 2,
    volunteer 5
Major programs: library, archives,
    museum, school programs, book
    publishing, newsletters/pamphlets,
    research
Period of collections: from 1783

HILLSBOROUGH

Hon. William Henry Steeves Home
24 Mill St.
Telephone: (506) 743-3102/734-3123
Mail to: P.O. Box 118, E0A 1X0
Claude Fales, Director
Questionnaire not received

HOPEWELL CAPE

**Albert County Historical
Society, Inc.**
Telephone: (506) 734-2003
Mail to: P.O. Box 51, E0A 1Y0
County agency
Founded in: 1951
Jean Waddy, Secretary
Number of members: 100
Staff: full time 3, part time 1,
    volunteer 10
Major programs: museum, school
    programs, exhibits, photographic
    collections
Period of collections: 1783-1918

KENT

**Société Historique de
Grande-Digue**
E0A 1S0
Telephone: (506) 576-6569
Town agency
Founded in: 1978
Assunta Bourgeois, Secretary
Number of members: 75
Major programs: school programs,
    manuscripts, historic preservation,
    research

MONCTON

Centre D'Etudes Acadiennes
Universite de Moncton, E1A 3E9
Telephone: (506) 858-4083
Staff: full time 8
Major programs: library, archives,
    manuscripts
Period of collections: 1492-present

Free Meeting House
140 Steadman St.
Mail to: 20 Mountain Rd., E1C 2J8
City agency
Founded in: 1821
Keith A. Wickens, Museum Director
Staff: full time 6, part time 2
Major programs: historic site(s),
    historic preservation
Period of collections: 1783-present

La Société historique acadienne
C.P. 2363 Succursale A, E1C 8J3
Founded in: 1961
Maurice A. Leger, President
Questionnaire not received

Lutz Mountain Heritage Foundation
R.R. 8, E1C 8T8
Telephone: (506) 384-7719
Mail to: P.O. Box 2952, Station A
Founded in: 1976
R. M. Kervin, President
Questionnaire not received

Moncton Museum, Inc.
20 Mountain Rd., E1C 2J8
Telephone: (506) 854-1001
City agency
Founded in: 1973
Keith A. Wickens, Director
Staff: full time 6, part time 2
Major programs: museum, school
    programs, newsletters/pamphlets,
    exhibits
Period of collections: 1800-1975

Musée Acadien
Université de Moncton, E1A 3E9
Telephone: (506) 858-4082
Private agency, authorized by the
    university
Founded in: 1886
Bernard LeBlanc, Director
Staff: full time 3, part time 4,
    volunteer 1
Major programs: museum, historic
    preservation, research, exhibits,
    photographic collections
Period of collections: 18th-20th
    centuries

NEWCASTLE

Miramichi Historical Society
318 Jane St., E1V 1Z3
Telephone: (506) 622-3119
Founded in: 1959
John B. McKay, President
Number of members: 50
Staff: volunteer 1
Major programs: archives, historic
    preservation, genealogy
Period of collections: 1765-1900

NEW DENMARK

New Denmark Historical Society
R.R. 2, E0J 1T0
Telephone: (506) 473-2394
Founded in: 1959
Robert Brinkman, President
Questionnaire not received

OROMOCTO

CFB Gagetown Military Museum
Telephone: (506) 357-8401
Mail to: Bldg. A-5, CFB Gagetown,
    E0G 2P0

J. Evans, Director
Questionnaire not received

Fort Hughes Military Blockhouse
Wharf Rd.
Telephone: (506) 357-3333
Mail to: P.O. Box 37, E2V 2G4
Bill Gay, Program Director

REXTON

Richibucto River Historical Society
Main St., E0A 2L0
Telephone: (506) 523-4408
Mail to: P.O. Box 211, E0A 2L0
Private agency
Founded in: 1970
John J. McCleave, President
Staff: part time 2, volunteer 3
Major programs: museum, exhibits
Period of collections: 19th century

ROBICHAUD

**Société Historique de la Mer
Rouge, Inc.**
R.R. 1, E0A 2S0
Founded in: 1980
Armand Robichaud, President
Number of members: 200
Magazine: *Sur L'Empremier*
Major programs: archives,
manuscripts, museum, historic
site(s), book publishing, historic
preservation, research

SACKVILLE

Mt. Allison University Archives
Mt. Allison University, E0A 3C0
Telephone: (506) 536-2040, ext. 384
Private agency, authorized by the
university
Founded in: 1970
Cheryl Ennals, Archivist
Staff: part time 1
Major programs: library, archives
Period of collections: 1845-present

Owens Art Gallery
Mt. Allison University, E0A 3C0
Telephone: (506) 536-2040, ext. 270
or 291
Authorized by the university
Founded in: 1889
T. Keilor Bentley, Director
Staff: full time 5, part time 5,
volunteer 10
Major programs: museum, historic
preservation, exhibits, fine art
Period of collections: 19th-20th
centuries

ST. ANDREWS

**Henry Phipps Ross and Sarah
Juliette Ross Memorial Museum**
188 Montague St.
Mail to: P.O. Box 603, E0G 2X0
Town agency
Ruth Spicer, Curator
Staff: full time 1, part time 5,
volunteer 15
Major programs: museum, research,
exhibits, decorative arts
Period of collections: pre-1945

Huntsman Marine Laboratory
E0G 2X0
Telephone: (506) 529-3979
Private agency

Founded in: 1969
Thomas W. Moon, Executive Director
Staff: full time 1
Major programs: museum, school
programs, newsletters/pamphlets,
research, exhibits, living history,
audiovisual programs

St. Andrews Civic Trust Inc.
Telephone: (506) 529-3927
Mail to: Box 484, E0G 2X0
Questionnaire not received

ST. JACQUES

Musée Automobile Museum
Les Jardins Provincial Parc
Telephone: (506) 739-7254
Mail to: c/o Madawaska Museum,
P.O. Box 462, Edmundston, E3V
3L1
Provincial agency
Founded in: 1976
Jean Pelletier, Director
Staff: part time 4
Major programs: historic
preservation, exhibits
Period of collections: 1905-present

ST. JOHN

**Association Museums New
Brunswick**
277 Douglas Ave., E2K 1E5
Telephone: (506) 642-5850
Provincial agency
Founded in: 1974
Rebecca Boyer, Executive Director
Number of members: 112
Staff: full time 1
Magazine: *Horizons*
Major programs: library,
newsletters/pamphlets, audiovisual
programs, museum education and
training programs

Barbour's General Store
Market Slip
Telephone: (506) 658-2990
Mail to: P.O. Box 1971, City Hall, E2L
4L1
Shirley Elliott, Tourist Officer
City agency, authorized by St. John
Visitor and Convention Bureau
Major programs: museum
Period of collections: 1840-1940

**Carleton Martello Tower National
Historic Park**
454 Whipple St., E2M 2R3
Telephone: (506) 674-2663
Mail to: P.O. Box 3946, Station B, E2M
5B6
Federal agency
Founded in: 1931
Fred A. Martin, Officer-in-Charge
Staff: full time 4, part time 1
Major programs: historic site(s),
historic preservation, exhibits
Period of collections: 1812-1944

Loyalist House Museum
120 Union St., E2L 1A3
Telephone: (506) 652-3590
Private agency
Founded in: 1874
Willard F. Merritt, Curator
Number of members: 366
Staff: full time 1, part time 3,
volunteer 1

Major programs: library, archives,
museum, historic site(s), tours, oral
history, school programs,
newsletters/pamphlets, historic
preservation, exhibits, living
history, genealogical services
Period of collections: 1810-present

New Brunswick Historical Society
120 Union St., E2L 1A3
Telephone: (506) 652-3590
Provincial agency
Founded in: 1874
Willard F. Merritt, Executive Secretary
Number of members: 300
Staff: full time 1, part time 3,
volunteer 3
Major programs: historic sites
preservation, markers,
tours/pilgrimages, books,
newsletters/pamphlets
Period of collections: 1874-1973

New Brunswick Museum
277 Douglas Ave., E2K 1E5
Telephone: (506) 693-1196
Founded in: 1842
Alan McNairn, Director
Number of members: 540
Staff: full time 32, part time 5,
volunteer 30
Major programs: library, archives,
museum, oral history, school
programs, book publishing,
newsletters/pamphlets, records
management, research, exhibits,
photographic collections,
genealogical services

Partridge Island Research Project
Telephone: (506) 693-2598
Mail to: P.O. Box 6326, Station A, E2L
4R7
Private agency
Founded in: 1977
Harold E. Wright, Coordinator
Staff: part time 1, volunteer 3
Major programs: historic site(s),
tours/pilgrimages, oral history,
school programs, book publishing,
historic preservation, records
management, research, exhibits,
living history, audiovisual
programs, photographic
collections, genealogical services,
field services
Period of collections: 1785-present

**St. John Branch, New Brunswick
Genealogical Society**
P.O. Box 3813, Station B, E2M 5C2
Private agency
Founded in: 1981
Jim McKenzie, President
Number of members: 65

St. John Heritage Trust, Inc.
76 Union St.
Telephone: (506) 693-5410
Mail to: P.O. Box 6622, Station A, E2L
4S1
Private agency
Founded in: 1972
Harold E. Wright, Research
Coordinator
Number of members: 100
Staff: part time 1, volunteer 3
Major programs: historic site(s),
school programs,
newsletters/pamphlets, historic

preservation, research,
photographic collections
Period of collections: from 1877

Signal Hill National Historic Park
Telephone: (709) 737-5364
Mail to: P.O. Box 5879, A1C 5X4
Founded in: 1958
M.E.A. Hall, Area Superintendent
Questionnaire not received

ST. JOSEPH

**Survival of the Acadians National
Historic Site**
Memramcook Institute, Edifice
Lefebvre
Telephone: (506) 758-9783/536-0720
Mail to: P.O. Box 3946, Station B, E2M
5E6
Federal agency, authorized by Parks
Canada
Founded in: 1982
Steven C. Ridlington,
Officer-in-Charge
Staff: part time 3
Major programs: historic site(s),
exhibits
Period of collections: 1755-present

ST. MARTINS

**Quaco Historical and Library
Society Inc.**
Main St., E0G 2Z0
Telephone: (506) 833-4768
Private agency
Founded in: 1971
Miriam Davidson, President
Number of members: 60
Staff: volunteer 20
Magazine: *Quaco Signal*
Major programs: library, archives,
manuscripts, museum, historic
site(s), markers, oral history, school
programs, newsletters/pamphlets,
historic preservation, exhibits,
photographic collections,
genealogical services
Period of collections: 1783-present

ST. STEPHEN

Charlotte County Museum
443 Milltown Blvd., E3L 1J9
Telephone: (506) 466-3295
Private agency, authorized by
Charlotte County Historical
Society, Inc.
Major programs: library, museum,
markers, tours, school programs,
historic preservation, records
management, research, exhibits
Period of collections: mid-late 19th
century

TABUSINTAC

**Tabusintac Centennial Memorial
Library and Museum**
Telephone: (506) 779-9261
Mail to: E0C 2A0
Bertha Stymiest, Director

TRACADIE

Musée historique de Tracadie
Telephone: (506) 395-3959
Mail to: C.P. 1221, rue du Couvent,
Académie Sainte-Famille,

Tracadie, Nouveau-Brunswick,
E0C 2B0
Soeur Dorina Frigault, Director
Questionnaire not received

WOODSTOCK

**Carleton County Historical
Society, Inc.**
Telephone: (506) 328-3273
Mail to: P.O. Box 898, E0J 2B0
Founded in: 1960
Patrick Karnes, President
Number of members: 64
Staff: full time 3, part time 4
Major programs: historic site(s),
historic preservation
Period of collections: 1785-present

NEWFOUNDLAND

BAY D'ESPOIR

Miawipukwik Micmac Museum
Telephone: (709) 882-2470
Mail to: Conne River, A0H 1J0
Jerry Wetzel, Director

BONAVISTA

Bonavista Museum
Telephone: (709) 468-2575/468-2880
Mail to: P.O. Box 882, A0C 1B0
Town agency
Marguerite Linthorne, Curator
Major programs: museum
Period of collections: late 1800s-early
1900s

BUCHANS

Buchans Miners Museum
Telephone: (709) 672-3356
Mail to: P.O. Box 219, R0H 1G0
Gary Gushie, Contact person
Questionnaire not received

CORNER BROOK

Humber-Bay of Islands Museum
Telephone: (709) 634-3972
Mail to: Suite 25, 19-21 West St.,
Corner Brook, A2H 2Y6
Questionnaire not received

COW HEAD

Tête de Vache Museum
Tête de Vache Library
Telephone: (709) 243-4526
Mail to: A0K 2A0
Ivy Payne, Chairman
Questionnaire not received

DURRELL

Durrell Museum
Arm Lads' Brigade Armoury, A0G 1Y0
Telephone: (709) 884-5496
Authorized by Durrell Museum
Association
Major programs: library, museum
Period of collections: early 1900s

FERRYLAND

Ferryland Historical Society
P.O. Box 7, A0A 2H0
Town agency
Founded in: 1964
Bernard J. Agriesti, Past President
Number of members: 50
Staff: full time 2, part time 1,
volunteer 5
Major programs: museum, historic
preservation
Period of collections: 18th century

Historic Ferryland Museum
Telephone: (709) 753-1200, local
2222
Mail to: A0A 2H0
Bernard Agriesti, President
Questionnaire not received

GRAND BANK

**Southern Newfoundland Seaman's
Museum**
Telephone: (709) 832-1484
Mail to: Marine Drive, A0E 1W0
Andrew Wilson, Curator

GRAND FALLS

**Mary March Regional Museum and
National Exhibition Centre**
Telephone: (709) 489-9331
Mail to: 22 St. Catherine St., A2A 2J9
Glenn Stroud, Director

GREENSPOND

Greenspond Museum
Telephone: (709) 269-3301
Mail to: P.O. Box 42, A0G 2N0
Stephen Mullins, Curator

HAPPY VALLEY

Them Days
3 Courte Manche
Telephone: (709) 896-8531
Mail to: P.O. Box 939, A0P 1E0
Private agency
Founded in: 1975
Doris Saunders, Editor
Staff: full time 2, volunteer 7
Magazine: *Them Days*
Major programs: library, archives,
manuscripts, oral history, book
publishing, records management,
research, exhibits, living history,
photographic collections,
genealogical services
Period of collections: 1800-1950

HARBOUR GRACE

Conception Bay Museum
Telephone: (709) 596-5465
Mail to: P.O. Box 442, A0E 2M0
William Parsons, Director
Questionnaire not received

HEART'S CONTENT

**Heart's Content Cable Station,
Provincial Historic Site**
Telephone: (709) 737-2460/583-2160
Mail to: c/o Newfoundland Museum,
287 Duckworth St., St. John's,
A1C 1G9
Martin Bowe, Director of Historic
Resources
Questionnaire not received

JERSEYSIDE

Castle Hill National Historic Park
3 km from Argentia Ferry, Placentia
  Bay
Telephone: (709) 227-2401
Mail to: P.O. Box 10, Placentia Bay,
  A0B 2G0
Federal agency, authorized by Parks
  Canada
Edna Hall, Area Superintendent
Major programs: historic
  preservation, interpretation
Period of collections: 1662-1811

MUSGRAVE HARBOUR

Fisherman's Museum
Marine Dr.
Telephone: (709) 655-2162/655-2119
Mail to: A0G 3J0
Walter Cuff, Director
Questionnaire not received

PORT DE GRAVE

Fishermen's Museum
Hibbs Cove
Telephone: (709) 786-3436/786-2170
Mail to: P.O. Box 1, A0A 3J0
George Dawe, Director
Questionnaire not received

POUCH COVE

Pouch Cove Museum
Main Hwy.
Telephone: (709) 335-2356
Mail to: P.O. Box 59, A0A 3L0
Questionnaire not received

ST. JOHN'S

**Museum Association of
  Newfoundland and Labrador**
253 Duckworth St., 3rd Floor
Telephone: (709) 722-9034
Mail to: P.O. Box 5785, A1C 5X3
Penny Houlden, Training Coordinator
Major programs: field services

Newfoundland Historical Society
Colonial Bldg., Room 15, AIC 2C9
Telephone: (708) 777-3191
Provincial agency, authorized by
  Department of Tourism and Culture
Founded in: 1905
Bobbie Robertson, Office Secretary
Number of members: 260
Staff: full time 1
Major programs: oral history,
  newsletters/pamphlets, historic
  preservation, living history
Period of collections: 1497-present

Newfoundland Museum
Telephone: (709) 737-2460
Mail to: 287 Duckworth St., A1C 1G9
Martin Bowe, Director
Questionnaire not received

**Newfoundland Naval and Military
  Museum**
Confederation Bldg., 11th Floor
Telephone: (709) 737-2834
Mail to: 281 Duckworth St., A1C 1G9
Martin Bowe, Director of Historic
  Resources
Questionnaire not received

Provincial Archives of Newfoundland and Labrador
Colonial Bldg., Military Rd., A1C 2C9
Telephone: (709) 753-9398
Provincial agency
Founded in: 1957
David J. Davis, Provincial Archivist
Staff: full time 12
Major programs: archives,
  manuscripts, records
  management, photographic
  collections, genealogical services
Period of collections: from 1750

Robert Jackman Collection
Telephone: (709) 726-9228
Mail to: P.O. Box 5682, A1C 5W8
Private agency
Founded in: 1983
Robert Jackman, Owner
Staff: full time 1
Major programs: archives,
  photographic collections

Signal Hill National Historic Park
Telephone: (709) 772-5367/772-4444
Mail to: P.O. Box 5879, A1C 5X4
Federal agency, authorized by
  Minister of the Environment, Parks
  Canada
Founded in: 1958
M.E.A. Hall, Area Superintendent
Staff: full time 22, part time 40
Major programs: historic site(s),
  historic preservation, interpretation
Period of collections: 1690s-1950

**United Church Archives,
  Newfoundland and Labrador
  Conference**
320 Elizabeth Ave., A1B 1T9
Telephone: (709) 754-0386
Private agency, authorized by the
  United Church of Canada
F. Burnham Gill, Conference Archivist
Staff: full time 3, part time 1,
  volunteer 100
Major programs: library, archives,
  manuscripts, museum, historic
  site(s), markers,
  newsletters/pamphlets, historic
  preservation, records
  management, research,
  photographic collections,
  genealogical services
Period of collections: 1765-present

SALVAGE

Salvage Fishermans Museum
Bishop Dr.
Telephone: (709) 677-2137
Mail to: P.O. Box 29, Eastport, A0G
  1Z0
Arthur Heffern, Chairman
Questionnaire not received

SPRINGDALE

H.V. Grant Heritage Centre
West end of Main St.
Telephone: (709) 673-3936
Mail to: A0J 1T0
A. Brett, Chairman
Questionnaire not received

STEPHENVILLE

**Port-au-Port—Bay St. George
  Heritage Association**
Kindale Library, 16 Glendale St., A2N
  2K3

Telephone: (709) 643-4262
Mail to: P.O. Box 314, A2N 2Z5
Private agency
Founded in: 1974
Gilbert E. Higgins, Chair
Number of members: 68
Staff: volunteer 6
Major programs: archives, exhibits,
  photographic collections
Period of collections: 1880-present

TRINITY

Trinity Museum and Archives
Telephone: (709) 464-3657/464-3720
Mail to: P.O. Box 54, A0C 2S0
Private agency
S.R. Morris, President
Major programs: archives, museum,
  historic preservation
Period of collections: late
  1700s-1800s

TWILLINGATE

Twillingate Museum
Telephone: (709) 884-5379
Mail to: P.O. Box 356, A0G 4M0
James Troke, Chairman
Questionnaire not received

WESLEYVILLE

**Bonavista North Regional Memorial
  Museum**
Telephone: (709) 536-2281
Mail to: Wesleyville Museum
  Committee, A0G 4R0
Alice Lacey, Chairman
Questionnaire not received

NORTHWEST TERRITORIES

FORT SMITH

**Northern Anthropological and
  Cultural Society Northern Life
  Museum and National Exhibition
  Centre**
110 King St.
Telephone: (401) 872-2859
Mail to: P.O. Box 371, X0E 0P0
Founded in: 1972
William R. Robbins, Director
Number of members: 26
Staff: full time 1, part time 2
Major programs: museum, galleries
  operating as National Exhibition
  Centre
Period of collections:
  prehistoric-present

FROBISHER BAY

Nunatta Sunaqutangit
P.O. Box 605, X0A 0H0
Telephone: (819) 979-5537
Authorized by Nunatta Sunaqutangit
  Museum Society
Major programs: museum, exhibits
Period of collections: 1960-1970

YELLOWKNIFE

Prince of Wales Northern Heritage Centre
c/o Government of the Northwest
  Territories, X1A 2L9
Telephone: (403) 873-7551
Territorial agency
Founded in: 1976
Robert R. Janes, Director
Staff: full time 21, part time 10
Major programs: library, archives,
  manuscripts, museum, historic
  site(s), markers, oral history, school
  programs, newsletters/pamphlets,
  historic preservation, research,
  exhibits, living history, archaeology
  programs, photographic
  collections, field services
Period of collections:
  prehistoric-present

NOVA SCOTIA

AMHERST

Cumberland County Museum Historical Society
150 Church St.
Mail to: 37 Clifford St., B4H 2G3
Questionnaire not received

ANNAPOLIS

Historic Restoration Enterprises Society and North Hills Museum
Telephone: (902) 532-2168
Mail to: c/o Ken Gilmour, Curator
  Branch Museums, Nova Scotia
  Museum,
1747 Summer St., Halifax, B0S 1A0
Shirley Carr, President

ANNAPOLIS ROYAL

Historical Association of Annapolis Royal
Telephone: (902) 532-2119
Mail to: P.O. Box 68, B0S 1A0
Founded in: 1919
J. B. Corston, President
Questionnaire not received

Historic Restoration Society of Annapolis County
St. George St.
Telephone: (902) 532-2041
Mail to: P.O. Box 503, B0S 1A0
County agency
Founded in: 1967
Harry Jost, President
Number of members: 150
Staff: full time 3, part time 1,
  volunteer 14
Major programs: museum,
  tours/pilgrimages, oral history,
  pamphlets, costume care
Period of collections: 1783-1918

ANTIGONISH

Heritage Association of Antigonish
42 West St., B2G 2H5
Telephone: (902) 863-6160 (summer
  only)

Mail to: P.O. Box 1492, B2G 2L7
County agency
Founded in: 1982
Bernadette Gillis, President
Number of members: 35
Staff: part time 1, volunteer 10
Major programs: research
Period of collections: 1800

ARCHAT

Le Noir Forge
Telephone: (902) 226-2051
Mail to: P.O. Box 239, B0E 1A0
Alexander Marchand, Chairman

ARMDALE

York Redoubt National Historic Site
Purcello Cove Rd.
Telephone: (902) 426-2335
Mail to: P.O. Box 17, Site 15, R.R. 5,
  B3L 4J5
John Belgrave, Area Superintendent

BADDECK

Alexander Graham Bell National Historic Park
Rt. 205, Chebucto St.
Telephone: (902) 295-2069
Mail to: P.O. Box 159, B0E 1B0
Federal agency, authorized by Parks
  Canada
Founded in: 1956
John W. Stephens, Superintendent
Staff: full time 8, part time 30
Major programs: museum, school
  programs, exhibits, audiovisual
  programs, photographic
  collections
Period of collections: 1860s-1920s

Victoria County Library Museum and Archives
Chebucto and Jones St.
Telephone: (902) 295-3397/295-2406
Mail to: c/o Curator, P.O. Box 75, B0E
  1B0
Private agency
Margot MacAulay, Curator
Major programs: library, archives,
  museum, historic preservation,
  research, photographic collections
Period of collections: 1820-present

BALMORAL MILLS

Balmoral Grist Mill
Telephone: (902) 429-4610
Mail to: c/o Person-in-Charge,
  Curator Branch Museums, Nova
  Scotia Museum, 1747
Summer St., Halifax, B3H 3A6
Ken Gilmour, Person in Charge

BARRINGTON PASSAGE

Cape Sable Historical Society
Telephone: (902) 637-3123
Mail to: P.O. Box 134, Barrington
  Passage, B0W 1G0
Founded in: 1933
Mary Snow, Corresponding Secretary
Number of members: 100
Staff: part time 7
Major programs: archives, museum,
  historic site(s),
  newsletters/pamphlets, historic

preservation, exhibits,
  genealogical services
Period of collections: from 1900

BARSS CORNER

Parkdale-Maplewood Community Museum
R.R. 1, B0R 1A0
Private agency
Muriel Wentzell, Co-curator
Staff: volunteer 2
Period of collections: 1750-1900

BEAR RIVER

Bear River Farmers' Museum
Telephone: (902) 467-3302
Mail to: B0S 1B0
Michael Susnick, Director
Questionnaire not received

BELL'S ISLAND

La Have Islands Marine Museum
R.R. 1, B0R 1C0
Telephone: (902) 688-2565
Private agency
Founded in: 1978
Lillian R. Romkey,
  Secretary/Treasurer
Number of members: 52
Major programs: museum
Period of collections: 1850-present

BRIDGEWATER

Bridgewater Heritage and Historical Society
55 Crescent, B4V 1L1
Telephone: (902) 543-3117
Town agency
Founded in: 1979
Florrie Little, President
Number of members: 14
Major programs: museum, school
  programs, research, photographic
  collections, genealogical services
Period of collections: 1850-1920

DesBrisay Museum and National Exhibition Centre
130 Jubilee Rd.
Telephone: (902) 543-4033
Mail to: P.O. Box 353, B4V 2W9
Town agency, authorized by Parks
  and Recreation Commission
Founded in: 1880
Gary Selig, Curator
Staff: full time 2
Major programs: library, archives,
  museum, school programs,
  exhibits, photographic collections
Period of collections: 1630-present

CANSO

Canso Museum
Whitman House, Union St.
Telephone: (902) 366-2322/366-2525
Mail to: c/o Neil McIsaac, Hazel Hill,
  R.R. 1, B0H 1H0
Neil McIsaac, President
Questionnaire not received

CAPE NORTH

North Highland Community Organization
Mail to: R.R. 1, Dingwall
Founded in: 1978

Evelyn M. Courtney,
Secretary/Treasurer
Number of members: 28
Staff: full time 2, part time 1,
volunteer 6
Major programs: archives,
manuscripts, museum, oral history,
historic preservation, records
management, research,
genealogical services
Period of collections: 1885-1930

CENTERVILLE

**Cape Sable Historical Society,
Archelaus Smith Branch**
Telephone: (902) 745-2478
Mail to: c/o McGray P.O. B0W 2G0
Founded in: 1970
Alfred M. Newell, President
Questionnaire not received

CHETICAMP

Musée Acadien
Telephone: (902) 224-2170
Mail to: C.P. 98, B0E 1H0
Authorized by Cooperative Artisanale
de Cheticamp Limitee
Luce Marie Boudreau, Directrice
Major programs: museum, school
programs, exhibits, living history,
demonstrations of carding,
spinning, weaving, dyeing of wool

CHURCH-POINT

Le Musée Sainte-Marie
Telephone: (902) 769-2832
Mail to: C.P. 28, B0W 1M0
Private agency
Philippe Belliveau, President
Major programs: museum,
tours/pilgrimages

CLARK'S HARBOR

Archelaus Smith Historical Society
Telephone: (902) 745-2478
Private agency
Alfred Newell, President
Number of members: 24
Major programs: museum
Period of collections: late 1800s-early
1900s

DARTMOUTH

**Cole Harbour Rural Heritage
Society**
471 Poplar Dr., Forest Hills, B2W 4LZ
Telephone: (902) 434-0222/434-1651
Mail to: R.R. 1, B2W 3X7
Private agency
Founded in: 1973
R. M. Eaton, Secretary
Number of members: 70
Staff: volunteer 15
Major programs: museum, markers,
oral history, school programs, book
publishing, newsletters/pamphlets,
historic preservation, research,
exhibits, living history, audiovisual
programs, photographic
collections
Period of collections: 1850-present

Dartmouth Heritage Museum
100 Wyse Rd., B3A 1M1
Telephone: (902) 421-2300/421-2199

City agency, authorized by
Dartmouth Museum Board
Founded in: 1967
G. S. Gosley, Director
Staff: full time 2, part time 5
Major programs: museum
Period of collections: 1750-1980

Dartmouth Museum Society
100 Wyse Rd., B3A 1M1
Telephone: (902) 421-2300
Private agency
Founded in: 1964
J. L. Harrison, President
Number of members: 115
Major programs: museum, historic
site(s), tours/pilgrimages, historic
preservation, exhibits
Period of collections: 1785-1920

**Halifax-Dartmouth Branch, United
Empire Loyalists' Association of
Canada**
7 Cathy Cross Dr., B2W 2R5
Telephone: (902) 434-7208
Private agency
Founded in: 1982
Lewis L. Perry, President
Number of members: 65
Staff: volunteer 12
Major programs: historic preservation
Period of collections: 1775-1800

GLACE BAY

Cape Breton Miners' Museum
Quarry Point, B1A 5T8
Telephone: (902) 849-4522
Founded in: 1964
Roger Hill, Director
Questionnaire not received

Miners' Museum
Birkley St., B1A 5T8
Telephone: (902) 849-4522
Private agency
Founded in: 1964
Roger Hill, Director
Staff: full time 4, part time 15,
volunteer 5
Major programs: library, museum
Period of collections: 1900-present

GRANVILLE FERRY

North Hills Museum
Telephone: (902) 532-2168
Mail to: c/o Curator Branch Museums,
Nova Scotia Museum, 1747
Summer St., Halifax, B0S 1A0
Founded in: 1974
Major programs: museum, historic
site(s)

GUYSBOROUGH

Guysborough Historical Society
Church St.
Telephone: (902) 533-4008
Mail to: P.O. Box 232, B0H 1N0
County agency
Founded in: 1972
Lesa A. George, Curator
Number of members: 60
Staff: full time 1, volunteer 15
Major programs: library, archives,
manuscripts, museum, historic
site(s), markers, tours/pilgrimages,
junior history, oral history, school
programs, book publishing,
newsletters/pamphlets, historic

preservation, records
management, research, exhibits,
living history, photographic
collections, genealogical services
Period of collections: 1780-1945

Old Court House Museum
Church St.
Telephone: (902) 533-4008
Mail to: P.O. Box 232, B0H 1N0
Lisa A. George, President
Authorized by Guysborough
Historical Society
Major programs: library, archives,
museum, historic site(s), markers,
tours/pilgrimages, school
programs, book publishing,
newsletters/pamphlets, historic
preservation, records
management, research,
photographic collections,
genealogical services

HALIFAX

The Army Museum, Halifax Citadel
Telephone: (902) 422-5979
Mail to: P.O. Box 3666, B3J 3K6
Founded in: 1953
D. E. Gravey, Curator and
Administrator
Questionnaire not received

Atlantic Canada Aviation Museum
Halifax International Airport
Telephone: (902) 861-3184
Mail to: 1747 Summer St., B3H 3A6
Private agency
Founded in: 1978
Bob Grantham, Founder
Number of members: 80
Staff: volunteer 20
Magazine: *Atlantic Wings*
Major programs: museum, oral
history, historic preservation,
research, exhibits, photographic
collections
Period of collections: 1909-present

Costume Society of Nova Scotia
5516 Spring Garden Rd., B3J 1G6
Telephone: (902) 423-4677
Private agency
Founded in: 1979
Clary Croft, Chair
Number of members: 100
Staff: volunteer 20
Major programs:
newsletters/pamphlets, historic
preservation, conservation and
preservation training, costume care
Period of collections: 1600-present

**Federation of Nova Scotian
Heritage**
5516 Spring Garden Road, Suite 305,
B3J 1G6
Telephone: (902) 423-4677
Provincial agency
Founded in: 1976
Elizabeth C. Ross, Executive Director
Number of members: 100
Staff: full time 3
Magazine: *Federation News*
Major programs: library,
newsletters/pamphlets, field
services, liaison with tourism
industry and resource development

Friends of the Citadel Society
P.O. Box 3116, B3J 3G6

Telephone: (902) 425-3923
Private agency
Founded in: 1980
Paul D. McNair, Executive Director
Number of members: 200
Staff: full time 1, part time 16
Major programs: book publishing,
newsletters/pamphlets, living
history

**Halifax Citadel National Historic
Park**
Telephone: (902) 426-5080
Mail to: P.O. Box 1480, N. Postal
Station, B3K 5H7
National agency
W. C. Ingram, Superintendent
Staff: full time 40, part time 9
Major programs: library, archives,
historic site(s), markers, historic
preservation, research, exhibits,
living history, audiovisual
programs, archaeology programs,
photographic collections
Period of collections: 1825-1900

Heritage Trust of Nova Scotia
1579 Dresden Row, B3H 3H1
Telephone: (902) 423-4807
Provincial agency
Founded in: 1959
Audrey Crawford, Executive
Secretary
Number of members: 550
Staff: part time 1, volunteer 28
Major programs: tours/pilgrimages,
oral history, book publishing,
historic preservation

**Historic Resources Research,
Parks Canada, Atlantic Region**
Historic Properties, Upper Water St.,
B3H 1S9
Telephone: (902) 426-7515
National agency
Founded in: 1975
Charles Lindsay, Chief
Staff: full time 14
Major programs: library, historic
site(s), markers,
newsletters/pamphlets, historic
preservation, research, exhibits,
archaeology programs
Period of collections: 1605-1945

Maritime Command Museum
Admiralty House, C.F.B. Halifax, B3K
2X0
Telephone: (902) 426-5210
National agency, authorized by
Department of National Defense
Founded in: 1974
Marilyn Gurney Smith, Curator
Staff: full time 2, part time 2
Major programs: library, archives,
museum, historic site(s), school
programs, research, exhibits
Period of collections: 1749-1945

Nova Scotia Museum
1747 Summer St., B3H 3A6
Telephone: (902) 429-4610
Founded in: 1868
J. Lynton Martin, Director
Questionnaire not received

Nova Scotia Sport Heritage Centre
1496 Lower Water St., Suite 300, B3J
1R9
Telephone: (902) 421-1266
Private agency

Founded in: 1983
Bill Robinson, Executive Director
Staff: full time 3
Major programs: archives, museum,
oral history, school programs,
newsletters/pamphlets, records
management, living history

Prescott House
Starrs Point
Telephone: (902) 5423984
Mail to: 1747 Summer St., B3H 3A6
Founded in: 1971
K. D. Gilmour, Curator, Branch
Museums
Staff: part time 7
Major programs: museum, historic
site(s), historic preservation
Period of collections: 1814

Public Archives of Nova Scotia
6016 University Ave., B3H 1W4
Provincial agency
Phyllis Blakeley, Provincial Archivist
Staff: full time 24, part time 22,
volunteer 5
Major programs: library, archives,
manuscripts, tours/pilgrimages,
junior history, oral history, records
management, research,
audiovisual programs,
photographic collections,
genealogical services
Period of collections: 1749-present

**Royal Nova Scotia Historical
Society**
Public Archives of Nova Scotia, 6016
University Ave., B3H 1W4
Telephone: (902) 423-9115
Private agency
Stephen F. Bedwell, President
Number of members: 316
Staff: volunteer 14
Major programs: library, archives,
manuscripts, historic site(s),
markers, tours/pilgrimages, historic
preservation, research,
genealogical services
Period of collections: 1604-present

Scotian Railroad Society, Inc.
Mail to: P.O. Box 798 Armdale Ptl.
Stn., B3L 4K5
Questionnaire not received

Telephone Historical Collection
Telephone: (902) 825-4911
Mail to: Maritime Centre, P.O. Box
880, B3J 2W3
J. Marshall, Historian/Archivist

Uniacke House
Rt. 1
Telephone: (902) 866-2560
Mail to: 1747 Summer St., B3H 3A6
Founded in: 1949
K. D. Gilmour, Curator, Branch
Museums
Staff: full time 2, part time 7
Major programs: museum, historic
site preservation
Period of collections: 1815

HALIFAX SOUTH

Army Museum
Halifax Citadel
Telephone: (902) 422-5979
Mail to: P.O. Box 3666, B3J 3K6
Private agency

Bruce F.Ellis, Curator
Major programs: historic site(s),
historic preservation, exhibits
Period of collections: 1730-present

HANTSPORT

**Churchill House—Marine Memorial
Room**
Main St.
Telephone: (902) 684-3461
Mail to: B0P 1P0
Private agency, authorized by
Hantsport Memorial Community
Centre
J. Porter, Administrator
Period of collections: 1860-1910

LA HAVE

**Lunenburg County Historical
Society—Fort Point Museum**
Telephone: (902) 688-2524
Mail to: B0R 1C0
Nancy Creaser, Honorary Curator

HEAD OF CHEZZETCOOK

Chezzetcook Historical Society
Mail to: P.O. Box 89
Questionnaire not received

INVERNESS

**Inverness Historical
Society/Inverness Miners
Museum**
Lower Railway St.
Telephone: (902) 258-2097
Mail to: P.O. Box 161, B0E 1N0
T. MacDonald, Director
Questionnaire not received

IONA

Nova Scotia Highland Village, Inc.
Telephone: (902) 622-2330
Mail to: P.O. Box 3, B0A 1L0
Founded in: 1959
Brian McCormack, Curator
Questionnaire not received

JEDDORE, OYSTER POND

Marine Highway Historical Society
B0J 1W0
Telephone: (902) 845-2294
Founded in: 1972
Helen M. Jennex, President
Questionnaire not received

KINGS COUNTY

Prescott House
Starrs Point
Telephone: (902) 542-3984
Mail to: 1747 Summer St., Halifax,
B3H 3A6
Founded in: 1971
K. D. Gilmour, Curator, Branch
Museums
Questionnaire not received

LIVERPOOL

Queens County Historical Society
Telephone: (902) 354-4058
Mail to: P.O. Box 1078, B0T 1K0
Founded in: 1929
G. C. Haslam, President
Number of members: 200

Staff: volunteer 20
Major programs: library, archives,
manuscripts, museum, historic
sites preservation, oral history,
genealogy
Period of collections: 1783-1918

Queens County Museum
115 Main St.
Telephone: (902) 354-4058
Mail to: P.O. Box 1078, B0T 1K0
County agency, authorized by
Queens County Historical Society
Founded in: 1929
Gary Hartlen, Curator/Director
Number of members: 225
Staff: full time 1, part time 4,
volunteer 25
Magazine: *The Simeon Perkins*
Major programs: library, archives,
manuscripts, museum, historic
site(s), markers, tours/pilgrimages,
junior history, oral history, school
programs, book publishing,
newsletters/pamphlets, historic
preservation, records
management, research, exhibits,
photographic collections,
genealogical services
Period of collections: 1800-1875

**Simon Perkins Museum and
Perkins House**
Main St.
Telephone: (902) 354-3058
Founded in: 1767
Gary Hartlen, House Curator
Staff: full time 4, part time 1
Major programs: museum, historic
sites preservation, pilgrimages,
oral history, genealogy
Period of collections: 1760-1929

LOCKEPORT

Little School Museum
B0T 1L0
Telephone: (902) 656-2338
Town agency
Founded in: 1967
William Suttle, Chair
Staff: full time 1, volunteer 6
Major programs: museum
Period of collections: 1845-present

Ragged Islands Historical Society
P.O. Box 287, B0T 1L0
Telephone: (902) 656-3468
Private agency
Founded in: 1984
Desmond Farrell, President
Number of members: 20
Major programs: historic
preservation, research,
photographic collections
Period of collections: 1750-1940

LOUISBOURG

**Fortress of Louisbourg National
Historic Park**
P.O. Box 160, B0A 1M0
Telephone: (902) 733-2280
National agency
Founded in: 1961
Roger Wilson, Superintendent
Staff: full time 132, part time 130,
volunteer 100
Major programs: library, archives,
museum, historic site(s), historic

preservation, research, exhibits,
living history, archaeology
programs, photographic
collections, genealogical services
Period of collections: 1713-1760

**Sydney and Louisburg Railway
Historical Society**
Telephone: (902) 733-2890
Mail to: P.O. Box 225, B0A 1M0
Private agency
Founded in: 1971
Guy M. Hiltz, President
Number of members: 400
Staff: full time 1, part time 1,
volunteer 5
Major programs: museum, oral
history, newsletters/pamphlets,
historic preservation, exhibits,
living history, photographic
collections
Period of collections: 1895-present

LUNENBURG

Fisheries Museum of the Atlantic
Lunenburg Waterfront
Telephone: (902) 634-4794
Mail to: P.O. Box 1363, B0J 2C0
Provincial agency, authorized by
Lunenburg Marine Museum Society
and Nova Scotia
Museum Department of Education
Founded in: 1967
A.S. Fox, Project Manager
Staff: full time 9, part time 29,
volunteer 1
Major programs: museum
Period of collections: 1910-present

Lunenburg Heritage Society
150 Brook St., B0J 2C0
Telephone: (902) 634-8575
Mail to: P.O. Box 674
Barbara M. Zwicker, President
Questionnaire not received

Lunenburg Marine Museum Society
P.O. Box 1363, B0J 2C0
Telephone: (902) 634-4794
Founded in: 1972
Neil Carleton, Project Manager
Questionnaire not received

South Shore Genealogical Society
120 Townsend St.
Telephone: (902) 634-8768
Mail to: P.O. Box 901, B0J 2C0
Private agency, authorized by The
Societies Act, Province of Nova
Scotia
Founded in: 1979
Gordon R. Mason, President
Number of members: 140
Staff: volunteer 8
Major programs: book publishing,
newsletters/pamphlets,
genealogical services
Period of collections: 1753-1950s

MABOU

**Mabou Gaelic and Historical
Society**
An Drochaid, B0E 1X0
Telephone: (902) 945-2311
Mail to: P.O. Box 175, B0E 1X0
Founded in: 1975
Margaret M. J. Beaton, President
Number of members: 65
Staff: volunteer 10

Major programs: archives, oral
history, newsletters/pamphlets,
living history, photographic
collections, genealogical services
Period of collections: 1830s-present

**Mabou Heritage Museum and
Society**
Telephone: (902) 945-2928
Mail to: B0E 1X0
Questionnaire not received

MAITLAND

East Hants Historical Society
Mail to: P.O. Box 41, Maitland, B0N
1T0
Private agency
Founded in: 1967
Wilma Densmore, President
Number of members: 93
Major programs: museum, markers,
photographic collections, artifacts
Period of collections: 1865-1950

W. D. Lawrence House
Rt. 215
Telephone: (902) 261-2628
Mail to: 1747 Summer St. Halifax, B3H
3A6
Founded in: 1967
K. D. Gilmour, Curator, Branch
Museums
Staff: part time 6
Major programs: museum, historic
sites preservation
Period of collections: 1870

MAPLEWOOD

**Parkwood-Maplewood Community
Museum**
Telephone: (902) 644-2790
Mail to: R.R. 1, Barss Corners, B0R
1A0
Loyd Wentzel, Curator

MARGAREE

Margaree Salmon Museum
N.E. Margaree, B0E 2H0
Telephone: (902) 248-2848
Private agency, authorized by
Margarett Anglers Association
Founded in: 1965
R. W. Watts, Secretary/Treasurer
Number of members: 50
Staff: full time 2, part time 1,
volunteer 3
Major programs: museum, historic
preservation, audiovisual programs
Period of collections: 1850-1980

Museum of Cape Breton Heritage
B0E 2H0
Telephone: (902) 248-2551
Private agency
Founded in: 1972
Mrs. Gerald Hart, Curator
Staff: full time 1, part time 2
Major programs: museum, exhibits
Period of collections: 1865-1918

METEGHAN RIVER

**Société Historique Acadienne La
Vieille Maison**
Telephone: (902) 769-2114, ext. 159
Mail to: B0W 2J0
Maurice J. Belliveau, President

MIDDLETON

Annapolis Valley Macdonald Museum
School St.
Telephone: (902) 825-6116
Mail to: P.O. Box 925, B0S 1P0
County agency, authorized by
Annapolis Valley Historical Society
Founded in: 1978
J. Michael Black, Curator
Number of members: 85
Staff: full time 2, part time 2,
volunteer 42
Major programs: library, archives,
museum, school programs,
newsletters/pamphlets, exhibits,
living history, audiovisual
programs, genealogical services
Period of collections: 1605-present

MINUDIE

King Seaman School Museum
Telephone: (902) 251-2041
Mail to: B0L 1G0
Lillian Arseneau, Chair

MOUNT UNIACKE

South Rawdon Museum
Telephone: (902) 757-2340
Mail to: R.R. 1, B0N 1Z0
H. Lawson, Curator

MUSQUODOBOIT HARBOUR

Friends of the Musquodoboit Railway
Musquodoboit Railway Museum, B0J 2L0
Telephone: (902) 889-2084
Founded in: 1974
David E. Stephens, Director/Curator
Questionnaire not received

NEW GLASGOW

Pictou County Historical Society Museum
Telephone: (902) 752-5583
Mail to: 86 Temperance St.
Helen Sproull, President
Questionnaire not received

NEW ROSS

New Ross District Museum Society—Ross Farm Museum of Agriculture
Rt. 12, B0J 2M0
Telephone: (902) 689-2210
Alan Hiltz, Curator
Major programs: museum, school
programs, historic preservation,
exhibits, living history
Period of collections: 1820-1900

PARRSBORO

Parrsboro Mineral and Gem Geological Museum
Eastern Ave.
Telephone: (902) 254-3266/254-2627
Mail to: P.O. Box 297, B0M 1S0
Private agency
Founded in: 1968
Marilyn F. Smith, Manager/Curator
Staff: full time 1, part time 3,
volunteer 10
Major programs: library, manuscripts,
museum, tours/pilgrimages, school
programs, book publishing,
exhibits, audiovisual programs,
photographic collections, geology
Period of collections:
prehistoric-present

PICTOU

Burning Bush Center and Museum
9 Prince St.
Telephone: (902) 485-4298
Mail to: P.O. Box 1003, B0K 1H0
Private agency, authorized by First
Presbyterian Church
Founded in: 1979
Lloyd A. Murdoch, Minister/Curator
Staff: part time 2, volunteer 7
Period of collections: 1767-present

Mic Mac Museum
Telephone: (902) 485-4723
Mail to: R.R. 1, B0K 1H0
Kenneth Hopps, Curator

Thomas McCulloch House—Hector Centre Trust National Exhibition Centre
Telephone: (902) 485-4563
Mail to: P.O. Box 1210, B0K 1H0
National agency, authorized by
Hector Centre Trust
J.L. Martin, Director
Major programs: archives, museum,
school programs, book publishing,
newsletters/pamphlets, research,
exhibits
Period of collections: 1895-1971

PORT HASTINGS

Port Hastings Historical Museum and Archives
Church St.
Telephone: (902) 625-1295
Mail to: P.O. Box 115, B0E 2T0
Authorized by Port Hastings
Historical Society
Founded in: 1979
Yvonne Fox, President
Number of members: 30
Staff: volunteer 6
Major programs: archives, museum,
oral history, newsletters/pamphlets,
research, photographic
collections, genealogical services

PORT HOOD

Chestico Museum and Historical Society
B0E 2W0
Telephone: (902) 787-3470
Private agency
Founded in: 1978
Vivien Tobey, President
Number of members: 70

Major programs: library, archives,
museum, oral history,
newsletters/pamphlets,
genealogical services
Period of collections: 1850-1920s

PUGWASH

North Cumberland Historical Society
P.O. Box 52, B0K 1L0
Telephone: (902) 243-2069
Founded in: 1963
John R. MacQuarrie, President
Carl O. Demings, Vice President
Number of members: 75
Staff: volunteer 10
Major programs: book publishing
Period of collections: 1783-present

ST. ANN'S

Giant Macaskill Highland Pioneers Museum
Telephone: (902) 295-2877
Mail to: P.O. Box 9, Baddeck, B0E 1B0
Leonard Jones, Director
Questionnaire not received

ST. PETER'S

Nicolas Denys Museum
Telephone: (902) 535-2175
Mail to: P.O. Box 249, B0E 3B0
Private agency, authorized by St.
Peter's Community Club
Jessie MacDonald, Curator
Major programs: library, museum,
markers, historic preservation,
records management, exhibits
Period of collections: 1650-1945

SEAFORTH

Chezzetcook Historical Society
P.O. Box 73, B0J 1N0
Telephone: (902) 827-2106
Private agency
Founded in: 1974
Margo Marshall, Treasurer
Number of members: 20
Major programs: markers, oral
history, school programs, book
publishing, research, exhibits,
genealogical services

SHEARWATER

Shearwater Aviation Museum
Telephone: (902) 463-5111, local 470
Mail to: C.F.B. Shearwater, B0J 3A0
National agency, authorized by
Department of National Defence,
Ottawa
Martin E. Hamilton, Curator
Major programs: museum, historic
site(s), historic preservation,
records management, research,
exhibits, photographic collections
Period of collections: 1918-present

SHELBURNE

Shelburne Historical Society and County Museum
Ross Thomson House, B0T 1W0
Founded in: 1949
Cathy Holmes, President
Number of members: 35

Staff: part time 4, volunteer 33
Major programs: archives, museum, school programs, book publishing, historic preservation, research, genealogical services
Period of collections: 1783-present

Shelburne Historical Society
P.O. Box 39, B0T 1W0
Telephone: (902) 875-3219
County agency
Founded in: 1949
Mrs. C. Holmes, President
Number of members: 35
Staff: volunteer 10
Major programs: library, archives, manuscripts, museum, historic site(s), oral history, school programs, book publishing, newsletters/pamphlets, historic preservation, records management, research, exhibits, audiovisual programs, photographic collections, genealogical services
Period of collections: 1783-1820

SHERBROOKE

Sherbrooke Restoration Commission
P.O. Box 285, B0J 3C0
Telephone: (902) 522-2400
Provincial agency, authorized by Nova Scotia Museum
Founded in: 1969
W. MacDonald Cruickshank, Project Director
Staff: full time 22, part time 73, volunteer 13
Major programs: museum, historic site(s), historic preservation, exhibits, living history, photographic collections
Period of collections: 1860-1914

Sherbrooke Village
Telephone: (902) 522-2400
Mail to: P.O. Box 285, B0J 3C0
W. M. Cruickshank, Director
Provincial agency, authorized by Nova Scotia Museum
Major programs: museum, historic site(s), historic preservation, records management, research, exhibits, living history, audiovisual programs
Period of collections: 1860-1914

SMITH'S COVE

Smith's Cove Historical Museum
Route 1 at Smith's Cove
Telephone: (902) 245-4063
Mail to: P.O. Box 10, B0S 1S0
David Irvine, President

SOUTH RAWDON

South Rawdon Museum Society, Inc.
S. Rawdon Rd., B0N 1Z0
Telephone: (902) 757-2342
Mail to: R.R. 1, Mt. Uniacke
Private agency
Founded in: 1965
Minnie McLearn, President
Number of members: 11
Staff: part time 2, volunteer 4
Major programs: museum

Period of collections: early 19th century-present

SPRINGHILL

Springhill Miner's Museum
Black River Rd.
Telephone: (902) 597-3449
Mail to: B0M 1X0
Guy Brown, Director
Questionnaire not received

SYDNEY

Old Sydney Society
The Esplanade
Telephone: (902) 564-4335
Mail to: P.O. Box 912
Founded in: 1966
M. J. Findlay, President
Questionnaire not received

TATAMAGOUCHE

North Shore Archives
B0K 1V0
County agency
Founded in: 1983
Anna Hamilton, President
Number of members: 30
Staff: volunteer 10
Major programs: archives, oral history, photographic collections, genealogical services
Period of collections: 1850-present

Tatamagouche Historical and Cultural Society
B0K 1V0
Telephone: (902) 657-2083
County agency
Sylvia Ross, President
Major programs: archives, school programs, historic preservation, research, exhibits, living history, audiovisual programs, photographic collections, genealogical services
Period of collections: 19th century

TRURO

Colchester Historical Museum
29 Young St.
Telephone: (902) 895-6284
Mail to: P.O. Box 412, B2N 5C5
Private agency, authorized by Colchester Historical Society
Founded in: 1954 (society); 1976 (museum)
Frances L. Langille, Curator
Staff: full time 1, volunteer 65
Major programs: museum, school programs, book publishing, newsletters/pamphlets, exhibits, photographic collections
Period of collections: 1770-present

Sunrise Trail Museum
24 Broad St., B2N 3G2
Questionnaire not received

TUPPERVILLE

Tupperville School Museum
Telephone: (902) 665-2427
Mail to: R.R. 3, Bridgetown, B0S 1C0
Private agency, authorized by Tupperville School Restoration Committee
Founded in: 1912

Carmen Inglis, President
Major programs: library, archives, museum, historic site(s), tours/pilgrimages, school programs, historic preservation, research, living history
Period of collections: 1865-1970

WEST BAY

Marble Mountain Community Museum
Telephone: (902) 756-2638
Mail to: Marble Mountain, R.R. 1, B0E 3K0
Jean McNicol, Curator

WEST PUBNICO

Le Musée acadien de Pubnico-Quest
Telephone: (902) 762-2966
Mail to: B0W 3S0
Questionnaire not received

WINDSOR

Haliburton House
Clifton Ave.
Telephone: (902) 795-2915
Mail to: 1747 Summer St., Halifax, B3H 3A6
Founded in: 1939
K. D. Gilmour, Curator, Branch Museums
Staff: full time 1, part time 7
Major programs: museum, historic sites preservation
Period of collections: 1836

West Hants Historical Society
Curry's Corner, B0N 1H0
Telephone: (902) 798-5265
Private agency
Founded in: 1973
Veronica Connelly, President
Number of members: 60
Staff: volunteer 10
Major programs: library, archives, manuscripts, museum, historic site(s), markers, tours/pilgrimages, oral history, school programs, book publishing, newsletters/pamphlets, historic preservation, records management, research, exhibits, photographic collections, genealogical services
Period of collections: 1750-1930

WOLFVILLE

Wolfville Historical Society
171 Main St.
Telephone: (902) 542-9775
Mail to: P.O. Box 38, B0P 1X0
Private agency
Founded in: 1941
James D. Davison, President
Number of members: 35
Staff: full time 2, volunteer 10
Major programs: museum, historic preservation
Period of collections: 19th century

YARMOUTH

Firefighters' Museum of Nova Scotia and National Exhibit Center
451 Main St., B5A 1G9

Telephone: (902) 742-5525
Provincial agency
Founded in: 1958
R. Bruce Hopkins, Curator
Number of members: 250
Staff: full time 2, part time 1,
  volunteer 75
Major programs: library, museum,
  school programs, records
  management, research, exhibits
Period of collections: 1819-1935

**Yarmouth County Historical
Society**
22 Collins St., B5A 3C8
Telephone: (902) 742-5539
Mail to: P.O. Box 39, B5A 4B1
Private agency
Founded in: 1935
Eric Ruff, Curator
Number of members: 300
Staff: full time 1, part time 2,
  volunteer 40
Major programs: library, archives,
  manuscripts, museum, historic
  site(s), junior history, oral history,
  school programs, book publishing,
  newsletters/pamphlets, records
  management, research, exhibits,
  photographic collections,
  genealogical services
Period of collections: 1850-1900

Yarmouth County Museum
22 Collins St.
Telephone: (902) 742-5539
Mail to: P.O. Box 39, B5A 4B1
Private agency, authorized by
  Yarmouth County Historical Society
Founded in: 1935
Eric J. Ruff, Curator
Number of members: 300
Staff: full time 1, part time 3,
  volunteer 40
Magazine: *Historigram*
Major programs: library, archives,
  manuscripts, museum, markers,
  school programs, book publishing,
  newsletters/pamphlets, research,
  exhibits, photographic collections,
  genealogical services
Period of collections: mid-late 1800s

ONTARIO

ALLISTON

South Simcoe Pioneer Museum
Riverdale Park
Telephone: (705) 435-7477
Mail to: c/o Town Municipal Office,
  L0M 1A0
John Ball, Chairman
Questionnaire not received

ALMONTE

**North Lanark Historical Society
Museum**
Mail to: c/o Sheila Symington, P.O.
  Box 218, K0A 1A0

ALVINSTON

A. W. Campbell House Museum
A. W. Campbell Conservation Area,
  R.R. 2

Telephone: (510) 245-3710
Mail to: 205 Mill Pond Crescent,
  Strathroy, N7G 3P9
David Nielsen, Director
Questionnaire not received

AMELIASBURGH

Ameliasburgh Historical Museum
County Road 19
Telephone: (613) 962-2782
Mail to: K0K 1A0
Vivian Swain, Director
Questionnaire not received

AMHERSTBURG

**Amherstburg Historic Sites
Association**
214 Dalhousie St., N9V 1W4
Telephone: (519) 736-2511
Private agency
Founded in: 1973
John Burkhart, President
Number of members: 50
Staff: part time 1, volunteer 8
Major programs: archives, museum,
  historic site(s), tours/pilgrimages,
  school programs, historic
  preservation, exhibits,
  genealogical services
Period of collections: 1799-1850

Ft. Malden National Historic Park
100 Laird Ave.
Telephone: (519) 736-5416
Mail to: P.O. Box 38, N9V 2Z2
National agency, authorized by Parks
  Canada, Department of the
  Environment
Founded in: 1939
Harry J. Bosveld, Superintendent
Staff: full time 11, part time 3
Major programs: museum, historic
  site(s), school programs
Period of collections: 1796-1860

ANCASTER

**Ancaster Township Historical
Society**
290 Harmony Rd., L9G 2T2
Telephone: (416) 648-2055
Questionnaire not received

APANEE

Allan Macpherson House
Lennox and Addington Historical
  Society
Telephone: (613) 354-4203
Mail to: P.O. Box 183, K7R 3M3
Founded in: 1967
Helen Hutchison, Executive Secretary
Questionnaire not received

ARNPRIOR

Arnprior and District Museum
35 Madawaska St., K7S 3H3
Telephone: (613) 623-4391/623-4902
Founded in: 1967
Helen Anglin, Curator
Staff: full time 1, part time 1
Major programs: manuscripts,
  museum, historic sites
  preservation, tours/pilgrimages,
  oral history, educational programs,
  historic preservation
Period of collections: 1825-1900

ATIKOKAN

**Atikokan Centennial Museum and
Historical Park**
P.O. Box 849, P0T 1C0
Telephone: (807) 597-6585
Founded in: 1967
Jo-Anne Lachapelle-Beyak,
  Director/Curator
Staff: full time 1, part time 1
Major programs: museum,
  educational programs
Period of collections: 1910-1960

AURORA

**Aurora and District Historical
Society, Inc.**
22 Church St.
Telephone: (416) 727-8991
Mail to: P.O. Box 356, L4G 3H4
Founded in: 1963
Alan Mitchell, President
Number of members: 200
Staff: full time 1, volunteer 10
Major programs: library, archives,
  museum, historic site(s), school
  programs, newsletters/pamphlets,
  research, exhibits, photographic
  collections, genealogical services
Period of collections: 1800-present

AYLMER

Aylmer and District Museum
Telephone: (519) 773-9723
Mail to: 14 East St., N5H 1W2
Town agency
Patricia Zimmer, Diretor
Major programs: archives, museum,
  tours/pilgrimages, junior history,
  oral history, school programs,
  pamphlets, historic preservation,
  records management, research,
  exhibits, photographic collections,
  genealogical services, tourism
  centre and programmes
Period of collections: 1850-1930

BANCROFT

Bancroft Historical Museum
Station St.
Telephone: (613) 332-1884
Mail to: P.O. Box 239, K0L 1C0
Town agency
Vilma Walker, Chair
Major programs: museum
Period of collections: mid-late 1800s

BARLOCHAN

Woodwinds Historical Museum
3 km off Hwy. 69 at Barlochan
Telephone: (705) 687-2498
Mail to: c/o Joyce Schell, R.R. 2,
  P.O. Box 55, P0C 1G0
Joyce Schell, Curator
Questionnaire not received

BARRIE

**Simcoe County Historical
Association**
Mail to: P.O. Box 144, L4M 4S9
Founded in: 1970
Questionnaire not received

**Simcoe County Museum and
Archives**
Hwy. 26
Telephone: (705) 728-3721

Mail to: R.R. 2, Minesing, L0L 1Y0
Founded in: 1928
Robert E. Fisher, Director
Questionnaire not received

BEACHVILLE

Beachville District Historical Society Museum
Country Road 9
Telephone: (519) 429-6367
Mail to: c/o Shirley Riddick, P.O. Box 6, N0J 1A0
Shirley Riddick, Secretary
Questionnaire not received

BEAVERTON

Beaver River Museum—Beaverton Thorah and Eldon Historical Society
P.O. Box 314, L0K IA0
Private agency
Founded in: 1976
Julienne Everett, Curator
Number of members: 110
Staff: volunteer 80
Major programs: archives, museum, book publishing, genealogical services
Period of collections: 1850-1900

BELLEVILLE

Hastings County Historical Society
257 Bridge St. E, K8N 1P4
Telephone: (613) 962-2329
Questionnaire not received

Moira River Conservation Authority
Telephone: (613) 968-8688
Mail to: 217 N. Front St., K8P 3C3
Founded in: 1947
B. A. Watson, Secretary-Treasurer
Staff: full time 4, part time 4
Major programs: museum, historic sites preservation
Period of collections: 1783-1865

BLIND RIVER

North Shore Museum
Hwy. 17 east of Blind River
Telephone: (705) 849-2433
Mail to: Algoma Mills, P0R 1A0
Blanch Mattaini, Curator
Questionnaire not received

Timber Village Museum
Hwy. 17-E
Telephone: (705) 356-7544
Mail to: P.O. Box 628, P0R 1B0
Town agency
Wolf Kirchmeir, Chair
Major programs: museum, oral history, historic preservation, exhibits
Period of collections: 1910-1960

BLOOMFIELD

United Empire Loyalist Museum
P.O. Box 215, K0K 1G0
Telephone: (613) 393-2869
Private agency
Mrs. M. Mackey, Museum Committee Chair
Major programs: library, archives, manuscripts, museum, tours/pilgrimages, junior history, school programs, book publishing,

historic preservation, research, exhibits, genealogical services, Loyalist family history
Period of collections: 1784-1884

BORDEN

Canadian Forces Base Borden Military Museum
Canadian Forces Base Borden, L0M 1C0
Telephone: (705) 424-1200 ext., 2331
Questionnaire not received

BOTHWELL

Fairfield Museum
Hwy. 2
Telephone: (519) 692-4397
Mail to: R.R. 3, N0P 1C0
Questionnaire not received

BOWMANVILLE

Bowmanville Museum
37 Silver St.
Mail to: P.O. Box 188
Founded in: 1961
Helen Knibb, Curator
Staff: full time 1
Major programs: museum
Period of collections: 1850-1930

Darlington Provincial Park Pioneer Home
Telephone: (416) 723-4341
Mail to: c/o Superintendent, Darlington Provincial Park, R.R. 2, L1C 3K3
Brian Swaile, Park Superintendent

BRACEBRIDGE

Muskoka Steamship and Historical Society
Ba9 St., Gravenhurst, P0C 1G0
Telephone: (705) 687-2612
Mail to: P.O. Box 1283, Gravenhurst
Questionnaire not received

BRANTFORD

Bell Homestead
94 Tutela Hghts. Rd., N3T 1A1
Telephone: (519) 756-6220
City agency
J. Brian Studier, Curator
Staff: full time 1, part time 3
Major programs: museum, historic site(s), school programs
Period of collections: 1870-1881

Brant Historical Society
57 Charlotte St.
Telephone: (519) 752-2483
Private agency
Founded in: 1908
Beth L. Hanna, Director/Curator
Number of members: 130
Major programs: library, archives, museum, school programs, book publishing
Period of collections: 1800-1918

BRIGHTON

Proctor House Museum
Yonge St. N
Telephone: (613) 475-2144
Mail to: P.O. Box 578, K0K 1H0
James Ogilvy, President
Questionnaire not received

BROCKVILLE

Brockville and District Historical Society
Mail to: P.O. Box 195
Founded in: 1911
Constance Ferguson, Corresponding Secretary
Number of members: 175
Staff: volunteer 12
Major programs: archives, museum, historic sites preservation, educational programs
Period of collections: prehistoric-present

Brockville Museum
5 Henry St., K6V 6M4
Telephone: (613) 342-4397
City agency
Founded in: 1980
Deborah Emerton, Director
Staff: full time 1, part time 3, volunteer 10
Major programs: archives, museum, school programs, exhibits, photographic collections
Period of collections: 1850-1910

Restoration Technology
St. Lawrence College of Applied Arts and Technology, 2288 Parkedale Ave., K6V 5X3
Telephone: (613) 345-0660
State agency, authorized by Ministry of Colleges and Universities
Founded in: 1973
John Silburn
Number of members: 25
Staff: full time 2, part time 4
Major programs: historic preservation, educational programs

BROUGHAM

Town of Pickering Museum: Greenwood
Telephone: (416) 683-2760, ext. 24
Mail to: Pickering Town Offices, Department of Parks and Recreation, 1710 Kingston Rd., L0H 1A0
Thomas Quinn, Director of Parks and Recreation

BRUCE MINES

Bruce Mines Museum
Taylor St., Hwy. 17, P0R 1C0
Telephone: (705) 785-3426
Town agency
Arthur Henderson, Curator
Major programs: archives, museum
Period of collections: 1846-1920

BURGESSVILLE

Oxford County Museum School
Telephone: (519) 424-9964/424-9815
Mail to: P.O. Box 40
Private agency
R. Cartmale, Director
Major programs: school programs
Period of collections: 1890-1920

BURLINGTON

Burlington Historical Society
555 Woodland Ave., L7R 2S3
Private agency
Eric Gudgeon, President

Major programs: markers,
tours/pilgrimages, book publishing,
newsletters/pamphlets, living
history

Joseph Brant Museum
1240 N. Shore Blvd., L7S 1C5
Telephone: (416) 634-3556
Founded in: 1942
Carlo T. Toccalino, Director
Number of members: 100
Staff: full time 2, part time 3,
volunteer 40
Major programs: museum,
educational programs
Period of collections: prehistoric-1970

Spruce Lane Farm
Bronte Creek Provincial Park
Telephone: (416) 827-6911/335-0023,
ext. 31
Mail to: 1219 Burloak Dr., L7R 2X5
Gordon Weedon, Manager
Questionnaire not received

CALEDONIA

Chiefwood
Hwy. 54
Telephone: (519) 445-2201
Mail to: Ohsweken Post Office,
Ohsweken, N0A 1M0
Betty Williams, Curator
Questionnaire not received

CALLANDER

North Himsworth Museum
107 Lansdowne St.
Telephone: (705) 752-2282
Mail to: P.O. Box 100, P0H 1H0
County agency
M. J. Wanamaker, Curator
Major programs: museum
Period of collections: 1880-1930s

CAYUGA

Haldimand County Museum
Court House Park
Telephone: (416) 772-5775
Mail to: c/o Ms. Rene Tunney,
Haldimand/Norfolk Regional
Museum Advisory Board, P.O. Box
38, N0A 1E0
Bob Vick, Chairman of the Museum
Advisory Board

CHAPLEAU

Chapleau Historical Museum
Monk St.
Telephone: (705) 864-1330
Mail to: P.O. Box 129, P0M 1K0
Town agency
Major programs: museum
Period of collections: 1885-present

CHATHAM

Chatham-Kent Museum
Telephone: (519) 352-8540
Mail to: 59 William St. N, N7M 4L3
Mary Creasey, Curator
Questionnaire not received

Fairfield Museum
R.R. 3, Rothwell
Telephone: (519) 692-4397
Questionnaire not received

CLARKSBURG

Beaver Valley Military Museum
Telephone: (519) 599-3031
Mail to: P.O. Box 40, N0H 1J0
W. MacKey, Chairman

COBALT

Cobalt's Northern Ontario Mining
24 Silver St.
Telephone: (705) 679-8301
Mail to: P.O. Box 215, P0J 1C0
Arnold Todd, Director

COCHRANE

**Cochrane Railway and Pioneer
Museum**
Union Station
Telephone: (705) 272-5171/272-4361
Mail to: P.O. Box 490, P0L 1C0
Juli Karam, Curator
Questionnaire not received

COLCHESTER SOUTH

**Southwestern Ontario Heritage
Village**
County Rd. 23
Telephone: (519) 776-6909
Mail to: P.O. Box 221, Harrow, N0R
1G0
Private agency, authorized by
Historic Vehicle Society of Ontario,
Windsor
Founded in: 1974
Christina Speer,
Administrator/Curator
Number of members: 60
Staff: full time 1, volunteer 10
Major programs: museum, school
programs, historic preservation,
records management, research,
exhibits, living history
Period of collections: 1875-1925

COLLINGWOOD

Collingwood Museum
St. Paul St., Memorial Park
Telephone: (705) 445-4811
Mail to: P.O. Box 556, L9Y 4B2
Town agency
Founded in: 1903
Barbara Arp, Curator
Staff: full time 1, part time 4
Major programs: museum
Period of collections: 1855-1970

COMBER

Tilbury West Agricultural Museum
Hwy. 77
Telephone: (519) 687-2240
Mail to: c/o Don McMillan, Township
Clerk's Office, P.O. Box 158, N0P
1J0
Don McMillan, Secretary-Treasurer
Questionnaire not received

COMBERMERE

Madonna House Pioneer Museum
Hwy. 517 (off Hwy. 62), K0J 1L0
Telephone: (613) 756-3713
Linda Lambeth, Director
Private agency
Major programs: museum
Period of collections: 1900-1940

COPPER CLIFF

Copper Cliff Museum
Telephone: (705) 682-2780
Mail to: c/o Mrs. A. McConnell, P.O.
Box 1000, Sudbury, P3E 4S5
R. Dow, Community Co-ordinator
Questionnaire not received

CORNWALL

**Stormont, Dundas and Glengarry
Historical Society**
Telephone: (613) 932-2381/938-9585
Mail to: P.O. Box 773, K6H 5T5
City agency
Founded in: 1920
Mrs. C. P. Proctor,
Secretary/Treasurer
Number of members: 320
Major programs: archives,
manuscripts, museum, historic
site(s), markers, junior history, oral
history, school programs,
newsletters/pamphlets, historic
preservation, research,
genealogical services
Period of collections: 1784-present

CORUNNA

Pilot House Museum
Sinclair Parkway 18
Telephone: (519) 344-6136
Mail to: c/o Malcolm McRae, 2012
Wayne Ave., Sarnia, N7T 7H5
Malcolm McRae, Director

CUMBERLAND

Cumberland Township Museum
Regional Rd. 34
Telephone: (613) 833-3059
Mail to: P.O. Box 159, K0A 1S0
E. A. Pilon, Director
Major programs: museum, school
programs, historic preservation
Period of collections: 1880-1935

DELHI

Ontario Tobacco Museum
200 Talbot Rd.
Telephone: (519) 582-0278
Mail to: c/o 192 Main St., N4B 2M2
Karen Harrison, Director
Questionnaire not received

DOWNSVIEW

Black Creek Pioneer Village
1000 Murray Ross Parkway (Jane St.
and Steeles Ave.)
Telephone: (416) 661-6600
Mail to: 5 Shoreham Dr., M3N 1S4
Russell Cooper, Director

DRESDEN

Uncle Tom's Cabin Museum
R.R. 5, N0P 1M0
Telephone: (519) 683-2978
Founded in: 1964
Dianne Jackson, Manager
Staff: full time 3, part time 3
Major programs: museum, historic
sites preservation, tours, oral
history
Period of collections: 1840-early
1900s

DRYDEN

Dryden District Museum
284 Government St., P8N 2P3
Telephone: (807) 223-4671/223-6192
Founded in: 1960
Louise M. Meloney
Questionnaire not received

DUNDAS

Dundas Historical Society Museum
Telephone: (416) 627-7412
Mail to: 139 Park St., W, L9H 5G1
Private agency
Olive Newcombe, Director
Major programs: archives, museum,
school programs, book publishing,
newsletters/pamphlets, exhibits
Period of collections: 1800-present

DUNVEGAN

Glengarry Museum
Telephone: (613) 527-5230
Mail to: P.O. Box 27, K0C 1J0
Private agency, authorized by
Glengarry Historical Society
R. B. Campbell, Chair
Major programs: manuscripts,
museum, historic site(s), historic
preservation, exhibits,
photographic collections,
genealogical services
Period of collections: 1850-1900

EAR FALLS

Ear Falls Museum
Hwy. 105
Telephone: (807) 222-3198
Mail to: P.O. Box 388, P0V 1T0
Joyce Appel, Contact person
Questionnaire not received

EGMONDVILLE

Van Egmond House
Telephone: (519) 527-0375
Mail to: c/o Mrs. R. Newnham, P.O.
Box 601, Seaforth, N0K 1W0
Mrs. R. Newnham, Contact person

ELLIOT LAKE

**Elliot Lake Nuclear and Mining
Museum**
Municipal Office Bldg.
Telephone: (705) 848-2287
Mail to: 45 Hillside Dr., N, P5A 1X5
Town agency
Robert Manuel, Curator
Major programs: museum,
tours/pilgrimages, exhibits
Period of collections: 1900-present

EMO

**Rainy River District Women's
Institute Museum**
Hwy. 71
Telephone: (807) 482-2007/482-2792
Mail to: P.O. Box 511, P0W 1E0
Private agency
Major programs: museum, historic
preservation
Period of collections: from 1880

ESSEX

**Essex Region Conservation
Authority**
360 Fairview Ave., W, N8M 1Y6

Telephone: (519) 738-2029
County agency, athorized by Essex
Region Conservation Authority
Founded in: 1973
David Guthrie, Curator
Staff: full time 3, volunteer 15
Major programs: museum, historic
site(s), tours, school programs,
historic preservation, living history,
audiovisual programs
Period of collections: 1850

**Southwestern Ontario Heritage
Village**
County Rd. 23 (Arner Town Line)
Telephone: (519) 776-6909
Mail to: c/o Chair, 94 Talbot St., N,
N8M 2C4
Private agency, authorized by
Historic Vehicle Society of Ontario,
Windsor
Ken Mackenzie, Chair
Major programs: museum, school
programs, research, exhibits
Period of collections: 1850-1905

ETOBICOKE

Montgomery's Inn
4709 Dundas St., W, Islington, M9A
1A8
Telephone: (416) 236-1046
City agency
Founded in: 1975
Shirley E. Hartt, Curator/Director
Staff: full time 4, part time 16,
volunteer 45
Major programs: museum, historic
site(s), school programs, living
history
Period of collections: 1830-1850

FENELON FALLS

Fenelon Falls and District Museum
50 Oak St.
Telephone: (705) 887-2336
Mail to: c/o Bessie Christian,
Secretary-Treasurer, 18 Francis St.
E, K0M 1N0
Wilfrid Jackett, Chairman
Questionnaire not received

FERGUS

Wellington County Museum
Telephone: (519) 846-5169
Mail to: Wellington Pl., R.R. 1,
N1M 2W3
Ken Seiling, Director

FLESHERTON

South Grey Museum
Memorial Park on Hwy. 10
Telephone: (519) 924-2948
Mail to: c/o Irene Field, P.O. Box 65,
N0C 1E0
Irene Field, Chairman
Questionnaire not received

FOREST

Forest-Lambton Museum
59 Broadway
Telephone: (510) 873-5884
Mail to: R.R. 1, N0N 1J0
Private agency
E. Powell, Curator
Major programs: archives, museum,
research, exhibits
Period of collections: 1880-present

FORT ERIE

Niagara Parks Commission
Oak Hall Administration Bldg., 7400
Portage Rd., S
Telephone: (416) 356-2241
Mail to: P.O. Box 150, Niagara Falls,
L2E 6T2
Provincial agency, authorized by
Niagara Parks Commission
M.S. Cushing, Assistant General
Manager
Staff: part time 17
Major programs: museum, historic
site(s), markers, tours/pilgrimages,
school programs, historic
preservation
Period of collections: 1783-1865

**Old Ft. Erie Historical Railroad and
Museum**
Oakes Park, Central Ave.
Telephone: (416) 871-1412
Mail to: P.O. Box 355, L2A 3M9
Town agency
John Jones, Director
Major programs: museum

FREELTON

Valens Log Cabin Museum
Hwy. 97
Telephone: (416) 659-7715
Mail to: P.O. Box 99, Ancaster,
L9G 3L3
James Anderson, Superintendent of
Conservation Area
Questionnaire not received

FRENCH LAKE

Quetico Provincial Park Museum
French Lake (off Hwy. 11)·
Telephone: (807) 929-3552
Mail to: Ministry of Natural Resources,
Atikokan, P0T 1C0
Provincial agency
Shan Walshe, Park Naturalist
Major programs: library, archives,
manuscripts, museum, historic
site(s), research, exhibits,
audiovisual programs, archaeology
programs, photographic
collections
Period of collections: prehistoric-fur
trade

GANAOQUE

Gananoque Historical Museum
10 King St. E
Telephone: (613) 382-4663
Malto: c/o Derrol Simpson, P.O. Box
293, K7G 2T7
Derrol Simpson, Chairman
Questionnaire not received

GODERICH

Huron County Pioneer Museum
110 North St., N7A 2T8
Telephone: (519) 524-9610
County agency
Founded in: 1951
Raymond Scotchmer,
Director/Curator
Staff: full time 4, part time 5
Major programs: archives, museum,
historic site(s), oral history, school
programs, exhibits
Period of collections: 1820

Huron Historic Gaol
Telephone: (519) 524-6971
Mail to: 181 Victoria St., N, N7A 2S8
Harold Erb, Curator
Private agency
Major programs: museum, school
  programs, historic preservation

GOLDEN LAKE

Golden Lake Algonquin Museum
Golden Lake Indian Reserve
Telephone: (613) 625-2027
Mail to: P.O. Box 28, K0J 1X0
Philip Commanda, Curator

GORE BAY

**Western Manitoulin Historical
Society**
Phipps St., P0P IH0
Telephone: (705) 282-2040
Town agency
Founded in: 1959
M. Bowman, Chair
Staff: full time 2
Major programs: archives,
  manuscripts, museum, junior
  history, oral history, educational
  programs, books,
  newsletters/pamphlets
Period of collections:
  prehistoric-present

GRAFTON

Barnum House Museum
3km west of Grafton on Hwy. 2
Telephone: (416) 349-2724
Mail to: P.O. Box 38, K0K 2G0
Gorman Young, Curator
Questionnaire not received

GRAND BEND

Lambton Heritage Museum
Telephone: (519) 243-2600
Mail to: R.R 2, N0M 1T0
County agency
Robert Tremain, Director
Major programs: museum, school
  programs, exhibits
Period of collections: 1850-1930

GRAVENHURST

Bethune Memorial House
John and Hughson Sts.
Telephone: (705) 687-4261
Mail to: P.O. Box 2160, P0C 1G0
National agency, authorized by Parks
  Canada
Margaret Evans, Superintendent
Major programs: historic site(s),
  tours/pilgrimages, historic
  preservation
Period of collections: 1890

Segwun Steamboat Museum
Gravenhurst Bay
Telephone: (706) 687-2612/687-2664
Mail to: P.O. Box 1283, P0C 1G0
Questionnaire not received

GRIMSBY

Grimsby Historical Society
Telephone: (416) 945-4982
Mail to: P.O. Box 294, L3M 4G1
Questionnaire not received

The Grimsby Museum
6 Murray St.
Mail to: P.O. Box 244, L3M 4G5
Town agency
Founded in: 1963
Wendy K. Evans, Curator/Director
Staff: full time 1, part time 1
Major programs: museum,
  educational programs, exhibits
Period of collections: 1783-1930

GUELPH

**Col. John McGrae Birthplace
Society**
Mail to: P.O. Box 601
Mrs. F. Cleghorn, Secretary
Questionnaire not received

HALIBURTON

Haliburton Highlands Museum
Hwy. 118
Telephone: (705) 457-2760
Mail to: c/o Director, P.O. Box 535,
  K0M 1S0
Town agency
R. D. Car, Chair
Major programs: museum, historic
  preservation, exhibits
Period of collections: 1860-present

HAMILTON

Dundurn Castle
York Blvd., L8R 3H1
Telephone: (416) 522-5313
Founded in: 1967
Marilynn Soules, Curator
Questionnaire not received

Hamilton History Association
Suite 32, 42 James S, L8N 3R1
Telephone: (416) 527-0999
Mail to: P.O. Box 985
William Rosart, President
Questionnaire not received

**Hamilton Museum of Steam and
Technology**
900 Woodward Ave., L8H 7N2
Telephone: (416) 549-5225
County agency, authorized by
  Regional Municipality of Hamilton,
  Wentworth
David Rollinson, Curator
Staff: full time 1, part time 2,
  volunteer 20
Major programs: museum, historic
  site(s)
Period of collections: 1850s-1900

**Head-of-the-Lake Historical
Society**
Mail to: P.O. Box 896, L8N 3P6
Founded in: 1944
Murray Aikman, President
Questionnaire not received

HARROW

**HEIRS (Harrow Early Immigrant
Research Society)**
Telephone: (519) 738-2500/738-2950
Mail to: P.O. Box 53, N0R 1G0
Private agency
Founded in: 1971
James R. Broadfoot, President
Number of members: 78

Major programs: archives, historic
  preservation, research,
  genealogical services
Period of collections: 1800-1920

John R. Park Homestead
Country Rd. 50 at Iler Rd.
Telephone: (519) 738-2029
Mail to: 360 Fairview Ave., W, Essex,
  N8M 1Y6
County agency, authorized by Essex
  Region Conservation Authority
Founded in: 1977
David Guthrie, Curator
Number of members: 1
Staff: full time 3, volunteer 15
Major programs: museum, historic
  site(s), tours, historic preservation,
  living history, audiovisual programs
Period of collections: 1850

HAVELOCK

Trent River Pioneer Museum
Telephone: (613) 397-3117
Mail to: R.R. 1, Wooler, K0K 3M0
Private agency
Ada Dalmas, Director
Major programs: museum
Period of collections: 1725-early
  1900s

HEATHCOTE

Grey County Historical Society
Telephone: (519) 599-5163
Mail to: Mrs. L. McNally, R.R. 1
  Clarksburg
Questionnaire not received

HOLLAND CENTRE

Comber Pioneer Village
4km north of Holland Centre
Telephone: (519) 794-3467
Mail to: R.R. 3, N0H 1R0
Robert Comber, Director

Queen's Bush Foundation
R.R. 3
Telephone: (519) 794-3231
Mail to: P.O. Box 148, N0H 1R0
Private agency
Founded in: 1984
Leonard David Hicks, Executive
  Coordinator
Staff: part time 1, volunteer 5
Major programs: museum, historic
  site(s), historic preservation
Period of collections: mid-late 1800s

HUNTSVILLE

**Muskoka Pioneer Village and
Museum**
Huntsville Park
Telephone: (705) 789-7576
Mail to: Brunel Rd., P0A 1K0
Town agency
Major programs: museum, school
  programs, exhibits, living history
Period of collections: 1860-1910

INNISVILLE

Innisville and District Museum
Hwy. 7
Telephone: (613) 257-2536
Mail to: c/o Mrs. John Rintoul, R.R. 1,
  Carleton Pl., K0A 1J0
Questionnaire not received

IRON BRIDGE

Iron Bridge Historical Museum
James St.
Telephone: (705) 843-2331
Mail to: P.O. Box 132, P0R 1H0
Town agency
Major programs: exhibits
Period of collections: 1890-1920

IROQUOIS

Carman House Museum
On the Carman Rd. to the Seaway
Locks off Hwy. 2
Telephone: (613) 652-4808
Mail to: c/o Reeve Frank Rooney, K0E
1K0
Mrs. Shelley Prins, Contact person
Questionnaire not received

IROQUOIS FALLS

Iroquois Falls Museum
Ontario Northlands Railroad Station,
Cambridge St.
Telephone: (613) 258-3730
Mail to: P.O. Box 448, P0K 1E0
Marie Peever, Director

ISLINGTON

Borough of York Museum
Centennial Bldg., 2694 Eglinton Ave.
W, at Keele
Telephone: (416) 653-2700, ext.
241/781-5531
Mail to: c/o Clerk's Department,
Borough of York, 2700 Eglinton
Ave. W, Toronto, M6M 1V1
William Easton, Chairman of the
Historical Committee
Questionnaire not received

City of York Historical Committee
2700 Eglington Ave., W, M6M 1V1
Telephone: (416) 653-2700
City agency
Mrs. N. Bradley, Secretary
Staff: part time 1, volunteer 20
Major programs: museum; historic
site(s)
Period of collections: 1918-present

Etobicoke Historical Society
4709 Dundas St. W, M9A 1A8
Questionnaire not received

Montgomery's Inn
Dundas St. at Islington Ave.
Telephone: (416) 236-1046
Mail to: 4709 Dundas St. W, M9A 1A8
Phil Dunning, Director
Questionnaire not received

JORDAN

Ball's Falls Conservation Area
R.R. 1
Telephone: (416) 892-2621/562-5235
Mail to: P.O. Box 460, 1440 Pelham
St., Fonthill, L0S 1E0
C. Leuty, Director
Questionnaire not received

**Jordan Historical Museum of the
Twenty**
Main St., P.O. Box 39, L0R 1S0
Telephone: (416) 562-5242
Founded in: 1953
H. Crowfoot, Director
Questionnaire not received

KAKABEKA

Hymers Museum
Mail to: R.R. 1, P0T 1W0
Orma Kempe, Curator
Questionnaire not received

KAPUSKASING

Ron Morel Memorial Museum
CN Station, Hwy. 11, N. Rt.
Telephone: (705) 335-5443/335-2733
Mail to: 25 Poplar Crescent, P5N 1Y2
Town agency
Pauline Martin, Curator
Major programs: museum, exhibits,
photographic collections
Period of collections: early 20th
century

KENORA

Lake of the Woods Museum
Main St., S
Telephone: (807) 468-8865
Mail to: P.O. Box 497, P9N 3X5
Town agency
Reg Reeve, Director
Major programs: archives, museum,
photographic collections
Period of collections: 1880-1920

KILLARNEY

Killarney Centennial Museum
Telephone: (705) 287-2466
Mail to: Charles St., P0M 2A0
Christine Pitfield, Curator

KINGSTON

**MacLachlan Woodworking
Museum**
1316 Princess St., K7L 4V8
Telephone: (613) 549-7000
Mail to: P.O. Box 186
Founded in: 1967
A. G. MacLachlan, Director
Questionnaire not received

**Marine Museum of the Great Lakes
at Kingston**
Telephone: (613) 542-2261
Mail to: 55 Ontario St., K7L 2Y2
Private agency
Maurice Smith, Curator
Major programs: library, archives,
museum, school programs,
research, exhibits
Period of collections: 1830s

Murney Tower Museum
Barrie and King Sts.
Mail to: P.O. Box 54, K7L 4V6
Private agency, authorized by
Kingston Historical Society and
Parks Canada
Major programs: museum, historic
site(s), school programs, exhibits

Old Ft. Henry
Junction Hwy. 2 and Hwy. 15
Telephone: (613) 542-7388
Mail to: P.O. Box 213, K7L 4V8
D. H. Clark, Manager
Major programs: library, museum,
living history, audiovisual programs
Period of collections: 1783-1901

Pump House Steam Museum
Telephone: (613) 546-4696
Mail to: 23 Ontario St., K7L 2Y2

City agency, authorized by
Department of Parks and
Recreation
F. Telgmann, Director
Major programs: museum, historic
site(s), historic preservation
Period of collections: 1849-present

KIRKLAND LAKE

**Museum of Northern History, Sir
Harry Oakes Chateau**
2 Chateau Dr., P.O. Box 966, P2N 3L1
Telephone: (705) 568-8800
Mail to: P.O. Box 730, P2N 3K1
Peter Tulumello, Director/Curator
Town agency
Major programs: archives, museum,
historic site(s), oral history, school
programs, book publishing,
newsletters/pamphlets, historic
preservation, research, exhibits,
audiovisual programs,
photographic collections
Period of collections: 1900-present

KITCHENER

Doon Pioneer Village
Telephone: (519) 893-1914
Mail to: R.R. 2, N2G 3W5
Regional agency
Marten Lewis, Director of Historic
Sites
Major programs: museum, historic
site(s), school programs, living
history
Period of collections: 1914

Waterloo Historical Society
P.O. Box 552, Station C, N2G 4A2
Founded in: 1912
Number of members: 550
Staff: volunteer 10
Magazine: *Waterloo Historical
Society Annual Volume*
Major programs: archives, markers,
books
Period of collections: 1918-present

Woodside National Historic Park
528 Wellington St., N, N2H 5L5
Telephone: (519) 742-5273
Federal agency, authorized by Parks
Canada
Founded in: 1954
J. Humphries, Area Superintendent
Staff: full time 4, part time 10
Major programs: historic site(s),
tours/pilgrimages, school
programs, historic preservation,
living history, audiovisual programs
Period of collections: 1890s

LAKEFIELD

Christ Church
62 Queen St.
Telephone: (705) 652-3614
Mail to: P.O. Box 926, K0L 2H0
Private agency, authorized by
Anglican Church of Canada
Founded in: 1853
Charles McDermott, Preservation
Committee Chair
Staff: volunteer 6
Major programs: museum, historic
site(s), tours/pilgrimages, school
programs, exhibits
Period of collections: 1855-1870

LANG

Century Village Museum
County of Peterborough
Telephone: (705) 295-6694,
    793-0380
Mail to: R.R. 3, Keene, K0L 2G0
County agency
Founded in: 1967
Margaret MacKelvie, Curator
Staff: full time 3, part time 30,
    volunteer 100
Major programs: library, archives,
    museum, school programs, historic
    preservation, records
    management, research, exhibits,
    living history
Period of collections: 1820-1899

Hope Sawmill
Telephone: (705) 745-5791
Mail to: c/o Otanabe Region
    Conservation Authority, 727
    Lansdowne St. W, Peterborough,
    K9J 1Z2
Elizabeth Wright, Contact person

LATCHFORD

House of Memories
Telephone: (705) 676-2417
Mail to: Drawer 10, P0J 1N0
Ed Garreau, President

LEAKSDALE

Country Heritage Museum
Telephone: (416) 852-3927
Mail to: R.R. 2, Uxbridge, L0C 1K0
Edward Brown, Co-Director

LINDSAY

Victoria County Historical Museum
435 Kent St. W
Telephone: (705) 324-4782
Mail to: 66 Colbourne St. W, K9V 3S9
John Wenzel, President
Questionnaire not received

LISTOWEL

**Historical Society of Perth-Queen's
    Bush**
Administration Bldg., N4W 1L3
Questionnaire not received

Queen's Bush Historical Society
330 Wallace Ave., N, N4W 1L7
Telephone: (519) 291-1688
Private agency
Founded in: 1972
Maurice Oliver, President
Number of members: 42
Staff: volunteer 6
Major programs: archives, historic
    site(s), oral history, school
    programs, historic preservation,
    research, genealogical services
Period of collections: 1850

LONDON

Fanshawe Pioneer Village
R.R. 6
Telephone: (519) 451-2800
Mail to: P.O. Box 6278, Station D,
    N5W 5S1
Authorized by Upper Thames River
    Conservation Authority
Founded in: 1959

Teresa Hollingsworth, Community
    Relations Coordinator
Staff: full time 3, part time 13,
    volunteer 5
Major programs: historic site(s),
    tours/pilgrimages, school
    programs
Period of collections: 1820-1920

**1st Hussars Regimental
    Association—Citizen Soldiers
    Museum**
399 Ridout St., N, N6A 2P1
Private agency
Founded in: 1983
Alastair L. Neely, Curator
Number of members: 300
Staff: part time 1, volunteer 20
Magazine: *1st Hussars Bulletin*
Major programs: archives, museum,
    oral history, newsletters/pamphlets,
    research, photographic collections
Period of collections: 1856-present

Gratton's Weldwood Museum
Hwy. 2 S.
Telephone: (519) 652-2810
Mail to: R.R. 4
Floyd Gratton, Director
Questionnaire not received

**London and Middlesex Historical
    Society**
P.O. Box 303, Station B, N6A 4W1
Private agency
Founded in: 1901
Number of members: 346
Magazine: *Transactions of the
    London and Middlesex Historical
    Society*
Major programs: library, archives,
    tours/pilgrimages, school
    programs, newsletters/pamphlets,
    historic preservation, research
Period of collections: 1865-1918

London Historical Museums
1017 Western Rd., N6G 1G5
Telephone: (519) 433-6171
Town agency
Founded in: 1958
Christopher Severance, Curator
Staff: full time 10, part time 8,
    volunteer 20
Magazine: *Access-Bulletin of London
    Public Libraries, Museums*
Major programs: library, museum,
    historic site(s), tours/pilgrimages,
    junior history, school programs,
    newsletters/pamphlets, records
    management, research, exhibits,
    photographic collections,
    genealogical services
Period of collections: late 19th
    century

**London Room, London Public
    Library and Art Museum**
305 Queens Ave., N6B 1X2
Telephone: (519) 432-7166, ext. 79
City agency
Founded in: 1967
W. Glen Curnoe, Librarian
Staff: full time 1
Major programs: library, archives,
    manuscripts, historic sites
    preservation, books
Period of collections: 1826-present

**Upper Thames River Conservation
    Authority**
P.O. Box 6278 Station D N5W 5S1
Telephone: (519) 451-2800
Founded in: 1947
Stephen Lane, Community Relations
    Coordinator
Staff: full time 3, part time 15,
    volunteer 5
Major programs: museum, historic
    sites preservation, educational
    programs, newsletters/pamphlets,
    historic preservation
Period of collections: 1850-1910

MAGNETAWAN

Magnetawan Historical Museum
Hwy. 520 at Biddy St., Magnetawan
    Lock
Telephone: (705) 387-3947
Mail to: c/o Arthur Raaflaub,
    Magnetawan Historical Museum
Arthur Raaflaub, Secretary-Treasurer
Questionnaire not received

MANITOWANING

Assiginack Historical Society
Albert St., P0P 1N0
Telephone: (705) 859-3196
Town agency
Founded in: 1952
David Smith, President
Number of members: 23
Staff: full time 3, volunteer 2
Major programs: archives, museum,
    historic sites preservation, oral
    history
Period of collections: 1865-present

MARKHAM

**Markham District Historical
    Museum**
Telephone: (416) 294-4576
Mail to: Main St. N, R.R. 2, L3P 3J3
John Lunau, Director
Questionnaire not received

MARTEN RIVER

Marten River Logging Museum
Marten River Provincial Park
Telephone: (705) 892-2200
Mail to: P0H 1T0
E. McIsaac, Park Superintendent

**Northern Ontario Trappers
    Museum**
Marten River, Hwy. 11
Telephone: (705) 892-2386
Mail to: P.O. Box 705, North Bay,
    P1B 8J8
Roger Betz, Director
Questionnaire not received

MASSEY

Massey Area Museum
Hwy. 17
Telephone: (705) 865-2266
Mail to: P.O. Box 237, P0P 1P0
Founded in: 1968
Mrs. T. Rainville, Curator
Staff: part time 6, volunteer 3
Major programs: museum, school
    programs, historic preservation,
    research, genealogical services
Period of collections: 1800-1920

MATHESON

Black River-Matheson Museum
4th St. S
Telephone: (705) 273-2325
Mail to: P0K 1N0
Thelma Miles, Director
Questionnaire not received

MEAFORD

Meaford Museum
111 Bayfield St.
Telephone: (519) 538-4779
Mail to: c/o Madeline Bennett, 57
Marshall St., N0H 1Y0
Madeline Bennett, Chairperson

MERRICKVILLE

Merrickville and District Historical Society
Telephone: (613) 283-1741
Mail to: P.O. Box 294, K0G 1N0
Founded in: 1966
Carolyn Walton, Secretary
Questionnaire not received

MIDDLEVILLE

Lanark Township Museum
Middleville
Mail to: R.R. 2, Lanark, K0G 1K0
William Croft, Curator

MIDLAND

Huronia Museum
Little Lake Park
Telephone: (705) 526 2844
Mail to: P.O. Box 638, L4R 4P4
Private agency
Jack Yelland, President
Major programs: museum, historic
site(s), tours/pilgrimages, exhibits,
audiovisual programs

Huron Indian Village
Little Lake Park (King St. Entrance)
Telephone: (705) 526-8757
Mail to: P.O. Box 638, L4R 4P4
Private agency
Major programs: historic site(s),
tours, audiovisual programs

Sainte Marie Among the Hurons
R.R. #1
Telephone: (705) 526-7838
Mail to: P.O. Box 160, L4R 4K8
Founded in: 1964
Bill Byrick, Manager
Questionnaire not received

MILFORD

Mariners' Park Museum
Telephone: (613) 476-4497
Mail to: R.R. 2, K0K 2P0
Howard Gyde, Chair
Major programs: museum, historic
preservation
Period of collections: 1800-1950

MILTON

Halton Region Museum
R.R. 3, L9T 2X7
Telephone: (416) 878-3232
County agency
Founded in: 1962
U. Ernest Buchner, Curator
Staff: full time 5, part time 9

Major programs: museum, school
programs, newsletters/pamphlets,
research, exhibits, archaeology
programs, genealogical services
Period of collections: 1806-1940

Ontario Agricultural Museum
144 Town Line
Telephone: (416) 878-8151
Mail to: P.O. Box 38, L9T 2Y3
Provincial agency, authorized by
Ontario Ministry of Agriculture and
Food
Founded in: 1973
John Wiley, General Manager
Staff: full time 19, part time 30
Major programs: library, archives,
museum, school programs,
research, exhibits, living history,
audiovisual programs,
photographic collections
Period of collections: 1885-1955

MINESING

Simcoe County Archives
R.R. 2, L0L 1Y0
Telephone: (705) 726-9331
County agency
Founded in: 1966
Peter P. Moran, County Archivist
Staff: full time 3
Major programs: archives,
manuscripts, oral history, school
programs, records management,
research, photographic
collections, genealogical services
Period of collections: 1850-1950

Simcoe County Museum
Hwy. 26
Telephone: (705) 728-3721
Mail to: R.R. 2, L0L 1Y0
County agency
Robert Fisher, Curator
Major programs: museum
Period of collections: prehistoric-1930

MISSISSAUGA

Bradley Museum
Orr Rd. at Meadowwood Rd.
Telephone: (416) 822-4884
Mail to: 1 City Centre Dr., L5B 1M2
Private agency, authorized by
Mississauga Heritage Foundation
Mary Lou Evans, Curator
Major programs: museum, school
programs, research, archaeology
programs, field services
Period of collections: 1830-1850

MOORETOWN

Moore Museum
94 William St., N0N 1M0
Telephone: (519) 867-2020
Gloria Leckie, Curator
Major programs: museum, school
programs
Period of collections: 1800s-1940s

MOOSE FACTORY

Moose Factory Centennial Museum
Telephone: (705) 567-4500
Mail to: c/o Roy Thompson, 521
Government Rd. W, Kirkland Lake
Roy Thompson, Director
Questionnaire not received

MORRISBURG

Upper Canada Village
Telephone: (613) 543-2911
Mail to: P.O. Box 740, K0C 1X0
Provincial agency, authorized by St.
Lawrence Parks Commission
Founded in: 1955
W. J. Patterson, Superintendent of
Historic Sites
Staff: full time 36, part time 150
Major programs: library, museum,
school programs, historic
preservation, exhibits, living history
Period of collections: 1800-1870

MT. BRYDGES

Ska-Nah-Dont Indian Village
R.R. 1, N0L 1W0
Telephone: (519) 264-2457
Authorized by Lower Thames Valley
Conservation Authority
Founded in: 1971
Janet Cobban, Co-ordinator
Staff: full time 1, part time 5
Major programs: museum, historic
site(s), school programs,
archaeology programs
Period of collections: A.D. 1200-A.D.
800

NANTICOKE

Wilson MacDonald Memorial School Museum
Telephone: (416) 776-2831/776-3319
Mail to: R.R. 1, Selkirk, N0A 1P0
City agency
Mrs. Gerald McKenzie, Curator
Major programs: library, museum,
historic site(s), tours/pilgrimages,
junior history, school programs,
historic preservation, photographic
collections, genealogical services
Period of collections: late
1800-present

NAPANEE

Lennox and Addington County Museum
97 Thomas St., E
Telephone: (613) 354-3027
Mail to: Postal Bag 1000, K7R 3S9
County agency
Founded in: 1976
Jane Foster, Director
Number of members: 180
Staff: full time 2, part time 2
Major programs: library, archives,
museum, school programs,
exhibits, photographic collections,
genealogical services
Period of collections: 1850-1920

Lennox and Addington Historical Society
Telephone: (613) 354-3027
Mail to: P.O. Box 392, K7R 3M3
Founded in: 1907
George Salsbury, Co-president
Number of members: 100
Staff: full time 2, part time 4
Major programs: library, archives,
museum, historic sites
preservation, markers,
tours/pilgrimages, oral history,
educational programs, books,
newsletters/pamphlets
Period of collections: 1783-present

NEWBORO

Skoryna Home Museum
Drummond and Simcoe Sts.
Telephone: (514) 935-3058
Mail to: c/o F. Emmons, K0G 1P0
Frederick Emmons, Curator

NIAGARA FALLS

Lundy's Lane Historical Museum
Telephone: (416) 358-5082
Mail to: 5810 Ferry St., L2G 1S9
City agency
Margaret Tabaka, Curator
Major programs: library, museum,
exhibits, audiovisual programs
Period of collections: 1812-present

The Niagara Parks Commission
Administration Bldg., Queen Victoria
Park, L2E 6T2
Telephone: (416) 356-2241
Mail to: P.O. Box 150
Founded in: 1885
M. S. Cushing, Assistant General
Manager
Questionnaire not received

Old Ft. Erie
Niagara River Parkway
Telephone: (416) 356-2241
Mail to: P.O. Box 150, L2E 6T2
Authorized by Niagara Parks
Commission
Major programs: tours/pilgrimages,
historic preservation

**Willoughby Township Historical
Museum**
9935 Niagara Parkway, at Weaver Rd.
Telephone: (416) 295-4036
Mail to: P.O. Box 138, R.R. 3, L2E 6S6
Ursula Bienzeisler, Curator

NIAGARA-ON-THE-LAKE

Ft. George National Historic Park
Telephone: (416) 468-4257
Mail to: P.O. Box 787, L0S 1J0
National agency
Founded in: 1950
Walter Haldorson, Superintendent
Staff: full time 9, part time 40
Major programs: museum, historic
site(s), school programs, historic
preservation, living history,
archaeology programs
Period of collections: 1797-1813

Niagara Historical Society Museum
43 Castlereagh St.
Mail to: P.O. Box 208, L0S 1J0
Private agency
Founded in: 1895
Staff: full time 2
Major programs: archives,
manuscripts, museum,
tours/pilgrimages, school
programs, newsletters/pamphlets,
records management, research,
exhibits, photographic collections
Period of collections: 1750-1920

NIPIGON

Nipigon Museum
2nd and Newton Sts.
Telephone: (807) 887-2727
Mail to: P.O. Box 208, P0T 2J0
Town agency
Roland Choiselat, Director

Major programs: museum,
photographic collections
Period of collections: 5000
B.C.-present

NIPISSING

Nipissing Township Museum
Hwy. 654
Telephone: (705) 724-5988
Mail to: P0H 1W0
Clare Hankinson, Curator
Questionnaire not received

NORTH BAY

North Bay and Area Museum
Riverbend Rd.
Mail to: P.O. Box 628, P1B 8J5
City, provincial, and national agency
Pamela Hanoley, Curator
Major programs: library, archives,
museum, school programs,
newsletters/pamphlets, historic
preservation, records
management, research, exhibits,
living history, audiovisual
programs, photographic
collections
Period of collections: 1890-1940

NORTH BUXTON

**Raleigh Township Centennial
Museum**
Concession 8, Raleigh Township
Telephone: (519) 452-4799
Mail to: R.R. 6, N0P 1Y0
Arlie Robbins, Curator

NORTH YORK

Black Creek Pioneer Village
Steeles Ave. and Jane St.
Telephone: (416) 736-1733
Mail to: 1000 Murray Ross Parkway,
M3J 2P3
Founded in: 1954
Authorized by Metropolitan Toronto
and Region Conservation Authority
Russell K. Cooper, Administrator
Number of members: 500
Staff: full time 31, part time 70
Major programs: museum, historic
site(s), school programs, historic
preservation, records
management, research, exhibits,
living history, audiovisual programs
Period of collections: 1793-1867

Gibson House
5172 Yonge St., M2N 5P6
Telephone: (416) 225-0146
City agency
Founded in: 1971
David Falconer, Administrator
Staff: full time 2, part time 7,
volunteer 41
Major programs: historic site(s),
historic preservation
Period of collections: 1851

North York Historical Society
P.O. Box 63, Station A, M2N 5S7
Telephone: (416) 222-5180
Private agency
Founded in: 1960
L. Cameron Cathcart, President
Number of members: 250
Staff: part time 1, volunteer 74

Major programs: archives, museum,
historic site(s), tours/pilgrimages,
oral history, book publishing,
newsletters/pamphlets, historic
preservation, exhibits,
photographic collections, political
advocacy
Period of collections: 1783-1867

NORWICH

**Norwich and District Historical
Museum**
Telephone: (519) 863-3638
Mail to: R.R. 3, N0J 1P0
Scott Gillies, Curator
Major programs: archives, museum,
school programs,
newsletters/pamphlets, research,
exhibits, photographic collections,
genealogical services

OAKVILLE

**Oakville Museums—Oakville
Historical Society**
8 Navy St.
Telephone: (416) 845-3952
Mail to: P.O. Box 395
Town agency
Founded in: 1953
Judith Margles, Curator/Administrator
Number of members: 600
Staff: full time 3, volunteer 20
Major programs: archives, museums,
school programs,
newsletters/pamphlets, historic
preservation, research, exhibits,
photographic collections,
genealogical services
Period of collections: 1783-1930

OIL SPRINGS

Oil Museum of Canada
Kelly Rd.
Telephone: (519) 834-2840
Mail to: R.R. 2, N0N 1P0
County agency
Founded in: 1960
Donna McGuire, Manager
Staff: full time 1, part time 4
Major programs: museum, historic
site(s), tours/pilgrimages, oral
history, school programs,
newsletters/pamphlets, records
management, exhibits, audiovisual
programs, photographic
collections
Period of collections: 1858-present

ORILLIA

Leacock Memorial Home Board
Old Brewery Bay, L3V 6K5
Telephone: (705) 326-9357
Mail to: P.O. Box 625
Founded in: 1958
Jean Cain, Chair
Questionnaire not received

**Orillia and District Historical
Society**
22 Tecumseth St., L3V 1X8
Telephone: (705) 325-7868
Questionnaire not received

ORONO

Clarke Museum and Archives
Corner of Church and Centre Sts.
Telephone: (416) 983-9425/786-2955
Mail to: P.O. Box 150, L0B 1M0
Dyana Layng, Registrar
Questionnaire not received

OSHAWA

Oshawa and District Historical Society—Oshawa Sydenham Museum: Henry House, Robinson House, Guy House
6 Henry St., L1H 7V5
Telephone: (416) 728-6331
City agency
Founded in: 1960
Eric Glenholmes, President
Number of members: 150
Staff: full time 1, part time 3
Major programs: archives, museum, historic site(s), school programs, book publishing, newsletters/pamphlets, historic preservation, records management, research, exhibits, photographic collections, genealogical services, field services
Period of collections: mid-late 1800s

OTTAWA

The Association for Preservation Technology
Telephone: (613) 238-1972
Mail to: P.O. Box 2487, Station D
Founded in: 1968
Ann Falkner, Executive Secretary
Questionnaire not received

Billings Estate Museum
2100 Cabot St., K1H 6K1
Telephone: (613) 563-3075
City agency
Founded in: 1975
Nancy E. M. Smith, Acting Manager/Curator
Staff: full time 4, part time 1, volunteer 30
Major programs: archives, museum, historic site(s), school programs, historic preservation, research, exhibits, archaeology programs, photographic collections
Period of collections: 1812-1975

Boy Scouts of Canada-Museum of Canadian Scouting
1345 Base Line Rd., K2C 3G7
Telephone: (613) 224-5131
Mail to: P.O. Box 5151, Stn. F
Founded in: 1951
Patrick M. O. Evans, Curator
Staff: part time 1
Major programs: museum, junior history
Period of collections: 1865-present
Questionnaire not received

Bytown Historical Museum
Ottawa Locks
Telephone: (613) 234-4570
Mail to: P.O. Box 523, Station B, K1P 5P6
Private agency
Vera Campbell, Curator

Major programs: library, archives, manuscripts, museum, historic site(s), tours/pilgrimages, school programs, historic preservation, research, exhibits, photographic collections
Period of collections: 1826-1926

Canadian Historical Association—Société historique du Canada
395 Wellington, K1A 0N3
Telephone: (613) 233-7885
Founded in: 1922
Susan Mann Trofimenkoff, President
Number of members: 2,200
Staff: full time 1, part time 12, volunteer 2
Magazine: *Historical Papers*
Major programs: educational programs, newsletters/pamphlets

◇**Canadian Museums Association**
280 Metcalfe, Suite 202, K2P 1R7
Telephone: (613) 233-5653
Founded in: 1947
John G. McAvity, Executive Director
Number of members: 2,000
Staff: full time 11, part time 1
Magazine: *Muse/Museogramme*
Major programs: library, book publishing, newsletters/pamphlets, correspondence course

Canadian Ski Museum/Musée canadien du ski
Telephone: (613) 233-5832
Mail to: 457A Sussex Dr., K1N 6Z4
Private agency
Rae Grinnell, Chair
Major programs: library, archives, museum

Canadian War Museum
330 Sussex Dr., K1A 0M8
Telephone: (613) 996-1420
National agency
Founded in: 1880
L. F. Murray, Chief Curator
Staff: full time 25
Major programs: library, museum, book publishing, exhibits, photographic collections
Period of collections: 19th-20th centuries

Heritage Canada
306 Metcalfe St.
Telephone: (613) 237-1066
Mail to: P.O. Box 1358, Station B, K1P 5R4
Private agency
Founded in: 1973
Jacques Dalibard, Executive Director
Number of members: 25,800
Staff: full time 27
Magazine: *Canadian Heritage*
Major programs: historic preservation

Historical Society of Ottawa
Telephone: (613) 234-4570
Mail to: P.O. Box 523, Station B
Private agency
Founded in: 1898
Clare Grandmaison, President
Number of members: 300
Staff: full time 1, volunteer 120
Major programs: library, archives, manuscripts, museum, historic site(s), tours/pilgrimages, oral history, school programs, book publishing, newsletters/pamphlets, historic preservation, research, exhibits, photographic collections
Period of collections: 1826-1926

ICOM Museums-Musées Canada
80 Metcalfe, Suite 202, K2P 1R7
Telephone: (613) 233-5653
Marie Couturier

La Société Canadienne d'Histoire de l'Englise Catholique
223 Main St., K1S 1C4
Telephone: (613) 235-1421
Founded in: 1933
Jean-Jacques Robillard, Chief Secretary
Number of members: 340
Staff: volunteer 4
Magazine: *Sessions d'étude*
Major programs: books
Period of collections: 1492-present

Laurier House
335 Laurier Ave. E, K1N 6R4
Telephone: (613) 992-8142
National agency, authorized by Public Archives of Canada
Founded in: 1951
Major programs: museum, tours/pilgrimages, school programs, historic preservation
Period of collections: 1922-1950

Musée National des Postes
Telephone: (613) 995-9904; 995-9905
Mail to: 180, Rue Wellington St., K1A 1C6
National agency, authorized by Canada Post Corporation
Mrs. M. Beaulieu, Director
Major programs: library, museum, school programs, research, exhibits, photographic collections
Period of collections: 17th century-present

Museum of Canadian Scouting, Boy Scouts of Canada
1345 Base Line Rd., K2C 3G7
Telephone: (613) 224-5131
Mail to: P.O. Box 5151, Station F
Private agency
Founded in: 1951
Staff: part time 1
Major programs: museum, junior history
Period of collections: 1865-present

National Aeronautical Collection
Rockcliffe Airport, K1A 0M8
Telephone: (613) 998-3814
Mail to: Aviation & Space Division, National Museum of Science & Technology
Founded in: 1966
Staff: full time 10

Major programs: museum, historic
  preservation
Period of collections: 1900-present

National Aviation Museum
Rockcliffe Airport, K1A 0MB
Telephone: (6l3) 993-2010
National agency
Founded in: 1960
Staff: full time 14
Major programs: museum, historic
  preservation, photographic
  collections
Period of collections: 1900-present

**National Museum of Man (Musée
national de l'Homme)—Musée
commémoratif Victoria Memorial
Museum**
Metcalfe and McLeod Sts., K1A 0MB
Telephone: (613) 992-3497
George F. MacDonald, Director
National agency, authorized by
  Department of Communications,
  National Museums of Canada
Major programs: museum, school
  programs, book publishing,
  newsletters/pamphlets, research,
  exhibits, archaeology programs,
  photographic collections,
  anthropology
Period of collections: 30,000
  B.C.-present

**National Postal Museum/Musée
national des Postes**
Telephone: (613) 995-9904/995-9905
Mail to: 180, rue Wellington St.,
  K1A 1C6
M. Lysack, Director
Questionnaire not received

**Organization of Military Museums
of Canada, Canadian War
Museum**
330 Promenade Sussex Dr., K1A 0M8
Telephone: (613) 996-1421
National agency, authorized by
  National Museums of Canada
L. F. Murray, Chief Curator
Major programs: library, museum,
  school programs, book publishing,
  records management, research,
  exhibits, photographic collections
Period of collections: 1850-1950

Ottawa City Archives
174 Stanley Ave., K1M 1P1
Telephone: (613) 563-3115
City agency
Founded in: 1975
Louise Roy Brochu, City Archivist
Staff: full time 9
Major programs: archives,
  manuscripts, museum, school
  programs, newsletters/pamphlets,
  records management, research,
  exhibits, audiovisual programs,
  photographic collections,
  genealogical services, Billings
  estate museum program
Period of collections: 1847-present

Public Archives of Canada
395 Wellington St., K1A 0N3
Telephone: (613) 995-5138
Founded in: 1872
Bernard Wielbrenner, Dominion
  Archivist
Magazine: *The Archivist*

Major programs: library, archives,
  manuscripts, oral history, records
  management, research, exhibits,
  photographic collections,
  genealogical services
Period of collections: 1492-present

**Regimental Museum, Governor
General's Foot Guards**
Drill Hall, Cartier Square, K1A 0K2
Telephone: (613) 992-3771
Founded in: 1955
W. L. Gault, Curator
Staff: volunteer 3
Magazine: *Guards Star*
Major programs: museum
Period of collections: 1861-present

**Société Franco-Ontarienne
d'Histoire et de Généalogie**
C.P. 720, Succ. B, K1J 8M4
Telephone: (613) 746-7786
Provincial agency
Founded in: 1981
Louise Décarie-Marier, Provincial
  President
Number of members: 475
Staff: volunteer 75
Magazine: *Le Chainon*
Major programs: library, archives,
  oral history, book publishing,
  newsletters/pamphlets, historic
  preservation, records
  management, research, exhibits,
  living history, genealogical
  services
Period of collections: 1608-present

OWEN SOUND

**The County of Grey-Owen Sound
Museum**
Telephone: (519) 376-3690
Mail to: 975-6th St. E
A. Landen, Curator
Questionnaire not received

PEMBROKE

Champlain Trail Museum
1032 Pembroke St., E, K8A 6Z2
Mail to: P.O. Box 985, K8A 7M5
District agency, authorized by
  Ontario Historical Society
Founded in: 1958
Number of members: 200
Staff: full time 2, part time 2
Major programs: archives, museum,
  junior history, oral history,
  newsletters/pamphlets
Period of collections: 1800-1975

PENETANGUISHENE

**Historic Naval and Military
Establishments**
Church St., L0K 1P0
Telephone: (705) 549-8064
Provincial agency, authorized by
  Ontario Ministry of Tourism and
  Recreation
Founded in: 1973
Burke Penny, Manager
Staff: full time 7, part time 42
Major programs: historic site(s),
  school programs, exhibits, living
  history
Period of collections: 1817-1856

PERTH

The Perth Museum
9 Gore St., K7H 1H4
Telephone: (613) 267-1947
Founded in: 1967
Mrs. Duncan MacDonald, Curator
Questionnaire not received

PETERBOROUGH

Hope Sawmill
727 Lansdowne St., W, K9J 1Z2
Telephone: (705) 745-5791
Judy Gilchrist, Community Relations
  Coordinator
Private agency, authorized by
  Otanabe Region Conservation
  Authority
Major programs: museum, historic
  site(s), living history
Period of collections: 1875-1890

**Peterborough Centennial Museum
and Archives**
Hunter St., E
Telephone: (705) 743-5180
Mail to: P.O. Box 143, K9J 6Y5
Founded in: 1967
Daniel O'Brien, Manager
Staff: full time 4, part time 6
Major programs: archives, museum,
  school programs, records
  management, costume care,
  industrial gallery
Period of collections: 1840-1890

**Peterborough Historical
Society—Hutchison House
Museum**
270 Brock St., K9H 2P9
Telephone: (705) 743-9710
Private agency
Founded in: 1953
Lynne Clifford-Ward, Curator,
  Hutchison House
Number of members: 375
Staff: full time 2, volunteer 90
Magazine: *Peterborough Historical
  Society Bulletin*
Major programs: historic sites
  preservation, educational
  programs, books,
  newsletters/pamphlets, historic
  preservation
Period of collections: 19th century

PICTON

**Macaulay Heritage Park—Prince
Edward County Museum**
Macaulay House, Church and Union
  Sts.
Tephone: (613) 476-3833
Mail to: P.O. Box 2150, K0K 2T0
District agency
Tom Kuglin, Director
Major programs: library, museum,
  historic site(s), tours/pilgrimages,
  oral history, school programs,
  historic preservation, records
  management, research, exhibits,
  living history, audiovisual
  programs, photographic
  collections, field services
Period of collections: 1615-W.W. II

PORT CARLING

Pt. Carling Pioneer Museum
Telephone: (705) 765-5367
Founded in: 1962
James M. Woodruff, President
Staff: part time 2, volunteer 14
Major programs: museum,
newsletters/pamphlets,
photographic collections
Period of collections: 1865-1918

PORT COLBORNE

**Port Colborne Historical and
Marine Museum**
280 King St.
Telephone: (416) 834-7604
Mail to: P.O. Box 572, L3K 4H1
Town agency
Jean Leitch, Chair
Major programs: museum, school
programs, exhibits
Period of collections: 1850-1925

PORT DOVER

Dover Mills Heritage Association
Telephone: (519) 583-1526
Mail to: P.O. Box 29, N0A 1N0
Founded in: 1976
William Gunn, President
Questionnaire not received

PORT HOPE

East Durham Historical Society
40 Mill St. N, L1A 2T2
Telephone: (416) 885-5044
Founded in: 1964
Mrs. S. E. Van Camp
Number of members: 88
Magazine: *Bulletin*
Major programs: library, manuscripts,
museum, tours/pilgrimages,
educational programs
Period of collections: 1763-present

PORT PERRY

Lake Scugog Historical Society
P.O. Box 419, L0B 1N0
Telephone: (416) 985-3589
Pat Holman, Curator
Questionnaire not received

PORT ROWAN

**Backus Conservation Area and
Historical Complex**
R. R. 1, N0E 1M0
Telephone: (519) 586-2201
Authorized by Long Point Region
Conservation Authority
Founded in: 1956
Sarah Weisman, Curator, Backus
Historical Complex
Staff: full time 1
Major programs: museum, historic
site(s), tours, school programs,
historic preservation, exhibits
Period of collections: 1790-1920

PRESCOTT

**Ft. Wellington National Historic
Park**
Telephone: (613) 925-2896
National agency
Ron Dale, Interpretation Officer, D. J.
Delaney, Superintendent

Staff: full time 5, part time 6,
volunteer 17
Major programs: museum, historic
sites preservation,
tours/pilgrimages, junior history,
oral history, educational programs
Period of collections: 1703-1885

**Grenville County Historical
Society, Inc.**
Heritage Hwy.
Telephone: (613) 348-3560
Mail to: P.O. Box 982, K0E 1T0
District agency, authorized by
Ontario Historical Society
Founded in: 1898
Mrs. G. Connell, Archivist
Number of members: 120
Magazine: *Sentinel/Pioneer People
and Places/Early Grenville*
Major programs: archives, museum,
historic site(s), markers, school
programs, newsletters/pamphlets,
historic preservation, research,
exhibits, photographic collections,
genealogical services
Period of collections: 1800-present

RENFREW

Heritage Renfrew
Telephone: (613) 432-3145
Mail to: P.O. Box 11, K7V 4A2
Founded in: 1974
Mrs. J. E. Lindsay, President
Questionnaire not received

RICHARDS LANDING

St. Joseph Island Museum Board
P0R 1J0
Telephone: (705) 246-2601
Founded in: 1963
Ada Tranter, Curator
Staff: part time 5
Period of collections: 1796-present

RIDGETOWN

**Ridgetown and District Historical
Society**
Erie St., S, N0P 2C0
Mail to: P.O. Box 297
Founded in: 1974
John F. Roy, President
Number of members: 160
Staff: full time 1, part time 1,
volunteer 30
Major programs: museum, historic
sites preservation,
tours/pilgrimages, historic
preservation
Period of collections: 1850-1930

RIDGEWAY

Ft. Erie Historical Museum
402 Ridge St.
Mail to: P.O. Box 242, L0S 1N0
Town agency
Major programs: museum,
tours/pilgrimages, school
programs, historic preservation,
exhibits
Period of collections: early
1800s-1920

ROCKTON

Wentworth Heritage Village
Hwy. 52, North of Hwy. 8

Mail to: P.O. Box 910, Hamilton, L8N
3V9
Founded in: 1964
Barry Lord, Curator
Staff: full time 2, part time 13,
volunteer 18
Major programs:
newsletters/pamphlets
Period of collections: 1783-1910

ROCKWOOD

**Ontario Electric Railway Historical
Association Museum**
Telephone: (519) 856-9802
Mail to: P.O. Box 121, Station A,
Scarborough, M1K 5B9
R. Johns, President

ST. CATHARINES

Historical Society of St. Catharines
Mail to: P.O. Box 1101, L2R 7A3
Founded in: 1927
Private agency, authorized by Ontario
Historical Society
Lorna Robson, Corresponding
Secretary
Number of members: 65
Major programs: book publishing,
historic preservation

St. Catharines Historical Museum
343 Merritt St., L2T 1K7
Telephone: (416) 227-2962
Founded in: 1965
City agency
Major programs: library, archives,
manuscripts, museum,
tours/pilgrimages, oral history,
school programs, book publishing,
newsletters/pamphlets, records
management, research, exhibits,
audiovisual programs,
photographic collections
Period of collections: 1800-present

ST. GEORGE

**Adelaide Hunter Hoodless
Homestead**
Telephone: (519) 442-3450
Mail to: c/o Mrs. J. Charlton,
Secretary, 5 Bayly Dr., Paris,
N3L 2R1

St. George Old School Museum
Mail to: c/o Mrs. E. Williams, 7
Elizabeth St., N0E 1N0
Melva Jackson, Staff

ST. JOSEPH ISLAND

St. Joseph Island Museum
Telephone: (705) 246-2601
Mail to: Richard's Landing, P0R 1J0
Ada Tranter, Director

ST. MARYS

St. Marys District Museum
177 Church St., S, N0M 2V0
Telephone: (519) 284-3556
Town agency
Major programs: museum, school
programs, research, audiovisual
programs, photographic
collections, genealogical services
Period of collections: from 1850s

ST. THOMAS

Elgin County Pioneer Museum
Telephone: (519) 631-6537
Mail to: 32 Talbot St., N5P 1A3
County agency
Deborah Herkimer, Director/Curator
Major programs: museum, school
programs, historic preservation

SARNIA

Lambton County Historical Society
728 Grove Ave., N7V 2Y1
Telephone: (519) 542-2373
Founded in: 1956
Lloyd Werden, President
Number of members: 60
Staff: volunteer 6
Major programs: library, archives,
book publishing, historic
preservation, exhibits
Period of collections: 19th-20th
centuries

SAULT STE. MARIE

**Sault Ste. Marie and 49th Field
Regt. R.C.A. Historical Society**
375 Pine St., P6A 5L8
Telephone: (705) 256-2566
Mail to: P.O. Box 309
Founded in: 1920
Patricia J. Speer, Curator
Questionnaire not received

Sault Ste. Marie Museum
107 East St., P6A 3C7
Telephone: (705) 256-2566
Private agency, authorized by Sault
Ste. Marie Historical Society
Founded in: 1950
Elizabeth B. Allaway, Executive
Director
Staff: full time 1, part time 1,
volunteer 46
Major programs: archives, museum,
school programs,
newsletters/pamphlets, records
management, exhibits
Period of collections: 1900-1940

SCARBOROUGH

**Scarborough Historical
Society—Cornell House Museum**
Thomson Memorial Park
Telephone: (416) 438-4826
Mail to: P.O. Box 593, Station A, M1K
5C4
Private agency
Sarah Walker, Chair
Major programs: archives, museum,
markers, oral history, school
programs, newsletters/pamphlets,
research, exhibits
Period of collections: 1850-1910

SHARON

Sharon Temple Museum
18062 Leslie St., L0G 1V0
Telephone: (416) 478-2389
Private agency, authorized by York
Pioneer and Historical Society
Edwin Hunt, Chair
Major programs: museum, historic
site(s)
Period of collections: 1820-1860

SHEGUINDAH

**The Little Current-Howland
Centennial Museum**
Hwy. 68
Telephone: (705) 368-2367
Mail to: c/o Boyne Heise, P0P 1W0
John Dunlop, Director
Questionnaire not received

SHELBURNE

**Dufferin County Historical Society
Museum**
Hyland Park
Telephone: (519) 925-5565
Mail to: c/o Harold Doan, P.O. Box
957, L0N 1S0
Harold Doan, Director

SIMCOE

Norfolk Historical Society
Eva Brook Donly Museum, 109
Norfolk St. S
Telephone: (519) 426-1583
Founded in: 1900
William Yeager, Curator
Questionnaire not received

SMITHS FALLS

Rideau Canal
12 Maple Ave., N, K7A 1Z5
National agency, authorized by Parks
Canada
Staff: full time 60, part time 60
Magazine: *Of Steam and Stone*
Major programs: library, historic
site(s), tours, school programs,
newsletters/pamphlets, historic
preservation, exhibits, living
history, audiovisual programs,
photographic collections
Period of collections: 1826-present

SOMBRA VILLAGE

**Sombra Township Historical
Society**
146 St. Clair, N0P 2H0
Telephone: (519) 892-3631
Mail to: P.O. Box 72
Founded in: 1958
Mrs. M. S. Dalgety, Director
Questionnaire not received

SOUTH BAYMOUTH

Tehkumsmah Township Museum
Hwy. 68
Telephone: (705) 859-3131
Mail to: c/o Coral Collins, P0P 1Z0
Ross Stillwagh, Chairman
Questionnaire not received

SOUTHAMPTON

Bruce County Historical Museum
33 Victoria St. N
Telephone: (519) 797-3644
Mail to: P.O. Box 180, N0H 2L0
Questionnaire not received

STONEY CREEK

Stoney Creek Battlefield House
77 King St., W
Telephone: (416) 662-8458
Mail to: Niagara Parks Commission,
P.O. Box 150, Niagara Falls, L2E
6T2

Provincial agency, authorized by the
Parks Commission
M. Cushing, Assistant General
Manager
Major programs: museum, historic
site(s), tours/pilgrimages, school
programs, historic preservation,
exhibits, audiovisual programs
Period of collections: 1830s

STRATFORD

Avon Valley Historical Society
24 St. Andrew St., N5A 1A3
Founded in: 1963
Private agency
Number of members: 125
Staff: volunteer 15
Major programs: historic site(s),
markers, tours/pilgrimages, oral
history, inn restoration program
Period of collections: 1820-present

Fryfogel Inn
40-24 St. Andrew St., N5A 1A3
J. Anderson, Archivist

**Perth County Branch, Ontario
Genealogical Society**
24 St. Andrew St., N5A 1A3
Telephone: (519) 273-0399
Private agency
Major programs: library,
newsletters/pamphlets,
genealogical services

Stratford-Perth Archives Board
24 St. Andrew St., N5A 1A3
Telephone: (519) 273-0399
County agency
Founded in: 1972
James Anderson, Archivist
Staff: full time 3, volunteer 3
Major programs: library, archives,
tours/pilgrimages, school
programs, records management,
research, photographic
collections, genealogical services
Period of collections: 1870-1950

STRATHROY

Strathroy Middlesex Museum
84 Oxford St., N7G 3A5
Telephone: (519) 245-0492
Founded in: 1971
Jean MacDonald, Director
Staff: full time 1, volunteer 10
Major programs: museum,
newsletters/pamphlets
Period of collections: 1832-1967
Questionnaire not received

STREETSVILLE

Streetsville Historical Society
Mail to: P.O. Box 598
Questionnaire not received

STURGEON FALLS

Sturgeon River House Museum
Hwy. 17, E
Mail to: P.O. Box 1390, P0H 2G0
Town agency
Armand Roy, Curator
Major programs: museum, historic
site(s), historic preservation,
records management, research,
exhibits, field services
Period of collections: 1879-1939

SUDBURY

Flour Mill Museum
514 Notre Dame St.
Telephone: (705) 674-2391
Mail to: c/o Alderman R. de la Riva,
222 Brebeuf St., P3C 5H1
Peter Philipow, Chairman

SUTTON WEST

Eildon Hall, Sibbald Memorial Museum
Telephone: (416) 722-3268
Mail to: Sibbald Point Provincial Park,
R.R. 2, L0E 1R0
Mary Brown, Curator
Major programs: museum, historic
preservation
Period of collections: 1850-1900

Georgina Village Museum
Civic Centre Rd.
Telephone: (416) 722-5680
Mail to: P.O. Box 495, L0E 1R0
Mrs. K. Marsden, Director

TEETERVILLE

Windham Township Pioneer Museum
Telephone: (519) 446-2557
Mail to: P.O. Box 45, N0E 1S0
William Evans, Director

THOROLD

Thorold and Beaverdams Historical Society
14 Ormond St. N, L2V 4J6
Telephone: (416) 227-5086
Mail to: P.O. Box 437
Founded in: 1894
John A. Nogas, President
Questionnaire not received

THUNDER BAY

Paipoonge Museum
R.R. 1, Hwy. 130 at Rosslyn Rd.
Telephone: (807) 557-6052
Mail to: c/o Addie Wing, R.R. 5,
P7C 5M9
Addie Wing, Curator

Thunder Bay Historical Museum Society
219 May St. S, P7E 1B5
Telephone: (807) 623-0801
Founded in: 1908
Gerrie Noble, Curator
Questionnaire not received

TILLSONBURG

Tillsonburg and District Historical Museum
Telephone: (519) 842-2294
Mail to: 8 Ross St., N4G 3N8
Helen Shearing, Director/Curator

TIVERTON

Bruce County Historical Society
Telephone: (519) 396-2205
Mail to: c/o Mary Anne Ellenton, P.O.
Box 182, N0G 2T0
Founded in: 1957
Mary Anne Ellenton, Secretary
Questionnaire not received

TOBERMORY

Peninsula and St. Edmunds Township Museum
Telephone: Tobermory 2479
Mail to: R.R. 1, N0H 2R0
Cora Wyonch, Curator
Questionnaire not received

TORONTO

Archives of Ontario
77 Grenville St., M7A 2R9
Telephone: (416) 965-4030
Founded in: 1903
William Ormsby, Archivist
Staff: full time 42
Major programs: library, archives,
manuscripts
Period of collections: 1783-present

Black Creek Pioneer Village
Steeles Ave. and Jane St.
Telephone: (416) 661-6600
Mail to: 5 Shoreham Dr. Downsview,
M3N 1S4
Founded in: 1954
Russell K. Cooper, Administrator
Number of members: 500
Staff: full time 31, part time 70
Major programs: museum, historic
sites preservation, educational
programs
Period of collections: 1793-1867

Borough of York Historical Committee
2700 Eglinton Ave. W., M6M 1V1
Telephone: (416) 653-2700
Mrs. N. Bradley, Secretary
Questionnaire not received

Canadian Friends Historical Association
60 Lowther Ave., M5R 1C7
Telephone: (416) 922-2632
Private agency, authorized by Society
of Friends
Founded in: 1972
Kathleen Hertzberg, Clerk
Number of members: 150
Staff: volunteer 3
Magazine: *Canadian Quaker History Newsletter*
Major programs: archives, oral
history, newsletters/pamphlets,
research
Period of collections: 1865-1918

Canadian Historical Collection, Art Gallery of Ontario and The Grange
317 Dundas St., W, M5T 1G4
Telephone: (416) 977-0414
National agency
Founded in: 1900
Elizabeth Addison, Manager,
Marketing/Public Relations
Number of members: 29,000
Staff: full time 195, part time 115,
volunteer 553
Major programs: library, archives,
historic site(s), tours/pilgrimages,
school programs, book publishing,
newsletters/pamphlets, historic
preservation, records
management, research, exhibits,
audiovisual programs,
photographic collections, field
services
Period of collections: 1790-1960

Colborne Lodge

Colborne Lodge Dr., High Park
Telephone: (416) 763-1534
Mail to: Stanley Barracks, Exhibition
Place, M6K 3C3
City agency, authorized by Toronto
Historical Board
Founded in: 1964
Ms. G. A. Karadi, Curator
Staff: full time 2, part time 2
Major programs: museum, school
programs, historic preservation
Period of collections: 1830-1880

Enoch Turner Schoolhouse
Telephone: (416) 863-0010
Mail to: 106 Trinity St., M5A 3C6
Donald Freeman, Curator

Gibson House
5172 Yonge St., Willowdale, M2N 5P6
Telephone: (416) 225-0146
Mail to: c/o Toronto Historical Board,
Stanley Barracks, Exhibition Place,
M6K 3C3
Founded in: 1971
David Falconer, Administrator
Questionnaire not received

Historic Ft. York
Garrison Rd.
Telephone: (416) 366-6127
Mail to: Stanley Barracks, Exhibition
Place, M6K 3C3
City agency, authorized by Toronto
Historical Board
Founded in: 1793
Staff: full time 6, part time 37
Major programs: museum,
educational programs
Period of collections: 1783-1865

Historical Society of Mecklenburg Upper Canada, Inc.
Telephone: (416) 270-5754
Mail to: P.O. Box 193, Station K, M4P
2G7
Founded in: 1972
Rolf A. Piro, President
Number of members: 200
Staff: volunteer 8
Magazine: *Canadiana Germanica*
Major programs: library, archives,
manuscripts, tours, educational
programs, books,
newsletters/pamphlets
Period of collections: 1600-present

Mackenzie House
82 Bond St.
Telephone: (416) 366-1371
Mail to: Stanley Barracks, Exhibition
Place, M6K 3C3
City agency, authorized by Toronto
Historical Board
Founded in: 1946
Ms. G. A. Karadi, Curator
Staff: full time 2, part time 6
Major programs: museum,
educational programs
Period of collections: 1783-1865

Marine Museum of Upper Canada
Exhibition Place
Telephone: (416) 595-1567
Mail to: Stanley Barracks, Exhibition
Place, M6K 3C3
City agency, authorized by Toronto
Historical Board
Founded in: 1959

Staff: full time 2, part time 2
Major programs: museum,
  educational programs
Period of collections: 1865-present

Ontario Genealogical Society
Mail to: P.O. Box 66, Station Q, M4T
  2L7
Private agency
Founded in: 1961
Number of members: 4,500
Magazine: *Families*
Major programs: library, manuscripts,
  book publishing,
  newsletters/pamphlets,
  genealogical services

Ontario Heritage Foundation
77 Bloor St., W, M7A 2R9
Provincial agency
Founded in: 1968
Robert G. Bowes, Secretary
Staff: full time 60, part time 5,
  volunteer 1
Magazine: *Ontario Heritage News:
  Keystone*
Major programs: museum, historic
  site(s), markers, tours/pilgrimages,
  book publishing,
  newsletters/pamphlets, historic
  preservation, research, exhibits,
  archaeology programs,
  architectural conservation, historic
  art collection
Period of collections: 1785-present

The Ontario Historical Society
78 Dunloe Rd. Rm. 207, M5P 2T6
Telephone: (416) 536-1353
Founded in: 1888
Sandra Morton, Executive Assistant
Number of members: 2,000
Staff: full time 1
Magazine: *Ontario History*
Major programs: educational
  programs, books,
  newsletters/pamphlets

Ontario Museum Association
38 Charles St., E, M4Y 1T1
Telephone: (416) 923-3868
Provincial agency
Founded in: 1971
Greg Baeker, Executive Director
Number of members: 1,300
Staff: full time 6, part time 1,
  volunteer 15
Magazine: *Museum Quarterly*
Major programs: museum, historic
  site(s), book publishing,
  newsletters/pamphlets, audiovisual
  programs

The Quetico Foundation
170 University Ave., M5H 3B5
Telephone: (416) 593-1391
Founded in: 1954
Quimby F. Hess and John W. Murray,
  Executive Secretaries
Staff: part time 2, volunteer 16
Magazine: *The Quetico Newsletter*
Major programs: historic sites
  preservation, markers, books,
  newsletters/pamphlets
Period of collections: 1492-present

Royal Ontario Museum
100 Queen's Park, M5S 2C6
Telephone: (416) 978-3690
Founded in: 1912

James E. Cruise, Director
Number of members: 10,080
Staff: part time 120, volunteer 520
Magazine: *Rotunda*
Major programs: library, archives,
  manuscripts, museum, educational
  programs, books,
  newsletters/pamphlets
Period of collections:
  prehistoric-present

**Salvation Army George Scott
  Railton Heritage Centre**
2130 Bayview Ave., M4N 3K6
Telephone: (416) 481-6635
Private agency, authorized by
  Governing Council, Salvation Army,
  Canada and Bermuda Territory
Founded in: 1882
William Brown, Director
Staff: full time 4, part time 3,
  volunteer 2
Major programs: library, archives,
  manuscripts, museum, oral history,
  photographic collections,
  genealogical services
Period of collections: 1884-present

Spadina
285 Spadina Rd.
Telephone: (416) 960-2115
Mail to: Stanley Barracks, Exhibition
  Place, M6K 3C3
City agency, authorized by Toronto
  Historical Board
Founded in: 1984
Ms. G. A. Karadi, Curator
Staff: full time 6, part time 10
Major programs: museum,
  educational programs
Period of collections: 1860-1935

Todmorden Mills Historic Site
67 Pottery Rd.
Mail to: 550 Mortimer Ave., M4J 2H2
City agency
Founded in: 1967

Ms. L.M.J. Scarrow, Curator/Manage
Staff: full time 1, part time 2,
  volunteer 35
Major programs: archives, museum,
  historic site(s), markers, school
  programs, historic preservation,
  records management, research,
  exhibits, audiovisual programs,
  photographic collections,
  genealogical services
Period of collections: 1793-1867

Toronto Historical Board
Stanley Barracks, Exhibition Place,
  M6K 3C3
Telephone: (416) 595-1567
City agency
Founded in: 1960
R. Scott James, Managing Director
Staff: full time 45, part time 70
Major programs: museum, historic
  site(s), markers, school programs,
  historic preservation, research,
  exhibits, living history, audiovisual
  programs
Period of collections: 1793-1940

**Toronto Jewish
  Congress—Canadian Jewish
  Congress, Ontario Region
  Archives**
4600 Bathurst St., M2R 3V2
Telephone: (416) 635-2883
Private agency
Founded in: 1973
Stephen A. Speisman, Director
Staff: full time 1, part time 1,
  volunteer 25
Major programs: archives
Period of collections: 1900-1960

**Ukrainian Canadian Research
  Foundation**
4 Island View Blvd., M8V 2P4
Telephone: (416) 255-9090
Founded in: 1965
S. T. Pawluk, President

Colborne Lodge, one of five museums operated by the Toronto Historical Board.—Toronto
Historical Board

Number of members: 129
Staff: volunteer 2
Major programs: library, archives,
 manuscripts, books
Period of collections: 1890-present

**Ukrainian Heritage Association and
 Museum of Canada**
1 Austin Terrace, Casa Loma, M5R
 1X8
Telephone: (416) 925-0924
Private agency
Founded in: 1969
Roman Radelicki, Curator
Staff: part time 1, volunteer 15
Major programs: library, archives,
 museum, newsletters/pamphlets,
 historic preservation, records
 management, research, exhibits,
 living history
Period of collections: late 19th
 century-present

**United Empire Loyalists'
 Association of Canada**
23 Prince Arthur Ave., M5R 1B2
Telephone: (416) 923-7921
Founded in: 1914
E. J. Chard, Chair
Number of members: 3,000
Staff: full time 2, part time 1
Magazine: *The Loyalist Gazette*
Major programs: library, historic
 site(s), markers, book publishing,
 research
Period of collections: 1776-1800

**Women's Canadian Historical
 Society**
153 Spadina Rd., M5R 2T9
Telephone: (416) 921-6159
Founded in: 1895
Mrs. Clendon A. P. McDowell,
 President
Questionnaire not received

York Pioneer and Historical Society
Telephone: (416) 481-8648
Mail to: P.O. Box 481, Station K, M4P
 2G9
Private agency
Founded in: 1869
Number of members: 500
Staff: part time 5, volunteer 20
Magazine: *The York Pioneer*
Major programs: museum, historic
 site(s), newsletters/pamphlets,
 historic preservation, heritage
 music festival
Period of collections: 1800-1875

UXBRIDGE

**Uxbridge-Scott Historical Society
 Museum**
Telephone: (416) 852-7493
Mail to: P.O. Box 704, L0C 1K0
Richard Hannah, Director
Major programs: archives, museum,
 historic preservation, exhibits,
 photographic collections,
 genealogical services
Period of collections: 1800s

VANDORF

Whitchurch Stouffville Museum
R.R. 1, Gormley, L0H 160
Telephone: (416) 727-8954
Town agency

Founded in: 1971
Mary T. Hopkins, Curator
Number of members: 100
Staff: full time 1, part time 1,
 volunteer 15
Major programs: museum, school
 programs, newsletters/pamphlets,
 historic preservation, research,
 exhibits, living history,
 genealogical services, field
 services, outreach education kits
Period of collections: 1800s-1925

VERNON

**Osgoode Township Historical
 Society and Museum**
Telephone: (613) 821-2858
Founded in: 1973
Harry M. Anderson, Secretary
Questionnaire not received

WALLACEBURG

**Wallaceburg and District Historical
 Society**
36 Grand Ave., N8A 4J9
Telephone: (519) 627-8776
Founded in: 1973
Joan Stearns, President
Number of members: 60
Staff: volunteer 12
Major programs: library, archives,
 museum
Period of collections: 1918-present

WASAGA BEACH

Nancy Island Historic Site
Mosley St.
Telephone: (705) 429-2728/429-2516
Mail to: Provincial Park, P.O. Box 183,
 L0L 2P0
Provincial agency, authorized by
 Ministry of Natural Resources
Gary Babcock, Park Superintendent
Major programs: museum, historic
 site(s)
Period of collections: War of 1812

WATERLOO

**The Pennsylvania German Folklore
 Society of Ontario**
43 Melbourne Cr. N2L 2M4
Telephone: (519) 886-6337
Founded in: 1951
Isaac High, President
Number of members: 280
Magazine: *Canadian German
 Folklore*
Major programs: library,
 tours/pilgrimages, educational
 programs, books,
 newsletters/pamphlets
Period of collections: 1865-present

WELLAND

Welland Historical Society
Mail to: P.O. Box 412
Wesley Laing, President
Number of members: 40
Staff: full time 1
Major programs: museum
Period of collections: 1865-1918

WELLINGTON

**Wellington Community Historical
 Museum**
Main St., K0K 3L0
Telephone: (613) 399-3041
Founded in: 1967
Ruth Armstrong, Curator/Director
Major programs: museum

WESTPORT

Rideau District Historical Society
Box 250 Main St. K0G 1X0
Telephone: (613) 273-2822
Founded in: 1965
Margaret I. Roberts, President
Number of members: 5
Staff: volunteer 15
Major programs: museum, historic
 sites preservation, markers
Period of collections: 1783-1865

WHITBY

Whitby Historical Society
Telephone: (416) 668-9490
Mail to: P.O. Box 281, L1N 5S1
Private agency
Brian Winter, Archivist
Major programs: archives, museum,
 school programs, records
 management, research, exhibits,
 photographic collections,
 genealogical services
Period of collections: 1800-pesent

WILLIAMSTOWN

Nor'Westers and Loyalist Museum
Telephone: (613) 347-3547
Mail to: P.O. Box 69, K0C 2J0
Private agency, authorized by
 Glengarry Historical Society
Joan Johnston, Curator
Major programs: museum
Period of collections: from 1784

WILLOWDALE

North York Historical Society
Mail to: P.O. Box 63, Station A, M2N
 5P0
Telephone: (416) 226-9283
Founded in: 1960
David J. Burnside, President
Number of members: 200
Staff: volunteer 75
Magazine: *Bulletin*
Major programs: archives, museum,
 tours/pilgrimages, junior history,
 oral history, educational programs,
 books, newsletters/pamphlets
Period of collections: 1783-1865

Ontario Historical Society
5151 Yonge St., M2N 5P5
Telephone: (416) 226-5011
Provincial agency
Founded in: 1888
Dorothy Duncan, Executive Director
Number of members: 3,000
Staff: full time 4, volunteer 10
Magazine: *Ontario History*
Major programs: junior history, oral
 history, book publishing,
 newsletters/pamphlets, historic
 preservation, research, field
 services

WINDSOR

Essex County Historical Society
254 Pitt St., W
Telephone: (519) 253-1812
Ian C. Pemberton, President
Number of members: 60
Staff: volunteer 9
Major programs: historic sites
   preservation, markers,
   tours/pilgrimages, educational
   programs, books,
   newsletters/pamphlets

Hiram Walker Historical Museum
254 Pitt St., W, N9A 5L5
Telephone: (519) 253-1812
City agency
Founded in: 1958
R. Alan Douglas, Curator
Staff: full time 3, part time 2
Major programs: museum
Period of collections: prehistoric-1965

Historic Vehicle Society of Ontario
Telephone: (519) 776-6909
Mail to: P.O. Box 221, Harrow, N0R
   1G0
Private agency
Founded in: 1959
Christina Speer, Administrator
Number of members: 60
Staff: volunteer 10
Major programs: museum, tours,
   school programs, historic
   preservation, records
   management, research, exhibits,
   photographic collections

WOODSTOCK

Oxford Museum
City Square, N4S 1C4
Telephone: (519) 537-8411
Private agency
Founded in: 1947
Sheila A. Johnson, Curator
Staff: full time 1
Major programs: museum, historic
   sites preservation,
   tours/pilgrimages,
   newsletters/pamphlets, exhibits
Period of collections: 1850-1910

PRINCE EDWARD ISLAND

ALBERTON

Alberton Museum
479 Church St., C0B 1B0
Telephone: (902) 853-2794
Private agency, authorized by
   Alberton Historical Preservation
   Foundation, Inc.
Founded in: 1982
Allan MacRae, Curator
Number of members: 200
Staff: part time 5, volunteer 8
Major programs: archives, museum,
   historic site(s), exhibits,
   photographic collections,
   genealogical services
Period of collections: 1880-1910

BASIN HEAD

Basin Head Fisheries Museum
Telephone: (902) 357-2966
Mail to: P.O. Box 248, C0A 2B0
Regan Paquet, Curator
Major programs: museum, school
   programs, historic preservation,
   exhibits, living history, archaeology
   programs, field services
Period of collections: 1850-present

CHARLOTTETOWN

**Prince Edward Island Museum and
   Heritage Foundation**
2 Kent St., C1A 1M6
Telephone: (902) 892-9127
Mail to: 2 Kent St.
Provincial agency
Founded in: 1970
Ian W. Scott, Director
Number of members: 1,200
Staff: full time 12, part time 7,
   volunteer 20
Magazine: *The Island Magazine*
Major programs: library, museum,
   historic site(s), markers, oral
   history, school programs, book
   publishing, newsletters/pamphlets,
   historic preservation, research,
   exhibits, living history, archaeology
   programs, photographic
   collections, genealogical services,
   field services
Period of collections: 1730-present

KENSINGTON

**Anne of Green Gables Museum at
   Silver Bush**
Telephone: (902) 886-2884
Mail to: R.R. 2, C0B 1M0
George Campbell, Director
Questionnaire not received

MISCOUCHE

**Musée acadien de
   Ile-du-Prince-Édouard à
   Miscouche**
Telephone: (902) 436-5614
Mail to: C0B 1T0
Soeur Marguerite Richard, Director
Questionnaire not received

MONT CARMEL

Village des pionniers acadiens
Telephone: (902) 854-2227
Mail to: C0B 2E0
Private agency
Major programs: historic site(s), living
   history
Period of collections: 1860-1890

MONTAGUE

Garden of the Gulf Museum
Telephone: (902) 838-2528/838-2467
Mail to: c/o Town Clerk, P.O. Box 324,
   C0A 1R0
Irma MacLaren, Curator
Questionnaire not received

MURRAY HARBOUR

Log Cabin Museum
Telephone: (902) 962-2201
Preston Robertson, Director
Questionnaire not received

NEW HAVEN

Strathgartney Homestead Museum
Route No. 1
Telephone: (902) 894-8618
Mail to: P.O. Box 550, Charlottetown,
   C1A 7L1
Mrs. Keith Picard, Director
Questionnaire not received

O'LEARY

O'Leary Museum
Telephone: (902) 859-2381
Mail to: C0B 1V0
L. Dewar, President
Major programs: library, museum,
   historic preservation, photographic
   collections
Period of collections: 19th-20th
   centuries

ORWELL CORNER

Orwell Corner Agricultural Museum
Telephone: (902) 651-2013
Mail to: R.R. 2, Vernon, C0A 2E0
Malcolm MacPherson, Director
Questionnaire not received

PORT HILL

Green Park Shipbuilding Museum
Telephone: (902) 831-2206
Mail to: Tyne Valley, C0B 2C0
Marven Moore, Director
Questionnaire not received

ROCKY POINT

Fort Amherst National Historic Park
Telephone: (902) 892-0203 or
   675-2220
Mail to: Parks Canada, P.O. Box 487,
   Charlottetown, C1A 7L1
Donald Harris, Parks Canada District
   Superintendent
Questionnaire not received

SUMMERSIDE

Old Mill Museum
Telephone: (506) 886-2757
Mail to: P.O. Box 1671, C1N 2V5
Layton Dunning, Director
Questionnaire not received

QUEBEC

ACTON VALE

Société d'histoire des Six Cantons
1093 rue St. André
Telephone: (514) 546-2093
Mail to: P.O. Box 236, J0H 1A0
Private agency
Founded in: 1977
Jean-Guy Brunelle, President
Number of members: 45
Staff: volunteer 5
Major programs: archives, school
   programs, historic preservation,
   photographic collections,
   genealogical services, annual
   historical picture calendar
Period of collections: from 1850

ALMA

Société Historique
54 St. Joseph Alma Lac-St. Jean,
G8B 3E4
Telephone: (418) 668-2606
Town agency
Founded in: 1954
Roger Lajoie, President
Staff: full time 1, volunteer 10
Major programs: archives,
manuscripts, museum, oral history,
school programs, historic
preservation, records
management, research, exhibits,
archaeology programs
Period of collections: 1885-present

AMOS

Société d'histoire d'Amos
341 rue Principale nord
Telephone: (819) 727-9935
Mail to: C.P. 626, J9T 3X2
Private agency
Founded in: 1952
Bernard Cossette, President
Number of members: 72
Staff: volunteer 2
Major programs: archives, oral
history, book publishing, exhibits,
audiovisual programs,
photographic collections
Period of collections: 1910-1960

ARTHABASKA

Musée Laurier
16 ouest, rue Laurler
Telephone: (819) 357-8655
Mail to: C.P. 306, Victoriaville, G6P
6S9
Denyse Poirier Lahaye, Director
Questionnaire not received

AYLMER

**Aylmer Heritage
Association—Association du
Patrimoine d'Aylmer**
P.O. Box 476, J9H 5E7
Telephone: (819) 684-0997
Private agency
Founded in: 1975
Laura Henderson, President
Number of members: 200
Major programs: archives,
tours/pilgrimages,
newsletters/pamphlets, historic
preservation, research
Period of collections: 1850s

BAIE-COMEAU

Société Historique De La Cote-Nord
C.P. 258 Baie-Comeau
Telephone: (418) 296-6283
Questionnaire not received

BATISCAN

**Musée du manoir du presbytère de
Batiscan**
Telephone: (418) 362-2051
Mail to: 340, rue Principale, route 138,
G0X 1A0
François Guibert, Directeur
Questionnaire not received

BEACONSFIELD

**Société Historique de
Beaurepaire—Beaconsfield
Historical Society**
303 Beaconsfield Blvd., H9W 4A7

BEAUMONT

Le Moulin de Beaumont
Telephone: (418) 833-1867/523-1012
Mail to: 2, route du Fleuve, G0R 1C0
Arthur Labrie, Director
Questionnaire not received

BEEBE

The Colby-Curtis Museum
Telephone: (819) 876-7322
Mail to: 110 Main St., J0B 1E0
Malcolm MacDonald, Contact person
Questionnaire not received

BERTHIERVILLE

Village du défricheur
Telephone: (514) 836-4539
Mail to: 1497, Grande Côte, Route
138, J0K 1A0
Jean-Noel Sylvestre, Collectionneur
Questionnaire not received

CABANO

Société Historique de Cabano, Inc.
Chemin Caldwell, C.P. 464, G0L 1E0
State agency, authorized by Ministere
des Affaires Culturelles
Founded in: 1971
Yves Bosse, President
Staff: full time 1, part time 3,
volunteer 7
Major programs: archives, historic
site(s), oral history,
newsletters/pamphlets, historic
preservation, archaeology
programs, photographic
collections

CAP-DE-LA-MADELEINE

**La Société d'Histoire du
Cap-de-la-Madeleine**
45 Dorval St.
Telephone: (819) 378-3388
Mail to: P.O. Box 212, G8T 7W2
Founded in: 1939
J. E. Biron, Archivist
Questionnaire not received

CAP-ROUGE

Société Historique du Cap-Rouge
4473 St. Felix, G0A 1K0
Telephone: (418) 651-1225
Private agency
Founded in: 1974
Jean-Marc Nicole, President
Number of members: 28
Major programs: archives,
manuscripts, book publishing,
historic preservation, archaeology
programs
Period of collections: 1534-present

CAP ST. IGNACE

**Société Historique des Bernier
d'Amérique, Inc.**
133 du Manoir Est, C.P. 82, G0R 1H0
Telephone: (418) 246-5383

Private agency
Founded in: 1958
Number of members: 1,000
Staff: full time 15
Magazine: *Journal Historique des
Bernier*
Major programs: archives, historic
preservation, living history

CAUGHNAWAGA

Musée Kateri Tekakwitha
Mission Saint-François-Xavier
Telephone: (514) 632-6030
Mail to: C.P. 70, J0L 1B0
Leon Lajoie, Director/Curator
Questionnaire not received

CHAMBLY

**Parc Historique National du Ft.
Chambly**
Telephone: (514) 658-1585
Mail to: C.P. 115, J3L 4B1
National agency, authorized by Parks
Canada
Major programs: historic site(s),
school programs, historic
preservation, exhibits
Period of collections: 1700-1750

**Société d'histoire de la Seigneurie
de Chambly**
Telephone: (514) 658-2067
Mail to: C.P. 142, J3L 4B1
Private agency
Founded in: 1979
Bernadette Laflamme, President
Number of members: I52
Staff: volunteer 10
Major programs: historic site(s),
tours/pilgrimages, book publishing,
photographic collections,
genealogical services
Period of collections: 1665-1920

CHARLESBOURG

**Société Historique de
Charlesbourg**
270 56e Rue Ouest, G1H 4Z6
Telephone: (418) 628-8278
Private agency
Founded in: 1983
Paul-Aimé Paiement, Secretary
Number of members: 125
Major programs: historic site(s),
tours/pilgrimages, historic
preservation, genealogical
services

CHARNY

L'Univers du Rail, Inc.
589 27e rue, G6W 5L6
Telephone: (418) 832-6602
Private agency
Founded in: 1978
Alain S. Amant, Secretary
Number of members: 30
Staff: volunteer 6
Major programs: archives, museum,
historic site(s), tours/pilgrimages,
book publishing, historic
preservation, exhibits

CHICOUTIMI

**Société Genealogique du
Saguenay, Inc.**
930 Jacques-Cartier est, G7H 2B1

Mail to: C.P. 814, G7H 5E8
Private agency
Founded in: 1980
Carmen Beaulieu-Tremblay,
    President
Number of members: 100
Staff: volunteer 7
Major programs: research,
    genealogical services

Société Historique du Saguenay
930 est, rue Jacques Cartier, C.P.
    456
Telephone: (418) 549-2805
Founded in: 1934
Roland Bélanger, Archivist
Staff: full time 1, part time 2,
    volunteer 2
Magazine: *Saguenayensia*
Major programs: library, archives,
    manuscripts, historic sites
    preservation, junior history, oral
    history, books
Period of collections: 1597-present

COATICOOK

Musée Beaulne
Château Norton
Telephone: (816) 849-6560/819-6560
Mail to: 96, rue Union, J1A 1Y9
Town agency, authorized by
    Ministère des Affaires culturelles
    du Québec
Pierre Jean, Director
Major programs: archives, museum,
    oral history, school programs,
    historic preservation, research,
    exhibits, audiovisual programs,
    photographic collections,
    ethnology
Period of collections: 1900-1930

COOKSHIRE

Compton County Museum
Telephone: (819) 875-5256/875-3600
Mail to: R.R. 3, J0B 1M0
Waymer Laberee, Director
Questionnaire not received

COTEAU-DU-LAC

**Parc Historique National de
    Coteau-du-Lac**
Telephone: (514) 763-5631
Mail to: C.P. 211, Coteau-du-Lac, J0P
    1B0
National agency, authorized by Parks
    Canada
Lorraine Neault, Director
Major programs: historic site(s),
    school programs, interpretation
Period of collections: 1779-mid 19th
    century

DRUMMONDVILLE

**Société Historique du Centre du
    Québec**
C.P. 188, 201 St. Jean J2B 5L2
Telephone: (819) 472-5245
Founded in: 1961
René Desrosiers, President
Questionnaire not received

EATON

**Compton County Historical and
    Museum Society**
Main St., J0B 1M0

Telephone: (819) 875-5256
Mail to: P.O. Box 44, J0B 1R0
Private agency
Founded in: 1959
Rodger Heatherington, President
Number of members: 209
Staff: volunteer 20
Major programs: archives, museum,
    historic site(s),
    newsletters/pamphlets, historic
    preservation, exhibits,
    genealogical services
Period of collections: 1865-1918

GASPÉ

Société Historique de la Gaspésie
80 Blvd. Gaspé
Telephone: (418) 368-5710
Mail to: C.P. 680, G0C 1R0
Private agency
Founded in: 1962
Jules Belanger, President
Number of members: 200
Staff: full time 4, part time 2,
    volunteer 10
Magazine: *Revue Gaspésie*
Major programs: library, archives,
    manuscripts, museum, oral history,
    book publishing, exhibits,
    photographic collections,
    genealogical services, art gallery
Period of collections: 19th-20th
    centuries

GODBOUT

**Musée amérindien et inuit de
    Godbout**
Chemin Pascal Comeau
Telephone: (418) 543-3467
Mail to: 48, Carillon, Chicoutimi-Nord,
    G7G 3J3
Claude Grenier, Director
Questionnaire not received

GRANBY

Société d'Histoire de Shefford
66 Dufferin, J2G 4W7
Telephone: (514) 372-4500
Private agency
Founded in: 1967
Benoit Lapierre, General Manager
Number of members: 53
Staff: full time 1, part time 2,
    volunteer 2
Major programs: archives, school
    programs, historic preservation,
    research, photographic
    collections, genealogical services
Period of collections: early 1800-1950

GRONDINES

Musée des Grondines
215, rue Principale
Telephone: (418) 268-8459
Mail to: C.P. 99, G0A 1W0
Daniel Miram, Director
Questionnaire not received

GUÉRIN

Musée plein air régional
Mail to: J0Z 2E0
Donat Martineau, Director
Questionnaire not received

HAVRE-AUBERT

Musée des Îles
Telephone: (418) 937-5711
Mail to: C.P. 69, Îles-de-la-Madeleine,
    G0B 1J0
Frederic Landry, Directeur
Questionnaire not received

HOWICK

**Société Historique de la Vallée de la
    Chateauguay**
51 Colville St. J0S 1G0
Mail to: P.O. Box 61
Founded in: 1963
J. Johnson, President
Number of members: 248
Staff: volunteer 12
Magazine: *Chateauguay Valley
    Historical Society Journal*
Major programs: archives,
    manuscripts, historic sites
    preservation, tours/pilgrimages,
    educational programs, books,
    newsletters/pamphlets
Period of collections: 1783-present

HULL

**Institut d'histoire et de Recherche
    sur l'Outaouais, Inc.**
C.P. 1875, Succ. B, J8X 3Z1
Telephone: (819) 777-2900
Private agency
Founded in: 1980
Beauvalet Dyanne, President
Number of members: 100
Staff: volunteer 10
Magazine: *Outaouais*
Major programs: archives, historic
    site(s), school programs, research

**Société de Genealogie de
    l'Outaouais, Inc.**
C.P. 2025, Succ. B, J8X 3Z2
Telephone: (819) 663-3744
County agency
Founded in: 1978
Number of members: 515
Staff: volunteer 9
Magazine: *L'Outaouais
    Genealogique*
Major programs: library, archives,
    manuscripts, tours/pilgrimages,
    book publishing research,
    genealogical services

**Société Historique de L'ouest du
    Québec, Inc.**
C.P. 1007, Place du Portage, J8X 3X5
Telephone: (819) 771-9447
Private agency
Founded in: 1968
L. M. Bourgoin, President
Number of members: 95
Magazine: *ASTICOU*
Major programs: library, archives,
    manuscripts, historic site(s),
    tours/pilgrimages, oral history,
    book publishing, historic
    preservation, research, exhibits,
    living history
Period of collections: 1800-present

ILE D'ORLEANS

Association des Familles Rouleau
P.O. Box 156, St. Laurent, G0A 3Z0
Telephone: (418) 828-2471

Federal agency
Founded in: 1978
René Rouleau, Secretary
Number of members: 200
Staff: volunteer 9
Magazine: *Je Veille et Roule au Grain*
Major programs:
newsletters/pamphlets,
photographic collections,
genealogical services
Period of collections: 1618-present

L'ISLET-SUR-MER

Musée Maritime Bernier
Telephone: (418) 247-5001
Mail to: 55 des Pionniers est, G0R
2B0
Major programs: archives, museum,
school programs, exhibits,
photographic collections

JOLIETTE

Société Historique de Joliette
2 St. Charles Borromee N
Telephone: (514) 759-2441
Mail to: P.O. Box 470
Founded in: 1929
Camille A. Roussin, President
Questionnaire not received

KNOWLTON

Brome County Historical Society
Lakeside
Telephone: (514) 243-6782
Mail to: P.O. Box 690, J0E 1V0
Private agency
Founded in: 1897
Marion L. Phelps, Curator
Number of members: 425
Staff: full time 1, part time 4,
volunteer 4
Major programs: archives,
manuscripts, museum, oral history,
research, photographic
collections, genealogical services
Period of collections: 1783-present

LACHINE

Musée de la Ville de Lachine
Telephone: (514) 634-9652
Mail to: 110 Chemin du Musée, H8S
2X1
Town agency
Jacques Toupin, Contact person
Major programs: archives, museum,
historic site(s), school programs,
historic preservation, exhibits,
photographic collections
Period of collections: 1669-present

LACHUTE

Musée de Carillon
a/s Société pour le comte
d'Argenteuil
Telephone: (514) 537-3861
Mail to: C.P. 5, J8G 3X2
Questionnaire not received

LA MALBAIE

Musée Regional Laure Conan
30 rue Patrick-Morgan
Telephone: (418) 665-4411
Mail to: C.P. 667, G0T 1J0
Private agency

François Tremblay, Director
Major programs: archives, museum,
book publishing,
newsletters/pamphlets, research,
exhibits, folk arts
Period of collections: early 20th
century

LA POCATIÉRE

**Société Historique de la
Côte-du-Sud**
100 Ave. Painchaud, G0R 1Z0
Telephone: (418) 856-3012
Founded in: 1948
Guy Théberge, Publicist
Number of members: 60
Staff: volunteer 4
Major programs: library, archives,
book publishing, photographic
collections
Period of collections: 1783-present

LAUZON

**GIRAM (Groupe d'Initiatives et de
Recherche Appliquées au Milieu)**
205 Mgr Bourget-CEGEP, G6V 6Z9
Private agency
Founded in: 1982
Gaston Cadrin, President
Major programs: research,
photographic collections
Period of collections: 17th
century-present

LAVAL

Société d'Histoire de l'ile Jésus
5495 Ouest Boul. St-Martin H7W 3S6
Founded in: 1963
Yves Ouimet, President
Questionnaire not received

LENNOXVILLE

**Eastern Townships Research
Centre**
Bishop's University, FAC Box 38, J1M
1Z7
Telephone: (819) 569-9551, local 300
Private agency, authorized by the
university
Founded in: 1982
Mrs. Andrée Chartrand Turgeon,
Coordinator
Staff: full time 1, volunteer 9
Major programs: archives, oral
history, newsletters/pamphlets,
genealogical services
Period of collections: late
1800s-present

**Lennoxville Ascot Historical and
Museum Society**
1 Belvidere
Telephone: (819) 569-1179
Mail to: P.O. Box 61, J1M 2A3
Town agency
Muriel Brand, President
Number of members: 65
Staff: volunteer 10
Major programs: archives, tours,
book publishing, exhibits,
audiovisual programs,
photographic collections
Period of collections: 1800-present

LEVIS

**Association des Familles
Ouellet-te, Inc.**
13 Garant, G6W 1N6
Telephone: (418) 835-1254
Mail to: C.P. 28, G0R 1Z0
Private agency
Founded in: 1966
Alphonse Ouellet, President
Number of members: 850
Staff: volunteer 12
Magazine: *Le Houallet*
Major programs: archives,
manuscripts, research,
photographic collections,
genealogical services

**Société d'histoire Régionale de
Levis**
C.P. 1303, Notre-Dame Station, G6V
6Z8
Telephone: (418) 833-0115
Private agency
Founded in: 1978
Number of members: 150
Staff: volunteer 9
Magazine: *La Seigneurie de Lauzon*
Major programs: historic site(s), oral
history, historic preservation, living
history
Period of collections: 1608-present

**Société Historique
Alphonse-Desjardins**
8 Ave. Mont-Marie, G6V 1V9
Telephone: (418) 835-2090
Private agency
Founded in: 1979
Staff: full time 3
Major programs: historic site(s),
research, exhibits, audiovisual
programs

LONGUEUIL

Musée Historique de l'Electricité
Telephone: (514) 670-2953
Mail to: C.P. 61, Succursale A, J4H
3W2
Private agency
François Beaudet, Director
Major programs: library, museum,
school programs, historic
preservation, exhibits, audiovisual
programs, photographic
collections
Period of collections: mid 19th-20th
centuries

Société Historique du Marigot, Inc.
440 Chemin de Chambly, J4H 3L7
Telephone: (514) 677-4573/670-7399
City agency
Founded in: 1978
Annette Laramée, President
Number of members: 125
Staff: volunteer 14
Major programs: library, archives,
tours/pilgrimages, junior history,
oral history, book publishing,
research, exhibits, audiovisual
programs, archaeology programs,
photographic collections,
genealogical services

LORETTEVILLE

Musée Kio-Warini
Telephone: (418) 843-5515
Mail to: Village Huron, G2B 3W5

François Vincent, Director
Questionnaire not received

MAGOG

Société Historique du lac Memphre Magog
446 Main, W
Telephone: (819) 843-1212
Mail to: P.O. Box 220, J1X 3W8
Private agency, authorized by
Ministry of Cultural Affairs, Quebec
Founded in: 1980
Boisvert Jacques, President
Staff: volunteer 3
Major programs: library, archives,
oral history, newsletters/pamphlets,
research, photographic
collections, diving and scuba
history

MATANE

Société d'Histoire et de Genealogie de Matane
C.P. 608, 2-C, G4W 3P6
Telephone: (418) 562-9766
Private agency
Founded in: 1949
Robert Lourmir, President
Number of members: 375
Staff: full time 9
Major programs: archives, museum,
historic preservation, research,
photographic collections,
genealogical services

MELBOURNE

Richmond County Historical Society
P.O. Box 280, J0B 2B0
Telephone: (819) 826-3645
Founded in: 1962
Alice Mellish, Corresponding
Secretary
Number of members: 280
Staff: part time 3, volunteer 25
Major programs: archives, museum,
historic sites preservation,
tours/pilgrimages, books,
newsletters/pamphlets, historic
preservation
Period of collections: 1800s

MONTRÉAL

Acadiens au Québec
8844E Blvd. Notre-Dame, H1L 3M4
Telephone: (514) 351-9310
Private agency
Founded in: 1974
Alonzo Le Blanc, Director
Number of members: 25
Staff: volunteer 3
Major programs: archives, historic
site(s), tours/pilgrimages, book
publishing, historic preservation,
research, exhibits, genealogical
services

Association des Archivistes du Québec, Inc.
7243 rue St. Denis, H2R 2E3
State agency, authorized by Loi des
compagnies
Founded in: 1967
Marcel Caya
Number of members: 600

Magazine: *Archives*
Major programs: archives, school
programs, book publishing,
newsletters/pamphlets, records
management, research

Association des Familles Hamel
Mail to: C.P. 482, H1H 5L5
Founded in: 1982
Monique Hamel Dansereau,
President
Number of members: 250
Staff: volunteer 25
Major programs: book publishing,
newsletters/pamphlets, research,
audiovisual programs,
photographic collections,
genealogical services

Association of Art Museum Directors
1130 Sherbrooke St., W, H3A 2R5
Telephone: (514) 842-3832
Private agency
Founded in: 1916
Millicent Hall Gaudieri, Administrator
Number of members: 153
Staff: full time 1
Major programs: museum, book
publishing

Atelier d'histoire Hochelaga-Maisonneuve
169l Blvd. Pie IX, H1V 2C3
Telephone: (514) 523-5930
Private agency
Founded in: 1978
Michel Roy, Treasurer
Number of members: 20
Staff: volunteer 5
Major programs: archives, oral
history, school programs, book
publishing, research, photographic
collections

Château Ramezay
280 Est, Notre Dame, H2Y 1C5
Telephone: (5l4) 861-7182
Founded in: 1862
Jacques Poulin, Director
Number of members: 200
Staff: full time 7, volunteer 50
Major programs: library, archives,
manuscripts, museum, educational
programs
Period of collections: 1492-1865

Fédération des Sociétés d'historique du Québec
1415, est, rue Jarry, H2E 2Z7
Telephone: (514) 347-4700
Mail to: Case postale 98; succursale
Rosemont; H1X 3B6
Founded in: 1963
Marc Beaudoin, President
Questionnaire not received

Fondation Robert Giguère, Inc.
25 Ouest Jarry, H2P 1S6
Telephone: (514) 387-2541
Founded in: 1979
Georges-Emile Giguere,
President/Founder
Number of members: 300
Staff: volunteer 11
Magazine: *La Giguererie*
Major programs: archives,
manuscripts, historic site(s),
tours/pilgrimages, oral history,
book publishing,

newsletters/pamphlets, research,
living history, audiovisual
programs, photographic
collections
Period of collections: 17th-18th
centuries

German-Canadian Historical Association, Inc.
193 Wildwood Park, R3T 0E2
Federal agency
Founded in: 1973
Gerhard Friesen, President
Number of members: 100
Staff: volunteer 10
Magazine: *Canadiana Germanica*
Major programs: library, archives,
book publishing,
newsletters/pamphlets, research
Period of collections: 1600-present

Head Office, Bank of Montreal
129 St. James St., H2Y 1L6
Telephone: (514) 877-6810
Founded in: 1817
Freeman Clowery, Archivist
Staff: full time 2, part time 1
Major programs: archives, museum,
exhibits, photographic collections,
numismatic history
Period of collections: 1817-present

Institut d'histoire de l'Amerique Française
261 Ave. Bloomfield, H2V 3R6
Telephone: (514) 271-4759
Founded in: 1947
Lise McNicoll, Directrice du
Secrétariat
Number of members: 2
Staff: full time 2, part time 1
Magazine: *Revue d'Histoire de
l'Amerique Française*
Major programs: library, archives,
manuscripts

McCord Museum
690 Sherbrooke St. W, H3A 1E9
Telephone: (514) 392-4778
Founded in: 1919
David Bourke, Interim Director
Staff: full time 10, part time 7,
volunteer 7
Major programs: museum

McGill University Archives
3459 rue McTavish, H3A 1Y1
Telephone: (514) 392-5356
Private agency, authorized by the
university
Founded in: 1962
Marcel Caya, University Archivist
Staff: full time 6
Major programs: archives,
manuscripts, records management
Period of collections: 1821-present

Musée de l'Eglise Notre-Dame
426 St. Sulpice, H2Y 2V5
Telephone: (514) 842-2925
Mail to: 116 Notre-Dame ouest, H2Y
1T2
Private agency
Founded in: 1937
Fernand Lecavalier, Pastor of
Notre-Dame Basilica
Staff: part time 1
Major programs: museum
Period of collections: 1492-present

Musée de Marguerite Bourgeoys
400 E. St. Paul, H2Y 1H4
Telephone: (514) 845-9991
Private agency
Founded in: 1951
Helene Perreault, Curator
Staff: part time 2
Major programs: museum
Period of collections: 1653-1700

Québec Museums Society
1193 Carré Phillips, H3B 3E1
Telephone: (514) 252-3391
Nicole Lemay, Director
Questionnaire not received

Recherches Amérindiennes au Québec
6200 de St. Vallier, H2S 2P5
Telephone: (514) 277-6178
Founded in: 1971
Claude Chapdelaine, President
Number of members: 531
Staff: full time 1, part time 1, volunteer 14
Major programs: library, book publishing, research, archaeology programs, conferences, colloquium
Period of collections: 1971-1976

Société Généalogique Canadienne Française
C.P. 335, Station Place D'Armes, H2Y 3H1
Telephone: (514) 272-7334
Founded in: 1943
Rév Julien Déziel, President
Number of members: 2,800
Staff: volunteer 25
Magazine: *Mémoires*
Major programs: library, archives, manuscripts, books, genealogical services

Society of the Montreal Military and Maritime Museum—St. Helen's Island Museum
Telephone: (514) 861-6738
Mail to: P.O. Box 1024, Station A, H3C 2W9
Founded in: 1955
B. D. Bolton, Manager
Number of members: 100
Staff: full time 18, part time 2, volunteer 20
Magazine: *The 4-M's*
Major programs: library, manuscripts, museum, educational programs, newsletters/pamphlets
Period of collections: 15th-20th centuries

NICOLET

Société d'histoire Regionale de Nicolet
2705 du Fleuve ouest, J0G IE0
Telephone: (819) 293-2213
Private agency
Founded in: 1978
Denis Fréchette, President
Staff: volunteer 5
Magazine: *Les Cahiers Nicoletains*
Major programs: archives, historic site(s), living history
Period of collections: 18th-20th centuries

OLD CHELSEA

Historical Society of the Gatineau
P.O. Box 143, J0X 2N0
County agency
Founded in: 1962
R.A.J. Phillips, President
Staff: volunteer 2
Magazine: *Up the Gatineau*
Major programs: historic site(s), oral history, book publishing, newsletters/pamphlets, historic preservation, research, exhibits
Period of collections: 18th century

OUTREMONT

Institut d'histoire de l'Amérique Française
261 Bloomfield, H2V 3R6
Telephone: (514) 271-4759
Private agency
Founded in: 1947
Lise McNicoll, Secretary to Director
Number of members: 850
Staff: full time 1, part time 1, volunteer 4
Major programs: archives, newsletters/pamphlets, research, yearly conference
Period of collections: 1500-present

La Société historique de Montreal
4499 av. de l'Esplanade, Annexe Aeguidius-Fauteux de la B.N.Q.
Telephone: (514) 270-2846
Mail to: 5251, avenue Durocher, H2V 3X9
Maurice Da Silva, Bibliothécaire

POINTE BLEUE

Société de'histoire et d'archéologie de Pointe-Bleue
Telephone: (418) 275-4842
Mail to: 406, Amisk, G0W 2H0
Carmen Gill Casavant, Director

POINTE CLAIRE

Quebec Family History Society
P.O. 1026 Postal Station, H9S 4H9
Private agency
Founded in: 1978
R.C.B. Garrity, President
Number of members: 450
Staff: volunteer 12
Magazine: *Connections*
Major programs: library, archives, tours/pilgrimages, newsletters/pamphlets, genealogical services, workshops, family history programs

POINTE JACQUES-CARTIER

Musée d'histoire et de Traditions Populaires de la Gaspésie
Baie de Gaspe
Telephone: (418) 368-5710
Mail to: C.P. 680, Gaspe, G0C 1R0
Private agency, authorized by Société Historique de la Gaspésie
Jean-Marie Fallu, Director
Major programs: library, archives, manuscripts, museum, book

publishing, newsletters/pamphlets, research, exhibits, photographic collections, genealogical services
Period of collections: prehistoric-present

QUÉBEC

Association des Archivistes du Québec Inc.
7243 rue St. Denis, H2R 2E3
State agency, authorized by Loi des compagnies
Founded in: 1967
Marcel Caya
Number of members: 600
Magazine: *Archives*
Major programs: archives, school programs, book publishing, newsletters/pamphlets, records management, research

Commission Nationale de Genealogie
9 Place Royale, G1K 4G3
Telephone: (418) 643-1616
Private agency, authorized by Association Québec-France
Founded in: 1979
Denis Cloutier, President
Number of members: 100
Staff: volunteer 7
Magazine: *Neuve-France/Mot-A-Mot*
Major programs: archives, tours/pilgrimages, research, genealogical services

Fondation de la Société Historique de Québec
C.P. 460, G1R 4R7
Telephone: (418) 694-9740
Private agency
Founded in: 1980
Staff: full time 4
Magazine: *Quebecensia*

Institut Québécois de Recherche Sur la Culture
93 rue St. Pierre, G1K 4A3
Telephone: (418) 643-4695
Provincial agency
Founded in: 1979
Fernand Dumont, President
Number of members: 50
Staff: full time 2, part time 1
Major programs: book publishing, research

L'Institut Canadien de Québec
37, rue Sainte-Angèle, GIR 4G5
Telephone: (418) 692-2135
Founded in: 1848
Philippe Sauvageau, Directeur général
Staff: full time 26, part time 32, volunteer35
Major programs: library, archives, tours/pilgrimages oral history
Period of collections: 1865-present

La Société Historique de Québec, Inc.
Sermiaire de Québec CP 460 G1R 4R7
Telephone: (418) 694-9740

Founded in: 1937
Goerges Gauthier-Larouche,
 Secretary
Number of members: 600
Magazine: *Cahier C'Histoire*
Major programs: archives,
 educational programs, books
Period of collections: 1783-present

Musée du Québec
Parc des Champs de Bataille, G1A
 1A3
Telephone: (418) 643-2150
Founded in: 1933
M. Pierre Lachapelle, Director
Staff: full time 50
Major programs: library, museum,
 educational programs
Period of collections: 1783-1865

**Société d'archéologie de
 Nouvelle-France**
410 Fatima, Les Saules, G1P 2C9
Telephone: (418) 871-3626
Mail to: C.P. 55, Haute-Ville, G1R 4M8
Private agency
Founded in: 1976
Richard Fiset, Administrator
Number of members: 85
Staff: part time 3, volunteer 12
Magazine: *Archeologie et
 Archeologie Quebec*
Major programs: historic site(s),
 newsletters/pamphlets, historic
 preservation, research, exhibits,
 archaeology programs, field
 services
Period of collections: from prehistoric

Société Historique de Québec
C.P. 460, G1R 4R7
Telephone: (418) 694-9740
Private agency
Founded in: 1937
Number of members: 600
Staff: volunteer 9
Magazine: *Quebecensia*
Major programs: library, archives,
 tours/pilgrimages, historic
 preservation, exhibits

RAWDON

Earle Moore's Canadiana Village
300 Lake Morgan Rd.
Telephone: (514) 834-2160; 457-5358
Mail to: 8455 Decarie Blvd., Montreal,
 H4P 2J3
Earle Moore, Director

RIMOUSKI

Musée Régional de Rimouski
Telephone: (418) 724-2272
Mail to: 35 ouest, rue Saint-Germain,
 G5L 4B4
Diane Paquin, Director

ROCK ISLAND

Barn Museum
Lee Farm, USA Border, Hwy. 143
Telephone: (819)

876-2578/876-5425/876-7322
Mail to: c/o Stanstead Historical
 Society, J0B 2K0
Malcolm MacDonald, President
Questionnaire not received

SAINTE-ANNE-DES-MONTS

**Société d'histoire et d'archéologie
 des Monts**
675 Chemin du Roy, La Pointe
Telephone: (418) 763-7871
Mail to: C.P. 1192, G0E 2G0
Private agency
Founded in: 1970
Roger Dumais, President
Number of members: 20
Staff: volunteer 9
Major programs: library, archives,
 manuscripts, museum, historic
 site(s), oral history, book
 publishing, newsletters/pamphlets,
 research, exhibits, archaeology
 programs, photographic
 collections, genealogical services,
 bookbinding, papermaking,
 printing
Period of collections: 1800-1950

ST. AUGUSTIN

Pavillon André-Coindre
5030 St. Felix, G0A 3E0
Private agency
Founded in: 1960
Major programs: archives, book
 publishing, historic preservation,
 research, genealogical services

ST. CONSTANT

**Canadian Railroad Historical
 Association**
122 St. Pierre St.
Telephone: (514) 632-2410
Mail to: P.O. Box 148, J0L 1X0
Founded in: 1932
David Johnson, President
Number of members: 1,700
Staff: full time 4, part time 6,
 volunteer 40
Magazine: *Canadian Rail*
Major programs: library, archives,
 museum, historic site(s), oral
 history, school programs,
 newsletters/pamphlets, historic
 preservation, research, exhibits,
 photographic collections
Period of collections: 1830-1980

SAINT-EUSTACHE

**APMAQ (Québec Old House
 Association)**
83 rue Chénier, Y7R 1W9
Telephone: (514) 473-0149
Private agency
Founded in: 1980
Thérèse Romer, Secretary General
Number of members: 450
Staff: part time 1, volunteer 3
Magazine: *La Lucarne*
Major programs: tours,
 newsletters/pamphlets, audiovisual
 programs, lectures and

educational courses on domestic
 architecture

**Société Quebecoise des Ponts
 Couverts, Inc.**
C.P. 102, J7R 4K5
Private agency
Founded in: 1981
Gaetan Forest, President
Number of members: 135
Staff: full time 6
Magazine: *Le Pontage*
Major programs: archives,
 newsletters/pamphlets,
 photographic collections
Period of collections: 1850-1950

ST. FRANCOIS

**Ralliement des Familles
 Bonneau, Inc.**
1 5e Rue
Telephone: (418) 259-7309
Mail to: P.O. Box 39, G0R 3A0
Private agency
Founded in: 1980
Louis-Philippe Bonneau, President
Number of members: 300
Magazine: *Le Bulletin du Ralliement
 des Familles Bonneau*
Major programs: archives,
 manuscripts, oral history,
 genealogical services
Period of collections: from 1670

SAINT-JEAN

Musée du Fort Saint-Jean Museum
Telephone: (514) 346-2131
Mail to: Royal Military College,
 J0J 1R0
S. Arseneault, Director
Questionnaire not received

ST-JEAN-SUR-RICHELIEU

**Société d'histoire du
 Haut-Richelieu, Inc.**
203 Jacques-Cartier nord, J3B 6T3
Telephone: (514) 348-8055
Mail to: C.P. 212, J3B 6Z4
Private agency
Founded in: 1965
Jean Marceau, President
Number of members: 80
Staff: volunteer 6
Magazine: *La Vigilante*
Major programs: historic
 preservation, genealogical
 services
Period of collections: from 1600

ST. JEROME

**Société de Genealogie des
 Laurentides**
C.P. 131, J7Z 5T7
Private agency
Founded in: 1984
Laliberté Serge, President
Number of members: 50
Staff: volunteer 7
Magazine: *Echos Généalogiques*
Major programs: genealogical
 services

Société d'histoire de la Rivière
160 Parent
Telephone: (514) 438-7313/432-3036
Mail to: C.P. 784, J7Z 5V4
Founded in: 1980
Francois Varin, President
Number of members: 52
Staff: volunteer 20
Major programs: archives,
 manuscripts, historic site(s),
 tours/pilgrimages, oral history,
 historic preservation, research,
 exhibits, photographic collections,
 genealogical services
Period of collections: from 1790

ST. JOSEPH EST

L'Institut Canadien de Québec
350 rue St. Joseph est, G1K 3B2
Telephone: (418) 529-0924
Founded in: 1948
Philippe Sauvageau, Directeur
 General
Staff: full time 40, part time 70,
 volunteer 35
Major programs: library, archives,
 tours/pilgrimages, oral history
Period of collections: 1865-present

SAINT-LAMBERT

Société d'histoire Mouillepied
31 Lorne, J4P 2G7
Telephone: (514) 672-4772
City agency
Founded in: 1984
Thérèse Parent, Chair

ST. LAURENT (ILE D'ORLEANS)

**Association des Familles
 Gosselin, Inc.**
1647 Chemin Royal, G0A 3Z0
Telephone: (418) 828-2896
State agency
Founded in: 1979
J. Simon Gosselin, President
Number of members: 200
Staff: volunteer 7
Major programs: book publishing,
 newsletters/pamphlets,
 genealogical services
Period of collections: 1652-present

ST. NICOLAS

Chalifour-Chalifoux-Chalufour
362 de la Corniche, G0S 2Z0
Telephone: (418) 831-1175
Private agency
Founded in: 1981
Jean Chalifour, President
Magazine: *Fête
 Chalifour-Chalifoux-Chalufour*

ST. ROCH DES AULNAIES

**Corporation Touristique de la
 Seigneurie des Aulnaies**
525 de la Seigneurie, G0R 4N0
Telephone: (418) 354-2800
Private agency
Founded in: 1967
Andrée Lapointe, Director
Number of members: 300
Staff: full time 2, part time 15,
 volunteer 10

Major programs: historic site(s),
 junior history, school programs,
 historic preservation, living history
Period of collections: 1650-1850

ST. SAUVEUR-DES-MONTS

**Société d'histoire des
 Pays-d'en-Haut, Inc.**
P.B. 1209, J0R 1R0
County agency
Jacques Gouin, President
Number of members: 150
Major programs: library, archives,
 manuscripts, markers, oral history,
 research, audiovisual programs,
 photographic collections
Period of collections: 1853-1953

ST. STANISLAS, COMTE
 CHAMPLAIN

Comité Historique St. Stanislas
232 Principale, G0X 3E0
Telephone: (418) 328-3255
Private agency
Founded in: 1976
Janine Trépanier-Massicotte,
 President/Founder
Number of members: 80
Staff: volunteer 17
Major programs: archives, historic
 site(s), book publishing, historic
 preservation, research, exhibits,
 living history, photographic
 collections, genealogical services
Period of collections: 1608-present

SAINTE-ANNE DE BEAUPRE

Musée historial
Boul. Sainte-Anne
Telephone: (418) 827-3781
Mail to: Basilique Sainte-Anne, G0A
 3C0
Père S. Baillargeon, Director
Questionnaire not received

LA SARRE

Musée d'histoire et d'archéologie
Ecole Polyno de La Sarre
Telephone: (514) 333-2512
Mail to: C.P. 115, avenue Principale,
 J9Z 2X4
Dominique Godbout, Director
Questionnaire not received

SEPT-ILES

Société Historique du Golfe, Inc.
649 Blvd. Laure, G4R 1X8
Telephone: (418) 962-3434
County agency
Founded in: 1970
Gaston Saint-Hilaire, President
Magazine: *Revue Histoire de la
 Cote-Nord*
Major programs: archives, oral
 history, historic preservation,
 research, living history,
 photographic collections

SHERBROOKE

**Société de Généalogie des Cantons
 de l'Est**
1831 King ouest
Telephone: (819) 562-7741
Mail to: C.P. 635, J1H 1W7

Founded in: 1969
Micheline Gilbert, President
Number of members: 300
Staff: volunteer 10
Magazine: *L'Entraide Généalogique*
Major programs: genealogical
 services

**Société d'Histoire des Cantons de
 l'Est—Eastern Townships
 Historical Society**
1304 Blvd. Portland, Pavillon 3,
 Domaine Howard, J1J 1S3
Telephone: (819) 562-0616
Mail to: C.P. 2117, J1J 3Y1
Private agency
Founded in: 1927
Andrée Désilets, President
Number of members: 223
Staff: full time 1, volunteer 3
Major programs: library, archives,
 manuscripts, museum, oral history,
 research, exhibits, living history,
 photographic collections
Period of collections: 1760-present

STANBRIDGE EAST

Missisquei Historical Society, Inc.
Telephone: (514) 248-3153
Mail to: P.O. Box 186, J0J 2H0
Private agency
Founded in: 1898
Number of members: 545
Staff: full time 1, part time 8,
 volunteer 75
Major programs: library, archives,
 manuscripts, museum, historic
 sites preservation, oral history,
 books
Period of collections: early 19th
 century

STANSTEAD

Stanstead Historical Society
Telephone: (819) 876-7322
Mail to: P.O. Box 268, J0B 3E0
County agency
Founded in: 1929
F. J. Bill Taylor, Executive Vice
 President
Number of members: 500
Staff: part time 6, volunteer 80
Magazine: *Stanstead Historical
 Society Journal*
Major programs: library, archives,
 museum, historic site(s), markers,
 tours/pilgrimages, historic
 preservation, research, exhibits,
 photographic collections,
 genealogical services
Period of collections: mid
 1800s-present

TERREBONNE

**Société d'histoire de la Région de
 Terrebonne**
C.P. 54, J6W 2M4
Telephone: (514) 471-3391
County agency
Founded in: 1975
Marguerite L. Desjardins, President
Number of members: 61
Magazine: *La Fournée*
Major programs: historic site(s),
 school programs, book publishing,
 newsletters/pamphlets, historic

preservation, research, exhibits,
living history, audiovisual
programs, archaeology programs,
photographic collections
Period of collections: 1673

THETFORD MINES

Megantic County Historical Society
P.O. Box 742, G6G 5V1
Telephone: (418) 335-6820
County agency
Founded in: 1971
Harold Brazel, Library Research
Number of members: 36
Staff: volunteer 5
Major programs: library, historic
site(s), markers, tours/pilgrimages,
newsletters/pamphlets, historic
preservation, research, living
history, photographic collections,
genealogical services,
preservation of pioneer cemeteries
Period of collections: from 1831

TROIS-PISTOLES

**Société Historique et Généalogique
de Trois-Pistoles, Inc.**
C.P. 1586, G0L 4K0
Telephone: (418) 851-3144
Private agency
Founded in: 1977
Emmanuel Rioux, President
Number of members: 210
Magazine: *L'Echo des Basques*
Major programs: library, archives,
book publishing,
newsletters/pamphlets, research,
exhibits, living history,
genealogical services

TROIS-RIVIÈRES

Musée Pierre Boucher
Telephone: (819) 375-7922
Mail to: 858 rue Laviolette, G9A 5J1
Yolande Lafleche, Director
Private agency
Major programs: museum, historic
site(s)
Period of collections: 1850

**Société de Généalogie de la
Mauricie et des Bois-Francs, Inc.**
C.P. 901, G9A 5K2
Provincial agency
Founded in: 1978
Jonathan Lemire, President
Number of members: 150
Staff: volunteer 9
Magazine: *Héritage*
Major programs: library, archives,
genealogical services

VALCOURT

Musée J. Armand Bombardier
1000, rue J. A. Bombardier
Mail to: C.P. 370, J0E 2L0
Private agency
France Bissonnette, Director
Major programs: exhibits

VAL D'OR

Société d'histoire de Val D'Or
600 7e Rue, J9P 3P3
Telephone: (819) 825-6352
Private agency
Founded in: 1976

Jean L'Houmeau, President
Staff: volunteer 3
Major programs: archives, historic
site(s), exhibits, photographic
collections
Period of collections: 1920

VAUDREUIL

Musée historique de Vaudreuil
Telephone: (514) 455-2092
Mail to: 431, boul. Roche, J7V 2N3
Louise Myette, Director
Questionnaire not received

**Musée Régional de
Vaudreuil-Soulanges**
431 Blvd. Roche, J7V 2N3
Telephone: (514) 455-2092
Private agency
Founded in: 1953
Ghislaine Lavoie, President
Number of members: 52
Staff: full time 2, part time 4,
volunteer 6
Major programs: archives, museum,
school programs, book publishing,
newsletters/pamphlets, historic
preservation, records
management, research, exhibits,
living history, audiovisual
programs, archaeology programs,
photographic collections

VILLE-MARIE

**Société d'histoire du
Témiscamimque**
9 rue Notre-Dame
Telephone: (819) 629-3533
Mail to: C.P. 1022, J0Z 3W0
County agency
Founded in: 1949
Gaétan Lemire, Historic Site Director
Number of members: 130
Staff: full time 1, part time 6,
volunteer 10
Magazine: *La Minerve*
Major programs: archives, historic
site(s), tours/pilgrimages, oral
history, school programs, book
publishing, research, photographic
collections
Period of collections: 1880-present

WESTMOUNT

Westmount Historical Association
4574 Sherbrooke St., W, H3Z 1G1
Private agency
Founded in: 1945
A. Henrietta Harvie, President
Number of members: 67
Major programs: archives,
manuscripts, historic site(s),
markers, tours/pilgrimages, oral
history, school programs,
newsletters/pamphlets, historic
preservation, exhibits, audiovisual
programs, photographic
collections
Period of collections: 1870-present

SASKATCHEWAN

ARCOLA

Arcola Museum
Corner of Carlyle St. and Railway Ave.
Telephone: (306) 455-2492/455-2258
Mail to: P.O. Box 181, S0C 0G0
G. Hislop, Director
Questionnaire not received

AVONLEA

Avonlea and District Museum
Main St.
Telephone: (306) 868-2221
Mail to: P.O. Box 401, S0H 0C0
Town agency, authorized by Village
of Avonlea
Founded in: 1980
Elaine Howse, Secretary
Number of members: 125
Staff: part time 1, volunteer 20
Major programs: museum
Period of collections: 1900-1940

BATTLEFORD

Battleford National Historic Park
Telephone: (306) 937-2621
Mail to: P.O. Box 70, S0M 0E0
Founded in: 1951
Mable Simpson, Area Superintendent
Staff: full time 9, part time 16
Major programs: library, historic sites
preservation, tours, historic
preservation
Period of collections: 1870-1924

BIGGAR

Biggar Museum and Gallery
202 3rd Ave., W
Telephone: (306) 948-3451
Mail to: P.O. Box 1598, S0K 0M0
Town agency
Founded in: 1972
Deborah Peterson, Curator
Staff: full time 1, volunteer 12
Major programs: archives, museum,
historic site(s), oral history, school
programs, historic preservation,
records management, research,
exhibits, living history,
photographic collections,
genealogical services
Period of collections: 1910-1940

Homestead Museum
Hwy. 51
Telephone: (306) 948-3427
Mail to: P.O. Box 542, S0K 0M0
Private agency
Roger Martin, Director
Major programs: museum, school
programs
Period of collections: 1910-1930

BROADVIEW

**Broadview Historical and Museum
Association, Inc.**
P.O. Box 556, S0G 0K0
Telephone: (306) 696-2286/696-2612
Private agency
Founded in: 1968
John J. Macmillan, Chair
Number of members: 25
Staff: volunteer 4

Major programs: archives, museum,
oral history, historic preservation,
exhibits, photographic collections
Period of collections: 1880-present

Broadview Museum
Telephone: (306) 696-5586/696-2624
Mail to: P.O. Box 556, S0G 0K0
John MacMillan, President
Questionnaire not received

BULYEA

Lakeside Museum
Telephone: (306) 725-4558
Mail to: R.R. 1, S0G 0L0
Robert Swanston, Director

CARLYLE

Rusty Relics Museum
Telephone: (306) 453-2500
Mail to: c/o Stella McLeod, P.O. Box
396, S0C 0R0
Gladys Nicholl, President
Questionnaire not received

CRAIK

Prairie Pioneer Museum
Old No. 11 highway in NE Craik
Telephone: (306) 734-2260
Mail to: c/o Mrs. H. Anderson, P.O.
Box 273, S0G 0V0
Mrs. H. Anderson, Director
Questionnaire not received

CUT KNIFE

Clayton McLain Memorial Museum
Hwy. 40
Telephone: (306) 398-2590
Mail to: P.O. Box 335, S0M 0N0
Mrs. E. McLain, Director
Period of collections: 1905-1930

DENARE BEACH

Northern Gateway Museum
Telephone: (306) 362-2123
Mail to: c/o Fred Shwaga, P.O. Box
430, Creighton, S0P 0A0
Anne Wiebe, Director
Questionnaire not received

DODSLAND

Dodsland Museum
2nd Ave.
Mail to: S0L 0V0
Town agency
Joan Meumeier, Director
Major programs: museum, exhibits
Period of collections: 1930

DUCK LAKE

Duck Lake Historical Museum
Telephone: (306) 467-2057
Mail to: P.O. Box 370, S0K 1J0
Private agency
Ron Bazylak, President
Major programs: museum, historic
site(s), tours/pilgrimages, school
programs, historic preservation,
research, exhibits
Period of collections: 1870-1905

Fort Carlton Historical Park
25km west of Duck Lake on Hwy. 212
Telephone: (306) 565-5879/467-4512

Mail to: c/o Supervisor Historic Parks,
Department of Culture and Youth,
11th Floor, Avord Tower, Regina,
S4P 3V7
Sharon Wood, Supervisor of
Historic Parks
Questionnaire not received

EARL GREY

Earl Grey Centennial Museum
Main St.
Telephone: (306) 939-2062/939-2008
Mail to: S0G 1J0
Helene Huber, Contact person
Questionnaire not received

ELBOW

**Elbow Museum and Historical
Society**
Telephone: (306) 854-4625
Mail to: P.O. Box 67, S0H 1J0
Elden Pfeffer, President
Questionnaire not received

ESTERHAZY

Esterhazy Community Museum
Maple St.
Telephone: (306) 745-3895
Mail to: S0A 0X0
Mrs. Dlouhy, Director
Questionnaire not received

ESTEVAN

Estevan National Exhibition Centre
118 4th St., S4A 0T4
Telephone: (306) 634-5007
Founded in: 1977
Colin Stevens, Director
Number of members: 50
Staff: full time 2, part time 1
Major programs: school programs,
newsletters/pamphlets, exhibits

ESTON

Prairie West Historical Society, Inc.
946 2nd St., SE, S0L 1A0
Telephone: (306) 962-3772
Provincial agency
Founded in: 1977
Lyle Williams, Chair
Number of members: 373
Staff: part time 3, volunteer 25
Major programs: museum, school
programs, historic preservation,
photographic collections
Period of collections: 1900-1945

FIR MOUNTAIN

**Wood Mountain Rodeo-Ranch
Museum and Historical Society**
Wood Mountain Regional Park
Telephone: (306) 266-4750
Mail to: c/o Thelma Poirier, S0H 1P0
Thelma Poirier, Director

FOAM LAKE

Foam Lake Pioneer Museum
Telephone: (306) 272-3265
Mail to: P.O. Box 91, S0A 1A0
Runa Helgason, Director

FROBISHER

Frobisher Thresherman's Museum
Telephone: (306) 486-2033

Mail to: S0C 0Y0
Lloyd Olson, President
Questionnaire not received

GRENFELL

Grenfell Community Museum
Wolseley Ave.
Telephone: (306) 697-2431
Mail to: P.O. Box 1156, S0G 2B0
Town agency, authorized by Grenfell
Museum Association, Inc.
Jeanie Kerr, Secretary
Major programs: manuscripts,
museum, historic preservation,
exhibits, photographic collections
Period of collections: 1880-1930

HERBERT

Old Homestead Museum
Telephone: (306) 784-2915
Mail to: P.O. Box 28, S0H 2A0
Peter E. Klassen, Director
Major programs: museum
Period of collections: 1900-1950

HUMBOLDT

**Humboldt and District Museum and
Gallery**
Main St. and 6th Ave.
Mail to: P.O. Box 2349, S0K 2A0
Town agency
Founded in: 1981
V. A. Campbell, Chair
Staff: part time 2, volunteer 30
Major programs: museum
Period of collections: 1885-1935

KERROBERT

Kerrobert and District Museum
Atlantic Ave. N
Telephone: (306) 834-2744
Mail to: P.O. Box 104, S0L 1R0
Mrs. M. Cholin, Co-Director
Questionnaire not received

KINCAID

Kincaid Museum
Telephone: (306) 264-3308
Mail to: c/o Mrs. A. Wald, P.O. Box 55,
S0H 2J0
Mrs. A. Wald, Chair
Questionnaire not received

KINDERSLEY

Kindersley Plains Museum
1st St., W, and Princess Ave., Baker
Park
Telephone: (306) 463-4141
Mail to: P.O. Box 599, S0L 1S0
Town agency
Jean Helfrich, Curator
Major programs: archives, museum,
historic preservation, photographic
collections
Period of collections: late 1800s-mid
1900s

KIPLING

**Kipling District Museum and
Historical Society**
4th St. S and Centennial Ave.
Mail to: c/o Olga Parker, S0G 2S0
Martin Kovacs, Director
Questionnaire not received

KISBEY

Kisbey Museum
Old Maitland School
Telephone: (306) 462-2164
Mail to: c/o Ella Snell, Museum
  Committee, P.O. Box 91, S0C 1L0
Clara Wilde, President

LASHBURN

Lashburn Centennial Museum
Telephone: (306) 285-3390
Mail to: c/o Northern Circle Women's
  Institute, S0M 1H0
Joyce Topley, Director
Questionnaire not received

LLOYDMINSTER

Barr Colony Museum
Weaver Park
Telephone: (403) 825-5655/875-9325
Mail to: c/o City Hall, 5011 49 Ave.,
  S9V 0T8
City agency
Richard Larsen, Director
Major programs: archives, museum,
  historic site(s), school programs,
  historic preservation, records
  management, exhibits,
  photographic collections

MANOR

Hewlett House Museum
13km north of Manor
Telephone: (306) 448-4428
Mail to: P.O. Box 211, S0C 1R0
A. Hewlett, Director

MAPLE CREEK

Ft. Walsh National Historic Park
P.O. Box 278, S0N 1N0
Telephone: (306) 662-2645
National agency, authorized by Parks
  Canada
Founded in: 1968
L. K. Roberts, Acting Operations
  Manager
Number of members: full time 3, part
  time 15
Major programs: historic site(s),
  school programs, exhibits, living
  history, audiovisual programs
Period of collections: 1873-1883

Old Timer's Museum
218 Jasper St.
Telephone: (306) 667-2474/667-2327
Mail to: Old Timer's Association, S0N
  1N0
Bob Evans, Curator
Questionnaire not received

MCCORD

McCord Museum
Main St.
Telephone: (306) 478-2538
Mail to: P.O. Box 62, S0H 2T0
Authorized by McCord and District
  Recreation Centre
Leila Belsher, Secretary
Major programs: museum, historic
  site(s), markers
Period of collections: 1930s

MELFORT

Pioneer Village Museum
Melfort Exhibition Grounds
Telephone: (306) 752-2240
Mail to: P.O. Box 520, S0E 1A0
Joan Mitchell, Director

MILDEN

Milden Community Museum
Saskatchewan Ave. and Centre St.
Telephone: (306) 935-4431
Mail to: S0L 2L0
G. Somerville, President

MOOSE JAW

**Moose Jaw Art Museum and
National Exhibition Centre**
Crescent Park, S6H 0X6
Telephone: (306) 692-4471
City agency, authorized by City of
  Moose Jaw
Founded in: 1966
Gerald Jessop, Director
Number of members: full time 4, part
  time 1, volunteer 9
Major programs: museum,
  tours/pilgrimages, oral history,
  school programs,
  newsletters/pamphlets, records
  management, exhibits
Period of collections: 1850-1950

**Prairie Pioneer Village and Museum
of Saskatchewan**
14km south of Moose Jaw on Hwy. 2
Telephone: (306) 692-4255/693-7315
Mail to: P.O. Box 1, Sub 1, S6H 5V0
C. Meacher, President
Questionnaire not received

**Saskatchewan History and Folklore
Society**
P.O. Box 1238, S6H 4P9
Telephone: (306) 693-6900
Provincial agency
Founded in: 1957
Richard J. Wood, Administrator
Number of members: 300
Staff: full time 1
Magazine: *Folklore*
Major programs: library, museum,
  tours/pilgrimages, oral history,
  newsletters/pamphlets, folklore
  programs
Period of collections: 1880-1939

MOOSOMIN

Jamieson Museum
306 Gertie St.
Telephone: (306) 435-3156
Mail to: P.O. Box 236, S0G 3N0
Private agency
Tim Jamieson, President
Major programs: museum
Period of collections: to 1900

NIPAWIN

**Nipawin and District Historical
Museum**
2nd Ave. E at 2nd St. E
Telephone: (306) 862-4867/862-4428
Mail to: P.O. Box 1917, S0E 1E0
Mike Mochoruk, President of the
  Board
Questionnaire not received

OXBOW

Ralph Allen Memorial Museum
802 Railway Ave. on Hwy. 18
Telephone: (306) 483-5082
Mail to: S0C 2B0
Mike Bartolf

PLENTY

Carscadden's Museum
8km south of Plenty on Hwy. 31
Telephone: (306) 932-4604
Mail to: S0L 2R0
Norman Carscadden, Director

PORCUPINE PLAIN

**Porcupine Plain and District
Museum**
Cultural Centre Building, Elm St.
Telephone: (306) 278-2317/278-2339
Mail to: P.O. Box 98, S0E 1H0
Town agency
Myrla Birch, Director
Major programs: museum, markers,
  exhibits
Period of collections: 1919-1959

PRELATE

**Blumenfeld and District Heritage
Site**
P.O. Box 220, S0N 2B0
Telephone: (306) 673-2200
District agency
Founded in: 1982
Roy Steier, Chair
Major programs: museum, historic
  site(s), tours/pilgrimages
Period of collections: 1912-1920s

St. Angela's Museum and Archives
P.O. Box 220, S0N 2B0
Telephone: (306) 673-2200
Private agency, authorized by
  Ursuline Sisters of Prelate
Founded in: 1969
Sister Philomena, Chair
Major programs: library, archives,
  museum, markers,
  tours/pilgrimages, oral history,
  historic preservation, photographic
  collections
Period of collections: early 1920s

PRINCE ALBERT

Little Gallery Committee
1010 Central Ave.
Telephone: (306) 922-9603
Mail to: 349 20th St., W, S6V 4G7
City agency
Founded in: 1978
Mrs. Ronnie Haner, Director
Staff: full time 1, part time 1,
  volunteer 17
Major programs: exhibits

**Prince Albert Historical Society
and Museum**
Central Ave. and River St.
Telephone: (306) 764-2992
Mail to: P.O. Box 531, S6V 5R8
City agency
Major programs: archives, museum,
  tours/pilgrimages, school
  programs, book publishing,
  exhibits, photographic collections
Period of collections: 1866-1945

RAYMORE

Raymore Pioneer Museum
P.O. Box 147, S0A 3J0
Telephone: (306) 746-4633
Founded in: 1965
David Birch, Secretary/Treasurer
Major programs: archives, museum, markers, school programs, historic preservation, photographic collections, genealogical services, field services
Period of collections: 1890-present

REGINA

Government House Historic Property
4607 Dewdney Ave., S4P 3V7
Telephone: (306) 565-5773
Provincial agency, authorized by Department of Culture and Recreation
Founded in: 1981
Marilyn Doolan, Manager
Staff: full time 3, part time 11
Major programs: museum, historic site(s), tours/pilgrimages, school programs, historic preservation
Period of collections: 1898-1910

Historical Collection, Saskatchewan Militia District Headquarters
1600 Elphinstone St.
Telephone: (306) 347-9351
Mail to: P.O. Box 5099, S4P 3M3
Authorized by Commander, Saskatchewan Militia District
Founded in: 1984
C. K. Inches, President
Staff: volunteer 5
Major programs: archives, museum
Period of collections: 1885-present

Museum of Natural History
Wascana Park, S4P 3V7
Telephone: (306) 565-2815
Founded in: 1906
John E. Storer, Director
Questionnaire not received

Plains Historical Museum
1801 Scarth St., S4P 2G9
Telephone: (306) 352-0844
Private agency
ounded in: 1960
Jan Morier, Director/Curator
Number of members: 260
Staff: part time 5, volunteer 60
Magazine: *Making History*
Major programs: museum, school programs, newsletters/pamphlets, exhibits, volunteer programs
Period of collections: 1880s-1930s

RCMP (Royal Canadian Mounted Police) Centennial Museum
P.O. Box 6500, S4P 3J7
Telephone: (306) 359-5836
National agency, authorized by Royal Canadian Mounted Police
Founded in: 1933
Malcolm J. H. Wake, Director
Staff: full time 4
Major programs: museum, tours/pilgrimages, research, exhibits, audiovisual programs, photographic collections
Period of collections: 1873-present

Saskatchewan Archives Board
University of Regina, S4S 0A2/University of Saskatchewan, Saskatoon, S7N 0W0
Telephone: (306) 787-4068/664-5832
Provincial agency
Founded in: 1945
Major programs: archives, manuscripts, oral history, book publishing, records management, photographic collections, genealogical services
Period of collections: 1875-present

Saskatchewan Museums Association
1870 Lorne St., S4P 2L7
Telephone: (306) 522-3651
Gayl Hipperson, Executive Director

Saskatchewan Provincial Historic Parks
3211 Albert St., S4S 5W6
Telephone: (306) 566-9573
Provincial agency, authorized by Department of Parks and Renewable Resources
Sharon Wood, Supervisor
Staff: full time 3, part time 15
Major programs: historic site(s)
Period of collections: to 1900

Saskatchewan Sports Hall of Fame
2205 Victoria Ave., S4P 0S4
Telephone: (306) 522-3651
Provincial agency
Founded in: 1966
Margaret J. Sandison, Executive Director
Number of members: 200
Staff: full time 2, part time 1
Major programs: library, archives, museum, tours/pilgrimages, school programs, newsletters/pamphlets, exhibits, audiovisual programs, photographic collections
Period of collections: late 19th-20th centuries

ROCANVILLE

Rocanville and District Museum
Corner of Qu'Appelle Ave. and St. Albert St.
Telephone: (306) 645-4308
Mail to: S0A 3L0
Everett Rice, President
Questionnaire not received

ROCKGLEN

Rolling Hills Historical Society
Railway
Telephone: (306) 476-2591
Mail to: P.O. Box 384, S0H 3R0
Private agency
Founded in: 1983
Charlie Yost, Director
Staff: volunteer 20
Magazine: *Rockglen Museum*
Major programs: archives, museum, exhibits
Period of collections: 1930

ST. WALBURG

St. Walburg and District Historical Museum, Inc.
S0M 2T0
Town agency

Founded in: 1984
Mary E. Stone, Secretary
Staff: volunteer 10
Major programs: museum, historic site(s), historic preservation, exhibits
Period of collections: to 1945

SASKATOON

Honorable John G. Diefenbaker Centre
University of Saskatchewan, S7N 0W0
Telephone: (806) 966-8382
Authorized by University Board of Governors
Founded in: 1980
Sharon D. Mitchell, Director
Number of members: 2
Staff: full time 6, part time 8
Major programs: archives, museum, historic site(s), oral history, school programs, historic preservation, research, exhibits, photographic collections
Period of collections: 1895-1979

Little Stone School
University of Saskatchewan Campus
Telephone: (306) 382-2504
Mail to: 3141 11th Street W, S7M 1K1
Ethel Hirsch, President
Questionnaire not received

Metis Museum
Telephone: (306) 244-1172
Mail to: 111 Avenue B South, S7M 1M2
Clarence Trotchie, President
Questionnaire not received

Saskatchewan Western Development Museums
2935 Melville St.
Telephone: (306) 934-1400
Mail to: P.O. Box 1910, S7K 3S5
Provincial agency
Founded in: 1949
David R. Richeson, Executive Director
Staff: full time 35, part time 10, volunteer 50
Magazine: *Sparks Off The Anvil*
Major programs: library, museum, educational programs, newsletters/pamphlets, historic preservation
Period of collections: 1870-present

Ukrainian Museum of Canada
910 Spadina Crescent, E, S7K 3H5
Telephone: (306) 244-3800
Private agency, authorized by Minister of Consumer and Corporate Affairs
Founded in: 1936
Albert Kachkowski, Director
Staff: full time 5, part time 4, volunteer 50
Major programs: library, museum, historic site(s), tours/pilgrimages, oral history, school programs, book publishing, newsletters/pamphlets, exhibits, audiovisual programs, photographic collections
Period of collections: 1895-1935

SHAUNAVON

Grand Coteau Heritage and Cultural Centre
P.O. Box 966, S0N 2M0
Telephone: (306) 297-3882
Town agency
Founded in: 1980
Ingrid Cazakoff, Curator
Staff: full time 1, volunteer 10
Major programs: museum, tours/pilgrimages

Grand Coteau Museum
Centre St.
Telephone: (306) 297-2561
Mail to: P.O. Box 1222, S0N 2M0
George Straub, Director

SPY HILL

Spy Hill Museum—Wolverine Hobby and Historical Society
Main St.
Telephone: (306) 534-2032
Mail to: P.O. Box 185, S0A 3W0
Private agency
Paul Magnusson, President
Major programs: archives, manuscripts, museum, markers, book publishing, newsletters/pamphlets, historic preservation, exhibits, photographic collections
Period of collections: 1883-1920

STAR CITY

Our Heritage
Corner of 4th St. and 2nd Ave.
Mail to: P.O. Box 371, S0E 1P0
Abner Garinger, President

STRASBOURG

Strasbourg and District Museum
CPR Station, Railway Ave.

Telephone: (306) 725-3049
Mail to: P.O. Box 446, S0G 4V0
Gerald Zealand, Director

SWIFT CURRENT

Swift Current Museum
105 Chaplin St., E, S9H 3X5
Telephone: (306) 773-9888
City agency
Founded in: 1937
Vera A. Wilson, Curator/Director
Staff: part time 2, volunteer 4
Major programs: museum, natural history

VANGUARD

Vanguard Library-Museum
S0N 2V0
Telephone: (306) 582-2244
Town agency
Founded in: 1974
Mrs. D. Saunderson, Chair
Staff: part time 1, volunteer 3
Major programs: library, museum
Period of collections: early 1900-present

VERIGIN

Doukhobor Society Museum
Telephone: (306) 542-3454
Mail to: S0A 4H0
P. Kabatoff, Director
Questionnaire not received

VERWOOD

Verwood Community Museum
Main St.
Telephone: (306) 642-5767
Mail to: c/o Helen Domes, Secretary, Museum Committee, S0H 4G0
Gerald Good, President
Questionnaire not received

WEEKES

Dunwell and Community Museum
Telephone: (306) 278-2906
Mail to: Weekes Centennial Community Hall, P.O. Box 120, S0E 1V0
Mrs. David Grisdale, Director

WEYBURN

Soo Line Historical Museum
411 Industrial Lane, Hwy. 39, E
Telephone: (306) 842-2922
Mail to: P.O. Box 1016, S4H 2L2
Lavine Stepp, Manager
Major programs: archives, museum, historic site(s), markers, book publishing, historic preservation, exhibits, photographic collections
Period of collections: early 1900s-1950

WILKIE

Wilkie and District Museum and Historical Society
1st St., E
Telephone: (306) 843-2717
Mail to: P.O. Box 868, S0K 4W0
Town agency
Founded in: 1976
Walter Andres, President
Number of members: 25
Major programs: historic preservation, records management
Period of collections: 1900-1950

WILLOW BUNCH

Willow Bunch Museum
Telephone: (306) 473-2267
Mail to: S0H 4K0
Jean Champigny, Custodian
Questionnaire not received

Willow Bunch Museum Society
Principal St., S0H 4K0
Authorized by Willow Bunch Museum Society
Founded in: 1972
Louise Boisvert, Custodian
Major programs: museum
Period of collections: 1890-1970

YORKTON

Western Development Museum
Hwy. 16, W
Telephone: (306) 783-8361
Mail to: P.O. Box 98, S3N 2V6
Private agency
Tom G. Waiser, Manager
Major programs: museum
Period of collections: 1900

Yorkton Arts Council
49 Smith St. E, S3N 1E2
Telephone: (306) 783-8722
Private agency
Founded in: 1965
Florence Slywka, Managing Secretary
Number of members: 225
Staff: full time 1, part time 1, volunteer 30
Major programs: exhibits

Immigrant family exhibition from the permanent collection of the Ukrainian Museum of Canada in Saskatoon.—Ukrainian Museum of Canada

YUKON TERRITORY

BURWASH LANDING

Kluane Museum of Natural History
Destruction Bay
Telephone: (403) 841-4541
Mail to: General Delivery, Y0B 1H0
Private agency
Founded in: 1968
Phil Temple, President
Number of members: 30
Staff: part time 3, volunteer 10
Major programs: museum, exhibits, audiovisual programs, natural history
Period of collections: 1895-present

DAWSON CITY

Dawson City Museum and Historical Society
5th Ave.
Telephone: (403) 993-5291
Mail to: P.O. Box 303, Y0B 1G0
Private agency
Founded in: 1959
Catherine Hines, Director
Number of members: 120
Staff: full time 1, part time 15, volunteer 10
Major programs: museum, research, audiovisual programs, photographic collections, genealogical services
Period of collections: 1898

Klondike National Historic Sites
P..O. Box 390, Y0B 1G0
Telephone: (403) 993-5462
National agency
Founded in: 1962
Staff: full time 20, part time 50
Major programs: historic site(s)
Period of collections: 1896-1918

KENO HILL

Keno Mining Museum
Telephone: (403) 995-3100
Mail to: General Delivery, Y0B 1J0
Private agency
Founded in: 1977
Drago Kokanov, President
Number of members: 10
Staff: volunteer 5
Major programs: museum, exhibits, photographic collections
Period of collections: 1895-1950s

MAYO

Mayo Historical Society
Telephone: (403) 996-2550
Mail to: P.O. Box 32, Y0B 1M0
Private agency
Founded in: 1981
L. MacDonald, Secretary
Number of members: 10
Staff: volunteer 10
Major programs: oral history, book publishing, research, photographic collections
Period of collections: 1901-1950

TESLIN

George Johnston Museum
Telephone: (403) 390-2550
Mail to: General Delivery, Y0A 1B0
Private agency
Founded in: 1975
S. Jeanne Foster, President
Number of members: 30
Staff: part time 5, volunteer 10
Major programs: museum, exhibits
Period of collections: 1898-1980s

WHITEHORSE

Heritage Branch
211 Hawkins St.
Telephone: (403) 667-5386

Mail to: P.O. Box 2703, Y1A 2C6
Territorial agency, authorized by Department of Economic Development and Tourism
Founded in: 1981
B. Dale Perry, Director
Staff: full time 6, part time 5
Major programs: museum assistance, historic site(s), archaeology programs

MacBride Centennial Museum
1st Ave. and Wood St.
Telephone: (403) 667-2709
Mail to: P.O. Box 4037, Y1A 3S9
Private agency, authorized by MacBride Museum Society
Laurent Cyr, President
Major programs: archives, manuscripts, museum, historic site(s), historic preservation
Period of collections: 1898-1970

Yukon Archives
2nd Ave. and Hanson St.
Telephone: (403) 667-5321
Mail to: P.O. Box 2703, Y1A 2C6
Territorial agency
Founded in: 1972
Miriam McTiernan, Director, Libraries and Archives
Staff: full time 7, part time 3
Major programs: library, archives, manuscripts, photographic collections, reference services
Period of collections: 1898-1953

Yukon Church Heritage Society
3rd Ave. and Elliot St.
Telephone: (403) 667-7746
Mail to: P.O. Box 4247, Y1A 3T3
Private agency, authorized by the Anglican Church, Diocese of Yukon
Founded in: 1982
Mrs. M. Almstrom, President
Number of members: 25
Staff: part time 6, volunteer 6
Major programs: archives, manuscripts, museum, historic site(s), newsletters/pamphlets, historic preservation, records management, research, exhibits, audiovisual programs
Period of collections: 1860-present

Yukon Historical and Museums Association
Telephone: (403) 667-4704
Mail to: P.O. Box 4357, Y1A 3T5
Private agency
Founded in: 1977
Shirley Foster, President
Number of members: 100
Staff: volunteer 10
Major programs: markers, tours/pilgrimages, book publishing, newsletters/pamphlets, historic preservation, research
Period of collections: 1900-present

This photograph was taken on May 18, 1923, and shows the steamer Canadian docked in Mayo, Yukon Territory, picking up a load of silver ore from the stockpile of Keno Hill ore on the Mayo waterfront.—Mayo Historical Society

Questionnaires Received after the Deadline

United States

ILLINOIS

CHICAGO

Swedish American Museum Association of Chicago
5248 N. Clark St.
Telephone: (312) 728-8111
Private agency, authorized by State of Illinois
Founded in: 1976
Sven Flodstrom, President
Number of members: 350
Staff: volunteer 3
Major programs: library, archives, museum, school programs, newsletters/pamphlets, historic preservation, exhibits, photographic collections, genealogical services
Period of collections: 1840-1930

IOWA

DUMONT

Dumont Historical Society
50625
Telephone: (515) 857-3565
Private agency
Founded in: 1976
Erna Clemens, President
Number of members: 30
Staff: volunteer 4
Major programs: library, manuscripts, museum, tours/pilgrimages, school programs, newsletters/pamphlets, historic preservation, exhibits, living history, photographic collections
Period of collections: 1879-1984

MARYLAND

COLLEGE PARK

Old Town College Park Preservation Association
7400 Dartmouth Ave., 20740
Telephone: (301) 864-6709
Private agency
Founded in: 1979
Number of members: 100
Staff: volunteer 8
Major programs: historic site(s), historic preservation

MASSACHUSETTS

BECKET

Becket Historical Commission
c/o Chair, Bancroft Rd., Chester, 01011
Telephone: (413) 623-5324
Town agency
Founded in: 1975
Esther Moulthrope, Chair
Staff: volunteer 7
Major programs: school programs, historic preservation
Period of collections: 1740-present

MICHIGAN

ANN ARBOR

Genealogical Society of Washtenaw County
Mail to: P.O. Box 7155, 48107
Private agency
Founded in: 1974
Karen Walker, President
Number of members: 250
Staff: volunteer 21
Magazine: *Family History Capers*
Major programs: library, genealogical services

MISSOURI

COLUMBIA

Boone County Historical Society
802 S. Edgewood Ave., 65203
Telephone: (314) 449-5876
Private agency
Founded in: 1965
Bill Thomas Crawford, President
Number of members: 250
Staff: volunteer 15
Major programs: museum, historic site(s), markers, tours/pilgrimages, book publishing, newsletters/pamphlets, historic preservation, genealogical services
Period of collections: 1835-present

NEW HAMPSHIRE

PLAISTOW

Plaistow Historical Society, Inc.
c/o Town Hall, Main St., 03865
Town agency
Founded in: 1974
Bernadine Fitzgerald, President
Number of members: 15
Major programs: museum, markers, oral history, historic preservation, records management, photographic collections
Period of collections: 1747-present

NEW JERSEY

MORRISTOWN

Morris County Trust for Historic Preservation, Inc.
45-A Macculloch Ave., 07960
Telephone: (201) 539-0366
Private agency
Founded in: 1979

Robert P. Guter, Chair
Number of members: 40
Staff: volunteer 6
Major programs: historic
   preservation, field services,
   easements acquisition

NEW YORK

CITY ISLAND

City Island Historical Society and Museum
190 Fordham St., 10464
Telephone: (212) 885-1616
Private agency, authorized by State
   Education Department
Founded in: 1964
Number of members: 125
Staff: part time 4, volunteer 10
Major programs: library, archives,
   manuscripts, museum, historic
   site(s), oral history, historic
   preservation, research, exhibits,
   living history, audiovisual
   programs, photographic
   collections, genealogical services
Period of collections: 1800-1930

TEXAS

CROCKETT

Downes-Aldrich House
206 N. Seventh St.
Telephone: (409) 544-4804
Mail to: 1003 Redbud, 75835

Private agency
Founded in: 1981
Olga Rabbit, President
Number of members: 150
Staff: volunteer 14
Major programs: tours/pilgrimages,
   historic preservation
Period of collections: 1890-1920

Monroe-Crook House
707 E. Houston, 75835
Telephone: (409) 544-5820
Private agency, authorized by
   George and Hallie M. Crook
   Foundation
Founded in: 1974
Albertine S. Dean, President
Number of members: 280
Staff: volunteer 65
Major programs: tours/pilgrimages,
   historic preservation
Period of collections: 1850s

VIRGINIA

ALEXANDRIA

Virginia Canals and Navigations Society
625 Pommander Walk, 22314
Telephone: (703) 836-7590
Private agency, authorized by
   Virginia Canal Society
Founded in: 1977
Samuel R. Hopper, President
Number of members: 330
Staff: volunteer 2
Magazine: *The Tiller*
Major programs:
   newsletters/pamphlets
Period of collections: 1780-1880

RICHMOND

American Canal Society
35 Towana Rd., 23226
Telephone: (804) 288-1334
Private agency
Founded in: 1972
Dr. William E. Trout, III, President
Number of members: 625
Staff: volunteer 4
Magazine: *American Canals*
Major programs:
   newsletters/pamphlets
Period of collections: 1780-1900

Canada

MANITOBA

WINNIPEG

Point Douglas Historical Society
No. 17, 21st Floor, 185 Smith St., R3C 3G4
Telephone: (204) 943-5907
Private agency, authorized by
   Province of Manitoba
Founded in: 1970
Stella Kozyniok, President
Number of members: 13
Major programs: junior history, oral
   history, school programs, historic
   preservation
Period of collections: 1812-present

General Index

A

A. M. and Welma Aikin, Jr., Regional Archives, Paris, TX 454

A.M. Chisholm Museum, Duluth, MN 228

AFAM (Air Force Armament Museum), Fort Walton Beach, FL 78

AIRCHIVE Association, Springfield, IL 116

APMAQ (Quebec Old House Association), Saint-Eustache, Quebec 561

APTA (Association for Preservation of Tennessee Antiquities), Nashville, TN 432

Aaron Burr Association, Hightstown, NJ 282

Abbeville County Historical Society, Abbeville, SC 413

Abbeville Historic Preservation Commission, Abbeville, SC 413

Abby Aldrich Rockefeller Folk Art Collection, Williamsburg, VA 481

Aberdeen Appearance and Preservation Commission, Aberdeen, MD 178

Abigail Adams Smith Museum, New York, NY 322

Abington Historical Commission, Abington, MA 187

abraham Lincoln Association, Springfield, IL 116

Abram Demaree Homestead, Closter, NJ 279

Acadian Genealogical and Historical Association of New Hampshire, Manchester, NH 273

Acadian Genealogy Exchange, Covington, KY 154

Acadian Heritage Society, Rumford-Mexico, ME 176

Acadiens au Québec, Montreal, Quebec 559

Acoma Tourist and Visitation Center, Acoma, NM 294

Acworth Silsby Library, Acworth, NH 269

Adair County Anquestors, Greenfield, IA 136

Adair County Historical Society, Greenfield, IA 136

Adams County Genealogical Society, Inc., West Union, OH 374

Adams County Historical Society, Brighton, CO 50

Adams County Historical Society, Gettysburg, PA 393

Adams County Historical Society, Hastings, NE 263

Adams County Historical Society, Inc., Decatur, IN 122

Adams County Historical Society Museum, Lind, WA 485

Adams National Historic Site, Quincy, MA 203

Addison Historical Society—Historical Museum of Addison, Addison, IL 99

Adel Historical Society, Adel, IA 131

Adena State Memorial, Chillicothe, OH 358

Adirondack Museum—Adirondack Historical Association, Blue Mountain Lake, NY 304

Admiral Nimitz State Historical Park, Fredericksburg, TX 446

Aerospace Museum and Park, Hampton, VA 474

Affton Historical Society, St. Louis, MO 253

African-American Cultural Alliance, Nashville, TN 432

African American Cultural Heritage Center—Children's Cultural Heritage Center and Museum, Dallas, TX 442

African American Museum of Art and History, Minneapolis, MN 232

Afro-American Communities Project, Washington, DC 71

Afro-American Heritage Association, Rome, NY 331

Afro-American Historical and Cultural Museum, Philadelphia, PA 400

Age of Steam Railroad Museum, Southwest Railroad Historical Society, Dallas, TX 442

Agricultural Hall of Fame, Bonner Springs, KS 143

Agricultural Heritage Museum, Brookings, SD 422

Agricultural History Society, Washington, D.C. 71

Aiken County Historical Commission, Aiken, SC 413

Aiken County Historical Society, Aiken, SC 413

Akwesasne Museum—Akwesasne Library and Culture Centre, Inc., Hogansburg, NY 315

Alabama Archaeological Society, Huntsville, AL 5

Alabama Baptist Historical Society—Special Collections, Samford University Library, Birmingham, AL 2

Alabama Department of Archives and History, Montgomery, AL 6

Alabama Division, United Daughters of the Confederacy, Albertville, AL 1

Alabama Historical Association, Birmingham AL 2

Alabama Historical Commission, Montgomery, AL 6

Alabama Mining Museum, Dora, AL 4

Alabama Pilgrimage Council, Montgomery, AL 6

Alabama Society, Daughters of the American Colonists, Mobile, AL 6

Alachua County Historical Commission, Gainesville, FL 78

Alamance Battleground, Burlington, NC 341

Alamance County Historic Properties Commission, Graham, NC 345

Alamance County Historical Museum, Burlington, NC 341

Alamo, The, San Antonio, TX 455

Alaska Association for Historic Preservation, Anchorage, AK 8

Alaska Historical and Transportation Museum, Inc., Palmer, AK 11

Alaska Historical Commission, Anchorage, AK 8

Alaska Historical Library, Juneau, AK 10

Alaska Historical Society, Anchorage, AK 9

Alaska State Archives, Juneau, AK 10

Alaska State Museum, Juneau, AK 10

Alaskana Collection and Archives, Anchorage, AK 9

Albany County Hall of Records, Albany, NY 300

Albany County Historical Association, Albany, NY 301

Albany County Historical Society, Laramie, WY 508

Albany Institute of History and Art, Albany, NY 301

Albemarle County Historical Society, Charlottesville, VA 471

Alberni District Historical Society, Port Alberni, British Columbia 520

Albert City Historical Association, Inc., Albert City, IA 131

Albert County Historical Society, Inc., Hopewell Cape, New Brunswick 529

Alberta Beach Museum, Alberta Beach, Alberta 510

Alberta Forest Service Museum, Hinton, Alberta 514

Alberta Historic Sites Service, Edmonton, Alberta 512

Alberta Historical Resources Foundation, Calgary, Alberta 510

Alberta Hospital Museum, Ponoka, Alberta 516

Alberta Museums Association, Edmonton, Alberta 512

Alberta Pioneer Railway Association, Edmonton, Alberta 512

Alberton Museum, The, Alberton, Prince Edward Island 555

Albion Historical Society, Albion, MI 209

Albuquerque Archaeological Society, Albuquerque, NM 294

Albuquerque Conservation Association, Albuquerque, NM 294

Alden Historical Society, Alden, NY 302
Alden Kindred of America, Inc., Duxbury, MA 194
Aldrich Public Library, Barre, VT 464
Alexander and Baldwin Sugar Museum, Puunene, HI 95
Alexander-Crawford Historical Society, Alexander,
    ME 168
Alexander Daugherty Chapter, United States Daughters
    of 1812, Midland, TX 452
Alexander Graham Bell National Historic Park,
    Baddeck, Nova Scotia 533
Alexander Ramsey House, St. Paul, MN 236
Alexander Young Log House, Washington, IA 141
Alexandria Archaeology, Alexandria, VA 469
Alexandria Library, Alexandria, VA 469
Alexandria Township Historical Society, Alexandria Bay,
    NY 302
Alexandria Urban Archaeology Program, Alexandria,
    VA 469
Alfalfa County Historical Society, Cherokee, OK 393
Alfred P. Sloan Museum, Flint, MI 215
Alger County Historical Society, Munising, MI 220
Aliceville Historical Preservation, Inc., Aliceville, AL 1
Alix-Clive Historical Club, Alix, Alberta 510
Allegan County Historical Society, Allegan, MI 209
Allegany Area Historical Association, Allegany, NY 302
Allegany County Historical Society, Belmont, NY 304
Allegany County Historical Society, Inc., Cumberland,
    MD 182
Alleghany Historical-Genealogical Society, Inc.—Floyd
    Crouse House, Sparta, NC 349
Allegheny-Kiski Valley Historical Society, Tarentum,
    PA 406
Allegheny Portage Railroad National Historic Site,
    Cresson, PA 391
Allen County—Ft. Wayne Historical Society, Ft. Wayne,
    IN 122
Allen County Historical Society and Museum, Lima,
    OH 366
Allen County Historical Society, Inc., Iola, KS 147
Allendale County Historical Society, Allendale, SC 413
Allentown-Upper Freehold Historical Society, Allentown,
    NJ 277
Alley Pond Environmental Center, New York, NY 322
Alliance Knight Museum, Alliance, NE 260
Allis-Bushnell House, Madison, CT 62
Alma Fire Department Museum, Alma, CO 49
Almond Historical Society, Inc., Almond, NY 302
Alpine Hills Historical Museum, Sugarcreek, OH 372
Alton Area Historical Society and Research Library,
    Alton, IL 99
Alton Area Landmarks Association, Inc., Alton, IL 99
Alton Museum of History and Art, Inc., Alton, IL 99
Amador County Historical Society, Jackson, CA 29
Amador-Livermore Valley Historical Society,
    Pleasanton, CA 36
Amalthea Historical Society, Westerville, OH 374
Amana Heritage Society and Museum of Amana
    History, Amana, IA 131
Amateur Softball Association Museum, Oklahoma City,
    OK 379
American Antiquarian Society, Worcester, MA 209
American Association for State and Local History,
    Nashville, TN 432
American Association for the Advancement of Science,
    Washington, DC 71
American Association of Botanical Gardens and
    Arboreta, Inc., Swarthmore, PA 406
American Association of Museums, Washington, DC 71
American Baptist Historical Society, Rochester, NY 330
American Canal Society, Inc., York, PA 408
American Canal Society, Richmond, VA 570
American Catholic Historical Association, Washington,
    DC 71
American Catholic Historical Society, Philadelphia,
    PA 400
American Clock and Watch Museum, Inc., Bristol,
    CT 58
American Craft Museum of the American Craft Council,
    New York, NY 322
American Division, Jesuit Historical Institute, Tucson,
    AZ 15
American Family Records Association, Kansas City,
    MO 247
American Heritage Center, Laramie, WY 508
American Historical Association, Washington, DC 71
American Historical Society of Germans from Russia,
    Lincoln, NE 264
American Indian Archaeological Institute, Washington,
    CT 68
American Institute for Conservation of Historic and
    Artistic Works, Washington, DC 71
American Institute of Architects Foundation—The
    Octagon Museum, Washington, DC 71
American Institute of the History of Pharmacy, Madison,
    WI 499
American Jewish Archives, Cincinnati, OH 358
American Jewish Historical Society, Waltham, MA 207
American Labor Museum—Botto House National
    Landmark, Haledon, NJ 282
American Merchant Marine Museum, Great Neck,
    NY 314
American Military Institute, Washington, DC 71
American Motley Association—Valley Forge Office
    Colony, Valley Forge, PA 407
American Museum—Hayden Planetarium, New York,
    NY 322
American Museum of Fly Fishing, Manchester, VT 467
American Museum of Immigration, New York, NY 322
American Museum of the Moving Image, New York,
    NY 322
American Numismatic Society Museum, New York,
    NY 322
American Police Center and Museum, Chicago, IL 102
American Radio Relay League Museum, Newington,
    CT 64
American Society for Legal History, Atlanta, GA 85
American Society of Military History, Los Angeles,
    CA 31
American Studies Association, Philadelphia, PA 400
American Swedish Historical Museum, Philadelphia,
    PA 400
American Swedish Institute, Minneapolis, MN 232
American Work Horse Museum, Paeonian Springs,
    VA 478
American-Canadian Genealogical Society, Manchester,
    NH 273
American-French Genealogical Society, Pawtucket,
    RI 411
Americana Manse, Whitney-Halsey Home, Belmont,
    NY 304
Americana Museum, Terra Alta, WV 474
Amerind Foundation, Inc., Dragoon, AZ 12
Amherst Historical Society, Amherst, MA 187
Amherst Historical Society, Amherst, OH 355
Amherstburg Historic Sites Association, Amherstburg,
    Ontario 539
Amistad Research Center, New Orleans, LA 165
Amityville Historical Society, Amityville, NY 302
Amon Carter Museum of Western Art, Fort Worth,
    TX 445
Amy B. Yerkes Museum of Hatboro Baptist Church,
    Hatboro, PA 394
Anadarko Philomathic Museum, Anadarko, OK 376
Anasazi Indian Village State Historical Monument,
    Boulder, UT 461
Ancestral Trails Historical Society, Vine Grove, KY 162

Anchorage Historical and Fine Arts Museum,
  Anchorage, AK 9
Anchorage Museum of History and Art, Anchorage,
  AK 9
Ancient and Honorable Artillery Company, Boston,
  MA 188
Anderson Heritage, Inc., Anderson, SC 413
Anderson House Museum of the Society of the
  Cincinnati, Washington, DC 72
Anderson Valley Historical Museum, Boonville, CA 24
Andersonville National Historic Site, Andersonville,
  GA 85
Andes Society for History and Culture, Andes, NY 302
Andover Historical Society, Andover, CT 57
Andover Historical Society, Andover, MA 187
Andover Historical Society, Andover, ME 168
Andrew County Historical Society, Savannah, MO 255
Andrew Johnson National Historic Site, Greeneville,
  TN 429
Andrew Pickens Chapter, Sons of the American
  Revolution, Greenville, SC 418
Androscoggin Historical Society, Auburn, ME 169
Angel Mounds State Memorial, Evansville, IN 122
Animas School Museum, Durango, CO 53
Ann Arbor Hands-On Museum, Ann Arbor, MI 210
Ann Arbor Historic District Commission, Ann Arbor,
  MI 210
Ann Arrundell County Historical Society, Severna Park,
  MD 185
Anna Miller Museum, Newcastle, WY 508
Annapolis Valley Macdonald Museum, Middleton, Nova
  Scotia 537
Anne Spencer Memorial Foundation, Lynchburg,
  VA 476
Annie Riggs Museum, Ft. Stockton, TX 445
Annie S. Kemerer Museum, Bethlehem, PA 388
Anniston Museum of Natural History, Anniston, AL 1
Anoka County Genealogical Society, Anoka, MN 226
Anoka County Historical Society, Anoka, MN 226
Anson County Historical Society, Wadesboro, NC 350
Anthro/Arts, Rockville, RI 412
Anthropology Museum, Northern Illinois University,
  DeKalb, IL 106
Anthropology Museum of the People of New York, New
  York, NY 322
Antiquarian and Landmarks Society, Inc., Hartford,
  CT 61
Antique Wireless Association, Inc., Holcomb, NY 315
Apalachicola Area Historical Society, Apalachicola,
  FL 76
Apopka Historical Society, Apopka, FL 76
Appalachian History of Medicine Society, Johnson City,
  TN 430
Appalachian Oral History Project, Pippa Passes, KY 161
Appling County Historical Society, Inc., Baxley, GA 86
Appomattox Courthouse National Historical Park,
  Appomattox, VA 470
Aquatic Hall of Fame and Museum of Canada,
  Winnipeg, Manitoba 525
Arbor Lodge State Historical Park, Nebraska City,
  NE 265
Arbuckle Historical Society, Davis, OK 376
Arch, Inc., Ft. Wayne, IN 123
Archaeological Committee, Wayne County Historical
  Society, Wooster, OH 375
Archaeological Society of Maryland, Inc., Silver Spring,
  MD 186
Archaeological Society of South Carolina, Columbia,
  SC 416
Archaeological Society of Virginia, Richmond, VA 479
Archaeological Survey Association of Southern
  California, Inc., Redlands, CA 37

Archelaus Smith Historical Society, Clark's Harbor,
  Nova Scotia 534
Archer County Historical Commission, Archer City,
  TX 437
Architectural Conservancy of Greenwich, Greenwich,
  CT 60
Archival Center, Mission Hills, CA 33
Archival Services, University of Akron, Akron, OH 354
Archives Branch, Denver Federal Archives and Records
  Center, Denver, CO 51
Archives and History Division, West Virginia State
  Museum, Charleston, WV 492
Archives and Museum, Mississippi University for
  Women, Columbus, MS 239
Archives and Records Division, Texas General Land
  Office, Austin, TX 437
Archives and Regional History Collections, Kalamazoo,
  MI 218
Archives and Special Collections, Harriet Irving Library,
  Fredericton, New Brunswick 528
Archives of American Art, Texas Project, Houston,
  TX 449
Archives of American Art, Washington, DC 72
Archives of DePauw University and Indiana United
  Methodism, Greencastle, IN 124
Archives of Labor and Urban Affairs, Detroit, MI 213
Archives of St. Luke's Hospital of Kansas City, Kansas
  City, MO 247
Archives of the American Camping Association,
  Martinsville, IN 127
Archives of the Archdiocese of Detroit, Detroit, MI 213
Archives of the Episcopal Church, Austin, TX 437
Archives of the Lutheran Church in America, Chicago,
  IL 102
Archives of the Mexican Baptist Convention of Texas,
  San Antonio, TX 455
Archives of the Moravian Church in America,
  Winston-Salem, NC 351
Archives of the North American Baptist Conference,
  Sioux Falls, SD 426
Ardmore Public Library, Ardmore, OK 376
Arenac County Historical Society, Au Gres, MI 211
Argonia and Western Somner County Historical Society
  and Museum, Argonia, KS 143
Arizona Archaeological and Historical Society, Tucson,
  AZ 15
Arizona Historical Foundation—Hayden Library, Arizona
  State University, Tempe, AZ 15
Arizona Historical Society, Tucson, AZ 15
Arizona Historical Society Century House Museum and
  Gardens, Yuma, AZ 16
Arizona Historical Society Fort Lowell Museum, Tucson,
  AZ 15
Arizona Historical Society Heritage Center, Tucson,
  AZ 15
Arizona Historical Society John C. Fremont
  House—Casa Del Governador, Tucson, AZ 15
Arizona Historical Society Museum of History, Phoenix,
  AZ 13
Arizona Historical Society Pioneer Museum, Flagstaff,
  AZ 12
Arizona Humanities Council, Phoenix, AZ 13
Arizona Jewish Historical Society, Phoenix Chapter,
  Phoenix, AZ 14
Arizona Museum, The, Phoenix, AZ 14
Arizona Pharmacy Historical Foundation, Glendale,
  AZ 12
Arizona State Department of Library, Archives and
  Public Records, Phoenix, AZ 14
Arizona State Genealogical Society, Tuscon, AZ 15
Arizona State Museum, Tucson, AZ 16
Arizona State Parks Board, Phoenix, AZ 14

Arkansas Archivists and Records Managers, Little Rock, AR 19
Arkansas Endowment for the Humanities, Little Rock, AR 19
Arkansas Historical Association, Fayetteville, AR 17
Arkansas History Commission, Little Rock, AR 19
Arkansas Museum Services, Little Rock, AR 19
Arkansas Museum of Science and History, Little Rock, AR 19
Arkansas Museums Association, Fort Smith, AR 18
Arkansas Oil and Brine Museum, Smackover, AR 22
Arkansas Post County Museum, Gillett, AR 18
Arkansas State University Museum, Jonesboro, AR 19
Arkansas Territorial Restoration, Little Rock, AR 19
Arlington Antebellum Home & Gardens, Birmingham, AL 2
Arlington Historical Society, Arlington, MA 187
Arlington Historical Society, Arlington, TX 437
Arlington Historical Society and Museums, Arlington, VA 470
Armand Bayou Nature Center, Houston, TX
Armed Forces Medical Museum, Washington, DC 72
Armenian Assembly of America, Washington, DC 72
Armstrong County Historical and Museum Society, Inc., Kittanning, PA 396
Army Museum, Halifax South, Nova Scotia 535
Arnprior and District Museum, Arnprior, Ontario 539
Aroostook Historical and Art Museum, Houlton, ME 172
Arrow Rock State Historic Site, Arrow Rock, MO 242
Art Conservation Department, State University College at Buffalo, Cooperstown, NY 308
Artesia Historical Museum and Art Center, Artesia, NM 296
Arthur J. Moore Methodist Museum, St. Simons Island, GA 92
Artifacts Center, Edmonton, Alberta 512
Arts and Humanities Council of Greater Baton Rouge, Baton Rouge, LA 163
Arvada Center for the Arts and Humanities Museum, Arvada, CO 49
Arvada Historical Society, Arvada, CO 49
Ashcroft Museum, Ashcroft, British Columbia 517
Ashfield Historical Society, Inc., Ashfield, MA 187
Ashland Anthracite Museum, Ashland, PA 387
Ashland County Historical Society, Ashland, OH 355
Ashland Historical Society, Ashland, MA 187
Ashland Historical Society—Whipple House Museum, Ashland, NH 269
Ashtabula County Historical Society, Jefferson, OH 366
Ashton Villa, Galveston, TX 446
Ashville Area Heritage Society, Ashville, OH 355
Asia Society, The, New York, NY 322
Asotin County Historical Society, Asotin, WA 482
Aspen Historical Society, Aspen, CO 49
Assiginack Historical Society, Manitowaning, Ontario 545
Association Canado-Americaine, Manchester, NH 273
Association Museums New Brunswick, Saint John, New Brunswick 530
Association Nouvelle-Angleterre/Acadie, Manchester, NH 273
Association des Archivistes du-Québec, Inc., Montreal, Quebec 559
Association des Familles Gosselin, Inc., St. Laurent, Quebec 562
Association des Familles Hamel, Montreal, Quebec 559
Association des Familles Landry d'Amérique, Caraquet, New Brunswick 527
Association des Familles Ouellet-Te, Inc., Levis, Quebec 558
Association des Familles Rouleau, Ile d'Orléans, Quebec 557
Association for Gravestone Studies, Needham, MA 199

Association for Northern California Records and Research, Chico, CA 25
Association for the Advancement of Dutch-American Studies, Grand Rapids, MI 216
Association for the Preservation of Historic Natchitoches, Natchitoches, LA 165
Association for the Preservation of Virginia Antiquities, Richmond, VA 479
Association of Art Museum Directors, Montreal, Quebec 559
Association of King County Historical Organizations, Seattle, WA 487
Association of Living History Farms and Museums, Washington, D.C. 72
Association of South Dakota Museums, Pierre, SD 425
Association of Utah Historians, Salt Lake City, UT 463
Atascadero Historical Society, Atascadero, CA 23
Atascosito Historical Society, Liberty, TX 451
Atelier d'histoire Hochelaga-Maisonneuve, Montreal, Quebec 559
Athenaeum of Philadelphia, Philadelphia, PA 400
Atheneum Society of Wilbraham, Wilbraham, MA 208
Athens-Clarke Heritage Foundation, Athens, GA 85
Athens County Historical Society and Museum, Athens, OH 355
Athens-Limestone County Arts Council, Athens, AL 1
Atikokan Centennial Museum and Historical Park, Atikokan, Ontario 539
Atlanta Historical Society, Inc., Atlanta, GA 85
Atlanta Preservation Center, Atlanta, GA 85
Atlantic Canada Aviation Museum, Halifax, Nova Scotia 534
Atlantic County Historical Society, Somers Point, NJ 291
Atlantic County Office of Cultural Affairs, Atlantic City, NJ 277
Atlantic Highlands Historical Society, Atlantic Highlands, NJ 277
Atlin Historical Museum, Atlin, British Columbia 517
Attleboro Area Industrial Museum, Attleboro, MA 187
Atwater Kent Museum, Philadelphia, PA 400
Au-Sable River Valley Historical Society, Mio, MI 220
AuSable-Oscoda Historical Society, Oscoda, MI 221
Auburn Automotive Heritage, Inc.—Auburn-Cord-Duesenberg Museum, Auburn, IN 120
Audie Murphy Room, W. Walworth Harrison Public Library, Greenville, TX 447
Audubon County Historical Society, Audubon, IA 131
Audrain County Historical Society, Mexico, MO 251
Audubon State Commemorative Area—Oakley Plantation, St. Francisville, LA 167
Augusta County Historical Society, Staunton, VA 480
Augusta Genealogical Society, Inc., Augusta, GA 86
Augusta Historical Museum, Augusta, KS 143
Augusta Richmond County Museum, Augusta, GA 86
Augustan Society, Inc., Torrance, CA 47
Augustana Historical Society, Rock Island, IL 115
Aurora Colony Historical Society, Aurora, OR 382
Aurora Historical Museum, Aurora, IL 100
Aurora Historical Society, Aurora, CO 49
Aurora Historical Society, Aurora, OH 355
Aurora Historical Society, Inc., East Aurora, NY 310
Aurora History Center, Aurora, CO 49
Aurora and District Historical Society, Inc., Aurora, Ontario 539
Austin History Center, City of Austin Library Department, Austin, TX 437
Autauga County Heritage Association, Prattville, AL 7
Avery Institute of Afro-American History and Culture, Charleston, SC 414
Aviation Hall of Fame of New Jersey, Teterboro, NJ 292
Avon Historical Society, Avon, OH 355
Avon Valley Historical Society, Stratford, Ontario 551

Avonlea and District Museum, Avonlea,
Saskatchewan 563
Aylmer Heritage Association—Association du
Patrimoine d'Aylmer, Aylmer, Quebec 556
Aylmer and District Museum, Aylmer, Ontario 539
Aztec Museum Association, Aztec, NM 296
Azusa Historical Society, Inc., Azusa, CA 23

B

B'nai B'rith Klutznick Museum, Washington, DC 72
Baca and Bloom Houses, Pioneer Museum, Trinidad,
CO 57
Backus Conservation Area and Historical Complex, Port
Rowan, Ontario 550
Bad Axe Historical Society, Bad Axe, MI 211
Badger Historical Society, Shullsburg, WI 504
Bainbridge Island Historical Society, Winslow, WA 491
Baker County Historical Society, Macclenny, FL 80
Baker Furniture Museum, Holland, MI 217
Baker-Cederberg Archives of the Rochester General
Hospital, Rochester NY 330
Bakken Library of Electricity in Life, Minneapolis,
MN 232
Balch Institute for Ethnic Studies, Philadelphia, PA 401
Baldwin County Historic Development Commission,
Montrose, AL 7
Baldwin County Historical Society, Stockton, AL 8
Baldwin Heritage Museum Association, Elberta, AL 4
Baldwin Historical Society, Inc. and Museum, Baldwin,
NY 303
Bale Grist Mill State Historic Park, Calistoga, CA 24
Ballestone Preservation Society, Baltimore, MD 180
Balmoral Grist Mill, Balmoral Mills, Nova Scotia 533
Baltimore Center for Urban Archaeology, Baltimore,
MD 180
Baltimore City Archives and Records Center, Baltimore,
MD 180
Baltimore Conference, United Methodist Historical
Society, Baltimore, MD 180
Baltimore Heritage, Inc., Baltimore, MD 180
Baltimore Museum of Industry, Baltimore, MD 180
Baltimore Public Works Museum, Inc., Baltimore,
MD 180
Balzekas Museum of Lithuanian Culture, Chicago,
IL 102
Bamberg County Historical and Genealogical Society,
Bamberg, SC 413
Bancroft Historical Museum, Bancroft, Ontario 539
Bancroft Library, The, Berkeley, CA 24
Bandar Log, Inc., Magdalena, NM 298
Bandera County Historical Commission, Bandera,
TX 438
Banff Centre School of Management, Banff, Alberta 510
Bangor Historical Society, Bangor, ME 169
Banneker-Douglas Museum of Afro-American Life and
History, Annapolis, MD 179
Banning Residence Museum, Wilmington, CA 48
Bantam Historical Society, Inc., Bantam, CT 57
Bar Harbor Historical Society, Bar Harbor, ME 169
Baraga County Historical Society, Inc., L'Anse, MI 218
Barbed Wire Museum, LaCrosse, KS 147
Barberton Historical Society, Barberton, OH 356
Barbour's General Store, St. John, New Brunswick 530
Barkerville Historic Park, Barkerville, British
Columbia 517
Barkhamsted Historical Society, Barkhamsted, CT 57
Barlow House, Canby, OR 382
Barlow Society for the History of Medicine, Los Angeles,
CA 31

Barnegat Light Historical Society, Barnegat Light,
NJ 277
Barnes County Historical Society, Inc., Valley City,
ND 354
Barnet Historical Society, Barnet, VT 464
Barnum Museum, Bridgeport, CT 58
Barr Colony Museum, Lloydminster, Saskatchewan 565
Barre Museum—Archives of Barre History, Barre,
VT 464
Barrhead and District Historical Society, Barrhead,
Alberta 510
Barrington Area Historical Society, Barrington, IL 100
Barrington Preservation Society, Barrington, RI 409
Barron's C & O Canal Museum, Sharpsburg, MD 185
Barrow County Historical Society, Winder, GA 94
Barry County Historical Society, Cassville, MO 244
Bartholomew County Historical Society, Columbus,
IN 121
Bartlett Historical Society, Bartlett, IL 100
Barton County Genealogical Society, Great Bend,
KS 146
Barton County Historical Society, Great Bend, KS 146
Barton County Historical Society, Lamar, MO 249
Basilian Fathers Museum, Mundare, Alberta 515
Basin Head Fisheries Museum, Basin Head, Prince
Edward Island 555
Basket Historical Society of the Upper Delaware Valley,
Long Eddy, NY 319
Bassett Hall, Williamsburg, VA 481
Batavia Depot Museum, Batavia, IL 100
Bath County Historical Society, Inc., Warm Springs,
VA 481
Bath Historic Committee, Bath, NY 303
Bath, Maine, Maritime Museum, Bath, ME 169
Battle of Lexington Historic Site, Lexington, MO 250
Battleford National Historic Park, Battleford,
Saskatchewan 563
Battleground Historical Society, Freehold, NJ 281
Battleship New Jersey Historical Museum Society,
Middletown, NJ 285
Battleship Texas State Historic Park, La Porte, TX 451
Baxter County Historical Society, Mountain Home,
AR 20
Bay Area Electric Railroad Association, Inc.—Western
Railway Museum, Suisun City, CA 46
Bay Area Heritage Society, Baytown, TX 439
Bay Area Museum, Seabrook, TX 457
Bay County Historical Society—Historical Museum of
Bay County, Bay City, MI 211
Bayard Taylor Memorial Library, Kennett Square,
PA 396
Baylor County Historical Museum, Seymour, TX 457
Baylor University Institute for Oral History, Waco,
TX 460
Bayou Bend Collection, Museum of Fine Arts, Houston,
TX 449
Bayport Heritage Association, Bayport, NY 303
Baytown Historical Museum, Baytown, TX 439
Beaufort Historical Association, Beaufort, NC 341
Beaumont Heritage Society, Beaumont, TX 439
Beauregard-Keyes House, New Orleans, LA 166
Beauvoir, Jefferson Davis Shrine, Biloxi, MS 239
Beaver Area Heritage Foundation, Beaver, PA 387
Beaver Falls Historical Society and Museum, Beaver
Falls, PA 388
Beaver Island Historical Society, St. James, MI 223
Beaver River Museum—Beaverton Thorah and Eldon
Historical Society, Beaverton, Ontario 540
Beaverhead County Museum, Dillon, MT 257
Beaverhead Museum Association, Dillon, MT 257
Becker County Historical Society, Detroit Lakes,
MN 228
Becket Historical Commission, Becket, MA 569

Beckoning Hills Museum, Boissevain, Manitoba 523
Bedford Historical Society, Bedford, NY 304
Bedford Historical Society, Bedford, OH 356
Bedford Historical Society, Inc., Bedford, VA 471
Beech Grove Confederate Cemetery, Beech Grove, TN 427
Beekman Historical Society, Poughquag, NY 329
Behringer-Crawford Museum, Covington, KY 154
Beiger Heritage Corporation, Mishawaka, IN 127
Belfast Historical Society, Inc., Belfast, ME 169
Belfast Museum, Inc., Belfast, ME 169
Belhaven Memorial Museum, Inc., Belhaven, NC 341
Belknap Mill Society, Laconia, NH 273
Bell County Historical Society, Inc., Middlesboro, KY 160
Bell Homestead, Brantford, Ontario 540
Belle Meade Mansion, Nashville, TN 432
Belleville Historical Society, Belleville, NJ 277
Bellevue-Harpeth Historical Society, Nashville, TN 432
Bellevue Valley Historical Society, Caledonia, MO 243
Bellflower Historical Society, Bellflower, IL 100
Bellport-Brookhaven Historical Society, Bellport, NY 304
Belmar Museum, Lakewood, CO 55
Belmont County Historical Society, Barnesville, OH 356
Belmont Historical Society, Belmont, MA 188
Belton Historical Society, Belton, MO 243
Beltrami County Historical Society, Bemidji, MN 226
Belvidere Historic Committee, Belvidere, NJ 277
Benicia Capitol State Historic Park, Benicia, CA 23
Benjamin F. Feinberg Library, State University College, Plattsburgh, NY 328
Bennett Place State Historic Site, Durham, NC 343
Bennington Museum and Peter Matteson Tavern, Bennington, VT 464
Bentley Historical Library, University of Michigan, Ann Arbor, MI 210
Benton County, Indiana Historical Society, Inc., Fowler, IN 123
Benton County Historical Society, Philomath, OR 384
Benton County Sesquicentennial Committee, Siloam Springs, AR 21
Bentonville Battleground State Historic Site, Newton Grove, NC 347
Berea College Appalachian Museum, Berea, KY 153
Bergen County Historical Society, River Edge, NJ 290
Bergen County Office of Cultural and Historic Affairs, Hackensack, NJ 282
Bergen Historical Society, Bergen, NY 304
Bergen Museum of Art and Science, Paramus, NJ 289
Bergenfield Museum Society, Bergenfield, NJ 278
Bergquist Pioneer Cabin Society, Moorhead, MN 233
Berkeley County Historical Preservation Commission, Cross, SC 418
Berkeley County Historical Society, Moncks Corner, SC 420
Berkeley Historical Society, Berkeley, CA 24
Berkshire Athenaeum, Local History and Literature Services, Pittsfield, MA 202
Berkshire County Historical Society, Pittsfield, MA 202
Berkshire Museum, The, Pittsfield, MA 202
Berlin Historical Society, Berlin, WI 495
Bernard Historical Society and Museum, Delton, MI 213
Bernice P. Bishop Museum, Honolulu, HI 95
Berrien County Historical Association, Inc., 1839 Courthouse Museum, Berrien Springs, MI 211
Berthoud Historical Society, Berthoud, CO 50
Bertrand Collection and Library, DeSoto National Wildlife Refuge Visitor Center, Missouri Valley, IA 139
Berwick Historical Society, Inc., Berwick, ME 169
Bethany Lutheran Theological Seminary, Mankato, MN 231
Bethel German Communal Colony, Inc., Bethel, MO 243

Bethel Historical Society, Inc., Bethel, ME 169
Bethune Memorial House, Gravenhurst, Ontario 543
Bethune Museum-Archives, Inc., Washington, DC 72
Bettendorf Museum, Bettendorf, IA 131
Betty D. Easton Historical Costume Collection, Department of Human Environment, Lexington, KY157 157
Beverly Historical Society, Beverly, MA 188
Bewley Family Association, Rineyville, KY 162
Bexley Historical Society, Bexley, OH 356
Bibb County Heritage Association, Brierfield, AL 3
Biblical Garden of the Cathedral of St. John the Divine, New York, NY 322
Bicentennial Heritage Corporation of Casey County, Inc., Liberty, KY 158
Bicentennial Restoration Committee for South River Meeting House, Lynchburg, VA 476
Bidwell Mansion Association, Chico, CA 25
Big Bear Valley Historical Society, Big Bear City, CA 24
Big Foot Wallace Museum, Big Foot, TX 439
Big Horn County Historical Society—Museum and Visitor Center, Hardin, MT 258
Big Sandy Valley Historical Society, Louisa, KY 158
Big Sioux River Valley Historical Society, Hawarden, IA 137
Big Thicket Association, Saratoga, TX 477
Big Thunder Gold Mine, Keystone, SD 424
Biggar Museum and Gallery, Biggar, Saskatchewan 563
Billings Estate Museum, Ottawa, Ontario 548
Billings Farm and Museum, Woodstock, VT 469
Billy Graham Center at Wheaton College, Wheaton, IL 119
Billy Graham Center Museum, Wheaton, IL 119
Billy the Kid Museum, Ft. Sumner, NM 297
Birmingham Historical Society, Birmingham, AL 2
Birmingham Public Library—Linn-Henley Research Library, Birmingham, AL 2
Birmingham-Jefferson Historical Association, Birmingham, AL 2
Birmingham-Jefferson Historical Society, Birmingham, AL 2
Bisbee Mining and Historical Museum, Bisbee, AZ 11
Bishop Hill Heritage Association, Bishop Hill, IL 100
Bishop Hill State Historic Site, Bishop Hill, IL 100
Bishop Museum and Historical Society, Bishop, CA 24
Bismarck-Mandan Historical and Genealogical Society, Bismarck, ND 352
Bitter Root Valley Historical Society, Hamilton, MT 258
Black Archives Research Center and Museum, Tallahassee, FL 83
Black Canyon of the Gunnison National Monument, Montrose, CO 56
Black Catholic History Project, Office of Black Catholics, Washington, DC 72
Black Civil War Tribute Committee, Nashville, TN 433
Black Creek Pioneer Village, North York, Ontario 547
Black Diamond Historical Society, Black Diamond, WA 483
Black Heritage Council, Montgomery, AL 6
Black Heritage Society of Washington State, Inc., Seattle, WA 487
Black River Historical Society, Inc., Ludlow, VT 467
Blackberry Historical Farm-Village, Aurora, IL 100
Blackstone Valley Historical Society, Lime Rock, RI 409
Blaine County Historical Society, Brewster, NE 261
Blaine County Historical Society, Chinook, MT 257
Blaine County Museum, Chinook, MT 257
Blaine County People and Place History, Inc., Watonga, OK 381
Blair County Historical Society, Altoona, PA 387
Blandwood Mansion, Greensboro, NC 345
Bleckley County Historical Society, Cochran, GA 87

Blissfield Historical Society—Victorsville School House, Blissfield, MI 211
Blithewold Gardens and Arboretum, Bristol, RI 409
Block Island Historical Society, Block Island, RI 409
Bloomfield Historical Society, Castalia, IA 132
Bloomington-Normal Genealogical Society, Bloomington, IL 100
Blount County Historical Society, Oneonta, AL 7
Blount County Historic Trust, Inc., Maryville, TN 431
Blount Mansion, Knoxville, TN 430
Blue Earth County Historical Society, Mankato, MN 231
Blue Grass Trust for Historic Preservation, Lexington, KY 157
Blue Island Historical Society, Blue Island, IL 101
Blue Ridge Institute—Blue Ridge Farm Museum, Ferrum, VA 473
Blue Ridge Parkway, Asheville, NC 340
Blue Ridge Preservation Association, Stanley, VA 480
Bluestem Genealogical Society, Eureka, KS 145
Bluffton Historical Preservation Society, Inc., Bluffton, SC 414
Blumenfeld and District Heritage Site, Prelate Province, Saskatchewan 565
Bolinas Historical Society, Bolinas, CA 24
Bolivar County Historical Society, Cleveland, MS 239
Bollinger Mill State Historic Site, Burfordville, MO 243
Bonavista Museum, Bonavista, Newfoundland 531
Bond County Historical Society, Inc., Greenville, IL 108
Boneyfiddle Association, Portsmouth, OH 371
Bonner County Historical Society, Inc., Sandpoint, ID 98
Bonneville County Historical Society, Idaho Falls, ID 97
Booker T. Washington National Monument, Hardy, VA 474
Boone County Genealogical Society, Boone, IA 132
Boone County Historical and Genealogical Society, Harrison, AR 18
Boone County Historical Society, Boone, IA 132
Boone County Historical Society, Columbia, MO 569
Boone Railroad Historical Society, Boone, IA 132
Boonsboro Museum of History, Boonsboro, MD 181
Boonslick Historical Society, Boonville, MO 243
Boot Hill Museum, Dodge City, KS 144
Boothbay Railway Village, Boothbay, ME 170
Boothbay Region Historical Society, Boothbay Harbor, ME 170
Boothe Memorial Park Museum, Stratford, CT 67
Bordentown Historical Society, Bordentown, NJ 278
Boscawen Historical Society, Inc., Boscawen, NH 269
Boscobel Restoration, Inc., Garrison-on-Hudson, NY 313
Bosque Memorial Museum, Clifton, TX 441
Boston Art Commission, Boston, MA 188
Boston Athenaeum, Boston, MA 188
Boston College, Newton, MA 200
Boston Landmarks Commission, Boston, MA 189
Boston Marine Society, Boston, MA 189
Boston National Historical Park, Boston, MA 189
Bostonian Society, Boston, MA 188
Bottineau Historical Society, Bottineau, ND 352
Boulder Historical Society and Museum, Boulder, CO 50
Boundary Museum Society, Grand Forks, British Columbia 518
Bourne Historical Society, Bourne, MA 191
Bourne Town Archives, Bourne, MA 191
Bowden Historical Society—Bowden Pioneer Museum, Bowden, Alberta 510
Bowdoin Park Historical and Archaeological Association, Wappingers Falls, NY 338
Bowen-Campbell House Association, Inc., Goodlettsville, TN 429
Bowmanville Museum, Bowmanville, Ontario 540
Bowne House Historical Society, Flushing, NY 31

Boyd County Historical Society and Public Library, Ashland, KY 153
Boyds-Clarksburg-Germantown Historical Society, Inc., Boyds, MD 181
Boyertown Museum of Historic Vehicles, Boyertown, PA 389
Boyhood Home of Robert E. Lee, Alexandria, VA 470
Boylston Historical Society, Inc., Boylston, MA 191
Braddock's Field Historical Society, Inc., Braddock, PA 389
Bradford County Historical Board of Trustees, Starke, FL 83
Bradford County Historical Society, Towanda, PA 406
Bradford Heritage Museum and Historical Society, Bradford, ME 170
Bradford Historical Society, Inc., Bradford, VT 464
Bradford Landmark Society, Bradford, PA 389
Bradley County Historical Society, Cleveland, TN 428
Bradley Museum, Mississauga, Ontario 546
Braintree Historical Society, Inc., Braintree, MA 191
Braintree Historical Society, Inc., Braintree, VT 464
Branch County Genealogical Society, Coldwater, MI 212
Brandon Museum, Brandon, Manitoba 523
Brandywine Battlefield Park, Chadds Ford, PA 390
Brandywine Conservancy, Chadds Ford, PA 390
Branford Electric Railway Association, East Haven, CT 59
Branford Historical Society, Branford, CT 58
Brant Historical Society, Brantford, Ontario 540
Brattleboro Historical Society, Brattleboro, VT 465
Brattleboro Museum and Art Center, Brattleboro, VT 465
Braxton Historical Society, Exchange, NV 268
Brazoria County Historical Museum, Angleton, TX 437
Brazos Valley Museum, Bryan-College Station, TX 440
Bremen Historical Society of Tinley Park, Tinley Park, IL 118
Bremer County Historical Society, Waverly, IA 142
Brennan House, The, Louisville, KY 158
Brenorsome Historical Society, Tokio, ND 354
Brethren in Christ Historical Society, Grantham, PA 393
Brevard Museum of History and Natural Science, Cocoa, FL 77
Brewer Historical Society, Brewer, ME 170
Brewster-Sugar Creek Township Historical Society, Brewster, OH 356
Brick House, Poughkeepsie, NY 329
Brick Store Museum, Kennebunk, ME 172
Bridge Memorial Library, Walpole, NH 276
Bridgewater Heritage and Historical Society, Bridgewater, Nova Scotia 533
Bridgewater Historical Society, Bridgewater, CT 58
Bridgton Historical Society, Bridgton, ME 170
Brierfield Ironworks Park, Brierfield, AL 3
Brighton Historical Society, Rochester, NY 330
Brimfield Memorial House Association, Inc., Kent, OH 366
Brimstone Historical Society, Sulphur, LA 168
Bristol Historical Society, Inc., Bristol, VT 465
British Columbia Farm Machinery and Agriculture Museum Association, Fort Langley, British Columbia 518
British Columbia Historical Federation, Vancouver, British Columbia 521
British Columbia Museums Association, Victoria, British Columbia 522
British Columbia Museum of Mining, Britannia Beach, British Columbia 517
British Columbia Provincial Museum, Victoria, British Columbia 522
British Columbia Sports Hall of Fame and Museum, Vancouver, British Columbia 521

Broad River Genealogical Society, Inc., Shelby, NC 349
Broadview Historical and Museum Association, Inc., Broadview, Saskatchewan 563
Broadwater County Museum and Library, Townsend, MT 260
Brockton Art Museum, Brockton, MA 191
Brockville Museum, Brockville, Ontario 540
Brockville and District Historical Society, Brockville, Ontario 540
Brodhead Historical Society, Brodhead, WI 495
Brome County Historical Society, Knowlton, Quebec 558
Bronson Museum, Attleboro, MA 187
Bronx County Historical Society, Bronx, NY 305
Brookings Area Genealogical Society, Brookings, SD 422
Brookline Historical Commission, Brookline, MA 191
Brookline Historical Society, Brookline, MA 191
Brookline New Hampshire Historical Society, Brookline, NH 269
Brooklyn Historic Railway Association, Brooklyn, NY 305
Brooklyn Historical Society, Brooklyn, CT 58
Brooklyn Historical Society, Brooklyn Center, MN 226
Brooklyn Historical Society, Brooklyn, OH 357
Brooks and District Museum, Brooks, Alberta 510
Brookville Historical Society, Brookville, OH 357
Broome County Historical Society, Binghamton, NY 304
Brown County Chapter, Ohio Genealogical Society, Georgetown, OH 364
Brown County Historical Society, Brownwood, TX 440
Brown County Historical Society, Green Bay, WI 497
Brown County Historical Society, Inc., Nashville, IN 127
Brown County Historical Society, New Ulm, MN 234
Brown County Territorial Pioneers, Aberdeen, SD 422
Brownsville Historical Association, Brownsville, TX 440
Brownville Historical Society, Brownville, NE 261
Bruce Mines Museum, Bruce Mines, Ontario 540
Brukner Nature Center, Troy, OH 373
Brule County Historical Society, Pukwana, SD 425
Brunnier Gallery—Farm House Museum, Ames, IA 131
Brunswick County Historical Society, Shallotte, NC 349
Bryan Lang Historical Library, Woodbine, GA 94
Bryant Cottage State Historic Site, Bement, IL 100
Buccleuch Mansion Museum, New Brunswick, NJ 287
Bucks County Genealogical Society, Doylestown, PA 391
Bucksport Historical Society, Inc., Bucksport, ME 170
Bucyrus Historical Society, Bucyrus, OH 357
Buechel Memorial LaKota Museum, St. Francis, SD 425
Buena Vista County Historical Society, Storm Lake, IA 141
Buffalo Bill Historical Center, Cody, WY 507
Buffalo Bill Memorial Museum, Denver, CO 51
Buffalo Bill Memorial Museum, Golden, CO 54
Buffalo Bill Museum of Le Claire, Inc., Le Claire, IA 138
Buffalo Bill's Ranch—State Historical Park, North Platte, NE 265
Buffalo County Historical Society, Kearney, NE 264
Buffalo Trails Museum, Epping, ND 352
Buffalo and Erie County Historical Society, Buffalo, NY 306
Bulkley Valley Museum, Smithers, British Columbia 521
Bunker Hill Monument, Boston, MA 189
Bureau County Historical Society, Princeton, IL 114
Bureau of Environmental Services, Ohio Department of Transportation, Columbus, OH 361
Bureau of Historic Preservation, Tallahassee, FL 83
Bureau of History and Archives, Roman Catholic Diocese of Harrisburg, Harrisburg, PA 394
Bureau of History, Michigan Department of State, Lansing, MI 218
Bureau of Indian Affairs—Navajo Area Office,

Environmental Quality Services, Window Rock, AZ 16
Burke County Historical Society, Morganton, NC 346
Burlington County Cultural and Heritage Commission, Mt. Holly, NJ 286
Burlington County Historical Society, Burlington, NJ 278
Burlington Historical Society, Burlington, Ontario 540
Burlington-Rock Island Railroad Museum, Teague, TX 458
Burnaby Village Museum, Burnaby, British Columbia 517
Burnett County Historical Society, Webster, WI 505
Burnham Tavern Museum, Machias, ME 173
Burning Bush Center and Museum, Pictou, Nova Scotia 537
Burpee Museum of Natural History, Rockford, IL 115
Burrard-Fraser Heritage Society, Port Moody, British Columbia 520
Burrillville Historical and Preservation Society, Pascoag, RI 411
Burritt Museum and Park, Huntsville, AL 5
Burt County Museum, Tekamah, NE 266
Burtner House Restoration, Inc., Natrona Heights, PA 399
Burton Historical Collection, Detroit Public Library, Detroit, MI 213
Bush House—Salem Art Association, Salem, OR 386
Bushnell Area Historical Society, Bushnell, IL 101
Bushy Run Battlefield, Jeannette, PA 396
Bustins Island, Maine, Historical Society, Bustins Island, ME 170
Butler County Historical Society, Butler, PA 389
Butler County Historical Society, David City, NE 262
Butler County Historical Society, El Dorado, KS 145
Butler County Historical Society, Hamilton, OH 365
Butler County Historical Society, Poplar Bluff, MO 252
Butte County Historical Society, Oroville, CA 35
Butte Historical Society, Butte, MT 256
Butte-Silver Bow Public Archives, Butte, MT 256
Butterfield Threshermen's Association, Butterfield, MN 227
Butterfield Trail Association—Logan County Historical Society, Russell Springs, KS 150
Byron R. Lewis Historical Library, Vincennes, IN 130
Bytown Historical Museum, Ottawa, Ontario 548

C

C. H. Nash Museum at Chucalissa, Memphis, TN 431
C.M. Russell Museum, Great Falls, MT 258
CEC-Seabee Museum, Port Hueneme, CA 36
CHIPS (Council of Historic Institutions and Preservation Societies in Summit and Portage Counties), Hudson, OH 365
CIGNA Corporation Museum, Philadelphia, PA 401
COMMA (Committee on Military Museums in America), Washington, DC 72
Cabool History Society, Cabool, MO 243
Cabrillo Historical Association, San Diego, CA 39
Cabrillo National Monument, San Diego, CA 39
Cache Valley Historical Society, Logan, UT 462
Cactus Park and Museum, George West, TX 447
Caddel-Smith Chapter, Daughters of the Republic of Texas, Uvalde, TX 459
Caddo Indian Territory Museum and Library, Caddo, OK 376
Caddo-Pine Island Oil and Historical Society Museum, Oil City, LA 167
Cahokia Courthouse State Historic Site, Cahokia, IL 101

Cahokia Mounds Museum Society, Collinsville, IL 105
Calaveras County Museum and Archives, San Andreas, CA 39
Calaveras Heritage Council, San Andreas, CA 39
Caldwell County Historical Society, Cameron, MO 243
Calhoun County Genies, Rockwell City, IA 141
Calhoun County Historical Commission, Port Lavaca, TX 454
Calhoun County Historical Society, Hardin, IL 108
Califon Historical Society, Califon, NJ 278
California Committee for the Promotion of History, Sacramento, CA 38
California Council for the Humanities, San Francisco, CA 40
California Department of Parks and Recreation, Friant, CA 28
California Genealogical Society, San Francisco, CA 40
California Heritage Council, California Trust for Historic Preservation, San Francisco, CA 40
California Historical Society, San Francisco, CA 40
California Museum of Photography, Riverside, CA 37
California Oil Museum, Santa Paula, CA 44
California State Archives, Sacramento, CA 38
California State Capitol Museum, Sacramento, CA 38
California State Department of Parks and Recreation, Sacramento, CA 38
California State Indian Museum, Sacramento, CA 38
California State Railroad Museum, Sacramento, CA 38
Callis P. Huntington Railroad Historical Society, Inc., Huntington, WV 493
Calumet Center, Nashville, TN 433
Calumet City Historical Society, Inc., Calumet City, IL 101
Calumet Regional Archives, Gary, IN 123
Calusa Valley Historical Society, Clewiston, FL 77
Calvert County Historic District Commission, Prince Frederick, MD 184
Calvert County Historical Society, Inc., Prince Frederick, MD 184
Calvert Marine Museum, Solomons, MD 186
Calvin Coolidge Memorial Foundation, Inc., Plymouth, VT 468
Camanche Historical Society, Camanche, IA 132
Cambria Historical Society, Lockport, NY 318
Cambridge Historical Commission, Cambridge, MA 192
Cambridge Historical Society, Cambridge, MA 192
Cambridge Museum, Cambridge, ID 97
Camden Archives, Camden, SC 414
Camden County Cultural and Heritage Commission, Haddon Township, NJ 282
Camden County Historical Society, Camden, NC 342
Camden District Heritage Foundation, Camden, SC 414
Camden Historical Commission, Camden, SC 414
Camden-Rockport Historical Society, Camden, ME 170
Camp Five Museums Foundation, Inc., Laona, WI 499
Campbell Center for Historic Preservation Studies, Mount Carroll, IL 111
Campbell Historical Museum, Campbell, CA 24
Campbell House Museum, St. Louis, MO 253
Campbell Museum, Camden, NJ 278
Campbell River and District Museum and Archives Society, Campbell River, British Columbia 517
Campus Martius Museum, Marietta, OH 367
Camron Stanford House Preservation Association, Oakland, CA 34
Camrose and District Museum Society, Camrose, Alberta 511
Canada's Aviation Hall of Fame, Edmonton, Alberta 512
Canadian Airborne Forces Museum, Lancaster Park, British Columbia 519
Canadian Friends Historical Association, Toronto, Ontario 552

Canadian Historical Association—Société historique du Canada, Ottawa, Ontario 548
Canadian Historical Collection, Art Gallery of Ontario and The Grange, Toronto, Ontario 552
Canadian Lacrosse Hall of Fame, New Westminster, British Columbia 520
Canadian Military Engineers Museum, Vedder Crossing, British Columbia 522
Canadian Museums Association, Ottawa, Ontario 548
Canadian Railroad Historical Association, St. Constant, Quebec 561
Canadian Rivers Historical Society, Geary, OK 377
Canadian Ski Museum/Musée canadien du ski, Ottawa, Ontario 548
Canadian War Museum, Ottawa, Ontario 548
Canajoharie Library and Art Gallery, Canajoharie, NY 306
Canal Center—Erie Canal Museum, Dewitt, NY 310
Canal Fulton Heritage Society, Canal Fulton, OH 357
Canal Museum and Hugh Moore Historical Park, Easton, PA 391
Canal Park Marine Museum, Duluth, MN 228
Canal Society of Indiana, Fort Wayne, IN 123
Canal Society of New Jersey, Morristown, NJ 286
Canal Society of New York State, Syracuse, NY 336
Canastota Canal Town Corporation—Canal Town Museum, Canastota, NY 306
Candler County Historical Society, Metter, GA 90
Cane Ridge Meeting House, Paris, KY 161
Caney Fork River Historical Association, Inc., Smithville, TN 435
Caney Valley Historical Society, Caney, KS 144
Canton Historical Commission, Canton, MI 212
Canton Historical Society Museum, Canton, MI 212
Canton Palace Theatre Association, Canton, OH 357
Canton Preservation Society, Canton, OH 357
Canyon County Historical Society, Nampa, ID 98
Canyonlands Natural History Association, Moab, UT 462
Cape Ann Historical Association, Gloucester, MA 195
Cape Coral Historical Society, Inc., Cape Coral, FL 76
Cape Hatteras National Seashore Library, Manteo, NC 346
Cape May County Historical and Genealogical Society, Cape May, NJ 279
Cape Sable Historical Society, Barrington Passage, Nova Scotia 533
Cape Vincent Historical Museum, Cape Vincent, NY 307
Capital Children's Museum, Washington, DC 72
Capital District Genealogical Society, Albany, NY 301
Capitol Reef National Park Museum, Torrey, UT 464
Capitol Restoration and Promotion, State Building Division, Nebraska State Capitol, Lincoln, NE 264
Caramoor Center for Music and the Arts, Inc., Katonah, NY 317
Carberry Plains Museum, Carberry, Manitoba 523
Carbon County Historical Society, Price, UT 463
Cardinal Spellman Philatelic Museum, Weston, MA 208
Caribou Historical Society, Inc., Soda Springs, ID 98
Carillon Park, Dayton, OH 362
Carl Sandburg Birthplace, Galesburg, IL 107
Carl Sandburg Home National Historic Site, Flat Rock, NC 344
Carleton County Historical Society, Inc., Woodstock, New Brunswick 531
Carleton Martello Tower National Historic Park, Saint John, New Brunswick 530
Carlisle Area Historical Society, Carlisle, OH 358
Carlton County Historical Society, Cloquet, MN 227
Carnegie Branch Library for Local History, Boulder, CO 50
Carnegie Cultural Arts Center, Oxnard, CA 35

Carnton Association, Inc., Franklin, TN 429

Carnton Mansion, Franklin, TN 429

Carousel Society of the Niagara Frontier, Inc., North Tonawanda, NY 326

Carrie M. McLain Memorial Museum, Nome, AK 10

Carroll County Farm Museum, Westminster, MD 186

Carroll County Historical Society, Carroll, IA 132

Carroll County Historical Society—Governor Gordon Browning Museum, McKenzie, TN 431

Carroll County Historical Society and Heritage Center, Berryville, AR 17

Carroll County Historical Society, Carrollon, OH 358

Carroll County Historical Society, Mount Carroll, IL 112

Carroll Mansion, Municipal Museum of Baltimore, Baltimore, MD 180

Carroll Reece Museum, Johnson City, TN 430

Carroll Society for the Preservation of Antiques, Carrollton, MS 239

Carson County Historical Survey Committee, Panhandle, TX 454

Carson County Square House Museum, Panhandle, TX 454

Carter House, A.P.T.A., Franklin, TN 429

Carter Presidential Materials Project, Atlanta, GA 85

Carteret Historical Research Association, Beaufort, NC 341

Carver County Historical Society, Inc., Waconia, MN 238

Cary Cottage, Cincinnati, OH 358

Cary Historical Society, Cary, NC 342

Casa Grande Ruins National Monument, Coolidge, AZ 12

Casa Grande Valley Historical Society, Casa Grande, AZ 12

Cascade County Historical Society, Great Falls, MT 258

Casemate Museum, Fort Monroe, VA 473

Cass County Historical Commission, Vandalia, MI 224

Cass County Historical Society, Inc., Harrisonville, MO 246

Cass County Historical Society, Logansport, IN 126

Cass County Historical Society, Plattsmouth, NE 266

Cass County Historical Society, Virginia, IL 118

Cass County Historical Society—Bonanzaville, USA, West Fargo, ND 354

Cassia County Historical Society, Inc., Burley, ID 96

Castile Historical Society, Castile, NY 307

Castillo de San Marcos—Fort Matanzas National Monument, St. Augustine, FL 82

Castine Scientific Society, Castine, ME 171

Castle Air Museum, Atwater, CA 23

Castle Clinton National Monument, New York, NY 322

Castle Hill National Historic Park, Jerseyside, Newfoundland 532

Castle Museum, Juliaetta, ID 97

Castle Piatt Mac-A-Cheek—Mac-Ochee Castle, West Liberty, OH 374

Castle and Museum at Inspiration Point, Eureka Springs, AR 17

Caswell County Historical Association, Inc., Yanceyville, NC 341

Catalina Island Museum Society, Inc., Avalon, CA 23

Catawba County Historical Association, Inc., Newton Grove, NC 347

Catholic Archives of Texas, Austin, TX 437

Catholic Historical Society of St. Paul, St. Paul, MN 236

Catholic Historical Society of the Diocese of Amarillo, Amarillo, TX 436

Catonsville Historical Society, Inc., Baltimore, MD 180

Catskill Fly Fishing Center, Roscoe, NY 331

Catskill Regional Folklife Program, Arkville, NY 302

Cattaraugus Area Historical Society, Cattaraugus, NY 307

Cavalier County Historical Society, Langdon, ND 353

Cavendish Historical Society, Cavendish, VT 466

Cayuga County Historian, Auburn, NY 302

Cayuga County Historical Society, Auburn, NY 303

Cayuga Museum of History and Art, Auburn, NY 303

Cayuga-Owasco Lakes Historical Society, Moravia, NY 321

Cedar Falls Historical Society, Cedar Falls, IA 133

Cedar Grove Historical Society, Cedar Grove, NJ 279

Cedar Key Historical Society, Cedar Key, FL 77

Cedar Swamp Historical Society, Cedar Swamp, NY 307

Centennial Valley Historical Association, Centennial, WY 506

Center City Historical Society, Center City, MN 227

Center for American Archeology—Kampsville Archeological Center, Kampsville, IL 109

Center for Anthropological Studies, Albuquerque, NM 294

Center for Archival Collections, Bowling Green, OH 356

Center for Arts Information, New York, NY 323

Center for Colorado Plateau Studies, Flagstaff, AZ 12

Center for Connecticut Studies—J. Eugene Smith Library, Willimantic, CT 68

Center for Cultural and Natural History, Mt. Pleasant, MI 220

Center for Environmental Study, Williams College, Williamstown, MA 208

Center for Historic Preservation, Fredericksburg, VA 473

Center for Historic Preservation, Murfreesboro, TN 432

Center for History of Louisiana Education, Natchitoches, LA 165

Center for Museum Studies, John F. Kennedy University, San Francisco, CA 40

Center for Southern Folklore, Memphis, TN 431

Center for Transportation and Commerce, Galveston, TX 446

Center for Voluntary Action Research, Memphis, TN 431

Center for Western Studies, Sioux Falls, SD 426

Center for Wooden Boats, Seattle, WA 487

Centerville Historical Society, Centerville, OH 358

Centerville Historical Society, Centerville, UT 461

Central City Opera House Association, Central City, CO 50

Central Community Historical Society of Clinton County, DeWitt, IA 134

Central Florida Genealogical and Historical Society, Inc., Orlando, FL 81

Central Jersey Chapter, American Italian Historical Association, Princeton, NJ 290

Central Minnesota Historical Center, St. Cloud, MN 236

Central Miramichi Historical Society, Doaktown, New Brunswick 528

Central Missouri State University Museum, Warrensburg, MO 255

Central New Brunswick Woodmen's Museum, Boiestown, New Brunswick 527

Central Ohio Alliance of Historical Societies, Columbus, OH 361

Central Texas Museum of Automotive History, Rosanky, TX 455

Centre County Historical Society—Centre Furnace Mansion, State College, PA 405

Centre County Library and Historical Museum, Bellefonte, PA 388

Centre D'Etudes Acadiennes, Moncton, New Brunswick 529

Century Village Museum, Lang, Ontario 545

Cercle de La Fleur de Lis, Gary, IN 123

Cernan Earth and Space Center—Triton College, River Grove, IL 114

Chaco Culture National Historical Park, Nore, NM 298
Chadds Ford Historical Society, Chadds Ford, PA 390
Chain Bridge Productions, Arlington, VA 470
Chalet of the Golden Fleece, New Glarus, WI 501
Chalifour-Chalifoux-Chalufour, St. Nicolas, Quebec 562
Chambers County Heritage Society, Mont Belvieu,
    TX 452
Champaign County Historical Museum, Inc.,
    Champaign, IL 102
Champlain Maritime Society, Burlington, VT 465
Champlain Trail Museum, Pembroke, Ontario 549
Champoeg State Park—Friends of Champoeg, St. Paul,
    OR 386
Chapleau Historical Museum, Chapleau, Ontario 541
Chapman Historical Museum of the Glens
    Falls-Queensbury Historical Association, Inc., Glens
    Falls, NY 313
Chapter 425, Children of the Confederacy, Shreveport,
    LA 168
Chariton County Historical Society, Salisbury, MO 254
Charles Dawson History Center of Harrison, New York,
    White Plains, NY 339
Charles M. Russell Log Cabin Studio, Great Falls,
    MT 258
Charles Mix County Historical Restoration Society,
    Geddes, SD 423
Charles Mix County Historical Society, Wagner, SD 427
Charles Towne Landing — 1670, Charleston, SC 414
Charles Towne Landing, Charleston, NC 342
Charles W. Bowers Memorial Museum, Santa Ana,
    CA 43
Charleston Chapter, South Carolina Genealogical
    Society, Charleston, SC 414
Charleston Historical Society, Charleston, NY 307
Charleston Library Society, Charleston, SC 414
Charleston Museum, The, Charleston, SC 414
Charlestown Navy Yard, Boston, MA 189
Charlotte County Museum, St. Stephen, New
    Brunswick 531
Charlotte-Genesee Lighthouse Historical Society,
    Rochester, NY 330
Charlton County Historical Society, Folkston, GA 88
Chase County Historical Society, Inc., Cottonwood
    Falls, KS 144
Chatham Historical Society, Chatham, NJ 279
Chattahoochee Valley Historical Society, Inc., Lanett,
    AL 6
Chattanooga Nature Center, Chattanooga, TN 427
Chaves County Historical Society, Roswell, NM 298
Cheboygan County Genealogical Society, Cheboygan,
    MI 212
Chelan County Historical Society, Cashmere, WA 483
Chelmsford Historical Society, Inc., Chelmsford, MA 192
Chelsea Historical Society, Inc., Chelsea, VT 466
Chelsea Public Library, Chelsea, MA 192
Chemung County Historical Society, Inc., Elmira,
    NY 311
Chemung Valley Old Timers Association, Inc.,
    Horseheads, NY 315
Chenango County Historical Society, Norwich, NY 326
Cheneaux Historical Association, Cedarville, MI 212
Cherokee Area Archives, Inc., Cherokee, IA 133
Cherokee County Historical Museum, Murphy, NC 347
Cherokee Heritage and Museum Association,
    Cherokee, CA 25
Cherokee Historical Association, Cherokee, NC 343
Cherokee National Historical Society, Inc., Tahlequah,
    OK 380
Cherokee Strip Museum of Alva, Alva, OK 375
Cherokee Strip Museum, Perry, OK 379
Cherokee-Red Clay Association, Cleveland, TN 428
Cherry County Historical Society, Valentine, NE 267

Cherry Creek Schoolhouse Museum, Englewood,
    CO 53
Cherry Creek Valley Historical Society, Inc., Aurora,
    CO 50
Cherry Valley Historical Association, Cherry Valley,
    NY 308
Cherryfield-Narraguagus Historical Society, Cherryfield,
    ME 171
Chesapeake Bay Maritime Museum, St. Michaels,
    MD 185
Chesapeake and Ohio Historical Society, Inc.,
    Alderson, WV 491
Chester County Historical Society, West Chester,
    PA 408
Chester Historical Society, Chester, NH 270
Chester Historical Society, Chester, NJ 279
Chesterfield County Historical Society, Chesterfield,
    VA 472
Chesterfield County Historic Preservation Commission,
    Cheraw, SC 416
Chesterfield Historical Society, Chesterfield, MA 192
Chesterfield Historical Society, Inc., Chesterfield,
    NH 270
Chesterwood, Stockbridge, MA 205
Chestico Museum and Historical Society, Port Hood,
    Nova Scotia 537
Chestnut Hill Historical Society, Philadelphia, PA 401
Cheyenne County Historical Association, Sidney,
    NE 266
Cheyenne County Historical Society, St. Francis, KS 150
Chezzetcook Historical Society, Seaforth, Nova
    Scotia 537
Chicago Architecture Foundation, Chicago, IL 102
Chicago Genealogical Society, Chicago, IL 102
Chicago Historical Society, Chicago, IL 102
Chicago Jewish Historical Society, Chicago, IL 102
Chicago Maritime Society, Chicago, IL 102
Chicamauga and Chattanooga National Military Park,
    Chattanooga, TN 427
Chickamauga and Chattanooga National Military Park,
    Fort Oglethorpe, GA 89
Chickasaw Council House Historic Site, Tishomingo,
    OK 381
Chickasaw County Genealogical Society, New
    Hampton, IA 140
Chief John Ross House, Rossville, GA 91
Chief Plenty Coups State Monument, Pryor, MT 259
Chief Wapello's Memorial Park, Agency, IA 131
Children's Museum of History, Natural History and
    Science, Utica, NY 338
Children's Museum of Oak Ridge, Oak Ridge, TN 435
Children's Museum, Indianapolis, IN 124
Childrens Museum, South Dartmouth, MA 205
Childrens Museums, Portsmouth, VA 478
Childress County Heritage Museum, Childress, TX 440
Chili Historical Society, Churchville, NY 308
Chilkat Valley Historical Society, Haines, AK 9
Chilliwack Museum and Historical Society, Chilliwack,
    British Columbia 517
Chilton County Historical Society and Archives, Inc.,
    Clanton, AL 3
Chimney Point Tavern, Addison, VT 464
China Historical Society, China, ME 171
Chinese Historical Society of America, San Francisco,
    CA 40
Chino Valley Historical Society, Chino, CA 25
Chippewa County Historical Society, Inc., Sault Sainte
    Marie, MI 223
Chippewa County Historical Society, Montevideo,
    MN 233
Chippewa Valley Museum, Eau Claire, WI 496
Chiricahua National Monument, Willcox, AZ 16

Chisago County Historical Society, Center City, MN 227
Chisholm Trail Historical Museum, Waurika, OK 381
Chisholm Trail Museum Corporation, Wellington, KS 152
Choctaw County Historical Society, Butler, AL 3
Christ Church, Lakefield, Ontario 544
Christian C. Sanderson Museum, Chadds Ford, PA 390
Christian County Historical Society, Hopkinsville, KY 157
Christian County Historical Society, Taylorville, IL 117
Christian County Museum and Historical Society, Ozark, MO 251
Christian Woman's Exchange—Hermann-Grima Historic House, New Orleans, LA 166
Churchill County Museum Association—Churchill County Museum and Archives, Fallon, NV 268
Churchill House—Marine Memorial Room, Hantsport, Nova Scotia 535
Cincinnati Art Museum, Cincinnati, OH 359
Cincinnati Fire Museum, Cincinnati, OH 359
Cincinnati Historical Society, Cincinnati, OH 359
Cincinnatus Area Heritage Society, Cincinnatus, NY 308
Circle District Museum—Circle District Historical Society, Inc., Central, AK 9
Circus City Festival, Inc., Peru, IN 128
Citadal Museum and Archives, Charleston, SC 415
Citizens' Committee for Historic Preservation, Las Vegas, NM 297
Citronelle Historical Preservation Society, Citronelle, AL 3
City History Club of New York, Bronx, NY 305
City Island Historical Society and Museum, City Island, NY 570
City Lights, Inc., New Orleans, LA 166
City of Burlington Historical Society, Burlington, NJ 278
City of DeKalb Landmark Commission, DeKalb, IL 106
City of Edmonton Archives, Edmonton, Alberta 512
City of Granite Falls—Andrew Volstead Home, Granite Falls, MN 230
City of Greeley Museums, Greeley, CO 55
City of Minnetonka Historical Society, Minnetonka, MN 233
City of Rochester Hills Museum at Van Hoosen Farm, Rochester, MI 222
City of San Bernardino Historical and Pioneer Society, San Bernardino, CA 39
City of San Buenaventura, Ventura, CA 47
City of White Rock Museum and Archives, White Rock, British Columbia 523
City of Wilson Historic Properties Commission, Wilson, NC 351
City of York Historical Committee, Islington, Ontario 544
Civil War Round Table Associates, Little Rock, AR 19
Civil War Round Table of Arkansas, Little Rock, AR 19
Clallam County Museum, Port Angeles, WA 486
Claremont Heritage, Claremont, CA 25
Clarion County Historical Society, Clarion, PA 390
Clark County Genealogical Society, Marshall, IL 111
Clark County Historical Association, Arkadelphia, AR 16
Clark County Historical Museum, Vancouver, WA 490
Clark County Historical Society, Clark, SD 423
Clark County Historical Society—Howard Steamboat Museum, Jeffersonville, IN 126
Clark County Historical Society, Kahoka, MO 247
Clark County Historical Society, Neillsville, WI 501
Clark County Historical Society—The Pioneer Museum, Ashland, KS 143
Clark County Historical Society, Winchester, KY 163
Clark Historical Society, Clark, NJ 279
Clarke County Historical Association, Berryville, VA 471
Clarke County Historical Society, Osceola, IA 140
Clarke Historical Library, Mt. Pleasant, MI 220
Clarke Memorial Museum, Eureka, CA 27

Clarksville-Montgomery County Historical Museum, Clarksville, TN 428
Clatsop County Historical Society, Astoria, OR 382
Clausen Memorial Museum, Petersburg, AK 11
Clawson Historical Museum, Clawson, MI 212
Clay County Division of Historic Sites, Kearney, MO 249
Clay County Genealogical Society, Inc., Brazil, IN 121
Clay County Historical Society, Clay Center, KS 144
Clay County Historical Society and Museum, Moorhead, MN 233
Clay County Museum Association, Liberty, MO 250
Clayton County Heritage Association, Morrow, GA 91
Clayton County Historical Society, Strawberry Point, IA 141
Clayton Historical Preservation Authority, Clayton, AL 3
Clayton McLain Memorial Museum, Cut Knife, Saskatchewan 564
Clear Creek Canyon Historical Society of Chaffee County, Inc., Granite, CO 55
Clear Lake Area Heritage Society, Seabrook, TX 457
Clear Spring District Historical Association, Clear Spring, MD 182
Clearfield County Historical Society, Clearfield, PA 390
Clearwater County Historical Society, Bagley, MN 226
Clermont County Historical Society, Batavia, OH 356
Clermont State Historic Park, Germantown, NY 313
Cleveland County Historical Association and Museum, Shelby, NC 349
Cleveland Landmarks Commission, Cleveland, OH 359
Cleveland Police Historical Society, Inc.—Cleveland Police Museum, Cleveland, OH 360
Clinton County Historical Association, Plattsburgh, NY 328
Clinton County Historical Commission, Lansing, MI 218
Clinton County Historical Society, Albany, KY 153
Clinton County Historical Society, St. Johns, MI 223
Clinton County Historical Society, Wilmington, OH 374
Clinton County Historical Society and Museum, Plattsburg, MO 252
Clinton Historical Museum Village, Clinton, NJ 279
Clinton Historical Society, Inc., Clinton, NY 308
Clinton Lake Historical Society, Inc., Overbrook, KS 150
Cliveden, Philadelphia, PA 401
Cloisters Children's Museum of Baltimore City, Brooklandville, MD 181
Cloud County Historical Museum, Concordia, KS 144
Cloud County Historical Society, Concordia, KS 144
Cloverdale Historical Society, Cloverdale, CA 25
Clyde Heritage League, Inc., Clyde, OH 360
Coast Artillery Museum at Fort Worden, Port Townsend, WA 486
Coast Guard Museum/Northwest, Seattle, WA 487
Coastal APDC Advisory Council on Historic Preservation, Brunswick, GA 86
Coastal Georgia Historical Society—Museum of Coastal History, St. Simons Island, GA 92
Coastal Heritage Society, Savannah, GA 92
Cobb County Genealogical Society, Marietta, GA 90
Cobb Memorial Archives, Lanett, AL 6
Cobblestone Farm Association, Ann Arbor, MI 210
Cobblestone Society Museum, Albion, NY 301
Cobden Museum, Cobden, IL 105
Cochise County Historical and Archaeological Society, Douglas, AZ 12
Cochrane Ranch, Cochrane, Alberta 512
Codington County Historical Society, Inc.—Kampeska Heritage Museum, Watertown, SD 427
Coe Hall at Planting Fields Arboretum, Oyster Bay, NY 327
Coeur d'Alene Mining District Museum, Wallace, ID 99
Coffee County Historical Society, Manchester, TN 431
Coffey County Genealogical Society, Inc., Burlington, KS 143

Coffey County Historical Society—County Museum, Burlington, KS 143

Coffeyville Historical Society, Inc., Coffeyville, KS 144

Coggeshall Farm Museum, Bristol, RI 409

Cohasset Historical Society, Cohasset, MA 192

Cohocton Historical Society, Cohocton, NY 308

Cokato Historical Society, Cokato, MN 227

Coke County Historical Commission, Robert Lee, TX 455

Colbert County Historical Landmarks Foundation, Inc., Tuscumbia, AL 8

Colborne Lodge, Toronto, Ontario 552

Colchester Historical Museum, Truro, Nova Scotia 538

Colchester Historical Society, Colchester, CT 58

Cole Camp Area Historical Society, Cole Camp, MO 244

Cole County Historical Society, Jefferson City, MO 247

Cole Harbour Rural Heritage Society, Cole Harbor, Nova Scotia 534

Colebrook Historical Society, Inc., Colebrook, CT 58

Coles County Historical Society, Charleston, IL 102

College Hill Historical Society, Cincinnati, OH 359

College Park Historical Society, Inc., College Park, GA 87

Collier County Museum, Naples, FL 81

Collin County Historical Society—Old Post Office Museum, McKinney, TX 452

Collingswood—Newton Colony Historical Society, Collingswood, NJ 279

Collingwood Museum, Collingwood, Ontario 541

Colonel John Ashley House, Ashley Falls, MA 187

Colonel William Bratton Chapter, Sons of American Revolution, York, SC 422

Colonel William Jones House, Gentryville, IN 123

Colonial Charlestown, Inc., Charlestown, MD 182

Colonial Infantry Albuquerque, Albuquerque, NM 295

Colonial National Historical Park: Jamestown Island and Yorktown Battlefield, Yorktown, VA 482

Colonial Philadelphia Historical Society, Philadelphia, PA 401

Colonial Society of Massachusetts, Boston, MA 189

Colonial Williamsburg Foundation, Williamsburg, VA 481

Colorado City Historical Museum, Colorado City, TX 441

Colorado Division of State Archives and Public Records, Denver, CO 51

Colorado Genealogical Society, Denver, CO 51

Colorado Midland Chapter, National Railroad Historical Society, Colorado Springs, CO 50

Colorado Railroad Historical Foundation, Inc., Golden, CO 54

Colorado Ski Museum—Ski Hall of Fame, Vail, CO 57

Colorado-Wyoming Association of Museums, Ft. Collins, CO 54

Colton Hall Museum of the City of Monterey, Monterey, CA 33

Colts Neck Historical Society, Colts Neck, NJ 279

Columbia Chapter, South Carolina Genealogical Society, Columbia, SC 416

Columbia County Historical Society, Kinderhook, NY 317

Columbia County Historical Society, Lake City, FL 79

Columbia Historical Society, Washington, DC 72

Columbia Museum, Columbia, SC 416

Columbia River Maritime Museum, Astoria, OR 382

Columbia State Historic Park, Columbia, CA 5

Columbiana County Chapter, Ohio Genealogical Society, Salem, OH 371

Columbiana-Fairfield Township Historical Society, Columbiana, OH 360

Columbus Chapel—Boal Mansion and Museum, Boalsburg, PA 388

Columbus Historical Society, Inc., Columbus, NM 296

Columbus Landmarks Foundation, Columbus, OH 361

Comanche County Historical and Museum, Comanche, TX 441

Comanche Crossing Historical Society, Strasburg, CO 57

Comfort Historical Society, Comfort, TX 441

Comité Historique St. Stanislas, St. Stanislas, Quebec 562

Comité des Archives de la Louisiane, Baton Rouge, LA 163

Comité Louisiane Francaise, Metairie, LA 165

Commandant's House, Boston, MA 189

Commerce Township Area Historical Society (CTAHS), Walled Lake, MI 224

Commission des Avoyelles, Inc., Hamburg, LA 164

Commission for Historical and Architectural Preservation, Baltimore, MD 180

Commission Nationale de Genealogie, Quebec, Quebec 560

Commission on Archives and History, Central Illinois Conference, United Methodist Church, Bloomington, IL 100

Commission on Archives and History, Minnesota Annual Conference, United Methodist Church, Minneapolis, MN 232

Commission on Archives and History, Peninsula Annual Conference, Frederica, DE 69

Commission on Archives and History, United Methodist Church, Madison, NJ 284

Commission on Chicago Historical and Architectural Landmarks, Chicago, IL 103

Committee to Preserve the Narcissa Prentiss House, Inc., Prattsburg, NY 329

Commonwealth Council for Arts and Culture, Saipan, Mariana Islands 509

Community Arts Center, Portsmouth, VA 478

Community Historical Society, Alden, MN 225

Community Historical Society, Colon, MI 212

Community Historical Society, Maxwell, IA 139

Community Memorial Museum of Sutter County, Yuba City, CA 49

Company of Military Historians, Westbrook, CT 68

Compton County Historical and Museum Society, Eaton, Quebec 557

Comstock Historic House Society, Moorhead, MN 233

Con Foster Museum, Traverse City, MI 224

Conant Public Library, Winchester, NH 276

Concord Antiquarian Museum, Concord, MA 193

Concord Historical Society, Springville, NY 335

Concord Public Library, Concord, NH 270

Concordia Historical Institute, St. Louis, MO 254

Conejo Valley Historical Society, Thousand Oaks, CA 46

Confederate Air Force, Harlingen, TX 448

Confederate Historical Institute, Little Rock, AR 19

Confederate Memorial State Historic Site, Higginsville, MO 246

Confederate Museum, Richmond, TX 455

Confederate Research Center and Museum, Hillsboro, TX 448

Confederation of South Carolina Local Historical Societies, Columbia, SC 416

Conference of California Historical Societies, Stockton, CA 46

Conference of Connecticut River Historical Societies in Connecticut, Inc., Rocky Hill, CT 65

Congregation Beth Ahabah Museum and Archives Trust, Richmond, VA 479

Congregational Christian Historical Society, Boston, MA 189

Congregational Library of the American Congregational Association, Boston, MA 189

Conneaut Railroad Museum, Conneaut, OH 362
Connecticut Firemen's Historical Society, Inc.,
    Manchester, CT 62
Connecticut Historical Commission, Hartford, CT 61
Connecticut Historical Society, Hartford, CT 61
Connecticut Humanities Council, Middletown, CT 62
Connecticut River Foundation, Essex, CT 60
Connecticut Society of Genealogists, Inc., Glastonbury,
    CT 60
Connecticut Trust for Historic Preservation, New Haven,
    CT 63
Connecticut Valley Historical Museum, Springfield,
    MA 205
Connecticut Valley Railroad Museum, Inc., Essex,
    CT 60
Conner Prairie Pioneer Settlement, Noblesville, IN 128
Conrad Mansion Historic Site Museum—Conrad
    Mansion Directors, Inc., Kalispell, MT 258
Conservation Center for Art and Historic Artifacts,
    Philadelphia, PA 401
Conservation Trust of Puerto Rico, San Juan, Puerto
    Rico 509
Constable Hall Association, Constableville, NY 308
Constitution Hall Park, Huntsville, AL 5
Constitution Island Association, West Point, NY 339
Contra Costa County Historical Society, Concord,
    CA 26
Conway Public Library, Conway, NH 270
Cook Inlet Historical Society—Anchorage Historical and
    Fine Arts Museum, Anchorage, AK 9
Cook Memorial Library, Tamworth, NH 276
Cook's Creek Heritage Museum, Cooks Creek,
    Manitoba 523
Cooke County Heritage Society, Inc., Gainesville,
    TX 446
Cookeville Committee to Preserve the Depot,
    Cookeville, TN 428
Coon Rapids Historical Commission, Coon Rapids,
    MN 227
Cooper Village Museum and Arts Center, Anaconda,
    MT 256
Cooper-Hewitt Museum, the Smithsonian Institution's
    National Museum of Design, New York, NY 323
Coos-County Historical Society Museum, North Bend,
    OR 384
Coosa River Valley Historical and Genealogical Society,
    Centre, AL 3
Copper King Mansion, Butte, MT 256
Coppertown USA, Calumet, MI 212
Coral Gables Historic Preservation Division, Coral
    Gables, FL 77
Cordova Historical Society, Inc., Cordova, AK 9
Cornell Plantations, Ithaca, NY 316
Corning Museum of Glass, Corning, NY 309
Corning-Painted Post Historical Society, Corning,
    NY 309
Cornish Historical Society, Cornish, NH 270
Coronado Historical Association, Inc., Coronado, CA 26
Coronado National Memorial, Hereford, AZ 12
Corporation Touristique de la Seigneurie des Aulnaies,
    St. Roch des Aulnaies, Quebec 562
Corpus Christi Museum, Corpus Christi, TX 441
Corry Area Historical Society, Corry, PA 390
Cortland County Historical Society, Cortland, NY 309
Corydon Capital State Memorial—Division of Historic
    Preservation, Department of Natural Resources,
    Corydon, IN 121
Coryell County Museum Foundation, Inc., Gatesville,
    TX 447
Costa Mesa Historical Society, Costa Mesa, CA 26
Costume Society of America, Englishtown, NJ 280
Costume Society of Nova Scotia, Halifax, Nova
    Scotia 534

Cottonlandia Museum, Greenwood, MS 240
Council for Museum Anthropology, Berkeley, CA 24
Council for Northeast Historical Archeology, Waterford,
    NY 338
Council on Abandoned Military Posts, USA, Inc.,
    Northern Virginia, VA 477
Council on America's Military Past, Fort Myer, VA 473
Country Doctor Museum, Bailey, NC 341
Country Music Foundation, Nashville, TN 433
Courtenay and District Historical Society, Courtenay,
    British Columbia 518
Courthouse-on-the-Square Museum, Denton, TX 443
Covington Historical Society, Andalusia, AL 1
Covington Historical Society, Pavilion, NY 328
Cowboy Artists of America Museum, Kerrville, TX 450
Cowboy Country Museum, Stamford, TX 457
Craigflower Heritage Site, Victoria, British Columbia 522
Craighead County Historical Society, Jonesboro, AR 19
Cranberry World Visitors Center, Plymouth, MA 202
Cranbrook Archives, Museum and Landmark
    Foundation, Cranbrook, British Columbia 518
Cranbury Historical and Preservation Society,
    Cranbury, NJ 280
Cranford Historical Society, Cranford, NJ 280
Cranston Historic District Commission, Cranston, RI 409
Crawford County Historical Society, Inc., Robinson,
    IL 115
Crawford County Historical Society, Meadville, PA 398
Crawford County Historical Society, Van Buren, AR 22
Crescent Bend: The Armstrong-Lockett House and
    Gardens, Knoxville, TN 430
Crescent-Shousetown Area Historical Association,
    Glenwillard, PA 393
Creston and District Historical and Museum Society,
    Creston, British Columbia 518
Creve Coeur-Chesterfield Historical Society, St. Louis,
    MO 254
Crittenden County Historical Society, Inc., Marion,
    KY 160
Crittenden County Historical Society, Inc., West
    Memphis, AR 22
Crockett County Museum, Ozona, TX 453
Crook County Historical Society—A.R. Bowman
    Museum, Prineville, OR 385
Crooks Council of the Minnehaha County Historical
    Society, Crooks, SD 423
Crosby County Pioneer Memorial Museum, Crosbyton,
    TX 442
Cross County Genealogical Society, Wynne, AR 22
Cross County Historical Society, Inc., Wynne, AR 22
Cross Plains—Berry Historical Society, Cross Plains,
    WI 495
Croton-on-Hudson Historical Society,
    Croton-on-Hudson, NY 309
Crow Wing County Historical Society, Brainerd,
    MN 226
Crystal City Historical Society, Crystal City, MO 245
Crystal River State Archaeological Site, Crystal, River,
    FL 77
Cudahy Historical Society, Cudahy, WI 495
Culbertson Mansion State Memorial, New Albany,
    IN 127
Cultural Heritage Foundation of Southern California,
    Inc., Los Angeles, CA 31
Cultural and Historical Resources, Maryland Forest,
    Park and Wildlife Service, Annapolis, MD 179
Cumberland County Cultural and Heritage Commission,
    Vineland, NJ 293
Cumberland County Historical Society, Greenup, IL 108
Cumberland County Historical Society, Greenwich,
    NJ 281
Cumberland County Historical Society—The Hamilton
    Library Association, Carlisle, PA 389

Cumberland Museum and Science Center, Nashville, TN 433

Cumberland Museum, Cumberland, British Columbia 518

Cumberland Township Museum, Cumberland, Ontario 541

Cumberland and Oxford Canal Association, Portland, ME 175

Cupertino Historical Society, Cupertino, CA 26

Curatorial Services Branch, National Park Service, Washington, DC 2

Curry County Historical Society, Gold Beach, OR 383

Custer Battlefield Historical and Museum Association, Crow Agency, MT 257

Custer Battlefield National Monument, Crow Agency, MT 257

Cuttyhunk Historical Society, Cuttyhunk, MA 193

Cuyuna Range Historical Society, Crosby, MN 227

Cypress College Local History Association, Cypress, CA 26

D

D.C. Preservation League, Washington, DC 72

Dacotah Prairie Museum, Aberdeen, SD 422

Dade Battlefield State Historic Site, Bushnell, FL 76

Dade County Missouri Historical Society, Greenfield, MO 246

Dade Heritage Trust, Inc., Miami, FL 80

Dahlonega Courthouse Gold Museum, Dahlonega, GA 88

Dakota County Historical Society, Dakota City, NE 262

Dakota County Historical Society, South St. Paul, MN 237

Dakota Territorial Museum, Yankton, SD 427

Dakotah Corral, Westerners International, Sioux Falls, SD 426

Dallam-Hartley Counties XIT Museum, Dalhart, TX 442

Dallas County Heritage Society, Inc., Dallas, TX 442

Dallas County Historical Commission, Dallas, TX 442

Dallas County Historical Society, Buffalo, MO 243

Dallas Historical Society, Dallas, TX 442

Dallas Landmark Committee, Dallas, TX 442

Dalnavert (Macdonald House Museum), Winnipeg, Manitoba 525

Dalton Historical Committee, Dalton, MA 193

Danbury Scott-Fanton Museum and Historical Society, Inc., Danbury, CT 59

Dane County Historical Society, Madison, WI 499

Daniel Boone Home, Defiance, MO 245

Daniel Boone Homestead, Birdsboro, PA 388

Daniel Parrish Witter Agricultural Museum, Syracuse, NY 336

Daniel Webster College, Nashua, NH 274

Danish American Fellowship, Minneapolis, MN 232

Danvers Alarm List Company, Inc,., Danvers, MA 193

Danvers Archival Center, Danvers, MA 193

Danvers Historical Society, Danvers, MA 193

Danville Museum of Fine Arts and History, Danville, VA 472

Darien Historical Society, Darien, IL 105

Darien Historical Society, Inc., Darien, CT 59

Darke County Historical Society, Greenville, OH 365

Darlington County Historical Commission, Darlington, SC 418

Darlington County Historical Society, Darlington, SC 418

Dartford Historical Society, Green Lake, WI 497

Dartmouth College Archives, Hanover, NH 272

Dartmouth Heritage Museum, Dartmouth, Nova Scotia 534

Dartmouth Museum Society, Dartmouth, Nova Scotia 534

Daughters of Hawaii—Queen Emma Summer Palace, Honolulu, HI 95

Daughters of Utah Pioneers Relic Hall, Montpelier, ID 98

Daughters of the American Revolution Library, Washington, DC 72

Daughters of the American Revolution Museum, Washington, DC 72

Dauphin County Historical Society, Harrisburg, PA 394

Davenport Historical Society, Davenport, NY 309

David Bradford House, Washington, PA 407

Davidson County Museum, Lexington, NC 346

Daviess County Historical Society, Gallatin, MO 246

Davis Family Association, Woodville, MS 242

Dawes Arboretum Museum, Newark, OH 369

Dawes County Historical Society, Chadron, NE 262

Dawson City Museum and Historical Society, Dawson City, Yukon Territory 568

Dawson County Historical Society, Lexington, NE 264

Dawson Creek Station Museum, Dawson Creek, British Columbia 518

Dayton-Montgomery County Park District, Dayton, OH 362

De Anza Trek Lancers Society, Cupertino, CA 26

De Smet Depot Museum, De Smet, SD 423

DeBolt and District Pioneer Museum Society, DeBolt, Alberta 512

DeKalb County Historical Society, DeKalb, IL 106

DeKalb Historical Society, Decatur, GA 88

DeWitt County Historical Museum, Cuero, TX 442

DeWitt Historical Society of Tompkins County, Inc., Ithaca, NY 316

DeWitt Wallace Decorative Arts Gallery, Williamsburg, VA 481

Deaf Smith County Museum, Hereford, TX 448

Dean and Creech Families of America, Morehead, KY 160

Dearborn Historical Museum, Dearborn, MI 212

Dearborn Historical Society—McFadden-Ross House, Dearborn, MI 212

Death Valley National Monument, Death Valley, CA 26

Decatur House Museum, Washington, DC 73

Dedham Historical Society, Dedham, MA 193

Deep River Historical Society, Inc., Deep River, CT 59

Deer Isle-Stonington Historical Society, Deer Isle, ME 171

Deer Lodge Abner Ross Memorial Center, Deer Lodge, TN 428

Deer Park Independent School District Historical Museum, Deer Park, TX 443

Deering Historical Society, Hillsboro, NH 272

Defiance County Chapter, Ohio Genealogy Society, Defiance, OH 362

Defiance County-Historical Society, Defiance, OH 363

Degenhart Paperweight and Glass Museum, Inc., Cambridge, OH 357

Dekalb County Historical Society, Auburn, IN 120

Delavan Community Historical Society, Delavan, IL 106

Delaware Agricultural Museum, Dover, DE 69

Delaware County Historical Association, Delhi, NY 310

Delaware County Historical Society, Chester, PA 390

Delaware County Historical Society, Hopkinton, IA 137

Delaware County Historical Society, Muncie, IN 127

Delaware Division of Historical and Cultural Affairs, Dover, DE 69

Delaware Society for the Preservation of Antiquities, Wilmington, DE 70

Delaware Valley Old Time Power and Equipment Association, Lambertville, NJ 284

Delaware Water Gap National Recreation Area, Bushkill, PA 389

Delhi Historical Society, Cincinnati, OH 359
Dells Country Historical Society, Wisconsin Dells, WI 506
Delray Beach Historical Society, Delray Beach, FL 77
Delta Blues Museum, Carnegie Public Library, Clarksdale, MS 239
Delta County Historical Society, Delta, CO 51
Delta Museum and Archives, Delta, British Columbia 518
Denver Art Museum, Denver, CO 51
Denver City Museum, Denver City, TX 443
Denver Museum of Natural History, Denver, CO 51
Department of Archives and History, Evangelical Lutheran Synod, Mankato, MN 232
Department of Archives and Manuscripts, Baton Rouge, LA 163
Department of Archives and Special Collections, Ohio University Libraries, Athens, OH 355
Department of Arkansas Natural and Cultural Heritage, Little Rock, AR 19
Department of Continuing Education and Community Services, Athens, AL 1
Department of Culture and History, State of West Virginia, Charleston, WV 492
Department of Fish, Wildlife, and Parks, Helena, MT 258
Department of Geology, University of New Mexico, Albuquerque, NM 295
Department of History and Archives, Nebraska Conference, United Church of Christ, Lincoln, NE 264
Department of History, Plymouth State College, Plymouth, NH 275
Department of History, University of Akron, Akron, OH 354
Department of Museums, City of Platteville, Platteville, WI 502
Department of the Interior Museum, Washington, DC 73
Depot Museum, Lake Wales, FL 80
Depot Museum: History Museum and Children's Discovery Center, Henderson, TX 448
Depot Park Museum, Sonoma, CA 45
Depreciation Lands Association, Allison Park, PA 387
Derby Historical Society, Inc., Derby, CT 59
Derby Historical Society, Inc., Derby, VT 466
Derry Historical Society and Museum, Derry, NH 271
Des Moines County Historical Society, Burlington, IA 132
Des Plaines Historical Society, Des Plaines, IL 106
DesBrisay Museum and National Exhibition Centre, Bridgewater, Nova Scotia 533
Deschutes County Historical Society, Bend, OR 382
Desert Caballeros Western Museum, Wickenburg, AZ 16
Desert Hot Springs Historical Society, Desert Hot Springs, CA 26
Desert Research Institute—Social Sciences Center, Reno, NV 268
Deserted Village at Allaire, Inc., Allaire, NJ 277
Desha County Museum Society, Dumas, AR 17
Destrehan Plantation, Destrehan, LA 164
Detroit Chapter, FCHSM (French-Canadian Heritage Society of Michigan), Detroit, MI 213
Detroit Historical Museum, Detroit, MI 213
Detroit Historical Society, Detroit, MI 213
Deutschheim State Historic Site, Hermann, MO 246
Devil's Den State Park, West Fork, AR 22
Dewey County Historical Society, Camargo, OK 376
Dewey Schoolhouse, Stockbridge, MI 224
Dexter Area Historical Society, Dexter, MI 214
Dexter Historical Museum, Dexter, IA 135
Dickinson County Historical Society, Abilene, KS 142
Dickson Mounds Museum, Lewistown, IL 109
Dighton Historical Society, Dighton, MA 194

Dillard Mill State Historic Site, Dillard, MO 245
Dinosaur Provincial Park, Patricia, Alberta 515
Diocese of Fredericton Archives, Fredericton, New Brunswick 528
Disciples of Christ Historical Society, Nashville, TN 433
Discovery Hall Museum, South Bend, IN 129
Discovery Museum, Essex Junction, VT 466
Division of Archaeology, Baton Rouge, LA 163
Division of Archives and Records, City of Charleston, Charleston, SC 415
Division of Historic Preservation, Baton Rouge, LA 163
Division of Historic Preservation, Fairfax County Park Authority, Annandale, VA 470
Division of Historic Properties, Doylestown, PA 391
Division of Historic Sites, Illinois Department of Conservation, Springfield, IL 116
Doak Historic Park, Doaktown, New Brunswick 528
Dobbs Ferry Historical Society, Dobbs Ferry, NY 310
Dodge County Historical Society, Beaver Dam, WI 495
Dodge County Historical Society, Fremont, NE 263
Dodsland Museum, Dodsland, Saskatchewan 564
Don F. Pratt Memorial Museum, Fort Campbell, KY 154
Donalda and District Museum Society, Donalda, Alberta 512
Donna Hooks Fletcher Historical Museum, Donna, TX 444
Doon Pioneer Village, Kitchener, Ontario 544
Dorchester County Historical Society, Inc., Cambridge, MD 182
Dorchester Heights Monument, Boston, MA 189
Dossin Great Lakes Museum, Belle Isle, MI 211
Douglas County Genealogical Society, Alexandria, MN 225
Douglas County Historical Society, Alexandria, MN 225
Douglas County Historical Society, Armour, SD 422
Douglas County Historical Society, Lawrence, KS 148
Douglas County Historical Society—General Crook House, Omaha, NE 265
Douglas County Museum of History and Natural History, Roseburg, OR 385
Douglass Historical Museum, Douglass, KS 145
Doukhobour Village Museum, Castlegar, British Columbia 517
Dover Historical Society—J.E. Reeves Home and Museum, Dover, OH 363
Dover Historical Society—Sawin Museum, Dover, MA 194
Dover-Foxcroft Historical Society—Blacksmith Shop Museum, Dover-Foxcroft, ME 171
Downers Grove Historical Society, Downers Grove, IL 106
Downes-Aldrich House, Crockett, TX 570
Downey Historical Society, Downey, CA 26
Downington Historical Commission, Downingtown, PA 391
Downingtown Historical Society, Downingtown, PA 391
Drake Well Museum, Titusville, PA 406
Drake's Midwest Phonograph Museum, Martinsville, IN 127
Draper Historical Society, Draper, UT 461
Drayton Hall, Charleston, SC 415
Drew County Historical Society and Museum, Monticello, AR 20
Drumheller and District Fossil Museum, Drumheller, Alberta 512
Drummer Boy Museum, Brewster, MA 191
Drummond Historical Society, Drummond, WI 496
Drummond Home, Hominy, OK 378
Drummond Island Historical Society, Drummond Island, MI 214
Du Page County Historical Society and Museum, Wheaton, IL 119
DuPont Historical Museum, DuPont, WA 483

DuSable Museum of African-American History, Chicago, IL 103

Duarte Historical Museum Society—Friends of the Duarte Library, Inc., Duarte, CA 26

Dublin Historical Society, Inc., Dublin, OH 363

Dublin-Laurens Museum, Dublin, GA 88

Dubuque County Historical Society—Mathias Ham House, Dubuque, IA 135

Duck Lake Historical Museum, Duck Lake, Saskatchewan 564

Duke Homestead State Historic Site and Tobacco Museum, Durham, NC 343

Dukes County Historical Society, Edgartown, MA 194

Dumbarton House, Washington, DC 73

Dumont Historical Society, Dumont, IA 569

Dundas Historical Society Museum, Dundas, Ontario 542

Dundee Township Historical Society, Inc., Dundee, IL 106

Dunedin Historical Society, Inc., Dunedin, FL 77

Duneland Historical Society, Inc., Chesterton, IN 121

Dunham Tavern Museum—Society of Collectors, Inc., Cleveland, OH 360

Dunklin County Museum, Kennett, MO 249

Dunn County Historical Society, Dunn Center, ND 352

Dunn County Historical Society, Menomonie, WI 500

Duplin County Historical Society—Leora H. McEachern Library of Local History, Rose Hill, NC 348

Durand-Hedden House and Garden Association, Maplewood, NJ 285

Durham Historic Association, Inc., Durham, NH 271

Durham Historical Society, Durham, CT 59

Durrell Museum, Durrell, Newfoundland 531

Dutchess County Genealogical Society, Poughkeepsie, NY 329

Dutchess County Historical Society, Poughkeepsie, NY 329

Duxbury Rural and Historical Society—Drew House, Duxbury, MA 194

Dwight D. Eisenhower Library, Abilene, KS 143

Dyer Library, Saco, ME 176

E

E.B. Black Historic House, Hereford, TX 448

ECHO (Essex Community Heritage Organization, Inc.), Essex, NY 311

Eagle County Historical Society, Inc., Eagle, CO 53

Eagle Grove Chapter, Wright County Historical Society, Eagle Grove, IA 135

Eagle Historical Society, Eagle City, AK 9

Eagle Rock Valley Historical Society, Eagle Rock, CA 27

Earle-Harrison House, Waco, TX 459

Early American Industries Association, Inc., Albany, NY 301

Early American Museum and Gardens, Mahomet, IL 110

East Bay Negro Historical Society, Inc., Oakland, CA 34

East Benton County Historical Society, Kennewick, WA 484

East Bridgewater Historical Commission, East Bridgewater, MA 194

East Chicago Historical Society, East Chicago, IN 122

East Feliciana Historical Preservation Society, Inc., Clinton, LA 164

East Feliciana Pilgrimage and Garden Club, Clinton, LA 164

East Hampton Historical Society, East Hampton, NY 310

East Hants Historical Society, Maitland, Nova Scotia 536

East Jersey Olde Towne, Inc., Piscataway, NJ 289

East Jordan Portside Art and Historical Museum Society, East Jordan, MI 214

East Liverpool Historical Society, East Liverpool, OH 363

East Longmeadow Historical Commission, East Longmeadow, MA 194

East Machias Historical Society, East Machias, ME 171

East Point Historical Society, Inc., East Point, GA 88

East Tennessee Historical Society, Knoxville, TN 430

east Texas Historical Association, Nacogdoches, TX 453

East Texas Oil Museum, Kilgore, TX 450

East Yuma County Historical Society, Wray, CO 57

Eastchester Historical Society, Eastchester, NY 310

Eastern Arizona Museum and Historical Society, Pima, AZ 14

Eastern Cabarrus Historical Society Museum, Mt. Pleasant, NC 347

Eastern Jasper County Historical Society, Sarcoxie, MO 255

Eastern Kentucky University Archives, Richmond, KY 161

Eastern Oregon Museum, Haines, OR 383

Eastern Shore of Virginia Historical Society, Onancock, VA 478

Eastern Townships Research Centre, Lennoxville, Quebec 558

Eastern Trails Museum, Inc., Vinita, OK 381

Eastern Washington State Historical Society—Cheney Cowles Memorial Museum, Spokane, WA 489

Eastham Historical Society, Inc., Eastham, MA 194

Easthampton Historical Commission, Easthampton, MA 194

Eaton Room, Manatee County Public Library System, Bradenton, FL 76

Eatonton-Putnam County Historical Society, Inc., Eatonton, GA 88

Eatonville Historical Society, Eatonville, WA 483

Eau Claire Landmarks Commission, Eau Claire, WI 496

Ebenezer Maxwell Mansion, Inc., Philadelphia, PA 401

Eckley Miners' Village, Hazleton, PA 395

Eckley Miners' Village, Weatherly, PA 408

Ector County Historical Commission, Odessa, TX 453

Edaville Railroad, South Carver, MA 205

Eden Historical Society, Eden, NY 310

Eden Historic Properties Commission, Eden, NC 343

Edenton Historical Commission, Edenton, NC 344

Edgar Allan Poe National Historic Site, Philadelphia, PA 401

Edgar County Historical Society, Paris, IL 113

Edge of the Cedars State Park, Blanding, UT 461

Edgecombe County Historical Society, Tarboro, NC 350

Edina Heritage Preservation Board, Edina, MN 228

Edina Historical Society, Edina, MN 228

Edison Birthplace Association, Inc., Milan, OH 368

Edison National Historic Site, West Orange, NJ 293

Edison Township Historical Society, Edison, NJ 280

Edmonds-South Snohomish County Historical Society, Inc., Edmonds, WA 483

Edmonton Space Sciences Foundation, Edmonton, Alberta 513

Edward Hopper Landmark Preservation Foundation—Hopper House, Nyack, NY 26

Edwards County Historical Society, Albion, IL 99

Edwards and Rose Genealogical Heritage, Irvine, KY 157

Edwin Langhart Museum—Healdsburg Historical Society, Healdsburg, CA 29

Edwin Smith Historical Museum, Westfield Athenaeum, Westfield, MA 208

Edwin Wolters Museum, Shiner, TX 457
Effigy Mounds National Monument, McGregor, IA 139
Effingham County Genealogical Society, Effingham,
    IL 106
Effingham Historical Society, Effingham, NH 271
Eighteen-ninety House, Cortland, NY 309
Eighteen-seventy-seven Peterson Station Museum,
    Peterson, MN 234
Eighteen-thirty-nine Williams Home, Galveston, TX 447
Eildon Hall, Sibbald Memorial Museum, Sutton West,
    Ontario 552
Eisenhower Birthplace State Historic Site, Denison,
    TX 443
Eisenhower National Historic Site, Gettysburg, PA 393
El Cajon Historical Society, El Cajon, CA 27
El Morro National Monument, Ramah, NM 298
El Paso Centennial Museum, El Paso, TX 444
El Paso County Historical Commission, El Paso, TX 444
El Paso County Historical Society, El Paso, TX 444
El Paso Jewish Historical Society, El Paso, TX 444
El Pueblo Museum, Pueblo, CO 56
El Pueblo de Los Angeles State Historic Park, Los
    Angeles, CA 31
Eleanor Roosevelt Center at Val-Kill, Hyde Park, NY 316
Electric Railway Historical Association of Southern
    California, Los Angeles, CA 31
Elgin Area Historical Society, Elgin, IL 106
Elgin County Pioneer Museum, St. Thomas, Ontario 551
Elgin Genealogical Society, Elgin, IL 107
Eli Whitney Museum, Hamden, CT 61
Elisabet Ney Museum, Austin, TX 437
Elizabeth II State Historic Site, Manteo, NC 346
Elizabeth M. Watkins Community Museum, Lawrence,
    KS 148
Elizabeth Sage Historic Costume Collection and
    Gallery, Bloomington, IN 120
Elizabeth Township Historical Society, Greenock,
    PA 393
Elizabethtown Heritage Society, Elizabeth, NJ 280
Elk County Historical Society, Ridgway, PA 404
Elk Creeks Preservation Society, Inc., Elkton, MD 183
Elkader Historical Society, Elkader, IA 136
Elkhart County Historical Society, Inc., Bristol, IN 121
Ella Sharp Museum Association of Jackson, Jackson,
    MI 217
Ellenville Public Library and Museum, Ellenville, NY 311
Ellicott City Restoration Foundation, Inc., Ellicott City,
    MD 183
Elliot Lake Nuclear and Mining Museum, Elliot Lake,
    Ontario 542
Ellis County Historical Society, Gage, OK 377
Ellis County Historical Society, Hays, KS 146
Ellsworth County Historical Society, Ellsworth, KS 145
Ellwood House Museum, DeKalb, IL 106
Elmhurst Historical Museum, Elmhurst, IL 107
Elmira Heights Historical Society, Inc., Elmira Heights,
    NY 311
Elmore County Historical Foundation, Inc., Mountain
    Home, ID 98
Elmwood Historical Society—Lorado Taft Museum,
    Elmwood, IL 107
Elsie Historical Society, Elsie, MI 214
Emery County Historical Society, Castle Dale, UT 461
Emmet County Historical Society, Inc., Estherville,
    IA 136
Endicott Historical and Preservation Society, Endicott,
    NY 311
Enfield Historical Society, Enfield, NH 271
Enfield Historical Society, Inc., Enfield, CT 59
Englewood Historical Society, Englewood, NJ 280
Enon Community Historical Society, Enon, OH 363
Ephrata Cloister Associates, Inc., Ephrata, PA 392
Erie Canal Museum, Syracuse, NY 336

Erie Canal Village, Rome, NY 331
Erie County Historical Federation, Cheektowaga,
    NY 307
Erie County Historical Society, Erie, PA 392
Erie County Historical Society, Sandusky, OH 371
Erie Historical Museum and Planetarium, Erie, PA 392
Ernest Hemingway Museum, Key West, FL 79
Ernie Pyle Public Library, Albuquerque, NM 295
Erwin-Painted Post Museum, Painted Post, NY 328
Escambia County Historical Society, Brewton, AL 2
Escondido Historical Society, Escondido, CA 27
Esko Historical Society, Esko, MN 229
Esperance Historical Society and Musuem, Esperance,
    NY 311
Essex County Historical Association, Salem, MA 203
Essex County Historical County, Elizabethtown, NY 310
Essex County Historical Society, Windsor, Ontario 555
Essex Historical Society—Essex Shipbuilding Museum,
    Essex, MA 195
Essex Historical Society, Inc., Essex, CT 60
Essex Institute, Salem, MA 203
Essex Region Conservation Authority, Essex,
    Ontario 542
Essex-Middle River Heritage Society, Baltimore, MD 180
Essley-Noble Museum, Aledo, IL 99
Estes Park Area Historical Museum, Estes Park, CO 53
Estevan National Exhibition Centre, Estevan,
    Saskatchewan 564
Ethnic Heritage Council of the Pacific Northwest,
    Seattle, WA 487
Etowah Historical Society, Gadsden, AL 2
Euclid Historical Society, Euclid, OH 363
Eudora Area Historical Society, Eudora, KS 145
Eufaula Heritage Association, Eufaula, AL 4
Eugene C. Barker Texas History Center, University of
    Texas at Austin, Austin, TX 437
Eugene Field House and Toy Museum, St. Louis,
    MO 254
Eureka Schoolhouse, Springfield, VT 469
Eureka Springs Preservation Society, Eureka Springs,
    AR 17
Evangeline Genealogical and Historical Society, Ville
    Platte, LA 168
Evanston Historical Society, Evanston, IL 107
Evansville Grove Society, Evansville, WI 496
Evansville Museum of Arts and Science, Evansville, IN 122
Evengelical and Reformed Historical Society,
    Lancaster, PA 396
Everest Community Historical Society, Everest, KS 145
Everett McKinley Dirksen Congressional Leadership
    Research Center, Pekin, IL 14
Evergreen House Foundation—John Work Garrett Rare
    Book Library, Baltimore, MD 180
Excelsior House, Jefferson, TX 450
Excelsior Springs Historical Museum, Excelsior Springs,
    MO 245
Excelsior-Lake Minnetonka Historical Society, Excelsior,
    MN 229
Exeter Historical Society, Exeter, NH 271
Experimental Aircraft Association, Oshkosh, WI 502
Ezra Meeker Historical Society, Inc., Puyallup, WA 486

F

Fabulous Koliba Home Museum, Columbus First Home
    Museum and Complex, Columbus, TX 441
Fair Haven Historical Society, Fair Haven, NJ 280
Fairfax County History Commission, Falls Church,
    VA 473
Fairfax Historical Society, Fairfax, VT 466
Fairfield County Historical Commission, Winnsboro,
    SC 421

Fairfield County Museum, Winnsboro, SC 421
Fairfield Heritage Association, Inc., Lancaster, PA 396
Fairfield Historical Society, Fairfield, CT 60
Fairlawn Museum—Douglas County Historical Society, Superior, WI 504
Fairport Harbor Historical Society, Fairport Harbor, OH 363
Fairview Museum of History and Art, Fairview, UT 462
Falkirk Community Cultural Center—Robert Dollar Estate, San Rafael, CA 43
Fall River County Historical Society, Hot Springs, SD 424
Fall River Historical Society, Fall River, MA 195
Fallbrook Historical Society, Fallbrook, CA 28
Fallowfield Historical Society, Coatesville, PA 390
Falls Village—Canaan Historical Society, Falls Village, CT 60
Falmouth Historical Society, Falmouth, MA 195
Fannin County Historical Museum, Bonham, TX 439
Fanshawe Pioneer Village, London, Ontario 545
Fargo Heritage Society, Inc., Fargo, ND 352
Faribault County Historical Society, Blue Earth, MN 226
Farmamerica—Minnesota Agricultural Interpretive Center, Waseca, MN 238
Farmers Branch Historical Park, Farmers Branch, TX 444
Farmers Museum, Inc., Cooperstown, NY 309
Farmersville Historical Society, Inc., Farmersville, OH 263
Farmingdale Historical Society, Farmingdale, NJ 281
Farmington Canal Corridor Association, Plainville, CT 65
Farmington Genealogical Society, Farmington, MI 214
Farmington Hills Historical Commission, Farmington Hills, MI 215
Farmington Historical Society, Farmington, CT 60
Farmington Museum, Farmington, NM 296
Father Leo E. Begin Chapter, American-Canadian Genealogical Society, Auburn-Lewiston, ME 169
Faulk County Historical Society, Faulkton, SD 423
Faulkner County Historical Society, Conway, AR 17
Fauquier Historical Society, Inc., Warrenton, VA 481
Favell Museum of Western Art and Indian Artifacts, Klamath Falls, OR 384
Fayette County Genealogical Society, Washington, Court House OH 373
Fayette County Helpers Club and Historical Society, West Union, IA 142
Fayette County Historical Society, Fayette, AL 4
Fayette County Historical Society, Inc., Fayetteville, GA 88
Fayette County Historical Society, Washington Court House, OH 373
Fayette State Historic Park, Garden, MI 215
Federal Hall National Memorial, New York, NY 323
Federation of Historical Services, Troy, NY 337
Federation of North Carolina Historical Societies, Raleigh, NC 348
Federation of Nova Scotian Heritage, Halifax, Nova Scotia 534
Felix Valle State Historic Site, Ste. Genevieve, MO 253
Fellow-Reeve Museum of History and Science, Wichita, KS 152
Fellowship for Metlar House, Piscataway, NJ 289
Fenton Historical Society, Jamestown, NY 317
Ferguson Historical Society, Ferguson, MO 245
Ferndale Museum, The, Ferndale, CA 28
Fernwood Botanic Garden, Nature Center—Arts and Crafts Center, Niles, MI 221
Ferro Monte Chapter, Daughters of the American Revolution, Succasunna, NJ 292
Ferryland Historical Society, Ferryland, Newfoundland 531

Field Museum of Natural History, Chicago, IL 103
Fielder Museum, Arlington, TX 437
Fikes Hall of Special Collections, DeGolyer Library, Dallas, TX 443
Fillmore County Historical Center, Preston, MN 235
Fillmore County Historical Society, Preston, MN 235
Fillmore Historical Society, Fillmore, CA 28
Filoli Center, Woodside, CA 48
Filson Club, The., Louisville, KY 158
Fine Arts Center, Cheekwood, Nashville, TN 433
Finn Creek Museum, New York Mills, MN 234
Finney County Historical Society, Garden City, KS 146
Fire Department Museum, Spokane, WA 489
Fire Fighters Historical Society of Winnipeg, Inc., Winnipeg, Manitoba 526
Firefighters' Museum of Nova Scotia and National Exhibit Center, Yarmouth, Nova Scotia 538
Firefighters Museum of Southern New Jersey, Pleasantville, NJ 290
Firelands Historical Society Museum, Norwalk, OH 370
First Baptist Church Archives, Blanchard, LA 164
First Baptist Church in America, Providence, RI 411
First Cavalry Division Museum, Fort Hood, TX 445
First Church of Christ, Lancaster, MA 197
First Hussars Regimental Association—Citizen Soldiers Museum, London, Ontario 545
First Missouri State Capitol, St. Charles, MO 252
First White House of the Confederacy, Montgomery, AL 7
Fischer-Hanlon House, Benicia, CA 24
Fisheries Museum of the Atlantic, Lunenburg, Nova Scotia 536
Fishermen's Museum, New Harbor, ME 174
Fitchburg Historical Society, Fitchburg, MA 195
Fitzwilliam Historical Society, Fitzwilliam, NH 271
Five Civilized Tribes Museum, Muskogee, OK 378
Flasher Historical Society, Flasher, ND 352
Flat River Historical Society and Museum, Greenville, MI 216
Flat Rock Historical Society, Flat Rock, MI 215
Flatbush Historical Society, Brooklyn, NY 305
Flathead Culture Committee, Confederated Salish and Kootenai Tribes, St. Ignatius, MT 259
Flickinger Foundation for American Studies Inc., Baltimore, MD 180
Flin Flon Community Archives, Flin Flon, Manitoba 523
Flint Hills Genealogical Society, Emporia, KS 145
Flint Historic Commission, Flint, MI 215
Florence Historical Board, Florence, AL 4
Florence Historical Society, Florence, KS 145
Florence Pioneer Museum and Historical Society, Florence, CO 54
Florida Aviation Historical Society, Indian, FL 78
Florida Baptist Historical Society, Deland, FL 77
Florida Caverns State Park, Marianna, FL 80
Florida Collection, State Library of Florida, Tallahassee, FL 83
Florida Folklife Programs, White Springs, FL 84
Florida Historical Society—University of South Florida Library, Tampa, FL 84
Florida Society for Genealogical Research, St. Petersburg, FL 83
Florida State Genealogical Society, Inc., Tallahassee, FL 83
Florida State Museum, Gainesville, FL 78
Florissant Fossil Beds, Florissant, CO 54
Floyd County Historical Museum, Floydada, TX 445
Floyd County Historical Society Museum, Charles City, IA 133
Floyd County Historical Society, New Albany, IN 128
Floyd County Museum, New Albany, IN 128
Flushing Area Historical Society, Flushing, MI 215
Foam Lake Pioneer Museum, Foam Lake, Saskatchewan 564

Foard County Museum—McAdams Ranch, Crowell, TX 442

Folger Shakespeare Library, Washington, DC 73

Follett House Museum, Sandusky, OH 371

Folsom Historical Society—Wells Fargo Building Museum, Folsom, CA 28

Fondation de la Société Historique de Québec, Quebec, Quebec 560

Fontaine House, Memphis, TN 431

Fontana Historical Society Corporation, Fontana, CA 28

Foothill Electronics Museum—DeForest Memorial Library, Los Altos Hills, CA 31

Forest History Society, Durham, NC 343

Forest-Lambton Museum, Forest, Ontario 542

Forney Historical Society, Birmingham, AL 2

Forney Transportation Museum, Denver, CO 52

Fort Abraham Lincoln State Park, Mandan, ND 353

Fort Atkinson Historical Society—Hoard Historical Museum, Fort Atkinson, WI 496

Fort Beausejour National Historic Park, Aulac, New Brunswick 527

Fort Bend County Museum, Richmond, TX 455

Fort Benton Museum, Ft. Benton, MT 258

Fort Bliss Replica Museum, Fort Bliss, TX 445

Fort Bridger State Historic Site, Fort Bridger, WY 507

Fort Caroline National Memorial, Jacksonville, FL 79

Fort Carson Museum, Colorado Springs, CO 50

Fort Caspar Museum, Casper, WY 506

Fort Churchill Historic State Monument, Silver Springs, NV 269

Fort Collins Historical Society, Fort Collins, CO 54

Fort Collins Museum, Fort Collins, CO 54

Fort Concho Museum, San Angelo, TX 455

Fort Croghan Museum—Burnet County Heritage Society, Burnet, TX 440

Fort Crook Historical Society, Fall River Mills, CA 28

Fort Davis National Historic Site, Fort Davis, TX 445

Fort Delaware Museum of Colonial History, Narrowsburg, NY 321

Fort Delaware Society, Wilmington, DE 70

Fort Dodge Chapter, Iowa Society for Preservation of Historic Landmarks, Fort Dodge, IA 136

Fort Dodge Historical Foundation—Fort Museum, Fort Dodge, IA 136

Fort Douglas Military Museum, Fort Douglas, UT 462

Fort Edmonton Park, Edmonton, Alberta 513

Fort Edward Historical Association, Fort Edward, NY 312

Fort Erie Historical Museum, Ridgeway, Ontario 550

Fort Fetterman State Historic Site, Douglas, WY 507

Fort Fisher State Historic Site, Kure Beach, NC 346

Fort Frederica National Monument, St. Simons Island, GA 92

Fort Garry Historical Society, Winnipeg, Manitoba 526

Fort George G. Meade Museum, Fort Meade, MD 183

Fort George National Historic Park, Niagara on the Lake, Ontario 547

Fort Gibson Military Park, Fort Gibson, OK 377

Fort Gordon Museum, U.S. Army Signal Center, Fort Gordon, GA 88

Fort Hall Replica Commission, Pocatello, ID 98

Fort Hamilton Historical Society, Brooklyn, NY 305

Fort Hartsuff State Historical Park, Burwell, NE 261

Fort Hill: John C. Calhoun Mansion, Clemson, SC 416

Fort Hunter Mansion and Park, Harrisburg, PA 394

Fort Jackson Museum, Fort Jackson, SC 418

Fort Jefferson National Monument, Key West, FL 79

Fort Kent Historical Society, Fort Kent, ME 172

Fort King George Historic Site, Darien, GA 88

Fort Klock Historic Restoration, St. Johnsville, NY 332

Fort Knox, Prospect, ME 175

Fort Lancaster State Historic Site, Sheffield, TX 457

Fort Langley National Historic Park, Fort Langley, British Columbia 518

Fort Laramie Historical Association—Fort Laramie National Historic Site, Fort Laramie, WY 507

Fort Laramie National Historic Site, Fort Laramie, WY 507

Fort Larned National Historic Site, Larned, KS 147

Fort Lauderdale Historic Preservation Board, Fort Lauderdale, FL 77

Fort Lauderdale Historical Society, Inc., Fort Lauderdale, FL 77

Fort Leavenworth Historical Society, Fort Leavenworth, KS 145

Fort Leavenworth Museum, Fort Leavenworth, KS 145

Fort Leonard Wood Museum, Fort Leonard Wood, MO 245

Fort Ligonier Memorial Foundation, Ligonier, PA 397

Fort Loudon Historical Society, Fort Loudon, PA 392

Fort Macleod Historical Association, Fort Macleod, Alberta 514

Fort Malden National Historic Park, Amherstburg, Ontario 539

Fort Massac Historic Site, Metropolis, IL 111

Fort McHenry National Monument and Historic Shrine, Baltimore, MD 180

Fort McKavett State Historic Site, Fort McKavett, TX 445

Fort McMurray Oil Sands Interpretive Centre, Ft. McMurray, Alberta 514

Fort Meigs State Memorial, Perrysburg, OH 370

Fort Morgan Heritage Foundation and Museum, Fort Morgan, CO 54

Fort Morgan Museum, Gulf Shores, AL 5

Fort Museum, Fort Macleod, Alberta 514

Fort Myers Historical Museum, Fort Myers, FL 78

Fort Nashborough, Nashville, TN 433

Fort Necessity National Battlefield, Farmington, PA 392

Fort Nisqually Museum, Tacoma, WA 489

Fort Ontario State Historic Site, Oswego, NY 327

Fort Osage Historic Site and Museum, Sibley, MO 255

Fort Pembina Historical Society, Pembina, ND 353

Fort Pike State Commemorative Area, New Orleans, LA 166

Fort Plain Museum, Fort Plain, NY 312

Fort Point National Historic Site, San Francisco, CA 40

Fort Point and Army Museum Association, San Francisco, CA 40

Fort Polk Military Museum, Fort Polk, LA 164

Fort Pulaski National Monument, Tybee Island, GA 94

Fort Raleigh National Historic Site, Manteo, NC 346

Fort Roberdeau, Hollidaysburg, PA 395

Fort Saint James National Historic Park, Fort St. James, British Columbia 518

Fort Saint-Jean Baptiste, Natchitoches, LA 165

Fort Saint Joseph Historical Association, Niles, MI 221

Fort Sam Houston Military Museum, San Antonio, TX 455

Fort Saskatchewan Historical Society, Fort Saskatchewan, Alberta 514

Fort Scott National Historic Site, Fort Scott, KS 145

Fort Selden State Monument, Radium Springs, NM 298

Fort Sheridan Museum, Fort Sheridan, IL 107

Fort Sherman Museum, Coeur d'Alene, ID 97

Fort Smith Historical Society, Inc., Fort Smith, AR 18

Fort Smith National Historic Site, Fort Smith, AR 18

Fort Stanwix National Monument, Rome, NY 331

Fort Steele Historic Park, Ft. Steele, British Columbia 518

Fort Stephenson Museum, Fremont, OH 364

Fort Stewart Museum, 24th Infantry Division, Fort Stewart, GA 89

Fort Stockton Historical Society, Fort Stockton, TX 445

Fort Sumter National Monument, Sullivan's Island, SC 421

Fort Ticonderoga, Fort Ticonderoga, NY 312

Fort Towson Historic Site, Fort Towson, OK 377

Fort Union National Monument, Watrous, NM 300

Fort Union Trading Post National Historic Site, Williston, ND 354
Fort Vancouver Historical Society of Clark County, Vancouver, WA 490
Fort Vancouver National Historic Site, Vancouver, WA 490
Fort Verde State Historical Park, Camp Verde, AZ 11
Fort Walla Walla Museum Complex, Walla Walla, WA 491
Fort Walsh National Historic Park, Maple Creek, Saskatchewan 565
Fort Ward Museum and Park, Alexandria, VA 470
Fort Washita, Durant, OK 377
Fort Wellington National Historic Park, Prescott, Ontario 550
Fort Western Museum, Augusta, ME 169
Fort Whoop-Up Interpretative Society, Lethbridge, Alberta 515
Fort Worth Museum of Science and History, Fort Worth, TX 445
Fortress of Louisbourg National Historic Park, Louisbourg, Nova Scotia 536
Fortuna Depot Museum, Fortuna, CA 28
Forty-fifth Infantry Division Museum, Oklahoma City, OK 379
Foster County Historical Society, Carrington, ND 352
Foster Preservation Society, Foster, RI 409
Fosterfields Living Historic Farm, Morristown, NJ 286
Fostoria Area Historical Society and Museum, Fostoria, OH 364
Fostoria Mausoleum Association, Fostoria, OH 364
Foundation Historical Association, Inc., Auburn, NY 303
Foundation Robert Giguère, Inc., Montreal, Quebec 559
Foundation for Historic Christ Church, Inc., Irvington, VA 475
Foundation for Historic Restoration in the Pendleton Area, Pendleton, SC 421
Foundation for Historical Louisiana, Inc., Baton Rouge, LA 163
Foundation for Restoration of Ste. Genevieve, Ste. Genevieve, MO 253
Foundation for San Francisco's Architectural Heritage, San Francisco, CA 41
Fountain County Historical Society, Kingman, IN 126
Fountain Elms/Munson-Williams-Proctor Institute Museum of Art, Utica, NY 338
Four Mile Historic Park, Denver, CO 52
Four River Valleys Historical Society, Carthage, NY 307
Fox Island Historical Society, Fox Island, WA 484
Francestown Improvement and Historical Society, Francestown, NH 271
Francis Vigo Chapter, Daughters of the American Revolution, Vincennes, IN 130
Franco-American Genealogical Society of York County, Biddeford, ME 170
Franco-American Genealogical Association, Albany, NY 301
Franco-American Heritage Center, Auburn-Lewiston, ME 169
Franco-American Heritage Center of New Hampshire, Manchester, NH 273
Frank H. McClung Museum, Knoxville, TN 430
Frank House, The, Kearney, NE 264
Frank Lloyd Wright Home and Studio Foundation, Oak Park, IL 113
Frank Phillips Home, Bartlesville, OK 376
Frank Slide Interpretive Centre, Frank (Crow's Nest Pass), Alberta 514
Frankenmuth Historical Museum, Frankenmuth, MI 215
Frankfort Area Historical Society and Museum, West Frankfort, IL 119
Franklin Area Historical Society, Franklin, OH 364
Franklin County Genealogical Society, Columbus, OH 361

Franklin County Heritage, Chambersburg, PA 390
Franklin County Historical Society, Benton, IL 100
Franklin County Historical Society, Columbus, OH 361
Franklin County Historical Society, Franklin, NE 262
Franklin County Historical Society, Hampton, IA 137
Franklin County Historical Society, Inc., Ottawa, KS 150
Franklin County Historical Society, Pasco, WA 486
Franklin County Historical Society, Rocky Mount, VA 480
Franklin County Historical Society, Winchester, TN 436
Franklin County Historical and Museum Society, Malone, NY 319
Franklin D. Roosevelt Library, Hyde Park, NY 316
Franklin Historical Commission, Franklin, MA 195
Franklin Square Historical Society, Franklin Square, NY 312
Frankston Depot Library and Museum, Inc., Frankston, TX 446
Fraunces Tavern Museum, New York, NY 323
Fred Hart Williams Genealogical Society, Detroit, MI 213
Frederick City Historic District Commission, Frederick, MD 183
Frederick County Landmarks Foundation, Frederick, MD 183
Frederick Law Olmsted National Historic Site, Brookline, MA 191
Fredericksburg and Spotsylvania County National Military Park, Fredericksburg, VA 473
Fredericton National Exhibition Centre, Fredericton, New Brunswick 528
Free Library of Philadelphia, Philadelphia, PA 401
Free Meeting House, Moncton, New Brunswick 529
Free State of Winston Historical Society, Double Springs, AL 4
Freeborn County Genealogical Society, Albert Lea, MN 225
Freeport Historical Society, Freeport, ME 172
Freestone County Historical Museum, Fairfield, TX 444
Fremont County Museums System, Lander, WY 508
Fremont County Pioneer Museum, Lander, WY 508
Fremont Historical Society, Fremont, NH 271
French Legation Museum, Austin, TX 437
French Library in Boston, Inc., Boston, MA 189
French-Canadian Genealogical Society of Connecticut, Rocky Hill, CT 66
French-Canadian Heritage Society of Michigan, Lansing, MI 218
Frenchboro Historical Society, Frenchboro, ME 172
Frick Collection, The, New York, NY 323
Friends Historical Association, Haverford, PA 394
Friends Historical Library of Swarthmore College, Swarthmore, PA 406
Friends of Adair Cabin, Inc., Osawatomie, KS 149
Friends of Arrow Rock, Arrow Rock, MO 242
Friends of Barclay Farmstead, Cherry Hill, NJ 279
Friends of Cabildo, New Orleans, LA 166
Friends of Clermont, Inc., Germantown, NY 313
Friends of Deepwood, Salem, OR 386
Friends of Devonian Botanic Garden, Edmonton, Alberta 513
Friends of Florida, Florida, MO 245
Friends of Hildene, Inc., Manchester, VT 467
Friends of Historic Boonville, Inc., Boonville, MO 243
Friends of Historic Meridian, Okemos, MI 221
Friends of History in Fulton, NY, Inc., Fulton, NY 312
Friends of Independence National Historical Park, Philadelphia, PA 401
Friends of 'Iolani Palace, Honolulu, HI 95
Friends of Jesse James Farm, Kearney, MO 249
Friends of John Jay Homestead State Historic Site, Katonah, NY 317
Friends of Keytesville, Inc., Keytesville, MO 249
Friends of Missouri Town 1855, Blue Springs, MO 243
Friends of North Carolina Archaeology, Inc., Raleigh, NC 348

Friends of Olana, Hudson, NY 315
Friends of Old Fort Stevens, Hammond, OR 383
Friends of Rocheport, Rocheport, MO 252
Friends of Rodgers Tavern, Perryville, MD 184
Friends of St. Mary's City, St. Mary's City, MD 185
Friends of the Adobes, Inc., San Miguel, CA 43
Friends of the Archives, Inc., Raleigh, NC 348
Friends of the Blue Hills Trust, Milton, MA 199
Friends of the Citadel Society, Halifax, Nova Scotia 534
Friends of the College Park Airport, College Park,
  MD 182
Friends of the Fort Lewis Military Museum—Fort Lewis
  Military Museum, Fort Lewis, WA 484
Friends of The Grange, Havertown, PA 394
Friends of the Governor's Mansion, Austin, TX 437
Friends of the Hermitage, Inc., Ho-Ho-Kus, NJ 283
Friends of the Mansion of Smithville, Mt. Holly, NJ 287
Friends of the Middle Border Museum, Mitchell, SD 424
Friends of the Nyacks, Inc., Nyack, NY 326
Friends of the Thomas Leiper House, Wallingford,
  PA 407
Friends of West Point, Durham, NC 343
Friendship Hill Association, New Geneva, PA 399
Friendship Hill National Historic Site, Point Marion,
  PA 404
Friendship Museum, Inc., Friendship, ME 172
Frontier Historical Park, Hays, KS 146
Frontier Historical Society and Museum, Glendwood
  Springs, CO 54
Frontier Museum, Williston, ND 354
Frontier Times Museum, Bandera, TX 438
Fruitlands Museums, Inc., Harvard, MA 196
Fryer Memorial Museum, Munnsville, NY 321
Fryfogel Inn, Stratford, Ontario 551
Frymire Weather Service and Museum, Irvington,
  KY 157
Fulda Heritage Society, Fulda, MN 229
Fullerton Arboretum—Heritage House, Fullerton, CA 28
Fulton County Historical Society, Inc., McConnellsburg,
  PA 398
Fulton County Historical Society, Inc., Rochester, IN 129
Fulton County Historical and Genealogical Society,
  Canton, IL 101
Fulton Mansion State Historic Structure, Fulton, TX 446

G

G.A.R. Memorial Hall Museum, Madison, WI 499
GAR (Grand Army of the Republic Hall)—Meeker
  County Museum, Litchfield, MN 231
GATEway to the Panhandle, Gate, OK 377
GIRAM (Groupe d'Initiatives et de Recherche
  Appliqués au Milieu), Lauzon, Quebec 558
Gadsby's Tavern Museum, Alexandria, VA 470
Gage County Historical Society, Beatrice, NE 261
Gahanna Historical Society, Gahanna, OH 364
Galen Historical Society, Clyde, NY 308
Galena-Jo Daviess County Historical Society, Galena,
  IL 107
Galena Mining and Historical Museum Association, Inc.,
  Galena, KS 146
Galeria de los Artesanos, Las Vegas, NM 297
Galesburg Historical Society, Inc., Galesburg, IL 107
Galion Historical Society, Inc., Galion, OH 364
Gallatin County Historical Society—Pioneer Museum,
  Bozeman, MT 256
Gallatin County Historical Society, Ridgway, IL 114
Gallery at the Old Post Office, Dayton, OH 362
Gallier House Museum, New Orleans, LA 166
Galveston County Historical Museum, Galveston,
  TX 447
Gann Museum of Saline County, Benton, AR 17
Garden Center, Valdosta, GA 94

Garden City Historical Commission, Garden City,
  MI 215
Garden Club of Georgia, Inc., Athens, GA 85
Garden Grove Historical Society, Garden Grove, CA 28
Gardner Museum of Architecture and Design, Quincy,
  IL 114
Garfield County Historical Society, Burwell, NE 261
Garfield County Museum, Jordan, MT 258
Garfield Farm and Tavern Museum, LaFox, IL 109
Garfield Park Conservatory, Chicago, IL 103
Garibaldi-Meucci Museum, Staten Island, NY 335
Garland County Historical Society, Hot Springs, AR 18
Garrett Historical Society, Garrett, IN 123
Garst Museum, Greenville, OH 365
Garza Historical Museum, Post, TX 454
Gasconade County Historical Society, Hermann,
  MO 246
Gaston County Museum of Art and History, Dallas,
  NC 343
Gates County Historical Society, Gatesville, NC 345
Gay 90 Button and Doll Museum, Eureka Springs, AR 17
Gay-Kimball Public Library, Troy, NH 276
Geauga County Historical Society, Burton, OH 357
Gem Village Museum, Bayfield, CO 50
Gene Stratton Porter Historic Site—Gene Stratton Porter
  Society, Rome City, IN 129
Genealogical Association of Southwestern Michigan, St.
  Joseph, MI 223
Genealogical Forum of Portland, Portland, OR 385
Genealogical Library, Church of Jesus Christ of
  Latter-Day Saints, Salt Lake City, UT 463
Genealogical Research Society of New Orleans, New
  Orleans, LA 166
Genealogical Section, Le Club Calumet, Augusta,
  ME 169
Genealogical Society of Broward County, Inc., Fort
  Lauderdale, FL 78
Genealogical Society of Harlan, Harlan, KY 156
Genealogical Society of Iredell County, Statesville,
  NC 349
Genealogical Society of Okaloosa County, Inc., Ft.
  Walton Beach, FL 78
Genealogical Society of Old Tryon County, Inc., Forest
  City, NC 344
Genealogical Society of Pennsylvania, Philadelphia,
  PA 401
Genealogical Society of Washtenau County, Ann Arbor,
  MI 569
Genealogy Club of the Albuquerque Public Library,
  Albuquerque, NM 295
General Adam Stephen Memorial Association, Inc.,
  Martinsburg, WV 493
General D. L. McBride Museum, Roswell, NM 298
General Francis Marion Chapter, Sons of the American
  Revolution, Bennettsville, SC 413
General John H. Forney Historical Society, Inc.,
  Gadsden, AL 5
General John J. Pershing Boyhood Home State Historic
  Site, Laclede, MO 249
General Society of Mayflower Descendants, Plymouth,
  MA 202
Genesee Country Museum, Rochester, NY 330
Genesee County Historical and Museum Society, Flint,
  MI 215
Genesee Heritage Society, Genesee Depot, WI 496
Geneva Historical Society, Geneva, IL 107
Geneva Historical Society and Museum, Geneva,
  NY 313
Geographical Center Historical Society, Rugby, ND 354
Geology Museum, The, Golden, CO 54
George C. Marshall Research Foundation, Lexington,
  VA 475
George C. Ruhle Library, West Glacier, MT 260
George Gamble Library, Danbury, NH 270

George Johnston Museum, Teslin, Yukon Territory 568
George Mason University Oral History Program, Fairfax, VA 472
George Tate House, Portland, ME 175
George Washington Masonic National Memorial, Alexandria, VA 470
George Wyth House Museum, Cedar Falls, IA 133
Georgetown County Historical Society, Georgetown, SC 418
Georgetown Society, Inc., Georgetown, CO 54
Georgia Agrirama Development Authority—State Museum of Agriculture, Tifton, GA 93
Georgia Baptist Historical Society, Macon, GA 90
Georgia Department of Archives and History, Atlanta, GA 85
Georgia Endowment for the Humanities, Atlanta, GA 85
Georgia Historical Society, Georgia, VT 466
Georgia Salzburger Society, Savannah, GA 92
Georgia Southern Museum, Statesboro, GA 93
Georgia Trust for Historic Preservation, Inc., Atlanta, GA 85
Gerald R. Ford Library, Ann Arbor, MI 210
Gerald R. Ford Museum, Grand Rapids, MI 216
German Village Society, Columbus, OH 61
German-Canadian Historical Association, Inc., Montreal, Quebec 559
Germans from Russia Heritage Society, Bismarck, ND 352
Germantown Historical, Inc., Germantown, WI 497
Germantown Historical Society, Philadelphia, PA 401
Germantown Mennonite Corporation, Philadelphia, PA 401
Gettysburg National Military Park, Gettysburg, PA 393
Ghost Ranch Living Museum, Abiquiu, NM 294
Gibbon Heritage Center, Gibbon, NE 263
Gibbs Farm Museum, Falcon Heights, MN 229
Gibson House Museum—Gibson Society, Inc., Boston, MA 189
Gibson House, North York, Ontario 547
Gila County Historical Society, Globe, AZ 12
Gilbert Stuart Memorial, Inc., Saunderstown, RI 412
Giles County Historical Society, Pulaski, TN 435
Gilman Museum, Hellertown, PA 395
Gilroy Historical Museum, Gilroy, CA 29
Gilroy Historical Society, Gilroy, CA 29
Gilsum Historical Society, Gilsum, NH 271
Gimli Historical Museum, Gimli, Manitoba 524
Girard Historical Society, Girard, OH 364
Gladding International Sport Fishing Museum, South Otselic, NY 334
Glass Museum, The, Dunkirk, IN 122
Glebe House Museum, Woodbury, CT 69
Glen Cove Historical Society, Glen Cove, NY 313
Glen Ellyn Historical Society, Glen Ellyn, IL 108
Glen Lillin Historical Society, Glen Lillin, ND 353
Glen Ridge Historical Society, Glen Ridge, NJ 281
Glenbow Museum, Glenbow-Alberta Institute, Calgary, Alberta 511
Glencoe Historical Society, Glencoe, IL 107
Glendale Arizona Historical Society, Glendale, AZ 12
Glengarry Museum, Dunvegan, Ontario 542
Glenn H. Curtiss Museum of Local History, Hammondsport, NY 314
Glensheen, Duluth, MN 228
Glenview Area Historical Society, Glenview, IL 108
Glocester Heritage Society, Chepachet, RI 409
Gloucester County Cultural and Heritage Commission, Woodbury, NJ 294
Gloucester County Historical Society, Woodbury, NJ 294
Goffstown Historical Society, Goffstown, NH 271
Goingsnake District Heritage Association, Westville, OK 381
Golden Ball Tavern Trust, Weston, MA 208

Golden District Historical Society, Golden, British Columbia 518
Golden Spike National Historic Site, Brigham City, UT 461
Golden Valley County Historical Society, Beach, ND 351
Goldendale Observatory State Park and Interpretation Center, Goldendale, WA 484
Goldie Paley Design Center, Philadelphia, PA 401
Goochland County Museum and Historical Center, Goochland, VA 474
Good Earth Association, Inc.—Living Farm Museum of the Ozarks, Pocahontas, AR 21
Goodhue County Historical Society, Red Wing, MN 235
Goodnow Museum and Historical Site, Manhattan, KS 148
Goodridge Area Historical Society, Inc., Goodridge, MN 229
Goodyear World of Rubber Museum, Akron, OH 354
Goschenhoppen Historians, Inc., Green Lane, PA 393
Goshen Historical Society, Goshen, CT 60
Goshen Historical Society, Inc., Goshen, IN 124
Gothenburg Historical Society, Gothenburg, NE 263
Government House Historic Property, Regina, Saskatchewan 566
Governor Bent Museum and Gallery, Taos, NM 300
Governor General's Foot Guard Museum, Ottawa, Ontario 548
Governor Hogg Shrine State Historical Park, Quitman, TX 454
Governor Lurleen B. Wallace Museum, Montgomery, AL 7
Governor Oglesby Mansion, Inc., Decatur, IL 105
Governor Stephen Hopkins House, Providence, RI 411
Gowanda Area Historical Society, Gowanda, NY 313
Gowrie Historical Society, Gowrie, IA 136
Grace and Holy Trinity Cathedral, Kansas City, MO 248
Gradenhutten Historical Society, Gradenhutten, OH 364
Grady County Historical Society, Chickasha, OK 376
Graeme Park, Horsham, PA 395
Grafton Historical Museum Society, Inc., Grafton, VT 466
Grand Banks Schooner Museum Trust, Boothbay Harbor, ME 170
Grand Blanc Heritage Association, Grand Blanc, MI 215
Grand Canyon Natural History Association, Grand Canyon, AZ 12
Grand Coteau Heritage and Cultural Centre, Shaunavon, Saskatchewan 567
Grand County Historical Association, Hot Sulphur Springs, CO 55
Grand Falls Historical Society, Inc.,—Société Historique de Grand Sault, Inc., Grand Falls, New Brunswick 529
Grand Forks County Historical Society, Grand Forks, ND 353
Grand Gulf Military Monument Commission, Port Gibson, MS 242
Grand Lake Area Historical Society, Grand Lake, CO 55
Grand Ledge Area Historical Society, Grand Ledge, MI 216
Grand Meadow Heritage Center, Washta, IA 142
Grand Opera House, Wilmington, DE 70
Grand Prairie Historical Commission, Grand Prairie, TX 447
Grand Prairie Historical Society, Gillett, AR 18
Grand Rapids Historical Society, Grand Rapids, MI 216
Grand Rapids Public Museum, Grand Rapids, MI 216
Grand River Historical Society and Museum, Chillicothe, MO 244
Grand Saline Public Library, Grand Saline, TX 447
Grand Valley Cap "M" Baller's Muzzleloading Gun Club, Wyoming, MI 225
Grand Village of the Natchez Indians, Natchez, MS 241
Grande Prairie Pioneer Museum, Grande Prairie, Alberta 514

Granger Homestead Society, Canandaigua, NY 306
Granite Falls Historical Society, Granite Falls, WA 484
Grant Cottage, Wilton, NY 340
Grant County Archaeological Society, Silver City, NM 299
Grant County Historical Society, Carson, ND 352
Grant County Historical Society, Elbow Lake, MN 228
Grant County Historical Society, Hyannis, NE 263
Grant County Historical Society, Inc., Petersburg, WV 494
Grant County Historical Society, Williamstown, KY 163
Grant County Museum Guild, Sheridan, AR 21
Grant County Museum, Sheridan, AR 21
Grant County Museum, Ulysses, KS 152
Grant Encampment Museum, Encampment, WY 507
Grant-Kohrs Ranch National Historic Site, Deer Lodge, MT 257
Granville Ohio Historical Museum, Inc., Granville, OH 365
Granville Slate Museum, Granville, NY 313
Gratiot County Historical Society, Ithaca, MI 217
Graue Mill and Museum, Oak Brook, IL 112
Gravesend Historical Society, Gravesend, NY 314
Grayson County Frontier Village, Inc., Denison, TX 443
Grayson County Historical Society, Leitchfield, KY 157
Great Falls Historical Society, Great Falls, VA 474
Great Harvard Area Historical Society, Harvard, IL 108
Great Lakes Historical Society, Vermilion, OH 373
Great Lakes Maritime Institute, Belle Isle, MI 211
Great Lakes Naval and Maritime Museum, Chicago, IL 103
Great Miami River Corridor Committee, Troy, OH 373
Great Plains Zoo and Museum, Sioux Falls, SD 426
Great Smoky Mountains National Park, Gatlinburg, TN 429
Greater Astoria Historical Society, New York, NY 323
Greater Latrobe Historical Society, Latrobe, PA 397
Greater Middletown Preservation Trust, Inc., Middletown, CT 62
Greater Milford Historical Association, Milford, NY 320
Greater New Orleans Archivists, New Orleans, LA 166
Greater Portland Landmarks, Inc., Portland, ME 175
Greater West Bloomfield Historical Society, Orchard Lake, MI 221
Greater Woodinville Historical Society, Woodinville, WA 491
Greeley County Historical Society, Tribune, KS 152
Green Bay Packer Hall of Fame, Green Bay, WI 487
Green County Historical Society, Inc., Greensburg, KY 156
Green County Historical Society, Monroe, WI 501
Green Oak Township Historical Society—Gage Museum, Brighton, MI 211
Greenbrier Historical Society, Lewisburg, WV 493
Greene County Chapter, Ohio Genealogical Society, Xenia, OH 375
Greene County Historical and Genealogical Society, Carrollton, IL 101
Greene County Historical Society, Coxackie, NY 309
Greene County Historical Society, Eutau, AL 4
Greene County Historical Society, Greensboro, GA 89
Greene County Historical Society, Jefferson, IA 138
Greene County Historical Society, Pittsburgh, PA 403
Greene County Historical Society, Xenia, OH 375
Greenfield Historic Commission, Greenfield, MA 195
Greenfield Historical Society, Greenfield, WI 487
Greenland Historical Society, Greenland, NH 272
Greenlawn-Centerport Historical Association and Museum, Greenlawn, NY 314
Greensboro Historical Museum, Inc., Greensboro, NC 345
Greensboro Historical Society, Greensboro, VT 466
Greenville Chapter, South Carolina Genealogical Society, Greenville, SC 418

Greenville County Historic Preservation Commission, Greenville, SC 418
Greenville County Historical Society, Greenville, SC 418
Greenwich Village Society for Historic Preservation, New York, NY 323
Greenwood County Historical Society, Eureka, KS 145
Greenwood Museum, Greenwood, British Columbia 519
Greers Ferry Visitor Center, Heber Springs, AR 18
Gregg County Historical Museum, Longview, TX 451
Gregg County Historical and Genealogical Society, Longview, TX 451
Gregory County Historical Society, Inc., Burke, SD 422
Grenfell Community Museum, Grenfell, Saskatchewan 564
Grenville County Historical Society, Inc., Prescott, Ontario 550
Gresham Historical Society, Gresham, OR 383
Grey Towers National Historic Landmark, Milford, PA 398
Griffin Historical and Preservation Society, Griffin, GA 89
Griggstown Historical Society, Griggstown, NJ 281
Grimsby Museum, The, Grimsby, Ontario 543
Grindstone Bluff Museum, Shreveport, LA 168
Grinnell Historical Museum, Grinnell, IA 137
Grinter House Museum, Kansas City, KS 147
Grosse Ile Historical Society, Grosse Ile, MI 216
Groton Historical Society, Groton, VT 466
Grout Museum of History and Science, Waterloo, IA 142
Grove National Historic Landmark, Glenview, IL 108
Grover Cleveland Birthplace, Caldwell, NJ 278
Grundy County Historical Society, Grundy Center, IA 137
Grundy County Historical Society, Trenton, MO 255
Guadalupe Historic Foundation, Santa Fe, NM 298
Guard House and Barrack Room, Fredericton, New Brunswick 528
Guernsey County Historical Society, Cambridge, OH 357
Guernsey State Park Museum, Guernsey, WY 508
Guilford Courthouse National Military Park, Greensboro, NC 345
Guilford Historical Society, Brattleboro, VT 465
Guilford Township Historical Collection, Plainfield Public Library, Plainfield, IN 128
Gulf Branch Nature Center, Arlington, VA 471
Gulf Coast Chapter, National Railway Historical Society, Inc., Houston, TX 449
Gulf Islands National Seashore, Pensacola, FL 82
Gulluh Gyap, Charleston, SC 415
Gunn Historical Museum, Washington, CT 68
Gunston Hall, Lorton, VA 476
Guthrie County Genealogical Society, Jamaica, IA 138
Guthrie County Historical Society, Guthrie Center, IA 137
Guysborough Historical Society, Guysborough, Nova Scotia 534
Guyton Historical Society, Guyton, GA 89
Gwinnett County Historical Society, Inc., Lawrenceville, GA 90

H

H. Earl Clack Memorial Museum, Havre, MT 258
H.P. Robinson Life-Style Museum, Granville, OH 365
HEIRS (Harrow Early Immigrant Research Society), Harrow, Ontario 543
Hackettstown Historical Society, Hackettstown, NJ 282
Hackley Heritage Association, Inc., Muskegon, MI 220
Hadley Historical Society, Inc., Hadley, MA 196
Hager House, Hagerstown, MD 183
Hagerman Valley Historical Society, Hagerman, ID 97
Haggin Museum, Stockton, CA 46

Hagley Museum and Library, Wilmington, DE 70
Hale Farm and Vilage, Bath, OH 356
Hale Springs Hotel, Rogersville, TN 435
Hales Corners Historical Society, Hales Corners, WI 497
Half-Shire Historical Society, Richland, NY 330
Haliburton Highlands Museum, Haliburton, Ontario 543
Haliburton House, Windsor, Nova Scotia 538
Halifax Citadel National Historic Park, Halifax, Nova
    Scotia 535
Halifax-Dartmouth Branch, United Empire Loyalists'
    Association of Canada, Dartmouth, Nova Scotia 534
Hall County Historical Society, Inc., Grand Island,
    NE 263
Hall of Fame—National Historical Fire Foundation,
    Phoenix, AZ 14
Halton Region Museum, Milton, Ontario 546
Hamburg Historical Society, Hamburg, NY 314
Hamilton County Chapter, Ohio Genealogical Society,
    Cincinnati, OH 359
Hamilton County Historical Society, Noblesville, IN 128
Hamilton Grange National Memorial, New York, NY 323
Hamilton Historical Society, Hamilton, MA 196
Hamilton House Museum, Clifton, NJ 279
Hamilton Museum of Steam and Technology, Hamilton,
    Ontario 543
Hamlin Historical Society, Hamlin, NY 314
Hammond Castle Museum, Inc., Gloucester, MA 195
Hammond Historical Society, Hammond, IN 124
Hammond-Harwood House Association, Annapolis,
    MD 179
Hammonton Historical Society, Hammonton, NJ 282
Hampden Historical Society, Hampden, ME 172
Hampden-Booth Theatre Library, New York, NY 323
Hampton Antiquarian and Historical Society, Hampton,
    CT 61
Hampton Center for the Arts and Humanities, Hampton,
    VA 474
Hampton County Historical Society, Hampton, SC 419
Hampton Historical Society, Hampton, IL 108
Hampton Mariners Museum, Beaufort, NC 341
Hampton National Historic Site, Towson, MD 186
Hampton Plantation State Park, McClellanville, SC 420
Hampton Roads Naval Museum, Norfolk, VA 477
Hampton University Museum, Hampton, VA 474
Hanalei Museum, Hanalei, HI 95
Hanchett-Bartlett Museum—Beloit Historical Society,
    Beloit, WI 495
Hancock County Historical Society, Carthage, IL 102
Hancock County Historical Society, Greenfield, IN 124
Hancock County Historical Society, Hawesville, KY 156
Hancock Historical Museum Association, Findlay,
    OH 364
Hancock Shaker Village, Inc., Pittsfield, MA 202
Hanford Mills Museum, East Meredith, NY 310
Hanford Science Center, Richland, WA 487
Hannah Lindahl Children's Museum, Mishawaka, IN 127
Hanover Area Historical Society, Hanover, PA 393
Hanover County Historical Society, Ashland, VA 471
Hanover Historical Commission, Hanover, MA 196
Hanover Historical Society, Hanover, MA 196
Haralson County Historical Society, Inc., Buchanan,
    GA 87
Hardanger Fiddle Association of America, Granite Falls,
    MN 230
Hardin County Chapter, Ohio Genealogy Society,
    Kenton, OH 366
Hardin County Historical Society, Eldora, IA 136
Hardin County Historical Society, Elizabethtown, KY 154
Hardin County Historical Society, Savannah, TN 435
Hardyston Heritage Society, Hamburg, NJ 282
Harlingen Hospital Museum—Rio Grande Valley
    Museum, Harlingen, TX 448
Harmonie Associates, Inc., Ambridge, PA 387

Harmonist Historic and Memorial Association, Harmony,
    PA 394
Harold B. Lee Library, Brigham Young University,
    Provo, UT 463
Harold Warp Pioneer Village Foundation, Minden,
    NE 264
Harper County Genealogical Society, Harper, KS 146
Harpswell Historical Society, Harpswell, ME 172
Harrington Park Historical Society, Harrington Park,
    NJ 282
Harris County Genealogical Society, Pasadena, TX 454
Harris County Heritage Society, Houston, TX 449
Harrison County Historical Society, Bethany, MO 243
Harrison County Historical Society, Clarksburg, WV 492
Harrison Township Historical Society, Mullica Hill,
    NJ 287
Harrisonburg-Rockingham Historical Society,
    Harrisonburg, VA 474
Harriton House, Bryn Mawr, PA 389
Harrodsburg Historical Society, Harrodsburg, KY 156
Harry S. Truman Birthplace, Lamar, MO 249
Harry S. Truman Courtroom and Office, Independence,
    MO 246
Harry S. Truman Library, Independence, MO 247
Hart County Historical Society, Munfordville, KY 160
Hart County, Georgia Historical Society, Atlanta, GA 86
Hartland Historical Society, Inc., East Hartland, CT 59
Hartsville Museum, Hartsville, SC 419
Hartung's Automotive Museum, Glenview, IL 108
Harvard Historical Society, Harvard, MA 196
Harvey County Historical Society, Newton, KS 149
Harwinton Historical Society, Inc., Harwinton, CT 62
Harwood Foundation, Taos, NM 300
Haskell County Historical Society, Sublette, KS 151
Hastings Historical Society, Hastings-on-Hudson,
    NY 314
Hastings Museum, Hastings, NE 263
Hatton-Eielson Museum, Hatton, ND 353
Hauberg Indian Museum, Black Hawk State Park, Rock
    Island, IL 115
Haverford Township Historical Society, Havertown,
    PA 394
Hawaii Bottle Museum, Honolulu, HI 95
Hawaii Chinese History Center, Honolulu, HI 95
Hawaii State Archives, Honolulu, HI 95
Hawaii State Historic Preservation Office, Honolulu,
    HI 96
Hawaiian Historical Society, Honolulu, HI 95
Hawaiian Mission Children's Society, Honolulu, HI 95
Hawks Inn Historical Society, Inc., Delafield, WI 496
Hay Creek Valley Historical Association, Geigertown,
    PA 393
Hay House, Macon, GA 90
Haynes Memorial Library, Alexandria, NH 269
Hayward Area Historical Society, Hayward, CA 29
Hazelwood Historic House, Green Bay, WI 497
Hazelwood Historical Society, Hazelwood, MO 246
Hazen Preservation Society, Hazen, NV 268
Head Office, Bank of Montreal, Montreal, Quebec 559
Head-Smashed-In Buffalo Jump Interpretive Centre,
    Fort Macleod, Alberta 514
Headquarters Museum and Library, National Society of
    Colonial Dames, New York, NY 323
Headwater's Heritage Museum, Three Forks, MT 260
Healdton Oil Museum, Healdton, OK 377
Healy House—Dexter Cabin, Leadville, CO 55
Heard Natural Science Museum and Wildlife Sanctuary,
    Inc., McKinney, TX 452
Hearne Heritage League, Hearne, TX 448
Heavener Runestone Recreation Area, Heavener,
    OK 377
Hebron Historical and Arts Society, Hebron, ND 353
Hebron Preservation Society, Hebron, NY 314

Heiltsuk Cultural Education Centre, Waglisla, British Columbia 522
Helen Keller Property Board, Tuscumbia, AL 8
Helper Mining Museum-Archives, Helper, UT 462
Henderson County Genealogical and Historical Society, Henderson, KY 156
Henderson County Historical Society, Lexington, TN 431
Hendricks County Museum, Danville, IN 122
Hennepin County Historical Society Museum, Minneapolis, MN 233
Henniker Historical Society, Henniker, NH 272
Henry B. Plant Museum, Tampa, FL 84
Henry Blommel Historic Automotive Data Collection, Connersville, IN 121
Henry County Historical Society, Abbeville, AL 1
Henry County Historical Society, Cambridge, IL 101
Henry County Historical Society, Mt. Pleasant, IA 139
Henry County Historical Society, New Castle, IN 128
Henry E. Simonds Memorial Archival Center, Winchester, MA 209
Henry Ford Estate—Fair Lane, Dearborn, MI 213
Henry Morrison Flagler Museum—Whitehall Historic House Museum, Palm Beach, FL 81
Henry Phipps Ross and Sarah Juliette Ross Memorial Museum, St. Andrews, New Brunswick 530
Henry S. Lane Place, Crawfordsville, IN 122
Henry Whitfield State Historical Museum, Guilford, CT 61
Herbert Hoover National Historic Site, West Branch, IA 142
Herbert Hoover Presidential Library, West Branch, IA 142
Heritage Association of Antigonish, Antigonish, Nova Scotia 533
Heritage Association of El Dorado County, Inc., Placerville, CA 36
Heritage Branch, Whitehorse, Yukon 568
Heritage Canada, Ottawa, Ontario 548
Heritage Center of Lancaster County, Inc., Lancaster, PA 396
Heritage Center, Inc., Pine Ridge, SD 425
Heritage Conservation Branch, Ministry of Provincial Affairs, Victoria, British Columbia 522
Heritage Farmstead—Plano Heritage Association, Plano, TX 454
Heritage Foundation of Arizona, Tempe, AZ 15
Heritage Foundation of Franklin and Williamson County, Franklin, TN 429
Heritage Foundation of Oswego County, Oswego, NY 327
Heritage Genealogical Society, Neodesha, KS 149
Heritage Hall Museum, Dubois, ID 97
Heritage Hill Association, Grand Rapids, MI 216
Heritage Hill State Park, Green Bay, WI 497
Heritage House Museum, Orange, TX 453
Heritage League of Greater Kansas City, Kansas, City, MO 248
Heritage Museum of Kappa Kappa Gamma, Columbus, OH 361
Heritage Park Society, Calgary, Alberta 511
Heritage Park—Historical Society of Ft. McMurray, Ft. McMurray, Alberta 514
Heritage Park—Pinellas County Historical Museum, Largo, FL 80
Heritage Plantation of Sandwich, Sandwich, MA 204
Heritage Preservation Commission, Fergus Falls, MN 229
Heritage Preservation Commission, Red Wing, MN 235
Heritage Searchers Genealogical Society, Willmar, MN 238
Heritage Trust of Nova Scotia, Halifax, Nova Scotia 535
Heritage Winnipeg, Inc., Winnipeg, Manitoba 526

Heritage and Genealogical Society of Montgomery County, Fonda, NY 312
Herkimer County Historical Society, Herkimer, NY 314
Herkimer Home State Historic Site, Little Falls, NY 318
Hermitage: Plantation Home of President Andrew Jackson, Hermitage, TN 429
Hermitage, The, Ho-Ho-Kus, NJ 283
Herrett Museum, Twin Falls, ID 99
Hershey Museum of American Life, Hershey, PA 395
Hezekiah Alexander Homesite, Charlotte, NC 342
Hi-Desert Nature Museum and Association, Yucca Valley, CA 49
Hialeah John F. Kennedy Library, Hialeah, FL 78
Hibbing Historical Society, Hibbing, MN 230
Hickman County Historical Society, Clinton, KY 154
Hickman Library and Museum, Big Lake, TX 439
Hidalgo County Historical Commission, McAllen, TX 452
Hidalgo County Historical Society, Edinburg, TX 444
Hidalgo County Historical Museum, Edinburg, TX 444
Higgins Armory Museum, Worcester, MA 209
High Cliff Historical Society, Sherwood, WI 504
High Plains Heritage Society, Spearfish, SD 426
High Plains Historical Foundation, Inc., Clovis, NM 296
High Plains Historical Society, McCook, NE 264
High Point Historical Society, Inc., High Point, NC 345
High Point Museum, High Point, NC 346
Highland County Historical Society, Hillsboro, OH 365
Highland Park Historical Society, Highland Park, IL 108
Highlands Historical Society, Fort Washington, PA 392
Highline School District Museum at Sunnydale, Seattle, WA 487
Hightstown East Windsor Historical Society, Hightstown, NJ 283
Hill-Hold, Campbell Hall, NY 306
Hill-Stead Museum, Farmington, CT 60
Hillforest Historical Foundation, Inc., Aurora, IN 120
Hillsboro Area Historical Society, Inc., Hillsboro, WI 497
Hillsborough County Historical Commission, Tampa, FL 84
Hillsborough Historical Society, Inc.—Franklin Pierce Homestead, Hillsborough, NH 272
Hillsborough Historical Society, Hillsborough, NC 346
Hillsborough Township Historic Commission, Neshanic, NJ 287
Hillsdale County Historical Society, Hillsdale, MI 217
Hillside Historical Society, Hillside, NJ 283
Hilton Head Island Historical Society, Hilton Head Island, SC 419
Hinckley Fire Museum, Hinckley, MN 217
Hinckley Foundation, The, Ithaca, NY 316
Hinsdale Historical Society, Hinsdale, IL 108
Hiram Township Historical Society, Inc., Hiram, OH 365
Hiram Walker Historical Museum, Windsor, Ontario 555
Historic Albany Foundation, Inc., Albany, NY 301
Historic Alexandria Foundation, Alexandria, VA 470
Historic Anchorage, Inc., Anchorage, AK 9
Historic Anderson, Inc., Anderson, TX 437
Historic Annapolis, Inc., Annapolis, MD 179
Historic Augusta, Inc., Augusta, GA 86
Historic Bath State Historic Site, Bath, NC 341
Historic Beaufort Foundation, Beaufort, SC 413
Historic Belmont Association, Nashville, TN 433
Historic Bethabara Park, Winston-Salem, NC 351
Historic Bethlehem, Inc., Bethlehem, PA 388
Historic Blooming Grove Historical Society, Madison, WI 499
Historic Boston, Inc., Boston, MA 189
Historic Boulder, Inc., Boulder, CO 50
Historic Burke Foundation, Inc., Morganton, NC 347
Historic Burlington County Prison Museum Association, Mt. Holly, NJ 287
Historic Burras House Foundation, Inc., Jamesville, NC 346

Historic Charleston Foundation, Charleston, SC 415
Historic Charlton Park Village and Museum, Hastings, MI 216
Historic Chattahoochee Commission, Eufaula, AL 4
Historic Cherry Hill, Albany, NY 301
Historic Columbia Foundation, Columbia, SC 416
Historic Columbus Foundation, Inc., Columbus, GA 87
Historic Crab Orchard Museum and Pioneer Park, Inc., Tazewell, VA 481
Historic Deerfield, Inc., Deerfield, MA 194
Historic Denver, Inc., Denver, CO 52
Historic District Commission, Cape May, NJ 279
Historic District Commission, City of Annapolis, Annapolis, MD 179
Historic District Commission, Muskegon, MI 220
Historic Dumfries Virginia, Inc., Dumfries, VA 472
Historic Dunvegan, Dunvegan, Alberta 512
Historic Edenton, Edenton, NC 344
Historic Ellicott City, Inc., Ellicott City, MD 183
Historic Elsah Foundation, Elsah, IL 107
Historic Fallsington, Inc., Fallsington, PA 392
Historic Fayetteville Foundation, Inc., Fayetteville, NC 344
Historic Fincastle, Inc., Fincastle, VA 473
Historic Flat Rock, Inc., Flat Rock, NC 344
Historic Florida Militia, St. Augustine, FL 82
Historic Florissant, Inc., Florissant, MO 245
Historic Fort Wayne, Detroit, MI 213
Historic Fort York, Toronto, Ontario 552
Historic Fredericksburg Foundation, Inc., Fredericksburg, VA 474
Historic Ft. Wayne, Inc., Fort Wayne, IN 123
Historic General Dodge House, Council Bluffs, IA 134
Historic Gettysburg-Adams County, Inc., Gettysburg, PA 393
Historic Governors' Mansion, Cheyenne, WY 506
Historic Halifax State Historic Site, Halifax, NC 345
Historic Hamilton Commission, Inc., Hamilton, NC 345
Historic Hawaii Foundation, Honolulu, HI 96
Historic Hermann, Inc., Hermann, MO 246
Historic Hiram Market Preservation Association, New Brunswick, NJ 288
Historic Homes Foundation, Inc., Louisville, KY 158
Historic Hope Foundation, Inc., Windsor, NC 351
Historic Huntsville Foundation, Inc., Huntsville, AL 5
Historic Ithaca and Tompkins County, Inc., Ithaca, NY 316
Historic Jasper, Inc., Jasper, IN 125
Historic Jefferson College, Washington, MS 242
Historic Kansas City Foundation, Kansas City, MO 248
Historic Key West Preservation Board, Key West, FL 79
Historic Landmarks and Preservation Districts Commission, Louisville, KY 158
Historic Landmarks Foundation of Indiana, Indianapolis, IN 124
Historic Liberty Jail Visitor's Center, Liberty, MO 250
Historic Lyme Village Association, Bellevue, OH 356
Historic Madison, Inc., Madison, IN 126
Historic Medley District, Inc., Poolesville, MD 184
Historic Merriam, Merriam, KS 149
Historic Middletown, Inc., Middletown, KY 160
Historic Mobile Preservation Society, Mobile, AL 6
Historic Nashville, Inc., Nashville, TN 433
Historic Natchez Foundation, Natchez, MS 241
Historic Naval and Military Establishments, Penetanguishene, Ontario 549
Historic Neighborhoods Foundation, Boston, MA 189
Historic New Harmony, Inc., New Harmony, IN 128
Historic New Orleans Collection, New Orleans, LA 166
Historic New Richmond, New Richmond, OH 370
Historic Newton Home, Decatur, MI 213
Historic Occoquan, Inc., Occoquan, VA 478
Historic Palmyra, Inc., Palmyra, NY 328

Historic Paulus Hook Association, Inc., Jersey City, NJ 283
Historic Pensacola Preservation Board of Trustees, Pensacola, FL 82
Historic Perrysburg, Inc., Perrysburg, OH 70
Historic Pipestone, Inc., Pipestone, MN 234
Historic Pittsford, Pittsford, NY 328
Historic Preservation Alliance of Arkansas, Little Rock, AR 20
Historic Preservation Association of Bourbon County, Inc., Ft. Scott, KS 151
Historic Preservation Council for Tarrant County, Texas, Inc., Fort Worth, TX 445
Historic Preservation Division, Office of Cultural Affairs, Santa Fe, NM 299
Historic Preservation Foundation of North Carolina, Inc., Raleigh, NC 348
Historic Preservation Fund of Edgecombe County, Inc., Tarboro, NC 350
Historic Preservation League of Oregon, Portland, OR 385
Historic Preservation of Shreveport, Shreveport, LA 168
Historic Preservation Office, Department of Parks and Recreation, Pago Pago, American Samoa 509
Historic Preservation Office, Upper Savannah Council of Governments, Greenwood, SC 419
Historic Preservation Section, Department of Natural Resources, Atlanta, GA 86
Historic Preservation Society of Social Circle, Inc., Social Circle, GA 92
Historic Preservation Trust of Lancaster County, Lancaster, PA 396
Historic Pullman Foundation, Inc., Chicago, IL 103
Historic Red Clay Valley, Inc., Wilmington, DE 70
Historic Renville Preservation Commission, Renville, MN 235
Historic Resources Branch, Winnipeg, Manitoba 526
Historic Resources Commission of Asheville and Buncombe County, Asheville, NC 340
Historic Resources Management, History Department, Riverside, CA 37
Historic Resources Research, Parks Canada, Atlantic Region, Halifax, Nova Scotia 535
Historic Restoration Society of Annapolis County, Annapolis Royal, Nova Scotia 533
Historic Restoration Trust of Nutley, Nutley, NJ 288
Historic Richmond Foundation, Richmond, VA 479
Historic Richmond Hill Law School Commission, Boonville, NC 341
Historic Rugby, Inc., Rugby, TN 435
Historic Saint Augustine Preservation Board, St. Augustine, FL 82
Historic Saint Mary's City, St. Mary's City, MD 185
Historic Salem Inc., Salem, MA 204
Historic Salisbury Foundation, Inc., Salisbury, NC 349
Historic Saranac Lake, Saranac Lake, NY 332
Historic Shepherdstown Commission, Shepherdstown, WV 494
Historic Sites Advisory Board, Hackensack, NJ 282
Historic Sites Service, Edmonton, Alberta 513
Historic Southwest Ohio, Inc., Cincinnati, OH 359
Historic Speedwell, Morristown, NJ 286
Historic Tallahassee Preservation Board, Tallahassee, FL 83
Historic Topeka, Inc., Topeka, KS 151
Historic Towson, Inc., Towson, MD 186
Historic Vehicle Society of Ontario, Windsor, Ontario 555
Historic Waco Foundation, Waco, TX 459
Historic Wichita—Sedgwick County, Inc., Wichita, KS 152
Historic Willard Society, Willard, UT 464

Historic Wilmington Foundation, Inc., Wilmington, NC 350
Historic York, Inc., York, PA 408
Historical and Genealogical Association of Mississippi, Jackson, MS 240
Historical and Genealogical Society of Indiana County, Indiana, PA 395
Historical Architecture Development, Walla Walla, WA 491
Historical Archives and Museum, Catholic Diocese of El Paso, El Paso, TX 444
Historical Archives, Langworthy Public Library, Hope Valley, RI 409
Historical Association and Society of Lewiston, Lewiston, NY 318
Historical Association of Greater Cape Girardeau, Inc., Cape Girardeau, MO 244
Historical Association of Southern Florida, Miami, FL 80
Historical Association of Greater St. Louis, St. Louis, MO 254
Historical Center, Mennonite Churches, Richfield, PA 404
Historical Center, Nebraska Wesleyan University, Lincoln, NE 264
Historical Collection, North Texas State University, Denton, TX 443
Historical Collection, Saskatchewan Militia District Headquarters, Regina, Saskatchewan 566
Historical Collections, Bridgeport Public Library, Bridgeport, CT 58
Historical Commission of Metropolitan Nashville-Davidson County, Nashville, TN 433
Historical Confederation of Kentucky, Frankfort, KY 155
Historical Crossroads Village—Huckleberry Railroad, Flint, MI 215
Historical Dental Museum, Temple University, Philadelphia, PA 401
Historical Department, Church of Jesus Christ of Latter-day Saints, Salt Lake City, UT 463
Historical Division, Chief of Engineers, Department of the Army, Fort Belvoir, VA 473
Historical Farm Association—Quiet Valley Living Historical Farm, Stroudsburg, PA 406
Historical Foundation of the Cumberland Presbyterian Church, Memphis,TN 431
Historical Foundation of the Presbyterian and Reformed Churches, Montreat, NC 346
Historical Jonesboro, Inc., Jonesboro, GA 89
Historical Museum at Ft. Missoula, Missoula, MT 259
Historical Museum of the Darwin R. Barker Library, Fredonia, NY 312
Historical Office, Federal Bureau of Investigation, Washington, DC 73
Historical Office, Washington National Guard, Tacoma, WA 490
Historical Old Salem, Inc., Catonsville, MD 182
Historical Projects of Houston County, Texas, Inc., Crockett, TX 441
Historical Research Center, Houston Academy of Medicine, Houston, TX 449
Historical Research, Inc., Minneapolis, MN 233
Historical Room of Stockbridge Library, Stockbridge, MA 205
Historical Society Museum, Valparaiso, FL 84
Historical Society and Avon Park Museum, Avon Park, FL 76
Historical Society and Museum of Arlington Heights, Arlington Heights, IL 100
Historical Society of Alma-Bacon County, Alma, GA 84
Historical Society of Alberta, Calgary, Alberta 511
Historical Society of Alpine County, Markleeville, CA 32
Historical Society of Amherst, Amherst, NH 269

Historical Society of Battle Creek—Kimball House Museum, Battle Creek, MI 211
Historical Society of Berks County, Reading, PA 404
Historical Society of Bloomfield, Bloomfield, NJ 278
Historical Society of Bridgeport, Bridgeport, MI 211
Historical Society of Carroll County, Inc., Westminster, MD 186
Historical Society of Cecil County, Elkton, MD 183
Historical Society of Cheboygan County, Inc., Cheboygan, MI 212
Historical Society of Cheshire County, Keene, NH 272
Historical Society of Decatur County, Inc., Greensburg, IN 124
Historical Society of Delaware, Wilmington, DE 70
Historical Society of Early American Decoration, Inc., Albany, NY 301
Historical Society of Easton, Inc., Easton, CT 59
Historical Society of Fairfax County, Fairfax, VA 473
Historical Society of Florham Park, Florham Park, NJ 281
Historical Society of Fort Washington, Fort Washington, PA 392
Historical Society of Frederick County, Inc., Frederick, MD 183
Historical Society of Glastonbury, Glastonbury, CT 60
Historical Society of Greater Peotone, Peotone, IL 114
Historical Society of Greater Port Jefferson, Port Jefferson, NY 329
Historical Society of Greenfield, Greenfield, MA 196
Historical Society of Grand Rapids, Grand Rapids, OH 364
Historical Society of Greece, Rochester, NY 330
Historical Society of Harford County, Inc., Bel Air, MD 181
Historical Society of Hopkins County, Inc., Madisonville, KY 159
Historical Society of Kent County, Inc., Chestertown, MD 182
Historical Society of Little Canada, Little Canada, MN 231
Historical Society of Long Beach, Long Beach, CA 31
Historical Society of Martin County, Stuart, FL 83
Historical Society of Michigan, Ann Arbor, MI 210
Historical Society of Millersburg and Upper Paxton Township, Millersburg, PA 398
Historical Society of Monterey Park, Monterey Park, CA 34
Historical Society of Moorestown, Moorestown, NJ 286
Historical Society of Montgomery County, Hillsboro, IL 108
Historical Society of Montgomery County, Norristown, PA 400
Historical Society of Newburgh Bay and the Highlands, Newburgh, NY 321
Historical Society of New Mexico, Santa Fe, NM 298
Historical Society of North Carolina, Raleigh, NC 348
Historical Society of Oak Park and River Forest, Oak Park, IL 113
Historical Society of Old Newbury—Cushing House Museum, Newburyport, MA 200
Historical Society of Old Randolph, Randolph, NJ 290
Historical Society of Ottawa, Ottawa, Ontario 548
Historical Society of Palm Beach County, Palm Beach, FL 81
Historical Society of Pennsylvania, Philadelphia, PA 401
Historical Society of Perry County, Newport, PA 399
Historical Society of Pomona Valley, Pomona, CA 36
Historical Society of Pottawattamie County, Council Bluffs, IA 134
Historical Society of Porter County, Inc.—Old Jail Museum, Valparaiso, IN 130
Historical Society of Princeton, Princeton, NJ 290

Historical Society of Quaker Hill and Pawling, Inc., Pawling, NY 328
Historical Society of Quincy and Adams County, Quincy, IL 114
Historical Society of Riverton, Riverton, NJ 290
Historical Society of Rockland County, New City, NY 321
Historical Society of Saginaw County, Saginaw, MI 222
Historical Society of Saint Catharines, St. Catharines, Ontario 550
Historical Society of Saratoga Springs, Saratoga Springs, NY 332
Historical Society of Scotch Plains and Fanwood, Scotch Plains, NJ 291
Historical Society of Schuylkill County, Pottsville, PA 404
Historical Society of Seabrook, Seabrook, NH 275
Historical Society of Southern California, Los Angeles, CA 31
Historical Society of Stanton County, Pilger, NE 266
Historical Society of Talbot County, Inc., Easton, MD 182
Historical Society of the Bellmores, Bellmore, NY 304
Historical Society of the South Georgia Conference, The United Methodist Church, St. Simons Island, GA 92
Historical Society of the Reformed Church in America, New Brunswick, NJ 287
Historical Society of the Fort Hill Country, Mundelein, IL 112
Historical Society of the Upper Baraboo Valley, Valton, WI 505
Historical Society of the Westburys, Westbury, NY 339
Historical Society of the Town of Greenwich, Inc., Cos Cob, CT 59
Historical Society of the Town of Hampden, Inc., Hampden, MA 196
Historical Society of the Cocalico Valley, Ephrata, PA 392
Historical Society of the Gatineau, Old Chelsea, Quebec 560
Historical Society of the Merricks, Merrick, NY 320
Historical Society of the Tarrytowns, Tarrytown, NY 337
Historical Society of the Tonawandas, Inc., Tonawanda, NY 337
Historical Society of University City, St. Louis, MO 254
Historical Society of Walden and Wallkill Valley, Walden, NY 338
Historical Society of Wells and Ogunquit, Wells, ME 178
Historical Society of West Caldwell, West Caldwell, NJ 293
Historical Society of Western Pennsylvania, Pittsburgh, PA 403
Historical Society of Windham County, Newfane, VT 468
Historical Society of York County, Tokio, ND 354
Historical Society of York County, York, PA 408
Historical Village and Pioneer Museum at Shandro, Willingdon, Alberta 517
History and Heritage Committee, American Society of Civil Engineers, Pittsburgh, PA 403
History and Traditions Museum, San Antonio, TX 456
History Department, Mint Museum, Charlotte, NC 342
History House Association, Skowhegan, ME 176
History Resources, Portland, OR 385
History Section, U.S. Forest Service, Washington, DC 73
Hitchcock County Historical Society, Trenton, NE 266
Hobart Historical Society, Inc., Hobart, IN 124
Holbert Family Association, Rineyville, KY 162
Holden Historical Society, Holden, MA 196
Holiday Cruises, Inc.—S.S. Clipper, Chicago, IL 103
Holland Historical Society, Inc., Holland, VT 466
Holland Purchase Historical Society, Batavia, NY 303

Hollis Historical Society, Hollis, NH 272
Holmes County Chapter, Ohio Genealogical Society, Millersburg, OH 369
Holmes County Historical Society, Millersburg, OH 369
Holocaust Council of New Jersey Professors, Lawrenceville, NJ 284
Holt County Historical Society, O'Neill, NE 265
Holt-Atherton Pacific Center for Western Studies, Stockton, CA 46
Holy Trinity (Old Swedes) Church Foundation, Inc., Wilmington, DE 71
Holy Trinity Orthodox Seminary Museum, Jordanville, NY 317
Home Sweet Home Museum—John Howard Payne Boyhood Home, East Hampton, NY 310
Homeplace-1850, The, Golden Pond, KY 156
Homer Historical Society, Homer, IL 109
Homer Historical Society, Homer, MI 217
Homer Society of Natural History—Pratt Museum, Homer, AK 10
Homestead Museum, Biggar, Saskatchewan 563
Homestead National Monument, Beatrice, NE 261
Homeville Museum, Homer, NY 315
Honey Creek Preservation Group, New Providence, IA 140
Honorable John G. Diefenbaker Centre, Saskatoon, Saskatchewan 566
Hoosick Township Historical Society—Louis Miller Museum, Hoosick Falls, NY 315
Hoover Historical Center, North Canton, OH 70
Hoover-Minthorn House Museum, Newberg, OR 384
Hope Historical Society, Hope, NJ 283
Hope Lodge—Mather Mill, Fort Washington, PA 392
Hope Museum, Hope, British Columbia 519
Hope Sawmill, Peterborough, Ontario 549
Hopewell Township Historic Sites Committee, Titusville, NJ 292
Hopewell Valley Historical Society, Pennington, NJ 289
Hopewell Village National Historic Site, Elverson, PA 392
Hopkins County Genealogical Society, Inc., Madisonville, KY 160
Hopkins County Museum and Heritage Park, Sulphur Springs, TX 458
Hopkins Forest Farm Museum, Williamstown, MA 208
Hopkins Historical Society, Hopkins, MN 230
Hopkinsville-Christian County Pride, Inc., Hopkinsville, KY 157
Hopkinton Historical Association, Hopkinton, RI 409
Hopsewee Plantation, Georgetown, SC 418
Horatio Colony House Museum, Keene, NH 273
Horner Museum, Corvallis, OR 382
Horry County Historic Preservation Commission, North Myrtle Beach, SC 420
Horry County Historical Society, Conway, SC 417
Horseheads Cultural Center and Historical Society, Inc., Horseheads, NY 315
Horseshoe Bend National Military Park, Dadeville, AL 3
Hot Spring County Historical Society, Malvern, AR 20
Hot Spring County Museum—The Boyle House, Malvern, AR 20
Hot Springs County Museum and Cultural Center, Thermopolis, WY 509
Houghton County Historical Society, Lake Linden, MI 218
House in the Horseshoe, Sanford, NC 349
House of Roses—Senator Wilson Home, Deadwood, SD 423
House of Seven Gables, Salem, MA 204
Houston Antique Museum, Chattanooga, TN 428
Houston County Historical Commission, Crockett, TX 441

Houston County Museum, Crockett, TX 442
Houston County Sesquicentennial Committee, Crockett, TX 441
Houston Metropolitan Research Center, Houston Public Library, Houston, TX 449
Houston Museum of Natural Science, Houston, TX 449
Howard County Historical Society, Inc., Ellicott City, MD 183
Howard County Historical Society, Inc., Kokomo, IN 126
Howard Dittrick Museum of Historical Medicine, Cleveland, OH 360
Howell Living Historical Farm, Hopewell Township, NJ 283
Howland Center for Cultural Exchange, Beacon, NY 304
Hoyt Sherman Place, Des Moines, IA 135
Hubbardston Historical Society, Hubbardston, MA 197
Hubbardton Battlefield, Hubbardton, VT 467
Hubbell Trading Post National Historic Site, Ganado, AZ 12
Huck's Museum and Trading Post, Blanding, UT 461
Hudson Athens Lighthouse Preservation Committee, Inc., Hudson, NY 315
Hudson Heritage Association, Hudson, OH 365
Hudson Historical Commission, Hudson, MA 197
Hudson Historical Society, Hudson, MA 197
Hudson Historical Society, Inc., Hudson, NH 272
Hudson Library and Historical Society, Hudson, OH 365
Hudson-Mohawk Industrial Gateway, Troy, NY 337
Hudson River Museum, Yonkers, NY 340
Hudson River Sloop Clearwater, Inc., Poughkeepsie, NY 329
Hudson Valley Studies, Annandale-on-Hudson, NY 302
Huguenot Historical Society, New Paltz, NY 321
Huguenot Society of America, New York, NY 323
Huilihee Palace, Kailua-Kona, HI 95
Hulmeville Historical Society, Inc., Hulmeville, PA 395
Humanities Foundation, Institute, WV 493
Humboldt County Historical Association, Humboldt, IA 137
Humboldt County Historical Society, Eureka, CA 27
Humboldt and District Museum and Gallery, Humboldt, Saskatchewan 564
Hummelstown Area Historical Society, Hummelstown, PA 395
Hundred Oaks Castle, Winchester, TN 436
Hunter-Dawson Home State Historic Site, New Madrid, MO 251
Hunter Museum of Art, Chattanooga, TN 428
Hunterdon County Cultural and Heritage Commission, Flemington, NJ 281
Hunterdon County Historical Society, Flemington, NJ 281
Huntingdon County Historical Society, Huntingdon, PA 395
Huntington Corral of Westerners International, San Marino, CA 43
Huntington County Historical Society, Huntington, IN 124
Huntington Historical Society, Huntington, NY 316
Huntington Historical Society, Inc., Huntington, CT 62
Huntley Project Museum of Irrigated Agriculture, Osborn, MT 259
Huntsman Marine Laboratory, St. Andrews, New Brunswick 530
Hurley Historical Society, Hurley, SD 424
Huron City Museum, Port Austin, MI 222
Huron County Pioneer Museum, Goderich, Ontario 542
Huron Historic Gaol, Goderich, Ontario 543
Huron Indian Village, Midland, Ontario 546
Huronia Museum, Midland, Ontario 546
Hustisford Historical Society, Hustisford, WI 498
Hutchinson County Museum—Boom Town Revisited, Borger, TX 439
Huxford Genealogical Society, Inc., Homerville, GA 89

Hyde County Historical Society, Englehard, NC 344
Hyde Park Historical Society, Hyde Park, MA 197
Hyde Park Historical Society, Hyde Park, NY 316
Hyrum City Museum, Hyrum, UT 462

I

ICOM (International Council of Museums Committee of the AAM), Washington, DC 73
ICOM Museums—Musées Canada, Ottawa, Ontario 548
IHRC (Immigration History Research Center), St. Paul, MN 236
Ice House Museum, Cedar Falls, IA 133
Ida County Historical Society, Ida Grove, IA 137
Idaho State Historical Society, Boise, ID 96
Illiana Genealogical and Historical Society, Danville, IL 105
Illinois Bell's Oliver P. Parks Telephone Museum, Springfield, IL 116
Illinois Canal Society, Lockport, IL 110
Illinois Heritage Association, Champaign, IL 102
Illinois Historic Preservation Agency, Springfield, IL 116
Illinois Historical Survey, Urbana, IL 118
Illinois Labor History Society, Chicago, IL 103
Illinois Pioneer Heritage Center, Inc., Monticello, IL 111
Illinois Railway Museum, Union, IL 118
Illinois State Archives, Springfield, IL 116
Illinois State Genealogical Society, Lincoln, IL 110
Illinois State Historical Library, Springfield, IL 116
Illinois State Museum, Springfield, IL 116
Illinois Terminal Railroad Historical Society, East Peoria, IL 106
Ilwaco Heritage Foundation, Ilwaco, WA 484
Imperial Calcasieu Museum, Inc., Lake Charles, LA 165
Independence County Historical Society, Batesville, AR 17
Independence National Historical Park, Philadelphia, PA 402
Index Historical Society, Index, WA 484
Indian City USA, Inc., Anadarko, OK 376
Indian Hill Historical Museum Association, Cincinnati, OH 359
Indian Pueblo Cultural Center, Albuquerque, NM 295
Indian and Colonial Research Center, Old Mystic, CT 65
Indiana Committee for the Humanities, Indianapolis, IN 124
Indiana Division, Historic Preservation and Archaeology, Indianapolis, IN 124
Indiana Dunes National Lakeshore, Porter, IN 129
Indiana Historical Bureau, Indianapolis, IN 125
Indiana Historical Society, Indianapolis, IN 125
Indiana Jewish Historical Society, Ft. Wayne, IN 123
Indiana Junior Historical Society, Indianapolis, IN 125
Indiana State Library, Indianapolis, IN 125
Indiana State Museum and Memorials, Indianapolis, IN 125
Indiana Transportation Museum, Noblesville, IN 128
Indianapolis Historic Preservation Commission, Indianapolis, IN 125
Indianapolis Motor Speedway Hall of Fame Museum, Indianapolis, IN 125
Indianapolis Museum of Art, Indianapolis, IN 125
Ingleside Historical Society, Ingleside, TX 450
Inman Park Restoration, Inc., Atlanta, GA 86
Innisfail and District Historical Society, Innisfail, Alberta 515
Institut Canado-Americaine, Manchester, NH 273
Institut Québécois de Recherche Sur la Culture, Quebec, Quebec 560
Institut d'histoire de l'Amérique Française, Outremont, Quebec 560

Institut d'histoire et de Recherche sur L'Outaouais, Inc., Hull, Quebec 557
Institute for Southern Studies, Columbia, SC 416
Institute of American Indian Arts Museum, Santa Fe, NM 299
Institute of Early American History and Culture, Williamsburg, VA 481
Institute of Local History, Manchester Community College, Manchester, CT 62
Institute of Texan Cultures, San Antonio, TX 456
Interlaken Historical Society, Interlaken, NY 316
International Museum of Cultures, Dallas, TX 443
International Museum of Photography—George Eastman House, Rochester, NY 330
International Museum of Surgery and Hall of Fame, Chicago, IL 103
International Tennis Hall of Fame—Tennis Museum, Middletown, RI 410
Interpretation and Exhibits Branch, Texas Parks and Wildlife Department, Austin, TX 438
Ionia County Historical Society, Ionia, MI 217
Iosco County Historical Museum, East Tawas, MI 214
Iowa Archaeological Society, Iowa City, IA 137
Iowa Chapter, Victorian Society in America, Des Moines, IA 135
Iowa Humanities Board, Iowa City, IA 137
Iowa Postal History Society, Cedar Rapids, IA 133
Iowa Society for the Preservation of Historic Landmarks, Des Moines, IA 135
Iowa State Historical Department, Des Moines, IA 135
Iowa State Historical Department, Iowa City Research Center, Iowa City, IA 137
Ipswich Historical Society—Whipple House, Ipswich, MA 197
Irish American Cultural Institute, St. Paul, MN 236
Iron & Steel Museum of Alabama—Tannehill Historical State Park, McCalla, AL 6
Iron Bridge Historical Museum, Iron Bridge, Ontario 544
Iron County Historical Society, Cedar City, UT 461
Iron County Historical Society, Hurley, WI 498
Iron County Historical and Museum Society, Caspian, MI 212
Iron Range Historical Society, Gilbert, MN 229
Iron Range Interpretative Center—Iron Range Research Center, Chisholm, MN 227
Iron Work Farm in Acton, Inc., Acton, MA 187
Iroquois County Genealogical Society, Watseka, IL 118
Iroquois County Historical Society, Watseka, IL 118
Irvine Historical Society and Museum, Irvine, CA 29
Irving House Historic Centre—New Westminster Museum, New Westminster, British Columbia 520
Irvington Historical Society, Irvington, NJ 283
Isanti County Historical Society, Cambridge, MN 227
Ischua Valley Historical Society, Franklinville, NY 312
Island County Historical Society, Coupeville, WA 483
Isle Royale National Park, Houghton, MI 217
Isle a la Cache Museum, Romeoville, IL 115
Islesboro Historical Society, Islesboro, ME 172
Israel Crane House Museum, Montclair, NJ 285
Issaquah Historical Society, Issaquah, WA 484
Italian Cultural Center, Stone Park, IL 117
Itasca County Historical Society, Grand Rapids, MN 230
Itawamba Historical Society, Inc., Mantachie, MS 241
Ivan Franko Museum, Winnipeg, Manitoba 526
Izard County Historical Society, Dolph, AR 17

J

J. B. Cain Archives of Mississippi Methodism, Jackson, MS 240
J. D. Sandefer Oil Annex, Breckenridge, TX 439
J. U. and Florence B. Fields Museum, Haskell, TX 448

J. Walter Thompson Company Archives, New York, NY 323
J.F.D. Lanier State Memorial, Madison, IN 127
JFK Special Warfare Museum, Fort Bragg, NC 344
Jacinto Foundation, Inc., Corinth, MS 239
Jack Lynn Memorial Museum, Horsefly, British Columbia 519
Jackson Assembly, Inc., Jackson, LA 165
Jackson Civil War Roundtable, Inc., Jackson, MS 240
Jackson County Genealogical Society, Jackson, MI 217
Jackson County Historical Association, Scottsboro, AL 7
Jackson County Historical Society, Holton, KS 147
Jackson County Historical Society, Independence, MO 247
Jackson County Historical Society, Jefferson, GA 89
Jackson County Historical Society, Murphysboro, IL 112
Jackson County Historical Society, Ripley, WV 494
Jackson Heritage Preservation Society, Jackson, NJ 283
Jackson Hole Museum, Jackson, WY 508
Jackson Homestead, Newton, MA 201
Jackson Township Historical Society, Massillon, OH 368
Jackson's Mill State 4-H Camp, Weston, WV 494
Jackson-Washabaugh County Historical Society, Kadoka, SD 424
Jacksonville Area Genealogical and Historical Society, Jacksonville, IL 109
Jacksonville Historic Landmarks Commission, Jacksonville, FL 79
Jacksonville Museum of Arts and Sciences, Jacksonville, FL 79
Jacobsburg Historical Society, Nazareth, PA 399
Jacques Timothe Boucher Sieur de Montbrun French Heritage Society, Louisville, KY 159
James Anderson House Archaeological Exhibit, Williamsburg, VA 481
James Buchanan Foundation for the Preservation of Wheatland, Lancaster, PA 396
James Iredell House State Historic Site, Edenton, NC 344
James K. Polk Memorial Association, Columbia, TN 428
James K. Polk Memorial, Pineville, NC 348
James Madison Museum, Orange, VA 478
James Millikin Homestead, Inc., Decatur, IL 105
James Monroe Law Office/Museum and Memorial Library, Fredericksburg, VA 474
Jamesburg Historical Association, Jamesburg, NJ 283
Jamestown Historical Society, Jamestown, RI 409
Jamestown-Yorktown Foundation, Williamsburg, VA 482
Jamieson Museum, Moosomin, Saskatchewan 565
Jane Addams' Hull-House, Chicago, IL 103
January 12th 1888 Blizzard Club, Lincoln, NE 264
Jarrell Plantation Historic Site, Juliette, GA 89
Jasper County Genealogical Society, Newton, IA 140
Jasper County Historical Foundation, Inc., Monticello, GA 91
Jasper County Historical Society, Newton, IA 140
Jay Historical Society, Jay, ME 172
Jedediah Smith Society, Stockton, CA 46
Jeff Matthews Memorial Museum, Galex, VA 474
Jefferson County Genealogical Society, Inc., Oskaloosa, KS 150
Jefferson County Historical Association, Monticello, FL 80
Jefferson County Historical Association and Genealogical Library, Steubenville, OH 372
Jefferson County Historical Development Commission, Birmingham, AL 2
Jefferson County Historical Society, Inc., Madison, IN 126
Jefferson County Historical Society, Mt. Vernon, IL 112
Jefferson County Historical Society, Oskaloosa, KS 150
Jefferson County Historical Society, Pine Bluff, AR 21

Jefferson County Historical Society, Port Townsend, WA 486

Jefferson County Historical Society, Watertown, NY 339

Jefferson County Office of Historic Preservation and Archives, Louisville, KY 158

Jefferson Davis Association, Houston, TX 449

Jefferson Davis Monument Shrine, Fairview, KY 154

Jefferson Historical Restoration and Preservation Corporation, Jefferson, TX 450

Jefferson Historical Society and Museum, Jefferson, TX 450

Jefferson Historical Society, Jefferson, NH 272

Jefferson National Expansion Memorial, St. Louis, MO 254

Jefferson Township Historical Society, Oak Ridge, NJ 288

Jekyll Island Museum, Jekyll Island, GA 89

Jensen-Alvarado Ranch Historic Park, Riverside, CA 38

Jericho Historical Society, Jericho, VT 467

Jerome County Historical Society, Jerome, ID 97

Jerome Historical Society, Jerome, AZ 13

Jersey Shore Historical Society, Jersey Shore, PA 396

Jessamine Historical Society, Nicholasville, KY 161

Jesse Besser Museum, Alpena, MI 209

Jesse James Bank Museum, Liberty, MO 250

Jesse James Home—Pony Express Historical Association, Inc., St. Joseph, MO 253

Jewish Genealogical Society of Illinois, Niles, IL 112

Jewish Historical Society of Central Jersey, New Brunswick, NJ 288

Jewish Historical Society of Greater Washington, Washington, DC 73

Jewish Historical Society of Maryland, Inc.—Jewish Heritage Center, Baltimore, MD 180

Jewish Historical Society of New York, Inc., New York, NY 324

Jewish Historical Society of Western Canada, Inc., Winnipeg, Manitoba 526

Jim Thorpe Home, Yale, OK 382

Jimmie Rodgers Memorial Festival, Inc., Meridian, MS 241

Johannes Schwalm Historical Association, Inc., Lyndhurst, OH 367

John Bartram Association—Bartram's Garden, Philadelphia, PA 402

John Brown Historical Association of Illinois, Inc, Chicago, IL 103

John E. Conner Museum, Kingsville, TX 450

John F. Kennedy National Historic Site, Brookline, MA 191

John F. Kennedy Presidential Library, Boston, MA 189

John G. Neihardt Center, Bancroft, NE 261

John J. Audubon Memorial Museum, Henderson, KY 156

John M. Browning Memorial Museum, Rock Island, IL 115

John Mark Verdier House Museum, Beaufort, SC 413

John Muir National Historic Site, Martinez, CA 32

John Nance Garner Home and Museum, Uvalde, TX 459

John Pelham Historical Association, Robertsdale, AL 7

John Perkins House—Wilson Museum, Castine, ME 171

John R. Park Homestead, Harrow, Ontario 543

John Walter Historic Site, Edmonton, Alberta 513

John Wesley Powell Memorial Museum, Page, AZ 13

John Whitmer Historical Association, Lamoni, IA 138

John Wilson Townsend Room, University Library, Richmond, KY 161

Johnson County Historical Museum and Society, Franklin, IN 123

Johnson County Historical Museum, Shawnee, KS 150

Johnson County Historical Society, Coralville, IA 134

Johnson County Historical Society, Paintsville, KY 161

Johnson Hall State Historic Site, Johnstown, NY 317

Johnston County Genealogical & Historical Society, Tishomingo, OK 381

Johnston County Genealogical Society, Smithfield, NC 349

Johnstown Flood Museum Association, Johnstown, PA 396

Joint Collection, University of Missouri Western Historical Manuscript Collection—Columbia and State Historical Society of Missouri Manuscripts, Columbia, MO 244

Joint Collection, University of Missouri Western Historical Manuscript Collection—State Historical Society of Missouri Manuscripts, Rolla, MO 252

Joint Collection, Western Historical Manuscript Collection—State Historical Society of Missouri Manuscripts, St. Louis, MO 254

Jollyville-Pond Springs Historical Association, Austin, TX 438

Jones County Iowa Historical Society, Inc., Monticello, IA 139

Jones Gallery of Glass and Ceramics, Sebago, ME 176

Jonesborough Civic Trust, Jonesborough, TN 430

Joplin Historical Society, Joplin, MO 247

Jose Antonio Navarro State Historic Site, San Antonio, TX 456

Joseph A. Tallman Museum, Cherokee, IA 133

Joseph Brant Museum, Burlington, Ontario 541

Joseph Smith Historic Center, Nauvoo, IL 112

Joshua's Tract Conservation and Historic Trust, Willimantic, CT 68

Jourdan Bachman Pioneer Farm, Austin, TX 438

Judaica Museum of Temple Beth Israel, Phoenix, AZ 14

Judge Roy Bean Visitor Center, Langtry, TX 451

Julia Morgan Association, Santa Cruz, CA 44

Juliette Gordon Low Girl Scout National Center, Savannah, GA 92

Junction City Historical Society, Junction City, OR 384

Jurica Nature Museum, Lisle, IL 110

Jurnpa Mountains Cultural Center, Riverside, CA 38

K

K.A.M. Isaiah Israel Congregation, Chicago, IL 103

Kalamazoo County Historical Society, Kalamazoo, MI 218

Kalamazoo Public Museum, Kalamazoo, MI 218

Kalamazoo Valley Genealogical Society, Kalamazoo, MI 218

Kalkaska County Historical Society, Kalkaska, MI 218

Kamloops Museum Association, Kamloops, British Columbia 519

Kamloops Museum and Archives, Kamloops, British Columbia 519

Kanabec County Historical Society and Museum, Mora, MN 233

Kanawha Valley Historical and Preservation Society, Charleston, WV 492

Kandiyohi County Historical Society, Willmar, MN 238

Kankakee County Historical Society Museum, Kankakee, IL 109

Kansas All-Sports Hall of Fame, Lawrence, KS 148

Kansas City Branch, National Archives, Kansas City, MO 248

Kansas City Museum, Kansas City, MO 248

Kansas City Posse—The Westerners, Kansas City, MO 248

Kansas Collection, University of Kansas Libraries, Lawrence, KS 148
Kansas Genealogical Society, Dodge City, KS 144
Kansas Health Museum, Halstead, KS 146
Kansas Museum of History, Topeka, KS 151
Kansas Museums Associations, Topeka, KS 151
Kansas State Historical Society—Center for Historical Research, Topeka, KS 151
Kauai Museum Association, Ltd., Lihue, HI 95
Kauffman Museum, North Newton, KS 149
Kearny Cottage Historical Association, Perth Amboy, NJ 289
Kearny Cottage, The, Perth Amboy, NJ 289
Kearny County Historical Society, Lakin, KS 147
Kearny Museum, Kearny, NJ 284
Keeler Tavern Preservation Society, Ridgefield, CT 65
Keillor House Museum, College Bridge, New Brunswick 528
Kelton House, Columbus, OH 361
Kempf House Center for Local History, Ann Arbor, MI 210
Kendall County Historical Society, Yorkville, IL 120
Kendall Whaling Museum, Sharon, MA 204
Kenilworth Historical Society, Kenilworth, IL 109
Kenmore Association, Inc., Fredericksburg, VA 474
Kennebunkport Historical Society, Kennebunkport, ME 172
Kennedy-Douglass, Florence, AL 4
Kennesaw Mountain National Battlefield Park, Marietta, GA 90
Keno Mining Museum, Keno Hill, Yukon 568
Kenosha County Historical Society, Kenosha, WI 498
Kensington Historical Society, Kensington, NH 273
Kensington Runestone Museum, Alexandria, MN 225
Kent County Council for Historic Preservation, Grand Rapids, MI 216
Kent County Genealogical and Historical Society, Jayton, TX 450
Kent Plantation House, Inc., Alexandria, LA 163
Kent State University Archives, Kent, OH 366
Kent-Delord House Museum, Plattsburgh, NY 328
Kenton County Historical Society, Covington, KY 154
Kenton County Public Library, Covington, KY 154
Kentucky Association of Museums, Covington, KY 154
Kentucky Association of Teachers of History, Georgetown, KY 156
Kentucky Baptist Historical Commission—Kentucky Baptist Historical Society, Middletown, KY 160
Kentucky Covered Bridge Association, Fort Thomas, KY 155
Kentucky Derby Museum Corporation, Louisville, KY 159
Kentucky Genealogical Society, Frankfort, KY 155
Kentucky Heritage Council, Frankfort, KY 155
Kentucky Heritage Quilt Society, Lexington, KY 157
Kentucky Historical Society, Frankfort, KY 155
Kentucky Horse Park, Lexington, KY 157
Kentucky Humanities Council, Lexington, KY 157
Kentucky Military History Museum, Frankfort, KY 155
Kentucky Museum and Library, Bowling Green, KY 153
Kentucky Oral History Commission, Frankfort, KY 155
Kentucky Railway Museum, Louisville, KY 159
Kentucky Room, Owensboro-Daviess County Public Library, Owensboro, KY 161
Keokuk Museum Commission, Keokuk, IA 138
Kern County Museum, Bakersfield, CA 23
Kern-Antelope Historical Society, Lancaster, CA 30
Kershaw County Historical Society, Camden, SC 414
Kewanee Historical Society, Inc., Kewanee, IL 109
Kewaskum Historical Society, Inc., Kewaskum, WI 498
Kewaunee County Historical Society, Kewaunee, WI 498

Keweenaw County Historical Society, Eagle Harbor, MI 214
Key City Genealogical Society, Dubuque, IA 135
Key West Art and Historical Society, Key West, FL 79
Keyport Historical Society, Keyport, NJ 284
Keystone Area Historical Society, Keystone, SD 424
Keystone Pioneer Museum, Roblin, Manitoba 524
Kilby Provincial Historic Park, Harrison Mills, British Columbia 519
Kindersley Plains Museum, Kindersley, Saskatchewan 564
King County Office of Historic Preservation, Seattle, WA 487
King Seaman School Museum, Minudie, Nova Scotia 537
King William Association, San Antonio, TX 456
King and Queen County Historical Society, King & Queen, VA 475
Kingdome Sports Museum, Seattle, WA 487
Kingman County Historical Museum, Kingman, KS 147
Kingman Museum of Natural History—Leila Arboretum, Battle Creek, MI 211
Kings County Historical and Archival Society, Inc., Hampton, New Brunswick 529
Kings Landing Corporation—Kings Landing Historical Settlement, Prince William, Fredericton, New Brunswick 528
Kings Mountain National Military Park, Blacksburg, SC 414
Kingston Improvement and Historical Society, Inc., Kingston, NH 273
Kirtland Temple Historic Center, Kirtland, OH 366
Kishwaukee Valley Heritage Society, Genoa, IL 107
Kit Carson Memorial Foundation, Inc., Taos, NM 300
Kit Carson Museum and Historical Society, Las Animas, CO 55
Kitimat Centennial Museum Association, Kitimat, British Columbia 519
Kitsap County Historical Society, Silverdale, WA 489
Kittery Historical and Naval Museum, Kittery, ME 173
Kittitas County Museum, Ellensburg, WA 483
Kittochtinny Historical Society, Chambersburg, PA 390
Kittson County Historical Society, Lake Bronson, MN 231
Klamath County Museum Complex, Klamath Falls, OR 384
Klamath National Forest, Yreka, CA 49
Klein Foundation Inc., Mobridge, SD 425
Klondike Gold Rush National Historical Park, Seattle, WA 487
Klondike National Historic Sites, Dawson City, Yukon 568
Kluane Museum of Natural History, Burwash Landing, Yukon 568
Knife River Indian Villages National Historic Site, Stanton, ND 354
Knights of Columbus Charities, Inc., New Haven, CT 63
Knights of Columbus Headquarters Museum, New Haven, CT 63
Knox County Historical Society, Barbourville, KY 153
Knox County Historical Society, Edina, MO 245
Knoxville-Knox County Archives, Knoxville, TN 430
Kodiak Historical Society, Kodiak, AK 10
Kona Historical Society, Kona, HI 95
Koochiching County Historical Society, International Falls, MN 230
Kootenay Museum Association and Historical Society—Nelson Museum, Nelson, British Columbia 520
Koshare Indian Museum, Inc., La Junta, CO 55
Kutztown Area Historical Society, Kutztown, PA 398

L

L'Anguille Valley Historical Association, Logansport, IN 126
L'Enfant Trust, The, Washington, DC 73
L'Institut Canadien de Quebec, Quebec, Quebec 560
L'Univers du Rail, Inc., Charny, Quebec 556
L. C. Bates Museum, Hinckley, ME 172
LSU Rural Life Museum, Baton Rouge, LA 164
La Crosse County Historical Society, Inc., La Crosse, WI 498
La Fourche Heritage Society, Thibodaux, LA 168
La Grange Area Historical Society, La Grange, IL 109
La Grange County Historical Society, Inc., La Grange, IN 126
La Have Islands Marine Museum, Bell's Island, Nova Scotia 533
La Jolla Historical Society, La Jolla, CA 30
La Mesa Historical Society, Inc., La Mesa, CA 30
La Paz Museum—Zapata County Historical Commission, San Ygnacio, TX 457
La Porte County Historical Society, La Porte, IN 126
La Puente Valley Historical Society, Inc., La Puente, CA 30
La Salle County Historical Society, Utica, IL 118
LaGuardia Archives, LaGuardia Community College, Long Island City, NY 319
Labor Archives and Research Center, San Francisco, CA 41
Lac qui Parle County Historical Society, Madison, MN 231
Lac Ste. Anne and District Pioneer Museum, Sangudo, Alberta 516
Lackawanna Historical Society, Scranton, PA 405
Laconia Historical Society, Laconia, NH 273
Lafayette County Genealogy Workshop, Inc., Shullsburg, WI 504
Lafayette County Historical Society, Darington, WI 496
Lafayette County Historical Society, Lewisville, AR 19
Lafayette Historical Society, Lafayette, CA 30
Lafayette Museum, Lafayette, LA 165
Lafayette Natural History Museum, Planetarium and Nature Station, Lafayette, LA 165
Lahaina Restoration Foundation, Lahaina, HI 95
Laird Norton Company Archives, Seattle, WA 487
Lajitas Museum and Desert Garden, Terlingua-Lajitas, TX 458
Lake Chelan Historical Society, Chelan, WA 483
Lake County Civic Center Association, Inc., Leadville, CO 55
Lake County Genealogical Society, Libertyville, IL 110
Lake County Genealogical Society, Painesville, OH 370
Lake County Historical Society, Lakeport, CA 30
Lake County Historical Society, Mentor, OH 368
Lake County Historical Society, Tavares, FL 84
Lake County Historical Society and Railroad Museum, Two Harbors, MN 237
Lake County Museum—Lake County Museum Association, Wauconda, IL 119
Lake County Parks and Recreation Department, Crown Point, IN 122
Lake Jackson Historical Association, Lake Jackson, TX 450
Lake Michigan Maritime Museum, South Haven, MI 223
Lake Odessa Area Historical Society, Lake Odessa, MI 218
Lake Shore Railway Historical Society, Inc., North East, PA 400
Lake Superior Museum of Transportation, Duluth, MN 228
Lake Wales Museum and Cultural Center, Lake Wales, FL 80

Lake of the Woods Historical Society, Baudette, MN 226
Lake of the Woods Museum, Kenora, Ontario 544
Lakeside Heritage Club, Inc., Lakeside, OH 366
Lakeside Museum, Bulyea, Saskatchewan 564
Lakewood Historical Society, Lakewood, CO 55
Lakewood Historical Society, Lakewood, OH 366
Lambton County Historical Society, Sarnia, Ontario 551
Lambton Heritage Museum, Grand Bend, Ontario 543
Lamesa-Dawson County Museum, Lamesa, TX 451
Lancaster County Historical Commission, Lancaster, SC 419
Lancaster County Historical Society, Lancaster, PA 397
Lancaster County Society for Historic Preservation, Inc., Lancaster, SC 419
Lancaster Historical Commission, Lancaster, MA 197
Lancaster Historical Society, Lancaster, NY 318
Lancaster League of Historical Societies, Leominster, MA 197
Lancaster Mennonite Historical Society, Lancaster, PA 397
Landmark Association of Bowling Green and Warren County, Inc., Bowling Green, KY 153
Landmark Center, St. Paul, MN 236
Landmark Commission, Township of Hanover, Whippany, NJ 294
Landmark Park, Dothan, AL 4
Landmark Society of Western New York, Inc., Rochester, NY 331
Landmark and Historical Society of Mt. Vernon, Mt. Vernon, NY 321
Landmarks Commission for Historic Preservation, Trenton, NJ 292
Landmarks Commission of Kansas City, Kansas City, MO 248
Landmarks Committee, Mountain Lakes, NJ 286
Landmarks Foundation—Old North Hull Historic District, Montgomery, AL 7
Landmarks Preservation Commission of Baltimore County, Towson, MD 186
Landmarks Preservation Council of Illinois, Chicago, IL 103
Landmarks Preservation Society of Southeast, Brewster, NY 305
Landmarks of DeKalb County, Inc., Fort Payne, AL 5
Lanesboro Historical Preservation Association, Lanesboro, MN 231
Langley Centennial Museum and National Exhibition Centre, Ft. Langley, British Columbia 518
Lanier Museum of Natural History, Buford, GA 87
Lansdowne Historical Society, Inc., Baltimore, MD 181
Lansing Historical Society, Lansing, IL 109
Lapham-Patterson House, Thomasville, GA 93
Laramie Plains Museum Association, Laramie, WY 508
Larchmont Historical Society, Larchmont, NY 318
Largo Area Historical Society, Largo, FL 80
Las Vegas Rough Rider and City Museum, Las Vegas, NM 297
Las Vegas—San Miguel Chamber of Commerce, Las Vegas, NM 297
Las Virgenes Historical Society, Agoura, CA 22
Lasalle Art-Historical Association, Trout, LA 168
Lassen County Historical Society, Susanville, CA 46
Latah County Historical Society, Inc., Moscow, ID 98
Laura Ingalls Wilder Memorial Society, Inc., De Smet, SD 423
Laura Ingalls Wilder Memorial Society, Inc., Pepin, WI 502
Laura Ingalls Wilder Museum and Tourist Information Center, Walnut Grove, MN 238
Laura Ingalls Wilder Park and Museum, Burr Oak, IA 132
Laurel County Historical Society, London, KY 158

Laurens County Historical Society, Inc., Dublin, GA 88
Laurens County Historical Society, Laurens, SC 420
Lauriano Cordova Memorial Museum, Vadito, NM 300
Laurier House, Ottawa, Ontario 548
Lava Beds National Monument, Tulelake, CA 47
Lawrence County Historical Society, Deadwood,
	SD 423
Lawrence County Historical Society, Ironton, OH 365
Lawrence County Historical Society, Lawrenceville,
	IL 109
Lawrence County Historical Society, Powhatan, AR 21
Lawrence County Regional Historical Society, Martha,
	KY 160
Lawrence Historical Society, Lawrenceville, NJ 284
Lawrence Sullivan Ross, United Daughters of
	Confederacy, Bryan, TX 440
Lawton Heritage Association, Lawton, OK 378
Lawton Public Library, Lawton, OK 378
Layland Museum, Cleburne, TX 441
Le Musée Sainte-Marie, Church-Point, Nova Scotia 534
Le Roy Historical Society, Le Roy, NY 318
Le Sueur County Historical Society and Museum,
	Elysian, MN 229
LeRoy Heritage Association, LeRoy Township, OH 366
LeSueur Historians, LeSueur, MN 231
Lea County Cowboy Hall of Fame, Hobbs, NM 297
Leadville Historical Association, Leadville, CO 56
Leavenworth Afro-American Historical Society, Ft.
	Leavenworth, KS 145
Leavenworth County Genealogical Society,
	Leavenworth, KS 148
Lebanon County Historical Society, Lebanon, PA 397
Lebanon Historical Society, Lebanon, IL 109
Lebanon Historical Society, Lebanon, ME 173
Lee Chapel, Lexington, VA 476
Lee County Historical Society, Keokuk, IA 138
Lee County Historical Society, Loachapoka, AL 6
Lee Historical Society, Durham, NH 271
Leelanau Historical Society, Inc., Leland, MI 219
Legislative Library, Winnipeg, Manitoba 526
Lehigh County Historical Society, Allentown, PA 386
Leisure World Historical Society of Laguna Hills, Inc.,
	Laguna Hills, CA 30
Leland Case Library, Spearfish, SD 426
Lenawee County Historical Society, Inc., Adrian, MI 209
Lennox and Addington County Museum, Napanee,
	Ontario 546
Lennox and Addington Historical Society, Napanee,
	Ontario 546
Lennox Area Historical Society, Lennox, SD 424
Lennoxville Ascot Historical and Museum Society,
	Lennoxville, Quebec 558
Lenoir Museum—Norris Dam State Park, Norris, TN 435
Lenox Historical Society, Inc., Jefferson, OH 366
Leominster Historical Commission, Leominster, MA 197
Leslie County Historical Society, Hyden, KY 157
Letchworth State Park Pioneer and Indian Museum,
	Castile, NY 307
Levi Coffin House Association, Fountain City, IN 123
Lewis County Historical Museum, Chehalis, WA 483
Lewis County Historical Society, Canton, MO 244
Lewis County Historical Society, Chehalis, WA 483
Lewis County Historical Society, Lyons Falls, NY 319
Lewis Research Center—National Aeronautics and
	Space Administration, Cleveland, OH 360
Lewis and Clark Interpretive Center, Fort Canby State
	Park, Ilwaco, WA 484
Lewiston Historical Commission, Lewiston, ME 173
Lexington Cemetery Company, Inc., Lexington, KY 157
Lexington County Historical Society, Lexington, SC 420
Lexington County Museum, Lexington, SC 420
Lexington Historical Society, Lexington, MA 197

Liberty Bell Shrine of Allentown, Inc., Allentown, PA 387
Liberty County Museum Association, Chester, MT 256
Liberty Hall Historic Center, Lamoni, IA 138
Liberty Hall—Orlando Brown House, Frankfort, KY 155
Liberty Memorial Association and Museum, Kansas
	City, MO 248
Libertyville-Mundelein Historical Society, Inc.,
	Libertyville, IL 110
Library Company of Philadelphia, Philadelphia, PA 402
Library and Archives Department, Kentucky Public
	Records Division, Frankfort, KY 155
Library of Michigan, Lansing, MI 218
Library, New Hampshire Votech College, Berlin, NH 269
Licking County Genealogical Society, Newark, OH 369
Lightner Museum, St. Augustine, FL 82
Ligonier Valley Historical Society—Compass Inn
	Museum, Ligonier, PA 397
Lillooet Museum, Lillooet, British Columbia 519
Lima Historical Society, Lima, NY 318
Limaville Historical Society, Inc., Limaville, OH 367
Limberlost State Historic Site, Geneva, IN 123
Limestone Chapter, Daughters of the American
	Revolution, Washington, KY 162
Limestone County Archives, Athens, AL 1
Limestone County Historical Society, Athens, AL 1
Lincoln Boyhood National Memorial, Lincoln City, IN 126
Lincoln County Cultural and Historical Association,
	Wicasset, ME 178
Lincoln County Heritage Trust, Lincoln, NM 297
Lincoln County Historical Society, Fayetteville, TN 429
Lincoln County Historical Society, Lincoln, KS 148
Lincoln County Historical Society—Lincoln County
	Museum, Hugo, CO 55
Lincoln Group of Boston, Hope Valley, RI 409
Lincoln Homestead State Park, Springfield, KY 162
Lincoln Log Cabin State Historic Site, Lerna, IL 109
Lincoln Memorial Shrine, Redlands, CA 37
Lincoln Parish Museum and Historical Society, Ruston,
	LA 167
Lincoln Park Conservatory, Chicago, IL 104
Lincoln Tomb State Historic Site, Springfield, IL 117
Lincoln's New Salem State Park, Petersburg, IL 114
Lincolnville Historical Society and Mini-Museum,
	Lincolnville, ME 173
Lindbergh Historic Site—Lindbergh State Park, Little
	Falls, MN 231
Linden Mills Historical Society, Linden, MI 219
Lindenhurst Historical Society, Lindenhurst, NY 318
Linn County Historical Society, Halsey, OR 383
Linn County Historical Society, Pleasanton, KS 150
Linn County Museum, Brownsville, OR 382
Litchfield Historical Society, Litchfield, CT 62
Lititz Historical Foundation, Inc., Lititz, PA 397
Little Beaver Historical Society, Inc., Darlington, PA 391
Little Beaver Museum, Darlington, PA 391
Little Compton Historical Society, Little Compton, RI 410
Little Falls Historical Society, Little Falls, NY 318
Little Falls Township Historical Society, Little Falls,
	NJ 284
Little Gallery Committee, Prince Albert,
	Saskatchewan 565
Little Landers Historical Society, Tujunga, CA 47
Little Nine Partners Historical Society, Pine Plains,
	NY 328
Little Norway, Inc., Blue Mounds, WI 495
Little Red Schoolhouse Museum, Denison, IA 134
Little Red Schoolhouse Museum, Farmington, ME 172
Little School Museum, Lockeport, Nova Scotia 536
Little Silver Historical Society, Little Silver, NJ 284
Littleton Historical Museum, Littleton, CO 56
Live-In-A-Landmark Council, Montgomery, AL 7
Livermore Heritage Guild, Livermore, CA 30

Liverpool Township Historical Society, Valley City, OH 373
Living Heritage Society, Van Buren, ME 177
Living History Farms, Des Moines, IA 135
Living Prairie Museum Park, Winnipeg, Manitoba 526
Livingston County Library, Chillicothe, MO 244
Livingston Historical Society, Livingston, NJ 284
Livonia Historic Preservation Commission, Livonia, MI 219
Livonia Historical Commission—Greenmead Historic Site, Livonia, MI 219
Lloyd Harbor Historical Society, Lloyd Harbor, NY 318
Loantaka Chapter, Daughters of the American Revolution, Madison, NJ 284
Local History Department, Joint Free Public Library of Morristown and Morris Township, Morristown, NJ 286
Local History and Genealogy Department, Toledo-Lucas County Public Library, Toledo, OH 373
Lock Museum of America, Inc., Terryville, CT 67
Lockwood-Mathews Mansion Museum, Norwalk, CT 64
Locust Creek Covered Bridge, Laclede, MO 249
Locust Grove Historic Home, Louisville, KY 159
Locust Valley Historical Society, Locust Valley, NY 319
Lodi Historical Society, Lodi, NY 319
Logan County Archeological and Historical Society, Bellefontaine, OH 356
Logan County Genealogical Society, Bellefontaine, OH 356
Logan County Genealogical Society, Inc., Russellville, KY 162
Logan County Genealogical Society, Lincoln, IL 110
Logan County Historical Society, Bellefontaine, OH 356
Logan County Historical Society, Guthrie, OK 377
Logan County Historical Society, Paris, AR 21
Lolo Pass Visitor Center, Lolo, MT 259
Lombard Historical Society, Inc., Lombard, IL 110
Lombardy Hall Foundation, Wilmington, DE 71
Lompoc Valley Historical Society, Inc., Lompoc, CA 30
Lon C. Hill Home Museum, Harlingen, TX 448
London Historical Museums, London, Ontario 545
London Room, London Public Library and Art Museum, London, Ontario 545
London Town Publik House and Gardens, Edgewater, MD 183
London and Middlesex Historical Society, London, Ontario 545
Londonderry Historical Society, Londonderry, NH 273
Londonderry Historical Society, Londonderry, VT 467
Lone Jack Civil War Museum, Lone Jack, MO 250
Long Beach Island Historical Association, Beach Haven, NJ 277
Long Branch Historical Museum, Long Branch, NJ 284
Long Grove Historical Society, Long Grove, IL 110
Long Island Archives Conference, Stony Brook, NY 336
Long Island Historical Society, Brooklyn, NY 305
Long Island Studies Council, Stony Brook, NY 336
Longfellow National Historic Site, Cambridge, MA 192
Longhorn Museum, Inc., Pleasanton, TX 454
Longmeadow Historical Society, Longmeadow, MA 197
Longmire Museum, Longmire, WA 485
Longmont Museum, Longmont, CO 56
Longstreet Farm, Holmdel, NJ 283
Longue Vue House and Gardens, New Orleans, LA 166
Longview Museum and Arts Center, Longview, TX 451
Longyear Historical Society and Museum, Brookline, MA 192
Lonoke County Historical Society, Lonoke, AR 20
Lopez Island Historical Society and Museum, Lopez Island, WA 485
Lorain County Chapter, Ohio Genealogy Society, Vermilion, OH 373
Lorain County Historical Society, Inc., Elyria, OH 363
Lord Selkirk Association of Rupert's Land, Winnipeg, Manitoba 526
Lorenzo State Historic Site, Cazenovia, NY 307
Los Alamos County Historical Museum and Society, Los Alamos, NM 297
Los Alamos National Laboratory Archives, Los Alamos, NM 297
Los Altos Hills Historical Society, Los Altos Hills, CA 31
Los Altos Historical Commission, Los Altos Hills, CA 31
Los Angeles State and County Arboretum, Arcadia, CA 23
Los Pobladores 200, Long Beach, CA 31
Lost City Museum of Archaeology, Overton, NV 268
Lou Tate Foundation, Inc.—The Little Loomhouse, Louisville, KY 159
Loudou Museum, Inc., Leesburg, VA 475
Louis A. Warren Lincoln Library and Museum, Fort Wayne, IN 123
Louisa May Alcott Memorial Association, Concord, MA 193
Louise Steinman von Hess Foundation, Columbia, PA 390
Louisiana Arts and Science Center, Baton Rouge, LA 163
Louisiana Collection Series of Books & Documents on Colonial Louisiana, Birmingham, AL 2
Louisiana Committee for the Humanities, New Orleans, LA 166
Louisiana Historical Association, Lafayette, LA 165
Louisiana Historical Association Confederate Museum, New Orleans, LA 166
Louisiana Historical Society, New Orleans, LA 166
Louisiana State Archives and Records Service, Baton Rouge, LA 163
Louisiana State Museum, New Orleans, LA 166
Louisville Area Historical-Preservation Society, Louisville, OH 367
Louisville Historical League, Louisville, KY 59
Loveland Historical Museum, Loveland, OH 367
Loveland Museum and Gallery, Loveland, CO 56
Lovely Lane Museum, Baltimore, MD 181
Lowden Historical Society, Lowden, IA 138
Lower Cape Fear Historical Society, Inc., Wilmington, NC 350
Lower Ft. Garry National Historic Park, Selkirk, Manitoba 525
Lower Hudson Conference: Historical Agencies and Museums, Elmsford, NY 311
Lower Merion Historical Society, Ardmore, PA 387
Lowndes County Historical Society, Valdosta, GA 94
Loxahatchee Historical Society, Inc., Jupiter, FL 79
Loyalist House Museum, St. John, New Brunswick 530
Lucas County Museum, Chariton, IA 133
Lula W. Dorsey Museum, Estes Park, CO 53
Lum and Abner Museum, Pine Ridge, AR 21
Lumberman's Museum, Patten, ME 175
Luna County Historical Society, Inc., Deming, NM 296
Lundy's Lane Historical Museum, Niagara Falls, Ontario 547
Luscher's Farm Relics of Yesterday, Frankfort, KY 155
Luther College Preus Library, Decorah, IA 134
Lutie Coal Miner's Museum, Wilburton, OK 381
Lutz Children's Museum, Manchester, CT 62
Lycoming County Historical Museum, Williamsport, PA 408
Lyman House Memorial Museum, Hilo, HI 94
Lyme Historical Society—Florence Griswold Museum, Old Lyme, CT 65
Lynchburg Museum System, Lynchburg, VA 476
Lyndhurst, Tarrytown, NY 337
Lyndon B. Johnson National Historical Park, Johnson City, TX 450

Lynn Historical Society, Lynn, MA 198
Lynnfield Historical Society, Inc., Lynnfield, MA 198
Lyon County Historical Society, Inc., Eddyville, KY 154
Lyon County Historical Society, Marshall, MN 232
Lyon County Historical Society, Rock Rapids, IA 140
Lyon County Historical Society and Museum, Emporia, KS 145
Lyons Historical Society, Lyons, CO 56

M

MALFA (Material Archives and Laboratory for Archaeology), Katonah, NY 317
MARC Pacific Collection, University of Guam, Mangilao, Guam 509
MIT (Massachusetts Institute of Technology) Museum, Cambridge, MA 192
Mabee-Gerrer Museum of Art, Shawnee, OK 380
Mabou Gaelic and Historical Society, Mabou, Nova Scotia 536
MacArthur Memorial, Norfolk, VA 477
Macaulay Heritage Park—Prince Edward County Museum, Picton, Ontario 549
Macaulay Museum of Dental History, Charleston, SC 415
MacBride Centennial Museum, Whitehorse, Yukon 568
Macculloch Hall Historical Museum, Morristown, NJ 286
MacDonald Farm Historical Park, Bartibog, New Brunswick 527
Machiasport Historical Society, Machiasport, ME 173
Mackenzie House, Toronto, Ontario 552
Mackinac Associates, Mackinac Island, MI 219
Mackinac Island State Park Commission, Mackinac Island, MI 219
Macomb County Historical Society, Mt. Clemens, MI 20
Macon County Historical Society, Franklin, NC 344
Macon County Historical Society, Lafayette, TN 430
Macon County Historical Society—Macon County Museum Complex, Decatur, IL 105
Macon Heritage Foundation, Inc., Macon, GA 90
Macoupin County Historical Society, Carlinville, IL 101
Madam Brett Homestead, Beacon, NY 304
Madawaska Historical Society, Madawaska, ME 173
Madbury Historical Society, Madbury, NH 273
Madera County Historical Society, Madera, CA 32
Madison County Historic Home, Anderson, IN 120
Madison County Historical Society, Inc., Anderson, IN 120
Madison County Historical Society, Inc., Edwardsville, IL 106
Madison County Historical Society, Oneida, NY 326
Madison County Historical Society, Richmond, KY 162
Madison County Historical Society, Winterset, IA 142
Madison County History Association, Sheridan, MT 259
Madison Historical Society, Madison, NH 273
Madison Historical Society, Madison, OH 367
Madison Parish Historical Society, Tallulah, LA168
Madison Township Historical Society, Matawan, NJ 285
Madonna House Pioneer Museum, Combermere, Ontario 541
Magevney House, Memphis, TN 431
Magnolia Mound Plantation, Baton Rouge, LA 164
Magoffin County Historical Society, Salyersville, KY 162
Mahaffie Farmstead and Stagecoach Stop, Olathe, KS 149
Mahanoy Valley Historical Society, Gordon, PA 393
Mahasha County Historical Society, Oskaloosa, IA 140
Mahnomen County Historical Society, Mahnomen, MN 231
Mahoning Valley Historical Society, Youngstown, OH 375

Main Street Association of Wickford, Wickford, RI 412
Main Street Preservation Society, Grafton, OH 364
Maine (N.B.) Connection, Alexander, ME 168
Maine Department of Conservation, Bureau of Parks and Recreation, Augusta, ME 169
Maine Historical Society, Portland, ME 175
Maine Humanities Council, Portland, ME 175
Maine Old Cemetery Association, Eliot, ME 171
Maine Society for the History of Medicine, Warren, ME 177
Maine State Museum, Augusta, ME 169
Makah Cultural and Research Center, Neah Bay, WA 485
Malabar Farm State Park, Lucas, OH 367
Malheur Country Historical Society, Ontario, OR 384
Mamaroneck Free Library, Mamaroneck, NY 319
Mamaroneck Historical Society, Mamaroneck, NY 319
Mamie Doud Eisenhower Birthplace Foundation, Inc., Boone, IA 132
Man and Telecommunications Museum, Alberta Government Telephones, Edmonton, Alberta 513
Manassas City Museum, Manassas, VA 476
Manchester Historic Association, Manchester, NH 274
Manchester Historical Society, Inc., Manchester, CT 62
Manchester Historical Society, Manchester, MA 198
Manito Historical Society, Manito, IL 110
Manitoba Historical Society, Winnipeg, Manitoba 526
Manitoba Museum of Man and Nature, Winnipeg, Manitoba 526
Manitou Springs Historical Society, Inc., Manitou Springs, CO 56
Manitowoc County Historical Society, Manitowoc, WI 499
Manitowoc Maritime Museum, Manitowoc, WI 499
Manlius Historical Society, Manlius, NY 320
Mann-Simons Cottage: Museum of African-American Culture, Columbia, SC 416
Mansfield Public Library, Temple, NH 276
Mansfield Township Historical Society, Columbus, NJ 279
Manship House, Jackson, MS 240
Mantorville Restoration Association, Mantorville, MN 232
Manuscript Department and Southern Historical Collection, Chapel Hill, NC 342
Manuscripts Department, University of Virginia Library, Charlottesville, VA 472
Maple Valley Historical Society and Museum, Inc., Maple Valley, WA 485
Marathon County Historical Society, Wausau, WI 505
Marble Historical Society, Marble, CO 56
Marble Rock Historical Society Museum, Marble Rock, IA 139
Marblehead Historical Society, Marblehead, MA 198
Marcus Whitman Historical Society, Gorham, NY 313
Marengo County Historical Society, Demopolis, AL 3
Margaree Salmon Museum, Margaree, Nova Scotia 536
Margaret Woodbury Strong Museum, Rochester, NY 331
Marianna-Lee County Museum, Marianna, AR 20
Marias Museum of History and Art, Shelby, MT 259
Maricopa County Historical Society, Wickenburg, AZ 16
Marietta Restoration Associates, Inc., Marietta, PA 398
Marilla Historical Society, Elma, NY 311
Marine Corps Historical Foundation, Washington, DC 73
Marine Historical Society of Detroit, Westland, MI 224
Marine Historical Society—Stone House Museum, Marine on St. Croix, MN 232
Marine Museum of the Great Lakes at Kingston, Kingston, Ontario 544
Marine Museum of Upper Canada, Toronto, Ontario 552
Mariners' Museum, Newport News, VA 477
Mariners' Park Museum, Milford, Ontario 546

Marinette County Historical Society, Marinette, WI 500
Marion County Genealogical and Historical Society, Salem, IL 116
Marion County Historical Society, Columbia, MS 239
Marion County Historical Society, Hannibal, MO 246
Marion County Historical Society, Marion, OH 367
Marion County Historical Society, Ocala, FL 81
Marion County Historical Society—Marion Museum of History, Salem, OR 386
Marion County-Indianapolis Historical Society, Indianapolis, IN 125
Marion County Museum, Marion, SC 420
Mariposa County Historical Society, Mariposa, CA 32
Marissa Historical and Genealogical Society, Marissa, IL 111
Maritime Command Museum, Halifax, Nova Scotia 535
Maritime Museum of British Columbia, Victoria, British Columbia 522
Maritime Research Society of San Diego, San Diego, CA 40
Mark Twain Birthplace Memorial, Stoutsville, MO 255
Mark Twain Birthplace State Historic Site, Florida, MO 245
Mark Twain Home Board, Hannibal, MO 246
Mark Twain Memorial, Hartford, CT 61
Marksville State Commemorative Area, Marksville, LA 165
Marlboro County Museums, Bennettsville, SC 414
Marlboro Township Historical Society, Alliance, OH 355
Marlborough County Historical Preservation Commission, Bennettsvile, SC 414
Marlborough Historical Society, Bennettsville, SC 414
Marquette County Historical Society, Marquette, MI 219
Marshall County Historical Society, Inc, Holly Springs, MS 240
Marshall County Historical Society, Inc., Plymouth, IN 128
Marshall County Historical Society, Lacon, IL 109
Marshall County Historical Society, Warren, MN 238
Marshall Gold Discovery State Historic Park, Coloma, CA 25
Marshall Historical Society, Inc., Marshall, MI 219
Martin County Historical Museum, Stanton, TX 458
Martin County Historical Society, Inc., Fairmont, MN 229
Martin County Historical Society, Inc., Shoals, IN 129
Martin Luther King, Jr., Center for Nonviolent Social Change, Atlanta, GA 86
Martin Luther King, Jr., National Historic Site, Atlanta, GA 86
Martin Van Buren National Historic Site, Kinderhook, NY 317
Martin and Osa Johnson Safari Museum, Inc., Chanute, KS 144
Mary Ball Washington Museum and Library, Inc., Lancaster, VA 475
Mary M. Arron Memorial Museum Association, Marysville, CA 33
Mary Walker Historical and Educational Foundation, Chattanooga, TN 428
Mary Washington Branch, Association for the Preservation of Virginia Antiquities, Fredericksburg, VA 474
Maryhill Museum of Art, Golendale, WA 484
Maryland Association of Historic District Commissions, Frederick, MD 183
Maryland Commission on Afro-American History and Culture, Annapolis, MD 179
Maryland Environmental Trust, Baltimore, MD 181
Maryland Historical Society, Baltimore, MD 181
Maryland State Archives, Hall of Records, Annapolis, MD 179
Marymoor Museum, Redmond, WA 487

Marymoor Museum, Redmond, WA 487
Mason City Historical Society, Mason, WV 493
Mason County Genealogical and Historical Society, Havana, IL 108
Mason County Historical Society, Belfair, WA 482
Mason County Historical Society, Ludington, MI 219
Mason County Museum—Maysville and Mason County Historical and Scientific Association, Maysville, KY 160
Mason Historical Society, Mason, NH 274
Masonic Library and Museum, New York, NY 324
Massac County Historical Society, Metropolis, IL 111
Massachusetts Archaeological Society, Inc., Attleboro, MA 187
Massachusetts Historical Commission, Boston, MA 190
Massachusetts Historical Society, Boston, MA 190
Massachusetts Society of Mayflower Descendants, Boston, MA 190
Massachusetts State Archives, Boston, MA 190
Massacoh Plantation, Simsbury, CT 66
Massasoit Historical Association, Warren, RI 412
Massey Area Museum, Massey, Ontario 545
Massillon Museum, The, Massillon, OH 368
Matagorda County Historical Museum, Bay City, TX 439
Matawan Historical Society, Matawan, NJ 285
Mather Training Center, Harpers Ferry, WV 493
Mathews County Historical Society, Inc., Mathews, VA 476
Mattatuck Historical Society, Waterbury, CT 68
Matteson Historical Society, Matteson, IL 111
Mattye Reed African Heritage Center, Greensboro, NC 345
Maturango Museum of the Indian Wells Valley, Ridgecrest, CA 37
Maui Historical Society and Museum, Wailuku, HI 95
Maumee Valley Historical Society, Maumee, OH 368
Maxwell Museum of Anthropology, Albuquerque, NM 295
Mayes County Historical Society, Inc.—Coo-Y-Yah Country Museum, Pryor, OK 380
Mayfield Historical Society, Mayfield, NY 320
Mayflower Society, North Abington, MA 201
Maymont Foundation, Richmond, VA 479
Maynard Historical Society, Maynard, MA 198
Mayne Island Museum, Mayne Island, British Columbia 519
Mayo Historical Society, Mayo, Yukon Territory 568
Mayo Historical Unit, Mayo Clinic, Rochester, MN 235
Mayville Historical Society, Mayville, MI 219
McCamey Junior Historians, McCamey, TX 452
McClain County Historical Society and Museum, Purcell, OK 380
McCone County Museum, Circle, MT 257
McCook County Historical Society, Salem, SD 425
McCord Museum, McCord, Saskatchewan 565
McCormick County Historical Society, McCormick, SC 420
McDowell House and Apothecary Shop, Danville, KY 154
McFaddin-Ward House, Beaumont, TX 439
McGill University Archives, Montreal, Quebec 559
McGregor Historical Society, McGregor, IA 139
McHenry County Historical Society, Union, IL 118
McHenry Museum, Modesto, CA 33
McIntosh County Historical Society, Ashley, ND 351
McKean County Historical Society, Smethport, PA 405
McKenzie County Museum and Historical Society, Inc., Watford City, ND 354
McKinley Museum of History, Science and Industry, Canton, OH 357
McKissick Museum, Columbia, SC 416
McLean County Historical Society, Bloomington, IL 101

McLean County Historical Society, Washburn, ND 354
McLeod County Historical Society, Hutchinson, MN 230
mcLoughlin Memorial Association, Oregon City, OR 384
McMinn County Living Heritage Museum, Athens,
   TN 427
McPherson County Historical Society, McPherson,
   KS 149
McPherson County Old Mill Museum and Park,
   Lindsborg, KS 148
Meadow Farm Museum, Richmond, VA 479
Meadowlands Museum, Rutherford, NJ 291
Meagher County Historical Association, White Sulphur
   Springs, MT 260
Mechanicsburg Museum Association, Mechanicsburg,
   PA 398
Mecklenburg Historical Association, Charlotte, NC 342
Medallion Home—Pioneer Park Association, Kermit,
   TX 450
Medfield Historical Society, Medfield, MA 198
Medical History Society of New Jersey, Lawrenceville,
   NJ 284
Medina Community Design Committee, Medina,
   OH 368
Medina County Historical Society, Medina, OH 368
Medina Historical Society, Medina, NY 320
Megantic County Historical Society, Thetford Mines,
   Quebec 563
Meigs County Genealogical Society, Pomeroy, OH 371
Meigs County Pioneer and Historical Society, Inc.,
   Pomeroy, OH 371
Mellette County Historical Society, White River, SD 427
Melrose Historical Commission, Melrose, MA 199
Melrose Historical Society, Melrose, MA 199
Melrose Park Historical Society, Melrose Park, IL 111
Memorabilia Museum, Inc., Coca-Cola Bottling
   Company of Elizabethtown, Elizabethtown, KY 154
Memphis Heritage, Inc., Memphis, TN 431
Memphis Pink Palace Museum, Memphis, TN 432
Menaul Historical Library, Albuquerque, NM 295
Mendocino County Museum, Willits, CA 48
Mendocino Historical Research, Inc., Mendocino,
   CA 33
Mendota-West St. Paul Chapter, Dakota County
   Historical Society, Mendota, MN 232
Menifee County Roots, Frenchburg, KY 156
Menninger Foundation Museum and Archives, Topeka,
   KS 151
Menno Simons Historical Library and Archives,
   Harrisonburg, VA 475
Mennonite Heritage Center, Metamora, IL 111
Mennonite Heritage Centre, Winnipeg, Manitoba 526
Mennonite Historical Society of Iowa, Inc., Kalona,
   IA 138
Mennonite Immigrant Historical Foundation, Goessel,
   KS 146
Mennonite Library and Archives, North Newton, KS 149
Mennonite Village Museum, Inc., Steinbach,
   Manitoba 525
Mentor Graham House, Blunt, SD 422
Merced County Historical Society, Merced, CA 33
Mercer County Chapter, Ohio Genealogical Society,
   Celina, OH 358
Mercer County Cultural and Heritage Commission,
   Trenton, NJ 292
Mercer County Historical Society, Beulah, ND 351
Mercer County Historical Society, Inc., and Museum,
   Celina, OH 358
Mercer County Historical Society, Mercer, PA 398
Mercer Museum of the Bucks County Historical Society,
   Doylestown, PA 391
Merchantville Historical Society, Merchantville, NJ 285
Meredith Historical Society, Meredith, NH 274

Meridian Restorations Foundation, Inc., Meridian,
   MS 241
Meriwether Lewis Monument, Hohenwald, TN 429
Merrick County Historical Museum, Central City, NE 262
Mesa Museum, Mesa, AZ 13
Metcalfe County Historical Society, Summer Shade,
   KY 162
Meux Home Museum Corporation, Fresno, CA 28
Mexican American Cultural Heritage Center, Dallas,
   TX 443
Miami Beach Public Library, Miami, FL 80
Miami County Historical Society, Inc., Peru, IN 128
Miami County Historical Society, Tipp City, OH 372
Miami Purchase Association for Historic Preservation,
   Cincinnati, OH 359
Miami Valley Council on Genealogy and History,
   Dayton, OH 362
Miami Valley Genealogical Society, Dayton, OH 362
Michigan Archaeological Society, Saginaw, MI 223
Michigan City Historical Society, Inc., Michigan City,
   IN 127
Michigan Council for the Humanities, East Lansing,
   MI 214
Michigan Museums Association, Frankenmuth, MI 215
Michigan State University Museum, East Lansing,
   MI 214
Mid-Atlantic Association of Museums, Newark, DE 70
Mid-Atlantic Center for the Arts, Cape May, NJ 279
Mid-Atlantic Regional Archives Conference, Garrison,
   NY 313
Mid-Continent Railway Historical Society and Museum,
   North Freedom, WI 502
Mid-Missouri Civil War Round Table, Jefferson City,
   MO 247
Middle Georgia Historical Society, Inc., Macon, GA 90
Middle Ohio River Chapter, Sons and Daughters of
   Pioneer Rivermen, Inc., Louisville, KY 159
Middle Tennessee Conference Afro-American Scholars,
   Nashville, TN 433
Middlesex Canal Association, Billerica, MA 188
Middlesex County Cultural and Heritage Commission,
   North Brunswick, NJ 288
Middlesex County Historical Society, Middletown, CT 62
Middleton Historical Society, Middleton, WI 500
Middleton Place Foundation, Charleston, SC 415
Middletown Historical Society, Middletown, OH 368
Middletown Landmarks Commission, Middletown,
   NJ 285
Middletown Springs Historical Society, Middletown
   Springs, VT 467
Midland County Historical Society, Midland, MI 220
Midland Genealogical Society, Midland, MI 220
Midland Historic District, Midland, MI 220
Midland Regional Airport Museum, Midland, TX 452
Midway Museum, Inc., Midway, GA 90
Midwest Historical and Genealogical Society, Inc.,
   Wichita, KS 152
Midwest Old Settlers and Threshers Association, Inc.,
   Mt. Pleasant, IA 139
Midwest Regional Office, National Trust for Historic
   Preservation, Chicago, IL 104
Midwest Riverboat Buffs, Keokuk, IA 138
Mifflinburg Buggy Museum Association, Mifflinburg,
   PA 398
Milaca Museum, Milaca, MN 232
Milan Historical Association, Milan, KS 149
Milan Historical Museum, Inc., Milan, OH 369
Milford Area Historical Society, Milford, OH 369
Milford Historical Commission, Milford, MA 199
Milford Historical Society, Milford, MI 220
Mill Valley Public Library, Mill Valley, CA 33
Millbrook Society, The, Hatboro, PA 394

Mille Lacs Lake Historical Society, Isle, MN 230
Miller-Cory House Museum, Westfield, NJ 293
Millicent Rogers Museum, Taos, NM 300
Million Dollar Museum, White's City, NM 300
Mills County Genealogical Society, Glenwood, IA 136
Mills Mansion State Historic Site, Staatsburg, NY 335
Milltown Historical Society, Milltown, NJ 285
Milton Historical Society, Milton, VT 467
Milton Historical Society, Milton, WI 500
Milwaukee County Historical Society, Milwaukee,
    WI 500
Milwaukee Public Museum, Milwaukee, WI 500
Mine Au Breton Historical Society, Potosi, MO 252
Mineral County Historical Society and Museum,
    Superior, MT 260
Mineral County Museum and Historical Society,
    Superior, MT 260
Mineral County Museum, Hawthorne, NV 268
Miners' Museum, Glace Bay, Nova Scotia 534
Minidoka County Historical Society, Inc., Rupert, ID 98
Mining Museum, Platteville, WI 502
Miniota Municipal Museum, Inc., Miniota, Manitoba 524
Minisink Valley Historical Society, Port Jervis, NY 329
Minneapolis History Collection, Minneapolis Public
    Library and Information Center, Minneapolis,
    MN 233
Minnehaha County Historical Society, Sioux Falls,
    SD 426
Minnesota Finnish-American Historical Society, Fergus
    Falls, MN 229
Minnesota Genealogical Society, St. Paul, MN 236
Minnesota Historical Society, St. Paul, MN 236
Minnesota Pioneer Park, Annandale, MN 225
Minnesota Society American Institute of Architects,
    Minneapolis, MN 233
Minnesota Transportation Museum, Inc., Minneapolis,
    MN 233
Minute Man National Historical Park, Concord, MA 193
Miramichi Historical Society, Newcastle, New
    Brunswick 529
Miramichi Natural History Association Museum,
    Chatham, New Brunswick 527
Miramont Castle Museum and Conference Center,
    Manitou Springs, CO 56
Miriam B. Wilson Foundation—Old Slave Mart Museum
    and Library, Charleston, SC 415
Mirror and District Museum Association, Mirror,
    Alberta 515
Mission House, The, Stockbridge, MA 205
Mission Inn Foundation, Riverside, CA 38
Mission Museum and Archives, Mission, British
    Columbia 519
Mission Nuestra Senora del Espiritu Santo de
    Zuniga—Goliad State Historical Park, Goliad,
    TX 447
Mission San Miguel, San Miguel, CA 43
Mission Trail—Los Pueblos Association, El Paso,
    TX 444
Mission Valley Heritage—Garden of the Rockies
    Museum, Ronan, MT 259
Missisquei Historical Society, Inc., Stanbridge East,
    Quebec 562
Missisquoi Valley Historical Society, North Troy, VT 468
Mississippi Agriculture and Forestry Museum—National
    Agricultural and Aviation Museum, Jackson, MS 240
Mississippi Baptist Historical Commission, Clinton,
    MS 239
Mississippi Committee for the Humanities, Jackson,
    MS 240
Mississippi Department of Archives and History,
    Jackson, MS 240
Mississippi Governor's Mansion, Jackson, MS 241

Mississippi Historical Society, Jackson, MS 241
Mississippi Military Museum, Jackson, MS 241
Mississippi Museums Association, Jackson, MS 241
Mississippi Museums Council, Jackson, MS 241
Mississippi River Museum, Memphis, TN 432
Mississippi Valley Collection, Special Collections
    Department, Memphis State University Libraries,
    Memphis, TN 432
Missouri and Arkansas Railroad Museum, Inc., Beaver,
    AR 17
Missouri Committee for the Humanities, Inc., Maryland
    Heights, MO 250
Missouri Cultural Heritage Center, Columbia, MO 244
Missouri Historical Society, St. Louis, MO 254
Missouri State Library, Jefferson City, MO 247
Missouri State Museum—Jefferson Landing State
    Historic Site, Jefferson City, MO 247
Missouri Town 1855, Blue Springs, MO 243
Missouri Valley Room, Kansas City Public Library,
    Kansas City, MO 248
Mitchell County Historical Society, Osage, IA 140
Mitchell Museum, Mount Vernon, IL 112
Mitchell Prehistoric Indian Village Preservation Society,
    Mitchell, SD 424
Mitchell Site National Historic Landmark, Mitchell,
    SD 424
Moab Museum, Moab, UT 462
Moanalua Gardens Foundation, Inc., Honolulu, HI 96
Mobile Historic Development Commission, Mobile, AL 6
Modern Woodmen of America, Rock Island, IL 115
Modoc County Historical Society and Museum, Alturas,
    CA 23
Moffat County Museum, Craig, CO 51
Mohave Museum of History and Arts—Mohave County
    Historical Society, Kingman, AZ 13
Mohawk Valley Historic Association, Mohawk, NY 320
Mojave River Valley Museum Association, Barstow,
    CA 23
Molly Brown House Museum, Denver, CO 52
MonDak Historical and Arts Society—MonDak Heritage
    Center, Sidney, MT 260
Moncton Museum, Inc., Moncton, New Brunswick 529
Moniteau County Historical Society, California, MO 243
Monmouth County Historical Association, Freehold,
    NJ 281
Monona Historical Society, Monona, IA 139
Monongalia Historical Society, New London, MN 234
Monroe County Historial Commission and Museum,
    Monroe, MI 220
Monroe County Historical Society and Museum,
    Bloomington, IN 120
Monroe County Historical Society, Aberdeen, MS 239
Monroe County Historical Society, Albia, IA 131
Monroe County Historical Society, Inc., Sparta, WI 504
Monroe County Historical Society, Stroudsburg, PA 406
Monroe County Historical Society, Woodsfield, OH 374
Monroe County Local History Room, Sparta, WI 504
Monroe County Museum Association, Stroudsburg,
    PA 406
Monroe Historical Preservation Society, Monroe, NY 320
Monroe-Crook House, Crockett, TX 570
Monroeville Historical Society, Monroeville, OH 369
Montague Association for the Restoration of Community
    History (MARCH), Montague, NJ 285
Montague Museum and Historical Association,
    Montague, MI 220
Montana Historical Society, Helena, MT 258
Montana Oral History Association, Helena, MT 258
Montana Women's History Project, Missoula, MT 259
Montauk, Clermont, IA 133
Montauk Historical Society, Montauk, NY 320
Monte Vista Historical Association, San Antonio, TX 456

Montecito History Committee, Montecito, CA 33

Monterey County Agricultural and Rural Life Museum, Salinas, CA 39

Monterey Historical Society, Monterey, MA 199

Monterey History and Art Association, Ltd., Monterey, CA 33

Montgomery County Chapter, Ohio Genealogical Society, Dayton, OH 362

Montgomery County Department of History and Archives, Fonda, NY 312

Montgomery County Genealogical Society, Coffeyville, KS 144

Montgomery County Genealogical Society, Litchfield, IL 110

Montgomery County Historical Society, Clarksville, TN 428

Montgomery County Historical Society, Dayton, OH 362

Montgomery County Historical Society, Montgomery City, MO 251

Montgomery County Historical Society, Red Oak, IA 140

Montgomery County Historical Society, Rockville, MD 185

Montgomery Historical Society, Montgomery, VT 467

Montgomery's Inn, Etobicoke, Ontario 542

Moody Museum, Taylor, TX 458

Moore County Historical Association, Southern Pines, NC 349

Moore County Historical Museum, Dumas, TX 444

Moore Museum, Mooretown, Ontario 546

Moores Creek National Battlefield, Currie, NC 343

Moorland-Spingarn Research Center, Washington, DC 73

Moose Jaw Art Museum and National Exhibition Centre, Moose Jaw, Saskatchewan 565

Moosehead Historical Society, Greenville, ME 172

Moraine Valley Oral History Association, Oak Lawn, IL 113

Moravian Archives, The, Bethlehem, PA 388

Moravian Historical Society, Nazareth, PA 399

Moravian Museums and Tours, Bethlehem, PA 388

Moravian Music Foundation, Inc., Winston-Salem, NC 351

Mordecai Square Historical Society, Inc., Raleigh, NC 348

Moreland Hills Historical Society, Moreland Hills, OH 369

Morgan County Foundation, Inc.—Madison-Morgan Cultural Center, Madison, GA 90

Morgan County Historical Society, Jacksonville, Il 109

Morgan County Historical Society, McConnelsville, OH 368

Moriarty Historical Society and Museum, Moriarty, NM 298

Morikami Museum of Japanese Culture, Delray Beach, FL 77

Mormon History Association, Provo, UT 463

Moross House, Home of the Detroit Garden Center, Detroit, MI 213

Morrice Farm Museum, Morrice, MI 220

Morris County Historical Society, Morristown, NJ 286

Morris County Trust for Historic Preservation, Inc., Morristown, NJ 569

Morris Historical Society, Morris, CT 63

Morris Library, Carbondale, IL 101

Morrison County Historical Society, Little Falls, MN 231

Morrison Historical Society, Morrison, IL 111

Morrison Museum Association, Islay, Alberta 515

Morristown-Hamblen Historical and Bicentennial Commission, Morristown, TN 432

Morristown National Historical Park, Morristown, NJ 286

Morrow County Historical Society, Mount Gilead, OH 369

Motor Bus Society, Inc., West Trenton, NJ 294

Moultonboro Public Library, Moultonboro, NH 274

Moultrie County Historical and Genealogical Society, Sullivan, IL 117

Mound City Group National Monument, Chillicothe, OH 358

Mound City Museum Association, Mound City, MO 251

Mount Dora Historical Society, Mount Dora, FL 80

Mount Prospect Historical Society of Elk Grove and Wheeling Townships, Mt. Prospect, IL 112

Mount Vernon Ladies' Association of the Union, Mount Vernon, VA 477

Mount Washington Historical Society, Mt. Washington, KY 160

Mountain Heritage Center, Cullowhee, NC 343

Mountain Lakes Historical Society, Mountain Lakes, NJ 286

Mountain View Museum, Olds, Alberta 515

Mountains-Plains Regional Office, National Trust for Historic Preservation, Denver, CO 52

Mt. Allison University Archives, Sackville, New Brunswick 530

Mt. Carmel Cultural and Historical Center, L'Ille, ME 173

Mt. Juliet-West Wilson County Historical Society, Mt. Juliet, TN 432

Mt. Pleasant Historical Society, Inc., Mt. Pleasant, OH 369

Multicultural Heritage Center, Stony Plain, Alberta 516

Mulvane Historical Society, Mulvane, KS 149

Municipal Museum of Baltimore, Baltimore, MD 181

Munroe Falls Historical Society, Munroe Falls, OH 369

Munroe Township Historical Society, Williamstown, NJ 294

Murfreesboro Historic Properties Commission, Murfreesboro, NC 347

Murfreesboro Historical Association, Murfreesboro, NC 347

Murney Tower Museum, Kingston, Ontario 544

Murphy's Landing, Shakopee, MN 237

Murray County Historical Society, Slayton, MN 237

Murray Lindsay Mansion, Lindsay, OK 378

Murrell Home, Tahlequah, OK 380

Musée Acadien, Caraquet, New Brunswick 527

Musée Acadien, Cheticamp, Nova Scotia 534

Musée Acadien, Moncton, NB 529

Musée Automobile Museum, St. Jacques, New Brunswick 530

Musée Beaulne, Coaticook, Quebec 557

Muséc d'histoire et de Traditions Populaires de la Gaspésie, Pointe Jacques-Cartier, Quebec 560

Musée de la Ville de Lachine, Lachine, Quebec 558

Musée de l'Eglise Notre-Dame, Montreal, Quebec 559

Musée de Marguerite Bourgeoys, Montreal, Quebec 560

Musée Historique de L'Electricité, Longueuil, Quebec 558

Musée J. Armand Bombardier, Valcourt, Quebec 563

Musée Maritime Bernier, L'Islet-Sur-Mer, Quebec 558

Musée National des Postes, Ottawa, Ontario 548

Musée Pierre Boucher, Trois-Rivieres, Quebec 563

Musée Régional Laure Conan, La Malbaie, Quebec 558

Musée Regional de Vaudreuil-Soulanges, Vaudreuil, Quebec 563

Musée Saint Joachim, La Broquerie, Manitoba 524

Muscatine Art Center, Muscatine, IA 139

Muscoot Farm Park, Katonah, NY 317

Museum and Archives of Georgia Education, Milledgeville, GA 90

Museum and Archives of the Big Bend, Alpine, TX 436

Museum Association of Newfoundland and Labrador, St. John's, Newfoundland 532

Museum Association of the American Frontier, Chadron, NE 262
Museum Computer Network, Inc., Stony Brook, NY 336
Museum in Memory of Virginia E. Randolph, Glen Allen, VA 474
Museum Lepanto U.S.A., Lepanto, AR 19
Museum Store Association, Inc., Doylestown, PA 391
Museum Village in Orange County, Monroe, NY 320
Museum of African American History, Detroit, MI 213
Museum of American Architecture and Decorative Arts, Houston, TX 449
Museum of American Folk Art, New York, NY 324
Museum of American Textile History, North Andover, MA 201
Museum of Anthropology, Highland Heights, KY 157
Museum of Anthropology, Pullman, WA 486
Museum of Appalachia, Norris, TN 435
Museum of Art, Rhode Island School of Design, Providence, RI 411
Museum of Art, Science, and Industry, Bridgeport, CT 58
Museum of Arts and History, Port Huron, MI 222
Museum of Broadcasting, New York, NY 324
Museum of Canadian Scouting, Boy Scouts of Canada, Ottawa, Ontario 548
Museum of Cape Breton Heritage, Margaree, Nova Scotia 536
Museum of Ceramics, East Liverpool, OH 363
Museum of Church History and Art, Salt Lake City, UT 463
Museum of Cultural History, Los Angeles, CA 31
Museum of Florida History, Tallahassee, FL 83
Museum of History and Art, Ontario, CA 34
Museum of History and Industry, Seattle, WA 487
Museum of History and Science, Louisville, KY 159
Museum of Holography, New York, NY 324
Museum of Independent Telephony, Abilene, KS 143
Museum of Indian Heritage, Indianapolis, IN 125
Museum of Missouri River History, Brownville, NE 261
Museum of Native American Cultures, Spokane, WA 489
Museum of Natural History, Eugene, OR 383
Museum of Natural and Cultural History, Oklahoma State University, Stillwater, OK 380
Museum of New Mexico, Santa Fe, NM 299
Museum of North Idaho, Inc., Coeur d'Alene, ID 97
Museum of Northern Arizona, Flagstaff, AZ 12
Museum of Northern History, Sir Harry Oakes Chateau, Kirkland Lake, Ontario 544
Museum of Oriental Cultures, Corpus Christi, TX 441
Museum of Our National Heritage, Lexington, MA 197
Museum of Peoples and Cultures, Provo, UT 463
Museum of Science and Industry, Chicago, IL 104
Museum of Sea and Ships, Seattle, WA 487
Museum of the Albemarle, Elizabeth City, NC 344
Museum of the American Indian, New York, NY 324
Museum of the American Numismatic Association, Colorado Springs, CO 51
Museum of the Americas, Brookfield, VT 465
Museum of the Baltimore College of Dental Surgery, Baltimore, MD 181
Museum of the Borough of Brooklyn at Brooklyn College, Brooklyn, NY 305
Museum of the Cherokee Strip, Enid, OK 377
Museum of the City of New York, New York, NY 324
Museum of the City of Washington, Washington, DC 73
museum of the Confederacy, Brockenbrough Library, Richmond, VA 479
Museum of the Fur Trade, Chadron, NE 262
Museum of the Great Plains, Lawton, OK 378
Museum of the Highwood, High River, Alberta 514
Museum of the Noncommissioned Officer, Fort Bliss, TX 445

Museum of the Ozarks, Springfield, MO 255
Museum of the Red River, Idabel, OK 378
Museum of the Rockies, Bozeman, MT 256
Museum of the Western Prairie, Altus, OK 375
Museum of the Yellowstone, West Yellowstone, MT 260
Museum of Tobacco Art and History, Nashville, TN 433
Museum of Waldensian Heritage, Valdese, NC 350
Museum of Western Colorado, Grand Junction, CO 54
Museum Services, Old St. Stephen's College, Edmonton, Alberta 513
Museum, The, Greenwood, SC 419
Museum, The, Texas Tech University, Lubbock, TX 451
Museums at Hartwick, Oneonta, NY 326
Museums at Stony Brook, Stony Brook, NY 336
Museums Collaborative, Inc., New York, NY 324
Museums Council of New Jersey, Trenton, NJ 292
Museums of the City of Mobile, Mobile, AL 6
Musical Museum, The, Deansboro, NY 309
Musical Wonder House, Wiscasset, ME 178
Muskegon County Genealogical Society, Muskegon, MI 220
Muskegon County Museum, Muskegon, MI 221
Muskingum County Genealogical Society, Zanesville, OH 375
Muskogee War Memorial Park, Muskogee, OK 378
Muskoka Pioneer Village and Museum, Huntsville, Ontario 543
Musselshell Valley Historical Museum, Roundup, MT 259
Mütter Museum, the College of Physicians of Philadelphia, Philadelphia, PA 402
Mystic River Historical Society, Stonington, CT 67
Mystic Seaport Museum, Mystic, CT 63

N

NASA—Johnson Space Center, Houston, TX 449
NICLOG (National Information Center for Local Government Records), Nashville, TN 433
Nanaimo and District Museum Society, Nanaimo, British Columbia 519
Nance County Historical Society, Fullerton, NE 263
Nancy Island Historic Site, Wasaga Beach, Ontario 554
Nanticoke Indian Association, Millsboro, DE 70
Nanticoke Valley Historical Society, Maine, NY 319
Nantucket Historical Association, Nantucket, MA 199
Napa County Historical Society, Napa, CA 34
Naperville Heritage Society—Naper Settlement, Naperville, IL 112
Nash County Historical Association, Inc., Rocky Mount, NC 348
Nashua Public Library, Nashua, NH 274
Nashville Room, Nashville Public Library, Nashville, TN 433
Nassau County Museum, Division of Museum Services, Syosset, NY 336
Natchez Pilgrimage Tours, Natchez, MS 41
Natchez Trace Genealogical Society, Florence, AL 4
Natick Historical Society, Natick, MA 199
National Afro-American Museum and Cultural Center, Columbus, OH 361
National Alliance of Preservation Commissions, Washington, DC 73
National Archives, Washington, DC 73
National Archives—Atlanta Branch, Atlanta, GA 86
National Archives—Boston Branch, Waltham, MA 207
National Archives—Chicago Branch, Chicago, IL 104
National Archives—Denver Branch, Denver, CO 52
National Archives—Fort Worth Branch, Ft. Worth, TX 446

National Archives—Kansas City Branch, Kansas City, MO 248

National Archives—Los Angeles Branch, Laguna Niguel, CA 32

National Archives—New York Branch, Bayonne, NJ 277

National Archives—Philadelphia Branch, Philadelphia, PA 402

National Archives—San Francisco Branch, San Bruno, CA 41

National Archives—Seattle Branch, Seattle, WA 488

National Association of Watch and Clock Collectors, Inc., Columbia, PA 390

National Atomic Museum, Albuquerque, NM 295

National Aviation Museum, Ottawa, Ontario 549

National Baseball Hall of Fame and Museum, Inc., Cooperstown, NY 309

National Bottle Museum, Ballston Spa, NY 303

National Broadcasters Hall of Fame, Freehold, NJ 281

National Center for the Study of History, Germantown, MD 183

National Colonial Farm of the Accokeek Foundation, Inc., Accokeek, MD 179

National Council on Public History, Morgantown, WV 494

National Cowgirl Hall of Fame, Hereford, TX 449

National Endowment for the Humanities, Washington, DC 73

National Federation of Franco-American Genealogical and Historical Societies, Manchester, NH 274

National Genealogical Society, Washington, DC 73

National Hispanic Museum, Los Angeles, CA 32

National Historical Society, Harrisburg, PA 394

National History Day, Cleveland, OH 360

National Humanities Alliance, Washington, DC 74

National Institute for the Conservation of Cultural Property, Inc., Washington, DC 74

National Inventors Hall of Fame Foundation, Inc., Washington, DC 74

National Maritime Museum, San Francisco—National Maritime Museum Association, San Francisco, CA 41

National Museum of American Jewish History, Philadelphia, PA 402

National Museum of Man (Musée national de l'Homme)—Musée commémoratif Victoria Memorial Museum, Ottawa, Ontario 549

National Museum of Racing, Inc., Saratoga Springs, NY 332

National Museum of Roller Skating, Lincoln, NE 264

National Museum of the Boy Scouts of America, Murray, KY 160

National Museum of Transport, St. Louis, MO 254

National Park Service History Collection, Office of Library and Archival Services, Harpers Ferry, WV 493

National Park Service, State of Alaska, Anchorage, AK 9

National Park Service, Washington, DC 74

National Portrait Gallery, Washington, DC 74

National Register of Historic Places, Washington, DC 74

National Road—Zane Grey Museum, Norwich, OH 370

National Ski Hall of Fame, Ishpeming, MI 217

National Soaring Museum, Elmira, NY 311

National Soccer Hall of Fame, Oneonta, NY 326

National Society of Andersonville, Andersonville, GA 85

National Society of Colonial Dames of America, Maine, Portland, ME 175

National Society of the Colonial Dames of America in the State of South Carolina, Charleston, SC 415

National Society of the Colonial Dames, Colorado Springs, CO 51

National Society, Children of the American Revolution, Washington, DC 74

National Society, Colonial Dames XVII Century, Washington, DC 74

National Society, Colonial Dames of America in the State of New Jersey, Mt. Holly, NJ 287

National Society, Daughters of Utah Pioneers, Salt Lake City, UT 463

National Society, Daughters of the American Revolution, Washington, DC 74

National Society, United States Daughters of 1812, Washington, DC 75

National Temple Hill Association, Vails Gate, NY 338

National Trust for Historic Preservation, Washington, DC 75

Native American Resource Center, Pembroke, NC 347

Native New Yorkers Historical Association, New York, NY 324

Natural History Museum of Los Angeles County, Los Angeles, CA 32

Naumkeag, Stockbridge, MA 205

Nauvoo Restoration, Inc., Nauvoo, IL 112

Navajo County Historical Society, Holbrook, AZ 13

Navajo Tribal Museum, Window Rock, AZ 16

Naval Aviation Museum, Pensacola, FL 82

Naval War College Museum, Newport, RI 410

Navarre-Bethlehem Township Historical Society, Navarre, OH 369

Navy Memorial Museum, Washington, DC 75

Neal Dow Memorial, Portland, ME 175

Nebraska Committee for the Humanities, Lincoln, NE 264

Nebraska Game and Parks Commission, Lincoln, NE 264

Nebraska State Historical Society, Lincoln, NE 264

Ned A. Hatathli Center Museum, Tsaile, AZ 15

Needham Historical Society, Inc., Needham, MA 199

Neill Cochran Museum House, Austin, TX 438

Nemaha County Historical Society, Inc., Seneca, KS 150

Nemours Mansion and Gardens, Wilmington, DE 71

Neosho Historical Society and Museum, Neosho, WI 501

Neptune Historical Museum, Neptune, NJ 287

Neptune Historical Society, Neptune, NJ 287

Ness County Historical Society, Ness City, KS 149

Netherland Inn Association, Kingsport, TN 430

Netherlands Museum, Holland, MI 217

Nevada County Historical Society, Nevada City, CA 34

Nevada Division of State Parks, Carson City, NV 267

Nevada Historical Society, Reno, NV 268

Nevada State Museum and Historical Society, Las Vegas, NV 268

Nevada State Museum, Carson City, NV 267

Neversink Valley Area Museum, Cuddebackville, NY 309

Neville Public Museum of Brown County, Green Bay, WI 497

New Albany-Plain Township Historical Society, New Albany, OH 269

New Baltimore Historical Society, New Baltimore, MI 221

New Bedford Glass Society, New Bedford, MA 200

New Bedford Whaling Museum, New Bedford, MA 200

New Berlin Heritage Association, New Berlin, PA 399

New Berlin Historical Society, New Berlin, WI 501

New Bern Historical Society Foundation, Inc., New Bern, NC 347

New Bern Preservation Foundation, Inc., New Bern, NC 347

New Bremen Historic Association, New Bremen, OH 369

New Brighton Area Historical Society, St. Paul, MN 236

New Britain Youth Museum, New Britain, CT 63

New Brunswick Genealogical Society, Fredericton, New Brunswick 528
New Brunswick Historical Society, Saint John, New Brunswick 530
New Brunswick Museum, Saint John, New Brunswick 530
New Brunswick Sports Hall of Fame, Fredericton, New Brunswick 528
New Canaan Historical Society, New Canaan, CT 63
New Castle Historical Society, Chappaqua, NY 307
New Castle Historical Society, New Castle, DE 70
New Durham Archives and Historical Collections, New Durham, NH 274
New England Air Museum, Windsor Locks, CT 69
New England Electric Railway Historical Society, Inc.—Kennebunkport, ME 173
New England Historic Genealogical Society, Boston, MA 190
New England Maple Museum, Rutland, VT 468
New England Museum Association, Boston, MA 190
New England Preservation Institute, New Bedford, MA 200
New England Ski Museum, Franconia, NH 271
New Glarus Historical Society—Swiss Historical Village, New Glarus, WI 501
New Gloucester, Maine, Historical Society, New Gloucester, ME 173
New Hampshire Antiquarian Society, Hopkinton, NH 272
New Hampshire Division of Records Management and Archives, Concord, NH 270
New Hampshire Farm Museum, Inc., Milton, NH 274
New Hampshire Historical Society, Concord, NH 270
New Hampshire State Historic Preservation Office, Department of Resources and Economic Development, Concord, NH 270
New Hanover County Museum of the Lower Cape Fear, Wilmington, NC 350
New Harmony Workingmen's Institute, New Harmony, IN 128
New Hartford Historical Society, New Hartford, NY 321
New Haven Colony Historical Society, New Haven, CT 64
New Haven Preservation Trust, New Haven, CT 64
New Holstein Historical Society, New Holstein, WI 501
New Jersey Bureau of Law and Reference Services, Trenton, NJ 292
New Jersey Committee for the Humanities, New Brunswick, NJ 288
New Jersey Folk Festival Association, New Brunswick, NJ 288
New Jersey Historical Commission, Trenton, NJ 292
New Jersey Historical Society, Newark, NJ 287
New Jersey Museum of Transportation, Inc., Farmingdale, NJ 281
New Jersey Postal History Society, Clementon, NJ 279
New Jersey Society, Sons of the American Revolution, Elizabeth, NJ 280
New Jersey State House, Department of State, Trenton, NJ 292
New Jersey State Museum, Trenton, NJ 292
New London County Historical Society, New London, CT 64
New London Heritage Historical Society, New London, WI 501
New London Historical Society, New London, NH 274
New London Landmarks—Union Railroad Station Trust, Inc., New London, CT 64
New Market Battlefield Park, New Market, VA 477
New Mexico Association of Museums, Santa Fe, NM 299
New Mexico Genealogical Society, Albuquerque, NM 295

New Mexico Historical Review, Albuquerque, NM 295
New Mexico Medical History Program, Albuquerque, NM 295
New Mexico Records Center and Archives, Santa Fe, NM 299
New Mexico Sons of Confederate Veterans, Albuquerque, NM 295
New Mexico Studies Association, Denton, TX 443
New Prague Historical Society, New Prague, MN 234
New River Historical Society, Radford, VA 479
New Ross District Museum Society—Ross Farm Museum of Agriculture, New Ross, Nova Scotia 537
New Westminster Historical Society, New Westminster, British Columbia 520
New Year's Shooters and Mummers Museum, Philadelphia, PA 402
New York Archival Society, New York City, NY 324
New York Central System Historical Society, Inc., Mentor, OH 368
New York Council for the Humanities, New York, NY 324
New York Genealogical and Biographical Society, New York, NY 324
New York Historical Resources Center, Ithaca, NY 316
New-York Historical Society, New York, NY 324
New York Public Library, Schomburg Center for Research in Black Culture, New York, NY 324
New York State Archaeological Association, Rochester, NY 331
New York State Archives, Albany, NY 301
New York State Historical Association, Cooperstown, NY 309
Newark Museum, The, Newark, NJ 287
Newark Preservation and Landmarks Committee, Newark, NJ 287
Newark Valley Historical Society, Newark Valley, NY 321
Newaygo County Society of History and Genealogy, White Cloud, MI 225
Newberry County Historical Society, Newberry, SC 420
Newberry Historical Restoration Association, Inc., Newberry, MI 221
Newberry Library, The, Chicago, IL 104
Newcastle Historical Society, Bellevue, WA 482
Newcomen Society of the United States, Exton, PA 392
Newfoundland Historical Society, St. John's, Newfoundland 532
Newington Historical Society and Trust, Inc., Newington, CT 64
Newkirk Historical Society, Newkirk, OK 378
Newnan-Coweta Historical Society, Newnan, GA 91
Newport Historical Society, Inc., Newport, RI 410
Newport Historical Society, Newport, RI 410
Newport Township Historical Society, Wadsworth, IL 118
Newstead Historical Society, Akron, NY 300
Newton County Historical and Genealogical Society, Jasper, AR 19
Newton County Historical Commission, Burkeville, TX 440
Newtown Association, Inc., Salisbury, MD 185
Newtown Historic Association, Newtown, PA 399
Newville Historical Society, Newville, PA 399
Nez Perce County Historical Society, Inc., Lewiston, ID 98
Nez Perce National Historical Park, Spalding, ID 98
Niagara County Historical Society, Inc., Lockport, NY 318
Niagara Falls Historical Society, Inc., Niagara Falls, NY 325
Niagara Historical Society Museum, Niagara-on-the-Lake, Ontario 547
Niagara Parks Commission, Fort Erie, Ontario 542
Nichols House Museum, Boston, MA 190
Nicolas Denys Museum, St. Peter's, Nova Scotia 537

Nicollet County Historical Society and Museum, St. Peter, MN 237

Nineteenth Louisiana Volunteer Infantry, Baton Rouge, LA 164

Niobrara Historical Society, Niobrara, NE 265

Nipigon Museum, Nipigon, Ontario 547

Nita Stewart Haley Memorial Library, Midland, TX 452

No Man's Land Historical Society and Museum, Goodwell, OK 377

Noah Webster Foundation—Historical Society of West Hartford, West Hartford, CT 68

Noank Historical Society, Noank, CT 64

Noble County Chapter, Ohio Genealogical Society, Caldwell, OH 357

Noble County Genealogical Society, Inc., Albion, IN 120

Noble County Historical Society, Albion, IN 120

Nobleboro Historical Society, Nobleboro, ME 174

Nodaway County Historical Society, Maryville, MO 250

Nome Community Historical Association, Inc., Nome, ND 353

Nor'Westers and Loyalist Museum, Williamstown, Ontario 554

Nordheim Historical Museum, Nordheim, TX 453

Nordic Heritage News, Seattle, WA 488

Norfolk County Historical Society of Chesapeake, Chesapeake, VA 472

Norfolk Historical Society, Inc., Norfolk, CT 65

Norlands Living History Center, Livermore, ME 173

Norman and Cleveland County Historical Museum, Norman, OK 378

Norman County Historical Area, Ada, MN 225

Norman Rockwell Museum at the Old Corner House, Stockbridge, MA 206

North American Society for Sport History, University Park, PA 406

North American Wildfowl Art Museum, Salisbury, MD 185

North Andover Historical Society, North Andover, MA 201

North Atlantic Regional Office, National Park Service, Boston, MA 190

North Bay and Area Museum, North Bay, Ontario 547

North Carolina Baptist Historical Collection, Winston-Salem, NC 351

North Carolina Chapter, Victorian Society in America, Raleigh, NC 348

North Carolina Collection, Chapel Hill, NC 342

North Carolina Division of Archives and History, Raleigh, NC 348

North Carolina Folklore Society, Boone, NC 341

North Carolina Genealogical Society, Raleigh, NC 348

North Carolina Humanities Committee, Durham, NC 343

North Carolina Literary and Historical Association, Raleigh, NC 348

North Carolina Museums Council, Wilmington, NC 350

North Carolina Synod, Lutheran Church in America, Salisbury, NC 349

North Castle Historical Society, Armonk, NY 302

North Central Kansas Genealogical Society and Library, Inc., Cawker City, KS 144

North Central Nevada Historical Society, Winnemucca, NV 269

North-Central Pennsylvania Historical Association, Milton, PA 398

North Central Washington Museum Association, Wenatchee, WA 491

North Cumberland Historical Society, Pugwash, Nova Scotia 537

North Dakota Historical Society, Inc., Coleharbor, ND 352

North Dakota Institute for Regional Studies, Fargo, ND 352

North Fork Historical Society, Paonia, CO 56

North Ft. Worth Historical Society, Fort Worth, TX 446

North Hampton Historical Society, North Hampton, NH 275

North Hampton Public Library, North Hampton, NH 275

North Highland Community Organization, Cape North, Nova Scotia 533

North Hills Museum, Granville Ferry, Nova Scotia 534

North Himsworth Museum, Callander, Ontario 541

North Jersey Electric Railway Historical Society, Rahway, NJ 290

North Jersey Highlands Historical Society, Ringwood, NJ 290

North Lee County Historical Society, Ft. Madison, IN 122

North Louisiana Genealogical Society, Ruston, LA 167

North Louisiana Historical Association, Shreveport, LA 168

North Manchester Historical Society, Inc., North Manchester, IN 128

North Platte Valley Historical Association, Inc., Gering, NE 263

North Seattle Community College Art Gallery, Seattle, WA 488

North Shore Archives, Tatamagouche, Nova Scotia 538

North Shore Museum and Archives, North Vancouver, British Columbia 520

North St. Paul Historical Society, North St. Paul, MN 234

North Suburban Genealogical Society, Winnetka, IL 119

North Western Illinois Chapter, National Railway Historical Society, Rockford, IL 115

North Yarmouth Historical Society, North Yarmouth, ME 174

North York Historical Society, North York, Ontario 547

Northampton County Historical and Genealogical Society, Easton, PA 391

Northampton Historical Society, Northampton, MA 201

Northborough Historical Society, Inc., Northborough, MA 201

Northeast Document Conservation Center, Andover, MA 187

Northeast Florida Anthropological Society, Jacksonville, FL 79

Northeast Folklore Society, Orono, ME 174

Northeast Georgia Area Planning and Development Commission, Athens, GA 85

Northeast Historical Society, Hurst, TX 450

Northeast Minnesota Historical Center, Duluth, MN 228

Northeastern Nevada Genealogical Society, Elko, NV 268

Northeastern Nevada Museum, Elko, NV 268

Northern Anthropological and Cultural Society Northern Life Museum and National Exhibition Centre, Fort Smith, Northwest Territories 532

Northern Arizona Pioneers' Historical Society, Inc., Flagstaff, AZ 12

Northern Illinois Historical Society, Grayslake, IL 108

Northern Indiana Historical Society, South Bend, IN 129

Northern Kentucky Historical Society, Fort Thomas, KY 155

Northern Montana College Collections, Havre, MT 258

Northern Neck of Virginia Historical Society, Montross, VA 477

Northern New York Agricultural Historical Society, Lafargeville, NY 317

Northern New York American-Canadian Genealogical Society, Keeseville, NY 317

Northern New York American-Canadian Genealogical Society, Plattsburgh, NY 329

Northern Virginia Association of Historians, Fairfax, VA 473

Northfield Historical Society, Northfield, MN 234

Northfield Historical Society, Northfield, VT 468

Northport Historical Society and Museum, Northport, NY 325

Northville Historical Society, Northville, MI 221
Northwest Chapter, Iowa Archaeological Society, Cherokee, IA 133
Northwest Ohio Historic Preservation Office, Bowling Green, OH 356
Northwest Suburban Council of Genealogists, Mt. Prospect, IL 112
Northwest Territory French and Canadian Heritage Institute, St. Louis Park, MN 236
Northwestern Memorial Hospital Archives, Chicago, IL 104
Norton County Historical Society, Norton, KS 149
Norwalk Historical Commission, Norwalk, CT 64
Norway Historical Society, Norway, ME 174
Norwegian-American Historical Association, Northfield, MN 234
Norwich and District Historical Museum, Norwich, Ontario 547
Nottingham Historical Society, Nottingham, NH 275
Nova Scotia Sport Heritage Centre, Halifax, Nova Scotia 535
Nuevo Santander Museum Complex, Laredo, TX 451
Nunatta Sunaqutangit, Frobisher Bay, Northwest Territories 532
Nutley Historical Society, Nutley, NJ 288
Nylander Museum, Caribou, ME 171

O

O. Henry Museum, Austin, TX 438
O'Brien County Historical Society, Primghar, IA 140
O'Leary Museum, O'Leary, Prince Edward Island 555
Oak Creek Historical Society, Oak Creek, WI 502
Oak Lawn Historical Society, Oak Lawn, IL 113
Oak Lawn Public Library, Oak Lawn, IL 113
Oak Summit School Historical Society, Frenchtown, NJ 281
Oakland County Pioneer and Historical Society, Pontiac, MI 221
Oakland Historical Society, Oakland, IA 140
Oakland Historical Society, Oakland, NJ 288
Oakland Museum Historical Society, Oakland, OR 384
Oakland Township Historical Society, Rochester, MI 222
Oaklands Association, Inc., Murfreesboro, TN 432
Oakville Museums—Oakville Historical Society, Oakville, Ontario 547
Oatlands Plantation, Leesburg, VA 475
Obion County Historical Society, Union City, TN 436
Oblate Archives, Saint Albert, Alberta 516
Ocean City Historical Museum, Ocean City, NJ 288
Ocean City Museum Society, Ocean City, MD 184
Ocean County Historical Society, Toms River, NJ 292
Ocmulgee National Monument, Macon, GA 90
Octorara Valley Historical Society, Parkesburg, PA 400
Odell Prairie Trails Historical and Genealogical Society, Odell, IL 113
Of Sea and Shore, Inc.—Museum of Seashells and Marine Life, Port Gammble, WA 486
Office of Archaeology and Historic Preservation, Colorado Historical Society, Denver, CO 52
Office of Historic Alexandria, City of Alexandria, Alexandria, VA 470
Office of Historic Preservation, Department of Parks and Recreation, Sacramento, CA 39
Office of Historic Preservation, Fall River, MA 195
Office of Historic Properties, Frankfort, KY 155
Office of History and Archaeology, Alaska Division of Parks and Outdoor Recreation, Anchorage, AK 9

Office of History, South Dakota State Historical Society, Pierre, SD 425
Office of Museum Programs, Wichita Public Schools, Wichita, KS 152
Office of Museums and Historic Sites, Onandaga County, Liverpool, NY 318
Office of the Curator, The White House, Washington, DC 75
Office of Vital Statistics, Frankfort, KY 155
Ogemaw Genealogical and Historical Society, West Branch, MI 224
Oglebay Institute—Mansion Museum, Wheeling, WV 494
Ohio Academy of History, Marion, OH 367
Ohio Association of Historical Societies and Museums, Columbus, OH 361
Ohio Baseball Hall of Fame and Museum, Maumee, OH 368
Ohio County Historical Society, Inc., Hartford, KY 156
Ohio County Historical Society, Inc., Rising Sun, IN 129
Ohio Covered Bridge Committee, Wyoming, OH 375
Ohio Genealogical Society, Mansfield, OH 367
Ohio Historic Preservation Office, Ohio Historical Society, Columbus, OH 361
Ohio Historical Society, Columbus, OH 361
Ohio Museums Association, Dayton, OH 362
Ohio Railway Museum, Worthington, OH 374
Ohio River Museum, Marietta, OH 367
Ohioana Library, Columbus, OH 361
Oil Museum of Canada, Oil Springs, Ontario 547
Ojai Valley Historical Society and Museum, Ojai, CA 34
Okanogan County Historical Society, Okanogan, WA 485
Okefenokee Heritage Center, Inc., Waycross, GA 94
Oklahoma County Historical Society, Oklahoma City, OK 379
Oklahoma Heritage Association, Oklahoma City, OK 379
Oklahoma Historic Fashions, Inc., Wagoner, OK 381
Oklahoma Historical Society, Oklahoma City, OK 379
Oklahoma Museums Association, Oklahoma City, OK 379
Oklahoma State Museum, Oklahoma City, OK 379
Oklahoma Steam Thresher Association, Pawnee, OK 379
Oklahoma Territorial Museum, Guthrie, OK 377
Oktibbeha County Heritage Museum, Starkville, MS 242
Olana State Historic Site, Hudson, NY 316
Old Abbeville District Historical Commission, Greenwood, SC 419
Old Barracks Association and Museum, Trenton, NJ 292
Old Bedford Village, Bedford, PA 383
Old Bethlehem Historical Society, Inc., Bethlehem, CT 58
Old Bohemia Historical Society, Inc., Warwick, MD 186
Old Bridge Historical Commission, Old Bridge, NJ 289
Old Bridgewater Historical Society, West Bridgewater, MA 207
Old Brown House Doll Museum, Gothenburg, NE 263
Old Brutus Historical Society, Inc., Weedsport, NY 339
Old Capitol, Iowa City, IA 137
Old Carratunk Historical Society, Bingham, ME 170
Old Castle Museum Complex, Baldwin City, KS 143
Old Central Museum of Higher Education, Stillwater, OK 380
Old Choctaw Chief's House, Swink, OK 380
Old Cienega Village Museum, Santa Fe, NM 299
Old Clinton Historical Society, Inc., Clinton, GA 87
Old Coal Mine Museum—Madrid Opera House, Madrid, NM 298
Old Colony Historical Society, Taunton, MA 206

Old Colony Planning Council, Brockton, MA 191
Old Constitution House, Windsor, VT 469
Old Court House Museum, Beaver, UT 461
Old Court House Museum, Guysborough, Nova
  Scotia 534
Old Cowtown Museum, Wichita, KS 152
Old Economy Village, Ambridge, PA 387
Old Exchange Building and Provost Dungeon,
  Charleston, SC 415
Old Fort Erie Historical Railroad and Museum, Ft. Erie,
  Ontario 542
Old Fort Harrod State Park, Harrodsburg, KY 156
Old Fort Henry, Kingston, Ontario 544
Old Fort Jackson, Savannah, GA 92
Old Fort Museum, Fort Smith, AR 18
Old Fort Niagara Association, Inc., Youngstown, NY 340
Old Fort Number Four Associates, Charlestown, NH 270
Old Fort Parker State Historic Site, Groesbeck, TX 448
Old Ft. Erie, Niagara Falls, Ontario 547
Old Greensborough Preservation Society, Greensboro,
  NC 345
Old Guard Museum, Fort Myer, VA 473
Old Homestead Museum, Herbert, Saskatchewan 564
Old House Guild of Sandusky, Sandusky, OH 371
Old Idaho Penitentiary, Boise, ID 96
Old Jail Art Center, Albany, TX 436
Old Jail Museum, Greenwood, AR 18
Old Jail Museum, Winchester, TN 436
Old Lighthouse Museum, Michigan City, IN 127
Old Logging Artifacts Museum, Cass Lake, MN 227
Old Market House State Historic Site, Galena, IL 107
Old Merchants House of New York, Inc., New York,
  NY 325
Old Mill Village Museum, New Milford, PA 399
Old Mines Area Historical Society, Old Mines, MO 251
Old Mint Museum, San Francisco, CA 41
Old Mission San Luis Obispo de Tolosa, San Luis
  Obispo, CA 42
Old Mobeetie Association—Mobeetie Jail Museum,
  Mobeetie, TX 452
Old Moheetie Association, Wheeler, TX 460
Old Molson Ghost Town and Museum, Molson, WA 485
Old Montana Prison, Deer Lodge, MT 257
Old Monterey Jail, Monterey, CA 33
Old North Church, Boston, MA 190
Old Northwest Corporation, Vincennes, IN 130
Old Post Office Museum—Collin County Historical
  Society, Inc., Frisco, TX 447
Old Rhinebeck Aerodrome, Inc., Rhinebeck, NY 330
Old Rock House, Santa Anna, TX 457
Old Rose Township Historical Society, Roseville,
  MN 235
Old Salem, Inc., Winston-Salem, NC 351
Old Saybrook Historical Society, Old Saybrook, CT 65
Old South Meeting House, Boston, MA 190
Old St. Mary's Historic Community Center, Cincinnati,
  OH 359
Old State House—Arkansas Commemorative
  Commission, Little Rock, AR 20
Old Stone Fort State Archaeological Park, Manchester,
  TN 431
Old Stone House, Washington, DC 75
Old Stone Prison, Decatur, TX 443
Old Sturbridge Village, Sturbridge, MA 206
Old Time Historical Association, Climax, NC 343
Old Town College Park Preservation Association,
  College Park, MD 569
Old Town Museum, Old Town, ME 174
Old Trail Driver's Association and Museum, San
  Antonio, TX 456
Old Trails Historical Society, Manchester, MO 250
Old Village Hall Museum, Lindenhurst, NY 318

Old Wall Historical Society, Wall, NJ 293
Old Washington Historic State Park, Washington, AR 22
Old West Museum, Chamberlain, SD 423
Old Westbury Gardens, Old Westbury, NY 326
Old World Wisconsin, Eagle, WI 496
Old York Historical Society, York, ME 178
Old York Road Historical Society, Jenkintown, PA 396
Oldest House and Tovar House, St. Augustine, FL 82
Oliver County Historical Society, Center, ND 352
Olivia Historic Preservation Corporation, Olivia, MN 234
Olivia Rodham Memorial Library, Nelson, NH 274
Olmsted County Genealogical Society, Rochester,
  MN 235
Oneida Historical Society, Utica, NY 338
Onondaga Historical Association, Syracuse, NY 336
Onslow County Historical Society, Jacksonville, NC 346
Ontario Agricultural Museum, Milton, Ontario 546
Ontario County Historical Society, Canandaigua,
  NY 306
Ontario Genealogical Society, Toronto, Ontario 553
Ontario Heritage Foundation, Toronto, Ontario 553
Ontario Historical Society, Ontario, NY 326
Ontario Historical Society, Willowdale, Ontario 554
Ontario Museum Association, Toronto, Ontario 553
Open Lands Project, Chicago, IL 104
Oracle Historical Society, Inc., Oracle, AZ 13
Oral History Office, Sangamon State University,
  Springfield, IL 117
Oral History Program, Fullerton, CA 28
Oral History Program, Little Rock, AR 20
Oral History Program, Plum Senior High School,
  Pittsburgh, PA 403
Oral History Program, University of Nevada, Reno,
  NV 269
Oral History Project, Social Science Research Institute,
  Honolulu, HI 96
Orange County Historical Commission, Orange, TX 420
Orange County Historical Commission, Santa Ana,
  CA 43
Orange County Historical Society, Inc., Orange,
  VA 478
Orange County Historical Society, Inc. and Museum,
  Orlando, FL 81
Orange Empire Railway Museum, Perris, CA 35
Orange Historical Society, Orange, CT 65
Orangeburg County Historical Society, Inc.,
  Orangeburg, SC 420
Orangeburgh German Swiss Genealogical Society,
  Charleston, SC 415
Orchard House, Home of the Alcotts, Concord, MA 193
Orchard Park Historical Society, Orchard Park, NY 327
Order of the Indian Wars, Little Rock, AR 20
Oregon-California Trails Association, Gerald, MO 246
Oregon Electric Railway Historical Society, Inc., Forest
  Grove, OR 383
Oregon Historical Society, Portland, OR 385
Oregon Lewis & Clark Heritage Foundation, Portland,
  OR 385
Oregon Military Museum, Clackamas, OR 382
Oregon Museum Park—Lane County Historical
  Museum, Eugene, OR 383
Oregon State Library, Salem, OR 386
Oregon Trail Museum Association, Baton Rouge,
  LA 164
Organization of American Historians, Bloomington,
  IN 121
Organization of Military Museums of Canada, Canadian
  War Museum, Ottawa, Ontario 549
Oriental Institute Museum, Chicago, IL 104
Orland Historical Society, Orland, ME 174
Orland Historical Society, Orland Park, IL 113
Orleans County Historical Association, Albion, NY 302

Orleans County Historical Society, Inc., Brownington, VT 465
Orleans Historical Society—Margaret Stranger House, Orleans, MA 201
Orma J. Smith Museum of Natural History, Caldwell, ID 97
Osage County Genealogical Society, Lyndon, KS 148
Osage County Historical Society, Pawhuska, OK 379
Osborne County Genealogical and Historical Society, Inc., Osborne, KS 149
Oscar Farris Agricultural Museum, Nashville, TN 434
Oscar Getz Museum of Whiskey History, Bardstown, KY 153
Oshawa and District Historical Society—Oshawa Sydenham Museum: Henry House, Robinson House, Guy House, Oshawa, Ontario 548
Oshkosh Public Museum, Oshkosh, WI 502
Osnaburg Historical Society, East Canton, OH 363
Ossining Historical Society and Museum, Ossining, NY 329
Osterville Historical Society, Osterville, MA 201
Oswego County Historical Society, Oswego, NY 327
Othello Community Museum, Othello, WA 486
Ottawa City Archives, Ottawa, Ontario 549
Otter Tail County Historical Society, Fergus Falls, MN 229
Outagamie County Historical Society, Inc., Appleton, WI 494
Overholser Mansion, Oklahoma City, OK 379
Overland Historical Society, Overland, MO 251
Overland Trail Museum, Sterling, CO 57
Owens Art Gallery, Sackville, New Brunswick 530
Owens-Thomas House Museum, Savannah, GA 92
Owensboro Area Museum, Owensboro, KY 161
Owls Head Transportation Museum, Owls Head, ME 174
Owyhee County Historical Society and Museum, Murphy, ID 98
Oxford County Museum School, Burgessville, Ontario 540
Oxford Historical Society, Inc., Oxford, CT 65
Oxford Museum, Woodstock, Ontario 555
Oyster Bay Historical Society, Oyster Bay, NY 327
Oyster Ponds Historical Society, Inc., Orient, NY 327
Ozark Folk Center, Mt. View, AR 20

P

P.K. Yonge Library of Florida History, Gainesville, FL 78
P.T. Boats, Inc., Memphis, TN 432
Pacific Coast Archaeological Society, Inc., Costa Mesa, CA 26
Pacific Coast Chapter, Railway and Locomotive Historical Society, Inc., San Francisco, CA 1
Pacific County Historical Society and Museum Foundation, South Bend, WA 489
Pacific Grove Heritage Society, Pacific Grove, CA 35
Pacific Northwest Chapter, National Railway Historical Society, Portland, OR 385
Pacific Northwest Conservation Laboratory, Port Orchard, WA 486
Pacific Northwest Historians Guild, Seattle, WA 488
Pacific Northwest Labor History Association, Seattle, WA 488
Pacific Palisades Historical Society, Pacific Palisades, CA 35
Pacific Railroad Society, Inc., Los Angeles, CA 32
Pacific Submarine Museum, Pearl Harbor, HI 96
Pacific University Museum, Old College Hall, Forest Grove, OR 383

Packwood House Museum, Lewisburg, PA 397
Paducah-McCracken County Growth, Inc. Paducah, KY 161
Pajaro Valley Historical Association, Watsonville, CA 48
Palace of the Governors, Santa Fe, NM 299
Palacios Area Historical Association, Palacios, TX 453
Palatine Historical Society, Palatine, IL 113
Palatine Settlement Society, St. Johnsville, NY 332
Palatka Public Library, Palatka, FL 81
Palm Beach County Genealogical Society, Inc., West Palm Beach, FL 84
Palm Beach Landmarks Preservation Commission, Palm Beach, FL 81
Palm Springs Historical Society, Palm Springs, CA 35
Palmer Historical Commission, Palmer, MA 201
Palmyra Historical Society, Palmyra, WI 502
Palo Alto Historical Association, Palo Alto, CA 35
Palo Pinto County Historical Association, Inc., Palo Pinto, TX 454
Panhandle Plains Historical Society and Museum, Canyon, TX 440
Paradise Fact and Folklore, Inc., Paradise, CA 35
Parc Historique National de Coteau-du-Lac, Coteau-du-Lac, Quebec 557
Parc Historique National du Fort Chambly, Chambly, Quebec 556
Pardee Home Foundation, Oakland, CA 34
Park City Historical Society, Park City, UT 463
Park City Museum, Park City, UT 463
Park College Historical Society, Parkville, MO 251
Park County Historical Society, Bailey, CO 50
Park County Historical Society, Livingston, MT 259
Park County Museum Association, Livingston, MT 259
Park Forest Historical Society, Park Forest, IL 113
Park-McCullough House Association, North Bennington, VT 468
Park Ridge Historical Society, Park Ridge, IL 114
Parkdale-Maplewood Community Museum, Barss Corner, Nova Scotia 533
Parke County Historical Society, Rockville, IN 129
Parker County Genealogical Society, Weatherford, TX 460
Parma Area Historical Society, Parma, OH 370
Parma Meetinghouse Museum, Hilton, NY 315
Parris Island Museum, Beaufort, SC 413
Parrsboro Mineral and Gem Geological Museum, Parrsboro, Nova Scotia 537
Partridge Island Research Project, Saint John, New Brunswick 530
Pas Historical and Heritage Society, Inc., The Pas, Manitoba 525
Pas-Ka-Poo Historical Park, Rimbey, British Columbia 520
Pasadena Historical Society, Pasadena, CA 35
Paso Real Stagecoach Inn Museum, Harlingen, TX 448
Pasquotank Historical and Genealogical Society, Elizabeth City, NC 344
Passaic County Historical Society, Paterson, NJ 289
Pate Museum of Transportation, Fort Worth, TX 446
Patee House Museum, St. Joseph, MO 253
Paterson Museum, Paterson, NJ 289
Patriots Point Development Authority, Mt. Pleasant, SC 420
Patterson Homestead, Dayton, OH 362
Patterson Township Historical Society, Patterson, CA 35
Patton Museum of Cavalry and Armor, Fort Knox, KY 154
Paul and Olive Bruner Museum, Valier, MT 260
Paul Revere House, Boston, MA 190
Pavillon André-Coindre, St. Augustin, Quebec 561
Pawlett Historical Society, Pawlett, VT 468
Pawnee County Historical Society, Pawnee, OK 379

Payne County Historical Society, Stillwater, OK 380
Paynesville Historical Society, Paynesville, MN 234
Pea River Historical and Genealogical Society,
    Enterprise, AL 4
Peabody Museum of Salem, Salem, MA 204
Peace River Centennial Museum, Peace River,
    Alberta 515
Peace River Valley Historical Society, Inc., Arcadia,
    FL 76
Peacham Historical Association, Peacham, VT 468
Pearl S. Buck Birthplace Foundation, Inc., Hillsboro,
    WV 493
Pearson Museum, The, Springfield, IL 117
Peary-MacMillan Arctic Museum, Brunswick, ME 170
Pecos National Monument, Pecos, NM 298
Pee Dee Heritage Center, Hartsville, SC 419
Peekskill Museum, Peekskill, NY 328
Peerless Rockville Historic Preservation, Ltd., Rockville,
    MD 185
Pejepscot Historical Society, Brunswick, ME 170
Pelham Historical Society, Pelham, NH 275
Pella Historical Society, Pella, IA 140
Pember Library and Museum, Granville, NY 313
Pemberton Hall Foundation, Inc., Salisbury, MD 185
Pemiscot County Historical Society, Caruthersville,
    MO 244
Pendleton Chapter, South Carolina Genealogical
    Society, Clemson, SC 416
Pendleton District Historical and Recreational
    Commission, Pendleton, SC 421
Peninsula Historical Society, Gig Harbor, WA 484
Peninsula Library and Historical Society, Peninsula,
    OH 370
Peninsular Archaeological Society, Inc., Holiday, FL 78
Pennsbury Manor, Morrisville, PA 399
Pennsylvania Dutch Folk Culture Society, Inc.,
    Lenhartsville, PA 397
Pennsylvania Farm Museum of Landis Valley,
    Lancaster, PA 397
Pennsylvania German Society, Bindsboro, PA 388
Pennsylvania Historical and Museum
    Commission—William Penn Memorial Museum,
    Harrisburg, PA 394
Pennsylvania Historical Association, University Park,
    PA 406
Pennsylvania Humanities Council, Philadelphia, PA 402
Pennsylvania Labor History Society, Philadelphia,
    PA 402
Pennsylvania Lumber Museum, Galeton, PA 393
Pennsylvania Military Museum, Boalsburg, PA 388
Pennsylvania Postal History Society, Paupack, PA 400
Pennsylvania Railway Museum Association,
    Inc.—Arden Trolley Museum, Washington, PA 407
Pennsylvania Society, Sons of the American Revolution,
    Quakertown, PA 404
Pennypacker Mills, Schwenksville, PA 405
Pennyroyal Area Museum, Hopkinsville, KY 157
Penobscot Marine Museum, Searsport, ME 176
Pensacola Historical Society, Pensacola, FL 82
Peoples of Utah Institute, Salt Lake City, UT 463
Peoria Historical Society, Peoria, IL 114
Perkins County Historical Society, Bison, SD 422
Permian Basin Petroleum Museum, Library, and Hall of
    Fame, Midland, TX 452
Permian Historical Society, Odessa, TX 453
Perquimans County Historical Society, Hertford, NC 345
Perry County Chapter, Ohio Genealogical Society,
    Junction City, OH 366
Perry County Genealogical and Historical Society, Inc.,
    Hazard, KY 156
Perry County Lutheran Historical Society, Altenburg,
    MO 242

Perry Historians, Newport, PA 399
Perry's Victory and International Peace Memorial,
    Put-in-Bay, OH 371
Perth County Branch, Ontario Genealogical Society,
    Stratford, Ontario 551
Peshtigo Historical Society, Peshtigo, WI 502
Petaluma Adobe State Historic Park, Petaluma, CA 35
Petaluma Museum and Historical Library, Petaluma,
    CA 5
Peter Conser House, Heavener, OK 378
Peter Wentz Farmstead, Worcester, PA 408
Peterborough Centennial Museum and Archives,
    Peterborough, Ontario 549
Peterborough Historical Society, Peterborough, NH 275
Peterborough Historical Society—Hutchison House
    Museum, Peterborough, Ontario 549
Peters Creek Historical Society, Finleyville, PA 392
Petersburg Museums, Petersburg, VA 478
Petersburg National Battlefield, Petersburg, VA 478
Petersham Historical Society, Inc., Petersham, MA 202
Peterson Heritage, Inc., Peterson, IA 140
Peterson Steamship Company—SS Keewatin, Douglas,
    MI 214
Pettaguamscatt Historical Society, Kingston, RI 409
Phelps County Genealogical Society, Rolla, MO 252
Phelps County Historical Society, Holdrege, NE 263
Phelps County Historical Society, Rolla, MO 252
Phi Alpha Theta International Honor Society in History,
    Allentown, PA 387
PhilaMatic Center, Boys Town, NE 261
Philadelphia Branch, National Archives, Philadelphia,
    PA 402
Philadelphia Historical Commission, Philadelphia,
    PA 402
Philadelphia Maritime Museum, Philadelphia, PA 402
Philadelphia Mummers Museum, Philadelphia, PA 402
Philadelphia Society for the Preservation of Landmarks,
    Philadelphia, PA 403
Philip Read Memorial Library, Plainfield, NH 275
Philipse Manor Hall State Historic Site, Yonkers, NY 340
Phillips County Museum, Helena, AR 18
Phillips House Museum, Rockville Centre, NY 331
Phippsburg Historical Society, Inc., Phippsburg,
    ME 175
Phoebe Apperson Hearst Historical Society, Inc., St.
    Clair, MO 253
Pickens County Historical Society, Pickens, SC 421
Pickwick Mill, Inc., Pickwick, MN 234
Piedmont Historical and Genealogical Society,
    Piedmont, AL 7
Pierce Brigade, Concord, NH 270
Pierce County Historical Society, Pierce, NE 266
Piermont Historical Society, Piermont, NH 275
Pike County Historical and Genealogical Society, Troy,
    AL 8
Pike County Historical Society, Pikeville, KY 161
Pike County Historical Society, Pittsfield, IL 114
Pike Heritage Museum, Waverly, OH 374
Pike Pioneer Museum, Troy, AL 8
Pilgrim John Howland Society—Howland House,
    Plymouth, MA 202
Pilgrim Society, Plymouth, MA 202
Pima Air Museum, Tucson, AZ 16
Pimeria Alta Historical Society, Nogales, AZ 13
Pincher Creek and District Historical Society—Pincher
    Creek Museum and Kootenzi Brown Historical
    Village, Pincher Creek, Alberta 515
Pinckney Area Historical Society, Pinckney, MI 221
Pine County Historical Society, Askou, MN 226
Pine Grove Historical Museum—Governor Moses
    Wisner Historic House and Grounds, Pontiac,
    MI 222

Pinellas County Historical Society, Largo, FL 80
Pinson Mounds State Archaeological Area, Pinson, TN 435
Pioneer Adobe House Museum, Hillsboro, KS 147
Pioneer America Society, Inc., Akron, OH 355
Pioneer and Historical Society of Muskingum County, Zanesville, OH 375
Pioneer Auto Museum and Antique Town, Murdo, SD 425
Pioneer City County Museum, Sweetwater, TX 458
Pioneer Farm and House Museum, Oxford, OH 370
Pioneer Farm and Village, Roseau, MN 235
Pioneer Farm Museum—The D.O.V.E. Center, Eatonville, WA 483
Pioneer Hall and Museum, San Antonio, TX 56
Pioneer Heritage Center, Shreveport, LA 168
Pioneer Historical Society, Inc., Farmington, IA 136
Pioneer Historical Society, Ponca City, OK 379
Pioneer Historical Society of Riverside, Riverside, CA 38
Pioneer Home Museum of Virden and District, Virden, Manitoba 525
Pioneer Memorial Museum, Darby, MT 257
Pioneer Museum and Art Center, Woodward, OK 381
Pioneer Museum and Historical Society of North Iowa, Mason City, IA 139
Pioneer Valley Planning Commission, West Springfield, MA 208
Pioneer Village, Farmington, UT 462
Pioneer Village Commission, Cedar Rapids, IA 133
Pioneer Woman Museum, Ponca City, OK 379
Pioneer's Cemetery Association, Inc., Phoenix, AZ 14
Pioneers' Museum, Colorado Springs, CO 51
Pioneers Texas Trail Drivers and Former Texas Rangers Corporation, Inc., San Antonio, TX 456
Pipe Spring National Monument, Moccasin, AZ 13
Pipestone County Historical Society, Pipestone, MN 235
Piqua Historical Society, Piqua, OH 371
Piscataway Cultural Arts Commission, Piscataway, NJ 289
Pittock Mansion, Portland, OR 385
Pittsburgh Children's Museum, Pittsburgh, PA 403
Pittsburgh History and Landmarks Foundation, Pittsburgh, PA 403
Placer County Historical Society, Auburn, CA 23
Placer County Museum, Auburn, CA 23
Plainfield Historical Society, Plainfield, NH 275
Plainfield Historical Society, Inc., Plainfield, MA 202
Plains Historical Museum, Regina, Saskatchewan 566
Plains Indians and Pioneer Historical Foundation, Woodward, OR 386
Plainsboro Historical Society, Plainsboro, NJ 289
Plainsman Museum, Aurora, NE 261
Plainville Historical Society, Inc., Plainville, CT 65
Plaistow Historical Society, Inc., Plaistow, NH 569
Plateau Sciences Society, Gallup, NM 297
Platt County Historical and Genealogical Society, Monticello, IL 111
Platte County Historical Society, Platte City, MO 251
Pleasant Valley Preservation Society, Holmdel, NJ 283
Plimoth Plantation, Inc., Plymouth, MA 202
Plumas County Museum, Quincy, CA 196
Plymouth Antiquarian Society, Plymouth, MA 203
Plymouth County Historical Museum, Le Mars, IA 138
Plymouth Historical Society, Plymouth, MI 221
Plymouth Meeting Historical Society, North Wales, PA 400
Pocahontas County Historical Society, Rolfe, IA 141
Pocahontas County Historical Society, Inc., Marlinton, WV 493
Pocumtuck Valley Memorial Association—Memorial Hall Museum, Deerfield, MA 194

Pohick Episcopal Church: Parish of Mt. Vernon and Gunston Hall, Lorton, VA 476
Point Douglas Historical Society, Winnipeg, Manitoba 570
Point Ellice House Museum, Victoria, British Columbia 522
Point of Honor, Lynchburg, VA 476
Polish American Historical Association, Chicago, IL 104
Polish Genealogical Society of Michigan, Detroit, MI 214
Polish Genealogical Society, Inc., Chicago, IL 104
Polish Historical Commission, Central Council of Polish Organizations, Pittsburgh, PA 404
Polish Museum of America, Chicago, IL 104
Polishville Cemetery and Grotto Association, Brighton, IA 132
Polk County Chapter, East Tennessee Historical Society, Cleveland, TN 428
Polk County Heritage Society, Livingston, TX 451
Polk County Historical and Genealogical Library, Bartow, FL 76
Polk County Historical Association, Bartow, FL 76
Polk County Historical Commission, Livingston, TX 451
Polk County Historical Society, Balsam Lake, WI 495
Polk County Historical Society, Cedartown, GA 87
Polk County Historical Society, Crookston, MN 227
Polk County Historical Society, Des Moines, IA 135
Poll Museum of Transportation, Holland, MI 217
Polson-Flathead Historic Museum, Polson, MT 259
Polson Park and Museum Historical Society, Hoquiam, WA 488
Ponca City Cultural Center and Museums, Ponca City, OK 380
Pontiac Area Historical and Genealogical Society, Pontiac, MI 222
Pony Express Museum, Marysville, KS 148
Pope County Historical Foundation, Russellville, AR 21
Pope County Historical Society and Museum, Glenwood, MN 229
Pope-Leighey House, Mount Vernon, VA 477
Porcupine Plain and District Museum, Porcupine Plain, Saskatchewan 565
Poricy Park Citizens Committee, Middletown, NJ 285
Port Carling Pioneer Museum, Pt. Carling, Ontario 550
Port Colborne Historical and Marine Museum, Port Colborne, Ontario 550
Port Deposit Heritage Corporation, Port Deposit, MD 184
Port Hastings Historical Museum and Archives, Port Hastings, Nova Scotia 537
Port Penn Museum—Port Penn Area Historical Society, Port Penn, DE 70
Port-au-Port—Bay St. George Heritage Association, Stephenville, Newfoundland 532
Portage Canal Society, Inc., Portage, WI 503
Portage County Chapter, Ohio Genealogical Society, Ravenna, OH 371
Portage County Historical Society, Stevens Point, WI 504
Portage County Historical Society, Inc., Ravenna, OH 371
Portal Heritage Society, Portal, GA 91
Porter-Phelps-Huntington Foundation, Inc., Hadley, MA 194
Porterville Museum, Porterville, CA 36
Portland Fire Museum, Portland, ME 175
Portland Museum, Louisville, KY 159
Portola Expedition Foundation, San Mateo, CA 43
Portsmouth Historical Society—John Paul Jones House, Portsmouth, NH 275
Portsmouth Lightship Museum, Portsmouth, VA 478
Portsmouth Museums, Portsmouth, VA 478
Portsmouth Naval Shipyard Museum, Portsmouth, VA 478

Portuguese Historical and Cultural Society, Sacramento, CA 39

Posey County Historical Society, Mt. Vernon, IN 127

Postville Courthouse State Historic Site, Lincoln, IL 110

Postville Historical Society, Postville, IA 140

Potrero-East County Museum Society, Potrero, CA 36

Potsdam Public Museum, Potsdam, NY 329

Potter County Historical Society, Coudersport, PA 391

Poudre Landmarks Foundation, Fort Collins, CO 54

Poughkeepsie Historical Society, Poughkeepsie, NY 329

Pound Ridge Historical Society, Pound Ridge, NY 329

Poway Historical and Memorial Society, Poway, CA 36

Powell County Museum, Deer Lodge, MT 257

Powers Museum, Carthage MO 244

Poweshiek County Historical and Genealogical Society, Montezuma, IA 139

Prairie County Historical Society, Hazen, AR 18

Prairie Grove Battlefield Historic State Park, Prairie Grove, AR 21

Prairie Historical Society, Inc., Madison, SD 424

Prairie Homestead, Philip, SD 425

Prairie Memories Museum, Irvine, Alberta 515

Prairie West Historical Society, Inc., Eston, Saskatchewan 564

Pratt County Historical Society, Pratt, KS 150

Preble County Historical Society, Eaton, OH 363

Presbyterian Historical Society, Philadelphia, PA 403

Prescott House, Halifax, Nova Scotia 535

Preservation Alliance of Louisville and Jefferson County, Inc., Louisville, KY 159

Preservation and Heritage Society of Scituate, Scituate, RI 412

Preservation Guild of Hancock County, Findlay, OH 364

Preservation, Inc., Chestertown, MD 182

Preservation New Jersey, Inc., Princeton, NJ 290

Preservation of Historic Winchester, Inc., Winchester, VA 482

Preservation Planning, City of Albuquerque, Albuquerque, NM 295

Preservation Society of Asheville and Buncombe County, Asheville, NC 341

Preservation Society of Charleston, Charleston, SC 415

Preservation Society of Fall River, Fall River, MA 195

Preservation Society of Newport County, Newport, RI 410

Preservation Technology Reference Center, Washington, DC 75

Preserve It Now, Fonda, NY 312

President Benjamin Harrison Memorial Home, Indianapolis, IN 125

President Harding's Home, Marion, OH 368

Presidential Museum, Odessa, TX 453

Presidio Army Museum, San Francisco, CA 41

Presidio La Bahia, Goliad, TX 447

Presidio Lancers, Albuquerque, NM 295

Presidio of Monterey Museum, Monterey, CA 33

Presque Isle County Historical Museum, Roger's City, MI 222

Preston County Historical Society, Kingwood, WV 493

Price County Historical Society, Fifield, WI 496

Price County Historical Society, Park Falls, WI 502

Prince Albert Historical Society and Museum, Prince Albert, Saskatchewan 565

Prince Edward Island Museum and Heritage Foundation, Charlottetown, Prince Edward Island 555

Prince George's County Historical Society, Riverdale, MD 184

Prince of Wales Northern Heritage Center, Yellowknife, Northwest Territories 533

Princess Patricia's Canadian Light Infantry, Regimental Museum, Calgary, Alberta 511

Princeton and District Pioneer Museum, Princeton, British Columbia 520

Princeton Historical Society, Inc., Princeton, WI 503

Princeton History Project, Princeton, NJ 290

Princetown Historical Society, Schenectady, NY 333

Private Caddo Indian Museum, Longview, TX 451

Pro Football Hall of Fame, Canton, OH 357

Promotion and Preservation of Iberville Parish, Inc., Plaquemine, LA 167

Prospect Park South Association, Brooklyn, NY 305

Providence Athenaeum, Providence, RI 411

Providence City Archives, Providence, RI 411

Providence Preservation Society, Providence, RI 411

Provincial Archives of Alberta, Provincial Government Department of Culture, Edmonton, Alberta 513

Provincial Archives of British Columbia, Victoria, British Columbia 522

Provincial Archives of Manitoba, Winnipeg, Manitoba 526

Provincial Archives of New Brunswick, Fredericton, New Brunswick 529

Provincial Archives of Newfoundland and Labrador, St. John's, Newfoundland 532

Provincial Museum of Alberta, Edmonton, Alberta 513

Prowers County Historical Society, Lamar, CO 55

Prudence Crandall Museum, Canterbury, CT 58

Public Archives of Canada, Ottawa, Ontario 549

Public Archives of Nova Scotia, Halifax, Nova Scotia 535

Public History Program, University of California, Santa Barbara, Santa Barbara, CA 43

Public Works Historical Society, Chicago, IL 194

Pueblo Grande Museum, Phoenix, AZ 14

Pulaski County Genealogy Society, Star City, IN 130

Pulaski County Historical Society, Little Rock, AR 20

Pulaski County Historical Society, Inc., Somerset, KY 162

Pulaski Historical Commission, Inc., Hawkinsville, GA 89

Pump House Steam Museum, Kingston, Ontario 544

Punxsutawney Area Historical and Genealogical Society, Punxsutawney, PA 404

Putnam County Archives and History Commission, Palatka, FL 81

Putnam County Historical Society, Cold Spring, NY 308

Putnam County Historical Society, Greencastle, IN 124

Putnam County Historical Society, Hennepin, IL 108

Putnam County Historical Society, Kalida, OH 366

Putnam Museum, Davenport, IA 134

Putney Historical Society, Putney, VT 468

Q

Quaco Historical and Library Society, Inc., St. Martins, New Brunswick 531

Quaker Collection, Haverford College, Haverford, PA 394

Quapaw Quarter Association, Little Rock, AR 20

Quebec Family History Society, Pointe Claire, Quebec 560

Quechan Indian Museum, Yuma, AZ 16

Queen Charlotte Islands Museum Society, Skidegate, British Columbia 521

Queen's Bush Foundation, Holland Centre, Ontario 543

Queen's Bush Historical Society, Listowel, Ontario 545

Queens County Farm Museum, New York, NY 325

Queens County Historical Society, Liverpool, Nova Scotia 535

Queens County Museum, Liverpool, Nova Scotia 536

Queens Historical Society, Flushing, NY 312

Queens Museum, The, Flushing, NY 312
Quetico Provincial Park Museum, French Lake, Ontario 542
Quincy Historical Society, Quincy, MA 203
Quincy Mine Hoist Association, Inc., Hancock, MI 216
Quivira Research Center, Albuquerque, NM 295

R

R. C. Baker Memorial Museum, Inc., Coalinga, CA 25
R. E. Olds Museum, Lansing, MI 218
R. H. Lowie Museum of Anthropology, Berkeley, CA 24
R. N. Atkinson Museum, Penticton, British Columbia 520
RCMP (Royal Canadian Mounted Police), Regina, Saskatchewan 566
Racine County Historical Society and Museum, Racine, WI 503
Ragged Islands Historical Society, Lockeport, Nova Scotia 536
Rahr-West Museum, Manitowoc, WI 500
Rail America, the National Railroad Museum, Green Bay, WI 497
Railroad and Pioneer Museum, Inc., Temple, TX 458
Railroad Museum of Pennsylvania, Strasburg, PA 405
Railroad Station Historical Society, Crete, NE 262
Railroader's Memorial Museum, Altoona, PA 387
Railroadians of America, Inc., Livingston, NJ 284
Rainy Hills Historical Society, Iddesleigh, Alberta 515
Rainy River District Women's Institute Museum, Emo, Ontario 542
Raleigh Historic Properties Commission, Inc., Raleigh, NC 348
Ralliement des Familles Bonneau, Inc., St. Francois, Quebec 561
Ralls County Historical Society, New London, MO 251
Ralph Foster Museum, Point Lookout, MO 252
Ramapogue Historical Society—The Day House, West Springfield, MA 208
Ramona Museum of California History, Los Angeles, CA 32
Ramona Pioneer Historical Society, Inc.—Guy B. Woodward Museum, Ramona, CA 36
Ramsey County Historical Society, St. Paul, MN 236
Ramsey Historical Association, Ramsey, NJ 290
Ranching Heritage Association, Lubbock, TX 452
Rancho Los Alamitos Associates, Long Beach, CA 31
Randolph County Historical Society, Asheboro, NC 340
Randolph County Historical Society, Moberly, MO 251
Randolph Historical Commission, Randolph, MA 203
Range Genealogical Society, Inc., Buhl, MN 227
Rankin County Historical Society, Inc., Brandon, MS 239
Rankin Museum Association, Rankin, TX 455
Rapid City Museum, Rapid City, Manitoba 524
Rare Book Department, Alderman Library, Charlottesville, VA 472
Raton Museum, Raton, NM 298
Rattlesnake Bomber Base Museum, Pyote, TX 454
Ravalli County Museum, Hamilton, MT 258
Ravalli Schoolhouse Restoration Society, Ravalli, MT 259
Ravenna Heritage, Ravenna, OH 371
Ravenswood—Lake View Historical Association, Chicago, IL 104
Rawlins County Historical Society, Atwood, KS 143
Raymore Pioneer Museum, Raymore, Saskatchewan 566
Raynham Hall Museum, Oyster Bay, NY 327
Reading Antiquarian Society, Reading, MA 203
Reading Historical Commission, Reading, MA 203

Reading Public Museum and Art Gallery, Reading, PA 404
Readsboro Historical Society, Readsboro, VT 468
Recherches Amérindiennes au Québec, Montreal, Quebec 560
Records and Information Center, Lutheran Council—Archives of Cooperative Lutheranism, New York, NY 325
Records Division, City of Portland, Portland, OR 385
Records Management Office, Portland Public Schools, Portland, OR 385
Records Management Program, Oneida Tribe of Indians of Wisconsin, Oneida, WI 502
Red Bank Historical Society, Inc., Red Bank, NJ 290
Red Clay State Historical Area, Cleveland, TN 428
Red Deer and District Museum and Archives, Red Deer, Alberta 516
Red Hill Shrine, Brookneal, VA 471
Red Lion Area Historical Society, Red Lion, PA 404
Red River Valley Heritage Society, Moorhead, MN 233
Red Rock Museum, Gallup, NM 297
Red Shirt Shrine, Oakley Park, Edgefield, SC 418
Redcliff Museum and Historical Society, Redcliff, Alberta 516
Redding Museum and Art Center, Redding, CA 37
Redwater and District Museum, Redwater, Alberta 516
Reed Gold Mine, Stanfield, NC 349
Reedley Historical Society, Reedley, CA 37
Refugio County Historical Society, Refugio, TX 455
Regimental Museum, Governor General's Foot Guards, Ottawa, Ontario 549
Regional Archives Branch, National Archives and Records Administration, Bayonne, NJ 277
Regional Conference of Historical Agencies, Syracuse, NY 336
Regional History Center, DeKalb, IL 106
Regional History Department, Community Library, Ketchum, ID 97
Regional History Programs, Marist College, Poughkeepsie, NY 329
Reina del Mar Parlor 126, Native Daughters of the Golden West, Santa Barbara, CA 43
Reitz Home Preservation Society, Inc., Evansville, IN 122
Remington Gun Museum, Ilion, NY 316
Remsen-Steuben Historical Society, Remsen, NY 330
Reno County Genealogical Society, Hutchinson, KS 147
Reno County Historical Society, Hutchinson, KS 147
Rensselaer County Historical Society, Troy, NY 337
Rensselaerville Historical Society, Rensselaerville, NY 330
Renton Historical Society and Museum, Renton, WA 487
Republic County Historical Society, Belleville, KS 143
Research Center for Dubuque Area History, Dubuque, IA 135
Resource and Research Center for Beaver County Local History, Beaver Falls, PA 388
Restigouche Regional Museum, Dalhouse, New Brunswick 528
Reston and District Historical Museum, Reston, Manitoba 524
Restoration Technology, Brockville, Ontario 540
Restoration of Kane County, St. Charles, IL 116
Restore our County, Inc., Dandridge, TN 428
Resurrection Bay Historical Society, Seward, AK 11
RevMex (Revolutionary Mexican Historical Society), Ozawkie, KS 150
Revelstoke Museum, Revelstoke, British Columbia 520
Reynolds Aviation Museum, Wetaskiwin, Alberta 517
Reynolds Community Museum, Reynolds, ND 353
Reynolds Homestead, Critz, VA 472
Reynolds Library Associates, Birmingham, AL 2

Rhoades Valley Camp, Daughters of Utah Pioneers, Kamas, UT 462
Rhode Island Black Heritage Society, Providence, RI 411
Rhode Island Committee for the Humanities, Providence, RI 411
Rhode Island Historical Preservation Commission, Providence, RI 412
Rhode Island Historical Society, Providence, RI 412
Rhode Island Jewish Historical Association, Providence, RI 412
Rhode Island State Archives, Providence, RI 412
Rialto Historical Society, Rialto, CA 37
Rice County Historical Society and Museum, Faribault, MN 229
Rice County Historical Society, Lyons, KS 148
Richard Caswell Memorial/CSS Neuse, Kinston, NC 346
Richard Montgomery Chapter, National Society, Sons of the American Revolution, Dayton, OH 362
Richey Historical Society, Richey, MT 259
Richfield Historical Society, Richfield, MN 235
Richibucto River Historical Society, Rexton, New Brunswick 530
Richland County Genealogical and Historical Society, Olney, IL 113
Richland County Historic Preservation Commission, Columbia, SC 416
Richland County Historical Society, Mansfield, OH 367
Richland County Historical Society, Wahpeton, ND 354
Richland West End Neighborhood Association, Inc., Nashville, TN 434
Richmond County Historical Society, Augusta, GA 86
Richmond Historical Society, Richmond, RI 412
Richmond Museum Association, Inc., Richmond, CA 37
Richmond National Battlefield Park, Richmond, VA 479
Ricketts Memorial Museum, Hamilton, MT 258
Rideau Canal, Smiths Falls, Ontario 551
Ridge Historical Society, Chicago, IL 104
Ridgewood Preservation, Inc., Canton, OH 358
Riley County Historical Society, Manhattan, KS 148
Ring House Galery, Edmonton, Alberta 513
Ringwood Manor House, Ringwood, NJ 290
Rio Grande County Museum, Del Norte, CO 51
Rio Vista Museum Association, Inc., Rio Vista, CA 37
Ripon Historical Society, Ripon, WI 503
River Road Historical Society, Destrehan, LA 164
Riverside Avondale Preservation, Inc., Jacksonville, FL 79
Riverside County Historical Commission, Riverside, CA 38
Riverside Municipal Museum, Riverside, CA 38
Riverview, the Historic Hobson House, Bowling Green, KY 153
Riviera Historical Museum, Riviera, TX 455
Roanoke Island Historical Association, Inc., Manteo, NC 346
Roanoke Museum of Fine Arts, Roanoke, VA 480
Roanoke River Museum, Prestwould Foundation, Clarksville, VA 472
Roanoke Transportation Museum, Roanoke, VA 480
Roanoke Valley Historical Society, Roanoke, VA 480
Robbins Hunter Museum, Granville, OH 365
Robert E. Lee Memorial Association, Inc., Stratford, VA 481
Robert Hull Fleming Museum, Burlington, VT 465
Robert Jackman Collection, St. John's, Newfoundland 532
Robert Toombs House, Washington, GA 94
Robinson State Museum, Pierre, SD 425
Rochester Association of Performing Arts, Webster, NY 339

Rochester Hills Historic District Commission, Rochester, MI 222
Rochester Historical Society, Rochester, NH 275
Rochester Historical Society, Rochester, NY 331
Rochester Museum and Science Center, Rochester, NY 331
Rock Castle Historic Home, Hendersonville, TN 429
Rock County Historical Society, Janesville, WI 498
Rock Creek Station State Historical Park, Fairbury, NE 262
Rock Creek Valley Historical Society and Museum, Westmoreland, KS 152
Rock Ford Plantation, Lancaster, PA 397
Rock Island Arsenal Historical Society, Rock Island, IL 115
Rock Island County Historical Society, Moline, IL 111
Rockdale County Historical Society, Conyers, GA 87
Rockford Area Historical Society, Rockford, MI 222
Rockford Museum Center and Midway Village, Rockford, IL 15
Rockingham County History Society, Wentworth, NC 350
Rockpile Museum, Gillette, WY 507
Rockwood Museum, Wilmington, DE 71
Rocky Hill Historical Society, Inc., Rocky Hill, CT 66
Rocky Lane School Museum, Ft. Vermilion, Alberta 514
Rocky Mount Historical Association, Piney Flats, TN 435
Rocky Mountain House National Historic Park, Rocky Mountain House, Alberta 516
Rocky Mountain Jewish Historical Society, Denver, CO 52
Rocky Mountain National Park, Estes Park, CO 53
Rocky Mountain Nature Association, Inc., Estes Park, CO 53
Rocky Reach Dam, Wenatchee, WA 491
Rocky River Historical Society, Rocky River, OH 371
Roebling Historical Society, Roebling, NJ 291
Roger Williams Park Museum of Natural History, Providence, RI 412
Rogers Historical Museum, Rogers, AR 21
Rolling Hills Historical Society, Rockglen, Saskatchewan 566
Rollo Jamison Museum, Platteville, WI 503
Rome Historical Society, Rome, NY 331
Romeo Historical Society, Romeo, MI 222
Romulus Historical Society, Romulus, MI 222
Ron Morel Memorial Museum, Kapuskasing, Ontario 544
Rooks County Historical Society, Stockton, KS 151
Roopville Historical Society and Archives, Roopville, GA 91
Roosevelt Campobello International Park Commission, Campobello Island, New Brunswick 527
Roosevelt County Genealogical and Historical Society, Portales, NM 298
Roosevelt's Little White House and Museum, Warm Springs, GA 94
Rosalie Daughters of the American Revolution, Natchez, MS 241
Roscoe Historical Society, Roscoe, TX 455
Roscoe Village Foundation, Coshocton, OH 362
Rose City Area Historical Society, Inc., Rose City, MI 222
Rose Hill Manor—Children's Museum and Carriage House, Frederick, MD 183
Rose Hill Mansion, Geneva, NY 313
Roseau County Historical Society Museum, Roseau, MN 235
Rosebud Centennial Museum, Rosebud, Alberta 516
Roselle Historical Society, Roselle, IL 115
Roselle Historical Society, Roselle, NJ 291
Roselle Park Historical Society, Roselle Park, NJ 291

Rosemead Library, Rosemead, CA 38
Rosemount Victorian House Museum, Pueblo, CO 56
Rosenbach Museum and Library, Philadelphia, PA 403
Roslyn Landmark Society, Roslyn, NY 331
Ross County Historical Society, Chillicothe, OH 358
Ross House Museum, Winnipeg, Manitoba 526
Ross Township Historical Society, Pittsburgh, PA 404
Roswell Historical Society, Roswell, GA 91
Rotch-Jones-Duff House and Garden Museum, New Bedford, MA 200
Rough Rider Memorial and City Museum, Las Vegas, NM 297
Rough and Tumble Engineers' Historical Association, Inc., Kinzers, PA 396
Rowan County Historic Properties Commission, Mt. Ulla, NC 347
Rowe Historical Society, Rowe, MA 203
Roxborough-Manayunk-Wissahickon Historical Society, Philadelphia, PA 403
Roxbury Burrough's Club, Roxbury, NY 332
Royal Arts Foundation—Belcourt Castle, Newport, RI 410
Royal Canadian Artillery Museum, Shilo, Manitoba 525
Royal Nova Scotia Historical Society, Halifax, Nova Scotia 535
Royal Ontario Museum, Toronto, Ontario 553
Royall House Association, Medford, MA 199
Royalston Historical Society, Royalston, MA 203
Rusk County Historical Foundation, Henderson, TX 448
Russell Cave National Monument, Bridgeport, AL 3
Russell County Historical Society, Russell, KS 150
Russell Vermontiana Collection, Martha Canfield Library, Arlington, VT 464
Rutherford B. Hayes Presidential Center, Fremont, OH 364
Rutherford County Historical Society, Murfreesboro, TN 432
Rutherford House Provincial Historic Site, Edmonton, Alberta 513
Rutland Historical Society, Rutland, VT 468
Rye Historical Society, Rye, NY 332

S

SARA (Southwest Arkansas Regional Archives), Washington, AR 22
SCOPS (All Southern Ohio Preservation Society), Chillicothe, OH 358
SIMAPC (Southwestern Illinois Metropolitan and Regional Planning Commission), Collinsville, IL 105
SPACES (Saving and Preserving Arts and Cultural Environments), Los Angeles, CA 32
SUNY-Binghamton, University Art Gallery, Binghamton, NY 304
Sac County Historical Society, Nemaha, IA 140
Sac Museum Memorial Society, Bellevue, NE 261
Sacket Harbor Battlefield State Historic Site, Sacket Harbor, NY 332
Sacramento County Historical Society, Sacramento, CA 39
Sacramento Mountains Historical Society, Inc., Cloudcraft, NM 296
Sacramento Museum and History Commission, Sacramento, CA 39
Saddleback Area Historical Society, El Toro, CA 27
Safety Harbor Museum of History and Fine Arts, Safety Harbor, FL 82
Sag Harbor Whaling and Historical Museum, Sag Harbor, NY 332
Sagadahoc Preservation, Inc., Bath, ME 169
Saginaw County Historical Society, Saginaw, MI 223

Saginaw Genealogical Society, Saginaw, MI 223
Saint Agatha Historical Society, St. Agatha, ME 176
Saint Albans Historical Society, St. Albans, VT 469
Saint Angela's Museum and Archives, Prelate, Saskatchewan 565
Saint Anne's Episcopal Church Historical Commission, Lowell, MA 198
Saint Augustine Historical Society, Saint Augustine, FL 83
Saint Catharines Historical Museum, St. Catharine's, Ontario 550
Saint Charles Avenue Association, New Orleans, LA 166
Saint Charles County Historical Society and Archives, St. Charles, MO 252
Saint Clair County Genealogical Society, Belleville, IL 100
Saint Clair County Historical Society, Belleville, IL 100
Saint Clair Shores Historical Commission, Saint Clair Shores, MI 223
Saint Croix County Historical Society, Hudson, WI 498
Saint Croix Landmarks Society, Frederiksted, Saint Croix, Virgin Islands 509
Saint Croix Valley Historical Research Center, River Falls, WI 503
Saint Elmo Historic Preservation, Buena Vista, CO 50
Saint-Gaudens National Historic Site, Cornish, NH 270
Saint Gertrude's Museum, Cottonwood, ID 97
Saint Helens Branch, Columbia County Historical Society, St. Helens, OR 386
Saint John Branch, New Brunswick Genealogical Society, Saint John, New Brunswick 530
Saint John Heritage Trust, Inc., Saint John, New Brunswick 530
Saint Joseph Island Museum Board, Richards Landing, Ontario 550
Saint Joseph Island Museum, Saint Joseph Island, Ontario 550
Saint Joseph Museum, Saint Joseph, MO 253
Saint Joseph State Hospital Psychiatric Museum, Saint Joseph, MO 253
Saint Lawrence County Historical Association, Canton, NY 306
Saint Louis County Department of Parks and Recreation, Clayton, MO 244
Saint Louis County Historical Society, Duluth, MN 228
Saint Louis Park Historical Society, St. Louis Park, MN 236
Saint Lucie Historical Commission, Ft. Pierce, FL 78
Saint Lucie Historical Society, Ft. Pierce, FL 78
Saint Mary's County Historical Society, Leonardtown, MD 184
Saint Marys District Museum, Saint Marys, Ontario 550
Saint Marys Historic Preservation Commission, St. Marys, GA 91
Saint Michael's Museum Association, Inc., Chatham, New Brunswick 527
Saint Michaels Historical Museum, St. Michaels, AZ 14
Saint Paul's National Historic Site, Mount Vernon, NY 321
Saint Petersburg Historical Society, Saint Petersburg, FL 83
Saint Photios Greek Orthodox National Shrine, St. Augustine, FL 83
Saint Vrain Historical Society, Longmont, CO 56
Saint Walburg and District Historical Museum, Inc., St. Walburg, Saskatchewan 566
Salamanca Rail Museum, Salamanca, NY 332
Salem County Historical Society, Salem, NJ 291
Salem-Crossroads Historical Restoration Society, Delmont, PA 391
Salem Historical Society and Museum, Salem, OH 371
Salem Maritime National Historic Site, Salem, MA 204
Salinas National Monument, Mountainair, NM 298

Saline County Historical Society, Inc., Salina, KS 150

Salisbury Association, Inc., Salisbury, CT 66

Salisbury Historic District Commission, Salisbury, NC 349

Salisbury Historical Society, Dolgeville, NY 310

Salisbury Hosue—Iowa State Education Association, Des Moines, IA 135

Salmon Arm Museum and Heritage Association, Salmon Arm, British Columbia 521

Salmon Brook Historical Society, Granby, CT 60

Salt Springville Community Restoration, Salt Springville, NY 332

Salvation Army Archives and Research Center, New York, NY 325

Salvation Army George Scott Railton Heritage Centre, Toronto, Ontario 553

Salvation Army Western Territorial Museum, Rancho Palos Verdes, CA 36

Sam Bell Maxey House State Historic Structure, Paris, TX 454

Sam Davis Memorial Association, Smyrna, TN 436

Sam Houston Memorial Museum, Huntsville, TX 449

Sam Houston Regional Library and Research Center, Liberty, TX 451

Sam Rayburn House, Bonham, TX 439

Sam Rayburn Library, Bonham, TX 439

Sam Waller Little Northern Museum, The Pas, Manitoba 525

Samford University, Birmingham, AL 2

Samson V. Maritime Museum, New Westminster, British Columbia 520

San Antonio Conservation Society, San Antonio, TX 456

San Antonio Missions National Historical Park, San Antonio, TX 456

San Antonio Museum Association, San Antonio, TX 456

San Antonio Valley Historical Association, King City, CA 29

San Benito County Historical Society, Hollister, CA 29

San Bernardino County Museum Association, Redlands, CA 37

San Clemente Historical Society, San Clemente, CA 39

San Diego Historical Society, San Diego, CA 40

San Fernando Valley Historical Society, Inc., Mission Hills, CA 33

San Francisco Fire Department Museum, St. Francisco Hook and Ladder Society, San Francisco, CA 41

San Francisco Lesbian and Gay History Project, San Francisco, CA 41

San Gabriel Historical Association, San Gabriel, CA 42

San Jacinto County Historical Commission and Heritage Society, Coldspring, TX 441

San Jacinto Museum of History Association, La Porte, TX 451

San Jacinto Valley Museum Association, Inc., San Jacinto, CA 42

San Joaquin County Historical Society and Museum, Lodi, CA 30

San Joaquin Pioneer and Historical Society, Stockton, CA 46

San Jose Historic Landmarks Commission, San Jose, CA 42

San Jose Historical Museum, San Jose, CA 42

San Juan Bautista Historical Society, San Juan Bautista, FL 83

San Juan County Archaeological Research Center and Library, Farmington, NM 96

San Juan County Historical Society, Silverton, CO 57

San Leandro Library—Historical Commission, San Leandro, CA 42

San Luis Obispo County Historical Society, San Luis Obispo, CA 42

San Marino Historical Society, San Marino, CA 43

San Mateo County Historical Association and Museum, San Mateo, CA 43

San Pablo Historical and Museum Society, San Pablo, CA 43

San Pedro Valley Arts and Historical Society, Benson, AZ 11

San Ramon Valley Historical Society, Danville, CA 26

Sand Lake Historical Society, Averill Park, NY 303

Sandoval County Historical Society, Bernalillo, NM 296

Sandusky County Historical Society, Fremont, OH 364

Sandwich Archives and Historical Center, Sandwich, MA 204

Sandwich Historical Commission, Sandwich, MA 204

Sandwich Historical Society and Glass Museum, Sandwich, MA 204

Sandy Bay Historical Society, Rockport, MA 203

Sandy Creek Covered Bridge State Historic Site, Hillsboro, MO 246

Sandy Hook Museum, Highlands, NJ 282

Sandy Spring Museum, Sandy Spring, MD 185

Sanford Historical Committee, Sanford, ME 176

Sanford Historical Society, Sanford, MI 223

Sanford Museum and Planetarium, Cherokee, IA 133

Sangamon County Genealogical Society, Springfield, IL 117

Sangamon County Historical Society, Springfield, IL 117

Sangamon Valley Collection, Lincoln Library, Springfield, IL 117

Sangre de Cristo Arts and Conference Center, Pueblo, CO 57

Sanilac County Historical Society, Port Sanilac, MI 222

Santa Barbara Historical Society, Santa Barbara, CA 43

Santa Barbara Trust for Historic Preservation, Santa Barbara, CA 44

Santa Clara County Historical and Genealogical Society, Santa Clara, CA 44

Santa Clara County Historical Heritage Commission, San Jose, CA 42

Santa Cruz County Society for Historic Preservation, Inc., Santa Cruz, CA 44

Santa Cruz Historical Society, Santa Cruz, CA 44

Santa Fe Area Historical Foundation, Inc., Arcadia, TX 437

Santa Fe Historical Society, Santa Fe, NM 299

Santa Fe Springs Historical Committee, Sante Fe Springs, CA 44

Santa Fe Trail Center, Larned, KS 148

Santa Fe Trail Historical, Inc., Baldwin City, KS 143

Santa Maria Valley Historical Society, Santa Maria, CA 44

Santa Monica Heritage Square Museum, Santa Monica, CA 44

Santa Monica Historical Society, Santa Monica, CA 44

Santa Ynez Valley Historical Society and Museum, Santa Ynez, CA 5

Santuit-Cotuit Historical Society, Cotuit, MA 193

Sappington House Foundation, Crestwood, MO 245

Sapulpa Historical Society, Inc., Sapulpa, OK 380

Saratoga County Historical Society, Ballston Spa, NY 303

Saratoga Historical Foundation, Saratoga, NY 332

Saratoga Museum Center, Saratoga, WY 508

Saratoga National Historical Park, Stillwater, NY 335

Saratoga Springs Preservation Foundation, Saratoga Springs, NY 332

Sargeant Memorial Room, Norfolk Public Library, Norfolk, VA 477

Sarpy County Historical Museum, Bellevue, NE 261

Saskatchewan Archives Board, Regina, Saskatchewan 566

Saskatchewan History and Folklore Society, Moose Jaw, Saskatchewan 565

Saskatchewan Museums Association, Regina, Saskatchewan 566

Saskatchewan Provincial Historic Parks, Regina, Saskatchewan 566

Saskatchewan Sports Hall of Fame, Regina, Saskatchewan 566

Saskatchewan Western Development Museums, Saskatoon, Saskatchewan 566

Sauder Farm and Craft Village, Archbold, OH 355

Sauk County Historical Society, Baraboo, WI 495

Sault Ste. Marie Museum, Sault Ste. Marie, Ontario 551

Sault de Ste. Marie Historical Sites, Inc., Sault Ste. Marie, MI 223

Saum Community Club, Inc., Saum, MN 237

Saunders County Historical Society, Wahoo, NE 267

Savannah-Yamacraw Branch, Association for the Study of Afro-American Life and History, Savannah, GA 92

Save Lucy Committee, Inc., Margate, NJ 285

Save Our Cemeteries, Inc., New Orleans, LA 166

Save Our Heritage Organization, San Diego, CA 40

Save the Tivoli, Inc., Washington, DC 75

Sawtooth Interpretive Association, Stanley, ID 99

Scarborough Historical Society—Cornell House Museum, Scarborough, Ontario 551

Scarsdale Historical Society, Scarsdale, NY 333

Schenectady County Historical Society, Schenectady, NY 333

Schenectady Museum, Schenectady, NY 333

Schiele Museum of Natural History—Living History Farm and Catawba Indian Village, Gastonia, NC 344

Schleicher County Museum, El Dorado, TX 444

Schminck Memorial Museum—Daughters of the American Revolution, Lakeview, OR 384

Schoenbrunn Village State Memorial, New Philadelphia, OH 370

Schoharie County Historical Society—Old Stone Fort Museum Complex, Schoharie, NY 333

Schoharie Crossing State Historic Site, Fort Hunter, NY 312

Schoharie Museum of the Iroquois Indian, Schoharie, NY 333

Schroon-North Hudson Historical Society, Inc., Schroon Lake, NY 333

Schuyler Historical Society, Schuyler, NE 266

Schuyler Mansion, State Historic Site, Albany, NY 301

Schuyler-Brown Historical Society, Rushville, IL 115

Schweinfurth Art Center, Auburn, NY 303

Schwenkfelder Library, Pennsburg, PA 400

Scioto Society, Inc., Chillicothe, OH 358

Scipio Society of Naval and Military History, Inc., Oyster Bay, NY 327

Scituate Historical Society, Scituate, MA 204

Scotland Historical Society, Scotland, SD 425

Scott County Genealogical Society, Georgetown, KY 156

Scott County Historical Society, Huntsville, TN 429

Scott County Historical Society, Scott City, KS 150

Scott County Historical Society, Inc., Eldridge, IA 136

Scottish Historic and Research Society of the Delaware Valley, Inc., Ardmore, PA 387

Scotts Bluff National Monument, Gering, NE 263

Scottsboro-Jackson Heritage Center, Scottsboro, AL 7

Scottsdale Historical Society, Scottsdale, AZ 14

Scouting Trail Museum, Seattle, WA 488

Scranton Anthracite Museum, Scranton, PA 405

Scurry County Museum, Snyder, TX 457

Sea Cliff Landmarks, Inc., Sea Cliff, NY 34

Sea Cliff Village Museum, Sea Cliff, NY 334

Seafood Industry Museum of Biloxi, Biloxi, MS 239

Seaford Historical Society, Inc., Seaford, DE 70

Searls Historical Library, Nevada City, CA 34

Seattle Branch, National Archives, Seattle, WA 488

Seaver Center for Western History Research, Natural

History Museum of Los Angeles County, Los Angeles, CA 32

Second Armored Division Museum, Fort Hood, TX 445

Second Rhode Island Regiment of the Continental Line, Pawtucket, RI 411

Second South Carolina Regiment, Columbia, SC 416

Sedgwick-Brooklin Historical Society, Sedgwick, ME 176

Selma-Dallas County Historic and Preservation Society, Selma, AL 8

Seminole Canyon State Historical Park, Comstock, TX 441

Seminole Nation Historical Society, Wewoka, OK 381

Seminole Valley Farm, Inc., Cedar Rapids, IA 133

Senate House State Historic Site, Kingston, NY 317

Seneca County Museum, Tiffin, OH 372

Seneca Falls Historical Society, Seneca Falls, NY 334

Seneca-Iroquois National Museum, Salamanca, NY 332

Sequim-Dungeness Museum, Sequim, WA 489

Sequoyah Home Site, Sallisaw, OK 380

Seventh Day Baptist Historical Society, Janesville, WI 498

Sewall-Belmont House, Washington, DC 75

Seward County Historical Society, Inc., Liberal, KS 148

Seymour Historical Society, Inc., Seymour, CT 66

Shadows-on-the-Teche, New Iberia, LA 165

Shafter Historical Society, Inc., Shafter, CA 45

Shaftsbury Historical Society, Shaftsbury, VT 468

Shaker Heritage Society, Albany, NY 301

Shaker Historical Museum, Shaker Heights, OH 372

Shaker Museum, Poland Spring, ME 175

Shaker Village, Inc., Canterbury, NH 270

Shakertown at Pleasant Hill, Inc., Harrodsburg, KY 156

Shakertown at South Union, South Union, KY 162

Sharlot Hall Historical Society—Prescott Historical Society, Prescott, AZ 14

Sharon Historical Society, Sharon Springs, NY 334

Sharon Temple Museum, Sharon, Ontario 551

Sharon Township Heritage Society, Sharon Center, OH 372

Sharpsteen Museum Association, Calistoga, CA 24

Shasta College Museum and Research Center, Redding, CA 37

Shawano County Historical Society Inc., Shawano, WI 503

Shawnee County Historical Society, Topeka, KS 152

Shawnee Historical Society, Inc.—Old Shawnee Town, Shawnee, KS 151

Shearwater Aviation Museum, Shearwater, Nova Scotia 537

Sheboygan County Historical Society, Sheboygan, WI 503

Sheffield Historical Society, Sheffield, MA 204

Shelburne Historical Society and County Museum, Shelburne, Nova Scotia 537

Shelburne Historical Society, Shelburne, Nova Scotia 538

Shelby County Historical Society, Harlan, IA 137

Shelby County Historical Society, Shelbyville, IN 129

Shelby County Historical Society, Shelbyville, KY 162

Shelby County Historical Society—Shelby County Archives and Museum, Columbiana, AL 3

Sheldon Historical Society—Prairie Museum, Sheldon, IA 141

Sheldon Jackson Museum, Sitka, AK 11

Sheldon Museum, Middlebury, VT 467

Sheldon Museum and Cultural Center, Haines, AK 10

Shenandoah Natural History Association, Inc., Luray, VA 476

Shepherd Area Historical Society, Shepherd, MI 223

Sherbrooke Restoration Commission, Sherbrooke, Nova Scotia 538

Sherbrooke Village, Sherbrooke, Nova Scotia 538

Sheridan County Historical Society, Inc., Hoxie, KS 147
Sheridan County Historical Society, Inc., Rushville, NE 266
Sherman County Historical Society, Moro, OR 384
Sherman County Historical Society, Inc., Stratford, TX 458
Sherman Hill Association, Des Moines, IA 135
Sherman Historical Museum, Sherman, TX 457
Sherman Historical Society, Sherman, CT 66
Sherman House, Lancaster, OH 366
Sherwood Forest Plantation, Charles City, VA 471
Shiawassee County Genealogical Society, Owosso, MI 221
Shiloh Museum, Springdale, AR 22
Shiloh National Military Park, Shiloh, TN 435
Ships of the Sea Museum, Savannah, GA 92
Shirley Historical Society, Shirley, MA 205
Shirley Plantation, Charles City, VA 471
Shoreline Historical Museum, Inc., Seattle, WA 488
Shrewsbury Historical Society, Inc., Shrewsbury, VT 468
Shrewsbury Historical Society, Shrewsbury, NJ 291
Shrine to Music Museum, Vermillion, SD 426
Sierra Historic Sites Association, Oakhurst, CA 34
Signal Hill National Historic Park, St. John's, Newfoundland 532
Silent Wings Museum, Terrell, TX 458
Siloam Springs Museum, Siloam Springs, AR 22
Silver City Museum, Silver City, NM 299
Silver Creek Historical Society, Silver Creek, NY 334
Simcoe County Archives, Minesing, Ontario 546
Simcoe County Museum, Minesing, Ontario 546
Simi Valley Historical Society, Simi Valley, CA 45
Simpson County Historical Society, Franklin, KY 155
Sinsinawa Dominican Archives, Dominican Sisters, Sinsinawa, WI 504
Sioux City Public Museum and Historical Association, Sioux City, IA 141
Sioux Empire Medical Museum, Sioux Falls, SD 426
Sioux Valley Genealogical Society, Sioux Falls, SD 426
Siouxland Heritage Museums, Sioux Falls, SD 426
Sippican Historical Society, Marion, MA 198
Sir Alexander Galt Museum and Archives, Lethbridge, Alberta 515
Siskiyou County Historical Society, Yreka, CA 49
Siskiyou County Historical Society and Museum, Yreka, CA 49
Sisters of the Holy Names of Jesus and Mary, Oregon Province, Marylhurst, OR 384
Sitka Historical Society, Sitka, AK 11
Siuslaw Pioneer Museum, Florence, OR 383
Sixteen ninety-nine Historical Committee, Ocean Springs, MS 241
Sixteen ninety-six Thomas Massey House, Broomall, PA 389
Ska-Nah-Dont Indian Village, Mt. Brydges, Ontario 546
Skagit County Historical Society, LaConner, WA 485
Skamania County Historical Society, Stevenson, WA 489
Skinner Museum, South Hadley, MA 205
Skokie Historical Society, Skokie, IL 116
Slate Belt Historical Society, Mt. Bethel, PA 399
Slate Run Living Historical Farm, Marcy, OH 367
Slater Memorial Museum and Converse Art Gallery, Norwich, CT 65
Slater Mill Historic Site, Pawtucket, RI 411
Sleepy Hollow Restorations, Inc., Tarrytown, NY 337
Slidell Museum, Slidell, LA 168
Sloss Furnaces, National Historical Landmark, Birmingham, AL 2
Slovak Museum and Archives, Middletown, PA 398
Smith County Historical Society and Historical Commission, Tyler, TX 459
Smith's Castle at Cocumscussoc, Wickford, RI 413

Smith-Harris House, East Lyme, CT 59
Smith-Zimmermann State Museum, Madison, SD 424
Smithfield Plantation, Blacksburg, VA 471
Smithtown Historical Society, Smithtown, NY 334
Smoky Hill Railway and Historical Society, Inc., Shawnee Mission, KS 151
Smoky Valley Genealogical Society and Library, Inc., Salina, KS 150
Smyth County Historical and Museum Society, Inc., Marion, VA 476
Snohomish County Museum and Historical Association, Everett, WA 484
Snoqualmie Valley Historical Society, North Bend, WA 485
Snyder Memorial Museum and Creative Arts Center, Bastrop, LA 163
Société Canadienne Francaise du Minnesota, Twin Cities, MN 237
Société d'archéologie de Nouvelle-France, Quebec, Quebec 560
Société d'Histoire des Cantons de l'Est—Eastern Townships Historical Society, Sherbrooke, Quebec 562
Société d'histoire Mouillepied, Saint-Lambert, Quebec 562
Société d'histoire Régionale de Lévis, Levis, Quebec 558
Société d'histoire Regionale de Nicolet, Nicolet, Quebec 560
Société d'histoire d'Amos, Amos, Quebec 556
Société d'histoire de la Région de Terrebonne, Terrebonne, Quebec 562
Société d'histoire de la Rivière Saint-Jean de Fredericton, Fredericton, New Brunswick 529
Société d'histoire de la Rivière, Saint Jerome, Quebec 562
Société d'histoire de la Seigneurie de Chambly, Chambly, Quebec 556
Société d'histoire de Shefford, Granby, Quebec 557
Société d'histoire de Val D'Or, Val D'Or, Quebec 563
Société d'histoire des Pays-d'en-Haut, Inc., St. Sauveur-des-Monts, Quebec 562
Société d'histoire des Six Cantons, Acton Vale, Quebec 555
Société d'histoire du Haut-Richelieu, Inc., St-Jean-sur-Richelieu, Quebec 561
Société d'histoire du Temiscamimque, Ville-Marie, Quebec 563
Société d'histoire et d'archéologie des Monts, Sainte-Anne-des-Monts, Quebec 561
Société d'histoire et de Genealogie de Matane, Matane, Quebec 559
Société de Généalogie de la Mauricie et des Bois-Francs, Inc., Trois-Rivieres, Quebec 563
Société de Genealogie de l'Outaouais, Inc., Hull, Quebec 557
Société de Généalogie des Cantons de l'Est, Sherbrooke, Quebec 562
Société de Genealogie des Laurentides, St. Jérôme, Quebec 561
Société Franco-Ontarienne d'Histoire et de Généalogie, Ottawa, Ontario 549
Société Généalogique Canadienne Francaise, Montreal, Quebec 560
Société Généalogique du Saguenay, Inc., Chicoutimi, Quebec 556
Société Historique Acadienne La Vieille Maison, Meteghan, Nova Scotia 536
Société Historique, Alma, Quebec 556
Société Historique Alphonse-Desjardins, Levis, Quebec 558
Société Historique de Beaurepaire—Beaconsfield Historical Society, Beaconsfield, Quebec 556

Société Historique de Cabano, Inc., Cabano, Quebec 556

Société Historique de Charlesbourg, Charlesbourg, Quebec 556

Société Historique de Grande-Digue, Kent, New Brunswick 529

Société Historique de l'ouest du Quebec, Inc., Hull, Quebec 557

Société Historique de la Côte-du-Sud, La Pocatiere, Quebec 558

Société Historique de la Gaspésie, Gaspé, Quebec 557

Société Historique de la Mer Rouge, Inc., Robichaud, New Brunswick 530

Société Historique de Québec, Quebec, Quebec 561

Société Historique de St. Boniface, Manitoba 524

Société Historique des Bernier d'Amérique, Inc., Cap St. Ignace, Quebec 556

Société Historique du Cap-Rouge, Cap-Rouge, Quebec 556

Société Historique du Golfe, Inc., Sept-Iles, Quebec 562

Société Historique du Lac Memphre Magog, Magog, Quebec 559

Société Historique du Madawaska, Inc., Edmundston, New Brunswick 528

Société Historique du Marigot, Inc., Longueuil, Quebec 558

Société Historique du Saguenay, Chicoutimi, Quebec 557

Société Historique et Généalogique de Trois-Pistoles, Inc., Trois-Pistoles, Quebec 563

Société Historique Franco-Américaine, Boston, MA 190

Société Historique Franco-Américaine, Woonsocket, RI 413

Société Historique Nicolas Denys, Bertrand, New Brunswick 527

Société Quebecoise des Ponts Couverts, Inc., Saint Eustache, Quebec 561

Sociedad Historica de la Tierra Amarilla, Los Ojos, NM 297

Society for Industrial Archaeology, Washington, DC 75

Society for the History of Technology, Durham, NC 343

Society for the Preservation and Appreciation of Antique Motor Fire Apparatus in America, Syracuse, NY 336

Society for the Preservation of Maryland Antiquities, Marriottsville, MD 184

Society for the Preservation of Federal Hill and Fell's Point, Baltimore, MD 181

Society for the Preservation of Long Island Antiquities, Setauket, NY 334

Society for the Preservation of Maryland Antiquities, Marriottsville, MD 184

Society for the Preservation of Minneota's Heritage, Minneota, MN 233

Society for the Preservation of New England Antiquities, Boston, MA 190

Society for the Preservation of Old Mills, Mishawaka, IN 127

Society for the Preservation of Weeksville and Bedford-Stuyvestant History—The Weeksville Society, Brooklyn, NY 305

Society of American Archivists, Chicago, IL 104

Society of American Historians, Manhattan, NY 319

Society of Biblical Literature, Denver, CO 53

Society of Boonesborough, Richmond, KY 162

Society of California Pioneers, San Francisco, CA 41

Society of Colonial Wars in the State of New Jersey, Elizabeth, NJ 280

Society of First Families of South Carolina, 1670-1700, Charleston, SC 415

Society of Georgia Archivists, Atlanta, GA 86

Society of Illustrators, New York, NY 325

Society of Indiana Archivists, Indianapolis, IN 125

Society of Indiana Pioneers, Indianapolis, IN 125

Society of Mareen Duvall Descendants, Upper Marlboro, MD 186

Society of Mayflower Descendants, Elizabeth City, NC 344

Society of North Carolina Archivists, Raleigh, NC 348

Society of Ohio Archivists, Columbus, OH 361

Society of Pioneer of Montgomery, Montgomery, AL 7

Society of Southwest Archivists, Lubbock, TX 452

Society of Systematic Zoology—Museum of Natural History, Washington, DC 75

Society of the Montreal Military and Maritime Museum—St. Helen's Island Museum, Montreal, Quebec 560

Socorro County Historical Society, Inc., Socorro, NM 299

Sod Buster Museum, Stanford, MT 260

Sod House, Aline, OK 375

Soldiers' Memorial Military Museum, St. Louis, MO 254

Solebury Township Historical Society, Solebury, PA 405

Solon Historical Society, Solon, OH 372

Somers Historical Society, Somers, CT 66

Somers Historical Society, Somers, NY 34

Somerset Historical Center, Somerset, PA 405

Somerset Place, Creswell, NC 343

Somerville Historical Museum, Somerville, MA 205

Somerville Preservation Commission, Somerville, AL 8

Sonnenberg Gardens and Mansion, Canandaigua, NY 06

Sonoma County Historical Society, Santa Rosa, CA 44

Sonoma County Museum, Santa Rosa, CA 44

Sonoma League for Historic Preservation, Sonoma, CA 45

Sons of Confederate Veterans, Hattiesburg, MS 240

Sons of Norway, Minneapolis, MN 233

Sons of the American Revolution Museum, Louisville, KY 159

Soo Line Historical Museum, Weyburn, Saskatchewan 567

Sooke Region Museum, Sooke, British Columbia 521

Sophienburg Memorial Association, Inc., New Braunfels, TX 453

Sourisseau Academy for California State and Local History, San Jose, CA 42

South Bannock County Historical Center, Lava Hot Springs, ID 97

South Box Elder Daughters of Utah Pioneers, Brigham City, UT 461

South Carolina Baptist Historical Society, Greenville, SC 419

South Carolina Committee for the Humanities, Columbia, SC 416

South Carolina Confederate Relic Room and Museum, Columbia, SC 417

South Carolina Criminal Justice Hall of Fame, Columbia, SC 417

South Carolina Department of Archives and History, Columbia, SC 417

South Carolina Department of Parks, Recreation and Tourism, Columbia, SC 417

South Carolina Heritage Trust Program, Columbia, SC 417

South Carolina Historical Association, Florence, SC 418

South Carolina Historical Association, Greenville, SC 419

South Carolina Historical Room for History and Genealogy, Greenville, SC 419

South Carolina Historical Society, Charleston, SC 415

South Carolina Institute of Archaeology and Anthropology, Columbia, SC 417

South Carolina Railroad Museum, Inc., Winnsboro, SC 421

South Carolina Society, Colonial Dames XVII Century, Aiken, SC 413

South Carolina Society, Sons of the American Revolution, Columbia, SC 417

South Carolina State Museum, Columbia, SC 417

South Carolina State Society, Daughters of the American Revolution, Greenville, SC 419

South Carolina State Society, National Society Daughters of the American Colonists, Columbia, SC 417

South Central Idaho Historical Council, Twin Falls, ID 99

South County Museum, Narragansett, RI 410

South Dakota Archaeological Society, Sioux Falls, SD 426

South Dakota Cowboy and Western Heritage Hall of Fame, Ft. Pierre, SD 423

South Dakota Division of Parks and Recreation, Pierre, SD 425

South Dakota Office of History, Pierre, SD 425

South Dakota State Archives, Pierre, SD 425

South Euclid Historical Society, South Euclid, OH 372

South Florida Museum and Bishop Planetarium, Bradenton, FL 76

South King County Genealogical Society, Kent, WA 485

South Lyon Area Historical Society, Inc., South Lyon, MI 224

South Lyon Historical Commission, South Lyon, MI 224

South Milwaukee Historical Society, South Milwaukee, WI 504

South Park City Museum, Fairplay, CO 53

South Park Historical Foundation, Inc., Fairplay, CO 54

South Pass City State Historic Site, South Pass City, WY 509

South Peace Historical Society, Dawson Creek, British Columbia 518

South Plainfield Historical Society, South Plainfield, NJ 291

South Rawdon Museum Society Inc., South Rawdon, Nova Scotia 538

South San Francisco History Room, South San Francisco, CA 45

South Sebastian County Historical Society, Greenwood, AR 18

South Shore Genealogical Society, Lunenburg, Nova Scotia 536

South Texas Museum, Alice, TX 436

South Thurston County Historical Society, Tenino, WA 490

South Wood County Historical Corporation, Wisconsin Rapids, WI 506

Southampton Historical Museum—Old Halsey Homestead, Southampton, NY 334

Southampton Historical Society, Vincentown, NJ 293

Southbury Historical Society, Inc., Southbury, CT 66

Southeast Arkansas Arts and Science Center, Pine Bluff, AR 21

Southeast Minnesota Historical Center, Winona, MN 238

Southeast Museum Association, Inc., Brewster, NY 305

Southeast Nebraska Genealogical Society, Beatrice, NE 261

Southeast Texas Genealogical and Historical Society, Beaumont, TX 439

Southeastern Railway Museum, Duluth, GA 88

Southern Appalachian Historical Association, Inc., Boone, NC 41

Southern Aroostook Historical Society, Houlton, ME 172

Southern Baptist Historical Library and Archives, Nashville, TN 434

Southern California Branch, California Historical Society, Los Angeles, CA 2

Southern Forest World, Inc., Waycross, GA 94

Southern Genealogist's Exchange Society, Inc., Jacksonville, FL 79

Southern Highland Handicraft Guild Museum and Library, Asheville, NC 341

Southern Historical Association, Athens, GA 85

Southern Jewish Historical Society, Valdosta, GA 94

Southern Lorain County Historical Society, Wellington, OH 374

Southern Minnesota Historical Center, Mankato, MN 232

Southern Ohio Museum and Cultural Center, Portsmouth, OH 371

Southern Oregon Historical Society, Jacksonville, OR 383

Southern Resources Unlimited, Nashville, TN 434

Southern Society of Genealogies, Centre, AL 3

Southington Historical Society, Southington, CT 66

Southold Historical Society and Museum, Southold, NY 334

Southport Historical Society, Southport, NC 349

Southwest Florida Historical Society, Inc., Fort Myers, FL 78

Southwest Franklin County Historical Society, Grove City, OH 365

Southwest Louisiana Genealogical Society, Lake Charles, LA 165

Southwest Minnesota Historical Center, Marshall, MN 232

Southwest Oklahoma Genealogical Society, Lawton, OK 378

Southwest Railroad Historical Society, Dallas, TX 443

Southwest Virginia Museum Historical State Park, Big Stone Gap, VA 471

Southwestern Antique Gas and Steam Engine Museum, Vista, CA 48

Southwestern Indiana Historical Society, Evansville, IN 122

Southwestern Mission Research Center—Arizona State Museum, Tucson, AZ 16

Southwestern Ontario Heritage Village, Colchester South, Ontario 541

Southwestern Ontario Heritage Village, Essex, Ontario 542

Southwestern Oral History Institute, Farmington, NM 296

Space Center—International Space Hall of Fame and Tombaugh Space Theater, Alamogordo, NM 294

Spadina, Toronto, Ontario 553

Spanishtown Historical Society, Half Moon Bay, CA 29

Special Collections and Archives, M.I. King Libraries, Lexington, KY 158

Special Collections Branch, Albuquerque Public Library, Albuquerque, NM 295

Special Collections Department, Library of the University of West Florida, Pensacola, FL 82

Special Collections Department, Tampa-Hillsborough County Public Library System, Tampa, FL 84

Special Collections Department, University of New Mexico, Albuquerque, NM 296

Special Collections, Library, Indiana University of Pennsylvania, Indiana, PA 395

Special Collections Library, Southern Utah State College, Cedar City, UT 461

Special Collections, Pan American University Library, Edinburg, TX 444

Spencer Historical Society, Spencer, NY 335

Spencer Shops, Spencer, NC 349

Spertus Museum of Judaica, Chicago, IL 105

Spillville Historic Action Group, Inc., Spillville, IA 141

Spindletop Museum, Beaumont, TX 439
Spotsylvania Historical Association, Inc., Spotsylvania, VA 480
Spring Lake Historical Society, Inc., Spring Lake, NJ 291
Spring Valley Community Historical Society, Inc., Spring Valley, MN 237
Springdale School, Westminster, MD 186
Springfield Armory National Historic Site, Springfield, MA 205
Springfield Art and Historical Society, Springfield, VT 469
Springfield Historical Commission, Springfield, OR 386
Springfield Historical Society, Inc., Springfield, NH 276
Springfield Historical Society, Springfield, SD 426
Springs Historical Society of the Casselman Valley, Springs, PA 405
Spy Hill Museum—Wolverine Hobby and Historical Society, Spy Hill, Saskatchewan 567
St. Ephrem Educational Center, Youngstown, OH 375
Stabler-Leadbeater Apothecary Shop Museum and Antique Shop, Alexandria, VA 470
Stafford County Historical and Genealogical Society, Stafford, KS 151
Stafford Historical Society, Inc., Stafford Springs, CT 66
Stagville Center, Durham, NC 343
Stamford Genealogical Society, Inc., Stamford, CT 67
Stamford Historical Society, Stamford, CT 67
Stan Hywet Hall and Gardens, Akron, OH 355
Stan Hywet Hall Foundation, Inc., Akron, OH 355
Standish Historical Society, Standish, ME 177
Stanford Historical Society, Stanfordville, NY 335
Stanley Area Historical Society and Museum, Stanley, WI 504
Stanley-Whitman House, Farmington, CT 60
Stanly County-Albemarle Historical Museum Association, Inc., Albemarle, NC 340
Stanly County Historic Properties Commission, Albemarle, NC 340
Stanstead Historical Society, Stanstead, Quebec 562
Star Mound School Museum, Snowflake, Manitoba 525
Star Valley Historical Society, Afton, WY 506
Star of the Republic Museum, Washington-on-the-Brazos State Historical Park, Washington, TX 460
Star-Spangled Banner Flag House—1812 Museum, Baltimore, MD 181
Stark County Historical Society, Canton, OH 358
Stark Preservation Alliance, Canton, OH 358
Starke County Historical Museum, Knox, IN 126
State Archaeological Center, Ft. Meade, SD 423
State Association of Texas Pioneers, San Antonio, TX 456
State Capital Publishing Museum, Guthrie, OK 377
State Capitol Historical Association, Olympia, WA 485
State Capitol Museum, Phoenix, AZ 14
State Capitol, Raleigh, NC 348
State Division of Archives and Records, Carson City, NV 267
State Division of Historic Preservation and Archaeology, Carson City, NV 267
State Foundation on Culture and the Arts, Honolulu, HI 96
State Historic Preservation Office, Cheyenne, WY 506
State Historic Preservation Office, Phoenix, AZ 14
State Historical Preservation Center, Vermillion, SD 426
State Historical Society of Colorado, Denver, CO 53
State Historical Society of Missouri, Columbia, MO 244
State Historical Society of North Dakota—North Dakota Heritage Center, Bismarck, ND 352
State Historical Society of Wisconsin, Madison, WI 49
State Library of Massachusetts, Boston, MA 190

State Museum of Pennsylvania, Harrisburg, PA 394
Staten Island Children's Museum, Staten Island, NY 335
Staten Island Historical Society—Richmondtown Restoration, Staten Island, NY 335
Staten Island Institute of Arts and Sciences, Staten Island, NY 335
Stationmasters' House Museum, Spearman, TX 457
Staunton River Historical Society—Willie Hodges Booth Museum, Brookneal, VA 471
Steamer Company Number 5, Richmond, VA 479
Steamship Historical Society of America, Inc., Baltimore, MD 181
Steamship Historical Society of America, Inc., Staten Island, NY 335
Stearns County Historical Society, Saint Cloud, MN 236
Steele County Historical Society, Hope, ND 353
Steele County Historical Society, Owatonna, MN 234
Steilacoom Historical Museum Association, Steilacoom, WA 489
Stenton—Home of James Logan, Philadelphia, PA 403
Stephansson House Provincial Historic Site, Markerville, Alberta 515
Stephen Foster Memorial, Pittsburgh, PA 404
Stephen Foster State Folk Culture Center, White Springs, FL 84
Stephens Museum of Natural History—United Methodist Historical Collection, Fayette, MO 245
Stephenson County Historical Society, Freeport, IL 107
Stephentown Historical Society, Stephentown, NY 335
Stephenville Historical House Museum, Stephenville, TX 458
Steppingstone Museum Association, Inc., Havre de Grace, MD 184
Sterling Historical Society, Inc., Sterling, MA 205
Sterne-Hoya Home, Nacogdoches, TX 453
Stettler Town and Country Museum, Stettler, Alberta 516
Stevens Coolidge Place, Trustees of Reservations, North Andover, MA 201
Stevens County Historical Society, Morris, MN 234
Stevens Museum, Salem, IN 129
Stewart County Historical Commission, Lumpkin, GA 90
Stewart M. Lord Memorial Historical Society, Burlington, ME 170
Still National Osteopathic Museum, Kirksville, MO 249
Stockholm Historical Society, Stockholm, ME 177
Stockton Archives, Cumberland University, Lebanon, TN 431
Stokes County Historical Society, Germanton, NC 345
Stone Hills Area Library Services Authority, Bloomington, IN 121
Stone Park Historical Society, Stone Park, IL 117
Stone's Trace Historical Society, Ligonier, IN 126
Stone-Tolan House, Rochester, NY 331
Stoneham Historical Society, Inc., Stoneham, MA 206
Stonewall Jackson House, Lexington, VA 476
Stoney Creek Battlefield House, Stoney Creek, Ontario 551
Stormont, Dundas and Glengarry Historical Society, Cornwall, Ontario 541
Storrowton Village Museum, West Springfield, MA 208
Stoughton Historical Society, Stoughton, MA 206
Stoughton Historical Society, Stoughton, WI 504
Stovall Museum of Science and History, Norman, OK 378
Stow Historical Commission, Stow, MA 206
Stow Historical Society, Stow, MA 206
Stow Historical Society, Stow, OH 372
Stow West School Society, Inc., Stow, MA 206
Stowe-Day Foundation, The, Hartford, CT 61
Stratford Hall Plantation, Stratford, VA 481
Stratford Historical Society, Strafford, CA 46
Stratford Historical Society, Stratford, CT 67

Stratford-Perth Archives Board, Stratford, Ontario 551
Strathcona Archaeological Centre, Edmonton, Alberta 513
Strawbery Banke, Portsmouth, NH 275
Streatorland Historical Society, Inc., Streator, IL 117
Strecker Museum, Waco, TX 459
Strongsville Historical Society, Inc., Strongsville, OH 372
Stuart House Museum, Mackinac Island, MI 219
Studebaker Family National Association, Tipp City, OH 372
Stuhr Museum of the Prairie Pioneer, Grand Island, NE 263
Sturgeon River House Museum, Sturgeon Falls, Ontario 551
Stuttgart Agricultural Museum, Stuttgart, AR 22
Sublette County Historical Society, Inc., Pinedale, WY 508
Submarine Memorial Association—USS Ling 297, Hackensack, NJ 282
Suffern Village Museum, Suffern, NY 336
Suffield Historical Society, Inc., Suffield, CT 67
Suffolk County Archaeological Association, Stony Brook, NY 336
Suffolk County Historic Trust—Suffolk County Division of Cultural and Historic Services, West Sayville, NY 339
Suffolk County Historical Society, Riverhead, NY 330
Suffolk Marine Museum, Sayville, NY 333
Suffolk Nansemond Historical Society, Suffolk, VA 481
Sugar Hill Historical Museum, Sugar Hill, NH 276
Sugar Land Heritage Society, Sugar Land, TX 458
Sugarloaf Regional Trails, Inc., Dickerson, MD 182
Sullivan-Johnson Museum of Hardin County, Kenton, OH 366
Sullivan-Sorrento Historical Society, Sullivan-Sorrento, ME 177
Summerland Museum and Arts Society, Summerland, British Columbia 521
Summersworth Historical Society, Somersworth, NH 276
Summerville Preservation Society, Summerville, SC 421
Summit County Historical Society, Akron, OH 355
Summit Historical Society, Dillon, CO 53
Sumner Historical Society, Sumner, WA 489
Sumter County Historical Commission, Sumter, SC 421
Sumter County Museum and Archives, Sumter, SC 421
Sun City Historical Society, Sun City, AZ 14
Sun House, The, Ukiah, CA 47
Sun Inn Preservation Association, Inc., Bethlehem, PA 388
Sun River Valley Historical Society, Sun River, MT 260
Sun Valley Center for the Arts and Humanities—Institute of the American West, Sun Valley, ID 99
Sunnyvale Historical Society and Museum Association, Sunnyvale, CA 46
Sunrise Museums, Charleston, WV 492
Superior Restorations, Inc.—Finnish Pioneer Crafts Guild, Greenbush, WI 497
Superstition Mountain Historical Society, Apache Junction, AZ 11
Suquamish Tribal Cultural Center and Museum, Suquamish, WA 489
Surratt Society, The, Clinton, MD 182
Surrey Museum, Surrey, British Columbia 521
Surveyors' Historical Society, Hayward, CA 29
Surveyors' Historical Society, Rancho Cordova, CA 36
Survival of the Acadians National Historic Site, St. Joseph, New Brunswick 531
Susan B. Anthony Memorial, Inc., Rochester, NY 331
Susquehanna County Historical Society and Free Library Association, Montrose, PA 398

Susquehanna Museum of Havre de Grace, Inc., Havre de Grace, MD 184
Sutter County Historical Society, Yuba City, CA 49
Sutter's Fort State Historic Park, Sacramento, CA 39
Swan River Valley Historical Society and Museum, Swan River, Manitoba 525
Swan Valley Museum, Swan River, Manitoba 525
Swansea Historical Society, Inc., Swansea, MA 206
Swarthmore College Peace Collection, Swarthmore, PA 406
Swedish American Museum Association of Chicago, Chicago, IL 569
Swedish Historical Society of Rockford, Rockford, IL 115
Swedish-American Historical Society, Chicago, IL 105
Sweetwater County Historical Society, Green River, WY 508
Sweetwater County Museum, Green River, WY 508
Swenson Memorial Museum of Stephens County, Breckenridge, TX 440
Swift County Historical Society, Benson, MN 226
Swift Current Museum, Swift Current, Saskatchewan 567
Swift River Valley Historical Society, Inc., New Salem, MA 200
Swigart Museum, Huntington, PA 395
Swiss Community Historical Society, Bluffton, OH 356
Swiss Mennonite Cultural and Historical Society, Hutchinson, KS 147
Sydney and Louisbourg Railway Historical Society, Louisbourg, Nova Scotia 536

T

T. T. Wentworth, Jr., Museum, Pensacola, FL 82
Tabernacle Historical Society, Tabernacle, NJ 392
Tabor Opera House, Leadville, CO 56
Taft Museum, The, Cincinnati, OH 359
Tales of Cape Cod, Inc., Barnstable, MA 188
Taliaferro County Historical Society, Inc., Crawfordville, GA 87
Talladega County Historical Association, Talladega, AL 8
Tallahassee Junior Museum, Tallahassee, FL 84
Tallman Restorations, Janesville, WI 498
Tama County Historical Society, Toledo, IA 141
Tanana-Yukon Historical Society, Fairbanks, AK 9
Taos County Historical Society, Taos, NM 300
Tappantown Historical Society, Tappan, NY 336
Tarboro Historic District Commission, Tarboro, NC 350
Tarrant County Black Historical and Genealogical Society, Inc., Ft. Worth, TX 446
Tatamagouche Historical and Cultural Society, Tatamagouche, Nova Scotia 538
Tattnall County Historic Preservation, Inc., Reidsville, GA 91
Taylor Conservation and Heritage Society, Taylor, TX 458
Taylor County Historical Society, Medford, WI 500
Taylors Falls Chapter, Chicago County Historical Society, Taylors Falls, MN 237
Tehama County Museum Foundation, Inc., Tehama, CA 46
Telecommunications Hall of Fame Museum, Alberta Government Telephones, Calgary, Alberta 511
Telephone Museum, San Francisco, CA 41
Telephone Pioneers of America, Albuquerque, NM 296
Telephone Pioneers of America, Seattle, WA 488
Telfair Academy of Arts and Sciences, Inc., Savannah, GA 92

Tell City Historical Society, Inc., Tell City, IN 130
Tempe Historical Society, Tempe, AZ 15
Temple Mound Museum, Fort Walton Beach, FL 78
Temporary State Commission on the Restoration of the Capitol, Albany, NY 301
Tennessee Association of Museums, Nashville, TN 434
Tennessee Baptist Historical Society, Brentwood, TN 427
Tennessee Historical Commission, Nashville, TN 434
Tennessee Historical Society, Nashville, TN 434
Tennessee Humanities Council, Inc., Nashville, TN 434
Tennessee State Library and Archives, Nashville, TN 434
Tennessee State Museum, Nashville, TN 434
Tennessee Valley Authority, Knoxville, TN 430
Tennessee Valley Historical Society, Sheffield, AL 8
Terrebonne Genealogical Society, Houma, LA 164
Terrebonne Historical and Cultural Society, Inc., Houma, LA 164
Terwilliger Museum, Waterloo, NY 338
Teton County Historical Research Center, Jackson, WY 508
Teutopolis Monastery Museum Committee, Teutopolis, IL 117
Texana Heritage Society, Edna, TX 444
Texarkana Historical Society and Museum, Texarkana, TX 458
Texas American Indian Museum, Granbury, TX 447
Texas Archeological Society, San Antonio, TX 456
Texas Association of Museums, Austin, TX 438
Texas Baptist Historical Center-Museum, Brenham, TX 440
Texas Barbed Wire Collectors Association, Austin, TX 438
Texas Catholic Historical Society, Inc., Austin, TX 438
Texas City Heritage Association, Texas City, TX 458
Texas Folklore Society, Nacogdoches, TX 453
Texas Forestry Museum, Lufkin, TX 452
Texas Gulf Historical Society, Beaumont, TX 439
Texas Heritage, Inc.—Thistle Hill, Fort Worth, TX 446
Texas Historical Commission, Austin, TX 438
Texas Historical Foundation, Austin, TX 438
Texas Old Missions and Forts Association, Waco, TX 459
Texas Oral History Association, Waco, TX 459
Texas Panhandle Heritage Foundation, Inc., Canyon, TX 440
Texas Pioneer Arts Association, Round Top, TX 455
Texas State Genealogical Society, Houston, TX 449
Texas State Library and Archives Commission, Austin, TX 438
Texas Tennis Museum and Hall of Fame—Texas Sports Hall of Champions, Waco, TX 460
Texas-Dallas History and Archives Division, Dallas Public Library, Dallas, TX 443
Texas-New Mexico Field Office, Ft. Worth, TX 446
Textile Conservation Workshop, Inc., South Salem, NY 335
Teysen's Woodland Indian Museum, Mackinaw City, MI 219
Thayer County Historical Society, Belvidere, NE 261
Theatre Historical Society of America, Chicago, IL 105
Them Days, Happy Valley, Newfoundland 531
Theodore Roosevelt Birthplace National Historic Site, New York, NY 325
Theodore Roosevelt Inaugural National Historic Site, Buffalo, NY 306
Theodore Roosevelt Nature and History Association, Medora, ND 353
Third Armored Cavalry Museum, Fort Bliss, TX 445
Thomas Burke Memorial Washington State Museum, Seattle, WA 488

Thomas Cole Foundation, Catskill, NY 307
Thomas County Historical Society and Museum, Colby, KS 144
Thomas County Historical Society, Inc., Thomasville, GA 93
Thomas Edison Winter Home and Museum, Ft. Myers, FL 78
Thomas Gilcrease Institute of American History and Art, Tulsa, OK 381
Thomas Hart Benton Home and Studio, Kansas City, MO 248
Thomas Jefferson Memorial Foundation, Charlottesville, VA 472
Thomas L. Kane Memorial Chapel, Kane, PA 396
Thomas McCulloch House—Hector Centre Trust National Exhibition Centre, Pictou, Nova Scotia 537
Thomas Warne Historical Museum and Library, Old Bridge, NJ 289
Thomas Wolfe Memorial, Asheville, NC 341
Thomasville Landmarks, Inc., Thomasville, GA 93
Thornton Historical Society, Thornton, IL 117
Thornton W. Burgess Museum, Sandwich, MA 204
Thousand Islands Craft School and Textile Museum, Clayton, NY 308
Thousand Islands Shipyard Museum, Clayton, NY 308
Three Creeks Historical Association, Lowell, IN 126
Three Island Crossing State Park, Glenns Ferry, ID 97
Three Rivers Historical Society, Hemingway, SC 419
Three Village Historical Society, East Setauket, NY 310
Thronateeska Heritage Foundation, Albany, GA 84
Ticonderoga Historical Society, Ticonderoga, NY 337
Tiffin Historic Trust, Tiffin, OH 372
Tigard Area Historical and Preservation Association, Portland, OR 385
Tillamook County Pioneer Museum, Tillamook, OR 386
Timber Lake and Area Historical Society, Timber Lake, SD 426
Timber Village Museum, Blind River, Ontario 540
Time Museum, The, Rockford, IL 115
Time Was Village Museum, Mendota, IL 111
Tioga County Historical Society, Owego, NY 327
Tioga County Historical Society, Wellsboro, PA 408
Tippecanoe Battlefield Museum, Battle Ground, IN 120
Tippecanoe County Historical Association, Lafayette, IN 126
Tisbury Museum, Vineyard Haven, MA 206
Titusville Historical Society, Titusville, PA 406
Toa Mo Ga Memorial Museum, Plains, TX 454
Tobias Community Historical Society, Tobias, NE 266
Todd County Historical Society, Inc., Long Prairie, MN 231
Todmorden Mills Historic Site, Toronto, Ontario 553
Tofield Historical Museum, Tofield, Alberta 517
Toledo Firefighter Museum, Inc., Toledo, OH 373
Toltec Mounds State Park, Scott, AR 21
Tom Green County Historical Society, San Angelo, TX 455
Tom Mix Museum, Dewey, OK 376
Tomales Elementary Local History Center, Tomales, CA 47
Tombstone Courthouse State Historic Park, Tombstone, AZ 15
Tome Parish Museum, Tome, NM 300
Toms River Seaport Society, Toms River, NJ 292
Tonawanda-Kenmore Historical Society, Tonawanda, NY 337
Tonganoxie Community Historical Society, Tonganoxie, KS 151
Tongass Historical Society, Inc., Ketchikan, AK 10
Top of Oklahoma Historical Society—Cherokee Outlet Museum, Blackwell, OK 376
Toppenish Museum, Toppenish, WA 490

Topsfield Historical Society, Topsfield, MA 206
Toronto Historical Board, Toronto, Ontario 553
Toronto Jewish Congress—Canadian Jewish Congress
    Ontario Region Archives, Toronto, Ontario 553
Torrance Historical Society, Torrance, CA 47
Torrington Historical Society, Inc., Torrington, CT 67
Totoket Historical Society, Inc., North Branford, CT 64
Towe Antique Ford Museum, Deer Lodge, MT 257
Town Creek Indian Mound State Historic Site, Mt.
    Gilead, NC 347
Town of Bethlehem Historical Association, Selkirk,
    NY 334
Town of Carmel Historical Society, Mahopac, NY 319
Town of Evans Historical Society, Angola, NY 302
Town of Maryland Historical Association, Schenevus,
    NY 333
Town of Massena Museum and Historian's Office,
    Massena, NY 20
Town of Middlefield Historical Association,
    Cooperstown, NY 309
Town of Norfolk Historical Museum, Norfolk, NY 325
Town of Perth Historical Society, Perth, NY 328
Town of Warren Historical Society, Jordanville, NY 317
Town of Yorktown Museum, Yorktown Heights, NY 340
Township of Randolph Landmarks Committee,
    Randolph, NJ 290
Trading Post Historical Museum, Trading Post, KS 152
Trail End Historic Center, Sheridan, WY 509
Trail of '98 Museum, Skagway, AK 11
Transport Museum Association, St. Louis, MO 254
Travellers' Rest Museum House 1799, Nashville, TN 434
Traverse County Historical Society, Wheaton, MN 238
Treasure Island Museum, San Francisco, CA 41
Tredyffrin Easttown History Club, Berwyn, PA 388
Tree Farm Archives, Shelton, CT 66
Trent River Pioneer Museum, Havelock, Ontario 543
Trenton Historical Commission, Trenton, MI 224
Trethewey House—Matsqui-Sumas-Abbotsford
    Museum Society, Abbotsford, British Columbia 517
Treutlen County Historical Society, Soperton, GA 93
Tri-Cities Historical Society, Grand Haven, MI 216
Tri-County Historical and Museum Society of King City,
    Inc., King City, MO 249
Tri-County Historical Society, Anaconda, MT 256
Tri-County Historical Society, Herington, KS 146
Tri-State Railway Historical Society, Inc., Morristown,
    NJ 286
Trimble County Historical Society, Bedford, KY 153
Trinity Museum and Archives, Trinity,
    Newfoundland 532
Trinity Museum, New York, NY 325
Trochu Valley Historical Society, Trochu, Alberta 517
Troup County Historical Society, Inc.—Archives,
    LaGrange, GA 89
Troy Historical Museum, Troy, MI 224
Truckee-Donner Historical Society, Inc., Truckee, CA 47
Truman G. Blocker, Jr. History of Medicine Collections,
    Moody Medical Library, Galveston, TX 447
Trumbull County Chapter, Ohio Genealogy Society,
    Warren, OH 373
Trumbull Historical Society, Trumbull, CT 67
Truro Historical Society, Inc., Truro, MA 206
Trustees of Reservations, Milton, MA 199
Tryon Palace Restoration Complex, New Bern, NC 347
Tubac Historical Society, Tubac, AZ 15
Tubac Presidio State Historic Museum, Tubac, AZ 15
Tucson Festival Society, Tucson, AZ 16
Tucumcari Historical Research Institute, Tucumcari,
    NM 300
Tuftonboro Historical Society, Melvin Village, NH 274
Tuftonboro Historical Society, Tuftonboro, NH 276

Tulare County Historical Society, Visalia, CA 48
Tularosa Basin Historical Society, Alamogordo, NM 294
Tularosa Village Historical Society, Tularosa, NM 300
Tully Area Historical Society, Tully, NY 337
Tulsa County Historical Society, Tulsa, OK 381
Tulsa County Historical Society Museum, Tulsa, OK 381
Tumwater Historical Association, Tumwater, WA 490
Tupperville School Museum, Tupperville, Nova
    Scotia 538
Tuscaloosa County Preservation Society, Tuscaloosa,
    AL 8
Tuscarora Township Historical Society, Laceyville,
    PA 396
Tuxedo Historical Society, Tuxedo, NY 337
Twenty-nine Palms Historical Society, Twenty-nine
    Palms, CA 47
Twinfield Historical Society, Plainfield, VT 468
Twinsburg Historical Society, Twinsburg, OH 373
Tyringham Historical Commission, Tyringham, MA 206

U

U.S. Air Force Historical Research Center, Montgomery,
    AL 7
U.S. Air Force in Utah Historical Society, Ogden,
    UT 463
U.S. Air Force Museum, Wright-Patterson Air Force
    Base, OH 375
U.S. Army Air Defense Artillery Association, Fort Bliss,
    TX 445
U.S. Army Air Defense Artillery Museum, Fort Bliss,
    TX 445
U.S. Army Aviation Museum, Fort Rucker, AL 5
U.S. Army Center of Military History, Washington, DC 75
U.S. Army Chaplain Museum, Fort Monmouth, NJ 281
U.S. Army Chemical Corps Museum, Fort McClellan,
    AL 5
U.S. Army Engineer Museum, Fort Belvoir, VA 473
U.S. Army Field Artillery and Fort Sill Museum, Fort Sill,
    OK 377
U.S. Army Finance Corps Museum, Indianapolis, IN 125
U.S. Army Military History Institute, Carlisle Barracks,
    PA 389
U.S. Army Military Police Corps Museum, Fort
    McClellan, AL 5
U.S. Army Ordnance Museum, Aberdeen, MD 179
U.S. Army Quartermaster Museum, Fort Lee, VA 473
U.S. Army Transportation Museum, Fort Eustis, VA 473
U.S. Capitol Historical Society, Washington, DC 75
U.S. Catholic Historical Society, Yonkers, NY 340
U.S. Cavalry Museum, Fort Riley, KS 145
U.S. Forest Service, Intermountain Region, Ogden,
    UT 463
U.S. Grant's Home State Historic Site, Galena, IL 107
U.S. Marine Corps Air-Ground Museum and Museums
    Branch Activities, Quantico, VA 478
U.S. Marine Corps Historical Center and Museum,
    Washington, DC 75
U.S. Senate Commission on Art and Antiquities,
    Washington, DC 75
U.S. Tobacco Museum, Greenwich, CT 61
US Naval Academy Museum, Annapolis, MD 179
USS Arizona Memorial, Pearl Harbor, HI 96
USS Cassin Young, Boston, MA 191
USS Constitution Museum Foundation, Inc., Boston,
    MA 191
USS North Carolina Battleship Memorial, Wilmington,
    NC 351
Ukrainian Canadian Research Foundation, Toronto,
    Ontario 553

Ukrainian Cultural Heritage Village, Edmonton, Alberta 513
Ukrainian Heritage Association and Museum of Canada, Toronto, Ontario 554
Ukrainian Museum-Archives, Inc., Cleveland, OH 360
Ukrainian Museum, New York, NY 325
Ukrainian Museum of Canada, Saskatoon, Saskatchewan 566
Ukrainian National Museum, Chicago, IL 105
Ulen Historical Recreation and Conservation Association, Inc., Ulen, MN 237
Ulysses Historical Society, Trumansburg, NY 337
Umatilla County Historical Society, Pendleton, OR 384
Unadilla Valley Historical Society, Mount Upton, NY 321
Uncle Tom's Cabin Museum, Dresden, Ontario 541
Underwater Archaeology Association, Elmira, NY 311
Uniacke House, Halifax, Nova Scotia 535
Union Cemetery Historical Society, Inc., Kansas City, MO 248
Union County Historical Society, Creston, IA 134
Union County Historical Society, Elizabeth, NJ 280
Union County Historical Society, Lewisburg, PA 397
Union County Office of Cultural and Heritage Affairs, Westfield, NJ 293
Union Covered Bridge State Historic Site, Paris, MO 251
Union Historical Society, Inc., Union, CT 67
Union Landing Historical Society, Brielle, NJ 278
Union Pacific Museum, Omaha, NE 265
Union Station Museums, Ogden, UT 462
Unitarian and Universalist Genealogical Society, Hunt Valley, MD 184
United Church Archives, Newfoundland and Labrador Conference, St. John's, Newfoundland 532
United Daughters of the Confederacy, Richmond, VA 479
United Empire Loyalist Museum, Bloomfield, Ontario 540
United Empire Loyalists' Association of Canada, Toronto, Ontario 554
United Methodist Archives, Delaware, OH 363
United Methodist Publishing House Library, Nashville, TN 434
United Society of Shakers, Sabbathday Lake, New Gloucester, ME 174
University Archives and Area Research Center, University of Wisconsin, Parkside, Kenosha, WI 498
University Archives and Historical Collections, East Lansing, MI 214
University Archives, University Library, Omaha, NE 265
University Archives, University of Louisville, Louisville, KY 159
University Museum, Carbondale, IL 101
University Museum, Las Cruces, NM 297
University Museum of Anthropology, Lexington, KY 158
University Museum, University of Arkansas, Fayetteville, AR 18
University Museum, The, Normal, IL 112
University Photographic Archives, Louisville, KY 159
University School Library, Ft. Lauderdale, FL 78
University South Caroliniana Society, Columbia, SC 417
University of Alberta Archives, Edmonton, Alberta 513
University of Alberta Dental Museum, Edmonton, Alberta 513
University of Alaska Museum, Fairbanks, AK 9
University of Calgary Archives, Calgary, Alberta 511
University of Colorado Museum, Boulder, Boulder, CO 50
University of Northern Iowa Museum, Cedar Falls, IA 133
University of Notre Dame Archives, Notre Dame, IN 128
University of Texas Winedale Historical Center, Round Top, TX 455
University of the South Archives, Sewanee, TN 435

Upper Canada Village, Morrisburg, Ontario 546
Upper Cumberland Humanities and Social Sciences Institute, Cookeville, TN 428
Upper Delaware Heritage Alliance, Callicoon, NY 306
Upper Snake River Valley Historical Society, Rexburg, ID 98
Upsala Area Historical Society, Upsala, MN 237
Urbain Baudreall Graveline Genealogical Association, Inc., Palmer, MA 202
Utah Endowment for the Humanities, Salt Lake City, UT 463
Utah Heritage Foundation, Salt Lake City, UT 464
Utah State Historical Society, Salt Lake City, UT 464
Ute Pass Historical Society—Ute Pass Trail Museum, Cascade, CO 50
Utica Historical and Museum Society, Utica, MT 260
Uvalde County Historical Commission, Uvalde, TX 459
Uxbridge-Scott Historical Society Museum, Uxbridge, Ontario 554

V

Vacaville Heritage Council, Vacaville, CA 47
Vachel Lindsay Association, Inc., Springfield, IL 117
Valdez Heritage Center, Valdez, AK 11
Valdres Samband, Granite Falls, MN 230
Valentine Museum, The, Richmond, VA 479
Vallejo Naval and Historical Museum, Vallejo, CA 47
Valley Center Historical and Cultural Society, Valley Center, KS 152
Valley Forge Historical Society, Valley Forge, PA 407
Valley Forge National Historical Park, Valley Forge, PA 407
Valley Historical Society, Sinclairville, NY 334
Valley Mills History Museum, Valley Mills, TX 459
Van Buren County Historical Society, Spencer, TN 436
Van Cortlandtville Historical Society, Peekskill, NY 328
Van Harlingen Historical Society of Montgomery, Inc., Belle Mead, NJ 277
Van Wert County Historical Society, Van Wert, OH 373
Vancouver Historical Society, Vancouver, British Columbia 521
Vancouver Maritime Museum, Vancouver, British Columbia 521
Vancouver Museum, Vancouver, British Columbia 521
Vandalia Historical Society, Vandalia, IL 118
Vandalia Statehouse State Historic Site, Vandalia, IL 118
Vanguard Library-Museum, Vanguard, Saskatchewan 567
Varner-Hogg State Historical Park, West Columbia, TX 460
Vashon Maury Island Heritage Association, Vashon, WA 491
Vassalboro Historical Society, East Vassalboro, ME 171
Venango County Historical Society, Franklin, PA 393
Ventura County Historical Society/Museum, Ventura, CA 48
Verdigre Heritage Museum, Verdigre, NE 267
Verendrye Museum, Fort Pierre, SD 423
Vermilion Interpretive Center, Ely, MN 228
Vermillion County Museum Society, Danville, IL 105
Vermont Council on the Humanities and Public Issues, Hyde Park, VT 467
Vermont Historical Society, Montpelier, VT 467
Vermont State Archives, Montpelier, VT 468
Verndale Historical Society, Verndale, MN 237
Vernon County Historical Society, Viroqua, WI 505
Vernon Historians, Inc., Vernon, VT 469
Vernon Historical Society, Vernon, NY 338
Vernon Township Historical Society, Vernon, NJ 293
Vesterheim-Norwegian-American Museum, Decorah, IA 134

Vicksburg Foundation for Historic Preservation, Vicksburg, MS 242
Vicksburg National Military Park, Vicksburg, MS 242
Vicksburg and Warren County Historical Society, Vicksburg, MS 467
Victor Historical Society—Valentown Museum, Fishers, NY 311
Victoria County Historical Commission, Victoria, TX 459
Victoria County Library Museum and Archives, Baddeck, Nova Scotia 533
Victoria Regional Museum Association, Inc./McNamara House Museum, Victoria, TX 459
Victoria Settlement Provincial Historic Site, Smoky Lake, Alberta 516
Victoria Society of Maine—The Victoria Mansion, Portland, ME 175
Victorian House Museum, Cedar Falls, IA 133
Victorian Military History Institute, Little Rock, AR 20
Victorian Society in America, Philadelphia, PA 403
Vigilance Club, Virginia City, MT 260
vigo County Historical Society, Terre Haute, IN 130
Viking Historical Society Museum, Viking, Alberta 517
Villa Louis Historic Site, Prairie du Chien, WI 503
Villa Montalvo Center for the Arts and Arboretum, Saratoga, CA 45
Villa Park Historical Society, Inc., Villa Park, IL 118
Village des pionniers acadiens, Mont Carmel, Prince Edward Island 555
Village Historical Society, Inc., Harrison, OH 365
Village of East Davenport Association, Inc., Davenport, IA 134
Village of Honeoye Falls—Town of Mendon Historical Society, Honeoye Falls, NY 315
Villagers, Inc., The, Miami, FL 80
Vinalhaven Historical Society, Inc., Vinalhaven, ME 177
Vincennes Historical and Antiquarian Society—Lewis Historical Collections Library, Vincennes, IN 130
Vineland Historical and Antiquarian Society, Vineland, NJ 293
Vinton County Historical Society, McArthur, OH 368
Violet Museum, Violet, TX 459
Virginia Area Historical Society—Heritage Center Museum, Virginia, MN 238
Virginia Association of Museums, Richmond, VA 479
Virginia Baptist Historical Society, Richmond, VA 480
Virginia Canals and Navigations Society, Alexandria, VA 570
Virginia Division of Historic Landmarks, Richmond, VA 480
Virginia Folklore Society, Charlottesville, VA 472
Virginia Genealogical Society, Richmond, VA 480
Virginia Historical Society, Richmond, VA 480
Virginia Historic Landmarks Commission, Research Center for Archaeology, Yorktown, VA 482
Virginia Military Institute Museum, Lexington, VA 476
Virginia Room, Fairfax City Regional Library—Fairfax County Public Library, Fairfax, VA 473
Virginia State Library, Richmond, VA 406
Virginia Trust for Historic Preservation—Lee-Fendall House Museum, Alexandria, VA 470
Virginia and Truckee Railroad Museum, Carson City, NV 268
Vizcaya Museum and Gardens, Miami, FL 80
Voigt House, Grand Rapids, MI 216

W

W. D. Lawrence House, Maitland, Nova Scotia 536
W. H. Over Museum, Vermillion, SD 427
WELS (Wisconsin Evangelical Lutheran Synod) Historical Institute, Milwaukee, WI 500
WHALE (Waterfront Historic Area League), New Bedford, MA 200
WHOM (Women Historians of the Midwest), St. Paul, MN 236
Wabasha County Historical Society, Lake City, MN 231
Wabaunsee County Historical Society Museum, Alma, KS 143
Wadsworth-Longfellow House, Portland, ME 175
Wagon Wheel Regional Museum, Alix, Alberta 510
Wailoa Center Advisory Committee, Hilo, HI 94
Wake Forest College Birthplace Society, Inc., Wake Forest, NC 350
Wakefield-Brookfield Historical Society, Wakefield, NH 276
Walker County Heritage Association, Jasper, AL 5
Wallace House—Old Dutch Parsonage, Somerville, NJ 291
Waller County Historical Commission, Hempstead, TX 448
Waller County Historical Museum, Brookshire, TX 440
Waller County Historical Society, Inc., Brookshire, TX 440
Wallingford Historical Society, Inc., Wallingford, CT 68
Wallisville Heritage Park, Wallisville, TX 460
Wallowa County Museum, Joseph, OR 384
Walnut Creek Historical Society, Walnut Creek, CA 48
Walnut Street Historic District, Inc., Florence, AL 4
Walpole Historical Society, Walpole, NH 276
Walsh County Historical Society, Minto, ND 353
Walt Disney Archives, Burbank, CA 24
Walt Whitman Association, Camden, NJ 278
Walt Whitman Birthplace Association, Huntington Station, NY 316
Walter Cecil Rawls Library and Museum, Courtland, VA 472
Walter Elwood Museum, Amsterdam, NY 302
Walter Wright Pioneer Village, Dawson Creek, British Columbia 518
Waltham Museum, Inc., Waltham, MA 207
Walworth County Historical Society, Elkhorn, WI 496
War Library and Museum, Military Order of the Loyal Legion of the United States, Philadelphia, PA 403
War Memorial Museum of Virginia, Newport News, VA 477
Ward M. Canaday Center, Toledo, OH 373
Waring Library Society, Charleston, SC 415
Warner Historical Society, Warner, NH 276
Warren County Cultural and Heritage Commission, Belvidere, NJ 277
Warren County Historical Society, Lebanon, OH 366
Warren County Historical Society, Warren, PA 407
Warren County Historical Society, Warrenton, MO 255
Warren County Historical and Genealogical Society, Belvidere, NJ 278
Warren Historical Society, Warren, ME 177
Warrick County Museum, Boonville, IN 121
Warrior Run Ft. Freeland Heritage Society, Turbotville, PA 404
Warrior Trail Association, Inc., Waynesburg, PA 407
Warsaw Historical Society, Warsaw, IL 118
Warwick Historical Society, Warwick, RI 412
Waseca County Historical Society, Waseca, MN 238
Washakie County Historical Society, Worland, WY 509
Washburn County Historical Society and Museum, Shell Lake, WI 503
Washington Archaeological Research Center, Pullman, WA 486
Washington Association of New Jersey, Morristown, NJ 286
Washington Commission for the Humanities, Olympia, WA 485
Washington County Chapter, Ohio Genealogical Society, Marietta, OH 367

Washington County Historical Association, Ft. Calhoun, NE 262
Washington County Historical Library and Museum, West Bend, WI 505
Washington County Historical Society, Fort Edward, NY 312
Washington County Historical Society, Hagerstown, MD 183
Washington County Historical Society, Inc., Bartlesville, OK 376
Washington County Historical Society, Nashville, IL 112
Washington County Historical Society, Salem, IN 129
Washington County Historical Society, Stillwater, MN 237
Washington County Historical Society, Washington, IA 142
Washington County Historical Society, Washington, KS 152
Washington County Historical Society, Washington, PA 407
Washington County Historical Society, West Bend, WI 505
Washington County Museum, Chatom, AL 3
Washington Crossing Foundation, Washington Crossing, PA 407
Washington Crossing Historic Park, Washington Crossing, PA 407
Washington Park Arboretum—The Arboretum Foundation, Seattle, WA 488
Washington State Archives Regional Branch, Seattle, WA 488
Washington State Heritage Council, Olympia, WA 486
Washington State Historical Society, Tacoma, WA 490
Washington Trust for Historic Preservation, Olympia, WA 486
Washington's Headquarters State Historic Site, Newburgh, NY 321
Washington's Headquarters—Elijah Miller Farmhouse, North White Plains, NY 326
Washington's Lands Museum, Ravenswood, WV 494
Washington-on-the-Brazos State Historical Park, Washington, TX 460
Washoe County Historical Society, Reno, NV 269
Washoe Heritage Council, Reno, NV 269
Washtenaw County Historical Society, Ann Arbor, MI 211
Washtenaw County History District Commission, Ann Arbor, MI 211
Wasilla-Knik-Willow-Creek Historical Society, Wasilla, AK 11
Water Mill Museum, Water Mill, NY 338
Waterford Foundation, Inc., Waterford, VA 481
Waterford Historical Society—Mary Gage Rice Museum—Waterford Village, Waterford, ME 177
Waterfront Awareness—Institute for Marine Studies, Seattle, WA 488
Waterloo Area Historical Society, Stockbridge, MI 224
Waterloo Area Historical Society, Waterloo, WI 505
Waterloo Historical Society, Kitchener, Ontario 544
Waterloo Memorial Day Museum, Waterloo, NY 338
Watermens Museum in Yorktown, Yorktown, VA 482
Watertown Historical Society, Watertown, WI 505
Watervliet Arsenal Museum, Watervliet, NY 339
Watkins Mill Association, Lawson, MO 249
Watkins Woolen Mill State Historic Site, Lawson, MO 250
Watkinsville Historical Society, Watkinsville, GA 94
Watonwan County Historical Society, Madelia, MN 231
Watrousville-Caro Area Historical Society, Caro, MI 212
Watters Smith Memorial State Park and Museum, Lost Creek, WV 493
Waukegan Historical Society, Waukegan, IL 119

Waukesha County Historical Museum, Waukesha, WI 505
Waupaca County Historical Society, Manawa, WI 499
Wauwatosa Historical Society, Wauwatosa, WI 505
Wax Museum of the Southwest, Grand Prairie, TX 447
Wayland Area Tree Tracers Genealogical Society, Wayland, MI 224
Wayland Historic District Commission, Wayland, MA 207
Wayne County Historical Society, Corydon, IA 134
Wayne County Historical Society, Honesdale, PA 395
Wayne County Historical Society, Lyons, NY 319
Wayne County Historical Society, Monticello, KY 160
Wayne County Historical Society, Wayne, NE 267
Wayne County Historical Society, Waynesboro, TN 436
Wayne County Historical Society, Wooster, OH 374
Wayne Township Historical Commission, Wayne, NJ 293
Waynesboro Historical Society, Waynesboro, PA 407
Weakley County Genealogical Society, Martin, TN 431
Webb City Preservation Committee, Webb City, MO 256
Webb County Heritage Foundation, Inc., Laredo, TX 451
Webb-Deane-Stevens Museum, The, Wethersfield, CT 68
Webster County Historical and Genealogical Society, Dixon, KY 154
Webster County Historical Museum, Red Cloud, NE 266
Webster Groves Historical Society, Webster Groves, MO 256
Webster Museum and Historical Society, Webster, NY 339
Weeping Water Valley Historical Society, Weeping Water, NE 267
Weld Historical Society, Inc., Weld, ME 177
Wellesley Historical Society, Inc., Wellesley, MA 207
Wellfleet Historical Society—Rider House, Wellfleet, MA 207
Wellington Community Historical Museum, Wellington, Ontario 554
Wells Auto Museum, Wells, ME 178
Wells County Historical Society, Bluffton, IN 121
Wells County Historical Society, Fessenden, ND 352
Wells Fargo Bank History Department, San Francisco, CA 42
Wells Museum and Sunset Theatre, Wells, British Columbia 523
Wenham Historic District Commission, Wenham, MA 207
Wenham Historical Association and Museum, Inc., Wenham, MA 207
Wesleyan Church Archives and Historical Library, Marion, IN 127
West Baton Rouge Historical Association, Port Allen, LA 167
West Bend Historical Society, West Bend, IA 142
West-Central Kentucky Family Research Association, Owensboro, KY 161
West Central Minnesota Historical Center, Morris, MN 234
West Chicago Historical Museum, West Chicago, IL 119
West Chicago Historical Society—Kruse House Museum, West Chicago, IL 119
West Des Moines Historical Society, West Des Moines, IA 142
West Feliciana Historical Society, St. Francisville, LA 167
West Hants Historical Society, Windsor, Nova Scotia 538
West Jefferson County Historical Society, Inc., Bessemer, AL 2
West Long Branch Historical Society, West Long Branch, NJ 293

West Milwaukee Historical Society, West Milwaukee, WI 506

West of the Pecos Museum, Pecos, TX 454

West Pasco Historical Society, Inc., New Port Richey, FL 81

West Point Museum, West Point, NY 339

West Salem Historical Society, West Salem, WI 506

West Seneca Historical Society and Museum, West Seneca, NY 339

West Springfield Historical Commission, West Springfield, MA 208

West Tennessee Historical Society, Memphis, TN 432

West Texas Historical Association, Abilene, TX 436

West Texas Pioneers and Old Settlers, Crosbyton, TX 442

West Whiteland Historical Commission, Exton, PA 392

Westborough Historical Commission, Westborough, MA 207

Westchester County Genealogical Society, White Plains, NY 339

Westchester County Historical Society, Valhalla, NY 338

Westchester Preservation League, Ossining, NY 327

Westerly Historical Society, Westerly, RI 412

Westerly Public Library Granite Collection, Westerly, RI 412

Western Archeological and Conservation Center Library, Tucson, AZ 16

Western Bayfield County Historical Society, Iron River, WI 498

Western Company Museum, Fort Worth, TX 446

Western Development Museum, Yorkton, Saskatchewan 567

Western Forest Industries Museum, Inc., Tacoma, WA 490

Western Frontier Museum, Puyallup, WA 486

Western Hampden Historical Society—Dewey House, Westfield, MA 208

Western Hennepin County Pioneer Association, Long Lake, MN 231

Western Heritage Center, Billings, MT 256

Western Historical Manuscript Collection-Kansas City, Kansas City, MO 249

Western History Association, Reno, NV 269

Western History Department, Denver Public Library, Denver, CO 53

Western Jewish History Center—Judah L. Magnes Memorial Museum, Berkeley, CA 24

Western Manitoulin Historical Society, Gore Bay, Ontario 543

Western Maryland Railway Historical Society, Inc., Union Bridge, MD 186

Western Minnesota Steam Threshers Reunion, Inc., Hawley, MN 230

Western Monroe Historical Society, Brockport, NY 305

Western Museum of Mining and Industry, Colorado Springs, CO 51

Western Museum, Macomb, IL 110

Western New Mexico University Museum, Silver City, NM 299

Western North Carolina Historical Association, Inc., Asheville, NC 341

Western Office, Division of Archives and History, Asheville, NC 341

Western Postal History Museum, Tucson, AZ 16

Western Research Room, Pueblo Library District, Pueblo, CO 57

Western Reserve Architectural Historians, Cleveland Heights, OH 360

Western Reserve Historical Society, Cleveland, OH 360

Western Rhode Island Civic Historical Society, North Scituate, RI 411

Western Sonoma County Historical Society, Sebastopol, CA 45

Western Springs Historical Society, Western Springs, IL 119

Western Trail Historical and Genealogical Society, Altus, OK 375

Westerville Historical Society, Westerville, OH 374

Westfield Historical Society, Westfield, NJ 293

Westford Historical Society, Inc., Westford, MA 208

Westminster Historical Society, Westminster, MA 208

Westminster Historical Society, Westminster, VT 469

Westmoreland County Historical Society, Greensburg, PA 393

Westmoreland-Fayette Historical Society, Scottdale, PA 405

Westmorland Historical Society—Keillor House Museum, Dorchester, New Brunswick 528

Westmount Historical Association, Westmount, Quebec 563

Weston County Historical Society, Newcastle, WY 508

Weston Historical Society, Weston, CT 68

Weston Historical Society, Weston, VT 469

Westport Historical Society, Inc., Westport, MA 208

Westport Historical Society, Kansas City, MO 249

Westport Historical Society, Westport, CT 68

Westville Historic Handicrafts, Inc., Lumpkin, GA 90

Wethersfield Historical Society, Wethersfield, CT 68

Wexford County Historical Society, Cadillac, MI 212

Weyerhaeuser Company Archives, Tacoma, WA 490

Whaley Historical House, Flint, MI 215

Wharton County Historical Museum and Association, Wharton, TX 460

Wharton Esherick Museum, Paoli, PA 400

Whatcom County Historical Society, Bellingham, WA 483

Wheaton Historical Association, Millville, NJ 285

Wheeler Historic Farm, Salt Lake City, UT 464

Wheelwright Museum of the American Indian, Santa Fe, NM 299

Whitby Historical Society, Whitby, Ontario 554

Whitchurch Stouffville Museum, Vandorf, Ontario 554

White County Historical Society, Carmi, IL 101

White County Retired Teachers' Association, Sparta, TN 436

White Deer Land Museum, Pampa, TX 454

White Hair Memorial, Ralston, OK 380

White House Association of the State of Alabama, Montgomery, AL 7

White House Historical Association, Washington, DC 76

White House Ranch Historic Site, Colorado Springs, CO 51

White River Valley Historical Society, Point Lookout, MO 252

White Settlement Historical Society, Inc., White Settlement, TX 460

Whiteface Historical Society, Whiteface, TX 460

Whitefield Historical Society, Whitefield, NH 276

Whitehall, Home of Bishop Berkeley, Middletown, RI 410

Whiteside County Genealogists, Sterling, IL 117

Whitfield-Murray Historical Society, Inc., Dalton, GA 88

Whiting-Robertsdale Historical Society, Whiting, IN 131

Whitley County Historical Museum and Society, Columbia City, IN 121

Whitman County Genealogical Society, Pullman, WA 486

Whitman Mission National Historic Site, Walla Walla, WA 491

Whitman Stafford Committee, Laurel Springs, NJ 284

Whittier Historical Society, Whittier, CA 48

Whoop-up Country Chapter, Historical Society of Alberta, Lethbridge, Alberta 515

Whyte Museum of the Canadian Rockies, Banff, Alberta 510
Wichita County Heritage Society, Wichita Falls, TX 460
Wichita Falls Museum and Art Center, Wichita Falls, TX 460
Wichita-Sedgwick County Historical Museum, Wichita, KS 152
Wickliffe Historical Society, Inc., Wickliffe, OH 374
Wickliffe Mounds Research Center, Wickliffe, KY 163
Wicomico Historical Society, Inc., Salisbury, MD 185
Wilber Czech Museum, Wilber, NE 267
Wild Rose Historical Society, Wild Rose, WI 506
Wilkie and District Museum and Historical Society, Wilkie, Saskatchewan 567
Will County Historical Society, Lockport, IL 110
Will Rogers Memorial, Claremore, OK 376
Willard Area Historical Society, Willard, OH 374
Willard House and Clock Museum, Inc., Grafton, MA 195
William A. Farnsworth Library and Art Museum, Rockland, ME 176
William Clark Market House Museum, Paducah, KY 161
William Cullen Bryant Homestead, Cummington, MA 193
William E. and Ophia D. Smith Library of Regional History, Oxford, OH 370
William Floyd Estate, Fire Island National Seashore, Mastic Beach, NY 320
William Hammond Mathers Museum, Bloomington, IN 121
William Henry Spencer Golden Owlettes, Inc., Columbus, GA 87
William Howard Taft National Historic Site, Cincinnati, OH 359
William K. Vanderbilt Historical Society, Oakdale, NY 326
William Penn Mott, Jr., Training Center, Pacific Grove, CA 35
William S. Harney Historical Society, Sullivan, MO 255
Williams County Historical Society, Montpelier, OH 269
Williamsburg County Historical Society, Kingstree, SC 419
Williamson County Genealogical Society, Round Rock, TX 455
Williamson County Historical Society, Marion, IL 110
Williston Historical Society, Williston, VT 469
Willoughby-Baylor House—Chrysler Museum, Norfolk, VA 477
Willow Bunch Museum Society, Willow Bunch, Saskatchewan 567
Wilmette Historical Museum and Society, Wilmette, IL 119
Wilmot Area Historical, Research and Restoration Association, Inc., Wilmot, OH 374
Wilmot Historical Society, Wilmot, NH 276
Wilson County Historical Society, Fredonia, KS 146
Wilson Historical Society, Wilson, NY 340
Wilson MacDonald Memorial School Museum, Nanticoke, Ontario 546
Wilson's Creek National Battlefield, Republic, MO 252
Wilton Historical Society, Inc., and Heritage Museum, Wilton, CT 69
Wilton Historical Society, Wilton, NH 276
Wilton Historical Society—Farm and Home Museum, Wilton, ME 178
Wilton House Museum, Richmond, VA 480
Winchendon Historical Society, Winchendon, MA 209
Winchester-Frederick County Historical Society, Winchester, VA 482
Winchester Historical Commission, Winchester, MA 209
Winchester Historical Society, Winsted, CT 69
Winchester Museum, Winchester, ID 99

Windham Historical Society, Inc., South Windham, ME 177
Windmill Gardens Museum Village, Fremont, MI 215
Windsor Historical Society, Windsor, CT 69
Windsor Locks Historical Society, Inc., Windsor Locks, CT 69
Winfield Historical Society, Winfield, IL 119
Wing Luke Memorial Museum, Seattle, WA 488
Wings and Things Museum, Inc., Delavan, IL 106
Winnebago Area Museum, Winnebago, MN 238
Winneconne Historical Society, Winneconne, WI 506
Winneshick County Historical Society, Decorah, IA 134
Winona County Historical Society, Inc., Winona, MN 238
Winston Churchill Memorial and Library, Fulton, MO 245
Winter Harbor Historical Society, Winter Harbor, ME 178
Winterport Historical Association, Winterport, ME 178
Winterthur in Odessa, Odessa, DE 70
Winterthur Museum and Gardens, Winterthur, DE 71
Wisconsin Archaeological Survey, Eau Claire, WI 496
Wisconsin Chapter, National Railway Historical Society, Inc., Milwaukee, WI 500
Wisconsin Humanities Committee, Madison, WI 499
Wisconsin Labor History Society, Milwaukee, WI 501
Wisconsin Marine Historical Society—Local History and Marine Room, Milwaukee, WI 501
Wisconsin Postal History Society, Oconomowoc, WI 502
Wisconsin Slovak Historical Society, Milwaukee, WI 501
Wisconsin State Genealogical Society, Inc., Monroe, WI 501
Wisconsin Veterans Museums, King, WI 498
Wistariahurst Museum, Holyoke, MA 197
Witte Museum, San Antonio, TX 456
Wittenberg Area Historical Society, Wittenberg, WI 506
Wolf Point Area Historical Society, Wolf Point, MT 260
Wolfville Historical Society, Wolfville, Nova Scotia 538
Women's Army Corps Museum, Fort McClellan, AL 4
Women's Rights National Historical Park, Seneca Falls, NY 334
Wood County Historical Society, Bowling Green, KY 153
Wood County Historical Society, Bowling Green, OH 356
Wood County Historical and Preservation Society, Inc., Parkersburg, WV 494
Wood Library—Museum of Anesthesiology, Park Ridge, IL 114
Woodford Mansion, Philadelphia, PA 403
Woodland Park Zoo—Family Farm, Seattle, WA 489
Woodlawn Plantation, Mount Vernon, VA 477
Woodrow Wilson Birthplace, Staunton, VA 480
Woodrow Wilson House Museum, Washington, DC 76
Woodside National Historic Park, Kitchener, Ontario 544
Woodstock Historical Society, Woodstock, CT 69
Woodstock Historical Society, Woodstock, VT 469
Woodstock Museum of Shenandoah County, Inc., Woodstock, VA 482
Woonsocket Historical Society, Woonsocket, RI 413
Worcester Art Museum, Worcester, MA 209
Worcester Historical Museum, Worcester, MA 209
Workman and Temple Homestead—Historical Perspectives, Inc., City of Industry, CA 25
World Heritage Museum, Champaign, IL 102
World Museum of Mining, Butte, MT 256
World War II Glider Pilots Association, Freehold, NJ 281
Wornall House Museum, Kansas City, MO 249
Worth County Historical Society, Allendale, MO 242
Wrather West Kentucky Museum, Murray, KY 161
Wrentham Historical Commission, Wrentham, MA 209
Wright Brothers National Memorial, Manteo, NC 346
Wright County Historical Society, Buffalo, MN 226
Wright County Historical Society, Clarion, IA 133
Wright State University Archives and Special Collections, Dayton, OH 362

Wrightsboro Quaker Community Foundation, Inc., Thomson, GA 93
Wyandotte County Historical Society and Museum, Bonner Springs, KS 143
Wyandotte Museum, Wyandotte, MI 225
Wyanet Historical Society, Wyanet, IL 119
Wynnewood Historical Society, Wynnewood, OK 382
Wyoming County Historical Society, Tunkhannock, PA 406
Wyoming Historical and Geological Society, Wilkes-Barre, PA 408
Wyoming Pioneer Memorial Museum, Douglas, WY 507
Wyoming State Archives, Museums and Historical Department, Cheyenne, WY 507
Wyoming State Museum and Art Gallery, Cheyenne, WY 507

Y

Yakima Nation Museum, Toppenish, WA 490
Yakima Valley Museum and Historical Association, Yakima, WA 491
Yale University Collection of Musical Instruments, New Haven, CT 64
Yankton County Historical Society, Yankton, SD 427
Yardley Historical Association, Inc., Yardley, PA 408
Yarmouth County Historical Society, Yarmouth, Nova Scotia 539
Yarmouth County Museum, Yarmouth, Nova Scotia 539
Yarmouth Historical Society—Museum of Yarmouth History, Yarmouth, ME 178
Yates County Genealogical and Historical Society, Inc., Penn Yan, NY 328
Yazoo Historical Society, Yazoo City, MS 242
Yell County Arkansas Historical and Genealogical Association, Russellville, AR 21
Yell County Historical and Genealogical Society, Dardanelle, AR 17
Yellow Medicine County Historical Society Museum, Granite Falls, MN 230

Yellow Springs Historical Society, Yellow Springs, OH 375
Yellowstone National Park—Albright Visitor Center, Yellowstone National Park, WY 509
Yeshiva University Museum, New York, NY 325
Yesteryear Museum, Whippany, NJ 294
Yoakum Heritage Museum, Yoakum, TX 461
York County Historical Commission, McConnells, SC 420
York Institute Museum, Saco, ME 176
York Pioneer and Historical Society, Toronto, Ontario 554
York-Sunbury Historical Society, Fredericton, New Brunswick 528
Yorkton Arts Council, Yorkton, Saskatchewan 567
Yosemite National Park Research Library, Yosemite, CA 49
Young Ideas Explorer Post 400, San Francisco, CA 42
Ypsilanti Historical Society, Ypsilanti, MI 225
Yugtarvik Regional Museum, Bethel, AK 9
Yukon Archives, Whitehorse, Yukon Territory 568
Yukon Church Heritage Society, Whitehorse, Yukon 568
Yukon Historical and Museums Association, Whitehorse, Yukon Territory 568
Yuma County Historical Society, Yuma, AZ 16

Z

Z. I. Hale Museum, Winters, TX 460
Zadock Pratt Museum, Inc., Prattsville, NY 329
Zebulon B. Vance Birthplace, Weaverville, NC 350
Zeeland Historical Society, Zeeland, MI 225
Zelienople Historical Society, Zelienople, PA 408
Ziebach County Historical Committee, Dupree, SD 423
Zion Historical Society, Zion, IL 120
Zionsville Historical Society, Inc., Zionsville, IN 131
Zoar Village State Memorial, Zoar, OH 375

Special Interest Index

AGRICULTURE

Agricultural Hall of Fame, Bonner Springs, KS 143
Agricultural Heritage Museum, Brookings, SD 422
Agricultural History Society, Washington, D.C. 71
Americana Museum, Terra Alta, WV 474
Andrew County Historical Society, Savannah, MO 255
Association of Living History Farms and Museums, Washington, D.C. 72
Audubon County Historical Society, Audubon, IA 131
Baldwin Heritage Museum Association, Elberta, AL 4
Barberton Historical Society, Barberton, OH 356
Beckoning Hills Museum, Boissevain, Manitoba 523
Belmar Museum, Lakewood, CO 55
Billings Farm and Museum, Woodstock, VT 469
British Columbia Farm Machinery and Agriculture Museum Association, Fort Langley, British Columbia 518
Brodhead Historical Society, Brodhead, WI 495
Burlington Historical Society, Burlington, Ontario 540
Burt County Museum, Tekamah, NE 266
Butterfield Threshermen's Association, Butterfield, MN 227
Carroll County Farm Museum, Westminster, MD 186
Center for Environmental Study, Williams College, Williamstown, MA 208
Chippewa County Historical Society, Montevideo, MN 233
Clinton Historical Museum Village, Clinton, NJ 279
Cobblestone Society Museum, Albion, NY 301
Cochrane Ranch, Cochrane, Alberta 512
Community Memorial Museum of Sutter County, Yuba City, CA 49
Corporation Touristique de la Seigneurie des Aulnaies, St. Roch des Aulnaies, Quebec 562
Covington Historical Society, Pavilion, NY 328
Cranberry World Visitors Center, Plymouth, MA 202
Dakota County Historical Society, South St. Paul, MN 237
Daniel Parrish Witter Agricultural Museum, Syracuse, NY 336
Delaware Agricultural Museum, Dover, DE 69
Delaware Valley Old Time Power and Equipment Association, Lambertville, NJ 284
Douglas County Historical Society, Armour, SD 422
Everest Community Historical Society, Everest, KS 145
Farmamerica—Minnesota Agricultural Interpretive Center, Waseca, MN 238
Farmers Museum, Inc., Cooperstown, NY 309
Fernwood Botanic Garden, Nature Center—Arts and Crafts Center, Niles, MI 221
Fort Kent Historical Society, Fort Kent, ME 172
Fort Walla Walla Museum Complex, Walla Walla, WA 491
Fosterfields Living Historic Farm, Morristown, NJ 286
Friends of Barclay Farmstead, Cherry Hill, NJ 279
Garfield Farm and Tavern Museum, LaFox, IL 109
Gibbs Farm Museum, Falcon Heights, MN 229
Good Earth Association, Inc.—Living Farm Museum of the Ozarks, Pocahontas, AR 21
Grand Forks County Historical Society, Grand Forks, ND 353
Haliburton Highlands Museum, Haliburton, Ontario 543
Hammonton Historical Society, Hammonton, NJ 282
Harrison County Historical Society, Bethany, MO 243

Heritage Farmstead—Plano Heritage Association, Plano, TX 454
Heritage Hill State Park, Green Bay, WI 497
Historical Farm Association—Quiet Valley Living Historical Farm, Stroudsburg, PA 406
Historical Society of University City, St. Louis, MO 254
History Section, U.S. Forest Service, Washington, DC 73
Hopkins Forest Farm Museum, Williamstown, MA 208
Hot Springs County Museum and Cultural Center, Thermopolis, WY 509
Howell Living Historical Farm, Hopewell Township, NJ 283
Huntley Project Museum of Irrigated Agriculture, Osborn, MT 259
Ice House Museum, Cedar Falls, IA 133
Indiana Dunes National Lakeshore, Porter, IN 129
Indiana State Museum and Memorials, Indianapolis, IN 125
Jackson's Mill State 4-H Camp, Weston, WV 494
Jerome County Historical Society, Jerome, ID 97
Kewaskum Historical Society, Inc., Kewaskum, WI 498
Keystone Pioneer Museum, Roblin, Manitoba 524
Klamath National Forest, Yreka, CA 49
Lenox Historical Society, Inc., Jefferson, OH 366
Lexington County Historical Society, Lexington, SC 420
Lexington County Museum, Lexington, SC 420
Living History Farms, Des Moines, IA 135
Lodi Historical Society, Lodi, NY 319
Logan County Archeological and Historical Society, Bellefontaine, OH 356
Longstreet Farm, Holmdel, NJ 283
Luscher's Farm Relics of Yesterday, Frankfort, KY 155
Madison County Historical Society, Oneida, NY 326
Madison Parish Historical Society, Tallulah, LA 168
Meadow Farm Museum, Richmond, VA 479
Midwest Old Settlers and Threshers Association, Inc., Mt. Pleasant, IA 139
Mississippi Agriculture and Forestry Museum—National Agricultural and Aviation Museum, Jackson, MS 240
Moross House, Home of the Detroit Garden Center, Detroit, MI 213
Morrice Farm Museum, Morrice, MI 220
Muscoot Farm Park, Katonah, NY 317
Musée Regional de Vaudreuil-Soulanges, Vaudreuil, Quebec 563
Muskegon County Museum, Muskegon, MI 221
National Colonial Farm of the Accokeek Foundation, Inc., Accokeek, MD 179
New Hampshire Farm Museum, Inc., Milton, NH 274
New Ross District Museum Society—Ross Farm Museum of Agriculture, New Ross, Nova Scotia 537
Newark Valley Historical Society, Newark Valley, NY 321
No Man's Land Historical Society and Museum, Goodwell, OK 377
Norlands Living History Center, Livermore, ME 173
Northern New York Agricultural Historical Society, Lafargeville, NY 317
Oklahoma Steam Thresher Association, Pawnee, OK 379
Oktibbeha County Heritage Museum, Starkville, MS 242
Old Colony Planning Council, Brockton, MA 191
Ontario Agricultural Museum, Milton, Ontario 546
Ontario Historical Society, Ontario, NY 326
Oscar Farris Agricultural Museum, Nashville, TN 434

Pajaro Valley Historical Association, Watsonville, CA 48
Park County Historical Society, Livingston, MT 259
Prairie County Historical Society, Hazen, AR 18
Prowers County Historical Society, Lamar, CO 55
Queens County Farm Museum, New York, NY 325
Ravalli County Museum, Hamilton, MT 258
Regional History Center, DeKalb, IL 106
Reno County Historical Society, Hutchinson, KS 147
Rio Vista Museum Association, Inc., Rio Vista, CA 37
Rough and Tumble Engineers' Historical Association,
    Inc., Kinzers, PA 396
Rutland Historical Society, Rutland, VT 468
Sac County Historical Society, Nemaha, IA 140
Saskatchewan Western Development Museums,
    Saskatoon, Saskatchewan 566
Shafter Historical Society, Inc., Shafter, CA 45
Slate Run Living Historical Farm, Marcy, OH 367
Sod House, Aline, OK 375
Somerset Place, Creswell, NC 343
South County Museum, Narragansett, RI 410
South Dakota Division of Parks and Recreation, Pierre,
    SD 425
Stuttgart Agricultural Museum, Stuttgart, AR 22
Sutter County Historical Society, Yuba City, CA 49
Swan Valley Museum, Swan River, Manitoba 525
The Southwestern Antique Gas and Steam Engine
    Museum, Vista, CA 48
The University Museums, Normal, IL 112
Wabasha County Historical Society, Lake City, MN 231
Warrior Trail Association, Inc., Waynesburg, PA 407
Waterford Historical Society—Mary Gage Rice
    Museum—Waterford Village, Waterford, ME 177
Watonwan County Historical Society, Madelia, MN 231
Western Minnesota Steam Threshers Reunion, Inc.,
    Hawley, MN 230
Wilton Historical Society, Wilton, NH 276
Woodland Park Zoo—Family Farm, Seattle, WA 489

ARCHAEOLOGY

Aiken County Historical Museum, Aiken, SC 413
Alabama Archaeological Society, Huntsville, AL 5
Albuquerque Archaeological Society, Albuquerque,
    NM 294
Alexandria Archaeology, Alexandria, VA 469
Alexandria Urban Archaeology Program, Alexandria,
    VA 469
Anasazi Indian Village State Historical Monument,
    Boulder, UT 461
Angel Mounds State Memorial, Evansville, IN 122
Archaeological Committee, Wayne County Historical
    Society, Wooster, OH 374
Archaeological Society of Maryland, Inc., Silver Spring,
    MD 186
Archaeological Society of South Carolina, Columbia,
    SC 416
Archaeological Society of Virginia, Richmond, VA 479
Archaeological Survey Association of Southern
    California, Inc., Redlands, CA 37
Archer County Historical Commission, Archer City,
    TX 437
Arizona Archaeological and Historical Society, Tucson,
    AZ 15
Arizona State Museum, Tucson, AZ 16
Baltimore Center for Urban Archaeology, Baltimore,
    MD 180
Barry County Historical Society, Cassville, MO 244
Bowdoin Park Historical and Archaeological
    Association, Wappingers Falls, NY 338

Brevard Museum of History and Natural Science,
    Cocoa, FL 77
Burpee Museum of Natural History, Rockford, IL 115
C. H. Nash Museum at Chucalissa, Memphis, TN 431
Cahokia Mounds Museum Society, Collinsville, IL 105
Casa Grande Ruins National Monument, Coolidge,
    AZ 12
Castine Scientific Society, Castine, ME 171
Center for American Archeology—Kampsville
    Archeological Center, Kampsville, IL 109
Center for Anthropological Studies, Albuquerque,
    NM 294
Chaco Culture National Historical Park, Nore, NM 298
Chelan County Historical Society, Cashmere, WA 483
Cherokee-Red Clay Association, Cleveland, TN 428
Cobden Museum, Cobden, IL 105
Cochise County Historical and Archaeological Society,
    Douglas, AZ 12
Council for Museum Anthropology, Berkeley, CA 24
Council for Northeast Historical Archeology, Waterford,
    NY 338
Crystal River State Archaeological Site, Crystal River,
    FL 77
Denver Museum of Natural History, Denver, CO 51
Desert Research Institute—Social Sciences Center,
    Reno, NV 268
Dickson Mounds Museum, Lewistown, IL 109
Division of Archaeology, Baton Rouge, LA 163
Drumheller and District Fossil Museum, Drumheller,
    Alberta 512
Edge of the Cedars State Park, Blanding, UT 461
Effigy Mounds National Monument, McGregor, IA 139
Florida State Museum, Gainesville, FL 78
Florissant Fossil Beds, Florissant, CO 54
Frank H. McClung Museum, Knoxville, TN 430
Friends of North Carolina Archaeology, Inc., Raleigh,
    NC 348
Friends of St. Mary's City, St. Mary's City, MD 185
Friends of the Blue Hills Trust, Milton, MA 199
Grant County Archaeological Society, Silver City,
    NM 299
Grindstone Bluff Museum, Shreveport, LA 168
H. Earl Clack Memorial Museum, Havre, MT 258
Head-Smashed-In Buffalo Jump Interpretive Centre,
    Fort Macleod, Alberta 514
Heritage Conservation Branch, Ministry of Provincial
    Affairs, Victoria, British Columbia 522
Historic Halifax State Historic Site, Halifax, NC 345
Houston Museum of Natural Science, Houston, TX 449
Illinois State Museum, Springfield, IL 116
Iowa Archaeological Society, Iowa City, IA 137
James Anderson House Archaeological Exhibit,
    Williamsburg, VA 481
Knife River Indian Villages National Historic Site,
    Stanton, ND 354
L. C. Bates Museum, Hinckley, ME 172
Lava Beds National Monument, Tulelake, CA 47
Lost City Museum of Archaeology, Overton, NV 268
MALFA (Material Archives and Laboratory for
    Archaeology), Katonah, NY 317
Marksville State Commemorative Area, Marksville,
    LA 165
Massachusetts Archaeological Society, Inc., Attleboro,
    MA 187
Maturango Museum of the Indian Wells Valley,
    Ridgecrest, CA 37
Maxwell Museum of Anthropology, Albuquerque,
    NM 295
Michigan Archaeological Society, Saginaw, MI 223
Mitchell Prehistoric Indian Village Preservation Society,
    Mitchell, SD 424
Mitchell Site National Historic Landmark, Mitchell,
    SD 424

Moffat County Museum, Craig, CO 51
Mound City Group National Monument, Chillicothe, OH 358
Museum of Anthropology, Highland Heights, KY 157
Museum of Anthropology, Pullman, WA 486
Museum of Florida History, Tallahassee, FL 83
Museum of Natural History, Eugene, OR 383
Museum of New Mexico, Santa Fe, NM 299
Museum of the Great Plains, Lawton, OK 378
Museum of the Red River, Idabel, OK 378
New York State Archaeological Association, Rochester, NY 331
Nipigon Museum, Nipigon, Ontario 547
Ocmulgee National Monument, Macon, GA 90
Office of Archaeology and Historic Preservation, Colorado Historical Society, Denver, CO 52
Old Stone Fort State Archaeological Park, Manchester, TN 431
Oriental Institute Museum, Chicago, IL 104
Orma J. Smith Museum of Natural History, Caldwell, ID 97
Pacific Coast Archaeological Society, Inc., Costa Mesa, CA 26
Peary-MacMillan Arctic Museum, Brunswick, ME 170
Pemberton Hall Foundation, Inc., Salisbury, MD 185
Peninsular Archaeological Society, Inc., Holiday, FL 78
Pinson Mounds State Archaeological Area, Pinson, TN 435
Pueblo Grande Museum, Phoenix, AZ 14
Quetico Provincial Park Museum, French Lake, Ontario 542
Quivira Research Center, Albuquerque, NM 295
R. H. Lowie Museum of Anthropology, Berkeley, CA 24
Robert Hull Fleming Museum, Burlington, VT 465
Rochester Museum and Science Center, Rochester, NY 331
Russell Cave National Monument, Bridgeport, AL 3
SCOPS (All Southern Ohio Preservation Society), Chillicothe, OH 358
Saginaw County Historical Society, Saginaw, MI 223
San Juan County Archaeological Research Center and Library, Farmington, NM 296
Société d'archéologie de Nouvelle-France, Quebec, Quebec 560
South Carolina Institute of Archaeology and Anthropology, Columbia, SC 417
South Dakota Archaeological Society, Sioux Falls, SD 426
South Florida Museum and Bishop Planetarium, Bradenton, FL 76
State Archaeological Center, Ft. Meade, SD 423
Stovall Museum of Science and History, Norman, OK 378
Strathcona Archaeological Centre, Edmonton, Alberta 513
Suffolk County Archaeological Association, Stony Brook, NY 336
Sullivan-Johnson Museum of Hardin County, Kenton, OH 366
Texas American Indian Museum, Granbury, TX 447
Texas Archeological Society, San Antonio, TX 456
The Amerind Foundation, Inc., Dragoon, AZ 12
The Bronson Museum, Attleboro, MA 187
The Herrett Museum, Twin Falls, ID 99
The University Museum, University of Arkansas, Fayetteville, AR 18
Thomas Burke Memorial Washington State Museum, Seattle, WA 488
Toltec Mounds State Park, Scott, AR 21
Town Creek Indian Mound State Historic Site, Mt. Gilead, NC 347
Underwater Archaeology Association, Elmira, NY 311

University Museum of Anthropology, Lexington, KY 158
University of Northern Iowa Museum, Cedar Falls, IA 133
Virginia Historic Landmarks Commission, Research Center for Archaeology, Yorktown, VA 482
Washington Archaeological Research Center, Pullman, WA 486
Wayne Township Historical Commission, Wayne, NJ 293
Western Archeological and Conservation Center Library, Tucson, AZ 16
Wickliffe Mounds Research Center, Wickliffe, KY 163
Winnebago Area Museum, Winnebago, MN 238

ETHNIC, RACIAL, RELIGIOUS

1877 Peterson Station Museum, Peterson, MN 234
Acadian Heritage Society, Rumford-Mexico, ME 176
African-American Cultural Alliance, Nashville, TN 432
African American Cultural Heritage Center—Children's Cultural Heritage Center and Museum, Dallas, TX 442
African American Museum of Art and History, Minneapolis, MN 232
Afro-American Communities Project, Washington, DC 71
Afro-American Heritage Association, Rome, NY 331
Afro-American Historical and Cultural Museum, Philadelphia, PA 400
Akwesasne Museum—Akwesasne Library and Culture Centre, Inc., Hogansburg, NY 315
Alabama Baptist Historical Society—Special Collections, Samford University Library, Birmingham, AL 2
Allendale County Historical Society, Allendale, SC 413
Amana Heritage Society and Museum of Amana History, Amana, IA 131
American Baptist Historical Society, Rochester, NY 330
American Catholic Historical Association, Washington, DC 71
American Catholic Historical Society, Philadelphia, PA 400
American Division, Jesuit Historical Institute, Tucson, AZ 15
American Jewish Archives, Cincinnati, OH 358
American Jewish Historical Society, Waltham, MA 207
American Swedish Historical Museum, Philadelphia, PA 400
American Swedish Institute, Minneapolis, MN 232
Amistad Research Center, New Orleans, LA 165
Amy B. Yerkes Museum of Hatboro Baptist Church, Hatboro, PA 394
Anthropology Museum, Northern Illinois University, DeKalb, IL 106
Archival Center, Mission Hills, CA 33
Archives of DePauw University and Indiana United Methodism, Greencastle, IN 124
Archives of the Lutheran Church in America, Chicago, IL 102
Archives of the Mexican Baptist Convention of Texas, San Antonio, TX 455
Archives of the Moravian Church in America, Winston-Salem, NC 351
Archives of the North American Baptist Conference, Sioux Falls, SD 426
Armenian Assembly of America, Washington, DC 72
Arthur J. Moore Methodist Museum, St. Simons Island, GA 92
Association Nouvelle-Angleterre/Acadie, Manchester, NH 273

Association for the Advancement of Dutch-American Studies, Grand Rapids, MI 216
Augustana Historical Society, Rock Island, IL 115
Avery Institute of Afro-American History and Culture, Charleston, SC 414
B'nai B'rith Klutznick Museum, Washington, DC 72
Balch Institute for Ethnic Studies, Philadelphia, PA 401
Balzekas Museum of Lithuanian Culture, Chicago, IL 102
Banneker-Douglas Museum of Afro-American Life and History, Annapolis, MD 179
Barre Museum—Archives of Barre History, Barre, VT 464
Basilian Fathers Museum, Mundare, Alberta 515
Bethany Lutheran Theological Seminary, Mankato, MN 231
Billy Graham Center at Wheaton College, Wheaton, IL 119
Billy Graham Center Museum, Wheaton, IL 119
Bishop Hill State Historic Site, Bishop Hill, IL 100
Black Archives Research Center and Museum, Tallahassee, FL 83
Black Catholic History Project, Office of Black Catholics, Washington, DC 72
Black Civil War Tribute Committee, Nashville, TN 433
Black Heritage Council, Montgomery, AL 6
Black Heritage Society of Washington State, Inc., Seattle, WA 487
brenorsome Historical Society, Tokio, ND 354
Brethren in Christ Historical Society, Grantham, PA 393
Buechel Memorial LaKota Museum, St. Francis, SD 425
Bureau of History and Archives, Roman Catholic Diocese of Harrisburg, Harrisburg, PA 394
Bureau of Indian Affairs—Navajo Area Office, Environmental Quality Services, Window Rock, AZ 16
California State Indian Museum, Sacramento, CA 38
Calumet Center, Nashville, TN 433
Canadian Friends Historical Association, Toronto, Ontario 552
Cane Ridge Meeting House, Paris, KY 161
Catholic Archives of Texas, Austin, TX 437
Catholic Historical Society of St. Paul, St. Paul, MN 236
Catholic Historical Society of the Diocese of Amarillo, Amarillo, TX 436
Center for Colorado Plateau Studies, Flagstaff, AZ 12
Center for Voluntary Action Research, Memphis, TN 431
Central Jersey Chapter, American Italian Historical Association, Princeton, NJ 290
Cercle de La Fleur de Lis, Gary, IN 123
Chain Bridge Productions, Arlington, VA 470
Chalet of the Golden Fleece, New Glarus, WI 501
Charles W. Bowers Memorial Museum, Santa Ana, CA 43
Cherokee National Historical Society, Inc., Tahlequah, OK 380
Chicago Jewish Historical Society, Chicago, IL 102
Chickasaw Council House Historic Site, Tishomingo, OK 381
Clarke Memorial Museum, Eureka, CA 27
Cokato Historical Society, Cokato, MN 227
Comité Louisiane Francaise, Metairie, LA 165
Commission on Archives and History, Peninsula Annual Conference, Frederica, DE 69
Commission on Archives and History, Central Illinois Conference, United Methodist Church, Bloomington, IL 100
Commission on Archives and History, United Methodist Church, Madison, NJ 284
Commonwealth Council for Arts and Culture, Saipan, The Mariana Islands 509

Commonwealth Council for Arts and Culture, Saipan, Mariana Islands 509
Concordia Historical Institute, St. Louis, MO 254
Congregation Beth Ahabah Museum and Archives Trust, Richmond, VA 479
Congregational Christian Historical Society, Boston, MA 189
Congregational Library of the American Congregational Association, Boston, MA 189
Cook's Creek Heritage Museum, Cooks Creek, Manitoba 523
Dade County Missouri Historical Society, Greenfield, MO 246
Daish American Fellowship, Minneapolis, MN 232
Delta Blues Museum, Carnegie Public Library, Clarksdale, MS 239
Department of History and Archives, Nebraska Conference, United Church of Christ, Lincoln, NE 264
Deutschheim State Historic Site, Hermann, MO 246
Disciples of Christ Historical Society, Nashville, TN 433
Doukhobour Village Museum, Castlegar, British Columbia 517
DuSable Museum of African-American History, Chicago, IL 103
Ethnic Heritage Council of the Pacific Northwest, Seattle, WA 487
Evengelical and Reformed Historical Society, Lancaster, PA 396
Fallowfield Historical Society, Coatesville, PA 390
First Baptist Church Archives, Blanchard, LA 164
First Church of Christ, Lancaster, MA 197
Flathead Culture Committee, Confederated Salish and Kootenai Tribes, St. Ignatius, MT 259
Florida Baptist Historical Society, Deland, FL 77
Franco-American Heritage Center, Auburn-Lewiston, ME 169
Franco-American Heritage Center of New Hampshire, Manchester, NH 273
Fred Hart Williams Genealogical Society, Detroit, MI 213
French Library in Boston, Inc., Boston, MA 189
Friends Historical Association, Haverford, PA 394
Galeria de los Artesanos, Las Vegas, NM 297
Garibaldi-Meucci Museum, Staten Island, NY 335
German-Canadian Historical Association, Inc., Montreal, Quebec 559
Germantown Mennonite Corporation, Philadelphia, PA 401
Gothenburg Historical Society, Gothenburg, NE 263
Grace and Holy Trinity Cathedral, Kansas City, MO 248
Hampton University Museum, Hampton, VA 474
Harmonie Associates, Inc., Ambridge, PA 387
Harwood Foundation, Taos, NM 300
Hauberg Indian Museum, Black Hawk State Park, Rock Island, IL 115
Hawaii Chinese History Center, Honolulu, HI 95
Heiltsuk Cultural Education Centre, Waglisla, British Columbia 522
Hershey Museum of American Life, Hershey, PA 395
Hillsboro Area Historical Society, Inc., Hillsboro, WI 497
Historical Archives and Museum, Catholic Diocese of El Paso, El Paso, TX 444
Historical Center, Nebraska Wesleyan University, Lincoln, NE 264
Historical Collection, North Texas State University, Denton, TX 443
Historical Department, Church of Jesus Christ of Latter-day Saints, Salt Lake City, UT 463
Historical Foundation of the Cumberland Presbyterian Church, Memphis, TN 431
Historical Foundation of the Presbyterian and Reformed Churches, Montreat, NC 346

Historical Society of New Mexico, Santa Fe, NM 298
Historical Society of the Reformed Church in America, New Brunswick, NJ 287
Historical Society of the South Georgia Conference, The United Methodist Church, St. Simons Island, GA 92
Holy Trinity Orthodox Seminary Museum, Jordanville, NY 317
Houghton County Historical Society, Lake Linden, MI 218
IHRC (Immigration History Research Center), St. Paul, MN 236
Indian City USA, Inc., Anadarko, OK 376
Indian and Colonial Research Center, Old Mystic, CT 65
Indiana Jewish Historical Society, Ft. Wayne, IN 123
Institut Canado-Americaine, Manchester, NH 273
Institut d'histoire de l'Amérique Française, Outremont, Quebec 560
Institut Québécois de Recherche Sur la Culture, Quebec, Quebec 560
Institute of American Indian Arts Museum, Santa Fe, NM 299
Institute of Texan Cultures, San Antonio, TX 456
International Museum of Cultures, Dallas, TX 443
Irish American Cultural Institute, St. Paul, MN 236
Isanti County Historical Society, Cambridge, MN 227
Italian Cultural Center, Stone Park, IL 117
Ivan Franko Museum, Winnipeg, Manitoba 526
J. B. Cain Archives of Mississippi Methodism, Jackson, MS 240
Jewish Historical Society of Maryland, Inc.—Jewish Heritage Center, Baltimore, MD 180
Jewish Historical Society of New York, Inc., New York, NY 324
Jewish Historical Society of Western Canada, Inc., Winnipeg, Manitoba 526
John Whitmer Historical Association, Lamoni, IA 138
K.A.M. Isaiah Israel Congregation, Chicago, IL 103
Kansas Collection, University of Kansas Libraries, Lawrence, KS 148
Kentucky Baptist Historical Commission—Kentucky Baptist Historical Society, Middletown, KY 160
Kirtland Temple Historic Center, Kirtland, OH 366
Knights of Columbus Charities, Inc., New Haven, CT 63
Koshare Indian Museum, Inc., La Junta, CO 55
Lac qui Parle County Historical Society, Madison, MN 231
Le Musée Sainte-Marie, Church-Point, Nova Scotia 534
Leavenworth Afro-American Historical Society, Ft. Leavenworth, KS 145
Liberty Hall Historic Center, Lamoni, IA 138
Loveland Museum and Gallery, Loveland, CO 56
Lovely Lane Museum, Baltimore, MD 181
Makah Cultural and Research Center, Neah Bay, WA 485
Mann-Simons Cottage: Museum of African-American Culture, Columbia, SC 416
Martin and Osa Johnson Safari Museum, Inc., Chanute, KS 144
Maryland Commission on Afro-American History and Culture, Annapolis, MD 179
Mattye Reed African Heritage Center, Greensboro, NC 345
McKissick Museum, Columbia, SC 416
Menaul Historical Library, Albuquerque, NM 295
Menno Simons Historical Library and Archives, Harrisonburg, VA 475
Mennonite Heritage Center, Metamora, IL 111
Mennonite Heritage Centre, Winnipeg, Manitoba 526
Mennonite Immigrant Historical Foundation, Goessel, KS 146
Mennonite Library and Archives, North Newton, KS 149
Mennonite Village Museum, Inc., Steinbach, Manitoba 525

Mexican American Cultural Heritage Center, Dallas, TX 443
Middle Tennessee Conference Afro-American Scholars, Nashville, TN 433
Minnesota Finnish-American Historical Society, Fergus Falls, MN 229
Miriam B. Wilson Foundation—Old Slave Mart Museum and Library, Charleston, SC 415
Mississippi Baptist Historical Commission, Clinton, MS 239
Moravian Museums and Tours, Bethlehem, PA 388
Moravian Music Foundation, Inc., Winston-Salem, NC 351
Morikami Museum of Japanese Culture, Delray Beach, FL 77
Mt. Carmel Cultural and Historical Center, L'Ille, ME 173
Multicultural Heritage Center, Stony Plain, Alberta 516
Musée Acadien, Moncton, NB 529
Musée d'histoire et de Traditions Populaires de la Gaspésie, Pointe Jacques-Cartier, Quebec 560
Musée de l'Eglise Notre-Dame, Montreal, Quebec 559
Musée Pierre Boucher, Trois-Rivieres, Quebec 563
Museum of African American History, Detroit, MI 213
Museum of Church History and Art, Salt Lake City, UT 463
Museum of Cultural History, Los Angeles, CA 31
Museum of Indian Heritage, Indianapolis, IN 125
Museum of Native American Cultures, Spokane, WA 489
Museum of Natural and Cultural History, Oklahoma State University, Stillwater, OK 380
Museum of Oriental Cultures, Corpus Christi, TX 441
Museum of Peoples and Cultures, Provo, UT 463
Museum of Waldensian Heritage, Valdese, NC 350
Museum of the Americas, Brookfield, VT 465
Museum of the American Indian, New York, NY 324
Museum of the Yellowstone, West Yellowstone, MT 260
Nanticoke Indian Association, Millsboro, DE 70
National Afro-American Museum and Cultural Center, Columbus, OH 361
National Federation of Franco-American Genealogical and Historical Societies, Manchester, NH 274
National Hispanic Museum, Los Angeles, CA 32
National Museum of American Jewish History, Philadelphia, PA 402
Native American Resource Center, Pembroke, NC 347
Navajo Tribal Museum, Window Rock, AZ 16
Ned A. Hatathli Center Museum, Tsaile, AZ 15
New Jersey Folk Festival Association, New Brunswick, NJ 288
New Mexico Association of Museums, Santa Fe, NM 299
New Mexico Studies Association, Denton, TX 443
New Prague Historical Society, New Prague, MN 234
New Year's Shooters and Mummers Museum, Philadelphia, PA 402
New York Public Library, Schomburg Center for Research in Black Culture, New York, NY 324
Nordic Heritage News, Seattle, WA 488
North Carolina Baptist Historical Collection, Winston-Salem, NC 351
North Carolina Synod, Lutheran Church in America, Salisbury, NC 349
Northern Montana College Collections, Havre, MT 258
Northwest Territory French and Canadian Heritage Institute, St. Louis Park, MN 236
Norwegian-American Historical Association, Northfield, MN 234
Old Choctaw Chief's House, Swink, OK 380
Old Economy Village, Ambridge, PA 387
Old Mines Area Historical Society, Old Mines, MO 251
Old Mission San Luis Obispo de Tolosa, San Luis Obispo, CA 42

Old World Wisconsin, Eagle, WI 496
Oral History Program, Fullerton, CA 28
Oral History Project, Social Science Research Institute, Honolulu, HI 96
Pella Historical Society, Pella, IA 140
Pennsylvania German Society, Bindsboro, PA 388
Peoples of Utah Institute, Salt Lake City, UT 463
Perry County Lutheran Historical Society, Altenburg, MO 242
Pioneer Adobe House Museum, Hillsboro, KS 147
Pohick Episcopal Church: Parish of Mt. Vernon and Gunston Hall, Lorton, VA 476
Polish Genealogical Society of Michigan, Detroit, MI 214
Polish Historical Commission, Central Council of Polish Organizations, Pittsburgh, PA 404
Polish Museum of America, Chicago, IL 104
Ponca City Cultural Center and Museums, Ponca City, OK 380
Portuguese Historical and Cultural Society, Sacramento, CA 39
Presbyterian Historical Society, Philadelphia, PA 403
Private Caddo Indian Museum, Longview, TX 451
Quaker Collection, Haverford College, Haverford, PA 394
Recherches Amérindiennes au Québec, Montreal, Quebec 560
Records Management Program, Oneida Tribe of Indians of Wisconsin, Oneida, WI 502
Records and Information Center, Lutheran Council—Archives of Cooperative Lutheranism, New York, NY 325
Red Rock Museum, Gallup, NM 297
Rhode Island Jewish Historical Association, Providence, RI 412
Rocky Mountain Jewish Historical Society, Denver, CO 52
Roger Williams Park Museum of Natural History, Providence, RI 412
Saint Anne's Episcopal Church Historical Commission, Lowell, MA 198
Saint Ephrem Educational Center, Youngstown, OH 375
Saint Michael's Museum Association, Inc., Chatham, New Brunswick 527
Saint Michaels Historical Museum, St. Michaels, AZ 14
Saint Photios Greek Orthodox National Shrine, St. Augustine, FL 83
Salinas National Monument, Mountainair, NM 298
Salvation Army Archives and Research Center, New York, NY 325
Salvation Army George Scott Railton Heritage Centre, Toronto, Ontario 553
San Luis Obispo County Historical Society, San Luis Obispo, CA 42
San Mateo County Historical Association and Museum, San Mateo, CA 43
Savannah-Yamacraw Branch, Association for the Study of Afro-American Life and History, Savannah, GA 92
Schoenbrunn Village State Memorial, New Philadelphia, OH 370
Schoharie Museum of the Iroquois Indian, Schoharie, NY 333
Schwenkfelder Library, Pennsburg, PA 400
Scottish Historic and Research Society of the Delaware Valley, Inc., Ardmore, PA 387
Seminole Nation Historical Society, Wewoka, OK 381
Seneca-Iroquois National Museum, Salamanca, NY 332
Shaker Museum, Poland Spring, ME 175
Shaker Village, Inc., Canterbury, NH 270
Sharon Temple Museum, Sharon, Ontario 551
Sheldon Jackson Museum, Sitka, AK 11
Sir Alexander Galt Museum and Archives, Lethbridge, Alberta 515

Sisters of the Holy Names of Jesus and Mary, Oregon Province, Marylhurst, OR 384
Ska-Nah-Dont Indian Village, Mt. Brydges, Ontario 546
Slovak Museum and Archives, Middletown, PA 398
Société Canadienne Francaise du Minnesota, Twin Cities, MN 237
Société Historique de l'ouest du Quebec, Inc., Hull, Quebec 557
Société Historique des Bernier d'Amérique, Inc., Cap St. Ignace, Quebec 556
Société Historique du Madawaska, Inc., Edmundston, New Brunswick 528
Société Historique Franco-Américaine, Boston, MA 190
Société Historique Franco-Américaine, Woonsocket, RI 413
Society of Biblical Literature, Denver, CO 53
Sons of Norway, Minneapolis, MN 233
Southern Jewish Historical Society, Valdosta, GA 94
Spertus Museum of Judaica, Chicago, IL 105
Spillville Historic Action Group, Inc., Spillville, IA 141
State Foundation on Culture and the Arts, Honolulu, HI 96
Superior Restorations, Inc.—Finnish Pioneer Crafts Guild, Greenbush, WI 497
Suquamish Tribal Cultural Center and Museum, Suquamish, WA 489
Survival of the Acadians National Historic Site, St. Joseph, New Brunswick 531
Swedish Historical Society of Rockford, Rockford, IL 115
Swedish-American Historical Society, Chicago, IL 105
Swiss Mennonite Cultural and Historical Society, Hutchinson, KS 147
Tarrant County Black Historical and Genealogical Society, Inc., Ft. Worth, TX 446
Tennessee Baptist Historical Society, Brentwood, TN 427
Teutopolis Monastery Museum Committee, Teutopolis, IL 117
Texas Catholic Historical Society, Inc., Austin, TX 438
The Moravian Archives, Bethlehem, PA 388
Thomas L. Kane Memorial Chapel, Kane, PA 396
Toronto Jewish Congress—Canadian Jewish Congress Ontario Region Archives, Toronto, Ontario 553
Trinity Museum, New York, NY 325
Tucson Festival Society, Tucson, AZ 16
U.S. Catholic Historical Society, Yonkers, NY 340
Ukrainian Canadian Research Foundation, Toronto, Ontario 553
Ukrainian Cultural Heritage Village, Edmonton, Alberta 513
Ukrainian Heritage Association and Museum of Canada, Toronto, Ontario 554
Ukrainian Museum of Canada, Saskatoon, Saskatchewan 566
Ukrainian Museum, New York, NY 325
Ukrainian Museum-Archives, Inc., Cleveland, OH 360
Ukrainian National Museum, Chicago, IL 105
United Methodist Archives, Delaware, OH 363
United Society of Shakers, Sabbathday Lake, New Gloucester, ME 174
University Museum, Carbondale, IL 101
University of Notre Dame Archives, Notre Dame, IN 128
University of Texas Winedale Historical Center, Round Top, TX 455
Utah Endowment for the Humanities, Salt Lake City, UT 463
Uvalde County Historical Commission, Uvalde, TX 459
Valdres Samband, Granite Falls, MN 230
Vesterheim-Norwegian-American Museum, Decorah, IA 134
Virginia Baptist Historical Society, Richmond, VA 480
WELS (Wisconsin Evangelical Lutheran Synod) Historical Institute, Milwaukee, WI 500

Wailoa Center Advisory Committee, Hilo, HI 94
Ward M. Canaday Center, Toledo, OH 373
Waupaca County Historical Society, Manawa, WI 499
Wesleyan Church Archives and Historical Library,
    Marion, IN 127
West Central Minnesota Historical Center, Morris,
    MN 234
Western Development Museum, Yorkton,
    Saskatchewan 567
Western Jewish History Center—Judah L. Magnes
    Memorial Museum, Berkeley, CA 24
Wheelwright Museum of the American Indian, Santa Fe,
    NM 299
White Hair Memorial, Ralston, OK 380
Wilber Czech Museum, Wilber, NE 267
Wisconsin Slovak Historical Society, Milwaukee, WI 501
Yakima Nation Museum, Toppenish, WA 490
Yeshiva University Museum, New York, NY 325
Yugtarvik Regional Museum, Bethel, AK 9
Yukon Church Heritage Society, Whitehorse, Yukon 568
Ziebach County Historical Committee, Dupree, SD 423
Zoar Village State Memorial, Zoar, OH 375

GENEALOGY

Acadian Genealogical and Historical Association of
    New Hampshire, Manchester, NH 273
Acadian Genealogy Exchange, Covington, KY 154
Acadiens au Québec, Montreal, Quebec 559
Adair County Anquestors, Greenfield, IA 136
Adams County Genealogical Society, Inc., West Union,
    OH 374
Albemarle County Historical Society, Charlottesville,
    VA 471
Albion Historical Society, Albion, MI 209
Alden Kindred of America, Inc., Duxbury, MA 194
Alexander Daugherty Chapter, United States Daughters
    of 1812, Midland, TX 452
Allegany County Historical Society, Belmont, NY 304
Alleghany Historical-Genealogical Society, Inc.—Floyd
    Crouse House, Sparta, NC 349
Almond Historical Society, Inc., Almond, NY 302
American Family Records Association, Kansas City,
    MO 247
American Historical Society of Germans from Russia,
    Lincoln, NE 264
American-Canadian Genealogical Society, Manchester,
    NH 273
American-French Genealogical Society, Pawtucket,
    RI 411
Ancestral Trails Historical Society, Vine Grove, KY 162
Andrew Pickens Chapter, Sons of the American
    Revolution, Greenville, SC 418
Anoka County Genealogical Society, Anoka, MN 226
Anoka County Historical Society, Anoka, MN 226
Archives and Records Division, Texas General Land
    Office, Austin, TX 437
Aspen Historical Society, Aspen, CO 49
Association for Northern California Records and
    Research, Chico, CA 25
Association Canado-Americaine, Manchester, NH 273
Association des Familles Gosselin, Inc., St. Laurent,
    Quebec 562
Association des Familles Hamel, Montreal, Quebec 559
Association des Familles Landry d'Amérique, Caraquet,
    New Brunswick 527
Association des Familles Ouellet-Te, Inc., Levis,
    Quebec 558
Association des Familles Rouleau, Ile d'Orléans,
    Quebec 557

Augusta Genealogical Society, Inc., Augusta, GA 86
Augusta Historical Museum, Augusta, KS 143
Barrow County Historical Society, Winder, GA 94
Barton County Genealogical Society, Great Bend,
    KS 146
Bell County Historical Society, Inc., Middlesboro,
    KY 160
Benton County, Indiana Historical Society, Inc., Fowler,
    IN 123
Bewley Family Association, Rineyville, KY 162
Bicentennial Heritage Corporation of Casey County,
    Inc., Liberty, KY 158
Bismarck-Mandan Historical and Genealogical Society,
    Bismarck, ND 352
Bloomington-Normal Genealogical Society,
    Bloomington, IL 100
Bluestem Genealogical Society, Eureka, KS 145
Boone County Genealogical Society, Boone, IA 132
Bradley County Historical Society, Cleveland, TN 428
Branch County Genealogical Society, Coldwater,
    MI 212
Broad River Genealogical Society, Inc., Shelby, NC 349
Brome County Historical Society, Knowlton,
    Quebec 558
Brookings Area Genealogical Society, Brookings,
    SD 422
Brown County Chapter, Ohio Genealogical Society,
    Georgetown, OH 364
Bucks County Genealogical Society, Doylestown,
    PA 391
Burlington County Historical Society, Burlington, NJ 278
Butler County Historical Society, Butler, PA 389
Caddel-Smith Chapter, Daughters of the Republic of
    Texas, Uvalde, TX 459
Calhoun County Genies, Rockwell City, IA 141
California Genealogical Society, San Francisco, CA 40
Calvert County Historical Society, Inc., Prince
    Frederick, MD 184
Camden Archives, Camden, SC 414
Caney Valley Historical Society, Caney, KS 144
Cape May County Historical and Genealogical Society,
    Cape May, NJ 279
Capital District Genealogical Society, Albany, NY 301
Castile Historical Society, Castile, NY 307
Cayuga County Historian, Auburn, NY 302
Cayuga-Owasco Lakes Historical Society, Moravia,
    NY 321
Centerville Historical Society, Centerville, OH 358
Central Florida Genealogical and Historical Society,
    Inc., Orlando, FL 81
Centre County Library and Historical Museum,
    Bellefonte, PA 388
Chalifour-Chalifoux-Chalufour, St. Nicolas, Quebec 562
Chambers County Heritage Society, Mont Belvieu,
    TX 452
Charleston Chapter, South Carolina Genealogical
    Society, Charleston, SC 414
Cheboygan County Genealogical Society, Cheboygan,
    MI 212
Cheneaux Historical Association, Cedarville, MI 212
Cherokee Area Archives, Inc., Cherokee, IA 133
Cherry Valley Historical Association, Cherry Valley,
    NY 308
Cherryfield-Narraguagus Historical Society, Cherryfield,
    ME 171
Chesterfield Historical Society, Chesterfield, MA 192
Chestico Museum and Historical Society, Port Hood,
    Nova Scotia 537
Chezzetcook Historical Society, Seaforth, Nova
    Scotia 537
Chicago Genealogical Society, Chicago, IL 102
Chickasaw County Genealogical Society, New
    Hampton, IA 140

Clark County Genealogical Society, Marshall, IL 111
Clay County Genealogical Society, Inc., Brazil, IN 121
Clayton County Historical Society, Strawberry Point, IA 141
Cobb County Genealogical Society, Marietta, GA 90
Coffey County Genealogical Society, Inc., Burlington, KS 143
Colorado Genealogical Society, Denver, CO 51
Colts Neck Historical Society, Colts Neck, NJ 279
Columbia Chapter, South Carolina Genealogical Society, Columbia, SC 416
Columbiana County Chapter, Ohio Genealogical Society, Salem, OH 371
Commission Nationale de Genealogie, Quebec, Quebec 560
Conant Public Library, Winchester, NH 276
Connecticut Historical Society, Hartford, CT 61
Connecticut Society of Genealogists, Inc., Glastonbury, CT 60
Coosa River Valley Historical and Genealogical Society, Centre, AL 3
Cross County Genealogical Society, Wynne, AR 22
Darlington County Historical Commission, Darlington, SC 418
Daughters of the American Revolution Library, Washington, DC 72
Davis Family Association, Woodville, MS 242
DeWitt County Historical Museum, Cuero, TX 442
Dean and Creech Families of America, Morehead, KY 160
Deer Isle-Stonington Historical Society, Deer Isle, ME 171
Defiance County Chapter, Ohio Genealogy Society, Defiance, OH 362
Delavan Community Historical Society, Delavan, IL 106
Delaware Society for the Preservation of Antiquities, Wilmington, DE 70
Detroit Chapter, FCHSM (French-Canadian Heritage Society of Michigan), Detroit, MI 213
Dexter Area Historical Society, Dexter, MI 214
Dexter Historical Museum, Dexter, IA 135
Douglas County Genealogical Society, Alexandria, MN 225
Duplin County Historical Society—Leora H. McEachern Library of Local History, Rose Hill, NC 348
Dutchess County Genealogical Society, Poughkeepsie, NY 329
Eastern Shore of Virginia Historical Society, Onancock, VA 478
Eastham Historical Society, Inc., Eastham, MA 194
Edwards County Historical Society, Albion, IL 99
Edwards and Rose Genealogical Heritage, Irvine, KY 157
Effingham County Genealogical Society, Effingham, IL 106
Elgin Genealogical Society, Elgin, IL 107
Elsie Historical Society, Elsie, MI 214
Evangeline Genealogical and Historical Society, Ville Platte, LA 168
Excelsior Springs Historical Museum, Excelsior Springs, MO 245
Farmington Genealogical Society, Farmington, MI 214
Father Leo E. Begin Chapter, American-Canadian Genealogical Society, Auburn-Lewiston, ME 169
Fayette County Genealogical Society, Washington, C.H. OH 373
Fayette County Helpers Club and Historical Society, West Union, IA 142
Ferro Monte Chapter, Daughters of the American Revolution, Succasunna, NJ 292
Flint Hills Genealogical Society, Emporia, KS 145
Florida Society for Genealogical Research, St. Petersburg, FL 83

Florida State Genealogical Society, Inc., Tallahassee, FL 83
Fort Atkinson Historical Society—Hoard Historical Museum, Fort Atkinson, WI 496
Franco-American Genealogical Association, Albany, NY 301
Franco-American Genealogical Society of York County, Biddeford, ME 170
Franklin County Genealogical Society, Columbus, OH 361
Freeborn County Genealogical Society, Albert Lea, MN 225
Fremont Historical Society, Fremont, NH 271
French-Canadian Genealogical Society of Connecticut, Rocky Hill, CT 66
French-Canadian Heritage Society of Michigan, Lansing, MI 218
Friends of the Archives, Inc., Raleigh, NC 348
Fulton County Historical Society, Inc., McConnellsburg, PA 398
Genealogical Association of Southwestern Michigan, St. Joseph, MI 223
Genealogical Forum of Portland, Portland, OR 385
Genealogical Library, Church of Jesus Christ of Latter-Day Saints, Salt Lake City, UT 463
Genealogical Research Society of New Orleans, New Orleans, LA 166
Genealogical Section, Le Club Calumet, Augusta, ME 169
Genealogical Society of Broward County, Inc., Fort Lauderdale, FL 78
Genealogical Society of Harlan, Harlan, KY 156
Genealogical Society of Okaloosa County, Inc., Ft. Walton Beach, FL 78
Genealogical Society of Old Tryon County, Inc., Forest City, NC 344
Genealogical Society of Washtenau County, Ann Arbor, MI 569
Genealogy Club of the Albuquerque Public Library, Albuquerque, NM 295
General Society of Mayflower Descendants, Plymouth, MA 202
Germans from Russia Heritage Society, Bismarck, ND 352
Giles County Historical Society, Pulaski, TN 435
Gloucester County Historical Society, Woodbury, NJ 294
Grand Blanc Heritage Association, Grand Blanc, MI 215
Gratiot County Historical Society, Ithaca, MI 217
Green County Historical Society, Inc., Greensburg, KY 156
Greenbrier Historical Society, Lewisburg, WV 493
Greene County Chapter, Ohio Genealogical Society, Xenia, OH 375
Greene County Historical and Genealogical Society, Carrollton, IL 101
Greenville Chapter, South Carolina Genealogical Society, Greenville, SC 418
Guilford Township Historical Collection, Plainfield Public Library, Plainfield, IN 128
Guthrie County Genealogical Society, Jamaica, IA 138
Guysborough Historical Society, Guysborough, Nova Scotia 534
Gwinnett County Historical Society, Inc., Lawrenceville, GA 90
HEIRS (Harrow Early Immigrant Research Society), Harrow, Ontario 543
Hackettstown Historical Society, Hackettstown, NJ 282
Hamilton County Chapter, Ohio Genealogical Society, Cincinnati, OH 359
Hamilton County Historical Society, Noblesville, IN 128
Hardin County Chapter, Ohio Genealogy Society, Kenton, OH 366

Harper County Genealogical Society, Harper, KS 146
Harris County Genealogical Society, Pasadena, TX 454
Harrisonburg-Rockingham Historical Society, Harrisonburg, VA 474
Hart County, Georgia Historical Society, Atlanta, GA 86
Harvard Historical Society, Harvard, MA 196
Hazelwood Historical Society, Hazelwood, MO 246
Headquarters Museum and Library, National Society of Colonial Dames, New York, NY 323
Henderson County Historical Society, Lexington, TN 431
Henry County Historical Society, Mt. Pleasant, IA 139
Heritage Genealogical Society, Neodesha, KS 149
Heritage Searchers Genealogical Society, Willmar, MN 238
Hickman County Historical Society, Clinton, KY 154
Historical Archives, Langworthy Public Library, Hope Valley, RI 409
Historical Center, Mennonite Churches, Richfield, PA 404
Historical Society of Alma-Bacon County, Alma, GA 84
Historical Society of Cecil County, Elkton, MD 183
Historical Society of Delaware, Wilmington, DE 70
Historical Society of Millersburg and Upper Paxton Township, Millersburg, PA 398
Historical Society of Wells and Ogunquit, Wells, ME 178
Historical and Genealogical Association of Mississippi, Jackson, MS 240
Holbert Family Association, Rineyville, KY 162
Holmes County Chapter, Ohio Genealogical Society, Millersburg, OH 369
Holy Trinity (Old Swedes) Church Foundation, Inc., Wilmington, DE 71
Hot Spring County Historical Society, Malvern, AR 20
Hudson Historical Society, Inc., Hudson, NH 272
Huguenot Society of America, New York, NY 323
Hunterdon County Historical Society, Flemington, NJ 281
Hurley Historical Society, Hurley, SD 424
Huxford Genealogical Society, Inc., Homerville, GA 89
Illiana Genealogical and Historical Society, Danville, IL 105
Illinois State Genealogical Society, Lincoln, IL 110
Indiana State Library, Indianapolis, IN 125
Interlaken Historical Society, Interlaken, NY 316
Iroquois County Genealogical Society, Watseka, IL 118
Itawamba Historical Society, Inc., Mantachie, MS 241
Jackson County Genealogical Society, Jackson, MI 217
Jackson County Historical Society, Murphysboro, IL 112
Jacksonville Area Genealogical and Historical Society, Jacksonville, IL 109
Jacques Timothe Boucher Sieur de Montbrun French Heritage Society, Louisville, KY 159
Jasper County Genealogical Society, Newton, IA 140
Jefferson County Genealogical Society, Inc., Oskaloosa, KS 150
Jefferson County Historical Association and Genealogical Library, Steubenville, OH 372
Jefferson Historical Society, Jefferson, NH 272
Jersey Shore Historical Society, Jersey Shore, PA 396
Jessamine Historical Society, Nicholasville, KY 161
Jewish Genealogical Society of Illinois, Niles, IL 112
Kalamazoo Valley Genealogical Society, Kalamazoo, MI 218
Kansas Genealogical Society, Dodge City, KS 144
Kennebunkport Historical Society, Kennebunkport, ME 172
Kent County Genealogical and Historical Society, Jayton, TX 450
Kenton County Public Library, Covington, KY 154
Kentucky Genealogical Society, Frankfort, KY 155
Kentucky Historical Society, Frankfort, KY 155

Kentucky Room, Owensboro-Daviess County Public Library, Owensboro, KY 161
Key City Genealogical Society, Dubuque, IA 135
Kings County Historical and Archival Society, Inc., Hampton, New Brunswick 529
Knox County Historical Society, Edina, MO 245
Lafayette County Genealogy Workshop, Inc., Shullsburg, WI 504
Lake County Genealogical Society, Painesville, OH 370
Lancaster Mennonite Historical Society, Lancaster, PA 397
Lawrence Sullivan Ross, United Daughters of Confederacy, Bryan, TX 440
Lawton Public Library, Lawton, OK 378
Le Roy Historical Society, Le Roy, NY 318
Leavenworth County Genealogical Society, Leavenworth, KS 148
Leslie County Historical Society, Hyden, KY 157
Lewis County Historical Society, Canton, MO 244
Lewis County Historical Society, Chehalis, WA 483
Library of Michigan, Lansing, MI 218
Licking County Genealogical Society, Newark, OH 369
Limestone Chapter, Daughters of the American Revolution, Washington, KY 162
Local History Department, Joint Free Public Library of Morristown and Morris Township, Morristown, NJ 286
Logan County Genealogical Society, Bellefontaine, OH 356
Logan County Genealogical Society, Inc., Russellville, KY 162
Logan County Genealogical Society, Lincoln, IL 110
Lorain County Chapter, Ohio Genealogy Society, Vermilion, OH 373
Lord Selkirk Association of Rupert's Land, Winnipeg, Manitoba 526
Lowndes County Historical Society, Valdosta, GA 94
Luther College Preus Library, Decorah, IA 134
Mabou Gaelic and Historical Society, Mabou, Nova Scotia 536
Magoffin County Historical Society, Salyersville, KY 162
Maine (N.B.) Connection, Alexander, ME 168
Manchester Historical Society, Manchester, MA 198
Mansfield Public Library, Temple, NH 276
Marion County Genealogical and Historical Society, Salem, IL 116
Marion County Museum, Marion, SC 420
Mason County Genealogical and Historical Society, Havana, IL 108
Massachusetts Society of Mayflower Descendants, Boston, MA 190
Matagorda County Historical Museum, Bay City, TX 439
Mayflower Society, North Abington, MA 201
Megantic County Historical Society, Thetford Mines, Quebec 563
Meigs County Genealogical Society, Pomeroy, OH 371
Menifee County Roots, Frenchburg, KY 156
Mercer County Chapter, Ohio Genealogical Society, Celina, OH 358
Metcalfe County Historical Society, Summer Shade, KY 162
Miami Valley Council on Genealogy and History, Dayton, OH 362
Miami Valley Genealogical Society, Dayton, OH 362
Middlesex County Historical Society, Middletown, CT 62
Middletown Springs Historical Society, Middletown Springs, VT 467
Midland Genealogical Society, Midland, MI 220
Midwest Historical and Genealogical Society, Inc., Wichita, KS 152
Mills County Genealogical Society, Glenwood, IA 136
Milton Historical Society, Milton, VT 467

Minnesota Genealogical Society, St. Paul, MN 236
Modern Woodmen of America, Rock Island, IL 115
Moniteau County Historical Society, California, MO 243
Monroe County Historical Society, Inc., Sparta, WI 504
Monroe County Local History Room, Sparta, WI 504
Montgomery County Chapter, Ohio Genealogical
  Society, Dayton, OH 362
Montgomery County Department of History and
  Archives, Fonda, NY 312
Montgomery County Genealogical Society, Coffeyville,
  KS 144
Montgomery County Genealogical Society, Litchfield,
  IL 110
Montgomery County Historical Society, Montgomery
  City, MO 251
Moultonboro Public Library, Moultonboro, NH 274
Moultrie County Historical and Genealogical Society,
  Sullivan, IL 117
Mt. Pleasant Historical Society, Inc., Mt. Pleasant,
  OH 369
Muskegon County Genealogical Society, Muskegon,
  MI 220
Muskingum County Genealogical Society, Zanesville,
  OH 375
Natchez Trace Genealogical Society, Florence, AL 4
National Genealogical Society, Washington, DC 73
National Society, Children of the American Revolution,
  Washington, DC 74
National Society, Colonial Dames of America in the
  State of New Jersey, Mt. Holly, NJ 287
National Society of Andersonville, Andersonville, GA 85
National Society of the Colonial Dames of America in
  the State of South Carolina, Charleston, SC 415
New Baltimore Historical Society, New Baltimore,
  MI 221
New Brunswick Genealogical Society, Fredericton, New
  Brunswick 528
New England Historic Genealogical Society, Boston,
  MA 190
New Jersey Society, Sons of the American Revolution,
  Elizabeth, NJ 280
New Mexico Genealogical Society, Albuquerque,
  NM 295
New York Genealogical and Biographical Society, New
  York, NY 324
New-York Historical Society, New York, NY 324
Newaygo County Society of History and Genealogy,
  White Cloud, MI 225
Newberry County Historical Society, Newberry, SC 420
Newberry Library, Chicago, IL 104
Newton County Historical and Genealogical Society,
  Jasper, AR 19
Noble County Chapter, Ohio Genealogical Society,
  Caldwell, OH 357
Noble County Genealogical Society, Inc., Albion, IN 120
Norfolk County Historical Society of Chesapeake,
  Chesapeake, VA 472
North Carolina Genealogical Society, Raleigh, NC 348
North Central Kansas Genealogical Society and Library,
  Inc., Cawker City, KS 144
North Highland Community Organization, Cape North,
  Nova Scotia 533
North Louisiana Genealogical Society, Ruston, LA 167
North Suburban Genealogical Society, Winnetka, IL 119
Northampton County Historical and Genealogical
  Society, Easton, PA 391
Northeastern Nevada Genealogical Society, Elko,
  NV 268
Northern New York American-Canadian Genealogical
  Society, Keeseville, NY 317
Northern New York American-Canadian Genealogical
  Society, Plattsburgh, NY 329

Northwest Suburban Council of Genealogists, Mt.
  Prospect, IL 112
Norwich and District Historical Museum, Norwich,
  Ontario 547
Odell Prairie Trails Historical and Genealogical Society,
  Odell, IL 113
Ogemaw Genealogical and Historical Society, West
  Branch, MI 224
Ohio Genealogical Society, Mansfield, OH 367
Ohioana Library, Columbus, OH 361
Old Bridgewater Historical Society, West Bridgewater,
  MA 207
Old Carratunk Historical Society, Bingham, ME 170
Olmsted County Genealogical Society, Rochester,
  MN 235
Ontario Genealogical Society, Toronto, Ontario 553
Oral History Program, Plum Senior High School,
  Pittsburgh, PA 403
Orange County Historical Commission, Orange, TX 420
Orangeburg County Historical Society, Inc.,
  Orangeburg, SC 420
Orangeburgh German Swiss Genealogical Society,
  Charleston, SC 415
Osage County Genealogical Society, Lyndon, KS 148
Osborne County Genealogical and Historical Society,
  Inc., Osborne, KS 149
Oshkosh Public Museum, Oshkosh, WI 502
Palacios Area Historical Association, Palacios, TX 453
Palatka Public Library, Palatka, FL 81
Palm Beach County Genealogical Society, Inc., West
  Palm Beach, FL 84
Parker County Genealogical Society, Weatherford,
  TX 460
Pasquotank Historical and Genealogical Society,
  Elizabeth City, NC 344
Paynesville Historical Society, Paynesville, MN 234
Pea River Historical and Genealogical Society,
  Enterprise, AL 4
Pendleton Chapter, South Carolina Genealogical
  Society, Clemson, SC 416
Pennsylvania Dutch Folk Culture Society, Inc.,
  Lenhartsville, PA 397
Perry County Chapter, Ohio Genealogical Society,
  Junction City, OH 366
Perry County Genealogical and Historical Society, Inc.,
  Hazard, KY 156
Perry Historians, Newport, PA 399
Perth County Branch, Ontario Genealogical Society,
  Stratford, Ontario 551
Peterborough Historical Society—Hutchison House
  Museum, Peterborough, Ontario 549
Petersham Historical Society, Inc., Petersham, MA 202
Pettaguamscatt Historical Society, Kingston, RI 409
Phelps County Genealogical Society, Rolla, MO 252
Philadelphia Branch, National Archives, Philadelphia,
  PA 402
Piedmont Historical and Genealogical Society,
  Piedmont, AL 7
Pike County Historical and Genealogical Society, Troy,
  AL 8
Platt County Historical and Genealogical Society,
  Monticello, IL 111
Platte County Historical Society, Platte City, MO 251
Polish Genealogical Society, Inc., Chicago, IL 104
Polk County Historical and Genealogical Library,
  Bartow, FL 76
Pontiac Area Historical and Genealogical Society,
  Pontiac, MI 222
Port Hastings Historical Museum and Archives, Port
  Hastings, Nova Scotia 537
Portage County Chapter, Ohio Genealogical Society,
  Ravenna, OH 371

Portage County Historical Society, Stevens Point, WI 504

Posey County Historical Society, Mt. Vernon, IN 127

Poweshiek County Historical and Genealogical Society, Montezuma, IA 139

Prince Edward Island Museum and Heritage Foundation, Charlottetown, Prince Edward Island 555

Providence City Archives, Providence, RI 411

Public Archives of Canada, Ottawa, Ontario 549

Public Archives of Nova Scotia, Halifax, Nova Scotia 535

Pulaski County Genealogy Society, Star City, IN 130

Pulaski County Historical Society, Inc., Somerset, KY 162

Putnam County Historical Society, Greencastle, IN 124

Putnam County Historical Society, Hennepin, IL 108

Racine County Historical Society and Museum, Racine, WI 503

Ralliement des Familles Bonneau, Inc., St. Francois, Quebec 561

Range Genealogical Society, Inc., Buhl, MN 227

Regional Archives Branch, National Archives and Records Administration, Bayonne, NJ 277

Remsen-Steuben Historical Society, Remsen, NY 330

Republic County Historical Society, Belleville, KS 143

Rhode Island State Archives, Providence, RI 412

Richland County Genealogical and Historical Society, Olney, IL 113

Richmond County Historical Society, Augusta, GA 86

Rosalie Daughters of the American Revolution, Natchez, MS 241

Rutland Historical Society, Rutland, VT 468

Saginaw Genealogical Society, Saginaw, MI 223

Saint Charles County Historical Society and Archives, St. Charles, MO 252

Saint Clair County Genealogical Society, Belleville, IL 100

Saint John Branch, New Brunswick Genealogical Society, Saint John, New Brunswick 530

Sangamon County Genealogical Society, Springfield, IL 117

Santa Clara County Historical and Genealogical Society, Santa Clara, CA 44

Sargeant Memorial Room, Norfolk Public Library, Norfolk, VA 477

Schuyler-Brown Historical Society, Rushville, IL 115

Scott County Genealogical Society, Georgetown, KY 156

Scott County Historical Society, Huntsville, TN 429

Seventh Day Baptist Historical Society, Janesville, WI 498

Shaftsbury Historical Society, Shaftsbury, VT 468

Shelburne Historical Society and County Museum, Shelburne, Nova Scotia 537

Shiawassee County Genealogical Society, Owosso, MI 221

Simpson County Historical Society, Franklin, KY 155

Sioux Valley Genealogical Society, Sioux Falls, SD 426

Smoky Valley Genealogical Society and Library, Inc., Salina, KS 150

Société de Généalogie de la Mauricie et des Bois-Francs, Inc., Trois-Rivieres, Quebec 563

Société de Genealogie de l'Outaouais, Inc., Hull, Quebec 557

Société de Généalogie des Cantons de l'Est, Sherbrooke, Quebec 562

Société de Genealogie des Laurentides, St. Jérôme, Quebec 561

Société d'histoire de Shefford, Granby, Quebec 557

Société d'histoire des Pays-d'en-Haut, Inc., St. Sauveur-des-Monts, Quebec 562

Société d'histoire du Haut-Richelieu, Inc., St-Jean-sur-Richelieu, Quebec 561

Société d'histoire et de Genealogie de Matane, Matane, Quebec 559

Société Franco-Ontarienne d'Histoire et de Généalogie, Ottawa, Ontario 549

Société Généalogique Canadienne Francaise, Montreal, Quebec 560

Société Genealogique du Saguenay, Inc., Chicoutimi, Quebec 556

Société Historique de Grande-Digue, Kent, New Brunswick 529

Société Historique de la Mer Rouge, Inc., Robichaud, New Brunswick 530

Société Historique et Généalogique de Trois-Pistoles, Inc., Trois-Pistoles, Quebec 563

Society of Colonial Wars in the State of New Jersey, Elizabeth, NJ 280

Society of First Families of South Carolina, 1670-1700, Charleston, SC 415

Society of Mareen Duvall Descendants, Upper Marlboro, MD 186

Society of Mayflower Descendants, Elizabeth City, NC 344

Society of Pioneer of Montgomery, Montgomery, AL 7

Somers Historical Society, Somers, NY 334

South Carolina Society, Colonial Dames XVII Century, Aiken, SC 413

South Carolina Society, Sons of the American Revolution, Columbia, SC 417

South Carolina State Society, Daughters of the American Revolution, Greenville, SC 419

South Carolina State Society, National Society Daughters of the American Colonists, Columbia, SC 417

South Dakota State Archives, Pierre, SD 425

South King County Genealogical Society, Kent, WA 485

South Shore Genealogical Society, Lunenburg, Nova Scotia 536

Southeast Nebraska Genealogical Society, Beatrice, NE 261

Southeast Texas Genealogical and Historical Society, Beaumont, TX 439

Southern Aroostook Historical Society, Houlton, ME 172

Southern Genealogist's Exchange Society, Inc., Jacksonville, FL 79

Southern Society of Genealogies, Centre, AL 3

Southwest Louisiana Genealogical Society, Lake Charles, LA 165

Southwest Minnesota Historical Center, Marshall, MN 232

Southwest Oklahoma Genealogical Society, Lawton, OK 378

Special Collections Department, Tampa-Hillsborough County Public Library System, Tampa, FL 84

Special Collections Branch, Albuquerque Public Library, Albuquerque, NM 295

Stamford Genealogical Society, Inc., Stamford, CT 67

Stevens Museum, Salem, IN 129

Studebaker Family National Association, Tipp City, OH 372

Suffolk County Historical Society, Riverhead, NY 330

Susquehanna County Historical Society and Free Library Association, Montrose, PA 398

Swift River Valley Historical Society, Inc., New Salem, MA 200

Taliaferro County Historical Society, Inc., Crawfordville, GA 87

Tama County Historical Society, Toledo, IA 141

Tennessee Historical Society, Nashville, TN 434

Terrebonne Genealogical Society, Houma, LA 164

Thayer County Historical Society, Belvidere, NE 261

Thomas McCulloch House—Hector Centre Trust
National Exhibition Centre, Pictou, Nova Scotia 537
Three Creeks Historical Association, Lowell, IN 126
Three Rivers Historical Society, Hemingway, SC 419
Tioga County Historical Society, Wellsboro, PA 408
Town of Bethlehem Historical Association, Selkirk,
NY 334
Town of Massena Museum and Historian's Office,
Massena, NY 320
Tuscarora Township Historical Society, Laceyville,
PA 396
Umatilla County Historical Society, Pendleton, OR 384
Unitarian and Universalist Genealogical Society, Hunt
Valley, MD 184
United Empire Loyalist Museum, Bloomfield,
Ontario 540
Urbain Baudreall Graveline Genealogical Association,
Inc., Palmer, MA 202
Uxbridge-Scott Historical Society Museum, Uxbridge,
Ontario 554
Van Buren County Historical Society, Spencer, TN 436
Verndale Historical Society, Verndale, MN 237
Vernon County Historical Society, Viroqua, WI 505
Virginia Area Historical Society—Heritage Center
Museum, Virginia, MN 238
Walker County Heritage Association, Jasper, AL 5
Washakie County Historical Society, Worland, WY 509
Washburn County Historical Society and Museum, Shell
Lake, WI 503
Washington County Chapter, Ohio Genealogical
Society, Marietta, OH 367
Washington County Historical Society, Salem, IN 129
Washington County Historical Society, West Bend,
WI 505
Washtenaw County Historical Society, Ann Arbor,
MI 211
Wayland Area Tree Tracers Genealogical Society,
Wayland, MI 224
Weakley County Genealogical Society, Martin, TN 431
Webster County Historical and Genealogical Society,
Dixon, KY 154
West Hants Historical Society, Windsor, Nova
Scotia 538
West Texas Pioneers and Old Settlers, Crosbyton,
TX 442
West-Central Kentucky Family Research Association,
Owensboro, KY 161
Westchester County Genealogical Society, White
Plains, NY 339
Whitby Historical Society, Whitby, Ontario 554
Whitefield Historical Society, Whitefield, NH 276
Whiteside County Genealogists, Sterling, IL 117
Whitman County Genealogical Society, Pullman,
WA 486
Wild Rose Historical Society, Wild Rose, WI 506
Williamson County Genealogical Society, Round Rock,
TX 455
Windham Historical Society, Inc., South Windham,
ME 177
Windsor Historical Society, Windsor, CT 69
Winter Harbor Historical Society, Winter Harbor, ME 178
Wisconsin State Genealogical Society, Inc., Monroe,
WI 501
Wyandotte Museum, Wyandotte, MI 225
Wyoming County Historical Society, Tunkhannock,
PA 406
Yarmouth County Museum, Yarmouth, Nova Scotia 539
Yell County Arkansas Historical and Genealogical
Association, Russellville, AR 21
Yell County Historical and Genealogical Society,
Dardanelle, AR 17

HISTORIC PERSON

A. M. and Welma Aikin, Jr., Regional Archives, Paris,
TX 454
Aaron Burr Association, Hightstown, NJ 282
Abraham Lincoln Association, Springfield, IL 116
Adams National Historic Site, Quincy, MA 203
Alexander Graham Bell National Historic Park,
Baddeck, Nova Scotia 533
Alexander Ramsey House, St. Paul, MN 236
Andrew Johnson National Historic Site, Greeneville,
TN 429
Anne Spencer Memorial Foundation, Lynchburg,
VA 476
Audie Murphy Room, W. Walworth Harrison Public
Library, Greenville, TX 447
Baca and Bloom Houses, Pioneer Museum, Trinidad,
CO 57
Banning Residence Museum, Wilmington, CA 48
Barnum Museum, Bridgeport, CT 58
Beauvoir, Jefferson Davis Shrine, Biloxi, MS 239
Bell Homestead, Brantford, Ontario 540
Belton Historical Society, Belton, MO 243
Bidwell Mansion Association, Chico, CA 25
Big Foot Wallace Museum, Big Foot, TX 439
Billy the Kid Museum, Ft. Sumner, NM 297
Blount Mansion, Knoxville, TN 430
Booker T. Washington National Monument, Hardy,
VA 474
Braintree Historical Society, Inc., Braintree, MA 191
Buffalo Bill Historical Center, Cody, WY 507
Buffalo Bill Memorial Museum, Denver, CO 51
Buffalo Bill Museum of Le Claire, Inc., Le Claire, IA 138
Buffalo Bill's Ranch—State Historical Park, North Platte,
NE 265
Cabool History Society, Cabool, MO 243
Cabrillo Historical Association, San Diego, CA 39
Calvin Coolidge Memorial Foundation, Inc., Plymouth,
VT 468
Carl Sandburg Birthplace, Galesburg, IL 107
Carl Sandburg Home National Historic Site, Flat Rock,
NC 344
Carroll Mansion, Municipal Museum of Baltimore,
Baltimore, MD 180
Carter Presidential Materials Project, Atlanta, GA 85
Castle Piatt Mac-A-Cheek—Mac-Ochee Castle, West
Liberty, OH 374
Charles M. Russell Log Cabin Studio, Great Falls,
MT 258
Chesterwood, Stockbridge, MA 205
Chief John Ross House, Rossville, GA 91
Colonel John Ashley House, Ashley Falls, MA 187
Committee to Preserve the Narcissa Prentiss House,
Inc., Prattsburg, NY 329
Comstock Historic House Society, Moorhead, MN 233
Concord Historical Society, Springville, NY 335
Copper King Mansion, Butte, MT 256
Coronado National Memorial, Hereford, AZ 12
Cumberland County Historical Society, Greenup, IL 108
Cypress College Local History Association, Cypress,
CA 26
Daniel Boone Homestead, Birdsboro, PA 388
Daughters of Hawaii—Queen Emma Summer Palace,
Honolulu, HI 95
Decatur House Museum, Washington, DC 73
Derry Historical Society and Museum, Derry, NH 271
Duke Homestead State Historic Site and Tobacco
Museum, Durham, NC 343
Dwight D. Eisenhower Library, Abilene, KS 143
Edgar Allan Poe National Historic Site, Philadelphia,
PA 401
Eighteen-thirty-nine Williams Home, Galveston, TX 447

Eisenhower Birthplace State Historic Site, Denison, TX 443
Eisenhower National Historic Site, Gettysburg, PA 393
Eleanor Roosevelt Center at Val-Kill, Hyde Park, NY 316
Elisabet Ney Museum, Austin, TX 437
Elmwood Historical Society—Lorado Taft Museum, Elmwood, IL 107
Ernest Hemingway Museum, Key West, FL 79
Ernie Pyle Public Library, Albuquerque, NM 295
Eugene Field House and Toy Museum, St. Louis, MO 254
Everett McKinley Dirksen Congressional Leadership Research Center, Pekin, IL 114
First White House of the Confederacy, Montgomery, AL 7
Forney Historical Society, Birmingham, AL 2
Fort Hill: John C. Calhoun Mansion, Clemson, SC 416
Foundation Historical Association, Inc., Auburn, NY 303
Foundation Robert Giguère, Inc., Montreal, Quebec 559
Franklin D. Roosevelt Library, Hyde Park, NY 316
Frederick Law Olmsted National Historic Site, Brookline, MA 191
Friends of Hildene, Inc., Manchester, VT 467
Friends of Keytesville, Inc., Keytesville, MO 249
Friends of Olana, Hudson, NY 315
Friends of Rodgers Tavern, Perryville, MD 184
Friends of the Governor's Mansion, Austin, TX 437
Friendship Hill Association, New Geneva, PA 399
Friendship Hill National Historic Site, Point Marion, PA 404
Fulton Mansion State Historic Structure, Fulton, TX 446
Gates County Historical Society, Gatesville, NC 345
Gene Stratton Porter Historic Site—Gene Stratton Porter Society, Rome City, IN 129
General Adam Stephen Memorial Association, Inc., Martinsburg, WV 493
General John H. Forney Historical Society, Inc., Gadsden, AL 5
General John J. Pershing Boyhood Home State Historic Site, Laclede, MO 249
George C. Marshall Research Foundation, Lexington, VA 475
George Johnston Museum, Teslin, Yukon Territory 568
Gerald R. Ford Library, Ann Arbor, MI 210
Gerald R. Ford Museum, Grand Rapids, MI 216
Glebe House Museum, Woodbury, CT 69
Glenn H. Curtiss Museum of Local History, Hammondsport, NY 314
Goodnow Museum and Historical Site, Manhattan, KS 148
Governor Hogg Shrine State Historical Park, Quitman, TX 454
Governor Lurleen B. Wallace Museum, Montgomery, AL 7
Governor Oglesby Mansion, Inc., Decatur, IL 105
Governor Stephen Hopkins House, Providence, RI 411
Graeme Park, Horsham, PA 395
Granger Homestead Society, Canandaigua, NY 306
Grant Cottage, Wilton, NY 340
Greater West Bloomfield Historical Society, Orchard Lake, MI 221
Grey Towers National Historic Landmark, Milford, PA 398
Grover Cleveland Birthplace, Caldwell, NJ 278
Gunston Hall, Lorton, VA 476
Hamilton Grange National Memorial, New York, NY 323
Harry S. Truman Birthplace, Lamar, MO 249
Harry S. Truman Courtroom and Office, Independence, MO 246
Harry S. Truman Library, Independence, MO 247
Head Office, Bank of Montreal, Montreal, Quebec 559
Henry Ford Estate—Fair Lane, Dearborn, MI 213

Henry Morrison Flagler Museum—Whitehall Historic House Museum, Palm Beach, FL 81
Henry S. Lane Place, Crawfordsville, IN 122
Herbert Hoover National Historic Site, West Branch, IA 142
Herkimer Home State Historic Site, Little Falls, NY 318
Hermitage: Plantation Home of President Andrew Jackson, Hermitage, TN 429
Hillsborough Historical Society, Inc.—Franklin Pierce Homestead, Hillsborough, NH 272
Historical Society of Amherst, Amherst, NH 269
Holt County Historical Society, O'Neill, NE 265
Home Sweet Home Museum—John Howard Payne Boyhood Home, East Hampton, NY 310
Honorable John G. Diefenbaker Centre, Saskatoon, Saskatchewan 566
Hoover-Minthorn House Museum, Newberg, OR 384
Hopsewee Plantation, Georgetown, SC 418
House in the Horseshoe, Sanford, NC 349
House of Roses—Senator Wilson Home, Deadwood, SD 423
Hubbell Trading Post National Historic Site, Ganado, AZ 12
Hundred Oaks Castle, Winchester, TN 436
Israel Crane House Museum, Montclair, NJ 285
J. U. and Florence B. Fields Museum, Haskell, TX 448
J.F.D. Lanier State Memorial, Madison, IN 127
James K. Polk Memorial Association, Columbia, TN 428
James K. Polk Memorial, Pineville, NC 348
James Madison Museum, Orange, VA 478
James Monroe Law Office/Museum and Memorial Library, Fredericksburg, VA 474
Jane Addams' Hull-House, Chicago, IL 103
Jefferson Davis Association, Houston, TX 449
Jefferson Davis Monument Shrine, Fairview, KY 154
Jesse James Bank Museum, Liberty, MO 250
Jim Thorpe Home, Yale, OK 382
John Bartram Association—Bartram's Garden, Philadelphia, PA 402
John Brown Historical Association of Illinois, Inc., Chicago, IL 103
John F. Kennedy National Historic Site, Brookline, MA 191
John F. Kennedy Presidential Library, Boston, MA 189
John G. Neihardt Center, Bancroft, NE 261
John J. Audubon Memorial Museum, Henderson, KY 156
John Muir National Historic Site, Martinez, CA 32
John Nance Garner Home and Museum, Uvalde, TX 459
John Pelham Historical Association, Robertsdale, AL 7
John Wesley Powell Memorial Museum, Page, AZ 13
Jose Antonio Navarro State Historic Site, San Antonio, TX 456
Joseph Smith Historic Center, Nauvoo, IL 112
Judge Roy Bean Visitor Center, Langtry, TX 451
Julia Morgan Association, Santa Cruz, CA 44
Juliette Gordon Low Girl Scout National Center, Savannah, GA 92
Justin Smith Morrill Homestead, Strafford, VT 469
Kansas All-Sports Hall of Fame, Lawrence, KS 148
Kearny Cottage, Perth Amboy, NJ 289
Kit Carson Memorial Foundation, Inc., Taos, NM 300
Kit Carson Museum and Historical Society, Las Animas, CO 55
Landmarks Commission of Kansas City, Kansas City, MO 248
Las Vegas Rough Rider and City Museum, Las Vegas, NM 297
Laura Ingalls Wilder Museum and Tourist Information Center, Walnut Grove, MN 238
Laurier House, Ottawa, Ontario 548

Lee Chapel, Lexington, VA 476
Levi Coffin House Association, Fountain City, IN 123
Limberlost State Historic Site, Geneva, IN 123
Lincoln Boyhood National Memorial, Lincoln City, IN 126
Lincoln Homestead State Park, Springfield, KY 162
Lincoln Tomb State Historic Site, Springfield, IL 117
Lindbergh Historic Site—Lindbergh State Park, Little
    Falls, MN 231
Locust Grove Historic Home, Louisville, KY 159
Longfellow National Historic Site, Cambridge, MA 192
Longyear Historical Society and Museum, Brookline,
    MA 192
Lorenzo State Historic Site, Cazenovia, NY 307
Louis A. Warren Lincoln Library and Museum, Fort
    Wayne, IN 123
MacArthur Memorial, Norfolk, VA 477
Madawaska Historical Society, Madawaska, ME 173
Magevney House, Memphis, TN 431
Malabar Farm State Park, Lucas, OH 367
Mamie Doud Eisenhower Birthplace Foundation, Inc.,
    Boone, IA 132
Mark Twain Birthplace Memorial, Stoutsville, MO 255
Mark Twain Birthplace State Historic Site, Florida,
    MO 245
Mark Twain Home Board, Hannibal, MO 246
Mark Twain Memorial, Hartford, CT 61
Marquette County Historical Society, Marquette, MI 219
Martin Luther King, Jr., Center for Nonviolent Social
    Change, Atlanta, GA 86
Martin Luther King, Jr., National Historic Site, Atlanta,
    GA 86
Martin Van Buren National Historic Site, Kinderhook,
    NY 317
Mary Washington Branch, Association for the
    Preservation of Virginia Antiquities, Fredericksburg,
    VA 474
Maryhill Museum of Art, Golendale, WA 484
Maumee Valley Historical Society, Maumee, OH 368
McDowell House and Apothecary Shop, Danville,
    KY 154
McKinley Museum of History, Science and Industry,
    Canton, OH 357
Mentor Graham House, Blunt, SD 422
Meriwether Lewis Monument, Hohenwald, TN 429
Millicent Rogers Museum, Taos, NM 300
Missisquoi Valley Historical Society, North Troy, VT 468
Molly Brown House Museum, Denver, CO 52
Montauk, Clermont, IA 133
Moorland-Spingarn Research Center, Washington,
    DC 73
Mount Vernon Ladies' Association of the Union, Mount
    Vernon, VA 477
National Portrait Gallery, Washington, DC 74
Neal Dow Memorial, Portland, ME 175
Norman Rockwell Museum at the Old Corner House,
    Stockbridge, MA 206
Northfield Historical Society, Northfield, MN 234
O. Henry Museum, Austin, TX 438
Olana State Historic Site, Hudson, NY 316
Orchard House, Home of the Alcotts, Concord, MA 193
Overholser Mansion, Oklahoma City, OK 379
Owens-Thomas House Museum, Savannah, GA 92
Palmyra Historical Society, Palmyra, WI 502
Paul Revere House, Boston, MA 190
Pavillon André-Coindre, St. Augustin, Quebec 561
Pennsbury Manor, Morrisville, PA 399
Peter Conser House, Heavener, OK 378
Peter Wentz Farmstead, Worcester, PA 408
Pierce Brigade, Concord, NH 270
Pine Grove Historical Museum—Governor Moses
    Wisner Historic House and Grounds, Pontiac,
    MI 222

Porter-Phelps-Huntington Foundation, Inc., Hadley,
    MA 196
President Benjamin Harrison Memorial Home,
    Indianapolis, IN 125
President Harding's Home, Marion, OH 368
Presidential Museum, Odessa, TX 453
Pro Football Hall of Fame, Canton, OH 357
Providence Athenaeum, Providence, RI 411
Prudence Crandall Museum, Canterbury, CT 58
Quincy Historical Society, Quincy, MA 203
R.E. Olds Museum, Lansing, MI 218
Red Hill Shrine, Brookneal, VA 471
Red Shirt Shrine, Oakley Park, Edgefield, SC 418
Reynolds Homestead, Critz, VA 472
Robert E. Lee Memorial Association, Inc., Stratford,
    VA 481
Robert Toombs House, Washington, GA 94
Rock Ford Plantation, Lancaster, PA 397
Roosevelt Campobello International Park Commission,
    Campobello Island, New Brunswick 527
Roosevelt's Little White House and Museum, Warm
    Springs, GA 94
Rough Rider Memorial and City Museum, Las Vegas,
    NM 297
Roxbury Burrough's Club, Roxbury, NY 332
Rutherford B. Hayes Presidential Center, Fremont,
    OH 364
Rutherford House Provincial Historic Site, Edmonton,
    Alberta 513
Saint Agatha Historical Society, St. Agatha, ME 176
Saint-Gaudens National Historic Site, Cornish, NH 270
Sam Bell Maxey House State Historic Structure, Paris,
    TX 454
Sam Houston Memorial Museum, Huntsville, TX 449
Sam Rayburn House, Bonham, TX 439
Sam Rayburn Library, Bonham, TX 439
San Clemente Historical Society, San Clemente, CA 39
San Jacinto Valley Museum Association, Inc., San
    Jacinto, CA 42
San Pablo Historical and Museum Society, San Pablo,
    CA 43
Schuyler Mansion, State Historic Site, Albany, NY 301
Scioto Society, Inc., Chillicothe, OH 358
Sequoyah Home Site, Sallisaw, OK 380
Sherman House, Lancaster, OH 366
Sherwood Forest Plantation, Charles City, VA 471
Shirley Historical Society, Shirley, MA 205
Société Historique Alphonse-Desjardins, Levis,
    Quebec 558
Société Historique de Cabano, Inc., Cabano,
    Quebec 556
Société historique de St. Boniface, St. Boniface,
    Manitoba 524
South Dakota Cowboy and Western Heritage Hall of
    Fame, Ft. Pierre, SD 423
Starke County Historical Museum, Knox, IN 126
Stenton—Home of James Logan, Philadelphia, PA 403
Stephansson House Provincial Historic Site, Markerville,
    Alberta 515
Stephen Foster Memorial, Pittsburgh, PA 404
Stonewall Jackson House, Lexington, VA 476
Stow Historical Society, Stow, MA 206
Sumter County Historical Commission, Sumter, SC 421
Sun House, Ukiah, CA 47
Sunnyvale Historical Society and Museum Association,
    Sunnyvale, CA 46
Sutter's Fort State Historic Park, Sacramento, CA 39
Theodore Roosevelt Birthplace National Historic Site,
    New York, NY 325
Theodore Roosevelt Inaugural National Historic Site,
    Buffalo, NY 306
Thomas Cole Foundation, Catskill, NY 307

Thomas Edison Winter Home and Museum, Ft. Myers, FL 78
Thomas Hart Benton Home and Studio, Kansas City, MO 248
Thomas Jefferson Memorial Foundation, Charlottesville, VA 472
Thomas Wolfe Memorial, Asheville, NC 341
Tom Mix Museum, Dewey, OK 376
U.S. Grant's Home State Historic Site, Galena, IL 107
Vachel Lindsay Association, Inc., Springfield, IL 117
Vernon Historians, Inc., Vernon, VT 469
Wadsworth-Longfellow House, Portland, ME 175
Walt Whitman Association, Camden, NJ 278
Walt Whitman Birthplace Association, Huntington Station, NY 316
Waltham Museum, Inc., Waltham, MA 207
Washington Crossing Foundation, Washington Crossing, PA 407
Washington's Headquarters State Historic Site, Newburgh, NY 321
Washington-on-the-Brazos State Historical Park, Washington, TX 460
West Des Moines Historical Society, West Des Moines, IA 142
West Salem Historical Society, West Salem, WI 506
Westerville Historical Society, Westerville, OH 374
Westport Historical Society, Kansas City, MO 249
Whaley Historical House, Flint, MI 215
Whitehall, Home of Bishop Berkeley, Middletown, RI 410
Will Rogers Memorial, Claremore, OK 376
Willard House and Clock Museum, Inc., Grafton, MA 195
William Cullen Bryant Homestead, Cummington, MA 193
William Howard Taft National Historic Site, Cincinnati, OH 359
William S. Harney Historical Society, Sullivan, MO 255
Winterthur in Odessa, Odessa, DE 70
Woodlawn Plantation, Mount Vernon, VA 477
Woodrow Wilson Birthplace, Staunton, VA 480
Woodrow Wilson House Museum, Washington, DC 76
Zadock Pratt Museum, Inc., Prattsville, NY 329
Zebulon B. Vance Birthplace, Weaverville, NC 350

HISTORY OF ERA

Abram Demaree Homestead, Closter, NJ 279
Adams County Historical Society Museum, Lind, WA 485
Alabama Department of Archives and History, Montgomery, AL 6
Alabama Division, United Daughters of the Confederacy, Albertville, AL 1
Alabama Society, Daughters of the American Colonists, Mobile, AL 1
Alamo, The, San Antonio, TX 455
Alexander and Baldwin Sugar Museum, Puunene, HI 95
Alexander-Crawford Historical Society, Alexander, ME 168
Allegany County Historical Society, Inc., Cumberland, MD 182
Amador County Historical Society, Jackson, CA 29
American Heritage Center, Laramie, WY 508
American Institute of Architects Foundation—The Octagon Museum, Washington, DC 71
American Museum of Immigration, New York, NY 322
American Work Horse Museum, Paeonian Springs, VA 478
Aderson Valley Historical Museum, Boonville, CA 24
Anna Miller Museum, Newcastle, WY 508

Anson County Historical Society, Wadesboro, NC 350
Apopka Historical Society, Apopka, FL 76
Appomattox Courthouse National Historical Park, Appomattox, VA 470
Arizona Historical Foundation—Hayden Library, Arizona State University, Tempe, AZ 15
Arizona Humanities Council, Phoenix, AZ 13
Armand Bayou Nature Center, Houston, TX 449
Arrow Rock State Historic Site, Arrow Rock, MO 242
Arvada Historical Society, Arvada, CO 49
Ashland Historical Society, Ashland, WI 495
Ashton Villa, Galveston, TX 446
Aurora Colony Historical Society, Aurora, OR 382
Aurora Historical Society, Inc., East Aurora, NY 310
Azusa Historical Society, Inc., Azusa, CA 23
Baraga County Historical Society, Inc., L'Anse, MI 218
Barnes County Historical Society, Inc., Valley City, ND 354
Bartlett Historical Society, Bartlett, IL 100
Battle of Lexington Historic Site, Lexington, MO 250
Bayard Taylor Memorial Library, Kennett Square, PA 396
Baylor University Institute for Oral History, Waco, TX 460
Baytown Historical Museum, Baytown, TX 439
Beaver Area Heritage Foundation, Beaver, PA 387
Bellport-Brookhaven Historical Society, Bellport, NY 304
Benicia Capitol State Historic Park, Benicia, CA 23
Bennington Museum and Peter Matteson Tavern, Bennington, VT 464
Benton County Sesquicentennial Committee, Siloam Springs, AR 21
Berkeley County Historical Society, Moncks Corner, SC 420
Berkshire Museum, The, Pittsfield, MA 202
Bertrand Collection and Library, DeSoto National Wildlife Refuge Visitor Center, Missouri Valley, IA 139
Bethune Museum-Archives, Inc., Washington, DC 72
Big Thunder Gold Mine, Keystone, SD 424
Birmingham Historical Society, Birmingham, AL 2
Blackberry Historical Farm-Village, Aurora, IL 100
Blaine County Museum, Chinook, MT 257
Bloomfield Historical Society, Castalia, IA 132
Blue Ridge Parkway, Asheville, NC 340
Bolivar County Historical Society, Cleveland, MS 239
Boone County Historical Society, Columbia, MO 569
Boot Hill Museum, Dodge City, KS 144
Boston National Historical Park, Boston, MA 189
Boundary Museum Society, Grand Forks, British Columbia 518
Bourne Historical Society, Bourne, MA 191
Bradford County Historical Society, Towanda, PA 406
Brennan House, The, Louisville, KY 158
Brighton Historical Society, Rochester, NY 330
Brimstone Historical Society, Sulphur, LA 168
Brooklyn Historical Society, Brooklyn, OH 357
Brooks and District Museum, Brooks, Alberta 510
Bryant Cottage State Historic Site, Bement, IL 100
Burnham Tavern Museum, Machias, ME 173
Burritt Museum and Park, Huntsville, AL 5
Bush House—Salem Art Association, Salem, OR 386
Butler County Historical Society, Poplar Bluff, MO 252
California Department of Parks and Recreation, Friant, CA 28
Camanche Historical Society, Camanche, IA 132
Canada's Aviation Hall of Fame, Edmonton, Alberta 512
Canal Fulton Heritage Society, Canal Fulton, OH 357
Canal Society of New Jersey, Morristown, NJ 286
Canastota Canal Town Corporation—Canal Town Museum, Canastota, NY 306
Canyonlands Natural History Association, Moab, UT 462

Cape Coral Historical Society, Inc., Cape Coral, FL 76
Cape Vincent Historical Museum, Cape Vincent, NY 307
Carlisle Area Historical Society, Carlisle, OH 358
Carlton County Historical Society, Cloquet, MN 227
Carnegie Cultural Arts Center, Oxnard, CA 35
Carousel Society of the Niagara Frontier, Inc., North Tonawanda, NY 326
Castle and Museum at Inspiration Point, Eureka Springs, AR 17
Catonsville Historical Society, Inc., Baltimore, MD 180
Cattaraugus Area Historical Society, Cattaraugus, NY 307
Cedar Falls Historical Society, Cedar Falls, IA 133
Cedar Key Historical Society, Cedar Key, FL 77
Centennial Valley Historical Association, Centennial, WY 506
Centerville Historical Society, Centerville, UT 461
Chapleau Historical Museum, Chapleau, Ontario 541
Chapter 425, Children of the Confederacy, Shreveport, LA 168
Charles Towne Landing, Charleston, NC 342
Charlton County Historical Society, Folkston, GA 88
Cherokee Historical Association, Cherokee, NC 343
Cherry Creek Schoolhouse Museum, Englewood, CO 53
Chestnut Hill Historical Society, Philadelphia, PA 401
Chino Valley Historical Society, Chino, CA 25
Chisholm Trail Historical Museum, Waurika, OK 381
Christian Woman's Exchange—Hermann-Grima Historic House, New Orleans, LA 166
Circle District Museum—Circle District Historical Society, Inc., Central, AK 9
Circus City Festival, Inc., Peru, IN 128
Civil War Round Table of Arkansas, Little Rock, AR 19
Clark County Historical Society—Howard Steamboat Museum, Jeffersonville, IN 126
Clinton County Historical Society, Albany, KY 153
Cliveden, Philadelphia, PA 401
Coast Artillery Museum at Fort Worden, Port Townsend, WA 486
Coe Hall at Planting Fields Arboretum, Oyster Bay, NY 327
Coggeshall Farm Museum, Bristol, RI 409
Coke County Historical Commission, Robert Lee, TX 455
Colonel William Bratton Chapter, Sons of American Revolution, York, SC 422
Colonial Society of Massachusetts, Boston, MA 189
Colorado City Historical Museum, Colorado City, TX 441
Colton Hall Museum of the City of Monterey, Monterey, CA 33
Confederate Historical Institute, Little Rock, AR 19
Confederate Research Center and Museum, Hillsboro, TX 448
Connecticut Valley Historical Museum, Springfield, MA 205
Conner Prairie Pioneer Settlement, Noblesville, IN 128
Constitution Hall Park, Huntsville, AL 5
Country Music Foundation, Nashville, TN 433
Courthouse-on-the-Square Museum, Denton, TX 443
Crescent-Shousetown Area Historical Association, Glenwillard, PA 393
Crittenden County Historical Society, Inc., West Memphis, AR 22
Cumberland Township Museum, Cumberland, Ontario 541
Curatorial Services Branch, National Park Service, Washington, DC 72
Cuyuna Range Historical Society, Crosby, MN 227
Dacotah Prairie Museum, Aberdeen, SD 422
Dade Battlefield State Historic Site, Bushnell, FL 76
Dallam-Hartley Counties XIT Museum, Dalhart, TX 442
Danvers Alarm List Company, Inc., Danvers, MA 193

Danville Museum of Fine Arts and History, Danville, VA 472
Dartmouth College Archives, Hanover, NH 272
David Bradford House, Washington, PA 407
De Anza Trek Lancers Society, Cupertino, CA 26
Deaf Smith County Museum, Hereford, TX 448
Deep River Historical Society, Inc., Deep River, CT 59
Department of History, Plymouth State College, Plymouth, NH 275
Depot Museum, Lake Wales, FL 80
Desert Caballeros Western Museum, Wickenburg, AZ 16
Desert Hot Springs Historical Society, Desert Hot Springs, CA 26
Devil's Den State Park, West Fork, AR 22
Dickinson County Historical Society, Abilene, KS 142
Dorchester County Historical Society, Inc., Cambridge, MD 182
Dover-Foxcroft Historical Society—Blacksmith Shop Museum, Dover-Foxcroft, ME 171
Downers Grove Historical Society, Downers Grove, IL 106
Downington Historical Commission, Downingtown, PA 391
Drake's Midwest Phonograph Museum, Martinsville, IN 127
Drew County Historical Society and Museum, Monticello, AR 20
Drummer Boy Museum, Brewster, MA 191
Drummond Historical Society, Drummond, WI 496
DuPont Historical Museum, DuPont, WA 483
Duck Lake Historical Museum, Duck Lake, Saskatchewan 564
Dunham Tavern Museum—Society of Collectors, Inc., Cleveland, OH 360
Dunn County Historical Society, Dunn Center, ND 352
Dunn County Historical Society, Menomonie, WI 500
Eagle Rock Valley Historical Society, Eagle Rock, CA 27
East Bay Negro Historical Society, Inc., Oakland, CA 34
East Texas Historical Association, Nacogdoches, TX 453
Ebenezer Maxwell Mansion, Inc., Philadelphia, PA 401
Eckley Miners' Village, Weatherly, PA 408
Edgar County Historical Society, Paris, IL 113
El Morro National Monument, Ramah, NM 298
El Paso County Historical Society, El Paso, TX 444
El Paso Jewish Historical Society, El Paso, TX 444
El Pueblo de Los Angeles State Historic Park, Los Angeles, CA 31
Elgin Area Historical Society, Elgin, IL 106
Eli Whitney Museum, Hamden, CT 61
Ellis County Historical Society, Gage, OK 377
Ellwood House Museum, DeKalb, IL 106
Emmet County Historical Society, Inc., Estherville, IA 136
Erie Canal Village, Rome, NY 331
Erwin-Painted Post Museum, Painted Post, NY 328
Euclid Historical Society, Euclid, OH 363
Excelsior-Lake Minnetonka Historical Society, Excelsior, MN 229
Fairview Museum of History and Art, Fairview, UT 462
Fallbrook Historical Society, Fallbrook, CA 28
Favell Museum of Western Art and Indian Artifacts, Klamath Falls, OR 384
Fayette County Historical Society, Inc., Fayetteville, GA 88
Fayette State Historic Park, Garden, MI 215
Fellow-Reeve Museum of History and Science, Wichita, KS 152
Fikes Hall of Special Collections, DeGolyer Library, Dallas, TX 443
Finn Creek Museum, New York Mills, MN 234

First Missouri State Capitol, St. Charles, MO 252
Fischer-Hanlon House, Benicia, CA 24
Five Civilized Tribes Museum, Muskogee, OK 378
Flickinger Foundation for American Studies Inc.,
   Baltimore, MD 180
Folger Shakespeare Library, Washington, DC 73
Fort Bridger State Historic Site, Fort Bridger, WY 507
Fort Caroline National Memorial, Jacksonville, FL 79
Fort Churchill Historic State Monument, Silver Springs,
   NV 269
Fort Concho Museum, San Angelo, TX 455
Fort Edmonton Park, Edmonton, Alberta 513
Fort Fetterman State Historic Site, Douglas, WY 507
Fort George National Historic Park, Niagara on the
   Lake, Ontario 547
Fort Hunter Mansion and Park, Harrisburg, PA 394
Fort Lauderdale Historic Preservation Board, Fort
   Lauderdale, FL 77
Fort Loudon Historical Society, Fort Loudon, PA 392
Fort Saint-Jean Baptiste, Natchitoches, LA 165
Fort Scott National Historic Site, Fort Scott, KS 145
Fort St. James National Historic Park, Fort St. James,
   British Columbia 518
Fort Ticonderoga, Fort Ticonderoga, NY 312
Fort Vancouver National Historic Site, Vancouver,
   WA 490
Fort Walsh National Historic Park, Maple Creek,
   Saskatchewan 565
Fort Whoop-Up Interpretative Society, Lethbridge,
   Alberta 515
Fortress of Louisbourg National Historic Park,
   Louisbourg, Nova Scotia 536
Fortuna Depot Museum, Fortuna, CA 28
Fountain Elms/Munson-Williams-Proctor Institute
   Museum of Art, Utica, NY 338
Fremont County Pioneer Museum, Lander, WY 508
French Legation Museum, Austin, TX 437
Friends of Cabildo, New Orleans, LA 166
Friends of Independence National Historical Park,
   Philadelphia, PA 401
Friends of Jesse James Farm, Kearney, MO 249
Friends of 'Iolani Palace, Honolulu, HI 95
Friends of the Middle Border Museum, Mitchell, SD 424
Fruitlands Museums, Inc., Harvard, MA 196
GAR (Grand Army of the Republic Hall)—Meeker
   County Museum, Litchfield, MN 231
Gadsby's Tavern Museum, Alexandria, VA 470
Galena Mining and Historical Museum Association, Inc.,
   Galena, KS 146
Galesburg Historical Society, Inc., Galesburg, IL 107
Galion Historical Society, Inc., Galion, OH 364
Gallier House Museum, New Orleans, LA 166
Garfield County Museum, Jordan, MT 258
Garst Museum, Greenville, OH 365
Garza Historical Museum, Post, TX 454
General Francis Marion Chapter, Sons of the American
   Revolution, Bennettsville, SC 413
Geology Museum, The, Golden, CO 54
George C. Ruhle Library, West Glacier, MT 260
George Mason University Oral History Program, Fairfax,
   VA 472
George Tate House, Portland, ME 175
George Washington Masonic National Memorial,
   Alexandria, VA 470
George Wyth House Museum, Cedar Falls, IA 133
Glencoe Historical Society, Glencoe, IL 107
Glensheen, Duluth, MN 228
Glenview Area Historical Society, Glenview, IL 108
Government House Historic Property, Regina,
   Saskatchewan 566
Grand County Historical Association, Hot Sulphur
   Springs, CO 55

Grand Falls Historical Society, Inc.,—Société Historique
   de Grand Sault, Inc., Grand Falls, New
   Brunswick 529
Grand Meadow Heritage Center, Washta, IA 142
Grand River Historical Society and Museum, Chillicothe,
   MO 244
Grand Saline Public Library, Grand Saline, TX 447
Grand Village of the Natchez Indians, Natchez, MS 241
Grant Encampment Museum, Encampment, WY 507
Grant-Kohrs Ranch National Historic Site, Deer Lodge,
   MT 257
Granville Slate Museum, Granville, NY 313
Great Falls Historical Society, Great Falls, VA 474
Green Oak Township Historical Society—Gage
   Museum, Brighton, MI 211
Greene County Historical Society, Pittsburgh, PA 403
Greenwood Museum, Greenwood, British Columbia 519
Grosse Ile Historical Society, Grosse Ile, MI 216
Grundy County Historical Society, Trenton, MO 255
Guernsey State Park Museum, Guernsey, WY 508
Halifax-Dartmouth Branch, United Empire Loyalists'
   Association of Canada, Dartmouth, Nova Scotia 534
Hall County Historical Society, Inc., Grand Island,
   NE 263
Hamilton House Museum, Clifton, NJ 279
Hammond Castle Museum, Inc., Gloucester, MA 195
Hancock County Historical Society, Hawesville, KY 156
Hanford Science Center, Richland, WA 487
Harlingen Hospital Museum—Rio Grande Valley
   Museum, Harlingen, TX 448
Hartsville Museum, Hartsville, SC 419
Haskell County Historical Society, Sublette, KS 151
Hatton-Eielson Museum, Hatton, ND 353
Hawaii State Archives, Honolulu, HI 95
Hawaiian Mission Children's Society, Honolulu, HI 95
Hay House, Macon, GA 90
Headwater's Heritage Museum, Three Forks, MT 260
Healy House—Dexter Cabin, Leadville, CO 55
Heavener Runestone Recreation Area, Heavener,
   OK 377
Hebron Historical and Arts Society, Hebron, ND 353
Henderson County Genealogical and Historical Society,
   Henderson, KY 156
Henry B. Plant Museum, Tampa, FL 84
Henry County Historical Society, New Castle, IN 128
Henry Whitfield State Historical Museum, Guilford,
   CT 61
Herbert Hoover Presidential Library, West Branch,
   IA 142
Heritage Association of El Dorado County, Inc.,
   Placerville, CA 36
Heritage Hall Museum, Dubois, ID 97
Heritage House Museum, Orange, TX 453
Heritage Museum of Kappa Kappa Gamma, Columbus,
   OH 361
Heritage Park Society, Calgary, Alberta 511
Heritage Plantation of Sandwich, Sandwich, MA 204
Hermitage, The, Ho-Ho-Kus, NJ 283
Hi-Desert Nature Museum and Association, Yucca
   Valley, CA 49
Hickman Library and Museum, Big Lake, TX 439
Higgins Armory Museum, Worcester, MA 209
High Cliff Historical Society, Sherwood, WI 504
Hill-Stead Museum, Farmington, CT 60
Hillsborough County Historical Commission, Tampa,
   FL 84
Hillsdale County Historical Society, Hillsdale, MI 217
Hilton Head Island Historical Society, Hilton Head
   Island, SC 419
Hinckley Fire Museum, Hinckley, MI 217
Hinckley Foundation, The, Ithaca, NY 316
Historic Anderson, Inc., Anderson, TX 437

Historic Bath State Historic Site, Bath, NC 341
Historic Charlton Park Village and Museum, Hastings, MI 216
Historic Cherry Hill, Albany, NY 301
Historic Governors' Mansion, Cheyenne, WY 506
Historic Jefferson College, Washington, MS 242
Historic St. Mary's City, St. Mary's City, MD 185
Historical Dental Museum, Temple University, Philadelphia, PA 401
Historical Jonesboro, Inc., Jonesboro, GA 89
Historical Society of Battle Creek—Kimball House Museum, Battle Creek, MI 211
Historical Society of Fort Washington, Fort Washington, PA 392
Historical Society of Monterey Park, Monterey Park, CA 34
Historical Society of Newburgh Bay and the Highlands, Newburgh, NY 321
Historical Society of Pennsylvania, Philadelphia, PA 401
Historical Society of Rockland County, New City, NY 321
Historical Society of the Bellmores, Bellmore, NY 304
Historical Society of Florham Park, Florham Park, NJ 281
Hitchcock County Historical Society, Trenton, NE 266
Holland Purchase Historical Society, Batavia, NY 303
Holmes County Historical Society, Millersburg, OH 369
Holocaust Council of New Jersey Professors, Lawrenceville, NJ 284
Homeplace-1850, The, Golden Pond, KY 156
Horner Museum, Corvallis, OR 382
Hot Spring County Museum—The Boyle House, Malvern, AR 20
Houston County Sesquicentennial Committee, Crockett, TX 441
Hoyt Sherman Place, Des Moines, IA 135
Huntington Corral of Westerners International, San Marino, CA 43
Huron Indian Village, Midland, Ontario 546
Hutchinson County Museum—Boom Town Revisited, Borger, TX 439
Hyde Park Historical Society, Hyde Park, MA 197
Illinois Historic Preservation Agency, Springfield, IL 116
Illinois State Archives, Springfield, IL 116
Illinois State Historical Library, Springfield, IL 116
Imperial Calcasieu Museum, Inc., Lake Charles, LA 165
Institute for Southern Studies, Columbia, SC 416
Institute of Early American History and Culture, Williamsburg, VA 481
Iosco County Historical Museum, East Tawas, MI 214
Iron Range Interpretative Center—Iron Range Research Center, Chisholm, MN 227
Isle a la Cache Museum, Romeoville, IL 115
Jackson Civil War Roundtable, Inc., Jackson, MS 240
Jackson Hole Museum, Jackson, WY 508
Jackson Homestead, Newton, MA 201
James Iredell House State Historic Site, Edenton, NC 344
Jamestown-Yorktown Foundation, Williamsburg, VA 482
January 12th 1888 Blizzard Club, Lincoln, NE 264
Jarrell Plantation Historic Site, Juliette, GA 89
Jay Historical Society, Jay, ME 172
Jeff Matthews Memorial Museum, Galex, VA 474
Jefferson National Expansion Memorial, St. Louis, MO 254
Jekyll Island Museum, Jekyll Island, GA 89
Jesse James Home—Pony Express Historical Association, Inc., St. Joseph, MO 253
John Wilson Townsend Room, University Library, Richmond, KY 161
Johnston County Genealogical & Historical Society, Tishomingo, OK 381

Joseph A. Tallman Museum, Cherokee, IA 133
Kalkaska County Historical Society, Kalkaska, MI 218
Kansas City Posse—The Westerners, Kansas City, MO 248
Kauai Museum Association, Ltd., Lihue, HI 95
Kauffman Museum, North Newton, KS 149
Kearny Cottage Historical Association, Perth Amboy, NJ 289
Keeler Tavern Preservation Society, Ridgefield, CT 65
Kenmore Association, Inc., Fredericksburg, VA 474
Kennedy-Douglass, Florence, AL 4
Kent County Council for Historic Preservation, Grand Rapids, MI 216
Kent Plantation House, Inc., Alexandria, LA 163
Keweenaw County Historical Society, Eagle Harbor, MI 214
Keyport Historical Society, Keyport, NJ 284
King and Queen County Historical Society, King & Queen, VA 475
Kings Landing Corporation—Kings Landing Historical Settlement, Prince William, Fredericton, New Brunswick 528
Kings Mountain National Military Park, Blacksburg, SC 414
Kittson County Historical Society, Lake Bronson, MN 231
Klondike Gold Rush National Historical Park, Seattle, WA 487
Klondike National Historic Sites, Dawson City, Yukon 568
Kutztown Area Historical Society, Kutztown, PA 396
LSU Rural Life Museum, Baton Rouge, LA 164
Lanesboro Historical Preservation Association, Lanesboro, MN 231
Lansdowne Historical Society, Inc., Baltimore, MD 181
Lawrence County Historical Society, Deadwood, SD 423
LeSueur Historians, LeSueur, MN 231
Leisure World Historical Society of Laguna Hills, Inc., Laguna Hills, CA 30
Leland Case Library, Spearfish, SD 426
Lewis and Clark Interpretive Center, Fort Canby State Park, Ilwaco, WA 484
Library Company of Philadelphia, Philadelphia, PA 402
Lightner Museum, St. Augustine, FL 82
Lillooet Museum, Lillooet, British Columbia 519
Lincoln County Historical Society—Lincoln County Museum, Hugo, CO 55
Lincoln Group of Boston, Hope Valley, RI 409
Lincoln Memorial Shrine, Redlands, CA 37
Lincoln's New Salem State Park, Petersburg, IL 114
Lititz Historical Foundation, Inc., Lititz, PA 397
Little Red Schoolhouse Museum, Farmington, ME 172
Loantaka Chapter, Daughters of the American Revolution, Madison, NJ 284
Lompoc Valley Historical Society, Inc., Lompoc, CA 30
Lon C. Hill Home Museum, Harlingen, TX 448
London Town Publik House and Gardens, Edgewater, MD 183
Londonderry Historical Society, Londonderry, VT 467
Longhorn Museum, Inc., Pleasanton, TX 454
Lonoke County Historical Society, Lonoke, AR 20
Los Alamos County Historical Museum and Society, Los Alamos, NM 297
Los Angeles State and County Arboretum, Arcadia, CA 23
Louisiana Arts and Science Center, Baton Rouge, LA 163
Louisiana Collection Series of Books & Documents on Colonial Louisiana, Birmingham, AL 2
Loxahatchee Historical Society, Inc., Jupiter, FL 79
Lutie Coal Miner's Museum, Wilburton, OK 381

Lyon County Historical Society, Marshall, MN 232
MARC Pacific Collection, University of Guam, Mangilao, Guam 509
Macaulay Heritage Park—Prince Edward County Museum, Picton, Ontario 549
Mackinac Island State Park Commission, Mackinac Island, MI 219
Madison County Historical Society, Richmond, KY 162
Magnolia Mound Plantation, Baton Rouge, LA 164
Mahaffie Farmstead and Stagecoach Stop, Olathe, KS 149
Mahanoy Valley Historical Society, Gordon, PA 393
Mahnomen County Historical Society, Mahnomen, MN 231
Margaret Woodbury Strong Museum, Rochester, NY 331
Marias Museum of History and Art, Shelby, MT 259
Marion County Historical Society, Hannibal, MO 246
Mariposa County Historical Society, Mariposa, CA 32
Martin County Historical Museum, Stanton, TX 458
Maryland State Archives, Hall of Records, Annapolis, MD 179
Marymoor Museum, Redmond, WA 487
Mason Historical Society, Mason, NH 274
Masonic Library and Museum, New York, NY 324
Massachusetts Historical Society, Boston, MA 190
Massacoh Plantation, Simsbury, CT 66
Massasoit Historical Association, Warren, RI 412
Maymont Foundation, Richmond, VA 479
McCone County Museum, Circle, MT 257
McFaddin-Ward House, Beaumont, TX 439
McPherson County Historical Society, McPherson, KS 149
Meadowlands Museum, Rutherford, NJ 291
Mecklenburg Historical Association, Charlotte, NC 342
Mercer County Historical Society, Beulah, ND 351
Merrick County Historical Museum, Central City, NE 262
Mesa Museum, Mesa, AZ 13
Mid-Missouri Civil War Round Table, Jefferson City, MO 247
Midland County Historical Society, Midland, MI 220
Milaca Museum, Milaca, MN 232
Milford Area Historical Society, Milford, OH 369
Miller-Cory House Museum, Westfield, NJ 293
Mills Mansion State Historic Site, Staatsburg, NY 335
Mission Inn Foundation, Riverside, CA 38
Mission Nuestra Senora del Espiritu Santo de Zuniga—Goliad State Historical Park, Goliad, TX 447
Mississippi Governor's Mansion, Jackson, MS 241
Mississippi River Museum, Memphis, TN 432
Missouri Cultural Heritage Center, Columbia, MO 244
Mojave River Valley Museum Association, Barstow, CA 23
Monroe County Historical Society, Albia, IA 131
Monroe-Crook House, Crockett, TX 570
Monroe Historical Preservation Society, Monroe, NY 320
Monroeville Historical Society, Monroeville, OH 369
Montecito History Committee, Montecito, CA 33
Montgomery's Inn, Etobicoke, Ontario 542
Moose Jaw Art Museum and National Exhibition Centre, Moose Jaw, Saskatchewan 565
Morgan County Historical Society, McConnelsville, OH 368
Mormon History Association, Provo, UT 463
Morristown National Historical Park, Morristown, NJ 286
Mount Washington Historical Society, Mt. Washington, KY 160
Murphy's Landing, Shakopee, MN 237
Murrell Home, Tahlequah, OK 380
Musée Acadien, Cheticamp, Nova Scotia 534
Musée Beaulne, Coaticook, Quebec 557
Museum Village in Orange County, Monroe, NY 320

Museum and Archives of Georgia Education, Milledgeville, GA 90
Museum of American Architecture and Decorative Arts, Houston, TX 449
Museum of Appalachia, Norris, TN 435
Museum of Canadian Scouting, Boy Scouts of Canada, Ottawa, Ontario 548
Museum of History and Art, Ontario, CA 34
Museum of Our National Heritage, Lexington, MA 197
Museum of Tobacco Art and History, Nashville, TN 433
Museum of the City of New York, New York, NY 324
Museum of the Confederacy, Brockenbrough Library, Richmond, VA 479
Museum of the Fur Trade, Chadron, NE 262
Museums at Hartwick, Oneonta, NY 326
Museums at Stony Brook, Stony Brook, NY 336
Nanaimo and District Museum Society, Nanaimo, British Columbia 519
Nancy Island Historic Site, Wasaga Beach, Ontario 554
National Soccer Hall of Fame, Oneonta, NY 326
National Society, United States Daughters of 1812, Washington, DC 75
Naumkeag, Stockbridge, MA 205
Navarre-Bethlehem Township Historical Society, Navarre, OH 369
Nebraska Game and Parks Commission, Lincoln, NE 264
Neill Cochran Museum House, Austin, TX 438
Nemaha County Historical Society, Inc., Seneca, KS 150
Nemours Mansion and Gardens, Wilmington, DE 71
Neptune Historical Museum, Neptune, NJ 287
Neptune Historical Society, Neptune, NJ 287
Ness County Historical Society, Ness City, KS 149
Netherland Inn Association, Kingsport, TN 430
Nevada State Museum and Historical Society, Las Vegas, NV 268
Neville Public Museum of Brown County, Green Bay, WI 497
New Canaan Historical Society, New Canaan, CT 63
New England Ski Museum, Franconia, NH 271
New Glarus Historical Society—Swiss Historical Village, New Glarus, WI 501
New Hampshire Historical Society, Concord, NH 270
New Harmony Workingmen's Institute, New Harmony, IN 128
New Jersey Committee for the Humanities, New Brunswick, NJ 288
New Jersey State House, Department of State, Trenton, NJ 292
New London Historical Society, New London, NH 274
New Market Battlefield Park, New Market, VA 477
New Mexico Sons of Confederate Veterans, Albuquerque, NM 295
Newport Township Historical Society, Wadsworth, IL 118
Niagara Historical Society Museum, Niagara-on-the-Lake, Ontario 547
Norman and Cleveland County Historical Museum, Norman, OK 378
North Carolina Chapter, Victorian Society in America, Raleigh, NC 348
North Central Washington Museum Association, Wenatchee, WA 491
North York Historical Society, North York, Ontario 547
Norton County Historical Society, Norton, KS 149
Oakland County Pioneer and Historical Society, Pontiac, MI 221
Oakland Historical Society, Oakland, IA 140
Oaklands Association, Inc., Murfreesboro, TN 432
Oblate Archives, Saint Albert, Alberta 516
Office of Museums and Historic Sites, Onandaga County, Liverpool, NY 318

Ohio Historical Society, Columbus, OH 361
Oklahoma Territorial Museum, Guthrie, OK 377
Old Bedford Village, Bedford, PA 388
Old Cienega Village Museum, Santa Fe, NM 299
Old Coal Mine Museum—Madrid Opera House, Madrid, NM 298
Old Exchange Building and Provost Dungeon, Charleston, SC 415
Old Fort Harrod State Park, Harrodsburg, KY 156
Old Fort Number Four Associates, Charlestown, NH 270
Old Fort Parker State Historic Site, Groesbeck, TX 448
Old Idaho Penitentiary, Boise, ID 96
Old Jail Museum, Winchester, TN 436
Old Mill Village Museum, New Milford, PA 399
Old Mint Museum, San Francisco, CA 41
Old Moheetie Association, Wheeler, TX 460
Old Montana Prison, Deer Lodge, MT 257
Old Sturbridge Village, Sturbridge, MA 206
Ontario Historical Society, Willowdale, Ontario 554
Oral History Office, Sangamon State University, Springfield, IL 117
Oral History Program, Little Rock, AR 20
Orchard Park Historical Society, Orchard Park, NY 327
Oregon Lewis & Clark Heritage Foundation, Portland, OR 385
Oregon Museum Park—Lane County Historical Museum, Eugene, OR 383
Oregon Trail Museum Association, Baton Rouge, LA 164
Organization of American Historians, Bloomington, IN 121
Osage County Historical Society, Pawhuska, OK 379
Overland Trail Museum, Sterling, CO 57
P.K. Yonge Library of Florida History, Gainesville, FL 78
Pacific Palisades Historical Society, Pacific Palisades, CA 35
Palace of the Governors, Santa Fe, NM 299
Park County Historical Society, Bailey, CO 50
Partridge Island Research Project, Saint John, New Brunswick 530
Paterson Museum, Paterson, NJ 289
Pecos National Monument, Pecos, NM 298
Pennsylvania Farm Museum of Landis Valley, Lancaster, PA 397
Pennsylvania Humanities Council, Philadelphia, PA 402
Pennsylvania Society, Sons of the American Revolution, Quakertown, PA 404
Pennypacker Mills, Schwenksville, PA 405
Petaluma Adobe State Historic Park, Petaluma, CA 35
Petersburg Museums, Petersburg, VA 478
Phelps County Historical Society, Rolla, MO 252
Philipse Manor Hall State Historic Site, Yonkers, NY 340
Pike County Historical Society, Pikeville, KY 161
Pilgrim John Howland Society—Howland House, Plymouth, MA 202
Pilgrim Society, Plymouth, MA 202
Pioneers Texas Trail Drivers and Former Texas Rangers Corporation, Inc., San Antonio, TX 456
Pipe Spring National Monument, Moccasin, AZ 13
Pittock Mansion, Portland, OR 385
Plainville Historical Society, Inc., Plainville, CT 65
Plimoth Plantation, Inc., Plymouth, MA 202
Point of Honor, Lynchburg, VA 476
Polk County Historical Commission, Livingston, TX 451
Polk County Historical Society, Des Moines, IA 135
Polson-Flathead Historic Museum, Polson, MT 259
Port-au-Port—Bay St. George Heritage Association, Stephenville, Newfoundland 532
Potsdam Public Museum, Potsdam, NY 329
Prairie Grove Battlefield Historic State Park, Prairie Grove, AR 21
Preservation Society of Fall River, Fall River, MA 195

Preservation Society of Newport County, Newport, RI 410
Presque Isle County Historical Museum, Roger's City, MI 222
Price County Historical Society, Park Falls, WI 502
Provincial Archives of British Columbia, Victoria, British Columbia 522
Public Works Historical Society, Chicago, IL 104
Quechan Indian Museum, Yuma, AZ 16
Ranching Heritage Association, Lubbock, TX 452
Randolph Historical Commission, Randolph, MA 203
Rawlins County Historical Society, Atwood, KS 143
Raynham Hall Museum, Oyster Bay, NY 327
Red Clay State Historical Area, Cleveland, TN 428
Resource and Research Center for Beaver County Local History, Beaver Falls, PA 388
RevMex (Revolutionary Mexican Historical Society), Ozawkie, KS 150
Reynolds Community Museum, Reynolds, ND 353
Rice County Historical Society, Lyons, KS 148
Richibucto River Historical Society, Rexton, New Brunswick 530
Richland County Historical Society, Mansfield, OH 367
Richmond National Battlefield Park, Richmond, VA 479
Ricketts Memorial Museum, Hamilton, MT 258
Rideau Canal, Smiths Falls, Ontario 551
Riverview, the Historic Hobson House, Bowling Green, KY 153
Roanoke Island Historical Association, Inc., Manteo, NC 346
Robbins Hunter Museum, Granville, OH 365
Rochester Historical Society, Rochester, NY 331
Rock Castle Historic Home, Hendersonville, TN 429
Rockford Museum Center and Midway Village, Rockford, IL 115
Rockpile Museum, Gillette, WY 507
Rockwood Museum, Wilmington, DE 71
Rocky Mountain House National Historic Park, Rocky Mountain House, Alberta 516
Rocky Mountain National Park, Estes Park, CO 53
Rogers Historical Museum, Rogers, AR 21
Roscoe Historical Society, Roscoe, TX 455
Rosenbach Museum and Library, Philadelphia, PA 403
Ross House Museum, Winnipeg, Manitoba 526
Ross Township Historical Society, Pittsburgh, PA 404
Royall House Association, Medford, MA 199
Royalston Historical Society, Royalston, MA 203
Saint Croix County Historical Society, Hudson, WI 498
Salamanca Rail Museum, Salamanca, NY 332
Salisbury Historical Society, Dolgeville, NY 310
San Jacinto Museum of History Association, La Porte, TX 451
San Jose Historical Museum, San Jose, CA 42
San Leandro Library—Historical Commission, San Leandro, CA 42
San Marino Historical Society, San Marino, CA 43
Sanford Historical Society, Sanford, MI 223
Sangre de Cristo Arts and Conference Center, Pueblo, CO 57
Santa Fe Trail Historical, Inc., Baldwin City, KS 143
Saskatchewan History and Folklore Society, Moose Jaw, Saskatchewan 565
Saum Community Club, Inc., Saum, MN 237
Schuyler Historical Society, Schuyler, NE 266
Selma-Dallas County Historic and Preservation Society, Selma, AL 8
Seneca County Museum, Tiffin, OH 372
Shadows-on-the-Teche, New Iberia, LA 165
Shaker Historical Museum, Shaker Heights, OH 372
Shakertown at Pleasant Hill, Inc., Harrodsburg, KY 156
Shakertown at South Union, South Union, KY 162
Sharpsteen Museum Association, Calistoga, CA 24

Shawano County Historical Society Inc., Shawano, WI 503

Sheffield Historical Society, Sheffield, MA 204

Sheridan County Historical Society, Inc., Rushville, NE 266

Shirley Plantation, Charles City, VA 471

Silver Creek Historical Society, Silver Creek, NY 334

Sixteen ninety-nine Historical Committee, Ocean Springs, MS 241

Smith-Harris House, East Lyme, CT 59

Smith-Zimmermann State Museum, Madison, SD 424

Société d'histoire de la rivière Saint-Jean de Fredericton, Fredericton, New Brunswick 529

Société d'histoire Régionale de Lévis, Levis, Quebec 558

Société Historique de la Gaspésie, Gaspé, Quebec 557

Société Historique de Québec, Quebec, Quebec 561

Société Historique du Lac Memphre Magog, Magog, Quebec 559

Société Quebecoise des Ponts Couverts, Inc., Saint Eustache, Quebec 561

Society for the Preservation of Minneota's Heritage, Minneota, MN 233

Socorro County Historical Society, Inc., Socorro, NM 299

Solebury Township Historical Society, Solebury, PA 405

Somerset Historical Center, Somerset, PA 405

Sonoma County Museum, Santa Rosa, CA 44

South Carolina Department of Archives and History, Columbia, SC 417

South Carolina Historical Association, Florence, SC 418

South Park City Museum, Fairplay, CO 53

South Pass City State Historic Site, South Pass City, WY 509

South Sebastian County Historical Society, Greenwood, AR 18

Southbury Historical Society, Inc., Southbury, CT 66

Southern Historical Association, Athens, GA 85

Southern Lorain County Historical Society, Wellington, OH 374

Southwestern Indiana Historical Society, Evansville, IN 122

Southwestern Ontario Heritage Village, Colchester South, Ontario 541

Special Collections Department, University of New Mexico, Albuquerque, NM 296

Stan Hywet Hall Foundation, Inc., Akron, OH 355

Star of the Republic Museum, Washington-on-the-Brazos State Historical Park, Washington, TX 460

State Capitol Museum, Phoenix, AZ 14

State Historical Society of Colorado, Denver, CO 53

State Library of Massachusetts, Boston, MA 190

Steppingstone Museum Association, Inc., Havre de Grace, MD 184

Stevens Coolidge Place, Trustees of Reservations, North Andover, MA 201

Stevens County Historical Society, Morris, MN 234

Still National Osteopathic Museum, Kirksville, MO 249

Stoney Creek Battlefield House, Stoney Creek, Ontario 551

Storrowton Village Museum, West Springfield, MA 208

Stowe-Day Foundation, The, Hartford, CT 61

Strecker Museum, Waco, TX 459

Stuart House Museum, Mackinac Island, MI 219

Sublette County Historical Society, Inc., Pinedale, WY 508

Suffolk Nansemond Historical Society, Suffolk, VA 481

Summerland Museum and Arts Society, Summerland, British Columbia 521

Sun River Valley Historical Society, Sun River, MT 260

Sunrise Museums, Charleston, WV 492

Surratt Society, The, Clinton, MD 182

Sweetwater County Historical Society, Green River, WY 508

Sydney and Louisbourg Railway Historical Society, Louisbourg, Nova Scotia 536

Tales of Cape Cod, Inc., Barnstable, MA 188

Tatamagouche Historical and Cultural Society, Tatamagouche, Nova Scotia 538

Terwilliger Museum, Waterloo, NY 338

Texas Baptist Historical Center-Museum, Brenham, TX 440

Texas Barbed Wire Collectors Association, Austin, TX 438

Texas Folklore Society, Nacogdoches, TX 453

Texas Heritage, Inc.—Thistle Hill, Fort Worth, TX 446

Teysen's Woodland Indian Museum, Mackinaw City, MI 219

Theodore Roosevelt Nature and History Association, Medora, ND 353

Time Was Village Museum, Mendota, IL 111

Tippecanoe Battlefield Museum, Battle Ground, IN 120

Tombstone Courthouse State Historic Park, Tombstone, AZ 15

Town of Middlefield Historical Association, Cooperstown, NY 309

Town of Yorktown Museum, Yorktown Heights, NY 340

Trail End Historic Center, Sheridan, WY 509

Trail of '98 Museum, Skagway, AK 11

Tree Farm Archives, Shelton, CT 66

Tri-County Historical Society, Herington, KS 146

Truckee-Donner Historical Society, Inc., Truckee, CA 47

Tryon Palace Restoration Complex, New Bern, NC 347

Tubac Presidio State Historic Museum, Tubac, AZ 15

Twinsburg Historical Society, Twinsburg, OH 373

Union County Historical Society, Creston, IA 134

Union County Historical Society, Elizabeth, NJ 280

Union Station Museums, Ogden, UT 462

United Daughters of the Confederacy, Richmond, VA 479

United Empire Loyalists' Association of Canada, Toronto, Ontario 554

University Photographic Archives, Louisville, KY 159

Valentine Museum, The, Richmond, VA 479

Valley Forge Historical Society, Valley Forge, PA 407

Valley Forge National Historical Park, Valley Forge, PA 407

Valley Historical Society, Sinclairville, NY 334

Vandalia Historical Society, Vandalia, IL 118

Vandalia Statehouse State Historic Site, Vandalia, IL 118

Varner-Hogg State Historical Park, West Columbia, TX 460

Vermont Historical Society, Montpelier, VT 467

Vicksburg and Warren County Historical Society, Vicksburg, MS 242

Victoria Society of Maine—The Victoria Mansion, Portland, ME 175

Victorian House Museum, Cedar Falls, IA 133

Victorian Society in America, Philadelphia, PA 403

Vigo County Historical Society, Terre Haute, IN 130

Villa Louis Historic Site, Prairie du Chien, WI 503

Village of East Davenport Association, Inc., Davenport, IA 134

Vinton County Historical Society, McArthur, OH 368

Voigt House, Grand Rapids, MI 216

Wallace House—Old Dutch Parsonage, Somerville, NJ 291

Washington Association of New Jersey, Morristown, NJ 286

Washington County Historical Society, Washington, IA 142

Waterloo Area Historical Society, Stockbridge, MI 224

Watrousville-Caro Area Historical Society, Caro, MI 212

Wax Museum of the Southwest, Grand Prairie, TX 447
Wenham Historical Association and Museum, Inc.,
Wenham, MA 207
West Baton Rouge Historical Association, Port Allen,
LA 167
West Jefferson County Historical Society, Inc.,
Bessemer, AL 2
West Pasco Historical Society, Inc., New Port Richey,
FL 81
Western History Association, Reno, NV 269
White County Retired Teachers' Association, Sparta,
TN 436
White House Association of the State of Alabama,
Montgomery, AL 7
White House Ranch Historic Site, Colorado Springs,
CO 51
Whitman Mission National Historic Site, Walla Walla,
WA 491
Wichita Falls Museum and Art Center, Wichita Falls,
TX 460
Wichita-Sedgwick County Historical Museum, Wichita,
KS 152
Willow Bunch Museum Society, Willow Bunch,
Saskatchewan 567
Windsor Locks Historical Society, Inc., Windsor Locks,
CT 69
Winterport Historical Association, Winterport, ME 178
Woodford Mansion, Philadelphia, PA 403
Woodside National Historic Park, Kitchener, Ontario 544
Workman and Temple Homestead—Historical
Perspectives, Inc., City of Industry, CA 25
World Heritage Museum, Champaign, IL 102
Wornall House Museum, Kansas City, MO 249
Wyoming State Archives, Museums and Historical
Department, Cheyenne, WY 507
Wyoming State Museum and Art Gallery, Cheyenne,
WY 507
Yarmouth County Historical Society, Yarmouth, Nova
Scotia 539
Yellow Springs Historical Society, Yellow Springs,
OH 375
Yesteryear Museum, Whippany, NJ 294
Yoakum Heritage Museum, Yoakum, TX 461
Zion Historical Society, Zion, IL 120

INDUSTRY

Alabama Mining Museum, Dora, AL 4
Alamance County Historical Museum, Burlington,
NC 341
Alberta Forest Service Museum, Hinton, Alberta 514
Aldrich Public Library, Barre, VT 464
Anthro/Arts, Rockville, RI 412
Arkansas Museum of Science and History, Little Rock,
AR 19
Arkansas Museum Services, Little Rock, AR 19
Arkansas Oil and Brine Museum, Smackover, AR 22
Ashland Anthracite Museum, Ashland, PA 387
Attleboro Area Industrial Museum, Attleboro, MA 187
Baltimore Museum of Industry, Baltimore, MD 180
Baltimore Public Works Museum, Inc., Baltimore,
MD 180
Barton County Historical Society, Great Bend, KS 146
Bisbee Mining and Historical Museum, Bisbee, AZ 11
Bollinger Mill State Historic Site, Burfordville, MO 243
Bradford Historical Society, Inc., Bradford, VT 464
Brattleboro Museum and Art Center, Brattleboro,
VT 465
Brierfield Ironworks Park, Brierfield, AL 3
British Columbia Museum of Mining, Britannia Beach,
British Columbia 517

Butte Historical Society, Butte, MT 256
California Oil Museum, Santa Paula, CA 44
Calumet Regional Archives, Gary, IN 123
Centre County Historical Society—Centre Furnace
Mansion, State College, PA 405
Coppertown USA, Calumet, MI 212
Corry Area Historical Society, Corry, PA 390
Cumberland Museum, Cumberland, British
Columbia 518
Deserted Village at Allaire, Inc., Allaire, NJ 277
Dillard Mill State Historic Site, Dillard, MO 245
Discovery Hall Museum, South Bend, IN 129
Drake Well Museum, Titusville, PA 406
Early American Industries Association, Inc., Albany,
NY 301
East Longmeadow Historical Commission, East
Longmeadow, MA 194
Elizabethtown Heritage Society, Elizabeth, NJ 280
Elkhart County Historical Society, Inc., Bristol, IN 121
Elliot Lake Nuclear and Mining Museum, Elliot Lake,
Ontario 542
Fishermen's Museum, New Harbor, ME 174
Fort King George Historic Site, Darien, GA 88
Fort McMurray Oil Sands Interpretive Centre, Ft.
McMurray, Alberta 514
Frank Slide Interpretive Centre, Frank (Crow's Nest
Pass), Alberta 514
Franklin County Heritage, Chambersburg, PA 390
Goodyear World of Rubber Museum, Akron, OH 354
Hagley Museum and Library, Wilmington, DE 70
Hamilton Museum of Steam and Technology, Hamilton,
Ontario 543
Hanford Mills Museum, East Meredith, NY 310
Healdton Oil Museum, Healdton, OK 377
Helper Mining Museum-Archives, Helper, UT 462
Hoover Historical Center, North Canton, OH 370
Hope Sawmill, Peterborough, Ontario 549
Hopewell Village National Historic Site, Elverson,
PA 392
Hudson-Mohawk Industrial Gateway, Troy, NY 337
Huron City Museum, Port Austin, MI 222
Illinois Bell's Oliver P. Parks Telephone Museum,
Springfield, IL 116
Illinois Canal Society, Lockport, IL 110
Iron County Historical and Museum Society, Caspian,
MI 212
J. D. Sandefer Oil Annex, Breckenridge, TX 439
J. Walter Thompson Company Archives, New York,
NY 323
L'Univers du Rail, Inc., Charny, Quebec 556
Laird Norton Company Archives, Seattle, WA 487
Lock Museum of America, Inc., Terryville, CT 67
Lou Tate Foundation, Inc.—The Little Loomhouse,
Louisville, KY 159
Lumberman's Museum, Patten, ME 175
Marinette County Historical Society, Marinette, WI 500
Massey Area Museum, Massey, Ontario 545
Mattatuck Historical Society, Waterbury, CT 68
Mayfield Historical Society, Mayfield, NY 320
Memorabilia Museum, Inc., Coca-Cola Bottling
Company of Elizabethtown, Elizabethtown, KY 154
Mifflinburg Buggy Museum Association, Mifflinburg,
PA 398
Milford Historical Commission, Milford, MA 199
Miners' Museum, Glace Bay, Nova Scotia 534
Mining Museum, Platteville, WI 502
Musée de la Ville de Lachine, Lachine, Quebec 558
Museum of American Textile History, North Andover,
MA 201
Museum of Art, Science, and Industry, Bridgeport,
CT 58
Museum of Ceramics, East Liverpool, OH 363

Museum of History and Science, Louisville, KY 159
Museum of Independent Telephony, Abilene, KS 143
New Bedford Glass Society, New Bedford, MA 200
Newcastle Historical Society, Bellevue, WA 482
Nita Stewart Haley Memorial Library, Midland, TX 452
North Jersey Highlands Historical Society, Ringwood, NJ 290
Oglebay Institute—Mansion Museum, Wheeling, WV 494
Oil Museum of Canada, Oil Springs, Ontario 547
Oscar Getz Museum of Whiskey History, Bardstown, KY 153
Outagamie County Historical Society, Inc., Appleton, WI 494
Peekskill Museum, Peekskill, NY 328
Pennsylvania Lumber Museum, Galeton, PA 393
Permian Basin Petroleum Museum, Library, and Hall of Fame, Midland, TX 452
Portal Heritage Society, Portal, GA 91
Quincy Mine Hoist Association, Inc., Hancock, MI 216
Remington Gun Museum, Ilion, NY 316
Roebling Historical Society, Roebling, NJ 291
Sandwich Historical Society and Glass Museum, Sandwich, MA 204
Schenectady Museum, Schenectady, NY 333
Shelby County Historical Society—Shelby County Archives and Museum, Columbiana, AL 3
Slater Mill Historic Site, Pawtucket, RI 411
Sloss Furnaces, National Historical Landmark, Birmingham, AL 2
Society for Industrial Archaeology, Washington, DC 75
State Capital Publishing Museum, Guthrie, OK 377
Telephone Pioneers of America, Albuquerque, NM 296
Tennessee Valley Authority, Knoxville, TN 430
Texas Forestry Museum, Lufkin, TX 452
Timber Village Museum, Blind River, Ontario 540
Torrington Historical Society, Inc., Torrington, CT 67
U.S. Tobacco Museum, Greenwich, CT 61
Watkins Mill Association, Lawson, MO 249
Watkins Woolen Mill State Historic Site, Lawson, MO 250
Wells Fargo Bank History Department, San Francisco, CA 42
Western Company Museum, Fort Worth, TX 446
Western Forest Industries Museum, Inc., Tacoma, WA 490
Western Museum of Mining and Industry, Colorado Springs, CO 51
Westmoreland-Fayette Historical Society, Scottdale, PA 405
Weyerhaeuser Company Archives, Tacoma, WA 490
Wheaton Historical Association, Millville, NJ 285
Winchester Museum, Winchester, ID 99
World Museum of Mining, Butte, MT 256
Young Ideas Explorer Post 400, San Francisco, CA 42

MARITIME

Adirondack Museum—Adirondack Historical Association, Blue Mountain Lake, NY 304
Albert County Historical Society, Inc., Hopewell Cape, New Brunswick 529
Alexandria Township Historical Society, Alexandria Bay, NY 302
American Merchant Marine Museum, Great Neck, NY 314
Barnegat Light Historical Society, Barnegat Light, NJ 277
Basin Head Fisheries Museum, Basin Head, Prince Edward Island 555
Bath, Maine, Maritime Museum, Bath, ME 169
Battleship New Jersey Historical Museum Society, Middletown, NJ 285
Boston Marine Society, Boston, MA 189
Bucksport Historical Society, Inc., Bucksport, ME 170
CIGNA Corporation Museum, Philadelphia, PA 401
Cabrillo National Monument, San Diego, CA 39
Calvert Marine Museum, Solomons, MD 186
Canal Center—Erie Canal Museum, Dewitt, NY 310
Canal Park Marine Museum, Duluth, MN 228
Center for Wooden Boats, Seattle, WA 487
Champlain Maritime Society, Burlington, VT 465
Charlotte-Genesee Lighthouse Historical Society, Rochester, NY 330
Chicago Maritime Society, Chicago, IL 102
Churchill House—Marine Memorial Room, Hantsport, Nova Scotia 535
Clatsop County Historical Society, Astoria, OR 382
Coast Guard Museum/Northwest, Seattle, WA 487
Columbia River Maritime Museum, Astoria, OR 382
Connecticut River Foundation, Essex, CT 60
Detroit Historical Museum, Detroit, MI 213
Dubuque County Historical Society—Mathias Ham House, Dubuque, IA 135
Elizabeth II State Historic Site, Manteo, NC 346
Erie Canal Museum, Syracuse, NY 336
Essex Historical Society—Essex Shipbuilding Museum, Essex, MA 195
Fairport Harbor Historical Society, Fairport Harbor, OH 363
Fisheries Museum of the Atlantic, Lunenburg, Nova Scotia 536
Gladding International Sport Fishing Museum, South Otselic, NY 334
Grand Banks Schooner Museum Trust, Boothbay Harbor, ME 170
Great Lakes Historical Society, Vermilion, OH 373
Great Lakes Naval and Maritime Museum, Chicago, IL 103
Gulf Islands National Seashore, Pensacola, FL 82
Hampton Mariners Museum, Beaufort, NC 341
Historic Naval and Military Establishments, Penetanguishene, Ontario 549
Holiday Cruises, Inc.—S.S. Clipper, Chicago, IL 103
Huntsman Marine Laboratory, St. Andrews, New Brunswick 530
Isle Royale National Park, Houghton, MI 217
Kendall Whaling Museum, Sharon, MA 204
Keokuk Museum Commission, Keokuk, IA 138
Key West Art and Historical Society, Key West, FL 79
Kittery Historical and Naval Museum, Kittery, ME 173
La Have Islands Marine Museum, Bell's Island, Nova Scotia 533
Lake Michigan Maritime Museum, South Haven, MI 223
Maine Historical Society, Portland, ME 175
Manitowoc Maritime Museum, Manitowoc, WI 499
Marine Museum of the Great Lakes at Kingston, Kingston, Ontario 544
Marine Museum of Upper Canada, Toronto, Ontario 552
Mariners' Museum, Newport News, VA 477
Maritime Command Museum, Halifax, Nova Scotia 535
Maritime Museum of British Columbia, Victoria, British Columbia 522
Maritime Research Society of San Diego, San Diego, CA 40
Michigan City Historical Society, Inc., Michigan City, IN 127
Miramichi Natural History Association Museum, Chatham, New Brunswick 527
Monterey History and Art Association, Ltd., Monterey, CA 33
Musée Maritime Bernier, L'Islet-Sur-Mer, Quebec 558
Museum of Missouri River History, Brownville, NE 261

Museum of Sea and Ships, Seattle, WA 487
Mystic Seaport Museum, Mystic, CT 63
National Maritime Museum, San Francisco—National Maritime Museum Association, San Francisco, CA 41
Naval War College Museum, Newport, RI 410
Noank Historical Society, Noank, CT 64
North American Wildfowl Art Museum, Salisbury, MD 185
Of Sea and Shore, Inc.—Museum of Seashells and Marine Life, Port Gammble, WA 486
Ohio River Museum, Marietta, OH 367
Old Lighthouse Museum, Michigan City, IN 127
Peabody Museum of Salem, Salem, MA 204
Penobscot Marine Museum, Searsport, ME 176
Peterson Steamship Company—SS Keewatin, Douglas, MI 214
Philadelphia Maritime Museum, Philadelphia, PA 402
Portsmouth Lightship Museum, Portsmouth, VA 478
Portsmouth Museums, Portsmouth, VA 478
Sag Harbor Whaling and Historical Museum, Sag Harbor, NY 332
Salem Maritime National Historic Site, Salem, MA 204
Samson V. Maritime Museum, New Westminster, British Columbia 520
Sault de Ste. Marie Historical Sites, Inc., Sault Ste. Marie, MI 223
Seafood Industry Museum of Biloxi, Biloxi, MS 239
Sippican Historical Society, Marion, MA 198
Society of the Montreal Military and Maritime Museum—St. Helen's Island Museum, Montreal, Quebec 560
Star-Spangled Banner Flag House—1812 Museum, Baltimore, MD 181
Steamship Historical Society of America, Inc., Baltimore, MD 181
Steamship Historical Society of America, Inc., Staten Island, NY 335
Suffolk Marine Museum, Sayville, NY 333
Susquehanna Museum of Havre de Grace, Inc., Havre de Grace, MD 184
Thousand Islands Shipyard Museum, Clayton, NY 308
Toms River Seaport Society, Toms River, NJ 292
USS Constitution Museum Foundation, Inc., Boston, MA 191
US Naval Academy Museum, Annapolis, MD 179
Vancouver Maritime Museum, Vancouver, British Columbia 521
Washington State Archives Regional Branch, Seattle, WA 488
Waterfront Awareness—Institute for Marine Studies, Seattle, WA 488
Watermens Museum in Yorktown, Yorktown, VA 482
Wisconsin Marine Historical Society—Local History and Marine Room, Milwaukee, WI 501

MILITARY

AFAM (Air Force Armament Museum), Fort Walton Beach, FL 78
Admiral Nimitz State Historical Park, Fredericksburg, TX 446
Aerospace Museum and Park, Hampton, VA 474
Alamance Battleground, Burlington, NC 341
American Military Institute, Washington, DC 71
American Society of Military History, Los Angeles, CA 31
Ancient and Honorable Artillery Company, Boston, MA 188
Andersonville National Historic Site, Andersonville, GA 85
Arizona Historical Society Fort Lowell Museum, Tucson, AZ 15
Battleship Texas State Historic Park, La Porte, TX 451
Bennett Place State Historic Site, Durham, NC 343
Bentonville Battleground State Historic Site, Newton Grove, NC 347
Brandywine Battlefield Park, Chadds Ford, PA 390
Bunker Hill Monument, Boston, MA 189
Bushy Run Battlefield, Jeannette, PA 396
CEC-Seabee Museum, Port Hueneme, CA 36
COMMA (Committee on Military Museums in America), Washington, DC 72
Camden District Heritage Foundation, Camden, SC 414
Canadian Airborne Forces Museum, Lancaster Park, British Columbia 519
Canadian Military Engineers Museum, Vedder Crossing, British Columbia 522
Canadian War Museum, Ottawa, Ontario 548
Carleton Martello Tower National Historic Park, Saint John, New Brunswick 530
Casemate Museum, Fort Monroe, VA 473
Castillo de San Marcos—Fort Matanzas National Monument, St. Augustine, FL 82
Charlestown Navy Yard, Boston, MA 189
Chicamauga and Chattanooga National Military Park, Chattanooga, TN 427
Chickamauga and Chattanooga National Military Park, Fort Oglethorpe, GA 89
Citadal Museum and Archives, Charleston, SC 415
Civil War Round Table Associates, Little Rock, AR 19
Coastal Heritage Society, Savannah, GA 92
Colonial Infantry Albuquerque, Albuquerque, NM 295
Commandant's House, Boston, MA 189
Company of Military Historians, Westbrook, CT 68
Confederate Air Force, Harlingen, TX 448
Confederate Memorial State Historic Site, Higginsville, MO 246
Coronado Historical Association, Inc., Coronado, CA 26
Costa Mesa Historical Society, Costa Mesa, CA 26
Council on America's Military Past, Fort Myer, VA 473
Custer Battlefield Historical and Museum Association, Crow Agency, MT 257
Custer Battlefield National Monument, Crow Agency, MT 257
Don F. Pratt Memorial Museum, Fort Campbell, KY 154
Dorchester Heights Monument, Boston, MA 189
First Cavalry Division Museum, Fort Hood, TX 445
First Hussars Regimental Association—Citizen Soldiers Museum, London, Ontario 545
Fort Abraham Lincoln State Park, Mandan, ND 353
Fort Beausejour National Historic Park, Aulac, New Brunswick 527
Fort Bliss Replica Museum, Fort Bliss, TX 445
Fort Carson Museum, Colorado Springs, CO 50
Fort Davis National Historic Site, Fort Davis, TX 445
Fort Dodge Historical Foundation—Fort Museum, Fort Dodge, IA 136
Fort Douglas Military Museum, Fort Douglas, UT 462
Fort Fisher State Historic Site, Kure Beach, NC 346
Fort Frederica National Monument, St. Simons Island, GA 92
Fort George G. Meade Museum, Fort Meade, MD 183
Fort Gibson Military Park, Fort Gibson, OK 377
Fort Gordon Museum, U.S. Army Signal Center, Fort Gordon, GA 88
Fort Hamilton Historical Society, Brooklyn, NY 305
Fort Hartsuff State Historical Park, Burwell, NE 261
Fort Jackson Museum, Fort Jackson, SC 418
Fort Knox, Prospect, ME 175
Fort Lancaster State Historic Site, Sheffield, TX 457
Fort Laramie Historical Association—Fort Laramie National Historic Site, Fort Laramie, WY 507

Fort Laramie National Historic Site, Fort Laramie, WY 507
Fort Larned National Historic Site, Larned, KS 147
Fort Leavenworth Historical Society, Fort Leavenworth, KS 145
Fort Leavenworth Museum, Fort Leavenworth, KS 145
Fort Leonard Wood Museum, Fort Leonard Wood, MO 245
Fort Ligonier Memorial Foundation, Ligonier, PA 397
Fort Malden National Historic Park, Amherstburg, Ontario 539
Fort McHenry National Monument and Historic Shrine, Baltimore, MD 180
Fort McKavett State Historic Site, Fort McKavett, TX 445
Fort Meigs State Memorial, Perrysburg, OH 370
Fort Morgan Museum, Gulf Shores, AL 5
Fort Ontario State Historic Site, Oswego, NY 327
Fort Osage Historic Site and Museum, Sibley, MO 255
Fort Pike State Commemorative Area, New Orleans, LA 166
Fort Point and Army Museum Association, San Francisco, CA 40
Fort Point National Historic Site, San Francisco, CA 40
Fort Polk Military Museum, Fort Polk, LA 164
Fort Pulaski National Monument, Tybee Island, GA 94
Fort Raleigh National Historic Site, Manteo, NC 346
Fort Roberdeau, Hollidaysburg, PA 395
Fort Sam Houston Museum, San Antonio, TX 455
Fort Selden State Monument, Radium Springs, NM 298
Fort Sheridan Museum, Fort Sheridan, IL 107
Fort Sherman Museum, Coeur d'Alene, ID 97
Fort Smith National Historic Site, Fort Smith, AR 18
Fort Stephenson Museum, Fremont, OH 364
Fort Stewart Museum, 24th Infantry Division, Fort Stewart, GA 89
Fort Sumter National Monument, Sullivan's Island, SC 421
Fort Towson Historic Site, Fort Towson, OK 377
Fort Union National Monument, Watrous, NM 300
Fort Verde State Historical Park, Camp Verde, AZ 11
Fort Ward Museum and Park, Alexandria, VA 470
Fort Washita, Durant, OK 377
Forty-fifth Infantry Division Museum, Oklahoma City, OK 379
Friends of Old Fort Stevens, Hammond, OR 383
Friends of the Fort Lewis Military Museum—Fort Lewis Military Museum, Fort Lewis, WA 484
Frontier Historical Park, Hays, KS 146
G.A.R. Memorial Hall Museum, Madison, WI 499
General D. L. McBride Museum, Roswell, NM 298
Gettysburg National Military Park, Gettysburg, PA 393
Governor General's Foot Guard Museum, Ottawa, Ontario 548
Guilford Courthouse National Military Park, Greensboro, NC 345
Halifax Citadel National Historic Park, Halifax, Nova Scotia 535
Hampton Roads Naval Museum, Norfolk, VA 477
Historic Florida Militia, St. Augustine, FL 82
Historic Fort Wayne, Detroit, MI 213
Historic Fort York, Toronto, Ontario 552
Historical Collection, Saskatchewan Militia District Headquarters, Regina, Saskatchewan 566
Historical Division, Chief of Engineers, Department of the Army, Fort Belvoir, VA 473
Historical Office, Washington National Guard, Tacoma, WA 490
Historical Society of the Fort Hill Country, Mundelein, IL 112
History and Traditions Museum, San Antonio, TX 456
Homeville Museum, Homer, NY 315
Horseshoe Bend National Military Park, Dadeville, AL 3
Hubbardton Battlefield, Hubbardton, VT 467

JFK Special Warfare Museum, Fort Bragg, NC 344
Johannes Schwalm Historical Association, Inc., Lyndhurst, OH 367
John M. Browning Memorial Museum, Rock Island, IL 115
Kennesaw Mountain National Battlefield Park, Marietta, GA 90
Kentucky Military History Museum, Frankfort, KY 155
L'Anguille Valley Historical Association, Logansport, IN 126
Liberty Bell Shrine of Allentown, Inc., Allentown, PA 387
Liberty Memorial Association and Museum, Kansas City, MO 248
Limestone County Historical Society, Athens, AL 1
Lone Jack Civil War Museum, Lone Jack, MO 250
Louisiana Historical Association Confederate Museum, New Orleans, LA 166
Manassas City Museum, Manassas, VA 476
Marine Corps Historical Foundation, Washington, DC 73
Minute Man National Historical Park, Concord, MA 193
Mississippi Military Museum, Jackson, MS 241
Moores Creek National Battlefield, Currie, NC 343
Museum of the Noncommissioned Officer, Fort Bliss, TX 445
Muskogee War Memorial Park, Muskogee, OK 378
National Archives, Washington, DC 73
Naval Aviation Museum, Pensacola, FL 82
Navy Memorial Museum, Washington, DC 75
Nineteenth Louisiana Volunteer Infantry, Baton Rouge, LA 164
Old Fort Henry, Kingston, Ontario 544
Old Fort Jackson, Savannah, GA 92
Old Fort Niagara Association, Inc., Youngstown, NY 340
Old Guard Museum, Fort Myer, VA 473
Order of the Indian Wars, Little Rock, AR 20
Oregon Military Museum, Clackamas, OR 382
Organization of Military Museums of Canada, Canadian War Museum, Ottawa, Ontario 549
P.T. Boats, Inc., Memphis, TN 432
Pacific Submarine Museum, Pearl Harbor, HI 96
Parc Historique National du Fort Chambly, Chambly, Quebec 556
Parris Island Museum, Beaufort, SC 413
Patriots Point Development Authority, Mt. Pleasant, SC 420
Patton Museum of Cavalry and Armor, Fort Knox, KY 154
Pennsylvania Military Museum, Boalsburg, PA 388
Perry's Victory and International Peace Memorial, Put-in-Bay, OH 371
Petersburg National Battlefield, Petersburg, VA 478
Portsmouth Naval Shipyard Museum, Portsmouth, VA 478
Presidio Army Museum, San Francisco, CA 41
Presidio La Bahia, Goliad, TX 447
Presidio Lancers, Albuquerque, NM 295
Princess Patricia's Canadian Light Infantry, Regimental Museum, Calgary, Alberta 511
RCMP (Royal Canadian Mounted Police), Regina, Saskatchewan 566
Richard Caswell Memorial/CSS Neuse, Kinston, NC 346
Richmond National Battlefield Park, Richmond, VA 479
Rock Island Arsenal Historical Society, Rock Island, IL 115
Royal Canadian Artillery Museum, Shilo, Manitoba 525
Sac Museum Memorial Society, Bellevue, NE 261
Sacket Harbor Battlefield State Historic Site, Sacket Harbor, NY 332
Saratoga National Historical Park, Stillwater, NY 335
Scipio Society of Naval and Military History, Inc., Oyster Bay, NY 327
Second Armored Division Museum, Fort Hood, TX 445

Second Rhode Island Regiment of the Continental Line, Pawtucket, RI 411

Second South Carolina Regiment, Columbia, SC 416

Shearwater Aviation Museum, Shearwater, Nova Scotia 537

Silent Wings Museum, Terrell, TX 458

Soldiers' Memorial Military Museum, St. Louis, MO 254

Sons of Confederate Veterans, Hattiesburg, MS 240

Sons of the American Revolution Museum, Louisville, KY 159

South Carolina Confederate Relic Room and Museum, Columbia,SC 417

Southwest Florida Historical Society, Inc., Fort Myers, FL 78

Springfield Armory National Historic Site, Springfield, MA 205

Submarine Memorial Association—USS Ling 297, Hackensack, NJ 282

Tennessee State Museum, Nashville, TN 434

Third Armored Cavalry Museum, Fort Bliss, TX 445

Toronto Historical Board, Toronto, Ontario 553

Treasure Island Museum, San Francisco, CA 41

U.S. Air Force Historical Research Center, Montgomery, AL 7

U.S. Air Force in Utah Historical Society, Ogden, UT 463

U.S. Air Force Museum, Wright-Patterson Air Force Base, OH 375

U.S. Army Air Defense Artillery Association, Fort Bliss, TX 445

U.S. Army Air Defense Artillery Museum, Fort Bliss, TX 445

U.S. Army Aviation Museum, Fort Rucker, AL 5

U.S. Army Center of Military History, Washington, DC 75

U.S. Army Chaplain Museum, Fort Monmouth, NJ 281

U.S. Army Chemical Corps Museum, Fort McClellan, AL 5

U.S. Army Engineer Museum, Fort Belvoir, VA 473

U.S. Army Field Artillery and Fort Sill Museum, Fort Sill, OK 377

U.S. Army Finance Corps Museum, Indianapolis, IN 125

U.S. Army Military History Institute, Carlisle Barracks, PA 389

U.S. Army Military Police Corps Museum, Fort McClellan, AL 5

U.S. Army Ordnance Museum, Aberdeen, MD 179

U.S. Army Quartermaster Museum, Fort Lee, VA 473

U.S. Cavalry Museum, Fort Riley, KS 145

U.S. Marine Corps Air-Ground Museum and Museums Branch Activities, Quantico, VA 478

U.S. Marine Corps Historical Center and Museum, Washington, DC 75

USS Arizona Memorial, Pearl Harbor, HI 96

USS Cassin Young, Boston, MA 191

USS North Carolina Battleship Memorial, Wilmington, NC 351

Vicksburg National Military Park, Vicksburg, MS 242

Victorian Military History Institute, Little Rock, AR 20

Virginia Military Institute Museum, Lexington, VA 476

War Library and Museum, Military Order of the Loyal Legion of the United States, Philadelphia, PA 403

War Memorial Museum of Virginia, Newport News, VA 477

Waterloo Memorial Day Museum, Waterloo, NY 338

Watervliet Arsenal Museum, Watervliet, NY 339

West Point Museum, West Point, NY 339

Wilson's Creek National Battlefield, Republic, MO 252

Wisconsin Veterans Museums, King, WI 498

Women's Army Corps Museum, Fort McClellan, AL 4

World War II Glider Pilots Association, Freehold, NJ 281

York-Sunbury Historical Society, Fredericton, New Brunswick 528

PIONEER

Alexander Young Log House, Washington, IA 141

Archives and Museum, Mississippi University for Women, Columbus, MS 239

Argonia and Western Somner County Historical Society and Museum, Argonia, KS 143

Arizona Historical Society, Tucson, AZ 15

Arlington Historical Society, Arlington, TX 437

Aztec Museum Association, Aztec, NM 296

Backus Conservation Area and Historical Complex, Port Rowan, Ontario 550

Bancroft Historical Museum, Bancroft, Ontario 539

Bandar Log, Inc., Magdalena, NM 298

Barbed Wire Museum, LaCrosse, KS 147

Barr Colony Museum, Lloydminster, Saskatchewan 565

Beltrami County Historical Society, Bemidji, MN 226

Bergquist Pioneer Cabin Society, Moorhead, MN 233

Birmingham-Jefferson Historical Association, Birmingham, AL 2

Bitter Root Valley Historical Society, Hamilton, MT 258

Black Creek Pioneer Village, North York, Ontario 547

Black Diamond Historical Society, Black Diamond, WA 483

Blaine County Historical Society, Brewster, NE 261

Blaine County Historical Society, Chinook, MT 257

Bleckley County Historical Society, Cochran, GA 87

Bosque Memorial Museum, Clifton, TX 441

Bowden Historical Society—Bowden Pioneer Museum, Bowden, Alberta 510

Brandon Museum, Brandon, Manitoba 523

Bremer County Historical Society, Waverly, IA 142

Broadview Historical and Museum Association, Inc., Broadview, Saskatchewan 563

Brown County Territorial Pioneers, Aberdeen, SD 422

Bruce Mines Museum, Bruce Mines, Ontario 540

Bulkley Valley Museum, Smithers, British Columbia 521

Cache Valley Historical Society, Logan, UT 462

Cactus Park and Museum, George West, TX 447

Camrose and District Museum Society, Camrose, Alberta 511

Capitol Reef National Park Museum, Torrey, UT 464

Carroll Reece Museum, Johnson City, TN 430

Cass County Historical Society—Bonanzaville, USA, West Fargo, ND 354

Center for Western Studies, Sioux Falls, SD 426

Century Village Museum, Lang, Ontario 545

Champoeg State Park—Friends of Champoeg, St. Paul, OR 386

Charles Mix County Historical Restoration Society, Geddes, SD 423

Charles Towne Landing — 1670, Charleston, SC 414

Cherokee County Historical Museum, Murphy, NC 347

Cherokee Heritage and Museum Association, Cherokee, CA 25

Chilliwack Museum and Historical Society, Chilliwack, British Columbia 517

Chiricahua National Monument, Willcox, AZ 16

Chisago County Historical Society, Center City, MN 227

Chisholm Trail Museum Corporation, Wellington, KS 152

Christian County Historical Society, Taylorville, IL 117

Churchill County Museum Association—Churchill County Museum and Archives, Fallon, NV 268

Clark County Historical Society, Clark, SD 423

Clark County Historical Society, Kahoka, MO 247

Clayton McLain Memorial Museum, Cut Knife, Saskatchewan 564

Cole County Historical Society, Jefferson City, MO 247

Colonel William Jones House, Gentryville, IN 123

Comanche County Historical and Museum, Comanche, TX 441

Conrad Mansion Historic Site Museum—Conrad Mansion Directors, Inc., Kalispell, MT 258

Craighead County Historical Society, Jonesboro, AR 19
Crosby County Pioneer Memorial Museum, Crosbyton, TX 442
Dakota Territorial Museum, Yankton, SD 427
Dallas County Heritage Society, Inc., Dallas, TX 442
Daniel Boone Home, Defiance, MO 245
Daughters of Utah Pioneers Relic Hall, Montpelier, ID 98
DeBolt and District Pioneer Museum Society, DeBolt, Alberta 512
Delta County Historical Society, Delta, CO 51
Depot Park Museum, Sonoma, CA 45
Deschutes County Historical Society, Bend, OR 382
Dewey Schoolhouse, Stockbridge, MI 224
Doak Historic Park, Doaktown, New Brunswick 528
Dodsland Museum, Dodsland, Saskatchewan 564
Doon Pioneer Village, Kitchener, Ontario 544
Early American Museum and Gardens, Mahomet, IL 110
East Point Historical Society, Inc., East Point, GA 88
Eastern Arizona Museum and Historical Society, Pima, AZ 14
Eastern Cabarrus Historical Society Museum, Mt. Pleasant, NC 347
Edwin Wolters Museum, Shiner, TX 457
Elgin County Pioneer Museum, St. Thomas, Ontario 551
Essex County Historical County, Elizabethtown, NY 310
Fanshawe Pioneer Village, London, Ontario 545
Florence Pioneer Museum and Historical Society, Florence, CO 54
Forest-Lambton Museum, Forest, Ontario 542
Fort Croghan Museum—Burnet County Heritage Society, Burnet, TX 440
Fort Erie Historical Museum, Ridgeway, Ontario 550
Fort Nashborough, Nashville, TN 433
Fort Nisqually Museum, Tacoma, WA 489
Four Mile Historic Park, Denver, CO 52
Frankfort Area Historical Society and Museum, West Frankfort, Il. 119
Freestone County Historical Museum, Fairfield, TX 444
Friends of the Adobes, Inc., San Miguel, CA 43
Frontier Historical Society and Museum, Glendwood Springs, CO 54
Frontier Museum, Williston, ND 354
Frontier Times Museum, Bandera, TX 438
Genesee County Historical and Museum Society, Flint, MI 215
Geographical Center Historical Society, Rugby, ND 354
Gimli Historical Museum, Gimli, Manitoba 524
Glenbow Museum, Glenbow-Alberta Institute, Calgary, Alberta 511
Glengarry Museum, Dunvegan, Ontario 542
Goingsnake District Heritage Association, Westville, OK 381
Golden District Historical Society, Golden, British Columbia 518
Golden Spike National Historic Site, Brigham City, UT 461
Gowrie Historical Society, Gowrie, IA 136
Grand Valley Cap "M" Baller's Muzzleloading Gun Club, Wyoming, MI 225
Granite Falls Historical Society, Granite Falls, WA 484
Grove National Historic Landmark, Glenview, IL 108
Gulf Branch Nature Center, Arlington, VA 471
Guthrie County Historical Society, Guthrie Center, IA 137
Harold Warp Pioneer Village Foundation, Minden, NE 264
High Plains Historical Foundation, Inc., Clovis, NM 296
High Plains Historical Society, McCook, NE 264
Historical Society Museum, Valparaiso, FL 84
Historical Society of Cheboygan County, Inc., Cheboygan, MI 212

Historical Village and Pioneer Museum at Shandro, Willingdon, Alberta 517
Homestead Museum, Biggar, Saskatchewan 563
Homestead National Monument, Beatrice, NE 261
Hope Museum, Hope, British Columbia 519
Hopkins County Museum and Heritage Park, Sulphur Springs, TX 458
Huron County Pioneer Museum, Goderich, Ontario 542
Huronia Museum, Midland, Ontario 546
Illinois Pioneer Heritage Center, Inc., Monticello, IL 111
Ingleside Historical Society, Ingleside, TX 450
Innisfail and District Historical Society, Innisfail, Alberta 515
Iowa Postal History Society, Cedar Rapids, IA 133
Iron Bridge Historical Museum, Iron Bridge, Ontario 544
Island County Historical Society, Coupeville, WA 483
Jamieson Museum, Moosomin, Saskatchewan 565
Jefferson County Historical Society, Oskaloosa, KS 150
John Walter Historic Site, Edmonton, Alberta 513
Jollyville-Pond Springs Historical Association, Austin, TX 438
Joplin Historical Society, Joplin, MO 247
Jurnpa Mountains Cultural Center, Riverside, CA 38
Kamloops Museum Association, Kamloops, British Columbia 519
Kansas City Museum, Kansas City, MO 248
Klein Foundation Inc., Mobridge, SD 425
Kluane Museum of Natural History, Burwash Landing, Yukon 568
Lac Ste. Anne and District Pioneer Museum, Sangudo, Alberta 516
Lake County Historical Society, Lakeport, CA 30
Lakewood Historical Society, Lakewood, CO 55
Lambton Heritage Museum, Grand Bend, Ontario 543
Lamesa-Dawson County Museum, Lamesa, TX 451
Lanier Museum of Natural History, Buford, GA 87
Laura Ingalls Wilder Memorial Society, Inc., De Smet, SD 423
Laura Ingalls Wilder Park and Museum, Burr Oak, IA 132
Lawrence County Regional Historical Society, Martha, KY 160
Layland Museum, Cleburne, TX 441
Lee County Historical Society, Loachapoka, AL 6
Lincoln Log Cabin State Historic Site, Lerna, IL 109
Linn County Historical Society, Halsey, OR 383
Living Heritage Society, Van Buren, ME 177
Long Grove Historical Society, Long Grove, IL 110
Lyons Historical Society, Lyons, CO 56
MacBride Centennial Museum, Whitehorse, Yukon 568
Madison County History Association, Sheridan, MT 259
Madonna House Pioneer Museum, Combermere, Ontario 541
Marcus Whitman Historical Society, Gorham, NY 313
Marshall County Historical Society, Warren, MN 238
Marshall Gold Discovery State Historic Park, Coloma, CA 25
Martin County Historical Society, Inc., Fairmont, MN 229
McCord Museum, McCord, Saskatchewan 565
McKenzie County Museum and Historical Society, Inc., Watford City, ND 354
Mellette County Historical Society, White River, SD 427
Mineral County Museum and Historical Society, Superior, MT 260
Miniota Municipal Museum, Inc., Miniota, Manitoba 524
Minnesota Pioneer Park, Annandale, MN 225
Mission Valley Heritage—Garden of the Rockies Museum, Ronan, MT 259
Monterey County Agricultural and Rural Life Museum, Salinas, CA 39
Moody Museum, Taylor, TX 458
Musée de Marguerite Bourgeoys, Montreal, Quebec 560

Museum Association of the American Frontier, Chadron, NE 262

Museum Lepanto U.S.A., Lepanto, AR 19

Museum of the Rockies, Bozeman, MT 256

Muskoka Pioneer Village and Museum, Huntsville, Ontario 543

National Cowgirl Hall of Fame, Hereford, TX 449

Nauvoo Restoration, Inc., Nauvoo, IL 112

New Berlin Historical Society, New Berlin, WI 501

Newkirk Historical Society, Newkirk, OK 378

Nez Perce County Historical Society, Inc., Lewiston, ID 98

Nicolas Denys Museum, St. Peter's, Nova Scotia 537

Nodaway County Historical Society, Maryville, MO 250

North Dakota Historical Society, Inc., Coleharbor, ND 352

North Himsworth Museum, Callander, Ontario 541

Northeast Historical Society, Hurst, TX 450

Northeastern Nevada Museum, Elko, NV 268

Northern Illinois Historical Society, Grayslake, IL 108

Oak Creek Historical Society, Oak Creek, WI 502

Oakland Museum Historical Society, Oakland, OR 384

Octorara Valley Historical Society, Parkesburg, PA 400

Ojai Valley Historical Society and Museum, Ojai, CA 34

Okanogan County Historical Society, Okanogan, WA 485

Old Castle Museum Complex, Baldwin City, KS 143

Old Homestead Museum, Herbert, Saskatchewan 564

Old Post Office Museum—Collin County Historical Society, Inc., Frisco, TX 447

Old Rock House, Santa Anna, TX 457

Old Trail Driver's Association and Museum, San Antonio, TX 456

Old West Museum, Chamberlain, SD 423

Orange County Historical Society, Inc. and Museum, Orlando, FL 81

Owyhee County Historical Society and Museum, Murphy, ID 98

Ozark Folk Center, Mt. View, AR 20

Pacific University Museum, Old College Hall, Forest Grove, OR 383

Parkdale-Maplewood Community Museum, Barss Corner, Nova Scotia 533

Pawnee County Historical Society, Pawnee, OK 379

Peace River Valley Historical Society, Inc., Arcadia, FL 76

Peterborough Centennial Museum and Archives, Peterborough, Ontario 549

Peterborough Historical Society—Hutchison House Museum, Peterborough, Ontario 549

Pike Pioneer Museum, Troy, AL 8

Pimeria Alta Historical Society, Nogales, AZ 13

Pincher Creek and District Historical Society—Pincher Creek Museum and Kootenzi Brown Historical Village, Pincher Creek, Alberta 515

Pioneer Auto Museum and Antique Town, Murdo, SD 425

Pioneer Farm and House Museum, Oxford, OH 370

Pioneer Farm and Village, Roseau, MN 235

Pioneer Hall and Museum, San Antonio, TX 456

Pioneer Home Museum of Virden and District, Virden, Manitoba 525

Pioneer Museum and Historical Society of North Iowa, Mason City, IA 139

Pioneer Village, Farmington, UT 462

Pioneer Woman Museum, Ponca City, OK 379

Pioneers' Museum, Colorado Springs, CO 51

Plainsman Museum, Aurora, NE 261

olk County Chapter, East Tennessee Historical Society, Cleveland, TN 428

Polk County Heritage Society, Livingston, TX 451

Polk County Historical Society, Crookston, MN 227

Pony Express Museum, Marysville, KS 148

Pope County Historical Foundation, Russellville, AR 21

Port Carling Pioneer Museum, Pt. Carling, Ontario 550

Prairie Homestead, Philip, SD 425

Prairie Memories Museum, Irvine, Alberta 515

Princeton and District Pioneer Museum, Princeton, British Columbia 520

Queen's Bush Foundation, Holland Centre, Ontario 543

Rainy River District Women's Institute Museum, Emo, Ontario 542

Raymore Pioneer Museum, Raymore, Saskatchewan 566

Reina del Mar Parlor 126, Native Daughters of the Golden West, Santa Barbara, CA 43

Reston and District Historical Museum, Reston, Manitoba 524

Rhoades Valley Camp, Daughters of Utah Pioneers, Kamas, UT 462

Richey Historical Society, Richey, MT 259

Rock Creek Station State Historical Park, Fairbury, NE 262

Rocky Lane School Museum, Ft. Vermilion, Alberta 514

Roselle Historical Society, Roselle, IL 115

Russell County Historical Society, Russell, KS 150

Saint Angela's Museum and Archives, Prelate, Saskatchewan 565

Saint Catharines Historical Museum, St. Catharine's, Ontario 550

Saint Helens Branch, Columbia County Historical Society, St. Helens, OR 386

Saint Vrain Historical Society, Longmont, CO 56

Saint Walburg and District Historical Museum, Inc., St. Walburg, Saskatchewan 566

Salvation Army Western Territorial Museum, Rancho Palos Verdes, CA 36

San Antonio Missions National Historical Park, San Antonio, TX 456

Santa Fe Springs Historical Committee, Sante Fe Springs, CA 44

Santa Fe Trail Center, Larned, KS 148

Santa Ynez Valley Historical Society and Museum, Santa Ynez, CA 45

Saratoga Museum Center, Saratoga, WY 508

Sarpy County Historical Museum, Bellevue, NE 261

Sauder Farm and Craft Village, Archbold, OH 355

Sauk County Historical Society, Baraboo, WI 495

Schiele Museum of Natural History—Living History Farm and Catawba Indian Village, Gastonia, NC 344

Scotland Historical Society, Scotland, SD 425

Scotts Bluff National Monument, Gering, NE 263

Sequim-Dungeness Museum, Sequim, WA 489

Seward County Historical Society, Inc., Liberal, KS 148

Sharlot Hall Historical Society—Prescott Historical Society, Prescott, AZ 14

Sheboygan County Historical Society, Sheboygan, WI 503

Simi Valley Historical Society, Simi Valley, CA 45

Siskiyou County Historical Society, Yreka, CA 49

Société d'histoire d'Amos, Amos, Quebec 556

Society of Boonesborough, Richmond, KY 162

Society of Indiana Pioneers, Indianapolis, IN 125

Sod Buster Museum, Stanford, MT 260

South Box Elder Daughters of Utah Pioneers, Brigham City, UT 461

Southwest Virginia Museum Historical State Park, Big Stone Gap, VA 471

Southwestern Ontario Heritage Village, Essex, Ontario 542

Stafford County Historical and Genealogical Society, Stafford, KS 151

Star Mound School Museum, Snowflake, Manitoba 525

State Association of Texas Pioneers, San Antonio, TX 456

Stationmasters' House Museum, Spearman, TX 457

Steele County Historical Society, Hope, ND 353
Steilacoom Historical Museum Association, Steilacoom, WA 489
Stewart M. Lord Memorial Historical Society, Burlington, ME 170
Stone's Trace Historical Society, Ligonier, IN 126
Stormont, Dundas and Glengarry Historical Society, Cornwall, Ontario 541
Stuhr Museum of the Prairie Pioneer, Grand Island, NE 263
Sturgeon River House Museum, Sturgeon Falls, Ontario 551
Superstition Mountain Historical Society, Apache Junction, AZ 11
Surrey Museum, Surrey, British Columbia 521
Swan River Valley Historical Society and Museum, Swan River, Manitoba 525
Swedish American Museum Association of Chicago, Chicago, IL 569
Taos County Historical Society, Taos, NM 300
Taylors Falls Chapter, Chicago County Historical Society, Taylors Falls, MN 237
Teton County Historical Research Center, Jackson, WY 508
Three Island Crossing State Park, Glenns Ferry, ID 97
Toa Mo Ga Memorial Museum, Plains, TX 454
Tonganoxie Community Historical Society, Tonganoxie, KS 151
Top of Oklahoma Historical Society—Cherokee Outlet Museum, Blackwell, OK 376
Trading Post Historical Museum, Trading Post, KS 152
Trent River Pioneer Museum, Havelock, Ontario 543
Tularosa Basin Historical Society, Alamogordo, NM 294
Upsala Area Historical Society, Upsala, MN 237
Utah State Historical Society, Salt Lake City, UT 464
Utica Historical and Museum Society, Utica, MT 260
Valdez Heritage Center, Valdez, AK 11
Valley Mills History Museum, Valley Mills, TX 459
Verendrye Museum, Fort Pierre, SD 423
Victoria County Library Museum and Archives, Baddeck, Nova Scotia 533
Victoria Settlement Provincial Historic Site, Smoky Lake, Alberta 516
Village des pionniers acadiens, Mont Carmel, Prince Edward Island 555
Vincennes Historical and Antiquarian Society—Lewis Historical Collections Library, Vincennes, IN 130
Wallowa County Museum, Joseph, OR 384
Washington Commission for the Humanities, Olympia, WA 485
Washington County Historical Association, Ft. Calhoun, NE 262
Washington County Historical Library and Museum, West Bend, WI 505
Washington County Historical Society, Washington, KS 152
Watters Smith Memorial State Park and Museum, Lost Creek, WV 493
Webster Museum and Historical Society, Webster, NY 339
Whitchurch Stouffville Museum, Vandorf, Ontario 554
Whiteface Historical Society, Whiteface, TX 460
Wilson County Historical Society, Fredonia, KS 146
Wyoming Pioneer Memorial Museum, Douglas, WY 507
York Pioneer and Historical Society, Toronto, Ontario 554
Z. I. Hale Museum, Winters, TX 460

PRESERVATION, RESTORATION

APMAQ (Quebec Old House Association), Saint-Eustache, Quebec 561
APTA (Association for Preservation of Tennessee Antiquities), Nashville, TN 432
Abbeville Historic Preservation Commission, Abbeville, SC 413
Aberdeen Appearance and Preservation Commission, Aberdeen, MD 178
Abigail Adams Smith Museum, New York, NY 322
Abington Historical Commission, Abington, MA 187
Acworth Silsby Library, Acworth, NH 269
Adair County Historical Society, Greenfield, IA 136
Adena State Memorial, Chillicothe, OH 358
Affton Historical Society, St. Louis, MO 253
Alabama Historical Commission, Montgomery, AL 6
Alabama Pilgrimage Council, Montgomery, AL 6
Alaska Association for Historic Preservation, Anchorage, AK 8
Alaska Historical Society, Anchorage, AK 9
Albert City Historical Association, inc., Albert City, IA 131
Alberta Historical Resources Foundation, Calgary, Alberta 510
Albuquerque Conservation Association, Albuquerque, NM 294
Alden Historical Society, Alden, NY 302
Aliceville Historical Preservation, Inc., Aliceville, AL 1
Allentown-Upper Freehold Historical Society, Allentown, NJ 277
Alley Pond Environmental Center, New York, NY 322
Alma Fire Department Museum, Alma, CO 49
Amador-Livermore Valley Historical Society, Pleasanton, CA 36
American Institute for Conservation of Historic and Artistic Works, Washington, DC 71
Amherstburg Historic Sites Association, Amherstburg, Ontario 539
Anderson Heritage Inc., Anderson, SC 413
Andes Society for History and Culture, Andes, NY 302
Androscoggin Historical Society, Auburn, ME 169
Ann Arbor Historic District Commission, Ann Arbor, MI 210
Antiquarian and Landmarks Society, Inc., Hartford, CT 61
Arbor Lodge State Historical Park, Nebraska City, NE 265
Arch, Inc., Ft. Wayne, IN 123
Architectural Conservancy of Greenwich, Greenwich, CT 60
Arkansas Territorial Restoration, Little Rock, AR 19
Army Museum, Halifax South, Nova Scotia 535
Artifacts Center, Edmonton, Alberta 512
Asotin County Historical Society, Asotin, WA 482
Association for Gravestone Studies, Needham, MA 199
Association for the Preservation of Historic Natchitoches, Natchitoches, LA 165
Association for the Preservation of Virginia Antiquities, Richmond, VA 479
Athenaeum of Philadelphia, Philadelphia, PA 400
Athens-Clarke Heritage Foundation, Athens, GA 85
Atlanta Preservation Center, Atlanta, GA 85
Atlantic Highlands Historical Society, Atlantic Highlands, NJ 277
Audubon State Commemorative Area—Oakley Plantation, St. Francisville, LA 167
Avon Valley Historical Society, Stratford, Ontario 551
Aylmer Heritage Association—Association du Patrimoine d'Aylmer, Aylmer, Quebec 556
Bad Axe Historical Society, Bad Axe, MI 211

Baldwin County Historic Development Commission, Montrose, AL 7

Baldwin County Historical Society, Stockton, AL 8

Bale Grist Mill State Historic Park, Calistoga, CA 24

Barlow House, Canby, OR 382

Bassett Hall, Williamsburg, VA 481

Bath Historic Committee, Bath, NY 303

Battleground Historical Society, Freehold, NJ 281

Bayou Bend Collection, Museum of Fine Arts, Houston, TX 449

Beaufort Historical Association, Beaufort, NC 341

Beaumont Heritage Society, Beaumont, TX 439

Beauregard-Keyes House, New Orleans, LA 166

Becket Historical Commission, Becket, MA 569

Beiger Heritage Corporation, Mishawaka, IN 127

Belknap Mill Society, Laconia, NH 273

Belle Meade Mansion, Nashville, TN 432

Bergen County Office of Cultural and Historic Affairs, Hackensack, NJ 282

Bethel German Communal Colony, Inc., Bethel, MO 243

Bethune Memorial House, Gravenhurst, Ontario 543

Betty D. Easton Historical Costume Collection, Department of Human Environment, Lexington, KY 157

Bicentennial Restoration Committee for South River Meeting House, Lynchburg, VA 476

Big Sioux River Valley Historical Society, Hawarden, IA 137

Blandwood Mansion, Greensboro, NC 345

Blissfield Historical Society—Victorsville School House, Blissfield, MI 211

Blithewold Gardens and Arboretum, Bristol, RI 409

Blount County Historic Trust, Inc., Maryville, TN 431

Blue Grass Trust for Historic Preservation, Lexington, KY 157

Blumenfeld and District Heritage Site, Prelate Province, Saskatchewan 565

Boneyfiddle Association, Portsmouth, OH 371

Boothe Memorial Park Museum, Stratford, CT 67

Boston Art Commission, Boston, MA 188

Boston College, Newton, MA 200

Boston Landmarks Commission, Boston, MA 189

Bottineau Historical Society, Bottineau, ND 352

Bowen-Campbell House Association, Inc., Goodlettsville, TN 429

Boyds-Clarksburg-Germantown Historical Society, Inc., Boyds, MD 181

Boylston Historical Society, Inc., Boylston, MA 191

Braddock's Field Historical Society, Inc., Braddock, PA 389

Bradford County Historical Board of Trustees, Starke, FL 83

Braintree Historical Society, Inc., Braintree, VT 464

Brandywine Conservancy, Chadds Ford, PA 390

Brewer Historical Society, Brewer, ME 170

Brick House, Poughkeepsie, NY 329

Brookline Historical Commission, Brookline, MA 191

Brooklyn Historic Railway Association, Brooklyn, NY 305

Brown County Historical Society, Green Bay, WI 497

Brownville Historical Society, Brownville, NE 261

Brunnier Gallery—Farm House Museum, Ames, IA 131

Buccleuch Mansion Museum, New Brunswick, NJ 287

Buena Vista County Historical Society, Storm Lake, IA 141

Bureau County Historical Society, Princeton, IL 114

Bureau of Historic Preservation, Tallahassee, FL 83

Burtner House Restoration, Inc., Natrona Heights, PA 399

Butler County Historical Society, David City, NE 262

Cahokia Courthouse State Historic Site, Cahokia, IL 101

Califon Historical Society, Califon, NJ 278

California Heritage Council, California Trust for Historic Preservation, San Francisco, CA 40

California State Capitol Museum, Sacramento, CA 38

California State Department of Parks and Recreation, Sacramento, CA 38

Cambridge Historical Commission, Cambridge, MA 192

Camden Historical Commission, Camden, SC 414

Campbell Center for Historic Preservation Studies, Mount Carroll, IL 111

Campbell House Museum, St. Louis, MO 253

Camron Stanford House Preservation Association, Oakland, CA 34

Canadian Historical Collection, Art Gallery of Ontario and The Grange, Toronto, Ontario 552

Canadian Rivers Historical Society, Geary, OK 377

Canton Palace Theatre Association, Canton, OH 357

Canton Preservation Society, Canton, OH 357

Capitol Restoration and Promotion, State Building Division, Nebraska State Capitol, Lincoln, NE 264

Cardinal Spellman Philatelic Museum, Weston, MA 208

Carnton Association, Inc., Franklin, TN 429

Carnton Mansion, Franklin, TN 429

Carroll County Historical Society, Mount Carroll 112

Carroll Society for the Preservation of Antiques, Carrollton, MS 239

Cary Cottage, Cincinnati, OH 358

Castle Air Museum, Atwater, CA 23

Castle Hill National Historic Park, Jerseyside, Newfoundland 532

Castle Museum, Juliaetta, ID 97

Catawba County Historical Association, Inc., Newton Grove, NC 347

Catskill Regional Folklife Program, Arkville, NY 302

Center City Historical Society, Center City, MN 227

Center for Historic Preservation, Fredericksburg, VA 473

Center for Historic Preservation, Murfreesboro, TN 432

Center for History of Louisiana Education, Natchitoches, LA 165

Central City Opera House Association, Central City, CO 50

Chadds Ford Historical Society, Chadds Ford, PA 390

Champlain Trail Museum, Pembroke, Ontario 549

Chariton County Historical Society, Salisbury, MO 254

Chaves County Historical Society, Roswell, NM 298

Chelsea Historical Society, Inc., Chelsea, VT 466

Chemung Valley Old Timers Association, Inc., Horseheads, NY 315

Cherokee Strip Museum of Alva, Alva, OK 375

Chester Historical Society, Chester, NJ 279

Chesterfield County Historic Preservation Commission, Cheraw, SC 416

Cheyenne County Historical Association, Sidney, NE 266

Chief Wapello's Memorial Park, Agency, IA 131

Chimney Point Tavern, Addison, VT 464

Cincinnatus Area Heritage Society, Cincinnatus, NY 308

Citizens' Committee for Historic Preservation, Las Vegas, NM 297

City Lights, Inc., New Orleans, LA 166

City of Burlington Historical Society, Burlington, NJ 278

City of San Buenaventura, Ventura, CA 47

Clark Historical Society, Clark, NJ 279

Clarke County Historical Society, Osceola, IA 140

Clay County Division of Historic Sites, Kearney, MO 249

Clayton County Heritage Association, Morrow, GA 91

Clayton Historical Preservation Authority, Clayton, AL 3

Clear Creek Canyon Historical Society of Chaffee County, Inc., Granite, CO 55

Clear Spring District Historical Association, Clear Spring, MD 182

Clermont State Historic Park, Germantown, NY 313

Cleveland Landmarks Commission, Cleveland, OH 359

Clinton County Historical Society and Museum, Plattsburg, MO 252

Cloud County Historical Museum, Concordia, KS 144
Coastal APDC Advisory Council on Historic Preservation, Brunswick, GA 86
Coffey County Historical Society—County Museum, Burlington, KS 143
Colbert County Historical Landmarks Foundation, Inc., Tuscumbia, AL 8
Colchester Historical Society, Colchester, CT 58
Colonial National Historical Park: Jamestown Island and Yorktown Battlefield, Yorktown, VA 482
Colonial Philadelphia Historical Society, Philadelphia, PA 401
Colonial Williamsburg Foundation, Williamsburg, VA 481
Columbia State Historic Park, Columbia, CA 25
Columbus Landmarks Foundation, Columbus, OH 361
Comanche Crossing Historical Society, Strasburg, CO 57
Comité des Archives de la Louisiane, Baton Rouge, LA 163
Commission des Avoyelles, Inc., Hamburg, LA 164
Commission for Historical and Architectural Preservation, Baltimore, MD 180
Commission on Chicago Historical and Architectural Landmarks, Chicago, IL 103
Community Historical Society, Alden, MN 225
Confederation of South Carolina Local Historical Societies, Columbia, SC 416
Connecticut Historical Commission, Hartford, CT 61
Connecticut Trust for Historic Preservation, New Haven, CT 63
Conservation Center for Art and Historic Artifacts, Philadelphia, PA 401
Constable Hall Association, Constableville, NY 308
Constitution Island Association, West Point, NY 339
Cookeville Committee to Preserve the Depot, Cookeville, TN 428
Coral Gables Historic Preservation Division, Coral Gables, FL 77
Corning Museum of Glass, Corning, NY 309
Corning-Painted Post Historical Society, Corning, NY 309
Crescent Bend: The Armstrong-Lockett House and Gardens, Knoxville, TN 430
Cross Plains—Berry Historical Society, Cross Plains, WI 495
Cultural Heritage Foundation of Southern California, Inc., Los Angeles, CA 31
Cupertino Historical Society, Cupertino, CA 26
D.C. Preservation League, Washington, DC 72
Dade Heritage Trust, Inc., Miami, FL 80
Dallas County Historical Commission, Dallas, TX 442
Darien Historical Society, Darien, IL 105
Dartmouth Museum Society, Dartmouth, Nova Scotia 534
Death Valley National Monument, Death Valley, CA 26
Deering Historical Society, Hillsboro, NH 272
Delaware County Historical Society, Muncie, IN 127
Dells Country Historical Society, Wisconsin Dells, WI 506
Delray Beach Historical Society, Delray Beach, FL 77
Denver Art Museum, Denver, CO 51
Department of Arkansas Natural and Cultural Heritage, Little Rock, AR 19
Department of Fish, Wildlife, and Parks, Helena, MT 258
Des Plaines Historical Society, Des Plaines, IL 106
Destrehan Plantation, Destrehan, LA 164
Detroit Historical Society, Detroit, MI 213
Dinosaur Provincial Park, Patricia, Alberta 515
Diocese of Fredericton Archives, Fredericton, New Brunswick 528
Division of Historic Preservation, Baton Rouge, LA 163
Division of Historic Properties, Doylestown, PA 391

Division of Historic Sites, Illinois Department of Conservation, Springfield, IL 116
Douglas County Historical Society—General Crook House, Omaha, NE 265
Downingtown Historical Society, Downingtown, PA 391
Drayton Hall, Charleston, SC 415
Drummond Island Historical Society, Drummond Island, MI 214
Dublin Historical Society, Inc., Dublin, OH 363
Dumbarton House, Washington, DC 73
Dunedin Historical Society, Inc., Dunedin, FL 77
ECHO (Essex Community Heritage Organization, Inc.), Essex, NY 311
Earle-Harrison House, Waco, TX 459
East Bridgewater Historical Commission, East Bridgewater, MA 194
East Feliciana Historical Preservation Society, Inc., Clinton, LA 164
East Feliciana Pilgrimage and Garden Club, Clinton, LA 164
East Hants Historical Society, Maitland, Nova Scotia 536
East Jersey Olde Towne, Inc., Piscataway, NJ 289
East Machias Historical Society, East Machias, ME 171
Eau Claire Landmarks Commission, Eau Claire, WI 496
Eden Historic Properties Commission, Eden, NC 343
Edenton Historical Commission, Edenton, NC 344
Edina Heritage Preservation Board, Edina, MN 228
Edward Hopper Landmark Preservation Foundation—Hopper House, Nyack, NY 326
Eighteen-ninety House, Cortland, NY 309
El Paso County Historical Commission, El Paso, TX 444
Elk Creeks Preservation Society, Inc., Elkton, MD 183
Ellicott City Restoration Foundation, Inc., Ellicott City, MD 183
Ellsworth County Historical Society, Ellsworth, KS 145
Elmore County Historical Foundation, Inc., Mountain Home, ID 98
Enfield Historical Society, Inc., Enfield, CT 59
Englewood Historical Society, Englewood, NJ 280
Essex Historical Society, Inc., Essex, CT 60
Essex Institute, Salem, MA 203
Essex Region Conservation Authority, Essex, Ontario 542
Eudora Area Historical Society, Eudora, KS 145
Eureka Schoolhouse, Springfield, VT 469
Eureka Springs Preservation Society, Eureka Springs, AR 17
Excelsior House, Jefferson, TX 450
Ezra Meeker Historical Society, Inc., Puyallup, WA 486
Faribault County Historical Society, Blue Earth, MN 226
Farmingdale Historical Society, Farmingdale, NJ 281
Faulk County Historical Society, Faulkton, SD 423
Faulkner County Historical Society, Conway, AR 17
Federal Hall National Memorial, New York, NY 323
Fellowship for Metlar House, Piscataway, NJ 289
Firefighters Museum of Southern New Jersey, Pleasantville, NJ 290
First Baptist Church in America, Providence, RI 411
Fitzwilliam Historical Society, Fitzwilliam, NH 271
Flint Historic Commission, Flint, MI 215
Florence Historical Board, Florence, AL 4
Florence Historical Society, Florence, KS 145
Florida Caverns State Park, Marianna, FL 80
Foard County Museum—McAdams Ranch, Crowell, TX 442
Fondation de la Société Historique de Québec, Quebec, Quebec 560
Fontaine House, Memphis, TN 431
Fort Delaware Society, Wilmington, DE 70
Fort Dodge Chapter, Iowa Society for Preservation of Historic Landmarks, Fort Dodge, IA 136

Fort Jefferson National Monument, Key West, FL 79
Fort Klock Historic Restoration, St. Johnsville, NY 332
Fort Stanwix National Monument, Rome, NY 331
Fort Steele Historic Park, Ft. Steele, British Columbia 518
Fostoria Mausoleum Association, Fostoria, OH 364
Foundation for Historical Louisiana, Inc., Baton Rouge, LA 163
Foundation for Historic Christ Church, Inc., Irvington, VA 475
Foundation for Historic Restoration in the Pendleton Area, Pendleton, SC 421
Foundation for Restoration of Ste. Genevieve, Ste. Genevieve, MO 253
Foundation for San Francisco's Architectural Heritage, San Francisco, CA 41
Francestown Improvement and Historical Society, Francestown, NH 271
Frank House, The, Kearney, NE 264
Frank Lloyd Wright Home and Studio Foundation, Oak Park, IL 113
Frank Phillips Home, Bartlesville, OK 376
Franklin County Historical Society, Hampton, IA 137
Frederick City Historic District Commission, Frederick, MD 183
Frederick County Landmarks Foundation, Frederick, MD 183
Free Meeting House, Moncton, New Brunswick 529
Free State of Winston Historical Society, Double Springs, AL 4
Friends of Arrow Rock, Arrow Rock, MO 242
Friends of Florida, Florida, MO 245
Friends of John Jay Homestead State Historic Site, Katonah, NY 317
Friends of Rocheport, Rocheport, MO 252
Friends of the Nyacks, Inc., Nyack, NY 326
Fullerton Arboretum—Heritage House, Fullerton, CA 28
GATEway to the Panhandle, Gate, OK 377
Gahanna Historical Society, Gahanna, OH 364
Gallatin County Historical Society, Ridgway, IL 114
Garden Center, Valdosta, GA 94
Gardner Museum of Architecture and Design, Quincy, IL 114
Gasconade County Historical Society, Hermann, MO 246
Genesee Country Museum, Rochester, NY 330
Georgetown Society, Inc., Georgetown, CO 54
Georgia Agrirama Development Authority—State Museum of Agriculture, Tifton, GA 93
Georgia Trust for Historic Preservation, Inc., Atlanta, GA 85
German Village Society, Columbus, OH 361
Gibson House Museum—Gibson Society, Inc., Boston, MA 189
Gibson House, North York, Ontario 547
Glen Ellyn Historical Society, Glen Ellyn, IL 108
Glen Ridge Historical Society, Glen Ridge, NJ 281
Glocester Heritage Society, Chepachet, RI 409
Golden Ball Tavern Trust, Weston, MA 208
Golden Valley County Historical Society, Beach, ND 351
Goodridge Area Historical Society, Inc., Goodridge, MN 229
Goshen Historical Society, Inc., Goshen, IN 124
Grand Gulf Military Monument Commission, Port Gibson, MS 242
Grand Lake Area Historical Society, Grand Lake, CO 55
Grand Ledge Area Historical Society, Grand Ledge, MI 216
Grand Opera House, Wilmington, DE 70
Grant County Historical Society, Carson, ND 352
Grant County Historical Society, Williamstown, KY 163
Grant County Museum Guild, Sheridan, AR 21

Grant County Museum, Sheridan, AR 21
Grayson County Frontier Village, Inc., Denison, TX 443
Grayson County Historical Society, Leitchfield, KY 157
Greater Middletown Preservation Trust, Inc., Middletown, CT 62
Greater Milford Historical Association, Milford, NY 320
Greater Portland Landmarks, Inc., Portland, ME 175
Greene County Historical Society, Eutau, AL 4
Greenville County Historical Society, Greenville, SC 418
Greenville County Historic Preservation Commission, Greenville, SC 418
Greenwich Village Society for Historic Preservation, New York, NY 323
Gregg County Historical and Genealogical Society, Longview, TX 451
Grenfell Community Museum, Grenfell, Saskatchewan 564
Griffin Historical and Preservation Society, Griffin, GA 89
Griggstown Historical Society, Griggstown, NJ 281
Grinter House Museum, Kansas City, KS 147
Guadalupe Historic Foundation, Santa Fe, NM 298
Guard House and Barrack Room, Fredericton, New Brunswick 528
Guernsey County Historical Society, Cambridge, OH 357
Guilford Historical Society, Brattleboro, VT 465
Gulluh Gyap, Charleston, SC 415
Hackley Heritage Association, Inc., Muskegon, MI 220
Hale Farm and Village, Bath, OH 356
Hale Springs Hotel, Rogersville, TN 435
Hampton Historical Society, Hampton, IL 108
Hampton Plantation State Park, McClellanville, SC 420
Hancock County Historical Society, Greenfield, IN 124
Hanover County Historical Society, Ashland, VA 471
Haralson County Historical Society, Inc., Buchanan, GA 87
Hardyston Heritage Society, Hamburg, NJ 282
Harpswell Historical Society, Harpswell, ME 172
Harrington Park Historical Society, Harrington Park, NJ 282
Harriton House, Bryn Mawr, PA 389
Harrodsburg Historical Society, Harrodsburg, KY 156
Hawaii State Historic Preservation Office, Honolulu, HI 96
Hawks Inn Historical Society, Inc., Delafield, WI 496
Hay Creek Valley Historical Association, Geigertown, PA 393
Hazen Preservation Society, Hazen, NV 268
Hebron Preservation Society, Hebron, NY 314
Helen Keller Property Board, Tuscumbia, AL 8
Hendricks County Museum, Danville, IN 122
Heritage and Genealogical Society of Montgomery County, Fonda, NY 312
Heritage Branch, Whitehorse, Yukon 568
Heritage Canada, Ottawa, Ontario 548
Heritage Foundation of Arizona, Tempe, AZ 15
Heritage Foundation of Franklin and Williamson County, Franklin, TN 429
Heritage Foundation of Oswego County, Oswego, NY 327
Heritage Hill Association, Grand Rapids, MI 216
Heritage Park—Historical Society of Ft. McMurray, Ft. McMurray, Alberta 514
Heritage Park—Pinellas County Historical Museum, Largo, FL 80
Heritage Preservation Commission, Fergus Falls, MN 229
Heritage Preservation Commission, Red Wing, MN 235
Heritage Trust of Nova Scotia, Halifax, Nova Scotia 535
Hidalgo County Historical Commission, McAllen, TX 452
Hill-Hold, Campbell Hall, NY 306

Hillside Historical Society, Hillside, NJ 283
Historic Albany Foundation, Inc., Albany, NY 301
Historic Alexandria Foundation, Alexandria, VA 470
Historic Anchorage, Inc., Anchorage, AK 9
Historic Annapolis, Inc., Annapolis, MD 179
Historic Beaufort Foundation, Beaufort, SC 413
Historic Belmont Association, Nashville, TN 433
Historic Blooming Grove Historical Society, Madison,
   WI 499
Historic Boston, Inc., Boston, MA 189
Historic Boulder, Inc., Boulder, CO 50
Historic Burke Foundation, Inc., Morganton, NC 347
Historic Burras House Foundation, Inc., Jamesville,
   NC 346
Historic Charleston Foundation, Charleston, SC 415
Historic Chattahoochee Commission, Eufaula, AL 4
Historic Columbus Foundation, Inc., Columbus, GA 87
Historic Columbia Foundation, Columbia, SC 416
Historic Denver, Inc., Denver, CO 52
Historic District Commission, Cape May, NJ 279
Historic District Commission, City of Annapolis,
   Annapolis, MD 179
Historic District Commission, Muskegon, MI 220
Historic Dumfries Virginia, Inc., Dumfries, VA 472
Historic Edenton, Edenton, NC 344
Historic Ellicott City, Inc., Ellicott City, MD 183
Historic Fayetteville Foundation, Inc., Fayetteville,
   NC 344
Historic Fincastle, Inc., Fincastle, VA 473
Historic Florissant, Inc., Florissant, MO 245
Historic Ft. Wayne, Inc., Fort Wayne, IN 123
Historic Gettysburg-Adams County, Inc., Gettysburg,
   PA 393
Historic Hamilton Commission, Inc., Hamilton, NC 345
Historic Hawaii Foundation, Honolulu, HI 96
Historic Hermann, Inc., Hermann, MO 246
Historic Homes Foundation, Inc., Louisville, KY 158
Historic Hope Foundation, Inc., Windsor, NC 351
Historic Huntsville Foundation, Inc., Huntsville, AL 5
Historic Ithaca and Tompkins County, Inc., Ithaca,
   NY 316
Historic Kansas City Foundation, Kansas City, MO 248
Historic Key West Preservation Board, Key West, FL 79
Historic Landmarks and Preservation Districts
   Commission, Louisville, KY 158
Historic Landmarks Foundation of Indiana, Indianapolis,
   IN 124
Historic Liberty Jail Visitor's Center, Liberty, MO 250
Historic Madison, Inc., Madison, IN 126
Historic Medley District, Inc., Poolesville, MD 184
Historic Mobile Preservation Society, Mobile, AL 6
Historic Nashville, Inc., Nashville, TN 433
Historic Natchez Foundation, Natchez, MS 241
Historic New Richmond, New Richmond, OH 370
Historic New Harmony, Inc., New Harmony, IN 128
Historic Newton Home, Decatur, MI 213
Historic Occoquan, Inc., Occoquan, VA 478
Historic Paulus Hook Association, Inc., Jersey City,
   NJ 283
Historic Perrysburg, Inc., Perrysburg, OH 370
Historic Pipestone, Inc., Pipestone, MN 234
Historic Pittsford, Pittsford, NY 328
Historic Preservation Alliance of Arkansas, Little Rock,
   AR 20
Historic Preservation Council for Tarrant County, Texas,
   Inc., Fort Worth, TX 445
Historic Preservation Division, Office of Cultural Affairs,
   Santa Fe, NM 299
Historic Preservation Foundation of North Carolina, Inc.,
   Raleigh, NC 348
Historic Preservation Fund of Edgecombe County, Inc.,
   Tarboro, NC 350

Historic Preservation League of Oregon, Portland,
   OR 385
Historic Preservation Office, Department of Parks and
   Recreation, Pago Pago, American Samoa 509
Historic Preservation Office, Upper Savannah Council
   of Governments, Greenwood, SC 419
Historic Preservation Section, Department of Natural
   Resources, Atlanta, GA 86
Historic Preservation of Shreveport, Shreveport, LA 168
Historic Preservation Society of Social Circle, Inc.,
   Social Circle, GA 92
Historic Preservation Trust of Lancaster County,
   Lancaster, PA 396
Historic Resources Branch, Winnipeg, Manitoba 526
Historic Resources Commission of Asheville and
   Buncombe County, Asheville, NC 340
Historic Resources Research, Parks Canada, Atlantic
   Region, Halifax, Nova Scotia 535
Historic Restoration Society of Annapolis County,
   Annapolis Royal, Nova Scotia 533
Historic Restoration Trust of Nutley, Nutley, NJ 288
Historic Richmond Foundation, Richmond, VA 479
Historic Richmond Hill Law School Commission,
   Boonville, NC 341
Historic Rugby, Inc., Rugby, TN 435
Historic Salisbury Foundation, Inc., Salisbury, NC 349
Historic Salem Inc., Salem, MA 204
Historic Saranac Lake, Saranac Lake, NY 332
Historic Sites Service, Edmonton, Alberta 513
Historic St. Augustine Preservation Board, St.
   Augustine, FL 82
Historic Tallahassee Preservation Board, Tallahassee,
   FL 83
Historic Topeka, Inc., Topeka, KS 151
Historic Towson, Inc., Towson, MD 186
Historic Waco Foundation, Waco, TX 459
Historic Willard Society, Willard, UT 464
Historic Wilmington Foundation, Inc., Wilmington,
   NC 350
Historic York, Inc., York, PA 408
Historical Architecture Development, Walla Walla,
   WA 491
Historical Association of Greater Cape Girardeau, Inc.,
   Cape Girardeau, MO 244
Historical Commission of Metropolitan
   Nashville-Davidson County, Nashville, TN 433
Historical Crossroads Village—Huckleberry Railroad,
   Flint, MI 215
Historical Old Salem, Inc., Catonsville, MD 182
Historical Research, Inc., Minneapolis, MN 233
Historical Society of Decatur County, Inc., Greensburg,
   IN 124
Historical Society of Greater Peotone, Peotone, IL 114
Historical Society of Moorestown, Moorestown, NJ 286
Historical Society of Quaker Hill and Pawling, Inc.,
   Pawling, NY 328
Historical Society of Pomona Valley, Pomona, CA 36
Historical Society of Pottawattamie County, Council
   Bluffs, IA 134
Historical Society of Riverton, Riverton, NJ 290
Historical Society of St. Catharines, St. Catharines,
   Ontario 550
Historical Society of Talbot County, Inc., Easton,
   MD 182
History House Association, Skowhegan, ME 176
History Resources, Portland, OR 385
Homer Historical Society, Homer, IL 109
Honey Creek Preservation Group, New Providence,
   IA 140
Hope Lodge—Mather Mill, Fort Washington, PA 392
Hopewell Township Historic Sites Committee, Titusville,
   NJ 292

Hopkinsville-Christian County Pride, Inc., Hopkinsville, KY 157
Hopkinton Historical Association, Hopkinton, RI 409
Hudson Athens Lighthouse Preservation Committee, Inc., Hudson, NY 315
Hudson Heritage Association, Hudson, OH 365
Hudson Historical Commission, Hudson, MA 197
Hudson River Sloop Clearwater, Inc., Poughkeepsie, NY 329
Huilihee Palace, Kailua-Kona, HI 95
Hulmeville Historical Society, Inc., Hulmeville, PA 395
Humboldt County Historical Association, Humboldt, IA 137
Hunter-Dawson Home State Historic Site, New Madrid, MO 251
Huron Historic Gaol, Goderich, Ontario 543
Ida County Historical Society, Ida Grove, IA 137
Independence National Historical Park, Philadelphia, PA 402
Indiana Division, Historic Preservation and Archaeology, Indianapolis, IN 124
Indianapolis Historic Preservation Commission, Indianapolis, IN 125
Indianapolis Museum of Art, Indianapolis, IN 125
Inman Park Restoration, Inc., Atlanta, GA 86
Iowa Society for the Preservation of Historic Landmarks, Des Moines, IA 135
Iowa State Historical Department, Des Moines, IA 135
Iron Work Farm in Acton, Inc., Acton, MA 187
Irving House Historic Centre—New Westminster Museum, New Westminster, British Columbia 520
Ischua Valley Historical Society, Franklinville, NY 312
Jacinto Foundation, Inc., Corinth, MS 239
Jackson Assembly, Inc., Jackson, LA 165
Jacksonville Historic Landmarks Commission, Jacksonville, FL 79
Jacobsburg Historical Society, Nazareth, PA 399
Jamesburg Historical Association, Jamesburg, NJ 283
Jefferson County Historical Development Commission, Birmingham, AL 2
Jefferson County Historical Society, Pine Bluff, AR 21
Jefferson Historical Restoration and Preservation Corporation, Jefferson, TX 450
Jensen-Alvarado Ranch Historic Park, Riverside, CA 38
John Mark Verdier House Museum, Beaufort, SC 413
John R. Park Homestead, Harrow, Ontario 543
Johnson Hall State Historic Site, Johnstown, NY 317
Jones County Iowa Historical Society, Inc., Monticello, IA 139
Jonesborough Civic Trust, Jonesborough, TN 430
Joshua's Tract Conservation and Historic Trust, Willimantic, CT 68
Kanawha Valley Historical and Preservation Society, Charleston, WV 492
Kelton House, Columbus, OH 361
Kempf House Center for Local History, Ann Arbor, MI 210
Kenilworth Historical Society, Kenilworth, IL 109
Kentucky Heritage Council, Frankfort, KY 155
Kentucky Heritage Quilt Society, Lexington, KY 157
Kershaw County Historical Society, Camden, SC 414
King County Office of Historic Preservation, Seattle, WA 487
King William Association, San Antonio, TX 456
Kingston Improvement and Historical Society, Inc., Kingston, NH 273
L'Enfant Trust, The, Washington, DC 73
La Grange County Historical Society, Inc., La Grange, IN 126
La Jolla Historical Society, La Jolla, CA 30
La Mesa Historical Society, Inc., La Mesa, CA 30
Lafayette Museum, Lafayette, LA 165

Lahaina Restoration Foundation, Lahaina, HI 95
Lake County Historical Society, Mentor, OH 368
Lake County Parks and Recreation Department, Crown Point, IN 122
Lancaster County Society for Historic Preservation, Inc., Lancaster, SC 419
Lancaster Historical Society, Lancaster, NY 318
Landmark Association of Bowling Green and Warren County, Inc., Bowling Green, KY 153
Landmark Center, St. Paul, MN 236
Landmark Commission, Township of Hanover, Whippany, NJ 294
Landmark Society of Western New York, Inc., Rochester, NY 331
Landmarks Commission for Historic Preservation, Trenton, NJ 292
Landmarks Preservation Commission of Baltimore County, Towson, MD 186
Landmarks Preservation Council of Illinois, Chicago, IL 103
Landmarks Preservation Society of Southeast, Brewster, NY 305
Landmarks of DeKalb County, Inc., Fort Payne, AL 5
Lapham-Patterson House, Thomasville, GA 93
Larchmont Historical Society, Larchmont, NY 318
Largo Area Historical Society, Largo, FL 80
Las Virgenes Historical Society, Agoura, CA 22
Laura Ingalls Wilder Memorial Society, Inc., Pepin, WI 502
Lauriano Cordova Memorial Museum, Vadito, NM 300
Lawrence County Historical Society, Ironton, OH 365
Lawrence Historical Society, Lawrenceville, NJ 284
Lawton Heritage Association, Lawton, OK 378
Le Sueur County Historical Society and Museum, Elysian, MN 229
Leadville Historical Association, Leadville, CO 56
Lebanon Historical Society, Lebanon, IL 109
Lee Historical Society, Durham, NH 271
Leelanau Historical Society, Inc., Leland, MI 219
Liberty Hall—Orlando Brown House, Frankfort, KY 155
Ligonier Valley Historical Society—Compass Inn Museum, Ligonier, PA 397
Limestone County Archives, Athens, AL 1
Lincoln County Cultural and Historical Association, Wicasset, ME 178
Lincoln County Heritage Trust, Lincoln, NM 297
Little Beaver Museum, Darlington, PA 391
Little Norway, Inc., Blue Mounds, WI 495
Little Red Schoolhouse Museum, Denison, IA 134
Littleton Historical Museum, Littleton, CO 56
Live-In-A-Landmark Council, Montgomery, AL 7
Liverpool Township Historical Society, Valley City, OH 373
Living Prairie Museum Park, Winnipeg, Manitoba 526
Livingston Historical Society, Livingston, NJ 284
Livonia Historic Preservation Commission, Livonia, MI 219
Lloyd Harbor Historical Society, Lloyd Harbor, NY 318
Lockwood-Mathews Mansion Museum, Norwalk, CT 64
Logan County Historical Society, Guthrie, OK 377
Longue Vue House and Gardens, New Orleans, LA 166
Los Pobladores 200, Long Beach, CA 31
Louise Steinman von Hess Foundation, Columbia, PA 390
Louisiana Historical Society, New Orleans, LA 166
Louisville Historical League, Louisville, KY 159
Lower Merion Historical Society, Ardmore, PA 387
Lucas County Museum, Chariton, IA 133
Lyman House Memorial Museum, Hilo, HI 94
Lyndhurst, Tarrytown, NY 337
Lyon County Historical Society, Inc., Eddyville, KY 154
Machiasport Historical Society, Machiasport, ME 173
Mackinac Associates, Mackinac Island, MI 219
Macomb County Historical Society, Mt. Clemens, MI 220

Macon Heritage Foundation, Inc., Macon, GA 90
Macoupin County Historical Society, Carlinville, IL 101
Madam Brett Homestead, Beacon, NY 304
Madison Historical Society, Madison, OH 367
Mahasha County Historical Society, Oskaloosa, IA 140
Main Street Preservation Society, Grafton, OH 364
Maine Department of Conservation, Bureau of Parks and Recreation, Augusta, ME 169
Maine Old Cemetery Association, Eliot, ME 171
Manito Historical Society, Manito, IL 110
Manship House, Jackson, MS 240
Mantorville Restoration Association, Mantorville, MN 232
Marengo County Historical Society, Demopolis, AL 3
Margaree Salmon Museum, Margaree, Nova Scotia 536
Marietta Restoration Associates, Inc., Marietta, PA 398
Marshall County Historical Society, Lacon, IL 109
Marshall Historical Society, Inc., Marshall, MI 219
Maryland Association of Historic District Commissions, Frederick, MD 183
Massachusetts Historical Commission, Boston, MA 190
Mather Training Center, Harpers Ferry, WV 493
McGregor Historical Society, McGregor, IA 139
McKean County Historical Society, Smethport, PA 405
McLean County Historical Society, Washburn, ND 354
Mechanicsburg Museum Association, Mechanicsburg, PA 398
Medallion Home—Pioneer Park Association, Kermit, TX 450
Medina Community Design Committee, Medina, OH 368
Melrose Historical Commission, Melrose, MA 199
Memphis Heritage, Inc., Memphis, TN 431
Meridian Restorations Foundation, Inc., Meridian, MS 241
Miami Purchase Association for Historic Preservation, Cincinnati, OH 359
Mid-Atlantic Center for the Arts, Cape May, NJ 279
Middleton Place Foundation, Charleston, SC 415
Middletown Landmarks Commission, Middletown, NJ 285
Midwest Regional Office, National Trust for Historic Preservation, Chicago, IL 104
Milan Historical Museum, Inc., Milan, OH 369
Millbrook Society, The, Hatboro, PA 394
Milltown Historical Society, Milltown, NJ 285
Mission San Miguel, San Miguel, CA 43
Mission Trail—Los Pueblos Association, El Paso, TX 444
Mississippi Museums Association, Jackson, MS 241
Mobile Historic Development Commission, Mobile, AL 6
Monroe County Museum Association, Stroudsburg, PA 406
Montague Museum and Historical Association, Montague, MI 220
Monte Vista Historical Association, San Antonio, TX 456
Montgomery County Historical Society, Rockville, MD 185
Montgomery Historical Society, Montgomery, VT 467
Mordecai Square Historical Society, Inc., Raleigh, NC 348
Morgan County Foundation, Inc.—Madison-Morgan Cultural Center, Madison, GA 90
Morgan County Historical Society, Jacksonville, IL 109
Morris County Trust for Historic Preservation, Inc., Morristown, NJ 569
Morris Historical Society, Morris, CT 63
Morris Library, Carbondale, IL 101
Mountains-Plains Regional Office, National Trust for Historic Preservation, Denver, CO 52
Munroe Township Historical Society, Williamstown, NJ 294
Murfreesboro Historical Association, Murfreesboro, NC 347
Murfreesboro Historic Properties Commission, Murfreesboro, NC 347
Nash County Historical Association, Inc., Rocky Mount, NC 348
Natchez Pilgrimage Tours, Natchez, MS 241
National Alliance of Preservation Commissions, Washington, DC 73
National Aviation Museum, Ottawa, Ontario 549
National Broadcasters Hall of Fame, Freehold, NJ 281
National Institute for the Conservation of Cultural Property, Inc., Washington, DC 74
National Park Service, State of Alaska, Anchorage, AK 9
National Park Service, Washington, DC 74
National Register of Historic Places, Washington, DC 74
National Temple Hill Association, Vails Gate, NY 338
National Trust for Historic Preservation, Washington, DC 75
Navajo County Historical Society, Holbrook, AZ 13
New Bern Historical Society Foundation, Inc., New Bern, NC 347
New Bern Preservation Foundation, Inc., New Bern, NC 347
New England Preservation Institute, New Bedford, MA 200
New Gloucester, Maine, Historical Society, New Gloucester, ME 173
New Hampshire Antiquarian Society, Hopkinton, NH 272
New Haven Preservation Trust, New Haven, CT 64
New London Heritage Historical Society, New London, WI 501
New London Landmarks—Union Railroad Station Trust, Inc., New London, CT 64
Newark Preservation and Landmarks Committee, Newark, NJ 287
Newtown Association, Inc., Salisbury, MD 185
Nez Perce National Historical Park, Spalding, ID 98
Niagara Parks Commission, Fort Erie, Ontario 542
north Atlantic Regional Office, National Park Service, Boston, MA 190
North Castle Historical Society, Armonk, NY 302
North Fork Historical Society, Paonia, CO 56
North Jersey Electric Railway Historical Society, Rahway, NJ 290
North Manchester Historical Society, Inc., North Manchester, IN 128
North Yarmouth Historical Society, North Yarmouth, ME 174
North-Central Pennsylvania Historical Association, Milton, PA 398
Northeast Florida Anthropological Society, Jacksonville, FL 79
Northeast Georgia Area Planning and Development Commission, Athens, GA 85
Northern Kentucky Historical Society, Fort Thomas, KY 155
Northville Historical Society, Northville, MI 221
Northwest Ohio Historic Preservation Office, Bowling Green, OH 356
O'Brien County Historical Society, Primghar, IA 140
Oatlands Plantation, Leesburg, VA 475
Ocean City Museum Society, Ocean City, MD 184
Office of Historic Preservation, Department of Parks and Recreation, Sacramento, CA 39
Office of Historic Preservation, Fall River, MA 195
Office of Historic Properties, Frankfort, KY 155
Oklahoma Historic Fashions, Inc., Wagoner, OK 381
Old Abbeville District Historical Commission, Greenwood, SC 419
Old Bethlehem Historical Society, Inc., Bethlehem, CT 58
Old Capitol, Iowa City, IA 137
Old Central Museum of Higher Education, Stillwater, OK 380
Old Constitution House, Windsor, VT 469
Old Court House Museum, Guysborough, Nova Scotia 534

Old Greensborough Preservation Society, Greensboro, NC 345
Old House Guild of Sandusky, Sandusky, OH 371
Old Merchants House of New York, Inc., New York, NY 325
Old Northwest Corporation, Vincennes, IN 130
Old South Meeting House, Boston, MA 190
Old St. Mary's Historic Community Center, Cincinnati, OH 359
Old Stone Prison, Decatur, TX 443
Old Time Historical Association, Climax, NC 343
Old Town College Park Preservation Association, College Park, MD 569
Old Washington Historic State Park, Washington, AR 22
Ontario Heritage Foundation, Toronto, Ontario 553
Open Lands Project, Chicago, IL 104
Oracle Historical Society, Inc., Oracle, AZ 13
Orange County Historical Commission, Santa Ana, CA 43
Oregon-California Trails Association, Gerald, MO 246
Overland Historical Society, Overland, MO 251
Owens Art Gallery, Sackville, New Brunswick 530
Oysterponds Historical Society, Inc., Orient, NY 327
Pacific County Historical Society and Museum Foundation, South Bend, WA 489
Pacific Northwest Chapter, National Railway Historical Society, Portland, OR 385
Pacific Northwest Conservation Laboratory, Port Orchard, WA 486
Paducah-McCracken County Growth, Inc., Paducah, KY 161
Palatine Historical Society, Palatine, IL 113
Palatine Settlement Society, St. Johnsville, NY 332
Palm Beach Landmarks Preservation Commission, Palm Beach, FL 81
Palo Pinto County Historical Association, Inc., Palo Pinto, TX 454
Parma Area Historical Society, Parma, OH 370
Pas-Ka-Poo Historical Park, Rimbey, British Columbia 520
Paso Real Stagecoach Inn Museum, Harlingen, TX 448
Peerless Rockville Historic Preservation, Ltd., Rockville, MD 185
Pennsylvania Historical and Museum Commission—William Penn Memorial Museum, Harrisburg, PA 394
Pennsylvania Railway Museum Association, Inc.—Arden Trolley Museum, Washington, PA 407
Perkins County Historical Society, Bison, SD 422
Peters Creek Historical Society, Finleyville, PA 392
Peterson Heritage, Inc., Peterson, IA 140
Philadelphia Historical Commission, Philadelphia, PA 402
Philadelphia Society for the Preservation of Landmarks, Philadelphia, PA 403
Pickwick Mill, Inc., Pickwick, MN 234
Pine County Historical Society, Askou, MN 226
Pinellas County Historical Society, Largo, FL 80
Pioneer Valley Planning Commission, West Springfield, MA 208
Pioneer Village Commission, Cedar Rapids, IA 133
Pioneer's Cemetery Association, Inc., Phoenix, AZ 14
Pittsburgh History and Landmarks Foundation, Pittsburgh, PA 403
Pleasant Valley Preservation Society, Holmdel, NJ 283
Plumas County Museum, Quincy, CA 36
Plymouth Antiquarian Society, Plymouth, MA 203
Plymouth Meeting Historical Society, North Wales, PA 400
Pocahontas County Historical Society, Rolfe, IA 141
Polishville Cemetery and Grotto Association, Brighton, IA 132
Pope County Historical Society and Museum, Glenwood, MN 229

Pope-Leighey House, Mount Vernon, VA 477
Poricy Park Citizens Committee, Middletown, NJ 285
Port Deposit Heritage Corporation, Port Deposit, MD 184
Portage Canal Society, Inc., Portage, WI 503
Portola Expedition Foundation, San Mateo, CA 43
Portsmouth Historical Society—John Paul Jones House, Portsmouth, NH 275
Poudre Landmarks Foundation, Fort Collins, CO 54
Prairie Historical Society, Inc., Madison, SD 424
Preble County Historical Society, Eaton, OH 363
Preservation Alliance of Louisville and Jefferson County, Inc., Louisville, KY 159
Preservation, Inc., Chestertown, MD 182
Preservation New Jersey, Inc., Princeton, NJ 290
Preservation of Historic Winchester, Inc., Winchester, VA 482
Preservation Planning, City of Albuquerque, Albuquerque, NM 295
Preservation Society of Asheville and Buncombe County, Asheville, NC 341
Preservation Society of Charleston, Charleston, SC 415
Preservation Technology Reference Center, Washington, DC 75
Preserve It Now, Fonda, NY 312
Prince of Wales Northern Heritage Center, Yellowknife, Northwest Territories 533
Promotion and Preservation of Iberville Parish, Inc., Plaquemine, LA 167
Public History Program, University of California, Santa Barbara, Santa Barbara, CA 43
Pulaski Historical Commission, Inc., Hawkinsville, GA 89
Pump House Steam Museum, Kingston, Ontario 544
Quapaw Quarter Association, Little Rock, AR 20
Raleigh Historic Properties Commission, Inc., Raleigh, NC 348
Ramapogue Historical Society—The Day House, West Springfield, MA 208
Ramona Museum of California History, Los Angeles, CA 32
Ramsey Historical Association, Ramsey, NJ 290
Ravalli Schoolhouse Restoration Society, Ravalli, MT 259
Ravenna Heritage, Ravenna, OH 371
Reading Historical Commission, Reading, MA 203
Redding Museum and Art Center, Redding, CA 37
Reed Gold Mine, Stanfield, NC 349
Reitz Home Preservation Society, Inc., Evansville, IN 122
Rensselaerville Historical Society, Rensselaerville, NY 330
Restoration Technology, Brockville, Ontario 540
Restorations of Kane County, St. Charles, IL 116
Restore our County, Inc., Dandridge, TN 428
Rhode Island Historical Preservation Commission, Providence, RI 412
Rialto Historical Society, Rialto, CA 37
Richard Montgomery Chapter, National Society, Sons of the American Revolution, Dayton, OH 362
Richland County Historic Preservation Commission, Columbia, SC 416
Richland West End Neighborhood Association, Inc., Nashville, TN 434
Ridgewood Preservation, Inc., Canton, OH 358
River Road Historical Society, Destrehan, LA 164
Riverside Avondale Preservation, Inc., Jacksonville, FL 79
Rochester Association of Performing Arts, Webster, NY 339
Rochester Hills Historic District Commission, Rochester, MI 222
Rock Creek Valley Historical Society and Museum, Westmoreland, KS 152
Rose City Area Historical Society, Inc., Rose City, MI 222
Rose Hill Mansion, Geneva, NY 313

Roslyn Landmark Society, Roslyn, NY 331
Roswell Historical Society, Roswell, GA 91
Rotch-Jones-Duff House and Garden Museum, New Bedford, MA 200
Rowan County Historic Properties Commission, Mt. Ulla, NC 347
Royal Arts Foundation—Belcourt Castle, Newport, RI 410
Rusk County Historical Foundation, Henderson, TX 448
Rutland Historical Society, Rutland, VT 468
SIMAPC (Southwestern Illinois Metropolitan and Regional Planning Commission), Collinsville, IL 105
Sagadahoc Preservation, Inc., Bath, ME 169
Saint Charles Avenue Association, New Orleans, LA 166
Saint Elmo Historic Preservation, Buena Vista, CO 50
Saint John Heritage Trust, Inc., Saint John, New Brunswick 530
Saint Louis County Department of Parks and Recreation, Clayton, MO 244
Saint Marys Historic Preservation Commission, St. Marys, GA 91
Salisbury Historic District Commission, Salisbury, NC 349
Salt Springville Community Restoration, Salt Springville, NY 332
San Antonio Conservation Society, San Antonio, TX 456
San Antonio Valley Historical Association, King City, CA 29
San Joaquin County Historical Society and Museum, Lodi, CA 30
San Jose Historic Landmarks Commission, San Jose, CA 42
San Juan County Historical Society, Silverton, CO 57
Sandy Creek Covered Bridge State Historic Site, Hillsboro, MO 246
Sandy Hook Museum, Highlands, NJ 282
Santa Barbara Trust for Historic Preservation, Santa Barbara, CA 44
Santa Clara County Historical Heritage Commission, San Jose, CA 42
Santa Cruz County Society for Historic Preservation, Inc., Santa Cruz, CA 44
Santa Fe Area Historical Foundation, Inc., Arcadia, TX 437
Santa Monica Heritage Square Museum, Santa Monica, CA 44
Saratoga Springs Preservation Foundation, Saratoga Springs, NY 332
Saskatchewan Provincial Historic Parks, Regina, Saskatchewan 566
Save Lucy Committee, Inc., Margate, NJ 285
Save Our Cemeteries, Inc., New Orleans, LA 166
Save Our Heritage Organization, San Diego, CA 40
Save the Tivoli, Inc., Washington, DC 75
Scarsdale Historical Society, Scarsdale, NY 333
Schleicher County Museum, El Dorado, TX 444
Sea Cliff Landmarks, Inc., Sea Cliff, NY 334
Seaford Historical Society, Inc., Seaford, DE 70
Seminole Canyon State Historical Park, Comstock, TX 441
Seminole Valley Farm, Inc., Cedar Rapids, IA 133
Shaftsbury Historical Society, Shaftsbury, VT 468
Shelby County Historical Society, Shelbyville, KY 162
Shepherd Area Historical Society, Shepherd, MI 223
Sherbrooke Restoration Commission, Sherbrooke, Nova Scotia 538
Sherbrooke Village, Sherbrooke, Nova Scotia 538
Sherman County Historical Society, Inc., Stratford, TX 458
Sherman Hill Association, Des Moines, IA 135
Signal Hill National Historic Park, St. John's, Newfoundland 532
Sinsinawa Dominican Archives, Dominican Sisters, Sinsinawa, WI 504
Sixteen ninety-six Thomas Massey House, Broomall, PA 389

Sleepy Hollow Restorations, Inc., Tarrytown, NY 337
Smith's Castle at Cocumscussoc, Wickford, RI 413
Smithfield Plantation, Blacksburg, VA 471
Smithtown Historical Society, Smithtown, NY 334
Smyth County Historical and Museum Society, Inc., Marion, VA 476
Society for the Preservation of Federal Hill and Fell's Point, Baltimore, MD 181
Society for the Preservation of Long Island Antiquities, Setauket, NY 334
Society for the Preservation of New England Antiquities, Boston, MA 190
Society for the Preservation of Old Mills, Mishawaka, IN 127
Society of Ohio Archivists, Columbus, OH 361
Somerville Preservation Commission, Somerville, AL 8
Sonnenberg Gardens and Mansion, Canandaigua, NY 306
Sonoma League for Historic Preservation, Sonoma, CA 45
South Carolina Department of Parks, Recreation and Tourism, Columbia, SC 417
South Carolina Heritage Trust Program, Columbia, SC 417
South Milwaukee Historical Society, South Milwaukee, WI 504
Southern Appalachian Historical Association, Inc., Boone, NC 341
Southern Highland Handicraft Guild Museum and Library, Asheville, NC 341
Southington Historical Society, Southington, CT 66
Springfield Art and Historical Society, Springfield, VT 469
Springfield Historical Society, Springfield, SD 426
Stagville Center, Durham, NC 343
Stan Hywet Hall and Gardens, Akron, OH 355
Stanly County Historic Properties Commission, Albemarle, NC 340
Stark Preservation Alliance, Canton, OH 358
State Division of Historic Preservation and Archaeology, Carson City, NV 267
State Historic Preservation Office, Cheyenne, WY 506
State Historic Preservation Office, Phoenix, AZ 14
State Historical Preservation Center, Vermillion, SD 426
Stephentown Historical Society, Stephentown, NY 335
Sterne-Hoya Home, Nacogdoches, TX 453
Stewart County Historical Commission, Lumpkin, GA 90
Stow Historical Commission, Stow, MA 206
Strawbery Banke, Portsmouth, NH 275
Summersworth Historical Society, Somersworth, NH 276
Summerville Preservation Society, Summerville, SC 421
Sumner Historical Society, Sumner, WA 489
Tabor Opera House, Leadville, CO 56
Taft Museum, The, Cincinnati, OH 359
Tarboro Historic District Commission, Tarboro, NC 350
Tattnall County Historic Preservation, Inc., Reidsville, GA 91
Taylor Conservation and Heritage Society, Taylor, TX 458
Taylor County Historical Society, Medford, WI 500
Telfair Academy of Arts and Sciences, Inc., Savannah, GA 92
Temporary State Commission on the Restoration of the Capitol, Albany, NY 301
Tennessee Historical Commission, Nashville, TN 434
Terrebonne Historical and Cultural Society, Inc., Houma, LA 164
Texana Heritage Society, Edna, TX 444
Texas Historical Commission, Austin, TX 438
Texas Historical Foundation, Austin, TX 438
Texas Oral History Association, Waco, TX 459
Texas Pioneer Arts Association, Round Top, TX 455
Texas-New Mexico Field Office, Ft. Worth, TX 446
Thomasville Landmarks, Inc., Thomasville, GA 93

Thousand Islands Craft School and Textile Museum, Clayton, NY 308

Tiffin Historic Trust, Tiffin, OH 372

Tigard Area Historical and Preservation Association, Portland, OR 385

Time Museum, The, Rockford, IL 115

Toledo Firefighter Museum, Inc., Toledo, OH 373

Town of Carmel Historical Society, Mahopac, NY 319

Travellers' Rest Museum House 1799, Nashville, TN 434

Trustees of Reservations, Milton, MA 199

Tubac Historical Society, Tubac, AZ 15

Tulare County Historical Society, Visalia, CA 48

Tumwater Historical Association, Tumwater, WA 490

Tuscaloosa County Preservation Society, Tuscaloosa, AL 8

Twinfield Historical Society, Plainfield, VT 468

Union Cemetery Historical Society, Inc., Kansas City, MO 248

Union County Office of Cultural and Heritage Affairs, Westfield, NJ 293

United Church Archives, Newfoundland and Labrador Conference, St. John's, Newfoundland 532

Upper Delaware Heritage Alliance, Callicoon, NY 306

Utah Heritage Foundation, Salt Lake City, UT 464

Vacaville Heritage Council, Vacaville, CA 47

Van Harlingen Historical Society of Montgomery, Inc., Belle Mead, NJ 277

Vicksburg Foundation for Historic Preservation, Vicksburg, MS 242

Victoria County Historical Commission, Victoria, TX 459

Village Historical Society, Inc., Harrison, OH 365

Village of Honeoye Falls—Town of Mendon Historical Society, Honeoye Falls, NY 315

Villagers, Inc., The, Miami, FL 80

Violet Museum, Violet, TX 459

Virginia Division of Historic Landmarks, Richmond, VA 480

Virginia Trust for Historic Preservation—Lee-Fendall House Museum, Alexandria, VA 470

WHALE (Waterfront Historic Area League), New Bedford, MA 200

Waller County Historical Museum, Brookshire, TX 440

Walnut Creek Historical Society, Walnut Creek, CA 48

Walnut Street Historic District, Inc., Florence, AL 4

Walpole Historical Society, Walpole, NH 276

Warren County Cultural and Heritage Commission, Belvidere, NJ 277

Warrior Run Ft. Freeland Heritage Society, Turbotville, PA 406

Washington Crossing Historic Park, Washington Crossing, PA 407

Washington Trust for Historic Preservation, Olympia, WA 486

Washoe Heritage Council, Reno, NV 269

Washtenaw County History District Commission, Ann Arbor, MI 211

Watertown Historical Society, Watertown, WI 505

Watkinsville Historical Society, Watkinsville, GA 94

Waukegan Historical Society, Waukegan, IL 119

Wayne County Historical Society, Corydon, IA 134

Wayne County Historical Society, Honesdale, PA 395

Waynesboro Historical Society, Waynesboro, PA 407

Webb City Preservation Committee, Webb City, MO 256

Webb County Heritage Foundation, Inc., Laredo, TX 451

Webb-Deane-Stevens Museum, The, Wethersfield, CT 68

Wellfleet Historical Society—Rider House, Wellfleet, MA 207

Wells County Historical Society, Fessenden, ND 352

Wenham Historic District Commission, Wenham, MA 207

West Whiteland Historical Commission, Exton, PA 392

Westborough Historical Commission, Westborough, MA 207

Westchester Preservation League, Ossining, NY 327

Westerly Historical Society, Westerly, RI 412

Western Sonoma County Historical Society, Sebastopol, CA 45

Westmorland Historical Society—Keillor House Museum, Dorchester, New Brunswick 528

Whitman Stafford Committee, Laurel Springs, NJ 284

Wilkie and District Museum and Historical Society, Wilkie, Saskatchewan 567

William A. Farnsworth Library and Art Museum, Rockland, ME 176

William Floyd Estate, Fire Island National Seashore, Mastic Beach, NY 320

Williamsburg County Historical Society, Kingstree, SC 419

Willoughby-Baylor House—Chrysler Museum, Norfolk, VA 477

Wilton House Museum, Richmond, VA 480

Winchester Historical Commission, Winchester, MA 209

Windmill Gardens Museum Village, Fremont, MI 215

Winterthur Museum and Gardens, Winterthur, DE 71

Witte Museum, San Antonio, TX 456

Woodstock Historical Society, Woodstock, VT 469

Worcester Art Museum, Worcester, MA 209

Worth County Historical Society, Allendale, MO 242

Wrightsboro Quaker Community Foundation, Inc., Thomson, GA 93

Yellowstone National Park—Albright Visitor Center, Yellowstone National Park, WY 509

York County Historical Commission, McConnells, SC 420

TRANSPORTATION

AIRCHIVE Association, Springfield, IL 116

Age of Steam Railroad Museum, Southwest Railroad Historical Society, Dallas, TX 442

Alaska Historical and Transportation Museum, Inc., Palmer, AK 11

Alberta Pioneer Railway Association, Edmonton, Alberta 512

Allegheny Portage Railroad National Historic Site, Cresson, PA 391

American Canal Society, Richmond, VA 570

Atlantic Canada Aviation Museum, Halifax, Nova Scotia 534

Auburn Automotive Heritage, Inc.—Auburn-Cord-Duesenberg Museum, Auburn, IN 120

Aviation Hall of Fame of New Jersey, Teterboro, NJ 292

Bay Area Electric Railroad Association, Inc.—Western Railway Museum, Suisun City, CA 46

Boone Railroad Historical Society, Boone, IA 132

Boonslick Historical Society, Boonville, MO 243

Boothbay Railway Village, Boothbay, ME 170

Boyertown Museum of Historic Vehicles, Boyertown, PA 389

Branford Electric Railway Association, East Haven, CT 59

Brewster-Sugar Creek Township Historical Society, Brewster, OH 356

buffalo County Historical Society, Kearney, NE 264

Bureau of Environmental Services, Ohio Department of Transportation, Columbus, OH 361

California State Railroad Museum, Sacramento, CA 38

Callis P. Huntington Railroad Historical Society, Inc., Huntington, WV 493

Camp Five Museums Foundation, Inc., Laona, WI 499

Canadian Railroad Historical Association, St. Constant, Quebec 561

Canal Museum and Hugh Moore Historical Park, Easton, PA 391

Canal Society of Indiana, Fort Wayne, IN 123

Center for Transportation and Commerce, Galveston, TX 446

Central Texas Museum of Automotive History, Rosanky, TX 455

Chesapeake and Ohio Historical Society, Inc., Alderson, WV 491

Citronelle Historical Preservation Society, Citronelle, AL 3

Colorado Midland Chapter, National Railroad Historical Society, Colorado Springs, CO 50

Colorado Railroad Historical Foundation, Inc., Golden, CO 54

Conneaut Railroad Museum, Conneaut, OH 362

Connecticut Valley Railroad Museum, Inc., Essex, CT 60

Cranbrook Archives, Museum and Landmark Foundation, Cranbrook, British Columbia 518

Cumberland and Oxford Canal Association, Portland, ME 175

Daniel Webster College, Nashua, NH 274

De Smet Depot Museum, De Smet, SD 423

Edaville Railroad, South Carver, MA 205

Edison Institute—Henry Ford Museum, Greenfield Village, Dearborn, MI 213

Electric Railway Historical Association of Southern California, Los Angeles, CA 31

Experimental Aircraft Association, Oshkosh, WI 502

Farmington Canal Corridor Association, Plainville, CT 65

Florida Aviation Historical Society, Indian, FL 78

Forney Transportation Museum, Denver, CO 52

Fort Benton Museum, Ft. Benton, MT 258

Fostoria Area Historical Society and Museum, Fostoria, OH 364

Friends of the College Park Airport, College Park, MD 182

Fulda Heritage Society, Fulda, MN 229

Garrett Historical Society, Garrett, IN 123

Great Miami River Corridor Committee, Troy, OH 373

Gulf Coast Chapter, National Railway Historical Society, Inc., Houston, TX 449

Hartung's Automotive Museum, Glenview, IL 108

Henry Blommel Historic Automotive Data Collection, Connersville, IN 121

Historic General Dodge House, Council Bluffs, IA 134

Historic Red Clay Valley, Inc., Wilmington, DE 70

Historic Vehicle Society of Ontario, Windsor, Ontario 555

Illinois Railway Museum, Union, IL 118

Illinois Terminal Railroad Historical Society, East Peoria, IL 106

Indiana Transportation Museum, Noblesville, IN 128

Indianapolis Motor Speedway Hall of Fame Museum, Indianapolis, IN 125

Jerome Historical Society, Jerome, AZ 13

Kentucky Railway Museum, Louisville, KY 159

Lake Shore Railway Historical Society, Inc., North East, PA 400

Lake Superior Museum of Transportation, Duluth, MN 228

Livermore Heritage Guild, Livermore, CA 30

Locust Creek Covered Bridge, Laclede, MO 249

Marine Historical Society of Detroit, Westland, MI 224

Mid-Continent Railway Historical Society and Museum, North Freedom, WI 502

Middle Ohio River Chapter, Sons and Daughters of Pioneer Rivermen, Inc., Louisville, KY 159

Middlesex Canal Association, Billerica, MA 188

Midland Regional Airport Museum, Midland, TX 452

Midwest Riverboat Buffs, Keokuk, IA 138

Minnesota Transportation Museum, Inc., Minneapolis, MN 233

Mirror and District Museum Association, Mirror, Alberta 515

Missouri and Arkansas Railroad Museum, Inc., Beaver, AR 17

Moncton Museum, Inc., Moncton, New Brunswick 529

Motor Bus Society, Inc., West Trenton, NJ 294

Musée Automobile Museum, St. Jacques, New Brunswick 530

National Museum of Transport, St. Louis, MO 254

National Road—Zane Grey Museum, Norwich, OH 370

Native New Yorkers Historical Association, New York, NY 324

New England Air Museum, Windsor Locks, CT 69

New England Electric Railway Historical Society, Inc.—Kennebunkport, ME 173

New Jersey Museum of Transportation, Inc., Farmingdale, NJ 281

New York Central System Historical Society, Inc., Mentor, OH 368

North Western Illinois Chapter, National Railway Historical Society, Rockford, IL 115

Ohio Covered Bridge Committee, Wyoming, OH 375

Ohio Railway Museum, Worthington, OH 374

Old Fort Erie Historical Railroad and Museum, Ft. Erie, Ontario 542

Old Rhinebeck Aerodrome, Inc., Rhinebeck, NY 330

Oregon Electric Railway Historical Society, Inc., Forest Grove, OR 383

Owls Head Transportation Museum, Owls Head, ME 174

Pacific Coast Chapter, Railway and Locomotive Historical Society, Inc., San Francisco, CA 41

Pacific Railroad Society, Inc., Los Angeles, CA 32

Parc Historique National de Coteau-du-Lac, Coteau-du-Lac, Quebec 557

Park County Museum Association, Livingston, MT 259

Pate Museum of Transportation, Fort Worth, TX 446

Patee House Museum, St. Joseph, MO 253

Pennyroyal Area Museum, Hopkinsville, KY 157

Pima Air Museum, Tucson, AZ 16

Poll Museum of Transportation, Holland, MI 217

Rail America, the National Railroad Museum, Green Bay, WI 497

Railroad Museum of Pennsylvania, Strasburg, PA 405

Railroad Station Historical Society, Crete, NE 262

Railroader's Memorial Museum, Altoona, PA 387

Railroadians of America, Inc., Livingston, NJ 284

Randolph County Historical Society, Moberly, MO 251

Reynolds Aviation Museum, Wetaskiwin, Alberta 517

Roanoke Transportation Museum, Roanoke, VA 480

Ron Morel Memorial Museum, Kapuskasing, Ontario 544

Rose Hill Manor—Children's Museum and Carriage House, Frederick, MD 183

Schoharie Crossing State Historic Site, Fort Hunter, NY 312

Smoky Hill Railway and Historical Society, Inc., Shawnee Mission, KS 151

Society for the Preservation and Appreciation of Antique Motor Fire Apparatus in America, Syracuse, NY 336

South Carolina Railroad Museum, Inc., Winnsboro, SC 421

Southeastern Railway Museum, Duluth, GA 88

Southwest Railroad Historical Society, Dallas, TX 443

Spencer Shops, Spencer, NC 349

Swigart Museum, Huntington, PA 395

Towe Antique Ford Museum, Deer Lodge, MT 257

Transport Museum Association, St. Louis, MO 254

Tri-State Railway Historical Society, Inc., Morristown, NJ 286

U.S. Army Transportation Museum, Fort Eustis, VA 473

Union Covered Bridge State Historic Site, Paris, MO 251
Union Pacific Museum, Omaha, NE 265
Virginia Canals and Navigations Society, Alexandria, VA 570
Virginia and Truckee Railroad Museum, Carson City, NV 268
Wells Auto Museum, Wells, ME 178
West Chicago Historical Museum, West Chicago, IL 119
Western Maryland Railway Historical Society, Inc., Union Bridge, MD 186
Willard Area Historical Society, Willard, OH 374
Wings and Things Museum, Inc., Delavan, IL 106
Wisconsin Chapter, National Railway Historical Society, Inc., Milwaukee, WI 500
Wright Brothers National Memorial, Manteo, NC 346

Historical and Archaeological Areas Administered by the National Park Service

ALABAMA

Horseshoe Bend National Military Park
Rt. 1, Box 103
Daviston, Al. 36256

Russell Cave National Monument
Rt. 1, Box 175
Bridgeport, Al. 35740

Tuskegee Institute National Historic Site
399 Old Montgomery Rd.
Tuskegee Institute, Al. 36088

ALASKA

Cape Krusenstern National Monument
General Delivery
Kotzebue, Ak. 99752

Klondike Gold Rush National Historical Park
P.O. Box 517
Skagway, Ak. 99840
(See also Washington)

Kobuk Valley National Park
General Delivery
Kotzebue, Ak. 99752

Sitka National Historical Park
Box 738
Sitka, Ak. 99835

Yukon-Charley Rivers National Preserve
P.O. Box 64
Eagle, Ak. 99738

ARIZONA

Canyon de Chelly National Monument
Box 588
Chinle, Az. 86503

Casa Grande National Monument
Box 518
Coolidge, Az. 85228

Coronado National Memorial
Rt. 1, Box 126
Hereford, Az. 85615

Fort Bowie National Historic Site
Box 158
Bowie, Az. 85605

Hohokam Pima National Monument
c/o Casa Grande National Monument
Box 518
Coolidge, Az. 85228

Hubbell Trading Post National Historic Site
Box 298
Ganado, Az. 86505

Montezuma Castle National Monument
Box 219
Campe Verde, Az. 86322

Navajo National Monument
Tonalea, Az. 86044

Pipe Spring National Monument
Moccasin, Az. 86022

Tonto National Monument
Box 707
Roosevelt, Az. 85545

Tumacacori National Monument
Box 67
Tumacacori, Az. 85640

Tuzigoot National Monument
Box 68
Clarkdale, Az. 86324

Walnut Canyon National Monument
Rt. 1, Box 25
Flagstaff, Az. 86001
m040.**Wupatki National Monument**
Tuba Star Rt.
Flagstaff, Az. 86001

ARKANSAS

Arkansas Post National Memorial
Rt. 1, Box 16
Gillett, Ar. 72055

Fort Smith National Historic Site
Box 1406
Fort Smith, Ar. 72902
(also in Oklahoma)

Pea Ridge National Military Park
Pea Ridge, Ar. 72751

CALIFORNIA

Cabrillo National Monument
Box 6175
San Diego, Ca. 92106

Death Valley National Monument
Death Valley, Ca. 92328
(Also in Nev.)

Eugene O'Neill National Historic Site
Eugene O'Neill Foundation
261 Livonia Heights Rd.
Alamo, Ca. 94507

Fort Point National Historic Site
Box 29333
Presidio of San Francisco, Ca. 94129

Golden Gate National Recreation Area
Fort Mason, San Francisco, Ca. 94123

John Muir National Historic Site
4202 Alhambra Ave.
Martinez, Ca. 94553

COLORADO

Bent's Old Fort National Historic Site
Box 581
La Junta, Co. 81050

Hovenweep National Monument
c/o Mesa Verde National Park, Co., 81330
(also in Utah)

Mesa Verde National Park
Mesa Verde National Park, Co. 81330

Yucca House National Monument
c/o Mesa Verde National Park
Mesa Verde National Park, Co. 81330

DISTRICT OF COLUMBIA

Chesapeake and Ohio Canal National Historical Park
Box 4
Sharpsburg, Md. 21782

Ford's Theatre National Historic Site
511 10th St., NW
Washington, D.C. 20004

Frederick Douglass Home
1411 W St., SE
Washington, D.C. 20020

Lincoln Memorial
National Capital Region, NPS
1100 Ohio Dr., SW
Washington, D.C. 20242

Lyndon Baines Johnson Memorial Grove on the Potomac
National Capital Region, NPS
1100 Ohio Dr., SW
Washington, D.C. 20242

National Capital Parks
1100 Ohio Dr., SW
Washington, D.C. 20242

National Mall
National Capital Region, NPS
1100 Ohio Dr., SW
Washington, D.C. 20242

Sewall-Belmont House National Historic Site
144 Constitution Ave., NE
Washington, D.C. 20002

Theodore Roosevelt Island
c/o George Washington Memorial Parkway
Turkey Run Park
McLean, Va. 22101

Thomas Jefferson Memorial
c/o National Capital Region, NPS
1100 Ohio Dr., SW
Washington, D.C. 20242

Vietnam Veterans Memorial
c/o National Capital Region, NPS
1100 Ohio Dr., SW
Washington, D.C. 20242

Washington Monument
c/o National Capital Region, NPS
1100 Ohio Dr., SW
Washington, D.C. 20242

White House
c/o National Capital Region, NPS
1100 Ohio Dr., SW
Washington, D.C. 20242

FLORIDA

Castillo de San Marcos National Monument
1 Castillo Dr.
St. Augustine, Fl. 32084

DeSoto National Memorial
75th St., NW
Bradenton, Fl. 33505

Fort Caroline National Memorial
12713 Fort Caroline Rd.
Jacksonville, Fl. 32225

Fort Jefferson National Monument
c/o Everglades National Park
Box 279
Homestead, Fl. 33030

Fort Matanzas National Monument
c/o Castillo de San Marcos National Monument
1 Castillo Dr.
St. Augustine, Fl. 32084

Gulf Islands National Seashore
P.O. Box 100
Gulf Breeze, Fl. 32561
(See also Mississippi)

GEORGIA

Andersonville National Historic Site
Andersonville, Ga. 31711

Chickamauga and Chattanooga National Military Park
Box 2126
Fort Oglethorpe, Ga. 30742
(also in Tennessee)

Fort Frederica National Monument
Rt. 4, Box 286C
St. Simons Island, Ga. 31522

Fort Pulaski National Monument
Box 98
Savannah Beach, Ga. 31328

Kennesaw Mountain National Battlefield Park
Box 1167
Marietta, Ga. 30061

**Martin Luther King, Jr., National Historic Site
Auburn Ave., NE
Atlanta, Ga. 30312**

Ocmulgee National Monument
1207 Emery Hwy.
Macon, Ga. 31201

GUAM

War in the Pacific National Historical Park
P.O. Box 3441
Agana, Gu. 96910

HAWAII

Kalaupapa National Historical Park
Kalaupapa, Hi. 96742

Kaloko-Honokohau National Historical Park
c/o Pacific Area Director
300 Ala Moana Blvd.
Honolulu, Hi. 96850

Pu'uhonua o Honaunau National Historical Park
P.O. Box 128
Honaunau, Kona, Hi. 96726

Puukohola Heiau National Historic Site
P.O. Box 4963
Kawaihae, Hi. 96743

U.S.S. Arizona Memorial
1 Arizona Memorial Place
Honolulu, Hi. 96818

IDAHO

Nez Perce National Historical Park
Box 93
Spalding, Id. 83551

ILLINOIS

Lincoln Home National Historic Site
526 S. 7th St.
Springfield, Il. 62703

INDIANA

George Rogers Clark National Historical Park
401 S. 2nd St.
Vincennes, In. 47591

Lincoln Boyhood National Memorial
Lincoln City, In. 47552

IOWA

Effigy Mounds National Monument
Box K
McGregor, Ia. 52157

Herbert Hoover National Historic Site
Box 607
West Branch, Ia. 52358

KANSAS

Fort Larned National Historic Site
Rt. 3
Larned, Ks. 67550

Fort Scott National Historic Site
Old Fort Blvd.
Fort Scott, Ks. 66701

KENTUCKY

Abraham Lincoln Birthplace National Historic Site
R.F.D. 1
Hodgenville, Ky. 42748

Cumberland Gap National Historical Park
Box 840
Middleboro, Ky. 40965
(also in Tennessee and Virginia)

LOUISIANA

Jean Lafitte National Historical Park and Preserve
400 Royal St., Room 200
New Orleans, La. 70130

MAINE

Saint Croix Island International Historic Site
c/o Acadia National Park
Rt. 1, Box 1
Bar Harbor, Me. 04609

MARYLAND

Antietam National Battlefield
Box 158
Sharpsburg, Md. 21782

Chesapeake and Ohio Canal National Historical Park
Box 4
Sharpsburg, Md. 21782

Clara Barton National Historic Site
5801 Oxford Rd.
Glen Echo, Md. 20768

Fort McHenry National Monument and Historic Shrine
Baltimore, Md. 21230

Fort Washington Park
National Capital Parks-East
5210 Indian Head Hwy.
Oxon Hill, Md. 20021

Hampton National Historic Site
525 Hampton Ln.
Towson, Md. 21204

Monocacy National Battlefield
c/o Antietam National Battlefield
Box 158
Sharpsburg, Md. 21782

Piscataway Park
National Capital Parks, East
5210 Indian Head Hwy.
Oxon Hill, Md. 20021

Thomas Stone National Historic Site
c/o George Washington
Birthplace National Monument
Washington's Birthplace, Va. 22575

MASSACHUSETTS

Adams National Historic Site
Box 531
Quincy, Ma. 02169

Boston National Historical Park
Charlestown Navy Yard
Boston, Ma. 02129

Frederick Law Olmsted National Historic Site
99 Warren St.
Brookline, Ma. 02146

John Fitzgerald Kennedy National Historic Site
83 Beals St.
Brookline, Ma. 02146

Longfellow National Historic Site
105 Brattle St.
Cambridge, Ma. 02138

Lowell National Historical Park
P.O. Box 1098
Lowell, Ma. 01853

Minute Man National Historical Park
Box 160
Concord, Ma. 01742

Salem Maritime National Historic Site
Custom House
174 Derby St.
Salem, Ma. 01970

Saugus Iron Works National Historic Site
244 Central St.
Saugus, Ma. 01906

Springfield Armory National Historic Site
Box 515
Springfield, Ma. 01101

MINNESOTA

Grand Portage National Monument
Box 666
Grand Marais, Mn. 55604

Pipestone National Monument
Box 727
Pipestone, Mn. 56164

Voyageurs National Park
P.O. Box 50
International Falls, Mn. 56649

MISSISSIPPI

Brices Cross Roads National Battlefield Site
c/o Natchez Trace Parkway
R.R. 1, N.T. 143
Tupelo, Ms. 38801

Gulf Islands National Seashore
4000 Hanley Rd.
Ocean Springs, Ms. 39564
(See also Florida)

Natchez Trace Parkway
R.R. 1, N.T. 143
Tupelo, Ms. 38801
(also in Alabama and Tennessee)

Tupelo National Battlefield
c/o Natchez Trace Parkway
R.R. 1, N.T. 143
Tupelo, Ms. 38801

Vicksburg National Military Park
Box 349
Vicksburg, Ms. 39180

MISSOURI

George Washington Carver National Monument
Box 38
Diamond, Mo. 64840

Harry S. Truman National Historic Site
P.O. Box 4139
Independence, Mo. 64050

Jefferson National Expansion Memorial National Historic Site
11 N. 4th St.
St. Louis, Mo. 63102

Wilson's Creek National Battlefield
Postal Drawer C
Republic, Mo. 65738

MONTANA

Big Hole National Battlefield
Box 237
Wisdom, Mt. 59761

Custer Battlefield National Monument
Box 39
Crow Agency, Mt. 59022

Grant-Kohrs Ranch National Historic Site
Box 790
Deer Lodge, Mt. 59722

NEBRASKA

Homestead National Monument of America
Rt. 3
Beatrice, Ne. 68310

Scotts Bluff National Monument
Box 427
Gering, Ne. 69341

NEW HAMPSHIRE

Saint-Gaudens National Historic Site
R.D. 2
Windsor, Vt. 05089

NEW JERSEY

Edison National Historic Site
Main St. and Lakeside Ave.
West Orange, N.J. 07052

Gateway National Recreation Area
P.O. Box 437
Highlands, N.J. 07732
(See also New York)

Morristown National Historical Park
Washington Place
Morristown, N.J. 07960

NEW MEXICO

Aztec Ruins National Monument
Box U
Aztec, N.M. 87410

Bandelier National Monument
Los Alamos, N.M. 87544

Chaco Culture National Historical Park
Star Rt. 4, Box 6500
Bloomfield, N.M. 87413

El Morro National Monument
Ramah, N.M. 87321

Fort Union National Monument
Watrous, N.M. 87753

Gila Cliff Dwellings National Monument
Gila Hot Springs
Rt. 11, Box 100
Silver City, N.M. 88061

Pecos National Monument
Drawer 11
Pecos, N.M. 87552

Salinas National Monument
Rt. 1
Mountainair, N.M. 87036

NEW YORK

Castle Clinton National Monument
Manhattan Sites, NPS
26 Wall St.
New York, N.Y. 10005

Eleanor Roosevelt National Historic Site
Hyde Park, N.Y. 12538

Federal Hall National Memorial
Manhattan Sites, NPS
26 Wall St.
New York, N.Y. 10005

Fort Stanwix National Monument
112 E. Park St.
Rome, N.Y. 13440

Gateway National Recreation Area
Bldg. 69, Floyd Bennett Field
Brooklyn, N.Y. 11234
(See also New Jersey)

General Grant National Memorial
c/o Manhattan Sites, NPS
26 Wall St.
New York, N.Y. 10005

Hamilton Grange National Memorial
287 Convent Ave.
New York, N.Y. 10031

Home of Franklin D. Roosevelt National Historic Site
Hyde Park, N.Y. 12538

Martin Van Buren National Historic Site
Box 214
Kinderhook, N.Y. 12106

Sagamore Hill National Historic Site
Cove Neck Rd., Box 304
Oyster Bay, N.Y. 11771

Saratoga National Historical Park
R.D. 1, Box 113-C
Stillwater, N.Y. 12170

Statue of Liberty National Monument
Liberty Island
New York, N.Y. 10004
(also in New Jersey)

Theodore Roosevelt Birthplace National Historic Site
28 E. 20th St.
New York, N.Y. 10003

Theodore Roosevelt Inaugural National Historic Site
641 Delaware Ave.
Buffalo, N.Y. 14209

Vanderbilt Mansion National Historic Site
Hyde Park, N.Y. 12538

Women's Rights National Historical Park
P.O. Box 70
Seneca Falls, N.Y. 13148

NORTH CAROLINA

Carl Sandburg Home National Historic Site
Box 395
Flat Rock, N.C. 28731

Fort Raleigh National Historic Site
c/o Cape Hatteras National Seashore
Rt. 1, Box 675
Manteo, N.C. 27954

Guilford Courthouse National Military Park
Box 9806
Greensboro, N.C. 27408

Moores Creek National Battlefield
Box 69
Currie, N.C. 28435

Wright Brothers National Memorial
c/o Cape Hatteras National Seashore
Rt. 1, Box 675
Manteo, N.C. 27954

NORTH DAKOTA

Fort Union Trading Post National Historic Site
Buford Rt.
Williston, N.D. 58801
(also in Montana)

Knife River Indian Villages National Historic Site
Box 175
Stanton, N.D. 58571

OHIO

Cuyahoga Valley National Recreational Area
P.O. Box 158
Peninsula, Oh. 44264

James A. Garfield National Historic Site
Lawnfield, 1950 Mentor Ave.
Mentor, Oh. 44060

Mound City Group National Monument
16062 State Rt. 104
Chillicothe, Oh. 45601

Perry's Victory and International Peace Memorial
Box 78
Put-in-Bay, Oh. 43456

William Howard Taft National Historic Site
2038 Auburn Ave.
Cincinnati, Oh. 45219

OREGON

Fort Clatsop National Memorial
Rt. 3, Box 604-FC
Astoria, Or. 97103

PENNSYLVANIA

Allegheny Portage Railroad National Historic Site
Box 247
Cresson, Pa. 16630

Edgar Allan Poe National Historic Site
c/o Independence National Historical Park
313 Walnut St.
Philadelphia, Pa. 19106

Eisenhower National Historic Site
c/o Gettysburg National Military Park
Gettysburg, Pa. 17325

Fort Necessity National Battlefield
Rt. 2, Box 528
Farmington, Pa. 15437

Friendship Hill National Historic Site
c/o Fort Necessity National Battlefield
Farmington, Pa. 15407

Gettysburg National Military Park
Gettysburg, Pa. 17325

Hopewell Furnace National Historic Site
R.D. 1, Box 345
Elverson, Pa. 19520

Independence National Historical Park
313 Walnut St.
Philadelphia, Pa. 19106

Johnstown Flood National Memorial
c/o Allegheny Portage Railroad
National Historic Site
Box 247
Cresson, Pa. 16630

Thaddeus Kosciuszko National Memorial
c/o Independence National Historical Park
313 Walnut St.
Philadelphia, Pa. 19106

Valley Forge National Historical Park
Valley Forge, Pa. 19481

PUERTO RICO

San Juan National Historic Site
Box 712
Old San Juan, P.R. 00902

RHODE ISLAND

Roger Williams National Memorial
Box 367, Annex Station
Providence, R.I. 02901

SOUTH CAROLINA

Cowpens National Battlefield
P.O. Box 308
Chesnee, S.C. 29323

Fort Sumter National Monument
1214 Middle St.
Sullivans Island, S.C. 29482

Kings Mountain National Military Park
Box 31
Kings Mountain, N.C. 28086

Ninety Six National Historic Site
Box 357
Ninety Six, S.C. 29666

SOUTH DAKOTA

Mount Rushmore National Memorial
Keystone, S.D. 57751

TENNESSEE

Andrew Johnson National Historic Site
Depot St.
Greeneville, Tn. 37743

Fort Donelson National Military Park
Box F
Dover, Tn. 37058

Shiloh National Military Park
Shiloh, Tn. 38376

Stones River National Battlefield
Rt. 10, Box 495
Murfreesboro, Tn. 37130

TEXAS

Alibates Flint Quarries National Monument
c/o Lake Meredith NRA
Box 1438
Fritch, Tx. 79036

Chamizal National Memorial
First City National Bank Bldg., Room 620
300 E. Main Dr.
El Paso, Tx. 79901

Fort Davis National Historic Site
Box 1456
Fort Davis, Tx. 79734

Lyndon B. Johnson National Historical Park
Box 329
Johnson City, Tx. 78636

Palo Alto Battlefield National Historic Site
P.O. Box 191
Brownsville, Tx. 78520

San Antonio Missions National Historical Park
727 E. Durango, Rm. A612
San Antonio, Tx. 78206

UTAH

Golden Spike National Historic Site
Box 394
Brigham City, Ut. 84302

VIRGIN ISLANDS

Christiansted National Historic Site
Box 160, Christiansted
St. Croix, V.I. 00820

Virgin Islands National Park
P.O. Box 806
Charlotte Amalie
St. Thomas, V.I. 00801

VIRGINIA

Appomattox Court House National Historical Park
Box 218
Appomattox, Va. 24522

**Arlington House
The Robert E. Lee Memorial**
c/o George Washington Memorial Pkwy.
Turkey Run Park
McLean, Va. 22101

Booker T. Washington National Monument
Rt. 1, Box 195
Hardy, Va. 24101

Colonial National Historical Park
Box 210
Yorktown, Va. 23690

**Fredericksburg and Spotsylvania County Battlefields
Memorial National Military Park**
Box 679
Fredericksburg, Va. 22401

George Washington Birthplace National Monument
Washington's Birthplace, Va. 22575

George Washington Memorial Parkway
Turkey Run Park
McLean, Va. 22101
(also in Maryland)

Maggie L. Walker National Historic Site
c/o Richmond National Battlefield Park
3215 E. Broad St.
Richmond, Va. 23223

Manassas National Battlefield Park
Box 1830
Manassas, Va. 22110

Petersburg National Battlefield
Box 549
Petersburg, Va. 23803

Richmond National Battlefield Park
3215 E. Broad St.
Richmond, Va. 23223

WASHINGTON

Fort Vancouver National Historic Site
Vancouver, Wa. 98661

Klondike Gold Rush National Historical Park
117 S. Main St.
Seattle, Wa. 98104

San Juan Island National Historical Park
Box 429
Friday Harbor, Wa. 98250

Whitman Mission National Historic Site
Rt. 2
Walla Walla, Wa. 99362

WEST VIRGINIA

Harpers Ferry National Historical Park
Box 65
Harpers Ferry, W.Va. 25425
(also in Maryland and Virginia)

New River Gorge National River
c/o Mid-Atlantic Regional Office
National Park Service
143 S. Third St.
Philadelphia, Pa. 19106

WYOMING

Fort Laramie National Historic Site
Fort Laramie, Wy. 82212

National Archives and Records Administration: National Archives Field Branches

CALIFORNIA

Los Angeles Branch
24000 Avila Rd.
Laguna Niguel, 92677-6719
Telephone: (714) 831-4220
Diane Nixon, Director

San Francisco Branch
1000 Commodore Dr.
San Bruno, 94066
Telephone: (415) 876-9009
Michael Anderson, Director

COLORADO

Denver Branch
Bldg. 48, Denver Federal Center
Denver, 80225
Telephone: (303) 236-0818
Joel Barker, Director

GEORGIA

Atlanta Branch
1557 St. Joseph Ave.
East Point, 30344
Telephone: (404) 763-7477
Gayle P. Peters, Director

ILLINOIS

Chicago Branch
7358 S. Pulaski Rd.
Chicago, 60629
Telephone: (312) 581-7816
Peter Bunce, Director

MASSACHUSETTS

Boston Branch
380 Trapelo Rd.
Waltham, 02154
Telephone: (617) 647-8100
James K. Owens, Director

MISSOURI

Kansas City Branch
2312 E. Bannister Rd.
Kansas City, 64131
Telephone: (816) 926-7271
R. Reed Whitaker, Director

NEW JERSEY

New York Branch
Bldg. 22, MOT
Bayonne, 07002-5388
Telephone: (201) 823-7545
Joel Buckwald, Director

PENNSYLVANIA

Philadelphia Branch
9th and Market Sts.
Philadelphia, 19107
Telephone: (215) 597-3000
Robert Plowman, Director

TEXAS

Fort Worth Branch
501 W. Felix St.
Fort Worth, 76115
Telephone: (817) 334-5525
Mail to: P.O. Box 6216
Kent C. Carter, Director

WASHINGTON

Seattle Branch
6125 Sand Point Way
Seattle, 98115
Telephone: (206) 526-6507
Phillip E. Lothyan, Director

The Essential Guide to Prescription Drugs

2004 Edition

The Essential Guide to Prescription Drugs

2004 Edition

James J. Rybacki, Pharm.D.

HarperResource

An Imprint of HarperCollins*Publishers*

To Dr. Jim Long, a brilliant man and the truest colleague and friend I've ever had.

To our families: Often as different as night and day, yet bound by a common genetic, social history, and legacy. The fabric of who we can and perhaps will become. Look to your family medical history to anticipate and prevent diseases and conditions. Help family members remember to take their medicines and then follow up to make sure the goals of the medicines are reached and maintained. Those pills won't do anyone any good if they simply stay in the bottle!

Designed by C. Linda Dingler

Library of Congress Catalog Card Number 87–657561
ISSN 0894–7058

ISBN 0-06-055410-X (pbk.)   03 04 RRD 10 9 8 7 6 5 4 3 2 1
ISBN 0-06-055409-6   03 04 RRD 10 9 8 7 6 5 4 3 2 1

Contents

Author's Note for the 2004 Edition   vii

Points for the Patient   xi

Points for the Pharmacist   xxi

Points for the Physician   xxvii

SECTION ONE

1. How to Use This Book   1
2. Guidelines for Safe and Effective Drug Use or How to Become a Powerful Patient   15

    Medicines and Pharmacy on the Internet   15

    Powerful Patients Do Not   16

    Powerful Patients Do   18

    Preventing Adverse Drug Reactions   20

    Medicines and People Over 65   22

    Measuring Drug Levels in Blood (Therapeutic Drug Monitoring)   25

3. True Breakthroughs in Medicines   28

SECTION TWO

Drug Profiles   33

SECTION THREE

The Leading Edge   1217

SECTION FOUR

Drug Classes   1225

SECTION FIVE

A Glossary of Drug-Related Terms   1251

SECTION SIX

Tables of Drug Information   1271

1. Medicines That May Adversely Affect the Fetus and
   Newborn Infant   1273
2. Medicines That May Increase Sensitivity to the Sun
   (Photosensitivity)   1274
3. Medicines That May Adversely Affect Behavior   1275
4. Medicines That May Adversely Affect Vision   1278
5. Medicines That May Cause Blood Cell Dysfunction or
   Damage   1280
6. Medicines That May Cause Heart Dysfunction or Damage   1283
7. Medicines That May Cause Lung Dysfunction or Damage   1285
8. Medicines That May Cause Liver Dysfunction or Damage   1287
9. Medicines That May Cause Kidney Dysfunction or Damage   1289
10. Medicines That May Cause Nerve Dysfunction or Damage   1291
11. Medicines That May Adversely Affect Sexuality   1293
12. Medicines That May Interact with Alcohol   1300
13. High-Potassium Foods   1304
14. Your Personal Drug Profile   1305
15. The Medication Map   1306
16. Medicines Removed from the Market   1307
17. Helpful, Balanced, and Objective Web Sites   1309
18. Powerful Patients and Home Test Kits   1313
19. Running a Risk: Recognizing and Regaining Control
    of Heart Disease Risk Factors   1314
20. Living Longer (Longevity) with Therapeutic Lifestyle
    Changes   1315
21. How to Get Your Family Help with the Cost of Medicines
    (Programs and Web Sites)   1316

Sources   1319
Index   1339
Controlled Drug Schedules   1377
Pregnancy Risk Categories   1379

Author's Note
for the 2004 Edition

Can we live longer? We may, and without doubt, medicines are part of the answer. Consider for a moment, however; it's better to take steps to PREVENT a disease or condition, BEFORE a medicine is needed. This relates to all of us by considering our family history and asking **what steps can be taken to check and then lower risk.** Please remember— YOU are the center of health care. Despite the busy doctor, receptionist, nurse, nurse practitioner, physicians assistant, and pharmacist—you always have been the center of activity, the focus of medicines and their results or outcomes. What we have so often collectively forgotten once we become patients is how to give ourselves and our loved ones permission to ask what problems we are at risk for, which conditions can be prevented, and, if not, why and how soon an effect is expected or what the goals of any treatment will be. Call on the strength of your family and loved ones to help get the best results from your medicines. Do this by asking for help remembering to take them, reaching goals, and by using this book to watch for any early side effects.

We receive care when we are sick, too late for prevention, too compromised and worried to reflect on what has happened. Far too often, the pills come in a stapled bag at the end of a busy day. STOP. STOP now and make a list of questions for your next visit to the doctor. I believe a sound approach covers a six-step continuum:

1. What diseases or conditions am I at risk for given my family history, and what tests are currently recommended to help define the degree of risk?
2. Given the risk I face, what steps can I take to lower the risk?
3. Understanding the conditions I now have, what research (evi-

dence base) SUPPORTS THE MEDICINES I AM NOW TAKING? Has this changed since my last visit (three months can be an eternity in cardiology)?

4. What are the goals of the medicines or prevention steps that I now take or have undertaken? What's a reasonable time frame to expect results from treatments or to recheck our success at prevention?
5. Given my health plan or insurance, how is information shared among the doctor's office or clinic, the pharmacy where I get my medicines, the hospital, and again my doctor's office or clinic? So often what we don't tell or share creates additional risk or blunts benefits.
6. Because the research always changes, once a year, start all over again and ask what diseases or conditions you now appear to be at risk for.

Once you make your list of questions, mail them to your doctor to be added to your medical chart and ask that they be discussed at your next office visit. A huge secret is that the chart is the center of the universe in the office, clinic, and hospital! Many doctors review charts the day before or the morning before YOU show up in the office. Sending your questions to your doctor ahead of time lets them THINK. Thinking is good because they want the best results for you. Health care as it now exists has simply so often contracted time and in effect has squeezed you out of the picture. Squeeze back in and partner with your doctor!

Getting back into the picture takes some planning, but remember, YOU are the center of health care. So often, an office visit results in a prescription. Does it have to? NO. A pill isn't always the answer. For example, if your cholesterol is only mildly increased and your pattern of good and bad cholesterol (particle size, etc.) is only a little out of range, your doctor may want to try diet and exercise before starting a medicine. If a medicine IS suggested, please be honest:

- Be honest about being able to afford the medicine.
- Be honest about being willing to take the medicine exactly as prescribed.
- Be honest about all of the nonprescription, prescription, and nutritional or herbal supplements that you now take.
- Be honest about how well you understand the goals of any treatment.
- Be honest in asking about when results will be checked.
- Be honest about how well your health care system talks to itself. Try to understand the relationship among the hospital, the doctor's office or clinic, your family and home, and the pharmacy or mail-order service where you actually get the medicines.

Affording medicines is one of the most daunting issues facing government and patients. Will there finally be a Medicare prescription drug benefit? I honestly do not know. I promise that I will work with the American Society of Clinical Pharmacists (ASCP) to talk to Congress to try to involve pharmacists in helping YOU get the most from your medicines. We've learned from many other countries (or should have) that simply giving the medicines away does NOT mean that people will take them!

Plan your medicines into your day (see the Medication Map provided in Table 15). **Plan your medicines into your insurance** (many doctors can check if a medicine is on formulary and will be covered, while you are still in the office). **Plan your medicines into your family budget** (Table 21 may help). One of the most difficult things is to remember to actually take your medicines. This year, I started a medicine to lower my cholesterol. It's a once-a-day pill, but I found myself forgetting. Since I involved my family, I haven't missed a pill. It's always a good idea to read about your medicines in this book and understand the mild and more serious possible side effects. Discussing these with your family will help them identify possible medicine-related problems. Finding problems early can be a lifesaver. If you are at all unsure that a new problem is related to a new or existing medicine, call your doctor. It's a good move and good medicine!

As noted in each previous edition, no claim is made that **all** known actions, uses, side effects, adverse effects, precautions, or interactions for a drug are included in the information provided in this book. Talk to your doctor before making any changes, additions, or deletions to the medicines that you already take. This book contains information about medicines and is not medical advice. Although diligent care has been taken to ensure the accuracy of the information provided during the preparation of this revision, the continued accuracy and currentness are ever subject to change relative to the dissemination of new information derived from drug research, development, and general usage.

James Joseph Rybacki, Pharm.D.

Points for the Patient

Regardless of what you do for a living, who you know, or what you know—when you become a patient, you are no longer the same person. **Dr. Jim Rybacki the author** and clinical pharmacist talks about adherence, compliance, and concordance—the critical importance of taking medicines EXACTLY as prescribed. **Jim Rybacki the patient** forgets to take his once-a-day cholesterol medicine and has to involve his family in order to remember to take that single pill.

Unfortunately, no one teaches you how to be a great patient. Too often, the hospital (a great facility where you have time to learn about your new disease or existing medical problem) is only oriented to treating and discharging. I can't begin to tell you how often I've heard a caring health care professional say something like, "I need a bed on two West." Did we forget the patient? When my mother was leaving the hospital after having had a stroke and carotid artery surgery, a very busy nurse came by and very quickly said, "Here's the medicines you were taking or are to take now. The stitches in your neck will have to be removed in about two weeks. There's a form that tells you the date and time of the follow-up appointment with your doctor in two weeks. Here's the sheets that tell about the meds. Here's the forms you have to take to the business office. Here's the lotion and other stuff from your admission. Someone will be by to take you to the business office on the way out. Do you have any questions?"

To me, being a great patient requires keeping yourself at the center of the system, and shaping the system to work for you. While the rapid-fire discharge method of my mother's nurse got the patient (my mother) out the door, it did nothing to encourage a stroke patient to take her medicines to prevent a second stroke. Did nothing to encourage a diabetic to keep her blood sugar under control, and it was probably confusing. The patient didn't skip a beat. She smiled at the busy nurse and said, "Well, you've gone very fast. I really want to get out of the hospital. I don't think

I understand these medicines, but I'll ask my son, Dr. Rybacki, if I have any questions." The nurse stopped, shook my hand—said she had a lot of patients and two more discharges—and then apologized for rushing. The obvious question here is what YOU can do if you don't have someone who can explain your medicines. TAKE THE TIME TO ASK. If you still don't understand once the nurse is done, ask the nurse to page your doctor or whoever is on call from his or her group. If you don't understand after your doctor is done, ask the question again! READ THIS BOOK WELL! Use it to start a valuable conversation with your doctor.

Understanding what you are facing can be half the battle in any situation. It's important to learn as much as you can about the new disease or condition you or a loved one has and how best to manage it. Ask your doctor and pharmacist for written information, visit reputable Web sites (see Table 17) to learn, and check your local libraries and national health organizations (such as the American Heart Association, American Diabetes Association, and National Cancer Institute) for pertinent publications. I try to help sort out information for you on my Web site, *www.medicineinfo.com*. Never be afraid to ask your nurse, doctor, or pharmacist questions about the disease or condition—you actually make their jobs easier when you help yourself. All competent health care professionals welcome the chance to help you understand your health, diseases or conditions, and medicines as they relate to their particular expertise—regardless of how busy they may be. Physicians and pharmacists are good examples. If they won't give you this critical time and these critical answers, find another physician or pharmacist.

We are all unique, and a critical factor in successful drug therapy is called tailoring. This means selecting each medicine for each patient and adjusting the medicine doses to each patient. In clothing, one size actually rarely fits all. In medicines, a "one dose fits all" approach can lead to perilous prescriptions. There is actually a new field called pharmacogenomics that seeks to tailor medicines to the genes that we have.

Once a medicine is prescribed, please **share the responsibility** for safe and effective drug treatment. Powerful patients help themselves by making sure every prescriber and pharmacist who helps provide your health care is aware of **all** the medicines you are taking. This sounds deceptively simple, but always include prescription, nonprescription, and any herbal or nutritional support you take.

Don't be afraid to take another list—I've had many patients do this and welcome the complete picture. Did you know that nonprescription medicines can blunt the benefits of your prescriptions? Millions of Americans now take herbal medicines. Talk to your doctor or pharmacist BEFORE combining any herbal medicine with any other medicine. REMEMBER, herbal medicines are NOT presently approved or regulated in the same way as prescription medicines. They fall under the Dietary Supplement Health and Education Act (DSHEA) of 1994. These products are more potent than ever. I believe it's time to regulate them as we do prescription medicines. They can have real benefits as well as serious interactions with prescription medicines. I've updated and broadened the possible herbal/prescription medicine interactions in the drug profiles to help protect you.

We all need to be there for our families—living in the best possible health. People do not exist alone. However you define family, you have a powerful and often underused resource to help you make medicines work! For example, it's okay to say that you feel like you have to take too many pills. With the progress in medicines today, there are many options. Whatever is chosen, I'll always end my upcoming new television program (*Medicines and Your Family*) with "Take your medicines and take care of your family." I'll continue to encourage you on the radio, on television, in my audiotapes, and on my Web site (www.medicineinfo. com) to ask questions and be a partner in your health care! Let's take a look at some specific ways to develop patient power.

When Your Doctor Prescribes a Drug for You

- POWERFUL PATIENTS ALWAYS find out about specific risk factors that go along with a new diagnosis. Take a look at Table 19 (Running a Risk: Recognizing and Regaining Control of Heart Disease Risk Factors) if you have a family history of heart disease. For other diseases or conditions, find out if risk factors can be modified to lower the chance of a repeat problem or to lessen the severity of an existing problem. For example, if you have a history of diabetes in your family and you are overweight, losing weight is one of those risk factors that you can change that can actually decrease your risk of diabetes. There is also a study (Diabetes Prevention Program) that says that lifestyle changes such as exercise as well as a medicine called metformin (Glucophage) can help PREVENT diabetes.
- POWERFUL PATIENTS ALWAYS ask if there is nutritional support that may be required if a new prescription is being considered. For example: HMG CoA reductase inhibitors may deplete coenzyme Q (co-Q) in some patients. If patients begin to feel tired after starting one of the high cholesterol medicines in that class, supplementation with co-Q may help restore quality of life. Another good example are corticosteroids such as prednisone (Deltasone, Orasone, and others), which can work to weaken bones by decreasing calcium absorption. Calcium supplements and a check of bone mineral density (by DEXA or PDEXA) are advisable if prednisone or similar corticosteroids are going to be taken on an ongoing basis.

When You Get a New Diagnosis Along with a Lifestyle Change or a New Prescription

- CHANGE? Yes, change. When a new disease or condition is identified, what you are really facing is change. For example, if your cholesterol is increased, the result by itself is simply a number. When your individual family and medical history are considered, the number becomes part of a reasonable series of steps that need to be taken over a specific time frame. High cholesterol is a great example. POWERFUL PATIENTS ALWAYS find out about specific risk factors that go along with a new diagnosis. For a closer look at where cholesterol fits in, visit Table 19 (Running a Risk: Recognizing and Regaining Control of Heart Disease Risk Factors). For people with small increases and few existing risk factors, TLC comes into play. We may think of this as tender loving care, but in the cholesterol arena, it means therapeutic lifestyle changes.

- POWERFUL PATIENTS ALWAYS ask if there is nutritional support that may be required if a new prescription is being considered. For example: HMG CoA reductase inhibitors may deplete coenzyme Q in some patients—particularly those who already have low coenzyme Q. If patients begin to feel tired after starting one of the high cholesterol medicines in that class, we first need to rule out (with a CK laboratory test) a muscle inflammation called myositis, then supplementation with co-Q may help restore quality of life. Another good example are corticosteroids such as prednisone (Deltasone, Orasone, and others), which can work to weaken bones by decreasing calcium absorption. Calcium supplements and a check of bone mineral density (by DEXA or PDEXA) are advisable if prednisone or similar corticosteroids are going to be taken on an ongoing basis. Powerful patients are proactive in preventing problems.

- POWERFUL PATIENTS ALWAYS ask what the goals of any existing or new treatment are, and how long it should take to reach them. In other words, the clock is ticking. If a new medicine is prescribed, the time for that medicine to work and then be checked should be told (disclosed) to you. For example, "Here is your new prescription for cholesterol, we'll see you again in three months." While this tells you that a return visit is needed, it is an example of a prescription, not patient-centered care. A much more desirable way is: Here is your new prescription to lower your cholesterol. It is called pravastatin and the brand name is Pravachol. Your pharmacist will give you printed information sheet on it. "Our goal is to have Pravachol work to lower your bad cholesterol (LDL) to 180 mg/dl in three months. It's critical to take it at the same time every day and to never miss a day. It's okay to get a fat or lipid panel or cholesterol rechecked in about four weeks if you happen to go to a health fair—but please make sure the results are sent to me. Do you have any questions for me?" Now this is valuable patient-centered information!

- POWERFUL PATIENTS ALWAYS ask what the goals of any existing or new treatment are. If your prescriber has done a good job, you will already know what the goals of treatment are! Beyond knowing the goals, POWERFUL PATIENTS ALWAYS ask if there are any lifestyle changes they can try to make that might help the medicine work harder. A good example here are the therapeutic lifestyle changes (TLC) found in the current National Cholesterol Guidelines (NCEP ATP 3) in addition to a medicine for cholesterol.

- POWERFUL PATIENTS ALWAYS ask what to do if goals of their medicines are not achieved in the time frame that they originally discussed with their doctor. Sometimes this means simply adjusting the dose. In any case, please do not wait until the last minute of an office visit to bring up the real reason you came to the office. I've seen this time after time, and while it's human nature to do this, it rarely gets the best results.

- Ask your doctor if he or she has an adherence assessment form (AAF) that can be placed in your medical chart. Explain to them that you would like to have adherence checked on every office visit and then charted (the medical term for adding it to your record) like a vital sign.

- Sound-alike and look-alike errors are unfortunately not unusual. Powerful patients protect themselves by ALWAYS asking that the prescription include both the **name of the drug** and the **disorder** for which the drug is taken. For example: Fosamax for osteoporosis or Zantac for heartburn. This helps avoid "sound-alike" errors. Over the phone, a person calling in Xanax may be misunderstood as saying Zantac. Zantac is for heartburn and ulcers. Xanax is for anxiety. If the disorder being treated is named on the label, it offers a second chance for a pharmacist or certified technician to discover a mistake.

- Ask your doctor to fill out the medication map from the back of this book while you're still in the office. This helps you fit the medicines realistically into your life. Taking this step may even show that a medicine being considered by your doctor might not really work out for you. The best medicine in the world does absolutely no good if you can't or won't be able to take it. Get the most from your health care dollars.

- Tell your doctor about any known drug allergies and of any prior drug-induced adverse effects. This will let the doctor check to see whether he or she has inadvertently prescribed a medicine from the same chemical family.

- POWERFUL PATIENTS ALWAYS honestly talk about **all other drugs** (prescription, nonprescription, herbal, or nutritional) that you are taking. Include alcohol, marijuana, and others. Remember that some herbal extracts contain the same ingredients found in prescription medicines and may lead to unforeseen toxicity, or may blunt prescription drug benefits. Interestingly, still other herbal medicines can help prescription medicines work or may even duplicate some prescription drug effects. Because of this, combining an herbal remedy with a prescription may actually require lower doses of the prescription drug. Powerful patients find out about possible interactions first. Make certain you talk to your doctor before you combine ANY medicines.

- Many medicines **require** special precautions. Examples include avoiding certain foods, alcohol, exposure to sun, certain medicines, or even hazardous activities.
- Be sure you understand how long to take a medicine. Talk with your prescriber about this and, if applicable, when and how to stop it. A hallmark of good prescribing is that goals and time frames are set at the time a medicine is first prescribed. Unfortunately, when people take several different medicines, mistakes can be made. I see many cases where patients thought they understood what to do and actually stopped the wrong medicine in a complicated regimen.
- Ask your doctor to give you a **written summary** about the drug prescribed. Few people can remember all of the information and instructions that have been talked about. A concept I have pioneered is the **medication map.** Very simple, but does YOUR DOCTOR have a chart tab that shows where HE or SHE mapped the medicines into YOUR life? WHY NOT? Many medicine errors are made because people forget, make incorrect combinations of medicines, mistake one pill for the other, or take medicine with food when it should not be. A medication map organizes all the medicines you are taking and tells you how much, when, and with what the medicines should be taken. Take the blank form from this book to your doctor or pharmacist and ask him or her to fill in the form with you. This will help you to clarify and verify pertinent information while taking the medicine itself in the best possible way. I've gotten a lot of smirks from mediocre minds who looked at the map and saw only paper. The power in a doctor's office is in the chart, and unfortunately, many national organizations simply do not know this.
- POWERFUL PATIENTS ALWAYS ask their doctor if the medicine prescribed offers the best balance of price and outcomes. This simple question will help a busy practitioner focus on his or her available choices. Remember to ask whether the dosing has been adjusted for any compromise in kidney or liver function or other chronic condition that you may have. Diseases can also "interact" with medicines.
- Many HMOs or health care insurers may not pay for some medicines. This can impact your doctor's prescribing authority and the pharmacist's ability to fill your prescription. Write the payer to complain. The Patient's Bill of Rights may restore your access to the medicine that will give the best results! I pray that the Medicare prescription drug benefit will involve community pharmacists and, perhaps more important, seamless inpatient-to-outpatient tracking by CLINICAL pharmacists to make sure that the drug you were prescribed is actually working for YOU.
- POWERFUL PATIENTS tell their doctor if new symptoms develop after they start taking the drug(s) prescribed. This can protect you from early stages of Bad Med Syndrome. Powerful patients know that some problems caused by medicines themselves are easily reversible if they are caught early. If you are found to have had a reaction to a medicine, ask your doctor to report the problem to the

Federal Drug Administration (FDA). This reporting is critical to maintaining safe and effective medicines for everyone.

- Keep follow-up appointments with your doctor and for laboratory tests. Many drugs must be monitored closely.
- If you go to any other health care provider, tell him or her of all medications you are taking currently—prescription and nonprescription. This is also a common source of problems: People often think that all doctors have all of their medical history simply because they are doctors. Doctors are not clairvoyant. Tell them your complete history in order to get the best possible results. Remember any herbal medicines you might be taking. Powerful patients never assume that every doctor knows all the medicines that they take.
- If the prescription you got was for pain management, remember that the Joint Commission on Accreditation of Healthcare Organizations has come forth with some novel and long-overdue pain management standards. From now on, when you go to the hospital, pain management will be a patient right. In time, you will see posters right in hospital hallways that help increase awareness of your basic right to effective pain management. Pain is now the fifth vital sign. In your doctor's office, you will not see the Joint Commission, but it is perfectly acceptable to demand effective pain management!
- This is controversial, but I think it is smart to ask your doctor if there is a gag rule he or she is working under that restricts him or her to a limited formulary and lower-cost medicines. There may be a conflict of interest in the advice he or she is giving you.

When You Get Your Prescription Medicine(s)

- POWERFUL PATIENTS OPEN THE BAG. This is especially valuable if you are able to get your prescription filled in a pharmacy. Unfortunately, many people don't use the considerable education and help that their pharmacist can provide. Many prescription bags are stapled shut, with the brief patient information sheet or even a Med Guide inside. You'll be glad if you open the bag! Powerful patients check to be sure. This gives you a chance (on a refill prescription) to see if the pills look the same as before. It is also a chance to look over the dose and make sure you know how often to take it. Make sure you understand this and ask your pharmacist questions. A few minutes reading the information about the medicine **can actually save your life.** If you are required or choose to use a mail-order pharmacy, once again, it is critical to check the bag and make certain that you have received the correct medicine—yet it is more difficult for you to get access to a pharmacist to confirm the medicine. The best way to go is to ask how you will have access to a pharmacist if you have medication questions. Insist on toll-free telephone numbers.
- POWERFUL PATIENTS READ THE LABEL and auxiliary labels carefully! It's time well spent. All prescription bottles MUST be

labeled with a minimum of information. Check that both the **name of the drug** and the **disorder** are specified. If these are missing, ask your pharmacist to call your doctor for permission to add them. For example, I've seen many patients who have become confused about which medicine is for what. Having a bottle for a cholesterol-lowering medicine labeled as rosuvastatin (Crestor) for cholesterol lowering is much better than simply having the name.

- Many managed-care organizations require pill splitting. Check with your pharmacist to see if this is something you will be expected to do. If so, ask if they will split the pills for you, or if they have a pill splitter for sale. This will help ensure that you will get an accurate dose of medicine.

- If this is a refill, check to see that the drug in the bottle is the same as the drug in your original supply. If it is not the same, ask your pharmacist to explain the difference. (Generic drug products from different manufacturers often vary in size, shape, color, etc.)

- There are more than 1,000 drug names that "look alike" in print or "sound alike" in speech. Examples: Celebrex—Celexa, cyclosporine—cycloserine, Prilosec—Prozac, Xanax—Zantac. Mistaking one drug for the other can lead to serious problems. "Sound-alikes" cause problems when a prescription is given by telephone. Listing the **disorder** on the prescription will help the pharmacist realize the mistake. Also, many of the most often prescribed drugs are pictured in the Color Chart insert in this book.

- Ask your pharmacist to give you **printed information sheets** about the drug(s) prescribed for you. Say YES if you are asked if you want counseling on your medicine! Make use of your pharmacist's training. Also ask this expert to fill out the **Medication Map** from the back of this book for you.

- Read the label. (I'm writing this again because it is so important.) I've seen people pay more attention to a peanut butter label than they do to their prescription label. These labels are a great opportunity to learn how to get the most from your medicines. They also tell about dosage forms that should not be altered (opened, crushed, or chewed) and about effects food may have.

- Use the same pharmacy for all of your medicines. Most pharmacies have a computer system. This can help prevent serious allergic reactions and significant drug interactions. Tell your pharmacist of all drugs (remember to include herbal remedies, megavitamins, alcohol, and nonprescription agents) you are currently taking.

Your Responsibilities—to Yourself—as a Patient

- POWERFUL PATIENTS know what the goals are for any medicine they take and how long it should take to reach those goals. If time goes by and the medicine does not help as it should, there are often many other options. Powerful patients give the medicine the time to work, and then work with their doctor and the medicine to reach goals.

- Know both the generic and brand name of all drugs prescribed for you.
- If you are taking more than one drug, be sure that the label of **each container** includes the **name of the drug** and the **condition it treats.**
- Remember that foods can react with medicines. Something as simple as grapefruit juice is now known to interact with some high blood pressure medicines. The best liquid to take with most medicines is water. Be aware.
- Take a moment to make sure you understand the directions for using a drug. Ask if you're not sure.
- Many nonprescription medicines were once available only by prescription. Talk with your pharmacist or physician **BEFORE** combining any two drugs.
- POWERFUL PATIENTS follow medicine instructions carefully and completely. **DO NOT** stop an antibiotic seven days into a 10-day prescription because you feel better. This can lead to serious illness. If you have trouble remembering to take your medications on time, ask for a dosing calendar or a weekly medication box.
- If you take medicines prescribed by more than one doctor, check the **generic names** for duplicate drugs with different brand names. This could cause serious overdoses.
- Ask your doctor and pharmacist if he or she offers "brown-bag sessions" for your medicines. Put all the medicines you currently take into a bag and have your pharmacist review them for potency, appropriateness, and dating.
- If you are looking at a new insurance plan or HMO, ask if there is a formulary. Find out if a mail-order pharmacy must be used. If so, ask who will regularly review your medicines and how you will be able to contact a pharmacist for questions.
- If you will be using an Internet pharmacy, look at the Guidelines for Safe and Effective Drug Use in Section One of this book. Expect pharmaceutical care, not just delivery of medicine.
- Be certain all drugs you take are "in date" (have not expired).
- Effective and timely control of pain is a basic right to which you are entitled. The Agency for Health Care Policy and Research has released *Clinical Practice Guidelines*, which outline management of cancer pain but also apply to management of pain in general. Demand that your pain be respected as much as a high fever. The American Pain Society has long asked that pain become the fifth vital sign, and this is finally a reality! The Joint Commission on Accreditation of Healthcare Organizations has developed an elaborate set of guidelines on pain management. You'll see more any time you go to a hospital.
- If you are facing a terminal illness, ask whether the hospital you are considering has a palliative care program as well as a hospice program.

Suggestions for Containing the Costs of Drug Therapy

- READ TABLE 21: How to Get Your Family Help with the Cost of Medicines. As always, I've tried to bring you information about the best programs, helpful tips, and balanced and objective Web sites that can help make a difference for you.

- TAKE YOUR MEDICINE IN THE RIGHT AMOUNT AT THE RIGHT TIME AND IN THE RIGHT WAY. This sounds so very basic, but it's a fundamental point where we fail time and time again. Unfortunately, if you skip doses, you may lose much of the possible benefit from many medicines. Additionally, your doctor could decide to add more medicine to the ones he thinks are not helping enough, further increasing your bill as well as chances for drug interactions.

- Cooperate fully with your doctor to ensure an accurate diagnosis. Many signs or symptoms can be embarrassing to talk about, but may be a critical part of the puzzle that could lead your doctor to an incorrect decision. An accurate and complete history helps ensure that any medicines needed will be as safe and effective as possible.

- Ask your doctor to prescribe the drug that is most appropriate for you, selecting the product that offers the best balance of price and outcomes. If you have several chronic diseases at the same time, what appears to be a more expensive antibiotic may have a better **outcome** for you than a less costly one. **Ask your doctor if a chosen medicine has a "cousin" in the same chemical family that may give the same results at a lower price!**

- Ask your doctor or pharmacist if an acceptable generic product is available.

- If your HMO or managed care organization requires you to split pills (a present controversy), ask if they will pay for a pill splitter so that you can accomplish this accurately. If they refuse to pay for a splitter, I strongly advise you to get one yourself. Please also write to your congressperson about the managed care organization's refusal.

- Ask your doctor if there are any vitamins or minerals that you should be taking based on family history (such as folic acid to help prevent some heart attacks or calcium for osteoporosis), or even because of the medicines themselves.

- Follow your doctor's and pharmacist's advice about your prescriptions. A medicine won't do you ANY GOOD AT ALL if it stays in the bottle.

- Many HMOs and physician groups use a concept called dual-product substitution. This is a measure that I agree with. For example, some prescription products are merely different names for the same medicine (Vanceril or Beclovent; Normodyne or Trandate). It makes perfect sense that the lowest-priced brand be freely substituted for a particular prescription. Ask your doctor about this idea when he or she is writing a prescription for you.

- Ask how the HMO or physician group measures up against other groups in your area. Remember, many groups are benchmarked or measured by groups such as the National Committee on Quality Assurance (on the Web at *www.ncqa.org*, or call them at 202-955-5697).

Points for the Pharmacist

Did you know that there are bills before the House and Senate that will provide pharmacists the opportunity to engage in medication therapy consults? While a specific fee schedule has not been created, this may be tagged to the internal medicine fees. If you have ever thought about developing your disease management expertise, this would be the year to augment your skills. I will try THIS YEAR to become involved (via ACCP) in bringing real national management of therapy to pharmacists!

As in previous years, I need to address adherence—yes, adherence. Half the people who get a prescription fail to take it correctly. WHY DO I HAVE TO SAY THIS YEAR AFTER YEAR? You can make a real difference by making sure that people understand how much to take, when to take it, and what to take it with. I've been working with the American Heart Association to involve pharmacists and pharmacies in more actively encouraging adherence and getting people quality information. My last paper (see Sources) talked about the great role pharmacists can have in helping decrease cardiovascular disease in women by increasing adherence! Some other pharmacist-oriented programs increased adherence rates by two to four times what had been found in some conventional health care delivery systems!

Do you encourage compliance at every initial prescription and refill? Do you call or e-mail the doctor if your patients are early or late for refills? Consider starting an adherence/compliance clinic. Start making a difference today. If you are a hospital pharmacist, find out about the American Heart Association's Get With The Guidelines program. It's a hospital-based program designed to identify champions in hospitals, identify patients who have had a first heart attack, and then help them get the best medicines in order to prevent a second heart attack. Learn more at www.americanheart.org.

Current estimates tell us that adverse drug events or Bad Med Syndrome costs **60–100 billion dollars a year**. Failure to individualize drug therapy is widespread and is something that you can help correct. Learn the current goals and time frames to achieve those goals in current objective guidelines (such as the American Heart Association's). Don't be afraid to keep your prescribers informed about goals and guidelines. Point-of-care testing, such as blood sugar and cholesterol checks (now available in the same machine), can be a valuable and compensated service. Many pharmacists are being paid for their expertise in medicines (cognitive services). There are many initiatives where you can help manage diabetes, compliance, asthma, and cholesterol problems and be reimbursed for the great help that you can give. I myself take appointments and help answer questions about medicines! I've also put a framework in this book for a wonderful new cognitive service: **Medication Mapping.** Use this form to make sure that newly prescribed medicines will actually work with their lives!

Many states have given pharmacists the opportunity to provide vaccinations, and large numbers of you are starting to offer them. In a setting where the pressure of time is less restrictive, you can make a great difference in helping prevent some common illnesses. It's always better to prevent a disease or condition than to have to treat it. Influenza is a great example. Pain management is another important problem. Hospital pharmacists will now see extensive Joint Commission on Accreditation of Healthcare Organizations (JCAHCO) guidelines relating to effective pain management. Pain is the fifth vital sign! This is a near-ideal opportunity to collaborate with your physician colleagues to make a real difference.

The American Heart Association has a Compliance Action Program under way. This bold initiative intends to help consumers, pharmacists, and prescribers understand how critical it is to work to reduce risk factors, develop evidence-based care, encourage and follow physician recommendations, and improve access to emergency care for people who have heart disease or have suffered a stroke.

Be a leader! Create a file of your prescribers who have office e-mail. Next, talk to your customers about the importance of your new adherence program. Explain that your pharmacy works closely with physicians to get the best results from medicines. Consider a patient adherence contract and offer a small discount for great adherence. Talk to your patients and tell them that your pharmacy actually e-mails your doctor when prescriptions are filled so that he or she knows that the new medicine is being put to work! Talk to your prescribers about this new system and explain how they can be e-mailed right at the office if their patients never fill or are early or late with their prescription refills.

Some pharmacists have made great inroads in clinical service by helping manage medicines for asthmatics, providing vaccines (where state law allows), offering smoking cessation groups, and helping monitor anticoagulation, asthma, blood sugar, and cholesterol. Call your state board of pharmacy for more information. It's okay to accept appointments and charge a fee for cognitive services. Many stores are getting high rates of reimbursement. No one wants to contract Bad Med Syndrome, and you can be there to help prevent it. Make your systems seamless. For example, work with your hospital pharmacy colleagues to create a seamless loop with Get With The Guidelines and follow-up care. An Adherence Assessment Form (AAF) can take 90 seconds to fill out and will keep your patients taking their medicines. Consider tracking existing medicines, start dates and dosing, and adherence via a form that follows your customers from the community to the hospital to the doctor's office and back again. The **Medication Map** in this book offers a perfect new service to help patients realistically fit medicines into their lives!

I advise consumers to take the fullest advantage of their pharmacist's training and experience. Get copies of the latest clinical guidelines for any disease state management services you are offering and keep your prescribers in the loop! The Agency for Health Care Policy and Research is advocating effective and timely control of pain as a basic human right. The American Pain Society and JCAHCO have made pain the fifth vital sign—and now JCAHO, the AMA, and NCQA are working together to develop quality measures (see True Breakthroughs). This is another clear opportunity for you to help in offering effective therapeutic options and superb pharmaceutical care. Call 1-800-422-6237 for more information on pain and cancer.

When You Fill a Prescription

- Clarify with the prescriber any prescription information that is illegible, uncertain, or a potential source for erroneous interpretation—by you or the patient. Remember the Institute of Medicine data—help your customers stay alive.
- Be alert to "look-alike" and "sound-alike" drug names. This is a significant cause of dispensing errors. In accepting prescriptions by telephone, confirm the brand with the generic name as a double check. If there is still some doubt, ask the caller to spell the name of the drug.
- Include both the **name of the drug** and the **disorder** on the label (for example, Fosamax for osteoporosis) if the patient does not object, and consult with the prescribing physician when necessary. This will help (1) reduce dispensing errors caused by "look-alike" and "sound-alike" drug names and (2) prevent confusion during concurrent use of multiple drugs: mistaken identity of drug and purpose, mistakenly altered dosing schedules, etc.
- Encourage your patients to look at the prescription label **with you**. Paper-clip the patient drug information to the bag. Take the lead in opening the bottle, showing the patient the medicine and making sure he or she understands how much and when to take the medicine. This also gives you a final chance to earn your place as the most trusted professional.
- Check the stock bottle for accurate identification and appropriate dating. If a technician fills the prescription, be certain you open the dispensing container as well as the completed prescription and check the drug personally.

When You Counsel the Patient as You Dispense the Filled Prescription

- Always follow up on existing medicines with an adherence or compliance check. Document this in the patient record. Ask patients to tell you how they are to take or give any new medicine. Hearing THEM tell YOU about their medicines is a great way to make sure they really understand. Clarify any points of confusion or misunderstanding. **Every refill is an opportunity to assess and encourage adherence. Don't fail your patients by forgetting to check the medicine itself. For those patients who have Internet access and who are at risk for heart disease—encourage them to sign up for American Heart Association programs to help patients (via patient-directed information on CAD, CHF, e-mail reminders, risk factor identification, and other measures) decrease their risk of heart attack and stroke. Tell them to visit www.americanheart.org!**
- Make sure that the patient recognizes the **name of the drug** and the **disorder being treated**. A simple way to start this important dialogue is to ask, "What did your doctor tell you this medicine was going to do for you?" Explain what the drug is supposed to do and when the expected therapeutic benefits are usually realized.
- Review the details of dosing instructions: how much to take, when to take it, and for how long. It doesn't do them any good if it stays in the bottle. A good question to ask is, "Tell me a little bit about how your doctor told you to take this medicine." See if your computer vendor has a module for medication maps. If not, ask the publisher for permission to use the map provided in this book. This can be a valuable cognitive service.
- If the medicine you are counseling patients about is for pain, encourage patients to view effective pain control as a basic right. If they were given a pain medicine in the hospital, they will have already seen signs posted in the hospital that address this issue, and will probably have had a visit from a pain management team.
- Talk about possible side effects or adverse effects that may occur. An easy way to broach this subject is to ask, "Did your doctor tell you about any possible side effects from this medicine?" Tell patients what to do if any of these occur. Encourage them to call their doctor if new signs or symptoms develop.
- Precautions are critical. This includes possible interactions with foods, beverages, drugs, or restricted activities.
- Provide **written information** about the drug(s) dispensed and the patient's **disorder** (if available).
- Clarify how best to store the medicine. Tell patients about refrigeration and avoiding the humidity of a medicine chest. If a non-childproof lid is dispensed, remind them to keep the drug out of reach whenever children are visiting.

- Remind patients that nonprescription (over-the-counter) drugs can interact with prescription drugs. Encourage them to call your pharmacy or their physician before combining any medicines.
- Always take a good medication history and repeat this at least every six months. On every visit, be certain to ask about new medicines and any herbal medicines or vitamins the patient may have added or may be considering.
- Encourage the patient to ask questions—at the time of dispensing and later—whenever the need arises. A good way to start this conversation is, "Now that we've talked, do you have any questions for me?" Encourage patients to call if they think of something later. This is often the case.
- Explain that drugs may not work in practice exactly as expected. Tell the patient to be alert to the possibility that a new symptom or sign *may* be drug related. If one of your patients does experience a novel adverse drug reaction, it is critical that you (or your technician/designate) call the FDA MedWatch at 1-800-332-1088.

Suggestions for Containing the Costs of Drug Therapy

- Assess and encourage compliance or adherence to medicines with every initial prescription and refill. The expense of nonadherence can be huge.
- As judgment dictates, fill the prescription with the most reasonably priced drug available—within legally possible and appropriate guidelines. Consult with the prescribing physician regarding generic substitution when feasible.
- If the patient is taking other drugs (prescribed by other physicians), look for drug duplications. Offer "brown-bag sessions" where patients can bring in all their medicines and get your expert help regarding possible problems.

Points for the Physician

I've been privileged to work side by side with many doctors. I've worked in hospitals, offices, and research. The changes in health care have been staggering and in many cases burdensome. Outcomes, goals, guidelines, seamless systems, benchmarking, and managed care: simple phrases that have significantly changed the way physicians practice medicine today. If you also add closed formularies and critical paths, in some senses clinical decision making has become more focused. I hope collaborative care will be welcomed by physicians. I think management of medicines is a daunting task. If there are certification criteria and protocols, I hope a team (with the patient at the center) and prescribers and pharmacists and nurses all working together for a common good will continue to evolve.

I believe that a renewed focus on outcomes simply creates an atmosphere of continuous improvement and is just good medicine. I've been advocating the concept of powerful patients in recent writings and interviews. One of the best colleagues to have in attaining the best results from any medicine is a fully informed patient. Unfortunately, many patients get less than balanced information from the Web. I bet I would be hard pressed to find a doctor who didn't have a patient show up with a fistful of printouts. I've augmented Table 17 this year in order to help provide balanced and objective Web sites. I believe that these are the sites where you can comfortably send patients. Perhaps the best new example are the patient profilers from the American Heart Association. Right now they offer objective and evidence-based information on treatment options for coronary artery disease as well as congestive heart failure. For the clinician, these profilers also offer you the ability to create virtual patient profiling. I think it's worth the time to visit www.american heart.org.

Hospital-based programs, right at one of the most teachable moments, offer a great way to get the medicines started that have the best data. Information about The Get With The Guidelines program (GWTG) is available at www.americanheart.org. GWTG is a hospital-based initiative that seeks to increase evidence-based therapy for secondary prevention of cardiovascular disease. If your patients are cared for by hospitalists if they suffer a heart attack—you may well find them returning to you with a form outlining new medicines.

Michael Weintraub, M.D., recognized the need for patient education back in 1991, when in his introduction to the *Yearbook of Drug Therapy* he stated, "In looking for trends in the medical literature, it is apparent that the need for the physician to be an educator of patients and their families is becoming greater and greater." In addition, citing an increased need for patient education, he summarized with the following opinion: "Treatment principles correctly applied by patients educated about their condition and involved in its management seem to be the wave of the future." More than ever before, the volume and characteristics of the drugs in use today require deliberate individualization of treatment. The overall effectiveness of any drug therapy depends on how carefully the medicine is selected, dispensed, and taken. Responsible communication between physician, pharmacist, nurse, and patient must be achieved to the greatest extent possible. This process begins with you, the physician. It is absolutely unacceptable that current estimates of the expense of adverse drug events and medical errors cost **more than 100 billion dollars a year**, more than is spent on diabetes in the United States.

Your office is most probably computerized. I've been doing work to help create a seamless patient flow sheet, which I call an Adherence Assessment Form (AAF). Create your own that lists current medicines, when they were started, and their dose and interval. Send this with the patient to the hospital and insist that it is updated on discharge. Many physicians delegate care to hospitalists and you can get the best results from them by having your AAF document augmentation of continuity of care. I wish that patients could or would use the same pharmacy, but the reality is they will shop. Make sure that your patients take or send the AAF to every pharmacy that fills prescriptions for them. Some exciting systems such as Allscripts will actually interface with office software to tell you in the exam room which medicines Jim Rybacki's insurance will pay for and what to go do next!

I've also told patients to "take your medicines and take care of your family" on TV programs (*Medicines and Your Family*), in my audiotapes, and on my Web site (*www.medicineinfo.com*). Rest assured that I will continue to encourage people to ask questions and to be partners in their health care. Don't be offended if patients bring Internet information to your office. It may be prudent to have your office staff search the Net for information on the 10 most common diagnoses that you make—and provide that data for those under your care. The good sites will tell patients that information is only to be used in conjunction with you, their doctor. I know that a six- to ten-minute patient visit can never explain all of the nuances of drug therapy; hopefully, this book can help patients partner with you and decrease some of the calls that you get!

When You Evaluate a Patient for Drug Therapy

- Because patients tend to save the real reason they came to see you for the end of an office visit, ask again why they scheduled an appointment before you start to review their medication history. "Tell me again about any other questions or problems that brought you to my office today." This kind of open-ended question may help circumvent derailing bombshells left for the end of the visit. Next, be certain to review the patient's drug history for known drug allergies and prior drug-induced adverse reactions.
- Ask if the patient is currently under treatment by other health care providers or if the patient has actually gotten any prescription medicines without a prescription on the Internet.
- Ask about all drugs used currently—prescription and over-the-counter. Remember that many over-the-counter agents were once prescription medicines. Herbal medicines are now widely used and can have beneficial as well as deleterious interactions. If some 10 billion dollars is spent each year on herbals, include a question about herbals in your routine questions. Rules about structure/function claims can be found at *http://vm.cfsan.gov/~llrd/fr000106.html*. Make certain that you do not gloss over medicines they can take without ever obtaining your guidance.
- Remember the prevalence of nutriceutical use. Include these substances in your questions. Complementary care can be valuable. A good example is getting a homocysteine level in patients in your practice with dementia or Alzheimer's. The National Institutes of Health (NIH) will be undertaking a study of B vitamin supplements in Alzheimer's patients.
- Consider a patient's history and lifestyle. Think about diseases or conditions for which the patient is at risk, and vitamins (such as folic acid for heart disease) or minerals (calcium to prevent osteoporosis and possibly reduce risk of some colon cancers) that may be used to prevent a disease or process. Rybacki's first recommendation: It is always better to prevent a disease or condition than to have to treat it. Part of NCEP ATP III actually repositions therapeutic lifestyle changes. Please also remember that some prescription medicines can negatively impact quality of life unless you recommend the appropriate nutritional support.
- Make certain that you are absolutely current. Many daily fax services are available that can be individualized to your practice and can easily be read after your morning rounds.
- Establish the nature and severity of the disorder under consideration for drug treatment.
- Elicit significant coexisting disorders—possible absolute contraindications for certain drugs.

- Evaluate any suspected or obvious organ dysfunction—possible relative contraindications for certain drugs. When creatinine values are available, take the time to calculate creatinine clearance. Many drugs have breakpoints for adjustment of dosage at various levels of renal impairment. Even though an older patient's creatinine is within the "normal limits," his or her clearance will not be. For example, a 72-year-old, 70-kg man with a 1.4 creatinine will have a creatinine clearance of about 48.6 ml/min. This is **below the level where doses or intervals of kidney- (renally) eliminated medicines must be adjusted**. Hepatic disease will also impact doses or intervals for many drugs, particularly those that are highly protein-bound or heavily metabolized.
- Assess the patient's potential for adherence or nonadherence with drug therapy. Remember the expense that a given prescription presents. The most brilliant prescription choice is totally ineffective if financial considerations prevent adherence with the medicine you choose. Once-a-day dosing is much easier to remember and, combined with a dosing calendar, gets excellent results. If a complicated regimen is required, there are also pager-based systems that can give patients a "beep" with the name of the medicine and instructions for using it. Find out where your patients get their prescriptions filled and partner with the pharmacy to have adherence checked on EVERY refill. If you have an e-mail service, ask to be e-mailed if they are early or late or if they miss a refill. See if the patient's pharmacist offers a medication mapping service. If not, map your patient's medicines yourself.

When Selecting Drugs for Therapy

- Try to match the drug's power to the patient's problem. Avoid over-prescribing—medicinal "overkill." For example, mild to moderate stress reactions (situational anxiety-tension states) respond well to antianxiety drugs; they do not require antipsychotic medication. An uncomplicated urinary tract infection with a broadly sensitive single organism does not require a broad-spectrum anti-infective drug.
- Get a copy of the *Agency for Health Care Policy and Research Clinical Practice Guidelines Number 9*. The AHCPR is advocating effective and timely pain control as a basic human right. Increase your awareness of the World Health Organization Pain Ladder and the use of the agents that are primary analgesics and adjuvants. AHCPR publications are great tools to help your patients understand their medicine and their disease. Thanks to JCAHO, pain is now the fifth vital sign in your hospital.
- Always check for drug–drug, drug–food, and drug–disease interactions. Remember to take a "new" drug history periodically.
- Many new oral anti-infectives are effective against pathogens that historically required intravenous therapy. Although this allows you

to avoid hospitalization, it makes the patient's adherence more critical.

- Consider the desired onset of drug action (immediate versus delayed) and the consequences or benefits of that effect.
- Choose the drug with the most favorable benefit-to-risk ratio: the best clinical effects with the fewest possible adverse reactions.
- When you prescribe narrow-therapeutic-window drugs that require periodic blood levels, be certain that blood sampling is done after the drug has reached its steady state (usually five half-lives). Understand which level is preferable to measure: "peak" level (as for theophylline), "trough" level (as for digoxin), and "peak and trough" for aminoglycosides (such as tobramycin). Many clinical pharmacists (the author included) will willingly calculate the best dose and interval for you and make a consultative recommendation. Remember that the peak-to-trough ratio can be a great indicator for true once-a-day dosing with oral medicines.
- Give due consideration to the patient's prior experience with other medicines similar to the one you are considering and prescribe accordingly. Prescribing a second drug from the same drug class to which a patient already has had an allergic reaction or adverse drug effect that required discontinuation of therapy or provided no therapeutic benefit is not prudent.
- Remember individual patient factors such as age, education, and cultural factors (including genetic effects on medication elimination).
- Think about the desired extent of effect (systemic or local). Some possible adverse effects can be limited by choosing an inhaled versus "pill" form.
- Set goals and time frames when you start any new medicine. Talk these over with your patient. It's amazing how many patients I see who really have no idea what their medicine is for. Frequently, dosing issues also arise, and, of course, an underdose can be just as dangerous as an overdose. If drug treatment fails after a reasonable trial with good adherence, change to a drug of another chemical class, or consider combination therapy with two medicines with different mechanisms of action. For example, if viral load decreases for a time and then increases in an AIDS patient, you MUST change treatment.
- Select the drugs you prescribe critically, utilizing independent, objective reviews of available information. The "most frequently prescribed" drug is not necessarily the best drug within its class. Slick, glossy detail pieces should always be confirmed by primary literature. Some clinical pharmacists (the author included) will provide a balanced overview of the current literature.
- Even "drugs of choice" in objective reviews can be poor choices when you consider the characteristics of individual patients. A renally compromised patient may better tolerate an "alternate drug" with dual elimination (hepatic and renal) than a "drug of choice" that is limited to renal elimination.

- Remember that possible pharmacokinetic and pharmacodynamic changes in those over 65 can lead to accumulation and excessive responses to "normal" doses and dosing intervals. In general, the possibility of side effects increases with increasing dose. Many medicines have "ceiling effects," above which dose increases act only to decrease quality of life and fail to add to therapeutic benefits.
- Be objective and discerning as you review the claims made for a newly released drug within a sizable class of drugs already available. Only a small percentage of newly approved drugs each year are classified by the FDA as truly innovative or more advantageous than similar drugs in current use. The remaining medicines are largely "me too" drugs with a limited history of use and a potential for "surprises" after a period of general use. It is best to select drugs with established records that show them to be the best in their class.

When You Issue Prescriptions in Writing or by Telephone

- When prescribing for outpatient use, slow down a little and give the pharmacist time to write. ALWAYS give both the brand and generic name, as this makes sense and can help YOU avoid a lawsuit arising from a "sound-alike" error. Consider the advantage of including both the **name of the drug** and the **therapeutic indication** (the patient's disorder) on the prescription label—for example, Vioxx (rofecoxib) for arthritis. Putting the disorder on the label will help (1) reduce dispensing errors caused by "look-alike" and "sound-alike" drug names and (2) prevent confusion that often occurs during concurrent use of multiple drugs, especially among the elderly: mistaken identity of drug and purpose, mistakenly altered dosing schedules, etc. Pain is now the fifth vital sign and a focus of new JCAHCO guidelines. If you work in a system where inpatient care is provided by hospitalists, be aware that they will in essence be charting the outcomes of YOUR outpatient pain management.
- Respect your patients' wishes as to whether they *want* the name of the disorder written on the prescription label. If they prefer you not include it, recommend that they write it on the label themselves *after* the prescription is filled.
- Keep dosing schedules as simple as possible. Once-a-day dosing improves adherence.
- Alert the pharmacist to "look-alike" and "sound-alike" drug names. Print the drug name and generic name on written prescriptions. Spell the drug name and include the generic name when prescribing by telephone.

When Counseling Patients About Drug Therapy

- ALWAYS stress the critical nature of adherence. If your patients are adherence-challenged, talk about pill boxes, bottle reminders, and even pager-based systems to make sure that they will take their medicines. Briefly explain the nature of the patient's disorder and its treatment. Use language that is readily understood by the average person. I've often found clinicians using language that is barely understood by the average doctor. If you use words that are on a sixth-grade level, you'll often have a patient colleague working to achieve the goals of treatment. The patient-profiler component of the American Heart Association Web site offers patients balanced information on CAD and CHF, repeat e-mail messages, and a real chance at continuing risk-lowering behaviors. Consider encouraging your office patients as a chance to get objective information and behavior reinforcement while they are in your office.

- Provide written information or references for educational material about the disorder. If the disorder is chronic in nature (diabetes, hypertension), explain the need to continue drug therapy indefinitely, possibly for life. It's no surprise that patients are visiting the Internet. Provide helpful Web sites (see Table 17) that give balanced information. Explain that some pharmaceutical company–provided sites may not give complete information, or may skew data to favor their products.

- Briefly explain the name and nature of the drugs you are prescribing. Again, stress the importance of strict adherence with the medicine. It is wise to tell the patient—in advance—about potential adverse effects. The patient who has such effects is more likely to be understanding and forgiving if they do not come as a surprise. Talk about possible options available if the goals of therapy are not achieved in the expected time frames.

- To supplement your discussion, **provide a printed document** that summarizes the essential information the patient needs to use the drug(s) safely and effectively. This is comforting and will save you an amazing number of telephone calls and pages. Be sure the patient knows what to do if a dose is missed. Look at an add-on program to your office-management program that prints out relevant information for your patients to take home. Such services can provide detailed descriptions of drugs, general guidelines for drug use, and personalized instructions. Unfortunately, your patient may run into a pill-splitting reality with many medicines. Be aware of what managed care organizations expect your patient to do. A pill splitter can be an important assurance of correct doses.

- Explain the need for follow-up visits to monitor the effects of drug treatment and the course of the disorder. If possible, empower the patient by self-testing. For example, a fructosamine finger stick test can augment the glycosylated hemoglobins (hemoglobin A1C) that you order and also give your diabetics better results from their medicines.

- Explain that drugs may not work in practice exactly as expected. Tell the patient to be alert to the possibility that a new symptom or sign *may* be drug related. Certainly tell the patient about probable effects and what to do about them. If one of your patients does experience a novel adverse drug reaction, it is CRITICAL that you (or your designate) call the FDA MedWatch at 1-800-332-1088.

- It is virtually impossible for the FDA to test new medicines against all possible multiple pill regimens. Calling MedWatch (1-800-332-1088) fulfills your voluntary obligation to Phase Four reporting and makes medication use safer for everyone. I admit that I am the one advocating mandatory reporting. Encourage the patient to call as needed regarding any aspect of drug treatment. Some of this call volume can be successfully shifted to pharmacists trained in specific disease management. Locate these pharmacy centers of excellence and work together to get the best results for your patients. Recognize the need to adjust drug selection and/or dosage regimens to accommodate individual variability.

- Give special attention to the older patient on drug therapy. The elderly (1) generally use multiple drugs concurrently and (2) are more prone to experience adverse drug effects.

- If you refer any of your patients to a specialist, be certain to take a repeat medication history when they are returned to your care. Check for duplications in medicines by cross-referencing brand or generic names.

- Every six months, ask your patients to bring in all the prescription, nonprescription, and herbal medicines that they routinely take. This kind of "brown bag session" can help you best understand all of the potential or actual interactions of therapies your patient is or will be taking. Remember: An informed patient can be your greatest ally in optimal therapeutics and the outcomes that will be benchmarked!

Suggestions for Containing the Costs of Drug Therapy

- When you have selected the most appropriate drug, consider its cost. LOOK AT TABLE 21 in this book and direct your patients to balanced and objective Web sites. While the government is presently considering a Medicare Prescription Drug Bill, we still need to get the most from the medicines that are prescribed. Canada as a socialized medicine system (see Avorn, J., in Sources) tells us that simply giving the medicines away does NOT get us the best results. If the patient requests an available generic product, direct the pharmacist to dispense one with certified bioequivalence. Because of generic product variability, caution the patient to have the prescription refilled with the identical generic (same manufacturer) each time.

- Avoid polypharmacy whenever possible. Limit the number of drugs that the patient is taking concurrently to the fewest required. Do not let the cure become the disease. Medicate serious, significant disorders; discourage the use of drugs for minor, transient complaints.

- Consider carefully any requests from patients for a prescription drug they have learned about through direct-to-consumer advertising. Explain to your patients the profit motive of the producer and assure them that you will prescribe the drug that, in your judgment, is the most appropriate for them.

- When circumstances permit, use home intravenous drug therapy in preference to hospitalization. If hospitalization is required, explore IV to PO switches and medication streamlining to help appropriately decrease length of stay.
- The move toward managed care and other health care reform initiatives brings increased scrutiny to the outcomes of your therapeutic and clinical decisions. Become more familiar with the expense of various medicinal options, as well as the specific patient populations where the benefit-to-risk and cost-to-outcome ratios make the most sense. Pharmacoeconomic and disease management approaches will bring the best balance of cost and outcome.
- Work with the pharmacy your patients use to create seamless systems. They have a lot of data, and you want to give the best care. If you have office e-mail, ask the pharmacy to e-mail if patients never fill or are early or late with their prescriptions. This gets you the information you need and can prompt a quick follow-up phone call from your office staff to your compliance-challenged patients. Finding out about nonadherence or noncompliance early can help prevent catastrophic events such as stroke or MI.

The Essential Guide to Prescription Drugs

2004 Edition

SECTION ONE

1
HOW TO USE THIS BOOK

2
GUIDELINES FOR SAFE AND EFFECTIVE DRUG USE OR HOW TO BECOME A POWERFUL PATIENT

3
TRUE BREAKTHROUGHS IN MEDICINES

1

How to Use This Book

When you're sick and finally make that decision to see your doctor, it's probably one of the worst times for you to think about the medicines you take now or even that new prescription. A visit to your physician's office can be a disconcerting experience. The reality of health care is that time has been contracted, patients may only be considered covered lives, and health care providers face severe time constraints. I think that the Institute of Medicine (IOM) report on medical errors will serve to increase awareness of systems problems in health care, but the reality will still remain that most patients will have the sense of their doctor needing—not wanting—to hurry out of the exam room to see the next patient. You may be left with a prescription for yourself or a loved one that no one told you anything—and certainly not everything—about.

Becoming a powerful patient means being well informed about the medicines you take and the goals of treatment. I can help you become a partner in your health care and will always try to supplement the direction and guidance your doctor will offer about your medicines. This principle is also ascribed to on my Web site (*www.medicineinfo.com*) via the Health On the Net Principles. Just like the site, this Guide seeks to augment, NOT to replace, the role of your doctor.

Your new book is arranged into six sections. The first section offers insight into modern drug therapy and gives you helpful tips on becoming a powerful patient. "True Breakthroughs in Medicines" will help identify new medicines that have gained FDA approval or that are the first new agents to treat an existing disease or condition. Section Two gives you detailed Drug Profiles covering more than 2,000 brand-name prescription drugs and nearly 400 widely used generic medicines. Selection of each drug is based on three criteria: the extent of its use, the urgency of the conditions it treats, and the volume and complexity of information essential to its proper use. You'll find that profiles are arranged alphabetically by

1

generic name. Read carefully to be sure you have the correct medicine. This section can really build up your medicine muscles (perhaps "brain" might be a better choice) and give you a basis for being a powerful patient.

Each profile is presented in the same way, and once you become familiar with the format, you'll be able to quickly find specific information on any drug. Unlike other imitators, each Essential Drug Profile contains up to 45 helpful categories of information. Let me introduce you to the other parts of your new book:

Herbal Medicines or Minerals

Because herbal medicines are so widely used, I developed a new section that included (where appropriate) important possible interactions between herbal and prescription medicines. Please remember that herbal products **are not regulated by the FDA as medicines. They fall under the Dietary Supplement Health and Education Act (DSHEA) of 1994**. Powerful patients then understand that this may mean that specific products have not been well studied—others rely on borrowed science—and certainly that these products can interact with prescription medicines. For example, ephedra (see *www.fda.gov*) has had a new warning label proposed, and found the American Heart Association recommending that it be removed from nonprescription products. Accordingly, I've broadened the data in your new Guide. You'll find that I'll tell you where combinations between herbs and prescription drugs may make sense, where they do not, and of course how to talk to your doctor before you move forward. This is a very dynamic area, and I'll update this section every year! There may also be information at *www.medicineinfo.com* that can help.

Year Introduced

At first glance, this may seem trivial, but remember, the longer the drug has been in general use, the more likely all of its actions are known and the less likely ongoing use will produce new problems. This will help you identify those medicines that are more likely to be more fully understood both because they have been used for a longer time period and because they have been widely used.

Drug Class

Drug classes are like families—in fact, some of the profiles giving information about medicines from the same class have been arranged into Medication Family Profiles. Many actions, reactions, and interactions with other drugs are often shared by drugs of the same class. For example, *if you are allergic to one member of the cephalosporin family, you most likely will be allergic to a second cephalosporin. By the same logic, if a medicine in a certain class has not helped you, it is likely that a second one from the same class will do you little good.* Pay close attention to this aspect of medicines, since this is an area that often leads to problems or lack of results.

Prescription Required

Just because a medicine does not require a prescription (over-the-counter) does not mean the medicine is weak or is free from possible drug interactions. Remember, over the last 15 years there has been a great shift in medicines from prescription to nonprescription. Current examples include medicines for yeast infections, patches and gum to help you stop smoking, as well as ulcer medicines (histamine H2 blockers) that can also be used to prevent or treat heartburn. Virtually all of these medicines were previously available only by prescription. Always mention nonprescription medicine use when asked about the "medicines" you take.

Controlled Drug

The Controlled Substances Act of 1970 assigned medicines with a potential for abuse to a specific schedule in the United States. A Canadian schedule is also given when applicable. A description of the schedules of controlled drugs is found at the back of your Guide.

Available for Purchase by Generic Name

In general, costs can be reduced by buying a generic equivalent of a brand-name product. The key word is "equivalent." It is important to make sure that "bioavailability and bioequivalence"—the comparative composition, quality, and effectiveness of the generic versus the brand-name drug product—are the same if a substitution is made. Further discussion of bioavailability and bioequivalence may be found in Section Five, the Glossary of Drug-Related Terms.

Brand Names

I realize that generic or chemical names of medicines can be complicated, so brand names are given to help. Brand names are listed for the United States and for Canada (W). A combination drug (one with more than one active ingredient) is identified by [CD] following the brand name. Be careful! In some cases THE SAME NAME used in both the United States and Canada will represent entirely different generic drugs (in a single drug product) or a significantly different mixture of generic medicines. If you travel between the two countries, make sure that the brand-name drug contains the same generic medicine(s).

Benefits versus Risks

The possible pros and cons for each drug are summarized. Capital letters emphasize the drug's principal benefits and risks, while lowercase letters are used for less critical benefits and risks. One look reveals the "comparative weights" of the two columns and gives a first impression about how a drug's benefits relate to its potential risks. This is meant to help you become more circumspect in your use of medicines—but is not to be the sole basis for deciding whether to use a drug. I find that the triad of **fail-**

ure to individualize drug selection and dose, failure to communicate goals of treatment, and lack of an effective system to repeatedly check, encourage, and follow up on how well people take their medicines (adherence) is the greatest weakness in current drug therapy and health care.

Principal Uses

A drug may be available as a single drug product or in combination with other drugs. The "As a Single Drug Product" section tells you the primary use(s) of the drug when it is used alone in a particular product. The "As a Combination Drug Product [CD]" section tells about the primary use(s) when an active medicine is combined with other drugs in the same pill. The uses are a consensus of the medical community and reflect current research. Where appropriate, the logic for combining certain drugs is explained.

In the Pipeline (A NEW SECTION!)

I've given a lot of interviews this year. Perhaps the most common question I've gotten relates to what new forms of a particular medicine are being studied, what new medicines are being studied for particular conditions, what studies are under way, and when the data/medicine/results will be available. While this information is often confidential, unpredictable, or unavailable, I'll do my best to fill you in on FDA applications that have been filed, research projects that have been publicized, or where preliminary research has been published. This section will not be present for every medicine, but will hopefully work to make you aware of progress that is being made and when results might be expected!

How This Drug Works

This section tells what a drug does to work. If a specific method of action has not been established, I will tell you about the current theory. This can be important in the sense that if you are taking two medicines that work in the same way or act on the same system, better combination therapy may be available.

Available Dosage Forms and Strengths

This gives you available manufacturers' dosage forms (tablets, capsules, elixirs, etc.) and strengths, without company identification. Dosage forms limited to hospital use are often not included. The section Dosage Forms and Strengths in the Glossary can help with those few abbreviations used to describe strengths of each dosage form.

Usual Adult Dosage Ranges

Dosing information represents a consensus by appropriate authorities and is the currently recommended standard. It is a guide showing how much of the drug can reasonably be expected to be both effective and safe. Under certain circumstances, your doctor may decide to modify the "standard" dose. Some dosage forms not covered (for example, extemporaneously made suppositories) may require different doses than those listed because of absorption at different routes.

Conditions Requiring Dosing Adjustments

Medical conditions can actually change the effect a medicine has on your body (technically called a drug-disease interaction). Powerful patients realize that this is a fact that is **often missed** in choosing a dose or in deciding how often a medicine should be taken (dosing interval)—and can lead to problems. For example, people over age 60 usually have an expected or "normal" age-related decline in kidney function. Throughout this book I refer to this as kidney compromise. What this means is that medicines removed by the kidneys may stay in the body longer than expected (increased half-life)—not because the kidneys are diseased but because they simply do not work as well as they used to. The real possible effect of this increased half-life is that a typically prescribed dose could in reality amount to an overdose. **While the exact age when this decline starts may vary—it is critical for people at or near 60 to ask their doctors if any prescribed medicine is removed by the kidneys—and if the dose or dosing interval has been adjusted for this kidney compromise.** I also include information on liver compromise (where appropriate) as well as information on other prevalent diseases or conditions that may impact dosing.

Dosing Instructions

Food and medicines can fight. Foods can actually change how much medicine gets into your body (increasing or decreasing absorption)—and this section tells you about them. Medicines can also irritate the lining of the stomach or intestines, and food can help ease this irritation. The dosing instruction section will also tell you about advisability of changing the form of the medicine itself. For example, sometimes, when medicine is urgently needed, you may have to crush the tablet or open the capsule and mix the contents with a food or beverage. On the other hand, many medicines should **NEVER** be crushed or altered to be taken. This information category identifies those forms of each drug that may be changed and those that should not be. A new feature of this section provides information on what to do if you forget your pill. If you are still uncertain—call your doctor. Another caveat on this: if you find yourself forgetting often, talk to your doctor and see if there is a medicine that might give the same benefits but not require so many doses! A good example is in the management of high blood pressure. Many patients may get great results from a newer medicine taken once or twice a day instead of one that has to be taken more frequently. There are also many reminder systems—even beeper-based ways—to help you take control of your disease or condition by taking your medicine right on time.

Usual Duration of Use

Many factors determine how long a medicine must be taken. This is often an area of great controversy and patient confusion. Factors such as the nature and severity of symptoms, drug form and strength, ability of the patient to respond, and use of other drugs come into play here. Some situations such as increased cholesterol or hyperlipidemia will need to be treated on an ongoing basis. It is always prudent to check results as well as problems on a regular basis. The main idea is for you and your clinician to give the medicine an appropriate amount of time to reach the goals of therapy, and to adjust the dose or even add or change the medicine if goals are not reached within the expected period of time. Where important, limitations in how long a medicine should be taken are outlined in this section.

Typical Treatment Goals and Measurements (Outcomes and Markers)

Powerful patients know the goals and actively work with their doctor to achieve them! One of the hallmarks of a good clinician lies in how well he or she sets and communicates, and then prescribes or adjusts, medicines to realize the goals of therapy. Unfortunately, I've often found this aspect of care to be sorely lacking. In order to help you understand what some reasonable expectations from treatment are, I've included typical goals, measurements, and results in ALL of this year's profiles. For example, the entries below pertain to blood sugar and cholesterol-lowering medicines that are taken by mouth.

- Blood Sugar: The general goal for blood sugar is to return it to the usual "normal" range (generally 70–120 mg/dl), while avoiding risks of excessively low blood sugar. One study (UKPDS) used a fasting plasma sugar (glucose) of less than 108 mg/dl.
- Cholesterol: The National Institutes of Health (NIH) has released ATP III—a new set of guidelines for treating people at risk for heart disease. This National Cholesterol Education Program (NCEP) effort has some changes versus the Adult Treatment Panel (ATP-2). Importantly, diabetes was added to the list of conditions that lead to increased heart disease risk. Total cholesterol targets remain at less than 200 mg/dl, but the guidelines recommend testing for the various components of total cholesterol, such as low-density lipoproteins (LDL) and high-density lipoproteins (HDL). New designations list 100 mg/dl of LDL to be optimal, 130–159 as borderline high, 160 mg as high, and 190 mg/dl as very high. A new focus has been placed on HDL, making the "too low" reading as 40 mg/dl for this "good" cholesterol. Because of all of these changes, instead of just a total cholesterol, ATP-3 suggests a lipid panel! I hope that this new feature on goals will let you be more involved in your health care, and will also encourage you to ask questions if the goals of your medicines are not achieved.

This Drug Should Not Be Taken If

These entries are the absolute contraindications to the use of the drug (see Contraindication in the Glossary). By consensus, these are circumstances where the medicine should NEVER be taken. Tell your doctor **immediately** if any information in this category applies to you.

Inform Your Physician Before Taking This Drug If

These entries tell you relative contraindications to a medicine. One way to think of this is as a relative benefit-to-risk decision. Again, tell your physician or other prescriber if these factors apply to you. For example, if you are taking a corticosteroid-type medicine and have unexplained hip or shoulder pain, it may be a sign of something more serious that should be evaluated.

Possible Side Effects

Here you can learn about natural, expected, and usually unavoidable medicine actions—the normal and anticipated consequences of taking it. This gives a realistic perspective, balancing side effects with goals of treatment. I emphasize that these are POSSIBLE side effects.

Possible Adverse Effects

These are unusual, unexpected, and infrequent drug effects that are often called adverse drug reactions or effects. These range from mild to serious. In order to more accurately define how frequently these effects happen, I've developed the following approach:

- Possible: An effect that has been documented for other drugs in the same family but not the profiled drug. Also assigned when the effect occurs in some limited patient populations and not in others.
- Case Reports: An effect that has been documented to happen, but has been seen only in isolated cases.
- Rare: An effect that is seen in less than 2 percent of patients. Another way to look at this is that 98 percent of people will take the medicine and NOT have the effect.
- Infrequent: An effect that is seen in 2 to 10 percent of patients.
- Frequent: Effects that happen in more than 10 percent of patients.

Powerful patients talk to their doctor if they suspect they may be having an adverse drug effect. **Serious adverse reactions may start with mild, unthreatening symptoms, and serious problems may be avoided if you call right away.** It's also possible to have an adverse reaction that has not yet been reported. Don't discount an adverse effect just because it's not listed. *A properly selected drug usually has a comparatively small chance of producing serious harm.* Knowing that a drug can cause a serious adverse reaction should not deter you from using it when it has been properly selected and its use will be carefully supervised.

Author's Note: A new feature will be integrated into this section where available. Number of patients evaluated for safety. For example: the new package insert for Plavix contains a notation "This drug has been evaluated for safety in more than 17,500 patients at the time of this writing." I'd like you to think of this as a rough measure of how well possible adverse effects from a given medicine might be known. While adverse reactions in general tend to be underreported, a medicine that has been used in 17,500 patients is more likely to have a more fully defined group of possible adverse reactions than a drug only evaluated in 3,500 patients. I'll build more of these details into subsequent editions.

If you have had a reaction to a medicine, make sure to remember to ask that your doctor REPORT THIS REACTION. One problem with our system of medicine surveillance is that reporting of adverse effect of medicines is VOLUNTARY for health care professionals. Less than 3 percent of serious adverse reactions are reported, and this can leave the next family vulnerable to the same undesirable experience. Your doctor (or his/her staff) can call 1-800-FDA-1088 (1-800-332-1088).

Possible Effects on Sexual Function

This information is often NOT something people want to discuss, or something that patients are told about. Currently available information (often inadequate and vague) from all reliable sources is presented. Both physician and patient are well advised to discuss frankly any potential effect that drug therapy could have on sexual expression.

Adverse Effects That May Appear Similar to Natural Diseases or Disorders

Medicines can actually cause effects similar to widely diagnosed diseases or disorders. Quite often this inadvertent error is compounded by prescribing another drug to relieve the "symptoms" of the first. My father was prescribed a medicine for his "arthritis" when he was actually having an adverse effect from a medicine for his heart rhythm. For milder symptoms (e.g., nasal congestion or diarrhea from reserpine), the oversight may not be too serious. But in the case of my father, the mistake was devastating. This section tells you about this common flaw.

Natural Diseases or Disorders That May Be Activated by This Drug

Many drugs can "activate" latent disorders that may not be recognized as drug induced. If a new and seemingly unrelated disorder starts during treatment with any new medicine, ask your doctor if it may be drug related.

Possible Effects on Laboratory Tests

Most drugs have significant effects on body chemistry and organ systems. Some effects are intended and beneficial (therapeutic); others are unintended, unavoidable, and potentially harmful. Timely use of laboratory tests lets us check how well a drug is working, detect early drug toxicity, assign some lab test changes to drug and lab test interactions, and also check the course of the condition being treated.

Caution

This category gives you information on aspects of drug actions and/or drug uses that require special emphasis. Occasionally, this section may actually relate to information provided in other categories. Once again, this is an important feature this Guide offers to help you take care of your family.

Precautions for Use: Infants and Children

Doses often MUST be changed for infants and children under 12 years of age, and some drugs and/or treatment situations call for special precautions. When administering any prescription or over-the-counter drug, it is best to ask your doctor or pharmacist about needed precautions. New FDA regulations will now require study of medicines in children where the drugs are specifically used in children.

Precautions for Use: Those Over 60 Years of Age

Our bodies do not remain the same over time, and people age at different rates and in different ways. Assessment of "age" must be based upon individual mental and physical condition, and never on years alone. Changes that accompany aging may affect the actions of the body on the drug, actions of the drug on the body—and even how well the medicine is removed. Appropriate precautions are outlined in this category.

Advisability of Use During Pregnancy: Pregnancy Category

Information about safe use of a particular drug during pregnancy was one of the most forceful concerns that led to the formal petitioning of the Food and Drug Administration in 1975 to make sure that information was disclosed to the public. The FDA definitions of the five pregnancy categories are listed at the back of this book. The FDA does not make the initial category assignment; this is the responsibility of the manufacturer that markets the drug. The initial designation is then subject to review and modification by the FDA. The "Pregnancy Category" designations presented in each profile were determined after thorough review of pertinent literature and consultation with appropriate authorities. They are offered at this time for initial guidance only. They may not be "official" and may not have the endorsement of either the manufacturer or the FDA. If controversy exists among researchers or manufacturers, you may find more than one pregnancy category for the same medicine.

Advisability of Use If Breast-Feeding

This section tells you about effects of the drug on milk production. You will also learn if the drug goes into human milk, and the possible effects of the drug on the nursing infant. Prudent recommendations are given where appropriate. Also included are impacts of disease where appropriate.

Suggested Periodic Examinations While Taking This Drug

Getting the best results from your medicines often means that your doctor may ask you to get tests while you take the drug(s) he or she has prescribed. Which exams and when they are made depend on your past and present medical history, the nature of the condition being treated, the dose and duration of drug use, and your doctor's observations of your response. For example, checking finger stick blood sugar and fructosamine or hemoglobin A1C while taking an oral glucose-lowering (oral hypoglycemic) medicine is critical. On the other hand, there may be many occasions when your doctor decides no examinations are necessary. Always tell your doctor about all developments you think may be drug related.

While Taking This Drug, Observe the Following: Herbal Medicines or Minerals

Since many millions of people are taking herbal medicines as well as minerals, I think it is critical to tell you about herbs and prescription or nonprescription medicines. I've tried to bring you timely data that tells about possible harmful combinations as well as situations where herbal medicines can actually increase beneficial effects of some prescription drugs. Complementary and beneficial use of herbal medicines may allow for lower prescription drug doses (this may be very beneficial, since it may also help you avoid side effects). Data have been difficult to come by, and you may find that not all profiles carry this kind of interaction or the same depth of coverage.

I have broadened the information since last year's groundbreaking inclusion of such information, and will continue to update this important aspect of care. POWERFUL PATIENTS DO NOT ASSUME that because it's herbal, it's natural and will not interact with your medicines. Because new prescription drug–herbal medicine interactions are always being discovered, NEVER combine any herbal or prescription or nonprescription drug without first talking to your pharmacist and doctor. I've also included the URLs of some helpful Web sites in the tables near the end of this book.

While Taking This Drug, Observe the Following: Marijuana Smoking

The widespread "social" use of marijuana by virtually all age groups and the approval of medicinal smoking of marijuana in two states have led to inquiries about interactions between the active chemicals in marijuana smoke and medicines in common use. Currently available literature on the health aspects of marijuana use contains very little practical information concerning the potential for drug interactions. The limited information presented in this category of selected Drug Profiles represents those possible interactions considered likely to occur in view of the known pharmacological effects of the principal components of marijuana and of the medicine reviewed in the profile. In most instances, the interaction statements are not based on documented evidence, since very little is available. The conclusions stated—derived by logical inductive reasoning—represent the concurrence of authorities with expertise in this field. There is a well-designed study of medical marijuana use under way at the time of this writing.

While Taking This Drug, Observe the Following: Other Drugs

Medicines can fight and powerful patients know this. While interactions can be a confusing and often controversial area of drug information, it is critical and is divided into five subcategories of possible interactions between drugs. Look carefully at the wording of each subcategory heading (see also Interaction in Glossary). Some of the drugs listed do not have a representative profile. If you are using one of these drugs, ask your doctor or pharmacist for help about potential interactions. A brand name (or names) that follows the generic name of an interacting drug is given as an example only. It is not intended to mean that the particular brand(s) named has interactions that are different from other brands of the same generic drug. If you are taking the generic drug, all brand names under which it is marketed MUST be considered as possible interactants. Medicines in the same or similar families may also interact.

Driving, Hazardous Activities

Clearly, medicines can change coordination and alertness. The information in this category applies not just to driving motor vehicles but to any activity of a dangerous nature, such as operating machinery, working on ladders, using power tools, and handling weapons. Your individual response and degree of reaction may vary from the way others react. Talk with your doctor or pharmacist if you take a medicine that may impair your abilities.

Aviation

Military pilots enjoy the expert guidance and surveillance provided by the flight surgeon, but no tightly structured control system exists for their civilian counterparts. The need for practical information regarding the possible effects of medicinal drugs on flight performance, however, is the same for pilots in all settings. This section can tell civilian pilots how a particular drug may affect their eligibility to fly and when it is advisable or necessary to consult a designated Aviation Medical Examiner or an FAA medical officer.

Occurrence of Unrelated Illness

Some medicines—for instance, "oral hypoglycemics" such as glipizide— require careful regulation of doses to maintain a constant drug effect within critical limits. In this section of your book, emphasis is given to those illnesses that might affect drug use. For example, if a body-wide infection were to occur, the oral hypoglycemic dose may not work and insulin injections may be temporarily required in order to maintain blood sugar in an appropriate range.

Discontinuation

How and when to stop a medicine are often as important as starting a medicine in the first place. Unfortunately, this aspect of drug use is often overlooked when a medicine is first discussed. Your doctor should always approach treatment with medicines with specific goals and time frames to reach those goals when the medicine is FIRST started, for example, reducing a blood pressure of 159/93 to 120/75 in two months using a particular medicine. Additionally, it is often mandatory that patients be fully informed on when to discontinue, when not to discontinue, and precisely how to stop use of the drug. In some cases, when one medicine is stopped, other drugs being taken at the same time may also need to be adjusted. The doctor who is primarily responsible for your overall medicine management must be kept informed of all the drugs you are taking at a given time and if and when any of them are stopped.

I believe that the remaining information categories in the Drug Profiles are self-explanatory, but I always welcome your letters and questions. I have also started a Web site called **Medicine Information** and can be reached at *www.medicineinfo.com*.

Section Three is called "The Leading Edge" and offers what are, in my opinion, medicines that show great promise and are just over the horizon from FDA approval. Some of these medicines may not actually be approved, but they give such significant hope that they're worth consideration. The information may let patients facing serious diseases ask to be included in scientific studies and get the medicine prior to actual approval.

Section Four is a presentation of Drug Classes arranged alphabetically by their chemical or therapeutic (generic) class. Because of chemical composition and biological activities, some drugs appear in two or more classes. For example, the drug product with the brand name Diuril will be represented by its generic name, chlorothiazide, in three drug classes: the Thiazide Diuretics (a chemical classification), the Diuretics (a drug action classification), and the Antihypertensives (a disease-oriented classification). Please use the Drug Classes to your advantage. I can't count the number of times I've seen busy physicians discover an allergy or problem with a particular medicine only to turn right around and prescribe a medicine **from the same class.** This section can protect you from this kind of error.

Frequently in the Drug Profiles in Section Two you are advised to "see [a particular] Drug Class." This alerts you to a possible drug contraindi-cation, or to possible interactions with certain foods, alcohol, or other drugs. In each case, you can find the more readily recognized brand names for each drug listed generically within a drug class by looking at the appropriate Drug Profile. Timely use of these references can help you avoid many possible hazards of medication.

Section Five is a Glossary of Drug-Related Terms used throughout the book. Powerful patients understand the language of medicines. The pre-ferred use of each term is explained. Frequent references to the Glossary are made in the Drug Profiles. Use of the Glossary will help you under-stand how to recognize and interpret significant drug effects.

Section Six offers **tables of drug and other information**. The title and introductory description explain the content and purpose of each table. The tables give you another source of ready reference. I've included a Medication Map as Table 15 because it is a way for you to use your doc-tor's or pharmacist's expertise to arrange all of the medicines you take into a reasonable schedule. It is also something I strongly advocate that you take to the hospital with you. If a new prescription or medicine is to be given, make sure that the prescriber knows about all of the "pills" you presently take. When it's time to go home from the hospital or to leave your doctor's office, take the time to have them help you get the most from your medicines.

Table 16 identifies medicines that have been removed from the mar-ket. This may help protect you from medicines that may still be available in other countries (or on the Internet) and not available on U.S. shelves. Please use the index of brand and generic names in the back of the book. It is a single alphabetical listing that provides page references to the appropriate Drug Profile(s) for all drugs found in this book. Read the introductory explanation of the special features of this combined index.

Because of the explosion of information on the Internet, I've also cre-ated a new table that tells you the URLs of a number of Web sites that I have found to be objective and valuable (Table 17) I've updated and broadened this part of the book for this edition. Powerful patients regard the Internet cautiously and know where to look for objective informa-tion. If you decide to buy medicines from the Net, make sure you have a prescription from your doctor and are then buying from a reputable company. Much has been heard this year about counterfeit medicines. You can actually call the National Association of Boards of Pharmacy at 847-698-6227 or visit them on the Web at *www.nabp.net* and find out if a site really does belong to a licensed pharmacy.

A clear trend in health care is the development of instruments and home test kits that can let patients themselves screen and even test and track serious illnesses. I've detailed some of the devices you are more likely to see in Table 18: Patient Power and Home Test Kits. Work with your doctor, pharmacist, or nurse practitioner to reach an agreement on which device or test makes sense for you.

Heart disease accounts for the greatest death toll of WOMEN and MEN in the United States. How do you know if you are at risk? It is clearly a role for doctors to explain which ones apply, but I believe that it is critical that powerful patients recognize risk factors and gain control of them. Table 19 will work with you to give you knowledge and power. The next step is to discuss risk factors with your doctor and figure out an individualized plan for what to do about them. The next table will also help you gain power over your heart!

One of the broadest set of national guidelines are the ones called NCEP ATP 3. Let me put that in English: National Cholesterol Education Program Adult Treatment Panel, number three. The changes versus the early version NCEP ATP II are detailed on my Web site at *www.medicineinfo. com*. What Table 20 will do is to describe various lifestyle changes that you can make that have been proven to help reduce risk of heart disease and stroke.

"How am I going to afford these medicines?" I can't begin to count the number of times that I've heard this question. We all know that medicines can be very expensive when you add up the total bill on an ongoing basis. Table 21, How to Get Help with the Cost of Medicines (Strategies, Programs, and Web Sites), is new for this edition, and I hope it will be a great help. In this table I've made a list of some successful strategies that are reasonable; listed the names, numbers, and the patient assistance programs for the 10 largest pharmaceutical companies; listed Web sites that I've found to be balanced and objective; and have identified sources that you may not have thought of—yet may be entitled to. This may be one of the most useful tables in the book!

2

Guidelines for Safe and Effective Drug Use or How to Become a Powerful Patient

MEDICINES AND PHARMACY ON THE INTERNET

There has been an explosion of e-mails, advertisements, health claims, prescription-less drug ordering, and even pharmacies on the Internet. While I cover some aspects in the Do and Do Not sections, I think this subject is important enough to break it out into a separate section. Mergers and changes in scope of service have occurred in pharmacy, as they have in other businesses. Amidst the change, there are still some common characteristics of appropriate pharmacies and medicines on the Internet. Powerful patients know that at a minimum these include:

- The pharmacy site requires a prescription for a prescription medicine and provides a way for you to prove that you have one. Given the present state of the Internet, it appears prudent to stick with "known" companies. The largest current online pharmacies are walgreens.com and cvs.com.
- The site requires a medication history. This history should include allergies, current weight and height, and illnesses as well as ALL prescription and nonprescription medications and herbal or nutritional supplements you are currently taking. This ensures that you will be getting appropriate pharmaceutical care (checking your medicines for interactions, errors, appropriate doses, etc.).

15

- Information on the site is referenced. This is critical; much of the Internet is unregulated. You should look for footnotes, endnotes, or parenthetical references or organization references placed appropriately relative to the information you have read. If such notes are not present, the information may be untrue, opinion, or inappropriately slanted. Make sure to talk to the person who prescribed any medicines for you BEFORE you make any changes based on information not provided by that prescriber—even from a well-referenced source.
- A statement disclosing how, with which references, and by whom your current prescription and any existing prescriptions will be checked for accuracy, possible drug interactions, and appropriate disease-, age-, or condition-related dosing changes. The site will also provide a way to talk to a human about questions about your medicines and possible adverse effects.
- Medicines arrive in an appropriate, labeled container that has any needed auxiliary labels on it as well. Please make sure to ask that the disease or condition being treated by the medicine is included on the label.
- Medicines can be obtained by anyone and can be shipped from anywhere. Unfortunately, not everyone has your best interests at heart. There have been a lot of news stories about counterfeit medicines—fake drugs or water substituted for expensive treatments. A real pharmacy with a board to inspect it and help ensure quality is a great idea. You can call the National Association of Boards of Pharmacy at 847-698-6227 or visit them on the Web at *www.nabp.net* to find out if a site really does belong to a licensed pharmacy.
- Information is a powerful ally when you are taking any medicine. When you look for information on a site, check to be sure that site has a date and date-revised section. This tells you that information is being reviewed and kept current.

POWERFUL PATIENTS DO NOT

- order a prescription medicine from the Internet without a prescription. Even if you can get the medicine, you will not have the benefit of your doctor's, pharmacist's, or nurse practitioner's training to help protect you. This can be a prescription for disaster. You also often have no way of knowing that what is supposed to be in the pill is actually what is there. Counterfeit medicines (particularly expensive formulations) have been repeatedly documented.
- automatically trust information that they get over the Internet. Appropriate information has references and at least a byline of a reputable person. If you find information that is troubling to you, talk to your doctor or pharmacist before you act on that information.
- pressure their doctor to prescribe drugs that, in his or her judgment, they do not need. A pill is not always the answer.
- blindly accept care from any provider. Ask your HMO or medical group how their results or outcomes compare to other groups in the area and the country.

- assume that all doctors know all the drugs they take. Always ask your doctor or pharmacist BEFORE combining any other medicine with medicines already prescribed.
- accept a stapled prescription bag. ALWAYS OPEN a stapled bag, check the brief patient information that may be inside the bag, and make sure you understand it. If there is a Med Guide with the prescription, read that carefully as well. While you are in the pharmacy, read the prescription label and make sure it makes sense. Look at the pills, and (especially on refill drugs) check to see that they look the same as they did before. On new prescriptions, ask that the prescription be checked to make sure it is the correct medicine.
- take prescription drugs on their own or on the advice of friends and neighbors because their symptoms are "just like theirs"—ESPECIALLY NOT FROM THE INTERNET WITHOUT A PRESCRIPTION. Drug therapy must be individualized, based on liver and/or kidney function, medicines you currently take, and many other factors.
- offer drugs prescribed for THEM to anyone else without a physician's guidance.
- change the dose or timing of any drug without the advice of their physician (except when the drug appears to be causing adverse effects).
- leave it to a guess that they've taken their medicine. ALWAYS get a dosing calendar or make one so that you can check off **each dose** as you take it.
- continue to take a drug that they feel is causing problems, until they are able to talk with their doctor.
- store their medicines in a bathroom medicine cabinet. This is often an area of high humidity, which can (even though the bottle is closed) enter the medicine and degrade the active drug. Select a lockable kitchen cabinet out of reach of children.
- take any drug (prescription or nonprescription) while pregnant or nursing an infant until they talk to their doctor or pharmacist. Many herbal combinations may have active ingredients similar to those found in prescription medicines.
- take any more medicines than are absolutely necessary. (The greater the number of drugs taken at the same time, the greater the likelihood of adverse effects.)
- withhold from their doctor information about previous prescription or nonprescription drug use. He or she will want to know what has helped and what has caused problems.
- take any drug in the dark. Identify every dose of medicine carefully in adequate light to be certain you are taking the intended drug.
- in general store drugs on a bedside table. In the dark and in a sleepy state, it's easy to get confused. Drugs for emergency use, such as nitroglycerin, are an exception. It is best to have only one such drug at the bedside for use during the night.

POWERFUL PATIENTS DO

- visit the FDA Web site at *www.fda.gov* on a regular basis to check medicines removed from the market and other press releases. Many parts of this site are now consumer friendly. Checking your medicines to make sure you are not continuing to take a medicine that has been removed from the market (see Table 16) is prudent.
- talk with their doctor about the results or outcomes expected from any medicine being considered. Understand that taking the medicine EXACTLY as it is prescribed is critical. Missing one pill in a three-times-a-day regimen may cause you to lose the benefits of all of the medicine.
- talk with their HMO or medical group every year about how their results or outcomes compare to other providers of health care in the area and in the country. This is especially important for businesses, because the preferred provider they choose impacts the health of many people.
- ask their HMO or medical group or pharmacy what their disease management programs are and how any specific disease or condition that they may have is addressed within the scope of their disease management plan. Find out how the results or outcomes of the program compare with other programs in the area or the country.
- know the name (and correct spelling) of the drug(s) they are taking. It is best to know both the brand name and the generic name.
- understand that finding information on the Internet is often only a starting point. Make sure you openly talk to your doctor before you take any action regarding medicines because you saw something on the Net.
- open the prescription bag and the bottle WHILE THEY ARE STILL IN THE PHARMACY. This will give you a chance to best use the training and experience of your pharmacist and will also let you make sure you understand how to best take your medicine. If the prescription is a refill, make sure the pills are the same as the ones originally prescribed. If they are not, ask why.
- read the package labels of all nonprescription drugs so that they know what is in them. This is especially critical when you realize that many of these medicines have names that do not reflect all of the active compounds that are in them.
- take the medicine exactly as prescribed. If you think there will be a change in your ability to take the medicine, call your doctor before you make any change. For example, taking one dose of a medicine that should be taken three times a day often will NOT give one third of the desired effect. I've been asked this kind of question often. Taking a medicine less frequently than prescribed will often give no beneficial effects, especially for those medicines that require a relatively constant blood level to work.
- put a dosing calendar or a reminder note on the refrigerator or near their car keys. Get a watch with an alarm and set it for the times when you need to take your medicine.

- thoroughly shake all liquid suspensions of drugs to ensure uniform distribution of ingredients.
- use a standardized measuring device for giving liquid medicines by mouth. The household "teaspoon" varies greatly in size.
- follow their doctor's advice on dietary or other measures designed to help the prescribed drugs work their best. For example, decreasing or eliminating salt when taking high blood pressure medicines may help you achieve desired drug effects with smaller doses.
- tell their anesthesiologist, surgeon, and dentist of *all* drugs they are taking, before any surgery.
- tell their doctor if they become pregnant while taking any drugs from any source.
- keep a written record of *all* drugs (prescription and nonprescription), vaccines, and herbal remedies they take during their entire pregnancy—name, dose, dates taken, and reasons for use.
- keep a written record of *all* drugs (and vaccines) to which they have become allergic or have an adverse reaction to. This should be done for each member of the family, especially the elderly or infirm.
- keep a written record of *all* drugs (and vaccines) to which their children become allergic or experience an adverse reaction to.
- fill out "Your Personal Drug Profile" (Table 14). Get the number of your Poison Control Center **today** and post it by your telephone. The worst time to try to find an emergency number is while there is a dire need for it. Fill in the Medication Map (Table 15) and ask your doctor if the times selected and combinations of medicines are appropriate.
- tell their doctor of all known or suspected allergies, especially allergies to drugs. Be sure that allergies are a part of your medical record. People with allergies are four times more prone to drug reactions.
- call their doctor immediately they think they are having an overdose, side effect, or adverse effect from a drug.
- ask if it is safe to drive a car, operate machinery, or engage in other hazardous activities while taking the drug(s) prescribed.
- ask if it is safe to drink alcoholic beverages while taking the drug(s) prescribed. We often forget that alcohol is a drug with its own pharmacology and drug-drug interactions.
- find out if any particular foods, beverages, or other prescription or nonprescription medicines should be avoided while taking the drug(s) prescribed.
- keep all appointments for follow-up examinations or laboratory tests.
- ask for help to understand any point that confuses them. If you are concerned about remembering information or instructions for use, ask for written materials.
- throw away all outdated drugs. Couple this with an annual visit to the medicine cabinet!
- ask their doctor if a prescribed medicine offers the best balance of cost and outcomes for them.
- store all drugs for intermittent use out of the reach of children. This is critical for those of you with grandchildren who visit frequently.

PREVENTING ADVERSE DRUG REACTIONS

Powerful patients know that it is always better to prevent a condition or disease than to have to treat it. This is especially true in the case of adverse drug reactions where the cure can become the disease. As our understanding of drug actions and reactions has expanded, we have learned that many adverse effects are, to some extent, predictable and preventable. Eleven contributing factors are now well recognized:

Previous Adverse Reaction to a Drug

People who have had an adverse drug reaction in the past are more likely to have adverse reactions to other drugs, even though the drugs are unrelated. This suggests that some people may have a genetic (inborn) predisposition to unusual or abnormal drug responses. *Always tell your doctor about any history of prior adverse drug experiences*.

Allergies

Some people are allergic by nature (have hay fever, asthma, eczema, hives) and are more likely to develop allergies to drugs. The allergic patient must be watched very closely when medicines are used. Known drug allergies must be written in the medical record. The patient must tell every health care provider that he or she is allergic by nature and is allergic to specific drugs. *Provide this information without waiting to be asked*. Your doctor will then be able to avoid prescribing those drugs that could provoke an allergic reaction, as well as related (cross-sensitivity) drugs.

Contraindications

Both patient and physician must strictly observe contraindications to any drug under consideration. *Absolute contraindications* include those conditions and situations that prohibit the use of the drug for any reason. *Relative contraindications* are those conditions that, in the judgment of the physician, do not preclude the use of the drug but make it essential that special care be given to its use. Often dosing adjustments, additional supportive measures, and close supervision are needed.

Precautions in Use

Patients should know any special precautions needed while taking a drug. This includes advisability of use during pregnancy or while nursing; precautions on sun exposure (or ultraviolet lamps); avoidance of extreme heat or cold; heavy physical exertion (such as with fluoroquinolone antibiotics); and so on.

Dose

It is important to take any medicine exactly as prescribed. *This is most important with drugs that have narrow margins of safety*. Even once-a-day medications should be taken at the same time of day or night to ensure the most constant blood levels. Call your doctor if nausea, vomiting, diarrhea, or other problems interfere with taking your medicine as prescribed.

Interactions

Some drugs can interact with foods (including vitamins and some herbal remedies), alcohol, and other drugs (prescription and nonprescription) to cause serious adverse effects. *The patient must be told about all likely interactants*. If, during the course of treatment, you feel you have discovered a new interaction, tell your doctor so that its full significance can be determined.

Warning Symptoms

Many drugs will cause symptoms that are early warnings of a developing adverse effect: for example, severe headaches or visual disturbances *before* a stroke in a woman taking oral contraceptives. *It is imperative that you know symptoms and signs that could be early warnings of adverse reactions*. The patient is then empowered to act in his or her own behalf by calling the doctor before taking another dose of the medicine. Adverse reactions should be reported to the FDA, following its current guidelines.

Examinations to Monitor Drug Effects

Many drugs in common use can damage vital body tissues (such as bone marrow, liver, kidney, and eye structures)—especially when these drugs are used for a long time or in high doses. Sometimes these adverse effects are not discovered until a newly approved drug has been in wide use for a long time. This damage may be reversible if found quickly. *Cooperate fully with your doctor when he or she asks for periodic exams to check for adverse drug effects*.

Advanced Age and Debility

When we age or as some disease processes progress, vital organs may not work as well and can greatly influence the body's response to drugs. These patients often poorly tolerate drugs with inherent toxic potential and frequently need smaller doses at longer intervals. *The effects of drugs on the elderly and severely ill are often unpredictable*. Great care must be taken to prevent or minimize adverse effects.

Appropriate Drug Choice

The use of any medicine is always a benefit-to-risk decision. The medication used should offer the best balance of overall cost (including lab tests) and outcomes (including quality of life). Many adverse reactions can be prevented if both physician and patient exercise good judgment and restraint.

Polypharmacy

Unfortunately, the cure can become the disease. Patients who are cared for by several physicians may end up with several drugs prescribed separately by more than one physician for different disorders—often without appropriate communication between patient and prescriber. This frequent practice can lead to serious drug-drug interactions. **Every patient should routinely talk to each health care provider about all the drugs—prescription and nonprescription—that he or she may be taking.** It is **mandatory** that each prescriber has this information before prescribing additional drugs.

DRUGS AND PEOPLE OVER 65

Powerful patients know that growing older is a wonderful thing, particularly when coupled with healthy aging. It is important to realize that regardless of your health status, advancing age brings changes that can alter how you (or I) will react to medicines. For example, an impaired digestive system may interfere with drug absorption. Declines in the ability of the kidney, and in some cases the liver, to remove and to change (metabolize) drugs may lead to toxic drug levels despite a "normal" dose. We slowly lose the ability to maintain "steady state" (or homeostasis) and face increased sensitivity of many tissues to the actions of drugs, even in "normal" drug doses. This has been termed homeostenosis by some clinicians. If aging causes a decline in understanding, memory, vision, or coordination, these patients may not always use drugs safely and effectively. Adverse reactions to drugs occur three times more frequently in the older population. An unwanted drug response can change an independent older person into a confused or helpless patient. For these reasons, drug treatment in the elderly must **always** be accompanied by the most careful consideration of the individual's health and tolerances. Powerful patients are advocates for once-daily dosing when it may be the only viable option for an individual patient.

Guidelines for the Use of Drugs by People Over 65

- Make sure that drug treatment is needed. Many health problems of the elderly can be managed **without** the use of drugs. A pill isn't always the answer.
- Avoid (if possible) the use of many drugs at one time.
- Dosing schedules should be as simple as possible. Once a medicine is selected, ask your doctor if a once- or twice-a-day formulation is available and appropriate. The balance here is convenience versus goals and time frames. For some patients, three doses a day may be required.
- Treatment with most drugs is often best started by using less-than-standard doses. Maintenance doses should be individualized and are often smaller for those over 65 years of age.

- Avoid large tablets and capsules if other dosage forms are available. Liquid forms are easier for the elderly or debilitated to swallow.
- Have all drug containers labeled with the drug name and directions for use in large, easy-to-read letters.
- Ask your pharmacist to package drugs in easy-to-open containers. Avoid childproof caps and stoppers (please remember this decision if grandchildren come to visit).
- Do not take any drug in the dark. Identify each dose of medicine carefully in adequate light to be certain you are taking the intended drug.
- To avoid taking the wrong drug or an extra dose, do not routinely leave medicines on a bedside table. Drugs for emergency use, such as nitroglycerin, are an exception. It is best to have only one such drug at the bedside for use during the night.
- Drug use by older people may require supervision; watch constantly to ensure safe and effective use.
- Powerful patients remember the adage: "Start low, go slow, and (when appropriate) learn to say no."

Drugs Best Avoided by the Elderly Because of Increased Possibility of Adverse Reactions (many of the medicines below were found to have been inappropriately prescribed in the most recent check of medication use in this population)

antacids (high sodium)*	estrogens	phenacetin
barbiturates*	indomethacin	phenylbutazone
benzodiazepines oxidase	tetracyclines*	(long-acting)
cyclophosphamide	(MAO) inhibitors*	monoamine
diethylstilbestrol	oxyphenbutazone	

Drugs That Should Be Used by the Elderly in Reduced Dosages Until Full Effect Has Been Determined

anticoagulants (oral)*	colchicine	narcotic drugs
antidepressants*	cortisone-like drugs*	prazosin
antidiabetic drugs*	cimetidine	pseudoephedrine
antihistamines*	digitalis preparations*	quinidine
antihypertensives*	diuretics* (all types)	sildenafil (Viagra)
anti-inflammatory	ephedrine	sleep inducers
drugs*	epinephrine	(hypnotics)*
barbiturates*	haloperidol	terbutaline
beta-blockers*	isoetharine	thyroid preparations
carvedilol (Coreg)	nalidixic acid	

*See Drug Classes, Section Four.

Drugs That May Cause Confusion and Behavioral Disturbances in the Elderly

acyclovir
albuterol
amantadine
anticholinergics*
antidepressants*
antidiabetic drugs*
antihistamines*
anti-inflammatory
  drugs*
asparaginase
atropine* (and drugs
  containing belladonna)
barbiturates*
benzodiazepines*

beta-blockers*
bromocriptine
carbamazepine
cimetidine
digitalis preparations*
diuretics*
ergoloid mesylates
famotidine
haloperidol
levodopa
meprobamate
methocarbamol
methyldopa
narcotic drugs

nizatidine
pentazocine
phenytoin
primidone
quinidine
ranitidine
reserpine
sedatives
sleep inducers (hyp-
  notics)*
thiothixene
tranquilizers (mild)*
trihexyphenidyl

Drugs That May Cause Orthostatic Hypotension in the Elderly

antidepressants*
antihypertensives*
diuretics* (all types)

neuroleptics*
sedatives
tranquilizers (mild)*

phenothiazines*
selegiline
vasodilators*

Drugs That May Cause Sluggishness, Unsteadiness, and Falling in the Elderly

barbiturates*
beta-blockers*
chlordiazepoxide
clorazepate

diazepam
diphenhydramine
flurazepam
halazepam

methyldopa
prazepam
sleep inducers
  (hypnotics)*

Drugs That May Cause Constipation and/or Retention of Urine in the Elderly

acebutolol
amantadine
amiodarone
androgens
anticholinergics*
antidepressants*
anti-parkinsonism
  drugs*

atropinelike drugs*
calcium
cholestyramine
epinephrine
ergoloid mesylates
famotidine
iron (some forms)
isoetharine

ketorolac
metoclopramide
narcotic drugs
phenothiazines*
ranitidine
sucralfate
terbutaline

Drugs That May Cause Loss of Bladder Control (Urinary Incontinence) in the Elderly

diuretics*
  (all types)
sedatives

sleep inducers
  (hypnotics)*
tacrine

thioridazine
tranquilizers (mild)*

*See Drug Classes, Section Four.

MEASURING DRUG LEVELS IN BLOOD
(THERAPEUTIC DRUG MONITORING)

People vary greatly in the nature and degree of their responses to medicines, and often, blood levels can help find the best dose. Frequently, the clinical response to a medicine shows that the drug is working as intended. For some drugs, however, especially those with narrow safety margins, toxic reactions may closely resemble the symptoms being treated. In many cases, the patient's expected response is not in keeping with his or her clinical condition.

By measuring blood levels at appropriate times, your doctor or clinical pharmacist can adjust dosing schedules, reduce the risk of toxicity, and achieve the best results or outcomes. These levels also tell the clinician if you've been taking your medicines as prescribed. Some medications require both a peak and trough level to ensure best results, and timing of blood sampling is critical.

In general, sampling should be avoided during the two hours after an oral dose, because during this absorption period, blood levels do not represent tissue levels of the drug, and the tissue is where many medicines actually work. The peak, or highest, level of the drug can measure several things: toxic levels within the body or how effectively bacteria are killed, for instance. The trough, or lowest, level tells how effectively a medicine is cleared from the body between doses. This can also be important, because if too much drug remains, toxicity can result, and if too little stays, it may not work well. Your doctor may also use peak-to-trough ratios to understand how often a particular medicine should be taken.

The following drugs are those most suitable for therapeutic drug monitoring. If you are using any of these on a regular basis, ask your doctor about checking blood levels. Let me remind you that these numbers are ranges where effects are usually seen, but people react differently. Therapeutic ranges listed are not absolute fixed levels where lack of effect or toxicity definitely occur. One patient may have a therapeutic response at a level lower than the low end of the range while another won't react at all. A blood level higher than the high end of the range is not always toxic but is a level higher than desirable, and dosing changes should be made. Fortunately, most clinicians "treat the patient, not the level." Powerful patients know this.

Generic Name/Brand Name	*Blood Level Range*
acetaminophen/Tylenol, etc.	10–20 mcg/ml
amikacin/Amikin	12–25 mcg/ml (peak)
	5–10 mcg/ml (trough)
amiodarone/Cordarone	0.8–2.8 mcg/ml (controversial—average level in supraventricular tachyarrhythmias was 1.9 mcg/ml in one study)

Generic Name/Brand Name	Blood Level Range
amitriptyline/Elavil, etc. (combined with nortriptyline)	120–250 ng/ml
amoxapine/Asendin	200–500 ng/ml
aspirin (other salicylates)	100–250 mcg/ml
carbamazepine/Tegretol	5–10 mcg/ml
chloramphenicol/Chloromycetin	10–25 mcg/ml
chlorpromazine/Thorazine	50–300 ng/ml
ciprofloxacin/Cipro	0.94–3.4 mcg/ml
clonazepam/Klonopin	10–50 mg/ml
cyclosporine/Sandimmune	100–150 ng/ml
desipramine/Norpramin, Pertofrane	150–300 ng/ml
digitoxin/Crystodigin	15–30 ng/ml
digoxin/Lanoxin	0.5–2.0 ng/ml (historic range) 0.5–0.8 ng/ml (Heart failure in men, controversial drug in heart failure in women)
diltiazem/Cardizem	0.1–0.4 mcg/ml
disopyramide/Norpace	2.0–4.5 mcg/ml
doxepin/Adapin, Sinequan	100–275 mg/ml
ethosuximide/Zarontin	40–100 mcg/ml
flecainide/Tambocor	0.2–1.0 mcg/ml
flucytosine/Ancobon	50–100 mcg/ml
gentamicin/Garamycin	4.0–10 mcg/ml (peak) less than 2 mcg/ml (trough)
gold salts/Auranofin, etc.	1.0–2.0 mcg/ml
imipramine/Janimine, Tofranil, etc.	150–300 ng/ml
kanamycin/Kantrex	25–35 mcg/ml
lidocaine/Xylocaine, etc.	1.4–6.0 mcg/ml
lithium/Lithobid, Lithotabs, etc.	0.3–1.3 MEq/L
mephobarbital/Mebaral	1–7 mcg/ml
methotrexate/Mexate	up to 0.1 mcmol/L
methsuximide/Celontin	up to 1.0 mcg/ml
metoprolol/Lopressor	20–200 ng/ml
mexiletine/Mexitil	0.75–2.0 mcg/ml
nifedipine/Procardia	25–100 ng/ml
nortriptyline/Aventyl, Pamelor	50–150 ng/ml
combined with amitriptyline	125–250 ng/ml
phenobarbital/Luminal, etc.	10–25 mcg/ml
phenytoin/Dilantin	10–18 mcg/ml
primidone/Mysoline	6–12 mcg/ml
procainamide/Pronestyl	4–10 mcg/ml
(NAPA metabolite)	4–10 mcg/ml
propafenone	0.06–1 mcg/ml
propranolol/Inderal	50–100 ng/ml
protriptyline/Vivactil	70–250 ng/ml
quinidine/Quinaglute, etc. (specific to quinidine test method)	1.0–4.0 mcg/ml

sulfadiazine/Microsulfon	100–120 mcg/ml
sulfamethoxazole/Gantanol	90–100 mcg/ml
theophylline/Aminophylline, etc.	10–20 mcg/ml
thioridazine/Mellaril	50–300 ng/ml
tobramycin/Nebcin	4.0–10 mcg/ml (peak)
	less than 2 mcg/ml (trough)
tocainide/Tonocard	5–12 mcg/ml
trimethadione/Tridione	10–30 mcg/ml
trimethoprim/Proloprim	1–3 mcg/ml
valproic acid/Depakene	50–100 mcg/ml
vancomycin/Vancocin	30–40 mcg/ml (peak)
	5–10 mcg/ml (trough)
verapamil/Calan	0.06–0.2 mcg/ml

3

True Breakthroughs in Medicines

Happily, every year we gain some great advances in medicines—this section tells you about some of the best, identifies novel treatment approaches, and gives truly new uses of existing medicines. I distinguish between "me too" products (that may simply be an existing drug with minor chemical changes) and forward-looking advances that powerful patients should know about. I believe that this section can help you make sure you are getting the very latest treatment. This data changes on a regular basis. One way to follow up on medicines themselves is to visit the FDA Web site at *www.fda.gov* and look at the type of approval the medicine was given. A "chemical type one" designation is a new molecular entity—something that has never existed before. "Chemical type four" designations are new combinations of medicines. These two categories coupled with the latest research can help you find the latest in therapy. I also have an Update on New Medicines report on my Web site at *www.medicineinfo.com*.

ACUTE CORONARY SYNDROMES AND THE CURE TRIAL

The CURE trial (Clopidogrel in Unstable Angina to prevent Recurrent Events) was reported at the American College of Cardiology meeting and was immediately termed a "blockbuster" clinical result by clinicians and researchers. One of the lead researchers estimated that widespread use of clopidogrel (Plavix) combined with aspirin in patients with acute coronary syndromes (ACS—such as unstable angina or non-Q-wave MI) could prevent 50,000 to 100,000 heart attacks, strokes, or deaths EACH YEAR in North America. I think of the great possible benefit this combination could have for my father had it only been available. One caution I want to tell you about is that there have been reports of some ACS patients who have had clopidogrel AND aspirin prescribed and have had this come up as a drug interaction in the pharmacy—causing confusion. If the combination has been prescribed, talk to your doctor about what to do if a pharmacy drug interactions program raises a red flag that in the ACS case simply does not apply.

ADHERENCE (COMPLIANCE) PROGRAMS

I've been the pharmacist representative to the Compliance Action Program (CAP) of the American Heart Association and have been working to get pharmacists and pharmacies more involved in helping people get great quality information and reminders to keep taking their medicines. You may have seen me talking on television about this. The focus is how well people take their medicines—in fact, the best medicine in the world will not do you any good at all if it stays in the bottle.

I have had many consults asking me why a given medicine failed to work, only to talk to the patient and find out that the medicine itself was either not being taken or was being taken as needed (when the patient felt bad). Two new patient profilers are available at *www.americanheart.org* that help you learn about coronary artery disease and also congestive heart failure and the importance of taking your medicine. Powerful patients can get a check of their treatment options—this is a prescription for success! You can also call the AHA at 1-800-242-8721 or fax them at 1-214-706-5233. I strongly encourage you to make a donation just like me.

AMA, JCAHO, AND NCQA PAIN INITIATIVE

Pain is the most common reason that people try to get medical care. Pain is now the fifth vital sign! This is a clear victory—but how does it translate to busy professionals? The Joint Commission on Accreditation of Healthcare Organizations made a bold move by elaborating new Pain Standards that in effect REQUIRE hospitals to address important issues in pain management. The fact that AMA, JCAHO, and NCQA will now work together to help doctors, health plans, and hospitals see how well they are doing (measure effectiveness) in their pain management programs tells us that pain management is FINALLY being taken seriously. What these groups are trying to do is to form a new alliance to improve the quality and consistency of pain management around the country. Interestingly, Purdue Pharma (a maker of pain medicines) has provided unrestricted funding to support development of the pain management measurement program (pain measure set). Congratulations to the three organizations and to Purdue for funding what I expect will be a most valuable body of work!

ASPIRIN

Yes—I include aspirin once again in this section. Previously I put it here because it can be one of the easiest ways to help limit the damage from a heart attack. This year I included it here because it was found to decrease (by 28 percent) the risk of a FIRST HEART ATTACK in otherwise healthy adults. Talk to your doctor to see if this makes sense for you. Please also remember that the current American Heart Association recommendation for people who appear to be suffering a heart attack (if they do not have any contraindications) is to give them a non-enteric full-dose aspirin (325 mg). This measure can help limit the size of the heart attack and possible heart muscle damage. If you have risk factors (see Table 19) for a first heart attack, talk to your doctor to see if he or she thinks it is a good idea for you to carry a non-enteric full dose (325 mg) with you in a plastic bag placed in your wallet or purse. Aspirin can also make great combination therapy sense for ACS patients who are taking clopidogrel (see CURE trial above or at *www.medicineinfo.com*). Aspirin may also have a role in preventing some kinds of cancers.

FUSION INHIBITOR

Historically, all of the available HIV treatments fell into the nucleoside reverse transcriptase inhibitor, non-nucleoside reverse transcriptase inhibitor, and protease inhibitor classes. A novel way to attack the AIDS virus was clearly needed and was discovered by Trimeris pharmaceutical. The new approach is called a fusion inhibitor—helping to keep HIV from entering cells and killing them. The first fusion inhibitor to be approved was previously known as T-20 and is now called efurvirtide (Fuseon) and is available (albeit channeled through a single pharmacy). I believe that fusion inhibitors will become an integral part of combination HIV therapy.

HUMAN GENOME

There are some 3 billion base pairs, and an estimated 40,000 genes in the human genome. Some 20 diseases cause more than 80 percent of deaths around the world. About 200–300 genes are responsible for these diseases. Amazingly, the human genome is now mostly known. Considering that about every three weeks we in essence get a new heart from the same set of genes, if controlling the genes becomes a reality, we can possibly knock out heart disease by knocking out the bad gene of a pair. Watch closely!

GET WITH THE GUIDELINES

You'd think that prescribing medicines and having patients take them after they've suffered a first heart attack would be well standardized and followed. Unfortunately, this is NOT the case! The situation is called secondary prevention (secondary prevention of cardiovascular disease). One data set found that only 37 percent of patients with increased cholesterol actually got a statin (HMG-CoA reductase inhibitor). The American Heart Association has launched a new program called Get With The Guidelines (GWTG) to address this problem. GWTG is a hospital-based initiative seeking to help patients and their families understand the goals of treatment and get the best medicines started. You can find out more by visiting *www.americanheart.org/getwiththeguidelines.html*. I am a spokesperson for this program. You can read my testimonial by visiting *www. americanheart.org/getwiththeguidelines/testimonials.html*.

NATIONAL POISON CONTROL PHONE NUMBER

If a loved one has taken an overdose of a medicine or toxic chemical, the last thing you want to do is search for your state's, or if you are visiting someone else, their state's 800 number for poison control. FINALLY, there is a National Poison Control number: 1-800-222-1222.

NIH CHOLESTEROL GUIDELINES

The National Institutes of Health (NIH) released ATP III as part of the update to the National Cholesterol Education Program, or NCEP. I include these guidelines again this year because I think that these guidelines are starting to be more widely followed and will save many, many lives. Key points in these new guidelines include acknowledging diabetes as one of the conditions that increases risk of heart disease. FINALLY, the relationship between these two critical health care problems has been put into important guidelines, and the American Diabetes Association (ADA) and the American Heart Association (AHA) are starting to work together to attack the common goal of decreasing risk of heart attack and stroke. Remember—these new guidelines also recommend a desirable total cholesterol of 200 mg/dl, as before, but change LDL to 100 mg/dl as optimal, 130–159 mg/dl as borderline high, 160 mg/dl as high, and 190 mg/dl as very high. "Good cholesterol," or HDL, has been made more important. The "too low" measure for HDL has been increased to 40 mg/dl. If you are NOT AT GOAL, powerful patients will talk to their doctor and decide what next steps need to be taken.

PRE-DIABETES

What comes before diabetes—logically, I think all of us could come up with pre-diabetes. The old term was impaired glucose tolerance, which would confuse most medical students. I believe that the Bush administration (Tommy Thompson from HHS in particular) and a panel from the American Diabetes Association (ADA) have worked well to create awareness and to get doctors to screen overweight patients over 45 for pre-diabetes. The importance of this? If you have blood sugar (glucose) levels in the pre-diabetes range—your heart attack risk increases by 50 percent. This is a staggering statistic. The ADA panel also said that even people younger than 45 who are overweight should be checked for pre-diabetes, especially if they: have high blood pressure; had diabetes when they were pregnant or had a baby that weighed more than 9 pounds; have increased triglycerides or an HDL less than 40 mg/dl; have a family history of diabetes; or are Pacific Islanders, Native American, black, Hispanic, or Asian, as these populations tend to be at increased risk for diabetes.

PRE-HYPERTENSION

What comes before high blood pressure—logically, I think all of us could come up with pre-hypertension. This term arose from the awareness that even what were once considered "normal blood pressures" can be associated with the beginnings of damage to our blood vessels. I believe that the Bush administration (Tommy Thompson from HHS in particular) and a panel from the National Heart, Lung, and Blood Institute known as JNC VII have worked brilliantly to create a new category of blood pressure and to further refine the awareness with the new High Blood Pressure guidelines. The importance of this? If you have blood pressure of more than 115/75 mm HG, the risk of death from stroke or heart disease increases. More important, the risk **DOUBLES** for each 20/10 increase that you have (see JNC VII in Glossary). Make this the year that you and your family get your weight and blood pressure under control!

DRUG PROFILES

Drugs Reviewed in This Section

Included are detailed and annually updated Drug Profiles of **more than 2,000 brands** and nearly 400 drugs of major importance. The criteria are that the medicine:

1. Is used to treat or prevent a prevalent, relatively serious significant disease or disorder.

2. Is recognized by experts to be among the "best choices" in its class.

3. Has a current benefit-to-risk ratio that compares favorably with those in its class or is the only available alternative therapy for those who cannot tolerate the first-line medicine.

4. May require special information and guidance for both the health care practitioner (physician, dentist, pharmacist, nurse) and the consumer (patient and family) for safe and effective use.

5. Is suitable (safe and practical) for use in an outpatient setting (home, work site, school, etc.). It can be self-administered or may require dosing by trained medical personnel (as with home intravenous therapy or free-standing cancer, emergency or pain centers).

ACARBOSE (A KAR BOZ)

Introduced: 1996   **Class:**   Alpha glucosidase inhibitor; antidiabetes agent, oral   **Prescription:**   USA: Yes   **Controlled Drug:**   USA: No; Canada: No   **Available as Generic:**   No
Brand Names: Glucobay, Precose, ✤Prandase

BENEFITS versus RISKS

Possible Benefits	*Possible Risks*
EFFECTIVE LOWERING OF BLOOD SUGAR	Gas (flatulence) and abdominal pain (often decreases over time)
DECREASES A SUDDEN RISE IN BLOOD SUGAR AFTER A MEAL	Increased liver function tests
DECREASED RISK OF HIGH BLOOD PRESSURE, BLINDNESS, HEART DISEASE, OR OTHER LONG-TERM DAMAGE OF UNCONTROLLED DIABETES (WITH BETTER OR TIGHTER CONTROL OF BLOOD SUGAR)	Combination use gives better results, but also increases risk of excessively low blood sugar (hypoglycemia) like other agents
MAY BE USED IN COMBINED TREATMENT WITH METFORMIN, INSULIN, OR A SULFONYLUREA IF NEEDED TO REACH BLOOD SUGAR CONTROL GOALS	
May help PREVENT type 2 diabetes in people with pre-diabetes.	

▷ **Principal Uses**

> *As a Single Drug Product:* Uses currently included in FDA-approved labeling: (1) Used with diet in diabetics who don't require insulin, yet don't have good (tight control of 80–120 mg/dl or as defined as acceptable by their doctor) blood sugar control with diet alone; (2) can be combined with a sulfonylurea (see Drug Classes) if diet plus acarbose or diet and sulfonylurea do not control blood sugar as well as needed; (3) can be combined with metformin or insulin if diet plus acarbose or diet plus sulfonylurea do not achieve blood sugar control goals.
> Other (unlabeled) generally accepted uses: (1) Combination treatment of diabetics (type one) who require insulin; (2) the Stop-NIDDM research on 1,368 patients found that acarbose worked to delay or prevent people with pre-diabetes from developing type 2 diabetes.

How This Drug Works: By blocking the chemicals (enzymes) called intestinal alpha glucosidases and pancreatic alpha amylase, this medicine impairs starch and sucrose digestion and actually keeps sugar low after meals.

Available Dosage Forms and Strengths
Tablets — 25 mg, 50 mg, 100 mg

▷ **Recommended Dosage Ranges** (Actual dose and schedule must be determined individually for each patient.)
Infants and Children: Safety and effectiveness not established in those less than 18 years old.

18 to 65 Years of Age: To start, 25 mg three times daily, taken at the start of each meal (after first bite). Dose increases are made at 4- to 8-week intervals to achieve blood sugar control while minimizing intestinal side effects (using 50 mg three times daily at the start of each meal). If response is not acceptable, patients weighing more than 132 pounds (60 kg) may be given doses up to 100 mg three times daily. Those weighing less than 60 kg should NOT be given more than 50 mg three times daily. If a dose increase doesn't give better sugar control, consider dose decrease.

Over 65 Years of Age: No specific recommendations unless kidney function is very limited, in which case *a* kidney specialist may be prudent.

Conditions Requiring Dosing Adjustments

Liver Function: Specific dosing changes do not appear to be needed. Enzymes found in the intestine and intestinal bacteria extensively contribute to removal of this medicine.

Kidney Function: Increases in drug levels may occur and dose decreases may be needed. Specific guidelines not available. The kidneys usually remove only about 2%.

▷ **Dosing Instructions:** Take this pill after starting to eat breakfast, lunch and dinner—after the first bite of a meal has been eaten. Dosing must be individualized. Gas (flatulence) or diarrhea is a common side effect, but often decreases over time. Limiting sucrose (read the food label) can also help.

If dose changes are made at 4- to 8-week intervals, the best sugar response and the least potential gas (flatulence) or diarrhea are realized. Often blood sugar is checked one hour after a meal (1 hr postprandial) and the dose adjusted to get the best balance of blood sugar and side effects (also avoiding too low a blood sugar). If you forget a dose but remember it while you are still eating, take it immediately. If you remember the dose just after finishing your meal, take the dose now (if you remember later than this, take your next dose with your next meal). Do not double doses or take acarbose between meals. Check your blood sugar as your doctor has instructed.

Usual Duration of Use: Use will be ongoing. Regular use is required for good blood sugar (glucose) control. DO NOT MISS DOSES. Keeping the sugar close to normal can decrease severity or risk of problems (such as blindness, heart disease, and undesirable circulation changes) often found in diabetes.

Typical Treatment Goals and Measurements (Outcomes and Markers)

Blood Sugar: The general goal for blood sugar is to return it to the usual "normal" range (generally 80–120 mg/dl), while avoiding risks of excessively low blood sugar. One study (UKPDS) used a fasting plasma sugar (glucose) of less than 108 mg/dl. Keeping blood sugar in the normal range helps avoid complications of diabetes.

Fructosamine and Glycosylated Hemoglobin: Fructosamine levels (a measure of the past two to three weeks of blood sugar control) should be less than or equal to 310 micromoles per liter. Glycosylated hemoglobin or hemoglobin A1C (a measure of the past 2–3 months of blood sugar control) should be less than or equal to 7.0%. Some clinicians advocate less than 6.5%. Diabetes is a CHD risk equivalent in NCEP ATP 3 (see Glossary). This means that diabetics face a significant risk of heart disease. EBCT (see Glossary) may help define risk.

Possible Advantages of This Drug

May be used in combination with oral hypoglycemics (such as sulfonylureas, insulin, or metformin (see Drug Classes) to get the best control of blood sugar. Uses a different (novel) mechanism than other oral hypoglycemic drugs. Please remember—the goal is to keep the blood sugar as close to normal as possible.

▷ **This Drug Should Not Be Taken If**

- you have had an allergic reaction to it previously.
- you are in diabetic ketoacidosis.
- your history includes intestinal obstruction or you have a partial obstruction of the intestine.
- you have inflammatory bowel disease or colon ulceration.
- you have cirrhosis of the liver.
- you have an intestinal condition that may worsen (such as a megacolon or bowel obstruction) if increased gas (flatus) forms.
- you have a long-standing (chronic) intestinal disease altering digestion or your ability to absorb materials from the intestine.
- you are pregnant or are breast-feeding your infant (no data exist on use in pregnancy or breast-feeding).
- you are less than 18 years old.

▷ **Inform Your Physician Before Taking This Drug If**

- you have an infection (insulin may be required).
- you do not know what the symptoms of hypoglycemia are.
- you have a history of kidney or liver disease.
- your liver function tests (LFTs) have become known to you and they are increased.
- you will have surgery with general anesthesia.
- you forgot to tell your doctor about all the drugs you take.
- you are also taking a sulfonylurea (increased risk of excessively low blood sugar).
- you are anemic (conflicting information here, but acarbose might lower iron levels).
- you are unsure of how much or how often to take acarbose.

Possible Side Effects (natural, expected, and unavoidable drug actions)

Gas (flatulence) or diarrhea (results from bacterial action on sugars) and tends to decrease over time.

▷ **Possible Adverse Effects** (unusual, unexpected, and infrequent reactions)

If any of the following develop, consult your physician promptly for guidance.

Mild Adverse Effects

Allergic reactions: skin redness (erythema), itching (urticaria).

Sleepiness, headache, dizziness—questionable cause (may really be blood sugar control signs or symptoms).

Pain or swelling of the belly (abdomen)—frequent.

Gas (flatulence) or diarrhea—frequent (often eases over time).

Serious Adverse Effects

Erythema multiforme—case report.

Low blood sugar if combined with sulfonylureas or other anti-diabetes medicines such as insulin—possible.

Anemia—rare in clinical approval trials, but not seen in later studies.

Increased liver enzymes up to necrosis of liver tissue—case reports (case reports developed this problem in 2–8 months—with an unclear relationship to the drug). Liver toxicity can be more common in women than in men. Call your doctor if you start to have nausea, fatigue, and light colored stools or pain in the right upper part of your abdomen.

Ileus—case reports and more likely in those with prior bowel blockage history.

Abnormal lipids (increased cholesterol and triglycerides)—case report.

▷ **Possible Effects on Sexual Function:** None reported.

Possible Effects on Laboratory Tests
Glycated protein (fructosamine): trending toward normal (good effect).
Hemoglobin A1C: trending more toward normal (good effect).
Blood sugar one hour after eating (postprandial): decreased.
Serum lipids: variable effect, but usually improved.
Liver enzymes: may be increased.

CAUTION
1. This medicine itself does not cause hypoglycemia. Low sugar may result if combined with metformin, insulin, or sulfonylureas.
2. Infections may cause loss of sugar control and require temporary insulin use.
3. This medicine is part of the total management of diabetes. A properly prescribed diet and regular exercise are still required for best control of blood sugar.
4. If your kidneys fail or worsen, tell your doctor.
5. Call your doctor if you have light colored stools, nausea, and pain in the upper right part of your abdomen.

Precautions for Use
By Infants and Children: Safety and effectiveness for those under 18 not established.
By Those Over 60 Years of Age: Specific changes are not made at this time.

▷ **Advisability of Use During Pregnancy**
Pregnancy Category: B. See Pregnancy Risk Categories at the back of this book.
Animal Studies: No significant increase in birth defects in rats or rabbits.
Human Studies: Adequate studies of pregnant women are not available. Insulin is often the drug of first choice for blood sugar control in pregnancy. Ask your doctor for help.

Advisability of Use If Breast-Feeding
Presence of this drug in breast milk: Yes, in rats. No human data available. Avoid drug or refrain from nursing.

Habit-Forming Potential: None.

Effects of Overdose: Temporary gas (flatus), abdominal discomfort, and diarrhea.

Possible Effects of Long-Term Use: Beneficial effects on blood sugar, lowered risk of cardiovascular disease and of high blood pressure with better sugar control.

Suggested Periodic Examinations While Taking This Drug (at physician's discretion)
Periodic blood sugar one hour after eating.
Glycated protein (fructosamine).

Hemoglobin A1C levels.

Liver function tests (transaminases)—checked every three months during the first year, then periodically thereafter. Patients taking other medicines that can be toxic to the liver should be tested more frequently.

Serum iron or iron-binding capacity prudent if anemia develops.

▷ **While Taking This Drug, Observe the Following**

Foods: Closely follow the diet your doctor has prescribed. Blood sugar control can help avoid or delay diabetes problems! Vitamin C in high dose may worsen blood sugar control.

Herbal Medicines or Minerals: Using chromium may change the way your body is able to use sugar. Some health food stores advocate vanadium as mimicking the actions of insulin, but possible toxicity and need for rigorous studies presently preclude recommending it. DHEA may change sensitivity to insulin or insulin resistance. Aloe, bitter melon, fenugreek, hawthorn, ginger, garlic, ginseng, glucomannan, guar gum, licorice, nettle, St. John's wort, and yohimbe may change blood sugar. Because these products can have an effect—talk to your doctor BEFORE combining any of these herbal medicines with acarbose. Echinacea purpurea (injectable) and blonde psyllium seed or husk should NOT be taken by people living with diabetes.

Beverages: No restrictions. May be taken with milk—mindful of the limits of the diet that your doctor has recommended.

▷ *Alcohol:* No interaction with acarbose. If you also take a sulfonylurea (see Drug Classes), alcohol can exaggerate lowering of blood sugar or cause a disulfiramlike (see Glossary) reaction.

Tobacco Smoking: No interactions expected, but I advise everyone to stop smoking.

▷ *Other Drugs*

Acarbose may *increase* the effects of

- insulins (see Drug Classes), further lowering blood sugar for patients who do not respond to acarbose alone (a beneficial effect when blood sugar is closely watched).
- metformin (Glucophage) may further lower blood sugar for patients who are not controlled by diet or acarbose alone (beneficial effect as above).
- sulfonylureas (see Drug Classes), causing further lowering of blood sugars (not an acarbose effect). This may be used for therapeutic benefit.
- warfarin (Coumadin)—INR testing more often is advisable.

Acarbose *taken concurrently* with

- activated charcoal (various) may blunt the benefits of acarbose.
- amylase (pancreatin) may blunt the benefits of acarbose.
- clofibrate (Atromid-S) may result in hypoglycemia.
- digestive enzyme products that contain amylase or lipase may result in loss of blood sugar control.
- digoxin (Lanoxin) may cause lower (subtherapeutic) blood levels of digoxin and loss of benefits (three case reports).
- disopyramide (Norpace) may result in hypoglycemia.
- fluoroquinolone antibiotics (such as ciprofloxacin-Cipro, gatifloxacin-Tequin, levofloxacin-Levaquin) may result in low blood sugar (hypoglycemia).
- high-dose aspirin or other salicylates and some NSAIDs (see Drug Classes) may result in hypoglycemia.

- monoamine oxidase (MAO) inhibitors (see Drug Classes) may increase glucose tolerance, leading to excessively low blood sugar.
- sulfonamide antibiotics (see Drug Classes) may pose an increased risk for low blood sugar (hypoglycemia).

The following drugs may *decrease* the effects of acarbose:
- adrenocorticosteroids (see Drug Classes).
- beta-blockers (see Drug Classes).
- calcium channel blockers (see Drug Classes).
- furosemide (Lasix) and bumetanide (Bumex).
- isoniazid (INH).
- nicotinic acid.
- pancreatin (or any medicines containing carbohydrate dividing enzymes such as amylase or pancreatin).
- phenytoin (Dilantin).
- rifampin (Rifadin, others).
- theophylline (Theo-Dur, others).
- thiazide diuretics (see Drug Classes).
- thyroid hormones (see Drug Classes).

▷ *Driving, Hazardous Activities:* Use caution until degree of drowsiness you may see is known.

Aviation Note: Diabetes *is a disqualification* for piloting. Consult a designated Aviation Medical Examiner.

Exposure to Sun: No restrictions.

Heavy Exercise or Exertion: Caution advised because this drug lowers peak in blood sugar after meals. Discuss dosing changes with your doctor.

Occurrence of Unrelated Illness: Illness can change blood sugar control and beneficial results from this medicine. Temporary use of insulin may be **required** if you are sick such as in the case of infection.

Discontinuation: **Never** stop acarbose before calling your doctor.

ACEBUTOLOL (a se BYU toh lohl)

Introduced: 1973   **Class:** Antihypertensive, beta-adrenergic blocker, heart rhythm regulator   **Prescription:** USA: Yes   **Controlled Drug:** USA: No; Canada: No   **Available as Generic:** Yes

Brand Names: ✤Apo-Acebutolol, ✤Gen-Acebutolol, ✤Med-Acebutolol, ✤†Monitan, ✤Rhotral, Sectral

```
┌─────────────────────────────────────────────────────────────────────┐
│                        BENEFITS versus RISKS                          │
│       Possible Benefits                    Possible Risks             │
│ EFFECTIVE ANTIHYPERTENSIVE        CONGESTIVE HEART FAILURE IN         │
│    (MILD–MODERATE HIGH               ADVANCED HEART DISEASE           │
│    PRESSURE) MAY BE USED           Masking of low blood sugar         │
│    ALONE OR IN COMBINATION           (hypoglycemia) in diabetics      │
│    WITH OTHER                      Rare lupus erythematosus syndrome  │
│    ANTIHYPERTENSIVES,                                                 │
│    ESPECIALLY DIURETICS                                               │
│ MAY DECREASE DEATHS                                                   │
│    OCCURRING AFTER HEART                                              │
│    ATTACK                                                             │
│ LONG-TERM USE CAN DECREASE                                           │
│    DEATH AND HEART PROBLEMS                                          │
│ HELPS PREVENT ABNORMAL                                               │
│    HEART RHYTHMS                                                     │
│ Because this drug also has intrinsic                                │
│    sympathomimetic activity it may                                  │
│    help in patients with high                                       │
│    cholesterol (dyslipidemia) because                              │
│    it avoids increases in serum                                     │
│    triglycerides                                                    │
│ May be particularly useful in people                               │
│    with asthma or diabetes (because of                             │
│    heart or cardioselectivity)                                     │
└─────────────────────────────────────────────────────────────────────┘
```

▷ **Principal Uses**
  As a Single Drug Product: Uses currently included in FDA-approved labeling:
      (1) Treats mild to moderate high blood pressure alone or in combination;
      (2) used to prevent premature ventricular heartbeats and ventricular
      arrhythmias.
      Other (unlabeled) generally accepted uses: (1) Stabilizes angina pectoris;
      (2) used after a heart attack to help prolong life.

  How This Drug Works: It blocks sympathetic nervous system effects and slows
      the rate and force of the heart, reducing the extent of blood vessel contrac-
      tion, expanding the walls and lowering blood pressure. Also slows nerve
      impulse speed through the heart, which helps ease some heart rhythm dis-
      orders.

  Available Dosage Forms and Strengths
      Capsules — 100 mg (in Canada), 200 mg, 400 mg
      Tablets — 100 mg, 200 mg and 400 mg (in Canada)

▷ **Recommended Dosage Ranges** (Actual dose and schedule must be determined
      for each patient individually.)
  Infants and Children: Not indicated.
  18 to 65 Years of Age: High blood pressure:200 mg a day works for some, but
      most patients require 400–800 mg a day, rarely 1,200 (given as 600 mg
      twice a day). Heart selectivity (beta one) decreases as doses increase.
      Arrhythmias: 400 mg daily, as 200 mg taken morning and evening (12 hours
      apart as a divided dose). Increased as needed and tolerated. 600–1200 mg
      a day is a typical effective dose. Total dose should not exceed 1,200 mg
      every 24 hours (600 mg twice a day).

Angina: 600 to 1,600 mg is divided into two or three equal doses given 8 to 12 hours apart.

Over 65 Years of Age: Bioavailability (amount taken into your body) doubles because of lower liver and kidney removal. Smaller ongoing doses are needed and 800 mg a day is a **maximum.**

Conditions Requiring Dosing Adjustments

Liver Function: Used with caution in compromised liver function.

Kidney Function: Dose must be decreased by up to 75% in severe kidney failure (dicetalol metabolite can accumulate).

▷ **Dosing Instructions:** May be taken without regard to eating. Capsule may be opened when taken. NEVER stop this drug abruptly. If you forget a dose: take it right away unless it's within 4 hours of your next regular dose. If it IS within 4 hours of the next dose, just take the scheduled dose. Do NOT double doses.

Usual Duration of Use: Use on a regular schedule for 5 to 14 days may be required to see peak benefits in lowering blood pressure or stopping premature heartbeats. Long-term use determined by sustained benefit and response to a combined program (weight decrease, salt restriction, smoking cessation, etc.) in high blood pressure and response of abnormal heart rhythm. Do NOT skip doses.

Typical Treatment Goals and Measurements (Outcomes and Markers)

Blood Pressure: The NEW guidelines (JNC VII) define normal blood pressure (BP) as **less than** 120/80. Because blood pressures that were once considered acceptable can actually lead to blood vessel damage, the committee from the National Institutes of Health, National Heart Lung and Blood Institute now have a new category called **Pre-hypertension**. This ranges from 120/80 to 139/89 and is intended to help your doctor encourage lifestyle changes (or in the case of people with a risk factor for high blood pressure, start treatment) much earlier—so that possible damage to blood vessels, your heart, kidneys, sexual potency, or eyes might be minimized or avoided altogether. The next two classes of high blood pressure are stage 1 hypertension: 140/90 to 159/99 and stage 2 hypertension equal to or greater than: 160/100 mm Hg. These guidelines also recommend that clinicians trying to control blood pressure work with their patients to agree on the goals and a plan of treatment. The first-ever guidelines for blood pressure (hypertension) in African Americans recommends that MOST black patients be started on TWO antihypertensive medicines with the goal of lowering blood pressure to 130/80 for those with high risk for heart and blood vessel disease or with diabetes. The American Diabetes Association recommends 130/80 as the target for people living with diabetes and less than 125/75 for those who spill more than one gram of protein into their urine. Most clinicians try to achieve a BP that confers the best balance of lower cardiovascular risk and avoids the problem of too low a blood pressure. Blood pressure duration is generally increased with beneficial restriction of sodium. The goals and time frame should be discussed with you when the prescription is written. If goals are not met, it is not unusual to intensify doses or add on medicines. You can find the new blood pressure guidelines at *www.nhlbi.hih.gocv/guidelines/hypertension/index.htm*. For the African American guidelines see Douglas J.G. in Sources.

Abnormal Heartbeats: The general goal is to return the heart to a normal rhythm or at least to markedly reduce the occurrence of abnormal heartbeats. In life-threatening arrhythmias, the goal is to abort the abnormal beats and return the pattern to normal. Success at ongoing suppression may involve ambulatory checks of heart rate and rhythm for a day (such as in Holter monitoring). This kind of testing involves placement of adhesive-backed temporary electrodes on the skin in several positions around the heart. A small heart rate and rhythm (EKG or ECG) recording device is carried around via a shoulder strap and records what the heart is doing over 24 hours. Once the recording is made, a scanning machine reviews the record, tallies abnormal heartbeats or rhythms and gives a close and extended look at how the heart is reacting or benefiting from the medicines that the patient is taking. Repeat measurements can be made if doses are changed to check the success at keeping the heart in normal sinus rhythm!

Possible Advantages of This Drug: Slows the heart less than most other beta-blocker drugs, and low doses are less likely to cause asthma attacks in asthmatics. May cause less frequent problems with blood vessels in the legs (peripheral vascular insufficiency) than non-selective beta blockers such as propranolol.

▷ **This Drug Should Not Be Taken If**
 • you have had an allergic reaction to it previously.
 • you are in heart failure (overt).
 • you have a severely slow (bradycardia) heart rate or serious heart block (second or third degree AV).

▷ **Inform Your Physician Before Taking This Drug If**
 • you have had an adverse reaction to any beta-blocker (see Drug Classes).
 • you have serious heart disease or episodes of heart failure (this drug may aggravate it).
 • you have disease of the mitral valve or aorta.
 • you have hay fever (allergic rhinitis), asthma, chronic bronchitis, or emphysema.
 • you have an overactive thyroid function (hyperthyroidism).
 • you have problems with circulation to your arms and legs (peripheral vascular disease or intermittent claudication).
 • you have a history of low blood sugar (hypoglycemia).
 • you have impaired liver or kidney function.
 • you have diabetes or myasthenia gravis.
 • you take digitalis, quinidine or reserpine, or any calcium blocker (see Drug Classes).
 • you will have surgery with general anesthesia.
 • you do not know how much or how often to take acebutolol.
 • you have not asked if the dose was adjusted for age-related kidney decline or kidney disease.

Possible Side Effects (natural, expected, and unavoidable drug actions)
 Lethargy and fatigability, cold extremities—rare; slow heart rate, light-headedness in upright position (see Orthostatic Hypotension in Glossary) possible.

▷ **Possible Adverse Effects** (unusual, unexpected, and infrequent reactions)
 If any of the following develop, consult your physician promptly for guidance.
 Mild Adverse Effects
 Allergic reactions: skin rash, itching—rare.
 Fatigue—frequent.
 Headache, dizziness, insomnia, fatigue, or abnormal dreams—infrequent.

Indigestion, nausea, constipation, diarrhea—infrequent.

Decreased tearing with long-term use—case reports.

Edema in the ankles—infrequent.

Increased frequency of urination or painful or nighttime urination—infrequent.

Joint and muscle discomfort—infrequent.

Serious Adverse Effects

Allergic reactions may be more severe or less responsive to epinephrine.

Mental depression or low blood sugar—rare.

Liver toxicity—case reports (may be a hypersensitivity reaction).

Chest pain, shortness of breath, precipitation of congestive heart failure—rare.

Rebound or withdrawal chest pain (angina) if this medicine is suddenly stopped—possible

Precipitation of intermittent claudication—possible in people with severe blood vessel spasm (vasospastic) disorders or severe Peripheral Artery Disease (PAD).

Bronchial asthma attack (in people with asthma)—possible, but less likely than some other beta blockers.

Positive ANA and lupus erythematosus—infrequent to frequent, up to 33%.

▷ **Possible Effects on Sexual Function:** Impotence, decreased libido, Peyronie's disease (see Glossary)—case reports to 2%.

Possible Effects on Laboratory Tests

Antinuclear antibodies (ANA) and LE cells: often positive after 3 to 6 months.

Free fatty acids (FFA): decreased.

Glucose tolerance test (GTT): decreased; abnormal tests at 60 and 120 minutes—possible.

Potassium: mild increases.

CAUTION

1. *Do not stop this drug suddenly* without the knowledge and help of your physician. Carry a note that says that you take this drug.
2. Nasal decongestants may cause sudden and SEVERE increases in blood pressure. Call your physician or pharmacist before using nasal decongestants and ask if they should ever be used.
3. Report any tendency to emotional depression.
4. This medicine may worsen preexisting kidney insufficiency.

Precautions for Use

By Infants and Children: Safety and effectiveness for those under 12 years not established. If this drug is used, watch for fainting as a sign of low blood sugar (hypoglycemia) if a meal is skipped.

By Those Over 60 Years of Age: All antihypertensive drugs used cautiously. High blood pressure should be lowered slowly, avoiding risks (such as stroke or heart attack) of excessively low blood pressure. Small doses and frequent blood pressure checks needed. The amount of medicine that gets into your body (bioavailability) from a given dose can increase by twofold in elderly people. Total daily dose should not exceed 800 mg. Watch for dizziness, falling, confusion, hallucinations, depression, or frequent urination.

▷ **Advisability of Use During Pregnancy**

Pregnancy Category: B. See Pregnancy Risk Categories at the back of this book.

Animal Studies: No significant increase in birth defects in rats or rabbits.

Human Studies: Adequate studies of pregnant women are not available.

Use this drug only if clearly needed. Ask your doctor for help.

Advisability of Use If Breast-Feeding
> Presence of this drug in breast milk: Yes, and concentrated.
> Avoid drug or refrain from nursing.

Habit-Forming Potential: None.

Effects of Overdose: Weakness, slow pulse, low blood pressure, fainting, cold and sweaty skin, congestive heart failure, possible coma, and convulsions.

Possible Effects of Long-Term Use: Decreased heart reserve and heart failure in some people with advanced heart disease.

Suggested Periodic Examinations While Taking This Drug (at physician's discretion)
> Blood pressure checks (treated to attain goals).
> Heart and liver function tests.
> May be prudent to check for hidden Peripheral Artery Disease (PAD) by checking ankle brachial index (ABI). ABI check (see Glossary) can help find PAD early, and avoid claudication that may result if this medication is taken by someone who has PAD but does not know it.
> ANA titer.

▷ **While Taking This Drug, Observe the Following**
> *Foods:* Follow a sensible low-cardiovascular-risk diet. Avoid excessive salt intake.
> *Herbal Medicines or Minerals:* Ginseng, hawthorn, saw palmetto, ma huang, guarana (caffeine), goldenseal, yohimbe, and licorice may also cause increased blood pressure. Dong quai may block the removal of this medicine from the body leading to toxic effects with "normal" doses. St. John's wort may increase removal of this medicine from the body leading to loss of benefits despite appropriate doses. Calcium and garlic may help lower blood pressure. Ginkgo benefits in helping peripheral artery disease are as yet, unproven. Indian snakeroot has a German Commission E monograph indication for hypertension—talk to your doctor. Eleuthero root and ephedra (ma huang) should be avoided by people living with hypertension.
> *Beverages:* No restrictions. May be taken with milk.

▷ *Alcohol:* Alcohol may exaggerate lowering of blood pressure and may increase its mild sedative effect.
> *Tobacco Smoking:* Nicotine may reduce this drug's effectiveness and can worsen closing of bronchial tubes seen in regular smokers. I advise everyone to quit smoking.
> *Marijuana Smoking:* Marijuana may increase blood pressure and reduce this drug's effectiveness. DO NOT COMBINE.

▷ *Other Drugs*
> Acebutolol may **increase** the effects of
> - other antihypertensive drugs, excessively lowering the blood pressure. Dose adjustments may be necessary.
> - reserpine (Ser-Ap-Es, etc.), causing sedation, depression, slow heart rate, and low blood pressure.
>
> Acebutolol **taken concurrently** with
> - alfentanil (Alfenta) or fentanyl may result in severe slowing of the heart leading to sinus arrest. Use with great caution.
> - alpha-one-adrenergic blockers (such as prazosin) may result in a severe drop in blood pressure (especially when patients stand) in response to a first dose of this medicine. Use with great caution.

- amiodarone (Cordarone) may result in severe slowing of the heart leading to sinus arrest. Use with great caution.
- calcium channel blockers such as mibefradil (Posicor) or verapamil (Calan) may lead to increased risk of abnormal heart rate or rhythm.
- clonidine (Catapres) may cause rebound high blood pressure if clonidine is withdrawn while acebutolol is still being taken.
- digoxin (Lanoxin) may change heart conduction.
- diltiazem (Cardizem) may result in increased acebutolol effects.
- fentanyl anesthesia (various) may lead to severe lowering of blood pressure.
- fluoxetine (Prozac), fluvoxamine (Luvox), paroxetine (Paxil), or venlafaxine (Effexor) may decrease removal of acebutolol from the body (not reported as yet). Caution is advised.
- insulin may cause low blood sugar (hypoglycemia).
- methyldopa (Aldomet) may lead to unexpected increases in blood pressure.
- NSAIDs (see Drug Classes) may result in decreased acebutolol benefits.
- oral antidiabetic drugs (see Drug Classes) may result in slow recovery from low blood sugar.
- ritonavir (Norvir) and perhaps other protease inhibitors may increase the metabolism of this medicine and blunt therapeutic benefits of acebutolol.

The following drugs may *decrease* the effects of acebutolol:

- indomethacin (Indocin) and some other "aspirin substitutes" (NSAIDs) can blunt acebutolol's antihypertensive effect.
- rifabutin (Mycobutin) and other drugs that may increase (induce) cytochrome P450 enzymes in the liver (the ones that help the body remove medicines like acebutolol) may result in loss of benefits of acebutolol even if every dose of acebutolol is being taken.

▷ *Driving, Hazardous Activities:* Use caution—may cause drowsiness.

Aviation Note: The use of this drug *is a disqualification* for piloting. Consult a designated Aviation Medical Examiner.

Exposure to Sun: No restrictions.

Exposure to Heat: Hot environments can exaggerate the effects of this drug.

Exposure to Cold: Elderly need to prevent hypothermia (see Glossary).

Heavy Exercise or Exertion: This drug can intensify increased blood pressure (hypertensive) response to isometric exercise. Talk to your doctor about how much and how to exercise.

Occurrence of Unrelated Illness: Fevers can lower blood pressure and require decreased doses. Nausea or vomiting may interrupt the dosing schedule. Ask your doctor for help.

Discontinuation: **DO NOT** stop the drug suddenly. Gradual dose decreases over 2–3 weeks (tapering) is needed. Stopping this medicine suddenly may lead to abnormal heart rhythm, heart attack or sudden death. Ask your doctor for help.

ACETAZOLAMIDE (a set a ZOHL a mide)

Introduced: 1953   **Class:**   Anticonvulsant, antiglaucoma, diuretic, sulfonamides

Brand Names: ♣Acetazolam, Diamox, Diamox Sequels, Diamox Sustained Release

---

BENEFITS versus RISKS

Possible Benefits	*Possible Risks*
REDUCTION OF INTERNAL EYE PRESSURE in some glaucoma cases	Rare bone marrow, liver or kidney injury
CONTROL OF ABSENCE (PETIT MAL) SEIZURES TREATMENT OF PERIODIC PARALYSIS	Acidosis with long-term use—possible
	Increased risk of kidney stones
	Tingling in the arms and legs (paresthesia)
REDUCES FLUID IN CONGESTIVE HEART FAILURE	Paralysis—rare
PREVENTION OR LESSENING OF SYMPTOMS OF ACUTE MOUNTAIN SICKNESS	Bone weakening (with long-term use)—possible

---

Author's Note: This profile has been further shortened to make room for more widely used medicines.

ACETIC ACIDS (Nonsteroidal Anti-Inflammatory Drug Family)

Diclofenac   (di KLOH fen ak)   **Etodolac** (e TOE doh lak)   **Indomethacin** (in doh METH a sin)   **Ketorolac**   (KEY tor o lak)   **Nabumetone**   (na BYU me tohn)   **Sulindac**   (sul IN dak)   **Tolmetin**   (TOHL met in)

Introduced: 1976, 1986, 1963, 1991, 1984, 1976, 1976, respectively
Class: Mild analgesic, NSAID   **Prescription:**   USA: Yes   **Controlled Drug:**   USA: No; Canada: No   **Available as Generic:**   USA: Yes, all.

Brand Names: Diclofenac, ✤Apo-Diclo, ✤Apo-Diclo SR, Arthrotec [CD], Cataflam, ✤Novo-Difenac, ✤Nu-Diclo, Voltaren, Voltaren Ophthalmic, Voltaren SR, Voltaren Timed Release, Voltaren XR; Etodolac, Lodine, Lodine XL; Indomethacin, ✤Apo-Indomethacin, Indameth, ✤Indocid, ✤Indocid-SR, ✤Indocid PDA, Indocin, Indocin-SR, ✤Novo-methacin, ✤Nu-Indo, Zendole; Ketorolac, Acular, Acular PF (ketorolac ophthalmic), ✤Apo-ketorolac, Toradol; Nabumetone, ✤Apo-Nabumetone, ✤Gen-Nabumetone ✤Novo-Nabumetone ✤Nu-Nabumetone ✤MS-Nabumetone, ✤Rhoxal-Nabumetone Relafen, Sulindac, ✤Apo-Sulin, Clinoril, ✤Novo-Sundac; Tolmetin, ✤Novo-Tolmetin, Tolectin, Tolectin DS, Tolectin 600

BENEFITS versus RISKS

Possible Benefits	*Possible Risks*
EFFECTIVE RELIEF OF MILD TO MODERATE PAIN AND INFLAMMATION	Gastrointestinal pain, ulceration, bleeding
Decreased stomach (GI) problems (etodolac and Arthrotec CD form)	Liver or kidney damage
	Fluid retention
	Bone marrow depression
	Pneumonitis (sulindac)
	Aseptic meningitis (diclofenac)
	Possible severe skin reactions (diclofenac, etodolac, nabumetone, and sulindac)

▷ **Principal Uses**

As a Single Drug Product: Uses currently included in FDA-approved labeling: (1) All of the drugs in this class except ketorolac are approved to treat osteoarthritis; (2) all of the drugs in this class except ketorolac is approved to relieve rheumatoid arthritis; (3) indomethacin, diclofenac, and sulindac are useful in ankylosing spondylitis; (4) sustained-release form of indomethacin as well as the immediate-release form of sulindac help symptoms of tendonitis, bursitis, and acute painful shoulder; (5) tolmetin eases symptoms of juvenile rheumatoid arthritis; (6) sulindac therapy is useful in acute gout; (7) ophthalmic form of diclofenac and ketorolac are useful after cataract surgery and after refractive surgery of the cornea (decreasing pain and sensitivity to light); (8) ketorolac is approved (oph-thalmic form) for use in seasonal allergic conjunctivitis; (9) Arthrotec is used in patients with osteo or rheumatoid arthritis who are at high risk for damage to the stomach or intestine (gastric or duodenal ulcer risk); (10) diclofenac is used to help dysmenorrhea.

Author's Note: Because of the approval and more widespread use of other medicines in this family (acetic acid NSAIDs) that can be taken by mouth (PO) and that have a more favorable benefit to risk profile, information on ketorolac intravenous and oral has been deleted from this profile. Ophthalmic ketorolac information remains.

Other (unlabeled) generally accepted uses: (1) Diclofenac used intramuscu-larly is effective in acute migraine headache and kidney colic; (2) indomethacin helps reduce systemic reactions in kidney transplants and addresses low-grade neonatal intraventricular hemorrhage; (3) sulindac is effective in treating colon polyps and easing diabetic neuropathic pain; (4) NSAIDs in general have shown conflicting results in preventing colon can-cer, but may have a beneficial preventive effect; (5) sulindac may be useful in lowering amounts of amniotic fluid (amnioreduction); (6) one study of 2,765 patients found NSAIDs of use in preventing decline of thinking abil-ity in older patients; (7) indomethacin was compared to ibuprofen in infants with patent ductus arteriosus. Results of the 148-infant study found that ibuprofen offered similar benefits while causing fewer cases of decreased urine output (oliguria); (8) NSAIDS may have a beneficial effect in reducing risk of Alzheimer's (cognitive decline).

As a Combination Drug Product [CD]: Diclofenac (50 mg) is combined with misoprostol (200 mcg in the Arthrotec form) in order to help ease side effects on the stomach.

How These Drugs Work: These drugs reduce prostaglandins (and related com-pounds), chemicals that cause inflammation and pain. Ketorolac may offer a morphine sparing action by an unknown mechanism. Arthrotec form combines diclofenac with the prostaglandin misoprostol in order to help protect the stomach from adverse effects (irritation, ulceration). How the beneficial effects of NSAIDS are conferred in possibly decreasing risk of colon cancer and/or Alzheimer's is not known.

Available Dosage Forms and Strengths

Diclofenac sodium:

Suppositories — 50 mg, 100 mg (Canada)
Tablets — 25 mg, 50 mg
Tablets-diclofenac/misoprostol — 50 mg or 75 mg diclofenac and 200 mcg misoprostol

Tablets (timed release),
           prolonged action — 50 mg, 75 mg, 100 mg (Canada)
           Ophthalmic solution — 1 mg/1 ml

Etodolac:
                      Capsules — 200 mg, 300 mg
           Tablets, extended-release form — 400 mg, 600 mg
Indomethacin:
                      Capsules — 25 mg, 50 mg, 75 mg
           Gelatin capsule (Canada) — 25 mg, 50 mg
           Capsules, SR (prolonged action) — 75 mg
                      Oral suspension — 25 mg/5 ml
                      Suppositories — 50 mg, 100 mg

Ketorolac:
                      Tablets — 10 mg
           Ophthalmic solution — 3 ml, 5 ml, 10 ml (0.5%)
                      Injection — 10 mg (Canada), 15 mg, 30 mg

Nabumetone:
                      Tablets — 500 mg, 750 mg, 1000 mg (Canada)

Sulindac:
                      Tablets — 150 mg, 200 mg

Tolmetin:
                      Capsules — 400 mg, 492 mg
           Gelatin capsules — 400 mg (Canada)
                      Tablets — 200 mg, 600 mg

▷ **Usual Adult Dosage Ranges**

Diclofenac potassium: Maximum daily dose is 200 mg.

Diclofenac sodium: 100 to 200 mg daily to start in two to five divided doses (for example: 25 mg four times a day). Reduction to the minimum effective dose is advisable. Maximum daily dose is 225 mg. The Voltaren XR form maximum dose is 100 mg twice a day. The Arthrotec form is 50 mg/200 mcg three times a day or 75 mg/200 mcg twice daily as tolerated (osteoarthritis).

Diclofenac ophthalmic: 1 drop of 1 mg per milliliter in the eye that underwent cataract surgery, four times a day, starting 24 hours AFTER surgery and continuing for 2 weeks.

Etodolac: For osteoarthritis: A starting dose of 800 to 1,200 mg is given in divided doses. The lowest effective dose is advisable, and effective treatment has been accomplished with 200 to 400 mg daily. In patients weighing less than 60 kg, the total dose in a day should not be more than 20 mg/kg.

Etodolac extended-release form (Lodine XL): Allows once-a-day dosing for many patients. Dosing range is 400 to 1,000 mg daily. Maximum dose is 1,000 mg daily. In patients weighing less than 60 kg, the total dose in a day should not be more than 20 mg/kg. Lowest effective dose should be used.

Indomethacin: For arthritis and related conditions: 25 to 50 mg two to four times daily. If needed and tolerated, dose may be increased by 25 or 50 mg per day at intervals of 1 week. For acute gout: 100 mg initially; then 50 mg three times per day until pain is relieved. Maximum daily dose is 200 mg.

Indomethacin SR form: 75 mg daily for ankylosing spondylitis or rheumatoid arthritis.

Ketorolac ophthalmic: One drop four times daily for allergic conjunctivitis.

Nabumetone: 1,000 mg daily as a single dose is given. Dose is increased as needed and tolerated to 1,500 mg daily. The lowest effective daily dose is advisable. Maximum daily dose is 2,000 mg. Some clinicians divide dosing into two equal daily doses.

Sulindac: Therapy is started with 150 to 200 mg twice daily taken 12 hours apart for ankylosing spondylitis. Maximum daily dose is 400 mg.

Tolmetin: 400 mg three times daily is started, with usual ongoing doses of 600 to 1,600 mg as needed and tolerated. Total daily dose should not exceed 1,800 mg. Children 2 years of age or older may be given 20 mg per kg of body mass orally, divided into three or four doses daily. The dose may be increased as needed and tolerated to a maximum daily dose of 30 mg per kg of body mass.

Note: Actual dose and dosing schedule must be determined for each patient individually.

Conditions Requiring Dosing Adjustments

Liver Function: These drugs are extensively metabolized in the liver. They should be used with caution in patients with liver compromise.

Kidney Function: All nonsteroidal anti-inflammatory drugs may inhibit prostaglandins and alter kidney blood flow in patients with kidney (renal) compromise. Use with caution or not at all in patients with kidney compromise.

▷ **Dosing Instructions:** Take with or following food to prevent stomach irritation. Take with a FULL GLASS of water and remain upright (do not lie down) for 30 minutes. Regular-release tablets may be crushed, but not extended-release forms. The regular capsules may be opened, but not the prolonged-action capsules. Food actually increases absorption of nabumetone. Ketorolac or diclofenac ophthalmic should NOT be used while contacts are worn. If you forget a dose: Take the missed dose right away. If it is almost time to take the next dose, skip the missed dose and continue the medicine on your regular schedule. DO NOT double doses.

Usual Duration of Use: Continual use on a regular schedule for 1 to 2 weeks is usually necessary to determine drug benefit in relieving arthritic discomfort. The usual length of treatment for bursitis or tendonitis for indomethacin or sulindac is 7 to 14 days. Ketorolac oral or IV when used is only for short-term pain treatment (a MAXIMUM of 5 days regardless of the way [route] that it is taken). Ophthalmic diclofenac and ketorolac dosing is started a day after cataract surgery and used for 14 days. Long-term use of the other agents in this class requires physician supervision.

Typical Treatment Goals and Measurements (Outcomes and Markers)

Pain: Most clinicians treating pain use a device called an algometer to check your pain. This looks like a small ruler, but lets the clinician better understand your pain. The goals of treatment then relate to where the level of pain started (for example, a rating of 7 on a 0–10 scale) and what the cause of the pain was. Pain medicines may also be used together (in combination) in order to get the best result or outcome. If your pain control is not acceptable to YOU (remember, in hospitals and outpatient settings, etc., pain control is a patient right) and if after a week of arthritis pain treatment results are not acceptable, be sure to call your doctor as you may need a different medicine or combination.

Arthritis: Control of arthritis symptoms (pain, loss of mobility, decreased ability to accomplish activities of daily living) is paramount in returning patient quality of life and to checking the results (beneficial outcomes) from these medicines. Many arthritis specialists use WOMAC (see Glossary) to measure results.

▷ **These Drugs Should Not Be Taken If**
- you have had an allergic reaction to them previously.
- you are subject to asthma or nasal polyps caused by aspirin or other NSAIDS.
- you are pregnant (all NSAIDs during the last 3 months of pregnancy). Arthrotec form is category X and should never be taken in pregnancy. These medicines are not recommended if you are breast-feeding.
- you have active peptic ulcer disease or any form of gastrointestinal ulceration or bleeding.
- you have active liver disease.
- you wear contact lenses and are prescribed an ophthalmic form.
- you have severe impairment of kidney function.
- you have severe aortic narrowing (coarctation).
- you have a history of rectal bleeding or proctitis (indomethacin suppositories).
- you have porphyria (diclofenac, indomethacin).

▷ **Inform Your Physician Before Taking This Drug If**
- you are allergic to aspirin or to other aspirin substitutes.
- you have an infection.
- you have a bleeding disorder or a blood cell disorder.
- you have a history of peptic ulcer disease, Crohn's disease, ulcerative colitis, or any type of bleeding disorder.
- you have a history of epilepsy, Parkinson's disease, or mental illness (psychosis).
- you have impaired liver or kidney function.
- you have high blood pressure or a history of heart failure.
- you are taking acetaminophen, aspirin or other aspirin substitutes, or anticoagulants.

Possible Side Effects (natural, expected, and unavoidable drug actions)
Drowsiness, ringing in ears, fluid retention. ALL NSAIDS can inhibit clotting (platelet effect) and thus have an effect in prolonging bleeding time.

▷ **Possible Adverse Effects** (unusual, unexpected, and infrequent reactions)
If any of the following develop, consult your physician promptly for guidance.
Mild Adverse Effects
Allergic reactions: skin rash, hives, itching, localized swellings of face and/or extremities.
Headache—infrequent (diclofenac and nabumetone) to frequent (indomethacin).
Dizziness, feelings of detachment—infrequent.
Mouth sores, indigestion, nausea, vomiting, diarrhea—infrequent.
Ringing in the ears (tinnitus)—possible.
Temporary loss of hair (indomethacin)—case reports.
Increased urination—infrequent (etodolac).
Serious Adverse Effects
Allergic reactions: worsening of asthma, difficult breathing (bronchospasm), mouth irritation—possible.
Angioneurotic edema (nabumetone)—rare.
Blurred vision, confusion, depression—rare.
Drug fever—case report (sulindac, tolmetin).

Active peptic ulcer, with or without bleeding, colon ulcers—possible.

Liver damage with jaundice (see Glossary)—case reports.

Kidney damage with painful urination, bloody urine, reduced urine formation—rare.

Pseudoporphyria (nabumetone)—case report.

Bone marrow depression (see Glossary): fatigue, fever, sore throat, bleeding or bruising—case reports.

Thrombophlebitis—frequent (intravenous diclofenac use).

Severe skin rash (Stevens-Johnson syndrome—diclofenac, etodolac, nabumetone, sulindac)—case reports.

Fluid retention, increased blood pressure or edema—possible with all.

Congestive heart failure worsening—possible.

Peripheral neuritis (see Glossary): numbness, pain in extremities (indomethacin)—rare.

Lung fibrosis (nabumetone)—case reports.

Pancreatitis (sulindac)—rare; (indomethacin)—case reports.

Pneumonitis (sulindac)—rare; (diclofenac)—case report.

Aseptic meningitis (diclofenac)—rare.

Seizures (indomethacin only)—case reports.

▷ **Possible Effects on Sexual Function:** Enlargement and tenderness of both male and female breasts (indomethacin, sulindac)—rare.

Nonmenstrual vaginal bleeding (indomethacin)—rare.

Impotence (indomethacin, nabumetone)—rare.

Decreased libido (indomethacin)—rare.

Uterine bleeding (sulindac)—rare.

Possible Delayed Adverse Effects: Mild anemia due to "silent" blood loss from the stomach.

Adverse Effects That May Mimic Natural Diseases or Disorders

Liver reactions may suggest viral hepatitis. Pancreatitis has occurred with sulindac.

Natural Diseases or Disorders That May Be Activated by These Drugs

Peptic ulcer disease, ulcerative colitis. Borderline clotting problems. Kidney disease.

Possible Effects on Laboratory Tests

Complete blood cell counts: decreased red cells, hemoglobin, white cells, and platelets—rare.

INR (prothrombin time): increased.

Tests of platelet aggregation: decreased aggregation.

Blood lithium level: increased.

Liver function tests: increased liver enzymes (ALT/GPT, AST/GOT, and alkaline phosphatase), increased bilirubin.

Blood sugar (glucose): increased (indomethacin only)—rare.

Kidney function tests: increased blood creatinine and urea nitrogen (BUN) levels (kidney damage).

Fecal occult blood test: positive.

Urine protein (tolmetin only): may be falsely positive.

CAUTION

1. The FDA requires a warning label on all nonprescription pain (analgesic) and fever (antipyretic) products that have aspirin or other salicylates, ibuprofen, naproxen sodium, ketoprofen, or acetaminophen in them (NSAIDs) that says: ALCOHOL WARNING: IF YOU CONSUME 3 OR MORE ALCO-

HOLIC DRINKS EVERY DAY, ASK YOUR DOCTOR WHETHER YOU SHOULD TAKE [THE MEDICINE IN QUESTION] OR OTHER PAIN RELIEVERS/FEVER REDUCERS. [THE INGREDIENT] MAY CAUSE STOMACH BLEEDING. This is a new warning intended to help protect patients from possible stomach or liver damage.

2. Dose should be limited to the smallest amount that produces reasonable improvement.
3. These drugs may mask early signs of infection. Tell your doctor if you think you are developing an infection of any kind.
4. Congestive heart failure in elderly patients may be unmasked or worsened. Risk appears to increase with use of higher doses.
5. Do NOT add non-prescription or prescription NSAIDS such as aspirin, ibuprofen (Advil or Motrin), or naproxen (Aleve) while you are taking these medicines. (The adverse stomach and intestinal effects will increase).

Precautions for Use

By Infants and Children:

Diclofenac, etodolac, nabumetone, sulindac: Safety and efficacy for those under 12 years of age not established.

Indomethacin: This drug frequently impairs kidney function in infants. Fatal liver reactions are possible in children between 6 and 12 years of age; avoid the use of this drug in this age group. Note: This medicine is used in infants (patent ductus arteriosus intravenously).

Ketorolac ophthalmic: Safety and efficacy for those 3 years of age and older for seasonal allergic conjunctivitis (eases itching) is established.

Tolmetin: Safety and efficacy for those under 2 years of age not established.

By Those Over 60 Years of Age: Small doses are advisable until tolerance is determined. Watch for any signs of liver or kidney toxicity, fluid retention, dizziness, confusion, impaired memory, depression, peptic ulcer, or diarrhea, often with rectal bleeding.

▷ **Advisability of Use During Pregnancy**

Pregnancy Category: Indomethacin, diclofenac, tolmetin B. Sulindac: B in first two trimesters. Nabumetone: C in first two trimesters. Not recommended in last trimester. Indomethacin, etodolac, nabumetone, and sulindac (D in last trimester): D. (Indomethacin is also category D if used after 34 weeks or for more than 48 hours.) Diclofenac to be avoided in late pregnancy. Arthrotec form is category X. See Pregnancy Risk Categories at the back of this book.

Animal Studies:

Indomethacin: significant toxicity and birth defects reported in mice and rats.

Diclofenac: Mouse, rat, and rabbit studies reveal toxic effects on the embryo but no birth defects.

Nabumetone, tolmetin: Rat and rabbit studies revealed no defects.

Human Studies:

Indomethacin: Adequate studies of pregnant women are not available. However, birth defects have been attributed to the use of this drug during pregnancy. The manufacturer recommends that indomethacin not be taken during pregnancy.

Diclofenac, nabumetone, sulindac, tolmetin: Adequate studies of pregnant women are not available. Avoid this drug completely during the last 3 months of pregnancy. Use it during the first 6 months only if clearly needed. Ask your doctor for guidance.

Etodolac: Adequate studies of pregnant women not available. The manufacturer advises that this drug be avoided during in late pregnancy.

Nabumetone: Fetal cardiovascular system adversely affected if used in the last trimester, so not recommended for last 3 months.

Advisability of Use If Breast-Feeding
Presence of these drugs in breast milk: Yes (all).
Avoid drugs or refrain from nursing (may have bad effects on infant's nervous system).

Habit-Forming Potential: None.

Effects of Overdose: Drowsiness, agitation, bleeding, confusion, nausea, vomiting, diarrhea, disorientation, seizures, coma.

Possible Effects of Long-Term Use: Indomethacin and tolmetin: eye changes—deposits in the cornea, alterations in the retina. Irritation of the stomach and intestine.

Suggested Periodic Examinations While Taking These Drugs (at physician's discretion)
Complete blood cell counts.
Liver and kidney function tests.
Complete eye examinations if vision is altered in any way.
Stool for hidden (occult) blood (may actually be positive from these drugs).

▷ **While Taking These Drugs, Observe the Following**
Foods: No restrictions. These medicines are taken with food to decrease stomach irritation.

Herbal Medicines or Minerals: Ginseng, ginkgo, alfalfa, clove oil, feverfew, cinchona bark, and garlic may also change clotting, so combining those herbals with these medicines is not recommended. Talk to your doctor BEFORE combining any medicines. NSAIDs may decrease feverfew effects. White willow bark (salicylates) can increase risk of stomach or intestinal adverse effects if combined. Since St. John's wort and some of these medicines may increase sensitivity to the sun, CAUTION IS ADVISED. Combined use of beta glucan and diclofenac, indomethacin, sulindac, and aspirin lead to severe reactions in lab animals (mice). Nabumetone did not appear to have severe reaction risk. Eucalyptus and skull cap may increase risk of undesirable effects on the liver. Hay flower, mistletoe herb, and white mustard seed carry German Commission E monograph indications for arthritis.

Nutritional Support: Indomethacin: Take 50 mg of vitamin C (ascorbic acid) daily.

Beverages: No restrictions. May be taken with milk.

▷ *Alcohol:* Used with caution: see FDA warning above. Alcohol can irritate the lining of the stomach. If excessive alcohol use is combined with the irritating effect of these medicines, risk of stomach and intestinal problems such as ulceration or bleeding can be increased.

Tobacco Smoking: No interactions expected. I advise everyone to quit smoking.

▷ *Other Drugs*
Medicines in this family may *increase* the effects of
- aminoglycoside antibiotics (amikacin, others—see Drug Classes) by increasing blood levels.
- anticoagulants such as warfarin (Coumadin) and increase the risk of bleeding; monitor INR (prothrombin time), adjust dose accordingly.
- cyclosporine (Sandimmune) and cause toxicity.

- digoxin (Lanoxin)—indomethacin only.
- eptifibatide (Integrilin) and increase risk of bleeding (benefit to risk decision).
- lithium and cause lithium toxicity (except sulindac, which may decrease lithium levels).
- methotrexate (Mexate, others) and cause toxic levels.
- phenytoin (Dilantin) because of increased drug levels.
- tacrolimus (Prograf) and increase risk of decreased kidney function.
- thrombolytics such as streptokinase or TPA.
- zidovudine (AZT) and lead to toxicity of either medicine (indomethacin).

Medications in this class may *decrease* the effects of
- ACE inhibitors (see Drug Classes).
- beta-blocker drugs (see Drug Classes) and reduce their antihypertensive effectiveness.
- bumetanide (Bumex).
- captopril (Capoten).
- ethacrynic acid (Edecrin).
- furosemide (Lasix) and other loop diuretics.
- thiazide diuretics (see Drug Classes).

Medications in this class *taken concurrently* with the following drugs may increase the risk of bleeding or serious side effects; avoid these combinations or use with great caution:
- aspirin or other NSAIDs (EVEN NONPRESCRIPTION FORMS).
- clopidogrel (Plavix).
- dicumarol.
- diflunisal (Dolobid).
- dipyridamole (Persantine).
- low-molecular-weight heparins (Lovenox, others).
- probenecid (Pro-Biosan, others).
- sulfinpyrazone (Anturane).
- valproic acid (Depakene).
- warfarin (Coumadin).

Medications in this class *taken concurrently* with:
- alendronate (Fosamax) may increase risk of stomach or intestinal irritation.
- colestipol and cholestyramine will reduce beneficial effects of the NSAIDs (diclofenac and sulindac).
- levofloxacin (Levaquin) and ofloxacin (Floxin) can increase risk of seizures.
- methotrexate (Mexate, others) may lead to increased methotrexate toxicity.
- ritonavir (Norvir) and other medicines that affect the cytochrome P-450 system in the liver will lead to altered blood levels of these medicines.

▷ *Driving, Hazardous Activities:* These drugs may cause drowsiness, dizziness, or impaired vision. Restrict activities as necessary.

Aviation Note: The use of these drugs *may be a disqualification* for piloting. Consult a designated Aviation Medical Examiner.

Exposure to Sun: Caution: Several medicines in this class have caused increased sensitivity (photosensitivity—see Glossary).

ADALIMUMAB (A dah lim you mab)

Other Name: D2E7 **Introduced:** 2003 **Class:** Disease Modifying Antirheumatic Drug (DMARD), human monoclonal antibodyto TNF alpha **Prescription:** USA: Yes **Controlled Drug:** USA: No; Canada: No **Available as Generic:** No

Brand Name: Humira

Author's Note: This newly approved medicine for rheumatoid arthritis offers the benefit of easier once every two week under the skin (subcutaneous) dosing. Current outcome measures such as quality of life, fatigue scales, acute phase reactant responses, ACR response and adverse effect profiles appear favorable at present. This is the first fully human tumor necrosis factor (TNF alpha) antibody. Information in this profile will broadened based on clinical research and continued favorable adverse effect profiles.

ALBUTEROL (al BYU ter ohl)

Other Name: Salbutamol **Introduced:** 1968 **Class:** Antiasthmatic, bronchodilator **Prescription:** USA: Yes **Controlled Drug:** USA: No; Canada: No **Available as Generic:** Yes

Brand Names: Accuneb, Airet, ✸Alti-Salbutamol, ✸Apo-Salvent, Combivent [CD], Diskhaler, ✸Novo-Salmol, PMS-Salbutamol, Proventil HFA, Proventil Inhaler, Proventil Repetabs, Proventil Tablets, Rotahaler, ✸Salbutamol, ✸Ventodisk Rotacaps, Ventolin HFA, Ventolin Inhaler, Ventolin Nebules, Ventolin Rotacaps, Ventolin Syrup, Ventolin Tablets, Volmax Sustained-Release Tablets, Volmax Timed-Release Tablets

BENEFITS versus RISKS	
Possible Benefits	*Possible Risks*
VERY EFFECTIVE RELIEF OF BRONCHOSPASM	Increased blood pressure or heart rate
	Fine hand tremor
	Potential hyperactivity in children under twelve
	Angina in patients with coronary artery disease
	Irregular heart rhythm and fatalities—possible, with excessive use
	Paradoxical spasm of the bronchi

▷ **Principal Uses**

As a Single Drug Product: Uses currently included in FDA-approved labeling: (1) Relieves acute bronchial asthma and reduces frequency and severity of chronic, recurrent asthmatic attacks; (2) helps prevent exercise-induced bronchospasm.

Other (unlabeled) generally accepted uses: (1) May have a role (nebulized) where blood potassium is too high; (2) limited use in patients with premature labor—especially if the cervix is dilated less than 3 centimeters.

As a Combination Drug Product [CD]: Combivent form has 120 mcg of albuterol and 21 mcg of ipratropium per press (actuation).

How This Drug Works: By acting on adenyl cyclase, a chemical called cyclic AMP is increased. In response to increased cyclic AMP, this drug relaxes muscle (smooth) that is found in the uterus, skeletal muscle blood vessels (vascular bed) and the bronchi. In some lung disease, albuterol also works to help the lungs move mucus and decreases chemical release from mast cells.

Available Dosage Forms and Strengths

Aerosol (actuation) — 90 mcg per press
— 100 mcg per press (Canada)
— 120 mcg per press

Capsules for inhalation
(technique is important) — 200 mcg, 400 mcg (Canada)
Nasal inhaler (Canada) — 100 mcg/dose
Solution for inhalation — 0.83% and 0.5%
Rotacaps — 200 mcg
Syrup — 2 mg/5 ml
— 2.4 mg/5 ml
Tablets — 2 mg, 4 mg
Tablets, sustained release — 4 mg, 4.8 mg, 8 mg, 9.6 mg
Tablets, timed release — 4 mg, 8 mg
Ventodisk (Canada) — 200 mcg and 400 mcg per disk

▷ **Recommended Dosage Ranges** (Actual dose and schedule must be determined for each patient individually.)

Capsules for inhalation (Rotahaler): Dose for children more than 4 years old and for adults is to use the contents of one capsule (200 mcg) via the Rotahaler device every 4 to 6 hours.

Metered dose inhaler—Adults and children 12 or older: Two inhalations (180 mcg) repeated every 4 to 6 hours. For some patients, one inhalation every 4 hours may be enough. Taking a larger number of inhalations is not recommended. If the dose that previously worked does not provide relief, call your doctor immediately. The status of your asthma must be examined.

Author's Note: Proventil Repetabs and Volmax are FDA-approved to treat bronchospasm in patients 6 years old or older. Treatments are best checked every 3–6 months and decreased in small steps if possible.

Preventing exercise-caused asthma: Two inhalations (180 mcg of Ventolin form) 15 minutes BEFORE exercise.

Tablets (immediate release) — 2 to 4 mg three to four times daily (every 8 to 6 hours).

Tablets (sustained release) — One or two tablets every 12 hours.

Do not exceed eight inhalations (720 mcg) or 32 mg (tablet form) every 24 hours. Some manufacturers limit tablets to 16 mg every 24 hours.

Conditions Requiring Dosing Adjustments

Liver Function: Low doses and caution needed in liver disease.
Kidney Function: No specific changes in dosing are available.
Heart (Coronary Artery) Disease: A maximum starting dose should be 1 mg in order to avoid chest pain (angina).
Thyroid Disease: People with low (hypoactive) thyroids may require increased doses.

▷ **Dosing Instructions:** May be taken on empty stomach or with food or milk. Nonsustained-release tablets may be crushed. Sustained-release forms should NEVER be crushed. For inhaler, follow the written instructions carefully. The Proventil inhaler should be primed FOUR TIMES before you first use it. If you have not used the Proventil inhalation aerosol for four days, please prime the aerosol twice before you use it. Do not use excessively. If you forget a dose: Use the inhaler as soon as possible. Do not double doses.

Usual Duration of Use: Do not use beyond the time necessary to stop episodes of asthma.

Typical Treatment Goals and Measurements (Outcomes and Markers)

Asthma: Short-acting beta agonists like albuterol are used to prevent or treat reversible spasms of the bronchial tubes. The peak effect happens 1 to 2 hours after dosing. Many clinicians use improved respiratory status (FEV1) to check benefits as well as no night time symptoms and ability to undertake usual activities and decreased need for hospitalizations. One center in London used measurement of peak flow (patients were asked to blow three times in quick succession into a special measuring meter) to help decide how long patients should remain in the hospital. Calculations between the first and last breath measurements were made. Patients who had a ratio of less than one were said to have a decreased peak flow (indicating inflammation) and were kept in the hospital for an additional 3 days. Patients with a ratio of more than one (acceptable peak flow and relative absence of inflammation) were successfully sent home from the hospital. In any patient, if the usual therapeutic response to this medicine is not seen, call your doctor right away.

▷ **This Drug Should Not Be Taken If**
- you have had an allergic reaction to any form of it.
- you have an irregular heart rhythm or a fast heartbeat (tachycardia—Volmax).
- you have a specific problem with the aorta (idiopathic hypertrophic subvalvular stenosis—Volmax form).
- you have an overactive thyroid (hyperthyroid).
- you are taking, or took in the past 2 weeks, any monoamine oxidase (MAO) type A inhibitor (see Drug Classes).

▷ **Inform Your Physician Before Taking This Drug If**
- you have a heart or circulatory disorder, especially high blood pressure, coronary heart disease or aneurysms.
- you have diabetes.
- you have pheochromocytoma.
- you take any form of digitalis or any stimulant drug.
- you take other prescription or nonprescription medications that weren't discussed when albuterol was prescribed.
- you are going to have a baby (this medicine may alter contractions).
- you are unsure how much or how often to take albuterol.

Possible Side Effects (natural, expected, and unavoidable drug actions)
Aerosol: dryness or irritation of mouth/throat, altered taste.
Tablet: nervousness, palpitation, fast heart rate (tachycardia)—infrequent.
Heart effect may not be seen with nebulized albuterol.

▷ **Possible Adverse Effects** (unusual, unexpected, and infrequent reactions)
If any of the following develop, consult your physician promptly for guidance.
Mild Adverse Effects
Itching—rare.
Headache, dizziness, restlessness, insomnia—infrequent.
Fine hand tremor—frequent.

Nausea—rare.
Leg cramps, flushing of skin—rare.
Difficulty urinating—rare.
Rapid heart rate—infrequent.
Decreased platelets—possible, but not clinically significant.

Serious Adverse Effects
Hypersensitivity reaction—case report.
Heart attack—case reports after intravenous or excessive inhalation use.
Abnormal heartbeats—possible.
Chest pain (angina)—possible with higher doses in patients with coronary artery disease.
Hallucinations or convulsions (with excessive dosing)—possible.
Decreased blood potassium (hypokalemia)—possible and dose related.
High blood sugar (hyperglycemia)—possible and more likely with intravenous use.

▷ **Possible Effects on Sexual Function:** None reported.

Natural Diseases or Disorders That May Be Activated by This Drug
Latent coronary artery disease, diabetes, or high blood pressure.

Possible Effects on Laboratory Tests
Blood aldosterone: increased.
Blood HDL cholesterol level: may be slightly increased.
Blood glucose level: increased.
Blood potassium: decreased.
Blood platelets: decreased (with high doses).
Blood magnesium: one study showed doses greater than 500 mcg lowered magnesium.

CAUTION
1. This drug may be dangerous if patients increase dose and/or frequency, as it may result in rapid or irregular heart rhythm and fatalities with overuse. A July 2001 report from the Dutch Centre for Human Drug Research found that when possible, high-dose inhaled albuterol may be best given with oxygen.
2. Use of this drug by inhalation with beclomethasone aerosol (Beclovent, Vanceril) may increase the risk of fluorocarbon propellant toxicity (fluorocarbons are being phased out). Use albuterol aerosol 20 to 30 minutes before beclomethasone aerosol to reduce toxicity and enhance the penetration of beclomethasone.
3. Serious heart rhythm problems or cardiac arrest can result from excessive or prolonged inhalation.
4. In general, women have been found to have higher peak blood levels (Cmax) after oral doses than men. Therefore, women may have an increased risk of adverse effects (like lowered potassium or tremor) even with "therapeutic or usual" doses.
5. One study (see Wolfenden, L.L. in Sources) of 4,005 patients found that many patients did not accurately describe their symptoms to their doctors. This lead to patients being under treated. Be honest with your doctor about the severity and frequency of your asthma so that the treatments can be tailored to the severity and frequency of asthma symptoms!
6. Call your doctor if you begin to increase the number of times you use this drug on a daily basis. Tolerance to the effects of this drug has been reported.

Precautions for Use

By Infants and Children: Dosing in children is often calculated on a mg per kg basis.

By Those Over 60 Years of Age: Avoid excessive and continual use. If asthma is not relieved promptly, other drugs will have to be tried. Watch for nervousness, palpitations, irregular heart rhythm, and muscle tremors. Doses of 2 mg by mouth three or four times daily are prudent.

▷ ## Advisability of Use During Pregnancy

Pregnancy Category: C. See Pregnancy Risk Categories at the back of this book.

Animal Studies: Cleft palate reported in mice.

Human Studies: Adequate studies of pregnant women are not available. Avoid use during first 3 months if possible.

Advisability of Use If Breast-Feeding

Presence of this drug in breast milk: Yes.
Avoid drug or refrain from nursing.

Habit-Forming Potential: A few cases of dependency and abuse have been described. These may be cases of use for the effect of the propellants (propellants are changing) or the drug itself.

Effects of Overdose: Nervousness, palpitation, rapid heart rate, life-threatening arrhythmias, sweating, headache, tremor, vomiting, chest pain.

Possible Effects of Long-Term Use: Loss of effectiveness.

Suggested Periodic Examinations While Taking This Drug (at physician's discretion)

Blood pressure measurements, evaluation of heart status, frequency of bronchospasms.

▷ ## While Taking This Drug, Observe the Following

Foods: No restrictions. Because this medicine may lead to minor lowering of potassium, talk to your doctor about possible need to increase potassium in your diet (see Table 13).

Herbal Medicines or Minerals: Using St. John's wort, ma huang, ephedrine-like compounds, guarana (caffeine), or kola while taking this medicine may result in unacceptable central nervous system stimulation. Talk to your doctor and pharmacist BEFORE making any combinations. Fir or pine needle oil should NOT be used by asthmatics. Ephedra alone does carry a German Commission E monograph indication for asthma treatment. If you are allergic to plants in the Asteraceae family (aster, chrysanthemum, daisy, or ragweed), you may also be allergic to echinacea, chamomile, feverfew, and St. John's wort.

Beverages: Avoid excessive caffeine as found in coffee, tea, cola, and chocolate.

▷ *Alcohol:* No interactions expected.

Tobacco Smoking: Smoking constricts airways. I advise everyone to quit.

▷ *Other Drugs*

Albuterol *taken concurrently* with

- amphetamines may worsen cardiovascular side effects.
- atomoxetine (Strattera) may worsen cardiovascular (increased blood pressure and heart rate) side effects.
- bendroflumethiazide (Corzide, Naturetin) and other thiazide and loop diuretics (see Drug Classes) may result in additive lowering of blood potassium.

- beta-blockers such as propranolol (Inderal) results in loss of effect of both medications.
- digoxin (Lanoxin) may lower blood levels, but clinical importance of the 16–22% lowering from one study is unclear.
- dopamine (Intropin) may worsen adverse effects on the heart. Avoid this combination.
- ephedrine (Bronkaid, Tedrigen) may result in excessive heart effects.
- ipratropium (Atrovent) can result in better (longer time) opening of the bronchi (beneficial interaction).
- isoproterenol (Isuprel) may result in worsening of heart (cardiac) side effects.
- monoamine oxidase (MAO) type A inhibitor drugs can cause very high blood pressure and undesirable heart stimulation.
- pancuronium (Pavulon) or vecuronium (Norcuron) may lead to bronchospasm and delayed recovery of neuromuscular function.
- phenylephrine (Dimetapp, Dristan, others) may worsen bad effects on the heart (adverse reaction), and the combination is not recommended.
- phenylpropanolamine (Acutrim, Alka-Seltzer Plus, Contac, others) may worsen bad effects on the heart (adverse reaction). Do not combine.
- pseudoephedrine (Sudafed, others) may worsen adverse heart effects. DO NOT COMBINE.
- theophylline (Theo-Dur, others) may result in rapid removal of theophylline and loss of therapeutic theophylline effect.
- tricyclic antidepressants (see Drug Classes) may cause a severe increase in blood pressure.

▷ *Driving, Hazardous Activities:* Use caution if excessive nervousness or dizziness occurs.

Aviation Note: The use of this drug *is a disqualification* for piloting. Consult a designated Aviation Medical Examiner.

Exposure to Sun: No restrictions.

Heavy Exercise or Exertion: Use caution. Excessive exercise can cause (induce) asthma in some asthmatics.

ALENDRONATE (a LEN druh nate)

Introduced: 1996   **Class:**   Second-generation bisphosphonate, Anti-osteoporotics   **Prescription:**   USA: Yes   **Controlled Drug:**   USA: No
Available as Generic: No
Brand Name: Fosamax

```
┌─────────────────────────────────────────────────────────────┐
│                    BENEFITS versus RISKS                      │
│        Possible Benefits              Possible Risks          │
│  EFFECTIVE TREATMENT OF MALE    Esophageal irritation         │
│    AND FEMALE OSTEOPOROSIS      Minor muscle pain             │
│  INCREASE IN BONE MASS                                        │
│  PREVENTION OF OSTEOPOROSIS                                   │
│  ONCE-WEEKLY TREATMENT                                        │
│    AND/OR PREVENTION OF                                       │
│    OSTEOPOROSIS                                               │
│  DECREASED RISK OF BONE                                       │
│    FRACTURES                                                  │
│  SYMPTOM RELIEF IN PAGET'S                                    │
│    DISEASE                                                    │
│  PREVENTION OF POST-                                          │
│    MENOPAUSAL OSTEOPOROSIS                                    │
│  PREVENTION OF OSTEOPOROSIS                                   │
│    IN THOSE TAKING                                            │
│    CORTICOSTEROID-TYPE                                        │
│    (STEROID) MEDICINES                                        │
└─────────────────────────────────────────────────────────────┘
```

▷ **Principal Uses**

As a Single Drug Product: Uses currently included in FDA-approved labeling: (1) Treatment of postmenopausal osteoporosis; (2) treatment of Paget's disease; (3) prevention of postmenopausal osteoporosis; (4) prevention of osteoporosis in people who take corticosteroid-type medicines; (5) once weekly prevention or treatment of osteoporosis; (6) treatment of osteoporosis in men.

Other (unlabeled) generally accepted uses: (1) approved in Canada in combination with hormone replacement therapy (estrogen or estrogen plus progesterone) to increase positive outcomes on increased bone mass; (2) may have a role in osteoporosis sometimes seen in HIV patients (antiretroviral induced); (3) could have a role intravenously in reflex sympathetic dystrophy syndrome (RSDS); (4) early research suggests a role in early treatment of osteonecrosis (avascular necrosis of bone); (5) prevents bone loss in women who stop hormone replacement therapy (HRT).

How This Drug Works: This medicine works at the brush border of the osteoclast cell (inhibiting enzymes in the mevalonate pathway). This prevents the cell from resorbing (gobbling up) bone while the osteoblast (bone-building cell) continues to work. The end result is bone-building and decreased fracture risk.

Available Dosage Forms and Strengths

Tablets — 5 mg, 10 mg, 35 mg, 40 mg, 70 mg

▷ **Recommended Dosage Ranges** (Actual dose and schedule must be determined for each patient individually.)

Infants and Children: Efficacy and safety are not established.

18 to 65 Years of Age: Treatment of osteoporosis in women after menopause: 70 mg once a week OR 10 mg taken once daily.

Osteoporosis prevention in women after menopause: 35 mg once a week OR 5 mg once daily. I strongly recommend an appropriate amount of dietary calcium and/or calcium supplementation to ensure adequate calcium every day. Discuss the need for vitamin D with your doctor. Calcium and vitamin D are critical in osteoporosis prevention and treatment.

Osteoporosis TREATMENT in women after menopause or in men: 70 mg once a week for women (can also be considered for men) OR 10 mg once daily. Calcium and vitamin D also should be added.

Prevention of glucocorticoid-induced osteoporosis: 5 mg daily in one study.

Treatment of glucocorticoid-induced osteoporosis: 5 mg once daily. In post-menopausal women who are NOT taking estrogen, the dose for this indication is 10 mg once daily.

Paget's disease: 40 mg once daily for 6 months. Repeat treatment after a 6 month evaluation period may be possible if patients relapse (increased serum alkaline phosphatase).

Over 65 Years of Age: Same as in those 18 to 65 years old.

Conditions Requiring Dosing Adjustments

Liver Function: No changes needed.

Kidney Function: Lower doses for patients with kidney compromise. Patients with creatinine clearances (see Glossary) less than 35 ml/min **should not** be given this medicine.

▷ **Dosing Instructions:** TAKE THIS MEDICINE WITH 6 TO 8 OUNCES OF TAP WATER TO GET THE BEST RESULTS. DO NOT take this drug with food or other drugs. The therapeutic benefit will be decreased. Take it at least half an hour before the first food or liquids (other than plain tap water) of the day. Avoiding food or drink for more than 30 minutes lets more medicine get into your body to go to work. **DO NOT** lie down for 30 minutes (preferably an hour) after taking this drug (decreases risk of irritation of the esophagus). If you forget a dose: Take the medicine right away, unless it is nearly time for your next dose. If you are taking it once weekly, call your doctor. DO NOT double doses.

Usual Duration of Use: In Paget's disease, this medicine is used once daily for 6 months, with recheck after that. In treating osteoporosis after menopause, many doctors get a bone mineral density test (DEXA or PDEXA presently most widely used) to help decide to start therapy and then get a second test 2 years later or order certain laboratory tests to check results or outcome of therapy. Further study is needed to find the best dosing strategies in long-term (greater than 5 years) use of alendronate (cyclic or ongoing).

Typical Treatment Goals and Measurements (Outcomes and Markers)

Fracture of bone is a critical issue when bones weaken and become osteoporotic. The World Health Organization has generated guidelines that establish weak bone (osteopenia) and osteoporosis based on certain patient populations. If this medicine is being used to prevent osteoporosis, a typical strategy would be to obtain a measure of bone mineral density such as a DEXA scan. The medicine would be started based on risk factors, medicines (such as glucocorticoids) that are being taken and the results of the DEXA scan itself. Laboratory tests (such as N-telopeptides) may be tested to augment treatment decisions. Once the medicine is started, a DEXA is often rechecked in 2 years to assess the beneficial effects of this medicine. Some clinicians will also recommend check of height (height loss) as well as an earlier repeat DEXA, PDEXA, ultrasound, and/or laboratory test in patients with a family history of rapid perimenopausal bone loss. In Paget's disease, this medicine is used once daily for 6 months, with recheck after that.

Possible Advantages of This Drug

This drug increases bone mass more than other available (anti-resorptive) drugs, which then decreases the risk of fractures. This medicine also helps form normal bone (microarchitecture). Alendronate also offers the adherence (taking the medicine as prescribed) benefits of once-weekly dosing. While the role in osteonecrosis is emerging, this medicine may offer an alternative to surgical approaches. Results of the EFFECT (Efficacy of Fosamax versus Evista Comparison Trial) showed that alendronate (70 mg once a week as compared to raloxifene 60 mg once a week) favored alendronate. This study was the first head to head research and revealed significantly larger increases at the hip and spine for alendronate versus raloxifene. A head to head study of alendronate (Fosamax 70 mg a week) versus risedronate (Actonel 35 mg a week) is currently being undertaken. Information from the FIT (Fracture Intervention Trial) showed that alendronate continued to have a beneficial effect on decreasing bone fractures for as long as five years. Alendronate was shown to protect against bone loss in women who stopped hormone replacement therapy (HRT).

▷ **This Drug Should Not Be Taken If**
- you are allergic to the drug or its components.
- you have a low blood calcium (hypocalcemia). Talk to your doctor.
- you have a significant kidney disease (medicine should NOT be taken if creatinine clearance less than 35 ml/min—no data).
- you are unable to sit or stand for 30 minutes after taking this medicine (increased risk of esophageal problems).
- you are pregnant or are nursing your infant.
- you have esophageal disease (abnormal esophagus) or difficulty emptying the esophagus.

▷ **Inform Your Physician Before Taking This Drug If**
- you have ulcers or inflammation of the duodenum.
- you have difficulty swallowing.
- you have a vitamin D deficiency.
- you have a diet poor in calcium (low calcium diet).

Possible Side Effects (natural, expected, and unavoidable drug actions)

Irritation of the esophagus and potential ulceration—rare. This effect is worsened if patients lie down soon after taking drug. Drug fever is common with intravenous use.

▷ **Possible Adverse Effects** (unusual, unexpected, and infrequent reactions)

If any of the following develop, consult your physician promptly for guidance.

Mild Adverse Effects

Allergic reactions: rare skin rash or redness.

Headache—infrequent.

Blurred vision (possible conjunctivitis)—rare.

Gas (flatulence), diarrhea, or constipation—infrequent.

Pain in the muscles or skeleton (musculoskeletal)—infrequent.

Mild calcium decrease—2% decrease (some patients at 10 mg daily).

Mild decrease in phosphorus—up to 6%.

Mild muscle pain—infrequent with the 10-mg dose.

Serious Adverse Effects

Allergic reactions: none reported.

Esophageal ulceration—rare. (Increased risk if you lie down after taking this drug. Best NOT to lie down for at least half an hour after taking this medicine.) One case report of a patient with a history of peptic ulcer disease who had stomach surgery and was also taking aspirin who developed an ulcer (anastamotic) and had mild hemorrhaging.

Liver toxicity—one case report.

Inflammation of the sclera (scleritis)—rare (probably idiosyncratic).

▷ **Possible Effects on Sexual Function:** None reported.

Possible Effects on Laboratory Tests

Serum calcium or phosphorus: lowered—infrequent.

Liver function tests: increased—rare (with intravenous form) (asymptomatic and transient).

CAUTION

1. A "dear doctor" letter was sent out by the FDA early after alendronate approval warning of increased occurrence of esophageal ulceration. This may have been caused by patients taking the medicine with less water than directed and by patients who took the medicine and went back to bed. Take this medicine with a full glass of tap water and DO NOT LIE DOWN for 30 minutes after taking this drug.
2. Patients who take more than 10 mg of alendronate a day may need to avoid aspirin and aspirin-containing compounds because upper gastrointestinal adverse effects may be increased in this situation if the medicines are combined (at any alendronate dose).
3. Other causes of osteoporosis besides estrogen or aging (secondary osteoporosis) must be ruled out.
4. Depression (long-standing) may be a risk factor for osteoporosis (probably diet related). Talk with your doctor about an osteoporosis test if depression is a problem for you.
5. Talk to your doctor if you develop eye symptoms while taking this medicine.

Precautions for Use

By Infants and Children: Safety and efficacy in this age group have not been established.

By Those Over 65 Years of Age: The amount that goes into the body (bioavailability) and the places alendronate goes (disposition) are similar to those less than 65. No specific dosing changes needed. Increased sensitivity to this drug is possible.

▷ **Advisability of Use During Pregnancy**

Pregnancy Category: C. See Pregnancy Risk Categories at the back of this book.

Animal Studies: Studies in rats have shown toxicity to the mother as well as neonatal death following dosing of alendronate during pregnancy.

Human Studies: Adequate studies of pregnant women are not available.

Avoid this medicine during pregnancy.

Advisability of Use If Breast-Feeding

Presence of this drug in breast milk: Yes in rats; unknown in humans.

Avoid drug or refrain from nursing.

Habit-Forming Potential: None.

Effects of Overdose: Nausea, vomiting, hypocalcemia, and hypophosphatemia. Heartburn, ulceration of the upper gastrointestinal tract.

Possible Effects of Long-Term Use: Increased bone density and decreased fracture risk (beneficial).

Suggested Periodic Examinations While Taking This Drug (at physician's discretion)

Tests of bone mineral density (DEXA, PDEXA, ultrasound, or QCT), check of lab tests of bone loss or formation.

Blood calcium.

Measurement of height.

Assessment of any eye irritation.

▷ **While Taking This Drug, Observe the Following**

Foods: DO NOT TAKE THIS DRUG WITH FOOD.

Herbal Medicines or Minerals: Soy or other plant-derived phytoestrogens may work to complement alendronate, but have not been studied. Ipriflavone is a synthetic flavonoid currently investigational for osteoporosis (which both inhibits bone resorption by reducing osteoclast recruitment and encourages osteoblast function). Combined use with alendronate has not been studied. Use with white willow bark (salicylates) may increase stomach irritation risk.

Adequate elemental calcium and vitamin D are needed. Calcium supplements should be taken at least half an hour after taking alendronate. Effervescent calcium (resulting in a solution) may be absorbed more rapidly and help avoid problems.

Beverages: ANY liquid other than water will DECREASE the amount of alendronate that gets into your body to help you. It is critical that this medicine only be taken with 6 to 8 ounces of water.

▷ *Alcohol:* Alcohol (especially in high doses) may act as a bone-forming cell (osteoblast) poison, and excessive use is a risk factor for osteoporosis. Alcohol may also irritate the stomach lining.

Tobacco Smoking: Smoking is a risk factor for osteoporosis. STOP SMOKING.

▷ *Other Drugs*

Alendronate *taken concurrently* with

- antacids may decrease the total absorption of alendronate and decrease its therapeutic benefit.
- aspirin or aspirin-containing products or salicylates may pose an increased risk of upper gastrointestinal adverse effects if more than 10 mg of alendronate is taken daily. Although other NSAIDs (see Drug Classes) were not presented as potential problems with alendronate doses greater than 10 mg, caution is advised for this benefit to risk decision.
- calcium products (various) will blunt absorption of alendronate. Wait at least half an hour after taking alendronate to take any other medicine including a calcium supplement. Effervescent calcium forms may offer an advantage considering their speed of absorption.
- estrogens (various) taken by a few women in clinical trials did not present problems. This combination is (both estrogen and/or estrogen plus a progestin) approved in Canada.
- foscarnet (Foscavir) may result in an additive decrease in calcium.
- magnesium (various) may increase stomach/intestine upset.
- medicines in general should NOT be taken at the same time as alendronate. Separate any dose of alendronate and any other medicine by at least half an hour.
- mesalamine or olsalazine may increase stomach/intestine upset.
- ranitidine (Zantac) (intravenous form and perhaps oral form) may double how much alendronate gets into your body. The clinical importance of this is not yet known.
- teriparatide (Forteo) may work in a beneficial way (and by a different mechanism of action) but has not yet been studied.

The following drugs may ***decrease*** the effects of alendronate:
- Because a small amount of alendronate gets into the body under the best conditions, take alendronate with a full 6 to 8 ounces of water. Take any other drugs at least half an hour after alendronate.

▷ *Driving, Hazardous Activities:* No specific limitations.

Aviation Note: The use of this drug is ***probably not a disqualification*** for piloting. Consult a designated Aviation Medical Examiner.

Exposure to Sun: No restrictions.

Heavy Exercise or Exertion: If your bone density is low, heavy aerobic exercise may not be a good idea. Discuss this with your doctor. In general, weight-bearing exercise stimulates receptors (mechanoreceptors) to release factors that result in increased bone strength.

Discontinuation: Talk with your doctor **before** stopping this medicine.

ALLOPURINOL (al oh PURE i nohl)

Introduced: 1963   **Class:**   Antigout, xanthine oxidase inhibitor
Prescription: USA: Yes   **Controlled Drug:**   USA: No; Canada: No
Available as Generic: USA: Yes; Canada: No

Brand Names: ✤Alloprin, ✤Apo-Allopurinol, Lopurin, ✤Novo-Purol, ✤Purinol, ✤Riva-Purinol, Zurinol, Zyloprim

---

BENEFITS versus RISKS

Possible Benefits	*Possible Risks*
EFFECTIVE CONTROL OF GOUT	Increased frequency of acute gout
CONTROL OF HIGH BLOOD URIC ACID DUE TO POLYCYTHEMIA, LEUKEMIA, CANCER, AND CHEMOTHERAPY	initially
	Peripheral neuritis
	Allergic reactions in skin, lung, blood vessels, and liver
More beneficial in patients who remove more than one gram of uric acid in a day	Bone marrow depression
	Kidney toxicity
May have a role in restoring blood vessel lining cells (endothelial cell) function in people with diabetes and mild high blood pressure	

▷ **Principal Uses**

As a Single Drug Product: Uses currently included in FDA-approved labeling: (1) Long-term gout therapy to prevent acute gout (does not relieve sudden gout attacks); (2) helps prevent high blood levels of uric acid in people who have recurrent uric acid or calcium oxalate kidney stones, people getting chemotherapy or radiation for cancer or who take thiazide diuretics (see Drug Classes).

Other (unlabeled) generally accepted uses: (1) May decrease pain and occurrence of mouth sores in people receiving 5-fluorouracil chemotherapy; (2) may help prostate swelling (nonbacterial prostatitis) not caused by bacteria; (3) early data show benefits in blood circulation damage (ischemic tissue damage); (4) may help Chagas' disease; (5) appears to ease refractive epilepsy in children; (6) effective in combination with quinine in treating malaria; (7) may have a role in helping restore how well the cells lining blood vessels (endothelial cells) work in people with diabetes and mild high blood pressure (300 mg a day in a 1-month study); (8) could have a role in some cases of mental illness (psychosis) where patients are resistant (refractory) to existing treatment (based on a small study of add on allopurinol).

How This Drug Works: Works to change chemicals called purines' removal (metabolism) by the body. This medicine does this without changing the ability of the body to make purines that are important to the body. Allopurinol blocks the enzyme xanthine oxidase, thereby decreasing uric acid formation that is the root cause of gout. It also uses a feedback mechanism to block purine synthesis (requires hypoxanthine guanine phosphoribosyltransferase).

Available Dosage Forms and Strengths
Tablets — 100 mg, 200 mg, 300 mg

▷ **Usual Adult Dosage Ranges:** Starts as 100 mg every 24 hours, then increased by 100 mg every 24 hours (1 week apart) until uric acid level is normal (6 mg/dl or less). Usual dose is 200–300 mg every 24 hours for mild gout, and 400 to 600 mg every 24 hours for moderate to severe gout. Daily doses of 300 mg or less may be taken as a single dose. Doses exceeding 300 mg daily should be divided into two or three equal portions. For high uric acid levels associated with cancer (to prevent uric acid nephropathy): 600–800 mg every 24 hours, divided into three equal portions (with high water intake). Kidney stone (calcium oxalate) recurrence prevention: 200–300 mg per day. Extemporaneously made mouthwash: 5–6 mg/ml suspension has been used several times a day to prevent 5-FU stomatitis.
   Note: Actual dosage and schedule must be determined for each patient individually.

Conditions Requiring Dosing Adjustments
   Liver Function: Dose adjustment in liver compromise is not documented.
   Kidney Function: Dosing must be adjusted in kidney compromise.
   Malnutrition: Malnourished or low-protein-diet patients will not remove this drug normally and are at risk for toxicity. Doses must be decreased.

▷ **Dosing Instructions:** Best taken with food or milk (or a meal) to reduce stomach irritation. Tablet may be crushed. Drink 2 to 3 quarts (10 to 12 glasses) of liquids daily if your doctor says it's ok (not contraindicated). If you forget a dose: Take the medicine as soon as you remember it, unless it is close to the time for the next dose—simply take the dose at the next scheduled time. Do NOT double doses.

Usual Duration of Use: Regular use for several months may be needed to prevent acute gout attacks. Ongoing use for years often needed for adequate control.

Typical Treatment Goals and Measurements (Outcomes and Markers)
   Uric Acid: Blood uric acid levels often decrease in 48 to 72 hours and may reach normal range in 1 to 3 weeks. Attacks of gout should become shorter and lessen in severity over time.

▷ **This Drug Should Not Be Taken If**
   • you have had an allergic reaction to it previously.
   • you are having an acute gout attack.

▷ **Inform Your Physician Before Taking This Drug If**
   • you have a family history of hemochromatosis.
   • you have a history of liver or kidney disease.

- you have had a blood cell or bone marrow disorder.
- you have a seizure or convulsive disorder (epilepsy—a slow withdrawal from this treatment is needed).
- you take other prescription or nonprescription medications not discussed when allopurinol was prescribed.
- you are unsure how much or how often to take allopurinol.
- you are on a low-protein diet.
- you do not drink very much water—talk to your doctor about this.
- you are pregnant.

Possible Side Effects (natural, expected, and unavoidable drug actions)

Acute gout may still occur during the first several weeks of therapy. Ask your doctor about using other medicines (such as colchicine) during this period.

▷ **Possible Adverse Effects** (unusual, unexpected, and infrequent reactions)
If any of the following develop, consult your physician promptly for guidance.

Mild Adverse Effects
Allergic reactions: skin rash, hives, itching—frequent; drug fever.
Confusion, agitation, headache, dizziness, drowsiness—rare.
Nausea, vomiting, diarrhea, stomach cramps—rare.
Taste disturbance—possible.
Loss of scalp hair—rare.

Serious Adverse Effects
Allergic reactions: severe skin reactions—infrequent.
High fever, chills, joint pains, swollen glands, kidney or liver damage—rare.
Idiosyncratic reaction: catatonia, paresthesia, agitation.
Hepatitis with or without jaundice (see Glossary): yellow eyes and skin, dark-colored urine, light-colored stools (may be part of allergy)—rare.
Kidney damage (acute tubular necrosis or interstitial nephritis)—case reports—rare.
Bone marrow depression (see Glossary)—rare.
Blood vessel inflammation/damage—rare (risk increased in kidney failure and thiazide diuretic use at the same time).
Peripheral neuritis—rare.
Bronchospasm (part of hypersensitivity)—rare.
Eye damage (macular), cataract formation—rare

▷ **Possible Effects on Sexual Function:** Rare cases of bladder inflammation have been reported.

Adverse Effects That May Mimic Natural Diseases or Disorders
Toxic liver reaction may suggest viral hepatitis.
Severe skin reactions may resemble the Stevens-Johnson Syndrome (erythema multiforme). One case report of Stevens-Johnson with combined allopurinol and captopril has been made.

Possible Effects on Laboratory Tests
Complete blood cell counts: decreased red cells, hemoglobin, and platelets; increased eosinophils.
Liver function tests: increased ALT/GPT, AST/GOT, and alkaline phosphatase.

CAUTION
1. Call your doctor immediately if you develop a rash. This can be the first sign of an allergic reaction. Prompt action may avoid a more serious reaction.

2. A patient with an allopurinol allergy had cross-allergenicity and allergic reaction to acyclovir (Zovirax).
3. In the first few weeks of therapy, frequency of gout attacks may increase. These subside with ongoing therapy.
4. Drug should not be started in acute gout. It does not help.
5. Vitamin C in doses of 2 g or more daily can increase the risk of kidney stone formation during the use of allopurinol.
6. Patients with kidney function decline are more likely to have allergic reactions to this drug.
7. Frequency of rash may be increased in patients also taking a penicillin.
8. Allergic-type kidney damage can result if thiazide diuretics (see Drug Classes) are taken with allopurinol. Avoid this combination.
9. Patients on low-protein diets will not eliminate allopurinol normally. Doses must be decreased.
10. Dosing MUST be adjusted to kidney function. If you are 60 or older, "normal" declines in kidney function may require decreased doses. Talk to your doctor.

Precautions for Use

By Infants and Children: Not used in children except for increased uric acid caused by malignant growths. Watch closely for allergic skin reactions and blood cell disorders. The toxicity of azathioprine (Imuran) or mercaptopurine (Purinethol) may be increased in children receiving chemotherapy. For this kind of secondary hyperuricemia: 150 mg per day in children less than 6. Response is checked in 2 days and the dose is adjusted to response. Those 6–10 years old receive 300 mg a day with the same response check and dose changes as required.

By Those Over 60 Years of Age: Smaller starting and ongoing doses of this drug must be used (age-related decrease in kidney function).

▷ **Advisability of Use During Pregnancy**
Pregnancy Category: C. See Pregnancy Risk Categories at the back of this book.
Animal Studies: Results are conflicting and inconclusive.
Human Studies: Adequate studies of pregnant women are not available.
Avoid use of drug during the first 3 months. Use during the last 6 months only if clearly needed.

Advisability of Use If Breast-Feeding
Presence of this drug in breast milk: Yes.
Avoid drug or refrain from nursing.

Habit-Forming Potential: None.

Effects of Overdose: Nausea, vomiting, or diarrhea. Hypersensitivity reactions, kidney and liver function decline.

Possible Effects of Long-Term Use: Beneficial decreases in uric acid.

Suggested Periodic Examinations While Taking This Drug (at physician's discretion)
Blood uric acid levels.
Complete blood cell counts.
Liver and kidney function tests.
Eye examinations (possible cataract formation or macular damage).

▷ **While Taking This Drug, Observe the Following**
Foods: Talk to your doctor about a low-purine diet (such as avoiding liver, lentils, anchovies, etc.). A low-protein diet may increase toxicity risk if dose isn't decreased.

Herbal Medicines or Minerals: Acerola is high in vitamin C. Inosine, like acerola, may increase uric acid levels. Aspen should be avoided in gout. Lipase may worsen gout (read the labels on all neutraceuticals). Goutweed (*Aegopodium podagraria*) does not have enough data to assess effectiveness.

Beverages: No restrictions. May be taken with milk.

▷ *Alcohol:* Alcohol can worsen gout. Best to avoid it.

Tobacco Smoking: No interactions expected. I advise everyone to quit smoking.

▷ *Other Drugs*

Allopurinol may *increase* the effects of
- azathioprine (Imuran) and mercaptopurine (Purinethol), making dose decreases necessary.
- didanosine (Videx) which was noted in a case report of two patients with impaired kidneys.
- oral anticoagulants (see Drug Classes) such as warfarin (Coumadin). INR should be checked more often.
- theophylline (aminophylline, Elixophyllin, Theo-Dur, etc.).

Allopurinol *taken concurrently* with
- ampicillin, amoxicillin (and perhaps other penicillins) may increase the incidence of skin rash.
- antacids containing aluminum will decrease the therapeutic effect of allopurinol.
- captopril (Capoten) or other ACE inhibitors (see Drug Classes) can increase the likelihood of allergic reactions. CAUTION.
- chlorpropamide (Diabinese)) can cause hypoglycemia.
- cyclophosphamide (Cytoxan, Neosar) may result in cyclophosphamide toxicity.
- cyclosporine (Sandimmune) can cause cyclosporine toxicity.
- iron salts may lead to excess liver iron. Avoid combining.
- mercaptopurine (Purinethol) increases toxicity risk.
- probenecid (Benemid, others) may increase probenecid levels.
- tamoxifen (Nolvadex) may result in increased allopurinol levels and increased risk of liver toxicity.
- thiazide diuretics (see Drug Classes) may decrease kidney function.
- theophylline (Theo-Dur, etc.) may cause toxic theophylline levels.
- vidarabine (Vira-A) may increase risk of neurotoxicity.

▷ *Driving, Hazardous Activities:* Drowsiness may occur in some people. Use caution.

Aviation Note: The use of this drug *may be a disqualification* for piloting. Consult a designated Aviation Medical Examiner.

Exposure to Sun: No restrictions.

Discontinuation: If you have a seizure disorder, this medicine dose should be slowly decreased and then stopped.

ALOSETRON (A LOH sah trahn)

Re-Introduced: 2002   **Class:**   Diarrhea predominant-Irritable Bowel Syndrome (IBS), type three serotonin receptor antagonist   **Prescription:** USA: Yes   **Controlled Drug:**   USA: No; Canada: No   **Available as Generic:**   No

Brand Names: Lotronex

Author's Note: This medicine was previously removed (see Table 17) from the U.S. market, but was re-approved WITH RESTRICTIONS under an sNDA. This profile will be broadened in subsequent editions if data warrant.

ALPRAZOLAM (al PRAY zoh lam)

Introduced: 1973, XR form 2002   **Class:**   Antianxiety drug, benzodiazepines   **Prescription:**   USA: Yes   **Controlled Drug:**   USA: C-IV*; Canada: No   **Available as Generic:**   Yes

Brand Names: Alprazolam Intensol, ✦Apo-Alpraz, ✦Med-Alprazolam, ✦Novo-Alprazol, ✦Nu-Alpraz, Xanax, Xanax XR

Warning: The brand names Xanax and Zantac are similar and can lead to serious medication errors. Xanax is alprazolam. Zantac is ranitidine, which treats peptic ulcers and heartburn. Make sure your prescription was filled correctly.

BENEFITS versus RISKS	
Possible Benefits	*Possible Risks*
RELIEF OF ANXIETY AND NERVOUS TENSION	Habit-forming potential with prolonged use
EFFECTIVE TREATMENT OF PANIC DISORDER	Minor impairment of mental functions with therapeutic doses
May have some action as an antidepressant	Tachycardia and palpitations

▷ **Principal Uses**

As a Single Drug Product: Uses currently included in FDA-approved labeling: (1) Used for short-term relief of mild to moderate anxiety and nervous tension; (2) helps relieve anxiety associated with neurosis; (3) decreases frequency and severity of panic disorder.

Other (unlabeled) generally accepted uses: (1) Can help control extreme PMS symptoms; (2) lessens a variety of types of cancer pain when given with various narcotics; (3) eases agoraphobia; (4) decreases symptoms in essential tremor; (5) decreases loudness of ear ringing in tinnitus; (6) can be helpful in alcohol withdrawal; (7) eases irritable bowel syndrome; (8) eases anxiety sometimes seen with depression; (9) helpful in reducing anticipatory vomiting from chemotherapy.

How This Drug Works: Calms by enhancing the action of the nerve transmitter gamma-aminobutyric acid (GABA), which in turn blocks higher brain centers.

Available Dosage Forms and Strengths

Tablets — 0.25 mg, 0.5 mg, 1 mg, 2 mg
Tablets, extended release (XR) — 0.5 mg, 1 mg, 2 mg, 3 mg
Oral solution — 0.25 mg, 0.5 mg, 1 mg/5 ml
— 0.25 mg/2.5 ml

▷ **Usual Adult Dosage Ranges: Regular release form:** *For anxiety and nervous tension:* 0.25–0.5 mg three times daily. Maximum dose is 4 mg every 24 hours, taken in divided doses—but the lowest effective dose should be used.

For panic disorder: Initially 0.5 mg three times daily; increase dose by 1 mg every 3 to 4 days as needed and tolerated. Some patients stopped having panic attacks with 6 mg a day. Maximum daily dose is 10 mg.

For treatment of alcohol withdrawal: Dosing is variable—one source reported a mean oral daily dose to be 2.2 mg.

XR Form: 3 to 6 mg once a day. Dosing is started with 0.5 to one mg a day. Doses can be increased as needed and tolerated once every 3–4 days in steps on as much as 1 mg. Slower stepwise increase may be prudent to allow the medicine a long enough time to go to work (full pharmacodynamic effect). **Note: Actual dosage and schedule must be determined for each patient individually.**

Conditions Requiring Dosing Adjustments

Liver Function: A starting dose of 0.25 mg is prudent in patients with advanced liver disease. Slow increase in dose only if needed.

Kidney Function: The manufacturer does not define specific-dose reductions.

Obesity: Takes a longer time to reach final concentrations in obese people. Doses should be calculated based on ideal rather than actual body weight.

Alcoholism: Because of some of the physiological and liver changes in alcoholism, removal of drug from the body may be delayed. Lower doses/longer times (intervals) between doses are needed.

▷ **Dosing Instructions:** Regular release form may be taken on empty stomach or with food or milk. Regular release tablets may be crushed. XR form should NOT be crushed and high fat meals given up to 2 hours before a dose of this form is taken increases how much gets into your body by roughly 25%. These XR tablets are best taken once a day in the morning. Do not stop this drug abruptly if taken for more than 4 weeks (stop slowly by decreasing 0.5 mg every 3 days or longer). If you forget a dose, but have missed by less than an hour, take the missed dose. If it is almost time for your next scheduled dose, skip the missed dose. Do NOT double doses.

Usual Duration of Use: Several days to several weeks. Continual use should not exceed 8 weeks without evaluation by your doctor.

Author's Note: The National Institute of Mental Health has a new information page on anxiety. It can be found on the World Wide Web (*www. nimh.nih.gov/anxiety*).

Typical Treatment Goals and Measurements (Outcomes and Markers)

Anxiety or panic: Goals for anxiety and panic tend to be more vague and subjective than hypertension or cholesterol. Frequently, the patient (in conjunction with physician assessment) will largely decide if anxiety has been modified to a successful extent. The Hamilton Depression Scale is widely used to assess depression. In the case of panic attacks, decreased number of trips to the hospital or ER visits may be a useful measure. In both cases, the ability of the patient to return to normal activities is a hallmark of successful treatment.

Possible Advantages of This Drug: XR form: May allow control of anxiety with reduced impact (pill burden) for patients.

▷ **This Drug Should Not Be Taken If**
- you have had an allergic reaction to it previously.
- you are pregnant (first 3 months).
- you have acute narrow-angle glaucoma.
- you have myasthenia gravis.

▷ **Inform Your Physician Before Taking This Drug If**
- your history includes palpitations or tachycardia (may be worsened).
- you are allergic to benzodiazepines (see Drug Classes).
- you are pregnant or planning pregnancy.
- you are breast-feeding your infant.
- you have a history of depression or serious mental illness (psychosis).
- you have a history of alcoholism or drug abuse.
- you have impaired liver or kidney function.
- you have open-angle glaucoma.
- you have a seizure disorder (epilepsy).
- you have severe chronic lung disease.
- you take other prescription or nonprescription medications that were not discussed when alprazolam was prescribed for you.
- you are unsure how much or how often to take alprazolam.

Possible Side Effects (natural, expected, and unavoidable drug actions)
Drowsiness, light-headedness—frequent.

▷ **Possible Adverse Effects** (unusual, unexpected, and infrequent reactions)
If any of the following develop, consult your physician promptly for guidance.

Mild Adverse Effects
Allergic reactions: skin rash, hives.
Headache, dizziness, fatigue, blurred vision, dry mouth—infrequent.
Drowsiness—frequent, up to 50%.
Nausea, vomiting, constipation—infrequent.
Increased salivation—infrequent.

Serious Adverse Effects
Confusion, hallucinations, depression, excitement, agitation (paradoxical reaction)—case reports to rare.
Tachycardia and palpitations—infrequent.
Increased liver enzymes—rare.
Increased white blood cells (leukocytosis) or decreased blood cells (pancytopenia)—case reports and of questionable causation.
Low blood pressure (hypotension)—case report.

▷ **Possible Effects on Sexual Function:** Rare but documented: inhibited female orgasm (5 mg/day); impaired ejaculation (3.5 mg/day); decreased libido, impaired erection (4.5 mg/day); altered timing and pattern of menstruation (0.75–4 mg/day).

Possible Effects on Laboratory Tests
Liver function tests: increased ALT/GPT, AST/GOT—rare and insignificant.
Urine screening tests for drug abuse: may be positive (depends upon amount of drug taken and testing method).

CAUTION
1. Do not stop taking this drug abruptly if it has been taken continually for more than 4 weeks.
2. Some nonprescription drugs with antihistamines (allergy and cold medicines, sleep aids) can cause excessive sedation.
3. This medicine is removed from the body by liver enzymes called cytochrome P450 3A4. Medicines that block this enzyme system will tend to increase alprazolam levels. Medicines that induce or increase P450 activity will tend to lower alprazolam levels and blunt effectiveness.

4. People with ongoing severe conditions such as cancer may not tolerate "typical" starting doses; 0.25 mg twice or three times a day as a starting dose is prudent. The dose may be increased as needed and tolerated.

Precautions for Use

By Infants and Children: Safety and effectiveness for those under 18 not established.

By Those Over 60 Years of Age: Starting dose should be 0.25 mg two or three times daily. Watch for excessive drowsiness, dizziness, unsteadiness, and incoordination (possible low blood pressure).

▷ **Advisability of Use During Pregnancy**

Pregnancy Category: D. See Pregnancy Risk Categories at the back of this book.

Animal Studies: Diazepam (a closely related benzodiazepine) can cause cleft palate in mice and skeletal defects in rats. No data on alprazolam.

Human Studies: Some studies suggest an association between diazepam use and cleft lip and heart deformities. Adequate studies in pregnant women are not available.

Avoid use during entire pregnancy if possible.

Advisability of Use If Breast-Feeding

Presence of this drug in breast milk: Yes.

Avoid drug or refrain from nursing.

Habit-Forming Potential: This drug can cause psychological and/or physical dependence (see Glossary), especially if used in large doses for an extended period of time.

Effects of Overdose: Marked drowsiness, weakness, feeling of drunkenness, staggering gait, tremor, stupor progressing to deep sleep or coma.

Possible Effects of Long-Term Use: Psychological and/or physical dependence.

Suggested Periodic Examinations While Taking This Drug (at physician's discretion)

None required for short-term use.

▷ **While Taking This Drug, Observe the Following**

Foods: No restrictions.

Herbal Medicines or Minerals: Kava, danshen (miltirone) and valerian may exacerbate central nervous system depression (avoid this combination). Kava is not presently recommended in Canada because of liver concerns. Kola nut, Siberian ginseng, mate, ephedra, guarana (caffeine), and ma huang may blunt the benefits of this medicine. While St. John's wort is indicated for anxiety, it is also thought to increase (induce) cytochrome P450 enzymes and will tend to blunt alprazolam effectiveness if combined with alprazolam. St. John's wort may also worsen sun sensitivity caused by alprazolam.

Beverages: Avoid excessive caffeine-containing beverages: coffee, tea, cola (counteracts effects). This drug may be taken with milk.

▷ *Alcohol:* Use with extreme caution. Alcohol may increase the sedative effects of alprazolam. Alprazolam may increase the intoxicating effects of alcohol. Avoid alcohol completely—throughout the day and night—if you find it necessary to drive or engage in any hazardous activity.

Tobacco Smoking: Heavy smoking may reduce calming. I advise quitting smoking.

Marijuana Smoking: Occasional (once or twice weekly): Increased sedative effect.

Daily: Marked increase in sedative effect.

▷   *Other Drugs*

Alprazolam may *increase* the effects of
• digoxin (Lanoxin) and cause digoxin toxicity.

Alprazolam may *decrease* the effects of
• levodopa (Sinemet, etc.) and reduce its effect in treating Parkinson's disease.

The following drugs may *increase* the effects of alprazolam:
• amprenavir (Agenerase).
• itraconazole or ketoconazole (azole antifungals).
• birth control pills (oral contraceptives—various kinds).
• cimetidine (Tagamet).
• delavirdine (Rescriptor).
• disulfiram (Antabuse).
• fluconazole (Diflucan).
• fluoxetine (Prozac).
• fluvoxamine (Luvox).
• isoniazid (INH, Rifamate, etc.).
• macrolide antibiotics (such as erythromycin, clarithromycin, or azithromycin—see Drug Classes).
• medicines that inhibit a liver enzyme (CYP3A4) will increase alprazolam levels (talk to your doctor and pharmacist).
• omeprazole (Prilosec).
• paroxetine (Paxil).
• propoxyphene (Darvon, etc.).
• ritonavir (Norvir) and perhaps other protease inhibitors (see Drug Classes).
• sertraline (Zoloft).
• valproic acid (Depakene).

The following drugs may *decrease* the effects of alprazolam:
• carbamazepine (Tegretol).
• rifampin (Rimactane, etc.).
• theophylline (aminophylline, Theo-Dur, etc.).

Alprazolam *taken concurrently* with
• alcohol (ethanol) will worsen coordination and mental abilities.
• benzodiazepines (see Drug Classes) can cause increased central nervous system (CNS) depression.
• buspirone (Buspar) can result in additive CNS depression.
• central nervous system active agents (see Antihistamine and Antipsychotic Drug Classes) can cause increased CNS depression.
• narcotics (morphine, etc.) cause additive CNS depression.
• medicines removed by the same cytochrome P450 3A4 enzyme (such as atorvastatin [Lipitor]) may lead to increased blood levels and added sedation.
• nefazodone (Serzone) may double the blood level.
• tricyclic and other kinds of antidepressants (see Drug Classes) results in additional CNS depression.

▷   *Driving, Hazardous Activities:* This drug can impair mental alertness, judgment, physical coordination, and reaction time. Avoid hazardous activities accordingly.

Aviation Note: The use of this drug *is a disqualification* for piloting. Consult a designated Aviation Medical Examiner.

Exposure to Sun: Use caution; rare photosensitivity reports (see Glossary).

Discontinuation: If this drug has been taken for an extended period of time, do not stop it abruptly. Various withdrawal schedules have been developed. Some clinicians decrease by 0.5 mg every three days. Another schedule uses dose reductions of 1 mg per week until a total daily dose of 4 mg is reached; by 0.5 mg per week until a total daily dose of 2 mg is reached; and then by 0.25 mg per week thereafter. Ask your doctor for help.

AMANTADINE (a MAN ta deen)

Introduced: 1966   **Class:**   Anti-Parkinsonism, antiviral   **Prescription:**   USA: Yes   **Controlled Drug:**   USA: No; Canada: No   **Available as Generic:**   USA: Yes; Canada: Yes
Brand Names: Antadine, Symadine, Symmetrel

BENEFITS versus RISKS	
Possible Benefits	*Possible Risks*
Partial relief of rigidity, tremor, and impaired motion in all forms of parkinsonis	Skin rashes, mild to severe
	Confusion, hallucinations
	Rare congestive heart failure
Combination treatment of hepatitis C that has failed to respond to interferon	Increased risk of prostatism (see Glossary)
Possible role in helping autism and other	Abnormally low white blood cell counts
Developmental disorders	
Prevention and treatment of respiratory infections caused by influenza type A viruses*	

▷ **Principal Uses**

As a Single Drug Product: Uses currently included in FDA-approved labeling: (1) Treats all forms of parkinsonism; (2) prevents or treats respiratory tract infections caused by influenza type A virus (rimantadine is the drug of first choice because of amantadine's more frequent CNS side effects); (3) eases movement problems caused by some phenothiazine type medicines (drug-induced extrapyramidal symptoms).

Other (unlabeled) generally accepted uses: (1) Role in managing behavioral problems in brain injuries, autism, others; (2) some success reversing symptoms of mild dementia; (3) eases some resistant myoclonic or absence seizures; (4) may help bed-wetting (enuresis) in children; (5) may ease fatigue in multiple sclerosis (MS) patients; (6) may give increased responses as part of combination therapy of hepatitis C—in both initial therapy and in interferon resistant cases.

How This Drug Works: It increases a nerve transmitter (dopamine) in some nerve centers and reduces muscular rigidity, tremor and impaired movement associated with Parkinsonism. May help some dyskinesias by blocking glutamate transmission in the globus pallidus. Helps wearing off or dyskinesia with advancing disease. By keeping the influenza from entering cells, it prevents the flu.

Available Dosage Forms and Strengths
> Capsules (gelatin and softgel) — 100 mg
> > Syrup — 50 mg/5 ml
> > Tablet — 100 mg

▷ **Usual Adult Dosage Ranges**

Anti-Parkinsonism: 100 mg once daily (for patients getting high doses of other antiparkinson medicines or who have serious sickness in addition to parkinsons. Other patients take 100 mg twice daily. Some patients may benefit from up to 400 mg daily. In general, many clinicians keep the total daily dose at 300 mg.

Antiviral: 200 mg once daily or 100 mg every 12 hours such as in flu (influenza) treatment. Dividing the total dose can help prevent side effects involving the central nervous system (CNS). (Hepatitis C cases with interferon alfa 2a for 12 months used 200 mg once daily.)

Children 1 to 9 years old: Treatment of type A flu: The CDC recommends 5 mg per kg per day up to 150 mg per day in order to prevent the flu, but decrease amantadine toxicity risk. This preventive "treatment" is best continued for 10 days after the exposure happened. The manufacturer gives a dosing range of: 4.4 to 8.8 mg per kg of body mass per day, up to a maximum of 150 mg once daily.

Children 10 and older: for those less than 40 kg, the CDC recommends 5 mg per kg per day (regardless of age). For those more than 40 kg, 100 mg twice daily is recommended.

Fatigue in multiple sclerosis: 100 mg two times a day for adults.

Note: Actual dose and schedule must be determined for each patient individually.

Conditions Requiring Dosing Adjustments

Liver Function: No dosing changes currently thought to be needed.

Kidney Function: Must be carefully adjusted to blood levels in people with kidney problems. Those with creatinine clearances of 30–50 ml/min should receive 100 mg daily. Those with 15–29 clearance should receive 100 mg every other day. Those with clearances less than 15 should receive 200 mg once a week.

Epilepsy: Doses of 200 mg/day should be avoided, as seizure risk may increase.

▷ **Dosing Instructions:** May be taken with or following meals. Can open the capsule to take it. If you forget a dose: Take the missed dose right away. If it is almost time to take the next dose, skip the missed dose and continue the medicine on your regular schedule. DO NOT double doses. If effectiveness is lost, the medicine can be gradually reduced (tapered) to zero and then restarted.

Usual Duration of Use: Use on a regular schedule for up to 2 weeks usually needed to see best effect in relieving Parkinson's symptoms. Long-term use (months to years) requires periodic check of response and dose changes. May allow for some levodopa decreases, but benefits may only last 6 months. See your doctor on a regular basis. Following exposure to influenza type A, protection requires continual daily doses for at least 10 days. During influenza epidemics, this drug may be given for 6 to 8 weeks.

Typical Treatment Goals and Measurements (Outcomes and Markers)

Parkinson's: The general goal is to ease movement problems and to allow for lowering of the levodopa dose. Benefits may be limited to about 6 months and therapy will then need to be adjusted.

Influenza (flu): Lessens the severity and length of time for the flu. PLEASE NOTE that a flu shot (or the new nasal spray "shot") is still the best way to deal with (PREVENT) the flu.

▷ **This Drug Should Not Be Taken If**
- you have had an allergic reaction to it previously.

▷ **Inform Your Physician Before Taking This Drug If**
- you have any type of seizure disorder.
- you have a history of a serious emotional or mental disorder.
- you have a history of heart disease, especially previous heart failure.
- you have impaired liver or kidney function.
- you have a history of lowering of blood pressure when you stand (orthostatic hypotension).
- you have a history of peptic ulcer disease.
- you have eczema or recurring eczemalike skin rashes.
- you are taking any drugs for emotional or mental disorders.
- you have angle closure glaucoma.
- you have a history of low white blood cell counts.
- you are unsure how much or how often to take this medicine.

Possible Side Effects (natural, expected, and unavoidable drug actions)
Light-headedness, dizziness, weakness, feeling faint (see Orthostatic Hypotension in Glossary). Dry mouth, constipation. Reddish-blue pattern or patchy skin discoloration on your legs or feet (livedo reticularis—transient and unimportant).

▷ **Possible Adverse Effects** (unusual, unexpected, and infrequent reactions)
If any of the following develop, consult your physician promptly for guidance.
Mild Adverse Effects
Allergic reaction: skin rash.
Headache, nervousness, irritability, inability to concentrate, insomnia, nightmares—rare to infrequent.
Unsteadiness, visual disturbances, slurred speech—infrequent.
Swelling (fluid retention) (arms, feet or ankles)—case report.
Difficulty breathing—possible.
Urine retention—rare.
Loss of appetite, nausea, vomiting—infrequent.
Serious Adverse Effects
Allergic reaction: severe eczemalike skin rashes.
Idiosyncratic reactions: confusion, depression, hallucinations, aggression—case reports to rare.
Neuroleptic malignant syndrome (NMS)—case reports when the medicine is stopped.
Increased seizure activity in epileptics—possible.
Congestive heart failure—rare.
Aggravation of prostatism (see Glossary)—possible.
SIADH (see Glossary)—case reports.
Elevated liver function tests—rare.
Low white blood cell counts: fever, sore throat, infection—rare.
Catatonia or seizures (if abruptly stopped).
Myasthenia gravis—case reports.

▷ **Possible Effects on Sexual Function:** None reported.

Adverse Effects That May Mimic Natural Diseases or Disorders

Mood changes, confusion or hallucinations may suggest a psychotic disorder. Swelling of the legs and feet may suggest (but not necessarily indicate) heart, liver or kidney disorder.

Natural Diseases or Disorders That May Be Activated by This Drug

Latent epilepsy, incipient congestive heart failure.

Possible Effects on Laboratory Tests

Liver function tests: increased (AST/GOT, alkaline phosphatase).
Kidney function tests: brief increase—blood urea nitrogen (BUN).

CAUTION

1. NARROW margin of safety. Maximum dose is 400 mg in 24 hours. Watch for adverse effects with doses over 200 mg a day.
2. Initial anti-Parkinsonism benefit may last 3 to 6 months. If this happens, ask your doctor if a new drug or dose is needed.
3. May increase susceptibility to German measles. Avoid exposure to anyone with active German measles.
4. Watch for early signs of congestive heart failure: shortness of breath on exertion or during the night, mild cough, swelling of feet or ankles. Report these promptly to your doctor.
5. May increase risk of seizures in people with epilepsy.
6. If you have been taking this medicine to help Parkinson's disease—do not stop it abruptly. Abruptly stopping this medicine may lead to Parkinsonian type crisis.

Precautions for Use

By Infants and Children: Safety and effectiveness for those under 18 not established.

By Those Over 60 Years of Age: Confusion, delirium, hallucinations, and disorderly conduct may develop. Prostatism may be aggravated.

▷ **Advisability of Use During Pregnancy**

Pregnancy Category: C. See Pregnancy Risk Categories at the back of this book.

Animal Studies: Birth defects reported in rat studies; no defects reported in rabbit studies.

Human Studies: Adequate studies of pregnant women are not available. Single case of heart lesions. Ask your doctor for help.

Advisability of Use If Breast-Feeding

Presence of this drug in breast milk: Yes.
Nursing infant may develop skin rash, vomiting, or urine retention. Avoid drug or refrain from nursing.

Habit-Forming Potential: This drug has a potential for abuse because of its ability to cause euphoria, hallucinations, and feelings of detachment.

Effects of Overdose: Hyperactivity, disorientation, confusion, visual hallucinations, aggressive behavior, severe toxic psychosis, seizures, heart rhythm disturbances, drop in blood pressure.

Possible Effects of Long-Term Use: Livedo reticularis (see "Possible Side Effects" on page 79). Congestive heart failure in predisposed people.

Suggested Periodic Examinations While Taking This Drug (at physician's discretion)

White blood cell counts.
Liver and kidney function tests.
Evaluation of heart function.

▷ **While Taking This Drug, Observe the Following**
Foods: No restrictions.
Herbal Medicines or Minerals: Calabar bean (chop nut, Fabia, ordeal nut, others) is unsafe when taken by mouth (physostigmine is the active ingredient) and should never be taken by people with Parkinson's disease. Betel nut contains cholinergic compounds—will lower anticholinergic effect of amantadine, hence the combination is not recommended. Kava kava may block the effectiveness of amantadine. Health Canada has told their citizens not to take kava. Echinacea purpurea should be avoided by those with multiple sclerosis.
Beverages: No restrictions. May be taken with milk.
▷ *Alcohol:* May impair mental function, lower blood pressure excessively.
Tobacco Smoking: No interactions expected. I advise everyone to quit smoking.
Marijuana Smoking: Added drowsiness.
▷ *Other Drugs*
Amantadine may *increase* the effects of
• atropinelike drugs used to treat Parkinsonism, especially benztropine (Cogentin), orphenadrine (Disipal) and trihexyphenidyl (Artane). Amantadine can increase results, but if doses are too large, these drugs (taken with amantadine) may cause confusion, delirium, hallucinations, and nightmares.
• levodopa (Dopar, Larodopa, Sinemet, etc.) and enhance results. Combination use with levodopa finds most clinicians limiting amantadine dose to 100 mg once or twice daily while they increase the levodopa dose to best patient results. Patients should be observed for sudden mental disturbances and doses adjusted accordingly.
The following drugs may *increase* the effects of amantadine:
• amphetamine and amphetaminelike stimulant drugs may cause excessive stimulation and adverse behavioral effects.
• hydrochlorothiazide with triamterene may increase the blood level of amantadine and cause toxicity.
Amantadine *taken concurrently* with
• cotrimoxazole may increase risk of CNS stimulation or arrhythmias.
• hydrochlorothiazide (Dyazide, Esidrix, others) may increase risk of amantadine toxicity.
• sulfamethoxazole may increase risk of CNS stimulation or arrhythmia.
• triamterene may increase risk of CNS toxicity.
• trimethoprim may increase risk of CNS toxicity.
• zotepine (Nipolept) may decrease amantadine benefits.
▷ *Driving, Hazardous Activities:* May cause drowsiness, dizziness, blurred vision, or confusion. If these drug effects occur, avoid hazardous activities.
Aviation Note: The use of this drug *may be a disqualification* for piloting. Consult a designated Aviation Medical Examiner.
Exposure to Sun: No restrictions.
Exposure to Cold: Use caution. Excessive chilling may enhance the development of livedo reticularis (see "Possible Side Effects" on page 79).
Discontinuation: When used to treat Parkinsonism, this drug should not be stopped abruptly (slowly tapering is prudent). Sudden discontinuation may cause an acute Parkinsonian crisis and cases of delirium or catatonia have been described. When treating influenza A infections, drug is continued for 48 hours after symptoms stop.

AMILORIDE (a MIL oh ride)

Introduced: 1967   **Class:** Diuretic, potassium sparing diuretic
Prescription: USA: Yes   **Controlled Drug:** USA: No; Canada: No
Available as Generic: Yes

Brand Names: ❧Apo-Amilzide, Midamor, ❧Moduret [CD], Moduretic [CD],
❧Novamilor [CD], ❧Nu-Amilzide [CD], ❧Riva-Amilzide [CD]

BENEFITS versus RISKS	
Possible Benefits	*Possible Risks*
EFFECTIVE DIURETIC WITH DECREASED POTASSIUM LOSS	ABNORMALLY HIGH BLOOD POTASSIUM WITH EXCESSIVE USE
	Rare heart arrhythmias
	Rare kidney toxicity
	Rare liver toxicity

▷ **Principal Uses**

As a Single Drug Product: Uses currently included in FDA-approved labeling: (1) Eliminates excessive fluid (edema) seen in congestive heart failure; (2) treats high blood pressure, especially those prone to low potassium; (3) thiazide-caused low blood potassium.

As a Combination Drug Product [CD]: Combined with other thiazide diuretics to prevent excess potassium loss.

Other (unlabeled) generally accepted uses: (1) May be able to help dissolve kidney stones in patients unable to tolerate surgery; (2) can help correct increased urination that occurs in patients taking lithium; (3) can help prevent lowered magnesium and potassium seen in patients who are given amphotericin B for serious fungal infections.

How This Drug Works: This drug promotes loss of sodium and water from the body and potassium retention by altering kidney enzymes that control urine formation.

Available Dosage Forms and Strengths

Tablets — 5 mg
Combination Tablets — 5 mg amiloride and 50 mg hydrochlorothiazide

▷ **Usual Adult Dosage Ranges:** One 5-mg dose a day, preferably in the morning. May increase up to 15 mg daily as needed and tolerated. Should not exceed 20 mg every 24 hours.

Note: Actual dose and schedule must be determined for each patient individually.

Conditions Requiring Dosing Adjustments

Liver Function: Extreme caution in patients with severe liver disease.
Kidney Function: Should NOT be used in patients who can't make urine or who have acute kidney failure or creatinine clearance less than 50 ml/min.

▷ **Dosing Instructions:** Best taken when you wake up, with food. Tablet may be crushed for administration. If you forget a dose: Take the medicine right away, unless it is nearly time for your next dose, then omit the missed dose and take the medicine when it was next scheduled. DO NOT double doses. Once excess fluid is removed, use may be intermittent in some patients.

Usual Duration of Use: Ongoing long-term use to treat high blood pressure. Some clinicians use this medicine as needed (PRN) to remove abnormal fluid accumulation. Use every other day also minimizes imbalance of sodium and potassium.

Typical Treatment Goals and Measurements (Outcomes and Markers)

Blood Pressure: The NEW guidelines (JNC VII) define normal blood pressure (BP) as **less than** 120/80. Because blood pressures that were once considered acceptable can actually lead to blood vessel damage, the committee from the National Institutes of Health, National Heart Lung and Blood Institute now have a new category called **Pre-hypertension**. This ranges from 120/80 to 139/89 and is intended to help your doctor encourage lifestyle changes (or in the case of people with a risk factor for high blood pressure, start treatment) much earlier—so that possible damage to blood vessels, your heart, kidneys, sexual potency, or eyes might be minimized or avoided altogether. The next two classes of high blood pressure are stage 1 hypertension: 140/90 to 159/99 and stage 2 hypertension equal to or greater than: 160/100 mm Hg. These guidelines also recommend that clinicians trying to control blood pressure work with their patients to agree on the goals and a plan of treatment. The first-ever guidelines for blood pressure (hypertension) in African Americans recommends that MOST black patients be started on TWO antihypertensive medicines with the goal of lowering blood pressure to 130/80 for those with high risk for heart and blood vessel disease or with diabetes. The American Diabetes Association recommends 130/80 as the target for people living with diabetes and less than 125/75 for those who spill more than one gram of protein into their urine. Most clinicians try to achieve a BP that confers the best balance of lower cardiovascular risk and avoids the problem of too low a blood pressure. Blood pressure duration is generally increased with beneficial restriction of sodium. The goals and time frame should be discussed with you when the prescription is written. If goals are not met, it is not unusual to intensify doses or add on medicines. You can find the new blood pressure guidelines at *www.nhlbi.nih.gov/guidelines/hypertension/index.htm*. For the African American guidelines see Douglas J.G. in Sources.

▷ **This Drug Should Not Be Taken If**
- you have had an allergic reaction to it before.
- your blood potassium level is greater than 5.5 MEq per liter and/or your serum creatinine is more than 1.5 mg/dl and your blood urea nitrogen (BUN) is more than 30 mg/dl (talk to your doctor about this).
- you have diabetic nerve damage (diabetic nephropathy).
- your kidneys are not making urine (anuria).

▷ **Inform Your Physician Before Taking This Drug If**
- you are allergic to any similar drug.
- you have diabetes or glaucoma.
- you have reason to believe that minerals such as potassium or chloride (electrolytes) are out of balance in your body.
- you have kidney disease or impaired kidney function.
- you take a different diuretic, blood pressure drug, digitalis, or lithium.
- you don't know how much to take or how often to take it.

Possible Side Effects (natural, expected, and unavoidable drug actions)
Abnormally high blood potassium level—infrequent.
Abnormally low blood sodium level, dehydration, decreased blood magnesium, constipation—possible.
Dizziness on standing (orthostatic hypotension)—possible.

▷ **Possible Adverse Effects** (unusual, unexpected, and infrequent reactions)
   If any of the following develop, consult your physician promptly for guidance.
   Mild Adverse Effects
   Allergic reactions: skin rash, itching—rare-infrequent.
   Headache—infrequent.
   Dizziness, weakness, fatigue, numbness and tingling—case reports (related to electrolyte problems).
   Dry mouth, nausea, vomiting, stomach pains, diarrhea—infrequent.
   Decreased ability to taste salt, bad taste—possible.
   Loss of scalp hair—rare.
   Serious Adverse Effects
   Idiosyncratic reactions: joint and muscle pains.
   Liver or kidney toxicity—rare.
   Abnormally low sodium or high potassium—possible.
   Increased internal eye pressure (of concern in glaucoma)—rare.
   Depression, visual disturbances, ringing in ears, tremors—infrequent.
   Bone marrow depression—rare (questionable cause).
   Palpitations and arrhythmias—rare.
   Decreased circulation to the legs (with combination furosemide use)—case reports.

▷ **Possible Effects on Sexual Function:** Does not appear to be a present side effect.

Adverse Effects That May Mimic Natural Diseases or Disorders
   Nervousness, confusion, or depression may mimic spontaneous mental disorder.

Natural Diseases or Disorders That May Be Activated by This Drug
   Preexisting peptic ulcer, latent glaucoma.

Possible Effects on Laboratory Tests
   Blood cholesterol level: decreased.
   Blood creatinine level: increased with long-term use.
   Blood potassium level: possibly increased.
   Blood uric acid level: decreased with long-term use.
   Blood sodium level: possibly decreased.

CAUTION
   1. Do **NOT** take potassium supplements or eat more high-potassium foods.
   2. More frequent potassium levels are needed if you take digitalis compounds.
   3. Do not stop this drug abruptly unless your doctor says you must.

Precautions for Use
   By Infants and Children: Oral dosing with 0.625 mg per kg of body mass daily has been used to promote water loss (diuresis) in young patients weighing from 6 to 20 kg.
   By Those Over 60 Years of Age: Declines in kidney function may make it likely that you will retain potassium. Limit use of this drug to periods of 2 to 3 weeks if possible. The dose MUST be reduced. May cause too much water loss, possible increased tendency of the blood to clot, and increased risk of clots (thrombosis, heart attack, stroke).

▷ **Advisability of Use During Pregnancy**
   Pregnancy Category: B. See Pregnancy Risk Categories at the back of this book.
   Animal Studies: No birth defects reported.
   Human Studies: Adequate studies of pregnant women are not available.
   Use only if clearly needed.

Advisability of Use If Breast-Feeding
   Presence of this drug in breast milk: Unknown, but probably present.
   This drug may suppress milk production. Avoid drug if possible. If use is necessary, watch nursing infant closely and stop drug or nursing if adverse effects develop.

Habit-Forming Potential: None.

Effects of Overdose: Thirst, drowsiness, fatigue, weakness, nausea, vomiting, confusion, numbness and tingling of face and extremities, irregular heart rhythm, shortness of breath.

Suggested Periodic Examinations While Taking This Drug (at physician's discretion)
   Complete blood counts.
   Blood levels of sodium, potassium, magnesium, and chloride.
   Kidney function tests.
   Easing of edema.

▷ **While Taking This Drug, Observe the Following**
   Foods: Avoid excessive salt restriction and high-potassium foods. Taking this drug with food may help nausea and stomach upset.
   Herbal Medicines or Minerals: Ginseng may increase blood pressure, blunting the benefits of this medicine. Arginine (a medicine used to treat metabolic alkalosis but also found as supplements) has led to severe increases in potassium in some patients who had previously (and recently) been given spironolactone. Eleuthero root, guarana (high caffeine dose), hawthorn, saw palmetto, ma huang (should not be combined), goldenseal, and licorice may cause increased blood pressure—blunting the beneficial effects of this medicine. Licorice may also increase hypokalemia risk. Couch grass may worsen edema due to heart or kidney problems. Indian snakeroot, calcium, and garlic may help lower blood pressure. Talk to your doctor and pharmacist BEFORE adding any herbal medicines.
   Beverages: Caffeine may increase blood pressure. Talk to your doctor about consumption. May be taken with milk.
▷ *Alcohol:* Use caution. Alcohol can exaggerate the blood-pressure-lowering effect of this drug and cause orthostatic hypotension (see Glossary).
   Tobacco Smoking: No interactions expected. I advise everyone to quit smoking.
▷ *Other Drugs*
   Amiloride may *increase* the effects of
   • other blood-pressure-lowering drugs. Dose decreases may be needed.
   Amiloride may *decrease* the effects of
   • digoxin (Lanoxin, etc.) and reduce its effect in treating heart failure.
   Amiloride *taken concurrently* with
   • ACE inhibitors (see Drug Classes) such as benazepril or angiotensin II antagonists (valsartan [Diovan], etc.) may result in abnormally high blood potassium.
   • arginine (various) may cause extreme and life-threatening potassium increases.
   • chlorpropamide (Diabinese) may lead to excessively low blood sodium.
   • cyclosporine (Sandimmune, others) may cause excessively high potassium levels.
   • digoxin (Lanoxin) may decrease benefits (positive inotropic effect) of digoxin.
   • dofetilide (Tikosyn) may cause serious irregular heartbeats. Combine only with great caution and careful patient monitoring.

- lithium (Lithobid) may cause lithium toxicity.
- metformin (Glucophage) may increase Glucophage levels and increase lactic acidosis (cationic drug interaction) or excessively lowered blood sugar (hypoglycemia) risk.
- NSAIDs (see Drug Classes) may decrease therapeutic effect.
- potassium supplements may result in extremely elevated blood potassium levels.
- quinidine (Quinaglute, others) may prolong the QRS interval and increase risk of abnormal heartbeats.
- spironolactone (Aldactone, Aldactazide) or triamterene (Dyrenium, Dyazide) may cause dangerous potassium levels. Avoid combining.
- tacrolimus (Prograf) may cause excessive potassium levels. Increased potassium checks are prudent.
- triamterene (Dyazide) may cause excessively high potassium levels and should not be combined.
- valsartan (Diovan) may cause excessively high potassium levels. Caution and more frequent checks of potassium are needed if this combination is undertaken.

▷ *Driving, Hazardous Activities:* May cause drowsiness, dizziness and orthostatic hypotension. If these drug effects occur, avoid hazardous activities.

Aviation Note: The use of this drug *may be a disqualification* for piloting. Consult a designated Aviation Medical Examiner.

Exposure to Sun: No restrictions.

Exposure to Heat: Caution is advised. Excessive sweating can cause water, sodium and potassium imbalance. Hot environments can cause lowering of blood pressure.

Occurrence of Unrelated Illness: Call your doctor if you contract an illness causing vomiting or diarrhea.

Discontinuation: With high doses or prolonged use, withdraw this drug gradually. Excessive potassium loss may occur with sudden withdrawal.

AMINOPHYLLINE (am in OFF i lin)

Other Name: Theophylline ethylenediamine

Introduced: 1910   **Class:**   Antiasthmatic, bronchodilator, xanthines
Prescription: USA: Yes   **Controlled Drug:**   USA: No; Canada: No
Available as Generic: Yes

Brand Names   Aminophyllin, Mudrane [CD], Mudrane GG [CD], ♣Palaron, Phyllocontin, Somophyllin, ♣Somophyllin-12, Truphylline

Author's Note: This drug is actually (79%) theophylline. See the theophylline profile for further details.

AMIODARONE (AM EE oh dur ohn)

Introduced: 1986   **Class:**   Antiarrhythmic, Class III agent   **Prescription:**   USA: Yes   **Controlled Drug:**   USA: No; Canada: No
Available as Generic: Yes

Brand Names: Cordarone, ♣Alti-Amiodarone, Braxan, ♣Gen-Amiodarone, ♣Med-Amiodarone, ♣Novo-Amiodarone, Pacerone

```
                    BENEFITS versus RISKS
      Possible Benefits                    Possible Risks
EFFECTIVE TREATMENT OF          SIGNIFICANT LIVER ENZYME
  SELECTED LIFE-THREATENING       (CYP3A) DRUG INTERACTIONS
  HEART RHYTHM DISORDERS        LUNG (PULMONARY) TOXICITY
TREATMENT OF ATRIAL             SLOWED HEART RATE
  FIBRILLATION (LOW MEDICINE      (BRADYCARDIA)
  DOSE)                         Some isolated cases of arrhythmia
PREVENTION OF ATRIAL             worsening
  FIBRILLATION RECURRENCE       Tingling in the extremities (peripheral
  (LOW DOSE)                      neuropathy)
BENEFICIAL EFFECTS ON HEART     Liver toxicity
  FAILURE                       Changes in thyroid gland function
INTRAVENOUS USE OF GREAT          (hypo or hyper)
  BENEFIT (NEWER DATA) IN       Heart conduction or rhythm
  CARDIAC ARREST AND IN           abnormalities
  ADVANCED CARDIAC LIFE         Microdeposits in the eye (cornea)
  SUPPORT (ACLS) WHEN           Very long half-life
  CARDIAC ARREST HAS
  RESULTED FROM (SECONDARY
  TO) VENTRICULAR
  ARRHYTHMIA
EFFECTIVE IN TREATING
  VENTRICULAR ARRHYTHMIAS
  AND FAST HEART RATE
  (TACHYCARDIA) THAT HAS
  FAILED TO RESPOND TO
  (REFRACTORY) TO OTHER
  AGENTS
Very long half-life
```

▷ **Principal Uses**

As a Single Drug Product: Uses currently included in FDA-approved labeling: (1) Treats abnormal rhythms in the heart ventricles (life-threatening ventricular arrhythmias such as recurrent hemodynamically unstable ventricular tachycardia).

Other (unlabeled) generally accepted uses: (1) Chest pain (angina pectoris); (2) suppression of abnormal heart rhythms in severe congestive heart failure (CHF) and may ease CHF itself; (3) effective in treating ventricular arrhythmias seen in heart inflammation patients (myocarditis) caused by Chagas' disease; (4) supraventricular arrhythmias (such as atrial fibrillation); (5) treats drug-induced (sotalol) Torsade de Pointes; (6) survivors of sudden heart attack (acute myocardial infarction) who have frequent or repetitive premature ventricular depolarizations (VPDs) may benefit from amiodarone therapy; (7) prevented repeat (recurrent) atrial fibrillation better than propafenone or sotalol in the Canadian CTAF study.

Author's Note: The manufacturer had a registry called the ARRIVE Registry (Advanced Resuscitation of Refractory VT/VF I.V. Amiodarone Evaluation. Further information is available at *www.cordarone.com/news/arrive.asp.*

How This Drug Works: Originally classified as a class three antiarrhythmic. Appears to work on the complete spectrum (blocks the sodium channel, slows heart rate and impedes the AV node by blocking beta-adrenergic receptors as well as calcium channels) of classes. It also lengthens ventricular and atrial repolarization time by inhibiting the potassium channel. These effects help restore normal heart rate and rhythm. Amiodarone also decreases cytokines (such as interleukin 6 or IL-6), which may explain its benefits in heart failure. Prior TNF alpha data does not appear to be explanatory of benefits.

Available Dosage Forms and Strengths

Injection — 50 mg/ml

Tablet — 200 mg, 400 mg

▷ **Usual Adult Dosage Ranges:** *Supraventricular arrhythmias:* Oral dosing has been started at 600–1,200 mg daily for one to two weeks, and then lowered (tapered) to 400–600 mg daily for one to three weeks and then lowered further to the lowest possible ongoing (maintenance) dose. The typical blood (serum) level in patients who have been successfully treated was 1.9 micrograms per milliliter and the median dose was 200 mg a day in one study. One Canadian study used 10 mg/kg per day for at least 14 days which was followed by 300 mg a day for 4 weeks, then 200 mg a day. Additional studies are needed. Some patients over 60 years old have gained control of their atrial fibrillation using 100 mg a day.

Ventricular arrhythmias: Oral doses are 800–1,600 mg per day as a loading dose for one to three weeks or longer (based on how well the heart rhythm problem responds), and then doses are gradually lowered to no more than 400 mg a day. Some European clinicians use generally lower ongoing doses. In the ALIVE trial, intravenous doses of 5 mg/kg were given versus 1.5 mg/kg of lidocaine. In hemodynamically unstable ventricular tachycardia or ventricular fibrillation, the manufacturer recommends loading doses as above. Giving the medicine with meals in divided doses if more than 1,000 mg is required is recommended. Once the heart rhythm is under control, doses can often then be lowered to 600–800 mg a day for a month, then to 400–600mg a day. Ongoing doses are then given once or twice a day depending on patient response.

Note: Actual dose and schedule must be determined for each patient individually.

Conditions Requiring Dosing Adjustments

Liver Function: Dosing hasn't been studied in liver failure, but since there is extensive liver metabolism, decreased doses and use of blood levels to guide dosing appear prudent in liver compromise. The medicine is also removed in the bile. Talk to your doctor if you have a block or periodic block in your bile duct (such as a gallstone) and this medicine is being considered.

Kidney Function: Dosing changes do NOT appear to be needed.

▷ **Dosing Instructions:** Tablets should be swallowed whole and may be taken with or following food to reduce stomach irritation. If you forget to take a dose: omit that dose and continue with the next scheduled dose. If you forget to take it for two or more days—call your doctor.

Usual Duration of Use: Regular use for 10 days may be required (with oral dosing) to begin to help ventricular tachycardia, but may take three to six weeks. Several months may be required to see the peak benefits. Long-term use requires supervision and ongoing evaluation by your doctor.

Typical Treatment Goals and Measurements (Outcomes and Markers)

Abnormal heartbeats: The general goal is to return the heart to a normal rhythm or at least to markedly reduce the occurrence of abnormal heartbeats. In life-threatening arrhythmias, the goal is to abort the abnormal beats and return the pattern to normal. Some increase in the QT interval (10–15% corrected for rate) may be seen when loading doses are being used, but is generally not a reliable prediction of serum amiodarone or desmethylamiodarone levels. Success at ongoing suppression may involve ambulatory checks of heart rate and rhythm for a day (such as in Holter monitoring). This kind of testing involves placement of adhesive-backed temporary electrodes on the skin in several positions around the heart. A small heart rate and rhythm (EKG or ECG) recording device is carried around via a shoulder strap and records what the heart is doing over 24 hours. Once the recording is made, a scanning machine reviews the record, tallies abnormal heartbeats or rhythms and gives a close and extended look at how the heart is reacting or benefiting from the medicines that the patient is taking. Repeat measurements can be made if doses are changed to check the success at keeping the heart in normal sinus rhythm! In cases where the heart stops (cardiac arrest) this medicine was nearly two times as effective as lidocaine (see ALIVE trial in sources).

Possible Advantages of This Drug: Other antiarrhythmics such as quinidine and procainamide can be associated with development of antinuclear antibodies (ANA). One study showed that amiodarone does NOT induce ANA. Because of its broad mechanism of action, amiodarone may be effective where other antiarrhythmics fail. Has additional direct beneficial effects on heart failure that other heart rhythm modifiers do not have. A sub study of the Atrial Fibrillation follow-up Investigation of Rhythm Management (AFFIRM) showed that amiodarone is the most effective medicine at keeping patients in normal sinus rhythm, helping them avoid cardioversion, staying alive and staying on the same medicine.

▷ **This Drug Should Not Be Taken If**
- you had an allergic reaction to amiodarone or similar drugs.
- you have second-degree, third-degree AV block (and do not have a pacemaker).
- you have "sick sinus" syndrome or severe heart slowing (sinus bradycardia—talk with your doctor).
- you are in heart (cardiogenic) shock.

▷ **Inform Your Physician Before Taking This Drug If**
- you have had unfavorable reactions to antiarrhythmic drugs.
- you have heart disease, especially "heart block."
- you have a history of heart attack, heart muscle changes (cardiomegaly), slow heartbeat or low blood pressure (especially with intravenous dosing).
- you have had a heart attack.
- you have impaired liver function.
- you have low blood platelets.
- your vision is impaired (this drug may cause microdeposits on the cornea).
- your blood electrolytes (such as potassium or magnesium) are not in balance.
- you have lung disease (pulmonary dysfunction).
- you live or will travel to a place where your heart rhythm cannot be checked (this medicine can help abnormal heartbeats, but may also worsen them and this must be checked when treatment is started).
- the left ventricle of your heart does not work correctly (left ventricular dysfunction).
- you have thyroid problems (hypo or hyper thyroidism).

- your job requires you to work outside in the sun or you already take other medicines that can increase sun sensitivity.

Possible Side Effects (natural, expected, and unavoidable drug actions)

Inflammation of the vein (with intravenous use)—possible.

Asymptomatic microdeposits in the cornea—frequent with long-term (more than six months) use.

▷ **Possible Adverse Effects** (unusual, unexpected, and infrequent reactions)

If any of the following develop, consult your physician promptly for guidance.

Mild Adverse Effects

Allergic reactions: skin rash, itching—case reports.

Blue-gray skin discoloration—rare to frequent (also sun sensitivity—see below).

Hair loss (alopecia)—rare to infrequent.

Headache, tiredness or sleep disturbances—rare-infrequent.

Movement problems (incoordination-ataxia), fatigue, dizziness—infrequent.

Lowered blood pressure (more common with the intravenous form)—up to frequent.

Swelling of the epididymis (epididymitis)—infrequent.

Increased serum creatinine—possible.

Cholesterol changes (increased in one study and lowered in another)—possible.

Increased liver function tests—infrequent to frequent (should be clinically monitored and dose lowered or medicine stopped if persistent).

Loss of appetite, taste disturbances, indigestion, nausea, vomiting—infrequent to frequent (usually responds to dosing adjustment or dividing).

Increased creatinine—case reports (usually happens during first six months of treatment).

Serious Adverse Effects

Allergic reaction—toxic epidermal necrolysis (TEN)—case report.

Neuropathy—frequent.

Abnormal thyroid function (hypo or hyper)—rare to frequent (may happen within one to 73 months).

Abnormal heart rhythm (such as excessive heart slowing-bradycardia)—infrequent.

Torsades de pointes—rare.

Lung toxicity (pulmonary)—rare to frequent (includes fatal cases).

High blood sugar (glucose)—rare (not seen in a small later study).

Abnormal blood sodium (syndrome of inappropriate antidiuretic hormone-SIADH)-case reports.

Abnormal movement (possible neurotoxic reaction)—may be frequent and may relate to large loading doses or ongoing doses more than 600 mg.

Jaundice (see Glossary) or liver toxicity—infrequent.

Optic neuritis, corneal changes—rare.

Abnormally low blood platelets, anemia, and pancytopenia—case reports-rare.

▷ **Possible Effects on Sexual Function:** Impotence or loss of libido—case reports. Swelling and tenderness of male breast tissue (gynecomastia)—case report.

Adverse Effects That May Mimic Natural Diseases or Disorders

Reversible jaundice may suggest viral hepatitis. Abnormal heart rhythms may mimic slow (brady) arrhythmias from other causes.

Natural Diseases or Disorders That May Be Activated by This Drug
> Abnormal heart rhythms, abnormal thyroid function, epididymal swelling may mimic infectious epididymitis.

Possible Effects on Laboratory Tests
> Blood platelets: rarely decreased.
> Liver function tests: increased liver enzymes (ALT/GPT, AST/GOT, and alkaline phosphatase), increased bilirubin.
> Abnormally low sodium (SIADH)—case reports.
> Blood urea nitrogen (BUN)—increased.
> Increased or decreased thyroid function.

CAUTION
1. Thorough heart exam (including electrocardiogram) is critical prior to using this drug.
2. Periodic heart exams are needed to follow drug responses. Some people may have heart rhythm or function declines. Close monitoring of heart rate, rhythm and overall performance is essential.
3. Dose must be individualized. Do not change your dose without your doctor's supervision.
4. Talk with your doctor about signs and symptoms of thyroid function changes. This medicine contains iodine; consequently protein-bound iodine (PBI) testing will NOT detect thyroid problems.
5. Do not take any other antiarrhythmic drug while taking this drug unless directed to do so by your doctor.

Precautions for Use
> *By Infants and Children:* In pediatric patients, amiodarone is given on a mg-per-kg-of-body-mass basis. Dose is then divided into equal doses, given at times determined by patient response. Some patients from one to four years old will receive 10 to 20 mg per kg of body mass per day, divided into equal doses and given every six hours. Initial use of this drug requires hospitalization and supervision by a qualified pediatrician.
> *By Those Over 60 Years of Age:* Watch closely for light-headedness, dizziness, unsteadiness and tendency to fall. Older patients may be more susceptible to problems from heart slowing and should be closely followed once this medicine is started.

▷ **Advisability of Use During Pregnancy**
> *Pregnancy Category:* D. See Pregnancy Risk Categories at the back of this book.
> *Animal Studies:* Can cause thyroid changes, maternal and embryo death in rabbits given 10 mg per kg or greater.
> *Human Studies:* Adequate studies of pregnant women are not available. This medicine should be used only if the potential benefit outweighs fetal risk.

Advisability of Use If Breast-Feeding
> Presence of this drug in breast milk: Yes.
> Refrain from nursing.

Habit-Forming Potential: None.

Effects of Overdose: Extremely slow heart rate (bradycardia), excessively low blood pressure, heart block (AV) and possibly cardiogenic shock as well as liver toxicity.

Possible Effects of Long-Term Use: Microdeposits in the cornea of the eye.

Suggested Periodic Examinations While Taking This Drug (at physician's discretion)

Liver function tests BEFORE starting treatment and every six months thereafter.

Electrocardiograms.

Complete blood counts.

Blood levels.

Vision checks periodically throughout therapy.

▷ **While Taking This Drug, Observe the Following**

Foods: No restrictions. Food may actually help avoid upset stomach.

Herbal Medicines or Minerals: Using St. John's wort, ma huang, ephedra, guarana, or kola while taking this medicine may result in unacceptable heart stimulation. Belladonna, henbane, *Scopolia*, pheasant's eye extract or lily-of-the-valley, or squill powdered extracts should NOT be taken if you have abnormal heart rhythms. Eucalyptus and skull cap may increase liver toxicity risk. Since St. John's wort and amiodarone may increase sun sensitivity, the combination is NOT advised. Pyridoxine may increase risk of phototoxicity.

Beverages: Your doctor may ask you to restrict caffeine intake. May be taken with milk.

▷ *Alcohol:* Use caution. Alcohol can increase the blood-pressure-lowering effects and may have an undesirable effect on heart rhythm in high doses.

Tobacco Smoking: Nicotine can irritate the heart, reducing effectiveness. I advise everyone to quit smoking.

▷ *Other Drugs*

Amiodarone may ***increase*** the effects of

- antihypertensive drugs and cause excessive lowering of blood pressure.
- atropinelike drugs (see Drug Classes).
- cyclosporine (Sandimmune, others) and lead to cyclosporine toxicity if cyclosporine doses are not lowered.
- digoxin (Lanoxin) by increasing blood level.
- procainamide (Procan SR, others) and NAPA.
- warfarin (Coumadin, etc.); check INR (prothrombin times) more often, and adjust dosing.

Amiodarone ***taken concurrently*** with

- amprenavir (Agenerase), indinavir (Crixivan), ritonavir (Norvir), and perhaps other protease inhibitors (see Drug Classes) may increase amiodarone blood levels and lead to toxicity.
- beta blockers (see Drug Classes) may result in abnormally low heart rates or sinus arrest. Extreme caution is advised.
- calcium channel blockers (see Drug Classes) should be avoided in patients with partial block (AV) or sick sinus syndrome.
- cimetidine (Tagamet) can increase amiodarone levels.
- cisapride (Propulsid) may lead to serious heart rhythm problems. DO NOT COMBINE.
- clonazepam (Klonopin) caused clonazepam toxicity in one case report. Caution is advised.
- digoxin (Lanoxin) can cause digoxin toxicity.
- disopyramide (Norpace) can prolong QT interval and lead to abnormal heart rhythms.
- dofetilide (Tikosyn) can lead to heart toxicity.
- dolasetron (Anzemet) can lead to heart toxicity.

- fentanyl (Actiq, Duragesic) may lead to low blood pressure, slow heart rate and lowered ability of the heart to work (cardiac output).
- flecainide (Tambocor) may allow lower flecainide dose to get the same effect.
- gatifloxacin (Tequin), levofloxacin (Levaquin), sparfloxacin (Zagam), and other quinolone antibiotics (see drug classes) may result in abnormal QT intervals and lead to abnormal heart rhythms. DO NOT COMBINE.
- halofantrine (Halfan) can lead to heart toxicity.
- ibutilide (Corvert) can lead to excessively refractory ventricles and atria of the heart.
- indinavir (Crixivan) can lead to amiodarone toxicity.
- insulin or oral antidiabetic drugs (see Drug Classes) may result in blunted blood sugar benefits.
- lidocaine (various) may lead to lidocaine toxicity. Extreme caution is advised.
- methotrexate (Rheumatrex, others) increases risk of methotrexate toxicity. Extreme caution is advised.
- mexiletine (Mexitil) may result in abnormal heart beats. Caution is advised.
- moxifloxacin (Avelox) may result in abnormal heart beats. DO NOT COMBINE.
- nelfinavir (Viracept) may result in amiodarone toxicity. DO NOT COMBINE.
- phenytoin (Dilantin) or fosphenytoin (Cerebyx) can result in phenytoin, phosphenytoin, and amiodarone toxicity.
- propafenone (Rythmol) may lead to propafenone toxicity. Reduced propafenone doses may be needed.
- quinidine can cause increases in quinidine levels.
- ritonavir (Norvir) may increase amiodarone levels and could result in abnormal heart beats. DO NOT COMBINE.
- sotalol (Betapace) may result in increased risk of abnormal heart rhythms because of prolongation of the QT interval. This combination is NOT recommended.
- verapamil (Calan, others) can precipitate or worsen congestive heart failure.
- ziprasidone (Geodon) may prolong the QT interval. DO NOT combine.

The following drugs may *decrease* the effects of amiodarone:

- cholestyramine (Questran, others) by increasing removal (enterohepatic elimination) of amiodarone.
- rifabutin (Mycobutin).
- rifampin (Rimactane, Rifadin).

▷ *Driving, Hazardous Activities:* May cause dizziness or blurred vision. Limit activities as needed.

Aviation Note: The use of this drug *may be a disqualification* for piloting. Consult a designated Aviation Medical Examiner.

Exposure to Sun: Use caution. This drug causes photosensitization (see Glossary).

Exposure to Heat: Use caution. The use of this drug in hot environments may increase the risk of heatstroke.

Occurrence of Unrelated Illness: Vomiting, diarrhea, or dehydration can affect this drug's action adversely. Report such developments promptly.

Discontinuation: This drug should not be stopped abruptly after long-term use. Ask your doctor for help regarding gradual dose reduction.

AMITRIPTYLINE (a mee TRIP ti leen)

Introduced: 1961   **Class:**   Antidepressant   **Prescription:**   USA:
Yes   **Controlled Drug:**   USA: No; Canada: No   **Available as Generic:**
Yes

Brand Names: Amitid, Amitril, ❧Apo-Amitriptyline, ❧Elatrol, Elavil,
❧Elavil Plus [CD], Emitrip, Endep, Enovil, ❧Entrafon-Plus [CD], Etrafon
[CD], ❧Etrafon-A [CD], ❧Etrafon-D [CD], Etrafon-Forte [CD], ❧Levate,
❧Novo-Triptyn, PMS-Levazine [CD], Limbitrol [CD], SK-Amitriptyline,
❧Triavil [CD]

BENEFITS versus RISKS

Possible Benefits	*Possible Risks*
EFFECTIVE RELIEF OF ENDOGENOUS DEPRESSION	ADVERSE BEHAVIORAL EFFECTS: Confusion, disorientation, hallucinations
Additive (adjunctive) therapy in some pain syndromes (such as peripheral neuropathic pain or pain after herpes infections—post-herpetic neuralgia)	CONVERSION OF DEPRESSION TO MANIA in manic-depressive disorders
	Irregular heart rhythms—possible
	Blood cell abnormalities—rare

▷ **Principal Uses**

As a Single Drug Product: Uses currently included in FDA-approved labeling:
(1) Eases symptoms of spontaneous (endogenous) depression; (2) helps
depression resistant (refractory) to a single medicine.

Other (unlabeled) generally accepted uses: (1) Additive (adjuvant) therapy in
chronic pain/pain syndromes (such as peripheral neuropathic pain); (2)
eases agitation; (3) helps diabetic nerve (neuropathy) pain; (4) is an alternative in intractable hiccups; (5) combined with other medicines to ease
the pain of postherpetic neuralgia; (6) some benefit easing pain of chronic
vulvar burning (vulvodynia); (7) used in fish (ciguatera) poisoning.

As a Combination Drug Product [CD]: Combined with chlordiazepoxide to relieve
anxiety and depression. Also available in combination with perphenazine, a
phenothiazine, to relieve severe agitation that may occur with depression.

How This Drug Works: Eases depression by restoring normal levels of two nerve
impulse chemicals (norepinephrine and serotonin).

Available Dosage Forms and Strengths

Injection — 10 mg/ml

Oral suspension — 10 mg/5 ml

Tablets — 10 mg, 25 mg, 50 mg, 75 mg, 100 mg, 150 mg

▷ **Usual Adult Dosage Ranges:** Intramuscular injection is given as 80 to 120 mg
per day divided into four doses. Switch to oral form made as soon as possible. Oral dosing starts with 25 mg two to three times daily. May be
increased cautiously as needed/tolerated by 10 to 25 mg daily at intervals
of 1 week with dose increases usually made later in the day or at bedtime.
Usual ongoing dose is 50 to 100 mg daily. Total dose should not exceed 150
mg daily. Once the best dose is found, it may be taken at bedtime as one
dose. Some clinicians start with 50 mg at bedtime.

**Note: Actual dose and schedule must be determined for each patient
individually.**

Conditions Requiring Dosing Adjustments
> *Liver Function:* Specific guidelines not available; however, low doses and a check of blood levels are prudent.
>
> *Kidney Function:* Lower doses and blood level checks are needed with kidney failure (18% of drug is removed this way).

▷ **Dosing Instructions:** May be taken without regard to meals. Immediate-release form tablets may be crushed to take it. DO NOT CRUSH SUSTAINED-RELEASE form (available in Great Britain). If you forget a dose: Take the medicine right away, unless it is nearly time for your next dose. If you only take one dose at bedtime, don't take the missed dose in the morning, skip the missed dose and take the next dose right on schedule. DO NOT double doses.

Usual Duration of Use: Some benefit in depression in 1 to 2 weeks, but peak benefit may take 30 days or longer. Some clinicians quicken the onset of tricyclic antidepressants like amitriptyline by adding thyroid supplements. This benefit seems to particularly work well in women. Long-term use of antidepressants should not exceed 6 months without follow-up evaluation. In a set of guidelines issued by the American College of Physicians, older and newer antidepressants were found to give equal results in treating depression, but the general characteristics were different. Older medicines were found to generally have more frequent constipation, dizziness, dry mouth, blurred vision, and tremors while newer medicines caused more diarrhea, headache, and nausea. The importance here is that many options are available and possible side effects can be somewhat tailored to try to avoid overlap. Start (onset) of benefits in pain management may happen more quickly than in depression.

Typical Treatment Goals and Measurements (Outcomes and Markers)
> *Depression:* The general goal: to lessen the degree and severity of depression, letting patients return to their daily lives. Specific measures of depression involve testing or inventories (such as the Hamilton Depression Inventory) and can be valuable in helping check benefits from this medicine.
>
> *Pain syndromes:* The general goal: to decrease pain to a manageable level. Pain should be appropriately checked (assessed), and progress defined based on lowering of overall pain level and improved quality of life. A PQRSTBG (see Glossary) and patient goal assessment should be made and rechecked.

▷ **This Drug Should Not Be Taken If**
- you are allergic to any of the brand names listed above.
- you are taking, or have taken within the past 14 days, any monoamine oxidase (MAO) type A inhibitor drug (see Drug Classes) or are taking cisapride.
- you are recovering from a recent heart attack (MI or myocardial infarction).
- you are pregnant.

▷ **Inform Your Physician Before Taking This Drug If**
- you have a history of diabetes, epilepsy (or other seizure disorder), glaucoma, heart disease, prostate gland enlargement (or urinary outflow problems), or overactive thyroid function.
- you will have surgery with general anesthesia.
- you have heart-induced chest pain (angina pectoris).
- you have a rapid heart rate that occurs spontaneously (paroxysmal tachycardia).
- you have narrow-angle glaucoma.
- you are unsure how much or how often to take this drug.
- you have a history of schizophrenia—this drug may worsen any paranoia.

- you have a history of prostate or sexual problems.
- you have a liver or kidney disorder.
- you have a blood cell disorder.
- you have a history of intestinal block (ileus).

Possible Side Effects (natural, expected, and unavoidable drug actions)
Drowsiness, blurred vision, dry mouth, constipation, impaired urination.

▷ **Possible Adverse Effects** (unusual, unexpected, and infrequent reactions)
If any of the following develop, consult your physician promptly for guidance.

Mild Adverse Effects

Allergic reactions: skin rash, hives, swelling of face or tongue, drug fever (see Glossary).

Headache, dizziness, weakness, fainting, unsteady gait, tremors—infrequent.

Ringing in the ears (tinnitus)—reported with other medicines in the same family.

Peculiar taste, irritation of tongue or mouth, nausea, indigestion—rare to infrequent.

Fluctuation of blood sugar levels—possible.

Increased dental cavities (caries)—increased risk.

Restlessness, nightmares—rare.

Change in the ability to perceive tones—case report.

Serious Adverse Effects

Allergic reactions: hepatitis (see Glossary).

Idiosyncratic reactions: neuroleptic malignant syndrome (see Glossary).

Confusion or hallucinations—may be more likely in older patients and with higher doses.

Bowel obstruction (ileus)—rare.

SIADH (see Glossary)—rare.

Excessively low blood pressure (hypotension)—possible.

Seizures—rare.

Severe eye or other movement problems—case reports.

Heart palpitation and irregular rhythm—rare and more likely with increasing doses or overdose.

Bone marrow depression (see Glossary): fatigue, weakness, fever, sore throat, abnormal bleeding or bruising—rare.

A lupus erythematosus–like syndrome has been reported.

Peripheral neuritis (see Glossary): numbness, tingling, pain, loss of arm or leg strength—possible.

Parkinson-like disorders (see Glossary): often mild and infrequent—more likely in the elderly.

Liver toxicity—rare.

Serotonin syndrome—possible.

Worsening of paranoid psychosis in schizophrenic patients—possible.

▷ **Possible Effects on Sexual Function:**

Decreased libido—rare.

Increased libido (possible antidepressant effect), inhibited female orgasm, inhibited ejaculation—case reports.

Male and female breast enlargement, milk production, swelling of testicles, impotence—case reports.

These effects usually disappear within 2 to 10 days after discontinuation of the drug.

Adverse Effects That May Mimic Natural Diseases or Disorders
Liver toxicity may suggest viral hepatitis.

Natural Diseases or Disorders That May Be Activated by This Drug
Latent diabetes, epilepsy, glaucoma, impaired urination due to prostate.

Possible Effects on Laboratory Tests
Complete blood counts: decreased white cells, and platelets; increased eosinophils.
Liver function tests: increased ALT/GPT, AST/GOT, alkaline phosphatase, increased bilirubin.
Blood glucose levels: increased or decreased (fluctuations).

CAUTION
1. Make sure you make follow-up visits to your doctor.
2. Best to withhold this drug if electroconvulsive therapy (ECT, "shock" treatment) is to be used.

Precautions for Use
By Infants and Children: Safety and effectiveness for those under 12 years old not established.
By Those Over 60 Years of Age: During the first 2 weeks watch for confusion, agitation, forgetfulness, delusions, and hallucinations. Decreased dose or stopping the drug may be needed. Unsteadiness may predispose to falling and injury. May worsen impaired urination seen with prostate gland enlargement (prostatism).

▷ **Advisability of Use During Pregnancy**
Pregnancy Category: C. See Pregnancy Risk Categories at the back of this book.
Animal Studies: Skull deformities reported in rabbits.
Human Studies: There have been reports of developmental delays, limb deformities, and central nervous system (CNS) problems in infants whose mothers had taken amitriptyline during pregnancy. Adequate studies of pregnant women are not available.
Use during pregnancy is a benefit-to-risk decision.

Advisability of Use If Breast-Feeding
Presence of this drug in breast milk: Yes.
One source says this medicine is NOT compatible with breast-feeding. Product insert notes levels of up to 151 ng/ml in breast milk—yet undetectable levels in the infant serum. Best to talk to your doctor about the benefits versus risks of breast feeding if you are taking this medicine.

Habit-Forming Potential: If prolonged therapy has been given, stopping this medicine suddenly can lead to headache, nausea, and weakness (malaise). Rare reports of hypomania or mania have been made 2 to 7 days after stopping therapy with tricyclic antidepressants.

Effects of Overdose: Confusion, hallucinations, marked drowsiness, heart palpitations, dilated pupils, tremors, stupor, deep sleep, coma, convulsions.

Suggested Periodic Examinations While Taking This Drug (at physician's discretion)
Complete blood cell counts.
Liver function tests.
Serial blood pressure readings and electrocardiograms.

▷ **While Taking This Drug, Observe the Following**
Foods: Excessive vitamin C can blunt therapeutic benefit of this drug. May also increase appetite and cause excessive weight gain.

Herbal Medicines or Minerals: Since amitriptyline and St. John's wort may act to increase serotonin, the combination is not advised. St. John's wort also increases sun sensitivity. Since part of the way ginseng works may be as a MAO inhibitor, do not combine with amitriptyline. Indian snakeroot, kava kava and yohimbe are also best avoided while taking this medicine.

Beverages: No restrictions. May be taken with milk.

▷ *Alcohol:* Even modest amounts of alcohol can lead to blackouts. Discuss any alcohol use with your doctor as this combination can markedly increase the intoxicating effects of alcohol and brain function depression. Many clinicians advise avoiding alcohol.

Tobacco Smoking: May hasten the removal of this drug from your body. I advise you to quit smoking.

▷ *Other Drugs*

Amitriptyline may ***increase*** the effects of
- albuterol or other direct sympathomimetic drugs (amphetamines, epinephrine).
- antihistamines (such as diphenhydramine—Benadryl, others), which can increase the risk of urinary retention, chronic glaucoma, and bowel obstruction (ileus). This is especially problematic in the elderly.
- atropinelike drugs (see Drug Classes).
- cimetidine (Tagamet).
- disulfiram (Antabuse), which can worsen the disulfiram effect if alcohol is consumed, but may also lead to decreased mental status.

Amitriptyline may ***decrease*** the effects of
- clonidine (Catapres).
- guanethidine (Ismelin).
- guanfacine (Tenex).
- methyldopa, which can result in reduced amitriptyline and/or methyldopa benefits.

Amitriptyline ***taken concurrently*** with
- amphetamines can cause excessive amitriptyline responses.
- amprenavir (Agenerase), ritonavir (Norvir) and perhaps other protease inhibitors (see Drug Classes) can lead to amitriptyline toxicity.
- anticoagulants such as warfarin (Coumadin) may cause an increased risk of bleeding.
- baclofen (Lioresal) may lead to muscle weakness and memory loss.
- bepridil (Vascor) can lead to heart rhythm problems. DO NOT COMBINE.
- carbamazepine (Tegretol) may decrease the blood level of amitriptyline.
- cisapride (Propulsid) can lead to heart rhythm problems. DO NOT COMBINE.
- diazepam (Valium) and perhaps other benzodiazepines (see Drug Classes) can result in additive loss of psychomotor skills.
- dofetilide (Tikosyn) can lead to heart rhythm problems. DO NOT COMBINE.
- enflurane (various) may increase seizure risk. DO NOT COMBINE.
- epinephrine may cause an increased risk of rapid heart rate and high blood pressure.
- estrogens (see Drug Classes) may increase amitriptyline drug levels.
- ethanol (alcohol) may give additive central nervous system toxicity.
- fluconazole (Diflucan) can result in very high levels of amitriptyline.
- fluoxetine (Prozac) can result in very high levels of amitriptyline.
- fluvoxamine (Luvox) can result in very high levels of amitriptyline.

- gatifloxacin (Tequin), grepafloxacin (Raxar), moxifloxacin (Avelox), or sparfloxacin (Zagam) may result in heart toxicity—DO NOT COMBINE.
- ibutilide (Corvert) may result in abnormal heart rhythms. DO NOT COMBINE.
- meperidine (Demerol) worsens breathing (respiratory) depression risk.
- monoamine oxidase (MAO) type A inhibitor drugs may cause high fever, delirium and convulsions (see Drug Classes).
- phenytoin (Dilantin) or fosphenytoin (Cerebyx) can lead to amitriptyline toxicity.
- potassium (various) may lead to ulceration from potassium as amitriptyline may slow the intestine.
- propafenone (Rhythmol) can result in increased antidepressant blood levels and possible toxicity (sedation, dry mouth, difficulty urinating, etc.).
- quinidine (Quinaglute, etc.) can result in increased antidepressant blood levels.
- S-adenosylmethionine (SAMe) may lead to serotonin syndrome. Combination is not recommended.
- salmeterol (Serevent) should be used with great care because of increased cardiovascular risk (changes in blood pressure, pulse, and electrocardiograms or EKGs).
- sertraline (Zoloft) can lead to heart rhythm problems. DO NOT COMBINE.
- thyroid preparations may impair heart rhythm and function, but may also help depression when used in combination. Ask your doctor for help with time frames for results in making depression better, adjustment of thyroid dose, and checks for changes in heart rhythm.
- tramadol (Ultram) may increase risk of seizures. This combination is not advised.
- venlafaxine (Effexor) can result in very high levels of amitriptyline.
- verapamil (Calan, others) can result in very high levels of amitriptyline.
- warfarin (Coumadin) may lead to increased bleeding risk. More frequent INRs are prudent.

▷ *Driving, Hazardous Activities:* This drug may impair mental alertness, judgment, physical coordination, and reaction time. Avoid hazardous activities.

Aviation Note: The use of this drug ***is a disqualification*** for piloting. Consult a designated Aviation Medical Examiner.

Exposure to Sun: This drug may cause photosensitivity (see Glossary).

Exposure to Heat: May inhibit sweating and impair the body's adaptation to hot environments, increasing risk of heatstroke. Avoid saunas.

Exposure to Cold: Older patients should avoid prolonged cold exposure (conducive to hypothermia—see Glossary).

Discontinuation: It is best to stop this drug gradually. Abrupt withdrawal after long-term use can cause a withdrawal syndrome (headache, malaise, and nausea).

AMLODIPINE (am LOH di peen)

Introduced: 1986   **Class:** Anti-anginal, antihypertensive, calcium channel blocker   **Prescription:** USA: Yes   **Controlled Drug:** USA: No; Canada: No   **Available as Generic:** No

Brand Names: Lotrel [CD], Norvasc

Controversies in Medicine: Medicines in this class have had many conflicting reports. Amlodipine got the first FDA approval to treat high blood pressure or angina in those with congestive heart failure. Some data appear to show that amlodipine lowers the risk of stroke or heart attack in people with coronary artery disease. CCBs are currently second-line agents for high blood pressure according to the JNC VII (see Glossary).

BENEFITS versus RISKS

Possible Benefits	*Possible Risks*
EFFECTIVE PREVENTION OF BOTH MAJOR TYPES OF ANGINA EFFECTIVE TREATMENT OF HYPERTENSION	DOSE-RELATED CHANGES IN HEART RHYTHM Peripheral edema (fluid retention in feet and ankles) Dose-related palpitations Other medicines in the same family have rare concern about depression, memory loss, or malignancy

---

▷ **Principal Uses**

As a Single Drug Product: Uses currently included in FDA-approved labeling: (1) Treats angina pectoris due to spontaneous coronary artery spasm (Prinzmetal's variant angina) that is not associated with exertion; (2) classical angina-of-effort (caused by "hardening" or atherosclerosis of coronary arteries) in people who don't respond or can't tolerate nitrates or beta-blockers; (3) mild to moderate hypertension.

Other (unlabeled) generally accepted uses: (1) May keep early atherosclerotic lesions from getting worse; (2) can help stop premature labor; (3) helps some symptoms in cases of lung (pulmonary) hypertension; (4) can work to lower blood pressure and decrease the amount of protein in the urine (microalbuminuria) of diabetics; (5) may ease silent myocardial ischemia in combination with a beta blocker; (6) some limited use in preventing migraines.

As a Combination Drug Product [CD]: In combination with benazepril offers the benefits of an ACE inhibitor and a calcium channel blocker.

How This Drug Works: This drug blocks normal passage of calcium through cell walls, inhibiting coronary artery and peripheral arteriole narrowing. As a result, this drug

- prevents spontaneous coronary artery spasm (Prinzmetal's angina).
- decreases heart rate and contraction force in exertion, making effort-induced angina less likely.
- opens contracted peripheral arterial walls, lowering blood pressure. (Also lessens heart work and helps prevent angina.)

May also offer dual receptor binding characteristics. The combination form (Lotrel) adds the benefits of inhibiting angiotensin converting enzyme (ACE) via the active benazeprilat form.

Available Dosage Forms and Strengths

Lotrel capsules — 2.5/10 mg, 5/10 mg and 5/20 mg
Tablets — 2.5 mg, 5 mg, 10 mg

▷ **Recommended Dosage Ranges** (Actual dose and schedule must be determined for each patient individually.)

Infants and Children: Dosage not established.

12 to 65 Years of Age: High blood pressure: 2.5 to 10 mg daily, in a single dose. The fixed combination (Lotrel form) is usually given as one to two capsules a day. In older (or frail patients) some clinicians limit the dose of the amlodipine component to 2.5 mg a day.

Chronic angina: 5 to 10 mg daily; 10 mg may improve exercise ability in stable angina patients.

Congestive heart failure: 5 mg once daily for 2 weeks with increase to 10 mg as needed and tolerated.

Over 65 Years of Age: Lower doses (2.5 mg for high blood pressure and 5 mg for angina) are prudent and effective.

Conditions Requiring Dosing Adjustments

Liver Function: Patients with damaged livers started on a daily 2.5-mg dose for high blood pressure, 5 mg for angina. Then dosing may be slowly increased as needed or tolerated.

Kidney Function: No adjustment in dosing is needed.

Low Protein or Starvation: This drug is moved around the body by a protein called albumin. If protein is low, in liver failure or starvation, increased effect may be seen with "normal" doses. Start therapy with low doses. Increase only if needed or tolerated.

▷ **Dosing Instructions:** May be taken with or following food to reduce stomach irritation. The tablet may be crushed. If you forget a dose: Take the medicine right away, unless it is nearly time for your next dose, then omit the missed dose and take the medicine when it was next scheduled. DO NOT double doses.

Usual Duration of Use: Regular use for 2 to 4 weeks often needed to see benefit in reducing angina frequency or severity of angina and in high blood pressure control. Best to use the lowest dose that works for long-term use (months to years). Periodic evaluation by your doctor is needed.

Typical Treatment Goals and Measurements (Outcomes and Markers)

Blood Pressure: The NEW guidelines (JNC VII) define normal blood pressure (BP) as **less than** 120/80. Because blood pressures that were once considered acceptable can actually lead to blood vessel damage, the committee from the National Institutes of Health, National Heart Lung and Blood Institute now have a new category called **Pre-hypertension**. This ranges from 120/80 to 139/89 and is intended to help your doctor encourage lifestyle changes (or in the case of people with a risk factor for high blood pressure, start treatment) much earlier—so that possible damage to blood vessels, your heart, kidneys, sexual potency, or eyes might be minimized or avoided altogether. The next two classes of high blood pressure are stage 1 hypertension: 140/90 to 159/99 and stage 2 hypertension equal to or greater than: 160/100 mm Hg. These guidelines also recommend that clinicians trying to control blood pressure work with their patients to agree on the goals and a plan of treatment. The first-ever guidelines for blood pressure (hypertension) in African Americans recommends that MOST black patients be started on TWO antihypertensive medicines with the goal of lowering blood pressure to 130/80 for those with high risk for heart and blood vessel disease or with diabetes. The American Diabetes Association recommends 130/80 as the target for people living with diabetes and less than 125/75 for those who spill more than one gram of protein into their urine. Most clinicians try to achieve a BP that confers the best balance of lower cardiovascular risk and avoids the problem of too low a blood pressure. Blood pressure duration is generally increased with beneficial restriction of sodium. The goals and time frame should be discussed with you when the prescription is written. If goals are not met, it is not unusual to intensify doses or add on medicines. You can find the new blood pressure guidelines at *www.nhlbi.nih.gov/guidelines/hypertension/index.htm*. For the African American guidelines see Douglas, J.G. in Sources.

Possible Advantages of This Drug

Slow onset and prolonged effect, allowing effective once-a-day treatment for both angina and high blood pressure. The combination form offers two distinct mechanisms of action to help lower blood pressure.

▷ **This Drug Should Not Be Taken If**

- you have had an allergic reaction to it previously.
- you have active liver disease.
- you have low blood pressure—systolic below 90 mm Hg.
- your left heart ventricle doesn't work well (dysfunctional).

▷ **Inform Your Physician Before Taking This Drug If**

- you have had a bad reaction to any calcium blocker.
- you take digitalis or a beta-blocker (see Drug Classes).
- you are taking any drugs that lower blood pressure.
- you have had congestive heart failure, heart attack, or stroke.
- you have a contracted or narrowed (stenosed) aorta.
- you are subject to disturbances of heart rhythm.
- you have a history of drug-induced liver damage.
- you develop a rash or other skin reaction while taking this medicine.
- you are unsure how much or how often to take this drug.
- you have circulation problems in your hands.
- you have muscular dystrophy.

Possible Side Effects (natural, expected, and unavoidable drug actions)

Swelling of feet and ankles, flushing (4.5% in women and 1.5% in men) and sensation of warmth.

Impaired sense of smell.

▷ **Possible Adverse Effects** (unusual, unexpected, and infrequent reactions)

If any of the following develop, consult your physician promptly for guidance.

Mild Adverse Effects

Allergic reaction: skin rash (call your doctor, as persistent rashes may become serious).

Headache (up to 12%), dizziness (dose related)—infrequent.

Fatigue, nausea, or constipation—infrequent.

Dose-related palpitations, low dose—rare; 10 mg—infrequent.

Overgrowth of the gums (gingival hyperplasia)—up to 40% with drugs in the same class.

Increased urge to urinate at night—rare.

Visual changes (eye pain, double vision)—rare.

Ringing in the ears (tinnitus)—rare.

Cough, muscle pain—infrequent.

Dose-related flushing (4.5% in women and 1.5% in men)—infrequent.

Elevated liver enzymes (may be a hypersensitivity, usually resolves)—rare.

Serious Adverse Effects

Allergic reactions: exfoliative dermatitis (very rare).

Idiosyncratic reactions: Parkinson-like symptoms—case report.

Dose-dependent edema (up to 6.2% in those over 65)—infrequent.

Exfoliative dermatitis or erythema multiforme—rare.

Agranulocytosis (only other medicines in this class)—case reports.
Rebound angina—if drug is abruptly stopped—possible.
Difficulty breathing (dyspnea)—infrequent (up to 15% in the PRAISE trial as pulmonary edema).

▷ **Possible Effects on Sexual Function:** Sexual dysfunction (both men and women)—1–2%.
Swelling and tenderness of male breast tissue (gynecomastia)—case report.

Adverse Effects That May Mimic Natural Diseases or Disorders
An allergic rash and swelling of the legs may resemble erysipelas.

Possible Effects on Laboratory Tests
Liver function tests: transient increases in liver enzymes.

CAUTION
1. Make sure all your health care providers know you take this drug. List this drug on a card in your purse or wallet.
2. Nitroglycerin or other nitrate drugs can be used as needed to ease acute angina pain. If your attacks become more frequent or intense, call your doctor promptly.

Precautions for Use
By Infants and Children: Safety and effectiveness for use by those under 12 not established.
By Those Over 60 Years of Age: May be more likely to be weak, dizzy or faint or fall. Be careful to prevent injury. Low starting doses are prudent.

▷ **Advisability of Use During Pregnancy**
Pregnancy Category: C. See Pregnancy Risk Categories at the back of this book.
Animal Studies: No information available.
Human Studies: Adequate studies of pregnant women are not available.
Avoid this drug during the first 3 months. Use during the last 6 months only if clearly needed. Ask your physician for guidance.

Advisability of Use If Breast-Feeding
Presence of this drug in breast milk: Unknown.
Avoid drug or refrain from nursing.

Habit-Forming Potential: None.

Effects of Overdose: Weakness, fainting, fast pulse, low blood pressure, slow heartbeat, metabolic acidosis, low potassium and calcium, sinus arrest, heart attack, seizures.

Possible Effects of Long-Term Use: Possible overgrowth of the gums.

Suggested Periodic Examinations While Taking This Drug (at physician's discretion)
Heart function tests: electrocardiograms; blood pressure check while supine, sitting, and standing.

▷ **While Taking This Drug, Observe the Following**
Foods: This medicine is increased by grapefruit or grapefruit juice. Avoid eating grapefruit for an hour after taking this medicine. Avoid excessive salt intake.
Herbal Medicines or Minerals: Ginseng may increase blood pressure, blunting the benefits of this medicine. Peppermint oil may work to decrease calcium channel effect (animal data) and lower drug benefits. Eleuthero root, hawthorn, saw palmetto, ma huang (should not be combined), guarana, goldenseal, and licorice may also cause increased blood pressure. Indian snakeroot, calcium, and garlic may help lower blood pressure. Ask your

doctor if calcium and/or garlic makes sense for you. St. John's wort may increase sun sensitivity and because of its effect on liver enzymes, may also decrease drug benefits in controlling blood pressure. Talk to your doctor BEFORE adding any herbal medicines.

Beverages: See foods above. May be taken with milk.

▷ *Alcohol:* Use caution. Alcohol may exaggerate the drop in blood pressure.

Tobacco Smoking: Nicotine may reduce the effectiveness of this drug. I advise everyone to quit smoking.

Marijuana Smoking: Possible reduced effectiveness of this drug; mild to moderate increase in angina; possible changes in electrocardiogram, confusing interpretation.

▷ *Other Drugs*

Amlodipine *taken concurrently* with

- adenosine (Adenocard) may cause extended problems with slow heart rate.
- amiodarone (Cordarone) may worsen AV block or cause further slowing of the heart in partial atrioventricular (AV) block or sick sinus syndrome.
- azole antifungals (such as fluconazole [Diflucan] or itraconazole [Sporanox]) and imidazoles (see Drug Classes) such as ketoconazole (Nizoral) may lead to toxic amlodipine blood levels.
- beta-blocker drugs or digitalis preparations (see Drug Classes) may cause heart rate and rhythm problems.
- cyclosporine (Sandimmune) causes increased cyclosporine blood levels and increased risk of toxicity.
- delavirdine (Rescriptor) may cause increased amlodipine levels and toxicity.
- dofetilide (Tikosyn) may cause dofetilide toxicity.
- medicines that inhibit cytochrome P450 3A4 will increase amlodipine blood levels and those that induce 3A4 will decrease amlodipine blood levels.
- NSAIDs or oral anticoagulants such as Coumadin (warfarin—see Drug Classes) may lead to increased risk of bleeding in the gastrointestinal (GI) tract.
- quinupristin/dalfopristin (Synercid) may cause extended amlodipine effects or toxicity.
- rifampin (Rifater, others) may result in decreased therapeutic benefit of amlodipine.
- ritonavir (Norvir) and probably other protease inhibitors (see Drug Classes) may lead to amlodipine toxicity.

The following drug may *increase* the effects of amlodipine

- cimetidine (Tagamet).

▷ *Driving, Hazardous Activities:* This drug may cause dizziness. Restrict activities as necessary.

Aviation Note: Coronary artery disease *is a disqualification* for piloting. Consult a designated Aviation Medical Examiner.

Exposure to Sun: Four case reports of phototoxicity have been made. Caution is advised.

Exposure to Heat: Caution is advised. Hot environments can exaggerate the blood-pressure-lowering effects of this drug. Observe for light-headedness or weakness.

Heavy Exercise or Exertion: This drug may improve your ability to be more active without resulting angina pain. Use caution.

Discontinuation: Do not stop this drug abruptly—gradual withdrawal is often prudent. Watch for development of rebound angina.

AMOXAPINE (a MOX a peen)

Introduced: 1970 **Class:** Antidepressant **Prescription:** USA: Yes **Controlled Drug:** USA: No; Canada: No **Available as Generic:** Yes

Brand Name: Asendin

BENEFITS versus RISKS	
Possible Benefits	*Possible Risks*
EFFECTIVE RELIEF OF PRIMARY DEPRESSIONS: ENDOGENOUS, NEUROTIC, REACTIVE	ADVERSE BEHAVIORAL EFFECTS: CONFUSION, DELUSIONS, DISORIENTATION, HALLUCINATIONS
	CONVERSION OF DEPRESSION TO MANIA IN MANIC-DEPRESSIVE DISORDERS
	Rare blood cell abnormalities
	Rare movement disorders
	Rare seizures
	Rare liver toxicity

Author's Note: Since use of this medicine has declined in favor of newer medicines, the information in this profile has been shortened.

AMOXICILLIN (a mox i SIL in)

AMOXICILLIN/CLAVULANATE (a mox i SIL in/KLAV yu lan ayt)

AMPICILLIN (am pi SIL in)

Please see the penicillin family profile for further information on amoxicillin, amoxicillin/clavulanate, or ampicillin.

ANAKINRA (ANN ah kin rah)

Other Names: Recombinant human interleukin-1 receptor antagonist. RhIL-1ra

Introduced: 2002 **Class:** Interleukin-1 receptor antagonist **Prescription:** USA: Yes **Controlled Drug:** USA: No; Canada: No **Available as Generic:** No

Brand Name: Kineret

BENEFITS versus RISKS

Possible Benefits	*Possible Risks*
USEFUL IN RHEUMATOID ARTHRITIS	INFECTIONS CAUSED BY IMMUNOSUPPRESSION FROM THE MEDICINE ITSELF
HAS A ROLE IN JUVENILE RHEUMATOID ARTHRITIS (ORPHAN DRUG)	Injection site reactions (usually mild)
	Possible development of antibodies
CAN BE USED IN COMBINATION WITH METHOTREXATE	Should NOT be started in people with active infections or lowered white blood cell counts
PREVENTION OF DISEASE PROGRESSION	
MAY GIVE A RESPONSE WHERE OTHER AGENTS HAVE FAILED	

▷ **Principal Uses**

As a Single Drug Product: Uses currently included in FDA-approved labeling: (1) Approved for treatment (alone or in combination with non-TNF therapies) of moderate to severe rheumatoid arthritis (RA) in people over 18, where one or more Disease Modifying Antirheumatic Drug (DMARD—see Glossary) has/have failed.

Other (unlabeled) generally accepted uses: (1) May have a role in graft-versus-host disease.

How This Drug Works: Binds competitively with two kinds of interleukin-1 receptors in the body (type 1 and 2). The effect of this binding is that the cellular responses that would have been seen from natural interleukin-1 alpha and beta is at least partially blocked.

Available Dosage Forms and Strengths

Injection — 100 mg/ml in a 1 ml prefilled syringe.

▷ **Recommended Dosage Ranges** (Actual dose and schedule must be determined for each patient individually.)

Infants and Children: Not studied in children.

Usual Adult Dosage Ranges: For rheumatoid arthritis (adults 18 and older):100 mg injected under the skin (subcutaneously), once a day. (Remember to change or rotate where you inject.)

Conditions Requiring Dosing Adjustments

Liver Function: No changes needed, as only small amounts are removed via the liver or gall bladder.

Kidney Function: Removal of anakinra from plasma is decreased 70–75% in people with creatinine clearance (see Glossary) less than 30 ml/min, but no guidelines for dosing changes are available as yet.

▷ **Dosing Instructions:** It is very important that you understand how to inject this drug under the skin (subcutaneously) and NOT intravenously. Please ask your doctor or pharmacist if you do not understand the patient information on injecting. Please also remember to change (rotate) where you inject (the injection site), and inject it at the same time every day (helps keep blood levels about the same). Combination use with TNF type therapies has not yet been studied. Talk to your doctor before injecting anakinra if you have an infection. If you forget a dose: Take the missed dose right away, unless it is nearly time for your next dose—if that is the case, skip the missed dose and take the next dose right on schedule. Call your doctor if you find yourself missing doses.

Usual Duration of Use: Use on a regular schedule determines benefit. In rheumatoid arthritis this drug usually goes to work in 1 to 3 weeks. Ongoing use (months to years) requires physician supervision and checks of ACR scores.

Typical Treatment Goals and Measurements (Outcomes and Markers):

Arthritis: Control of arthritis symptoms (pain, loss of mobility, decreased ability to accomplish activities of daily living, range of motion, etc.) is paramount in returning patient quality of life and to checking the results (beneficial outcomes) from this medicine. The American College of Rheumatology has a set of criteria for positive results in treating rheumatoid arthritis (you may hear this referred to as ACR 20, 50, or 70). Many arthritis management or pain centers use interdisciplinary teams (physicians from several specialties, nurses, physician's assistants, physical and occupational therapists, pharmacotherapists, psychotherapists, social workers, and others) to get the best results. Specific mobility goals are often set by the physician and administered by a physical/occupational therapist. The arthritis foundation has additional information at *www.arthritis.org*.

Possible Advantages of This Drug Uses: A novel mechanism (against interleukin-1) to fight rheumatoid arthritis. May give relief where other agents have failed.

▷ **This Drug Should Not Be Taken If**
- you have had an allergic reaction to it or to proteins that come from a bacteria called *E. coli*.
- you currently have an active infection.

▷ **Inform Your Physician Before Taking This Drug If**
- you have moderate to severe kidney (renal) compromise (removal of the medicine will be lowered by up to 75%).
- you develop a new infection while taking this medicine.
- you have recently received a live virus vaccine.
- you have a white blood cell count less than 2,000 (ask your doctor about leukopenia).
- you have a disease or condition that weakens your immune system (are immunosuppressed).
- you are pregnant or planning pregnancy in the near future.
- you are breast-feeding your infant.
- you are taking a tumor necrosis blocking agent (not studied yet).
- you have a history of allergies to other medicines.

Possible Side Effects (natural, expected, and unavoidable drug actions)
Report such developments to your physician promptly.
Discomfort at the injection site.

▷ **Possible Adverse Effects** (unusual, unexpected, and infrequent reactions)
If any of the following develop, consult your physician promptly for guidance.

Mild Adverse Effects
Allergic reaction: skin rash at the injection site—possible.
Headache—frequent.
Sinusitis—up to 7% in clinical trials.
Nausea—may be frequent.

Serious Adverse Effects
Allergic reactions—possible.
Lowering of a specific kind of white blood cell (neutrophil)—neutropenia—rare.
Infections—may be frequent.

▷ **Possible Effects on Sexual Function:** None reported.

Possible Delayed Adverse Effects: Possible development of anti-anakinra antibodies. Long-term effects on response and benefits from anakinra are not fully understood.

Possible Effects on Laboratory Tests
Anti-anakinra antibodies: positive.

CAUTION
1. This drug must be monitored carefully by a qualified physician.
2. Make certain you understand how to inject this medicine under the skin.
3. Live-virus vaccines should be avoided during use of this drug. Live-virus vaccines could actually produce infection rather than stimulate an immune response.
5. The manufacturer advises against using this medicine if you have an active infection.
6. Patients should be followed closely if they develop an infection while taking this medicine, and treatment should be STOPPED in patients with serious infections or sepsis.

Precautions for Use
By Those Over 60 Years of Age: Specific changes are not indicated at present.

▷ **Advisability of Use During Pregnancy**
Pregnancy Category: B. See Pregnancy Risk Categories at the back of this book.
Human Studies: Adequate studies are NOT available.
Talk to your doctor about benefits versus risks of use.

Advisability of Use If Breast-Feeding
Presence of this drug in breast milk: Unknown.
Avoid drug or refrain from nursing.

Habit-Forming Potential: None.

Effects of Overdose: Symptomatic management indicated.

Possible Effects of Long-Term Use: Positive anti-anakinra antibodies—significance not presently known.

Suggested Periodic Examinations While Taking This Drug (at physician's discretion)
Beneficial response to the medicine (ACR criteria).
Sedimentation rate (ESR) and rheumatoid factor or C-reactive protein.
If used in congestive heart failure, tests of heart function and symptom-free walking time.

▷ **While Taking This Drug, Observe the Following**
Foods: No specific recommendations.
Herbal Medicines or Minerals: There is NO DATA on combined use of this drug with glucosamine or hay flower, mistletoe herb, or white mustard seed. Echinacea may actually blunt the immune response if used on an ongoing basis, and therefore combination is not advisable. Talk to your doctor before combining any herbal medicine with anakinra.
Beverages: No restrictions.
▷ *Alcohol:* No specific recommendations.
Tobacco Smoking: No interactions expected. I advise everyone to quit smoking.
Marijuana Smoking: May impair immunity.
▷ *Other Drugs*
Anakinra *taken concurrently* with
• medicines that blunt the immune system may lead to additive immune system depression if combined with etanercept.

- TNF blocking agents (such as etanercept (Enbrel) or infliximab (Remicade) has not been well studied, but may lead to increased risk of infection.
- yellow fever, pneumococcal, smallpox, or any other live vaccine may result in decreased immune response to the vaccine as well as possible transmission of the infection BY the vaccine.

▷ *Driving, Hazardous Activities:* No restrictions.

Aviation Note: The use of this drug is ***probably not a disqualification*** for piloting, but the condition being treated may be. Consult a designated Aviation Medical Examiner.

Exposure to Sun: No restrictions.

Occurrence of Unrelated Illness: Call your doctor to report any sign of infection.

Discontinuation: No specific recommendations. Ask your doctor before stopping any drug for any reason.

Special Storage Instructions: Keep this medicine in the refrigerator, but do not freeze it.

ANASTROZOLE (Ann AZ troh zoal)

Other Names: ZD 1033, ICID1033

Introduced: 2002 **Class:** Aromatase inhibitor, selective aromatase inhibitor, cancer chemotherapy antagonist **Prescription:** USA: Yes **Controlled Drug:** USA: No; Canada: No **Available as Generic:** No **Brand Name:** Arimidex

BENEFITS versus RISKS	
Possible Benefits	*Possible Risks*
FIRST-LINE TREATMENT OF BREAST CANCER IN POST-MENOPAUSAL WOMEN SECOND-LINE TREATMENT OF ADVANCED BREAST CANCER IN WOMEN WHO HAVE HAD A RELAPSE OF BREAST CANCER AFTER HAVING BEEN TREATED FIRST WITH TAMOXIFEN MORE FAVORABLE RESULTS AND SIDE EFFECT PROFILE THAN TAMOXIFEN IN WOMEN AFTER MENOPAUSE	BLOOD CLOTS (thromboembolic events)—less than 4.1% HOT FLASHES (FLUSHES) JOINT OR BONE PAIN Increased risk of bone fracture Fluid buildup (edema)

▷ **Principal Uses**

As a Single Drug Product: Uses currently included in FDA-approved labeling: (1) Approved for first-line treatment of postmenopausal women who have early breast cancer that is hormone receptor positive or receptor unknown cancer which is either advanced on a local basis or is metastatic; (2) second-line treatment for women with advanced breast cancer that has continued to grow (progressed) after having first been treated with tamoxifen.

Other (unlabeled) generally accepted uses: Not defined as yet.

Author's Note: Data presented from the ATAC (Arimidex, Tamoxifen Alone or in Combination) study was presented in Barcelona, Spain. The study, which involves more than 9,000 women showed that anastrozole out-performed tamoxifen (lower occurrence of hot flushes, blood clots, and cancer of the uterus) and also showed a 58% lower risk in development of a new tumor in the other breast. The company received fast track designation by the FDA for approval for use in early breast cancer.

How This Drug Works: This medicine works to lower estrogen levels in women after menopause by interfering with the conversion of androstenedione to estrone in peripheral tissues. This is accomplished by blocking an enzyme called aromatase.

Available Dosage Forms and Strengths
Tablets — 1 mg

▷ **Usual Adult Dosage Ranges:** *Breast cancer or advanced breast cancer in women after menopause:* One mg is given once daily. In first-line treatment of advanced breast cancer, the treatment is continued until the tumor progresses.

Note: Actual dose and schedule must be determined for each patient individually.

Conditions Requiring Dosing Adjustments
Liver Function: Doses may accumulate in mild to moderate liver disease, however no dosing changes are yet defined.
Kidney Function: Dose decreases are not thought to be needed in kidney disease (only 10% is removed that way).

▷ **Dosing Instructions:** The tablet may be crushed and taken either on an empty stomach or with food. If you forget a dose: Take the missed dose as soon as you remember it, unless it's nearly time for your next dose—if that is the case, skip the missed dose and take the next dose right on schedule. DO NOT double up on doses. Talk with your doctor if you find yourself missing doses—there are effective beeper-based systems to help you remember your medicine.

Usual Duration of Use: Use on a regular schedule for 2 weeks usually finds the peak response. The ideal (optimal) length of treatment is not fully defined (approval was based on study of patients for a median two and a half years). Ongoing use (months to years) requires physician supervision and periodic evaluation.

Typical Treatment Goals and Measurements (Outcomes and Markers)
Breast cancer: Treatment of existing cancer seeks to attain a complete remission. The minimum goal is to shrink (regress) the size of the tumor and decrease the probability of spread. Talk to your doctor about the goals of treatment when this medicine is prescribed.

▷ **This Drug Should Not Be Taken If**
• you had a serious allergic or adverse reaction to it before.
• you are pregnant.

▷ **Inform Your Physician Before Taking This Drug If**
• you have a history of pulmonary embolism.
• you have a history of stroke or blood clots.
• you have a history of edema.
• you have impaired liver function.
• you have high cholesterol.
• you plan to have surgery in the near future.

Possible Side Effects (natural, expected, and unavoidable drug actions)
> Hot flashes—frequent.
> Fluid retention (edema), weight gain.

▷ **Possible Adverse Effects** (unusual, unexpected, and infrequent reactions)
> **If any of the following develop, consult your physician promptly for guidance.**
> *Mild Adverse Effects*
> Allergic reaction: skin rash.
> Sweating—infrequent.
> Joint pain (arthralgia) or arthritis—frequent.
> Increased cholesterol—infrequent.
> Headache, dizziness, drowsiness, fatigue, insomnia—infrequent.
> Nausea, vomiting, diarrhea—frequent.
> Urinary tract infection, vaginal dryness—infrequent.
> *Serious Adverse Effects*
> Osteoporosis—infrequent.
> Development of clots (thromboembolic disease)—increased risk.
> Depression—may be frequent.
> Liver toxicity—rare.

▷ **Possible Effects on Sexual Function:** Vaginal dryness may lead to discomfort during intercourse. A lubricant may be prudent.

Possible Effects on Laboratory Tests
> Liver function tests: increased liver enzyme (AST/GOT).
> Cholesterol: may be increased.

CAUTION
> 1. This medicine is presently used ONLY used after menopause.
> 2. Case reports of undesirable lipid changes (increased cholesterol) have been made. Periodic checks are prudent.

▷ **Advisability of Use During Pregnancy**
> *Pregnancy Category:* D. See Pregnancy Risk Categories at the back of this book.
> *Animal Studies:* No birth defects due to this drug reported.
> *Human Studies:* Adequate studies of pregnant women are not available.
> It should not be used during pregnancy.

Advisability of Use If Breast-Feeding
> Presence of this drug in breast milk: Unknown.
> Avoid drug or refrain from nursing.

Habit-Forming Potential: None.

Effects of Overdose: Severe extension of the pharmacological effects.

Possible Effects of Long-Term Use: Osteoporosis.

Suggested Periodic Examinations While Taking This Drug (at physician's discretion)
> Measurement of bone mineral density.
> Check of Hamilton Depression scale.

▷ **While Taking This Drug, Observe the Following**
> *Foods:* Food appears to change how much medicine gets into your body, but the maker of this drug has not supplied any specific guidelines.
> *Herbal Medicines or Minerals:* Some patients use echinacea to attempt to boost their immune systems. Unfortunately, use of echinacea is not recommended in people with damaged immune systems. This herb may also actually weaken any immune system if it is used too often or for too long a

time. Black cohosh estrogenic effects may have an undesirable effect—do not combine. Talk to your doctor to find out about further research and BEFORE combining any herbal or neutraceutical product with this medicine.

Beverages: No restrictions. May be taken with milk.

▷   *Alcohol:* No interactions expected.

Tobacco Smoking: No interactions expected. I advise everyone to quit smoking.

Marijuana Smoking: Animal Studies show an increased suppression of the immune system; significance in humans is not known.

▷   *Other Drugs*

The following drugs may *decrease* the effects of anastrozole:

• estrogens.

• oral contraceptives (those that contain estrogens).

Anastrozole *taken concurrently* with

• tamoxifen (Nolvadex) is not recommended by the manufacturer (lowers anastrozole blood levels).

▷   *Driving, Hazardous Activities:* This drug may cause dizziness or drowsiness. Restrict activities as necessary.

Aviation Note: The use of this drug *may be a disqualification* for piloting. Consult a designated Aviation Medical Examiner.

Exposure to Sun: No restrictions.

ANGIOTENSIN CONVERTING ENZYME (ACE) INHIBITOR FAMILY

Benazepril   (ben AY ze pril)   **Captopril**   (KAP toh pril)   **Enalapril** (e NAL a pril)   **Fosinopril**   (Foh SIN oh pril)   **Lisinopril**   (li SIN oh pril)   **Quinapril**   (KWIN a pril)   **Ramipril**   (RAH mi pril)

Other Names: ACEIs

Introduced: 1985, 1979, 1981, 1986, 1988, 1984, 1985, respectively **Class:**   ACE inhibitor, antihypertensive   **Prescription:**   USA: Yes **Controlled Drug:**   USA: No; Canada: No   **Available as Generic:**   Yes (captopril, enalapril, lisinopril)

Brand Names: Benazepril: Lotensin, Lotensin HCT [CD], Lotrel [CD], Captopril: Acediur [CD], ✤Alti-Captopril, ✤Apo-Capto, Capoten, Capozide [CD], ✤Novo-Captopril, ✤Nu-Capto, ✤Syn-Captopril, Enalapril: Lexxel [CD], ✤Vaseretic (also in U.S.) [CD], Vasotec, Fosinopril: ✤Lin-Fosinopril, Monopril, Monopril HCT, Lisinopril: Prinivil, Prinzide [CD], Zestoretic [CD], Zestril, Quinapril: Accupril, Accuretic, Ramipril: Altace, ✤Ramace

Author's Note: Ramipril (Altace) plus felodipine is available as a combination product in Canada only. Perindopril (Aceon), moexipril (Univasc), moexipril/hydrochlorothiazide (Uniretic), trandolapril (Mavik), and trandolapril/verapamil (Tarka) information will be added to this profile in future editions if differential benefits emerge from clinical studies. Data from a study in the British Medical Journal found that combination of ramipril (Altace) plus a water pill (thiazide diuretic) used by patients who had previous transient ischemic attacks (TIAs) or strokes helped prevent a first or a repeat stroke. The interesting finding was that for some patients, the protective benefits happened even though blood pressure was reduced only slightly.

BENEFITS versus RISKS	
Possible Benefits	*Possible Risks*
RAMIPRIL HAS DATA SHOWING THAT IT CAN DECREASE THE RISK OF HEART ATTACK AND STROKE (lowered cardiovascular events by 22% in the HOPE trial; lisinopril also approved for use after heart attack)	Impaired white blood cell production—rare (not for ramipril)
	Bone marrow depression—rare (not for ramipril)
	Allergic swelling of face, tongue, throat, vocal cords—possible
EFFECTIVE CONTROL OF MILD TO SEVERE HIGH BLOOD PRESSURE	Kidney damage—rare (enalapril, lisinopril, quinapril, and ramipril lower risk)
USEFUL ADJUNCTIVE TREATMENT FOR CONGESTIVE HEART FAILURE	Liver damage—rare (not for ramipril)
MAY DECREASE RISK OF KIDNEY PROBLEMS IN DIABETICS TAKING INSULIN (CAPTOPRIL)	
MAY REDUCE RISK OF DEATH AND/OR CONGESTIVE HEART FAILURE AFTER HEART ATTACK (several ACES are approved for this)	
MAY BE DRUGS OF FIRST CHOICE FOR PATIENTS WITH HIGH BLOOD PRESSURE WHO EXERCISE	
COMBINATION USE OF PERINDOPRIL WITH INDAPAMIDE REDUCED RISK OF RECURRENT STROKE BY NEARLY HALF IN ONE STUDY	
USE OF RAMIPRIL AND A THIAZIDE DIURETIC LOWERED STROKE RISK BY 32% AND FATAL STROKE RISK BY 61%	
LISINOPRIL HAS BEEN SHOWN TO REDUCE THE FREQUENCY, SEVERITY AND DURATION OF MIGRAINES	
Quinapril has been shown to stimulate growth of new blood vessels in laboratory animals	

▷ **Principal Uses**

As Single Drug Products: Uses currently included in FDA-approved labeling: (1) Treats all degrees of high blood pressure; (2) helps prevent death after heart attacks (ramipril, lisinopril); (3) used in advanced heart failure; (4) used in diabetics who have kidney problems (decreases or controls amount of protein in urine); (5) helps people live longer (improves survival) in cases of congestive heart failure; (6) ramipril approved to lower risk of heart and blood vessel disease (cardiovascular) in people with coronary artery disease, stroke, diabetes or peripheral vascular disease who have one or more risk factors (for example—high cholesterol or blood pressure); (7) captopril used if undesirable increases in red blood cells happen after a kidney transplant.

Author's Note: Enalapril was studied in the ABCD trial and was found to control blood pressure and also decrease risk of heart attack in people living with diabetes. Follow-up research is pending.

Other (unlabeled) generally accepted uses: (1) Helps relieve symptoms of cystinuria (captopril); (2) may ease rheumatoid arthritis symptoms (captopril or enalapril); (3) can help Raynaud's phenomenon symptoms (captopril); (4) enalapril and lisinopril help prevent migraines (prophylaxis); (5) enalapril and quinapril may be helpful in aortic regurgitation; (6) helps treat increased blood pressure resulting from blood vessel problems in the kidneys (renovascular hypertension) in people who can't have angioplasty or surgery; (7) combination use of indapamide with perindopril (Aceon) reduced risk of repeat stroke by nearly 50% in one study. A study (see Bosch, J in Sources) undertaken in England found that use of ramipril plus a thiazide diuretic lowered risk for all strokes by 32% and for fatal strokes by 61%. These benefits occurred despite small lowering of blood pressure. Both studies will probably lead to use of ramipril and a thiazide to help prevent first or repeat strokes in patients at risk for stroke. The goal then of therapy will focus on stroke prevention rather than lowering of blood pressure; (8) lisinopril lowered the percentage of people who had retinopathy (retinopathy score) increases in the EUCLID research.

Author's Note: One large study found that patients using captopril had similar low rates of nonfatal and fatal heart (cardiovascular) events to patients taking beta-blockers or diuretics. Another study showed that fosinopril cut the risk of heart attack or stroke by 51% in people who have high blood pressure and diabetes.

As Combination Drug Products [CD]: In combination with hydrochlorothiazide, captopril, enalapril, fosinopril, lisinopril, and benazepril offer the benefits of an ACE inhibitor and a diuretic. Benazepril has also been combined with amlodipine, a calcium channel blocker (Lotrel form).

How These Drugs Work: By blocking an enzyme system (angiotensin converting enzyme or ACE), these drugs relax arterial walls and lower pressure. This decreases the work a heart has to do and improves performance. Benefits after heart attack come from blunting reaction to catecholamines, scavenging free-radicals and increasing prostacyclin or bradykinin. Some members of this class must be converted by the liver to the active drug form. Combined therapy with diuretics helps ease fluid load. Combination with a calcium channel blocker works by blocking calcium channels and acts primarily on peripheral circulation to lower blood pressure. Amlodipine offers the further advantage of getting into the body well (bioavailability) and increased binding when blood flow is compromised (ischemic conditions and low pH). Ramipril plus a thiazide may help prevent strokes by acting in decreasing plaque rupturing, blood vessel blockage, lowered proliferation of smooth muscle in blood vessels, and through encouraging fibrin degradation (fibrinolysis).

Available Dosage Forms and Strengths
Benazepril:

Capsules — 2.5 mg of amlodipine with 10 mg of benazepril, 5 mg of amlodipine with 10 mg of benazepril and 5 mg of amlodipine with 20 mg of benazepril (Lotrel form)

Tablets — 5 mg, 10 mg, 20 mg, 40 mg (Lotensin)

Captopril:

Tablets — 6.25 mg, 12.5 mg, 25 mg, 50 mg, 100 mg

Tablet, combination (Capozide) — 25 or 50 mg captopril with 15 or 25 mg of hydrochlorothiazide

Enalapril:

Injection — 1.25 mg/ml

Tablets — 2.5 mg, 5 mg, 10 mg, 20 mg

Tablets (Vaseretic) — 10 mg enalapril and 25 mg of hydrochlorothiazide

Fosinopril:

Tablets — 5 mg, 10 mg, 20 mg, 40 mg

Lisinopril:

Tablets — 2.5 mg, 5 mg, 10 mg, 20 mg, 30 mg, 40 mg

Tablet, combination — 20 mg lisinopril with 12.5 or
(Prinzide, Zestoretic)   25 mg of hydrochlorothiazide

Quinapril:

Tablets — 5 mg, 10 mg, 20 mg, 40 mg

Tablet, combination (Accuretic) — 10 or 20 mg of quinapril with 12.5 or 25 mg of hydrochlorothiazide

Ramipril:

Capsules (gelcaps in Canada) — 1.25 mg, 2.5 mg, 5 mg, 10 mg

▷ **Usual Dosage Ranges for Infants and Children**
Captopril: One study used a starting dose of 0.01 to 0.25 mg per kg of body mass every 12 hours in infants; 0.05 to 0.5 mg per kg of body mass three times daily has been used in older children. Maximum dose is 2 mg/kg per dose up to three times a day.

Enalapril: Malignant Hypertension: 0.625–1.25 mg per dose, given every 6 hours. Maximum dose is 5 mg every 6 hours intravenously. In hypertension 0.08 mg per kg of body weight daily.

Quinapril, benazepril, ramipril, fosinopril, and lisinopril: Dosage not established in infants and children.

▷ **Usual Adult Dosage Ranges**
For high blood pressure:
Captopril: 25 mg two or three times daily for 1–2 weeks. If pressure goals are not met—dose may be increased to 50 mg three times daily if needed. If blood pressure still not acceptable, a diuretic (low dose similar to 25 mg of hydrochlorothiazide) or change to a combination form may be needed. Maximum daily dose is 450 mg.

Enalapril (if not also taking a diuretic): 5 mg once daily starting dose. Usual ongoing dose is 10 to 40 mg daily in a single dose or divided into two equal doses. Total daily dose should not exceed 40 mg if kidney function is impaired. If pressure goals are not met by enalapril alone, a diuretic can be added (pill burden is decreased by fixed dose combinations).

Fosinopril (18 to 60 years of age): For hypertension, initially 10 mg once daily. Usual maintenance dose is 20 to 40 mg daily taken in a single dose. Total daily dosage should not exceed 80 mg.

Quinapril, benazepril, lisinopril (12 to 60 years of age): 10 mg once daily for those not taking a diuretic; 5 mg once daily if taking a diuretic. Usual ongoing dose is 20 to 40 mg daily, taken in a single dose. If once-a-day dosing does not give stable blood pressure control over the day, divide the dose equally into morning and evening doses. Some studies have found better blood pressure control despite some data for full 24 hour coverage for some ACE inhibitors.

Ramipril: Initially 2.5 mg once daily for 2 to 4 weeks. Usual ongoing dose is 2.5 to 20 mg daily in a single dose or two divided doses. If taking diuretics, either stop diuretic for 3 days before starting this drug or begin treatment with 1.25 mg of this drug.

For congestive heart failure (CHF):

Captopril: A test dose of 6.25 to 12.5 mg three times a day is used by some clinicians to reduce risk of undesirably low blood pressure. If needed and tolerated, doses of 25 mg three times daily are started.

Enalapril: 2.5 to 10 mg once or twice daily. Usually combined with other medications. Maximum is 40 mg daily.

Fosinopril: Starting doses of 5 mg (especially for dehydrated patients or those who have kidney failure) to 10 mg have been recommended. Some studies have used once-daily dosing. Dosing must be individualized.

Ramipril: Test dose of 1.25 mg, then a dose of 2.5 to 5 mg twice a day.

To decrease cardiovascular risk:

Ramipril: Starting dose 2.5 mg a day, followed by 5 to 10 mg daily.

After a heart attack:

Captopril: A test dose of 6.25 mg is given to see if excessive lowering of the blood pressure occurs. Test usually delayed until 3 days after heart attack. If the test is tolerated, 12.5 mg is given three times a day. This dose is then increased toward a goal blood pressure or an ongoing dose of 50 mg three times a day.

Enalapril: Test dose of 2.5 mg (24 hours after a heart attack), followed by 2.5 mg twice a day, with increase (titration) to 20 mg as quickly as tolerated (in the EDEN study).

Lisinopril (when hemodynamically stable): Often a test dose of 5 mg may be given within 24 hours after symptoms started. If this dose is tolerated, a repeat dose is given 24 hours later and then increased to 10 mg a day. Therapy continues for at least 6 weeks, but may be ongoing.

Ramipril: 10 mg a day started within 24 hours has been used. Protocol driven systems have used 1.25 mg to start, then 2.5 mg given 12 hours later, followed by daily interval increases to 10 mg once a day.

Diabetic kidney problems (nephropathy) and eye problems (retinopathy):

Captopril: Success has been achieved with 50 mg twice daily in two large studies. The manufacturer suggests a starting dose of 25 mg three times a day.

Over 60 Years of Age:

Captopril: Dosing interval is adjusted to any age-related decrease in creatinine clearance or glomerular filtration rate. The initial change (cut point) is from 75 to 35 ml/minute: dose every 12 to 24 hours. Dosing is started once a day and increased as needed and tolerated.

Enalapril: Same as in younger patients, with dosing corrected for age-related decline in kidney function.

Benazepril: Same as 12 to 60 years of age, if kidney function is normal. If kidney function is significantly impaired, reduce dose by 50%. Total daily maximum is 40 mg in those with impaired kidneys.

Fosinopril: Same as 18 to 60 years of age, but these patients may be more sensitive to fosinopril. Smaller and more gradual dose increases are prudent as needed and tolerated.

Lisinopril: Exercise tolerance was improved by 2.5 to 20 mg daily. Any needed dose increases should be made at longer intervals between adjustments.

Quinapril: Same as 12 to 60 years of age, if kidney function is normal. If kidney function is significantly impaired, reduce dose by 50%. The total daily dose should not exceed 40 mg.

Ramipril: Small doses are advisable until tolerance has been determined. Sudden and excessive lowering of blood pressure can predispose to stroke or heart attack in those with impaired brain circulation or coronary artery heart disease.

Note: Actual dose and schedule must be determined for each patient individually.

Conditions Requiring Dosing Adjustments

Liver Function:

Captopril: Must be used with extreme caution and started at a lower dose in liver failure.

Enalapril: In patients with liver compromise, the dose may need to be **increased** because less of the drug is activated.

Fosinopril: Is a prodrug and is changed into fosinoprilat (the active form) by the liver. Use with caution and in lower doses by patients with liver compromise.

Quinapril, benazepril and lisinopril: The liver is minimally involved in removing these drugs.

Ramipril: Close monitoring for adverse effects is prudent.

Kidney Function:

Benazepril: For people with creatinine clearances of less than 30 ml/min, or serum creatinine greater than 3 mg/dl (ask your doctor), the starting dose should be 5 mg once daily.

Captopril: Increased blood level and risk of adverse effects (low blood counts and protein in the urine) if used in kidney failure. **Must** decrease dose according to decreases in creatinine clearance. The lowest effective dose must be used.

Enalapril: Patients with mild to moderate kidney failure can be given 5 mg/day. In severe kidney failure, maximum dose is 2.5 mg/day.

Fosinopril: This drug undergoes liver and bile (dual hepatobiliary) and kidney (renal) elimination. Patients with renal compromise (especially those with renal artery stenosis) should start on a decreased dose, with slow dose increases if needed.

Lisinopril: Patients with moderate kidney failure should be started on 5 mg daily. In severe kidney failure, the patient can take 2.5 mg of lisinopril daily. This drug is contraindicated in kidney blood flow problems (renal artery stenosis). Combination (with hydrochlorothiazide) drugs (fixed dose products) should NOT be used in kidney failure as loop (see Drug Classes) diuretics are more effective.

Quinapril: Patients with mild kidney failure can take 10 mg daily. Those with moderate kidney failure should take 5 mg daily. In severe kidney failure, 2.5 mg per day may be taken. If needed and tolerated, dose increases should only be made every 2 weeks.

Ramipril: For patients with moderate kidney failure or creatinine values of greater than 2.5 mg/dl, 1.25 mg of ramipril can be taken daily.

Diabetes:

Enalapril: Patients with diabetes with decreased creatinine clearance and protein in the urine (proteinuria) should be given decreased doses.

▷ **Dosing Instructions**

Captopril: Best taken on empty stomach, 1 hour before meals.

Enalapril, quinapril, benazepril, ramipril, fosinopril, and lisinopril: May be taken without regard to food. All ACE drugs should be taken at the same time each day, and all ACE tablets at the time of this writing may be crushed if needed to make them easier to take. If extended-release forms are present when you read this profile—talk to your doctor and pharmacist before crushing any dosage form. If you forget a dose: Take the medicine right away, unless it is nearly time for your next dose, then skip or omit the missed dose and take the medicine when it was next scheduled. DO NOT double doses.

Usual Duration of Use: Several weeks of use on a regular schedule may be required to see best benefits in lowering high blood pressure and for other uses. Use in treating high blood pressure is often a partnership for life for taking control of high blood pressure and when used in kidney disease. Reach the goal and stay on target!

Typical Treatment Goals and Measurements (Outcomes and Markers)

Blood Pressure: The NEW guidelines (JNC VII) define normal blood pressure (BP) as **less than** 120/80. Because blood pressures that were once considered acceptable can actually lead to blood vessel damage, the committee from the National Institutes of Health, National Heart Lung and Blood Institute now have a new category called **Pre-hypertension**. This ranges from 120/80 to 139/89 and is intended to help your doctor encourage lifestyle changes (or in the case of people with a risk factor for high blood pressure, start treatment) much earlier—so that possible damage to blood vessels, your heart, kidneys, sexual potency, or eyes might be minimized or avoided altogether. The next two classes of high blood pressure are stage 1 hypertension: 140/90 to 159/99 and stage 2 hypertension equal to or greater than: 160/100 mm Hg. These guidelines also recommend that clinicians trying to control blood pressure work with their patients to agree on the goals and a plan of treatment. The first-ever guidelines for blood pressure (hypertension) in African Americans recommends that MOST black patients be started on TWO antihypertensive medicines with the goal of lowering blood pressure to 130/80 for those with high risk for heart and blood vessel disease or with diabetes. The American Diabetes Association recommends 130/80 as the target for people living with diabetes and less than 125/75 for those who spill more than one gram of protein into their urine. Most clinicians try to achieve a BP that confers the best balance of lower cardiovascular risk and avoids the problem of too low a blood pressure. Blood pressure duration is generally increased with beneficial restriction of sodium. The goals and time frame should be discussed with you when the prescription is written. If goals are not met, it is not unusual to intensify doses or add on medicines. You can find the new blood pressure guidelines at *www.nhlbi.nih.gov/guidelines/hypertension/index.htm*. For the African American guidelines see Douglas, J.G. in Sources.

Stroke Prevention: Combination use of ramipril and a thiazide diuretic for patients at high risk for stroke (even those with normal blood pressure) will not use the typical blood pressure goals outlined above. The goal of the combination is to prevent the frequency of TIAs and non-fatal or fatal stoke.

Possible Advantages of These Drugs

Quinapril, benazepril, ramipril, fosinopril, and lisinopril control blood pressure effectively with one daily dose with relatively low incidence of adverse effects (ramipril at present has the most favorable data). No adverse influence on asthma, cholesterol blood levels, or diabetes. Sudden withdrawal does not result in a rapid increase in blood pressure. Fosinopril can decrease total cholesterol by 10% in patients with both high blood pressure and protein in the urine.

Captopril has a special chemical (sulfhydryl group) at its active site. This may help it ease intolerance to nitrates. Lisinopril and captopril DO NOT require activation by the liver to work. They may be drugs of choice in situations where an ACE inhibitor is desirable and liver compromise is also present. Quinapril goes into tissues well and may have a future role in treating or preventing problems (dysfunction) of the lining (endothelium) of blood vessels. Quinapril also has some laboratory data showing it to be able to stimulate growth of new blood vessels in laboratory animals. The Joint National Committee number seven (see JNC VII in Glossary) advocates ACE inhibitors as preferred medicines in diabetics with high blood pressure who have protein in their urine.

Ramipril has important and robust data to show it decreases risk of heart attack and stroke! The HOPE trial showed ramipril to decrease risk of death from any heart (cardiovascular) event by 25%, nonfatal heart attack by 20% and nonfatal stroke by 32%. This is remarkable by itself, yet dramatic when coupled with a 30% lowering of development of diabetes and kidney disease in people living with diabetes.

ACE inhibitors in general are drugs of first choice in African Americans who are at risk for or who have kidney (renal) problems (dysfunction). The African American Study of Kidney Disease and Hypertension research showed that African Americans with nephrosclerosis and hypertension who took ramipril (Altace) were found to have a 41% lower risk of end-stage kidney disease and death than those taking amlodipine (a calcium channel blocker). A new analysis (meta analysis) of existing studies (see Shekelle in Sources and the AIRE, CONSENSUS, SAVE, SMILE, SOLVD, and TRACE studies) found that ACE inhibitors benefit most patients with heart failure.

▷ **These Drugs Should Not Be Taken If**
- you have had an allergic reaction to them.
- you develop swelling of the tongue, face or throat while taking this drug or with a previous ACE inhibitor (angioedema). Call your doctor immediately if this effect starts while taking this medicine.
- you are pregnant (last 6 months especially).
- you currently have a blood cell or bone marrow disorder.
- you have an abnormally high level of blood potassium (talk to your doctor).

▷ **Inform Your Physician Before Taking These Drugs If**
- you develop swelling of the tongue, face, or throat while taking this drug. Call your doctor immediately.
- you are planning pregnancy or to breast-feed your child.
- you have kidney disease or impaired kidney function.
- you have had an allergic reaction while undergoing desensitization for bee stings (ask your doctor).

- you have scleroderma or systemic lupus erythematosus.
- you have any form of heart or liver disease.
- you have diabetes.
- you have an elevated potassium level.
- you have a blood cell disorder.
- you take other antihypertensives, diuretics, nitrates, allopurinol (Zyloprim), Indocin, or potassium supplements.
- you will have surgery with general anesthesia.
- you have renal artery or aortic stenosis (ask your doctor).
- you are taking medicines that suppress the immune system.
- you are unsure how much to take or how often to take it.

Possible Side Effects (natural, expected and unavoidable drug actions)

Dizziness, light-headedness, fainting (excessive drop in blood pressure). Increased heart rate on standing (captopril).

Scalded mouth sensation for some class members.

Impaired sense of smell—case reports for enalapril.

Nausea or constipation, increased blood potassium—all rare.

Cough—rare to infrequent (captopril, enalapril [highest withdrawal rate at 10%], fosinopril 2–10 %. Lisinopril 3.5%, quinapril 1–4%, ramipril 3–12% [greatest with delapril and least with quinapril and less than 5% overall] may start in as little as a day or up to 10 months).

▷ **Possible Adverse Effects** (unusual, unexpected and infrequent reactions)

If any of the following develop, consult your physician promptly for guidance.

Mild Adverse Effects

Allergic reactions: skin rash, psoriasis—rare to infrequent.

Swelling of face, hands or feet; fever—rare.

Ringing in the ears (tinnitus)—lisinopril—rare.

Lost or altered (metallic or salty) taste, mouth or tongue sores—case reports.

Hair loss—captopril—possible.

Headache—infrequent-relatively frequent.

Nightmares, joint pain—rare.

Increased temperature (hyperthermia)—case reports (captopril).

Low blood sugar—case reports (idiosyncratic?—and limited clinical effect)—captopril and enalapril.

Rapid heart rate on standing—case reports.

Serious Adverse Effects

Allergic reactions: swelling (angioedema) of face, tongue and/or vocal cords—rare; can be life-threatening—case reports.

Bone marrow depression (neutropenia, anemia, aplastic anemia): weakness, fever, sore throat, bleeding or bruising—rare (infrequent in kidney failure and collagen vascular disease) (not reported for ramipril).

Hemolytic or aplastic anemia—case reports (not for ramipril).

Kidney damage: water retention (edema)—case reports to rare (first 8 months usually for captopril).

Elevated blood potassium (hyperkalemia)—case reports.

Rare fluid formation around the heart (pericarditis)—case reports (captopril).

Hallucinations—rare (captopril, quinapril, and enalapril).

Stevens-Johnson Syndrome, lupus erythematosus, or other serious skin conditions (some members of this class)—rare.

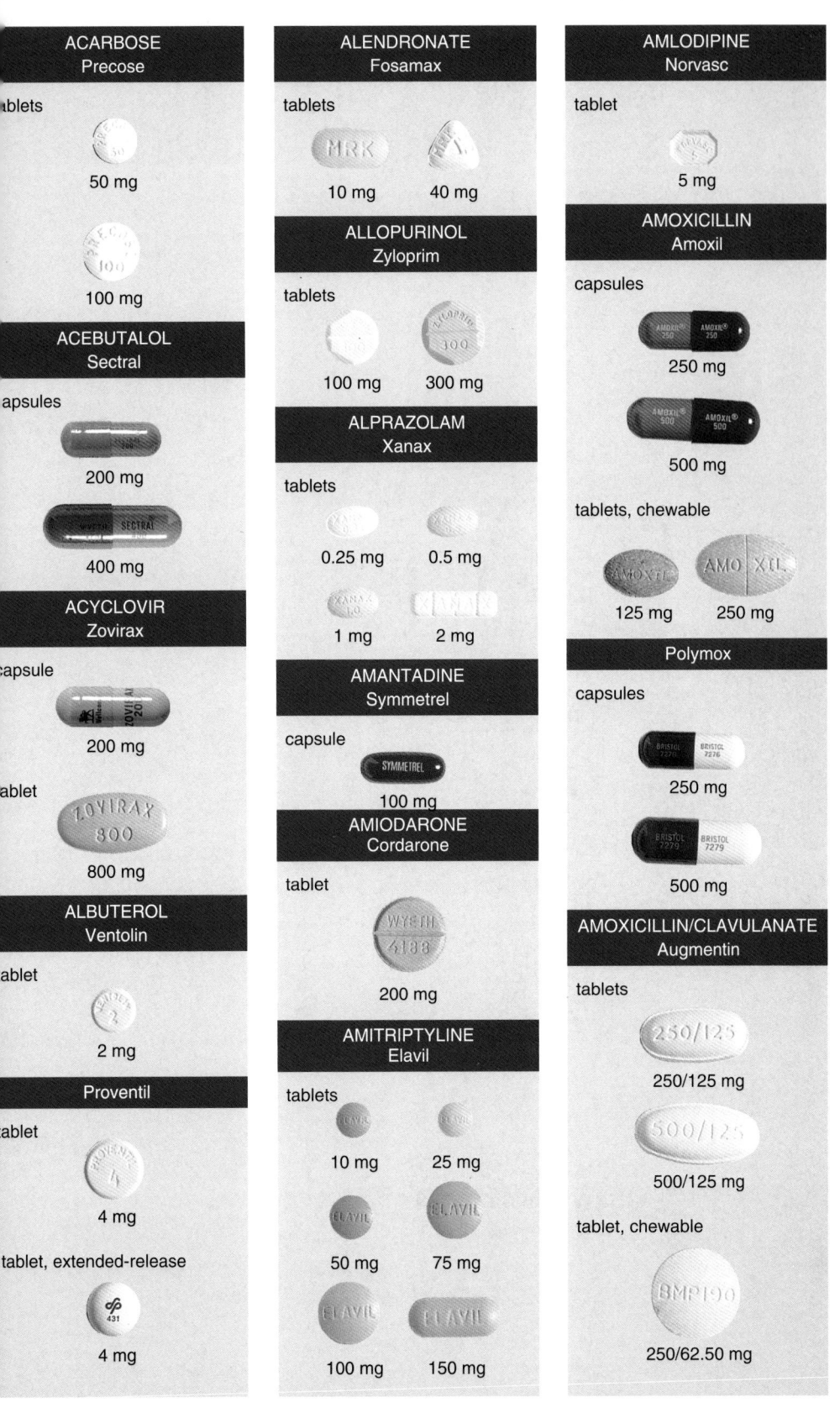

ACARBOSE
Precose

tablets

50 mg

100 mg

ACEBUTALOL
Sectral

capsules

200 mg

400 mg

ACYCLOVIR
Zovirax

capsule

200 mg

tablet

800 mg

ALBUTEROL
Ventolin

tablet

2 mg

Proventil

tablet

4 mg

tablet, extended-release

4 mg

ALENDRONATE
Fosamax

tablets

10 mg   40 mg

ALLOPURINOL
Zyloprim

tablets

100 mg   300 mg

ALPRAZOLAM
Xanax

tablets

0.25 mg   0.5 mg

1 mg   2 mg

AMANTADINE
Symmetrel

capsule

100 mg

AMIODARONE
Cordarone

tablet

200 mg

AMITRIPTYLINE
Elavil

tablets

10 mg   25 mg

50 mg   75 mg

100 mg   150 mg

AMLODIPINE
Norvasc

tablet

5 mg

AMOXICILLIN
Amoxil

capsules

250 mg

500 mg

tablets, chewable

125 mg   250 mg

Polymox

capsules

250 mg

500 mg

AMOXICILLIN/CLAVULANATE
Augmentin

tablets

250/125 mg

500/125 mg

tablet, chewable

250/62.50 mg

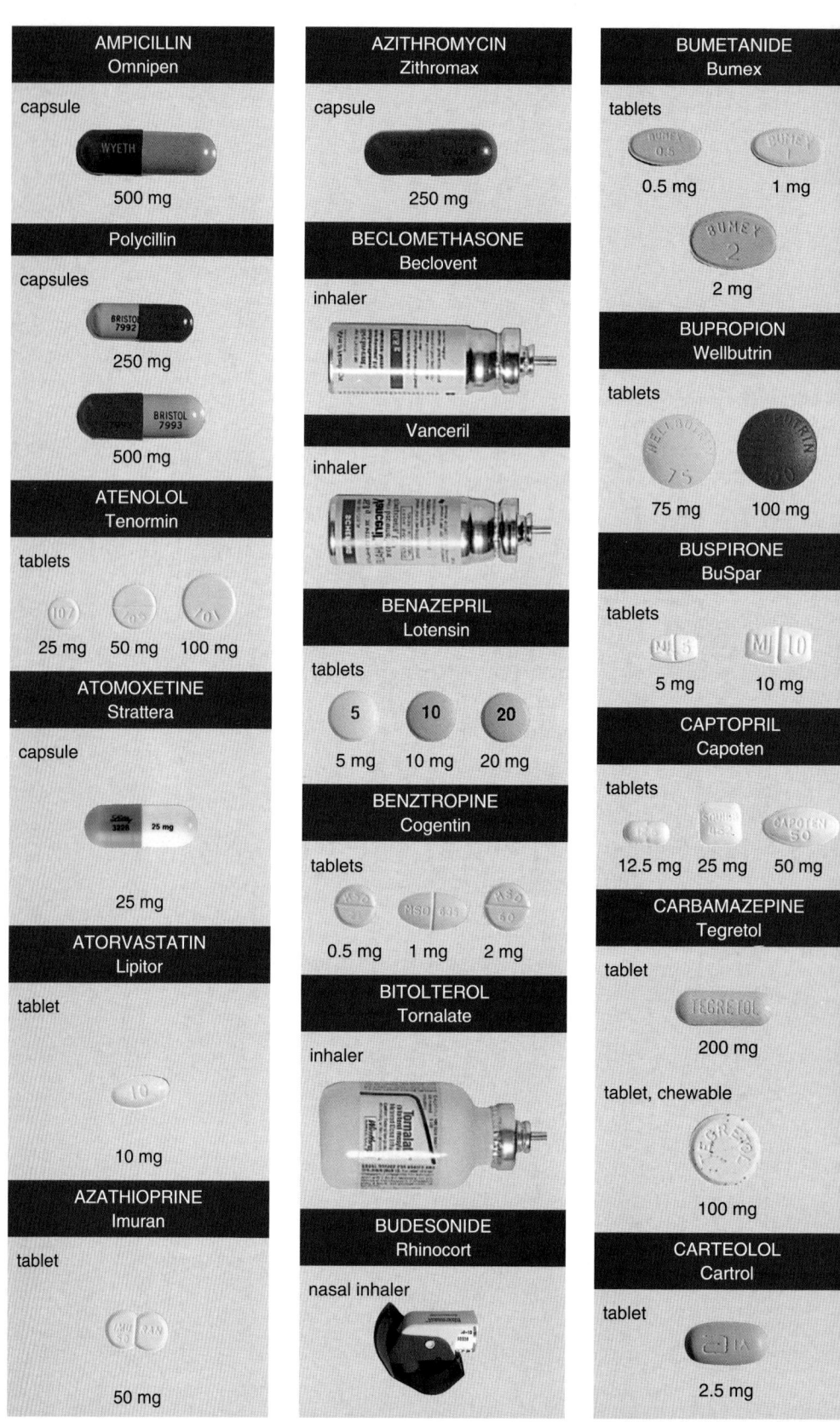

AMPICILLIN
Omnipen

capsule

500 mg

Polycillin

capsules

250 mg

500 mg

ATENOLOL
Tenormin

tablets

25 mg   50 mg   100 mg

ATOMOXETINE
Strattera

capsule

25 mg

ATORVASTATIN
Lipitor

tablet

10 mg

AZATHIOPRINE
Imuran

tablet

50 mg

AZITHROMYCIN
Zithromax

capsule

250 mg

BECLOMETHASONE
Beclovent

inhaler

Vanceril

inhaler

BENAZEPRIL
Lotensin

tablets

5   10   20

5 mg   10 mg   20 mg

BENZTROPINE
Cogentin

tablets

0.5 mg   1 mg   2 mg

BITOLTEROL
Tornalate

inhaler

BUDESONIDE
Rhinocort

nasal inhaler

BUMETANIDE
Bumex

tablets

0.5 mg   1 mg

2 mg

BUPROPION
Wellbutrin

tablets

75 mg   100 mg

BUSPIRONE
BuSpar

tablets

5 mg   10 mg

CAPTOPRIL
Capoten

tablets

12.5 mg   25 mg   50 mg

CARBAMAZEPINE
Tegretol

tablet

200 mg

tablet, chewable

100 mg

CARTEOLOL
Cartrol

tablet

2.5 mg

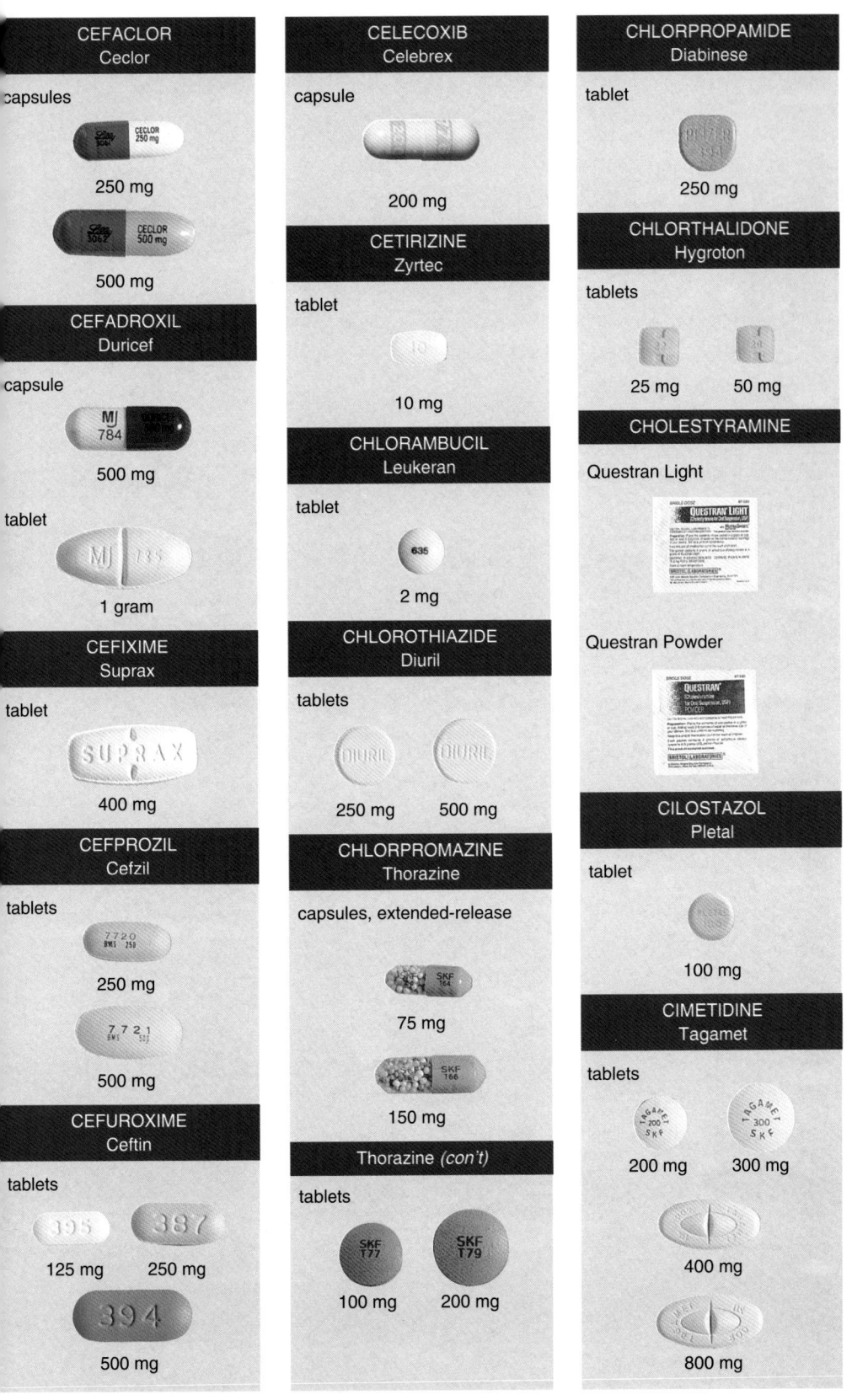

CEFACLOR
Ceclor

capsules

250 mg

500 mg

CEFADROXIL
Duricef

capsule

500 mg

tablet

1 gram

CEFIXIME
Suprax

tablet

SUPRAX

400 mg

CEFPROZIL
Cefzil

tablets

250 mg

500 mg

CEFUROXIME
Ceftin

tablets

125 mg   250 mg

500 mg

CELECOXIB
Celebrex

capsule

200 mg

CETIRIZINE
Zyrtec

tablet

10 mg

CHLORAMBUCIL
Leukeran

tablet

2 mg

CHLOROTHIAZIDE
Diuril

tablets

250 mg   500 mg

CHLORPROMAZINE
Thorazine

capsules, extended-release

75 mg

150 mg

Thorazine (con't)

tablets

100 mg   200 mg

CHLORPROPAMIDE
Diabinese

tablet

250 mg

CHLORTHALIDONE
Hygroton

tablets

25 mg   50 mg

CHOLESTYRAMINE

Questran Light

Questran Powder

CILOSTAZOL
Pletal

tablet

100 mg

CIMETIDINE
Tagamet

tablets

200 mg   300 mg

400 mg

800 mg

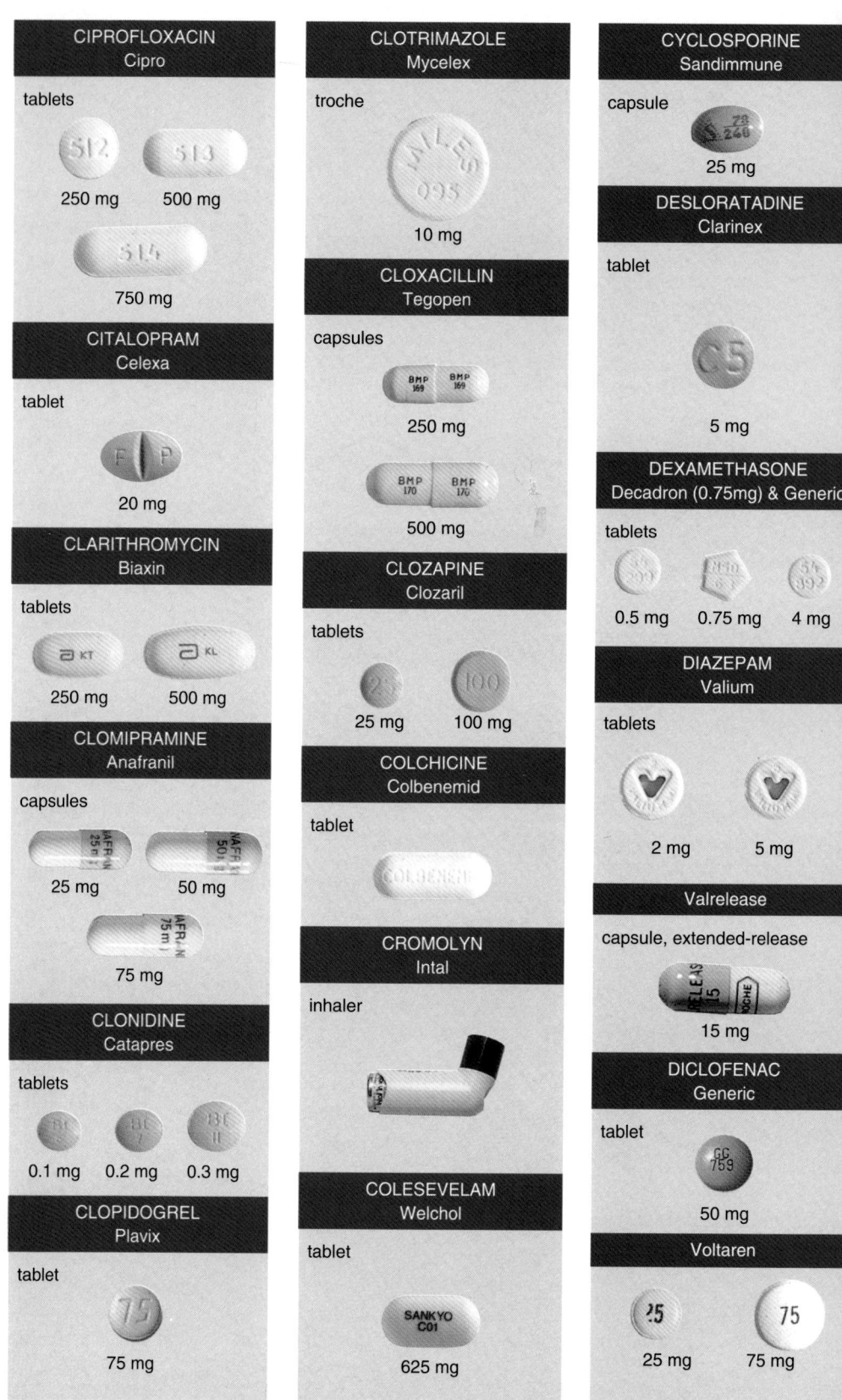

CIPROFLOXACIN
Cipro

tablets

250 mg   500 mg

750 mg

CITALOPRAM
Celexa

tablet

20 mg

CLARITHROMYCIN
Biaxin

tablets

250 mg   500 mg

CLOMIPRAMINE
Anafranil

capsules

25 mg   50 mg

75 mg

CLONIDINE
Catapres

tablets

0.1 mg   0.2 mg   0.3 mg

CLOPIDOGREL
Plavix

tablet

75 mg

CLOTRIMAZOLE
Mycelex

troche

10 mg

CLOXACILLIN
Tegopen

capsules

250 mg

500 mg

CLOZAPINE
Clozaril

tablets

25 mg   100 mg

COLCHICINE
Colbenemid

tablet

CROMOLYN
Intal

inhaler

COLESEVELAM
Welchol

tablet

625 mg

CYCLOSPORINE
Sandimmune

capsule

25 mg

DESLORATADINE
Clarinex

tablet

5 mg

DEXAMETHASONE
Decadron (0.75mg) & Generic

tablets

0.5 mg   0.75 mg   4 mg

DIAZEPAM
Valium

tablets

2 mg   5 mg

Valrelease

capsule, extended-release

15 mg

DICLOFENAC
Generic

tablet

50 mg

Voltaren

25 mg   75 mg

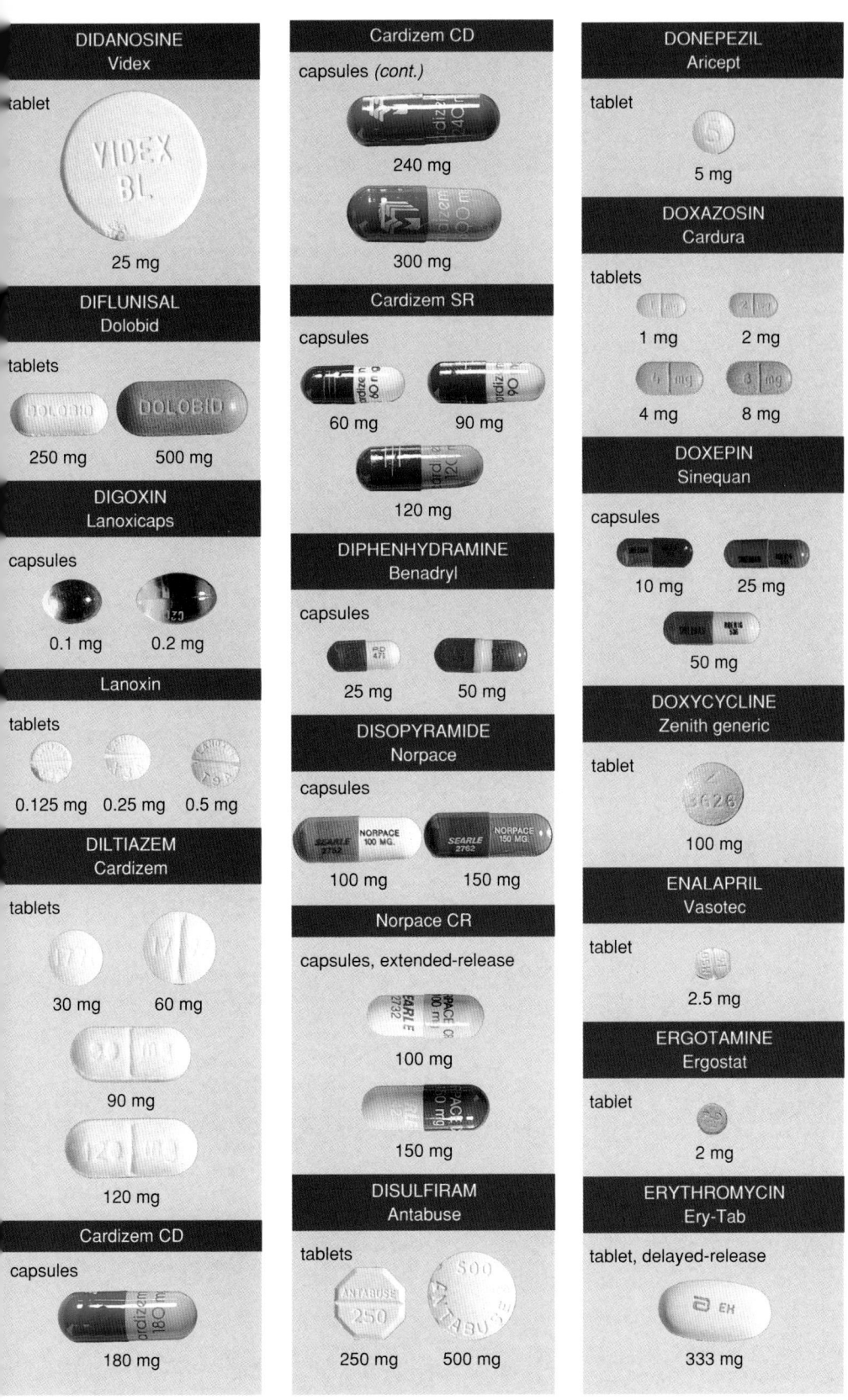

DIDANOSINE
Videx

tablet

VIDEX BL.

25 mg

DIFLUNISAL
Dolobid

tablets

DOLOBID — 250 mg

DOLOBID — 500 mg

DIGOXIN
Lanoxicaps

capsules

0.1 mg

0.2 mg

Lanoxin

tablets

0.125 mg   0.25 mg   0.5 mg

DILTIAZEM
Cardizem

tablets

30 mg

60 mg

90 mg

120 mg

Cardizem CD

capsules

180 mg

Cardizem CD
capsules *(cont.)*

240 mg

300 mg

Cardizem SR

capsules

60 mg

90 mg

120 mg

DIPHENHYDRAMINE
Benadryl

capsules

25 mg

50 mg

DISOPYRAMIDE
Norpace

capsules

SEARLE 2762 — NORPACE 100 MG.

SEARLE 2762 — NORPACE 150 MG.

100 mg

150 mg

Norpace CR

capsules, extended-release

NORPACE CR 100 mg — SEARLE 2732

100 mg

NORPACE CR 150 mg

150 mg

DISULFIRAM
Antabuse

tablets

ANTABUSE 250

500 ANTABUSE

250 mg

500 mg

DONEPEZIL
Aricept

tablet

5

5 mg

DOXAZOSIN
Cardura

tablets

1 mg

2 mg

4 mg

8 mg

DOXEPIN
Sinequan

capsules

10 mg

25 mg

50 mg

DOXYCYCLINE
Zenith generic

tablet

3626

100 mg

ENALAPRIL
Vasotec

tablet

2.5 mg

ERGOTAMINE
Ergostat

tablet

2 mg

ERYTHROMYCIN
Ery-Tab

tablet, delayed-release

EH

333 mg

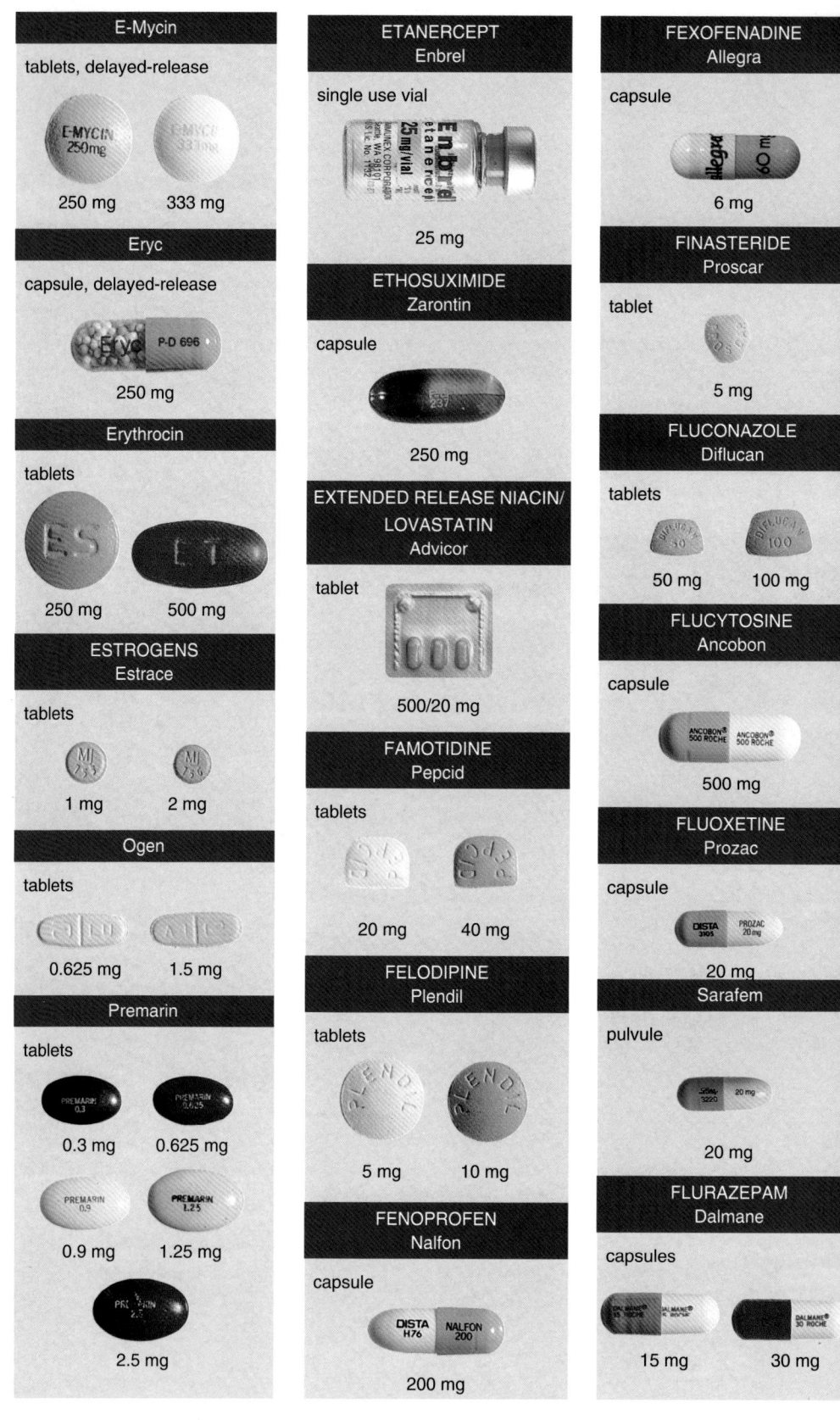

E-Mycin

tablets, delayed-release

250 mg — 333 mg

Eryc

capsule, delayed-release

250 mg

Erythrocin

tablets

250 mg — 500 mg

ESTROGENS
Estrace

tablets

1 mg — 2 mg

Ogen

tablets

0.625 mg — 1.5 mg

Premarin

tablets

0.3 mg — 0.625 mg

0.9 mg — 1.25 mg

2.5 mg

ETANERCEPT
Enbrel

single use vial

25 mg

ETHOSUXIMIDE
Zarontin

capsule

250 mg

EXTENDED RELEASE NIACIN/ LOVASTATIN
Advicor

tablet

500/20 mg

FAMOTIDINE
Pepcid

tablets

20 mg — 40 mg

FELODIPINE
Plendil

tablets

5 mg — 10 mg

FENOPROFEN
Nalfon

capsule

200 mg

FEXOFENADINE
Allegra

capsule

6 mg

FINASTERIDE
Proscar

tablet

5 mg

FLUCONAZOLE
Diflucan

tablets

50 mg — 100 mg

FLUCYTOSINE
Ancobon

capsule

500 mg

FLUOXETINE
Prozac

capsule

20 mg

Sarafem

pulvule

20 mg

FLURAZEPAM
Dalmane

capsules

15 mg — 30 mg

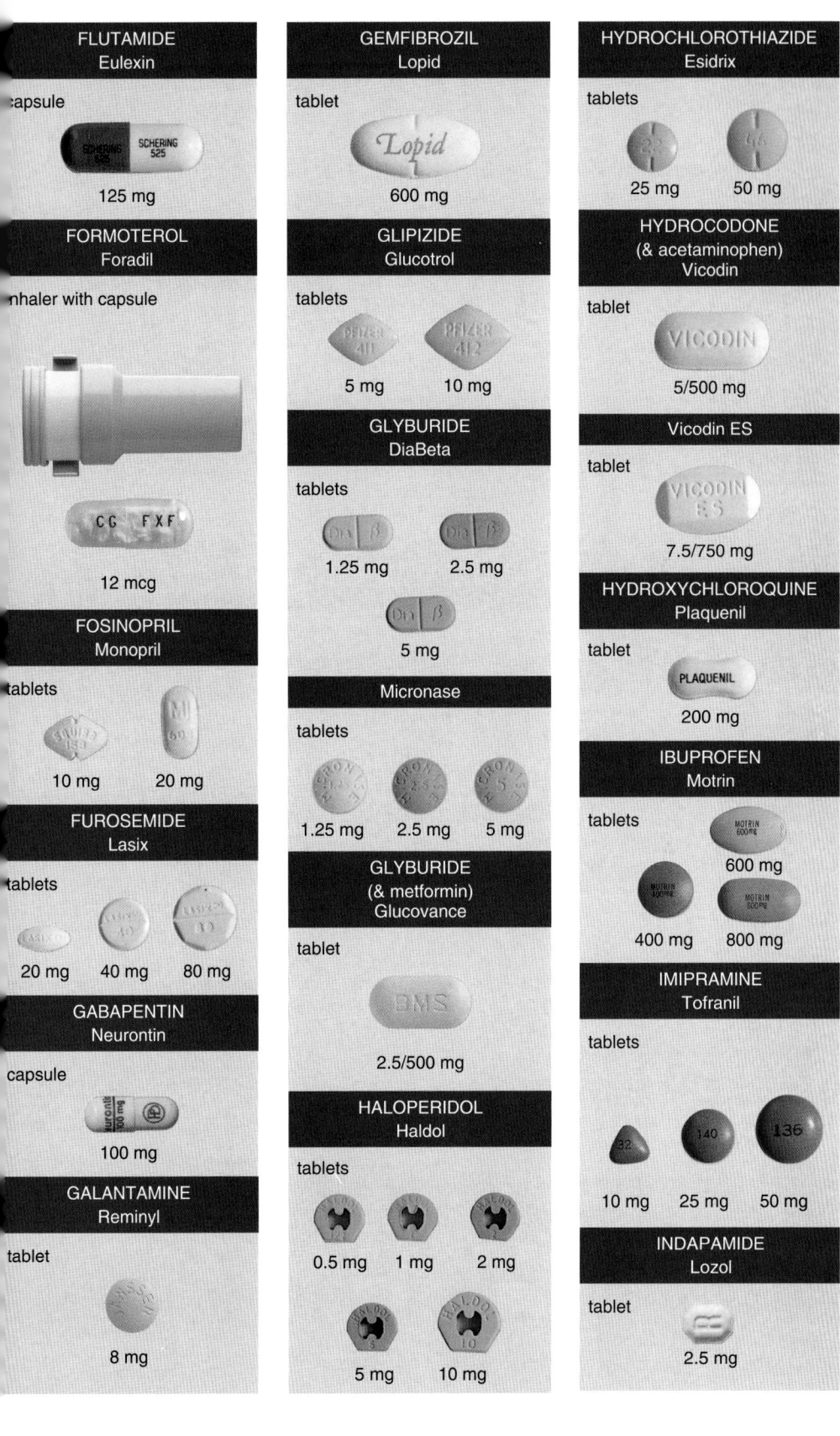

FLUTAMIDE
Eulexin

capsule

125 mg

FORMOTEROL
Foradil

inhaler with capsule

C G   F X F

12 mcg

FOSINOPRIL
Monopril

tablets

10 mg   20 mg

FUROSEMIDE
Lasix

tablets

20 mg   40 mg   80 mg

GABAPENTIN
Neurontin

capsule

100 mg

GALANTAMINE
Reminyl

tablet

8 mg

GEMFIBROZIL
Lopid

tablet

Lopid

600 mg

GLIPIZIDE
Glucotrol

tablets

PFIZER 411   PFIZER 412

5 mg   10 mg

GLYBURIDE
DiaBeta

tablets

1.25 mg   2.5 mg

5 mg

Micronase

tablets

1.25 mg   2.5 mg   5 mg

GLYBURIDE
(& metformin)
Glucovance

tablet

BMS

2.5/500 mg

HALOPERIDOL
Haldol

tablets

0.5 mg   1 mg   2 mg

5 mg   10 mg

HYDROCHLOROTHIAZIDE
Esidrix

tablets

25 mg   50 mg

HYDROCODONE
(& acetaminophen)
Vicodin

tablet

VICODIN

5/500 mg

Vicodin ES

tablet

VICODIN ES

7.5/750 mg

HYDROXYCHLOROQUINE
Plaquenil

tablet

PLAQUENIL

200 mg

IBUPROFEN
Motrin

tablets

MOTRIN 600mg

600 mg

MOTRIN 400mg   MOTRIN 800mg

400 mg   800 mg

IMIPRAMINE
Tofranil

tablets

32   140   136

10 mg   25 mg   50 mg

INDAPAMIDE
Lozol

tablet

2.5 mg

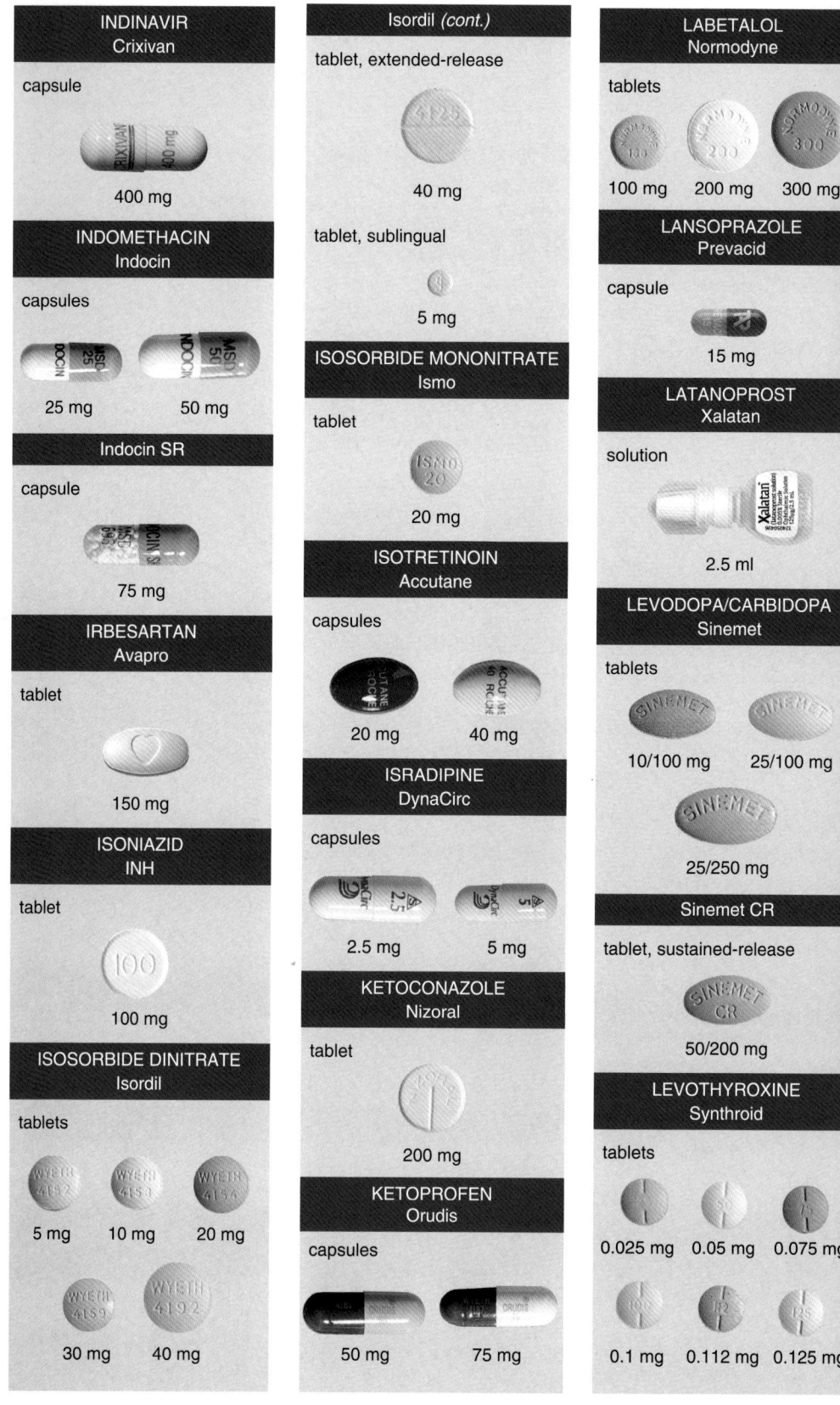

INDINAVIR
Crixivan

capsule

400 mg

INDOMETHACIN
Indocin

capsules

25 mg   50 mg

Indocin SR

capsule

75 mg

IRBESARTAN
Avapro

tablet

150 mg

ISONIAZID
INH

tablet

100 mg

ISOSORBIDE DINITRATE
Isordil

tablets

5 mg   10 mg   20 mg

30 mg   40 mg

Isordil *(cont.)*

tablet, extended-release

40 mg

tablet, sublingual

5 mg

ISOSORBIDE MONONITRATE
Ismo

tablet

20 mg

ISOTRETINOIN
Accutane

capsules

20 mg   40 mg

ISRADIPINE
DynaCirc

capsules

2.5 mg   5 mg

KETOCONAZOLE
Nizoral

tablet

200 mg

KETOPROFEN
Orudis

capsules

50 mg   75 mg

LABETALOL
Normodyne

tablets

100 mg   200 mg   300 mg

LANSOPRAZOLE
Prevacid

capsule

15 mg

LATANOPROST
Xalatan

solution

2.5 ml

LEVODOPA/CARBIDOPA
Sinemet

tablets

10/100 mg   25/100 mg

25/250 mg

Sinemet CR

tablet, sustained-release

50/200 mg

LEVOTHYROXINE
Synthroid

tablets

0.025 mg   0.05 mg   0.075 mg

0.1 mg   0.112 mg   0.125 mg

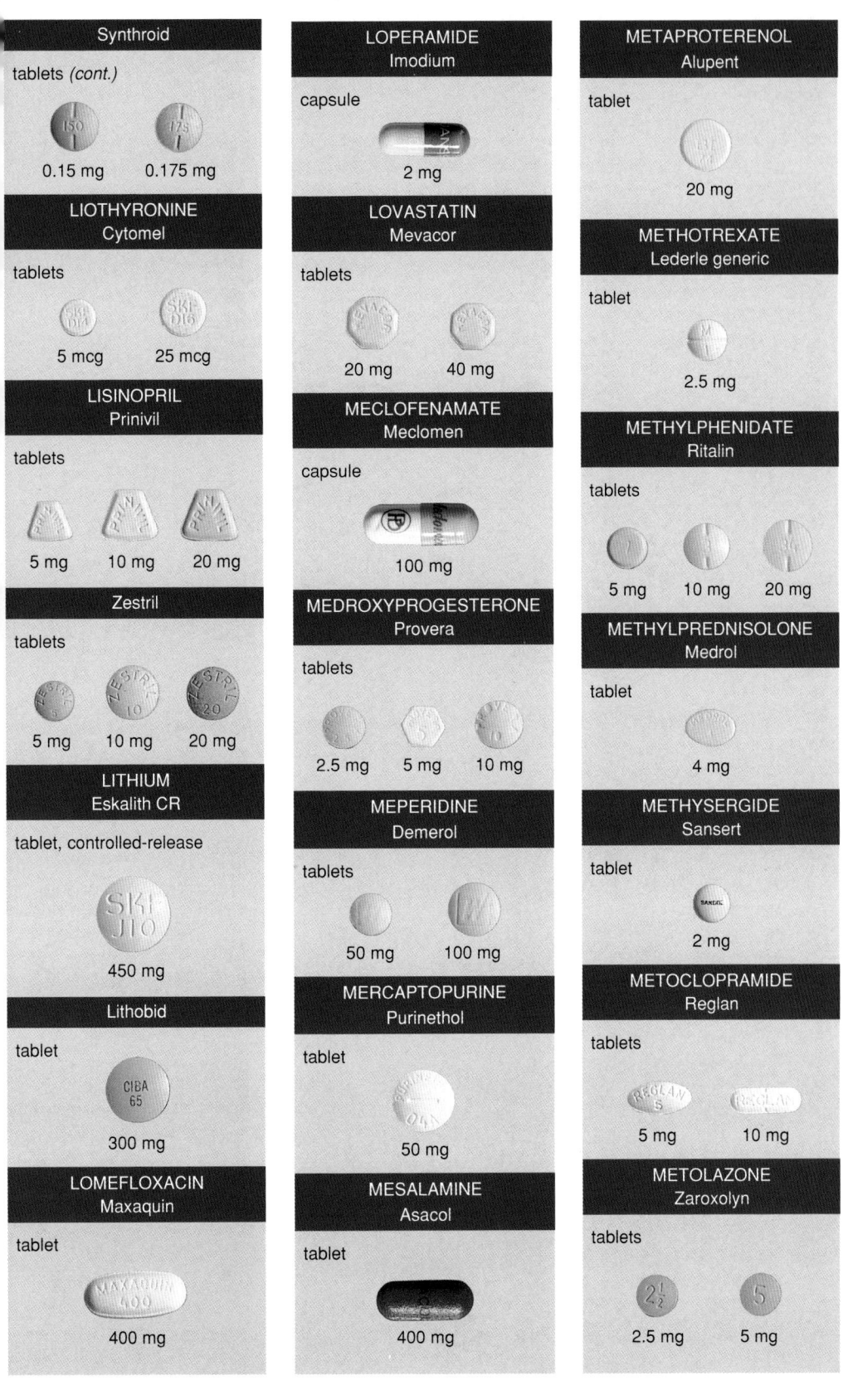

Synthroid

tablets *(cont.)*

0.15 mg   0.175 mg

LIOTHYRONINE
Cytomel

tablets

5 mcg   25 mcg

LISINOPRIL
Prinivil

tablets

5 mg   10 mg   20 mg

Zestril

tablets

5 mg   10 mg   20 mg

LITHIUM
Eskalith CR

tablet, controlled-release

450 mg

Lithobid

tablet

300 mg

LOMEFLOXACIN
Maxaquin

tablet

400 mg

LOPERAMIDE
Imodium

capsule

2 mg

LOVASTATIN
Mevacor

tablets

20 mg   40 mg

MECLOFENAMATE
Meclomen

capsule

100 mg

MEDROXYPROGESTERONE
Provera

tablets

2.5 mg   5 mg   10 mg

MEPERIDINE
Demerol

tablets

50 mg   100 mg

MERCAPTOPURINE
Purinethol

tablet

50 mg

MESALAMINE
Asacol

tablet

400 mg

METAPROTERENOL
Alupent

tablet

20 mg

METHOTREXATE
Lederle generic

tablet

2.5 mg

METHYLPHENIDATE
Ritalin

tablets

5 mg   10 mg   20 mg

METHYLPREDNISOLONE
Medrol

tablet

4 mg

METHYSERGIDE
Sansert

tablet

2 mg

METOCLOPRAMIDE
Reglan

tablets

5 mg   10 mg

METOLAZONE
Zaroxolyn

tablets

2.5 mg   5 mg

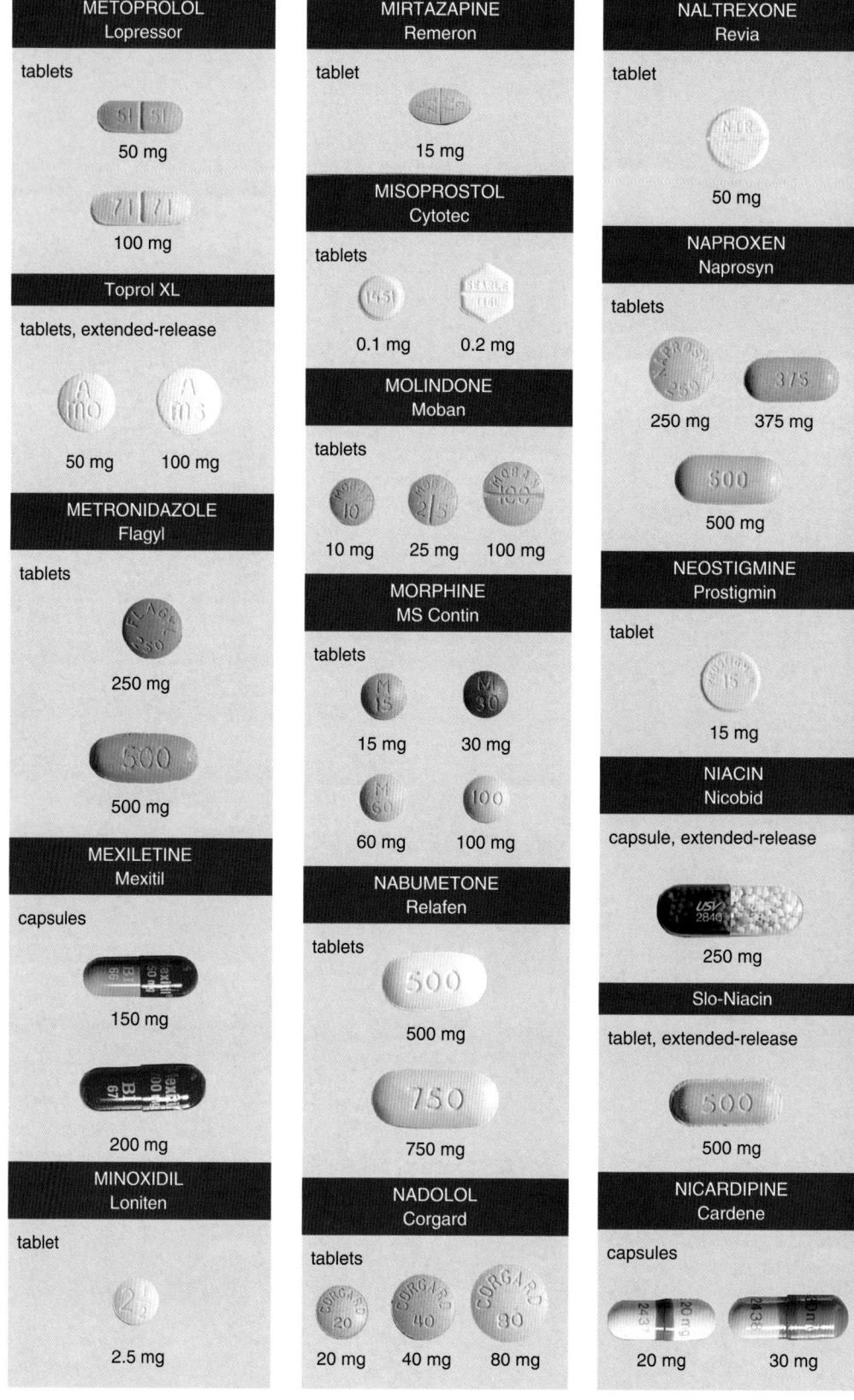

METOPROLOL
Lopressor

tablets

51 51
50 mg

71 71
100 mg

Toprol XL

tablets, extended-release

A mo
50 mg

A ms
100 mg

METRONIDAZOLE
Flagyl

tablets

FLAGYL 250
250 mg

500
500 mg

MEXILETINE
Mexitil

capsules

150 mg

200 mg

MINOXIDIL
Loniten

tablet

2.5 mg

MIRTAZAPINE
Remeron

tablet

15 mg

MISOPROSTOL
Cytotec

tablets

1451
0.1 mg

SEARLE 1461
0.2 mg

MOLINDONE
Moban

tablets

MOBAN 10
10 mg

MOBAN 25
25 mg

MOBAN 100
100 mg

MORPHINE
MS Contin

tablets

M 15
15 mg

M 30
30 mg

M 60
60 mg

100
100 mg

NABUMETONE
Relafen

tablets

500
500 mg

750
750 mg

NADOLOL
Corgard

tablets

CORGARD 20
20 mg

CORGARD 40
40 mg

CORGARD 80
80 mg

NALTREXONE
Revia

tablet

NTR
50 mg

NAPROXEN
Naprosyn

tablets

NAPROSYN 250
250 mg

375
375 mg

500
500 mg

NEOSTIGMINE
Prostigmin

tablet

15
15 mg

NIACIN
Nicobid

capsule, extended-release

USV 2846
250 mg

Slo-Niacin

tablet, extended-release

500
500 mg

NICARDIPINE
Cardene

capsules

20 mg

30 mg

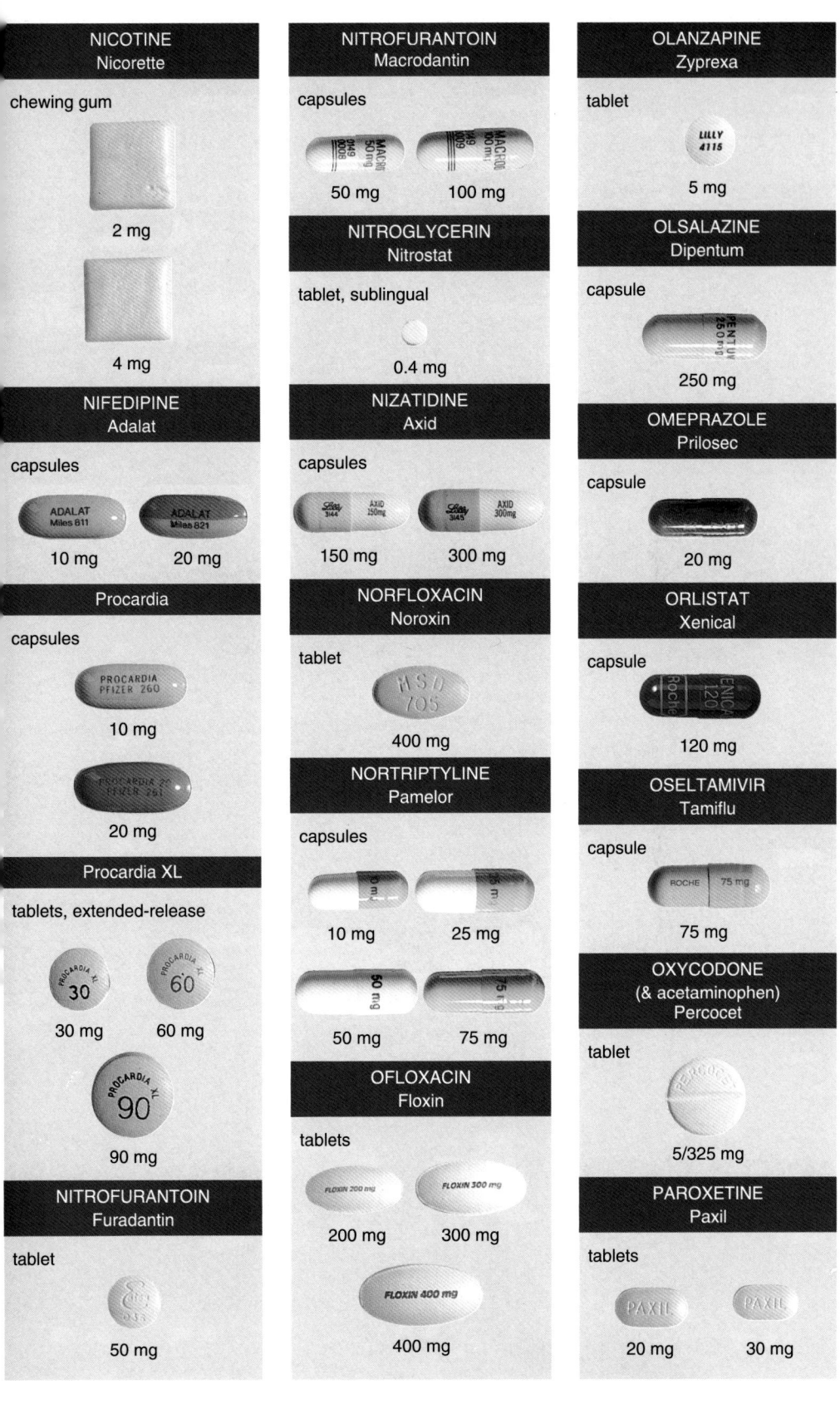

NICOTINE
Nicorette

chewing gum

2 mg

4 mg

NIFEDIPINE
Adalat

capsules

ADALAT
Miles 811

ADALAT
Miles 821

10 mg

20 mg

Procardia

capsules

PROCARDIA
PFIZER 260

10 mg

PROCARDIA 20
PFIZER 261

20 mg

Procardia XL

tablets, extended-release

PROCARDIA XL
30

PROCARDIA XL
60

30 mg

60 mg

PROCARDIA XL
90

90 mg

NITROFURANTOIN
Furadantin

tablet

50 mg

NITROFURANTOIN
Macrodantin

capsules

MACRO
50 mg

MACRO
100 mg

50 mg

100 mg

NITROGLYCERIN
Nitrostat

tablet, sublingual

0.4 mg

NIZATIDINE
Axid

capsules

Lilly
3144

AXID
150mg

Lilly
3145

AXID
300mg

150 mg

300 mg

NORFLOXACIN
Noroxin

tablet

MSD
705

400 mg

NORTRIPTYLINE
Pamelor

capsules

10 mg

25 mg

50 mg

75 mg

OFLOXACIN
Floxin

tablets

FLOXIN 200 mg

FLOXIN 300 mg

200 mg

300 mg

FLOXIN 400 mg

400 mg

OLANZAPINE
Zyprexa

tablet

LILLY
4115

5 mg

OLSALAZINE
Dipentum

capsule

IPENT UV
25.0 mg

250 mg

OMEPRAZOLE
Prilosec

capsule

20 mg

ORLISTAT
Xenical

capsule

Roche

XENICAL
120

120 mg

OSELTAMIVIR
Tamiflu

capsule

ROCHE

75 mg

75 mg

OXYCODONE
(& acetaminophen)
Percocet

tablet

PERCOCET

5/325 mg

PAROXETINE
Paxil

tablets

PAXIL

PAXIL

20 mg

30 mg

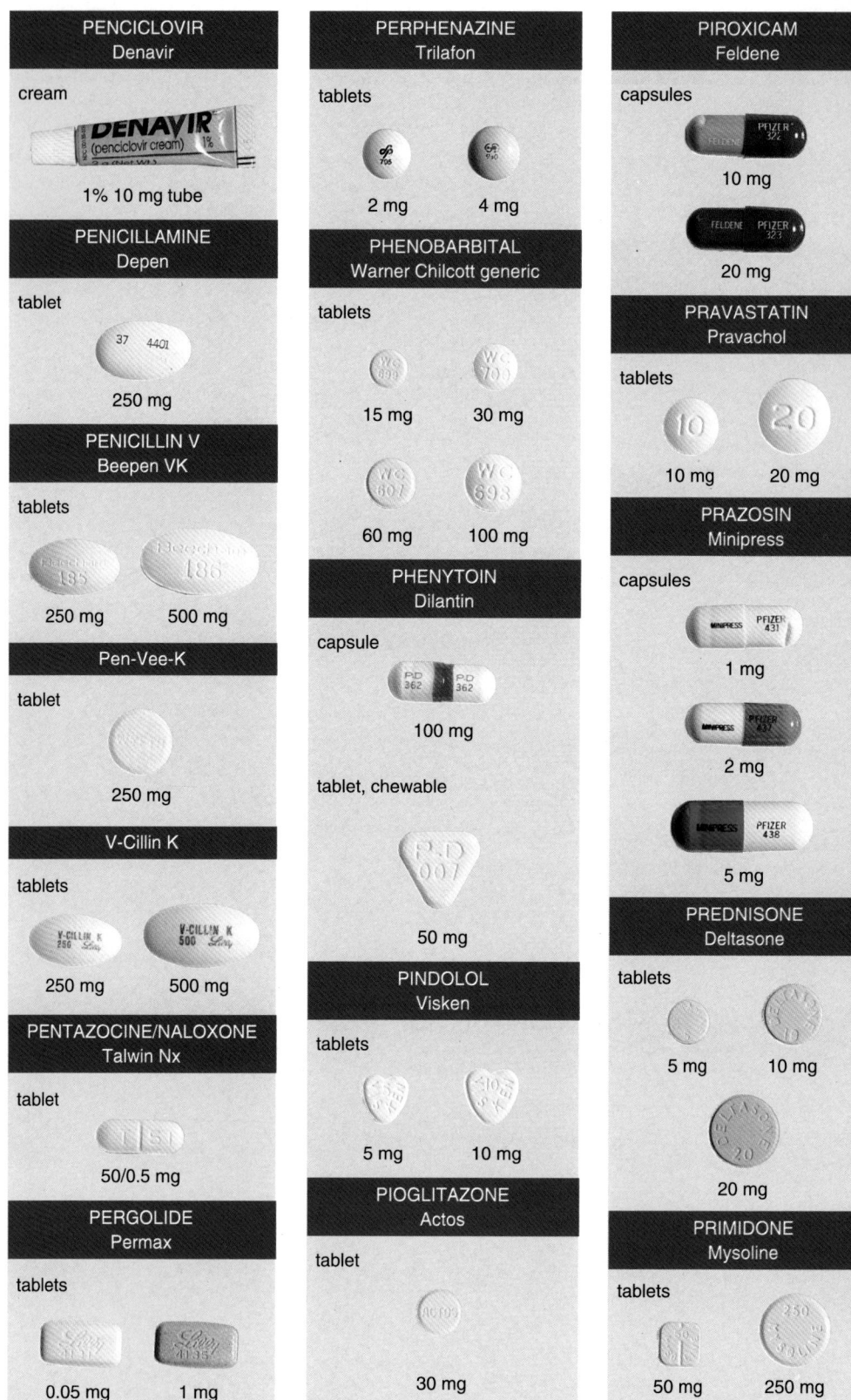

PENCICLOVIR
Denavir

cream

1% 10 mg tube

PENICILLAMINE
Depen

tablet

250 mg

PENICILLIN V
Beepen VK

tablets

250 mg   500 mg

Pen-Vee-K

tablet

250 mg

V-Cillin K

tablets

250 mg   500 mg

PENTAZOCINE/NALOXONE
Talwin Nx

tablet

50/0.5 mg

PERGOLIDE
Permax

tablets

0.05 mg   1 mg

PERPHENAZINE
Trilafon

tablets

2 mg   4 mg

PHENOBARBITAL
Warner Chilcott generic

tablets

15 mg   30 mg

60 mg   100 mg

PHENYTOIN
Dilantin

capsule

100 mg

tablet, chewable

50 mg

PINDOLOL
Visken

tablets

5 mg   10 mg

PIOGLITAZONE
Actos

tablet

30 mg

PIROXICAM
Feldene

capsules

10 mg

20 mg

PRAVASTATIN
Pravachol

tablets

10 mg   20 mg

PRAZOSIN
Minipress

capsules

1 mg

2 mg

5 mg

PREDNISONE
Deltasone

tablets

5 mg   10 mg

20 mg

PRIMIDONE
Mysoline

tablets

50 mg   250 mg

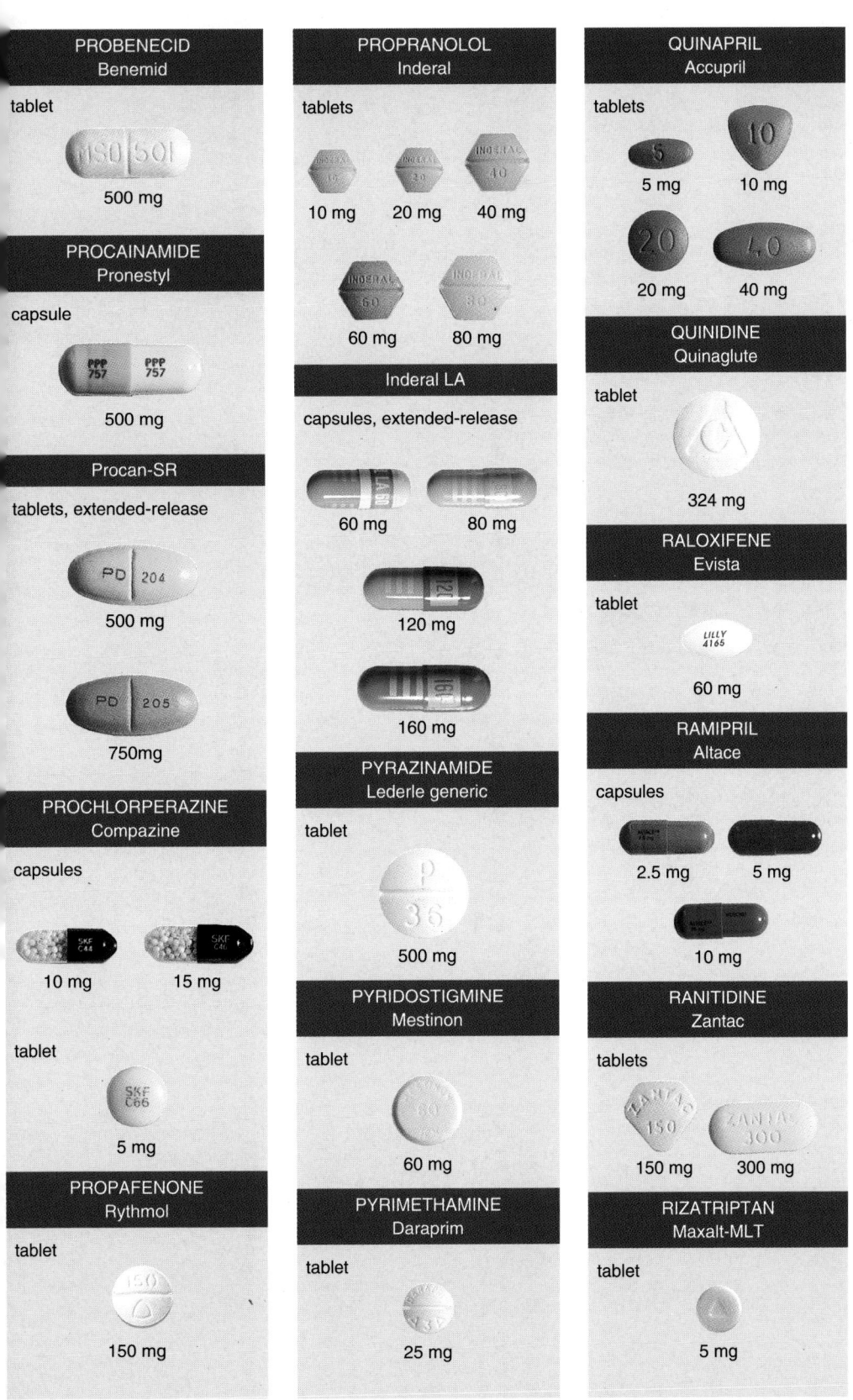

PROBENECID
Benemid

tablet

500 mg

PROCAINAMIDE
Pronestyl

capsule

500 mg

Procan-SR

tablets, extended-release

500 mg

750mg

PROCHLORPERAZINE
Compazine

capsules

10 mg   15 mg

tablet

5 mg

PROPAFENONE
Rythmol

tablet

150 mg

PROPRANOLOL
Inderal

tablets

10 mg   20 mg   40 mg

60 mg   80 mg

Inderal LA

capsules, extended-release

60 mg   80 mg

120 mg

160 mg

PYRAZINAMIDE
Lederle generic

tablet

500 mg

PYRIDOSTIGMINE
Mestinon

tablet

60 mg

PYRIMETHAMINE
Daraprim

tablet

25 mg

QUINAPRIL
Accupril

tablets

5 mg   10 mg

20 mg   40 mg

QUINIDINE
Quinaglute

tablet

324 mg

RALOXIFENE
Evista

tablet

60 mg

RAMIPRIL
Altace

capsules

2.5 mg   5 mg

10 mg

RANITIDINE
Zantac

tablets

150 mg   300 mg

RIZATRIPTAN
Maxalt-MLT

tablet

5 mg

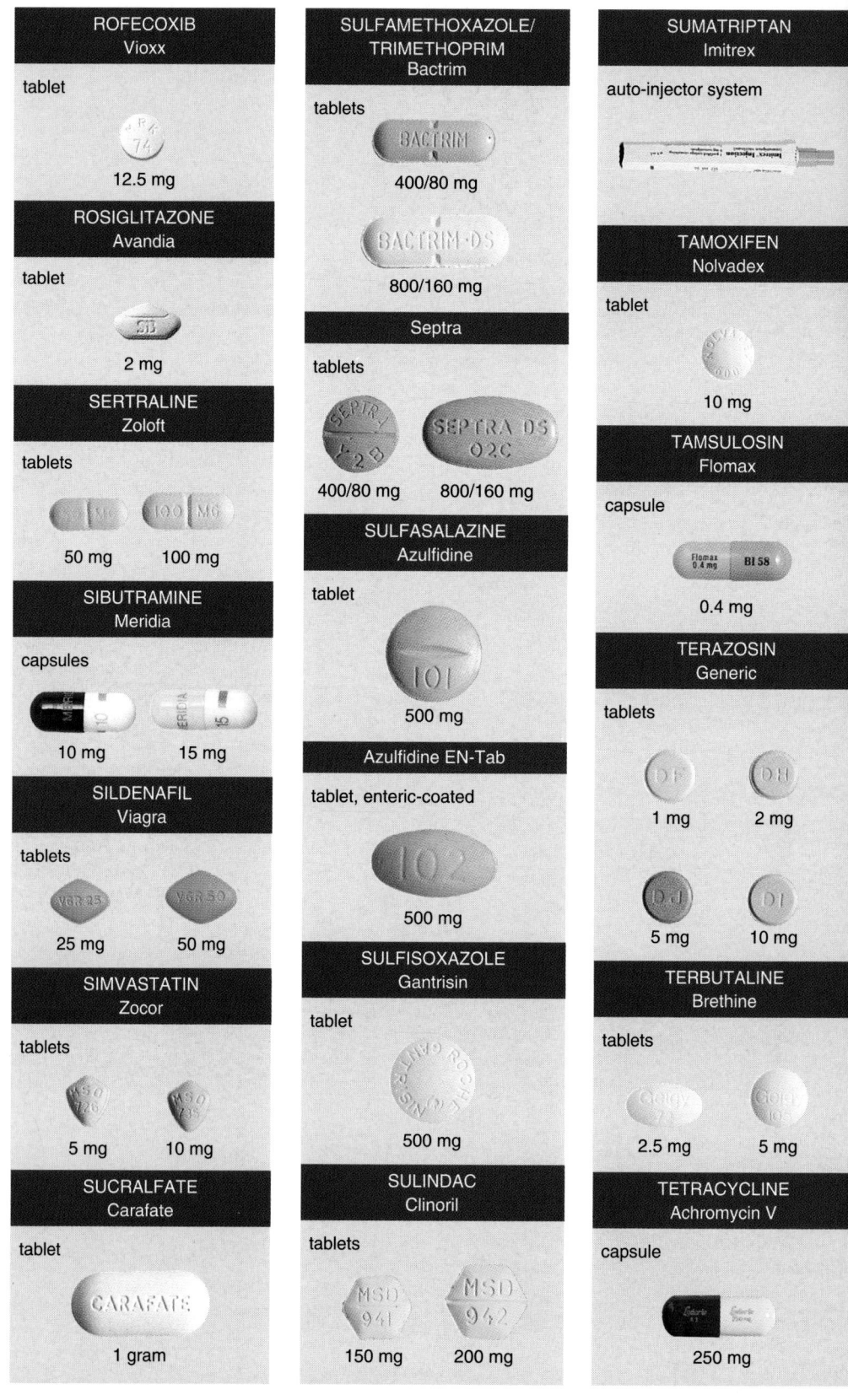

ROFECOXIB
Vioxx

tablet

12.5 mg

ROSIGLITAZONE
Avandia

tablet

2 mg

SERTRALINE
Zoloft

tablets

50 mg   100 mg

SIBUTRAMINE
Meridia

capsules

10 mg   15 mg

SILDENAFIL
Viagra

tablets

25 mg   50 mg

SIMVASTATIN
Zocor

tablets

5 mg   10 mg

SUCRALFATE
Carafate

tablet

1 gram

**SULFAMETHOXAZOLE/
TRIMETHOPRIM**
Bactrim

tablets

400/80 mg

800/160 mg

Septra

tablets

400/80 mg   800/160 mg

SULFASALAZINE
Azulfidine

tablet

500 mg

Azulfidine EN-Tab

tablet, enteric-coated

500 mg

SULFISOXAZOLE
Gantrisin

tablet

500 mg

SULINDAC
Clinoril

tablets

150 mg   200 mg

SUMATRIPTAN
Imitrex

auto-injector system

TAMOXIFEN
Nolvadex

tablet

10 mg

TAMSULOSIN
Flomax

capsule

0.4 mg

TERAZOSIN
Generic

tablets

1 mg   2 mg

5 mg   10 mg

TERBUTALINE
Brethine

tablets

2.5 mg   5 mg

TETRACYCLINE
Achromycin V

capsule

250 mg

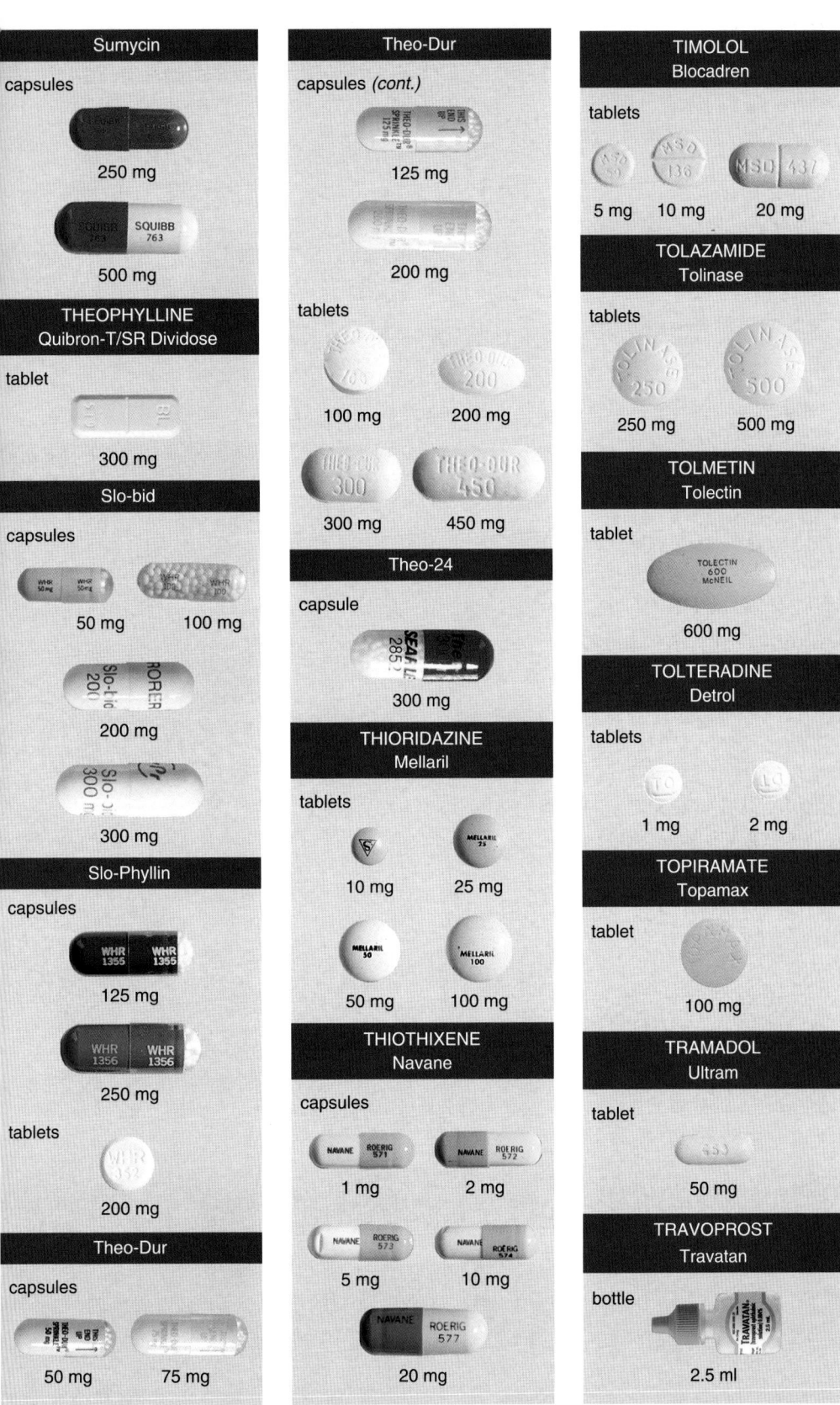

Sumycin

capsules

250 mg

500 mg

THEOPHYLLINE
Quibron-T/SR Dividose

tablet

300 mg

Slo-bid

capsules

50 mg   100 mg

200 mg

300 mg

Slo-Phyllin

capsules

125 mg

250 mg

tablets

200 mg

Theo-Dur

capsules

50 mg   75 mg

Theo-Dur

capsules *(cont.)*

125 mg

200 mg

tablets

100 mg   200 mg

300 mg   450 mg

Theo-24

capsule

300 mg

THIORIDAZINE
Mellaril

tablets

10 mg   25 mg

50 mg   100 mg

THIOTHIXENE
Navane

capsules

1 mg   2 mg

5 mg   10 mg

20 mg

TIMOLOL
Blocadren

tablets

5 mg   10 mg   20 mg

TOLAZAMIDE
Tolinase

tablets

250 mg   500 mg

TOLMETIN
Tolectin

tablet

600 mg

TOLTERADINE
Detrol

tablets

1 mg   2 mg

TOPIRAMATE
Topamax

tablet

100 mg

TRAMADOL
Ultram

tablet

50 mg

TRAVOPROST
Travatan

bottle

2.5 ml

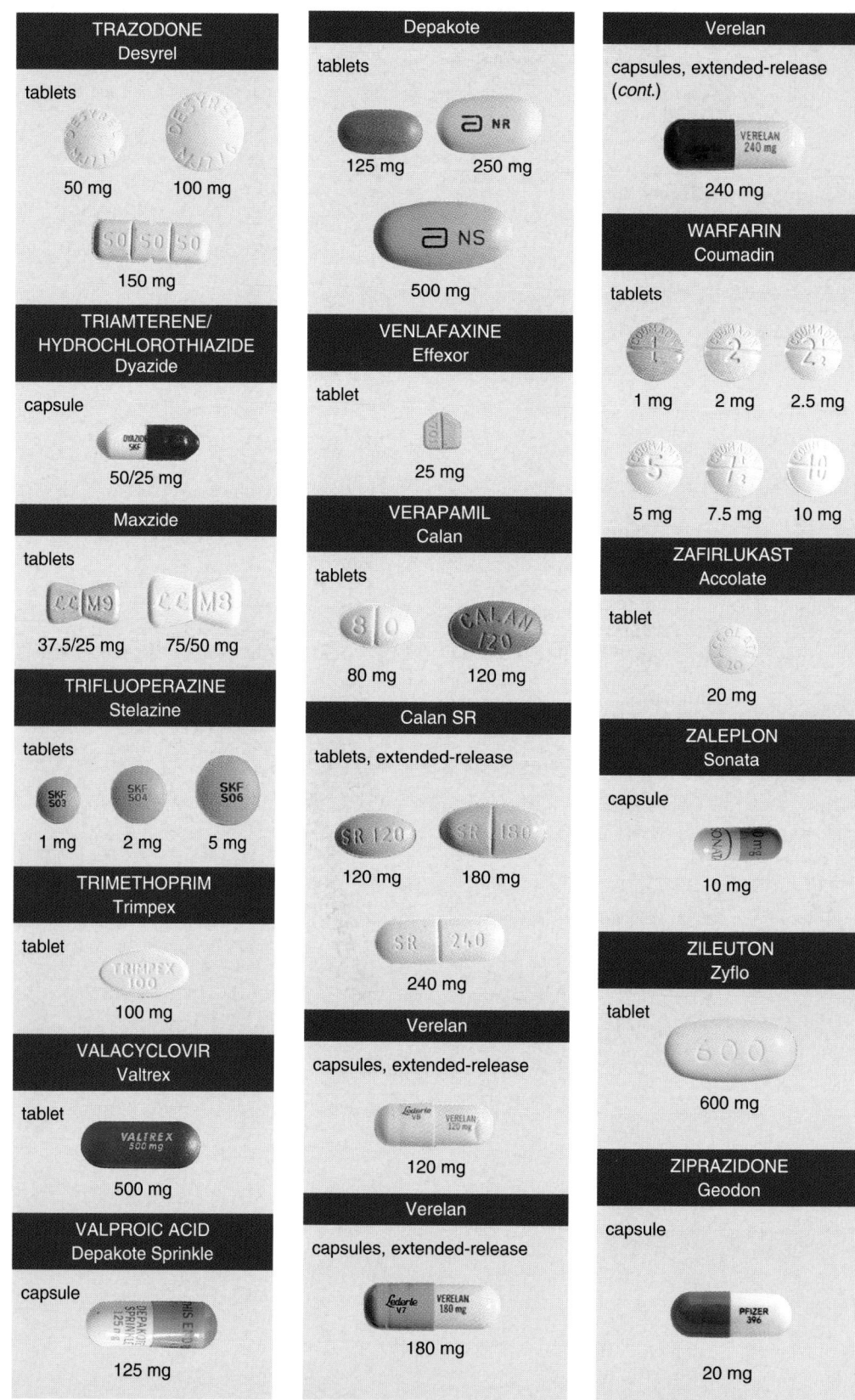

TRAZODONE
Desyrel

tablets

50 mg   100 mg

150 mg

TRIAMTERENE/ HYDROCHLOROTHIAZIDE
Dyazide

capsule

50/25 mg

Maxzide

tablets

37.5/25 mg   75/50 mg

TRIFLUOPERAZINE
Stelazine

tablets

1 mg   2 mg   5 mg

TRIMETHOPRIM
Trimpex

tablet

100 mg

VALACYCLOVIR
Valtrex

tablet

500 mg

VALPROIC ACID
Depakote Sprinkle

capsule

125 mg

Depakote

tablets

125 mg   250 mg

500 mg

VENLAFAXINE
Effexor

tablet

25 mg

VERAPAMIL
Calan

tablets

80 mg   120 mg

Calan SR

tablets, extended-release

120 mg   180 mg

240 mg

Verelan

capsules, extended-release

120 mg

Verelan

capsules, extended-release

180 mg

Verelan

capsules, extended-release (*cont.*)

240 mg

WARFARIN
Coumadin

tablets

1 mg   2 mg   2.5 mg

5 mg   7.5 mg   10 mg

ZAFIRLUKAST
Accolate

tablet

20 mg

ZALEPLON
Sonata

capsule

10 mg

ZILEUTON
Zyflo

tablet

600 mg

ZIPRAZIDONE
Geodon

capsule

20 mg

Pancreatitis—case reports with some members of this class.

Liver damage (with or without jaundice)—rare but may be fulminant (lisino-pril) and has been seen in as little as 5 days and up to 3 years after starting treatment (watch for dark urine, clay colored stools, yellow eyes or skin and abdominal pain or tenderness).

▷ **Possible Effects on Sexual Function:** Decreased male libido—rare (captopril, lisinopril and perindopril). Impotence. Swelling and tenderness of male breast tissue (gynecomastia)—rare (enalapril and captopril). Vulvovaginal itching-case report for enalapril.

Possible Effects on Laboratory Tests

Complete blood counts: decreased red cells, hemoglobin, white cells, and platelets; increased eosinophils.

Blood antinuclear antibodies (ANA): increased (captopril, lisinopril, quinapril).

Blood cholesterol (decreased-fosinopril) and triglycerides: decreased (benazepril).

Blood sodium level: decreased.

Blood urea nitrogen level (BUN): increased.

Blood uric acid level: may be increased (ramipril).

Insulin sensitivity: increased—captopril.

Blood potassium level: may be increased.

Liver function tests: increased liver enzymes (alkaline phosphatase, AST/GOT, LDH), increased bilirubin—possible.

Urine ketone tests: false positive results with Keto-Diastix and Chemstrip-6 (captopril).

Blood sugar (glucose): decreased—case reports (captopril, enalapril).

Venereal Disease Research Laboratory (VDRL): rare false-positive results (captopril).

Digoxin blood level: may read falsely low with fosinopril.

IgA deficiency: case report captopril.

CAUTION

1. If possible, may be best to stop all other antihypertensive drugs (especially diuretics) for 1 week before starting these medicines.
2. **Tell your doctor immediately if you become pregnant.** These drugs should not be taken after the first 3 months of pregnancy.
3. **Report promptly** any signs of infection (fever, sore throat) and any indications of water retention (weight gain, swollen feet or ankles).
4. Many salt substitutes contain potassium; ask your doctor before using.
5. Laboratory tests are needed (see below) **before taking these medicines.**
6. The FDA has started to evaluate blood levels of ACE inhibitors (trough to peak ratios—T/P—see Glossary) to check how these medicines should be dosed best. Talk to your doctor about this concept.
7. One observational epidemiologic study found that ACE inhibitors were often prescribed in lower than recommended doses and were also underused. Check your ACE inhibitor dose, and ask if an ACE inhibitor is appropriate if you are NOT currently taking one.
8. High blood pressure rarely has symptoms. If this medicine is controlling your blood pressure, STAY ON IT—even if you never felt sick from your prior high blood pressure.

Precautions for Use

By Infants and Children: Benazepril, fosinopril, lisinopril, quinapril, and ramipril: Safety and effectiveness not established.

By Those Over 60 Years of Age: Smaller starting doses advisable. Sudden or excessive lowering of blood pressure can cause stroke or heart attack.

▷ **Advisability of Use During Pregnancy**

Pregnancy Category: C during the first 3 months; **D during the last 6 months** (last two trimesters). See Pregnancy Risk Categories at the back of this book.

Animal Studies: Birth defects found in some animals for some ACE inhibitors.

Human Studies: The use of ACE inhibitor drugs during the last 6 months of pregnancy is known to possibly cause very serious injury and possible death to the fetus; skull and limb malformations, lung defects, and kidney failure have been reported in over 50 cases (captopril) worldwide.

Avoid these drugs completely during the last 6 months. During the first 3 months of pregnancy, use this drug only if clearly needed. Ask your doctor for guidance.

Advisability of Use If Breast-Feeding

Presence of this drug in breast milk: Yes, in small amounts (captopril, enalapril, and ramipril); benazepril—in very small amounts; lisinopril, quinapril, fosinopril—unknown.

Monitor nursing infant closely, and discontinue drug or nursing if adverse effects develop. Breast-feeding while taking ramipril is not recommended. Breast feeding with benazepril and enalapril is probably safe, but fixed dose combinations with hydrochlorothiazide and amlodipine (such as Lotensin HCT or Lotrel) are NOT recommended.

Habit-Forming Potential: None.

Effects of Overdose: Excessive drop in blood pressure—light-headedness, dizziness, fainting.

Possible Effects of Long-Term Use: Gradual increase in blood potassium level, cough.

Suggested Periodic Examinations While Taking These Drugs (at physician's discretion)

Before drug is started: complete blood cell count, urine analysis, creatinine BUN and electrolytes.

Once started: Blood counts during the first 3 months, then periodically. Congestive heart failure patients may need more frequent testing. Urine protein prudent every month for the first 9 months, then periodically. Periodic blood potassium tests. ANA titer for some ACEs. Blood pressure goals should be checked and results evaluated.

▷ **While Taking This Drug, Observe the Following**

Foods: Talk to your doctor about salt intake.

Herbal Medicines or Minerals: Ginseng may increase blood pressure, blunting the benefits of this medicine. Hawthorn, guarana, saw palmetto, ma huang (contraindicated in hypertension), goldenseal, and licorice may also cause increased blood pressure. Excessive caffeine from coffee, mate, or guarana may also increase blood pressure. Calcium and garlic may help lower blood pressure. One case report of excessively low zinc in a (polycystic kidney) patient for captopril. Talk with your doctor before combining any herbal medicine with your current prescriptions.

Nutritional Support: **Do not** take potassium supplements unless directed by your doctor. Case reports of zinc deficiency have been made (captopril). Large amounts of garlic, soy, and calcium may lower blood pressure. A small study by Hong at Sungkyukwan University in Seoul found that use of 256 mg of iron daily over a 4-week treatment period found all of the treatment group to have their cough improved with three patients nearly stopping this adverse effect. Further research is needed. Talk to your doctor to find out if additional research has been done, if this iron benefit only applies to patients with low iron or if a consensus has developed that rational use of iron while avoiding iron side effects makes sense for you.

Beverages: Grapefruit juice may increase amlodipine in the Lotrel form. May be taken with milk or water.

▷ *Alcohol:* Alcohol can further lower blood pressure. Use with caution.

Tobacco Smoking: Smoking can certainly irritate the airways and since these medicines can also lead to cough, smoking is not advisable. I advise everyone to quit smoking.

▷ *Other Drugs*

These medicines *taken concurrently* with

- allopurinol (Zyloprim) may increase risk of serious skin reactions.
- azathioprine (Imuran) may result in severe anemia.
- capsaicin (Zostrix, others) may increase risk of cough.
- clomipramine (Anafranil, others) may result in clomipramine toxicity and confusion, mood changes and irritability. Lower doses may be required if these medicines are combined.
- cyclosporine (Sandimmune) may result in kidney failure that takes a while to appear (delayed acute renal dysfunction).
- dalfopristin (Synercid) may result in increased amlodipine levels with Lotrel form.
- erythropoietin (various) may result in lowered erythropoietin benefits and require a higher dose to reach the same hematocrit.
- fluconazole and any imidazole or triazole antifungal (itraconazole and ketoconazole) may increase amlodipine levels with the Lotrel form.
- iron (various) may result in decreased ACE inhibitor absorption and blunted benefits. Separate dosing by 1 to 2 hours.
- interferons (alpha and beta) may greatly increase risk of blood problems with some members of this class. Monitor blood counts if combination must be used (captopril, lisinopril, quinapril, benazepril—case reports).
- lithium (Lithobid, others) may result in toxic blood lithium levels and **toxicity.**
- loop diuretics (such as Lasix or Bumex; see Drug Classes) may cause excessively low blood pressure on standing (postural hypotension) but may also be therapeutically needed.
- metformin (Glucophage) lead to high potassium levels and lactic acidosis in a diabetic patient with kidney compromise who combined metformin and enalapril.
- nesiritide (Natrecor) may increase risk of excessively low blood pressure (hypotension).
- oral hypoglycemic agents (glyburide—Glynase, others) may result in decreased insulin resistance and the need to decrease the dose of the oral hypoglycemic agent (enalapril only).
- pergolide (Permax, others) has a single case report of hypotension with lisinopril—caution is advised.
- phenothiazines (see Drug Classes) may result in postural hypotension.
- potassium preparations (K-Lyte, Slow-K, etc.) will increase blood potassium with risk of serious heart rhythm disturbances.
- potassium-sparing diuretics—amiloride (Moduretic), spironolactone (Aldactazide), triamterene (Dyazide)—may increase blood levels of potassium with risk of serious heart rhythm disturbances.

- quinupristin (Synercid) may result in increased amlodipine levels with Lotrel form.
- rifampin (Rifadin) or rifabutin (Mycobutin) may cause decreased therapeutic benefit from enalapril.
- saquinavir (Invirase) may result in increased amlodipine levels with Lotrel form.
- thiazide diuretics (hydrochlorothiazide, others) may result (especially in older people) in increased levels of enalaprilat (the active medicine) and increased reduction in blood pressure. May be used to therapeutic benefit.
- cotrimoxazole (trimethoprim component; Bactrim, Trimpex, others) may increase blood potassium (risk of serious heart rhythm disturbances).

The following drugs may *decrease* the effects of these medicines:
- antacids—by decreasing captopril (and perhaps other ACEs) absorption. Separate doses by 2 hours.
- COX-II inhibitors (celecoxib, rofecoxib and valdecoxib).
- ibuprofen (Motrin), indomethacin (Indocin) or other NSAIDs (see Drug Classes).
- naloxone (Narcan).
- salicylates (aspirin, etc.) or other NSAIDs (see Drug Classes).

▷ *Driving, Hazardous Activities:* Usually no restrictions. Be aware of possible drops in blood pressure with resultant dizziness or faintness.

Aviation Note: The use of these drugs *may be a disqualification* for piloting. Consult a designated Aviation Medical Examiner.

Exposure to Sun: Caution is advised. Some drugs in this class can cause photosensitivity (captopril, enalapril, moexipril, ramipril, and trandolapril).

Exposure to Heat: Caution is advised. Excessive perspiring may drop blood pressure.

Occurrence of Unrelated Illness: Call your doctor to report any disorder causing vomiting or diarrhea. Fluid and chemical imbalances must be corrected as soon as possible.

Discontinuation: Captopril, lisinopril, quinapril, fosinopril, and benazepril have been stopped abruptly without causing a sudden increase in blood pressure (though not recommended). Ask your doctor before stopping any drug for any reason.

ANGIOTENSIN II RECEPTOR ANTAGONIST FAMILY

Candesartan   (KAN da sar tan)   **Eprosartan**   (Eh PRO sar tan)
Irbesartan   (Ir BAH sar tan)   **Losartan**   (LOW sar tan)   **Telmisartan**   (TELL mih sar tan)   **Valsartan**   (VAL sar tan)

Other Names: ARBs

Introduced: 1998, 1999, 1997, 1995, 1998, 1997, respectively   **Class:** Angiotensin II antagonists (ARBs)   **Prescription:**   USA: Yes   **Controlled Drug**   USA: No; Canada: No   **Available as Generic:** USA: irbesartan and hydrochlorothiazide Yes, others No; Canada: No

Brand Names: *Candesartan:* Atacand, Atacand HCT [CD]; *Eprosartan:* Teveten; *Irbesartan:* Avapro, Avalide [CD]; *Losartan:* Cozaar, Hyzaar [CD]; *Telmisartan:* Micardis; *Valsartan:* Diovan, Diovan HCT [CD]

Author's Note: Information in this profile will be broadened in subsequent editions to include data on eprosartan and telmisartan if the data war-

rant inclusion. One early study showed that using eprosartan WITH an ACE inhibitor reduced blood pressure (diastolic—the bottom blood pressure number) in people with chronic heart failure—yet did NOT increase heart rate as an undesirable effect. Emerging information on combination use of ACE inhibitors (ACEIs) and ARBs in people with compromised kidneys appears to have increased benefits. Some data shows that two of the medicines in this family did not work as well as in African Americans as other high blood pressure medicines. A recent study (see Mancia in Sources) found that irbesartan (Avapro) lowered blood pressure to a greater degree than valsartan in people with high blood pressure. An additional head to head trial found that maximum doses of candesartan lowered blood pressure to a greater degree than did losartan. A new approval for losartan gives it FDA approval to prevent stroke.

BENEFITS versus RISKS

Possible Benefits	*Possible Risks*
EFFECTIVE CONTROL OF HIGH BLOOD PRESSURE	Increased liver function tests (all except irbesartan)
DECREASED NUMBER OF DEATHS FROM CONGESTIVE HEART FAILURE (LOSARTAN)	
USE IN (LOSARTAN) PEOPLE LIVING WITH DIABETES TO HELP THEIR KIDNEYS (NEPHROPATHY)	
DECREASED RISK OF STROKE, HEART ATTACK, AND DEATH IN SERIOUSLY ILL HEART PATIENTS (LOSARTAN)	
LOSARTAN IS NEWLY FDA APPROVED TO PREVENT STROKE IN PATIENTS WITH HIGH BLOOD PRESSURE AND LEFT-SIDED HEART ENLARGEMENT	
DECREASED RISK OF NEW ONSET DIABETES (BY 25% IN THE LIFE STUDY-LOSARTAN)	
Decreased cough side effect versus ACE inhibitors	
Candesartan increases insulin sensitivity	

▷ **Principal Uses**

As a Single Drug Product: Uses currently included in FDA-approved labeling: (1) Treatment of high blood pressure; (2) decreases abnormal size of the left ventricle (left ventricular hypertrophy) (losartan); (3) candesartan works to increase insulin sensitivity; (4) losartan, irbesartan approved in type 2 diabetics with a specific kidney problem (nephropathy); (5) losartan is newly approved to prevent stroke in people with high blood pressure and left sided heart enlargement (left ventricular hypertrophy), (6) valsartan approved for use in congestive heart failure (CHF).

Author's Note: The JNC VI (see Glossary) report placed use of these medicines as appropriate in patients who have indications for ACE therapy but do not tolerate those medicines (such as intolerable ACE inhibitor–induced cough). JNC VII on equal ground with ACEs. The International Society for Hypertension recommended this class of medicines as first-line treatment in patients with heart failure. Some early data show some reversal of fibrosis in animals treated with losartan. Because of trials such as LIFE (see Dahlof in Sources), where there were clear data from a large study showing decreased heart attack, stroke, death, and diabetes risk with use of losartan, I expect that losartan will have much broader use.

Other (unlabeled) generally accepted uses: (1) The ELITE study compared losartan to an ACE inhibitor (in patients over 65 with ejection fraction mean of 30%) and found a significant decrease in deaths for any reason (all-cause death) in treating congestive heart failure; (2) congestive heart failure (CHF); (3) excessive protein excretion in diabetic patients (nephropathy); (4) one study of hypertensive men with sexual dysfunction found improved sexual satisfaction and erections (erectile function) after 12 weeks of losartan treatment; (4) may have a role (new data) in helping prevent migraine headaches; (5) losartan may work to ease sexual dysfunction; (6) irbesartan in combination with amiodarone was more effective in easing atrial fibrillation than amiodarone alone in one small study.

As Combination Drug Products [CD]: These medicines have been combined with hydrochlorothiazide in fixed-dose forms. These drugs complement each other, making the combination a more effective antihypertensive used if blood pressure control is not achieved with initial therapy.

How These Drugs Work: They block the effects of angiotensin II by binding to a specific site (the AT1 receptor). This helps the blood vessels stay open and lowers blood pressure. These drugs and some of their metabolites also block aldosterone, something of benefit in congestive heart failure. When combined with hydrochlorothiazide, these medicines have the added benefit of removing excessive accumulation of body water.

Available Dosage Forms and Strengths

Candesartan:

Tablet — 4 mg, 8 mg, 16 mg and 32 mg

Tablet (*Atacand HCT*) — candesartan 16mg or 32 mg and hydrochlorothiazide (HCTZ) 12.5 mg

Irbesartan:

Tablet — 75 mg, 150 mg, 300 mg

Tablet (*Avalide* irbesartan and HCTZ) — irbesartan 150 or 300 mg and HCTZ 12.5 mg

Losartan:

Tablet — 25 mg, 50 mg, 100 mg

Tablet (*Hyzaar*) — losartan 50 mg and HCTZ 12.5 mg

Tablet (*Hyzaar*) — losartan 100 mg and HCTZ 25 mg

Valsartan:

Tablet — 80 mg and 160 mg

Tablet (*Diovan HCT*) — valsartan 80 mg and HCTZ 12.5 mg

— valsartan 160 mg and HCTZ 12.5 mg

— valsartan 160 mg and HCTZ 25 mg

▷ **Recommended Dosage Ranges** (Actual dose and schedule must be determined for each patient individually.)

Infants and Children: Not recommended for use in this age group.

18 to 60 Years of Age:

High blood pressure (hypertension):

  Candesartan: Starting dose of 16 mg A DAY in patients who have normal blood volume (normovolemic). Hypovolemic patients are given lower starting doses. Total dose can be divided into two doses and given twice a day or given in a single dose. Some European countries use lower starting doses in all patients and a maximum of 8 mg. Doses may be increased as needed and tolerated to 32 mg once daily.

  Irbesartan: Starting dose of 150 mg daily. This dose may be increased as needed and tolerated to 300 mg daily. A starting dose of 75 mg daily is used in people also taking hydrochlorothiazide.

  Losartan: A starting dose of 50 mg daily is used. If the blood pressure response is not sufficient, the same dose may be divided into two equal doses and given twice daily. The dose may also be increased as needed and tolerated and taken in two divided doses daily. The maximum daily dose is 100 mg. In people who are hypovolemic or who are on water pills (diuretics), the starting dose is 25 mg. Peak effects may not be seen for 3 to 6 weeks once dosing changes are made. Maximum daily doses are lower in those taking diuretics and hypovolemics.

  Valsartan: Starting dose is 80 mg daily. Dosing may be increased to 160 mg, then a maximum of 320 mg once daily as needed and tolerated. Many clinicians will change to a combination HCTZ form if goals are not met with a 160-mg dose of the single-ingredient product.

Over 60 Years of Age:

  Candesartan: No initial dose change needed, but some older patients may be more sensitive than younger ones.

  Irbesartan: No age-related changes needed.

  Losartan: Patients who are dehydrated or have a decreased intravascular volume should take 25 mg once daily as a starting dose.

  Valsartan: No clinically relevant changes.

  Author's Note: Combination forms containing hydrochlorothiazide (HCTZ) are used only after target goals for blood pressure are not met with the ARB alone. Dosing is then usually started with the lowest available combination dose and increased as needed and tolerated. Hydrochlorothiazide (HCTZ) side effects may be a mixture of rare dose-independent (such as pancreatitis) and dose-dependent problems (such as excessive lowering of potassium, which is largely avoided using low-HCTZ forms).

Diabetic Nephropathy:

  Irbesartan: 300 mg once a day (in type 2 diabetics).

  Losartan: 50 mg once a day (in type 2 diabetics). Dose can be increased as needed and tolerated to 100 mg daily.

Congestive Heart Failure:

  Valsartan: 40 mg twice a day. Dose can be increased as needed and tolerated to 80-160 mg twice daily.

Conditions Requiring Dosing Adjustments

Liver Function:

  Candesartan: No changes in mild liver compromise. Some European clinicians start at 2 mg daily.

Irbesartan: No changes needed.

Losartan: This drug is extensively changed (metabolized) in the liver to an active metabolite. The starting dose should be 25 mg. Dosing is then increased as needed and tolerated at weekly intervals. The fixed-dose drug Hyzaar should not be used by patients with liver failure.

Valsartan: Maximum starting dose is 80 mg in mild to moderate liver failure. Drug has not been used in severe liver failure.

Kidney Function:

Candesartan: No change in starting dose in mild kidney compromise.

Irbesartan: No changes needed.

Losartan: No dosing changes appear to be needed. The fixed-dose combination Hyzaar should not be used by patients with creatinine clearances (see Glossary) less than 30 ml/min.

Valsartan: Some clinical trials started dosing at 40 mg daily with increase to 80 mg after 28 days as needed and tolerated.

▷ **Dosing Instructions:** Food slows the absorption of losartan and valsartan but does not decrease the total absorption. Irbesartan and candesartan can be taken with or without food. If you forget a dose: take it right away unless it's nearly time for your next regular dose. If it is nearly dosing time, just take the scheduled dose. DO NOT double doses.

Usual Duration of Use: Regular use for 3 to 4 weeks is usually needed to determine peak effectiveness in controlling high blood pressure. Long-term use (months to years) requires periodic evaluation of response and dose adjustment. See your doctor on a regular basis and stay on target with pressure goals!

Typical Treatment Goals and Measurements (Outcomes and Markers)

Blood Pressure: The NEW guidelines (JNC VII) define normal blood pressure (BP) as **less than** 120/80. Because blood pressures that were once considered acceptable can actually lead to blood vessel damage, the committee from the National Institutes of Health, National Heart Lung and Blood Institute now have a new category called **Pre-hypertension**. This ranges from 120/80 to 139/89 and is intended to help your doctor encourage lifestyle changes (or in the case of people with a risk factor for high blood pressure, start treatment) much earlier—so that possible damage to blood vessels, your heart, kidneys, sexual potency, or eyes might be minimized or avoided altogether. The next two classes of high blood pressure are stage 1 hypertension: 140/90 to 159/99 and stage 2 hypertension equal to or greater than: 160/100 mm Hg. These guidelines also recommend that clinicians trying to control blood pressure work with their patients to agree on the goals and a plan of treatment. The first-ever guidelines for blood pressure (hypertension) in African Americans recommends that MOST black patients be started on TWO antihypertensive medicines with the goal of lowering blood pressure to 130/80 for those with high risk for heart and blood vessel disease or with diabetes. The American Diabetes Association recommends 130/80 as the target for people living with diabetes and less than 125/75 for those who spill more than one gram of protein into their urine. Most clinicians try to achieve a BP that confers the best balance of lower cardiovascular risk and avoids the problem of too low a blood pressure. Blood pressure duration is generally increased with beneficial restriction of sodium. The goals and time frame should be discussed with you when the prescription is written. If goals are not met, it is not unusual to intensify doses or add on medicines. You can find the new blood pressure guidelines at *www.nhlbi.nih.gov/guidelines/hypertension/index.htm*. For the African American guidelines, see Douglas, J.G. in Sources.

Possible Advantages of These Drugs

A different mechanism of action in treating high blood pressure than diuretics or beta blockers. Lower rate of cough side effect than ACE inhibitors. Candesartan has NOT been associated with dry cough in any clinical trial. Once-daily dosing can improve patient compliance. Irbesartan: dosing changes NOT needed in those over 60 or in people with kidney or liver disease. Candesartan: The cytochrome P-450 system is NOT involved in removal of the medicine. Candesartan appears to avoid dry cough side effect and also works to increase sensitivity to insulin, making it a preferred agent for patients with high blood pressure who also have insulin resistance. Irbesartan appears to avoid potential of liver damage. Losartan has critically important new data showing decreased risk of heart attack, stroke, diabetes and death in seriously ill heart patients. The LIFE study compared patients with left ventricular hypertrophy taking losartan versus atenolol (a beta blocker) with positive results. One small head to head trial of mild to moderate hypertension found that irbesartan/hctz (Avalide) was better at lowering blood pressure than losartan/hctz (Hyzaar). Irbesartan has shown a most favorable duration of action of angiotensin II inhibition versus losartan or valsartan. Once a day dosing helps people take their medicines well (adherence)! If migraine prevention data holds up, this could be a great new use for these medicines as they are better tolerated than some other drugs currently used to prevent migraines.

▷ **These Drugs Should Not Be Taken If**
- you had an allergic reaction to them previously (note: HCTZ combinations should also be avoided by people with sulfonamide allergies).
- you have stenosis of the kidney arteries on both sides (bilateral) renal artery stenosis (candesartan).
- you have primary hyperaldosteronism (candesartan).
- you are pregnant.

▷ **Inform Your Physician Before Taking These Drugs If**
- you have a history of liver or kidney disease.
- you have a history of circulation problems in the brain.
- you are breast-feeding your infant.
- you have a history of lupus erythematosus (losartan).
- you have a history of aspirin or penicillin allergy (losartan).
- you have a history of disease in the blood vessels that supply the heart (coronary artery disease) or aortic or mitral valve stenosis or stenosis of one kidney artery.
- you have abnormal heart rhythms (cardiac).
- you develop swelling of the face, glottis, or tongue (angioedema). Call your doctor immediately.
- you are taking a diuretic (doses will need to be lowered).
- you are going to have general anesthesia (these medicines require more careful use of induction agents to avoid excessive lowering of the blood pressure.

Possible Side Effects (natural, expected, and unavoidable drug actions) Taste disorders.

Candesartan may cause flushing and/or excessive sweating in some patients.

Headache is possible with any of these medicines—though less than placebo for some.

First-dose excessive lowering of blood pressure is probably possible with all of these medicines (reported first for losartan).

▷ **Possible Adverse Effects** (unusual, unexpected, and infrequent reactions)
  If any of the following develop, consult your physician promptly for guidance.

Mild Adverse Effects
  Allergic reaction: skin rash.
  Dizziness, headache, or sleep disturbances—infrequent.
  Taste disorders—case reports for losartan.
  Fatigue or muscle cramps—infrequent.
  Nose bleed—case reports for candesartan and valsartan (questionable causation).
  Cough—possible for some members (up to 3.4% losartan, 2.8% irbesartan, 0.8% valsartan and not reported with candesartan in clinical trials).
  Diarrhea—infrequent.

Serious Adverse Effects
  Allergic reactions: not defined.
  Swelling of the face and lips (angioedema)—case reports for losartan, valsartan, and irbesartan probably possible for all.
  Migraine headaches—rare.
  Gout—rare and of questionable cause (losartan).
  Liver toxicity—case reports (irbesartan, losartan, valsartan).
  Kidney toxicity—possible (see Caution).
  Pancreatitis—case reports for losartan.
  Dose-related increase in blood potassium (hyperkalemia).
  Anemia—case reports, minimal clinical significance (candesartan, losartan, valsartan).
  Neutropenia—rare (valsartan).
  Movement problem (ataxia)—rare (valsartan).

▷ **Possible Effects on Sexual Function:** Decreased libido, impotence—both rare (losartan and valsartan).

Possible Delayed Adverse Effects: None reported.

▷ **Adverse Effects That May Mimic Natural Diseases or Disorders**
  Increases in liver function tests may mimic infectious hepatitis (candesartan, irbesartan, losartan, and valsartan).

Natural Diseases or Disorders That May Be Activated by These Drugs: None reported.

Possible Effects on Laboratory Tests
  Losartan, irbesartan, candesartan, and valsartan: Liver function tests: increased.
  Potassium level: may be increased.
  Increased kidney function tests: creatinine possible with candesartan, irbesartan, losartan, and valsartan.

CAUTION
  1. Goals are set in the current approach to antihypertensive therapy. If the blood pressure lowering goals are not met in a reasonable amount of time, dosing changes and/or new medicines must be started.
  2. Patients with low renin levels (often the case in African American patients) may get a lessened benefit from these medicines.
  3. These drugs should not be taken during pregnancy. Losartan manufacturer says to stop it once pregnancy is identified.
  4. Case reports of kidney problems emphasized the need for periodic checking of kidney function and withdrawal of therapy if kidney problems (dysfunction) begin.
  5. Losartan undergoes a significant change (first pass effect) in the liver. Because of this activation to the active medicine, inhibitors of the liver

enzyme system (CYP 3A4) such as grapefruit juice may block conversion to active drug and blunt the effectiveness of the medicine.

Precautions for Use

By Infants and Children: Safety and effectiveness for use by those under 18 years of age have not been established.

By Those Over 60 Years of Age: People in this age group may be more sensitive to the effects of medicines that lower blood pressure. Lower starting doses are indicated for patients who are dehydrated.

▷ **Advisability of Use During Pregnancy**

Pregnancy Category: C in the first 3 months, **D in the fourth month through birth.** See Pregnancy Risk Categories at the back of this book.

Animal Studies: Rat studies have produced kidney toxicity and death in fetuses.

Human Studies: Information from adequate studies of pregnant women is not available.

If pregnancy is detected, these medicines should be stopped as soon as possible.

Advisability of Use If Breast-Feeding

Presence of this drug in breast milk: Unknown, but expected (losartan and valsartan), yes in rats (candesartan and irbesartan).

Avoid drug or refrain from nursing.

Habit-Forming Potential: None.

Effects of Overdose: Severe decreases in blood pressure and dizziness. Possible increased or decreased heart rate.

Possible Effects of Long-Term Use: Not defined.

Suggested Periodic Examinations While Taking This Drug (at physician's discretion)

Periodic checks of blood pressure (high blood pressure is treated to a target lowering of blood pressure and should be kept there).

Liver function tests (irbesartan, losartan, and valsartan). May be prudent for all these medicines as they are structurally similar.

Kidney function tests when starting and at two and four weeks into treatment. Some clinicians also check kidney function after any dose increases as well. Case reporting advocated immediate withdrawal of ARB treatment if kidney (renal) impairment starts while taking an ARB.

▷ **While Taking This Drug, Observe the Following**

Foods: Follow the diet that your doctor has prescribed. Grapefruit may blunt the benefits of losartan, and further research is required to define the clinical significance of this.

Herbal Medicines or Minerals: Ginseng, guarana, hawthorn, saw palmetto, ma huang, goldenseal, yohimbe, and licorice may also increase blood pressure. Calcium and garlic may help lower blood pressure and could be part of complementary care. Use of calcium to excess (7.5 to 10 grams) with combination thiazide diuretics can lead to excessive calcium levels. Talk to your doctor about how much calcium to take. Indian snakeroot has a German Commission E monograph indication for hypertension—talk to your doctor. Eleuthero root and ephedra should be avoided by people living with hypertension. St. John's wort can cause sun sensitivity. Since some of these medicines can cause sun sensitivity also—caution is advised. Because some members of this family (losartan, irbesartan, and valsartan) and kava kava has/have had recent case reports of adverse effects on the liver, the combination should be voided.

Nutritional Support: Specific measures are not indicated.

Beverages: Avoid excessive caffeine intake. Grapefruit juice may blunt losartan benefits.

▷ *Alcohol:* Alcohol may intensify the blood pressure lowering effects of this medicine. Ask your doctor for guidance.

Tobacco Smoking: No interactions expected. I advise everyone to quit smoking.

Marijuana Smoking: May increase the blood pressure lowering effects of this drug.

▷ *Other Drugs*

These medicines ***taken concurrently*** with

- ACE inhibitors (see Drug Classes) when combined with CD HCTZ forms may lead to severe first-dose lowering of blood pressure (hypotension). Low-dose ACE and caution are critical—yet the combination is also therapeutically useful.
- corticosteroids (methylprednisolone, others—see Drug Classes) may lead to excessive loss of potassium when used with the HCTZ combination forms of these medicines. Caution is advised.
- fluconazole (Diflucan) may blunt clinical benefits of losartan by blocking conversion to an active chemical. If these medicines are combined—watch for changes in therapeutic benefits.
- hydrochlorothiazide (various) may increase clinical benefits (redundant with CD forms unless extra fluid loss desired and HCTZ dose less than maximum).
- lithium (Lithobid, others) (case reports for some HCTZ combinations) resulted in lithium toxicity. Caution is advised.
- moxonidine (Cynt, available in Germany) may result in additive lowering of blood pressure.
- rifampin (various) may lower losartan blood levels. Blood pressure should be checked and dosing adjusted as needed.
- ritonavir (Norvir) may change losartan blood levels.

Losartan and valsartan ***taken concurrently*** with

- amiloride, spironolactone and triamterene (potassium-sparing diuretics) may lead to undesirable increases in potassium.

Candesartan ***taken concurrently*** with

- insulin and perhaps other oral hypoglycemic agents may increase response to insulin or oral agents because of increased insulin sensitivity. This may be used to clinical advantage.

Losartan ***taken concurrently*** with

- inhibitors of cytochrome P450 3A4 may blunt therapeutic benefits of this medicine by blocking an activation step to the active medicines. Examples to be avoided are use with grapefruit juice, erythromycin, and antifungal agents such as ketoconazole.

▷ *Driving, Hazardous Activities:* These drugs may cause confusion or dizziness. Restrict activities as necessary.

Aviation Note: The use of these drugs ***may be a disqualification*** for piloting. Consult a designated Aviation Medical Examiner.

Exposure to Sun: Caution is advised. Isolated cases of photosensitivity have been reported.

Exposure to Heat: Caution: Excessive sweating (perspiration) may lead to dehydration and an excessive blood pressure lowering effect of these drugs.

Discontinuation: Talk with your doctor before stopping these medicines for any reason.

ANTI-ALZHEIMER'S DRUG FAMILY

Donepezil   (DON ep a zill)   **Rivastigmine**   (REEVA stig meen)
Tacrine   (TA kreen)   **Galantamine**   (GAH lan tah meen)

Introduced: 1993, 2000, 1996, 2001   **Class:**   Acetylcholinesterase
inhibitor, anti-Alzheimer's drug, nicotinic acid receptor blocker (galantamine
only)   **Prescription:**   USA: Yes   **Controlled Drug:**   USA: No;
Canada: No   **Available as Generic:**   USA: Pending for donepezil at the
time of this writing, No for others

Brand Names: *Donepezil:* Aricept; *Rivastigmine:* Exelon; *Tacrine:* Cognex;
    Galantamine: Reminyl

**Author's Note: Information on rivastigmine will not be broadened in this
    edition. CAUTION: in Canada felodipine, a calcium channel blocker, car-
    ries the brand name Renedil. Because this is so similar sounding a name,
    errors may occur during a telephone prescription.**

BENEFITS versus RISKS

Possible Benefits	*Possible Risks*
IMPROVEMENT OF MEMORY IN MILD TO MODERATE ALZHEIMER'S DISEASE	LIVER TOXICITY (TACRINE-dose related)
IMPROVEMENT OF SYMPTOMS IN MILD TO MODERATE ALZHEIMER'S DISEASE	Nausea (A CAUTION FOR RIVASTIGMINE)
MILD TO MODERATE ALZHEIMER'S PATIENTS CONTINUED TO BENEFIT FROM SUSTAINED TREATMENT FOR MORE THAN ONE YEAR (DONEPEZIL)	Dizziness
WORKS ON ACETYLCHOLINESTERASE AND ALLOSTERIC NICOTINIC RECEPTORS (GALANTAMINE ONLY)	
ONCE-DAILY DOSING (DONEPEZIL) MAKES IT EASIER FOR CAREGIVERS AND PATIENTS TO KEEP TAKING THE MEDICINE	
GALANTAMINE WAS RECENTLY FOUND TO BE USEFUL IN PEOPLE WHO HAVE CEREBROVASCULAR DISEASE	
Galantamine is available as an oral solution	
Donepezil was shown to work to fight sleepiness from morphine in a small study of cancer patients	

▷ **Principal Uses**

As a Single Drug Product: Uses currently included in FDA-approved labeling: Treats mild to moderate Alzheimer's disease symptoms (all these medicines).

Author's Note: Guidelines (*www.psych.org/clin_res/pg_dementia.cfm*) **from the American Psychiatric Association (APA) recommend use of vitamin E alone or in combination with donepezil as first-line therapy for delaying symptoms of patients with mild to moderate Alzheimer's. Some studies of the herbal medicine called ginkgo biloba have also shown benefits, but the two medicines have not been studied together. Galantamine may need to undergo comparative trials to further define its place in therapy.**

Other (unlabeled) generally accepted uses: (1) Donepezil may have a role in people who have memory problems after brain injuries; (2) galantamine works in people with cerebrovascular disease; (3) donepezil had moderate benefits in fighting sleepiness (sedation) in a small study of cancer patients who were taking morphine.

How These Drugs Work: Alzheimer's disease is thought to be caused by a loss of nerve cells that make a nerve transmitter (acetylcholine). Donepezil and tacrine act to increase levels of a neurotransmitter (acetylcholine) in the brain. Galantamine also works to increase levels of acetylcholine and has been found to have activity at nicotinic acid receptors as well.

Available Dosage Forms and Strengths

Donepezil:
>   Tablets — 5 mg, 10 mg

Galantamine:
>   Oral solution — 4 mg per ml
>   Tablets — 4 mg, 8 mg and 12 mg

Tacrine:
>   Capsules — 10 mg, 20 mg, 30 mg, 40 mg

▷ **Recommended Dosage Ranges** (Actual dosage and schedule must be determined for each patient individually.)

Infants and Children: No data are available on use of these drugs in infants and children.

18 to 60 Years of Age:

Donepezil: Start with 5 mg once daily at bedtime, and keep at this dose for 6 weeks. As needed and tolerated increase to 10 mg. The 10-mg dose has had increased GI side effects.

Tacrine: Start at 10 mg four times a day (between meals). This can be increased at 4-week intervals if needed and tolerated. Maximum daily dose is 160 mg.

Galantamine: Dosing is usually started at 4 mg twice a day. If this dose is well tolerated, the dose should be increased to 8 mg twice a day. An additional increase to 12 mg twice a day should be attempted only after an additional 4 weeks at the 8 mg dose has been found to be tolerated. One placebo compared trial found that an ongoing (maintenance) dose of 24–32 mg had generally better results on thinking than lower doses.

Over 60 Years of Age: Same as 18 to 60 years of age.

Conditions Requiring Dosing Adjustments

Liver Function:

Donepezil: Lower doses and blood levels prudent in liver disease.

Tacrine: Not used at all with previous liver toxicity (bilirubin more than 3 mg per dl) and used with caution in liver compromise.

Galantamine: Not used at all in severe liver disease (Child-Pugh 10–15) and used with caution, with more time between dose increases and a maximum 16 mg dose in moderate in liver compromise (Child-Pugh score of 7–9).

Kidney Function: Dose decreases in kidney compromise not now indicated for donepezil or tacrine. Galantamine should NOT be used in people with creatinine clearance (see Glossary) less than or equal to 9 ml /min. In mild kidney compromise (renal function decline), dose increases should be made slowly and with great care.

▷ **Dosing Instructions:** The donepezil tablet may be crushed and is not affected by food. The tacrine capsule may be opened and best taken 1 hour before meals. Food decreases tacrine body levels by 30 to 40%. Liver function tests should be checked while this medicine is being taken. Galantamine is best taken with milk or food (morning and evening meals often works well). The oral liquid form of galantamine should be measured in a dose cup or measuring spoon. If you forget a dose: take it right away unless it's nearly time for your next regular dose. If it IS nearly time, just take the scheduled dose. DO NOT double doses.

Usual Duration of Use: Regular use for 3 to 4 weeks may be needed to see improvement from these medicines. Dose increases are made at 4- to 6-week intervals. Long-term use (months to years) requires periodic evaluation of response and dose. If benefits do not occur within 6 weeks, patients or family members should talk with the prescriber about stopping these drugs. Research shows that donepezil benefits continue for more than a year with regular use.

Typical Treatment Goals and Measurements (Outcomes and Markers)

Thinking and cognition: Improvement in the Mini-Mental State Examination (sMMSE), Alzheimer's Disease Assessment Scale (ADAS-cog) and/or global function using the Clinician Interview Based Assessment of Change. Assessments should be made periodically as benefits from these medicines will decay over time.

Possible Advantages of These Drugs

Improvement of memory and other symptoms of mild to moderate Alzheimer's with fewer side effects than other agents. Donepezil has a more favorable side effect profile than tacrine, offers once-a-day dosing and also avoids liver damage. Donepezil benefits continue for more than 140 weeks with regular use. Galantamine has Alzheimer's improvement data for 52 weeks (newer medicine) and is available in an oral solution form. New data shows galantamine helps in cerebrovascular disease. Galantamine also has data that shows effectiveness in people who were previously given different acetylcholinesterase inhibitors.

Currently a "Drug of Choice"

Donepezil is preferred for treatment of symptoms in mild to moderate Alzheimer's disease. Galantamine is preferred in people with cerebrovascular disease, but may become the preferred agent as additional studies are completed.

▷ **These Drugs Should Not Be Taken If**

Donepezil:
• you have had an allergic reaction to it previously.

Tacrine:
• you have had an allergic reaction to it previously.
• you have bronchial asthma.

- you had tacrine liver toxicity and bilirubin levels greater than 3 mg/dl.
- you have an overly active thyroid (hyperthyroidism).
- you have peptic ulcer disease.
- you have an intestinal or urinary tract obstruction.

Galantamine:

- you have had an allergic reaction to it previously.
- your liver or kidneys are severely impaired.

▷ **Inform Your Physician Before Taking These Drugs If**
- you have a history of seizure disorder.
- you have had liver disease.
- you have a history of peptic ulcer disease.
- you have a slow heartbeat (bradycardia), abnormal electrical conduction in your heart (AV conduction defect), or excessively low blood pressure.
- you take an NSAID (see Drug Classes).
- you take muscle relaxants.
- you have glaucoma (angle closure).
- you have asthma.
- you are pregnant.
- you are anemic or have low blood platelets.
- you will be having surgery (donepezil may enhance some muscle relaxants).

Possible Side Effects (natural, expected, and unavoidable drug actions)

Symptoms of cholinergic excess (abdominal upset, agitation). Weight loss—up to 11% in one galantamine study. Indigestion (dyspepsia) is the most common adverse effect of galantamine.

▷ **Possible Adverse Effects** (unusual, unexpected, and infrequent reactions)
If any of the following develop, consult your physician promptly for guidance.

Mild Adverse Effects

Allergic reactions: skin rash, itching.

Increased sweating—rare.

Increased salivation—may be frequent with galantamine.

Increased urination—infrequent.

Muscle aches—infrequent.

Pisa syndrome (abnormal body posturing)—case reports (donepezil).

Abnormal dreams—possible (donepezil).

Insomnia—frequent (galantamine).

Increased risk of passing out or syncope (galantamine—dose related)—possible.

Lowered blood pressure—possible.

Nausea/vomiting, diarrhea, decreased appetite—infrequent to frequent (dose dependent with donepezil).

Dizziness, confusion, insomnia—infrequent to frequent (frequent with galantamine).

Serious Adverse Effects

Allergic reactions: anaphylactoid reactions.

Dose-related increase in liver function tests (starts 6 to 8 weeks after therapy begins)—frequent (tacrine only).

Hallucinations—case report (tacrine).

Inner ear problems—rare (tacrine).

Purpura—infrequent (tacrine).

Aggravation of asthma in asthmatics, bronchospasm or pulmonary edema—

possible (increased acetylcholine because of the way that these medicines work).

Severe decrease in white blood cells—one tacrine case report.

Anemia or low blood platelets—infrequent (donepezil).

Slow heart rate (bradycardia) or abnormal rhythm—possible to rare.

Seizures—case reports (tacrine).

▷ **Possible Effects on Sexual Function:** Very rare effect of causing lactation (tacrine). Donepezil has had case reports of INCREASED libido.

Possible Delayed Adverse Effects: Liver toxicity (tacrine only), rash, low white blood cell count (tacrine only).

Adverse Effects That May Mimic Natural Diseases or Disorders
Liver toxicity of tacrine may mimic acute hepatitis.

Natural Diseases or Disorders That May Be Activated by These Drugs
Tacrine, galantamine, and donepezil may worsen bronchial asthma, precipitate seizures (may be dose-related), and could exacerbate peptic ulcer disease because of their mechanism of action.

Possible Effects on Laboratory Tests
Tacrine:
Liver function tests: increased SGOT, SGPT, and CPK.
Complete blood count: decreased white blood cells.
Donepezil: decreased hematocrit or platelets.

CAUTION
1. These drugs should **NOT** be stopped abruptly. Sudden decline in thinking may happen (acute deterioration of cognitive abilities).
2. Changes in color of stools (light or very black—tacrine) should be promptly reported to your doctor.
3. These drugs do **NOT** alter the course of Alzheimer's disease. Over time, benefits may be lost.
4. The dose of tacrine **must** be lowered by 40 mg per day if liver function tests (transaminases) rise three to five times the upper normal value.
5. Females achieve 50% higher tacrine blood levels than men. Dose-related side effects may occur sooner (with lower doses) in women than in men. Beneficial doses may be lower for women than men.
6. Donepezil shows benefits for more than 140 weeks with regular ongoing use. Interruption of therapy is NOT appropriate for that time span.
7. Galantamine is removed by two widely used liver enzymes (cytochrome P-450 2D6 and 3A4). Medicines that inhibit these enzymes will increase blood levels of galantamine, which may lead to toxic effects—requiring galantamine dosing decreases while or if the medicines are combined. Because galantamine is derived from daffodils—talk to your doctor if you are allergic to daffodils.

Precautions for Use
By Infants and Children: Safety and effectiveness for those under 18 years of age not established.
By Those Over 60 Years of Age: No specific changes are presently indicated.

▷ **Advisability of Use During Pregnancy**
Pregnancy Category: B for galantamine, C for donepezil and tacrine. See Pregnancy Risk Categories at the back of this book.
Animal Studies: Data not available.
Human Studies: Adequate studies of pregnant women are not available.
Consult your doctor.

Advisability of Use If Breast-Feeding

Presence of these drugs in breast milk: Unknown.

Monitor nursing infant closely, and discontinue drug or nursing if adverse effects develop.

Habit-Forming Potential: None.

Effects of Overdose: May precipitate a cholinergic crisis—severe nausea and vomiting, slow heartbeat, low blood pressure, extreme muscle weakness, collapse, and convulsions.

Suggested Periodic Examinations While Taking These Drugs (at physician's discretion)

Assessment of mental status: periodically—check benefits or loss of benefits as Alzheimer's progresses.

For tacrine, liver function tests should be checked every other week for the first 16 weeks of treatment, then every 3 months ongoing if the same dose is used. If medicine is stopped for more than 4 weeks, the liver tests should be repeated again on the same schedule.

Tacrine and donepezil patients need complete blood counts periodically or if symptoms of low blood count occur.

Homocysteine levels.

▷ **While Taking These Drugs, Observe the Following**

Foods: Tacrine is best NOT taken with food. Donepezil is not affected by food. Galantamine is best taken WITH FOOD. Homocysteine appears to have a role in dementia. Current data shows that people with high homocysteine levels are twice as likely to develop Alzheimer's or some form of dementia. A check of homocysteine levels and certainly augmented B vitamins is prudent and good complimentary care. The NIH is planning a large study to look at the effect of using folic acid, vitamin B12, and vitamin B6 to decrease homocysteine and the rate of thinking (cognitive) decline in Alzheimer's patients.

Herbal Medicines or Minerals: Data from appropriate scientific studies about combination of these medicines with ginkgo biloba is not available and cannot be recommended. A well-designed study of ginkgo biloba DID show it to be effective in mild to moderate Alzheimer's. Because galantamine is derived from daffodils, talk to your doctor if you have a daffodil allergy before taking this medicine.

Beverages: No restrictions.

▷ *Alcohol:* Occasional small amounts of alcohol are okay. Frequent use may worsen memory problems and affect the liver.

Tobacco Smoking: No interactions expected. I advise everyone to quit smoking.

Marijuana Smoking: Additive dizziness may occur.

▷ *Other Drugs*

These medicines may ***increase*** the effects of
- bethanechol (Duvoid, others).
- theophylline (Theo-Dur, others) by doubling the drug level (reported for tacrine).
- succinylcholine (Anectine, others).

These medicines may ***decrease*** the effects of
- anticholinergic medications (see Drug Classes).

The following drug may ***increase*** the effects of tacrine and galantamine:
- cimetidine (Tagamet).

These medicines ***taken concurrently*** with
- carbamazepine (Tegretol), dexamethasone, phenobarbital, fosphenytoin

(Cerebyx), phenytoin (Dilantin), or rifampin (Rifater, others) may decrease therapeutic benefits of the anti-Alzheimer drugs.

- dexamethasone (various) may blunt donepezil benefits.
- erythromycin (various) or paroxetine (Paxil) increases blood levels of these medicines. Caution and close patient follow up for signs or symptoms of dose excess is needed.
- ibuprofen (Motrin, others) was associated with delirium in one case report on tacrine.
- ketoconazole, quinidine, and perhaps ritonavir (Norvir) or other protease inhibitors (see Drug Classes) may lead to increased risk of donepezil or tacrine toxicity (decreased removal by two liver enzymes. Caution and close patient follow up is advised.
- medicines removed by cytochrome P-450 enzymes (2D6 and 3A4) or that inhibit those enzymes may lead to toxic levels of all of these medicines. Caution is advised.
- NSAIDs (see Drug Classes) may cause additive stomach upset.
- riluzole (Rilutek) may increase risk of tacrine toxicity (both drugs removed by P450 1A2).

▷ *Driving, Hazardous Activities:* These drugs may cause confusion or dizziness. Restrict activities as necessary.

Aviation Note: The use of these drugs *may be a disqualification* for piloting. See a designated Aviation Medical Examiner.

Exposure to Sun: No restrictions.

Exposure to Heat: Increased sweating may occur rarely with tacrine. The combination of increased sweating and hot environments may lead to more rapid dehydration.

Discontinuation: These drugs should NOT be abruptly stopped. Some adverse effects are dose related and may abate if the dose is decreased. Slow withdrawal of the drug is indicated if it is not tolerated. A discontinuation syndrome has been reported for donepezil.

ANTI-LEUKOTRIENE FAMILY

Montelukast: (mon TELL oo cast) **Zafirlukast** (zah FUR lew kast) **Zileuton** (ZEYE loo ton)

Introduced: 1998, 1996, 1997 **Class:** Antiasthmatic, anti-leukotriene, 5-lipoxygenase inhibitor (zileuton) **Prescription:** USA: Yes **Controlled Drug:** USA: No; Canada: No **Available as Generic:** No

Brand Names: *Montelukast:* Singulair; *Zafirlukast:* Accolate; *Zileuton:* Zyflo

---

BENEFITS versus RISKS

Possible Benefits	*Possible Risks*
EFFECTIVE PREVENTION AND CHRONIC TREATMENT OF BRONCHIAL ASTHMA	Headache Nausea Liver enzyme increase
TREATS HAY FEVER (montelukast)	
May have a role in treating bronchospasm caused by exercise (montelukast, zafirlukast)	
May have a role in preventing or treating allergies to cats (zafirlukast)	

▷ **Principal Uses**

As a Single Drug Product: Uses currently included in FDA-approved labeling: (1) Prevent recurrence of asthmatic episodes; (2) chronically treat asthmatic episodes; (3) zafirlukast is approved to prevent and for long-term treatment of asthma in patients 5 years old or older; (4) montelukast is approved to prevent and treat ongoing asthma in adults and in pediatric patients who are 2 years old or older as well as for use in preventing asthma induced by exercise; (5) montelukast approved for allergic rhinitis.

Author's Note: These medicines are indicated as Step Two medicines (alternatives to low-dose inhaled steroids, cromolyn or nedocromil in mild persistent asthma) in the National Institutes of Health's (NIH, NHLBI) "Guidelines for Diagnosis and Management of Asthma."

Other (unlabeled) generally accepted uses: (1) montelukast and zafirlukast may have a role in preventing spasm of the bronchi caused by exercise; (2) zileuton may have a role in preventing allergic rhinitis or aspirin-sensitive asthma; (3) zafirlukast combined with loratadine yielded superb results in treating hay fever symptoms in a study of 458 patients; (4) zafirlukast may help prevent allergic reactions to cats; (5) montelukast could have a role in preventing migraines; (6) montelukast eases delayed pressure urticaria; (7) leukotrienes in general would be expected to have steroid sparing effects in asthma and may have a role in psoriasis.

How These Drugs Work: Zafirlukast and montelukast work by blocking (leukotriene receptor antagonist) action of chemicals called leukotrienes (slow-reacting substances of anaphylaxis). Zileuton works by blocking creation of (leukotriene pathway inhibitor) leukotrienes themselves. By inhibiting action or formation of leukotrienes, all medicines help keep the airways open.

Available Dosage Forms and Strengths

Montelukast:
Chewable tablets — 4 mg and 5 mg
Tablet — 10 mg

Zafirlukast:
Tablet — 10 mg and 20 mg

Zileuton:
Tablet — 600 mg

▷ **Recommended Dosage Ranges** (Actual dosage and schedule must be determined for each patient individually.)

Children 12 to 23 months:
   Montelukast only: One 4-mg packet of oral granules or one 4 mg chewable
      tablet in the evening.
Children 2 to 5:
   Montelukast only: One 4-mg chewable tablet in the evening.
Children 5 to 11:
   Zafirlukast: 10 mg in the morning and evening.
Children 6 to 14:
   Montelukast only: One 5-mg chewable tablet in the evening.
People 12 to 60 Years of Age:
   Zafirlukast: 20 mg twice daily.
   Zileuton: 600 mg four times a day.
People 15 to 60 years of age:
   Montelukast: 10 mg once a day, taken in the evening.
Over 60 Years of Age:
   Montelukast: No difference in safety or efficacy, but increased sensitivity to
      the drug can't yet be ruled out.
   Zafirlukast: Maximum blood level can be twice that of younger patients. Pru-
      dent to lower doses, but specific guidelines have not been developed. Pack-
      age insert notes that using typical dose did not result in adverse effects in
      clinical trials.
   Zileuton: Same as those for 12 to 60 years old.
   **Author's Note: These medicines may be continued during an acute
      worsening (exacerbation) of asthma, but are not to be used to treat a
      sudden (acute) asthma attack.**
Conditions Requiring Dosing Adjustments
   Liver Function:
      Montelukast has NOT been studied in liver compromise, but is removed by
         liver (CYP450 3A4, 2C9 and 2A6) therefore lower doses may be prudent.
      Zafirlukast stays in the body up to 60% longer in patients with alcoholic cir-
         rhosis. Lower doses and blood levels appear prudent.
      Zileuton should not be given if active liver disease is present.
   Kidney Function: Dosage changes not needed for the medicines in this class.
▷ **Dosing Instructions:** Montelukast should be taken in the evening. Zafirlukast
   should be taken on an empty stomach, 1 hour before or 2 hours after a
   meal. Zileuton may be given with or without food. It's important to note
   that these medicines are NOT to be used to stop a sudden (acute) asthma
   attack, but are usually continued during exacerbation (worsening) of
   asthma if they have already been started. If you forget a dose: take it right
   away unless it's nearly time for your next regular dose. If it IS nearly time,
   just take the scheduled dose. DO NOT double doses.

Usual Duration of Use: Both zafirlukast and zileuton start to work in half an
   hour. Montelukast peaks and also starts to work in 3–4 hours. It lasts for 24
   hours. Zafirlukast significantly relaxes bronchi in 30 minutes, and lasts for
   12 hours after a typical dose. Zileuton peaks in 2–4 hours, and with multiple doses may last up to 7 days. Ongoing use requires periodic follow-up
   with your doctor.

Typical Treatment Goals and Measurements (Outcomes and Markers)
   Asthma: The frequency of asthma attacks as well as the severity of asthma
      attacks that occur (such as those requiring an emergency department visit)
      are a benchmark of effectiveness. Pulmonary function tests such as FEV1
      are valuable measures to assess response. Some clinicians also use the

number of times a rescue inhaler must be used as well as daily and night (nocturnal) symptom scores as clinical fine points. Prednisone dose decreases (physician supervised) may also indicate that the medicine is working. Goals should be communicated and checked.

Possible Advantages of These Drugs

A completely new mechanism of action in preventing asthma and some allergic reactions. Once-daily dosing can improve how well people take these medicines (patient adherence or compliance).

▷ **These Drugs Should Not Be Taken If**
- you have had an allergic reaction to one of the medicines in this family.
- you have active liver disease or increased liver enzymes (transaminases) greater than three times the upper normal limit (zileuton).

▷ **Inform Your Physician Before Taking These Drugs If**
- you have a liver disease (montelukast or zafirlukast).
- you are having a sudden (acute) asthma attack.
- you are a child less than 12 years old (zafirlukast).
- you are taking warfarin (zafirlukast).
- you have impaired kidney function (zafirlukast or zileuton).
- you drink large amounts of alcohol (zileuton).
- you develop a rash, tingling of the arms or legs, flu-like symptoms, or sinusitis.
- you are pregnant or are breast-feeding your baby.

Possible Side Effects (natural, expected, and unavoidable drug actions)

Not defined at present.

▷ **Possible Adverse Effects** (unusual, unexpected, and infrequent reactions)

If any of the following develop, consult your physician promptly for guidance.

Mild Adverse Effects

Allergic reactions: skin rash, hives.

Headache—frequent (montelukast, zafirlukast).

Fatigue, weakness—infrequent.

Dizziness—rare for zafirlukast, infrequent for zileuton.

Nausea or abdominal pain—infrequent.

Muscle pain—rare for zafirlukast, infrequent for zileuton.

Serious Adverse Effects

Allergic reactions: possible.

Idiosyncratic reactions: drug-induced lupus erythematosus—case reports.

Liver toxicity (increased enzyme tests)—rare for zafirlukast, less frequent for montelukast, infrequent for zileuton.

Decreases in steroid doses may be followed by onset of Churg-Strauss syndrome (montelukast and zafirlukast, possibly zileuton)—rare.

▷ **Possible Effects on Sexual Function:** None reported.

Natural Diseases or Disorders That May Be Activated by These Drugs: Since all three medicines may increase liver enzymes, hidden (subclinical) liver problems may be activated.

Possible Effects on Laboratory Tests

Liver function tests (SGPT, SGOT, LDH): may be increased.

CAUTION

1. The chewable montelukast tablet has phenylalanine (0.842 mg per 5-mg tablet). People with phenylketonuria (PKU) must be advised.

2. Talk with your doctor about continuing other asthma drugs once you start one of these medicines.
3. Since these medicines can affect the liver, it is critical that you have lab tests of liver function as your doctor orders them.
4. One case report of drug fever for zafirlukast.
6. All these medicines may be rare causes of Churg-Strauss syndrome. Call your doctor if you develop a rash, tingling of the arms or legs, flu-like symptoms, or sinusitis.
7. One study (see Wolfenden, L.L. in Sources) of 4,005 patients found that many patients did not accurately describe their symptoms to their doctors. This lead to patients being under treated. Be honest with your doctor about the severity and frequency of your asthma so that the treatments can be tailored to the severity and frequency of asthma symptoms!

Precautions for Use
By Children: Make certain that these medicines are taken in the amount and for the number of times they are ordered.
By Those Over 65 Years of Age: Zafirlukast goes to higher peak blood levels and remains in the body longer in those over 65, so smaller starting doses are indicated. Montelukast and zileuton are not changed by age.

▷ **Advisability of Use During Pregnancy**
Pregnancy Category: Montelukast and zafirlukast: B; zileuton: C. See Pregnancy Risk Categories at the back of this book.
Animal Studies: Montelukast—no teratogenicity at 320 times the maximum human dose in rats. Zafirlukast—no teratogenicity up to 160 times maximum recommended human dose given to mice. Zileuton—adverse effects were seen in rats given 18 times the typical human dose.
Human Studies: Adequate studies of pregnant women are not available. Ask your doctor for guidance.

Advisability of Use If Breast-Feeding
Presence of this drug in breast milk: Yes (zafirlukast); unknown (montelukast [but yes in rats], zileuton).
Avoid drug or refrain from nursing.

Habit-Forming Potential: None.

Effects of Overdose: No overdose experience in humans for montelukast (900 mg a day was given for a week in one study without any adverse effects) or zafirlukast. Zileuton overdose experience is limited. One patient received 6.6 to 9.0 g of zileuton, which caused vomiting, but recovered without ill effects.

Possible Effects of Long-Term Use: Possible increased liver enzymes.

Suggested Periodic Examinations While Taking This Drug (at physician's discretion)
Periodic liver function tests, lung (pulmonary) function tests.

▷ **While Taking This Drug, Observe the Following**
Foods: Zafirlukast should be taken on an empty stomach; no restrictions for montelukast or zileuton.
Herbal Medicines or Minerals: Using St. John's wort with zafirlukast or montelukast may cause a problem as St. John's wort has known interactions with CYP 3A4 and 2C9—the enzymes that remove zafirlukast and probably montelukast and zileuton. Fir or pine needle oil should NOT be used by asthmatics. Ephedra alone does carry a German Commission E monograph indication for asthma treatment. Talk to your doctor as this has not

been studied with leukotriene inhibitors. If you are allergic to plants in the Asteraceae family (aster, chrysanthemum, daisy, or ragweed), you may also be allergic to echinacea, chamomile, feverfew, and St. John's wort.

Beverages: No restrictions.

▷ *Alcohol:* May worsen drowsiness.

Tobacco Smoking: Smoking may lower levels of zileuton and is NOT advisable for anyone, least of all people living with asthma. I advise everyone to quit smoking.

Marijuana Smoking: May cause additive drowsiness.

▷ *Other Drugs*

These medicines *taken concurrently* with

- aspirin (various brands) may cause zafirlukast toxicity.
- astemizole (Hismanal—no longer on the U.S. market) may lead to heart toxicity with zileuton.
- beta-blocker drugs (see Drug Classes) may cause beta-blocker toxicity if combined with zileuton.
- dofetilide (Tikosyn) may increase dofetilide blood levels if taken with zafirlukast.
- erythromycin (E-Mycin, etc.) may decrease zafirlukast's benefits.
- phenobarbital (various) may lower montelukast blood levels.
- prednisone (montelukast report only) lead to severe accumulation of fluid (peripheral edema) in one patient. Close patient follow up and caution is prudent. The other members of this class may be corticosteroid sparing.
- propranolol (Inderal) and perhaps other beta-blockers (see Drug Classes) cause excessive/undesirable beta blockage.
- rifampin (Rifater) may lower montelukast blood levels.
- terfenadine (Seldane—no longer on the U.S. market) may decrease zafirlukast blood levels and its therapeutic benefits. Zileuton may decrease terfenadine (and perhaps other similarly structured minimally sedating antihistamine levels) and lead to toxicity. DO NOT combine.
- theophylline (Theo-Dur, others) may decrease zafirlukast blood levels and its therapeutic benefits. Zileuton may result in doubling of theophylline levels and require reduced theophylline doses.
- warfarin (Coumadin) may lead to increased risk of bleeding (zafirlukast and zileuton). More frequent INRs are needed.

▷ *Driving, Hazardous Activities:* These drugs may cause dizziness. Restrict activities as necessary.

Aviation Note: The use of these drugs *may be a disqualification* for piloting. Consult a designated Aviation Medical Examiner.

Exposure to Sun: No restrictions.

Discontinuation: Do not stop these medicines without first talking with your doctor.

APREPITANT (AH prep in tant)

Introduced: 2003 **Class:** Antiemetic; Substance P blocker **Prescription:** USA: Yes **Controlled Drug:** USA: No; Canada: No **Available as Generic:** USA: No; Canada: No

Brand Name: Emend

Author's Note: Information in this profile will be broadened as clinical study results and comparative data warrant.

ARIPIPRAZOLE (AIR ih pip rah zohl)

Introduced: 2002 **Class:** Antipsychotic; Atypical antipsychotic agent, dopamine system stabilizer; partial agonist **Prescription:** USA: Yes **Controlled Drug:** USA: No; Canada: No **Available as Generic:** USA: No; Canada: No

Brand Name: Abilify

As a Single Drug Product: Uses currently included in FDA-approved labeling: (1) Treatment of schizophrenia.

Other (unlabeled) generally accepted uses: (1) A well-designed clinical trial presented at the American Psychiatric meeting found rapid onset of benefit (as soon as day four) in treating sudden (acute) bipolar mania using 30 mg of aripiprazole a day, with the option to decrease to 15 mg daily. Patients showed improved Young Mania Rating Scale (Y-MRS) results and improved Clinical Global Impression-Bipolar Disorder (CGI-BP), Positive and Negative Syndrome Scaled (PANSS)-total (PANNSS-total) as well as the PANSS hostility subscale.

Author's Note: Information in this profile will be broadened as clinical data warrant.

ASPIRIN* (AS pir in)

Other Names: acetylsalicylic acid, ASA

Introduced: 1899 **Class:** Analgesics, mild; antiplatelet, antipyretic, NSAIDs, salicylates **Prescription:** USA: No **Controlled Drug:** USA: No; Canada: No **Available as Generic:** Yes

Brand Names: Added Strength Analgesic Pain Reliever, Adult Strength Pain Reliever [CD], Aggrenox [CD], Alka-Seltzer Effervescent Pain Reliever and Antacid [CD], Alka-Seltzer Night Time [CD], Alka-Seltzer Plus [CD], Alka-Seltzer Plus Cold [CD], Anacin [CD], Anacin Maximum Strength [CD], ♣Anacin w/Codeine [CD], ♣Ancasal, APC [CD], APC w/Codeine [CD], ♣APO-ASA, Arthritis Pain Formula [CD], Arthritis Strength Bufferin, A.S.A. Enseals, ♣Asasantine [CD], Ascriptin [CD], Ascriptin A/D [CD], Aspergum, ♣Aspirin,* Aspirin PROTECT, Asprimox, ♣Astrin, Axotal [CD], Azdone [CD], Bayer Aspirin, Bayer Children's Chewable Aspirin, Bayer Enteric Aspirin, Bayer Back & Body Pain, Bayer Plus, Bayer PM Extra Strength, BC Powder, Buffaprin, Bufferin [CD], Bufferin Arthritis Strength [CD], Bufferin Extra Strength [CD], Bufferin w/Codeine [CD], Cama Arthritis Pain Reliever [CD], Cardioprin, Carisoprodol Compound [CD], Cope [CD], Coricidin [CD], ♣Coryphen, ♣Coryphen-Codeine [CD], ♣C2 Buffered [CD], Darvon Compound [CD], Direct Formulary Aspirin, ♣Dristan [CD], Easprin, Ecotrin, 8-Hour Bayer, Empirin, Empirin w/Codeine No. 2, 4 [CD], ♣Entrophen, Excedrin [CD], Excedrin Extra Strength Geltabs [CD], Excedrin Migraine* [CD], Fiorinal [CD], ♣Fiorinal-C [Q],-C [h] [CD], Fiorinal w/Codeine [CD], Genacote, Genprin, Goody's Headache Powder [CD], Halprin, Hepto [CD], Lortab ASA [CD], Low Dose Adult Chewable Aspirin, Marnal [CD], Maximum Bayer Aspirin, Measurin, Midol Caplets [CD], Momentum [CD], Norgesic [CD], Norgesic Forte [CD], Norwich Aspirin, ♣Novasen, Orphenadrine [CD], PAP w/Codeine [CD], Percodan [CD], Percodan-Demi [CD], ♣Phenaphen [CD], ♣Phenaphen

No. 2, 3, 4 [CD], Propoxyphene Compound [CD], ✤Riphen-10, Robaxisal [CD], ✤Robaxisal-C [CD], Roxiprin [CD], ✤692 [CD], SK-65 Compound [CD], Soma Compound [CD], St. Joseph Children's Aspirin, ✤Supasa, Synalgos [CD], Synalgos-DC [CD], Talwin Compound [CD], Talwin Compound-50 [CD], ✤Tecnal Tablet [CD], ✤Triaphen-10, ✤217 [CD], ✤217 Strong [CD], ✤292 [CD], Vanquish [CD], Verin, Wesprin, Zorprin

---

BENEFITS versus RISKS

EFFECTIVE RELIEF OF MILD TO MODERATE PAIN AND INFLAMMATION	*Possible Risks*

EFFECTIVE RELIEF OF MILD TO
MODERATE PAIN AND
INFLAMMATION
REDUCTION OF FEVER
PREVENTION OF BLOOD CLOTS
PREVENTION OF HEART ATTACK
(a benefit when satisfactory blood
pressure control has been achieved
prior to starting aspirin)
PREVENTION OF STROKE
PREVENTION OF COLON CANCER
ACTS TO LIMIT THE SIZE AND
SEVERITY OF HEART ATTACKS
ONCE THEY HAVE STARTED
TREATMENT OF MIGRAINE HEAD-
ACHES (EXCEDRIN MIGRAINE
ONLY)
PREVENTION OF COLON CANCER
(COLORECTAL ADENOMAS) IN
PEOPLE WITH PREVIOUS
COLORECTAL CANCER
PREVENTION OF STROKE IN
PEOPLE WITH ATRIAL
FIBRILLATION
PREVENTION OF ADVERSE
OUTCOMES IN ACUTE
CORONARY SYNDROME
PATIENTS WHEN COMBINED
WITH CLOPIDOGREL
(PLAVIX)

Possible Risks
Stomach irritation, bleeding, and/or
ulceration
Decreased numbers of white blood
cells and platelets
Hemolytic anemia—rare
Liver toxicity—rare
Bronchospasm in asthmatics-possible
Ringing in the ears (tinitis) possible as
toxicity sign
Hemorrhagic strokes—case
reports/increased risk
Full-dose use (not low-dose) carries
an increased risk of hospitalization
for congestive heart failure in the el-
derly (NSAIDs as a class effect)

▷ **Principal Uses**

As a Single Drug Product: Uses currently included in FDA-approved labeling: (1) Relieves mild to moderate pain and eases symptoms in conditions causing inflammation or high fever. Treats musculoskeletal disorders, especially acute and chronic arthritis, as well as painful menstruation (dysmenorrhea). Used selectively to: (2) reduce risk of first heart attack; (3) reduce the risk of repeat heart attack; (4) prevent platelet embolism to the brain (in men); (5) reduce risk of clots (thromboembolism) after heart attack and in people with artificial heart valves and after hip surgery (see Blood Platelets in Glossary); (6) help prevent a second stroke in people who have had a stroke; (7) help prevent strokes in people with transient ischemic attack (TIA) history; (8) help prevent migraine headaches (Excedrin Migraine only); (9) treat TIA in women and men; (10) treat sudden heart attack (acute myocardial infarction or AMI) in men and women;

(11) decrease risk of heart attack in patients with unstable angina; (12) treat pleurisy associated with systemic lupus erythematosus; (13) used in some patients after coronary angioplasty; (14) used in combination with clopidogrel (Plavix) in some patients with acute coronary syndromes (see CURE trial reference and unstable angina).

Other (unlabeled) generally accepted uses: (1) Long-term use may decrease the risk of colon polyps or colon cancer in women AND MEN. New data also shows benefits in preventing colorectal adenomas in people who have already had colon or rectal cancer; (2) may limit size and severity of a heart attack if aspirin is taken immediately after symptoms are recognized and is continued for at least 30 days after the heart attack; (3) can help reduce flushing caused by niacin; (4) used after carotid artery surgery (endarterectomy) to prevent TIA or stroke; (5) general data supporting NSAID use and decreased Alzheimer's risk; (6) one 1999 study found that low dose (100 mg) of aspirin given 8 hours after waking or at bedtime worked to decrease blood pressure in women at risk for gestational hypertension or preeclampsia; (7) used in some atrial fibrillation patients (intolerant of anticoagulant treatment) to help prevent strokes; (8) ADA recommendation for prevention strategy for people living with diabetes who are also at risk for cardiovascular disease; (9) a survey of 14,000 women appears to show that long-term aspirin use may decrease risk of lung cancer.

As a Combination Drug Product [CD]: Frequently combined with other mild or strong analgesic drugs to enhance pain relief. Also combined with antihistamines and decongestants in many cold preparations to relieve headache and general discomfort. Aggrenox combines 200 mg of dipyridamole with 25 mg of aspirin.

How This Drug Works: Reduces prostaglandins, chemicals involved in the production of inflammation and pain. By modifying the temperature-regulating center in the brain, dilating blood vessels and increasing sweating, aspirin reduces fever. Works on blood clotting elements called platelets to inactivate prostaglandin G/H synthase. This inactivation leads to almost complete suppression of platelet ability to make thromboxanes. By preventing the production of thromboxane in blood platelets, aspirin inhibits formation of blood clots.

Available Dosage Forms and Strengths

Capsules, enteric coated — 500 mg
Capsules, enteric-coated granules — 325 mg
Gum tablets — 227.5 mg
Suppositories — 60 mg, 120 mg, 125 mg, 130 mg, 195 mg, 200 mg, 300 mg, 325 mg, 600 mg, 650 mg, 1.2 g
Tablets — 65 mg, 81 mg, 165 mg, 325 mg, 496 mg, 500 mg
Tablets, chewable — 81 mg
Tablets, enteric coated — 81 mg, 165 mg, 325 mg, 500 mg, 650 mg, 975 mg
Tablets, prolonged action — 80 mg (Canada), 650 mg, 800 mg, 975 mg

▷ **Usual Adult Dosage Ranges:** *In men or women having a heart attack:* One (325 mg) nonenteric-coated aspirin (then call 911). If only enteric-coated aspirin is available, it should be chewed in order to make it enter the body faster. Aspirin is then continued for 30 days after the heart attack. Some studies have continued it for up to 2 years.

In stroke: 50–325 mg showed a benefit in the CAST study.

In preventing transient ischemic attacks (TIA): 325–900 mg a day has been used. Low-dose treatment of TIA has used 50–325 mg. For the Aggrenox combination form: Prevention of stroke in people who have had transient brain blood flow problems (ischemia) or those who have suffered an ischemic stroke from a clot (thrombosis)—one capsule in the morning and in the evening has been used.

For pain or fever: 325 to 650 mg every 4 hours and as needed for fever (ongoing pain or fever use should be medically supervised).

Arthritis (and related conditions): 3,600 to 5,400 mg daily in divided doses.

Prevention of blood clots: 80–162 mg daily or every other day. Low-dose, long-term daily aspirin may also decrease risk of colon cancer or heart attacks. FDA advocates 75–325 mg daily for unstable angina or a previous heart attack to reduce risk of death or another heart attack. The U.S. Preventive Services Task Force recommends that clinicians consider low-dose aspirin use in patients who are 40 or older who have significantly increased risk of heart attack (myocardial infarction or MI) and who are not contraindicated low-dose aspirin. A phenomenon called **aspirin resistance** has been described in several studies. The practical implication of this research is that some patients may be more resistant to the beneficial effects of aspirin in preventing blood clots than others. Some clinicians use tests of how well blood elements called platelets clump (aggregate) in order to check results from aspirin and to adjust dosing.

Note: For long-term use, actual dosage and schedule must be determined for each patient individually.

Conditions Requiring Dosing Adjustments

Liver Function: This medication should be avoided in severe liver disease.

Kidney Function: Avoided or used with caution in patients with kidney problems. NOT to be used in severe (creatinine clearance less than 10 ml/min) kidney failure.

Glucose-6-Phosphate Dehydrogenase (G6PD) Deficiency: May cause destruction of red blood cells in patients with G6PD deficiency.

▷ **Dosing Instructions:** Take with food, milk or a full glass of water to reduce stomach upset. Regular tablets may be crushed and capsules opened for administration. Enteric-coated tablets, prolonged-action tablets, A.S.A. Enseals, Cama tablets, and Ecotrin tablets should not be crushed. If you forget a dose: take it right away unless it's nearly time for your next regular dose. Aggrenox capsules SHOULD NOT be chewed. If it IS nearly time, just take the scheduled dose. DO NOT double dose.

Usual Duration of Use: Short-term use is recommended—3 to 5 days for fever or cold symptoms. Daily use should not exceed 10 days without physician supervision. Use on a regular schedule for 1 week usually needed to see benefit in relieving chronic arthritis symptoms. Response must be evaluated and dose adjusted in long-term use. Ongoing use for prevention of heart attack, colon cancer, or stroke REQUIRES ongoing supervision by your doctor, even though aspirin is not a prescription drug.

Typical Treatment Goals and Measurements (Outcomes and Markers)

Pain: Most clinicians treating pain use a device called an algometer to check your pain. This looks like a small ruler, but lets the clinician better understand your pain. The goals of treatment then relate to where the level of pain started (for example, a rating of 7 on a zero to ten scale) and what the cause of the pain was. Pain medicines may also be used together (in combination) in order to get the best result or outcome. If your pain control is not acceptable to YOU after a week of arthritis pain treatment, be sure to call your doctor as you may need a different medicine or combination.

Cardiovascular disorders (strokes and heart attacks): The clear marker here is prevention of a first or second stroke or heart attack. Measures of 11-dehydro thromboxane B2 in the urine (see Eikelboom in Sources) and use of the PFA-100 may help define people who have more clotting propensity to overcome or who activate their platelets by a pathway different than cyclooxygenase (such as Thrombin). These tests may help identify "aspirin resistant patients."

Possible Advantages of This Drug: Inexpensive medicine that treats a wide variety of conditions and can also help prevent heart attacks, colon cancer, and strokes. A recent study found that one baby aspirin (81 mg) daily decreased risk of a first heart attack in high risk, otherwise healthy patients. Your doctor should decide if this makes sense for you. Bayer Back & Body Pain has a Micro-coating (Toleraid) that makes it more easily swallowed.

▷ **This Drug Should Not Be Taken If**
  • you have had an allergic reaction to any form of aspirin.
  • you have a history of urticaria/angioedema or spasm of the bronchi with rhinoconjunctivitis with aspirin, other NSAID or selective COX II inhibitor (adults who developed nasal polyps, asthma, chronic rhinitis, or ongoing angioedema or urticaria make these reactions more likely).
  • you have any type of bleeding disorder (such as hemophilia).
  • you have active peptic ulcer disease.
  • you are a child or even teenager with a viral infection (use in viral illnesses in those populations increases the risk of Reye's syndrome—see Glossary).
  • it smells like vinegar. This indicates decomposition of aspirin.

▷ **Inform Your Physician Before Taking This Drug If**
  • you are taking any anticoagulant drug or have a history of blood clotting difficulties (such as low vitamin K or prothrombin).
  • you are taking a COX II inhibitor and this medicine is prescribed.
  • you are taking oral antidiabetic drugs.
  • you have a history of peptic ulcer (FDA advisory committee notes that people who take 3 or more alcohol containing drinks a day, increased risk of stomach bleeding occurs).
  • you have gout.
  • you have lupus erythematosus.
  • you are pregnant (particularly third trimester) or planning pregnancy.
  • you have asthma, carditis or nasal polyps.
  • you plan to have surgery of any kind (used in different doses before some kinds of surgery and not at all before others).
  • you take prescription or nonprescription medications not discussed when aspirin was recommended for you.
  • you are unsure how much to take or how often to take it.
  • you have a history of liver or kidney problems.
  • you have low glucose-6-phosphate dehydrogenase (G6PD).
  • you drink three or more alcoholic drinks a day (see Caution).

Possible Side Effects (natural, expected, and unavoidable drug actions)
  Mild drowsiness in sensitive patients.
  Interference with usual blood clotting.

▷ **Possible Adverse Effects** (unusual, unexpected, and infrequent reactions)
If any of the following develop, consult your physician promptly for guidance.

Mild Adverse Effects

Allergic reactions: skin rash, hives, nasal discharge (resembling hay fever), nasal polyps.

Stomach irritation, heartburn, nausea, vomiting, constipation—infrequent to frequent.

Ringing in the ears (tinnitus)—a sign of excessive doses or dose sensitivity-call your doctor if this happens (see serious adverse effects)—possible.

Lowering of the blood sugar—rare.

Serious Adverse Effects

Allergic reactions: acute anaphylactic reaction (see Glossary), allergic destruction of blood platelets (see Glossary) and bruising—rare.

Idiosyncratic reactions: hemolytic anemia (see Glossary)—rare.

Stevens-Johnson syndrome—possible.

Hemorrhagic stroke in some populations—case reports.

Erosion of stomach lining, with silent bleeding—may be dose and frequency related.

Activation of peptic ulcer, with or without hemorrhage—frequent with long-term non-enteric-coated use.

Bone marrow depression (see Glossary): fatigue, weakness, fever, sore throat, abnormal bleeding or bruising—possible.

Hepatitis with jaundice (see Glossary): yellow skin and eyes, dark-colored urine, light-colored stool—possible, especially with daily use of more than 2 grams (2,000 mg)—dose related.

Hearing toxicity (ototoxicity, tinnitus)—more common with higher doses and long-term use.

Kidney function decline—possible in kidney failure patients who depend on prostaglandins for their kidneys to work.

Bronchospasm when used in patients with nasal polyps, asthma—possible.

May worsen angina attacks (Prinzmetal's) and increase their frequency—possible.

Reye's syndrome if used during viral illness—DO NOT USE in children or teenagers with viral illnesses.

▷ **Possible Effects on Sexual Function:** None reported.

Adverse Effects That May Mimic Natural Diseases or Disorders: Liver damage may suggest viral hepatitis or reveal (unmask) low-level (subclinical) liver disease. May lead to decline in kidney function in people with borderline kidney disease.

Possible Effects on Laboratory Tests

Complete blood counts: decreased red cells, hemoglobin, white cells, and platelets.

Bleeding time: prolonged.

INR (prothrombin time): increased by large doses; decreased by small doses.

Blood glucose level: decreased.

Blood uric acid level: increased by small doses; decreased by large doses.

Liver function tests: increased ALT/GPT, AST/GOT, alkaline phosphatase.

Thyroid function tests: increased T3 uptake, free T3, and free T4; decreased TSH, T3, T4, and free thyroid index (FTI).

Urine sugar tests: false positive with Clinitest or Benedict's solution.

Fecal occult blood test: positive with large doses of aspirin.

CAUTION
1. The FDA now requires a warning noting that people who have three or more alcoholic drinks a day may have increased risk of stomach bleeding if they also use aspirin (problems may also occur with lower alcohol use).
2. **Aspirin is a drug.** We tend to have an unrealistic sense of its safety and its potential for adverse effects. TALK TO YOUR DOCTOR TO SEE IF BENEFITS OUTWEIGH RISKS OF REGULAR ASPIRIN USE. A meta-analysis of 55,462 patients and 16 clinical trials found an increased risk of stroke (12 strokes for every 10,000 patients). The study concluded that benefits may outweigh risks for many populations. A recent study found that aspirin use can decrease risk of some cardiovascular problems by 28% in otherwise healthy people. Talk to your doctor.
3. Talk to your doctor about dosing of aspirin BEFORE you take it and also before undertaking any ongoing use of aspirin.
4. An outcome study of 5,499 men found that the risk of stroke with aspirin treatment related to blood pressure. One conclusion is that blood pressure should be satisfactorily controlled BEFORE aspirin therapy for prevention of CHD is started.
5. Remember that aspirin can
   • cause new illnesses.
   • complicate existing illnesses.
   • complicate pregnancy.
   • complicate surgery.
   • interact unfavorably with other drugs.
   • When a health care professional asks, "Are you taking any drugs?" the answer is "yes" if you are taking aspirin. This also applies to *any* non-prescription drug you may be taking (see Over-the-Counter Drugs in the Glossary).
6. Some patients may be "aspirin resistant." This term is used to help identify people who still have platelets that clump to their usual extent, despite appropriate low-dose aspirin treatment.
   • **Controversies in Medicine: Some clinicians think that aspirin will remove some of the benefits of ACE inhibitors (see Drug Classes) if these two medicines are taken together.**
   • Aspirin tends to be underused in people with diabetes and in patients with coronary artery disease (one study found only 26% use), others even less. If you are living with diabetes, or have coronary artery disease, ask your doctor if aspirin makes sense for you.
7. A study by MacDonald (see Sources) found that ibuprofen (not diclofenac, acetaminophen, or rofecoxib) can inhibit beneficial (cardioprotective) effects of aspirin. His conclusion was that aspirin should be taken two hours before ibuprofen so that aspirin can go to work first. Other clinicians recommended avoiding ongoing use of ibuprofen in patients receiving aspirin for heart protection.

Precautions for Use
By Infants and Children: Reye's syndrome (brain and liver damage in children, often fatal) can follow flu or chickenpox in children and teenagers. Some reports suggest that the use of aspirin by children with flu or chickenpox can increase the risk of developing this complication. Consult your physician before giving aspirin to a child or teenager with chickenpox, flu, or similar infection.

Usual dosage schedule for children (Up to 2 years of age—consult physician):
- 2 to 4 years of age — 160 mg/4 hours, up to 5 doses/24 hours.
- 4 to 6 years of age — 240 mg/4 hours, up to 5 doses/24 hours.
- 6 to 9 years of age — 320 mg/4 hours, up to 5 doses/24 hours.
- 9 to 11 years of age — 400 mg/4 hours, up to 5 doses/24 hours.
- 11 to 12 years of age — 480 mg/4 hours, up to 5 doses/24 hours.

Do not exceed 5 days of continual use without talking to your doctor. Give all doses with food, milk or a full glass of water.

By Those Over 60 Years of Age: Watch for signs of high blood level: irritability, ringing in the ears, deafness, confusion, nausea or stomach upset. Aspirin can cause serious stomach bleeding. This can occur as "silent" bleeding of small amounts over a long time. Sudden hemorrhage can occur, even without a history of stomach ulcer. Watch for gray- to black-colored stools, an indication of stomach bleeding.

▷ **Advisability of Use During Pregnancy**

Pregnancy Category: C/**D**. See Pregnancy Risk Categories at the back of this book.

Animal Studies: Significant birth defects due to this drug have been reported.

Human Studies: Information from studies of pregnant women indicates no increased risk of birth defects in 32,164 pregnancies exposed to aspirin. Studies show, however, that the regular use of aspirin during pregnancy is often detrimental to the health of the mother and the welfare of the fetus. Anemia, hemorrhage before and after delivery and an increased incidence of stillbirths and newborn deaths have been reported. There are data that support use of aspirin in low doses to prevent toxemia of pregnancy in some women with a history of this problem.

Ask your doctor for help. Avoid aspirin altogether during the last 3 months unless your doctor prescribes it.

Advisability of Use If Breast-Feeding

Presence of this drug in breast milk: Yes.

Avoid drug or refrain from nursing.

Habit-Forming Potential: Extended high-dose use may cause a psychological dependence (see Glossary).

Effects of Overdose: Stomach distress, nausea, vomiting, ringing in the ears, dizziness, impaired hearing, blood chemistry imbalance, stupor, fever, deep and rapid breathing, twitching, delirium, shock, hallucinations, convulsions.

Possible Effects of Long-Term Use

A form of psychological dependence (see Glossary). Anemia due to chronic blood loss from erosion of stomach lining. The development of stomach ulcer. The development of "aspirin allergy"—nasal discharge, nasal polyps, asthma. Kidney damage. Prolonged bleeding time, critical in the event of injury or surgery.

Suggested Periodic Examinations While Taking This Drug (at physician's discretion)

Complete blood cell counts.

Kidney function tests and urine analyses.

Liver function tests.

▷ **While Taking This Drug, Observe the Following**

Foods: May decrease the total amount of aspirin per dose that is absorbed.

Herbal Medicines or Minerals: Many herbal medicines may interact with aspirin. Examples include evening primrose oil (EPO), ginkgo, garlic, ginger, ginseng, guggul, and feverfew. St. John's wort may increase sensitivity to the sun, and caution is advised as additive sensitivity may develop. White willow bark contains salicylates. Adding products that contain that herb add additional aspirin and are not advised.

Nutritional Support: Do not take large doses of vitamin C while taking aspirin regularly.

Beverages: No restrictions. May be taken with milk.

▷ *Alcohol:* Use of alcohol and aspirin at the same time may increase risk of stomach damage and may prolong bleeding time (see cautions).

Tobacco Smoking: No interactions expected. I advise everyone to quit smoking.

▷ *Other Drugs*

Aspirin may ***increase*** the effects of

- adrenocortical steroids (see Drug Classes), leading to additive stomach irritation and possible bleeding.
- insulin (various brands including insulin lispro) and require dosage adjustment when more than 650 mg of aspirin is taken daily.
- heparin and cause abnormal bleeding.
- methotrexate and increase its toxic effects.
- oral anticoagulants (see Drug Classes) such as low-molecular-weight heparins (see Drug Classes) and warfarin (Coumadin) and cause abnormal bleeding.
- oral antidiabetic drugs (see Drug Classes) and cause hypoglycemia. Dosage adjustments are often necessary—particularly with first-generation agents.
- ticlodipine (Ticlid) may increase bleeding risk. Careful monitoring of blood counts is prudent.
- tiludronate (Skelid) by increasing blood levels by 50%.
- thrombolytics such as TPA and reteplase (Retavase). Careful monitoring is advised if these medicines are combined.
- valproic acid (Depakene).

Aspirin may ***decrease*** the effects of

- ACE inhibitors—since vein opening or vasodilator prostaglandins may account for some of the ACE beneficial effects and aspirin inhibits prostaglandins, aspirin may blunt ACE inhibitor benefits. Still, many clinicians feel that the benefits of aspirin and ACE use after a heart attack outweigh any blunting effect.
- beta-adrenergic-blocking drugs (see Drug Classes).
- captopril (Capoten).
- enalapril (Vasotec) by decreasing enalapril's beneficial increase in heart (cardiac) output.
- furosemide (Lasix).
- other NSAIDs (see Drug Classes).
- phenytoin (Dilantin) and fosphenytoin (Cerebyx) by decreasing phenytoin or fosphenytoin blood levels (high aspirin doses).
- probenecid (Benemid) and reduce its effectiveness in the treatment of gout—with aspirin doses of less than 2 g every 24 hours.
- spironolactone (Aldactazide, Aldactone, others) and reduce its diuretic effect.
- sulfinpyrazone (Anturane) and reduce its effectiveness in the treatment of gout—with aspirin doses of less than 2 g every 24 hours.
- tiludronate (Skelid) by decreasing the amount getting into the body.

Aspirin ***taken concurrently*** with

- alendronate (Fosamax) or other bisphosphonates (tiludronate or Skelid or risedronate or Actonel) may result in increased risk of stomach upset/diarrhea and decreases bisphosphonate.

- capsaicin (Zostrix and others) increases risk of bleeding.
- celecoxib (Celebrex), etoricoxib (investigational), rofecoxib (Vioxx), or valdecoxib (Bextra) (see Cox II Inhibitors in Drug Classes) increases risk of stomach ulcers. Benefits versus risks of low dose (such as 81 mg) aspirin in combination may favor benefits in many patients. Talk to your doctor.
- cilostazol (Pletal) changed platelet clumping (aggregation) in one study but the clinical significance of the change found is unknown. Caution is prudent.
- clopidogrel (Plavix) is a benefit-to-risk decision because of increased risk of bleeding. Talk to your doctor to see if the benefits (see CURE trial above) of combining aspirin and clopidogrel outweigh any increased bleeding risk.
- cortisonelike drugs (see Drug Classes) increases risk of stomach ulcers.
- diltiazem (Cardizem) may result in increased risk of bleeding.
- eptifibatide (Integrilin) increases risk of bleeding.
- high blood pressure (antihypertensive) medicines may blunt their therapeutic benefit, especially those that are diuretics such as furosemide (Lasix), spironolactone, or thiazides (see Drug Classes).
- ibuprofen (Motrin, others) may result in blunting of cardioprotective effects of aspirin. If mini-dose aspirin is being taken, the aspirin should be taken two hours BEFORE the ibuprofen. Ongoing use of ibuprofen in patients using aspirin for heart protective benefits should probably be avoided until further data are available.
- intrauterine devices (IUDs) may result in decreased IUD effectiveness.
- lithium (Lithobid) may increase lithium blood levels.
- low-molecular-weight heparins (Lovenox, Fragmin, others) increases the risk of bleeding.
- methotrexate (Mexate) may cause toxicity.
- niacin (various) may BENEFICIALLY decrease flushing from niacin.
- quinidine (Quinaglute, others) may increase risk of bleeding.
- tirofiban (Aggrastat) may increase bleeding risk. Careful monitoring of blood counts is prudent.
- valproic acid (Depakote) may cause toxic blood levels.
- varicella vaccine (Varivax) may result in Reye's syndrome. **Avoid aspirin and other salicylates for 6 weeks following Varivax inoculation**.
- verapamil (Calan, others) may cause increased bleeding risk.
- zafirlukast (Accolate) may increase zafirlukast blood levels and increase adverse effects.

The following drugs may *increase* the effects of aspirin:
- acetazolamide (Diamox).
- cimetidine (Tagamet).
- para-aminobenzoic acid (Pabalate).

The following drugs may *decrease* the effects of aspirin:
- antacids, with regular continual use.
- cholestyramine (Questran, others)—will decrease the amount of aspirin that goes to work; separate doses by 30 minutes.
- cortisonelike drugs (see Drug Classes).
- urinary alkalinizers (sodium bicarbonate, sodium citrate).

▷ *Driving, Hazardous Activities:* No restrictions or precautions.

Aviation Note: It is advisable to watch for mild drowsiness and restrict activities accordingly.

Exposure to Sun: Use caution, may cause photosensitivity.

Discontinuation: Aspirin should be stopped 1 week before some kinds of surgery. There are some data for use of low-dose aspirin in some cases (such as in carotid endarterectomy).

ATAZANAVIR (at ah ZAN ah veer)

Introduced: 2004 **Class:** Anti-viral, Anti-HIV, antiviral **Prescription:** USA: Yes **Controlled Drug:** USA: No; Canada: No **Available as Generic:** Yes

Brand Names: Reyataz

Author's Note: Please see the protease inhibitor family profile for further preliminary information on this medicine.

ATENOLOL (a TEN oh lohl)

Introduced: 1973 **Class:** Anti-anginal, antihypertensive, beta-adrenergic blocker **Prescription:** USA: Yes **Controlled Drug:** USA: No; Canada: No **Available as Generic:** Yes

Brand Names: ❦Apo-Atenolol, ❦Novo-Atenolol, ❦Nu-Atenolol,❦PMS-Atenolol, Tenoretic [CD], Tenormin

---

BENEFITS versus RISKS

Possible Benefits	*Possible Risks*
EFFECTIVE ANTI-ANGINAL DRUG in the management of effort-induced angina	CONGESTIVE HEART FAILURE in advanced heart disease
EFFECTIVE, WELL-TOLERATED ANTIHYPERTENSIVE in mild to moderate high blood pressure	Worsening of angina in coronary heart disease (abrupt withdrawal)
DECREASES RISK OF DYING AFTER A HEART ATTACK	May lead to low blood sugar in type one diabetics
DECREASES RISK OF PROBLEMS (MORBIDITY) AFTER A HEART ATTACK	Masking of low blood sugar (hypoglycemia) in drug-treated diabetes
HELPS PREVENT MIGRAINE HEADACHES	May provoke bronchial asthma in people with asthma when used in high doses
Probable role in decreasing risk of death (morbidity) or problems (morbidity) when taken before bypass (CABG) surgery	

▷ **Principal Uses**

As a Single Drug Product: Uses currently included in FDA-approved labeling: (1) Treats classical, effort-induced angina pectoris; (2) used for mild to moderately severe high blood pressure (may be used alone or in combination with other antihypertensive drugs, such as diuretics); (3) used following heart attacks to prolong life, help decrease risk of a second heart attack, decrease the size of the heart attack, and reduce risk of abnormal heartbeats.

Other (unlabeled) generally accepted uses: (1) Can help people with stage fright; (2) may have a role in preventing migraine headaches; (3) can have an adjunctive role in alcohol withdrawal; (4) helps congestive heart failure when used with fosinopril (Monopril); (5) taken before and after surgery, this drug can help maintain blood flow to the heart and decrease death; (6) decreases preeclampsia in women at risk for this; (7) a May 2002 study from Duke (see Ferguso, et al. in Sources) found that people who get beta blockers before heart bypass surgery (CABG) have better results than those who do not take those medicines.

As a Combination Drug Product [CD]: Used in combination with a thiazide diuretic (chlorthalidone) to combine the benefits of a beta-blocker with the excess-fluid-losing properties of a thiazide. This attacks high blood pressure using two different mechanisms.

How This Drug Works: It blocks some actions of the sympathetic nervous system, reducing heart rate and contraction force and reducing oxygen needs as the heart works, and it reduces blood vessel contraction, resulting in opening and lowering of blood pressure.

Available Dosage Forms and Strengths

Injection — 5 mg/10 ml

Tablets — 25 mg, 50 mg, 100 mg

Tablets, combination — 50 mg, 100 mg of atenolol with 25 mg of chlorthalidone

▷ **Usual Adult Dosage Ranges**

Hypertension: Initially 50 mg once daily. Dose may be increased gradually at intervals of 7 to 10 days as needed and tolerated up to 100 mg every 24 hours. The usual maintenance dose is 50 to 100 mg every 24 hours. The total dose should not exceed 100 mg every 24 hours.

Angina: Starting dose is 50 mg once daily. May be gradually increased at 7- to 10-day intervals as needed and tolerated up to 100 mg every 24 hours. Usual ongoing dose is 50 to 100 mg every 24 hours. Some patients require 200 mg daily.

After a heart attack (post-MI): Within 12 hours after the attack, 5 mg of this drug is given intravenously. This is followed by a second 5-mg intravenous dose 10 minutes later. Twelve hours after the second intravenous dose, 50 mg is given orally, followed by a second 50 mg 12 hours later. Oral dosing is continued at 100 mg orally for the next 10 days.

Note: Actual dose and schedule must be determined for each patient individually.

Conditions Requiring Dosing Adjustments

Liver Function: No decreases needed (liver has a small removal role).

Kidney Function: The dose must be decreased, with 25 mg a day as a maximum dose in some people.

▷ **Dosing Instructions:** Food decreases the amount of drug that gets into your body by up to 20%. Better taken on an empty stomach. Tablet may be crushed to take it. **DO NOT** stop this drug abruptly. If you forget a dose: take it right away unless it's within 8 hours of your next regular dose. If it IS within 8 hours of the next dose, just take the scheduled dose. DO NOT double doses.

Usual Duration of Use: Regular use for 3 to 7 days usually needed to see this drug's benefits in lowering blood pressure. Peak benefits may take two weeks. Meeting blood pressure goals will decide long-term use. Medicines are often coupled to an overall program of weight reduction, salt restriction, smoking cessation, etc. May take 3 months for peak chest pain benefits. See your doctor regularly.

Typical Treatment Goals and Measurements (Outcomes and Markers)

Blood Pressure: The NEW guidelines (JNC VII) define normal blood pressure (BP) as **less than** 120/80. Because blood pressures that were once considered acceptable can actually lead to blood vessel damage, the committee from the National Institutes of Health, National Heart Lung and Blood Institute now have a new category called **Pre-hypertension**. This ranges from 120/80 to 139/89 and is intended to help your doctor encourage lifestyle changes (or in the case of people with a risk factor for high blood pressure, start treatment) much earlier—so that possible damage to blood vessels, your heart, kidneys, sexual potency, or eyes might be minimized or avoided altogether. The next two classes of high blood pressure are stage 1 hypertension: 140/90 to 159/99 and stage 2 hypertension equal to or greater than: 160/100 mm Hg. These guidelines also recommend that clinicians trying to control blood pressure work with their patients to agree on the goals and a plan of treatment. The first-ever guidelines for blood pressure (hypertension) in African Americans recommends that MOST black patients be started on TWO antihypertensive medicines with the goal of lowering blood pressure to 130/80 for those with high risk for heart and blood vessel disease or with diabetes. The American Diabetes Association recommends 130/80 as the target for people living with diabetes and less than 125/75 for those who spill more than one gram of protein into their urine. Most clinicians try to achieve a BP that confers the best balance of lower cardiovascular risk and avoids the problem of too low a blood pressure. Blood pressure duration is generally increased with beneficial restriction of sodium. The goals and time frame should be discussed with you when the prescription is written. If goals are not met, it is not unusual to intensify doses or add on medicines. You can find the new blood pressure guidelines at *www.nhlbi.nih.gov/guidelines/hypertension/index.htm*. For the African American guidelines see Douglas, J.G. in Sources.

Possible Advantages of This Drug: Least likely of all beta-blocker drugs to cause central nervous system adverse effects: confusion, hallucinations, nervousness, nightmares. This medicine (unlike metoprolol or propranolol) has minimal involvement using the liver for removal from the body. May be a drug of choice in patients with liver compromise who require a beta blocker.

▷ **This Drug Should Not Be Taken If**
  • you have had an allergic reaction to it previously.
  • you are in heart failure (overt).
  • you have an abnormally slow heart rate or a serious form of heart block.
  • you are taking, or have taken within the past 14 days, any monoamine oxidase (MAO) type A inhibitor drug (see Drug Classes).
  • you are in cardiogenic shock.

▷ **Inform Your Physician Before Taking This Drug If**
  • you've had beta-blocker adverse reactions (see Drug Classes).
  • you have a history of serious heart disease, with or without episodes of heart failure.
  • you have a history of hay fever (allergic rhinitis), asthma, chronic bronchitis, chronic obstructive pulmonary disease (COPD), or emphysema.
  • you have been taking clonidine.
  • you have a history of overactive thyroid function (hyperthyroidism).
  • you have low blood sugar (hypoglycemia) or diabetes—may hide some symptoms of hypoglycemia.
  • you have impaired liver or kidney function.
  • you have diabetes or myasthenia gravis.
  • you take digitalis, quinidine, reserpine, or any calcium blocker (see Drug Classes).

- you take clonidine (atenolol should be stopped a few days before stopping clonidine).
- you will have surgery with general anesthesia.
- you take prescription or nonprescription drugs not discussed when atenolol was prescribed.
- you are unsure how much or how often to take this drug.

Possible Side Effects (natural, expected, and unavoidable drug actions)

Lethargy, fatigability, cold extremities, slow heart rate, light-headedness in upright position (see Orthostatic Hypotension in Glossary)—all reported during treatment.

▷ **Possible Adverse Effects** (unusual, unexpected, and infrequent reactions)

If any of the following develop, consult your physician promptly for guidance.

Mild Adverse Effects

Allergic reactions: skin rash, itching.

Headache, abnormal dreams—infrequent.

Dizziness, tiredness or depression—rare to frequent.

Indigestion, nausea, diarrhea—infrequent.

Joint and muscle discomfort, fluid retention (edema)—possible.

Serious Adverse Effects

Allergic reactions: may contribute to seriousness and refractory allergic reactions.

Chest pain, shortness of breath, can lead to congestive heart failure—rare.

May lead to an asthma attack (in asthmatic people)—possible.

Angina or rebound hypertension—if abruptly stopped.

Difficulty walking (intermittent claudication)—controversial.

Psychosis—case reports.

Systemic lupus erythematosus—case reports.

▷ **Possible Effects on Sexual Function:** Decreased libido and impaired potency (50 to 100 mg per day). This drug is less likely to cause lowered ability to achieve a completely firm penis (reduced erectile capacity) than most drugs of its class. Impotence—rare.

Possible Effects on Laboratory Tests

Blood cholesterol, LDL and VLDL cholesterol levels: no effect with doses of 50 mg/day; increased with doses of 100 mg/day.

ANA titer: increased.

Blood triglyceride levels: no effect with doses of 50 mg/day; increased with doses of 100 mg/day.

Blood HDL cholesterol levels: no effect with doses of 50 mg/day; decreased with doses of 100 mg/day.

CAUTION

1. Control your high blood pressure for life! Even though it usually does not have any signs or symptoms, high blood pressure does damage. Control your pressure and take your medicine. Visit www.americanheart.org for more information.
2. ***DO NOT stop this drug suddenly*** without the guidance of your doctor. Carry a note in your purse or wallet that says you take this drug.
3. Talk to your doctor or pharmacist BEFORE using nasal spray or pill decongestants. These may cause sudden increases in blood pressure when combined with beta-blocker drugs.
4. Report any tendency to emotional depression to your doctor.

Precautions for Use

By Infants and Children: Safety and effectiveness by those under 12 years of age not established. However, if this drug is used, watch for development of low blood sugar (hypoglycemia), especially if meals are skipped.

By Those Over 60 Years of Age: Proceed ***cautiously*** with all antihypertensive drugs. High blood pressure should be reduced slowly, avoiding excessively low blood pressure. Small doses and frequent blood pressure checks are needed. Sudden and excessive decrease in blood pressure can predispose to stroke or heart attack. Watch for dizziness, unsteadiness, tendency to fall, confusion, hallucinations, depression, or urinary frequency.

▷ **Advisability of Use During Pregnancy**

Pregnancy Category: **D.** See Pregnancy Risk Categories at the back of this book.

Animal Studies: Increased resorptions of embryo and fetus reported in rats, but no birth defects.

Human Studies: Adequate studies of pregnant women are not available, but the drug has caused fetal harm. This drug has been used during the last 3 months of pregnancy; however, fetal growth may be slowed and the child may be born with low blood pressure and temperature.

Ask your doctor for guidance.

Advisability of Use If Breast-Feeding

Yes.

Avoid drug if possible. If drug is necessary, observe nursing infant for slow heart rate and indications of low blood sugar.

Habit-Forming Potential: None.

Effects of Overdose: Weakness, slow pulse, low blood pressure, fainting, cold sweaty skin, congestive heart failure, coma, and convulsions.

Possible Effects of Long-Term Use: Reduced heart reserve or heart failure in some people with advanced heart disease.

Suggested Periodic Examinations While Taking This Drug (at physician's discretion)

Measurements of blood pressure (checks at health fairs or pharmacies are a great idea).

Valuation of heart function.

ANA titer.

▷ **While Taking This Drug, Observe the Following**

Foods: Can decrease total atenolol absorption by 20%. Best to avoid excessive salt intake.

Herbal Medicines or Minerals: Ginseng, guarana, hawthorn, saw palmetto, ma huang, goldenseal, yohimbe, and licorice may cause increased blood pressure. Calcium and garlic may help lower blood pressure. Indian snakeroot has a German Commission E monograph indication for hypertension—talk to your doctor. Eleuthero root and ephedra should be avoided by people living with hypertension.

Beverages: No restrictions. May be taken with milk.

▷ *Alcohol:* Use caution. Alcohol may exaggerate this drug's ability to lower blood pressure and may increase its mild sedative effect.

Tobacco Smoking: Nicotine may reduce this drug's effectiveness. I advise everyone to quit smoking.

▷ *Other Drugs*

Atenolol may ***increase*** the effects of

- other antihypertensive drugs and cause excessive lowering of blood pressure. Dosage adjustments may be necessary.

- reserpine (Ser-Ap-Es, etc.) and cause sedation, depression, slowing of heart rate, and lowering of blood pressure.

Atenolol *taken concurrently* with

- amiodarone (Cordarone) may result in cardiac arrest.
- ampicillin or bacampicillin may result in lower blood levels of atenolol.
- calcium (various) may result in *large decreases* in atenolol blood levels.
- calcium channel blockers (dihydropyridine forms—various) may result in heart impairment or severe lowering of blood pressure. Caution is advised with this combination, but it may have good therapeutic use.
- clonidine (Catapres) requires close monitoring for rebound high blood pressure if clonidine is stopped while atenolol is still being taken.
- digoxin (Lanoxin) may result in very slow heart rates.
- dolasetron (Anzemet) may result in slow heart beat, low blood pressure, or headache from accumulation of a metabolite of dolasetron.
- fentanyl anesthesia (various) may cause excessive lowering of the blood pressure.
- insulin requires close monitoring to avoid undetected hypoglycemia (see Glossary).
- oral antidiabetic drugs (see Drug Classes) may result in prolonged low blood sugar.
- phenothiazines (see Drug Classes) may increase the effects of both agents and result in phenothiazine toxicity or excessively low blood pressure.
- quinidine (Quinaglute) may cause additive lowering of the blood pressure.
- ritodrine (Yutopar) may blunt ritodrine benefits.
- verapamil can result in undesirable slowing of the heart rate and excessively low blood pressure.

The following drugs may *decrease* the effects of atenolol:

- antacids—decrease atenolol absorption.
- aspirin (various).
- indomethacin (Indocin), and possibly other "aspirin substitutes," or NSAIDs, which may impair atenolol's blood pressure lowering (antihypertensive) effect.

▷ *Driving, Hazardous Activities:* Use caution until the full extent of drowsiness, lethargy and blood pressure change has been determined.

Aviation Note: The use of this drug is *a disqualification* for piloting. Consult a designated Aviation Medical Examiner.

Exposure to Sun: No restrictions.

Exposure to Heat: Caution is advised. Hot environments can lower blood pressure and exaggerate the effects of this drug.

Exposure to Cold: Caution is advised. Can enhance the circulatory deficiency that may occur with this drug. The elderly should be careful to prevent hypothermia (see Glossary).

Heavy Exercise or Exertion: Avoid exertion that causes light-headedness, excessive fatigue or muscle cramping. This drug may worsen the blood pressure response to isometric exercise.

Occurrence of Unrelated Illness: Fever can lower blood pressure and require a decreased dose. Nausea or vomiting may interrupt the dosing schedule. Ask your physician for help.

Discontinuation: Avoid stopping this drug suddenly. If possible, gradual reduction of dose over a period of 2 to 3 weeks is recommended. During such reduction, physical activity is best kept to a minimum. Ask your doctor for help.

ATOMOXETINE (STRAH tare ah)

Introduced: 2003 **Class:** Norepinephrine reuptake inhibitor, anti-attention-deficit-disorder drug **Prescription:** USA: Yes **Controlled Drug:** USA: No; Canada: No **Available as Generic:** USA: No; Canada: No

Brand Names: Strattera

BENEFITS versus RISKS

Possible Benefits	Possible Risks
EFFECTIVE IN ATTENTION DEFICIT HYPERACTIVITY	ANOREXIA
May be useful in some cases of depression	Sleepiness
	Insomnia

▷ **Principal Uses**

As a Single Drug Product: Uses currently included in FDA-approved labeling: Treats (1) Attention deficit hyperactivity disorder (ADHD).

Other (unlabeled) generally accepted uses: (1) May treat mild to moderate depression.

Author's Note: This medicine is NOT a cure for ADHD. Some sources estimate that about 60% of people with ADHD in childhood will also have in as an adult. The largest study in adults with ADHD was presented at the June 2003 American Psychiatric Association meeting. The study involved 31 sites and showed very strong outcomes.

How This Drug Works: The exact way in which it benefits people with ADHD is unclear at present. The medicine acts as a selective (presynaptic) norepinephrine reuptake inhibitor. Changes in this nerve transmitter are thought to help control impulsivity, hyperactivity, and being inattentive.

Available Dosage Forms and Strengths

Capsules — 10 mg, 18 mg, 25 mg, 40 mg and 60 mg

▷ **Recommended Dosage Ranges:**

Attention deficit disorder: Pediatric dosing: *Children over 6 years old or adolescents weighing less than 70 kg (154 pounds):* are given 0.5 mg per kg per day. This dose is then increased after three days to a goal dose of 1.2 mg per kg. The 1.2 mg per kg dose can be given as a single dose in the morning or as equally divided doses given in the morning and late afternoon or early evening. The total dose in children and adolescents should NOT exceed 1.4 mg per kg or 100 mg (whichever is less).

*Children over 6 years old, adolescents **or adults** weighing more than 70 kg (154 pounds):* The starting dose is 40 mg. This initial dose is increased after at least three days to 80 mg. The 80 mg dose can be given as a single dose in the morning or as two equally divided doses—one in the morning and one in the late afternoon or early evening. After 14 days, the dose may be increased (if outcome goals are not met) as needed and as tolerated to 100 mg. 100 mg is the maximum dose. SEE CYP 2D6 dosing instructions in Caution and While Taking this Drug sections below.

Note: Actual dose and schedule must be determined for each patient individually.

Conditions Requiring Dosing Adjustments

Liver Function: People with moderate (Child-Pugh class B) liver (hepatic) compromise should be given 50% of the usual initial and goal (target) doses.

Those with severe (Child-Pugh class C) liver compromise should have the initial and target doses decreased by 25%.

Kidney Function: No changes currently thought to be needed.

▷ **Dosing Instructions:** The capsules SHOULD NOT be broken or sprinkled on food (take whole, and don't crush or alter). It is best to take medicines with a full glass of water. If you forget a dose: Take the missed dose as soon as you remember it, unless it's nearly time for your next dose—if that is the case, skip the missed dose and take the next dose right on schedule. Talk with your doctor if you find yourself missing doses.

Usual Duration of Use: Regular use for one week in children and in 2 weeks is adults usually determines benefits in improving ADHD. If there is no improvement 4 weeks with use of methylphenidate, the manufacturer recommends discontinuation. There is not presently such a recommendation for atomoxetine, and discontinuation will be a clinician decision. Long-term need for treatment of ADHD is generally acknowledged, however, benefits of therapy using this medicine for longer than 9 weeks and safety for more than a year have not been studied. Ongoing use requires supervision by your doctor.

Typical Treatment Goals and Measurements (Outcomes and Markers)

Attention Deficit: The general goal is to achieve the ability to "stay on task." This medicine can also help decrease impulsiveness and socially appropriate behavior. Specific measures of cognitive function, motor performance and educational tasking may help assess response. Treatment guidelines from AHCPR and DSM-IV criteria from the American Psychiatric Association are widely used. The American Academy of Pediatricians has an important set of guidelines. Please remember that these are guidelines and therapy must still be individualized. The guidelines can be found at www.pediatrics.org (see also sources and American Academy of Pediatrics). Clinical trials used the Attention-Deficit hyperactivity Disorder rating Scale (ADHDrs) to check results of treatment. In adults, the Conners' Adult ADHD Rating Scale (CAARS) is often used.

Possible Advantages of This Drug: The first non-stimulant medicine to be approved to treat ADHD.

▷ **This Drug Should Not Be Taken If**
- you have had an allergic reaction to it previously.
- you have taken a monoamine oxidase inhibitor (MAOI-see Drug Classes) in the last 14 days.
- you have narrow angle glaucoma and this medicine has been prescribed for you (causes pupil dilation—mydriasis).

▷ **Inform Your Physician Before Taking This Drug If**
- you are experiencing a period of severe anxiety, nervous tension, or emotional depression.
- you have a seizure disorder or bipolar disorder.
- you have a history of abnormal heartbeats.
- you have high blood pressure, angina, or epilepsy.
- you are less than 6 years old (not studied).

Possible Side Effects (natural, expected, and unavoidable drug actions)
Anxiety or insomnia. Reduced appetite (7–12%), weight loss. Growth should be monitored during ongoing use (there are no data on atomoxetine effects

on growth). Slight increase in heart rate and/or blood pressure. Dilation of the pupil of the eye (mydriasis).

▷ **Possible Adverse Effects** (unusual, unexpected, and infrequent reactions)
 If any of the following develop, consult your physician promptly for guidance.
 Mild Adverse Effects
 Allergic reactions: skin rash, hives—possible.
 Sleepiness and dizziness (may be dose related)—possible.
 Headache—possible.
 Nausea or vomiting—infrequent.
 Urinary retention—infrequent (adults).
 Serious Adverse Effects
 Allergic reactions: possible.
 Palpitations or chest pain—rare.

▷ **Possible Effects on Sexual Function:** Decreased libido, ejaculatory problems.
 Painful or difficult menstruation (Dysmenorrhea)—infrequent.

Natural Diseases or Disorders That May Be Activated by This Drug
 Because this medicine can dilate the pupil, it should not be used in narrow angle glaucoma.

Possible Effects on Laboratory Tests
 Not defined at present.

CAUTION
 1. This drug should be used ONLY AFTER a careful assessment by a qualified specialist is made. True attention deficit disorder requires careful assessment to differentiate it from behavior problems arising from family tensions or other conditions that do not require atomoxetine therapy.
 2. Some people remove this medicine from their bodies poorly (are poor metabolizers found in about 7% of the population). A lower dose may be prudent.
 3. The American Academy of Pediatricians has an important set of guidelines. Please remember that these are guidelines and therapy must still be individualized. The guidelines can be found at *www.pediatrics.org* (see also Sources and American Academy of Pediatrics).
 4. Careful dose adjustments on an individual basis are mandatory.

Precautions for Use
 By Infants and Children: Safety and effectiveness for those under 6 years of age are not established. See Poor Metabolizer note above. If methylphenidate is not beneficial in managing an attention deficit disorder after a trial of 1 month, it should be stopped. Specific guidelines for this medicine are not established and are a clinical judgment. During ongoing use, monitor the child for ongoing benefits.
 By Those Over 60 Years of Age: Not studied in this population.

▷ **Advisability of Use During Pregnancy**
 Pregnancy Category: C. See Pregnancy Risk Categories at the back of this book.
 Animal Studies: No birth defects found in mouse studies.
 Human Studies: Adequate studies of pregnant women are not available.
 Ask your doctor for guidance.

Advisability of Use If Breast-Feeding
 Presence of this drug in breast milk: Unknown in humans, yes in rats.
 Avoid drug or refrain from nursing.

Habit-Forming Potential: This drug is NOT a stimulant type medicine or amphetaminelike drug like methylphenidate (Ritalin). The abuse potential of atomoxetine has not been established.

Effects of Overdose: Experience with more than twice the maximum daily dose is not present. Headache, vomiting, and other extensions of expected increased norepinephrine levels would drive symptoms and management.

Possible Effects of Long-Term Use: Not fully defined.

Suggested Periodic Examinations While Taking This Drug (at physician's discretion)

Blood pressure and pulse measurements.

Height and weight.

Follow up evaluation for beneficial effects of treatment.

▷ **While Taking This Drug, Observe the Following**

Herbal Medicines or Minerals: Using St. John's wort, guarana, ma huang, or kola while taking this medicine may result in unacceptable central nervous system stimulation.

Beverages: Avoid beverages prepared from meat or meat extracts. This drug may be taken with milk.

▷ *Alcohol:* Avoid beer, Chianti wines, and vermouth (may have high tyramine contents).

Tobacco Smoking: No interactions expected. I advise everyone to quit smoking.

▷ *Other Drugs*

Atomoxetine may ***increase*** the effects of

• albuterol (and other beta two agonists see Drug Classes) and enhance their actions on the heart and blood vessels (cardiovascular system). Combined with caution

Atomoxetine ***taken concurrently*** with

• medicines that increase CYP 2D6 enzyme levels in the liver will blunt atomoxetine benefits. Medicines that decrease or inhibit CYP 2D6 (such as paroxetine—Paxil, fluoxetine—Prozac or quinidine—Quinaglute, others) may lead to toxic atomoxetine levels.

• monoamine oxidase (MAO) type A inhibitors (see Drug Classes) may cause a significant rise in blood pressure; avoid the concurrent use of these drugs.

▷ *Driving, Hazardous Activities:* This drug may cause dizziness or drowsiness. Restrict activities as necessary.

Aviation Note: The use of this drug ***may be a disqualification*** for piloting. Consult a designated Aviation Medical Examiner.

Exposure to Sun: No restrictions.

Discontinuation: A specific withdrawal syndrome has NOT been identified as yet. Talk to your doctor if you are considering stopping it for any reason.

ATORVASTATIN (a TOR va stat in)

Introduced: 1996   **Class:** Cholesterol-lowering agent, HMG-CoA reductase inhibitor   **Prescription:** USA: Yes   **Controlled Drug:** USA: No; Canada: No   **Available as Generic:** No

Brand Name: Lipitor

BENEFITS versus RISKS

Possible Benefits	*Possible Risks*
REDUCTION OF TOTAL AND LDL CHOLESTEROL	Drug-induced hepatitis (without jaundice)—rare
DECREASED TRIGLYCERIDES	Drug-induced myositis (muscle inflammation)—rare
INCREASES HDL-C (GOOD CHOLESTEROL) IN PEOPLE WITH PRIMARY HYPER-CHOLESTEROLEMIA AND MIXED DYSLIPIDEMIA	Decreased coenzyme Q10
	Possible easing of benefit over time
MAY LOWER THE RISK OF REPEATED PROBLEMS (ISCHEMIC EVENTS) ONCE A PATIENT HAS HAD A SUDDEN CORONORY SYNDROME	
BENEFICIAL EFFECT ON C-REACTIVE PROTEIN LEVELS	
BENEFICIAL EFFECT ON THE PATTERN OF UNDESIRABLE CHOLESTEROL	
May help prevent bone loss in type 2 diabetics and/or osteoporosis	
May help prevent Alzheimer's	
May help prevent cancer	

▷ **Principal Uses**

As a Single Drug Product: Uses currently included in FDA-approved labeling: (1) Treats high blood cholesterol (in people with Types IIa and IIb hypercholesterolemia) due to increased fractions of low-density lipoprotein (LDL) cholesterol; (2) also works in primary dysbetalipoproteinemia (Fredrickson Type III) and in patients with elevated serum triglycerides (Fredrickson Type IV). Used in conjunction with a cholesterol-lowering diet. Should not be used until an adequate trial of nondrug methods has proved to be ineffective. NCEP ATP 3 (see Glossary) recognizes therapeutic lifestyle changes (TLC) as very important; (3) also helps familial hypercholesterolemia; (4) approved to increase HDL-C (good cholesterol) in people with primary hypercholesterolemia and mixed dyslipidemia.

Other (unlabeled) generally accepted uses: (1) a *New England Journal of Medicine* study found that atorvastatin was as effective as getting an angioplasty when it was used to treat stable heart (coronary) artery disease; (2) prevention of coronary heart disease; (3) treats abnormal fat (lipid) changes caused by protease inhibitors; (4) may help prevent bone loss (osteoporosis) in type two diabetics and osteoporosis in general; (5) may help prevent clogging (restenosis) of tubes (stents) placed in coronary arteries; (6) starting atorvastatin quickly after a sudden coronary problem (see acute coronary syndromes in Glossary) may help lower the risk of circulatory events (recurrent ischemic events) based on results of the MIRACL trial; (7) ongoing use may help lower the risk of dementia (such as Alzheimer's disease); (8) one case-control study found a 20% reduction in cancer risk by "statin type" medicines. Further research is needed.

How This Drug Works: Blocks a liver enzyme that starts making cholesterol. Lowers low-density lipoproteins (LDL), the cholesterol fraction thought to increase risk of coronary heart disease. Since the amount of cholesterol is reduced in the liver, the VLDL fraction may also be decreased. There is a growing body of evidence that "statins" also have beneficial changes on what is in the blood, blood flow and even the blood vessel walls themselves (some of this may account for benefits in decreasing Alzheimer's risk). Specific compounds or effects of platelet derived growth factor (PDGF), undesirable blood clotting via thrombin-antithrombin III, thrombomodulin, and other chemicals may be beneficially lowered or effects mitigated by statins.

Available Dosage Forms and Strengths
Tablets — 10 mg, 20 mg, 40 mg, 80 mg

▷ **Recommended Dosage Ranges** (Actual dosage and schedule must be determined for each patient individually.)

Infants and Children: Data are not available.

18 to 65 Years of Age:
Cholesterol management: Patients are started on a typical low cholesterol diet (see *www.americanheart.org*). Atorvastatin dosing is started with 10 mg once daily. Patients who require more than a 45% decrease in LDL can be started at 40 mg once a day. The starting dose is increased (dose intensified) as needed and tolerated to a maximum of 80 mg daily. Lipid levels best rechecked within 2 to 4 weeks of starting or changing the dose. Some clinicians are studying weekly divided dosing, but conclusions are not yet made.

Acute Coronary Syndromes: (based on MIRACL data): 80 mg once a day is started 24–96 hours after the patient goes into the hospital (along with other medicines such as aspirin, beta blockers, nitrates, and heparin).

Over 65 Years of Age: Some research shows that usual doses may result in higher levels than seen in younger patients. It appears prudent that the lowest dose (10 mg) should be used and LDL-C levels be checked to guide any dose increases. Dose increases must be made after weighing the benefits and risks, mindful that any given dose may result in a higher than expected blood level.

Conditions Requiring Dosing Adjustments

Liver Function: Caution should be used in patients with liver compromise. In those with liver damage caused by alcohol, removal from the body has been prolonged. A 10-mg dose appears prudent. Like other HMG-CoA medicines, atorvastatin should not be given during active liver disease.

Kidney Function: The manufacturer does not recommend dosing changes.

▷ **Dosing Instructions:** The tablet may be crushed or split. Better taken on an empty stomach. Since cholesterol is made at the fastest rate between midnight and 5 a.m., many clinicians advise patients to take such medicines at bedtime. If you forget a dose, take it immediately unless it is almost time for your next dose. If your next dose is shortly due, skip the missed dose and just take the next scheduled dose. DO NOT double doses.

Usual Duration of Use: Use on a regular schedule for 2 to 4 weeks usually determines the effectiveness of this drug in reducing blood levels of total and LDL-C cholesterol. Increases in good cholesterol (HDL) may take longer. Use is usually ongoing. Long-term use (months to years) requires periodic physician evaluation and follow-up.

Typical Treatment Goals and Measurements (Outcomes and Markers)

Cholesterol: The National Institutes of Health Adult Treatment Panel has released ATP III as part of the update to the National Cholesterol Education Program or NCEP. Key points in these guidelines include acknowledging diabetes as one of the conditions that increases risk of heart disease, modifying risk factors, therapeutic lifestyle changes (TLC), and recommending routine testing for all of the cholesterol fractions (lipoprotein profile) versus total cholesterol alone.

Current NCEP guidelines recommend a desirable total cholesterol of 200 mg/dl, and optimal bad cholesterol (LDL) as 100 mg/dl, 130–159 mg/dl as borderline high, 160 mg/dl as high and 190 mg/dl as very high. Did you know that there are at least five different kinds of "good cholesterol" or HDL? The "too low" measure for HDL is still 40mg/dl, but in order to learn more about cholesterol types some doctors are starting to order lipid panels. There are at least seven different kinds of "bad cholesterol." The new panels tell doctors about the kinds of cholesterol that your body makes. This is important because some kinds (small dense particles) tend to stick to blood vessels (are highly atherogenic). Take your medicine to reach your goals!

Two additional tests you will hear about will be electron beam computed tomography (EBCT) and CRP. EBCT is an important tool used in conjunction with laboratory studies. Findings show that even patients who meet cholesterol goals (particularly females over 55) can still be at significant cardiovascular risk. EBCT then defines risk by giving a calcium score and a "virtual tour" of the coronary arteries. C Reactive Protein or CRP is a new and apparently independent predictor of heart disease risk. A large study (see Ridker, P.M. in Sources) found that CRP predicted heart disease risk independently of bad cholesterol (low density lipoprotein).

Talk to your doctor about this new laboratory test and ask about current guidelines for who should be tested (see Pearson, T.A. in Sources).

Possible Advantages of This Drug: Studies indicate that drugs of this class (HMG-CoA reductase inhibitors) are more effective and better tolerated than other drugs currently available for reducing total and LDL-C cholesterol. Atorvastatin decreased LDL by up to 51% in one study (the most of any medicine in this family). Another study showed this medicine to be as effective as angioplasty when used to treat coronary artery disease that is stable. This medicine is easily split, although pill splitting—certainly forced pill splitting is an area of controversy. At the time of this writing, the price is the same for a 20 or 80 mg tablet. Splitting tablets (get a pill splitter for accuracy) can lower costs a lot. One short-term outcome study of changing other statins to this medicine (therapeutic interchange of atorvastatin for simvastatin or pravastatin) found that both significant lowering of LDL and cost savings occurred.

This Drug Should Not Be Taken If
- you have had an allergic reaction to it previously.
- you have active liver disease or increased liver function tests that are unexplained.
- you are pregnant or are breast-feeding your infant.

Inform Your Physician Before Taking This Drug If
- you have previously taken and have not tolerated other drugs in this class such as: lovastatin (Mevacor), simvastatin (Zocor) (see Drug Classes).
- you have liver disease or impaired liver function.
- you have kidney disease.
- you are not using any method of birth control or you are planning pregnancy.
- you regularly consume substantial amounts of alcohol.

- you develop unexplained muscle weakness, pain or tenderness.
- you have any type of chronic muscular disorder.
- goals were set by another doctor and have not been met using this medicine.

Possible Side Effects (natural, expected, and unavoidable drug actions)
None with usual doses.

Possible Adverse Effects (unusual, unexpected, and infrequent reactions)
If any of the following develop, consult your physician promptly for guidance.

Mild Adverse Effects
Allergic reaction: skin rash—infrequent.
Headache—infrequent to frequent, rare drowsiness.
Vision changes—case report.
Flu-like syndrome—infrequent.
Reversible hair loss (alopecia)—case report.
Diarrhea, constipation or gas (flatulence)—infrequent.
Muscle pain (myalgia)—infrequent with 20-mg dose (tell your doctor right away if this happens).

Serious Adverse Effects
Allergic reactions: not reported as yet.
Neuropathy—reported for a different member of this class.
Marked and persistent abnormal liver function tests (with or without jaundice)—case reports to rare.
Lowered blood platelets (thrombocytopenia)—rare.
Acute myositis (muscle pain and tenderness)—rare to infrequent with 10- to 80-mg doses.
Rhabdomyolysis with sudden kidney failure—rare with HMG-CoA medicines.
One case report of euphoria, confusion, and short-term memory problems.

Possible Effects on Sexual Function: Case reports of impotence.

Possible Delayed Adverse Effects: Increased liver enzymes. Decreased coenzyme Q10 (co-Q10 or ubiquinone).

Natural Diseases or Disorders That May Be Activated by This Drug
Latent liver disease.

Possible Effects on Laboratory Tests
Blood total cholesterol, LDL cholesterol and triglyceride levels: decreased.
HDL: increased.

CAUTION
1. If pregnancy occurs while taking this drug, stop drug immediately and call your doctor.
2. Report promptly any development of unexplained muscle pain or tenderness, especially if accompanied by fever or weakness (malaise).
3. Report promptly the development of altered or impaired vision so that appropriate evaluation can be made.
4. If liver enzymes (ALT or AST) increase to more than three times the upper limit of normal and persist, the dose should be lowered and/or the medicine should be stopped.
5. A study in Circulation (see Heeschen in Sources) found that stopping "statin" type medicines in patients with acute coronary syndrome symptoms can lead to a three-fold increase risk of non-fatal heart attack (MI) or death.

6. A chart review showed a trend of peak benefit in lowering LDL. Some 220 days after peak benefits were achieved, an increase in LDL of about 15% and plateau of benefit. One source concluded that this may represent a tachyphylaxis.

Precautions for Use

By Infants and Children: Safety and effectiveness for those under 18 years of age not established.

By Those Over 60 Years of Age: Blood levels for those over 65 may be higher than those reached by the same dose in younger people.

Advisability of Use During Pregnancy

Pregnancy Category: X. See Pregnancy Risk Categories at the back of this book.

Animal Studies: Rat studies reveal decreased pup survival and maturity with high-dose studies.

Human Studies: Adequate studies of pregnant women are not available.

This drug should be avoided during entire pregnancy.

Advisability of Use If Breast-Feeding

Presence of this drug in breast milk: Yes, in rats; expected in humans.

Avoid drug or refrain from nursing.

Habit-Forming Potential: None.

Effects of Overdose: Increased indigestion, stomach distress, nausea, diarrhea with other HMG-CoA medicines.

Possible Effects of Long-Term Use: Abnormal liver function tests. Decreased coenzyme Q10 (co-Q10 or ubiquinone). Loss of beneficial effects—reported with some statin type medicines.

Suggested Periodic Examinations While Taking This Drug (at physician's discretion)

Blood cholesterol studies: total cholesterol, HDL and LDL fractions. This may be especially important with this medicine as one retrospective chart review appeared to show a tachyphylaxis.

Liver function tests before treatment, at 12 weeks (the same for any dose increases) and then semiannually (every 6 months) thereafter. If the ALT or AST increases to more than three times the upper limit of normal and persist, the dose should be lowered and or the drug stopped. Ask your doctor for guidance.

Checks of the pattern of HDL and LDL (cholesterol subtypes). This helps the clinician determine how well cholesterol is being taken back to the liver (reverse cholesterol transport by HDL) and how likely the cholesterol that your body makes is to stick to blood vessels (small particles are highly atherogenic).

C-reactive Protein (CRP).

Author's Note: A related medicine called cerivastatin (Baycol) was removed from the market because of liver changes. At the time of this writing, the FDA has not asked for more frequent checks of liver function for atorvastatin.

Electron beam computed tomography (EBCT) can help predict silent ischemia and other problems with blood vessels that supply the heart itself. This also may help define the results (outcomes) you are getting from this medicine.

▷ **While Taking This Drug, Observe the Following**

Foods: Follow a standard low-cholesterol diet. Your doctor may also recommend some specific foods such as increased vegetables or functional foods such as Benecol. Three well-designed studies were published in early April 2002 found that both in women and men and before and after a heart attack, people who ate more fish (2–4 servings a week) appeared to avoid heart disease. Additionally putting supplements containing Omega 3 polyunsaturated fatty acids (PUFA) into the diet also appeared to protect against abnormal heart rhythms and sudden death from heart attack. The studies appeared in *JAMA*, *Circulation* and the *New England Journal of Medicine*. Increasing oat bran in the diet may be of additional help in lowering cholesterol, but can decrease the amount of medicine that gets into your body. Take oat bran two hours before atorvastatin or four to six hours after. Your doctor may also recommend increasing B vitamins. See Tables 19 and 20 about lifestyle changes and risk factors you can fix!

Herbal Medicines or Minerals: No data exist from well-designed clinical studies about garlic and atorvastatin combinations and cannot presently be recommended. Additionally, garlic may inhibit blood clotting (platelet) aggregation—something to consider if you are already taking a platelet inhibitor. The FDA has allowed one dietary supplement called Cholestin to continue to be sold. This preparation actually contains lovastatin. Since use of two HMG-CoA inhibitors may increase risk of rhabdomyolysis or myopathy, the combination is NOT advised. Some products containing plant sterols (Benecol) may be useful as complementary care. Soy (milk, tofu, etc.) contains phytoestrogens that have led to an FDA-approved health claim for reducing risk of heart disease (if they have at least 6.25 grams of soy protein per serving). Substituting soy for some of the meat in your diet can help avoid cardiovascular problems. Lastly, because atorvastatin can deplete coenzyme Q10, supplementation may be needed.

Beverages: DO NOT take this medicine with grapefruit juice. Excessive blood levels and increased risk of muscle damage may occur. May be taken with water or milk.

▷ *Alcohol:* Excessive alcohol not recommended.

Tobacco Smoking: No interactions expected. I advise everyone to quit smoking.

▷ *Other Drugs*

Atorvastatin may ***increase*** the effects of
- clofibrate (Atromid-S) and other fibric acid derivatives—has been associated with increased risk of muscle damage (rhabdomyolysis).

Atorvastatin ***taken concurrently*** with
- amprenavir (Agenerase) and ritonavir (Norvir), saquinavir (Invirase) and perhaps other protease inhibitors may increase atorvastatin levels and the risk of muscle damage (myopathy).
- antacids decreases the amount of atorvastatin that gets into your body.
- azole antifungals (such as itraconazole or Sporanox) may increase the risk for muscle damage (myopathy).
- birth control pills (oral contraceptives) may increase the levels of the contraceptives (certain kinds) and may increase risk of adverse effects.
- clopidogrel (Plavix) may blunt the benefits of clopidogrel. This is a new drug interaction. The degree of clinical effect of this interaction is not presently known. It appears prudent that testing of platelet aggregation be undertaken if these medicines must be combined. If this is not possible, pravastatin (Pravachol) or rosuvastatin (Crestor—investigational) should be considered as they do not use the same liver pathway.
- colesevelam (Welchol) results in better lowering of LDL-C.
- colestipol (Colestid) results in lowered atorvastatin blood levels, but better lowering of LDL-C.

- cyclosporine (Sandimmune) may increase the risk for myopathy.
- digoxin (Lanoxin, others) can increase digoxin levels (and possibly lead to toxic effects).
- erythromycin (and perhaps other macrolide antibiotics) may increase the risk for myopathy.
- ezetimibe (Zetia) increases beneficial effects on cholesterol.
- fluconazole (Diflucan) or itraconazole (Sporanox) or ketoconazole (Nizoral) will increase risk of myopathy. Extreme caution is advised.
- fosphenytoin (Cerebyx) and phenytoin (Dilantin) may blunt atorvastatin therapeutic effects.
- gemfibrozil (Lopid) may increase the risk of muscle damage (myopathy).
- medicines that change cytochrome P450 3A4 (inhibitors will increase atorvastatin levels and inducers will blunt atorvastatin therapeutic effects).
- nefazodone (Serzone) may lead to atorvastatin toxicity.
- niacin (various) may increase the risk for myopathy. Niacin may also increase homocysteine levels—a risk factor for heart disease.
- oral contraceptive (norethindrone and ethinyl estradiol) level increases are likely. Increased monitoring for adverse effects is prudent.
- quinupristin/dalfopristin (Synercid) may increase the risk for myopathy by increasing atorvastatin blood levels.

▷ *Driving, Hazardous Activities:* This drug may cause drowsiness. Restrict activities as necessary.

Aviation Note: The use of this drug *may be a disqualification* for piloting. Consult a designated Aviation Medical Examiner.

Exposure to Sun: No restrictions.

Occurrence of Unrelated Illness: Call your doctor if another physician (such as a specialist) diagnoses a sudden liver problem.

Discontinuation: Do not stop this drug without your doctor's knowledge and help. There may be a significant increase in blood cholesterol levels if this medicine is stopped. Patients who have acute coronary syndromes or ACS (such as unstable angina, heart attack [non-p; Q-wave myocardial infarction], and Q-wave myocardial infarction) were reviewed as part of the Platelet Receptor Inhibitor in Ischemic Syndrome Management (PRISM) study. It was found that pretreatment with statin type medicines (HMG-CoA reductase inhibitors such as the medicine in this profile) significantly lowered risk during the first 30 days after ACS symptoms started. Most importantly, it was found that if a statin type medicine is stopped in ACS patients, there was a three-fold increased risk of non-fatal heart attack or death (see Heeschen, C in Sources). Talk with your doctor BEFORE stopping any statin type medicine.

AURANOFIN (aw RAY noh fin)

Introduced: 1976 **Class:** Antiarthritic **Prescription:** USA: Yes **Controlled Drug:** USA: No; Canada: No **Available as Generic:** Yes

Brand Name: Ridaura

BENEFITS versus RISKS

Possible Benefits	*Possible Risks*
REDUCTION OF JOINT PAIN, TENDERNESS, AND SWELLING IN ACTIVE, SEVERE RHEUMATOID ARTHRITIS	SIGNIFICANTLY REDUCED LEVELS OF RED AND WHITE BLOOD CELLS AND BLOOD PLATELETS
Effective when taken by mouth	LIVER DAMAGE WITH JAUNDICE
	Diarrhea
	Ulcerative colitis
	Skin rash
	Mouth sores
	Kidney toxicity (protein in the urine)
	Lung damage

Author's Note: Given the FDA approval of DMARDS (see Glossary), this profile has been shortened to make room for more widely used medicines.

AZATHIOPRINE (ay za THI oh preen)

Introduced: 1965 **Class:** Antiarthritic, immunosuppressive **Prescription:** USA: Yes **Controlled Drug:** USA: No; Canada: No **Available as Generic:** Yes

Brand Name: Imuran, ✤Med-azathioprine, ✤Riva-azathioprine

BENEFITS versus RISKS

Possible Benefits	*Possible Risks*
PREVENTION OF REJECTION IN KIDNEY (RENAL) TRANSPLANT	UNACCEPTABLE ADVERSE EFFECTS IN 15% OF USERS
Reduction of joint pain in active, severe, resistant heumatoid arthritis	REDUCED LEVELS OF WHITE BLOOD CELLS
	REDUCED LEVELS OF RED BLOOD CELLS AND PLATELETS
	LIVER DAMAGE WITH JAUNDICE
	POSSIBLE INCREASED RISK OF MALIGNANCY

▷ **Principal Uses**

As a Single Drug Product: Uses currently included in FDA-approved labeling: (1) Helps prevent transplanted kidney rejection (adjunctive use); (2) also used in active, severe rheumatoid arthritis (in adults) failing conventional treatment.

Other (unlabeled) generally accepted uses: (1) Used to treat actinic dermatitis.

How This Drug Works: It impairs metabolism of purines, DNA, and RNA. This blunts the immune reaction responsible for rheumatoid arthritis, lupus erythematosus, etc.

Available Dosage Forms and Strengths

Injection — 100 mg per 20-ml vial

Tablets — 50 mg

▷ **Usual Adult Dosage Ranges:** *As immunosuppressant:* 3–5 mg per kg of body mass daily, 1 to 3 days before transplantation surgery; for ongoing postoperative use—1–3 mg per kg of body mass daily, but the amount needed to have minimal toxicity yet prevent rejection will vary from patient to patient. Careful follow up is required.

▷ **While Taking This Drug, Observe the Following**

Foods: No restrictions and may help stomach upset.

Herbal Medicines or Minerals: Some patients use echinacea to attempt to boost their immune systems. Unfortunately, use of echinacea is not recommended in people with damaged immune systems. This herb may also actually weaken any immune system if it is used too often or for too long a time.

Beverages: No restrictions. May be taken with milk.

▷ *Alcohol:* No interactions expected, but excessive drinking will also blunt the immune system.

Tobacco Smoking: No interactions expected. I advise everyone to quit smoking.

Marijuana Smoking: May contain infectious agents (such as toxoplasmosis) which may be more likely to cause infections in a person with a blunted immune system.

▷ *Other Drugs*

Azathioprine may ***decrease*** the effects of
• certain muscle relaxants (gallamine, pancuronium, tubocurarine) and make it necessary to increase their dosage.
• oral anticoagulants (warfarin, etc.) and requires increased doses.

The following drug may ***increase*** the effects of azathioprine:
• allopurinol (Zyloprim)—may increase its activity and toxicity and make it necessary to reduce its dosage.

Azathioprine ***taken concurrently*** with
• ACE inhibitors (see Drug Classes) such as captopril or enalapril may cause severe white blood cell count lowering or anemia.
• cotrimoxazole (Bactrim, others) can cause severe lowering of white blood cell counts.
• cyclosporine (Sandimmune, others) may lead to decreased cyclosporine levels, requiring more frequent blood level checks and dosing adjustments.
• prednisolone will result in lower prednisolone blood levels and risk of decreased therapeutic benefit.
• vaccines (live—various) may result in abnormal patient responses to the vaccines and risk of infection by the live vaccine itself.
• warfarin (Coumadin) may result in decreased anticoagulant effectiveness.

▷ *Driving, Hazardous Activities:* No restrictions.

Aviation Note: The use of this drug ***may be a disqualification*** for piloting. Consult a designated Aviation Medical Examiner.

Exposure to Sun: No restrictions.

Discontinuation: A gradual reduction in dosage is preferable. Consult your physician for a withdrawal schedule.

Author's Note: Information in this profile has been truncated to make room for more widely used medicines.

AZITHROMYCIN (a zith roh MY sin)

See the macrolide antibiotics profile for further information.

BACAMPICILLIN (bak am pi SIL in)

See the new penicillins profile for further information.

BECLOMETHASONE (be kloh METH a sohn)

Introduced: 1976   **Class:** Antiasthmatic, cortisonelike drugs   **Prescription:** USA: Yes   **Controlled Drug:** USA: No; Canada: No   **Available as Generic:** No

Brand Names: ❦Apo-Beclomethasone-AQ, ❦Beclodisk, ❦Becloforte, Beclovent, ❦Beclovent Rotacaps, ❦Beclovent Rotahaler, Beconase AQ Nasal Spray, Beconase Nasal Inhaler, ❦Med-Beclomethasone-AQ, ❦Nu-Beclomethasone, ❦Propaderm, ❦Propaderm-C, QVAR, Vancenase AQ Nasal Spray, Vancenase Nasal Inhaler, Vanceril

BENEFITS versus RISKS	
Possible Benefits	*Possible Risks*
EFFECTIVE RELIEF OF ALLERGIC RHINITIS	FUNGUS INFECTIONS OF THE MOUTH AND THROAT
EFFECTIVE CONTROL OF SEVERE, CHRONIC ASTHMA	Localized areas of "allergic" pneumonia
HELPS PREVENT NASAL POYLPS	Changes in lining of the nose (nasal mucosa)
	Increased cataract risk
	Possible osteoporosis

▷ **Principal Uses**

As a Single Drug Product: Uses currently included in FDA-approved labeling: (1) Bronchial asthma in people who don't have sufficient response to bronchodilators and need cortisonelike drugs for asthma control; (2) prevents nasal polyp return after surgical removal; (3) treats seasonal and perennial rhinitis in children and adults (AQ nasal forms).

Other (unlabeled) generally accepted uses: (1) Helps lung disease (bronchopulmonary dysplasia) allowing smaller daily prednisone doses; (2) helps hoarseness seen in LE and juvenile rheumatoid arthritis.

How This Drug Works: It increases cyclic AMP, thus increasing epinephrine, which opens bronchial tubes and fights asthma. Also reduces local lung inflammation in the respiratory tract.

Available Dosage Forms and Strengths

Inhalant — 17 g (50 mcg)

Nasal inhaler — 16.8 g (42 or 82 mcg each)

Nasal spray — 0.042%, 42 mcg and 84 mcg per spray (52 mcg in Canada)

Oral inhaler — 16.8 g (200 doses of 42 mcg each, 50 mcg in Canada)

Rotacaps (Canada) — 100- and 200-mcg capsules

Topical lotion (Canada) — 0.025%

▷ **Usual Adult Dosage Ranges**

Infants and Children: Data are not available for infants. Children 6–12 years old may receive: Nasal spray—one (42 mcg) dose in each nostril twice a day.

Oral inhalation (42 mcg)—one to two inhalations, three or four times a day depending on the response. Some clinicians use 4 inhalations twice daily. Oral inhalation (double strength—84 mcg)—2 inhalations twice a day. Maximum is 5 inhalations (420 mcg for Vanceril Double Strength).

18 to 65 Years of Age: Nasal spray—one to two sprays (42–84 mcg) in each nostril twice daily. Oral inhaler (double strength)—two inhalations (of 84 mcg) twice daily. For severe asthma—6 to 8 inhalations daily. Nasal polyp prevention after surgery: 42 or 84 mcg in each nostril twice a day (Beconase AQ form).

Those Over 65 Years of Age: Doses similar to those used in younger patients have been effective and safe. In some cases, oral-steroid-dependent patients have been able to slowly taper and then stop oral steroids while taking beclomethasone.

Note: Actual dose and schedule must be determined for each patient individually.

Conditions Requiring Dosing Adjustments

Liver Function: Use with caution in patients with liver compromise.

Kidney Function: No adjustments in dosing expected to be needed.

▷ **Dosing Instructions:** May be used without regard to eating. Instructions are supplied with this product—read them carefully in order to get the most benefit from this medicine. Shake the inhaler well before you use it. Rinse the mouth and throat (gargle) with water thoroughly after each inhalation. If you forget a dose: Use the inhaler as soon as possible. DO NOT double doses.

Usual Duration of Use: Regular use for 1 to 3 weeks is usually needed to see this drug's effectiveness in relieving severe, chronic allergic rhinitis and in controlling severe, chronic asthma. Up to 2 weeks may be needed to relieve rhinitis by nasal inhalation. If signs and symptoms have not improved in 21 days, beclomethasone should be discontinued. Long-term use must be physician-supervised. See your doctor regularly.

Typical Treatment Goals and Measurements (Outcomes and Markers)

Asthma: This medicine is NOT useful in a sudden asthma attack, but is used to decrease the severity and frequency of attacks. Some clinicians also use the number of times a rescue inhaler is used as another clinical benchmark. FEV1 (a lung function test) is widely used to check results when available. While using this medicine—call your doctor immediately if it becomes less beneficial (helps less than it used to).

Possible Advantages of This Drug: Inhaled beclomethasone does not suppress or causes minimal suppression of the HPA axis versus medicines such as fluticasone (which causes greater suppression than other agents).

Currently a "Drug of Choice"

The "nose" (intranasal) form is a first choice in allergic rhinitis.

▷ **This Drug Should Not Be Taken If**
- you have had an allergic reaction to any form of this drug.
- you are having severe acute asthma or status asthmaticus (requires more intense and prompt treatment).
- other antiasthmatic drugs can control your asthma that are not related to cortisone.
- you have a form of nonallergic bronchitis with asthmatic features.

▷ **Inform Your Physician Before Taking This Drug If**
- you take or recently took any cortisone-related drug (including ACTH by injection) for any reason (see Drug Classes).

- you have a history of tuberculosis of the lungs.
- you have chronic bronchitis or bronchiectasis.
- you think you have an active infection of any kind, especially a respiratory infection.
- you have recently been exposed to chickenpox or other viral illnesses.
- you are prone to nosebleeds (epistaxis) (nasal forms).
- you are unsure how much to take or how often to take this drug.

Possible Side Effects (natural, expected, and unavoidable drug actions)
Fungus infections (thrush) of the mouth and throat. Headache. Changes in ability to taste.

▷ **Possible Adverse Effects** (unusual, unexpected, and infrequent reactions)
If any of the following develop, consult your physician promptly for guidance.

Mild Adverse Effects
Allergic reaction: skin rash—rare.
Dryness of mouth, hoarseness, sore throat, cough—possible.
Nosebleeds (epistaxis)—infrequent.
May decrease growth rate in children—possible.

Serious Adverse Effects
Allergic reaction: localized areas of "allergic" pneumonitis (lung inflammation), angioedema-possible.
Bronchospasm, asthmatic wheezing—rare.
Shrinking of the nasal tissues (nasal atrophy)—possible.
Yeast infections (up to 41%)—frequent.
Severe chicken pox—case reports with intranasal form.
Increased risk of cataracts with long-term (chronic) use—possible.
Suppression of the adrenal gland (HFA axis)—possible in sensitive individuals.
Increased pressure in the head (pseudotumor cerebri)—possible.
Osteoporosis (any corticosteroid can cause this)—possible.

▷ **Possible Effects on Sexual Function:** None reported.

Natural Diseases or Disorders That May Be Activated by This Drug
Cortisone-related drugs having systemic effects impair immunity and lead to reactivation of "healed" or dormant tuberculosis. People with a history of tuberculosis must be watched closely while using this drug.

Possible Effects on Laboratory Tests
Blood cortisol levels: decreased.
Bone mineral density: possibly decreased with chronic use although much less likely than with systemic forms.

CAUTION
1. This drug should not be relied upon for immediate relief of acute asthma.
2. If you required cortisonelike drugs *before* starting this inhaler, you may again require a cortisonelike drug if you are injured, have an infection or need surgery.
3. If severe asthma returns while using this drug, call your doctor immediately. Cortisonelike drugs may be required.
4. Carry an ID card saying that you have used (if true) cortisone-related drugs in the past year.
5. Wait 5 to 10 minutes after using a bronchodilator inhaler such as epinephrine, isoetharine or isoproterenol (which should be used first) before this drug. This permits greater penetration of beclomethasone into the lung. The time between inhalations also reduces risk of adverse propellant effects.

6. This drug does NOT replace systemic steroids, but may allow dosage decreases in some patients.
7. If this drug is used long-term, a bone mineral density test before treatment and every two years is prudent.
8. Unlike other corticosteroids, reports of osteonecrosis (avascular necrosis or aseptic necrosis) have not been made for this medicine. Caution is prudent, and patients should report any unexplained joint (such as knee, hip, or shoulder) pain to their doctor.

Precautions for Use

By Infants and Children: Safety and effectiveness for use of the nasal inhaler or oral inhaler by those under 6 years of age has not been established. Maximum daily dose in children 6 to 12 years of age varies with the products being used.

By Those Over 60 Years of Age: People with bronchiectasis should be watched closely for the development of lung infections.

▷ Advisability of Use During Pregnancy

Pregnancy Category: C. See Pregnancy Risk Categories at the back of this book.
Animal Studies: Mouse, rat, and rabbit studies reveal significant birth defects due to this drug.
Human Studies: Adequate studies of pregnant women are not available.
Avoid drug during the first 3 months. Use infrequently and only as clearly needed during the last 6 months.

Advisability of Use If Breast-Feeding

Presence of this drug in breast milk: Probably yes.
Avoid drug or refrain from nursing.

Habit-Forming Potential: With recommended dosage, a state of functional dependence (see Glossary) is not likely to develop. There have been a small number of cases reported where the aerosol was abused for the fluorocarbon propellants.

Effects of Overdose: Indications of cortisone excess (due to systemic absorption)—fluid retention, flushing of the face, stomach irritation, nervousness.

Suggested Periodic Examinations While Taking This Drug (at physician's discretion)

Inspection of nose, mouth and throat for fungus infection.
Inspection of the nose tissues for nasal atrophy.
Assessment of adrenal function in people using cortisone-related drugs for an extended time prior to this drug.
Lung X-ray if a prior history of tuberculosis.
Measures of bone mineral density (DEXA or PDEXA) and cataract check.

▷ While Taking This Drug, Observe the Following

Foods: No specific restrictions beyond those advised by your physician.
Herbal Medicines or Minerals: Fir or pine needle oil should NOT be used by asthmatics. Ephedra alone does carry a German Commission E monograph indication for asthma treatment. If you are allergic to plants in the Asteraceae family (aster, chrysanthemum, daisy, or ragweed), you may also be allergic to echinacea, chamomile, feverfew, and St. John's wort. Talk to your doctor BEFORE adding it to any medicines that you already take.
Beverages: No specific restrictions.
▷ *Alcohol:* No interactions expected.

Tobacco Smoking: Smoking can reduce the benefits of this drug. I advise every-one to quit smoking.

▷ *Other Drugs*

The following drugs may **increase** the effects of beclomethasone:
- some antiepileptic medicines such as phenytoin (Dilantin)—may increase risk of osteoporosis.
- flunisolide (Nasalide).
- inhalant bronchodilators—epinephrine, isoetharine, isoproterenol.
- oral bronchodilators—aminophylline, ephedrine, terbutaline, theophylline, etc.

Beclomethasone **taken concurrently** with
- alendronate (Fosamax) helps prevent steroid-induced osteoporosis.

▷ *Driving, Hazardous Activities:* No restrictions.

Aviation Note: The use of this drug and the disorder for which this drug is pre-scribed **may be disqualifications** for piloting. Consult a designated Avia-tion Medical Examiner.

Exposure to Sun: No restrictions.

Occurrence of Unrelated Illness: Acute infections, serious injuries, and surgery can create an urgent need for cortisone-related drugs. Call your doctor immediately in the event of new illness or injury.

Discontinuation: If this drug has made it possible to reduce or stop ongoing cortisonelike drugs, do not stop this drug abruptly. If you must stop this drug, call your doctor. You may need to resume cortisone medicines.

Special Storage Instructions: Store at room temperature. Avoid exposure to temperatures above 120 degrees F. (49 degrees C.). Do not store or use this inhaler near heat or open flame. Protect from light.

BENAZEPRIL (ben AY ze pril)

Class: ACE inhibitor, antihypertensive

Please see the new angiotensin converting enzyme (ACE) inhibitor family profile for more information.

BENZTROPINE (BENZ troh peen)

Introduced: 1954   **Class:**   Anti-Parkinsonism,   atropinelike   drugs
Prescription: USA: Yes   **Controlled Drug:**   USA: No; Canada: No
Available as Generic: USA: Yes; Canada: Yes

Brand Names: ✤Apo-Benztropine, ✤Bensylate, Cogentin ✤PMS Benz-tropine

BENEFITS versus RISKS	
Possible Benefits	*Possible Risks*
PARTIAL RELIEF OF SYMPTOMS OF PARKINSON'S DISEASE RELIEF OF DRUG-INDUCED EXTRAPYRAMIDAL REACTIONS	Atropinelike side effects: blurred vision, dry mouth, constipation, impaired urination Toxic psychosis—rare Tardive dyskinesia—rare

▷ **Principal Uses**

As a Single Drug Product: Uses currently included in FDA-approved labeling: (1) Used in combination to treat all types of Parkinsonism (if relief is inadequate supplemental medicines are used); (2) controls Parkinsonian reactions from many antipsychotic drugs; (3) eases Parkinsonian symptoms after encephalitis.

Other (unlabeled) generally accepted uses: (1) helps sweating caused by other drugs (such as venlafaxine); (2) can help drooling (sialorrhea) in developmentally disabled patients.

Author's Note: Some clinicians are using higher-dose vitamin E for decreasing Parkinsonian symptoms seen with some antipsychotic medicines. Some use it in combination with benztropine.

How This Drug Works: Restores a more normal balance of two brain chemicals (acetylcholine and dopamine), thereby decreasing Parkinsonism symptoms.

Available Dosage Forms and Strengths

Injection — 1 mg/ml, 2 mg/ml

Tablets — 0.5 mg, 1 mg, 2 mg

▷ **Usual Adult Dosage Ranges:** *For Parkinson's disease:* 1–2 mg daily, taken in a single dose by mouth at bedtime. *For drug-induced Parkinsonian reactions:* 1 to 4 mg once or twice a day. The total daily dose should not exceed 6 mg. *For Parkinson's symptoms after encephalitis:* Starting doses of 2 mg/day are used. May then be increased as needed or tolerated to 4 to 6 mg per day.

Note: Actual dosage and schedule must be determined for each patient individually.

Conditions Requiring Dosing Adjustments

Liver Function: Use with **Caution** In patients with impaired liver function.

Kidney Function: **Caution:** Decreased kidney function may lead to an increased blood level and an increased risk of adverse effects.

▷ **Dosing Instructions:** May be taken with or following food to reduce stomach irritation. Tablet may be crushed. If you forget a dose, take the missed dose as soon as possible. If it is nearly time for your next dose, skip the missed dose and continue benztropine on its regular schedule. DO NOT double doses.

Usual Duration of Use: Regular use for 2 to 4 weeks usually needed to see peak benefit relieving symptoms of Parkinsonism. Long-term use (months to years) requires physician supervision.

Typical Treatment Goals and Measurements (Outcomes and Markers)

Parkinson's: This medicine helps treat symptoms of Parkinson's disease, but does NOT halt its progression and combination therapy is often required. Usual goals are to decrease symptom severity and improve quality of life. Regular physician assessment is required as symptoms change or exacerbate.

▷ **This Drug Should Not Be Taken If**

- you have had an allergic reaction to it.
- you are a child under 3 years of age.
- you have tardive dyskinesia.
- you have narrow-angle glaucoma (untreated).

▷ **Inform Your Physician Before Taking This Drug If**

- you have had an unfavorable reaction to atropine or atropinelike drugs.
- you have glaucoma or myasthenia gravis.

- you have heart disease or high blood pressure.
- you have a history of liver or kidney disease.
- you have difficulty emptying the urinary bladder, especially if due to an enlarged prostate gland.
- you are taking, or took in the past 2 weeks, any monoamine oxidase (MAO) type A inhibitor (see Drug Classes).
- you take prescription or nonprescription medicines not discussed when benztropine was prescribed for you.
- you are unsure how much to take or how often to take it.
- you will be exposed to extreme heat for extended periods, such as some iron smelters or those who must work outdoors in tropical climates.
- you have a history of bowel obstructions.

Possible Side Effects (natural, expected, and unavoidable drug actions)
Nervousness, blurring of vision, dryness of mouth, constipation, impaired urination. (These often subside as drug use continues.) Heat intolerance.

▷ **Possible Adverse Effects** (unusual, unexpected, and infrequent reactions)
If any of the following develop, consult your physician promptly for guidance.
Mild Adverse Effects
Allergic reaction: skin rashes—rare.
Headache, dizziness, drowsiness, muscle cramps—possible.
Indigestion, nausea, vomiting—reported.
Fast heart rate (tachycardia)—infrequent.
Memory problems—possible.
Serious Adverse Effects
Idiosyncratic reactions: abnormal behavior, confusion, delusions, hallucinations, toxic psychosis—case reports.
Tardive dyskinesia—case reports.
Dystonia—rare.
Bowel obstruction—case reports.
Abnormal temperature (hyperthermia)—case reports.

▷ **Possible Effects on Sexual Function:** Reversal of male impotence due to the use of fluphenazine (a phenothiazine antipsychotic drug).
Male infertility (0.5 to 6 mg per day).
May help treat priapism.

Natural Diseases or Disorders That May Be Activated by This Drug
Latent glaucoma, latent myasthenia gravis.

Possible Effects on Laboratory Tests
Prolactin: may be increased (especially if taken with haloperidol).

CAUTION
1. Many over-the-counter (OTC) drugs for allergies, colds, and coughs should NOT be combined with benztropine. Ask your doctor or pharmacist for help.
2. This drug may aggravate tardive dyskinesia (see Glossary). Ask your physician for guidance.
3. If you exercise or use a sauna or hot tub, caution is advised as this medicine will make you less able to sweat and your body may overheat.
4. If you develop a rash while taking this medicine, talk to your doctor (medicine should be discontinued if the dose is lowered and the rash continues).

Precautions for Use

By Infants and Children: Safety and effectiveness for those under 3 years of age not established. Children are especially susceptible to the atropinelike effects.

By Those Over 60 Years of Age: Small starting doses are prudent. Increased risk of confusion, nightmares, hallucinations, increased internal eye pressure (glaucoma) and impaired urination associated with prostate gland enlargement (prostatism).

▷ **Advisability of Use During Pregnancy**

Pregnancy Category: C. See Pregnancy Risk Categories at the back of this book.

Animal Studies: No data available.

Human Studies: Adequate studies of pregnant women are not available.

Avoid use if possible, especially close to delivery. This drug can impair the infant's intestinal tract following birth.

Advisability of Use If Breast-Feeding

Presence of this drug in breast milk: Unknown.

Ask your doctor for help.

Habit-Forming Potential: Occasional reports of anti-Parkinsonian drug abuse have been made. Sudden withdrawal of benztropine may lead to craving, restlessness, nervousness, and depression. Propranolol (20–80 mg three times daily) or diazepam (Valium, others) has been used to ease these symptoms.

Effects of Overdose: Weakness; drowsiness; stupor; impaired vision; rapid pulse; excitement; confusion; hallucinations; dry; hot skin; skin rash; dilated pupils.

Possible Effects of Long-Term Use: Increased internal eye pressure—possible glaucoma, especially in the elderly.

Suggested Periodic Examinations While Taking This Drug (at physician's discretion)

Measurement of internal eye pressure at regular intervals. Check of continued effectiveness of the drug itself.

▷ **While Taking This Drug, Observe the Following**

Foods: No restrictions.

Herbal Medicines or Minerals: See marijuana below. Additionally, talk to your doctor BEFORE adding any herbs to any medicines that you already take. Phenylalanine (200–500 mg daily) has been used by some clinicians to ease Parkinson's. Calabar bean (chop nut or ordeal bean) and octacosanol should be AVOIDED by people living with Parkinson's. Betel nut may impair benztropine benefits.

Beverages: No restrictions.

▷ *Alcohol:* Use caution. Alcohol may increase the sedative effects.

Tobacco Smoking: No interactions expected, but I advise everyone to quit smoking.

Marijuana Smoking: May increase heart rate to unacceptable levels. Avoid completely if this increased heart rate will be a problem for you.

▷ *Other Drugs*

Benztropine may *decrease* the effects of

- phenothiazines (Haloperidol, Thorazine, others).

The following drugs may *increase* the effects of benztropine:

- antihistamines may add to the dryness of mouth and throat.
- monoamine oxidase (MAO) type A inhibitor drugs may intensify all effects of this drug (see Drug Classes).

- tricyclic antidepressants (Elavil, etc.) may add to eye effects and further increase internal eye pressure (dangerous in glaucoma).

Benztropine *taken concurrently* with

- amantadine (Symmetrel) may cause increased confusion and possible hallucinations.
- belladonna (contains atropine, L-hyoscyamine and scopolamine) may cause increased risk of excessive anticholinergic side effects such as weakness, confusion and possible hallucinations.
- clozapine (Clozaril) can cause increased risk of elevated temperatures, neurological adverse effects and bowel obstruction (ileus).
- procainamide (Procanbid, etc.) may increase risk of heart conduction problems.

▷ *Driving, Hazardous Activities:* Drowsiness and dizziness may occur. Avoid hazardous activities until full effects and tolerance have been determined.

Aviation Note: The use of this drug *is a disqualification* for piloting. Consult a designated Aviation Medical Examiner.

Exposure to Sun: No restrictions.

Exposure to Heat: Use caution. This drug may reduce sweating, cause an increase in body temperature and increase risk of heatstroke.

Heavy Exercise or Exertion: Use caution. Avoid in hot environments.

Discontinuation: Do not stop this drug abruptly. Ask your doctor how to reduce the dose gradually.

BETAXOLOL (be TAX oh lohl)

Introduced: 1983   **Class:**   Antihypertensive, beta-adrenergic blocker
Prescription: USA: Yes   **Controlled Drug:**   USA: No; Canada: No
Available as Generic: Yes (ophthalmic)

Brand Names: Betoptic, Betoptic-Pilo [CD], Betoptic-S, Kerlone, ✤Novo-Betaxolol

---

BENEFITS versus RISKS

Possible Benefits	Possible Risks
EFFECTIVE, WELL-TOLERATED ANTIHYPERTENSIVE IN MILD TO MODERATE HIGH BLOOD PRESSURE	CONGESTIVE HEART FAILURE in advanced heart disease
EFFECTIVE TREATMENT OF CHRONIC, OPEN-ANGLE GLAUCOMA	Worsening of angina in coronary heart disease (abrupt withdrawal)
PROLONGATION OF LIFE AFTER HEART ATTACK	Masking of low blood sugar (hypoglycemia) in diabetes
TREATMENT OF OCULAR HYPERTENSION	Provocation of bronchial asthma (with high doses)
	Rare anemia and low blood platelets (above risks for systemic form)

▷ **Principal Uses**

As a Single Drug Product: Uses currently included in FDA-approved labeling: Used to treat (1) mild to moderate high blood pressure (alone or combined with other antihypertensive drugs, such as diuretics); (2) chronic open-angle glaucoma (eyedrops); (3) ocular hypertension (ophthalmic forms);

(4) Betoptic-Pilo—reduces elevated eye pressure in primary open-angle glaucoma who have failed Betoptic-S therapy.

Other (unlabeled) generally accepted uses: (1) The oral form may help decrease death (mortality) from a heart attack; (2) helps decrease incidence and severity of chest pain (angina); (3) can ease aggressive behavior or movement disorders in some psychiatric patients; (4) can treat selected cases of stuttering.

How This Drug Works: By blocking some sympathetic nervous system actions, it reduces heart rate and contraction force, lowers blood ejection pressure and reduces oxygen needed by the heart. Relaxes blood vessel walls, resulting in expansion and lower blood pressure. Reduces internal eye pressure.

Available Dosage Forms and Strengths

Eyedrops (solution) — 2.8 mg/ml, 5.6 mg/ml

Eyedrops (suspension) — 0.25%

— 0.25%/1.75% (Betoptic-Pilo)

Tablets — 10 mg, 20 mg

▷ **Usual Adult Dosage Ranges:**

Hypertension: Initially 10 mg once daily. Dose may be increased at intervals of 7 to 14 days as needed and tolerated up to 20 mg every 24 hours. Usual ongoing dose is 10 to 15 mg daily. Some people tolerate 40 mg, but had no further blood pressure effects. Total maximum is 20 mg daily.

For use in glaucoma: One or two drops of the 2.8 mg/ml solution or one drop of the 5.6 mg/ml twice daily.

Betoptic-Pilo (betaxolol/pilocarpine) used to lower eye pressure in primary open-angle glaucoma when Betoptic-S fails: Follow doctor and label instructions.

Note: Actual dose and schedule must be determined for each patient individually.

Conditions Requiring Dosing Adjustments

Liver Function: Use with caution; this drug is metabolized in the liver. Dose decreases not routinely needed.

Kidney Function: Starting dose is 5 mg. The dose is increased as needed and tolerated by 5 mg every 2 weeks for a maximum of 20 mg daily.

▷ **Dosing Instructions:** May be taken without regard to eating. The tablet may be crushed. Do not stop this drug abruptly. If you forget a dose: take it right away unless it's within 8 hours of your next regular dose. If it IS within 8 hours of the next dose, just take the scheduled dose. DO NOT double doses. Wash your hands with water and soap BEFORE using the eye drops. Talk to your doctor about how to use the drops. Ophthalmic suspension should be re-suspended (see package instructions) before instilling it in your eye. Many ophthalmologists want patients to use their index finger to pull out the lower eye lid to form a pocket, then drop the required number of drops into the pocket.

Usual Duration of Use: Regular use for 10 to 14 days usually needed to see this drug's effectiveness in lowering blood pressure. Long-term use determined by success in lowering blood pressure and response to overall treatment program (weight reduction, salt restriction, smoking cessation, etc.). See your doctor regularly. Use for glaucoma will be ongoing and may take two weeks to reach its maximum benefit.

Typical Treatment Goals and Measurements (Outcomes and Markers)

Blood Pressure: The NEW guidelines (JNC VII) define normal blood pressure (BP) as **less than** 120/80. Because blood pressures that were once considered acceptable can actually lead to blood vessel damage, the committee from the National Institutes of Health, National Heart Lung and Blood Institute now have a new category called **Pre-hypertension**. This ranges from 120/80 to 139/89 and is intended to help your doctor encourage lifestyle changes (or in the case of people with a risk factor for high blood pressure, start treatment) much earlier—so that possible damage to blood vessels, your heart, kidneys, sexual potency, or eyes might be minimized or avoided altogether. The next two classes of high blood pressure are stage 1 hypertension: 140/90 to 159/99 and stage 2 hypertension equal to or greater than: 160/100 mm Hg. These guidelines also recommend that clinicians trying to control blood pressure work with their patients to agree on the goals and a plan of treatment. The first-ever guidelines for blood pressure (hypertension) in African Americans recommends that MOST black patients be started on TWO antihypertensive medicines with the goal of lowering blood pressure to 130/80 for those with high risk for heart and blood vessel disease or with diabetes. The American Diabetes Association recommends 130/80 as the target for people living with diabetes and less than 125/75 for those who spill more than one gram of protein into their urine. Most clinicians try to achieve a BP that confers the best balance of lower cardiovascular risk and avoids the problem of too low a blood pressure. Blood pressure duration is generally increased with beneficial restriction of sodium. The goals and time frame should be discussed with you when the prescription is written. If goals are not met, it is not unusual to intensify doses or add on medicines. You can find the new blood pressure guidelines at *www.nhlbi.nih.gov/guidelines/hypertension/index.htm*. For the African American guidelines see Douglas, J.G. in Sources.

Glaucoma: Return of eye pressure (intraocular pressure) to normal and avoidance of consequences of increased pressure. If this medicine does not work well enough by itself, combination treatment is typical.

Possible Advantages of This Drug: Usually effective and well-tolerated with a single dose daily, which is easier to remember to take. Twice-daily dosing for glaucoma also enhances taking the medicine (adherence). Suspension form may be better tolerated than the solution form.

▷ **This Drug Should Not Be Taken If**
- you have had an allergic reaction to it previously.
- you have heart (overt) failure or cardiogenic shock.
- you have an abnormally slow heart rate (bradycardia) or a serious heart block (second or third degree).
- you take, or took in the past 14 days, any monoamine oxidase (MAO) type A inhibitor (see Drug Classes).

▷ **Inform Your Physician Before Taking This Drug If**
- you have had an adverse reaction to any beta-blocker (see Drug Classes).
- you have serious heart disease or episodes of heart failure.
- you have a history of hay fever (allergic rhinitis), asthma, chronic bronchitis, or emphysema. Some drugs in this class are contraindicated in asthmatics.
- you have overactive thyroid function (hyperthyroidism).
- you have a history of low blood sugar (hypoglycemia) or diabetes.
- you have impaired liver or kidney function.
- you have narrowing of the vessels in your legs or arms (peripheral vascular disease). Discuss this with your doctor.
- you have myasthenia gravis.

- you take digitalis, quinidine or reserpine, or any calcium blocker drug (see Drug Classes).
- you will have surgery with general anesthesia.
- you take prescription or nonprescription medications not discussed when betaxolol was prescribed for you.

Possible Side Effects (natural, expected, and unavoidable drug actions)

Lethargy, fatigue (up to 10%), cold extremities—rare; slow heart rate, light-headedness in upright position (see Orthostatic Hypotension in Glossary), rebound hypertension if drug is stopped suddenly.

Possible Adverse Effects (unusual, unexpected, and infrequent reactions)

If any of the following develop, consult your physician promptly for guidance.

Mild Adverse Effects

Allergic reactions: skin rash, itching—rare.
Hair loss—case reports (even with ophthalmic use).
Headache (up to 15%)—frequent.
Dizziness, fatigue—infrequent.
Insomnia or abnormal dreams—infrequent.
Indigestion, nausea, diarrhea—infrequent.
Joint and muscle discomfort—infrequent.
Fluid retention (edema)—rare.
Difficulty breathing—infrequent.

Serious Adverse Effects

Allergic reactions: may make allergic reactions more difficult to treat (refractory to epinephrine).
Mental depression or anxiety—rare.
Increased blood sugar (hyperglycemia) in non-insulin-dependent diabetics—possible.
Chest pain, shortness of breath, congestive heart failure—rare.
Induction of bronchial asthma (in asthmatic patients)—possible.
Low blood platelets and anemia—rare.
Systemic Lupus erythematosus—case report.
Angina (if pill form abruptly stopped).
Slow heart rate (bradycardia)—infrequent.
Intermittent problems walking (intermittent claudication)—possible.
Heart attack (myocardial infarction)—rare.
Author's Note: Adverse effects from eye drops happen rarely versus "pill" form.

▷ **Possible Effects on Sexual Function:** Decreased libido, impotence—rare and less frequent than other medicines in this class.

Altered menstrual patterns (reported rarely with other medicines in this class)—possible.

Adverse Effects That May Mimic Natural Diseases or Disorders

Reduced blood flow to extremities may mimic Raynaud's disease (see Glossary).

Possible Effects on Laboratory Tests

Glaucoma-screening test (measurement of internal eye pressure): pressure is decreased (false low or normal value).
Antinuclear antibodies (ANA) test: case report.
Blood potassium: slightly increased.
Blood platelet counts and hemoglobin: decreased—rare.
Blood glucose: increased in non-insulin-dependent diabetics.

CAUTION
1. Do not stop this drug suddenly without calling your doctor. Always carry a note with you that says you are taking this drug.
2. Ask your physician or pharmacist before using nasal decongestants. These can cause sudden increases in blood pressure when combined with beta-blocker drugs.
3. Levobetaxolol (Betaxon) is NOT the same medicine as betaxolol.
4. Report any tendency to emotional depression.
5. Eye (ophthalmic) form may cause additive effects on blood pressure if taken with the pill form.

Precautions for Use

By Infants and Children: Safety and effectiveness for those under 12 years of age not established.

By Those Over 60 Years of Age: Caution: High blood pressure should be slowly reduced, avoiding risks associated with excessively low blood pressure. Treatment should be started with 5 mg daily and blood pressure checked often. Sudden, rapid and excessive reduction of blood pressure can cause stroke or heart attack. Total daily dosage should not exceed 10 to 15 mg. Watch for dizziness, unsteadiness, tendency to fall, confusion, hallucinations, depression, or urinary frequency. This age group is more prone to develop excessively slow heart rates and hypothermia.

▷ **Advisability of Use During Pregnancy**

Pregnancy Category: C. C/**D** from one researcher. See Pregnancy Risk Categories at the back of this book.

Animal Studies: Rat studies reveal increased resorptions of embryo and fetus, retarded growth and development of newborn, and mild skeletal defects.

Human Studies: Adequate studies of pregnant women are not available.

Avoid use of drug during the first 3 months if possible. Avoid use during labor and delivery because of the possible effects on the newborn infant.

Advisability of Use If Breast-Feeding

Presence of this drug in breast milk: Yes.

Avoid drug if possible. If drug is necessary, observe nursing infant for slow heart rate and indications of low blood sugar.

Habit-Forming Potential: None.

Effects of Overdose: Weakness, slow pulse, low blood pressure, fainting, cold and sweaty skin, congestive heart failure, possible coma, and convulsions.

Possible Effects of Long-Term Use: Reduced heart reserve and eventual heart failure in susceptible individuals with advanced heart disease. Case reports of carpal tunnel syndrome with some medicines in this family.

Suggested Periodic Examinations While Taking This Drug (at physician's discretion)

Measurements of blood pressure.

Evaluation of heart function. Checks of intraocular pressure (ophthalmic use).

▷ **While Taking This Drug, Observe the Following**

Foods: No restrictions. Avoid excessive salt intake.

Herbal Medicines or Minerals: Ginseng may increase blood pressure, blunting the benefits of this medicine. Hawthorn, saw palmetto, ma huang, goldenseal, yohimbe, and licorice may also increase blood pressure. Calcium and garlic may help lower blood pressure. Indian snakeroot has a German Commission E monograph indication for hypertension—talk to your doctor. Eleuthero root and ephedra should be avoided by people living with hypertension. Belladonna, ephedra, henbane leaf, and scopolia root should be avoided by people living with glaucoma. Dong Quai may lead to higher than expected blood levels. St. John's wort may lower blood levels and blunt therapeutic benefits.

Beverages: No restrictions. May be taken with milk.

▷ *Alcohol:* Use with caution. Alcohol may exaggerate oral form lowering of blood pressure and may increase its mild sedative effect.

Tobacco Smoking: Nicotine may reduce this drug's effectiveness. High drug doses worsen bronchial constriction caused by regular smoking. I advise everyone to quit smoking.

▷ *Other Drugs*

Betaxolol may ***increase*** the effects of
- other antihypertensive drugs and cause excessive lowering of blood pressure. Dosage decreases may be necessary.
- reserpine (Ser-Ap-Es, etc.) and cause sedation, depression, slowing of heart rate and lowering of blood pressure (light-headedness, fainting).
- verapamil and cause additive risk of congestive heart failure and slow heart rate (bradycardia).

Betaxolol ***taken concurrently*** with
- amiodarone (Cordarone) may result in extremely slow heart rate and arrest.
- calcium channel blockers (Diltiazem, etc. or other dihydropyridine forms) may severely lower blood pressure.
- clonidine (Catapres) requires close monitoring for rebound high blood pressure if clonidine is stopped while betaxolol is still being taken.
- digoxin (Lanoxin) may prolong AV conduction time and digoxin toxicity.
- fluoroquinolone (see Drug Classes) antibiotics may cause an increase in betaxolol blood levels and lead to toxicity.
- fluvoxamine (Luvox) may cause excessive slowing of the heart and very low blood pressure.
- insulin requires close supervision to avoid hidden hypoglycemia (see Glossary).
- methyldopa (various) may lead to an exaggerated hypertensive response to stress.
- oral antidiabetic (hypoglycemic) drugs (see Drug Classes) may prolong recovery from low blood sugars.
- phenothiazines (see Drug Classes) may result in additive blood pressure lowering effects.
- rifabutin (Mycobutin) may decrease betaxolol benefits.
- ritonavir (Norvir) and perhaps other protease inhibitors (see Drug Classes) may decrease betaxolol benefits.
- venlafaxine (Effexor) may cause excessive slowing of the heart and very low blood pressure.
- zileuton (Zyflo) may cause excessive blood pressure lowering.

The following drugs may ***decrease*** the effects of betaxolol:
- indomethacin (Indocin) and possibly other "aspirin substitutes," or NSAIDs, may impair betaxolol's antihypertensive effect.

▷ *Driving, Hazardous Activities:* Use caution until the full extent of drowsiness, lethargy, and blood pressure change has been determined.

Aviation Note: The use of this drug *is a disqualification* for piloting. Consult a designated Aviation Medical Examiner.

Exposure to Sun: No restrictions.

Exposure to Heat: Caution is advised. Hot environments can lower blood pressure and exaggerate the effects of this drug.

Exposure to Cold: Caution is advised. Cold environments can enhance the circulatory deficiency in the extremities that may occur with this drug. The elderly should be careful to prevent hypothermia (see Glossary).

Heavy Exercise or Exertion: Talk with your doctor about an exercise program that is right for you, mindful of this medicine and your physical condition.

Occurrence of Unrelated Illness: Fever can lower blood pressure and require dosing changes. Nausea or vomiting may interrupt dosing. Ask your doctor for help.

Discontinuation: DO NOT stop this drug suddenly. Gradual physician-supervised dose reduction over 2 to 3 weeks is recommended.

BITOLTEROL (bi TOHL ter ohl)

Introduced: 1985 **Class:** Antiasthmatic, bronchodilator **Prescription:** Yes **Controlled Drug:** No **Available as Generic:** No

Brand Name: Tornalate

Author's Note: This medicine is no longer available in the inhaler form. The information in this profile has been truncated to make room for more widely used medicines.

BROMOCRIPTINE (broh moh KRIP teen)

Introduced: 1975 **Class:** Anti-Parkinsonism, ergot derivative **Prescription:** USA: Yes **Controlled Drug:** USA: No; Canada: No **Available as Generic:** No

Brand Names: Normatine, Parlodel

Author's Note: This profile has been shortened to make room for more widely used medicines.

BUDESONIDE (byou DES oh nyde)

Introduced: 1994 (Rhinocort), 1997 (Turbuhaler) **Class:** Antiasthmatic, cortisonelike drugs **Prescription:** USA: Yes **Controlled Drug:** USA: No; Canada: No **Available as Generic:** No

Brand Names: ✦Entocort, Entocort EC, ✦Gen-Budesonide-AQ, Pulmicort, ✦Pulmicort Nebuamp, Pulmicort Respules and Turbuhaler, Rhinocort Aqua, Rhinocort Turbuhaler

```
                         BENEFITS versus RISKS
         Possible Benefits                    Possible Risks
EFFECTIVE RELIEF OF ALLERGIC      FUNGUS INFECTIONS OF THE
   RHINITIS                          MOUTH AND THROAT
EFFECTIVE CONTROL OF ASTHMA       Changes in lining of the nose (nasal
TENDS TO HAVE MORE LOCAL            mucosa)
   THAN SYSTEMIC EFFECTS          Increased cataract risk
   (HIGH RATIO)                   Osteoporosis risk
THE NEW ENTOCORT EC FORM IS
   SPECIFICALLY APPROVED TO
   TREAT SUDDEN (ACUTE) FLARE
   UPS OF CROHN'S DISEASE
   WHILE AVOIDING MANY
   SYSTEMIC EFFECTS OF OTHER
   STEROIDS
```

▷ **Principal Uses**

As a Single Drug Product: Uses currently included in FDA-approved labeling: (1) Ongoing treatment of bronchial asthma in people who don't have sufficient response to bronchodilators and need cortisonelike drugs for asthma control; (2) treats seasonal and perennial rhinitis in children and adults (nasal form); (3) Entocort EC form is a form taken by mouth specifically for mild to moderate Crohn's disease that effects the ileum or ascending colon.

Other (unlabeled) generally accepted uses: (1) Eases nasal polyps (nasal polyposis).

How This Drug Works: It reduces inflammation (arachidonic acid pathway) and decreases response to immediate and delayed hypersensitivity. Also reduces local lung inflammation in the respiratory tract. The Entocort EC form is released in the small intestine and ascending colon where is works to decrease inflammation. Systemic effects are minimized because it next goes to the liver where it is transformed.

Available Dosage Forms and Strengths

Enteric Capsules (EC) — 3 mg

Nasal inhaler — 7 g (32 mcg per press)

Nasal spray — 200-dose canister (50 mcg per dose) (Canada)

Oral inhaler — 200 doses of 1 or 4 mg per ml

Spacer form — same as above (200 doses of 1 or 4 mg per ml)

Turbuhaler — 200 mcg (100 and 400 mcg in Canada)

▷ **Recommended Dosage Ranges**

Infants and Children:

Seasonal rhinitis (children 6 or older): Pressurized nasal inhaler—two inhalations in each nostril twice a day, morning and evening, or 4 inhalations in each nostril in the morning (256 mcg maximum).

Perennial allergic rhinitis: Same dose, but see Caution section.

Seasonal and perennial rhinitis (for those 12 or older): Nonaerosol pump nasal spray—one puff (50 mcg) in each nostril twice daily. This may be increased to 2 puffs twice daily if required (256 mcg maximum).

Asthma: Oral inhalation form (in those more than 6 and based on prior treatment): (a) Bronchodilators alone—200 mcg twice a day; (b) inhaled corticosteroids—200 mcg twice daily; (c) oral corticosteroids—400 mcg twice daily. Children under 12 years old are given one puff or 0.2 mg twice a day with a maximum of 2 puffs a day (0.8 mg). Some clinicians use 400 mcg per square meter.

Author's Note: Use in pediatrics may slow a child's rate of growth.

Adults:

Seasonal rhinitis: Non-aerosol pump spray form—one puff (equals 50 mcg) in each nostril twice a day. Dosing can be increased to 2 puffs in each nostril twice daily if needed and tolerated. The effect should be checked in 3 to 7 days and the medicine stopped in 3 weeks if an adequate response isn't achieved.

Perennial rhinitis: Same dose as seasonal rhinitis, but see Caution section. Once adequate benefits have been seen, the dose is then slowly decreased to the lowest dose that works. If symptoms return while doses are being lowered, the dose may be increased back to the starting dose (briefly) and then decreased back to the dose that worked before the symptoms returned.

Asthma (use in is based on prior treatment): Oral inhaler—people receiving (a) bronchodilators alone—200–400 mcg twice a day; (b) inhaled corticosteroids—200–400 mcg twice daily; (c) oral corticosteroids—400–800 mcg twice daily. If asthma has been controlled by corticosteroids taken by mouth, the budesonide inhaler must be used at the same time as the oral corticosteroids for about 1 week. After a week, the oral corticosteroid can be SLOWLY tapered. The patient should be closely watched for the return of asthma or other effects (see Caution section).

Crohn's disease (Entocort EC form): Used for sudden (acute) flare ups of Crohn's disease that involves the ileum or ascending colon: Three capsules taken once a day in the morning for up to eight weeks. Dosing is decreased (tapered) to 6 mg a day for 14 days before it is stopped.

Those Over 65 Years of Age: Doses similar to those used in younger patients have been effective and safe.

Note: Actual dose and schedule must be determined for each patient individually.

Conditions Requiring Dosing Adjustments

Liver Function: Use with caution in patients with liver compromise. This drug may stay in the body longer in people with liver damage, and lower doses appear prudent. The Entocort EC form is rapidly transformed (metabolized) in the liver, but was not studied in severe liver dysfunction and can not be recommended in that population.

Kidney Function: No adjustments in dosing appear to be required.

▷ **Dosing Instructions:** May be used without regard to eating. Rinse the mouth and throat (gargle) with water thoroughly after each inhalation. If you forget a dose: Use the inhaler or spray as soon as possible. DO NOT double doses. Entocort EC form should NOT be crushed, chewed, or altered.

Usual Duration of Use: Regular use for 1 to 2 weeks is often needed to see the best response from the oral inhalation form in asthma, but Pulmicort form may work in a day in some patients. The nasal inhalation form may go to work in 3–7 days. This is why results are checked after 3–7 days and at 3 weeks. If acceptable relief isn't seen in 3 weeks, the drug should be stopped. Once relief is achieved, the dose should be decreased at 2- to 4-week intervals to the minimum effective dose. Long-term use must be physician-supervised. See your doctor regularly. For Entocort EC form, dosing in continued for up to eight weeks. A repeat episode of active Crohn's can be treated with a repeat eight-week course.

Typical Treatment Goals and Measurements (Outcomes and Markers)

Asthma: Frequency and severity of asthma attacks should ease. Some clinicians also use decreased frequency of rescue inhaler use as a further clinical indicator. It is critical that this medicine is used regularly to get the best results. An additional goal of therapy is to use the lowest effective dose. Some people keep their improvements when doses are lowered, while others relapse. Those with a less than 2-fold improvement in airway response and people who stay in the moderate to severe asthma range despite high budesonide doses may be more likely to relapse. If the usual benefit is not realized, call your doctor.

Allergic rhinitis: Symptoms such as itchy, runny nose, sore throat, and postnasal drip should all ease once this medicine begins to work. Because there may be some seasonality to the pollen or molds that can cause rhinitis, talk to your doctor about exactly how you should use this medicine.

Crohn's Disease: Flare ups involving the ileum or ascending colon are brought under control.

Possible Advantages of This Drug

Turbuhaler form avoids pressurized metered dose inhaler CFCs as well as increased amount of drug in the lung. Intranasal form causes less depression of free cortisol. Inhaled forms cause less of a systemic effect than the same medicine taken by mouth. Medicines in this class are considered first-line treatment by many clinicians in allergic rhinitis because they slow (attenuate) early-phase reactions and suppress late-phase allergic reactions (they may also cost less). In asthma, inhaled steroids have been recommended in revised guidelines for those with more than infrequent or mild asthma. Entocort EC form releases the active drug in the small intestine and part of the colon (ascending) and eases inflammation. The drug is subsequently quickly transformed (metabolized) in the liver so that only a small amount goes out the whole body (systemic circulation).

▷ **This Drug Should Not Be Taken If**
- you have had an allergic reaction to any form of this drug.
- you are having severe acute asthma or status asthmaticus (requires intense treatment for prompt relief).
- other antiasthmatic drugs can control your asthma that are not related to cortisone.
- your asthma requires cortisonelike drugs infrequently for control.

▷ **Inform Your Physician Before Taking This Drug If**
- you take or recently took any cortisone-related drug (including ACTH by injection) for any reason (see Drug Classes).
- you have a history of tuberculosis of the lungs.
- you have chronic bronchitis or bronchiectasis.
- you think you have an active infection of any kind, especially a respiratory infection or herpes of the eye.
- you have recently been exposed to chickenpox or other viral illnesses.
- you are prone to nosebleeds (epistaxis) or have nose ulcers or have had nose surgery (nasal forms).
- you are unsure how much to take or how often to take this drug.
- you are a child and your growth rate has not been checked.

Possible Side Effects (natural, expected, and unavoidable drug actions)

Author's Note: The new Entocort EC form is released in the intestines and quickly deactivated in the liver. Because very little drug actually reached the general circulation (systemic), whole body effects such

as suppression of the adrenal gland, acne, moon face, and other changes are minimized or absent.

Fungus infections (thrush) of the mouth and throat. Voice changes (dysphonia).

Suppression of the adrenal glands—possible.

Stinging of nasal tissues (nasal form)—possible.

▷ **Possible Adverse Effects** (unusual, unexpected, and infrequent reactions)

If any of the following develop, consult your physician promptly for guidance.

Mild Adverse Effects

Allergic reaction: skin rash (contact dermatitis)—infrequent.

Headache—frequent (oral inhalation).

Dryness of mouth, hoarseness, sore throat, cough—possible.

Nosebleeds (epistaxis)—infrequent.

Weight gain—infrequent.

Serious Adverse Effects

Allergic reaction: localized areas of "allergic" pneumonitis (lung inflammation), immediate type hypersensitivity reactions.

Bronchospasm, asthmatic wheezing—rare.

Behavioral changes—case reports.

Nose perforation (septal)—rare.

Hyperglycemia (dose related)—case report.

Increased susceptibility to chickenpox—possible.

Growth slowing (growth retardation)—possible.

Increased risk of cataracts with long-term (chronic) use.

Osteoporosis (any corticosteroid can cause this)—possible.

▷ **Possible Effects on Sexual Function:** None reported.

Natural Diseases or Disorders That May Be Activated by This Drug

Cortisone-related drugs having systemic effects impair immunity and lead to reactivation of "healed" or dormant tuberculosis. People with a history of tuberculosis must be watched closely while using this drug.

Possible Effects on Laboratory Tests

Blood cortisol levels: decreased.

HDL and blood sugar may increase.

Bone mineral density: may be decreased with chronic use.

CAUTION

1. The substance (sorbitan trioleate) that this medicine is delivered in (vehicle) may cause symptoms that are like rhinitis. Doses early in treatment may suppress these symptoms, and they may slowly come back once the dose is lowered. If this occurs and the dose can't be lowered, other treatment may be needed.

2. The maker of the pressurized nasal inhaler uses the amount of drug released from the nasal adapter (32 mcg) to determine the dose. The nasal inhaler actually releases 50 mcg.

3. Use in people with asthma REQUIRES regular use to get the best results. Please do not skip doses.

4. This drug should not be relied upon for immediate relief of acute asthma.

5. The inhaled powder form does not prevent asthma precipitated by exercise.

6. If you required cortisonelike drugs before starting this inhaler, you may again require a cortisonelike drug if you are injured, have an infection

or need surgery. Extreme care must be taken if you are being changed from corticosteroids that work in the whole body (systemically active) to this medicine.

7. If severe asthma returns while using this drug, call your doctor immediately. Cortisonelike drugs may be required.
8. Carry a personal ID card saying that you have used (if true) cortisone-related drugs in the past year.
9. This drug may allow dosage decreases in some patients.
10. If this medicine is to be used long-term, a bone mineral density test before treatment and every 2 years is prudent.
11. Entocort EC form should NOT be used for ongoing (chronic) therapy. DO NOT drink grapefruit while this form is being taken.
12. Unlike other corticosteroids, reports of osteonecrosis (avascular necrosis or aseptic necrosis) have not been made for this medicine. Caution is prudent, and patients should report any unexplained joint (such as knee, hip or shoulder) pain to their doctor.

Precautions for Use
By Infants and Children: Safety and effectiveness as described above. Children may be more susceptible to adverse effects of this drug and should be watched closely.
By Those Over 60 Years of Age: People with bronchiectasis should be watched closely for the development of lung infections.

▷ **Advisability of Use During Pregnancy**
Pregnancy Category: C. See Pregnancy Risk Categories at the back of this book.
Animal Studies: Mouse, rat, and rabbit studies reveal significant birth defects due to this drug.
Human Studies: Adequate studies of pregnant women are not available.
Talk with your doctor.

Advisability of Use If Breast-Feeding
Presence of this drug in breast milk: Amount not determined.
Controversial. Discontinue nursing or the medicine. Discuss this with your doctor.

Habit-Forming Potential: With recommended dosage, a state of functional dependence (see Glossary) is not likely to develop.

Effects of Overdose: Indications of cortisone excess (due to systemic absorption)—fluid retention, flushing of the face, stomach irritation, nervousness.

Suggested Periodic Examinations While Taking This Drug (at physician's discretion)
Inspection of nose, mouth and throat for fungus infection.
Inspection of the nose tissues for damage.
Assessment of adrenal function in people using cortisone-related drugs for an extended time prior to this drug.
Lung X-ray if a prior history of tuberculosis.
Measures of bone mineral density (DEXA, ultrasound, or PDEXA) and cataract check.

▷ **While Taking This Drug, Observe the Following**
Foods: Follow specific restrictions advised by your physician. Grapefruit can change the ability of the body to remove this medicine—DO NOT eat this—particularly with the Entocort EC form.

Herbal Medicines or Minerals: Fir or pine needle oil should NOT be used by asthmatics. Ephedra alone does carry a German Commission E monograph indication for asthma treatment. If you are allergic to plants in the Asteraceae family (aster, chrysanthemum, daisy, or ragweed), you may also be allergic to echinacea, chamomile, feverfew, and St. John's wort. Taking added calcium and vitamin D while taking this medicine is prudent. Talk to your doctor BEFORE adding any herbals to this medicine.

Beverages: Avoid grapefruit juice as it increases blood levels of the non-EC form and will also increase the chance of whole body effects of even the EC form. DO NOT drink grapefruit juice while taking this medicine.

▷ *Alcohol:* No interactions expected.

Tobacco Smoking: Smoking can reduce the benefits of this drug. I advise everyone to quit smoking.

▷ *Other Drugs*

The following drugs may ***increase*** the effects of budesonide:

- some antiepileptic medicines such as phenytoin (Dilantin) may increase risk of osteoporosis.
- inhalant bronchodilators—epinephrine, isoetharine, isoproterenol.
- methylphenidate (Ritalin) may cause increased growth suppression.
- oral bronchodilators—aminophylline, ephedrine, terbutaline, theophylline, etc.

Budesonide ***taken concurrently*** with:

- amiodarone (Cordarone) may cause increased risk of Cushing's syndrome (because of liver enzyme-CYP450 3A4 inhibition). Careful clinical follow-up is needed.
- ketoconazole (Nizoral), itraconazole, erythromycin, ritonavir, and other inhibitors of CYP450 3A4 may cause increased budesonide levels. Caution is advised.

▷ *Driving, Hazardous Activities:* No restrictions.

Aviation Note: The use of this drug and the disorder for which this drug is prescribed ***may be disqualifications*** for piloting. Consult a designated Aviation Medical Examiner.

Exposure to Sun: No restrictions.

Occurrence of Unrelated Illness: Acute infections, serious injuries, and surgery can create an urgent need for cortisone-related drugs. Call your doctor immediately in the event of new illness or injury.

Discontinuation: If this drug has made it possible to reduce or stop ongoing cortisonelike drugs, ***do not*** stop this drug abruptly. If you must stop this drug, call your doctor. You may need to resume cortisone medicines. The Entocort EC form is tapered to 6 mg daily for 14 days before it is stopped.

BUMETANIDE (byu MET a nide)

Introduced: 1983 **Class:** Diuretic **Prescription:** USA: Yes; Canada: No **Controlled Drug:** USA: No **Available as Generic:** Yes

Brand Names: Bumex, Burinex

```
┌─────────────────────────────────────────────────────────────┐
│                    BENEFITS versus RISKS                      │
│      Possible Benefits              Possible Risks            │
│ POTENT, EFFECTIVE DIURETIC BY   ABNORMALLY LOW BLOOD          │
│    MOUTH OR INJECTION              POTASSIUM with excessive use│
│ TREATS CONGESTIVE HEART         Decreased magnesium with chronic│
│    FAILURE, HIGH BLOOD             therapy                    │
│    PRESSURE, AND FLUID BUILDUP  Blood disorders—rare          │
│    IN KIDNEY FAILURE            Possible bone weakening with  │
│                                    prolonged use              │
└─────────────────────────────────────────────────────────────┘
```

▷ **Principal Uses**

   As a Single Drug Product: Uses currently included in FDA-approved labeling: (1) Removes fluid excess in patients with congestive heart failure, kidney or liver disease; (2) eases edema in people who fail to respond to or will not tolerate furosemide (Lasix).

   Other (unlabeled) generally accepted uses: (1) Used as an adjunct to other therapy in high blood pressure (hypertension); (2) can help older people decrease the number of times they must get up at night to urinate (nocturia); (3) eases the amount of fluid that can build up in the lungs (pulmonary edema).

In the Pipeline: The Health and Human Services secretary has identified a group of medicines to be tested for use in children. Bumetanide was on that list of the 12 highest priority medicines to be studied in children (find out more at *www.hhs.gov/news/press/2003pres/20030121.html*).

How This Drug Works: Increases removal of salt and water from the body (through increased urine production). Reduces sodium and amount of fluid in the blood.

Available Dosage Forms and Strengths

   Injection — 0.25 mg/aml (2-ml ampules)

   Tablets — 0.5 mg, 1 mg, 2 mg

▷ **Usual Adult Dosage Ranges:** 0.5 to 2 mg daily, usually taken in the morning as a single dose. If needed, an additional second or third dose may be taken later in the day at 4- to 5-hour intervals. The total daily dose should not exceed 10 mg. Ongoing (maintenance) doses should be given intermittently (every other day) and typically have been the safest way to control edema.

   Note: Actual dose and schedule must be determined for each patient individually.

Conditions Requiring Dosing Adjustments

   Liver Function: Rapid body fluid removal can cause a coma in liver failure patients. Use of loop diuretics only done under close medical supervision (hospital or outpatient care center).

   Kidney Function: NOT recommended for use in progressive renal failure.

▷ **Dosing Instructions:** May be crushed when taken and given with or following food to reduce stomach irritation. If you forget a dose: take it right away unless it's nearly time for your next regular dose. If it IS nearly time for the next dose, just take the scheduled dose. DO NOT double doses.

Usual Duration of Use: Two to three days of regular use often needed to see peak effect relieving fluid buildup (edema). Once peak benefit is realized, intermittent use reduces risk of sodium, potassium, magnesium, and water imbalance. Long-term use requires supervision by your doctor.

Typical Treatment Goals and Measurements (Outcomes and Markers)

Blood Pressure: The NEW guidelines (JNC VII) define normal blood pressure (BP) as **less than** 120/80. Because blood pressures that were once considered acceptable can actually lead to blood vessel damage, the committee from the National Institutes of Health, National Heart Lung and Blood Institute now have a new category called **Pre-hypertension**. This ranges from 120/80 to 139/89 and is intended to help your doctor encourage lifestyle changes (or in the case of people with a risk factor for high blood pressure, start treatment) much earlier—so that possible damage to blood vessels, your heart, kidneys, sexual potency, or eyes might be minimized or avoided altogether. The next two classes of high blood pressure are stage 1 hypertension: 140/90 to 159/99 and stage 2 hypertension equal to or greater than: 160/100 mm Hg. These guidelines also recommend that clinicians trying to control blood pressure work with their patients to agree on the goals and a plan of treatment. The first-ever guidelines for blood pressure (hypertension) in African Americans recommends that MOST black patients be started on TWO antihypertensive medicines with the goal of lowering blood pressure to 130/80 for those with high risk for heart and blood vessel disease or with diabetes. The American Diabetes Association recommends 130/80 as the target for people living with diabetes and less than 125/75 for those who spill more than one gram of protein into their urine. Most clinicians try to achieve a BP that confers the best balance of lower cardiovascular risk and avoids the problem of too low a blood pressure. Blood pressure duration is generally increased with beneficial restriction of sodium. The goals and time frame should be discussed with you when the prescription is written. If goals are not met, it is not unusual to intensify doses or add on medicines. You can find the new blood pressure guidelines at *www.nhlbi.hih.gov/guidelines/hypertension/index.htm*. For the African American guidelines see Douglas, J.G. in Sources.

Congestive heart failure: Used to remove excessive fluid which builds up in the body. Typical treatment markers include resolution of ankle swelling and increased output of fluid (diuresis).

Possible Advantages of This Drug

Diuretic effect is usually complete in 4 hours; diuretic effect of furosemide usually lasts from 6 to 8 hours. Hearing impairment (ototoxicity) is probably less than that with furosemide (Lasix).

▷ **This Drug Should Not Be Taken If**
- you have had an allergic reaction to sulfonamides or to bumetanide.
- coma caused by liver failure is present (a point for caregivers).
- severe electrolyte or fluid imbalance.
- you have developed a marked increase in creatinine or blood urea nitrogen (BUN) while taking this drug.
- your kidneys are unable to produce adequate urine (oliguria).

▷ **Inform Your Physician Before Taking This Drug If**
- you are allergic to any form of sulfa drug.
- you are pregnant or planning pregnancy.
- you have a blood disorder.
- you have impaired liver or kidney function.
- you have diabetes, a diabetic tendency, or a history of gout.
- you have impaired hearing or develop hearing loss during therapy.

- you have low blood platelets.
- you are taking: cortisone, digitalis, oral antidiabetic drugs, insulin, probenecid (Benemid), indomethacin (Indocin), lithium, or aminoglycoside antibiotics.
- you will have surgery with general anesthesia.
- you are unsure how much to take or how often to take it.

Possible Side Effects (natural, expected, and unavoidable drug actions)
Light-headedness on arising from sitting or lying position (see Orthostatic Hypotension in Glossary).
Hearing impairment (ototoxicity)—rare.
Increase in level of blood sugar, affecting control of diabetes.
Increase in level of blood uric acid, affecting control of gout.
Decreased blood potassium and sodium with muscle weakness and cramping.
Decreased blood magnesium. Increased calcium loss in the urine (calciuria).

▷ **Possible Adverse Effects** (unusual, unexpected, and infrequent reactions)
If any of the following develop, consult your physician promptly for guidance.
Mild Adverse Effects
Allergic reactions: skin rashes, hives, itching.
Headache, dizziness, vertigo, fatigue, weakness, sweating, earache—rare.
Nausea, vomiting, stomach pain, diarrhea—infrequent.
Breast nipple tenderness, joint and muscle pains or cramps—rare.
Serious Adverse Effects
Serious skin rash (Stevens-Johnson Syndrome)—case reports.
Liver coma (in preexisting liver disease)—possible.
Abnormally low magnesium, potassium and sodium (electrolytes): possible with long-term or high-dose use—rare to frequent.
Low white blood cells and platelets (leukopenia and thrombocytopenia)—rare.
Kidney failure—rare.
Pseudoporphyuria—case report.
Pancreatitis—case reports.
Elevated blood glucose—infrequent.
Lung fibrosis—case reports.
Hearing toxicity (ototoxicity)—rare.

▷ **Possible Effects on Sexual Function:** Difficulty maintaining an erection; premature ejaculation (0.5 to 2 mg daily)—rare.
Male breast enlargement and tenderness (gynecomastia)—case reports.

Natural Diseases or Disorders That May Be Activated by This Drug
Latent diabetes, gout.

Possible Effects on Laboratory Tests
White blood cell counts: increased—usual; decreased—rare.
Blood platelets: decreased.
Blood sugar (glucose): increased.
Blood lithium or uric acid levels: increased.
Blood potassium, magnesium or chloride: decreased.

CAUTION
1. High doses can cause excessive excretion of water, sodium, and potassium, with loss of appetite, nausea, weakness, confusion, and profound drop in blood pressure (circulatory collapse). Magnesium may also be lost and should be checked and replaced as needed.

2. May cause digitalis toxicity by depleting potassium. If you are taking a digitalis preparation (digitoxin, digoxin), ensure an adequate intake of high-potassium foods.
3. People with cirrhosis of the liver must never increase their dose unless told to do so by their doctor. Excess dosing can cause liver coma.
4. People who take lithium may experience lithium toxicity.
5. Use with aminoglycoside antibiotics may increase risk of ear problems (ototoxicity).

Precautions for Use

By Infants and Children: Safety and effectiveness for those under 18 years of age not established.

By Those Over 60 Years of Age: Small starting doses are advisable. You may be more susceptible to the development of impaired thinking, orthostatic hypotension, potassium loss, and elevation of blood sugar. Overdose and prolonged use can cause excessive loss of body water, thickening of the blood, and an increased risk of blood clots, stroke, heart attack, or thrombophlebitis.

▷ Advisability of Use During Pregnancy

Pregnancy Category: C, D by one researcher. See Pregnancy Risk Categories at the back of this book.

Animal Studies: Ten times the maximum therapeutic human dose caused bone defects in rabbits.

Human Studies: Adequate studies of pregnant women are not available.

Only used in pregnancy if a very serious complication of pregnancy occurs for which this drug is significantly beneficial.

Advisability of Use If Breast-Feeding

Presence of this drug in breast milk: Unknown.
Avoid drug or refrain from nursing.

Habit-Forming Potential: None.

Effects of Overdose: Weakness, lethargy, dizziness, confusion, nausea, vomiting, muscle cramps, thirst, electrolyte disturbances, drowsiness progressing to deep sleep or coma, weak and rapid pulse.

Possible Effects of Long-Term Use: Impaired balance of water, magnesium, salt, and potassium in blood and body tissues. Dehydration with possible increased blood viscosity and potential for abnormal clotting. Increased blood sugar in some patients. Osteoporosis due to increased calcium loss in the urine.

Suggested Periodic Examinations While Taking This Drug (at physician's discretion)

Complete blood counts.
Blood levels of sodium, potassium, magnesium, chloride, sugar, uric acid.
Liver and kidney function tests.
Bone mineral density tests (with long term use).

▷ While Taking This Drug, Observe the Following

Foods: Salt restriction and a high-potassium diet may be needed. Ask your doctor. See Table 13, High-Potassium Foods.

Herbal Medicines or Minerals: Ginseng, hawthorn, saw palmetto, ma huang, goldenseal, guarana, and licorice may cause increased blood pressure. Calcium and garlic may help lower blood pressure. Dandelion root has diuretic properties. Talk to your doctor BEFORE combining any herbals with this medicine.

Beverages: No restrictions unless directed by your doctor. May be taken with milk.

▷ *Alcohol:* Alcohol can exaggerate the blood pressure lowering effect of this drug and cause orthostatic hypotension (see Glossary).

Tobacco Smoking: No interactions expected. I advise everyone to quit smoking.

▷ *Other Drugs*

Bumetanide may ***increase*** the effects of:
- antihypertensive drugs. Careful decreases in dose are needed to prevent excessive lowering of the blood pressure.

Bumetanide ***taken concurrently*** with:
- ACE inhibitors (see Drug Classes) may result in severe lowering of blood pressure on standing (postural or orthostatic hypotension).
- aminoglycoside antibiotics (amikacin, gentamicin, kanamycin, neomycin, streptomycin, tobramycin, viomycin) increases the risk of hearing loss (ototoxicity).
- cephalosporins (see Drug Classes) may increase risk of kidney toxicity.
- cortisone-related drugs may cause excessive potassium loss and also blunted therapeutic benefits.
- digitalis-related drugs (digoxin-Lanoxin, others—see Drug Classes) requires very careful monitoring to prevent serious disturbances of heart rhythm.
- lithium (Lithobid, others) may increase lithium toxicity risk.

The following drugs may ***decrease*** the effects of bumetanide:
- indomethacin (Indocin) or other NSAIDs (see Drug Classes) may reduce its diuretic effect.

▷ *Driving, Hazardous Activities:* Caution: Varying degrees of dizziness, weakness, or orthostatic hypotension (see Glossary) may occur.

Aviation Note: The use of this drug ***may be a disqualification*** for piloting. Consult a designated Aviation Medical Examiner.

Exposure to Sun: No restrictions.

Occurrence of Unrelated Illness: Report vomiting or diarrhea promptly to your doctor.

Discontinuation: It may be advisable to stop this drug 5 to 7 days before major surgery. Ask your doctor for help.

BUPROPION (byu PROH pee on)

Other Name: Amfebutamone **Introduced:** 1986 **Class:** Antidepressant **Prescription:** USA: Yes **Controlled Drug:** USA: No; Canada: No **Available as Generic:** USA: Yes

Brand Names: Wellbutrin, Wellbutrin SR, Zyban

```
                        BENEFITS versus RISKS
        Possible Benefits                    Possible Risks
EFFECTIVE IN SMOKING                DRUG-INDUCED SEIZURES—RARE
  CESSATION (ZYBAN)                 Excessive mental stimulation:
EFFECTIVE TREATMENT OF                excitement, anxiety, confusion,
  MAJOR DEPRESSIVE                    hallucinations, insomnia
  DISORDERS                         Conversion of depression to mania in
SEXUAL DESIRE MAY BE                  manic-depressive disorders
  INCREASED IN SOME PEOPLE          57 case reports of people who smoked
  AND USED IN TREATMENT               and who took Zyban and died have
MAY HELP ADHD IN ADULTS               been made in the United Kingdom
Offers a different class than tricyclic,  (reports contained both seizures
  MAO or SSRI antidepressants          and heart attacks)
```

▷ **Principal Uses**

As a Single Drug Product: Uses currently included in FDA-approved labeling: (1) Helps smokers quit smoking (Zyban); (2) treatment of major depressive disorders.

Other (unlabeled) generally accepted uses: (1) May ease chronic fatigue syndrome symptoms; (2) can reduce cocaine craving when combined with psychotherapy; (3) drug of choice in people who have significant weight gain while taking tricyclic antidepressants; (4) can help some cases of low back pain not responding to other agents; (5) increased sexual desire in 77% of patients in one study; (6) an Alabama Veterans Affairs medical center study found this drug to be effective in post-traumatic stress disorder; (7) works to help people stop using smokeless tobacco; (8) is an alternative to stimulant-type medicines to treat attention deficit hyperactivity disorder (ADHD) based on one cohort study with variable dosing (both in children and in adults); (8) useful in chronic fatigue syndrome; (9) eases periodic limb movement disorder.

How This Drug Works: Bupropion increases levels of two nerve transmitters (norepinephrine and dopamine). It is biochemically unique and works differently from other antidepressants (may be a benefit if other medicines have failed). How it works in quitting smoking is unknown.

Available Dosage Forms and Strengths

Tablets, immediate release — 75 mg, 100 mg

Tablets, sustained release — 50 mg (Canada), 100 mg, 150 mg, 200 mg

Zyban Tablets, sustained release only — 150 mg

▷ **Recommended Dosage Ranges** (Actual dose and schedule must be determined for each patient individually.)

Infants and Children: Dosage not established for those under 18 years of age.

18 to 60 Years of Age:

Depression: For first 3 days, 100 mg in the morning and evening. On the fourth day, dose may be increased to 100 mg in the morning, at noon, and in the evening; total daily dose of 300 mg. This schedule of 100 mg, three times daily, 6 hours apart, is used for 3 to 4 weeks. If needed and beneficial, dose may be slowly increased to a maximum of 450 mg daily. Increases should not exceed 100 mg per day in a period of 3 days. No single dose should exceed 150 mg. If daily dose is 450 mg, take 150 mg in the morning, then 100 mg every 4 hours for three more doses. The lowest effective dose should be used. Drug should be stopped if significant improvement is not seen after a trial of 450 mg daily. Doses higher than 450 mg daily may only increase risk of seizures. For the sustained release (SR) form, the starting dose is 150 mg in the morning.

Smoking cessation: 150 mg once a day for 3 days, then 150 mg twice daily for 7 to 12 weeks. If progress has not been made in 7 weeks, talk with your doctor.

ADHD in adults: 100 to 200 mg of the SR form twice daily.

Over 60 Years of Age: Same as 18 to 60 years of age.

Conditions Requiring Dosing Adjustments

Liver Function: Lower dosages and caution in monitoring should be used.

Kidney Function: Not specifically studied in Zyban form; however, prudent to decrease the dose in people with damaged kidneys or who develop kidney damage while taking this drug.

Dosing Instructions: May be taken with food to reduce stomach upset. Best to swallow the tablet whole, not chewing or crushing it; this drug has a bitter taste and a local numbing effect on the lining of the mouth. Sustained-release forms should never be crushed or altered. If you forget a dose (and you take the regular-release tablets): Take the medicine right away, unless it is nearly time for your next dose. When this medicine is being used to help stop smoking, it takes about a week to achieve needed blood levels. The medicine should be started while the patient is still smoking and a quit date decided on by both patient and doctor in the second week. For the sustained-release forms: If you miss a dose, don't take the missed dose, simply take the next scheduled dose. DO NOT double doses. Call your doctor if you miss more than one dose. Some doctors use combined therapy with bupropion and nicotine "patches" (transdermals).

Usual Duration of Use: Regular use for 3–4 weeks needed to realize benefits in depression. Long-term use (months to years) requires periodic evaluation of response and dose. Some clinical guidelines suggest that 4–9 months of treatment should continue after the symptoms of depression go away. Some clinicians use lower ongoing doses to prevent depression. People who take their medicine regularly are least likely to have a recurrence.

For use in quitting smoking: Use for 7–12 weeks (although likelihood of quitting decreases if little progress occurs after 7 weeks). Some cases of success where 300 mg was used for 6 months have been reported. ADHD treatment continues into adulthood for many (some studies indicate 60%) patients. See your doctor regularly.

Typical Treatment Goals and Measurements (Outcomes and Markers)

Depression: The general goal: to help lessen the degree and severity of depression, letting patients return to their daily lives. In a set of guidelines issued by the American College of Physicians, older and newer antidepressants were found to give equal results in treating depression. Older medicines were found to generally have more frequent constipation, dizziness, dry mouth, blurred vision, and tremors while newer medicines caused more diarrhea, headache and nausea. The importance here is that many options are available and possible side effects can be somewhat tailored to try to avoid overlap. Activities of living (ADLs) and interest level can help tell patients when the medicine is starting to show benefits. The Hamilton Depression Scale is a useful measure of success in depression treatment for clinicians.

Smoking Cessation: The general goal: to stop smoking. Combination with a "quit smoking" course and/or support group can increase beneficial results.

▷ **Possible Advantages of This Drug**

Causes less atropinelike side effects: blurred vision, dry mouth, constipation, or impaired urination than other antidepressants. Does not cause sedation or orthostatic hypotension (see Glossary). Some clinicians use it for add on therapy for existing depression treatments. May cause **weight loss** instead of weight gain like other antidepressants. Avoids stimulant effects possible with stimulant type medicine for ADHD such as methylphenidate (Ritalin).

▷ **This Drug Should Not Be Taken If**

• you have had an allergic reaction to it previously.
• you have a history of anorexia nervosa or bulimia (may be associated with increased seizure risk).
• you have a seizure disorder of any kind (while not a disorder, this includes people who have recently had to suddenly stop sedatives [such as Valium—diazepam] or alcohol).
• you are taking, or took in the past 14 days, any monoamine oxidase (MAO) type A inhibitor (see Drug Classes).

▷ **Inform Your Physician Before Taking This Drug If**

• you have had any adverse effects from antidepressant drugs.
• you are pregnant or planning pregnancy.
• you are breast-feeding your infant.
• you have a history of mental illness, head injury, or brain tumor.
• you have a history of alcoholism or drug abuse.
• you have any kind of heart disease, especially a recent heart attack.
• you have impaired liver or kidney function.
• you take prescription or nonprescription drugs not discussed when bupropion was prescribed for you.
• you take other medicines that can make seizures more likely.

Possible Side Effects (natural, expected, and unavoidable drug actions)

Nervousness, anxiety, confusion, insomnia (may be frequent), tremor.
Weight loss of more than 5 pounds—frequent (19–28% depending on the product).

▷ **Possible Adverse Effects** (unusual, unexpected, and infrequent reactions)

If any of the following develop, consult your physician promptly for guidance.

Mild Adverse Effects

Allergic reactions: skin rash, itching—rare to infrequent.
Headache, dizziness, tremor (dose related), agitation (9.7% more than placebo) or blurred vision (4.3% more than placebo)—infrequent.
Agitation—common.
Vivid dreaming—possible (more likely with higher doses).
Indigestion, nausea and vomiting, constipation—infrequent.
Dry mouth or edema—frequent.
Taste disorders (taste perversion)—infrequent and may be dose related.
Excessive sweating (diaphoresis)—frequent.
Bruising (ecchymosis)—possible (prudent to tell your doctor if this happens).
Ringing in the ears (tinnitus)—possible.
Palpitations—frequent.
Increased blood pressure—possible to infrequent.

Serious Adverse Effects

Drug-induced seizures—rare, more common with high doses (roughly 0.4% with 400 mg a day of Wellbutrin SR).

Change of depression to mania in manic-depressive disorders—possible.

Psychosis in patients with psychotic predisposition—possible.

Migraine headache—may be common.

Increased blood pressure (hypertension)—infrequent but may be significant In people who had high blood pressure before starting bupropion.

Decreased (leukopenia) or increased (leukocytosis) white blood cell counts or low platelets—case reports.

Liver toxicity—case reports.

Rhabdomyolysis—case report.

Movement disorders—possible, but not causally proven.

Heart attack/arrhythmia—case reports (in the United Kingdom—238 reports of chest pain and 134 cases of chest tightness were reported—call your doctor if you have these signs or symptoms).

▷ **Possible Effects on Sexual Function:** A study at the University of Alabama found 77% of patients experienced increased sexual desire. Clitoral priapism was reported in one case report.

Impotence—infrequent; however, another study reported a decrease in sexual dysfunction when patients were switched from fluoxetine (Prozac) to bupropion.

Altered menstruation up to 3.6% more than placebo in clinical trials—infrequent.

Possible Delayed Adverse Effects: Tardive dyskinesia.

Natural Diseases or Disorders That May Be Activated by This Drug

Latent epilepsy, latent psychosis, manic phase of bipolar affective disorder.

Possible Effects on Laboratory Tests

White blood cell or platelet counts: increased or decreased.

CAUTION

1. Take exactly the amount prescribed; rapid dose increases can cause seizures. Watch closely for excessive stimulation.
2. Ask your doctor or pharmacist BEFORE taking any other prescription or nonprescription drug.
2. Do not take any monoamine oxidase (MAO) type A inhibitor while taking this drug (see Drug Classes). If you have taken a MAO inhibitor, wait 2 weeks before starting bupropion
3. 57 case reports of people who smoked and who also took Zyban and died have been made in the United Kingdom (reports contained both seizures and heart attacks).

Precautions for Use

By Infants and Children: Safety and effectiveness for those under 18 years of age not established.

By Those Over 60 Years of Age: Age-related liver or kidney function decline may require dose decreases.

▷ **Advisability of Use During Pregnancy**

Pregnancy Category: B. See Pregnancy Risk Categories at the back of this book.

Animal Studies: Rat and rabbit studies reveal no significant birth defects.

Human Studies: Adequate studies of pregnant women are not available.

Use this drug only if clearly needed. Ask your doctor for help. A pregnancy registry has been established at 888-825-5249. Encourage your doctor to register you if you have taken this medicine while pregnant.

Advisability of Use If Breast-Feeding
Presence of this drug in breast milk: Yes.
Avoid drug or refrain from nursing.

Habit-Forming Potential: Remote with use of recommended doses. Slight potential for abuse by those who abuse stimulant drugs.

Effects of Overdose: Headache, agitation, confusion, hallucinations, seizures, loss of consciousness.

Possible Effects of Long-Term Use: Not reported.

Suggested Periodic Examinations While Taking This Drug (at physician's discretion)
Liver and/or kidney function tests as appropriate. Check of weight and blood pressure.

▷ **While Taking This Drug, Observe the Following**
Foods: No restrictions.
Herbal Medicines or Minerals: Ginseng, ma huang, yohimbe, and St. John's wort may interact with antidepressants, so combining those herbals with this medicine is not recommended.
Beverages: No restrictions. May be taken with milk.
▷ *Alcohol:* Avoid completely. Alcohol may predispose to the development of seizures.
Tobacco Smoking: I advise everyone to quit smoking.
Marijuana Smoking: Avoid completely; it may lead to psychotic behavior.
▷ *Other Drugs*
The following drugs *taken concurrently* with bupropion may *increase* the risk of major seizures:
• antidepressants (tricyclic) or other bupropion-containing medicines.
• clozapine (Clozaril).
• fluoxetine (Prozac).
• guanfacine (Tenex).
• haloperidol (Haldol).
• lithium (Lithobid, others).
• loxapine (Loxitane).
• maprotiline (Ludiomil).
• molindone (Moban).
• phenothiazines (see Drug Classes).
• thioxanthenes (see Xanthine Drug Class).
• trazodone (Desyrel).
Bupropion *taken concurrently* with
• carbamazepine (Tegretol) may result in lowered carbamazepine levels.
• cimetidine (Tagamet) may lead to increased bupropion levels.
• flecainide (Tambocor) may lead to increased flecainide levels (interference with P450 2D6). The manufacturer suggests that flecainide doses be used at the lower end of the dose range if these medicines are combined. Flecainide blood levels are prudent.
• levodopa results in increased nausea, restlessness and tremor.
• MAO inhibitors (see Drug Classes) can lead to sudden toxicity. Do not combine.
• metoprolol (Toprol XL, others) can lead to toxicity. Lower metoprolol doses are prudent.
• phenobarbital may result in decreased levels.

- phenytoin (Dilantin) or fosphenytoin (Cerebyx) may result in decreased phenytoin or fosphenytoin levels.
- propafenone (Rythmol) can lead to toxicity. Lower propafenone doses and blood levels are prudent.
- risperidone (Risperdal), sertraline (Zoloft) and other medicines removed from the body by P450 2D6 may lead to increased blood levels of the medicine removed by P450 2D6. Lower doses and careful patient follow-up are prudent if these medicines are combined.
- ritonavir (Norvir) and probably other protease inhibitors may lead to increased blood levels of bupropion and toxicity—DO NOT COMBINE.
- zolpidem (Ambien) may lead to hallucinations.

▷ *Driving, Hazardous Activities:* This drug may cause dizziness, drowsiness or seizures. Restrict activities as necessary.

Aviation Note: The use of this drug *is a disqualification* for piloting. Consult a designated Aviation Medical Examiner.

Exposure to Sun: No restrictions.

Discontinuation: Do not stop this drug abruptly. Ask your doctor for help.

BUSPIRONE (byu SPI rohn)

Introduced: 1979 **Class:** Antianxiety drug **Prescription:** USA: Yes **Controlled Drug:** USA: No; Canada: No **Available as Generic:** Yes

Brand Names: ❧Apo-buspirone, Buspar, Buspar Dividose, ❧Buspirex, ❧Med-buspirone, ❧Buspirex, Censpar, Sorbon

BENEFITS versus RISKS	
Possible Benefits	*Possible Risks*
EFFECTIVE RELIEF OF MILD TO MODERATE ANXIETY	Mild dizziness, faintness, or headache—uncommon
DECREASED RISK OF SEDATION OR DEPENDENCE THAN OTHER AGENTS	Tachycardia—rare
	Restlessness, depression, tremor, or rigidity (with high doses)—rare

▷ **Principal Uses**

As a Single Drug Product: Uses currently included in FDA-approved labeling: (1) Relieves mild to moderate anxiety and nervous tension (useful in elderly, alcoholics and addiction-prone people because of its lack of significant sedative effects or abuse potential); (2) helps control self-injurious behaviors or aggression in developmentally disabled adults.

Other (unlabeled) generally accepted uses: (1) May reduce alcohol craving in alcoholics; (2) can help aggression or hyperactivity in people living with autism; (3) may decrease symptoms in obsessive-compulsive disorder; (4) can help in sexual dysfunction in people with generalized anxiety disorder; (5) may help decrease smoking urge in smokers; (6) can help prevent chronic tension headaches and migraines; (7) some data with success in treatment resistant depression and for those with anxiety and depression; (8) may have a role in preventing (prophylaxis) of migraines; (9) could have a role in easing post-traumatic stress disorder.

How This Drug Works: Changes brain chemicals (dopamine, norepinephrine, serotonin), resulting in a calming effect. Decreases actions of serotonin using nerve cells (neurons) in part of the brain (nuclei raphe). Also a partial agonist at serotonin reuptake sites (5HT1A).

Available Dosage Forms and Strengths

Tablets — 5 mg, 10 mg, 15 mg, 30 mg
Tablets scored (Dividose) — 15 mg, 30 mg

▷ **Usual Adult Dosage Ranges:** Initially 7.5 mg twice daily; if needed, dose can be increased by 5 mg/day every 2 or 3 days as needed and tolerated. Some patients respond well to total daily doses of 20–30 mg which are divided into two or three equal doses. Maximum daily dose is 60 mg.

Note: Actual dose and schedule must be determined for each patient individually.

Conditions Requiring Dosing Adjustments

Liver Function: Doses should be decreased in people with compromised livers. The manufacturer does NOT support use in people with compromised liver function.

Kidney Function: One study based on kinetics suggested a the dose should be lowered to 25–50% of normal dose in people with mild to severe kidney compromise. The manufacturer does NOT recommend this medicine for people with severely impaired kidneys.

▷ **Dosing Instructions:** The tablet may be crushed and taken without regard to food—however, it is best to always take it with or without food in order to help keep blood levels steady. DO NOT take this medicine with grapefruit juice—take it with water. If you forget a dose, but have missed by less than an hour, take the missed dose. If it is almost time for your next scheduled dose, skip the missed dose and simply take the next scheduled dose. DO NOT double doses. Some researchers have reported this medicine to be equal to diazepam (Valium) in treating anxiety. If this medicine is meant to replace previous benzodiazepine use such as diazepam, the benzodiazepine should be slowly withdrawn (tapered) before the buspirone is started.

Usual Duration of Use: Regular use for 7 to 14 days may be needed to see full benefit in relieving anxiety and nervous tension. Continual use should not exceed 8 weeks without evaluation by your doctor.

Author's Note: The National Institute of Mental Health has a good information page on anxiety, and anxious reactions to terrorism. It can be found on the World Wide Web (*www.nimh.nih.gov/anxiety*).

Typical Treatment Goals and Measurements (Outcomes and Markers)

Anxiety or panic: Goals for anxiety and panic tend to be more vague and subjective than hypertension or cholesterol. Frequently, the patient (in conjunction with physician assessment) will largely decide if anxiety has been modified to a successful extent. In the case of panic attacks, decreased number of trips to the hospital or emergency department visits may be a useful measure. In both cases, the ability of the patient to return to normal activities is a hallmark of successful treatment. The Hamilton Anxiety Scale is used by many physicians.

Possible Advantages of This Drug: Relieves anxiety or tension without severe sedation or impaired thinking. Low abuse potential compared to benzodiazepines. May be a drug of choice in patients prone to getting addicted and also in people with lung disease.

▷ **This Drug Should Not Be Taken If**
  • you have had an allergic reaction to this medicine.
  • you take, or took in the last 2 weeks, a MAO inhibitor (see Drug Classes). May increase blood pressure.

▷ **Inform Your Physician Before Taking This Drug If**
  • you take other drugs that affect the brain or nervous system: tranquilizers, sedatives, hypnotics, analgesics, narcotics, antidepressants, antipsychotic drugs, anticonvulsants, or anti-Parkinsonism drugs.
  • you have impaired liver or kidney function.
  • you take fluoxetine (Prozac) for depression.
  • you are prone to fast heart rate (tachycardia).

Possible Side Effects (natural, expected, and unavoidable drug actions)
  Mild drowsiness (less than with benzodiazepines) (may be more likely with higher doses up to 8%)—infrequent; lethargy is possible. Infrequent dry mouth. Case reports of bed-wetting (enuresis).

▷ **Possible Adverse Effects** (unusual, unexpected, and infrequent reactions)
  If any of the following develop, consult your physician promptly for guidance.
  Mild Adverse Effects
  Headache, faintness, paradoxical excitement—infrequent.
  Nervousness—infrequent.
  Dizziness—infrequent.
  Tingling and touch sensation changes (paresthesias)—rare.
  Insomnia and dream disturbances, racing thoughts, or depression—possible.
  Increased blood pressure—case reports.
  Nausea—infrequent.
  Serious Adverse Effects
  Tachycardia or palpitations—infrequent but greater than seen with diazepam.
  With high doses: dysphoria, restlessness, rigidity, tremors—possible (may be more likely with high doses).
  Movement disorders—case reports.
  Apnea increases (in some patients with sleep apnea)—possible.

▷ **Possible Effects on Sexual Function:** Difficult or absent orgasm—case report.
  May increase prolactin; however, no cases of male breast tenderness or enlargement have been reported. One case of painful and sustained erection (priapism).

Possible Effects on Laboratory Tests
  Growth hormone: Conflicting increases or lack of effect on growth hormone levels.
  Blood prolactin levels: dose-related increase.
  May or may not change (increase delta or theta waves) on the EEG.

CAUTION
  1. This drug is reported to have very mild sedative effects and no abuse potential; however, it should be used with caution and only when clearly needed. Actual dysphoria has been reported with higher doses and may preclude its recreational use.
  2. Best to take this medicine the same way (with or without food) to help keep the blood levels steady.

Precautions for Use
  By Infants and Children: Safety and effectiveness for those under 18 years of age not established.

By Those Over 60 Years of Age: Expected to be tolerated much better than benzodiazepines and barbiturates. Watch for increased dizziness or weakness and avoid falls.

▷ **Advisability of Use During Pregnancy**
Pregnancy Category: B. See Pregnancy Risk Categories at the back of this book.
Animal Studies: No birth defects found in rat and rabbit studies.
Human Studies: Adequate studies of pregnant women are not available.
Discuss any use of this drug during pregnancy with your doctor.

Advisability of Use If Breast-Feeding
Presence of this drug in breast milk: Excreted in rat milk; probably also in humans.
Avoid drug or refrain from nursing.

Habit-Forming Potential: Does not appear to cause addiction; however, more studies are needed. Higher doses result in a dysphoric reaction, which may keep it from becoming a drug involved in recreational use.

Effects of Overdose: Drowsiness, fatigue, nausea, dysphoria, tingling sensations (paresthesias), and a rare chance of seizures.

Possible Effects of Long-Term Use: None reported.

Suggested Periodic Examinations While Taking This Drug (at physician's discretion)
Periodic check of heart rate and of course, success in controlling anxiety.

▷ **While Taking This Drug, Observe the Following**
Foods: No restrictions; taking with food may result in a clinically insignificant increase in absorption of this drug.
Herbal Medicines or Minerals: Hawthorn, guarana, and ephedra may react antagonistically to buspirone. Avoid those medicines. Valerian may interact additively (drowsiness) and has not been recommended because of liver toxicity concerns. Hops, Indian snakeroot, passionflower herb, and St. John's wort carry German Commission E monograph indications for anxiety. Indian snakeroot and kava kava (not recommended in Canada) are contraindicated in depression and well-designed studies in anxiety combined with this medicine are not available. Talk to your doctor BEFORE you take any herbal medicine with buspirone.
Beverages: No restrictions.
▷ *Alcohol:* Milder problems than diazepam (Valium), but avoid the combination.
Tobacco Smoking: No interactions expected. I advise everyone to quit smoking.
Marijuana Smoking: Additive increase in drowsiness.
▷ *Other Drugs:*
Buspirone ***taken concurrently*** with
• citalopram (Celexa) may result in serotonin syndrome. This combination is not advisable.
• clozapine (Clozaril) may result in serious lowering of blood sugar and stomach bleeding.
• diazepam (Valium) may increase risk of headache, dizziness, and nausea.
• diltiazem (Cardizem, etc.) may increase buspirone drug concentrations. Watch for increased drowsiness—lower buspirone doses may be needed.
• dofetilide (Tikosyn) may increase blood levels of dofetilide and risk of adverse effects. If this combination must be used, low doses of dofetilide and careful patient follow-up are critical.
• erythromycin (various) may increase blood levels of buspirone and risk of adverse effects.

- fluoxetine (Prozac) may increase underlying anxiety or mental disorder such as obsessive-compulsive disorder. Combination is best avoided, but if deemed clinically necessary, patients should be closely watched for worsening of symptoms.
- fluvoxamine (Luvox) resulted in serious slowing of the heart (bradycardia) in one case report (peak buspirone level was doubled). A later trial in healthy volunteers found elevated blood levels, but no clinical changes. Caution is advised.
- itraconazole (and perhaps other similar antifungals) may increase blood levels of buspirone and risk of adverse effects.
- MAO inhibitors (see Drug Classes) such as phenelzine (Nardil) may result in large blood pressure increases. DO NOT COMBINE.
- narcotics such as oxycodone (Percodan) may result in additive sedation and potential decreases in breathing (respiratory depression).
- nefazodone (Serzone) may increase blood levels of buspirone and risk of adverse effects. If this combination must be used, low doses of buspirone and careful patient follow-up are critical.
- paroxetine (Paxil) may increase blood levels of buspirone and risk of adverse effects. If this combination must be used, lower doses of buspirone and careful patient follow-up are critical.
- rifampin (Rifater, others) may decrease buspirone blood levels. If this combination must be used, buspirone doses may need to be increased.
- trazodone (Desyrel) may lead to liver toxicity. Liver tests should be obtained regularly if the two drugs are combined.
- venlafaxine (Effexor) may lead to decreased buspirone benefits or venlafaxine toxicity.
- verapamil (Calan, etc.) may increase blood levels of buspirone and risk of adverse effects.

▷ *Driving, Hazardous Activities:* This drug may cause dizziness, faintness, or fatigue. Restrict activities as necessary.

Aviation Note: The use of this drug *may be a disqualification* for piloting. Consult a designated Aviation Medical Examiner.

Exposure to Sun: No restrictions.

CALCITONIN (kal si TOH nin)

Other Names: Salcatonin, thyrocalcitonin

Introduced: 1977, 1995 (nasal spray form)   **Class:**   Anti-osteoporotic, hormone **Prescription:**   USA: Yes   **Controlled Drug:**   USA: No; Canada: No   **Available as Generic:**   USA: Yes (one injectable form); Canada: No

Brand Names: Calcimar, Cibacalcin, Miacalcin Injection, Miacalcin Nasal Spray

---

BENEFITS versus RISKS

Possible Benefits	*Possible Risks*
PARTIAL RELIEF OF SYMPTOMS OF PAGET'S DISEASE OF BONE	Nausea (with or without vomiting) Allergic reactions
NASAL FORM CAN INCREASE BONE MASS	
Effective adjunctive treatment of postmenopausal osteoporosis	
Effective adjunctive treatment of abnormally high blood calcium levels (associated with malignant disease)	

Author's Note: Information in this profile has been shortened to make room for more widely used medicines.

CAPECITABINE (CAP eh sit ah been)

Introduced: 2001 for colon cancer **Class:** Antineoplastic **Prescription:** USA: Yes **Controlled Drug:** USA: No; Canada: No **Available as Generic:** No

Brand Names: Xeloda

Author's Note: This medicine was first approved for treatment of breast cancer, and now has been approved for treatment of metastatic colorectal cancer. This first treatment for such cancers to be available taken by mouth (oral), capecitabine is changed (metabolized) into 5-fluorouracil in the body. Capecitabine causes fewer mouth ulcers and less diarrhea and nausea, but seems to cause pain and swelling of the hands and feet more frequently than other therapies. Information in this profile will be broadened further when more specific information becomes available. An excellent and evidence based review of cancer treatments is available from *www.cancer.gov/cancerinfo/pdq/treatment/colon/HealthProfessional.*

CAPTOPRIL (KAP toh pril)

Introduced: 1979 **Class:** ACE inhibitor, antihypertensive

Please see the new angiotensin converting enzyme (ACE) inhibitor family profile for more information.

CARBAMAZEPINE (kar ba MAZ e peen)

Introduced: 1962 **Class:** Anticonvulsant, antineuralgic, pain syndrome modifier, mood stabilizer **Prescription:** USA: Yes **Controlled Drug:** USA: No; Canada: No **Available as Generic:** Yes

Brand Names: ✤Apo-Carbamazepine, Carbitrol Extended Release, ✤ Dom-carbamazepine-CR, Epitol, ✤Gen-Carbamazepine CR, ✤Mazepine, ✤Novo-Carbamaz, ✤PMS Carbamazepine, Taro-carbamazepine CR, Tegretol, Tegretol Chewable Tablet, ✤Tegretol-CR, Tegretol-XR

BENEFITS versus RISKS

Possible Benefits	*Possible Risks*
RELIEF OF PAIN IN TRIGEMINAL NEURALGIA	BONE MARROW DEPRESSION (reduced formation of all blood
EFFECTIVE CONTROL OF CERTAIN TYPES OF EPILEPTIC SEIZURES	cells)—RARE Liver damage with jaundice—rare
EFFECTIVE IN SUDDEN ONSET AND IN PREVENTING BIPOLAR DISORDER	
Relief of pain in some rare forms of nerve pain (neuralgia)	

▷ **Principal Uses**

As a Single Drug Product: Uses currently included in FDA-approved labeling: (1) pain relief in true trigeminal neuralgia (tic douloureux) or glossopharyngeal neuralgia; (2) for control of several types of epilepsy (grand mal, tonic-clonic, psychomotor/temporal lobe, complex partial and mixed seizure patterns as well as infantile spasms or myoclonic-astatic seizures). Precise diagnosis and careful management are mandatory.

Other (unlabeled) generally accepted uses: Beneficial in (1) bipolar affective disorders; (2) schizoaffective disorders; (3) resistant schizophrenia; (4) post-traumatic stress disorder; (5) tabes dorsalis; (6) diabetic neuropathy; (7) hemifacial spasm; (8) cocaine withdrawal; (9) aggression in some Alzheimer's patients; (10) helping hiccups and belching associated with flutter of the diaphragm; (11) treating nerve problems from thiamine deficiency; (12) has a role in pain that occurs when an arm or leg is amputated (phantom limb pain) and pain associated with depression; (13) easing a perceived repetitive ear noise called clicking tinnitus; (14) case reports of being helpful in people having difficulty making purposeful movements even though they have normal coordination and muscle power (apraxia).

How This Drug Works: Reduces impulses at certain nerve terminals and relieves pain (of trigeminal neuralgia). Also reduces excitability of nerve fibers in the brain, decreasing likelihood, frequency, and severity of seizures.

Available Dosage Forms and Strengths

Oral suspension — 100 mg/5 ml, 200 mg/5 ml

Tablets — 200 mg (400 mg in Canada)

Tablets, chewable — 100 mg, 200 mg

Tablets, controlled release — 200 mg, 400 mg

Tablets, extended release — 100 mg, 200 mg, 300 mg, 400 mg

▷ **Recommended Dosage Ranges:**

Epilepsy: Initially 200 mg every 12 hours (regular or extended-release tablets). Suspension is started at 100 mg four times a day. Dose may be increased at weekly intervals by 200 mg daily as needed and tolerated and as guided by drug levels. The dose is given twice daily for the extended-release tablets (in general, extended-release forms are given in the same total daily dose—but are given less often). The regular release tablets are given three times daily. Because suspensions give higher peak blood levels in the body, they are generally given in smaller, more frequent doses. Total daily dosage should generally not exceed 1,200 mg, but rare uses of 1,600 mg have been required.

Migraine prevention (prophylaxis): 10–20 mg per kg of body weight per day separated into two equal daily doses has been used.

Trigeminal neuralgia: 50 mg of the suspension four times daily or 100 mg twice daily (tablets or extended release form). Dose is then increased as needed and tolerated to 400–800 mg daily with a 1,200 mg maximum. Every three months you and your doctor should try to lower the dose to the minimum dose that works (minimum effective dose) and to discontinue the medicine.

Bipolar disorder: Required doses have been in the 2,000–3,000 mg a day, but most people respond to 600–1,600 mg a day. Patients who go from mania to depression quickly (rapid cycling patients) may need 1,000–2,000 mg a day to help ease the swings in mood.

Infants and Children: Children under age 6 are given 10–20 mg per kg of body mass. This dose is divided into two to three equal doses and is given two to three times daily. The suspension dosing is the same daily dose divided into 4 equal doses given four times daily. Increased as needed or tolerated based on clinical response and blood levels, with a maximum dose of 35 mg/kg/day. Children over 12 are given 200 mg twice daily or 100 mg of the suspension four times daily. The dose can then be increased by 200 mg a day after a week, as needed and tolerated—guided by blood levels and clinical response. The typical dose that works is in the range of 17–25 mg/kg/day. Maximum is 1,000 mg or lower.

Note: Actual dosage and schedule must be determined for each patient individually. Dosing must be guided by blood levels.

Conditions Requiring Dosing Adjustments

Liver Function: Use with extreme caution, in lower doses and closely watched. Should NOT be used in active liver disease or in worsened liver compromise.

Kidney Function: May be toxic to kidneys. Used with caution.

Heart Attack: Changes in blood distribution (perfusion) and protein binding may give much higher than expected blood levels. More frequent lab tests are needed to guide dosing and avoid toxicity.

▷ **Dosing Instructions:** Take at same time each day, with or following food to reduce stomach irritation. Regular-release tablet may be crushed for administration. Extended-release tablet should not be altered or taken if they are broken. The suspension SHOULD NOT be given at the same time as other medicines or diluents. The suspension will generally give higher peak levels than an equal dose of a tablet form. Patients changed from the tablet to the suspension may be asked to take the same number of milligrams a day, but to take smaller doses more often. If you forget a dose: Take the medicine as soon as you remember it, unless it is close to the time for the next dose—simply take the dose at the next scheduled time. DO NOT double doses. Call your doctor if you miss more than one dose.

Usual Duration of Use: Regular use for 3 months may be needed to see effect in easing of trigeminal neuralgia. Longer periods, with dose changes, may be required for control of epileptic seizures. Careful evaluation of tolerance and response should be made every 3 months during long-term treatment. Every three months, the minimum effective dose should be tried to be found and/or the medicine attempted to be stopped if it is being used to treat trigeminal neuralgia.

Typical Treatment Goals and Measurements (Outcomes and Markers)

Seizures: The general goal for this medicine is effective seizure control. Neurologists tend to define effective on a case-by-case basis depending on the seizure type and patient factors.

Currently a "Drug of Choice"
> For patients with partial seizures (without or with secondary generalization).

▷ **This Drug Should Not Be Taken If**
- you have had an allergic reaction to it previously.
- you have active liver disease.
- you currently have a blood cell or bone marrow disorder.
- you currently take, or have taken within the past 14 days, a monoamine oxidase (MAO) type A inhibitor (see Drug Classes).

▷ **Inform Your Physician Before Taking This Drug If**
- you have had an allergic reaction to any tricyclic antidepressant drug (see Drug Classes).
- you have taken this drug in the past.
- you have had any blood or bone marrow disorder, especially drug induced.
- you have a history of liver or kidney disease.
- you have depression or other mental disorder.
- you have had thrombophlebitis.
- you have high blood pressure, heart disease, increased eye pressure, or glaucoma.
- you take more than two alcoholic drinks a day.
- you take prescription or nonprescription drugs not discussed when carbamazepine was prescribed for you.
- you are unsure how much to take or how often to take it.
- you are pregnant or are breast-feeding your baby.

Possible Side Effects (natural, expected, and unavoidable drug actions)
> Dry mouth and throat, constipation, impaired urination.

▷ **Possible Adverse Effects** (unusual, unexpected, and infrequent reactions)
> **If any of the following develop, consult your physician promptly for guidance.**

Mild Adverse Effects
> Allergic reactions: skin rash, hives, itching, drug fever—rare to infrequent.
> Idiosyncratic reactions (cough or shortness of breath)—possible.
> Dizziness, drowsiness, unsteadiness—may be frequent when therapy is started (often eases).
> Fatigue, blurred vision, confusion—infrequent.
> Exaggerated hearing, ringing in ears—case reports.
> Loss of appetite, nausea, vomiting, indigestion, diarrhea—may be frequent when starting therapy.
> Hair loss—case reports.
> Decreased sense of taste—possible.
> Aching of muscles and joints, leg cramps—case reports.

Serious Adverse Effects
> Allergic reactions: severe dermatitis with peeling of skin (including toxic epidermal necrolysis-TEN and Stevens Johnson Syndrome), irritation of mouth and tongue, swelling of lymph glands—case reports.
> Idiosyncratic reactions: lung inflammation (pneumonitis), may also be an aseptic meningitis mechanism.
> Agranulocytosis may also be idiosyncratic—case reports.
> Pure red cell aplasia—case reports.
> Lowering of white blood cells (leukopenia): may be up to 10%—infrequent.
> Aplastic anemia—rare.

Abnormally low blood platelets—thrombocytopenia (clotting elements on blood)—rare, but tends to happen 2–3 weeks after the medicine is started.

Low thyroid hormones—rare.

Bone marrow depression (see Glossary) (agranulocytosis, hemolytic or aplastic anemia) or thrombocytopenia: fatigue, weakness, fever, sore throat, abnormal bleeding, or bruising—case reports.

Pseudolymphoma or systemic lupus erythematosus—case reports.

Abnormal heartbeats—case reports.

Aggravation of disease of the coronary arteries (CAD)—possible.

Liver damage with jaundice (see Glossary): yellow eyes or skin, dark-colored urine, light-colored stools—case reports.

Kidney damage or porphyria—case reports.

Mental depression or agitation/psychosis or paradoxical increase in seizures—case reports.

Abnormally elevated urine output (SIADH)—case reports.

Neuroleptic malignant syndrome—case reports.

Abnormal movement and muscle contractions—case reports.

Pancreatitis—case reports.

Retinopathy, visual hallucinations, peripheral neuritis (see Glossary)—case reports.

Vitamin D deficiency (especially if other risk factors are present). This may lead to osteoporosis.

▷ **Possible Effects on Sexual Function:**
Decreased libido and/or impotence—case reports.

Possible male infertility.

This drug is used to control hypersexuality (exaggerated sexual behavior) that can result from injury to the temporal lobe of the brain.

Adverse Effects That May Mimic Natural Diseases or Disorders
Liver reactions may suggest viral hepatitis. Lung reactions may suggest interstitial pneumonitis. SLE syndrome mimics SLE.

Natural Diseases or Disorders That May Be Activated by This Drug
Latent psychosis, systemic lupus erythematosus, osteoporosis, heart disease (see homocysteine note below).

Possible Effects on Laboratory Tests
Complete blood cell: decreased red cells, hemoglobin, white cells, and platelets; increased eosinophils, increased white cells.

Blood calcium level: decreased.

Blood sodium: may be lowered in SIADH.

INR (prothrombin time): decreased.

Thyroid hormones: decreased blood levels.

Blood urea nitrogen level (BUN): increased.

Liver function tests: increased liver enzymes (ALT/GPT, AST/GOT, and alkaline phosphatase), increased bilirubin.

Urine pregnancy tests: false negative or inconclusive results with Prepurex, Predictor, Gonavislide, Pregnosticon.

ANA: positive if SLE effect begins.

CAUTION
1. This drug should be used only after less toxic drugs have failed.
2. *Before* the first dose is taken, blood cell counts, liver function tests and kidney function tests should be obtained.

3. Careful periodic testing for blood cell or bone marrow toxicity is ***mandatory***.
4. ***This drug should not be used*** to prevent recurrence of trigeminal neuralgia when it is in remission.
5. ***Do not stop this drug suddenly*** if it is being used to control seizures.
6. If exposed to humidity, tablet hardens, resulting in poor absorption and erratic control of seizures. Store in a cool, dry place; avoid bathrooms. Try a locking kitchen cabinet.
7. Case reports have been made about an allergic (atypical cross-sensitivity) reaction in people who are allergic to phenytoin who are given carbamazepine. Talk to your doctor if you have this allergy and carbamazepine is prescribed for you.
8. If you are prescribed the suspension, usually the same total dose is given, but smaller and more frequent doses are used because the suspension gives a higher peak level.
9. Because of some carbamazepine caused (drug induced) lowering of pyridoxal 5-phosphate and folate, homocysteine levels are increased with this therapy. See foods below.
10. There are reports of people who are allergic to oxcarbazepine also being allergic to carbamazepine (25–30%). This can also happen with phenytoin as noted in number 7 above.
11. Grapefruit and grapefruit juice can lead to toxicity from this medicine. Do not eat grapefruit or drink grapefruit juice while taking this medicine.

Precautions for Use
By Infants and Children: Careful testing of blood production and liver and kidney function must be performed regularly. This drug can reduce the effectiveness of other anticonvulsant drugs. Blood levels of all anticonvulsant drugs should be checked if this drug is added to the treatment program.
By Those Over 60 Years of Age: Can cause confusion and agitation. Watch for aggravation of glaucoma, coronary artery disease (angina), or prostatism (see Glossary).

▷ **Advisability of Use During Pregnancy**
Pregnancy Category: **D.** See Pregnancy Risk Categories at the back of this book.
Animal Studies: Rat studies reveal significant birth defects.
Human Studies: Adequate studies of pregnant women are not available.
Avoid completely during the first 3 months. Use during the last 6 months only if clearly needed.

Advisability of Use If Breast-Feeding
Presence of this drug in breast milk: Yes.
Levels in breast milk appear to be 24 to almost 70% of the mother's plasma level. Discuss avoiding drug or refrain from nursing with your doctor.

Habit-Forming Potential: None.

Effects of Overdose: Dizziness, drowsiness, disorientation, tremor, involuntary movements, nausea, vomiting, flushed skin, dilated pupils, stupor progressing to coma, cardiac arrest.

Possible Effects of Long-Term Use: Water retention (edema), impaired liver function, possible jaundice, possible osteoporosis.

Suggested Periodic Examinations While Taking This Drug (at physician's discretion)
Complete blood counts weekly during the first 3 months and then monthly.

Liver and kidney function tests.

Eye examinations.

Serum iron levels.

Blood levels of the medicine.

Thyroid hormone levels.

Bone mineral density tests (for osteoporosis) and/or check of height.

Homocysteine levels.

▷ **While Taking This Drug, Observe the Following**

Foods: DO NOT eat grapefruit while taking this medicine. There may be a minor increase in absorption if taken with food. Because of drug effects on B vitamins, homocysteine levels are prudent and supplementation with B vitamins while this drug is being taken is also prudent.

Herbal Medicines or Minerals: Using kola, guarana, or ma huang may result in unacceptable central nervous system stimulation. Valerian and kava kava (not recommended in Canada) may interact to increase drowsiness. St. John's wort may increase carbamazepine blood levels and also cause increased sun sensitivity—caution is advised. Some ginkgo products (depending on the amount of 4-o-methylpyridoxine in them) may increase risk of seizures.

Beverages: DO NOT drink grapefruit juice while taking this medicine. May be taken with milk.

▷ *Alcohol:* Avoid alcohol, unless your doctor approves alcohol use.

Tobacco Smoking: No interactions expected. I advise everyone to quit smoking.

▷ *Other Drugs*

Carbamazepine may ***increase*** the effects of

- medicines that increase heart block such at adenosine (Adenocard). Where possible, carbamazepine should not be given until adenosine has cleared from the body (roughly 4.32 or 5 half-lives, which is 4 days).
- sedatives, tranquilizers, hypnotics and narcotics, and enhance their sedative effects.
- voriconazole (Vfend) and lead to much higher than expected blood levels.

Carbamazepine may ***decrease*** the effects of

- adrenocortical steroids (see Drug Classes).
- alprazolam (Xanax).
- amprenavir (Agenerase).
- antidepressants (see Drug Classes).
- bupropion (Wellbutrin, Zyban).
- caspofungin (Cancidas).
- corticosteroids (such as prednisone or cortisone; see Drug Classes).
- cyclosporine (Sandimmune).
- doxycycline (Doxy-II, Vibramycin, etc.).
- felodipine (Plendil).
- haloperidol (Haldol) or other phenothiazines.
- isradipine (DynaCirc).
- lamotrigine (Lamictal).
- methylphenidate (Ritalin, others).
- midazolam (Versed).
- nelfinavir (Viracept).
- olanzapine (Zyprexa).
- quetiapine (Seroquel).
- sirolimus (Rapamune) blood levels and dosing adjusted to blood sirolimus levels is prudent.

- tacrolimus (Prograf) blood levels and dosing adjusted to tacrolimus levels is prudent.
- tetracyclines (see Drug Classes).
- tramadol (Ultram) and cause loss of tramadol efficacy.
- valproic acid (Depakene, etc.).
- vincristin (Oncovin).
- warfarin (Coumadin). Increased frequency of INR testing is indicated.

Carbamazepine *taken concurrently* with

- acetaminophen (Tylenol, others) may increase risk of acetaminophen liver toxicity.
- activated charcoal (various) will bind this drug and lower benefits.
- birth control pills (oral contraceptives) may lower blood levels of the birth control pills and result in pregnancy.
- chlorpromazine (Thorazine) solution may form a rubbery orange precipitate that is passed in the stool. DO NOT combine.
- cisplatin (Platinol, others).
- clozapine (Clozaril) may result in serious bone marrow suppression.
- delavirdine (Rescriptor) may lower trough levels of delavirdine.
- doxorubicin (Doxil, others).
- felbamate (Felbatol) may result in decreased carbamazepine levels and seizures.
- itraconazole (Sporanox) may cause loss of itraconazole benefits.
- ketorolac (Toradol) may blunt carbamazepine benefits.
- lithium (Lithobid, others) may cause serious neurological problems: confusion, drowsiness, weakness, unsteadiness, tremors, and twitching.
- monoamine oxidase (MAO) type A inhibitor drugs (see Drug Classes) may cause severe toxic reactions.
- N-acetylcysteine (various) may blunt seizure control.
- phenytoin (Dilantin, etc.) and fosphenytoin (Cerebyx) may cause unpredictable fluctuations of blood levels of both drugs and impair seizure control.
- primidone (Mysoline) may blunt carbamazepine effectiveness.
- sildenafil (Viagra) may result in changes in blood levels.
- terfenadine (Seldane), and perhaps other nonsedating antihistamines, may result in carbamazepine toxicity.
- theophylline (Theo-Dur, etc.) may reduce the effects of both drugs.
- thioridazine (Mellaril) solution may form a rubbery orange precipitate that is passed in the stool. DO NOT combine.

The following drugs may *increase* the effects of carbamazepine:

- cimetidine (Tagamet).
- danazol (Danocrine).
- diltiazem (Cardizem)—and perhaps other calcium channel blockers.
- flu shots (influenza vaccine).
- fluoxetine (Prozac); may lead to toxicity.
- fluvoxamine (Luvox); may result in toxicity.
- isoniazid (INH).
- ketoconazole (Nizoral) and fluconazole (Diflucan).
- macrolide antibiotics—erythromycins, clarithromycin, or troleandomycin (not azithromycin).
- nefazodone (Serzone).
- nicotinamide (nicotinic acid amide).
- omeprazole (Prilosec).

- propoxyphene (Darvon, Darvocet, etc.).
- quinupristin/dalfopristin (Synercid) may lead to increased blood levels of carbamazepine and toxicity. Blood levels are prudent and carbamazepine dose decreases may be required.
- rifampin (Rifampicin) may result in toxicity.
- ritonavir (Norvir) and perhaps other protease inhibitors such as amprenavir (Agenerase) (see Drug Classes).
- verapamil (Calan, Isoptin).

▷ *Driving, Hazardous Activities:* Can cause dizziness, drowsiness, or blurred vision. Adjust activities.

Aviation Note: The use of this drug *is a disqualification* for piloting. Consult a designated Aviation Medical Examiner.

Exposure to Sun: This drug can cause photosensitivity (see Glossary). Use caution until sensitivity to sun is known.

Heavy Exercise or Exertion: Use caution if you have coronary artery disease. Can intensify angina and reduce tolerance for physical activity.

Occurrence of Unrelated Illness: You MUST tell all health care providers that you take this drug.

Discontinuation: If treating trigeminal neuralgia, attempts to reduce the maintenance dose or to stop this drug are needed every 3 months. If used to control epilepsy, this drug *must not be stopped abruptly*.

Special Storage Instructions: Store tablets in a cool, dry place. Protect from humid conditions (**DO NOT store in a bathroom medicine cabinet**) as humidity can decrease potency of both brand or generic forms to a serious degree (significant percentage degradation of drug).

CARTEOLOL (KAR tee oh lohl)

Introduced: 1983   **Class:**   Antihypertensive, beta-adrenergic blocker
Prescription: USA: Yes   **Controlled Drug:**   USA: No; Canada: No
Available as Generic: Yes (ophthalmic)
Brand Names: Cartrol, Ocupress, Occupress

BENEFITS versus RISKS	
Possible Benefits	*Possible Risks*
EFFECTIVE, WELL-TOLERATED ANTIHYPERTENSIVE	Congestive heart failure worsening (in some patients)
EFFECTIVE GLAUCOMA TREATMENT	Worsening of angina in coronary heart disease (abrupt withdrawal)
Prevention of angina	Possible masking of low blood sugar (hypoglycemia) in drug-treated type 2 diabetics
May help prevent complications and left ventricle damage after a heart attack	Provocation of asthma in asthmatics
May help prevent tolerance to nitrates	

▷ **Principal Uses**

As a Single Drug Product: Uses currently included in FDA-approved labeling: (1) Treats mild to moderate high blood pressure, alone or in combination with other drugs, such as diuretics; (2) helps lower eye (intraocular) pressure in people with glaucoma or increased eye pressure (ocular hypertension).

Other (unlabeled) generally accepted uses: (1) Increases amount of exercise that can be performed before angina occurs; (2) can help decrease aggressive behavior; (3) decreases risk of abnormal heart rhythms; (4) has shown benefits after heart attacks—preserving left heart ventricle function and preventing second heart attacks; (5) may help lessen panic attacks.

How This Drug Works: Blocks certain actions of the sympathetic nervous system. Reduces the heart rate and contraction force, lowering ejection pressure of blood leaving the heart. Reduces extent of blood vessel wall contraction, relaxing the walls, and lowering blood pressure. Reduces elevated eye pressure (intraocular) and relieves glaucoma symptoms.

Available Dosage Forms and Strengths

Ophthalmic solution — 5 ml, 10 ml (1%)

Tablets — 2.5 mg, 5 mg

▷ **Usual Adult Dosage Ranges:** *High blood pressure (hypertension):* Starts with 2.5 mg daily (by itself or combined with a water pill or diuretic) once a day. If needed because blood pressure goals are not reached, the dose can be gradually (peak benefits from a given dose may take several days up to several weeks) increased to 5 or 10 mg a day. This medicine has a maximum dose effect (ceiling effect), and doses above 10 mg are not likely to give added benefit in controlling high blood pressure—yet may increase how often side effects happen.

For angina: A wide range of effective doses from 2.5 to a maximum of 60 mg has been used. Most commonly, 20–40 mg once a day has been reported to control pressure for many patients.

For glaucoma or eye (ocular) hypertension: One drop in the affected eye or eyes two times a day.

Note: Actual dose and schedule must be determined for each patient individually.

Conditions Requiring Dosing Adjustments

Liver Function: Liver does play a role in removing this medicine, but how much of a role is not defined. Decreased doses are probably needed in severe liver failure.

Kidney Function: Dosing interval **MUST** be decreased in kidney compromise. For example, in severe compromise (creatinine clearance less than 10), 5 mg is given every 48 to 72 hours.

▷ **Dosing Instructions:** Tablet may be crushed and taken without regard to eating. Do not stop this drug abruptly. If you forget a dose: take it right away unless it's nearly time for your next daily dose. If it IS within 8 hours of the regular dose, skip the missed dose and just take the scheduled dose. DO NOT double doses. It is important to wash your hands BEFORE using the eye drops. Make sure you understand how your doctor wants you to place (instill) the eye drops. Your vision may be cloudy or blurry for a little while after you place the eye drops in the eyes.

Usual Duration of Use: Regular use for up to 3 weeks may be needed to see effectiveness in lowering blood pressure, and the medicine should be given this reasonable therapeutic trial before it is discontinued or dose escalated. Long-term use (months to years) is determined by lowering of blood pressure and response to a overall program (weight reduction, salt restriction, smoking cessation, etc.). See your doctor on a regular basis. For the eye drops, use is usually ongoing with follow up checks of eye pressure (intraocular pressure or IOP) helping decide additional therapy or dose adjustments.

Typical Treatment Goals and Measurements (Outcomes and Markers)

Blood Pressure: The NEW guidelines (JNC VII) define normal blood pressure (BP) as **less than** 120/80. Because blood pressures that were once considered acceptable can actually lead to blood vessel damage, the committee from the National Institutes of Health, National Heart Lung and Blood Institute now have a new category called **Pre-hypertension**. This ranges from 120/80 to 139/89 and is intended to help your doctor encourage lifestyle changes (or in the case of people with a risk factor for high blood pressure, start treatment) much earlier—so that possible damage to blood vessels, your heart, kidneys, sexual potency, or eyes might be minimized or avoided altogether. The next two classes of high blood pressure are stage 1 hypertension: 140/90 to 159/99 and stage 2 hypertension equal to or greater than: 160/100 mm Hg. These guidelines also recommend that clinicians trying to control blood pressure work with their patients to agree on the goals and a plan of treatment. The first-ever guidelines for blood pressure (hypertension) in African Americans recommends that MOST black patients be started on TWO antihypertensive medicines with the goal of lowering blood pressure to 130/80 for those with high risk for heart and blood vessel disease or with diabetes. The American Diabetes Association recommends 130/80 as the target for people living with diabetes and less than 125/75 for those who spill more than one gram of protein into their urine. Most clinicians try to achieve a BP that confers the best balance of lower cardiovascular risk and avoids the problem of too low a blood pressure. Blood pressure duration is generally increased with beneficial restriction of sodium. The goals and time frame should be discussed with you when the prescription is written. If goals are not met, it is not unusual to intensify doses or add on medicines. You can find the new blood pressure guidelines at *www.nhlbi.nih.gov/guidelines/hypertension/index.htm*. For the African American guidelines see Douglas, J.G. in Sources.

Possible Advantages of This Drug: Adequate control of blood pressure with a single daily dose helps adherence or compliance. Causes less slowing of the heart rate than most other beta-blocker drugs.

▷ **This Drug Should Not Be Taken If**
- you have bronchial asthma and/or obstructive lung (pulmonary) disease.
- you have had an allergic reaction to it previously.
- you have congestive heart failure (overt) or are in shock of heart origin (cardiogenic shock).
- you have an abnormally slow heart rate (bradycardia) or a serious heart block (second- or third-degree AV).

▷ **Inform Your Physician Before Taking This Drug If**
- you have had an adverse reaction to any beta blocker (see Drug Classes).
- you have serious heart disease or episodes of heart failure.
- you have had hay fever (allergic rhinitis), asthma, chronic bronchitis, or emphysema.
- you have a history of overactive thyroid function (hyperthyroidism).
- you have a history of low blood sugar (hypoglycemia), diabetes (particularly type 1), or myasthenia gravis.
- you have impaired liver or kidney function.
- you have a circulation problem (Raynaud's phenomenon, claudication, pains in legs).

- you take any form of digitalis, quinidine or reserpine, or any calcium blocker drug (see Drug Classes).
- you will have surgery with general anesthesia.

Possible Side Effects (natural, expected, and unavoidable drug actions)

Lethargy and fatigability, cold extremities, slow heart rate. Rebound angina if this medicine is stopped abruptly. Short-term itching or eye tearing with the ophthalmic drops—frequent.

▷ **Possible Adverse Effects** (unusual, unexpected, and infrequent reactions)

If any of the following develop, consult your physician promptly for guidance.

Mild Adverse Effects

Allergic reactions: skin rash—rare.

Headache, dizziness, nervousness, drowsiness—infrequent to frequent.

Indigestion, nausea, vomiting, constipation, diarrhea—infrequent.

Slight increase in blood potassium—possible.

Cough, wheezing or sinusitis—rare.

Joint and muscle discomfort, numbness of fingers or toes—rare.

Carpal tunnel syndrome—case reports with other medicines in this class.

Episodic difficulty walking (intermittent claudication with peripheral vascular disease)—possible.

Tearing and irritation (with eye use)—infrequent to frequent.

Serious Adverse Effects

Mental depression—possible, but less likely than some other beta blockers.

Chest pain, irregular heartbeat, shortness of breath; can cause congestive heart failure—possible.

Induction of bronchial asthma (in asthmatic patients)—possible.

Aggravation of myasthenia gravis—possible.

May hide symptoms of low blood sugar.

▷ **Possible Effects on Sexual Function:** Decreased libido, impotence—case reports.

Adverse Effects That May Mimic Natural Diseases or Disorders

Decreased extremity blood flow may mimic Raynaud's phenomenon (see Glossary).

Natural Diseases or Disorders That May Be Activated by This Drug

Raynaud's disease, intermittent claudication, myasthenia gravis.

Possible Effects on Laboratory Tests

Blood creatine kinase level: increased.

Blood potassium: slight increase.

CAUTION

1. ***Do not stop this drug suddenly*** without the knowledge of your doctor. Carry a note that says you are taking this drug.
2. Ask your physician or pharmacist before using nasal decongestants. These can cause sudden increases in blood pressure when combined with beta-blocker drugs.
3. Report any new tendency to emotional depression.
4. Use of the eye (ophthalmic) form may lead to additive lowering of blood pressure with other beta blockers.

Precautions for Use

By Infants and Children: Safety and effectiveness by those under 12 years of age not established.

By Those Over 60 Years of Age: **Caution**: Unacceptably high blood pressure should be reduced without creating excessively low blood pressure. Small doses and frequent blood pressure checks are needed. Sudden/excessive blood pressure lowering can cause stroke or heart attack. Watch for dizziness, confusion, depression, or urinary frequency.

▷ **Advisability of Use During Pregnancy**
Pregnancy Category: C. See Pregnancy Risk Categories at the back of this book.
Animal Studies: No birth defects found in rat or rabbit studies.
Human Studies: Adequate studies of pregnant women are not available.
Use this drug only if clearly needed. Ask your physician for guidance.

Advisability of Use If Breast-Feeding
Presence of this drug in breast milk: Unknown in humans; yes in animals.
Avoid drug or refrain from nursing.

Habit-Forming Potential: None.

Effects of Overdose: Weakness, slow pulse, low blood pressure, fainting, cold and sweaty skin, congestive heart failure, possible coma, and convulsions.

Possible Effects of Long-Term Use: Reduced heart reserve and eventual heart failure in susceptible individuals with advanced heart disease.

Suggested Periodic Examinations While Taking This Drug (at physician's discretion)
Measurements of blood pressure (treated to pressure goal within a set time frame).
Evaluation of heart function. Recheck of eye pressure.

▷ **While Taking This Drug, Observe the Following**
Foods: No specific restrictions, but losing weight can help meet blood pressure goals. Avoid excessive salt intake.
Herbal Medicines or Minerals: Ginseng, guarana, hawthorn, saw palmetto, ma huang, goldenseal, yohimbe, and licorice may cause increased blood pressure. St. John's wort can change liver removal of medicines and is not recommended for people taking beta blockers. Calcium and garlic may help lower blood pressure, and the dose has to be individualized with a standardized extract. Dong quai can change the removal of medicines by the liver—caution is advised for excessive lowering of blood pressure. Ginger, vanadium, and nettle may also change blood sugar, an effect that may be hidden by some of the actions of this medicine. Indian snakeroot has a German Commission E monograph indication for hypertension—talk to your doctor. Eleuthero root and ephedra should be avoided by people living with hypertension. Talk to your doctor BEFORE adding any herbals.
Beverages: No restrictions. May be taken with milk.
▷ *Alcohol:* Use caution. Alcohol may exaggerate blood pressure lowering and also increase its mild sedative effect.
Tobacco Smoking: Nicotine may reduce benefits in treating high blood pressure. High doses may worsen bronchial constriction caused by regular smoking. I advise everyone to quit smoking.
▷ *Other Drugs*
Carteolol may ***increase*** the effects of
• other antihypertensive drugs and cause excessive lowering of the blood pressure. Dosage adjustments may be necessary.
• reserpine (Ser-Ap-Es, etc.) and cause sedation, depression, slowing of the heart rate, and low blood pressure. This combination is best avoided.
• theophyllines (aminophylline, dyphylline, oxtriphylline, etc.).
• verapamil (Calan, Isoptin) and cause excessive depression of heart function; monitor this combination closely.

Carteolol *taken concurrently* with
- amiodarone (Cordarone) may cause severe slowing of the heart and sinus arrest. Do not combine these agents.
- clonidine (Catapres) requires close monitoring for rebound high blood pressure if clonidine is stopped while carteolol is still being taken. Severe rebound hypertension may occur.
- digoxin (Lanoxin) may lead to abnormal heart conduction. Caution is prudent.
- diltiazem (Cardizem) and other dihydropyridine type calcium channel blockers (like verapamil) may be very helpful in patients with normal heart function, but may result in AV conduction problems.
- epinephrine (Adrenalin, etc.) may cause sudden rise in blood pressure followed by slowing of the heart rate. Avoid this combination.
- ergot preparations (ergotamine, methysergide, etc.) may enhance serious ergot-induced constriction of peripheral circulation.
- fluoxetine (Prozac) may result in dangerous slowing of the heart or dangerously low blood pressure.
- fluvoxamine (Luvox) may result in dangerous slowing of the heart or dangerously low blood pressure.
- insulin requires close monitoring to avoid hypoglycemia (see Glossary).
- nifedipine (and perhaps other dihydroperidine calcium channel blockers) may result in excessive lowering of the blood pressure.
- oral antidiabetic drugs (see Drug Classes) may cause prolonged recovery from hypoglycemia should it occur.
- phenothiazines (see Drug Classes) can cause increased effects of both drugs.
- rifabutin (Mycobutin) may reduce carteolol's effectiveness.
- ritodrine (Yutopar) may block Yutopar actions. Maker of ritodrine does NOT recommend this combination.
- sibutramine (Meridia) may lead to increases in blood pressure.
- venlafaxine (Effexor) may lead to toxicity from either drug.
- zileuton (Zyflo) may result in increased toxicity risk from carteolol. Caution is advised.

The following drugs may *decrease* the effects of carteolol:
- indomethacin (Indocin), and possibly other "aspirin substitutes" or NSAIDs, and may impair carteolol's antihypertensive effect.

▷ *Driving, Hazardous Activities:* Use caution until the full extent of fatigue, dizziness, and blood pressure change have been determined.

Aviation Note: The use of this drug *is a disqualification* for piloting. Consult a designated Aviation Medical Examiner.

Exposure to Sun: No restrictions.

Exposure to Heat: Caution is advised. Hot environments can lower the blood pressure and exaggerate the effects of this drug.

Exposure to Cold: Caution is advised. The elderly should take precautions to prevent hypothermia (see Glossary).

Heavy Exercise or Exertion: Avoid exertion that produces light-headedness, excessive fatigue, or muscle cramping.

Occurrence of Unrelated Illness: Fever can lower blood pressure and require decreased doses. Illnesses that cause nausea or vomiting may interrupt the regular dosage schedule. Ask your physician for guidance.

Discontinuation: **DO NOT STOP this drug suddenly**. If possible, gradual reduction of dose over a period of 2 to 3 weeks is recommended. Ask your physician for help.

CARVEDILOL (KAR vi die lohl)

Introduced: 1997   **Class:**   Alpha adrenergic blocker, antihypertensive, beta-adrenergic blocker   **Prescription:**   USA: Yes   **Controlled Drug:** USA: No; Canada: No   **Available as Generic:**   No

Brand Names: Coreg, ♣Dilatrend, ♣Eucardic, ♣Proreg

BENEFITS versus RISKS

Possible Benefits	*Possible Risks*
EFFECTIVE, WELL-TOLERATED ANTIHYPERTENSIVE	Worsening of heart failure (often responds to dose changes)
IMPROVES CONGESTIVE HEART FAILURE (mild–severe)	Slow heartbeat
CONFERS SIGNIFICANT SURVIVAL BENEFITS IN PATIENTS WITH ADVANCED CONGESTIVE HEART FAILURE	Masking of low blood sugar (hypoglycemia) in drug-treated diabetics (possible)
	Provocation of asthma in asthmatics
DECREASES RISK OF DEATH IN HEART ATTACK PATIENTS WITH HEARTS THAT DO NOT WORK PROPERLY (IMPAIRED CARDIAC FUNCTION)	
WORKS ON TWO KINDS OF BETA RECEPTORS (B1 AND B2) AND ALPHA [ALPHA 1]) RECEPTORS AS WELL	

▷ **Principal Uses**

As a Single Drug Product: Uses currently included in FDA-approved labeling: (1) Treats mild to moderate high blood pressure, alone or in combination with other drugs; (2) improves congestive heart failure or CHF (one of two beta blockers along with metoprolol XL form approved for CHF). Approved for mild to severe CHF; (3) lowers risk of death (23%) in heart attack victims who have hearts that no longer have their usual heart function (impaired cardiac function).

Other unlabeled, generally accepted uses: (1) Eases frequency and severity of angina; (2) may help prevent loss of benefits from nitroglycerin (nitrate tolerance) when that medicine is used to ease angina pain; (3) may be of help in people with increased blood pressure in the liver blood circulation that stems from liver disease (portal hypertension).

In the Pipeline: The COMET (Carvedilol or Metoprolol European Trial) is the first study to make a head to head (drug to drug) comparison of two beta blockers in people with ongoing (chronic) heart failure (CHF). This research was designed to look at the effect of the two medicines on survival. The chair of the study is Professor Philip Poole-Wilson of the Imperial College in London. One early report sited a survival benefit for carvedilol. This study will involve more than 10,000 patient years of followup (large number of patients who were studied for a significant time) and is expected to be published in the summer of 2003.

How This Drug Works: Blocks certain actions of the sympathetic nervous system and:

- reduces the heart rate and contraction force, lowering ejection pressure of blood leaving the heart.
- reduces extent of blood vessel wall contraction, relaxing the walls and lowering blood pressure.
- after a heart attack, works to prevent inappropriate changes (remodeling) in the left ventricle, prevent repeat heart attacks and also appears to help decrease the size of the heart attack (infarct size in animals).

Carvedilol also is able to open (dilate) blood vessels in the periphery because of alpha-1 receptor blockade. This medicine acts as an antioxidant and inhibits programmed cell death, benefiting blood vessel lining (endothelial) function.

Available Dosage Forms and Strengths
   Tablets — 3.125, 6.25, 12.5, 25 mg
   Tablets — 25 mg, 50 mg (Dilatrend)

▷ **Usual Adult Dosage Ranges**
   For high blood pressure (hypertension): Starts with 6.25 mg twice daily. Dose may be increased to 12.5 mg twice daily and then to 25 mg twice daily at intervals of 2 weeks, as needed and tolerated. This medicine should be taken with food in order to decrease the risk of postural hypotension (see Glossary).
   For angina: 25 to 50 mg twice a day (benefits are dose related).
   For congestive heart failure: 3.125 mg twice a day. After 2 weeks, this dose may be increased to 6.25 mg twice daily as needed and tolerated. The dose can be subsequently doubled every 14 days to a maximum of 25 mg twice daily (for those less than 85 kg) or to 50 mg twice daily for people weighing more than 85 kg. When the dose is changed, patients should be watched for dizziness (for 2 hours after the first dose at the new level). Carvedilol should be taken with food to slow the speed at which it enters the body (see note in dosing instructions below regarding heart failure).
   Note: Actual dose and schedule must be determined for each patient individually.

Conditions Requiring Dosing Adjustments
   Liver Function: Twenty percent of the usual dose is given in people with cirrhosis of the liver. Carvedilol should NOT be used in severe liver failure.
   Kidney Function: No changes thought to be needed.

▷ **Dosing Instructions:** Tablet may be crushed. Doses should be taken with food in order to decrease the risk of abnormally low blood pressure when standing up (orthostatic hypotension). Do not stop this drug abruptly. When the medicine is used in congestive heart failure, if the heart failure worsens— water pill doses (diuretics) should be increased and the dose of carvedilol not increased any further until the situation stabilizes. Talk to your doctor about how he or she wants you to manage this. If you forget a dose, take it right away unless it's nearly time for your next dose. If it is nearly time, just take the scheduled dose. DO NOT double doses.

Usual Duration of Use: Regular use brings the best results in lowering blood pressure. DO NOT SKIP DOSES. This medicine may reach its peak benefit with the first dose. Long-term use (months to years) is determined by lowering of blood pressure and response to a overall program (weight reduction, salt restriction, smoking cessation, etc). See your doctor on a regular basis.

Typical Treatment Goals and Measurements (Outcomes and Markers)
   Blood Pressure: The NEW guidelines (JNC VII) define normal blood pressure (BP) as **less than** 120/80. Because blood pressures that were once considered acceptable can actually lead to blood vessel damage, the committee

from the National Institutes of Health, National Heart Lung and Blood Institute now have a new category called **Pre-hypertension**. This ranges from 120/80 to 139/89 and is intended to help your doctor encourage lifestyle changes (or in the case of people with a risk factor for high blood pressure, start treatment) much earlier—so that possible damage to blood vessels, heart, kidneys, sexual potency, or eyes might be minimized or avoided altogether. The next two classes of high blood pressure are stage 1 hypertension: 140/90 to 159/99 and stage 2 hypertension equal to or greater than: 160/100 mm Hg. These guidelines also recommend that clinicians trying to control blood pressure work with their patients to agree on the goals and a plan of treatment. The first-ever guidelines for blood pressure (hypertension) in African Americans recommends that MOST black patients be started on TWO antihypertensive medicines with the goal of lowering blood pressure to 130/80 for those with high risk for heart and blood vessel disease or with diabetes. The American Diabetes Association recommends 130/80 as the target for people living with diabetes and less than 125/75 for those who spill more than one gram of protein into their urine. Most clinicians try to achieve a BP that confers the best balance of lower cardiovascular risk and avoids the problem of too low a blood pressure. Blood pressure duration is generally increased with beneficial restriction of sodium. The goals and time frame should be discussed with you when the prescription is written. If goals are not met, it is not unusual to intensify doses or add on medicines. You can find the new blood pressure guidelines at *www.nhlbi.nih.gov/guidelines/hypertension/index.htm*. For the African American guidelines see Douglas J.G. in Sources!

Possible Advantages of This Drug

Works on two kinds of beta receptors and alpha receptors as well. May reach its peak benefit with the first dose. Based on the COPERNICUS (Carvedilol Prospective Randomized Cumulative Survival Study), carvedilol confers marked survival benefits in advanced heart failure. A 2001 study of 2,289 patients (with severe heart failure—ejection fraction less than 25%) undertaken at Columbia University found that carvedilol reduced death by 35%. An economic evaluation of the US Carvedilol Heart Failure Trials published in August of 2001 in *Pharmacotherapy* found carvedilol to reduce mortality and also save costs. A meta analysis of heart failure studies found that many if not most patients with heart failure would benefit from a beta blocker (see Shekelle, PG 2003). Carvedilol may have a more desirable effect on insulin sensitivity than other beta blockers.

▷ This Drug Should Not Be Taken If

- you have bronchial asthma and/or obstructive lung (pulmonary) disease.
- you have had an allergic reaction to it previously.
- you have sick sinus syndrome (ask your doctor).
- you have decompensated heart failure (NYHA Class four).
- you have a severely slow heart rate (bradycardia) or a serious heart block (second or third degree).

▷ Inform Your Physician Before Taking This Drug If

- you have had an adverse reaction to any beta blocker (see Drug Classes).
- you have serious heart disease or episodes of heart failure.
- you have had hay fever (allergic rhinitis), asthma, chronic bronchitis, or emphysema.
- you have a history of overactive thyroid function (hyperthyroidism).
- you have pheochromocytoma.

- you have a history of low blood sugar (hypoglycemia), diabetes, or myasthenia gravis.
- you have impaired liver or kidney function.
- you have a circulation problem (Raynaud's phenomenon, claudication pains in legs).
- you have low blood platelets.
- you take any form of digitalis, quinidine, or reserpine, or any calcium blocker drug (see Drug Classes).
- you will have surgery with general anesthesia.

Possible Side Effects (natural, expected, and unavoidable drug actions)

Lethargy and fatigability, cold extremities, slow heart rate, light-headedness in upright position (see Orthostatic Hypotension in Glossary)—rare when treating hypertension, infrequent when treating congestive heart failure. Rebound hypertension if this medicine is stopped abruptly.

Dizziness—frequent in congestive heart failure.

▷ **Possible Adverse Effects** (unusual, unexpected, and infrequent reactions)

If any of the following develop, consult your physician promptly for guidance.

Mild Adverse Effects

Allergic reaction: skin rash—rare.

Headache, dizziness, nervousness, drowsiness—infrequent to frequent.

Indigestion, nausea, vomiting, constipation, diarrhea—infrequent.

Urination at night (nocturia) or difficulty urinating—reported with other beta blockers.

Cough, wheezing, or sinusitis—reported with other beta blockers.

Episodic difficulty walking (intermittent claudication with peripheral vascular disease)—possible.

Muscle aches or back pain—case reports.

Visual changes—infrequent.

Serious Adverse Effects

Allergic reactions: One case report of Stevens-Johnson Syndrome.

Lowering of blood platelets—rare and questionable cause.

Slow heartbeat (bradycardia)—possible with higher doses.

Fainting (syncope)—possible.

Edema (dependent and peripheral)—rare in hypertension and infrequent in CHF.

Increased blood sugar—possible.

May hide symptoms of low blood sugar.

Chest pain, irregular heartbeat, shortness of breath; can cause congestive heart failure—possible.

Induction of bronchial asthma (in asthmatic patients)—possible.

Liver toxicity (hepatotoxicity)—infrequent.

Aggravation of myasthenia gravis—possible.

Resistance to epinephrine in hypersensitivity or other similar treatment—possible.

▷ **Possible Effects on Sexual Function:** Impotence—case reports with other beta blockers. This rare effect is less common with heart selectivity and low fat (lipid) solubility.

Adverse Effects That May Mimic Natural Diseases or Disorders

Decreased extremity blood flow may mimic Raynaud's phenomenon (see Glossary).

Natural Diseases or Disorders That May Be Activated by This Drug

Intermittent claudication, diabetes.

Possible Effects on Laboratory Tests
Blood sugar: increased or decreased in diabetics.
CAUTION
- ***Do not stop this drug suddenly*** without the knowledge of your doctor (may cause dangerous increases in blood pressure or angina). Carry a note that says you are taking this drug.
- Ask your physician or pharmacist before using nasal decongestants. These can cause sudden increases in blood pressure when combined with beta-blocker drugs.
- May worsen positional blood pressure lowering (postural hypotension) in the elderly.
- Report any new tendency to emotional depression.
- Because dizziness is a common side effect, make sure you know the extent and severity of this possible effect before undertaking activities that may be hazardous.

Precautions for Use
By Infants and Children: Safety and effectiveness in children not established.
*By Those Over 60 Years of Age: **Caution:*** Unacceptably high blood pressure should be reduced without creating excessively low blood pressure. Small doses and frequent blood pressure checks are needed.
Sudden/excessive blood pressure lowering can cause stroke or heart attack. Watch for dizziness, confusion, depression, or urinary frequency.

▷ **Advisability of Use During Pregnancy**
Pregnancy Category: C. See Pregnancy Risk Categories at the back of this book.
Animal Studies: No birth defects found in rat or rabbit studies.
Human Studies: Adequate studies of pregnant women are not available.
Use this drug only if clearly needed. Ask your physician for guidance.

Advisability of Use If Breast-Feeding
Presence of this drug in breast milk: Unknown in humans, but expected (large volume of distribution and is fat soluble or lipophillic).
Avoid drug or refrain from nursing.

Habit-Forming Potential: None.

Effects of Overdose: Weakness, slow pulse, low blood pressure, fainting, cold and sweaty skin, congestive heart failure, possible coma, and convulsions.

Possible Effects of Long-Term Use: Not defined.

Suggested Periodic Examinations While Taking This Drug (at physician's discretion): Measurements of blood pressure and treatment to goals within a set time frame, blood sugar, periodic evaluation liver, heart, and visual function.

▷ **While Taking This Drug, Observe the Following**
Foods: No restrictions. Avoid excessive salt intake.
Herbal Medicines or Minerals: Ginseng, guarana, hawthorn, saw palmetto, ma huang, goldenseal, yohimbe, and licorice may cause increased blood pressure. St. John's wort can change liver removal of medicines and is not recommended for people taking beta blockers. Calcium and garlic may help lower blood pressure, and the dose has to be individualized with a standardized extract. Dong quai can change the removal of medicines by the liver—caution is advised for excessive lowering of blood pressure. Ginger, vanadium, and nettle may also change blood sugar, an effect that may be hidden by some of the actions of this medicine. Indian snakeroot has a German Commission E monograph indication for hypertension—talk to your doctor. Eleuthero root and ephedra should be avoided by people living with hypertension. Talk to your doctor BEFORE adding any herbals.

Beverages: No restrictions. May be taken with milk.

▷ *Alcohol:* Use caution. Alcohol may exaggerate blood pressure lowering and also increase its mild sedative effect.

Tobacco Smoking: Nicotine may reduce benefits in treating high blood pressure. High doses may worsen bronchial constriction caused by regular smoking. I advise everyone to quit smoking.

▷ *Other Drugs*

Carvedilol may *increase* the effects of

- cyclosporine (Sandimmune, others) requiring cyclosporine dose decreases.
- other antihypertensive drugs, and cause excessive lowering of the blood pressure. Dosage adjustments may be necessary.
- reserpine (Ser-Ap-Es, etc.), and cause sedation, depression, slowing of the heart rate, and low blood pressure. This combination is best avoided.
- verapamil (Calan, Isoptin), and cause excessive depression of heart function; monitor this combination closely.

Carvedilol *taken concurrently* with

- amiodarone (Cordarone) may cause severe slowing of the heart and sinus arrest. Do not combine this agent.
- cimetidine (Tagamet) may lead to excessive levels of carvedilol and possible toxic effects.
- clonidine (Catapres) requires close monitoring for rebound high blood pressure if clonidine is stopped while carvedilol is still being taken. Severe rebound hypertension may occur.
- digoxin (Lanoxin) may lead to abnormal heart conduction and increased blood digoxin levels. Caution is prudent. A small study in children from 14 days to 8 years old found that this combination slowed the removal of digoxin by 50%. Lower doses and more frequent blood levels are prudent if this combination must be used—particularly in children.
- diltiazem (Cardizem) (like verapamil) may be very helpful in patients with normal heart function, but may result in AV conduction problems.
- epinephrine (Adrenalin, etc.) may cause sudden rise in blood pressure followed by slowing of the heart rate. Avoid this combination.
- insulin requires close monitoring to avoid hypoglycemia (see Glossary).
- medicines that increase CYP 2D6 or 2 C9 will blunt carvedilol benefits while those that inhibit those liver enzymes will increase effects of carvedilol.
- nifedipine (dihydroperidine) may result in excessive lowering of the blood pressure.
- oral antidiabetic drugs (see Drug Classes) may cause prolonged recovery from hypoglycemia should it occur.
- rifabutin (Mycobutin) may reduce carvedilol's effectiveness.
- ritodrine (Yutopar) may block Yutopar actions. Maker of ritodrine does NOT recommend this combination.
- sibutramine (Meridia) may lead to increases in blood pressure.
- zileuton (Zyflo) may result in increased toxicity risk from carvedilol. Caution is advised.

The following drugs may *decrease* the effects of carvedilol:

- indomethacin (Indocin), and possibly other "aspirin substitutes" or NSAIDs, may impair carvedilol's antihypertensive effect.

▷ *Driving, Hazardous Activities:* Use caution until the full extent of fatigue, dizziness, and blood pressure change has been determined. Dizziness is more common in congestive heart failure patients.

Aviation Note: The use of this drug *is a disqualification* for piloting. Consult a designated Aviation Medical Examiner.

Exposure to Sun: No restrictions.

Exposure to Heat: Caution is advised. Hot environments can lower the blood pressure and exaggerate the effects of this drug.

Exposure to Cold: Caution is advised. The elderly should take precautions to prevent hypothermia (see Glossary).

Heavy Exercise or Exertion: Avoid exertion that produces light-headedness, excessive fatigue, or muscle cramping.

Occurrence of Unrelated Illness: Fever can lower blood pressure and require decreased doses. Illnesses that cause nausea or vomiting may interrupt the regular dosage schedule. Ask your physician for guidance.

Discontinuation: **DO NOT STOP this drug suddenly.** If possible, gradual reduction of dose over a period of 2 to 3 weeks is recommended. Ask your physician for help.

CEPHALOSPORIN ANTIBIOTIC FAMILY
(SEF a low spoar ins)

Cefaclor (SEF a klor)   **Cefadroxil** (SEF a drox il)   **Cefixime** (SE fix eem)   **Cefprozil** (SEF proh zil)   **Ceftriaxone** (SEF try ax own)   **Cefuroxime** (SEF yur ox eem)   **Cephalexin** (SEF ah lex in)   **Loracarbef** (lor ah KAR bef)

Introduced: 1979, 1977, 1986, 1991, 1984, 1974, 1969, 1992, respectively **Class:** Antibiotics, cephalosporins **Prescription:** USA: Yes **Controlled Drugs:** USA: No; Canada: No **Available as Generic:** *Cefaclor:* yes; *Cefadroxil:* yes; *Cefixime:* no; *Cefprozil:* no; *Ceftriaxone:* no; *Cefuroxime:* yes; *Cephalexin:* yes; *Loracarbef:* no

Brand Names: *Cefaclor:* Ceclor; *Cefadroxil:* Duricef, Ultracef; *Cefixime:* Suprax; *Cefprozil:* Cefzil; *Ceftriaxone:* Rocephin; *Cefuroxime:* Ceftin, Kefurox, Zinacef; *Cephalexin:* ✤Apo-Cephalex, Cefanex, ✤Ceporex, Keflet, Keflex, Keftab, ✤Novo-Lexin, ✤Nu-Cephalex; *Loracarbef:* Lorabid

---

BENEFITS versus RISKS

Possible Benefits	*Possible Risks*
EFFECTIVE TREATMENT OF INFECTIONS DUE TO SUSCEPTIBLE MICRO-ORGANISMS	ALLERGIC REACTIONS, MILD TO SEVERE (MAY ALSO BE SEEN IN THOSE ALLERGIC TO PENICILLIN)
HOME INTRAVENOUS TREATMENT OF SERIOUS INFECTIONS (ceftriaxone)	Drug-induced colitis—rare
	Superinfections (see Glossary)
ONE-INJECTION TREATMENT OF SOME CHILDHOOD EAR INFECTIONS	Low white blood cell or platelet counts (cefixime or ceftriaxone)—rare
	Anemia (ceftriaxone)—rare

▷ **Principal Uses**

As a Single Drug Product: Uses currently included in FDA-approved labeling: (1) To treat some infections of the skin and skin structures, the upper and lower respiratory tract (including middle ear infections—ceftriaxone has a one-dose indication for bacterial otitis media—and "strep" throat), some urinary tract and some postoperative wound infections; (2) treatment of advanced Lyme disease (stage 2 or 3) via home intravenous (home IV) services (ceftriaxone); (3) treatment of serious bone infections (osteomyelitis) via home IV; (4) treatment of gonorrhea (cefuroxime).

Other unlabeled, generally accepted uses: (1) May have an alternative role in helping prevent rheumatic fever if the bacteria are resistant to erythromycin (cefaclor); (2) may help treat resistant cervical infections (cefixime); (3) part of combination treatment of Whipple's disease (cefixime); (4) treats sexual assault cases and chancroid (ceftriaxone); (5) used in *Shigella* infections; (6) used to change from an intravenous medicine to one taken by mouth in order to shorten hospital stays and preserve results (cefuroxime).

How These Drugs Work: These drugs destroy susceptible infecting bacteria by interfering with their ability to produce new protective cell walls as they multiply and grow.

Available Dosage Forms and Strengths

Cefaclor:
Capsules — 250 mg, 500 mg
Oral suspension — 125 mg, 187 mg, 250 mg, 375 mg/5 ml

Cefadroxil:
Capsules — 500 mg, 1,000 mg
Gelatin capsules (Canada) — 500 mg
Oral suspension — 125 mg, 250 mg, 500 mg/5 ml
Tablets — 1,000 mg (1 g)

Cefixime:
Oral suspension — 100 mg/5 ml
Tablets — 200 mg, 400 mg

Cefprozil:
Oral suspension — 125 mg, 250 mg/5 ml
Tablets — 250 mg, 500 mg

Ceftriaxone:
250 mg of Rocephin — Boxes of 1 or 10 vial(s)
500 mg of Rocephin — Boxes of 1 or 10 vial(s)
1 g of Rocephin — Boxes of 1 or 10 vial(s) or piggyback bottles of 10
2 g of Rocephin — Boxes of 10 vials, or piggyback bottles of 10
10 g of Rocephin — Box of one 1 g or 2 g ADD-Vantage packaging

Cefuroxime:
Intravenous — 750 mg/10 ml
— 750 mg/50 ml
— 750 mg/100 ml
— 1.5 g/100 ml
— 1.5 g/50 ml
— 1.5 g/20 ml
— 7.5 g/127 ml
Oral suspension — 125 mg/5 ml, 250 mg/5 ml
Tablets — 125 mg, 250 mg, 500 mg

Cephalexin:
Capsules — 250 mg, 500 mg
Oral suspension — 125 mg, 250 mg/5 ml
Pediatric oral suspension — 100 mg/ml
Tablets — 250 mg, 500 mg, 1,000 mg (1 g)

Loracarbef:
>   Capsules — 200 mg and 400 mg
>   Oral suspension — 100 mg or 200 mg/5 ml

▷ **Recommended Dosage Ranges**

Cefaclor: For FDA labeled uses. 250 mg every 8 hours for susceptible infections, up to 500 mg every 8 hours for severe infections. Maximum daily dose is 2 g (2,000 mg).

Cefadroxil: Skin infections—500 mg every 12 hours, or 1 g daily. "Strep" throat—500 mg every 12 hours for 10 days. Urinary tract infections—500 mg to 1 g every 12 hours, or 1 to 2 g daily. Maximum daily dose 6 g (6,000 mg).

Cefixime: 400 mg daily, taken as a single dose or as 200 mg every 12 hours. For treatment of multidrug-resistant *Salmonella*—20 mg per kg of body mass per day in equal doses every 12 hours, for at least 12 days. Uncomplicated gonorrhea—400 to 800 mg as a single dose.

Cefuroxime: See general dosing below. Blood levels in pregnancy are up to 50% lower than in non-pregnant females. Dosing in pregnancy should be adjusted to achieve the usual peak to MIC ratio needed to kill the infecting organism.

Cephalexin: 250 to 500 mg every 6 hours. Total daily dose should not exceed 4 g.

Loracarbef: 200–400 mg every 12 hours for 7–14 days depending on the infection being treated.

Infants and Children:

Cefaclor: 20 to 40 mg per kg of body mass per day is given in divided doses every 8 hours. Maximum dose is 1 g (1,000 mg) daily.

Cefadroxil: 30 mg per kg of body mass per day, given in divided doses every 12 hours.

Cefixime (for children over 6 months of age): 8 mg per kg of body mass per day, all in one dose or divided into two doses.

Cefprozil: For otitis media (6 months to 12 years of age)—15 mg per kg of body mass every 12 hours, for 10 days.

Ceftriaxone: For neonates and children less than 12 for treatment of serious infections caused by susceptible organisms (other than CNS infections such as meningitis)—50–75 mg per kg of body mass per day, given in two equally divided doses 12 hours apart (not to exceed 2 g daily). Some clinicians use 50 mg per kg of body weight per day for neonates 1 week old or younger; neonates older than 1 week and weighing 2 kg or less also receive 50 mg per kg of body mass per day; neonates older than 1 week and weighing more than 2 kg receive 50–75 mg per kg of body mass per day.

For meningitis (caused by susceptible organisms)—the dose for neonates and children 12 or younger is 100 mg per kg of body mass (no more than 4 grams or 4,000 mg) daily, divided into two equal doses given every 12 hours. The American Academy of Pediatrics suggests 80–100 mg per kg of body mass be given once daily or in two equally divided doses every 12 hours for children older than 1 month. Because the once-daily regimen is relatively new, I suggest that the 12-hour regimen be used. For serious CNS disease—children can be treated with 75–100 mg per kg of body mass IV daily for 21 days.

For heart (cardiac disease)—children can be given 75–100 mg per kg of body mass per day IV. Treatment of serious Lyme arthritis, cardiac or neurologic complications of early or late (stage 2 or 3) Lyme disease: Arthritis: 75–100 mg per kg of body mass per day IV. One recent article advocated a single dose of ceftriaxone for some childhood ear infections. For otitis media: 75–100 mg per kg of body mass per day, in four divided doses.

Cefuroxime: Oral (for children over 2)—125 mg twice a day, 250 mg twice daily for treatment of otitis media. Intravenous—Those over 3 months should be given 50 to 100 mg per kg of body mass per day, divided every 6 to 8 hours. Maximum dose is 4 g.

Cephalexin: 25 to 50 mg per kg of body mass per day in two to four divided doses. Maximum dose is 4 g (4,000 mg).

Loracarbef: For ear infection (otitis media)—30 mg per kg per day given in equal doses, taken every 12 hours for 10 days (suspension only—capsules should NOT be substituted for suspension).

12 to 60 Years of Age:

Cefprozil: Pharyngitis or tonsillitis—500 mg every 24 hours (once daily), for 10 days. Acute or chronic bronchitis—500 mg every 12 hours, for 10 days. Bacterial pneumonia—250 mg three times a day for 14 days. Skin or skin structure infections—250 to 500 mg every 12 to 24 hours, for 10 days.

Ceftriaxone: For most infections (caused by susceptible organisms)—1–2 g daily or in equally divided doses two times a day depending on the type and severity of the infection. Children over 12 are given the adult dose. Some clinicians use 4 g daily in CNS infections in adults. This is the maximum adult dosage recommended by the manufacturer. Uncomplicated gonorrhea caused by penicillinase-producing strains of *Neisseria gonorrhea* (PPNG) or non-penicillinase-producing strains—Single IM 250-mg dose. Disseminated gonococcal infection should be treated by 1 g of ceftriaxone IV or IM once a day for 7 days. Acute sexually transmitted epididymitis in adults—Single 250-mg IM dose, followed by 7 days of oral tetracycline or erythromycin. For treatment of acute pelvic inflammatory disease (PID)—Single 250-mg IM dose, followed by 100 mg of oral doxycycline two times a day for 10–14 days. Treatment of serious Lyme arthritis, cardiac or neurologic complications of early or late (stage 2 or 3) Lyme disease: Arthritis—2 g IV daily. Serious CNS disease—2 g IV daily for 21 days. Cardiac disease—2 g IV per day for 21 days.

Cefuroxime: Oral—250 to 500 mg every 12 hours. Total daily dosage should not exceed 4 g. Intravenous—750 mg to 1.5 g every 8 hours.

Over 60 Years of Age:

Cefprozil: No specific age-related changes. Decreased dose in kidney failure.

Ceftriaxone: No specific changes needed.

Loracarbef: Same as adult dose unless kidney function has declined.

Note: Actual dosage and schedule must be determined for each patient individually for ALL of these medicines.

Conditions Requiring Dosing Adjustments

Liver Function:

Cefaclor, cefixime, cefprozil, cefuroxime, cephalexin, or loracarbef: No changes in dosing needed at present.

Cefadroxil: The liver is involved to a minimal degree, and no dosing changes are anticipated in liver compromise.

Ceftriaxone: Patients with both liver and kidney problems should have blood levels checked and a maximum dose of 2 g given.

Kidney Function:

Cefaclor: 40–80% eliminated by the kidney. For creatinine clearances (CrCl) of 10–50 ml/min, 50–100% of the usual dose at the normal interval is used. For creatinine clearances of less than 10 ml/min, 50% of the usual dose at the usual time is given.

Cefadroxil: With creatinine clearances of 10–50 ml/min, use the usual doses every 12–24 hours. For CrCl less than 10 ml/min, usual doses are given every 24–48 hours.

Cefixime: Dose **must be decreased** in mild to moderate kidney problems. In severe failure, a single dose every 48 hours is often used.

Cefprozil: With severe kidney failure, **half** the dose can be given at the usual time.

Ceftriaxone: Patients with kidney compromise must be carefully followed for adverse effects.

Cefuroxime: 750 mg once daily for most kidney compromise. Dose must be repeated after dialysis, as this medicine is dialyzable.

Cephalexin: For creatinine clearances of 10–50 ml/min, usual dose every 6 hours. For creatinine clearances less than 10 ml/min, usual dose every 8–12 hours.

Loracarbef: Usual dose for CrCl 50 ml/minute or greater. If the CrCl is 10–49 ml/min half the usual dose is given at the usual time.

Phenylketonuria (PKU): Cefprozil only: The suspension has 28 mg of phenylalanine in every 5 ml. This may preclude use of this drug in these patients.

▷ **Dosing Instructions:** May be taken on an empty stomach or with food if stomach upset occurs. Loracarbef must be taken on an empty stomach. Capsule (cefaclor, cefadroxil) may be opened and tablet forms crushed. Cefuroxime tablet can give a bitter taste that lingers. Shake suspension forms well before measuring dose (use a measured dose cup or calibrated dose measure). Intravenous forms should be brought to room temperature if they are refrigerated. Take the full course prescribed. If you forget a dose: Take the missed dose as soon as you remember it, and take any remaining doses for the day at evenly spaced time periods. If you miss more than one dose, please call your doctor.

Usual Duration of Use: Regular use for 3–5 days is usually needed to see effectiveness of these drugs in controlling the infection. Response varies with the infection. Treatment time will vary from 1 week (for some minor infections) to 6 weeks (as in some bone infections). Some cases **require 10–14 consecutive days** of treatment to prevent rheumatic fever. Follow your doctor's instructions carefully. Many clinicians ask you to call them if symptoms worsen or fever persists for 24–48 hours after you start to take these medicines.

Typical Treatment Goals and Measurements (Outcomes and Markers)

Infections: The most commonly used measures of serious infections are white blood cell counts and differentials (the kind of blood cells that occur most often in your blood) and temperature. Many clinicians look for positive changes in 24–48 hours. NEVER stop an antibiotic because you start to feel better. For many infections, a full 14 days is REQUIRED to kill the bacteria. The goals and time frame (see peak benefits above) should be discussed with you when the prescription is written.

Possible Advantages of These Drugs

One-time dosing (injection) of ceftriaxone guarantees that the medicine will be taken (adherence) by children with one kind of ear infection (acute otitis media).

These Drugs Should Not Be Taken If

• you are allergic to any cephalosporin (see Drug Classes).
• you have pseudomembranous colitis.

▷ **Inform Your Physician Before Taking These Drugs If**
  - you have a history of allergy to any penicillin (see Drug Classes).
  - you have a history of regional enteritis or ulcerative colitis.
  - you have impaired kidney function.
  - you have a history of blood clotting disorders.
  - you have a history of low platelets or white blood cell count (cefprozil, cefixime, or ceftriaxone).

Possible Side Effects (natural, expected, and unavoidable drug actions)
  Superinfections (see Glossary).

▷ **Possible Adverse Effects** (unusual, unexpected, and infrequent reactions)
  If any of the following develop, consult your physician promptly for guidance.

  Mild Adverse Effects
  Allergic reactions: skin rash, itching, hives.
  Nausea and vomiting or mild diarrhea—most common adverse effects.
  Sore mouth or tongue—possible.
  Mild and reversible decrease in white blood cells (neutrophils) (cefaclor).
  Confusion, nervousness, insomnia, dizziness—rare.

  Serious Adverse Effects
  Allergic reactions: drug fever (see Glossary), anaphylactic reaction (see Glossary), Stevens-Johnson Syndrome—rare.
  Idiosyncratic reactions: lowered white blood cell counts or platelets (cefixime, ceftriaxone, cefuroxime)—rare and idiosyncratic (cephalexin).
  Extended time for blood to clot (reported with chronic use of other second- or third-generation cephalosporins in debilitated patients and for loracarbef)—case reports to rare.
  Genital itching (may represent a fungus superinfection)—possible.
  Serum sickness (itching, joint pain and irritated swellings)—rare.
  Increased blood urea nitrogen (BUN) or serum creatinine—rare.
  Gallbladder concretions (ceftriaxone)—rare.
  Severe diarrhea may be drug-induced colitis—rare.
  Increases in liver enzymes (cefadroxil and loracarbef) and jaundice (cholestatic) (cefaclor)—rare.

▷ **Possible Effects on Sexual Function:** None reported.

Adverse Effects That May Mimic Natural Diseases or Disorders
  Skin rash and fever may resemble measles.

Possible Effects on Laboratory Tests
  Blood platelet counts: decreased—rare (see above).
  INR:may be increased (cefixime, ceftriaxone)—rare.
  PTT:extended (cefprozil)—rare.
  Liver enzymes: increased (cefaclor, cefuroxime, cefprozil, ceftriaxone)—rare.
  BUN and creatinine: increased (cefaclor, cefprozil, cefuroxime, ceftriaxone)—rare.
  White blood cell counts: decreased (cefprozil, cefixime, cefuroxime, ceftriaxone, cephalexin, loracarbef)—rare.
  A specific kind of white blood cell increased (eosinophils): loracarbef-rare.

CAUTION
  - ***Do not stop these drugs*** without the knowledge of your doctor (may cause dangerous bacterial resistance).
  - Some drugs in this class can cause a false-positive test result for urine sugar when using Clinitest tablets, Benedict's solution, or Fehling's solution, but not with Tes-Tape.

- Cefuroxime suspension and tablets DO NOT get into the body to the same extent (bioavailability). They should not be substituted on a mg of ingredient to mg of ingredient basis.

Precautions for Use

By Infants and Children: Not recommended for use in infants less than 1 month old (cefaclor) or 1 year old (cephalexin). The maximal dose in children should not exceed 1 g every 24 hours (cefaclor). Dosing of other medicines in this class is based on weight. Follow the dosing instructions exactly. Safety and effectiveness for those under 6 months not established (cefixime, cefprozil).

By Those Over 60 Years of Age: Dosage must be carefully individualized and based upon evaluation of kidney function. Natural changes in the skin may predispose to severe and prolonged itching reactions in the genital and anal regions. Such reactions should be reported promptly. The natural decline in kidney function often requires a decrease in dose and achieves the same effect as a larger dose (all but ceftriaxone).

▷ **Advisability of Use During Pregnancy**

Pregnancy Category: B. See Pregnancy Risk Categories at the back of this book.
Animal Studies: No birth defects reported.
Human Studies: Information from adequate studies of pregnant women is not available.
Generally considered to be safe. Ask your physician for guidance. See dosing in pregnancy above for cefuroxime.

Advisability of Use If Breast-Feeding

Presence of these drugs in breast milk: Yes, in small amounts (cefaclor, cefadroxil, ceftriaxone, cefuroxime, and cephalexin); unknown (cefixime, cefprozil, and loracarbef).
Ask your doctor for advice.

Habit-Forming Potential: None.

Effects of Overdose: Nausea, vomiting, stomach cramps, and/or diarrhea.

Possible Effects of Long-Term Use: Superinfections (see Glossary).

Suggested Periodic Examinations While Taking These Drugs (at physician's discretion)
Complete blood cell counts.
Liver enzymes.
INR or PTT (for some of these medicines).
BUN and creatinine with long-term therapy.

▷ **While Taking These Drugs, Observe the Following**

Foods: Delays the absorption of these drugs and may result in decreased antibiotic effect: cefaclor and loracarbef—take these 1 hour before or 2 hours after eating. No restrictions: cefadroxil, cefprozil, cefixime, ceftriaxone, cefuroxime, or cephalexin.

Herbal Medicines or Minerals: Echinacea: Some patients use echinacea to attempt to boost their immune systems. Unfortunately, use of echinacea is not recommended in people with damaged immune systems. This herb may also actually weaken any immune system if it is used too often or for too long a time. Do NOT take mistletoe herb, oak bark or F.C. of marshmallow root, and licorice.

Beverages: No restrictions. May be taken with milk.

▷ *Alcohol:* Ceftriaxone: May cause severe nausea and vomiting.

Others: No interactions expected, but large amounts of alcohol may blunt the immune system.

Tobacco Smoking: No interactions expected. I advise everyone to quit smoking.

▷ *Other Drugs*

These medicines *taken concurrently* with

- any aminoglycoside antibiotic (see Drug Classes) may result in increased kidney (renal) toxicity.
- anticoagulants (blood thinners) such as heparin or warfarin (Coumadin) may have anticoagulant effects increased by some medicines in this class.
- birth control pills (oral contraceptives) may result in **decreased effectiveness** in preventing conception and pregnancy.
- cholestyramine may decrease cephalexin (and perhaps other drugs in this class) absorption and blunt the beneficial effects in fighting infection.
- cyclosporine (Sandimmune, others) may lead to cyclosporine toxicity with some members of this family. More frequent cyclosporine levels are prudent.
- live typhoid vaccine (Vivotif Berna) may blunt the response to the vaccine if taken with some of these medicines. Separate the last dose of antibiotic and vaccination by 24 hours.
- loop diuretics such as ethacrynic acid may result in increased risk of kidney toxicity.
- nilvadipine (Escor) may increase cephalosporin blood levels.
- probenecid (Benemid) will slow the elimination of these drugs, resulting in higher blood levels and prolonged effect.

▷ *Driving, Hazardous Activities:* Usually no restrictions.

Aviation Note: The use of these drugs *may be a disqualification* for piloting. Consult a designated Aviation Medical Examiner.

Exposure to Sun: No restrictions.

Special Storage Instructions: Oral suspension should be kept at room temperature (cefixime or loracarbef). Oral suspensions should be refrigerated (cefaclor, cefadroxil, cefprozil, cephalexin, ceftriaxone IV form). Cefuroxime may be stored at room temperature or in the refrigerator.

Observe the Following Expiration Times: Do not take the oral suspension of this drug if it is older than 14 days (cefaclor, cefadroxil, cefprozil, cephalexin, or loracarbef) or 10 days (cefuroxime).

CERIVASTATIN (SIR iv a sta tin)

Brand Name: Baycol

Author's Note: This medicine has been voluntarily removed from the market by the manufacturer because of reports of fatal muscle damage (see Table 16 for more information).

CHLORAMBUCIL (klor AM byu sil)

Introduced: 1974   **Class:** Anticancer, immunosuppressant   **Prescription:** USA: Yes   **Controlled Drug:** USA: No; Canada: No   **Available as Generic:** USA: No; Canada: No

Brand Names: Leukeran, ✽Alti-Chlorambucil

```
                    BENEFITS versus RISKS
       Possible Benefits              Possible Risks
EFFECTIVE PALLIATIVE          BONE MARROW DEPRESSION (see
  TREATMENT FOR CHRONIC         Glossary)
  LYMPHOCYTIC LEUKEMIA        INCREASED SUSCEPTIBILITY TO
EFFECTIVE PALLIATIVE            INFECTIONS
  TREATMENT FOR HODGKIN'S     CENTRAL Nervous SYSTEM
  DISEASE AND OTHER             TOXICITY
  LYMPHOMAS                   Male and female sterility
Immunosuppression of nephrotic  Drug-induced liver or lung damage
  syndrome                    Development of secondary cancers
Immunosuppression of rheumatoid
  arthritis
```

▷ **Principal Uses**

As a Single Drug Product: Uses currently included in FDA-approved labeling: Treats (1) chronic lymphocytic leukemia; (2) Hodgkin's lymphoma and other malignant lymphomas.

Other (unlabeled) generally accepted uses: (1) Hairy cell leukemia; (2) multiple myeloma; (3) Letterer-Siwe disease; (4) nephrotic syndrome; (5) ovarian cancer; (6) combined with methylprednisolone in one study to stabilize kidney disease of unknown cause (idiopathic membranous nephropathy); (7) case reports of combination treatment with corticosteroids in Sjögren's syndrome.

How This Drug Works: This drug blocks genetic activity (impairs DNA and RNA) and inhibits production of essential proteins. This kills cancerous cells.

Available Dosage Forms and Strengths

Tablets — 2 mg, 5 mg

▷ **Usual Adult Dosage Ranges:** *For leukemia and lymphoma:* Dosing is started with 0.1 to 0.2 milligrams per kilogram of body weight per day (4–10 mg per day for an average sized patient). Those with chronic lymphocytic leukemia often only need 0.1 mg/kg/day which is given all at one time. This dosing is continued for three to six weeks. Dosing is carefully adjusted according to individual patient reaction and is lowered once the white blood cell count abruptly falls. Some clinicians use twice weekly or once a month dosing schedules. Such interrupted dosing schedules usually start with one dose of 0.4 mg/kg, and dosing is increased by 0.1 mg per kg until desired control of white blood cells (lymphocytes) or toxicity is seen. After this, following doses are adjusted to result in mild blood (hematologic) toxicity. Many clinicians think that this kind of intermittant or pulse dosing is safer.

For immunosuppression: 0.1–0.2 mg/kg of body mass daily, given in a single dose, then adjusted (titrated) based on response and toxicity.

Note: Actual dose and schedule must be determined for each patient individually. Strategies for combination use are fluid and tend to evolve based on emerging research. Visit for updates!

Conditions Requiring Dosing Adjustments

Liver Function: Can cause liver damage. Use with extreme caution in liver compromise. Extensively metabolized.

Kidney Function: Can cause bladder inflammation; caution is advised in cases of compromised urine outflow.

▷ **Dosing Instructions:** Best to swallow the tablet whole—do NOT crush it. May be taken with food; however, food may decrease absorption by up to 20%. See your doctor if vomiting prevents you from taking chlorambucil. It is best to drink 6–8 glasses of water a day while you are taking this medicine. If you forget a dose: Take the dose immediately, unless it is nearly time for your next dose—then skip the missed dose and take the next dose on schedule. DO NOT DOUBLE DOSES. If you miss more than one dose, call your doctor. Remember to ask about needed vaccinations, timing of vaccinations and vaccinations to avoid.

Usual Duration of Use: Regular use for 3 to 4 weeks is usually required to see benefits in controlling leukemia or lymphoma. See dosing above and comment on pulse dosing. Repeat laboratory studies (such as complete blood counts or CBCs, uric acid, and perhaps bone marrow aspirations will help guide both results and dosing adjustments.

Typical Treatment Goals and Measurements (Outcomes and Markers)
Leukemia (chronic lymphocytic): Many clinicians use lowering of lymphocyte count and easing of lymph swelling (lymphadenopathy) as markers of response to treatment. Pulse dosing is a balance off toxicity and beneficial outcomes.

▷ **This Drug Should Not Be Taken If**
- you have had an allergic reaction or no benefit from it previously.
- you currently have an uncontrolled infection.

▷ **Inform Your Physician Before Taking This Drug If**
- you are allergic to melphalan (Alkeran).
- you are pregnant, planning pregnancy, or breast-feeding.
- you have had bone marrow depression or blood cell disorders.
- you had full-course radiation therapy less than 4 weeks ago.
- you have a history of gout or urate kidney stones.
- you develop a skin reaction while taking this drug.
- you have a seizure disorder of any kind.
- you have a history of porphyria.
- you have impaired liver or kidney function.
- you have had cancer chemotherapy or radiation therapy.
- you are taking drugs that can impair your immunity.
- you had or recently were exposed to chickenpox or herpes zoster.

Possible Side Effects (natural, expected, and unavoidable drug actions)
Decreased white blood cell and platelet counts. Decreased immunity; susceptibility to infections. Increased blood levels of uric acid, formation of kidney stones. Nausea, vomiting, or diarrhea.

▷ **Possible Adverse Effects** (unusual, unexpected, and infrequent reactions)
If any of the following develop, consult your physician promptly for guidance.
Mild Adverse Effects
Allergic reactions: skin rash, itching, drug fever (see Glossary)—rare.
Mouth and lip sores, nausea, vomiting—infrequent.
Serious Adverse Effects
Allergic reactions: drug-induced hepatitis with jaundice—case reports.
Delayed allergic reaction erythema multiforme, TEN and Stevens-Johnson Syndrome.

Cataract formation with high-dose usage—case reports.

Blindness—case reports.

Central nervous system toxicity: agitation, confusion, hallucinations, twitching, seizures, tremors, paralysis—case reports.

Peripheral neuritis (see Glossary), movement disorders (ataxia)—possible.

Lung damage (pulmonary fibrosis): cough, shortness of breath—case reports.

Bone marrow damage, aplastic anemia (see Glossary)—possible (dose-related and can be dose limiting).

Leukemia (may depend on dose and length of treatment)—possible.

Liver damage (hepatotoxicity and jaundice)—case reports.

Severe skin damage (toxic epidermal necrolysis-TEN)—case reports.

▷ **Possible Effects on Sexual Function:** Can inhibit reproduction: stops sperm production (male sterility); alters menstrual patterns (amenorrhea, others), blocks ovulation and menstruation (female sterility)—possible.

Possible Delayed Adverse Effects

Severe bone marrow depression (even after drug is stopped). Secondary cancers (especially leukemia) have been reported. Lung damage (pulmonary fibrosis). Delayed allergic reaction.

Adverse Effects That May Mimic Natural Diseases or Disorders

Drug-induced seizures may suggest epilepsy. Drug-induced jaundice may suggest viral hepatitis.

Natural Diseases or Disorders That May Be Activated by This Drug

Gout, urate kidney stones, porphyria, latent epilepsy.

Possible Effects on Laboratory Tests

Complete blood counts: decreased red cells, hemoglobin, white cells, and platelets.

Bone marrow: normalization of bone marrow prep.

Blood uric acid level: increased.

Liver function tests: increased liver enzymes (ALT/GPT, AST/GOT), increased bilirubin, increased icterus index.

Sperm counts: decreased or absent.

CAUTION

1. Long-term, ongoing use has been replaced by pulse dosing. Use of this drug in noncancerous conditions requires extreme caution. Risks include permanent sterility, lung damage and the development of secondary cancers. It should only be used where less toxic medicines have failed.
2. Periodic check for leukemia is appropriate.
3. Four weeks should pass after a full course of radiation therapy or chemotherapy before chlorambucil is started.
4. Have dental work prior starting drug. Bone marrow depression could lead to gum infection, bleeding and delayed healing.
5. If gout develops, allopurinol is the drug of choice for chlorambucil-caused gout symptoms.
6. Both killed or live virus vaccines will not work while you take this drug. Live virus vaccines may actually cause infection. It may take 3 months to a year for the immune system to recover after stopping this or similar drugs. People in close contact with chlorambucil patients should not get oral poliovirus vaccine. This eliminates risk of accidental exposure.

7. Immediately report: Infection, unusual bruising or bleeding, excessive fatigue, tremors or muscle twitching, trouble walking, loss of appetite with nausea or vomiting. The lowering of white blood cells (neutrophils) may continue for 10 days after the last dose of this medicine.
8. It is advisable to avoid pregnancy while taking this drug. A nonhormonal method of contraception is recommended. Call your doctor promptly if you think pregnancy has occurred.
9. High-dose treatment increases risk of seizures.

Precautions for Use
By Infants and Children: Dosage schedules and treatment monitoring should be supervised by a qualified pediatrician. Children with nephrotic syndrome can be more prone to drug-induced seizures.
By Those Over 60 Years of Age: Watch for central nervous system toxicity.

▷ **Advisability of Use During Pregnancy**
Pregnancy Category: D. See Pregnancy Risk Categories at the back of this book.
Animal Studies: Rat studies reveal drug-associated defects of the nervous system, palate, skeleton, and urogenital system.
Human Studies: Adequate studies of pregnant women are not available. There are two known cases of an infant born with an absent kidney and ureter following exposure to this drug during early pregnancy.
If possible, this drug should be avoided during pregnancy, especially the first 3 months. A nonhormonal contraceptive is generally advisable during treatment with this and similar drugs.

Advisability of Use If Breast-Feeding
Presence of this drug in breast milk: Unknown.
Avoid drug or refrain from nursing.

Habit-Forming Potential: None.

Effects of Overdose: Fatigue, weakness, fever, sore throat, bruising, agitation, unstable gait, bone marrow depression, seizures.

Possible Effects of Long-Term Use: Permanent sterility, secondary cancers (leukemia), lung damage (pulmonary fibrosis).

Suggested Periodic Examinations While Taking This Drug (at physician's discretion)
Before drug treatment and periodically during drug use: Complete blood counts, uric acid levels, liver function tests. Sperm counts in men.

▷ **While Taking This Drug, Observe the Following**
Foods: No restrictions.
Herbal Medicines or Minerals: Echinacea: Some patients use echinacea to attempt to boost their immune systems. Unfortunately, use of echinacea is not recommended in people with damaged immune systems. This herb may also actually weaken any immune system if it is used too often or for too long a time.
Beverages: No restrictions. May be taken with milk. Drinking 2 to 3 quarts of liquids daily can reduce kidney stone risk. Ask your doctor.
▷ *Alcohol:* Use with caution. Avoid if platelet counts are low and there is a risk of stomach bleeding.
Tobacco Smoking: No interactions expected. I advise everyone to quit smoking.
Marijuana Smoking: Best avoided. Increases risk of central nervous system toxicity. Some fungal infections (toxoplasmosis) may be contracted from marijuana itself if the immune system is weak.

▷ *Other Drugs*
    Chlorambucil *taken concurrently* with
    • amphotericin B (Abelcet) may increase risk of bronchial spasm, low blood pressure and kidney (nephrotoxicity) toxicity.
    • antidepressant or antipsychotic (neuroleptic) drugs requires careful monitoring; these drugs lower the seizure threshold and increase the risk of chlorambucil-induced seizures.
    • aspirin may increase the risk of bruising or bleeding; the platelet-reduction effects of chlorambucil and the antiplatelet action of aspirin are additive. Avoid aspirin while taking chlorambucil.
    • other immunosuppressant drugs can increase the risk of infection and the development of secondary cancers.
    • tramadol (Ultram) may increase risk of seizures.
    • live virus vaccines (such as MMWR) may result in overwhelming infections.
▷ *Driving, Hazardous Activities:* This drug may cause nervous agitation, confusion, hallucinations or seizures. Restrict activities as necessary.
    Aviation Note: The use of this drug *may be a disqualification* for piloting. Consult a designated Aviation Medical Examiner.
    Exposure to Sun: No restrictions.
    Discontinuation: Many factors will determine when and how this drug should be stopped. Follow your doctor's advice to get the best results.

CHLORAMPHENICOL (KLOR am fen ih coll)

Introduced: 1947 **Class:** Antibiotic **Prescription:** USA: Yes
Controlled Drug: USA: No; Canada: No **Available as Generic:** USA: Yes; Canada: No

Brand Names: Ak-Chlor, Chloracol, Chlorofair, Chloromycetin, Chloroptic, Chloroptic SOP, Econochlor, ✤Elase-Chloromycetin, I-Chlor, ✤Isopto Fenicol, ✤Minims, ✤Nova-Phenicol, ✤Novochlorocap, ✤Ocu-Chlor, Ophthochlor, ✤Ophtho-Chloram, Ophthocort, ✤PMS-Chloramphenicol, ✤Sopamycetin, ✤Sopamycetin/HC

BENEFITS versus RISKS	
Possible Benefits	*Possible Risks*
VERY EFFECTIVE TREATMENT OF INFECTIONS DUE TO SUSCEPTIBLE MICROORGANISMS	BONE MARROW DEPRESSION APLASTIC ANEMIA (see Glossary) Peripheral neuritis (see Glossary) Liver damage, jaundice

Author's Note: Risks are largely as defined for systemic use, not for ophthalmic use.

▷ **Principal Uses**
    As a Single Drug Product: Uses currently included in FDA-approved labeling: (1) Very effective in a broad spectrum of serious infections—however, because of serious toxicity (fatal aplastic anemia), it is now reserved for life-threatening infections (such as meningitis) caused by resistant organisms and for infections in people who cannot tolerate other appropriate anti-infective drugs; (2) used in eye (intraocular) infections.

Available Dosage Forms and Strengths
Previously available capsules and oral suspensions are no longer made.
Cream — 1%
Eye/ear solutions — 0.5%
Eye ointment — 1%
Injection — 100 mg/ml
Ophthalmic/otic suspension — 2 mg/ml

▷ **Usual Adult Dosage Ranges:** Ophthalmic: Chloramphenicol plus hydrocortisone suspension or solution is given as two drops to the affected eye every 3 hours day and night for 48 hours. After this, the time between doses is usually lengthened and therapy continued until 48 hours after the eye appears normal.
Note: Actual dose and schedule must be determined for each patient individually.
Author's Note: Because use of this medicine is largely limited to ophthalmic use, this profile has been shortened to make room for more widely used medicines.

CHLOROQUINE (KLOR oh kwin)

Introduced: 1964 **Class:** Amebecide, antimalarial **Prescription:**
USA: Yes **Controlled Drug:** USA: No; Canada: No   Available as
Generic: USA: Yes; Canada: No
Brand Names: Aralen, Kronofed-A-JR, ✚Novo-Chloroquine

Warning: The brand names Aralen and Arlidin are similar and can be mistaken for each other; this can lead to serious medication errors. These names represent very different drugs. Verify that you are taking the correct drug.

BENEFITS versus RISKS	
Possible Benefits	*Possible Risks*
EFFECTIVE PREVENTION AND TREATMENT OF CERTAIN FORMS OF MALARIA	INFREQUENT BUT SERIOUS DAMAGE OF CORNEAL AND RETINAL EYE TISSUES
EFFECTIVE COMBINATION TREATMENT OF SOME FORMS OF AMEBIC INFECTION	RARE BUT SERIOUS BONE MARROW DEPRESSION; aplastic anemia, deficient white blood cells, and platelets
Possibly effective in palindromic rheumatism	Heart muscle damage—rare
Possibly effective in short-term treatment of systemic lupus erythematosus	Ear damage; hearing loss, ringing in ears—rare
Can be of help in refractory Rheumatoid arthritis	Eye damage—rare

Author's Note: Because this medicine is not as widely used as other medicines, this profile has been shortened to make room for more widely used drugs. New combination data for this medicine combined with azithromycin (Zithromax) lead to 96% of malaria patients being symptom free.

CHLOROTHIAZIDE (klor oh THI a zide)

Please see the thiazide diuretic family profile.

CHLORPROMAZINE (klor PROH ma zeen)

Introduced: 1952 **Class:** Antipsychotic, phenothiazines, strong tranquilizer **Prescription:** USA: Yes **Controlled Drug:** USA: No; Canada: No **Available as Generic:** Yes

Brand Names: ✤Chlorpromanyl, ✤Largactil, ✤Novochlorpromazine, Ormazine, Thora-Dex, Thorazine, Thorazine SR

BENEFITS versus RISKS
Possible Benefits	*Possible Risks*
EFFECTIVE CONTROL OF ACUTE MENTAL DISORDERS	Toxic effects on the brain with long-term use—rare but possible
Beneficial effects on thinking, mood, and behavior	Liver damage with jaundice—rare
Moderately effective control of nausea and vomiting	Rare blood disorders: hemolytic anemia, abnormally low white blood cell count
	Eye toxicity

▷ **Principal Uses**

As a Single Drug Product: Uses currently included in FDA-approved labeling: (1) Treats acute and chronic psychotic disorders such as agitated depression, schizophrenia and mania; (2) can be used for presurgical anxiety; (3) helps reduce symptoms in porphyrias and tetanus; (4) is used to stop prolonged hiccups; (5) lessens or stops vomiting caused by toxic chemotherapy or a potent drug used to treat fungal infections (amphotericin B).

Other (unlabeled) generally accepted uses: (1) Can be of help in complicated drug withdrawal cases; (2) lessens the symptoms of Tourette's syndrome; (3) may be of help in combination therapy of tuberculosis; (4) can be used intravenously after some heart surgeries.

Author's Note: The information in this profile has been shortened to make room for more widely used medicines.

CHLORPROPAMIDE (klor PROH pa mide)

Introduced: 1958 **Class:** Antidiabetic, sulfonylureas **Prescription:** USA: Yes **Controlled Drug:** USA: No; Canada: No **Available as Generic:** Yes

Brand Names: ✤Apo-Chlorpropamide, ✤Chloronase, Diabinese, Glucamide

BENEFITS versus RISKS	
Possible Benefits	*Possible Risks*
Helps in regulating blood sugar in non-insulin-dependent diabetes (adjunctive to appropriate diet and weight control)	HYPOGLYCEMIA, severe and prolonged
	Allergic skin reactions (some severe)
	Water retention
Tight blood sugar control may avoid or delay blood vessel, heart, nerve, and vision damage possible with uncontrolled increase in blood sugar	Liver damage or blood cell and bone marrow disorders—rare

Author's Note: The information in this profile has been shortened to make room for more widely used medicines.

CHLORTHALIDONE (klor THAL i dohn)

Please see the thiazide diuretics family profile.

CHOLESTYRAMINE (koh LES tir a meen)

Introduced: 1959   **Class:** Anticholesterol   **Prescription:** USA: Yes   **Controlled Drug:** USA: No; Canada: No   **Available as Generic:** USA: No; Canada: No

Brand Names: Questran, Questran Light, ✽Novo-Cholamine, ✽Novo-Cholamine Light, Prevalite

Author's Note: Questran and Questran Light were proposed to the FDA to be changed from prescription to nonprescription status. Approval was not granted.

BENEFITS versus RISKS	
Possible Benefits	*Possible Risks*
EFFECTIVE REDUCTION OF TOTAL CHOLESTEROL AND LOW-DENSITY CHOLESTEROL IN TYPE IIA CHOLESTEROL DISORDERS	Constipation (may be severe)
	Reduced absorption of fat-soluble vitamins (A, D, E, K), folic acid, and niacin
Reduction of total cholesterol and LDL cholesterol	May increase triglycerides
EFFECTIVE RELIEF OF ITCHING associated with biliary obstruction	Reduced formation of prothrombin with possible bleeding
Effective binding of medicines in some drug overdoses	
Helps remove leflunomide (Arava) in patients desiring pregnancy	

▷ **Principal Uses**

As a Single Drug Product: Uses currently included in FDA-approved labeling: (1) Reduces high blood levels of total cholesterol and low-density (LDL)

cholesterol in Type IIa cholesterol disorders; (2) relieves itching due to the deposit of bile acids in the skin associated with partial biliary obstruction; (3) reduces risk of heart disease in type II hyperlipoproteinemia; (4) reduces progression of disease in coronary arteries in people with type II hyperlipoproteinemia.

Other (unlabeled) generally accepted uses: (1) Because leflunomide (Arava) stays in the body for a very long time, cholestyramine has been used by some clinicians to help remove the medicine in patients desiring to become pregnant or who are having problems with the drug; (2) may help biliary fistulas and skin irritations seen in colostomy; (3) helps lower thyroid hormone levels if too much thyroid hormone is given; (4) treats cholesterol ester storage disease (CESD); (5) treats relapses of resistant diarrhea (pseudomembranous colitis); (6) eases diarrhea caused by quinidine.

Author's Note: Information in this profile has been shortened to make room for more widely used medicines.

CILOSTAZOL (SIGH low stay zahl)

Introduced: 1999 **Class:** Blood flow agent, phosphodiesterase (type III) inhibitor **Prescription:** USA: Yes **Controlled Drug:** USA: No; Canada: No **Available as Generic:** No

Brand Name: Pletal

BENEFITS versus RISKS	
Possible Benefits	*Possible Risks*
IMPROVED BLOOD FLOW IN PERIPHERAL ARTERIAL DISEASE	Worsening of congestive heart failure (CHF) (never to be used in CHF)
REDUCES PAIN OF INTERMITTENT CLAUDICATION	Palpitation
DATA FROM A STUDY OF 1,052 PATIENTS FOUND A SIGNIFICANT RELATIVE RISK REDUCTION (41.7%) IN RECURRENT STROKES	Diarrhea
	Headache
Some increase in force of contraction of the heart	
May have a role in improving function of blood vessel linings in smokers	

▷ **Principal Uses**

As a Single Drug Product: Uses currently included in FDA-approved labeling: Management of peripheral obstructive arterial disease to improve arterial blood flow and reduce frequency and severity of muscle pain due to intermittent claudication.

Other (unlabeled) generally accepted uses: (1) May be used as part of combination treatment of problems in small vessels (microangiopathic hemolytic anemia) in graft-versus-host disease; (2) could have a role in angioplasty (percutaneous transluminal coronary) in helping keep the blood vessel from having problems after the procedure (postprocedure restenosis); (3) May have a role in preventing repeat (recurrent) strokes in people who have suffered a first stroke; (4) early data seems to show a benefit in helping control clogging of arteries (atherosclerosis) in people with type 2 diabetes; (5) appears to improve blood vessel function (by improving how well the lining or endothelium works) in people who smoke.

How This Drug Works: Acts as a selective inhibitor (type three) of phosphodiesterase. Works to keep platelets from clumping directed by arachidonic acid, epinephrine, thromboxane A2, platelet activating factor, ADP or collagen. Works to dilate the bronchi and decreases thrombomodulin in diabetics. Works to prevent repeat blockage of coronary arteries in dogs after a clot buster (thrombolytic) has been used (unknown in humans). Improves blood vessel response (vasodilation) by an unknown mechanism that probably involves the lining (endothelium) of blood vessels in smokers.

Available Dosage Forms and Strengths
Tablets — 50 mg, 100 mg

▷ **Usual Adult Dosage Ranges:** *Intermittent claudication:* 100 mg twice daily, taken half an hour before or two hours after breakfast and dinner.
Preventing a second stroke: One study used 100 mg twice daily and appeared to provide nearly a 42% decrease in repeat (recurrent) strokes (cerebral infarction).
Note: Actual dose and schedule must be determined for each patient individually.

Conditions Requiring Dosing Adjustments
Liver Function: No apparent changes in mild liver impairment. This drug has NOT been studied in moderate to severe liver impairment, but this medicine should be used with caution and patients closely monitored.
Kidney Function: No changes thought to be needed.

▷ **Dosing Instructions:** Take cilostazol at the same time each day, one half hour before or two hours after breakfast and dinner. It is taken this way because food (especially a high-fat meal) INCREASES the amount that gets into your body. If you forget a dose: Take it as soon as you remember it, unless it's nearly time for your next dose, then simply take the next scheduled dose. DO NOT double doses.

Usual Duration of Use: Regular use for 2–4 weeks may show benefits, but up to 12 weeks may be required to see the full benefit of cilostazol in preventing or delaying intermittent claudication pain when walking. Long-term use (months to years) requires follow-up with your doctor and checks of progression of blood vessel problems.

Typical Treatment Goals and Measurements (Outcomes and Markers)
Claudication: Many clinicians use distance a patient can walk without leg pain as a way to standardize response. Another measure is absence of leg pain. Ankle/brachial index (ABI) is used to check peripheral artery disease or PVD (normal value is more than one, and less than 0.9 suggests PVD). Roughly a third (33%) of people with PVD have intermittent claudication (see McDermott, M.M. et al. in Sources).

Possible Advantages of This Drug
Works on both blood vessel (vascular) beds and on heart function. Keeps platelets from clumping and may also have good effects on blood lipoproteins which adversely effect blood vessels. Good cholesterol (HDL) has been increased in some patients.

▷ **This Drug Should Not Be Taken If**
  • you have had an allergic reaction to it previously.
  • you have an active hemorrhage.
  • you have congestive heart failure.

▷ **Inform Your Physician Before Taking This Drug If**
  • you have impaired liver or kidney function.
  • you have low blood pressure or arrhythmias.
  • you get migraines.
  • you are pregnant.
  • you have a bleeding problem or low blood platelets.
  • you smoke tobacco.
  • you are taking any antihypertensive drugs, antiplatelet medicines, or anti-coagulants or medicines that change liver enzyme levels (CYP 3A4 or CYP 2C19) or block them (see drug interactions below).

Possible Side Effects (natural, expected, and unavoidable drug actions)
  Prolonged bleeding time (one investigator).

▷ **Possible Adverse Effects** (unusual, unexpected, and infrequent reactions)
  If any of the following develop, consult your physician promptly for guidance.
  Mild Adverse Effects
  Allergic reaction: Skin rash.
  Headache (mild to severe)—frequent.
  Dizziness or vertigo—rare to infrequent.
  Flushing of the face—infrequent.
  Runny nose—infrequent to frequent.
  Edema (peripheral)—infrequent.
  Back pain or muscle aches—infrequent.
  Nausea—infrequent.
  Diarrhea—infrequent to frequent.
  Palpitations or fast heart rate—possible to infrequent.
  Blood sugar changes—possible but do appear clinically significant.
  Serious Adverse Effects
  Development of heart rhythm disorders, chest pain, and heart attack—case reports.
  Increased bleeding risk with low blood platelets—possible.

▷ **Possible Effects on Sexual Function:** None reported.

Possible Effects on Laboratory Tests
  Bleeding time: extended.
  Complete blood cell counts: rarely lowers red cells.
  Blood sugar: variable changes.
  Triglycerides: decreased (beneficial effect).
  May increase HDL (beneficial effect).

CAUTION
  1. May worsen migraines.
  2. DO NOT USE IF YOU HAVE CONGESTIVE HEART FAILURE.

Precautions for Use
  By Infants and Children: Safety and effectiveness for those less than 18 years of age not established. Use by this age group is not anticipated.
  By Those Over 60 Years of Age: You may be more susceptible to effects of this medicine. Observe closely for any adverse effects and report these promptly.

▷ **Advisability of Use During Pregnancy**
Pregnancy Category: C. See Pregnancy Risk Categories at the back of this book.
Animal Studies: Increased fetal cardiovascular, kidney and skeletal problems.
Human Studies: Adequate studies of pregnant women are not available.
Talk to your doctor.

Advisability of Use If Breast-Feeding
Presence of this drug in breast milk: Yes in rats, expected in humans.
Avoid drug or refrain from nursing.

Habit-Forming Potential: None.

Effects of Overdose: Limited data: severe headache, diarrhea, low blood pressure, fast heart rate, and possible abnormal heartbeats.

Possible Effects of Long-Term Use: None reported.

Suggested Periodic Examinations While Taking This Drug (at physician's discretion)
Blood pressure measurements.
Evaluation of heart and blood vessel status. Check of HDL and triglycerides.

▷ **While Taking This Drug, Observe the Following**
Foods: Best taken on an empty stomach. Some data finds L-arginine to be helpful in intermittent claudication, but head to head trials are needed.
Herbal Medicines or Minerals: Many herbal medicines may interact with cilostazol because of its potential action on blood clotting. Examples include ginkgo, garlic, ginger, ginseng, white willow bark, and feverfew. DO NOT COMBINE THESE HERBAL MEDICINES WITH CILOSTAZOL. Capsaicin (Zostrix, others) and evening primrose oil may increase bleeding risk.
Beverages: DO NOT TAKE WITH GRAPEFRUIT JUICE.
▷ *Alcohol:* Alcohol may increase the blood pressure lowering effect of this drug.
Tobacco Smoking: Smoking decreases cilostazol benefits. Avoid tobacco.
▷ *Other Drugs*
Cilostazol may *increase* the effects of
• antihypertensive drugs and cause excessive lowering of blood pressure.
• aspirin on blood clotting, but clinical significance is not known.
The following drugs may *increase* the effects of cilostazol:
• any medicine that interferes with cytochrome (CYP3A4-major or 2C9-minor) will potentially increase cilostazol blood levels (such as sibutramine [Meridia] that uses CYP3A4). In some cases, I expect that cilostazol dosing will need to be adjusted, and in others, the combination should be avoided.
• cimetidine (Tagamet).
• diltiazem (Cardizem).
• erythromycins (see Drug Classes erythromycin and clarithromycin).
• fluconazole (Diflucan).
• itraconazole (Sporanox).
• ketoconazole (Nizoral).
• metronidazole (Flagyl).
• miconazole (Monistat).
• nefazodone (Serzone).
• nelfinavir (Viracept) and perhaps other protease inhibitors (see Drug Classes), which may increase cilostazol blood levels and effects.
• sertraline (Zoloft).

Cilostazol *taken concurrently* with
- CYP-3A4 (diltiazem-Cardizem, erythromycin). Itraconazole, others or CYP 2C19 inhibitors such as omeprazole (Prilosec) may result in excessively high cilostazol levels and increased risk of cilostazol toxicity unless doses are lowered.
- glipizide (Glucotrol) or other medicines that lower blood sugar may result in excessively low blood sugar.
- omeprazole (Prilosec) may lead to increased adverse effects if the cilostazol dose is not reduced to 50 mg twice daily.
- warfarin (Coumadin, etc.) finds that multiple dosing effects are not known.

The following drugs may *decrease* the effects of cilostazol:
- carbamazepine (Tegretol).
- phenytoin (Dilantin).
- rifabutin (Mycobutin).
- rifampin (Rifadin, Rimactane).

▷ *Driving, Hazardous Activities:* This drug may cause dizziness. Restrict activities as necessary.

Aviation Note: The use of this drug *may be a disqualification* for piloting. Consult a designated Aviation Medical Examiner.

Exposure to Sun: No restrictions.

CIMETIDINE (si MET i deen)

Please see the histamine (H2) blocking drug family profile.

CIPROFLOXACIN (sip roh FLOX a sin)

Please see the fluoroquinolone antibiotic family profile.

CISAPRIDE (SIS a pryde)

Introduced: 1993 **Class:** Gastrointestinal drug **Prescription:** USA: Yes **Controlled Drug:** USA: No; Canada: No **Available as Generic:** USA: No; Canada: No

Brand Names: ♣Prepulsid, Propulsid

Author's Note: This medicine is only available under severely restricted medication guidelines and as such is no longer covered as a full profile— the information in this profile has been shortened.

CITALOPRAM (SIH tal oh prahm)

Introduced: 1998 **Class:** Antidepressant **Prescription:** USA: Yes **Controlled Drug:** USA: No **Available as Generic:** USA: No

Brand Name: Celexa

BENEFITS versus RISKS

Possible Benefits	*Possible Risks*
EFFECTIVE TREATMENT OF DEPRESSION	Headache
	Dry mouth
Rapidly goes to work (reaches steady state)	Sleepiness
	Constipation

▷ **Principal Uses**

As a Single Drug Product: Uses currently included in FDA-approved labeling: (1) Treats depression.

Other (unlabeled) generally accepted uses: (1) may have a role in alcohol abuse; (2) can ease the frequency and intensity of tension headaches; (3) may have a role in obsessive-compulsive disorder; (4) relieves symptoms of premenstrual dysphoria syndrome (PDS); (5) eases depression that can occur after a stroke; (6) effective in panic disorder—particularly useful where headache is also seen; (7) one small study found improvement in seven 12–18 year old patients with post-traumatic stress disorder (PTSD) which warrants additional research.

How This Drug Works: It restores normal levels of a nerve transmitter (serotonin) by selectively inhibiting the reuptake of serotonin.

Available Dosage Forms and Strengths

Oral solution — 10 mg per 5 ml
Tablets — 10 mg, 20 mg, 40 mg

▷ **Usual Adult Dosage Ranges:** *Depression:* Starts with 20 mg, if no improvement after a week, dose may be increased by 20 mg/day as needed and tolerated. Most people don't have to take more than 40 mg a day, but the dose can be increased up to a maximum of 60 mg daily.

Alcohol abuse: 40 mg once daily.

Depression or crying after a stroke: 20 mg once daily with lower doses being used in older patients.

Obsessive-compulsive disorder: 20 mg to 60 mg once daily.

Infants and Children: Safety and efficacy not established.

Note: Actual dose and schedule must be determined for each patient individually.

Conditions Requiring Dosing Adjustments

Liver Function: The dose should be decreased to 20 mg daily in treating depression. One drug maker in Germany suggests a limit of 30 mg a day in liver dysfunction.

Kidney Function: Dosing changes do not appear to be needed. Patients with mild to moderate kidney failure should be closely watched for adverse effects as less than 15% of the original (parent) drug and 20% of metabolites are removed by the kidneys. Use of this medicine in people with severe kidney failure has not been studied.

▷ **Dosing Instructions:** The capsule may be opened and the contents mixed with any convenient food. The contents may be mixed with orange juice or apple juice (NOT GRAPEFRUIT JUICE). The liquid form should always be measured with a dosing spoon. Some clinicians have patients take this medicine at night in order to avoid possible drowsiness, while others have patients take this drug in the morning. If you forget a dose: Take the dose right away, unless it is nearly time for your next dose—then simply take the next scheduled dose. DO NOT double doses. Call your doctor if you find yourself forgetting doses.

Usual Duration of Use: Use on a regular schedule for 1 week may reveal start of benefits in depression. Up to 6 weeks may be needed for peak effects in (1) relieving depression and (2) the pattern of both favorable and unfavorable effects. Since there are active metabolites and a long half-life, it may take several weeks before the benefits of a change in dose are seen. Long-term use requires periodic physician evaluation. Some clinical guidelines suggest that 4–9 months of treatment should continue after the symptoms of depression go away. Some clinicians use lower ongoing doses to prevent depression. People who take their medicine regularly are least likely to have a recurrence.

Typical Treatment Goals and Measurements (Outcomes and Markers)

Depression: The general goal: to at least help lessen the degree and severity of depression, letting patients return to their daily lives. Specific measures of depression involve testing or inventories (such as the Hamilton Depression Scale-HAMD) can be valuable in helping check benefits from this medicine.

Possible Advantages of This Drug: Does not cause weight gain, a common side effect of tricyclic antidepressants. Less likely to cause dry mouth, constipation, urinary retention, orthostatic hypotension (see Glossary), and heart rhythm disturbances than tricyclic antidepressants. Since a large National Cancer Institute study found that those who suffer depression for 6 years or more have a generally increased risk of cancer, one benefit of effective treatment of depression with this drug may be a generally reduced risk of cancer.

▷ **This Drug Should Not Be Taken If**
  • you had an allergic reaction to it previously.
  • you take, or took in the last 14 days, a monoamine oxidase (MAO) type A inhibitor (see Drug Classes).

▷ **Inform Your Physician Before Taking This Drug If**
  • you have had any adverse effects from antidepressant drugs.
  • you have impaired liver or kidney function.
  • you have a seizure disorder.
  • you have a history of suicide attempt.
  • you are pregnant or plan pregnancy while taking this drug.

Possible Side Effects (natural, expected, and unavoidable drug actions)
  Increased sweating or cough—may be frequent.
  Weight loss.
  Withdrawal symptoms if this medicine is stopped suddenly (best to slowly decrease or taper the dose over 2–4 weeks or longer).
  Excessive lowering of the blood pressure upon standing (orthostatic hypotension; see Glossary)—may be frequent.

▷ **Possible Adverse Effects** (unusual, unexpected, and infrequent reactions)
  If any of the following develop, consult your physician promptly for guidance.
  Mild Adverse Effects
  Allergic reactions: skin rash, itching—may be frequent.
  Headache, insomnia, drowsiness, tremor, dizziness—infrequent to frequent (these central nervous system symptoms tend to diminish over time).
  Agitation/anxiety syndrome (acathesia like)—may be frequent.
  Altered taste, increased saliva, or nausea—frequent.

Increased appetite or gas (flatulence)—may be frequent.
Nausea, vomiting, constipation—infrequent to frequent.
Increased heart rate—frequent.
Slowing of the heart rate—case reports.
Increased urination—frequent.
Increased liver enzymes—possible.
Blurred vision—infrequent.
Excessive sweating (diaphoresis)—frequent.

Serious Adverse Effects
Allergic reactions: not reported.
Drug-induced seizures—rare and questionable cause and effect.
Changes in sodium levels—possible (SIADH or low sodium).
Suicidal preoccupation—possible.
Serotonin syndrome—case reports.
Activation of mania/hypomania—possible.
This medicine caused some degeneration of the retina in rats. The significance of this for humans is not known.

▷ **Possible Effects on Sexual Function:** Inhibition of ejaculation or inhibited orgasm in men and women—infrequent.
Amenorrhea—frequent.

Natural Diseases or Disorders That May Be Activated by This Drug
Latent epilepsy.

Possible Effects on Laboratory Tests
Blood sodium level: possibly decreased.

CAUTION
1. If dry mouth develops and persists for more than 2 weeks, consult your dentist for help.
2. Ask your doctor or pharmacist before taking any other prescription or over-the-counter drug while taking this medicine
3. A withdrawal syndrome can happen if this medicine is stopped suddenly. Best to slowly decrease this medicine (taper) over 2–4 weeks or more.
4. If you must start any monoamine oxidase (MAO) type A inhibitor (see Drug Classes), allow an interval of 5–6 weeks after stopping this drug before starting the MAO inhibitor.

Precautions for Use
By Infants and Children: Safety and effectiveness are not established.
By Those Over 60 Years of Age: Lower or less frequent doses are recommended by the German manufacturer with a maximum dose of 40 mg daily.

▷ **Advisability of Use During Pregnancy**
Pregnancy Category: C. See Pregnancy Risk Categories at the back of this book.
Animal Studies: No birth defects due to this drug found in rat or rabbit studies.
Human Studies: Adequate studies of pregnant women are not available.
Use this drug in pregnancy is a benefit-to-risk decision that MUST be discussed with your doctor.

Advisability of Use If Breast-Feeding
Presence of this drug in breast milk: Yes.
Use is a benefit-to-risk decision. There have been a few reports of weight loss, excessive somnolence and decreased feeding in babies breast-fed while the mother was taking citalopram.

Habit-Forming Potential: Not systematically studied, but a withdrawal syndrome is possible.

Effects of Overdose: Post-marketing reports of drug overdoses that included citalopram include 12 fatalities. Symptoms include agitation, sweating, tremor, nausea, vomiting, seizures, ECG changes, and one possible case of Torsades de Pointes.

Possible Effects of Long-Term Use: None reported.

Suggested Periodic Examinations While Taking This Drug (at physician's discretion)
Check of electrolytes if symptoms of SIADH begin.

▷ **While Taking This Drug, Observe the Following**
Foods: No specific guidance.
Beverages: Best taken with milk or water.
Herbal Medicines or Minerals: Since citalopram and St. John's wort may act to increase serotonin, the combination is not advised. St. John's wort also increases sun sensitivity. Ginkgo may have some MAO activity—hence this combination cannot be recommended. Ma huang, yohimbe, Indian snakeroot, and kava kava are also best avoided while taking this medicine.
▷ *Alcohol:* This combination is NOT advisable.
Tobacco Smoking: No interactions expected, but I advise everyone to quit smoking.
Marijuana Smoking or injestion: Mania resulted from combination of a selective serotonin reuptake inhibitor (fluoxetine) and marijuana in one report.

▷ *Other Drugs*
Citalopram may *increase* the effects of
• dofetilide (Tikosyn) requiring dosing decreases.
• imipramine (Tofranil).
• metoprolol (Toprol, Lopressor, others) by increasing metoprolol blood levels.
• sildenafil (Viagra) by competing for CYP3A4. Caution is advised.
Citalopram *taken concurrently* with
• azole antifungals (such as fluconazole, itraconazole, and ketoconazole) may lead to higher than expected citalopram blood levels and increased risk of adverse effects.
• buspirone (Buspar) may lead to serotonin syndrome. Avoid the combination.
• carbamazepine (Tegretol, others) may blunt benefits of citalopram, however, this combination has been used where the carbamazepine is used as a mood stabolizer.
• cimetidine (Tagamet) may theoretically lead to increased citalopram levels.
• cisapride (Propulsid) may lead to excessive cisapride levels and risk of serotonin syndrome.
• clarithromycin (Biaxin) may lead to citalopram toxicity—avoid the combination.
• delavirdine (Rescriptor) may lead to citalopram toxicity.
• dextromethorphan (a cough suppressant in many "DM"-labeled nonprescription cough medicines) has resulted in visual hallucinations when combined with fluoxetine, a related medicine. Caution is advised if these drugs are combined.
• diltiazem (Cardizem) may lead to excessive citalopram levels and possible serotonin syndrome.
• fenfluramine (Pondimin) may lead to serotonin syndrome—DO NOT combine.

- lithium (Lithobid, others) may increase risk of enhanced effects from serotonin. Caution is advised.
- medicines that inhibit CYP3A4 or CYP2C19 may lead to higher than expected citalopram blood levels and increased citalopram toxicity risk.
- monoamine oxidase (MAO) type A inhibitor drugs (see Drug Classes) may cause confusion, agitation, high fever, seizures, and dangerous elevations of blood pressure. Avoid combining these drugs.
- naratriptan (Amerge), rizatriptan (Maxalt), sumatriptan (Imitrex), almotgriptan (Axert), or zolmitriptan (Zomig) may lead to increased risk of incoordination, weakness or excessive reflex responses.
- selegiline (Eldepryl) can result in serotonin toxicity syndrome. Avoid this combination.
- sibutramine (Meridia) may lead to serotonin syndrome—AVOID COMBINING.
- tryptophan will result in central nervous system toxicity. Avoid the combination.
- any tricyclic antidepressant (amitriptyline, nortriptyline, etc.) may result in increased antidepressant drug levels and serotonin syndrome. Extreme caution is advised.
- tramadol (Ultram) may increase seizure risk. DO NOT COMBINE.
- verapamil (Calan) may lead to excessive citalopram levels and possible serotonin syndrome.

▷ *Driving, Hazardous Activities:* This drug may cause drowsiness, dizziness, impaired judgment, and delayed reaction time. Restrict activities as necessary.

Aviation Note: The use of this drug *is a disqualification* for piloting. Consult a designated Aviation Medical Examiner.

Exposure to Sun: No restrictions.

Discontinuation: Best to slowly decrease (taper) the medicine over 2–4 weeks or longer. Call your doctor if you plan to stop this drug for any reason.

Controversies in Drug Management: A review of relevant literature on the subject of depression and suicide reveals that the development or intensification of suicidal thoughts during treatment (regardless of the severity of depression) has been documented repeatedly for many patients who were also taking some of the antidepressant drugs in wide use. If you or a loved one are taking this medicine talk to your doctor immediately if suicidal thinking begins.

CLARITHROMYCIN (klar ith roh MY sin)

Please see the macrolide antibiotic family profile.

CLINDAMYCIN (klin da MY sin)

Introduced: 1973 **Class:** Antibiotic **Prescription:** USA: Yes
Controlled Drug: USA: No; Canada: No **Available as Generic:** USA: Yes; Canada: No

Brand Names: Cleocin, Cleocin Pediatric, Cleocin T, Cleocin Vaginal Cream, ✤Dalacin C, ✤Dalacin T

> **BENEFITS versus RISKS**

Possible Benefits	*Possible Risks*
EFFECTIVE TREATMENT FOR SERIOUS INFECTIONS OF THE LOWER RESPIRATORY TRACT, ABDOMINAL CAVITY, GENITAL TRACT IN WOMEN, BLOODSTREAM (SEPTICEMIA), SKIN, AND RELATED TISSUES CAUSED BY SUSCEPTIBLE ORGANISMS	SEVERE DRUG-INDUCED COLITIS (FATALITIES REPORTED— SYSTEMIC USE)
Combination treatment of *Pneumocystis carinii* pneumonia	Liver injury with jaundice—rare
Effective for local treatment of acne	Reduction in white blood cell and platelet counts—rare

▷ **Principal Uses**

As a Single Drug Product: Uses currently included in FDA-approved labeling: (1) Treats serious and unusual infections of the lungs and bronchial tubes, organs and tissues within the abdominal cavity, the genital tract, and pelvic organs in women, the skin and soft tissue structures and generalized infections involving the bloodstream; (2) used in topical form to treat acne.

Other (unlabeled) generally accepted uses: (1) Treatment of resistant gum disease and malaria; (2) prevention of infection of the heart; (3) combination treatment of *Pneumocystis carinii* pneumonia (PCP), an infection associated with AIDS; (4) may have a role in combination therapy of toxoplasmosis infections of the brain in AIDS patients.

Author's Note: This profile has been shortened to make room for more widely used medicines.

CLOMIPRAMINE (kloh MI pra meen)

Introduced: 1970 **Class:** Antidepressant **Prescription:** USA: Yes **Controlled Drug:** USA: No; Canada: No **Available as Generic:** Yes

Brand Names: Anafranil, ✦Apo-Clomipramine, ✦Novo-Clopamine, Maronil

BENEFITS versus RISKS

Possible Benefits	*Possible Risks*
EFFECTIVE TREATMENT OF SEVERE OBSESSIVE-COMPULSIVE NEUROSIS	DRUG-INDUCED SEIZURES ADVERSE BEHAVIORAL EFFECTS
Effective relief of symptoms of some types of depression	Conversion of depression to mania in manic-depressive (bipolar) disorders
Relief in some pain syndromes	Aggravation of schizophrenia
	Liver toxicity
	Bone marrow depression and blood cell disorders

▷ **Principal Uses**

As a Single Drug Product: Uses currently included in FDA-approved labeling: Relieves severe, disabling obsessive-compulsive disorder.

Other (unlabeled) generally accepted uses: (1) eases depression; (2) relieves symptoms of panic attacks; (3) helps some phobias; (4) may help repetitive symptoms in autistics; (5) could have a role in diabetic neuropathy and some low back pain problems; (6) can help premature ejaculation; (7) may relieve severity of hair-pulling (trichotillomania), nail-biting, or arm-burning in obsessive-compulsive patients; (8) can ease symptoms in severe premenstrual syndrome.

How This Drug Works: By increasing brain nerve transmitters (mostly serotonin), it reduces frequency/intensity of obsessive-compulsive behavior.

Available Dosage Forms and Strengths

Capsules — 10 mg (Canada only), 25 mg, 50 mg, 75 mg
Tablet, sustained release — 75 mg

▷ **Usual Adult Dosage Ranges:** Starts at 25 mg daily in the evening. If needed, may be increased by 25 mg daily at 3- to 4-day intervals up to 100 mg daily (reached in 2 weeks). The 100 mg should be divided and taken after meals. Usual maintenance dose is 50 mg to 150 mg daily. Maximum daily dose is 250 mg. (Once identified, the daily dose may be given at bedtime as a single dose to help ease sleepiness problems during the day and confer sleep at night.)

Note: Actual dose and schedule must be determined for each patient individually.

Conditions Requiring Dosing Adjustments

Liver Function: The dose should be decreased in patients with liver compromise.

Kidney Function: Changes in dose are not usually needed.

▷ **Dosing Instructions:** May be taken without regard to meals, but when starting this medicine it is smart to take this medicine with meals to lower GI problems. If needed, the capsule may be opened and mixed with soft goods such as applesauce—but the beads of medicine should NOT be chewed. If you forget a dose: Take the missed dose right away, unless it's nearly time for your next dose. If you only take one dose at bedtime, call your doctor. DO NOT double doses.

Usual Duration of Use: Regular use for 4 to 10 weeks often needed to see benefits in controlling obsessive-compulsive behavior. Intravenous dosing gives an initial response in less than 6 days. Long-term use (months to years) requires periodic evaluation.

Typical Treatment Goals and Measurements (Outcomes and Markers)
Obsessive-compulsive disorder: The general goal is to ease the severity of the OCD in order to let the patient resume his or her usual activities. There should involve less time spent with prior obsessions or compulsions. Blood levels of 100 to 250 ng/ml plus 230 to 550 ng/ml for desmethylclomipramine (an active chemical that your body changes this medicine into) have been designated as the therapeutic range, but the effective level varies patient to patient.

Possible Advantages of This Drug: Used as first line treatment of obsessive compulsive disorder. May be beneficial in people who also have one kind of movement disorder (akathisia) or problems sleeping.

▷ **This Drug Should Not Be Taken If**
- you have had an allergic reaction to it previously.
- you are taking, or have taken within the past 14 days, any monoamine oxidase (MAO) type A inhibitor drug (see Drug Classes).
- you have active bone marrow depression or a current blood cell disorder.
- you have had a recent heart attack (myocardial infarction).

▷ **Inform Your Physician Before Taking This Drug If**
- you have had an adverse reaction to an antidepressant drug, especially one of the tricyclic class.
- you have a history of bone marrow or blood cell disorder.
- you have any type of seizure disorder.
- you have any type of heart disease, especially coronary artery disease or a heart rhythm disorder.
- you are subject to bronchial asthma.
- you have impaired liver or kidney function.
- you have any type of thyroid disorder or are taking thyroid medication.
- you have a history of suicide attempts.
- you have an adrenaline-producing tumor.
- you are pregnant.
- you have prostatism (see Glossary).
- you have a history of alcoholism.
- you will have surgery with general anesthesia.

Possible Side Effects (natural, expected, and unavoidable drug actions)
Drowsiness, increased sweating, light-headedness, blurred vision, dry mouth, constipation, impaired urination.

▷ **Possible Adverse Effects** (unusual, unexpected, and infrequent reactions)
If any of the following develop, consult your physician promptly for guidance.

Mild Adverse Effects
Allergic reactions: skin rash, itching, drug fever (see Glossary)—case reports.
Headache, dizziness, nervousness, impaired memory, weakness, tremors, insomnia, muscle cramps, flushing—infrequent.
Tremor—frequent.
Sweating—infrequent.
Increased appetite, weight gain—infrequent.
Altered taste, indigestion, nausea, vomiting, diarrhea—infrequent.

Serious Adverse Effects
Allergic reactions: drug-induced hepatitis, with or without jaundice—case reports.
Idiosyncratic reactions: hyperthermia, neuroleptic malignant syndrome (see Glossary)—case reports.
Adverse behavioral effects: confusion, delirium, delusions, hallucinations, paranoia—case reports.
Seizures, reduced control of epilepsy—case reports to rare.
Aggravated paranoid psychoses or schizophrenia—case reports.
Heart rhythm disturbances—case report.
Bone marrow depression (see Glossary): fatigue, weakness, fever, sore throat, infections, abnormal bleeding or bruising—case reports.
SIADH and severe lowering of blood sodium—case reports.
Liver toxicity—infrequent.
Serotonin syndrome—case reports.

▷ **Possible Effects on Sexual Function:** Altered libido, impaired (delayed) ejaculation, impotence, inhibited male orgasm, inhibited female orgasm, abnormal sperm formation, female breast enlargement with milk production (galactorrhea), absence of menstruation—case reports. The delay in ejaculation is useful in males who are troubled by premature ejaculation.

Adverse Effects That May Mimic Natural Diseases or Disorders
Liver toxicity may suggest viral hepatitis.

Natural Diseases or Disorders That May Be Activated by This Drug
Latent epilepsy, glaucoma, prostatism, schizophrenia.

Possible Effects on Laboratory Tests
Complete blood cell counts: decreased red cells, hemoglobin, white cells, and platelets.
Liver function tests: increased liver enzymes (ALT/GPT, AST/GOT)—liver damage.
Thyroid function tests: decreased TT3 and FT3.
Blood sodium: severely lowered in cases of drug-induced SIADH.

CAUTION
1. Watch for toxicity: confusion, agitation, rapid heart rate, heart irregularity. Blood levels clarify the situation.
2. Use with caution in schizophrenia. Watch closely for deterioration of thinking or behavior.
3. Use with caution in epilepsy. Watch for any change in the frequency or severity of seizures.
4. Complete blood counts should be obtained in patients who develop sore throat or fever while taking this medicine.

Precautions for Use
By Infants and Children: Safety and effectiveness for those under 10 years of age not established. Dose and management should be supervised by a properly trained pediatrician. Dosing is started at 25 mg daily and is then increased over 2 weeks to 200 mg or 3 mg per kg of body mass, whichever number is smaller.
By Those Over 60 Years of Age: Started with 10 mg at bedtime. Dose is increased as needed and tolerated to 75 mg daily in divided doses. During first 2 weeks, watch for behavioral reactions: restlessness, agitation, forgetfulness, disorientation, hallucinations. Unsteadiness or instability may predispose to falling. Prostate problems may also be aggravated.

▷ **Advisability of Use During Pregnancy**
Pregnancy Category: C. See Pregnancy Risk Categories at the back of this book.
Animal Studies: No drug-induced birth defects seen in mouse or rat studies.
Human Studies: Adequate studies of pregnant women are not available.
Use only if clearly needed. Avoid use during the last 3 months, if possible, to prevent withdrawal symptoms in the newborn infant: irritability, tremors, and seizures.

Advisability of Use If Breast-Feeding
Presence of this drug in breast milk: Yes.
Talk with your doctor about this benefit to risk decision.

Habit-Forming Potential: Withdrawal symptoms have been reported (nausea, vomiting, dizziness, headache, and temperature changes), and the drug should be tapered if it is to be stopped.

Effects of Overdose: Confusion, delirium, hallucinations, drowsiness, tremors, unsteadiness, heart irregularity, seizures, stupor, sweating, fever.

Possible Effects of Long-Term Use: Neuroleptic malignant syndrome (see Glossary): Fever, fast or irregular heartbeat, fast breathing, sweating, weakness, muscle stiffness, seizures, loss of bladder control.

Suggested Periodic Examinations While Taking This Drug (at physician's discretion)

Monitoring of blood drug levels as appropriate.

Complete blood cell counts.

Liver and kidney function tests.

Serial blood pressure readings and electrocardiograms.

Visual acuity checks.

▷ **While Taking This Drug, Observe the Following**

Foods: No specific restrictions. May need to limit food intake to avoid excessive weight gain.

Herbal Medicines or Minerals: Since clomipramine and St. John's wort may act to increase serotonin, the combination is not advised. St. John's wort also increases sun sensitivity. Since part of the way ginkgo biloba works may be as a MAO inhibitor, do not combine with this medicine. Ma huang and yohimbe are best avoided while taking clomipramine. Indian snakeroot and kava kava (kava is no longer recommended in Canada) are also best avoided while taking this medicine.

Beverages: No restrictions. May be taken with milk.

▷ *Alcohol:* Avoid completely. This drug can markedly increase the intoxicating effects of alcohol; the combination can depress brain function significantly.

Tobacco Smoking: May delay the elimination of this drug and require dosage adjustment. I advise everyone to quit smoking.

Marijuana Smoking or injestion: Increased drowsiness and mouth dryness; reduced effectiveness and increased cardiovascular problems.

▷ *Other Drugs*

Clomipramine may *increase* the effects of

• all drugs with atropinelike effects (see Drug Classes).

• all sedating drugs. Watch for excessive sedation.

Clomipramine may *decrease* the effects of

• clonidine (Catapres).

• guanadrel (Hylorel).

• guanethidine (Ismelin, Esimil).

Clomipramine *taken concurrently* with

• anticonvulsants (see Drug Classes) such as carbamazepine (Tegretol) requires careful monitoring for changes in seizure patterns and the need to adjust anticonvulsant dosage.

• bepridil (Vascor) may lead to dangerous heart rhythms.

• cisapride (Propulsid) may lead to dangerous heart rhythms.

• dofetilide (Tikosyn) may lead to dangerous heart rhythms. Do not combine.

• gatifloxacin (Tequin), grepafloxacin (Raxar), moxifloxacin (Avelox), or sparfloxacin (Zagam) may lead to dangerous heart rhythms. Combination is NOT recommended.

• medicines that affect the QTc interval of the heart may worsen the QTc interval changes if combined with clomipramine.

• monoamine oxidase (MAO) type A inhibitor drugs (see Drug Classes) may cause high fever, seizures and hypertension. Avoid combining these drugs—14 days should separate doses of either.

- phenytoin (Dilantin) or fosphenytoin (Cerebyx) may lead to phenytoin or fosphenytoin toxicity.
- SAMe (S-adenosylmethionine) may lead to serotonin syndrome (mental status changes, muscle movement problems, high temperature, and high blood pressure).
- stimulant drugs (amphetamine, cocaine, epinephrine, methylphenidate, etc.) may cause severe high blood pressure and/or high fever.
- thyroid preparations may increase risk of heart rhythm disorders.
- tramadol (Ultram) may increase seizure risk.
- valproic acid (Depakote) may lead to clomipramine toxicity. Clomipramine doses should be lowered if these two medicines must be combined.
- venlafaxine (Effexor) may lead to venlafaxine and clomipramine toxicity.
- warfarin (Coumadin) may cause an increased warfarin effect and bleeding. More frequent INR (prothrombin time) testing is needed.

The following drugs may **_increase_** the effects of clomipramine:
- ACE inhibitors (see Drug Classes).
- birth control pills (oral contraceptives).
- cimetidine (Tagamet).
- enalapril (Vasotec, Vaseretic).
- estrogens (various).
- fluoxetine (Prozac).
- fluvoxamine (Luvox).
- haloperidol (Haldol).
- medicines that interfere with or inhibit cytochrome P450 2D6, a liver enzyme that is responsible for removing clomipramine from the body.
- methylphenidate (Ritalin).
- modafinil (Provigil).
- paroxetine (Paxil).
- phenothiazines (see Drug Classes).
- propafenone (Rythmol).
- quinidine (Quinaglute).
- ranitidine (Zantac).
- ritonavir (Norvir) and perhaps other protease inhibitors (see Drug Classes).
- sertraline (Zoloft).
- verapamil (Calan, others).

The following drugs may **_decrease_** the effects of clomipramine:
- barbiturates (see Drug Classes).
- carbamazepine (Tegretol).
- chloral hydrate (Noctec, Somnos, etc.).
- lithium (Lithobid, Lithotab, etc.).
- reserpine (Serpasil, Ser-Ap-Es, etc.).

▷ _Driving, Hazardous Activities:_ This drug may cause seizures and impair alertness, judgment, physical coordination and reaction time. Restrict activities as necessary.

Aviation Note: The use of this drug **_is a disqualification_** for piloting. Consult a designated Aviation Medical Examiner.

Exposure to Sun: No restrictions.

Exposure to Heat: Use caution. This drug may impair the body's adaptation to hot environments, increasing the risk of heatstroke. Avoid saunas.

Exposure to Environmental Chemicals: This drug may mask the symptoms of poisoning due to handling certain insecticides (organophosphorous types). Read their labels carefully.

Discontinuation: It is best to slowly reduce the dose over 3 to 4 weeks. Abrupt withdrawal after prolonged use may cause nausea, vomiting, diarrhea, headache, dizziness, malaise, disturbed sleep, and irritability. Obsessive-compulsive behavior may worsen if drug is stopped. Other drug doses may need to be changed to adjust.

CLONAZEPAM (kloh NA ze pam)

Introduced: 1977   **Class:** Anticonvulsant, benzodiazepines   **Prescription:** USA: Yes   **Controlled Drug:** USA: C-IV*; Canada: No   **Available as Generic:** Yes

Brand Names: ✤Apo-clonazepam, Klonopin, Klonopin Wafers, ✤Medclonazepam, ✤Novo-clonazepam, ✤Rhoxal-clonazepam, ✤Rivotril

Warning: Klonopin and the generic clonidine have similar names and can be mistaken for each other—a serious error. Make sure you are taking the correct drug.

BENEFITS versus RISKS	
Possible Benefits	*Possible Risks*
EFFECTIVE CONTROL OF SOME TYPES OF PETIT MAL, AKINETIC AND MYOCLONIC SEIZURES	Paradoxical reactions: excitement, agitation, and hallucinations
EFFECTIVE IN MANAGING PANIC DISORDER	Minor impairment of mental functions
ORPHAN DRUG FOR STARTLE DISEASE	Blood cell disorders: anemia, abnormally low white blood cell and platelet counts—rare
Can help restless leg syndrome	Increased salivation (difficult in people with chronic lung disese)
Klonopin Wafers offers the ability to take the drug without water	

▷ **Principal Uses**

As a Single Drug Product: Uses currently included in FDA-approved labeling: (1) Treats several types of epilepsy: petit mal variations, akinetic, myoclonic, and absence seizure patterns; (2) effective in panic disorder; (3) an orphan drug for startle disease (hyperekplexia).

Other (unlabeled) generally accepted uses: (1) Eases symptoms of Tourette's syndrome; (2) relieves trigeminal neuralgia; (3) helps resistant depression; (4) can ease drug-induced mania; (5) may be of help in restless leg syndrome (Ekbom syndrome); (6) may help essential tremor symptoms; (7) eases alprazolam withdrawal.

How This Drug Works: Increases the action of a nerve transmitter (gamma-aminobutyric acid or GABA), which blocks seizures.

Available Dosage Forms and Strengths

Orally disintegrating tablets — 0.125 mg, 0.25 mg, 0.5 mg, 1 mg and 2 mg (Wafers)

Tablets — 0.125 mg, 0.25 mg, 0.5 mg, 1 mg, 2 mg

*See Schedules of Controlled Drugs at the back of this book.

▷ **Usual Adult Dosage Ranges**
  Seizures: Starts with 0.5 mg three times daily. Increased by 0.5 mg to 1.0 mg
    every 3 days, as needed and tolerated. Maximum daily dose 20 mg.
  Panic disorder: Not established for those less than 18 years old.
    **Note: Actual dose and schedule must be determined for each patient
    individually**.

Conditions Requiring Dosing Adjustments
  Liver Function: The dose must be decreased in liver compromise.
  Kidney Function: Watch for signs and symptoms of accumulation (see "Effects
    of Overdose" below).

▷ **Dosing Instructions:** May be taken on empty stomach or with food or milk.
    Klonopin Wafers are orally disintegrating tablets that dissolve without
    water. The tablet may be crushed. Do not stop this drug abruptly if taken
    for seizure control, or if taken for more than 4 weeks to control panic
    attacks. If your forget a dose: take the dose as soon as you remember it,
    unless it's nearly time for your next dose—if that is the case, skip the missed
    dose and simply take the next scheduled dose. DO NOT double doses.

Usual Duration of Use: Regular use for 2 to 3 weeks may be needed to see bene-
    fit in reducing frequency or severity of seizures. Peak control requires dose
    adjustments over several months. Long-term use (months to years)
    requires evaluation by your doctor.

Typical Treatment Goals and Measurements (Outcomes and Markers)
  Seizures: The general goal for this medicine is effective seizure control. Neurol-
    ogists tend to define effective on a case-by-case basis depending on the
    seizure type and patient factors. IF goals have not been reached, combina-
    tion treatment may be needed.
  Panic: Goals for panic tend to be more vague and subjective than for hyperten-
    sion or cholesterol. Frequently, the patient (in conjunction with physician
    assessment) will largely decide if panic has been successfully controlled.
    Additional markers include: decreased number of trips to the hospital or
    ER visits may be a useful measure. The ability of the patient to return to
    normal activities is a hallmark of successful treatment.

Possible Advantages of This Drug: The new wafer form may be particularly
    suited to treatment of panic attacks, offering a medicine that goes to work
    quickly (rapid onset) and does not require water to take it.

▷ **This Drug Should Not Be Taken If**
  • you have had an allergic reaction to it previously.
  • you have sudden (acute) narrow-angle glaucoma.
  • you have active liver disease.

▷ **Inform Your Physician Before Taking This Drug If**
  • you are allergic to any benzodiazepine (see Drug Classes).
  • you have a history of alcoholism or drug abuse.
  • you are pregnant or planning pregnancy.
  • you have palpitations, as this drug may worsen palpitations.
  • you have impaired liver or kidney function.
  • you have a history of serious depression or mental disorder.
  • you have asthma, emphysema, chronic bronchitis, or myasthenia gravis.
  • you have acute intermittent porphyria or lung disease.

Possible Side Effects (natural, expected, and unavoidable drug actions)
    Drowsiness—frequent (may diminish with time).
    Increased salivation.

▷ **Possible Adverse Effects** (unusual, unexpected, and infrequent reactions)
If any of the following develop, consult your physician promptly for guidance.

Mild Adverse Effects

Allergic reactions: skin rash, hives, itching.

Ataxia—frequent.

A feeling that the mouth is burning (burning mouth syndrome)—case report.

Weight gain—frequent.

Headache, dizziness, blurred vision, double vision, slurred speech, impaired memory, confusion, depression—possible.

Muscle weakness, uncontrolled body movements—possible.

Palpitations or hair loss—rare.

Nausea, vomiting, constipation, diarrhea, impaired urination, incontinence—case reports in older patients.

Serious Adverse Effects

Idiosyncratic reactions: paradoxical responses of excitement, hyperactivity, agitation, anger, hostility—case reports.

Hallucinations, seizures—case reports.

Blood disorders: abnormally low platelet counts—case reports.

Porphyria—case reports.

Increased secretions and breathing problems, especially in those with chronic lung disease—case reports.

▷ **Possible Effects on Sexual Function:** Increased libido, enlargement of male breasts. May cause abnormally early (precocious) secondary sex characteristics in children—case reports.

Possible Effects on Laboratory Tests

Complete blood cell counts: low red or white cells, hemoglobin, or platelets.

Urine tests for drug abuse: may be positive. (Results depend on amount of drug taken and test method.)

Liver function tests: increased.

CAUTION

1. Drug should not be stopped abruptly if used to control seizures (rebound seizures may occur), and should be slowly decreased (see discontinuation) if it must be stopped.
2. Some over-the-counter products containing antihistamines (allergy and cold preparations, sleep aids) can cause excessive sedation if combined with clonazepam.
3. Adverse behavioral reactions are more common in people with brain damage, mental retardation or psychiatric disorders.
4. Decreased drug response seen in about 30% of users 3 months after therapy starts. Dose increase often needed to restore seizure control.

Precautions for Use

By Infants and Children: This drug has data for use in infants and children of all ages. Careful dosage adjustment based on weight and age is mandatory. Abnormal behavioral responses are more common in children.

By Those Over 60 Years of Age: Smaller doses and longer intervals are suggested. Watch for lethargy, indifference, fatigue, unsteadiness, disturbing dreams, paradoxical excitement, agitation, anger, hostility, or rage.

▷ **Advisability of Use During Pregnancy**

Pregnancy Category: C. See Pregnancy Risk Categories at the back of this book.

Animal Studies: This drug causes cleft palates, open eyelids, fused rib structures, and limb defects in rabbits.

Human Studies: Adequate studies of pregnant women are not available.

Avoid drug during the first 3 months if possible. Frequent use in late pregnancy may cause the "floppy infant" syndrome in newborns: weakness, lethargy, unresponsiveness, low body temperature, depressed breathing.

Advisability of Use If Breast-Feeding
Presence of this drug in breast milk: Yes.
Avoid drug or refrain from nursing.

Habit-Forming Potential: This drug can produce psychological and/or physical dependence (see Glossary), especially with large doses for extended periods.

Effects of Overdose: Marked drowsiness, weakness, confusion, slurred speech, staggering gait, tremor, stupor progressing to deep sleep or coma.

Possible Effects of Long-Term Use: Benefits versus risks must be considered carefully.

Suggested Periodic Examinations While Taking This Drug (at physician's discretion)
During long-term use: Complete blood cell counts; liver function tests.

▷ **While Taking This Drug, Observe the Following**
Foods: No restrictions.
Herbal Medicines or Minerals: Hawthorn may react antagonistically to clonazepam. Valerian and kava kava may interact additively (drowsiness). Avoid these combinations. Kola nut, Siberian ginseng, mate, ephedra, and ma huang may blunt the benefits of this medicine. While St. John's wort is indicated for anxiety, it is also thought to increase (induce) cytochrome P450 enzymes and will tend to blunt clonazepam effectiveness if combined with clonazepam. Evening primrose oil may increase risk of seizures and is not recommended. Some forms of ginkgo are contaminated with 4'-O-methylpyridoxine which can be toxic to nerves. Caution is advised.
Beverages: No restrictions. May be taken with milk.
▷ *Alcohol:* Use with extreme caution. Alcohol may increase the depressant effects of this drug on the brain. It is advisable to avoid alcohol completely—throughout the day and night—if it is necessary to drive or to engage in any hazardous activity.
Tobacco Smoking: No interactions expected. I advise everyone to quit smoking.
Marijuana Smoking: Increased sedation and significant impairment of intellectual and physical performance.
▷ *Other Drugs*
Clonazepam *taken concurrently* with
- amiodarone (Cordarone) may decrease elimination of clonazepam and also worsen toxicity by causing low thyroid function.
- carbamazepine (Tegretol) may decrease blood levels and hence benefits of both medications.
- desipramine, imipramine and other tricyclic antidepressants (see Drug Classes) can decrease the tricyclic antidepressant blood level and lessen its therapeutic benefit.
- MAO inhibitors (see Drug Classes) may result in very low blood pressure and worsening of sedation and respiratory depression.
- phenytoin (Dilantin) or fosphenytoin (Cerebyx) may result in decreased phenytoin or fosphenytoin levels.
- primidone (Mysoline) may lead to excessive drowsiness.
- ritonavir (Norvir), and perhaps other protease inhibitors (see Drug Classes), may lead to clonazepam toxicity.

- valproic acid (Depakene, etc.) may cause continuous absence seizures, and is a benefit to risk decision.

The following drugs may *increase* the effects of clonazepam:

- antifungal medicines such as itraconazole (Sporanox) and ketoconazole (Nizoral).
- cimetidine (Tagamet).
- disulfiram (Antabuse).
- macrolide antibiotics such as azithromycin, clarithromycin, or erythromycin (see Drug Classes).
- omeprazole (Prilosec).
- oral contraceptives (birth control pills).

The following drugs may *decrease* the effects of clonazepam:

- rifampin (Rifater) or rifabutin (Mycobutin).
- theophylline (aminophylline, Theo-Dur, etc.).

▷ *Driving, Hazardous Activities:* This drug can impair mental alertness, judgment, physical coordination, and reaction time. Avoid hazardous activities accordingly.

Aviation Note: The use of this drug *is a disqualification* for piloting. Consult a designated Aviation Medical Examiner.

Exposure to Sun: No restrictions.

Discontinuation: Do not stop clonazepam suddenly if it was controlling any type of seizure, or if it was taken for more than 4 weeks. Dosing should be slowly decreased (tapered) to prevent a withdrawal syndrome.

CLONIDINE (KLOH ni deen)

Introduced: 1969 **Class:** Antihypertensive, analgesic **Prescription:** USA: Yes **Controlled Drug:** USA: No; Canada: No **Available as Generic:** USA: Yes; Canada: No

Brand Names: ✚Apo-Clonidine, Catapres, Catapres-TTS, Combipres [CD], ✚Dixarit, Duraclon, ✚Novo-Clonidine, ✚Nu-Clonidine

BENEFITS versus RISKS	
Possible Benefits	*Possible Risks*
EFFECTIVE ANTIHYPERTENSIVE IN MILD TO MODERATE HIGH BLOOD PRESSURE	ACUTE WITHDRAWAL SYNDROME (rebound hypertension) with abrupt discontinuation
Effective control of menopausal hot flashes (in selected cases)	Raynaud's phenomenon (cold fingers or toes)
Effective help in narcotic withdrawal	
Has an anesthetic sparing effect in some cases	
May have a role as a second-line medicine for people who are trying to quit smoking	

▷ **Principal Uses**

As a Single Drug Product: Uses currently included in FDA-approved labeling:
(1) Used in combination with other medicines to treat mild to moderate

high blood pressure; (2) helpful in adjunctive treatment of cancer pain (helps narcotics or opioids work better).

Other (unlabeled) generally accepted uses: (1) Helps prevent migraine headache; (2) helps improve outcomes in some head injuries (may be a drug of choice there); (3) can aid menopausal hot flashes and severe menstrual cramps; (4) lessens symptoms of alcohol or narcotic drug withdrawal; (5) helped atrial fibrillation in one study; (6) second-line drug in controlling high blood pressure in congestive heart failure patients; (7) case reports of benefits in water contact pain (aquadynia); (8) useful in some diabetic nerve damage (peripheral neuropathy) and cancer pain; (9) may have a use protecting the kidneys (renal protective) from cyclosporine or in coronary artery bypass surgery; (10) useful in Tourette's syndrome; (11) second-line agent in quitting smoking; (12) given preoperatively, it was shone to lower pain coming from propofol injection in gynecological laparotomy.

As a Combination Drug Product [CD]: Available in combination with chlorthalidone. The different ways in which these drugs work complement each other, making the combination a more effective antihypertensive.

How This Drug Works: Decreases action of the brain (vasomotor center), limiting the sympathetic nervous system's constriction of blood vessels and blood pressure increases. Chlorthalidone combination helps remove excess water from the body that contributes to high blood pressure.

Available Dosage Forms and Strengths
Patches — 2.5 mg, 5.0 mg, 7.5 mg
Tablets — 0.1 mg, 0.2 mg, 0.3 mg
Tablets, combination — 0.1 mg, 0.2 mg and 0.3 mg of clonidine with 15 mg chlorthalidone

▷ **Usual Adult Dosage Ranges:** *Tablets:* Initially 0.1 mg twice daily. Increased by 0.1 to 0.2 mg daily as needed and tolerated. Usual range is 0.2 to 0.6 mg daily, taken in two doses. Maximum daily dose is 2.4 mg. Some clinicians set maximum of 1.2 mg daily. *Patches:* Applied once a week. Dosing begins with the 0.1mg a day system (Catapres TTS-1) Dosing greater than a 0.6 milligram daily dose does not often result in added therapeutic effects.

Note: Actual dose and schedule must be determined for each patient individually.

Conditions Requiring Dosing Adjustments
Liver Function: This drug is changed into six active forms. The dose must be decreased in liver compromise.
Kidney Function: Some kidney patients may require higher ongoing doses to get the best blood pressure.

▷ **Dosing Instructions:** Tablets may be taken without regard to eating. The tablet may be crushed. Patches should not be altered. If you forget a dose: For the patch form—put the patch on as soon as you remember it. If you are more than 3 days late, call your doctor. If you forget a regular release tablet, take the missed dose right away unless it is nearly time for your next dose, then skip the missed dose and take the regularly scheduled dose. DO NOT double doses. If you have trouble remembering this medicine, talk with your doctor. If a change is being made from oral treatment to the patches, it's important to remember that the blood pressure lowering effect often does not start for 2–3 days. The maker of this medicine recommends placing the patch, then on day one taking 100% of the usual dose, on day two taking 50% of the usual dose and on day three taking 25% of the usual dose. Your doctor will decide which strength patch to give you based on how large your oral dose is.

Usual Duration of Use: Use on a regular schedule for 2 to 3 weeks may be needed to see this drug's full benefit in lowering high blood pressure. If target goals are not met by the expected time frame, changes should be made. Long-term use (months to years) requires physician supervision and guidance.

Typical Treatment Goals and Measurements (Outcomes and Markers)

Blood Pressure: The NEW guidelines (JNC VII) define normal blood pressure (BP) as **less than** 120/80. Because blood pressures that were once considered acceptable can actually lead to blood vessel damage, the committee from the National Institutes of Health, National Heart Lung and Blood Institute now have a new category called **Pre-hypertension**. This ranges from 120/80 to 139/89 and is intended to help your doctor encourage lifestyle changes (or in the case of people with a risk factor for high blood pressure, start treatment) much earlier—so that possible damage to blood vessels, your heart, kidneys, sexual potency, or eyes might be minimized or avoided altogether. The next two classes of high blood pressure are stage 1 hypertension: 140/90 to 159/99 and stage 2 hypertension equal to or greater than: 160/100 mm Hg. These guidelines also recommend that clinicians trying to control blood pressure work with their patients to agree on the goals and a plan of treatment. The first-ever guidelines for blood pressure (hypertension) in African Americans recommends that MOST black patients be started on TWO antihypertensive medicines with the goal of lowering blood pressure to 130/80 for those with high risk for heart and blood vessel disease or with diabetes. The American Diabetes Association recommends 130/80 as the target for people living with diabetes and less than 125/75 for those who spill more than one gram of protein into their urine. Most clinicians try to achieve a BP that confers the best balance of lower cardiovascular risk and avoids the problem of too low a blood pressure. Blood pressure duration is generally increased with beneficial restriction of sodium. The goals and time frame should be discussed with you when the prescription is written. If goals are not met, it is not unusual to intensify doses or add on medicines. You can find the new blood pressure guidelines at *www.nhlbi.nih.gov/guidelines/hypertension/index.htm*. For the African American guidelines see Douglas J.G. in Sources!

▷ **This Drug Should Not Be Taken If**
- you have had an allergic reaction to it previously.
- you have a problem in your heart that impacts the timing of the heartbeat or transmission of electrical impulses through the heart.

▷ **Inform Your Physician Before Taking This Drug If**
- you have a circulatory disorder of the brain.
- you have angina or coronary artery disease.
- you recently had a heart attack (MI).
- you have or have had serious emotional depression.
- you have a very slow heart rate.
- you have kidney failure.
- you have Buerger's disease or Raynaud's phenomenon.
- you are taking a tricyclic antidepressant (see Drug Classes).

- you are taking any sedative or hypnotic drugs or an antidepressant.
- you will have surgery with general anesthesia.

Possible Side Effects (natural, expected, and unavoidable drug actions)
Drowsiness, dry nose and mouth, constipation—common.
Decreased heart rate, mild orthostatic hypotension (see Glossary).
Serious abnormal heartbeats possible if drug is stopped suddenly. Skin irritation (contact dermatitis) with the patch—infrequent to frequent.

▷ **Possible Adverse Effects** (unusual, unexpected, and infrequent reactions)
If any of the following develop, consult your physician promptly for guidance.
Mild Adverse Effects
Allergic reactions: skin rash, hives, localized swellings, itching—rare to infrequent.
Drowsiness—infrequent to frequent.
Headache, dizziness, fatigue, anxiety, sleep disorders (nightmares or vivid dreaming), dry and burning eyes—possible.
Painful parotid (salivary) gland, nausea, vomiting—case reports.
Dry mouth—frequent.
Urination at night—rare.
Increased liver function tests—case reports.
Serious Adverse Effects
Idiosyncratic reaction: Raynaud's phenomenon (see Glossary)—case reports.
Aggravation of congestive heart failure, heart rhythm disorders—case reports.
Depression, hallucinations or psychosis—case reports.

▷ **Possible Effects on Sexual Function:** Decreased libido or impotence—infrequent.
Enlargement of male breasts (gynecomastia)—rare.
Precocious puberty in females—case report.

Possible Effects on Laboratory Tests
Blood cholesterol or triglyceride levels: no consistent or significant effects.
Blood sodium level: increased.
Liver function: rare increases of enzymes (ALT/GPT, AST/GOT, alkaline phosphatase).

CAUTION
1. ***Do not stop this drug suddenly***. Sudden withdrawal can cause a severe and possibly fatal reaction.
2. Hot weather or fever can reduce blood pressure significantly. Dose adjustments may be necessary.
3. Report any tendency to depression.
4. Lowered response to the beneficial effects on blood pressure may happen over time (tolerance). This may require alternate medicines for blood pressure control.

Precautions for Use
By Infants and Children: Initial doses of 5–10 mcg per kg of body mass per day, divided into two or three doses, have been used. A larger evening dose and smaller morning dose can help minimize sedation during school hours when used for attention deficit hyperactivity disorder (ADHD).
By Those Over 60 Years of Age: ***Proceed cautiously*** with this drug. High blood pressure should be reduced slowly without the risks associated with excessively low blood pressure. Low initial doses and frequent blood pressure

checks are needed. Watch for development of light-headedness, dizziness, unsteadiness, fainting, and falling. Sedation and dry mouth occur in 50% of elderly users. Promptly report any changes in mood or behavior: depression, delusions, hallucinations.

▷ **Advisability of Use During Pregnancy**

Pregnancy Category: C. See Pregnancy Risk Categories at the back of this book.

Animal Studies: No birth defects reported. However, this drug is toxic to the embryo in low dosage.

Human Studies: Adequate studies of pregnant women are not available. The manufacturer recommends that women who are or who may become pregnant avoid this drug. Ask your doctor for help.

Advisability of Use If Breast-Feeding

Presence of this drug in breast milk: Yes.

This drug may impair milk production. Monitor nursing infant closely. Stop drug or nursing if adverse effects begin.

Habit-Forming Potential: A small number of reports regarding abuse of this drug have surfaced. It may cause extreme grogginess and lethargy when combined with diazepam (Valium). It may produce (with large doses of 1–3 mg) an altered mental state (nod effect) which may have lead to some abuse of this medicine. A withdrawal syndrome (rebound hypertension) is possible if this medicine is stopped suddenly, but is not withdrawal as it is used relative to opioids.

Effects of Overdose: Marked drowsiness, weakness, dry mouth, slow pulse, low blood pressure, vomiting, stupor progressing to coma.

Possible Effects of Long-Term Use: Development of tolerance (see Glossary) with loss of drug effect; weight gain due to salt and water retention; temporary sexual impotence.

Suggested Periodic Examinations While Taking This Drug (at physician's discretion)

Blood pressure measurements.

Monitoring of body weight.

▷ **While Taking This Drug, Observe the Following**

Foods: Avoid excessive salt and ask your doctor for help with salt restriction.

Herbal Medicines or Minerals: Ginseng, guarana, hawthorn, saw palmetto, ma huang, goldenseal, yohimbe, and licorice may cause increased blood pressure. Calcium and garlic may help lower blood pressure and Indian snakeroot has a German Commission E monograph indication for hypertension—talk to your doctor to see if those combinations may allow some lowering of prescription medicine doses. Eleuthero root and ephedra should be avoided by people living with hypertension.

Beverages: No restrictions. May be taken with milk.

▷ *Alcohol:* Use with extreme caution. Combined effects can cause marked drowsiness and exaggerated reduction of blood pressure.

Tobacco Smoking: No expected interactions. I advise everyone to quit smoking.

▷ *Other Drugs*

Clonidine may **decrease** the effects of

• levodopa (Larodopa, Sinemet, etc.), causing an increase in Parkinsonism symptoms.

Clonidine **taken concurrently** with

• beta-adrenergic blocking drugs (Inderal, Lopressor, Coreg, etc.) may increase rebound hypertension risk if clonidine is stopped first. It is best to stop the beta-blocker first and then withdraw clonidine gradually.

- cyclosporine (Sandimmune) may lead to cyclosporine toxicity.
- ephedrine (various) may dangerously increase the blood pressure raising effect of ephedrine.
- mirtazapine (Remeron) resulted in a large increase in blood pressure in one case report. Caution is advised.
- naloxone (Narcan, Talwin NX) may blunt the therapeutic effect of clonidine and result in a hypertensive response.
- niacin may decrease the facial-flushing side effect of niacin.
- nonsteroidal anti-inflammatory drugs (NSAIDs—see Drug Classes) may blunt blood pressure lowering benefits of clonidine.
- verapamil (Calan, others) may lead to problems in conduction of the heart.

The following drugs may **decrease** the effects of clonidine:

- nonsteroidal anti-inflammatory drugs (NSAIDs—see Drug Classes).
- tricyclic antidepressants (Elavil, Sinequan, etc.—see Drug Classes), possibly reducing clonidine's effectiveness in lowering blood pressure.

▷ *Driving, Hazardous Activities:* Use caution. Can cause drowsiness and impair alertness, judgment, and coordination.

Aviation Note: Hypertension (high blood pressure) *is a disqualification* for piloting. Consult a designated Aviation Medical Examiner.

Exposure to Sun: No restrictions.

Exposure to Heat: Use caution. Hot environments may reduce blood pressure, making orthostatic hypotension (see Glossary) more likely.

Exposure to Cold: Use caution. May cause painful blanching and numbness of the hands and feet on exposure to cold air or water (Raynaud's phenomenon).

Heavy Exercise or Exertion: Use caution. This drug may intensify the hypertensive response to isometric exercise. Ask your doctor for help.

Occurrence of Unrelated Illness: Fever may lower blood pressure. Repeated vomiting may prevent the regular use of this drug and cause an acute withdrawal reaction. Consult your physician.

Discontinuation: **Do not stop this drug suddenly.** A severe withdrawal reaction can occur within 12 to 48 hours after the last dose. It is best to gradually decrease the dose over 3 to 4 days, and check blood pressure often.

CLOPIDOGREL (KLOH pi doh grel)

Introduced: 1998   **Class:**   Antiplatelet (platelet aggregation inhibitor)
Prescription: USA: Yes   **Controlled Drug:**   USA: No; Canada: No
Available as Generic: No
Brand Name: Plavix

BENEFITS versus RISKS

Possible Benefits	*Possible Risks*
PREVENTION OF HEART ATTACK (CARDIOVASCULAR EVENTS IN PEOPLE WITH USTABLE ANGINA)	Stomach irritation, bleeding, and/or ulceration (less than aspirin)
EFFECTIVE PREVENTION OF ATHEROSCLEROTIC EVENTS	Lowered white blood cells
PREVENTION OF BLOOD CLOTS	Liver toxicity
PREVENTION OF HEART ATTACK	Thrombotic thrombocytopenic purpura
PREVENTION OF STROKE	
PREVENTION OF VASCULAR DEATH	
PREVENTION OF CARDIOVASCULAR COMPLICATIONS (SUCH AS STROKE, HEART ATTACK, OR CARDIOVASCULAR DEATH IN PEOPLE WITH ACUTE CORONARY SYNDROMES (UNSTABLE ANGINA AND NON-Q-WAVE MI) WHEN COMBINED WITH ASPIRIN	
LONG-TERM BENEFIT (THREE YEARS IN THE CAPRIE STUDY) IN PREVENTING DEATH, HEART ATTACK, OR STROKE	

▷ **Principal Uses**

As a Single Drug Product: Uses currently included in FDA-approved labeling: (1) Reduces atherosclerotic events (vascular death, stroke or heart attack, [MI]) in people who have atherosclerosis (shown by recent MI, peripheral artery disease or stroke); (2) used to lower the number of repeat problems (events) caused by clogging of the arteries (atherosclerosis) such as stroke, heart attack, or vascular death in people who have artery clogging (atherosclerosis) which is documented by a recent stroke, heart attack, or peripheral artery disease; (3) FDA approved this medicine in the first quarter of 2002 to prevent cardiovascular problems (events such as heart attack, cardiovascular death, or stroke) in patients with acute coronary syndrome (unstable angina/non-Q-wave MI) in combination with 75–325 mg of aspirin once daily.

Other (unlabeled) generally accepted uses: (1) Combined use of clopidogrel with dalteparin or when used alone helped heal wounds (refractory venous stasis ulcers); (2) Used for up to one year in the Clopidogrel for the Reduction of Events During Observation (CREDO) study in patients after percutaneous coronary intervention (PCI) showing that long-term use gave a 38% reduction in heart attack, stroke, or death.

How This Drug Works: Permanently (irreversibly) inhibits adenosine diphosphate (ADP)-induced platelet clumping (aggregation). Combination of clopidogrel with aspirin decreases a compound important to platelet function (down regulates P-selectin expression) and also decreases C Reactive Protein (CRP) in stroke (acute ischemic).

Available Dosage Forms and Strengths: Tablets—75 mg

▷ **Usual Adult Dosage Ranges**

In patients with *Acute Coronary Syndromes or ACS* (unstable angina/non-Q-wave Myocardial Infarction):300 mg is given as a priming (loading dose) to quickly gain the therapeutic effect, and then 75 mg is given by mouth each day. Aspirin (75-325 mg once a day) should also be started and used together with clopidogrel. In this population, therapy must clearly be individualized. In the CURE trial most patients were also given heparin.

After a heart attack or stroke: 75 mg once a day by mouth. This approach may take 2–3 days to have a full anti-clot effect.

In coronary stenting with gamma radiation: In the WRIST PLUS trial, a 300 mg clopidogrel dose before the procedure was given. Patients were given aspirin. In the WRIST PLUS study, patients continued 75 mg of clopidogrel for six months after their procedure.

In percutaneous coronary intervention (PCI): 300 mg given as a loading dose from three to 24 hours before the procedure. After PCI, 75 mg a day was continued for up to one year.

Conditions Requiring Dosing Adjustments

Liver Function: No change needed in mild to moderate cirrhosis (Child-Pugh class A or B). Dose lowering may be needed in moderate to severe liver disease and the drug used with caution.

Kidney Function: No changes thought to be needed.

▷ **Dosing Instructions:** May be taken with or without food. Talk to your doctor or pharmacist BEFORE combining this medicine with any other pill, herbal or nutritional medicine. If you forget a dose: take the missed dose as soon as you remember it, unless it is nearly time for your next dose. If this is the case, skip the missed dose and simply take the next scheduled dose. DO NOT double doses.

Usual Duration of Use: Ongoing use for prevention of atherosclerotic events MUST continue until your doctor tells you to stop this medicine. In Acute Coronary Syndrome (this includes unstable angina/Non-Q-wave MI). The latest FDA approval is for COMBINED USE WITH ASPIRIN and includes people who are going to be managed with medicines and those who have percutaneous coronary intervention (with or without a stent) or coronary artery bypass graft (CABG). The ongoing dose (75 mg) of clopidogrel in ACS patients is given WITH aspirin (75-325 mg) once a day for a duration of up to a year (CURE trial). The Caprie trial showed benefits for up to three years. The Clopidogrel for the Reduction of Events During Observation (CREDO) trail showed the benefit (38% decrease in heart attack, stroke or death) with a loading dose followed by 75 mg daily for up to a year. Ongoing physician supervision is required.

Typical Treatment Goals and Measurements (Outcomes and Markers)

Atherosclerotic events: Most clinicians view preventing, rather than treating an atherosclerotic event such as stroke or heart attack, as the ultimate goal of this therapy. Measurement then becomes straightforward in that fewer than expected (based on the severity of the atherosclerosis that you face) heart attack or stroke occurrences is the end point of therapy. Electron beam computed tomography (EBCT) may help define the severity of circulatory compromise.

Unstable angina: Avoidance of a cardiovascular problem (event) such as a heart attack, cardiovascular death, or a stroke.

Possible Advantages of This Drug: Combined use of clopidogrel with aspirin showed dramatic results in the CURE (Clopidogrel in Unstable angina to prevent Recurrent Events) trial. One researcher estimated that 50,000 to 100,000 strokes, heart attacks or deaths in patients with acute coronary syndromes could be prevented EACH YEAR with combined aspirin and clopidogrel use. As a result of a New Drug Application (NDA 20-839/S-019) clopidogrel was approved to use in Acute Coronary Syndrome (this includes unstable angina/Non-Q-wave MI). The added approval includes people who are going to be managed with medicines and those who have percutaneous coronary intervention (with or without a stent) or coronary artery bypass graft (CABG). The advantage of this use is that clopidogrel decreased the rate of measures (combined endpoints) of cardiovascular death, MI or stroke as well as cardiovascular death, MI, stroke or resistant lowering of circulation (refractory ischemia). The CREDO (see above) trial showed a 38% reduction in heart attack (MI), stroke and death when a loading dose and up to a year of clopidogrel was used. The CAPRIE trial showed clopidogrel benefits for up to three years. A novel, hospital-based program called STRIVE (Strategies and Therapies for Reducing Ischemic and Vascular Events) was created by the makers of this medicine. This program is a unique advantage in that it gives hospital clinicians the tools needed to most appropriately treat acute coronary syndromes (unstable angina-UA and non-ST-segment elevation myocardial infarction-NSTEMI) in the hospital where they work.

▷ **This Drug Should Not Be Taken If**
- you have had an allergic reaction to this drug or to any substance in the pill.
- you have any type of bleeding disorder (such as hemophilia).
- you are actively bleeding, such as from an ulcer or hemorrhage in the head (intracranial).

▷ **Inform Your Physician Before Taking This Drug If**
- you are taking any anticoagulant drug or you have an increased risk of bleeding.
- you are pregnant or planning pregnancy.
- you have high blood pressure.
- you plan to have general surgery (drug is usually stopped 5–7 days BEFORE major surgery). The exception to this in PCI where the medicine is given in a loading dose and continued for up to a year.
- you have a low white blood cell count.
- you have a history of liver problems.

Possible Side Effects (natural, expected, and unavoidable drug actions)
Interference with usual blood clotting.

▷ **Possible Adverse Effects** (unusual, unexpected, and infrequent reactions)
SAFETY DATA: This drug has been evaluated for safety in more than 17,500 patients at the time of this writing.
If any of the following develop, consult your physician promptly for guidance
Mild Adverse Effects
Allergic reactions: skin rash, itching—infrequent.
Headache, fatigue, depression, or dizziness—infrequent.
Flu-like symptoms—infrequent.

Loss of taste (ageusia)—case reports.

Nose bleeds—infrequent.

Sudden (acute) arthritis—case reports.

Cough—infrequent.

Increased cholesterol—infrequent.

Stomach irritation, nausea, vomiting, or diarrhea—infrequent to frequent.

Increased blood pressure—infrequent.

Serious Adverse Effects

Allergic reactions: possible.

Erosion of stomach lining, with silent bleeding—possible.

Bone marrow depression (see Glossary): fatigue, weakness, fever, sore throat, abnormal bleeding or bruising—possible.

Thrombotic thrombocytopenic purpura (low blood platelets, anemia, fever, nerve and kidney changes)—20 cases reported to date (onset mostly within 2 weeks after treatment was started).

Hemothorax—rare.

Hemolytic uremic syndrome—case report.

Ischemic necrosis—rare.

Hepatitis with jaundice (see Glossary): yellow skin and eyes, dark-colored urine, light-colored stool—possible.

Intracranial bleeding—possible.

▷ **Possible Effects on Sexual Function:** Excessive menstrual flow (menorrhagia)—case reports.

Adverse Effects That May Mimic Natural Diseases or Disorders

Liver damage may suggest viral hepatitis or reveal (unmask) low-level (subclinical) liver disease.

Possible Effects on Laboratory Tests

Bleeding time: prolonged.

Cholesterol: possibly increased.

Complete blood counts: decreased white blood cells (agranulocytosis, neutropenia, or granulocytopenia)—possible.

Liver function tests: increased ALT/GPT, AST/GOT, alkaline phosphatase.

CAUTION

1. You may take longer than usual to stop bleeding.
2. Since this medicine is indicated for preventing problems in people with atherosclerosis, the atherosclerosis needs to be diagnosed by: recent heart attack or stroke or established peripheral artery disease. Make certain you also understand the goal of the cholesterol-lowering medicine you are taking.
3. If you are planning surgery, talk to your doctor about how soon before surgery they want you to stop this medicine (usually 7 days in zero antiplatelet effect is desired).
4. Call your doctor if you start to develop infections more often than usual.

Precautions for Use

By Infants and Children: Safety and efficacy not evaluated.

By Those Over 60 Years of Age: The blood levels achieved with the standard dose are significantly higher than those in younger patients, but no dosing changes are presently thought to be needed. Watch for gray- to black-colored stools, an indication of stomach bleeding.

▷ **Advisability of Use During Pregnancy**

Pregnancy Category: B. See Pregnancy Risk Categories at the back of this book.

Animal Studies: No changes in rats at up to 78 times the human dose.

Human Studies: Adequate human studies are not available. Talk to your doctor to see if benefit outweighs the risk.

Advisability of Use If Breast-Feeding
Presence of this drug in breast milk: Yes in rats, unknown in humans. Avoid drug or refrain from nursing.

Habit-Forming Potential: None.

Effects of Overdose: One overdose (1,050 mg) resulted in no special treatment or adverse effects.

Possible Effects of Long-Term Use: Prolonged bleeding time, critical in the event of injury or surgery.

Suggested Periodic Examinations While Taking This Drug (at physician's discretion)
Complete blood cell counts.
Liver function tests.

▷ **While Taking This Drug, Observe the Following**
Foods: No effect by food on how much gets into your body.
Herbal Medicines or Minerals: Many herbal medicines may interact with clopidogrel. Examples include capsaicin, primrose oil (EPO), ginkgo, garlic, ginger, ginseng, guggul, anise, skull cap, white willow bark, and feverfew. Combining those medicines with clopidogrel is not recommended. Talk to your doctor BEFORE adding any herbal medicine.
Beverages: No restrictions. May be taken with milk.
▷ *Alcohol:* Use of alcohol and clopidogrel at the same time may increase risk of stomach damage and may prolong bleeding time.
Tobacco Smoking: No interactions expected, but I advise everyone to quit smoking.
▷ *Other Drugs*
Clopidogrel may *increase* the effects of
- aspirin (various), posing an increased bleeding risk—however the CURE trial showed a dramatic benefit in Acute Coronary Syndrome patients where aspirin was combined with clopidogrel. Some pharmacy drug interactions programs do not yet have this information or have confusing extra (auxiliary labels) that are put on the prescription bottles about combined use with aspirin. The indication for clopidogrel is for COMBINED USE WITH ASPIRIN for people with acute coronary syndromes (unstable angina/non Q wave heart attack-MI). See dosing above. The ongoing dose (75 mg) of clopidogrel in those patients is given WITH aspirin (75-325 mg) once a day for a duration of up to a year. Talk to your doctor about this important combination and what he or she wants you to do if any conflicting information arises from a pharmacy computer.
- eptifibatide (Integrilin), leading to an increased bleeding risk.
- fluvastatin (Lescol) (blood levels may be increased because of overlapping liver removal-CYP-2C9).
- heparin, leading to increased bleeding risk (used with caution).
- medicines removed by cytochrome P450 2C9 may be increased if combined with clopidogrel (an inhibitor of this enzyme).
- oral anticoagulants (see Drug Classes) such as warfarin (Coumadin), low molecular weight heparins (see Drug Classes) and cause abnormal bleeding.
- phenytoin (Dilantin) and fosphenytoin (Cerebyx). More frequent blood levels and dosage adjustments are prudent.

- tamoxifen (Nolvadex), leading to tamoxifen toxicity.
- tolbutamide (Orinase), leading to tolbutamide toxicity.

Clopidogrel *taken concurrently* with

- alendronate (Fosamax) may result in increased risk of stomach upset/diarrhea.
- atorvastatin (Lipitor) may blunt the benefits of clopidogrel. This is a new drug interaction. The degree of clinical effect of this interaction is not presently known. It appears prudent that testing of platelet aggregation be undertaken if these medicines must be combined. If this is not possible, pravastatin (Pravachol) or rosuvastatin (Crestor—investigational) should be considered as they do not use the same liver pathway.
- capsaicin (Zostrix, others) may increase bleeding risk because of overlapping effects on platelets.
- cortisonelike drugs (see Drug Classes) increases risk of stomach ulcers.
- high blood pressure medicines (antihypertensives) may lessen lowering of elevated blood pressure.
- thrombolytic agents (such as TPA, streptokinase, TNKase, others) may lead to increased bleeding risk.
- torsemide (Demadex), leading to excessive torsemide effect.
- zafirlukast (Accolate) may cause additive inhibition of the CYP2C9 isoenzyme, possibly increasing blood levels of other medicines removed by CYP2C9.

The following drug may *decrease* the effects of clopidogrel:

- cholestyramine (Questran, others) might decrease the amount of clopidogrel that goes to work—separate doses by 30 minutes.

▷ *Driving, Hazardous Activities:* No restrictions or precautions.

Aviation Note: It is advisable to watch for dizziness and fatigue and restrict activities accordingly.

Exposure to Sun: No reports of problems.

Discontinuation: Talk to your doctor before stopping this medicine for any reason.

CLOTRIMAZOLE (kloh TRIM a zohl)

Introduced: 1976   **Class:**   Antifungal   **Prescription**: USA: Yes, though some are nonprescription   **Controlled Drug:**   USA: No; Canada: No   **Available as Generic:**   USA: Yes; Canada: No

Brand Names: ✤Canesten, Clotrimaderm, ✤Desenex, Desenex AF, Femcare, Femzol-7, Gyne-Lotrimin (1% cream and insert are nonprescription), ✤Lotriderm, Lotrimin, Lotrimin AF (nonprescription), Lotrisone, Mycelex (1% vaginal cream is nonprescription), Mycelex-G, Mycelex-7, ✤Myclo, ✤Myclo-Gyne, ✤Neo-Zol

Warning: The brand names Mycelex and Myoflex sound similar. This can lead to serious errors. Make sure you are using the correct drug.

BENEFITS versus RISKS

Possible Benefits	*Possible Risks*
EFFECTIVE TREATMENT AND PREVENTION OF *CANDIDA* (YEAST) INFECTIONS OF THE MOUTH AND THROAT (THRUSH)	Skin and mucous membrane irritation due to sensitization (drug-induced allergy)
EFFECTIVE TREATMENT OF *CANDIDA* (YEAST) INFECTIONS OF THE SKIN	Nausea, vomiting, stomach cramping, diarrhea (when swallowed)
EFFECTIVE TREATMENT OF *CANDIDA* (YEAST) INFECTIONS OF THE VULVA AND VAGINA	
EFFECTIVE TREATMENT OF TINEA (RINGWORM) INFECTIONS OF THE SKIN	

▷ **Principal Uses**

As a Single Drug Product: Uses currently included in FDA-approved labeling: (1) Treats *Candida* (yeast) infections of skin, mouth, throat, vulva, and vagina; (2) treats tinea and related infections: ringworm of the body, groin (jock itch), or feet (athlete's foot), due to susceptible fungi; (3) treats pityriasis.

Other (unlabeled) generally accepted uses: (1) Prevention of *Candida* (yeast) infections of the mouth and throat in the management of HIV; an orphan drug for treatment of sickle cell disease.

How This Drug Works: It damages cell walls and blocks critical enzymes, inhibiting fungal growth (with low drug levels) and kills fungus (with high drug concentrations).

Available Dosage Forms and Strengths

Cream — 1% (10 mg/g)
Lotion — 1% (10 mg/g)
Mouth lozenges — 10 mg
Topical solution — 1% (10 mg/ml)
Vaginal cream — 1% (10 mg/g), 2% (20 mg/g)
Vaginal tablets — 100 mg, 200 mg, 500 mg

▷ **Recommended Dosage Ranges** (Actual dosage and schedule must be determined for each patient individually.)

Infants and Children: Use of lozenges not recommended for children under 5 years of age; for 5 years and older, dissolve one lozenge slowly and completely in mouth five times a day for 14 days, longer if necessary.

12 to 60 Years of Age:

For Candida infections of mouth and throat: Dissolve 1 lozenge slowly and completely in mouth five times a day for 14 days; extended treatment will be necessary for people with AIDS.

For PREVENTING Candida infections of mouth and throat: One lozenge (troche) is dissolved in the mouth three times a day while patients are getting medicines that blunt the immune system (such as in kidney transplants, leukemia, and some tumors). Your doctor will decide when to stop the prophylactic use.

For Candida and tinea infections of skin: Apply cream, lotion, or solution to infected areas twice a day, morning and evening. Make certain that you use this product for the length of time specified by your doctor (if a prescription form) or by the label if you are using a nonprescription form.

For Candida infections of vulva and vagina: One applicatorful (5 g) of cream intravaginally at bedtime for 7 consecutive days; or one 100-mg tablet intravaginally at bedtime for 7 days; or one- 200-mg tablet intravaginally at bedtime for 3 days; or as a single-dose treatment, one 500-mg tablet intravaginally at bedtime, one time only.

Over 60 Years of Age: Same as 12 to 60 years of age.

Conditions Requiring Dosing Adjustments

Liver Function: This drug is removed via the bile—dose should be decreased if bile duct is blocked.

Kidney Function: Dosing changes are not needed.

▷ **Dosing Instructions:** Dissolve lozenge in mouth completely, swallowing saliva as it accumulates. Do not chew the lozenge or swallow it whole. Take full course prescribed. Vaginal forms will seep out of the vagina. It's prudent to wear a minipad to protect your clothing. If symptoms persist after or worsen during a course of nonprescription forms, see your doctor. Many clinicians prefer multiple-day regimens for more complicated or severe vulvovaginal yeast infections. If you forget a dose: Take the missed dose right away, unless it is nearly time for your next dose—then skip the missed dose and just take the next scheduled dose. DO NOT double doses.

Usual Duration of Use: Regular use for a weeks usually needed to see benefit in controlling yeast or tinea infection. Some single-, 3- or 7-day courses are appropriate for some creams or tablets. Long-term use (as in AIDS management) requires periodic physician evaluation. Treatment failure may indicate need for new combination HIV therapy in HIV positive patients.

Typical Treatment Goals and Measurements (Outcomes and Markers)

Infections: The most commonly used measures of serious infections are white blood cell counts and differentials (the kind of blood cells that occur most often in your blood) and temperature. For uncomplicated vaginal yeast infections, many clinicians look for positive changes in 48 hours. If this is a multi-day course, NEVER stop an antifungal because you start to feel better. The goals and time frame (see peak benefits above) should be discussed with you when the prescription is written.

Possible Advantages of This Drug

Reasonably effective with minimal toxicity. More palatable than nystatin.

▷ **This Drug Should Not Be Taken If**
- you have had an allergic reaction to it previously.

▷ **Inform Your Physician Before Taking This Drug If**
- you are allergic to related antifungal drugs: fluconazole, itraconazole, ketoconazole, miconazole.
- you have liver problems and take oral clotrimazole troche.
- you think you are pregnant.

Possible Side Effects (natural, expected, and unavoidable drug actions)
None.

▷ **Possible Adverse Effects** (unusual, unexpected, and infrequent reactions)
If any of the following develop, consult your physician promptly for guidance.

Mild Adverse Effects

Allergic reactions: skin rash, hives, itching, burning, swelling, blistering (not present prior to treatment)—possible.

Depression, disorientation, or drowsiness—may be frequent with oral therapy.

Nausea, vomiting, stomach cramping, diarrhea (when swallowed)—frequent.

Serious Adverse Effects

Allergic reactions: sensitization of tissues (where applied locally) that will react allergically with future drug application—possible.

Inverted T waves on the ECG—case report.

Liver toxicity (with oral form)—infrequent.

Author's Note: Side effects with topical forms are rare.

▷ **Possible Effects on Sexual Function:** None.

Possible Delayed Adverse Effects: Local tissue sensitization to this drug.

Possible Effects on Laboratory Tests

Liver function tests: increased liver enzyme AST/GOT in 15% of oral form users.

CAUTION

1. Avoid contact of cream, lotion, and solution with the eyes.
2. Do not cover applied cream or lotion with an occlusive dressing.
3. Failure of treatment may mean resistant fungi.
4. Failure of treatment in AIDS patients may mean resistant HIV.

Precautions for Use

By Infants and Children: Use of lozenges by those under 5 years of age is not recommended.

By Those Over 60 Years of Age: No specific problems reported.

▷ **Advisability of Use During Pregnancy**

Pregnancy Category: B for vaginal or topical use. C for troches. See Pregnancy Risk Categories at the back of this book.

Animal Studies: No drug-induced birth defects were found in mouse, rat, or rabbit studies.

Human Studies: Adequate studies of pregnant women are not available.

Ask your physician for guidance.

Advisability of Use If Breast-Feeding

Presence of this drug in breast milk: Unknown.

Watch infant closely. Stop drug or nursing if adverse effects.

Habit-Forming Potential: None.

Effects of Overdose: Excessive use of lozenges may cause nausea, vomiting, or diarrhea.

Possible Effects of Long-Term Use: None reported.

Suggested Periodic Examinations While Taking This Drug (at physician's discretion)

Ongoing oral use: liver function tests.

▷ **While Taking This Drug, Observe the Following**

Foods: No restrictions.

Herbal Medicines or Minerals: Echinacea: Some patients use echinacea to attempt to boost their immune systems. Unfortunately, use of echinacea is not recommended in people with damaged immune systems. This herb may also actually weaken any immune system if it is used too often or for too long a time. Do NOT take mistletoe herb, oak bark or F.C. of marshmallow root, and licorice.

Beverages: No restrictions.

▷ *Alcohol:* No interactions expected.

Tobacco Smoking: No interactions expected. I advise everyone to quit smoking.

▷ *Other Drugs:*

Clotrimazole (oral dosage forms) ***taken concurrently*** with

- amphotericin B lipid complex (Abelcet) may blunt benefits.
- aspirin (various) may lead to additive stomach and intestinal (GI upset, bleeding) problems.
- betamethasone (Betaderm, Diprolene, others) resulted in enhanced fungal growth (Majocchi's granulomas) in one case report.
- cyclosporine (Sandimmune) may result in cyclosporine toxicity.
- dofetilide (Tikosyn) may result in dofetilide toxicity.
- sirolimus (Rapamune) and tacrolimus (Prograf) can result in increased sirolimus or tacrolimus levels and increased risk of kidney toxicity and increased potassium and glucose.
- trimetrexate (Neutrexin) may result in trimexate toxicity.

▷ *Driving, Hazardous Activities:* No restrictions.

Aviation Note: No restrictions.

Exposure to Sun: No restrictions.

Discontinuation: As directed by your doctor.

CLOXACILLIN (klox a SIL in)

Please see the penicillin family profile.

CLOZAPINE (KLOH za peen)

Introduced: 1975   **Class:**   Antipsychotic, atypical · antipsychotic
Prescription: USA: Yes   **Controlled Drug:**   USA: No   **Available as Generic:**   USA: Yes

Brand Names: ✤Apo-Clozaril, Clozaril

Author's Note: In the United States, this drug is available only by special arrangement through the Clozaril National Registry. Your doctor will call 800-448-5938 to register you and then a form is filled out by the MD and pharmacy, which is faxed to 800-648-6015. The medicine can then be ordered directly from the pharmacy wholesaler. This is to make certain that required blood tests are obtained, and proper follow up undertaken. Ask your doctor for help.

BENEFITS versus RISKS	
Possible Benefits	*Possible Risks*
EFFECTIVE CONTROL OF SEVERE SCHIZOPHRENIA THAT HAS FAILED TO RESPOND ADEQUATELY TO OTHER APPROPRIATE DRUGS	SERIOUS BLOOD CELL DISORDERS: ABNORMALLY LOW WHITE BLOOD CELL AND PLATELET COUNTS
Improvement in many refractory cases	DRUG-INDUCED SEIZURES (DEPENDING ON SIZE OF DOSE)
Useful in patients who have tardive dyskinesia	HEART MUSCLE INFLAMMATION (MYOCARDITIS)
This class of medicines may be drugs of choice in older adults	

▷ **Principal Uses**

As a Single Drug Product: Uses currently included in FDA-approved labeling: (1) Manages severe schizophrenia that fails to respond to adequate trials of other standard antipsychotic medicines. Because of potential for serious blood cell disorders and seizures, its use is reserved for severely ill schizophrenic patients; (2) helps control suicidal behavior.

Other (unlabeled) generally accepted uses: (1) Severe and refractory bipolar disorder; (2) severe tardive dyskinesia (dystonic subtype)—a syndrome that can happen after some medicines are used to treat psychosis; (3) psychosis occurring after labor with lactation; (4) may help excessive urination (polydipsia) caused by other neuroleptic agents.

How This Drug Works: By blocking the place (receptor) where dopamine works, this drug corrects an imbalance of nerve impulses causing schizophrenic thought disorders.

Available Dosage Forms and Strengths

Tablets — 25 mg, 100 mg

▷ **Usual Adult Dosage Ranges:** *Resistant schizophrenia:* Starts with 12.5 mg (half of a 25 mg tablet) once or two times a day; the dose is gradually increased by 25 mg to 50 mg daily, as tolerated, to reach a dose of 300 mg to 450 mg daily (divided into three doses) by the end of 2 weeks. Later increases should be limited to 100 mg one or two times a week. For ongoing (maintenance) doses, the lowest effective dose should be used. One researcher commented on dosing ranges from 50 to 900 mg daily.

Note: Actual dose and schedule must be determined for each patient individually.

Conditions Requiring Dosing Adjustments

Liver Function: Eliminated in the liver; however, no specific dosing guidelines are available.

Kidney Function: Patients with kidney failure should be watched closely for adverse effects.

▷ **Dosing Instructions:** White blood cell checks are MANDATORY with this medicine. May be taken without regard to meals or with food if necessary to reduce stomach irritation. The tablet may be crushed. If you forget a dose: Take the missed dose as soon as you remember it, unless it is nearly time for the next scheduled dose—then skip the missed dose and take the scheduled dose on time. DO NOT double doses.

Usual Duration of Use: Benefits may be seen after 2 to 4 weeks of regular use. Peak effect may require 3 to 12 months. If no significant benefit is seen, many clinicians stop the drug. Long-term use requires periodic evaluation for desirable results, laboratory testing and checks to see if lower doses and continued treatment is needed.

Typical Treatment Goals and Measurements (Outcomes and Markers)

Schizophrenia: The general goal: to ease the severity of symptoms in order to let the patient resume his or her usual activities. There should be lessened time spent with prior intrusions of abnormal thinking into more normal life. This improved quality of life (QOL) and the patient perception of QOL may be measured by the Quality of Life Enjoyment and Satisfaction Questionnaire. Numerous clinical ratings such as the Brief Psychiatric Rating Scale (BPRS24) and the Physician Global rating Scale (PhGRS) as well as dimensions of temperament such as the tridimensional personality questionnaire (TPQ) have been used to check results of therapy. The Minnesota Multiphasic personality Inventory and several subscales are also used.

Possible Advantages of This Drug: Rarely causes significant sexual dysfunction. Low incidence of Parkinson-like reactions (see Glossary). Only case reports of tardive dyskinesia (see Glossary). Medicines in this class are probably drugs of choice in older adults. Additional information is available at *www.clozapineregistry.com, www.nimh.gov*.

Currently a Drug of Choice: For treatment of severe schizophrenia in patients who have not responded to other standard antipsychotic drugs.

▷ **This Drug Should Not Be Taken If**
- you have had an allergic reaction to it previously.
- you have had severe bone marrow depression (impaired white blood cell production) with previous use of this drug.
- you have a bone marrow or blood cell disorder.
- you have epilepsy that is not controlled.
- you have severe kidney failure.
- you take any other drug that can cause bone marrow depression (see Glossary).

▷ **Inform Your Physician Before Taking This Drug If**
- you have a history of any type of seizure disorder.
- you have a history of narrow-angle glaucoma.
- you have any type of heart or circulatory disorder, especially heart rhythm abnormalities or hypertension.
- you have diabetes or glucose intolerance.
- your body is very depleted (cachectic).
- you have impaired liver or kidney function.
- you have prostatism (see Glossary).

Possible Side Effects (natural, expected, and unavoidable drug actions)
Drowsiness, sedation—frequent.
Weight gain—frequent.
Dizziness, light-headedness—infrequent to frequent.
Orthostatic hypotension (see Glossary)—possible.
Blurred vision, salivation, dry mouth, impaired urination, constipation—possible.

▷ **Possible Adverse Effects** (unusual, unexpected, and infrequent reactions)
If any of the following develop, consult your physician promptly for guidance.
Mild Adverse Effects
Allergic reactions: skin rash; drug fever (see Glossary), which usually occurs within the first 3 weeks of treatment and is self-limiting—rare.
Headache, tremor, fainting, sleep disorders, restlessness, confusion, depression—rare.
Edema (in the ankles and around the eyes)—rare.
Increased salivation—frequent.
Rapid heartbeat (tachycardia), hypertension, chest pain—rare to infrequent.
Nausea, indigestion, vomiting, diarrhea—rare.

Serious Adverse Effects
Allergic reactions: asthmatic-type respiratory reaction—case reports.
Bone marrow depression: specific impairment of white blood cell production with potential for serious infection—rare.
Increased eosinophils (a type of white blood cell) above 4,000 per cubic millimeter—rare.
Systemic lupus erythematosus like reaction—case reports.
Glucose intolerance—case reports.

Build up of lactic acid (lactic acidosis)—case reports.

Drug-induced seizures, dose-related—rare.

Tardive dyskinesia—case reports.

Heart muscle inflammation (myocarditis-now in a boxed warning in the FDA labeling)—possible

Lung clot (pulmonary thromboembolism)—case reports.

Anticholinergic syndrome—rare.

Neuroleptic malignant syndrome—case reports.

▷ **Possible Effects on Sexual Function:** Decreased libido and impotence—infrequent and dose-related (over 150 mg).

Abnormal ejaculation or priapism (see Glossary)—rare.

Adverse Effects That May Mimic Natural Diseases or Disorders

Drug-induced fever may suggest systemic infection. Because of the risk of bone marrow depression and secondary infection, any occurrence of fever must be carefully evaluated. Drug-induced seizures may suggest the possibility of epilepsy.

Natural Diseases or Disorders That May Be Activated by This Drug

Latent glaucoma, prostatism, diabetes.

Possible Effects on Laboratory Tests

White blood cell counts: decreased.

Eosinophils: may be rarely increased significantly.

CAUTION

1. Baseline white blood cell counts must be checked before clozapine treatment is started; follow-up counts must be made every week during the entire course of treatment and for 4 weeks after discontinuation of clozapine.
2. Promptly report any signs of infection: fever, sore throat, flu-like symptoms, skin infections, painful urination, etc.
3. Report promptly light-headedness or dizziness on rising from a sitting or lying position—this could be orthostatic hypotension (see Glossary).
4. There have been case reports of glucose intolerance and diabetes mellitus with this medicine.
5. Call your doctor before taking any other medication. (ANY prescription or over-the-counter drug.)

Precautions for Use

By Infants and Children: Safety and effectiveness have NOT been established.

By Those Over 60 Years of Age: Starting doses of 6.25 to 12.5 mg are prudent with required increases not exceeding 25 mg a day. There is an increased risk of orthostatic hypotension, confusion, blood problems, and prostatism. Report related symptoms promptly.

▷ **Advisability of Use During Pregnancy**

Pregnancy Category: B. See Pregnancy Risk Categories at the back of this book.

Animal Studies: No birth defects due to this drug reported.

Human Studies: Adequate studies of pregnant women are not available.

Use this drug only if clearly needed.

Advisability of Use If Breast-Feeding

Presence of this drug in breast milk: Yes, in animal studies.

Avoid drug or refrain from nursing.

Habit-Forming Potential: None, but a withdrawal syndrome has been reported after suddenly stopping long-term therapy.

Effects of Overdose: Marked drowsiness, delirium, hallucinations, rapid and irregular heartbeat, irregular breathing, fainting.

Possible Effects of Long-Term Use: Tardive dyskinesia—case report.

Suggested Periodic Examinations While Taking This Drug (at physician's discretion)

  White blood and differential counts prior to starting therapy, every week during therapy, and for 4 weeks after stopping therapy.

  Serial blood pressure measurements and electrocardiograms.

  Plasma drug levels (controversial)—350–420 micrograms per liter.

▷ **While Taking This Drug, Observe the Following**

  Foods: Because many non-prescription diet aids have large amounts of caffeine, make certain that you carefully read the label and talk to your doctor and pharmacist before combining such a product with clozapine. Dehydroepiandrosterone (DHEA) supplementation may lower benefits from clozapine.

  Herbal Medicines or Minerals: Kava and valerian may worsen drowsiness. Since part of the way that ginkgo biloba may work is as a MAO inhibitor, combination with this medicine is not advisable. Evening primrose has some case reports of increasing seizure risk when combined with medicines that are structurally similar to clozapine. St. John's wort may increase the removal of clozapine from the body—combined use is NOT recommended. Because the active ingredient of guarana and mate is caffeine—these products should be avoided.

  Beverages: The caffeine in coffee can block the removal of clozapine if 400 to 1000 mg of caffeine a day is taken. For this reason, guarana, and mate should be avoided. May be taken with milk.

▷ *Alcohol:* Avoid completely. Alcohol increases clozapine-induced sedation and can worsen possible undesirable side effects of clozapine on blood pressure and brain function.

  Tobacco Smoking: May accelerate the elimination of this drug and require increased dosage. I advise everyone to quit smoking.

  Marijuana Smoking: Moderate increase in drowsiness, worsening of orthostatic hypotension, increased risk of aggravating psychosis.

▷ *Other Drugs*

  Clozapine may *increase* the effects of

  • antihypertensive drugs; observe for excessive lowering of blood pressure.
  • drugs with atropinelike actions (see Drug Classes).
  • drugs with sedative actions (see benzodiazepines, etc.); observe for excessive sedation.

  Clozapine *taken concurrently* with

  • other bone marrow depressant drugs, such as carbamazepine (Tegretol), may increase the risk of impaired white blood cell production.
  • amprenavir (Agenerase) may lead to increased clozapine levels. Caution is advised.
  • buspirone (Buspar) may excessively elevate blood sugar and also lead to bleeding.
  • carbamazepine (Tegretol) may increase risk of low white blood cells.
  • cimetidine (Tagamet) can result in a toxic level of clozapine.
  • erythromycin (E-Mycin, others) can result in increased clozapine concentrations and potential toxicity. This has been seen in a single case report, but caution is advised.
  • fluoxetine (Prozac) can result in clozapine toxicity.
  • fluvoxamine (Luvox) can result in clozapine toxicity.
  • lithium (Lithobid, Lithotab, etc.) may increase the risk of confusional states, seizures and neuroleptic malignant syndrome (see Glossary).

- monoamine oxidase inhibitors (MAO inhibitors; see Drug Class) may cause abnormally low blood pressure and exaggerated central nervous system response.
- nefazodone (Serzone) may lead to clozapine toxicity.
- other medicines that interfere with cytochrome P450 3A4 may increase clozapine levels and increase risk of clozapine side effects or toxicity.
- paroxetine (Paxil) may lead to toxicity from either medicine.
- phenytoin (Dilantin) and fosphenytoin (Cerebyx) can cause a decreased clozapine level and result in breakthrough schizophrenia.
- risperidone (Risperdal) may lead to increased risperidone levels.
- ritonavir (Norvir), and perhaps other protease inhibitors (see Drug Classes), may lead to increased risk of blood adverse effects or other adverse effects. DO NOT COMBINE.
- sertraline (Zoloft) can result in clozapine toxicity.
- tramadol (Ultram) may increase seizure risks.
- venlafaxine (Effexor) may lead to clozapine toxicity.
- zotepine (Nipolept) may increase seizure risk.

▷ *Driving, Hazardous Activities:* This drug may cause drowsiness, dizziness, blurred vision, confusion, and seizures. Restrict activities as necessary.

Aviation Note: The use of this drug *is a disqualification* for piloting. Consult a designated Aviation Medical Examiner.

Exposure to Sun: No restrictions except for heat adaptation (see below).

Exposure to Heat: Use caution. This drug can cause fever and can impair the body's adaptation to heat.

Occurrence of Unrelated Illness: Infections must be vigorously treated. White blood cell response to infection must be followed closely.

Discontinuation: If possible, this drug should be discontinued gradually over a period of 1 to 2 weeks. If abrupt withdrawal is necessary, observe carefully for recurrence of psychotic symptoms, and headache, diarrhea, nausea, and vomiting are frequent.

CODEINE (KOH deen)

Introduced: 1886 **Class:** Analgesic, narcotic, opioid **Prescription:** USA: Yes **Controlled Drug:** USA: C-II*; Canada: No **Available as Generic:** Yes

Brand Names: A.B.C. Compound w/Codeine [CD], AC&C [CD], Accopain, Actagen-C [CD], Actifed w/Codeine [CD], Afed-C [CD], Alamine-C [CD], Alamine Expectorant [CD], Ambenyl Expectorant [CD], Ambenyl Syrup [CD], Anacin 3 w/Codeine #2–4, Anacin w/Codeine [CD], APC w/Codeine [CD], Atasol-8,-15,-30 [CD], Ban-Tuiss C [CD], Benylin Syrup w/Codeine [CD], Bitex [CD], Bromanyl Cough Syrup [CD], Bromotuss, Bromphen DC [CD], Brontex [CD], Bufferin w/Codeine [CD], Butalbital Compound [CD], Chemdal Expectorant [CD], Chem-Tuss NE [CD], Cheracol [CD], Chlor-Trimeton Expectorant [CD], Coactifed [CD], Codecon-C [CD], Codehist DH, Codehist Elixir, ✦Codeine Contin (timed release), ✦Coricidin w/Codeine [CD], ✦Coryphen-Codeine [CD], ✦C2 Buffered, ✦C2 w/Codeine, Deproist [CD], Dimetane Cough Syrup-DC [CD], Dimetane Expectorant-C [CD], Dimetapp-C [CD], Dimetapp w/Codeine [CD], Empirin w/Codeine No. 2, 4 [CD], ✦Empracet-30,-60 [CD], Empracet w/Codeine No. 3, 4 [CD], ✦Emtec-30 [CD], ✦Exdol-8,-15,-30 [CD], ✦Extra Strength Acetaminophen with Codeine [CD], ✦Fiorinal-C ¼,-C ½ [CD], Fiorinal w/Codeine No. 1, 2, 3 [CD], Gecil [CD], Glydeine, Isoclor Expectorant [CD], ✦Lenoltec w/Codeine No. 1,

2, 3, 4 [CD], ❧Mersyndol, Naldecon-CX [CD], Normatane [CD], Novadyne DH [CD], ❧Novahistex C [CD], ❧Novo-Gesic, Nucochem [CD], Nucofed [CD], ❧Omni-Tuss [CD], Oridol-C [CD], Panadol w/Codeine [CD], ❧Paveral, Pediacof [CD], Penntuss [CD], ❧Phenaphen No. 2, 3, 4 [CD], Phenaphen w/Codeine No. 2, 3, 4 [CD], Phenergan w/Codeine [CD], Poly-Histine [CD], Promethazine CS [CD], Pyra-Phed [CD], ❧Robaxacet-8, Robaxisal-C [CD], ❧Rounox w/Codeine [CD], SK-Apap [CD], Tamine Expectorant DC [CD], ❧Tecnal C [CD], Terpin Hydrate and Codeine [CD], ❧318 AC&C [CD], Triafed w/Codeine [CD], Triaminic Expectorant w/Codeine [CD], ❧Triatec-8, 30 [CD], ❧Tussaminic C Forte [CD], ❧Tussaminic C Ped [CD], ❧Tussi-Organidin [CD], ❧222 [CD], ❧282 [CD], ❧292 [CD], ❧Tylenol w/Codeine [CD], Tylenol w/Codeine No. 1, 2, 3, 4 [CD], Tylenol w/Codeine Elixir [CD], ❧VC Expectorant w/Codeine, ❧Veganin [CD]

BENEFITS versus RISKS	
Possible Benefits	*Possible Risks*
RELIEF OF MILD TO MODERATE PAIN	Potential for habit formation (dependence)
VERY EFFECTIVE CONTROL OF COUGH	Mild allergic reactions—infrequent Nausea, constipation

▷ **Principal Uses**

As a Single Drug Product: Uses currently included in FDA-approved labeling: (1) Relieves mild to moderate pain; (2) controls cough—its widest use is as an ingredient in analgesic preparations and cough remedies.

Other (unlabeled) generally accepted uses: (1) Limited role in controlling diarrhea; (2) migraine during pregnancy.

As a Combination Drug Product [CD]: Codeine is combined with other analgesics (aspirin and acetaminophen) on the World Health Organization pain ladder to increase overall pain control. It is also added to cough mixtures containing antihistamines, decongestants, and expectorants.

How This Drug Works: By depressing some brain functions, this drug decreases pain perception, calms emotional responses to pain, and reduces cough reflex sensitivity.

Available Dosage Forms and Strengths

Combination form — 15mg codeine, 300 mg acetaminophen (number 2)
— 30 mg codeine, 300 mg acetaminophen (number 3)
— 60 mg codeine, 300 mg acetaminophen (number 4)
Injection — 30 mg/ml, 60 mg/ml
Tablets — 15 mg, 30 mg, 60 mg
Tablets, soluble — 15 mg, 30 mg, 60 mg

▷ **Usual Adult Dosage Ranges:** *As analgesic:* 15 to 60 mg (dosed as the codeine content) every 4 hours.

Author's Note: Current pain treatment theory calls for timed or scheduled dosing. This tends to prevent pain, rather than allowing pain to recur and then having to be treated. Some clinicians will use timed dosing immediately after surgery and then revert to as-needed dosing once the most severe period of pain has passed. Pain is now the fifth vital sign.

For cough (non-combination forms): 10 to 20 mg every 4 to 6 hours as needed. Maximum daily dose 200 mg for pain, 120 mg for cough.

Note: Actual dose and schedule must be determined for each patient individually.

Conditions Requiring Dosing Adjustments
Liver Function: The dose must be decreased in liver compromise.
Kidney Function: Dose decreased by up to 50% in moderate to severe failure.

▷ **Dosing Instructions:** Tablet may be crushed and then taken with or following food to reduce stomach irritation or nausea. If you forget a dose: take it as soon as you remember, unless it's nearly time for your next dose—then omit the dose you forgot and take the next scheduled dose. DO NOT double doses.

Usual Duration of Use: As long as it is needed to control cough (usually the shortest time required). Use for pain should not exceed 5 to 7 days without reassessment of need.

Typical Treatment Goals and Measurements (Outcomes and Markers)
Pain: Most clinicians treating pain use a device called an algometer to check your pain. This looks like a small ruler, but lets the clinician better understand your pain. The goals of treatment then relate to where the level of pain started (for example, a rating of 7 on a 0–10 scale) and what the cause of the pain was. Pain medicines may also be used together (in combination) in order to get the best result or outcome. If your pain control is not acceptable to YOU (remember, in hospitals and outpatient settings, etc., pain control is a patient right) and if after a week of pain treatment, results are not acceptable, be sure to call your doctor as you may need a different medicine or combination.

Cough: The frequency and severity of cough should decrease as discussed with you by your physician. If coughing persists at its prior level, it is prudent to call your doctor.

▷ **This Drug Should Not Be Taken If**
- you have had an allergic reaction to any form of it.
- you are having an acute attack of asthma.
- your breathing is depressed (respiratory depression).

▷ **Inform Your Physician Before Taking This Drug If**
- you have a history of drug abuse or alcoholism.
- you have impaired liver or kidney function.
- you have gallbladder disease, a seizure disorder or an underactive thyroid gland.
- you have chronic obstructive pulmonary disease (COPD) or other lung problems such as asthma.
- you have low blood calcium (increased sensitivity to this medicine).
- you have a history of porphyria.
- you tend to be constipated.
- you are taking any other drugs that have a sedative effect.
- you will have surgery with general anesthesia.

Possible Side Effects (natural, expected, and unavoidable drug actions)
Drowsiness, light-headedness, dry mouth, urinary retention—possible.
Constipation—frequent and dose-related. (Best to start a stool softener or related medicine before codeine is started if you are prone to constipation.)

▷ **Possible Adverse Effects** (unusual, unexpected, and infrequent reactions)
If any of the following develop, consult your physician promptly for guidance.
Mild Adverse Effects
Allergic reactions: skin rash, hives, itching—case reports.
Dizziness, impaired concentration, sensation of drunkenness, confusion, depression, blurred or double vision—infrequent.
Nausea, vomiting—frequent and may be dose-related.

Serious Adverse Effects
Allergic reactions: anaphylaxis, severe skin reactions—case reports.
Idiosyncratic reactions: delirium, hallucinations, excitement, increased pain sensitivity once the medicine wears off.
Seizures—rare.
Impaired breathing—dose-related (children and people with low calcium levels may be more sensitive to this medicine).
Porphyria—case reports.
Pancreatitis—case reports (all patients had previously had their gallbladders removed).
Liver or kidney toxicity—case reports.

▷ **Possible Effects on Sexual Function:** Opiates have a variety of effects on sexual response. These may range from blunting of sexual response to increased response if anxiety has been a factor inhibiting response—case reports.

Adverse Effects That May Mimic Natural Diseases or Disorders
Paradoxical behavioral disturbances may suggest psychotic disorder.

Possible Effects on Laboratory Tests
Blood platelet counts: decreased.
Blood amylase and lipase levels: increased (natural side effect).
Urine screening tests for drug abuse: may be positive. (Test results depend upon amount of drug taken and testing method used.)

CAUTION
1. If you have asthma, chronic bronchitis, or emphysema, use of this drug may cause respiratory difficulty, thickening of secretions, and decrease of needed cough reflex.
2. Combining this drug with atropinelike drugs can increase the risk of urinary retention and reduced intestinal function.
3. Do not take this drug following acute head injury.
4. It is easy to forget about the acetaminophen in combination codeine products and also in many other products. Make sure to add up ALL the acetaminophen you are taking and stay with the 4,000 mg a day limit.

Precautions for Use
By Infants and Children: Do not use this drug in children under 2 years of age (possible life-threatening respiratory depression). Children 2 to 6 years old can receive 1 mg per kg of body mass per day, divided into four equal doses. Maximum dose is 30 mg per day. Children 6 to 12 years of age can receive 5 to 10 mg per dose every 4 to 6 hours, to a maximum of 60 mg every 24 hours.
By Those Over 60 Years of Age: Small starting doses and short-term use is indicated. Expect increased risk of drowsiness, dizziness, unsteadiness, falling, urinary retention, and constipation (often leading to fecal impaction).

▷ **Advisability of Use During Pregnancy**
Pregnancy Category: C; D if used in high doses or for prolonged periods near the time the baby is about to be born. See Pregnancy Risk Categories at the back of this book.
Animal Studies: Skull defects reported in hamster studies.
Human Studies: Adequate studies of pregnant women are not available. Some studies suggest an increase in significant birth defects when this drug is taken during the first 6 months of pregnancy. Codeine taken during the last few weeks before delivery can cause withdrawal symptoms in the newborn.
Use only if clearly needed and in small, infrequent doses.

▷ **Advisability of Use If Breast-Feeding**
    Presence of this drug in breast milk: Yes, in small amounts.
    Discuss this benefit to risk decision with your doctor.

▷ **Habit-Forming Potential:** Psychological and/or physical dependence can
    develop with use of large doses for an extended period of time. True
    dependence is infrequent, however, and unlikely with prudent use.

Effects of Overdose: Drowsiness, restlessness, agitation, nausea, vomiting, dry
    mouth, vertigo, weakness, lethargy, stupor, coma, seizures.

Possible Effects of Long-Term Use: Psychological and physical dependence,
    chronic constipation.

Suggested Periodic Examinations While Taking This Drug (at physician's dis-
    cretion)
    Periodic check for constipation, especially in older patients.

▷ **While Taking This Drug, Observe the Following**
    Foods: No restrictions.
    Herbal Medicines or Minerals: Valerian and kava kava may interact additively
    (drowsiness). Avoid these combinations. St. John's wort can change
    (inducing or increasing) P450 3A4 enzymes, blunting the effects of this
    medicine. Talk to your doctor BEFORE you combine any herbals with
    codeine.
    Beverages: No restrictions. May be taken with milk.

▷ *Alcohol:* DO NOT COMBINE. Codeine intensifies alcohol, and alcohol intensi-
    fies codeine depressant effects on brain function, breathing, and circula-
    tion.
    Tobacco Smoking: Tobacco smoking may cause decreased pain tolerance and
    require an increased or more frequent dose of codeine. I advise everyone
    to quit smoking.
    Marijuana Smoking: Increases drowsiness and pain relief. Mental and physical
    performance will be impaired.

▷ *Other Drugs*
    Codeine may ***increase*** the effects of
    • atropinelike drugs and increase the risk of constipation and urinary reten-
      tion.
    • monoamine oxidase (MAO) inhibitors and also increase central nervous
      system symptoms and depression.
    • other drugs with sedative effects.
    • tramadol (Ultram).
    Codeine ***taken concurrently*** with
    • acetaminophen (Tylenol, others) may lead to overlap of acetaminophen
      dose and exceed the 4 gram daily limit. This can increase risk of liver toxi-
      city. Read the label, total the acetaminophen and keep it at 4,000 mg or
      less.
    • naltrexone (ReVia, others) may lead to withdrawal symptoms.
    • quinidine may decrease codeine pain control.
    • rifabutin (Mycobutin) may decrease codeine effectiveness.
    • ritonavir (Norvir) may blunt codeine benefits.

▷ *Driving, Hazardous Activities:* This drug can impair mental alertness, judg-
    ment, reaction time, and physical coordination. Avoid hazardous activities
    accordingly.
    Aviation Note: The use of this drug ***is a disqualification*** for piloting. Consult a
    designated Aviation Medical Examiner.

Exposure to Sun: No restrictions.

Discontinuation: Best to limit use to short-term. If extended use occurs, gradual decreases in dose are prudent to minimize possible withdrawal (usually mild with codeine).

COLCHICINE (KOL chi seen)

Introduced: 1763   **Class:**   Antigout   **Prescription:**   USA: Yes
Controlled Drug: USA: No; Canada: No   **Available as Generic:**   Yes
Brand Names: Colbenemid [CD], Col-Probenecid [CD], Colsalide, Proben-C [CD]

BENEFITS versus RISKS	
Possible Benefits	*Possible Risks*
EFFECTIVE RELIEF OF ACUTE GOUT SYMPTOMS	Loss of hair
	Rare bone marrow depression (see Glossary)
Prevention of recurrent gout attacks	
Prevention of attacks of Mediterranean fever	Rare peripheral neuritis (see Glossary)
	Rare liver damage

▷ **Principal Uses**

As a Single Drug Product: Uses currently included in FDA-approved labeling: (1) Reduces pain, swelling, and inflammation seen in acute gout attacks (many clinicians prefer NSAIDs [see Drug Classes] as drugs of first choice in acute gout); (2) also used in smaller doses to prevent recurrent gout attacks.

Other (unlabeled) generally accepted uses: (1) Prevention and control of attacks of familial Mediterranean fever; (2) may have a role in easing symptoms of Behçet's disease; (3) some use in biliary cirrhosis of the liver and in hepatitis B patients who can't tolerate usual interferon treatment; (4) may have a role in recurrent pericarditis; (5) can be of help in pseudogout; (6) treats some cases of refractory immune thrombocytopenic purpura.

As a Combination Drug Product [CD]: Colchicine combined with probenecid enhances its ability to prevent recurrent attacks of gout. Colchicine is most effective in relieving acute gout; it has some effect in preventing recurrent and chronic discomfort. Probenecid increases removal of uric acid by the kidneys and reduces risk of acute gout. This dual action is more effective than either drug used alone in long-term management of gout.

How This Drug Works: Decreasing joint tissue acid, lowering painful uric acid deposits and acute inflammation and pain. (Colchicine does not lower uric acid in the blood or increase urine removal.)

Available Dosage Forms and Strengths

Granules — 0.5 mg

Injection — 1 mg/2 ml

Tablets — 0.5 mg, 0.6 mg, 0.65 mg (also 1 mg in Canada)

▷ **Usual Adult Dosage Ranges:** *For acute attack:* 1.0 to 1.2 mg, followed by 0.5 to 0.65 mg every 2 hours until pain eases or nausea, vomiting, or diarrhea occurs. Maximum total dose is 8 mg per attack. *For preventing recurrent* *attacks:* If you have had less than one attack a year, 0.5 to 0.65 mg per day, taken three or four times a week. If you have more than one attack a year, 0.5 to 0.65 mg per day. The maximum dose in preventing gout is 0.5 to 0.65 taken two or three times a day. *Pericarditis:* 3 mg daily to start, followed by 0.5 mg up to one mg daily.

Note: Actual dose and schedule must be determined for each patient individually.

Conditions Requiring Dosing Adjustments

Liver Function: Caution must be used, and the dose decreased, if there is a bile obstruction. This drug should NOT be used in people with both liver and kidney compromise.

Kidney Function: For creatinine clearance of 10 to 50 ml/min (see Glossary), up to 0.6 mg every other day is given. Ongoing preventive use NOT prudent in moderate (creatinine clearance less than 50 ml/min) kidney problems. In severe kidney failure, the medicine should not be given.

▷ **Dosing Instructions:** The tablet may be crushed and then either taken on an empty stomach or with food to reduce nausea or stomach irritation. Talk to your doctor about how much water you should drink. Some clinicians recommend 8–10 full glasses a day. Start this medicine at the first sign of an acute attack. Take the exact dose prescribed. While dosing should be individualized, once the dose needed to abort a sudden (acute) attack is identified, the patient should keep that supply on hand in order to stop an acute attack. Remember that if diarrhea or stomach and intestine (gastrointestinal) side effects happen, the drug needs to be stopped. If you forget a dose: take the dose you forgot as soon as you remember it, unless it's nearly time for your next dose. If it's nearly time for your next dose, skip the dose you missed and simply take the next scheduled dose. DO NOT double doses.

Usual Duration of Use: For acute attack, stop the drug when pain is relieved or when nausea, vomiting or diarrhea occurs; do not restart this drug for 3 days without asking your doctor. Total doses of 8 mg should not be exceeded. For prevention, use the smallest dose that works. Ask your doctor about dosing.

Typical Treatment Goals and Measurements (Outcomes and Markers)

Gout: Blood uric acid levels are not changed by this medicine (tissue deposits are), but gout pain decreases (lowered by ongoing use of this drug as in dosing section) or limiting nausea defines response or highest tolerable dose of colchicine. Call your doctor if an acute attack of gout is not stopped or if you have reached dose-limiting nausea or vomiting.

▷ **This Drug Should Not Be Taken If**
- you have had an allergic reaction to it previously.
- you have an active stomach or duodenal ulcer.
- you have active ulcerative colitis.
- you have a severe kidney or liver disorder.
- you have a serious heart disorder.
- you are pregnant.
- you have a history of blood cell disorders.

▷ **Inform Your Physician Before Taking This Drug If**
- you have peptic ulcer disease or ulcerative colitis.
- you develop diarrhea and vomiting while taking this drug.
- you have any type of heart disease.
- you have impaired liver or kidney function.
- you plan to have surgery in the near future.

Possible Side Effects (natural, expected, and unavoidable drug actions)
Nausea, vomiting, abdominal cramping, diarrhea—frequent, especially with maximum doses.

▷ **Possible Adverse Effects** (unusual, unexpected, and infrequent reactions)
If any of the following develop, consult your physician promptly for guidance.

Mild Adverse Effects
Allergic reactions: skin rash, hives, fever—rare.
Hair loss—reported after overdoses.

Serious Adverse Effects
Allergic reaction: anaphylactic reaction (see Glossary)—case reports.
Bone marrow depression (see Glossary): fatigue, weakness, fever, sore throat, abnormal bleeding, or bruising—case reports.
Peripheral neuritis (see Glossary): numbness, tingling, pain, weakness in hands and/or feet or myopathy with nerve symptoms (facial palsy and weakness, especially with long-term use in patients with declines in kidney function)—case reports.
Rhabdomyolysis—case reports.
Porphyria—case reports.
Drooping of the eyes (ptosis)—case reports.
Inflammation of colon with bloody diarrhea—case reports.
Thrombophlebitis with intravenous use—case reports.

▷ **Possible Effects on Sexual Function:** Reversible absence of sperm (azoospermia).

Possible Delayed Adverse Effects: Impaired production of sperm, possibly resulting in birth defects.
A rare combined muscle and nerve damage syndrome.

Natural Diseases or Disorders That May Be Activated by This Drug
Peptic ulcer disease, ulcerative colitis.

Possible Effects on Laboratory Tests
Complete blood cell counts: decreased red cells, hemoglobin, white cells, and platelets; increased white cells (follows initial decrease).
Prothrombin time: decreased (with concurrent use of warfarin).
Blood vitamin B12 level: decreased.
Liver function tests: increased liver enzymes (ALT/GPT, AST/GOT, and alkaline phosphatase), increased bilirubin.
Fecal occult blood test: positive.
Sperm counts: decreased (may be marked).

CAUTION
1. If this drug causes vomiting and/or diarrhea before relief of joint pain, stop it and call your doctor.
2. Try to limit each course of treatment for acute gout to 4 to 8 mg. Do not exceed 3 mg every 24 hours or a total of 8 mg per course.
3. Omit drug for 3 days between courses to avoid toxicity.
4. Carry this drug with you while traveling if you are subject to attacks of acute gout.
5. Surgical stress can cause a gout attack. Ask your doctor how much colchicine should be taken before and after surgery to prevent gout.
6. This medicine may inhibit healing of the cornea. Talk to your doctor about this if you will have eye surgery.

Precautions for Use
By Infants and Children: Use for preventing (prophylaxis) familial Mediterranean fever in children 5 years old or older: 0.5 mg twice per day and

increased by 0.5 mg per day, to symptom control or a maximum of 2 mg per day. Safety and efficacy have not been established for conditions other than familial Mediterranean fever.

By Those Over 60 Years of Age: Because the dosage needed to relieve acute gout often causes vomiting and/or diarrhea, extreme caution is advised if you have heart or circulatory disorders, reduced liver or kidney function, or general debility.

▷ **Advisability of Use During Pregnancy**

Pregnancy Category: C by one manufacturer, and D by another source. See Pregnancy Risk Categories at the back of this book.

Animal Studies: This drug causes significant birth defects in hamsters and rabbits.

Human Studies: Adequate studies of pregnant women are not available. However, it is reported that colchicine can cause harm to the fetus.

Avoid during entire pregnancy if possible. Ask your physician for guidance.

Advisability of Use If Breast-Feeding

Presence of this drug in breast milk: Yes.

Ask your doctor for help. The American Academy of Pediatrics considers this medicine compatible with breast-feeding.

Habit-Forming Potential: None.

Effects of Overdose: Nausea, vomiting, abdominal cramping, diarrhea (may be bloody), burning sensation in throat and skin, weak and rapid pulse, progressive paralysis, inability to breathe.

Possible Effects of Long-Term Use: Hair loss, aplastic anemia (see Glossary), peripheral neuritis (see Glossary).

Suggested Periodic Examinations While Taking This Drug (at physician's discretion)

Complete blood cell counts.

Uric acid blood levels to monitor status of gout.

Sperm analysis for quantity and condition.

Liver function tests.

▷ **While Taking This Drug, Observe the Following**

Foods: Follow your doctor's advice about a low-purine diet.

Herbal Medicines or Minerals: Acerola is high in vitamin C. Inosine, like acerola, may increase uric acid levels. Aspen should be avoided in gout. Lipase may worsen gout. Goutweed (*Aegopodium podagraria*) does not have enough data to assess effectiveness. Some "herbal teas" (promoted as being beneficial for arthritis) contain phenylbutazone and other potentially toxic ingredients. Avoid herbal teas if you are not certain of their source, content, and medicinal effects. This drug is derived from a plant called Colchicum autumnale. Carefully read the labels of any herbal products you take to make sure autumn crocus or meadow saffron are not in the product. If they are, you may be unknowingly adding extra doses of this medicine.

Beverages: Drink at least 3 quarts of liquids every 24 hours. This drug may be taken with milk.

▷ *Alcohol:* No interactions expected. Combination may increase the risk of gastrointestinal irritation or bleeding and raise uric acid blood levels.

Tobacco Smoking: No interactions expected. I advise everyone to quit smoking.

▷   *Other Drugs*
      Colchicine *taken concurrently* with
      • allopurinol (Zyloprim), probenecid (Benemid), or sulfinpyrazone (Antu-
        rane) can prevent attacks of acute gout that often occur when treatment
        with these drugs is first started.
      • cyanocobalamin will decrease absorption of the vitamin B12. Higher doses
        of oral cyanocobalamin may be required by patients on colchicine.
      • cyclosporine (Sandimmune) may increase cyclosporine levels and result in
        toxicity.
      • erythromycins (E.E.S., clarithromycin) can result in toxic colchicine blood
        levels.
      • insulin may inhibit the response (biphasic) of the body to sugar.
      • interferon alfa-2A may blunt the antiviral benefits of the interferon.
▷   *Driving, Hazardous Activities:* Usually no restrictions when taken continually in
        small (preventive) doses.
      May cause nausea, vomiting, and/or diarrhea when taken in larger (treat-
        ment) doses.
   Aviation Note: The use of this drug *may be a disqualification* for piloting. Con-
        sult a designated Aviation Medical Examiner.
   Exposure to Sun: No restrictions.
   Exposure to Cold: This drug can lower body temperature. Use caution to prevent
        excessive lowering (hypothermia), especially in those over 60 years of age.
   Occurrence of Unrelated Illness: Acute attacks of gout may result from injury or
        illness. Call your doctor for dosing adjustment if injury or new illness
        occurs.

COLD SORE AND GENITAL HERPES TREATMENT
FAMILY (KOLD sore)

Acyclovir   (ay SI kloh veer)   **Famciclovir**   (fam SEYE klo veer)
Penciclovir   (PEN SI kloh veer)   **Valacyclovir**   (val a SY klo veer)
Docosanol cream (Abreva)   (a BREE vah):

**Author's Note: Once head-to-head trials have been conducted with pre-
scription antivirals and this new non-prescription medicine for cold
sores, a decision will be made as to inclusion in this profile. (Docosanol
needs to be applied 12 hours after itching or redness and appears to work
by inhibiting fusion between the skin membrane and the herpes virus
envelope.)**

Other Name: *Acyclovir*: Acycloguanosine, *penciclovir:* BRL-39123, *valacyclovir:* BW256U87   **Introduced:**   1979, 1994, 1997, 1996   **Class:**
Antiviral, cold sore medicines, anti-herpes virus   **Prescription:**   USA: Yes
Controlled Drug: USA: No; Canada: No   **Available as Generic:**   Yes
acyclovir: (capsule, suspension, and tablets). No for famciclovir, penciclovir, valacyclovir

Brand Names: *Ayclovir*: ✤Apo-Acyclovir, ✤Gen-Acyclovir, Zovirax; *Famciclovir*: Famvir; *Penciclovir*: Denavir; *Valacyclovir*: Valtrex

BENEFITS versus RISKS

Possible Benefits   *Possible Risks*

Acyclovir: *Acyclovir systemic use*:
TREATMENT OF ENCEPHALITIS   Nausea, vomiting, diarrhea
  CAUSED BY HERPES SIMPLEX   Joint and muscle pain
TREATMENT OF CHICKENPOX   Seizures or coma with IV use—rare
Acyclovir, famciclovir, and valacyclovir: *Famciclovir*:
FASTER RECOVERY FROM INITIAL   Purpura
  EPISODE OF GENITAL HERPES   Paresthesias
TREATMENT OF SUDDEN (ACUTE)   *Valacyclovir*:
  SHINGLES (HERPES ZOSTER)   Rare reports of thrombotic
PREVENTION OF RECURRENCE   thrombocytopenic purpura (TTP) in
  OF GENITAL HERPES   HIV and bone marrow or kidney
Valacyclovir: transplant patients
ORAL (BY MOUTH) DOSING   *Valacyclovir, acyclovir, and penciclovir*
  ACHIEVES BLOOD LEVELS   *topical use*:
  SIMILAR TO THOSE OBTAINED   Skin redness or irritation
  FROM INTRAVENOUS DOSING
3-DAY DOSING OF VALACYCLOVIR
  IN RECURRENT GENITAL
  HERPES WILL HELP PEOPLE
  TAKE IT (ADHERENCE)
Acyclovir, famciclovir, and penciclovir:
TREATMENT OF HERPES SIMPLEX
  OF THE LIPS (COLD SORES OR
  MUCOCUTANEOUS HERPES)

Author's Note: Acyclovir has been rejected by the FDA for a change to nonprescription "over-the-counter" (OTC) status. This was based on fear of development of viral resistance—NOT on safety issues.

▷ **Principal Uses**

As a Single Drug Product: Uses currently included in FDA-approved labeling:

Acyclovir only: (1) Used to treat varicella (chickenpox) in children over a year old who have a chronic lung disease or skin condition, who take aspirin regularly, who are receiving short courses of corticosteroids via the lungs, or are over 13 years old and are otherwise healthy (must be started within 24 hours of signs and symptoms); (2) used to treat brain infections caused by herpes simplex (encephalitis); (3) used to prevent herpes simplex virus infections in bone marrow transplant patients.

Acyclovir, famciclovir and valacyclovir: (1) Treats or helps prevent (suppress) genital herpes; (2) treats shingles (herpes zoster).

Acyclovir and famciclovir: (1) treats skin and mucous membrane infections (mucocutaneous) caused by herpes simplex in patients with immune problems (immunocompromised); (2) treatment of cold sores (mucocutaneous herpes) of the lips and face.

Penciclovir: (1) treatment of cold sores (mucocutaneous herpes) of the lips and face.

Famciclovir only: used in severe damage to the retina (retinal necrosis syndrome) in cases where acyclovir has failed to work.

Other (unlabeled) generally accepted uses: (1) Acyclovir helps treat herpes simplex infections of the eye and rectum (proctitis), and pneumonia caused by the chickenpox (varicella) virus; (2) some data support acyclovir use in nonmalignant skin growths in the throat (laryngeal papillomatosis); (3) prevention of repeat episodes of herpes eye infections; (4) penciclovir may have a role in herpes infections of the genitals—phase three trials have started in treating herpes simplex skin infections in immunocompromised patients; (5) famciclovir may help treat hepatitis B; (6) some combination data with interferon alpha and famciclovir in treating polyarteritis nodosa are promising; (7) valacyclovir may have a role in erythema multiforme and in decreasing risk of cytomegalovirus disease in kidney and heart transplant patients; (8) famciclovir has some use in hepatitis B.

Author's Note: A study of 455 patients reported in JAMA found that when famciclovir was correctly taken for 1 year to suppress herpes simplex virus (HSV), nearly 75% of those patients did NOT have any HSV outbreaks during that year.

How These Drugs Work: By blocking genetic material formation of the herpes simplex virus, these drugs stop viral multiplication and spread, reducing severity and duration of the herpes infection. Use at the first sign of infection (such as the "itch" of a cold sore) can prevent a full blown lesion. Famciclovir is changed in the body to penciclovir. Valacyclovir is rapidly changed into acyclovir in the body and enters the body to a much greater extent than acyclovir. Docosanol prevents fusion between the skin and the virus.

Available Dosage Forms and Strengths
Acyclovir:
>   Capsules — 200 mg, 400 mg, 800 mg
>   Intravenous — 500 mg, 1 g
>   Oral suspension — 200 mg/5 ml
>   Tablets — 200 mg, 400 mg, 500 mg, 800 mg
>   Ointment — 5%, 50 mg/g (Canada)

Famciclovir:
>   Tablets — 125 mg, 250 mg, 500 mg

Penciclovir:
>   Ointment — 1%

Valacyclovir:
>   Caplets — 500 mg, 1,000 mg
>   Coated tablets — 500 mg (Canada)

▷ **Recommended Dosage Ranges** (Actual dose and schedule must be determined for each patient individually.)

Infants and Children:

Acyclovir: In children less than 12 who have deficient immune systems (immunocompromised), intravenous acyclovir has been used (250 mg per square meter given over 1 hour) every 8 hours in a week-long treatment for skin and mouth herpes simplex infections. Safety and efficacy of oral use in children younger than 6 weeks of age have NOT been established.

Famciclovir, penciclovir, and valacyclovir: Safety and efficacy in infants and children not established.

18 to 65 Years of Age:

Acyclovir: For first episode of genital herpes: 200 mg every 4 hours for a total of five capsules daily for 7 to 10 days (or until what your doctor describes as "clinical resolution" happens). Some clinicians use 400 mg three times a day for 7 to 10 days. Initial cases of herpes proctitis may require 400–800 mg five times daily by mouth (orally) for 10 days or until clinical resolution or 800 mg three times daily for 7–10 days until clinical resolution.

For intermittent recurrence: 200 mg every 4 hours for a total of five capsules daily for 5 consecutive days (total dose of 25 capsules) or 400 mg three times a day for 5 days. Start treatment at the earliest sign of recurrence.

For prevention of frequent recurrence: 400 mg taken twice daily for up to 12 months and then evaluation of ongoing need for this medicine.

For the ointment form: Cover all infected areas every 3 hours for a total of six times daily for 7 consecutive days. Start treatment at the earliest sign of infection (this can avoid a full-blown lesion).

In attempting to decrease the pain of herpes zoster: 800 mg five times daily (every 4 hours) for 7–10 days. Ointment use six times a day for 10 days helps the crusts form sooner.

Treatment of chickenpox: For those over 12 months old with a long-standing skin or lung condition, those being given aerosolized steroids, those taking long-term salicylates or those 13 years old (otherwise healthy as outlined by the American Academy of Pediatrics): In those 2 or older: 20 mg per kg of body mass (do not exceed 800 mg) orally, four times a day for 5 days. If over 40 kg: 800 mg four times daily for 5 days. Start treatment at the first symptom or sign.

Treatment of herpes infections of the eye: 400 mg by mouth five times a day for at least 5 days.

Prevention of repeat herpes eye infections: One study used 400 mg twice a day (decreased recurrence by 45%).

Famciclovir: Shingles (herpes zoster): 500 mg is given every 8 hours for 7 days. It is important to start this medicine promptly after the diagnosis is made (within 48 hours of rash is best).

Recurrent genital herpes: 125 mg twice a day for 5 days. Once the initial infection is controlled, 250 mg twice a day has been given for up to a year (for suppression).

Hepatitis B: 500 mg three times daily.

Penciclovir: For the cream form: Cover all infected areas every 2 hours for a total of six times daily (during waking hours) for 4 consecutive days. Start treatment at the earliest sign of infection.

Valacyclovir: Herpes zoster (shingles): Best started within 48 hours of the zoster rash; 1 g (1,000 mg) three times a day for 7 days. Genital herpes simplex: This medicine is best started within 48 hours of the onset of symptoms and is taken as 1,000 mg twice daily for 7–10 days. It has not been shown to work if started more than 72 hours after symptoms start.

Recurrent genital herpes simplex: 500 mg twice a day for 3–5 days.

Suppression of genital herpes:1 gram taken once a day. Some clinicians use 500 mg once a day in patients who have nine *or fewer recurrences a year. Safety and efficacy have not been established for use more than a year.*

Over 65 Years of Age (all four medicines): The dose must be adjusted if the kidneys are impaired.

Conditions Requiring Dosing Adjustments

Liver Function: All medicines: Specific adjustment in liver dysfunction is not defined. Valacyclovir is NOT recommended in people with cirrhosis.

Kidney Function:

Acyclovir: The dose MUST be adjusted in people with compromised kidney function. For example: Creatinine clearance of 25–50 ml/min gets usual dose every 12 hours; 10–25 ml/min gets usual dose once daily.

Famciclovir: In people with mild kidney compromise (creatinine clearance greater than 60 ml/min), 500 mg is given every 8 hours. Mild to moderate compromise (creatinine clearance 40 to 59 ml/min) receives 500 mg every

12 hours. Moderate to severe (creatinine clearance 20 to 39 ml/min) receives 500 mg every 24 hours.

Penciclovir: Dosing may need to be lowered in ongoing dosing cases of oral dosing. Topical use generally results in no detectable drug in the blood.

Valacyclovir: Dosing changes MUST be made in patients with compromised kidneys (500 mg once a day for creatinine clearance less than 30 ml/min).

Obesity: Acyclovir: Dosing (intravenous form) should be made on ideal body weight and given as 10 mg per kg of body mass. Maximum dose is 500 mg per square meter every 8 hours.

▷ **Dosing Instructions:**

Acyclovir, famciclovir and valacyclovir: May be taken without regard to food. Acyclovir only: Capsule may be opened. The maker of acyclovir recommends drinking 1 liter of water for each gram (1,000 mg) taken.

All medicines: Take or apply the full course of the exact dose prescribed—interrupted therapy can make the virus smarter (lead to resistant viruses). Apply ointment forms to the lesions every 2 hours while you are awake. Start treatment at the earliest sign of infection. Use a finger cot or rubber glove to apply the ointment forms. If you forget a dose: Take or apply the missed dose as soon as you remember it, unless it is nearly time for your next dose—if that is the case, simply take the next dose right on schedule. DO NOT double doses.

Usual Duration of Use:

Acyclovir: Use on a regular schedule for 10 days is usually needed to see this drug's effect in reducing the severity and duration of the initial infection. Continual use for 6 months may be needed to prevent frequent recurrence of herpes eruptions.

Famciclovir: For herpes zoster: Regular use for 2 days determines effectiveness. Then the medicine is typically continued for 7 days. Your doctor should decide when to stop the medicine.

For recurrent genital herpes: Start at first sign of recurrence and dosing is continued for 5 days.

Penciclovir: Use on a regular schedule for 4 days usually needed to see this drug's effect in reducing the severity and duration of the infection.

Valacyclovir: Best started within 48 hours of onset of the zoster rash. Use on a regular schedule for 7 days for herpes zoster has been effective. Start therapy within 24 hours of signs of genital herpes; regular use for 10 days is appropriate for initial cases. Take the full course as prescribed. Missing doses may lead to resistance. For recurrent genital herpes, 500 mg twice a day for 3 days is a NEW shorter treatment.

If you forget a dose: Apply the cream or ointment form as soon as you remember, but skip the missed dose if it is nearly time for your next dose. If you are taking the "pill" forms, take the missed dose as soon as you remember it, unless it is nearly time for your next dose—then skip the missed dose and continue with your next scheduled dose. DO NOT double doses.

Typical Treatment Goals and Measurements (Outcomes and Markers)

Infections: The most commonly used measures of serious infections are white blood cell counts and differentials (the kind of blood cells that occur most often in your blood) and temperature. With herpes infections, clinicians look for positive changes in the appearance of the infection (shortened time to crusting, etc.) as well as shortened time for postherpetic neuralgia. Suppressive use finds decreased frequency of outbreaks (for example, with genital herpes) and shorter duration of any recurrences as a goal.

Possible Advantages of These Drugs: Valacyclovir: Achieves blood levels similar to INTRAVENOUS acyclovir with a medicine taken by mouth (the oral route). Patients do not have to take it as many times a day as acyclovir (should help people stay on the medicine-adherence). Newer dosing for vala-cyclovir in recurrent genital herpes should also help adherence. Famciclovir also offers less frequent dosing (three times a day) in shingles versus acy-clovir. Penciclovir may give results even if started later in a "cold sore" case.

▷ **These Drugs Should Not Be Taken If**
  • you have had an allergic reaction to them previously.

▷ **Inform Your Physician Before Taking These Drugs If**
  Valacyclovir:
  • your immune system is compromised (immunocompromised patients) or you have shingles (herpes zoster) that has spread (disseminated). Valacy-clovir benefits not established in this population.
  • you have advanced HIV disease or have had a bone marrow or kidney transplant (increased risk of thrombotic thrombocytopenic purpura).
  Acyclovir and valacyclovir:
  • you take other medicines that may cause kidney damage.
  • you think you are dehydrated and can't or will not drink water.
  Famciclovir:
  • you have a first episode of genital herpes or your immune system is com-promised (immunocompromised) and you have shingles (herpes zoster).
  All medicines:
  • your liver (hepatic), kidney (renal) or nerve (neurologic) function is impaired.
  • you are unsure of how much or how often to take them.

Possible Side Effects (natural, expected, and unavoidable drug actions)
  Acyclovir and valacyclovir:
  Possible increased sensitivity to light (photophobia).
  With IV acyclovir—possible irritation of the vein (thrombophlebitis) up to 9%. Tissue death (necrosis) can occur if this acyclovir form is given in a vein and the vein "blows" letting the drug into the tissue around the IV site. A special IV line (peripherally inserted central catheter) is prudent.
  All medicines with ointment forms:
  With use of ointment—mild pain or stinging at site of application.

▷ **Possible Adverse Effects** (unusual, unexpected, and infrequent reactions)
  If any of the following develop, consult your physician promptly for guidance.
  Mild Adverse Effects: Allergic reaction: skin rash, itching.
  Acyclovir: Headache (valacyclovir, penciclovir, famciclovir as well and may be frequent), dizziness, nervousness, confusion, insomnia, depression, fatigue—rare. Nausea, vomiting, diarrhea—infrequent with IV form. Joint pains, muscle cramps—rare. Acne, hair loss—rare.
  Famciclovir: Nausea or diarrhea—infrequent to frequent.
  Valacyclovir: fast heart rate—case reports.
  Serious Adverse Effects
  Acyclovir: Superficial thrombophlebitis—infrequent with IV form. Seizures, hallucinations or coma with IV use—rare. Kidney problems—rare (espe-cially if adequate water is taken). Low platelets or red or white blood cells—case reports—rare. Colitis—case reports.
  Famciclovir: Purpura or paresthesias—case reports. Rigors or movement disorders—case reports to rare. Increased breast cancer in male rats given extremely high doses. Does not appear to increase risk in humans.

Valacyclovir: Thrombotic thrombocytopenic purpura—rare and in immuno-compromised patients.

Aseptic meningitis (stiff neck, disorientation, sleepiness, and incontinence)—case report. Erythema multiforme—case report.

▷ **Possible Effects on Sexual Function:** None reported for these medicines.

Possible Effects on Laboratory Tests

Acyclovir and valacyclovir: Complete blood cell counts: decreased red or white cells or hemoglobin—rare.

Blood urea nitrogen (BUN)/creatinine: increased—rare.

Liver function tests: increased—rare.

CAUTION

1. These drugs do not eliminate all herpes virus and are not a cure. The infection often returns. Restart treatment at the earliest sign of infection.
2. Avoid intercourse if herpes blisters and swelling are present.
3. Do not exceed the prescribed dose.
4. If severity/frequency of infections don't improve, call your doctor.
5. The manufacturer recommends drinking 1 liter (1,000 ml) of fluid for each gram (1,000 mg) of oral or intravenous form taken of acyclovir.
6. Other medicines that can form damaging crystals in the urine may lead to added kidney problem risk if combined with acyclovir.
7. Some managed care organizations suggest pill splitting (valacyclovir is an example). If you are required to split pills, get a pill splitter to help ensure accuracy.

Precautions for Use

By Infants and Children: Acyclovir: Specific dosing required. Fluid intake must be adequate.

Famciclovir, penciclovir, and valacyclovir: Safety and efficacy not established.

By Those Over 60 Years of Age: Acyclovir and valacyclovir:

Avoid dehydration. Talk to your doctor about how much water you should take or can tolerate. Make sure dosing is adjusted for age-related decline in kidney function.

Famciclovir and penciclovir: Age-related declines in kidney function may require dosing adjustment.

▷ **Advisability of Use During Pregnancy**

Pregnancy Category:

Acyclovir: B for the oral and intravenous forms. C for the topical form. See Pregnancy Risk Categories at the back of this book.

Famciclovir, penciclovir, and valacyclovir: B. See Pregnancy Risk Categories at the back of this book.

Animal Studies:

Acyclovir: No birth defects found in mouse, rat, or rabbit studies.

Famciclovir and penciclovir: No birth defects found in animals.

Valacyclovir: NOT teratogenic in rabbits or rats (up to 10 times the human dose).

Human Studies:

Acyclovir: The pregnancy registry has followed more than 600 cases to date. Sixteen birth defects occurred, with no pattern. Widespread (disseminated) or life-threatening herpes virus infections may warrant use of this medicine during pregnancy. Talk with your doctor about use.

Famciclovir and penciclovir: Studies not available.

Valacyclovir: Adequate studies of pregnant women are not available. A vala-cyclovir pregnancy registry can be accessed by physicians at 1-800-722-9292, extension 39437.

Advisability of Use If Breast-Feeding

Presence of this drug in breast milk: Acyclovir: Yes. *Famciclovir:* yes in lab ani-mals, unknown in humans. *Penciclovir:* unknown. *Valacyclovir:* Yes (docu-mented in two women; 0.6 to 4.1 times the plasma levels).

Ask your physician for guidance: Acyclovir: often okay to breast-feed. While the drug is in the milk, it is in small amounts. *Famciclovir:* stop nursing or dis-continue drug. *Valacyclovir:* Discuss discontinuing the medicine or stop-ping nursing with your doctor. Discuss benefits and risk factors with your doctor for other medicines in this profile also.

Habit-Forming Potential: None.

Effects of Overdose: Possible impairment of kidney function with acyclovir and valacyclovir, not defined or symptomatic management for famciclovir or penciclovir.

Possible Effects of Long-Term Use: Resistant strains of herpes virus may emerge. See your doctor.

Suggested Periodic Examinations While Taking This Drug (at physician's dis-cretion)

Kidney function tests for acyclovir and valacyclovir, not defined for famci-clovir or penciclovir.

▷ **While Taking This Drug, Observe the Following**

Foods: No restrictions. Some claims have been made for lysine (an amino acid) in cold sores, but specific scientifically rigorous studies have not been made.

Herbal Medicines or Minerals: Some patients use echinacea to attempt to boost their immune systems. Unfortunately, use of echinacea is not recom-mended in people with damaged immune systems. This herb may also actually weaken any immune system if it is used too often or for too long a time. Since St. John's wort and valacyclovir can increase sensitivity to the sun—caution is advised.

Beverages: No restrictions. Acyclovir may be taken with milk. Drink 2 to 3 quarts of liquids daily (if not contraindicated for you) when you take acy-clovir or valacyclovir.

▷ *Alcohol:* Acyclovir and valacyclovir: Use caution; dizziness or fatigue may be accentuated. Penciclovir and famciclovir: No restrictions.

Tobacco Smoking: No interactions expected. I advise everyone to quit smoking.

▷ *Other Drugs*

Penciclovir: No significant interactions for the cream as it results in unde-tectable blood levels.

The following drugs may ***increase*** the effects of acyclovir and valacyclovir:

• cyclosporine (Sandimmune)—use may result in increased risk of kidney toxicity.

• probenecid (Benemid)—may delay acyclovir or valacyclovir elimination.

Acyclovir or valacyclovir ***taken concurrently*** with or by

• a patient with an allopurinol (Zyloprim) allergy may result in cross-allergenicity and allergic reaction.

• cimetidine (Tagamet) increases risk of antiviral toxicity.

• fosphenytoin (Cerebyx) or phenytoin (Dilantin) may cause loss of seizure control (lower blood levels of this seizure medicine).

• meperidine (Demerol) may result in neurologic problems.

• valproic acid (Depakote) may cause loss of seizure control (lower valproic blood levels).

- varicella vaccine (Varivax) will blunt the vaccine effectiveness.
- zidovudine (AZT) may result in severe fatigue and lethargy.

Famciclovir **taken concurrently** with

- digoxin (Lanoxin) may increase peak digoxin blood level slightly.
- probenecid (Benemid) may increase famciclovir blood levels as both medicines are removed from the body by active tubular secretion in the kidney.

▷ *Driving, Hazardous Activities:* Use caution if dizziness or fatigue occurs from acyclovir, or famciclovir. Caution is advised if significant headache results from these medicines.

Aviation Note: The use of acyclovir, famciclovir, or valacyclovir **may be a disqualification** for piloting. Penciclovir is probably not a disqualification. Consult a designated Aviation Medical Examiner.

Exposure to Sun: No restrictions; however, some data indicate that sun exposure may trigger release of herpes simplex from its dormant state (from the optic nerve).

COLESEVELAM (koh lee SEV eh lamb)

Introduced: 2000 **Class:** Anticholesterol **Prescription:** USA: Yes **Controlled Drug:** USA: No; Canada: No **Available as Generic:** USA: No; Canada: No
Brand Name: Welchol

BENEFITS versus RISKS
Possible Benefits	*Possible Risks*
EFFECTIVE REDUCTION OF TOTAL CHOLESTEROL AND LOW-DENSITY CHOLESTEROL IN TYPE IIA CHOLESTEROL DISORDERS	Constipation
	Reduced absorption of fat, fat-soluble vitamins (A, D, E, and K, etc.)
ADDITIVE EFFECTS WHEN COMBINED WITH HMG-CoA REDUCTASE INHIBITORS	

▷ **Principal Uses**

As a Single Drug Product: Uses currently included in FDA-approved labeling: (1) Used in combination with diet and exercise to decrease blood cholesterol and low-density (LDL) cholesterol in Type IIa cholesterol disorders; (2) used in combination with "statin" type (see Drug Classes) medicines to achieve cholesterol lowering goals.

Other (unlabeled) generally accepted uses: None at present.

How This Drug Works: Cross-linked hydrogel polymer that holds onto (binds) bile acids in the intestine, which prevents them from being absorbed. Because bile acids are not absorbed, more cholesterol is converted to bile acids. This effect works to lower cholesterol (upregulate the LDL receptor) by removing cholesterol from the blood (plasma).

Available Dosage Forms and Strengths

Tablets — 625 mg

▷ **Usual Adult Dosage Ranges:** *When used alone:* This medicine is started with three tablets twice a day (with meals) or six tablets once a day with a meal.

The dose can then be increased if goals are not met to seven tablets a day (4,375 mg a day maximum).

Combination therapy (with an HMG-CoA inhibitor-see Drug Classes): Four to six tablets per day has worked. To gain maximum effect, 3 colesevelam tablets twice a day with meals or 6 tablets a day with a meal combined with a statin has been used.

Note: Actual dose and schedule must be determined for each patient individually.

Conditions Requiring Dosing Adjustments

Liver Function: No changes needed (zero to minimal absorption).

Kidney Function: No changes needed (zero to minimal absorption).

▷ **Dosing Instructions:** Always take just before or with a meal and with liquids. If you forget a dose: Take the missed dose as soon as you remember it, unless it is nearly time for the next dose. DO NOT DOUBLE DOSES. Call your doctor if you find yourself forgetting doses. While not included in official FDA labeling, the recent National Cholesterol Education Program (NCEP) ATP 3 guidelines call for use of TLC or therapeutic lifestyle changes (see Glossary) in order to augment results in achieving cholesterol goals.

Usual Duration of Use: Initial response often occurs in 2 weeks. Regular use for up to a month may be needed to see peak benefits in lowering cholesterol. If no acceptable response in 3 months with peak doses, combination therapy with an HMG-CoA is advisable. Long-term use (months to years) requires periodic follow-up with your doctor. Treat cholesterol for life!

Typical Treatment Goals and Measurements (Outcomes and Markers)

Cholesterol: The National Institutes of Health Adult Treatment Panel has released ATP III as part of the update to the National Cholesterol Education Program or NCEP. Key points in these new guidelines include acknowledging diabetes as one of the conditions that increases risk of heart disease, modifying risk factors, therapeutic lifestyle changes (TLC), and recommending routine testing for all of the cholesterol fractions (lipoprotein profile) versus total cholesterol alone.

Current NCEP guidelines recommend a desirable total cholesterol of 200 mg/dl, and optimal bad cholesterol (LDL) as 100 mg/dl, 130–159 mg/dl as borderline high, 160 mg/dl as high and 190 mg/dl as very high. Did you know that there are at least five different kinds of "good cholesterol" or HDL? The "too low" measure for HDL is still 40 mg/dl, but in order to learn more about cholesterol types some doctors are starting to order lipid panels. There are at least seven different kinds of "bad cholesterol." The new panels tell doctors about the kinds of cholesterol that your body makes. This is important because some kinds (small dense particles) tend to stick to blood vessels (are highly atherogenic). Take your medicine to reach your goals!

Two additional tests you will hear about will be electron beam computed tomography (EBCT) and CRP. EBCT is an important tool used in conjunction with laboratory studies. Findings show that even patients who meet: cholesterol goals (particularly females over 55) can still be at significant cardiovascular risk. EBCT then defines risk by giving a calcium score and a "virtual tour" of the coronary arteries. C Reactive Protein or CRP is a new and apparently independent predictor of heart disease risk. A large study (see Ridker, P.M. in Sources) found that CRP predicted heart disease risk independently of bad cholesterol (low density lipoprotein).

Talk to your doctor about this new laboratory test and ask about current guidelines for who should be tested (see Pearson, T.A. in Sources).

▷ **This Drug Should Not Be Taken If**
- you have had an allergic reaction to it previously.
- you have a bowel block (obstruction).

▷ **Inform Your Physician Before Taking This Drug If**
- you are prone to constipation.
- you have low thyroid function (hypothyroidism).
- you have stomach or intestinal problems (gastrointestinal disorders).
- you have a bleeding disorder of any kind.
- you have a fat soluble vitamin (especially vitamin K) deficiency.

Possible Side Effects (natural, expected, and unavoidable drug actions)
Constipation; interference with normal fat digestion and absorption; reduced absorption of vitamins A, D, E, and K and folic acid. Binds to vitamin B12-intrinsic factor complex.

▷ **Possible Adverse Effects** (unusual, unexpected, and infrequent reactions)
If any of the following develop, consult your physician promptly for guidance.
Mild Adverse Effects
Allergic reactions: not reported as yet.
Joint pains or muscle aches (myalgia)—possible.
Constipation or indigestion (dyspepsia)—most frequent.
Loss of appetite, indigestion, heartburn, abdominal discomfort, excessive gas, nausea, vomiting, diarrhea—case reports.
Serious Adverse Effects
Fat-soluble vitamin deficiency—possible.

▷ **Possible Effects on Sexual Function:** None reported.

Natural Diseases or Disorders That May Be Activated by This Drug
Fat-soluble vitamin deficiency.

Possible Effects on Laboratory Tests
Blood cholesterol and triglyceride levels: decreased (therapeutic effect).

CAUTION
1. Watch carefully for constipation; use stool softeners and laxatives as needed.

Precautions for Use
By Infants and Children: Safety and effectiveness for those under 12 years of age not established.
By Those Over 60 Years of Age: Increased risk of severe constipation.

▷ **Advisability of Use During Pregnancy**
Pregnancy Category: B. See Pregnancy Risk Categories at the back of this book.
Animal Studies: No information available.
Human Studies: Adequate studies of pregnant women are not available.
Use this drug only if clearly needed. Ensure adequate intake of vitamins and minerals to satisfy needs of mother and fetus.

Advisability of Use If Breast-Feeding
Presence of this drug in breast milk: None.
Breast-feeding is permitted.

Habit-Forming Potential: None.

Effects of Overdose: Progressive constipation.

Possible Effects of Long-Term Use: Deficiencies of vitamins A, D, E, and K and folic acid. Binding of the B12-intrinsic factor complex may lead to blood cell problems.

Suggested Periodic Examinations While Taking This Drug (at physician's discretion)

Measurements of blood levels of total cholesterol, low-density (LDL) cholesterol and high-density (HDL) cholesterol. HDL and LDL patterns, CRP.

▷ **While Taking This Drug, Observe the Following**

Foods: Avoid foods that tend to constipate (cheeses, etc.). Talk to your doctor if you are considering adding soy milk or other soy products to your diet. Follow a standard low-cholesterol diet. Your doctor may also recommend some specific foods such as increased vegetables or functional foods such as Benecol (see TLC in Glossary). Three well-designed studies were published in April 2002 found that both in women and men and before and after a heart attack, people who ate more fish (2–4 servings a week) appeared to avoid heart disease. Additionally, putting supplements containing Omega 3 polyunsaturated fatty acids (PUFA) into the diet also appeared to protect against abnormal heart rhythms and sudden death from heart attack. Your doctor may also recommend increasing B vitamins. See Tables 19 and 20 about lifestyle changes and risk factors you can fix.

Herbal Medicines or Minerals: Some studies show garlic to reduce cholesterol. Since it probably works by a different mechanism than colesevelam, the combination use may be reasonable if dosing is separated. Discuss this with your doctor. Soy milk may also offer some lowering of cholesterol. Current cholesterol therapy sets a goal for treatment, and these herbs may help reach that goal when combined with this prescription medicine. Talk to your doctor before combining any herbals with colesevelam.

Nutritional Support: Ask your doctor if you need supplements of vitamins A, D, E, and K, folic acid and calcium.

Beverages: Ensure adequate liquid intake (up to 2 quarts daily). This drug may be taken with milk.

▷ *Alcohol:* No interactions expected.

Tobacco Smoking: No interactions expected. I advise everyone to quit smoking.

▷ *Other Drugs*

Colesevelam may **decrease** the effects of
- alendronate (Fosamax); take 2 hours before colesevelam.
- fibrates (Tricor, others); take 2 hours before colestipol or 4 to 6 hours after colestipol.
- verapamil (Calan, others). Caution and careful patient follow up is prudent.
- vitamin B12 and fat-soluble vitamins.

Colesevelam may **increase** the effects of
- atorvastatin (Lipitor), lovastatin (Mevacor), and simvastatin (Zocor), and other statins (see Drug Classes) [desirable and beneficial effect].

▷ *Driving, Hazardous Activities:* No restrictions.

Aviation Note: The use of this drug is usually not a disqualification for piloting. Consult a designated Aviation Medical Examiner.

Exposure to Sun: No restrictions.

Discontinuation: Once colesevelam is stopped, cholesterol levels usually return to pretreatment levels in 1 month.

COLESTIPOL (koh LES ti pohl)

Introduced: 1974   **Class:**   Anticholesterol   **Prescription:**   USA:
Yes   **Controlled Drug:**   USA: No; Canada: No   **Available as Generic:**
USA: No; Canada: No
Brand Names: Colestid, Lestid

```
┌─────────────────────────────────────────────────────────────────────────┐
│                        BENEFITS versus RISKS                              │
│            Possible Benefits              Possible Risks                  │
│  EFFECTIVE REDUCTION OF TOTAL     Constipation (may be severe)            │
│    CHOLESTEROL AND LOW-           Reduced absorption of fat, fat-soluble  │
│    DENSITY CHOLESTEROL IN           vitamins (A, D, E, and K) and folic   │
│    TYPE IIA CHOLESTEROL             acid                                  │
│    DISORDERS                      Reduced formation of prothrombin        │
│  EFFECTIVE RELIEF OF ITCHING        with possible bleeding                │
│    associated with biliary obstruction                                    │
│  Treatment of some                                                        │
│    pseudomembranous colitis cases                                         │
└─────────────────────────────────────────────────────────────────────────┘
```

▷ **Principal Uses**

As a Single Drug Product: Uses currently included in FDA-approved labeling:
(1) Used in combination with diet changes to decrease blood cholesterol
and low-density (LDL) cholesterol in Type IIa cholesterol disorders; (2)
eases itching due to deposit of bile acids in skin.

Other (unlabeled) generally accepted uses: (1) Data from one study showed
that colestipol in combination with lovastatin actually caused regression
of plaque buildup (atherosclerosis) inside blood vessels; (2) some data
show that colestipol is useful in pseudomembranous colitis.

How This Drug Works: Binds bile acids and is removed in feces. Removal of bile
acids stimulates conversion of cholesterol to bile acids, which then
reduces cholesterol. By reducing levels of bile acids, this drug hastens
removal of bile acids in the skin and relieves itching.

Available Dosage Forms and Strengths

Bottles — 250g, 500g
Flavored Colestid
granules for oral
suspension — 5 g per dose (7.5 grams in Canada)
Packets — 5 g
Tablet, coated — 1 g

▷ **Usual Adult Dosage Ranges:** Starts with 5 g of powder mixed in an approved
liquid (such as orange juice, apple juice, water, or grape juice) and taken
three times daily. May be increased slowly as needed and tolerated to 30 g
daily in two to four divided doses. The tablet form is taken as two to 16
grams a day as a single dose or divided into several equal doses. Dose is
increased as needed and tolerated every 30–60 days.

**Note: Actual dose and schedule must be determined for each patient
individually.**

Conditions Requiring Dosing Adjustments

Liver Function: No changes needed.
Kidney Function: No changes needed.

▷ **Dosing Instructions:** Always take just before or with a meal; drug does not work if taken without food. Mix the powder thoroughly in 4 to 6 ounces of water, fruit juice, tomato juice, milk, thin soup or a soft food such as applesauce. **Do not take the powder in its dry form.** If you forget a dose, take the missed dose as soon as you remember it, unless it is nearly time for the next dose. DO NOT DOUBLE DOSES. Call your doctor if you find yourself forgetting doses. The tablet form should be swallowed whole and taken with a liquid such as water.

Usual Duration of Use: Regular use for up to a month may be needed to see peak benefits in lowering cholesterol. If no acceptable response in 3 months, combination treatment with an HMG-CoA inhibitor should be considered. Long-term use (months to years) requires periodic follow-up with your doctor as cholesterol tends to increase as we age.

Typical Treatment Goals and Measurements (Outcomes and Markers)

Cholesterol: The National Institutes of Health Adult Treatment Panel has released ATP III as part of the update to the National Cholesterol Education Program or NCEP. Key points in these new guidelines include acknowledging diabetes as one of the conditions that increases risk of heart disease, modifying risk factors, therapeutic lifestyle changes (TLC) and recommending routine testing for all of the cholesterol fractions (lipoprotein profile) versus total cholesterol alone.

Current NCEP guidelines recommend a desirable total cholesterol of 200 mg/dl, and optimal bad cholesterol (LDL) as 100 mg/dl, 130–159 mg/dl as borderline high, 160 mg/dl as high and 190 mg/dl as very high. Did you know that there are at least five different kinds of "good cholesterol" or HDL? The "too low" measure for HDL is still 40 mg/dl, but in order to learn more about cholesterol types some doctors are starting to order lipid panels. There are at least seven different kinds of "bad cholesterol." The new panels tell doctors about the kinds of cholesterol that your body makes. This is important because some kinds (small dense particles) tend to stick to blood vessels (are highly atherogenic). Take your medicine to reach your goals!

Two additional tests you will hear about will be electron beam computed tomography (EBCT) and CRP. EBCT is an important tool used in conjunction with laboratory studies. Findings show that even patients who meet cholesterol goals (particularly females over 55) can still be at significant cardiovascular risk. EBCT then defines risk by giving a calcium score and a "virtual tour" of the coronary arteries. C Reactive Protein or CRP is a new and apparently independent predictor of heart disease risk. A large study (see Ridker, P.M. in Sources) found that CRP predicted heart disease risk independently of bad cholesterol (low density lipoprotein).

Talk to your doctor about this new laboratory test and ask about current guidelines for who should be tested (see Pearson, T.A. in Sources).

▷ **This Drug Should Not Be Taken If**
- you have had an allergic reaction to it previously.
- you have complete biliary obstruction.

▷ **Inform Your Physician Before Taking This Drug If**
- you are prone to constipation.
- you have low thyroid function (hypothyroidism).
- you have peptic ulcer disease.
- you have a bleeding disorder of any kind.
- you have impaired kidney function.

Possible Side Effects (natural, expected, and unavoidable drug actions)

Constipation; interference with normal fat digestion and absorption; reduced absorption of vitamins A, D, E, and K and folic acid. Binds to vitamin B12-intrinsic factor complex.

▷ **Possible Adverse Effects** (unusual, unexpected, and infrequent reactions)

If any of the following develop, consult your physician promptly for guidance.

Mild Adverse Effects

Allergic reactions: skin rash—rare; hives, tongue irritation, anal itching—case reports.

Headache, dizziness, weakness, muscle and joint pains—possible.

Constipation—most frequent.

Loss of appetite, indigestion, heartburn, abdominal discomfort, excessive gas, nausea, vomiting, diarrhea—case reports.

Serious Adverse Effects

Vitamin K deficiency and increased bleeding tendency—possible.

Impaired absorption of calcium; predisposition to osteoporosis—possible.

Hypothyroidism—possible.

Disruption of normal acid-base balance of the body (metabolic acidosis)—possible with long-term use.

▷ **Possible Effects on Sexual Function:** None reported.

Natural Diseases or Disorders That May Be Activated by This Drug

Peptic ulcer disease; steatorrhea (excessive fat in stools) with large doses.

Possible Effects on Laboratory Tests

Blood cholesterol and triglyceride levels: decreased (therapeutic effect).

Blood thyroxine (T4) level: decreased when colestipol and niacin are taken concurrently (in presence of normal thyroid function).

CAUTION

1. Never take the dry powder; always mix thoroughly with a suitable liquid before swallowing.
2. Watch carefully for constipation; use stool softeners and laxatives as needed.
3. This drug may bind other drugs taken concurrently and impair their absorption. It is advisable to take all other drugs 1 to 2 hours before or 4 to 6 hours after taking this drug.
4. If triglycerides rise significantly, the dose may need to be decreased (talk to your doctor).

Precautions for Use

By Infants and Children: Safety and effectiveness for those under 12 years of age not established. Watch carefully for the possible development of acidosis and vitamin A or folic acid deficiency. (Ask your physician for guidance.)

By Those Over 60 Years of Age: Increased risk of severe constipation. Impaired kidney function may predispose to the development of acidosis.

▷ **Advisability of Use During Pregnancy**

Pregnancy Category: not established, B2 in Australia. See Pregnancy Risk Categories at the back of this book.

Animal Studies: No information available.

Human Studies: Adequate studies of pregnant women are not available.

Use this drug only if clearly needed. Ensure adequate intake of vitamins and minerals to satisfy needs of mother and fetus.

Advisability of Use If Breast-Feeding

Presence of this drug in breast milk: Not known.

Talk to your doctor about breast-feeding.

Habit-Forming Potential: None.

Effects of Overdose: Progressive constipation, skin changes (skin drying).

Possible Effects of Long-Term Use: Deficiencies of vitamins A, D, E, and K and folic acid. Calcium deficiency, osteoporosis. Acidosis due to excessive retention of chloride. Binding of the B12-intrinsic factor complex may lead to blood cell problems such as macrocytic anemia.

Suggested Periodic Examinations While Taking This Drug (at physician's discretion)

Appropriate testing to rule out low thyroid, diabetes, or other causes (secondary) of hypercholesterolemia before the medicine is started.

Measurements of blood levels of total cholesterol, low-density (LDL) cholesterol and high-density (HDL) cholesterol, HDL and LDL fraction testing, and CRP.

Hemoglobin and red blood cell studies for possible anemia.

Thyroid function tests.

▷ **While Taking This Drug, Observe the Following**

Foods: Avoid foods that tend to constipate (cheeses, etc.). Follow a standard low-cholesterol diet. Your doctor may also recommend some specific foods such as increased vegetables or functional foods such as Benecol. Three well-designed studies were published in April 2002 found that both in women and men and before and after a heart attack, people who ate more fish (2–4 servings a week) appeared to avoid heart disease. Additionally putting supplements containing Omega 3 polyunsaturated fatty acids (PUFA) into the diet also appeared to protect against abnormal heart rhythms and sudden death from heart attack. Your doctor may also recommend increasing B vitamins. See Tables 19 and 20 about lifestyle changes and risk factors you can fix.

Herbal Medicines or Minerals: Some studies show garlic to reduce cholesterol. Since it probably works by a different mechanism than colestipol, the combination use may be reasonable if dosing is separated. Discuss this with your doctor. Soy milk may also offer some lowering of cholesterol. Current cholesterol therapy sets a goal for treatment, and these herbs may help reach that goal when combined with this prescription medicine. Talk to your doctor before combining any herbals with colestipol.

Nutritional Support: Ask your doctor if you need supplements of vitamins A, D, E, and K, folic acid and calcium.

Beverages: Ensure adequate liquid intake (up to 2 quarts daily). This drug may be taken with milk.

▷ *Alcohol:* No interactions expected.

Tobacco Smoking: No interactions expected. I advise everyone to quit smoking.

▷ *Other Drugs*

Colestipol may ***decrease*** the effects of

- acetaminophen (Tylenol); take 2 hours before colestipol.
- alendronate (Fosamax); take 2 hours before colestipol.
- aspirin; take 2 hours before colestipol.
- atorvastatin (Lipitor); take 2 hours before colestipol.
- cephalexin (Keflex); take 2 hours before colestipol.
- diclofenac (various); take 2 hours before colestipol.
- digitoxin and digoxin (Lanoxin); take 2 hours before colestipol.

- fibrates (Tricor, others); take 2 hours before colestipol or 4 to 6 hours after colestipol.
- folic acid; take 2 hours before colestipol.
- furosemide (Lasix); take 2 hours before colestipol or 4 to 6 hours after colestipol.
- hydrocortisone; take 2 hours before colestipol.
- iron preparations; take 2 to 3 hours before colestipol.
- leflunomide (Arava); take 2 hours before colestipol.
- penicillin G (Pentids); take 2 hours before colestipol.
- phenobarbital; take 2 hours before colestipol.
- pravastatin (Pravachol); take 2 hours before colestipol.
- oral antidiabetic drugs (see Drug Classes).
- raloxifene (Evista); take 2 hours before colestipol.
- tetracycline (various); take 2 hours before or 3 hours after colestipol.
- thiazide diuretics (see Drug Classes); take 2 hours before colestipol.
- thyroxine (see Thyroid Hormones Drug Class); take 5 hours before colestipol.
- vancomycin (various oral forms); take 2 hours before colestipol or 4 to 6 hours after colestipol.
- vitamin B12.

▷ *Driving, Hazardous Activities:* No restrictions.
Aviation Note: The use of this drug is usually ***not a disqualification*** for piloting. Consult a designated Aviation Medical Examiner.
Exposure to Sun: No restrictions.
Discontinuation: The dose of any toxic drug combined with colestipol must be reduced when this drug is stopped. Once colestipol is stopped, cholesterol levels usually return to pretreatment levels in 1 month.

COX II INHIBITOR FAMILY (KOX too)

Celecoxib   (SELL ah kox ib)   **Rofecoxib**   (ROW fah kox ib)

Introduced: 1999, 1999   **Class:**   COX II Inhibitor, selective NSAID
Prescription: USA: Yes   **Controlled Drug:**   USA: No; Canada: No
Available as Generic: No

Brand Names: *Celecoxib:* Celebrex; *Rofecoxib:* Vioxx, *Valdecoxib:* Bextra, *Etoricoxib:* Arcoxia (investigational)

Author's Note: Some sound-alike errors have been made with Celexa and Celebrex. One drug is an antidepressant, while the other is a COX II inhibitor. Caution is advised. Information on Bextra will be included in subsequent editions if clinical data and use warrant inclusion.

BENEFITS versus RISKS	
Possible Benefits	*Possible Risks*
EFFECTIVE TREATMENT OF OSTEOARTHRITIS	INCREASED BLOOD PRESSURE
EFFECTIVE RELIEF OF INFLAMMATION	ROFECOXIB USED WITH CAUTION IN PEOPLE WITH ISHEMIC HEART DISEASE
EFFECTIVE SHORT-TERM RELIEF OF SUDDEN (ACUTE) NONARTHRITIC PAIN	Stomach irritation, bleeding, and/or ulceration—possible but less likely than earlier NSAIDS
TREATMENT OF PRIMARY DYSMENORRHEA	Anemia—rare
REDUCTION OF ADENOMATOUS COLON POLYPS IN FAMILIAL ADENOMATOUS POLYPOSIS (FAP) (CELECOXIB ONLY)	Bronchospasm in asthmatics— possible
	CELECOXIB only—allergic reactions in people allergic to sulfa drugs
TREATMENT OF RHEUMATOID ARTHRITIS PAIN	
ROFECOXIB NOW HAS LABELING THAT SAYS IT HAS A BETTER STOMACH AND INTESTINAL SIDE EFFECT PROFILE THAN NAPROXEN	
May have a role in treating a kind of bladder cancer (carcinoma *in situ*)	
Both medicines reduce fevers	
Rofecoxib may have a role in acute migraines	
Both may have a role in Alzheimer's	

▷ **Principal Uses**

As a Single Drug Product: Uses currently included in FDA-approved labeling: (1) Both medicines relieve sudden (acute) nonarthritic pain in adults (orthopedic and dental pain); (2) relieves signs and symptoms of osteoarthritis (both medicines); (3) treats primary dysmenorrhea; (4) relieves signs and symptoms of rheumatoid arthritis; (5) celecoxib reduces the number of adenomatous colorectal polyps in familial adenomatous polyposis (FAP).

Other (unlabeled) generally accepted uses: (1) Based on the way that they work, both could have a role in Alzheimer's disease; (2) may have a role in treating carcinoma *in situ* of the bladder; (3) could be useful in ankylosing spondylitis; (4) rofecoxib may have a role in sudden (acute) migraines.

How These Drugs Work: Inhibit cyclooxygenase (COX) II. Since COX II is the COX type (isoform) that is mostly responsible for inflammation and pain, this results in relief of pain and inflammation. COX II also causes fever in humans (along with other compounds), so these medicines work to lower fevers if they occur. Because COX I works to maintain kidney function and has a protective role in the stomach, lack of inhibition of this isoform by both medicines should result in a much more favorable gastrointestinal side effect profile than nonselective NSAIDs for most patients.

Available Dosage Forms and Strengths
Celecoxib:
Capsules — 100 mg, 200 mg
Rofecoxib:
Oral suspension — 12.5 mg/5 ml, 25 mg/5 ml
Tablets — 12.5 mg, 25 mg, 50 mg

▷ **Usual Adult Dosage Ranges**
Celecoxib:
Osteoarthritis: 100 mg twice daily or 200 mg once a day.
Rheumatoid arthritis: 100 mg twice a day, increased as needed and tolerated to 200 mg twice daily.
Sudden pain or primary dysmenorrhea: acute pain treatment is started with 400 mg right away (stat) an option for an additional 200 mg on the first day. Dosing is continued at 200 mg twice a day if needed.
FAP: 400 mg twice a day (taken with food).
Rofecoxib:
Osteoarthritis: Dosing is started at 12.5 mg once daily. The dose may be increased as needed and tolerated to 25 mg daily. The lowest effective dose should be used.
Rheumatoid arthritis: 25 mg once a day is appropriate and is also the maximum dose.
Sudden pain or primary dysmenorrhea: 50 mg once daily is used (use for more than 5 days). May have an opioid sparing effect in patients taking opioids (medicines such as morphine).
Note: Actual dosage and schedule must be determined for each patient individually.

Conditions Requiring Dosing Adjustments
Liver Function: Celecoxib: Lower doses recommended for celecoxib in moderate liver compromise. Lowering usual doses by half (50%) is appropriate. Not recommended for use in severe liver (hepatic) problems. Rofecoxib: Use in mild (Child-Pugh score of less than 6) liver problems (dysfunction) showed that rofecoxib achieves similar blood levels as in healthy patients. A small amount of data in moderate (Child-Pugh 7–9) liver disease shows that blood levels are roughly 53% increased. Dose decreases by half (50%) appear prudent, and the lowest possible dose should be used. This medicine has NOT been studied in severe liver failure.
Kidney Function: Rofecoxib and celecoxib have not been studied in advanced kidney (renal) disease and are NOT recommended for use in those situations.

▷ **Dosing Instructions:** Celecoxib and rofecoxib: May be taken with or without food. Higher doses of celecoxib are best taken with food to increase how much gets into the body. Taking these medicines with a full glass of water is a good idea. Use of rofecoxib in treating pain or in primary dysmenorrhea has only been studied for up to 5 days. An oral rofecoxib suspension is available if you have trouble swallowing pills. The suspension should be shaken well before a dose is taken. The pill and suspension form give the benefit of equal dosing (are bioequivalent). For both medicines: If you forget a dose: take the missed dose as soon as you remember it, unless its nearly time for your next scheduled dose—if this is the case, skip the missed dose and simply take the regularly scheduled dose. DO NOT double doses.

Usual Duration of Use: Celecoxib may generally take 1–2 weeks of regular use to work in osteoarthritis and 2 weeks in rheumatoid arthritis. Onset for the treatment of more complicated Familial Adenomatous Polyposis (FAP) may require 6 months. In any case, use on a regular basis delivers the best results.

Short-term use of rofecoxib is recommended (up to 5 days) for nonarthritic pain or dysmenorrhea. The medicine usually goes to work in 30 minutes but may take up to an hour. Use on a regular schedule for 1 week usually needed to see benefit in relieving osteoarthritis symptoms. Use of the 50 mg rofecoxib dose on an ongoing (chronic) basis is not recommended. Both medicines are best used in the smallest possible dose and for the shortest possible length of time (minimizes the possibility of GI adverse effects). Treatment of osteo or rheumatoid arthritis duration will be decided by your doctor. Follow up with your doctor on a regular basis is needed.

Typical Treatment Goals and Measurements (Outcomes and Markers)

Pain: Most clinicians treating pain use a device called an algometer to check your pain. This looks like a small ruler, but lets the clinician better understand your pain. The goals of treatment then relate to where the level of pain started (for example, a rating of 7 on a 0–10 scale) and what the cause of the pain was. Pain medicines may also be used together (in combination) in order to get the best result or outcome. For example, many clinicians use acetaminophen (Tylenol, others) rescue doses (NOT NSAID rescue) to help breakthrough pain previously controlled by a COX II inhibitor. If your pain control is not acceptable to YOU (remember, in hospitals and outpatient settings, etc., pain control is a patient right and the fifth vital sign) and if after a week of arthritis pain treatment, results are not what you expect, be sure to call your doctor. It is not unusual to combine medicines or change them to get the best results.

Arthritis: Control of arthritis symptoms (pain, loss of mobility, decreased ability to accomplish activities of daily living, range of motion, etc.) is paramount in returning patient quality of life and to checking the results (beneficial outcomes) from these medicines. Clinicians use the WOMAC osteoarthritis index (see Glossary) to globally assess the health status of people living with osteoarthritis. Many arthritis management or pain centers use interdisciplinary teams (physicians from several specialties, nurses, physician's assistants, physical and occupational therapists, pharmacotherapists, psychotherapists, social workers, and others) to get the best results. Laboratory measures of results for rheumatoid arthritis include decreases in chemicals released by the body (acute phase reactants) such as C-reactive protein. A more general test to roughly measure inflammation is a sed rate (erythrocyte sedimentation rate). In rheumatoid arthritis (RA), the American College of Rheumatologists (ACR) has a scoring system ACR 20, etc. that gives a measure of the degree of response. The higher the ACR number, the better the response.

Possible Advantages of These Drugs: Both compounds: Do NOT inhibit the COX I isoenzyme. Rofecoxib is now the only COX II inhibitor that can claim better gastrointestinal safety based on approved FDA labeling. Rofecoxib: Is NOT a sulfonamide compound and avoids possible allergic sulfonamide reactions of celecoxib. Metabolic differences are present between the medicines in this profile. Rofecoxib is mainly removed by cycotosolic enzymes, versus CYP 450 2C9 removal of celecoxib. Because of the mechanism of both medicines, combined use of low-dose (81 mg) aspirin may be advisable for patients who have already suffered a heart attack. The GI effects of this combination are not fully defined, but are expected to increase the risk of ulcers versus the medicines taken alone, therefore this issue should be discussed with your doctor. In a head-to-head study of 382 arthritis patients, rofecoxib was reported to relieve pain at night more effectively than celecoxib. In a head-to-head trial of 800 patients with osteoarthritis and high blood pressure, only 6% of celecoxib versus 12% of rofecoxib patients developed higher blood pressure. Rofecoxib offers dosing flexibility with a suspension form (offers an easy way to take the medicine for those who have trouble swallowing).

▷ **These Drugs Should Not Be Taken If**
• you have had an allergic reaction to any COX II inhibitor or NSAID.
• you have active peptic ulcer disease.
• you are in the last 3 months of pregnancy.
• you have severe liver disease (not studied).
• you have a history of urticaria/angioedema or spasm of the bronchi with rhinoconjunctivitis with aspirin or other NSAID (adults who developed nasal polyps, asthma, chronic rhinitis, or ongoing angioedema or urticaria make these reactions more likely).

▷ **Inform Your Physician Before Taking These Drugs If**
• you smoke, have ulcerative colitis, take corticosteroids or abuse alcohol.
• you have a bleeding disorder.
• you have a history of peptic ulcer disease.
• you have a history of heart disease or high blood pressure.
• you have ischemic heart disease (rofecoxib only).
• you are pregnant or planning pregnancy.
• you have asthma, carditis or nasal polyps.
• you have a history of liver or kidney problems.
• you drink three or more alcoholic drinks a day (see Caution).

Possible Side Effects (natural, expected, and unavoidable drug actions)
Not defined at present.

▷ **Possible Adverse Effects** (unusual, unexpected, and infrequent reactions)
If any of the following develop, consult your physician promptly for guidance.
Mild Adverse Effects
Allergic reactions: skin rash, itching.
Dizziness—infrequent.
Auditory hallucinations (celecoxib)—case report.
Stomach irritation, heartburn—infrequent.
Increased liver enzymes—up to 15% of people who take NSAIDs. (This was a rare effect for rofecoxib in clinical trials, and 6% of people had this effect.)
Diarrhea—infrequent.
Edema/fluid accumulation (call your doctor if you develop swelling in your legs or ankles)—infrequent.
Serious Adverse Effects
Allergic reactions: acute anaphylactic reaction (see Glossary)—not reported, but possible based on NSAID experience.
Erosion of stomach lining, with silent bleeding—possible (rofecoxib has labeling minimizing this risk).
Gastrointestinal (GI) bleeding, ulceration or perforation (call your doctor if you have a black, tarry stool, unexplained stomach pain, or vomit that has a coffee ground look)—possible to infrequent.
Anemia—rare.
Kidney function decline—possible similar to other NSAIDs.

Liver function changes with possible severe reactions—rare.

Lowered white blood cells, platelets, or bone marrow suppression—rare (rofecoxib).

Bronchospasm when used in patients with nasal polyps, asthma—possible.

May worsen angina attacks and increase their frequency—possible (because of fluid retention and increased heart work).

Clot related (thrombotic) cardiovascular problems (events)—rofecoxib (from the VIGOR study) appeared to have increased risk and the label was changed. Celecoxib has had four cases of blood clots (thrombosis) when used in patients with connective tissue diseases.

▷ **Possible Effects on Sexual Function:** None reported.

Adverse Effects That May Mimic Natural Diseases or Disorders

Increased liver enzymes may suggest viral hepatitis. Other NSAIDs have led to decline in kidney function in people with borderline kidney disease. Accumulation of fluid may mimic worsening of congestive heart failure.

Possible Effects on Laboratory Tests

Complete blood counts: decreased red cells or hemoglobin.

Liver function tests: increased ALT/GPT, AST/GOT, alkaline phosphatase.

Fecal occult blood test: may be positive.

CAUTION

1. The FDA requires a warning noting that people who have three or more alcoholic drinks a day may have increased risk of stomach bleeding if they also use NSAIDs (problems may also occur with lower alcohol use).

2. NSAIDs should be used with extreme caution in people with a previous history of gastrointestinal bleeding or ulcer disease.

3. People with asthma may have aspirin-sensitive asthma. Cross-reactivity between aspirin and these medicines may be possible.

4. When NSAIDs are taken long term, kidney damage is possible. Caution is needed if these medicines are to be used in a patient with kidney damage or in one who is dehydrated (should be rehydrated BEFORE these medicines are started).

5. Rofecoxib and celecoxib may lead to anemia. Patients should be evaluated if they are taking rofecoxib and start to show signs or symptoms of anemia.

6. Part of the removal of rofecoxib from the body happens in a way that can become full or saturated. This means a small change in dose could result in a larger than expected increase in blood level. Take this medicine exactly as prescribed.

7. People who take NSAIDS such as these medicines can develop serious stomach or intestinal (gastrointestinal) problems. Elderly people or patients with debilitating diseases or conditions may be at increased risk for gastrointestinal problems from these medicines. The FDA recently ruled that data on rofecoxib (VIGOR) supported favorable modification (but not removal) of the gastrointestinal side effect labeling. To lower risk of possible GI problems, the lowest effective dose should be used for rofecoxib or celecoxib for the shortest amount of time.

8. These medicines may cause fluid retention, complicating high blood pressure or heart failure treatment—this effect may generally be managed by an inexpensive and well-tolerated water pill (diuretic) such as low-dose hydrochlorothiazide.

9. Rofecoxib has new FDA labeling saying that it should be used with caution in people with ischemic heart disease.

10. It is important to realize that while the lack of effect on platelets is a benefit, it is also a challenge. In patients who require prevention of cardiovascular problems (prophylaxis), rofecoxib is NOT a substitute for a cardioprotective drug.
11. Celecoxib is primarily removed by a liver enzyme called P450 2C9. Caution is advised if consideration is being given to medicines that effect this enzyme. Celecoxib also acts as an inhibitor of a liver enzyme called P450 2D6. Caution should be used in considering prescribing celecoxib for patients already receiving a medicine removed by 2D6.

Precautions for Use

By Infants and Children: Safety and efficacy in those less than 18 years old have NOT been established.

By Those Over 60 Years of Age: Clinical studies included many patients who were more than 75 years old. These patients showed no difference in drug levels from younger patients. For people less than 50 kg, the lowest dose of celecoxib should be used to start treatment. Rofecoxib has new labeling saying that doctors should use caution in prescribing it for patients with ischemic heart disease.

▷ **Advisability of Use During Pregnancy**

Pregnancy Category: C for both medicines. See Pregnancy Risk Categories at the back of this book.

Animal Studies: Slight increase in vertebral malformations in rabbits for rofecoxib. Celecoxib caused skeletal defects at two times the usual human dose.

Human Studies: Adequate studies of pregnant women have NOT been performed.

These medicines should be avoided in pregnancy because of possible premature closure of the ductus arteriosus.

Advisability of Use If Breast-Feeding

Presence of this drug in breast milk: Yes for both medicines in rats, unknown in humans.

Avoid drug or refrain from nursing.

Habit-Forming Potential: None.

Effects of Overdose: No overdose data were reported in clinical trials. Supportive measures consistent with patient symptoms as well as removal of unabsorbed drug from the stomach is reasonable.

Possible Effects of Long-Term Use: Anemia due to chronic blood loss from erosion of stomach lining.

Suggested Periodic Examinations While Taking These Drugs (at physician's discretion)

Check for signs or symptoms of serious GI toxicity.

Complete blood cell counts.

Liver function tests if signs or symptoms of liver problems begin.

Increased range of motion and decreased pain in arthritis.

▷ **While Taking These Drugs, Observe the Following**

Foods: May be taken with or without food (take it with food if the medicine upsets your stomach).

Herbal Medicines or Minerals: Ginseng, ginkgo, alfalfa, clove oil, feverfew, cinchona bark, white willow bark, and garlic may change clotting, so combining those herbals with these medicines is not recommended. NSAIDs may decrease feverfew effects. Hay flower, mistletoe herb, and white mustard seed carry German Commission E monograph indications for arthritis and may be complementary. White willow bark contains salicylate (aspirin) and may increase GI toxicity risk. Talk to your doctor BEFORE combining any herbal medicines or prescription medicines.

Beverages: No restrictions. May be taken with milk.

▷ *Alcohol:* Use of alcohol and these medicines at the same time may increase risk of stomach irritation. See alcohol/NSAIDs warning in Cautions.

Tobacco Smoking: May increase risk of stomach irritation. I advise everyone to quit smoking.

▷ *Other Drugs*

These medicines may ***increase*** the effects of

- adrenocortical steroids (see Drug Classes), which may lead to additive stomach irritation and bleeding.
- methotrexate—not by increasing blood levels, but by possible increased GI effects.
- oral anticoagulants (see Drug Classes) such as warfarin (Coumadin) and require more frequent INR testing.

The following drugs may ***decrease*** the effects of these medicines:

- cholestyramine (Questran, others) may decrease the amount of drug that goes to work (not reported, but possible in theory). Separate doses by 30 minutes.

These medicines ***taken concurrently*** with

- ACE inhibitors—since vein-opening or vasodilator prostaglandins may account for some of the ACE beneficial effects and since data from combined use with benazepril (Lotensin) showed blunting of beneficial effects from benazepril, caution with all ACE inhibitors is prudent.
- alendronate (Fosamax) may blunt alendronate absorption and may also result in increased risk of stomach upset/diarrhea (not reported, but theoretically possible).
- cortisonelike drugs (see Drug Classes) increase risk of stomach ulcers.
- high blood pressure (antihypertensive) medicines may blunt their therapeutic benefit, especially those that are diuretics such as furosemide (Lasix) or other loop diuretics, spironolactone, or thiazides (see Drug Classes).
- lithium (Lithobid) may increase lithium blood levels.
- other NSAIDs (see Drug Classes) (such as aspirin) may increase risk of stomach or intestine (GI) toxicity. The benefit-to-risk decision of combined use of aspirin with these medicines in patients who have had a heart attack (secondary prevention) may be desirable because of the lack of a needed effect on platelets or to overcome a possible effect of these medicines on clotting. Further study is needed.

The following drugs may ***increase*** the effects of celecoxib:

- any medicine that inhibits the liver enzyme that removes celecoxib from the body (CYP 2C9).
- fluconazole (Diflucan) by inhibiting liver enzymes that remove celecoxib from the body. Celecoxib dose decreases are prudent if these medicines are to be combined.
- fluoxetine (Prozac) by inhibiting liver enzymes that remove celecoxib from the body. Celecoxib dose decreases may be prudent if these medicines are to be combined.
- propafenone (Rythmol) by inhibiting liver enzymes that remove celecoxib from the body. Celecoxib dose decreases may be prudent if these medicines are to be combined.

- ritonavir (Norvir) and perhaps other protease inhibitors by inhibiting liver enzymes that remove celecoxib from the body. Celecoxib dose decreases may be prudent if these medicines are to be combined.
- sertraline (Zoloft) by inhibiting liver enzymes that remove celecoxib from the body. Celecoxib dose decreases may be prudent if these medicines are to be combined.

The following drugs may **decrease** the effects of celecoxib:

- carbamazepine (Tegretol), phenytoin (Dilantin) and rifampin (Rifater, others) by increasing the liver enzyme that removes it from the body (not yet reported, but these medicines are known CYP 2C9 inducers).

The following drugs **taken concurrently with** celecoxib:

- diltiazem (Cardizem, others) may lead to increased blood pressure. Careful monitoring of blood pressure is prudent.

▷ *Driving, Hazardous Activities:* May cause dizziness. Use caution until full effects are known.

Aviation Note: The use of these drugs **may be a disqualification** for piloting. Consult a designated Aviation Medical Examiner.

Exposure to Sun: No reported problems.

Discontinuation: May be stopped abruptly, but talk to your doctor before making any changes in your medicines.

CROMOLYN (KROH moh lin)

Other Names: Cromolyn sodium, sodium cromoglycate

Introduced: 1968 **Class:** Antiasthmatic drug, mast cell stabilizing agent, asthma attack preventive **Prescription:** USA: Yes **Controlled Drug:** USA: No; Canada: No **Available as Generic:** USA: Yes; Canada: Yes

Brand Names: Children's Nasalcrom, Crolom, Fisoneb [CD], Gastrocrom, Intal, ✦Gen-cromolyn ✦Intal Spincaps, ✦Intal Syncroner, ✦Nalcrom, Nasalcrom, ✦Novo-cromolyn, Opticrom, ✦Rynacrom, Vistacrom

Author's Note: Cromolyn sodium (4%) as Nasalcrom is available without a prescription.

BENEFITS versus RISKS

Possible Benefits	*Possible Risks*
LONG-TERM PREVENTION OF RECURRENT ASTHMA ATTACKS	Anaphylactic reaction (see Glossary)
Prevention of acute asthma due to allergens or exercise	Spasm of bronchial tubes, increased wheezing
Prevention and treatment of allergic rhinitis	Allergic pneumonitis (allergic reaction in lung tissue)
Prevention of bronchospasm	
RELIEF OF ALLERGIC EYE INFLAMMATION- (CONJUNCTIVITIS)	
Treatment of giant papillary conjunctivitis	

▷ **Principal Uses**

As a Single Drug Product: Uses currently included in FDA-approved labeling: (1) Prevents allergic reactions in the nose (allergic rhinitis, hay fever) and the bronchial tubes (bronchial asthma); (2) used to treat eye inflammation (allergic conjunctivitis); (3) helps prevent exercise- or environmental-induced asthma; (4) treats mastocytosis and manages several allergy-related skin disorders.

Other (unlabeled) generally accepted uses: (1) Can be used to help stop cough from ACE inhibitors (see Drug Classes); (2) helps modify the reactions in food allergies; (3) may have a small part in therapy of Bell's palsy.

How This Drug Works: Blocks the release of histamine (and other chemicals) from mast cells that worsens allergic reactions. Prevents sequence of events leading to swelling, itching and constriction of bronchial tubes (asthma).

Available Dosage Forms and Strengths

Capsules, oral — 20 mg, 100 mg
Eyedrops — 2% (such as Vistacrom) and 4%
Inhalation aerosol — 0.8 mg per metered spray
Inhalation capsules (powder) — 20 mg
Inhalation solution — 20 mg per ampule
Nasal insufflation (powder) — 10 mg per cartridge
Nasal solution — 40 mg/ml
Nasal spray — 5.2 mg per spray in a 26 ml bottle

▷ **Usual Adult Dosage Ranges**

Eyedrops: One to two drops of the 4% solution in each eye four to six times daily at regular intervals.

Inhalation aerosol: 1.6 mg (two inhalations) four times daily at regular intervals for prevention of asthma, or two inhalations 10 to 15 minutes before exposure to prevent allergen- or exercise-induced asthma.

Inhalation powder: 20 mg (one capsule) four times daily at regular intervals for long-term prevention of asthma; 20 mg (one capsule) as a single dose 10 to 15 minutes before exposure to prevent acute allergen- or exercise-induced asthma. Total daily maximum dosage is 160 mg (eight capsules).

Inhalation solution: Same as inhalation powder.

Nasal insufflation: Initially 10 mg in each nostril every 4 to 6 hours as needed; reduce to every 8 to 12 hours for maintenance.

Nasal solution: 5.2 mg in each nostril three to six times daily as needed.

Oral powder: ALL of the contents of capsules for oral use are poured into a half glass of hot water. This is stirred, and a half glass of cold water is added while mixing. Drink all the liquid and add more water to be sure you drink any leftover medicine. Mix cromolyn with water only, not with fruit juice, milk or foods.

Note: Actual dose and schedule must be determined for each patient individually.

Conditions Requiring Dosing Adjustments

Liver Function: If the bile duct is damaged by liver disease, the dose must be decreased.

Kidney Function: The dose should be decreased in kidney failure.

▷ **Dosing Instructions:** Follow instructions provided with all of the dosage forms, especially inhalers and eyedrops. Do not swallow capsules intended for inhalation. (If the capsule is accidentally swallowed, drug will cause no beneficial or adverse effects.) Capsules for mouth (oral) use can be poured into 4 ounces (one half glass) of hot water as above. If you forget a dose, take it right away unless it's nearly time for your next regular dose. If it IS nearly time, just take the scheduled dose. DO NOT double doses. The Nasalcrom form if best used 1–2 weeks BEFORE you are going to be exposed to something that you are allergic to (allergen).

Usual Duration of Use: Regular use for 6 weeks or more is often needed for benefits in preventing asthma attacks. Onset in perennial allergic rhinitis can be 1 to 2 weeks. Eye use (ophthalmic) may work in a few days up to 6 weeks. Long-term use (months to years) requires periodic evaluation.

Typical Treatment Goals and Measurements (Outcomes and Markers)

Asthma: The frequency of asthma attacks as well as the severity of asthma attacks that occur (such as those requiring an emergency department visit) are a benchmark of effectiveness. Some clinicians also use the number of times a rescue inhaler must be used as a clinical fine point. Pulmonary function tests such as FEV1 may also be used. Goals should be communicated and checked.

Possible Advantages of This Drug

May be quite effective in young asthmatics. Well tolerated. Serious adverse effects are very rare. Works against immediate responses to allergens as well as late nasal responses and isolated late nasal responses. Usually regarded as the drug of choice in adding medicines to step one of current asthma treatments for children under five years old.

▷ **This Drug Should Not Be Taken If**
- you have had an allergic reaction to any dosage form of it previously.

▷ **Inform Your Physician Before Taking This Drug If**
- you are allergic to milk, milk products, or lactose. (The inhalation powder contains lactose.)
- you have impaired liver or kidney function.
- you have soft contact lenses (these should not be worn while using the eye-drops).
- you have angina or a heart rhythm disorder. (Some inhalation aerosol forms have propellants that could be hazardous).

Possible Side Effects (natural, expected, and unavoidable drug actions)

Unpleasant taste with use of inhalation aerosol. Mild throat irritation, hoarseness, cough (minimized by a few swallows of water after each powder inhalation). Painful or difficult urination (dysuria)—rare. For the eye (ocular) form—the most common problem (adverse reaction) is stinging or burning.

▷ **Possible Adverse Effects** (unusual, unexpected, and infrequent reactions)

If any of the following develop, consult your physician promptly for guidance. (Frequency and probable severity of adverse effects is greatly reduced or not applicable for the eye [ophthalmic] form).

Mild Adverse Effects

Allergic reactions: skin rash, hives, itching—possible.
Headache, dizziness, drowsiness—rare.
Nausea, vomiting, urinary urgency and pain (dysuria), joint pain—infrequent.
Muscle pain (myositis)—rare.
Stinging or burning of the eyes with ophthalmic use—possible.
Cough and bronchial irritation—rare.
Nosebleed or itching with nasal solution use—rare.

Serious Adverse Effects

Allergic reactions: rare anaphylactic reaction (see Glossary).
Allergic pneumonitis (allergic reaction in lung tissue)—case reports.

Propellants in the metered dose inhaler may cause problems in patients with disease of the heart arteries or a history of abnormal heart rhythms—possible.

Pericarditis—case report.

Inflammation of the arteries—case reports.

▷ **Possible Effects on Sexual Function:** None reported.

Possible Effects on Laboratory Tests
None reported.

CAUTION
1. This drug only helps **prevent** bronchial asthma—use **before** the start of acute bronchial constriction (asthmatic wheezing).
2. *Do not* use during an acute asthma attack—may worsen and prolong asthmatic wheezing.
3. This drug does not block the benefits of drugs that relieve acute asthma attacks after they start. Cromolyn is used *before and between* acute attacks to help keep them from starting; bronchodilators are used during acute attacks.
4. If you are using a bronchodilator drug by inhalation, it is best to take it about 5 minutes before inhaling cromolyn.
5. If this drug has allowed you to decrease or eliminate steroids and you are unable to tolerate cromolyn, ask your doctor about the need to start steroids once again.

Precautions for Use
By Infants and Children: Safety and effectiveness for those under 5 years of age not established for the metered dose inhaler. Inhalation capsules: For children 2 years and older—20 mg (contents of one capsule) inhaled four times a day. Young children may find a nebulized solution easier than the powder.
By Those Over 60 Years of Age: This drug does not work in the management of chronic bronchitis or emphysema.

▷ **Advisability of Use During Pregnancy**
Pregnancy Category: B. See Pregnancy Risk Categories at the back of this book.
Animal Studies: Mouse, rat and rabbit studies revealed no birth defects due to this drug.
Human Studies: Adequate studies of pregnant women are not available.
Use this drug only if clearly needed.

Advisability of Use If Breast-Feeding
Presence of this drug in breast milk: Unknown.
Avoid drug or refrain from nursing.

Habit-Forming Potential: None.

Effects of Overdose: No significant effects reported.

Possible Effects of Long-Term Use: Allergic reaction of lung tissue (allergic pneumonitis)—very rare.

Suggested Periodic Examinations While Taking This Drug (at physician's discretion) sputum analysis and X-ray if symptoms suggest allergic pneumonitis. FEV1.

▷ **While Taking This Drug, Observe the Following**
Foods: Follow physician-prescribed diet. Avoid all foods to which you are allergic.

Herbal Medicines or Minerals: If you are allergic to plants in the Asteraceae family (aster, chrysanthemum, daisy, or ragweed), you may also be allergic to echinacea, chamomile, feverfew, and St. John's wort. Fir or pine needle oil should NOT be used by asthmatics. Ephedra alone does carry a German Commission E monograph indication for asthma treatment. Talk to your doctor before using any herbal medicine.

Beverages: Avoid all beverages to which you may be allergic.

▷ *Alcohol:* No interactions expected.

Tobacco Smoking: No interactions with the medicine, but smoking can irritate your airways. I advise everyone to quit smoking.

▷ *Other Drugs:* Cromolyn may allow reduced dosage of cortisonelike drugs in the management of chronic asthma. Ask your doctor about dosage adjustment.

▷ *Driving, Hazardous Activities:* This drug may cause dizziness. Restrict activities as necessary.

Aviation Note: The use of this drug **may be a disqualification** for piloting. Consult a designated Aviation Medical Examiner.

Exposure to Sun: No restrictions.

Heavy Exercise or Exertion: This drug may prevent exercise-induced asthma if taken 10 to 15 minutes before exertion. It is most effective in young people.

Discontinuation: If cromolyn has made it possible to reduce or stop maintenance doses of cortisonelike drugs and you find it necessary to discontinue cromolyn, watch closely for a sudden return of asthma. A slow withdrawal (over a week) is advisable. You may have to start a cortisonelike drug as well as take other measures to control asthma and prevent a recurrence if this medicine is stopped.

Special Storage Instructions: Keep the powder cartridges in a dry, tightly closed container. Store in a cool place, but not in the refrigerator. Do not handle the cartridges or the inhaler when hands are wet.

CYCLOPHOSPHAMIDE (si kloh FOSS fa mide)

Introduced: 1959   **Class:**   Anticancer,   immunosuppressive   **Prescription:**   USA: Yes   **Controlled Drug:**   USA: No; Canada: No
Available as Generic: Yes

Brand Names: Cycloblastin, Cytoxan, Neosar, ✤Procytox

BENEFITS versus RISKS	
Possible Benefits	*Possible Risks*
CURE OR CONTROL OF CERTAIN TYPES OF CANCER	REDUCED WHITE BLOOD CELL COUNT
PREVENTION OF REJECTION IN ORGAN TRANSPLANTATION	SECONDARY INFECTION
	URINARY BLADDER
Possibly beneficial in rheumatoid arthritis or lupus erythematosus	BLEEDING HEART
	LUNG, LIVER OR KIDNEY DAMAGE
May help selected cases of childhood nephrotic syndrome	Loss of hair

▷ **Principal Uses**

As a Single Drug Product: Uses currently included in FDA-approved labeling: (1) Combination treatment of various cancers: malignant lymphomas, multiple myeloma, sarcomas, retinoblastomas, leukemias, as well as breast and ovarian cancer; (2) also used to prevent rejection in organ transplantation and in some autoimmune disorders; (3) treats some resistant forms of nephrotic syndrome.

Other (unlabeled) generally accepted uses: (1) Used to prepare patients for autologous bone marrow transplants; (2) part of several combination chemotherapy regimens; (3) helps overall survival in combination therapy of lung or fallopian tube cancer; (4) can be part of combination therapy for Ewing's sarcoma; (5) may be of help in patients with lupus erythematosus who have interstitial lung disease or nephritis; (6) secondary role in prostate cancer; (7) high-dose therapy of anemia (aplastic anemia); (8) helps in resistant rheumatoid arthritis or RA (and in pachymeningitis associated with RA); (9) may have a role in drug-induced serious skin reactions (such as Stevens-Johnson syndrome or toxic epidermal necrolysis, etc.).

How This Drug Works: Kills cancer cells during all phases of development. Suppresses primary growth and secondary spread (metastasis) of some types of cancer.

Available Dosage Forms and Strengths
Injection — vials of 100 mg, 200 mg, 500 mg, 1 g, and 2 g
Tablets — 25 mg, 50 mg

▷ **Usual Adult Dosage Ranges:** *Oral form:* Many different ways of using and dosing this medicine have been reported. In general, doses range from one to five mg/kg of body weight per day through starting (induction) phases and ongoing (maintenance) dosing. Doses are adjusted individually to the response of the tumor as well as to development of toxicity such as low white blood cell count (leukopenia). Some clinicians use 60 to 120 mg per square meter of body surface area daily or 400 mg per square meter of body surface area on days 1 to 5, every 3 to 4 weeks. Once again as therapy continues, the dose is adjusted according to how the tumor responds or unacceptable low white blood cell counts develop. *Intravenous:* 1,000 to 1,500 mg per square meter every 3 to 4 weeks, adjusted the same as the oral form. Current experimental approaches for combination therapy can be found at *www.cancer.org* and *www.clinicaltrials.gov*.

Note: Actual dose and schedule must be determined for each patient individually.

Conditions Requiring Dosing Adjustments
Liver Function: Dose changes are not required in liver compromise. Toxicity may be more likely in people with liver failure.
Kidney Function: In moderate to severe kidney problems, the dose is decreased by 25–50%.

▷ **Dosing Instructions:** Tablets may be crushed and are best taken on an empty stomach. If nausea or indigestion occurs, may be taken with or following food. Liquid intake should be no less than 3 quarts every 24 hours to reduce risk of bladder irritation and help keep your kidneys flushed. If you forget a dose, take it right away unless it's nearly time for your next regular dose. If it IS nearly time, just take the scheduled dose. DO NOT double doses.

Usual Duration of Use: Use on a regular schedule is required to achieve and maintain a significant cancer remission. Initial response often happens in 1 to 3 weeks. Duration depends on response of the cancer and patient tolerance of the drug. Your doctor will help decide.

Typical Treatment Goals and Measurements (Outcomes and Markers)

Cancer chemotherapy: The balance here is a difficult one of killing cancer cells versus toxic effects of the medicine itself (bone marrow suppression, heart and others). Complete blood cell counts, assessment of the cancer (as in disappearance of soft tissue bumps or masses in multiple myeloma) and resolution of increased calcium are typical markers.

▷ **This Drug Should Not Be Taken If**
- you have had an allergic reaction to it previously.
- you have an active infection of any kind, or your bone marrow is severely suppressed.
- you have bloody urine for any reason.
- you are pregnant (exposure through a sexual partner may also cause fetal damage) or are breast-feeding your infant.

▷ **Inform Your Physician Before Taking This Drug If**
- you have impaired liver, heart or kidney function.
- you have a blood cell or bone marrow disorder.
- you have had previous chemotherapy or X-ray therapy for any type of cancer.
- you take, or have taken within the past year, any cortisonelike drug (adrenal corticosteroids).
- you have diabetes.
- you will have surgery with general anesthesia.

Possible Side Effects (natural, expected, and unavoidable drug actions)

Bone marrow depression (see Glossary)—low production of white blood cells and, to a lesser degree, red blood cells, and blood platelets (see Glossary). Fever, chills, sore throat, fatigue, weakness, abnormal bleeding, or bruising. Leukemia has been reported following cyclophosphamide therapy. Impairment of natural resistance (immunity) to infection. Weakening of the heart muscle (cardiomyopathy). Excessive urination (SIADH). Cystitis or hemorrhagic cystitis. Up to ninefold increase in bladder cancer risk. Some combination regimens (such as cyclophosphamide, methotrexate, and fluorouracil-CMF) have been associated with changes in thinking (mental status change).

▷ **Possible Adverse Effects** (unusual, unexpected, and infrequent reactions)

If any of the following develop, consult your physician promptly for guidance.

Mild Adverse Effects

Allergic reaction: skin rash—rare.

Headache, dizziness, blurred vision—possible.

Loss of scalp hair (50% of users), darkening of skin and fingernails, transverse ridging of nails.

Nausea, vomiting (dose-related)—frequent.

Ulceration of mouth, diarrhea (may be bloody)—possible.

Serious Adverse Effects

Idiosyncratic reaction: hemolytic anemia—case reports.

Allergic reaction: anaphylaxis—possible.

Heart damage (cardiomyopathy)—possible and associated with higher doses (18-270 mg/kg).

Liver damage with jaundice: yellow eyes and skin, dark-colored urine, light-colored stools—rare.

Kidney damage: impaired kidney function, reduced urine volume, bloody urine—case reports.

Lowered white blood cell (granulocyte) colony formation—possible even with rheumatoid arthritis use.

Leukemia—reported.

Severe inflammation of bladder: painful urination, bloody urine—infrequent to frequent.

Syndrome of inappropriate antidiuretic hormone secretion (SIADH)—rare.

Increased potassium (hyperkalemia)—possible.

Intestinal or stomach bleeding (hemorrhagic colitis or GI bleed)—possible.

Drug-induced damage of heart and lung (interstitial pneumonitis) tissue—case reports.

Pancreatitis—case reports.

▷ **Possible Effects on Sexual Function:** Suppression of ovarian function—irregular menstrual pattern or cessation of menstruation (amenorrhea): 18 to 57%, depending upon dose and duration of use.

Testicular suppression—reduced or no sperm production (100% of users).

Possible Delayed Adverse Effects: Development of other types of cancer (secondary malignancies). Development of severe cystitis with bleeding from the bladder wall (may occur many months after the last dose).

Possible Effects on Laboratory Tests

Complete blood cell counts: decreased red cells, hemoglobin, white cells, and platelets.

Blood sodium levels: decreased in SIADH (rare).

Blood potassium: may be increased.

INR (prothrombin time): increased.

Liver function tests: increased liver enzymes (ALT/GPT, AST/GOT, and alkaline phosphatase), increased bilirubin.

CAUTION

1. This drug may interfere with the normal healing of wounds.
2. This drug can cause significant changes in genetic material in both men and women (sperm and eggs or ova). Patients taking this drug must understand the potential for serious defects in children that are conceived during or following the course of medication.
3. This drug can suppress natural resistance (immunity) to infection, resulting in life-threatening illness.
4. Avoid live-virus vaccines while taking this drug (talk with your doctor about this).

Precautions for Use

By Infants and Children: This drug should not be given if the child is dehydrated. Adequate fluid intake to ensure a copious urine volume for 4 hours following each dose is needed. Prevent exposure of child to anyone with active chickenpox or shingles. This drug may cause ovarian or testicular sterility.

By Those Over 60 Years of Age: Increased risk of serious bladder problems (chemical cystitis). Patients MUST drink large amounts of water in order to keep the bladder flushed. This may increase the risk of urinary retention in men with prostatism (see Glossary).

▷ **Advisability of Use During Pregnancy**

Pregnancy Category: D. See Pregnancy Risk Categories at the back of this book.

Animal Studies: Significant birth defects reported in mice, rat, and rabbit studies.

Human Studies: Information from studies of pregnant women indicates that this drug can cause serious birth defects or fetal death.

Avoid completely during the first 3 months. Use of this drug during the last 6 months must be carefully individualized.

Advisability of Use If Breast-Feeding
Presence of this drug in breast milk: Yes.
Avoid drug or refrain from nursing.

Habit-Forming Potential: None.

Effects of Overdose: Nausea, vomiting, diarrhea, bloody urine, water retention, weight gain, severe bone marrow depression, severe infections.

Possible Effects of Long-Term Use: Development of fibrous tissue in lungs; secondary malignancies.

Suggested Periodic Examinations While Taking This Drug (at physician's discretion)
Complete blood cell counts, every 2 to 4 days during initial treatment and then every 3 to 4 weeks during maintenance treatment. Signs and symptoms of bleeding.
Liver and kidney function tests, potassium.
Thyroid function tests (if symptoms warrant).

▷ **While Taking This Drug, Observe the Following**
Foods: No restrictions.
Herbal Medicines or Minerals: Echinacea: Some patients use echinacea to attempt to boost their immune systems. Unfortunately, use of echinacea is not recommended in people with damaged immune systems. This herb may also actually weaken any immune system if it is used too often or for too long a time. Talk to your doctor before taking any herbal medicine with cyclophosphamide.
Beverages: No restrictions. May be taken with milk.
▷ *Alcohol:* No interactions expected.
Tobacco Smoking: No interactions expected. I advise everyone to quit smoking.
▷ *Other Drugs*
Cyclophosphamide *taken concurrently* with
- allopurinol (Zyloprim) may increase the extent of bone marrow depression.
- amphotericin (Abelcet and others) may increase risk of kidney toxicity.
- chloramphenicol can decrease cyclophosphamide effectiveness.
- ciprofloxacin (Cipro) can result in lowered ciprofloxacin levels and the need for a larger than usual dose.
- digoxin may decrease digoxin absorption and impair digoxin's effectiveness.
- flu (influenza) vaccine, and perhaps other vaccines, may decrease the vaccine's ability to confer immunity.
- hydrochlorothiazide and other thiazide diuretics (see Drug Classes) may worsen the lowering of white blood cells (myelosuppression) caused by cyclophosphamide. Watch for combination blood pressure pills that may contain "hidden thiazides."
- indomethacin (Indocin) can cause fluid retention.
- live-virus vaccines should be avoided.
- ondansetron (Zofran) may blunt benefits of cyclophosphamide.
- pentostatin may cause fatal heart damage.
- ritonavir (Norvir) may lead to cyclophosphamide toxicity.
- succinylcholine can result in succinylcholine toxicity.

- tamoxifen (Nolvadex) can increase blood clot risk.
- traztuzumab (Herceptin) may increase the risk of heart problems (congestive heart failure or ventricular dysfunction).

▷ *Driving, Hazardous Activities:* Use caution if dizziness occurs.
Aviation Note: The use of this drug *may be a disqualification* for piloting. Consult a designated Aviation Medical Examiner.
Exposure to Sun: No restrictions.
Occurrence of Unrelated Illness: Any signs of infection—fever, chills, sore throat, cough, or flu-like symptoms—must be promptly reported. This drug may have to be stopped until the infection is controlled. Consult your physician.

CYCLOSPORINE (SI kloh spor een)

Other Names: Ciclosporin, cyclosporin A

Introduced: 1983   **Class:**   Immunosuppressant   **Prescription:**
USA: Yes   **Controlled Drug:**   USA: No; Canada: No   **Available as**
Generic: USA: Yes; Canada: No
Brand Names: Neoral, Sandimmune, SangCya, Sangstat

BENEFITS versus RISKS	
Possible Benefits	*Possible Risks*
EFFECTIVE PREVENTION AND TREATMENT OF REJECTION IN ORGAN TRANSPLANTATION	MARKED KIDNEY TOXICITY DEVELOPMENT OF HYPERTENSION
Some use treating severe rheumatoid arthritis, psoriasis, and other inflammatory (autoimmune) conditions	HIGH BLOOD PRESSURE Liver toxicity Low white blood cell count Development of lymphoma Excessive hair growth Blunted response to vaccines (best given 3–4 weeks BEFORE cyclosporine is started)

▷ **Principal Uses**
As a Single Drug Product: Uses included in FDA-approved labeling: (1) Helps prevent (in conjunction with cortisonelike drugs) organ rejection in kidney, liver and heart transplantation; (2) helps treat rejection crisis; (3) the Neoral microemulsion form and Sandimmune treats severe active rheumatoid arthritis; (4) treats refractory psoriasis.
Other (unlabeled) generally accepted uses: (1) Used in transplantation of the bone marrow; (2) used investigationally in a variety of diseases involving the immune system such as: Sjögren's, Crohn's, and Grave's diseases; ulcerative colitis; psoriasis; myasthenia gravis; bullous pemphigoid; pulmonary fibrosis associated with rheumatoid arthritis; Sweet's syndrome; insulin-dependent diabetes; systemic lupus erythematosus (SLE); large granular lymphocytic leukemia; and some anemias; (3) severe, steroid-dependent asthma; (4) treats severe skin reactions (toxic epidermal necrolysis) to phenytoin (Dilantin).

How This Drug Works: By inhibiting some lymphocytes (white blood cells) and their growth factors, this drug suppresses the rejection of transplanted organs.

Available Dosage Forms and Strengths
Capsules, soft gelatin — 25 mg, 100 mg
Injection, intravenous — 50 mg/ml
Oral solution — 100 mg/ml (Note: The microemulsion Neoral is NOT the same as Sandimmune.)

▷ **Usual Adult Dosage Ranges:** *Transplantation:* Initially 15 mg per kg of body mass intravenously (some clinicians use higher doses, but this is not common), the chosen dose is given 4–12 hours prior to transplantation surgery. The drug is then continued after surgery at the same dose for up to 14 days. Clinicians use the lowest blood levels (trough) to adjust dosing. After this, the dose is usually lowered (tapered) by 5% per week to an ongoing dose taken by mouth that is equal to 5–10 mg per kg of body weight each day. Sandimmune should be given with corticosteroids.

If a conversion is made from oral Sandimmune to Neoral, Neoral dose is usually started at the same daily dose as Sandimmune, given at the same time each day in two equally divided doses. Cyclosporine trough levels should be measured twice weekly in people who were taking more than 10 mg per kg of body mass per day of Sandimmune. Dosing of SangCya and Neoral is always given in two divided doses.

Crohn's disease or severe/refractory ulcerative colitis: Therapy is started with 8–10 mg/kg/day with the medicine adjusted to response and a maximum treatment length of 6 months.

Note: Actual dose and schedule must be determined for each patient individually.

Conditions Requiring Dosing Adjustments
Liver Function: The dose must be adjusted (based on blood levels) in liver compromise. Much of the drug is eliminated in the bile.

Kidney Function: This drug is capable of causing marked kidney toxicity. Caution is critical. One set of guidelines for rheumatoid arthritis suggested that cyclosporine dosing should be adjusted to serum creatinine. For example, if serum creatinine increases more than 30% above the starting level (baseline) in two tests taken a week apart, then the cyclosporine dose is lowered by 0.5 to 0.75 mg/kg/day. If the creatinine returns to less than 30% of the starting level—cyclosporine can be continued. If the serum creatinine stays up, cyclosporine is stopped for 30 days and is restarted if creatinine decreases to 15% of the starting level. As in other cases of increasing creatinine, the medicines being taken at the same time should be evaluated for possible adverse impact on kidney function.

Diabetes: People who are diabetic and subsequently have kidney or pancreatic transplants will need larger than usual doses.

Hypercholesterolemia: If the blood cholesterol is 50% above normal, the dose must be decreased by 50% in order to avoid toxicity.

Obesity: Dosing **must** be based on ideal (a calculation that helps eliminate the weight that is fat) body weight.

Cystic Fibrosis: It is very difficult to appropriately dose this medication in patients who have this disease. Some patients will require as much as two times the usual dose. The dose should be adjusted to drug levels.

Multiple Organ Transplants: Patients with multiple transplants (such as pancreas and kidney) often need an increased dose of cyclosporine in order to achieve the desired effect. The dose should be determined based on blood levels.

▷ **Dosing Instructions:** Preferably taken with or immediately following food to reduce stomach irritation. The capsule should be swallowed whole; do not open, crush, or chew. The oral solution should carefully measure and can be mixed with milk, chocolate milk or orange juice (at room temperature) in a glass or ceramic cup; do not use a wax-lined or plastic cup or container. Stir well and drink immediately. Use the same liquid to dilute the dose, because different liquids may change the amount that gets into your body. Blood levels are important. DO NOT take this medicine with grapefruit juice. It is also best to take this drug at the same time each day to maintain steady blood levels.

Usual Duration of Use: Use on a regular schedule for several weeks is usually needed to prevent organ rejection or stop rejection already underway. Benefits in psoriasis or rheumatoid arthritis may take 4 to 8 weeks. Long-term use (months to years) requires follow-up by your doctor. If you forget a dose: Take the dose you missed as soon as possible, unless it's nearly time for your next dose. If that is the case, skip the missed dose and take the next scheduled dose. DO NOT double doses. If you find yourself missing doses, talk to your doctor.

▷ **This Drug Should Not Be Taken If**
- you have had an allergic reaction to it previously. Attention should be paid to the ingredients also present in many forms of this medicine (such as castor oil).
- you are getting radiation treatment.
- you have uncontrolled high blood pressure and are taking this medicine to treat rheumatoid arthritis.
- you have an active lymphoma or a malignancy of any type.
- you are taking this medicine to control psoriasis and are getting PUVA treatment.
- you have an active, uncontrolled infection, especially chickenpox or shingles.

▷ **Inform Your Physician Before Taking This Drug If**
- you are taking any immunosuppressant drug other than cortisonelike preparations.
- you are pregnant or breast-feeding.
- you have a history of liver or kidney disease or impaired liver or kidney function.
- you have a history of hypertension or gout.
- you have a chronic gastrointestinal disorder.
- you are taking a potassium supplement or drugs that can raise the blood level of potassium.
- you have a seizure disorder.
- you have a history of a blood cell disorder.
- you take other medicines toxic to the kidney.

Possible Side Effects (natural, expected, and unavoidable drug actions)
Predisposition to infections (such as pneumocystis). Drug fever—possible.

▷ **Possible Adverse Effects** (unusual, unexpected, and infrequent reactions)
If any of the following develop, consult your physician promptly for guidance.
Mild Adverse Effects
Allergic reactions: skin rash, itching—case reports.
Excessive hair growth—frequent in transplant patients.
Acne—rare.

Headache, confusion, anxiety, or mood alterations—infrequent.

Tremors (dose dependent)—frequent.

Mouth sores—rare.

Gum overgrowth—frequent in some reports.

Nausea/vomiting, diarrhea—infrequent.

Changes in facial features (dysmorphosis)—possible with longer-term therapy.

Serious Adverse Effects

Allergic reactions: anaphylactic reaction (see Glossary) to intravenous solution—case reports.

Kidney injury (25% kidney transplant, 37% liver and 38% heart)—frequent.

Hypertension, mild to severe (up to half of patients getting this drug)—frequent.

Blood total cholesterol: increased (while HDL decreased).

Seizures—rare to frequent (kidney, 1.8%; bone marrow, 5.5%; up to 25% of liver transplant patients).

Cortical blindness—case reports.

Hearing loss (ototoxicity)—rare.

Hallucinations, movement problems (catatonia), dementia or coma (may all derive from encephalopathy)—case reports.

Nerve damage (neurotoxicity)—possible and usually reversible when the medicine is stopped, but may be permanent.

Liver injury—infrequent and dose dependent.

Pancreatitis—rare.

Low white blood cell count (leukopenia)—infrequent.

Low blood platelets (thrombocytopenia)—rare.

Abnormal blood clots (thromboembolic complications)—case reports (usually in the first week, but up to 30 days after the medicine was started).

High blood potassium levels, blood sugar (glucose) increases, uric acid levels (and gout), increased blood cholesterol, or low blood magnesium—all possible.

Lymphoma, possibly drug-induced—rare to infrequent.

Relapse of lupus erythematosus—case reports.

Increased risk of skin cancers (risk increased by sun or UV light exposure).

▷ **Possible Effects on Sexual Function:** Enlargement and tenderness of male breast (gynecomastia-1 to 4%)—rare to infrequent.

Adverse Effects That May Mimic Natural Diseases or Disorders

Liver toxicity may suggest viral hepatitis.

Natural Diseases or Disorders That May Be Activated by This Drug

Latent infections, hypertension, gout.

Possible Effects on Laboratory Tests

Complete blood cell counts: decreased red cells, hemoglobin, and white cells.

Blood potassium level or uric acid level: increased.

Blood platelets, white cells, magnesium: decreased.

Liver function tests: increased liver enzymes (ALT/GPT, AST/GOT, and alkaline phosphatase), increased bilirubin.

Kidney function tests: blood creatinine and urea nitrogen levels (BUN) increased; urine casts present.

Total cholesterol: increased. HDL: decreased.

CAUTION

1. Report promptly any indications of infection of any kind.
2. Promptly report swollen glands, sores or lumps in the skin, abnormal bleeding or bruising.

3. Call your doctor immediately if you become pregnant.
4. Periodic laboratory tests are mandatory.
5. It is best to avoid live virus vaccines, and contact with people who have recently taken them (such as oral poliovirus vaccine). Other shots (vaccines) should be given 3–4 weeks BEFORE cyclosporine is started in order to get the best results from them.

Precautions for Use

By Infants and Children: This drug has been used successfully and safely in children of all ages. Dosing is made on the adult schedule in some cases, while others require increased dosing.

By Those Over 60 Years of Age: The dose must be adjusted to any decline in kidney function.

▷ **Advisability of Use During Pregnancy**

Pregnancy Category: C. See Pregnancy Risk Categories at the back of this book.

Animal Studies: Rat and rabbit studies reveal that this drug is toxic to the embryo and fetus. No drug-induced birth defects were found.

Human Studies: Adequate studies of pregnant women are not available.

Avoid this drug during entire pregnancy unless it is clearly needed.

Advisability of Use If Breast-Feeding

Presence of this drug in breast milk: Yes.

Avoid drug or refrain from nursing.

Habit-Forming Potential: None.

Effects of Overdose: Headache, pain, facial flushing, gum soreness and bleeding, high blood pressure, atrial fibrillation, respiratory distress, seizures, coma, hallucinations, neurotoxicity, electrolyte disturbances, liver toxicity.

Possible Effects of Long-Term Use: Irreversible kidney damage, severe hypertension, abnormal growth of gums.

Suggested Periodic Examinations While Taking This Drug (at physician's discretion)

Cyclosporine blood levels.

Complete blood counts.

Liver and kidney function tests.

Magnesium, potassium, and uric acid blood levels.

Cholesterol with fractions (including LDL fractions).

Blood pressure checks.

▷ **While Taking This Drug, Observe the Following**

Foods: Food may increase the peak blood level of cyclosporine.

Herbal Medicines or Minerals: Some patients use echinacea to attempt to boost their immune systems when they are ill. Use of echinacea is not recommended in people taking medicines to suppress their immune systems. Do NOT take mistletoe herb, oak bark or F.C. of marshmallow root, and licorice. There have been case reports of heart transplant rejection with combined use of cyclosporine and St. John's wort. DO NOT COMBINE THESE. Cyclosporine may deplete magnesium from the body. Ask your doctor if supplementation with magnesium makes sense for you. Potassium levels may be increased by cyclosporine. Avoid excessive intake of high-potassium foods. See Table 13.

Beverages: Grapefruit juice and other fruit juices increase blood levels. Milk may increase blood levels.

▷ *Alcohol:* Large amounts of alcohol may increase cyclosporine levels.

Tobacco Smoking: This interaction has not been well studied. I advise everyone to quit smoking.

▷   *Other Drugs*

Cyclosporine *taken concurrently* **with**

- ACE inhibitors (see Drug Classes) may increase the risk of kidney problems.
- acyclovir (Zovirax) may lead to increased cyclosporine levels. CAREFUL check of cyclosporine blood levels are recommended.
- aminoglycoside antibiotics (see Drug Classes) may increase kidney toxicity.
- amphotericin B (Abelcet, others) can cause serious kidney toxicity.
- amprenavir (Agenerase) may increase blood levels, resulting in cyclosporine toxicity. More frequent cyclosporine blood levels are prudent.
- aspirin substitutes (nonsteroidal anti-inflammatory drugs or NSAIDs) may increase kidney toxicity.
- atorvastatin (Lipitor), fluvastatin (Lescol), lovastatin (Mevacor, Advicor), and simvastatin (Zocor) may result in increased risk of muscle damage or rhabdomyolysis. If a patient requires combination therapy, very close patient follow up and education regarding immediately reporting unexplained muscle pain, weakness, or tenderness should be given along with instructions as to who to call.
- azathioprine (Imuran) may increase immunosuppression.
- calcium channel blockers (see Drug Classes) may result in cyclosporine toxicity.
- clonidine (Catapres) can increase risk of kidney problems.
- ciprofloxacin (Cipro), and other fluoroquinolones—(see Drug Classes) may increase risk of kidney toxicity.
- cotrimoxazole (Bactrim, others) may result in decreased cyclosporine effectiveness as well as kidney toxicity.
- cyclophosphamide (Cytoxan) may increase immunosuppression.
- digoxin (Lanoxin) may result in serious digoxin toxicity.
- furosemide (Lasix) may result in increased risk of gout.
- ganciclovir (Cytovene) may result in increased kidney toxicity.
- histamine (H2) inhibitors (see Drug Classes) and ketoconazole may experience decreased cyclosporine blood levels.
- imipenem/cilastatin (Primaxin) may result in neurotoxicity.
- methylprednisolone (Medrol) may cause seizures.
- metronidazole (Flagyl) may result in increased cyclosporine levels and toxicity.
- nifedipine (Adalat) may worsen abnormal gum growth (gingival hyperplasia) and also cause nifedipine toxicity (low blood pressure and abnormal heartbeats).
- propafenone (Rythmol) may increase risk of cyclosporine toxicity.
- pravastatin (Pravachol) increased blood levels of pravastatin and an increased risk of muscle damage. Some later studies did not find muscle problems. Given this variable result, it appears prudent to generally not combine the medicines. If a patient requires combined treatment, the 10 mg pravastatin dose should be used and the patient carefully followed with creatinine kinase levels. The patient should also be taught to self-monitor for unexplained muscle tenderness, weakness or pain.
- saquinavir (Fortovase, Invirase) may increase risk of cyclosporine toxicity.
- sirolimus (Rapamune) can cause sirolimus toxicity. Separate dosing by four hours.

- spironolactone (various) may increase risk of excessive potassium levels.
- sulfamethoxazole and/or trimethoprim (Septra) may increase kidney toxicity.
- tacrolimus (Prograf) can cause kidney toxicity.
- thiazide diuretics (see Drug Classes) may increase adverse effects on the blood (myelosuppression).
- triamterene (various) may increase risk of excessive potassium levels.
- vaccines may blunt the benefit of the vaccine. Vaccines are best given 3–4 weeks BEFORE cyclosporine is started.
- valproic acid (Depakene, others) lead to liver toxicity in one patient.
- verapamil (Calan) may increase immunosuppression.
- warfarin (Coumadin) may lower anticoagulant benefits of warfarin.

The following drugs may increase the effects of cyclosporine:
- acetazolamide.
- allopurinol (Zyloprim).
- amiodarone (Cordarone).
- ceftriaxone (Rocephin).
- cimetidine (Tagamet).
- cisapride (Propulsid).
- clarithromycin (Biaxin).
- clotrimazole (Mycelex, Gyne-Lotrimin, others).
- colchicine (Colbenemid).
- dalfopristin (Synercid or quinupristin/dalfopristin).
- danazol or other anabolic steroids.
- diltiazem (Cardizem).
- econazole (Spectazole).
- erythromycin (E.E.S., others).
- fluconazole (Diflucan).
- fluvoxamine (Luvox).
- glipizide (Glucotrol) or glyburide (Diabeta).
- grepafloxacin (Raxar).
- imatinib (Gleevec).
- itraconazole (Sporanox).
- ketoconazole (Nizoral).
- medicines that inhibit cytochrome P-450 3A4 liver enzymes. Caution is advised.
- methotrexate (Rheumatrex).
- methyltestosterone (various).
- metoclopramide (Reglan).
- miconazole (Lotrimin, Micatin).
- nonsteroidal anti-inflammatory agents (see Drug Classes).
- oral contraceptives (birth control pills).
- ritonavir (Norvir).
- tamoxifen (Nolvadex).
- terconazole (Terazol).
- ticarcillin/clavulanic acid (Timentin).

The following drugs may *decrease* the effects of cyclosporine:
- carbamazepine (Tegretol).
- carvedilol (Coreg).
- clindamycin (various).
- isoniazid (INH).
- nafcillin.
- octreotide (Sandostatin).

- orlistat (Xenical).
- omeprazole (Prilosec).
- phenobarbital.
- phenytoin (Dilantin) or fosphenytoin (Cerebyx).
- quinine.
- rifabutin (Mycobutin).
- rifampin (Rifadin).
- sulfadimidine, sulfadiazine and/or trimethoprim.
- ticlopidine (Ticlid).
- warfarin (Coumadin).

▷ *Driving, Hazardous Activities:* This drug may cause confusion or seizures. Restrict activities as necessary.

Aviation Note: The use of this drug **may be a disqualification** for piloting. Consult a designated Aviation Medical Examiner.

Exposure to Sun: Exposure to sunlight or other ultraviolet (UV) radiation may increase the risk of skin cancer.

Discontinuation: Do not stop this drug without your physician's guidance.

Special Storage Instructions: Keep the gelatin capsules in the blister packets until ready for use. Store below 77 degrees F. (25 degrees C.). Keep the oral solution in a tightly closed container. Store below 86 degrees F. (30 degrees C.). Do not refrigerate or freeze it.

Observe the Following Expiration Times: The oral solution must be used within 2 months after opening.

DESIPRAMINE (des IP ra meen)

Introduced: 1964 **Class:** Antidepressant **Prescription:** USA: Yes **Controlled Drug:** USA: No; Canada: No **Available as Generic:** USA: Yes; Canada: Yes

Brand Names: ❦Apo-desipramine, Deprexan, Norpramin, Pertofrane

Author's Note: Information in this profile has been shortened to make room for more widely used medicines.

DEXAMETHASONE (dex a METH a sohn)

Introduced: 1958 **Class:** Cortisonelike drugs **Prescription:** USA: Yes **Controlled Drug:** USA: No; Canada: No **Available as Generic:** USA: Yes; Canada: Yes

Brand Names: Aeroseb-Dex, ❦Ak-Dex, Ak-Trol [CD], Baldex, Dalalone, Dalalone DP, Dalalone LA, Decaderm, Decadron, Decadron Nasal Spray, Decadron-LA, Decadron Phosphate Ophthalmic, Decadron Phosphate Respihaler, Decadron Phosphate Turbinaire, Decadron w/Xylocaine [CD], Decadron dose pack, Decaject, Decaject LA, Decaspray, Deenar [CD], Deone-LA, ❦Deronil, Dex-4, Dexacen-4, Dexacen LA-8, Dexacidin [CD], Dexacort, Dexameth, Dexasone, Dexasone-LA, Dexo-LA, Dexon, Dexone-E, Dexone-4, Dexone-LA, Dexsone, Dexsone-E, Dexsone-LA, Dezone, Duo-dezone, Gammacorten, Hexadrol, Maxidex, Mymethasone, ❦Neodecadron Eye-Ear, Neodexair, Neomycin-Dex, Ocu-Trol [CD], ❦Oradexon, ❦PMS-Dexamethasone, ❦SK-Dexamethasone, ❦Sofracort, Solurex, Solurex-LA, ❦Spersadex, Tobradex [CD], Turbinaire

---

BENEFITS versus RISKS

Possible Benefits	*Possible Risks*
EFFECTIVE RELIEF OF SYMPTOMS IN A WIDE VARIETY OF INFLAMMATORY AND ALLERGIC DISORDERS	Ongoing systemic use (variable onset) can be associated with increased possible emergence of effects such as: ALTERED OR CHANGED MOOD AND PERSONALITY, CATARACTS, GLAUCOMA, HYPERTENSION, ARRHYTHMIAS, PEPTIC ULCERS, PANCREATITIS, OSTEOPOROSIS, INCREASED SUSCEPTIBILITY TO INFECTIONS, AND OTHERS
EFFECTIVE IMMUNOSUP-PRESSION IN SELECTED BENIGN AND MALIGNANT DISORDERS	
COMBINED WITH TOBRAMYCIN TO FIGHT BOTH INFECTION AND INFLAMMATION IN THE EYE	ASCEPTIC BONE NECROSIS (OSTEONECROSIS) IS AN AREA OF CONTROVERSY, UNCLEAR ONSET, PATIENT RISK FACTORS, AND CORRELATION VERSUS CAUSATION (SEE CONTROVER-SIES IN MEDICINE)

▷ **Principal Uses**

As a Single Drug Product: Uses currently included in FDA-approved labeling: (1) Used to manage serious skin disorders (such as Stevens-Johnson Syndrome, exfoliative dermatitis, etc.), asthma, allergic rhinitis, lymphoma, brain edema, shock, systemic lupus erythematosus, and all types of major rheumatic disorders including bursitis, tendonitis, and most forms of arthritis; (2) ulcerative disease of the colon; (3) topical cream is used to treat eczema, psoriasis, dermatitis, and lichen planus; (4) used in conjunction with antibiotics in meningitis; (5) helps ease swelling in otitis media.

Other (unlabeled) generally accepted uses: (1) Adrenal insufficiency; (2) acute airway obstruction; (3) mountain sickness; (4) vomiting caused by chemotherapy; (5) cardiopulmonary bypass; (6) refractory depression; (7) relief of brain cancer symptoms; (8) combination with other drugs in multiple myeloma; (9) cases of *Pneumocystis carinii* pneumonia; (10) can help suppress male hormones (androgens) in women with acne, hirsutism, or hair loss (androgenic alopecia) caused by androgens; (11) eases vomiting after cancer treatment (chemotherapy); (12) single doses may have a role in croup.

How This Drug Works: Inhibits defensive functions of certain white blood cells. It reduces the production of lymphocytes and some antibodies and acts as an immunosuppressant. When combined with tobramycin or other antibiotics in the eye, it helps relieve inflammation and pain while the antibiotic kills the infection.

Available Dosage Forms and Strengths

Aerosol — 0.01% and 0.04%
Aerosol inhaler — 84 mcg per spray
Cream — 0.1%
Elixir — 0.5 mg/5 ml
Eye ointment — 0.05%
Eye solution — 0.1%
Eye suspension — 0.1% dexamethasone, 0.3% tobramycin

Gel — 0.1%
Injection — 4 mg/ml, 8 mg/ml, 10 mg/ml, 16 mg/ml, 20 mg/ml, 24 mg/ml
Oral solution — 0.5 mg/0.5 ml, 0.5 mg/5 ml
Solution — 0.1%
Spray, topical — 10 mg/25 g
Suspension — 0.1%
Tablets — 0.25 mg, 0.5 mg, 0.75 mg, 1 mg, 1.5 mg, 2 mg, 4 mg, 6 mg

▷ **Usual Adult Dosage Ranges**

Respihaler: For asthma, three inhalations taken three to four times a day in asthmatics whose asthma is unresponsive to other medicines.

Turbinaire form: Two sprays in each nostril two or three times daily. Twelve sprays is the daily maximum.

Decadron dose pack form: On the first day, 1 or 2 ml is given as an intramuscular injection (IM). On the second day, four tablets are taken—divided into two equal doses (such as two in the morning at 9 A.M. and two at 9 P.M.). The third day, the same tablet dose is given, the fourth day two tablets are given in two equal doses, the fifth and sixth day one tablet a day is given and treatment is stopped on the seventh day (tapering schedule).

Ophthalmic: Tobradex form is often started as one to two drops into the eye sac or sacs (conjunctival) every 2 hours during the first day or two of treatment. The dosing frequency is then gradually decreased to one or two drops every 4–6 hours depending on the severity and response of the infection to treatment.

Oral: 0.75 to 9 mg daily divided into two to four doses—depending on the condition.

Topical (0.1% cream): Apply thin film of medicine on the affected area three or four times a day.

Oral dose for children: 0.03 to 0.15 mg per kg of body mass per day, divided into equal doses given every 6 to 12 hours, or 1–5 mg per square meter divided into equal doses and given every 6 to 12 hours.

Note: Actual dose and schedule must be determined for each patient individually.

Conditions Requiring Dosing Adjustments

Liver Function: This drug is eliminated via the liver; however, no specific guidelines for dosing adjustments are available.

Kidney Function: Use with caution as it can cause alkalosis (a change toward a more basic condition in the body's chemistry).

Obesity: Dosing on a mg-per-kg-of-body-mass-per-day basis is recommended. It is best to measure free urinary cortisol as well.

▷ **Dosing Instructions:** Tablet may be crushed and taken with or following food to prevent stomach irritation, preferably in the morning. If you forget a dose: (suspension, solution): take the missed dose right after you remember it. If it is nearly time for your next scheduled dose, skip the missed dose and continue with the scheduled dose. DO NOT double doses. If you only take this medicine every other day, take the dose you forgot right away, unless it's late in the day. If you only remember late in the day, wait until the next morning to take the missed dose and then continue on your every other day schedule. If you forget a dose of the shot (IM injection), call your doctor for instructions.

Usual Duration of Use: Varies with the problem: 4 to 10 days generally. Dose, patient reaction to tapering, disease flare and other factors must be considered.

For chronic disorders: varies. Length of therapy should not exceed time needed for adequate symptomatic relief in sudden (acute) self-limiting conditions or time required to stabilize a chronic condition and permit gradual and appropriate individualized withdrawal.

Typical Treatment Goals and Measurements (Outcomes and Markers)

Inflammation: The general goal is to relieve the swelling and the inflammatory response. Use in asthma should help decrease the frequency and severity of acute attacks. Some clinicians use decreased frequency of rescue inhaler use as a measure of success. Lung (pulmonary function) testing and improvement in those tests also helps define results in asthma. Lastly, clinical signs and symptoms such as wheezing, tightness in the chest, and exercise tolerance should all move in favorable directions.

▷ **This Drug Should Not Be Taken If**
  • you have had an allergic reaction to it previously.
  • you have active peptic ulcer disease.
  • you have an active herpes simplex, fungal or mycobacterial infection of the eye, or fungal ear infection.
  • you have a systemic fungal infection (talk with your doctor).
  • your sputum consistently grows *Candida albicans* (a yeast that may grow very quickly if steroids suppress your immune system).
  • you have a psychoneurosis or psychosis.
  • you have active tuberculosis.

▷ **Inform Your Physician Before Taking This Drug If**
  • you have had unfavorable reactions to cortisonelike drugs.
  • you have a history of peptic ulcer disease, thrombophlebitis, low blood platelets, or tuberculosis.
  • you have diabetes, glaucoma, high blood pressure, deficient thyroid function, or myasthenia gravis.
  • you start to have restricted motion, unexplained or increased pain (as in knees, hips, or shoulders, fever, or joint swelling while taking or after taking this medicine—may be early signs of aseptic necrosis (osteonecrosis). Call your doctor right away.
  • you have osteoporosis.
  • you are taking an "in the nose form" (intranasal) and you have ongoing irritation of the nose.
  • you have recently had a heart attack (may have a serious effect on the wall of the left ventricle).
  • you plan to have surgery of any kind in the near future.

▷ **Possible Side Effects** (natural, expected, and unavoidable drug actions)

Increased appetite, weight gain, retention of salt and water, benign increase in head (intracranial) pressure—rare, but more likely with long-term use, excretion of potassium, increased susceptibility to infection (yeast infections can be frequent in cancer patients treated with a corticosteroid)-superinfection due to immune system suppression. Increased facial hair. Increased white blood cell count (release from the bone marrow versus a sign of infection). Nose irritation with nasal forms. **All of the possible and mild or serious adverse effects may happen with inhaled or even ophthalmic steroid use, but generally to a much reduced extent and/or severity.**

▷ **Possible Adverse Effects** (unusual, unexpected, and infrequent reactions)

If any of the following develop, consult your physician promptly for guidance.

Mild Adverse Effects

Allergic reaction: skin rash—case reports.

Headache, dizziness, insomnia—possible.

Mild depression or euphoria—most common possible central nervous system (CNS) effects.

High blood pressure (may be lessened by alternate-day therapy): more likely in older patients and those who already have high blood pressure—possible.

Acid indigestion, abdominal distention—possible.

Muscle cramping and weakness—case reports.

Slowing of growth in infants—possible and minimized by use of lowest effective dose and or alternate day treatment if possible.

Easy bruising (ecchymosis) or acne lesions—common after long-term high dose use.

Vaginal itching—may be frequent with intravenous dosing.

Serious Adverse Effects

Allergic reaction: anaphylaxis—case reports.

Mental and emotional disturbances of serious magnitude—infrequent.

Reactivation of latent tuberculosis—possible.

Pneumocystis carinii pneumonia—possible with immunosuppression and chronic use.

Development of peptic ulcer—rare, but risk increases with higher doses and preexisting ulcers.

Inflammation of the pancreas (pancreatitis)—rare.

Thrombophlebitis (inflammation of a vein with the formation of blood clot): pain or tenderness in thigh or leg or swelling of the foot, ankle, or leg—possible with intravenous use.

Abnormal lipids (cholesterol-mean increase 88mg/dl, triglyceride-mean increase 30 mg/ml, LDLs)—possible (may need to be addressed by lowest possible dose, diet, exercise, and even added medicines.

Abnormal heart rhythm—case reports.

Cushing's syndrome—possible with chronic use and high doses (supraphysiologic).

Suppression of the adrenal gland—possible with chronic use and more common with larger doses.

High blood sugar—risk increases with use in pre-diabetes, patients with family history of diabetes, with higher doses and longer treatment duration.

Excessively low blood potassium—case reports.

Abnormally slow heartbeat in infants—case reports.

Increased pressure in the eye or cataracts or glaucoma—rare to frequent.

Precipitation of porphyria—case reports.

Excessive thyroid function (questionable causality)—case reports.

Fluid build up in the lungs (pulmonary edema)-possible (more likely with combined ritodrine and dexamethasone treatment in threatened premature labor.

Muscle changes (myopathy)—infrequent, but more likely with higher doses and some steroids.

Bone death (aseptic necrosis, osteonecrosis or avascular necrosis)—Questions remain as to correlation versus causation, but may be more likely with high initial doses, long-term treatment and cumulative doses of 4.32 grams. May also happen with short-term modest doses. Individual patient risk factors appear to be important. See controversies in medicine below.

Osteoporosis—more likely with long-term and higher-dose use.

▷ **Possible Effects on Sexual Function:** Altered timing and pattern of menstruation—case reports.

Adverse Effects That May Mimic Natural Diseases or Disorders
Pattern of symptoms and signs resembling Cushing's syndrome.

Natural Diseases or Disorders That May Be Activated by This Drug
Latent diabetes, glaucoma, peptic ulcer disease, tuberculosis.

Possible Effects on Laboratory Tests
Blood amylase level: increased (possible pancreatitis).
Blood glucose level: increased.
Digoxin testing: may falsely increase digoxin results.
Glucose tolerance test (GTT): increased.
Blood potassium level: decreased.
Thyroid function tests: may be increased (questionable causation).
Cholesterol, LDL, triglycerides: increased.

CAUTION
1. It is best to carry a card noting that you are taking this drug, if your course of treatment is to exceed 1 week.
2. Do not stop this drug abruptly if it is used for long-term treatment.
3. If vaccination against measles, rabies, smallpox or yellow fever is required, stop this drug 72 hours before vaccination and do not resume it for at least 14 days after vaccination.
4. Children may be more sensitive to topical application because there is a larger skin surface area to body weight ratio.
5. A variety of patient risk factors appear to be important in possible development of osteonecrosis. Talk to your doctor about the current list.

Controversies in Medicine: Medicines in this class have had conflicting reports regarding correlation with or causation of aseptic bone necrosis (osteonecrosis-ON). There appear to be patient risk factors, possible delayed onset with occurrence even after the medicine is stopped, and some diseases or conditions where corticosteroids are often used and ON is more frequent than the general population. It is unclear if this is because of the disease or condition or the use of corticosteroids. Previous data regarding cumulative dosing (4.32 grams) appears controversial, with more recent case reports of 6-days of treatment with some doses being associated with ON. Some existing and emerging patient risk factors include alcohol use versus abuse, initial high doses, HIV positive patients who weight trained, Systemic Lupus Erythematosus, some clotting disorders, and high homocysteine levels amongst others appear to increase risk. Early research regarding use of alendronate (Fosamax) to treat ON appears to show that it is important for patients to quickly return to their doctors if unexplained joint pain (such as in the hip or knee) happens. Some centers note that ON has been poorly studied, and while the weight of data in growing, it is yet too early to say more than ON is correlated with corticosteroid use.

Precautions for Use
Infants and Children: Avoid prolonged use if possible. During long-term use, watch for suppression of normal growth and the possibility of increased intracranial pressure. Following long-term use, the child may be at risk for adrenal gland deficiency during stress for as long as 18 months after cessation.

By Those Over 60 Years of Age: Avoid prolonged use of this drug if possible. Continual use (even in small doses) can increase the severity of diabetes, enhance fluid retention, raise blood pressure, weaken resistance to infection, induce stomach ulcer, and accelerate the development of cataracts and osteoporosis.

▷ **Advisability of Use During Pregnancy**

Pregnancy Category: C. See Pregnancy Risk Categories at the back of this book.
Animal Studies: Birth defects reported in mice, rats and rabbits.
Human Studies: Adequate studies of pregnant women are not available.

Avoid completely during the first 3 months. Limit use during the last 6 months as much as possible. If used, examine infant for possible deficiency of adrenal gland function.

Advisability of Use If Breast-Feeding

Presence of this drug in breast milk: Yes.
Avoid drug or refrain from nursing.

Habit-Forming Potential: Use to suppress symptoms over an extended period of time may produce a state of functional dependence (see Glossary). In treating asthma and rheumatoid arthritis, it is best to keep the dose as small as possible and to attempt drug withdrawal after periods of reasonable improvement. Such procedures may reduce the degree of "steroid rebound"—the return of symptoms as the drug is withdrawn.

Effects of Overdose: Fatigue, muscle weakness, stomach irritation, acid indigestion, excessive sweating, facial flushing, fluid retention, swelling of extremities, increased blood pressure.

Possible Effects of Long-Term Use: Increased blood sugar (possible diabetes), increased fat deposits on the trunk of the body ("buffalo hump"), rounding of the face ("moon face"), thinning and fragility of skin, loss of texture and strength of bones (osteoporosis, aseptic necrosis-questionable correlation versus causation), cataracts, glaucoma, increased body hair (hirsutism), retarded growth and development in children.

Suggested Periodic Examinations While Taking This Drug (at physician's discretion)

Measurements of blood pressure, blood sugar and potassium levels.
Complete eye examinations at regular intervals.
Chest X-ray if history of tuberculosis.
Determination of the rate of development of the growing child to detect retardation of normal growth.
Bone mineral density testing to assess risk of osteoporosis or thinning of bones.
Check on patient visit for unexplained joint pain (such as in the knee, hip, or shoulder). Further evaluation of any such development by MRI is prudent.
Homocysteine level (increased Homocysteine levels appear to be a risk factor for osteonecrosis).

▷ **While Taking This Drug, Observe the Following**

Foods: No interactions expected. Ask your physician about salt restriction or need for potassium-rich foods. During long-term use of this drug, it is advisable to eat a high-protein diet.

Herbal Medicines or Minerals: Hawthorn, ginger, garlic, ma huang, ginseng, and nettle may change blood sugar. Since dexamethasone may also change blood sugar control, caution is advised. Licorice may interfere with removal of this medicine—dexamethasone doses may need to be decreased and the combination is not recommended.

Fir or pine needle oil should NOT be used by asthmatics. Ephedra alone does carry a German Commission E monograph indication for asthma treatment. If you are allergic to plants in the Asteraceae family (aster, chrysanthemum, daisy, or ragweed), you may also be allergic to echinacea, chamomile, feverfew, and St. John's wort. Echinacea and ginseng may reverse some of the desired immunosuppression from this medicine. Combination is not advised.

During long-term use, take a vitamin D supplement and increase calcium. During wound repair, take a zinc supplement. Talk to your doctor BEFORE adding any herbal to any other medicines that you already take.

Beverages: No restrictions. Drink all forms of milk liberally.

▷ *Alcohol:* Alcohol use is a risk factor seen in osteonecrosis cases. Talk to your doctor about how they would like you to approach any alcohol use. Caution needed as well if you are prone to peptic ulcer disease.

Tobacco Smoking: Nicotine increases the blood levels of naturally produced cortisone and related hormones. Heavy smoking may add to the expected actions of this drug and requires close observation for excessive effects. I advise everyone to quit smoking.

Marijuana Smoking: May cause additional impairment of immunity and also is a risk factor for toxoplasmosis.

▷ *Other Drugs*

Dexamethasone may ***decrease*** the effects of
- amprenavir (Agenerase) and indinavir (Crixivan).
- caspofungin (Cancidas), requiring dosing increases in caspofungin.
- donepezil (Aricept). A different steroid should be used in patients on donepezil.
- insulin (various), requiring dosing changes of insulin.
- isoniazid (INH, Niconyl, etc.).
- quetiapine (Seroquel).
- salicylates (aspirin, sodium salicylate, etc.), increasing ulcer risk.
- vaccines (such as flu vaccine), by blunting the immune response to them.

Dexamethasone ***taken concurrently*** with
- aspirin (various) and other NSAIDS (see Drug Classes) increases the risk of stomach and intestinal (gastrointestinal) ulceration.
- birth control pills (oral contraceptives) may increase dexamethasone's therapeutic effects.
- carbamazepine (Tegretol) will reduce the effectiveness of dexamethasone.
- irinotecan (Camptosar) may increase risk of low white blood cells (lymphocytopenia) and increase hyperglycemia risk. Caution and close patient monitoring advisable.
- loop diuretics such as furosemide (Lasix) or bumetanide (Bumex) can result in additive potassium loss.
- oral anticoagulants may either increase or decrease their effectiveness; ask your doctor about increased INR testing and dose adjustment.
- oral antidiabetic drugs (see Drug Classes) will decrease their effectiveness.
- neuromuscular blocking agents (such as pancuronium [Pavulon] or vecuronium [Norcuron] may antagonize the neuromuscular blockade, increasing risk or severity of flaccid paralysis. Dose adjustments or unparalyzed periods may be advisable.
- ritodrine (Yutopar) increases the risk of pulmonary edema. Extreme caution and close patient monitoring are needed if this combination must be used.

- ritonavir (Norvir), saquinavir (Fortovase) and possibly other protease inhibitors (PI—see Drug Classes) may decrease PI blood levels and increase dexamethasone blood levels.
- thalidomide (various) increases risk of a serious skin problem (TEN). Combination not advisable except in closely followed clinical trials.
- thiazide diuretics (see Drug Classes) will decrease their blood-pressure-lowering ability.

The following drugs may *decrease* the effects of dexamethasone:

- antacids—may reduce its absorption.
- barbiturates (Amytal, Butisol, phenobarbital, etc.).
- fosphenytoin (Cerebyx).
- phenytoin (Dilantin, etc.).
- primidone (Mysoline).
- rifabutin (Mycobutin).
- rifampin (Rifadin, Rimactane, etc.).

▷ *Driving, Hazardous Activities:* Usually no restrictions. Be alert to the rare occurrence of dizziness.

Aviation Note: The use of this drug *may be a disqualification* for piloting. Consult a designated Aviation Medical Examiner.

Exposure to Sun: No restrictions.

Occurrence of Unrelated Illness: This drug may decrease natural resistance to infection. Call your doctor if you develop an infection of any kind. It may also reduce your body's ability to respond to the stress of acute illness, injury, or surgery. Keep your physician fully informed of any significant health changes.

Discontinuation: Do not stop this drug abruptly after chronic use. Ask your doctor for help about gradual, individualized withdrawal. Some clinicians change from daily to every other day therapy for four weeks BEFORE starting to lower the dose in a stepwise fashion. Many patients tolerate dose reductions of 2.5 mg of prednisone (other steroids are calculated on the basis of prednisone equivalents) with those decreases made every 3–7 days. If a disease flare occurs (worsening of symptoms), the dose should be increased to the last dose before the disease flare and should be tapered more slowly down to 5-10 mg or lower. Some clinicians use 8 AM predose plasma cortisol to guide tapering. If this lab test is less than 10 mcg/deciliter, tapering is continued until the daily prednisone equivalent is 2-5 mg. In general, if long-term treatment or high doses were used, prednisone equivalents should be tapered over 9–12 months. For up to 2 years after stopping this drug, you may require it again if you have an injury, surgery, or an illness.

DEXMETHYLPHENIDATE (DEX meth il FEN i dayt)

Introduced: 2001   **Class:** Amphetaminelike drug, anti-attention-deficit-disorder drug   **Prescription:** USA: Yes   **Controlled Drug:** USA: C-II*; Canada: Yes   **Available as Generic:** USA: Yes; Canada: Yes

Brand Names: Focalin

Author's Note: Focalin is a new treatment for ADHD. This medicine is NOT the same as methylphenidate. This drug is dexmethylphenidate. The usual dose is only half of the methylphenidate dose. Information on Focalin will be broadened if ongoing studies and results warrant this.

*See Schedules of Controlled Drugs at the back of this book.

DIAZEPAM (di AZ e pam)

Introduced: 1963 **Class:** Antianxiety drug, benzodiazepines, mild tranquilizer **Prescription:** USA: Yes **Controlled Drug:** USA: C-IV*; Canada: No **Available as Generic:** Yes

Brand Names: ✳Apo-Diazepam, Diastat, ✳Diazemuls, Diazepam Intensol Oral Solution, Dizac, E-Pam, ✳Meval, ✳Novo-Dipam, Q-pam, ✳Rival, T-Quil, Valcaps, Valium, Valrelease, Vazepam, ✳Vivol, Zetran

---

BENEFITS versus RISKS

Possible Benefits	Possible Risks
RELIEF OF ANXIETY AND NERVOUS TENSION	Habit-forming potential with prolonged use
Wide margin of safety with therapeutic doses	Minor impairment of mental functions
	Respiratory depression
	Jaundice—very rare

▷ **Principal Uses**

As a Single Drug Product: Uses included in FDA-approved labeling: (1) Provides short-term relief of mild to moderate anxiety; (2) relieves the symptoms of acute alcohol withdrawal: agitation, tremors, hallucinations, incipient delirium tremens; (3) eases skeletal muscle spasm; (4) provides short-term control of certain types of seizures (epilepsy, fever-induced and status epilepticus); (5) short-term relief of insomnia; (6) adjunctive use in endoscopic procedures; (7) decreases anxiety prior to electrical defibrillation of the heart (cardioversion); (8) eases severe muscle spasms; (9) rectal gel is approved as an orphan drug for intermittent sudden (acute) seizure control in some patients who fail to respond to other treatments.

Other (unlabeled) generally accepted uses: (1) Helps prevent LSD flashbacks; (2) short-term treatment of sleepwalking; (3) treatment of persistent hiccups; (4) adjunctive treatment of catatonia; (5) helpful in easing chest pain in patients who have taken cocaine and have acute heart (coronary) syndromes; (6) further study is needed to define use in movement disorder caused by antipsychotic medicines (akathisia).

How This Drug Works: This drug calms higher brain centers by enhancing a nerve transmitter (gamma-aminobutyric acid or GABA).

Available Dosage Forms and Strengths

Capsules, prolonged action (sustained release) — 15 mg

Concentrate — 5 mg/ml

Injection — 5 mg/ml

Oral solution — 1 mg/ ml, 5 mg/5 ml, 10 mg/10 ml

Rectal gel — 2.5 mg, 5 mg, 10 mg, 15 mg, 20 mg

Tablets — 2 mg, 5 mg, 10 mg

▷ **Usual Adult Dosage Ranges:** *For anxiety:* 2 to 10 mg, two to four times daily. Dose may be increased cautiously as needed and tolerated. After 1 week of continual use, the total daily dose may be taken at bedtime. Maximum

---

*See Schedules of Controlled Drugs at the back of this book.

daily dose is 60 mg. Sustained-release form can be given once daily (15 mg) if it is replacing use of the immediate-release form that has been taken as a total daily dose of 15 mg divided into 5-mg doses three times a day.

Seizures: 2–10 mg two to four times daily.

Alcohol withdrawal: 10 mg given every eight hours up to every 6 hours during the first day. This is then lowered to 5 mg three or four times daily as needed and tolerated.

Note: Actual dose and schedule must be determined for each patient individually.

Conditions Requiring Dosing Adjustments

Liver Function: The dose must be decreased by 50% in patients with liver compromise.

Kidney Function: Caution—if 15 mg or more is given daily, diazepam metabolites may accumulate.

Obesity: Obese patients may take longer than nonobese patients to accumulate this medicine. The time that it takes to remove diazepam (elimination half-life) is prolonged in obese people. This means that obese people may take a much longer time to get the peak effect of diazepam and will also take a longer time to remove the drug from their bodies.

▷ **Dosing Instructions:** The tablet may be crushed and taken on empty stomach or with food or milk. The prolonged-action capsule should not be opened, broken or chewed. Always use a measuring spoon for oral liquid forms to get the correct dose. Do not stop this drug abruptly if taken for more than 4 weeks (medicine should be slowly withdrawn or tapered). If you forget a dose, take the dose as soon as you remember it, unless it's nearly time for your next dose. If you remember when it's nearly time for your next dose, skip the missed dose and take the next dose right on schedule. DO NOT double doses.

Usual Duration of Use: Regular use for 3 to 5 days is usually needed to see benefits in relieving moderate anxiety. Severity and probability of addiction (physical dependence) is associated with increasing dose and ongoing nature of use. Best to limit continual use to 1 to 3 weeks. Avoid uninterrupted and prolonged use if possible. Use for seizures may be ongoing, and appropriate cautions taken.

Author's Note: The National Institute of Mental Health has an information page on anxiety. It can be found on the World Wide Web (*www.nimh.nih.gov/anxiety*).

Typical Treatment Goals and Measurements (Outcomes and Markers)

Goals for anxiety tend to be more vague and subjective than hypertension or cholesterol. Frequently, the patient (in conjunction with physician assessment) will largely decide if anxiety has been modified to a successful extent. The ability of the patient to return to normal activities is a hallmark of successful treatment. The Hamilton Anxiety Scale is a useful measurement tool.

▷ **This Drug Should Not Be Taken If**
- you have had an allergic reaction to any dosage form of it previously.
- you have acute narrow-angle glaucoma.
- it is prescribed for a child under 6 months of age.

▷ **Inform Your Physician Before Taking This Drug If**
- you are allergic to any benzodiazepine (see Drug Classes).
- you have a history of alcoholism or drug abuse.
- you are pregnant or planning pregnancy.
- you have impaired liver or kidney function.

- you have a history of serious depression or a mental disorder.
- you have asthma, emphysema or other lung problems which limit appropriate breathing (limited pulmonary reserve), epilepsy or myasthenia gravis.

Possible Side Effects (natural, expected, and unavoidable drug actions)
Drowsiness—frequent.
Lethargy, unsteadiness—rare. Irritation of the vein with the intravenous form—possible.
"Hangover" effects on the day following bedtime use.

▷ **Possible Adverse Effects** (unusual, unexpected, and infrequent reactions)
If any of the following develop, consult your physician promptly for guidance.
Mild Adverse Effects
Allergic reactions: rashes, hives—rare.
Dizziness, fainting, blurred or double vision, slurred speech, sweating, nausea—possible.
Increased liver enzymes—case report.
Ringing in the ears—case reports.
Impaired motor skills (dose-related to some extent)—frequency varies.
Serious Adverse Effects
Allergic reactions: liver damage with jaundice (see Glossary), kidney damage, abnormally low blood platelet count, anaphylaxis—case reports.
Respiratory depression—dose-related.
Bone marrow depression: low white blood cells, fever, sore throat—case reports.
Severe lowering of blood pressure, slow heart rate, and cardiac arrest have been reported after rapid intravenous dosing—case reports.
Hip fracture—possible indirect effect of the medicine arising from unsteadiness.
Amnesia—dose-related.
Vein irritation and or blood clots—possible with intravenous (IV) form.
Heart arrhythmia (intravenous form)—possible.
Obsessive-compulsive disorder following extended use and abrupt withdrawal—possible.
Paradoxical responses of excitement, agitation, anger, rage—case reports.

▷ **Possible Effects on Sexual Function:**
Altered timing and pattern of menstruation.
Small doses (2 to 5 mg/day) may help the anxiety seen in many cases of impotence in men and inhibited sexual responsiveness in women. Larger doses (10 mg/day or more) can decrease libido, impair potency in men, and inhibit orgasm in women.
Swelling and tenderness of male breast tissue (gynecomastia).
Abnormally prolonged erections (priapism)—case reports.

Adverse Effects That May Mimic Natural Diseases or Disorders
Liver reaction with jaundice may suggest viral hepatitis.

Possible Effects on Laboratory Tests
White blood cell counts: decreased.
Blood thyroxine (T4) level: decreased.
Liver function tests: increased liver enzymes (ALT/GPT, AST/GOT, and alkaline phosphatase), increased bilirubin—all rare.
Urine sugar tests: no drug effect with Tes-Tape; low test results with Clinistix and Diastix.

Urine screening tests for drug abuse may be positive. (Test results depend upon amount of drug taken and testing method used.)

CAUTION
1. This drug should not be stopped abruptly if it has been taken continually for more than 4 weeks.
2. Some nonprescription (over-the-counter or OTC) drug products that contain antihistamines (allergy and cold preparations, sleep aids) can cause excessive sedation if combined with diazepam.

Precautions for Use

By Infants and Children: This drug should not be used in hyperactive or psychotic children. Watch for excessive sedation and incoordination. Usual dose in children for muscle relaxation or sedation is 0.1 to 0.8 mg per kg of body mass per day, divided into equal doses and given every 8 hours or as often as every 6 hours. The drug has been used intravenously to help seizures in neonates.

By Those Over 60 Years of Age: Small doses are indicated (two to 2.5 mg once or twice a day). Watch for lethargy, indifference, fatigue, weakness, unsteadiness, disturbing dreams, nightmares, and paradoxical reactions of excitement, agitation, anger, hostility, and rage.

▷ **Advisability of Use During Pregnancy**

Pregnancy Category: D. See Pregnancy Risk Categories at the back of this book.
Animal Studies: Cleft palate reported in mice; skeletal defects in rats.
Human Studies: Available information is conflicting and inconclusive. Some findings of increased serious birth defects. Other studies have found no significant increase in birth defects.

Frequent use in late pregnancy can cause the "floppy infant" syndrome in the newborn: weakness, lethargy, unresponsiveness, depressed breathing, low body temperature. Avoid use during entire pregnancy.

Advisability of Use If Breast-Feeding

Presence of this drug in breast milk: Yes.
Avoid drug or refrain from nursing.

Habit-Forming Potential: This drug can produce psychological and/or physical dependence (see Glossary), especially if used in large doses for an extended period of time.

Effects of Overdose: Marked drowsiness, weakness, feeling of drunkenness, staggering gait, tremor, stupor progressing to deep sleep or coma.

Possible Effects of Long-Term Use: Psychological and/or physical dependence, rare blood cell disorders.

Suggested Periodic Examinations While Taking This Drug (at physician's discretion)
Complete blood cell counts during long-term use.

▷ **While Taking This Drug, Observe the Following**

Foods: Grapefruit and grapefruit juice can increase diazepam concentrations. Caution and moderation advised.

Herbal Medicines or Minerals: Kava, skull cap, and valerian may exacerbate central nervous system depression (avoid this combination). Kola nut, Siberian ginseng, guarana, mate, ephedra, hawthorn, and ma huang may blunt the benefits of this medicine. While St. John's wort is indicated for anxiety, it is also thought to increase (induce) cytochrome P450 enzymes and will tend to blunt diazepam effectiveness if combined with diazepam. Dong quai inhibits removal of diazepam in some animal models. Evening primrose oil increased seizure risk in some patients. If diazepam is being used to treat a seizure disorder, this combination is not recommended. Ginkgo is also not recommended in seizure patients as some extracts have a contaminant (4'-O-methylpyridoxine) which may blunt anticonvulsant benefits. Do not combine any herbal medicines without talking to your doctor first.

Beverages: Avoid excessive intake of caffeine-containing beverages: coffee, tea, cola. May be taken with milk. Caffeine use may be recommended by your doctor to ease some cases of excessive diazepam-caused drowsiness. Grapefruit juice will concentrate substances in grapefruit that can inhibit removal of diazepam from the body. Better to take this medicine with water.

▷ *Alcohol:* Avoid this combination. Alcohol increases the absorption of this drug and adds to its depressant effects on the brain. It is advisable to avoid alcohol completely—throughout the day and night—if it is necessary to drive or to engage in any hazardous activity.

Tobacco Smoking: Heavy smoking may reduce the calming action of this drug. I advise everyone to quit smoking.

Marijuana Smoking: Increased sedation and impairment of intellectual and physical performance.

▷ *Other Drugs*

Diazepam may ***increase*** the effects of
- digoxin (Lanoxin) and cause digoxin toxicity.
- phenytoin (Dilantin) or fosphenytoin (Cerebyx) and cause toxicity.

Diazepam may ***decrease*** the effects of
- levodopa (Sinemet, etc.) and reduce its effectiveness in treating Parkinson's disease.

Diazepam ***taken concurrently*** with
- fluoxetine (Prozac) may lead to diazepam toxicity.
- fluvoxamine (Luvox) can result in serious accumulation of diazepam and toxicity.
- macrolide antibiotics (see Drug Classes) may lead to toxicity. Lowering doses by half to 75% may be prudent.
- MAO inhibitors (see Drug Classes) may exaggerate breathing depression.
- mirtazapine (Remeron) may worsen motor skills. Avoid operating dangerous machinery or tasks requiring coordination.
- narcotics or other centrally active medicines may cause additive respiratory depression or decreased levels of consciousness.
- olanzapine (Zyprexa) may cause blood pressure lowering when you stand (orthostatic hypotension).
- propoxyphene (various) may lead to benzodiazepine (diazepam) intoxication.
- quinupristin/dalfopristin (Synercid) may lead to diazepam toxicity.

The following drugs may ***increase*** the effects of diazepam:
- amprenavir (Agenerase).
- birth control pills (oral contraceptives).
- cimetidine (Tagamet).
- cisapride (Propulsid).
- disulfiram (Antabuse).
- isoniazid (INH, Rifamate, etc.).
- itraconazole (Sporanox), ketoconazole (Nizoral) or other azole antifungals.
- macrolide antibiotics such as erythromycin or clarithromycin.

- omeprazole (Prilosec).
- ritonavir (Norvir) and other protease inhibitors (see Drug Classes).
- sertraline (Zoloft).
- valproic acid (Depakene, Depakote).

The following drugs may *decrease* the effects of diazepam:

- ranitidine (Zantac).
- rifampin (Rimactane, etc.).
- rifabutin (Mycobutin).
- theophylline (aminophylline, Theo-Dur, etc.).

▷ *Driving, Hazardous Activities:* This drug can impair mental alertness, judgment, physical coordination, and reaction time. Avoid hazardous activities accordingly.

Aviation Note: The use of this drug **is a disqualification** for piloting. Consult a designated Aviation Medical Examiner.

Exposure to Sun: No restrictions.

Exposure to Heat: Because of reduced urine volume, this drug may accumulate in the body and produce effects of overdose.

Discontinuation: Avoid stopping this drug suddenly if taken for over 4 weeks. Prudent to taper gradually to prevent a withdrawal syndrome (sweating, tremor, depression, hallucinations, seizures, and vomiting).

DICLOFENAC (di KLOH fen ak)

Please see the acetic acid (nonsteroidal anti-inflammatory drug) family profile.

DIDANOSINE (di DAN oh seen)

Other Names: DDI, dideoxyinosine

Introduced: 1991   **Class:** Antiviral   **Prescription:** USA: Yes
Controlled Drug: USA: No; Canada: No   **Available as Generic:**   USA: No; Canada: No

Brand Names: Videx, Videx EC

BENEFITS versus RISKS	
Possible Benefits	*Possible Risks*
DELAYED PROGRESSION OF DISEASE IN HIV-POSITIVE PATIENTS	DRUG-INDUCED PANCREATITIS DRUG-INDUCED PERIPHERAL NEURITIS
USE IN COMBINATION THERAPY OF AIDS	Drug-induced seizures
ONCE or TWICE-DAILY DOSING	Liver damage—rare

▷ **Principal Uses**

As a Single Drug Product: Uses currently included in FDA-approved labeling: (1) Combination treatment of human immunodeficiency virus (HIV) infections in adults and children (6 months of age or older).

Author's Note: Adherence or taking medicines for HIV exactly on time and in the right amount is ABSOLUTELY critical to getting the best possible results or outcomes (see STI note).

Antiretroviral therapy guidelines from NIAID take into account how easily the medicine treating HIV can fit into a patient's life.

Other (unlabeled) generally accepted uses: None at present.

How This Drug Works: By interfering with essential HIV enzyme systems, this drug prevents growth and reproduction of HIV particles in infected cells, limiting the severity and extent of HIV infection.

Available Dosage Forms and Strengths

Capsules, extended release — 125 mg, 200 mg, 250 mg, 400 mg

Powder for oral solution (bottle) — 2 g, 4 g

Powder for oral solution (packet) — 100 mg, 167 mg, 250 mg, 375 mg

Tablets, chewable/dispersible — 25 mg, 50 mg, 100 mg, 150 mg, 200 mg

▷ **Recommended Dosage Ranges** (Actual dose and schedule must be determined for each patient individually.)

Infants and Children: For those 2 weeks to 8 months is 100 mg per square meter. Eight months of age or older, dose is based on drug form and body surface area with 120 mg per square meter twice daily used. Once-daily dosing HAS NOT been studied as yet in children.

12 to 60 Years of Age: (Twice daily dosing is preferred for all forms). Chewable/dispersible tablets: 400 mg once a day or 200 mg every 12 hours for those weighing more than 60 kg; 250 mg once daily or 125 mg every 12 hours for those weighing less than 60 kg.

EC form: 200-mg EC tablets are only part of a 400-mg once-daily regimen and dosing is based on a mg per kg of body weight basis. For example—if a patient weighs more than 60 kg, 400 mg of Videx EC should be taken daily.

Over 60 Years of Age: Same as 12 to 60 group, but the dose should be reduced if there is an age-related decline in kidney function.

Conditions Requiring Dosing Adjustments

Liver Function: Increased risk of liver toxicity if used in people with compromised liver. Doses must be decreased in liver failure.

Kidney Function: Dose must be decreased in mild to moderate kidney failure. For example: those with creatinine clearance of 30–59 ml/min who weigh 60 kg or more would receive 100 mg twice daily or 200 mg each day of the oral tablets, 100 mg twice daily of the buffered powder and 200 mg each day of Videx EC. Care must also be taken as there is an increased risk of magnesium toxicity (chewable dispersible tablets have 8.6 MEQ of magnesium each). Risk of drug-induced pancreatitis also increases in patients with kidney problems.

▷ **Dosing Instructions:** Best taken on an empty stomach, 30 minutes before or 2 hours after eating. Patients MUST take at least two of the needed chewable/dispersible tablets at each dose in order to make sure that there is adequate buffer present. This actually protects the drug itself from being destroyed by stomach acid. The Videx EC should be swallowed whole (not crushed or altered).

Pediatric oral solution first reconstituted with water and then combined with equal amounts of antacid (such as Mylanta or Maalox). Shake this mixture thoroughly BEFORE you measure each dose.

Adult oral solution is made by stirring one packet into 120 ml (4 ounces) of water until the powder is dissolved; this may take up to 3 minutes. Do not mix powder with fruit juice or other acidic liquid. Swallow all of the 4-ounce solution immediately.

The chewable/dispersible buffered tablets should be thoroughly chewed, crushed or dispersed in water before swallowing. To disperse the tablet(s), stir in at least 30 ml (1 ounce) of water until all the medicine is in the water. Swallow all of preparation immediately. The mandarin orange flavor formulation of Videx disperses in water in as little as 2 minutes. These tablets are dropped whole into a glass of water and are stirred to speed dispersion in the water. If you forget a dose: take the missed dose as soon as you remember it, unless it's nearly time for your next dose—then skip the missed dose and take the next scheduled dose right on time. DO NOT double doses. Talk openly with your doctor if you are having trouble remembering doses. Some patients benefit greatly from beeper-based reminder systems.

Author's Note: Current HIV therapy involves combination use of agents from different drug classes to attack the AIDS virus from different points and delay resistance. Clinicians use viral load (see Glossary) to indicate success or failure of therapy.

Usual Duration of Use: Regular use for several months with repeat viral load and CD4 tests are needed check benefits in slowing HIV progression. Long-term use requires follow-up with your doctor.

Typical Treatment Goals and Measurements (Outcomes and Markers)

HIV: Goals for HIV treatment presently are maximum suppression of viral replication, maximum lowering of the amount of virus in your body (viral load or burden), and maximum patient survival. Markers of successful therapy include undetectable viral load, increased CD4 cells, absence of indicator or opportunistic infections (OIs) and in the case of the HIV-positive patient, delay of the infection to progress to AIDS.

Possible Advantages of This Drug

Does not cause serious bone marrow depression (production of blood cells). Less frequent liver toxicity than some other antiretrovirals. Once-daily dosing can be a great advantage in adherence.

This Drug Should Not Be Taken If

- you have had an allergic reaction to it previously.
- you have active liver disease.
- you have had pancreatitis recently.

▷ **Inform Your Physician Before Taking This Drug If**

- you have had allergic reactions to any drugs in the past.
- you are taking any other drugs currently.
- you have a history of pancreatitis or peripheral neuritis.
- you have a history of gout or high blood uric acid level.
- you have a history of alcoholism.
- you have a history of eye problems.
- you have a history of diarrhea.
- you have had nerve damage (peripheral neuropathy) from other medicines.
- you have a history of phenylketonuria (PKU).
- you have a history of low blood platelets or blood disorder.
- you are pregnant—increased chance of metabolic problems (lactic acidosis risk).
- you have a history of low blood potassium.
- you have a history of heart failure.
- you have a seizure disorder.
- you have impaired liver or kidney function.

Possible Side Effects (natural, expected, and unavoidable drug actions)

Mild decreases in red blood cell, white blood cell, and platelet counts in adults.

Mild increases in blood uric acid levels. Increased sodium load (each buffered powder packet has 1,380 mg of sodium).

Increased magnesium levels in patients with kidney problems.

▷ **Possible Adverse Effects** (unusual, unexpected, and infrequent reactions)

If any of the following develop, consult your physician promptly for guidance.

Mild Adverse Effects

Allergic reactions: skin rash and itching—occasional in adults and common in pediatric patients.

Headache, dizziness, insomnia, nervousness, confusion—infrequent.

Visual disturbances—rare.

Nausea, vomiting—may be frequent in pediatrics.

Stomach pain and diarrhea (25% of adults and frequent in pediatric patients), dry mouth and altered taste, yeast infection of mouth—rare to infrequent.

Lowered blood pressure—rare to infrequent.

Loss of color in the retina (retinal depigmentation)—case reports.

Nose bleeds—frequent in clinical trials in children.

Increased urination—infrequent in pediatric patients.

Cough—infrequent.

Loss of hair, muscle and joint pains—rare to infrequent.

Serious Adverse Effects

Skin reaction: Stevens-Johnson Syndrome—case report.

Drug-induced pancreatitis, usually seen in the first 6 months—infrequent.

Drug-induced peripheral neuritis (see Glossary), usually occurring after 2 to 6 months of treatment (this effect also appears to be dose-related)—infrequent to frequent.

Muscle damage (myalgia and/or rhabdomyolysis including sudden kidney failure)—case reports.

Electrolyte imbalance (low potassium or calcium)—variable.

Increased triglycerides—frequent.

Asthma—frequent in children.

Abnormal heart rhythm, heart failure—rare.

High blood sugar—possible.

Excessive lowering of blood pressure and passing out (syncope)—case reports to infrequent.

Serious skin rash (Stevens-Johnson Syndrome)—case report.

Seizures (may be due to electrolyte problems)—rare.

Lowered white blood cell counts, lowered granulocyte (a specific white blood cell) counts and lowered blood platelets (69%) in pediatric patients—infrequent to frequent.

Lactic acidosis—case reports.

Optic neuritis and blindness—case reports.

Liver damage—rare to infrequent.

Kidney damage—rare.

▷ **Possible Effects on Sexual Function:** Gynecomastia—case report.

Adverse Effects That May Mimic Natural Diseases or Disorders

Drug-induced liver reaction—rare at less than 0.2%—may suggest viral hepatitis.

Possible Effects on Laboratory Tests
>   Complete blood cell counts: decreased red cells and white cells—variable; decreased platelets—infrequent.
>   Blood amylase or uric acid level: increased—infrequent.
>   Blood electrolytes: low calcium, potassium and magnesium.
>   Liver function tests: increased liver enzymes (ALT/GPT, AST/GOT, and alkaline phosphatase), increased bilirubin—infrequent in adults, higher in pediatric patients.

CAUTION
1. This drug **does not cure HIV infection.** Ongoing CD4 and viral load tests are prudent. The AIDS virus may still be passed to other people while you are taking this medicine.
2. Report stomach pain with nausea and vomiting to your doctor; this could indicate pancreatitis.
3. Report pain, numbness, tingling, or burning in the hands or feet—could be peripheral neuritis. Drug may need to be stopped.
4. If your kidneys are damaged or your creatinine elevated, ask your doctor if accumulating magnesium will be a problem for you.
5. One current therapy approach uses STI or structured therapy interruptions also called structured interruptions in therapy (SIT) by one group to carefully attempt to evoke an immune response to HIV. This approach is presently controversial and should NOT be attempted without the supervision of your doctor.

Precautions for Use
>   *By Infants and Children:* Safety and effectiveness for those under 6 months of age not established. Children are also at risk for developing pancreatitis and peripheral neuritis. It is recommended that detailed eye examinations be performed every 6 months and at any time that visual disturbance occurs.
>   *By Those Over 60 Years of Age:* Reduced kidney function may require dose reduction.

▷ **Advisability of Use During Pregnancy**
>   *Pregnancy Category:* B. See Pregnancy Risk Categories at the back of this book.
>   *Animal Studies:* Rat and rabbit studies show no birth defects.
>   *Human Studies:* Adequate studies of pregnant women not available.
>   Consult your physician for specific guidance.

Advisability of Use If Breast-Feeding
>   Presence of this drug in breast milk: Yes in rats, unknown in humans.
>   Avoid drug or refrain from nursing.
>   **Note: HIV has been found in human breast milk. Breast-feeding may result in transmission of HIV infection to the nursing infant.**

Habit-Forming Potential: None.

Effects of Overdose: Nausea, vomiting, stomach pain, diarrhea, pain in hands and feet, irritability, confusion.

Possible Effects of Long-Term Use: Peripheral neuritis (see Glossary).

Suggested Periodic Examinations While Taking This Drug (at physician's discretion)
>   Complete blood cell counts before starting treatment and weekly thereafter until tolerance is established.
>   Electrolytes.

Blood amylase levels, fractionated for salivary gland and pancreatic origin.
Liver and kidney function tests.
Viral load or viral burden in order to assess success of treatment.
CD4 counts.

▷ **While Taking This Drug, Observe the Following**

Foods: Best taken on an empty stomach.

Herbal Medicines or Minerals: Echinacea: Some patients use echinacea to attempt to boost their immune systems. Unfortunately, use of echinacea is not recommended in people with damaged immune systems. This herb may also actually weaken any immune system if it is used too often or for too long a time. Some cancer patients are looking to mistletoe (Iscador) to boost their immune systems. This HAS NOT been studied in HIV-positive patients.

Beverages: Do not take with acidic fruit juices.

▷ *Alcohol:* No interactions expected.

Tobacco Smoking: No interactions expected. I advise everyone to quit smoking.

▷ *Other Drugs*

Didanosine may *increase* the effects of
- zidovudine (Retrovir) and enhance its antiviral effect against HIV.

Didanosine may *decrease* the effects of
- amprenavir (Agenerase) and indinavir (Crixivan) and blunt therapeutic benefits; separate dosing by 2 hours.
- ciprofloxacin (Cipro) and other fluoroquinolones (gatifloxacin [Tequin] and grepafloxacin [Raxar], levofloxacin [Levaquin] and see Drug Classes), if taken at the same time; take fluoroquinolones at least 4 hours before taking didanosine buffered solution, tablets, or the oral powder.
- dapsone and render it ineffective; avoid concurrent use.
- itraconazole (Sporanox). Separate dosing by at least 2 hours.
- ketoconazole (Nizoral), if taken at the same time; take ketoconazole at least 2 hours before taking didanosine.
- tetracyclines (see Drug Classes), if taken at the same time; take tetracyclines at least 2 hours before taking didanosine.

Didanosine *taken concurrently* with
- allopurinol (various) increased didanosine absorption in two patients with damaged kidneys. Caution and blood levels are prudent if this medicine is used in patients with kidney failure.
- amprenavir (Agenerase) will probably decrease amprenavir absorption. Separate doses by at least 1 hour.
- antacids will decrease didanosine absorption and lower its therapeutic benefit.
- delavirdine (Rescriptor) may lower both drug levels. Separate doses by an hour.
- fluconazole (Diflucan) and other azole antifungals may decrease fluconazole benefits.
- histamine (H2) blocking drugs (see Drug Classes)—cimetidine, etc.—may increase didanosine toxicity.
- hydroxyurea (Droxia) and increase risk of pancreatitis or liver toxicity. Careful patient monitoring is critical.
- pentamidine or sulfamethoxazole may increase the risk of drug-induced pancreatitis; watch for significant symptoms.
- ritonavir (Norvir) will inactivate both medicines. Separate doses by 2[h] to 3 hours.
- tenofovir (Viread) increases didanosine levels by up to 60% (particularly if taken with a light meal)—possibly leading to didanosine toxicity. If the

medicines must be combined, dosing changes appear prudent. Talk to your doctor.
- zalcitabine (Hivid) may cause increased neurotoxicity.

▷ *Driving, Hazardous Activities:* This drug may cause dizziness and impaired vision. Restrict activities as necessary.

Aviation Note: The use of this drug *is a disqualification* for piloting. Consult a designated Aviation Medical Examiner.

Exposure to Sun: No restrictions.

Discontinuation: Do not stop this drug without your physician's knowledge and guidance.

DIFLUNISAL (di FLU ni sal)

Please see the acetic acid (nonsteroidal anti-inflammatory drug) family profile.

DIGITOXIN (di ji TOX in)

See the digoxin profile for further information.

DIGOXIN (di JOX in)

Introduced: 1934 **Class:** Digitalis preparations **Prescription:** USA: Yes **Controlled Drug:** USA: No; Canada: No **Available as Generic:** Yes

Brand Names: ❧Digitaline Nativelle, Digitek, Lanoxicaps, Lanoxin, ⚘Novodigoxin, SK-Digoxin

BENEFITS versus RISKS	
Possible Benefits	*Possible Risks*
EFFECTIVE HEART STIMULANT IN CONGESTIVE HEART FAILURE	NARROW TREATMENT RANGE
EFFECTIVE PREVENTION AND TREATMENT OF CERTAIN HEART RHYTHM DISORDERS	Frequent and sometimes serious disturbances of heart rhythm
	Controversial in heart failure in women (may relate to levels)

▷ **Principal Uses**

As a Single Drug Product: Uses in current FDA-approved labeling: (1) Treats congestive heart failure; (2) restores and helps keep normal heart rate and rhythm in cases of atrial fibrillation and flutter, is a second-line agent behind verapamil [drug of choice in Paroxysmal Atrial Tachycardia].

Controversies in Medicine: Some clinicians found that lower than previously advocated levels of digoxin (0.5-0.8 ng/ml) reduced death (mortality) in heart failure patients. One research group found 0.5-0.8 mg/ml to be ideal (optimal) for men in stable heart failure who have normal heart rhythm (see Rosenberg, J. in Sources). A group at Yale questioned the safety of digoxin in treating heart failure in women. Further research on blood levels is required (see Ratthore,

S.S. in Sources). **A most recent study in JAMA found the lower levels of digoxin (0.5-0.8 ng/ml to reduce death in heart failure patients.**
Other (unlabeled) generally accepted uses: (1) Postoperative arrhythmias; (2) helps to increase left ventricular function in patients with pacemakers; (3) may have a role in treating Wolff-Parkinson-White syndrome.

How This Drug Works: Increases force of heart muscle contraction. Delays electrical transmission through the heart, helping restore normal rate and rhythm.

Available Dosage Forms and Strengths
> Capsules — 0.05 mg, 0.1 mg, 0.2 mg
> Elixir — 0.25 mg/5 ml, 0.125 mg/5 ml
> Elixir, pediatric — 0.05 mg/ml
> Injection — 0.1 mg/ml, 0.25 mg/ml
> Tablets — 0.0625 mg (Canada), 0.125 mg, 0.25 mg, 0.5 mg

Author's Note: Dosing and timing of doses are critical for this medicine. The difference between toxic blood levels and therapeutic blood levels is small. Be CERTAIN you understand how and when to take this medicine.

▷ **Usual Adult Dosage Ranges:** For loading dose, 10 mcg per kilogram of lean body mass (some clinicians use ideal body weight as the math is less complicated); 8–12 mcg per kg of body mass may be needed if digoxin is being used to control abnormal heart rhythms (such as atrial fibrillation); 8–12 mcg per kg is typical if this medicine is being used for heart failure (0.75 to 1.25 mg by mouth-orally). Loading dose can be given orally or intravenously. Once decided, is often given as 50% in the first dose with remainder divided into smaller doses and given at 6- to 8-hour intervals until the desired response is achieved. Usual ongoing dose after loading is 0.125 to 0.5 mg per day, and is calculated by a specific formula. Divided versus once daily dosing is recommended for patients who are likely to have toxic levels, in those who require 300 mcg a day or more and in people who have had digoxin toxicity previously. Newer guidance on lower ongoing blood levels may lead to lower loading and ongoing doses. Further research is needed. In neonatal and pediatric patients, a similar loading and ongoing strategy is used, but the amount on a mg-per-kg-of-body-mass basis is very different.
Note: Actual dose and schedule must be determined for each patient individually.

Conditions Requiring Dosing Adjustments
Liver Function: Use with caution; blood levels should be obtained more frequently.
Kidney Function: Dose **must** be adjusted in kidney compromise. Smaller doses and some cases of dosing every other day may be needed.

▷ **Dosing Instructions:** Tablet may be crushed and is best taken at the same time each day (to help keep blood levels about the same) on an empty stomach. The elixir form can be useful if swallowing is a problem, and should be measured using a dosing spoon or measured medicine cup. Can be taken with or following food; milk and dairy products may delay absorption but do not reduce the amount of drug absorbed. The capsule should be swallowed whole. If you forget a dose: Take the dose you missed as soon as you remember it, unless you are more than 12 hours late. If that is the case, skip the missed dose and simply take the next scheduled dose. DO NOT double doses. If you forget your medicine for 2 days, call your doctor for directions.

Usual Duration of Use: Regular use for 7 to 10 days needed to see benefits in relieving heart failure or controlling heart rhythm disorders. Long-term use requires physician supervision and checks of blood levels. Treatment of heart rhythm disorders and congestive heart failure will usually be ongoing.

Typical Treatment Goals and Measurements (Outcomes and Markers)

Heart failure: Because the level of this medicine in the blood must be kept in a certain range, blood levels are used to help guide dosing. When this medicine is in the correct range, it helps the heart beat more strongly, increasing the amount of work that it can do (see controversies in medicines above). Your doctor may use terms like cardiac output (the amount of work that your heart can do in a given amount of time), contractile force (the strength of your heart action) and edematous decrease (lowered ankle swelling) to describe how much better your heart is working. Surrogate end points (a marker that offers vital information about how well a patient is responding to a treatment) is useful to clinicians. Two possible surrogate markers for CHF are left ventricular end diastolic volume (LVEDV) and b-type natriuretic peptide (BNP). These will be updated as more information becomes available. The goals and time frame should be discussed with you when the prescription is written.

▷ **This Drug Should Not Be Taken If**
- you have had an allergic reaction to any form of it.
- you are in ventricular fibrillation (a life-threatening heart rhythm).

▷ **Inform Your Physician Before Taking This Drug If**
- you have had an unfavorable reaction to digitalis.
- you have taken digitalis in the past 2 weeks.
- you take (or have recently taken) any diuretic drug.
- you have a history of severe lung disease.
- you have abnormal heart rhythms (such as severe slowing or bradycardia), sick sinus syndrome, rapid rate arising in the ventricles (ventricular tachycardia), or certain aortic problems.
- you have had damage to the heart muscle (myocardium), such as in a heart attack or myocarditis.
- you have ongoing (chronic) inflammation of part of the heart (constrictive pericarditis).
- you have a history of low blood potassium or magnesium.
- you have impaired liver or kidney function or develop impaired function while taking this medicine.
- you have a history of thyroid function disorder.

Possible Side Effects (natural, expected, and unavoidable drug actions)
Slow heart rate.
May cause blackening of feces.
Enlargement or sensitivity of the male breast—rare.

▷ **Possible Adverse Effects** (unusual, unexpected, and infrequent reactions)
If any of the following develop, consult your physician promptly for guidance.
Mild Adverse Effects
Allergic reactions: skin rash, hives-rare.
Headache, drowsiness, lethargy, confusion, changes in vision: "halo" effect, blurring, spots, double vision, yellow-green vision—infrequent.
Changes in vaginal tissue (vaginal cornification)—case reports.
Nightmares—case reports.

Loss of appetite, nausea, vomiting, diarrhea (can be early signs of adult toxicity)—frequent.

Serious Adverse Effects

Idiosyncratic reactions: hallucinations, facial neuralgias, peripheral neuralgias, blindness—case reports.

Low blood platelets (thrombocytopenia)—case reports and probably an immune reaction.

Psychosis and hallucinations—associated with toxic levels.

Seizures—rare.

Serious skin rash (Stevens-Johnson Syndrome)—rare.

Disorientation—most common in the elderly.

Trigeminal neuralgia—case report.

Heart rhythm disturbances—possible and dose-related.

▷ **Possible Effects on Sexual Function:**

Decreased libido and impotence in 35% of male users. Enlargement and tenderness of male breasts (gynecomastia)—case reports. Both effects are attributed to digoxin's estrogenlike action. May cause cornification of the vagina in women after menopause. Caution is advised, as this has been mistaken for cancer (endometrial).

Adverse Effects That May Mimic Natural Diseases or Disorders

Drug-induced mental changes may be mistaken for senile dementia or psychosis. May cause cornification of the vagina in women after menopause. Caution is advised as this has been mistaken for cancer (endometrial).

Possible Effects on Laboratory Tests

Blood platelet counts: rarely decreased.

Blood testosterone level: may be decreased with long-term use.

CAUTION

1. Take this medicine EXACTLY as prescribed.
2. If you take calcium supplements, ask your physician for help. May be prudent to avoid large doses.
3. Prudent to carry a card that says you are taking this drug.
4. Avoid over-the-counter antacids and cold, cough, or allergy remedies without first asking your doctor or pharmacist.
5. Because blood levels are so important, make sure you stay on the same brand or generic form that you are started on. If you are changed from one form or one generic to the other, blood level checks are usually prudent. If your blood potassium is lowered you can have signs and symptoms of toxicity with a "therapeutic level and a normal dose."
6. May cause changes (cornification) in the vagina in women after menopause. Caution is advised, as this has been mistaken for cancer (endometrial).

Precautions for Use

By Infants and Children: Watch for indications of toxicity: slow heart rate (below 60 beats/min), irregular heart rhythms.

By Those Over 60 Years of Age: Reduced drug tolerance; smaller doses are prudent. Watch for toxicity: headache, dizziness, fatigue, weakness, lethargy, depression, confusion, nervousness, agitation, delusions, difficulty with reading. Call your doctor if these happen.

▷ **Advisability of Use During Pregnancy**

Pregnancy Category: C. See Pregnancy Risk Categories at the back of this book.

Animal Studies: No birth defects reported.

Human Studies: Adequate studies of pregnant women not available. However, no birth defects from the therapeutic use of this drug have been reported. Use this drug only if clearly needed. Overdose can be harmful to the fetus.

Advisability of Use If Breast-Feeding
Presence of this drug in breast milk: Yes.
Monitor nursing infant closely and discontinue drug or nursing if adverse effects develop.

Habit-Forming Potential: None.

Effects of Overdose: Loss of appetite, excessive saliva, nausea, vomiting, diarrhea, serious disturbances of heart rate and rhythm, intestinal bleeding, drowsiness, headache, confusion, delirium, hallucinations, convulsions.

Possible Effects of Long-Term Use: May cause cornification of the vagina in women after menopause. Caution is advised, as this has been mistaken for cancer (endometrial).

Suggested Periodic Examinations While Taking This Drug (at physician's discretion)
Measurements of blood levels of digoxin, calcium, magnesium and potassium. (Time to sample blood for digoxin level:6–8 hours after last dose or just before next dose). Recommended broad therapeutic range: 0.5–2.0 ng/ml., but 5-0.8 ng/ml has been recommended for heart failure patients—see above controversies in medicine note).
Electrocardiograms.

▷ **While Taking This Drug, Observe the Following**
Foods: Talk to your doctor about high-potassium foods. The peak level and rate that digoxin enters your body will decrease if taken with food.
Herbal Medicines or Minerals: Hawthorn and co-enzyme Q10 (co-Q10) can affect the way the heart works. Issues remain regarding optimum doses, monitoring strategies and possible interactions. One objective review recognized co-Q10 as adjunctive therapy for congestive heart failure. BE CERTAIN to tell your doctor that you are taking or are considering taking these herbs if you are taking digoxin or if a digoxin prescription is being considered for you or a loved one. Co-Q10 may also interact badly with aspirin. Soy (milk, tofu, etc.) contains phytoestrogens that have led to an FDA-approved health claim for reducing risk of heart disease (if they have at least 6.25 grams of soy protein per serving). It is important that potassium and magnesium levels be kept in the normal range while you are taking digoxin. Aloe can work as a laxative and can cause excess potassium loss—caution is advised as low potassium or magnesium can lead to digoxin toxicity with "normal" dosing and blood levels.
St. John's wort appears to lower digoxin levels by about 25%. This decrease may lead to loss of digoxin benefits and can be a very serious drug interaction. Couch grass or nettle should NOT be taken by patients who have increased fluid (edema) caused by heart weakness. Patients taking digoxin should NOT take lily of the valley herb, pheasant's eye, or squill. Hawthorn (Crataegus variety) has been used to help heart failure, but should not be combined with heart medicines as combination use has not been studied. Use of intravenous calcium may cause a fatal interaction with digoxin. A case report of ginseng falsely elevating digoxin test levels has been made.
Beverages: Avoid excessive amounts of caffeine-containing beverages or herbs: coffee, tea, cola. May be taken with milk.

▷ *Alcohol:* No interactions expected.

Tobacco Smoking: Nicotine can cause heart muscle irritability and predispose to serious rhythm disturbances. I advise everyone to quit smoking.

Marijuana Smoking: Possible accentuation of heart failure; reduced digoxin effect; possible changes in electrocardiogram, confusing interpretation.

▷ *Other Drugs*

Digoxin **taken concurrently** with

- acarbose (Precose) may result in decreased digoxin blood levels and loss of digoxin's benefits.
- calcium (intravenously) may cause a fatal interaction.
- digoxin immune Fab (Digibind) will result in decreased blood levels. This is used to therapeutic advantage in digoxin toxicity.
- diuretics (except spironolactone or triamterene) can cause serious heart rhythm problems due to loss of potassium.
- dofetilide (Tikosyn) has been found to result in increased occurrence of an abnormal heart effect (Torsades de pointes). Presently, it is unclear if this is an interaction or is a result of medicines used in sicker patients. Caution is advised.
- metformin (Glucophage) may increase metformin levels and lead to excessively low blood sugar.
- pancuronium (Pavulon) or vecuronium (Norcuron) may cause abnormal heartbeats (arrhythmia).
- propranolol or other beta-blocking medicines (see Drug Classes) may cause very slow heart rate.
- quinidine may result in decreased digoxin effectiveness and increased digoxin toxicity; careful dose adjustments are needed.
- succinylcholine may lead to abnormal heart rhythms.

The following drugs may **increase** the effects of digoxin:

- alprazolam (Xanax).
- amiloride (Midamor).
- amiodarone (Cordarone).
- amphotericin B (Abelcet, Fungizone).
- atorvastatin (Lipitor), simvastatin (Zocor) blood levels should be checked more frequently and digoxin dosing adjusted as needed.
- benzodiazepines (Librium, Valium, etc.; see Drug Classes).
- captopril (Capoten, Capozide).
- carvedilol (Coreg) may lead to abnormal heart conduction and increased blood digoxin levels. Caution is prudent. A small study in children from 14 days to 8 years old found that this combination slowed the removal of digoxin by 50%. Lower doses and more frequent blood levels are prudent if this combination must be used—particularly in children.
- cotrimoxazole (various).
- cyclosporine (Sandimmune).
- diltiazem (Cardizem) and other calcium channel blockers (see Drug Classes).
- disopyramide (Norpace).
- erythromycin (E.E.S., Erythrocin, etc.). May also occur with clarithromycin and azithromycin.
- ethacrynic acid.
- esomeprazole (Nexium), omeprazole (Prilosec).
- flecainide (Tambocor).
- fluoxetine (Prozac, Sarafem) and fluvoxamine (Luvox).
- gatifloxacin (Tequin).

- hydroxychloroquine.
- ibuprofen (Advil, Medipren, Motrin, Nuprin, etc.).
- indomethacin (Indocin) and other NSAIDs.
- itraconazole (Sporanox).
- methimazole (Tapazole).
- mibefradil (Posicor).
- nefazodone (Serzone).
- nifedipine (Adalat, Procardia).
- omeprazole (Prilosec), rabeprazole (Aciphex).
- phenytoin (Dilantin).
- propafenone (Rythmol) (30–100% increased blood level).
- propylthiouracil (Propacil).
- quinine.
- quinupristin/dalfopristin (Synercid).
- ritonavir (Norvir).
- spironolactone (Aldactone).
- telmisartan (Micardis).
- tetracyclines (see Drug Classes).
- tolbutamide (Orinase).
- tramadol (Ultram).
- trazodone (Desyrel).
- trimethoprim (Septra, others).
- verapamil (Calan, Verelan, others).

The following drugs may *decrease* the effects of digoxin:
- activated charcoal (various).
- aluminum, magnesium hydroxide and magnesium trisilicate-containing antacids (Amphojel, Maalox, Mylanta, etc.).
- bleomycin (Blenoxane).
- carmustine (BiCNU).
- cholestyramine (Questran).
- colestipol (Colestid).
- cyclophosphamide (Cytoxan).
- cytarabine (Cytosar).
- doxorubicin (Adriamycin).
- fluvoxamine (Luvox).
- kaolin/pectin (Donnagel, others).
- methotrexate (Mexate).
- metoclopramide (Reglan).
- miglitol (Glyset).
- neomycin.
- penicillamine (Cuprimine, Depen).
- procarbazine (Matulane).
- rifampin or rifabutin.
- St. John's wort (hypericum).
- sucralfate (Carafate).
- sulfa antibiotics or sulfasalazine.
- thyroid hormones.
- vincristine (Oncovin).

▷ *Driving, Hazardous Activities:* Usually no restrictions. This drug may cause drowsiness, vision changes and nausea. Restrict activities as necessary.

Aviation Note: Heart function disorders *are a disqualification* for piloting. Consult a designated Aviation Medical Examiner.

Exposure to Sun: No restrictions.

Occurrence of Unrelated Illness: Vomiting or diarrhea can seriously alter this drug's effectiveness. Notify your physician promptly.

Discontinuation: This drug may be continued indefinitely. Do not stop it without consulting your physician.

DILTIAZEM (dil TI a zem)

Introduced: 1977   **Class:** Anti-anginal, antihypertensive, calcium channel blocker   **Prescription:** USA: Yes   **Controlled Drug:** USA: No; Canada: No   **Available as Generic:** Yes

Brand Names: ✤Abert Diltiazem CD, ✤Apo-Diltiaz, ✤Alti-Diltiazem, Cardizem, Cardizem CD, Cardizem LA, Cardizem SR, Cartia XT, Dilacor XR, Diltia XT, Diltiazem, Diltiazem ER, Med Diltiazem SR, ✤Novo-Diltiazem, ✤Nu-Diltiaz, Pharma-Diltiaz, ✤Syn-Diltiazem, Teczem [CD], Tiamate, Tiazac

Controversies in Medicine: Medicines in this class have had many conflicting reports. The FDA has held hearings on the calcium channel blocker (CCB) class. Research at New York University found that nifedipine is a cause of reversible male infertility. CCBs are currently second-line agents for high blood pressure according to the JNC VII (see Glossary).

BENEFITS versus RISKS	
Possible Benefits	*Possible Risks*
EFFECTIVE PREVENTION OF BOTH MAJOR TYPES OF ANGINA	Depression, confusion
EFFECTIVE CONTROL OF MILD TO MODERATE HYPERTENSION	Low blood pressure
	Heart rhythm disturbance
HELPS CONTROL ATRIAL FIBRILLATION	Fluid retention-possible worsening of CHF
May help prevent repeat blockage of coronary arteries in heart transplant patients	Liver damage—case reports
	Muscle damage—case reports
May inhibit the inflammatory response of the body in heart bypass patients	
Reduces frequency of slowed heart circulation in patients with end-stage kidney disease	
CARDIZEM LA FORM MAY GIVE ENHANCED ANGINA CONTROL WHEN TAKEN AT BEDTIME	

▷ **Principal Uses**

As a Single Drug Product: Uses currently included in FDA-approved labeling: Treats (1) angina pectoris (coronary artery spasm or spontaneous Prinzmetal's variant angina) or associated with exertion; (2) classical angina-of-effort (due to atherosclerotic disease); (3) mild to moderate hypertension; (4) atrial fibrillation.

Other (unlabeled) generally accepted uses: (1) Unstable angina; (2) congestive heart failure; (3) migraine prophylaxis; (4) prevention of abnormal protein excretion in the urine; (5) abnormal heart rhythms; (6) treats abnormal plaques inside blood vessels (atherosclerosis); (7) may help prevent abnormal growth of the left side of the heart (left ventricular hypertrophy) after a heart attack; (8) treats some esophageal disorders; (9) eases symptoms of an overactive thyroid gland (hyperthyroidism); (10) can ease symptoms of Raynaud's phenomenon; (11) can have a role in preserving function in kidney and heart transplant patients; (12) may protect against heart attacks or variant or unstable angina that can occur after (postoperatively) coronary artery bypass grafting; (13) could have a role in slowing the advance of low tension glaucoma; (14) may help prevent repeat blockage (restenosis) in heart transplant patients; (15) appears to reduce the frequency of heart blood flow decreases in patients with end-stage kidney disease.

How This Drug Works: This drug blocks normal passage of calcium through cell walls, inhibiting coronary artery and peripheral arteriole narrowing. As a result, this drug

- prevents spontaneous coronary artery spasm (Prinzmetal's angina).
- decreases heart rate and contraction force in exertion, making effort-induced angina less likely.
- opens contracted peripheral arterial walls, lowering blood pressure (also lessens heart work and helps prevent angina).

Appears to work as an antiinflammatory drug (inhibits IL-6) in people getting a heart bypass.

Available Dosage Forms and Strengths

Capsules, extended release — 120 mg, 180 mg, 240 mg, 300 mg
Capsules, extended release (Tiazac only) — 120, 180, 240, 300, 360, 420 mg
Capsules, sustained release — 60 mg, 90 mg, 120 mg
Tablets, immediate release — 30 mg, 60 mg, 90 mg, 120 mg

▷ **Usual Adult Dosage Ranges:** High blood pressure: Sustained-release capsules are started at 60 to 120 mg twice daily or 180 to 240 mg daily (for example, Cardizem LA is started at 180–240 mg when used alone). Effective dose for many patients is 120 to 180 mg twice a day. Daily maximum is 360 mg a day for Cardizem SR. Extended release capsules (Dilacor XR) are started at 120 to 240 mg once a day. Many patients benefit from 240–360 mg daily. Maximum dose is 540 mg once a day. *Angina:* Extended release (such as Cardizem CD, Dilacor XR or Tiazac) forms may be started at 120 to 180 mg daily. The dose can then be increased as needed and tolerated to 480 mg over 1 to 2 weeks. Maximum dose is 540 mg.

Note: Actual dose and schedule must be determined for each patient individually.

Conditions Requiring Dosing Adjustments

Liver Function: Maximum daily dose in patients with liver compromise should be 90 mg. Rarely causes hepatoxicity, and a benefit-to-risk decision must be made.

Kidney Function: May be one of the best calcium channel blockers to use in kidney compromise (large liver and fecal removal). Caution must still be used. Drug can be a rare cause of kidney compromise.

▷ **Dosing Instructions:** Immediate-release form may be crushed and is best taken before meals and at bedtime. Extended-release forms should NEVER be crushed or altered. Tiazac form may be taken with or without food. Tiazac capsules have been cautiously opened and the contents sprinkled on applesauce. This mixture is then swallowed without chewing. Dilacor XR form is best taken on an empty stomach in the morning. Cardizem LA form has new data finding more than a 200% improvement in angina control when taken at bedtime (see Glasser, S.P. in Sources, and talk to your doctor). If you forget a dose, take it as soon as you remember it, unless it is nearly time for your next dose—then skip the missed dose and take the next dose right on schedule. DO NOT double doses. If you find yourself forgetting doses, please talk to your doctor about possible reminder systems to help.

Usual Duration of Use: Use for 2 to 4 weeks is required to see effectiveness in decreasing angina frequency and severity and in lowering blood pressure. Smallest effective dose should be used in long-term therapy (months to years). Take control of your blood pressure for life!

Typical Treatment Goals and Measurements (Outcomes and Markers)

Blood Pressure: The NEW guidelines (JNC VII) define normal blood pressure (BP) as **less than** 120/80. Because blood pressures that were once considered acceptable can actually lead to blood vessel damage, the committee from the National Institutes of Health, National Heart Lung and Blood Institute now have a new category called **Pre-hypertension**. This ranges from 120/80 to 139/89 and is intended to help your doctor encourage lifestyle changes (or in the case of people with a risk factor for high blood pressure, start treatment) much earlier—so that possible damage to blood vessels, your heart, kidneys, sexual potency, or eyes might be minimized or avoided altogether. The next two classes of high blood pressure are stage 1 hypertension: 140/90 to 159/99 and stage 2 hypertension equal to or greater than: 160/100 mm Hg. These guidelines also recommend that clinicians trying to control blood pressure work with their patients to agree on the goals and a plan of treatment. The first-ever guidelines for blood pressure (hypertension) in African Americans recommends that MOST black patients be started on TWO antihypertensive medicines with the goal of lowering blood pressure to 130/80 for those with high risk for heart and blood vessel disease or with diabetes. The American Diabetes Association recommends 130/80 as the target for people living with diabetes and less than 125/75 for those who spill more than one gram of protein into their urine. Most clinicians try to achieve a BP that confers the best balance of lower cardiovascular risk and avoids the problem of too low a blood pressure. Blood pressure duration is generally increased with beneficial restriction of sodium. The goals and time frame should be discussed with you when the prescription is written. If goals are not met, it is not unusual to intensify doses or add on medicines. You can find the new blood pressure guidelines at *www.nhlbi.hih.gov/guidelines/hypertension/index.htm*. For the African American guidelines, see Douglas J.G. in Sources.

Possible Advantages of This Drug

Minimal kidney removal may make this a drug of choice in people with kidney damage who require a calcium channel blocker. Works in ongoing suppressive treatment in patients who will not tolerate beta blockers. New Cardizem LA form offered a 200% improvement in angina control when taken at bedtime.

▷ **This Drug Should Not Be Taken If**
- you have had an allergic reaction to it previously.
- you have "sick sinus" syndrome, second or third degree heart block (and do not have an artificial pacemaker).
- you've recently had a heart attack and your lungs are not working well (acute MI with pulmonary congestion).

- you have atrial fibrillation or flutter and an IV form is being considered.
- you have a particular kind of fast heart rate (ventricular tachycardia with a wide [QRS more than 0.12 sec] complex and an IV form is being considered).
- you have low blood pressure—systolic pressure below 90.

▷ **Inform Your Physician Before Taking This Drug If**
- you had an unfavorable response to any calcium blocker drug.
- you take digitalis or a beta-blocker (see Drug Classes).
- you have a history of or have congestive heart failure.
- you have a narrowing or stenosis of the aorta.
- you have atrial fibrillation (talk with your doctor).
- you have impaired liver or kidney function.
- your blood pressure is excessively low.
- you have a blockage in your stomach or intestines or they are moving excessively (gastrointestinal obstruction or hypermotility).
- you develop a skin rash.
- you have a history of drug-induced liver damage.

Possible Side Effects (natural, expected, and unavoidable drug actions)
Fatigue—rare.
Light-headedness, heart rate and rhythm changes in some people—rare.
Excessive growth of gum tissue (gingival hyperplasia)—possible.
Difficulty breathing or cough—possible.
Drug fever—one case report—possible.

▷ **Possible Adverse Effects** (unusual, unexpected, and infrequent reactions)
If any of the following develop, consult your physician promptly for guidance.
Mild Adverse Effects
Allergic reactions: skin rash, hives, itching—rare.
Headache—may be self-limiting but frequent.
Drowsiness, dizziness—occasional and dose-related.
Nervousness, sleep problems, depression, confusion, hallucinations—case reports.
Overgrowth of the gums (gingival hyperplasia)—may be frequent.
Impaired sense of smell or taste—possible.
Increased urination—rare.
Flushing, palpitations, fainting, slow heart rate, low blood pressure—rare.
Edema—infrequent (up to 8% with Diltiazem LA form).
Nausea, indigestion, heartburn, vomiting, diarrhea, constipation—rare to infrequent.
Serious Adverse Effects
Serious skin rashes (Stevens-Johnson Syndrome, others).
Movement disorder (akathisia)—case report.
Serious disturbances of heart rate and/or rhythm, fluid retention (edema), congestive heart failure—rare.
Drug-induced myopathy or liver damage—rare.
Lowering of a specific kind of white blood cell (granulocytes)—case reports with this and other calcium channel blockers.
Lowering of blood platelets or function—case reports.
Sudden kidney failure—case reports to rare.
Systemic lupus erythematosus—rare.

▷ **Possible Effects on Sexual Function:** Impotence—rare.
Swelling or tenderness of the male breast tissue (gynecomastia)—case reports.

One reported case of heavy vaginal bleeding. 1–2% male sexual dysfunction reported with other calcium antagonists.

Possible Effects on Laboratory Tests

Blood total cholesterol and triglyceride levels: no effects.
Blood HDL cholesterol level: increased (beneficial).
Blood LDL and VLDL cholesterol levels: no effects.

CAUTION

1. Tell health care providers that you take this drug. Carry a card in your purse or wallet saying you take diltiazem.
2. Nitroglycerin and other nitrate drugs as needed may still be used to relieve acute angina pain. If your angina attacks become more frequent or intense, call your doctor promptly.

Precautions for Use

By Infants and Children: Safety and effectiveness for those under 12 years of age not established.

By Those Over 60 Years of Age: May be more likely to have weakness, dizziness, fainting and falling. Take necessary precautions to prevent injury. Report promptly any changes in your pattern of thirst and urination.

▷ **Advisability of Use During Pregnancy**

Pregnancy Category: C. See Pregnancy Risk Categories at the back of this book.
Animal Studies: Embryo and fetal deaths and skeletal birth defects reported in mice, rats, and rabbits.
Human Studies: Adequate studies of pregnant women not available.
Avoid this drug during the first 3 months. Use during the last 6 months only if clearly needed. Ask your physician for help.

Advisability of Use If Breast-Feeding

Presence of this drug in breast milk: Yes.
Avoid drug or refrain from nursing.

Habit-Forming Potential: None.

Effects of Overdose: Weakness, light-headedness, fainting, slow pulse, low blood pressure, shortness of breath, congestive heart failure.

Possible Effects of Long-Term Use: None reported.

Suggested Periodic Examinations While Taking This Drug (at physician's discretion)
Evaluations of heart function, including electrocardiograms.
Liver and kidney function tests, with long-term use.

▷ **While Taking This Drug, Observe the Following**

Foods: May increase absorption and cause a 30% increase in blood levels. Avoid excessive salt intake.

Herbal Medicines or Minerals: Ginseng, guarana, hawthorn, saw palmetto, ma huang, goldenseal, yohimbe, and licorice may also cause increased blood pressure. Garlic and calcium may work to lower blood pressure. The combination may work to require lower diltiazem doses. St. John's wort may work to lower calcium channel blocker levels (because it increases P-glycoprotein in the gut). This combination may also increase sun sensitivity. Guggul and gugulipid will reduce effectiveness of diltiazem—do not combine. Eleuthero root, and ephedra should be avoided by people living with hypertension.
Indian snakeroot has a German Commission E monograph indication for hypertension—talk to your doctor. Discuss any plans for herbal medicines or minerals with your doctor.

Beverages: No restrictions. May be taken with milk.

▷   Alcohol: Use with caution. Alcohol may exaggerate the drop in blood pressure.

Tobacco Smoking: Nicotine reduces benefits. I advise everyone to quit smoking.

Marijuana Smoking: Possible reduced effectiveness of this drug; mild to moderate increase in angina; possible changes in electrocardiogram, confusing interpretation.

▷   *Other Drugs*

Diltiazem **taken concurrently** with

- alfentanil (various) may lead to accumulation of alfentanil. Caution and lower doses of alfentanil are prudent.
- amiodarone (Cordarone) may lead to abnormal heart rhythm.
- anticoagulants (see Drug Classes) may lead to stomach or intestinal bleeding.
- aspirin can result in prolonged bleeding time or hemorrhage. This is a benefit to risk decision.
- beta-blocker drugs or digitalis preparations (see Drug Classes) may affect heart rate and rhythm. Careful patient monitoring is necessary if these drugs are combined.
- carbamazepine (Tegretol) may result in toxicity and seizures.
- celecoxib (Celebrex) or rofecoxib (Vioxx) may increase blood pressure secondary to fluid retention.
- cilostazol (Pletal) may result in cilostazol toxicity. Lower cilostazol doses are prudent.
- cisapride (Propulsid) may lead to heart toxicity.
- cyclosporine (Sandimmune) may result in cyclosporine toxicity and kidney failure.
- digoxin (Lanoxin) can result in digoxin toxicity.
- dofetilide (Tikosyn) may result in dofetilide toxicity. Checks of dofetilide levels and dosing adjustments to levels are prudent.
- lithium (Lithobid, others) can result in psychosis and neurotoxicity.
- lovastatin (Mevacor), simvastatin (Zocor) may increase these (and perhaps other) HMG CoA reductase inhibitor levels that rely on CYP 450 3A4 for removal, and increase risk of muscle damage. Lower HMG CoA doses and careful patient monitoring are prudent.
- midazolam (Versed) may result in midazolam toxicity. Lower doses (by 50%) and careful patient monitoring are critical.
- nifedipine (various) may result in nifedipine toxicity. Alternative medicines or nifedipine dosing adjusted to blood levels is prudent.
- nonsteroidal anti-inflammatory drugs (NSAIDs—see Drug Classes) may lead to stomach or intestinal bleeding.
- oral anticoagulants (warfarin—Coumadin, others) may result in higher than expected anticoagulation. Increased INRs and careful patient following are prudent.
- oral antidiabetic drugs (see Drug Classes) such as glipizide Glucotrol) may result in greater than expected lowering of blood sugar and hypoglycemia.
- phenytoin (Dilantin) and fosphenytoin (Cerebyx) decreases phenytoin and fosphenytoin metabolism and may cause toxicity. Lower doses and blood level checks are prudent.
- quinidine (Quinaglute, others) may lead to quinidine toxicity.
- rifabutin (Mycobutin) may decrease diltiazem blood levels.
- rifampin (Rifadin) may result in decreased diltiazem effectiveness.
- ritonavir (Norvir) and other protease inhibitors (see Drug Profiles) may lead to diltiazem toxicity.
- Sirolimus (Rapamune) or tacrolimus (Prograf) may result in serolimus or

tacrolimus accumulation and toxicity. Blood levels and dosing adjustments as needed are prudent.
- theophylline (Theo-Dur, others) may lead to theophylline toxicity.
- tretinoin (Vesanoid, others) may lead to tretinoin toxicity.
- triazolam (Halcion) may lead to triazolam toxicity.

The following drugs may *increase* the effects of diltiazem:
- amprenavir (Agenerase).
- cimetidine (Tagamet).
- fluoxetine (Prozac).
- fluvoxamine (Luvox).
- quinupristin/dalfopristin (Synercid).
- ranitidine (Zantac).
- sertraline (Zoloft).
- voriconazole (Vfend).

▷ *Driving, Hazardous Activities:* Usually no restrictions. This drug may cause drowsiness or dizziness. Limit activities as necessary.

Aviation Note: Coronary artery disease *is a disqualification* for piloting. Consult a designated Aviation Medical Examiner.

Exposure to Sun: This drug may cause photosensitivity (see Glossary).

Exposure to Heat: Caution is advised. Hot environments can exaggerate the blood-pressure-lowering effects of this drug. Observe for light-headedness or weakness.

Heavy Exercise or Exertion: May improve ability to be more active without angina pain. Use caution, and avoid exercise that might be excessive and yet not result in warning pain.

Discontinuation: **Do not stop this drug abruptly.** Ask your doctor about gradual withdrawal.

DIPHENHYDRAMINE (di fen HI dra meen)

Introduced: 1946 **Class:** Antihistamine (ethanolamine type), hypnotic **Prescription:** USA: Varies with dose(50 mg is prescription form) **Controlled Drug:** USA: No*; Canada: No **Available as Generic:** Yes

Author's Note: This medicine is available without a prescription in lower doses and is found in many products.

Brand Names: Acetaminophen-PM, AID to Sleep, Allerdryl, Allergy Capsules, Allergy Formula, Allermax, ✽Ambenyl Expectorant [CD], Ambenyl Syrup [CD], Anacin P.M. Aspirin-Free, Banophen, Bayer Select, Beldin Syrup, Bena-D, Benadryl, Benadryl 25, Benadryl Allergy, Benahist, Benylin, ✽Benylin Decongestant [CD], ✽Benylin Pediatric Syrup, ✽Benylin Syrup w/Codeine [CD], ✽Caladryl [CD], Caldyphen Lotion, Children's Complete Allergy, Complete Allergy Medication, Compoz, Dermarest, Di-Delamine, Dihydrex, Diphendryl, Diphenhist, Dormarex 2, ✽Ergodryl [CD], Excedrin P.M. [CD], Extra Strength Tylenol PM, Gecil, Genahist, Gen-D-Phen, Hydramine, ✽Insomnal, Kolex, ✽Mandrax [CD], Maximum Strength Nytol, Medi-Phedryl, Midol-PM, Nervine Nighttime Sleep, Nidryl Elixir, Nighttime Cold Medicine [CD], Nite-Time, Noradryl [CD], Noradryl 25, Nytol, Pain Relief PM [CD], Pathadryl, ✽PMS-Diphenhydramine, Sinutab Maximum Strength, SK-Diphenhydramine, Sleep, ✽Sleep-Eze D, Sleep-Eze 3, Sominex, Sominex 2, Theraflu Cold Medicine (Nighttime Strength), Twilite, Tylenol PM Extra

Strength, Unisom Sleepgels, Valdrene, Valu-Dryl Allergy Medicine [CD], Wal-Ben, Wal-Dryl, Wehydryl

---

BENEFITS versus RISKS

Possible Benefits	*Possible Risks*
EFFECTIVE RELIEF OF ALLERGIC RHINITIS AND ALLERGIC SKIN DISORDERS	Marked sedation
	Atropinelike effects
EFFECTIVE, NONADDICTIVE SEDATIVE AND HYPNOTIC	Accentuation of prostatism (see Glossary)
Treatment of anaphylaxis	Difficulty driving or operating hazardous machinery
Prevention and relief of motion sickness	
Partial relief of symptoms of Parkinson's disease	

▷ **Principal Uses**

As a Single Drug Product: Uses currently included in FDA-approved labeling: (1) Prevention or treatment of motion sickness (control of dizziness, nausea, and vomiting); (2) treatment of drug-induced Parkinsonian reactions, especially in children or the elderly; (3) treatment of conditions caused by histamine release (such as allergic drug reactions and allergic rhinitis (hay fever)); (4) used as a short-term sleep aid; (5) helps hives (urticaria) that have an unknown cause (idiopathic); (6) approved to help treat symptoms of the common cold.

Other (unlabeled) generally accepted uses: (1) Cough suppression; (2) can have a role in easing the discomfort of mucositis caused by radiation therapy; (3) used in combination with metoclopramide (Reglan) to help stop vomiting caused by chemotherapy (moderately emetogenic); (4) intravenous or intramuscular use can help serious eye spasm (oculogyric crisis).

As a Combination Drug Product [CD]: This drug may have a mild suppressant effect on coughing. It is combined with expectorants and codeine or dextromethorphan in some cough products.

How This Drug Works: Blocks the action of histamine. Its natural side effects are used to advantage: sedative action used to help people fall asleep; atropine-like action used in motion sickness and Parkinson-related disorders.

Available Dosage Forms and Strengths

Capsules, nonprescription — 5 mg
Capsules, prescription — 50 mg
Cream — 1%
Elixir — 12.5 mg/5 ml (14% alcohol)
Spray — 1%
Syrup — 12.5 mg/5 ml and 13.3 mg/5 ml
Tablets, nonprescription — 25 mg
Tablets, prescription — 50 mg

▷ **Usual Adult Dosage Ranges:** *Antihistamine, to prevent motion sickness, or in parkinsonism:* 25 to 50 mg every 6 to 8 hours. Maximum daily dose is 300 mg. Cough control (antitussive): 25 mg every 4 to 6 hours. Maximum daily dose is 150 mg. *As a sleep aid (hypnotic):* 50 mg at bedtime is often used. To prevent vomiting from chemotherapy: 50 mg of diphenhydramine combined with 50 mg of metoclopramide every 6 hours for 2 to 4 days.

Note: Actual dose and schedule must be determined for each patient individually.

Conditions Requiring Dosing Adjustments

Liver Function: Caution—single doses are not expected to be a problem; however, the use of multiple doses in patients with liver compromise has not been studied.

Kidney Function: In mild kidney failure (creatinine clearance more than 50 ml/min), usual dose is given every 6 hours; every 6–12 hours in mild-moderate failure; and every 12–18 hours in severe kidney failure.

▷ **Dosing Instructions:** Tablet may be crushed and capsule may be opened and is best taken with or following food. Elixirs are available if swallowing is a difficulty, and should be measured with a dosing spoon or medicine cup. If you forget a dose, take the missed dose as soon as you remember unless it is almost time for your next dose—if that is the case, simply skip the missed dose and take the next dose right on schedule. DO NOT double doses.

Usual Duration of Use: Regular use for 2 to 3 days is needed to see effectiveness in easing allergic rhinitis and dermatosis symptoms. If it doesn't work after 5 days, this drug should be stopped. As a bedtime sedative (hypnotic), use only as needed. Avoid long-term use.

▷ **This Drug Should Not Be Taken If**
- you have had an allergic reaction to it previously.
- you are nursing your infant.
- you are taking, or took during the past 2 weeks, any monoamine oxidase (MAO) type A inhibitor (see Drug Classes).
- cream (topical 1%) should NOT be used on the eye lids or in the eyes.

▷ **Inform Your Physician Before Taking This Drug If**
- you have had an unfavorable response to any antihistamine.
- you have narrow-angle glaucoma.
- you have peptic ulcer disease, with any degree of pyloric obstruction.
- you have chickenpox and are considering the topical form of this medicine.
- you have prostatism (see Glossary).
- you are subject to bronchial asthma or seizures (epilepsy).
- you have difficulty urinating.
- you have glucose-6-phosphate dehydrogenase (G6PD) deficiency.

Possible Side Effects (natural, expected, and unavoidable drug actions)

Drowsiness (diphenhydramine is the most sedating antihistamine); weakness; dryness of nose, mouth, and throat; constipation; thickening of bronchial secretions.

▷ **Possible Adverse Effects** (unusual, unexpected, and infrequent reactions)

If any of the following develop, consult your physician promptly for guidance.

Mild Adverse Effects

Allergic reactions: skin rash, hives—rare.

Headache, dizziness, inability to concentrate, blurred or double vision, difficult urination—infrequent.

Reduced tolerance for contact lenses—possible.

Nausea, vomiting, diarrhea—possible.

Serious Adverse Effects

Allergic reaction: anaphylactic reaction (see Glossary)—case reports.

Idiosyncratic reactions: insomnia, excitement, hallucinations, confusion—case reports.

Severe constriction of blood vessels (vasoconstriction)—possible with injection use as a local anesthetic.

Hemolytic anemia (see Glossary) or porphyria—case reports.

Reduced white blood cell count: fever, sore throat, infections, or blood platelet destruction (abnormal bleeding or bruising; see Glossary)—case reports.

Movement disorders (dyskinesias, dystonias)—case reports.

Impaired reaction time—dose related and greater impairment than 0.1% blood alcohol in some people.

Hip fractures—case reports resulting in older patients from unsteadiness from the drug versus the drug itself.

▷ **Possible Effects on Sexual Function:** Shortened menstrual cycle (early arrival of expected menstrual onset).

Natural Diseases or Disorders That May Be Activated by This Drug
Latent epilepsy, glaucoma, prostatism.

Possible Effects on Laboratory Tests
Red blood cell counts and hemoglobin: decreased—possible.

Urine screening tests for drug abuse: initial test result may be falsely **positive;** confirmatory test result will be **negative.** (Test results depend upon amount of drug taken and testing method used.)

CAUTION
1. Stop this drug 5 days before diagnostic skin testing procedures in order to prevent false-negative test results.
2. Do not use if you have active bronchial asthma, bronchitis, or pneumonia
3. May lead to unsteadiness in older patients (generally more sensitive to this drug), resulting in falls. Caution is advised.
4. Benylin Elixir has 19 mg (0.8 MEQ) of sodium in each 5 ml.

Precautions for Use
By Infants and Children: This drug should not be used in premature or full-term newborn infants. Doses for children should be small, as the young child is especially sensitive to the effects of antihistamines on the brain and nervous system. For use to decrease coughing (antitussive) in children 6 to 12 years old: 12.5 mg every 4 to 6 hours. The maximum daily dose here is 75 mg/day. Avoid the use of this drug in the child with chickenpox or a flu-like infection—may lead to altered mental status and loss of coordination.

By Those Over 60 Years of Age: Increased risk of drowsiness, dizziness, unsteadiness, and impairment of thinking, judgment, and memory. Can increase the degree of impaired urination associated with prostate enlargement (prostatism). Sedative effects may be misinterpreted as senility or emotional depression.

▷ **Advisability of Use During Pregnancy**
Pregnancy Category: B by the manufacturer. See Pregnancy Risk Categories at the back of this book.

Animal Studies: No birth defects reported in rats or rabbits.

Human Studies: Some case reports of fetal toxicity have been made. Information from studies of pregnant women is not available. A withdrawal syndrome of tremor and diarrhea was reported in a 5-day-old infant whose mother used this drug (150 mg daily) during pregnancy.

Use is a benefit-to-risk decision. Ask your doctor for help.

Advisability of Use If Breast-Feeding
Presence of this drug in breast milk: Yes.

Avoid drug or refrain from nursing.

Habit-Forming Potential: Combination use of pentazocine and diphenhydramine has become an abused intravenous drug combination. There have been rare reports of a withdrawal syndrome after use of high doses. Intravenous use has led to some rare cases of drug abuse.

Effects of Overdose: Marked drowsiness, confusion, incoordination, muscle tremors, fever, dilated pupils, stupor, coma, seizures.

Possible Effects of Long-Term Use: The development of tolerance (see Glossary) and reduced effectiveness of drug.

Suggested Periodic Examinations While Taking This Drug (at physician's discretion)

Complete blood cell counts.

▷ **While Taking This Drug, Observe the Following**

Foods: No restrictions.

Herbal Medicines or Minerals: Valerian and kava kava (kava no longer recommended in Canada) may interact additively (drowsiness). Avoid these combinations. Ginkgo biloba leaf extract has a German Commission E indication for vertigo, but has not been studied in combination with antihistamines and cannot presently be recommended. Talk to your doctor BEFORE adding any herbal medicines.

Beverages: No restrictions. May be taken with milk.

▷ *Alcohol:* Use extreme caution. The combination of alcohol and antihistamines can cause rapid and marked sedation.

Tobacco Smoking: No interactions expected. I advise everyone to quit smoking.

Marijuana Smoking: Increased drowsiness and mouth dryness; accentuation of impaired thinking.

▷ *Other Drugs*

Diphenhydramine may ***increase*** the effects of
- all drugs with a sedative effect such as benzodiazepines, tricyclic antidepressants and narcotics (see Drug Classes) and cause oversedation.
- amitriptyline (Elavil) and cause increased urinary retention.
- atropine and atropinelike drugs (see Drug Classes).
- metaproterenol (Alupent, others) leading to increased risk of metaproterenol toxicity.
- tramadol (Ultram), leading to increased sedation risk.

The following drugs may ***increase*** the effects of diphenhydramine:
- monoamine oxidase (MAO) type A inhibitor drugs (see Drug Classes); can delay elimination, exaggerating and prolonging its action.

Diphenhydramine ***taken concurrently*** with
- metoprolol (see Drug Profiles) may result in increased risk of metoprolol toxicity. Careful patient follow up and dose changes are prudent.
- phenothiazines (see Drug Classes) may result in increased difficulty urinating, intestinal obstruction or glaucoma, especially in those over 70 years old.
- temazepam (Restoril) in pregnancy may increase risk of death of the fetus.
- tricyclic antidepressants (see Drug Classes) may cause increased risk of urinary retention.

▷ *Driving, Hazardous Activities:* This drug may impair alertness, judgment, coordination and reaction time. Restrict activities as necessary.

Aviation Note: The use of this drug ***is a disqualification*** for piloting. Consult a designated Aviation Medical Examiner.

Exposure to Sun: Caution—this drug may cause phototoxicity (eczematous eruptions) if the lotion is applied and you go in the sun (see Glossary).

Exposure to Environmental Chemicals: The insecticides Aldrin, Dieldrin and Chlordane may decrease the effectiveness of this drug. Sevin may increase the sedative effects of this drug.

DISOPYRAMIDE (di so PEER a mide)

Introduced: 1969 **Class**: Antiarrhythmic (group or class 1A) **Prescription:** USA: Yes **Controlled Drug:** USA: No; Canada: No **Available as Generic:** USA: Yes; Canada: No

Brand Names: Norpace, Norpace CR, Pisopyramide, Rythmical, ✿Rythmodan, ✿Rythmodan-LA

BENEFITS versus RISKS

Possible Benefits	*Possible Risks*
EFFECTIVE TREATMENT OF SELECTED HEART RHYTHM DISORDERS	NARROW TREATMENT RANGE LOW BLOOD PRESSURE LOW BLOOD SUGAR (INFREQUENT) AGRANULOCYTOSIS—RARE Peripheral neuropathy Liver toxicity Heart conduction and rhythm abnormalities Frequent atropinelike side effects

---

▷ **Principal Uses**

As a Single Drug Product: Uses currently included in FDA-approved labeling: Treats abnormal rhythms in the heart ventricles (ventricular arrhythmias). It is classified as a Type 1A antiarrhythmic agent.

Other (unlabeled) generally accepted uses: (1) Abolishes and prevents recurrence of premature heartbeats in the atria (upper chambers) and ventricles (lower heart chambers); (2) treats and prevents abnormally rapid heart rates (tachycardia) beginning in the atria or the ventricles; (3) eases arrhythmias and abnormal heart pressures arising from cardiomyopathy or subaortic stenosis.

Author's Note: Information in this profile has been shortened to make room for more widely used medicines.

DISULFIRAM (di SULF i ram)

Introduced: 1948 **Class:** Antialcoholism **Prescription:** USA: Yes **Controlled Drug:** USA: No; Canada: No **Available as Generic:** USA: Yes; Canada: No

Brand Name: Antabuse

```
┌─────────────────────────────────────────────────────────────────┐
│                     BENEFITS versus RISKS                         │
│      Possible Benefits                    Possible Risks          │
│   EFFECTIVE ADJUNCT IN THE        DANGEROUS REACTIONS WITH        │
│     TREATMENT OF CHRONIC            ALCOHOL INGESTION             │
│     ALCOHOLISM                     Acute psychotic reactions       │
│                                    Drug-induced liver damage       │
│                                    Drug-induced optic and/or peripheral │
│                                       neuritis                     │
│                                    Low blood platelets             │
└─────────────────────────────────────────────────────────────────┘
```

▷ **Principal Uses**
  As a Single Drug Product: Uses currently included in FDA-approved labeling: Deters abusive drinking of alcoholic beverages. It does not abolish the craving or impulse to drink.
    Other (unlabeled) generally accepted uses: (1) Limited use in helping skin problems (dermatitis) caused by nickel exposure; (2) some data showing benefit in people addicted to narcotics who subsequently abused cocaine.

How This Drug Works: This drug blocks normal liver enzyme activity after alcohol is changed to acetaldehyde. This causes accumulation of acetaldehyde and causes the disulfiram (Antabuse) reaction (see Glossary).

Available Dosage Forms and Strengths
  Tablets — 250 mg, 500 mg

▷ **Usual Adult Dosage Ranges:** Once all signs of intoxication are gone and no less than 12 hours after the last alcohol drink, therapy begins with 500 mg/day for 1 to 2 weeks, followed by an ongoing dose of 250 mg/day. Range is 125 mg to 500 mg daily and is individually determined. Maximum daily dose is 500 mg.
  Note: Actual dose and schedule must be determined for each patient individually.

Conditions Requiring Dosing Adjustments
  Liver Function: This drug is a benefit-to-risk decision in mild liver compromise. Disulfiram is clearly contraindicated in portal hypertension and active hepatitis.
  Kidney Function: Dosing adjustments are not indicated.
  Diabetes: People with diabetes who take disulfiram can be at increased risk for diabetic blood vessel (micro- and macrovascular) problems. The risk is worsened by potential adverse drug effects such as increased cholesterol levels and peripheral neuropathy.
  Lung Disease: Accumulation of a metabolite may occur in severe lung problems. Drug levels or dose reduction will be needed.

▷ **Dosing Instructions:** The tablet may be crushed and taken with or following food to decrease stomach irritation. The dose can be given in the evening if sleepiness from the drug is a problem. If you forget a dose: take the missed dose right away, unless it is 12 hours after you should have taken the dose—if that is the case, simply take the next scheduled dose. DO NOT double doses.

Usual Duration of Use: Use on a regular schedule for several months is needed to see effectiveness in deterring alcohol use. If tolerated well, use should continue until self-control and sobriety are ongoing (use is highly individualized, but may be required for years).

Typical Treatment Goals and Measurements (Outcomes and Markers)

Alcoholism: This medicine does NOT cure alcoholism, but reduces the desire to drink. The goal is to stop drinking and return self-control and sobriety. Combination of this medicine with psychological help (psychotherapy) gets the best results.

▷ **This Drug Should Not Be Taken If**
- you have had a severe allergic reaction to disulfiram. (Note: The interaction of disulfiram and alcohol is not an allergic reaction.)
- you have taken any form of alcohol within the past 12 hours.
- you are pregnant.
- you have a history of psychosis.
- you are taking paraldehyde.
- you have significant exposure to ethylene dibromide where you live or work. Disulfiram inhibits the removal of this chemical and enhances the ability of ethylene dibromide to cause cancer.
- you are taking (or have taken recently) metronidazole (Flagyl).
- you have coronary blood vessel occlusion (block in a coronary artery) or a serious heart rhythm disorder.

▷ **Inform Your Physician Before Taking This Drug If**
- you are allergic to rubber (contact dermatitis form it).
- you have used disulfiram in the past.
- you do not intend to avoid alcohol completely while taking this drug.
- you do not understand what will happen if you drink alcohol while taking this drug.
- you are planning pregnancy in the near future.
- you have a history of diabetes, epilepsy, or kidney or liver disease.
- you take oral anticoagulants, digitalis, isoniazid, paraldehyde, or phenytoin (Dilantin).
- you have a history of low thyroid function (hypothyroidism).
- you have a history of lung disease.
- you plan to have surgery under general anesthesia while taking this drug.

Possible Side Effects (natural, expected, and unavoidable drug actions)

Drowsiness, lethargy during early use.

Offensive breath and body odor.

▷ **Possible Adverse Effects** (unusual, unexpected, and infrequent reactions)

If any of the following develop, consult your physician promptly for guidance.

Mild Adverse Effects

Allergic reactions: skin rash, hives—case reports.

Headache, dizziness, restlessness, tremor—infrequent.

Metallic or garlic-like taste, indigestion (usually subsides in 2 weeks).

Increased cholesterol after 3–6 weeks of treatment—possible (taking 50 mg per day of pyridoxine appears to stop this).

Decreased or increased blood pressure—possible.

Serious Adverse Effects

Allergic reactions: severe skin rashes, drug-induced hepatitis—rare.

Idiosyncratic reaction: acute toxic effect on brain, including abnormal movements and psychotic behavior—case reports.

Optic or peripheral neuritis (see Glossary)—case reports.

Seizures or catatonia—case reports.

Movement changes (akinesia)—case report.

Decreased thyroid gland function—possible.

May increase risk for blood vessel problems in people with diabetes or cause low blood platelets—case reports.

Carpal tunnel syndrome, peripheral neuropathy—case reports.

▷ **Possible Effects on Sexual Function:** Decreased libido and/or impaired erection in users taking recommended doses of 125 to 500 mg daily—case reports.

Adverse Effects That May Mimic Natural Diseases or Disorders

Liver reaction may suggest viral hepatitis.

Brain toxicity may suggest spontaneous psychosis.

Possible Effects on Laboratory Tests

Blood cholesterol level: increased.

INR (prothrombin time): increased (taken concurrently with warfarin).

Liver function tests: liver enzymes increased (ALT/GPT, AST/GOT, and alkaline phosphatase), increased bilirubin.

CAUTION

1. No one intoxicated with alcohol should take this drug.
2. Patients must be fully informed about purpose and actions of this drug **before** treatment is started.
3. Long-term use requires exam for reduced thyroid function.
4. Carry a personal identification card noting you are taking this drug.
5. Many liquid herbal medicines contain alcohol—do not combine.

Precautions for Use

By Infants and Children: Safety and effectiveness for those under 12 years of age not established.

By Those Over 60 Years of Age: Watch for excessive sedation when the drug is started. **Do not** perform an "alcohol trial" to see the effects of this drug.

▷ **Advisability of Use During Pregnancy**

Pregnancy Category: C. See Pregnancy Risk Categories at the back of this book.

Animal Studies: No defects reported in rats and hamsters.

Human Studies: Two reports indicate that four of eight fetuses exposed had serious birth defects. Adequate studies of pregnant women are not available.

Avoid this drug completely if possible.

Advisability of Use If Breast-Feeding

Presence of this drug in breast milk: Unknown.

Talk with your doctor, as this is a question of benefit of the drug versus the risk of adverse effects to the fetus.

Habit-Forming Potential: None.

Effects of Overdose: Marked lethargy, impaired memory, altered behavior, confusion, unsteadiness, weakness, stomach pain, nausea, vomiting, diarrhea.

Possible Effects of Long-Term Use: Decreased function of thyroid gland.

Suggested Periodic Examinations While Taking This Drug (at physician's discretion)

Visual acuity.

Liver function tests.

Thyroid function tests.

▷ **While Taking This Drug, Observe the Following**

Foods: Avoid all foods prepared with alcohol, including sauces, marinades, vinegars, desserts, etc. Ask when dining out about use of alcohol in cooking food. Increased cholesterol after 3–6 weeks of treatment is possible.

Taking 50 mg per day of pyridoxine seems to stop this side effect. Talk to
your doctor.

Herbal Medicines or Minerals: Many liquid herbal medicines such as ginseng
and echinacea contain alcohol. DO NOT combine them with disulfiram.
Using St. John's wort, guarana, ma huang, ephedrine-like compounds, or
kola while trying to stop drinking may worsen jitteriness and anxiety.

Beverages: Avoid all punches, fruit drinks, etc., that may contain alcohol. This
drug may be taken with milk.

▷ *Alcohol:* ***Avoid completely in all forms*** while taking this drug and for 14 days
after the last dose. Disulfiram and alcohol—even in small amounts—
produces the disulfiram (Antabuse) reaction. This starts 5 to 10 minutes
after alcohol: intense flushing, severe headache, shortness of breath, chest
pains, nausea, repeated vomiting, sweating, and weakness. If large amounts
of alcohol, reaction may progress to blurred vision, vertigo, confusion,
severely low blood pressure, and loss of consciousness. May go on to convulsions and death. Reaction may last from 30 minutes to hours, depending
upon amount of alcohol and disulfiram.

Tobacco Smoking: No interactions expected. I advise everyone to quit smoking.

Marijuana Smoking: Possible increase in drowsiness or lethargy and one case
report of hypomania.

▷ *Other Drugs*

Disulfiram may ***increase*** the effects of
- chlordiazepoxide (Librium) and diazepam (Valium) and cause oversedation. Other benzodiazepines such as alprazolam, clonazepam, clorazepate,
  flurazepam, halazepam, prazepam, or triazolam may also be subject to
  this interaction.
- oral anticoagulants (warfarin, etc.) and increase the risk of bleeding; dose
  adjustments may be necessary.
- paraldehyde and cause excessive depression of brain function.
- phenytoin (Dilantin) or fosphenytoin (Cerebyx) and cause toxicity; dose
  must be decreased.

Disulfiram may ***decrease*** the effects of
- perphenazine (Trilafon, etc.).

Disulfiram ***taken concurrently*** with
- amprenavir (Agenerase) has propylene glycol in the oral solution. Combined use with disulfiram can lead to toxicity. Do not combine.
- bacampicillin (Spectrobid) can theoretically cause a disulfiram reaction,
  but no cases have been reported.
- cisplatin (Platinol) can increase risk of toxicity of cisplatin.
- cyclosporine (Sandimmune) may result in a disulfiram reaction, as there is
  alcohol in the intravenous and oral forms of cyclosporine.
- isoniazid (INH, etc.) may cause acute mental problems and incoordination.
- metronidazole (Flagyl) may cause acute mental and behavioral disturbances, making it necessary to stop treatment.
- omeprazole (Prilosec) and possibly esomeprazole (Nexium) may result in
  increased disulfiram levels and toxicity.
- over-the-counter (OTC) cough syrups, tonics, etc., containing alcohol may
  cause a disulfiram (Antabuse) reaction; avoid concurrent use (see Over-
  the-Counter Drugs in Glossary).
- paraldehyde may result in a disulfiram reaction.
- theophylline (Theo-Dur, others) can lead to theophylline toxicity because
  the metabolism of theophylline is decreased.

- tranylcypromine (Parnate) can increase risk of hallucinations, disorientation, and agitation. Monitor the patient closely if these two medicines must be used together.
- warfarin will result in an increased risk of bleeding. More frequent INR testing is recommended.

The following drugs may *increase* the effects of disulfiram:

- amitriptyline (Elavil) and perhaps other tricyclic antidepressants may enhance the disulfiram-alcohol interaction; avoid concurrent use of these drugs.

▷ *Driving, Hazardous Activities:* This drug may cause drowsiness or dizziness. Limit activities as necessary.

Aviation Note: Alcoholism *is a disqualification* for piloting. Consult a designated Aviation Medical Examiner.

Exposure to Sun: No restrictions.

Exposure to Environmental Chemicals: Thiram, a pesticide, and carbon disulfide, a pesticide and industrial solvent, can have additive toxic effects. Watch for toxic effects on the brain and nervous system.

Discontinuation: This medicine is only part of your program. Do not stop it unless you have talked with your doctor. Even if it is stopped, no alcohol should be ingested for 14 days.

DOFETILIDE (Doh FET ill eyed)

Introduced: 1999 **Class:** Antiarrhythmic **Prescription:** USA: Yes **Controlled Drug:** USA: No; Canada: No **Available as Generic:** USA: No; Canada: No

Brand Name: Tikosyn

Author's Note: Information on this medicine will be broadened in subsequent editions as clinical use and medication benefits warrant.

DORNASE ALPHA (Door nase AL fa)

Introduced: 1994 **Class:** Anti-cystic-fibrosis agent **Prescription:** USA: Yes **Controlled Drug:** USA: No; Canada: No **Available as Generic:** USA: No; Canada: No

Brand Name: Pulmozyme

BENEFITS versus RISKS	
Possible Benefits	*Possible Risks*
DECREASED MUCUS VISCOSITY	Hoarseness
IMPROVED LUNG FUNCTION	Antibodies to DNA
DECREASED OCCURRENCE OF RESPIRATORY INFECTIONS	Facial swelling (edema)
DECREASED NUMBER OF HOSPITALIZATIONS	

▷ **Principal Uses**

As a Single Drug Product: Uses currently included in FDA-approved labeling: Eases symptoms of cystic fibrosis (used with standard therapies).

Other (unlabeled) generally accepted uses: None at present.

How This Drug Works: Large amounts of DNA are found in sputum of people with cystic fibrosis, making it thicker than normal. Dornase breaks the DNA down, making the sputum easier to remove. Other undiscovered mechanisms may also account for its benefits.

Available Dosage Forms and Strengths
Solution — 2.5-ml ampules of 1.0 mg/ml dornase alpha (2.5 mg)

▷ **Recommended Dosage Ranges** (Actual dose and schedule must be determined for each patient individually.)
Infants and Children: Now approved for patients 3 months to less than 5 years of age. Rashes, cough, and runny nose (rhinitis) may happen at a higher rate in this population than in older patients.
5 to 60 Years of Age: One 2.5-mg dose administered by one of the tested nebulizers each day. Some selected patients (FVC greater than 85%) may benefit from twice-daily dosing.
Over 60 Years of Age: Same as 5 to 60 years of age.

Conditions Requiring Dosing Adjustments
Liver Function: Not defined.
Kidney Function: Not defined.

▷ **Dosing Instructions:** Solution must be refrigerated and protected from strong light. The drug should not be used if it is cloudy or discolored. Do **not** mix dornase with other medicines. Clinical trials have only been conducted with the Hudson T Up-Draft 2, Marquest Acorn II and Pulmo-Aide compressor. The reusable PARI LC Jet nebulizer and PARI PRONEB compressor were also tested. Do not use with other equipment. If you forget a dose, administer the missed dose as soon as you remember it, unless it is almost time for your next dose—if that is the case, simply administer the next scheduled dose. DO NOT double doses.

Usual Duration of Use: Regular use for up to 8 days may be needed in cystic fibrosis. Long-term use (up to 12 months has been studied) requires periodic physician evaluation.

Typical Treatment Goals and Measurements (Outcomes and Markers)
Cystic fibrosis: Lung (pulmonary) function tests (FEV1 or FEC) are used to measure the success of treatment. Improvements in these tests may be seen in as little as 3 days. Patient clinical signs and symptoms of cystic fibrosis (such as easing of breathing difficulty or dyspnea and clearing of sputum) may also be a measure of treatment results. If the usual benefit is not realized, call your doctor.

Possible Advantages of This Drug
Reduction in number of infections, use of antibiotics and hospitalizations with minimal side effects.

▷ **This Drug Should Not Be Taken If**
• you have had an allergic reaction to it.
• you have an allergy to Chinese hamster ovary cells.

▷ **Inform Your Physician Before Taking This Drug If**
• you had a rash after the last dose was taken.
• you are uncertain how to use the nebulizer or compressor.
• you are uncertain how much to take or how often to take it.

Possible Side Effects (natural, expected, and unavoidable drug actions)
Hoarseness—may be frequent.

▷ **Possible Adverse Effects** (unusual, unexpected, and infrequent reactions)
   If any of the following develop, consult your physician promptly for guidance.
   Mild Adverse Effects
      Allergic reactions: rash or itching—infrequent to frequent (may be more likely in those 3 months to less than 5 years old).
      Cough or runny nose—infrequent (may be more likely in those 3 months to less than 5 years old).
      Mild pharyngitis or laryngitis—frequent.
      Conjunctivitis—infrequent.
      Chest pain—has been reported.
      Facial swelling—rare.
   Serious Adverse Effects
      Allergic reactions: none defined at present.
      Antibodies to DNA (2–4%).
▷ **Possible Effects on Sexual Function:** None reported.
Possible Delayed Adverse Effects: None reported.
Possible Effects on Laboratory Tests
   Antibodies to DNA.
CAUTION
   1. This drug should only be used with one of the studied nebulizers and compressors.
   2. Do not use the drug if it is cloudy or discolored.
Precautions for Use
   By Infants and Children: Rash, cough, and runny nose may be more likely in those 3 months to 5 years old.
   By Those Over 60 Years of Age: No changes or precautions.
▷ **Advisability of Use During Pregnancy**
   Pregnancy Category: B. See Pregnancy Risk Categories at the back of this book.
   Animal Studies: Studies in rats and rabbits at up to 600 times the usual human dose have not revealed any harm to the fetus.
   Human Studies: Adequate studies of pregnant women are not available.
      Ask your doctor for guidance.
Advisability of Use If Breast-Feeding
   Presence of this drug in breast milk: Unknown.
   Avoid drug or refrain from nursing.
Habit-Forming Potential: None.
Effects of Overdose: Single doses of up to 180 times the usual human dose in rats and monkeys have been well tolerated.
Possible Effects of Long-Term Use: Not defined.
Suggested Periodic Examinations While Taking This Drug (at physician's discretion)
Periodic pulmonary function tests. Improved clearing of sputum.
▷ **While Taking This Drug, Observe the Following**
   Foods: No restrictions.
   Herbal Medicines or Minerals: Some herbals such as anise seed and fennel oil have German commission E monograph indications for catarrh or upper respiratory tract difficulties, but since no studies have been performed in combination with this medicine, they cannot be recommended.
   Nutritional Support: Continued enzyme and nutritional support is still needed.
   Beverages: No specific restrictions.

▷ *Alcohol:* Follow your doctor's advice relative to alcohol use.

Tobacco Smoking: No interaction, but smoking irritates airways. I advise everyone to quit smoking.

▷ *Other Drugs*

Clinical studies have revealed that dornase is compatible with medicines typically used to manage cystic fibrosis. Specific drug interactions are not documented at present.

▷ *Driving, Hazardous Activities:* Specific limitations because of drug effects are not defined at present.

Aviation Note: The use of this drug **may be a disqualification** for piloting. Consult a designated Aviation Medical Examiner.

Exposure to Sun: No restrictions.

Discontinuation: This drug's benefits stop soon after its regular use is stopped. It must be continued indefinitely to maintain benefit.

Special Storage Instructions: This drug should be stored at 36–46 degrees F. and should be protected from light. Unused ampules should be stored in their protective pouch in the refrigerator.

DOXAZOSIN (dox AY zoh sin)

Introduced: 1986 **Class:** Antihypertensive **Prescription:** USA: Yes **Controlled Drug:** USA: No **Available as Generic:** Yes

Brand Names: ❧Apo-Doxazosin, Cardura, Cardura-1, Doxaloc, ❧Gen-Doxazosin, ❧Med-Doxazosin

Author's Note: Data from the ALLHAT trial found that alpha blockers are not drugs of first choice in high blood pressure. A recent FDA panel decided not to change the product label. Information in this profile has been truncated to make room for more widely used medicines.

DOXEPIN (DOX e pin)

Introduced: 1969 **Class:** Antidepressant **Prescription:** USA: Yes **Controlled Drug:** USA: No; Canada: No **Available as Generic:** USA: Yes; Canada: No

Brand Names: Adapin, Sinequan, ❧Triadapin, Zonalon

BENEFITS versus RISKS	
Possible Benefits	*Possible Risks*
EFFECTIVE RELIEF OF ENDOGENOUS DEPRESSION	ADVERSE BEHAVIORAL EFFECTS: Confusion, disorientation, hallucinations, delusions
EFFECTIVE RELIEF OF ANXIETY AND NERVOUS TENSION	CONVERSION OF DEPRESSION TO MANIA in manic-depressive (bipolar) disorders
EFFECTIVE RELIEF OF SOME KINDS OF ITCHING (TOPICAL FORM)	Aggravation of schizophrenia and paranoia
Possibly beneficial in other depressive disorders	Rare blood cell disorders
	Rare liver toxicity
	Low blood pressure on standing

Author's Note: Information in this profile has been truncated to make room for more widely used medicines.

EFAVIRENZ (e FAV i rinz)

Introduced: 1998 **Class:** Non-nucleoside reverse transcriptase inhibitor, antiretroviral, antiviral **Prescription:** USA: Yes **Controlled Drug:** USA: No; Canada: No **Available as Generic:** USA: No; Canada: No

Brand Name: Sustiva

BENEFITS versus RISKS	
Possible Benefits	*Possible Risks*
EFFECTIVE COMBINATION TREATMENT OF HIV IS PART OF THE STRONGLY RECOMMENDED MEDICINES IN THE NEW NIAID GUIDELINES May be the most effective non-nucleoside reverse transcriptase inhibitor currently available when used in combination with other antiretrovirals. Convenient once-daily dosing schedule decreases pill burden and will improve adherence.	SIGNIFICANT CENTRAL NERVOUS SYSTEM EFFECTS Rash

Author's Note: Information in this profile will be broadened or shortened as more information and outcomes become available.

ENALAPRIL (e NAL a pril)

Class: Antihypertensive, ACE inhibitor

Please see the angiotensin converting enzyme (ACE) inhibitor family profile.

ENFUVIRTIDE (En FOO vur tyde)

Introduced: 2003 **Class:** Fusion inhibitor, antiretroviral, antiviral **Prescription:** USA: Yes **Controlled Drug:** USA: No; Canada: No **Available as Generic:** USA: No; Canada: No

Brand Name: Fuzeon

Author's Note: This new HIV treatment is the first in a class of medicines that keeps the virus out of immune system cells. Information on this drug will be broadened as more information becomes available.

EPINEPHRINE (ep ih NEF rin)

Other Name: Adrenaline **Introduced:** 1900 **Class:** Antiasthmatic, antiglaucoma, decongestant **Prescription:** USA: Varies **Controlled Drug:** USA: No; Canada: No **Available as Generic:** USA: Yes; Canada: No

Brand Names: Adrenalin, Adreno-Mist, Ana-Kit, Asthmahaler, Asthmanephrine, Bronkaid Mist, ✤Bronkaid Mistometer, ✤Citanest Forte, Duranest [CD], ✤Dysne-Inhal, Epifrin, E-Pilo Preparations [CD], Epinal Ophthalmic, EpiPen, Epitrate, Marcaine, Medihaler-Epi Preparations, Micronephrine, Norocaine, Octocaine, P1E1, P2E1, P3E1, P4E1, P6E1, Primatene Mist, Propine Ophthalmic, Sensorcaine, Sus-Phrine, Thalfed [CD], Therex [CD], ✤Ultracaine, Vaponefrin, Xylocaine

---

BENEFITS versus RISKS

Possible Benefits	*Possible Risks*
EFFECTIVE RELIEF OF SEVERE ALLERGIC (ANAPHYLACTIC) REACTIONS	Significant increase in blood pressure (in sensitive people)
TEMPORARY RELIEF OF ACUTE BRONCHIAL ASTHMA	Idiosyncratic reaction: Pulmonary edema (fluid formation in lungs)
Reduction of internal eye pressure (treatment of glaucoma)	Heart rhythm disorders (in sensitive people)
Relief of allergic congestion of the nose and sinuses	

▷ **Principal Uses**

As a Single Drug Product: Uses currently included in FDA-approved labeling: (1) Inhalation to relieve acute attacks of bronchial asthma; (2) as a decongestant for symptomatic relief of allergic nasal congestion and as eyedrops in the management of glaucoma; (3) treats anaphylactic shock; (4) emergency treatment of abnormal heart rhythms (such as ventricular fibrillation) and in cardiopulmonary resuscitation; (5) increases beneficial effects of topical anesthetics.

Other (unlabeled) generally accepted uses: (1) Septic shock; (2) wheezing in infants; (3) croup; (4) can have a role in easing painful erections (priapism); (5) may be used in cataract surgery.

How This Drug Works: By stimulating some nerve (sympathetic) terminals, this drug:

- contracts blood vessel walls, raising blood pressure.
- inhibits histamine release into skin and internal organs.
- dilates constricted bronchial tubes, increasing the size of the airways and improving the ability to breathe.
- decreases fluid formation in the eye, increases its outflow and reduces internal eye pressure.
- decreases blood flow in the nose, shrinking swelling (decongestion) and expanding nasal airways.

Available Dosage Forms and Strengths

Aerosol — 0.2, 0.27, and 0.3 mg per spray
Eyedrops — 0.1%, 0.25%, 0.5%, 1%, 2%
Injection — 0.01, 0.1, 1, and 5 mg/ml

Nose drops — 0.1%
Solution for nebulizer — 1%, 1.25%, 2.25%

▷ **Usual Adult Dosage Ranges**

Aerosols: One inhalation, repeated in 1 to 2 minutes if needed; wait 4 hours before next inhalation.

Eyedrops: One drop every 12 hours. Dose may vary with product; follow printed instructions and label directions.

Note: Actual dose and schedule must be determined for each patient individually.

Conditions Requiring Dosing Adjustments

Liver Function: Dose reduction is not needed in liver compromise.

Kidney Function: Dose adjustment is not defined in kidney compromise.

Diabetes: People with diabetes benefit more from standard-dose epinephrine when they are undergoing cardiopulmonary resuscitation (CPR) than they do from high dose.

▷ **Dosing Instructions:** Aerosols and inhalation solutions: Do not use Adrenalin solutions if they are discolored (possibly pink to brown) or if they contain particles (precipitates). For inhalers: After first inhalation, wait 1 to 2 minutes to see if a second inhalation is needed. If relief does not occur within 20 minutes of use, stop this drug and seek medical attention **promptly. Avoid prolonged and excessive use.** Eyedrops: Place one drop of the 0.25% to 2.0 % solution in the eye. During instillation of drops and for 2 minutes after, press finger against the tear sac (inner corner of eye) to prevent rapid absorption of drug into body. If you forget a dose: take (instill) the missed dose as soon as you remember it, unless it is nearly time for your next dose— then simply skip the missed dose and instill the next dose right on schedule.

Usual Duration of Use: According to individual needs. Long-term use requires physician supervision.

Typical Treatment Goals and Measurements (Outcomes and Markers)

Asthma: Short-acting sympathomimetics like epinephrine are used to prevent or treat reversible spasms of the bronchial tubes. The peak effect happens 1 to 2 hours after dosing. Goals are to return bronchial status to more acceptable status (relief of respiratory distress) FEV1 is useful. If the usual benefit to your breathing is not realized, call your doctor right away.

▷ **This Drug Should Not Be Taken If**

- you have had an allergic reaction to it previously.
- you have narrow-angle glaucoma.
- you are in shock.
- you have organic brain damage.
- you are in labor—it may delay the second stage of labor.
- you are to undergo general anesthesia with cyclopropane or halogenated hydrocarbons.
- your heart is dilated and you have a coronary deficiency.
- you have experienced a recent stroke or heart attack.

▷ **Inform Your Physician Before Taking This Drug If**

- you have any degree of high blood pressure.
- you have any form of heart disease, especially coronary heart disease (with or without angina) or a heart rhythm disorder.
- you have diabetes or overactive thyroid function (hyperthyroidism).
- you have a history of stroke.
- you have ongoing (chronic lung disease).

- you take monoamine oxidase (MAO) type A inhibitors, phenothiazines (see Drug Classes), digitalis preparations or quinidine.

Possible Side Effects (natural, expected, and unavoidable drug actions)

In some people—restlessness, anxiety, headache, tremor, palpitation, cold hands and feet, dryness of mouth and throat (with use of aerosol). Temporary increase in blood platelets. Discoloration of soft contact lenses—possible.

▷ **Possible Adverse Effects** (unusual, unexpected, and infrequent reactions)

If any of the following develop, consult your physician promptly for guidance.

Mild Adverse Effects

Allergic reactions: skin rash; eyedrops may cause redness, swelling, and itching of the eyelids.

Weakness, dizziness, pallor.

Serious Adverse Effects

Idiosyncratic reaction: sudden development of excessive fluid in the lungs (pulmonary edema).

Gas gangrene after injection into a muscle (intramuscular)—possible.

In predisposed people—excessive rise in blood pressure with risk of stroke (cerebral hemorrhage).

Rapid heart rate and arrhythmias and heart attack—case reports.

Passing out (syncope)—possible.

Seizures or porphyria—rare.

Pulmonary edema—case reports.

Constriction of the bowel (mesenteric) blood vessels leading to necrosis—possible.

Pigmentation of the eye—case reports.

Kidney toxicity—rare.

▷ **Possible Effects on Sexual Function:** May ease painful and abnormally prolonged erections (priapism).

Possible Effects on Laboratory Tests

Complete blood counts: red cells and white cells increased; eosinophils decreased.

Blood glucose level: increased.

Urine sugar tests: false low or negative results with Clinistix; true positive with Benedict's or Fehling's solution.

Acidosis—possible.

Blood platelets: temporarily increased.

CAUTION

1. Medication failure can result from frequent repeat use at short intervals. If this develops, avoid use for 12 hours, and a normal response should return.

2. Excessive use of aerosol preparations in asthmatics has been associated with sudden death.

3. May cause significant irritability of nerve pathways (conduction system) and heart muscle, predisposing to serious heart rhythm disorders. Talk with your doctor about this.

4. This drug can increase blood sugar level. If you have diabetes, test for sugar often to detect significant changes.

5. If this drug no longer works for you and you substitute isoproterenol (Isuprel), allow 4 hours between drugs.

6. Promptly throw this drug away if a pinkish-red to brown coloration or cloudiness (precipitation) occurs.

Precautions for Use

By Infants and Children: Use cautiously in small doses until tolerance is determined. Watch for weakness, light-headedness or fainting.

By Those Over 60 Years of Age: Small doses are prudent. Watch for nervousness, headache, tremor, rapid heart rate. If you have hardening of the arteries (arteriosclerosis), heart disease, high blood pressure, Parkinson's disease, or prostatism (see Glossary), this drug may aggravate your disorder. Ask your doctor for help.

▷ **Advisability of Use During Pregnancy**

Pregnancy Category: C. See Pregnancy Risk Categories at the back of this book.

Animal Studies: Birth defects reported in rats.

Human Studies: Adequate studies of pregnant women are not available.

This drug can cause significant reduction of oxygen supply to the fetus. Use it only if clearly needed and in small, infrequent doses. Avoid during the first 3 months and during labor and delivery.

Advisability of Use If Breast-Feeding

Presence of this drug in breast milk: Yes.

Avoid drug or refrain from nursing.

Habit-Forming Potential: Tolerance to this drug (see Glossary) can develop with frequent use, but dependence does not occur.

Effects of Overdose: Nervousness, throbbing headache, dizziness, tremor, palpitation, disturbance of heart rhythm, difficult breathing, abdominal pain, vomiting of blood.

Possible Effects of Long-Term Use: "Epinephrine fastness": loss of ability to respond to this drug's bronchodilator effect. With long-term treatment of glaucoma: pigment deposits on eyeballs and eyelids, possible damage to retina, impaired vision, blockage of tear ducts.

Suggested Periodic Examinations While Taking This Drug (at physician's discretion)

Blood pressure measurements.

Blood or urine sugar measurements in diabetics.

Vision testing and measurement of internal eye pressure in glaucoma.

▷ **While Taking This Drug, Observe the Following**

Foods: No restrictions, except those that cause you to have an asthma attack.

Herbal Medicines or Minerals: Using St. John's wort, ma huang, guarana, paullinia, ephedrine-like compounds, or kola while taking this medicine may result in unacceptable central nervous system stimulation. Fir or pine needle oil should NOT be used by asthmatics. Ephedra alone does carry a German Commission E monograph indication for asthma treatment, but combining it with this medicine would be like using two medicines from the same family and does not make sense. If you are allergic to plants in the Asteraceae family (aster, chrysanthemum, daisy, or ragweed), you may also be allergic to echinacea, chamomile, feverfew, and St. John's wort. Talk to your doctor BEFORE combining herbal meds with epinephrine.

Beverages: No restrictions.

▷ *Alcohol:* Alcoholic beverages can increase the urinary excretion of this drug.

Tobacco Smoking: No interactions expected. I advise everyone to quit smoking.

▷ *Other Drugs*

Epinephrine *taken concurrently* with

• some beta-blockers (carvedilol, carteolol, nadolol, propranolol) may cause increased blood pressure response to epinephrine and decreased heart rate and resistance to epinephrine if it is used in anaphylaxis.

- chlorpromazine (Thorazine) or other phenothiazines (see Drug Classes) may cause decreased blood pressure and increased heart rate.
- dihydroergotamine (D.H.E.) may cause extreme increases in blood pressure.
- furazolidone (Furoxone) may cause increased blood pressure.
- guanethidine (Esimil, Ismelin) may cause increased blood pressure.
- halothane may cause abnormal heartbeats (ventricular arrhythmia).
- monoamine oxidase (MAO) inhibitors (see Drug Classes) may lead to large and undesirable increases in blood pressure.
- pilocarpine (Ocusert) may cause increased myopia.
- tricyclic antidepressants (amitriptyline, etc.) may cause increased blood pressure and heart rhythm disturbances.
- zotepine (Nipolept) may lead to low blood pressure and reversal of epinephrine benefits.

▷ *Driving, Hazardous Activities:* This drug may cause dizziness or nervousness. Limit activities as necessary.

Aviation Note: The use of this drug *may be a disqualification* for piloting. Consult a designated Aviation Medical Examiner.

Exposure to Sun: No restrictions.

Heavy Exercise or Exertion: No interactions expected, but exercise can induce asthma in sensitive individuals.

Occurrence of Unrelated Illness: Use caution in severe burns. This drug can increase drainage from burned tissue and cause serious loss of tissue fluids and blood proteins.

Special Storage Instructions: Protect drug from exposure to air, light, and heat. Keep in a cool place, preferably in the refrigerator.

Discontinuation: If this drug fails after an adequate trial, stop using it and call your doctor. It is dangerous to increase the dose or frequency.

ERGOTAMINE (er GOT a meen)

Introduced: 1926 **Class:** Antimigraine, ergot derivative **Prescription:** USA: Yes **Controlled Drug:** USA: No; Canada: No **Available as Generic:** Yes

Brand Names: Bellamine [CD], Bellaspas [CD], ✤Bellergal [CD], Bellergal-S [CD], ✤Bellergal Spacetabs [CD], Cafergot [CD], Cafergot P-B [CD], Cafetrate [CD], Drummergal [CD], Duragal-S [CD], Ercaf [CD], Ergobel [CD], Ergocaf [CD], ✤Ergodryl [CD], Ergomar, Ergostat, Genergen, ✤Gravergol [CD], ✤Gynergen, Medihaler Ergotamine, ✤Megral [CD], Oxoid, Phenerbrel-S [CD], Spastrin [CD], Wigraine [CD], ✤Wigraine [CD], Wigrettes

---

BENEFITS versus RISKS

Possible Benefits	*Possible Risks*
PREVENTION AND RELIEF OF CLUSTER HEADACHES	GANGRENE OF THE FINGERS, TOES, OR INTESTINE
RELIEF OF MIGRAINE HEADACHE	AGGRAVATION OF CORONARY ARTERY DISEASE (ANGINA)
	INCREASED RISK OF ABORTION (if used during pregnancy)

▷ **Principal Uses**

    As a Single Drug Product: Uses currently included in FDA-approved labeling: Treats vascular headaches, especially migraine and "cluster" headaches. Often effective in stopping headache if taken in the first hour following start of pain. Short-term basis use is a valid attempt to prevent or abort "cluster" headaches. The inhalation form provides rapid onset of action.

    Other (unlabeled) generally accepted uses: None at present.

    As a Combination Drug Product [CD]: Combined with caffeine to enhance its absorption. This makes a smaller dose of ergotamine effective and reduces risk of adverse effects with repeated use. This drug is also combined with belladonna (atropine) and barbiturates to help premenstrual tension and the menopausal syndrome—nervousness, nausea, hot flushes, and sweating.

How This Drug Works: It constricts blood vessel walls in the head, preventing or relieving dilation that causes pain of migrainelike headaches.

Available Dosage Forms and Strengths

    Aerosol — 9 mg/ml (0.36 mg/inhalation)

    Nasal inhaler (Canada) — 9 mg/ml (360 mcg/dose)

    Suppositories — 2 mg (in combination with 100 mg of caffeine)

    Tablets, sublingual — 2 mg

▷ **Usual Adult Dosage Ranges:** *Inhalation:* One spray (0.36 mg) when headache starts; repeat 1 spray after 30 to 60 minutes as needed for relief, up to a maximum of 6 sprays every 24 hours. Do not exceed 15 sprays (5.4 mg) per week. *Oral dose:* 1–2 mg immediately, then 1–2 mg every 30–60 minutes. Dosing up to 6 mg in 24 hours or 10 mg per week. *Sublingual tablets:* Dissolve 2 mg under tongue at the start of headache; repeat 2 mg in 30 minutes as needed, up to a maximum of 6 mg per day. Do not exceed 6 mg every 24 hours or 10 mg/week.

    Note: Actual dose and schedule must be determined for each patient individually.

Conditions Requiring Dosing Adjustments

    Liver Function: Should be used with caution by patients with liver compromise.

    Kidney Function: This drug is a rare cause of acute renal failure and should be used with caution by patients with compromised kidneys.

▷ **Dosing Instructions:** Follow written instructions and doses **carefully.** The regular tablets (combination drug) may be crushed; sustained-release tablets should be taken whole (not crushed). Sublingual tablets should be dissolved under the tongue, not swallowed. If you forget a dose: Call your doctor as this medicine gets the best results if you take it at the first sign of migraine.

Usual Duration of Use: Regular use for several headache episodes often needed to see effectiveness in aborting or relieving vascular headache. Do not exceed recommended schedules. If headaches are not controlled after several trials of maximal doses, ask your doctor about other treatments. There are also a variety of medicines to prevent (prophylactic use) for migraines.

Typical Treatment Goals and Measurements (Outcomes and Markers)

    Pain: Most clinicians treating pain use a device called an algometer to check your pain. This looks like a small ruler, but lets the clinician better understand your pain. The goals of treatment then relate to where the level of pain started (for example, a rating of 7 on a 0 to 10 scale) and what the cause of the pain was. Pain medicines may also be used together (in combination) in order to get the best result or outcome. Specific results to migraine relate to stopping (aborting) an attack or easing the severity of an attack. Once again, the role of prophylactic medicines is clear in helping some patients avoid attacks altogether.

▷ **This Drug Should Not Be Taken If**
- you have had an allergic reaction to any dose form.
- you are pregnant or are breast-feeding.
- you have a severe infection (sepsis).
- you have any of the following conditions:
  angina pectoris (coronary artery disease)
  Buerger's disease
  hardening of the arteries (arteriosclerosis)
  high blood pressure (severe hypertension)
  ischemic heart disease or angina
  stroke
  peptic ulcer
  malnutrition
  kidney disease or impaired kidney function
  liver disease or impaired liver function
  Raynaud's phenomenon
  thrombophlebitis
  glaucoma

▷ **Inform Your Physician Before Taking This Drug If**
- you are allergic or overly sensitive to any ergot preparation.
- you have a prolonged aura and migraines (aura may be further prolonged).
- you are planning to have a face-lift (rhytidectomy) or other plastic surgery. This drug may cause serious skin flap problems.

Possible Side Effects (natural, expected, and unavoidable drug actions)
Usually infrequent and mild with recommended doses.
Some people may have cold hands and feet, with mild numbness and tingling.

▷ **Possible Adverse Effects** (unusual, unexpected, and infrequent reactions)
If any of the following develop, consult your physician promptly for guidance.
Mild Adverse Effects
Allergic reactions: localized swellings (angioedema), itching—case reports.
Headache, drowsiness, dizziness, confusion—possible.
Chest pain, abdominal pain, numbness and tingling of fingers and toes, muscle pains in arms or legs—infrequent.
Nausea, vomiting, diarrhea—possible.
Serious Adverse Effects
Gangrene of the extremities: coldness; numbness; pain; dark discoloration; eventual loss of fingers, toes, or feet—possible.
Gangrene of the intestine: severe abdominal pain and swelling; emergency surgery required—case reports.
Retroperitoneal fibrosis—case reports.
Fibrous changes in the lung (pleuropulmonary fibrosis)—case reports.
Pain syndromes (reflex sympathetic dystrophy)—possible.
Insufficient blood flow to the heart (myocardial ischemia) or arrhythmias—case reports.
Clots in a large artery (superior mesenteric)—case reports.
Decreased heart circulation (myocardial ischemia)—case reports and dangerous in ischemic or occult/hidden heart disease.

Fibrous changes in the heart (myocardial fibrosis) or porphyria—case reports.

Lesions of the rectum or anus (anorectal lesions)—case reports.

Kidney failure—case reports.

▷ **Possible Effects on Sexual Function:** None reported.

Natural Diseases or Disorders That May Be Activated by This Drug
Angina pectoris (coronary artery insufficiency), Buerger's disease, Pheochromocytoma (hypertensive crisis), Raynaud's phenomenon.

Possible Effects on Laboratory Tests: None reported.

CAUTION
1. Excessive use of this drug can actually provoke migraines and increase their frequency.
2. Do not exceed a total dose of 6 mg daily or 10 mg/week of the oral form.
3. Individual drug sensitivity varies greatly. Some may have early toxic effects while taking recommended doses. Promptly report numbness in fingers or toes, muscle cramping or chest pain.

Precautions for Use
By Infants and Children: Safety and effectiveness for those under 12 years of age are not established.
By Those Over 60 Years of Age: Natural circulation changes may make you more susceptible to adverse effects of this drug. See the preceding list of disorders that are contraindications for the use of this drug.

▷ **Advisability of Use During Pregnancy**
Pregnancy Category: X. See Pregnancy Risk Categories at the back of this book.
Animal Studies: Fetal deaths reported due to this drug.
Human Studies: Information from studies of pregnant women indicates that this drug can cause abortion.
This drug should be avoided during the entire pregnancy.

Advisability of Use If Breast-Feeding
Presence of this drug in breast milk: Yes.
Avoid drug or refrain from nursing. May also suppress prolactin secretion.

Habit-Forming Potential: Functional dependence is possible with a withdrawal syndrome (nausea, vomiting and headache) reported. This has been treated with naproxen (500 mg twice a day).

Effects of Overdose: "Ergotism": cold skin, severe muscle pain, tingling or burning pain in hands and feet, loss of blood supply to extremities resulting in tissue death (gangrene) in fingers and toes. Acute ergot poisoning: nausea, vomiting, diarrhea, cold skin, numbness of extremities, confusion, seizures, coma.

Possible Effects of Long-Term Use: A form of functional dependence (see Glossary) may develop, resulting in withdrawal headaches if the drug is stopped. Tolerance to beneficial effects.

Suggested Periodic Examinations While Taking This Drug (at physician's discretion)
Evaluation of circulation (blood flow) to the extremities.
Observation for emergence of tolerance. Headache diaries can be very helpful in identifying triggers.

▷ **While Taking This Drug, Observe the Following**
Foods: No interactions expected. Avoid all foods to which you are allergic; some migraine headaches are due to food allergies. There are also often "trigger" foods. Keep a diary and try to identify, then avoid these.

Herbal Medicines or Minerals: Using ma huang or ephedrine-like compounds (ephedra) may result in additive and undesirable vasoconstriction. If you are allergic to plants in the Asteraceae family (aster, chrysanthemum, daisy, or ragweed), you may also be allergic to echinacea, chamomile, feverfew, and St. John's wort. St. John's wort can cause changes in the liver enzymes that help remove this medicine—talk to your doctor before combining any herbal medicine or mineral with ergotamine.

Beverages: No restrictions.

▷ *Alcohol:* Best avoided; alcohol can intensify vascular headache.

Tobacco Smoking: Best avoided; nicotine can further reduce the restricted blood flow produced by this drug.

Marijuana Smoking: Best avoided; additive effects can increase the coldness of hands and feet.

▷ *Other Drugs*

Ergotamine may ***decrease*** the effects of
* nitroglycerin and reduce its effectiveness in preventing or relieving angina pain.

The following drugs may ***increase*** the effects of ergotamine:
* amprenavir (Agenerase), indinavir (Crixivan), nelfinavir (Viracept), ritonavir (Norvir), saquinavir (Fortovase), and efavirenz (Sustiva) are removed by the same enzymes that remove ergotamine. Ritonavir actually has had reports of sudden (acute) ergotism. These combinations are to be avoided.
* beta-blockers (see Drug Classes).
* delavirdine (Rescriptor).
* dopamine (Intropin).
* erythromycins: clarithromycin (Biaxin), dirithromycin (Dynabac), or E-Mycin, ERYC, etc. Azithromycin (Zithromax) has not been reported to cause this effect.
* medicines that inhibit cytochrome P450 3A4 or compete for elimination by it will lead to increased ergotamine levels (such as fluconazole (Diflucan) or voriconazole (Vfend)—do not combine, increasing toxicity risk, and those that induce P450 3A4 (such as St. John's wort) will blunt therapeutic effects.
* troleandomycin (TAO).

Ergotamine ***taken concurrently*** with
* triptans (naratriptan [Amerge], rizatriptan [Maxalt], sumatriptan [Imitrex], or zolmitriptan [Zomig]) may lead to prolonged vasospastic reaction. One day should pass between an ergotamine dose and triptan use.

▷ *Driving, Hazardous Activities:* This drug may cause drowsiness or dizziness. Restrict activities as necessary.

Aviation Note: Vascular headache ***is a disqualification*** for piloting. Consult a designated Aviation Medical Examiner.

Exposure to Sun: No restrictions.

Exposure to Cold: Avoid as much as possible. Cold further reduces restricted blood flow to the extremities.

Discontinuation: Following long-term use, it may be necessary to withdraw this drug gradually to prevent withdrawal headache. Ask your doctor for help.

ERYTHROMYCIN (er ith roh MY sin)

Please see the macrolide antibiotic family profile.

ESCITALOPRAM (EH sih tal oh pram)

Introduced: 2002 **Class:** Antidepressant, SSRI **Prescription:** USA: Yes **Controlled Drug:** USA: No **Available as Generic:** USA: No

Brand Name: Lexapro

Author's Note: This medicine is a different chemical form (isomer) of citalopram (Celexa). Additional clinical study is needed to define the role of this medicine versus other SSRIs, but it appears to offer decreased side effects and increased beneficial results. Information in this profile will be broadened in subsequent editions if clinical benefits warrant.

ESTROGENS (es TROH jenz)

Other Names: Chlorotrianisene, conjugated estrogens, esterified estrogens, estradiol, estriol, estrone, estropipate, quinestrol

Introduced: 1933, 2000, 2003 (low dose Prempro form) **Class:** Female sex hormones **Prescription:** USA: Yes **Controlled Drug:** USA: No; Canada: No **Available as Generic:** USA: Yes; Canada: No

Brand Names: Activella, Alora, ✤C.E.S., ✤Climacteron, Climara, ✤Climestrone, ✤Congest, Delestrogen, Depo-Estradiol, DV, Esclim, Estinyl, Estrace, Estraderm, Estraguard, Estratab, Estrovis, Feminone, ✤Femogen, ✤Femogex, Femhrt, Gynetone, Gynodiol, Gynogen LA, Menest, Menotab, Menotab-M, Menrium [CD], Milprem [CD], ✤Minestrin, ✤Neo-Pause, ✤Oesclim, ✤Oestrilin, Ogen, PMB [CD], Ortho-Prefest, PMS-Estradiol, Premarin, Premphase [CD], Prempro [CD], (a lower dose Prempro was approved March, 2003), Progynon Pellet, TACE, Valergen-10, Vivelle, Vivelle-Dot, White Premarin

Author's Note: Controversy about estrogen therapy (ERT) and use of combination hormone replacement therapy (HRT) started with the HERS (Heart and Estrogen/progestin Replacement Study). HERS negated the role of estrogen/progestin in preventing a second heart attack. A large study called WISDOM is continuing to study estrogen alone. The Women's Health Initiative (WHI) combination arm was stopped early (see *www.whi.org;* July 17, 2002 JAMA article, especially Table 4; *www.acog.org;* and *www.menopause.org.*) Importantly, the WHI data showed that if 10,000 women took the 0.626 mg conjugated estrogens and 2.5 mg medroxy-progesterone daily (as in Prempro), versus not taking it: 8 more women would develop invasive breast cancer, 7 more would have a heart attack or other coronary, and 8 more would have blood clots in the lungs or a stroke. Five fewer would have hip fracture and 6 fewer would have colorectal cancers. The WHIMS group (Women's Health Initiative Memory Study) of the WHI (May 27, 2003—see FDA talk paper T03-39 in Sources) found that this medicine should NOT be used to help prevent dementia or Alzheimer's, and for the data analyzed, showed an increased risk of undesirable mental status change (dementia) in women over 65 who used the combination for longer periods. A two month time frame of use was recommended by the WHI panel (shortest period and in the lowest dose to meet treatment goals).

A continued analysis of the 16,608 women from the Women's Health Initiative (WHI), published in the July 25, 2003 issue of JAMA reported that in women who used the combination of estrogen plus progesterone who developed breast cancer, the tumors tended to be larger than women who did not take the combination. Additionally, 25.4 % of the combined product users who developed breast cancer had tumors that had begun to spread. In general, women who took the combination formulation had a 24% increased breast cancer risk. Increased risk did not become apparent in the first two years of those studied. Some question regarding difficulty of discovering tumors because of increased breast density caused by the hormone progestin has been postulated.

The new low-dose Prempro contains 0.45 mg of conjugated estrogens and 1.5 mg of medroxyprogesterone acetate. This new combination form is indicated for use by women who have a uterus and is used to treat moderate to severe vasomotor symptoms (night sweats and hot flashes) as well as moderate to severe vulvar and vaginal changes (atrophy) which may show as vaginal dryness. Topical forms should be considered if the combination is only being used for vulvar and vaginal atrophy. Alternatives for patients who can't take estrogen currently include: clonidine, fluoxetine (Prozac), gabapentin (Neurontin), and venlafaxine (Effexor).

BENEFITS versus RISKS

Possible Benefits	*Possible Risks*
COMBINATION WITH SIMVASTATIN MAY REDUCE UNDESIRABLE CLOTTING FACTORS AND INFLAMMATION	INCREASED RISK OF INVASIVE BREAST CANCER (combo form with time frame of use uncertain, yet showing after 2 years)
RELIEF OF MENOPAUSAL HOT FLASHES AND NIGHT SWEATS	INCREASED RISK OF HEART ATTACK
PREVENTION OR RELIEF OF ATROPHIC VAGINITIS, ATROPHY OF THE VULVA AND URETHRA	INCREASED RISK OF STROKE INCREASED RISK OF LONG OR DEEP VEIN CLOTS (THROMBOSIS
PREVENTION OF POSTMENOPAUSAL OSTEOPOROSIS	INCREASED RISK OF CANCER OF THE UTERUS (endometrium— possible and risk increases with
PATCH FORM MAY GIVE UP TO A WEEK OF ESTROGEN	longer use)
DECREASED RISK OF HIP FRACTURE	Accelerated growth of preexisting fibroid tumors of the uterus
DECREASED RISK OF COLORECTAL CANCER	Fluid retention
Prevention of thinning of the skin	Postmenopausal bleeding
	Increased gall stone risk
	Increased blood pressure risk
	Decreased sugar tolerance (glucose)

▷ **Principal Uses**

As a Single Drug Product: Uses currently included in FDA-approved labeling: "replacement" therapy in (1) ovarian failure or surgical removal; (2) the menopausal syndrome; (3) postmenopausal atrophy of genital tissues; (4) postmenopausal osteoporosis; (5) selected cases of breast cancer and prostate cancer; (6) treats difficulty having sexual intercourse (dysparunia) caused by vaginal secretion drying (topical forms may be most desirable).

Other (unlabeled) generally accepted uses: (1) Used in combination with simvastatin (Zocor) (in one study of women averaging 57 years old) lowered LDL, increased HDL, reduced undesirable blood clotting factors and inflammation; (2) may have a role in some selected cases of Turner's syndrome (beneficial changes in blood vessels and sensitivity to insulin).

As a Combination Drug Product [CD]: Estrogen is available in combination with chlordiazepoxide (Librium) and with meprobamate (Equanil, Miltown). These drugs provide a calming effect and ease symptoms in selected cases of menopause. See oral contraceptives profile for a discussion of estrogens and progestins.

In the Pipeline: Prempro product with 0.3 mg of conjugated estrogens and 1.5 mg of MPA is being studied and has been submitted to the FDA.

How This Drug Works: When used to correct hormonal deficiency states, estrogens restore normal cellular activity by increasing nuclear material and protein synthesis. Frequency and intensity of menopausal symptoms are reduced when normal levels of estrogen are restored. Blood vessel effects appear to work through both nongenetic and genetic ways. Estrogen may modify inflammation that encourages buildup of plaque on vessels (atherosclerosis), relaxes the heart muscle and increases sensitivity to insulin. The precise mechanism of estrogen in protecting brain cells (neurons) from oxidative stress or amyloid protein is unknown, but the end result appears to be some protection from development of Alzheimer's disease.

Available Dosage Forms and Strengths
        Capsules — 12 mg, 25 mg
      Capsules (TACE) — 72 mg
  Combination form — 0.45 conjugated estrogens/1.5 mg medroxyprogesterone acetate (new)
  Combination form — 0.625 mg conjugated estrogens/1.5 mg medroxyprogesterone acetate
      Tablets — 0.02 mg, 0.05 mg, 0.1 mg, 0.3 mg,
           — 0.5 mg, 0.625 mg, 0.9 mg, 1.25 mg, 2.5 mg
  Transdermal patch — 0.01 mg per day, 0.05 mg per day, 0.025 mg per day, 0.075 mg per day,
           — 0.0375 mg per day, 1.5 mg, 2.3 mg, 3 mg
  Transdermal patch — 10, 20, and 30 mg (Canada only)
     Vaginal cream — 0.1, 0.625, 1.5 mg/g

▷ **Usual Adult Dosage Ranges:** *For conjugated and esterified estrogens:* lowest doses that will control moderate to severe vasomotor symptoms that happen in menopause should be used for the shortest amount of time: Starting doses of 0.45 mg with increases up to 1.25 mg daily are used. Cenestin product notes attempts to lower doses or taper the medicine should be made. Premarin product notes use of 1.25 mg daily for treatment of moderate to severe vasomotor symptoms. Dosing is undertaken for 21 days with 1 week off. Addition of a progestin for the last 10–14 days of the cycle is recommended to lower the occurrence of effects (endometrial hyperplasia or carcinoma) caused by estrogen alone (unopposed). Some studies suggested that combined estrogen and progestin use actually increases breast cancer risk. For other forms of estrogen: Ask your doctor. Patch forms give a week of estrogen replacement in a small patch.

Note: Actual dose and schedule must be determined for each patient individually.

Conditions Requiring Dosing Adjustments

Liver Function: The dose should probably be decreased in mild liver disease as they are poorly removed (metabolized). Estrogens should not be used in acute or severe liver compromise. This drug can be lithogenic (capable of causing stones) in bile.

Kidney Function: In severe kidney compromise requiring dialysis, blood levels are higher than in those with normal kidneys. Lower doses appear prudent.

▷ **Dosing Instructions:** The tablets may be crushed and taken without regard to food. The capsules should be taken whole. If you forget a dose, take the dose you forgot as soon as you remember it, unless it is nearly time for your next dose—if that is the case, simply skip the missed dose and take the next dose right on schedule. DO NOT double doses. Talk to your doctor if you find yourself forgetting doses.

Usual Duration of Use: Transdermal products such as Climara, Estroderm and Vivelle increase estradiol levels above the starting point (baseline) in about 4 hours. Regular use for 10 to 20 days needed to see effectiveness in easing menopausal symptoms. These medicines should be used in the lowest possible dose for the shortest amount of time in order to reach the goals and avoid the risks of treatment. Use requires periodic evaluation by your doctor (individualized) to see if the benefits of this medicine are being realized (depending on the use) and if it is still needed.

Typical Treatment Goals and Measurements (Outcomes and Markers)

Menopause: Most clinicians treating menopause seek goals of reduction or cessation of hot flashes, and avoidance of rapid bone loss (which can also be measured by some lab tests and DEXA testing).

▷ **This Drug Should Not Be Taken If**

- you have had an allergic reaction to the medicine or the substances in the pills previously.
- you have a history of thrombophlebitis, embolism, heart attack, or stroke.
- you have seriously impaired liver function or recent onset of liver disease.
- you are trying to prevent heart and blood vessel (cardiovascular) disease.
- you have abnormal and unexplained genital/vaginal bleeding.
- you are pregnant.
- you have sickle cell disease.
- you have or are suspected to have breast cancer (may be used to treat some kinds of breast cancer), or cancer of the uterus.
- you have known or suspected estrogen-dependent cancer (your doctor will determine this)—except in selected patients being treated for cancer.

▷ **Inform Your Physician Before Taking This Drug If**

- you have had an unfavorable reaction to estrogen therapy previously or if you have an allergy to horses.
- you have a history of breast or reproductive organ cancer.
- you have fibrocystic breast changes, fibroid tumors or bleeding of the uterus, endometriosis, migraine headaches, epilepsy, asthma, vision disturbances, high blood pressure, gallbladder disease, diabetes, or porphyria.
- you tend to retain fluid.
- you have low calcium or kidney disease.
- you smoke tobacco on a regular basis.
- you have a history of blood-clotting (increased likelihood of forming blood clots-hypercoagulability) disorders.
- you plan to have surgery in the near future.
- you are depressed or have a history of depression.

Possible Side Effects (natural, expected, and unavoidable drug actions)

Fluid retention, weight gain, "breakthrough" bleeding (spotting in middle of menstrual cycle), altered menstrual pattern, resumption of menstrual flow ("periods") after natural cessation (postmenopausal bleeding), increased yeast infection susceptibility of the genitals.

▷ **Possible Adverse Effects** (unusual, unexpected, and infrequent reactions)

If any of the following develop, consult your physician promptly for guidance.

Mild Adverse Effects

Allergic reactions: skin rash, hives, itching—rare.

Headache, nervous tension/anxiety, irritability, depression, accentuation of migraine headaches—infrequent.

Nausea, vomiting, bloating, diarrhea—infrequent to frequent.

Tannish pigmentation of the face—possible.

Serious Adverse Effects

Allergic reactions: anaphylaxis—case reports.

Idiosyncratic reaction: cutaneous porphyria—fragility and scarring of the skin.

Erythema multiforme or nodosum—reported.

Can produce or worsen high blood pressure—more likely with higher doses.

Gallbladder disease, pancreatitis, benign liver tumors, jaundice, rise in blood sugar—case reports.

Erosion of uterine cervix, enlargement of uterine fibroid tumors—possible.

Thrombophlebitis (inflammation of a vein with formation of blood clot): pain or tenderness in thigh or leg, with or without swelling of foot or leg—low dose has minimal increased risk; higher doses may carry more risk.

Thromboembolism—increased risk of stroke and blood clots in the veins or lung in women after menopause who have a uterus (risk was greater than benefits for estrogen plus progestin) (see WHI note above).

Pulmonary embolism (movement of blood clot to lung): sudden shortness of breath, pain in chest, coughing, bloody sputum—increased risk (see WHI note above).

Benign liver tumors (adenomas)—possible.

Systemic lupus erythematosus or porphyria—rare.

Stroke (blood clot in brain): headaches, blackout, sudden weakness or paralysis of any part of the body, severe dizziness, altered vision, slurred speech, inability to speak—increased risk (see WHI note above).

Endometrial cancer—increased risk (risk from using estrogen alone (unopposed estrogen) may be 2 to 12 times greater than people who do not use estrogen. Many studies do not show an increased endometrial cancer risk if estrogens are used for less than a year. Risk with longer term use may persist for 8-15 years after estrogen treatment is stopped.

Ovarian cancer—Short term, combined estrogen-progestin use didn't appear to increase risk, but increased risk based on years of use was found once age, oral contraceptive use and menopause type was considered with a 7% increase in rate ratio per year that estrogen alone was used (found in patients in the Breast Cancer Detection Demonstration Project).

Retinal thrombosis (blood clot in eye vessels): sudden impairment or loss of vision—case reports.

Heart attack (blood clot in coronary artery)—sudden pain in chest, neck, jaw, or arm; weakness; sweating; nausea—increased risk (see WHI note above).

Severe hypercalcaemia—reported in patients with breast cancer that spread to the bone.

Breast cancer—increased risk with combination form use. The Women's Health Initiative (WHI) found a 26% increase in invasive breast cancer in women with a uterus who took estrogen plus progestin treatment (see WHI note above). A re-analysis of the WHI data found that increased tumor risk did not appear in the first two years that the combination form was used (see Chlepowski, R.T. in Sources). A subset analysis of 975 women from 65–79 found that the greatest risk of breast cancer was seen in women who used the combination for at least five years (see Li, C.I. in Sources). Patients using estrogen alone (data women who have had a hysterectomy and for use as long as 25 years did not show any appreciable increased risk of breast cancer.

▷ **Possible Effects on Sexual Function:** Swelling and tenderness of breasts, milk production.

Increased vaginal secretions. Gynecomastia in males exposed to custom compounded cream used by a parent—case report.

Possible Delayed Adverse Effects: Estrogens taken during pregnancy may predispose a female child to the later development of cancer of the vagina or cervix following puberty.

▷ **Adverse Effects That May Mimic Natural Diseases or Disorders**

Liver reactions may suggest viral hepatitis.

Natural Diseases or Disorders That May Be Activated by This Drug

Latent hypertension, diabetes mellitus, acute intermittent porphyria.

Possible Effects on Laboratory Tests

Arginine test of the pituitary (human growth hormone increase)—falsely increased.

Red blood cells, hemoglobin and platelets: decreased.

Blood calcium level: increased.

Blood total cholesterol level: decreased (treatment effect); increased in postmenopausal women.

Blood LDL cholesterol level: decreased in postmenopausal women.

Blood triglyceride level: increased.

HDL: increased.

Blood glucose level: increased.

Glucose tolerance test (GTT): decreased.

Blood thyroid hormone (T3 and T4) levels: increased.

Blood uric acid level: decreased.

Liver function tests: increased liver enzymes (ALT/GPT, AST/GOT, and alkaline phosphatase), increased bilirubin.

CAUTION

1. To avoid prolonged (uninterrupted) stimulation of breast and uterine tissues, estrogen should be taken in cycles of 3 weeks on and 1 week off of medication.

2. The estrogen in estrogen vaginal creams is absorbed systemically. It may also be absorbed through the penis during sexual intercourse and can cause enlargement and tenderness of male breast tissue.

3. Some patients may benefit from lower or may require higher than usual doses to prevent osteoporosis. Bone mineral density tests (DEXA or PDEXA) are prudent to see whether a selected dose is working.

4. See WHI note above regarding breast cancer, heart disease, blood clots, etc. Best to take this medicine as a benefit to risk decision in its present dosing for the shortest possible time consistent with treatment goals. Results and continued need should be quickly assessed.

5. Patch forms should not be stored above 86 degrees—be careful when traveling in the summer.
6. The active ingredient of many forms of estrogen replacement comes from pregnant horse urine. Talk to your doctor if you are allergic to horses.

Precautions for Use

By Those Over 60 Years of Age: Thinking has changed on use of estrogen in older populations and benefits have been shown in the eighth decade of life. In this age group, it is advisable to attempt relief of hot flashes with non-estrogenic medicines, yet benefits have been shown in osteoporosis. During use, report promptly any indications of impaired circulation: speech disturbances, altered vision, sudden hearing loss, vertigo, sudden weakness or paralysis, angina, leg pains.

▷ **Advisability of Use During Pregnancy**

Pregnancy Category: X. See Pregnancy Risk Categories at the back of this book.
Animal Studies: Genital defects reported in mice and guinea pigs; cleft palate reported in rodents.
Human Studies: Information from studies of pregnant women indicates that estrogens can masculinize the female fetus. In addition, limb defects and heart malformations have been reported.

It is now known that estrogens taken during pregnancy can predispose the female child to the development of cancer of the vagina or cervix following puberty. **Avoid estrogens completely during entire pregnancy.**

Advisability of Use If Breast-Feeding

Presence of this drug in breast milk: Yes, in minute amounts.
Estrogens in large doses can suppress milk formation. Breast-feeding is considered to be safe during the use of estrogens. Malnourished mothers may have unacceptable decreases in protein and nitrogen in their breast milk if this drug is used while breast-feeding. Discuss benefits and risks with your doctor. The infant should be closely followed and growth checked.

Habit-Forming Potential: There has been some suggestion of estrogens having potential for psychological dependence and tolerance because of their mood-elevating properties, but clinical reports have not been presented.

Effects of Overdose: Headache, drowsiness, nausea, vomiting, fluid retention, abnormal vaginal bleeding, breast enlargement, and discomfort.

Possible Effects of Long-Term Use: Long term use of combination form is no longer recommended. Ongoing study of the WHI is ongoing for estrogens alone. Prudence dictates that women with intact uteri should use estrogens only when symptoms justify it and with proper supervision and attempts every 3–6 months to assess continued need and possible discontinuation.

Suggested Periodic Examinations While Taking This Drug (at physician's discretion)

Checks every 3-6 months for benefits and continued need. Regular evaluation of the breasts (self exam) and annual mammography). Check of pelvic organs including Pap smears, and check for urinary tract infection. Periodic lipid panels and blood pressure checks are prudent. Liver function tests as indicated.

▷ **While Taking This Drug, Observe the Following**

Foods: Avoid excessive use of salt if fluid retention occurs. Combining DHEA with estrogen can lead to signs and symptoms (such as nausea, colitis, or breakthrough bleeding) of excess estrogen.

Herbal Medicines or Minerals: Black cohosh appears to work by: (1) suppressing lutenizing hormone; (2) binding to estrogen receptors in the pituitary; and (3) inhibiting lutenizing hormone release. The net effect is that this herb eases symptoms of menopause, but little is known about long-term use or heart and bone protective effects. This herb may interfere with the benefits of estrogen replacement therapy. Talk to your doctor before starting black cohosh if you are currently taking estrogen. Other herbal or integrative approaches to women's health are always best discussed with your doctor to develop an evidence-based approach to overall therapy and avoid possible undesirable additive or side effects.

Use of St. John's wort, echinacea or ginkgo completely blocked or lowered the ability of sperm to penetrate eggs in one study. DO NOT use these herbs if you are using a conjugated estrogen product to augment mucus quality and help infertility. Combined use of calcium and vitamin D can be a further step to help avoid osteoporosis. St. John's wort may lead to additive sun sensitivity. Talk to your doctor BEFORE adding any herbal medicines.

Beverages: Caffeine levels will be increased—limited consumption of caffeine is prudent. May be taken with milk.

▷ *Alcohol:* No interactions expected.

Tobacco Smoking: Some studies show that heavy smoking (15 or more cigarettes daily) in association with use of estrogen-containing oral contraceptives significantly increases risk of heart attack (coronary thrombosis). I advise everyone to stop smoking.

▷ *Other Drugs*

Estrogens *taken concurrently* with

- alendronate (Fosamax) have not been well studied. One small clinical study suggested the combination was beneficial in preventing post-menopausal osteoporosis. The combination of alendronate and hormone replacement therapy (HRT) is now approved in Canada because of excellent combination results.
- amprenavir (Agenerase) may blunt benefits of amprenavir in fighting HIV, and may also result in loss of contraceptive benefits (efficacy). Other protease inhibitors such as nelfinavir (Viracept) may lead to contraceptive failure also.
- atorvastatin (Lipitor) may lead to increased birth control pill medicine levels.
- fluconazole (Diflucan) may increase contraceptive medicine blood levels (ethinyl estradiol).
- lamotrigene (Lamictal) may increase or decrease lamotrigene levels. More frequent blood level checks are needed with doses adjusted accordingly.
- naratriptan (Amerge) may increase naratriptan as well as zolmitriptan (Zomig) blood levels. Patients should be closely followed for increased naratriptan or zolmitriptan adverse effects.
- oral antidiabetic drugs (see Drug Classes) or oral blood-sugar-lowering medicines may cause loss of glucose control and high blood sugars.
- progestins (various) may increase risk of breast cancer versus estrogen use by itself.
- tacrine (Cognex) increases the risk of tacrine adverse effects.
- thyroid hormones may increase the bound (inactive) drug and require an increase in thyroid dose.
- tricyclic antidepressants (Elavil, Sinequan, etc.) may enhance their adverse effects and reduce their antidepressant effectiveness.

- vitamin C (ascorbic acid, various brands) in higher doses may result in increased estrogen effects. A lower dose of estrogens may be indicated if higher-dose vitamin C will be taken on an ongoing basis.
- warfarin (Coumadin) may cause alterations of prothrombin activity. Increased doses may be needed.

The following drugs may *decrease* the effects of estrogens:

- carbamazepine (Tegretol).
- penicillin (various) may blunt contraceptive benefits.
- phenobarbital (Belladonna, others).
- phenytoin (Dilantin), fosphenytoin (Cerebyx).
- primidone (Mysoline).
- rifampin (Rifadin, Rimactane).

▷ *Driving, Hazardous Activities:* Usually no restrictions. Consult your physician for assessment of individual risk and for guidance regarding specific restrictions.

Aviation Note: Usually no restrictions, but watch for the rare occurrence of disturbed vision and restrict activities accordingly. Consult a designated Aviation Medical Examiner.

Exposure to Sun: Caution—may cause photosensitivity (see Glossary).

Discontinuation: Best to use estrogens in the smallest effective dose, for the shortest amount of time consistent with the benefit to risk profile of the patient and the goals of treatment. If used to control menopausal symptoms, the dose is reduced gradually to prevent acute withdrawal hot flashes. Avoid continual, uninterrupted use of large doses. Ask your doctor for help.

ETANERCEPT (ee TAN err sept)

Other Names: TNFR: Fc (Tumor necrosis factor receptor p75 Fc fusion protein)

Introduced: 1998   **Class:**   Disease-modifying   antirheumatic   drug (DMARD), biologic response modifier   **Prescription:**   USA: Yes   **Controlled Drug:**   USA: No; Canada: No   **Available as Generic:**   No

Brand Name: Enbrel

```
┌─────────────────────────────────────────────────────────────────┐
│                      BENEFITS versus RISKS                        │
│      Possible Benefits                    Possible Risks          │
│  USEFUL IN RHEUMATOID            INFECTIONS CAUSED BY             │
│    ARTHRITIS                       IMMUNOSUPPRESSION FROM         │
│  HAS A ROLE IN MANY CASES OF       THE MEDICINE ITSELF           │
│    JUVENILE RHEUMATOID           Injection site reactions        │
│    ARTHRITIS                     Possible development of antibodies│
│  CAN BE USED IN COMBINATION      Questionable cause of heart failure or│
│    WITH METHOTREXATE               worsening of existing failure  │
│  MAY GIVE A RESPONSE WHERE                                        │
│    OTHER AGENTS HAVE FAILED                                       │
│  THE FIRST PRODUCT TO BE                                          │
│    APPROVED FOR PSORIATIC                                         │
│    ARTHRITIS (either alone or in                                  │
│    combination with methotrexate)                                 │
│  APPROVED JULY 2003 FOR                                           │
│    ANKYLOSING SPONDYLITIS                                         │
│  One recent study found this drug to                              │
│    provide short-term relief in                                   │
│    ankylosing spondylitis                                         │
│  New data may evolve into a role for                              │
│    this drug in immune                                            │
│    thrombocytopenic purpura                                       │
└─────────────────────────────────────────────────────────────────┘
```

▷ **Principal Uses**

As a Single Drug Product: Uses currently included in FDA-approved labeling: (1) Approved for INITIAL treatment of rheumatoid arthritis (RA) where previously it was used in treatment of moderate to severe rheumatoid arthritis (RA) in patients who have not responded to one or more disease-modifying antirheumatic drugs (DMARD); (2) approved for use in RA in children over 4 years old (juvenile rheumatoid arthritis); (3) treats psoriatic arthritis (either alone or in combination with methotrexate); (4) treats ankylosing spondylitis.

Other (unlabeled) generally accepted uses: (1) May have a role in some kinds of wasting (cachexia) where tumor necrosis factor (TNF) is involved; (2) data from the cholesterol and recurrent events (CARE) trial found that decreasing tumor necrosis factor (TNF) (see how this drug works, below) reduces risk of repeat heart attacks; (3) appears to have a role in ongoing (chronic) nerve problems (demyelinating polyneuropathy); (4) early data showed a complete recovery from resistant (refractory) platelet problems (immune thrombocytopenic purpura).

How This Drug Works: Binds with tumor necrosis factor alpha (TNF-alpha) in the body, as well as to lymphotoxin alpha (TNF-beta), and stops their biologic actions. This drug also works to change the body's responses that are caused or regulated by TNF, such as increased levels of matrix metalloproteinase-3, serum levels of cytokines and release of substances that control white blood cell migration.

Available Dosage Forms and Strengths

Injection — 25 mg with a syringe containing 1 ml of bacteriostatic water.

▷ **Recommended Dosage Ranges** (Actual dose and schedule must be determined for each patient individually.)

Infants and Children: Not studied in children less than 4 years old.

Children 4–17 years old who have moderate to severely active juvenile rheumatoid arthritis (JRA) and who did not respond to or tolerate methotrexate were given 0.4 mg/kg up to a maximum of 25 mg twice a week (subcutaneously). Twice-weekly dosing is best, given 72 to 96 hours apart.

Usual Adult Dosage Ranges: For rheumatoid arthritis (adults): 25 mg injected under the skin (subcutaneously), twice a week. (Remember to change or rotate where you inject.)

Author's Note: A new production facility called BioNext is being developed to encompass cell culture manufacturing for etanercept. A medicine also used in rheumatoid arthritis (infliximab or Remicade) has added a black box (more stringent) warning about increased risk of infections in patients who use that medicine. Etanercept now has a bold warning about infections in post-marketing reports. Enbrel should be stopped if the patient develops a serious infection while taking this medicine. Members of an FDA advisory panel found that more data was required for the three existing TNF blockers (adalimumab-Humira, etanercept-Enbrel, and infliximab-Remicade) relative to their possible role in causing lymphoma in patients that use them.

Conditions Requiring Dosing Adjustments

Liver Function: No changes needed, as the drug is removed by the reticuloendothelial system.

Kidney Function: Dosing changes are not known to be needed in people with kidney problems.

▷ **Dosing Instructions:** It is very important that you understand how to inject this drug under the skin (subcutaneously) and NOT intravenously. Please ask your doctor or pharmacist if you do not understand the patient information on injecting. Please also remember to change (rotate) where you inject (the injection site). Do not use places where the skin is tender, red, or puffy. Talk to your doctor before injecting etanercept if you have an infection. If you forget a dose, take the missed dose right away, unless it is nearly time for your next dose—if that is the case, skip the missed dose and take the next dose right on schedule. Call your doctor if you find yourself missing doses.

Usual Duration of Use: Use on a regular schedule determines benefit. In rheumatoid arthritis this drug usually goes to work in 1 to 4 weeks. Long-term use (months to years) requires physician supervision. Data for use as long as five years has accumulated for this medicine.

Typical Treatment Goals and Measurements (Outcomes and Markers)

Arthritis: Control of arthritis symptoms (pain, loss of mobility, decreased ability to accomplish activities of daily living, range of motion, etc.) is paramount in returning patient quality of life and to checking the results (beneficial outcomes) from this medicine. The American College of Rheumatology uses scales that define the degree of benefit from a medicine treating rheumatoid arthritis. You will hear these mentioned as ACR 20, 50, and 70. Many arthritis management or pain centers use interdisciplinary teams (physicians from several specialties, nurses, physician's assistants, physical and occupational therapists, pharmacotherapists, psychotherapists, social workers, and others) to get the best results. Specific mobility goals are often set by the physician and administered by a physical/occupational therapist. Laboratory tests include C Reactive Protein-(CRP), rheumatoid factor or "sed rate (erythrocyte sedimentation rate or

ESR). The arthritis foundation has additional information at *www. arthritis.org.*

Possible Advantages of This Drug Uses: A novel mechanism (against TNF) to fight arthritis. Works to prevent joint damage better than methotrexate and also eases symptoms faster than methotrexate. Convenient dosing schedule. A new enrollment program has been started and can be entered by patients by calling 1-888-4EN-BREL. The only agent FDA approved to treat psoriatic arthritis.

▷ **This Drug Should Not Be Taken If**
  • you have had an allergic reaction to it previously.
  • you currently have an active infection (including chronic or localized infections).

▷ **Inform Your Physician Before Taking This Drug If**
  • you have poorly controlled diabetes or a suppression of the immune system or any other disease or condition that predisposes you to infections.
  • you develop a serious infection or sepsis while taking this medicine (the drug should be stopped).
  • you have recently received a live virus vaccine.
  • you have a history of malignancy.
  • you are pregnant or planning pregnancy in the near future.
  • you are breast-feeding your infant.
  • you have an allergy to latex.
  • you develop signs and symptoms of heart failure while taking this medicine or have a history of heart failure.
  • you have impaired kidney function.
  • you have a history of asthma or allergies to other medicines.

Possible Side Effects (natural, expected, and unavoidable drug actions)

Report such developments to your physician promptly.
  Discomfort at the injection site. Immune system suppression. Emergence of latent or quiescent tuberculosis in patients previously exposed.

▷ **Possible Adverse Effects** (unusual, unexpected, and infrequent reactions)
  If any of the following develop, consult your physician promptly for guidance.
  Mild Adverse Effects
  Allergic reactions: skin rash at the injection site—possible.
  Development of antinuclear antibodies—infrequent to frequent.
  Cough—frequent.
  Sinusitis—possible.
  Upper respiratory infections—up to 29%.
  Vomiting—may be frequent in some children.
  Serious Adverse Effects
  Allergic reactions: anaphylaxis—possible.
  Central nervous system damage (demyelination)—case reports with unclear causality.
  Suppression of the immune system/cells (pancytopenia/aplastic anemia)—possible.
  Emergence of tuberculosis in patients previously exposed.
  Systemic lupus erythematosus—case reports.
  Lymphoma—questionable correlation or causation for all three TNF blockers.
  Skin cancer (squamous cell carcinoma)—case reports.

Development of or worsening of heart failure—47 patient case reports receiving etanercept or infliximab).

Excessive activity of the thyroid (hyperthyroidism)—case report.

▷ **Possible Effects on Sexual Function:** None reported.

Possible Delayed Adverse Effects: Possible development of antinuclear antibodies. Long-term effects on infections and malignancies is not fully understood.

Possible Effects on Laboratory Tests

Antinuclear antibodies (ANA): positive.

CAUTION

1. This drug must be monitored carefully by a qualified physician.
2. Make certain you understand how to inject this medicine under the skin.
3. Live-virus vaccines should be avoided during use of this drug. Live-virus vaccines could actually produce infection rather than stimulate an immune response.
4. Positive antinuclear antibodies (ANA) have been reported, but the clinical importance is not yet known.
5. The manufacturer advises against using this medicine if you have an active infection.
6. Patients should be followed closely if they develop an infection while taking etanercept, and treatment should be STOPPED in patients with serious infections or sepsis.
7. All three TNF blockers have come into question relative to correlation or causative agents in lymphoma.

Precautions for Use

By Those Over 60 Years of Age: Specific changes are not indicated at present.

▷ **Advisability of Use During Pregnancy**

Pregnancy Category: B. See Pregnancy Risk Categories at the back of this book. *Human Studies:* Adequate studies are NOT available.

Talk to your doctor about benefits versus risks of use.

Advisability of Use If Breast-Feeding

Presence of this drug in breast milk: Unknown.

Avoid drug or refrain from nursing.

Habit-Forming Potential: None.

Effects of Overdose: One patient injected 62 mg twice a week for 3 weeks without any significant adverse effects.

Possible Effects of Long-Term Use: Positive antinuclear antibodies—significance not presently known. One case of diabetes mellitus.

Suggested Periodic Examinations While Taking This Drug (at physician's discretion)

Beneficial response to the medicine (ACR category).

Sedimentation rate (ESR) and rheumatoid factor or C-reactive protein.

CBC with differential (see lymphoma note above).

ANA and fasting glucose tests.

If used in congestive heart failure, tests of heart function and symptom-free walking time.

▷ **While Taking This Drug, Observe the Following**

Foods: No specific recommendations.

Herbal Medicines or Minerals: There is NO DATA on combined use of etanercept with glucosamine. There are also no data on use of etanercept with hay flower, mistletoe herb, or white mustard seed. Echinacea may actually blunt the immune response if used on an ongoing basis, and therefore combination with etanercept is not advisable. Talk to your doctor before combining any herbal medicine with etanercept.

Beverages: No restrictions.

▷ *Alcohol:* No specific recommendations.

Tobacco Smoking: No interactions expected. I advise everyone to quit smoking.

Marijuana Smoking: May cause impairment of immunity.

▷ *Other Drugs*

Etanercept *taken concurrently* with

- anakinra (Kineret) may pose an increased risk of infections, and combined use had NOT been decided.
- medicines that blunt the immune system may lead to additive immune system depression if combined with etanercept.
- yellow fever, pneumococcal, smallpox, or any other live vaccine may result in decreased immune response to the vaccine as well as possible transmission of the infection BY the vaccine.

▷ *Driving, Hazardous Activities:* No restrictions.

Aviation Note: The use of this drug is *probably not a disqualification* for piloting, but the condition being treated may be. Consult a designated Aviation Medical Examiner.

Exposure to Sun: No restrictions.

ETHAMBUTOL (eth AM byu tohl)

Introduced: 1971 Class: Anti-infective, antituberculosis drug **Prescription:** USA: Yes **Controlled Drug:** USA: No; Canada: No **Available as Generic:** USA: No; Canada: No

Brand Names: ✤Etibi, Myambutol

BENEFITS versus RISKS	
Possible Benefits	*Possible Risks*
EFFECTIVE ADJUNCTIVE TREATMENT OF PULMONARY TUBERCULOSIS	RARE OPTIC NEURITIS WITH IMPAIRMENT OR LOSS OF VISION
EFFECTIVE ADJUNCTIVE TREATMENT OF AIDS-RELATED *MYCOBACTERIUM AVIUM-INTRACELLULARE* COMPLEX INFECTIONS	Rare peripheral neuritis (see Glossary)
	Activation of gout
Possibly effective treatment of tuberculous meningitis	

▷ **Principal Uses**

As a Single Drug Product: Uses currently included in FDA-approved labeling: Treats lung (pulmonary) tuberculosis. Used with other antitubercular drugs (currently three other medicines are added to ethambutol).

Other (unlabeled) generally accepted uses: (1) Treatment of tuberculous meningitis; (2) treatment of AIDS-related *Mycobacterium avium-intracellulare* (MAI) complex infections, in combination with other antimycobacterial drugs.

Available Dosage Forms and Strengths
  Tablets — 100 mg, 400 mg

▷ **Recommended Dosage Ranges** (Actual dose and schedule must be determined for each patient individually.)
  Infants and Children: Dose not established. Some authorities recommend that children under 13 years of age not be given this drug.
  13 to 60 Years of Age: To start—15 mg per kg of body mass, once daily. Daily maximum is 500–1,500 mg.
    For retreatment of tuberculosis—25 mg per kg of body mass, once daily for 60 days; then 15 mg per kg of body mass. Total daily dose should not exceed 900–2,500 mg. A variety of dosing schedules have been used, but all of them depend on clinical judgment and a balance of the organism being treated and the ability of the patient to keep taking the medicine.
    For tuberculous meningitis or AIDS-related MAI infections—15 mg per kg of body mass, once daily in combination with other medicines.
  Over 60 Years of Age: Same as 13 to 60 years of age.

▷ **This Drug Should Not Be Taken If**
  • you have had an allergic reaction to it previously.
  • you currently have optic neuritis or peripheral neuritis.
  • you currently have active gout.
  • you are not able to have visual acuity testing.
  Author's Note: The information in this profile has been shortened to make room for more widely used medicines.

ETHANOL (ETH an all)

Other Names: **Prescription:**   None

Nonprescription: Moonshine, alcohol, jack, white lightning, wine, beer, whiskey, vodka, others

Introduced: 1980 (prescription); 6,000 years ago (nonprescription)
Class: Antianxiety drug (nonprescription form)   **Prescription:**   USA: Yes (IV)   **Controlled Drug:**   USA: No; Canada: Yes (IV)   **Available as Generic:**   USA: Yes; Canada: Yes

Brand Names: **Prescription:**   ❖Dilusol (38.7%), Eskaphen B, Novahistine DMX Liquid, Nyquil Nighttime Cold Medicine, Temaril (5.7%), Tuss-Ornade (5%), Vicks Formula 44D (often used as part of liquid combination medicines) **Nonprescription:** Robert Alison Chardonnay (12% by volume), Bud Dry, Glenlivet, Smirnoff (40% by volume), Cabernet, others

Warning: Clinical use is limited to intravenous treatment of methanol and antifreeze (ethylene glycol) poisoning and as a preservative. Many products contain alcohol. Ask your pharmacist for help if you must avoid alcohol. Widely used in nonprescription form as an antianxiety agent. Some data show heart (cardiac) benefit of moderate use—however, other data show increased cancer risks. Data from the UK show that heavy drinking may actually DOUBLE the risk of strokes. Some people may not have any mental or physical changes even though a breath or blood alcohol test shows they are "legally drunk."

BENEFITS versus RISKS	
Possible Benefits	*Possible Risks*
EFFECTIVE TREATMENT OF METHANOL OR ETHYLENE GLYCOL POISONING	WITHDRAWAL SYMPTOMS SEIZURES
MODERATE USE MAY DECREASE HEART DISEASE/HEART ATTACK RISK	LIVER DAMAGE (with prolonged use)
LIGHT TO MODERATE USE (AS LITTLE AS ONE DRINK PER WEEK) MAY DECREASE RISK OF STROKE AND ISCHEMIC STROKE IN MEN	Possible increased cancer risk
	Heavy drinking may increase the risk of type 2 diabetes
	Pancreatitis
	Encephalopathy
	Low white blood cell counts and anemia
Moderate drinking may lower the risk of type 2 diabetes	Myopathy

▷ **Principal Uses**

As a Single Drug Product: Uses currently included in FDA-approved labeling: (1) Intravenously (as 10% ethanol and 5% dextrose) in very specific depletion cases as a calorie source.

Other (unlabeled) generally accepted uses: (1) Treatment of methanol or antifreeze (ethylene glycol) poisoning; (2) adjunctive treatment of cancer pain; (3) intravenous treatment of DTs (delirium tremens); (4) used to sclerose esophageal varices and stop bleeding; (5) treatment of hepatocellular cancer where severe liver problems preclude surgery; (6) used to sclerose thyroid cysts; (7) used to destroy nerve tissue (neurolytic block) in chronic pain therapy; (8) widely used in nonprescription form as an antianxiety agent; (9) one large study appears to show that use ranging up to moderate (and NO GREATER than 0.7 mg per kg of body mass for 3 days in a row) may actually help prevent coronary heart disease and heart attacks; (10) a large study of more than 22,000 men showed that light to moderate use (as little as one drink per week) appears to decrease risk of stroke and ischemic stroke in men; (11) moderate drinking (one to two drinks per day) appears to lower the risk of type 2 diabetes; (12) ethanol injection may have a role in managing benign prostatic hypertrophy (BPH); (13) injected (Percutaneous Ethanol Injection or PEI) therapy of liver carcinoid tumors that had spread (metastasized) and use of PEI combined with transcatheter arterial chemoembolization therapy (TAE) has been helpful in cases of unresectable cancer (hepatocellular carcinoma) of the liver.

As a Combination Drug Product [CD]: Uses currently included in FDA-approved labeling: Widely present in elixirs and other liquid vehicles for drugs as a preservative and partial drug action enhancer.

How This Drug Works: In antifreeze (ethylene glycol) or methanol poisoning, ethanol prevents ethylene glycol or methanol from being changed (metabolized) into toxic chemicals, letting the body remove antifreeze or methanol harmlessly. If used in nonprescription form in excess, it depresses nerve function, leading to emotional changes and disturbances of perception, coordination, and intoxication. Nonprescription use of up to moderate amounts appears to decrease risk of heart and blood vessel disease, but how it works is unknown. Theories include increased HDL, decreased ADP, antioxidant levels in red wine, fibrinolytic system (anticoagulant) effects, and increased levels of prostacyclin have all been presented. Some researchers found that red wine–particularly Cabernet has the greatest protective value. Antioxidant substances are postulated to be active in some reports of cardioprotective effects. One report found that beer containing vitamin B6 helps protect against heart disease by lowering homocysteine-a risk factor for heart disease.

Available Dosage Forms and Strengths
>   Intravenous — 5%, 10%, 95%
>   Nonprescription — Each ounce of 100-proof whiskey has 15 ml of ethanol
>   — 6 ounces (12%) wine has 22 ml of ethanol
>   — 12 ounces of beer (4.9%) has 18 ml of ethanol

▷ **Recommended Dosage Ranges** (Actual dose and schedule must be determined for each patient individually.)

Infants and Children: Methanol or ethylene glycol poisoning: 40 ml per kg of body mass per day.

18 to 60 Years of Age: Ethylene glycol poisoning: A loading dose of 0.6 to 0.7 grams per kg of body mass is given (by mouth, NG tube or intravenously) and followed by 66 to 154 mg per kg of body mass per hour intravenously to maintain a blood level of 100 to 200 mg/dl (milligrams per deciliter) until ethylene glycol levels are undetectable. Methanol poisoning: 0.80 to 1 ml per kg by mouth of 95% ethanol in 6 ounces of orange juice over 30 minutes. Some centers use 1.5 to 2 milliliters per kilogram by mouth of 40% v/v ethanol given in 6 ounces of orange juice over 30 minutes. Dosing is continued to keep a blood level as above until methylene glycol levels are less than 10 mg/dl and/or metabolic changes (such as acidosis, amylase, bicarb, and clinical findings) have resolved.

Coronary heart disease or heart attack prevention: It appears that use of moderate amounts (up to 0.8 mg per kg of body mass per day or no more than 0.7 mg per kg of body mass per day for 3 days in a row) of alcohol may help in preventing risk of this kind of blood vessel disease and myocardial infarctions.

Ischemic stroke or stroke prevention: It appears that as little as one drink per week decreases risk.

Over 60 Years of Age: Same as 18 to 60 years of age for poisonings. Older people may be less able to tolerate the same amount as a younger person for the nonprescription forms. A smaller dose will generally cause an equal or greater loss of coordination or mental ability. Hypothermia risk is also increased.

Conditions Requiring Dosing Adjustments

Liver Function: Ethanol is extensively metabolized in the liver to acetaldehyde and acetyl CoA. The drug is also a clear cause of liver toxicity. The dose must be decreased in liver compromise.

Kidney Function: Kidneys are minimally involved. No changes needed.

▷ **Dosing Instructions:** If methanol or ethylene glycol poisoning is suspected: The nearest poison control center should be contacted (new national number is 800-222-1222). Oral dosing (use vodka mixed in orange juice) may be of benefit, depending on distance from a hospital or free-standing emergency center.

For nonprescription antianxiety use: Dose of this drug and the blood alcohol level varies with many factors. Critical ones are weight, metabolic activity of the liver, how much food is in the stomach, strength of alcohol in the beverage, number of "drinks" consumed over a given period of time, and how well hydrated (whether there has been extreme exercise and fluid loss) you are. In general, most of the ethanol consumed is absorbed in the small intestine in fasting patients and the remaining 20% of ethanol is absorbed in the stomach. Food does not change absorption from the small intestine, but delays absorption in the stomach by 2-6 hours.

A blood or breath alcohol test is a marker for mental or physical changes, some people may not have physical or mental changes and will actually have a blood or breath alcohol level in the state-defined range of "legally drunk." Specific levels of blood or breath alcohol do not absolutely predict impairment. Each 10 ml of ethanol increases blood ethanol of an average 150-lb (70-kg) person by 16.6 mg percent (3.6 mmol/L).

The legal definition of intoxication varies state to state, but generally, the legal definition of intoxication is a blood alcohol level of 0.10% or 100 mg/dl. "Under the influence" in Maryland is 0.07% or 70 mg/dl. Driving impairment may occur at blood levels of 0.05% (50 mg/dl) or lower.

Usual Duration of Use: Use on a regular schedule for 48 hours determines effectiveness in methanol overdose. Long-term excessive use as an antianxiety agent is NOT recommended. If you forget a dose: not applicable. Small daily doses appear to have heart protective effects.

Typical Treatment Goals and Measurements (Outcomes and Markers)
Prevention of coronary heart disease: Information from big and small studies shows that taking two or fewer (see dosing above) drinks per day can help decrease the risk of coronary heart disease. Red wine appears to have the most data, but some recent information appears to show a benefit from vitamin B6-containing beer. Goals then relate to probability of a coronary problem, and time gained without experiencing a coronary problem.

▷ **This Drug Should Not Be Taken If**
- you have had an allergic reaction to any dose form of it previously.
- you have epilepsy.
- you have a history of alcohol addiction.
- you have a urinary tract infection.
- you are pregnant.
- you are in diabetic coma.

▷ **Inform Your Physician Before Taking This Drug If**
- you are in shock or have had surgery on the head (cranium).
- you have liver or kidney compromise.
- you have gout.
- you are prone to low blood sugars.
- you are a diabetic.
- you have congestive heart failure.

Possible Side Effects (natural, expected, and unavoidable drug actions)
Intoxication, perception, coordination, and mood changes.

▷ **Possible Adverse Effects** (unusual, unexpected, and infrequent reactions)
If any of the following develop, consult your physician promptly for guidance.
Mild Adverse Effects
Allergic reactions: itching, rash, hives, and flushing.
Headache "hangover": nausea, headache, and malaise—dose-related.
Sedation—dose-dependent.
Disorientation, memory loss—dose-dependent.
Color blindness or neuropathy (tingling, burning, or numbness)—with chronic use.

Vitamin deficiency or muscle changes (myopathy)—with chronic use.

Stomach irritation—frequent.

Serious Adverse Effects

Allergic reactions: anaphylaxis (rash, swelling of tongue, breathing problems, flushing)—case reports.

Bronchospasm (asthmatics at increased risk)—case reports.

Respiratory depression—dose-related.

Elevated or decreased white blood cell count—possible.

Increased or decreased platelets—case reports.

Anemia with large red blood cells (megaloblastic)—possible and dose related.

Heart dysfunction (myopathy) or anemia (megaloblastic)—possible with chronic-particularly high dose use.

High blood pressure—possible to frequent.

Abnormal heart rhythms (atrial and ventricular) or chest pain (angina)—increased risk.

Liver toxicity—cirrhosis possible with chronic use.

Liver cancer—may be a relationship to heavy drinking.

Osteoporosis—increased risk with chronic use.

Pancreatitis—increased risk with chronic higher-dose use.

Encephalopathy or cerebrovascular bleeding—increased risk with higher-dose chronic use.

Nerve damage (peripheral neuropathy)—commonly seen in alcoholism.

Low blood sugar or ketoacidosis—especially if meals are missed or with chronic or high dose "binge" use.

Vitamin deficiency (folic acid, vitamins B1 and B6) or low magnesium—with chronic use.

Low potassium (especially with acute intoxication in children)—possible.

Gout (precipitated by alcohol use in those with gout)—possible.

Tolerance (with chronic use)—possible.

Withdrawal: nausea, fever, rapid heart rate, hallucinations. May progress to delirium tremens (5%): profound confusion, hallucinations, etc.—possible.

Breast cancer—controversial (some case studies found an association while others did not, some data for more dose related effect in women).

Gastroesophageal (tongue, mouth, oral pharynx, hypopharynx and the esophagus) and/or liver cancer—increased associated with heavy drinking.

▷ **Possible Effects on Sexual Function:** Decreased libido, impotence (with excessive chronic use). Difficulty achieving an erection in males and decreased vaginal dilation in females. Chronic alcohol use may lead to tenderness and swelling of male and female breast tissue, testicular atrophy, low sperm counts, decreased menstrual blood flow, and diminished capability for orgasm in females. Patients with carcinomas, Hodgkin's disease, lymphoma, and some non-malignant conditions have described intense pain associated with drinking alcohol.

Possible Delayed Adverse Effects: Liver toxicity, anemia, low or high platelets, vitamin deficiency.

▷ **Adverse Effects That May Mimic Natural Diseases or Disorders**

Alcoholic cirrhosis may mimic hepatitis.

Natural Diseases or Disorders That May Be Activated by This Drug

Peptic ulcer disease.

Possible Effects on Laboratory Tests

Liver function tests: elevated ALT.

Complete blood count: decreased white blood cells, decreased hemoglobin, increased or decreased platelets, large (macrocytic) red blood cells, macrocytic anemia.

Amylase: elevated.

Acidosis: possible.

Sperm count: decreased with chronic use.

Sodium and phosphorous: decreased.

Magnesium: decreased with chronic use.

Iron: increased serum iron levels.

Uric acid: increased.

CAUTION

1. The FDA now requires a warning label on all nonprescription pain (analgesic) and fever (antipyretic) products that have aspirin or other salicylates, ibuprofen, naproxen sodium, ketoprofen, or acetaminophen in them (NSAIDs) that says:

   Alcohol Warning: If you consume 3 or more alcoholic drinks every day, ask your doctor whether you should take [the medicine in question] or other pain relievers/fever reducers. [The ingredient] may cause stomach bleeding.

   This is a new warning intended to help protect patients from possible stomach or liver damage.

2. Nonprescription form may cause FATAL increases in blood pressure if combined with cocaine.

3. With high doses (nearly pure "grain" alcohol) or many drinks (frequent dosing) over a short period of time, FATAL blood alcohol levels may be reached with the nonprescription form.

4. Some alcoholic beverages have tyramine in them. Combination of these beverages with MAO inhibitors (see Drug Classes) may lead to extreme increases in blood pressure (hypertensive crisis).

5. Data from a study of 5,766 men over more than 21 years showed that heavy drinking may DOUBLE the risk of strokes.

6. Data from a study of more than 22,000 men showed that light to moderate use (from one drink per week up to one drink per day) of alcohol decreased the risk of stroke or ischemic stroke. Having more than one drink per day DID NOT further decrease risk.

7. Some data says that drinking alcohol (dose related or heavy use according to different researchers) while taking a corticosteroid (see drug classes) type medicine increases risk of bone death (osteonecrosis or avascular necrosis). Talk to your doctor to see how he or she wants to advise you on this. If you do drink alcohol while taking Corticosteroids, promptly report any unexplained joint (such as hip, knee, or shoulder) pain.

Precautions for Use

By Infants and Children: Safety and effectiveness for those under 12 years of age not established. Accidental and unsupervised drinking of the nonprescription form may result in severe consequences in children. Seriously low blood sugar may happen and be delayed up to 6 hours after drinking. Low potassium may also occur with high ethanol levels. Therapy is guided by blood sugar, potassium, and blood alcohol (ethanol) levels. Fatality caused by low blood sugar was reported in a 4-year-old child who drank 12 ounces of a mouthwash that contained 10% ethanol.

By Those Over 60 Years of Age: Poisoning with methanol or ethylene glycol is an emergency situation, and while there may be an increased sensitivity to effects, dosing is adjusted to blood levels. The nonprescription form dosing (number of drinks) tolerated would be expected to decrease with increasing age.

▷ **Advisability of Use During Pregnancy**

Pregnancy Category: D, X if used for long periods. See Pregnancy Risk Categories at the back of this book.

Human Studies: Fetal alcohol syndrome—a collection of limb, neurological and behavioral defects—occurs with excessive alcohol use.

Avoid use of this drug during your **entire** pregnancy.

Advisability of Use If Breast-Feeding

Presence of this drug in breast milk: Yes.

Avoid drug or refrain from nursing.

Habit-Forming Potential: Clearly defined alcoholism exists and occurs. Tolerance also occurs. Severe withdrawal (delirium tremens or DTs) is well documented.

Effects of Overdose: Toxic levels result in ataxia, loss of consciousness progressing to coma, anesthesia, respiratory failure, and death. Levels of 150 to 300 mg/dl may result in exaggerated emotional states, confusion, and incoordination. Fatalities most often result with blood concentrations greater than 400 mg/dl. Fatal blood levels vary greatly, however, and death has been reported following levels as low as 260 mg/dl. Once again, some people will not have any mental or physical changes with an alcohol level that is in the "legally drunk" range and even with higher levels.

Possible Effects of Long-Term Use: Liver toxicity, anemia, esophageal varices, low white blood cell counts, compromised heart function, high blood pressure, depression, peripheral neuropathy, seizures, cerebrovascular accident (with acute high levels), water intoxication, vitamin and electrolyte disturbances, gastritis or ulcers, pancreatitis, some cancers (see above) muscle pain, osteoporosis, tolerance, and withdrawal.

Suggested Periodic Examinations While Taking This Drug (at physician's discretion)

Blood alcohol levels and methanol or ethylene glycol levels guide therapy in poisonings.

Chronic alcohol abuse: Complete blood counts, liver function tests, amylase, and lipase, Bone mineral density test such as DEXA, electrocardiograms.

▷ **While Taking This Drug, Observe the Following**

Foods: Food may decrease the absorption of ethanol from the stomach and reduce chances of intoxication.

Nutritional Support: Vitamin support, particularly thiamin (B1), folic acid, B6 and vitamin A are needed with chronic use. Vitamin C may help eliminate ethanol.

Herbal Medicines or Minerals: Valerian and kava kava (kava is now not recommended in Canada because of possible liver damage) may interact additively (drowsiness). Avoid these combinations. Magnesium replacement may be needed.

Tobacco Smoking: No interactions expected. I advise everyone to quit smoking.

Marijuana Smoking: Additive central nervous system depression and possible increases in ethanol blood levels.

▷ *Other Drugs*

Ethanol may ***increase*** the effects of

• some antibiotics (such as doxycycline, others).

- central nervous system depressants, such as benzodiazepines, barbiturates, opioids (codeine, oxycodone, morphine, others), and anesthetic agents.
- chlorpromazine (Thorazine) and will result in increased sedation.
- cocaine and result in dangerous increases in blood pressure.
- cyclosporine (Sandimmune)—with large amounts of ethanol.
- diphenhydramine (Benadryl, others) and will increase sedation.
- paroxetine (Paxil) and venlafaxine (Effexor) and other antidepressants and may increase CNS effects of both drugs.
- warfarin (Coumadin) and require more frequent INR testing and possible dose changes.

Ethanol may *decrease* the effects of
- phenytoin (Dilantin) or fosphenytoin (Cerebyx) by reducing blood levels.
- propranolol (Inderal) by increasing propranolol elimination.

Ethanol taken concurrently with
- abacavir (Ziagen) may result in increased blood levels of abacavir and possibly an increased risk of toxicity.
- acetaminophen (Tylenol) poses an increased risk of liver damage.
- some antihistamines may increase sedation.
- amprenavir (Agenerase) solution may carry a risk of propylene glycol toxicity. Combination is NOT recommended.
- aspirin may result in increased blood loss from the stomach.
- bupropion (Wellbutrin) lowers the seizure threshold in chronic alcohol users. This combination should at least be minimized and better avoided.
- cefamandole (Mandol), cefotetan (Cefotan), metronidazole (Flagyl), cotrimoxazole, sulfamethoxazole, and cefoperazone (Cefobid) may result in disulfiramlike reaction (see Glossary).
- cimetidine (Zantac) may decrease the amount of alcohol that it takes to make you drunk (intoxicated).
- cisapride (Propulsid) may increase ethanol blood levels.
- corticosteroids (various) may increase risk of bone death (aseptic necrosis, avascular necrosis or osteonecrosis. Talk to your doctor about drinking BEFORE you take any alcoholic beverage.
- disulfiram (Antabuse) will result in severe vomiting and intolerance.
- dronabinol (Marinol) may increase ethanol levels.
- escitalopram (Lexapro) is NOT recommended by the manufacturer.
- fexofenadine (Allegra) showed NO driving performance decrease in one study of 24 healthy men.
- griseofulvin (Fulvicin) can increase the effects of alcohol.
- insulin (various, see insulin profile) may result in potential severe hypoglycemia.
- isoniazid may result in elevated isoniazid levels.
- ketoconazole (Nizoral) may result in disulfiramlike reactions.
- lithium (Lithobid) may result in worsened impairment of coordination and intoxication.
- metformin (Glucophage) may increase risk of lactic acidosis with ongoing or excessive ethanol use.
- methotrexate (Rheumatrex, others) may increase risk of liver damage (especially with long-term ethanol use).
- metronidazole (Flagyl) may result in a disulfiramlike reaction.
- mirtazapine (Remeron) may lead to increased risk of psychomotor impairment.
- nitroglycerin (Nitrostat, others) may result in excessive decreases in blood pressure.

- nonsteroidal anti-inflammatory drugs (NSAIDs; see Drug Classes) may lead to increased risk of stomach bleeding or liver damage.
- olanzapine (Zyprexa) may lead to excessive depression of the central nervous system.
- oral hypoglycemic agents (see Drug Classes) poses an increased risk of seriously low glucose levels.
- quetiapine (Seroquel) may worsen thinking and motor skill depression caused by ethanol.
- ranitidine (Zantac) lead to increased ethanol levels in one study. Ethanol intake is best minimized in patients taking ranitidine.
- sibutramine (Meridia) is not recommended by the manufacturer.
- sulfonylurea oral hypoglycemic agents (such as glipizide, glyburide, others; see Drug Classes) poses an increased risk of seriously low glucose levels and disulfiram-like reactions.
- tramadol (Ultram) may lead to excessive depression of the central nervous system.
- tricyclic antidepressants (see Drug Classes) may result in increased antidepressant levels and toxicity.
- trimethoprim/sulfamethoxazole (Cotrimoxazole, Septra, Bactrim, others) may lead to a disulfiram-like reaction.
- valproic acid (Depakene, Depakote, others) may enhance central nervous depression from ethanol.
- venlafaxine (Effexor) is not advised by the manufacturer.
- verapamil (Calan, others) may increase the amount of time ethanol stays in the body and may pose an increased risk of intoxication.
- zaleplon (Sonata) may result in increased additive central nervous depression (impairing psychomotor functions). Combination should be avoided.
- zolpidem (Ambien) may result in increased additive central nervous depression (impairing psychomotor functions). Combination should be avoided.

▷ *Driving, Hazardous Activities:* This drug may cause drowsiness, mental impairment and coordination problems. Driving skill may be impaired at very low blood levels with the perception that capabilities are *not* reduced. Drinking and driving is not recommended. Restrict activities as necessary.

Aviation Note: The use of this drug *is a disqualification* for piloting. Consult a designated Aviation Medical Examiner.

Exposure to Sun: May result in additive dehydration.

Heavy Exercise or Exertion: May worsen the adverse effects of this drug.

Discontinuation: Abrupt discontinuation after chronic use may result in a serious withdrawal syndrome known as DT or delirium tremens.

ETHOSUXIMIDE (eth oh SUX i myde)

Introduced: 1960   **Class:** Anticonvulsant   **Prescription:** USA: Yes
Controlled Drug: USA: No; Canada: No   **Available as Generic:** Yes
Brand Name: Zarontin

BENEFITS versus RISKS

Possible Benefits	*Possible Risks*
EFFECTIVE CONTROL OF ABSENCE SEIZURES (PETIT MAL EPILEPSY)	RARE APLASTIC ANEMIA (see Aplastic Anemia and Bone Marrow Depression in Glossary)
EFFECTIVE CONTROL OF MYOCLONIC AND AKINETIC EPILEPSY IN SOME PATIENTS	Rare decrease in white blood cells and blood platelets

---

▷ **Principal Uses**

As a Single Drug Product: Uses currently included in FDA-approved labeling: Used to treat petit mal epilepsy and is a drug of choice in absence seizures. Other (unlabeled) generally accepted uses: None at present.

How This Drug Works: Alters some nerve impulses, suppressing abnormal electrical activity that causes absence seizures (petit mal epilepsy). In general succinimides inhibit (suppress) paroxysmal three-cycle per second wave activity that is seen (associated) with lapses of consciousness in absence seizures. Ethosuximide action is possible related to inhibition at the synapse, which is caused by GABA (GABA mediated chloride conductants).

Available Dosage Forms and Strengths

Capsules or
Gelcaps — 250 mg
Solution — 250 mg/5 ml
Syrup — 250 mg/5 ml

▷ **Usual Adult Dosage Ranges:** Dosing starts with 500 mg daily and can be increased by 250 mg every 4 to 7 days until acceptable control is achieved. Ending dose may be 20 to 30 mg per kg daily. Daily maximum is 1,500 mg. IMPORTANT: Blood levels increase more quickly in females than males. *For children 3 to 6 years old:* Usual starting dose is 250 mg per day. May increase by 250-mg doses every 4 to 7 days as needed. Usually 20–30 mg per kg is the once-daily dose. *More than 6 years old with absence seizures:* Same as adults.

Note: Actual dose and schedule must be determined for each patient individually.

Conditions Requiring Dosing Adjustments

Liver Function: Blood levels are recommended if the liver is damaged.
Kidney Function: No specific changes needed, but a more frequent check of blood levels may be prudent.

▷ **Dosing Instructions:** Capsule may be opened and taken with food to reduce stomach irritation. If you forget a dose: take the dose you missed as soon as you remember it, unless it is nearly time for your next dose—if that is the case, simply skip the missed dose and take the next scheduled dose right on schedule. DO NOT double doses.

Usual Duration of Use: Regular use for 1 to 2 weeks may be needed to identify the best dose and reduce frequency of absence seizures. Long-term use requires physician supervision and use is ongoing.

Typical Treatment Goals and Measurements (Outcomes and Markers)

Seizures: The general goal for this medicine is effective seizure control. Neurologists tend to define effective on a case-by-case basis depending on the seizure type and patient factors. Blood levels can help guide dosing. If this medicine is being used to treat absence seizures, EEG can be used to check clinical progress.

Currently a Drug of Choice
For ongoing (maintenance) therapy of absence seizures.

▷ **This Drug Should Not Be Taken If**
- you are allergic to any succinimide anticonvulsant (see Drug Classes).
- you currently have a blood cell or bone marrow disorder.

▷ **Inform Your Physician Before Taking This Drug If**
- you have a history of or active liver or kidney disease.
- you have any type of blood disorder, especially one caused by drugs.
- you have serious depression or mental illness.

Possible Side Effects (natural, expected, and unavoidable drug actions)
Drowsiness, lethargy, fatigue.

▷ **Possible Adverse Effects** (unusual, unexpected, and infrequent reactions)
If any of the following develop, consult your physician promptly for guidance.
Mild Adverse Effects
Allergic reactions: skin rash, hives—case reports.
Headache, unsteadiness, euphoria, impaired vision, numbness and tingling in extremities—infrequent.
Loss of appetite, nausea, vomiting, dizziness, hiccups, stomach pain, diarrhea—infrequent to frequent.
Thickening and overgrowth of gums—possible.
Serious Adverse Effects
Allergic Reaction: Swelling of tongue—case reports.
Severe skin eruptions (Stevens-Johnson Syndrome, erythema multiforme)—occasional.
Aggravation of emotional depression and paranoid mental disorders—case reports.
Severe bone marrow depression: fatigue, fever, sore throat, abnormal bleeding or bruising—case reports.
Porphyria, myasthenia gravis or systemic lupus erythematosus—rare.

▷ **Possible Effects on Sexual Function:** Increased libido (questionable); nonmenstrual vaginal bleeding—case reports.

Natural Diseases or Disorders That May Be Activated by This Drug
Latent psychosis, systemic lupus erythematosus.

Possible Effects on Laboratory Tests
Complete blood cell counts: decreased red cells, hemoglobin, white cells, and platelets; increased eosinophils.
Blood aspartate aminotransferase (AST) level: increased in 33% of users.
Blood bilirubin level: increased (rare liver damage).
Blood lupus erythematosus (LE) cells: positive—rare.
Kidney function tests: increased blood urea nitrogen (BUN) level, increased urine protein content.

CAUTION
1. May increase the frequency of grand mal seizures in people with mixed seizure disorders.
2. Periodic blood counts and other tests are mandatory.
3. Plasma levels increase faster in women than men.

Precautions for Use

By Infants and Children: If a single daily dose causes nausea or vomiting, give in two or three divided doses 8 to 12 hours apart. Large differences in response occur and require blood levels. Watch for a lupuslike reaction: fever, rash, arthritis.

By Those Over 60 Years of Age: Rarely used in this age group.

▷ **Advisability of Use During Pregnancy**

Pregnancy Category: C. See Pregnancy Risk Categories at the back of this book.

Animal Studies: Bone defects reported in rodents.

Human Studies: Three instances of birth defects have been reported. Adequate studies of pregnant women are not available.

Avoid during first 3 months. Use only if clearly needed during the final 6 months.

Advisability of Use If Breast-Feeding

Presence of this drug in breast milk: Yes, but not usually a significant level.

Watch nursing infant closely and discontinue drug or nursing if adverse effects develop. If mother requires high doses, refrain from nursing. Ask your doctor for help.

Habit-Forming Potential: None, but sudden withdrawal may lead to seizures.

Effects of Overdose: Drowsiness, lethargy, dizziness, nausea, vomiting, stupor progressing to coma.

Possible Effects of Long-Term Use: Systemic lupus erythematosus.

Suggested Periodic Examinations While Taking This Drug (at physician's discretion)

Complete blood counts every 2 weeks during the first months of use and then monthly thereafter.

Liver and kidney function tests.

▷ **While Taking This Drug, Observe the Following**

Foods: No restrictions.

Herbal Medicines or Minerals: Valerian and kava kava may interact additively (drowsiness). Avoid these combinations. Kava is no longer recommended in Canada due to liver problems. Evening primrose oil should not be used in people with seizures. A contaminant (4'-o-methylpyridoxine) in some ginkgo preparations can increase seizure risk. Talk to your doctor about this benefit to risk decision.

Beverages: No restrictions. May be taken with milk.

▷ *Alcohol:* Use caution—this drug may increase the sedative effects of alcohol. Excessive alcohol may precipitate seizures.

Tobacco Smoking: No interactions expected. I advise everyone to quit smoking.

▷ **Other Drugs**

Ethosuximide may *increase* the effects of

- phenytoin (Dilantin) and fosphenytoin (Cerebyx), by slowing elimination.

Ethosuximide *taken concurrently* with

- carbamazepine (Tegretol) may change ethosuximide blood levels.
- phenobarbital may decrease seizure control success.
- ritonavir (Norvir) and perhaps other protease inhibitors (see Drug Classes) may lead to toxicity.
- tramadol (Ultram) may increase seizure risk.
- valproic acid (Depakene, Depakote) may unpredictably alter ethosuximide effects.

The following drug may *increase* the effects of ethosuximide:
- isoniazid (INH, Niconyl, etc.).

▷ *Driving, Hazardous Activities:* This drug may cause drowsiness, dizziness, unsteadiness, and impaired vision. Restrict activities as necessary.

Aviation Note: Seizure disorders and the use of this drug *are disqualifications* for piloting. Consult a designated Aviation Medical Examiner.

Exposure to Sun: No restrictions.

Discontinuation: Do not stop taking this drug abruptly as sudden withdrawal may lead to seizures. Slow and stepwise lowering is prudent (over at least three months). Some clinicians have obtained superb results by lowering the dose in increments of three months and discontinuing the medicine over 9 months. Ask your physician for help with gradual dose reduction.

ETIDRONATE (e ti DROH nate)

Introduced: 1976 **Class:** Anti-osteoporotic **Prescription:**
USA: Yes **Controlled Drug:** USA: No; Canada: No **Available as**
Generic: USA: No; Canada: No
Brand Name: Didronel

BENEFITS versus RISKS	
Possible Benefits	*Possible Risks*
PARTIAL RELIEF OF SYMPTOMS OF PAGET'S DISEASE OF BONE	Increased bone pain
	Bone fractures
EFFECTIVE PREVENTION AND TREATMENT OF ABNORMAL CALCIFICATION	Kidney failure
	Focal osteomalacia
Effective adjunctive treatment of abnormally high blood calcium levels (associated with malignant disease)	
Treatment of postmenopausal osteoporosis	

▷ **Principal Uses**

As a Single Drug Product: Uses currently included in FDA-approved labeling: (1) Treatment of symptomatic Paget's disease of bone (excessive bone growth of skull, spine, and long bones); (2) prevention and treatment of abnormal bone formation (ossification) following total hip replacement or spinal cord injury; (3) adjunctive treatment of excessively high blood calcium levels due to malignant bone disease.

Other (unlabeled) generally accepted uses: (1) treatment of Paget's disease of bone that is not yet causing symptoms; (2) treatment of abnormal calcium levels that may result from prolonged immobilization; (3) helps hyperparathyroidism; (4) helps pulmonary alveolar microlithiasis (PAM); (5) treatment (with cyclic dosing) of postmenopausal osteoporosis.

How This Drug Works: This drug attaches to the surface of bone and slows the abnormally accelerated processes of "bone turnover" that occur in Paget's disease. In malignant bone disease, this drug slows bone destruction and reduces excessive transfer of calcium from bone to blood.

Available Dosage Forms and Strengths
  Injection — 50 mg/ml
  Tablets — 200 mg, 400 mg
▷ **Recommended Dosage Ranges** (Actual dose and schedule must be determined for each patient individually.)
  Infants and Children: Dose not established.
  12 to 60 Years of Age:
    For Paget's disease: Initially 5 mg per kg of body mass daily, as a single dose, for up to 6 months. Discontinue for a drug-free period of 6 months. As needed, repeat, alternating 6-month courses of drug treatment and abstention. Doses above 10 mg per kg of body mass per day are only used if there is a critical need to decrease increased work output of the heart or to quickly slow down increased bone turnover.
    For ossification associated with hip replacement: 20 mg per kg of body mass daily for 1 month before and 3 months after surgery.
    For ossification associated with spinal cord injury: Initially 20 mg per kg of body mass daily for 2 weeks after injury; then decrease dose to 10 mg per kg of body mass daily for an additional 10 weeks.
    For high blood calcium associated with malignant bone disease: 20 mg per kg of body mass daily for 30 days; if needed and tolerated, continue for a maximum of 90 days. The total daily dose should not exceed 20 mg per kg of body mass.
  Over 60 Years of Age: Same as 12 to 60 years of age.
  Author's Note: The information in this profile has been shortened to allow room for more widely used medicines.

ETODOLAC (e TOE do lak)

Please see the acetic acids (nonsteroidal anti-inflammatory drug) family profile.

ETRETINATE (e TRET i nayt)

Introduced: 1976 **Class:** Antipsoriasis
Brand Name: Tegison
Author's Note: The manufacturer has stopped marketing this medicine.

EXTENDED RELEASE NIACIN/LOVASTATIN
(NIGH a sin/loh VAH sta tin)

Introduced: 2002 **Class:** Anticholesterol, cholesterol lowering medicine, vasodilator **Prescription:** USA: Yes **Controlled Drug:** USA: No **Available as Generic:** USA: No; Canada: No
Brand Name: Advicor

BENEFITS versus RISKS	
Possible Benefits	**Possible Risks**
EFFECTIVE REDUCTION OF TOTAL BLOOD CHOLESTEROL, LOW DENSITY LIPOPROTEINS (LDL), AND TRIGLYCERIDES IN TYPES II, III, IV, AND FIVE CHOLESTEROL DISORDERS	FLUSHING (minimized by taking aspirin 30 minutes before this product and also by taking at bedtime)
PREVENTS CORONARY HEART DISEASE IN PATIENTS WHO DO NOT HAVE SYMPTOMS, BUT HAVE INCREASED TOTAL CHOLESTEROL, LDL-C, AND LOW HDL-C	Drug-induced hepatitis (without jaundice)
INCREASES HIGH DENSITY LIPOPROTEINS (HDL)	Drug-induced myositis (muscle inflammation)
DECREASES Lp (a)	Decreased co-enxyme Q10 (possible effect of the lovastatin component)
SLOWS PROGRESSION OF HEART (CORONARY) ATHEROSCLEROSIS	Possible aggravation of diabetes or gout
May reduce risk of stroke, like other medicines in this class	
May lower the risk of some cancers	

▷ **Principal Uses**

As a Single Drug Product: Uses currently included in FDA-approved labeling: (1) Reduces abnormally high total blood cholesterol levels in people with primary hypercholesterolemia (heterozygous familial and nonfamilial increased cholesterol) as well as mixed dyslipidemia (otherwise known as Frederickson Types IIa and IIb) where the patients have (1) attempted a low cholesterol diet and other nonpharmacologic measures and have: (2) been treated with lovastatin, but need to have their triglycerides lowered more or their HDL raised or (3) who would benefit from taking niacin. Additionally, this combination drug should be used in people who have been taking niacin—yet require to have their LDL lowered more and who would benefit from taking lovastatin.

Other (unlabeled) generally accepted uses: (1) None at present.

How This Drug Works: The combination of these two distinct medicines offers the benefit of niacin actions and while not completely understood, it is thought that: (1) the niacin part of this combination increases lipoprotein lipase activity which then quickens removal of triglyceride (via chylomicrons) from the plasma; (2) decreases the speed that the liver makes LDL and VLDL; (3) may inhibit release of free fatty acids from fat (adipose tissue). Via the lovastatin component, this medicine blocks a liver enzyme that starts making cholesterol. It decreases low-density lipoproteins (LDL), the fraction of total blood cholesterol that increases risk of coronary heart disease. Since the amount of cholesterol is reduced in the liver, the VLDL fraction may also be decreased. There is a growing body of evidence that "statins" also have beneficial effects on undesirable compounds in the blood, on blood flow and even on the blood vessel walls themselves. Specific compounds or effects on platelet derived growth factor (PDGF), undesirable clotting via thrombin-antithrombin III, thrombomodulin, and other chemicals are probably changed in desirable ways by statins. The original (prodrug) form of this medicine increases CDKI P21 and P27 and may account for the ability of lovastatin to lower the risk of cancer.

Available Dosage Forms and Strengths

Tablets, extended action niacin/lovastatin — 500 mg niacin/20 mg lovastatin

— 750 mg niacin/20 mg lovastatin

— 1,000 mg niacin/20 mg lovastatin.

▷ **Usual Adult Dosage Ranges:** *For cholesterol disorders:* Usual Niaspan starting dose is 500 mg taken at bedtime. People who already take Niaspan can be switched directly to the appropriate (niacin equivalent) dose of Advicor. The typical lovastatin starting dose is 20 mg daily. Increases are made at 4 week intervals as needed to reach goals and tolerated. One 500/20 mg tablet at bedtime, which is increased as needed and tolerated at four-week intervals to 750 and 1,000 mg daily. Taking more than 2000 mg/40 mg daily is NOT recommended. If Advicor is stopped for more than 7 days, it should be restarted at the lowest dose and increased as above all over again (re-titrated).

Note: Actual dose and dosing schedule must be determined for each patient individually.

Conditions Requiring Dosing Adjustments

Liver Function: Both medicines in this combination are removed via the liver and have not been studied in liver compromised populations. Advicor is contraindicated in liver disease/dysfunction.

Kidney Function: Specific dosing adjustments for the combination medicine are not available, but great caution should be used in considering doses above 20 mg per day of the lovastatin component for patients with severe kidney problems (creatinine clearance less than 30 ml/min).

▷ **Dosing Instructions:** Other (secondary causes) of hypercholesterolemia (such as low thyroid function, poorly controlled diabetes, alcoholism, or certain kidney problems) should be ruled out before a cholesterol lowering medicine is started. Take at night with a low fat snack to help prevent stomach irritation and avoid the problem of flushing (a common side effect). Taking aspirin half an hour before taking this medicine can help prevent facial flushing and itching. Taking hot drinks close to the time this medicine is taken may worsen the feeling of flushing. This medicine should not be crushed or altered. If you forget a dose, take the missed dose as soon as you remember it, unless it's nearly time for your next dose—if that is the case, skip the missed dose and take the next dose right on schedule. Talk with your doctor if you find yourself missing doses.

Usual Duration of Use: Use on a regular schedule for 3 to 5 weeks determines benefit in reducing levels of cholesterol and triglycerides. Long-term use (months to years) requires periodic physician evaluation. Treatment of high cholesterol is an ongoing therapy in order to help avoid heart disease and stroke.

Typical Treatment Goals and Measurements (Outcomes and Markers)

Cholesterol: The National Institutes of Health Adult Treatment Panel has released ATP III as part of the update to the National Cholesterol Education Program or NCEP. Key points in these guidelines include acknowledging diabetes as one of the conditions that increases risk of heart disease, modifying risk factors, therapeutic lifestyle changes (TLC) and recommending routine testing for all of the cholesterol fractions (lipoprotein profile) versus total cholesterol alone.

Current NCEP guidelines recommend a desirable total cholesterol of 200 mg/dl, and optimal bad cholesterol (LDL) as 100 mg/dl, 130–159 mg/dl as borderline high, 160 mg/dl as high and 190 mg/dl as very high. Did you know that there are at least five different kinds of "good cholesterol" or HDL? The "too low" measure for HDL is still 40 mg/dl, but in order to learn more about cholesterol types some doctors are starting to order lipid panels. There are at least seven different kinds of "bad cholesterol." The new panels tell doctors about the kinds of cholesterol that your body makes. This is important because some kinds (small dense particles) tend to stick to blood vessels (are highly atherogenic). Take your medicine to reach your goals!

Two additional tests you will hear about will be electron beam computed tomography (EBCT) and CRP. EBCT is an important tool used in conjunction with laboratory studies. Findings show that even patients who meet cholesterol goals (particularly females over 55) can still be at significant cardiovascular risk. EBCT then defines risk by giving a calcium score and a "virtual tour" of the coronary arteries. C Reactive Protein or CRP is a new and apparently independent predictor of heart disease risk. A large study (see Ridker, PM in Sources) found that CRP predicted heart disease risk independently of bad cholesterol (low density lipoprotein). Talk to your doctor about this new laboratory test and ask about current guidelines for who should be tested (see Pearson, TA in Sources).

Author's Note: the Advicor Versus Other Cholesterol-modifying Agents Trial Evaluation (ADVOCATE) study showed significant advantage of this medicine over 16 weeks versus atorvastatin (Lipitor) and simvastatin (Zocor). Comparison was made with checks of LDL, HDL, triglycerides, and Lp(a) and the Advicor 1000/40 versus Lipitor and Zocor 20mg).

Possible Advantages of This Drug Combination

Provides benefits of two proven medicines, which work both to lower cholesterol and increase reverse cholesterol transport via an increase in HDL. May have specific benefits in women who are having trouble meeting their cholesterol lowering goals. Advicor benefits lipid profiles in both sexes, but has a significantly larger beneficial effect in women than in men. Lovastatin portion of this medicine increases some substances that may reduce the risk of cancer.

▷ **This Drug Should Not Be Taken If**
- you have had an allergic reaction to any component of it previously.
- you have active peptic ulcer disease.
- you have active liver disease or unexplained increases in liver enzymes.
- you are bleeding from an artery.

▷ **Inform Your Physician Before Taking This Drug If**
- you are prone to low blood pressure.
- you regularly drink substantial amounts of alcohol.
- you have cataracts or impaired vision.
- you have a heart rhythm disorder of any kind.
- you have a history of peptic ulcer disease, inflammatory bowel disease, liver disease, jaundice, or gallbladder disease.
- you have any type of chronic muscular disorder.
- you are not using any method of birth control or you are planning pregnancy.
- you have diabetes or gout.

Possible Side Effects (natural, expected, and unavoidable drug actions)

Flushing, itching, tingling, and feeling of warmth, usually in the face and neck. Sensitive people may experience orthostatic hypotension (see Glossary). Development of abnormal liver function tests without associated symptoms. Increases CDKI P21 and P27 and may decrease cancer risk.

▷ **Possible Adverse Effects** (unusual, unexpected, and infrequent reactions)
If any of the following develop, consult your physician promptly for guidance.

Mild Adverse Effects

Allergic reactions: skin rash, itching, hives.

Headache, dizziness, faintness, impaired vision—infrequent to frequent.

Indigestion, nausea, altered taste, impaired sense of smell, excessive gas, vomiting, and diarrhea—rare-infrequent.

Flushing and tingling—infrequent to frequent (modified by this new form of niacin and can be further modified by taking aspirin 30 minutes before Advicor.

Dryness of skin, grayish-black pigmentation of skin folds—infrequent.

Prolonged protime—possible.

Gum pain—case reports with one component.

Serious Adverse Effects

Drug-induced hepatitis with jaundice (see Glossary): yellow eyes and skin, dark-colored urine, light-colored stools—case reports with lovastatin. Hypersensitivity syndrome (positive ANA, anaphylaxis, angioedema, arthritis, fever, toxic epidermal necrolysis, or other features) has been reported.

Worsening of diabetes (hyperglycemia) and gout—possible.

Neuropathy or systemic lupus erythematosus-like syndrome-case reports with the single ingredient lovastatin.

Blood clotting problem (increased prothrombin time) and/or low blood platelets (thrombocytopenia)—case reports.

Development of heart rhythm disorders—case reports to infrequent.

Sudden unexplained muscle pain and tenderness (myopathy) or rhabdomyolysis—case reports with lovastatin, no reports in clinical trials at doses up to 2,000/40 mg Advicor for two years.

Peptic ulcers—case reports.

Vision changes (macular edema)—case reports with lovastatin.

▷ **Possible Effects on Sexual Function:** None reported.

▷ **Adverse Effects That May Mimic Natural Diseases or Disorders**
Liver reactions may suggest viral hepatitis.

Possible Delayed Adverse Effects: Myopathy.

Natural Diseases or Disorders That May Be Activated by This Drug
Latent diabetes, gout, inflammatory bowel disease or peptic ulcer.

Possible Effects on Laboratory Tests
Complete blood cell counts: decreased eosinophils and lymphocytes.

Platelet counts: may be decreased (more likely in men).

Blood total cholesterol, LDL cholesterol, triglyceride, and Lp(a) levels: decreased.

Blood phosphorous levels: may be decreased.

Blood HDL cholesterol level: increased.

Blood glucose level: increased.

Glucose tolerance test (GTT): decreased.

Blood uric acid level: increased.

Liver function tests: increased enzymes (ALT/GPT, AST/GOT, alkaline phosphatase) or bilirubin.

Urine sugar tests: inaccurate test results with Benedict's solution.

INR (PT) may be increased.

CAUTION

1. Periodic measurements of blood cholesterol and triglyceride levels are essential for monitoring response and determining the need for changes in dose or medication. Talk to your doctor if goals are not reached.
2. Stop the drug immediately and call your doctor if you become pregnant.
3. Muscle problems and rhabdomyolysis have been seen when niacin (some release forms not used in the Advicor combination) has been used in combination with lovastatin. Risk of these problems is increased with high levels of lovastatin in the body. Because of this, careful attention should be paid to taking medicines (see drug interactions) that can block a liver enzyme called P450 3A4.
4. Call your doctor is you have unexplained muscle tenderness, weakness or pain—especially during the first month of treatment. It is prudent to check a lab test called creatine kinase during the first month of treatment and if the dose of this medicine is increased. While checking this test periodically is prudent, no assurance is present that such testing will prevent muscle problems (myopathy).
5. In people who have just had a heart attack (acute MI phase) and in patients with unstable angina, this combination of medicines should be used with caution—especially if they are already being given medicines that work to dilate blood vessels (such as adrenergic blockers, calcium channel blockers, or nitrates.)
6. A study in Circulation (see Heeschen in sources) found that stopping "statin" type medicines in patients with acute coronary syndrome symptoms can lead to a three-fold increase risk of non-fatal heart attack (MI) or death. This must be balanced against the caution in number 4.
7. This medicine should be stopped a few days before elective major surgery.
8. The Advicor combination product should NOT be exchanged (substituted) for immediate release (crystalline) niacin. This switch can be made, but treatment in those cases should be started with the 500/20 mg Advicor dose.

Precautions for Use

By Infants and Children: Safety and effectiveness for use by those less than 18 years of age have not been established.

By Those Over 60 Years of Age: Watch for possible development of low blood pressure (light-headedness, dizziness, faintness) and heart rhythm changes.

▷ **Advisability of Use During Pregnancy**

Pregnancy Category: X. See Pregnancy Risk Categories at the back of this book.

Animal Studies: Significant birth defects due to one component of this drug were found in chicks. Mouse and rat studies reveal skeletal birth defects due to the lovastatin part of this medicine.

Human Studies: Adequate studies of pregnant women are not available.

Should NOT be used in pregnancy. Given to women of childbearing potential only after careful instruction about contraception and where they are highly unlikely to get pregnant. If a pregnancy occurs, the drug should be stopped immediately and your doctor notified.

Advisability of Use If Breast-Feeding

Presence of this drug in breast milk: Yes for one component, probably for another.

Avoid drug or refrain from nursing.

Habit-Forming Potential: None.

Effects of Overdose: Generalized flushing, nausea, vomiting, stomach cramps, diarrhea, weakness, fainting, low blood pressure (reported for the niacin component).

Possible Effects of Long-Term Use: Increased blood levels of sugar and uric acid; increased liver enzymes. Studies in rats with three to four times the human lovastatin dose resulted in increases in hepatocellular carcinoma (cancer). Clinical significance in human is not known. Research published in July 2002 in the *National Academy of Sciences Proceedings* shows that the lovastatin component of this medicine increases cyclin-dependent kinase inhibitors P21 and P27. This effect may reduce cancer risk in general in humans.

Suggested Periodic Examinations While Taking This Drug (at physician's discretion)

Measurements of blood levels of total cholesterol, HDL and LDL cholesterol fractions, triglycerides, sugar, and uric acid.

Liver function tests and creatine kinase (CK). CK testing is prudent particularly during the first month of treatment.

▷ **While Taking This Drug, Observe the Following**

Foods: Follow the low-cholesterol diet prescribed by your doctor. Your doctor may also recommend some specific foods such as increased vegetables or functional foods such as Benecol. Three well-designed studies published in early April 2002 found that both in women and men and before and after a heart attack, people who ate more fish (2–4 servings a week) appeared to avoid heart disease. Additionally putting supplements containing Omega 3 polyunsaturated fatty acids (PUFA) into the diet also appeared to protect against abnormal heart rhythms and sudden death from heart attack. The studies appeared in *JAMA, Circulation,* and the *New England Journal of Medicine.* Vitamins that have a large amount of niacin or niacin-like compounds may increase the effects of this medicine.

Herbal Medicines or Minerals: The FDA has allowed one dietary supplement called Cholestin to continue to be sold. This preparation actually contains lovastatin, or lovastatin like compounds and since increasing the amount of HMG-CoA inhibitor may increase risk of muscle problems, the combination is NOT advised. Be on the look out for red rice yeast products as they are similar. No data exist from well-designed clinical studies about garlic and this product, but the combination is probably complementary in lowering cholesterol. One other consideration is that garlic may inhibit blood-clotting (platelet) aggregation—something to consider if you are already taking a platelet inhibitor.

Soy products (milk, tofu, etc.) contain phytoestrogens that have led to an FDA-approved health claim for reducing risk of heart disease (if they have at least 6.25 g of soy protein per serving). Use of soy products have been proven to lower cholesterol. Talk to your doctor to see if this makes sense for you. Because the lovastatin part of this medicine may lower coenzyme Q 10, supplementation may be needed.

Beverages: Grapefruit juice may increase the lovastatin portion of this medicine. Prudent NOT to combine. May be taken with milk or water.

▷ *Alcohol:* Use with caution. Alcohol used with large doses of this drug may cause excessive lowering of blood pressure and may also increase flushing or itching. There has been one case report of delirium.

Tobacco Smoking: May increase risk of flushing and dizziness. I advise everyone to quit smoking.

▷ *Other Drugs*

Niacin may *increase* the effects of

- some antihypertensive drugs and cause excessive lowering of blood pressure.

Niacin may *decrease* the effects of

- antidiabetic drugs (insulin and oral antidiabetic drugs; see Drug Classes), by raising the level of blood sugar.
- aspirin (various), which may decrease flushing but may also increase niacin blood levels; talk to your doctor.
- probenecid (Benemid) and sulfinpyrazone (Anturane), by raising the level of blood uric acid.

Niacin *taken concurrently* with

- isoniazid (INH) may result in decreased niacin levels and require increased niacin dosing.
- cholestyramine (Cholybar, Questran) or colestipol (Colestid) may result in decreased niacin levels and require increased niacin dosing. Separate dosing by 4–6 hours.
- lovastatin and other HMG-CoA type medicines does increase the chance of muscle problems (myositis or even rhabdomyolysis). Your doctor will make this a benefit-to-risk decision.
- nicotine (particularly transdermal) may result in increased risk of flushing and dizziness

▷ *Other Drugs*

Lovastatin *taken concurrently* with

- amprenavir (Agenerase) may lead to lovastatin toxicity (damage muscles (rhabdomyolysis).
- clofibrate (Atromid-S, others) may damage muscles (rhabdomyolysis).
- colesevelam (Welchol) can help further lower cholesterol.
- cyclosporine (Sandimmune) can cause a severe myopathy.
- diltiazem (Cardizem) may increase risk of myopathy.
- erythromycin (E.E.S.) and other macrolide antibiotics clarithromycin (Biaxin) or dirithromycin may result in severe rhabdomyolysis.
- fluconazole (Diflucan), itraconazole (Sporanox), ketoconazole (Nizoral), and voriconazole (Vfend) may increase risk of muscle damage (rhabdomyolysis).
- gemfibrozil (Lopid) and other fibrates may cause myopathy and the combination is not recommended.
- levothyroxine (various) may decrease thyroxine benefits.
- medicines that change the liver enzyme cytochrome P450 3A4 will change the levels of lovastatin and could lead to a subtherapeutic effect or toxicity. Talk to your doctor and pharmacist before adding other medicines.
- nefazodone (Serzone) may lead to myopathy.
- quinupristin/dalfopristin (Synercid) may increase risk of muscle damage (rhabdomyolysis).
- ritonavir (Norvir), amprenavir (Agenerase), indinavir (Crixivan), and perhaps other protease inhibitors may lead to lovastatin toxicity.
- warfarin (Coumadin, others) may result in bleeding; increased frequency of INR (prothrombin time or protime) testing is suggested.

▷ *Driving, Hazardous Activities:* This drug may cause dizziness or impaired vision. Restrict activities as necessary.

Aviation Note: The use of this drug *may be a disqualification* for piloting. Consult a designated Aviation Medical Examiner.

Exposure to Sun: No restrictions.

Discontinuation: Do not stop this drug without your physician's knowledge and guidance. Patients who have acute coronary syndromes or ACS (such as unstable angina, heart attack [non-p; Q-wave myocardial infarction], and Q-wave myocardial infarction) were reviewed as part of the Platelet Receptor Inhibitor in Ischemic Syndrome Management (PRISM) study. It was found that pretreatment with statin type medicines (HMG-CoA reductase inhibitors such as the medicine in this profile) significantly lowered risk during the first 30 days after ACS symptoms started. Most importantly, it was found that if a statin type medicine is stopped in ACS patients, there was a three-fold increased risk of non-fatal heart attack or death (see Heeschen, C in Sources). Talk with your doctor BEFORE stopping any statin type medicine.

EZETIMIBE (Ee ZET ih mybe)

Introduced: 2003   **Class:** Anticholesterol, selective cholesterol absorption inhibitor   **Prescription:**   USA: Yes   **Controlled Drug:** USA: No   **Available as Generic:**   No

Brand Name: Zetia

Author's Note: This medicine is presently approved for add-on therapy (for example, in people who do not reach their cholesterol lowering or cholesterol goals with their present medicine. Early data appears to show a well-tolerated medicine with excellent combined (as with a statin-type medicine) results in lowering cholesterol. While present strategy is for add on treatment, conjecture remains as to possible benefits in earlier add-on in order to avoid HMG-CoA reductase (statin) dosing increases and possible adverse effects. Information in this profile will be broadened in subsequent editions if ongoing research and comparative trials warrant.

FAMOTIDINE (fa MOH te deen)

Please see the histamine (H2) drug family profile.

FELODIPINE (feh LOH di peen)

Introduced: 1986   **Class:** Antihypertensive, dihydropyridine derivative calcium channel blocker   **Prescription:**   USA: Yes   **Controlled Drug:**   USA: No   **Available as Generic:**   No

Brand Names: Plendil, Altace plus felodipine [CD], Lexxel [CD], ✤Logimax [CD], ✤Renedil

Controversies in Medicine: Medicines in this class have had many conflicting reports. The FDA has held hearings on the calcium channel blocker (CCB) class. Amlodipine got the first FDA approval to treat high blood pressure or angina in people with congestive heart failure. Early research at NYU found that nifedipine is a cause of reversible male infertility. CCBs are currently second-line agents for high blood pressure according to the JNC VII (see Glossary).

```
┌─────────────────────────────────────────────────────────────┐
│                    BENEFITS versus RISKS                      │
│       Possible Benefits              Possible Risks           │
│  EFFECTIVE TREATMENT OF MILD    Peripheral edema (fluid retention in │
│   TO MODERATE HYPERTENSION       feet and ankles)             │
└─────────────────────────────────────────────────────────────┘
```

▷ **Principal Uses**

As a Single Drug Product: Uses currently included in FDA-approved labeling: Treats mild to moderate hypertension.

Other (unlabeled) generally accepted uses: (1) Treats angina; (2) arrhythmias; (3) may inhibit progression of atherosclerosis; (4) can be used in some cases of premature labor; (5) may have a role in kidney disease in diabetes (diabetic nephropathy); (6) helps kidney toxicity caused by cyclosporine (nephropathy).

As a Combination Drug Product [CD]: Available combined with enalapril (an ACE inhibitor) as the brand name Lexxel. The combination puts two different actions to work to lower blood pressure. Logimax combines felodipine with metoprolol, and Altace plus felodipine combines ramipril (an ACE inhibitor) with felodipine.

How This Drug Works: Blocks normal passage of calcium through some cell walls. This slows spread of electrical activity and reduces contraction of peripheral arterial walls, lowering blood pressure. Combination form adds the benefits of an ACE inhibitor to this calcium blocker.

Available Dosage Forms and Strengths

Tablets, sustained release — 5 mg, 10 mg

Coated tablet (Lexxel) — 5 mg enalapril and 2.5 mg or 5 mg felodipine

Extended-release tablet (Plendil) — 2.5 mg, 5 mg and 10 mg felodipine

Sustained-release tablet (Logimax) — 5 mg felodipine and 47.5 mg metoprolol

Author's Note: information in this profile has been truncated pending a combination family profile based on utilization and clinical data for the next edition.

FENAMATE (NONSTEROIDAL ANTI-INFLAMMATORY DRUG) FAMILY

Meclofenamate   (MEK low fen a mate)   **Mefenamic Acid**   (MEF en amik a sid)

Introduced: 1977, 1966 **Class:** Analgesic, mild; NSAIDs **Prescription:** USA: Yes **Controlled Drug:** USA: No; Canada: No **Available as Generic:** Yes

Brand Names: *Meclofenamate:* Meclodium, Meclofenaf, Meclomen; *Mefenamic Acid:* ✣Apo-Mefanamic, ✣Novo-Mefanamic, Ponstel, ✣Ponstan

BENEFITS versus RISKS	
Possible Benefits	*Possible Risks*
EFFECTIVE RELIEF OF MILD TO MODERATE PAIN AND INFLAMMATION	Diarrhea (frequent for meclofenamate)
	Gastrointestinal pain, ulceration, bleeding
	Kidney damage
	Fluid retention
	Bone marrow depression (mefenamic acid)
	Hemolytic anemia (mefenamic acid)
	Systemic lupus erythematosus (mefenamic acid)
	Pancreatitis (mefenamic acid)

Author's Note: Information in this profile has been truncated to make room for more widely used medicines.

FENOPROFEN (fen oh PROH fen)

Please see the propionic acid (nonsteroidal anti-inflammatory drug) family profile.

FENTANYL (FEN ta nil)

Introduced: 1991   Class: Analgesic, strong   Prescription: USA: Yes   Controlled Drug: USA: C-II*; Canada: Yes   Available as Generic: USA: No; Canada: No

Brand Names: Actiq, Duragesic, ✦Innovar, Oralet, Sublimaze

Author's Note: An investigational form of fentanyl is being studied and is sprayed into the mouth (buccal dosing see *www.medicineinfo.com*). The company that makes Duragesic has an excellent personal pain diary available from their web site at *www.duragesic.com/files/pain=_diary=_other.pdf*

BENEFITS versus RISKS	
Possible Benefits	*Possible Risks*
EFFECTIVE PAIN RELIEF	Habit-forming potential with prolonged use
SKIN PATCH APPLICATION NEEDED ONLY ONCE EVERY 3 DAYS	Impairment of mental function
	Methemoglobinemia
EFFECTIVE RELIEF OF BREAKTHROUGH CANCER PAIN WITH A MEDICINE TAKEN BY MOUTH (Actiq)	Respiratory depression

▷ Principal Uses

As a Single Drug Product: Uses currently included in FDA-approved labeling: (1) Treatment of chronic pain; (2) Actiq approved for treatment of breakthrough cancer pain (contains the same medicine as Oralet) for people ALREADY taking or who are tolerant to opioid therapy for cancer pain; (3)

balanced anesthesia and cardiac and neurosurgery anesthesia (injection form); (4) anesthesia induction (injection form); (5) premedication (Oralet); (6) transdermal or epidural form is approved for chronic pain.
Other (unlabeled) generally accepted uses: None at present.

How This Drug Works: Acts at specific pain receptors (Mu agonist) to block pain.

Available Dosage Forms and Strengths

Buccal lozenge (Actiq) — 400 mcg, 600 mcg, 800 mcg, 1,200 mcg, 1,600 mcg

Transdermal patch — 2.5 mg (25 mcg/hour), 5 mg (50 mcg/hour), 7.5 mg (75 mcg/hour), 10 mg (100 mcg/hour)

Lozenge on a handle — 100 mcg, 200 mcg, 300 mcg, 400 mcg

Author's Note: Injectable forms are not presented in this profile.

▷ **Recommended Dosage Ranges** (Actual dose and schedule *must* be determined for each patient individually.)

Children: Lozenge on a handle form: Based on weight. For those more than 40 kg may need 5-15 mcg/kg and those less than 40 kg may need 10–15 mcg/kg range as a premedication to lower anxiety and give pain relief before surgery.

18 to 60 Years of Age:

Patch (transdermal): Not generally indicated for patients less than 12 or those 18 years old who weigh less than 50 kg (110 lb). In patients who are not opioid tolerant, the 25 mcg/hour (10 cm) patch has been used. In people who used opioids previously, the amount needed to control pain on a 24-hour basis is calculated, converted to an equal amount of morphine (morphine equianalgesic dose) and then converted to fentanyl. It is important for patients to have the benefit of a judicious amount of short acting opioid during the first 24 hours after the patch is applied. After this, a "rescue dose" of short acting opioids is used. A circumspect review of rescue dose use should be made, and subsequently used to decide if any increases in the fentanyl patch is needed. Some centers use intravenous fentanyl and make a transition to a patch that is equal to the final ongoing fentanyl infusion rate. In that case, the continuous infusion fentanyl was lowered by half (50%) six hours after the patch was applied, and was stopped 12 hours after the patch was first applied. Patches are generally replaced every 72 hours, but some patients require replacement every 48 hours.

Oralet form: Used to treat pain/anxiety before surgery; 400 mcg for those with a body mass of 50 kg or more.

Buccal lozenge (Actiq)—used for patients with breakthrough cancer pain: 200 mcg (in cancer patients already receiving and who are tolerant to opioid (such as morphine) treatment—as defined by taking at least 50 mcg of transdermal fentanyl per hour, 60 mg of morphine a day or an equianalgesic dose of a different opioid for 7 days or longer). They can subsequently be given another of the same dose (IF NEEDED) in 30 minutes. No more than 2 units should be taken for each breakthrough cancer pain episode. When the medicine is being added to the baseline opioid and a dose that works is found, patients should take no more than 4 units in a single day. Current pain treatment dictates that if more than 4 units are needed, the dose of the ongoing long-acting opioid should be evaluated, the cause of increasing assessed and then dose increased as appropriate.

Over 60 Years of Age: Should receive 25 mcg per hour (2.5 mg) patch, unless already receiving equivalent of 135 mg of oral morphine or an equivalent opioid dose daily. Intravenous fentanyl clears more slowly in those over 60 than in younger patients. Watch carefully for overdose. If a decision is made to use the Actiq form, 200 mcg is used as a starting dose, and those over 75 generally require lower total doses than younger patients.

Conditions Requiring Dosing Adjustments

Liver Function: The dose must be decreased in liver compromise.

Kidney Function: In moderate to severe kidney failure, 75% of the usual dose. Dose reduced by 50% in severe kidney failure. People in end-stage kidney disease may be more sensitive to this medicine.

Dosing Instructions

Patch: Take the patch from pouch. Remove stiff protective liner from sticky side of patch. Do not cut the system. Place sticky side on a hair-free, dry area (back, chest, side, or upper arm). Avoid burned, irritated, or oily areas. Hold the patch in place for 30 seconds, paying close attention to the edges of the patch. Wash hands after patch is applied. Apply a new patch to a different area after 3 days. Fold the old patch onto itself and flush it down the toilet. Avoid heat such as electric blankets or heating pads.

Lozenge or sucker: Slowly dissolve in the mouth. Do not bite or chew it. For Actiq, place medicine between cheek and lower gum, and rotate occasionally using the handle.

If the patient feels sleepy or otherwise has signs of excessive fentanyl effects, the medicine should be removed. Subsequent doses MUST be decreased if the above effects occur.

Usual Duration of Use:
Regular use for 1 to 3 days determines benefits in pain control. Immediate-release morphine or similar drug should be available while this drug reaches peak effect (patch form). Long-term use requires evaluation by your doctor. If you forget a dose: apply the missed patch as soon as you remember it, and then continue on the same three-day schedule or on the schedule that your doctor has prescribed. Make sure you tell your doctor as your use of rescue medication may increase. DO NOT double doses or apply two patches at the same time unless your doctor has told you to do so.

Typical Treatment Goals and Measurements (Outcomes and Markers)

Pain: Most clinicians treating pain use a device called an algometer to check your pain. This looks like a small ruler, but lets the clinician better understand your pain. The goals of treatment then relate to where the level of pain started (for example, a rating of 7 on a zero to ten scale) and what the cause of the pain was. I use the PQRSTG system. Pain medicines may also be used together (in combination) in order to get the best result or outcome. If your pain control is not acceptable to YOU (remember, in hospitals and outpatient settings, etc., pain control is a patient right and the fifth vital sign) or if after applying the patch or using the sucker form, and if there is no other pain contingency, ask your doctor about a different rescue medicine. If pain treatment results are not what you expect, be sure to call your doctor as you may need a different medicine or combination. Cancer pain can vary, and it is not unusual to need different doses.

Possible Advantages of This Drug

Effective pain relief with patch placement once every 3 days and no injections. Effective pain relief with a medicine used by mouth. Effective rescue pain relief.

▷ **This Drug Should Not Be Taken If**
- you had an allergic reaction to any form of it previously.
- you have had an allergic reaction to the adhesive in the patch.
- you are less than 12 years old. Oralet should NOT be used in children weighing less than 22 pounds (10 kg).
- you are at home and a Fentanyl Oralet is prescribed—these are only to be used in hospital settings.
- you weigh less than 50 kg and are less than 18 years old.
- you have mild pain.
- you have acute or postoperative pain without opportunity for proper dose adjustment.

▷ **Inform Your Physician Before Taking This Drug If**
- you have liver or kidney compromise.
- you have chronic lung disease (such as COPD).
- you have an abnormally slow heartbeat or other heart disease.
- you develop a high fever.
- you have not taken narcotic pain medicines before and you are given a dose more than 25 mcg per hour.
- you take, or took in the last two weeks, an MAO inhibitor (see Drug Classes).
- you have a brain tumor or seizure disorder.
- you are elderly or debilitated.
- a benzodiazepine (such as diazepam or Valium—see Drug Classes) has been prescribed for you.
- you are anemic or have heart disease.
- you have a history of alcoholism or drug abuse.
- you take prescription or nonprescription drugs not discussed with your doctor when fentanyl was prescribed.

Possible Side Effects (natural, expected, and unavoidable drug actions)
Constipation, dry mouth. Dose related respiratory depression.
Sleepiness (somnolence) or euphoria—infrequent to frequent.

▷ **Possible Adverse Effects** (unusual, unexpected, and infrequent reactions)
If any of the following develop, consult your physician promptly for guidance.
Mild Adverse Effects
Allergic reactions: skin rash and itching.
Blurred vision or amblyopia—rare to infrequent.
Nausea or vomiting—infrequent.
Urinary retention—infrequent.
Tremor or muscular rigidity—possible.
Sweating or itching (transdermal)—infrequent to frequent.
Serious Adverse Effects
Allergic reactions: exfoliative dermatitis and/or anaphylactic reactions—case reports.
Arrhythmias—rare.
Paranoid reaction, depersonalization, speech problems (aphasia)—rare, dose-related.
Increased or decreased blood pressure—possible.
Benign increases in pressure in the head (pseudotumor cerebri)—possible.
Seizures or hallucinations—case reports.
Methemoglobinemia or porphyrias—rare.
Paresthesias—rare.

Respiratory depression (this effect may last longer than the pain-relieving effect)—dose-related and possible.
▷ **Possible Effects on Sexual Function:** Impotence and blunted orgasm sensation in men. Irregular menstrual periods and blunted orgasm sensation in women.

Possible Delayed Adverse Effects: Dependence and tolerance.

Possible Effects on Laboratory Tests
Screening tests for opioids: positive.

CAUTION

1. Extreme caution should be used if this drug is combined with other opioids, narcotic drugs, benzodiazepines or alcohol.
2. May cause serious constipation in older patients. Many clinicians use an appropriate drug to PREVENT constipation in older patients or those prone to constipation by starting a medicine to keep the bowels open (such as Senokot) when the medicine is started.
3. Do not expose the patch site to external sources of heat such as heating pads or electric blankets, as an increased rate of drug release may occur.
4. If there are children living in the same house as someone using Actiq or any form of fentanyl, great care must be taken to avoid accidentally having a child take one of the lozenges, or other dosage form as the dose would be fatal. A child-resistant container is provided in case a lozenge is not fully taken.
5. If this medicine is to be stopped, gradual withdrawal is required.
6. Dosing is individualized based on numerous factors such as: underlying conditions or diseases, age and weight, physical status, other ongoing medicines, liver function, any anesthesia that may be used and others.

Precautions for Use
By Infants and Children: Safety and effectiveness for those less than 12 years of age are not established.
By Those Over 60 Years of Age: The 2.5-mg patch should NOT be used as a starting dose unless you are already taking more than 135 mg of morphine daily. Those with cardiac, respiratory, kidney, or liver compromise or dehydration should be given low doses and carefully monitored.

▷ **Advisability of Use During Pregnancy**
Pregnancy Category: C, D if used in high doses when the baby is born or for prolonged periods. See Pregnancy Risk Categories at the back of this book.
Animal Studies: Some fetal death data with intravenous use in rats.
Human Studies: Adequate studies of pregnant women are not available.
Ask your doctor for guidance.

Advisability of Use If Breast-Feeding
Presence of this drug in breast milk: Yes.
Avoid drug or refrain from nursing.

Habit-Forming Potential: Fentanyl is a Schedule II narcotic and can cause dependence similar to morphine dependence. Physical and psychological dependence and tolerance can occur with repeated use.

Effects of Overdose: Dizziness, amnesia and stupor. Respiratory depression and apnea may occur.

Possible Effects of Long-Term Use: Tolerance and physical or psychological dependence.

Suggested Periodic Examinations While Taking This Drug (at physician's discretion)

PQRSTG assessment of pain (see Glossary). Liver function tests. Check for constipation.

▷ **While Taking This Drug, Observe the Following**

Foods: No restrictions.

Herbal Medicines or Minerals: Valerian and kava kava may interact additively (drowsiness). Avoid these combinations. Kava is no longer recommended in Canada at the time of this writing because of liver damage reports. St. John's wort can change (inducing or increasing) P450 3A4 or 2D6 enzymes, blunting the effects of fentanyl. Talk to your doctor BEFORE you combine any herbal medicines with fentanyl.

Beverages: No restrictions.

▷ *Alcohol:* **DO NOT DRINK ALCOHOL** while you are taking this drug—leads to additive loss of mental status, respiratory depression and confusion.

Tobacco Smoking: No interactions expected. I advise everyone to quit smoking.

Marijuana Smoking: Additive adverse effects; however, marijuana may block the vomiting effect of fentanyl.

▷ *Other Drugs*

Fentanyl may *increase* the effects of
- benzodiazepines such as diazepam (Valium) and alprazolam (Xanax).
- central nervous system depressants such as opiates, barbiturates, tranquilizers, and tricyclic antidepressants.

Fentanyl *taken concurrently* with
- amiodarone (Cordarone) may result in heart (cardiac) toxicity.
- clonidine (Catapres, others) may result in greater than expected fentanyl effects. The fentanyl dose may need to be decreased if these medicines are to be combined.
- MAO inhibitors (see Drug Classes) may worsen the lowering of blood pressure and depression of breathing seen with fentanyl.
- rifabutin (Mycobutin) and rifampin may decrease pain control by fentanyl.
- medicines which block (inhibit) or use cytochrome P-450 3A4 to get out of the body (such as ketoconazole or voriconazole or macrolide antibiotics such as erythromycin) will increase effects of fentanyl and medicines that induce cytochrome P-450 3A4 in the liver (such as fosphenytoin-Cerebyx or phenytoin-Dilantin) will blunt the benefits of fentanyl.
- ritonavir (Norvir) and perhaps other protease inhibitors (see Drug Classes) can lead to major fentanyl toxicity by inhibiting removal of this medicine from the body.
- sibutramine (Meridia) may increase risk of serotonin syndrome. DO NOT COMBINE.
- sildenafil (Viagra) may lead to changes in sildenafil or in fentanyl levels. Caution is advised (both drugs are removed by CYP450 3A4).

▷ *Driving, Hazardous Activities:* This drug may cause drowsiness, sedation, and respiratory depression. Restrict activities as necessary.

Aviation Note: The use of this drug *is a disqualification* for piloting. Consult a designated Aviation Medical Examiner.

Exposure to Sun: No restrictions.

Discontinuation: Once the patch is removed, fentanyl will still be released from the site for 17 hours or more. If pain medicine is still needed, the alternative should be substituted once the fentanyl level is low enough. The level from the lozenge declines more rapidly, and replacement medicine is required sooner if the fentanyl lozenge is stopped. If the lozenge has been used routinely, the drug should be slowly tapered, NOT stopped abruptly.

FILGRASTIM (fil GRA stim)

Other Name: Recombinant G-CSF

Introduced: 1991   **Class:**   Hematopoietic agent   **Prescription:**
USA: Yes   **Controlled Drug:**   USA: No; Canada: No   **Available as**
Generic: USA: No; Canada: No

Brand Name: Neupogen

Author's Note: Pegfilgrastim (Neulasta) is NOT the same as filgrastim. Pegfilgrastim is given in a dose of 6 mg under the skin per each cycle of
chemotherapy.

BENEFITS versus RISKS

Possible Benefits	*Possible Risks*
PREVENTION OF INFECTIONS	Bone pain
DUE TO LOWERED WHITE	Changes in heart waves
BLOOD CELL COUNTS:	
FOLLOWING CHEMOTHERAPY	
FOLLOWING BONE MARROW	
TRANSPLANT	
IN PATIENTS WITH CHRONIC OR	
CYCLIC NEUTROPENIA	
INCREASED BLOOD CELLS IN	
AIDS PATIENTS	
CORRECTION OF DRUG-INDUCED	
LOWERING OF WHITE BLOOD	
CELLS	

▷ **Principal Uses**

As a Single Drug Product: Uses currently included in FDA-approved labeling:
(1) Used to help white blood cell counts recover after bone marrow transplants; (2) used subcutaneously or intravenously to reduce or prevent low
white blood cell counts that occur after cancer chemotherapy; (3) treats
patients who have an absence of white blood cells at birth; (4) used to help
patients with Kostmann syndrome have improved white blood cell counts;
(5) used to help patients who have low white blood cell counts (neutropenia) of unknown cause (idiopathic); (6) helps cyclic low white blood cells
(cyclic neutropenia); (7) used in adults to move blood-forming cells
(hematopoietic progenitors) into the blood stream (peripheral blood) so
that they can be collected by leukopharesis.

Other (unlabeled) generally accepted uses: (1) Helps patients recover from a
particular kind of lack of white blood cells (agranulocytosis) that has been
caused by medicines (drug-induced); (2) used in AIDS (orphan drug status) patients (taking ganciclovir) to help restore white blood cell counts;
(3) used to treat patients with severe long-term (chronic) low white blood
cell counts; (4) used to treat patients with abnormally low white blood cell
and neutrophil counts (myelodysplastic syndrome).

In the Pipeline: A phase three study comparing 5 or 10 mcg/kg per day for mobilization with chemotherapy, followed by autologous transplantation in
patients with nonmyeloid malignancies is underway (see Andre, M. in
Sources). One case report was made for patients resistant to other antipsy-

chotics who developed white blood cell problems with clozapine, who were successfully managed with filgrastim so that they could take clozapine (see Hagg, S et al. in Sources). In leukemia patients treated with imatinib (Gleevec), filgrastim was successfully used to mobilize peripheral blood stem cells (PBSC) in people who achieved complete cytogenetic response (CCR). The yield of CD 34+ cells was improved when imatinib was withheld temporarily (see Hui, CH in Sources).

How This Drug Works: Regulates proliferation and release of early (progenitor) forms of white blood cells. In effect, this medicine can tell bone marrow (where important blood cells are actually made) to increase the rate at which it makes white blood cells. Filgrastim may also work with other factors to increase the production of blood platelets.

Available Dosage Forms and Strengths

Solution for injection — 300 mcg/ml (supplied as a 300- or 480-mcg vial), 600 mcg/ml

How to Store

The prepared solution should be stored at 36 to 46 degrees F. (2 to 8 degrees C.). This medicine should not be frozen. Some centers draw up a 7-day supply of syringes that are then stored in a refrigerator.

▷ **Recommended Dosage Ranges** (Actual dose and schedule must be determined for each patient individually.)

Infants and Children: Studied doses of 0.6 to 120 mcg per kg of body mass per day for up to 3 years have been well tolerated in children 3 months to 18 years of age. In low blood cells (neutropenia) that occur after chemotherapy, a starting dose of 5 mcg/kg per day has been used by giving 15–30-minute intravenous infusions or via ongoing infusions. Doses are subsequently increased in steps of 5 mcg/kg/day while the patient is getting a cycle of chemotherapy. Dosing is adjusted in response to the severity and length of time that the lowest point (nadir) of the neutrophil count. In the studies leading to approval (phase III), 4–8 mcg/day were typically successful. In chronic low white blood cell counts (chronic neutropenia), doses of 5 to 10 mcg per kg of body mass per day have been used. Safety and efficacy in pediatric patients with neutropenia that is a result of one's own immune system working against oneself (autoimmune) have not been established.

18 to 60 Years of Age: Patients having bone marrow destroyed (myeloablative treatment) and getting a bone marrow transplant: Wait 24 hours after chemo was given and 24 hours after bone marrow transplant. Then 10 mcg per kg of body mass per day to start. The dose is given over 4 to 24 hours. Ongoing daily dosing is adjusted to increase of white blood cells (absolute neutrophil count).

Patients receiving bone marrow suppression should wait until 24 hours after or before the chemotherapy is given. Filgrastim is started with 5 mcg per kg of body mass per day, increased by 5 mcg per kg per day for each cycle of chemotherapy. Dosing is based on severity of white blood cell count decrease (nadir) and how long lowered white cell (absolute neutrophil) count lasts. Drug can be given daily for up to 14 days.

Guidelines released by the Infectious Disease Society of America talk about using this medicine (on a non-routine basis) to reverse low white blood cell counts (neutropenia) associated with HIV infection. The dose noted there was 5–10 mcg/kg per day subcutaneously or 250 mcg/square meter intravenously infused over 2 hours each day. The use period listed was 2 to 4 weeks.

Peripheral blood progenitor cell mobilization: Conflicting data about once versus twice a day dosing in this unique donor situation. One group received 6 mcg per kg intravenously every 12 hours and another received 12 mcg/kg intravenously once daily for 3 days before leukopharesis. In this study, each patient then received 6 mcg/kg on the fourth day within 2 hours before the first leukopharesis. The results in harvesting the needed donor cells were roughly (statistically) the same.

Over 60 Years of Age: Same as 18 to 60 years of age.

Conditions Requiring Dosing Adjustments

Liver Function: Not significantly involved in the elimination of this drug.

Kidney Function: Roughly 90% of a given filgrastim dose is eliminated by the kidneys. Changes in dosing are not defined.

▷ **Dosing Instructions:** The solution in the reconstituted vial should be colorless and clear. Once your doctor or nurse has taught you how to inject the medicine:
- Make certain the solution has not expired (check the expiration date).
- Make certain that albumin (human) has been added to the 2 mg per ml Neupogen to protect it from attaching (adsorbing) to the plastic material of the container.
- Make certain you have the correct kind of syringe (talk this over with your doctor, nurse or nurse practitioner).
- Follow the provided patient instructions carefully, not using saline to dilute, and not diluting to a final concentration of less than 5 mcg/ml.
- If you are using a syringe, make certain you inject the medicine under the skin (subcutaneously or Sub Q), not into a vein.
- This medicine can also be given intravenously over a period of 15 to 30 minutes.
- If you forget a dose: call your doctor and ask what he or she would like you to do.

Usual Duration of Use: Ten to 14 days of regular use may be needed to see benefits in correcting low white blood cell (absolute neutrophil) counts after chemotherapy. Bone marrow transplant patients may take still longer to respond. Long-term problems with white blood cells (such as chronic neutropenia) may require years of therapy. Long-term use requires periodic evaluation of response and dose adjustment. See your doctor on a regular basis.

Typical Treatment Goals and Measurements (Outcomes and Markers)

Neutropenia: Most clinicians will check laboratory tests (white blood cell counts with differentials) two to three times per week and adjust dosing to results. Additionally, bone marrow tests (aspiration) will be done periodically to check granulocyte-macrophage counts, morphology, myeloid/erythroid ratios and even colony-forming unit counts.

Possible Advantages of This Drug

Effective recombinant product with few side effects.

▷ **This Drug Should Not Be Taken If**
- you had an allergic reaction to it previously.
- you have a known allergy to products derived from *E. coli* (a bacteria).

▷ **Inform Your Physician Before Taking This Drug If**
- you have a history of gout or psoriasis.
- you have received chemotherapy within the last 24 hours.
- you have a history of heart problems (heart rhythm should be closely monitored).

- you have a history of leukemia (myeloid type). The safety and efficacy of this medicine are not established in that condition.
- you have a history of cancer (with myeloid characteristics). There is a possibility that this drug may act as a growth factor for these tumors. Use, however, in a small number of leukemia patients has not resulted in worsening of their leukemia.
- you have an excessive increase in white blood cells (leukocytosis).

Possible Side Effects (natural, expected, and unavoidable drug actions)

Pain on injection.

Bone pain (up to 33%).

Extreme sensitivity to light (photophobia) possible and dose limiting with 30-100,000 mcg/square meter daily.

▷ **Possible Adverse Effects** (unusual, unexpected, and infrequent reactions)

If any of the following develop, consult your physician promptly for guidance.

Mild Adverse Effects

Allergic reactions: skin rash or itching—infrequent.

Mild decreases in blood pressure or increases in uric acid—case reports.

Drug-induced fever—infrequent to frequent.

Headache—infrequent.

Nausea and anorexia—rare.

Irritation of the eye (iridocyclitis, conjunctival erythema)—case reports.

Enlargement of the spleen: reported in patients with chronic lowering of the white blood cells (chronic neutropenia)—frequent, though asymptomatic in these patients.

Taste disorders—case reports.

Serious Adverse Effects

Allergic reactions: anaphylaxis—case report.

Sweet syndrome (acute neutrophilic dermatosis)—possible.

Worsening of psoriasis—case report.

Low oxygen in the blood (hypoxemia)—very rare.

Anemia—possible (happened in peripheral blood progenitor donations).

Low blood platelets—infrequent to frequent.

Depression of part of the heart action (ST depression)—rare to infrequent.

Myocardial infarction (heart attack)—happened in 11 of 375 cancer patients in one study, but the relationship to filgrastim is unclear.

Liver or kidney toxicity—case reports and of unclear relationship.

Potential for this medicine to act as a growth factor for certain cancers: breast, colon, lung, and lymphoma—possible (use in preleukemia is an area of controversy.

Myelodysplastic syndrome (MDS) or acute myeloid leukemia—annual rate of 2% and cumulative rate of 16.5% when patients with congenital neutropenia are treated.

Capillary leak syndrome—possible, case reports.

Respiratory distress syndrome in patients with serious (septic) infections, because white blood cells may travel to the infected area—possible.

Hypothyroidism—case report.

▷ **Possible Effects on Sexual Function:** None reported.

Possible Delayed Adverse Effects: Increased uric acid. Formation of neutralizing antibodies.

▷ **Adverse Effects That May Mimic Natural Diseases or Disorders**

None reported.

Natural Diseases or Disorders That May Be Activated by This Drug
Gout.

Possible Effects on Laboratory Tests
Absolute neutrophil count: increased.
Alkaline phosphatase: increased markedly.
Uric acid: increased mildly.
Lactate dehydrogenase (LDH): increased.
Formation of neutralizing antibodies—possible.

CAUTION
1. Bone pain may be prevented by taking acetaminophen (Tylenol, others) BEFORE this medicine is injected.
2. Call your doctor if you have chills, fever or any other sign of infection.
3. Be certain to follow up with your laboratory testing as scheduled.
4. The solution in the vial should be clear. Do not inject any discolored or cloudy solution.
5. Make sure you have the correct kind of syringe before you inject this medicine.
6. This medicine can be given intravenously when it is appropriately prepared. If your doctor has instructed you on how to give yourself an injection using a syringe, the medicine should be given under the skin. Be certain you understand the technique.
7. Always change the site in which you inject this medicine, as your doctor instructed.

Precautions for Use
By Infants and Children: This medicine has been used in children with long-term lowering of white blood cell counts (chronic neutropenia) in doses of 5 to 10 mcg per kg of body mass per day.
By Those Over 60 Years of Age: No specific precautions.

▷ **Advisability of Use During Pregnancy**
Pregnancy Category: C. See Pregnancy Risk Categories at the back of this book.
Animal Studies: In rabbits given 80 mcg per kg of body mass per day (very high doses), increased abortion and death of embryos were observed.
Human Studies: Information from adequate studies of pregnant women is not available.
Ask your doctor for help with this benefit-to-risk decision.

Advisability of Use If Breast-Feeding
Presence of this drug in breast milk: Unknown.
Ask your doctor for guidance.

Habit-Forming Potential: None.

Effects of Overdose: No maximum tolerated dose has been identified.

Possible Effects of Long-Term Use: Enlarged spleens may occur in up to 25% of patients (splenomegaly) with severe chronic neutropenia. Skin rashes may occur in up to 6% of patients.

Suggested Periodic Examinations While Taking This Drug (at physician's discretion)
Complete blood cell counts and platelet counts should be obtained prior to chemotherapy and twice weekly during filgrastim therapy.

▷ **While Taking This Drug, Observe the Following**
Foods: No restrictions.
Herbal Medicines or Minerals: Echinacea: Some patients use echinacea to attempt to boost their immune systems. Unfortunately, use of echinacea is not recommended in people with damaged immune systems. This herb may also

actually weaken any immune system if it is used too often or for too long a time. **Caution:** St. John's wort may also cause extreme reactions to the sun. Additive photosensitivity may be possible—combination is not advised.

Beverages: No restrictions.

▷ *Alcohol:* No restrictions.

Tobacco Smoking: No interactions expected. I advise everyone to quit smoking.

▷ *Other Drugs*

Filgrastim **taken concurrently** with

- lithium (Lithobid, others) may (in theory) result in additive release of white blood cells.
- topotecan (Hycamtin) may cause extended low white blood cells.
- vincristine (Oncovin) has led to nerve problems (peripheral neuropathy).

▷ *Driving, Hazardous Activities:* No restrictions presently attributed to this medicine.

Aviation Note: The use of this drug is **probably not a disqualification** for piloting. Consult a designated Aviation Medical Examiner.

Exposure to Sun: SEVERE intolerance of sunlight (photophobia) has been a treatment-limiting factor. **Caution:** See the Herbal Medicines note on St. John's wort above.

Occurrence of Unrelated Illness: Report development of chills, fever or other signs or symptoms of infection immediately to your doctor.

Discontinuation: In people taking bone marrow suppressing drugs: Filgrastim is usually stopped when white blood cell (absolute neutrophil count) reaches 10,000 per cubic mm (once the lowest white blood cell count was reached for the chemotherapy given).

In people taking bone marrow destroying medicine who then have a bone marrow transplant: The drug is started as described above. If white blood cell count reaches 1,000 per cubic mm, dose is decreased to 5 mcg per kg of body mass per day. Once white cell count reaches 1,000 per cubic mm for 6 consecutive days, filgrastim can be stopped.

Special Storage Instructions: This drug should be stored at 36 to 46 degrees F. (2 to 8 degrees C.) in the refrigerator once it has been mixed with the diluent (reconstituted). Care should be taken **not to shake** the prepared drug, as it may lose activity. Care should also be taken **not to freeze** the prepared medicine, as it will clump and lose therapeutic activity.

Observe the Following Expiration Times: Once the medicine is prepared, it is stable for 1 day (24 hours) if it is refrigerated. If the drug is stored at room temperature, it is stable for 6 hours. Medicine left at room temperature for more than 6 hours should be returned.

FINASTERIDE (fin ASS tur ide)

Introduced: 1992 **Class:** 5-alpha reductase inhibitor **Prescription:** USA: Yes **Controlled Drug:** USA: No; Canada: No **Available as Generic:** USA: No; Canada: No

Brand Names: Propecia, Proscar

Author's Note: A study called the Prostate Cancer Prevention Trial (see Thompson, IM in Sources) looked at 18,882 men. From the study results, it appeared that finasteride offers a 25% reduction of prostate cancer which must be balanced against the risk of higher grade (more aggressive or advanced) cancers if a cancer does occur.

```
┌─────────────────────────────────────────────────────────────────────┐
│                         BENEFITS versus RISKS                         │
│        Possible Benefits                    Possible Risks            │
│   NONSURGICAL TREATMENT OF          Impotence (small percentage)      │
│     SYMPTOMATIC BENIGN              Decreased libido (small percentage)│
│     PROSTATIC HYPERPLASIA           Gynecomastia (rare)               │
│   Shrinkage of prostatic tissue and HIGHER GRADE CANCER IF IT         │
│     increase in urine flow            HAPPENS                         │
│   RETENTION OF HAIR OR                                                │
│     INCREASED HAIR GROWTH IN                                          │
│     MEN                                                               │
│   25% DECREASE IN PROSTATE                                            │
│     CANCER                                                            │
└─────────────────────────────────────────────────────────────────────┘
```

▷ **Principal Uses**

As a Single Drug Product: Uses currently included in FDA-approved labeling: (1) Treats symptomatic benign prostatic hyperplasia (BPH)—peak decrease in prostate size has occurred after 6 months of therapy; (2) approved to decrease risk of urine retention and need for prostate surgery in BPH; (3) used as Propecia brand (1 mg) to retain or regrow hair.

Other (unlabeled) generally accepted uses: Reduces excessive hair in women (hirsutism).

How This Drug Works: Blocks an enzyme (5-alpha reductase) that decreases change of testosterone to dihydrotestosterone (in liver); this causes the prostate to shrink. Symptoms such as urgency and trouble urinating improve. Inhibiting 5-alpha reductase also leads to hair growth.

Available Dosage Forms and Strengths

Proscar tablets — 5 mg

Propecia tablets — 1 mg

▷ **Recommended Dosage Ranges** (Actual dose and schedule must be determined for each patient individually.)

Infants and Children: Not indicated.

12 to 60 Years of Age: Symptomatic benign prostatic hyperplasia often does not occur in the younger end of this adult dosing range; however, the dose for this age range is 5 mg each day, taken by mouth.

Hair-restoring agent: 1 mg daily dose.

Over 60 Years of Age: Same as 12 to 60 years of age, unless liver function has decreased.

Conditions Requiring Dosing Adjustments

Liver Function: People with abnormal liver tests should be closely followed by their doctors.

Kidney Function: No changes thought to be needed.

▷ **Dosing Instructions:** May be taken without regard to food. Food changes time to peak blood concentration only. If you forget a dose: Take the missed dose as soon as you remember it, unless it is nearly time for your next dose—if that is the case, omit the missed dose and take the next scheduled dose right on schedule. DO NOT double doses.

Usual Duration of Use: Use on a regular schedule for at least 6 months is needed to see this drug's peak benefit in shrinking the prostate and decreasing symptoms. Use for five years has been documented. Use for 1 year may be required to demonstrate hair regrowth.

Typical Treatment Goals and Measurements (Outcomes and Markers)

Hair loss: Most clinicians use hair counts, or lack of further hair loss, to define results. Use for that indication will be ongoing.

BPH: Urologists use improvement in urinary flow as well as subjective measures such as relief of difficulty urinating and lowered feeling of urgency. Digital rectal examination for prostate cancer should be done prior to therapy and periodically.

Possible Advantages of This Drug: May give you symptomatic relief of benign prostatic hyperplasia (BPH) without surgery. May be more effective than other available agents in helping hair regrowth. Few clinically significant drug interactions. Twenty-five percent decrease in prostate cancer in a recent study.

▷ **This Drug Should Not Be Taken If**
- you had an allergic reaction to it previously and you are a woman or child.
- you are pregnant.

▷ **Inform Your Physician Before Taking This Drug If**
- you have impaired liver function or liver disease.
- you are a woman or a child.
- you have kidney problems of any nature.
- your sexual partner is pregnant.

Possible Side Effects (natural, expected, and unavoidable drug actions)

May or may not increase testosterone levels; however, the significance of this effect is not known.

▷ **Possible Adverse Effects** (unusual, unexpected, and infrequent reactions)

If any of the following develop, consult your physician promptly for guidance.

Mild Adverse Effects

Allergic reactions: skin rash, hives—rare.

Plasma testosterone—decreased.

Headaches—infrequent.

Serious Adverse Effects

Allergic reactions: hypersensitivity reactions—case reports.

Handling Propecia or Proscar tablets by pregnant females may harm male fetuses.

Muscle changes (myopathy—progressive leg or arm weakness)—case report.

Low blood platelets (thrombocytopenia)—case report.

Higher grade prostate cancer—possible associated higher grade cancers if a cancer does happen.

Possible increase in more aggressive tumors if cancer (neoplasm) does happen—possible.

▷ **Possible Effects on Sexual Function:** Impotence, decreased libido or decreased volume of ejaculate—infrequent. Adverse sexual effects may resolve in more than 60% of patients who continue this medication.

Possible Delayed Adverse Effects: Possible enlargement of male breast tissue (gynecomastia), decreased libido, impotence, and decreased volume of ejaculate—infrequent.

Possible Effects on Laboratory Tests

Decreased PSA (prostate specific antigen).

CAUTION

1. A digital rectal exam and other prostate cancer exams are prudent before this medicine is started and periodically thereafter. PSA will be falsely

decreased by this medicine. More frequent checks may be prudent given the Thompson data.

2. If you have a change in liver function, inform your doctor.
3. If your sexual partner is pregnant, avoid exposing your partner to your semen. Exposure to finasteride-containing semen may cause genital abnormalities in male offspring.
4. If cancer of the prostate does happen, it may be more aggressive.

Precautions for Use
By Infants and Children: Safety and effectiveness for infants and children are not established.

By Those Over 60 Years of Age: No specific precautions other than changes related to decreased liver function.

▷ ### Advisability of Use During Pregnancy
Pregnancy Category: X. See Pregnancy Risk Categories at the back of this book.

Animal Studies: When administered to pregnant rats, the male offspring developed hypospadias. The offspring experienced decreased prostatic and seminal vesicular weight, slow preputial separation, and transient nipple problems.

Human Studies: Contraindicated in women who are pregnant or who plan to become pregnant. Women who are pregnant must avoid exposure to crushed tablets and semen of a sexual partner who is on finasteride.

Ask your physician for guidance.

Advisability of Use If Breast-Feeding
Refrain from nursing if you have been exposed to finasteride or finasteride-containing semen.

Habit-Forming Potential: None.

Effects of Overdose: Multiple doses of up to 80 mg per day have been taken without adverse effect.

Possible Effects of Long-Term Use: Adverse effects of long-term use are similar to short-term use effects.

Suggested Periodic Examinations While Taking This Drug (at physician's discretion)
Patients should be monitored for signs and symptoms of hypersensitivity.

Periodic digital rectal exam and PSA.

Patients should be monitored for improvement in symptoms of BPH.

▷ ### While Taking This Drug, Observe the Following
Foods: This medicine is best taken on an empty stomach.

Herbal Medicines or Minerals: Saw palmetto works by anti-androgenic and anti-inflammatory actions. The combination of this herb and finasteride has not been studied, but both drugs appear to work by different mechanisms. Talk to your doctor before combining. Autumn crocus should be avoided in alopecia.

Beverages: No restrictions.

▷ *Alcohol:* No restrictions.

Tobacco Smoking: No interactions expected. I advise everyone to quit smoking.

Marijuana Smoking: No interactions expected.

▷ *Other Drugs*
Finasteride *taken concurrently* with
- tirilazad (Freedox) will be increased by up to 29% if combined with finasteride. Caution is advised.

▷ *Driving, Hazardous Activities:* No restrictions.
Aviation Note: No restrictions.
Exposure to Sun: No restrictions.
Special Storage Instructions: Keep at room temperature. Avoid exposure to extreme humidity.

FLUCONAZOLE (flu KOHN a zohl)

Introduced: 1985 **Class:** Antifungal (triazole) **Prescription:**
USA: Yes **Controlled Drug:** USA: No; Canada: No **Available as**
Generic: USA: No; Canada: No

Brand Names: ❦Apo-Fluconazole, Diflucan, ❦Dom-Fluconazole, ❦Gen-Fluconazole, ❦Nu-Flucon

BENEFITS versus RISKS	
Possible Benefits	*Possible Risks*
EFFECTIVE PREVENTION OF YEAST (CANDIDIASIS) INFECTIONS	Severe skin reactions
	Possible liver damage
	Many possible drug interactions
EFFECTIVE TREATMENT AND SUPPRESSION OF CRYPTOCOCCAL MENINGITIS	
EFFECTIVE TREATMENT OF *CANDIDA* INFECTIONS OF THE MOUTH, THROAT, AND ESOPHAGUS	
EFFECTIVE TREATMENT OF SYSTEMIC *CANDIDA* INFECTIONS	
EFFECTIVE SINGLE-DOSE TREATMENT OF VAGINAL YEAST INFECTIONS	

▷ **Principal Uses**
As a Single Drug Product: Uses currently included in FDA-approved labeling: (1) *Candida* (yeast) infections of the mouth, throat, esophagus (may be AIDS related); (2) systemic *Candida* infections: lungs, peritonitis, urinary tract infections (may be AIDS related); (3) treats vaginal yeast infections (approved for single use); (4) treatment of cryptococcal meningitis in HIV-positive patients.
Other (unlabeled) generally accepted uses: (1) Prevention of yeast infections in patients with low white blood cell counts or cancer or those taking steroids; (2) treatment of some fungal eye infections (endophthalmitis); (3) treatment of Aspergillus pneumonia; (4) treatment of candidal urinary tract infections; (5) used to treat some fungal infections that may occur in people who have received transplanted organs; (6) may be a drug of choice for Sporothrix schenckii infections or for prevention of relapse of some Histoplasma infections; (7) some use as an alternative to amphotericin B in presumptive (empiric) treatment of cancer patients with prolonged fever and low white blood cell counts.

How This Drug Works: By damaging cell walls and blocking essential cell enzymes, this drug inhibits cell growth and reproduction (with low drug concentrations) and destroys fungal cells (with high drug concentrations).

Available Dosage Forms and Strengths

        Injection — 2 mg in 1 ml

        Tablets — 50 mg, 100 mg, 150 mg, 200 mg

    Oral suspension — 10 mg in 5 ml,

           — 40 mg in 5 ml

▷ **Recommended Dosage Ranges** (Actual dose and schedule must be determined for each patient individually.)

Infants and Children: From 3 to 13 years of age: 3–6 mg per kg of body mass daily, depending on the kind and site of infection. Intravenous use should be infused over 2 hours in this population.

Cryptococcal meningitis: 12 mg per kg on the first day and then 6 mg per kg daily for 10 to 12 weeks after cerebrospinal fluid culture becomes negative.

13 to 60 Years of Age: Cryptococcal meningitis: 400 mg once daily until improvement occurs; then 200 to 400 mg once daily for 10 to 12 weeks after cerebrospinal fluid culture becomes negative.

Suppression of cryptococcal meningitis: 50–200 mg once daily for up to 21 months have been used.

Candida infections of mouth and throat: 200 mg first day and then 100 mg once daily for 2 weeks.

Candida infection of the esophagus: 200 mg first day and then 100 mg once daily for at least 3 weeks; treat for 2 weeks after all signs of infection are gone. Doses up to 400 mg daily may be used. Some patients with chronic mucocutaneous *Candida* infections have benefited from 50 mg/day of this medicine.

Systemic *Candida* infections: 400 mg daily for at least 4 weeks; treating for 2 weeks after all symptoms of infection are gone.

Vaginal yeast infections (*Candida*): One 150-mg tablet by mouth.

Over 60 Years of Age: Same as 13 to 60, adjusted if kidneys are impaired.

Conditions Requiring Dosing Adjustments

Liver Function: Caution: Rare cause of hepatitis.

Kidney Function: Mild to moderate failure—usual dose every 48 hours. In severe kidney failure—half (50%) of usual dose every 48 hours.

▷ **Dosing Instructions:** The tablet may be crushed; may be taken with or after food to reduce stomach upset. Suspension forms are available if swallowing is a problem. Shake them well before dosing and use a measuring spoon for suspension forms. If you forget a dose, take the missed dose as soon as you remember it—unless it is nearly time for your next dose. If that is the case, skip the missed dose and take the next pill right on schedule. DO NOT double doses. Fungal infections will return if you do not take this medicine as long as you are supposed to.

Usual Duration of Use: Use on a regular schedule for 2 to 4 weeks is usually needed to see this drug's benefit in controlling candidal or cryptococcal infections. Actual cures or long-term suppression often require continual treatment for many months. May be continuous therapy in AIDS patients.

Typical Treatment Goals and Measurements (Outcomes and Markers)

Candida *infections:* Goals for treatment of infections include resolution of signs and symptoms (such as sore throat and white coloration in candidal throat infections), return of white blood cell count and differential to normal (for systemic infections), negative growth of fungus in appropriate cultures and failure of the infection to return in prophylactic use.

Currently a "Drug of Choice"

For maintenance therapy to prevent relapse following control of AIDS-related candidal esophagitis. Because oral absorption is so complete, oral and intravenous dosing are the same.

▷ **This Drug Should Not Be Taken If**
- you have had an allergic reaction to it previously.
- you have active liver disease.

▷ **Inform Your Physician Before Taking This Drug If**
- you are allergic to clotrimazole, itraconazole, ketoconazole, or miconazole.
- you have impaired liver or kidney function.
- you develop light stools, unexplained abdominal pain, dark urine, nausea, or yellow eyes (signs of liver problems).
- you tend to have low blood potassium.
- you get a skin rash while taking this medicine.

Mild Adverse Effects

Allergic reactions: skin rash—rare.

Hair loss—very rare with usual doses. Reversible hair loss (alopecia) may be more common with high doses of fluconazole given for 2 months or longer.

Headache—rare.

Nausea, vomiting, stomach pain, diarrhea—frequent.

Serious Adverse Effects

Allergic reactions: severe dermatitis (Stevens-Johnson Syndrome)—very rare.

Anaphylactic reactions—case reports.

Liver toxicity—rare.

Abnormally low platelet counts: abnormal bruising/bleeding or low white blood cell counts—rare.

Seizures or adrenal suppression—case reports, rare.

Low blood potassium (hypokalemia)—case reports in 3 acute myeloid leukemia patients.

Abnormal heart rhythm (Torsades de Pointes)—case report.

▷ **Possible Effects on Sexual Function:** Amenorrhea—one case report.

Possible Delayed Adverse Effects: Liver toxicity.

▷ **Adverse Effects That May Mimic Natural Diseases or Disorders**

Possible liver reaction may suggest viral hepatitis.

Possible Effects on Laboratory Tests

Blood platelet counts: decreased.

Liver function tests: increased liver enzymes (ALT/GPT, AST/GOT, and alkaline phosphatase), increased bilirubin.

Blood potassium: lowered—case reports.

Precautions for Use

By Infants and Children: Safety and effectiveness for those under 13 years of age are not established, but any infusions for age-appropriate patients should be given over 2 hours.

By Those Over 60 Years of Age: Age-related decrease in kidney function may require adjustment of dose.

▷ **Advisability of Use During Pregnancy**

Pregnancy Category: C. See Pregnancy Risk Categories at the back of this book.

Animal Studies: Rat studies revealed significant abnormalities in bone growth and development.

Human Studies: Adequate studies of pregnant women are not available. Use this drug only if clearly needed. Ask your doctor for help.

Advisability of Use If Breast-Feeding
Presence of this drug in breast milk: Yes.
Avoid drug or refrain from nursing.

Habit-Forming Potential: None.

Effects of Overdose: Possible nausea, vomiting, diarrhea.

Possible Effects of Long-Term Use: None reported.

Suggested Periodic Examinations While Taking This Drug (at physician's discretion)
Liver function tests (medicine should be stopped in patients who have signs and symptoms of liver disease while taking this medicine). Kidney function tests, potassium levels in patients with one kind of leukemia (acute myeloid).
Check for skin rashes.

▷ **While Taking This Drug, Observe the Following**
Foods: Caution is advised regarding grapefruit or grapefruit juice. Avoid eating grapefruit.
Herbal Medicines or Minerals: Echinacea: Some patients use echinacea to attempt to boost their immune systems. Unfortunately, use of echinacea is not recommended in people with damaged immune systems. This herb may also actually weaken any immune system if it is used too often or for too long a time. Eucalyptus may increase risk of liver toxicity. Kava is no longer recommended in Canada because of liver toxicity.
Beverages: Grapefruit juice should be avoided. May be taken with milk or water.
▷ *Alcohol:* No interactions expected.
Tobacco Smoking: No interactions expected. I advise everyone to quit smoking.
▷ *Other Drugs*
Fluconazole may ***increase*** the effects of
- benzodiazepines (see Drug Classes).
- birth control pills (oral contraceptives with ethinyl estradiol and levonorgestrel) may lead to adverse effects.
- celecoxib (Celebrex).
- cyclosporine (Sandimmune).
- dofetilide (Tikosyn).
- felodipine (Plendil).
- nicardipine (Cardene) and nifedipine (Adalat, others) leading to excessively low blood pressure. Lower doses of one or both drugs are prudent with careful patient follow up.
- oral antidiabetic drugs (chlorpropamide, glipizide, glyburide, tolbutamide, others) and cause hypoglycemia; check sugar levels carefully.
- phenytoin (Dilantin, etc.) or fosphenytoin (Cerebyx) and cause toxicity, monitor blood levels.
- sirolimus (Rapamune), and tacrolimus (Prograf). Sirolimus and tacrolimus levels should be used to guide dosing.
- triazolam (Halcion), leading to toxicity.
- tricyclic antidepressants (see Drug Classes).
- trimetrexate (Neutrexin).
- warfarin (Coumadin) and cause unwanted bleeding. Dosing changes and more frequent INRs are prudent.
- zidovudine (AZT) and result in toxicity. The zidovudine dose may need to be decreased if this combination is to be continued.

- zolpidem (Ambien) and result in toxicity. The zolpidem dose may need to be decreased if this combination is to be continued.

The following drugs may *decrease* the effects of fluconazole:
- cimetidine (Tagamet).
- rifampin (Rifadin, Rimactane, etc.).

Fluconazole *taken concurrently* with
- amphotericin B (Amphotec, others) may decrease amphotericin benefits.
- astemizole (Hismanal—now removed from the US market) may result in fatal toxicity to the heart.
- atorvastatin (Lipitor), and other HMG-CoA inhibitors, may increase risk of muscle toxicity.
- cisapride (Propulsid) may lead to adverse effects on the heart. DO NOT COMBINE.
- cotrimoxazole (various) may lead to adverse effects on the heart. DO NOT COMBINE.
- ergot-type medicines (Cafergot, others) may lead to increased ergotism risk. DO NOT COMBINE.
- hydrochlorothiazide (Esidrix, others) may increase potassium loss.
- loratadine (Claritin) may result in increased blood levels of loratadine, but to date, toxicity to the heart has not been reported. Since blood levels may be increased if combined use is undertaken, it is prudent to decrease the dose of loratadine.
- losartan (Cozaar) may blunt blood pressure control.
- oral contraceptives (birth control pills) may blunt contraception and result in pregnancy.
- prednisone (various) may lead to increased removal (metabolism) of prednisone if the two medicines are taken at the same time, then the fluconazole is stopped and the prednisone dose is left the same.
- quetiapine (Seroquel) may lead to quetiapine toxicity.
- ritonavir (Norvir) may increase ritonavir blood levels.
- terfenadine (Seldane—now removed from the US market) may result in toxicity to the heart.
- ziprasidone (Geodon) may result in toxicity to the heart (QT prolongation—see Glossary). DO NOT combine.

▷ *Driving, Hazardous Activities:* No restrictions.
Aviation Note: The use of this drug *is probably not a disqualification* for piloting. Consult a designated Aviation Medical Examiner.
Exposure to Sun: No restrictions.
Discontinuation: Take all of the medicine. Ongoing therapy for months may be needed. Ask your doctor when it is okay to stop this medicine.

FLUCYTOSINE (flu SI toh seen)

Other Names: 5-fluorocytosine, 5-FC **Introduced:** 1977 **Class:** Antifungal **Prescription:** USA: Yes **Controlled Drug:** USA: No; Canada: No **Available as Generic:** USA: No; Canada: No
Brand Names: Ancobon, ✦Ancotil, ✦Novo-triphyl

```
┌─────────────────────────────────────────────────────────────────┐
│                     BENEFITS versus RISKS                         │
│        Possible Benefits              Possible Risks              │
│  EFFECTIVE ADJUNCTIVE           BONE MARROW DEPRESSION            │
│    TREATMENT OF CERTAIN         DRUG-INDUCED LIVER DAMAGE         │
│    INFECTIONS CAUSED BY         Peripheral neuritis               │
│    CANDIDA, CRYPTOCOCCUS                                          │
│    FUNGI, AND ASPERGILLUS                                         │
│  Effective adjunctive treatment of                               │
│    chromomycosis infection                                       │
└─────────────────────────────────────────────────────────────────┘
```

▷ **Principal Uses**
  As a Single Drug Product: Uses currently included in FDA-approved labeling:
    (1) Treats endocarditis, osteomyelitis, arthritis, meningitis, pneumonia,
    septicemia, and urinary tract infections caused by *Candida*; (2) treats
    meningitis, pneumonia, septicemia, endocarditis, and urinary tract infec-
    tions caused by *Cryptococcus*.
  Other (unlabeled) generally accepted uses: (1) Treatment of disseminated
    candidiasis, chromoblastomycosis and cryptococcosis (these infections
    may be AIDS related); (2) treatment of general fungal infections.
  **Author's Note: Flucytosine is usually used together with amphotericin
  B to treat widely distributed (disseminated) fungal infections.**

How This Drug Works: This drug goes into fungal cells and blocks production of
  RNA and DNA, inhibiting fungal development and reproduction.

Available Dosage Forms and Strengths
    Capsules — 200 mg, 250 mg, 500 mg
    Injection — 2.5 grams/250 ml

▷ **Recommended Dosage Ranges** (Actual dose and schedule must be determined
    for each patient individually.)
  Infants and Children: Safety and efficacy in children have not been established.
  12 to 60 Years of Age: 50 to 150 mg per kg of body mass, divided into equal
    doses and given every 6 hours. Some severe infections have required 250
    mg per kg of body mass per day. Capsules are often taken a few at a time
    and the total dose taken over 15 minutes.
  Over 60 Years of Age: Same as 12 to 60 years of age. If kidney function is
    impaired, dose reduction is mandatory.

Conditions Requiring Dosing Adjustments
  Liver Function: No changes needed in mild to moderate liver compromise. This
    drug may cause liver toxicity (with blood levels greater than 100 mcg/ml).
    Used with caution in liver compromise.
  Kidney Function: In mild to moderate kidney failure, the usual dose can be
    given every 12–24 hours (GFR 10–50 ml/min). In severe kidney failure the
    usual dose can be given every 24–48 hours.

▷ **Dosing Instructions:** If a single dose requires more than one capsule, space
    doses over a period of 15 minutes to reduce stomach upset and nausea.
    The capsule may be opened and taken with or after food. If you forget a
    dose: Take the omitted dose as soon as you remember it, unless it is nearly
    time for your next dose—if that is the case, skip the missed dose and take
    the next scheduled dose right on time. DO NOT double doses.

Usual Duration of Use: Use on a regular schedule for 4 to 6 weeks is needed to see effectiveness in controlling *Candida* or cryptococcal infection. Long-term use requires physician evaluation.

Typical Treatment Goals and Measurements (Outcomes and Markers)
Fungal infections: Goals for treatment of infections include resolution of signs and symptoms, return of white blood cell count and differential to normal (for systemic infections), and checks of blood levels of flucytosine (levels more than 100–125 mcg/ml increase toxicity risk).

Currently a "Drug of Choice"
For the treatment of Chromomycosis with or without amphotericin B.

▷ **This Drug Should Not Be Taken If**
 • you have had an allergic reaction to it previously.
 • you have an active blood cell or bone marrow disorder.
 • you have active liver disease.

▷ **Inform Your Physician Before Taking This Drug If**
 • you have a history of drug-induced bone marrow depression.
 • you have a history of peripheral neuritis.
 • you have impaired liver or kidney function.

Possible Side Effects (natural, expected, and unavoidable drug actions)
Dose-related nausea and vomiting.

▷ **Possible Adverse Effects** (unusual, unexpected, and infrequent reactions)
If any of the following develop, consult your physician promptly for guidance.
Mild Adverse Effects
Allergic reactions: skin rash, itching.
Headache, dizziness, drowsiness, confusion, hallucinations—infrequent.
Loss of appetite, nausea, vomiting, stomach pain, diarrhea—possible and dose-related.
Serious Adverse Effects
Allergic reactions: anaphylactic reactions, toxic epidermal necrolysis—case reports.
Bone marrow depression (see Glossary): fatigue, weakness, fever, sore throat, abnormal bleeding or bruising—rare.
Liver toxicity, with or without jaundice (see Glossary)—may be frequent.
Peripheral neuritis (see Glossary)—possible.
Hallucinations—case reports.
Bowel perforation or kidney damage—rare.
Heart toxicity (ventricular dysfunction, toxicity, or cardiac arrest)—infrequent.

▷ **Possible Effects on Sexual Function:** None reported.

▷ **Adverse Effects That May Mimic Natural Diseases or Disorders**
Drug-induced hepatitis may suggest viral hepatitis.

Natural Diseases or Disorders That May Be Activated by This Drug
Crohn's disease, ulcerative colitis.

Possible Effects on Laboratory Tests
Complete blood counts: decreased red cells, hemoglobin, white cells, and platelets.
Liver function tests: increased liver enzymes (ALT/GPT, AST/GOT, and alkaline phosphatase), increased bilirubin.
Kidney function tests: increased blood urea nitrogen (BUN) and creatinine.
Serum creatinine: may be falsely increased if tested by some methods.

CAUTION
1. When this drug is used alone, resistance can occur rapidly. It is usually used concurrently with amphotericin B (Abelcet) (given intravenously).
2. This drug may cause false increases in creatinine laboratory values tested by the Ektachem method. DuPont ACA does not appear to have this problem.

Precautions for Use
By Infants and Children: No information available.
By Those Over 60 Years of Age: If necessary, adjust dose for age-related decrease in kidney function.

▷ **Advisability of Use During Pregnancy**
Pregnancy Category: C. See Pregnancy Risk Categories at the back of this book.
Animal Studies: Rat studies reveal drug-induced birth defects.
Human Studies: Adequate studies of pregnant women are not available.
Use this drug only if clearly needed. Ask your physician for guidance.

Advisability of Use If Breast-Feeding
Presence of this drug in breast milk: Yes.
Avoid drug or refrain from nursing.

Habit-Forming Potential: None.

Effects of Overdose: Nausea, vomiting, stomach pain, diarrhea, confusion.

Possible Effects of Long-Term Use: Bone marrow depression, liver or kidney damage.

Suggested Periodic Examinations While Taking This Drug (at physician's discretion)
Measurement of blood levels of flucytosine.
Complete blood cell counts.
Liver and kidney function tests.

▷ **While Taking This Drug, Observe the Following**
Foods: No restrictions.
Herbal Medicines or Minerals: Echinacea: Some patients use echinacea to attempt to boost their immune systems. Unfortunately, use of echinacea is not recommended in people with damaged immune systems. This herb may also actually weaken any immune system if it is used too often or for too long a time. **Caution:** St. John's wort may also cause extreme reactions to the sun. Additive photosensitivity may be possible. Eucalyptus may increase risk of liver toxicity. Kava is no longer recommended in Canada because of liver toxicity.
Beverages: No restrictions. May be taken with milk.
▷ *Alcohol:* No interactions expected.
Tobacco Smoking: No interactions expected. I advise everyone to quit smoking.
▷ *Other Drugs*
The following drugs may *decrease* the effects of flucytosine:
- antacids.
- cytarabine (Cytosar).

Flucytosine *taken concurrently* with
- amphotericin B may result in increased risk of kidney toxicity; lipid-associated form (Abelcet) may help avoid this.
- zidovudine (AZT) may result in additive and serious blood (hematological) toxicity.

▷ *Driving, Hazardous Activities:* This drug may cause dizziness, drowsiness, or confusion. Limit activities as necessary.

Aviation Note: The use of this drug *may be a disqualification* for piloting. Consult a designated Aviation Medical Examiner.

Exposure to Sun: Use caution—may cause photosensitivity (see Glossary). See Herbal Medicines note on page 451.

Discontinuation: This drug may be needed for an extended period. Your doctor must decide when to stop it.

FLUNISOLIDE (flu NIS oh lide)

Introduced: 1980   **Class:** Antiasthmatic, cortisonelike drugs   **Prescription:** USA: Yes   **Controlled Drug:** USA: No; Canada: No   **Available as Generic:** No

Brand Names: AeroBid, AeroBid-M, ✤Bronalide, Nasalide, Nasarel, ✤Nu-Flunisolide, ✤Rhinalar

---

BENEFITS versus RISKS

Possible Benefits	*Possible Risks*
EFFECTIVE CONTROL OF SEVERE,CHRONIC BRONCHIAL ASTHMA	Yeast infections of mouth and throat (inhaler form)
FIRST-LINE TREATMENT OF ALLERGIC RHINITIS WITH INTRANASAL FORM	Increased susceptibility to respiratory tract infections (inhaler form)
	Localized areas of "allergic" pneumonia (inhaler form)
	Possible osteoporosis with long-term use

Principal Uses

As a Single Drug Product: Uses currently included in FDA-approved labeling: (1) Treats chronic bronchial asthma in people requiring cortisonelike drugs for asthma control; (2) treats various kinds of "hay fever" (seasonal or perennial allergic rhinitis).

Other (unlabeled) generally accepted uses: (1) Treatment of nasal polyps; (2) treats bronchopulmonary dysplasia; (3) may have a role in acute or chronic sinusitis in combination with an antibiotic (amoxicillin/clavulanate in one study).

How This Drug Works: Increases cyclic AMP, which may increase epinephrine, an effective bronchodilator and antiasthmatic. Also reduces local allergic reaction and inflammation.

Available Dosage Forms and Strengths

Inhalation aerosol — 0.25 mg (250 mcg) per metered spray

Nasal solution — 25 mcg per actuation

▷ **Recommended Dosage Ranges** (Actual dose and schedule must be determined for each patient individually.)

Infants and Children:

Oral inhalation: Less than 6 years old—not recommended. Six to 15 years old—two inhalations which are 500 mcg twice a day. Maximum daily dose is 1 mg.

Nasal inhalation: Up to 6 years old—not recommended. Six to 15 years old—0.25 mcg (one spray in each nostril) three times a day. Once the peak effect is seen, the dose should be reduced to the smallest dose and frequency that works. Maximum is four sprays in each nostril (200 mcg/day).

Aqueous nasal form: Up to 6 years old—not recommended. Six to 14 years old—two sprays in each nostril twice daily or one spray in each nostril three times a day. Once the peak effect is seen, the dose should be reduced to the smallest dose and frequency that works.

15 to 60 Years of Age:

Oral inhalation: 0.5 to 1 mg (2 to 4 metered sprays) twice a day, morning and evening. Limit total daily dose to 2 mg (four inhalations twice daily). Once the peak effect is seen, the dose should be reduced to the smallest dose and frequency that works.

Nasal inhalation: Two sprays (50 mcg) per nostril twice a day. The dose may be increased to two sprays in each nostril three times a day (300 mcg/day) if required. Maximum dose with this route is eight sprays (400 mcg) in each nostril daily. Once the peak effect is seen, the dose should be reduced to the smallest dose and frequency that works.

Aqueous nasal form: Two sprays in each nostril twice daily to start. Maintenance dosing is continued with the lowest dose that is effective. This may be as low as one spray in each nostril daily.

Over 60 Years of Age: Same as 15 to 60 years of age.

Conditions Requiring Dosing Adjustments

Liver Function: Specific guidelines are not available.

Kidney Function: No specific changes needed—dual kidney and fecal elimination (Nasalide).

▷ **Dosing Instructions:** May be used as needed without regard to eating. Shake the container well before using. Carefully follow the printed patient instructions provided with the inhaler; rinse the mouth and throat (gargle) with water thoroughly after each inhalation. A decongestant is prudent BEFORE flunisolide is used in people with blocked nose (nasal) passages. If you forget a dose: take the next dose as soon as you remember it, unless it is nearly time for your next dose—if that is the case, skip the dose you forgot, and take the next dose right on schedule. DO NOT double doses. Once the peak benefit is seen, the dose should be lowered to the smallest dose that works.

Usual Duration of Use: Use on a regular schedule for 1 to 3 weeks is necessary to see effectiveness in controlling allergic rhinitis. It may take 4 weeks to see the greatest benefit in severe, chronic asthma. In patients who are dependent on systemic steroids, changing to oral flunisolide inhalations may be more difficult since recovering from suppressed adrenal gland function can be slow. When therapy is started, the inhaler form is typically used at the same time as the prior systemic steroid and continued for 7–14 days. After this, gradual reductions of the daily dose of the previous steroid are undertaken. As with other steroids, if severe asthma attacks or stress, systemic steroids may need to be restarted. Ongoing use requires physician supervision and guidance.

Typical Treatment Goals and Measurements (Outcomes and Markers)

Asthma: Frequency and severity of asthma attacks should ease. Some clinicians also use decreased frequency of rescue inhaler use as a further clinical indicator. It is critical that this medicine is used regularly to get the best results. An additional goal of therapy is to use the lowest effective dose. Some people keep their improvements when doses are lowered, while others relapse. Specific testing goals include improvement in PEFR and other lung (pulmonary) function tests. Wheezing and difficulty breathing (Dyspnea) should ease as well as asthma caused (induced) by exercise. If the usual benefit is not realized, call your doctor.

Allergic rhinitis: Signs and symptoms of allergic rhinitis such as runny or stuffy nose, postnasal drip and sneezing should ease. Scratch testing for a specific immune substance (IgE) can also be done to check progress at a cellular level.

Possible Advantages of These Dosage Forms and Medicines: Intranasal or inhaled flunisolide has not been reported to be related to suppression of the adrenal gland. The localized nature of the dosing appears, the dose amount and/or the medicine to offer systemic exposure or medicine action different than other approaches to corticosteroids use.

▷ **This Drug Should Not Be Taken If**
- you have had an allergic reaction to it previously.
- you are having severe acute asthma or status asthmaticus that requires more intense treatment for prompt relief.
- you have been taking this medicine and have repeat nosebleeds.
- you have a form of nonallergic bronchitis with asthmatic features.

▷ **Inform Your Physician Before Taking This Drug If**
- you are now taking or have recently taken any cortisone-related drug (including ACTH by injection; see Drug Classes) for any reason.
- you have a history of tuberculosis (inhalation form).
- you have herpes simplex infection of the eye.
- you have chicken pox or measles or have been exposed to them.
- you have had recent surgery of the nose or have ulcers of the nose or nosebleeds—this medicine should be used cautiously until the site has healed.
- you are a child and your growth has slowed.
- you have chronic bronchitis or bronchiectasis.
- you think you may have an active infection of any kind, especially a respiratory infection (such as tuberculosis).

Possible Side Effects (natural, expected, and unavoidable drug actions)
Yeast infections (thrush) of the mouth and throat. Suppression of the adrenal gland (possible and more likely with higher doses).
Unpleasant taste. Orally inhaled flunisolide can cause flu-like symptoms occasionally in people taking the drug by oral inhalation. The most frequent adverse effect of the nasal form is irritation of the nose (nasal mucosa).

▷ **Possible Adverse Effects** (unusual, unexpected, and infrequent reactions)
If any of the following develop, consult your physician promptly for guidance.
Mild Adverse Effects
Allergic reactions: skin rash, hives, itching.
Headache, dizziness, nervousness, moodiness, insomnia, loss of smell or taste—rare to infrequent.
Aftertaste (nasal form)—frequent.
Upper respiratory infections, cough—possible.
Heart palpitation, increased blood pressure, swelling of feet and ankles (inhalation form)—possible to infrequent.
Loss of appetite, indigestion, nausea, vomiting, stomach pain, diarrhea—infrequent.
Sore throat, stinging of the nose—infrequent to frequent.
Nasal irritation—infrequent to frequent (less common with the aqueous form).
Slowing of growth rate in children—possible.
Impaired sense of smell—possible.

Serious Adverse Effects

Allergic reaction: localized areas of "allergic" pneumonitis (lung inflammation).

Bronchospasm, asthmatic wheezing—rare with the inhalation form.

Tachycardia or hypertension—rare with the inhalation form.

Osteoporosis—possible with long-term use, even in people who do not usually get osteoporosis, such as men, blacks, and women before menopause. Cumulative dose and how long the corticosteroids have been used impacts this problem, but exact cumulative doses (cut point) are not known (often greatest in the first 6 months of treatment and in the spine and ribs—alendronate or raloxifene plus calcium replacement may prevent this). The British Royal College of Physicians recommends that patients at high risk for osteoporosis should also start bone protective treatment at the same time.

Increased risk of cataracts (posterior subcapsular)—possible, though less likely than with other corticosteroid dosing strategies.

▷ **Possible Effects on Sexual Function:** None reported.

Natural Diseases or Disorders That May Be Activated by This Drug

Cortisone-related drugs (used by inhalation) that produce systemic effects can impair immunity and lead to reactivation of "healed" or quiescent tuberculosis. People with a history of tuberculosis should be watched closely during use of cortisonelike drugs by inhalation.

Possible Effects on Laboratory Tests

None reported.

CAUTION

1. Does NOT act primarily as a bronchodilator. **Should not be used for immediate relief of acute asthma**.

2. If you were using any cortisone-related drugs for treatment of your asthma before changing to this inhaler, the cortisone-related drug may be required if you are injured, have an infection or require surgery. Tell your doctor about prior use of cortisone-related drugs. Slow downward adjustment of the prior steroid is typical. For example, if prednisone was being taken, 2.5 mg per week decreases in prednisone (as outlined above) would be a usual occurrence.

3. If severe asthma returns while using this drug, call your doctor immediately.

4. If you have used cortisone-related drugs in the past year, carry a card that says so.

5. Five to ten minutes should separate the inhalation of bronchodilators, such as albuterol, epinephrine, pirbuterol, etc. (which should be used first), and the inhalation of this drug. This lets more flunisolide reach the bronchial tubes and reduces risk of adverse effects from the propellants used in the two inhalers.

6. A decongestant may be a good idea in people with blocked nasal passages. Talk with your doctor or pharmacist.

7. Osteoporosis risk is increased with long-term use of this medicine. Bone mineral density (BMD) tests are prudent as well as the use of alendronate (Fosamax) as a preventive (prophylactic) medicine in some high-risk patients (based on BMD results).

8. Unlike other corticosteroids, reports of osteonecrosis (avascular necrosis or aseptic necrosis) have not been made for this medicine. Caution is prudent, and patients should report any unexplained joint (such as knee, hip, or shoulder) pain to their doctor.

9. Up to 50% of an intranasal dose may reach the rest of the body (systemic circulation).

Precautions for Use

By Infants and Children: Safety and effectiveness for those under 4 years of age are not established. To obtain maximal benefit, the use of a spacer device is recommended for inhalation therapy in children.

By Those Over 60 Years of Age: People with chronic bronchitis or bronchiectasis should be watched closely for the development of lung infections.

▷ **Advisability of Use During Pregnancy**

Pregnancy Category: C. See Pregnancy Risk Categories at the back of this book.

Animal Studies: Rat and rabbit studies reveal significant birth defects due to this drug.

Human Studies: Adequate studies of pregnant women are not available.

Avoid drug during the first 3 months. Use infrequently and only as clearly needed during the final 6 months.

Advisability of Use If Breast-Feeding

Presence of this drug in breast milk: Unknown.

Avoid drug or refrain from nursing.

Habit-Forming Potential: With recommended dose, a state of functional dependence (see Glossary) is not likely to develop.

Effects of Overdose: Indications of cortisone excess (due to systemic absorption)—fluid retention, flushing of the face, stomach irritation, nervousness.

Possible Effects of Long-Term Use: Development of acne, cataracts, altered menstrual pattern. Osteoporosis (periodic bone mineral density tests are prudent).

Suggested Periodic Examinations While Taking This Drug (at physician's discretion)

Inspection of mouth and throat for evidence of yeast infection.

Check of adrenal function in people who have used cortisone-related drugs for an extended period of time before using this drug.

X-ray of the lungs of people with a prior history of tuberculosis.

Bone mineral density testing (osteoporosis test DEXA or PDEXA) with long-term use.

▷ **While Taking This Drug, Observe the Following**

Foods: No specific restrictions beyond those advised by your physician.

Herbal Medicines or Minerals: Fir or pine needle oil should NOT be used by asthmatics. Ephedra alone does carry a German Commission E monograph indication for asthma treatment. If you are allergic to plants in the Asteraceae family (aster, chrysanthemum, daisy, or ragweed), you may also be allergic to echinacea, chamomile, feverfew, and St. John's wort. Increased calcium and vitamin D are prudent while taking this medicine. Talk to your doctor BEFORE adding any herbals to this medicine.

Beverages: No specific restrictions.

▷ *Alcohol:* No direct interactions expected, but excessive alcohol use may be a risk factor for osteoporosis. Since long-term use of this medicine may lead to osteoporosis, excessive use of alcohol must be avoided.

Tobacco Smoking: No direct drug interactions expected; however, smoking can worsen asthma and reduce benefits of flunisolide. I advise everyone to quit smoking.

▷   *Other Drugs*
  The following drugs may *increase* the effects of flunisolide:
  • inhalant bronchodilators—albuterol, bitolterol, epinephrine, etc.
  • oral bronchodilators—aminophylline, ephedrine, terbutaline, theophylline, etc.
  Flunisolide *taken concurrently* with
  • stanozolol (Winstrol) may result in increased risk of acne or edema.
  • some antiepileptic medicines such as phenytoin (Dilantin) may increase risk of osteoporosis.
  • inhalant bronchodilators—epinephrine, isoetharine, isoproterenol—may offer improved results in asthma treatment.
▷   *Driving, Hazardous Activities:* No restrictions.
  Aviation Note: The use of this drug and the disorder for which this drug is prescribed *may be disqualifications* for piloting. Consult a designated Aviation Medical Examiner.
  Exposure to Sun: No restrictions.
  Occurrence of Unrelated Illness: Acute infections, serious injuries or surgical procedures can create an urgent need for cortisone-related drugs given by mouth and/or injection. Call your doctor immediately in the event of new illness or injury.
  Special Storage Instructions: Store at room temperature. Avoid exposure to temperatures above 120 degrees F. (49 degrees C.). Do not store or use this inhaler near heat or open flame.
  Discontinuation: If this drug has made it possible to reduce or discontinue cortisonelike drugs by mouth, do not stop this drug abruptly. If you must stop this drug, call your doctor promptly. Cortisone preparations and other measures may be necessary.

FLUOROQUINOLONE ANTIBIOTIC FAMILY

Ciprofloxacin   (sip roh FLOX a sin)   **Gatifloxacin**   (GAT ih flox a sin)
Grepafloxacin   (GREP ah flox a sin)   **Levofloxacin**   (leev oh FLOX a sin)   **Lomefloxacin**   (loh me FLOX a sin)   **Norfloxacin**   (nor FLOX a sin)   **Ofloxacin**   (oh FLOX a sin)   **Sparfloxacin**   (SPAR flox a sin)
Trovafloxacin   (TROV ah flox a sin)

Introduced: 1984, 2000, 1997, 1996, 1992, 1986, 1984, 1996, 1997, respectively   **Class:**   Anti-infective, fluoroquinolone   **Prescription:**   USA: Yes   **Controlled Drug:**   USA: No   **Available as Generic:**   USA: Yes, ciprofloxacin, no, others; Canada: Yes (IV)

Brand Names: *Ciprofloxacin*: Ciloxan, Cipro, Cipro Cystitis pack, Cipro HC [CD]; *Gatifloxacin*: Tequin; *Grepafloxacin* (removed from the market); *Levofloxacin:* Levaquin, Maxaquin, Quixin; *Moxifloxacin:* Avelox; *Norfloxacin*: Chibroxin, Noroxin, Noroxin Ophthalmic; *Ofloxacin*: ✤Apo-Oflox, Floxin, Floxin Otic, Floxin Uropak, Ocuflox, ✤Ofloxacine; *Sparfloxacin:* Zagam; *Trovafloxacin*: Trovan, Trovan/Zithromax Compliance Pak

Author's Note: Information in this profile will be broadened to include data on gatifloxacin and moxifloxacin once more data are available. It does carry a precautionary note regarding QTc interval prolongation and avoidance in people with QTc prolongation and in those taking other medicines that can cause QTc prolongation.

Warning: Some prescribers use "Norflox" to identify norfloxacin. This is not an accepted name in any setting for any reason. Using this name has

resulted in serious medication errors—that is, the dispensing of Norflex, the generic drug orphenadrine, a skeletal muscle relaxant. Check to be sure you get the right drug.

Warning: There have been reports for some drugs in this class that find tendon rupture as a rare adverse effect. Ask your doctor about limits on strenuous exercise while you are taking this medicine. A rare idiosyncratic reaction has also been reported that presents as mental confusion and disorientation. Use of these medicines after head trauma may be a risk factor. If you have suffered a fall, ask your doctor if a medicine in a different antibiotic class should be substituted. If you are taking this drug and notice a change in your thinking, call your doctor. THE FDA HAS RESTRICTED TROVAFLOXACIN USE TO EMERGENCIES AND THE DRUG IS NO LONGER BEING SOLD IN DRUGSTORES. The CDC has stopped recommending quinolones to treat gonorrhea in Hawaii and California due to resistant gonorrhea.

BENEFITS versus RISKS	
Possible Benefits	*Possible Risks*
HIGHLY EFFECTIVE TREATMENT FOR INFECTIONS OF THE LOWER RESPIRATORY TRACT (ciprofloxacin and ofloxacin), URINARY TRACT, BONES, JOINTS AND SKIN TISSUES due to susceptible organisms	TROVAFLOXACIN PATIENTS WERE WARNED (IN EUROPE) TO STOP TROVAFLOXACIN IF THEY DEVELOP SKIN RASH OR HIVES, YELLOWING OF THE SKIN OR EYES, DARK URINE, OR NAUSEA AND VOMITING WITH STOMACH PAIN; THE DRUG IS NO LONGER SOLD IN DRUG STORES
EFFECTIVE TREATMENT OF BACTERIAL (EYE) INFECTIONS	
Effective treatment for some forms of bacterial gastroenteritis (diarrhea)	SOME OF THESE MEDICINES CAN CAUSE SEVERE SUN SENSITIVITY
Effective treatment for some infections of the prostate gland	PROLONGATION OF THE QT INTERVAL with some Nausea, Indigestion Drug-induced colitis Hallucination or seizure Tendon rupture

▷ **Principal Uses**

As a Single Drug Product: Uses currently included in FDA-approved labeling: Treats responsive infections (in adults) of (1) the lower respiratory tract (lungs and bronchial tubes); (2) the urinary tract (kidneys, bladder, urethra [including uncomplicated gonorrhea], and prostate gland); (3) the digestive tract (small intestine and colon); (4) bones and joints (ciprofloxacin; ofloxacin—unlabeled); (5) skin and related tissues; (6) used in ophthalmic preparations to treat bacterial conjunctivitis caused by susceptible organisms; (7) ciprofloxacin has been approved to treat mild to moderate acute sinusitis caused by *Streptococcus pneumoniae, Haemophilus influenzae,* or *Moraxella catarrhalis;* (8) sparfloxacin is very active against Streptococcus; (9) ciprofloxacin/hydrocortisone is used for sudden infections of the outside of the ear (*acute otitis externa*); (10) ciprofloxacin is used in postexposure anthrax cases; (11) gatifloxacin is approved for a short course (5-day regimen) for acute exacerbation of chronic bacterial bronchitis; Cipro

XR form is approved for uncomplicated bladder (cystitis) as once-a-day treatment for three days.

Other (unlabeled) generally accepted uses: (1) Can have a role in treating cholera where the organisms are resistant to doxycycline (ciprofloxacin); (2) lessens symptoms or prevents traveler's diarrhea; (3) ciprofloxacin can be of use in treating some unusual organisms such as Aeromonas, cat-scratch fever or chancroid; (4) ofloxacin and sparfloxacin may help in combination therapy of leprosy; (5) levofloxacin is listed as an alternative medicine for treating chlamydia or gonorrhea (where the gonorrhea did NOT come from the Pacific or Asia—resistance problem).

Author's Note: A study in Britain of 3,315 first-time heart attack victims found that people who had been given fluoroquinolones had a 55% lower risk for a first heart attack. More research is needed. Given the restricted use of trovafloxacin, information on that medicine will be truncated.

As a Combination Drug Product [CD]: Combined with hydrocortisone in the Cipro HC form to give the benefit of a corticosteroid in reducing inflammation and the antibiotic ciprofloxacin to kill the causative bacteria.

How These Drugs Work: These medicines block the bacterial enzyme DNA gyrase (required for DNA synthesis and cell reproduction), arrest bacterial growth (in low concentrations) and kill bacteria (in high concentrations).

Available Dosage Forms and Strengths

Ciprofloxacin:
Ophthalmic solution — 0.3%
Otic suspension — 2 mg/ml ciprofloxacin and 10 mg/ml hydrocortisone
Suspension — 250 mg and 500 mg per 5 ml
Tablets — 250 mg, 500 mg, 750 mg
Tablets, XR — 500 mg
Tablets Ciprocystitis pack — 100 mg

Levofloxacin:
Ophthalmic solution — 0.5%
Solution for injection — 5 mg per ml, 25 mg per ml
Tablets — 250 mg, 500 mg, 750 mg

Lomefloxacin:
Tablets — 400 mg

Norfloxacin:
Ophthalmic solution — 3 mg/ml
Tablets — 400 mg

Ofloxacin:
Ophthalmic solution — 3 mg/ml
Otic solution — 0.3%
Tablets — 200 mg, 300 mg, 400 mg

Sparfloxacin:
Tablet — 200 mg

▷ **Recommended Dosage Ranges** (Actual dose and schedule for all these medicines must be determined for each patient individually.)

Infants and Children: None of these medicines are recommended.

18 to 60 Years of Age:
Ciprofloxacin: 250 mg to 750 mg every 12 hours (depends on nature and severity of infection). Daily maximum is 1,500 mg. Mild to moderate sinusitis (caused by organisms outlined above) treated with 500 mg every

12 hours for 10 days in adults. Cipro XR form is used for uncomplicated bladder (cystitis) infections with 500 mg once a day for 3 days.

Anthrax (after exposure): 500 mg by mouth every 12 hours (started as soon as possible after exposure) and continued **for 60 days. Please note, the 60-day time frame is critical. Amazingly, many patients who thought they were exposed did NOT continue the medicine as directed according to some sources.**

Ophthalmic—one or two drops instilled in the eye every 2 hours while awake for 2 days and then one or two drops for 5 more days (given every 4 hours while awake). *Otic:* After shaking the bottle well and warming it in your hand, children one year and older and adults should be given 3 drops of the suspension into the affected ear twice a day for seven days.

Levofloxacin: 500 mg orally every 24 hours for 7–14 days for community-acquired pneumonia, 500 mg a day for 7 days for chlamydia in people who can't take azithromycin or doxycycline.

Ophthalmic: On the first and second day—one to two drops in the affected eye every 2 hours (up to 8 times a day) while you are awake. On the 3rd through 7th day—1–2 drops every 4 hours (up to 4 times a day) while you are awake.

Lomefloxacin: For bronchitis—400 mg daily for 10 days. For bladder infections (cystitis)—400 mg daily for 10 days. For complicated urinary tract infections—400 mg daily for 14 days. For preoperative prevention of urinary tract infection—400 mg (single dose) taken 2 to 6 hours before surgery.

Norfloxacin: Uncomplicated urinary tract infections—400 mg every 12 hours for 3 days. Complicated urinary tract infections—400 mg every 12 hours for 10 to 21 days. Total daily dose should not exceed 800 mg. Ophthalmic dosing—1 to 2 drops to the affected eye 4 times daily.

Ofloxacin: 200 mg to 400 mg every 12 hours (for 10 days for lower respiratory infections), depending on nature and severity of infection. Daily maximum is 800 mg. Ophthalmic dosing (conjunctivitis)—1 to 2 drops every 2 to 4 hours for 2 days and then four times a day for 7 to 10 days. Otic: For patients 12 or older, the Floxin Otic form is used to treat otitis externa and 10 drops are placed into the affected ear twice a day for 10 days (in otitis media that is ongoing and suppurative, the same dose is used for 14 days).

Sparfloxacin: 400 mg now; then 200 mg a day for 10 days for pneumonia.

Over 60 Years of Age: Same as 18 to 60 years of age unless kidney function is an issue.

Conditions Requiring Dosing Adjustments

Liver Function: Use ciprofloxacin, norfloxacin used with caution in severe liver failure. No changes for levofloxacin, ofloxacin or sparfloxacin. Because of possible liver toxicity trovafloxacin use not prudent in liver compromise.

Kidney Function: Ciprofloxacin, levofloxacin, lomefloxacin, norfloxacin, ofloxacin, and sparfloxacin **must** be decreased (or time between doses increased) in kidney compromise. For moderate to severe kidney compromise, ofloxacin dose is decreased to 400 mg daily. For patients with moderate kidney failure, the usual ofloxacin dose can be taken every 24 hours. For patients with severe failure, one-half the usual dose should be taken every 24 hours. Since some of these medicines can form crystals in urine, drink adequate quantities of water.

Cystic Fibrosis: A loading dose for ciprofloxacin, as well as ongoing doses of 750 mg every 8 hours, is taken by cystic fibrosis patients. This dosing gives blood levels that are more aggressive versus the bacteria that usually cause infections in these patients. No changes for the other drugs are presented.

▷ **Dosing Instructions:** Ciprofloxacin, levofloxacin, lomefloxacin, norfloxacin, or sparfloxacin may be taken with or without food (NOT dairy products), and all immediate release forms may be crushed. Extended release forms should NOT be crushed, chewed, or changed and should be taken whole. Ofloxacin is best taken 2 hours after eating. Drink large amounts of fluids while taking any of these drugs. For suspension forms, shake them well BEFORE taking them to resuspend the medicine and measure the dose with a dosing spoon or calibrated medicine measuring cup. Avoid aluminum or magnesium antacids, iron, zinc, or calcium for 2 hours before and after drug doses. If you forget a dose: take the missed dose as soon as you remember it, unless it is nearly time for your next dose—then skip the missed dose and take the next dose right on schedule. Then return to your usual schedule. If you are taking one of the every-12-hour quinolones, take any remaining doses for the day at an evenly spaced time period. If you miss more than one dose, please call your doctor. The otic ciprofloxacin suspension should be warmed by rolling the container in your hand for several minutes.

Usual Duration of Use: Regular use for 7 to 14 days is needed to see benefits in eradicating infection. Dosing should be continued for at least 2 days after all indications of infection have disappeared. Bone and joint infections (ciprofloxacin or ofloxacin) or prostate gland infections may be treated for 6 weeks or longer. Anthrax treatment using ciprofloxacin REQUIRES 60 days of treatment. Long-term use requires periodic evaluation of response by a physician. Cipro XR form is used once a day for three days for uncomplicated bladder infections (cystitis).

Typical Treatment Goals and Measurements (Outcomes and Markers)

Infections: The most commonly used measures of serious infections are white blood cell counts and differentials (the kind of blood cells that occur most often in your blood), and temperature. Many clinicians look for positive changes in 24–48 hours. NEVER stop an antibiotic because you start to feel better. For many infections, a full 14 days is REQUIRED to kill the bacteria. The goals and time frame (see benefits) should be discussed with you when the prescription is written. Response to eye (ophthalmic) and ear (otic) forms can be assessed by reduced redness and itching of the eye and reduced swelling of the ear (auditory) canal and lessened severity and subsequent disappearance of earache.

Possible Advantages of These Drugs: Ciprofloxacin and ofloxacin have very broad spectrums of antibacterial activity of all currently available oral antimicrobial drugs. Highly effective in treating numerous types of infection caused by a wide spectrum of bacteria. Provide effective drug levels in the prostate gland (a difficult place to penetrate). Lomefloxacin has not had significant effects on kidney function. Sparfloxacin has better gram positive (Strep and Staph) activity than other medicines in this family. Cipro XR form treats uncomplicated bladder infections (cystitis) with only a once-a-day dose taken for three days. Ciprofloxacin and levofloxacin offer the opportunity to change (streamline) from intravenous to pill forms taken by mouth once clinically appropriate. This can offer treatment with a very potent antibiotic without the use of an intravenous line, and also allow treatment at home, shortening hospital stay.

▷ **These Drugs Should Not Be Taken If**
  • you take an antiarrhythmic drug (see Drug Classes) or have a prolonged QTc (heartbeat interval) or take medicines known to cause Torsades de

pointes. Talk with your doctor (gatifloxacin, levofloxacin, moxifloxacin, sparfloxacin—perhaps others).
• you had an allergic reaction to any quinolone antibiotic.
• you have swelling (inflammation), pain or bursting (rupture) of a tendon.
• you are pregnant or breast-feeding.
• you have a poorly controlled seizure disorder.
• you are less than 18 years of age.

▷ **Inform Your Physician Before Taking These Drugs If**
• you are allergic to cinoxacin (Cinobac), naladixic acid (NegGram), or other quinolone drugs.
• you have a seizure disorder or a brain circulatory disorder.
• you have increased lipids (dyslipidemia) as this may increase risk of tendonitis.
• you have impaired liver or kidney function.
• you have a history of mental disorders (psychosis).
• you are taking any form of probenecid, theophylline, or steroids.
• your work requires you to be in the sun. Sparfloxacin can cause severe phototoxicity, ciprofloxacin increases sensitivity as well.
• your urine is alkaline (talk to your doctor) as this may increase risk of crystals in the urine from some members of this medicine family.
• your work requires heavy manual labor. (Several cases of tendon rupture have been reported with fluoroquinolone use. Heavy exercise or work may be contraindicated. Call your doctor immediately if you develop inflammation or pain in a tendon.

Possible Side Effects (natural, expected, and unavoidable drug actions)
Superinfections (see Glossary). Permanent greenish tooth discoloration if used in infants (ciprofloxacin). Photosensitivity.

▷ **Possible Adverse Effects** (unusual, unexpected, and infrequent reactions)
If any of the following develop, consult your physician promptly for guidance.
Mild Adverse Effects
Allergic reaction: rash, itching, localized swelling—rare.
Dizziness, headache (frequent with lomefloxacin), weakness, migraine, anxiety, abnormal vision—rare.
Nausea, diarrhea, vomiting, indigestion—rare to frequent.
Muscle aches—case reports.
Burning feeling in the eye when the ophthalmic solutions are used—possible.
Decreased vision (with ophthalmic use)—case reports.
Serious Adverse Effects
Allergic reaction: anaphylaxis—case reports.
Serious skin rashes—case reports for some (for example, ciprofloxacin has a case report of bullous pemphigoid, ofloxacin has a report as a probable cause of toxic epidermal necrolysis [TEN], and levofloxacin has a case report for TEN also). Call your doctor immediately if you develop a rash.
Idiosyncratic reactions—central nervous system stimulation (restlessness, tremor, confusion, hallucinations, seizures (lowers seizure threshold). One medication of this class has had reports of severe neurological compromise. Stop the drug immediately and call your doctor if you become confused or have trouble speaking while taking this drug—case reports. An idiosyncratic reaction between levofloxacin and warfarin leading to increased INR has been reported. Careful consideration of alternative antibiotics is advisable, more frequent INR checks and patient instruction

on self-monitoring of possible bleeding is prudent if those medicines must be combined.

Kidney disease (interstitial nephritis)—case reports.

Tendon rupture—case reports for some family members (talk to your doctor about how much if at all to exercise or undertake strenuous work). Risk may be increased for people with high cholesterol or triglycerides, those who have kidney (renal) failure, those taking corticosteroids and in people over 60 years old.

Abnormal heartbeats (even Torsades de Pointes) or palpitations—rare, but may be additive or worse if these medicines are taken with other medicines that change QT interval.

Liver toxicity—rare (trovafloxacin availability changed because of this).

Blood sugar disturbances—possible (more likely in diabetics taking insulin or an oral hypoglycemic medicine).

Bone marrow depression—case reports with ciprofloxacin, norfloxacin, and levofloxacin.

Intracranial hypertension (ciprofloxacin or ofloxacin)—case reports.

Worsening of myasthenia gravis—case reports.

▷ **Possible Effects on Sexual Function:** Vaginitis with discharge has been reported. Painful menstruation, excessive menstrual bleeding (ofloxacin only), urethral bleeding (ciprofloxacin)—case reports. Intermenstrual bleeding—case reports (lomefloxacin).

Natural Diseases or Disorders That May Be Activated by These Drugs

Latent epilepsy, latent gout.

Possible Effects on Laboratory Tests

Kidney function: increased blood creatinine and urea nitrogen (BUN)—rare.

Liver function tests: increased as a sign of liver toxicity—rare.

Red and white blood cell counts: rarely decreased (norfloxacin and ciprofloxacin)—case reports.

Blood glucose levels: rare fluctuations.

CAUTION

1. If you develop skin rash, hives, fatigue, or skin yellowing with nausea and vomiting while taking these medicines (especially trovafloxacin), call your doctor immediately.

2. With high doses or prolonged use, crystal formation in the kidneys may occur. This can be prevented by drinking large amounts of water, up to 2 quarts daily.

3. These drugs may decrease saliva formation, making dental cavities or gum disease more likely. Consult your dentist if dry mouth persists.

4. Changes in heart rhythm have been reported (QT interval). Sparfloxacin, gatifloxacin and moxifloxacin appear to cause this problem more often than ciprofloxacin. Only polymorphic ventricular tachycardia reported for levofloxacin.

5. Strenuous exercise is NOT recommended while these medicines are being taken.

6. If a sudden change in mental status is noticed, call your doctor immediately.

7. The ciprofloxacin suspension must be reconstituted with the special diluent that comes with the powder. DO NOT reconstitute with water.

8. Case reports of bone marrow depression have been made in patients taking some of the medicines in this family. The drug should be suspect if white blood cell counts and platelets fall while taking this medicine.

9. Sun sensitivity which may be severe (phototoxicity) is possible with sparfloxacin (Zagam), lomefloxacin (Maxaquin), levofloxacin (Levaquin), and ciprofloxacin (Cipro). Sun should be avoided while sparfloxacin is being taken and for 5 days after the medicine is stopped. Sun sensitivity may be minimized by taking lomefloxacin in the evening.

Precautions for Use
By Infants and Children: Avoid the use of these drugs completely. Impairs normal bone growth and development.
By Those Over 60 Years of Age: Impaired kidney function may require dose reduction.

▷ ## Advisability of Use During Pregnancy
Pregnancy Category: C. See Pregnancy Risk Categories at the back of this book.
Animal Studies: Rabbit studies showed maternal weight loss and increased abortions (ciprofloxacin). Mild skeletal defects due to ofloxacin were found in rat studies; toxic effects on the fetus were shown in rat and rabbit studies. These drugs can impair normal bone development in immature dogs.
Human Studies: Adequate studies of pregnant women are not available.
The potential for adverse effects on fetal bone development contraindicates the use of these drugs during entire pregnancy.

Advisability of Use If Breast-Feeding
Presence of these drugs in breast milk: yes for levofloxacin, ofloxacin, and ciprofloxacin—probably for the rest.
Avoid drug or refrain from nursing.

Habit-Forming Potential: None.

Effects of Overdose: Confusion, headache, abdominal pain, diarrhea, liver toxicity, seizures, kidney toxicity, hallucinations.

Possible Effects of Long-Term Use: Superinfections (see Glossary); crystal formation in kidneys.

Suggested Periodic Examinations While Taking These Drugs (at physician's discretion)
Liver function tests. (Specific baseline and follow-up liver function tests prudent for trovafloxacin and perhaps others in this class.)
Urine analysis.

While Taking These Drugs, Observe the Following
Foods: Caffeine may remain in your system longer than usual. Use care in the amount of caffeine consumed. Dairy foods (such as milk and cheese) will decrease the effectiveness of these drugs by decreasing the amount absorbed. Separate 2 hours before or 6 hours after a dose.
Herbal Medicines or Minerals: Calcium supplements, iron pills, or zinc will decrease the amount of these medicines that go to work fighting infection. Separate doses by 2 hours before or 6 hours after the antibiotic. Some dandelion preparations may have a high enough concentration of metal ions to bind these medicines and blunt their benefits. Fennel seeds may have enough cations to also blunt benefits of these antibiotics. Separation by 2 hours before or 4–6 hours after is recommended. Use of St. John's wort may lead to additive sensitivity to the sun. Some patients use echinacea to attempt to boost their immune systems. Unfortunately, use of echinacea is not recommended in people with damaged immune systems. This herb may also actually weaken any immune system if it is used too often or for

too long a time. Do NOT take mistletoe herb, oak bark or F.C. of marsh-mallow root, and licorice.

Beverages: No restrictions (see Foods note on caffeine page 464).

▷ *Alcohol:* No interactions expected, but since heavy alcohol intake can blunt the immune system, limit alcohol if you are ill enough to require an antibiotic.

Tobacco Smoking: No interactions expected. I advise everyone to quit smoking.

▷ *Other Drugs*

The following drug may ***increase*** the effects of fluoroquinolones:
- probenecid (Benemid).

Fluoroquinolones ***taken concurrently*** with
- amiodarone (Cordarone) may lead to heart toxicity.
- azlocillin may result in toxicity.
- caffeine will result in increased caffeine levels.
- corticosteroids (such as methylprednisolone, prednisone, and others) may result in increased risk of tendon rupture.
- cyclosporine (Sandimmune) may result in increased risk of kidney toxicity.
- dofetilide (Tikosyn) may lead to prolonged QT intervals and even possible Torsades de pointes.
- foscarnet (Foscavir) may result in an increased risk of seizures.
- ibutilide (Corvert) may lead to prolonged QT intervals and even possible Torsades de pointes.
- lithium led to lithium toxicity in one patient who took it with levofloxacin.
- live typhoid vaccine (Vivotif Bernia) may lead to blunted immunological response.
- olanzapine (Zyprexa) may lead to increased olanzapine levels (reported for ciprofloxacin, but caution advised for all quinolones acting on CYP1A2).
- phenytoin (Dilantin) or fosphenytoin (Cerebyx) may result in increased or decreased phenytoin levels.
- riluzole (Rilutek) combined with ofloxacin (because of P450 1A2 inhibition) may lead to riluzole toxicity. Riluzole doses may need to be lowered.
- theophylline (Theo-Dur, others) may lead to theophylline toxicity over time (norfloxacin or ciprofloxacin).
- warfarin (Coumadin) can result in increased risk of bleeding or blunted warfarin response. More frequent INR testing is needed and prudent.

The following drugs may ***decrease*** the effects of fluoroquinolones:
- antacids containing aluminum or magnesium, reducing absorption and lessening effectiveness.
- calcium supplements.
- didanosine (ciprofloxacin only).
- iron salts.
- magnesium, decreasing therapeutic benefits.
- morphine (only reported for trovafloxacin).
- nitrofurantoin (Macrodantin, etc.), which may antagonize the antibacterial action in the urinary tract. Avoid this combination.
- sucralfate (Carafate).
- zinc salts.

Sparfloxacin ***taken concurrently*** with the following drugs may cause abnormal heartbeats (also to be used with extreme caution with any new medicines that can prolong the QTc interval):
- amiodarone (Cordarone).
- astemizole (Hismanal).

- bepridil (Vascor).
- beta blockers (see Drug Classes).
- chlorpromazine (Thorazine).
- cisapride (Propulsid).
- disopyramide (Norpace).
- macrolide antibiotics (erythromycin, dirithromycin, others).
- phenothiazines (see Drug Classes).
- procainamide (Pronestyl) (see Drug Classes).
- quinidine (Quinaglute, various).
- tricyclic antidepressants (see Drug Classes).

Moxifloxacin *taken concurrently* with
- class 1A or class III antiarrhythmic agents (see Drug Classes) may lead to abnormal heart changes (QT prolongation or even Torsades de Pointes). DO NOT combine.

Norfloxacin *taken concurrently* with
- dofetilide (Tikosyn) may lead to dofetilide toxicity via inhibition of CYP 3A4.

▷ *Driving, Hazardous Activities:* May cause dizziness or impair vision. Restrict activities as necessary.

Aviation Note: The use of these drugs *may be a disqualification* for piloting. Consult a designated Aviation Medical Examiner.

Exposure to Sun: Some members of this class have caused photosensitivity (see Glossary) and have limiting sun warnings. Sunglasses are advised if eyes are overly sensitive to bright light. A strong sun block is advised for your skin. Sparfloxacin users should avoid the sun while taking that medicine and for 5 days after the medicine is stopped. Lomefloxacin sun sensitivity may be reduced by taking the medicine at night. Excessive sun exposure should be avoided by levofloxacin users.

Heavy Exercise or Exertion: Several reports have surfaced regarding tendon rupture in patients with some of the medicines in this class. It is prudent to avoid heavy exercise or exertion while you are taking a fluoro-quinolone.

Discontinuation: If you experience no adverse effects from these drugs, take the full course prescribed for best results. Ask your doctor when to stop treatment.

FLUOXETINE (flu OX e teen)

Introduced: 1978, 2001 **Class:** Antidepressant **Prescription:** USA: Yes **Controlled Drug:** USA: No **Available as Generic:** USA: Yes

Brand Names: ❦Alti-Fluoxetine, ❦Apo-Fluoxetine, ❦Gen-Fluoxetine, ❦Med-Fluoxetine, Prozac, Prozac Weekly, Sarafem

```
┌─────────────────────────────────────────────────────────────────────┐
│                     BENEFITS versus RISKS                             │
│        Possible Benefits                  Possible Risks              │
│  EFFECTIVE TREATMENT OF          Serious allergic reactions           │
│    MAJOR DEPRESSIVE              Conversion of depression to mania in  │
│    DISORDERS                       manic-depressive (bipolar)         │
│  EFFECTIVE PREVENTION OF           disorders                          │
│    RECURRENCE OF DEPRESSION                                           │
│  EFFECTIVE IN SEVERE PMS                                              │
│    (premenstrual dysphoric syndrome                                   │
│    or PMDS)                                                           │
│  TREATS BULIMIA NERVOSA                                               │
│  TREATS OBSESSIVE-COMPULSIVE                                          │
│    DISORDER                                                           │
│  ONCE-WEEKLY FORMULATION                                              │
│    FOR DEPRESSION WILL HELP                                           │
│    ADHERENCE                                                          │
│  APPROVED FOR PREMENSTRUAL                                            │
│    DYSPHORIC THERAPY WHEN                                             │
│    USED 14 DAYS BEFORE THE                                            │
│    PERIOD WILL START                                                  │
│  May reduce hot flashes in some                                      │
│    cancer survivors                                                   │
└─────────────────────────────────────────────────────────────────────┘
```

▷ **Principal Uses**

As a Single Drug Product: Uses currently included in FDA-approved labeling: Treats (1) major forms of depression (including depression in HIV-positive patients and in geriatric depression); (2) obsessive-compulsive disorder; (3) bulimia; (4) approved for use in severe PMS (PMDS either every day or for the 14 days before menstruation is expected to start).

Other (unlabeled) generally accepted uses: (1) Refractory diabetic neuropathy; (2) may help control kleptomania; (3) can be of help in treating obesity, especially when obesity is accompanied by depression; (4) eases symptoms of panic attacks; (5) used to treat seasonal affective disorder (such as depression limited to winter months); (6) treats some forms of sexual problems; (7) some data for use of childhood anxiety disorder; (8) may ease ringing in the ears (tinnitus) that has not responded to other medicines; (9) may reduce the severity and frequency of hot flashes (by about half) in cancer survivors; (10) could have a role after a stroke in decreasing emotionalism and improving motor performance; (11) may have a role in anorexia nervosa when weight is returned to prior levels in order to help prevent relapse; (12) improved some measures of thinking in a small trial of patients with traumatic brain injury.

How This Drug Works: It restores normal levels of a nerve transmitter (serotonin). May work to stimulate Brain Derived Neurotrophic Factor (BDNF) and a specific receptor (tyrosine kinase receptor) resulting in remodeling of nerves. While this mechanism is derived from rat data, early clinical trials show improved performance in some small studies where fluoxetine gained improvements in thinking in adults who had suffered traumatic injuries.

Available Dosage Forms and Strengths

Capsules — 10 mg, 20 mg, 40 mg
Capsules — 90 mg (Prozac Weekly form)

Capsules — 10 mg and 20 mg (28-pill blister packs Sarafem form)

Oral solution — 20 mg/5 ml

Tablet — 10 mg

▷ **Usual Adult Dosage Ranges:**

Depression: Starts with 20 mg in the morning; if no improvement after several weeks, dose may be increased by 20 mg/day. Doses over 20 mg/day should be divided into two equal doses and taken twice daily. Maximum daily dose is 80 mg. Prozac Weekly form is intended for people who are already stabilized on the daily 20 mg form. The once weekly form is started seven days after the last 20 mg dose was given and is continued at 90 mg per week.

Bulimia: 60 mg once daily in the morning.

PMDS (severe PMS): A 28-pill blister pack is available (Sarafem form). In clinical studies, some patients used 20–60 mg during the entire month to check sign and symptom decreases (this is the recommended dose in current labeling). One part of the clinical study group obtained an 86% symptom reduction using 20 mg a day on days 14–28 of each menstrual cycle. Your doctor may adjust dosing strategies to the severity of your symptoms. This drug is now approved in PMDS for use only in the 14 days (luteal phase) BEFORE menstruation is expected to start.

Hot flashes in cancer survivors: 20 mg per day.

Obsessive-compulsive disorder: 20 to 80 mg daily.

Note: Actual dose and schedule must be determined for each patient individually.

Conditions Requiring Dosing Adjustments

Liver Function: The dose should be decreased or the dosing interval lengthened for patients with liver compromise. Some clinicians decrease the dose by 50% in compensated cirrhosis. This drug is also a rare cause of liver toxicity and should be used with caution by this patient population.

Kidney Function: Dosing changes are needed for severely impaired kidney function. Patients should be closely watched for adverse effects.

▷ **Dosing Instructions:** The capsule may be opened and the contents mixed with any convenient food. To make smaller doses, the contents may be mixed with orange juice or apple juice (NOT GRAPEFRUIT JUICE) and refrigerated; doses of 5–10 mg may prove effective and better tolerated. If you forget a dose: take the dose you missed as soon as you remember it, unless it is nearly time for your next dose—if that is the case, skip the missed dose and take the next dose right on schedule. DO NOT DOUBLE DOSES. If you find yourself missing doses, talk to your doctor.

Usual Duration of Use: Use on a regular schedule for 1 to 2 weeks may reveal start of benefits in depression. Up to 4 weeks may be needed for peak effects in (1) relieving depression and (2) the pattern of both favorable and unfavorable effects. A recent article in the *American Journal of Psychiatry* (see Quitkin, F.M. in Sources) advocated that 8 weeks of treatment should be undertaken BEFORE this medicine in treatment of depression is assessed and declared unsuccessful. Since there is an active metabolite and a long half-life, it may take several weeks before the benefits of a change in dose are seen. Benefits in obsessive-compulsive disorder may take 5 weeks or even longer in some cases. Long-term use (months to years) requires periodic physician evaluation. Some clinical guidelines suggest that 4 to 9 months of treatment should continue after the symptoms of depression go away. Some clinicians use lower doses to prevent or use as prophylaxis of depression. People who take their medicine regularly are least likely to have a recurrence. Will often take several weeks to work in reducing hot flashes in cancer survivors. PMDS use is recommended as 20 mg per day in the package insert, but acknowledges the need for reassessment of ongoing patient need. Bulimia treatment is often ongoing, however, there should be periodic checks to see if the medicine is still needed.

Typical Treatment Goals and Measurements (Outcomes and Markers)

Depression: The general goal is to lessen the degree and severity of depression, letting patients return to their daily lives. Specific measures of depression involve testing or inventories and can be valuable in helping check benefits from this medicine. The Hamilton Depression Scale (HAM-D) is widely used to assess depression. In the case of PMDS, control of irritability and decreased number and/or severity of symptoms and the ability of the patient to return to normal activities or not have them interrupted is a hallmark of successful treatment.

PMDS: The goal is to lessen the degree and severity of menstrual difficulties (such as pain, irritability, etc.) or to prevent menstruation-associated problems altogether.

Possible Advantages of This Drug

Does not cause weight gain, a common side effect of tricyclic antidepressants. May actually cause weight loss. Less likely to cause dry mouth, constipation, urinary retention, or orthostatic hypotension (see Glossary) than tricyclic antidepressants. Since a large National Cancer Institute study found that those who suffer depression for 6 years or more have a generally increased risk of cancer, one benefit of effective treatment of depression with this drug may be a generally reduced risk of cancer.

▷ **This Drug Should Not Be Taken If**
- you had an allergic reaction to it previously.
- you take, or took in the last 14 days, a monoamine oxidase (MAO) type A inhibitor (see Drug Classes).

▷ **Inform Your Physician Before Taking This Drug If**
- you have had any adverse effects from antidepressant drugs.
- you have impaired liver or kidney function.
- you have Parkinson's disease.
- you have a seizure disorder.
- you have a history of psychosis.
- you have a history of SIADH (talk with your doctor).
- you are pregnant or plan pregnancy while taking this drug.

Possible Side Effects (natural, expected, and unavoidable drug actions)
Decreased appetite, weight loss.
Case reports of orthostatic hypotension (see Glossary).

▷ **Possible Adverse Effects** (unusual, unexpected, and infrequent reactions)
If any of the following develop, consult your physician promptly for guidance.

Mild Adverse Effects
Allergic reactions: skin rash, hives, itching—rare.
Headache, nervousness, insomnia, drowsiness, tremor, dizziness, tingling of extremities—rare.
Vivid nightmares—case reports.
Altered taste, nausea—frequent.
Vomiting, diarrhea—possible to rare.
Bruising or nosebleeds—rare.
Hair loss—case reports.

Fast heart rate (tachycardia) or palpitations—rare.

Blurred vision—infrequent.

Excessive sweating—frequent.

Serious Adverse Effects

Allergic reactions: serum-sickness-like syndrome (fever, weakness, joint pain and swelling, swollen lymph glands, fluid retention, skin rash, and/or hives).

Drug-induced seizures—rare.

Worsening of Parkinson's disease—possible.

Parkinson-like reactions (extrapyramidal effects)—rare.

Neuroleptic malignant syndrome—case reports.

Intense suicidal preoccupation in severe depression that does not respond to this drug—case reports.

Mania or hypomania and psychosis or hallucinations—rare.

Aplastic anemia—case report.

Abnormal and excessive urination (SIADH)—case reports.

Abnormal heartbeats (even Torsades de Pointes) or palpitations—rare, but may be additive or worse with other medicines that change QT interval.

Liver toxicity—rare.

▷ **Possible Effects on Sexual Function:** Impaired erection (1.9%), inhibition of ejaculation or inhibited orgasm in men and women—case reports. Worsening of fibrocystic breast disease in a female—case report. Spontaneous and persistent milk production (galactorrhea)—case reports during post-marketing period.

Natural Diseases or Disorders That May Be Activated by This Drug

Latent epilepsy.

Possible Effects on Laboratory Tests

Blood glucose level: decreased.

Blood sodium level: decreased.

CAUTION

1. If any skin reaction develops (rash, hives, etc.), stop this drug and inform your physician promptly.
2. If dry mouth develops and persists for more than 2 weeks, consult your dentist for help.
3. Ask your doctor or pharmacist before taking any other prescription or over-the-counter drug while taking fluoxetine.
4. If you must start any monoamine oxidase (MAO) type A inhibitor (see Drug Classes), allow an interval of 5–6 weeks after stopping this drug before starting the MAO inhibitor.
5. This drug should be withheld if electroconvulsive therapy (ECT, "shock" treatment) is to be used.
6. Be honest with your doctor about how well this medicine is helping you. There are many antidepressants available, and the first one that is tried may or may not work. Call your doctor immediately if you have thoughts of suicide.
7. A study (see above and Quitkin, F.M. in Sources) advocated that 8 weeks of treatment be undertaken before assessing this medicine to be unsuccessful.

Precautions for Use

By Infants and Children: Safety and effectiveness for those under 7 years of age are not established.

For those 7 to 18 years old, some clinicians have used 5–10 mg per day or 10 mg three times a week. The dose is subsequently increased as needed and tolerated to a maximum of 20 mg per day.

By Those Over 60 Years of Age: Lower or less frequent doses are recommended by the manufacturer.

▷ **Advisability of Use During Pregnancy**

Pregnancy Category: C. See Pregnancy Risk Categories at the back of this book.

Animal Studies: No birth defects due to this drug found in rat or rabbit studies.

Human Studies: Adequate studies of pregnant women are not available. Of the SSRIs, this medicine probably has the largest amount of data on women who have taken fluoxetine during pregnancy without adverse effects. One study of 228 women appeared to show that it was safer to take fluoxetine in the first two trimesters of pregnancy and discontinue it during the last trimester.

Use of this drug during pregnancy is a benefit-to-risk decision that must be discussed with your doctor.

Advisability of Use If Breast-Feeding

Presence of this drug in breast milk: Yes.

Avoid drug or refrain from nursing.

Habit-Forming Potential: Reports of patients using excess doses of fluoxetine or combining the drug with alcohol have surfaced. It appears possible that a euphoric effect and abuse potential exists.

Effects of Overdose: Agitation, restlessness, excitement, nausea, vomiting, seizures.

Possible Effects of Long-Term Use: None reported.

Suggested Periodic Examinations While Taking This Drug (at physician's discretion)

None.

▷ **While Taking This Drug, Observe the Following**

Foods: No restrictions (see Beverages below).

Beverages: Grapefruit juice may lead to increased blood levels. AVOID IT. May be taken with milk.

Herbal Medicines or Minerals: Since fluoxetine and St. John's wort may act to increase serotonin, the combination is not advised. Since part of the way ginseng works may be as an MAO inhibitor, do not combine with fluoxetine. Ma huang, yohimbe, Indian snakeroot, and kava kava (kava no longer recommended in Canada) are also best avoided while taking this medicine. Calcium now has excellent data (1,200–1,600 mg per day unless contraindicated) in helping prevent premenstrual dysphoric syndrome (PMS). This may be an intelligent first-line therapy or valuable adjunctive use. Talk to your doctor to see if this makes sense for you.

▷ *Alcohol:* Does not appear to increase the central nervous system effects of fluoxetine or change the metabolism of alcohol.

Tobacco Smoking: No interactions expected, but I advise everyone to quit smoking.

Marijuana Smoking: Led to one case of mania in a patient who combined the two drugs.

▷ *Other Drugs*

Fluoxetine may *increase* the effects of
- beta blockers (see Drug Classes).
- diazepam (Valium) and other benzodiazepines (see Drug Classes).
- digitalis preparations (digitoxin, digoxin).

- diltiazem (Cardizem).
- dofetilide (Tikosyn), requiring dosing decreases.
- ergot derivatives (Cafergot, various) may increase risk of ergotism and is NOT advisable.
- flecainide (Tambocor).
- phenytoin (Dilantin), or fosphenytoin (Cerebyx) by increasing the phenytoin or fosphenytoin levels.
- propafenone (Rythmol).
- propranolol (Inderal).
- quinidine (Quinaglute).
- sildenafil (Viagra), by inhibiting CYP3A4.
- valproic acid (Depakote, others).
- warfarin (Coumadin) and related oral anticoagulants. Test INR more often.

Fluoxetine *taken concurrently* with

- antidiabetic drugs (insulin, oral hypoglycemics) may increase the risk of hypoglycemic reactions; monitor blood sugar levels carefully.
- aspirin (various) caused hives to reappear in a patient allergic to fluoxetine.
- astemizole (Hismanal), terfenadine (Seldane) (no longer on the US market) or similar drugs may result in increased antihistamine levels and risk of heart arrhythmias. **Avoid** combining.
- azole antifungals (such as fluconazole, itraconazole, and ketoconazole) may lead to higher than expected fluoxetine blood levels and increased risk of adverse effects.
- buspirone (Buspar) may increase underlying anxiety. Combination is best avoided, but if deemed clinically necessary, patients should be closely watched for worsening of symptoms.
- carbamazepine (Tegretol) will increase the carbamazepine level. Drug levels are critical if the drugs are combined.
- cimetidine (Tagamet) may theoretically lead to increased fluoxetine levels.
- clarithromycin (Biaxin) may lead to fluoxetine toxicity—avoid the combination.
- clozapine (Clozaril) may result in increased levels of clozapine. The clozapine dose may need to be decreased if both medicines are to be used at the same time.
- cotrimoxazole (Bactrim) or cyclobenzaprine (Flexaril) may lead to changes in the heart pattern (QTc interval) and are NOT recommended.
- delavirdine (Rescriptor) may lead to delavirdine toxicity.
- dextromethorphan (a cough suppressant in many "DM"-labeled nonprescription cough medicines) may result in visual hallucinations if these drugs are combined. DO NOT COMBINE.
- fenfluramine (Pondimin) may lead to serotonin syndrome—DO NOT COMBINE.
- haloperidol (Haldol) will increase haloperidol levels. Dose decrease and blood levels are needed.
- ketorolac (Toradol) may result in hallucinations. DO NOT COMBINE.
- lithium (Lithobid, etc.) will result in increased lithium levels and increased risk of neurotoxicity. AVOID COMBINING.
- loratadine (Claritin) may result in increased loratadine levels. It may be prudent to decrease the loratadine dose if these medicines are to be combined. Unlike some of the other nonsedating antihistamines (see Drug Classes), loratadine has not (to date) resulted in abnormal heart rhythms.

- medicines that inhibit liver metabolism (removal) of this medicine may lead to higher than expected fluoxetine blood levels and increased toxicity risk.
- monoamine oxidase (MAO) type A inhibitor drugs (see Drug Classes) may cause confusion, agitation, high fever, seizures, and dangerous elevations of blood pressure. AVOID COMBINING.
- morphine (various) blunted pain management benefits of morphine in one case report.
- naratriptan (Amerge), rizatriptan (Maxalt), sumatriptan (Imitrex), zolmitriptan, almotriptan (Axert), or other triptans may lead to incoordination and abnormal reflexes. Caution is advised.
- olanzapine (Zyprexa) may lead to worsening of depression. Extreme caution is advised.
- ondansetron (Zofran) may have undesirable effects on the heart (QT prolongation). DO NOT COMBINE.
- selegiline (Eldepryl) can result in serotonin toxicity syndrome. AVOID COMBINING.
- sibutramine (Meridia) may lead to serotonin syndrome. AVOID COMBINING.
- sulfamethoxazole (various) may increase abnormal heartbeat risk (QTc interval changes). DO NOT COMBINE.
- thioridazine (Mellaril) may increase abnormal heartbeat risk. DO NOT COMBINE.
- tramadol (Ultram) may increase seizure risk. DO NOT COMBINE.
- any tricyclic antidepressant (amitriptyline, nortriptyline, etc.) will result in increased antidepressant drug levels that will persist for weeks. Avoid the combination.
- trimethoprim (Septra, others) may increase abnormal heartbeat risk (QTc interval changes). DO NOT COMBINE.
- tryptophan will result in central nervous system toxicity. AVOID COMBINING.
- ziprasidone (Geodon) may increase abnormal heartbeat risk (QTc interval changes). DO NOT COMBINE.
- zolpidem (Ambien) may increase risk of hallucinations.

▷ *Driving, Hazardous Activities:* This drug may cause drowsiness, dizziness, impaired judgment, and delayed reaction time. Restrict activities as necessary.

Aviation Note: The use of this drug *is a disqualification* for piloting. Consult a designated Aviation Medical Examiner.

Exposure to Sun: No restrictions.

Discontinuation: Slow drug elimination makes withdrawal effects unlikely, but call your doctor if you plan to stop this drug for any reason.

FLUPHENAZINE (flu FEN a zeen)

Introduced: 1959 **Class:** Strong tranquilizer, phenothiazines **Prescription:** USA: Yes **Controlled Drug:** USA: No; Canada: No **Available as Generic:** USA: Yes; Canada: Yes

Brand Names: ✤Apo-Fluphenazine, ✤Modecate, ✤Moditan, Permitil, PMS-Fluphenazine, Prolixin

---

BENEFITS versus RISKS

Possible Benefits	*Possible Risks*
EFFECTIVE CONTROL OF ACUTE MENTAL DISORDERS	SERIOUS TOXIC EFFECTS ON BRAIN with long-term use
Beneficial effects on thinking, mood, and behavior	Liver damage with jaundice
Decanoate injection gives long-lasting benefit with one shot	Blood cell disorders: abnormally low white blood cell counts

---

Author's Note: The information in this profile has been shortened to make room for more widely used medicines.

FLURAZEPAM (flur AZ e pam)

Introduced: 1970   **Class:** Hypnotic, benzodiazepines   **Prescription:** USA: Yes   **Controlled Drug:** USA: C-IV*; Canada: No   **Available as Generic:** USA: Yes; Canada: Yes

Brand Names: ✿Apo-Flurazepam, Dalmane, Durapam, ✿Novo-Flupam, ✝Somnol

---

BENEFITS versus RISKS

Possible Benefits	*Possible Risks*
EFFECTIVE HYPNOTIC	Habit-forming potential with long-term use
NO SUPPRESSION OF REM (RAPID EYE MOVEMENT) SLEEP	Minor impairment of mental functions ("hangover" effect)
NO REM SLEEP REBOUND after discontinuation	Jaundice
Wide margin of safety with therapeutic doses	Blood cell disorder
	–Suppression of stage 4 sleep with reduced "quality" of sleep

---

▷ **Principal Uses**

As a Single Drug Product: Uses currently included in FDA-approved labeling: Short-term treatment of insomnia consisting of difficulty in falling asleep, frequent nighttime awakenings and/or early morning awakenings.

Other (unlabeled) generally accepted uses: None at present.

Author's Note: Information in this profile has been shortened to make room for more widely used medicines.

Author's Note: The National Institute of Mental Health has an information Web page on anxiety. It can be found at *www.nimh.nih.gov/anxiety*.

FLURBIPROFEN (flur BI proh fen)

Please see the propionic acids (nonsteroidal anti-inflammatory drug) family profile.

*See Schedules of Controlled Drugs at the back of this book.

FLUTAMIDE (FLUTE a myde)

Introduced: 1983 **Class:** Anticancer (antineoplastic), nonsteroidal nonhormonal antiandrogenic **Prescription:** USA: Yes **Controlled Drug:** USA: No; Canada: No **Available as Generic:** USA: Yes; Canada: Yes

Brand Names: ✲Apo-flutamide, ✲Euflex, Eulexin, Flutamex (Germany)

BENEFITS versus RISKS

Possible Benefits	*Possible Risks*
EFFECTIVE ADJUNCTIVE TREATMENT OF PROSTATE CANCER	Rare drug-induced hepatitis
	Breast enlargement and tenderness (gynecomastia)
	Hot flashes

▷ **Principal Uses**

As a Single Drug Product: Uses currently included in FDA-approved labeling: Treatment of metastatic prostate cancer, used concurrently with leuprolide (given by injection), goserelin, or with removal of the testicles (orchiectomy).

Other (unlabeled) generally accepted uses: (1) Some early data on use in bulimia; (2) can help excessive hair growth in women (hirsutism); (3) combination use (with fludrocortisone, reduced hydrocortisone and testolactone helped a group of children with adrenal gland problems present at birth (congenital adrenal hyperplasia; (4) may have a place in improving flow to the uterus in polycystic ovary syndrome (PCOS).

How This Drug Works: Flutamide suppresses effects of dihydrotestosterone (a male sex hormone also called DHT) and testosterone by blocking uptake and binding target tissues (such as the prostate gland). Used in conjunction with leuprolide (a drug that suppresses testosterone from testicles by damping the pituitary gland's testicular stimulation). The combination of these two drug actions—chemical castration by leuprolide and testosterone blockage by flutamide—significantly reduces hormonal stimulation of cancerous prostate tissue.

Available Dosage Forms and Strengths

Capsules — 125 mg (US)
Tablets — 250 mg (Canada, Germany)

▷ **Recommended Dosage Ranges** (Actual dose and schedule must be determined for each patient individually.)

Infants and Children: Not used in this age group.

12 to 60 Years of Age: In stage B2-C prostate cancer (a measure of the cancer severity): 250 mg by mouth every 8 hours. Flutamide is to be taken at the same time as an LHRH agonist such as leuprolide; the usual dose of leuprolide is 7.5 mg given by injection once a month, starting 8 weeks before radiation treatment. The medicine is also continued during radiation treatment.

Stage D2 prostate cancer: 250 mg by mouth every 8 hours in conjunction with an LHRH agonist. It is continued until there is evidence of progression.

Over 60 Years of Age: Same as 12 to 60 years of age.

Conditions Requiring Dosing Adjustments

Liver Function: Use with caution by patients with liver compromise. It is also a rare cause of cholestatic jaundice.

Kidney Function: Primarily eliminated by the kidneys. Use with caution in kidney compromise.

▷ **Dosing Instructions:** May be taken without regard to food. The capsule may be opened, and the tablet may be crushed. If you forget a dose: take the missed dose as soon as you remember it, unless it is nearly time for your next dose—if that is the case, skip the missed dose and take the next dose right on schedule. DO NOT double doses. Use a condom to keep your semen from contacting your sexual partner.

Warning: Since this medicine is a kind of cancer-killing medicine (antineoplastic agent), proper disposal of urine or vomit MUST be undertaken (ask your doctor).

Usual Duration of Use: Regular use for 2 to 4 months usually needed to see drug's benefits in controlling prostate cancer (tumor response) although symptom relief may happen in 12–28 days. Long-term use (months to years and up to 2.5 years has been reported) requires periodic physician evaluation and check for relapse.

Typical Treatment Goals and Measurements (Outcomes and Markers)

Prostate Cancer: The goal is to decrease bone pain, increase urine outflow and increase survival time in D2 prostate cancer. Remissions have been gained from this medicine. Monthly bone and liver scans, chest X-ray, excretory urograms, and liver tests are typically obtained for the 4 months of treatment and periodically after that. PSA may also serve as a marker of success. Physical examination and follow-up on bone pain are important. Appropriate therapy and pain medicines to manage pain are critical.

Possible Advantages of This Drug

Ease of use. Less toxicity than other chemotherapeutic drugs.

Currently a "Drug of Choice"

For the management of prostate cancer (in combination with leuprolide) and coupled with castration.

▷ **This Drug Should Not Be Taken If**
- you have had an allergic reaction to it previously.
- your liver transaminases levels (ALT) are twice the upper laboratory normal limit.

▷ **Inform Your Physician Before Taking This Drug If**
- you have a history of liver disease or impaired liver function.
- you have high blood pressure (hypertension).
- you have a history of anemia, low white blood cells, or low blood platelets.
- you have not had a PSA or one has not been checked on a regular basis since starting this medicine.
- you have a history of lupus erythematosus.

Possible Side Effects (natural, expected, and unavoidable drug actions)

Hot flashes (61%), loss of libido (with combination LHRH therapy), impotence, breast enlargement and tenderness. Bright yellow urine color. Sun sensitivity.

▷ **Possible Adverse Effects** (unusual, unexpected, and infrequent reactions)
   If any of the following develop, consult your physician promptly for guidance.
   Mild Adverse Effects
   Allergic reaction: skin rash.
   Drowsiness, confusion, nervousness, depression—rare.
   Indigestion, nausea/vomiting, diarrhea—infrequent.
   Blurred vision—rare.
   Fluid retention (edema) of legs—possible.
   Serious Adverse Effects
   Drug-induced hepatitis with jaundice (see Glossary)—rare to infrequent.
   Manic-like mental changes (syndrome)—case reports.
   Low blood platelets, white blood cells, or anemia—rare.
   Lupus erythematosus-like skin rash—case reports.
   Hypertension—rare.
   Heart attack—rare.
   Methemoglobinemia—case report.
▷ **Possible Effects on Sexual Function:** See Possible Side Effects on page 476.
   Flutamide itself does not presently appear to change libido, sexual performance or the ability to have an erection. Combination therapy does appear to carry the risks of these adverse effects (medicines such as Viagra and Levitra may be of some help here). Swelling and tenderness of male breast tissue (gynecomastia) may be frequent.
▷ **Adverse Effects That May Mimic Natural Diseases or Disorders**
   Drug-induced hepatitis may suggest viral hepatitis.

Possible Effects on Laboratory Tests
   Complete blood counts: decreased red and white cells, hemoglobin, and platelets.
   Liver function tests: increased liver enzymes (ALT/GPT, AST/GOT, and alkaline phosphatase), increased bilirubin.
   PSA: reduced (a marker for cancer treatment results).
   Sperm counts and testosterone levels: decreased.

CAUTION
   1. For best results, flutamide and leuprolide should be started together and continued for the duration of therapy.
   2. During combination therapy with flutamide and leuprolide, symptoms of prostate cancer (difficult urination, bone pain, etc.) may worsen temporarily; these are transient and not significant.
   3. This medicine is not used in women.
   4. Call your doctor immediately if you have light-colored stools, dark urine, yellowing of the eyes or skin, or unexplained weakness or abdominal pain while taking this medicine (may be early signs of liver problems and can be reversible if caught early).
   5. Liver enzyme testing (ALT) should be checked BEFORE starting therapy. Therapy should NOT be started if ALT is twice the upper normal limit.

Precautions for Use
   By Those Over 60 Years of Age: Drug is more slowly excreted. If digestive symptoms or edema are troublesome, ask your doctor about adjusting dose.
▷ **Advisability of Use During Pregnancy**
   Pregnancy Category: D. See Pregnancy Risk Categories at the back of this book.

Animal Studies: Rat studies reveal malformation of bone structures and feminization of male fetuses.

Human Studies: Adequate studies of pregnant women are not available. Discuss this benefit-to-risk decision with your doctor.

Advisability of Use If Breast-Feeding
Presence of this drug in breast milk: Unknown, but not intended for women. Stop nursing.

Habit-Forming Potential: None.

Effects of Overdose: Possible drowsiness, unsteadiness, nausea, vomiting.

Possible Effects of Long-Term Use: None reported.

Suggested Periodic Examinations While Taking This Drug (at physician's discretion)
Prostate-specific antigen (PSA) assays.
Complete blood cell counts.
Liver function tests (see "Caution" note). Digital rectal exam and check for any metastasis (such as bone and liver scans).

▷ **While Taking This Drug, Observe the Following**
Foods: No restrictions.

Herbal Medicines: Since St. John's wort may also lead to increased sensitivity to the sun, DO NOT COMBINE. There are no data about use of echinacea with this medicine and the combination cannot be recommended. Herbal products that may be relatively toxic to the liver could increase liver toxicity risk if combined (such as eucalyptus, kava, or valerian).

Beverages: No restrictions. May be taken with milk.

▷ *Alcohol:* No interactions expected.

Tobacco Smoking: No interactions expected, but I advise everyone to quit smoking.

Marijuana Smoking: Animal studies have shown this combination to result in additive suppression of the immune system. The combination therefore is not advisable.

▷ *Other Drugs*
Flutamide *taken concurrently* with
• influenza, pneumococcal, or yellow fever vaccine may result in blunting of immune response to the vaccine.
• warfarin (Coumadin, others) may cause an increased bleeding risk. More frequent INRs are prudent.

▷ *Driving, Hazardous Activities:* This drug may cause drowsiness. Restrict activities as necessary.

Aviation Note: The use of this drug *may be a disqualification* for piloting. Consult a designated Aviation Medical Examiner.

Exposure to Sun: This drug may cause photosensitivity (see Glossary).

Discontinuation: To be determined by your physician.

FLUTICASONE (flu TIC a zone)

Introduced: 1994 **Class:** Adrenocortical steroids **Prescription:** USA: Yes **Controlled Drug:** USA: No; Canada: No **Available as Generic:** USA: No; Canada: No

Brand Names: ♣Advair [CD], Advair Diskus [CD], Cutivate, Flonase, Flovent, Flovent Diskus, Flovent Rotadisc

Author's Note: Some of the side effects are specific to or more likely with a particular dosing form (product).

BENEFITS versus RISKS	
Possible Benefits	*Possible Risks*
EFFECTIVE, ONCE-DAILY RELIEF OF SEASONAL ALLERGIC RHINITIS	Reversible adrenal gland suppression Yeast infections of the mouth and throat
EFFECTIVE ONCE-DAILY ECZEMA TREATMENT	Possible osteoporosis with long-term use
EFFECTIVE ASTHMA TREATMENT	Irritation of the nose (nasal form)

▷ **Principal Uses**

As a Single Drug Product: Uses currently included in FDA-approved labeling: (1) Helps perennial and seasonal (hay fever) allergic or nonallergic rhinitis in adults or children who are 12 years of age or older; (2) the topical form is used for a variety of skin conditions from sunburn to eczema or psoriasis; (3) asthma (inhaler form); (4) cream approved for once-daily treatment of eczema.

Other (unlabeled) generally accepted uses: (1) Oral form may have a role in Chronic Obstructive Pulmonary disease (COPD); (2) may have a role in combination treatment of vitiligo using the fluticasone cream plus UV light.

As a Combination Drug Product [CD]: Combined with salmeterol (see drug profile of salmeterol later in this book). These drugs complement each other, making the combination a more effective antiasthmatic.

How This Drug Works: Corticosteroid-type medicines work to ease inflammation, suppress reaction of certain cells and slow the inflammatory process. Halomethyl carbothionates have very potent anti-inflammatory and blood vessel–contracting (vasoconstrictive) activity.

Available Dosage Forms and Strengths

Amber glass bottle — 16 g (120 actuations) and 9 g (60 actuations)

Cream — 0.05 mg/g

Inhalation — 44 mcg, 110 mcg, 220 mcg

Inhalation powder — 50 mcg of salmeterol and 100, 250 or 500 mcg

(US, Canada)   fluticasone per actuation

ointment — 0.005%

Nasal spray — 50 mcg per 100 mg

▷ **Recommended Dosage Ranges** (Actual dose and schedule must be determined for each patient individually.)

Infants and Children: Safety and efficacy for those less than 4 have not yet been defined. Nasal dosing for those 4 to 12—start with one spray (50 mcg in each spray) in each nostril (total 100 mcg) once a day. If symptoms are severe, the dose can be increased to two sprays in each nostril (50 mcg each spray) or 200 micrograms a day (for Flovent Rotadisc and fluticasone Rotadisc). After a few days, the dose should be reduced to 50 micrograms in each nostril once daily.

12 to 60 Years of Age:

Nasal dosing: Started with two sprays (50 mcg in each spray) in each nostril once a day when allergic or non-allergic rhinitis is being treated. The same dose can also be given as 100 mcg twice daily (8 A.M. and 8 P.M.). After a few days, the dose can often be decreased to 100 mcg (one spray in each nostril) daily.

Inhalation for asthma: For those 12 and older: Starting dose is 88 mcg twice a day for patients who were previously treated with bronchodilators alone. Maximum daily dose is 440 mcg. Patients who required an inhaled corticosteroid previously are given 88 to 220 mcg a day. This dose is increased up to 440 mcg twice a day as needed and tolerated. Those taking a corticosteroid by mouth are given 880 mcg twice daily. Once the asthma is under control, the dose is reduced to the lowest effective dose.

Fluticasone/salmeterol combination: The starting dose is 100 mcg fluticasone and 50 mcg of salmeterol in people who are not presently taking an inhaled steroid (corticosteroid). If they are taking an inhaled corticosteroid such as budesonide and the steroid dose is less than or equal to 400 mcg a day, then the combination inhaler containing 100 mcg of fluticasone and 50 mcg of salmeterol is substituted and is taken twice a day. Other doses of budesonide or other corticosteroids require different combinations of fluticasone/salmeterol to get the best results.

Over 60 Years of Age: Same as 12 to 60 years of age.

Conditions Requiring Dosing Adjustments

Liver Function: This drug is extensively changed in the liver; however, no specific dosing changes are defined for patients with compromised livers.

Kidney Function: No changes in dosing are needed.

▷ **Dosing Instructions:** A patient instruction sheet will always accompany this medicine. The instructions should be followed closely as a limited amount of medicine reaches the lungs with the best inhaler technique. Your doctor should be called if the condition being treated worsens or does not improve. Once an inhalation treatment is completed, rinse your mouth with water. If you forget a dose: use the spray or inhaler as soon as you remember it, unless it's nearly time for your next dose—if this is the case, skip the missed dose and just take the next scheduled dose right on time. DO NOT double doses. This medicine is not used for sudden asthma episodes or status asthmaticus.

Usual Duration of Use: Continual use on a regular schedule for several days is usually necessary to determine this drug's effectiveness in treating seasonal and perennial allergic rhinitis. For the inhaled form, a beneficial response may happen in a day, but it may take two weeks to realize the maximum benefits. Long-term use (months to years) requires periodic evaluation of response and dose adjustment (to the minimum effective dose). Keep appointments with your doctor.

Typical Treatment Goals and Measurements (Outcomes and Markers)

Asthma: Frequency and severity of asthma attacks should ease. Some clinicians also use decreased frequency of rescue inhaler use as a further clinical indicator. It is critical that this medicine is used regularly to get the best results. An additional goal of therapy is to use the lowest effective dose. Some people keep their improvements when doses are lowered, while others relapse. Specific testing goals include improvement in PEFR, FEV1, and other lung (pulmonary) function tests. Wheezing and difficulty breathing (dyspnea) should ease as well as asthma caused (induced) by exercise. If the usual benefit is not realized, call your doctor.

Allergic rhinitis: Signs and symptoms of allergic rhinitis such as runny or stuffy nose, postnasal drip and sneezing should ease. Scratch testing for a specific immune substance (IgE) can also be done to check progress at a cellular level.

Possible Advantages of This Drug

Once-a-day dosing for the nasal form, and small (roughly 2%) systemic absorption.

▷ **This Drug Should Not Be Taken If**
- you have had an allergic reaction to any dose form of it previously.
- you have sudden onset asthma or status asthmaticus. (Fluticasone or fluticasone/salmeterol WON'T WORK.)

▷ **Inform Your Physician Before Taking This Drug If**
- you are already taking systemic prednisone.
- you are exposed to measles or chicken pox.
- you are unsure how much to take or how often to take it.
- you take prescription or nonprescription medicines not discussed when fluticasone was prescribed.
- you have diabetes.
- you have signs or symptoms of an infection in your nose.
- your skin is shrunken (atrophied) or you have acne, warts, or other skin problems (topical form).
- you've had fungal infections, herpes simplex of the eye, tuberculosis, or other infections.
- you have damage from an accident or surgery to your nose while you are taking this medicine.
- your allergic rhinitis does not improve or worsens.
- you have unexplained joint pain such as knee, hip, or shoulder pain. While not reported for this particular corticosteroid, other medicines in the same family have caused osteonecrosis (aseptic necrosis or avascular necrosis) and caution is prudent.

Possible Side Effects (natural, expected and unavoidable drug actions)

Irritation of the nose, nosebleeds. Systemic steroid effects—possible. Development of yeast infections of the mouth or throat.

▷ **Possible Adverse Effects** (unusual, unexpected and infrequent reactions)
If any of the following develop, consult your physician promptly for guidance.

Mild Adverse Effects

Allergic reactions: contact dermatitis.
Nosebleeds or nasal burning—case reports to infrequent.
Dizziness or headache—rare to infrequent.
Unpleasant taste, nausea or vomiting—rare.
Increased heart rate—case reports.

Serious Adverse Effects

Allergic reactions: anaphylaxis—case report.
Suppression of the hypothalamic pituitary adrenal (HPA) axis—rare.
Increased risk from viral infections—possible.
Increased pressure in the head (more likely in children)—possible.
Yeast infections of the nose—rare.
Blood vessel inflammation (vasculitis) including Churg-Strauss Like syndrome—case reports, but of questionable cause.
Loss of control of blood sugar—possible in diabetics and others.
Glaucoma or cataracts—case reports (inhaled form)—increased risk.
Cushing's syndrome (with excessive doses or very sensitive patients)—possible.
Growth suppression in children—possible.
Osteoporosis—increased risk with long-term use.

▷ **Possible Effects on Sexual Function:** None defined.

Possible Delayed Adverse Effects: Yeast infections of the nose—rare. Osteo-porosis—increased risk.

▷ **Adverse Effects That May Mimic Natural Diseases or Disorders**
None defined.

Natural Diseases or Disorders That May Be Activated by This Drug
If systemic effects occur, the patient may be more susceptible to infections, or dormant infections may become active. This drug increases osteoporo-sis risk even in those not predisposed to developing osteoporosis.

Possible Effects on Laboratory Tests
Cortisol levels: decreased.
Eosinophils: increased in rare case reports.

CAUTION
1. Call your doctor if you are exposed to measles or chicken pox.
2. Long-term use requires periodic evaluation for yeast infection of the nose.
3. Call your doctor if your condition does not improve or worsens.
4. Children are in general at greater risk for adrenal gland suppression (HPA axis suppression) and are at greater risk for inadequate levels once therapy is withdrawn. Careful patient follow-up by a qualified specialist is needed.

Precautions for Use
By Infants and Children: Safety and effectiveness for use by those under 12 years of age have not been established for the intranasal form. Many ado-lescents can be started successfully with one spray in each nostril per day (100 mcg). Maximum total daily dose should not exceed 200 mcg. Children in general are at greater risk for suppression of the HPA axis and glucocor-ticosteroid insufficiency than adults.
By Those Over 60 Years of Age: No specific precautions.

▷ **Advisability of Use During Pregnancy**
Pregnancy Category: C. See Pregnancy Risk Categories at the back of this book.
Animal Studies: High-dose studies in rats revealed fetal toxicity consistent with changes caused by other steroids.
Human Studies: Information from adequate studies of pregnant women is not available.
Ask your doctor for guidance.

Advisability of Use If Breast-Feeding
Presence of this drug in breast milk: Unknown.
Monitor nursing infant closely and discontinue drug or nursing if adverse effects develop.

Habit-Forming Potential: Not defined.

Effects of Overdose: Not defined.

Possible Effects of Long-Term Use: Rare nasal yeast infections.

Suggested Periodic Examinations While Taking This Drug (at physician's dis-cretion)
Nasal exams, check for osteoporosis (DEXA, PDEXA) with long-term use, periodic CBCs.

▷ **While Taking This Drug, Observe the Following**
Foods: No restrictions.
Herbal Medicines or Minerals: Fir or pine needle oil should NOT be used by asthmatics. Ephedra alone does carry a German Commission E mono-graph indication for asthma treatment. If you are allergic to plants in the

Asteraceae family (aster, chrysanthemum, daisy, or ragweed), you may also be allergic to echinacea, chamomile, feverfew, and St. John's wort. Increased calcium and vitamin D are prudent while taking this medicine. Talk to your doctor BEFORE adding any herbals to this medicine.

Beverages: No restrictions.

▷ *Alcohol:* No interactions expected.

Tobacco Smoking: No interactions expected. I advise everyone to quit smoking.

▷ *Other Drugs*

Fluticasone *taken concurrently* with

- ketoconazole (Nizoral) and perhaps other azole antifungals may increase fluticasone blood levels.
- medicines that inhibit CYP 3A4 (such as ketoconazole) will lead to increased fluticasone effects and those that induce 3A4 will decrease fluticasone benefits.
- ritonavir (Norvir) may increase fluticasone blood levels and lead to Cushing's syndrome. A check of cortisol levels may help make the diagnosis.
- systemic steroids (such as prednisone) may increase the likelihood of suppression of the hypothalamic pituitary adrenal (HPA) axis.

▷ *Driving, Hazardous Activities:* This drug may cause dizziness. Restrict activities as necessary.

Aviation Note: The use of this drug *may be a disqualification* for piloting. Consult a designated Aviation Medical Examiner.

Exposure to Sun: No restrictions.

Discontinuation: This medicine should not be stopped abruptly. Talk with your doctor before stopping this drug.

FLUVASTATIN (flu va STAT in)

Introduced: 1994 **Class:** Cholesterol-reducing drug, HMG-CoA reductase inhibitor **Prescription:** USA: Yes **Controlled Drug:** USA: No; Canada: No **Available as Generic:** USA: No; Canada: No

Brand Names: Lescol, Lescol XL

BENEFITS versus RISKS	
Possible Benefits	*Possible Risks*
EFFECTIVE REDUCTION OF TOTAL BLOOD CHOLESTEROL	Increased liver enzymes
REDUCES TRIGLYCERIDES AND APOLIPOPROTEIN B	Muscle pain or weakness
SLOWS PROGRESSION OF CORONARY ATHEROSCLEROSIS	Decreased coenzyme Q10
Reduces the number of coronary events in patients with coronary heart disease	
May decrease osteoporosis risk	
May decrease risk of Alzheimer's	
May decrease cancer risk	

▷ **Principal Uses**

As a Single Drug Product: Uses currently included in FDA-approved labeling: (1) Manages abnormally high cholesterol and triglycerides and apolipoprotein B in people with type 2 hypercholesterolemia; (2) slows progression of atherosclerosis in patients with coronary heart disease.

Other (unlabeled) generally accepted uses: (1) One case of blue toe syndrome was successfully reversed; (2) worked to lower LDL cholesterol in one study of Type II hyperlipoproteinemia; (3) may have a role in stroke prevention, or deep vein clot (thrombosis) prevention but further studies are needed; (4) helps prevent clogging (restenosis) of coronary stents or bypasses; (5) like other HMG-CoA reductase inhibitors, may have a role in reducing risk of bone fractures; (6) decreases the number of coronary events in patients with coronary heart disease; (7) could have a role in decreasing risk of dementia; (8) may help decrease fracture risk/osteoporosis; (9) one case-control study found a 20% reduction in cancer risk by "statin-type" medicines. Further research is needed.

How This Drug Works: This medicine is changed (hydrolyzed) to a beta-hydroxy-acid form. The beta-hydroxy-acid inhibits HMG-CoA reductase. This enzyme is critical for cholesterol formation. Once inhibited, cholesterol formation slows. Since the amount of cholesterol is reduced in the liver, the VLDL fraction may also be decreased. There is a growing body of evidence that "statins" also have beneficial changes on what is in the blood, blood flow and even the blood vessel walls themselves. Specific compounds or effects of platelet-derived growth factor (PDGF), undesirable blood clotting via thrombin-antithrombin III, thrombomodulin and other chemicals may be beneficially lowered or effects mitigated by statins.

Available Dosage Forms and Strengths
Tablets — 10 mg, 20 mg, 40 mg

Tablets extended release — 80 mg

▷ **Recommended Dosage Ranges** (Actual dose and schedule must be determined for each patient individually.)

Infants and Children: Safety and efficacy for those less than 18 years of age have not been established.

18 to 60 Years of Age: Hypercholesterolemia: Dosing is started with 20 mg a day, taken with the evening meal or simply in the evening. This dose is increased as needed and tolerated to 80 mg with each evening (24 hours apart) meal. Any needed increases are made at intervals of 4 weeks. Patients who take immunosuppressant medicines are started on 10 mg of lovastatin daily and should not receive more than 20 mg daily with the evening meal. If 80 mg is required to achieve cholesterol and HDL goals, a single evening dose of 80 mg of the Lescol XL form can be taken.

Atherosclerosis: Dosing of 20 mg twice a day was used in a study called the Lipoprotein and Coronary Atherosclerosis Study (LCAS).

Over 60 Years of Age: Same as 18 to 60 years of age.

Conditions Requiring Dosing Adjustments

Liver Function: This drug is extensively changed in the liver. Lower doses appear prudent in liver disease.

Kidney Function: Patients with severe failure (creatinine clearance less than 30 ml/min) should be closely followed if given over 20 mg daily.

▷ **Dosing Instructions:** This medicine is best taken in the EVENING (such as with the evening MEAL), as it produces the best cholesterol-lowering results or outcomes. If you forget a dose: Take the next dose as soon as you remember it, unless it is nearly time for your next dose—then skip the dose you missed and just take the next scheduled dose. DO NOT double doses. If you find yourself omitting doses, call your doctor for some added ways to help remember your medicine.

Usual Duration of Use: Continual use on a regular schedule for 3 to 4 weeks may be needed to determine this drug's effectiveness in helping lower low-density lipoprotein (LDL) level. Long-term use may be needed to lead to beneficial effects on the pattern of HDL and LDL. Ongoing (months to years) use requires evaluation of response by your doctor. Know your cholesterol numbers and try to achieve NCEP goals. Take control of cholesterol for life!

Typical Treatment Goals and Measurements (Outcomes and Markers)

Cholesterol: The National Institutes of Health Adult Treatment Panel has released ATP III as part of the update to the National Cholesterol Education Program, or NCEP. Key points in these new guidelines include acknowledging diabetes as one of the conditions that increases risk of heart disease, modifying risk factors, therapeutic lifestyle changes (TLC) and recommending routine testing for all of the cholesterol fractions (lipoprotein profile) versus total cholesterol alone.

Current NCEP guidelines recommend a desirable total cholesterol of 200 mg/dl, and optimal bad cholesterol (LDL) as 100 mg/dl, 130–159 mg/dl as borderline high, 160 mg/dl as high and 190 mg/dl as very high. Did you know that there are at least five different kinds of "good cholesterol," or HDL? The "too low" measure for HDL is still 40 mg/dl, but in order to learn more about cholesterol types, some doctors are starting to order lipid panels. There are at least 7 different kinds of "bad cholesterol." The new panels tell doctors about the kinds of cholesterol that your body makes. This is important because some kinds (small, dense particles) tend to stick to blood vessels (are highly atherogenic). Take your medicine to reach your goals!

Two additional tests you will hear about will be electron beam computed tomography (EBCT) and CRP. EBCT is an important tool used in conjunction with laboratory studies. Findings show that even patients who meet cholesterol goals (particularly females over 55) can still be at significant cardiovascular risk. EBCT then defines risk by giving a calcium score and a "virtual tour" of the coronary arteries. C Reactive Protein, or CRP, is a new and apparently independent predictor of heart disease risk. A large study (see Ridker, P.M. in Sources) found that CRP predicted heart disease risk independently of bad cholesterol (low-density lipoprotein).

Talk to your doctor about this new laboratory test and ask about current guidelines for who should be tested (see Pearson, T.A. in Sources).

Possible Advantages of This Drug

May give a more favorable time of medicine exposure than other medicines of the same family. Clinical significance of the inability to cross the blood brain barrier and not being changed into active compounds (active metabolites) have not been clinically demonstrated.

▷ **This Drug Should Not Be Taken If**
- you had an allergic reaction to it previously.
- you have active liver disease or your liver enzymes become elevated (talk to your doctor).
- you are pregnant or breast-feeding your infant.

▷ **Inform Your Physician Before Taking This Drug If**
- you have previously taken any other drugs in this class: lovastatin (Mevacor), pravastatin (Pravachol).

- another doctor prescribes niacin, cyclosporine, erythromycin, or fibrate-type medicines.
- you have a history of liver disease or impaired liver function.
- you are not using birth control or you are planning pregnancy.
- you regularly consume substantial amounts of alcohol.
- you have cataracts or impaired vision.
- you have any type of chronic muscular disorder.
- you develop muscle pain, weakness or soreness that is unexplained while taking this medicine.
- you plan to have major surgery in the near future.

Possible Side Effects (natural, expected, and unavoidable drug actions)
Development of abnormal liver function tests without associated symptoms.
Decreased ubiquinone (Co-Q10).

▷ **Possible Adverse Effects** (unusual, unexpected, and infrequent reactions)
If any of the following develop, consult your physician promptly for guidance.

Mild Adverse Effects
Allergic reactions: rash.
Headache, insomnia or dizziness—infrequent.
Indigestion, nausea, excessive gas, constipation, diarrhea—infrequent.
Lowering of the blood pressure—possible.

Serious Adverse Effects
Marked and persistent abnormal liver function tests with focal hepatitis (without jaundice)—case reports.
Acute myositis (muscle pain and tenderness)—occurred rarely during long-term use.
Rhabdomyolysis (simvastatin, atorvastatin, pravastatin, lovastatin, and fluvastatin from highest to lowest probability)—rare.
Sudden kidney failure—rare.
Vision changes—possible, case report.
Lichen planus skin rash—rare.
Neuropathy—case reports.
Systemic lupus erythematosus–like syndrome—case reports.

▷ **Possible Effects on Sexual Function:** None reported.

Possible Delayed Adverse Effects: Vision change. Doses of 15 to 33 times the human dose of another drug in this class given to rats caused an increase in liver cancers.

Natural Diseases or Disorders That May Be Activated by This Drug
Latent liver disease.

Possible Effects on Laboratory Tests
Blood alanine aminotransferase (ALT) enzyme level: increased (with higher doses of drug).
Blood total cholesterol, LDL cholesterol and triglyceride levels: decreased.
Blood HDL cholesterol level: increased. Beneficial changes in pattern of HDL and LDL.

CAUTION
1. If pregnancy occurs while taking this drug, stop taking the drug immediately and call your doctor.
2. Promptly report any development of muscle pain or tenderness, especially if accompanied by fever or weakness (malaise).
3. Promptly report altered or impaired vision so that appropriate evaluation can be made.

4. A study in *Circulation* (see Heeschen, C. et al. in Sources) found that stopping "statin"-type medicines in patients with acute coronary syndrome symptoms can lead to a three fold increase risk of non-fatal heart attack (MI) or death.

Precautions for Use

By Infants and Children: Safety and effectiveness for those under 20 years of age are not established.

By Those Over 60 Years of Age: Tell your doctor about any personal or family history of vision problems. If periodic eye examinations are recommended, get them. Promptly report any vision changes.

▷ **Advisability of Use During Pregnancy**

Pregnancy Category: X. See Pregnancy Risk Categories at the back of this book.

Animal Studies: Mouse and rat studies reveal skeletal birth defects due to a closely related drug of this class.

Human Studies: Adequate studies of pregnant women are not available.

This drug should be avoided during entire pregnancy.

Advisability of Use If Breast-Feeding

Presence of this drug in breast milk: Unknown, but not thought to be safe. Avoid drug or refrain from nursing.

Habit-Forming Potential: None.

Effects of Overdose: Increased indigestion, stomach distress, nausea, diarrhea.

Possible Effects of Long-Term Use: Abnormal liver function with focal hepatitis. Abnormal liver function tests. Decreased coenzyme Q10 (Co-Q10 or ubiquinone). Loss of beneficial effects—reported with some statin-type medicines.

Suggested Periodic Examinations While Taking This Drug (at physician's discretion)

Blood cholesterol studies: total cholesterol, HDL and LDL fractions (usually every 4 weeks with dose changes). SLE test.

Liver function tests before treatment, 12 weeks after the medicine is started and 12 weeks after any increase in dose.

Complete eye examination at beginning of treatment and at any time that significant change in vision occurs. Ask your physician for guidance.

Electron beam computed tomography (EBCT) can help predict silent ischemia and other problems with blood vessels that supply the heart itself. This also may help define the results (outcomes) you are getting from this medicine.

Ubiquinone levels.

▷ **While Taking This Drug, Observe the Following**

Foods: Follow a standard low-cholesterol diet. Your doctor may also recommend some specific foods such as increased vegetables or functional foods such as Benecol. Three well-designed studies published in early April 2002 found that both in women and men and before and after a heart attack, people who ate more fish (2–4 servings a week) appeared to avoid heart disease. Additionally, putting supplements containing Omega 3 polyunsaturated fatty acids (PUFA) into the diet also appeared to protect against abnormal heart rhythms and sudden death from heart attack. The studies appeared in *JAMA*, *Circulation* and the *New England Journal of Medicine*.

Herbal Medicines or Minerals: No data exist from well-designed clinical studies about garlic and fluvastatin combinations and cannot presently be recommended. Additionally, garlic may inhibit blood clotting (platelet) aggregation—something to consider if you are already taking a platelet inhibitor. Herbal medicines that can be toxic to the liver such as kava and valerian should be avoided. The FDA will allow one dietary supplement called Cholestin to be sold. Because this product actually contains lovastatin, and the use of two HMG-Co-A inhibitors may increase risk of rhabdomyolysis or myopathy, the combination is NOT advised. Some products containing plant sterols (Benecol) may be useful as complementary care to lower total and LDL cholesterol. Substituting soy for some of the meat in your diet can help avoid cardiovascular problems. Lastly, because this medicine can deplete Co-Q10, supplementation may be needed.

Beverages: No restrictions. May be taken with milk.

▷ *Alcohol:* No interactions expected. Use sparingly.

Tobacco Smoking: No interactions expected. I advise everyone to quit smoking.

▷ *Other Drugs*

Fluvastatin may ***increase*** the effects of

- digoxin (Lanoxin).
- warfarin (Coumadin); more frequent testing of INR (prothrombin time) will be needed.

Fluvastatin ***taken concurrently*** with

- amprenavir (Agenerase) and ritonavir (Norvir) and perhaps other protease inhibitors may increase fluvastatin levels and the risk of muscle damage (myopathy).
- clofibrate (Atromid-S) or other fibrate compounds may result in increased risk of serious muscle toxicity.
- clopidogrel (Plavix) may result in increased fluvastatin levels (because of possible CYP 450 2C9 inhibition. Careful patient follow-up is prudent.
- cyclosporine (Sandimmune) can result in kidney failure and myopathy.
- erythromycin and perhaps other macrolide antibiotics (see Drug Classes) may increase risk of muscle damage (myopathy or rhabdomyolysis).
- fluconazole (Diflucan), itraconazole (Sporanox) or ketoconazole (Nizoral) increases myopathy or rhabdomyolysis risk.
- gemfibrozil (Lopid) may alter the absorption and excretion of fluvastatin; these drugs should not be taken concurrently.
- levothyroxine (various) may blunt the effects of levothyroxine.
- medicines that change cytochrome P450 3A4 (inhibitors will increase fluvastatin levels and inducers will blunt fluvastatin therapeutic effects).
- niacin may cause an increased frequency of muscle problems (myopathy) when combined with a related medicine (lovastatin). Caution is advised. Niacin may also increase homocysteine levels—a risk factor for heart disease.
- omeprazole (Prilosec) and possible esomeprazole (Nexium) may increase fluvastatin levels and lead to toxicity.
- quinupristin/dalfopristin (Synercid) may increase the risk for myopathy by increasing cerivastatin blood levels.
- ranitidine (Zantac) may increase peak blood levels of fluvastatin.
- ritonavir (Norvir) may lead to fluvastatin toxicity.
- sildenafil (Viagra) may change levels of either drug as they both use CYP3A4 to be removed from the body.

The following drug may ***decrease*** the effects of fluvastatin:

- cholestyramine (Questran), by possibly reducing absorption of fluvastatin; take fluvastatin 1 hour before or 4 hours after cholestyramine.

▷　*Driving, Hazardous Activities:* No restrictions.
　Aviation Note: No restrictions.
　Exposure to Sun: No restrictions.
　Discontinuation: Do not stop this drug without your doctor's knowledge and
　　help. There may be a significant increase in blood cholesterol levels if this
　　medicine is stopped. Patients who have acute coronary syndromes, or ACS
　　(such as unstable angina, heart attack [non-p; Q-wave myocardial infarc-
　　tion], and Q-wave myocardial infarction), were reviewed as part of the
　　Platelet Receptor Inhibitor in Ischemic Syndrome Management (PRISM)
　　study. It was found that pretreatment with statin-type medicines (HMG-
　　CoA reductase inhibitors such as the medicine in this profile) significantly
　　lowered risk during the first 30 days after ACS symptoms started. Most
　　importantly, it was found that if a statin-type medicine is stopped in ACS
　　patients, there is a threefold increased risk of non-fatal heart attack or
　　death (see Heeschen, C in Sources). Talk with your doctor BEFORE stop-
　　ping any statin-type medicine.

FLUVOXAMINE (FLU vox a meen)

Introduced:　1995　**Class:**　Antidepressant, selective serotonin reuptake
inhibitor　**Prescription:**　USA: Yes　**Controlled Drug:**　USA: No;
Canada: No　**Available as Generic:**　USA: Yes; Canada: Yes

Brand Names:　✤Apo-Fluvoxamine, ✤Gen-Fluvoxamine, Luvox, ✤Novo-
Fluvoxamine, ✤PMS-Fluvoxamine, ✤Riva-Fluvoxamine

**Warning: Do not combine this medicine with terfenadine (Seldane) or
astemizole (Hismanal). No longer on the US market, but may still be in
some foreign countries.**

BENEFITS versus RISKS	
Possible Benefits	*Possible Risks*
TREATMENT OF OBSESSIVE-COMPULSIVE DISORDER IN ADULTS	Nausea and vomiting (often resolve with time)
TREATMENT OF OBSESSIVE-COMPULSIVE DISORDER IN CHILDREN (over 8)	
Treatment of depression	
Treatment of panic disorder	
May have a role in helping to control binge eating	
May have a role in helping to treat social anxiety disorder	

▷ **Principal Uses**
　As a Single Drug Product: Uses currently included in FDA-approved labeling:
　　Treatment of obsessive-compulsive disorder in adults and children.
　　Other (unlabeled) generally accepted uses: (1) May have a role in helping
　　compulsive exhibitionism; (2) treats depression; (3) may be useful in eat-
　　ing problems where binge behaviors are a key factor; (4) can help panic
　　attacks; (5) helps prevent long-standing (chronic) tension headaches; (6)
　　eases social anxiety disorder; (7) may help pathological gambling.

How This Drug Works: Inhibits reuptake of the neurotransmitter 5-HT, easing symptoms of treated behaviors or conditions.

Available Dosage Forms and Strengths
Tablets — 25 mg, 50 mg, 100 mg

▷ **Recommended Dosage Ranges** (Actual dose and schedule must be determined for each patient individually.)

Infants and Children: For children 8 years old or older with obsessive-compulsive disorder: Dosing is started with 25 mg at bedtime for 3 days. The dose is then increased by 25-mg steps every 3 to 4 days as needed and tolerated until a maximum of 200 mg is reached. If the required dose is larger than 75 mg, the total daily dose is divided into two equal doses and given twice daily.

18 to 60 Years of Age: Therapy is started with 50 mg taken at bedtime. The dose may then be increased as needed and tolerated by 50-mg intervals every 4 to 7 days to a maximum dose of 300 mg daily. The prescriber should remember that the drug may take from 4 to 14 days to begin to work. If patient needs a daily dose greater than 100 mg, dose is divided in half and taken twice daily.

Over 60 Years of Age: This medicine is removed half as slowly as in younger patients. Plasma concentrations are also roughly 40% higher than in younger patients. Slower time frames for any increases beyond the starting dose and lower maintenance doses are prudent.

Conditions Requiring Dosing Adjustments

Liver Function: This drug is extensively changed by the liver. If it is used by patients with liver disease, lower starting doses, slow dose increases and careful patient monitoring are indicated.

Kidney Function: A lower starting dose and careful patient monitoring are needed.

▷ **Dosing Instructions:** Take this medicine exactly as prescribed and at the same time each time you take it. This medicine may be taken with or without food. Call your doctor if vomiting (a possible side effect) continues for more than 2 days after you start treatment. If you forget a dose: take the missed dose as soon as you remember it, unless it's nearly time for your next dose—if that is the case, skip the missed dose and take the next dose right on time. DO NOT double doses.

Usual Duration of Use: Continual use on a regular schedule for 4 to 14 days is usually necessary to determine effectiveness in helping obsessive-compulsive disorder. Long-term use (months to years) requires evaluation by your doctor.

Typical Treatment Goals and Measurements (Outcomes and Markers)

Obsessive-compulsive disorder: The general goal: to lessen the degree and severity of obsessions or compulsive behavior, letting patients return to their daily lives. Specific measures of this condition involve testing or inventories (such as the Yale-Brown Obsessive-Compulsive Scale, or Y-BOCS) and can be valuable in checking benefits from this medicine.

Possible Advantages of This Drug
Offers once-daily dosing and has a good side-effect profile.

▷ **This Drug Should Not Be Taken If**
- you had an allergic reaction to it previously.
- you are taking cisapride (Propulsid).

▷ **Inform Your Physician Before Taking This Drug If**
- you continue to have a problem with vomiting 2 days after starting this medicine.
- you feel light-headed when you get up from a sitting position.
- you have a history of seizures.
- you are unsure how much to take or how often to take it.
- you have taken an MAO inhibitor (see Drug Classes) within the last 14 days.
- you have a history of heart problems.
- you take prescription or nonprescription medicines not discussed when fluvoxamine was prescribed.

Possible Side Effects (natural, expected, and unavoidable drug actions)
Nausea and vomiting (usually stops after a few days of treatment). This may be avoided by slowly increasing the dose of this medicine. Dose-related orthostatic hypotension.

▷ **Possible Adverse Effects** (unusual, unexpected, and infrequent reactions)
If any of the following develop, consult your physician promptly for guidance.
Mild Adverse Effects
Allergic reaction: skin rash.
Somnolence, headache, agitation, sleep disorders—infrequent to frequent.
Change in heart waves (R-R, QT and QTc intervals).
Bruising or nosebleeds—possible (may be stopped by 500 mg of vitamin C daily), usually resolves over time.
Liver toxicity—rare.
Patchy baldness (alopecia)—case report.
Dry mouth, anorexia, or constipation—possible to frequent.
Serious Adverse Effects
Allergic reactions: anaphylactic reaction—case reports.
Serious skin rash (toxic epidermal necrolysis (TEN) or Stevens Johnson Syndrome)—case reports.
Liver toxicity—rare.
Prolonged bleeding time, rectal bleeding or nose bleeds—stopped by 500 mg of vitamin C daily in one case and usually resolves over time, but the medicine should be stopped if bleeding is significant and does not stop.
Seizures or mania—rare.
Parkinson-like reactions—case reports with SSRI-type medicines.
Tourette's syndrome—case reports.
Serotonin syndrome—case report.
Excessive urination (SIADH)—case reports.

▷ **Possible Effects on Sexual Function:** Delayed or absent orgasm, failure to ejaculate—case reports.
Impotence 2–8%. Galactorrhea—case reports with SSRIs.

Possible Delayed Adverse Effects: Not reported.

▷ **Adverse Effects That May Mimic Natural Diseases or Disorders**
Increased liver enzymes may mimic hepatitis.

Natural Diseases or Disorders That May Be Activated by This Drug
None defined.

Possible Effects on Laboratory Tests
Liver function tests: increased.
Melatonin level: increased.

CAUTION
1. This medicine has several important drug-drug interactions. Be certain to tell all health care professionals that you take this medicine.
2. If nausea and vomiting continue for more than 2 days after you start this medicine, call your doctor.

Precautions for Use
By Infants and Children: Safety and effectiveness for use by those under 18 years of age have not been established.
By Those Over 60 Years of Age: Lowering starting and maintenance doses is indicated.

▷ **Advisability of Use During Pregnancy**
Pregnancy Category: C. See Pregnancy Risk Categories at the back of this book.
Animal studies: Consistent with category C.
Human studies: Information from adequate studies of pregnant women is not available.
Ask your doctor for help.

Advisability of Use If Breast-Feeding
Presence of this drug in breast milk: Yes, in small amounts.
Monitor nursing infant closely and discontinue drug or nursing if adverse effects develop.

Habit-Forming Potential: None, but a withdrawal syndrome has been reported if the medicine is stopped abruptly (moderate to high occurrence rate).

Effects of Overdose: Nausea, vomiting, seizures.

Possible Effects of Long-Term Use: Not defined.

Suggested Periodic Examinations While Taking This Drug (at physician's discretion)
Liver function tests.

▷ **While Taking This Drug, Observe the Following**
Foods: No restrictions. Vitamin C (500 mg daily) may stop bruising that is possible with this medicine.
Herbal Medicines or Minerals: Since fluvoxamine and St. John's wort may both act to increase serotonin, the combination is not advised. Since part of the way ginseng and ginkgo work may be as MAO inhibitors, do not combine with fluvoxamine. Ma huang and yohimbe are also best avoided while taking this medicine. Valerian and kava kava (kava is no longer recommended in Canada) may interact additively (drowsiness). Avoid these combinations. Indian snakeroot and dehydroepiandrosterone (DHEA) are also best avoided while taking this medicine. Since fluvoxamine can inhibit a compound that helps remove caffeine from your system, caution with caffeine-containing products such as guarana is advised. Fluvoxamine may also inhibit melatonin removal. Talk to your doctor BEFORE combining any herbal medicine with this medicine.
Beverages: May inhibit an enzyme that removes caffeine—-use caution.
▷ *Alcohol:* May worsen drowsiness. Ask your doctor for guidance.
Tobacco Smoking: Fluvoxamine stays in the body of smokers up to one-quarter less time than in nonsmokers, and fluvoxamine benefits may be blunted. I advise everyone to quit smoking.
Marijuana Smoking: Additive sleepiness and one case of mania with an SSRI.
▷ *Other Drugs*
Fluvoxamine *taken concurrently* with
• amitriptyline (Elavil, others) can result in amitriptyline toxicity.

- astemizole (Hismanal) may cause *serious heart arrhythmias*. DO NOT COMBINE.
- benzodiazepines (see Drug Classes) may result in benzodiazepine toxicity.
- beta blockers (see Drug Classes) may result in decreased drug clearance and toxicity.
- buspirone (Buspar) may lead to very slow heart rates in some patients. One later study found doubling of buspirone levels but no clinical effects. The combination is best avoided, but if deemed clinically necessary, clinical effects on the patient should be closely followed.
- carbamazepine (Tegretol) may cause toxicity. More frequent checks of drug levels needed.
- cimetidine (Tagamet) may lead to toxicity.
- cisapride (Propulsid) may cause heart toxicity. DO NOT COMBINE.
- clomipramine (Anafranil) may cause toxicity.
- clozapine (Clozaril) can result in higher clozapine levels and toxicity.
- cyclosporine (Sandimmune, others) may increase cyclosporine levels.
- dextromethorphan may cause hallucinations (reported with similar medicines).
- diltiazem (Cardizem) may cause diltiazem toxicity.
- dofetilide (Tikosyn) may lead to dofetilide toxicity via inhibition of CYP 3A4 inhibition.
- ergot derivative (such as Cafergot) may lead to toxicity. DO NOT COMBINE.
- imipramine (Tofranil, others) may result in imipramine toxicity.
- lithium (Lithobid) can cause serotonin syndrome.
- MAO inhibitors (see Drug Classes) can cause toxicity. DO NOT COMBINE.
- maprotiline can cause maprotiline toxicity.
- methadone may result in increased opioid effects.
- monoamine oxidase inhibitors (see Drug Classes) may lead to central nervous system toxicity or frank serotonin syndrome.
- olanzapine (Zyprexa) may lead to olanzapine toxicity via inhibition of CYP 1A2.
- oral antidiabetic drugs (see Drug Classes) may remain in the body longer than expected, requiring a dose decrease. This has not been reported with fluvoxamine, but has been reported with sertraline, a medicine in the same pharmacological family.
- phenytoin (Dilantin) or fosphenytoin (Cerebyx) may lead to toxicity. Patients should be watched closely for problems walking (ataxia) or drowsiness (early toxicity signs), and their doctor notified at once if these occur.
- ritonavir (Norvir) and perhaps other protease inhibitors may lead to toxicity.
- sibutramine (Meridia) may lead to serotonin syndrome.
- sumatriptan (Imitrex), naratriptan, almotriptan, zolmitriptan, and any other triptan-type medicines may lead to weakness and confusion—caution is required.
- tacrine (Cognex) may lead to tacrine toxicity.
- terfenadine (Seldane) may cause *serious heart arrhythmias*. DO NOT COMBINE.
- theophylline may result in theophylline toxicity.
- tramadol (Ultram) may increase seizure risk. DO NOT COMBINE.
- tricyclic antidepressants (imipramine, others) may lead to tricyclic toxicity.
- triptans, such as naratriptan (Amerge), rizatriptan (Maxalt), sumatriptan (Imitrex), or zolmitriptan (Zomig), may lead to weakness and incoordination.
- tryptophan may increase serotonin effects of fluvoxamine and cause severe vomiting.

- warfarin (Coumadin) can result in increased warfarin concentrations and may lead to bleeding; more frequent INR testing is needed.

▷ *Driving, Hazardous Activities:* This drug may cause drowsiness. Restrict activities as necessary.

Aviation Note: The use of this drug **is probably a disqualification** for piloting. Consult a designated Aviation Medical Examiner.

Exposure to Sun: No restrictions.

Discontinuation: A withdrawal syndrome has been reported if this medicine is abruptly stopped. The doses should be slowly tapered.

FORMOTEROL (for MOT er all)

Introduced: 2001 **Class:** Bronchodilator **Prescription:** USA: Yes **Controlled Drug:** USA: No; Canada: Not available in Canada **Available as Generic:** USA: No

Brand Name: Foradil Aerolizer

Author's Note: Information in this profile will be broadened in subsequent editions if evolving patient benefit and research data warrant.

FOSINOPRIL (FOH sin oh pril)

Introduced: 1986 **Class:** Antihypertensive, ACE inhibitor

Please see the angiotensin converting enzyme (ACE) inhibitor family profile.

FUROSEMIDE (fur OH se mide)

Introduced: 1964 **Class:** Antihypertensive, diuretic **Prescription:** USA: Yes **Controlled Drug:** USA: No; Canada: No **Available as Generic:** USA: Yes; Canada: Yes

Brand Names: ✤Albert Furosemide, ✤Apo-Furosemide, Fumide MD, Furocot, Furomide MD, Furose, Furosemide-10, ✤Furoside, Lasaject, Lasimide, Lasix, ✤Lasix Special, Lo-Aqua, Luramide, Myrosemide, Novo-Semide, Ro-Semide, SK-Furosemide, ✤Uritol

BENEFITS versus RISKS	
Possible Benefits	*Possible Risks*
PROMPT, EFFECTIVE, RELIABLE DIURETIC	WATER AND ELECTROLYTE DEPLETION with excessive use
MODEST ANTIHYPERTENSIVE IN MILD TO MODERATE HYPERTENSION	Excessive potassium and magnesium loss
ENHANCES EFFECTIVENESS OF OTHER ANTIHYPERTENSIVES	Increased blood sugar level
	Decreased blood calcium level
	Liver damage
	Blood cell disorder

▷ **Principal Uses**

As a Single Drug Product: Uses currently included in FDA-approved labeling: (1) Increases urine and removes excessive water (edema), as in congestive heart failure or some forms of liver, lung, and kidney disease; (2) lowers high blood pressure, usually with other drugs.

Other (unlabeled) generally accepted uses: (1) Inhaled furosemide may help protect the lungs in people with asthma; (2) can have a role in helping infants with lung problems (chronic bronchopulmonary dysplasia); (3) one study found furosemide beneficial in helping lung mechanics of infants after heart surgery; (4) aborted migraine aura in a small number of case reports.

In the Pipeline: The Health and Human Services secretary has identified a group of medicines to be tested for use in children. Furosemide was on that list of the 12 highest priority medicines to be studied in children (find out more at *www.hhs.gov/news/press/2003pres/20030121.html*).

How This Drug Works: By increasing the elimination of salt and water through increased urine production, this drug reduces fluid in the blood and body tissues. These changes also contribute to lowering blood pressure.

Available Dosage Forms and Strengths
   Injection — 10 mg/ml
   Solution — 10 mg/ml
   Tablets — 20 mg, 40 mg, 80 mg

▷ **Usual Adult Dosage Ranges:** *As antihypertensive:* 40 mg every 12 hours initially. Doses have historically been increased as needed and tolerated. If the response does not meet therapeutic goals, other blood pressure medicines should be added, rather than going above 80 mg a day. *As "water pill" (diuretic):* 20 to 80 mg in a single dose initially; if necessary, increase the dose by 20 to 40 mg every 6 to 8 hours. The smallest effective dose should be used. Daily maximum is 600 mg in treating severe edematous states—but the usual ongoing dose is 40–120 mg a day. Edema removal is often effectively accomplished using intermittent dosing schedules, such as use of furosemide 2 to 4 days in a row each week.

Note: Actual dose and schedule must be determined for each patient individually.

Conditions Requiring Dosing Adjustments
   Liver Function: Larger doses may be needed for patients with liver compromise, and extreme care must be used to maintain critical electrolytes.
   Kidney Function: Larger initial doses may be needed before any benefit is seen. Drug may cause kidney stones and protein in urine.
   Cystic Fibrosis: Patients with this disease may be more sensitive to the drug, and smaller starting doses are indicated.

▷ **Dosing Instructions:** The tablet may be crushed and taken with or following meals to reduce stomach irritation. Best taken in the morning to avoid nighttime urination. Be certain to measure the oral liquid with a measuring spoon. If you forget a dose: take the missed dose as soon as you remember it, unless it's nearly time for your next dose—if that is the case, skip the missed dose and take the next dose right on time. DO NOT double doses. Call your doctor if you find yourself having problems remembering to use this medicine.

Usual Duration of Use: Use on a regular schedule for 2 to 3 weeks may be required to see effectiveness in lowering high blood pressure. Long-term use (months to years) requires periodic physician evaluation of response. Some cases of mild hypertension may remain normal after therapy with furosemide, lowering blood pressure to goals and allowing gradual furosemide withdrawal.

Typical Treatment Goals and Measurements (Outcomes and Markers)

Blood Pressure: The NEW guidelines (JNC VII) define normal blood pressure (BP) as **less than** 120/80. Because blood pressures that were once considered acceptable can actually lead to blood vessel damage, the committee from the National Institutes of Health, National Heart, Lung and Blood Institute now have a new category called **Pre-hypertension**. This ranges from 120/80 to 139/89 and is intended to help your doctor encourage lifestyle changes (or in the case of people with a risk factor for high blood pressure, start treatment) much earlier so that possible damage to blood vessels, your heart, kidneys, sexual potency, or eyes might be minimized or avoided altogether. The next two classes of high blood pressure are stage 1 hypertension: 140/90 to 159/99, and stage 2 hypertension equal to or greater than: 160/100 mm Hg. These guidelines also recommend that clinicians trying to control blood pressure work with their patients to agree on the goals and a plan of treatment. The first-ever guidelines for blood pressure (hypertension) in African Americans recommend that MOST black patients be started on TWO antihypertensive medicines with the goal of lowering blood pressure to 130/80 for those with high risk for heart and blood vessel disease or with diabetes. The American Diabetes Association recommends 130/80 as the target for people living with diabetes and less than 125/75 for those who spill more than one gram of protein into their urine. Most clinicians try to achieve a BP that confers the best balance of lower cardiovascular risk and avoids the problem of too low a blood pressure. Blood pressure duration is generally increased with beneficial restriction of sodium. The goals and time frame should be discussed with you when the prescription is written. If goals are not met, it is not unusual to intensify doses or add on medicines. You can find the new blood pressure guidelines at *www.nhlbi.nih.gov/guidelines/hypertension/index.htm*. For the African American guidelines see Douglas, J.G. in Sources.

Congestive heart failure: Used to remove excessive fluid which builds up in the body. Typical treatment markers include resolution of ankle swelling and increased output of fluid (diuresis) as well as improved ease of breathing. Successful withdrawal of furosemide is possible in many elderly heart failure patients.

▷ **This Drug Should Not Be Taken If**
- you had an allergic reaction to it previously.
- you have extremely low potassium or sodium.
- your kidneys are not making urine.
- you have severe fluid depletion (hypovolemia) with or without excessively low blood pressure.
- you are in a coma caused by liver failure.

▷ **Inform Your Physician Before Taking This Drug If**
- you are allergic to any form of sulfa drug.
- you are pregnant or planning pregnancy.
- you have a history of kidney or liver disease.
- you have diabetes, gout or lupus erythematosus.
- you have impaired hearing.
- you have low blood potassium or other electrolytes (talk with your doctor).
- you take cortisone, digitalis, oral antidiabetic drugs, or insulin.
- you will have surgery with general anesthesia.

Possible Side Effects (natural, expected, and unavoidable drug actions)

Light-headedness on rising from sitting or lying position (see orthostatic hypotension in Glossary).

Increase in blood sugar level, affecting control of diabetes.

Increase in blood uric acid level, affecting control of gout.

Increased cholesterol (may be related to intravascular volume).

Decrease in blood potassium level, causing muscle weakness and cramping.

Decreased magnesium level.

▷ **Possible Adverse Effects** (unusual, unexpected, and infrequent reactions)
If any of the following develop, consult your physician promptly for guidance.

Mild Adverse Effects

Allergic reactions: skin rashes, hives, drug fever—case reports.

Headache, dizziness, blurred or yellow vision, ringing in ears, numbness and tingling—rare to infrequent.

Reduced appetite, indigestion, nausea, vomiting, diarrhea—possible.

Metabolic alkalosis—possible.

Serious Adverse Effects

Allergic reactions: hepatitis with jaundice (see Glossary), anaphylactic reaction (see Glossary), severe skin reactions—case reports.

Idiosyncratic reaction: fluid in lungs—case reports.

Temporary hearing loss—case reports.

Inflammation of the pancreas (severe abdominal pain)—rare.

Bone marrow depression (see Glossary): fatigue, weakness, fever, sore throat, abnormal bleeding or bruising—case reports.

Low blood pressure on standing or abnormal heartbeats (arrhythmias)—rare.

Drug-induced porphyria or excessive parathyroid gland action (hyperparathyroidism)—case reports.

Low blood potassium or magnesium—possible.

Vitamin deficiency (thiamine)—possible.

Kidney stones (calcium-containing)—case reports.

Liver toxicity (cholestatic jaundice)—rare.

Fever in infants—case reports.

Skin lesions (erythema multiforme or Stevens-Johnson Syndrome)—case reports.

Hip fractures (may increase risk).

▷ **Possible Effects on Sexual Function:** Impotence—infrequent.

▷ **Adverse Effects That May Mimic Natural Diseases or Disorders**

Liver reaction may suggest viral hepatitis.

Natural Diseases or Disorders That May Be Activated by This Drug

Diabetes, gout, systemic lupus erythematosus.

Possible Effects on Laboratory Tests

Complete blood counts: reduced red cells, hemoglobin, white cells, and platelets.

Blood amylase and lipase levels: increased (possible pancreatitis).

Blood sodium and chloride levels: decreased.

Blood levels of total cholesterol, LDL and VLDL cholesterol, and triglycerides: increased.

Blood glucose level: increased.

Glucose tolerance test (GTT): decreased tolerance.

Blood potassium or magnesium level: decreased.

Blood thyroid hormone (T3 and T4) levels: decreased.

Blood uric acid level or blood urea nitrogen (BUN): increased.

Urine sugar tests: no drug effect (Tes-Tape); false low (Clinistix, Diastix).

CAUTION
1. Take exactly the dose that was prescribed. Increased doses can cause serious loss of sodium and potassium, with resultant loss of appetite, nausea, fatigue, weakness, confusion, and tingling in the extremities.
2. If you take a digitalis preparation (digitoxin, digoxin), ensure an adequate intake of high potassium foods to prevent potassium deficiency. (See Table 13, High Potassium Foods, Section Six.) Magnesium is also important.
3. Intravenous furosemide should be replaced with oral dosing as soon as possible.

Precautions for Use
By Infants and Children: Significant potassium loss can occur within the first 2 weeks of drug use.

By Those Over 60 Years of Age: Small starting doses are critical. Increased risk of impaired thinking, orthostatic hypotension, potassium loss, and blood sugar increase. Overdose and extended use of this drug can cause excessive loss of body water, thickening (increased viscosity) of the blood and an increased tendency for the blood to clot, predisposing to stroke, heart attack, or thrombophlebitis (vein inflammation with blood clot).

▷ **Advisability of Use During Pregnancy**
Pregnancy Category: C. See Pregnancy Risk Categories at the back of this book.
Animal Studies: Significant birth defects have been reported.
Human Studies: Adequate studies of pregnant women are not available.
It should not be used during pregnancy unless a very serious complication occurs for which this drug is significantly beneficial. Avoid completely during the first 3 months. Ask your physician for guidance.

Advisability of Use If Breast-Feeding
Presence of this drug in breast milk: Yes.
Avoid drug or refrain from nursing.

Habit-Forming Potential: None.

Effects of Overdose: Dry mouth, thirst, lethargy, weakness, muscle cramping, nausea, vomiting, drowsiness progressing to stupor or coma.

Possible Effects of Long-Term Use: Impaired water, salt, magnesium, and potassium balance; dehydration and increased blood coagulability, with risk of blood clots.
Development of glucose intolerance or hyperglycemia in predisposed individuals.

Suggested Periodic Examinations While Taking This Drug (at physician's discretion)
Complete blood counts.
Measurements of blood levels of sodium, potassium, chloride, sugar, and uric acid.
Kidney and liver function tests.

▷ **While Taking This Drug, Observe the Following**
Foods: Ask your doctor if it would benefit you to eat foods rich in potassium. If so advised, see Table 13, High Potassium Foods, Section Six. Follow your physician's advice regarding the use of salt. Food decreases absorption of furosemide by up to 30%. Take this medicine 1 hour before or 2 hours after a meal.

Herbal Medicines or Minerals: Ginseng, guarana, eleuthero root, hawthorn, saw palmetto, ma huang, goldenseal, and licorice may also cause increased blood pressure. Couch grass may worsen edema due to heart or kidney problems. Indian snakeroot, calcium, and garlic may help lower blood pressure. CAUTION: St. John's wort may also lead to photosensitivity. Yohimbe may blunt the blood pressure–lowering benefits of this medicine. Magnesium levels should be checked and magnesium replaced if needed. Talk to your doctor BEFORE adding any herbal medicines or minerals.

Beverages: No restrictions. This drug may be taken with milk.

▷ *Alcohol:* Use with caution—alcohol may exaggerate the blood pressure–lowering effects of this drug and cause orthostatic hypotension.

Tobacco Smoking: No interactions expected. I advise everyone to quit smoking.

▷ *Other Drugs*

Furosemide may increase the effects of

- other antihypertensive drugs; dose adjustments may be necessary to prevent excessive lowering of blood pressure.
- digoxin (Lanoxin) and result in digoxin toxicity.
- lithium (Lithobid, others) and cause lithium toxicity.

Furosemide may *decrease* the effects of

- oral antidiabetic drugs (sulfonylureas); dose adjustments may be necessary for proper control of blood sugar.

Furosemide *taken concurrently with*

- activated charcoal (various) will blunt absorption of oral furosemide.
- adrenocortical steroids (see Drug Classes) may cause additive loss of potassium.
- amikacin, gentamicin, tobramycin, or other aminoglycosides may increase risk of hearing toxicity (ototoxicity).
- bepridil (Vascor) may lead to abnormal heart effects if potassium is low.
- cephalosporin antibiotics (see Drug Classes) may increase risk of kidney problems (nephrotoxicity).
- cholestyramine (Questran) may cause loss of furosemide effectiveness.
- clofibrate (Atromid-S) may lead to muscle stiffness and increased diuretic effects.
- colestipol (Colestid) may cause loss of furosemide effectiveness.
- cortisone (various corticosteroids) may lead to excessive potassium loss.
- cyclosporine (Sandimmune) may cause elevated uric acid levels (hyperuricemia) and gout.
- digitalis preparations (digitoxin, digoxin) require blood tests or dose changes to maintain potassium levels and avoid heart rhythm problems.
- lomefloxacin (Maxaquin) may increase lomefloxacin levels and lead to toxicity.
- metformin (Glucophage) may increase metformin and decrease furosemide effects.
- NSAIDs (see Drug Classes) may cause loss of diuretic effectiveness.
- phenytoin (Dilantin) or fosphenytoin (Cerebyx) may decrease furosemide diuretic effects.

▷ *Driving, Hazardous Activities:* Use caution until the possible occurrence of orthostatic hypotension, dizziness or impaired vision has been determined.

Aviation Note: The use of this drug *may be a disqualification* for piloting. Consult a designated Aviation Medical Examiner.

Exposure to Sun: Use caution—this drug may cause photosensitivity (see Glossary). See Herbal Medicines warning on St. John's wort above.

Exposure to Heat: Avoid excessive perspiring, which could cause additional loss of salt and water from the body.

Heavy Exercise or Exertion: Avoid exertion that produces light-headedness, excessive fatigue or muscle cramping. Ask your doctor for help about participation in exercise.

Occurrence of Unrelated Illness: Vomiting or diarrhea can produce a serious imbalance of important body chemistry. Ask your doctor for guidance.

Discontinuation: It may be best to discontinue this drug 5 to 7 days before major surgery. Ask your physician, surgeon and/or anesthesiologist for guidance regarding dose adjustment or drug withdrawal.

GABAPENTIN (GAB ah pen tin)

Introduced: 1981   **Class:**   Anticonvulsant, pain syndrome modifier, mood stabilizer   **Prescription:**   USA: Yes **Controlled Drug:** USA: No; Canada: No   **Available as Generic:**   USA: No; Canada: No

Brand Name: Neurontin

BENEFITS versus RISKS	
Possible Benefits	*Possible Risks*
ADJUNCTIVE THERAPY OF PARTIAL SEIZURES	Sleepiness
	Movement problems
EFFECTIVE TREATMENT OF A VARIETY OF PAIN SYNDROMES	
PREVENTION OF MIGRAINES	
MAY HAVE A ROLE AS A MOOD STABILIZER/ANXIOLYTIC	
May have a role in reducing symptoms of social phobia	

▷ **Principal Uses**

As a Single Drug Product: Uses currently included in FDA-approved labeling: (1) As an antiepileptic drug adjunctive to other medicines to control partial seizures; (2) treats postherpetic neuralgia pain in adults.

Other (unlabeled) generally accepted uses: (1) widely used in chronic pain syndromes, such as diabetic nerve damage (diabetic neuropathy); (2) may have a role in spasticity; (3) possible role in combination treatment of resistant bipolar disorder; (4) low-dose gabapentin eased spasms seen in multiple sclerosis in one study; (5) a small study found that gabapentin reduced symptoms of social phobia; (6) may be of help in essential tremor; (7) helps prevent migraines; (8) case reports of gabapentin easing difficult-to-treat hot flashes in prostate cancer cases; (9) one report of gabapentin easing nicotine addiction.

How This Drug Works: Similar in chemistry to an inhibitory substance called gamma-aminobutyric acid (GABA). Gabapentin appears to increase GABA levels in the brain. Works in preventing migraines by stabilizing actions of the nerves.

Available Dosage Forms and Strengths

Capsules — 100 mg, 300 mg, 400 mg

Oral solution — 250 mg/5 ml

Tablets — 100 mg, 300 mg, 400 mg, 600 mg and 800 mg

▷ **Usual Adult Dosage Ranges**

Seizures: Initially 300 mg 3 times a day. Dose may be increased to 900 mg a day by the third day. Doses up to 2,400 mg have been well tolerated and 3,600 mg used in some patients.

Pain syndromes: 100 mg a day, increased as needed and tolerated. Maximum doses are as those seen in seizure patients.

Postherpetic neuralgia: 300 mg on the first day followed by 300 mg twice a day on the second day and 300 mg 3 times daily on the third day. Further dosing is adjusted as needed and tolerated up to 600 mg 3 times a day.

Note: Actual dose and schedule must be determined for each patient individually.

Conditions Requiring Dosing Adjustments

Liver Function: Not changed by the liver. No dosing changes needed.

Kidney Function: 300 mg twice daily is given to those with a creatinine clearance of 30–60 ml/min. For creatinine clearance of 15–30 ml/min, 300 mg is given daily.

▷ **Dosing Instructions:** May be taken with or after food to reduce stomach irritation. The capsule may be opened, and the tablet may be crushed. The liquid should be measured with a measuring spoon or measuring dose cup. If you forget a dose: take the missed dose as soon as you remember it, unless it's nearly time for your next dose—if that is the case, skip the missed dose and take the next dose right on time. DO NOT double doses. Call your doctor if you find yourself having problems remembering this medicine or if you miss two doses.

Usual Duration of Use: Use on a regular schedule for 2 to 3 weeks usually determines benefit in reducing frequency and severity of seizures. Optimal control will require careful dose adjustments. Use in pain syndromes may take a similar time. Long-term use requires ongoing physician supervision.

Typical Treatment Goals and Measurements (Outcomes and Markers)

Pain: Most clinicians treating pain use a device called an algometer to check your pain. This looks like a small ruler, but lets the clinician better understand your pain. The goals of treatment then relate to where the level of pain started (for example, a rating of 7 on a 0 to 10 scale) and what the cause of the pain was. Pain medicines may also be used together (in combination) in order to get the best result or outcome. I use the PQRSTG method. If your pain control is not acceptable to YOU (remember, in hospitals and outpatient settings, etc. pain control is a patient right) and if after a week of pain treatment results are not acceptable, be sure to call your doctor as you may need a different medicine or combination.

▷ **This Drug Should Not Be Taken If**
- you have pancreatitis.
- you have had an allergic reaction to this drug.

▷ **Inform Your Physician Before Taking This Drug If**
- you are taking any other drugs at this time.
- you have a history of kidney disease or impaired kidney function.
- you are less than 12 years old (not studied).
- you have low blood pressure.

Possible Side Effects (natural, expected, and unavoidable drug actions)
Mild fatigue, sluggishness, drowsiness, dizziness—may be frequent.

▷ **Possible Adverse Effects** (unusual, unexpected, and infrequent reactions)
If any of the following develop, consult your physician promptly for guidance.
Mild Adverse Effects
Allergic reactions: skin rashes, hives—possible.
Acne—occasional.

Weight gain or loss—infrequent.

Accumulation of fluid in the ankles (edema)—infrequent.

Nausea, vomiting, constipation—infrequent.

Vision changes—infrequent.

Slurred speech—possible and more likely during the first three days after the medicine is started.

Purpura—may be frequent.

Lowering or increasing of blood pressure—infrequent.

Bed-wetting—case reports, mild and resolved with ongoing therapy.

Serious Adverse Effects

Allergic reactions: Severe skin rash (Stevens-Johnson Syndrome)—case reports.

Idiosyncratic reactions: none reported.

Seizures or paresthesia—case reports.

Disturbed mood (hostility, mania, labile emotions, and/or depression)—reported (case report for mania).

Amnesia—case reports.

Movement disorders (ataxia)—possible (case reports) and more likely in the first three days after starting therapy—careful follow-up for cogging is important.

Lowered white blood cell counts—rare.

Pancreatitis—case report.

▷ **Possible Effects on Sexual Function:** Impotence—rare. Swelling and tenderness of male breast tissue—gynecomastia—reported.

▷ **Adverse Effects That May Mimic Natural Diseases or Disorders**

Drug-induced hepatitis may suggest viral hepatitis.

Skin reactions may resemble lupus erythematosus.

Natural Diseases or Disorders That May Be Activated by This Drug

Partial seizures.

Possible Effects on Laboratory Tests

Complete blood cell counts: decreased white cells—rare.

CAUTION

1. When used for the treatment of epilepsy, **this drug must not be stopped abruptly.**
2. Taking this medicine exactly as prescribed is essential. Take this drug at the same time each day to help keep the blood level about the same.
3. Carry a personal identification card noting that you are taking this drug.

Precautions for Use

By Infants and Children: Not indicated unless 3 or older. Patients 3–12 for adjunctive partial seizure treatment are given 10–15 mg/kg of body weight per day. The total dose is divided into 3 equal doses and given 3 times a day.

By Those Over 60 Years of Age: You may be more sensitive to all of the actions of this drug and require smaller doses. Some clinicians start with 100 mg at bedtime and slowly increase the dose as needed and tolerated. Watch closely for any adverse effects: drowsiness, fatigue, confusion, "cogging" of arms, vision changes.

▷ **Advisability of Use During Pregnancy**

Pregnancy Category: C. See Pregnancy Risk Categories at the back of this book.

Human Studies: Information from adequate studies of pregnant women is not available. Discuss use of this drug during pregnancy with your doctor.

Advisability of Use If Breast-Feeding
Presence of this drug in breast milk: Unknown.
Monitor nursing infant closely and discontinue drug or nursing if adverse effects develop.

Habit-Forming Potential: None.

Effects of Overdose: Drowsiness, slurred speech, double vision, and diarrhea.

Possible Effects of Long-Term Use: None defined.

Suggested Periodic Examinations While Taking This Drug (at physician's discretion)
Checks of seizure control. Check for "cogging" of arms. For pain assessment, I use the PQRSTG method.

▷ **While Taking This Drug, Observe the Following**
Foods: No restrictions.
Herbal Medicines or Minerals: Ma huang and guarana may cause increased blood pressure and excessive sympathetic stimulation. Ginseng, eleuthero root, hawthorn, saw palmetto, goldenseal, and licorice may also cause increased blood pressure. Evening primrose oil may increase risk of seizures and should be avoided. Some forms of ginkgo have been found to contain a contaminant which is actually a neurotoxin (4'-O-methylpyridoxine). Prudent to avoid ginkgo unless each lot of the product can be checked for this contaminant.
Nutritional Support: None required.
Beverages: No restrictions. May be taken with milk.
▷ *Alcohol:* Use extreme caution. Alcohol (in large quantities or with continual use) may reduce effectiveness in preventing seizures.
Tobacco Smoking: No interactions expected. I advise everyone to quit smoking.
▷ *Other Drugs*
Gabapentin **taken concurrently** with
- antacids (various) may lower beneficial effects.
- cimetidine (Tagamet) may increase blood levels of gabapentin.
- morphine (various) may increase CNS side effects and increase gabapentin concentrations. Doses of either or both medicines should be lowered.
- naproxen (Anaprox, others) may increase gabapentin levels slightly.
- phenytoin (Dilantin) or fosphenytoin (Cerebyx) may lead to phenytoin or fosphenytoin toxicity.
- tramadol (Ultram) may increase seizure risk if gabapentin is being used to treat seizures.
▷ *Driving, Hazardous Activities:* This drug may impair mental alertness, vision, and coordination. Restrict activities as necessary.
Aviation Note: The use of this drug **is a disqualification** for piloting. Consult a designated Aviation Medical Examiner.
Exposure to Sun: No restrictions at present.
Discontinuation: **This drug must not be discontinued abruptly.** Sudden withdrawal can precipitate severe and repeated seizures. If this drug is to be discontinued, gradual reduction in dose should be made. Discuss this with your doctor.

GALANTAMINE (ga LAN tah meen)

Author's Note: please see the Anti-Alzheimer's Drug Family combination profile for further information.

GANCICLOVIR (gan SIGH klo veer)

Introduced: 1995 (tablet) **Class:** Antiviral **Prescription:**
USA: Yes **Controlled Drug:** USA: No; Canada: No **Available as**
Generic: USA: No; Canada: No
Brand Names: Cytovene, Vitrasert

Warning: The oral form of this medicine should be used only by patients who are not candidates for intravenous dosing and for whom the risk of more rapid cytomegalovirus (CMV) retinitis progression is outweighed by the benefit of avoiding the intravenous route.

BENEFITS versus RISKS

Possible Benefits	*Possible Risks*
Oral, intravenous or implanted treatment of cytomegalovirus (CMV) retinitis	More rapid progression of CMV disease (capsules)
Decreased side effects with the oral form	Bone marrow suppression
Transition to an oral form following intravenous induction	Reproductive toxicity (see "Infants and Children" section)
	Possible increased cancer risk (see "Infants and Children" section)

▷ **Principal Uses**

As a Single Drug Product: Uses currently included in FDA-approved labeling: (1) Treatment of cytomegalovirus (CMV) retinitis; (2) prevention of CMV retinitis in a variety of patients such as liver, kidney, lung, bone marrow and heart transplant patients; (3) implantation of the ocular implant into the diseased area—this form may work for 5 months or more; (4) prevention of CMV disease in patients with advanced HIV infection.

Other (unlabeled) generally accepted uses: (1) Treatment of pediatric CMV; (2) may have a role in treating Epstein-Barr virus infection; (3) can have a role in treating leukoplakia; (4) may help outer retinal necrosis; (5) could have a role in some acyclovir-resistant herpes simplex and varicella zoster virus.

How This Drug Works: Changed to an active (triphosphate) form in infected cells. The active form interferes with DNA and the survival of the virus. May be synergistic with some other antiviral medicines (such as foscarnet).

Available Dosage Forms and Strengths

Capsules — 250 mg, 500 mg
Intravenous — 500 mg/10 ml
Intravitreal insert — 4.5 mg

▷ **Recommended Dosage Ranges** (Actual dose and schedule must be determined for each patient individually.)

Infants and Children: **Author's Note: This drug has potential for reproductive toxicity and the risk of causing cancer. It is used in children only after careful evaluation of benefit to risk and with extreme caution.**

Induction: 2.5 mg per kg of body mass given intravenously three times daily.
Maintenance dose: 6.5 mg per kg of body mass given intravenously once daily 5 to 7 times a week.

12 to 60 Years of Age:
Induction: 5 mg per kg of body mass intravenously (infused over 1 hour) every 12 hours for 14 to 21 days.

Maintenance dose: 2.1 to 6 mg per kg of body mass infused into a vein over 1 hour each day. Some centers have used 6 mg per kg of body mass given once daily 5 days per week. If retinitis progresses, the patient can be restarted on the twice-daily-dosing approach. Maximum dose is 6 mg per kg of body mass infused over 1 hour.

Oral: Once the intravenous induction dosing has been accomplished, oral ganciclovir is given at 1,000 mg 3 times daily. Some centers have opted for 500 mg 6 times per day, given every 3 hours while the patient is awake. If retinitis progresses, intravenous induction therapy should be given.

Intravitreous: This device is surgically implanted and has been effective for 5 or more months. Use not established in patients younger than 9.

Over 60 Years of Age: Kidney function must be checked, and the dose appropriately adjusted.

Conditions Requiring Dosing Adjustments

Liver Function: The liver is only minimally involved in the elimination of this drug, and dosing changes in liver compromise are not needed.

Kidney Function: The dose must be decreased in kidney compromise. This adjustment is accomplished based on creatinine clearance (see Glossary).

Induction: 5 mg per kg of body mass every 12 hours (70 ml/min or higher); 2.5 mg per kg of body mass every 12 hours (50–69); 2.5 mg per kg of body mass every 24 hours (25–49); 1.25 mg per kg of body mass every 24 hours (10–24); 1.25 mg per kg of body mass 3 times per week (less than 10).

Maintenance: 5 mg per kg of body mass every 24 hours (70 ml/min or higher); 2.5 mg per kg of body mass every 24 hours (50–69); 1.25 mg per kg of body mass every 24 hours (25–49); 0.625 mg per kg of body mass every 24 hours (10–24); 0.625 mg per kg of body mass 3 times per week (less than 10).

▷ **Dosing Instructions:** This medicine should be taken with food if taken by mouth (orally). It is best to take the medicine at the same time each day. Capsule form should not be opened or crushed, because you may have adverse reactions from the toxic powder. If you are taking the capsule form and your vision declines, call your doctor immediately. If you miss a dose: take it as soon as you remember it, unless it's nearly time for your next dose—if that is the case, skip the missed dose and return to taking the medicine on your usual schedule. DO NOT double doses. Call your doctor if you miss more than one dose.

Usual Duration of Use: Continual use on a regular schedule for up to 16 days is usually needed to determine this drug's effectiveness in treating retinitis. Because of a very high frequency of relapse, most centers recommend ongoing maintenance therapy for life. If patients have an ongoing (durable) response to combination antiretroviral therapy (HAART) and CD4 cells improve to more than 100–150 per microliter for more than 6 months, some centers have stopped this medicine. Long-term use (months to years) requires periodic evaluation of response and dose adjustment. The ocular implant form may work for 5 months or more. Keep your follow-up appointments with your doctor.

Typical Treatment Goals and Measurements (Outcomes and Markers)

CMV infections: Goals for treatment of CMV include response to the treatment and avoidance of bone marrow depression and kidney problems. Markers for the infection itself include eyesight improvement, eye exam for retinopathy, slit lamp tests, and eye pressure. Additionally, many patients have been found to gain weight and improve albumin levels.

Possible Advantages of This Drug
> Transition from the intravenous form to the oral form (if successful in treatment) offers a clear quality-of-life advantage.

Currently a "Drug of Choice"
> For patients with liver failure and CMV.

▷ **This Drug Should Not Be Taken If**
- you had an allergic reaction to it previously.
- your absolute neutrophil count (a specific kind of white blood cell) is less than 500 per cubic mm.
- your platelet count is less than 25,000 per cubic mm.

▷ **Inform Your Physician Before Taking This Drug If**
- you think you are dehydrated (this drug is primarily removed by the kidneys).
- you have a sore throat or fever.
- you have a history of blood cell disorders.
- you are planning pregnancy.
- you are male and are planning pregnancy (attempted conception should be avoided for at least 3 months after ganciclovir therapy).
- you are uncertain of how much ganciclovir to take, how often to take it, how to handle the intravenous solution or if you have the insert form and your vision has not cleared in 14 days.
- you take other prescription or nonprescription medicines that were not discussed with your doctor when ganciclovir was prescribed. This includes natural extracts or herbal remedies and "underground" therapies for AIDS.

Possible Side Effects (natural, expected, and unavoidable drug actions)
> Pain at the injection site with the IV form. Possible phlebitis. Visual acuity loss for the first 60 days after the insert form is put in (up to 20% of people lose 3 lines or more).

▷ **Possible Adverse Effects** (unusual, unexpected, and infrequent reactions)
> **If any of the following develop, consult your physician promptly for guidance.**

Mild Adverse Effects
> Allergic reactions: skin rash and itching.
> Confusion, headache, nervousness, tremor, somnolence, abnormal dreams, ataxia, "pins-and-needles" sensations of the hands (paresthesias)—infrequent.
> Muscle aches—rare.
> Fever—may be frequent with oral therapy.
> Decreased blood glucose or potassium—rare.
> Nausea, vomiting, or diarrhea—infrequent to frequent.

Serious Adverse Effects
> Allergic reactions: anaphylactic reaction—case reports.
> Bone marrow suppression—rare.
> Lowered white blood cell (neutropenia) counts—frequent.
> Lowered blood platelets—infrequent.
> Arrhythmias—rare.
> Coma, psychosis or seizures—case reports.
> Neuropathy—infrequent to frequent.
> Liver toxicity—rare to infrequent.
> Retinal detachment—infrequent.
> Visual decline—infrequent to frequent with intravitreal implant.
> This drug is a potential cancer-causing (carcinogenic) agent—no percentage defined.

▷ **Possible Effects on Sexual Function:** Reversible infertility in men.

Possible Delayed Adverse Effects: Lowered white blood cell counts or platelets.

▷ **Adverse Effects That May Mimic Natural Diseases or Disorders**
Increased liver enzymes may mimic hepatitis.

Natural Diseases or Disorders That May Be Activated by This Drug
None defined.

Possible Effects on Laboratory Tests
Liver enzymes: increased.
Serum bilirubin or creatinine: increased.
Blood glucose, platelets or white blood cells: decreased.

CAUTION
1. The oral form may be less effective than the intravenous form. Call your doctor immediately if your vision declines.
2. May cause bone marrow suppression. Call your doctor if you get a sore throat, start to bruise easily or develop fever.

Precautions for Use
By Infants and Children: Safety and effectiveness for use by those under `18 years of age have not been established. The drug has been used selectively in patients as young as 36 weeks.
By Those Over 60 Years of Age: Because of the age-related decline in kidney function, a creatinine clearance should be obtained and dosing adjusted appropriately.

▷ **Advisability of Use During Pregnancy**
Pregnancy Category: C. See Pregnancy Risk Categories at the back of this book.
Animal Studies: Rabbits have developed cleft palate, exhibited poorly developed organs, and have experienced fetal death.
Human Studies: Information from adequate studies of pregnant women is not available.
Use of this drug during pregnancy is not recommended.

Advisability of Use If Breast-Feeding
Presence of this drug in breast milk: Unknown.
HIV may be present in breast milk. Avoid drug or refrain from nursing.

Habit-Forming Potential: None.

Effects of Overdose: Nausea and vomiting, excessive salivation, increased liver function tests, bone marrow suppression, kidney failure.

Possible Effects of Long-Term Use: Not defined.

Suggested Periodic Examinations While Taking This Drug (at physician's discretion)
Platelet counts and complete blood counts: every 2 days during induction and weekly thereafter.
Liver function tests: monthly.
Kidney function tests: every 2 weeks.
Eye (ophthalmologic) exams: weekly during induction and every 2 weeks thereafter. These exams may be needed more frequently if the optic nerve or macula of the eye is involved.

▷ **While Taking This Drug, Observe the Following**
Foods: No restrictions—the oral form should be taken with food.
Herbal Medicines or Minerals: Some patients use echinacea to attempt to boost their immune systems. Unfortunately, use of echinacea is not recommended in people with damaged immune systems. This herb may also

actually weaken any immune system if it is used too often or for too long a time. **Caution:** St. John's wort may also cause extreme reactions to the sun. Additive photosensitivity may be possible.

Beverages: No restrictions.

▷ *Alcohol:* No restrictions; however, alcohol may blunt the immune system.

Tobacco Smoking: No interactions expected. I advise everyone to quit smoking.

Marijuana Smoking: May increase somnolence.

▷ *Other Drugs*

Ganciclovir *taken concurrently* with

- amphotericin B (Fungizone, Abelcet) may result in increased bone marrow suppression.
- cancer chemotherapy may result in additive bone marrow suppression.
- cotrimoxazole (Septra) may result in added bone marrow suppression problems.
- cyclosporine (Sandimmune) can result in increased kidney toxicity.
- dapsone is a benefit-to-risk decision, as additive bone marrow suppression may occur.
- didanosine (Videx) can result in increased risk of didanosine toxicity (pancreatitis, nerve damage (neuropathy) or diarrhea.
- flucytosine (Ancobon) can cause additive bone marrow toxicity.
- imipenem/cilastatin (Primaxin) can cause seizures.
- pentamidine may result in additive bone marrow suppression.
- tacrolimus (Prograf) can result in increased risk of kidney toxicity.
- zidovudine (AZT) will often cause a serious increase in bone marrow suppression.

The following drug may *increase* the effects of ganciclovir:

- probenecid (Benemid)—by interfering with elimination by the kidney.

▷ *Driving, Hazardous Activities:* This drug may cause somnolence. Restrict activities as necessary.

Aviation Note: The use of this drug *may be a disqualification* for piloting. Consult a designated Aviation Medical Examiner.

Exposure to Sun: Caution is advised. Photosensitivity has been reported (with IV or oral use). See Herbal Medicines caution on St. John's wort above.

Discontinuation: Talk with your doctor before stopping this medicine.

Special Storage Instructions: Store the intravenous form at 39 degrees F. (4 degrees C.) and use within 12 hours after it has been reconstituted.

Observe the Following Expiration Times: The intravenous form will be stamped or labeled with a specific expiration time if this has been provided by a home infusion company; it should be used within 12 hours after it has been reconstituted.

GEMFIBROZIL (jem FI broh zil)

Introduced: 1976 **Class:** Anticholesterol **Prescription:** USA: Yes **Controlled Drug:** USA: No; Canada: No **Available as Generic:** USA: Yes; Canada: Yes

Brand Names: ✤Apo-Gemfibrozil, Gemcor, ✤Gem-Gemfibrozil, Lopid, ✤Med-Gemfibrozil, ✤Novo-Gemfibrozil, ✤PMS-Gemfibrozil, ✤Riva-Gemfibrozil

---

BENEFITS versus RISKS

Possible Benefits	*Possible Risks*
EFFECTIVE REDUCTION OF TRIGLYCERIDE BLOOD LEVELS	Possible myopathy or rhabdomyolysis
INCREASE IN HIGH-DENSITY LIPOPROTEIN (HDL) BLOOD LEVELS	
REDUCES RISK OF CORONARY HEART DISEASE	

▷ **Principal Uses**

As a Single Drug Product: Uses currently included in FDA-approved labeling: (1) Reduces abnormally high blood levels of triglycerides in Types IV and V blood lipid (fat) disorders or Type IIb patients who do not have symptoms or history of existing heart disease (coronary); (2) decreases risk for developing coronary artery heart disease.

Other (unlabeled) generally accepted uses: Could lower the risk of stroke in people with decreased HDL.

How This Drug Works: Reduces triglycerides by inhibiting the liver from making them. Reduces secretion of VLDL and LDL and inhibits VLDL carrier apoproteins. Decreases triglycerides by interfering with liver (hepatic) extraction of free fatty acids and also inhibits peripheral lipolysis. Increases HDL production and does so more than clofibrate. Also appears to increase liver production of more desirable kinds of HDL (small HDL particles).

Available Dosage Forms and Strengths

Capsules — 300 mg

Tablets — 600 mg

▷ **Usual Adult Dosage Ranges:** 1,200 to 1,600 mg daily in two divided doses (30 minutes before the morning and evening meals). The average dose is 1,200 mg daily. Dose increases should be made gradually over a period of 2 to 3 months. These doses improve lipids and appear to offer a 34% decrease in coronary heart disease after the second year of treatment. **Note: Actual dose and schedule must be determined for each patient individually.**

Conditions Requiring Dosing Adjustments

Liver Function: This drug should not be taken (is contraindicated) in primary biliary cirrhosis and severe liver failure.

Kidney Function: For patients with moderate kidney failure (GFR 10–50 ml/min), 50% of the usual dose should be taken at the usual interval. Patients with severe kidney failure should take 25% of the usual dose at the usual dosing interval.

▷ **Dosing Instructions:** The capsule may be opened and taken 30 minutes before the morning and evening meals. If you forget a dose: take it as soon as you remember it, unless it's nearly time for your next dose—if that is the case, skip the missed dose and return to taking the medicine on your usual schedule. DO NOT double doses. Call your doctor if you find yourself missing doses.

Usual Duration of Use: Regular use for 4 to 8 weeks determines effectiveness in reducing triglycerides. Results in reducing coronary heart disease showed up during the second year of treatment in one study. Long-term use (months to years) requires periodic evaluation by your doctor.

Typical Treatment Goals and Measurements (Outcomes and Markers)

Cholesterol: The National Institutes of Health Adult Treatment Panel has released ATP III as part of the update to the National Cholesterol Education Program, or NCEP. Key points in these new guidelines include acknowledging diabetes as one of the conditions that increases risk of heart disease, modifying risk factors, therapeutic lifestyle changes (TLC) and recommending routine testing for all of the cholesterol fractions (lipoprotein profile) versus total cholesterol alone.

Current NCEP guidelines recommend a desirable total cholesterol of 200 mg/dl, and optimal bad cholesterol (LDL) as 100 mg/dl, 130–159 mg/dl as borderline high, 160 mg/dl as high and 190 mg/dl as very high. Did you know that there are at least five different kinds of "good cholesterol," or HDL? The "too low" measure for HDL is still 40 mg/dl, but in order to learn more about cholesterol types, some doctors are starting to order lipid panels. There are at least seven different kinds of "bad cholesterol." The new panels tell doctors about the kinds of cholesterol that your body makes. This is important because some kinds (small, dense particles) tend to stick to blood vessels (are highly atherogenic). Take your medicine to reach your goals!

Two additional tests you will hear about will be electron beam computed tomography (EBCT) and CRP. EBCT is an important tool used in conjunction with laboratory studies. Findings show that even patients who meet cholesterol goals (particularly females over 55) can still be at significant cardiovascular risk. EBCT then defines risk by giving a calcium score and a "virtual tour" of the coronary arteries. C Reactive Protein, or CRP, is a new and apparently independent predictor of heart disease risk. A large study (see Ridker, P.M. in Sources) found that CRP predicted heart disease risk independently of bad cholesterol (low density lipoprotein).

Talk to your doctor about this new laboratory test and ask about current guidelines for who should be tested (see Pearson, T.A. in Sources).

Possible Advantages of This Drug

Stronger effect than other fibrates in increasing HDL, decreased risk of death (mortality) from non-heart (noncardiac) causes than other fibric acids. Does not appear to increase homocysteine levels like fenofibrate.

▷ This Drug Should Not Be Taken If

- you have had an allergic reaction to it previously.
- you have biliary cirrhosis of the liver or liver disease.
- you have gallbladder disease.
- you have severe kidney compromise.

▷ Inform Your Physician Before Taking This Drug If

- you have impaired liver or kidney function.
- you have gallbladder disease or gallstones.
- you are a diabetic.
- you are obese and increased exercise and diet have not been attempted.
- you have a type IIa cholesterol problem and only have high LDL.
- you are taking an anticoagulant medicine.
- you have an underactive thyroid (hypothyroidism).

Possible Side Effects (natural, expected, and unavoidable drug actions)

Moderate increase in blood sugar levels.

▷ **Possible Adverse Effects** (unusual, unexpected, and infrequent reactions)
 If any of the following develop, consult your physician promptly for guidance.

Mild Adverse Effects
 Allergic reactions: skin rash, hives, itching.
 Headache, dizziness, blurred vision, fatigue, muscle aches and cramps—infrequent.
 Indigestion, excessive gas, stomach discomfort, nausea, vomiting, diarrhea—rare to infrequent.
 Paresthesias—very rare.

Serious Adverse Effects
 Abnormally low white blood cell count: fever, chills, sore throat—rare.
 Formation of gallstones with long-term use—possible.
 Low blood potassium—possible.
 Raynaud's phenomenon—case report.
 Liver toxicity—possible.
 Myopathy (muscle weakness) or rhabdomyolysis (inability to walk)—case reports to rare.
 Kidney failure with muscle damage (rhabdomyolysis with renal failure)—case reports.

▷ **Possible Effects on Sexual Function:** Decreased libido or impotence—rare to infrequent.

Natural Diseases or Disorders That May Be Activated by This Drug
 Latent diabetes, latent urinary tract infections.

Possible Effects on Laboratory Tests
 Complete blood counts: decreased red cells, hemoglobin, white cells, and platelets.
 Blood HDL cholesterol levels: increased.
 Blood triglyceride levels: decreased.
 Liver function tests: increased liver enzymes (ALT/GPT, AST/GOT, and alkaline phosphatase), increased bilirubin.

CAUTION
 1. Gemfibrozil is used only after diet has NOT worked to lower triglyceride levels.
 2. If you used the drug clofibrate (Atromid-S) in the past, tell your physician fully about how this worked or affected you.
 3. Periodic triglyceride and cholesterol levels are critical.

Precautions for Use
 By Infants and Children: Safety and effectiveness for those under 12 years of age are not established.
 By Those Over 60 Years of Age: Watch for increased tendency to infection; treat all infections promptly.

▷ **Advisability of Use During Pregnancy**
 Pregnancy Category: C. See Pregnancy Risk Categories at the back of this book.
 Animal Studies: Produces adverse effects in rabbits and rats.
 Human Studies: Adequate studies of pregnant women are not available.
 Ask your physician for guidance.

Advisability of Use If Breast-Feeding
 Presence of this drug in breast milk: Yes.
 Avoid drug or refrain from nursing.

Habit-Forming Potential: None.

Effects of Overdose: Abdominal pain, nausea, vomiting, diarrhea.

Possible Effects of Long-Term Use: Formation of gallstones.

Suggested Periodic Examinations While Taking This Drug (at physician's discretion)

    Complete blood cell counts (during the first year of treatment then periodically) and liver function tests.

    Measurements of blood levels of total cholesterol, HDL and LDL cholesterol fractions, triglycerides, and sugar.

▷ **While Taking This Drug, Observe the Following**

    Foods: Follow the diet prescribed by your physician. Your doctor may also recommend some specific foods such as increased vegetables or functional foods such as Benecol. Three well-designed studies published in early April 2002 found that both in women and men and before and after a heart attack, people who ate more fish (2–4 servings a week) appeared to avoid heart disease. Additionally, putting supplements containing Omega 3 polyunsaturated fatty acids (PUFA) into the diet also appeared to protect against abnormal heart rhythms and sudden death from heart attack. The studies appeared in *JAMA, Circulation* and the *New England Journal of Medicine.*

    Herbal Medicines or Minerals: No data exist from well-designed clinical studies about garlic and gemfibrozil combinations and cannot presently be recommended. The FDA allowed one dietary supplement called Cholestin to continue to be sold. This preparation actually contains lovastatin. Since use of an HMG-CoA inhibitor with gemfibrozil may increase risk of rhabdomyolysis or myopathy, the combination is NOT advised. Talk to your doctor before combining any herbal products with this medicine.

    Beverages: No restrictions. May be taken with milk.

▷   *Alcohol:* No interactions expected.

    Tobacco Smoking: No interactions expected. I advise everyone to quit smoking.

▷   *Other Drugs*

    Gemfibrozil *taken concurrently* with

    • ezetimibe (Zetia) may risk muscle damage or rhabdomyolysis. Combination is not recommended, but if combined, careful monitoring and CK levels are required.

    • ritonavir (Norvir) may risk gemfibrozil toxicity.

    Gemfibrozil may *increase* the effects of

    • glyburide (Micronase) and other oral antidiabetic drugs (see Drug Classes).

    • lovastatin and other HMG-CoA-type drugs (see Drug Classes), which may increase muscle damage risk (myopathy) if taken at the same time.

    • warfarin (Coumadin) and increase the risk of bleeding; increased frequency of INR (prothrombin time, or protime) measurements and dose changes based on results are critical.

    Gemfibrozil may *decrease* the effects of

    • chenodiol (Chenix), reducing its benefit in gallstone therapy.

    • colestipol (Colestid); separate doses by two hours.

▷   *Driving, Hazardous Activities:* This drug may cause dizziness and blurred vision. Restrict activities as necessary.

    Aviation Note: The use of this drug *is usually not a disqualification* for piloting. Consult a designated Aviation Medical Examiner.

    Exposure to Sun: No restrictions.

    Discontinuation: If triglyceride-lowering does not occur after 3 months, this drug should be stopped.

GLIMEPIRIDE (glim EP er ide)

Introduced: 1996 **Class:** Antidiabetic, sulfonylureas **Prescription:** USA: Yes **Controlled Drug:** USA: No **Available as Generic:** No

Brand Name: Amaryl

BENEFITS versus RISKS
Possible Benefits

TIGHTER CONTROL OF BLOOD
 SUGAR (added to by appropriate
 diet and weight control)
DECREASED RISK OF HEART
 DISEASE, KIDNEY DISEASE,
 ETC., BY ATTAINING TIGHTER
 CONTROL OF BLOOD SUGAR
ONCE-A-DAY DOSING
DECREASED RISK OF INCREASED
 INSULIN LEVELS
DECREASED RISK OF
 HYPOGLYCEMIA
MAY BE COMBINED WITH
 METFORMIN IF BLOOD SUGAR
 GOALS ARE NOT ACHIEVED
 WITH SINGLE MEDICINE
 TREATMENT
MAY BE USED IN COMBINATION
 WITH INSULIN IN SECONDARY
 FAILURE
Inhibits platelet aggregation and
 probably decreases risk of
 abnormal clots

Possible Risks

Allergic skin reactions
Possible increased risk of heart
 (cardiovascular) mortality

▷ **Principal Uses**

As a Single Drug Product: Uses currently included in FDA-approved labeling: (1) Used in type 2 diabetes (adult, maturity-onset) not requiring insulin, but not adequately controlled by diet alone; (2) approved for combination use with insulin or metformin if diet and exercise and this drug are not adequate and in secondary failures (USED WITH INSULIN).

Other (unlabeled) generally accepted uses: None at present.

How This Drug Works: This drug (1) stimulates insulin secretion from the pancreas; (2) enhances use of insulin by tissues (increased sensitivity); and (3) binds to a receptor on the pancreas (beta cell sulfonylurea-inhibiting K-ATP) and activating the L-type calcium channel. Glimepiride works on platelets to inhibit collagen and ADP-caused aggregation. The effect possibly lowers blood vessel complications such as blood clots. One study showed a beneficial effect on Homocysteine and LP(a), but the cause and effect relationship is uncertain.

Available Dosage Forms and Strengths

Tablets — 1 mg, 2 mg, 3 mg (Switzerland), 4 mg, 6 mg

▷ **Usual Adult Dosage Ranges:** Started with 1 or 2 mg once daily, with breakfast or the first meal. Once a dose of 2 mg is reached, further dose increases should be made at 1- to 2-week intervals in increments of no more than 2 mg; the maximum daily dose is 8 mg. Typical ongoing doses have ranged from 1 to 4 mg a day. If target blood sugar goals are not met, combination treatment with metformin (glucophage) can be started. The minimum effective dose of both medicines should be used. In patients who fail treatment with an oral blood sugar–lowering agent, consideration is given to combined glimepiride and insulin therapy. If fasting blood sugar (glucose) is greater than 150 mg/dl and insulin/glimepiride is used, 8 mg is taken with the first main meal. Low-dose insulin is started and adjusted as needed/tolerated weekly based on blood sugar and A1C results.

Note: Actual dose and schedule must be determined for each patient individually.

Conditions Requiring Dosing Adjustments

Liver Function: Starting dose is 1 mg daily in mild liver failure. Further dose changes are based on results of blood sugar testing. No data on use in more severe liver compromise.

Kidney Function: Starting dose is 1 mg daily. Further dose changes are based on results of blood sugar testing.

▷ **Dosing Instructions:** The tablet may be crushed. Follow closely doctor's instructions about dosing and diet. If meals are skipped, hypoglycemia may result. Know the signs and symptoms of hypoglycemia (such as confusion, drowsiness, shakiness, weakness, hunger, blurred vision, headache, and fast heartbeat).

Usual Duration of Use: Use on a regular schedule for 1 to 2 weeks determines effectiveness in controlling diabetes. Failure to respond to maximal doses within 1 month constitutes a primary failure. Insulin or metformin may then be combined with glimepiride to reach blood sugar goals. Blood sugars must be measured, and your doctor will decide if the drug should be continued. If you forget a dose: take it as soon as you remember it, unless it's nearly time for your next dose—if that is the case, skip the missed dose and return to taking the medicine on your usual schedule. DO NOT double doses. Call your doctor if you find yourself missing doses. There are reminder services (beeper-based) that can help.

Typical Treatment Goals and Measurements (Outcomes and Markers)

Blood sugar: The general goal for blood sugar is to return it to the usual "normal" range (generally 80–120 mg/dl), while avoiding risks of excessively low blood sugar. One study (UKPDS) used a fasting plasma sugar (glucose) of less than 108 mg/dl. This medicine generally decreases fasting blood sugar by 60 mg per deciliter.

Fructosamine and glycosylated hemoglobin: Fructosamine levels (a measure of the past 2 to 3 weeks of blood sugar control) should be less than or equal to 310 micromoles per liter. Glycosylated hemoglobin or hemoglobin A1C (a measure of the past 2–3 months of blood sugar control) should be less than or equal to 7.0%. Some clinicians advocate A1C of 6.5%. This medicine generally decreases A1C by 1.5 to 2%.

Possible Advantages of This Drug

Effective with once-daily dosing.

May be less likely to cause excessive lowering of the blood sugar (hypoglycemia).

May cause less excessive insulin in the bloodstream (hyperinsulinemia).

May be combined with insulin in secondary failure. Works on platelets to inhibit aggregation, and probably decreases the risk of blood vessel (vascular) complications.

May beneficially change homocysteine and Lp(a) [risk factors for heart disease), but the direct effect of the medicine in the study that found this result is uncertain.

▷ **This Drug Should Not Be Taken If**
  • you have had an allergic reaction to it previously.
  • you have diabetic ketoacidosis (insulin is the drug of choice).

▷ **Inform Your Physician Before Taking This Drug If**
  • you are allergic to other sulfonylurea drugs or to sulfa drugs.
  • you have been experiencing prolonged vomiting.
  • you are pregnant or are breast-feeding your infant.
  • you do not know how to recognize or treat hypoglycemia (see Glossary).
  • you will have surgery or have had trauma.
  • you have a history of congestive heart failure, peptic ulcer disease, cirrhosis of the liver, kidney disease, or hypothyroidism.
  • your blood sugar starts to trend upward (may be a sign of secondary failure).
  • you are malnourished or have a high fever, infection, or pituitary or adrenal insufficiency.

Possible Side Effects (natural, expected, and unavoidable drug actions)
Hypoglycemia will occur if drug dose is excessive or if meals are missed or inadequate. The risk of hypoglycemia may be increased if this medicine is combined with insulin.

▷ **Possible Adverse Effects** (unusual, unexpected, and infrequent reactions)
If any of the following develop, consult your physician promptly for guidance.
Mild Adverse Effects
Allergic reactions: skin rash, hives, itching (may subside over time).
Headache, dizziness, or blurred vision—rare.
Nausea—rare.
Increased liver enzymes—infrequent.
Serious Adverse Effects
Allergic reactions: not reported to date.
Lowering of sodium—case reports.
Low blood sugar (hypoglycemia)—possible.

▷ **Possible Effects on Sexual Function:** None reported. Diabetes is a possible cause of impotence.

▷ **Adverse Effects That May Mimic Natural Diseases or Disorders**
Increased liver enzymes may suggest viral hepatitis.

Possible Effects on Laboratory Tests
Hemoglobin A1C (glycosylated hemoglobin): trending toward normal if tight control of blood sugar has been achieved.
Glycated hemoglobin (fructosamine) checks will trend toward normal.
Blood glucose levels: decreased.
Liver function tests: increased liver enzymes (ALT/GPT, AST/GOT, and alkaline phosphatase), increased bilirubin.

CAUTION
  1. This drug is only one part of a diabetes program. It is not a substitute for a proper diet and regular exercise.

2. Over time (usually several months) this drug may not work. Periodic follow-up examinations are mandatory.

3. Checking your blood sugar by getting blood from your finger or forearm has become a standard of care. A new device called a GlucoWatch is also available. (See the new Table 18: Patient Power and Home Test Kits.)

4. The American Diabetic Association (ADA) now says that a person is considered diabetic if two fasting blood sugars in a row are more than 125 mg/dl. This more conservative approach reflects new information saying that complications start at lower blood sugar levels than previously thought. The concept of Pre-diabetes (formerly impaired glucose tolerance) is described in the Glossary. Some new British data advocate that statin-type medicines could cut the risk of heart attack and stroke by a third (even in people with "normal" cholesterol)—yet these medicines are underused in diabetics. Talk to your doctor about this.

Precautions for Use

By Infants and Children: Safety and effectiveness in pediatrics have not been established.

By Those Over 60 Years of Age: Use with caution, and start with 1 mg/day. Dose should be increased slowly as needed and tolerated and glucose checked often. Repeated hypoglycemia in the elderly can cause brain damage.

▷ Advisability of Use During Pregnancy

Pregnancy Category: C. See Pregnancy Risk Categories at the back of this book.

Human Studies: Adequate studies of pregnant women are not available.

Because uncontrolled blood sugar levels during pregnancy are dangerous for the fetus, many experts recommend insulin instead of an oral agent.

Advisability of Use If Breast-Feeding

Presence of this drug in breast milk: Yes, in animal data; unknown in humans.

Avoid drug or refrain from nursing.

Habit-Forming Potential: None.

Effects of Overdose: Symptoms of mild to severe hypoglycemia: headache, light-headedness, faintness, nervousness, confusion, tremor, sweating, heart palpitation, weakness, hunger, nausea, vomiting, stupor progressing to coma.

Possible Effects of Long-Term Use: Reports of increased frequency and severity of heart and blood vessel diseases with long-term use of this class of drugs are highly controversial and inconclusive. A direct cause-and-effect relationship (see Glossary) is tenuous—yet all carry this boxed warning. Ask your doctor for help.

Suggested Periodic Examinations While Taking This Drug (at physician's discretion)

Hemoglobin A1C and/or fructosamine.

Liver function tests.

Evaluation of heart and circulatory system.

Blood sugar levels (via finger sticks and periodic lab checks).

▷ While Taking This Drug, Observe the Following

Foods: Follow the diabetic diet and portion control. Rice bran has been checked in a small (57-subject) study of type 1 and type 2 diabetics. The benefit was a 30% lowering of sugar. This might be a new complementary care option.

Herbal Medicines or Minerals: Using chromium may change the way your body is able to use sugar. Some health food stores advocate vanadium as mimicking the actions of insulin, but possible toxicity and need for rigorous studies presently preclude recommending it. Caution: St. John's wort may lower blood sugar and also cause photosensitivity, and this drug may also have these effects. Caution is advised in overlapping.

DHEA may change sensitivity to insulin or insulin resistance. Fenugreek, aloe, bitter melon, hawthorn, ginger, garlic, ginseng, glucomannan, guar gum, licorice, nettle, and yohimbe may change blood sugar. Since this may require adjustment of hypoglycemic medicine dosing, talk to your doctor BEFORE combining any herbal medicines with this medicine. Echinacea pupurea (injectable) and blonde psyllium seed or husk should NOT be taken by people living with diabetes. Psyllium increases risk of excessively low blood sugar. Surprisingly, boiled stems of the prickly pear cactus (Optuntia streptacantha) appear to be able to lower blood sugar. Ongoing effects and effects on A1C are not known. Red sage is used for blood sugar effects, but is unproven. Rice bran has been checked in a small study of type 1 and type 2 diabetics. The benefit was a 30% lowering of sugar. This might be a new complementary care option.

Beverages: As directed in the diabetic diet. May be taken with milk.

▷ *Alcohol:* Use with extreme caution—alcohol can prolong this drug's hypoglycemic effect. Other drugs in this class can also cause a disulfiramlike reaction (see Glossary).

Tobacco Smoking: No interactions expected. I advise everyone to quit smoking.

▷ *Other Drugs*

The following drugs may ***increase*** the effects of glimepiride:
- aspirin and other salicylates.
- chloramphenicol.
- cotrimoxazole (Septra).
- fenfluramine (Pondimin).
- miconazole (Lotrimin).
- monoamine oxidase (MAO) type A inhibitors (see Drug Classes).
- NSAIDs (see Drug Classes).
- probenecid (SK-Probenecid).
- sulfa drugs such as Septra.

The following drugs may ***decrease*** the effects of glimepiride:
- beta-blocker drugs (see Drug Classes).
- bumetanide (Bumex).
- diazoxide (Proglycem).
- ethacrynic acid (Edecrin).
- furosemide (Lasix).
- phenothiazines (see Drug Classes).
- phenytoin (Dilantin) or fosphenytoin (Cerebyx).
- rifampin (Rifadin, others).
- steroids (betamethasone, prednisone, others).
- thiazide diuretics (see Drug Classes).

Glimepiride ***taken concurrently*** with
- antacids (magnesium hydroxide–containing) may result in increased risk of excessively lowered blood sugar.
- antifungal agents (such as itraconazole or other azoles) may result in severe lowering of blood sugar.
- calcium channel blockers (see Drug Classes) may cause excessive lowering of blood glucose.

- gatifloxacin (Tequin) or levofloxacin (Levaquin) may result in blood sugar changes. Careful checks of blood sugar and dosing adjustments in response to changes are prudent.

▷ *Driving, Hazardous Activities:* Dosing schedule, eating schedule and physical activities must be coordinated to prevent hypoglycemia. Know the early symptoms of hypoglycemia so that you can avoid hazardous activities and take corrective measures.

Aviation Note: Diabetes *is a disqualification* for piloting. Consult a designated Aviation Medical Examiner.

Exposure to Sun: Some drugs of this class can cause photosensitivity (see Glossary).

Occurrence of Unrelated Illness: Acute infections, vomiting or diarrhea, serious injuries and surgical procedures can worsen diabetic control and may require insulin. If any of these conditions occur, call your doctor.

Discontinuation: Because of secondary failures, the continued benefit of this drug should be evaluated every 6 months.

GLIPIZIDE (GLIP i zide)

Introduced: 1972 **Class:** Antidiabetic, sulfonylureas **Prescription:** USA: Yes **Controlled Drug:** USA: No **Available as Generic:** Yes

Brand Names: Glucotrol, Glucotrol XL, Metaglip [CD]

BENEFITS versus RISKS	
Possible Benefits	*Possible Risks*
TIGHTER CONTROL OF BLOOD SUGAR (adjunctive to appropriate diet and weight control)	HYPOGLYCEMIA, extent varies with patient status
DECREASED RISK OF HEART DISEASE, KIDNEY DISEASE, ETC., BY ATTAINING TIGHTER CONTROL OF BLOOD SUGAR	Allergic skin reactions (some severe)
	Blood cell and bone marrow disorders
	Possible increased risk of heart (cardiovascular) mortality (a warning label that all sulfonylureas carry based on a different medicine
ONCE-A-DAY DOSING	
NEW COMBINATION WITH METFORMIN OFFERS TIGHTER SUGAR CONTROL AND LESS RISK OF LOW BLOOD SUGAR	

▷ **Principal Uses**

As a Single Drug Product: Uses currently included in FDA-approved labeling: (1) Type 2 diabetes (adult, maturity-onset) not requiring insulin but not adequately controlled by diet alone, (2) combination form (Metaglip or glipizide/metformin) is used in people who do not meet blood sugar goals using diet and single medicine treatment with metformin or a sulfonylurea.

Other (unlabeled) generally accepted uses: (1) may help reverse abnormal changes in capillaries (very small blood vessels) if given early in diabetes.

As a Combination Drug Product [CD]: Newly combined with metformin (Metaglip) which offers the added benefits/mechanism of action (how it works) of metformin in controlling blood sugar.

How This Drug Works: This drug (1) stimulates the secretion of insulin and (2) enhances the use of insulin by appropriate tissues. The combination form (Metaglip) also decreases sugar (glucose) production in the liver and increases sensitivity of the body to insulin.

Available Dosage Forms and Strengths

> Tablets, combination (Metaglip) — 2.5 mg glipizide and 250 mg or 500 mg of metformin, 5 mg glipizide and 500 mg metformin
> Tablets — 5 mg, 10 mg
> Tablets, extended release — 2.5 mg, 5 mg, 10 mg

▷ **Usual Adult Dosage Ranges:** Immediate release form: Starts with 5 mg daily—taken 30 minutes before a meal. At 3- to 7-day intervals, dose may be increased (by 2.5 to 5 mg daily) as needed and tolerated. Daily maximum is 40 mg. If the daily dose is more than 15 mg, it should be divided into two equal doses given twice a day (immediate release form). Extended release form starts at 5 mg, taken with breakfast. Dose increases are made at 7-day intervals. Most patients have a favorable response to 10 mg daily. Maximum daily extended release–form dose is 20 mg. Combination form (Metaglip) is started at 2.5/250 mg once a day with a meal. If the starting blood sugar is 280–320 mg/dl, the starting dose is 2.5/500 mg. The dose is increased as needed and tolerated every 14 days to 10/2000 in equally divided doses with morning and evening meals.

Note: Actual dose and schedule must be determined for each patient individually.

Conditions Requiring Dosing Adjustments

Liver Function: Patients with liver failure should take a starting dose of 2.5 mg and be closely followed. The combination form SHOULD NOT be used in liver compromise (hepatic insufficiency) because of increased risk of lactic acidosis.

Kidney Function: Patients should be monitored closely if the drug is used in mild to moderate renal (kidney) compromise. It is a rare cause of kidney stones. The combination form SHOULD NOT be taken in kidney compromise because the risk of lactic acidosis increases.

▷ **Dosing Instructions:** If the daily maintenance dose is found to be 15 mg or more (immediate release form), the total dose should be divided into two equal doses—the first taken with the morning meal, the second with the evening meal. The immediate release–form tablet may be crushed. If you forget a dose: take it as soon as you remember it, unless it's nearly time for your next dose—if that is the case, skip the missed dose and return to taking the medicine on your usual schedule. DO NOT double doses. Call your doctor if you find yourself missing doses because the best results are achieved by taking exactly the right dose and keeping your blood sugar in "tight" control.

Usual Duration of Use: Use on a regular schedule for 1 to 2 weeks determines effectiveness in controlling diabetes. Failure to respond to maximal doses within 1 month constitutes a primary failure. Up to 10% who respond initially may fail later (secondary failure). Blood sugars must be checked. Better (tight) sugar control is best!

Typical Treatment Goals and Measurements (Outcomes and Markers)

Blood sugar: The general goal for blood sugar is to return it to the usual "normal" range (generally 80–120 mg/dl), while avoiding risks of excessively low blood sugar. One study (UKPDS) used a fasting plasma sugar (glucose) of less than 108 mg/dl.

Fructosamine and glycosylated hemoglobin: Fructosamine levels (a measure of the past 2 to 3 weeks of blood sugar control) should be less than or equal to 310 micromoles per liter. Glycosylated hemoglobin or hemoglobin A1C (a measure of the past 2–3 months of blood sugar control) should be less than or equal to 7.0%. Some clinicians advocate 6.5%.

Possible Advantages of This Drug
Effective with once-daily dosing.
Onset of action within 30 minutes. Near-normal insulin response to eating.
Well tolerated by the elderly diabetic. No substantiated reports of liver toxicity.
Combination form offers fewer pills (better adherence to taking the medicine) and two different mechanisms of action for better blood sugar control.
Advantages of the combination form with metformin may confer:
Overcoming insulin resistance
Avoidance of weight gain

▷ **This Drug Should Not Be Taken If**
• you have had an allergic reaction to it previously.
• you have diabetic ketoacidosis
For the Metaglip form:
• you had an allergic reaction to it previously.
• you have impaired kidneys (serum creatinine greater than 1.4 for females or 1.5 for males) as this potentially increases risk of lactic acidosis.
• you have congestive heart failure (CHF) and take medicines to treat it (increases risk of lactic acidosis).
• you have liver disease.
• you are an alcoholic.
• you have a heart or lung insufficiency (increased lactic acidosis risk).
• you are going to have a radiology test that uses iodinated contrast media (ask your doctor).
• you have chronic metabolic acidosis or ketoacidosis.
• you are breast-feeding your infant.

▷ **Inform Your Physician Before Taking This Drug If**
• you are allergic to other sulfonylurea drugs or to sulfa drugs.
• your diabetes has been unstable or "brittle" in the past.
• you do not know how to recognize or treat hypoglycemia (see Glossary).
• you have severe impairment of liver or kidney function.
• you have an infection or fever or are going to have surgery. Insulin may be required.
• you are pregnant.
• you have a history of congestive heart failure, peptic ulcer disease, cirrhosis of the liver, bone marrow depression, hypothyroidism, or porphyria.
For Metaglip form:
• you are planning to have surgery soon.
• you have a serious infection (increases risk of lactic acidosis).
• you drink excessive amounts of alcohol (talk with your doctor) or are elderly (increases lactic acidosis risk).
• you have a history of megaloblastic anemia.
• you are pregnant (insulin is the drug of choice).
• you have seen another doctor and ketoacidosis was diagnosed.
• you are unsure how much to take or how often to take it.

Possible Side Effects (natural, expected, and unavoidable drug actions)
If drug dose is excessive or if meals are missed or inadequate, abnormally low blood sugar (hypoglycemia) will occur as a drug effect.

▷ **Possible Adverse Effects** (unusual, unexpected, and infrequent reactions)
If any of the following develop, consult your physician promptly for guidance.

Mild Adverse Effects

Allergic reactions: skin rash, hives, itching.

Headache, drowsiness, dizziness, fatigue, sweating—rare to infrequent.

Indigestion, nausea, vomiting, diarrhea—rare to infrequent.

Increased liver enzymes—case reports (questionable causation).

Serious Adverse Effects

Allergic reactions: severe skin reactions—case reports.

Idiosyncratic reaction: hemolytic anemia (see Glossary).

Disulfiramlike reaction (see Glossary) with alcohol use.

Low blood sodium or drug-induced urinary stones—possible.

Bone marrow depression (see Glossary): fatigue, weakness, fever, sore throat, abnormal bleeding or bruising—case reports.

Risk of cardiovascular mortality (based on an old study—UGDP—with a different drug)—possible.

For Metaglip form additional possibilities include:

Lactic acidosis—very rare (Less than 0.1%, but more likely if used in patients with kidney disease or congestive heart failure that requires medicines, which is why current FDA labeling warns against use in those patients. Lactic acidosis is usually not dramatic in signs or symptoms—breathing difficulty [respiratory distress], low body temp [hypothermia], vague abdominal pain, muscle aches [myalgias], and/or increasing sleepiness).

Lowered vitamin B12 levels and resultant anemia (megaloblastic)—rare.

Destruction of red blood cells (hemolysis)—case report.

Drug-induced porphyria—case reports.

Liver toxicity—two case reports.

▷ **Possible Effects on Sexual Function:** None reported.

▷ **Adverse Effects That May Mimic Natural Diseases or Disorders**

Liver reaction may suggest viral hepatitis.

Possible Effects on Laboratory Tests

Complete blood counts: decreased red cells, hemoglobin, white cells, and platelets.

Glycated hemoglobin or protein: trending toward normal.

Blood glucose levels: decreased.

Liver function tests: increased liver enzymes (ALT/GPT, AST/GOT, and alkaline phosphatase), increased bilirubin.

CAUTION

1. This drug is only part of a diabetes program. It is not a substitute for a proper diet and regular exercise.
2. Over time (usually months), this drug may not work. Periodic follow-up examinations are needed.
3. If you develop an infection, insulin may be required to control your blood sugar.
4. The American Diabetic Association (ADA) now says that a person is considered diabetic if 2 fasting blood sugars in a row are more than 125 mg/dl. This more conservative approach reflects new information saying that complications start at lower blood sugar levels than previously thought. The concept of Pre-diabetes (formerly impaired glucose tolerance) is described in the Glossary. Some new British data advocated that statin-type medicines could cut the risk of heart attack and stroke by a

third (even in people with "normal" cholesterol)—yet these medicines are underused in diabetics. Talk to your doctor about this.

Precautions for Use

By Infants and Children: This drug does not work in type 1 (juvenile, growth-onset) insulin-dependent diabetes.

By Those Over 60 Years of Age: Use with caution, and start with 2.5 mg/day. Dose should be increased slowly and glucose checked often. Repeated hypoglycemia in the elderly can cause brain damage.

▷ **Advisability of Use During Pregnancy**

Pregnancy Category: C. See Pregnancy Risk Categories at the back of this book.

Animal Studies: No birth defects reported in rats and rabbits.

Human Studies: Adequate studies of pregnant women are not available.

Because uncontrolled blood sugar levels during pregnancy are associated with a higher incidence of birth defects, many experts recommend that insulin (instead of an oral agent) be used as necessary to control diabetes during the entire pregnancy.

Advisability of Use If Breast-Feeding

Presence of this drug in breast milk: Unknown.

Avoid drug or refrain from nursing.

Habit-Forming Potential: None.

Effects of Overdose: Symptoms of mild to severe hypoglycemia: headache, light-headedness, faintness, nervousness, confusion, tremor, sweating, heart palpitation, weakness, hunger, nausea, vomiting, stupor progressing to coma.

Possible Effects of Long-Term Use: Reduced thyroid function (hypothyroidism). Reports of increased frequency and severity of heart and blood vessel diseases with long-term use of this class of drugs are highly controversial and inconclusive. A direct cause-and-effect relationship (see Glossary) is tenuous. Ask your doctor for help.

Suggested Periodic Examinations While Taking This Drug (at physician's discretion)

Hemoglobin A1C and/or fructosamine.

Blood sugar checks (via finger stick and periodically in the laboratory)

Complete blood cell counts.

Liver function tests.

Thyroid function tests.

Periodic evaluation of heart and circulatory system.

▷ **While Taking This Drug, Observe the Following**

Foods: Follow the diabetic diet prescribed by your physician. Rice bran has been checked in a small (57-subject) study of type 1 and type 2 diabetics. The benefit was a 30% lowering of sugar. This might be a new complementary care option.

Herbal Medicines or Minerals: Using chromium may change the way your body is able to use sugar. Some health food stores advocate vanadium as mimicking the actions of insulin, but possible toxicity and need for rigorous studies presently preclude recommending it. Caution: St. John's wort may cause photosensitivity, and this drug may too. DHEA may change sensitivity to insulin or insulin resistance. Fenugreek, Hawthorn, ginger, garlic, ginseng, guar gum, licorice, nettle, and yohimbe may change blood sugar. Since this may require adjustment of hypoglycemic medicine dosing, talk to your doctor BEFORE combining any of these herbal medicines with this medicine. Echinacea pupurea (injectable) and blonde psyllium seed or husk should NOT be taken by people living with diabetes. Psyllium increases risk of excessively low blood sugar. Surprisingly, boiled stems of the Optuntia streptacantha form of prickly pear cactus appear to be able to lower blood sugar. Ongoing effects and effects on A1C are not known. Red sage is used for blood sugar effects, but is unproven. Rice bran has been checked in a small (57-subject) study of type 1 and type 2 diabetics. The benefit was a 30% lowering of sugar. This might be a new complementary care option.

Beverages: As directed in the diabetic diet. May be taken with milk.

▷ *Alcohol:* Use with extreme caution—alcohol can prolong this drug's hypoglycemic effect. This drug can also cause a disulfiramlike reaction (see Glossary): facial flushing, sweating, palpitation.

Tobacco Smoking: No interactions expected. I advise everyone to quit smoking.

▷ *Other Drugs*

The following drugs may *increase* the effects of glipizide:
- acarbose (Precose) may increase risk of excessive lowering of blood sugar.
- aspirin and other salicylates.
- chloramphenicol (Chloromycetin).
- cimetidine (Tagamet).
- clofibrate (Atromid-S).
- cotrimoxazole (Septra).
- fenfluramine (Pondimin).
- itraconazole (Sporanox) and other azole antifungal medicines.
- levothyroxine (and other thyroid products).
- magnesium (increased absorption into the body).
- monoamine oxidase (MAO) type A inhibitors (see Drug Classes).
- NSAIDs (see Drug Classes).
- probenecid (Benemid).
- ranitidine (Zantac).
- sulfa drugs such as trimethoprim/sulfamethoxazole (Septra) or erythromycin/sulfisoxazole (Pediazole).

The following drugs may *decrease* the effects of glipizide:
- beta-blocker drugs (see Drug Classes).
- bumetanide (Bumex).
- cholestyramine (Questran).
- diazoxide (Proglycem).
- ethacrynic acid (Edecrin).
- furosemide (Lasix).
- phenothiazines (see Drug Classes).
- phenytoin (Dilantin).
- rifampin (Rifadin, others).
- ritonavir (Norvir).
- steroids (betamethasone, prednisone, others).
- thiazide diuretics (see Drug Classes).

Glipizide *taken concurrently* with
- antacids (containing magnesium hydroxide) may result in increased risk of excessively lowered blood sugar.
- antifungal agents (such as itraconazole or other azoles) may result in severe lowering of blood sugar.
- calcium channel blockers (see Drug Classes) may cause excessive lowering of blood glucose.

- cyclosporine (Sandimmune) may result in cyclosporine toxicity.
- gatifloxacin (Tequin) or levofloxacin (Levaquin) may result in blood sugar changes. Careful checks of blood sugar and dosing adjustments in response to changes are prudent.
- sildenafil (Viagra) one case report of an interaction. Talk to your doctor about current data regarding combined use.
- warfarin (Coumadin) can cause an increased hypoglycemic effect.

Metaglip form *taken concurrently* with

- cationic drugs (cotrimoxazole, digoxin (Lanoxin), dofetilide (Tikosyn), procainamide, quinidine, quinine, vancomycin, and others) may increase risk of lactic acidosis.
- contrast media for certain X-ray studies may increase risk of lactic acidosis. Metformin should not be combined with these agents. Some clinicians substitute a different agent to control blood sugar, stop the metformin 48 hours before the X-ray, and then stop the substituted agent and restart metformin once kidney function is tested and found to be normal.
- cotrimoxazole (Bactrim, others) may increase risk of lactic acidosis.
- dofetilide (Tikosyn) may pose a problem because it is a cationic drug and uses the same removal (elimination) pathway that metformin does. This may lead to increased risk of dofetilide toxicity.

▷ *Driving, Hazardous Activities:* Dosing schedule, eating schedule and physical activities must be coordinated to prevent hypoglycemia. Know the early symptoms of hypoglycemia so that you can avoid hazardous activities and take corrective measures.

Aviation Note: Diabetes *is a disqualification* for piloting. Consult a designated Aviation Medical Examiner.

Exposure to Sun: Some drugs of this class can cause photosensitivity (see Glossary).

Occurrence of Unrelated Illness: Acute infections, vomiting or diarrhea, serious injuries, and surgical procedures can worsen diabetic control and may require insulin. If any of these conditions occur, call your doctor.

Discontinuation: Because of secondary failures, the continued benefit of this drug should be evaluated every 6 months.

GLYBURIDE (GLI byoor ide)

OtherName: Glibenclamide   **Introduced:**   1970   **Class:**   Antidiabetic, sulfonylureas   **Prescription:**   USA: Yes   **Controlled   Drug:** USA: No; Canada: No   **Available as Generic:**   Yes

Brand Names: ✤Albert-Glyburide, ✤Apo-Glyburide, Diabeta, ✤Euglucon, ✤Gen-Glybe, Glubate, Glucovance [CD], Glynase Prestab, Micronase, ✤Novo-Glyburide

---

BENEFITS versus RISKS

Possible Benefits	*Possible Risks*
HELPS REGULATE BLOOD SUGAR IN TYPE 2 DIABETES (NON-INSULIN DEPENDENT DIABETES) ADJUNCTIVE TO APPROPRIATE DIET AND WEIGHT CONTROL	HYPOGLYCEMIA, SEVERE AND PROLONGED
	LACTIC ACIDOSIS (A RARE RISK WITH GLUCOVANCE FORM)
	Possible anemia with long-term use (added as a rare risk with Glucovance form)
COMBINED WITH METFORMIN IN THE GLUCOVANCE FORM TO GIVE ADDED AND TIGHTER BLOOD SUGAR (GLUCOSE) CONTROL	Liver damage
	Blood cell and bone marrow disorders
	Allergic skin reactions (some severe)
	Possible increased risk of heart (cardiovascular) mortality based on an old study with a different drug

---

▷ **Principal Uses**

As a Single Drug Product: Uses currently included in FDA-approved labeling: (1) Type 2 diabetes mellitus (adult, maturity-onset) that does not require insulin but can't be adequately controlled by diet alone; (2) combination form (Glucovancep or glyburide/metformin) is used in people who do not meet blood sugar goals using diet and single medicine treatment with metformin or a sulfonylurea.

Other (unlabeled) generally accepted uses: None.

How This Drug Works: This drug (1) stimulates the secretion of insulin, (2) decreases glucose production in the liver and (3) enhances insulin use. The combination form (with metformin): overlaps in some of the way that it works and also increases sensitivity of the body to insulin.

Available Dosage Forms and Strengths

Tablets — 1.25 mg, 1.5 mg, 2.5 mg, 3 mg, 5 mg, 6 mg

Tablets, combination — 250 mg metformin and 1.25 mg glyburide, 500 mg metformin and 2.5 or 5.0 mg glyburide (Glucovance form).

▷ **Usual Adult Dosage Ranges:** *Regular-release products:* 2.5 to 5 mg daily with breakfast. At 7-day intervals the dose may be increased by increments of 2.5 mg daily as needed and tolerated. Total daily dose should not exceed 20 mg. Prudent to start sensitive patients on 1.25 mg daily.

Micronized products: 1.5 to 3 mg daily taken with breakfast. (Patients more sensitive to oral agents should be started at 0.75 mg daily.) If the daily dose required is more than 6 mg daily, twice daily dosing may be needed. Maximum dose is 12 mg daily.

Combination form (Glucovance): For people who do not meet blood sugar goals with their existing regimen of exercise and medicine: the beginning dose is 1.25 mg glyburide/250 mg metformin once a day. If patients have fasting plasma blood sugar (glucose) greater than 200 mg/dl or a hemoglobin A1C (glycosylated hemoglobin) more than 9%, the 1.25 mg/250 mg dose can be given with the morning and evening meals. Dosing can be increased as needed and tolerated until goals of treatment are met up to a maximum of 10 mg glyburide/2000 mg metformin.

Note: Actual dose and schedule must be determined for each patient individually.

Conditions Requiring Dosing Adjustments

Liver Function: Glyburide may cause catastrophic hypoglycemia (low blood sugar) if it is used by patients with liver disease. Very low starting doses should be taken and the patient closely followed. It is also a rare cause of hepatitis and cholestatic jaundice. The Glucovance combination form SHOULD NOT be used in liver compromise (hepatic insufficiency) because of increased risk of lactic acidosis.

Kidney Function: Glyburide should be used with caution in mild renal compromise, with low initial doses and careful patient monitoring. The drug SHOULD NOT be used by patients with moderate kidney failure (creatinine clearances less than 50 ml/min) or in severe kidney failure. The combination form SHOULD NOT be taken in kidney compromise because the risk of lactic acidosis increases.

▷ **Dosing Instructions:** If the daily maintenance dose is 10 mg or more, the total dose should be divided into two equal doses: the first taken with the morning meal, the second with the evening meal. The tablet may be crushed. If you forget a dose: take it as soon as you remember it, unless it's nearly time for your next dose—if that is the case, skip the missed dose and return to taking the medicine on your usual schedule. DO NOT double doses. Call your doctor if you find yourself missing doses—the best results are achieved by taking exactly the right dose and keeping your blood sugar in "tight" control.

Usual Duration of Use: Use on a regular schedule for 1 to 2 weeks determines effectiveness in controlling diabetes. No response to peak doses in 1 month constitutes a primary failure. Up to 10% of those who respond initially may develop secondary failure. The duration of effective use can only be determined by periodic measurement of the blood sugar.

Typical Treatment Goals and Measurements (Outcomes and Markers)

Blood sugar: The general goal for blood sugar is to return it to the usual "normal" range (generally 80–120 mg/dl), while avoiding risks of excessively low blood sugar. One study (UKPDS) used a fasting plasma sugar (glucose) of less than 108 mg/dl.

Fructosamine and glycosylated hemoglobin: Fructosamine levels (a measure of the past 2 to 3 weeks of blood sugar control) should be less than or equal to 310 micromoles per liter. Glycosylated hemoglobin or hemoglobin A1C (a measure of the past 2–3 months of blood sugar control) should be less than or equal to 7.0%. Some clinicians recommend 6.5%.

Possible Advantages of This Drug

Advantages of the combination form with metformin may confer:
Overcoming insulin resistance
Improved glucose control and adherence with a single pill.

▷ **This Drug Should Not Be Taken If**
- you have had an allergic reaction to it previously.
- you have severe impairment of liver and kidney function.
- you have diabetic ketoacidosis.
- you are pregnant.

For the Glucovance form:
- you had an allergic reaction to it previously.
- you have impaired kidneys (serum creatinine greater than 1.4 for females or 1.5 for males) as this potentially increases risk of lactic acidosis.
- you have congestive heart failure (CHF) and take medicines to treat it (increases risk of lactic acidosis).

- you have liver disease.
- you are an alcoholic.
- you have a heart or lung insufficiency (increased lactic acidosis risk).
- you are going to have a radiology test that uses iodinated contrast media (ask your doctor).
- you have chronic metabolic acidosis or ketoacidosis.
- you are breast-feeding your infant.

▷ **Inform Your Physician Before Taking This Drug If**
- you are allergic to other sulfonylurea drugs or to "sulfa" drugs.
- your diabetes has been unstable or "brittle" in the past.
- you do not know how to recognize or treat hypoglycemia (see Glossary).
- you have a history of problems with blood clotting or have a glucose-6-phosphate dehydrogenase (G6PD) deficiency.
- you have a history of congestive heart failure, peptic ulcer disease, cirrhosis of the liver, hypothyroidism or porphyria.
- you have an infection or a fever.

For the Glucovance form:
- you are planning to have surgery soon.
- you have a serious infection (increases risk of lactic acidosis).
- you drink excessive amounts of alcohol (talk with your doctor) or are elderly (increases lactic acidosis risk).
- you have a history of megaloblastic anemia.
- you are pregnant (insulin is the drug of choice).
- you have seen another doctor and ketoacidosis was diagnosed.
- you are unsure how much to take or how often to take it.

Possible Side Effects (natural, expected, and unavoidable drug actions)

If drug dose is excessive or food intake is delayed or inadequate, abnormally low blood sugar (hypoglycemia) will occur as a predictable drug effect.

▷ **Possible Adverse Effects** (unusual, unexpected, and infrequent reactions)

If any of the following develop, consult your physician promptly for guidance.

Mild Adverse Effects

Allergic reactions: skin rash, hives, itching.

Headache, drowsiness, dizziness, fatigue—possible.

Indigestion, heartburn, nausea—rare.

Bed-wetting at night (nocturnal enuresis), especially in young adults—case reports.

Serious Adverse Effects

Allergic reactions: hepatitis with jaundice (see Glossary), severe skin reactions (exfoliative dermatitis)—case reports.

Idiosyncratic reaction: hemolytic anemia (see Glossary).

Disulfiramlike reaction with concurrent use of alcohol (see Glossary)—possible.

Bone marrow depression (see Glossary): fatigue, fever, sore throat, abnormal bleeding—case reports.

Thrombocytopenic purpura—case report.

Liver toxicity (granulomatous or intrahepatic cholestasis)—case reports.

Blood clotting defects (coagulation)—rare.

Cardiovascular mortality (based on an old study of a different medicine)—increased risk.

For Metaglip form additional possibilities include:

Lactic acidosis—very rare (Less than 0.1%, but more likely if used in patients with kidney disease or congestive heart failure that requires medicines, which is why current FDA labeling warns against use in those patients. Lactic acidosis is usually not dramatic in signs or symptoms—breathing difficulty [respiratory distress], low body temp [hypothermia], vague abdominal pain, muscle aches [myalgias], and/or increasing sleepiness).

Lowered vitamin B12 levels and resultant anemia (megaloblastic)—rare.

Destruction of red blood cells (hemolysis)—case report.

Drug-induced porphyria—case reports.

Liver toxicity—two case reports (metformin component).

▷ **Possible Effects on Sexual Function:** None reported.

▷ **Adverse Effects That May Mimic Natural Diseases or Disorders**

Liver reactions may suggest viral hepatitis.

Possible Effects on Laboratory Tests

Blood platelet counts: decreased.

Blood cholesterol and triglyceride levels: decreased.

Glycated hemoglobin or protein: trending toward normal.

Blood glucose levels: decreased.

Liver function tests: increased liver enzymes (ALT/GPT, AST/GOT, and alkaline phosphatase).

CAUTION

1. This drug is only part of diabetes management. Much of the damage from diabetes can be delayed or avoided if you keep your blood sugar in the normal range. Ask your doctor about a proper diet and regular exercise.

2. Over time (usually many months), this drug may not work. Periodic follow-up examinations are necessary.

3. The American Diabetic Association (ADA) now says that a person is considered diabetic if 2 fasting blood sugars in a row are more than 125 mg/dl. This more conservative approach reflects new information saying that complications start at lower blood sugar levels than previously thought. The concept of Pre-diabetes (formerly impaired glucose tolerance) is described in the Glossary. Some new British data advocates that statin-type medicines could cut the risk of heart attack and stroke by a third (even in people with "normal" cholesterol)—yet these medicines are underused in diabetics. Talk to your doctor about this.

Precautions for Use

By Infants and Children: This drug does not work in type 1 (juvenile, growth-onset) insulin-dependent diabetes.

By Those Over 60 Years of Age: Use with caution, and start with 1.25 mg/day of the regular form. Dose should be slowly increased and glucose closely followed. Repeated hypoglycemia in the elderly can cause brain damage.

▷ **Advisability of Use During Pregnancy**

Pregnancy Category: C: Glyburide, B: Glyburide/metformin. See Pregnancy Risk Categories at the back of this book.

Animal Studies: No birth defects reported in rats and rabbits.

Human Studies: Adequate studies of pregnant women are not available.

Uncontrolled blood sugar levels during pregnancy are associated with a higher incidence of birth defects, so many experts recommend insulin (instead of an oral agent) to control diabetes during the entire pregnancy.

Advisability of Use If Breast-Feeding
>   Presence of this drug in breast milk: Unknown.
>   Avoid drug or refrain from nursing.

Habit-Forming Potential: None.

Effects of Overdose: Symptoms of mild to severe hypoglycemia: headache, light-headedness, faintness, nervousness, confusion, tremor, sweating, heart palpitation, weakness, hunger, nausea, vomiting, stupor progressing to coma.

Possible Effects of Long-Term Use: Reduced thyroid gland function (hypothyroidism). Reports of increased frequency and severity of heart and blood vessel diseases associated with long-term use of this class of drugs are highly controversial and inconclusive. A direct cause-and-effect relationship (see Glossary) is tenuous. Ask your physician for guidance.

Suggested Periodic Examinations While Taking This Drug (at physician's discretion)
>   Complete blood cell counts.
>   Liver function tests.
>   Thyroid function tests.
>   Periodic evaluation of heart and circulatory system.
>   Self assessment (finger stick) of blood sugar is prudent as well as periodic glycosylated hemoglobin and/or fructosamine tests.

▷ **While Taking This Drug, Observe the Following**
>   *Foods:* Follow the diabetic diet prescribed by your physician.
>   *Herbal Medicines or Minerals:* Using chromium may change the way your body is able to use sugar. Some health food stores advocate vanadium as mimicking the actions of insulin, but possible toxicity and need for rigorous studies presently preclude recommending it. Caution: St. John's wort may cause photosensitivity, and this drug may too.
>   DHEA may change sensitivity to insulin or insulin resistance. Fenugreek, glucomannan, hawthorn, ginger, garlic, ginseng guar gum, licorice, nettle, and yohimbe may change blood sugar. Since this may require adjustment of hypoglycemic medicine dosing, talk to your doctor BEFORE combining any of these herbal medicines with this medicine. Echinacea pupurea (injectable) and blonde psyllium seed or husk should NOT be taken by people living with diabetes. Psyllium increases risk of excessively low blood sugar. Surprisingly, boiled stems of the Optuntia streptacantha, or prickly pear cactus, appear to be able to lower blood sugar. Ongoing effects and effects on A1C are not known. Red sage is used for blood sugar effects, but is unproven. Rice bran has been checked in a small (57-subject) study of type 1 and type 2 diabetics. The benefit was a 30% lowering of sugar. This might be a new complementary care option.
>   *Beverages:* As directed in the diabetic diet. May be taken with milk.
▷   *Alcohol:* Use with extreme caution—alcohol can exaggerate this drug's hypoglycemic effect. This drug can cause a disulfiramlike reaction (see Glossary): facial flushing, sweating, palpitation.
>   *Tobacco Smoking:* No interactions expected. I advise everyone to quit smoking.
▷   *Other Drugs*
>   The following drugs may **increase** the effects of glyburide:
>   • acarbose (Precose).
>   • aspirin and other salicylates (aspirin may also block disulfiram effect).
>   • chloramphenicol (Chloromycetin).

- cimetidine (Tagamet).
- ciprofloxacin (Cipro).
- clofibrate (Atromid-S).
- cotrimoxazole (various).
- fenfluramine (Pondimin).
- gemfibrozil (Lopid).
- monoamine oxidase (MAO) type A inhibitors (see Drug Classes).
- phenylbutazone (Butazolidin).
- ranitidine (Zantac).
- ritonavir (Norvir).
- sulfa drugs such as trimethoprim/sulfamethoxazole (Septra) or erythromy-cin/sulfisoxazole (Pediazole).

The following drugs may *decrease* the effects of glyburide:
- beta-blocker drugs (see Drug Classes).
- bumetanide (Bumex).
- diazoxide (Proglycem).
- ethacrynic acid (Edecrin).
- furosemide (Lasix).
- phenytoin (Dilantin).
- rifampin (Rifadin, others) and rifabutin (Mycobutin).
- thiazide diuretics (see Drug Classes).
- thyroid hormones (see Drug Classes).

Glyburide *taken concurrently* with
- antacids (containing magnesium hydroxide) or magnesium supplements may result in increased risk of excessively lowered blood sugar.
- antifungal agents (such as itraconazole, voriconazole [Vfend], or other azoles) may result in severe lowering of blood sugar.
- cyclosporine (Sandimmune) may increase cyclosporine levels by up to 57%.
- enalapril (Vasotec) may enhance blood sugar–lowering effect.
- gatifloxacin (Tequin) or levofloxacin (Levaquin) may result in blood sugar changes. Careful checks of blood sugar and dosing adjustments in response to changes are prudent.
- MAO inhibitors (see Drug Classes) may increase risk of hyperglycemia.
- steroids (betamethasone, prednisone, others) blunt glyburide benefits.
- warfarin (Coumadin) may result in bleeding; more frequent INR (prothrombin time) testing is needed.

Glucovance form *taken concurrently* with
- cationic drugs (cotrimoxazole, digoxin (Lanoxin), dofetilide (Tikosyn), procainamide, quinidine, quinine, vancomycin, and others) may increase risk of lactic acidosis.
- contrast media for certain X-ray studies may increase risk of lactic acidosis. Metformin should not be combined with these agents. Some clinicians substitute a different agent to control blood sugar, stop the metformin 48 hours before the X-ray, and then stop the substituted agent and restart metformin once kidney function is tested and found to be normal.
- cotrimoxazole (Bactrim, others) may increase risk of lactic acidosis.
- dofetilide (Tikosyn) may pose a problem because it is a cationic drug and uses the same removal (elimination) pathway that metformin does. This may lead to increased risk of dofetilide toxicity.

▷ *Driving, Hazardous Activities:* Regulate dosing, eating and physical activities carefully to prevent hypoglycemia. Know the early symptoms of hypoglycemia so that you can avoid hazardous activities and take corrective measures.

Aviation Note: Diabetes *is a disqualification* for piloting. Consult a designated Aviation Medical Examiner.

Exposure to Sun: Use caution until sensitivity has been determined. Some drugs of this class can cause photosensitivity (see Glossary).

Occurrence of Unrelated Illness: Acute infections, vomiting or diarrhea, serious injuries and surgical procedures can worsen diabetic control and may require insulin. If any of these conditions occur, consult your physician promptly.

Discontinuation: Because of the possibility of secondary failure, it is advisable to evaluate the continued benefit of this drug every 6 months.

GUANFACINE (GWAHN fa seen)

Introduced: 1980   **Class:** Antihypertensive   **Prescription:** USA: Yes   **Controlled Drug:** USA: No   **Available as Generic:** USA: Yes

Brand Name: Tenex

Author's Note: Information in this profile has been shortened to make room for more widely used medicines.

HALOPERIDOL (hal oh PER i dohl)

Introduced: 1958   **Class:** Antipsychotic; tranquilizer, strong   **Prescription:** USA: Yes   **Controlled Drug:** USA: No; Canada: No   **Available as Generic:** USA: Yes; Canada: Yes

Brand Names: ✱Alti-Haloperidol, ✱Apo-Haloperidol, Haldol, ✱Haldol LA, Halperon, ✱Novo-Peridol, ✱Peridol, ✱PMS Haloperidol

BENEFITS versus RISKS	
Possible Benefits	*Possible Risks*
EFFECTIVE CONTROL OF PSYCHOSES	FREQUENT PARKINSON-LIKE side effects
BENEFICIAL EFFECTS ON THINKING, MOOD, AND BEHAVIOR	SERIOUS TOXIC EFFECTS ON BRAIN with long-term use
EFFECTIVE CONTROL OF SOME CASES OF TOURETTE'S SYNDROME	Rare blood cell disorders
Beneficial in management of some hyperactive children	Abnormally low white blood cell count
Decanoate form treats schizophrenia for a month with a single injection	

▷ **Principal Uses**

As a Single Drug Product: Uses currently included in FDA-approved labeling: (1) Helps control psychotic thinking and abnormal behavior in acute psychosis of unknown nature, acute schizophrenia, paranoid states, and the manic phase of manic-depressive disorders; (2) helps control outbursts of aggression and agitation; (3) used to treat Tourette's syndrome; (4) approved for use in children 3 years old or older who have unexplained (unprovoked) explosive and combative hyperexcitability.

Other (unlabeled) generally accepted uses: (1) Helps control refractory hiccups; (2) used to lessen delirium in LSD flashbacks and phencyclidine intoxication; (3) used as combination (adjuvant) therapy in chronic pain syndromes; (4) may be helpful in autistic patients; (5) may have a role in refractory vomiting caused by cancer chemotherapy; (6) can ease symptoms in refractory sneezing; (7) may be helpful as adjunctive therapy in stuttering.

How This Drug Works: By interfering with a nerve impulse transmitter (dopamine), this drug reduces anxiety and agitation, improves coherence and thinking, and abolishes delusions and hallucinations.

Available Dosage Forms and Strengths

Concentrate — 2 mg/ml

Injection — 5 mg/ml, 50 mg/ml, and 100 mg/ml

Tablets — 0.5 mg, 1 mg, 1.5 mg, 2 mg, 5 mg, 10 mg, 20 mg

▷ **Usual Adult Dosage Ranges:** Initially this medicine can be started at 1 to 6 milligrams a day to help control moderate symptoms and at 6 to 15 mg a day in severe cases. Doses are divided into equal amounts and given 2 to 3 times a day. Dosing is increased as needed and tolerated. Some patients require increases of up to 100 mg a day. Ongoing doses are highly individualized. Decanoate form may relieve schizophrenia for a month with a single injection. The typical change (conversion) to the decanoate form is 10 to 20 times the previous dose (in oral haloperidol equivalents), but not more than a maximum starting decanoate-form dose of 100 mg. If in some cases, the starting conversion dose is greater than 100 mg, the first dose should be 100 mg of decanoate, followed by the rest of the dose in 3 to 7 days.

Note: Actual dose and schedule must be determined for each patient individually.

Conditions Requiring Dosing Adjustments

Liver Function: The dose, dosing interval and titration interval (time to adjust the drug to desired effect) should be adjusted for liver compromise.

Kidney Function: High doses used with caution in kidney compromise.

▷ **Dosing Instructions:** The tablet may be crushed and taken with or following food to reduce stomach irritation. The concentrate may be diluted in 2 ounces of water or fruit juice (do not add it to coffee or tea), and should be measured using a medicine spoon or calibrated dose cup. If you forget a dose: take it as soon as you remember it, unless it's nearly time for your next dose—if that is the case, skip the missed dose and return to taking the medicine on your usual schedule. DO NOT double doses. Call your doctor if you find yourself forgetting doses.

Usual Duration of Use: Use on a regular schedule for several weeks determines this drug's effectiveness in controlling psychotic behavior. If it doesn't provide significant benefit in 6 weeks, it should be stopped. Long-term use requires supervision and periodic physician evaluation.

Typical Treatment Goals and Measurements (Outcomes and Markers)

Psychosis: The general goal: to lessen the degree and severity of abnormal thinking, letting patients return to their daily lives. Specific measures of psychosis may involve testing or inventories and can be valuable in helping check benefits from this medicine.

This Drug Should Not Be Taken If

• you had an allergic reaction to it previously.

• you are experiencing severe mental depression.

- you have any form of Parkinson's disease.
- you have severe active liver disease.
- you are presently experiencing central nervous system (CNS) depression due to alcohol or narcotics.
- you currently have a bone marrow or blood cell disorder.

▷ **Inform Your Physician Before Taking This Drug If**
- you are allergic or abnormally sensitive to phenothiazine drugs.
- you have a history of mental depression.
- you have any type of heart disease.
- you have impaired liver or kidney function.
- you have cancer of the breast.
- you have thyroid disease.
- you are allergic to the dye tartrazine.
- you are pregnant or are planning pregnancy.
- you have a history of neuroleptic malignant syndrome.
- you have low blood pressure, epilepsy, or glaucoma.
- you are taking any drugs with a sedative effect.
- you plan to have surgery and general or spinal anesthesia soon.

Possible Side Effects (natural, expected, and unavoidable drug actions)
Mild drowsiness, low blood pressure, blurred vision, dry mouth, constipation, marked and frequent Parkinson-like reactions (see Glossary).

▷ **Possible Adverse Effects** (unusual, unexpected, and infrequent reactions)
If any of the following develop, consult your physician promptly for guidance.

Mild Adverse Effects
Allergic reactions: skin rash, hives.
Dizziness, weakness, agitation, insomnia—case reports to infrequent.
Loss of appetite, indigestion, nausea, vomiting, diarrhea—case reports.
Decreased white blood cell count—possible.

Serious Adverse Effects
Allergic reactions: rare liver reaction with jaundice, asthma, spasm of vocal cords.
Idiosyncratic reactions: Neuroleptic malignant syndrome (see Glossary).
Nervous system reactions: rigidity of extremities, tremors, seizures, constant movement, facial grimacing, eye-rolling, spasm of neck muscles, tardive dyskinesia (see Glossary)—case reports to infrequent.
Rhabdomyolysis—case report.
Abnormal heartbeat (premature ventricular contractions)—possible with aggressive dosing.
Torsades de pointes—possible.
Worsening of psychosis—possible.
Low blood sugar or abnormal and frequent urination (SIADH)—case reports.
Liver toxicity—possible.
Bronchospasm or myasthenia gravis—case reports.

▷ **Possible Effects on Sexual Function:** Decreased libido; impotence—infrequent to frequent; painful ejaculation; priapism (see Glossary). Tender and enlarged breast tissue in men (gynecomastia); breast enlargement with milk production in women.
Altered timing and pattern of menstruation—case reports.

▷ **Adverse Effects That May Mimic Natural Diseases or Disorders**
Liver reaction may suggest viral hepatitis. Nervous system reactions may suggest Parkinson's disease or Reye's syndrome.

Natural Diseases or Disorders That May Be Activated by This Drug
Latent epilepsy, glaucoma, diabetes.

Possible Effects on Laboratory Tests
Complete blood counts: decreased red cells, hemoglobin, and white cells; increased eosinophils.
INR (prothrombin time): decreased.
Blood cholesterol level: decreased.
Blood glucose level: increased.
Liver function tests: increased liver enzymes (ALT/GPT, AST/GOT, and alkaline phosphatase), increased bilirubin.

CAUTION
1 The smallest effective dose should be used for long-term therapy.
2. Use with extreme caution in epilepsy; can alter seizure patterns.
3. Those with lupus erythematosus or who are taking prednisone have more nervous system reactions.
4. Levodopa should not be used to treat Parkinson-like reactions; it can cause agitation and worsening of the psychotic disorder.
5. Obtain prompt evaluation of any change or disturbance in vision.

Precautions for Use
By Infants and Children: This drug should not be used in children under 3 years of age or 15 kg in weight. While the dose is not well established in children 3–6 years old, 0.05–0.15 mg per kg of body weight daily for psychotic disorders is the usual range. The total daily dose is separated into 2 or 3 equal oral doses. Avoid this drug in the presence of symptoms suggestive of Reye's syndrome. Side effects are usually similar to the ones seen in adults.
By Those Over 60 Years of Age: Small doses are indicated when therapy is started. This drug can cause significant changes in mood and behavior; watch for confusion, disorientation, agitation, restlessness, aggression, and paranoia. You may be more susceptible to the development of drowsiness, lethargy, orthostatic hypotension (see Glossary), hypothermia (see Glossary), Parkinson-like reactions, and prostatism (see Glossary).

▷ **Advisability of Use During Pregnancy**
Pregnancy Category: C. See Pregnancy Risk Categories at the back of this book.
Animal Studies: Cleft palate reported in mouse studies.
Human Studies: No increase in birth defects reported in 100 exposures. Adequate studies of pregnant women are not available.
Avoid during the first 3 months (trimester). Use only if clearly needed. Ask your physician for guidance.

Advisability of Use If Breast-Feeding
Presence of this drug in breast milk: Yes.
Use is controversial. Monitor nursing infant closely and discontinue drug or nursing if adverse effects develop.

Habit-Forming Potential: Reports of recreational use have been made. If the drug is stopped suddenly, patients may experience a withdrawal syndrome.

Effects of Overdose: Marked drowsiness, weakness, tremor, unsteadiness, agitation, stupor, coma, convulsions.

Possible Effects of Long-Term Use: Eye damage—deposits in cornea, lens, or retina; tardive dyskinesia (see Glossary).

Suggested Periodic Examinations While Taking This Drug (at physician's discretion)

Complete blood counts.

Liver function tests.

Eye examinations.

Electrocardiograms.

The tongue should be watched for fine, involuntary, wavelike movements that could be the beginning of tardive dyskinesia. The Abnormal Involuntary Movement Scale (AIMS) should be checked every 6 months.

▷ **While Taking This Drug, Observe the Following**

Foods: No restrictions.

Herbal Medicines or Minerals: St. John's wort may also lead to increased sensitivity to the sun—DO NOT COMBINE. Evening primrose oil may work to lower the threshold for seizures. Combination with haloperidol may increase seizure risk—DO NOT COMBINE. Since part of the way ginseng works may be as an MAO inhibitor, do not combine. Because chasteberry acts as a dopamine agonist, it may actually work against the action of haloperidol—caution is advised. Betel nut appeared to increase movement problems (extrapyramidal side effects) when it was chewed by patients taking a similar medicine—combination is not advisable.

Beverages: No restrictions. May be taken with milk.

▷ *Alcohol:* Avoid completely. Alcohol can increase the sedative action of haloperidol and accentuate its depressant effects on brain function. Haloperidol can increase the intoxicating effects of alcohol.

Tobacco Smoking: Combination with nicotine actually increased suppression of tics in Tourette's syndrome in one study. I advise everyone to quit smoking.

Marijuana Smoking: Moderate increase in drowsiness; accentuation of orthostatic hypotension; increased risk of precipitating latent psychosis, confusing interpretation of mental status and of drug response.

▷ *Other Drugs*

Haloperidol may ***increase*** the effects of

- all drugs with sedative actions and cause excessive sedation.
- some antihypertensive drugs and cause excessive lowering of blood pressure; monitor the combined effects carefully.
- fluvoxamine (Luvox) and result in toxicity (altered mental status, GI side effects).

Haloperidol may ***decrease*** the effects of

- guanethidine (Esimil, Ismelin) and reduce its antihypertensive effect.

Haloperidol ***taken concurrently*** with

- anticholinergic drugs (see Drug Classes) can cause additive anticholinergic effects (dry mouth, constipation or sedation).
- beta-blocker drugs may cause excessive lowering of blood pressure.
- bupropion (Zyban, Wellbutrin) can be cautiously combined, but careful patient follow up and lower haloperidol doses are required.
- buspirone (Buspar) may gradually increase haloperidol levels and lead to toxicity. Careful patient follow-up and adjustment of dose is prudent.
- dextromethorphan (**common cough suppressant in cough medicines**) may lead to dextromethorphan toxicity.
- fluoxetine (Prozac) can result in an increased risk of haloperidol toxicity.
- fluvoxamine (Luvox) can result in an increased risk of haloperidol toxicity.
- lithium (Lithobid, others) may cause toxic effects on the brain and nervous system.

- MAO inhibitors (see Drug Classes) may exaggerate low blood pressure and brain (CNS) effects.
- methyldopa (Aldomet) may cause serious dementia.
- olanzapine (Zyprexa) may lead to Parkinson-like symptoms.
- paroxetine (Paxil) may lead to haloperidol toxicity.
- quinidine (Quinaglute, others) may lead to haloperidol toxicity.
- QT interval–prolonging medicines (see Glossary) such as some fluoro-quinolone antibiotics, quinidine (Quinaglute), Ziprasidone (Geodon), and others should NOT be combined.
- ritonavir (Norvir) and perhaps other protease inhibitors (see Drug Classes) may lead to toxicity.
- sertraline (Zoloft) may lead to haloperidol toxicity.
- sparfloxacin (Zagam) may lead to abnormal heartbeats.
- tacrine (Cognex) may lead to Parkinson-like symptoms.
- tramadol (Ultram) may lead to seizures.
- venlafaxine (Effexor) may lead to haloperidol toxicity.
- zotepine (Nipolept) may lead to seizures.

The following drugs may *decrease* the effects of haloperidol:

- antacids containing aluminum and/or magnesium, which may reduce its absorption.
- barbiturates.
- benztropine (Cogentin).
- carbamazepine (Tegretol).
- phenytoin (Dilantin) or fosphenytoin (Cerebyx).
- rifampin (Rifater, others).
- trihexyphenidyl (Artane).

▷ *Driving, Hazardous Activities:* This drug may impair mental alertness, judgment and physical coordination. Restrict activities as necessary.

Aviation Note: The use of this drug *is a disqualification* for piloting. Consult a designated Aviation Medical Examiner.

Exposure to Sun: Use caution—this drug can cause photosensitivity. See Herbal Medicines note on St. John's wort on page 535.

Exposure to Heat: Use caution in hot environments. This drug may impair the regulation of body temperature and increase the risk of heatstroke.

Exposure to Cold: This drug can increase the risk of hypothermia (see Glossary) in the elderly.

Discontinuation: This drug should not be stopped abruptly following long-term use. Gradual withdrawal over a period of 2 to 3 weeks is advised. Ask your doctor for help.

HISTAMINE (H2)-BLOCKING DRUG FAMILY

Cimetidine   (si MET i deen)   **Famotidine**   (fa MOH te deen)   **Niza-tidine**   (ni ZA te deen)   **Ranitidine**   (ra NI te deen)

Introduced: 1977, 1986, 1988, 1983, respectively   **Class:**   Histamine (H2)-blocking drugs   **Prescription:**   USA: Yes   **Controlled Drug:** USA: No; Canada: No   **Available as Generic:**   USA: Yes (prescription forms cimetidine and ranitidine) and Tagamet HB; Canada: Yes

Brand Names: *Cimetidine:*   ♣Apo-Cimetidine, ♣Enlon, ♣Novo-Cimetine, ♣Nu-Cimet, ♣Peptol, Tagamet [nonprescription: Tagamet HB 200, Acid Reducer 200, Acid Reducer Cimetidine, Heartburn 200, Heartburn Relief 200]; *Famotidine:* Pepcid [nonprescription: Pepcid AC, Pepcid Complete (CD), ✤Acid Control, Acid Controller], ✤Alti-famotidine; *Nizatidine:* ✤Apo-Nizatidine, Axid, ✤Novo-Nizatidine [nonprescription: Axid AR]; *Ranitidine:* ✤Alti-ranitidine, ✤ Apo-Ranitidine, Novo-Ranidine, Nu-Ranit, Zantac, ✤Zantac-C [nonprescription: Zantac 75, Zantac 75 EFFERdose, Acid Reducer]

Warning: The brand names Zantac and Xanax are similar and can be mistaken. These are very different drugs, and a mix-up can lead to serious problems. Check the color chart insert of drugs and verify that you are taking the correct drug.

BENEFITS versus RISKS

Possible Benefits	*Possible Risks*
EFFECTIVE TREATMENT OF GERD AND PEPTIC ULCERS IN CHILDREN (FAMOTIDINE ONLY)	Drug-induced hepatitis
	Bone marrow depression (lowered white blood cells or hemoglobin)
EFFECTIVE TREATMENT OF PEPTIC ULCER DISEASE: relief of symptoms, acceleration of healing, prevention of recurrence	Confusion (particularly in compromised elderly with some of these drugs)
CONTROL OF HYPERSECRETORY STOMACH DISORDERS	Low blood platelet counts
	(All of the above are case report to rare effects for prescription forms; occasional use of nonprescription forms makes them even less likely)
TREATMENT OF REFLUX ESOPHAGITIS	
TREATMENT OF HEARTBURN	
PREVENTION OF HEARTBURN (cimetidine, ranitidine, famotidine, and nizatidine)	

Author's Note: The nonprescription heartburn-preventing or treating forms of these medicines have, in general, side effects or adverse effects that occur less frequently or not at all when compared to the already well-tolerated prescription forms. Some doctors are using proton pump inhibitors (see Drug Classes) during the day combined with a dose of a histamine H2 blocker at night in order to gain improved acid control.

▷ **Principal Uses**

As a Single Drug Product: Uses currently included in FDA-approved labeling: (1) Treatment and prevention of repeat (recurrence) of peptic ulcer in adults; (2) all are used for both duodenal and gastric ulcers; (3) cimetidine, ranitidine, and famotidine are used in conditions where extreme production of stomach acid occurs (Zollinger-Ellison syndrome); (4) all four medicines are used to control excess acid moving from the stomach into the lower throat (gastroesophageal reflux disease—GERD); (5) cimetidine is approved for use in preventing upper stomach/intestinal bleeding (stress ulcer prophylaxis); (6) all have been used with antibiotics and bismuth compounds (Pepto-Bismol and others) in refractory ulcers where *Helicobacter pylori* has been found; (7) cimetidine is approved to prevent ulcers caused by stress (stress ulcer prophylaxis); (8) all are approved in nonprescription forms for treatment of heartburn—cimetidine (Tagamet HB 200), famotidine (Pepcid AC), and nizatidine (Axid AR) are also approved for prevention of heartburn; (9) famotidine, ranitidine are approved for treatment of stomach (peptic) ulcers and GERD in children; (10) cimetidine if approved to treat abnormal growths which can increase acid release (multiple endocrine adenomas, systemic mastocytosis).

Other (unlabeled) generally accepted uses: (1) Ranitidine, famotidine, and nizatidine have been used in the prevention of upper stomach/intestinal bleeding; (2) cimetidine has been used prior to surgery to prevent aspiration pneumonitis caused by anesthesia, and ranitidine has shown some benefit here as well; (3) ranitidine and famotidine have been used to help prevent ulcers that may occur in acutely and seriously ill patients; (4) cimetidine appears to have a role in helping patients with colorectal cancer and some other cancers live longer, but further research is needed; (5) famotidine may have a role in treating anaphylactic reactions; (6) cimetidine also may have a role in helping recurrent and resistant warts in some children; (7) cimetidine intravenously has been helpful in some cases of severe drug reactions (resistant drug-induced anaphylactic shock); (8) nizatidine may help by inhibiting weight gain (earlier plateau) in people taking olanzapine (Zyprexa).

How These Drugs Work: They block the action of histamine and, by doing this, inhibit the ability of the stomach to make acid. Once acid is decreased, the body is able to heal itself. Ulcers resistant to healing have now been shown to have an infectious component (Helicobacter pylori), and antibiotics combined with a histamine (H2)-blocking drug can work.

Available Dosage Forms and Strengths

Cimetidine:

Injection — 300 mg/2 ml, 300 mg/50 ml (single dose in 0.9% sodium chloride)

Liquid — 300 mg/5 ml (2.8% alcohol)

Oral solution — 300 mg/5 ml

Tablets — 100 mg, 200 mg, 300 mg, 400 mg, 600 mg, 800 mg

Tablets (nonprescription) — 200 mg

Famotidine:

Injection — 10 mg/ml (in 2- and 4-ml vials)

Oral suspension — 40 mg/5 ml

Tablets — 20 mg, 40 mg

Tablets (nonprescription) — 10 mg

Nizatidine:

Pulvules (capsules) — 75 mg, 150 mg, 300 mg

Tablets (nonprescription) — 75 mg

Ranitidine:

Gelcap — 168 mg, 336 mg (Canada only)

GELdose capsules — 150 mg, 300 mg

Injection — 0.5 mg/ml (single dose in 100 ml)

— 25 mg/ml (in 2-, 10- and 40-ml vials and 2-ml syringes)

Oral solution (Canada) — 84 mg/5 ml

Syrup — 15 mg/ml (7.5% alcohol)

Tablets — 150 mg, 300 mg (effervescent)

— 150 mg

Tablets (nonprescription) — 5 mg

▷ **Recommended Dosage Ranges** (Actual dose and schedule must be determined for each patient individually.)

Infants and Children:

Cimetidine: Routine use is not recommended in those less than 16 years old. Doses of 20 to 40 mg per kg of body mass per day have been used.

Famotidine: GERD—1 mg per kg per day separated into two equal daily doses. Peptic ulcer—0.5 mg per kg of body mass at bedtime or divided into two equal doses up to a total of 40 mg per day (children).

Nizatidine: No data.

Ranitidine: GERD: For those 2 to 18 years old—1.25 to 2 mg per kg of body mass per dose given every 12 hours, or 37.5 mg per dose.

16 to 60 Years of Age:

Peptic ulcer and hypersecretory states:

Cimetidine: 300 mg by mouth 4 times daily, taken with meals and at bedtime, or 800 mg at bedtime. A maintenance dose of 400 mg at bedtime is useful for some patients.

Famotidine: 40 mg by mouth at bedtime for 4 or up to 8 weeks. Maintenance doses of 20 mg at bedtime have been used. Up to 640 mg daily for hypersecretory states.

Nizatidine: 300 mg by mouth at bedtime, or 150 mg twice a day for up to 8 weeks. A maintenance dose of 150 mg at bedtime is useful for some patients. Not used for hypersecretory states.

Ranitidine: 150 mg by mouth twice daily. Maintenance doses of 150 mg at bedtime may be of benefit for some patients. Up to 6 g in hypersecretory states.

Heartburn (nonprescription forms):

Cimetidine: 200 mg by mouth 30 minutes or less before eating foods or drinking liquids that cause you problems. May also be taken once heartburn has started.

Famotidine: 10 mg by mouth before eating foods or drinking liquids that cause you problems or once heartburn has started.

Nizatidine: 75 mg up to twice daily before eating foods or drinking liquids that cause you problems, or once heartburn has started.

Ranitidine: 75 mg by mouth.

Over 60 Years of Age:

Cimetidine: Half the usual adult dose to start. Cimetidine may be more likely to cause confusion in the elderly than the other medicines in this family.

Ranitidine, famotidine, and nizatidine: Same dose as 16 to 60 years of age. All pose a risk for formation of masses (phytobezoars) of undigested vegetable fibers. Watch for nervousness, confusion, loss of appetite, stomach fullness, nausea, and vomiting.

Conditions Requiring Dosing Adjustments:

Liver Function: Cimetidine and famotidine are most dependent on the liver for elimination. Dose must be decreased in liver failure.

Kidney Function: All of these H2 blockers are primarily eliminated by the kidneys. Doses must be decreased in moderate kidney failure.

▷ **Dosing Instructions:** Cimetidine and ranitidine should be taken immediately after meals to obtain the longest decrease in stomach acid when treating peptic ulcers. Cimetidine, ranitidine, and famotidine should be taken after meals when used in hypersecretory states. If you forget a dose: take it as soon as you remember it, unless it's nearly time for your next dose—if that is the case, skip the missed dose and return to taking the medicine on your usual schedule. DO NOT double doses. Call your doctor if you find yourself forgetting doses.

Usual Duration of Use: Use on a regular schedule for 4 to 6 weeks usually determines effectiveness in healing active peptic ulcer disease. Long-term use (months to years) for prevention requires periodic individualized consideration by your physician. Continual use for 6 to 12 weeks is needed to heal the esophagus when cimetidine, ranitidine, famotidine, or nizatidine are used in gastroesophageal reflux disease (GERD). Since nonprescription forms are available for heartburn, if heartburn relief has not occurred in 2 hours, call your doctor, as there may be another medical reason for your signs and symptoms.

Typical Treatment Goals and Measurements (Outcomes and Markers)

Ulcers: The role of *Helicobacter pylori* in ulcers is no longer controversial—and omeprazole (a proton pump inhibitor) is widely recognized as the standard for short-term treatment of stomach ulcers. When *H. pylori* is present, single-medicine therapy is not recommended. Additionally, an antibiotic is often used with other agents. The goal is to heal the ulcer area and prevent re-occurrence of the ulceration. Sign and symptom relief as well as endoscopic examination help define success of treatment.

Heartburn: The general goal: to lessen the degree or severity of or to prevent heartburn. Some patients take the nonprescription forms BEFORE they eat foods that historically have given them heartburn. This issue of self-treatment should be discussed with your doctor, and if heartburn continues beyond the time you and your doctor have decided is reasonable, call your doctor.

Possible Advantages of These Drugs: Nonprescription forms offer relief of heartburn discomfort and the opportunity for effective self-care.

These Drugs Should Not Be Taken If
• you had an allergic reaction to the medicine itself or to the ingredients in the pill previously.

▷ **Inform Your Physician Before Taking These Drugs If**
• you have impaired liver or kidney function.
• you have a low sperm count (cimetidine).
• you are taking any anticoagulant drug.
• you do not tolerate or should not take phenylalanine (ranitidine EFFER-dose tablets or granules).
• you have had low white blood cell counts.
• you have a history of acute porphyria (ranitidine).

Possible Side Effects (natural, expected, and unavoidable drug actions)
None reported.

▷ **Possible Adverse Effects** (unusual, unexpected, and infrequent reactions)
If any of the following develop, consult your physician promptly for guidance.

Mild Adverse Effects
Allergic reactions: skin rash, hives.
Headache: ranitidine—rare; cimetidine—rare; famotidine—infrequent; nizatidine—frequent.
Abnormal dreams: nizatidine—rare.
Diarrhea: ranitidine, nizatidine, cimetidine, famotidine—all rare.
Joint pain (arthralgia): cimetidine, ranitidine, famotidine—all rare.
Depression: cimetidine—case reports.
Muscle pain: cimetidine, nizatidine, famotidine—rare.

Serious Adverse Effects
Allergic reactions: cimetidine and ranitidine can be rare causes of pancreatitis and anemia. Cimetidine and nizatidine can cause exfoliative dermatitis. There have been some case reports of serious skin rashes with all of these medicines, including toxic epidermal necrolysis (TEN).
Anaphylactic reactions: cimetidine, nizatidine—rare.
Idiosyncratic reactions: nervousness, confusion, hallucinations.
Worsening of Alzheimer's: cimetidine—case reports.
Liver damage—case reports.
Abnormal heart rhythm changes (slow heartbeat or atrioventricular block)—case reports.
Bone marrow depression: cimetidine, ranitidine, famotidine—rare.
Decreased platelets: cimetidine, ranitidine, nizatidine—rare; famotidine—case reports.
Bronchospasm: cimetidine and ranitidine—rare; famotidine—rare and questionable.

▷ **Possible Effects on Sexual Function:** Impotence: ranitidine, famotidine, cimetidine, nizatidine—case reports.
Decreased libido: cimetidine—rare.
Male breast enlargement (gynecomastia): nizatidine, cimetidine—case reports.

Possible Delayed Adverse Effects: Male breast enlargement (nizatidine and cimetidine).

▷ **Adverse Effects That May Mimic Natural Diseases or Disorders**
Liver changes may mimic viral hepatitis. Mental status changes from cimetidine in older patients may mimic organic causes.

Possible Effects on Laboratory Tests
Blood platelet counts: may be decreased by all histamine (H2) blockers.
Complete blood counts: rare white blood cell (granulocytes) decrease by cimetidine, ranitidine, and famotidine.
Urine protein tests (Multistix): false positive with ranitidine use.
Urine urobilinogen: false positive with nizatidine.
Thyroid hormones: T4, free T4 may be low with ranitidine use.
Liver enzymes (SGPT, OT, etc.): can be increased with liver damage.
Sperm count: decreased with cimetidine.

CAUTION
1. Ulcer rebound/perforation may occur if you stop these drugs abruptly when they are being used to treat ulcers.
2. Once medicines are stopped, call your doctor promptly if symptoms recur.
3. Use of these medicines and symptom relief does not absolutely remove possibility of cancer of the stomach (gastric malignancy).
4. The nonprescription forms of these medicines should NOT be used to treat ulcers.
5. Some of cimetidine is removed by hemodialysis. Additional doses are needed.
6. Cimetidine may worsen thinking ability (mental status) in those older patients with pre-existing mental status problems.

Precautions for Use
By Infants and Children:
Cimetidine: Routine use is not recommended in those less than 16 years old. Doses of 20 to 40 mg per kg of body mass per day have been used.

Famotidine: 0.5 mg per kg of body mass twice a day for 8 weeks in those 6 to 15 years old.

Nizatidine: No data.

Ranitidine: For those 2 to 18 years old—1.25 to 2 mg per kg of body mass per dose given every 12 hours, or 37.5 mg per dose.

By Those Over 60 Years of Age: Increased risk of masses of partially digested vegetable fibers (phytobezoars), especially in people who can't chew well. Watch closely for decreased appetite, stomach fullness, nausea, and vomiting. Watch those in this age range who are taking cimetidine for changes in thinking (mental status changes).

▷ **Advisability of Use During Pregnancy**

Pregnancy Category: B for all. See Pregnancy Risk Categories at the back of this book.

Animal Studies: No birth defects for cimetidine, ranitidine, and famotidine. Rabbit studies of nizatidine showed abortions, while rat studies showed no effects.

Human Studies: Adequate studies of pregnant women are not available. Use only if clearly needed. Ask your doctor for advice.

Advisability of Use If Breast-Feeding

Presence of these drugs in breast milk: Yes.

Avoid drugs or refrain from nursing.

Habit-Forming Potential: None.

Effects of Overdose:

Cimetidine (rarely documented): confusion, tachycardia, sweating, drowsiness, muscle twitching, seizures, respiratory failure, severe CNS symptoms such as coma (after 20–40 g).

Nizatidine (rarely documented): increased tearing of the eyes, salivation, vomiting, and diarrhea.

Ranitidine and famotidine: no documentation of overdose changes. Adverse effects of the usual dose. Symptomatic and supportive care would be indicated (nonprescription forms do not have documentation of overdoses).

Possible Effects of Long-Term Use: Rare liver damage with cimetidine, ranitidine, and nizatidine. Swelling and tenderness of breast tissue with cimetidine, ranitidine and nizatidine.

Suggested Periodic Examinations While Taking These Drugs (at physician's discretion)

Complete blood counts.

Liver and kidney function tests.

More frequent tests of INR (prothrombin time) if an anticoagulant is also taken.

Sperm counts (cimetidine).

Thinking ability (mental status check).

▷ **While Taking These Drugs, Observe the Following**

Foods: Protein-rich foods increase stomach acid secretion. Garlic, onions, citrus fruits, and tomatoes may also increase acid secretion. Many people know the kinds of foods that are likely to result in significant heartburn. Ask your doctor or pharmacist for help in timing the dose of a nonprescription agent for heartburn.

Herbal Medicines or Minerals: Kola and ma huang may increase stomach acid, blunting the benefits of these medicines. Black cohosh root, ginkgo, and squill are contraindicated in gastrointestinal disturbances. Licorice root has a German Commission E monograph indication for gastrointestinal ulcers, but use with H2 blockers has not been studied. Some members of this family have increased sun sensitivity. Caution is advised if St. John's wort is being considered. Talk to your doctor BEFORE adding any herbals to these medicines.

Nutritional Support: Diet as prescribed by your doctor.

Beverages: The caffeine in caffeine-containing beverages such as coffee, tea, and some sodas may stay in the body up to 50% longer than usual with cimetidine (Tagamet) use. Milk may increase acid secretion.

▷ *Alcohol:* Stomach acidity is increased by alcohol—avoid use. Cimetidine may produce a drug interaction with higher-than-expected levels.

Tobacco Smoking: Smoking is a clear risk factor for peptic ulcer disease. I advise everyone to quit smoking.

Marijuana Smoking: Possible additive reduction in sperm counts with cimetidine use.

▷ *Other Drugs*

Cimetidine may ***increase*** the effects of

- amiodarone (Cordarone).
- amitriptyline (Elavil) and perhaps other tricyclic antidepressants (see Drug Classes). Decreased doses may be needed if the medicines are to be combined.
- amoxapine (Ascendin).
- amprenavir (Agenerase).
- benzodiazepines (Librium, Valium, etc.; see Drug Classes).
- carbamazepine (Tegretol), with increased toxicity risk. Blood level checks are recommended and ongoing carbamazepine doses adjusted to blood levels.
- carvedilol (Coreg) and increased patient monitoring is prudent.
- cyclosporine (Sandimmune, others) may result in increased blood levels and cyclosporine toxicity.
- dofetilide (Tikosyn) may result in increased blood levels and dofetilide toxicity.
- flecainide (Tambocor) and require dosing changes and more frequent blood level checks.
- loratadine (Claritin), by causing a large increase in blood levels. A study did NOT report any adverse effects on the heart from these levels, but since excessive blood levels of any medicine may be more likely to cause undesirable effects, it appears prudent to lower loratadine doses if these medicines are to be combined.
- meperidine (Demerol, others) and result in toxicity with potential respiratory depression, and low blood pressure.
- metformin (Glucophage) (increasing risk of lactic acidosis)—reduced doses are prudent.
- metoprolol (Lopressor, others), and perhaps other beta blockers (see Drug Classes), and result in very slow heartbeat and excessively low blood pressure.
- morphine (MS Contin, MSIR, others) and result in central nervous system depression and respiratory depression.
- oral anticoagulants, with increased risk of bleeding; increased frequency of INR testing is recommended.
- pentoxifylline (Trental) [excessively low blood pressure, sweating, seizures].
- phenytoin (Dilantin).
- procainamide (Procan, Pronestyl).
- propranolol (Inderal).

- quetiapine (Seroquel).
- quinidine (Quinaglute).
- sertraline (Zoloft).
- sildenafil (Viagra) may increase blood levels of sildenafil by up to 56% (800 mg cimetidine dose). Talk to your doctor about this BEFORE using these medicines together.
- sirolimus (Rapamune) may result in increased blood levels and sirolimus toxicity.
- some statin-type medicines for cholesterol (fluvastatin-Lescol and perhaps others removed from the body in similar fashion) may result in increased blood levels and fluvastatin toxicity. Watch patient for unexplained muscle ache, weakness, and call your doctor if these occur.
- tacrolimus (Prograf) may result in increased blood levels and tacrolimus toxicity.
- tamsulosin (Flomax) may result in increased blood levels and tamsulosin.
- terbinafine (Lamisil).
- theophylline (Theo-Dur, etc.).
- venlafaxine (Effexor).
- warfarin (Coumadin).
- zaleplon (Sonata) may result in increased blood levels and zaleplon toxicity. A 5 mg dose of zaleplon is prudent in people who require both medicines.
- zolmitriptan (Zomig) may result in increased blood levels and zolmitriptan toxicity.

Ranitidine may *increase* the effects of
- diazepam (Valium).
- fluvastatin (Lescol).
- glipizide (Glucotrol) and perhaps other oral antidiabetic drugs (see Drug Classes).
- metformin (Glucophage).
- midazolam (Versed).
- procainamide (Procan, Pronestyl).
- theophylline (Theo-Dur, etc.).
- warfarin (Coumadin)—rarely; increased INR testing is recommended.

Nizatidine, ranitidine and famotidine (prescription forms) may *increase* the effects of
- amoxicillin.
- high-dose aspirin (may increase level and toxicity risk).
- pentoxifylline (Trental); however, this interaction has only been documented with cimetidine.
- theophylline (Theo-Dur, others); ongoing theophylline dosing should be based on more frequent blood levels if these medicines are to be taken together.

Cimetidine *taken concurrently* with
- most calcium channel blockers (see Drug Classes) may result in increased blood levels of the calcium channel blockers and potential toxicity; decreased calcium channel–blocker doses may be needed. This may also occur with other H2 blockers, and caution is advised.
- carmustine (BiCNU) may cause severe bone marrow depression.
- carvedilol (Coreg) may result in increased blood levels and carvedilol toxicity.
- chloroquine may result in toxicity and may cause cardiac arrest.

- cisapride (Propulsid) may result in increased cisapride levels and a potentially serious increase in heart rate.
- clozapine (Clozaril) may result in increased blood levels and clozapine toxicity.
- digoxin (Lanoxin) may result in changes in digoxin levels.
- oral hypoglycemic agents such as glipizide (Glucotrol), glyburide (DiaBeta, Micronase), and tolbutamide (Tolinase, others) may result in severe low blood sugars and seizures.
- paroxetine (Paxil) and perhaps other SSRI antidepressants (see Drug Classes) may result in increased blood levels of the SSRI and require dosing changes.
- pentoxifylline (Trental) may result in increases in blood levels of pentoxifylline; pentoxifylline dose changes may be needed.
- ritonavir (Norvir), amprenavir (Agenerase), and perhaps other protease inhibitors may result in increased cimetidine levels.
- zalcitabine (Hivid) may result in increased blood levels of zalcitabine and result in toxicity; decreased doses of zalcitabine may be needed.

Cimetidine, ranitidine, famotidine and nizatidine *taken concurrently* with
- antacids will result in a decreased histamine-blocker level; it may be prudent to separate the dosing of these medicines (prescription forms) by an hour.
- delavirdine (Rescriptor) will result in a decreased amount of delavirdine getting into the body. Ongoing use of this combination of medicines is not advisable.

Cimetidine may *decrease* the effects of
- indomethacin (Indocin) and perhaps other NSAIDs, by decreasing absorption.
- iron salts, by decreasing absorption.
- ketoconazole, itraconazole, and fluconazole—taking cimetidine two hours after these medicines coupled with careful patient follow-up is prudent. The uncomplicated way to address this is to talk to your doctor about taking the antifungal with a cola beverage (low pH).
- tetracyclines, by decreasing absorption.

Ranitidine, nizatidine and famotidine may *decrease* the effects of
- indomethacin, by decreasing absorption.
- ketoconazole, itraconazole, and fluconazole. The uncomplicated way to address this is to talk to your doctor about taking the antifungal with a cola beverage (low pH).
- sucralfate (Carafate).

▷ *Driving, Hazardous Activities:* Use caution until the degree of confusion, dizziness, or other effect is seen.

Aviation Note: The use of these drugs (prescription forms) *may be a disqualification* for piloting. Consult a designated Aviation Medical Examiner.

Exposure to Sun: Rare and questionable association with some medicines in this family. Use caution with sun exposure when first starting this medicine.

Occurrence of Unrelated Illness: Idiopathic thrombocytopenic purpura (ITP), a rare lowering of blood platelets, is a contraindication for use of any of these medicines. Aplastic anemia, whatever the cause, may be worsened by cimetidine. If symptoms of heartburn get worse, you experience unexplained weight loss and are over 45 years old, talk with your doctor—this may be an indication of stomach cancer.

Discontinuation: **Do not stop these medicines suddenly if they are being taken for peptic ulcer disease.** Ask your doctor for withdrawal instructions. Be alert to the recurrence of ulcers any time after these drugs are stopped. Recurrent or refractory ulcers may also represent an infectious disease caused by Helicobacter pylori. If this is the case, combination therapy with an antibiotic may be indicated.

HYDRALAZINE (hi DRAL a zeen)

Introduced: 1950 **Class:** Antihypertensive **Prescription:** USA: Yes **Controlled Drug:** USA: No; Canada: No **Available as Generic:** USA: Yes; Canada: No

Brand Names: Alazine, Alphapress, Apo-Hydralazine, Apresazide [CD], Apresoline, Apresoline-Esidrix [CD], Cam-Ap-Es, Dralserp, Dralzine, H-H-R, Hydroserpine [CD], Hyserp [CD], Lo-Ten, Marpres, Novo-Hylazin, Nu-Hydral, Ser-A-Gen [CD], Ser-Ap-Es [CD], Serpasil-Apresoline [CD], Serprex [CD], Supres [CD], Tri-Hydroserpine, Unipres [CD], Uniserp [CD]

Author's Note: The information in this profile has been shortened to make room for more widely used medicines.

HYDROCHLOROTHIAZIDE (hi droh klor oh THI a zide)

Please see the thiazide diuretics family profile.

HYDROCODONE (hi droh KOH dohn)

Other Name: Dihydrocodeinone **Introduced:** 1951 **Class:** Analgesic, strong; cough suppressant; opioid **Prescription:** USA: Yes **Controlled Drug:** USA: C-III*; Canada: Yes **Available as Generic:** USA: Yes, hydrocodone/APAP; Canada: No

Brand Names: Allay [CD], Alor 5/500 [CD], Anaplex, Anexsia [CD], Anexsia 7.5 [CD], Anolor DH5, Atuss [CD], Azdone [CD], Ban-Tuss-HC [CD], ♣Biohisdex DHC [CD], ♣Biohisdine DHC [CD], Chemdal-HD [CD], Codone, Detussin [CD], DHC Plus, Dicoril, Dimetane Expectorant-DC [CD], Dolacet [CD], Duocet [CD], Duratuss HD [CD], Endagen HD [CD], Endal-HD, Entuss-D, Histinex-HC [CD], Histussin HC [CD], ♣Hycodan, Hycodan [CD], ♣Hycomine [CD], Hycomine Compound [CD], Hycomine Pediatric Syrup [CD], ♣Hycomine-S [CD], Hycomine Syrup [CD], Hyco-tuss Expectorant [CD], Lorcet-HD [CD], Lorcet Plus [CD], Lortab [CD], Lortab ASA [CD], Medipain 5, Norcet 7 [CD], ♣Novahistex DH [CD], ♣Novahistine DH [CD], Polygesic, Protuss, ♣Robidone, Ru-Tuss [CD], T-Gesic [CD], Triaminic Expectorant DH [CD], ♣Tussaminic Expectorant DH [CD], Tussend [CD], Tussend Expectorant [CD], Tussionex [CD], Tycolet [CD], Vanex [CD], Vicodin [CD], Vicodin ES [CD], Vicoprofen [CD], Zydone [CD]

*See Schedules of Controlled Drugs at the back of this book.

BENEFITS versus RISKS

Possible Benefits	*Possible Risks*
EFFECTIVE RELIEF OF MILD TO MODERATE PAIN	Mild allergic reactions—infrequent
	Nausea, constipation
EFFECTIVE CONTROL OF COUGH	Potential for addiction apparently greater than codeine

---

▷ **Principal Uses**

As a Single Drug Product: Uses currently included in FDA-approved labeling: (1) Controls cough; (2) relieves mild to moderate pain.

Other (unlabeled) generally accepted uses: May be a benefit for some patients with chronic obstructive lung disease (COPD).

As a Combination Drug Product [CD]: Often added to cough mixtures containing antihistamines, decongestants and expectorants to increase effectiveness in reducing cough. Also combined with analgesics, such as acetaminophen and aspirin and other nonsteroidal anti-inflammatory (NSAID) compounds, to enhance pain relief.

Author's Note: Information in this profile has been shortened to make room for more widely used medicines.

HYDROXYCHLOROQUINE (hi drox ee KLOR oh kwin)

Introduced: 1967   **Class:** Antimalarial, immunosuppressant   **Prescription:** USA: Yes   **Controlled Drug:** USA: No; Canada: No
Available as Generic: USA: Yes; Canada: No
Brand Names: ✤Dermoplast, Plaquenil

BENEFITS versus RISKS

Possible Benefits	*Possible Risks*
EFFECTIVE PREVENTION AND TREATMENT OF CERTAIN FORMS OF MALARIA	INFREQUENT DAMAGE OF CORNEAL AND RETINAL EYE TISSUES
Effective in the management of acute and chronic rheumatoid arthritis in adults who have not responded to less toxic medicines	BONE MARROW DEPRESSION
	Heart muscle damage
	Ear damage: hearing loss, ringing in ears
Possibly effective in management of chronic discoid and systemic lupus erythematosus	

▷ **Principal Uses**

As a Single Drug Product: Uses currently included in FDA-approved labeling: (1) Prevention and therapy of acute attacks of certain types of malaria; (2) reduces disease activity in rheumatoid arthritis in adults who have not responded to less toxic medicines; (3) suppresses disease activity in chronic discoid and systemic lupus erythematosus.

Other (unlabeled) generally accepted uses: (1) Treatment of Sjögren's syndrome; (2) treats refractory Lyme arthritis; (3) therapy of sarcoidosis, polymorphous light eruption, porphyria, solar urticaria, and chronic vasculitis; (4) may help decrease steroid requirements in asthma; (5) can help decrease insulin needs when an oral hypoglycemic agent is taken with insulin; (6) combination therapy of Weber-Christian disease.

How This Drug Works: In malaria, this drug impairs DNA in the organisms. As an antiarthritic and antilupus drug, acts as a mild immunosuppressant. Accumulates in white blood cells and inhibits many enzymes involved in tissue destruction.

Available Dosage Forms and Strengths

Tablets — 200 mg

▷ **Usual Adult Dosage Ranges**

For malaria suppression: 400 mg once every 7 days. Treatment starts 2 weeks before entering an area where malaria is present and continues for 8 weeks after returning. If treatment is not started before going into an area where malaria is likely (endemic), 800 mg should be the initial dose (can be given as two 400 mg doses 6 hours apart).

For malaria treatment: (1) 800 mg as a single dose or (2) initially 800 mg, followed by 400 mg in 6 to 8 hours; then 400 mg once a day on the second and third days.

For pediatric malaria treatment: 10 mg per kg of body mass followed in 6 hours by 5 mg per kg of body mass, with 5 mg per kg of body mass given 18 hours after the second dose; then 5 mg per kg of body mass taken 24 hours after the first dose.

For lupus erythematosus: 400 mg once or twice daily. This is used for several weeks or cautiously until remission. Ongoing dose is 200–400 mg daily.

For rheumatoid arthritis: Starting dose of 400 to 600 mg and an ongoing dose of 200–400 mg a day.

Note: Actual dose and schedule must be determined for each patient individually.

Conditions Requiring Dosing Adjustments

Liver Function: Benefit-to-risk decision by patients with liver compromise or who take liver-toxic drugs.

Kidney Function: Use with caution in kidney compromise.

▷ **Dosing Instructions:** Take with food or milk to reduce stomach irritation. The tablet may be crushed and mixed with jam, jelly, or gelatin. Take it exactly as prescribed.

Author's Note: For malaria prevention, begin medication 2 weeks before entering malarious area; continue medication while in the area and for 8 weeks after leaving the area.

For treating arthritis and lupus, take medication on a regular schedule daily; continual use for 6 months may be necessary to determine maximal benefit. If you forget a dose: take it as soon as you remember it, unless it's nearly time for your next dose—if that is the case, skip the missed dose and return to taking the medicine on your usual schedule. DO NOT double doses. If you only take one dose a week, call your doctor for instructions.

Usual Duration of Use: Use on a regular schedule for 2 weeks before exposure, during period of exposure and 8 weeks after exposure determines this drug's effectiveness in preventing attacks of malaria. Use on a regular schedule for up to 6 months may be required to evaluate benefits in reducing rheumatoid arthritis and lupus erythematosus. If significant improvement is not achieved in 6 months of treatment in rheumatoid arthritis, this drug should be stopped. Long-term use (months to years) requires periodic physician evaluation.

Possible Advantages of This Drug
Considered to have less potential for retinal toxicity than chloroquine.

Typical Treatment Goals and Measurements (Outcomes and Markers)
Rheumatoid arthritis: Most rheumatologists use sign and symptom control, joint mobility and pain as indicators of success of therapy. For clinicians treating pain, a device called an algometer is used to check your pain. This looks like a small ruler, but lets the clinician better understand your pain. The goals of treatment then relate to where the level of pain started (for example, a rating of 7 on a 0 to 10 scale) and what the cause of the pain was. Pain medicines may also be used together (in combination) in order to get the best result or outcome. If your pain control is not acceptable to YOU (remember, in hospitals and outpatient settings, etc. pain control is a patient right) and if results are not acceptable, be sure to call your doctor as you may need a different medicine or combination.

Currently a Drug of Choice
For the treatment of chronic discoid and systemic lupus erythematosus.

▷ **This Drug Should Not Be Taken If**
• you had past allergies to chloroquine or hydroxychloroquine.
• you have an active bone marrow or blood cell disorder.
• it was prescribed for long-term treatment in children (should not be used in that way).

▷ **Inform Your Physician Before Taking This Drug If**
• you are pregnant or planning pregnancy.
• you have had bone marrow depression or a blood cell disorder.
• you have a deficiency of glucose-6-phosphate dehydrogenase (G6PD)—talk with your doctor.
• you have any disorder of the eyes, especially disease of the cornea or retina or visual field changes.
• you have impaired hearing or ringing in the ears.
• you have a seizure disorder of any kind.
• you have a history of peripheral neuritis.
• you have low blood pressure or a heart rhythm disorder.
• you have peptic ulcer disease, Crohn's disease or ulcerative colitis.
• you have impaired liver or kidney function.
• you have a history of porphyria.
• you have any form of psoriasis.
• you are taking antacids, cimetidine, digoxin, or penicillamine.

Possible Side Effects (natural, expected, and unavoidable drug actions)
Light-headedness (low blood pressure); blue-black discoloration of skin, fingernails, or mouth lining with long-term use.

▷ **Possible Adverse Effects** (unusual, unexpected, and infrequent reactions)
If any of the following develop, consult your physician promptly for guidance.
Mild Adverse Effects
Allergic reactions: skin rash, itching (more common in African Americans).
Loss of hair color, loss of hair.
Headache, blurring of near vision (reading), ringing in ears—possible to infrequent.
Loss of appetite, nausea, vomiting, stomach cramps, diarrhea—infrequent.
Dizziness—case reports.

Serious Adverse Effects

Allergic reactions: severe skin rash, exfoliative dermatitis.

Idiosyncratic reactions: hemolytic anemia in those with glucose-6-phosphate dehydrogenase (G6PD) deficiency in red blood cells.

Emotional or psychotic mental changes; seizures—case reports.

Loss of hearing, porphyria—case reports.

Eye tissue damage, specifically cornea and retina, with significant impairment of vision—case reports.

Aplastic anemia (see Glossary): abnormally low red blood cell counts (fatigue and weakness); abnormally low white blood cell counts (fever, sore throat, infections); abnormally low platelet counts (abnormal bruising or bleeding)—case reports.

Muscle damage (myopathy)—case report.

▷ **Possible Effects on Sexual Function:** None reported.

Possible Delayed Adverse Effects: Irreversible eye (retinal) damage has developed 7 years after discontinuation of chloroquine, a closely related drug. Retinal damage is more likely to occur following high-dose and/or long-term use.

▷ **Adverse Effects That May Mimic Natural Diseases or Disorders**

Central nervous system toxicity may suggest unrelated neuropsychiatric disorder. Seizures may suggest the onset of epilepsy.

Natural Diseases or Disorders That May Be Activated by This Drug

Porphyria, psoriasis.

Possible Effects on Laboratory Tests

Complete blood cell counts: decreased red cells, hemoglobin, white cells, and platelets.

Liver function tests: increased liver enzymes (ALT/GPT, AST/GOT, and alkaline phosphatase), increased bilirubin.

Electrocardiogram: conduction abnormalities, prolonged QRS interval, T-wave changes, and heart block have all been reported for chloroquine, a closely related drug.

CAUTION

1. Does not prevent relapses in certain types of malaria.
2. High-dose and/or long-term use of this drug may cause irreversible retinal damage, significant visual impairment, or hearing loss due to nerve damage. Report promptly any changes in vision or hearing so appropriate evaluation can be made.
3. If toxic signs and symptoms happen, ammonium chloride in a dose of 8 grams a day divided into equal doses may help removal of this drug in adults.

Precautions for Use

By Infants and Children: This age group is very sensitive to the effects of this drug. Doses should be determined and therapy should be monitored by a qualified pediatrician.

By Those Over 60 Years of Age: Tolerance for this drug may be reduced. Watch for behavioral changes, low blood pressure, heart rhythm disturbances, muscle weakness, and changes in vision or hearing.

▷ **Advisability of Use During Pregnancy**

Pregnancy Category: C. See Pregnancy Risk Categories at the back of this book.

Animal Studies: No information available.

Human Studies: Adequate studies of pregnant women are not available. However, closely related drugs of this class are known to cause abnormal retinal pigmentation and hemorrhage and congenital deafness in the fetus.

Avoid use during pregnancy except for the suppression or treatment of malaria. Other use is a benefit-to-risk decision.

Advisability of Use If Breast-Feeding

Presence of this drug in breast milk: Yes.

Avoid drug or refrain from nursing (controversial).

Habit-Forming Potential: None.

Effects of Overdose: Drowsiness, headache, blurred vision, excitability, low blood pressure, seizures, coma.

Possible Effects of Long-Term Use: Irreversible eye damage (cornea and retina), hearing loss, muscle weakness, aplastic anemia.

Suggested Periodic Examinations While Taking This Drug (at physician's discretion)

Complete blood cell counts.

Liver and kidney function tests.

Serial blood pressure readings and electrocardiograms.

Neurological examinations for significant muscle weakness.

Complete eye examinations before starting high-dose and/or long-term treatment and every 3 to 6 months during drug use.

Hearing tests as indicated.

▷ **While Taking This Drug, Observe the Following**

Foods: No restrictions.

Herbal Medicines or Minerals: Caution: St. John's wort may also cause extreme reactions to the sun. Additive photosensitivity may be possible. Hay flower, mistletoe herb, and white mustard seed carry German Commission E monograph indications for arthritis, but have not been studied with this medicine. Talk to your doctor BEFORE combining any herb with hydroxychloroquine.

Beverages: No restrictions. May be taken with milk.

▷ *Alcohol:* Use sparingly to minimize stomach irritation.

Tobacco Smoking: No interactions expected, but I advise everyone to quit smoking.

▷ *Other Drugs*

Hydroxychloroquine may *increase* the effects of

• aurothioglucose (Solganol), which increases risk of blood problems.

• digoxin (Lanoxin) and increase its toxic potential.

• metoprolol (Lopressor). Close follow-up of blood pressure and potential decrease in dose is prudent.

• penicillamine (Cuprimine, Depen) and increase its toxic potential.

The following drug may *increase* the effects of hydroxychloroquine:

• cimetidine (Tagamet).

The following drugs may **decrease** the effects of hydroxychloroquine:

• magnesium salts and antacids.

▷ *Driving, Hazardous Activities:* This drug may cause light-headedness, blurred vision, or impaired hearing. Restrict activities as necessary.

Aviation Note: The use of this drug *may be a disqualification* for piloting. Consult a designated Aviation Medical Examiner.

Exposure to Sun: Use caution until sensitivity has been determined. Closely related drugs of this class may cause photosensitivity (see Glossary and on page 551 Herbal Medicines note on St. John's wort).

Discontinuation: This drug should be stopped and prompt evaluation should be made if any of the following develop—changes in vision or hearing, seizures, unusual muscle weakness, indications of infection (fever, sore throat, etc.), abnormal bruising or bleeding.

HYDROXYUREA (hi DROX EE yur ia)

Introduced: 1995 (AIDS or sickle cell)   **Class:**   Anti-AIDS, anticancer, anti–sickle-cell anemia   **Prescription:**   USA: Yes   **Controlled Drug:** USA: No; Canada: No   **Available as Generic:**   USA: Yes; Canada: No

Brand Names: Droxia, Hydrea, Mylocel

Warning: This drug is a cytotoxic agent. Appropriate precautions must be taken, as with other chemotherapy.

BENEFITS versus RISKS	
Possible Benefits	*Possible Risks*
COMBINATION TREATMENT OF AIDS	BONE MARROW SUPPRESSION
DECREASED SEVERITY AND FREQUENCY OF SICKLE-CELL CRISES	Hepatitis
Treatment of chronic myelocytic leukemia, melanoma, and other cancers	Possible secondary leukemia-causing agent (long-term 7–10 years of therapy)

▷ **Principal Uses**

As a Single Drug Product: Uses currently included in FDA-approved labeling: (1) Blast crisis; (2) chronic myelogenous leukemia; (3) head, neck, and ovarian cancers; (4) chronic leukemias; (5) cancers of certain cell types (squamous cell); (6) decreases frequency and severity of sickle-cell crises; (7) malignant melanoma.

Other (unlabeled) generally accepted uses: (1) Used to treat certain diseases of the red blood cells (polycythemia vera); (2) used in combination with other medicines to treat HIV-positive patients (possible first-line or salvage therapy); (3) brain cancer.

Author's Note: Combination therapy has become a standard of care. NIAID antiretroviral therapy guidelines take into account how easily HIV therapy can fit into a patient's life. The ATIS Guidelines (AIDS Treatment Information Service—*www.hivatis.org/guidelines/adult/May23_02/AAMay23.pdf*) tell us that therapy should be supervised by an expert, and cover considerations of when to start therapy in both asymptomatic and established HIV infections. Adherence or taking medicines for HIV exactly on time and in the right amount is ABSOLUTELY critical to getting the best possible results or outcomes. Structured therapy interruptions (STI) or structured interruptions of therapy (SIT) are still controversial.

How This Drug Works: When used in cancer, this medicine is a cell-cycle-specific drug. It works in the S phase of mitosis. When used in HIV-positive patients, the exact mechanism of action is not fully understood. When used in sickle-cell patients, the specific mechanism has not been identified.

Available Dosage Forms and Strengths
Capsules (Droxia) — 200 mg, 300 mg, 400 mg
Capsule (Hydrea) — 500 mg
Tablet (Mylocel) — 1,000 mg

▷ **Recommended Dosage Ranges** (Actual dose and schedule must be determined for each patient individually.)

Infants and Children: Safety and effectiveness have not been defined in this age group.

18 to 60 Years of Age: All doses are decided based on ideal or actual body mass, whichever is less.

Oral dosing: Usual oral doses range from 20 to 30 mg per kg of body mass per day, which is given as a single daily dose. Some centers give 80 mg per kg of body mass every third day. If a patient is in blast crisis, up to 12 g per day has been given to rapidly decrease white blood cell counts.

In sickle-cell anemia: Starting dose of 15 mg per kg of body mass. Depending on the blood (hematologic) response, the dose is increased by 5 mg per kg of body mass every 12 weeks (unless toxicity occurs) to the maximum dose of 35 mg per kg of body mass per day or to the maximum dose less than 35 mg per kg that is tolerated.

In HIV/AIDS: The protocols are still changing.

Over 60 Years of Age: Same as 18 to 60 years of age.

Conditions Requiring Dosing Adjustments
Liver Function: No changes in dosing are anticipated.
Kidney Function: The dose must be decreased for patients with kidney compromise. Decreases of up to 80% are needed in severe compromise.

▷ **Dosing Instructions:** This medicine is best taken on an empty stomach. Do not crush, open or alter the capsules. Call your doctor if you vomit after taking this medicine. If you forget a dose: take it as soon as you remember it, unless it's nearly time for your next dose—if that is the case, skip the missed dose and return to taking the medicine on your usual schedule. DO NOT double doses. Adherence with this medicine is very important. Follow-up with required laboratory testing is also critical. Call your doctor if you find yourself forgetting doses.

Usual Duration of Use: Continual use on a regular schedule for up to 16 weeks may be needed to treat cancers of the head and neck. Treatment in sickle-cell disease is ongoing, using the lowest effective dose.

Treatment in HIV-positive patients is yet to be defined.

Long-term use (months to years) requires periodic evaluation of response and dose adjustment. Consult your physician on a regular basis.

Typical Treatment Goals and Measurements (Outcomes and Markers)
Sickle-cell anemia: The severity and number of sickle-cell attacks is used as a marker for success when treating sickle-cell anemia. This medicine can also help decrease the number of sudden (acute) visits to the emergency room and subsequent hospitalizations for sickle-cell crisis.

Currently a Drug of Choice
For reducing the frequency and severity of sickle-cell crises in patients with sickle-cell disease.

▷ **This Drug Should Not Be Taken If**
• you had an allergic reaction to it previously.
• you have severely depressed bone marrow. This is seen in very low white

blood cell, platelet, or hemoglobin levels (neutrophils less than 2,000, platelets less than 100,000 or severe anemia).

▷ **Inform Your Physician Before Taking This Drug If**
- you have signs or symptoms of cancer.
- you are considering pregnancy (males or females).
- you have had chemotherapy or radiation therapy previously.
- you have compromised kidneys.
- you have herpes zoster (shingles).
- you have recently been exposed to chicken pox.
- you are having unusual bruising or bleeding.
- you are unsure how to dispose of urine or vomit.
- you are unsure how much to take or how often to take it.
- you plan to breast-feed your baby.
- you take prescription or nonprescription medicines not discussed when hydroxyurea was prescribed.

Possible Side Effects (natural, expected, and unavoidable drug actions)
Hair loss, painful mouth sores, sensitivity to the sun, hair loss—rare.

▷ **Possible Adverse Effects** (unusual, unexpected, and infrequent reactions)
If any of the following develop, consult your physician promptly for guidance.
Mild Adverse Effects
Allergic reactions: skin rash and itching or fever.
Dizziness, disorientation, headaches, or fever—rare.
Nausea, vomiting, or diarrhea—frequent (vomiting usually mild).
Difficulty urinating—rare.
Ulceration of the skin—rare.
Serious Adverse Effects
Allergic reactions: skin ulceration—case reports.
Idiosyncratic reactions: not reported.
Bone marrow depression—possible.
Convulsions or hallucinations—rare.
Hepatitis or kidney problems—rare.
Drug-induced lupus erythematosus—case report.
Lung problems (acute interstitial lung disease)—rare.
Squamous cancer (carcinoma) or leukemia—possible increased risk.

▷ **Possible Effects on Sexual Function:** None reported.

Possible Delayed Adverse Effects: Bone marrow suppression, temporary decrease in kidney function.

▷ **Adverse Effects That May Mimic Natural Diseases or Disorders**
Liver toxicity may be similar to acute hepatitis.

Natural Diseases or Disorders That May Be Activated by This Drug
Not defined.

Possible Effects on Laboratory Tests
Liver function tests: increased.
Complete blood counts: decreases in several components.

CAUTION
1. This medicine is toxic to cells. Be certain your doctor has carefully explained how to dispose of urine or vomit.
2. Call your doctor at once if you have a seizure.
3. Both women and men should avoid conception for several months after taking this medicine.

4. Wash your hands after taking this medicine before you touch your eyes or your nose.

Precautions for Use

By Infants and Children: Safety and effectiveness for use by those under 18 years of age have not been established.

By Those Over 60 Years of Age: Lower doses are prudent, as increased sensitivity to any dose may occur. Natural declines in kidney function may require dose decrease.

▷ **Advisability of Use During Pregnancy**

Pregnancy Category: D. See Pregnancy Risk Categories at the back of this book.

Animal Studies: Causes birth defects in animals.

Human Studies: Adequate studies of pregnant women are not available.

Talk with your doctor about this benefit-to-risk decision.

Advisability of Use If Breast-Feeding

Presence of this drug in breast milk: Yes.

Avoid drug or refrain from nursing.

Habit-Forming Potential: None.

Effects of Overdose: Bone marrow depression, increased heart rate, liver cell and testicular damage.

Possible Effects of Long-Term Use: Bone marrow depression.

Suggested Periodic Examinations While Taking This Drug (at physician's discretion)

Complete blood cell counts.

Dental exams.

▷ **While Taking This Drug, Observe the Following**

Foods: No restrictions, but folic acid is recommended with Droxia treatment.

Herbal Medicines or Minerals: Some patients use echinacea to attempt to boost their immune systems. Unfortunately, use of echinacea is not recommended in people with damaged immune systems. This herb may also actually weaken any immune system if it is used too often or for too long a time. **Caution:** St. John's wort may also cause extreme reactions to the sun. Additive photosensitivity may be possible.

Beverages: No restrictions. May be taken with milk.

▷ *Alcohol:* Do not drink alcohol.

Tobacco Smoking: No interactions expected. I advise everyone to quit smoking.

▷ *Other Drugs*

Hydroxyurea *taken concurrently* with

- amphotericin (Abelcet) may increase risk of kidney toxicity and spasm of bronchi.
- didanosine (DDI) may increase risk of lactic acidosis.
- fluorouracil (Efudil) may increase toxicity to nerves.
- other medicines that cause bone marrow depression (see Table 5, Section Six) may lead to additive toxicity to bone marrow.
- stavudine (Zerit) may increase risk of lactic acidosis.
- vaccines (live virus, such as smallpox vaccine) may result in undesirable or life-threatening effects if immune system is depressed.

▷ *Driving, Hazardous Activities:* This drug may cause light-headedness, blurred vision, or impaired hearing. Restrict activities as necessary.

Aviation Note: The use of this drug *may be a disqualification* for piloting. Consult a designated Aviation Medical Examiner.

Exposure to Sun: Use caution until sensitivity has been determined. Closely related drugs of this class may cause photosensitivity (see Glossary). See Herbal Medicines caution on St. John's wort on page 555.

Discontinuation: This drug should be stopped and prompt evaluation should be made if any of the following develop—changes in vision or hearing, seizures, unusual muscle weakness, indications of infection (fever, sore throat, etc.), abnormal bruising or bleeding.

IBANDRONATE (ih BAN droh nate)

Recently approved by the FDA for once-daily treatment of osteoporosis with the original name of Boniva (being changed due to a similarity in name with a different medicine at the time of this writing). Further research is being undertaken by the company to see if giving this medicine less often (such as every 14–21 days) will still have beneficial effects. This profile will be broadened in future editions as clinical research warrants.

IBUPROFEN (i byu PROH fen is official pronunciation, EYE byu proh fen is the common one)

Please see the propionic acid (nonsteroidal anti-inflammatory drug) family profile.

IMATINIB (im ah TIN ib)

Introduced: 2001, February 2002 for GIST tumors   **Class:**   Protein-tyrosine kinase inhibitor, signal transduction inhibitor, pharmacogenomic, anti-cancer   **Prescription:**   USA: Yes   **Controlled Drug:**   USA: No; Canada: No   **Available as Generic:**   No
Brand Name: Gleevec

BENEFITS versus RISKS

Possible Benefits	*Possible Risks*
EFFECTIVE TREATMENT OF CHRONIC MYELOID LEUKEMIA (IN BLAST CRISIS, ACCELERATED PHASE OR IN CHRONIC PHASE AFTER FAILURE OF INTERFERON-ALPHA THERAPY)	HEMATOLOGICAL TOXICITY EDEMA (MAY BE SEVERE) Liver toxicity Opportunistic infections (with long-term use in animals)
APPROVED FOR TREATING KIT (CD117) POSITIVE GASTROINTESTINAL STROMAL TUMORS (GIST) THAT ARE NOT RESECTABLE OR HAVE SPREAD (METASTATIC)	
TREATS PEDIATRIC PATIENTS WITH Ph+ PHILADELPHIA POSITIVE CHRONIC MYELOID LEUKEMIA IN CHRONIC PHASE	

▷ **Principal Uses**

As a Single Drug Product: Uses currently included in FDA-approved labeling: (1) Treats patients with chronic myeloid leukemia (CML) who are in blast crisis, accelerated phase or who are in chronic phase after failure of interferon-alpha therapy; (2) works in gastrointestinal stromal tumors (GIST) that are unresectable or that have spread (metastasized); (3) Treats pediatric patients who are Ph+ (Philadelphia chromosome positive) in chronic phase (for children who have had the disease happen again (recur) after stem cell transplant or in those children who are resistant to interferon treatment.

Other (unlabeled) generally accepted uses: (1) One small study of use in myeloid dysplasia with further study needed.

In the Pipeline: In leukemia patients treated with imatinib (Gleevec), filgrastim was successfully used to mobilize peripheral blood stem cells (PBSC) in people who achieved complete cytogenetic response (CCR). The yield of CD 34+ cells was improved when imatinib was withheld temporarily (see Hui, CH in Sources).

How This Drug Works: By inhibiting protein kinase, this medicine inhibits the Bcr-Abl abnormal kinase required by Philadelphia chromosome–positive chronic myelogenous leukemia cells. This works to stop the abnormal and excessive number of white blood cells seen in that kind of leukemia. In GIST tumors, this signal transduction inhibitor (STI) interferes with a gene named c-kit which makes cells divide and multiply when the gene is stuck in the "on" position.

Available Dosage Forms and Strengths

Capsules — 50 mg (Canada), 100 mg

▷ **Usual Adult Dosage Ranges**

Chronic phase chronic myelogenous leukemia (CML): 400 mg is given daily. This dose should be taken at the same time each day with a meal and a large glass of water. In patients who do not get an acceptable initial response (see below) dose increases have been used, with ongoing chronic phase dose of 600 mg once daily.

Blast crisis or accelerated phase CML: 600 mg daily. The dose should be taken at the same time each day with a meal and a large glass of water. If patients fail to get an acceptable response, dose increase to 800 mg (given as 400 mg twice a day) has been used by some clinicians.

Unresectable and/or metastatic, malignant GIST: CD 117–positive patients are given 400 mg to 600 mg a day as a starting dose. Careful dosing adjustment should be made by a qualified specialist (for example, in people also getting medicines that increase the liver enzymes that remove this drug-CYP 450 3A4 inducers).

Note: Actual dose and schedule must be determined for each patient individually.

Conditions Requiring Dosing Adjustments

Liver Function: Not studied in patients with compromised liver function. If liver bilirubin increases by 3 times the upper limit of normal (ULN), or if other liver function tests (liver transaminases) increase by 5 times the ULN, imatinib should be held until bilirubin levels have lowered to 1.5 ULN or transaminase levels to less than 2.5 ULN. Once those conditions are met, therapy can continue at a reduced daily dose.

Kidney Function: Not studied in patients with decreased kidney (renal) function. Clinical trials specifically excluded those with serum creatinine levels more than 2 times the upper limit of normal. Metabolites and imatinib itself are not significantly removed by the kidney.

▷ **Dosing Instructions:** Doses should be taken at the same time each day with a meal and a large glass of water (lessens gastrointestinal tract irritation). If increases in bilirubin or liver enzymes develop, dosing instructions above should be followed. If severe lowering of white blood cells (neutropenia) or severe lowering of platelets happens, specific steps MUST be taken (see "Caution"). If you forget a dose: take it as soon as you remember it, unless it's nearly time for your next dose—if that is the case, skip the missed dose and return to taking the medicine on your usual schedule. DO NOT double doses. Call your doctor for instructions if you miss more than one dose.

Usual Duration of Use: Duration of use will be decided by your doctor based on response of the condition being treated. For example, in CML, resolution of blast crisis and lowering of abnormally elevated white blood cell counts as well as development of any adverse effects will determine the course of therapy. In GIST, tumor response and adverse effect development will determine therapy steps to be taken. Follow-up of many patients treated with this medicine has been short (less than 6 months). The medicine is generally continued as long as the patient continues to have benefits from it. Long-term safety information of treatment with this medicine is still emerging. Talk to your doctor on a regular basis.

Typical Treatment Goals and Measurements (Outcomes and Markers)

CML: The number and type of white blood cells are used to describe the kind of leukemia. For example, in blast crisis, a certain amount and a certain kind of white blood cell predominates the cells seen in the blood/bone marrow. Resolution of the kind and number of cells toward normal levels indicates response of the condition to the medicine. Usual terms used are: no evidence of leukemia (NEL) or return to chronic phase of CML.

GIST: Shrinkage of the tumor and lack of tumor progression are indicators that the situation is resolving.

Possible Advantages of This Drug

Response of GIST where responses to other chemotherapy were poor. Response of CML where other treatment has failed and blast crisis resulted and return to chronic phase is an excellent result.

Currently a "Drug of Choice"

For use in CML in blast crisis, accelerated phase or chronic phase after interferon-alpha failure. For kit (CD 117)-positive GIST tumors.

▷ **This Drug Should Not Be Taken If**
- you have had an allergic reaction to it previously.
- your absolute neutrophil count and/or platelets have dropped or bilirubin or liver transaminases have increased to unacceptable levels.

▷ **Inform Your Physician Before Taking This Drug If**
- you have an increase in bilirubin or liver transaminases that your doctor is not aware of.
- your white blood cells (neutrophils) have lowered to less than 1.0×10^9 per liter or your platelets have dropped to less than 50×10^9 per liter.
- you are taking medicines that change or are removed by cytochrome P450 3A4 or 2C9.
- you have any type of heart disease, especially congestive heart failure that may be worsened by fluid accumulation.
- you have impaired liver or kidney function.
- you are pregnant or are breast-feeding your infant.
- you develop swelling of the ankles while taking this medicine.
- you have a history of alcoholism.

Possible Side Effects (natural, expected, and unavoidable drug actions)

Weakness and headache—possible (may be more pronounced in women). Weight gain (because of fluid retention). Rapid increases in weight should be promptly evaluated, probably represent fluid increases in the body and are generally treated with water pills (diuretics) and/or decreases in doses. Return of hair color (repigmentation).

▷ **Possible Adverse Effects** (unusual, unexpected, and infrequent reactions)

If any of the following develop, consult your physician promptly for guidance.

Mild Adverse Effects

Allergic reactions—possible.

Nausea, vomiting, diarrhea—possible to infrequent.

Fluid retention/edema—may be frequent.

Muscle cramps—frequent.

Fever—infrequent.

Serious Adverse Effects

Allergic reactions—possible.

Idiosyncratic reactions—not reported as yet.

Liver or kidney toxicity—infrequent.

Rupture of the spleen (splenic rupture)—case reports.

Carcinogenicity studies not yet performed, but positive genotoxic effects were seen in an in vitro mammalian cell assay (Chinese hamster ovary).

Fluid retention/edema (including rapid weight gain, and/or pulmonary edema, and/or fluid around the eye-periorbital edema—possible (some cases have been life threatening) and periorbital edema may be frequent.

Abnormally low white blood cell and platelet counts: fever, sore throat, infections, abnormal bleeding or bruising—possible and dose related.

▷ **Possible Effects on Sexual Function:** Not reported.

▷ **Adverse Effects That May Mimic Natural Diseases or Disorders**

Liver toxicity may suggest viral hepatitis.

Natural Diseases or Disorders That May Be Activated by This Drug

Not defined.

Possible Effects on Laboratory Tests

Complete blood cell counts: decreased white cells (neutropenia) and platelets (depends on the stage of the disease).

Kidney function tests: increased BUN or creatinine.

Liver function tests: increased liver enzymes (ALT/GPT, AST/GOT, and alkaline phosphatase), increased bilirubin.

CAUTION

1. Look for early signs of liver, kidney, or hematologic toxicity.
2. If a different doctor than the one prescribing imatinib wants to start a new prescription medicine, make certain you tell him or her that you are taking this medicine.
3. Talk to your doctor if you have an unexplained weight gain or swelling of the ankles.
4. Be certain to keep appointments for any follow-up laboratory testing that your doctor orders.
5. Specific interruptions of therapy steps should be taken if platelet counts or the absolute neutrophil count (ANC) are in the range of: white blood cells (neutrophils) have lowered to less than 1.0×10^9 per liter or your platelets have dropped to less than 50×10^9 per liter.

Precautions for Use

By Infants and Children: New indication for pediatrics in Ph+ (Philadelphia chromosome—positive) patients with chronic myeloid leukemia who have had their disease come back (recur) after stem cell transplant or in those who are resistant to interferon treatment.

By Those Over 60 Years of Age: Results (efficacy) were similar to younger patients. Edema happened more often in older patients than younger ones.

▷ **Advisability of Use During Pregnancy**

Pregnancy Category: D. See Pregnancy Risk Categories at the back of this book.

Human Studies: Information from adequate studies of pregnant women is not available.

Talk to your doctor if you become pregnant while taking this medicine and ask your doctor for guidance about the risk of fetal damage versus the benefits this medicine brings to you.

Advisability of Use If Breast-Feeding

Presence of this drug in breast milk: Yes, estimated at 1.5%.

Breast-feeding is NOT recommended.

Habit-Forming Potential: Not defined, not expected.

Effects of Overdose: Limited experience. An oral dose of 2.5 times the human dose given to rats was not lethal after 14 days. A dose equal to 7.5 times the human dose was lethal to rats after 7–10 days.

Possible Effects of Long-Term Use: Hematologic toxicity—possible; immunosuppression, liver or kidney toxicity.

Suggested Periodic Examinations While Taking This Drug (at physician's discretion)

Complete blood cell counts.

Liver and kidney function tests.

Weight.

Pedal edema checks.

Check of GIST tumor progression or regression.

▷ **While Taking This Drug, Observe the Following**

Foods: No specific restrictions, and food may help lessen GI irritation.

Herbal Medicines or Minerals: Some people take echinacea or mistletoe to try to boost their immune systems. Since neither herb was studied with imatinib, this is NOT recommended. Because St. John's wort acts on the cytochrome P450 system, DO NOT COMBINE. Talk to your doctor BEFORE combining any herbal medicine with imatinib.

Beverages: No restrictions. Should be taken with a full glass of water.

▷ *Alcohol:* May increase stomach and intestinal irritation that can be caused by this drug. Talk to your doctor about this.

Tobacco Smoking: No specific interactions, but I advise everyone to quit.

Marijuana Smoking: Increased chance of opportunistic fungal infections and possible drug level changes.

▷ *Other Drugs*

Imatinib may ***increase*** the effects of

- carbamazepine (Tegretol).
- dihydropyridine calcium channel blockers.
- dofetilide (Tikosyn).
- medicines removed by cytochrome P450 2C9.
- triazole benzodiazepines.

- warfarin (Coumadin). Patients who require a blood thinner (anticoagulant) would more prudently be given a low molecular weight heparin (see Drug Classes).

Imatinib *taken concurrently* with

- all drugs requiring cytochrome P450 3A4 for removal from the body or inhibiting (such as clarithromycin and voriconazole) or inducing (such as phenytoin-Dilantin) that enzyme would be expected to increase or decrease blood levels of imatinib.
- anticonvulsants requires careful monitoring for changes in seizure patterns and need to adjust anticonvulsant dose.
- cyclosporine (Sandimmune) should have more frequent cyclosporine blood levels and dosing adjusted to blood levels.
- fosphenytoin (Cerebyx) or phenytoin (Dilantin) may excessively lower the blood level of imatinib.
- medicines with hematologic toxicity may lead to additive toxicity if combined with imatinib.
- ritonavir (Norvir) and perhaps other protease inhibitors (see Drug Classes) may lead to toxicity.
- "statin"-type medicines (see Drug Classes)—such as simvastatin or Zocor—may lead to toxicity. Lower doses of all are prudent. Pravastatin (Pravachol) may be a drug of choice if a statin is needed because it does not rely on the P450 3A4 system.

The following drugs may *increase* the effects of imatinib:

- azole antifungals (such as fluconazole, itraconazole and ketoconazole) may lead to higher-than-expected imatinib blood levels and increased risk of adverse effects.
- macrolide antibiotics (Erythromycin [various] or clarithromycin [Biaxin]).

The following drugs may *decrease* the effects of imatinib:

- barbiturates (see Drug Classes).
- carbamazepine (Tegretol).
- dexamethasone (various).
- fosphenytoin (Cerebyx) or phenytoin (Dilantin) may excessively lower the blood level of imatinib.
- rifampin (various).

▷ *Driving, Hazardous Activities:* Fatigue from this medicine or from the underlying condition may make operating hazardous equipment dangerous. Restrict activities as necessary.

Aviation Note: The use of this drug *is probably a disqualification* for piloting. Consult a designated Aviation Medical Examiner.

Exposure to Heat: Use caution. This drug can cause temperature increases.

Discontinuation: Talk to your doctor before stopping this medicine for any reason.

IMIPRAMINE (im IP ra meen)

Introduced: 1955   **Class:** Antidepressant   **Prescription:** USA: Yes
Controlled Drug: USA: No; Canada: No   **Available as Generic:**   USA: Yes; Canada: Yes

Brand Names: Antipress, ✤Apo-Imipramine, ✤Impril, Imprin, Janimine, ✤Novo-Pramine, ✤PMS Imipramine, Presamoine, SK-Pramine, Tipramine, Tofranil, Tofranil-PM, W.D.D.

BENEFITS versus RISKS

Possible Benefits	*Possible Risks*
EFFECTIVE RELIEF OF NEUROSES AND PSYCHOTIC DEPRESSION	ADVERSE BEHAVIORAL EFFECTS
EFFECTIVE TREATMENT FOR CHILDHOOD BED-WETTING (enuresis)	CONVERSION OF DEPRESSION TO MANIA in manic-depressive (bipolar) disorders
Helps manage chronic, severe pain	Aggravation of schizophrenia and paranoia
Aids cocaine withdrawal	Induction of serious heart rhythm abnormalities
Relieves symptoms of attention deficit disorder	Abnormally low white blood cell and platelet counts
Helps prevent panic attacks	
Helps control binge eating and purging in bulimia	

▷ **Principal Uses**

As a Single Drug Product: Uses currently included in FDA-approved labeling: (1) Relieves severe emotional depression and initiates gradual restoration of normal mood; (2) helps prevent childhood bed-wetting in children over 6 years of age; (3) used to treat delusions.

Other (unlabeled) generally accepted uses: (1) Helps treat agoraphobia; (2) some case evidence of help in treating aspermia; (3) can be of help in chronic pain syndromes; (4) eases diabetic neuropathy; (5) inappropriate emotionalism (such as pathological crying) can be controlled by this drug; (6) of use in globus hystericus; (7) may have a role in treating panic disorder; (8) can help post-traumatic stress disorder; (9) may help control retrograde ejaculation; (10) can be of adjunctive benefit in helping control schizophrenia; (11) shows some benefit in patients who fail ear, nose, or throat surgery or weight reduction as treatment of sleep apnea; (12) may be of help as a second-line agent in attention deficit disorder (ADD).

Author's Note: Information in this profile has been shortened to make room for more widely used medicines.

INDAPAMIDE (in DAP a mide)

Introduced: 1974   **Class:** Antihypertensive, diuretic   **Prescription:** USA: Yes   **Controlled Drug:** USA: No; Canada: No   **Available as Generic:** Yes

Brand Names: ✚Apo-Indapamide, ✚Biprel [CD] indapamide and perindopril, Dom-Indapamide, ✚Dom-Indapamide, ✚Gen-Indapamide, ✚Lozide, Lozol, ✚PMS-Indapamide

BENEFITS versus RISKS

Possible Benefits	*Possible Risks*
EFFECTIVE ONCE-A-DAY TREATMENT OF MILD TO MODERATE HYPERTENSION	Excessive loss of blood potassium or magnesium
EFFECTIVE, MILD DIURETIC	Increased blood sugar level
COMBINATION USE WITH AN ACE INHIBITOR (PERINDOPRIL OR ACEON) REDUCED RISK OF RECURRENT STROKE BY NEARLY HALF IN ONE STUDY	Increased blood uric acid level

▷ **Principal Uses**

As a Single Drug Product: Uses currently included in FDA-approved labeling: (1) Increases urine output (diuresis) to correct fluid retention seen in congestive heart failure (edema); (2) used as starting therapy in high blood pressure (hypertension).

Other (unlabeled) generally accepted uses: (1) Helps ease the excessive elimination of calcium in the urine (hypercalciuria); (2) may help protect the heart after blood-flow problems (preserves ischemic heart from reperfusion injury); (3) combination use with perindopril (Aceon) reduced risk of repeat stroke by nearly 50% in one study.

As a Combination Drug Product [CD]: Available in combination with the ACE inhibitor perindopril in Canada.

How This Drug Works: Increases elimination of salt and water (through increased urine production). Also works directly on the blood vessel walls and relaxes the walls of smaller arteries and decreases pressure reactions (calcium channel action). The combined effects lower blood pressure.

Available Dosage Forms and Strengths

Tablets — 1.25 mg, 2.5 mg

Tablets, combination — 1.25 mg indapamide, 4 mg perindopril

▷ **Usual Adult Dosage Ranges:** *Hypertension:* 1.25 mg per day, as a single dose in the morning. If needed, the dose may be increased to 2.5 mg/day after 4 weeks, and up to 5 mg if needed and tolerated. Use in treating edema may require a starting dose of 2.5 mg. Maximum total daily dose is 5 mg. (In Canada, the total daily dose limit is given as 2.5 mg.)

Note: Actual dose and dosing schedule must be determined for each individual patient.

Conditions Requiring Dosing Adjustments

Liver Function: Should be used with caution and in decreased doses by patients with liver problems. Blood chemistry (electrolytes) should be closely followed.

Kidney Function: Used with caution and must be stopped if kidney failure progresses after indapamide is started.

▷ **Dosing Instructions:** The immediate release tablet may be crushed and taken with or following food to reduce stomach upset. Sustained release forms should never be crushed. This medicine is best taken in the morning to avoid nighttime urination. If you forget a dose: take it as soon as you remember it, unless it's nearly time for your next dose—if that is the case, skip the missed dose and return to taking the medicine on your usual schedule. DO NOT double doses. Call your doctor for instructions if you miss more than one dose.

Usual Duration of Use: Use on a regular schedule for 2 to 4 weeks determines peak effect in lowering blood pressure. Long-term use (months to years) requires periodic physician evaluation. Make certain you maintain pre-hypertension or hypertension goals!

Typical Treatment Goals and Measurements (Outcomes and Markers)

Blood Pressure: The NEW guidelines (JNC VII) define normal blood pressure (BP) as **less than** 120/80. Because blood pressures that were once considered acceptable can actually lead to blood vessel damage, the committee from the National Institutes of Health, National Heart, Lung, and Blood Institute now have a new category called **Pre-hypertension**. This ranges from 120/80 to 139/89 and is intended to help your doctor encourage lifestyle changes (or in the case of people with a risk factor for high blood pressure, start treatment) much earlier, so that possible damage to blood vessels, your heart, kidneys, sexual potency, or eyes might be minimized or avoided altogether. The next 2 classes of high blood pressure are stage 1 hypertension: 140/90 to 159/99; and stage 2 hypertension equal to or greater than: 160/100 mm Hg. These guidelines also recommend that clinicians trying to control blood pressure work with their patients to agree on the goals and a plan of treatment. The first-ever guidelines for blood pressure (hypertension) in African Americans recommends that MOST black patients be started on TWO antihypertensive medicines with the goal of lowering blood pressure to 130/80 for those with high risk for heart and blood vessel disease or with diabetes. The American Diabetes Association recommends 130/80 as the target for people living with diabetes and less than 125/75 for those who spill more than one gram of protein into their urine. Most clinicians try to achieve a BP that confers the best balance of lower cardiovascular risk and avoids the problem of too low a blood pressure. Blood pressure duration is generally increased with beneficial restriction of sodium. The goals and time frame should be discussed with you when the prescription is written. If goals are not met, it is not unusual to intensify doses or add on medicines. You can find the new blood pressure guidelines at *www.nhlbi.nih.gov/guidelines/hypertension/index.htm*. For the African American guidelines see Douglas, J.G. in Sources.

Possible Advantages of This Drug

Causes no significant increase in blood cholesterol levels. Less likely to cause significant loss of potassium. Increases good cholesterol (HDL). ONCE-DAILY DOSING will encourage people to take this medicine regularly. Works directly on blood vessels while also working as a "water pill," or diuretic. If there are no compelling reasons for other medicines, diuretics are drugs of choice for starting high blood pressure treatment according to JNC VII.

▷ **This Drug Should Not Be Taken If**
- you have had an allergic reaction to it previously or to a sulfonamide-type medicine or chemical.
- your kidneys are not making any urine.

▷ **Inform Your Physician Before Taking This Drug If**
- you are allergic to any form of "sulfa" drug.
- you are pregnant or planning pregnancy.
- you presently have an excessively low blood potassium.
- you have a history of kidney or liver disease.
- you have diabetes, gout or systemic lupus erythematosus.

- you take any form of cortisone, digoxin, oral antidiabetic drug, or insulin.
- you have had a sympathectomy.
- you plan to have surgery under general anesthesia in the near future.

Possible Side Effects (natural, expected, and unavoidable drug actions)

Light-headedness on rising from sitting or lying position (see orthostatic hypotension in Glossary). Increase in blood sugar level, affecting control of diabetes. Increase in blood uric acid level, affecting control of gout. Decrease in blood potassium level, causing muscle weakness and cramping. Low blood sodium and magnesium.

▷ **Possible Adverse Effects** (unusual, unexpected, and infrequent reactions)

If any of the following develop, consult your physician promptly for guidance.

Mild Adverse Effects

Allergic reactions: skin rashes, hives, itching—infrequent.

Headache, dizziness, drowsiness, weakness, lethargy, visual disturbance—case reports.

Reduced appetite, indigestion, nausea, vomiting, diarrhea—rare.

Paresthesias—rare.

Urination at night—possible, especially with evening dosing.

Serious Adverse Effects

Serious skin rashes (Stevens-Johnson Syndrome, toxic epidermal necrolysis)—case reports.

Abnormal heartbeat (premature ventricular contractions)—rare.

Liver or kidney toxicity—rare.

Inhibition of platelet aggregation—possible.

▷ **Possible Effects on Sexual Function:** Decreased libido—infrequent; impotence—rare.

Natural Diseases or Disorders That May Be Activated by This Drug

Diabetes, gout, systemic lupus erythematosus.

Possible Effects on Laboratory Tests

Total cholesterol and LDL cholesterol levels: no effect or slightly decreased.

Blood HDL cholesterol level: increased.

Blood potassium, magnesium, or sodium level: decreased.

Blood uric acid level or blood sugar (glucose): increased.

CAUTION

1. Take exactly as prescribed—excessive doses can cause excessive sodium and potassium loss (decreased appetite, nausea, fatigue, confusion, or tingling extremities).
2. If you take a digitalis preparation (digitoxin, digoxin), ensure intake of high-potassium foods to help avoid digitalis toxicity (see Table 13, "High-Potassium Foods"). Magnesium should also be checked and replaced as needed.

Precautions for Use

By Infants and Children: Safety and effectiveness for those under 12 years of age are not established.

By Those Over 60 Years of Age: It is best to start with small doses. You may be more susceptible to impaired thinking, orthostatic hypotension, potassium loss, and blood sugar increase. Overdose or extended use causes excessive loss of body water, thickening (increased viscosity) of blood, and an increased tendency for the blood to clot—predisposing to stroke, heart attack, or thrombophlebitis (vein inflammation with blood clot).

▷ **Advisability of Use During Pregnancy**

Pregnancy Category: B. D by one researcher. See Pregnancy Risk Categories at the back of this book.

Animal Studies: No birth defects reported.

Human Studies: Data from studies of pregnant women are not available.

This drug should not be used during pregnancy unless a very serious complication occurs for which this drug is significantly beneficial. Ask your physician for guidance.

Advisability of Use If Breast-Feeding

Presence of this drug in breast milk: Unknown.

Avoid drug or refrain from nursing.

Habit-Forming Potential: None.

Effects of Overdose: Dry mouth, thirst, lethargy, weakness, muscle cramping, nausea, vomiting, drowsiness progressing to stupor or coma.

Possible Effects of Long-Term Use: Impaired balance of water, salt, and potassium in blood and body tissues. Development of diabetes in predisposed individuals.

Suggested Periodic Examinations While Taking This Drug (at physician's discretion)

Measurements of blood levels of sodium, potassium, chloride, sugar, and uric acid.

▷ **While Taking This Drug, Observe the Following**

Foods: Ask your doctor about a high-potassium diet. If so advised, see Table 13, High-Potassium Foods, in Section Six. Follow your doctor's advice about salt use.

Herbal Medicines or Minerals: Ginseng, hawthorn, saw palmetto, ma huang, guarana (caffeine), goldenseal, yohimbe, and licorice may also cause increased blood pressure. Calcium and garlic may help lower blood pressure. Ginkgo benefits in helping peripheral artery disease are, as yet, unproven. Indian snakeroot has a German Commission E monograph indication for hypertension—talk to your doctor. Eleuthero root and ephedra (ma huang) should be avoided by people living with hypertension. Magnesium and potassium replacement may be needed.

Beverages: No restrictions. This drug may be taken with milk.

▷ *Alcohol:* Alcohol may exaggerate the blood pressure–lowering effects of this drug and cause orthostatic hypotension.

Tobacco Smoking: No interactions expected. I advise everyone to quit smoking.

▷ *Other Drugs*

Indapamide may *increase* the effects of

• ACE inhibitors (see Drug Classes) and cause SEVERE lowering of blood pressure on standing (postural hypotension).

• other antihypertensive drugs; dose adjustments may be necessary to prevent excessive lowering of blood pressure.

• lithium (Lithobid, others) and cause lithium toxicity.

Indapamide may *decrease* the effects of

• oral antidiabetic drugs (sulfonylureas); dose adjustments may be needed for proper control of blood sugar.

Indapamide *taken concurrently* with

• digitalis preparations (digitoxin, digoxin) must be followed closely and adjustments made to prevent fluctuations of blood potassium levels and serious disturbances of heart rhythm.

- NSAIDs (see Drug Classes) may blunt the therapeutic benefit of indapamide.

The following drugs may **_decrease_** the effects of indapamide:
- cholestyramine (Cuemid, Questran)—may interfere with its absorption.
- colestipol (Colestid)—may interfere with its absorption.

Take cholestyramine and colestipol 1 hour before any oral diuretic.

▷ _Driving, Hazardous Activities:_ Use caution until the possible occurrence of orthostatic hypotension, drowsiness, dizziness or impaired vision has been determined.

Aviation Note: The use of this drug **_may be a disqualification_** for piloting. Consult a designated Aviation Medical Examiner.

Exposure to Sun: No restrictions.

Exposure to Heat: Excessive perspiring could cause additional loss of salt and water.

Heavy Exercise or Exertion: Isometric exercises can raise blood pressure significantly. Ask your physician for help.

Occurrence of Unrelated Illness: Vomiting or diarrhea can produce a serious imbalance of important body chemistry. Consult your physician for guidance.

Discontinuation: It may be advisable to discontinue this drug 5 to 7 days before major surgery. Ask your physician, surgeon and/or anesthesiologist for guidance.

INDOMETHACIN (in doh METH a sin)

Please see the acetic acid (nonsteroidal anti-inflammatory drug) family profile.

INFLIXIMAB (IN FLIX ih mab)

Other Names: Anti-TNF monoclonal antibody, chimeric monoclonal antibody to TNF alpha, cA2

Introduced: 1998-Crohn's, 1999 rheumatoid arthritis combination approval, 2002 improved function in RA   **Class:**   Disease-modifying antirheumatic drug (DMARD), biologic response modifier   **Prescription:**   USA: Yes   **Controlled Drug:**   USA: No; Canada: No   **Available as Generic:**   No

Brand Name: Remicade

```
╔══════════════════════════════════════════════════════════════╗
                      BENEFITS versus RISKS
       Possible Benefits                    Possible Risks
 GIVEN ORPHAN PRODUCT             POSSIBLE LOWERED RESISTANCE
   DESIGNATION FOR USE IN           TO INFECTIONS AND
   CROHN'S DISEASE                  OPPORTUNISTIC INFECTIONS
 EASES RHEUMATOID ARTHRITIS       Injection site reactions
   (RA) IN COMBINATION WITH       Possible development of antibodies
   METHOTREXATE                   May have a role in causing lymphoma
 MAY GIVE A RESPONSE IN RA
   WHERE OTHER AGENTS HAVE
   FAILED
 COULD HAVE A ROLE IN
   CONGESTIVE HEART FAILURE
   AND IN DECREASING RISK OF
   REPEAT HEART ATTACKS
 FIRST MEDICINE APPROVED TO
   IMPROVE PHYSICAL FUNCTION
   IN RA
╚══════════════════════════════════════════════════════════════╝
```

▷ **Principal Uses**

As a Single Drug Product: Uses currently included in FDA-approved labeling: (1) Treatment of moderately to severely active Crohn's disease or fistulizing Crohn's disease; (2) Use in combination with methotrexate in rheumatoid arthritis (RA) patients to lower signs and symptoms when patients have not responded to methotrexate alone; (3) improves physical function in RA.

Other (unlabeled) generally accepted uses: (1) May have a role in some kinds of wasting (cachexia) where tumor necrosis factor (TNF) is involved; (2) data from the cholesterol and recurrent events (CARE) trial found that decreasing tumor necrosis factor (TNF) (see How This Drug Works on page 569) reduces risk of repeat heart attacks; (3) may ease congestive heart failure.

How This Drug Works: Binds with both soluble and transmembrane tumor necrosis factor alpha (TNF alpha) in the body. Inhibits binding of existing TNF alpha to p55 and p75 receptors. Both effects act to stop the biologic actions of TNF alpha. Works to change the body's responses that are caused or regulated by TNF, such as increased levels of matrix metalloproteinase-3, serum levels of cytokines and release of substances that control white blood cell migration.

Author's Note: The company that makes this product has added a more stringent (black-box) warning about opportunistic infections to the product label. Information in this profile may be broadened in subsequent editions if warranted. Members of an FDA advisory panel found that more data was required for the 3 existing TNF blockers (adalimumab-Humira, etanercept-Enbrel, and infliximab-Remicade) relative to their possible role in causing lymphoma in patients who use them.

INFLUENZA VACCINE (IN flu en za VAX ceen)

Other Name: Flu vaccine

Introduced: Specific formulation for each year. 2003 for FluMist   **Class:**

Antiviral **Prescription:** USA: Yes **Controlled Drug:** USA: No;
Canada: No **Available as Generic:** USA: No; Canada: No

Brand Names: Flu-Immune, FluMist, Fluoge, Flu-Shield, Fluzone

**Author's Note: For the 2003–2004 flu season, the shot (vaccine) will have 3
strains: H1N1, A/New Caledonia/20/99; H3N2, A/Panama/2007/99, which is
an A/Moscow/10/99-like virus and B/Hong Kong/330/2001-like virus strain.
Like last year, the Advisory Committee suggests that people ages 50–64 get
a flu shot. From 20,000 to 40,000 people die from the flu each year. Don't
become a statistic. New data from nearly 150,000 patients found that *elderly people who got flu shots benefited from fewer admissions to the hospital
for heart disease and stroke* (see Nichol, KL in sources)! The American Diabetes Association (*www.diabetes.org* or 1-877-CDC-DIAB for more information) recommends that people living with diabetes get both a flu and
pneumococcal shot (vaccine). If you would like a copy of the ACIP recommendations, call 1-888-232-3228. Information on current general shot (vaccine) recommendations can be found at *www.cdc.gov/nip/recs/child-
schedule.htm*. This year, additional concerns about SARS make it especially
prudent to get a flu shot to help ease fears that an emerging case of the flu
might be SARS.**

BENEFITS versus RISKS

Possible Benefits	*Possible Risks*
PREVENTION OF INFLUENZA CAUSED BY THE MOST SERIOUS OR PREVALENT VIRAL STRAINS IDENTIFIED FOR A GIVEN YEAR	GUILLAIN-BARRÉ SYNDROME (questionable causation for previous shot form)
FLUMIST FORM AVOIDS INJECTION AND IS A NASAL SPRAY	Hypersensitivity
Possible cross-protection from other similar virus strains	

▷ **Principal Uses**

As a Single Drug Product: Uses currently included in FDA-approved labeling:
Prevention of influenza.

Other (unlabeled) generally accepted uses: (1) Used in patients with compromised immune systems (such as HIV-positive, cancer and bone marrow
transplant patients); (2) can be of use in isolated outbreaks such as in nursing homes or military camps; (3) may decrease the number of middle ear
infections in children who attend day-care centers; (4) FluMist form is
approved for those 5–49 years old to prevent types A and B influenza.

How This Drug Works: Vaccine made of purified parts of the virus surface,
split virus or whole virus, which has been inactivated. When injected, it
stimulates the immune system to make antibodies. The antibodies
(appearing roughly 2 weeks after vaccination) act to reduce disease
severity or decrease probability of infection by the expected flu viruses.
The FluMist form is a live virus vaccine that provokes an immune
response using the whole virus. It appears that influenza-specific T cells,
mucosal antibodies, and serum antibodies also play a role in conferring
immunity to the flu.

Available Dosage Forms and Strengths

Typical split virus: 15 mcg/0.5 ml of each of the 3 selected strains.

Nasal spray live vaccine form (Flumist): Package of 10 single-use sprayers containing 0.5 ml in each.

▷ **Recommended Dosage Ranges** (Actual dose and schedule must be determined for each patient and each flu season individually.)

Infants and Children: For the shot form: Those 6 to 35 months old should be given 0.25 ml of a split-dose vaccine shot. If this is the first vaccination, two doses should be given 1 month apart. Split dose is suggested for children because it tends to cause fewer undesirable effects. For infants and young children, the vaccine is usually given in the thigh muscle.

Children 3 to 8 years old should be given 0.5 ml of the selected split-virus vaccine shot. Children in this age range who have not been previously vaccinated should be given two vaccinations, 1 month apart.

Children: FluMist: For children 5 to 8 years old: For children not previously vaccinated using FluMist for the first time: Two doses of 0.5 ml each (0.25 ml in each nostril) are needed. The first dose is given (0.25 ml in each nostril as in the dosing instruction section), then a second dose (0.25 ml in each nostril) should be given within 14 days of the first one. For children 9 and older for FluMist: 0.25 ml in each nostril each flu season.

For previously available shots (vaccinations): those 9 years old or older should be given a single vaccination of 0.5 ml of split-virus vaccine in the deltoid muscle.

9 to 49 Years of Age Using FluMist: Should be given 0.5 ml of FluMist as 0.25 ml in each nostril every flu season.

13 to 60 Years of Age Using Shot Form: Should be given 0.5 ml of whole- or split-virus vaccine in the deltoid muscle.

Over 60 Years of Age: Same as 13 to 60 years of age for the shot form. FluMist form should NOT be used.

Note: Dosing for all appropriate patients is best accomplished in October through November of the flu season for which you are seeking protection. A shot from a prior year will NOT protect you.

Conditions Requiring Dosing Adjustments
Liver Function: Not involved.
Kidney Function: Not involved.

▷ **Dosing Instructions:** Prior vaccination **does not** mean you are immune to the current year's virus strains. People at increased risk for complications from the flu (50 or older, those with asthma or other ongoing chronic lung problems, cardiovascular disease, immunosuppression, women in the 6th to 9th months [second or third trimester] of pregnancy, etc.). Some tenderness at the injection site is possible. Because of SARS, it is particularly prudent to get an influenza vaccine in order to help avoid the stress and confusion that may result. Fever and muscular aches or pains are possible from the injected vaccine and may be pretreated and treated with acetaminophen (Tylenol, others). If you forget to get the shot: timing of vaccination (enough time to let your body build up immunity) before the flu season is important. The FluMist form may range from colorless to pale yellow, and the liquid may by clear to slightly cloudy. Half of the dose of FluMist is given to each nostril while the patient sits upright. The person giving the spray inserts the tip of the sprayer just inside the nose, and pushes the plunger to give the spray. Once the first nostril is sprayed, the dose-dividing clip is removed from the sprayer and the second half of the dose is given into the unsprayed nostril. If you get the flu because you did

NOT get vaccinated, a neuramidase inhibitor (see drug profiles) may be an option for you. Talk to your doctor.

Usual Duration of Use: Single vaccination confers relative immunity to the expected viral strains in 2 weeks. This does not confer immunity to all strains of virus capable of causing an influenzalike (flu-like) syndrome. Annual vaccination is strongly suggested.

Typical Treatment Goals and Measurements (Outcomes and Markers)

Influenza: Prevention of a serious viral illness. **In a typical season some 20,000 Americans die from influenza. Years with virulent strains can see 40,000 people lose their lives.** This vaccination can help you avoid illness, hospitalization, and death.

Possible Advantages of This Drug

Allows the prevention of a viral syndrome that can cause loss of several weeks of work in younger, otherwise healthy patients or serious illness in older or compromised patients. Given the SARS problem, a flu shot may help avoid stress and confusion. The new FluMist form is a nasal spray and will most probably replace an injection for otherwise healthy people. A large review found that elderly people who get a flu shot avoid a significant number of hospitalizations for stroke and heart disease!

Currently a "Drug of Choice"

For prevention of types A and B influenza due to the viral strains that are of the greatest concern in the current flu season.

▷ **This Drug Should Not Be Taken If**

- you have had an allergic reaction to any dose form of it previously or to any vaccine components.
- you are allergic to eggs (the virus is grown on eggs).
- you have an acute illness and a fever.

FluMist Form:

- you have an asthma or reactive airway disease (safety and efficacy not established)
- you are over 50 (safety and efficacy not established)
- you have an ongoing (chronic) medical condition that predisposes you to severe flu infections (injected form of influenza vaccine is needed).
- you have an immunosuppression (either disease such as AIDS or immune deficiency disease or are taking a medicine that causes immunosuppression). Like other live virus vaccines, FluMist should not be taken.

▷ **Inform Your Physician Before Taking This Drug If**

- you are HIV positive (shot form).
- you have a history of blood disorders or active nerve problem (neurologic disorder).
- you have had Guillain-Barré syndrome.
- you have a history of seizures or of a latex allergy.
- you have been receiving cancer therapy (chemotherapy).

Possible Side Effects (natural, expected, and unavoidable drug actions)

Pain at the vaccination site. Muscle aches, fever, or bothersome tiredness (malaise). This is **not** the flu. The vaccine contains viral fragments or non-infectious (dead) virus. These symptoms are a reaction to the components of the vaccine.

▷ **Possible Adverse Effects** (unusual, unexpected, and infrequent reactions)
If any of the following develop, consult your physician promptly for guidance.

Mild Adverse Effects
Allergic reactions: swelling and redness—possible.
Muscle aches or fever—infrequent.
Fatigue, nausea, and headache—infrequent.
Vasculitis (joint pain, weakness, fever, and rash)—rare.

Serious Adverse Effects
Allergic reactions: anaphylactic reactions.
Low blood platelets or pericarditis—case reports.
Guillain-Barré syndrome (only reported during the 1976–1977 flu season and of questionable causation).
Kidney toxicity—case report.
Vision changes—case report.

▷ **Possible Effects on Sexual Function:** None reported.

Possible Delayed Adverse Effects: Guillain-Barré syndrome during one flu season.

▷ **Adverse Effects That May Mimic Natural Diseases or Disorders**
Reaction to vaccine contents may mimic the flu.

Natural Diseases or Disorders That May Be Activated by This Drug
None reported.

Possible Effects on Laboratory Tests
Hepatitis B test: false positive.
Hepatitis C test: false positive.
HTLV-1 test: false positive.

CAUTION
1. A vaccine in the previous year **does not** confer immunity to the flu in following years.
2. The flu vaccine confers immunity to viruses predicted to cause influenza in a particular flu season. Vaccine does not confer immunity to all strains of virus capable of causing a flu-like syndrome.
3. If muscle aches or fever occur after vaccination, acetaminophen (Tylenol, others) is recommended. **Do not** take aspirin, and especially do not give aspirin to children. It may be prudent to take acetaminophen BEFORE vaccination to prevent such reactions.
4. Call your doctor immediately if you develop hives, facial swelling, or difficulty breathing after the vaccination.
5. It is ALWAYS better to prevent a disease or condition than to have to treat it. Additionally, **when the type A flu is prevalent, some 20,000 people usually die** from the flu or its complications in that particular flu season. Talk with your doctor or pharmacist. If you do not have a medical reason for avoiding flu vaccination—get the shot! In many states, your pharmacist can actually give you a flu shot.

Precautions for Use
By Infants and Children: Safety and effectiveness for use by those under 6 months of age have not been established.
By Those Over 60 Years of Age: The vaccine is especially **valuable** in this age group, as the effects of the flu may be devastating.

▷ **Advisability of Use During Pregnancy**
  Pregnancy Category: C. See Pregnancy Risk Categories at the back of this book.
  Animal Studies: Animal studies have not been conducted.
  Human Studies: Information from adequate studies of pregnant women is not
    available.
  Ask your doctor for guidance.

Advisability of Use If Breast-Feeding
  Presence of this drug in breast milk: Not defined.
  Monitor nursing infant closely and contact your doctor if adverse effects
    develop. The CDC has not listed breast-feeding as a precaution against
    receiving this vaccine.

Habit-Forming Potential: None.

Effects of Overdose: No specific cases reported. Treatment would be consistent
    with any symptoms of the patient.

Possible Effects of Long-Term Use: Not indicated for long-term use.

Suggested Periodic Examinations While Taking This Drug (at physician's dis-
    cretion)
  None indicated.

▷ **While Taking This Drug, Observe the Following**
  Foods: No restrictions.
  Herbal Medicines or Minerals: Some patients use echinacea to attempt to boost
    their immune systems. Unfortunately, use of echinacea is not recom-
    mended in people with damaged immune systems. This herb may also
    actually weaken any immune system if it is used too often or for too long a
    time.
  Beverages: No restrictions.
▷ *Alcohol:* No restrictions.
  Tobacco Smoking: No interactions expected. I advise everyone to quit smoking.
▷ *Other Drugs*
  Influenza vaccine may ***increase*** the effects of
  • carbamazepine (Tegretol), by decreasing the elimination of the drug.
  • phenobarbital, by increasing the half-life of the drug.
  • theophylline (Theo-Dur, others), by increasing the blood level of the
    drug.
  • warfarin (Coumadin) and pose an increased risk of bleeding; more fre-
    quent INR (prothrombin time or protime) testing is suggested.
  Influenza vaccine ***taken concurrently*** with
  • cyclosporine (Sandimmune) can cause blunting of the immune response
    to the vaccine.
  • immunosuppressive agents (chemotherapy, corticosteroids) may impair or
    blunt immune response to the vaccine.
  • medicines for which use of live virus vaccine is not recommended (talk
    with your doctor), such as medicines that suppress the immune system.
    FluMist form should not be given (is contraindicated).
  • methotrexate (Rheumatrex) can result in blunting of the immune response
    to the shot.
  • neuramidase inhibitors (see Drug Classes) have not been found to cause
    differences in hemagglutination inhibition antibody levels (titers).
  • phenytoin (Dilantin) and fosphenytoin (Cerebyx) have had variable effects
    on the blood levels of this drug.

▷ *Driving, Hazardous Activities:* This drug may cause excessive tiredness and
    muscle aches. Restrict activities as necessary.

Aviation Note: The use of this drug **may be a short-term disqualification** for
piloting. Consult a designated Aviation Medical Examiner.

Exposure to Sun: No restrictions.

Exposure to Heat: Since this vaccine may cause short-duration fevers, it is wise
to avoid hot environments for a day after vaccination.

Heavy Exercise or Exertion: A fever may result, and it is wise to avoid strenuous
exercise for a day after vaccination.

Special Storage Instructions: This vaccine is ideally stored in the refrigerator. If
this is how storage is accomplished, the outdate specified by the manufacturer is valid. If the vaccine is stored at room temperature, it is stable for
up to 7 days.

Observe the Following Expiration Times: If the vaccine is stored at room temperature, it is stable for up to 7 days.

**Author's Note: There is a Vaccine Adverse Event Reporting System
(VAERS). The toll-free number is 1-800-822-7967.**

INSULIN (IN suh lin)

Introduced: 1922; insulin lispro, 1996; insulin glargine, 2000; insulin aspart,
2000 **Class:**   Antidiabetic **Prescription:**   USA: No   **Controlled
Drug:**   USA: No; Canada: No   **Available as Generic:**   Yes

Brand Names: Humalog, Humalog Mix 75/25, Humulin BR, Humulin L,
Humulin N, Humulin R, Humulin 70/30, Humulin 30/70, Humulin U,
Humulin U Ultralente, Iletin I NPH, Iletin II Pork, Iletin U—40, Iletin U—
500, ✤Initard, Insulatard NPH, insulin aspart (NovoLog), ✤Insulin
Human, ✤Insulin-Toronto, Lantus (insulin glargine), Lente Iletin I, Lente
Iletin II Pork, Lente Insulin, Lente Purified Pork, Mixtard, Mixtard Human
70/30, NovoLog, Novolin L, ✤Novolin-Lente, Novolin N, ✤Novolin-NPH,
NovolinPen, Novolin R, ✤Novolinset, ✤Novolinset NPH, ✤Novolinset
30/70, ✤Novolinset Toronto, Novolin—70/30, Novolin 70/30, Novolin 70/30
Penfill, Novolin 30/70, ✤Novolin-Toronto, ✤Novolin-Ultralente, NPH
Iletin I, NPH Iletin II Pork, NPH Insulin, NPH Purified Pork, Protamine,
Zinc & Iletin I, Protamine, Protamine, Zinc & Iletin II Pork, Regular Con-
centrated Iletin II, Regular Iletin I, Regular Iletin II Pork, Regular Iletin II
U—500, Regular Insulin, Regular Purified Pork Insulin, Semilente Iletin I,
Semilente Insulin, Semilente Purified Pork, Ultralente Iletin I, Ultralente
Insulin, Velosulin, ✤Velosulin Cartridge, Velosulin Human

Author's Note: Not all listed forms may still be available in the U.S.

BENEFITS versus RISKS

Possible Benefits	*Possible Risks*
EFFECTIVE CONTROL OF TYPE 1 (INSULIN-DEPENDENT) DIABETES MELLITUS	HYPOGLYCEMIA WITH EXCESSIVE DOSE
EFFECTIVE COMBINATION OF TYPE 2 DIABETES THAT DOES NOT RESPOND (MEET BLOOD SUGAR GOALS) TO DIET AND ORAL HYPOGLYCEMIC AGENT ALONE	Infrequent allergic reactions Lipodystrophy
EXTREMELY QUICK ONSET (ASPART FORM)	
EFFECTIVE CONTROL OF A TYPE OF BLOOD SUGAR PROBLEM (GESTATIONAL DIABETES) THAT HAPPENS IN PREGNANCY	
TIGHT CONTROL OF BLOOD SUGAR MAY AVOID OR DELAY DEVELOPMENT OF HIGH BLOOD PRESSURE AND KIDNEY, HEART, NERVE, EYE, OR OTHER DAMAGE THAT HAPPENS WHEN BLOOD SUGAR IS OUT OF CONTROL	
INTENSIVE INSULIN THERAPY THAT ACHIEVES NEAR NORMAL A1C LOWERED MICROVASCULAR PROBLEMS IN TYPE 1 DAIBETICS	
ONCE-DAILY DOSING (Lantus form—insulin glargine only)	
NOVOLOG FORM APPROVED FOR USE IN INSULIN PUMPS	

▷ **Principal Uses**

As a Single Drug Product: Uses currently included in FDA-approved labeling: (1) Used in diabetes mellitus that is insulin-dependent and by people who have non-insulin-dependent diabetes who are experiencing stress such as illness or who do not meet blood sugar goals; (2) used to control blood sugar in critically ill patients who are being fed by intravenous nutrient mixtures; (3) used to control blood sugar in pregnancy (gestational diabetes as a drug of choice).

Other (unlabeled) generally accepted uses: (1) Insulin in combination with glucagon has been used in alcoholic hepatitis; (2) may have a role in combination therapy with an oral hypoglycemic agent in some diabetics; (3) helps diabetic ketoacidosis; (4) can help diabetic neuropathy and retinopathy; (5) can be of help in critically ill patients with maple syrup urine disease; (6) used in implantable pumps to control blood sugar; (7) intensive therapy (more than 3 injections daily) may decrease risk of small blood vessel disease, retinopathy, and kidney problems (nephropathy); (8) one study used a combination of insulin and sugar (glucose) intravenously after a heart attack and found that death decreased by 30% in the following year.

Author's Note: Controversies in Medicines: Some clinicians are advocating use of insulin in type 2 diabetics. The clear goal is to help keep blood sugar in the normal range and avoid complications of diabetes. Perhaps the first best hope for realistically having patients accept this concept is a "mouth spray insulin" (buccal) that is in clinical trials (see Insulin, Oral in the Leading Edge section).

How This Drug Works: Insulin is a hormone that is made in a body organ called the pancreas. It helps sugar get through the cell wall to the inside of the cell (it actually interacts with an insulin receptor [a glycoprotein complex in the cell membrane] and then: a) the activated receptor turns on a messenger protein inside the cell, b) the activated messenger bumps into a glucose transporter four (GLUT-4), c) the GLUT-4 vesicle goes (translocates) to the cell surface and actually unfolds into the cell and acts like a taxi to bring sugar into the cell where it is used for energy.

Available Dosage Forms and Strengths
Buccal (mouth) spray — still investigational
Injections — 40, 100 and 500 units per ml
Penfill cartridges — 100 units per ml

▷ **Usual Adult Dosage Ranges:** According to individual requirements for the best regulation of blood sugar on a 24-hour basis. It is not unusual to use a long-acting insulin to provide what is called basal insulin, in addition to a rapidly acting insulin to "cover" and food or sugar that is eaten.

Note: Actual dose and schedule must be determined for each patient individually.

Conditions Requiring Dosing Adjustments
Liver Function: Specific adjustment guidelines are not available.
Kidney Function: Caution should be used by patients with compromised kidneys. Requirements become extremely variable.
Thyrotoxicosis: Glucose utilization is typically increased, and insulin requirements may actually decrease.

▷ **Dosing Instructions:** Inject insulin subcutaneously according to the schedule prescribed by your physician. The timing and frequency of injections will vary with the type of insulin prescribed. The following table of insulin actions (according to type) will help you understand the treatment schedule prescribed for you. If you forget a dose: Please call your doctor. People with type 1 diabetes must also use a long-acting insulin if NovoLog is prescribed. If you are combining a longer-acting insulin with insulin aspart, draw up the insulin aspart into the syringe first. If you are using an insulin pump, make certain you understand how to program it. It is critical that this medicine be taken exactly as prescribed.

Insulin Type	Action Onset	Peak	Duration
Insulin aspart	0.15 hr	0.45–1.5 hrs	3–5 hrs
Insulin (buccal)	hr	hrs	hrs
Insulin glargine	1.0 hr	none	24 hrs
Insulin lispro	0.25 hr	0.5–1.5 hrs	3–4 hrs
Regular	0.5–1 hr	2–4 hrs	5–7 hrs
Isophane (NPH)	3–4 hrs	6–12 hrs	18–28 hrs
Regular 30%/NPH 70%	0.5 hr	4–8 hrs	24 hrs
Semilente	1–3 hrs	2–8 hrs	12–16 hrs
Lente	1–3 hrs	8–12 hrs	18–28 hrs
Ultralente	4–6 hrs	18–24 hrs	36 hrs
Protamine Zinc	4–6 hrs	14–24 hrs	36 hrs

Usual Duration of Use: In type 1 insulin-dependent (juvenile-onset) diabetes mellitus, insulin therapy is usually required for life. Type 2 non-insulin-dependent (maturity-onset) diabetes may be controlled by oral antidiabetic drugs and/or diet, but can require insulin when you have a serious infection, injuries, burns, surgical procedures, and other physical stress. The advent of buccal insulin may find increased use of insulin in type 2 diabetes based on patient acceptance. Type 4, or diabetes in pregnancy (gestational), often finds insulin being stopped as appropriate after the baby is born. See your doctor on a regular basis.

Typical Treatment Goals and Measurements (Outcomes and Markers)

Blood sugar: The general goal for blood sugar is to return it to the usual "normal" range (generally 80–120 mg/dl), while avoiding risks of excessively low blood sugar. One study (UKPDS) used a fasting plasma sugar (glucose) of less than 108 mg/dl.

Fructosamine and glycosylated hemoglobin: Fructosamine levels (a measure of the past 2 to 3 weeks of blood sugar control) should be less than or equal to 310 micromoles per liter. Glycosylated hemoglobin or hemoglobin A1C (a measure of the past 2–3 months of blood sugar control) should be less than or equal to 7.0%. Some clinicians are advocating 6.5% as the target, but others note an increased risk of hypoglycemia with this very strict target.

Possible Advantages of This Drug: Allows tight control of blood sugar that can help avoid microvascular, visual, kidney and cardiovascular effects of diabetes. The insulin lispro provides a rapid onset, which may be more forgiving in the sense of timing of the shot itself (goes to work faster) as well as offering a more physiologic response to blood sugar. The insulin aspart (NovoLog) has the quickest onset of all. Insulin glargine actually does NOT have a peak effect. The kinetics of that insulin glargine offer a great advantage in providing a relatively constant (baseline) insulin level. Some prescribers use Lantus as a baseline insulin and Humalog with meals—avoiding use of a pump in some patients. An experimental form of insulin sprayed into the mouth (Oralin) is now poised to enter phase three studies (see Insulin, Oral in the Leading Edge section). The Diabetes Control and Complications Trial (DCCT) showed that intensive insulin treatment that attains a near normal A1C lowers risk of microvascular problems in type 1 diabetics.

▷ **This Drug Should Not Be Taken If**
- the need for insulin and its dose schedule have not been established by a qualified clinician.
- you are hypoglycemic.
- you are using insulin aspart and it is cloudy or thickened.

▷ **Inform Your Physician Before Taking This Drug If**
- you have an insulin allergy.
- you do not know how to recognize and treat abnormally low blood sugar (see Hypoglycemia in Glossary).
- you have been newly diagnosed with kidney or liver disease or low thyroid (hypothyroidism).
- you are pregnant.
- you have an illness that is causing diarrhea or vomiting.
- you take aspirin, beta-blockers, fenfluramine (Pondimin), or monoamine oxidase (MAO) type A inhibitors (see Drug Classes).

Possible Side Effects (natural, expected, and unavoidable drug actions)

Hypoglycemia is the most common side effect of insulin treatment. This effect is made more likely when diet, physical activity and other factors are incorrectly balanced and maintained. In unstable ("brittle") diabetes, unexpected drops in blood sugar levels can occur, resulting in hypoglycemia (see Glossary). Weight gain.

▷ **Possible Adverse Effects** (unusual, unexpected, and infrequent reactions)

If any of the following develop, consult your physician promptly for guidance.

Mild Adverse Effects

Allergic reactions: local redness, swelling, and itching at site of injection or hives—infrequent.

Taste disorders—possible.

Thinning of subcutaneous tissue at sites of injection (lipodystrophy)—infrequent.

Serious Adverse Effects

Allergic reaction: anaphylactic reactions (see Glossary).

Severe, prolonged hypoglycemia—possible to infrequent.

Inflammation of the parotid (parotitis)—case reports.

Hemolytic anemia or porphyria—case reports.

Arrhythmias (such as premature ventricular contractions)—associated with hypoglycemia) or very fast heart rate (with intravenous use)—case reports.

Insulin resistance—possible to rare.

▷ **Possible Effects on Sexual Function:** May resolve sexual problems (dysfunction) in patients who have this prior to starting insulin therapy. May also cause decrease in libido and erectile dysfunction—case reports (may also be a result of nerve/blood vessel damage as part of diabetes progressive effect).

▷ **Adverse Effects That May Mimic Natural Diseases or Disorders**

The early signs of hypoglycemia may be mistaken for alcoholic intoxication.

Possible Effects on Laboratory Tests

Blood cholesterol level: decreased.

Blood glucose level: decreased.

Blood potassium level: decreased.

Glycosylated hemoglobin (hemoglobin A1C) or fructosamine: decreased.

CAUTION

1. Carry a card in your purse or wallet saying that you have diabetes and are taking insulin.
2. Know how to recognize hypoglycemia and how to treat it. Always carry a readily available form of sugar, such as hard candy or sugar cubes. Report all episodes of hypoglycemia to your doctor.
3. Your vision may improve during the first few weeks of insulin therapy. Postpone eye exams for eyeglasses for 6 weeks after starting insulin.
4. Insulin is absorbed more quickly or slowly depending on where it is injected. Absorption is 80% greater from the abdominal wall than from the leg and 30% greater than from the arm. It is advisable to rotate the injection site within the same body region than from one site to another.
5. Insulin glargine is CLEAR, not cloudy. This may be confusing to some patients because in the past, diabetics have been taught that short-acting insulins are clear and long-acting insulins are cloudy. Lantus form should NOT be mixed with other insulins. Insulin aspart is clear and colorless.

6. The American Diabetic Association (ADA) now says that a person is considered diabetic if two fasting blood sugars in a row are more than 125 mg/dl. This more conservative approach reflects new information saying that complications start at lower blood sugar levels than previously thought. The concept of Pre-diabetes (formerly impaired glucose tolerance) is described in the Glossary. Some new British data advocates that statin-type medicines could cut the risk of heart attack and stroke by a third (even in people with "normal" cholesterol), yet these medicines are underused in diabetics. Talk to your doctor about this.

7. If metformin is used in combination with insulin (added to existing insulin treatment), the insulin dose is continued at the level used prior to adding metformin. When fasting plasma sugar (glucose) falls below 120 mg/deciliter, the insulin dose should be lowered by 10 to 25%. Ongoing dose adjustments will be determined by goals and blood sugar checks.

8. Newer targets of A1C (glycosylated hemoglobin) of 6.5 are prudent in helping to avoid complications, but also carry the increased risk of excessively low blood sugar (hypoglycemia). Make sure you understand the signs and symptoms of hypoglycemia if more aggressive goals have been chosen.

Precautions for Use

By Infants and Children: Insulin doses and schedules are modified according to patient's size. Adhere strictly to the physician's prescribed routine. Some of the insulins, such as insulin aspart (NovoLog), are NOT approved in children.

By Those Over 60 Years of Age: Insulin needs may change with age. Periodic individual evaluation is needed to identify the best dose and schedule. The aging brain adapts well to higher blood sugar levels. Rigid attempts at "tight" sugar control may result in hypoglycemia that shows as confusion and abnormal behavior. Repeated hypoglycemia (especially if severe) may cause brain damage.

▷ **Advisability of Use During Pregnancy**

Pregnancy Category: B. See Pregnancy Risk Categories at the back of this book.
Animal studies: Inconclusive.
Human studies: Adequate studies of pregnant women are not available. Birth defects occur 2 to 4 times more frequently in infants of diabetic mothers than in infants of mothers who do not have diabetes. The exact causes of this are not known.

Insulin is the drug of choice for managing diabetes during pregnancy. To preserve the health of the mother and fetus, every effort must be made to establish the best dose of insulin necessary for "good control" and to prevent episodes of hypoglycemia.

Advisability of Use If Breast-Feeding

Presence of this drug in breast milk: No data.
Insulin treatment of the mother has no adverse effect on the nursing infant. Breast-feeding may decrease insulin requirements; dose adjustment may be necessary.

Habit-Forming Potential: None, but cases of surreptitious insulin injection have been reported.

Effects of Overdose: Hypoglycemia: fatigue, weakness, headache, nervousness, irritability, sweating, tremors, hunger, confusion, delirium, abnormal behavior (resembling alcoholic intoxication), loss of consciousness, seizures.

Possible Effects of Long-Term Use: Thinning of subcutaneous fat tissue at sites of insulin injection. Insulin resistance.

Suggested Periodic Examinations While Taking This Drug (at physician's discretion)

Routine testing of blood sugar levels at intervals recommended by your physician is prudent. Historically, estimates of blood sugar were obtained by checking urine sugar. This method has been replaced by finger stick testing of blood glucose. Finger stick testing accurately reflects the blood sugar and helps ensure better control (tighter control) of blood glucose. A new device uses a laser to "stick" the finger (see *www.cellrobotics.com*). The laser is painless and appears to avoid toughening the skin like a lancet. One new blood sugar machine can also test glycated protein (fructosamine). If you are ill, increased frequency of finger stick blood glucose testing may be indicated. A new handheld machine called A1cNow enables pharmacists and physicians to check hemoglobin A1C in the office or pharmacy in 8 minutes! Additionally, a device called a Glucowatch Biographer uses a pad and a watchlike device to painlessly check blood sugar (see *www.cygnus.com*).

▷ **While Taking This Drug, Observe the Following**

Foods: Follow your diabetic diet conscientiously. Taking a diabetes education course is very smart and can teach you about portion control, what to do on sick days and other important concepts. Blood sugar control can help avoid or delay diabetes problems! Vitamin C in high dose may worsen blood sugar control. Do not omit snack foods in mid-afternoon or at bedtime if they help prevent hypoglycemia. Rice bran has been checked in a small (57-subject) study of type 1 and type 2 diabetics. The benefit was a 30% lowering of sugar. This might be a new complementary care option.

Herbal Medicines or Minerals: Using chromium may change the way your body is able to use sugar. Some health food stores advocate vanadium as mimicking the actions of insulin, but possible toxicity and need for rigorous studies presently preclude recommending it. DHEA may change sensitivity to insulin or insulin resistance. Aloe, bitter melon, eucalyptus, fenugreek, ginger, garlic, ginseng, glucomannan, guar gum, hawthorn, licorice, nettle, and yohimbe may change blood sugar. Surprisingly, boiled stems of the Optuntia streptacantha prickly pear cactus appear to be able to lower blood sugar. Ongoing effects and effects on A1C are not known. Red sage is used for blood sugar effects, but is unproven. Psyllium increases risk of excessively low blood sugar. Since so many of these products may require adjustment of insulin dosing, talk to your doctor BEFORE combining any of these herbal medicines with this medicine. Echinacea pupurea (injectable) and blonde psyllium seed or husk should NOT be taken by people living with diabetes.

Beverages: Use according to prescribed diabetic diet.

▷ *Alcohol:* Used excessively, alcohol can cause severe hypoglycemia, resulting in brain damage.

Tobacco Smoking: Regular smoking can decrease insulin absorption and increase insulin requirements by 30%. It is advisable to stop smoking altogether.

Marijuana Smoking: Possible increase in blood sugar levels.

▷ *Other Drugs*

The following drugs may ***increase*** the effects of insulin:

• acarbose (Precose)—by decreasing the amount of sugar that insulin has to work on.

- aspirin and other salicylates.
- some beta-blocker drugs (especially the nonselective ones; see Drug Classes)—may prolong insulin-induced hypoglycemia.
- clofibrate (Atromid-S).
- disopyramide (Norpace).
- fenfluramine (Pondimin).
- monoamine oxidase (MAO) type A inhibitors (see Drug Classes).
- oral antidiabetic drugs (see Drug Classes)—results in additive hypoglycemia.

The following drugs may *decrease* the effects of insulin (by raising blood sugar levels):

- birth control pills (oral contraceptives).
- chlorthalidone (Hygroton).
- cortisonelike (corticosteroid) drugs (see Drug Classes).
- furosemide (Lasix).
- phenytoin (Dilantin, etc.) or fosphenytoin (Cerebyx).
- thiazide diuretics (see Drug Classes).
- thyroid preparations (various).

▷ *Driving, Hazardous Activities:* Be prepared to stop and take corrective action if hypoglycemia develops.

Aviation Note: Diabetes and the use of this drug *are disqualifications* for piloting. Consult a designated Aviation Medical Examiner.

Exposure to Sun: No restrictions.

Exposure to Heat: Use caution. Sauna baths can significantly increase the rate of insulin absorption and cause hypoglycemia.

Heavy Exercise or Exertion: Use caution. Periods of unusual or unplanned heavy physical activity will use up sugar more quickly and predispose to hypoglycemia.

Occurrence of Unrelated Illness: Omission of meals as a result of nausea, vomiting, or injury may lead to hypoglycemia. Infections can increase insulin needs. Ask your doctor for help.

Discontinuation: Do not stop this drug without asking your doctor. Omission of insulin may result in life-threatening coma.

Special Storage Instructions: Keep in a cool place, preferably in the refrigerator. Protect from freezing. Protect from strong light and high temperatures when not refrigerated.

Observe the Following Expiration Times: Do not use this drug if it is older than the expiration date on the vial. Always use fresh, "within date" insulin.

IPRATROPIUM (i pra TROH pee um)

Introduced: 1975 **Class:** Bronchodilator **Prescription:** USA: Yes **Controlled Drug:** USA: No; Canada: No **Available as Generic:** USA: No; Canada: No

Brand Names: Atrovent (single ingredient US), Atrovent [CD other countries], ✽Alti-Atrovent, ✽Apo-Atrovent, Atrovent Nasal Spray, Combivent [CD], Dom-Ipratropium, Ipratropium Novaplus, PMS-Ipratropium

```
┌─────────────────────────────────────────────────────────────────┐
│                    BENEFITS versus RISKS                          │
│      Possible Benefits              Possible Risks                │
│  EFFECTIVE BRONCHODILATOR       Mild and infrequent adverse effects│
│    FOR TREATMENT OF CHRONIC       (see Possible Adverse Effects on │
│    BRONCHITIS AND EMPHYSEMA       page 584)                        │
│  EFFECTIVE TREATMENT OF                                            │
│    RUNNY NOSE (RHINORRHEA)                                         │
│  Effective adjunctive treatment in                                │
│    some bronchial asthma                                           │
└─────────────────────────────────────────────────────────────────┘
```

▷ **Principal Uses**

As a Single Drug Product: Uses currently included in FDA-approved labeling: (1) Helps prevent or relieve episodes of difficult breathing in chronic bronchitis, chronic obstructive pulmonary disease (COPD) and emphysema (should not be used to treat acute attacks of asthma because it takes a while to work); (2) used in nasal spray to relieve symptoms of runny nose (rhinorrhea) from allergic or nonallergic perennial rhinitis (including runny nose from colds) in adults and children over 12 years old.

Other (unlabeled) generally accepted uses: (1) Relief of asthma symptoms; (2) lung symptoms of congestive heart failure.

As a Combination Drug Product [CD]: Available in combination with fenoterol (Combivent form in other countries), a beta-adrenergic agonist that works in a different way. Also available with albuterol (Combivent form in the US). These combinations are more effective than either drug used alone. Different ingredients with the same brand name are also a good example of how the same name in different countries can contain different active ingredients. This profile will focus on the single-ingredient forms.

How This Drug Works: Through its atropinelike (anticholinergic) action, it blocks bronchial constriction and opens bronchi. Nasal form keeps acetylcholine from working (antagonizes it) and decreases production and secretion of mucus.

Available Dosage Forms and Strengths

Inhalation aerosol — 14 g metered dose inhaler; 18 mcg per inhalation

Nasal inhaler — 20 mcg per actuation

Nasal spray — 0.03 and 0.06%

Nebulizer — 250 mcg/ml solution

▷ **Usual Adult Dosage Ranges:** *Inhalation form:* Initially two inhalations (36 mcg) 4 times a day, 4 hours apart. If needed, the dose may be increased to 4 inhalations (72 mcg) at one time to get the best (optimal) relief. Maintain 4-hour intervals between doses. Maximum daily dose is 12 inhalations (216 mcg). *Nasal spray:* for use in runny nose (rhinorrhea) seen with the common cold: 0.03%—two sprays (21 mcg each) in each nostril 2 to 3 times a day for up to 4 days; 0.06%—2 sprays (42 mcg each) in each nostril 3 to 4 times a day for up to 4 days.

Note: Actual dose and dosing schedule must be determined for each patient individually.

Conditions Requiring Dosing Adjustments

Liver Function: Specific guidelines not developed.

Kidney Function: Used with caution by patients with bladder neck obstructions.

▷ **Dosing Instructions:** Carefully follow the patient instructions provided with the inhaler because a small amount of medicine reaches the lungs with the best technique. Shake well before using. Many people do NOT take the time to learn the best inhaler technique—take the time to do this. Carefully follow the patient instructions on the nasal form: the pump of the nasal form must be primed before the unit is used. Read the package insert carefully, and ask your pharmacist for help if you don't understand the directions. If you forget a dose: use the inhaler or nasal spray as soon as you remember it, unless it's nearly time for your next dose—then skip the missed dose, space the remaining doses for the day at regularly separated times and continue the next day right on schedule. DO NOT double doses. Call your doctor if you find yourself missing doses or if you do not get the usual benefits from this medicine.

Usual Duration of Use:
Inhalation form: Continual use on a regular schedule for 48 to 72 hours is usually necessary to determine this drug's effectiveness. Long-term use (months to years) requires check of response and dose adjustment. See your doctor.

Nasal spray: The nasal form helps some people feel better right away and may take a week or so for others. The nasal spray may only be used for up to 4 days.

Typical Treatment Goals and Measurements (Outcomes and Markers)
Asthma: Frequency and severity of asthma attacks should ease. Some clinicians also use decreased frequency of rescue inhaler use as a further clinical indicator. Lung function (pulmonary function) tests such as FEV1 are typical for more involved testing. It is critical that this medicine is used regularly to get the best results. If the usual benefit is not realized, call your doctor.

Runny nose (rhinorrhea) from a cold: Decreased need to blow your nose. Resolution of runny nose.

Possible Advantages of This Drug
Inhalation form produces a greater degree of bronchodilation than theophylline in patients with chronic bronchitis and emphysema. Causes minimal adverse effects. Repeated use does not lead to tolerance and loss of effectiveness. Suitable for long-term maintenance therapy.

Nasal spray eases a very annoying symptom (rhinorrhea, or runny nose) seen with common cold.

Currently a "Drug of Choice"
For difficult breathing associated with chronic bronchitis and emphysema. Nasal form makes the common cold much easier to deal with.

▷ **This Drug Should Not Be Taken If**
- you have had an allergic reaction to it previously.
- you are allergic to soybeans or peanuts (inhalation form).
- you are allergic to atropine or to aerosol propellants (fluorocarbons) (inhalation form).
- you are allergic to benzalkonium chloride or edetate disodium (nasal spray).

▷ **Inform Your Physician Before Taking This Drug If**
- you have had an adverse effect from any belladonna-type chemical (derivative) previously.
- you have a history of glaucoma.
- you have any form of urinary retention or prostatism (see Glossary).

Possible Side Effects (natural, expected, and unavoidable drug actions)
Throat dryness, cough, irritation from aerosol—rare.
Blurred vision, dry mouth.
Bad or bitter taste—frequent.

▷ **Possible Adverse Effects** (unusual, unexpected, and infrequent reactions)
If any of the following develop, consult your physician promptly for guidance.
Mild Adverse Effects
Allergic reactions: skin rash, hives—rare.
Headache, dizziness, nervousness—rare.
Palpitations—rare.
Nosebleeds (with nasal spray)—infrequent to frequent.
Serious Adverse Effects
Allergic reactions: rare first-dose angioedema or bronchospasm.
Author's Note: Other than the rare allergic reactions, the nasal spray does not appear to have any serious adverse effects.
Abnormal heartbeat (supraventricular tachycardia)—case report.
Intraocular pressure changes—rare.

▷ **Possible Effects on Sexual Function:** None reported.

Natural Diseases or Disorders That May Be Activated by This Drug
Angle-closure glaucoma, prostatism (see Glossary).

Possible Effects on Laboratory Tests: None reported.

CAUTION
1. This drug won't start to work for 5 to 15 minutes. It should not be used alone to treat acute attacks of asthma needing a fast result.
2. When used as combination therapy with beta-adrenergic antiasthmatic drugs (albuterol, terbutaline, metaproterenol, etc.), the beta-adrenergic aerosol should be used about 5 minutes before using ipratropium to prevent fluorocarbon toxicity.
3. When used as an adjunct to steroid or cromolyn aerosols (beclomethasone, Intal), ipratropium should be used about 5 minutes before using the steroid or cromolyn aerosol to prevent fluorocarbon toxicity.
4. Contact with the eyes can cause temporary blurring of vision.
5. Call your doctor if you are using the nasal spray and your runny nose (rhinorrhea) continues or gets worse and you develop a fever.

Precautions for Use
By Infants and Children: Nasal spray is now approved for use for those 6 to 11 years old. Dosing is the same as for adults for the 0.03% form. Safety and effectiveness for those under 6 are not established.
By Those Over 60 Years of Age: Watch for possible development of prostatism and adjust dose as necessary.

▷ **Advisability of Use During Pregnancy**
Pregnancy Category: B. See Pregnancy Risk Categories at the back of this book.
Animal studies: No drug-induced birth defects in mouse, rat, or rabbit studies.
Human studies: Adequate studies of pregnant women are not available.
Use this drug during pregnancy only if clearly needed.

Advisability of Use If Breast-Feeding
Presence of this drug in breast milk: Possibly yes, but in very small amounts.
Watch nursing infant closely and stop drug or nursing if adverse effects start.

Habit-Forming Potential: None.

Effects of Overdose: This drug is not well absorbed into the circulation when it is taken by aerosol inhalation. No systemic effects of overdose are expected.

Possible Effects of Long-Term Use: Drying of the nose with nasal form.

Suggested Periodic Examinations While Taking This Drug (at physician's discretion)

Internal eye pressure measurements if appropriate.

▷ **While Taking This Drug, Observe the Following**

Foods: No restrictions.

Herbal Medicines or Minerals: Fir or pine needle oil should NOT be used by asthmatics. Betel nut may lower the beneficial effects of ipratropium in treating asthma. Ephedra alone does carry a German Commission E monograph indication for asthma treatment. If you are allergic to plants in the Asteraceae family (aster, chrysanthemum, daisy, or ragweed), you may also be allergic to echinacea, chamomile, feverfew, and St. John's wort. Talk to your doctor BEFORE adding any herbals to this medicine.

Beverages: No restrictions.

▷ *Alcohol:* No interactions expected.

Tobacco Smoking: No interactions expected, but smoking should be avoided completely if you have chronic bronchitis or emphysema. I advise everyone to quit smoking.

Marijuana Smoking: Possible excessive increase in heart rate (tachycardia).

▷ *Other Drugs*

Ipratropium may *increase* the effects of
- albuterol (Proventil, others).
- other atropinelike drugs (see Drug Classes).

Ipratropium *taken concurrently* with
- belladonna (various) may lead to excessive anticholinergic action (fast heart rate, blurred vision, constipation, weakness, etc.).
- cisapride (Propulsid) may lessen benefits of cisapride.
- procainamide (Procan, others) may lead to additive effects on the vagal nerve and heart conduction (atrioventricular).
- tricyclic antidepressants (see Drug Classes) may result in additive anticholinergic effects.

▷ *Driving, Hazardous Activities:* May cause dizziness or blurred vision. Restrict activities as necessary.

Aviation Note: The use of this drug *may be a disqualification* for piloting. Consult a designated Aviation Medical Examiner.

Exposure to Sun: No restrictions.

Exposure to Cold: Inhaling cold air may cause bronchospasm and induce asthmatic breathing and cough; dose adjustment of this drug may be necessary.

Heavy Exercise or Exertion: This drug is not considered to be consistently effective in preventing or treating exercise-induced asthma.

Discontinuation: Ask your doctor for help. Substitute medication may be advisable.

IRINOTECAN (ear in oh TEE kan)

Other Name: Camptothecin-11 **Introduced:** 2000 **Class:** Antineoplastic, chemotherapy, topoisomerase I inhibitor **Prescription:** USA: Yes **Controlled Drug:** USA: No; Canada: No **Available as Generic:** USA: No; Canada: No

Brand Name: Camptosar

Warning: You may not expect a non-prescription herbal product to create a problem, but St. John's wort lowered blood levels of irinotecan by 40% in a small study in the Netherlands. Make sure you are getting the most from your chemotherapy and avoid even combination products that have hypericin, hypericum, hypervorin, or similar ingredients. If a generic name of an herbal "shotgun" product sounds similar, talk to your doctor or pharmacist to be sure that an innocent-sounding treatment for depression isn't blocking your "chemo" and letting the cancer continue.

Author's Note: Irinotecan is a first-line treatment for colorectal cancer, and is the first such agent to be FDA approved in more than 40 years. It is approved for use in combination with 5-FU/LV to treat colorectal cancer that has spread (metastatic), and for people who have had their cancer recur or progress after being given 5-FU-based treatment. Information in this profile will be broadened in subsequent editions as data warrants.

ISONIAZID (i soh NI a zid)

Other Names: Isonicotinic acid hydrazide, INH

Introduced: 1956   **Class:**   Antituberculosis   **Prescription:** USA: Yes   **Controlled Drug:**   USA: No; Canada: No   **Available as Generic:**   USA: Yes; Canada: Yes

Brand Names: INH, ✤Isotamine, Laniazid, Nydrazid, Pasna Tri-Pack 300 [CD], P-I-N Forte [CD], ✤PMS-Isoniazid, Rifamate [CD], Rifater [CD], Rimactane/INH Dual Pack [CD], Seromycin w/Isoniazid [CD], Teebaconin, Teebaconin and Vitamin B6 [CD]

BENEFITS versus RISKS

Possible Benefits	*Possible Risks*
EFFECTIVE PREVENTION AND TREATMENT OF ACTIVE TUBERCULOSIS (TREATS TB IN COMBINATION)	ALLERGIC LIVER REACTION— RARE Peripheral neuropathy (see Glossary) Bone marrow depression (see Glossary) Mental and behavioral disturbances

---

Principal Uses

As a Single Drug Product: Uses currently included in FDA-approved labeling: (1) Used alone to prevent the development of tuberculous infection (prophylaxis) in people who are at high risk because of exposure to infection or recent conversion of a negative tuberculin skin test to positive; (2) used in combination with other drugs to treat tuberculosis in a variety of body sites.

Other (unlabeled) generally accepted uses: (1) Could have a role in some high-risk patients as part of a methadone maintenance designed to prevent tuberculosis in high-risk patients; (2) may have a role in part of a regimen used to treat local (superficial) bladder cancer (Bacillus Calmette-Guerin—BCG).

As a Combination Drug Product [CD]: Available in combination with rifampin, another antitubercular drug that works in a different way. This combination is more effective than either drug used alone and also encourages patients to take their medicine (adherence). Isoniazid can cause low pyridoxine (vitamin B6); for this reason, a combination of the two drugs is available in tablet and granule form.

How This Drug Works: By interfering with metabolism or cell walls, this drug kills (bactericidal) or inhibits (bacteriostatic) susceptible tuberculosis organisms.

Available Dosage Forms and Strengths
Injection — 100 mg/ml
Packet — 100 mg pyridoxine, 10 mg pyridoxine, 4.5 grams
aminosalicylate
Syrup — 50 mg/5 ml
Tablets — 50 mg, 100 mg, 300 mg

▷ **Usual Adult Dosage Ranges:** *For prevention:* 300 mg once daily (usually for 6 to 12 months). *For treatment:* 5 mg per kg of body mass daily. The total daily dose should not exceed 300 mg. Some clinicians use 5 mg/kg daily (up to 300 mg) for 2 weeks and then give 15 mg per kg (up to 900 mg) 2 to 3 times weekly. *Latent TB:* 5 mg per kg of body mass once a day (up to 300 mg a day) for 9 months is suggested by the American Thoracic Society to treat latent TB in HIV-negative or HIV-positive patients.
Note: Actual dose and dosing schedule must be determined on an individual basis.

Conditions Requiring Dosing Adjustments
Liver Function: This drug should not be used in sudden (acute) liver disease. It should be discontinued if liver function tests become increased to 3 times the normal value.
Kidney Function: This drug is a rare cause of nephrosis. For severe kidney failure (creatinine clearance less than 10 ml/min), daily dose is lowered by 50%.

▷ **Dosing Instructions:** The tablet may be crushed and taken with food to prevent stomach irritation. Make sure you use a measuring cup or spoon if you are taking the liquid form. If you forget a dose: take the missed dose as soon as you remember it, unless it's nearly time for your next dose, then skip the missed dose and take the next dose right on schedule. DO NOT double doses. Call your doctor if you find yourself missing doses.

Usual Duration of Use: Use on a regular schedule for 1 year or more is often necessary, depending upon the nature of the infection. Shorter courses of intermittent high doses may work, but the medicine must be taken for months. See your doctor regularly.

Typical Treatment Goals and Measurements (Outcomes and Markers)
Infections: The most commonly used measures of serious infections are white blood cell counts and differentials (the kind of blood cells that occur most often in your blood), and temperature or night sweats. Because of the nature of this infection, therapy will be long-term. NEVER stop a medicine for tuberculosis because you start to feel better. The goals and time frame should be discussed with you when the prescription is written.

▷ **This Drug Should Not Be Taken If**
  - you have had an allergic reaction (especially a liver reaction) to any dose form of it previously.
  - you have active liver disease.

▷ **Inform Your Physician Before Taking This Drug If**
  - you have serious impairment of liver or kidney function.
  - you drink an alcoholic beverage daily.
  - you are an alcoholic.
  - you are pregnant or breast-feeding your baby.
  - you have a seizure disorder.
  - you take other drugs on a long-term basis, especially phenytoin (Dilantin).
  - you plan to have surgery under general anesthesia in the near future.

Possible Side Effects (natural, expected, and unavoidable drug actions)
  Toxic fever—rare.

▷ **Possible Adverse Effects** (unusual, unexpected, and infrequent reactions)
  If any of the following develop, consult your physician promptly for guidance.

Mild Adverse Effects
  Allergic reactions: skin rash, fever, swollen glands, painful muscles and joints.
  Dizziness, indigestion, nausea, vomiting.
  Peripheral neuritis (see Glossary): numbness, tingling, pain, weakness in hands and/or feet—frequent in adults, rare in children (may be prevented with pyridoxine).

Serious Adverse Effects
  Allergic reactions: drug-induced hepatitis (see Glossary) [loss of appetite, nausea, fatigue, itching, dark-colored urine, yellowing of eyes and skin]—may be fulminant and fatal, hypersensitivity, meningitis—case reports.
  Severe skin reactions (Stevens-Johnson Syndrome, pellagra)—case reports.
  Acute mental/behavioral disturbances, psychosis, impaired vision, increase in epileptic seizures—rare.
  Movement disorders (ataxia)—case reports in patients not receiving supplemental pyridoxine.
  High or low blood sugars (hyperglycemia or hypoglycemia)—possible.
  Porphyria, pancreatitis, or kidney toxicity—case reports.
  Lupus erythematosus–like syndrome or abnormal muscle changes (rhabdomyolysis)—case reports.
  Pellagra—rare.
  Disseminated intravascular coagulation (DIC)—case report.
  Bone marrow depression (see Glossary): fatigue, weakness, fever, sore throat, abnormal bleeding or bruising—case reports.

▷ **Possible Effects on Sexual Function:** Male breast enlargement and tenderness (gynecomastia)—rare.

Possible Delayed Adverse Effects: Increased frequency of liver cirrhosis has been reported.

▷ **Adverse Effects That May Mimic Natural Diseases or Disorders**
  Drug-induced hepatitis may suggest viral hepatitis. Collagen vascular changes may mimic rheumatoid arthritis or systemic lupus erythematosus. Pseudolymphoma may occur.

Natural Diseases or Disorders That May Be Activated by This Drug
  Latent epilepsy, systemic lupus erythematosus (questionable).

Possible Effects on Laboratory Tests

Complete blood cell counts: decreased red cells, hemoglobin, white cells, and platelets; increased eosinophils (allergic reaction).

Blood amylase level: increased (possible pancreatitis).

Blood antinuclear antibodies (ANA): positive.

Blood lupus erythematosus (LE) cells: positive.

Blood glucose level: increased (with large doses).

Liver function tests: increased liver enzymes (ALT/GPT, AST/GOT, and alkaline phosphatase), increased bilirubin.

Urine sugar tests: increased; false positive results with Benedict's solution and Clinitest.

CAUTION

1. **The FDA has required a new warning for Laniazid: "A recent report suggests an increased risk of fatal hepatitis associated with isoniazid among women, particularly African American and Hispanic women. The risk may also be increased during the postpartum period."** Increased laboratory testing is also suggested.

2. Ask your doctor about determining if you are a "slow" or "rapid" inactivator (acetylator) of isoniazid. This has a bearing on your predisposition to developing adverse effects.

3. Copper sulfate tests for urine sugar may give a false-positive test result. (Diabetics, please note.)

4. Because multidrug-resistant (MDR) tuberculosis is now more common in many areas, four-drug combination therapy (isoniazid, pyrazinamide, ethambutol, and rifampin) is often used.

Precautions for Use

By Infants and Children: Use with caution in children with seizure disorders. "Slow acetylators" are more prone to adverse drug effects. It is advisable to give supplemental pyridoxine (vitamin B6).

Prevention: Infants and children are given 10 mg per kg per day up to 300 mg for 6–12 months.

By Those Over 60 Years of Age: There is a greater incidence of liver damage in this age group, and liver status should be closely watched. Watch for any indications of an "acute brain syndrome" which will show up as confusion, delirium, and seizures.

▷ **Advisability of Use During Pregnancy**

Pregnancy Category: C. See Pregnancy Risk Categories at the back of this book.

Animal Studies: No birth defects reported in mice, rats, or rabbits.

Human Studies: Data from adequate studies of pregnant women are not available.

If clearly needed, this drug is now used at any time during pregnancy. Ask your physician for guidance.

Advisability of Use If Breast-Feeding

Presence of this drug in breast milk: Yes.

Talk to your doctor about benefits and risks.

Habit-Forming Potential: None.

Effects of Overdose: Nausea, vomiting, dizziness, blurred vision, hallucinations, slurred speech, stupor, coma, seizures.

Possible Effects of Long-Term Use: Peripheral neuritis due to a deficiency of pyridoxine (vitamin B6).

Suggested Periodic Examinations While Taking This Drug (at physician's discretion)

Complete blood cell counts.

Liver function tests.

Complete eye examinations, repeat sputum cultures. Chest X-rays.

▷ **While Taking This Drug, Observe the Following**

Foods: Eat the following foods cautiously until your tolerance is determined: Swiss and Cheshire cheeses, tuna fish, skipjack fish, and Sardinella species. These may interact with the drug to produce skin rash, itching, sweating, chills, headache, light-headedness, or rapid heart rate. Taking this drug with food also acts to decrease absorption and lessen therapeutic benefits. Some red wines and aged cheeses also contain high levels of tyramine. This may result in an undesirable increase in blood pressure if consumed. Avoid this combination.

Nutritional Support: It is advisable to take a supplement of pyridoxine (vitamin B_6) to prevent peripheral neuritis. Ask your physician for help.

Herbal Medicines or Minerals: Echinacea: Some patients use echinacea to attempt to boost their immune systems. Unfortunately, use of echinacea is not recommended in people with damaged immune systems. This herb may also actually weaken any immune system if it is used too often or for too long a time (more than 8 weeks). DO NOT take mistletoe herb, oak bark or F.C. of marshmallow root, and licorice.

Beverages: No restrictions. May be taken with milk.

▷ *Alcohol:* Alcohol may reduce the effectiveness of this drug and increase the risk of liver toxicity, and possibly lead to disulfiram reactions.

Tobacco Smoking: No interactions expected. I advise everyone to quit smoking.

▷ *Other Drugs*

Isoniazid may ***increase*** the effects of

- carbamazepine (Tegretol) and cause toxicity.
- disulfiram (Antabuse) and change behavior.
- phenytoin (Dilantin) or fosphenytoin (Cerebyx) and cause toxicity.

The following drugs may ***decrease*** the effects of isoniazid:

- cortisonelike drugs (see Drug Classes).

Isoniazid ***taken concurrently*** with

- acetaminophen (Tylenol) may increase the risk of liver damage (hepatoxicity).
- antacids may decrease the absorption of this medicine. Separate antacid dosing by 2 hours from dosing of this medicine.
- BCG vaccine will result in decreased vaccine effectiveness.
- cyclosporine (Sandimmune) may blunt cyclosporine benefits.
- diazepam and perhaps other benzodiazepines (see Drug Classes) may result in increased blood levels and toxicity.
- ketoconazole, itraconazole, voriconazole (Vfend), or related compounds may result in decreased therapeutic benefits of the antifungal.
- meperidine (Demerol) may result in excessive lowering of blood pressure.
- niacin (various) may lead to a need for increased niacin.
- oral antidiabetic drugs (see Drug Classes) may result in loss of control of blood glucose.
- propranolol (Inderal, others) may lead to isoniazid toxicity.
- rifampin (Rifadin, others) can result in a serious increased risk of liver toxicity.
- theophylline (Theodur, others) may result in theophylline toxicity.
- valproic acid (Depakene) can result in isoniazid or valproic acid toxicity.

- warfarin (Coumadin) may result in increased bleeding risk; more frequent INR (prothrombin time or protime) testing is needed.

▷ *Driving, Hazardous Activities:* This drug may cause dizziness. Restrict activities as necessary.

Aviation Note: The use of this drug **may be a disqualification** for piloting. Consult a designated Aviation Medical Examiner.

Exposure to Sun: No restrictions.

Discontinuation: Long-term treatment is required. Do not stop this drug without asking your physician.

ISOSORBIDE DINITRATE (i soh SOHR bide di NI trayt)

Other Name: Sorbide nitrate **Introduced:** 1959 **Class:** Anti-anginal, nitrates **Prescription:** USA: Yes **Controlled Drug:** USA: No; Canada: No **Available as Generic:** USA: Yes; Canada: No

Brand Names: Angipec, ✽Apo-ISDN, ✽Cedocard-SR, ✽Coradur, ✽Coronex, Dilatrate-SR, Iso-BID, Isochron, Isonate, Isordil, Isordil Tembids, Isordil Titradose, Isotrate Timecelles, ✽Novo-Sorbide, Sorbitrate, Sorbitrate-SA

Warning: The brand names Isordil and Isuprel sound similar; this can lead to serious errors. Isordil is isosorbide dinitrate, used to treat angina. Isuprel is isoproterenol, used for asthma. Make sure you are taking the correct drug.

BENEFITS versus RISKS	
Possible Benefits	*Possible Risks*
EFFECTIVE RELIEF AND PREVENTION OF ANGINA	Orthostatic hypotension (see Glossary)
EFFECTIVE ADJUNCTIVE TREATMENT IN SOME CASES OF CONGESTIVE HEART FAILURE	Rare skin reactions (severe peeling)

▷ **Principal Uses**

As a Single Drug Product: Uses currently included in FDA-approved labeling: (1) The sublingual (under-the-tongue) tablets and the chewable tablets are used to prevent and relieve acute attacks of anginal pain; (2) the longer-acting tablets and capsules are used to prevent the development of angina, but are not effective in relieving acute episodes of anginal pain (nitroglycerin is the drug of choice in those cases).

Other (unlabeled) generally accepted uses: (1) This drug is also used to improve heart function in selected cases of congestive heart failure; (2) can help ease the pressure in esophageal varices in alcoholics; (3) can help painful leg cramping (intermittent claudication); (4) may be of use topically as an ointment to avoid surgery (sphincterotomy) or to ease symptoms of anal fissures; (5) may help diagnose syndrome X (angina resulting from exercise in people with normal epicardial coronary arteries); (6) used after a heart attack intravenously to help address congestive heart failure; (7) sublingual dosing may help achalasia.

How This Drug Works: This drug relaxes and dilates arteries and veins. Benefits in treating angina and heart failure are due to dilation of coronary arteries and dilation of systemic veins. Net effects are improved heart blood flow and reduced workload.

Available Dosage Forms and Strengths

Capsules — 40 mg

Capsules, prolonged action — 40 mg

Tablets — 5 mg, 10 mg, 20 mg, 30 mg, 40 mg

Tablets, chewable — 5 mg, 10 mg

Tablets, prolonged action — 20 mg, 40 mg

Tablets, sublingual — 2.5 mg, 5 mg, 10 mg

▷ **Recommended Dosage Ranges** (Actual dose and schedule must be determined for each patient individually.)

Infants and Children: Dose not established.

12 to 60 Years of Age:

Sublingual tablets: 5 to 10 mg dissolved under tongue every 2 to 3 hours; use for relief of acute attack and for prevention of anticipated attack.

Chewable tablets: initially 5 mg chewed to evaluate tolerance; increase dose to 5 or 10 mg every 2 to 3 hours as needed and tolerated. Use for relief of acute attack and for prevention of anticipated attack.

Tablets: 5 to 20 mg 4 times daily to prevent acute attack, with at least a 12-hour nitrate-free period.

Prolonged-action capsules and tablets: 40 mg to start and then 40–80 mg every 8 to 12 hours as needed to prevent acute attacks.

Author's Note: Dosing for all forms is set up to give a 12-hour nitrate-free period in order to avoid tolerance to the therapeutic benefits of this medicine.

Over 60 Years of Age: Same as 12 to 60 years of age, although excessive lowering of blood pressure on standing (postural hypotension) may be more likely in this population.

Conditions Requiring Dosing Adjustments

Liver Function: Used with caution and in decreased doses by patients with liver compromise, as increased blood levels will occur.

Kidney Function: No specific dosing changes are needed for compromised kidneys. This drug can discolor urine (brown to black).

▷ **Dosing Instructions:** Capsules and tablets to be swallowed are best taken on an empty stomach to achieve maximal blood levels. Regular tablets may be crushed; prolonged-action capsules and tablets should be taken whole, NOT chewed, crushed, or altered. If you forget a dose: take the missed dose as soon as you remember it, unless it's nearly time for your next dose—if this is the case, skip the missed dose, take the next dose right on schedule. DO NOT double doses. Call your doctor if you find yourself missing doses.

Usual Duration of Use: Use on a regular schedule for 3 to 7 days is needed to (1) identify this drug's peak effect in preventing or relieving acute anginal pain and (2) to find the optimal dose schedule. Long-term use (months to years) requires physician supervision. Ask your doctor what he or she wants you to do if the frequency or severity of angina increases or is not relieved by previously effective doses.

Typical Treatment Goals and Measurements (Outcomes and Markers)

Angina: The most commonly used markers are prevention or relief of chest pain (angina). Many cardiologists look for easing of frequency and severity of angina attacks as well as pulmonary capillary wedge pressure as measures of successful therapy. If your chest pain does not go away after using the maximum dose at the recommended time interval, have someone drive you to the hospital or call 911. Ask your doctor on the next office visit if it would make sense for you to chew a regular release full-dose aspirin prior to going to the hospital if that situation occurs.

▷ **This Drug Should Not Be Taken If**
- you had an allergic reaction to any form of it previously.
- you have severe anemia.
- you have increased intraocular pressure.
- you have suffered trauma to the head.
- you have an overactive thyroid gland.
- you have abnormal growth of the heart muscle (hypertrophic cardiomyopathy).
- you have already taken or take sildenafil (Viagra).
- you have had a very recent heart attack (myocardial infarction) and have elevated blood pressure or very rapid heart rate (tachycardia).

▷ **Inform Your Physician Before Taking This Drug If**
- you have had an unfavorable response to other nitrate drugs or vasodilators in the past or have an allergy to tartrazine dye (in some forms of this medicine).
- you have a history of low blood pressure.
- you are anemic and are being prescribed the under-the-tongue (sublingual) form.
- you have any form of glaucoma.
- you have had a cerebral hemorrhage recently.
- you are pregnant or are planning pregnancy.
- you are allergic to the dye tartrazine.
- you have a glucose-6-phosphate dehydrogenase (G6PD) deficiency (ask your doctor).
- you have excessive thyroid function (hyperthyroidism), cardiomyopathy, or have suffered head trauma.

Possible Side Effects (natural, expected, and unavoidable drug actions)
Flushing of face, throbbing in head, palpitation, rapid heart rate, orthostatic hypotension (see Glossary).

▷ **Possible Adverse Effects** (unusual, unexpected, and infrequent reactions)
If any of the following develop, consult your physician promptly for guidance.
Mild Adverse Effects
Allergic reaction: skin rash.
Headache (may be severe and persistent)—infrequent to frequent.
Dizziness, fainting—possible.
Nausea, vomiting—possible.
Bad breath (halitosis)—case reports.
Urine discoloration—possible and not clinically significant.
Serious Adverse Effects
Allergic reaction: severe dermatitis with peeling of skin—case reports.
Transient ischemic attacks (TIAs) in presence of impaired circulation within the brain: dizziness, fainting, impaired vision or speech, localized numbness or weakness—possible.
Anemia (in those with G6PD deficiency)—possible.
Abnormal heart rates or conduction—case reports.
Abnormally low blood pressure on standing (postural hypotension)—possible.
Myocardial ischemia (with abrupt withdrawal) or infarction—possible.
Methemoglobinemia—case report.

Tolerance—possible with 24-hour use (daily 12-hour drug-free period is used to prevent this).

▷ **Possible Effects on Sexual Function:** None reported.

▷ **Adverse Effects That May Mimic Natural Diseases or Disorders**

Spells of low blood pressure (due to this drug) may mimic late-onset epilepsy.

Possible Effects on Laboratory Tests

Methemoglobin: increased.

CAUTION

1. Tolerance (see Glossary) to long-acting forms of nitrates may cause sublingual tablets of nitroglycerin to be less effective in relieving acute anginal attacks. Anti-anginal effectiveness is restored after 1 week of abstinence from long-acting nitrates. Daily 12-hour periods without use of the drug are needed.
2. Many over-the-counter (OTC) medicines for allergies, colds, and coughs contain drugs that may counteract the desired drug effects. Ask your physician or pharmacist for help before using such medicines.

Precautions for Use

By Those Over 60 Years of Age: Small starting doses are advisable. You may be more susceptible to the development of low blood pressure and associated "blackout" spells, fainting, and falling. Throbbing headaches and flushing may be more apparent.

▷ **Advisability of Use During Pregnancy**

Pregnancy Category: C. See Pregnancy Risk Categories at the back of this book.

Animal Studies: No information available.

Human Studies: Adequate studies of pregnant women are not available.

Use this drug only if clearly needed.

Advisability of Use If Breast-Feeding

Presence of this drug in breast milk: Unknown.

If this drug is thought to be necessary, monitor the nursing infant for low blood pressure and poor feeding.

Habit-Forming Potential: None.

Effects of Overdose: Headache, dizziness, marked flushing of face and skin, vomiting, weakness, fainting, difficult breathing, coma.

Possible Effects of Long-Term Use: Development of tolerance with temporary loss of effectiveness at recommended doses. Development of abnormal hemoglobin (red blood cell pigment).

Suggested Periodic Examinations While Taking This Drug (at physician's discretion)

Measurement of internal eye pressure.

Red cell counts and hemoglobin and methemoglobin tests.

▷ **While Taking This Drug, Observe the Following**

Foods: Oral doses are best taken on an empty stomach to ensure quick absorption. Vitamin C may help ease nitrate tolerance. More study is needed. Your doctor may also recommend some specific foods such as increased vegetables or functional foods such as Benecol. Three well-designed studies published in early April 2002 found that both in women and men and before and after a heart attack, people who ate more fish (2–4 servings a week) appeared to avoid heart disease. Additionally, putting supplements containing Omega 3 polyunsaturated fatty acids (PUFA) into the diet also appeared to protect against abnormal heart rhythms and sudden death from heart attack. The studies appeared in *JAMA*, *Circulation* and the *New England Journal of Medicine*. Increasing oat bran in the diet may be of additional help in lowering cholesterol, but might decrease the amount of medicine that gets into your body. Take oat bran 2 hours before or 4 to 6 hours after. Your doctor may also recommend increasing B vitamins. See Tables 19 and 20 about lifestyle changes and risk factors you can fix!

Herbal Medicines or Minerals: Hawthorn and co-enzyme Q10 (co-Q10) can affect the way the heart works. Co-Q10 may also interact badly with aspirin. Soy (milk, tofu, etc.) contains phytoestrogens that have led to an FDA-approved health claim for reducing risk of heart disease (if they have at least 6.25 grams of soy protein per serving). Couch grass or nettle should NOT be taken by patients who have increased fluid (edema) caused by heart weakness. Hawthorn (Crataegus variety) has been used to help heart failure, but should not be combined with heart medicines as combination use has not been studied. BE CERTAIN to tell your doctor that you are taking or are considering taking these herbs if you are taking a nitrate.

Beverages: No restrictions. May be taken with milk.

▷ *Alcohol:* Use extreme caution and avoid alcohol completely in the presence of any side effects or adverse effects of this drug. Alcohol may exaggerate the blood pressure–lowering effect of this drug.

Tobacco Smoking: Nicotine can reduce benefits. Avoid all forms of tobacco.

Marijuana Smoking: Possible reduced effectiveness of this drug; mild to moderate increase in angina; possible changes in electrocardiogram, confusing interpretation.

▷ *Other Drugs*

Isosorbide dinitrate **taken concurrently** with

- antihypertensive drugs may cause excessive lowering of blood pressure; dose adjustments may be necessary.
- hydralazine (Apresoline) may work well to help control angina.
- propranolol (Inderal) can help improve exercise time without angina.
- sildenafil (Viagra) may result in LIFE-THREATENING lowering of blood pressure. NEVER COMBINE.

▷ *Driving, Hazardous Activities:* Usually no restrictions. This drug may cause dizziness or spells of low blood pressure. Restrict activities as necessary.

Aviation Note: Coronary artery disease **is a disqualification** for piloting. Consult a designated Aviation Medical Examiner.

Exposure to Sun: No restrictions.

Exposure to Heat: Use caution. Hot environments can cause a significant drop in blood pressure.

Exposure to Cold: Cold environments can increase the need for this drug and limit its benefits.

Heavy Exercise or Exertion: This drug may improve your ability to be more active without anginal pain. Use caution and avoid excessive exertion.

Discontinuation: It is advisable to gradually withdraw this drug after long-term use. DO NOT abruptly withdraw this medicine. Dose and frequency of prolonged-action dose forms should be reduced gradually over a period of 4 to 6 weeks.

ISOSORBIDE MONONITRATE (i soh SOHR bide mon oh NI trayt)

Introduced: 1983 **Class:** Anti-anginal, nitrates **Prescription:** USA: Yes **Controlled Drug:** USA: No **Available as Generic:** USA: Yes

Brand Names: Elan (Italy), Elantan, Imdur, Ismo, Monoket

BENEFITS versus RISKS	
Possible Benefits	*Possible Risks*
EFFECTIVE PREVENTION OF ANGINA	Orthostatic hypotension (see Glossary) Headache

▷ **Principal Uses**

As a Single Drug Product: Uses currently included in FDA-approved labeling: (1) To reduce the frequency and severity of recurrent angina; not effective in acute anginal pain.

Other (unlabeled) generally accepted uses: (1) May have a role in treating congestive heart failure (intravenous); (2) can help in decreasing the number of attacks and time spent in silent myocardial ischemia; (3) may be of help in heart attacks (myocardial infarction); (4) may help stomach bleeding in people with cirrhosis of the liver.

How This Drug Works: Relaxes and dilates arteries and veins. Benefits in angina are due to dilation of coronary arteries and dilation of systemic veins. Net effects are improved blood flow to the heart and reduced workload of the heart.

Available Dosage Forms and Strengths

Capsules, sustained release — 60 mg
Capsules, sustained release (Italy) — 50 mg
Tablets — 10 mg, 20 mg
Tablets, sustained release — 30 mg, 60 mg, 120 mg

▷ **Recommended Dosage Ranges** (Actual dose and schedule must be determined for each patient individually.)

Infants and Children: Dose not established.

12 to 60 Years of Age:

Regular release: 20 mg (one tablet), taken twice daily. Take the first tablet when you wake up; take the second tablet 7 hours later. Do not take additional doses during the balance of the day. Total daily dose should not exceed 40 mg.

Author's Note: Dosing is set up to give a 12-hour nitrate-free period to avoid tolerance to the therapeutic benefits of this medicine.

Sustained release: 30 mg (one half-tablet) or 60 mg (a whole tablet) once daily, taken in the morning when you get up. The dose can be increased in steps over several days to 120 mg once a day, and then increased farther if needed and tolerated. Total daily dose should not exceed 240 mg.

Over 60 Years of Age: Same as 12 to 60 years of age.

Conditions Requiring Dosing Adjustments

Liver Function: This drug should be used with caution by patients with liver compromise. No specific guidelines for dose reduction are available.

Kidney Function: No dosing changes in kidney compromise. Drug turns urine brown to black in color.

▷ **Dosing Instructions:** The immediate release tablet may be crushed and is preferably taken on an empty stomach to achieve the best blood levels. Sustained release forms should not be chewed or crushed. If you forget a dose: take the missed dose as soon as you remember it, unless it's nearly time for your next dose, then skip the missed dose and take the next dose right on schedule. DO NOT double doses. Call your doctor if you find yourself missing doses.

Usual Duration of Use: Use on a regular schedule for 3 to 7 days is needed to (1) identify this drug's peak effect in preventing or relieving acute anginal pain and (2) to find the optimal dose schedule. Long-term use (months to years) requires physician supervision.

Typical Treatment Goals and Measurements (Outcomes and Markers)

Angina: The most commonly used markers are prevention or relief of chest pain (angina). Many cardiologists look for easing of frequency and severity of angina attacks as well as pulmonary capillary wedge pressure as measures of successful therapy. If your chest pain does not go away after using the maximum dose at the recommended time interval, have someone drive you to the hospital or call 911. Plan for this possibility and ask your doctor on the next office visit if it would make sense for you to chew a regular release full-dose aspirin prior to going to the hospital if you do not get relief from maximum nitrate doses and have to go to the hospital.

Possible Advantages of This Drug

Designed to provide the best possible prevention of acute angina with minimal development of tolerance (loss of effectiveness—see Glossary). The nitrate-free interval during the evening and night prevents the development of tolerance.

▷ **This Drug Should Not Be Taken If**
- you have had an allergic reaction to it previously.
- you currently have congestive heart failure or a severe anemia.
- you have taken or are currently taking sildenafil (Viagra).
- your thyroid is overactive.
- you have a hypertrophic cardiomyopathy.

▷ **Inform Your Physician Before Taking This Drug If**
- you have had an unfavorable response to other nitrate drugs or vasodilators in the past.
- you have a history of low blood pressure or your body is fluid depleted (hypovolemic).
- you have had a very recent heart attack (myocardial infarction) and your heart is beating quickly (tachycardia) or your blood pressure is excessively high.
- you have had a cerebral hemorrhage recently.
- you are pregnant or planning pregnancy or breast-feeding your baby.
- you have any form of glaucoma.
- you have excessive thyroid function (hyperthyroidism) or cardiomyopathy or have suffered head trauma.

Possible Side Effects (natural, expected, and unavoidable drug actions)

Flushing of face, throbbing in head, palpitation, rapid heart rate, orthostatic hypotension (see Glossary).

▷ **Possible Adverse Effects** (unusual, unexpected, and infrequent reactions)

If any of the following develop, consult your physician promptly for guidance.

Mild Adverse Effects

Allergic reactions: skin rash, itching—infrequent.

Headache—frequent, but decreases over time.

Dizziness, fainting or blurred vision—possible.

Nausea, vomiting or bad breath (halitosis seen with isosorbide dinitrate)—possible.

Urine discoloration—possible and not clinically significant.

Increased liver enzymes—possible.

Serious Adverse Effects

Transient ischemic attacks (TIAs) in presence of impaired circulation within the brain: dizziness, fainting, impaired vision or speech, localized numbness or weakness—possible.

Bone marrow depression—infrequent and of uncertain relationship.

Anemia (in patients with glucose-6-phosphate dehydrogenase [G6PD] deficiency)—possible.

Abnormally low blood pressure—possible.

Abnormal heartbeat—case reports.

Tolerance—possible with 24-hour use (daily 12-hour drug-free period is used to prevent this).

Worsening of angina or abnormal heartbeats—case reports.

▷ **Possible Effects on Sexual Function:** Decreased libido and impotence—infrequent.

▷ **Adverse Effects That May Mimic Natural Diseases or Disorders**

Spells of low blood pressure with fainting (due to this drug) may be mistaken for late-onset epilepsy.

Possible Effects on Laboratory Tests

Liver function tests: increased.

CAUTION

1. Take this drug exactly as prescribed. If headaches are frequent or troublesome, call your doctor. Aspirin or acetaminophen may be taken to relieve headaches.

2. Many over-the-counter (OTC) medicines for allergies, colds, and coughs contain drugs that may counteract the desired effects of this drug. Ask your doctor or pharmacist for help before using such medicines.

Precautions for Use

By Those Over 60 Years of Age: Small starting doses are advisable. Increased risk of low blood pressure and associated "blackout" spells, fainting, and falling. Throbbing headaches and flushing may be more apparent.

▷ **Advisability of Use During Pregnancy**

Pregnancy Category: Ismo: C. Imdur: B. Monoket: B. See Pregnancy Risk Categories at the back of this book.

Animal Studies: Rat and rabbit studies reveal embryo deaths due to large doses of Ismo. Rat and rabbit studies did not reveal embryo deaths from Imdur.

Human Studies: Adequate studies of pregnant women are not available.

Use this drug only if clearly needed. Ask your physician for guidance.

Advisability of Use If Breast-Feeding

Presence of this drug in breast milk: Unknown.

If this drug is thought to be necessary, watch the nursing infant for low blood pressure and poor feeding.

Habit-Forming Potential: None.

Effects of Overdose: Headache, dizziness, marked flushing of face and skin, vomiting, weakness, fainting, difficult breathing, coma.

Possible Effects of Long-Term Use: Development of abnormal hemoglobin (red blood cell pigment).

Suggested Periodic Examinations While Taking This Drug (at physician's discretion)

Measurement of internal eye pressure.

▷ **While Taking This Drug, Observe the Following**

Foods: No restrictions. Vitamin C may help ease nitrate tolerance. More study is needed. Your doctor may also recommend some specific foods such as increased vegetables or functional foods such as Benecol. Three well-designed studies published in early April 2002 found that both in women and men and before and after a heart attack, people who ate more fish (2–4 servings a week) appeared to avoid heart disease. Additionally putting supplements containing Omega 3 polyunsaturated fatty acids (PUFA) into the diet also appeared to protect against abnormal heart rhythms and sudden death from heart attack. The studies appeared in *JAMA, Circulation* and the *New England Journal of Medicine.* Increasing oat bran in the diet may be of additional help in lowering cholesterol, but may decrease the amount of medicine that gets into your body. Take oat bran 2 hours before or 4 to 6 hours after. Your doctor may also recommend increasing B vitamins. See Tables 19 and 20 about lifestyle changes and risk factors you can fix!

Herbal Medicines or Minerals: Hawthorn and co-enzyme Q10 (co-Q10) can affect the way the heart works. Co-Q10 may also interact badly with aspirin. Soy (milk, tofu, etc.) contains phytoestrogens that have led to an FDA-approved health claim for reducing risk of heart disease (if they have at least 6.25 grams of soy protein per serving). Couch grass or nettle should NOT be taken by patients who have increased fluid (edema) caused by heart weakness. Hawthorn (*Crataegus* variety) has been used to help heart failure, but should not be combined with heart medicines as combination use has not been studied. BE CERTAIN to tell your doctor that you are taking or are considering taking these herbs if you are taking a nitrate.

Beverages: No restrictions. May be taken with milk.

▷ *Alcohol:* Use extreme caution. Avoid alcohol completely in the presence of any side effects or adverse effects of this drug. Alcohol may exaggerate the blood pressure–lowering effect of this drug.

Tobacco Smoking: Nicotine can reduce effectiveness. Avoid all forms of tobacco.

Marijuana Smoking: Possible reduced effectiveness of this drug; mild to moderate increase in angina and possible changes in electrocardiogram confusing interpretation.

▷ *Other Drugs*

Isosorbide mononitrate *taken concurrently* with

- antihypertensive drugs may cause excessive lowering of blood pressure; dose adjustments may be necessary.
- calcium channel–blocking drugs (see Drug Classes) may cause marked orthostatic hypotension (see Glossary).
- hydralazine (Apresoline) may work well to help control angina.
- propranolol (Inderal) can help improve exercise time without angina.
- sildenafil (Viagra) may result in LIFE-THREATENING lowering of blood pressure. NEVER COMBINE.

▷ *Driving, Hazardous Activities:* Usually no restrictions. This drug may cause dizziness or spells of low blood pressure. Restrict activities as necessary.

Aviation Note: Coronary artery disease *is a disqualification* for piloting. Consult a designated Aviation Medical Examiner.

Exposure to Sun: No restrictions.

Exposure to Heat: Use caution. Hot environments can cause a significant drop in blood pressure.

Exposure to Cold: Cold environments can increase the need for this drug and limit its effectiveness.

Heavy Exercise or Exertion: This drug may improve your ability to be more active without anginal pain. Use caution and avoid excessive exertion.

Discontinuation: It is best to withdraw this drug gradually (over a period of 2 to 4 weeks) after long-term use.

ISOTRETINOIN (i soh TRET i noy in)

Introduced: 1979   **Class:** Antiacne, vitamin A analog   **Prescription:** USA: Yes   **Controlled Drug:** USA: No; Canada: No   **Available as Generic:** Yes

Brand Names: Accutane, Amnesteem

Author's Note: This medicine has serious benefit-to-risk considerations. Make CERTAIN that you read the specific Medication Guide that is dispensed with the medicine itself. Guidance for this medicine and specific required patient follow-ups have changed over time; but include such serious adverse effects as possible birth defects if this medicine is taken by pregnant women and cases where patients have developed serious depression while taking or shortly after stopping this medicine. See Possible Adverse Effects on page 602 for more information and check *www.fda. gov/medwatch/safety/2002/accutaine_deardoc_10-202.htm.*

BENEFITS versus RISKS

Possible Benefits	*Possible Risks*
EFFECTIVE TREATMENT OF SEVERE CYSTIC ACNE	DEPRESSION
Treatment of other skin conditions of serious and resistant nature	MAJOR BIRTH DEFECTS
	ELEVATED LIPIDS (HYPERTRIGLYCERIDEMIA)
	PANCREATITIS
	HEARING IMPAIRMENT
	Initial worsening of acne (Transient)
	Dry skin, nose, and mouth
	Musculoskeletal discomfort
	Corneal opacities

▷ **Principal Uses**

As a Single Drug Product: Uses currently included in FDA-approved labeling: (1) Reserved to treat severe, disfiguring nodular, and cystic acne that has failed to respond to all other forms of therapy—*it should not be used to treat mild forms of acne;* (2) it is also used to treat some less common conditions of the skin that are due to disorders of keratin production.

Other (unlabeled) generally accepted uses: (1) May be helpful in refractory hypertrophic lupus erythematosus; (2) can help control resistant oral leukoplakia; (3) used in Apert's syndrome facial treatment; (4) used adjunctively to surgery in some cervical cancers; (5) treats mycosis fungoides; (6) eases symptoms in Darier's disease; (7) may have a role in treating dysplastic nevi; (8) can help treat the abnormal gum growth (gingival hyperplasia) that can occur with phenytoin therapy; (9) treats severe and refractory rosacea; (10) has been combined with interferon alpha treatment in squamous cell skin cancer.

How This Drug Works: Reduces the size of sebaceous glands and inhibits sebum (skin oil) production. This helps to correct acne and complications.

Available Dosage Forms and Strengths

Capsules — 10 mg, 20 mg, 40 mg

▷ **Usual Adult Dosage Ranges:** Starting dose is based on the patient's weight and severity of acne; the usual dose is 0.5 to 2 mg per kg of body mass daily, taken in 2 divided doses for 15 to 20 weeks. After weeks of treatment, the dose should be adjusted according to response of the acne and the development of adverse effects. After 15 to 20 weeks of therapy, if the cyst count has been lowered by more than 70%, the medicine can be stopped (discuss this with your doctor).

Note: Actual dose and schedule must be determined for each patient individually.

Conditions Requiring Dosing Adjustments

Liver Function: The dose should be empirically decreased when isotretinoin is used by patients with compromised livers.

Kidney Function: Isotretinoin should be used with caution in kidney compromise.

Dosing Instructions: Two forms of contraception should be used at the same time for a month before, during therapy and for a month after treatment with this medicine. Begin treatment only on the second or third day of your next normal menstrual period. Serum pregnancy test should be checked BEFORE treatment is started and monthly while taking this medicine. Take this medicine with meals (morning and evening) to achieve optimal blood levels. The capsule should not be opened for administration. If you forget a dose: take the missed dose as soon as you remember it, unless it's nearly time for your next dose, then skip the missed dose and take the next dose right on schedule. DO NOT double doses. Call your doctor if you find yourself missing doses.

Author's Note: A patient consent form must be filled out before starting this medicine. The form will ask you to tell your doctor if you or family members have had symptoms of depression and/or other psychological symptoms. Female patients will also be reminded about pregnancy risks (severe birth defects) possible if they become pregnant while taking this medicine. *Monthly pregnancy tests are required.* Only 30 days' worth of this medicine will be dispensed at a time. Stronger warnings are now present in labeling about depression and suicide and aggressive behavior in patients taking Accutane.

Usual Duration of Use: Use on a regular schedule for 15 to 20 weeks best determines effectiveness in clearing or improving severe cystic acne. The drug may be stopped earlier if the total cyst count is reduced by more than 70%. If a repeat course of treatment is necessary, it should not be started for 2 months. Long-term use (months to years) requires physician supervision.

Typical Treatment Goals and Measurements (Outcomes and Markers)

Acne: Many dermatologists look for improvement or decrease in the lesions being treated as the measure of response (see cyst count above). Blood fat (lipid) levels are tested before isotretinoin is given and then are rechecked periodically until reaction to the medicine is seen (often in a month).

▷ **This Drug Should Not Be Taken If**
- you have had an allergic reaction to it previously.
- you are allergic to parabens (preservatives used in this drug product).
- you have mild acne.
- you are not able or willing to follow contraception measures to avoid pregnancy and have not taken 2 forms of contraception for the previous month (unless abstinence is the way pregnancy is chosen to be avoided or if the patient has had a hysterectomy).
- you have not gotten verbal and written warnings about this medicine and fetal damage. You have not read, understood, and signed the consent form required for this medicine.
- you have not had a negative urine or serum pregnancy test (at least 50 mIU/ml sensitivity) when your doctor decided you were eligible for treatment and you did not have a second pregnancy test which was also negative which was a urine or serum pregnancy test on the second day of the next usual menstrual period (or 11 days after the last time you had unprotected sexual intercourse). You will not be able to comply with monthly pregnancy tests that are required.
- you are pregnant or planning pregnancy.
- you are not starting treatment on the second or third day of a subsequent normal menstrual period.

▷ **Inform Your Physician Before Taking This Drug If**
- you have a history of depression or become depressed while taking this medicine.
- you start to notice a hearing loss or ringing in the ears while you are taking this medicine. If this happens, stop the medicine and call your doctor.
- you had an allergic reaction to vitamin A in the past.
- you routinely take a nonprescription form of vitamin A.
- you have diabetes mellitus.
- you are considering giving blood (you will NOT be eligible for 1 month after the last isotretinoin dose).
- you have a cholesterol or triglyceride disorder, or if signs and symptoms of pancreatitis start while you are taking this medicine.
- you are considering having a child or are breast-feeding your infant.
- you wear contact lenses (your ability to wear these lenses [tolerance] may decrease while you take this medicine).
- you have a change in vision while taking this medicine. The medicine should be stopped and an eye (ophthalmological) exam obtained immediately.
- you have a history of liver or kidney disease.

Possible Side Effects (natural, expected, and unavoidable drug actions)

Frequent dryness of the nose and mouth (often results in nosebleeds or epistaxis), inflammation of the lips (cheilitis), dryness of the skin with itching, peeling of the palms and soles. Decreased night vision, dose-related irritation of the eye (conjunctivitis) may be frequent. Dose-related increase in triglycerides—frequent.

▷ **Possible Adverse Effects** (unusual, unexpected, and infrequent reactions)

If any of the following develop, consult your physician promptly for guidance.

Mild Adverse Effects

Allergic reaction: skin rash—may resemble pityriasis rosea.

Thinning of hair, conjunctivitis, intolerance of contact lenses, decreased night vision, muscular aches, headache, fatigue, indigestion—infrequent.

Insomnia—infrequent.

Increased blood sugar—infrequent.

Back or joint pain—frequent.

Chest pain (usually reversible if medicine is stopped)—rare.

Serious Adverse Effects

Depression—case reports to infrequent.

Psychosis—case reports.

Suicidal ideation and suicide attempts—rare.

Skin infections, arthritis flare, inflammatory bowel disorders—case reports.

Abnormal acceleration of bone development/growth arrest in children— possible.

Development of opacities in the cornea of the eye/cataracts, retinopathy— possible.

Reduced red blood cell and white blood cell counts; decreased blood platelet count—infrequent, but medicine should be stopped if significant lowering of the white blood cell count happens.

Seizures—case reports.

Aggressive and/or violent behavior—reported.

Hearing loss—reported.

Myopathy—case reports.

Tendonitis (Achilles)—case reports.

Kidney toxicity, liver toxicity or pancreatitis—rare.

Inflammatory bowel disease (severe diarrhea, abdominal pain, rectal bleeding—case reports.

Abnormal blood glucose control—infrequent.

Increased pressure within the head (pseudotumor cerebri-headache, visual disturbances, nausea/vomiting)—case reports.

Increased triglycerides—frequent.

Pancreatitis (secondary to increased triglycerides)—case reports.

▷ **Possible Effects on Sexual Function:** Decreased male or female libido—possible.

Ejaculatory failure—case report.

Decreased vaginal secretions—possible.

Altered timing and pattern of menstruation—case reports.

Possible Effects on Laboratory Tests

Complete blood cell counts: infrequently decreased red cells and white cells.

Blood platelets: increased or decreased.

Sedimentation rate (ESR): increased.

Blood total cholesterol, LDL cholesterol, VLDL cholesterol, and triglyceride levels: increased.

Blood HDL cholesterol levels: decreased.

Blood thyroid hormones (T3, T4, and free T4 index): decreased.

Liver function tests: infrequently increased liver enzymes (ALT/GPT, AST/GOT, and alkaline phosphatase), increased bilirubin.

Blood calcium level: increased.

Protein in the urine: positive, though infrequent.

CAUTION

1. This medicine has caused a number of verified cases of depression. Your prescriber should ask you about mood changes at each office visit, and you should call if depression starts.

2. This drug should not be used to treat mild forms of acne.

3. Worsening of your acne may occur during the first few weeks of treatment; this will subside with continued use of the drug.

4. Do not take any other form of vitamin A while taking this drug. (Check contents of multiple vitamin preparations.)

5. Women who may become pregnant should have a blood pregnancy test 2 weeks before taking this drug, take 2 forms of contraception for the month prior to starting this medicine, have a repeat negative pregnancy test (see timing mentioned earlier), and need 2 effective forms of contraception simultaneously during its use. Contraception should be continued until normal menstruation resumes after stopping this drug.

6. May increase blood levels of cholesterol and triglycerides. Your doctor must get a supply of Accutane Qualification stickers and read the booklet called the SMART (System to Manage Accutane Related Teratogenicity) guide to best practices.

7. If repeated courses of this drug are prescribed, wait a minimum of 2 months between courses before resuming medication.

8. DO NOT give blood for 1 month after this medicine is stopped.

9. This medicine may lead to bone problems (such as osteoporosis). Caution is to be used if people taking this medicine play sports with repeated impacts.

10. DO NOT share this medicine with anyone else.

Precautions for Use

By Infants and Children: Long-term use (6 to 12 months) may cause abnormal acceleration of bone growth and development. Your physician can monitor this possibility by periodic X-ray examination of long bones.

▷ Advisability of Use During Pregnancy

Pregnancy Category: X. See Pregnancy Risk Categories at the back of this book.

Animal Studies: Birth defects of skull, brain and vertebral column found in rats; skeletal birth defects found in rabbits.

Human Studies: Adequate studies of pregnant women are not available. However, many serious birth defects (thought to be due to this drug) have been reported. These include major abnormalities of the head, brain, heart, blood vessels, and hormone-producing glands.

Avoid this drug completely during entire pregnancy.

Advisability of Use If Breast-Feeding

Presence of this drug in breast milk: Unknown.

Avoid drug or refrain from nursing.

Habit-Forming Potential: None.

Effects of Overdose: Increased blood pressure, lethargy, nausea, vomiting, mild gastrointestinal bleeding, elevated blood calcium, hallucinations, and psychosis.

Suggested Periodic Examinations While Taking This Drug (at physician's discretion)

Monthly pregnancy tests are required by the FDA while taking this medicine.

Complete blood cell counts, including platelet counts.

Measurements of blood cholesterol and triglyceride levels.

Complete eye and hearing examinations.

Growth chart checks in children.

May be prudent to get baseline and periodic Bone Mineral Density tests in high-risk patients.

Assessment of mood/depression.

Liver and kidney function tests.

▷ **While Taking This Drug, Observe the Following**

Foods: Increases absorption and may be a good mechanism to maintain blood levels.

Herbal Medicines or Minerals: **Caution:** St. John's wort may also cause extreme reactions to the sun. Additive photosensitivity may be possible. Medicinal yeast has a German Commission E monograph indication for acne, but has not been studied with isotretinoin. Talk to your doctor BEFORE combining any herbals with prescription medicines.

Beverages: No restrictions.

▷ *Alcohol:* A disulfiramlike reaction was described in 1 case report. Heavy alcohol intake may increase the risk of osteoporosis and is not advisable while taking this medicine.

Tobacco Smoking: Smoking may increase risk of osteoporosis and is not advisable while taking this medicine. I advise everyone to quit smoking.

▷ *Other Drugs*

Isotretinoin *taken concurrently* with

- carbamazepine (Tegretol) may cause subtherapeutic carbamazepine levels.
- medicines known to increase sensitivity to the sun (see Table 2) as these do may additively increase sun sensitivity if taken with isotretinoin.
- medicines known to increase osteoporosis risk (such as corticosteroids [methylprednisolone, prednisone, and others] and phenytoin-Dilantin) may additively increase risk of osteoporosis if combined with isotretinoin.
- micro-dosed Progesterone (Minipills) for birth control may not be effective enough alone in preventing pregnancy while taking this medicine. Two forms of contraception should be taken at the same time while taking this medicine.
- minocycline may increase risk of severe headache, papilledema, and visual changes.
- tetracyclines may cause increased risk of pseudotumor cerebri.

▷ *Driving, Hazardous Activities:* No restrictions.

Exposure to Sun: Caution: This drug can cause photosensitivity (see Glossary). See "Herbal Medicines" caution above.

ISRADIPINE (is RA di peen)

Introduced: 1984   **Class:**   Antihypertensive, calcium channel blocker
Prescription: USA: Yes   **Controlled Drug:**   USA: No   **Available as Generic:**   USA: No

Brand Names: DynaCirc, DynaCirc CR

Controversies in Medicine: Medicines in this class have had many conflicting reports. The FDA has held hearings on the calcium channel–blocker (CCB) class. Amlodipine got the first FDA approval to treat high blood pressure or angina in people with congestive heart failure. CCBs are currently second-line agents for high blood pressure according to the JNC VII (see Glossary).

BENEFITS versus RISKS

Possible Benefits	*Possible Risks*
EFFECTIVE TREATMENT OF MILD TO MODERATE HYPERTENSION	Headache, dizziness, fluid retention, palpitations
May prevent progression of early atherosclerotic damage in blood vessels	
Might slow how quickly new atherosclerotic lesions are developed	

▷ **Principal Uses**

As a Single Drug Product: Uses currently included in FDA-approved labeling: (1) Treats mild to moderate hypertension, alone or in combination.

Other (unlabeled) generally accepted uses: (1) Treatment of chronic, stable angina; (2) may help prevent progression of early lesions and rate of development of new lesions in atherosclerosis.

How This Drug Works: Blocks passage of calcium through cell walls, inhibiting contraction of coronary arteries and peripheral arterioles. As a result:
- promotes dilation of the coronary arteries (anti-anginal effect);
- reduces the degree of contraction of peripheral arterial walls, resulting in lowering of blood pressure. This further reduces heart workload and helps prevent angina. Isradipine inhibits platelet clumping and thus may have a protective role against heart attack and stroke.

Available Dosage Forms and Strengths

Capsules — 2.5 mg, 5 mg

Tablets (timed release) — 5 mg and 10 mg

▷ **Usual Adult Dosage Ranges:** *Hypertension:* Initially 2.5 mg twice daily, 12 hours apart, for a trial period of 2 to 4 weeks. If needed, the dose may be increased by 5 mg per day at intervals of 2 to 4 weeks. The usual maintenance dose is 5 to 10 mg daily. The total daily dose should not exceed 20 mg. Timed release form is started at 5 mg once a day and increased slowly (2- to 4-week intervals) if needed.

Note: Actual dose and dosing schedule must be determined for each patient individually.

Conditions Requiring Dosing Adjustments

Liver Function: Empiric decreases in dosing are prudent in liver damage. Careful patient follow-up is needed.

Kidney Function: Use with caution in kidney compromise. Initial dose should be 2.5 mg twice a day or 5 mg once daily (sustained release), with careful patient follow-up.

▷ **Dosing Instructions:** May be taken with or following food to reduce stomach irritation. Swallow the capsule or tablet whole. Even though you take the sustained release tablets correctly, you may see a shell of the tablet which no longer has any medicine in it in your stool. If you forget a dose: take the missed dose as soon as you remember it, unless it's nearly time for your next dose—if that is the case, skip the missed dose and take the next dose right on schedule. DO NOT double doses. Call your doctor if you find yourself missing doses as there are pager and timer reminder systems to help get the right dose on time.

Usual Duration of Use: Use on a regular schedule for 2 to 4 weeks determines this drug's effectiveness in controlling hypertension or in reducing the frequency and severity of angina. The smallest effective dose should be used for long-term (months to years) therapy. Periodic physician evaluation is essential to make sure your blood pressure is lowered into the target range and kept there.

Typical Treatment Goals and Measurements (Outcomes and Markers)

Blood Pressure: The NEW guidelines (JNC VII) define normal blood pressure (BP) as **less than** 120/80. Because blood pressures that were once considered acceptable can actually lead to blood vessel damage, the committee from the National Institutes of Health, National Heart, Lung and Blood Institute now have a new category called **Pre-hypertension**. This ranges from 120/80 to 139/89 and is intended to help your doctor encourage lifestyle changes (or in the case of people with a risk factor for high blood pressure, start treatment) much earlier—so that possible damage to blood vessels, your heart, kidneys, sexual potency, or eyes might be minimized or avoided altogether. The next 2 classes of high blood pressure are stage 1 hypertension: 140/90 to 159/99; and stage 2 hypertension equal to or greater than: 160/100 mm Hg. These guidelines also recommend that clinicians trying to control blood pressure work with their patients to agree on the goals and a plan of treatment. The first-ever guidelines for blood pressure (hypertension) in African Americans recommend that MOST black patients be started on TWO antihypertensive medicines with the goal of lowering blood pressure to 130/80 for those with high risk for heart and blood vessel disease or with diabetes. The American Diabetes Association recommends 130/80 as the target for people living with diabetes and less than 125/75 for those who spill more than 1 gram of protein into their urine. Most clinicians try to achieve a BP that confers the best balance of lower cardiovascular risk and avoids the problem of too low a blood pressure. Blood pressure duration is generally increased with beneficial restriction of sodium. The goals and time frame should be discussed with you when the prescription is written. If goals are not met, it is not unusual to intensify doses or add on medicines. You can find the new blood pressure guidelines at *www.nhlbi.nih.gov/guidelines/hypertension/index.htm*. For the African American guidelines see Douglas, J.G. in Sources.

Possible Advantages of This Drug

Does not cause orthostatic hypotension (see Glossary). Inhibits platelet clumping (aggregation) more than nifedipine and therefore may have the most desirable effect of those 2 calcium channel blockers on preventing undesirable blood clots and thus strokes and heart attacks.

▷ **This Drug Should Not Be Taken If**
- you have had an allergic reaction to it previously.
- you have symptomatic low blood pressure (hypotension).
- you have severe problems in the left side of your heart (left ventricular dysfunction).

▷ **Inform Your Physician Before Taking This Drug If**
- you have had an unfavorable response to any calcium channel–blocker drug in the past (see Drug Classes).
- you take any beta-blocker drug (see Drug Classes).
- you are taking any drugs that lower blood pressure.

- you have a history of congestive heart failure, heart attack, or stroke.
- you have narrowing of the aorta.
- you are subject to disturbances of heart rhythm.
- you have muscular dystrophy or myasthenia gravis.
- you develop a skin reaction while taking this drug (call your doctor as this may be an early sign of a significant skin reaction).
- you have impaired liver or kidney function.
- you will have surgery with general anesthesia in the near future.

Possible Side Effects (natural, expected, and unavoidable drug actions)

Flushing, gum overgrowth—infrequent.

Swelling of the feet and ankles, cough, flushing, and sensation of warmth—infrequent.

Small weight loss—possible.

▷ **Possible Adverse Effects** (unusual, unexpected, and infrequent reactions)

If any of the following develop, consult your physician promptly for guidance.

Mild Adverse Effects

Allergic reactions: skin rash—infrequent; hives, itching—rare.

Headache—frequent.

Dizziness, weakness—infrequent.

Nervousness, blurred vision, or eye pain—rare.

Decreased skin sensation—rare.

Palpitation, shortness of breath—infrequent.

Indigestion, nausea, vomiting, constipation—infrequent.

Increased liver enzymes (usually mild and transient)—possible.

Cramps in legs and feet—rare.

Increased urination—rare.

Abnormal growth of the gums (gingival hyperplasia)—frequent with some drugs in the same class.

Serious Adverse Effects

Allergic reactions: erythema multiforme, exfoliative dermatitis—case reports.

Heart rhythm disturbances—infrequent.

Increased frequency or severity of angina (when therapy is started or dose increased)—possible.

Marked drop in blood pressure with fainting—rare.

Low white blood cell counts—rare.

▷ **Possible Effects on Sexual Function:** Decreased libido, impotence (less than 1%).

▷ **Adverse Effects That May Mimic Natural Diseases or Disorders**

Flushing and warmth may resemble menopausal "hot flashes."

Possible Effects on Laboratory Tests

White blood cell counts: decreased (less than 1% of users).

Liver function tests: increased enzyme levels—infrequent.

Electrocardiogram: slight increase in QT interval.

CAUTION

1. If you check your blood pressure, check it just before each dose and 2 to 3 hours after each dose. Even though high blood pressure usually has no symptoms, high blood pressure MUST be treated to avoid serious complications.
2. Tell health care professionals who treat you that you take this drug. List this drug on a card in your purse or wallet.
3. Nitroglycerin and other nitrate drugs may be used as needed to relieve

acute episodes of angina pain. However, if your angina attacks are becoming more frequent or intense, notify your physician promptly.

Precautions for Use

By Infants and Children: Safety and effectiveness under 18 years of age not established.

By Those Over 60 Years of Age: Usually well tolerated by this age group. However, watch for weakness, dizziness, fainting, and falling. Take necessary precautions to prevent injury.

▷ **Advisability of Use During Pregnancy**

Pregnancy Category: C. See Pregnancy Risk Categories at the back of this book.

Animal Studies: Embryo and fetal toxicity reported in small animals, but no birth defects due to this drug.

Human Studies: Adequate studies of pregnant women are not available.

Avoid this drug during the first 3 months. Use during the final 6 months only if clearly needed. Ask your physician for guidance.

Advisability of Use If Breast-Feeding

Presence of this drug in breast milk: Unknown.

Avoid drug or refrain from nursing.

Habit-Forming Potential: None. Abrupt withdrawal has led to an increased frequency of angina if this medicine has been used to treat angina.

Effects of Overdose: Weakness, light-headedness, fainting, fast pulse, low blood pressure, shortness of breath, flushed and warm skin, tremors, abnormal heartbeats.

Possible Effects of Long-Term Use: None reported.

Suggested Periodic Examinations While Taking This Drug (at physician's discretion)

Evaluations of heart function, including electrocardiograms.

Measurements of blood pressure in supine, sitting, and standing positions.

▷ **While Taking This Drug, Observe the Following**

Foods: DO NOT take this medicine with grapefruit or grapefruit juice. Avoid excessive salt intake.

Herbal Medicines or Minerals: Ginseng, guarana, hawthorn, saw palmetto, ma huang, goldenseal, yohimbe, and licorice may also increase blood pressure. Calcium and garlic may help lower blood pressure. Indian snakeroot has a German Commission E monograph indication for hypertension—talk to your doctor. Eleuthero root and ephedra should be avoided by people living with hypertension. Talk to your doctor before combining any herbal medicine or mineral with isradipine.

Beverages: DO NOT take this medicine with grapefruit or grapefruit juice. May be taken with milk.

▷ *Alcohol:* Use caution. Alcohol may exaggerate the drop in blood pressure in some people.

Tobacco Smoking: Nicotine may reduce the effectiveness of this drug. I advise everyone to quit smoking.

Marijuana Smoking: Possible reduced effectiveness; mild to moderate increase in angina; possible changes in electrocardiogram, confusing interpretation.

▷ *Other Drugs*

Isradipine *taken concurrently* with

- amiodarone (Cordarone) should be avoided in people with certain kinds of heart conduction problems (partial atrioventricular block or "sick sinus" syndrome).

- amprenavir (Agenerase) may increase blood levels of isradipine. Careful patient follow-up and possible decreased doses are prudent.
- antifungals (triazoles) such as fluconazole (Diflucan), itraconazole (Sporanox), ketoconazole (Nizoral), or voriconazole (Vfend) may lead to toxicity.
- beta-blocker drugs or digitalis preparations (see Drug Classes) may affect heart rate and rhythm adversely. Careful monitoring by your physician is needed if these drugs are taken concurrently.
- carbamazepine (Tegretol) has resulted in decreased blood levels of carbamazepine with calcium channel blockers from the same pharmacological family. Caution is advised.
- cimetidine (Tagamet) may lead to isradipine toxicity, careful patient follow-up is advisable.
- class I, IA and class III antiarrhythmics (see Drug Classes) may prolong the QT interval and lead to dangerous arrhythmias (such as Torsades de Pointes or even cardiac arrest). DO NOT combine.
- cotrimoxazole (various) may lead to additive QT prolongation and arrhythmias. DO NOT combine.
- delavirdine (Rescriptor) may lead to isradipine toxicity.
- digoxin (Lanoxin) may increase blood levels. Laboratory testing of blood levels should be performed more often if these drugs are combined.
- erythromycin (various and combination erythromycin forms) may increase the free (active) form of isradipine, and may prolong the QT interval. DO NOT combine.
- magnesium (various)—especially in doses used in premature labor, can cause very low and abnormal blood pressure.
- nonsteroidal anti-inflammatory drugs (NSAIDs; see Drug Classes) may blunt benefits of isradipine.
- oral anticoagulant medicines (such as Coumadin or warfarin) may lead to increased risk of bleeding from the stomach or intestines.
- phenytoin (Dilantin) may result in loss of isradipine's effectiveness. Caution is advised.
- quinupristin/dalfopristin (Synercid) may increase blood levels of isradipine. Careful patient follow-up and possible decreased doses are prudent.
- rifampin (Rifadin, others) may result in a decreased therapeutic benefit from isradipine.
- ritonavir (Norvir), saquinavir (Invirase) and perhaps other protease inhibitors (see Drug Classes) can lead to toxicity.
- trimethoprim (Septra, various) may lead to QT prolongation and arrhythmias. DO NOT combine.
- vasopressin (various) may lead to QT prolongation and arrhythmias. DO NOT combine.
- zolmitriptan (Zomig) and any other QT prolonging medicines (see Glossary) may lead to QT prolongation and arrhythmias. DO NOT combine.

▷ *Driving, Hazardous Activities:* Usually no restrictions. This drug may cause drowsiness or dizziness. Restrict activities as necessary.

Aviation Note: Coronary artery disease and hypertension *are disqualifications* for piloting. Consult a designated Aviation Medical Examiner.

Exposure to Sun: No restrictions.

Exposure to Heat: Caution is advised. Hot environments can exaggerate the blood pressure–lowering effects of this drug. Observe for light-headedness or weakness.

Heavy Exercise or Exertion: This drug may improve your ability to be more active without resulting in angina pain. Use caution and avoid excessive exercise that could impair heart function in the absence of warning pain.

Discontinuation: Do not stop this drug abruptly. Ask your doctor about gradual withdrawal. Watch for the development of rebound angina.

KETOCONAZOLE (kee toh KOHN a zohl)

Introduced: 1981   **Class:** Antifungal   **Prescription:** USA: Yes
Controlled Drug: USA: No; Canada: No   **Available as Generic:** USA: Yes; Canada: No

Brand Names: ✿Apo-Ketoconazole, Nizoral, Nizoral A-D, ✿Novo-Ketocon, ✿Nu-Ketocon

---

BENEFITS versus RISKS

Possible Benefits	*Possible Risks*
EFFECTIVE TREATMENT OF THE FOLLOWING FUNGUS INFECTIONS: blastomycosis, candidiasis, chromomycosis, coccidioidomycosis, histoplasmosis, paracoccidioidomycosis, tinea (ringworm)	SERIOUS DRUG-INDUCED LIVER DAMAGE
	Allergic reactions
	Low blood platelets and anemia
	Some serious drug interactions
Beneficial short-term treatment of advanced prostate cancer	
Beneficial auxiliary treatment of Cushing's syndrome	

▷ **Principal Uses**

As a Single Drug Product: Uses currently included in FDA-approved labeling: Treatment of (1) lung and systemic blastomycosis; (2) *Candida* (yeast) infections of the skin, mouth, throat, and esophagus (may be AIDS-related); (3) systemic *Candida* infections—pneumonia, peritonitis, urinary tract infections (may be AIDS-related); (4) chromomycosis (auxiliary); (5) lung and systemic coccidioidomycosis; (6) lung and systemic histoplasmosis; (7) paracoccidioidomycosis; (8) tinea infections—groin (jock itch) and feet (athlete's foot) using the cream form; (9) tinea versicolor (pityriasis); (10) fungal dandruff (topical).

Other (unlabeled) generally accepted uses: Treatment of (1) *Candida* infections of the vulva and vagina; (2) alternative short-term prostate cancer treatment combined with prednisone; (3) Cushing's syndrome (excessive adrenal hormones); (4) systemic sporotrichosis; (5) fungal toenail infections; (6) visceral leishmaniasis.

How This Drug Works: As an antifungal: By damaging cell walls and impairing critical cell enzymes, this drug inhibits cell growth and reproduction (with low drug levels) and destroys fungal cells (with high drug concentrations).

In treating prostate cancer: Decreases testosterone (male hormone) levels—and prostate cancer needs testosterone to grow.

In treating Cushing's syndrome: This drug suppresses the excessive production of adrenal corticosteroid hormones.

Available Dosage Forms and Strengths

Cream — 2% (for local application to *Candida* or tinea skin infections)

Oral suspension — 100 mg/5 ml (Canada)

Shampoo — 2%

Tablets — 200 mg (US and Canada)

▷ **Recommended Dosage Ranges** (Actual dose and schedule must be determined for each patient individually.)

Infants and Children: Up to 2 years of age—Dose not established.

Over 2 years of age—3.3 to 6.6 mg per kg of body mass, once daily; the dose depends upon the nature of the infection.

12 to 60 Years of Age: For fungus infections—200 to 400 mg once daily; 800 mg maximum daily dose.

For prostate cancer—400 mg 3 times daily; 1,200 mg maximum daily dose.

For Cushing's syndrome—600 to 1,200 mg once daily; total daily dose should not exceed 1,200 mg.

Topical for dandruff: 2% shampoo is used twice a week for 4 weeks.

Over 60 Years of Age: Same as 12 to 60 years of age.

Conditions Requiring Dosing Adjustments

Liver Function: Dose empirically decreased for patients with liver compromise.

Kidney Function: Decreased doses are not needed in kidney compromise.

Achlorhydria (lack of acid in the stomach): This medicine requires an acid environment in the stomach to be absorbed. Talk with your doctor about making a dilute acid solution or taking a cola drink (acid pH) prior to taking the tablet form.

▷ **Dosing Instructions:** The tablet may be crushed and is best taken with or after food to enhance absorption and reduce stomach irritation. The bottle of suspension form should be shaken well and a measuring cup or measuring spoon used to get the right dose. Do not take with antacids. Take the full course prescribed. If you forget a dose: Take the missed dose as soon as you remember it, unless it's nearly time for your next dose—if that is the case, skip the missed dose and take the next dose right on schedule. Talk with your doctor if you find yourself missing doses.

Usual Duration of Use: Use on a regular schedule for 2 to 4 weeks determines effectiveness in controlling fungal infections. Actual cures (up to 83 days in one patient with mouth yeast infection [oral candidiasis] or use for long-term suppression often require continual treatment for many months. Periodic physician evaluation of response and dose adjustment are essential. Fungal cultures take a long time to grow and it is not unusual for anti-fungal sensitivity patterns to take a long time to be reported.

Typical Treatment Goals and Measurements (Outcomes and Markers)

Fungal infections: Resolution of signs and symptoms of infection (such as sore throat and white coloration in candidal throat infections), return of white blood cell count and differential to normal (for systemic infections), and failure of the infection to return in prophylactic use. Blood levels can be used to guide dosing in serious infections or in the case of relapses.

▷ **This Drug Should Not Be Taken If**
  - you have had an allergic reaction to it previously.
  - you have active liver disease.
  - you take astemizole, cisapride, sildenafil, or triazolam.

▷ **Inform Your Physician Before Taking This Drug If**
  - you are allergic to related antifungal drugs: clotrimazole, fluconazole, itraconazole, or miconazole.
  - you have a liver disease or impaired liver function.
  - you take loratadine. Heart problems have not been reported as with other nonsedating antihistamines, but the blood level does increase if the drugs are combined; the dose of loratadine may need to be decreased.
  - you have a history of adrenal gland problems (adrenal insufficiency).
  - you have a history of low blood platelets or anemia.
  - you have a history of alcoholism.
  - you have a deficiency of stomach hydrochloric acid.
  - you are taking any other drugs currently.

Possible Side Effects (natural, expected, and unavoidable drug actions)
  Suppression of testosterone and adrenal corticosteroid hormone production (more pronounced with high drug doses).

▷ **Possible Adverse Effects** (unusual, unexpected, and infrequent reactions)
  If any of the following develop, consult your physician promptly for guidance.
  Mild Adverse Effects
  Allergic reactions: skin rash, hives, itching—rare.
  Headache, dizziness, drowsiness, photophobia—infrequent.
  Nausea (helped by taking with meals) and vomiting, stomach pain, diarrhea—rare.
  Increased blood pressure—possible.
  Hair loss (alopecia) or ringing in the ears—case reports.
  Muscle and joint aches—infrequent.
  Serious Adverse Effects
  Allergic reactions: anaphylactic reaction (see Glossary).
  Severe liver toxicity: loss of appetite, nausea, yellow skin or eyes, dark urine, light-colored stools (see Jaundice in Glossary)—rare.
  Suppression of the adrenal gland or low thyroid function—case reports.
  Mental depression—rare.
  Hemolytic anemia or abnormally low platelet counts (abnormal bruising or bleeding)—rare.

▷ **Possible Effects on Sexual Function:** Decreased testosterone blood levels: reduced sperm counts, decreased libido, impotence, male breast enlargement and tenderness (gynecomastia)—case reports.
  Altered menstrual patterns—case reports.

Possible Delayed Adverse Effects: Deficiency of adrenal corticosteroid hormones (cortisone related); this could be serious during stress resulting from illness or injury and require corticosteroids replacement.

▷ **Adverse Effects That May Mimic Natural Diseases or Disorders**
  Drug-induced liver reaction may suggest viral hepatitis.

Possible Effects on Laboratory Tests
  Complete blood cell counts: decreased red cells, white cells and platelets.
  Liver function tests: increased liver enzymes (ALT/GPT, AST/GOT, and alkaline phosphatase), increased bilirubin.

Thyroid function tests: decreased—rare.
Adrenal corticosteroid blood levels: decreased.
Testosterone blood levels: decreased.
Cholesterol levels: case report of increases.

CAUTION
1. This drug inhibits several liver enzymes (CYP3A4, 1A2, 2C9 and 2C19). If you combine medicines with ketoconazole that are removed by these liver enzymes, there may be serious increases in effect or blood levels (toxicity) of those drugs.

Precautions for Use
By Infants and Children: Safety and effectiveness for under 2 years old not established.
By Those Over 60 Years of Age: This drug requires an acid stomach to enter the body. Talk with your doctor if achlorhydria (gastric) has been diagnosed.

▷ **Advisability of Use During Pregnancy**
Pregnancy Category: C. See Pregnancy Risk Categories at the back of this book.
Animal Studies: Rat studies revealed significant embryo toxicity and birth defects due to this drug.
Human Studies: Adequate studies of pregnant women are not available.
Use this drug only if clearly needed. Ask your physician for guidance.

Advisability of Use If Breast-Feeding
Presence of this drug in breast milk: Yes.
Avoid drug or refrain from nursing.

Habit-Forming Potential: None.

Effects of Overdose: Possible nausea, vomiting, diarrhea.

Possible Effects of Long-Term Use: Suppression of adrenal corticosteroid hormone production, requiring replacement therapy during periods of stress.

Suggested Periodic Examinations While Taking This Drug (at physician's discretion)
Liver function tests should be obtained BEFORE long-term therapy is started and checked monthly during treatment.
Adrenal function tests are prudent with long-term therapy.
Sperm counts.

▷ **While Taking This Drug, Observe the Following**
Foods: No restrictions.
Herbal Medicines or Minerals: Some patients use echinacea to attempt to boost their immune systems. Unfortunately, use of echinacea is not recommended in people with damaged immune systems. This herb may also actually weaken any immune system if it is used too often or for too long a time. If you are considering St. John's wort, caution is advised as it can alter the liver enzymes involved in ketoconazole removal and can also cause sun sensitivity. Herbals that can be toxic to the liver such as kava, valerian and eucalyptus should NOT be combined with ketoconazole.
Beverages: No restrictions. May be taken with milk.
▷ *Alcohol:* Avoid completely. Alcohol can cause a disulfiramlike reaction (see Glossary). In addition, alcohol may cause liver toxicity.
Tobacco Smoking: No interactions expected. I advise everyone to quit smoking.

▷ *Other Drugs*

Ketoconazole may *increase* the effects of

- almotriptan (Axert) by inhibiting liver enzyme (2D6) removal of almotriptan.
- alprazolam (Xanax) and other benzodiazepines (see Drug Classes).
- carbamazepine (Tegretol).
- cortisonelike drugs (budesonide, fluticasone, prednisone, etc.).
- cyclosporine (Sandimmune).
- delavirdine (Rescriptor).
- dihydropyridine calcium channel blockers (nifedipine, nicardipine, amlodipine, isradipine, and felodipine). Caution is advised.
- donepezil (Aricept) and galantamine (Reminyl)—careful patient follow-up is needed.
- ergot derivatives (Cafergot, others)—DO NOT COMBINE.
- fluticasone (Flonase) patients should be carefully watched for adverse effects from increased ketoconazole levels and unexpectedly great suppression of the adrenal (HPA).
- granisetron (Kytril)—careful patient follow-up is needed.
- HMG-CoA reductase inhibitors (atorvastatin, lovastatin, simvastatin, etc.; see Drug Classes), increasing risk of myopathy. Pravastatin (Pravachol) may be the safest medicine in this class to use with ketoconazole.
- imatinib (Gleevec)—careful patient follow-up is needed, perhaps coupled with decreased imatinib doses.
- irinotecan (Camptosar)—careful patient follow-up and decreased doses are needed.
- loratadine (Claritin) and fexofenadine (Allegra), which are minimally sedating antihistamines, but HAVE NOT been associated with heart rhythm problems when combined with ketoconazole. The blood level does appear to increase, and lower doses of both medicines may be prudent if these medicines are to be combined.
- oral antidiabetic drugs (see Drug Classes) and result in very low blood sugars.
- medicines removed by liver cytochrome P450 3A4 because ketoconazole inhibits this medicine-removing enzyme system. Extreme caution is advised.
- nonsedating antihistamines, such as astemizole (Hismanal) and terfenadine (Seldane) (now removed from the US market) and may cause large increases in blood levels and result in serious heart rhythm problems. DO NOT COMBINE.
- protease inhibitors (see Drug Classes).
- quetiapine (Seroquel).
- quinidine (Quinaglute) and cause toxicity; blood levels are needed.
- ritonavir (Norvir) and other liver-removed (such as amprenavir [Agenerase]) protease inhibitors.
- sibutramine (Meridia) can lead to sibutramine toxicity. Caution is advised.
- sildenafil (Viagra)—talk to your doctor BEFORE using these medicines together.
- sirolimus (Rapamune) or tacrolimus (Prograf) can lead to sirolimus or tacrolimus toxicity. More frequent blood levels and dosing adjustments are prudent.
- sucralfate (Carafate), which may decrease the blood levels of ketoconazole.
- tolterodine (Detrol) can lead to tolterodine toxicity. Caution is advised.

- tretinoin (Vesanoid), which may increase risk of tretinoin toxicity.
- trimexate (Neutrexin).
- warfarin (Coumadin) and cause bleeding; increased testing of INR (prothrombin time or protime) is needed.
- zolpidem (Ambien) can lead to zolpidem toxicity. Caution is advised.

Ketoconazole may *decrease* the effects of

- amphotericin B (Abelcet).
- didanosine (Videx).
- theophyllines (aminophylline, Theo-Dur, etc.).

The following drugs may *decrease* the effects of ketoconazole:

- antacids; if needed, take antacids 2 hours after ketoconazole.
- didanosine (Videx)—take ketoconazole dose first and separate doses by 2 hours.
- histamine (H2)-blocking drugs: cimetidine, famotidine, nizatidine, ranitidine; if needed, take 2 hours after ketoconazole.
- isoniazid (Laniazid, Nydrazid, etc.).
- lansoprazole (Prevacid).
- omeprazole (Prilosec), or other proton pump inhibitors.
- rifampin (Rifadin, Rifater, Rimactane, etc.).

Ketoconazole *taken concurrently* with

- amprenavir (Agenerase) may increase ketoconazole levels and decrease amprenavir slightly.
- cisapride (Propulsid) can lead to serious heart toxicity. DO NOT COMBINE.
- dofetilide (Tikosyn) can lead to serious heart toxicity. DO NOT COMBINE.
- miconazole (Monistat) may increase the blood levels of ketoconazole or miconazole.
- phenytoin (Dilantin) or fosphenytoin (Cerebyx) may change the levels of both drugs.

▷ *Driving, Hazardous Activities:* This drug may cause dizziness or drowsiness. Restrict activities as necessary.

Aviation Note: The use of this drug *may be a disqualification* for piloting. Consult a designated Aviation Medical Examiner.

Exposure to Sun: This drug may cause photophobia; wear sunglasses if appropriate.

Discontinuation: Take the full course prescribed. Continual treatment for several months may be needed. Ask your doctor when the drug should be stopped.

KETOPROFEN (kee toh PROH fen)

Please see the propionic acid (nonsteroidal anti-inflammatory drug) family profile.

LABETALOL (la BET a lohl)

Introduced: 1978 **Class:** Antihypertensive alpha-and-beta-adrenergic blocker **Prescription:** USA: Yes **Controlled Drug:** USA: No; Canada: No **Available as Generic:** Yes

Brand Names: Normodyne, Normozide [CD], Trandate, Trandate HCT [CD]

```
┌──────────────────────────────────────────────────────────────┐
│                    BENEFITS versus RISKS                       │
│      Possible Benefits                   Possible Risks        │
│ EFFECTIVE, WELL-TOLERATED        CONGESTIVE HEART FAILURE in    │
│   ANTIHYPERTENSIVE in mild to      advanced heart disease      │
│   moderate high blood pressure   Worsening of angina in coronary│
│ PROLONGS LIFE AFTER A HEART        heart disease (if drug is abruptly│
│   ATTACK                           withdrawn)                  │
│                                  Masking of low blood sugar    │
│                                    (hypoglycemia) in drug-treated│
│                                    diabetes                    │
│                                  Liver toxicity                │
└──────────────────────────────────────────────────────────────┘
```

▷ **Principal Uses**

As a Single Drug Product: Uses currently included in FDA-approved labeling: (1) Treats mild to moderate high blood pressure.

Other (unlabeled) generally accepted uses: (1) Combination therapy of hypertension in heart attacks (acute MI)—beta blockers have also been shown to decrease the risk of repeat heart attacks, limit the size of the original heart attack damage, and help control arrhythmias; (2) treatment of cocaine overdose; (3) therapy of phobic anxiety reactions; (4) treatment of angina; (5) therapy of pheochromocytoma, a tumor that releases compounds that increase blood pressure (controversial); (6) eases blood pressure in severely high blood pressure (hypertensive emergency).

As a Combination Drug Product [CD]: This drug has been combined with hydrochlorothiazide (a thiazide diuretic) to attack high blood pressure in 2 different ways.

How This Drug Works: By blocking part of the sympathetic nervous system, this drug:
- reduces the rate and contraction force of the heart, thus lowering the ejection pressure of blood leaving the heart.
- reduces the degree of contraction of blood vessel walls, resulting in their expansion and lowering of blood pressure.

Available Dosage Forms and Strengths

Injection — 5 mg/ml

Tablets — 100 mg, 200 mg, 300 mg

Tablets, combination — 100 mg, 200 mg, 300 mg of labetalol with 25 mg hydrochlorothiazide

▷ **Usual Adult Dosage Ranges:** *High blood pressure*: Initially 100 mg twice daily, 12 hours apart; the dose may be increased by 100 mg twice daily every 2 to 3 days as needed to reduce blood pressure. The usual ongoing dose is 200 to 400 mg twice daily. Maximum daily dose is 3,200 mg in sudden (acute) and ongoing high blood pressure. For moderate high blood pressure, 400–800 mg is the usual effective dose.

Stable angina: 100 to 400 mg by mouth 2 to 3 times daily. Low doses (100 mg) are usually used in people who have normal blood pressure to help avoid excessively low blood pressure on standing up.

Note: Actual dose and dosing schedule must be determined individually.

Conditions Requiring Dosing Adjustments

Liver Function: The dose must be decreased in liver disease. Average dose for people with long-standing liver disease is 50% of the usual dose. This drug is a rare cause of liver injury.

· *Kidney Function:* No changes presently needed (only 1% removal of the medicine).

▷ **Dosing Instructions:** Immediate release tablet may be crushed and is best taken at the same time daily, ideally following morning and evening meals. Do not stop this drug abruptly. If you forget a dose: take the missed dose as soon as you remember it, unless it's within 8 hours of the next scheduled dose—if that is the case, skip the missed dose and take the next dose right on schedule. Talk with your doctor if you find yourself missing doses.

Usual Duration of Use: Use on a regular schedule for 10 to 14 days determines peak effectiveness in lowering blood pressure. Long-term use (months to years) is determined by individual response to this drug and a program (weight reduction, salt restriction, smoking cessation, etc.).

Typical Treatment Goals and Measurements (Outcomes and Markers)

Blood Pressure: The NEW guidelines (JNC VII) define normal blood pressure (BP) as **less than** 120/80. Because blood pressures that were once considered acceptable can actually lead to blood vessel damage, the committee from the National Institutes of Health, National Heart, Lung and Blood Institute now have a new category called **Pre-hypertension**. This ranges from 120/80 to 139/89 and is intended to help your doctor encourage lifestyle changes (or in the case of people with a risk factor for high blood pressure, start treatment) much earlier—so that possible damage to blood vessels, your heart, kidneys, sexual potency, or eyes might be minimized or avoided altogether. The next 2 classes of high blood pressure are stage 1 hypertension: 140/90 to 159/99; and stage 2 hypertension equal to or greater than: 160/100 mm Hg. These guidelines also recommend that clinicians trying to control blood pressure work with their patients to agree on the goals and a plan of treatment. The first-ever guidelines for blood pressure (hypertension) in African Americans recommend that MOST black patients be started on TWO antihypertensive medicines with the goal of lowering blood pressure to 130/80 for those with high risk for heart and blood vessel disease or with diabetes. The American Diabetes Association recommends 130/80 as the target for people living with diabetes and less than 125/75 for those who spill more than one gram of protein into their urine. Most clinicians try to achieve a BP that confers the best balance of lower cardiovascular risk and avoids the problem of too low a blood pressure. Blood pressure duration is generally increased with beneficial restriction of sodium. The goals and time frame should be discussed with you when the prescription is written. If goals are not met, it is not unusual to intensify doses or add on medicines. You can find the new blood pressure guidelines at *www.nhlbi.nih.gov/guidelines/hypertension/index.htm.* For the African American guidelines see Douglas, J.G. in Sources.

Possible Advantages of This Drug

Decreases blood pressure more rapidly than other beta-blocker drugs. Can be used to treat hypertensive emergencies.

▷ **This Drug Should Not Be Taken If**

- you have had an allergic reaction to it previously.
- you have active bronchial asthma.
- you have congestive heart failure.
- you are in cardiogenic shock.
- your blood pressure is very low or you have a condition that causes severe lowering of blood pressure for a long time.

- you have an abnormally slow heart rate (bradycardia) or a serious form of heart block (second- or third-degree AV).

▷ **Inform Your Physician Before Taking This Drug If**
- you have had an adverse reaction to any beta-blocker drug (see Drug Classes).
- you have a history of serious heart disease.
- you have a history of hay fever (allergic rhinitis), asthma, chronic bronchitis, or emphysema.
- you have a history of overactive thyroid function (hyperthyroidism) or pheochromocytoma.
- you have a history of low blood sugar (hypoglycemia).
- you have sporadic cramping of the leg muscles (intermittent claudication).
- you have a history of spasms of the bronchi of the lungs.
- you have impaired liver or kidney function.
- you have diabetes or myasthenia gravis.
- you take any form of digitalis, quinidine, or reserpine or any calcium channel–blocker drug (see Drug Classes).
- you will have surgery with general anesthesia.

Possible Side Effects (natural, expected, and unavoidable drug actions)
Lethargy and fatigability—frequent.
Light-headedness in upright position (see orthostatic hypotension in Glossary).

▷ **Possible Adverse Effects** (unusual, unexpected, and infrequent reactions)
If any of the following develop, consult your physician promptly for guidance.
Mild Adverse Effects
Allergic reactions: skin rash, itching.
Headache, drowsiness, dizziness—frequent.
Scalp tingling (during early treatment)—possible.
Vivid dreams, nightmares, depression—infrequent.
Urine retention, difficulty urinating—case reports.
Indigestion, nausea, diarrhea—infrequent.
Joint and muscle discomfort, carpal tunnel syndrome, fluid retention (edema)—rare.
Serious Adverse Effects
Allergic reactions: anaphylaxis—case reports.
Chest pain, shortness of breath, precipitation of congestive heart failure—possible.
Induction of bronchial asthma (in asthmatic individuals)—possible.
Hypertensive crisis in people with pheochromocytoma—case reports.
Lichen planus—case reports.
Muscle toxicity (toxic myopathy, worsening of intermittent claudication)—possible.
Drug-induced systemic lupus erythematosus—rare.
Aggravation of myasthenia gravis—case reports.
Liver damage with jaundice—rare and often reversible (call your doctor immediately if you have dark urine, loss of appetite, unexplained tiredness, or abdominal pain, jaundice, or light-colored stools.

▷ **Possible Effects on Sexual Function:** Impotence, inhibited ejaculation, prolonged erection following orgasm (related to higher doses), Peyronie's disease (see Glossary)—rare to infrequent.

Decreased vaginal secretions (with low doses), inhibited female orgasm (higher doses)—possible.

Possible Effects on Laboratory Tests

Blood potassium or glucose: slight increase.

Liver function tests: rare increases.

CAUTION

1. ***Do not stop this drug suddenly*** without the knowledge and help of your doctor. Carry a note or wear a labetalol drug-identification bracelet.
2. Ask your physician or pharmacist before using nasal decongestants, which are usually present in over-the-counter cold preparations and nose drops. These can cause sudden increases in blood pressure if combined with labetalol.
3. Report the development of any tendency to emotional depression.
4. Sound-alike errors involving Lamictal have been reported. Lamictal is a seizure medicine. Make certain you have the correct medicine.
5. Dosing is usually started at 100 mg twice a day in order to keep blood pressure from becoming too low when you stand up (orthostatic hypotension).

Precautions for Use

By Infants and Children: Safety and effectiveness for those under 12 years of age are not established. If this drug is used, however, watch for low blood sugar (hypoglycemia) during periods of reduced food intake.

By Those Over 60 Years of Age: Proceed **cautiously** with all antihypertensive drugs. Therapy should be started with small doses, with frequent checks of blood pressure. Sudden, rapid or excessive lowering of blood pressure can increase stroke or heart attack risk. Watch for dizziness, unsteadiness, tendency to fall, confusion, hallucinations, depression, or urinary frequency.

▷ **Advisability of Use During Pregnancy**

Pregnancy Category: C. See Pregnancy Risk Categories at the back of this book.

Animal Studies: No significant increase in birth defects found in rats or rabbits; some increase in fetal deaths reported.

Human Studies: Adequate studies of pregnant women are not available.

Use this drug only if clearly needed. Ask your physician for guidance.

Advisability of Use If Breast-Feeding

Presence of this drug in breast milk: Yes, in very small, but variable amounts. Listed as safe in one source. Talk to your doctor.

Habit-Forming Potential: None. Rebound increases in blood pressure have been reported if the medicine is stopped suddenly. This is a physiologic response, not addiction.

Effects of Overdose: Weakness, slow pulse, low blood pressure, fainting, cold and sweaty skin, congestive heart failure, possible coma, and convulsions.

Possible Effects of Long-Term Use: Reduced heart reserve and eventual heart failure in susceptible individuals with advanced heart disease.

Suggested Periodic Examinations While Taking This Drug (at physician's discretion)

Measurements of blood pressure (take advantage of health fairs or your local pharmacy).

Evaluation of heart and liver function.

Antinuclear antibody (ANA) every 3 months.

May be prudent to check for hidden Peripheral Artery Disease (PAD) by checking ankle brachial index (ABI). ABI check (see Glossary) can help find PAD early, and avoid claudication that may result if this medication is taken by someone who has PAD but does not know it.

▷ **While Taking This Drug, Observe the Following**

Foods: May increase the absorption of labetalol and result in a larger-than-expected blood level. Patients taking this medicine should also avoid excessive salt intake.

Herbal Medicines or Minerals: Ginseng may increase blood pressure, blunting the benefits of this medicine. Hawthorn, saw palmetto, ma huang, guarana (caffeine), goldenseal, yohimbe, and licorice may also cause increased blood pressure. Dong quai may block the removal of this medicine from the body, leading to toxic effects with "normal" doses. St. John's wort may increase removal of this medicine from the body, leading to loss of benefits despite appropriate doses. Calcium and garlic may help lower blood pressure. Ginkgo benefits in helping peripheral artery disease are, as yet, unproven. Indian snakeroot has a German Commission E monograph indication for hypertension—talk to your doctor. Eleuthero root and ephedra (ma huang) should be avoided by people living with hypertension.

Beverages: No restrictions. May be taken with milk.

▷ *Alcohol:* Use with caution. Alcohol may exaggerate this drug's ability to lower blood pressure and may increase its mild sedative effect.

Tobacco Smoking: Nicotine may reduce this drug's effectiveness. I advise everyone to quit smoking.

▷ *Other Drugs*

Labetalol may ***increase*** the effects of

- oral antidiabetic drugs (see Drug Classes) and prolong recovery from any hypoglycemia (low blood sugar) that may occur.
- other antihypertensive drugs and cause excessive lowering of blood pressure. Dose adjustments may be necessary.

Labetalol ***taken concurrently*** with

- amiodarone (Cordarone) may result in extremely slow heart rates and cardiac arrest.
- cimetidine (Tagamet) can cause elevated labetalol levels and low blood pressure or heart rate.
- clonidine (Catapres) must be closely watched for rebound high blood pressure if clonidine is withdrawn while labetalol is still being taken.
- digoxin's (Lanoxin) atrioventricular node conduction time extension may cause heart block and digoxin toxicity.
- dihydropyridine calcium channel blockers (nifedipine, others) may lead to impaired heart performance or excessively lowered blood pressure.
- epinephrine may result in severe increases in blood pressure.
- fluoxetine (Prozac) may increase labetalol effects.
- fluvoxamine (Luvox) may result in excessive lowering of blood pressure or excessive slowing of the heart.
- imipramine and other tricyclic antidepressants may result in increases in antidepressant blood levels and toxicity.
- insulin must be watched for development of hypoglycemia (see Glossary).
- NSAIDs (see Drug Classes) may result in blunting of the therapeutic effects of labetalol.
- paroxetine (Paxil) may increase labetalol effects.
- phenothiazines (see Drug Classes) may cause additive lowering of the blood pressure.
- ritodrine (Yutopar) may blunt the beneficial effects of ritodrine.

- venlafaxine (Effexor) may increase labetalol effects.
- zileuton (Zyflo) may increase labetalol effects.

▷ *Driving, Hazardous Activities:* Use caution until the full extent of fatigue, dizziness, and blood pressure change has been determined.

Aviation Note: The use of this drug ***is a disqualification*** for piloting. Consult a designated Aviation Medical Examiner.

Exposure to Sun: No restrictions.

Exposure to Heat: Caution is advised. Hot environments can lower the blood pressure and exaggerate the effects of this drug.

Exposure to Cold: Caution is advised. Cold environments can increase blood flow problems in the extremities that may occur with beta-blocker drugs. The elderly should take precautions to prevent hypothermia (see Glossary).

Heavy Exercise or Exertion: It is prudent to avoid exertion that produces lightheadedness, excessive fatigue, or muscle cramping. Use of this drug may intensify hypertensive response to isometric exercise.

Occurrence of Unrelated Illness: Fever can lower blood pressure and require decreased doses. Nausea or vomiting may interrupt scheduled doses. Ask your doctor for help.

Discontinuation: If possible, gradual reduction of dose over a period of 2 to 3 weeks is recommended—otherwise rebound increases in blood pressure may occur. Ask your doctor for help.

LAMIVUDINE (LAM iv u deen)

Introduced: 1995   **Class:** Antiviral, antiretroviral, reverse transcriptase inhibitor, nucleoside analog   **Prescription:** USA: Yes   **Controlled Drug:** USA: No   **Available as Generic:** No

Brand Names: Combivir [CD], Epivir, Epivir HBV, Trizivir [CD]

BENEFITS versus RISKS	
Possible Benefits	*Possible Risks*
IMPRESSIVE SUPPRESSION OF VIRAL LOAD WHEN USED IN COMBINATION THERAPY TREATING HIV	DECREASED WHITE BLOOD CELL COUNTS
	Peripheral neuropathy
	Pancreatitis
DOES NOT LEAD TO SUPPRESSION OF THE BONE MARROW	Lactic acidosis
EFFECTIVE TREATMENT OF HEPATITIS B INFECTION	Because of abacavir in the Trizivir form, caution for severe rash and reporting of any rash are required

▷ **Principal Uses**

As a Single Drug Product: Uses currently included in FDA-approved labeling: (1) Used to treat HIV infection. Used in combination because of possible resistance; this medicine is now available in combination with 3 drugs used together in one pill—abacavir, lamivudine, and zidovudine (Trizivir); (2) Used with zidovudine (AZT) and other antiretrovirals to reduce the risk of disease progression and death in HIV; (3) FDA-approved (in a lower dose than that used for treating HIV) to treat hepatitis B.

Author's Note: **Combination therapy has become a standard of care. NIAID antiretroviral therapy guidelines take into account how easily HIV therapy can fit into a patient's life. The ATIS Guidelines (AIDS Treatment Information Service**—*www.hivatis.org/guidelines/adult/ May23_02/AAMay23.pdf*) **tell us that therapy should be supervised by an expert, and cover considerations of when to start therapy in both asymptomatic and established HIV infections. Adherence or taking medicines for HIV exactly on time and in the right amount is ABSOLUTELY critical to getting the best possible results or outcomes. Structured therapy interruptions (STI) or structured interruptions of therapy (SIT) are still controversial.**
Other (unlabeled) generally accepted uses: Possible combination use in post-exposure prevention (prophylaxis).
As a Combination Drug Product [CD]: Available in combination with zidovudine, a nucleoside analog. This combination along with a protease inhibitor (indinavir) was one of the first regimens to decrease HIV viral burden to undetectable levels. A newer form which is a combination of abacavir, lamivudine, and zidovudine (Trizivir) gives benefits of triple combination therapy and a protease inhibitor sparing effect.

How This Drug Works: Potent reverse transcriptase inhibitor—interferes with ability of HIV and the hepatitis B virus to create genetic material.

Available Dosage Forms and Strengths
Solution (Epivir) — 10 mg/ml
Solution (Epivir HBV) — 5 mg/ml
Tablets (Combivir) — 150 mg lamivudine and 300 mg zidovudine
Tablets (Trizivir) — 150 mg lamivudine, 300 mg zidovudine and abacavir 300 mg
Tablets (Epivir) — 150 mg
Tablets (Epivir HBV) — 100 mg

▷ **Recommended Dosage Ranges** (Actual dose and schedule must be determined for each patient individually.)
Infants and Children: 3 months to 12 years old: 4 mg per kg of body mass twice daily (300 mg maximum a day).
Combivir (for those over 12 years old): One tablet twice a day.
12 to 65 Years of Age:
    HIV: Usual dose is 150 mg twice daily. Two mg per kg of body mass twice daily for adults weighing less than 110 lb, or 50 kg.
    Combivir: One tablet twice a day.
    Trizivir: One tablet twice a day.
    Hepatitis B (Epivir HBV): 100 mg daily.
Over 65 Years of Age: If decision is made to use it in this population, blood levels may be prudent, as up to 70% is removed by the kidneys.

Conditions Requiring Dosing Adjustments
Liver Function: No changes expected.
Kidney Function: Up to 70% of a given dose is removed by the kidneys. Those with creatinine clearances (see Glossary) of 5 to 14 ml/min should take a first dose of 150 mg and then 50 mg once daily. This will limit use of fixed-dose combination forms.

▷ **Dosing Instructions:** Lamivudine tablets and solution can be taken without regard to meals. A solution is available for patients who can't swallow the tablets. Make certain you use a measuring spoon or calibrated dosing cup for the solution. If you forget a dose: take the missed dose as soon as you remember it, unless it's nearly time for your next dose—if that is the case, skip the missed dose and take the next dose right on schedule. Talk with your doctor if you find yourself missing doses.

> **Author's Note: Adherence to taking medicines for HIV exactly on time and in the right amount is ABSOLUTELY critical to getting the best possible results or outcomes. The new antiretroviral therapy guidelines from NIAID take into account how easily the medicine treating HIV can fit into a patient's life. Structured therapy interruptions (also known as structured interruptions in therapy) are controversial.**

Usual Duration of Use: *HIV*: Measurement of viral load (burden) and/or CD4 counts are used to decide the effectiveness of treatment and help in the decision to continue or change medications.

Hepatitis B: Clinical studies saw use of lamivudine for 1 year. The optimal duration of use is yet decided. The question of combination treatment (such as with interferon) of hepatitis B also has yet to be decided.

Typical Treatment Goals and Measurements (Outcomes and Markers)

HIV: Goals for HIV treatment presently are maximum suppression of viral replication, maximum lowering of the amount of virus in your body (viral load or burden), and maximum patient survival. Markers of successful therapy include durable undetectable viral load, increased CD4 cells, absence of indicator or opportunistic infections (OIs) and in the case of the HIV-positive patient, failure of the infection to progress to AIDS.

Hepatitis B: Hepatitis B antigen, hepatitis B antibodies and liver function tests such as serum alanine aminotransferase (ALT) are used to show that liver damage is resolving and the body is responding to the beneficial effects of the medicine.

Possible Advantages of This Drug

Offers reasonably durable HIV suppression in retroviral naive patients. May work where other combinations have failed (salvage therapy). Trizivir form can reserve protease inhibitor–containing regimens and avoid their metabolic complications.

Possible Side Effects (natural, expected, and unavoidable drug actions)

Paresthesias and/or peripheral neuropathy (12% in a study in children taking lamivudine monotherapy). Trizivir form has the drug abacavir in the pill. Discuss rash issues with your doctor and what to do if a rash or signs and symptoms of allergy happen if you are taking the Trizivir form.

▷ **Possible Adverse Effects** (unusual, unexpected, and infrequent reactions)

If any of the following develop, consult your physician promptly for guidance.

Mild Adverse Effects

Skin rash—infrequent.

Headache—frequent.

Dizziness—infrequent.

Sleep disorders—infrequent to frequent.

Nausea, vomiting or diarrhea—infrequent to frequent.

Cough—frequent.

Muscle aches—infrequent.

Serious Adverse Effects

Severe and dangerous skin rashes—possible due to the abacavir present in the Trizivir form.

Lowered white blood cell counts—infrequent in adults, frequent in pediatrics.

Lowered red blood cell counts (pure red cell aplasia)—case reports.

Lactic acid buildup (Lactic acidosis)—possible.

Pancreatitis (more common in children receiving lamivudine monotherapy)—rare to infrequent.

Fat redistribution—possible and associated with this and other antiretroviral treatment.

Liver toxicity—infrequent but may be severe (risk factors appear to involve prolonged nucleoside therapy and obesity). The majority of cases have happened in women.

Seizures—case reports.

▷ **Possible Effects on Sexual Function:** None reported.

Possible Delayed Adverse Effects: Anemia or lowering of white blood cell counts. Pancreatitis. Peripheral neuropathy.

▷ **Adverse Effects That May Mimic Natural Diseases or Disorders**: Seizures may suggest the possibility of epilepsy.

Possible Effects on Laboratory Tests
Complete blood cell counts: decreased red cells.
Increased amylase and lipase (if pancreatitis occurs).
Lactic acidosis—possible.

CAUTION
1. This drug is not a cure for HIV or AIDS; nor does it protect completely against other infections or complications. Follow your doctor's instructions. Take exactly as prescribed.
2. HIV can still be spread through sexual contact or blood. Use of an effective condom is mandatory. Don't share needles.

Precautions for Use
By Infants and Children: Patients from 3 months to 12 years old are dosed on a mg-per-kg-of-body-mass basis.
By Those Over 60 Years of Age: Probable age-related decline in kidney function requires blood levels to check need for dose reduction.

▷ **Advisability of Use During Pregnancy**
Pregnancy Category: C. See Pregnancy Risk Categories at the back of this book.
Animal Studies: Rat and rabbit studies reveal no birth defects.
Human Studies: Adequate studies of pregnant women are not available.
Your physician should call 1-800-722-9292, ext. 38465, if the decision is made to use this medicine while you are pregnant.

Advisability of Use If Breast-Feeding
Presence of this drug in breast milk: Mean concentration varied from less than 5 mcg/ml to 6.06 mcg/ml.
Refrain from nursing (HIV may be transferred via breast milk).

Habit-Forming Potential: None.

Effects of Overdose: Nausea, vomiting, diarrhea, bone marrow depression.

Possible Effects of Long-Term Use: Anemia and loss of white blood cells.
Pancreatitis or peripheral neuropathy.

Suggested Periodic Examinations While Taking This Drug (at physician's discretion)
Complete blood counts.

Periodic CD4 counts or viral load tests are needed. Increasing viral load or decreasing CD4 are indicators that therapy is failing and you should demand change of antiretroviral therapy.

Amylase and lipase. Check for peripheral neuropathy.

Tests for lactic acidosis. Liver function tests.

Liver biopsy may need to be taken periodically to assess the success of this medicine in treating hepatitis. Slightly more than half of patients responded in clinical trials.

▷ **While Taking This Drug, Observe the Following**

Foods: No restrictions.

Herbal Medicines or Minerals: Milk thistle has some data to support its role as an antioxidant and may help promote liver cell regeneration. Talk to your doctor if lamivudine is being used to treat the infection of hepatitis B and you are considering milk thistle. Echinacea: Some patients use echinacea to attempt to boost their immune systems. Unfortunately, use of echinacea is not recommended in people with damaged immune systems. This herb may also actually weaken any immune system if it is used too often or for too long a time.

Beverages: No restrictions. May be taken with milk.

▷ *Alcohol:* No interactions expected with lamivudine. The abacavir combination form will find abacavir remaining in the system longer than expected. Careful patient follow-up is needed.

Tobacco Smoking: No interactions expected. I advise everyone to quit smoking.

▷ *Other Drugs*

Lamivudine *taken concurrently* with

• cotrimoxazole (Septra, Bactrim) may increase lamivudine blood levels.

• indinavir (Crixivan) and zidovudine (AZT) resulted in undetectable HIV levels in some HIV-positive patients (beneficial effect of combination treatment).

• nelfinavir (Viracept) may increase lamivudine levels.

• other medicines capable of causing pancreatitis may result in increased pancreatitis risk.

• other medicines capable of lowering white or red cell counts may cause additive risks.

• ribavirin (Rebetron) may lead to lactic acidosis. A careful and cautious analysis of the benefit-to-risk aspects of this combination should be considered. Careful patient monitoring is prudent if this combination must be used.

• sulfamethoxazole (various) may increase lamivudine levels.

• trimethoprim (various) may increase lamivudine levels.

• trimexate (Mexate) may cause additive blood (hematological) toxicity.

▷ *Driving, Hazardous Activities:* This drug may cause dizziness or fainting. Restrict activities as necessary.

Aviation Note: The use of this drug *is a disqualification* for piloting. Consult a designated Aviation Medical Examiner.

Exposure to Sun: No restrictions.

Discontinuation: Do not stop this drug without your physician's knowledge and guidance.

LAMOTRIGINE (la MOH tri jean)

Introduced: 1995 **Class:** Anticonvulsant, phenyltriazine, mood stabilizer **Prescription:** USA: Yes **Controlled Drug:** USA: No; Canada: No **Available as Generic:** USA: No

Brand Names: ❦Alti-Lamotrigine, ❦Apo-Lamotrigine, Lamictal, ❦PMS-Lamotrigine, ❦Ratio-Lamotrigine

BENEFITS versus RISKS	
Possible Benefits	*Possible Risks*
EFFECTIVE MANAGEMENT OF SEIZURES THAT RESIST THERAPY	RASHES THAT CAN BE LIFE-THREATENING
	Changes in vision
INCREASE IN SEIZURE-FREE DAYS	Dizziness
MANAGEMENT OF PARTIAL SEIZURES	
MANAGEMENT OF SEIZURES ASSOCIATED WITH LENNOX-GASTAUT SYNDROME	

▷ **Principal Uses**

As a Single Drug Product: Uses currently included in FDA-approved labeling: (1) Adjunctive combination therapy of partial seizures in adults who have not responded to treatment with other medicines; (2) used to treat Lennox-Gastaut syndrome as add-on therapy.

Other (unlabeled) generally accepted uses: (1) May have a role in treating epilepsy in children who have not responded to more established treatment; (2) could have a role in treating status epilepticus; (3) could have a role in some pain syndromes (trigeminal neuralgia); (4) used in rapid cycling bipolar disorder as a mood stabilizer; (5) case reports of resolving of impotence in epileptic men who took this medicine.

How This Drug Works: The exact mechanism of action is not known, but animal models appear to show that this medicine blocks voltage-dependent sodium channels. This causes a decreased amount of glutamate and aspartate transmitters and a decreased likelihood of seizures.

Available Dosage Forms and Strengths

Chewable tablets — 2 mg, 5 mg, 25 mg
Tablets — 25 mg, 100 mg, 150 mg, 200 mg

▷ **Recommended Dosage Ranges** (Actual dose and schedule must be determined for each patient individually.)

Infants and Children: Safety and efficacy in those under 16 years old have not been established except for Lennox-Gastaut syndrome patients. Dosing is based on weight and whole tablets (chewable) should be used. Dosing should be rounded DOWN to the nearest whole tablet dose. As in adults, dosing is adjusted if medicines known to interact with lamotrigine are also being taken.

16 to 65 Years of Age: In patients receiving medicines known to interact (phenytoin, primidone, carbamazepine or phenobarbital, but not valproic acid), starting dose is 50 mg a day for 2 weeks and then 50 mg twice a day as needed or tolerated (increases made at 100 mg a day each week). Most patients end up taking 300–500 mg a day in 2 equal doses. Some centers have used doses as high as 700 mg a day.

Patients only taking valproic acid and/or the above drugs: 25 mg every other day for 2 weeks and then 25 mg once daily for 2 weeks, with increases of 25 to 50 mg per day at 1- to 2-week intervals to a maximum of 150 mg daily as needed and tolerated. Usual ongoing dose is 100–400 mg daily. If taking valproic acid alone, dose is usually 100–200 mg a day.

Over 65 Years of Age: Same dosing as 16 to 65 (single-dose pharmacokinetics were similar to younger adults). Few patients over 65 were included during premarketing studies.

Conditions Requiring Dosing Adjustments

Liver Function: This drug is mostly changed in the liver. In people with moderate liver (hepatic dysfunction) compromise (Child-Pugh Grade B), the starting dose, dose increases and ongoing doses should be 50% lower than in people with normal liver function. Caution and clinical response as well as drug levels (even though levels are still not well established) should be used to guide the need for any increases. In severe liver compromise (Child-Pugh C), the beginning dose, step increases and ongoing (maintenance) doses should be lowered by 75%.

Kidney Function: Most of this medicine (once changed or glucuronidated) is removed by the kidneys. Used with caution and with more frequent blood levels (in severe kidney failure).

▷ **Dosing Instructions:** Take this medicine exactly as prescribed. Food does not affect how much medicine gets into your body. Swallow the tablet form whole. In pediatrics, dosing is ROUNDED DOWN to the nearest whole chewable tablet. The chewable form can be swallowed whole or can even be dissolved in a teaspoon of water and swallowed after it is given a minute to dissolve. Talk with your doctor IMMEDIATELY if you get a rash, swollen lymph glands and fever. If you forget a dose: take the missed dose as soon as you remember it, unless it's nearly time for your next dose—if that is the case, skip the missed dose and take the next dose right on schedule. Talk with your doctor if you find yourself missing doses.

Usual Duration of Use: Regular use for 3 months in children with resistant seizures may be needed to see peak benefits. Long-term use (months to years) will be determined by individual response.

Typical Treatment Goals and Measurements (Outcomes and Markers)

Seizures: The general goal for this medicine is effective seizure control. Neurologists tend to define effective results on a case-by-case basis depending on the seizure type and patient factors.

Possible Advantages of This Drug

May work where single medicines have failed.

▷ **This Drug Should Not Be Taken If**
- you have developed a rash with swollen lymph glands while taking this medicine.
- you are allergic to this medicine or ones similar to it.

▷ **Inform Your Physician Before Taking This Drug If**
- you develop a rash. If this happens, stop the medicine and call your doctor immediately as the rash needs to be evaluated and a different seizure medicine needs to be started right away.
- your heart function is compromised.
- you do not understand how much or how often to take it.
- you have liver or kidney damage.

Possible Side Effects (natural, expected, and unavoidable drug actions)
Somnolence.
Weight gain, blurred vision (may be frequent).

▷ **Possible Adverse Effects** (unusual, unexpected, and infrequent reactions)
If any of the following develop, consult your physician promptly for guidance.

Mild Adverse Effects
Allergic reactions: skin rash (should be reported to your doctor), itching—infrequent.
Dizziness and headache—most common adverse effects.
Problems coordinating movements (ataxia)—infrequent.
Muscle tremor, chills, or nerve tingling (peripheral neuropathy)—infrequent.
Nausea and vomiting—dose-related and may be frequent.
Blurred vision—dose-related
Double vision—frequent.
Increased liver enzymes—case reports.

Serious Adverse Effects
Allergic reactions: anaphylaxis, increased liver enzymes—case reports.
Serious rashes (Stevens-Johnson Syndrome, toxic epidermal necrolysis)—case reports.
Hostility—rare.
Lowered blood platelets (thrombocytopenia) or increased platelets (thrombocytosis), low white blood cells (leukopenia) or sudden (acute) disseminated intravascular coagulation—case reports.
Anemia (aplastic and hemolytic)—case reports and questioned cause.
Pure red cell aplasia (PRCA)—case report.
Blood in the urine—infrequent.
Movement problems (ataxia)—infrequent.
Myopathy or rhabdomyolysis—case reports.
Tourette's syndrome—case reports and dose related.
Peripheral neuropathy—rare and of questionable cause.
Sudden unexplained death (SUDEP). The rate of SUDEP was similar to that of another agent also tested and appears to be a population effect—case reports.

▷ **Possible Effects on Sexual Function:** Case reports of lamotrigine controlling seizures and easing impotence in some epileptic men.

Possible Effects on Laboratory Tests: Blood levels of interacting medicines may be changed, sodium may be lowered.

CAUTION
1. **DO NOT** stop this medicine suddenly, as seizures may occur. If it must be stopped because of a rash, your doctor must be called and another medicine started.
2. Sound-alike errors involving labetalol have been reported. Labetalol is a high blood pressure medicine. Make certain you have the correct medicine.
3. Dosing in children is ROUNDED DOWN to the nearest whole chewable tablet.

Precautions for Use
By Infants and Children: This medicine is approved for add-on therapy in children over 16 years of age.
By Those Over 60 Years of Age: No specific changes.

▷ **Advisability of Use During Pregnancy**

Pregnancy Category: C. See Pregnancy Risk Categories at the back of this book.

Animal Studies: No evidence of drug-related changes were found in mice or rabbits that were given up to 1.2 times the human dose.

Human Studies: This medicine has been shown to cause toxicity to the mother and, because of this, toxicity to the fetus. Adequate studies of pregnant women are not available.

Discuss benefits and risks with your doctor.

Advisability of Use If Breast-Feeding

Presence of this drug in breast milk: Yes.

Avoid drug or refrain from nursing.

Habit-Forming Potential: None.

Effects of Overdose: Sleepiness, changes in muscular reflexes, coma. Keep a seizure diary to check for decrease in seizure frequency.

Possible Effects of Long-Term Use: Weight gain.

Suggested Periodic Examinations While Taking This Drug (at physician's discretion)

Examinations for nystagmus, muscular coordination.

Blood counts.

Check for rash.

Sodium.

▷ **While Taking This Drug, Observe the Following**

Foods: No restrictions. Can be taken with or without food.

Herbal Medicines or Minerals: Using St. John's wort, ma huang, guarana, or kola may result in unacceptable central nervous system stimulation and worsen possible nervousness as a side effect of lamotrigine. Since part of the way that ginseng may work is as an MAO inhibitor, and because some gingko products have been found to be contaminated with 4'-O-methylpyridoxine, which can increase seizures, combination with this medicine is not recommended. Valerian and kava kava (not recommended in Canada) may interact to increase drowsiness. Evening primrose oil increased seizure risk and is not recommended.

Beverages: No restrictions. May be taken with milk.

▷ *Alcohol:* Avoid alcohol use, unless you discuss this with your doctor.

Tobacco Smoking: No interactions expected. I advise everyone to quit smoking.

▷ *Other Drugs*

Lamotrigine *taken concurrently* with

- long-standing use of acetaminophen (Tylenol, others) may result in decreases in blood levels caused by this medicine and a potential decrease in seizure control. Periodic use should not cause problems.
- birth control pills (combination forms of oral contraceptives—various) may increase the removal of lamotrigine from the body and require dosing changes in lamotrigine.
- carbamazepine (Tegretol) may increase the removal of lamotrigine from the body and require dosing adjustments.
- phenobarbital may result in faster removal of lamotrigine from the body and require dosing changes.
- phenytoin (Dilantin) and fosphenytoin (Cerebyx) may result in faster removal of lamotrigine from the body and require dosing changes.
- primidone (Mysoline) may result in faster removal of lamotrigine from the body and require dosing changes.

- rifampin (Rifater, others) and ritonavir (Norvir) may lead to decreased lamotrigine levels and increased risk of seizure.
- sertraline (Zoloft) may lead to lamotrigine toxicity.
- tramadol (Ultram) may increase seizure risk and is not recommended.
- valproic acid (Depakene) may slow removal of lamotrigine from the body, requiring lamotrigine dose decreases to avoid toxicity.

▷ *Driving, Hazardous Activities:* Use caution until the full extent of fatigue, dizziness, or coordination or vision changes have been determined.

Aviation Note: The use of this drug *is a disqualification* for piloting. Consult a designated Aviation Medical Examiner.

Exposure to Sun: No restrictions.

Exposure to Heat: Use caution. Muscular coordination problems may be worsened by excessive heat.

Discontinuation: DO NOT stop this medicine abruptly without talking with your doctor first. Abrupt discontinuation without first starting another antiseizure medicine may result in seizures. The dose is usually decreased by half (50%) a week over at least 2 weeks. If there are patient safety concerns, clinicians have withdrawn this medicine more rapidly.

LANSOPRAZOLE (lan SO pra sole)

Introduced: 1995   **Class:**   Anti-ulcer, proton pump inhibitor   **Prescription:**   USA: Yes   **Controlled Drug:**   USA: No; Canada: No   **Available as Generic:**   USA: No; Canada: No

Brand Names: Prevacid, Prevacid delayed release oral suspension, Prevpac [CD]

BENEFITS versus RISKS

Possible Benefits	*Possible Risks*
VERY EFFECTIVE TREATMENT OF CONDITIONS ASSOCIATED WITH EXCESSIVE PRODUCTION OF STOMACH (GASTRIC) ACID: ZOLLINGER-ELLISON SYNDROME, MASTOCYTOSIS, ENDOCRINE ADENOMA	Liver enzyme increases protein in the urine
VERY EFFECTIVE TREATMENT OF REFLUX ESOPHAGITIS	
VERY EFFECTIVE TREATMENT OF DUODENAL ULCER	
DELAYED RELEASE SUSPENSION FORM OFFERS EASIER-TO-SWALLOW MEDICINE	
EFFECTIVE MAINTENANCE THERAPY OF HEALED DUODENAL ULCERS	
COMBINATION PRODUCT (PREVPAC) ENCOURAGES ADHERENCE	

▷ **Principal Uses**

As a Single Drug Product: Uses currently included in FDA-approved labeling: (1) Used to treat duodenal and stomach (gastric) ulcers; (2) treats erosive esophagitis; (3) used in syndromes (such as Zollinger-Ellison) where excessive amounts of stomach acid are produced; (4) maintains healed duodenal ulcers; (5) treats heartburn (gastroesophageal reflux disease, or GERD); (6) part of dual (with amoxicillin) or triple (with amoxicillin and clarithromycin) treatment of *Helicobacter pylori*.

Other (unlabeled) generally accepted uses: (1) may increase fat absorption in cystic fibrosis.

As a Combination Drug Product [CD]: This drug is available in combination with two antibiotics—clarithromycin and amoxicillin (Prevpac). Since refractory ulcers are often actually *Helicobacter pylori* infections, the combination works to kill the bacteria and lower acid production.

How This Drug Works: Inhibits an enzyme system (H/K adenosine triphosphate) in the stomach (parietal cells) lining and stops production of stomach acid. By doing this, it eliminates the principal cause of ulcers or esophagitis and creates an environment conducive to healing. Taking this medicine 15–30 minutes before the morning meal makes best use of the fact that this will allow the medicine to be at its peak just when the largest number of proton pumps are working. Use of this drug with 1 or 2 antibiotics attacks *Helicobacter pylori* and also decreases acid. The delayed release oral suspension offers a more convenient dosing form and beneficial release characteristics (kinetics).

Available Dosage Forms and Strengths

Capsules — 15 mg, 30 mg

Capsules (Prevpac) — 30 mg lansoprazole, 500 mg amoxicillin and clarithromycin

Suspension (Prevacid Delayed — 15 or 30 mg packets Release Oral Suspension)

▷ **Recommended Dosage Ranges** (Actual dose and schedule must be determined for each patient individually.)

Infants and Children: Not studied in this age group.

18 to 60 Years of Age: For duodenal ulcer: 15 mg daily, taken before a meal. Some patients require 30 mg daily. Four weeks of therapy are needed, and treatment has been used for 8 weeks in some patients.

For ongoing therapy of healed duodenal ulcers: 15 mg daily.

For erosive esophagitis: 30 mg daily, taken before a meal. Up to 8 weeks of treatment can be given. If healing does not occur, an additional 8 weeks may be considered.

For excessive acid production syndromes: Dosing is started at 60 mg daily. The dose is increased as needed and tolerated. Doses up to 90 mg twice daily have been used. Once the condition is under control, dose is usually slowly reduced to 30 mg a day.

For *Helicobacter pylori*: Seven-day regimen for duodenal ulcers and *H. pylori* of lansoprazole 30 mg twice daily, plus amoxicillin 1,000 mg twice daily, plus clarithromycin 500 mg twice daily. Three-day quadruple treatment: bismuth subcitrate, 240 mg; clarithromycin, 500 mg; lansoprazole, 30 mg; and metronidazole, 400 mg twice a day.

Eradication: The above regimen is used for 14 days.

Over 60 Years of Age: Same as 18 to 60 years of age.

Conditions Requiring Dosing Adjustments

Liver Function: The manufacturer strongly suggests a dose of 15 mg daily for people with significant liver problems.

Kidney Function: No dosing changes are needed.

▷ **Dosing Instructions:** The capsules contain enteric-coated granules that protect the medicine in the stomach's acid. Take the capsules whole if possible. Some studies have found that lansoprazole **taken in the morning** works best in controlling stomach acid. It should be taken 15–30 minutes before the morning meal so that the peak level of lansoprazole happens just when the largest number of proton pumps are working. If swallowing is a problem, the capsule may be opened and the intact granules sprinkled into applesauce, yogurt, strained pears, and even ENSURE pudding. Once opened, it should be taken right away. The oral suspension form comes as 15 or 30 mg. The contents of the packet should be emptied into a container holding 2 tablespoons of water, then stirred well and drunk immediately. If you forget a dose: take the missed dose as soon as you remember it, unless it's nearly time for your next dose—if that is the case, skip the missed dose and take the next dose right on schedule. Talk with your doctor if you find yourself missing doses.

Usual Duration of Use: Use on a regular schedule for 7 days resulted in a 90–94% decrease in acid release. Patients with stomach (gastric) or duodenal ulcers had a decrease in symptoms in about 1 week—this DOES NOT mean that the ulcer is gone. Especially with maintenance of healing of duodenal ulcers, therapy may be ongoing. Eradication regimen with 3 drugs (see previous page) took 14 days. People with reflux esophagitis had decreases in heartburn after 7 to 28 days. Some esophagitis patients needed a second 8-week course to bring symptoms under control. Long-term use requires periodic physician follow-up.

Typical Treatment Goals and Measurements (Outcomes and Markers)

Ulcers: The role of *Helicobacter pylori* in ulcers is no longer questioned and a proton pump inhibitor is widely recognized as the standard for short-term treatment of stomach ulcers. When *H. pylori* is present, single-medicine therapy is not recommended (an antibiotic is often used with other agents). The goal is to heal the ulcer area and prevent re-occurrence of the ulceration. Sign and symptom relief (stomach pain, etc.) as well as endoscopic examination help define success of treatment.

▷ **This Drug Should Not Be Taken If**
- you are allergic to the medicine or any of its components.

▷ **Inform Your Physician Before Taking This Drug If**
- you have a history of liver disease (or kidney compromise if taking the combination product).
- you smoke and expect to continue smoking (worsens acid secretion).

Possible Side Effects (natural, expected, and unavoidable drug actions)

Increased serum gastrin levels (clinical significance is unknown). There have been 6 cases of black tongue and mouth inflammation reported in people who took antibiotics and lansoprazole to treat *Helicobacter pylori*.

▷ **Possible Adverse Effects** (unusual, unexpected, and infrequent reactions)

If any of the following develop, consult your physician promptly for guidance.

Mild Adverse Effects

Allergic reaction: skin rash.

Headache (may be common), dizziness, or tiredness—infrequent.

Diarrhea or nausea—infrequent.

Ringing in the ears—rare.

Serious Adverse Effects

Allergic reaction: not defined.

Protein in the urine—rare.

Liver toxicity or low blood platelets—rare and of questionable cause.

▷ **Possible Effects on Sexual Function:** None reported.

▷ **Adverse Effects That May Mimic Natural Diseases or Disorders**

Drug-induced liver reaction may suggest viral hepatitis.

Possible Effects on Laboratory Tests

Liver function tests: increased.

CAUTION

1. Follow your doctor's advice on how long to take this drug.
2. This drug effectively treats ulcers but does not preclude the chance of cancer of the stomach.

Precautions for Use

By Infants and Children: Not indicated in this age group.

By Those Over 60 Years of Age: This medicine may cause dizziness. Use caution until you've seen the effects it has on you.

▷ **Advisability of Use During Pregnancy**

Pregnancy Category: B. See Pregnancy Risk Categories at the back of this book.

Advisability of Use If Breast-Feeding

Presence of this drug in breast milk: Unknown.

Avoid drug or refrain from nursing.

Habit-Forming Potential: None.

Effects of Overdose: Possible nausea, vomiting, dizziness, lethargy and abdominal pain.

Possible Effects of Long-Term Use: Serum gastrin levels are increased by this medicine, but the clinical significance is not known. Presently it is indicated for a maximum of 2 8-week courses in erosive esophagitis. Maintenance of healed ulcers will further define effects of longer-term treatment.

Suggested Periodic Examinations While Taking This Drug (at physician's discretion)

Complete blood counts.

Liver function tests.

▷ **While Taking This Drug, Observe the Following**

Foods: Lansoprazole is best taken on an empty stomach. Follow your doctor's instructions regarding the types of foods you eat.

Herbal Medicines or Minerals: Kola, guarana, and ma huang may increase stomach acid, blunting the benefits of this medicine. Black cohosh root, ginkgo, and squill are contraindicated in gastrointestinal disturbances. Licorice root has a German Commission E monograph indication for gastrointestinal ulcers, but use with proton pump inhibitors has not been studied. Talk to your doctor BEFORE adding any herbals to a proton pump inhibitor.

Beverages: No restrictions.

▷ *Alcohol:* No specific interactions, but alcohol stimulates the secretion of stomach acid and may lessen the therapeutic benefits of this medicine.

Tobacco Smoking: Smoking can stimulate stomach acid and lessen benefits of this drug. I advise everyone to quit smoking.

▷ *Other Drugs*

Lansoprazole **taken concurrently** with

* antacids may blunt how much lansoprazole gets into your body, blunting lansoprazole benefits.
* clarithromycin (Biaxin) may lead to a blackening of the tongue or stomatitis. Lower lansoprazole doses and stopping the clarithromycin may be required.
* corticosteroids may irritate the stomach and blunt the benefits of lansoprazole.
* itraconazole (Sporonox), ketoconazole (Nizoral) absorption and blood levels may be changed and benefit of antifungal lost. Careful check of treatment progress is needed.
* ritonavir (Norvir) may change lansoprazole blood levels.
* sucralfate (Carafate) may decrease lansoprazole absorption; separate doses by 2 hours.
* theophylline (Theo-Dur, others) may decrease blood theophylline level, requiring dosing adjustments.

▷ *Driving, Hazardous Activities:* Caution—this medicine may cause drowsiness. Limit activities as necessary.

Aviation Note: The use of this drug **may be a disqualification** for piloting. Consult a designated Aviation Medical Examiner.

Exposure to Sun: No restrictions.

Discontinuation: Talk with your doctor before stopping this medicine for any reason. Taking the medicine for a shorter time than needed may result in incomplete ulcer healing and continuation of the original problem.

LATANOPROST (la TAN oh prost)

Introduced: 1996   **Class:**   Prostaglandin F2-alpha analogue, antiglaucoma agent   **Prescription:**   USA: Yes   **Controlled Drug:**   USA: No; Canada: No   **Available as Generic:**   No

Brand Names: ✤Xalacom [CD], Xalatan

BENEFITS versus RISKS	
Possible Benefits	*Possible Risks*
EFFECTIVE REDUCTION OF INTERNAL EYE PRESSURE FOR CONTROL OF ACUTE AND CHRONIC GLAUCOMA	Mild side effects with systemic absorption
	Joint or back pain
	Minor eye discomfort
CONTROL OF OCULAR HYPERTENSION	Altered vision
	Iris pigmentation
Formation of eyelashes	

▷ **Principal Uses**

As a Single Drug Product: Uses currently included in FDA-approved labeling: (1) Used to manage glaucoma; (2) lowers increased pressure in the eye (intraocular pressure).

Other (unlabeled) generally accepted uses: (1) Used to attempt to encourage eyelash formation in patients who previously did not have any.

As a Combination Drug Product [CD]: This drug is available in combination with a beta blocker called timilol. The combination offers 2 different mechanisms of action to help lower pressure (intraocular pressure) in the eye.

How This Drug Works: This medicine lowers pressure in the eye by increasing outflow from the uveoscleral area without changing aqueous flow.

Available Dosage Forms and Strengths

Combination Eyedrop solutions — 50 mcg per ml of latanoprost and 5 mg/ml of timolol

Eyedrop solutions — 0.005% or 50 mcg per ml

▷ **Usual Adult Dosage Ranges:** For open-angle glaucoma or ocular hypertension: One drop (0.005%) in the eye each evening.

Note: Actual dose and dosing schedule must be determined for each patient individually.

Conditions Requiring Dosing Adjustments

Liver Function: The drug is changed in the liver and removed by the kidneys. Dose changes in liver disease are not defined.

Kidney Function: Changed drug (metabolites) removed by the kidney, but dosing changes in kidney failure are not defined.

▷ **Dosing Instructions:** Remove contact lenses and do not replace them for at least 15 minutes after putting this medicine into your eye. To avoid excessive absorption into the body, press finger against inner corner of the eye (to close off the tear duct) during and for 1 minute after dropping the medicine in. Be careful not to touch the dropper to the eye. If you forget a dose: Take the missed dose as soon as you remember it, unless it's nearly time for your next dose—if that is the case, skip the missed dose and take the next dose right on schedule. DO NOT double doses. Talk with your doctor if you find yourself missing doses.

Usual Duration of Use: Use on a regular schedule for a day usually sees an effect in lowering the pressure in the eye. A week may be required for the full benefits of the medicine to be realized. Long-term use (months to years) requires physician supervision and may require combination therapy if pressure rises again.

Typical Treatment Goals and Measurements (Outcomes and Markers)

Glaucoma: Ophthalmologists measure intraocular pressure (IOP), and then check IOP-lowering once this medicine is started. The chamber angle can be checked prior to treatment. A 6–8 mm of HG drop in intraocular pressure is common during ongoing use.

▷ **This Drug Should Not Be Taken If**
- you have had an eye infection with herpes simplex (case report authors suggest avoiding latanoprost).
- you have had an allergic reaction to it previously or to the benzalkonium chloride that is in it.

▷ **Inform Your Physician Before Taking This Drug If**
- you wear contact lenses.
- you have had an eye infection in the last 3 months.
- you have some of the risk factors for fluid accumulation in the macula (macular edema). Talk to your doctor about this.
- you have sudden (acute) angle closure of the eye.

Possible Side Effects (natural, expected, and unavoidable drug actions)
> Burning of the eyes or irritation—frequent (usually mild).
> Pigmentation of the eye (iridial) has been reported.
> Growth of eyelashes in patients who previously did not have any has been reported.

▷ **Possible Adverse Effects** (unusual, unexpected, and infrequent reactions)
> **If any of the following develop, consult your physician promptly for guidance.**
> *Mild Adverse Effects*
> Allergic reactions: itching of the eyes, eyelid itching and/or swelling, or rash.
> Headache—infrequent.
> Nausea—case reports.
> Muscle or back pain—rare to infrequent.
> *Serious Adverse Effects*
> Pigmentation of the iris—infrequent, though may be frequent (up to 16%) with therapy ongoing for more than a year.
> Hypertension—2 case reports.
> Choroidal detachment of effusion—case reports.
> Angina pectorus and/or chest pain—rare.

▷ **Possible Effects on Sexual Function:** None reported.

Natural Diseases or Disorders That May Be Activated by This Drug
> Herpes infection in the skin around the eye may be reactivated in patients who have already had this problem.

Possible Effects on Laboratory Tests
> None reported.

Precautions for Use
> *By Those Over 60 Years of Age:* No age-specific changes presently needed.

▷ **Advisability of Use During Pregnancy**
> *Pregnancy Category:* C. See Pregnancy Risk Categories at the end of book.
> *Human Studies:* Adequate studies of pregnant women are not available.
> Discuss use with your doctor BEFORE using this drug.

Advisability of Use If Breast-Feeding
> Presence of this drug in breast milk: Unknown.
> Watch infant closely and stop drug or nursing if adverse effects develop.

Habit-Forming Potential: None.

Effects of Overdose: Not defined.

Possible Effects of Long-Term Use: Pigmentation of the iris.

Suggested Periodic Examinations While Taking This Drug (at physician's discretion)
> Measurement of internal eye pressure on a regular basis.
> Check for early signs of pigmentation.

▷ **While Taking This Drug, Observe the Following**
> *Foods:* No restrictions.
> *Herbal Medicines or Minerals:* Scopolia root has glaucoma as a possible side effect. DO NOT COMBINE. Henbane, ephedra, and belladonna should also be avoided.
> *Beverages:* No restrictions.
▷ *Alcohol:* No restrictions except prudence in alcohol use.
> *Tobacco Smoking:* No interactions expected. I advise everyone to quit smoking.

Marijuana Smoking: Sustained additional decrease in internal eye pressure.
▷ *Other Drugs*
   Latanoprost **taken concurrently** with
   • pilocarpine (various) may blunt latanoprost benefits. Dose pilocarpine 1 hour after latanoprost.
   • thimerosal (various) can cause a precipitation. DO NOT combine eyedrops containing thimerosal with latanoprost. Separate doses by 5 minutes or more.
▷ *Driving, Hazardous Activities:* This drug may cause blurry vision for a time. Restrict activities as necessary.
   Aviation Note: The use of this drug **may be a disqualification** for piloting. Consult a designated Aviation Medical Examiner.
   Exposure to Sun: This medicine may make your eyes sensitive to the sun. Wear sunglasses. See the table in the back of this book about other medicines that may cause such sensitivity—effects may be additive if these medicines are combined.
   Discontinuation: Do not stop regular use of this drug without consulting your physician.

LEFLUNOMIDE (LEH flew no myde)

Introduced: 1998   **Class:** Disease-modifying antirheumatic drug (DMARD), pyrimidine synthesis inhibitor, immunosuppressant (Tcell)   **Prescription:**   USA: Yes   **Controlled Drug:**   USA: No; Canada: No   **Available as Generic:**   No

Brand Name: Arava

Author's Note: Considerable controversy has erupted regarding reports of sudden liver problems (acute hepatotoxicity with liver necrosis). Additional considerations of a very long half-life and possible toxicity as well as other considerations mean that until further data are available regarding incidence, testing strategy and other data are available, the information in this profile has been shortened to make room for more widely used medicines.

LEVODOPA (lee voh DOH pa)

Introduced: 1967   **Class:**   Anti-Parkinsonism, dopamine pro-drug   **Prescription:**   USA: Yes   **Controlled Drug:**   USA: No; Canada: No   **Available as Generic:**   USA: Yes; Canada: Yes

Brand Names: ✦Apo-Levocarb, Bendopa, Biodopa, Dopar, Larodopa, ✦Prolopa [CD], Sinemet [CD], Sinemet CR [CD]

BENEFITS versus RISKS	
Possible Benefits	*Possible Risks*
EFFECTIVE SYMPTOM RELIEF IN IDIOPATHIC PARKINSON'S DISEASE	Emotional depression, confusion, abnormal thinking and behavior
Helpful in Parkinsonism after encephalitis	Abnormal involuntary movements
Roughly 6-month benefit in Parkinsonism after manganese poisoning	Heart rhythm disturbance Urinary bladder retention Induction of peptic ulcer Blood abnormalities: hemolytic anemia, reduced white blood cell count

▷ **Principal Uses**

As a Single Drug Product: Uses currently included in FDA-approved labeling: Treats major types of Parkinson's disease: paralysis agitans ("shaking palsy" of unknown cause), the type that follows encephalitis, Parkinsonism that develops with aging (associated with hardening of the brain arteries) and the Parkinsonism that follows poisoning by carbon monoxide or manganese.

Other (unlabeled) generally accepted uses: (1) May have a limited role in treating catatonic stupor; (2) can improve conscious level in coma caused by liver failure; (3) can help restless leg or periodic limb movements in sleep; (4) could be helpful in treating severe congestive heart failure.

As a Combination Drug Product [CD]: This drug is available in combination with carbidopa, a chemical that prevents the breakdown of levodopa before it reaches its site of action. The addition of carbidopa reduces levodopa requirements by 75% and also decreases the frequency and severity of adverse effects. Prolopa form has both levodopa and benserazide (12.5 mg) as a decarboxylase inhibitor to help prevent breakdown of levodopa.

How This Drug Works: Levodopa enters the brain tissue and is converted to dopamine. After sufficient dose, this corrects the dopamine deficiency (thought to be the cause of Parkinsonism) and restores a more normal brain chemistry. Carbidopa blocks an enzyme (decarboxylase) that degrades levodopa before it reaches the brain. This allows a lower dose to have a greater benefit. Products containing carbidopa also have fewer adverse effects.

Available Dosage Forms and Strengths

Capsules — 100 mg, 250 mg, 500 mg
Sinemet CR, sustained release tablets — 25/100 mg, 50/200 mg
Sinemet tablets — 10/100 mg, 25/100 mg, 25/250 mg
Tablets — 100 mg, 250 mg, 500 mg

▷ **Usual Adult Dosage Ranges:** Initially 250 mg 2 to 4 times daily. Dose may be increased by increments of 100 to 750 mg at 3- to 7-day intervals as needed and tolerated. Total dose should not exceed 8,000 mg daily. If the combination drug Sinemet is used, the total levodopa requirement will be considerably less. For someone who has not taken levodopa before (levodopa-naive and using the sustained release form): one 50/200 mg tablet twice daily, no more frequently than every 6 hours while awake. The dose is then increased as needed and tolerated by either daily or every-other-day dosing of one tablet, to a maximum of 8 tablets daily.

Note: Actual dose and schedule must be determined for each patient individually.

Conditions Requiring Dosing Adjustments

Liver Function: Dosing changes are not indicated in liver compromise.

Kidney Function: Possible urine retention requires that patients with urine outflow problems should be closely watched. No dose decreases are needed in kidney failure.

Intestinal Parasites: A report of large increases in doses needed by patients with Strongyloides stercoralis has been filed. Cure of this intestinal parasite allowed the levodopa dose to be decreased by 33%.

▷ **Dosing Instructions:** Immediate release form may be crushed and is best taken with or following carbohydrate foods to reduce stomach upset. When possible, don't take this drug with high-protein foods. Sustained release tablet (Sinemet CR) may be cut in half, but it should not be crushed or chewed. The last daily dose should be taken before 7 P.M. in order to avoid problems with normal sleeping patterns. "Drug holidays" (periods when no medicine is taken) are controversial, and not all patients benefit from this approach to therapy. If you forget a dose: take the missed dose as soon as you remember it, unless it's nearly time for your next dose—if that is the case, skip the missed dose and take the next dose right on schedule. Talk with your doctor if you find yourself missing doses.

Usual Duration of Use: Use on a regular schedule for 2 to 3 weeks determines effectiveness in relieving the major symptoms of Parkinsonism. Peak benefits may require continual use for 6 months. Long-term use (months to years) requires physician supervision.

Typical Treatment Goals and Measurements (Outcomes and Markers)

Parkinson's disease: The general goal is to minimize symptoms (tremor, sluggish movements, analysis of walking or gait, etc.) to the fullest extent possible. Additionally, many neurologists use Hahn-Yahr scores and the time it takes to maximum amount of finger tapping as indicators of the benefits of this drug.

Possible Advantages of This Drug

The slow-release formulation of Sinemet CR allows a 25% to 50% reduction in dosing frequency.

The wearing-off phenomenon and end-of-dose failure seen with standard Sinemet may be reduced or eliminated.

▷ **This Drug Should Not Be Taken If**
- you are allergic to any of the brands listed.
- you have narrow-angle glaucoma (inadequately controlled).
- you have a history of melanoma or skin lesions that have not been diagnosed.
- you are taking, or have taken within the past 14 days, any monoamine oxidase (MAO) type A inhibitor drug (see Drug Classes).

▷ **Inform Your Physician Before Taking This Drug If**
- you have diabetes, epilepsy, heart disease, high blood pressure, or chronic lung disease.
- you have impaired liver or kidney function.
- you have problems making blood (hematopoiesis).
- you have had a heart attack and have some abnormal heart rhythms.
- you have a history of ongoing (chronic) wide-angle glaucoma.
- you have a history of depression or other mental illness.
- you have a history of peptic ulcer disease or malignant melanoma.
- you will have surgery with general anesthesia.

Possible Side Effects (natural, expected, and unavoidable drug actions)

Fatigue, lethargy.

Altered taste, offensive body odor.

Orthostatic hypotension (see Glossary).

Pink- to red-colored urine, which turns black on exposure to air (of no significance).

Gout.

▷ **Possible Adverse Effects** (unusual, unexpected, and infrequent reactions)

If any of the following develop, consult your physician promptly for guidance.

Mild Adverse Effects

Allergic reactions: skin rash, itching.

Headache, dizziness, numbness, insomnia, nightmares, blurred or double vision—infrequent.

Nausea and vomiting—frequent.

Dry mouth, difficult swallowing, gas, diarrhea, constipation—infrequent.

Decreased taste sensation—possible.

More rapid rate of nail growth—possible.

Loss of hair or changes in hair color—case reports.

Serious Adverse Effects

Idiosyncratic reactions: hemolytic anemia (see Glossary).

Neuroleptic malignant syndrome (see Glossary), high blood pressure—case reports.

Confusion, hallucinations, paranoia, depression—infrequent to frequent.

Psychotic episodes, seizures—rare.

Congestive heart failure—rare.

Mania or seizures—rare.

Abnormal involuntary movements of the head, face and extremities—frequent.

Disturbances of heart rhythm—infrequent; low blood pressure—rare.

Development of peptic ulcer, gastrointestinal bleeding—case reports.

Urinary bladder retention—case reports.

Low white blood cell count: increased infection risk, sore throat (transient, but may require you to stop this medicine until the condition clears), low blood platelets, or hemolytic anemia—case reports to rare.

Systemic lupus erythematosus—case reports.

▷ **Possible Effects on Sexual Function:** Increased male or female libido—infrequent.

Inhibited ejaculation, priapism (see Glossary), postmenopausal bleeding—all rare.

▷ **Adverse Effects That May Mimic Natural Diseases or Disorders**

Mental reactions may resemble idiopathic psychosis.

Natural Diseases or Disorders That May Be Activated by This Drug

Latent peptic ulcer, gout.

Possible Effects on Laboratory Tests

Complete blood cell counts: occasionally decreased white cells; occasionally increased eosinophils (without symptoms).

Blood thyroxine (T4) level: increased.

Liver function tests: may be increased.

Urine sugar tests: no effect with Tes-Tape; false negative with Clinistix; false positive with Clinitest.

Urine ketone tests: false positive with Ketostix and Phenistix.

Blood uric acid, growth hormone: increased.

Blood potassium or sodium: may be decreased.

CAUTION

1. It is best to begin treatment with small doses, increasing gradually until desired response is achieved.
2. As improvement occurs, avoid excessive and hurried activity (often causes falls and injury).

Precautions for Use

By Infants and Children: This drug can cause precocious puberty in prepubertal boys. Watch for hypersexual behavior and premature growth of genital organs.

By Those Over 60 Years of Age: Therapy should start with half the usual adult dose; dose increases should be made in small increments as needed and tolerated. Watch for significant behavioral changes: depression or inappropriate elation, acute confusion, agitation, paranoia, dementia, nightmares, and hallucinations. Abnormal involuntary movements may also occur.

▷ **Advisability of Use During Pregnancy**

Pregnancy Category: C. See Pregnancy Risk Categories at the back of this book.

Animal Studies: Significant birth defects reported in rodent studies.

Human Studies: Adequate studies of pregnant women are not available.

Avoid use of drug during the first 3 months. Use only if clearly needed during the final 6 months.

Advisability of Use If Breast-Feeding

Presence of this drug in breast milk: Yes, at low levels.

Avoid drug or refrain from nursing.

Habit-Forming Potential: None.

Effects of Overdose: Muscle twitching, spastic closure of eyelids, nausea, vomiting, diarrhea, weakness, fainting, confusion, agitation, hallucinations.

Possible Effects of Long-Term Use: Development of abnormal involuntary movements involving the head, face, mouth, and extremities. May be reversible and gradually subside as the drug is withdrawn.

Suggested Periodic Examinations While Taking This Drug (at physician's discretion)

Complete blood cell counts.

Measurements of internal eye pressure.

Blood pressure measurements in lying, sitting, and standing positions.

▷ **While Taking This Drug, Observe the Following**

Foods: Insofar as possible, do not take concurrently with protein foods; proteins compete for absorption.

Herbal Medicines or Minerals: Calabar bean (chop nut, Fabia, ordeal nut, others) is unsafe when taken by mouth (physostigmine is the active ingredient) and should never be taken by people with Parkinson's disease. Octacosanol (a cousin of vitamin E) can worsen movement problems and should also be avoided.

Nutritional Support: If taken alone (without carbidopa), watch for tingling of the extremities (peripheral neuritis). Small (10 mg or less) doses of pyridoxine (vitamin B6) may help. Larger doses can decrease the effectiveness of levodopa. If taking Sinemet, supplemental pyridoxine is not required. Rare reports of vitamin C (ascorbic acid) decreasing nausea and other side effects have been made.

Beverages: No restrictions. May be taken with milk.
▷ *Alcohol:* No interactions expected.
Tobacco Smoking: No interactions expected. I advise everyone to quit smoking.
Marijuana Smoking: Increased fatigue and lethargy; possible accentuation of orthostatic hypotension (see Glossary).
▷ *Other Drugs*
Levodopa **taken concurrently** with
- benzodiazepines (see Drug Classes) may blunt the therapeutic benefit of levodopa.
- bromocriptine (Parlodel) may result in decreased blood levels of bromocriptine.
- bupropion (Wellbutrin, Zyban) may increase adverse effects.
- cisapride (Propulsid) may increase adverse effects.
- clonidine (Catapres) can result in decreased therapeutic benefit of levodopa; avoid this combination.
- entacapone (Comtan) may enhance therapeutic effects and be used beneficially.
- fentanyl/droperidol (Innovar) can cause muscular rigidity.
- indinavir (Crixivan) may lead to severe movement problems (dyskinesias).
- isoniazid (INH) may cause flushing, worsening of symptoms, or increased blood pressure. DO NOT COMBINE.
- metoclopramide (Reglan) may increase chance of movement problems (extrapyramidal symptoms). Combination is not recommended.
- monoamine oxidase (MAO) type A inhibitor drugs (see Drug Classes) can cause a dangerous rise in blood pressure and body temperature; do not combine these drugs.
- phenothiazines (see Drug Classes) may blunt therapeutic benefits of levodopa. DO NOT COMBINE.
- reserpine (Naquival, others) may blunt the therapeutic benefits of levodopa; avoid this combination.
- risperidone (Risperdal) can blunt the therapeutic benefits of levodopa; avoid this combination.
- tolcapone (Tasmar) may lead to vitiligo (skin lesions).
- tricyclic antidepressants (see Drug Classes) may decrease the therapeutic effect of levodopa.
- zotepine (Nipolept) may decrease the therapeutic effect of levodopa.

The following drugs may **decrease** the effects of levodopa:
- amoxapine (Asendin).
- chlordiazepoxide (Librium) or other benzodiazepines (see Drug Classes).
- iron salts.
- olanzapine (Zyprexa) may blunt therapeutic benefits of levodopa, but the clinical degree of this is not known.
- papaverine (Cerespan, Pavabid, Vasospan, etc.).
- phenytoin (Dilantin, etc.) or fosphenytoin (Cerebyx).
- pyridoxine (vitamin B6).
- risperidone (Risperdal).

▷ *Driving, Hazardous Activities:* May cause dizziness, impaired vision, and orthostatic hypotension. Restrict activities as necessary.
Aviation Note: Parkinson's disease **is a disqualification** for piloting. Consult a designated Aviation Medical Examiner.
Exposure to Sun: No restrictions.
Exposure to Heat: Use caution. This drug can cause flushing and excessive sweating and predispose to heat exhaustion.

Occurrence of Unrelated Illness: Dark-colored skin lesions should be evaluated carefully by your doctor, as they may be malignant melanoma. White blood cell counts should be closely followed if you develop an infection.

LEVOTHYROXINE (lee voh thi ROX een)

Other Names: L-thyroxine, thyroxine, T-4

Introduced: 1953 **Class:** Thyroid hormones **Prescription:** USA: Yes **Controlled Drug:** USA: No; Canada: No **Available as Generic:** USA: Yes; Canada: No

Brand Names: Alti-Thyroxine, Armour Thyroid, ✤Eltroxin, Euthroid [CD], Euthyrox, Levo-T, Levotabs, Levothroid, Levoxine, Levoxyl, L-Thyroxine, ✤Proloid, Synthroid, Synthrox, Syroxine, Thyroid USP, Thyrolar [CD], Unithroid, V-Throid

---

BENEFITS versus RISKS

Possible Benefits	*Possible Risks*
EFFECTIVE REPLACEMENT THERAPY IN STATES OF THYROID HORMONE DEFICIENCY (HYPOTHYROIDISM) EFFECTIVE TREATMENT OF SIMPLE GOITER, CHRONIC THYROIDITIS, AND THYROID GLAND CANCER	Intensification of angina in presence of coronary artery disease Drug-induced hyperthyroidism (with excessive dose) Spasm of the coronary vessels

---

▷ **Principal Uses**

As a Single Drug Product: Uses currently included in FDA-approved labeling: (1) Replacement therapy to correct thyroid deficiency (drug-induced, hypothyroidism, cretinism, myxedema); (2) treatment of simple (nonendemic) goiter and benign thyroid nodules; (3) treatment of Hashimoto's thyroiditis; (4) adjunctive prevention and treatment of thyroid cancer; (5) treats Grave's disease.

Author's Note: Concern has arisen over levothyroxine medicines that were never approved under current FDA regulations. On July 16, 2001, the FDA issued guidance that said that manufacturers of unapproved hypothyroidism drugs will have to stop distributing their products. See *www.fda.gov/bbs/topics/ANSWERS/2001/ANSO1089.html.*

Other (unlabeled) generally accepted uses: (1) Helps amenorrhea caused by (secondary to) low thyroid function; (2) may help fetal lung tissue mature in premature babies; (3) could help long-standing (chronic) hives (urticaria); (4) some clinicians use levothyroxine in combination with triiodothyronine (10–12.5 mcg of triiodothyronine and lowering the levothyroxine dose by 50 mcg); (5) may have a role in easing carpal tunnel syndrome (CTS) in patients who have underactive thyroid glands; (6) some clinicians use this medicine as a way to intensify treatment for certain psychiatric problems (such as depression).

As a Combination Drug Product [CD]: This thyroid hormone is available in combination with the other principal thyroid hormone, liothyronine, in a preparation (generic name: liotrix) that resembles the natural hormone material produced by the thyroid gland.

How This Drug Works: Alters cellular chemistry, making more energy available and increases metabolism of all tissues. Thyroid hormones are essential to normal growth and development, especially the development of infant brain and nervous systems.

Available Dosage Forms and Strengths
 Injections — 100 mcg/ml, 200 mcg/ml, 500 mcg/ml
  Tablets — 0.0125 mg, 0.025 mg, 0.037 mg, 0.05 mg, 0.075 mg, 0.088 mg, 0.1 mg, 0.112 mg, 0.125 mg, 0.15 mg, 0.175 mg, 0.2 mg, 0.3 mg

▷ **Recommended Dosage Ranges** (Actual dose and schedule must be determined for each patient individually.)

Infants and Children: Up to 6 months of age—8 to 10 mcg per kg of body mass, in a single daily dose.

6 to 12 months of age—6 to 8 mcg per kg of body mass, in a single daily dose.

1 to 5 years of age—5 to 6 mcg per kg of body mass, in a single daily dose.

6 to 12 years of age—4 to 5 mcg per kg of body mass, in a single daily dose.

Over 12 years of age—2 to 3 mcg per kg of body mass, in a single daily dose, until the usual adult daily dose is reached (150 to 200 mcg).

12 to 60 Years of Age: In younger patients with heart and blood vessel (cardiovascular) disease or in older patients, dosing is started at 12.5 to 50 mcg once a day. Adjustments to this dose are usually made by 12.5 to 25 micrograms every 3 to 6 weeks as needed and tolerated. Clinicians use TSH becoming normal as a marker. One hundred to 200 mcg per day is the usual ongoing dose range from the maker of Levothroid. For many patients, the dose relates to weight as 1.6 micrograms/kilogram per day. Few people require more than 200 mcg per day. If response is not seen at this level, absorption problems or misunderstanding in taking the medicine (adherence) should be evaluated.

Over 60 Years of Age: Initially 12.5 mcg as a single daily dose; increase gradually at intervals of 3 to 4 weeks, as needed and tolerated. The usual maintenance dose is approximately 75 mcg (0.075 mg) daily.

Author's Note: A University of California Medical Center at San Francisco study found the generic to be as effective as the brand name at savings of 50% of the cost of the brand. One key principle is to keep taking the same generic or brand to avoid fluctuations.

Conditions Requiring Dosing Adjustments
Liver Function: Dosing changes are not needed.
Kidney Function: Dosing changes are not indicated in kidney compromise.

▷ **Dosing Instructions:** The tablets may be crushed and are best taken in the morning on an empty stomach. Take the medicine at the same time every day. If you forget a dose: take the missed dose as soon as you remember it, unless it's nearly time for your next dose—if that is the case, skip the missed dose and take the next dose right on schedule. Talk with your doctor if you find yourself missing doses.

Usual Duration of Use: Use on a regular schedule for 4 to 6 weeks determines effectiveness in correcting the symptoms of thyroid deficiency. Repeat checks of laboratory tests are required. Long-term use (months to years, possibly for life) requires physician supervision.

Typical Treatment Goals and Measurements (Outcomes and Markers)

Hypothyroidism: The goal is to return the thyroid hormone level to normal or euthyroid. Clinicians check easing of low thyroid signs and symptoms (low energy, weight gain, sluggishness, etc.) as well as checking very specific laboratory tests. Tests often used include the thyroid stimulating hormone (TSH) and T3 and T4 as well as the thyrotropin test. Adjunctive tests include total cholesterol.

Currently a "Drug of Choice"

For treatment of hypothyroidism.

▷ **This Drug Should Not Be Taken If**

- you have had an allergic reaction to it previously.
- you are recovering from a heart attack; ask your doctor for help.
- you have an adrenal insufficiency, angina, high blood pressure, or thyrotoxicosis that has not been corrected.
- you are using it to lose weight and your thyroid function is normal (no deficiency).

▷ **Inform Your Physician Before Taking This Drug If**

- you have high blood pressure, any form of heart disease or diabetes.
- you have a history of Addison's disease or adrenal gland deficiency.
- you are taking any antiasthmatic medications.
- you are taking an anticoagulant.

Possible Side Effects (natural, expected, and unavoidable drug actions)

Aggravation of cardiovascular problems.

▷ **Possible Adverse Effects** (unusual, unexpected, and infrequent reactions)

If any of the following develop, consult your physician promptly for guidance.

Mild Adverse Effects

Allergic reactions: skin rash, hives.

Headache in sensitive people, even with proper dose adjustment—may be frequent.

Serious Adverse Effects

Increased frequency or intensity of angina in people with coronary artery disease—possible.

Spasm of the arteries that supply blood to the heart and heart attack—rare.

Seizures, pseudotumor cerebri, drug-induced porphyria, or myasthenia gravis—case reports to rare.

Decrease in IgA immune concentration—rare.

May be a part of the development of osteoporosis. Bone mineral density testing is recommended.

Note: Other adverse effects are manifestations of excessive dose. See Effects of Overdose on page 647.

▷ **Possible Effects on Sexual Function:** Altered menstrual pattern during dose adjustments.

Possibly beneficial in treating impaired sexual function that is associated with true hypothyroidism.

Natural Diseases or Disorders That May Be Activated by This Drug

Latent coronary artery insufficiency (angina), diabetes, osteopenia may progress to osteoporosis.

Possible Effects on Laboratory Tests

Prothrombin time: increased (when taken concurrently with warfarin).

Blood total cholesterol, HDL and LDL cholesterol levels: decreased.

Blood triglyceride levels: no effect.

Blood glucose level: increased.

Blood thyroid hormone levels: increased T3, T4 and free T4.

Blood thyroid-stimulating hormone (TSH) level: decreased.

CAUTION

1. Careful supervision of individual response is needed to identify correct dose. Do not change dosing or drug products without asking your physician.
2. This drug should not be used to treat nonspecific fatigue, obesity, infertility, or slow growth. Such use is inappropriate and could be harmful.
3. If combination levothyroxine and triiodothyronine dosing is used, the levothyroxine dose is lowered by 50 mcg.
4. If a combination levothyroxine and triiodothyronine dosing is used, thyroid extract should be avoided, as it has an elevated amount of T3, which can lead to tremors or palpitations.

Precautions for Use

By Infants and Children: Thyroid-deficient children often require higher doses than adults. Transient hair loss may occur during the early months of treatment. Follow the child's response to thyroid therapy by periodic measurements of bone age, growth and mental and physical development.

By Those Over 60 Years of Age: Usually requirements for thyroid hormone replacement are about 25% lower than in younger adults. Watch closely for any indications of toxicity.

▷ **Advisability of Use During Pregnancy**

Pregnancy Category: A. See Pregnancy Risk Categories at the back of this book.

Animal Studies: Cataract formation reported in rat studies. Other defects reported in rabbit and guinea pig studies.

Human Studies: Thyroid hormones do not reach the fetus (cross the placenta) in significant amounts. Clinical experience has shown that appropriate use of thyroid hormones causes no adverse effects on the fetus.

Use this drug only if clearly needed and with carefully adjusted dose.

Advisability of Use If Breast-Feeding

Presence of this drug in breast milk: Yes, in minimal amounts (roughly 10% of the mother's dose).

Talk to your doctor about the advisability of breast-feeding.

Habit-Forming Potential: None. One case report of abuse of this medicine was made in a bulimic patient. Caution and vigilance for abuse in bulimics is warranted.

Effects of Overdose: Headache, sense of increased body heat, nervousness, increased sweating, hand tremors, insomnia, rapid and irregular heart action, diarrhea, muscle cramping, weight loss, heart attack.

Possible Effects of Long-Term Use: Bone loss (osteoporosis) in the lumbar vertebrae (spine). Worsening of abnormal growth of the left side of the heart.

Suggested Periodic Examinations While Taking This Drug (at physician's discretion)

Measurement of thyroid hormone levels in blood.

Bone mineral density testing.

▷ **While Taking This Drug, Observe the Following**

Foods: Enteral formulas for nutrition support that contain soybeans may increase the fecal elimination of thyroxine.

Herbal Medicines or Minerals: Horseradish root might worsen low thyroid (hypothyroidism) or blunt effectiveness of therapy. Calcium doses (if taken) should be separated from levothyroxine doses by 4 hours. Cabbage and iodine may worsen goiters and exacerbate hypothyroidism. Gamma oryzanol (extracted from rice bran oil) can lower thyroid stimulating hormone (TSH) and change test results. Tiratricol is a naturally occurring metabolite of thyroxine and triiodothyronine. In theory, tiratricol may enhance the adverse action and effects of bungleweed, wild thyme and balm leaf. Soy may decrease the absorption of levothyroxine. Kelp products contain iodine and can change thyroid gland function. Talk to your doctor BEFORE adding any herbal medicines to levothyroxine.

Beverages: No restrictions.

▷ *Alcohol:* No interactions expected.

Tobacco Smoking: No interactions expected. I advise everyone to quit smoking.

▷ *Other Drugs*

Levothyroxine may ***increase*** the effects of
- warfarin (Coumadin) and increase the risk of bleeding; decreased anticoagulant dose is usually needed. More frequent INR testing (prothrombin time or protime) is needed.

Levothyroxine may ***decrease*** the effects of
- digoxin (Lanoxin), when correcting hypothyroidism; a larger dose of digoxin may be needed.

Levothyroxine ***taken concurrently*** with
- antacids may cause decreased levothyroxine absorption and a decreased therapeutic effect.
- all antidiabetic drugs (insulin and oral hypoglycemic agents) may require an increased dose to obtain proper control of blood sugar levels.
- benzodiazepines (Librium and others) can enhance the toxic or therapeutic effects of both drugs.
- calcium carbonate may cause decreased levothyroxine absorption and a decreased therapeutic effect.
- conjugated estrogens (Premarin) may require an increased levothyroxine dose.
- tricyclic antidepressants (see Drug Classes) may cause an increase in activity of both drugs.

The following drugs may ***decrease*** the effects of levothyroxine:
- cholestyramine (Cuemid, Questran)—may reduce its absorption; intake of the 2 drugs should be separated by 5 hours.
- colestipol (Colestid).
- iron salts—by decreasing absorption.
- lovastatin (Mevacor).
- phenytoin (Dilantin) or fosphenytoin (Cerebyx)—can increase levothyroxine removal (clearance).
- rifampin (Rifater, others).
- ritonavir (Norvir).
- sodium polystyrene sulfonate (Kayexalate).
- sucralfate (Carafate).

▷ *Driving, Hazardous Activities:* No restrictions.

Aviation Note: The use of this drug is ***probably not a disqualification*** for piloting. Consult a designated Aviation Medical Examiner.

Exposure to Sun: No restrictions.

Exposure to Heat: This drug may decrease individual tolerance to warm environments, increasing discomfort due to heat. Consult your physician if you develop symptoms of overdose during the warm months of the year.

Heavy Exercise or Exertion: Use caution if you have angina (coronary artery disease). This drug may increase the frequency or severity of angina during physical activity.

Discontinuation: Must be taken continually on a regular schedule to correct thyroid deficiency. Never stop it without talking to your doctor.

LIDOCAINE (LYE doh kane)

Other Names: None

Introduced: Patch form 1999 **Class:** Analgesic, antiarrhythmic
Prescription: USA: Yes **Controlled Drug:** USA: No; Canada: No
Available as Generic: USA: No; Canada: No

Brand Names: Lidoderm

BENEFITS versus RISKS	
Possible Benefits	*Possible Risks*
EFFECTIVE TREATMENT/PREVENTION OF THE PAIN WHICH HAPPENS AFTER SHINGLES (POSTHERPETIC NEURALGIA)	Interactions are possible—drug is used with caution in people who are taking other Class I (such as mexiletine or tocainide) antiarrhythmic drugs
WHEN USED AS DIRECTED, ROUGHLY 2% OF THE APPLIED DOSE REACHES THE BODY CIRCULATION	Skin irritation where the patch is applied
	Possible allergic reaction (rare)

▷ **Principal Uses**

As a Single Drug Product: Uses currently included in FDA-approved labeling: (1) Pain relief for pain associated with postherpetic neuralgia.

Other (unlabeled) generally accepted uses: None at present.

Author's Note: This brief profile focused on the only specifically FDA-approved treatment for pain after shingles (postherpetic neuralgia)—not the antiarrhythmic use. This profile will be broadened in future editions if warranted.

LIOTHYRONINE (li oh THI roh neen)

Other Names: Triiodothyronine, T-3

Introduced: 1956 **Class:** Thyroid hormone **Prescription:** USA: Yes **Controlled Drug:** USA: No; Canada: No **Available as Generic:** USA: Yes; Canada: No

Brand Names: Cytomel, Euthroid [CD], ✚Proloid, Thyroid USP, ✚Thyrolar [CD], Thyrolar ¼, ½, 1, 2 and 3 [CD], Triostat

```
BENEFITS versus RISKS
```
Possible Benefits	*Possible Risks*
EFFECTIVE REPLACEMENT THERAPY IN STATES OF THYROID HORMONE DEFICIENCY (HYPOTHYROIDISM)	Intensification of angina in presence of coronary artery disease
	Drug-induced hyperthyroidism (with excessive dosing)
	Rapid heartbeat
EFFECTIVE TREATMENT OF SIMPLE GOITER, CHRONIC THYROIDITIS, AND THYROID GLAND CANCER	Heart attack

▷ **Principal Uses**

As a Single Drug Product: Uses currently included in FDA-approved labeling: (1) Replacement therapy to correct thyroid deficiency (hypothyroidism); (2) treatment of simple (nonendemic) goiter and benign thyroid nodules; (3) treatment of Hashimoto's thyroiditis; (4) adjunctive prevention and treatment of thyroid cancer; (5) therapy of cretinism; (6) used to help diagnose different kinds of thyroid problems; (7) treats low thyroid that comes from medicines.

Other (unlabeled) generally accepted uses: (1) Can help infertility caused by low thyroid function; (2) thyroid replacement of choice for thyroid cancer; (3) may have a role in some kinds of heart problems (cardiomyopathy); (4) may have a role in some cases of resistant (refractory) depression; (5) could be helpful in supplementing Selective Serotonin Reuptake Inhibitor–treatment of posttraumatic stress disorder (PTSD); (6) used by some clinicians for medication intensification in resistant depression.

As a Combination Drug Product [CD]: This thyroid hormone is available in combination with the other principal thyroid hormone, levothyroxine, in a preparation (generic name: liotrix) that resembles the natural hormone material produced by the thyroid gland.

How This Drug Works: Alters cellular chemistry, making more energy available. Increases cellular metabolism in all tissues. Thyroid hormones are essential to normal growth and development, especially the development of the infant's brain and nervous system.

Available Dosage Forms and Strengths

Injection — 10 mcg/ml

Tablets — 5 mcg, 25 mcg, 50 mcg

▷ **Recommended Dosage Ranges** (Actual dose and schedule must be determined for each patient individually.)

Infants and Children: Infants several months old may need 20 mcg a day. When they reach 1 year, 50 mcg a day may be needed. Children over 3 years old may need the full adult dose.

12 to 60 Years of Age: For mild hypothyroidism—initially 25 mcg daily; increase by 12.5 to 25 mcg every 1 to 2 weeks as needed and tolerated. The usual maintenance dose is 25 to 75 mcg daily.

For severe hypothyroidism—initially 2.5 to 5 mcg daily; increase by 5 to 10 mcg at intervals of 1 to 2 weeks. When a dose of 25 mcg is reached, increase by 12.5 to 25 mcg at intervals of 1 to 2 weeks, as needed and tolerated. The usual maintenance dose is 50 to 100 mcg daily.

For simple goiter—initially 5 mcg daily; increase by 5 to 10 mcg at intervals of 1 to 2 weeks. When a dose of 25 mcg is reached, increase by 12.5 to 25 mcg at intervals of 1 week, as needed and tolerated. The usual maintenance dose is 50 to 100 mcg daily.

Over 60 Years of Age: Initially 5 mcg as a single daily dose; increase by 5 mcg at intervals of 1 to 2 weeks, as needed and tolerated. The usual maintenance dose is 12.5 to 37.5 mcg daily.

Conditions Requiring Dosing Adjustments

Liver Function: Dosing changes are not indicated for patients with liver compromise.

Kidney Function: Dosing changes are not indicated in renal compromise. Caution should be used when increasing the dose of this medicine for those with kidney problems.

▷ **Dosing Instructions:** The tablets may be crushed and are preferably taken in the morning on an empty stomach to ensure maximal absorption and uniform results. If you forget a dose: take the missed dose as soon as you remember it, unless it's nearly time for your next dose—if that is the case, skip the missed dose and take the next dose right on schedule. Talk with your doctor if you find yourself missing doses.

Usual Duration of Use: Use on a regular schedule for 2 to 4 days determines effectiveness in correcting the symptoms of thyroid deficiency. Long-term use (months to years, possibly for life) requires physician supervision and checks of thyroid status.

Typical Treatment Goals and Measurements (Outcomes and Markers)

Hypothyroidism: The goal is to return the thyroid hormone level to normal or euthyroid. Clinicians check easing of low thyroid signs and symptoms (low energy, weight gain, sluggishness, etc.) as well as checking very specific laboratory tests. Tests often used include the thyroid stimulating hormone (TSH) and T3 and T4 as well as the thyrotropin test. Adjunctive tests include total cholesterol.

▷ **This Drug Should Not Be Taken If**
  • you have had an allergic reaction to it previously.
  • you are recovering from a heart attack; ask your doctor for guidance.
  • you have an uncorrected adrenal cortical deficiency.
  • you are using it to lose weight and your thyroid function is normal.

▷ **Inform Your Physician Before Taking This Drug If**
  • you have high blood pressure, any form of heart disease or diabetes.
  • you have a history of Addison's disease, adrenal gland deficiency, or thyrotoxicosis.
  • you are taking any antiasthmatic medications.
  • you take digoxin.
  • you are taking an anticoagulant.

Possible Side Effects (natural, expected, and unavoidable drug actions)
  Fast heartbeat (tachycardia).

▷ **Possible Adverse Effects** (unusual, unexpected, and infrequent reactions)
  If any of the following develop, consult your physician promptly for guidance.
  Mild Adverse Effects
  Allergic reactions: skin rash, hives.
  Headache in sensitive patients, even with proper dose adjustment—may be frequent.

Rapid heart rate (tachycardia)—infrequent.

Hair loss—case reports.

Serious Adverse Effects

Allergic reactions: erythema, bullae, and papules.

Increased frequency or intensity of angina or abnormal heartbeat—possible to infrequent.

Lowering of blood pressure—rare.

Heart attack—rare.

Osteoporosis—possible increased risk (bone mineral density testing is recommended).

Hyperthyroidism—possible with improper dosing.

Drug fever or drug-induced myasthenia gravis—case reports.

Author's Note: Other adverse effects are manifestations of excessive dose. See Effects of Overdose on page 653.

▷ **Possible Effects on Sexual Function:** Altered menstrual pattern during dose adjustments.

Possibly beneficial in treating impaired sexual function that is associated with true hypothyroidism.

Natural Diseases or Disorders That May Be Activated by This Drug

Latent coronary artery insufficiency (angina), diabetes.

Possible Effects on Laboratory Tests

Prothrombin time: increased (when taken concurrently with warfarin).

Blood total cholesterol, HDL and LDL cholesterol levels: decreased.

Blood triglyceride levels: no effect.

Blood glucose level: increased.

Blood thyroid hormone levels: increased T3.

Blood thyroid stimulating hormone (TSH) level: decreased.

CAUTION

1. Careful supervision of individual response is needed to identify correct dose. Do not change dosing schedule without asking your doctor.
2. This drug should not be used to treat nonspecific fatigue, obesity, infertility, or slow growth. Such use is inappropriate and could be harmful.

Precautions for Use

By Infants and Children: Not recommended for treatment of this age group. It must reach the brain and nervous system, and this drug may not do that. Levothyroxine is the drug of choice to treat thyroid deficiency in infants and children.

By Those Over 60 Years of Age: Needs for thyroid hormone are usually about 25% lower than in younger adults. Watch closely for any toxicity.

▷ **Advisability of Use During Pregnancy**

Pregnancy Category: A. See Pregnancy Risk Categories at the back of this book.

Animal Studies: No information available.

Human Studies: Thyroid hormones do not reach the fetus (cross the placenta) in significant amounts. Clinical experience has shown that appropriate use of thyroid hormones causes no adverse effects on the fetus.

Use this drug only if clearly needed and with carefully adjusted dose.

Advisability of Use If Breast-Feeding

Presence of this drug in breast milk: Yes, in minimal amounts.

Talk to your doctor as this decision must be cautiously made (benefit-to-risk).

Habit-Forming Potential: None.

Effects of Overdose: Headache, sense of increased body heat, nervousness, increased sweating, hand tremors, insomnia, rapid and irregular heart action, diarrhea, muscle cramping, weight loss, heart attack.

Possible Effects of Long-Term Use: Bone loss (osteoporosis) in the lumbar vertebrae (spine). Bone mineral density testing is recommended.

Suggested Periodic Examinations While Taking This Drug (at physician's discretion)

Measurement of thyroid hormone levels in blood.

Bone mineral density testing.

▷ **While Taking This Drug, Observe the Following**

Foods: No restrictions.

Herbal Medicines or Minerals: Horseradish root might worsen low thyroid (hypothyroidism) or blunt effectiveness of therapy. Calcium doses (if taken) should be separated from levothyroxine doses by 4 hours. Cabbage and iodine may worsen goiters and exacerbate hypothyroidism. Gamma oryzanol (extracted from rice bran oil) can lower thyroid stimulating hormone (TSH) and change test results. Tiratricol is a naturally occurring metabolite of thyroxine and triiodothyronine. In theory, tiratricol may enhance the adverse action and effects of bungleweed, wild thyme, and balm leaf. Soy may decrease the absorption of levothyroxine. Kelp products contain iodine and can change thyroid gland function. Talk to your doctor BEFORE adding any herbal medicines to liothyronine.

Beverages: No restrictions.

▷ *Alcohol:* No interactions expected.

Tobacco Smoking: No interactions expected. I advise everyone to quit smoking.

▷ *Other Drugs*

Liothyronine may *increase* the effects of

- warfarin (Coumadin) and increase the risk of bleeding; more frequent INR (prothrombin time or protime) tests are needed (in general, anticoagulant effect is increased in hyperthyroidism and decreased in hypothyroidism).

Liothyronine may *decrease* the effects of

- digoxin (Lanoxin) when correcting hypothyroidism; a larger dose of digoxin may be needed.

Liothyronine *taken concurrently* with

- all antidiabetic drugs (insulin and oral hypoglycemic agents) may require an increased dose to obtain proper control of blood sugar because liothyronine increases insulin.
- estrogens (including birth control pills and Premarin) may require increased doses of liothyronine.
- monoamine oxidase (MAO) inhibitors (see Drug Classes) may increase the therapeutic benefits of the antidepressant.
- tricyclic antidepressants (see Drug Classes) may cause an increase in the activity of both drugs; watch for signs of toxicity.

The following drugs may *decrease* the effects of liothyronine:

- carbamazepine (Tegretol, others) may decrease free serums T4 and T3.
- cholestyramine (Cuemid, Questran), and perhaps other cholesterol-lowering resins, may reduce its absorption; intake of the two drugs should be separated by 5 hours.

▷ *Driving, Hazardous Activities:* No restrictions.

Aviation Note: The use of this drug is *probably not a disqualification* for piloting. Consult a designated Aviation Medical Examiner.

Exposure to Sun: No restrictions.

Exposure to Heat: This drug may decrease individual tolerance to warm environments, increasing discomfort due to heat. Consult your physician if you develop symptoms of overdose during the warm months of the year.

Heavy Exercise or Exertion: Use caution if you have angina (coronary artery disease). This drug may increase the frequency or severity of angina during physical activity.

Discontinuation: This drug must be taken continually on a regular schedule to correct thyroid deficiency. Do not stop it without consulting your physician.

LISINOPRIL (Li SIN oh pril)

Introduced: 1988   **Class:** Antihypertensive, ACE inhibitor
Please see the angiotensin converting enzyme (ACE) inhibitor family profile.

LITHIUM (LITH i um)

Introduced: 1949   **Class:** Antidepressant, mood stabilizer **Prescription:** USA: Yes   **Controlled Drug:** USA: No; Canada: No   **Available as Generic:** USA: Yes; Canada: No

Brand Names: ✤Carbolith, Cibalith-S, ✤Duralith, Eskalith, Eskalith CR, Liskonium, Lithane, ✤Lithizine, Lithobid, Lithonate, Lithotabs

BENEFITS versus RISKS	
Possible Benefits	*Possible Risks*
RAPID REVERSAL OF ACUTE MANIA	VERY NARROW MARGIN OF TREATMENT
STABILIZATION OF MOOD	POTENTIALLY FATAL TOXICITY WITH INADEQUATE MONITORING
Prevention of recurrent depression in "responders"	Infrequent induction of diabetes mellitus, hypothyroidism
	Diabetes insipidus–like syndrome (excessive dilute urine)

▷ **Principal Uses**

As a Single Drug Product: Uses currently included in FDA-approved labeling: (1) Manages bipolar disorder (promptly corrects acute mania and also reduces frequency and severity of recurrent manic-depressive mood swings); (2) used to treat mania; (3) helps control mania.

Other (unlabeled) generally accepted uses: (1) May be helpful in chronic hair-pulling (trichotillomania); (2) can help prevent cluster headaches; (3) may help control aggressive behavior; (4) can have a role in treating Fanconi's aplastic anemia; (5) may be of use in patients who have mood problems that also affect their sex drive.

In the Pipeline: The Health and Human Services secretary has identified a group of medicines to be tested for use in children. Lithium was on that list of the

12 highest-priority medicines to be studied in children (find out more at *www.hhs.gov/news/press/2003pres/20030121.html*). A finding published in the *Journal of Molecular Psychiatry* reported a flawed gene (GRK3) as being related to development of bipolar disorder. This may serve as a new target for treatment of the *cause* of bipolar disorder!

How This Drug Works: Lithium changes the way nerve signals are transmitted and interpreted, influencing emotional status and behavior.

Available Dosage Forms and Strengths

Capsules — 150 mg, 300 mg, 600 mg

Syrup — 8 mEq/5 ml

Tablets — 300 mg

Tablets, prolonged action — 300 mg, 450 mg

▷ **Usual Adult Dosage Ranges:** Mania: 1,800 mg per day, divided into 3 equal doses. Dosing is individualized to get the desired clinical response and a general blood level of 1–1.5 mmol/L.

Usual maintenance dose: When manic symptoms ease, the dose is lowered to obtain blood levels of 0.6 to 1.2 millimole per liter. Typical ongoing doses are 900 to 1,200 mg a day. This total daily dose is divided into equal doses that are given (immediate release forms) 3 or 4 times daily, and sustained release forms are given less often—only TWICE daily.

Note: Actual dose and dosing schedule must be determined for each patient individually.

Conditions Requiring Dosing Adjustments

Liver Function: The liver is minimally involved in the elimination of lithium.

Kidney Function: Frequent and careful side effect monitoring, decreased doses, and more frequent blood levels are prudent. In moderate to severe kidney failure (creatinine clearance of 10–50 ml/min), 50–75% of the usual dose is taken. In severe kidney failure, 25–50% of the usual dose is taken.

▷ **Dosing Instructions:** The capsules may be opened, and regular tablets crushed, and taken with or after meals to reduce stomach upset. The prolonged-action tablets should be swallowed whole and not altered. Always use a measuring cup or measuring spoon for the liguid form. If you forget a dose: take the missed dose as soon as you remember it, unless it's nearly time for your next dose—if that is the case, skip the missed dose and take the next dose right on schedule. Talk with your doctor if you find yourself missing doses.

Usual Duration of Use: Use on a regular schedule for 1 to 3 weeks determines effectiveness in correcting acute mania; several months of continual treatment may be required to correct swings in mood. Long-term use (months to years) requires physician supervision and periodic evaluation of blood levels.

Typical Treatment Goals and Measurements (Outcomes and Markers)

Bipolar disorder: Helps even out the highs and lows often seen in bipolar problems. The general goal is to create a situation where excessive highs or lows no longer feel "normal" and patients are able to return to their appropriate quality of life. Blood levels are kept in a tight range (0.6 to 1.5 mmol/L). Levels are usually checked every 2 months. Thyroid function tests are checked every 3 to 6 months.

Currently a "Drug of Choice"

For the treatment of acute mania in bipolar manic-depressive disorders.

Author's Note: The American Psychiatric Association updated their

1994 treatment guidelines for bipolar disorder (see *AMJP* in References). Lithium and valproate are recommended first for most people.

▷ **This Drug Should Not Be Taken If**
- you had an allergic reaction to it previously.
- you have uncontrolled diabetes or uncorrected hypothyroidism.
- you are breast-feeding your infant.
- you will be unable to comply with the need for regular monitoring of lithium blood levels.
- you have severe kidney failure or heart disease.

▷ **Inform Your Physician Before Taking This Drug If**
- you have a history of a schizophreniclike thought disorder.
- you have any type of organic brain disease or a history of grand mal epilepsy.
- you have diabetes, heart disease, hypothyroidism, or impaired kidney function.
- you are on a salt-restricted diet.
- you are pregnant or planning pregnancy.
- you are taking any diuretic drug or a cortisonelike steroid preparation.
- your blood sodium level is low.
- you will have surgery with general anesthesia or electroconvulsive (ECT) therapy.

Possible Side Effects (natural, expected, and unavoidable drug actions)

Increased thirst and urine volume in 60% of initial users and in 20% of long-term users.

Weight gain in first few months of use.

Drowsiness and lethargy in sensitive individuals.

Metallic taste.

Increased white blood cells—not a sign of infection, but an effect of lithium.

Heart block—frequent but does not usually lead to the medicine being stopped.

Tremor (fine)—frequent (may respond to a beta blocker).

▷ **Possible Adverse Effects** (unusual, unexpected, and infrequent reactions)

If any of the following develop, consult your physician promptly for guidance.

Mild Adverse Effects

Allergic reactions: skin rashes, generalized itching.

Skin dryness, loss of hair—case reports.

Headache, joint pain, dizziness, weakness, blurred vision, ringing in ears, unsteadiness—infrequent.

Sleepwalking or restless leg syndrome—case reports.

Nausea, vomiting, diarrhea—frequent.

Metallic taste—possible.

Edema—possible.

Serious Adverse Effects

"Blackout" spells, confusion, stupor, slurred speech, spasmodic movements of extremities, epilepticlike seizures—case reports to rare.

Abnormal fixed eye position (oculogyric crisis)—case reports.

Abnormal changes in heart rate, rhythm, and wave forms—frequent.

Loss of bladder or rectal control—infrequent.

Diabetes insipidus–like syndrome: excessive dilute urine—infrequent to frequent.

Abnormal movements (may be a sign of toxicity)—rare.
Cerebellar atrophy or neuroleptic malignant syndrome—case reports.
Inflammation of the heart muscle (myocarditis)—case reports.
Pseudotumor cerebri, myasthenia gravis, or systemic lupus erythematosus—
case reports.
Increased platelet counts—possible.
Low thyroid function or abnormally high thyroid function—possible to case
reports.
Elevated blood calcium or blood sugar—rare.
Porphyria or inflammation of the parotid gland—case reports.
Seizures—case reports and certainly with toxicity.
Drug-induced low or high potassium—possible.

▷ **Possible Effects on Sexual Function:**
Decreased libido (blood level of 0.7 to 0.9 mEq/L in one study)—case reports.
Inhibited erection (0.5 to 0.9 mEq/L in one study)—frequent.
Male infertility.
Female breast swelling with milk production—case reports.

▷ **Adverse Effects That May Mimic Natural Diseases or Disorders**
Painful discoloration and coldness of the hands and feet may resemble Raynaud's phenomenon.

Natural Diseases or Disorders That May Be Activated by This Drug
Diabetes mellitus may be worsened. Psoriasis may be intensified. Myasthenia gravis may be induced (one case).

Possible Effects on Laboratory Tests
White blood cell and platelet counts: increased.
Blood alkaline phosphatase (bone isoenzyme): markedly increased in up to
66% of users.
Blood cholesterol level: increased.
Blood parathyroid hormone level: increased.
Blood thyroid stimulating hormone (TSH) level: increased.
Blood thyroid hormone (T3 and T4) levels: decreased.
Blood uric acid level: decreased.
Blood bromide, calcium or glucose levels: increased.
Blood potassium level: increased or decreased.

CAUTION
1. The blood level required for this drug to work is close to the level that can
   cause toxic effects. Periodic blood lithium levels are mandatory. Follow
   instructions about drug dose and periodic blood tests.
2. Lithium should be stopped at the first signs of toxicity: drowsiness, sluggishness, unsteadiness, tremor, muscle twitching, vomiting, or diarrhea.
3. Some major causes of lithium toxicity are:
   • accidental overdose (may be due to inadequate blood level checks)
   • impaired kidney function
   • salt restriction
   • inadequate fluid intake, dehydration
   • concurrent use of diuretics
   • intercurrent illness
   • childbirth (rapid decrease in kidney clearance of lithium)
   • initiation of treatment with a new drug
   • over-the-counter preparations that contain iodides (some cough prod-
     ucts and vitamin-mineral supplements) should be avoided because of
     the added antithyroid effect when taken with lithium.

- low blood sodium can lead to toxic lithium effects with a "normal" lithium level.

Precautions for Use

By Infants and Children: Safety and effectiveness for those under 12 years of age are not established. Follow your physician's instructions exactly.

By Those Over 60 Years of Age: Treatment should start with a "test" dose of 75 to 150 mg daily. Observe closely for early indications of toxic effects, especially if on a low-salt diet and using diuretics. Increased risk of Parkinsonian reactions (abnormal gait and movements); coma can develop without warning symptoms.

▷ **Advisability of Use During Pregnancy**

Pregnancy Category: D. See Pregnancy Risk Categories at the back of this book.

Animal Studies: Cleft palate reported in mice; eye, ear, and palate defects reported in rats.

Human Studies: Adequate studies of pregnant women are not available, but cardiovascular defects and goiter in newborn infants (of mothers using lithium) have been reported. If the infant's blood level of lithium approaches the toxic range before delivery, the newborn may suffer the "floppy infant" syndrome: weakness, lethargy, unresponsiveness, low body temperature, weak cry, and poor feeding ability.

Avoid use of drug during the first 3 months. Use only if clearly necessary during the final 6 months. Monitor mother's blood lithium levels carefully to avoid possible toxicity.

Advisability of Use If Breast-Feeding

Presence of this drug in breast milk: Yes, in significant amounts.

Avoid drug or refrain from nursing.

Habit-Forming Potential: None.

Effects of Overdose: Drowsiness, weakness, lack of coordination, nausea, vomiting, diarrhea, muscle spasms, blurred vision, dizziness, staggering gait, slurred speech, confusion, stupor, coma, cerebellar atrophy, seizures.

Possible Effects of Long-Term Use: Hypothyroidism (5%), goiter, reduced sugar tolerance, diabetes insipidus–like syndrome, serious kidney damage.

Suggested Periodic Examinations While Taking This Drug (at physician's discretion)

Regular determinations of blood lithium levels are absolutely essential. Time to sample blood for lithium level: 12 hours after evening dose or in the morning, just before next dose. Therapeutic range: 0.8 to 1.5 MEq/L (acute) and 0.6 to 1.2 (maintenance). Levels should be checked every 2 months.

Periodic evaluation of thyroid gland size and function.

Complete blood cell counts.

Kidney function tests.

▷ **While Taking This Drug, Observe the Following**

Foods: Maintain a normal diet; do not restrict your use of salt.

Herbal Medicines or Minerals: This drug may cause increased calcium. Talk to your doctor BEFORE taking any calcium supplements. Herbs that have a diuretic or potassium-losing effect may lead to lithium toxicity. Many herbal products are actually combination products: read labels carefully to look for guarana and mate as they contain caffeine which may lower lithium levels.

Beverages: Excessive caffeine may lower lithium levels. It is prudent to drink at least 8 to 12 glasses of water or other liquids daily. This drug may be taken with milk.

▷ *Alcohol:* Use with caution. May have an increased intoxicating effect. Avoid alcohol completely if any symptoms of lithium toxicity develop.

Tobacco Smoking: Lithium may increase sensitivity to nicotine. I advise everyone to quit smoking.

Marijuana Smoking: Possible increase in apathy, lethargy, drowsiness, or sluggishness; accentuation of lithium-induced tremor; possible increased risk of precipitating psychotic behavior.

▷ *Other Drugs*

Lithium may ***increase*** the effects of
- tricyclic antidepressants (see Drug Classes).

Lithium ***taken concurrently*** with
- ACE inhibitors (see Drug Classes) such as captopril (Capoten) may increase lithium levels by as much as 3 times the level prior to combination therapy.
- calcium channel blockers (see Drug Classes), such as diltiazem, may cause neurotoxicity or mania.
- carbamazepine (Tegretol) may result in neurotoxicity.
- chlorpromazine (Thorazine, etc.) and other phenothiazines (see Drug Classes) may decrease lithium or phenothiazine therapeutic effects.
- cisplatin may cause changes in lithium levels; level checks are prudent.
- citalopram (Celexa) may enhance the effect of citalopram on serotonin.
- clozapine (Clozaril) may result in serious agranulocytosis, delirium, and neuroleptic malignant syndrome; do not combine these medicines.
- diazepam (Valium) may cause hypothermia.
- diuretics (see Diuretic Drug Classes) may lead to lithium toxicity.
- filgrastim (Neupogen) may result in a greater-than-expected increase in white blood cell numbers.
- fludrocortisone (Florinef) may result in loss of the mineralocorticoid benefits of fludrocortisone.
- fluoxetine (Prozac) may result in neurotoxicity.
- fluvoxamine (Luvox) may result in increased lithium levels and toxicity.
- haloperidol (Haldol) or with other neuroleptics may result in decreased beneficial effects from both medicines.
- levofloxacin (Levaquin) may lead to kidney impairment and increased lithium levels and toxicity.
- methyldopa (Aldomet, etc.) is usually well tolerated; however, it may cause a severe neurotoxic reaction in susceptible individuals. These combinations should be used very cautiously.
- metronidazole (Flagyl) may lead to lithium toxicity.
- monoamine oxidase (MAO) inhibitors (see Drug Classes) may result in serotonin syndrome and potential fatality.
- nicotine (various brands) may cause supersensitivity to nicotine.
- sibutramine (Meridia) may cause an increased risk of serotonin syndrome. DO NOT COMBINE.
- vasartan (Diovan) may cause lithium toxicity. Careful follow-up of lithium levels and patient condition are very important.
- verapamil (Calan, Isoptin) may cause unpredictable effects; both lithium toxicity and decreased lithium blood levels have been reported.

The following drugs may ***increase*** the effects of lithium:
- aspirin (various).

- bumetanide (Bumex).
- celecoxib (Celebrex), rofecoxib (Vioxx) or valdecoxib (Bextra).
- ethacrynic acid (Edecrin).
- fluoxetine (Prozac).
- furosemide (Lasix, etc.).
- ibuprofen (Motrin, others), indomethacin (Indocin) and other nonsteroidal anti-inflammatory drugs (NSAIDs).
- losartan (Cozaar, Hyzaar) and perhaps other angiotensin II inhibitors.
- piroxicam (Feldene) or any nonsteroidal anti-inflammatory drug (NSAID—see Drug Classes).
- thiazide diuretics (see Drug Classes).

The following drugs may *decrease* the effects of lithium:

- acetazolamide (Diamox, etc.).
- calcitonin (various).
- sodium bicarbonate.
- theophylline (Theo-Dur, etc.) and related drugs.

▷ *Driving, Hazardous Activities:* This drug may impair mental alertness, judgment, physical coordination and reaction time. Restrict activities as necessary.

Aviation Note: The use of this drug *is a disqualification* for piloting. Consult a designated Aviation Medical Examiner.

Exposure to Sun: No restrictions.

Exposure to Heat: Excessive sweating can cause significant depletion of salt and water and resultant lithium toxicity. Avoid sauna baths.

Occurrence of Unrelated Illness: Fever, sweating, vomiting or diarrhea can result in significant alterations of blood and tissue lithium concentrations. Close monitoring of your physical condition and blood lithium levels is needed to prevent serious toxicity.

Discontinuation: Sudden discontinuation does not cause withdrawal symptoms. Avoid premature discontinuation; some individuals may require continual treatment for up to a year to achieve maximal response. Discontinuation by "responders" may result in recurrence of either mania or depression. Lithium should be discontinued if symptoms of brain toxicity appear or if an uncorrectable diabetes insipidus–like syndrome develops.

LOMEFLOXACIN (loh me FLOX a sin)

Please see the fluoroquinolone antibiotic family profile.

LOPERAMIDE (loh PER a mide)

Introduced: 1977   **Class:** Antidiarrheal   **Prescription:** USA: Yes   **Controlled Drug:** USA: No; Canada: No   **Available as Generic:** Yes

Brand Names: Anti-Diarrheal, Apo-loperamide, Diarrid, ♣Dom-Loperamide, Imodium, Imodium AD, ♣Imodium Advanced, Kaopectate 1-D, Maalox A/D, Pepto Diarrhea Control

BENEFITS versus RISKS	
Possible Benefits	*Possible Risks*
EFFECTIVE RELIEF OF INTESTINAL CRAMPING AND DIARRHEA	Drowsiness
	Constipation
	May cause serious colon problems (toxic megacolon)

▷ **Principal Uses**

As a Single Drug Product: Uses currently included in FDA-approved labeling: (1) Control of cramping and diarrhea associated with acute gastroenteritis and chronic enteritis and colitis and chronic diarrhea; (2) used to reduce the volume of discharge from ileostomies; (3) irritable bowel syndrome that has failed to respond to dietary supplements; (4) traveler's diarrhea.

Other (unlabeled) generally accepted uses: (1) decreases unformed stools in Shigella diarrhea.

As a Combination Drug Product [CD]: Loperamide is available in Canada combined with simethicone. Simethicone works to decrease gas.

How This Drug Works: Acts directly on the nerve supply of the gastrointestinal tract, decreases secretions and relieves cramping and diarrhea. When combined with simethicone, simethicone acts to stop gas.

Available Dosage Forms and Strengths

Capsules — 2 mg

Liquid (4.07% alcohol) — 0.2 mg/5 ml

Liquid (5.25% alcohol) — 1 mg/5 ml

Tablets, combination — 2 mg simethicone, 125 mg of simethicone

Tablets — 2 mg

▷ **Recommended Dosage Ranges:** *For acute diarrhea*: 4 mg initially (2 capsules) and then 2 mg after each unformed stool until diarrhea is controlled. Stop the medicine and call your doctor if the diarrrhea does not decrease in 48 hours (medicine should be stopped if this happens).

For chronic diarrhea: 4 mg immediately, then 2 mg taken after each unformed stool until the diarrhea is successfully controlled. The dosing should then be individualized. Maximum daily dose is 16 mg. If your diarrhea is not controlled after 10 days of the maximum dose of 16 mg, call your doctor.

Pediatric dosing: NOT recommended for children under 2 years old. Two- to 5-year-olds can be given 1 mg 3 times a day on the first day (13–30 kg); 6- to 8-year-olds can have 2 mg twice daily on the first day (20–30 kg); 8- to 12-year-olds can have 2 mg 3 times daily (greater than 30 kg). Follow-up doses on the next day are 1 mg per 10 kg of body mass, up to the maximum daily doses on day 1. If diarrhea persists, call your doctor.

Note: Actual dose and schedule must be determined for each patient individually.

Conditions Requiring Dosing Adjustments

Liver Function: Dosing adjustments for patients with liver compromise are not needed. Half of a given dose is removed unchanged in the feces.

Kidney Function: Changes in dosing are not indicated in kidney compromise.

▷ **Dosing Instructions:** The capsule may be opened and taken on an empty stomach or with food if stomach upset occurs. Liquid form should be taken using a medicine spoon or calibrated medicine dosing cup. If you forget a dose: Take the missed dose as soon as you remember it, unless it's nearly time for your next dose—if that is the case, skip the missed dose and take the next dose right on schedule. Talk with your doctor if you find yourself missing doses.

Usual Duration of Use: Use on a regular schedule for 48 hours determines effectiveness in controlling acute diarrhea; continual use for 10 days may be needed to evaluate its effectiveness in controlling chronic diarrhea. If diarrhea persists, call your doctor.

Typical Treatment Goals and Measurements (Outcomes and Markers)

Diarrhea: The goal is to at least decrease the frequency of stools and ideally to return "normal" bowel patterns and stool consistency. In patients with ostomies, the amount of drainage should decrease.

▷ **This Drug Should Not Be Taken If**
- you have had an allergic reaction to it previously.
- constipation is never acceptable for you.
- it is prescribed for a child under 2 years of age.

▷ **Inform Your Physician Before Taking This Drug If**
- you have a history of liver disease or impaired liver function.
- you have regional enteritis or ulcerative colitis.
- you have swelling of the abdomen, or become constipated.
- you develop swelling (distention) of the abdomen while taking this medicine.
- you have acute dysentery (increased temperature and blood in the stools).

Possible Side Effects (natural, expected, and unavoidable drug actions)

Drowsiness, constipation. Retention of urine.

▷ **Possible Adverse Effects** (unusual, unexpected, and infrequent reactions)

If any of the following develop, consult your physician promptly for guidance.

Mild Adverse Effects

Allergic reaction: skin rash.

Fatigue, dizziness—rare.

Reduced appetite, cramps, dry mouth, nausea, vomiting, stomach pain, bloating—infrequent.

Serious Adverse Effects

"Toxic megacolon" (distended, immobile colon with fluid retention) may develop while treating acute ulcerative colitis—possible.

Hallucinations—case reports.

Movement disorders (akathisia, tardive dyskinesia, acute dystonia)—case reports.

Increased blood sugar—possible.

Necrotizing enterocolitis or paralytic ileus—rare.

▷ **Possible Effects on Sexual Function:** None reported.

Possible Effects on Laboratory Tests: None reported.

CAUTION

1. Do not exceed recommended doses.
2. If treating chronic diarrhea, promptly report development of bloating, abdominal distention, nausea, vomiting, constipation, or abdominal pain.

Precautions for Use

By Infants and Children: Do not use in those under 2 years of age. Follow your physician's instructions exactly regarding dose. Watch for drowsiness, irritability, personality changes, and altered behavior.

By Those Over 60 Years of Age: Small starting doses are needed, as you may be more sensitive to the sedative and constipating effects of this drug.

▷ **Advisability of Use During Pregnancy**
Pregnancy Category: B. See Pregnancy Risk Categories at the back of this book.
Animal Studies: No birth defects found in rat and rabbit studies.
Human Studies: Adequate studies of pregnant women are not available.
   Use sparingly and only if clearly needed. Ask your physician for guidance.

Advisability of Use If Breast-Feeding
Presence of this drug in breast milk: Small, clinically insignificant amounts.
Talk with your doctor about the BENEFITS versus RISKS of using this medicine and nursing. Described as safe by one source.

Habit-Forming Potential: Physical dependence has occurred in monkeys, but there have been no reports in humans.

Effects of Overdose: Drowsiness, lethargy, depression, dry mouth.

Possible Effects of Long-Term Use: None identified.

Suggested Periodic Examinations While Taking This Drug (at physician's discretion)
Decreased frequency of stools within 48 hours. Check for movement disorders with chronic use.

▷ **While Taking This Drug, Observe the Following**
Foods: No restrictions. Follow prescribed diet.
Herbal Medicines or Minerals: Numerous herbal medicines have German Commission E monograph indications for diarrhea. Examples include: bilberry fruit, oak bark, psyllium seed husk, tormentil root, and uzara root. Use of these herbals with loperamide has not been studied. Electrolyte replacement (sodium, potassium, etc.) can be critical in ongoing diarrhea, especially if you are taking digoxin and other electrolyte-sensitive medicines. St. John's wort led to a case of delirium in one patient. Talk to your doctor BEFORE adding any herbal medicine to loperamide therapy.
Beverages: No restrictions, other than your doctor's recommendations regarding diet.
▷ *Alcohol:* Use with caution. This drug may increase the depressant action of alcohol on the brain.
Tobacco Smoking: No interactions expected. I advise everyone to quit smoking.
▷ *Other Drugs* No significant drug interactions reported.
▷ *Driving, Hazardous Activities:* This drug may cause drowsiness or dizziness. Restrict activities as necessary.
Aviation Note: The use of this drug *is a disqualification* for piloting. Consult a designated Aviation Medical Examiner.
Exposure to Sun: No restrictions.

LORATADINE (lor AT a deen)

Introduced: 1992   **Class:**   Antihistamines, nonsedating
Please see the minimally sedating antihistamines family profile.

LORAZEPAM (lor A za pam)

Introduced: 1977   **Class:**   Anxiolytic, mild tranquilizer, hypnotic, benzodiazepine   **Prescription:**   USA: Yes   **Controlled Drug:**   USA: C-IV*; Canada: No   **Available as Generic:**   USA: Yes; Canada: Yes

Brand Names: Alzapam, ✿Apo-Lorazepam, Ativan, ✿Dom-Lorazepam, Loraz, Lorazepam Intensol, ✿Novo-Lorazepam, ✿Nu-Loraz, ✿PMS-Loraz

---

BENEFITS versus RISKS

Possible Benefits	*Possible Risks*
RELIEF OF ANXIETY AND NERVOUS TENSION	Habit-forming potential with prolonged use
NOT CHANGED SIGNIFICANTLY INTO ACTIVE DRUG FORMS IN THE LIVER	Minor impairment of mental functions
Wide margin of safety with therapeutic doses	Blood cell, movement or liver disorders
	Dose-related respiratory depression
	Withdrawal symptoms if abruptly stopped

▷ **Principal Uses**

  As a Single Drug Product: Uses currently included in FDA-approved labeling: (1) Helps treat anxiety; (2) used in surgical cases to help in delivering effective anesthesia; (3) used intravenously as a sedative.

  Other (unlabeled) generally accepted uses: (1) Used to help prevent the severe symptoms of alcohol detoxification (delirium tremens or DTs); (2) used under the tongue to treat serial seizures in children; (3) can be used to promote amnesia in patients who must take chemotherapy and have suffered vomiting; (4) used to relieve insomnia.

  In the Pipeline: The Health and Human Services secretary has identified a group of medicines to be tested for use in children. Lorazepam was on that list of the 12 highest-priority medicines to be studied in children (find out more at *www.hhs.gov/news/press/2003021.htm*).

How This Drug Works: Attaches to a specific site (GABA-A receptor) in the brain and enables gamma-aminobutyric acid to inhibit activity of nervous tissue. Drugs in this class also reduce the time it takes to fall asleep and the number of awakenings during the night.

Available Dosage Forms and Strengths

  Injection — 2 mg/ml, 4 mg/ml
  Oral solution — 2 mg/ml
  Sublingual tablet — 0.5 mg, 1 mg, 2 mg
  Tablet — 0.5 mg, 1 mg, 2 mg

▷ **Recommended Dosage Ranges** (Actual dose and dosing schedule must be determined for each patient individually.)

  Infants and Children: Safety and effectiveness in those under 18 years of age are not established for injection. Has been used in 1- to 4-mg doses under the tongue for treatment of serial seizures in children.

---

*See Schedules of Controlled Drugs at the back of this book.

18 to 60 Years of Age:

Sedation and anxiety: Therapy is started with 1 to 2 mg per day in 2 to 3 divided doses. Doses may be increased as needed and tolerated to the usual maintenance dose of 2 to 6 mg daily in divided doses. The maximum dose is 10 mg daily in 2 to 3 divided doses.

Insomnia: 1 to 3 mg at bedtime.

Over 60 Years of Age:

Sedation and anxiety: Therapy is started with 0.5 to 1 mg in divided doses. The initial dose should not exceed 2 mg daily.

Insomnia: 0.5 to 1 mg at bedtime.

Conditions Requiring Dosing Adjustments

Liver Function: The dose must be decreased in liver compromise, and the drug should not be used in liver failure. Use of the lowest effective dose is recommended for those with mild to moderate liver failure.

Kidney Function: The drug should not be used in kidney failure. In mild to moderate kidney compromise, the dose must be decreased and the lowest effective dose is recommended.

▷ **Dosing Instructions:** The tablet may be crushed and taken on an empty stomach or with milk or food. Do not stop this drug abruptly if it has been taken for more than 4 weeks. Oral solution should be dosed using a measured dose cup or measuring spoon. If you forget a dose: take the missed dose as soon as you remember it, unless it's nearly time for your next dose—if that is the case, skip the missed dose and take the next dose right on schedule. DO NOT double doses. Talk with your doctor if you find yourself missing doses.

Usual Duration of Use: Use on a regular schedule for 3 to 5 days usually determines effectiveness in relieving moderate anxiety or insomnia. Continual use should be limited to 1 to 3 weeks. Consult your physician on a regular basis.

Author's Note: The National Institute of Mental Health has a new information page on anxiety. It can be found on the World Wide Web (*www.nimh.nih.gov/anxiety*).

Typical Treatment Goals and Measurements (Outcomes and Markers)

Anxiety: Goals for anxiety tend to be more vague and subjective than hypertension or cholesterol. Frequently, the patient (in conjunction with physician assessment) will largely decide if anxiety has been modified to a successful extent. Sleep patterns typically improve with decreased anxiety. The ability of the patient to return to normal activities is a hallmark of successful treatment.

Possible Advantages of This Drug

More direct elimination and lack of active forms may be of benefit in the elderly. Increased lipid solubility is of benefit when the drug is used to treat acute alcohol withdrawal.

▷ **This Drug Should Not Be Taken If**

- you have had an allergic reaction to any dose form or any component of the dose previously.
- you have a primary depression or psychosis.
- you have excessively low blood pressure.
- you have narrow-angle glaucoma.

▷ **Inform Your Physician Before Taking This Drug If**

- you are allergic to any benzodiazepine (see Drug Classes).
- you have a history of alcoholism or drug abuse.

- you are prone to respiratory depression.
- you are pregnant or planning pregnancy.
- you have impaired liver or kidney function.
- you have a history of low white blood cell counts.
- you have asthma, emphysema, epilepsy, or myasthenia gravis.
- you take other prescription or nonprescription medicines that were not discussed with your doctor when lorazepam was prescribed.

Possible Side Effects (natural, expected, and unavoidable drug actions)
Sedation, "hangover" effects on the day following bedtime use.

▷ **Possible Adverse Effects** (unusual, unexpected, and infrequent reactions)
If any of the following develop, consult your physician promptly for guidance.
Mild Adverse Effects
Allergic reactions: rashes, hives—rare.
Dizziness, amnesia, insomnia (rebound), fainting, confusion, blurred vision, slurred speech, constipation, and sweating—infrequent.
Ringing in the ears (associated with withdrawal), decreased hearing ability—infrequent.
Serious Adverse Effects
Allergic reactions: liver damage with jaundice (see Glossary)—case reports.
Low white blood cell counts (leukopenia)—rare.
Paradoxical excitement and rage—case reports.
Low blood pressure—rare.
Hallucinations (transient)—rare.
Porphyria, seizures, or abnormal body movements—case reports.
Respiratory depression—dose-related.

▷ **Possible Effects on Sexual Function:** Decreased male libido or impotence—case reports.

Possible Effects on Laboratory Tests
White blood cell counts: decreased.
Liver function tests: increased SGPT, SGOT, and LDH.

CAUTION
1. This drug should **not** be stopped abruptly if it has been taken continually for more than 4 weeks.
2. Over-the-counter medicines with antihistamines can cause excessive sedation if taken with lorazepam.
3. Lorazepam should **not** be combined with alcohol. This combination will worsen adverse mental and coordination decreases and increase lorazepam levels.

Precautions for Use
By Infants and Children: Safety and effectiveness for those under 18 years of age are not established. Lorazepam has been used under the tongue in children with serial seizures.
By Those Over 60 Years of Age: Small doses are indicated. Watch for lethargy, fatigue, weakness, and paradoxical agitation, anger, hostility, and rage.

▷ **Advisability of Use During Pregnancy**
Pregnancy Category: D. See Pregnancy Risk Categories at the back of this book.
Animal Studies: Cleft palate has been reported in mice; skeletal defects in rats with similar drugs in this class.

Human Studies: Adequate studies of pregnant women are not available.

Frequent use in late pregnancy can result in "floppy infant" syndrome in the newborn: weakness, depressed breathing, and low body temperature. Avoid use during the entire pregnancy.

Advisability of Use If Breast-Feeding

Presence of this drug in breast milk: Yes.

Avoid drug or refrain from nursing. Discuss premedication use with your doctor.

Habit-Forming Potential: This drug can cause psychological and/or physical dependence (see Glossary).

Effects of Overdose: Marked drowsiness, weakness, feeling of drunkenness, staggering gait, depression of breathing, stupor progressing to coma.

Possible Effects of Long-Term Use: Psychological or physical dependence, rare liver toxicity.

Suggested Periodic Examinations While Taking This Drug (at physician's discretion)

Liver function tests.

Complete blood cell counts. Mental status check. Respiratory status check in children.

▷ **While Taking This Drug, Observe the Following**

Foods: No restrictions.

Herbal Medicines or Minerals: Kava, danshen, skull cap, and valerian may exacerbate central nervous system depression (avoid this combination). Dong Quai may slow removal of lorazepam from the body and increase risk of central nervous system depression. Kola nut, Siberian ginseng, guarana, mate, ephedra, hawthorn, and ma huang may blunt the benefits of this medicine. While St. John's wort is indicated for anxiety, it is also thought to increase (induce) cytochrome P450 enzymes and will tend to blunt lorazepam effectiveness.

Beverages: Avoid excessive caffeine-containing beverages: coffee, tea and cola.

▷ *Alcohol:* Avoid this combination. Alcohol increases depression of mental function, further worsens coordination, and causes increased lorazepam levels.

Tobacco Smoking: Heavy smoking may reduce the calming action of this drug. I advise everyone to quit smoking.

Marijuana Smoking: Additive drowsiness and impaired physical performance.

▷ *Other Drugs*

Lorazepam *taken concurrently* with

- clozapine (Clozaril) may result in marked sedation and muscular incoordination.
- heparin may result in increased effects of lorazepam (increased free fraction).
- lithium (Lithobid, others) may result in a lowering of body temperature (hypothermic reaction).
- oxycodone (Percocet, others) and other central nervous system depressants may result in additive CNS or respiratory depression.
- phenytoin (Dilantin) or fosphenytoin (Cerebyx) may result in altered phenytoin or lorazepam levels.
- quetiapine (Seroquel) may increase lorazepam levels. Watch for increased drowsiness, dizziness, or movement trouble.

The following drugs may *increase* the effects of lorazepam:
- macrolide antibiotics (see Drug Classes).
- probenecid (Benemid)—may result in a 50% increased lorazepam level; decreased lorazepam doses or an increased time between doses are indicated.
- valproic acid (Depakene)—decreased doses or an increased time between doses may be needed.

The following drugs may *decrease* the effects of lorazepam:
- birth control pills (oral contraceptives).
- caffeine, amphetamines, or other stimulants.
- theophylline (Theo-Dur, others).

▷ *Driving, Hazardous Activities:* This drug can impair alertness and coordination. Restrict activities as necessary.

Aviation Note: The use of this drug *is a disqualification* for piloting. Consult a designated Aviation Medical Examiner.

Exposure to Sun: No restrictions.

Discontinuation: Do **not** stop this drug suddenly if it has been taken for over 4 weeks. Consult your doctor about a gradual tapering of dose.

LOSARTAN (loh SAR tan)

Please see the angiotensin II receptor antagonist family profile.

LOVASTATIN (loh vah STA tin)

Author's Note: Because of the release of the ADVOCATE study (see References) and other data, the newly available niacin/lovastatin (Advicor) will replace lovastatin.

LOW-MOLECULAR-WEIGHT HEPARINS (HEP ar inz)

Introduced: (Europe 1991) 1998, (includes latest PI approval data)   **Class:** Anticoagulant   **Prescription:**   USA: Yes   **Controlled Drug:**   USA: No; Canada: No   **Available as Generic:**   USA: No; Canada: No

Brand Names: Ardeparin: Normiflo; Dalteparin: Fragmin; Enoxaparin: Lovenox; Tinzaparin: Innohep

Author's Note: Because potential outpatient use trends are increasing, information in this profile will be broadened in subsequent editions. A statement has been released from the American Heart Association on heparin use with low-molecular-weight heparins.

MACROLIDE ANTIBIOTIC FAMILY (ma KRO lied)

Azithromycin (a zith roh MY sin) **Clarithromycin** (KLAR ith roh my sin) **Erythromycin** (er ith roh MY sin)

Introduced: 1991, 1991, 1952, respectively   **Class:**   Anti-infective, antibiotic, macrolide antibiotic   **Prescription:**   USA: Yes   **Controlled**

Drug: USA: No; Canada: No   **Available as Generic:**   Azithromycin: No; clarithromycin: No; erythromycin: Yes

Brand Names: Azithromycin: Zithromax; Clarithromycin: Biaxin, Biaxin XL (Biaxin XL Pac), Prevpac [CD]; Erythromycin: AK-Mycin Ophthalmic, Akne-Mycin, ✤Apo-Erythro Base, ✤Apo-Erythro E-C, ✤Apo-Erythro-ES, ✤Apo-Erythro-S, A/T/S, Benzamycin [CD], C-Solve 2, E.E.S., E.E.S. 200, E.E.S. 400, Emgel, E-Mycin, E-Mycin Controlled Release, E-Mycin E, E-Mycin 333, Eramycin, ✤Erybid, ERYC, Erycette, Eryderm, Erygel, Erymax, EryPed, Eryphar, Ery-Tab, Erythrocin, ✤Erythromid, E-Solve 2, Ethril, ETS-2%, Ilosone, Ilotycin, ✤Novo-Rythro, PCE, Pediamycin, ✤Pediazole [CD], ✤PMS-Erythromycin, Robimycin, Sans-Acne, SK-Erythromycin, Staticin, ✤Stievamycin, T-Stat, ✤Wyamycin E, Wyamycin S

BENEFITS versus RISKS

Possible Benefits	*Possible Risks*
EFFECTIVE TREATMENT OF INFECTIONS due to susceptible microorganisms	Allergic reactions, mild and infrequent
MAY ACTUALLY HAVE A ROLE IN PREVENTING OR TREATING SOME HEART ATTACKS WHERE *CHLAMYDIA PNEUMONIAE* IS PRESENT	Liver reaction (most common with erythromycin estolate)
	Mild gastrointestinal symptoms
	Drug-induced colitis
	Superinfections

▷ **Principal Uses**

As a Single Drug Product: Uses currently included in FDA-approved labeling: Treatment of (1) skin and skin structure infections (such as acne and *Streptococcus*); (2) upper and lower respiratory tract infections, including "strep" throat, diphtheria, and several types of pneumonia; (3) gonorrhea and syphilis; (4) amebic dysentery (erythromycin); (5) Legionnaire's disease (erythromycin); (6) long-term prevention of recurrences of rheumatic fever (erythromycin)—effective use requires the precise identification of the causative organism and determination of its sensitivity to a macrolide antibiotic; (7) treatment of mycoplasma pneumonia; (8) listeriosis; (9) neonatal conjunctivitis (erythromycin); (10) treatment of ear infections (otitis media) (all); (11) treatment of AIDS-related *Mycobacterium avium-intracellulare* (all); (12) treatment of *Chlamydia trachomatis* urethritis (azithromycin); (13) therapy of *Helicobacter pylori* duodenal ulcers in combination with omeprazole (clarithromycin); (14) prevention of bacterial endocarditis in people allergic to penicillin.

Author's Note: An Agency for Health Care Policy and Research (AHCPR) study found that most patients who were 60 or younger obtained the same outcomes and significantly reduced costs when erythromycin was used to treat community-acquired pneumonia versus other antibiotics. Biaxin XL is presently only approved for bronchitis, maxillary sinusitis, and community-acquired pneumonia due to susceptible organisms in adults. Please note that resistant *Streptococcus* is a growing threat. In some areas, half of these bacteria are resistant to macrolide antibiotics.

Other (unlabeled) generally accepted uses: (1) Treatment of early Lyme disease (erythromycin; azithromycin is an alternative drug); (2) erythromycin helps sterilize the bowel before surgical procedures; (3) may help threatened preterm labor if the cause is Ureaplasma organisms (erythromycin);

(4) helps impetigo (erythromycin); (5) azithromycin or clarithromycin are second choices for Legionnaire's disease; (6) early azithromycin therapy can reduce severity of gum (gingival) hyperplasia caused by cyclosporine; (7) can help some cases of stomach slowness in diabetics (gastroparesis); (8) may treat or prevent some heart attacks where *Chlamydia pneumoniae* is present; (9) erythromycin has shown some efficacy in cholera; (10) combined use of clarithromycin with a proton pump inhibitor (see Drug Classes) may work to eradicate *Helicobacter pylori* in its role in causing ulcers; (11) **new combination treatment results of azithromycin (Zithromax) taken with chloroquine in malaria patients led to a 96% symptom prevention**.

As a Combination Drug Product [CD]: Clarithromycin is available in combination with amoxicillin and lansoprazole. Since refractory ulcers are often actually *Helicobacter pylori* infections, the combination works to kill the bacteria and lower acid production. Erythromycin is available in combination with sulfisoxazole (Pediazole). This combination can be useful in patients who are allergic to penicillin.

In the Pipeline: Clarithromycin in combination with 20 mg of rabeprazole (Aciphex) twice daily worked to eradicate *Helicobacter pylori* in 91.4% of patients in one study (see Mario, F.D. in Sources). A larger study (1,200 patients) will be undertaken by Pfizer to assess the effects of combination therapy of malaria using chloroquine and azithromycin (Zithromax).

How These Drugs Work: They prevent growth and multiplication of susceptible organisms by interfering with their formation of essential proteins.

Available Dosage Forms and Strengths

Azithromycin:
Oral suspension — 100 mg/5 ml, 200 mg/5 ml
Tablet — 600 mg

Clarithromycin:
Oral suspension granules — 125 mg/5 ml, 185.5 mg/5ml or 250 mg/5 ml
Tablets — 250 mg, 500 mg
Tablets, extended release — 500 mg

Erythromycin:
Capsules — 125 mg, 250 mg
Capsules, enteric coated — 125 mg, 250 mg
Drops — 100 mg/ml
Eye ointment — 5 mg/g
Gel — 2%
Oral suspension — 125 mg/5 ml, 250 mg/5 ml
Skin ointment — 2%
Tablets — 250 mg, 500 mg
Tablets, chewable — 125 mg, 200 mg, 250 mg
Tablets, delayed release — 250 mg, 333 mg
Tablets, dispersible (Canada) — 500 mg
Tablets, enteric coated — 250 mg, 333 mg, 500 mg
Tablets, film coated — 250 mg, 500 mg
Topical solution — 1.5%, 2%

▷ **Recommended Dosage Ranges** (Actual dose and schedule must be determined for each patient individually.)

Infants and Children:

Azithromycin: For otitis media (6 months and older)—New dosing provides for a single dose regimen of 30 mg per kg of the suspension form. For example: a 22-pound child would be dosed based on a 10 kg weight and would be given a 7.5 ml (one-and-a-half teaspoonful) dose of the 200 mg/5 ml suspension (300 mg total dose); or a 3-day regimen of 10 mg per kg of body mass for 3 days. Other options include 10 mg per kg of body mass as a single dose on the first day (up to 500 mg), followed by 5 mg per kg of body mass (up to 250 mg) on days 2–5. For pharyngitis—12 mg per kg of body mass (up to 500 mg) daily for 5 days.

Clarithromycin: When used to treat otitis media (caused by *Haemophilus influenzae, M. catarrhalis* or *Strep. pneumoniae*) in children, the dose is 7.5 mg per kg of body mass twice daily, up to a maximum of 500 mg twice a day for 10 days. For Mycobacterium avium-intracellulare complex infections in HIV-positive children, the dose is 7.5 mg per kg of body mass twice daily, to a maximum of 500 mg twice a day. If this dose is successful, therapy is continued for life. Extended release (XL) form has not yet been evaluated in children.

Erythromycin: In pediatrics, oral erythromycin is usually given at a dose of 30 to 50 mg per kg of body mass per day and is divided into 3 or 4 doses. For some very severe infections, the dose is doubled.

12 to 60 Years of Age:

Azithromycin (16 to 60 years of age): For pharyngitis/tonsillitis, bronchitis, pneumonia and skin infections—500 mg as a single dose on the first day and then 250 mg once daily on days 2–4 for a total dose of 1.5 g. For *Helicobacter pylori*—500 mg daily for 7 days. For nongonococcal urethritis and cervicitis—a single 1 g (1,000 mg) dose.

Clarithromycin: For pharyngitis/tonsillitis—250 mg every 12 hours for 10 days. For maxillary sinusitis—500 mg every 12 hours for 14 days. For acute bronchitis—250 to 500 mg every 12 hours for 7 to 14 days. For pneumonia—250–500 mg every 12 hours for 7 to 14 days. For skin infections—250 mg every 12 hours for 7 to 14 days. Biaxin XL treats bronchitis (sudden or acute exacerbation of chronic bronchitis) in adults with two 500 mg tablets (1,000 mg), once a day for 7 days. Sudden or acute maxillary sinusitis is treated using two 500 mg tablets for 14 days.

Erythromycin: 250 mg every 6 hours, or 500 mg every 12 hours according to nature and severity of infection. Total daily dose should not exceed 4 g. For endocarditis prophylaxis (stearate oral form): 1 gram is given 2 hours before procedure and 500 mg 6 hours later.

Over 60 Years of Age:

Azithromycin: Same as 16 to 60 years of age. If liver or kidney function is limited, the dose must be reduced.

Clarithromycin: Same as 12 to 60 years of age. Dose must be reduced in kidney compromise.

Erythromycin: Same as usual adult dosing range. If liver or kidney function is limited, dose must be reduced.

Conditions Requiring Dosing Adjustments

Liver Function: These drugs are metabolized in the liver and will accumulate in patients with liver compromise. Decreased doses may be needed. They should be used with caution by patients with biliary tract disease. Clarithromycin does not need to be adjusted for patients with liver problems if kidney function is normal.

Kidney Function: No dosing changes are needed for azithromycin. The dose of clarithromycin must be decreased or the time between doses (dosing interval) prolonged for patients with compromised kidneys (for example, if the CrCl is less than 30 ml/min, one-half of the usual dose could be used in the usual dosing interval). Patients with severe kidney failure can take 50–75% of the usual erythromycin dose at the usual time. Azithromycin and erythromycin are rare causes of interstitial nephritis (inflammation of a specific part of the kidney).

▷ **Dosing Instructions:** Nonenteric-coated preparations should be taken 1 hour before or 2 hours after eating. Enteric-coated preparations may be taken without regard to food. Azithromycin may be better tolerated if taken with food. The amount that gets into your body increases if the suspension is taken with food, but decreases if the capsules are taken with food. Do not take azithromycin with antacids containing aluminum or magnesium. Regular uncoated capsules may be opened, and tablets may be crushed; coated and prolonged-action preparations should be swallowed whole. Azithromycin suspension should be shaken before giving a dose and should also be dosed using a measuring cup or measuring spoon. Biaxin XL should be taken WITH food to help increase absorption. Ask your pharmacist for help. If you forget a dose: Take the missed dose as soon as you remember it, unless it's nearly time for your next dose—if that is the case, skip the missed dose and take the next dose right on schedule. Talk with your doctor if you find yourself missing doses.

Usual Duration of Use: Use on a regular schedule for the full schedule is necessary to determine this drug's effectiveness in controlling infections and preventing emergence of resistant bacteria. For streptococcal infections, the full course is very important without interruption of any multiple-day course to reduce the possibility of developing rheumatic fever or glomerulonephritis. The duration of use should not exceed the time required to eliminate the infection.

Typical Treatment Goals and Measurements (Outcomes and Markers)
Infections: The most commonly used measures of serious infections are white blood cell counts, differentials (the kind of blood cells that occur most often in your blood) and temperature. Many clinicians look for positive changes in 24–48 hours. NEVER stop an antibiotic because you start to feel better. For many infections, a full 14 days is REQUIRED to kill the bacteria. The goals and time frame (see benefits above) should be discussed with you when the prescription is written.

Possible Advantages of These Drugs
Azithromycin and clarithromycin: Broader spectrum of infectious microorganism coverage; equivalent to erythromycin, some penicillins, and some cephalosporins. Effective with fewer doses (only 1 dose for azithromycin, 2 for clarithromycin, and once daily for the Biaxin XL form), which may help pill-taking or adherence. Azithromycin and clarithromycin are very well tolerated; infrequent and minor adverse effects.

▷ **These Drugs Should Not Be Taken If**
- you had an allergic reaction to a macrolide previously.
- you have active liver disease (erythromycin estolate form).
- you are pregnant or planning pregnancy (some forms).
- you are allergic to *para*-aminobenzoic-acid-type anesthetics (intramuscular form of erythromycin).

▷ **Inform Your Physician Before Taking These Drugs If**
- you have a history of a previous "reaction" to any macrolide antibiotic.
- you are allergic by nature: hay fever, asthma, hives, eczema.
- you have a blood disorder.

- you have an abnormal heart rhythm.
- you have a history of porphyria.
- you have a history of kidney disorder.
- you have myasthenia gravis.
- you have a hearing disorder.
- you are taking a blood thinner (oral anticoagulant) (clarithromycin).
- you have a history of low blood platelets (some macrolides).
- you have taken the estolate form of erythromycin previously.

Possible Side Effects (natural, expected, and unavoidable drug actions)
Superinfections (see Glossary).

▷ **Possible Adverse Effects** (unusual, unexpected, and infrequent reactions)
If any of the following develop, consult your physician promptly for guidance.

Mild Adverse Effects
Allergic reactions: skin rash, hives, itching—rare.
Nausea, vomiting, diarrhea, abdominal cramping—infrequent.
Headache—rare.
Visual hallucinations—case report for clarithromycin.
Drug-induced increased liver enzymes (see Jaundice in Glossary)—rare.

Serious Adverse Effects
Allergic reaction: anaphylactic reaction (see Glossary)—rare. Stevens-Johnson Syndrome (erythromycin)—case report.
Idiosyncratic reactions: liver reaction—nausea, vomiting, fever, jaundice (usually, but not exclusively, associated with erythromycin estolate).
Prolonging of the QT interval (Torsade de Pointes or ventricular tachycardia)—possible.
Abnormal heart rhythm—rare.
Decreased white blood cells (erythromycin)—rare.
Hemolytic anemia (erythromycin)—case report.
Lowered blood platelets (clarithromycin)—case report.
Worsening of myasthenia gravis—case reports.
Low body temperature (hypothermia)—rare.
Pseudomembranous colitis—rare.
Pancreatitis (erythromycin)—rare.
Kidney problems (interstitial nephritis) (azithromycin, erythromycin)—case reports.
Abnormal urination (SIADH)—case reports for azithromycin.
Hearing loss (ototoxicity)—case reports.

▷ **Possible Effects on Sexual Function:** None reported.

▷ **Adverse Effects That May Mimic Natural Diseases or Disorders**
Liver toxicity may resemble acute gallbladder disease or viral hepatitis.

Possible Effects on Laboratory Tests
Complete blood cell counts: white cells may increase or decrease; eosinophils increased (allergic reaction); platelets decreased.
INR (prothrombin time): increased (drugs taken concurrently with warfarin).
Liver function tests: liver enzymes increased (ALT/GPT, AST/GOT, and alkaline phosphatase), increased bilirubin.

CAUTION
1. Take the **full dose prescribed** to help prevent resistant bacteria.
2. If you have a history of liver disease or impaired liver function, avoid any form of erythromycin estolate.

3. If diarrhea develops and continues for more than 24 hours, consult your physician promptly.

Precautions for Use

By Infants and Children: Watch allergic children closely for indications of developing allergy to this drug. Observe also for evidence of gastrointestinal irritation. Dosing based on body mass is critical.

By Those Over 60 Years of Age: Watch for itching reactions in the genital and anal regions, often due to yeast superinfections. Observe also for evidence of hearing loss. Report such developments promptly. If liver or kidney function is impaired, dose decreases must be considered.

▷ **Advisability of Use During Pregnancy**

Pregnancy Category: C for clarithromycin. B for others. See Pregnancy Risk Categories at the back of this book.

Animal Studies: Studies of rats are inconclusive for erythromycin. Monkey, rabbit, and rat studies have shown problems in pregnancy outcomes and fetal development.

Human Studies: Information from adequate studies of pregnant women is not available.

Generally thought to be safe during entire pregnancy, except for erythromycin estolate; this form of erythromycin can cause toxic liver reactions during pregnancy and should be avoided. Clarithromycin should be avoided unless no other antibiotic option is available.

Advisability of Use If Breast-Feeding

Presence of this drug in breast milk: Yes for others; clarithromycin unknown. Watch nursing infant closely and discontinue drug or nursing if adverse effects develop.

Habit-Forming Potential: None.

Effects of Overdose: Possible nausea, vomiting, hallucinations (clarithromycin), diarrhea, and abdominal discomfort.

Possible Effects of Long-Term Use: Superinfections (see Glossary).

Suggested Periodic Examinations While Taking These Drugs (at physician's discretion)

Liver function tests if the erythromycin estolate form is used.
Complete blood counts to measure response of infection.

▷ **While Taking These Drugs, Observe the Following**

Foods: New formulation absorption is decreased by more than 70% (especially with high-fat meals) and effectiveness may be seriously compromised for erythromycin. Azithromycin suspension is increased, while capsules are decreased. Clarithromycin immediate release is not affected. Biaxin XL form is best taken with food.

Herbal Medicines or Minerals: Echinacea: Some patients use echinacea to attempt to boost their immune systems. Unfortunately, use of echinacea is not recommended in people with damaged immune systems. This herb may also actually weaken any immune system if it is used too often or for too long a time. DO NOT take mistletoe herb, oak bark or F.C. of marshmallow root, and licorice. **Caution:** St. John's wort may also cause extreme reactions to the sun. Additive photosensitivity may be possible.

Beverages: Avoid fruit juices and carbonated beverages for 1 hour after taking any nonenteric-coated preparation of erythromycin. May be taken with milk.

▷   *Alcohol:* Avoid if you have impaired liver function or are taking the estolate form of erythromycin.

Tobacco Smoking: No interactions expected. I advise everyone to quit smoking.

▷   *Other Drugs*

Clarithromycin and erythromycin may ***increase*** the effects of

- amprenavir (Agenerase).
- benzodiazepines (see Drug Classes).
- buspirone (Buspar) (erythromycin only).
- carbamazepine (Tegretol) and cause toxicity.
- cilostazol (Pletal). Patients should be watched for increased heart rate, blood pressure, and complete blood counts taken in order to check for possible toxicity if these medicines must be combined.
- cisapride (Propulsid).
- clozapine (Clozaril).
- digoxin (Lanoxin) and cause toxicity.
- entacapone (Comtan) leading to increased entacapone adverse effects (movement problems, diarrhea).
- ergotamine (Cafergot, Ergostat, etc.) and cause impaired circulation to extremities/ergotism. DO NOT combine.
- imatinib (Gleevec) and cause excess imatinib effects or toxicity.
- medicines that have an effect on the QTc interval of the heart (see glossary) such as class I, IA or class III antiarrhythmic drugs such as flecainide (Tambocor) and medicines such as ziprasidone (Zyprexa) may lead to serious toxicity such as Torsades de Pointes. DO NOT COMBINE these medicines.
- methylprednisolone (Medrol) and prednisone and cause excess steroid effects.
- phenytoin (Dilantin or fosphenytoin [Cerebyx]).
- quetiapine (Seroquel).
- quinidine (Quinaglute, others).
- sibutramine (Meridia) [erythromycin and clarithromycin].
- sildenafil (Viagra)—reported up to 182% increased blood level (clarithromycin and erythromycin only).
- tacrolimus (Prograf) or sirolimus (Rapamune).
- theophylline (aminophylline, Theo-Dur, etc.) and cause toxicity.
- tretinoin (Vesanoid).
- valproic acid (Depakote).
- vinblastine (Velban) erythromycin and clarithromycin.
- warfarin (Coumadin) and increase the risk of bleeding (azithromycin also).

These medicines may ***decrease*** the effects of

- clindamycin.
- lincomycin.
- penicillins.

These medicines ***taken concurrently*** with

- astemizole (Hismanal—now off the US market) may cause serious arrhythmias.
- atorvastatin (Lipitor), pravastatin (Pravachol), simvastatin (Zocor), and other HMG-CoA reductase inhibitors INCREASE RISK OF MYOPATHY (serious muscle damage) if used with erythromycin or clarithromycin. Combination is NOT recommended.
- birth control pills (oral contraceptives) can cause loss of effectiveness and result in pregnancy (erythromycin).

- cyclosporine (Sandimmune) may result in cyclosporine toxicity if taken with erythromycin.
- disopyramide may cause heart (cardiac) arrhythmias.
- dofetilide (Tikosyn) may lead to dofetilide toxicity.
- fluoxetine (Prozac) may lead to fluoxetine toxicity.
- grepafloxacin (Raxar) and perhaps gatifloxacin (Tequin) may lead to heartbeat changes (prolonged QTc interval) if combined with erythromycin.
- lansoprazole (Prevacid) may lead to black tongue if combined with clarithromycin.
- loratadine (Claritin) may result in increased loratadine levels (also with fexofenadine [Allegra]), but it does not appear to cause the serious arrhythmia of some of the other nonsedating antihistamines. Since loratadine or fexofenadine levels may be increased, it may be prudent to decrease doses while taking erythromycin.
- midazolam (and probably other benzodiazepines) (see Drug Classes) may lead to excessive central nervous system depression.
- nevirapine (Viramune), delavirdine (Rescriptor) or efavirenz (Sustiva) may lead to nevirapine, efavirenz or delavirdine toxicity.
- omeprazole, esomepraxole and perhaps other proton pump inhibitors may increase levels of both erythromycin and clarithromycin.
- prednisone and other corticosteroids may lead to corticosteroid toxicity if combined with clarithromycin or erythromycin.
- rifabutin (Mycobutin) increases risk of low white blood cells (neutropenia) if combined with azithromycin or clarithromycin; clarithromycin also increases risk of rifabutin rash.
- ritonavir (Norvir) and perhaps other protease inhibitors (see Drug Classes) may lead to toxicity.
- sparfloxacin (Zagam) may lead to heartbeat changes (prolonged QTc interval) if combined with erythromycin.
- terfenadine (Seldane—now off the US market) can cause cardiac (heart) arrhythmias.
- triazolam may cause toxicity.
- trimexate (Mexate) can decrease trimexate metabolism and can lead to toxicity.
- valproic acid (Depakene, Depakote) can lead to toxic blood levels.
- zafirlukast (Accolate) and blunt zafirlukast benefits.
- zidovudine (AZT) may lead to decreased levels and lack of zidovudine effectiveness (clarithromycin and erythromycin).

▷ *Driving, Hazardous Activities:* This drug may cause nausea and/or diarrhea. Restrict activities as necessary.

Aviation Note: The use of these drugs *may be a disqualification* for piloting. Consult a designated Aviation Medical Examiner.

Exposure to Sun: Use caution; some medicines in this class have caused increased sensitivity to the sun (photosensitivity).

Special Storage Instructions: Keep liquid forms refrigerated.

Observe the Following Expiration Times: Freshly mixed oral suspension—14 days for clarithromycin (DO NOT refrigerate). Freshly mixed oral suspensions of erythromycin should be refrigerated to preserve taste. These go bad (outdate) in 14 days. Single-dose azithromycin suspension should be mixed with water and taken right away. Ask your pharmacist for help.

MAPROTILINE (ma PROH ti leen)

Introduced: 1974 **Class:** Antidepressant **Prescription:** USA: Yes **Controlled Drug:** USA: No; Canada: No **Available as Generic:** Yes

Brand Name: Ludiomil

Author's Note: Because use of this medicine has declined in favor of newer medicines, the information in this profile has been abbreviated.

MECLOFENAMATE (me kloh fen AM ayt)

Please see the fenamate (nonsteroidal anti-inflammatory drug) family profile.

MEDROXYPROGESTERONE (me DROX e proh jess te rohn)

Introduced: 1959 **Class:** Female sex hormones, progestins **Prescription:** USA: Yes **Controlled Drug:** USA: No; Canada: No **Available as Generic:** Yes

Brand Names: ✣Alti-MPA, Amen, Curretab, Cycrin, Depo-Provera, Premphase, Prempro, ✣PMS-Medroxyprogesterone, ✣Premelle, ✣Proclim, Provera, ✣Riva-Medrone

Author's Note: This profile will focus on the single medicine medroxyprogesterone forms.

BENEFITS versus RISKS

Possible Benefits

EFFECTIVE TREATMENT OF ABSENT OR ABNORMAL MENSTRUATION due to hormone imbalance

EFFECTIVE CONTRACEPTION when given by injection

USED IN ADJUNCTIVE AND PALLIATIVE TREATMENT OF INOPERABLE, RECURRING, AND METASTATIC ENDOMETRIAL AND KIDNEY CANCER

Possible Risks

Thrombophlebitis

Pulmonary embolism

Liver reaction with jaundice

Drug-induced birth defects

▷ **Principal Uses**

As a Single Drug Product: Uses currently included in FDA-approved labeling: (1) Used to initiate and regulate menstruation and correct abnormal patterns of menstrual bleeding caused by hormonal imbalance (and not by organic disease); (2) used in combination to treat metastatic, inoperable or recurrent endometrial carcinoma; (3) treatment of renal cell carcinoma; (4) used as a contraceptive injected into the muscle, once every 3 months; (5) helps dysfunctional uterine bleeding; (6) used to help infants with alveolar hypoventilation syndrome.

Other (unlabeled) generally accepted uses: (1) Used as a part of combination therapy in breast, refractory prostate, lung and ovarian cancers; (2) therapy of endometriosis; (3) helps abnormal hair growth in women (hirsutism); (4) can help breast pain (mastodynia); (5) used in combination with estrogen to help symptoms of menopause; (6) can be of use in pelvic congestion and pickwickian syndrome; (7) may help severe PMS; (8) can be of use in male hypersexuality.

How This Drug Works: By inducing and maintaining a lining in the uterus that resembles pregnancy, this drug can prevent uterine bleeding until it is withdrawn. By suppressing the release of the pituitary gland hormone that induces ovulation and by stimulating the secretion of mucus by the uterine cervix (to resist the passage of sperm), this drug can prevent pregnancy.

Available Dosage Forms and Strengths
Injection — 100, 150 and 400 mg/ml
Injection (single-dose vials) — 150 mg
Tablets — 2.5 mg, 5 mg, 10 mg

▷ **Usual Adult Dosage Ranges:** *To initiate menstruation*: 5 to 10 mg daily for 5 to 10 days, started at any time.

To correct abnormal bleeding: 5 to 10 mg daily for 5 to 10 days, started on the 16th or 21st day of the menstrual cycle. Withdrawal bleeding usually begins within 3 to 7 days after stopping the drug.

As a contraceptive: Intramuscular injections of 150 mg every 3 months are needed.

Author's Note: Controversy about estrogen therapy (ERT) and use of combination hormone replacement therapy (HRT) is fully outlined in the estrogen profile presented earlier in this book. The Women's Health Initiative raised important questions regarding use of the combined form of estrogen and progestin (Premphase and Prempro forms are listed for completeness).

Conditions Requiring Dosing Adjustments
Liver Function: This drug should be used with caution and the dose empirically decreased, by patients with liver compromise.
Kidney Function: No dosing changes thought to be needed.

▷ **Dosing Instructions:** The tablet may be crushed and taken on an empty stomach or with food to prevent nausea. If you forget a dose: take the missed dose as soon as you remember it, unless it's nearly time for your next dose—if that is the case, skip the missed dose and take the next dose right on schedule. If you miss a contraceptive injection, call your doctor about alternative forms of birth control. Talk with your doctor if you find yourself missing doses.

Usual Duration of Use: Use on a regular schedule for 2 or 3 menstrual cycles determines effectiveness in correcting abnormal patterns of menstrual bleeding. See your doctor on a regular basis.

Typical Treatment Goals and Measurements (Outcomes and Markers)
Contraception: Used to prevent conception with an injection once every 13 weeks. Ongoing use is required to avoid becoming pregnant.

Possible Advantages of This Drug
Effective contraception with a shot once every 13 weeks.

▷ **This Drug Should Not Be Taken If**
- you have had an allergic reaction to it previously.
- you are pregnant.

- you have experienced a missed abortion.
- you have impaired liver function/liver disease.
- you have a history of cancer of the breast or reproductive organs.
- you have a history of thrombophlebitis, embolism or stroke.
- you have abnormal and unexplained vaginal bleeding.

▷ **Inform Your Physician Before Taking This Drug If**
- you have impaired kidney function.
- you have any of the following disorders: asthma, diabetes, emotional depression, epilepsy, heart disease, migraine headaches.

Possible Side Effects (natural, expected, and unavoidable drug actions)
Fluid retention, weight gain (when injected as a contraceptive by increasing deposition of fat), changes in menstrual timing and flow, spotting between periods.

▷ **Possible Adverse Effects** (unusual, unexpected, and infrequent reactions)
If any of the following develop, consult your physician promptly for guidance.
Mild Adverse Effects
Allergic reactions: skin rash, hives, itching.
Fatigue, weakness, nausea—infrequent.
Conflicting reports on blood lipids.
Acne, excessive hair growth, hair loss—case reports.
Serious Adverse Effects
Allergic reaction: anaphylactic reaction (see Glossary)—rare. Stevens-Johnson Syndrome.
Liver toxicity with jaundice (see Glossary): yellow eyes/skin, dark-colored urine, light-colored stools—possible.
Thrombophlebitis (inflammation of a vein with blood clot formation): pain or tenderness in thigh or leg, with or without swelling of the foot, ankle, or leg—case reports.
Pulmonary embolism (movement of blood clot to lung): sudden shortness of breath, chest pain, cough, bloody sputum—case reports.
Stroke (blood clot in the brain): sudden headache, weakness or paralysis of any part of the body—possible.
Cushing's Syndrome—case reports.
Retinal thrombosis (blood clot in the eye): sudden impairment or loss of vision—case reports.
Drug-induced pseudotumor cerebri—possible.
Arachnoiditis (with intrathecal injection)—case reports.
Pneumonitis, especially in patients who have received radiation therapy—case reports.
Medroxyprogesterone was NOT found to increase risk of breast cancer in a World Health Organization study of 12,759 women. It was also found NOT to increase risk of ovarian or uterine cancer in a study of 5,000 African American women who received it as a contraceptive for 10 years.
A study in mice found that when progesterone was used in large doses for prolonged periods, it acted as a co-carcinogen.
Cervical cancer—weak or no association in case-control studies.

▷ **Possible Effects on Sexual Function:** Altered timing and pattern of menstruation. Female breast tenderness and secretion (galactorrhea). Decreased vaginal secretions. Infertility—case reports.

▷ **Adverse Effects That May Mimic Natural Diseases or Disorders**
Liver toxicity may suggest viral hepatitis.

Possible Effects on Laboratory Tests
Blood total cholesterol, HDL cholesterol, LDL cholesterol, and triglyceride levels: variable results.
Glucose tolerance test (GTT): decreased.

CAUTION
1. There is an increased risk of birth defects in children whose mothers take this drug during the first 4 months of pregnancy.
2. Inform your physician promptly if you think you may be pregnant.
3. This drug should not be used as a test for pregnancy.

Precautions for Use
By Infants and Children: Not used in this age group.
By Those Over 60 Years of Age: Used as adjunctive therapy in cancer of the breast, uterus, prostate, and kidney. Watch for excessive fluid retention.

▷ **Advisability of Use During Pregnancy**
Pregnancy Category: X. See Pregnancy Risk Categories at the back of this book.
Animal Studies: Genital defects reported in rat and rabbit studies; masculinization of the female rodent fetus; various defects in chick embryos and rabbits.
Human Studies: In a study of 1,016 pregnancies, oral doses of 80–120 mg daily used from the 5th to 7th week of pregnancy up to the 18th week were not associated with teratogenic effects. Other data show masculinization of the female genitals: enlargement of the clitoris, fusion of the labia. Increased risk of heart, nervous system, and limb defects when used in the second and third trimesters of pregnancy.
The drug is used as a benefit-to-risk decision in the first 3 months of pregnancy. Avoid this drug completely during the final 6 months of pregnancy.

Advisability of Use If Breast-Feeding
Presence of this drug in breast milk: Yes.
Avoid drug or refrain from nursing.

Habit-Forming Potential: None.

Effects of Overdose: Nausea, vomiting, fluid retention, breast enlargement and discomfort, abnormal vaginal bleeding.

Possible Effects of Long-Term Use: There has been considerable controversy regarding use of this drug and cancer. The most recent large patient studies do not show an increased relative risk that is statistically significant.

Suggested Periodic Examinations While Taking This Drug (at physician's discretion)
Regular examinations (every 6 to 12 months) of the breasts and reproductive organs (pelvic examination of the uterus and ovaries, including Pap smear).

▷ **While Taking This Drug, Observe the Following**
Foods: No restrictions.
Herbal Medicines or Minerals: Black cohosh appears to work by (1) suppressing luteinizing hormone; (2) binding to estrogen receptors in the pituitary and inhibiting luteinizing hormone release and (3) binding to estrogen receptors in the pituitary. The net effect is that this herb eases symptoms of

menopause, but little is known about long-term use or heart and bone protective effects. Talk to your doctor before starting black cohosh if you are
currently taking medroxyprogesterone—particularly if you take it for
PMS. Calcium may help ease some PMS symptoms.

Beverages: Do not take this medicine with grapefruit juice. Grapefruit juice
inhibits CYP3A4, which helps remove this drug from the body.

▷ *Alcohol:* No interactions expected.

Tobacco Smoking: No direct drug interactions expected. I advise everyone to
quit smoking.

▷ *Other Drugs*

The following drugs may ***decrease*** the effects of medroxyprogesterone:
• nevirapine (Viramune).
• rifampin (Rifadin, Rimactane, etc.) may hasten its elimination.

Medroxyprogesterone ***taken concurrently*** with
• CYP3A4 inhibitors (such as erythromycin, fluoxetine, fluvoxamine, itraconazole, ketoconazole, virconazole, ritonavir, and others) may lead to
increased medroxyprogesterone levels.
• digitoxin may result in slightly higher-than-expected digoxin levels.
• estrogens (Premphase, Prempro) have a very different benefit-to-risk profile (see earlier estrogens profile in this book).
• nevirapine (Viramune) may lower medroxyprogesterone levels and blunt
contraceptive or other benefits.
• ritonavir (Norvir) and perhaps other protease inhibitors (see Drug Classes)
may lead to toxicity.
• tamoxifen (Nolvadex) may result in blunting of the therapeutic benefits of
tamoxifen.
• warfarin (Coumadin) may increase warfarin effects; increased lab INR
(prothrombin time or protime) testing is needed.

▷ *Driving, Hazardous Activities:* Usually no restrictions. Ask your doctor about
your individual risk and for guidance regarding specific restrictions.

Aviation Note: The use of this drug ***may be a disqualification*** for piloting. Consult a designated Aviation Medical Examiner.

Exposure to Sun: No restrictions.

MEFENAMIC ACID (me FEN am ik A sid)

**Please see the fenamate (nonsteroidal anti-inflammatory drug) family
profile.**

MEPERIDINE (me PER i deen)

Other Name: Pethidine **Introduced:** 1939 **Class:** Strong
analgesic, opioids **Prescription:** USA: Yes **Controlled Drug:** USA:
C-II*; Canada: Yes **Available as Generic:** Yes

Brand Names: Demerol, Demerol APAP [CD], Mepergan, Pethadol, ✤Pethi-
dine

*See Schedules of Controlled Drugs at the back of this book.

BENEFITS versus RISKS

Possible Benefits	*Possible Risks*
EFFECTIVE RELIEF OF MODERATE TO SEVERE PAIN NORMEPERIDINE METABOLITE	POTENTIAL FOR HABIT FORMATION (DEPENDENCE) ADVERSE REACTIONS: Weakness, fainting, Disorientation, hallucinations, Interference with urination, Constipation

---

Author's Note: This profile has been shortened to make room for more effective medicines.

MERCAPTOPURINE (mer kap toh PYUR een)

Other Names: 6-mercaptopurine, 6-MP

Introduced: 1960   **Class:**   Anticancer (antineoplastic), immunosuppressant   **Prescription:**   USA: Yes   **Controlled Drug:**   USA: No; Canada: No   **Available as Generic:**   USA: No; Canada: No

Brand Names: ❦Alti-Mercaptopurine, Purinethol

BENEFITS versus RISKS

Possible Benefits	*Possible Risks*
EFFECTIVE TREATMENT OF CERTAIN ACUTE AND CHRONIC LEUKEMIAS AND LYMPHOMAS Effective treatment of polycythemia vera Possibly effective treatment of Crohn's disease and ulcerative colitis	BONE MARROW DEPRESSION (see Glossary) DRUG-INDUCED LIVER DAMAGE Rare gastrointestinal ulceration

---

▷ **Principal Uses**

As a Single Drug Product: Uses currently included in FDA-approved labeling: Combination treatment of acute lymphocytic leukemia.

Other (unlabeled) generally accepted uses: Treatment of (1) inflammatory bowel diseases (Crohn's disease and ulcerative colitis).

How This Drug Works: This drug interferes with specific stages of cell reproduction (tissue growth) by inhibiting the formation of DNA and RNA.

Available Dosage Forms and Strengths

Tablets — 50 mg

▷ **Recommended Dosage Ranges** (Actual dose and schedule must be determined for each patient individually.)

Infants and Children: For acute lymphoblastic leukemia (induction dose)—2.5 mg per kg of body mass (to the nearest 25 mg) daily (roughly 50 mg for the average 5-year-old), in single or divided doses. If the platelets and white blood cell counts do not fall and clinical improvement is not acceptable after 4 weeks of the induction dosing, the dose may be increased to 5 mg per kg of body mass per day. If there is still no response, some centers give mercaptopurine as 75 mg per square meter on days 29–42. This is combined with vincristine, prednisone, and methotrexate. Maintenance therapy then occurs as in adult dosing.

12 to 60 Years of Age: For leukemia (induction)—initially 2.5 mg per kg of body mass (to the nearest 25 mg, usually 100–200 mg) daily, in single or divided doses, for 4 weeks. If the white blood cell or platelet counts do not fall and there is no clinical improvement, the dose may be increased as needed and tolerated to 5 mg per kg of body mass daily. For ongoing dose (maintenance): 1.5 to 2.5 mg per kg of body mass daily.

For inflammatory bowel disease (Crohn's)—1.5 mg per kg of body mass daily. The dose is subsequently adjusted to keep the platelet count above 100,000 and the white blood cell count above 4,500.

Over 60 Years of Age: Same as 12 to 60 years of age.

Author's Note: If mercaptopurine is given with allopurinol, the mercaptopurine dose should be lowered to a fourth or a third of the usual dose.

Conditions Requiring Dosing Adjustments

Liver Function: Used with caution and in decreased doses by patients with liver compromise. It is also a rare cause of liver toxicity.

Kidney Function: Dose should be decreased in kidney (renal) compromise. It is a rare cause of drug crystals in urine.

TPMT Negatives: Some patients do not have an enzyme called thiopurine methyltransferase (TPMT). The mercaptopurine dose is decreased by 10% for these patients.

▷ **Dosing Instructions:** The tablet may be crushed and taken with or following food to reduce stomach upset. Increasing the amount of water that you drink while taking this medicine can help avoid kidney problems. Talk to your doctor about the amount he or she would like you to drink. This medicine can lead to serious harm of a fetus. Talk to your doctor about appropriate contraception if you are a female of child-bearing age. If you forget a dose: take the missed dose as soon as you remember it, unless it's nearly time for your next dose—if that is the case, skip the missed dose and take the next dose right on schedule. DO NOT double doses. Talk with your doctor if you find yourself missing doses.

Usual Duration of Use: Use on a regular schedule for 4 to 6 weeks determines effectiveness in inducing remission in leukemia; continual use for 2 to 3 months determines benefit in treating inflammatory bowel disease. Long-term use requires periodic physician evaluation.

Typical Treatment Goals and Measurements (Outcomes and Markers)

Leukemia: The goal is to improve clinical signs and symptoms, and control leukemia while avoiding myelosuppression and liver toxicity. Checks of blood platelets, hematocrits, and white blood cell counts are required. Periodic checks of liver function tests help detect liver problems early. Bone marrow tests help define changes in peripheral blood.

▷ **This Drug Should Not Be Taken If**
- you have had an allergic reaction to it previously.
- you have a solid tumor or lymphoma (this drug is not indicated).
- you have prior resistance to the drug.
- you are pregnant. (Ask your physician for guidance.)

▷ **Inform Your Physician Before Taking This Drug If**
- you have a history of drug-induced bone marrow depression.
- you have impaired liver or kidney function.

- you are not using any contraception.
- you have gout.
- you are taking allopurinol (the mercaptopurine dose must be reduced).
- you have inflammatory bowel disease.
- you do not understand the steps needed to dispose of any vomit or urine.
- you have been exposed recently to chicken pox or herpes zoster (shingles).
- you are taking any of the following drugs: allopurinol, probenecid, sulfinpyrazone, anticoagulants, immunosuppressants.

Possible Side Effects (natural, expected, and unavoidable drug actions)

Bone marrow depression (see Glossary). Abnormally increased blood uric acid levels; possible urate kidney stones, hyperpigmentation of the skin. Possible drug fever. Serum sickness.

▷ **Possible Adverse Effects** (unusual, unexpected, and infrequent reactions)

If any of the following develop, consult your physician promptly for guidance.

Mild Adverse Effects

Allergic reactions: skin rash, itching, joint pain—case reports.

Headache, weakness—infrequent.

Loss of appetite, mouth and lip sores, nausea, vomiting, diarrhea—infrequent.

Serious Adverse Effects

Liver damage with jaundice (see Glossary)—infrequent.

Kidney damage: fever, cloudy or bloody urine—rare.

Pancreatitis (especially in patients taking this medicine for inflammatory bowel disease)—infrequent.

Gastrointestinal ulceration: stomach pain, bloody or black stools.

Increased cancer risk (carcinogen): one case report of cancer in a patient with bowel disease—possible.

▷ **Possible Effects on Sexual Function:** Suppression of sperm production.

Cessation of menstruation—case reports.

Possible Delayed Adverse Effects: Bone marrow depression may not be apparent during early treatment.

▷ **Adverse Effects That May Mimic Natural Diseases or Disorders**

Drug-induced liver damage may suggest viral hepatitis.

Natural Diseases or Disorders That May Be Activated by This Drug

Latent gout, peptic ulcer disease, inflammatory bowel disease.

Possible Effects on Laboratory Tests

Complete blood cell counts: decreased red cells, hemoglobin, white cells, and platelets.

Blood glucose levels: falsely increased with SMA testing.

Blood uric acid levels: increased.

Liver function tests: increased enzymes (ALT/GPT, AST/GOT, and alkaline phosphatase) or bilirubin.

Kidney function tests: increased blood urea nitrogen (BUN) and creatinine.

Sperm counts: decreased.

CAUTION

1. Make sure you get all laboratory tests ordered.
2. Call your doctor at the first sign of infection or abnormal bleeding or bruising.
3. Inform your physician promptly if you become pregnant.

4. It is best to avoid immunizations while taking this drug and to avoid contact with people who have recently taken oral poliovirus vaccine. If possible, the vaccinations can be given BEFORE therapy is started.
5. Call your doctor if you see a different doctor who finds a significant fall in your blood tests (this medicine must usually then be stopped if the test was accurate).

Precautions for Use
By Infants and Children: No specific problems anticipated.
By Those Over 60 Years of Age: Increased risk of bone marrow depression. Periodic blood counts are mandatory.

▷ **Advisability of Use During Pregnancy**
Pregnancy Category: D. See Pregnancy Risk Categories at the back of this book.
Animal Studies: Rat studies reveal toxic effects on the embryo.
Human Studies: Adequate studies of pregnant women are not available. Known to cause abortions and premature births.
Avoid drug during entire pregnancy if possible. Use a nonhormonal method of contraception.

Advisability of Use If Breast-Feeding
Presence of this drug in breast milk: Unknown.
Avoid drug or refrain from nursing.

Habit-Forming Potential: None.

Effects of Overdose: Headache, dizziness, abdominal pain, nausea.

Possible Effects of Long-Term Use: Development of new malignant diseases.

Suggested Periodic Examinations While Taking This Drug (at physician's discretion)
Complete blood cell counts.
Blood uric acid levels.
Amylase and lipase.
Liver and kidney function tests.

▷ **While Taking This Drug, Observe the Following**
Foods: No restrictions.
Herbal Medicines or Minerals: Echinacea: Some patients use echinacea to attempt to boost their immune systems. Unfortunately, use of echinacea is not recommended in people with damaged immune systems. This herb may also actually weaken any immune system if it is used too often or for too long a time. Herbals that have known toxic effects on the liver (such as kava, eucalyptus, and valerian) should be avoided as they could lead to additive toxicity.
Beverages: No restrictions. Drink liquids liberally, up to 2 quarts daily. Ask your doctor about the specific amount he or she wants you to drink.
▷ *Alcohol:* Avoid completely.
Tobacco Smoking: No interactions expected. I advise everyone to quit smoking.
▷ *Other Drugs*
Mercaptopurine may ***decrease*** the effects of
• warfarin (Coumadin); the INR (prothrombin time or protime) should be checked more frequently.
The following drug may ***increase*** the effects of mercaptopurine:
• allopurinol (Zyloprim). Doses must be reduced to 33% or even as low as 25% of the usual dose if these two medicines are to be combined.
Mercaptopurine ***taken concurrently*** with
• amphotericin B (Abelcet) may increase risk of kidney toxicity or spasm of the bronchi.

- live-virus vaccines (such as smallpox) may lead to life-threatening infections.
- methotrexate (Rheumatrex, Mexate) can result in mercaptopurine toxicity.
- olsalazine (Dipentum) may increase risk of bone marrow depression.

▷ *Driving, Hazardous Activities:* No restrictions.
Aviation Note: The use of this drug *may be a disqualification* for piloting. Consult a designated Aviation Medical Examiner.
Exposure to Sun: No restrictions.
Discontinuation: To be determined by your physician.

MESALAMINE (me SAL a meen)

Other Names: Mesalazine, 5-aminosalicylic acid, 5-ASA

Introduced: 1982   **Class:**   Bowel anti-inflammatory   **Prescription:**
USA: Yes   **Controlled Drug:**   USA: No; Canada: No   **Available as**
Generic: USA: No; Canada: No

Brand Names: Asacol, ✤Mesasal, Pentasa, ✤Quintasa, Rowasa, ✤Salofalk

BENEFITS versus RISKS	
Possible Benefits	*Possible Risks*
EFFECTIVE SUPPRESSION OF INFLAMMATORY BOWEL DISEASE	Allergic reactions: acute intolerance syndrome, drug-induced kidney damage

▷ **Principal Uses**
As a Single Drug Product: Uses currently included in FDA-approved labeling: Treatment of active mild to moderate ulcerative colitis, proctosigmoiditis, and proctitis.
   Other (unlabeled) generally accepted uses: (1) May help improve semen quality that had been damaged by prior sulfasalazine treatment; (2) can ease canker sores (aphthous ulcers); (3) has a steroid-sparing effect in Crohn's disease; (4) used to maintain remission in ulcerative colitis.

How This Drug Works: Suppresses prostaglandin (and related compounds) formation, chemicals causing inflammation, tissue destruction, and diarrhea—the main problems in ulcerative colitis and proctitis.

Available Dosage Forms and Strengths
      Capsules, timed-release — 400 mg
            Rectal suspension — 4 g per 60-ml unit
      Suppositories (Canada) — 250 mg
            Suppositories — 500 mg
            (US and Canada)
      Tablets, enteric coated — 250 mg, 500 mg
      Tablets, sustained release — 250 mg, 500 mg

▷ **Recommended Dosage Ranges** (Actual dose and schedule must be determined for each patient individually.)
Infants and Children: Dose not established.
12 to 60 Years of Age: Active ulcerative colitis: Immediate release (Asacol)—800 mg 3 times a day for 6 weeks. Controlled release (Pentasa)—1,000 mg 4 times a day for up to 8 weeks.

Maintenance of ulcerative colitis remission: Immediate release (Asacol)—
1,600 mg divided into equal doses.

Crohn's disease (Pentasa): 1,000 mg taken 3 times a day.

Over 60 Years of Age: Same as 12 to 60 years of age.

Conditions Requiring Dosing Adjustments

Liver Function: Guidelines for dose adjustment not available. Drug changed by
the liver and colon wall to Ac-5-ASA.

Kidney Function: This drug should be used with caution in kidney compromise.

▷ **Dosing Instructions**

Rectal suspension: Use as a retention enema at bedtime. If possible, empty
the rectum before inserting suspension; try to retain the suspension all
night.

Tablets: Best taken with 8 ounces of water on an empty stomach, 1 hour before
or 2 hours after eating. Also can be taken with or following food to reduce
stomach upset. Sustained release tablet should be swallowed whole without alteration. If you forget a dose: take the missed dose as soon as you
remember it, unless it's nearly time for your next dose—if that is the case,
skip the missed dose and take the next dose right on schedule. Talk with
your doctor if you find yourself missing doses.

Usual Duration of Use: Regular use for 1 to 3 weeks determines benefits controlling ulcerative colitis. Long-term use (months to years) requires periodic physician evaluation.

Typical Treatment Goals and Measurements (Outcomes and Markers)

Inflammatory bowel disease: The goal is to cause (induce) a remission and
maintain it. Symptoms that will resolve include rectal bleeding and diarrhea. More involved exams will reveal an absence of bowel ulceration and
easing of friability or granularity of the bowel itself.

Possible Advantages of This Drug

Does not cause bone marrow or blood cell disorders. Does not inhibit sperm
production or function. Better side effect profile than sulfasalazine. May
actually (5-ASA form) help prevent risk of colorectal cancer.

▷ **This Drug Should Not Be Taken If**

- you have had an allergic reaction to it previously.
- you have severely impaired kidney function.
- you have a known sulfite allergy. (Rectal suspension should NOT be used.)
- you have active ulcer disease.

▷ **Inform Your Physician Before Taking This Drug If**

- you are allergic to aspirin (or other salicylates), olsalazine, or sulfasalazine.
- you are allergic by nature: history of hay fever, asthma, hives, eczema.
- you have impaired liver or kidney function.
- you have a history of a blood-clotting (coagulation) disorder.
- you develop chest pain or trouble while taking this medicine (pericarditis
happens rarely).
- you have a history of low white blood cell counts.
- you are taking other medicines that effect the bone marrow. Discuss this
with your doctor.
- you are currently taking sulfasalazine (Azulfidine).

Possible Side Effects (natural, expected, and unavoidable drug actions)

Anal irritation (with use of rectal suspension or suppositories). Flu-like syndrome with oral mesalamine use.

▷ **Possible Adverse Effects** (unusual, unexpected, and infrequent reactions)
If any of the following develop, consult your physician promptly for guidance.

Mild Adverse Effects
Allergic reaction: skin rash.
Headache (may be dose related), hair loss—rare.
Blurred vision, ringing in the ears—possible.
Paresthesias, neck and joint pain, dizziness, cough—infrequent.
Nausea, stomach pain, excessive gas—infrequent.

Serious Adverse Effects
Allergic reactions: acute intolerance syndrome (fever, skin rash, severe headache, severe stomach pain, bloody diarrhea).
Depression or confusion—reported.
Kidney damage (nephrosis, interstitial nephritis)—rare.
Peripheral neuropathy—rare.
Pancreatitis, peptic ulcers or hepatitis—rare.
Low white blood cell or platelet counts or anemia—rare.
Heart toxicity (myocarditis, pericarditis, pericardial effusions)—case reports.
Lung toxicity (interstitial infiltrates)—case report.

▷ **Possible Effects on Sexual Function:** Oligospermia and infertility have been reported with sulfasalazine, but NOT with mesalamine.

Possible Effects on Laboratory Tests
Increased liver function tests.

CAUTION
1. Report promptly any signs of acute intolerance syndrome. Stop taking drug.
2. Shake the rectal suspension thoroughly before administering.
3. This medicine is a salicylate and as such is a cousin of aspirin. Avoid taking this medicine in combination with other medicines or during other conditions in which aspirin is contraindicated. Salicylate toxicity is possible.
4. Mesalamine and other medicines that belong to the sulfasalazine family have been implicated as possible causes of heart toxicity in case reports. Call your doctor if you are taking mesalamine or a medicine related to sulfasalazine and start to have difficulty breathing and/or pain in the chest.

Precautions for Use
By Infants and Children: Safety and effectiveness by those under 12 years of age are not established.
By Those Over 60 Years of Age: None.

▷ **Advisability of Use During Pregnancy**
Pregnancy Category: B. See Pregnancy Risk Categories at the back of this book.
Animal Studies: No drug-induced birth defects found in rat or rabbit studies.
Human Studies: Adequate studies of pregnant women are not available.
Use this drug only if clearly needed. Ask your physician for guidance.

Advisability of Use If Breast-Feeding
Presence of this drug in breast milk: Yes.
Avoid drug or refrain from nursing.

Habit-Forming Potential: None.

Effects of Overdose: Headache, dizziness, nausea, vomiting, abdominal cramping.

Possible Effects of Long-Term Use: None reported.

Suggested Periodic Examinations While Taking This Drug (at physician's discretion)
Kidney function tests.
Urinalysis.

▷ **While Taking This Drug, Observe the Following**
Foods: Decreases 5-ASA levels. Follow prescribed diet.
Herbal Medicines or Minerals: Flaxseed, peppermint oil, and psyllium husk have Commission E monograph indications for irritable bowel syndrome. This is NOT the same as ulcerative colitis, and those products have not been studied in ulcerative colitis. Aloe, buckhorn berry or bark, cascara sagrada bark, rhubarb root, and senna should not be taken by people living with ulcerative colitis.
Beverages: No restrictions. May be taken with milk.
▷ *Alcohol:* No interactions expected.
Tobacco Smoking: No interactions expected. I advise everyone to quit smoking.
▷ *Other Drugs*
Mesalamine *taken concurrently* with
- alendronate (Fosamax) may increase stomach or intestinal upset risks (because of salicylate).
- ardeparin (Normiflo), dalteparin (Fragmin), enoxaparin (Lovenox), or other low molecular weight heparins may increase risk of bleeding (hemorrhage).
- aspirin or other salicylates may increase risk of salicylate toxicity.
- varicella vaccine (Varivax) may result in Reye's syndrome; avoid taking this medicine for 6 weeks following varicella vaccine.
- warfarin (Coumadin) may blunt warfarin effectiveness. More frequent INRs are prudent.
▷ *Driving, Hazardous Activities:* No restrictions.
Aviation Note: The use of this drug is *probably not a disqualification* for piloting. Consult a designated Aviation Medical Examiner.
Exposure to Sun: No restrictions.

METAPROTERENOL (met a proh TER e nohl)

Other Name: Orciprenaline

Introduced: 1964   **Class:**   Antiasthmatic, bronchodilator   **Prescription:**   USA: Yes   **Controlled Drug:**   USA: No; Canada: No   **Available as Generic:**   Yes

Brand Names: ✤Alti-Orciprenaline, Alupent, Arm-a-Med, Dey-Dose, Dey-Lute, Metaprel, Metaprel Nasal Inhaler, Prometa

BENEFITS versus RISKS	
Possible Benefits	*Possible Risks*
VERY EFFECTIVE RELIEF OF BRONCHOSPASM	Increased blood pressure
	Fine hand tremor
	Fast heart rate
	Irregular heart rhythm (with excessive use)

▷ **Principal Uses**

As a Single Drug Product: Uses currently included in FDA-approved labeling: (1) Relieves acute bronchial asthma and reduces the frequency and severity of chronic, recurrent asthmatic attacks; (2) used to relieve reversible bronchospasm associated with chronic bronchitis and emphysema; (3) eases symptoms in obstructive bronchial disease.

Other (unlabeled) generally accepted uses: Some use in stopping premature labor (threatened abortion).

How This Drug Works: Dilates those bronchial tubes that are in sustained constriction, increasing the size of airways and improving breathing.

Available Dosage Forms and Strengths

Nasal inhaler — 0.65 mg per metered dose
Oral suspension — 10 mg/5 ml
Powder for inhalation — 0.65 mg per inhalation
Solution for nebulizer — 0.4%, 0.6%, 5%
Syrup — 10 mg/5 ml
Tablets — 10 mg, 20 mg

▷ **Usual Adult Dosage Ranges:** Inhaler: 2 or 3 inhalations as often as every 3 to 4 hours; do not exceed 12 inhalations daily.

Hand nebulizer: 5 to 15 inhalations every 4 hours; do not exceed 40 inhalations daily.

Syrup and tablets: 20 mg up to every 6 to 8 hours.

Note: Actual dose and schedule must be determined for each patient individually.

Conditions Requiring Dosing Adjustments

Liver Function: Specific guidelines for dosing adjustment for patients with liver compromise are not usually indicated.

Kidney Function: Dosing changes are not indicated in kidney compromise.

▷ **Dosing Instructions:** May be taken on empty stomach or with food or milk. Tablets should not be crushed. For aerosol and nebulizer, follow the written instructions carefully in order to get the needed dose. Do not overuse. If symptoms are not controlled with most-frequent dosing, call your doctor. If you forget a dose: take the missed dose as soon as you remember it, then take the remaining daily doses at evenly spaced intervals. If it's nearly time for your next dose, skip the missed dose and take the next dose right on schedule. Talk with your doctor if you find yourself missing doses.

Usual Duration of Use: According to individual requirements. Do not use beyond the time necessary to stop episodes of asthma.

Typical Treatment Goals and Measurements (Outcomes and Markers)

Asthma: Beta-adrenergic medicines like this one are used to prevent or treat reversible spasms of the bronchial tubes. The peak effect happens 2 to 4 hours after dosing. Inhaled use often gives improvement in FEV-1 in 5 to 30 minutes. Patient signs such as wheeze and symptoms like rales and rhonchi should ease. If the usual benefit is not realized, call your doctor.

▷ **This Drug Should Not Be Taken If**
- you had an allergic reaction to it previously.
- you currently have an irregular heart rhythm.
- you are taking, or have taken within the past 2 weeks, any monoamine oxidase (MAO) type A inhibitor drug (see Drug Classes).

▷ **Inform Your Physician Before Taking This Drug If**
- you are overly sensitive to other sympathetic stimulant drugs.
- you currently use epinephrine (Adrenalin, Primatene Mist, etc.) to relieve asthmatic breathing.
- you have any type of heart or circulatory disorder, especially high blood pressure or coronary heart disease.
- you have diabetes or an overactive thyroid gland (hyperthyroidism).
- you are taking any form of digitalis or any stimulant drug.

Possible Side Effects (natural, expected, and unavoidable drug actions)
Aerosol—dryness or irritation of mouth or throat, altered taste, nervousness. Tablet—nervousness, palpitation.

▷ **Possible Adverse Effects** (unusual, unexpected, and infrequent reactions)
If any of the following develop, consult your physician promptly for guidance.
Mild Adverse Effects
Headache, dizziness, restlessness, insomnia, fine tremor of hands—possible to infrequent.
Increased sweating; muscle cramps in arms and legs—case reports.
Nausea, heartburn, vomiting—possible.
Serious Adverse Effects
Rapid or irregular heart rhythm, intensification of angina, increased blood pressure—possible.
Hallucinations and psychosis—rare.
Paradoxical spasm of the bronchi (bronchospasm)—rare.

▷ **Possible Effects on Sexual Function:** None reported.

Natural Diseases or Disorders That May Be Activated by This Drug
Latent coronary artery disease, diabetes or high blood pressure.

Possible Effects on Laboratory Tests
Urine sugar tests: positive (unreliable results with Benedict's solution).

CAUTION
1. Combined use of this drug by aerosol inhalation with beclomethasone aerosol (Beclovent, Vanceril) may increase the risk of toxicity due to fluorocarbon propellants (these propellants are being phased out). Use this aerosol 20 to 30 minutes before beclomethasone aerosol, as this will reduce the risk of toxicity and enhance the penetration of beclomethasone.
2. *Avoid excessive use of aerosol inhalation.* Excessive or prolonged use of this drug by inhalation can reduce its effectiveness and cause serious heart rhythm disturbances, including cardiac arrest.
3. Do not combine this drug with epinephrine. These 2 drugs may be used alternately if an interval of 4 hours is allowed between doses.
4. If you do not respond to your usually effective dose, ask your doctor for help. Do not increase the size or frequency of the dose without your physician's approval.

Precautions for Use
By Infants and Children: Safety and effectiveness of the aerosol and nebulized solution are not established for children under 12 years of age.
Oral dosing in children 2–6 years old—1.3 to 2.6 mg per kg of body mass per day, divided into equal doses and given 3 to 4 times a day. In children 6 to 9 years old or less than 60 pounds—10 mg per dose 3 to 4 times a

day. Children over 9 years old or over 60 pounds—20 mg 3 or 4 times a day.

Safety and effectiveness of the syrup and tablet are not established for children under 6 years of age.

By Those Over 60 Years of Age: Avoid excessive and continual use. If acute asthma is not relieved promptly, other drugs will have to be tried. Watch for nervousness, palpitations, irregular heart rhythm, and muscle tremors. Use with extreme caution if you have hardening of the arteries, heart disease, or high blood pressure.

▷ **Advisability of Use During Pregnancy**

Pregnancy Category: C. See Pregnancy Risk Categories at the back of this book.

Animal Studies: Significant birth defects reported in rabbit studies.

Human Studies: Adequate studies of pregnant women are not available.

Avoid during first 3 months. Use in final 6 months only if clearly needed.

Advisability of Use If Breast-Feeding

Presence of this drug in breast milk: Unknown.

Avoid drug or refrain from nursing.

Habit-Forming Potential: None.

Effects of Overdose: Nervousness, palpitation, rapid heart rate, sweating, headache, tremor, vomiting, chest pain.

Possible Effects of Long-Term Use: Loss of effectiveness (see Caution on page 691).

Suggested Periodic Examinations While Taking This Drug (at physician's discretion)

Blood pressure measurements.

Evaluation of heart status.

▷ **While Taking This Drug, Observe the Following**

Foods: No restrictions.

Herbal Medicines or Minerals: Using St. John's wort, guarana, ma huang, ephedrine-like compounds, or kola while taking this medicine may result in unacceptable central nervous system stimulation. Fir or pine needle oil should NOT be used by asthmatics. Ephedra alone does carry a German Commission E monograph indication for asthma treatment. If you are allergic to plants in the Asteraceae family (aster, chrysanthemum, daisy, or ragweed), you may also be allergic to echinacea, chamomile, feverfew, and St. John's wort.

Beverages: Avoid excessive use of caffeine-containing beverages: coffee, tea, cola, chocolate.

▷ *Alcohol:* No interactions expected.

Tobacco Smoking: No interactions expected. I advise everyone to quit smoking.

▷ *Other Drugs*

Metaproterenol *taken concurrently* with

• albuterol (Proventil, others) may result in increased heart (cardiovascular) side effects.

• monoamine oxidase (MAO) type A inhibitors (see Drug Classes) may cause excessive increase in blood pressure and undesirable heart stimulation.

• phenothiazines (see Drug Classes) may blunt some effects of this drug.

▷ *Driving, Hazardous Activities:* Usually no restrictions. Use caution if excessive nervousness or dizziness occurs.

Aviation Note: The use of this drug *is a disqualification* for piloting. Consult a designated Aviation Medical Examiner.

Exposure to Sun: No restrictions.
Heavy Exercise or Exertion: Use caution. Excessive exercise can induce asthma
   in sensitive individuals.

METFORMIN (met FOR min)

Introduced: 1995 **Class:** Antidiabetes drug, oral; biguanide **Pre-
scription:** USA: Yes **Controlled Drug:** USA: No; Canada: No
Available as Generic: USA: Yes (new Geneva extended release generic);
Canada: Yes

Brand Names: ♣Apo-Metformin, Avandamet [CD], ♣Dom-Metformin, Glucophage, Glucophage XR, Glucovance [CD], ♣Glycon, Metaglip [CD],
   ♣Novo-Metformin, PMS-Metformin, Riva-Metformin

**Warning: Avoid excessive alcohol. Alcohol can cause lactic acidosis, a con-
dition that metformin can also rarely cause. (See note in Conditions Requiring Dosage Adjustments on page 695.)**

BENEFITS versus RISKS

Possible Benefits	*Possible Risks*
USE IN HIGH-RISK PATIENTS MAY ACTUALLY PREVENT DIABETES (31% IN A LARGE STUDY)	LACTIC ACIDOSIS (see Caution on page 697)
COMBINATION USE WITH ROSIGLITAZONE (AVANDIA) MAY SLOW THE PROGRESSION OF DIABETES	Possible anemia with long-term use (most likely due to decreased B12)
COMBINATION USE WITH ROSIGLITAZONE MAY PREVENT LONG-TERM COMPLICATIONS OF DIABETES	
EFFECTIVE GLUCOSE CONTROL WITHOUT INSULIN INJECTION	
A PRESENTATION AT AN AMERICAN DIABETES CONFERENCE FOUND EXCELLENT RESULTS WHEN METFORMIN WAS COMBINED WITH AN INSULIN SPRAYED INTO THE MOUTH (ORALIN)	
MAY BE USED CONCURRENTLY WITH A SULFONYLUREA	
DOES NOT LEAD TO WEIGHT GAIN	
TAKEN BY MOUTH, VERSUS INJECTION OF INSULIN	
COMBINATION WITH GLIPIZIDE OFFERS IMPROVED BLOOD SUGAR CONTROL	
Usually avoids excessive lowering of blood sugar	
Favorable effects on lipids	

▷ **Principal Uses**

As a Single Drug Product: Uses currently included in FDA-approved labeling: (1) Used in combination with diet restrictions to treat non-insulin-dependent diabetes (type 2); (2) can be combined with a sulfonylurea (see Drug Classes) for patients who do not have an adequate response to diet restrictions. May also be combined with insulin.

Other (unlabeled) generally accepted uses: (1) May be used as single-agent therapy to overcome insulin resistance; (2) could help nondiabetic, obese women with high blood pressure in helping improve blood pressure and lipid profile; (3) may help insulin-dependent (type 1) diabetics decrease insulin requirements; (4) may have a role in treating polycystic ovary syndrome (PCOS); (5) combination use with rosiglitazone may slow the progression of diabetes; (6) use in patients at risk for diabetes may PREVENT diabetes from happening (31% decrease in a large study—see Knowler, W.C. in Sources).

As a Combination Drug Product [CD]: Metformin is available combined with glyburide (Glucovance) as initial treatment of type 2 diabetes or when blood sugar (glucose) control goals are not met by either medicine alone. Also available combined with glipizide (Metaglip).

How This Drug Works: Decreases sugar (glucose) production in the liver. It also increases sensitivity of the body to insulin.

Available Dosage Forms and Strengths

Tablets — 500 mg, 850 mg, 1,000 mg

Tablets, combination (Glucovance) — 250 mg metformin and 1.25 mg glyburide, 500 mg metformin and 2.5 or 5.0 mg glyburide

Tablets, combination (Metaglip) — 250 mg metformin and 2.5 mg glipizide, 500 mg metformin and 5.0 mg glipizide

Tablets, combination (Avandamet) — 500 mg metformin and 2 mg rosiglitazone

Tablets, extended release — 500 mg

▷ **Recommended Dosage Ranges** (Actual dose and schedule must be determined for each patient individually.)

Infants and Children: Immediate release metformin is NOT recommended for children under 10 years old. For ages 10 to 16 years, the starting dose is 500 mg twice daily with meals. Dosing can be increasd as needed and tolerated by 500 mg every 7 days to a maximum of 2,000 mg a day. Doses of this size are separated into equal doses and given 2 or 3 times a day based on results and patient tolerance. The safety and effectiveness for the XR form have not been established in that population.

16 to 60 Years of Age: Dosing is started at 500 mg twice daily. It is best to take this medicine with the morning and evening meals. Doses can be increased as needed and tolerated by 500 mg increments every 7 days. Some clinicians use 850 mg once daily. If the 850 mg dose is used, dosing is increased as needed and tolerated at 14-day intervals. Maximum dose is 2,500 mg if the 500 mg tablets are used, and 2,550 mg if the 850 mg tablets are used. Doses up to 2,000 mg are separated into 2 doses, but doses higher than this are best divided into 3 daily doses.

Extended Release Form: Dosing is started with 500 mg once daily with the evening meal. With this form, doses can be increased as needed and toleratd by 500 mg a day every 7 days up to a maximum of 2,000 mg a day. If the 2,000 mg daily dose does not achieve goals (see below), some patients benefit from 1,000 mg twice daily. If after 28 days of regular medicine use (good adherence), goals are still not met, a sulfonylurea (see Drug Classes) may be added. Each medicine dose should be carefully changed to obtain the best control of blood sugar. Once again, good control is critical. If 1 to 3 months of maximum metformin and sulfonylurea doses does not meet goals, the next step is to start insulin treatment, with or without metformin.

Combination form: (Avandamet): Fasting plasma sugar (glucose) is checked. For patients not well controlled on metformin alone: Dosing is started with a total daily dose of 4 mg of rosiglitasone plus the previous daily dose of metformin. For example, for people previously getting 1,000mg of metformin a day, dosing is started with 1 of the 2 mg rosiglitazone/500 mg metformin tablets twice a day.

Combination form: (Glucovance): Dosing is started with the 1.25 glyburide and 250 mg metformin once a day with meals in people who have a fasting blood sugar more than 200 mg/dl or a glycosylated hemoglobin (hemoglobin A1C) more than 9%.

Combination form: (Metaglip): Dosing is started with the 1.25 glyburide and 250 mg metformin once a day with breakfast. The dose is increased as needed and tolerated every 14 days to 10/2000 in equally divided doses with morning and evening meals.

Over 60 Years of Age: Some patients may have acceptable blood sugar control with as little as 500 mg daily. If this dose is used, take it with the morning meal. Dose may be slowly increased if needed.

Conditions Requiring Dosing Adjustments

Liver Function: This drug should not be used by patients with liver compromise. This is a risk factor for lactic acidosis.

Kidney Function: NOT to be used in kidney disease (renal dysfunction) defined as females with steady-state creatinine levels greater than 1.4 or males with levels greater than 1.5.

▷ **Dosing Instructions:** This drug should be taken with the morning and evening meals if it has been prescribed on a twice-daily basis. One study found that use of metformin with insulin at bedtime not only lowered risk of excessively low blood sugar (hypoglycemia), but also prevented weight gain. If you forget a dose: take the missed dose as soon as you remember it, unless it's nearly time for your next dose—if that is the case, skip the missed dose and take the next dose right on schedule. Talk with your doctor if you find yourself missing doses. Follow-up of benefits of this medicine involve finger stick blood sugar testing. Talk to your doctor about how often to check your blood sugar and what to check it with. (See the new Table 18—Patient Power and Home Test Kits).

Usual Duration of Use: Continual use on a regular schedule for a week is usually necessary to determine this drug's effectiveness in establishing tight glucose control. A month or more of continuous use will be needed before an effect on glycosylated hemoglobin (a measure of past success of glucose control) is seen. Long-term use (months to years) requires periodic evaluation of response and dose adjustment. See your doctor on a regular basis.

Typical Treatment Goals and Measurements (Outcomes and Markers)

Blood sugar: The general goal for blood sugar is to return it to the usual "normal" range (generally 80–120 mg/dl), while avoiding risks of excessively low blood sugar. One study (UKPDS) used a fasting plasma sugar (glucose) of less than 108 mg/dl. DCCT found that tight control of blood sugar helped avoid long-term diabetic complications (see Sources). For Pre-diabetes (see below): one goal of the use of this medicine may actually be to PREVENT development of diabetes.

Fructosamine and glycosylated hemoglobin: Fructosamine levels (a measure of the past 2 to 3 weeks of blood sugar control) should be less than or equal to 310 micromoles per liter. Glycosylated hemoglobin or hemoglobin A1C (a measure of the past 2–3 months of blood sugar control) should be less than or equal to 7.0%. Some clinicians recommend 6.5% with the caveat that you must be more aware of the signs and symptoms of low blood sugar and know what to do if this happens.

Possible Advantages of This Drug

Does not lead to weight gain.

Can be used (because of its mechanism of action) in combination with a sulfonylurea.

Can be used to overcome insulin resistance.

Can be used in combination with rosiglitazone to slow diabetes progression and help avoid long-term diabetes complications.

Does not cause excessive lowering of blood sugar (hypoglycemia) when used as monotherapy.

Combined with glipizide (Metaglip) to offer better (tighter) blood sugar control while being less likely to lead to prolonged low blood sugar like some other possible combinations.

Data from the Diabetes Prevention Program (DPP) showed that use of metformin in high-risk patients PREVENTED diabetes in 31% of those studied!

Currently a "Drug of Choice"

For helping to PREVENT development of diabetes. Also a "drug of choice" for treatment of hyperglycemia in the elderly.

▷ This Drug Should Not Be Taken If

- you had an allergic reaction to it previously.
- you have impaired kidneys (serum creatinine greater than 1.4 for females or 1.5 for males) as this potentially increases the risk of lactic acidosis).
- you have congestive heart failure (CHF) and take medicines to treat it (increases risk of lactic acidosis).
- you have liver disease.
- you are an alcoholic.
- you have a heart or lung insufficiency (increased lactic acidosis risk).
- you are going to have a radiology test that uses iodinated contrast media (ask your doctor because this medicine should be stopped before or at the time of the test, then kidney function checked and found to be in the normal range; then metformin can be started 48 hours after).
- you have chronic metabolic acidosis or ketoacidosis.
- you are breast-feeding your infant.

▷ Inform Your Physician Before Taking This Drug If

- you are planning to have surgery soon.
- you have a serious infection (increases risk of lactic acidosis).
- you drink excessive amounts of alcohol (talk with your doctor) or are elderly (increases lactic acidosis risk).
- you have a history of megaloblastic anemia.
- you are pregnant (insulin is the drug of choice).
- you have seen another doctor and ketoacidosis was diagnosed.
- you are unsure how much to take or how often to take it.

Possible Side Effects (natural, expected, and unavoidable drug actions)
Low blood sugar (hypoglycemia) if meals are skipped or if you exercise strenuously without eating. Blocking of absorption of vitamin B12 and development of anemia (some 7% have lowered B12 with no anemia).

▷ **Possible Adverse Effects** (unusual, unexpected, and infrequent reactions)
If any of the following develop, consult your physician promptly for guidance.

Mild Adverse Effects
Allergic reaction: rare rash.
Metallic taste—infrequent and usually resolves.
Anorexia, nausea, vomiting, or diarrhea—up to 30% when started and then they often subside.
Headache, nervousness, dizziness, or tiredness—infrequent.

Serious Adverse Effects
Allergic reactions: not reported.
Idiosyncratic reactions: liver toxicity—rare.
Lactic acidosis—very rare (Less than 0.1%, but more likely if used in patients with kidney disease or congestive heart failure that requires medicines—which is why current FDA labeling warns against use in those patients. Lactic acidosis is usually not dramatic in signs or symptoms—breathing difficulty [respiratory distress], low body temp [hypothermia], vague abdominal pain, muscle aches [myalgias], and/or increasing sleepiness).
Lowered vitamin B12 levels and resultant anemia (megaloblastic)—rare.
Destruction of red blood cells (hemolysis)—case report.
Drug-induced porphyria—case reports.
All oral hypoglycemic agents carry a label indicating that they may increase risk of cardiovascular death (based on a 1975 study of tolbutamide and phenformin)—possible.
Liver toxicity—2 case reports.

▷ **Possible Effects on Sexual Function:** None reported.

Possible Delayed Adverse Effects: Low vitamin B12 levels and anemia (megaloblastic).

▷ **Adverse Effects That May Mimic Natural Diseases or Disorders**
Acidosis may mimic ketoacidosis, which is seen in diabetics.

Natural Diseases or Disorders That May Be Activated by This Drug
None reported.

Possible Effects on Laboratory Tests
Blood glucose: decreased.
A1C: trending toward 7 or 6.5 %—a beneficial effect!
Vitamin B12: lowered.
Liver function tests: possibly increased.

CAUTION
1. This drug may cause lactic acidosis. Ask your doctor for signs or symptoms that may occur.
2. Drugs in this class (phenformin or tolbutamide) were reported to increase risk of cardiovascular death based on an old study. Although there is no data to support that effect for this medicine, patients should be closely followed.
3. The risk of lactic acidosis is increased if this medicine is used in patients with kidney disease or heart failure that requires medicine. The current

drug label says that metformin should not be used in those patients (black box warning).

4. You should know the signs and symptoms of lactic acidosis (breathing difficulty [respiratory distress], low body temp [hypothermia], vague abdominal pain, muscle aches [myalgias], and/or increasing sleepiness) and should stop the medicine and immediately call your doctor if any develop while taking this medicine.

5. The American Diabetic Association (ADA) now says that a person is considered diabetic if 2 fasting blood sugars in a row are more than 125 mg/dl. This more conservative approach reflects new information saying that complications start at lower blood sugar levels than previously thought. The concept of Pre-diabetes (formerly impaired glucose tolerance) is described in the Glossary. Some new British data advocate that statin-type medicines could cut the risk of heart attack and stroke by a third (even in people with "normal" cholesterol), yet these medicines are underused in diabetics. Talk to your doctor about this.

Precautions for Use

By Infants and Children: Safety and effectiveness for use by those under 10 years of age have not been established. See dosing information on page 695 for those 10 or older for the regular form. Safety and effectiveness for the Metformin XR form in the pediatric population have not been established.

By Those Over 60 Years of Age: Smaller starting doses (500 mg daily) are indicated. People in this age group tend to have an age-related decline in kidney function as well as a more compromised ability to tolerate lower blood sugar levels. Some patients have had great blood sugar control with 500 mg a day, but doses up to 3,000 mg have been used. Patients who are over 80 should have a laboratory test called a MEASURED CREATININE clearance to check how well their kidneys work before this medicine is used. If the test result is within the normal limits, this medicine can be given with the same lower dose caveat dscribed above.

▷ **Advisability of Use During Pregnancy**

Pregnancy Category: B. See Pregnancy Risk Categories at the back of this book.
Animal Studies: No birth defects in rats at 2 times the typical human dose.
Human Studies: Information from adequate studies of pregnant women is not available. The manufacturer does not recommend the use of this drug in pregnancy.
Insulin is still considered the "drug of choice" to control blood sugar in pregnancy.

Advisability of Use If Breast-Feeding

Presence of this drug in breast milk: Unknown.
Avoid drug or refrain from nursing.

Habit-Forming Potential: None.

Effects of Overdose: Nausea and vomiting, pulmonary edema, hemorrhage from the stomach, lactic acidosis, seizures, intractable lowering of blood pressure, coma.

Possible Effects of Long-Term Use: Lowering of vitamin B12 and resultant anemia (megaloblastic). Possible malabsorption of folic acid and amino acids.

Suggested Periodic Examinations While Taking This Drug (at physician's discretion)
Vitamin B12 levels (particularly in those likely to have low B12), but at least every 2 to 3 years. Annual complete blood count (CBC).

Tests of kidney and liver function before treatment is started and yearly at least.

Hemoglobin A1C.

▷ **While Taking This Drug, Observe the Following**

Foods: Follow the ADA diet your doctor recommends. Taking a well-formulated multivitamin that contains B12 is prudent. Rice bran has been checked in a small (57-subject) study of type 1 and type 2 diabetics. The benefit was a 30% lowering of sugar. This might be a new complementary care option.

Herbal Medicines or Minerals: Using chromium may change the way your body is able to use sugar. Some health food stores advocate vanadium as mimicking the actions of insulin, but possible toxicity and need for rigorous studies presently preclude recommending it. DHEA may change sensitivity to insulin or insulin resistance. Aloe, bitter melon, eucalyptus, fenugreek, ginger, garlic, ginseng, glucomannan, guar gum, hawthorn, licorice, nettle, and yohimbe may change blood sugar. Surprisingly, boiled stems of the Optuntia streptacantha prickly pear cactus appear to be able to lower blood sugar. Ongoing effects and effects on A1C are not known. Red sage is used for blood sugar effects, but is unproven. Psyllium increases risk of excessively low blood sugar. Since so many of these products may require adjustment of insulin dosing, talk to your doctor BEFORE combining any of these herbal medicines with this medicine. Echinacea pupurea (injectable) and blonde psyllium seed or husk should NOT be taken by people living with diabetes.

Nutritional Support: Diet as prescribed by your doctor. Check of vitamin B12 levels determines need for support. A multivitamin that has B12 in it may be prudent!

Beverages: No restrictions.

▷ *Alcohol:* Use with extreme caution. Alcohol worsens the effect of metformin on lactate. Avoid alcohol in excessive amounts.

Tobacco Smoking: No interactions expected, but I advise everyone to quit smoking.

Marijuana Smoking: May worsen dizziness.

▷ *Other Drugs*

Metformin may ***increase*** the effects of

- insulin, in the sense that the lowering of blood sugar will be increased; this may be used to therapeutic advantage in some insulin-dependent diabetics.

Metformin ***taken concurrently*** with

- ACE inhibitors (see Drug Classes) may increase lowering of blood sugar to an undesirable extent.
- azole antifungals (see Drug Classes) may increase lowering of blood sugar to an undesirable extent.
- beta blockers (see Drug Classes) may slow recovery from any hypoglycemia that occurs and can also block symptoms of low blood sugar.
- cationic drugs (cotrimoxazole, procainamide, quinidine, quinine, vancomycin, and others) may increase risk of lactic acidosis.
- contrast media for certain X-ray studies may increase risk of lactic acidosis. Metformin should not be combined with these agents. Some clinicians substitute a different agent to control blood sugar, stop the metformin 48 hours before the X-ray and then stop the substituted agent and restart metformin once kidney function is tested and found to be normal.
- cotrimoxazole (Bactrim, others) may increase risk of lactic acidosis.

- digoxin (Lanoxin, others) may pose a problem because it is a cationic drug and may lead to excess metformin levels.
- dofetilide (Tikosyn) may pose a problem because it is a cationic drug and uses the same removal (elimination) pathway that metformin does. This may lead to increased risk of dofetilide toxicity.
- gatifloxacin (Tequin), levofloxacin (Levaquin) can have variable effects on blood sugar. Close patient follow-up and blood sugar checks are prudent if these medicines must be combined.
- itraconazole (Sporanox), voriconazole (Vfend), or other azole antifungal agents can result in severe lowering of the blood sugar.
- procainamide (Pronestyl) may lead to toxicity.
- quinidine (Quinaglute) may lead to toxicity.
- thyroid hormones (see Drug Classes) can result in blunting of metformin's therapeutic effect.

The following drugs may *increase* the effects of metformin:
- cimetidine (Tagamet)—may result in toxicity.
- monoamine oxidase inhibitors (see Drug Classes) can result in severe lowering of the blood sugar.
- morphine (various)—may lead to toxicity.
- nifedipine (Adalat)—may lead to toxicity.
- oral antidiabetic drugs (see Drug Classes)—this effect may be used to therapeutic advantage.
- ranitidine (Zantac)—may lead to toxicity.
- trimethoprim (Septra)—may lead to toxicity.

▷ *Driving, Hazardous Activities:* This drug may cause drowsiness or dizziness. Restrict activities as necessary.

Aviation Note: Diabetes *is a disqualification for piloting.* Consult a designated Aviation Medical Examiner.

Exposure to Sun: Use caution. Some medicines that are similar in chemical structure can cause increased sensitivity to the sun.

Heavy Exercise or Exertion: Heavy exercise will tend to use up sugar faster than usual. This drug will have an effect on lowering the blood sugar. Be alert to the symptoms of low blood sugar.

Occurrence of Unrelated Illness: Infections or other illness may still require use of insulin to achieve acceptable blood sugar control.

Discontinuation: Periodic physician evaluations of the continued benefit of this medicine are needed in order to get the best results. It is not unusual to change doses or to combine this medicine with other medicines. Do not stop this medicine without talking to your doctor.

METHOTREXATE (meth oh TREX ayt)

Other Names: Amethopterin, MTX

Introduced: 1948   **Class:**   Chemotherapy, Anticancer drugs, antipsoriasis   **Prescription:**   USA: Yes   **Controlled Drug:**   USA: No; Canada: No   **Available as Generic:**   Yes

Brand Names: Abitrexate, Folex, Folex PFS, Mexate, Mexate AQ, Rheumatrex Dose Pack, Trexall

```
┌─────────────────────────────────────────────────────────────┐
│                    BENEFITS versus RISKS                       │
│      Possible Benefits              Possible Risks             │
│  EFFECTIVE TREATMENT OF SOME    GASTROINTESTINAL ULCERATION    │
│    CASES OF SEVERE DISABLING      AND BLEEDING MOUTH AND       │
│    PSORIASIS                      THROAT ULCERATION            │
│  EFFECTIVE TREATMENT OF         SEVERE BONE MARROW            │
│    CERTAIN ADULT AND              DEPRESSION                   │
│    CHILDHOOD CANCERS            DAMAGE TO LUNGS, LIVER OR      │
│  PREVENTION OF REJECTION OF       KIDNEYS                      │
│    BONE MARROW TRANSPLANTS      Loss of hair                   │
│  USEFUL IN RHEUMATOID                                         │
│    ARTHRITIS AND RELATED                                      │
│    DISORDERS                                                  │
└─────────────────────────────────────────────────────────────┘
```

▷ **Principal Uses**

As a Single Drug Product: Uses currently included in FDA-approved labeling: (1) Combination therapy of acute lymphocytic leukemia; (2) combination therapy of various types of adult and childhood cancer; (3) severe and widespread forms of disabling psoriasis that have failed to respond to all standard treatment procedures; (4) various types of both adult and childhood cancer; (5) used to prevent rejection of transplanted bone marrow; (6) used in the treatment of connective tissue disorders such as rheumatoid arthritis and related conditions (its use in rheumatoid arthritis is restricted to the treatment of selected adults and children with severe active disease [particular] that has failed to respond to conventional therapy); (7) used in COMBINATION with sulfasalazine or hydroxychloroquin in some cases of refractory rheumatoid arthritis. Also used in combination with infliximab and some of the other DMARDs in rheumatoid arthritis patients who do not have successful response to methotrexate alone.

Other (unlabeled) generally accepted uses: (1) Used in a variety of neoplastic syndromes in combination therapy; (2) may have a role in helping decrease steroid use in steroid-dependent asthma; (3) helps lessen neutropenia in Felty's syndrome; (4) used in combination with misoprostol to cause abortion; (5) can be of help in chronic granulomatous hepatitis of unknown cause (idiopathic); (6) used in some cases of systemic lupus erythematosus.

How This Drug Works: Blocks normal use of folic acid in cell reproduction and slows abnormally rapid tissue growth (as in psoriasis and cancer). How this works in rheumatoid arthritis is not presently known, but probably works by fighting inflammation and by slowing down the immune system (immunosuppresion).

Available Dosage Forms and Strengths

Injections — 2.5 mg/ml, 10 mg/ml, 25 mg/ml

Injections, preservative free — 25 mg/ml, 50 mg/ml, 100 mg/ml, 250 mg/ml

Powder, intrathecal cryodessicated — 20 mg, 50 mg, 100 mg

Tablets — 2.5 mg

▷ **Usual Adult Dosage Ranges:** *For psoriasis (alternate schedules):* (1) 10 to 25 mg once a week taken by mouth (orally); (2) a test dose of 5 to 10 mg is given, then if the laboratory test results are normal, 7 days later, 2.5 to 5 mg every 12 hours for 3 doses per week can be given. Doses can be increased as needed and tolerated by 2.5 to 5 mg every 7 days. The maximum dose is 20 mg per week on this divided schedule.

For rheumatoid arthritis (alternate schedules): (1) single oral dose of 7.5 mg once weekly; (2) divided doses of 2.5 mg every 12 hours for 3 doses per week. Dose may be increased gradually as needed and tolerated. Do not exceed a weekly dose of 20 mg. Intramuscular injections of 7.5 to 15 mg per week have been used. Once people respond to the medicine, the dose should be gradually lowered to the lowest dose that still works. The length of treatment is not known.

For acute lymphocytic leukemia (ALL): Induction—3.3 mg per square meter in combination with corticosteroid treatment is usually taken daily for 4 to 6 weeks. Maintenance—a total weekly dose of 30 mg per square meter is given as 2 divided oral or intramuscular injections. Some centers also use 2.5 mg per kg of body mass intravenously every 14 days. The tablets can be substituted for the solution. Injections beneath the skin (subcutaneous) can be substituted for injection into the muscle (intramuscular).

Note: Actual dose and schedule must be determined for each patient individually.

Conditions Requiring Dosing Adjustments

Liver Function: Used with caution and in decreased dose in liver disease. Some clinicians use laboratory tests as a guide—for example, when dose is due, if bilirubin is less than 3 mg % and AST (SGOT) is less than 180 IU, 100% of the scheduled dose can be given. If bilirubin is greater than 5.0 mg %, dose SHOULD NOT be given.

Kidney Function: Methotrexate is a benefit-to-risk decision. Increased adverse effects are possible with damaged kidneys. Do not take with severe kidney failure (creatinine clearance less than 10 ml/min). For moderate failure, 50% of the usual dose should be taken in the usual dosing interval.

▷ **Dosing Instructions:** The tablet may be crushed and taken with food to reduce stomach irritation. Drink at least 2 to 3 quarts of liquids daily. Many clinicians using methotrexate in rheumatoid arthritis also give folic acid in order to minimize methotrexate toxicity. If you forget a dose: take the missed dose as soon as you remember it, unless it's nearly time for your next dose—if that is the case, skip the missed dose and take the next dose right on schedule. Two forms of birth control should be used by women who can have children while they are taking this medicine and for 3 months after treatment ends. Talk with your doctor if you find yourself missing doses of methotrexate. Ask your doctor BEFORE getting any vaccinations. Some shots can be given before treatment is started, others should be avoided.

Usual Duration of Use: Use on a regular schedule for several weeks determines benefit in reducing the severity and extent of psoriasis. Response in rheumatoid arthritis usually begins after 3 to 6 weeks of treatment. Dose should be reduced to smallest amount that will maintain acceptable improvement. Long-term use (months to years) requires physician supervision. The ideal length of treatment is not presently known for rheumatoid arthritis.

Typical Treatment Goals and Measurements (Outcomes and Markers)

Rheumatoid arthritis: Control of arthritis symptoms (severity of pain, number of swollen joints, loss of mobility, decreased ability to accomplish activities of daily living, range of motion, early morning stiffness [EMS], etc.) is paramount in returning patient quality of life and to checking the results (beneficial outcomes) from this medicine. A scale called the ACR response is widely used. Many arthritis management or pain centers use interdisciplinary teams (physicians from several specialties, nurses, physician's assistants, physical and occupational therapists, pharmacotherapists, psychotherapists, social workers, and others) to get the best results. Blood levels of methotrexate are used to help avoid toxicity. In rheumatoid arthritis, C-reactive protein, or sedimentation rate also measures results.

▷ **This Drug Should Not Be Taken If**
- you have had an allergic reaction to it previously.
- you currently have, or have had a recent exposure to, either chicken pox or shingles (herpes zoster).
- you are pregnant or planning pregnancy in the near future and you are taking this drug to treat psoriasis or rheumatoid arthritis.
- you are breast-feeding your infant.
- you have alcoholic liver disease.
- you have an immune deficiency.
- you have fluid in the pleura of the lung (pleural effusions).
- you have active liver disease, peptic ulcer, regional enteritis, or ulcerative colitis.
- you are making very small amounts of urine or your creatinine clearance (see Glossary) is less than 40 ml/min.
- you currently have a blood cell or bone marrow disorder.

▷ **Inform Your Physician Before Taking This Drug If**
- you have a chronic infection of any kind.
- you do not understand how to handle vomit or urine while taking chemotherapy.
- you have impaired liver or kidney function.
- you have a history of bone marrow impairment of any kind, especially drug-induced bone marrow depression.
- your white blood cell count is less than 1,500 or your platelet count is less than 75,000.
- you start to have a skin reaction while taking this drug.
- you are dehydrated.
- you have a history of gout, peptic ulcer disease, regional enteritis, or ulcerative colitis.

Possible Side Effects (natural, expected, and unavoidable drug actions)
The following are due to the pharmacological actions of this drug. **Report such developments to your physician promptly.**
Sores on the lips, in the mouth or throat.
Vomiting.
Photoxicity with sun exposure.
Intestinal cramping.
Diarrhea (may be bloody).
Painful urination.
Eye irritation (conjunctivitis).
Bloody urine.
Superinfections (may be lung-respiratory such as pneumocystis pneumonia, or PCP, and case reports of histoplasmosis have been made).
Reduced resistance to infection, fatigue, weakness, fever, abnormal bleeding or bruising (bone marrow depression).

▷ **Possible Adverse Effects** (unusual, unexpected, and infrequent reactions)
 If any of the following develop, consult your physician promptly for guidance.
  Mild Adverse Effects
   Allergic reactions: skin rash, hives, itching.
   Headache, drowsiness, blurred vision, conjunctivitis—infrequent.
   Loss of appetite, nausea, vomiting—infrequent to frequent.
   Muscle pain—rare.
   Loss of hair, loss of skin pigmentation, acne—infrequent.
   Impaired sense of smell or taste—possible.
  Serious Adverse Effects
   Allergic reactions: drug-induced pneumonia (cough, chest pain, shortness of breath).
   Anaphylaxis.
   Asthma-like reaction—possible (may require dosing interval extensions).
   Nervous system toxicity: speech disturbances, paralysis, seizures—infrequent.
   Liver toxicity with jaundice (see Glossary)—case reports.
   Kidney toxicity: reduced urine volume, kidney failure—more likely with higher doses.
   Accumulation of fluid around the heart (pericardial effusion and pericarditis)—possible and some may require leucovorin rescue.
   Clogging of the arteries (atherosclerotic vascular disease)—possibly increased.
   Colitis or toxic megacolon—case report.
   Tumor lysis syndrome: uric acid nephropathy; very low potassium, magnesium, and calcium—possible.
   Fluid buildup in the lung pleura (pleural effusion)—possible.
   Immune suppression and subsequent infection with Pneumocystis carinii pneumonia—possible.
   Bone toxicity (osteopathy)—case reports (6 month- to 8.5-year onset with usual or even low-dose treatment).
   Severe skin reactions (toxic epidermal necrolysis)—case reports.
   Chromosomal damage (from occupational exposure)—possible.
▷ **Possible Effects on Sexual Function:** Altered timing and pattern of menstruation. Swelling and tenderness of the male breast tissue (gynecomastia)—case reports. Impotence—case reports.

Possible Delayed Adverse Effects: Some reports suggest that methotrexate therapy may contribute to the later development of secondary cancers. Other studies have not confirmed this.

Possible Effects on Laboratory Tests
  Complete blood cell counts: decreased red cells, hemoglobin, white cells, and platelets.
  Blood uric acid level: increased.
  Liver function tests: increased liver enzymes (ALT/GPT, AST/GOT, and alkaline phosphatase) or bilirubin.
  Kidney function tests: increased blood urea nitrogen (BUN) level; increased urine creatinine.
  Fecal occult blood test: positive.
  Sperm count: decreased.

CAUTION
  1. This drug must be monitored carefully by a qualified physician. Request the Patient Package Insert (Rheumatrex Dose Pack) and read it thoroughly.

2. When methotrexate is used to treat rheumatoid arthritis, folic acid can minimize toxicity.
3. Appropriate laboratory examinations, performed before and during the use of this drug, are mandatory.
4. Women with potential for pregnancy should have a pregnancy test before taking this drug and should use 2 forms of birth control while taking this medicine and for 3 months after stopping it.
5. Live-virus vaccines should be avoided during use of this drug. Live-virus vaccines could actually produce infection rather than stimulate an immune response.
6. Try to avoid people with obvious infections like the flu or colds because this medicine lowers the strength of your immune system and you will be more likely to catch them.

Precautions for Use

By Those Over 60 Years of Age: Careful evaluation of kidney function should be made before starting treatment and during the entire course of therapy.

▷ **Advisability of Use During Pregnancy**

Pregnancy Category: X. See Pregnancy Risk Categories at the back of this book.
Animal Studies: Skull and facial defects reported in mice.
Human Studies: This drug is known to cause fetal deaths and birth defects. Its use during pregnancy to treat psoriasis or rheumatoid arthritis cannot be justified.

Advisability of Use If Breast-Feeding

Presence of this drug in breast milk: Yes.
Avoid drug or refrain from nursing.

Habit-Forming Potential: None.

Effects of Overdose: The side effects and adverse effects listed on the previous page develop earlier and with greater severity.

Possible Effects of Long-Term Use: Liver compromise (fibrosis and cirrhosis) occurs in 3–5% of long-term users (35 to 49 months).

Suggested Periodic Examinations While Taking This Drug (at physician's discretion)

Complete blood cell counts (CBCs). When methotrexate is used in rheumatoid arthritis, complete blood counts are checked after the first, second and fourth weeks of use. If the CBC is acceptable, after 2 weeks, the dose can be increased to 7.5 mg a week. Usually the CBC is checked each month after this.

Liver and kidney function tests.

Blood uric acid levels.

Blood methotrexate levels in high-risk patients (some examples include those with dehydration, compromised kidneys, pleural effusion, prior treatment with cysplatin and acites).

Chest X-ray examinations.

▷ **While Taking This Drug, Observe the Following**

Foods: Avoid highly seasoned foods that could be irritating. Between courses of treatment, eat liberally of the following foods: beef, chicken, lamb, and pork liver, asparagus, navy beans, kale, and spinach. Any food will reduce the peak methotrexate level obtained. Folic acid supplementation is suggested for people who will take this medicine on an ongoing basis.

Herbal Medicines or Minerals: Some patients use echinacea to attempt to boost their immune systems. Unfortunately, use of echinacea is not recommended in people with damaged immune systems (even if a medicine caused the damage). This herb may also actually weaken any immune system if it is used too often or for too long a time. Like methotrexate, St. John's wort may cause sensitivity to the sun. Avoid this combination. There are no data regarding combined use of hay flower, mistletoe herb,or white mustard seed with methotrexate in rheumatoid arthritis. Herbals such as kava, valerian, and eucalyptus may have additive effects on liver toxicity and should be avoided.

Beverages: No restrictions. This drug may be taken with milk.

▷ *Alcohol:* Markedly lower how much you drink or avoid completely (increases risk of liver damage).

Tobacco Smoking: No interactions expected. I advise everyone to quit smoking.

Marijuana Smoking: May cause additional impairment of immunity.

▷ *Other Drugs*

Methotrexate may *decrease* the effects of
- digoxin (Lanoxin).
- folate (various) by blocking the change (conversion) of folate to folic acid.
- phenytoin (Dilantin) or fosphenytoin (Cerebyx).

The following drugs may *increase* the effects of methotrexate and enhance its toxicity:
- aspirin and other salicylates.
- diuretics (see Drug Classes) may result in methotrexate-enhanced lowering of granulocyte-type white blood cells (myelosuppression).
- NSAIDs (see Drug Classes) (especially with higher NSAID doses).
- omeprazole (Prilosec).
- probenecid (Benemid).
- rofecoxib (Vioxx).

Methotrexate *taken concurrently* with
- amiodarone (Cordarone) may result in methotrexate toxicity.
- asparaginase (Elspar, others) may result in blunted methotrexate activity.
- bismuth subsalicylate (Pepto-Bismol, others) may result in methotrexate toxicity.
- carbenicillin (Geocillin, others) and other penicillins (see Drug Classes) may lead to methotrexate toxicity.
- cholestyramine (Questran, others) and other cholesterol-lowering resins may result in decreased methotrexate effectiveness.
- cotrimoxazole (Bactrim) may result in lowering of all blood cells (pancytopenia).
- cyclosporine (Sandimmune) can result in increased toxicity from both drugs. This combination should be avoided.
- doxycycline (various) may result in methotrexate toxicity.
- etretinate (Tegison) results in increased liver toxicity.
- influenzae (flu) vaccine may blunt benefits of the vaccine.
- leflunomide (Arava) may result in liver toxicity.
- live-virus vaccines (such as MMWR) may lead to severe infections.
- mercaptopurine (Purinethol) may lead to mercaptopurine toxicity.
- neomycin (various) may result in decreased methotrexate benefits.
- penicillins (see Drug Classes) may result in serious methotrexate toxicity. If these medicines must be combined, lower methotrexate doses, blood levels of methotrexate and extremely careful patient follow-up are required.
- pneumococcal or smallpox vaccine may result in decreased immune response to the vaccine.

- sulfa drugs, such as sulfamethoxazole, can result in increased hematological toxicity.
- tamoxifen (Nolvadex) may increase risk of blood clots (thromboembolism)—part of a combination regimen that leads to this.
- thiazide diuretics (see Drug Classes) may increase risk of myelosuppression.
- theophylline (Theo-Dur, others) may result in theophylline toxicity; decreased theophylline doses may be needed.
- triamterene (Dyazide, others) may increase risk of bone marrow problems (myelosuppression).
- trimethoprim (Septra, others) may increase risk of toxicity.
- yellow fever vaccine can result in blunted response and benefit from the vaccine.

▷ *Driving, Hazardous Activities:* This drug may cause drowsiness, dizziness, or blurred vision. Restrict activities as necessary.

Aviation Note: The use of this drug *is a disqualification* for piloting. Consult a designated Aviation Medical Examiner.

Exposure to Sun: Use caution—this drug can cause photosensitivity. Avoid ultraviolet lamps.

METHYCLOTHIAZIDE (METH i kloh thi a zide)

Please see the thiazide diuretics family profile.

METHYLPHENIDATE (meth il FEN i dayt)

Introduced: 1956 **Class:** Amphetaminelike drug, anti–attention deficit disorder drug **Prescription:** USA: Yes **Controlled Drug:** USA: C-II*; Canada: Yes **Available as Generic:** USA: Yes; Canada: Yes

Brand Names: Concerta, Metadate CD and ER, Methylin ER, ♣PMS-Methylphenidate, Ritalin, Ritalin-LA and SR

Author's Note: Focalin is a relatively new treatment for ADHD. This medicine is NOT the same as methylphenidate. This drug is DEX-methylphenidate. The usual dose is only half of the methylphenidate dose. Information on Focalin will be included in a broader dex-methylphenidate profile if ongoing studies and results warrant this.

*See Schedules of Controlled Drugs at the back of this book.

BENEFITS versus RISKS	
Possible Benefits	*Possible Risks*
EFFECTIVE CONTROL OF NARCOLEPSY	POTENTIAL FOR SERIOUS PSYCHOLOGICAL DEPENDENCE
USEFUL AS ADJUNCTIVE TREATMENT IN ATTENTION DEFICIT DISORDERS	(oral dosing reaches brain levels slowly and appears to avoid this effect)
CONCERTA FORM OFFERS ONCE-DAILY DOSING	SUPPRESSION OF GROWTH IN CHILDHOOD (recovers when
Adjunctive treatment in ADHD	medicine is stopped)
Useful in treatment of mild to moderate depression	Abnormal behavior
	Rare blood cell disorders
Useful in some cases of emotional withdrawal in the elderly	
May have a role in some chronic pain cases	

▷ **Principal Uses**

As a Single Drug Product: Uses currently included in FDA-approved labeling: Treats (1) narcolepsy—recurrent spells of uncontrollable drowsiness and sleep; (2) attention deficit disorders of childhood, formerly known as the hyperactive child syndrome, with minimal brain damage and minimal brain dysfunction.

Other (unlabeled) generally accepted uses: (1) Treats mild to moderate depression; (2) manages apathetic and withdrawal states in the elderly; (3) combination therapy of chronic pain, particularly cancer pain; (4) could have a role in autism; (5) may help passing out (recurrent neurocardiogenic syncope).

How This Drug Works: Activates the brain stem, improves alertness and concentration, increases learning ability and attention span. A study in *Science* found that levels of the nerve transmitter serotonin are increased by this medicine, restoring a proper balance between serotonin and other brain chemicals.

Available Dosage Forms and Strengths

Capsule, extended release (Metadate CD) — 20 mg
Tablets — 5 mg, 10 mg, 20 mg
Tablets, prolonged action — 20 mg, 30 mg and 40 mg
Tablet, extended osmotic release (Concerta) — 18 mg, 27 mg, 36 mg, 54 mg
Tablet, extended release (Metadate ER) — 10 mg, 20 mg

▷ **Recommended Dosage Ranges:** *Narcolepsy*: 10 to 60 mg daily, divided into equal doses, given 2 to 3 times daily. Ideally, given 30 to 45 minutes before meals.

Attention deficit disorder: Pediatric dosing: Children over 6 years old (regular release form)—5 mg before breakfast and lunch (twice daily). Some clinicians use 0.25 mg per kg per day divided into 2 doses as a starting dose. Dose is increased as needed and tolerated (weekly intervals) to daily maximum of dose of 60 mg. Sustained release form lasts 8 hours. The Metadate CD form is started at 20 mg once a day before breakfast. Osmotic release form (Concerta) is given once daily in the morning. A specific conversion table is used when people are changed from the immediate release forms to the Concerta form. For example: If 5 mg of immediate release (IR) was being taken 2 or 3 times daily or if 20 mg of the SR form was being taken daily, 18 mg of the Concerta form is taken in the morning.

Pain management: Some clinicians use methylphenidate added onto opioid pain relievers (analgesics) using 10 mg in the morning and 5 mg at lunch.

Note: Actual dose and schedule must be determined for each patient individually.

Conditions Requiring Dosing Adjustments

Liver Function: Used with caution and prudent to decrease dose in liver disease.

Kidney Function: No changes currently thought to be needed.

▷ **Dosing Instructions:** The regular tablet may be crushed and taken 30 to 45 minutes before meals. The prolonged-action tablet, the osmotic controlled release form (Concerta) and any other extended release forms should be taken whole, not crushed. It is best to take this medicine with a full glass of water, juice, or milk. The Ritalin LA capsules can be opened and the contents sprinkled over a spoonful of room temperature or cold (not warm) applesauce. Once so prepared, ALL of the applesauce/ritalin mixture should be taken right away. If you forget a dose: take the missed dose as soon as you remember it, unless it's nearly time for your next dose—if that is the case, skip the missed dose and take the next dose right on schedule. Talk with your doctor if you find yourself missing doses.

▷ **Usual Duration of Use:** Regular use for 3 to 4 weeks determines benefits in easing the symptoms of narcolepsy or improving behavior of attention deficit children. If there is no improvement after this time, the drug should be stopped. Long-term use (months to years) requires supervision by your doctor.

Typical Treatment Goals and Measurements (Outcomes and Markers)

Attention Deficit: The general goal is to achieve the ability to "stay on task." This medicine can also help decrease impulsiveness and increase socially appropriate behavior. Specific measures of cognitive function, motor performance, and educational tasking may help assess response. Treatment guidelines from AHCPR and DSM-IV criteria from the American Psychiatric Association are widely used. The American Academy of Pediatricians has an important set of guidelines. Please remember that these are guidelines and therapy must still be individualized. The guidelines can be found at *www.pediatrics.org* (see also Sources and American Academy of Pediatrics).

▷ **This Drug Should Not Be Taken If**
- you have had an allergic reaction to it previously.
- you have glaucoma.
- you have taken a monoamine oxidase inhibitor (MAOI—see Drug Classes) in the last 14 days.
- you have Tourette's syndrome or experience tics while using this medicine.
- you are experiencing a period of severe anxiety, nervous tension, or emotional depression.

▷ **Inform Your Physician Before Taking This Drug If**
- you have a history of mental illness.
- you have a seizure disorder.
- you have a history of abnormal heartbeats.
- you have high blood pressure, angina, or epilepsy.
- you are under 6 years old (usually avoided).

Possible Side Effects (natural, expected, and unavoidable drug actions)
Nervousness, excitement, insomnia. Reduced appetite. Growth suppression (stopping the medicine in the summer is used to allow a growth spurt). Slight increase in heart rate.

▷ **Possible Adverse Effects** (unusual, unexpected, and infrequent reactions)
If any of the following develop, consult your physician promptly for guidance.
Mild Adverse Effects
Allergic reactions: skin rash, hives, drug fever, joint pains—possible.
Headache, dizziness, rapid and forceful heart palpitation—infrequent.
Nausea, abdominal discomfort—infrequent.
Stuttering and hallucinations—case reports.
Serious Adverse Effects
Allergic reactions: severe skin reactions, extensive bruising (allergic destruction of platelets)—case reports.
Idiosyncratic reactions: abnormal patterns of behavior.
Cerebral vasculitis (tingling and numbness followed by movement disorders)—case report.
Porphyria or muscle damage (rhabdomyolysis)—rare.
Liver toxicity—case reports.
Precipitation of Tourette's syndrome—case reports.

▷ **Possible Effects on Sexual Function:** None reported.

Natural Diseases or Disorders That May Be Activated by This Drug
Latent epilepsy. Increased eye pressure unmasking glaucoma.

Possible Effects on Laboratory Tests
Eosinophils: Increased (IV abuse).

CAUTION
1. This drug should be used ONLY AFTER a careful assessment by a qualified specialist is made. True attention deficit disorder requires careful assessment to differentiate it from behavior problems arising from family tensions or other conditions that do not require methylphenidate therapy.
2. A February 2000 study of 200,000 children coordinated by the University of Maryland found a large increase in Ritalin, Prozac, and clonidine prescriptions in patients under 4 years old. This retrospective review of Medicaid and HMO records may represent better ability to diagnose, but may also reflect excessive use. The American Academy of Pediatricians has an important set of guidelines. Please remember that these are guidelines and therapy must still be individualized. The guidelines can be found at *www.pediatrics.org* (see also Sources and American Academy of Pediatrics).
3. Careful dose adjustments on an individual basis are mandatory.
4. Paradoxical reactions (see Glossary) can occur, causing aggravation of initial symptoms for which this drug was prescribed.

Precautions for Use
By Infants and Children: Safety and effectiveness for those under 6 years of age are not established. If this drug is not beneficial in managing attention deficit disorder after a trial of 1 month, it should be stopped. During long-term use, monitor the child for normal growth and development.
By Those Over 60 Years of Age: Start with small doses. Those in this group may be at increased risk for nervousness, agitation, insomnia, high blood pressure, angina, or disturbance of heart rhythm.

▷ **Advisability of Use During Pregnancy**
Pregnancy Category: C. See Pregnancy Risk Categories at the back of this book.
Animal Studies: No birth defects found in mouse studies.
Human Studies: Adequate studies of pregnant women are not available.
Ask your physician for guidance.

Advisability of Use If Breast-Feeding
Presence of this drug in breast milk: Unknown.
Avoid drug or refrain from nursing.

Habit-Forming Potential: This drug can produce tolerance and cause serious
psychological dependence (see Glossary), a potentially dangerous characteristic of amphetaminelike drugs (see Drug Classes). The street name for
this medicine is R-ball or Vitamin-R. It is one of the top prescription drugs
stolen in the United States for recreational use. Caution is needed. If you
start to feel like the medicine is not working, call your doctor. One study of
abuse of methylphenidate on a college campus described this as a potentially serious public health issue (see Teter, C.J. in Sources).

Effects of Overdose: Headache, vomiting, agitation, tremors, dry mouth, sweating, fever, confusion, hallucinations, seizures, coma.

Possible Effects of Long-Term Use: Suppression of growth (in weight and/or
height) occurs. Many patients are taken off the drug during summer vaca-
tions.

Suggested Periodic Examinations While Taking This Drug (at physician's dis-
cretion)
Complete blood cell counts.
Blood pressure measurements.
Height and weight.
Follow-up evaluation for beneficial effects of treatment.

▷ **While Taking This Drug, Observe the Following**
Herbal Medicines or Minerals: Using St. John's wort, guarana, ma huang, or
kola while taking this medicine may result in unacceptable central nervous
system stimulation.
Beverages: Avoid beverages prepared from meat or meat extracts. This drug
may be taken with milk.
▷ *Alcohol:* Avoid beer, Chianti wines and vermouth (may have high tyramine contents).
Tobacco Smoking: No interactions expected. I advise everyone to quit smoking.
▷ *Other Drugs*
Methylphenidate may *increase* the effects of
• tricyclic antidepressants (see Drug Classes) and enhance their toxic effects.
Methylphenidate may *decrease* the effects of
• guanethidine (Ismelin) and impair its ability to lower blood pressure.
Methylphenidate *taken concurrently* with
• anticonvulsants (such as carbamazepine or fosphenytoin or phenytoin)
may cause a significant change in the pattern of epileptic seizures; dose
adjustments may be necessary for proper control.
• monoamine oxidase (MAO) type A inhibitors (see Drug Classes) may cause
a significant rise in blood pressure; avoid the concurrent use of these
drugs.
• morphine may be used to great therapeutic benefit to increase alertness,
especially if high doses of morphine must be used.
• tricyclic antidepressants (see Drug Classes) may result in undesirable
increases in blood pressure.

▷ *Driving, Hazardous Activities:* This drug may cause dizziness or drowsiness. Restrict activities as necessary.

Aviation Note: The use of this drug **is a disqualification** for piloting. Consult a designated Aviation Medical Examiner.

Exposure to Sun: No restrictions.

Discontinuation: If the drug has been taken for a long time, do not stop it abruptly. Talk to your doctor about how to slowly decrease doses.

METHYLPREDNISOLONE (meth il pred NIS oh lohn)

Introduced: 1957   **Class:** Cortisonelike drugs   **Prescription:** USA: Yes   **Controlled Drug:** USA: No; Canada: No   **Available as Generic:** USA: Yes; Canada: Yes

Brand Names: A-Methapred, Depmedalone-40, Depmedalone-80, Depo-Medrol, Enpak Refill, Mar-Pred 40, Medrol, ✤Medrol Acne Lotion, Medrol Enpak, ✤Medrol Veriderm Cream, Meprolone, ✤Neo-Medrol Acne Lotion, ✤Neo-Medrol Veriderm, Pre-Dep 40, 80, Rep-Pred 80, Solu-Medrol

BENEFITS versus RISKS	
Possible Benefits	*Possible Risks*
EFFECTIVE RELIEF OF SYMPTOMS IN A WIDE VARIETY OF INFLAMMATORY AND ALLERGIC DISORDERS	Ongoing systemic use or exposure (variable onset) can be associated with increased possible emergence of effects such as:
EFFECTIVE IMMUNO-SUPPRESSION IN SELECTED BENIGN AND MALIGNANT DISORDERS	ALTERED MOOD AND PERSONALITY
	CATARACTS, GLAUCOMA
	HYPERTENSION
	OSTEOPOROSIS
	INCREASED SUSCEPTIBILITY TO INFECTIONS, AND OTHERS
	ASCEPTIC BONE NECROSIS (OSTEONECROSIS) IS AN AREA OF CONTROVERSY, UNCLEAR ONSET. PATIENT RISK FACTORS AND CORRELATION VERSUS CAUSATION (SEE "CONTROVER-SIES IN MEDICINE" ON PAGE 716)

▷ **Principal Uses**

As a Single Drug Product: Uses currently included in FDA-approved labeling: (1) Treats a wide variety of allergic and inflammatory conditions (used most commonly in the management of serious skin disorders, asthma, regional enteritis, multiple sclerosis, lupus erythematosus, ulcerative colitis, and all types of major rheumatic disorders including bursitis, tendonitis, and most forms of arthritis); (2) helps treat low platelet counts of unknown cause (idiopathic thrombocytopenic purpura); (3) treats shock due to adrenal gland insufficiency—Addisonian shock; (4) plays an adjunctive role in anaphylactic shock; (5) used in acute lymphocytic leukemia as part of chemotherapy treatment.

Other (unlabeled) generally accepted uses: (1) Treats refractory anemia; (2) used in therapy of chronic obstructive pulmonary disease; (3) used in combination therapy of severe vomiting caused by chemotherapy; (4) helps prevent rejection of transplanted organs; (5) combination therapy of *Pneumocystis carinii* pneumonia in AIDS patients; (6) helps treat bone cysts in children; (7) has a role in treating croup; (8) can help symptoms in Still's disease; (9) used by intramuscular injection to treat polymyalgia rheumatica and some carpal tunnel cases; (10) used to help control cancer pain, especially where inflammation is involved.

How This Drug Works: Anti-inflammatory effect is due to its ability to block normal defensive functions of certain white blood cells. Immunosuppressant effect comes from reduced production of lymphocytes (a kind of white blood cell) and antibodies.

Available Dosage Forms and Strengths
Injection, solution (per vial) — 40 mg, 125 mg, 500 mg, 1 g
Injection, suspension — 40 mg/ml, 80 mg/ml
Ointment — 0.25%, 1%
Retention enema (per bottle) — 40 mg
Tablets — 2 mg, 4 mg, 8 mg, 16 mg, 24 mg, 32 mg

▷ **Usual Adult Dosage Ranges:** 4 to 48 mg daily as a single (oral) dose or in divided doses. Medrol dosepaks are a card with 4 mg tablets of methylprednisolone in them. On the first day, 2 tablets are taken before breakfast, 1 tablet after the noon and evening meals and then 2 tablets are taken at bedtime. Patients should then follow the ongoing instructions on the card for the remaining days (6 days total).
Note: Actual dose and schedule must be determined for each patient individually.

Conditions Requiring Dosing Adjustments
Liver Function: Specific dose adjustments in liver compromise are not defined. This drug is a rare cause of liver changes (hepatomegaly).
Kidney Function: This drug can worsen existing kidney compromise. A benefit-to-risk decision must be made regarding the use of methylprednisolone by these patients.
Obesity: The amount of time this medicine stays in the body is extended in obese patients. Dosing should be calculated based on ideal body weight.

▷ **Dosing Instructions:** The tablet may be crushed and taken with or following food to prevent stomach irritation, preferably in the morning. If you forget a dose: Call your doctor for instructions. Follow the specific instructions from your doctor and as outlined on the Medrol DosePak if that form is used.

Usual Duration of Use: For sudden (acute) disorders, 4 to 10 days. Need for tapering, patient reaction, possible disease flare are all factors to be considered. Medrol DosePaks are a pre-planned 6-day course. For long-standing (chronic) disorders, this medicine is used according to individual and condition requirements. Duration of use should not exceed the time necessary to obtain adequate symptomatic relief in acute self-limiting conditions, then permit appropriate withdrawal or the time required to stabilize a chronic condition and permit appropriate withdrawal. Because of its intermediate duration of action, this drug may be appropriate for alternate-day use in some cases. See your doctor on a regular basis.

Typical Treatment Goals and Measurements (Outcomes and Markers)

Inflammation: The general goal is to decrease inflammation. Physical signs and symptoms such as hives (urticaria), rash, difficulty breathing, and swelling should ease. Representative tests may include sedimentation rate, cortisol, peak expiratory flow rate, FEV1 for respiratory conditions.

Asthma: Frequency and severity of asthma attacks should ease. Some clinicians also use decreased frequency of rescue inhaler use as a further clinical indicator. It is critical that this medicine is used regularly to get the best results. An additional goal of therapy is to use the lowest effective dose. Some people keep their improvements when doses are lowered, while others relapse. Specific testing goals include improvement in PEFR, FEV1, and other lung (pulmonary) function tests. Wheezing and difficulty breathing (dyspnea) should ease as well as asthma caused (induced) by exercise. If the usual benefit is not realized, call your doctor.

▷ **This Drug Should Not Be Taken If**
- you had an allergic reaction to it previously.
- you have active peptic ulcer disease.
- you have had recent bowel surgery where an anastomosis was performed.
- you have a premature infant and the injection form is ordered (contains benzyl alcohol).
- you have an active eye infection from herpes simplex virus.
- you have active tuberculosis or a full-body (systemic) fungus infection.

▷ **Inform Your Physician Before Taking This Drug If**
- you have had a reaction to any cortisonelike drug.
- you have a history of peptic ulcer disease, colitis, thrombophlebitis, or tuberculosis.
- you have diabetes, glaucoma, high blood pressure, deficient thyroid function, or myasthenia gravis.
- you have been exposed to measles or chicken pox or other viral illness.
- you have osteoporosis, kidney disease, or have a history of threadworm (Strongyloides) infection.
- you start to have restricted motion, increased and/or unexplained pain (such as in the knees, hips, or shoulders), fever, or swelling of joints while taking or after taking this medicine—these may be early signs of aseptic necrosis (osteonecrosis). Call your doctor right away.
- you plan to have surgery of any kind in the near future.
- you have liver compromise.

Possible Side Effects (natural, expected, and unavoidable drug actions)

Increased appetite, weight gain, retention of salt and water, excretion of potassium, increased susceptibility to infection. Decreased wound healing. Adrenal gland suppression. Growth retardation with chronic use in children. Increased eye pressure (intraocular). Easy bruising (ecchymosis). Increased white blood cell count (not a sign of infection, but an effect of the medicine). Suppression of the immune system leading to possible opportunistic infections or increased chance of infections in general.

▷ **Possible Adverse Effects** (unusual, unexpected, and infrequent reactions)
If any of the following develop, consult your physician promptly for guidance.

Mild Adverse Effects
Allergic reaction: skin rash.
Headache, dizziness, insomnia—infrequent.

Acid indigestion, abdominal distention—infrequent.

Muscle cramping, weakness, and joint pain—possible.

Acne, excessive growth of facial hair—case reports.

Serious Adverse Effects

Allergic reactions: anaphylaxis.

Mental and emotional disturbances—infrequent.

Reactivation of latent tuberculosis, *Pneumocystis carinii* pneumonia— possible, case reports.

Development of peptic ulcer—case reports.

Seizures—possible.

Toxic megacolon—case reports.

Liver or kidney compromise—rare.

Blindness, opportunistic infections of the eye, cataracts—case reports.

Changes in white blood cell counts—possible.

Cushing's syndrome with chronic use (central obesity, buffalo hump, and moon-shaped face)—possible.

Osteoporosis—possible with long-term use.

Bone death (aseptic necrosis, osteonecrosis, or avascular necrosis)— questions remain as to correlation versus causation, but may be more likely with high initial doses, long-term treatment, and cumulative doses of 4.32 grams. May also happen after short-term modest use. Individual patient risk factors appear to be important. See Controversies in Medicine on page 716. Call your doctor if unexplained joint pain happens.

Increased blood sugar (hyperglycemia)—possible and dose-related.

Muscle changes (myopathy) or pancreatitis—case reports.

Increased blood pressure—case reports.

Abnormal heartbeat (arrhythmias)—case reports.

Development of inflammation of the pancreas—case reports.

Thrombophlebitis (inflammation of a vein with the formation of blood clot): pain or tenderness in thigh or leg, with or without swelling of the foot, ankle, or leg—case reports.

Pulmonary embolism (movement of a blood clot to the lung): sudden short- ness of breath, pain in the chest, coughing, bloody sputum—case reports.

▷ **Possible Effects on Sexual Function:** Altered timing and pattern of menstrua- tion—infrequent.

▷ **Adverse Effects That May Mimic Natural Diseases or Disorders**

Pattern of symptoms and signs resembling Cushing's syndrome.

Natural Diseases or Disorders That May Be Activated by This Drug

Latent diabetes, glaucoma, peptic ulcer disease, tuberculosis.

Possible Effects on Laboratory Tests

Blood amylase and lipase levels: increased (possible pancreatitis).

Glucose tolerance test (GTT): decreased.

Blood potassium or testosterone level: decreased.

Cholesterol and LDL: increased.

HDL: decreased.

CAUTION

1. If your treatment will exceed 1 week, carry a card in your purse or wallet that says you take this drug. Suppression of the adrenal gland may con- tinue for months even after this medicine is stopped (adrenocortical insufficiency), and replacement therapy (with quick-acting steroids) can be needed during stress (such as serious illness or surgery).

2. You have an increased risk of severe infection from viral illnesses, such as measles or chicken pox. Try to avoid being exposed, and call your doctor if exposure occurs.
3. Growth and development of children receiving chronic steroids should be carefully followed.
4. Do not stop this drug abruptly after long-term treatment (the medicine should be slowly tapered).
5. If vaccination against measles, rabies, smallpox, or yellow fever is required, stop drug 72 hours before vaccination and do not resume it for at least 14 days.
6. Dermatitis around the mouth may occur. Talk with your doctor if this happens.
7. A variety of patient risk factors appear to be important in possible development of osteonecrosis. Talk to your doctor about the current list.

Controversies in Medicine: Medicines in this class have had conflicting reports regarding correlation with or causation of aseptic bone necrosis (osteonecrosis, or ON). There appear to be patient risk factors, possible delayed onset with occurrence even after the medicine is stopped, and some diseases or conditions where corticosteroids are often used and ON is more frequent than the general population. It is unclear if this is because of the disease or condition or the use of corticosteroids. Previous data regarding cumulative dosing (4.32 grams) appears controversial, with more recent case reports of 6 days of treatment with some doses being associated with ON. Some existing and emerging patient risk factors include alcohol use versus abuse, initial high doses, HIV-positive patients who weight trained, Systemic Lupus Erythematosus, some clotting disorders, and high homocysteine levels amongst others appear to increase risk. Early research regarding use of alendronate (Fosamax) to treat ON appears to show that it is important for patients to quickly return to their doctors if unexplained joint pain (such as in the hip or knee) happens. Some centers note that ON has been poorly studied, and while the weight of data is growing, it is yet too early to say more than that ON is correlated with corticosteroid use.

Precautions for Use
By Infants and Children: Avoid prolonged use if possible. Watch for growth suppression. Long-term use also increases risk of adrenal gland deficiency during stress (up to 18 months after drug is stopped). Pressure in the brain may increase.

By Those Over 60 Years of Age: Cortisonelike drugs should be used very sparingly after 60 and only when the disorder under treatment is unresponsive to adequate trials of unrelated drugs. Avoid prolonged use of this drug where possible. Continual use (even in small doses) can increase the severity of diabetes, enhance fluid retention, raise blood pressure, weaken resistance to infection, induce stomach ulcer, and accelerate the development of cataract and osteoporosis or other bone problems.

▷ **Advisability of Use During Pregnancy**
Pregnancy Category: C. See Pregnancy Risk Categories at the back of this book.
Animal Studies: Birth defects reported in mice, rats, and rabbits.
Human Studies: Adequate studies of pregnant women are not available. Avoid completely during the first 3 months. Limit use during the final 6 months as much as possible. If used, the infant should be examined for possible deficiency of adrenal gland function.

Advisability of Use If Breast-Feeding
Presence of this drug in breast milk: Yes.
The amount that the infant is exposd to can be decreased by avoiding breast-feeding for 3 to 4 hours after methylprednisolone is given. Talk to your doctor about this benefit-to-risk decision.

Habit-Forming Potential: Use of this drug over an extended period of time may produce a state of functional dependence (see Glossary). Treating asthma and rheumatoid arthritis, the dose should be kept as small as possible, and withdrawal should be attempted after periods of reasonable improvement. Such procedures may reduce "steroid rebound"—return of symptoms as the drug is withdrawn.

Effects of Overdose: Fatigue, muscle weakness, stomach irritation, acid indigestion, excessive sweating, facial flushing, fluid retention, swelling of extremities, increased blood pressure.

Possible Effects of Long-Term Use: Increased blood sugar (possible diabetes), increased fat deposits on the trunk of the body ("buffalo hump"), rounding of the face ("moon face"), thinning and fragility of skin, loss of texture and strength of bones (osteoporosis, aseptic necrosis—questionable causation versus correlation), cataracts, glaucoma, retarded growth and development in children.

Suggested Periodic Examinations While Taking This Drug (at physician's discretion)
Measurements of blood pressure.
Blood sugar and potassium levels.
Complete eye examinations at regular intervals.
Chest X-ray if history of tuberculosis.
Determination of the rate of development of the growing child to detect retardation of normal growth.
Bone mineral density testing to assess osteoporosis and fracture risk. Any unexplained joint pain (such as knee, hip, or shoulder) should be evaluated (possible ON and need for MRI).
Homocysteine levels are prudent (appear to be a risk factor for osteonecrosis).

▷ **While Taking This Drug, Observe the Following**
Foods: See grapefruit note under "Beverages." Ask your physician regarding need to restrict salt intake or to eat potassium-rich foods. During long-term use, higher protein diet may be prudent.
Herbal Medicines or Minerals: Hawthorn, ginger, garlic, ma huang, ginseng, guar gum, fenugreek, and nettle may change blood sugar. Since methylprednisolone may also change blood sugar control, caution is advised. Fir or pine needle oil should NOT be used by asthmatics. Ephedra alone does carry a German Commission E monograph indication for asthma treatment, and may blunt benefits of this drug. Because ma huang contains ephedra, it may do the same thing. If you are allergic to plants in the Asteraceae family (aster, chrysanthemum, daisy, or ragweed), you may also be allergic to echinacea, chamomile, feverfew, and St. John's wort. Licorice may increase methylprednisolone blood levels and lead to excessive effects. Added calcium and vitamin D while taking this medicine is prudent. Combination use of glucosamine has not been studied, but the combined use in cases of post-traumatic osteoarthritis may be beneficial. During wound repair, zinc supplementation may be prudent. Using echinacea or ginseng may boost the immune system and blunt the benefits of methylprednisolone. Talk to your doctor BEFORE adding any herbals to this medicine.

Beverages: Grapefruit juice will increase the plasma levels of methylprednisolone—water is a better liquid to take this medicine with. Drink all forms of milk liberally (as a calcium and vitamin D source).

▷ *Alcohol:* Alcohol use is a risk factor seen in osteonecrosis cases. Talk to your doctor about how he or she would like you to approach any alcohol use. Caution needed as well if you are prone to peptic ulcer disease.

Tobacco Smoking: Nicotine increases the blood levels of naturally produced cortisone and related hormones. I advise everyone to quit smoking.

Marijuana Smoking: May cause additional impairment of immunity.

▷ *Other Drugs*

Methylprednisolone may ***decrease*** the effects of
- insulin and require higher doses.
- isoniazid (INH, Niconyl, etc.).
- salicylates (aspirin, sodium salicylate, etc.).
- vaccines by blunting immune response to them.

Methylprednisolone ***taken concurrently*** with
- amphotericin B (Fungizone) may increase risk of potassium loss.
- carbamazepine (Tegretol) may blunt methylprednisolone benefits.
- cholestyramine (Questran) may decrease the amount of medicine that is absorbed into your body.
- clarithromycin (Biaxin) can result in increased methylprednisolone levels and toxicity.
- cyclosporine (Sandimmune) can result in increased steroid levels and cyclosporine toxicity.
- ketoconazole (Nizoral) (and other azole antifungals) may increase blood levels of methylprednisolone and result in toxicity (abnormal heartbeats or psychiatric reactions).
- loop diuretics, such as furosemide (Lasix) or bumetanide (Bumex), may result in increased risk of potassium loss.
- neuromuscular blocking agents (such as pancuronium [Pavulon], vecuronium [Norcuron], others) can result in increased risk and/or severity of muscle problems (myopathy and flaccid paralysis) and can also antagonize blockade from these medicines. Caution and unparalyzed periods are prudent.
- NSAIDs (such as aspirin, ibuprofen or others—see Drug Classes) may cause increased risk of ulceration of the stomach or intestine.
- oral anticoagulants (warfarin [Coumadin]) may either increase or decrease their effectiveness; consult your physician regarding the need for prothrombin time testing and dose adjustment.
- oral antidiabetic drugs (see Drug Classes) or insulin may result in loss of control of blood sugar and require higher doses or more frequent dosing of oral hypoglycemics or insulin in order to control blood sugar.
- primidone (Mysoline) may lead to increased metabolism of methylprednisolone and decreased therapeutic benefits of methylprednisolone.
- quinupristin/dalfopristin (Synercid) can result in increased steroid levels and toxicity.
- rifampin (Rifadin, others) may lead to increased metabolism of methylprednisolone and decreased therapeutic benefits of methylprednisolone.
- ritonavir (Norvir) and perhaps other protease inhibitors (see Drug Classes) may change therapeutic benefits of methylprednisolone.
- tacrolimus (Prograf) can result in increased tacrolimus levels and tacrolimus toxicity.

- theophylline (Theo-Dur) results in variable changes in blood levels; more frequent theophylline blood levels are indicated.
- thiazide diuretics (see Drug Classes) can result in additive potassium loss.
- vaccines (such as flu or pneumococcal) may result in a blunting of the immune response to the vaccine.

The following drugs may **decrease** the effects of methylprednisolone:

- antacids—may reduce its absorption.
- barbiturates (Amytal, Butisol, phenobarbital, etc.).
- phenytoin (Dilantin, etc.) or fosphenytoin (Cerebyx).
- rifampin (Rifadin, Rimactane, etc.).

▷ *Driving, Hazardous Activities:* Usually no restrictions. Be alert to the rare occurrence of dizziness.

Aviation Note: The use of this drug **may be a disqualification** for piloting. Consult a designated Aviation Medical Examiner.

Exposure to Sun: No restrictions.

Occurrence of Unrelated Illness: Decreases resistance to infection. Tell your doctor if you get an infection of any kind. May also reduce ability to respond to stress of acute illness, injury or surgery. Tell your doctor about any significant changes in your state of health.

Discontinuation: Do not stop this drug abruptly after chronic use. Ask your doctor for help with gradual, individualized withdrawal. Some clinicians change from daily to every-other-day therapy for 4 weeks BEFORE starting to lower the dose in a stepwise fashion. Many patients tolerate dose reductions of 2.5 mg of prednisone (other steroids are calculated on the basis of prednisone equivalents) with those decreases made every 3–7 days. If a disease flare occurs (worsening of symptoms), the dose should be increased to the last dose before the disease flare and should be tapered more slowly down to 5–10 mg or lower. Some clinicians use 8 A.M. predose plasma cortisol to guide tapering. If this lab test is less than 10 mcg/deciliter, tapering is continued until the daily prednisone equivalent is 2–5 mg. In general, if long-term treatment or high doses were used, prednisone equivalents should be tapered over 9–12 months. For up to 2 years after stopping this drug, you may require it again if you have an injury, surgery or an illness.

METHYSERGIDE (meth i SER jide)

Introduced: 1961 **Class:** Antimigraine drug, ergot derivative **Prescription:** USA: Yes **Controlled Drug:** USA: No; Canada: No **Available as Generic:** USA: No; Canada: No
Brand Name: Sansert

```
┌─────────────────────────────────────────────────────────────────┐
│                     BENEFITS versus RISKS                         │
│      Possible Benefits              Possible Risks                │
│  EFFECTIVE PREVENTION OF       FIBROSIS (SCARRING) INSIDE         │
│    MIGRAINE AND CLUSTER          CHEST AND ABDOMINAL              │
│    HEADACHES                     CAVITIES, OF HEART AND LUNG      │
│                                  TISSUES, ADJACENT TO MAJOR       │
│                                  BLOOD VESSELS AND INTERNAL       │
│                                  ORGANS (see "Possible Effects of │
│                                  Long-Term Use" on page 722)      │
│                                Aggravation of hypertension,       │
│                                  coronary artery disease and      │
│                                  peripheral vascular disease      │
└─────────────────────────────────────────────────────────────────┘
```

▷ **Principal Uses**

As a Single Drug Product: Uses currently included in FDA-approved labeling: Prevention of frequent and/or disabling vascular headaches (migraine and cluster neuralgia) that have not responded to other conventional treatment. Other (unlabeled) generally accepted uses: None at present.

How This Drug Works: Blocks serotonin inflammatory and vasoconstrictor effects, easing blood vessel constriction that causes vascular headaches. (Competitive 5-HT blocker and also stabilizes platelet release of 5-HT.)

Available Dosage Forms and Strengths

Tablets — 2 mg

▷ **Recommended Dosage Ranges** (Actual dose and schedule must be determined for each patient individually.)

Infants and Children: Safety and efficacy are not established—use of this drug is not recommended.

18 to 60 Years of Age: 4 to 8 mg daily, in divided doses with meals. A medication-free period of 3 to 4 weeks is REQUIRED after every 6-month course.

Over 60 Years of Age: 2 to 4 mg daily, in divided doses. Use very cautiously, with frequent monitoring for adverse effects.

Conditions Requiring Dosing Adjustments

Liver Function: This drug should not be used by patients with liver compromise.

Kidney Function: This drug should not be used by patients with renal compromise.

▷ **Dosing Instructions:** The tablet may be crushed and taken with food or milk to reduce stomach irritation. Uninterrupted use is limited to 6 months; avoid drug completely for 3 to 4 weeks between courses. If you forget a dose: Call your doctor. It is extremely important that you take this medicine exactly as directed.

▷ **Usual Duration of Use:** Use on a regular schedule for 3 weeks usually determines effectiveness in preventing recurrence of vascular headache. If significant benefit does not occur during this trial, this drug should be stopped. None of this medicine can be given for 3 to 4 weeks after every 6-month course of treatment. Periodic long-term use (months to years) requires periodic physician evaluation.

Typical Treatment Goals and Measurements (Outcomes and Markers)

Pain: Most clinicians treating pain use a device called an algometer to check your pain. This looks like a small ruler, but lets the clinician better understand your pain. The goals of treatment then relate to where the level of pain started (for example, a rating of 7 on a 0 to 10 scale) and what the cause of the pain was. Specific results in migraine therapy and this medicine relate to decreasing the frequency and/or severity of headaches or avoiding them altogether.

▷ **This Drug Should Not Be Taken If**
- you have had an allergic reaction to it previously.
- you are pregnant.
- you currently have a severe infection.
- you have any of the following conditions:
  - angina pectoris
  - Buerger's disease
  - cellulitis of the lower legs
  - chronic lung disease
  - connective tissue (collagen) disease
  - coronary artery disease
  - hardening of the arteries (arteriosclerosis)
  - heart valve disease
  - high blood pressure (significant hypertension)
  - kidney disease or significantly impaired kidney function
  - liver disease or significantly impaired liver function
  - active peptic ulcer disease
  - peripheral vascular disease
  - phlebitis of any kind
  - Raynaud's disease or phenomenon

▷ **Inform Your Physician Before Taking This Drug If**
- you had an adverse reaction to any ergot.
- you have a history of peptic ulcer disease or heart disease.

Possible Side Effects (natural, expected, and unavoidable drug actions)
Fluid retention, weight gain. Impaired circulation to the extremities (peripheral ischemia).

▷ **Possible Adverse Effects** (unusual, unexpected, and infrequent reactions)
If any of the following develop, consult your physician promptly for guidance.
Mild Adverse Effects
Allergic reactions: skin rashes, flushing of the face, transient loss of scalp hair.
Dizziness, drowsiness, agitation, unsteadiness, altered vision—infrequent to frequent.
Heartburn, nausea, vomiting, diarrhea—infrequent.
Transient muscle and joint pains—infrequent.
Serious Adverse Effects
Idiosyncratic reactions: nightmares, hallucinations, acute mental disturbances.
Fibrosis (scar tissue formation) involving the chest and/or abdominal cavities, heart, heart valves, lungs, kidneys, major blood vessels—case reports.
Spasm and narrowing of coronary and peripheral arteries: anginal chest pain, cold and painful extremities, leg cramps on walking—case reports.
Hemolytic anemia (see Glossary) or abnormally low platelet or white blood cell counts—case reports.
Heart attack (myocardial infarction)—case reports.

▷ **Possible Effects on Sexual Function:** Fibrosis of penile tissues—case reports.

▷ **Adverse Effects That May Mimic Natural Diseases or Disorders**

> Swelling of the hands, lower legs, feet, and ankles (peripheral edema) may suggest heart or kidney dysfunction.

Natural Diseases or Disorders That May Be Activated by This Drug

> Latent coronary artery insufficiency (angina), Buerger's disease, Raynaud's disease, peptic ulcer disease.

Possible Effects on Laboratory Tests

> Complete blood cell counts: decreased white cells (lymphocytes).
> Stomach hydrochloric acid: increased.
> Kidney function tests: increased blood urea nitrogen (BUN).

CAUTION

> 1. Continual use limited to 6 months. Gradual dose reduction is prudent during last 2 to 3 weeks of each course to prevent headache rebound. Omit drug for a period of 3 to 4 weeks before resuming. Mandatory "drug-free" period reduces fibrosis risk.
> 2. Promptly report fatigue, fever, chest pain, difficult breathing, stomach/flank pain, or urinary changes.
> 3. Useful only for prevention of recurring vascular headaches. NOT recommended for sudden (acute) headaches. Not effective for tension headaches.

Precautions for Use

> *By Infants and Children:* Use of this drug is not recommended.
> *By Those Over 60 Years of Age:* The age-related changes in blood vessels, circulatory functions and kidney function can make you more susceptible to the serious adverse effects of this drug. See the list of diseases and disorders on the previous page that are contraindications to the use of this drug. Ask your doctor for help.

▷ **Advisability of Use During Pregnancy**

> *Pregnancy Category:* X. See Pregnancy Risk Categories at the back of this book.
> *Animal Studies:* No information is available.
> *Human Studies:* Adequate studies of pregnant women are not available.
> The manufacturer states that this drug is contraindicated during entire pregnancy.

Advisability of Use If Breast-Feeding

> Presence of this drug in breast milk: Yes.
> Avoid drug or refrain from nursing.

Habit-Forming Potential: None.

Effects of Overdose: Nausea, vomiting, stomach pain, diarrhea, dizziness, excitement, cold hands and feet.

Possible Effects of Long-Term Use: Formation of scar tissue (fibrosis) inside chest cavity and/or abdominal cavity, on heart valves, in lung tissues and surrounding major blood vessels and internal organs. Requires close and continual medical supervision.

Suggested Periodic Examinations While Taking This Drug (at physician's discretion)

> Careful examination at regular intervals (6 to 12 months) for scar tissue formation or circulatory complications.
> Complete blood cell counts.
> Kidney function tests.

▷ **While Taking This Drug, Observe the Following**

    Foods: No restrictions except foods you are allergic to. Some vascular headaches are due to food allergy, or have specific food triggers. A headache diary can help you identify triggers and then avoid them.

    Herbal Medicines or Minerals: Since methysergide and St. John's wort may act on serotonin, the combination is not advised. Using ma huang or ephedrine-like compounds (ephedra) may result in additive and undesirable vasoconstriction. If you are allergic to plants in the *Asteraceae* family (aster, chrysanthemum, daisy, or ragweed), you may also be allergic to echinacea, chamomile, feverfew, and St. John's wort. St. John's wort can cause changes in the liver enzymes that help remove this medicine—talk to your doctor before combining any herbal medicine or mineral with methysergide.

    Beverages: No restrictions.

▷   *Alcohol:* No interactions expected. Observe closely to determine if alcoholic beverages can initiate a migrainelike headache.

    Tobacco Smoking: Avoid completely.

▷   *Other Drugs*

    Methysergide *taken concurrently* with

- beta-blocker drugs (see Drug Classes) may cause hazardous constriction of peripheral arteries; watch combined effects on circulation in the extremities. Careful patient monitoring and a selective beta blocker (such as atenolol) are prudent.
- clarithromycin, erythromcin (macrolide antibiotics) may lead to egotism. DO NOT combine.
- efavirenz (Sustiva) increases risk of methysergide toxicity.
- medicines removed by the cytochrome P450 3A4 enzymes as well as those that inhibit CYP 3A4 may lead to methysergide toxicity. Medicines that increase CYP3A4 will blunt methysergide benefits.
- sibutramine (Meridia) increases serotonin syndrome risk.
- sildenafil (Viagra) may increase risk of methysergide toxicity.
- sumatriptan (Imitrex) and other triptans, such as naratriptan, zolmitriptan, almotriptan, or rizatriptan, may cause prolonged spasm of blood vessels—DO NOT COMBINE or use within 24 hours of a "triptan" dose.

▷   *Driving, Hazardous Activities:* This drug may cause dizziness, drowsiness, or impaired vision. Restrict activities as necessary.

    Aviation Note: The use of this drug *is a disqualification* for piloting. Consult a designated Aviation Medical Examiner.

    Exposure to Sun: No restrictions.

    Exposure to Cold: Use caution. Cold environments may increase the occurrence of reduced circulation (blood flow) to the extremities.

    Discontinuation: Do not stop it abruptly if drug has been taken for a long time. Slowly lowering (tapering) the dose over 2 to 3 weeks can prevent rebound vascular headaches.

METOCLOPRAMIDE (met oh KLOH pra mide)

Introduced: 1973   **Class:** Gastrointestinal drug, antinausea (antiemetic)
Prescription: USA: Yes   **Controlled Drug:** USA: No; Canada: No
Available as Generic: Yes
Brand Names: ✤Apo-Metoclop, ✤Clopra, ✤Emex, ✤Gastrobid, ✤Maxeran, Maxolon, Octamide, Reclomide, Reglan

```
┌─────────────────────────────────────────────────────────────────────┐
│                        BENEFITS versus RISKS                          │
│        Possible Benefits                    Possible Risks            │
│ EFFECTIVE STOMACH STIMULANT   Sedation and fatigue                    │
│   FOR CORRECTING DELAYED      Parkinson-like reactions                │
│   EMPTYING                    Tardive dyskinesia                      │
│ Symptomatic relief in reflux                                          │
│   esophagitis                                                         │
│ Relief of nausea and vomiting                                         │
│   associated with migraine headache                                   │
└─────────────────────────────────────────────────────────────────────┘
```

▷ **Principal Uses**

As a Single Drug Product: Uses currently included in FDA-approved labeling: Helps (1) stomach retention (gastroparesis) associated with diabetes; (2) acid reflux from the stomach into the esophagus (esophagitis); (3) nausea and vomiting associated with migraine headaches; (4) nausea and vomiting induced by anticancer drugs (chemotherapy); (5) decrease the time needed to place a tube in the intestine; (6) used prior to cesarean section to decrease postdelivery or postsurgical nausea or vomiting; (7) used in some X-ray (radiologic) tests or tube placements (intubations).

Other (unlabeled) generally accepted uses: (1) Used as a preparatory drug in stomach hemorrhage; (2) may help gastrointestinal symptoms in anorexia nervosa; (3) eases drug-induced slowed functioning of the intestine (adynamic ileus); (4) decreases the frequency of accumulations of food in the stomach (bezoars); (5) can be of benefit in migraine attacks; (6) can help tongue protrusion in resistant tardive dyskinesia cases.

How This Drug Works: Inhibits relaxation of stomach muscles and enhances parasympathetic nervous system (responsible for stomach muscle contractions) stimulation, which accelerates emptying of stomach contents into the intestine.

Available Dosage Forms and Strengths

Injection — 5 mg/ml, 10 mg/ml

Intranasal — available in Italy as Pramdin, (investigational in the US)

Solution — 10 mg/ml

Syrup — 5 mg/5 ml

Tablets — 5 mg, 10 mg

▷ **Usual Adult Dosage Ranges:** Diabetic gastroparesis: 10 mg, taken 30 minutes before breakfast, lunch, and dinner and at bedtime (4 times a day) for 2 to 8 weeks. Daily maximum is 0.5 mg per kg of body mass.

Note: Actual dose and schedule must be determined for each patient individually.

Conditions Requiring Dosing Adjustments

Liver Function: No changes appear to be needed.

Kidney Function: For patients with moderate kidney failure, 75% of the usual dose can be taken at the usual dosing interval. In severe kidney failure, 50% of the usual dose can be taken at the usual dosing interval. A benefit-to-risk decision must be made.

▷ **Dosing Instructions:** Take tablet or syrup 30 minutes before each meal and at bedtime. The tablet may be crushed. Use a calibrated medication spoon or dosing cup for the liquid form. If you forget a dose: take the missed dose as soon as you remember it, unless it's nearly time for your next dose—if that is the case, skip the missed dose and take the next dose right on schedule. Talk with your doctor if you find yourself missing doses.

Usual Duration of Use: Use on a regular schedule for 5 to 7 days determines benefit in accelerating stomach emptying and relieving symptoms of heartburn, fullness and belching. Long-term use (2 to 8 weeks) requires physician supervision. Repeat cycles of the medicine are possible.

Typical Treatment Goals and Measurements (Outcomes and Markers)
> *Gastroparesis*: The general goal is to decrease feeling of stomach fullness by increasing stomach (gastric) emptying. For other uses, nausea and vomiting are decreased.

▷ **This Drug Should Not Be Taken If**
- you have had an allergic reaction to it previously.
- you have a seizure disorder of any kind.
- you have active gastrointestinal bleeding.
- you are taking, or have taken within the last 14 days, an MAO inhibitor (see Drug Classes).
- you are taking tricyclic antidepressants.
- you have a pheochromocytoma (adrenaline-producing tumor).

▷ **Inform Your Physician Before Taking This Drug If**
- you are allergic or overly sensitive to procaine or procainamide.
- you have impaired liver or kidney function.
- you have Parkinson's disease.
- you have epilepsy.
- you have high blood pressure.
- you have a history of depression.
- you are taking atropinelike drugs, antipsychotics, or opioid analgesics (see Drug Classes).

Possible Side Effects (natural, expected, and unavoidable drug actions)
> Drowsiness and lethargy, breast tenderness and swelling, milk production.

▷ **Possible Adverse Effects** (unusual, unexpected, and infrequent reactions)
If any of the following develop, consult your physician promptly for guidance.

Mild Adverse Effects
> Allergic reaction: skin rash. Mild decreases in blood pressure.
> Headache, dizziness, restlessness, depression, insomnia—infrequent.
> Dry mouth, nausea, diarrhea, constipation—infrequent to frequent.
> Urinary retention or incontinence—possible.

Serious Adverse Effects
> Idiosyncratic reactions: neuroleptic malignant syndrome (see Glossary), bronchospastic reactions in asthmatics.
> Parkinson-like reactions (see Glossary) or tardive dyskinesia (see Glossary— may be more likely in females and with longer treatment)—case reports.
> Abnormal fixed positioning of the eyes (oculogyric crisis)—case reports.
> Movement disorders (extrapyramidal symptoms)—rare.
> Depression—case reports.
> Severe decrease in white blood cells (agranulocytosis)—case report.
> Abnormal heartbeat—possible, case reports with intravenous use.
> Severe increases in blood pressure (hypertensive crisis)—case reports.
> Drug-induced porphyria—case reports.
> Methemoglobinemia—case report in an overdose case.

▷ **Possible Effects on Sexual Function:** Decreased libido, impaired erection, decreased sperm count, sustained painful erection (priapism). Sudden milk production by a non-pregnant woman (galactorrhea)—case reports. Altered timing and pattern of menstruation—case reports to infrequent.

Possible Effects on Laboratory Tests
   Blood lithium level: increased.
   Blood thyroid stimulating hormone (TSH) level: increased.

Precautions for Use
   By Infants and Children: Watch for development of Parkinson-like reactions soon after starting therapy. Use of the smallest effective dose can minimize such reactions. For diabetic gastroparesis, 0.5 mg per kg of body mass per day, divided into 3 equal doses given every 8 hours has been used. Children under 6 years old should NOT receive single doses more than 0.1 mg per kg of body mass.
   By Those Over 60 Years of Age: Parkinson-like reactions and tardive dyskinesias are more likely to occur with the use of high doses over an extended period of time. The smallest effective dose should be identified and used only when clearly needed.

▷ **Advisability of Use During Pregnancy**
   Pregnancy Category: B. See Pregnancy Risk Categories at the back of this book.
   Animal Studies: No birth defects found due to this drug.
   Human Studies: Adequate studies of pregnant women are not available.
   Use this drug only if clearly needed.

Advisability of Use If Breast-Feeding
   Presence of this drug in breast milk: Yes.
   But blood levels appear to avoid therapeutic 500 mcg/kg/day in children. Talk to your doctor about BENEFITS versus RISKS and watch your infant closely.

Habit-Forming Potential: None.

Effects of Overdose: Marked drowsiness, confusion, muscle spasms, jerking movements of head and face, tremors, shuffling gait. Methemoglobinemia.

Possible Effects of Long-Term Use: Parkinson-like reactions may appear within several months of use. Tardive dyskinesias usually occur after a year of continual use; they may persist after this drug is discontinued.

Suggested Periodic Examinations While Taking This Drug (at physician's discretion)
   During long-term use, observe for the development of fine, wormlike movements on the surface of the tongue; these may be the first indications of an emerging tardive dyskinesia.

▷ **While Taking This Drug, Observe the Following**
   Foods: No restrictions.
   Herbal Medicines or Minerals: Valerian and kava kava may intensify drowsiness (no longer recommended because of liver questions. Aloe, cascara, and senna may increase possibility of diarrhea. Using chromium may change the way your body is able to use sugar. Some health food stores advocate vanadium as mimicking the actions of insulin, but possible toxicity and need for rigorous studies presently preclude recommending it. DHEA may change sensitivity to insulin or insulin resistance. Hawthorn, ginger, garlic, ginseng and licorice, nettle, and yohimbe may change blood sugar. Since this may require adjustment of hypoglycemic medicine dosing, talk to your doctor BEFORE combining any of these herbal medicines with meto-

clopramide. Echinacea pupurea (injectable) and blonde psyllium seed or husk should NOT be taken by people living with diabetes.

Beverages: No restrictions. May be taken with milk.

▷ *Alcohol:* Combined effects can result in excessive sedation and marked intoxication because of increased alcohol absorption. Alcohol is best avoided.

Tobacco Smoking: No interactions expected. I advise everyone to quit smoking.

▷ *Other Drugs*

Metoclopramide may *decrease* the effects of

- cimetidine (Tagamet).
- digoxin (slow-dissolving dose forms) and reduce their effectiveness.

Metoclopramide *taken concurrently* with

- acetaminophen may increase the absorption of this drug; decreased doses are prudent if chronic acetaminophen use will continue with metoclopramide therapy.
- major antipsychotic drugs (phenothiazines, thiothixenes, haloperidol, etc.) may increase the risk of developing Parkinson-like reactions.
- cyclosporine (Sandimmune) may result in increased cyclosporine levels and toxicity.
- morphine (slow release) may result in faster onset and increased sedation.
- neuromuscular blocking agents (such as pancuronium-Pavulon, vecuronium-Norcuron, others) can result in extended recovery times from blockade. Caution is prudent.
- penicillin may result in decreased therapeutic benefits of the antibiotic; increased doses may be needed.
- quinidine (Quinaglute, others) may result in decreased therapeutic benefits from quinidine; increased blood level testing and adjustment of dosing to levels is indicated.
- serolimus (Rapamune) or tacrolimus (Prograf) may result in toxicity. Checks of serolimus or tacrolimus levels are prudent.
- sertraline (Zoloft) may increase risk of movement disorders.
- zalcitabine (Hivid) may blunt zalcitabine levels and benefits.

The following drugs may *decrease* the effects of metoclopramide:

- atropinelike drugs.
- opioid analgesics (see Drug Classes).
- ritonavir (Norvir).

▷ *Driving, Hazardous Activities:* This drug may cause drowsiness and dizziness. Restrict activities as necessary.

Aviation Note: The use of this drug *may be a disqualification* for piloting. Consult a designated Aviation Medical Examiner.

Exposure to Sun: No restrictions.

METOLAZONE (me TOHL a zohn)

Please see the thiazide diuretics family profile.

METOPROLOL (me TOH proh lohl)

Introduced: 1974 **Class:** Antihypertensive, beta-adrenergic blocker
Prescription: USA: Yes **Controlled Drug:** USA: No; Canada: No
Available as Generic: Yes

Brand Names: ✤Apo-Metoprolol, ✤Betaloc, ✤Co-Betaloc [CD], ✤Logimax [CD], Lopressor, Lopressor Delayed-Release, Lopressor HCT [CD], Lopressor OROS, ✤Novo-Metoprol, ✤Nu-Metop, Toprol, Toprol XL

BENEFITS versus RISKS

Possible Benefits	*Possible Risks*
EFFECTIVE, WELL-TOLERATED ANTIHYPERTENSIVE in mild to moderate high blood pressure	Worsening of angina in coronary heart disease (abrupt withdrawal)
MAY HELP REDUCE DEATH FROM HEART ATTACKS	Masking of low blood sugar (hypoglycemia) in drug-treated diabetes
APPROVED (Toprol XL form) TO TREAT CONGESTIVE HEART FAILURE	Provocation of asthma (with high doses in asthmatics)
REDUCES DEATH AND DISABILITY AFTER A HEART ATTACK	
EFFECTIVE TREATMENT OF ANGINA	

▷ **Principal Uses**

As a Single Drug Product: Uses currently included in FDA-approved labeling: (1) Treats mild to moderate high blood pressure, alone or with other drugs; (2) helps reduce the frequency and severity of angina; (3) used to reduce the risk of a second heart attack; (4) approved (Toprol XL form) to treat congestive heart failure (carvedilol, or Coreg, is the only other beta blocker approved for this use).

Other (unlabeled) generally accepted uses: (1) Reduces symptoms of heart muscle damage (dilated cardiomyopathy); (2) second-line drug in panic attacks; (3) used to decrease pressure in the eye (intraocular pressure) in open-angle glaucoma; (4) helps prevent migraine headaches; (5) A May 2002 study from Duke (see Ferguson, et al. in Sources) found that people who get beta blockers before heart bypass surgery (CABG) have better results than those who do not take those medicines.

As a Combination Drug Product [CD]: Metoprolol is available combined with hydrochlorothiazide (Lopressor HCT) which gives the benefits of both a beta blocker and a thiazide diuretic. Also available as Logimax in Canada which offers the benefits of metoprolol and a calcium channel blocker called felodipine.

In the Pipeline: The COMET (Carvedilol or Metoprolol European Trial) is the first study to make a head-to-head (drug-to-drug) comparison of 2 beta blockers in people with ongoing (chronic) heart failure (CHF). This research was designed to look at the effect of the 2 medicines on survival. The chair of the study is Professor Philip Poole-Wilson of the Imperial College in London. One early report sited a survival benefit for carvedilol. This study involved more than 10,000 patient years of follow-up (large number of patients who were studied for a significant time) and was published in the summer of 2003.

How This Drug Works: Blocks some actions of the sympathetic nervous system:
- reducing rate, contraction force and ejection pressure of the heart.
- reducing contraction of blood vessels, resulting in lowering of blood pressure.

- prolonging conduction time of nerve impulses through the heart, managing certain heart rhythm disorders.

In heart failure, lowered remodeling of the left side of the heart (left ventricular remodeling) as well as lowered heart rate and action of the renin-angiotensin system may all work to help.

Available Dosage Forms and Strengths

Injection — 1 mg/ml

Tablets — 50 mg, 100 mg

Tablets, prolonged action — 25 mg, 50 mg, 100 mg, 200 mg

▷ **Usual Adult Dosage Ranges:** *Hypertension:* Starts with 50 mg once or twice daily (12 hours apart). Dose may be increased gradually at intervals of 7 to 10 days as needed and tolerated, up to 300 mg/day. For ongoing use (maintenance), 100 mg twice a day. The total daily dose should not exceed 450 mg. The sustained release form is only given once daily.

Angina: Dosing is started at 50 mg twice a day taken with meals or right after eating. The XL form is a sustained release dosage and can be taken as 100 mg once a day. Doses can be carefully increased as needed and tolerated to 400 mg a day. The selectiveness of this medicine for the heart goes away as the dose increases.

Migraine prevention: 50 to 200 mg a day.

Heart failure (NYHA Class II or III—once symptoms are stable for 2–4 weeks): Clinicians may start patients with the Toprol XL form (plus other evidence-based medicines such as ACE inhibitors, water pills—diuretics and digoxin) on a low dose such as 25 mg once a day for 14 days in class II patients. For more severe heart failure, 12.5 mg once a day. The dose then can be doubled every 2 weeks as needed and tolerated up to 200 mg a day. Other medicines used in combination should be adjusted as needed and tolerated.

After a heart attack: People who are able to handle (tolerate) the full 15 mg intravenous dosing, 50 mg of oral metoprolol is given 15 minutes after the last intravenous dose and continued every 6 hours for 48 hours. Ongoing doses are 100 mg twice a day (some clinicians continue this for 1–3 years).

Note: Actual dose and schedule must be determined for each patient individually.

Conditions Requiring Dosing Adjustments

Liver Function: Used with caution by patients with liver compromise.

Kidney Function: No changes thought to be needed.

▷ **Dosing Instructions:** The regular tablet may be crushed and taken without regard to eating. In general, prolonged-action forms should be swallowed whole (not altered). Toprol XL brand now comes in an updated 25 mg form that is scored so that heart failure patients can take a 12.5 mg dose (talk to your doctor about this). While it is OK to split the XL tablet, do not crush the half-tablet to take it as it will change how quickly the medicine is released into your body. Do not stop this drug abruptly. If you forget a dose: take the missed dose as soon as you remember it, unless it's within 4 hours (regular release) or 8 hours (extended release form) of your next dose—if that is the case, skip the missed dose and take the next dose right on schedule. Talk with your doctor if you find yourself missing doses.

Usual Duration of Use: Regular use for 10 to 14 days determines benefits in lowering blood pressure. The long-term use in controlling blood pressure will be determined by your response to a treatment program (weight reduction, restricted salt, smoking cessation, etc.). Secondary cardiovascular disease prevention use (after a heart attack) and use in heart failure will be ongoing. See your doctor regularly.

Typical Treatment Goals and Measurements (Outcomes and Markers)

Blood Pressure: The NEW guidelines (JNC VII) define normal blood pressure (BP) as **less than** 120/80. Because blood pressures that were once considered acceptable can actually lead to blood vessel damage, the committee from the National Institutes of Health, National Heart, Lung and Blood Institute now have a new category called **Pre-hypertension**. This ranges from 120/80 to 139/89 and is intended to help your doctor encourage lifestyle changes (or in the case of people with a risk factor for high blood pressure, start treatment) much earlier—so that possible damage to blood vessels, your heart, kidneys, sexual potency, or eyes might be minimized or avoided altogether. The next 2 classes of high blood pressure are stage 1 hypertension:140/90 to 159/99; and stage 2 hypertension equal to or greater than: 160/100 mm Hg. These guidelines also recommend that clinicians trying to control blood pressure work with their patients to agree on the goals and a plan of treatment. The first-ever guidelines for blood pressure (hypertension) in African Americans recommends that MOST black patients be started on TWO antihypertensive medicines with the goal of lowering blood pressure to 130/80 for those with high risk for heart and blood vessel disease or with diabetes. The American Diabetes Association recommends 130/80 as the target for people living with diabetes and less than 125/75 for those who spill more than 1 gram of protein into their urine. Most clinicians try to achieve a BP that confers the best balance of lower cardiovascular risk and avoids the problem of too low a blood pressure. Blood pressure duration is generally increased with beneficial restriction of sodium. The goals and time frame should be discussed with you when the prescription is written. If goals are not met, it is not unusual to intensify doses or add on medicines. You can find the new blood pressure guidelines at *www.nhlbi.nih.gov/guidelines/hypertension/index.htm*. For the African American guidelines see Douglas, J.G. in Sources.

Migraine prevention: Specific results in migraine therapy and this medicine relate to decreasing the frequency and/or severity of headaches or avoiding them altogether.

Possible Advantages of This Drug: Generic form offers beta-blocker advantages at a lower cost than some other medicines in the same class. A small study in the journal *Circulation* found no difference between the generic version of metoprolol and the more expensive carvedilol. The Oros brand of metoprolol works to reduce exercise-induced angina and daily lowering of heart blood flow (ischemia). The Toprol XL form is FDA-approved for use in heart failure.

Currently a "Drug of Choice"

For starting hypertension therapy with one drug, especially for those with bronchial asthma or diabetes and to lower cardiovascular morbidity and mortality.

▷ **This Drug Should Not Be Taken If**
- you have had an allergic reaction to it previously.
- you have had a heart attack and your heart rate is less than 45 beats/min.
- you have an abnormally slow heart rate or a serious form of heart block (second or third degree).
- you are in cardiogenic shock.

- you took any monoamine oxidase (MAO) type A drug (see Drug Classes) in the last 14 days.

▷ **Inform Your Physician Before Taking This Drug If**
- you had an adverse reaction to any beta blocker (see Drug Classes).
- you have a history of serious heart disease.
- you have a history of hay fever (allergic rhinitis), asthma, chronic bronchitis or emphysema. (People with bronchial asthma should generally not take beta blockers. This drug is somewhat heart selective and may be used with caution by asthmatics.)
- you have a history of overactive thyroid function (hyperthyroidism).
- you have a history of low blood sugar (hypoglycemia).
- you have impaired liver or kidney function.
- you have diabetes or myasthenia gravis.
- you currently take digitalis, quinidine or reserpine or any calcium channel-blocker drug (see Drug Classes).
- you have a history of poor circulation to the extremities (peripheral vascular disease).
- you have a history of periodic cramps of your legs (intermittent claudication).
- you will have surgery with general anesthesia.

Possible Side Effects (natural, expected, and unavoidable drug actions)

Lethargy and fatigability, cold extremities, slow heart rate, light-headedness in upright position (see orthostatic hypotension in Glossary). Abnormally slow heartbeat (bradycardia). Mild increase in potassium.

▷ **Possible Adverse Effects** (unusual, unexpected, and infrequent reactions)

If any of the following develop, consult your physician promptly for guidance.

Mild Adverse Effects

Allergic reactions: skin rash, itching.

Worsening of psoriasis—case reports.

Headache, fatigue, dizziness, insomnia, abnormal dreams—infrequent.

Indigestion, nausea, vomiting, constipation, diarrhea—infrequent.

Eye and joint pain—case reports.

Joint and muscle discomfort, fluid retention (edema)—possible.

Serious Adverse Effects

Mental depression, hallucinations, anxiety—infrequent.

Chest pain, shortness of breath, precipitation of congestive heart failure—case reports.

Intermittant claudication—possible. May be prudent to check for hidden Peripheral Artery Disease (PAD) by checking ankle brachial index (ABI). ABI check (see Glossary) can help find PAD early, and avoid claudication that may result if this medication is taken by someone who has PAD but does not know it.

Induction of bronchial asthma (in asthmatic patients)—possible.

Rebound hypertension—if the drug is abruptly stopped.

Precipitation of myasthenia gravis—case reports.

Carpal tunnel syndrome—case reports.

Low or high blood sugar (hypoglycemia or hyperglycemia)—possible and more likely in type 1 diabetics.

Liver compromise (hepatitis)—case report.

▷ **Possible Effects on Sexual Function:** Decreased libido (4 times more common in men); impaired erection (less common with this drug than with most other beta blockers); Peyronie's disease (see Glossary)—case reports.

Possible Effects on Laboratory Tests
Blood HDL cholesterol level: decreased.
Blood LDL and VLDL cholesterol level: decreased.
Blood glucose level: increased.
Blood triglyceride levels: increased.

CAUTION
1. ***Do not stop this drug suddenly*** without the knowledge and help of your physician. Carry a note with you that says you take this drug.
2. Ask your doctor or pharmacist before using any nasal decongestants. These are often found in nonprescription cold medicines and nose drops. They may increase blood pressure.
3. Report development of emotional depression.
4. When patients are changed from an immediate release to a sustained release form, the same total dose is used and is then increased as needed and tolerated.
5. As the dose of this medicine is increased, the heart (beta one) selectivity is lost.

Precautions for Use
By Infants and Children: Safety and effectiveness for use by those under 12 years of age have not been established, but if this drug is used, observe for the development of low blood sugar (hypoglycemia) during periods of reduced food intake.
By Those Over 60 Years of Age: Proceed cautiously with all antihypertensive drugs. Unacceptably high blood pressure should be reduced slowly, to avoid the risks associated with excessively low blood pressure. Therapy should be started with small doses and the blood pressure checked often. Sudden, rapid, and excessive reduction of blood pressure can predispose to stroke or heart attack. Watch for dizziness, unsteadiness, tendency to fall, confusion, hallucinations, depression, or urinary frequency.

▷ **Advisability of Use During Pregnancy**
Pregnancy Category: C. See Pregnancy Risk Categories at the back of this book.
Animal Studies: No significant increase in birth defects due to this drug.
Human Studies: Adequate studies of pregnant women are not available.
Use this drug only if clearly needed. Ask your physician for guidance.

Advisability of Use If Breast-Feeding
Presence of this drug in breast milk: Yes.
Discuss BENEFITS versus RISKS with your doctor.

Habit-Forming Potential: None.

Effects of Overdose: Weakness, slow pulse, low blood pressure, cold and sweaty skin, congestive heart failure, possible coma, and convulsions.

Possible Effects of Long-Term Use: Reduced heart reserve and eventual heart failure in susceptible individuals with advanced heart disease.

Suggested Periodic Examinations While Taking This Drug (at physician's discretion)
Measurements of blood pressure.
Evaluation of heart function, check of frequency of angina. When used after a heart attack, the function of the left side of the heart, size of the damaged area (infarct size), and heart rate should be checked.

▷ **While Taking This Drug, Observe the Following**
Foods: Peak drug concentration and peak effect will increase if taken with food. Avoid excessive salt intake. Migraines often have specific food triggers. Keep a headache diary, and then avoid the triggering foods.

Herbal Medicines or Minerals: Valerian and kava kava (no longer recommended in Canada) may intensify drowsiness. Ginseng may increase blood pressure, and St. John's wort may increase removal of this medicine from the body, blunting the benefit of this medicine. Guarana, hawthorn, saw palmetto, ma huang (do not take if hypertensive), goldenseal, yohimbe, and licorice may also increase blood pressure. Calcium and garlic may help lower blood pressure and could be part of complementary care. Use of calcium to excess (7.5 to 10 grams) with combination thiazide diuretics can lead to excessive calcium levels. Talk to your doctor about how much calcium to take. Indian snakeroot has a German Commission E monograph indication for hypertension—talk to your doctor. Eleuthero root and ephedra should be avoided by people living with hypertension.

Beverages: No restrictions. May be taken with milk.

▷ *Alcohol:* Use with caution. Alcohol may exaggerate this drug's ability to lower the blood pressure and may increase its mild sedative effect.

Tobacco Smoking: Nicotine may reduce this drug's benefit in treating high blood pressure. I advise everyone to quit smoking.

▷ *Other Drugs*

Metoprolol may ***increase*** the effects of

- other antihypertensive drugs, causing excessive lowering of blood pressure; dose adjustments may be necessary.
- reserpine (Ser-Ap-Es, etc.) and cause sedation, depression, slowing of the heart rate, and lowering of the blood pressure.
- verapamil (Calan, Isoptin) and cause excessive depression of heart function; monitor this combination closely.

Metoprolol ***taken concurrently*** with

- amiodarone (Cordarone) may result in extremely slow heartbeat and cardiac arrest—NOT ADVISED.
- clonidine (Catapres) requires close monitoring for rebound high blood pressure if clonidine is withdrawn while metoprolol is still being taken.
- digoxin (Lanoxin, others) may increase heart slowing.
- fluoxetine (Prozac) may cause metoprolol toxicity.
- fluvoxamine (Luvox) may lead to metoprolol toxicity.
- insulin requires close monitoring to avoid undetected hypoglycemia (see Glossary).
- lidocaine can lead to lidocaine toxicity (cardiac arrest).
- methyldopa (Aldomet, others) can have a rare paradoxical hypertensive response—caution is advised.
- nifedipine (Adalat, Procardia, others) may result in heart failure.
- oral antidiabetic drugs (see Drug Classes) can result in prolonged hypoglycemia if it occurs.
- phenothiazines (see Drug Classes) can result in low blood pressure or toxicity due to the phenothiazine.
- quinidine (Quinaglute, others) can lead to abnormally slow heartbeat and shortness of breath.
- ritonavir (Norvir) and perhaps other protease inhibitors (see Drug Classes) may cause toxicity.
- tocainide (Tonocard) may lead to depressed contraction ability of the heart (myocardial contractility).
- venlafaxine (Effexor) may lead to metabolic changes and toxic blood levels of both medicines.

The following drugs may ***increase*** the effects of metoprolol:

- alpha one adrenergic blockers, such as prazosin (Minipres).

- bupropion (Zyban). Metoprolol doses at the lower end of the dosing range are prudent if these drugs must be used together.
- cimetidine (Tagamet).
- ciprofloxacin (Cipro).
- diltiazem (Cardizem) and other dihydroperidine calcium blockers— especially in people with decreased function of the left ventricle.
- MAO inhibitors (see Drug Classes).
- methimazole (Tapazole).
- oral contraceptives (birth control pills); a different (non–first pass) beta blocker is advisable.
- propafenone (Rythmol).
- propoxyphene (Darvocet, others).
- propylthiouracil (Propacil).
- zafirlukast (Accolate) or zileuton (Zyflo); dose decreases of metoprolol may be needed.

The following drugs may *decrease* the effects of metoprolol:
- barbiturates (phenobarbital, etc.).
- indomethacin (Indocin) and possibly other aspirin substitutes or NSAIDs—may impair metoprolol's antihypertensive effect.
- rifampin (Rifadin, Rimactane).

▷ *Driving, Hazardous Activities:* Use caution until the full extent of drowsiness, lethargy and blood pressure change has been determined.

Aviation Note: The use of this drug *is a disqualification* for piloting. Consult a designated Aviation Medical Examiner.

Exposure to Sun: No restrictions.

Exposure to Heat: Caution is advised. Hot environments can lower the blood pressure and exaggerate the effects of this drug.

Exposure to Cold: Caution: Cold environments can increase circulatory deficiency in extremities. The elderly should take care to prevent hypothermia (see Glossary).

Heavy Exercise or Exertion: Best to avoid exertion that produces lightheadedness, excessive fatigue or muscle cramping. This drug may intensify the blood pressure response to isometric exercise.

Occurrence of Unrelated Illness: Fever can lower the blood pressure and require adjustment of dose. Nausea or vomiting may interrupt the regular dose schedule. Ask your doctor for help.

Discontinuation: **Do not stop this drug suddenly.** Gradual dose lowering over 1 to 2 weeks is recommended. Ask your doctor for help.

METRONIDAZOLE (me troh NI da zohl)

Introduced: 1960 **Class:** Anti-infective **Prescription:** USA: Yes **Controlled Drug:** USA: No; Canada: No **Available as Generic:** Yes

Brand Names: ✽Apo-Metronidazole, Femazole, Flagyl, Flagyl ER (extended release form), Flagystatin [CD], Helidac [CD], Lagyl, Losec Helicopak [CD], Metizol, MetroGel, Metro IV, Metryl, ✽Neo-Tric, ✽Noritate cream, ✽Novo-Nidazole, ✽PMS-Metronidazole, Protostat, ✽Rho-Metrostatin, SK-Metronidazole, ✽Trikacide

BENEFITS versus RISKS	
Possible Benefits	*Possible Risks*
EFFECTIVE TREATMENT FOR *TRICHOMONAS* INFECTIONS, AMEBIC DYSENTERY AND GIARDIASIS AND SOME ANAEROBIC BACTERIAL INFECTIONS TREATMENT OF BACTERIAL VAGINOSIS (ER FORM) Effective local treatment for rosacea	Superinfection with yeast organisms Peripheral neuropathy Abnormally low white blood cell count (transient) Colitis Aggravation of epilepsy

▷ **Principal Uses**

As a Single Drug Product: Uses currently included in FDA-approved labeling: (1) Treats *Trichomonas* infections of the vaginal canal and cervix and of the male urethra; (2) also used to treat amebic dysentery and liver abscess, *Giardia* infections of the intestine, and serious infections caused by certain strains of anaerobic bacteria; (3) treats *Gardnerella* infections of the vagina; (4) treatment of acne rosacea with local application of a gel dose form; (5) used in therapy of pseudomembranous colitis in adults; (6) has a role in treating bed sores (decubitus ulcers); (7) can help prevent infection (prophylaxis) in gynecological, appendectomy or colorectal surgery; (8) ER form used in bacterial vaginosis.

Other (unlabeled) generally accepted uses: (1) Combination therapy with gentamicin in treating intra-abdominal infections; (2) combination antibiotic treatment of duodenal ulcers caused by *Helicobacter pylori;* (3) can help treat infections caused by *Giardia lamblia;* (4) used to help heal the lesions in Crohn's disease; (5) may help abnormal gum growth (gingival hyperplasia) caused by cyclosporine; (6) often used to treat pseudomembranous colitis.

As a Combination Drug Product [CD]: Metronidazole is available combined with 20 mg of omeprazole, 500 mg of amoxicillin and 400 mg of metronidazole for combination treatment of *Helicobacter pylori*. Also available in Canada combined with nystatin for yeast infections as a vaginal insert.

How This Drug Works: Interacts with DNA, destroying essential component (nucleus) that is needed for life and growth of infecting organisms.

Available Dosage Forms and Strengths

Capsules — 375 mg

Gel — 0.75%

Injection — 500 mg/100 ml

Tablets — 250 mg, 500 mg

Tablets, extended release — 750 mg

Vaginal cream — 10%

Vaginal insert — 500 mg/100,000 U (Canada)

▷ **Usual Adult Dosage Ranges:** *For bacterial vaginosis* (ER form): 750 mg once a day for 7 days in a row.

For trichomoniasis: 1-day course — 2 g as a single dose or 1 g for 2 doses 12 hours apart. 7-day course — 250 mg 3 times a day for 7 consecutive days. (The 7-day course is preferred.)

For amebiasis: 500 to 750 mg 3 times a day for 5 to 10 consecutive days.

For giardiasis: 2 g once daily for 3 days, or 250 to 500 mg 3 times a day for 5 to 7 days.

For Helicobacter pylori: The Helidac kit has 14 blister cards. One metronidazole and tetracycline tablet are taken once a day and 2 bismuth subsalicylate tablets are taken 4 times daily for a total regimen of 14 consecutive days. An H2 antagonist is also added to this combination. The total daily dose should not exceed 4 g (4,000 mg).

Note: Actual dose and schedule must be determined for each patient individually.

Conditions Requiring Dosing Adjustments

Liver Function: Dose is decreased by one-third in mild to moderate liver disease. Should not be used in severe liver compromise.

Kidney Function: In severe kidney failure, 50% of the normal dose can be taken at the usual dosing interval. A benefit-to-risk decision must be made for these patients, as there is a risk of systemic lupus erythematosus (SLE) from the metabolites of this drug.

▷ **Dosing Instructions:** The tablet may be crushed and taken with or following food to reduce stomach irritation. If you forget a dose: take the missed dose as soon as you remember it, unless it's nearly time for your next dose—if that is the case, skip the missed dose and take the next dose right on schedule. Talk with your doctor if you find yourself missing doses. Continue to take the full course of this medicine as prescribed even if you start to feel better.

Usual Duration of Use: Use on a regular schedule as outlined is needed to ensure effectiveness. Do not repeat the course of treatment without your physician's approval.

Typical Treatment Goals and Measurements (Outcomes and Markers)

Infections: The most commonly used measures of serious infections are white blood cell counts and differentials (the kind of blood cells that occur most often in your blood), and temperature. Many clinicians look for positive changes in 24–48 hours. NEVER stop an antibiotic because you start to feel better. For many infections, a full 14 days is REQUIRED to kill the bacteria. The goals and time frame (see benefits on page 735) should be discussed with you when the prescription is written.

▷ **This Drug Should Not Be Taken If**
  • you have had an allergic reaction to it or any of the parabens contained in the gel form.
  • you are pregnant (first 3 months).
  • you currently have a bone marrow or blood cell disorder.
  • you have any type of central nervous system disorder, including epilepsy.

▷ **Inform Your Physician Before Taking This Drug If**
  • you have a history of any type of blood cell disorder, especially one caused by drugs.
  • you have a history of seizures or peripheral neuropathy.
  • you have impaired liver or kidney function.
  • you are taking a form applied on the skin (topical) and develop a rash after applying it.
  • you have a history of alcoholism.
  • you are pregnant or breast-feeding.

Possible Side Effects (natural, expected, and unavoidable drug actions)
  A sharp, metallic, unpleasant taste. Dark discoloration of the urine (of no

clinical significance). Superinfection (see Glossary) by yeast organisms in the mouth or vagina. Pseudomembranous colitis.

▷ **Possible Adverse Effects** (unusual, unexpected, and infrequent reactions)
If any of the following develop, consult your physician promptly for guidance.

Mild Adverse Effects

Allergic reactions: skin rash, hives, flushing, itching.

Headache, dizziness, incoordination, unsteadiness, incontinence—infrequent.

Loss of appetite, nausea, vomiting, abdominal cramps, diarrhea—infrequent.

Irritation of mouth and tongue, possibly due to yeast infection—possible.

Serious Adverse Effects

Idiosyncratic reactions: abnormal behavior; confusion; depression; Jarisch-Herxheimer's reaction (sweating, diarrhea, vomiting, scalding urination, joint pain, and itching)—case reports.

Peripheral neuropathy (see Glossary)—case reports.

Abnormally low white blood cell count (transient): fever, sore throat, infections—case reports.

Disulfiram-type reaction (nausea, vomiting) if alcoholic beverages are consumed—possible.

Seizures—case reports.

Drug-induced pneumonitis, porphyria or pancreatitis—case reports.

Hemolytic-uremic syndrome—case reports.

▷ **Possible Effects on Sexual Function:** Decreased libido; decreased vaginal secretions (difficult or painful intercourse)—case reports.

Abnormal swelling of male breast tissue (gynecomastia)—case report.

Possible Delayed Adverse Effects: Studies have shown that this drug can cause cancer in mice and possibly in rats. Two researchers concluded that the carcinogenic risk is low in doses used to treat episodic vaginitis. High-dose, long-term use may carry increased cancer risk. Follow your doctor's instructions exactly. Avoid unnecessary or prolonged use.

▷ **Adverse Effects That May Mimic Natural Diseases or Disorders**

Behavioral changes may suggest spontaneous psychosis.

Natural Diseases or Disorders That May Be Activated by This Drug

Latent yeast infections.

Possible Effects on Laboratory Tests

White blood cell counts: decreased.

INR (prothrombin time): increased.

Blood theophylline levels: falsely increased by some methods.

CAUTION

1. Troublesome and persistent diarrhea can develop. If diarrhea persists for more than 24 hours, stop this drug and call your physician.
2. Stop this drug immediately if you develop any signs of toxic effects on the brain or nervous system: confusion, irritability, dizziness, incoordination, unsteady stance or gait, muscle jerking or twitching, numbness or weakness in the extremities.
3. Don't get the topical cream form in your eyes.
4. If this medicine is being taken for an infection of the genitals, it is important to make certain that your partner(s) also get treated.
5. Do not drink alcoholic beverages while taking this medicine. The combination of alcohol and this medicine leads to flushing, vomiting, and other signs and symptoms (disulfiram reaction).

Precautions for Use
> *By Infants and Children:* Avoid use in those with a history of bone marrow or blood cell disorders.
> *By Those Over 60 Years of Age:* Natural changes in the skin may predispose to yeast infections in the genital and anal regions. Report the development of rashes and itching promptly.

▷ **Advisability of Use During Pregnancy**
> *Pregnancy Category:* B. See Pregnancy Risk Categories at the back of this book.
> *Animal Studies:* No birth defects reported in rat studies, but this drug is known to cause cancer in mice and possibly in rats.
> *Human Studies:* No increase in birth defects reported in 206 exposures to this drug during the first 3 months. However, information from adequate studies of pregnant women is not available.
> The manufacturer advises against the use of this drug during the first 3 months. Use during the final 6 months is not advised unless it is absolutely essential to the mother's health.

Advisability of Use If Breast-Feeding
> Presence of this drug in breast milk: Yes.
> Avoid drug or refrain from nursing.

Habit-Forming Potential: None.

Effects of Overdose: Weakness, stomach irritation, nausea, vomiting, confusion, disorientation.

Possible Effects of Long-Term Use: None reported. Avoid long-term use.

Suggested Periodic Examinations While Taking This Drug (at physician's discretion)
> Complete blood cell counts.

▷ **While Taking This Drug, Observe the Following**
> *Foods:* No restrictions.
> *Herbal Medicines or Minerals:* Some patients use echinacea to attempt to boost their immune systems. Unfortunately, use of echinacea is not recommended in people with damaged immune systems (even if a medicine caused the damage). This herb may also actually weaken any immune system if it is used too often or for too long a time. DO NOT take mistletoe herb, oak bark or F.C. of marshmallow root, and licorice.
> *Beverages:* No restrictions. May be taken with milk.
▷ *Alcohol:* A disulfiramlike reaction has been reported (see Glossary). It is NOT advisable to drink alcohol while taking metronidazole.
> *Tobacco Smoking:* No interactions expected. I advise everyone to quit smoking.
▷ *Other Drugs*
> Metronidazole may ***increase*** the effects of
> • carbamazepine (Tegretol) and lead to toxicity.
> • warfarin (Coumadin, etc.) and cause abnormal bleeding; the INR (prothrombin time or protime) should be monitored closely, especially during the first 10 days of concurrent use.
> Metronidazole ***taken concurrently*** with
> • antacids may decrease absorption of metronidazole.
> • birth control pills (oral contraceptives) may block the effectiveness of contraception and result in pregnancy.
> • cholestyramine (Questran) or other cholesterol-lowering resins may decrease metronidazole absorption and lower its therapeutic effect.

- cotrimoxazole or other sulfa drugs may result in a disulfiramlike effect.
- cyclosporine (Sandimmune) can lead to cyclosporine toxicity.
- disulfiram (Antabuse) may cause severe emotional and behavioral disturbances.
- lithium (Lithobid, others) can cause lithium toxicity.
- phenytoin (Dilantin) or fosphenytoin (Cerebyx) may result in increased blood levels of phenytoin; more frequent blood level testing is needed, and the phenytoin dose should be adjusted to blood levels.
- ritonavir (Norvir) may increase blood levels of metronidazole.
- sirolimus (Rapamune) or tacrolimus (Prograf) may increase risk of sirolimus toxicity.
- sulfamethoxazole (Septra, others) and perhaps other sulfa drugs may lead to a disulfiramlike reaction.
- trimethoprim (Septra, others) and perhaps other sulfa drugs may lead to a disulfiramlike reaction.

▷ *Driving, Hazardous Activities:* This drug may cause dizziness or incoordination. Restrict activities as necessary.

Aviation Note: The use of this drug *may be a disqualification* for piloting. Consult a designated Aviation Medical Examiner.

Exposure to Sun: No restrictions.

MEXILETINE (mex IL e teen)

Introduced: 1973 **Class:** Antiarrhythmic (Class or Group One)
Prescription: USA: Yes **Controlled Drug:** USA: No; Canada: No
Available as **Generic:** Yes
Brand Name: Mexitil

BENEFITS versus RISKS	
Possible Benefits	*Possible Risks*
EFFECTIVE TREATMENT IN SELECTED HEART RHYTHM DISORDERS	NARROW TREATMENT RANGE FREQUENT ADVERSE EFFECTS WORSENING OF SOME ARRHYTHMIAS (class one antiarrhythmics have increased risk of death when used in non–life threatening arrhythmias) Rare seizures, liver injury, and reduced white blood cell count

▷ **Principal Uses**

As a Single Drug Product: Uses currently included in FDA-approved labeling: Helps correct premature beats that arise in the ventricles (lower heart chambers).

Other (unlabeled) generally accepted uses: (1) Used before breast cancer surgery in one small study before surgery (preemptive analgesia) and was found to decrease pain medicine requirements (analgesic) after surgery.

How This Drug Works: Slows transmission of electrical impulses in the heart, restoring normal heart rate and rhythm in selected types of arrhythmia.

Available Dosage Forms and Strengths
Capsules — 150 mg, 200 mg, 250 mg
Gelcap — 100 mg
Gelcap (Canada) — 200 mg
Tablet — 250 mg

▷ **Usual Adult Dosage Ranges:** When rapid control of life-threatening ventricular arrhythmias is required, the manufacturer suggests a loading dose of 400 mg, then 200 mg every 8 hours. Dose can be increased (every 2 to 3 days), as needed and tolerated in 50- or 100-mg steps. Daily maximum is 1,200 mg (doses greater than this can have undesirable central nervous system side effects). If rapid control of abnormal heartbeats is not required, starting doses of 200 mg given every eight hours can be used. Some clinicians try to improve how well patients take this medicine by using an every-12-hours dosing strategy. The strategy is to arrive at an every-8-hours approach (for example, 300 mg every 8 hours). If that dose (or less) works to control abnormal heartbeats, the same dose is given every 12 hours with careful follow-up for rhythm control. Dosing can then be adjusted as needed and tolerated based on individual patient response as far as 450 mg every 12 hours. Testing blood levels is advised to guide dosing.
Note: Actual dose and schedule must be determined for each patient individually.

Conditions Requiring Dosing Adjustments
Liver Function: Dose should be decreased by one-fourth to one-third in liver disease.
Kidney Function: Dose is decreased and blood levels obtained more often.

▷ **Dosing Instructions:** The capsule may be opened and taken with food or antacid to reduce stomach irritation. DO NOT change extended release forms (Britain). Take at same times each day to obtain uniform results (even blood levels). If you forget a dose: and you take this medicine twice a day, take the missed dose as soon as you remember it, unless you are more than 6 hours late—if that is the case, skip the missed dose and take the next dose right on schedule. If you take the mexiletine three times a day, take the missed dose once you remember it, unless you are more than 4 hours late—if that is the case, skip the missed dose and return to your usual schedule. Talk with your doctor if you find yourself missing doses.

Usual Duration of Use: Effect of the loading dose strategy is usually seen in 30 to 120 minutes. Use on a regular schedule for 1 to 2 weeks determines effectiveness in correcting or preventing responsive rhythm disorders— particularly if a loading dose approach is used. Long-term use requires physician supervision.

Typical Treatment Goals and Measurements (Outcomes and Markers)
Abnormal Heartbeats: The general goal is to return the heart to a normal rhythm or at least to markedly reduce the occurrence of abnormal heartbeats. For example, when a loading dose is used to help control ventricular arrhythmias, the effect is usually seen in 30 to 150 minutes. In life-threatening arrhythmias, the goal is to abort the abnormal beats and return the heart rhythm pattern to normal. 24-hour heart monitors such as Holter monitors are often used to check success over a full day in controlling abnormal heartbeats. An early study found that sudden and short-term benefits of this medicine in controlling rapid heartbeat rate (ventricular tachycardia), was predictive of long-term results of this medicine.

▷ **This Drug Should Not Be Taken If**
  - you have had an allergic reaction to it previously.
  - you have shock resulting from the heart (cardiogenic shock).
  - you have second- or third-degree heart block (determined by electrocardiogram), uncorrected by a pacemaker.

▷ **Inform Your Physician Before Taking This Drug If**
  - you had adverse reactions to other antiarrhythmic drugs.
  - you have a history of heart disease of any kind, especially "heart block" or heart failure AND YOU DO NOT HAVE A PACEMAKER.
  - you have a blood disorder that lowers white blood cells (agranulocytosis or leukopenia) or platelets (thrombocytopenia).
  - you have impaired liver function.
  - you have Parkinson's disease.
  - another doctor has prescribed a medicine to make your urine basic (alkalinization) as this can keep mexilitine in your body longer.
  - you are prone to low blood pressure or have a seizure disorder of any kind.
  - you take digitalis, a potassium supplement or any diuretic drug that can cause potassium loss (ask your doctor).

Possible Side Effects (natural, expected, and unavoidable drug actions)
  Nervousness, light-headedness. Unpleasant taste.

▷ **Possible Adverse Effects** (unusual, unexpected, and infrequent reactions)
  If any of the following develop, consult your physician promptly for guidance.

  Mild Adverse Effects
  Allergic reaction: skin rash.
  Headache, dizziness, visual disturbance, fatigue, weakness, tremor—infrequent.
  Loss of appetite, indigestion, nausea, vomiting, constipation, diarrhea, joint or abdominal pain—rare.
  Hesitation of urine stream (urinary hesitancy)—case reports.

  Serious Adverse Effects
  Idiosyncratic reactions: depression, confusion, amnesia, hallucinations, seizures—all rare.
  Drug-induced heart rhythm disorders: shortness of breath, palpitations, chest pain, swelling—rare.
  Myelofibrosis—case reeports.
  Systemic lupus erythematosus (SLE)—(increased ANA rarely [two in 10,000 patients] and SLE in roughly 4 of 10,000 patients—rare.
  Seizures—case reports.
  Psychological changes (depression, hallucinations, or psychosis)—reported.
  Ataxia and confusion—reported.
  Congestive heart failure and sinus arrest—rare.
  Urinary retention—possible.
  Bleeding in the stomach or intestines (gastrointestinal tract)—rare.
  Liver damage with jaundice (see Glossary)—case reports.
  Low white blood cell or platelet counts: fever, sore throat, abnormal bleeding/bruising—case reports.

▷ **Possible Effects on Sexual Function:** Decreased libido, impotence—rare.

▷ **Adverse Effects That May Mimic Natural Diseases or Disorders**
  Liver toxicity may suggest viral hepatitis.

Natural Diseases or Disorders That May Be Activated by This Drug
  Latent epilepsy.

Possible Effects on Laboratory Tests
Blood white cell and platelet counts: decreased.
Liver function tests: increased liver enzymes (ALT/GPT, AST/GOT)—increased in less than 1% of users.

CAUTION
1. Thorough evaluation of your heart function (including electrocardiograms) is necessary prior to using this drug.
2. Periodic evaluation of your heart function is needed to determine your response to this drug. Some individuals may experience worsening of their heart rhythm disorder and/or deterioration of heart function. Close monitoring of heart rate, rhythm, and overall performance is essential.
3. Dose must be adjusted carefully for each person. Do not change your dose without talking to your doctor.
4. Do not take any other antiarrhythmic drug while taking this drug unless you are directed to do so by your physician.
5. Carry a card in your purse or wallet saying that you take this drug. Tell health care providers that you take it.

Precautions for Use
By Infants and Children: Safety and effectiveness for those under 12 years of age are not established. Initial use of this drug requires hospitalization and supervision by a qualified cardiologist.
By Those Over 60 Years of Age: Reduced liver function may require reduction in dose. Watch carefully for light-headedness, dizziness, unsteadiness, and tendency to fall.

▷ ## Advisability of Use During Pregnancy
Pregnancy Category: C. See Pregnancy Risk Categories at the back of this book.
Animal Studies: No birth defects reported in mice, rats, or rabbits, but an increased rate of fetal resorption was found.
Human Studies: Adequate studies of pregnant women are not available. Avoid during first 3 months. Use this drug only if clearly needed. Ask your physician for guidance.

Advisability of Use If Breast-Feeding
Presence of this drug in breast milk: Yes.
Avoid drug or refrain from nursing.

Habit-Forming Potential: None.

Effects of Overdose: Impaired urination, constipation, marked drop in blood pressure, abnormal heart rhythms, congestive heart failure, dizziness, incoordination, seizures.

Possible Effects of Long-Term Use: None reported.

Suggested Periodic Examinations While Taking This Drug (at physician's discretion)
Electrocardiograms.
Complete blood cell counts.
Liver function tests.
Mexiletine blood levels. Check of beneficial outcomes on the heart with 24-hour monitoring (such as Holter monitors).

▷ ## While Taking This Drug, Observe the Following
Foods: No restrictions. Ask your physician regarding need for salt restriction.
Herbal Medicines or Minerals: Using St. John's wort, ma huang, ephedra, guarana, or kola while taking this medicine may result in unacceptable heart stimulation. Belladonna, henbane, scopolia, pheasant's eye extract or

lily-of-the-valley, or squill powdered extracts should NOT be taken if you have abnormal heart rhythms.

Beverages: Caffeine may have an effect on heart rate and may not be desirable. Talk to your doctor about caffeine. Can be taken with milk.

▷ *Alcohol:* Use caution. Alcohol can increase the blood pressure–lowering effects of this drug.

Tobacco Smoking: Nicotine irritates the heart, reducing drug effectiveness. I advise everyone to quit smoking.

▷ *Other Drugs*

Mexiletine may ***increase*** the effects of
- antihypertensive drugs and cause excessive lowering of blood pressure.
- beta-blocker drugs (see Drug Classes).
- disopyramide (Norpace).
- lidocaine (various).
- quinidine (Quinaglute, various).
- theophylline (Theo-Dur, others), leading to theophylline toxicity and seizures.

Mexiletine ***taken concurrently*** with
- amiodarone (Cordarone) may lead to abnormal heartbeat or rhythm (QT changes and torsades de pointes).
- dofetilide (Tikosyn) and other medicines such as class I, IA or III antiarrhythmics, clarithromycin, cotrimoxazole, ondansetron, ziprazidone, and others may lead to prolongation of the QTc interval and undesirable effects. Combination is not recommended.
- drugs that inhibit or are removed by CYP 2D6 (talk to your doctor) may increase mexiletine effects.
- ritonavir (Norvir) and perhaps other protease inhibitors (see Drug Classes) may lead to toxicity.

The following drugs may ***decrease*** the effects of mexiletine:
- phenytoin (Dilantin, etc.) or fosphenytoin (Cerebyx).
- rifampin (Rifadin, Rimactane).

▷ *Driving, Hazardous Activities:* This drug may cause weakness, dizziness, or blurred vision. Restrict activities as necessary.

Aviation Note: The use of this drug ***may be a disqualification*** for piloting. Consult a designated Aviation Medical Examiner.

Exposure to Sun: No restrictions.

Occurrence of Unrelated Illness: Vomiting, diarrhea, or dehydration can affect this drug's action adversely. Report such developments promptly.

Discontinuation: Should not be stopped abruptly after long-term use. Ask your doctor about slowly reducing the dose.

MIBEFRADIL (mi BEF rah dill)

Introduced: 1997   **Class:**   Antihypertensive, calcium channel blocker
Author's Note: This medicine has been withdrawn from the market.

MIGLITOL (MIG lit all)

Introduced: 1999   **Class:**   Antidiabetic, Second generation alpha-glucosidase inhibitor   **Prescription:**   USA: Yes   **Controlled Drug:** USA: No; Canada: No   **Available as Generic:**   No
Brand Name: Glyset

```
┌─────────────────────────────────────────────────────────────────────┐
│                      BENEFITS versus RISKS                            │
│        Possible Benefits                    Possible Risks            │
│ EFFECTIVE LOWERING OF BLOOD    Gas and abdominal pain (often          │
│   SUGAR                          decreases over time)                 │
│ USE IN TYPE 1 OR TYPE 2                                               │
│   DIABETICS                                                           │
│ DECREASED RISK OF HIGH                                                │
│   BLOOD PRESSURE, HEART                                               │
│   DISEASE, OR OTHER LONG-                                             │
│   TERM DAMAGE OF HIGH BLOOD                                           │
│   SUGAR (WITH BETTER                                                  │
│   GLUCOSE CONTROL)                                                    │
│ COMBINED TREATMENT WITH                                               │
│   SULFONYLUREA IF NEEDED                                              │
└─────────────────────────────────────────────────────────────────────┘
```

▷ **Principal Uses**

As a Single Drug Product: Uses currently included in FDA-approved labeling: (1) Used with diet in diabetics who don't require insulin, yet don't have good blood sugar control with diet alone; (2) can be combined with a sulfonylurea (see Drug Classes) if diet plus miglitol or diet and sulfonylurea do not control blood sugar as well as needed.

Other (unlabeled) generally accepted uses: None at present.

How This Drug Works: By blocking intestinal alpha glucosidase and pancreatic alpha amylase (two enzymes), this medicine impairs sugar digestion and actually keeps sugar low after meals.

Available Dosage Forms and Strengths

Tablets — 25 mg, 50 mg, 100 mg (Canada)
Tablets, coated — 25 mg, 50 mg, 100 mg

▷ **Recommended Dosage Ranges** (Actual dose and schedule must be determined individually for each patient.)

Infants and Children: Safety and effectiveness not established in those less than 18 years old.

18 to 65 Years of Age: The most conservative starting dose is 25 mg once a day with the first bite of the first meal of the day. Subsequently, as needed and tolerated, the dose can be increased to 25 mg three times daily, taken at the start of each meal (after first bite). Dose increases are made at 4-to-8 week intervals to achieve blood sugar control while minimizing intestinal side effects (using 50 mg three times daily at the start of each meal). If response is not acceptable, dose may be increased to 50 mg three times daily. After three months of therapy, an A1C (glycosylated hemoglobin) should be checked. If this is still abnormal, dose may be increased to 100 mg three times daily. If a dose increase doesn't give better sugar control, dose decreases are usually considered because side effects tend to increase with increasing doses. 50-100 mg three times daily is often successful when this medicine is used by itself (monotherapy).

Over 65 Years of Age: No specific recommendations unless kidney function is very limited. Smaller doses are prudent.

Conditions Requiring Dosing Adjustments

Liver Function: Specific dosing changes do not appear to be needed.
Kidney Function: Use NOT recommended in kidney disease.

▷ **Dosing Instructions:** Take this pill after starting breakfast, lunch, and dinner—after the first bite of a meal has been eaten. Gas (flatulence) and diarrhea are common side effects but often decrease over time. Limiting the sugar sucrose can also help. If dose changes are made at 4- to 8-week intervals, the best sugar response and the least potential gas (flatulence) or diarrhea are realized. Often blood sugar is checked one hour after a meal (1 hr post-prandial) and the dose adjusted to get the best balance of blood sugar and side effects. If you forget a dose: Take the missed dose as soon as you remember it, if you are still eating your meal. If you've finished eating, the most conservative course is to check your blood sugar and ask the doctor what to do. DO NOT double doses. Return to the next dose right on schedule. Talk with your doctor if you find yourself missing doses.

Usual Duration of Use: Dosing must be individualized. Peak drug response happens in about an hour. Dosing changes are made at 4- to 8-week intervals if needed. Regular use required to give better blood glucose control. Since non-insulin–dependent diabetes is a chronic condition, use of miglitol will be ongoing. Periodic hemoglobin A1C (glycosylated hemoglobin) tests and physician follow-up are needed. Keeping the sugar close to normal can minimize diabetic problems.

Typical Treatment Goals and Measurements (Outcomes and Markers)

Blood Sugar: The general goal for blood sugar is to return it to the usual "normal" range (generally 80–120 mg/dl), while avoiding risks of excessively low blood sugar. One study (UKPDS) used a fasting plasma sugar (glucose) of less than 108 mg/dl. Fasting plasma sugar (glucose) is generally decreased by 20-30 mg/dl.

Fructosamine and Glycosylated Hemoglobin: Fructosamine levels (a measure of the past two to three weeks of blood sugar control) should be less than or equal to 310 micromoles per liter. Glycosylated hemoglobin or hemoglobin A1C (a measure of the past 2–3 months of blood sugar control) should be less than or equal to 7.0%. Some clinicians are advocating 6.5 % as the target, but others note an increased risk of hypoglycemia with this very strict target. A1C is often lowered by 0.7 to 1% by miglitol.

Possible Advantages of This Drug

May be used in combination with sulfonylurea oral hypoglycemics (see Drug Classes) to get the best control of blood sugar. This second generation alpha-glucosidase inhibitor has a chemical structure similar to sugar (glucose) and is well absorbed by the body—generally upsetting the stomach and intestines to a lesser degree. May also be more potent than acarbose (Precose) on a mg-to-mg basis.

▷ **This Drug Should Not Be Taken If**
- you have had an allergic reaction to it previously.
- you are in diabetic ketoacidosis.
- your history includes intestinal obstruction or you have a partial obstruction of the intestine.
- you have inflammatory bowel disease or colon ulceration.
- you have an intestinal condition that may worsen (such as a megacolon or bowel obstruction) if increased gas (flatus) forms.
- you have a long-standing (chronic) intestinal disease altering digestion or your ability to absorb materials from the intestine.

▷ **Inform Your Physician Before Taking This Drug If**
- you do not know what the symptoms of hypoglycemia are.
- you have an infection (insulin may be required).

- you are pregnant or are breast-feeding your infant (no data exists on use in pregnancy or breast-feeding).
- you have a history of kidney or liver disease.
- you will have surgery with general anesthesia or have a serious infection (insulin may be required).
- you forgot to tell your doctor about all the drugs you take.
- you are unsure of how much to take or how often to take it.

Possible Side Effects (natural, expected, and unavoidable drug actions)

Gas (flatulence) or diarrhea results from bacterial action on sugars and tends to decrease over time.

▷ **Possible Adverse Effects** (unusual, unexpected, and infrequent reactions)

If any of the following develop, consult your physician promptly for guidance.

Mild Adverse Effects

Allergic reactions: skin rash, itching.

Sleepiness, headache, dizziness—of questionable causation.

Pain or swelling of the belly (abdomen)—frequent.

Gas (flatulence) or diarrhea—frequent (often eases).

Low serum iron—infrequent.

Serious Adverse Effects

Low blood sugar if combined with sulfonylureas—possible.

Anemia—possible.

Ileus—case reports and in those with prior bowel blockage history.

▷ **Possible Effects on Sexual Function:** None reported.

Possible Effects on Laboratory Tests

Hemoglobin A1C: trending more toward normal (good effect).

Blood sugar one hour after eating (postprandial): decreased.

Liver enzymes: no change in one short-term study.

CAUTION

1. This medicine itself does not cause hypoglycemia. Low sugar may result if combined with insulin or sulfonylureas.
2. Infections may cause loss of sugar control and require temporary insulin use.
3. This medicine is part of the total management of diabetes. A properly prescribed diet and regular exercise are still required for best control of blood sugar.
4. **If** your kidneys fail or worsen, tell your doctor. This drug is generally not used if serum creatinine is greater than 2 mg/dl.

Precautions for Use

By Infants and Children: Safety and effectiveness for those under 18 not established.

By Those Over 60 Years of Age: Specific recommendations are not made at this time.

▷ **Advisability of Use During Pregnancy**

Pregnancy Category: B. See Pregnancy Risk Categories at the back of this book.

Human Studies: Adequate studies of pregnant women are not available.

Insulin is often the drug of first choice for blood sugar control in pregnancy. Ask your doctor for help.

Advisability of Use If Breast-Feeding

Presence of this drug in breast milk: Yes, in very small amounts.

Avoid drug or refrain from nursing.

Habit-Forming Potential: None.

Effects of Overdose: Temporary gas (flatus), abdominal discomfort, and diarrhea.

Possible Effects of Long-Term Use: Beneficial effects on blood sugar.

Suggested Periodic Examinations While Taking This Drug (at physician's discretion)

Routine testing of blood sugar levels at intervals recommended by your physician is prudent. Historically, estimates of blood sugar were obtained by checking urine sugar. This method has been replaced by finger stick testing of blood glucose. Finger stick testing accurately reflects the blood sugar and helps ensure better control (tighter control) of blood glucose. A new device uses a laser to "stick" the finger (see *www.cellrobotics.com*). The laser is painless and appears to avoid toughening the skin like a lancet. One new blood sugar machine can also test glycated protein (fructosamine). If you are ill, increased frequency of finger stick blood glucose testing may be indicated. Periodic checks of blood sugar one hour after eating are prudent. A new handheld machine called A1cNow enables pharmacists and physicians to check hemoglobin A1C in the office or pharmacy in 8 minutes. Additionally, a device called a Glucowatch Biographer uses a pad and a watch-like device to painlessly check blood sugar (see *www.cygnus.com*). With this medicine a periodic complete blood count is prudent—with serum iron or iron-binding capacity if anemia develops. Liver function tests (transaminases) do not appear to be required based on one study.

▷ **While Taking This Drug, Observe the Following**

Foods: Follow your diabetic diet conscientiously. Taking a diabetes education course is very smart and can teach you about portion control, what to do on sick days and other important concepts. Blood sugar control can help avoid or delay diabetes problems. Vitamin C in high dose may worsen blood sugar control. Do not omit snack foods in mid-afternoon or at bedtime if they help prevent hypoglycemia. Rice bran has been checked in a small (57 subject) study of type 1 and type 2 diabetics. The benefit was a 30% lowering of sugar. This might be a new complementary care option.

Herbal Medicines or Minerals: Using chromium may change the way your body is able to use sugar. Some health food stores advocate vanadium as mimicking the actions of insulin, but possible toxicity and need for rigorous studies presently preclude recommending it. DHEA may change sensitivity to insulin or insulin resistance. Aloe, eucalyptus, fenugreek, ginger, garlic, ginseng, glucomannan, guar gum, hawthorn, licorice, nettle, and yohimbe may change blood sugar. Surprisingly, boiled stems of the Optuntia streptacantha prickly pear cactus appears to be able to lower blood sugar. Ongoing effects and effects on A1C are not known. Red sage is used for blood sugar effects, but is unproven. Psyllium increases risk of excessively low blood sugar. Since so many of these products may require adjustment of insulin dosing, talk to your doctor BEFORE combining any of these herbal medicines with this medicine. Echinacea pupurea (injectable) and blonde psyllium seed or husk should NOT be taken by people living with diabetes.

Beverages: No restrictions. May be taken with milk.

▷ *Alcohol:* No interaction with miglitol. If you also take a sulfonylurea (see Drug Classes), alcohol can exaggerate lowering of blood sugar or cause a disulfiramlike (see Glossary) reaction.

Tobacco Smoking: No interactions expected. I advise everyone to stop smoking.
▷ *Other Drugs*
Miglitol may *increase* the effects of
- sulfonylureas (see Drug Classes), causing a lower blood sugar (not a miglitol effect); this may be used for therapeutic benefit.

Miglitol *taken concurrently* with
- clofibrate (Atromid-S) may result in hypoglycemia.
- digestive enzyme products that contain amylase or lipase may result in loss of blood sugar control.
- digoxin (Lanoxin) may lead to low digoxin levels and benefits.
- disopyramide (Norpace) may result in hypoglycemia.
- gatifloxacin (Tequin) or levofloxacin (Levaquin) may increase or decrease blood sugar. Caution and close follow-up on blood sugar are required.
- high-dose aspirin or other salicylates and some NSAIDs (see Drug Classes) may result in hypoglycemia.
- insulin (see profile) increases risk of low blood sugar.
- ranitidine (Zantac) may blunt the benefits of ranitidine.
- sulfonamide antibiotics (see Drug Classes) may pose an increased risk for low blood sugar (hypoglycemia).

The following drugs may *decrease* the effects of miglitol:
- adrenocorticosteroids (see Drug Classes).
- beta blockers (see Drug Classes).
- calcium channel blockers (see Drug Classes).
- furosemide (Lasix) and bumetanide (Bumex).
- isoniazid (INH).
- monoamine oxidase (MAO) inhibitors (see Drug Classes).
- nicotinic acid.
- pancreatin (various).
- phenytoin (Dilantin).
- rifampin (Rifadin, others).
- theophylline (Theo-Dur, others).
- thiazide diuretics (see Drug Classes).
- thyroid hormones (see Drug Classes).

▷ *Driving, Hazardous Activities:* Use caution until degree of drowsiness you may experience is known.
Aviation Note: Diabetes *is a disqualification* for piloting. Consult a designated Aviation Medical Examiner.
Exposure to Sun: No restrictions.
Heavy Exercise or Exertion: Caution advised because this drug lowers peak in blood sugar after meals. Talk over dosing changes with your doctor.
Occurrence of Unrelated Illness: Illness can change blood sugar control. Temporary use of insulin may be required.
Discontinuation: Never stop miglitol before calling your doctor.

MINIMALLY SEDATING ANTIHISTAMINES

Cetirizine   (sa TEER a zeen)   **Desloratadine**   (DEZ lor AT a deen)
Fexofenadine   (fex oh FEN a deen)   **Loratadine**   (lor AT a deen)

Introduced: 1996, 2002, 1996, 1992, respectively   **Class:**   Antihistamines, minimally sedating   **Prescription:**   USA: Yes   **Controlled Drug:** USA: No; Canada: No   **Available as Generic:**   U.S.: cetirizine: No; desloratidine: No; fexofenadine: No; loratadine: Yes; Canada: Same as U.S.

Brand Names: *Cetirizine:* ✤Apo-Cetirizine, ✤Reactine Zyrtec, Zyrtec D [CD], *Desloratadine:* Clarinex, *Fexofenadine:* Allegra, Allegra-D [CD], *Loratadine:* Alavert (nonprescription), ✤Allertin, ✤Chlor-Tripolon ND [CD], ✤Claritin Extra, Claritin Reditabs [CD], ✤Novo-Loratadine.

Author's Note: Astemizole and terfenadine data have been removed. Loratadine is now available as Alavert in a nonprescription 10 mg orally disintegrating tablet form (can be taken with or without water). Fexofenadine (Allegra) still requires a prescription at the time of this writing. Information on desloratadine (Clarinex) is included in this edition.

```
                    BENEFITS versus RISKS
     Possible Benefits                Possible Risks
EFFECTIVE AND LONG-LASTING     RARE HEART RHYTHM
  RELIEF OF ALLERGIC RHINITIS    DISTURBANCES (HAVE
EFFECTIVE RELIEF OF SOME         OCCURRED AS A DRUG
  ALLERGIC SKIN DISORDERS        INTERACTION EFFECT OR AS A
MINIMAL DROWSINESS               DRUG EFFECT) fexofenadine has
MINOR TO NO ANTICHOLINERGIC      one case report, loratadine
  SIDE EFFECTS                  Low white blood cell count
                                   (leukopenia) (1.4% of fexofenadine
                                   patients)
                                Slight atropinelike effects (some
                                   medicines in this class)
                                Mild sedation or fatigue
```

▷ **Principal Uses**

As a Single Drug Product: Uses currently included in FDA-approved labeling: (1) Used to treat non-nasal and nasal symptoms of seasonal allergic rhinitis (hay fever); (2) helps ease symptoms of rhinitis; (3) used to treat swellings of unknown origin (idiopathic urticaria) (cetirizine, loratadine); (4) helps ease symptoms of pollen-induced asthma (cetirizine, loratadine).

Other (unlabeled) generally accepted uses: (1) chronic idiopathic urticaria (loratadine); (4) food allergies (cetirizine).

As a Combination Drug Product [CD]: Allegra-D, Claritin-D and Zyrtec-D contain the original minimally sedating antihistamine and add the benefits of pseudoephedrine. Caution should be used when taking the "D" forms if you are also taking a medicine that interacts with pseudoephedrine.

How These Drugs Work: These medicines block histamine, stopping symptoms (caused by histamine), such as swelling and itching of the eyes.

Available Dosage Forms and Strengths

Cetirizine:
Solution — 5 mg/ml
Tablets — 5 mg, 10 mg
Tablets (Canada only) — 20 mg

Desloratadine:
Tablets — 5 mg

Fexofenadine:
Capsules — 60 mg
Tablet — 30 mg, 60 mg, 180 mg
Tablets, extended-release — 60 mg fexofenadine,
— 120 mg pseudoephedrine

Loratadine:

Syrup — 1 mg/ml
Tablets — 10 mg
Tablets, extended-release (Claritin-D 24-Hour) — 10 mg loratadine, 240 mg pseudoephedrine
Tablets, rapidly disintegrating (micronized — 10 mg loratadine)
Tablets, repeat-action (Claritin-D [CD]) — 5 mg loratadine, 120 mg pseudoephedrine

▷ **Recommended Dosage Ranges** (Actual dose and schedule must be determined for each patient individually.)

Infants and Children: **Safety and efficacy in children younger than 12 years old have been established only for fexofenadine and cetirizine, not for the rest of the medicines in this family.**

Cetirizine (Zyrtec) is approved for children 2 to 5 years old who have seasonal or perennial allergic rhinitis or hives (idiopathic urticaria) of unknown cause.

Fexofenadine (Allegra) is newly approved for children 6 to 11 years old who have seasonal or perennial allergic rhinitis or hives (idiopathic urticaria) of unknown cause using 30 mg twice daily.

12 to 60 Years of Age:

Cetirizine: The starting dose is 5 mg (depending on severity, may be 10 mg) and is increased as needed and tolerated to a maximum of 20 mg daily.

Desloratadine: A single 5-mg tablet once a day. (5 mg every other day if liver or kidneys are impaired).

Fexofenadine:

Seasonal allergic rhinitis: 60 mg twice daily or 180 mg once daily.

Chronic idiopathic urticaria: 60 mg twice daily.

Loratadine: A single 10-mg tablet (of the nonrepeat action, noncombination product) is taken once daily.

Loratadine/pseudoephedrine (5 mg/120 mg nonrepeat action): One tablet twice daily.

Loratadine/pseudoephedrine (10 mg/240 mg repeat action): One tablet daily.

Over 60 Years of Age:

Dosing changes for fexofenadine and loratadine (Claritin-D and Claritin-D 24-Hour forms) do not appear to be needed. Prudent to decrease cetirizine doses, as it is slowly removed from the body at this age.

Conditions Requiring Dosing Adjustments

Liver Function: Cetirizine: A 5-mg dose is recommended.

Fexofenadine: Dosing changes do not appear to be needed.

Desloratadine: 5 mg every other day.

Loratadine: Patients with liver compromise take a dose of 10 mg (of the non-repeat action, noncombination product) every other day.

Kidney Function: Cetirizine: Patients with moderate kidney decline (creatinine clearance 11–31 ml/min) may take 5 mg daily.

Desloratadine: 5 mg every other day.

Fexofenadine: A daily dose of 60 mg once daily is recommended.

Loratadine: Patients with moderate kidney failure (creatinine clearance less than 30 ml/min) get a starting dose of 10 mg (of nonrepeat action, non-combination product) every other day.

▷ **Dosing Instructions:** Loratadine is best taken on an empty stomach. Once the rapidly disintegrating (Reditab) form has dissolved, water may be used to help patients swallow the contents of the pill. The other medicines in this class may be taken with food. Extended-release forms of these medicines should never be crushed. If you forget a dose: Take the missed dose as soon as you remember it, unless it's nearly time for your next dose—if that is the case, skip the missed dose and take the next dose right on schedule. DO NOT double doses. Talk with your doctor if you find yourself missing doses.

Usual Duration of Use: Although all of these medicines may go to work immediately, regular use for up to 1 day (fexofenadine), up to 2 days (astemizole or cetirizine) or up to 3 days (loratadine) may be needed to see substantial symptom improvement. Long-term use requires evaluation of response by your doctor.

Typical Treatment Goals and Measurements (Outcomes and Markers):

Seasonal Allergic Rhinitis: The general goal is to decrease or eliminate hay fever symptoms such as watery eyes, sneezing, and itchy feelings in the throat or eyes, and runny nose.

Possible Advantages of These Drugs: Less sedating than previously available antihistamines. Once-daily dosing for some agents in this class. Some medicines in this class do not interact with certain antifungals and macrolide antibiotics (see Drug Classes) or do interact but do not appear to cause side effects on the heart or change the safety profile. Cetirizine has NOT had ANY case reports of QTc prolongation. Tachyphylaxis or tolerance may be less likely to occur to these medicines than with earlier agents. Reditabs do not require water to take them. Fexofenadine did NOT exhibit any driving performance decrease in one study of 24 healthy men when fexofenadine was combined with ethanol. Once a day dosing is a distinct advantage.

Currently "Drugs of Choice"

For patients who must take antihistamine-type medicines and require the best possible balance of symptom relief and minimal sedation.

▷ **These Drugs Should Not Be Taken If**
- you have had an allergic reaction to any dose form of these medicines or any of the ingredients in them previously.
- you are presently being tested (using skin tests) for allergies.
- you are taking medicines that prolong the QT interval, such as quinidine, pentamidine, disopyramide, or others (for cetirizine and fexofenadine).
- you have urinary retention, liver disease, severe disease of the arteries of the heart (coronary artery disease), or narrow-angle glaucoma (loratadine combination products that contain pseudoephedrine).

▷ **Inform Your Physician Before Taking These Drugs If**
- you have asthma.
- you are at risk for drowsiness or fainting (syncope).
- you have a history of a heart rhythm disorder.
- your electrolytes are not in balance.
- you are taking other medicines metabolized by or that change CYP 3A4 levels (ask your doctor) and one of these medicines is removed by that enzyme.
- you are taking other medicines (especially antifungal or macrolide antibiotics). Blood levels of loratadine or fexofenadine may be increased. Decreases in loratadine and fexofenadine doses may be prudent.
- you have a history of liver or kidney compromise.
- you are pregnant.
- your work REQUIRES mental alertness.

Possible Side Effects (natural, expected, and unavoidable drug actions)
Dry nose, mouth, or throat, somnolence (drowsiness): cetirizine—frequent, fexofenadine—rare, loratadine—infrequent.

▷ **Possible Adverse Effects** (unusual, unexpected, and infrequent reactions)
If any of the following develop, consult your physician promptly for guidance.

Mild Adverse Effects
Allergic reactions: skin rash, itching.
Headache, fatigue or dizziness—infrequent to frequent, depending on the agent.
Dry mouth—possible to infrequent.
Leg cramps, muscle aches (loratadine)—rare.
Weight gain (cetirizine)—uncommon.
Fast heart rate (tachycardia) (loratadine)—rare.
Prolonged QTc interval (fexofenadine)—possible if used in people with existing heart disease, case report(s).
Lowering of the blood pressure (loratadine)—rare.
Vision changes (loratadine)—rare.

Serious Adverse Effects
Allergic reactions: anaphylaxis (loratadine)—rare.
Idiosyncratic reactions: not reported.
Serious heart rhythm disorders: fexofenadine—case report.
Tachycardia—rare.
Lowering of the white blood cell count (fexofenadine)—rare.
Abnormal liver function (loratadine)—case reports.
Depression, confusion, paresthesias—rare.
Passing out (syncope)—rare.

▷ **Possible Effects on Sexual Function:** Vaginitis, painful menses (dysmenorrhea), breast enlargement or breast pain (loratadine)—case reports.
Menstrual disorders (loratadine, fexofenadine)—case reports to rare.
Galactorrhea (loratadine)—case reports.
Impotence (loratadine)—case reports.

Possible Delayed Adverse Effects: None reported.

▷ **Adverse Effects That May Mimic Natural Diseases or Disorders**
Increased liver enzymes may mimic hepatitis of infectious origin.

Natural Diseases or Disorders That May Be Activated by These Drugs
None reported.

Possible Effects on Laboratory Tests
Skin tests for allergies will be blunted and less diagnostic.
Liver function tests: may be increased (loratadine, fexofenadine [mildly].
White blood cell counts: decreased (leukopenia)—rare in clinical trials (fexofenadine).

CAUTION
1. Loratadine does interact with some antifungals and some macrolide antibiotics—but appears to be free of the heart (cardiac) effects, even though blood levels of loratadine may increase if it is taken with these interacting medicines. Talk to your doctor or pharmacist before taking any medicines that were not discussed when loratadine was prescribed.
2. Some of these medicines HAVE LIFE-THREATENING DRUG INTERACTIONS. Talk to your doctor or pharmacist BEFORE combining any pre-

scription, nonprescription or herbal remedies with medicines in this class.

3. Report dizziness, heart palpitation, or chest pain promptly when using any of these medicines.

4. Fexofenadine (Allegra) levels may be decreased by roughly 70% if it is taken with orange, apple, or grapefruit juice. Current thinking holds that this is due to fruit juice inhibiting a drug "taxi" (transporter) called OATP.

Precautions for Use

By Infants and Children: Safety and effectiveness for use by those under 12 years of age have not been established.

By Those Over 60 Years of Age: Smaller starting and maintenance doses are needed. Longer dosing intervals may be needed as well.

▷ **Advisability of Use During Pregnancy**

Pregnancy Category: B (cetirizine, loratadine); C (fexofenadine). See Pregnancy Risk Categories at the back of this book.

Animal Studies: No birth defects reported.

Human Studies: Information from adequate studies of pregnant women is not available. **These medicines should be used during pregnancy only if clearly needed. Discuss the BENEFITS versus RISKS with your doctor.**

Advisability of Use If Breast-Feeding

Presence of this drug in breast milk: No data (cetirizine, fexofenadine); yes (loratadine).

Ask your doctor for guidance regarding stopping the drug or stopping nursing (cetirizine, fexofenadine, or loratadine).

Habit-Forming Potential: None.

Effects of Overdose: With overdoses greater than 10 mg (40–80 mg): tachycardia, somnolence, and headache (loratadine). Usual antihistamine protocols (cetirizine or fexofenadine).

Possible Effects of Long-Term Use: None defined.

Suggested Periodic Examinations While Taking These Drugs (at physician's discretion)

Examination for relief of the condition(s) being treated.

If palpitations, unexplained dizziness, or chest pain or discomfort happens, an electrocardiogram (ECG) and heart pattern (QT interval, etc.) should be checked.

▷ **While Taking These Drugs, Observe the Following**

Foods: Astemizole and loratadine are best taken on an empty stomach. DO NOT combine with grapefruit.

Herbal Medicines or Minerals: Valerian and kava kava may intensify drowsiness. St. John's wort may lead to photosensitivity. Combination with medicines in this class that also cause photosensitivity is NOT advised. If you are allergic to plants in the *Asteraceae* family (aster, chrysanthemum, daisy, or ragweed), you may also be allergic to echinacea, chamomile, feverfew, and St. John's wort. A well-designed study of 125 patients (see Schapowal in sources) found that an herb called butterbur was comparable to cetirizine in seasonal allergic rhinitis. Talk to your doctor to see if this makes sense for you.

Beverages: Grapefruit juice may lead to increased blood levels of astemizole and loratadine, leading to toxicity. Fexofenadine (Allegra) levels may be decreased by roughly 70% if it is taken with orange, apple, or grapefruit juice. Current thinking holds that this is due to fruit juice inhibiting a drug "taxi" (transporter) called OATP. Water is the best liquid with to take the medicines in this family.

▷ *Alcohol:* May cause excessive drowsiness (central nervous system depression).

Tobacco Smoking: No interactions expected. I advise everyone to quit smoking.

Marijuana Smoking: May cause additive drowsiness or lethargy.

▷ *Other Drugs*

These medicines *taken concurrently* with

- cimetidine (Tagamet) may produce a significant increase in loratadine blood levels. No serious drug effects have been reported, but since in general the frequency of adverse effects increases with increasing blood levels, it appears prudent to decrease the dose of loratadine if these medicines are to be taken at the same time because of possible loratadine toxicity. The loratadine dose should certainly be decreased if increased frequency of adverse effects occurs if these medicines are combined in usual doses. Cetirizine is mostly removed by the kidneys.
- fluoxetine (Prozac) produced a serious heart rhythm problem in a patient taking terfenadine—DO NOT COMBINE THESE MEDICINES. Caution is advised for the other drugs in this class.
- fluvoxamine (Luvox) may result in increased blood levels of cetirizine or loratadine. Caution is advised.
- grepafloxacin (Raxar) may increase risk of heart rhythm problems (astemizole)—DO NOT COMBINE.
- indinavir (Crixivan) and perhaps ritonavir, saquinavir or nelfinavir may decrease metabolism of astemizole and should NEVER BE COMBINED. Loratadine levels may be increased, and doses may need to be lowered. Other drugs in this family may also be affected.
- itraconazole (and perhaps other similarly structured antifungals, such as ketoconazole) should NEVER BE COMBINED with astemizole. These drugs may cause increased blood levels of loratadine or fexofenadine. Although no serious heart rhythm toxicity has been reported to date with this medicine, caution is advised, and it appears prudent to lower the dose of loratadine or fexofenadine.
- macrolide antibiotics such as clarithromycin or erythromycin—while no serious heart rhythm toxicity has been reported to date with loratadine or fexofenadine, caution is advised, as excessive blood levels of any medicine may increase risk of adverse effects; it may be prudent to lower the dose of loratadine.
- medicines that prolong the QT interval should be avoided (such as disopyramide, ibutilide, quinolones [grepafloxacin, sparfloxacin], others); cetirizine and loratadine and desloratadine (very new medicine) are the medicines in this class without any reports of QTc interval changes.
- nefazodone (Serzone) may lead to life-threatening heart problems if combined with astemizole.
- paroxetine (Paxil) may inhibit the enzymes needed to remove cetirizine or loratadine. Caution is advised.
- quinidine (Quinaglute, others) may result in a change in the effect of quinidine and result in undesirable effects on the heart. Caution is advised.
- ritonavir (Norvir) and perhaps other protease inhibitors (see Drug Classes) may increase blood levels and toxicity.
- sertraline (Zoloft) may lead to life-threatening heart problems if combined with astemizole. DO NOT COMBINE.
- sotalol (Betapace) may cause additive adverse effects (QT interval prolon-

gation) on the heart by these medicines—this combination is not recommended.

- theophylline (Theo-Dur, others) may decrease cetirizine clearance. Patients should be closely followed for signs of excessive cetirizine levels.
- zafirlukast (Accolate), and perhaps zileuton (Zyflo) if combined with astemizole, may decrease zafirlukast levels and blunt the therapeutic benefits of zafirlukast.

▷ *Driving, Hazardous Activities:* Although these medicines are much less likely than earlier antihistamines to cause drowsiness, caution should be used until your individual reaction to these medicines is determined. Restrict activities as necessary.

Aviation Note: The use of these drugs is probably not a disqualification for piloting. Consult a designated Aviation Medical Examiner.

Exposure to Sun: Rare cases of photosensitivity have been reported with some medicines (astemizole, loratadine) in this class. Use caution.

MINOXIDIL (min OX i dil)

Introduced: 1972 **Class:** Antihypertensive, hair growth stimulant
Prescription: USA: Yes **Controlled Drug:** USA: No; Canada: No
Available as Generic: Yes

Brand Names: Alostil, ✦Apo-Gain, ✦Hairgro, Kresse, Loniten, ✦Med-Minoxidil, Minocalve 5, Minodyl, Minoximen, Rogaine, Rogaine Extra Strength, Rogaine 5

Author's Note: Rogaine treatment for baldness is available without a prescription.

BENEFITS versus RISKS

Possible Benefits	*Possible Risks*
POTENT, LONG-ACTING ANTIHYPERTENSIVE	EXCESSIVE BODY HAIR GROWTH
EFFECTIVE IN CASES OF SEVERE HYPERTENSION, ACCELERATED AND MALIGNANT HYPERTENSION	SALT AND WATER RETENTION
	Excessively rapid heart rate
	Aggravation of angina
Moderately effective in treating male pattern baldness and female baldness (alopecia androgenica)	Local scalp irritation (topical use)

▷ **Principal Uses**

As a Single Drug Product: Uses currently included in FDA-approved labeling: (1) Treats severe high blood pressure not controlled by conventional therapy; (2) treats female androgenic baldness or male pattern baldness; (3) effective in patients with high blood pressure and kidney failure.

Other (unlabeled) generally accepted uses: (1) Supportive therapy in hair transplants.

How This Drug Works: (1) Relaxes constricted muscles in walls of small arteries and permits expansion of the arteries and lower blood pressure. (2) May act directly on the hair follicle, may increase size of previously closed small scalp blood vessels, restoring blood flow and returning small hair follicles to normal size and activity.

Available Dosage Forms and Strengths
Tablets — 2.5 mg, 10 mg
Topical solution — 2%,
— 5% (Extra-Strength)

▷ **Usual Adult Dosage Ranges:** *For hypertension:* In severe cases, initially 5 mg once a day. The dose is then gradually increased as needed and tolerated to 10 mg, 20 mg and then 40 mg every 24 hours, taken in one or two divided doses daily. The usual ongoing dose is 10 to 40 mg daily.
For Male Pattern Baldness: Apply thinly 1 ml of topical solution to the balding area of the scalp twice a day (for example in the morning and at bedtime). The total daily dose should not exceed 2 ml.
Note: Actual dose and schedule must be determined for each patient individually.

Conditions Requiring Dosing Adjustments
Liver Function: This drug is metabolized (90%) in the liver. It should be used with caution by patients with liver compromise.
Kidney Function: In moderate kidney failure, the dose should be decreased empirically.

▷ **Dosing Instructions:** For hypertension: Tablets may be crushed and taken with or following food to prevent nausea. Take at the same time each day. If you forget a dose: Take or apply the missed dose as soon as you remember it, unless it's nearly time for your next dose—if that is the case, skip the missed dose and take or apply the next dose right on schedule. Talk with your doctor if you find yourself missing doses.
For baldness: The topical solution is for external, local use only; it is not to be swallowed. Begin application at the center of the bald area; apply thinly to cover the entire area. The scalp and hair must be dry at the time of application. Follow instructions carefully.

Usual Duration of Use: Use on a regular schedule for 3 to 7 days usually determines effectiveness in controlling severe hypertension. Continual use of the topical solution for at least 4 months is needed to determine its ability to promote hair growth. Growth usually continues for up to a year of treatment. Long-term use (months to years) of both dose forms requires physician supervision.

Typical Treatment Goals and Measurements (Outcomes and Markers)
Baldness: The goal is to regain hair and maintain existing hair. Some dermatologists use hair counts to assess progress and peak benefits. Initial regrowth may be uncolored and soft in texture. Continued use of topical form finds development of hair of the same texture and color as the original hair.
Blood Pressure: The NEW guidelines (JNC VII) define normal blood pressure (BP) as **less than** 120/80. Because blood pressures that were once considered acceptable can actually lead to blood vessel damage, the committee from the National Institutes of Health, National Heart Lung and Blood Institute now have a new category called **Pre-hypertension**. This ranges from 120/80 to 139/89 and is intended to help your doctor encourage lifestyle changes (or in the case of people with a risk factor for high blood pressure, start treatment) much earlier—so that possible damage to blood vessels, your heart, kidneys, sexual potency, or eyes might be minimized or avoided altogether. The next two classes of high blood pressure are stage 1 hypertension: 140/90 to 159/99 and stage 2 hypertension equal to or greater than: 160/100 mm Hg. These guidelines also recommend that clinicians trying to control blood pressure work with their patients to agree on

the goals and a plan of treatment. The first-ever guidelines for blood pressure (hypertension) in African Americans recommends that MOST black patients be started on TWO antihypertensive medicines with the goal of lowering blood pressure to 130/80 for those with high risk for heart and blood vessel disease or with diabetes. The American Diabetes Association recommends 130/80 as the target for people living with diabetes and less than 125/75 for those who spill more than one gram of protein into their urine. Most clinicians try to achieve a BP that confers the best balance of lower cardiovascular risk and avoids the problem of too low a blood pressure. Blood pressure duration is generally increased with beneficial restriction of sodium. The goals and time frame should be discussed with you when the prescription is written. If goals are not met, it is not unusual to intensify doses or add on medicines. You can find the new blood pressure guidelines at *www.nhlbi.nih.gov/guidelines/hypertension/index.htm*. For the African American guidelines see Douglas J.G. in Sources.

▷ **This Drug Should Not Be Taken If**
- you have had an allergic reaction to it previously.
- you are known to have a pheochromocytoma (an adrenaline-producing tumor).
- you have pulmonary hypertension due to mitral valve stenosis.
- the topical dosing form should not be used with products that can increase absorption in the skin. Combined use of vasoline (petrolatum), retinoids, and topical corticosteroids should be avoided.

▷ **Inform Your Physician Before Taking This Drug If**
- you are pregnant or planning pregnancy.
- you are breast-feeding your infant.
- you have had a heart attack in the last month or have swelling around the heart (pericarditis).
- you have angina attacks.
- you have existing blood vessel disease in your head (cerebrovascular disease).
- you have a history of coronary artery disease (and are not taking a water pill–diuretic) or impaired heart function.
- you have a history of stroke or impaired brain circulation.
- you have impaired liver or kidney function.

Possible Side Effects (natural, expected, and unavoidable drug actions)
Increased heart rate, fluid retention with weight gain, excessive hair growth on face, arms, legs, and back (frequent).

▷ **Possible Adverse Effects** (unusual, unexpected, and infrequent reactions)
If any of the following develop, consult your physician promptly for guidance.
Mild Adverse Effects
Allergic reaction: skin rash.
Localized dermatitis at site of application of topical solution—rare.
Headache, dizziness, fainting—rare.
Nausea, increased thirst—infrequent.
Hair growth and changes in hair color—case reports.
Weight gain—possible (may be due to fluid if this drug is used without a water pill (diuretic).
Mild increase in liver enzymes—infrequent.
Serious Adverse Effects
Allergic reactions: serious skin rash (Stevens-Johnson Syndrome).
Idiosyncratic reaction: fluid formation around the heart (pericardial effusion).

Development of angina pectoris; high blood pressure in the lungs (pulmonary hypertension)—case reports.

Systemic lupus erythematosus—case reports.

Low white blood cells or platelets—rare and transient.

Author's Note: Topical use of this medicine for hair growth avoids most of these adverse effects.

▷ **Possible Effects on Sexual Function:** Male breast tenderness (gynecomastia)—case reports. Some data to support that this drug balances the male ability to ejaculate and have a healthy sex drive that may have been blunted by other drugs that treat high blood pressure.

Natural Diseases or Disorders That May Be Activated by This Drug

Latent coronary artery disease with symptomatic angina.

Possible Effects on Laboratory Tests

Blood HDL cholesterol level: increased.

Blood LDL cholesterol level: decreased.

CAUTION

1. Long-term use for hypertension usually requires use of a diuretic to counteract salt and water retention.
2. The long-term use of this drug for hypertension may require concurrent use of a beta-blocker drug to control excessive acceleration of the heart.
3. It is best to avoid combining this drug and guanethidine; the combination can cause severe orthostatic hypotension (see Glossary).
4. Consult your physician regarding the advisability of using a "no-salt-added" diet.
5. Little of this drug is absorbed into the general circulation when the topical solution is applied to the scalp. However, some systemic effects have been reported. Inform your physician promptly if you experience any unusual symptoms while using the topical solution.
6. The topical form contains alcohol. Avoid getting this baldness medicine into your eyes.

Precautions for Use

By Infants and Children: Dose schedules should be determined by a qualified pediatrician. In children under 12 years old, starting dose is 0.2 mg per kg of body mass in a single dose. Dose is then increased as needed and tolerated by 0.1 to 0.2 mg per kg per day at 3-day intervals. Children over 12 are given the adult dose. Monitor closely for salt and water retention.

By Those Over 60 Years of Age: Treatment with small doses and a limit of total daily dose to 75 mg is indicated. Headache, palpitation, and rapid heart rate due to this drug are more common in this age group and can mimic acute anxiety states. Observe for dizziness, unsteadiness, fainting, and falling.

▷ **Advisability of Use During Pregnancy**

Pregnancy Category: C. See Pregnancy Risk Categories at the back of this book.

Animal Studies: No birth defects reported in rats or rabbits, but studies did reveal decreased fertility and increased fetal deaths.

Human Studies: Adequate studies of pregnant women are not available.

Avoid during the first 3 months. Use only if clearly needed during the final 6 months.

Advisability of Use If Breast-Feeding

Presence of this drug in breast milk: Yes.

Avoid drug or refrain from nursing.

Habit-Forming Potential: None.

Effects of Overdose: Headache, dizziness, weakness, nausea, marked low blood pressure, weak and rapid pulse, loss of consciousness.

Possible Effects of Long-Term Use: Excessive growth of body hair occurs in 80% of users after 1 to 2 months of continual treatment for hypertension. Close to 100% of users will experience this effect after 1 year of continual treatment. This may be accompanied by darkening of the skin and coarsening of facial features.

Suggested Periodic Examinations While Taking This Drug (at physician's discretion)

Body weight measurement for insidious gain due to water retention.
Electrocardiographic and echocardiographic heart examinations.

▷ **While Taking This Drug, Observe the Following**

Foods: Avoid excessive salt and heavily salted foods.

Herbal Medicines or Minerals: Hawthorn, ginseng, saw palmetto, ma huang, guarana, goldenseal, yohimbe, and licorice may cause increased blood pressure, blunting the benefits of this medicine. St. John's wort can change liver removal of medicines. Careful patient follow-up for decreased benefit from minoxidil is prudent. Calcium and garlic may help lower blood pressure, and the dose has to be individualized with a standardized extract. Dong quai can change the removal of medicines by the liver—caution is advised for excessive lowering of blood pressure. Indian snakeroot has a German Commission E monograph indication for hypertension—talk to your doctor. Eleuthero root and ephedra should be avoided by people living with hypertension. Talk to your doctor BEFORE adding any herbals. Autumn crocus should be avoided in alopecia.

Beverages: No restrictions. May be taken with milk.

▷ *Alcohol:* Use with extreme caution. Alcohol can exaggerate the blood pressure–lowering effects of this drug when it is taken orally.

Tobacco Smoking: Best avoided. Nicotine can contribute significantly to angina. I advise everyone to quit smoking.

▷ *Other Drugs*

Minoxidil may *increase* the effects of
- all other antihypertensive drugs; careful dose adjustments are mandatory.

Minoxidil *taken concurrently* with
- clonidine (Catapres TTS, others) may help ease fast heart rate and increased sympathetic nervous system activity caused by minoxidil.
- guanethidine (Ismelin, Esimil) may cause severe orthostatic hypotension; avoid this combination.
- NSAIDs may blunt the therapeutic benefit of minoxidil.
- vitamin E (one report of high-dose use) reversing hair growth.

▷ *Driving, Hazardous Activities:* This drug may cause dizziness and fatigue. Restrict activities as necessary.

Aviation Note: The use of this drug *is a disqualification* for piloting. Consult a designated Aviation Medical Examiner.

Exposure to Sun: No restrictions.

Discontinuation: This drug should not be stopped abruptly. If it is to be discontinued, consult your physician regarding gradual reduction in dose and appropriate replacement with other drugs for the management of hypertension. Following discontinuation of the topical solution, the pretreatment pattern of baldness may return within 3 to 4 months.

MIRTAZAPINE (mur TAZ a peen)

Introduced: 1996   **Class:** Antidepressant, piperazinoazepine, norepi-nephrine, serotonin reuptake inhibitor   **Prescription:** USA: Yes   **Controlled Drug:** USA: No; Canada: No   **Available as Generic:** USA: Yes; Canada: Yes

Brand Names: Remeron, Remeron Sol Tab

BENEFITS versus RISKS

Possible Benefits	*Possible Risks*
EFFECTIVE TREATMENT OF DEPRESSION	Sleepiness
	Weight gain
BENEFICIAL ACTION ON SLEEP	Lowering of white blood cells
HELPS PATIENTS WITH DEPRESSION WHO ALSO HAVE PROBLEMS SLEEPING AND ARE ANXIOUS	
AVAILABLE IN A TABLET THAT MELTS ON THE TONGUE AND CAN BE TAKEN EASILY	

▷ **Principal Uses**

As a Single Drug Product: Uses currently included in FDA-approved labeling: Treatment of depression.

Other (unlabeled) generally accepted uses: (1) Eases presurgical insomnia; (2) may help antidepressant (SSRI–see drug classes)-induced sexual problems (dysfunction); (3) could be useful in tremor or pain syndromes; (4) helpful in a small study of post–traumatic stress disorder (PTSD); (5) has antianxiety effects which need to be further studied.

How This Drug Works: Works on antihistaminic (H1) and subtypes of the sero-tonin receptor (5-HT2 and 5-HT-3). Works to decrease the time it takes to fall asleep (sleep latency), but the mechanism isn't clear at present.

Available Dosage Forms and Strengths

Tablets — 15 mg, 30 mg, 45 mg

▷ **Recommended Dosage Ranges** (Actual dose and schedule must be determined for each patient individually.)

Infants and Children: Dose not established.

Adults to Age 60: For treatment of adult depression, 15 to 45 mg at bedtime. Dosing is started at 15 mg. Increases in dose (as needed and tolerated) are made at seven-to-fourteen–day intervals.

Over 60 Years of Age: Removed more slowly from the body, and slower still by males versus females. Lower doses are prudent.

Conditions Requiring Dosing Adjustments

Liver Function: Lower doses and slow dose increases are needed. Doses may need to be decreased by half of the usual dose in severe liver compromise.

Kidney Function: Lower doses and slow dose increases are needed. Patients should be closely followed.

▷ **Dosing Instructions:** The original tablet form may be crushed and can be taken with or without food. Take it at the same time daily. The Soltab is made to fall apart in your mouth and should NOT be crushed or chewed. This dosage form does not need to be taken with water. Make certain to take it once you remove it from the compartment (blister pack). Because any form of this medicine can cause drowsiness, it is usually taken at bedtime. If you forget a dose: Take the missed dose as soon as you remember it, unless it's morning when you remember it—if that is the case, skip the missed dose and take the next dose right on schedule. Talk with your doctor if you find yourself missing doses. Continue to take this medicine after you start to feel better.

Usual Duration of Use: Use on a regular schedule for 1 week will usually start to show benefits in relieving depression. Peak effect may take several weeks to be seen. Long-term use (months to years) requires follow-up by your doctor. Controversy exists as to the length of time to take an antidepressant once problems resolve, but many clinicians advocate 4–9 months and individualized treatment.

Typical Treatment Goals and Measurements (Outcomes and Markers)
Depression: The general goal: to lessen the degree and severity of depression, letting patients return to their daily lives. Specific measures of depression (Hamilton Depression or Ham-D) involve testing or inventories and can be valuable in helping check benefits from this medicine.
Pain Syndromes: The general goal: to decrease pain to a manageable level. Pain should be appropriately assessed, and progress defined based on lowering of overall pain level.

Possible Advantages of This Drug
Less likely to cause dry mouth, constipation, urinary retention, orthostatic hypotension (see Glossary), and heart rhythm disturbances than tricyclic antidepressants. Does not cause Parkinson-like reactions. Has been successfully used in people who were depressed, had sexual problems from medicines in the selective serotonin reuptake inhibitor (SSRI) family. The Soltab form can be taken without water. May go to work faster than other medicines for depression.

▷ **This Drug Should Not Be Taken If**
- you have had an allergic reaction to it previously.
- you are currently taking, or have taken within the past 14 days, any monoamine oxidase (MAO) type A inhibitor drug (see Drug Classes).

▷ **Inform Your Physician Before Taking This Drug If**
- you have experienced any adverse effects from antidepressant drugs.
- you have impaired liver or kidney function.
- you have Parkinson's disease.
- you have had a recent heart attack or have heart disease.
- you have a seizure disorder.
- you have phenylketonuria (PKU) as the Soltab has 2.6 mg of phenylalanine in each 15 mg tablet.
- you are pregnant or plan pregnancy while taking this drug.

Possible Side Effects (natural, expected, and unavoidable drug actions)
Increased appetite, weight gain. Lower blood pressure on standing (see postural hypotension in Glossary).

▷ **Possible Adverse Effects** (unusual, unexpected, and infrequent reactions)
If any of the following develop, consult your physician promptly for guidance.
Mild Adverse Effects
Allergic reactions: skin rash, itching—rare.
Headache, nervousness, insomnia—rare to infrequent.

Somnolence—frequent (may be up to 54%—this is why the medicine is taken at night).

Ringing in the ears, excessive noise sensitivity, and decreased hearing ability—reported.

Fatigue and dry mouth or constipation—frequent.

Tremor, dizziness, abnormal dreams—rare.

Muscle or joint pain—rare.

Abnormal vision, numbness and tingling—rare.

Confusion—rare.

Fluid accumulation (edema)—rare.

Chest pain and increased blood pressure—rare.

Increased heart rate—infrequent.

Altered taste, nausea, vomiting, diarrhea—rare to infrequent.

Serious Adverse Effects

Allergic reactions: dermatitis (various forms)—rare.

Drug—induced seizures—case reports.

Hallucinations, paranoid reactions—rare.

Movement problems (akathisia [feeling that you have to keep moving], dysarthrias)—infrequent.

Diabetes or thyroid problems—rare.

Increased blood cholesterol (hypercholesterolemia)—infrequent.

Liver cirrhosis or pancreatitis—rare in controlled studies.

Agranulocytosis—case reports.

▷ **Possible Effects on Sexual Function:** Male sexual dysfunction: delayed ejaculation—infrequent. Has been successfully used in people who could not tolerate SSRIs due to sexual dysfunction caused by the drug itself.

Female sexual dysfunction: inhibited orgasm—rare.

Swelling and tenderness of male and female breast tissue—case reports.

Dysmenorrhea—rare.

Natural Diseases or Disorders That May Be Activated by This Drug

Latent epilepsy.

Possible Effects on Laboratory Tests

Blood total cholesterol and triglyceride levels: increased—infrequent.

Liver function tests: increased liver enzymes (ALT/GPT, AST/GOT, and alkaline phosphatase).

Blood cell counts: decreased (aplastic anemia)—case reports.

Blood sodium: decreased (with rare SIADH).

CAUTION

1. If any type of skin reaction develops (rash, hives, etc.), discontinue this drug and inform your physician promptly.
2. If dryness of the mouth develops and persists for more than 2 weeks, consult your dentist for guidance.
3. Ask your doctor or pharmacist before taking any other prescription or over-the-counter drug while taking mirtazapine.
4. If you are advised to take any monoamine oxidase (MAO) type A inhibitor (see Drug Classes), allow an interval of 5 weeks after discontinuing this drug before starting the MAO inhibitor.
5. It is advisable to withhold this drug if electroconvulsive therapy (ECT, or "shock" treatment) is to be used to treat your depression.

Precautions for Use

By Infants and Children: Safety and effectiveness for those under 12 years of age are not established.

By Those Over 60 Years of Age: The lowest effective dose should be used for maintenance treatment and adjusted as needed for reduced kidney function.

▷ **Advisability of Use During Pregnancy**
Pregnancy Category: C. See Pregnancy Risk Categories at the back of this book.
Animal Studies: Delayed bone development due to this drug found in rat and rabbit studies.
Human Studies: Adequate studies of pregnant women are not available.
Use this drug only if clearly needed. Ask your physician for guidance.

Advisability of Use If Breast-Feeding
Presence of this drug in breast milk: Unknown.
Avoid drug or refrain from nursing.

Habit-Forming Potential: None, however, a withdrawal syndrome (nausea, anxiety, paresthesia, and panic attack) has been reported after abrupt discontinuation.

Effects of Overdose: Agitation, restlessness, excitement, nausea, vomiting, seizures.

Possible Effects of Long-Term Use: None reported.

Suggested Periodic Examinations While Taking This Drug (at physician's discretion)
Periodic complete blood counts and liver function tests. Because of lipid effects, a baseline lipid panel and periodic checks appear prudent.

▷ **While Taking This Drug, Observe the Following**
Foods: No restrictions.
Herbal Medicines or Minerals: Since part of the way ginseng works may be as a MAO inhibitor, do not combine ginseng with mirtazapine. Valerian and kava kava may interact additively (drowsiness). Avoid these combinations. St. John's wort may lead to dangerously increased serotonin activity as well as additive sensitivity to the sun. Indian snakeroot, ma huang, and yohimbe are also best avoided while taking this medicine.
Beverages: No restrictions. May be taken with milk.
▷ *Alcohol:* Avoid completely.
Tobacco Smoking: No interactions expected. I advise everyone to quit smoking.
▷ *Other Drugs*
Mirtazapine *taken concurrently* with
• diazepam (Valium) and perhaps other benzodiazepines (see Drug Classes) may impair movement ability.
• inhibitors of cytochrome CYP 2D6, such as amiodarone, fluoxetine, and zileuton, may lead to excessive blood levels and mirtazapine toxicity.
• monoamine oxidase (MAO) type A inhibitor drugs may cause confusion, agitation, high fever, seizures, and dangerous elevations of blood pressure; avoid the concurrent use of these drugs.
• ritonavir (Norvir) and perhaps other protease inhibitors (see Drug Classes) may lead to toxicity.
▷ *Driving, Hazardous Activities:* This drug may cause drowsiness, dizziness, impaired judgment and altered vision. Restrict activities as necessary.
Aviation Note: The use of this drug *is a disqualification* for piloting. Consult a designated Aviation Medical Examiner.
Exposure to Sun: Use caution—this drug may (rarely) cause photosensitivity (see Glossary).

Discontinuation: The slow elimination of this drug from the body makes it unlikely that any withdrawal effects will result from abrupt discontinuation. However, case reports of a withdrawal syndrome have been made. It appears prudent to slowly decrease (taper) the dose if you and your doctor have decided to stop this medicine. Call your doctor if you plan to stop this drug for any reason.

MISOPROSTOL (mi soh PROH stohl)

Introduced: 1987   **Class:** Gastrointestinal drug (ulcer preventive), prostaglandin analog   **Prescription:** USA: Yes   **Controlled Drug:** USA: No; Canada: No   **Available as Generic:**   USA: No; Canada: No

Brand Names: ✤Apo-Misoprostol, Arthrotec [CD], Cytotec, ✤Novo-Misoprostol, ✤PMS-Misoprostol

---

BENEFITS versus RISKS

Possible Benefits	*Possible Risks*
EFFECTIVE PREVENTION OF STOMACH ULCERATION WHILE TAKING ANTI-INFLAMMATORY DRUGS	INCREASED RISK OF ABORTION (IF USED DURING PREGNANCY) Diarrhea (transient) Neuropathy
GEL FORM IS USED TO "RIPEN" THE CERVIX DURING LABOR	
Effective treatment of duodenal ulcer	

▷ **Principal Uses**

As a Single Drug Product: Uses currently included in FDA-approved labeling: (1) Prevents development of stomach ulcers during long-term use of anti-inflammatory drugs as therapy for arthritis and related conditions; (2) treatment of duodenal ulcers.

Other (unlabeled) generally accepted uses: (1) Used (in Canada and other countries) for treatment of active duodenal ulcer unrelated to use of anti-inflammatory drugs; (2) has some use in inducing abortions; (3) used in combination with cyclosporine or prednisone to decrease transplanted organ rejection; (4) widely used to help "ripen" or prime the cervix in preparation for a vaginal delivery.

As a Combination Drug Product [CD]: Available in combination with diclofenac, an NSAID (see Drug Classes). The misoprostol is used to prevent stomach (gastric) irritation or ulceration from the NSAID.

How This Drug Works: Protects lining of the stomach and duodenum by (1) replacing tissue prostaglandins depleted by anti-inflammatory drugs; (2) inhibiting secretion of stomach acid; (3) increasing local production of bicarbonate (to neutralize acids) and mucus (to protect stomach and duodenal tissues). Combined effects prevent new ulcers and promote healing of existing ulcer(s).

Arthrotec form: This combination uses the above mechanism of misoprostol to protect from possible ulcers caused by the NSAID diclofenac.

Available Dosage Forms and Strengths

Tablets — 100 mcg, 200 mcg

Tablets (Arthrotec) — misoprostol 0.2 mg (200 mcg) and diclofenac 50 mg

Conditions Requiring Dosing Adjustments

Liver Function: Specific dose adjustments in liver compromise are not defined.

Kidney Function: The dose of misoprostol should be decreased in kidney disease. (See the diclofenac profile for information on diclofenac.)

▷ **Usual Adult Dosage Ranges:** *Prevention of stomach ulcer:* 200 mcg four times daily with food, taken concurrently during the use of any anti-inflammatory drug (see Antiarthritic or NSAIDs Drug Classes).

Treatment of Duodenal Ulcer: 200 mcg four times daily for 4 to 8 weeks.

Combination Abortions: RU-496 600 mg taken once, followed by 400–600 mcg of misoprostol in one dose or two equal doses.

*Rheumatoid Arthritis (Arthrotec Form):*one tablet 2 to 4 times daily.

Cervical Ripening: 100 mcg of extemporaneous gel vaginally with repeat doses of 100 mcg by mouth every two hours until they have 3 contractions in ten minutes.

Note: Actual dose and schedule must be determined for each patient individually.

▷ **Dosing Instructions:** The regular, noncombination tablet may be crushed and taken with each of three daily meals; take the last (fourth) dose of the day with food at bedtime. Arthrotec form should be taken right after a meal or with food or milk. DO NOT crush or alter. If you forget a dose: Take the missed dose as soon as you remember it, unless it's nearly time for your next dose—if that is the case, skip the missed dose and take the next dose right on schedule. DO NOT double doses. Talk with your doctor if you find yourself missing doses. The intravaginal gel is made in the hospital.

Usual Duration of Use: For prevention of stomach ulcer, use is recommended for the entire period of anti-inflammatory drug use. For treatment of duodenal ulcer, continual use on a regular schedule for 4 weeks is recommended; if ulcer healing is not complete, a second course of 4 weeks is advised. Long-term use (months to years) requires periodic physician evaluation of response and dose adjustment.

Typical Treatment Goals and Measurements (Outcomes and Markers)

Prevention of ulcers: The goal is to prevent ulceration from anti-inflammatory drug use, or to heal the ulcer area and prevent re-occurrence of the ulceration. Sign and symptom prevention or relief as well as endoscopic examination help define success of ulcer treatment or prevention.

Induction of labor: In an early comparative study of causing (inducing) labor, 100 mcg of misoprostol versus intravenous oxytocin (one miliunit per minute) were compared in 126 pregnant women. Misoprostol shortened the time until labor more effectively than oxytocin.

Possible Advantages of This Drug: Significantly more effective than histamine (H2) blocking drugs (cimetidine, famotidine, nizatidine, ranitidine) or sucralfate in preventing the development of stomach ulcers. Arthrotec form may increase adherence (having people take it as directed). Use to help ripen the cervix shortens the time until labor better than a previously used medicine called oxytocin.

▷ **This Drug Should Not Be Taken If**

• you have had an allergic reaction to it previously.

• you are allergic to any type of prostaglandin.

• you are pregnant (unless this medicine is being used in the hospital to help "ripen" the cervix).

- you are breast-feeding your infant.
- you are not able or willing to use effective contraception (oral contraceptives or intrauterine device) while taking this drug.

▷ **Inform Your Physician Before Taking This Drug If**
- you have a history of peptic ulcer disease or Crohn's disease.
- you have inflammatory bowel disease.
- you have impaired kidney function.
- you have a seizure disorder.

Possible Side Effects (natural, expected, and unavoidable drug actions)
Diarrhea (14–40% of users), usually beginning after 13 days of use and subsiding spontaneously after 8 days.
Abortion (miscarriage) of pregnancy (11% of users); this is often incomplete and accompanied by serious uterine bleeding that may require hospitalization and urgent treatment.

▷ **Possible Adverse Effects** (unusual, unexpected, and infrequent reactions)
If any of the following develop, consult your physician promptly for guidance.
Mild Adverse Effects
Allergic reaction: skin rash.
Headache, dizziness—infrequent.
Anxiety, depression—rare.
Hair loss with long-term use—case reports.
Ringing in the ears (tinnitus)—case reports.
Joint pain and muscle aches—rare.
Passing out (syncope)—rare.
Abdominal pain, indigestion, nausea, vomiting, flatulence, constipation—rare to infrequent.
Serious Adverse Effects
Allergic reactions: anaphylaxis—rare.
Anemia and low blood platelets—rare.
Blood in the urine—rare.
Uterine complications (excessive action of the uterus or tachysystole)—frequent.
Bronchospasm—rare.
Neuropathy—rare.
Autonomic dysreflexia (Arthotec form)—case reports.
Abortion (if taken while pregnant—NOT for cervical ripening).

▷ **Possible Effects on Sexual Function:** Menstrual irregularity, menstrual cramps, heavy menstrual flow, spotting between periods—all rare.
Postmenopausal vaginal bleeding; this may require further evaluation.
Reduced libido and impotence—rare and causal relationship not established.

▷ **Natural Diseases or Disorders That May Be Activated by This Drug**
Latent epilepsy.

Possible Effects on Laboratory Tests
Mild increase in liver function enzymes.

CAUTION
1. Do not take this drug if you are pregnant. It can cause abortion (see cervical ripening note).
2. Do not make this drug available to others who may be pregnant or who may become pregnant.

3. If this drug is prescribed, it is advisable that you have a negative serum pregnancy test within 2 weeks before starting treatment.
4. Start taking this drug only on the second or third day of your next normal menstrual period.
5. Initiate effective contraceptive measures when you begin to take this drug. Discuss the use of oral contraceptives or intrauterine devices with your physician.
6. Should you become pregnant, stop the drug immediately and call your doctor.

Precautions for Use

By Infants and Children: Safety and effectiveness for those under 18 years of age not established.

By Those Over 60 Years of Age: This drug is usually well tolerated by this age group, but some forms of prostaglandins can cause drops in blood pressure; watch for light-headedness or faintness that may indicate low blood pressure. Report any such development to your physician.

▷ **Advisability of Use During Pregnancy**

Pregnancy Category: X. See Pregnancy Risk Categories at the back of this book.

Animal Studies: No birth defects due to this drug found in rat or rabbit studies.

Human Studies: Information from studies of pregnant women confirms that this drug can cause abortion, sometimes incomplete; unpassed products of conception can cause life-threatening complications.

Avoid this drug completely.

Author's Note: Because of widespread use of a specific dosage (intravaginal gel) form of this medicine to ripen the cervix, labeling regarding use in pregnancy was modified by the FDA.

Advisability of Use If Breast-Feeding

Presence of this drug in breast milk: Unknown.

Avoid drug or refrain from nursing.

Habit-Forming Potential: None.

Effects of Overdose: Abdominal pain, diarrhea, fever, drowsiness, weakness, tremor, convulsions, difficult breathing.

Possible Effects of Long-Term Use: Unknown at this time.

Suggested Periodic Examinations While Taking This Drug (at physician's discretion)

Monitoring for accidental pregnancy.

▷ **While Taking This Drug, Observe the Following**

Foods: High-fat meals may reduce peak blood concentration.

Herbal Medicines or Minerals: Kola, guarana, and ma huang may increase stomach acid, blunting the benefits of the combination use in Arthrotec form. Black cohosh root, ginkgo, and squill are contraindicated in gastrointestinal disturbances. Licorice root has a Commission E monograph indication for gastrointestinal ulcers, but use with misoprostol has not been studied. Talk to your doctor BEFORE adding any herbals to this medicine.

Beverages: No restrictions. May be taken with milk.

▷ *Alcohol:* No interactions expected, but alcohol can promote the development of stomach ulcer and reduce the effectiveness of this drug.

Tobacco Smoking: No interactions expected. Nicotine is conducive to stomach ulcers. I advise everyone to quit smoking.

▷ *Other Drugs*
   Misoprostol *taken concurrently* with
   * antacids that contain magnesium may increase the risk of diarrhea; avoid this combination. Antacids in general may decrease misoprostol absorption and lessen its therapeutic benefits.
   * phenylbutazone may result in neurosensory problems (movement problems, tingling, etc.).

▷ *Driving, Hazardous Activities:* This drug may cause dizziness, light-headedness, stomach pain, or diarrhea. Restrict activities as necessary.
   Aviation Note: The use of this drug *may be a disqualification* for piloting. Consult a designated Aviation Medical Examiner.
   Exposure to Sun: No restrictions.
   Discontinuation: This drug should be taken as combination therapy while you are taking antiarthritic/anti-inflammatory drugs that can cause stomach ulceration. Call your doctor if you have reason to stop it prematurely.

MODAFINIL (moh DAF in ihl)

Introduced: 1998   **Class:** Central nervous system stimulant   **Prescription:** USA: Yes   **Controlled Drug:** USA: Yes C-IV*; Canada: Yes   **Available as Generic:** No

Brand Name: Provigil

Author's Note: Information in this profile will be broadened in subsequent editions if warranted.

MOLINDONE (moh LIN dohn)

Introduced: 1971   **Class:** Antipsychotic   **Prescription:** USA: Yes   **Controlled Drug:** USA: No; Canada: No   **Available as Generic:** No

Brand Name: Moban

Author's Note: Information in this profile has been truncated to make room for more widely used medicines.

MORPHINE (MOR feen)

Other Name: MS (morphine sulfate)

Introduced: 1806, Avinza form 2002   **Class:** Strong analgesic, opioids   **Prescription:** USA: Yes   **Controlled Drug:** USA: C-II*; Canada: Yes   **Available as Generic:** Yes

Brand Names: ✤Alti-Morphine, Astramorph, Astramorph PF, Avinza, Duramorph, ✤Epimorph, Infumorph, Kadian, ✤M-Eslon, ✤Morphine H.P., ✤Morphitec, ✤M.O.S., ✤M.O.S.-S.R., MS Contin, MS-IR, OMS Concentrate, Opium Tincture, Oramorph SR, Paregoric, RMS Uniserts, Roxanol, Roxanol 100, Roxanol SR, ✤Statex

*See Schedules of Controlled Drugs at the back of this book.

```
┌─────────────────────────────────────────────────────────────────┐
│                    BENEFITS versus RISKS                          │
│      Possible Benefits              Possible Risks                │
│  EFFECTIVE RELIEF OF            POTENTIAL FOR HABIT               │
│    MODERATE TO SEVERE             FORMATION (DEPENDENCE)          │
│    PAIN WHEN IT IS DOSED        Respiratory depression (dose and  │
│    CORRECTLY                      patient dependent)              │
│  EXTENDED-RELEASE FORMS         Disorientation, hallucinations    │
│    OFFER TWICE OR ONCE DAILY    Constipation                      │
│    DOSES AND INCREASED          Problems urinating                │
│    ADHERENCE                                                      │
└─────────────────────────────────────────────────────────────────┘
```

▷ **Principal Uses**

As a Single Drug Product: Uses currently included in FDA-approved labeling: (1) Given by mouth, suppository or injection to relieve moderate to severe pain of heart attack, cancer, surgical procedures/operations, fluid on the lungs, and other causes; (2) used as an adjunct to anesthesia; (3) used in treatment-resistant (intractable) cough.

Other (unlabeled) generally accepted uses: (1) Therapy of pain in sickle cell crisis; (2) used in patient-controlled analgesia pumps to fight pain.

Author's Note: The FDA and Purdue Pharmaceuticals have worked together to strengthen warnings for a related strong opioid called OxyContin because of continuing reports of abuse and diversion of this medicine. A "Dear Healthcare Professional" letter has been sent out that explains the strengthening of the labeling, including proper prescribing information, and also highlights the problems associated with abuse and diversion of OxyContin. An important factor that MUST be considered when OxyContin is prescribed is the severity of the pain that is being treated, not simply the disease that is the root cause of the painful symptoms. The company has also responsibly undertaken a "Profiles in Pain Management" series in the *Pharmacy Today* journal of the American Pharmaceutical Association to increase awareness of prescription medication abuse. Because ALL opioids (like morphine) are subject to abuse, the FDA is also encouraging all makers of opioids sold in the US to voluntarily review and revise product labeling as needed to help ensure adequate warnings and precautions regarding risks of abuse, misuse, and diversion are presented and that responsible prescribing practices are promoted.

How This Drug Works: Acting primarily as a depressant of certain brain functions, this drug suppresses the perception of pain and calms the emotional response to pain. There are a variety of brain places (receptors) where morphine works to have both beneficial and undesirable effects. Widely quoted is the mu receptor where much like endorphins, morphine acts to block pain. Avinza form actually has two components. One part goes to work right away (immediate release), and the second part is an extended-release form (Spheroidal Oral Drug Absorption System or SODAS).

Available Dosage Forms and Strengths

Capsules, extended-release (Avinza) — 30 mg, 60 mg, 90 mg and 120 mg

Capsules, sustained-release (Kadian) — 20 mg, 30 mg, 50 mg, 60 mg, 100 mg

Injection — 0.5 mg/ml, 1 mg/ml, 2 mg/ml,
4 mg/ml, 5 mg/ml, 8 mg/ml,
10 mg/ml, 15 mg/ml, 25 mg/ml,
50 mg/ml
Oral solution — 20 mg/ml; 10 mg/5 ml, 20 mg/5 ml,
100 mg/5 ml
Suppositories — 5 mg, 10 mg, 20 mg, 30 mg
Syrup — 1 mg/ml, 5 mg/ml, 10 mg/ml,
20 mg/ml
Syrup (Canada only) — 50 mg/ml
Tablets — 5 mg, 10 mg, 15 mg, 25 mg, 30 mg,
50 mg
Tablets, soluble — 10 mg, 15 mg, 30 mg
Tablets, sustained-release — 15 mg, 30 mg, 60 mg, 100 mg,
200 mg
Tablets, timed-release — 15 mg, 30 mg, 60 mg, 100 mg,
200 mg

▷ **Recommended Dosage Ranges** (Actual dose and schedule must be determined for each patient individually.)

Infants and Children: 0.05 to 0.1 mg per kg of body mass have been used every 4 hours for the immediate-release form. Single dose should not exceed 15 mg, and dosing is adjusted (titrated to pain control goals). Infants and small children should be approached cautiously as they are generally more sensitive to narcotic (opioid) medicines dosed on a body weight basis.

17 to 60 Years of Age: By injection (IV form is used where naloxone [Narcan] and assisted breathing are available): Requirements for analgesia vary with the patient and with the painful condition being treated. For example: after a heart attack (Acute Myocardial Infarction or MI): When patient symptoms are not helped by 3 appropriately spaced nitroglycerin tablets taken under the tongue or in patients who have symptoms come back (recur) after such treatment: IV morphine 1–5 mg is given every 5 to 30 minutes until the pain is controlled. Limiting factors include patient intolerance or excessive lowering of blood pressure. For general intravenous pain relief (analgesia): 2–10 mg given over 4–5 minutes. Repeat dosing is guided by pain control goals and patient effects. In sickle cell crisis some clinicians have used Patient-Controlled Analgesia (PCA) with or without a constant IV infusion. Constant infusions of 10 to 75 mg per hour were detailed in one case study where the patient had not responded to IV injections. PCA dosing usually combines a loading dose (determined by patient weight, pain being treated and other individual factors) and subsequent patient-administered doses (usually a lesser amount than the loading dose with a lock out interval [such as fifteen minutes] to allow for the peak effect of the prior dose to be reached before another dose is given.

By mouth (regular solution, syrup and tablets) — 5 to 30 mg every 4 hours.

By mouth (sustained-release forms) — 30 mg every 12 hours.

By mouth (Kadian brand sustained-release form and the Avinza extended-released form)—once daily. Dosing here is usually made after pain relief requirements are defined by an immediate-release form of morphine. An immediate-release form should still be made available in order to provide relief and (rescue) to the patient from pain.

By suppository — 10 to 30 mg every 4 hours.

Over 60 Years of Age: Same as 12 to 60 years of age, using smaller doses to start. Dose is slowly increased if needed. Many clinicians treat constipation in this age group once the morphine is started.

Author's Note: Current pain treatment theory calls for timed or scheduled dosing. This tends to prevent pain, rather than allowing pain to recur and then having to be treated. Some clinicians will use timed dosing immediately after surgery and then change to regular pain assessment with Patient-Controlled Analgesia (PCA), then to regular pain assessment with oral dosing once the most severe period of pain has passed. Pain is now the fifth vital sign and should be checked regularly.

Conditions Requiring Dosing Adjustments

Liver Function: The dose and frequency **must** be adjusted (decreased) with liver compromise. This medicine is removed (metabolized) by the liver to morphine-6-glucuronide.

Kidney Function: Dose and frequency are prudently reduced in kidney compromise.

▷ **Dosing Instructions:** The regular tablet may be crushed and taken with or following food to reduce stomach irritation or nausea. Extended-release (such as Kadian or Avinza) or sustained-release forms should be swallowed whole; do not break, crush, or chew them. Oral liquid form may be mixed with fruit juice to improve taste. If you forget a dose: Take the missed dose as soon as you remember it, unless it's nearly time for your next dose—if that is the case, skip the missed dose and take the next dose right on schedule. DO NOT double dose. Talk with your doctor if you find yourself missing doses. If you are uncertain about any dose, call your doctor.

Usual Duration of Use: Used to control pain, hence the duration will be determined by the source of the pain. For short-term, self-limiting conditions, continual use should not exceed 5 to 7 days without reassessment of need. For the long-term management of severe chronic pain, it is advisable to determine a fixed dose schedule with rescue dose contingency schedule. It is not unusual for additional (adjuvant) medicines such as those usually used for seizures or for depression to be combined with morphine in chronic pain situations.

Typical Treatment Goals and Measurements (Outcomes and Markers)

Pain: Most clinicians treating pain use a device called an algometer to check your pain. This looks like a small ruler, but lets the clinician better understand your pain. The goals of treatment then relate to where the level of pain started (for example, a rating of 7 on a 0–10 scale) and what the cause of the pain was. I use the PQRSTBG (see Glossary) system. Pain medicines may also be used together (in combination) in order to get the best result or outcome. If your pain control is not acceptable to YOU (remember, in hospitals and outpatient settings, etc. pain control is a patient right and the fifth vital sign), call your doctor. It is not unusual to have an immediate-release rescue dose available and then some percentage of previous-day use added back to an extended-release form. Pain can be dynamic and adjustments are often required.

▷ **This Drug Should Not Be Taken If**
- you had an allergic reaction to it previously.
- you are having an acute attack of asthma or your upper airway is blocked (obstructed).

- you have a specific bowel problem (paralytic ileus).
- you have acute respiratory depression.

▷ **Inform Your Physician Before Taking This Drug If**
- you took a monoamine oxidase (MAO) type A inhibitor drug (see Drug Classes) in the last 14 days.
- you are taking atropinelike drugs, antihypertensives, metoclopramide (Reglan), or zidovudine (AZT).
- you are taking any other drugs that have a sedative effect.
- you have a history of drug abuse or alcoholism.
- you have impaired liver, bile tract, or kidney function.
- you have prostate gland enlargement (see prostatism in Glossary).
- you have a history of asthma, emphysema, epilepsy, gallbladder disease, or inflammatory bowel disease.
- you are dehydrated.
- you have a tendency toward constipation.
- you have a history of head injury or a seizure disorder.
- you have a history of sickle cell anemia.
- you have a history of low blood pressure.
- you plan to have surgery under general anesthesia in the near future.

Possible Side Effects (natural, expected, and unavoidable drug actions)
Drowsiness, light-headedness, weakness, euphoria, dry mouth, urinary retention, dose-related constipation. Temperature changes. Miosis or pinpoint pupils. Histamine release if morphine is injected too quickly.

▷ **Possible Adverse Effects** (unusual, unexpected, and infrequent reactions)
If any of the following develop, consult your physician promptly for guidance.
Mild Adverse Effects
Allergic reactions: skin rash, hives, itching (especially if the intravenous form is injected too quickly).
Headache, dizziness, impaired concentration, sensation of drunkenness, confusion, depression, blurred or double vision—infrequent to frequent and may be dose-related.
Facial flushing, sweating, heart palpitation—possible.
Nausea, vomiting—possible and may be dose-related.
Spasm of the biliary tract—possible.
Urine retention—possible.
Serious Adverse Effects
Allergic reactions: swelling of throat or vocal cords, spasm of larynx or bronchial tubes—rare.
Hallucinations, psychosis—case reports.
Drop in blood pressure, causing severe weakness and fainting—possible.
Disorientation, hallucinations, unstable gait, tremor, muscle twitching—possible.
Drug-induced myasthenia gravis—case reports.
Respiratory depression—dose-related.
Seizures—possible.

▷ **Possible Effects on Sexual Function:** Reduced libido and/or potency.
Amenorrhea and disruption of ovulation—case reports.

▷ **Adverse Effects That May Mimic Natural Diseases or Disorders**
Paradoxical behavioral disturbances may suggest psychotic disorder.

Possible Effects on Laboratory Tests
Blood amylase and lipase levels: increased (natural side effects).

Liver function tests: increased liver enzymes (ALT/GPT, AST/GOT, and alkaline phosphatase), increased bilirubin.

Urine screening tests for drug abuse: may be positive. (Test results depend upon amount of drug taken and testing method used.)

CAUTION
1. If you have asthma, chronic bronchitis, or emphysema, excessive use of this drug may cause significant respiratory difficulty, thickening of bronchial secretions, and suppression of coughing.
2. Taking this drug with atropinelike drugs can increase the risk of urinary retention and reduced intestinal function.
3. Constipation can be a serious problem, particularly in older patients (as bowel function tends to slow down). Many clinicians prescribe a medicine (such as Senokot-S) to promote bowel movements at the same time that morphine is prescribed.
4. Do not take this drug following acute head injury.

Precautions for Use
By Infants and Children: Use very cautiously in infants under 2 years of age because of their vulnerability to life-threatening respiratory depression. Watch for paradoxical excitement in this age group.
By Those Over 60 Years of Age: Small doses and short-term use are indicated. There may be increased risk of drowsiness, dizziness, unsteadiness, falling, urinary retention, and constipation (often leading to fecal impaction).

▷ **Advisability of Use During Pregnancy**
Pregnancy Category: C. D if used long-term or in high doses at term. See Pregnancy Risk Categories at the back of this book.
Animal Studies: Significant skeletal birth defects reported in mouse and hamster studies.
Human Studies: Adequate studies of pregnant women are not available, but no significant increase in birth defects was found in one report of 448 exposures to this drug.
Avoid during the first 3 months. Use sparingly and in small doses during the final 6 months only if clearly needed.

Advisability of Use If Breast-Feeding
Presence of this drug in breast milk: Yes.
Avoid drug or refrain from nursing.

Habit-Forming Potential: This drug can cause psychological and physical dependence (see Glossary).

Effects of Overdose: Marked drowsiness, dizziness, confusion, restlessness, depressed breathing, tremors, convulsions, stupor progressing to coma.

Possible Effects of Long-Term Use: Psychological and physical dependence, chronic constipation.

Suggested Periodic Examinations While Taking This Drug (at physician's discretion)
Ask the patient about his or her bowel habits.

▷ **While Taking This Drug, Observe the Following**
Foods: No restrictions.
Herbal Medicines or Minerals: Valerian and kava kava (no longer recommended in Canada) may interact additively (drowsiness). Avoid these combinations. St. John's wort can change (inducing or increasing) P450 3A4

enzymes, blunting the effects of morphine. Yohimbe may increase adverse effects as well as increase the pain-relieving effects of morphine. Talk to your doctor BEFORE you combine any herbal medicines with morphine.

Beverages: No restrictions. May be taken with milk.

▷ *Alcohol:* Alcohol is best avoided. Opioid analgesics can intensify the intoxicating effects of alcohol and alcohol can intensify the depressant effects of opioids on brain function, breathing and circulation.

Tobacco Smoking: No interactions expected. I advise everyone to quit smoking.

Marijuana Smoking: Increase in drowsiness and pain relief; impairment of mental and physical performance.

▷ *Other Drugs*

Morphine may ***increase*** the effects of

- antihypertensives and cause excessive lowering of blood pressure.
- atropinelike drugs and increase the risk of constipation and urinary retention.
- metformin (Glucophage).
- other drugs with sedative effects.

Morphine may ***decrease*** the effects of

- metoclopramide (Reglan).

Morphine ***taken concurrently*** with

- benzodiazepines (see Drug Classes) may result in increased risk of respiratory depression.
- cimetidine (Tagamet) may result in morphine toxicity.
- fluoxetine (Prozac) may antagonize morphine's pain-relieving effect.
- hydroxyzine (Vistaril) can increase pain relief but carries the risk of increased respiratory depression.
- medicines that increase CYP 3A4 will blunt morphine benefits and those that inhibit or use 3A4 for removal from the body may increase morphine blood levels. Caution and dosing adjustments are prudent.
- metoclopramide (Reglan) may lead to increased morphine effects.
- monoamine oxidase (MAO) type A inhibitors (see Drug Classes) may cause the equivalent of an acute narcotic overdose: unconsciousness and severe depression of breathing, heart rate and circulation. A variation can be excitability, convulsions, high fever and rapid heart action.
- naltrexone (ReVia or Narcan) may lead to sudden withdrawal symptoms.
- phenothiazines (see Drug Classes) may cause excessive and prolonged depression of brain functions, breathing and circulation.
- rifampin (Rifater, others) may lower morphine benefits.
- ritonavir (Norvir) may lead to lower morphine benefits.
- tramadol (Ultram) may increase CNS side effects.
- trovafloxacin (Trovan) may blunt trovafloxacin benefits.
- zidovudine (AZT) may increase the toxicity of both drugs; avoid concurrent use.

▷ *Driving, Hazardous Activities:* This drug can impair mental alertness, judgment, reaction time and physical coordination. Avoid hazardous activities.

Aviation Note: The use of this drug ***is a disqualification*** for piloting. Consult a designated Aviation Medical Examiner.

Exposure to Sun: No restrictions.

Discontinuation: Where possible, it is advisable to limit this drug to short-term use. Longer-term use requires gradual tapering (decreasing) of doses to minimize possible effects of withdrawal: body aches, fever, sweating, nervousness, trembling, weakness, runny nose, sneezing, rapid heart rate, nausea, vomiting, stomach cramps, diarrhea.

MUPIROCIN (myu PEER oh sin)

Introduced: 1987   **Class:** Antibiotic, topical   **Prescription:** USA:
Yes   **Controlled Drug:**   USA: No; Canada: No   **Available as Generic:**
USA: No; Canada: No
Brand Names: Bactroban, Bactroban Nasal

BENEFITS versus RISKS

Possible Benefits	*Possible Risks*
EFFECTIVE TOPICAL TREATMENT OF *STAPHYLOCOCCUS* AND *STREPTOCOCCUS* SKIN INFECTIONS	Skin irritation
EFFECTIVE ERADICATION OF *STAPHYLOCOCCUS AUREUS* FROM THE NOSE	

▷ **Principal Uses**
  As a Single Drug Product: Uses currently included in FDA-approved labeling:
    (1) Used to treat skin infections caused by staphylococcal and streptococ-
    cal infections such as ecthyma or impetigo; (2) the intranasal form is
    specifically formulated to kill *Staphylococcus aureus* bacteria that are liv-
    ing (have colonized) in the nasal passages; (3) treats secondary skin infec-
    tions caused by Strep or Staph; (4) treats skin lesions that are traumatic.
  Other (unlabeled) generally accepted uses: (1) Used in burns where resistant
    Staphylococcus aureus is causing infection; (2) helps prevent opportunistic
    infections of venous access devices, such as intravascular cannulas; (3)
    treats cellulitis caused by Gram-positive organisms; (4) has been used in
    some specific situations in skin surgery to prevent infections; (5) used to
    eradicate vaginal *Staphylococcus* infections.

How This Drug Works: Binds to an enzyme (isoleucyl transfer-RNA synthetase)
  and stops susceptible bacteria from being able to make critical proteins
  and kills them.

Available Dosage Forms and Strengths
        Intranasal form (Bactroban Nasal) — 2%
              Topical cream — 2.15%
        Topical ointment (Bactroban) — 2%
      Topical ointment (Bactroban, Canada) — 20 mg/g

▷ **Recommended Dosage Ranges** (Actual dose and schedule must be determined
  for each patient individually.)
  Infants and Children: Cream (3 months to 16 years)—follow your pediatrician's
    recommendations.
    Nasal (children 12 or over)—one-half of the ointment from the single-use
    tube of mupirocin is applied into one nostril and the other half is applied
    to the second nostril, twice daily, in the morning and evening, for 5 con-
    secutive days. One study found that application of this medicine to both
    nostrils (nares) three times daily for up to 21 days removed resistant Staph
    (methicillin-resistant *Staphylococcus aureus* (MRSA) in 62.5% of infants in
    a small study.
  16 to 60 Years of Age: 2% ointment—apply three times daily for 5 to 14 days.
    Some more involved or extensive infections have been treated for longer

periods. If the infection in question has not resolved after the initial course of the ointment, the site should be evaluated by a physician and full body (systemic) antibiotics or other treatment considered.

2% topical cream—for traumatic skin infections caused by *Strep pyogenes* or *Staph aureus*, apply (small amount) three times daily for 10 days.

Intranasal—one-half of the ointment from the single-use tube of mupirocin is applied into one nostril and the other half is applied to the second nostril, twice daily in the morning and evening for 5 consecutive days.

Over 60 Years of Age: Same as 16 to 60 years of age.

Conditions Requiring Dosing Adjustments

Liver Function: Little of this ointment is usually absorbed into the body. No guidelines exist for liver disease adjustments.

Kidney Function: A substance in this formulation (polyethylene glycol) may be toxic to the kidneys if the ointment is applied over an extensive burn or wound area.

▷ **Dosing Instructions:** This medicine should be applied as a thin film or as described by your doctor. Call your doctor if the condition has not improved or worsens during the course of treatment. Do **not** combine this medicine with other ointments or treatments unless your doctor has prescribed this approach. Please remember that if you are going to use this medicine in the nose, you should have Bactroban Nasal. Using the Bactroban ointment in the nose (polyethylene glycol base) is more likely to cause irritation. As with other medicines, applying this medicine right on time is critical. If you forget a dose: Apply the missed dose as soon as you remember it, unless it's nearly time for your next dose—if that is the case, skip the missed dose and apply the next dose right on schedule. Talk with your doctor if you find yourself missing doses.

Usual Duration of Use: Continual use on a regular schedule for several days is usually necessary to determine this drug's effectiveness in treating skin infections. Wounds not responding in 3 to 5 days must be evaluated by your doctor. Longer-term use requires physician evaluation.

Typical Treatment Goals and Measurements (Outcomes and Markers)

Staph Colonization or Other Infection: The goal is to kill the colonizing or infecting organism. Markers for improvement include improvement in signs and symptoms of the infection or in the case of colonization—negative repeat cultures.

Possible Advantages of This Drug

Effective topical treatment of skin infections. Intranasal form can help people who have been colonized by infectious bacteria stop spreading it to other people.

▷ **This Drug Should Not Be Taken If**
- you had an allergic reaction to any form of it previously.
- you have extensive burns or open wounds.

▷ **Inform Your Physician Before Taking This Drug If**
- several days have passed since this medicine was started and there has been no change or worsening of the wound.
- pain at the site of the infection or severe irritation occurs.
- you are unsure how much to apply or how often to apply mupirocin.

Possible Side Effects (natural, expected, and unavoidable drug actions)

Irritation at the site of infection caused by the polyethylene glycol component.

▷ **Possible Adverse Effects** (unusual, unexpected, and infrequent reactions)
  If any of the following develop, consult your physician promptly for guidance.
  Mild Adverse Effects
  Allergic reactions: skin rash and irritation at the infection site.
  Soreness, stinging or pain at the infection site—possible.
  Headache or taste changes—infrequent (intranasal only).
  Serious Adverse Effects
  Allergic reactions: contact dermatitis—rare.
  If this medicine is applied to an extensive skin area, polyethylene glycol may be absorbed and cause kidney toxicity—possible.

▷ **Possible Effects on Sexual Function:** Not reported.

  Possible Delayed Adverse Effects: This medicine is indicated for short-term use.

▷ **Adverse Effects That May Mimic Natural Diseases or Disorders**
  None reported.

  Natural Diseases or Disorders That May Be Activated by This Drug
  None reported.

  Possible Effects on Laboratory Tests
  None reported.

  CAUTION
  1. Do not apply this medicine to an area of skin larger than what your doctor prescribed.
  2. Because the Bactroban ointment uses a polyethylene glycol base and may cause irritation, the calcium mupirocin (Bactroban Nasal) is recommended for intranasal use.

  Precautions for Use
  By Infants and Children: Safety and effectiveness for use by some age groups varies with the product.
  By Those Over 60 Years of Age: No special changes are needed.

▷ **Advisability of Use During Pregnancy**
  Pregnancy Category: B. See Pregnancy Risk Categories at the back of this book.
  Animal Studies: No fetal problems defined.
  Human Studies: Information from adequate studies of pregnant women is not available.

  Advisability of Use If Breast-Feeding
  Presence of this drug in breast milk: Unknown.
  Avoid drug or refrain from nursing.

  Habit-Forming Potential: None.

  Effects of Overdose: If this medicine is applied to an extensive area of skin, excessive amounts of polyethylene glycol may be absorbed and cause kidney toxicity.

  Possible Effects of Long-Term Use: None defined.

  Suggested Periodic Examinations While Taking This Drug (at physician's discretion)
  Follow-up bacterial cultures of the nose with intranasal form.

▷ **While Taking This Drug, Observe the Following**
  Foods: No restrictions.
  Herbal Medicines or Minerals: Echinacea: Some patients use echinacea to attempt to boost their immune systems. Unfortunately, use of echinacea is

not recommended in people with damaged immune systems. This herb may also actually weaken any immune system if it is used too often or for too long a time. DO NOT take mistletoe herb, oak bark or F.C. of marshmallow root, and licorice.

Beverages: No restrictions.

▷ *Alcohol:* No restrictions.

Tobacco Smoking: No interactions expected. I advise everyone to quit smoking.

▷ *Other Drugs*

Mupirocin **taken concurrently** with
• other medications that are toxic to the kidneys may result in additive kidney toxicity if mupirocin is applied to a large area of skin.

Aviation Note: The use of this drug **does not appear to be a restriction** for piloting. Consult a designated Aviation Medical Examiner.

Exposure to Sun: Increased sensitivity (photosensitivity) has NOT been reported with topical application. No restrictions.

NABUMETONE (na BYU me tohn)

Please see the acetic acid (nonsteroidal anti-inflammatory drug) family profile.

NADOLOL (NAY doh lohl)

Introduced: 1976   **Class:** Antianginal, antihypertensive, beta blocker
Prescription: USA: Yes   **Controlled Drug:** USA: No; Canada: No
Available as Generic: Yes

Brand Names: ✿Alti-Nadol, ✿Apo-Nadol, Corgard, Corzide [CD], ✿Novo-Nadolol, ✿Ratio-Nadol, Syn-Nadol

BENEFITS versus RISKS	
Possible Benefits	*Possible Risks*
EFFECTIVE, WELL-TOLERATED ANTIHYPERTENSIVE for mild to moderate high blood pressure EFFECTIVE ANTIANGINAL DRUG IN CLASSIC CORONARY ARTERY DISEASE with moderate to severe angina	CONGESTIVE HEART FAILURE in advanced heart disease Provocation of asthma (in predisposed patients) Masking of hypoglycemia in drug-dependent diabetes Worsening of angina following abrupt withdrawal

▷ **Principal Uses**

As a Single Drug Product: Uses currently included in FDA-approved labeling: (1) Treats high blood pressure; (2) helps prevent attacks of effort-induced angina (should not be used in Prinzmetal's vasospastic angina).

Other (unlabeled) generally accepted uses: (1) Helps prevent hemorrhage from bulging veins (esophageal varices) in cirrhosis; (2) may have an adjunctive role in helping prevent and reduce migraine severity; (3) may have a role in helping prevent death after a heart attack (myocardial infarction) similar to other beta blockers; (4) may help ease tremor in patients taking lithium; (5) helps decrease risk of ruptured blood vessels in the esophagus (esophageal varices) in patients with cirrhosis; (6) can ease aggressive behavior for some patients (BPRS scores improve).

As a Combination Drug Product [CD]: Available in combination with bendroflumethiazide, a diuretic antihypertensive drug. This combination product works better and is more convenient for long-term use.

How This Drug Works: By blocking certain actions of the sympathetic nervous system, this drug:

- reduces the rate and contraction force of the heart, lowering oxygen needs of heart muscle and reducing ejection pressure of blood leaving the heart. This reduces frequency of angina and lowers blood pressure.
- reduces contraction of blood vessel walls, lowering blood pressure.
- prolongs conduction time of nerve impulses through the heart, which is of benefit in the management of certain heart rhythm disorders.

May use a vasodilating effect (possible involving dopamine) to preserve kidney blood flow and glomerular filtration.

Available Dosage Forms and Strengths

Tablets — 20 mg, 40 mg, 80 mg, 100 mg, 120 mg, 160 mg
Tablets, combination — 40 mg or 80 mg of nadolol with 5 mg
bendroflumethiazide

▷ **Usual Adult Dosage Ranges:** For hypertension: Start with 40 mg daily; this may be increased gradually (in steps of 40–80 mg at 14-day intervals) as needed and tolerated, up to 320 mg daily. The usual ongoing dose is 80 to 320 mg daily. Daily maximum is 320 mg.

For Angina: Initially 40 mg daily; increased gradually at intervals of 3 to 7 days as needed and tolerated until the best control is achieved or there is unacceptable slowing of the heart (to 240 mg daily). Usual ongoing dose is 80 to 240 mg every 24 hours. Daily maximum is 240 mg of nadolol.

Note: Actual dose and schedule must be determined for each patient individually.

Conditions Requiring Dosing Adjustments

Liver Function: No dosing changes needed.

Kidney Function: For patients with moderate kidney failure, the usual dose should be taken every 24 to 36 hours. For patients with severe kidney failure, the dose can be taken every 40 to 60 hours.

▷ **Dosing Instructions:** Immediate-release tablet may be crushed and taken without regard to eating. Do not stop this drug abruptly. If you forget a dose: Take the missed dose as soon as you remember it, unless it's 8 hours or less until your next scheduled dose—if that is the case, skip the missed dose and take the next dose right on schedule. Talk with your doctor if you find yourself missing doses.

Usual Duration of Use: Use on a regular schedule for up to 14 days determines this drug's effectiveness in lowering blood pressure and preventing angina. The long-term use of this drug (months to years) will be determined by your response to an overall treatment program (weight reduction, salt restriction, smoking cessation, etc.). Keep follow-up appointments with your doctor.

Typical Treatment Goals and Measurements (Outcomes and Markers)

Blood Pressure: The NEW guidelines (JNC VII) define normal blood pressure (BP) as **less than** 120/80. Because blood pressures that were once considered acceptable can actually lead to blood vessel damage, the committee from the National Institutes of Health, National Heart Lung and Blood Institute now have a new category called **Pre-hypertension**. This ranges from 120/80 to 139/89 and is intended to help your doctor to encourage lifestyle changes (or in the case of people with a risk factor for high blood pressure, start treatment) much earlier—so that possible damage to blood vessels, your heart, kidneys, sexual potency, or eyes might be minimized or avoided altogether. The next two classes of high blood pressure are stage 1 hypertension: 140/90 to 159/99 and stage 2 hypertension equal to or greater than: 160/100 mm Hg. These guidelines also recommend that clinicians trying to control blood pressure work with their patients to agree on the goals and a plan of treatment. The first-ever guidelines for blood pressure (hypertension) in African Americans recommends that MOST black patients be started on TWO antihypertensive medicines with the goal of lowering blood pressure to 130/80 for those with high risk for heart and blood vessel disease or with diabetes. The American Diabetes Association recommends 130/80 as the target for people living with diabetes and less than 125/75 for those who spill more than one gram of protein into their urine. Most clinicians try to achieve a BP that confers the best balance of lower cardiovascular risk and avoids the problem of too low a blood pressure. Blood pressure duration is generally increased with beneficial restriction of sodium. The goals and time frame should be discussed with you when the prescription is written. If goals are not met, it is not unusual to intensify doses or add on medicines. You can find the new blood pressure guidelines at *www.nhlbi.nih.gov/guidelines/hypertension/index.htm*. For the African American guidelines see Douglas J.G. in Sources.

Possible Advantages of This Drug

Does not reduce blood flow to the kidney. Can be used with other drugs that may reduce blood flow to the kidney (such as most anti-inflammatory aspirin substitutes). May be taken without regard to meals. Once-daily dosing encourages patients to take their medicine (adherence). May have positive effects on lipid peroxidation which then could block processes leading to atherosclerosis.

▷ **This Drug Should Not Be Taken If**
- you have had an allergic reaction to it previously.
- you have heart shock (cardiogenic).
- you have an abnormally slow heart rate or a serious form of heart block (2nd or 3rd degree AV).
- you have ongoing obstructive lung disease (COPD) or bronchial asthma.

▷ **Inform Your Physician Before Taking This Drug If**
- you have had an adverse reaction to any beta blocker (see Drug Classes).
- you have a history of serious heart disease/heart failure.
- you have a history of hay fever (allergic rhinitis), asthma, chronic bronchitis, or emphysema.
- you have a history of overactive thyroid function (hyperthyroidism).
- you have a history of low blood sugar (hypoglycemia).
- you have impaired liver or kidney function.
- you have diabetes or myasthenia gravis.
- you are pregnant or breast-feeding your infant.
- you have difficulty with blood circulation to the periphery (peripheral vascular disease).
- you are currently taking any form of digitalis, quinidine, or reserpine, or any calcium-channel-blocker drug (see Drug Classes).
- you will have surgery with general anesthesia.

Possible Side Effects (natural, expected, and unavoidable drug actions)
> Lethargy and fatigability, cold extremities, slow heart rate, light-headedness in upright position (see orthostatic hypotension in Glossary).

▷ **Possible Adverse Effects** (unusual, unexpected, and infrequent reactions)
> **If any of the following develop, consult your physician promptly for guidance.**

Mild Adverse Effects
> Allergic reactions: skin rash, itching, drug fever.
> Headache, dizziness, vivid dreaming, visual disturbances, ringing in ears, slurred speech, paresthesia—case reports to infrequent.
> Hair loss and sweating—case reports to infrequent.
> Bleeding gums (gingival bleeding)—case report.
> Cough, indigestion, nausea, vomiting, diarrhea, abdominal pain—infrequent.
> Increased blood potassium—possible.
> Numbness and tingling of extremities—case reports.

Serious Adverse Effects
> Allergic reactions: facial swelling, anaphylaxis.
> Chest pain, shortness of breath, precipitation of congestive heart failure—possible.
> Intensification of heart block or severe slowing of the heart—case reports and may be dose-related.
> Bronchospasm—rare.
> Carpal tunnel syndrome or pancreatitis—case reports.
> Precipitation of bronchial asthma (in people already living with asthma)—possible and dose-related.
> Masking of warning indications of acute hypoglycemia in drug-treated diabetes—possible.
> May precipitate cramping when walking (intermittent claudication)—possible. May be prudent to check for hidden Peripheral Artery Disease (PAD) by checking ankle brachial index (ABI). ABI check (see Glossary) can help find PAD early, and avoid claudication that may result if this medication is taken by someone who has PAD but does not know it.
> Excessively low blood pressure—possible.

▷ **Possible Effects on Sexual Function:** Decreased libido, impotence, impaired erection—case reports to frequent.

▷ **Adverse Effects That May Mimic Natural Diseases or Disorders**
> Impaired circulation to the extremities may resemble Raynaud's phenomenon.

Natural Diseases or Disorders That May Be Activated by This Drug
> Bronchial asthma, Prinzmetal's variant (vasospastic) angina, latent Raynaud's disease, myasthenia gravis (questionable).

Possible Effects on Laboratory Tests
> Blood HDL cholesterol level: decreased.
> Blood VLDL cholesterol level: increased.
> Blood triglyceride levels: increased.

CAUTION
> 1. ***Do not stop this drug suddenly*** without the knowledge and help of your doctor. Carry a note stating that you are taking this drug.
> 2. Ask your physician or pharmacist before using nasal decongestants, which are usually present in over-the-counter cold preparations and nose

drops. These can cause rapid blood pressure increases when combined with beta-blocker drugs.

3. Report the development of any tendency to emotional depression.

Precautions for Use

By Infants and Children: Safety and effectiveness for those under 12 years of age are not established. However, if this drug is used, observe for the development of low blood sugar (hypoglycemia) during periods of reduced food intake.

By Those Over 60 Years of Age: Unacceptably high blood pressure should be reduced without creating the risks associated with excessively low blood pressure. Small doses and frequent blood pressure checks are needed. Sudden, rapid, and excessive reduction of blood pressure can predispose to stroke or heart attack. Watch for dizziness, unsteadiness, tendency to fall, confusion, hallucinations, depression, or urinary frequency.

▷ **Advisability of Use During Pregnancy**

Pregnancy Category: C. See Pregnancy Risk Categories at the back of this book.

Animal Studies: No significant increase in birth defects due to this drug, but embryotoxicity reported in rabbits.

Human Studies: Adequate studies of pregnant women are not available. Avoid use during the first 3 months if possible. Use this drug only if clearly needed. Ask your physician for guidance.

Advisability of Use If Breast-Feeding

Presence of this drug in breast milk: Yes.

Avoid drug or refrain from nursing.

Habit-Forming Potential: None.

Effects of Overdose: Weakness, slow pulse, low blood pressure, fainting, cold and sweaty skin, congestive heart failure, possible coma, and convulsions.

Possible Effects of Long-Term Use: Reduced heart reserve and possible heart failure in susceptible individuals with advanced heart disease.

Suggested Periodic Examinations While Taking This Drug (at physician's discretion)

Measurements of blood pressure.

Evaluation of heart function, check of lipid panel.

▷ **While Taking This Drug, Observe the Following**

Foods: Follow the diet your doctor prescribes. Avoid excessive salt intake.

Herbal Medicines or Minerals: Valerian and kava kava (no longer recommended in Canada) may intensify drowsiness. Dong quai may make this medicine stay in the body longer than expected, while St. John's wort may increase removal of this medicine from the body, blunting the benefit of this medicine. Ginseng, guarana, hawthorn, saw palmetto, ma huang (do not take if hypertensive), goldenseal, yohimbe, and licorice may also increase blood pressure. Calcium and garlic may help lower blood pressure and could be part of complementary care. Use of calcium to excess (7.5 to 10 grams) with combination thiazide diuretics can lead to excessive calcium levels. Talk to your doctor about how much calcium to take. Indian snakeroot has a German Commission E monograph indication for hypertension—talk to your doctor. Eleuthero root and ephedra should be avoided by people living with hypertension.

Beverages: No restrictions. May be taken with milk.

▷ *Alcohol:* Use with caution. Alcohol may exaggerate this drug's ability to lower blood pressure and may increase its mild sedative effect.

Tobacco Smoking: Nicotine may reduce this drug's effectiveness. I advise everyone to quit smoking.

▷ *Other Drugs*

Nadolol may ***increase*** the effects of

- other antihypertensive drugs and cause excessive lowering of blood pressure; dose adjustments may be necessary.
- reserpine (Ser-Ap-Es, etc.) and cause sedation, depression, slowing of the heart rate, and lowering of blood pressure.
- verapamil (Calan, Isoptin) or other calcium channel blockers (see Drug Classes) and cause excessive depression of heart function; monitor this combination closely.

Nadolol may ***decrease*** the effects of

- ritodrine (Yutopar), and may result in undesirable heart effects.
- theophyllines (Aminophyllin, Theo-Dur, etc.) and reduce their effectiveness in treating asthma.

Nadolol ***taken concurrently*** with

- amiodarone (Cordarone) can cause severe slowing of the heart and potentially stop the heart (cardiac arrest).
- antacids containing aluminum can block absorption of this medicine and lessen therapeutic nadolol effects.
- clonidine (Catapres) requires close monitoring for rebound high blood pressure if clonidine is withdrawn while nadolol is still being taken.
- digoxin (Lanoxin) may result in undesirable heart effects.
- dihydropyridine calcium channel blockers may result in undesirable heart effects (bradycardia) or excessively low blood pressure.
- epinephrine can cause serious hypertension and slowing of the heart and, should anaphylaxis occur, epinephrine resistance.
- ergot derivatives (see Drug Classes) can cause decreased blood flow to the extremities (peripheral ischemia).
- insulin requires close monitoring to avoid undetected hypoglycemia (see Glossary).
- lidocaine can lead to lidocaine toxicity (depressed heart function, cardiac arrest).
- oral antidiabetic drugs (see Drug Classes) can cause slowed recovery from any hypoglycemia that may occur.

The following drug may ***decrease*** the effects of nadolol:

- indomethacin (Indocin), and possibly other "aspirin substitutes," or NSAIDs, and may impair nadolol's antihypertensive effect.

▷ *Driving, Hazardous Activities:* Use caution until the full extent of drowsiness, lethargy, and blood pressure change has been determined.

Aviation Note: The use of this drug ***is a disqualification*** for piloting. Consult a designated Aviation Medical Examiner.

Exposure to Sun: No restrictions.

Exposure to Heat: Caution is advised. Hot environments can lower blood pressure and exaggerate the effects of this drug.

Exposure to Cold: Caution is advised. Cold environments can enhance the circulatory deficiency in the extremities that may occur with this drug. The elderly should take precautions to prevent hypothermia (see Glossary).

Heavy Exercise or Exertion: Prudent to avoid exertion that produces light-headedness, excessive fatigue, or muscle cramping.

Occurrence of Unrelated Illness: Fever can lower blood pressure, requiring dose decreases. Nausea or vomiting may interrupt dosing. Ask your doctor for help.

Discontinuation: Best not to stop this drug suddenly. Gradual lowering of doses (tapering) over 2 to 3 weeks is recommended.

NAFARELIN (NAF a re lin)

Introduced: 1984   **Class:** Hormones, miscellaneous   **Prescription:** USA: Yes   **Controlled Drug:** USA: No; Canada: No   **Available as Generic:** USA: No

Brand Name: Synarel

BENEFITS versus RISKS	
Possible Benefits	*Possible Risks*
VERY EFFECTIVE TREATMENT OF ENDOMETRIOSIS (alternative to oophorectomy)	Symptoms of estrogen deficiency (during treatment)
	Masculinizing effects (during treatment)
	Loss of bone density
	White blood cell count lowering

▷ **Principal Uses**

As a Single Drug Product: Uses currently included in FDA-approved labeling: (1) Treats endometriosis: reduction in the size and activity of endometrial implants within the pelvis; relief of pelvic pain associated with menstruation; (2) also used to treat precocious puberty due to excessive production of gonadotropic hormones.

Other (unlabeled) generally accepted uses: (1) Intranasal dosing helps control abnormal hair growth in women; (2) can be injected below the skin (subcutaneously) to help benign prostatic hyperplasia; (3) may be used before surgery to help decrease size of some tumors (myomas); (4) low-dose use for in vitro fertilization.

How This Drug Works: Stimulates the pituitary gland to release two additional hormones that regulate production of estrogen by the ovaries. With continued use, estrogen levels suppress (by a feedback mechanism) ovary-stimulating hormones—thereby lowering estrogen levels. The implants of endometrium (from the lining of the uterus) that are attached to the pelvic wall are stimulated by the rise and fall of estrogen in menstruation. When this drug suppresses estrogen production, the displaced endometrial tissue (endometriosis) becomes dormant and the premenstrual and menstrual pain no longer happens.

Available Dosage Forms and Strengths

Nasal solution (10-ml bottle) — 2 mg/ml

▷ **Usual Adult Dosage Ranges:** *Endometriosis:* Pregnancy MUST be excluded prior to starting therapy. Dosing starts with 400 mcg daily. Spray one dose of 200 mcg into one nostril in the morning and one dose of 200 mcg into the other nostril in the evening, 12 hours apart. Start taking this medicine between days 2 and 4 of the menstrual cycle. If menstruation persists after 2 months of treatment, the dose may be increased to 800 mcg daily: one spray into each nostril (a total of two sprays, 400 mcg) in the morning and again in the evening.

Note: Actual dose and schedule must be determined for each patient individually.

Conditions Requiring Dosing Adjustments

Liver Function: No dosing changes needed.

Kidney Function: Specific guidelines are not available for dosing. Decreases may be needed in kidney compromise.

▷ **Dosing Instructions:** Carefully read and follow the patient instructions provided with this drug. The solution is to be sprayed directly into the nostrils; it is not to be swallowed. Time the start of therapy and daily dosing exactly as directed. A nasal decongestant (spray or drops) should not be used for at least 30 minutes after dosing with the nafarelin spray; earlier use could impair absorption of nafarelin. If you forget a dose: Take the missed dose as soon as you remember it, unless it's nearly time for your next dose—if that is the case, skip the missed dose and take the next dose right on schedule. DO NOT double doses. Talk with your doctor if you find yourself missing doses.

Usual Duration of Use: Regular use for 2 to 3 months usually determines benefits in easing endometriosis symptoms. The standard course of treatment is limited to 6 months. Safety data does not exist for re-treatment and is not advised by the maker.

Typical Treatment Goals and Measurements (Outcomes and Markers)

Endometriosis: The goal most gynecologists use is the resolution of active endometriosis lesions as well as patient relief from pelvic pain, difficulty having intercourse, and painful menstruation (dysmenorrhea). A laboratory test (estradiol levels) can be used (when they go below 30 pg/ml) as a guide to expecting patient response.

Possible Advantages of This Drug

Causes fewer masculinizing effects than danazol. Less tendency than danazol to increase blood cholesterol levels. Unlike danazol, this drug does not cause abnormally low HDL cholesterol levels or abnormally high LDL cholesterol levels. Superb alternative to oophorectomy.

Currently a Drug of Choice

For management of symptoms associated with endometriosis.

▷ **This Drug Should Not Be Taken If**

- you have had an allergic reaction to it previously.
- you are pregnant or breast-feeding.
- you have abnormal vaginal bleeding of unknown cause.

▷ **Inform Your Physician Before Taking This Drug If**

- you have used this drug, danazol, or similar drugs previously.
- you are taking any type of estrogen, progesterone, or oral contraceptive.
- you are planning pregnancy in the near future.
- you have a family history of osteoporosis or have low bone mass (osteopenia).
- you use alcohol or tobacco regularly.
- you have a history of low white blood cells.
- you are using anticonvulsants or cortisonelike drugs.
- you are subject to allergic or infectious rhinitis and use nasal decongestants frequently.

Possible Side Effects (natural, expected, and unavoidable drug actions)

Effects due to reduced estrogen production: hot flashes (90%), headaches, emotional lability, insomnia. Masculinizing effects: acne, muscle aches, fluid retention, increased skin oil, weight gain, excessive hair growth—rare.

▷ **Possible Adverse Effects** (unusual, unexpected, and infrequent reactions)
   If any of the following develop, consult your physician promptly for guidance.
   Mild Adverse Effects
      Allergic reactions: skin rash, hives—rare.
      Nasal irritation—frequent.
      Vaginal dryness—infrequent to frequent.
      Depression—rare.
      Hot flashes—when used in men with prostate problems (BPH).
   Serious Adverse Effects
      Loss of vertebral bone density: at completion of 6 months of treatment, bone density decreases an average of 8.7% and bone mass decreases an average of 4.3%; partial recovery during the post treatment period restores bone density loss to 4.9% and bone mass loss to 3.3%.
      Lowering of the white blood cell count (leukopenia)—case reports.
      Transient prostate enlargement—possible.
      Uterine bleeding—case report.

▷ **Possible Effects on Sexual Function:** Decreased libido, vaginal dryness, reduced breast size—infrequent to frequent. Milk production in women who are not pregnant (galactorrhea)—case reports. Uterine bleeding—case reports. Impotence occurred in all men in one study using this drug for prostate problems; hot flashes also occurred in all of them.

Natural Diseases or Disorders That May Be Activated by This Drug
   Worsening or increased progression of osteoporosis.

Possible Effects on Laboratory Tests
   Blood testosterone level: decreased in men with benign enlargement of prostate gland.
   Blood estradiol: decreased.
   Blood progesterone: decreased to less than 4 mg/ml.
   Alkaline phosphatase: increased.
   Serum estrone: decreased.

CAUTION
   1. With continual use of this drug, menstruation will stop. If regular menstruation persists, call your doctor. Dose changes may be needed.
   2. Use this drug consistently on a regular basis. Missed doses can result in breakthrough bleeding and ovulation.
   3. It is advisable to avoid pregnancy during the course of treatment. Use a nonhormonal method of birth control; do not use oral contraceptives. Inform your physician promptly if you think you may be pregnant.
   4. If you need to use nasal decongestant sprays or drops, delay their use for at least 30 minutes after the intranasal spray of nafarelin.

Precautions for Use
   By Infants and Children: Safety and effectiveness for those under 18 years of age are not established.
   By Those Over 60 Years of Age: If used for prostatism, impotence is a common side effect. Depression and hot flashes were also often reported.

▷ **Advisability of Use During Pregnancy**
   Pregnancy Category: X. See Pregnancy Risk Categories at the back of this book.
   Animal Studies: Major fetal abnormalities and increased fetal deaths due to this drug have been demonstrated in rat studies.
   Human Studies: Adequate studies of pregnant women are not available.
   Avoid this drug during entire pregnancy.

Advisability of Use If Breast-Feeding
> Presence of this drug in breast milk: Unknown.
> Avoid drug or refrain from nursing.

Habit-Forming Potential: None.

Effects of Overdose: No significant effects expected.

Possible Effects of Long-Term Use: Continual use should be limited to 6 months.

Suggested Periodic Examinations While Taking This Drug (at physician's discretion)
> Blood cholesterol and triglyceride profiles.
> Bone mineral density measurements.

▷ **While Taking This Drug, Observe the Following**

Foods: No restrictions.

Herbal Medicines or Minerals: Black cohosh appears to work by: (1) suppressing luteinizing hormone; (2) binding to estrogen receptors in the pituitary and inhibiting luteinizing hormone release; and (3) binding to estrogen receptors in the pituitary. Talk to your doctor before starting black cohosh or any other herbal products if you are currently taking nafarelin.

Beverages: No restrictions.

▷ *Alcohol:* No interactions expected.

Tobacco Smoking: No interactions expected. I advise everyone to quit smoking.

▷ *Other Drugs*
> The following drugs will ***decrease*** the effects of nafarelin:
> - birth control pills (oral contraceptives).
> - estrogens.

▷ *Driving, Hazardous Activities:* No restrictions.

Aviation Note: The use of this drug ***is not a disqualification*** for piloting. Consult a designated Aviation Medical Examiner for confirmation.

Exposure to Sun: No restrictions.

Special Storage Instructions: Store in an upright position at room temperature. Protect from light.

Discontinuation: Normal ovarian function (ovulation, menstruation, etc.) is usually restored within 4 to 8 weeks after discontinuation of this drug.

NALTREXONE (nahl TREX ohn)

Introduced: 1995   **Class:** Antialcoholism, opioid antagonist   **Prescription:** USA: Yes   **Controlled Drug:** USA: No; Canada: No   **Available as Generic:** USA: Yes; Canada: Yes

Brand Names: Depade, Trexan, ReVia

Warning: This medication can cause liver damage if taken in excessive doses. If abdominal pain, white stools, or yellowing of the eyes or skin occurs, call your doctor immediately.

BENEFITS versus RISKS	
Possible Benefits	*Possible Risks*
CONTROL OF CRAVING FOR ALCOHOL	LIVER DAMAGE IF EXCESSIVE DOSES TAKEN
PART OF AN EFFECTIVE COMBINATION APPROACH TO ALCOHOLISM	
ONCE-DAILY DOSING	

▷ **Principal Uses**

As a Single Drug Product: Uses currently included in FDA-approved labeling: (1) Used as part of a comprehensive program to help alcohol dependence; (2) used to treat narcotic addiction.

Other (unlabeled) generally accepted uses: (1) May help women with a specific type of cessation of menstruation (hypothalamic amenorrhea); (2) helps itching in hemodialysis patients; (3) incidental reports from a detoxification program may yield a use for this drug in smoking cessation.

How This Drug Works: In narcotic addiction, this medicine antagonizes the effects of opioid medicines and blocks the perceived benefit of the drug to the addicted patient. In alcohol addiction, it may interfere with the body's own opioids that are released in response to drinking alcoholic beverages. If the effect of the body's own opioids (endogenous) is blocked, the craving for alcohol is then reduced.

Available Dosage Forms and Strengths

Tablets — 50 mg

▷ **Recommended Dosage Ranges** (Actual dose and schedule must be determined for each patient individually.)

Infants and Children: Not indicated.

18 to 60 Years of Age: 50 mg daily. The best results are gained when this medicine is used as part of a comprehensive approach to curbing alcohol use.

Over 60 Years of Age: Same as 18 to 60 years of age.

Conditions Requiring Dosing Adjustments

Liver Function: This drug is extensively metabolized in the liver and is contraindicated in acute hepatitis or liver failure.

Kidney Function: Metabolites of this drug are removed by the kidneys, but specific guidelines for dosing changes are not available.

▷ **Dosing Instructions:** If there is any question of opioid dependence, a Narcan challenge test must be performed. Naltrexone is almost completely absorbed after oral dosing. This medicine may be taken with or without food. If you forget a dose: Take the missed dose as soon as you remember it, unless it's nearly time for your next dose—if that is the case, skip the missed dose and take the next dose right on schedule. Talk with your doctor if you find yourself missing doses.

Usual Duration of Use: Continual use on a regular schedule for 12 weeks is usually necessary to determine this drug's effectiveness in treating alcoholism. This drug should be a part of a comprehensive alcohol treatment program. Long-term use (months to years) requires periodic evaluation of response and dose adjustment. Consult your physician on a regular basis.

Typical Treatment Goals and Measurements (Outcomes and Markers)

Alcohol or Narcotic Abuse: The general goal is to gain a patient defined (subjective) decrease in desire for alcohol or narcotics (opioids). Specific markers may include an alcohol abstinence diary or specific urine or blood tests for narcotics.

Possible Advantages of This Drug

Actually decreases the craving for alcohol versus aversive therapy with antabuse (leads to vomiting).

▷ **This Drug Should Not Be Taken If**

• you had an allergic reaction to any form of it previously.

• you have liver failure or acute hepatitis.

- you are in opioid withdrawal.
- you are physically dependent on narcotics.

▷ **Inform Your Physician Before Taking This Drug If**
- you have a history of viral hepatitis.
- you are planning surgery or a diagnostic procedure requiring anesthesia.
- you are unsure how much to take or how often to take it.
- you take prescription or nonprescription medicines not discussed with your doctor when naltrexone was prescribed.

Possible Side Effects (natural, expected, and unavoidable drug actions)
None.

▷ **Possible Adverse Effects** (unusual, unexpected, and infrequent reactions)
If any of the following develop, consult your physician promptly for guidance.
Mild Adverse Effects
Allergic reaction: rash.
Oily skin, itching, hair loss—case reports.
Nosebleeds—possible.
Joint and muscle pain—infrequent to frequent.
Anorexia, weight loss, fatigue, anxiety, nervousness—case reports to frequent.
Sleep disturbances—infrequent.
Depression—case reports.
Serious Adverse Effects
Allergic reactions: none reported.
Idiosyncratic reactions: none reported.
Liver toxicity (hepatocellular injury)—case reports and reported with large doses.
Muscle damage (rhabdomyolysis)—case report.
Precipitation of acute withdrawal syndrome in patients dependent on narcotics.
Suicidal ideation—case reports.
Abnormal platelet function (idiopathic thrombocytopenic purpura)—case reports.

▷ **Possible Effects on Sexual Function:** Delayed ejaculation—infrequent.

Possible Delayed Adverse Effects: None reported.

▷ **Adverse Effects That May Mimic Natural Diseases or Disorders**
Liver problems may mimic acute hepatitis.

Natural Diseases or Disorders That May Be Activated by This Drug
None.

Possible Effects on Laboratory Tests
Liver function tests: increased.
Gonadotropins (LH, FSH, ACTH, catecholamines, and cortisol): increased.

CAUTION
1. The therapeutic dose and doses that can cause liver damage may be fairly close in some patients. Make certain that you understand how much to take and how often to take it.
2. Self-administration of any narcotic drug may be fatal.
3. If you are taking ongoing narcotic or opioid treatment for pain, this drug could precipitate an acute withdrawal syndrome.

Precautions for Use
By Infants and Children: Safety and effectiveness for use by those under 18 years of age have not been established.
By Those Over 60 Years of Age: None.

▷ **Advisability of Use During Pregnancy**
   Pregnancy Category: C. See Pregnancy Risk Categories at the back of this book.
   Animal Studies: This drug has been shown to be embryocidal in rats and rabbits at roughly 140 times the typical human dose.
   Human Studies: Information from adequate studies of pregnant women is not available.
   Ask your doctor for help with this benefit-to-risk decision.

Advisability of Use If Breast-Feeding
   Presence of this drug in breast milk: Unknown.
   Avoid drug or refrain from nursing.

Habit-Forming Potential: None.

Effects of Overdose: Human subjects who received over 800 mg daily for a week showed no adverse effects.

Possible Effects of Long-Term Use: None defined.

Suggested Periodic Examinations While Taking This Drug (at physician's discretion)
   Liver function tests.

▷ **While Taking This Drug, Observe the Following**
   Foods: No restrictions.
   Herbal Medicines or Minerals: Ephedra, guarana, kola, or yohimbe may worsen anxiety associated with abstaining from alcohol. Valerian or kava kava (no longer recommended in Canada because of possible toxic liver effects) may ease anxiety or difficulty falling asleep, but has not been studied with naltrexone. Given the possible effects on the liver of those herbs and naltrexone, this combination is not recommended. Talk to your doctor BEFORE you add any herbal medicine.
   Beverages: No restrictions.
▷ *Alcohol:* Obviously not recommended, as this medication is part of a combination approach to help problem drinkers.
   Tobacco Smoking: No interactions expected. I advise everyone to quit smoking.
   Marijuana Smoking: Should not be attempted.
▷ *Other Drugs*
      Naltrexone *taken concurrently* with
      • narcotic medicines may result in a severe reaction.
      • other drugs that are toxic to the liver may result in increased risk of liver toxicity.
      • thioridazine (Mellaril) may result in somnolence and lethargy.
▷ *Driving, Hazardous Activities:* This drug may cause fatigue. Restrict activities as necessary.
   Aviation Note: Alcoholism *is a disqualification* for piloting. Consult a designated Aviation Medical Examiner.
   Exposure to Sun: No restrictions.
   Discontinuation: Do not stop this medicine without the knowledge of your doctor.

NAPROXEN (na PROX en)

Please see the propionic acid (nonsteroidal anti-inflammatory drug) family profile.

NATEGLINIDE (na TAG lyn ide)

Introduced: 2000   **Class:**   Antidiabetic, D-phenylalanine derivative
Prescription: USA: Yes   **Controlled Drug:**   USA: No; Canada: No
Available as Generic: No
Brand Name: Starlix

BENEFITS versus RISKS

Possible Benefits	*Possible Risks*
HELPS REGULATE BLOOD SUGAR in TYPE 2 DIABETES (adjunctive to appropriate diet and weight control) MAY BE COMBINED WITH METFORMIN IF BLOOD SUGAR CONTROL IS NOT ACCEPTABLE Absorbed well and cleared quickly from the blood More selective for beta cells in the pancreas than nateglinide	Hypoglycemia (less common than repaglinide or sulfonylureas) Possible increased risk of heart (cardiovascular) problems (based on a 1970 UGDP study)

▷ **Principal Uses**

As a Single Drug Product: Uses currently included in FDA-approved labeling: (1) Type 2 diabetes mellitus (adult, maturity-onset) that does not require insulin but can't be adequately controlled by diet alone; (2) combination treatment with metformin in people who do not have an adequate blood sugar response from nateglinide alone.

Other (unlabeled) generally accepted uses: (1) One small study of combined use with rosiglitasone found very favorable results in controlling blood sugar and A1C.

How This Drug Works: Stimulates secretion of insulin by the pancreas (closes ATP-sensitive potassium channels in beta cells leading to an influx of calcium and increased release of insulin). This mechanism is like the sulfonylureas, but nateglinide works faster.

Available Dosage Forms and Strengths

Tablets — 60 mg, 120 mg, 180 mg

▷ **Usual Adult Dosage Ranges:** Dosing is started at 120 mg given three times a day between one and 30 minutes before meals. *People with a hemoglobin A1C (HGB A1C or glycosylated hemoglobin) who are near the treatment goal can be started on 60 mg taken before meals as above.* If goals are not met with the 60 mg dose, it can be increased to 120 mg as above. If goals are still not met, this medicine can be combined with metformin.

Note: Actual dose and schedule must be determined for each patient individually.

Conditions Requiring Dosing Adjustments

Liver Function: Current thinking is that dosing changes are not needed in mild liver compromise. Studies are limited in more severe compromise (moderate to severe), but generally, dosing changes are not thought to be needed for mild to moderate liver compromised people. More frequent blood sugar checks are prudent in this patient population until the full effects are individually known.

Kidney Function: Dosing changes are not required in mild to severe kidney compromise.

▷ **Dosing Instructions:** It is important to take this medicine before meals. You can take it up to 30 minutes before a meal, but ten appears to be best. If you skip a meal, then skip the dose of nateglinide. This medicine rarely causes low blood sugar (hypoglycemia), and you should talk to your doctor about what he wants you to do if symptoms (unexplained weakness, tiredness, nervousness, sweating, trouble concentrating, and headache) occur. At present there is no sustained-release form, so the immediate-release tablet may be crushed. If you forget a dose: Skip the missed dose and take the next dose right on schedule. DO NOT double doses. Talk with your doctor if you find yourself missing doses. Staying on schedule helps keep tight blood sugar control and can help you avoid diabetic complications.

Usual Duration of Use: This medicine goes to work quickly (about 15 minutes). Use on a regular schedule for 1 to 2 weeks determines effectiveness in controlling diabetes. Checking blood sugar by finger stick is the best way to make sure you are getting the best results from this medicine. Some patients will have control of their blood sugar for a while and then the medicine will not continue to work and will need to be changed. Diabetes is now recognized as a risk factor for cardiovascular disease. Take control of your blood sugar and help your heart.

Typical Treatment Goals and Measurements (Outcomes and Markers)
Blood Sugar: The general goal for blood sugar is to return it to the usual "normal" range (generally 80–120 mg/dl), while avoiding risks of excessively low blood sugar. One study (UKPDS) used a fasting plasma sugar (glucose) of less than 108 mg/dl. Tight control helps avoid diabetic complications.
Fructosamine and glycosylated hemoglobin: Fructosamine levels (a measure of the past two to three weeks of blood sugar control) should be less than or equal to 310 micromoles per liter. Glycosylated hemoglobin or hemoglobin A1C (a measure of the past 2–3 months of blood sugar control) should be less than or equal to 7.0%. One group of clinicians advocates less than or equal to 6.5% as a target.

Possible Advantages of This Drug
The risk of excesively low blood sugar (hypoglycemia) is expected to be less than with other agents. Goes to work more quickly than repaglinide. Safety and results (efficacy) in patients more than 65 years old is the same as in younger patients. A study of combined use with rosiglitasone found improvement in insulin release and the benefit of lower increases in sugar after meals (postprandial).

▷ **This Drug Should Not Be Taken If**
• you have had an allergic reaction to it previously.
• you have diabetic ketoacidosis.
• you are pregnant.
• you have the kind of diabetes that requires insulin.

▷ **Inform Your Physician Before Taking This Drug If**
• your blood sugar begins to drift up. This may be a sign of failure and require a change in medicine.
• you do not know how to recognize or treat hypoglycemia (see Glossary).
• you have a history of congestive heart failure, cirrhosis of the liver, or hypothyroidism.
• you have an infection or a fever—insulin may be required.

Possible Side Effects (natural, expected, and unavoidable drug actions)
If drug dose is excessive or food intake is delayed or inadequate, abnormally low blood sugar (hypoglycemia) will occur. Mild hypoglycemia happened in 2-3% of people using this medicine in reported studies.

▷ **Possible Adverse Effects** (unusual, unexpected, and infrequent reactions)
If any of the following develop, consult your physician promptly for guidance.
Mild Adverse Effects
Allergic reactions: skin rash, hives, itching.
Headache, drowsiness, dizziness, fatigue—possible.
Nausea, vomiting, diarrhea, heartburn—infrequent.
Serious Adverse Effects
Allergic reactions: not defined.
Idiosyncratic reactions: not reported.
Hypoglycemia—possible but less than sulfonylureas such as glyburide.
Cardiovascular mortality (based on an old study of a different medicine)—possible increased risk.

▷ **Possible Effects on Sexual Function:** None reported.
▷ **Adverse Effects That May Mimic Natural Diseases or Disorders**
Not defined.

Possible Effects on Laboratory Tests
Blood glucose levels: decreased.
Glycated hemoglobin or protein: trending toward normal.

CAUTION
1. This drug is only part of diabetes management. Much of the damage from diabetes can be delayed or avoided if you keep your blood sugar in the normal range. Ask your doctor about a proper diet and regular exercise.
2. Over time, this drug, like other oral medicines for type 2 diabetes may not work. Periodic follow-up examinations are necessary.
3. If you develop an infection, insulin may be required to control your blood sugar.

Precautions for Use
By Infants and Children: Safety and efficacy not defined.
By Those Over 65 Years of Age: No differences in pharmacokinetics in this age group in clinical trials. People in this population may be more sensitive to this medicine, and careful patient follow-up and more frequent blood sugar checks are prudent when nateglinide is started.

▷ **Advisability of Use During Pregnancy**
Pregnancy Category: C. See Pregnancy Risk Categories at the back of this book.
Animal Studies: No birth defects reported in rats and rabbits.
Human Studies: Adequate studies of pregnant women are not available.
Uncontrolled blood sugar levels during pregnancy are associated with a higher incidence of birth defects, so many experts recommend insulin (instead of an oral agent) to control diabetes during the entire pregnancy.

Advisability of Use If Breast-Feeding
Presence of this drug in breast milk: Unknown.
Avoid drug or refrain from nursing.

Habit-Forming Potential: None.

Effects of Overdose: Symptoms of mild to severe hypoglycemia: headache, light-headedness, faintness, nervousness, confusion, tremor, sweating, heart palpitation, weakness, hunger, nausea, vomiting, stupor progressing to coma.

Possible Effects of Long-Term Use: More normal hemoglobin A1C.

Suggested Periodic Examinations While Taking This Drug (at physician's discretion)

Periodic evaluation of heart and circulatory system. Check of lipid panel (because diabetes is a significant risk factor for heart disease).

Self-assessment of blood sugar is prudent as well as periodic glycosylated hemoglobin tests and/or fructosamine tests.

▷ **While Taking This Drug, Observe the Following**

Foods: Follow your diabetic diet conscientiously. Taking a diabetes education course is very smart and can teach you about portion control, what to do on sick days and other important concepts. Blood sugar control can help avoid or delay diabetes problems. Vitamin C in high dose may worsen blood sugar control. Do not omit snack foods in mid-afternoon or at bedtime if they help prevent hypoglycemia. Rice bran has been checked in a small (57 subject) study of type 1 and type 2 diabetics. The benefit was a 30% lowering of sugar. This might be a new complementary care option.

Herbal Medicines or Minerals: Using chromium may change the way your body is able to use sugar. Some health food stores advocate vanadium as mimicking the actions of insulin, but possible toxicity and need for rigorous studies presently preclude recommending it. DHEA may change sensitivity to insulin or insulin resistance. Aloe, bitter melon, eucalyptus, fenugreek, ginger, garlic, ginseng, glucomannan, guar gum, hawthorn, licorice, nettle, and yohimbe may change blood sugar. Surprisingly, boiled stems of the Optuntia streptacantha prickly pear cactus appears to be able to lower blood sugar. Ongoing effects and effects on A1C are not known. Red sage is used for blood sugar effects, but is unproven. Psyllium increases risk of excessively low blood sugar. Since so many of these products may require adjustment of insulin dosing, talk to your doctor BEFORE combining any of these herbal medicines with this medicine. Echinacea purpurea (injectable) and blonde psyllium seed or husk should NOT be taken by people living with diabetes.

Beverages: As directed in the diabetic diet. May be taken with milk.

▷ *Alcohol:* Use with extreme caution—alcohol can exaggerate this drug's hypoglycemic effect.

Tobacco Smoking: No interactions expected. I advise everyone to quit smoking.

▷ *Other Drugs*

The following drugs may ***increase*** the effects of nateglinide:

- cimetidine (Tagamet).
- erythromycins (see Drug Classes).
- itraconazole (Sporanox).
- ketoconazole (Nizoral).
- medicines that inhibit or compete for CYP3A4 or 2C9 (liver enzymes) may increase nateglinide because it is removed by that enzyme.
- nelfinavir (Viracept) and perhaps other protease inhibitors (see Drug Classes)—may increase blood levels.
- sildenafil (Viagra), since both drugs are removed by CYP3A4.
- Any medicine that interferes with cytochrome CYP3A4 or 2C9—will potentially increase nateglinide blood levels; in some cases, I expect that nateglinide dosing will need to be adjusted.

The following drugs may ***decrease*** the effects of nateglinide:

- carbamazepine (Tegretol), since it induces CYP3A4, which removes nateglinide from the body.
- corticosteroids (see Drug Classes).

- rifabutin (Mycobutin).
- rifampin (Rifadin, Rimactane).

▷ *Driving, Hazardous Activities:* This drug may cause dizziness, drowsiness, impaired vision, and impaired hearing. Restrict activities as necessary.

Aviation Note: Diabetes *is a disqualification* for piloting. Consult a designated Aviation Medical Examiner.

Exposure to Sun: No restrictions.

Discontinuation: It is advisable not to interrupt or stop this drug without consulting your physician.

NEDOCROMIL (na DOK ra mil)

Introduced: 1992 **Class:** Antiasthmatic, preventive **Prescription:** USA: Yes **Controlled Drug:** USA: No; Canada: No **Available as Generic:** USA: No; Canada: No

Brand Names: Alocril, Tilade, Tilade Nebulizer Solution

BENEFITS versus RISKS	
Possible Benefits	*Possible Risks*
EFFECTIVE PREVENTION OF RECURRENT ASTHMA	Acute bronchospasm—rare
	Taste disorder
Prevention of exercise-induced asthma	

▷ **Principal Uses**

As a Single Drug Product: Uses currently included in FDA-approved labeling: (1) Ongoing therapy of mild to moderate asthma; (2) steroid-sparing effect that may allow reduction or elimination of oral steroids; (3) helps manage asthmatic bronchitis; (4) eases allergic conjunctivitis.

Other (unlabeled) generally accepted uses: (1) May have a role in helping ease allergic rhinitis.

How This Drug Works: Inhibits release of inflammatory chemical mediators such as histamine, prostaglandins and leukotrienes that constrict the bronchi and cause inflammation seen in acute asthma.

Author's Note: Information in this profile has been shortened to make room for more widely used medicines.

NEFAZODONE (na FAZ oh dohn)

Introduced: 1994 **Class:** Antidepressant **Prescription:** USA: Yes **Controlled Drug:** USA: No; Canada: No **Available as Generic:** USA: No; Canada: No

Brand Names: ✤Lin-Nefazodone, Serzone, ✤Serzone 5HT2

Author's Note: Case reports of Serzone (nefazodone) being mistaken (heard incorrectly) for Seroquel (quetiapine) and vice versa are being made. Soundalike mistakes are dangerous. Make certain that you check the pills that you are given. Information in this profile has been shortened to make room for more widely used medicines.

NEOSTIGMINE (nee oh STIG meen)

Introduced: 1931 **Class:** Antimyasthenic **Prescription:** USA:
Yes **Controlled Drug:** USA: No; Canada: No **Available as Generic:**
USA: Yes; Canada: Yes
Brand Names: ♣PMS-Neostigmine, Prostigmin

BENEFITS versus RISKS

Possible Benefits	*Possible Risks*
MODERATELY EFFECTIVE TREATMENT OF OCULAR AND MILD FORMS OF MYASTHENIA GRAVIS (symptomatic relief of muscle weakness)	Cholinergic crisis (overdose): excessive salivation, nausea, vomiting, stomach cramps, diarrhea, shortness of breath (asthmalike wheezing), weakness.
Eases postoperative bowel slowing or block (paralytic ileus)	

Author's Note: Information in this profile has been shortened to make room for more widely used medicines.

NESIRITIDE (Neh SEAR ih tyde)

Introduced: 2001 **Class:** Cardiac hormone **Prescription:** USA:
Yes **Controlled Drug:** USA: No; Canada: No **Available as Generic:**
No
Brand Name: Natrecor (NAH trah core)

BENEFITS versus RISKS

Possible Benefits	*Possible Risks*
EFFECTIVE TREATMENT IN CONGESTIVE HEART FAILURE	Lowering of blood pressure (hypotension)
EFFECTIVE PREVENTION AND TREATMENT OF CERTAIN HEART RHYTHM DISORDERS	Mild increase in heart rate

---

▷ **Principal Uses**

   As a Single Drug Product: Uses in current FDA-approved labeling: (1) Treats congestive heart failure.

   Other (unlabeled) generally accepted uses: (1) None at present.

How This Drug Works: Binds to specific receptors (guanylate cyclase linked natriuretic peptide A/B) which works to increase specific beneficial chemicals such as guanosine 3, 5-cyclic monophosphate (cGMP). The overall effect is to cause both coronary conductance and resistance vessels to dilate. This leads to an increase in blood flow and uptake of oxygen in the heart.

Available Dosage Forms and Strengths

   Injection — 1.5 mg/vial

   Author's Note: Information in this profile will be broadened as more information and clinical studies become available. A new study of

this medicine called FUSION (Management of Patients with CHF After Hospitalization with Follow Up Serial Infusions Of Natrecor has started enrolling patients and should provide an excellent opportunity to further define the use of this medicine.

NEURAMIDASE INHIBITOR FAMILY (Nur AM ih dayce)

Oseltamivir   (Oss uhl TAM ih veer)   **Zanamivir**   (Zah NAM ih veer)

Introduced: 1999   **Class:**   Antiviral, anti-influenza   **Prescription:** USA: Yes   **Controlled Drug:**   USA: No; Canada: No   **Available as Generic:**   USA: No; Canada: No

Brand Names: Oseltamivir: Tamiflu, Zanamivir: Relenza

BENEFITS versus RISKS	
Possible Benefits	*Possible Risks*
DECREASED COMPLICATIONS FROM TYPE A OR B FLU (INFLUENZA) DECREASED FLU SEVERITY	Triggering of bronchospasm by zanamivir (may be more likely in those with underlying airway diseases)

▷ **Principal Uses**

As a Single Drug Product: Uses currently included in FDA-approved labeling: (1) Treatment or prevention of type A or B influenza in people 13 or older (for oseltamivir) or people 7 or older (for zanamivir).

Other (unlabeled) generally accepted uses: (1) oseltamivir reduced complications (secondary) from the flu in one study.

How These Drugs Work: These medicines preferentially inhibit a critical chemical called neuramidase in type A or B flu (influenza) viruses. When neuramidase is blocked, newly formed virus is not released from infected cells (because sialic acid cleavage is inhibited from cell surface glycoconjugates) and the flu virus is kept from spreading across the respiratory tract (mucous lining). Oseltamivir is the ester prodrug of GS 4071.

Available Dosage Forms and Strengths

Oseltamivir

Capsule — 75 mg

Solution — see dosing in mg per ml to get the total dose needed

Suspension — see dosing in mg per ml to get the total dose needed (Canada)

Zanamivir

Dry powder inhaler — 5 mg per inhalation

▷ **Usual Adult Dosage Ranges:**

Oseltamivir: Treatment: Adults: 75 mg is taken twice a day (BID) for 5 days. Best if started within 24 hours of flu symptoms (up to 48 hours still helps-confers benefits). For the solution or suspension form: children as young as one year old based on weight (see mg per kg of body weight dosing on page 799.).

Prevention *(Prophylaxis):* FDA-approved for patients 13 or older (following close contact with an infected person) is 75 mg once daily for at least seven days. During a community outbreak, 75 mg once a day for up to six weeks has been used.

Zanamivir: Treatment of adults or children more than 7 years old: Two doses are used on the first day that this medicine is started. Take the first dose once you get the medicine, then wait at least two hours and inhale the second dose. After this, take two inhalations (5 mg each, total 10 mg) twice a day (12 hours apart) for a total of 5 days. Better started within 30 hours after symptoms start and in patients who had a fever (were febrile).

Note: Actual dose and schedule must be determined for each patient individually.

Conditions Requiring Dosing Adjustments

Liver Function: No dosing changes currently thought to be needed.

Kidney Function: Oseltamivir: Must be carefully adjusted in people with kidney problems. Those with creatinine clearances of less than 30 ml/min should receive 75 mg daily for five days. Those with clearances less than 10 ml/min have not been studied and can not be recommended.

Zanamivir: This medicine is absorbed into the body (systemically) to a limited extent—therefore even though it is primarily removed by the kidneys, dosing changes probably are not needed.

▷ **Dosing Instructions:** May be taken with or following meals. Can open the oseltamivir capsule to take it. The oseltamivir suspension should be shaken well before dosing, both suspension and solution should be given using the dosing syringe to measure the correct dose. Zanamivir is used with a device called a Diskhaler. Make sure you understand how to use this product in order to get the medicine into your lungs. If your symptoms worsen or do not improve, call your doctor. If you forget a dose: Take or use the missed dose as soon as you remember it, unless it's nearly time for your next dose—if that is the case, skip the missed dose and take the next dose right on schedule. DO NOT double doses. Talk with your doctor if you find yourself missing doses.

Usual Duration of Use: Best results come from starting oseltamivir or zanamivir within a day of flu symptoms, but benefits are gained if started within 48 hours. Use as prescribed for five days is REQUIRED to get results. During influenza epidemics (for example, if flu vaccine is NOT available), oseltamivir was given for 6 weeks in one study.

Typical Treatment Goals and Measurements (Outcomes and Markers)

Influenza: The general goal is to ease the severity of the flu (lessening of muscle aches, headache, vomiting, sore throat, fever, and others). Prophylactic use of oseltamivir or zanamivir (investigational) seeks to avoid or prevent a "full blown" case of the flu if possible. **If you would like a copy of the ACIP (flu shot and other) recommendations, call 1-888-232-3228.**

▷ **These Drugs Should Not Be Taken If**
  • you have had an allergic reaction to them previously.

▷ **Inform Your Physician Before Taking This Drug If**
  • you have a history of kidney impairment (oseltamivir).
  • you have high-risk medical conditions (zanamivir).
  • you have a compromised immune system.
  • you have severe or decompensated ongoing and obstructive lung disease (COPD) or asthma (zanamivir).
  • you are pregnant (oseltamivir and zanamivir).

Possible Side Effects (natural, expected, and unavoidable drug actions)
  Not defined.

▷ **Possible Adverse Effects** (unusual, unexpected, and infrequent reactions)
   If any of the following develop, consult your physician promptly for guidance.
   Mild Adverse Effects
   Allergic reaction: Not defined.
   Headache, nervousness, irritability, inability to concentrate, insomnia—rare to infrequent (oseltamivir).
   Unsteadiness, dizziness—infrequent (oseltamivir).
   Loss of appetite, nausea, vomiting—infrequent to frequent (oseltamivir).
   Serious Adverse Effects
   Allergic reaction—toxic epidermal necrolysis (questionable causality— oseltamivir).
   Arrhythmia—causality not defined (oseltamivir).
   Aggravation of existing diabetes—case reports—causality not defined (oseltamivir).
   Bronchospasm/respiratory distress—reported for zanamivir and in people with underlying COPD or asthma.

▷ **Possible Effects on Sexual Function:** None reported.

Adverse Effects That May Mimic Natural Diseases or Disorders
   Not defined.

Natural Diseases or Disorders That May Be Activated by These Drugs
   Possible aggravation of diabetes and change in heart rhythm for oseltamivir, but of questionable causation. Underlying respiratory disease such as COPD or asthma may be associated with an increased risk of bronchospasm or decline in lung function (zanamivir).

Possible Effects on Laboratory Tests
   Not defined.

CAUTION
   1. These medicines may be very helpful for high-risk patients who are unable to prevent the flu with a shot and need to decrease the amount of time that they have the flu and also to decrease adverse outcomes from the flu.
   2. Zanamivir may not work in Chronic Obstructive Pulmonary Disease (COPD) and can pose a safety risk in asthmatics.

Precautions for Use
   By Infants and Children: Safety and effectiveness for those under 13 (oseltamivir) for prophylaxis have not been established. Prophylactic dosing: for those 13 or older is 75 mg daily for 7 days. Flu treatment: for oseltamivir: for children one year and older (must be started within 48 hours): based on body weight: For example—Less than 15 kg: 30 mg, twice daily for seven days. For influenza treatment using zanamivir: Dosing for those under 7 (zanamivir) not established. For those 7 or over, see adult dosing above. For prophylaxis: zanamivir is not FDA-approved.
   By Those Over 60 Years of Age: Special considerations not defined at present.

▷ **Advisability of Use During Pregnancy**
   Pregnancy Category: C for both medicines. See Pregnancy Risk Categories at the back of this book.
   Human Studies: Adequate studies of pregnant women (both drugs) are not available. Ask your doctor for help.

Advisability of Use If Breast-Feeding
Presence of this drug in breast milk: Yes in animals for oseltamivir; unknown for zanamivir.
Talk to your doctor about this benefit-to-risk decision.

Habit-Forming Potential: None.

Effects of Overdose: Single doses of roughly 1,000 mg of oseltamivir have resulted in vomiting. No data for zanamivir. Supportive care and contact of a poison control center are indicated for both medicines.

Possible Effects of Long-Term Use: Not defined.

Suggested Periodic Examinations While Taking This Drug (at physician's discretion)
Rapid influenza test.

▷ **While Taking This Drug, Observe the Following**
Foods: No restrictions.
Herbal Medicines or Minerals: Echinacea: Some patients use echinacea to attempt to boost their immune systems. Unfortunately, use of echinacea is not recommended in people with damaged immune systems. This herb may also actually weaken any immune system if it is used too often or for too long a time.
Beverages: No restrictions. May be taken with milk.
▷ *Alcohol:* No interactions expected.
Tobacco Smoking: No interactions expected, but smoking may further irritate airways. I advise everyone to quit smoking.
Marijuana Smoking: Added dizziness (oseltamivir).
▷ *Other Drugs*
Oseltamivir *taken concurrently* with
• Probenecid (various) may increase blood levels of oseltamivir, but adverse effects are not defined.
Zanamivir *taken concurrently* with
• other inhaled medicines has NOT been studied.
▷ *Driving, Hazardous Activities:* Oseltamivir may cause dizziness. Avoid hazardous activities until the extent of this effect is known.
Aviation Note: The use of this drug *may be a disqualification* for piloting. Consult a designated Aviation Medical Examiner.
Exposure to Sun: No restrictions.

NIACIN (NI a sin)

Other Names: Nicotinic acid, vitamin B3

Introduced: 1937   **Class:**   Anticholesterol, vasodilator   **Prescription:**
USA: tablets and liquid: No; capsules: Yes   **Controlled Drug:**   USA: No;
Canada: No   **Available as Generic:**   USA: Yes; Canada: Yes

Brand Names: ✤Antivert [CD], Endur-Acin, Niac, Niacels, Niacin SR, Niacin TR, Niacor, Niacor-B, Nia-Bid, Niaplus, Niaspan, Nicobid, Nico-400, Nicolar, Nicotinex, ✤Novoniacin, SK-Niacin, Slo-Niacin, Span-Niacin-150, Tega-Span, Tri-B3

Author's Note: Because of the ADVOCATE study and other data, the combination product Advicor (extended-release niacin/lovastatin has replaced the niacin profile.

NICARDIPINE (ni KAR de peen)

Introduced: 1984 **Class:** Antianginal, antihypertensive, calcium channel blocker **Prescription:** USA: Yes **Controlled Drug:** USA: No; Canada: No **Available as Generic:** USA: Yes

Brand Names: Cardene, Cardene SR

Controversies in Medicine: Medicines in this class have had many conflicting reports. The FDA has held hearings on the calcium channel blocker (CCB) class. Research at New York University found that nifedipine (a member of the same class) is a cause of reversible male infertility. CCBs are currently second-line agents for high blood pressure according to the JNC VII (see Glossary).

Author's Note: Information in this profile has been truncated in order to make room for more widely used medicines.

NICOTINE (NIK oh teen)

Introduced: 1992, 1996, 1997 **Class:** Smoking cessation adjunct, nicotine replacement therapy **Prescription:** USA: Both Nicorettes (2 mg and 4 mg) are now available without a prescription for those over 18 years old. Nicotine patches are FDA-approved for nonprescription use. The nicotine inhaler and nasal spray are only available with a prescription. **Controlled Drug:** USA: No; Canada: No **Available as Generic:** USA: Yes; Canada: Yes

Brand Names: Habitrol, Clear Nicoderm CQ, ✤Nicoderm, Nicorette, Nicorette DS, Nicotine Transdermal System, Nicotrol, Nicotrol Inhaler, Nicotrol NS, Prostep, Prostep Transdermal System

Author's Note: Representative Henry Waxman urged the halt of making and selling nicotine-containing lollipops in the United States. The lollipops (sold as NicoPop and Likatine) contained nicotine salicylate. They became an area of controversy, and the FDA declared them illegal on April 11, 2002. A new medicine is in trials called varenicline (see the Leading Edge section of this book) which works in a different way to help smokers quit smoking.

BENEFITS versus RISKS

Possible Benefits	*Possible Risks*
EFFECTIVE REDUCTION OF NICOTINE CRAVING AND WITHDRAWAL EFFECTS WHEN USED ADJUNCTIVELY IN SMOKING-CESSATION TREATMENT PROGRAMS	Aggravation of existing angina, heart rhythm disorders, hypertension, insulin-dependent diabetes, peptic ulcer, and vascular diseases Increased risk of abortion (if used during pregnancy)

▷ **Principal Uses**

As a Single Drug Product: Uses currently included in FDA-approved labeling: Nicotine chewing gum, nicotine transdermal systems, inhaler, and nasal spray are used adjunctively in behavior modification programs to help cig-arette smokers who wish to stop smoking.

Author's Note: The American Lung Association has an excellent resource called the "Quit Smoking Action Plan." If you are planning

to stop smoking (and I hope that you are), call them at 1-800-LUNG-USA (1-800-586-4872) or find them at the Web site listed in Table 17 at the back of this book. The American Heart Association guidelines for primary and secondary prevention of cardiovascular disease once again tell people that smoking is a risk factor for heart attacks and that you should immediately STOP. Visit *www.americanheart.org* for more information.

Other (unlabeled) generally accepted uses: (1) Gum and nasal spray have been used to increase nicotine levels in the blood and help ease sudden cravings; (2) a study using nicotine patches along with haloperidol (see drug profile) lead to better overall results in children with Tourette's syndrome compared to haloperidol alone (Yale Global Tic Severity Scale-YGTSS).

How This Drug Works: By providing an alternate source of nicotine (for nicotine-dependent smokers), the appropriate use of these drug products can reduce nicotine craving and lessen smoking withdrawal effects, such as irritability, nervousness, headache, fatigue, sleep disturbances, and drowsiness.

Available Dosage Forms and Strengths

> Inhaler (per cartridge) — 10 mg
> Nasal spray (10-ml bottle) — 10 mg/ml
> Nicotine chewing gum tablets — 2 mg (nonprescription)
> Nicorette (U.S., Canada) — 2 mg
> Nicorette (Canada) — 4 mg
> Nicorette DS (U.S., Canada) — 4 mg

Transdermal systems:

> 16-hour systems, U.S. only — 5 mg, 10 mg, 15 mg
> 24-hour systems — 7 mg (U.S., Canada), 11 mg (U.S.), 14 mg (U.S., Canada), 21 mg (U.S., Canada), 22 mg (U.S.)

How to Store

Store nicotine gum at room temperature and protect from light. Store nicotine patches at room temperature and be especially careful to avoid exposing the patches to temperatures greater than 86 degrees F. (30 degrees C.). Do not store unpouched. Once opened, patches should be used promptly because they may lose their strength.

▷ **Recommended Dosage Ranges** (Actual dose and schedule must be determined for each patient individually.)

Infants and Children: Avoid use completely in children. Avoid accidental exposure to patches.

18 to 60 Years of Age: For chewing gum tablets: Initially one piece every hour while awake (10 to 12 pieces daily); supplement with one additional piece if and when needed to control urge to smoke. Total daily dose should not exceed 30 pieces (60 mg).

For inhaler form: Dosing is divided into two parts (phases). At first (weeks one to 12), 6–16 cartridges a day. Dosing is individualized to control smoking urges, excess nicotine, or withdrawal. During the second phase (weeks 13-24), a quit date is set, patients are told to use the inhaler less often, and the dose is gradually decreased. Maximum daily dose is 16 cartridges. If a particular patient is not able to quit smoking after 4 weeks, treatment should be stopped, and a "break" (therapeutic holiday) given before another attempt to stop is made.

For nasal spray: Two sprays, one in each nostril. Starting dose is usually two to four sprays each hour. Dosing follows a 14-week pattern: In the weeks one to eight, one or two doses are used per hour and at least 8 doses daily. When weeks 9-14 are reached: dosing is gradually reduced (as in second phase of the inhaler form protocol). Maximum is 5 doses per hour (5 mg) and 40 doses per day (40 mg or 80 sprays).

For transdermal systems: Dose depends upon patient characteristics and product used:

For those weighing 100 lb. or more, smoking 10 or more cigarettes daily, and without cardiovascular disease: The 16-hour system (Nicotrol) is started with one 15-mg patch applied for 16 hours daily for 6 weeks. The patch is taken off at bedtime. The 24-hour system (Nicoderm CQ) is started with one 21-mg patch applied daily for weeks one to 6. For those who have abstained from smoking, reduce dose to one 14-mg patch daily for the next 2 weeks and then to one 7-mg patch daily for weeks 9-10.

For those weighing less than 100 lb. smoking less than 10 cigarettes daily, or with cardiovascular disease: The 24-hour system (Habitrol) is started with one 14-mg patch applied daily for 1 to 6 weeks. For those who have abstained from smoking, reduce dose to one 7-mg patch daily for the next 2 weeks.

Over 60 Years of Age: Same as 12 to 60 years of age in those without diseases that pose as risk factors (such as cardiovascular problems—see cautions).

Conditions Requiring Dosing Adjustments

Liver Function: Lower starting doses are prudent in liver disease.

Kidney Function: Doses are decreased in severe kidney compromise.

Cardiovascular Disease: See above.

▷ **Dosing Instructions:** Carefully follow the manufacturer's directions provided with each product.

For Chewing Gum: Limit use to one piece of gum at a time. While it is called gum, it is much harder than typical chewing gum. Be careful of any dental work that you should not put much pressure on. Chew each piece slowly and intermittently for 30 minutes. A tingling of your gum tissue or peppery taste means the nicotine is being released. Try to gradually reduce the number of pieces chewed each day by using it only when there is an urge to smoke. When trying to quit smoking, always have the gum available.

For Transdermal Systems: Apply a new patch at the same time each day. Do not alter the patch in any way. Apply the patch to the upper arm or body where the skin is clean, dry, and free of hair, oil, scars, and irritation of any kind; alternate sites of application. Press the patch firmly in place for 10 seconds; ensure good contact throughout. Wash your hands when you have finished applying the patch. Replace patches that are dislodged by showering, bathing, or swimming.

For Spray: DO NOT swallow, inhale, or sniff when spraying the spray. The nasal route may best mimic the effect of using a cigarette to deliver nicotine.

For the Inhaler: Follow the patient package insert exactly. Make sure you understand how to use this product.

For All: If you can't quit by the fourth week, treatment should be stopped. It's best to have a therapeutic holiday before trying to quit again.

If you Forget a Dose: Take the missed dose as soon as you remember it, unless it's nearly time for your next dose—if that is the case, skip the missed dose and take the next dose right on schedule. DO NOT double doses. Talk with your doctor if you find yourself missing doses.

Usual Duration of Use: Use on a regular schedule as described above determines effectiveness in achieving lasting cessation of smoking. Nicotine chewing gum should not be used for more than 6 months; transdermal systems, nasal spray, and inhaler form are used according to the guidelines (protocols) on page 803. It's smart to involve your family and friends to help in this difficult process. Use of the prescription forms requires periodic physician evaluation of response and dose adjustment. It's smart to involve your doctor in the use and selection for the nonprescription forms as well.

Typical Treatment Goals and Measurements (Outcomes and Markers)

Smoking Cessation: The goal is to ease or eliminate signs or symptoms of tobacco withdrawal, encouraging patients to stop smoking. Replacing the nicotine that smokers previously received from tobacco products avoids the life-threatening by-products of tobacco smoke while replacing the chemical that a smoker has become addicted to. Once the replacement has occurred, the patch, nasal inhalation, or inhaled nicotine dose can be gradually decreased, and then replacement stopped altogether.

Author's Note: There are NO DATA to show that smoking is good for you. Please make every effort to stop. I firmly believe that my father would be alive today if he had been able to stop smoking. A study in Iceland (Iceland has an abundance of genetic and family data) found that combining two methods of nicotine replacement (such as a patch and the spray) worked better than using a single method. The American Lung Association has a Quit Smoking Action Plan that can be very helpful. Find them on the web at *www.lungusa.org*. Once again—-please involve your friends, family, pharmacist, and doctor in this critical effort to quit. Be persistent—you can do it!

Possible Advantages of These Drugs

Provides control and flexibility of gradual nicotine withdrawal for use in supervised smoking-cessation programs. Avoids the possible cancer causing components- "excipients" of cigarette smoke.

Currently a "Drug of Choice"

For people who are motivated to stop smoking. Since many forms are now available without a prescription, be sure to talk with your doctor or pharmacist about how to best use these medicines. Many pharmacists also offer programs to help you quit.

▷ **This Drug Should Not Be Taken If**
- you had an allergic reaction to any form of it previously or to any of the ingredients in the dosage form (read the label carefully).
- you have severe or uncontrolled or a pattern of worsening angina (physician's discretion)
- you keep smoking or using other tobacco products (yes, chewing tobacco or tobacco pouches count—in general if it is a product that has nicotine—it should be stopped).
- you have uncontrolled, life-threatening heart rhythm disorders.
- you have had a recent heart attack.

▷ **Inform Your Physician Before Taking This Drug If**
- you have any form of angina (coronary heart disease).
- you have had a heart attack at any time.
- you are subject to heart rhythm disorders.
- you have insulin-dependent diabetes.
- you have hypertension (high blood pressure).
- you have hyperthyroidism (overactive thyroid function).

- you have a pheochromocytoma (adrenaline-producing tumor).
- you have a history of esophagitis or peptic ulcer disease.
- you have a history of Buerger's disease or Raynaud's phenomenon.
- you currently have any dental problems or skin disorders.
- you have a history of kidney or liver disease.
- you have an increase in cardiovascular effects while you are taking this medicine.
- you have already taken a 3-month course of the patch.
- you use birth control pills (oral contraceptives).
- you think you are pregnant or plan to become pregnant.
- you are unsure how much to take or how often to take this medicine.

Possible Side Effects (natural, expected, and unavoidable drug actions)

Increased blood pressure.

For chewing gum: mouth or throat irritation; injury to teeth or dental repairs.

For transdermal systems: redness, itching, or burning at site of application (mild and transient).

For nasal spray: runny nose, nasal irritation.

For inhaler: coughing and nose irritation—frequent.

▷ **Possible Adverse Effects** (unusual, unexpected, and infrequent reactions)

If any of the following develop, consult your physician promptly for guidance.

Mild Adverse Effects

Allergic reactions: skin rash, hives, itching, local or generalized swellings.

Headache, light-headedness, dizziness, drowsiness, irritability, nervousness, insomnia, joint pain, muscle aches, abnormal dreams—possible to infrequent and some may be dose-related.

Rapid heartbeat, palpitation, increased sweating—infrequent to frequent, dose-related.

Increased or decreased appetite, nausea, dry mouth, indigestion, constipation, or diarrhea—infrequent.

Serious Adverse Effects

Irregular heart rhythms, chest pain (angina), edema—infrequent.

Stroke—case report.

Depression—case report.

Worsening of myasthenia gravis—case report.

Heart attack—related in time, but of inconclusive cause.

See Effects of Overdose on page 807.

▷ **Possible Effects on Sexual Function:** There are some data questioning an effect on sperm (diminished penetration), but a distinct demonstration of an effect is lacking.

Natural Diseases or Disorders That May Be Activated by This Drug

Latent angina, atrial fibrillation, hypertension, peptic ulcer disease, temporomandibular joint (TMJ) disorder (by chewing gum).

Possible Effects on Laboratory Tests

Free fatty acids (FFA blood level): increased.

Blood glucose: increased.

Prothrombin time (INR): decreased.

Urine screening test for drug abuse: no effect.

CAUTION

1. For these drug products to be safe and effective, it is mandatory that all smoking be stopped immediately at the beginning of drug treatment.

2. Extended use of chewing gum may cause damage to mouth tissues and teeth, loosen fillings, stick to dentures, and initiate or aggravate TMJ dysfunction.

3. Smoking cessation and the use of these drug products can result in increased blood levels of insulin (in insulin-dependent diabetics); dose reduction of insulin may be necessary to prevent hypoglycemic reactions.

4. If you are taking any of the following drugs, consult your physician regarding the need to reduce their dose while participating in a smoking-cessation program: aminophylline, beta-blocker drugs, imipramine, oxazepam, oxtriphylline, pentazocine, prazosin, propoxyphene, theophylline.

5. If you are taking any of the following drugs, consult your physician regarding the need to increase their dose while participating in a smoking-cessation program: isoproterenol, phenylephrine.

6. Used patches should be folded in half with the adhesive sides sealed together; place them in the original pouch or aluminum foil and dispose of them promptly; keep out of reach of animals and children.

7. Use of antacids, such as Tums, prior to chewing nicotine gum can increase the amount of nicotine absorbed from the gum.

8. Patches have improved benefits when they are part of a complete smoking-cessation program that includes counseling.

9. The Centers for Disease Control (CDC) has many excellent publications available to give you more information on stopping smoking. Call 1-800-232-1311 for more information.

10. The possibility of becoming dependent on these replacement products also exists. The chance of this happening may be greater for the nasal spray than for the transdermal or "gum" products.

Precautions for Use

By Infants and Children: Safety and effectiveness for those under 12 years of age are not established for the gum, and for those under 18 not established for other forms.

By Those Over 60 Years of Age: Because of the increased possibility of cardiovascular disorders in this age group, treatment should be cautiously started. Watch closely for adverse effects.

▷ **Advisability of Use During Pregnancy**

Pregnancy Category: For nicotine chewing gum: C. For nicotine transdermal systems, nasal spray, and inhaler: D. See Pregnancy Risk Categories at the back of this book.

Animal Studies: Impaired fertility found in mouse, rat, and rabbit studies. Birth defects found in high-dose studies of mice.

Human Studies: Adequate studies of pregnant women are not available, but it is known that cigarette smoking during pregnancy may cause low birth weight, increased risk of abortion, and increased risk of newborn death.

The use of these drug products is not recommended during pregnancy.

Advisability of Use If Breast-Feeding

Presence of this drug in breast milk: Yes.

Avoid drug or refrain from nursing.

Habit-Forming Potential: The prolonged use of these drug products may perpetuate the physical dependence of nicotine-dependent smokers. Patches should have the lowest potential for dependence. Potential exists for abuse of nonprescription forms of this medicine.

Effects of Overdose: Nausea, vomiting, increased salivation, stomach cramps, diarrhea, headache, dizziness, impaired vision and hearing, weakness, confusion, fainting, difficult breathing, seizures.

Possible Effects of Long-Term Use: If not slowly lowered in dose, perpetuation of nicotine dependence.

Suggested Periodic Examinations While Taking This Drug (at physician's discretion)
Evaluation of patient's ability to abstain from smoking.
Evaluation of patient's blood pressure and heart function.

▷ **While Taking This Drug, Observe the Following**
Foods: Avoid any food with a nicotine content.
Herbal Medicines or Minerals: Using ephedra, ma huang, guarana, kola, or similar products may accentuate nervousness and anxiety people have when trying to quit smoking. Talk to your doctor BEFORE combining any herbal medicine with nicotine.
Beverages: No restrictions.
▷ *Alcohol:* May cause an increase in heart and blood vessel (cardiovascular) effects.
Tobacco Smoking: Avoid all forms of tobacco completely.
Marijuana Smoking: Avoid completely.
▷ *Other Drugs*
Nicotine may *increase* the effects of
• adenosine.
The following drugs may **increase** the effects of nicotine:
• antacids such as Tums used prior to chewing nicotine-containing gum—may increase the absorption of nicotine from the gum.
• cimetidine (Tagamet).
• lithium (Lithobid).
• ranitidine (Zantac).
Nicotine *taken concurrently* with
• niacin (Nicobid, others) can cause severe facial flushing.
▷ *Driving, Hazardous Activities:* This drug may cause dizziness or drowsiness. Restrict activities as necessary.
Aviation Note: The use of this drug *may be a disqualification* for piloting. Consult a designated Aviation Medical Examiner.
Exposure to Sun: No restrictions.
Exposure to Cold: Use caution until tolerance is determined. Cold environments may enhance the vasospastic action of nicotine.
Heavy Exercise or Exertion: Patients with angina, coronary artery disease, or hypertension should use this drug with caution.
Special Storage Instructions: Store nicotine gum at room temperature and protect from light. Store nicotine patches at room temperature, and be especially careful to avoid exposing the patches to temperatures greater than 86 degrees F. (30 degrees C.). Do not store unpouched. Once opened, patches should be used promptly because they may lose their strength.
Discontinuation: As soon as a lasting cessation of smoking has been achieved, these drugs should be gradually reduced in dose and then discontinued. Continual use of the chewing gum or inhaler should not exceed 6 months, the nasal spray form no longer than 3 months, and the transdermal system no more than 20 weeks.

NIFEDIPINE (ni FED i peen)

Introduced: 1972 **Class:** Antianginal, antihypertensive, calcium channel blocker **Prescription:** USA: Yes **Controlled Drug:** USA: No; Canada: No **Available as Generic:** Yes

Brand Names: Adalat, Adalat CC, ✦Adalat FT, XL, ✦Adalat P.A., ✦Apo-Nifed, ✦Gen-Nifedipine, ✦Novo-Nifedin, ✦Nu-Nifed, Procardia, Procardia XL, ✦Scheinpharm Nifedipine XL

Controversies in Medicine: Medicines in this class have had many conflicting reports. The FDA has held hearings on the calcium channel blocker (CCB) class. Research at New York University found that nifedipine is a cause of reversible male infertility. CCBs are currently second-line agents for high blood pressure according to the JNC VII (see Glossary).

BENEFITS versus RISKS

Possible Benefits	*Possible Risks*
EFFECTIVE PREVENTION OF CLASSICAL ANGINA OF EFFORT AND OTHER ANGINA TYPES	Rare increase in angina upon starting treatment
SECOND-LINE TREATMENT OF HYPERTENSION (sustained-release form)	Rare precipitation of congestive heart failure
NIFEDIPINE CR FORM MAY HELP AVOID A MORNING SURGE IN BLOOD PRESSURE IF IT IS TAKEN RIGHT AFTER YOU WAKE UP	Rare anemia and low white blood cell counts
	Very rare drug-induced hepatitis
	Fainting

▷ **Principal Uses**

As a Single Drug Product: Uses currently included in FDA-approved labeling: Treats (1) angina pectoris due to coronary artery spasm (Prinzmetal's variant angina) that occurs spontaneously and is not associated with exertion; (2) classical angina of effort (due to atherosclerotic disease of the coronary arteries) in people who have not responded to or cannot tolerate the nitrates and beta-blocker drugs customarily used to treat this disorder (sustained-release form); (3) mild to moderate hypertension (extended-release forms).

Author's Note: A chart review found the immediate-release form of this medicine IS NOT recommended for use in treating hypertension, heart attack, hypertensive crisis, and acute coronary syndrome. This lead to FDA label changes (see below).

Other (unlabeled) generally accepted uses: (1) Treats symptoms of Raynaud's phenomenon; (2) may stop some early atherosclerosis; (3) can have a role in treating pulmonary hypertension; (4) helps decrease risk of heart attack after coronary artery bypass grafting; (5) could have a role in some neurologically based pain disorders; (6) can help itching (urticaria) of unknown cause; (7) therapy of achalasia or esophageal spasm; (8) helps intractable hiccups; (9) helps amaurosis fugax; (10) helps abnormal reactions to cold (chilblains).

How This Drug Works: Blocks passage of calcium through certain cell walls (needed for nerve and muscle tissue function), slowing electrical activity through the heart (post excitation phase) and inhibits contraction of coronary arteries and peripheral arterioles. As a result:

- prevents spontaneous spasm of coronary arteries (Prinzmetal's angina).
- reduces heart rate and force during exertion, decreasing oxygen needs of heart muscle and reducing occurrence of effort-induced angina (classical angina pectoris).
- reduces the degree of contraction of peripheral arterial walls, lowering blood pressure. This further reduces the work of the heart during exertion and helps prevent angina.

Some data has shown that this medicine helps red blood cells bend (RBC deformability) by decreasing the amount of calcium in the red cells.

Author's Note: One study found that nifedipine restored the function of the lining of blood vessels (endothelium).

Available Dosage Forms and Strengths

Capsules — 5 mg (Canada), 10 mg (U.S. and Canada), 20 mg (U.S.)

Tablets — 10 mg, 20 mg (Canada)

Tablets, extended-release — 10 mg, 20 mg (Canada), 30 mg, 60 mg, 90 mg (U.S.)

Tablets, sustained-release — 30 mg, 60 mg, 90 mg

▷ **Recommended Dosage Ranges** (Actual dose and schedule must be determined for each patient individually.)

Infants and Children: Dose not established.

Adults up to 60 Years of Age: Chronic stable angina or vasospastic (Prinzmetal's) angina: Immediate-release form: Dosing is started with 10 mg three times a day. Most people respond to 10–20 mg three times a day. Change to extended-release forms can be accomplished on a same dose to same dose (mg to mg) basis. *Extended-release form for high blood pressure:* Initially 30 mg once daily. Dose may be increased gradually at 7- to 14-day intervals (as needed and tolerated) up to 60 mg. Maximum total daily dose should not exceed 90 mg.

Sublingual for hypertensive crisis: **FDA labeling for the immediate-release form of this medicine says that it is NOT recommended for use in treating acute hypertensive crisis, ongoing (chronic) hypertension, acute myocardial infarction (heart attack), and acute coronary syndrome.**

Over 60 Years of Age: **Nifedipine immediate-release capsules have revised FDA labeling recommendations against use in people with acute coronary syndrome, heart attack (acute myocardial infarction), hypertensive crisis and ongoing (chronic) hypertension. Use of the immediate-release form by those over 71 has been associated with almost a fourfold increase in risk for all-cause death when compared to ACE inhibitors, beta blockers, or other calcium channel blockers. Extended-release tablets adjusted between 10–20 mg twice daily gave significant response rate in that group.**

Conditions Requiring Dosing Adjustments

Liver Function: Lower doses are prudent in liver disease. This drug is also a rare cause of liver toxicity (allergic hepatitis) and should be used with caution. Also a potential cause of portal hypertension and should NOT be used by patients with portal hypertension.

Kidney Function: For patients with compromised kidneys, nifedipine is a benefit-to-risk decision, as it can lead to kidney toxicity.

▷ **Dosing Instructions:** May be taken with or following food to reduce stomach irritation. Take this medicine with water. DO NOT take this medicine with grapefruit juice or eat grapefruit while you are taking this medicine. The capsule and the sustained-release tablet should be swallowed whole (not altered). DO NOT be frightened if you see part of the tablet in your stools—while it looks like something wrong happened, the form that you see is simply what remains after your body has taken out all the medicine. As with other medicines, it is critical to take the right dose, right on time. One study found that the nifedipine CR form helped prevent a surge in blood pressure if it was taken right after the patients woke up. Talk to your doctor about this. If you forget a dose: Take the missed dose as soon as you remember it, unless it's nearly time for your next dose—if that is the case, skip the missed dose and take the next dose right on schedule. DON'T take two doses at the same time. Talk with your doctor if you find yourself missing doses.

Usual Duration of Use: Use on a regular schedule for 2 to 4 weeks determines effectiveness in reducing the frequency and severity of angina and in controlling hypertension. For long-term use (months to years), the smallest effective dose should be used. Supervision and periodic physician evaluation are essential.

Typical Treatment Goals and Measurements (Outcomes and Markers)

Blood Pressure The NEW guidelines (JNC VII) define normal blood pressure (BP) as **less than** 120/80. Because blood pressures that were once considered acceptable can actually lead to blood vessel damage, the committee from the National Institutes of Health, National Heart Lung and Blood Institute now have a new category called **Pre-hypertension**. This ranges from 120/80 to 139/89 and is intended to help your doctor encourage lifestyle changes (or in the case of people with a risk factor for high blood pressure, start treatment) much earlier—so that possible damage to blood vessels, your heart, kidneys, sexual potency, or eyes might be minimized or avoided altogether. The next two classes of high blood pressure are stage 1 hypertension: 140/90 to 159/99 and stage 2 hypertension equal to or greater than: 160/100 mm Hg. These guidelines also recommend that clinicians trying to control blood pressure work with their patients to agree on the goals and a plan of treatment. The first-ever guidelines for blood pressure (hypertension) in African Americans recommends that MOST black patients be started on TWO antihypertensive medicines with the goal of lowering blood pressure to 130/80 for those with high risk for heart and blood vessel disease or with diabetes. The American Diabetes Association recommends 130/80 as the target for people living with diabetes and less than 125/75 for those who spill more than one gram of protein into their urine. Most clinicians try to achieve a BP that confers the best balance of lower cardiovascular risk and avoids the problem of too low a blood pressure. Blood pressure duration is generally increased with beneficial restriction of sodium. The goals and time frame should be discussed with you when the prescription is written. If goals are not met, it is not unusual to intensify doses or add on medicines. You can find the new blood pressure guidelines at *www.nhlbi.nih.gov/guidelines/hypertension/index.htm*. For the African American guidelines see Douglas J.G. in Sources.

Possible Advantages of This Drug

The sustained-release form offers effective once-a-day treatment for both angina and hypertension. Little or no effect on depressing the SA or AV node of the heart. Greater effect as a peripheral vasodilator than others.

▷ **This Drug Should Not Be Taken If**
- you have had an allergic reaction to it previously.
- you have active liver disease or had a heart attack in the last month.
- you are over 71 and have been prescribed the immediate-release form of nifedipine.
- you have low blood pressure—systolic pressure below 90—or you have had a heart attack in the last 4 weeks.
- you have significant narrowing of your aorta (aortic stenosis). Ask your doctor.
- you have been prescribed nifedipine immediate-release capsules and have acute coronary syndrome, heart attack (acute myocardial infarction), hypertensive crisis, and ongoing hypertension. Ask your doctor.

▷ **Inform Your Physician Before Taking This Drug If**
- you had an adverse response to any calcium channel blocker.
- you take any form of digitalis or a beta blocker (see Drug Classes).
- you are taking any drugs that lower blood pressure.
- you have a history of congestive heart failure, heart attack, or stroke.
- you are subject to disturbances of heart rhythm.
- you have cardiomyopathy (nonobstructive) or aortic stenosis.
- you have impaired liver or kidney function.
- you have abnormal circulation to your fingers.
- you have atrial fibrillation.
- you develop a skin condition while taking this medicine.
- you have diabetes or Duchenne muscular dystrophy.
- you have a history of drug-induced liver damage.

Possible Side Effects (natural, expected, and unavoidable drug actions)

Low blood pressure, rapid heart rate, swelling of the feet and ankles, flushing and sensation of warmth, sweating.

▷ **Possible Adverse Effects:** (unusual, unexpected, and infrequent reactions)

If any of the following develop, consult your physician promptly for guidance.

Mild Adverse Effects

Allergic reactions: skin rash, hives, itching, fever.

Headache, dizziness, weakness, nervousness, blurred vision, eye pain, or swelling around eyes—infrequent.

Pedal edema—frequent.

Depression—rare.

Abnormal growth of the gums (gingival hyperplasia)—rare.

Taste disturbances—possible.

Ringing in the ears (tinnitus)—case reports.

Sleep disturbances or bedwetting—case reports.

Increased or decreased blood potassium—possible.

Palpitation, shortness of breath, wheezing, cough—infrequent.

Impaired sense of smell—possible.

Heartburn, nausea, taste disturbances, cramps, diarrhea—rare.

Tremors, muscle cramps—possible.

Serious Adverse Effects

Allergic reaction: drug-induced hepatitis—very rare; drug eruptions and erysipelaslike reactions and exfoliative dermatitis or erythema multiforme.

Idiosyncratic reactions: joint stiffness and inflammation.

Increased frequency or severity of angina on initiation of treatment following an increase in dose.

Abnormal muscle movements (myoclonus)—case reports.

Kidney toxicity or pulmonary edema—case reports.
Bezoars—rare (seen with sustained-release forms).
Acute psychosis—case report.
Worsening of circulation to the fingers—possible.
Marked drop in blood pressure with fainting—possible.
Low white blood cells, platelets, and hemoglobin—case reports.

▷ **Possible Effects on Sexual Function:** Altered timing and pattern of menstruation; excessive menstrual bleeding. Tenderness and swelling of male breast tissue (gynecomastia)—case reports.

▷ **Adverse Effects That May Mimic Natural Diseases or Disorders**
Allergic rash and swelling of the legs may resemble erysipelas. Drug-induced hepatitis may suggest viral hepatitis. Transient increases in liver function tests may suggest infectious hepatitis.

Possible Effects on Laboratory Tests
Bleeding time: increased.
Liver function tests: transient increases.
Blood total cholesterol level: no effect in those under 60 years old; decreased in those over 60 years old.
Blood HDL cholesterol level: no effect or lowered slightly.
Blood LDL and VLDL cholesterol levels: no effect.
Blood triglyceride levels: no effect or decreased.

CAUTION
1. Tell health care providers that you take this drug. Note nifedipine use on a card in your purse or wallet.
2. You may use nitroglycerin and other nitrate drugs as needed to relieve acute angina pain. If angina attacks become more frequent or intense, call your doctor.
3. Nifedipine immediate-release capsules have revised FDA labeling recommendations against use in people with acute coronary syndrome, heart attack (acute myocardial infarction), hypertensive crisis, and ongoing hypertension. Use of the immediate-release form by those over 71 has been associated with almost a fourfold increase in risk for all-cause death when compared to ACE inhibitors, beta blockers, or other calcium channel blockers.

Precautions for Use
By Infants and Children: Safety and effectiveness for those under 12 years of age are not established.
By Those Over 60 Years of Age: You may be more susceptible to the development of weakness, dizziness, fainting, and falling. Take necessary precautions to prevent injury. Report promptly any changes in your pattern of thirst and urination.

▷ **Advisability of Use During Pregnancy**
Pregnancy Category: C. See Pregnancy Risk Categories at the back of this book.
Animal Studies: Embryo and fetal deaths reported in mice, rats, and rabbits; birth defects reported in rats.
Human Studies: Adequate studies of pregnant women are not available.
Avoid this drug during the first 3 months. Use during the final 6 months only if clearly needed. Ask your physician for guidance.

Advisability of Use If Breast-Feeding
Presence of this drug in breast milk: Yes.
Avoid drug or refrain from nursing.

Habit-Forming Potential: None.

Effects of Overdose: Weakness, light-headedness, fainting, fast pulse, low blood pressure, shortness of breath, flushed and warm skin, tremors.

Possible Effects of Long-Term Use: None reported.

Suggested Periodic Examinations While Taking This Drug (at physician's discretion)

Evaluations of heart function, including electrocardiograms.

Measurements of blood pressure in supine, sitting, and standing positions.

▷ **While Taking This Drug, Observe the Following**

Foods: Do not eat grapefruit while you are taking this medicine. It is also prudent to avoid excessive salt intake.

Herbal Medicines or Minerals: Valerian and kava kava (no longer recommended in Canada) may intensify drowsiness. Dong quai may make nifedipine stay in the body longer than expected while St. John's wort may increase removal of this medicine from the body, blunting the benefit of this medicine (also increases sun sensitivity). Ginseng, guarana, hawthorn, saw palmetto, ma huang (do not take if hypertensive), goldenseal, yohimbe, and licorice may also increase blood pressure. Calcium and garlic may help lower blood pressure and could be part of complementary care. Use of calcium to excess (7.5 to 10 grams) with combination thiazide diuretics can lead to excessive calcium levels. Talk to your doctor about how much calcium to take. Indian snakeroot has a German Commission E monograph indication for hypertension—talk to your doctor. Eleuthero root and ephedra should be avoided by people living with hypertension.

Beverages: Grapefruit juice may greatly increase the absorption (bioavailability) of nifedipine and result in an exaggerated therapeutic effect. Water is the best liquid to take this medicine with. May be taken with milk.

▷ *Alcohol:* Use with caution. Alcohol may exaggerate the drop in blood pressure experienced by some people.

Tobacco Smoking: Nicotine may reduce the effectiveness of this drug. I advise everyone to quit smoking.

Marijuana Smoking: Possible reduced effectiveness of this drug; mild to moderate increase in angina; possible changes in electrocardiogram, confusing interpretation.

▷ *Other Drugs*

Nifedipine *taken* **concurrently** with

• amiodarone (Cordarone) may cause the heart to stop.

• beta-blocker drugs or digitalis preparations (see Drug Classes) may affect heart rate and rhythm adversely; careful monitoring by your physician is necessary if these drugs are taken concurrently.

• cyclosporine (Sandimmune) can lead to nifedipine toxicity.

• digoxin (Lanoxin) may lead to digoxin toxicity.

• diltiazem (Cardizem) may lead to nifedipine toxicity.

• magnesium can cause additive lowering of the blood pressure.

• oral blood thinners (anticoagulant drugs–see Drug Classes) may increase risk of bleeding.

• oral antidiabetic drugs (see Drug Classes) or insulin may result in loss of glucose control.

• phenytoin (Dilantin) or fosphenytoin (Cerebyx) can cause phenytoin or fosphenytoin toxicity.

• quinupristin/dalfopristin (Synercid) can cause nifedipine toxicity.

• rifampin (Rifadin) can decrease nifedipine's effectiveness.

- tacrolimus (Prograf) may lead to tacrolimus toxicity.
- theophylline can reduce the therapeutic benefits of nifedipine and may lead to theophylline toxicity as well.
- vincristine (Oncovin) can cause vincristine toxicity.

The following drugs may *increase* the effects of nifedipine:

- some antifungals (fluconazole, itraconazole, ketoconazole, and voriconazole)—may increase nifedipine blood levels and lead to toxicity.
- cimetidine (Tagamet).
- quinidine (Quinaglute, others)—can lead to nifedipine toxicity as well as decreased quinidine effectiveness.
- ranitidine (Zantac).
- ritonavir (Norvir) and other protease inhibitors (such as amprenavir which is also removed by the same liver enzyme).

▷ *Driving, Hazardous Activities:* Usually no restrictions. This drug may cause drowsiness or dizziness. Restrict activities as necessary.

Aviation Note: Coronary artery disease *is a disqualification* for piloting. Consult a designated Aviation Medical Examiner.

Exposure to Sun: Caution—rare cases of phototoxicity have been reported.

Exposure to Heat: Caution is advised. Hot environments can exaggerate the blood pressure–lowering effects of this drug. Observe for light-headedness or weakness.

Heavy Exercise or Exertion: This drug may improve your ability to be more active without resulting angina pain. Use caution and avoid excessive exercise that could impair heart function in the absence of warning pain.

Discontinuation: Do not stop this drug abruptly. Consult your physician regarding gradual withdrawal. Observe for the possible development of rebound angina.

NISOLDIPINE (ni SOLD i peen)

Introduced: 1996 **Class:** Antianginal, antihypertensive, calcium channel blocker **Prescription:** USA: Yes **Controlled Drug:** USA: No; Canada: No **Available as Generic:** No

Brand Name: Sular

Author's Note: Information in this profile will be broadened in subsequent editions if data warrant.

NITROGLYCERIN (ni troh GLIS er in)

Introduced: 1847 **Class:** Antianginal, nitrates **Prescription:** USA: Yes **Controlled Drug:** USA: No; Canada: No **Available as Generic:** Yes

Brand Names: Corobid, Deponit, Minitran Transdermal Delivery System, Nitrek, Nitro-Bid, Nitrocap TD, Nitrocine Timecaps, Nitrocine Transdermal, Nitrodisc, Nitro-Dur, Nitro-Dur II, Nitrogard, ✤Nitrogard-SR, Nitroglyn, Nitrol, Nitrolin, Nitrolingual Spray, ✤Nitrol TSAR Kit, Nitrong, ✤Nitrong SR, Nitroquick, Nitrospan, ✤Nitrostabilin, Nitrostat, Nitro Transdermal System, NTS Transdermal Patch, Transderm-Nitro, ✤Trates S.R., Tridil

BENEFITS versus RISKS	
Possible Benefits	*Possible Risks*
EFFECTIVE RELIEF AND PREVENTION OF ANGINA	Orthostatic hypotension with and without fainting
EFFECTIVE ADJUNCTIVE TREATMENT IN SELECTED CASES OF CONGESTIVE HEART FAILURE	Skin rash—rare
	Altered hemoglobin with large doses—very rare
	Low blood platelets—rare

▷ **Principal Uses**

As a Single Drug Product: Uses currently included in FDA-approved labeling: (1) Treats symptomatic coronary artery disease (rapid-action forms are used to relieve acute attacks of anginal pain; sustained-action forms prevent development of angina, translingual spray is used in acute treatment and acute prevention); (2) helps improve breathing difficulty caused by heart failure (left ventricle); (3) intravenous form used in surgery to control blood pressure; (4) relieves congestive heart failure after heart attacks.

Other (unlabeled) generally accepted uses: (1) May help ease spasms of the Oddi's sphincter; (2) topical use may help in impotence; (3) can help reduce the extent of heart damage if given following a heart attack (myocardial infarction); (4) helps relax cocaine-constricted heart arteries; (5) eases the pain of peripheral neuropathy; (6) may be of help in easing esophageal problems (achalasia); (7) when the anal sphincter does not work correctly, this drug can help reduce the muscle pressure and ease constipation; (8) nitroglycerin in combination with vasopressin may be of use in stopping bleeding esophageal varices; (9) can help loss of vision that has been caused by a clot in the retinal artery; (10) if ergot medications (see Drug Classes) have shut down circulation to the extremities, nitroglycerin can open up the circulation; (11) used to delay contractions in order to rotate an abnormally positioned fetus; (12) may help diabetics with nerve damage (diabetic neuropathy); (13) helps relax the uterus when the placenta has been retained; (14) relaxes the uterus in cases where a fetus's head is trapped or there is a second fetus.

How This Drug Works: Relaxes and dilates both arteries and veins. Beneficial effects in angina are due to (1) dilation of narrowed coronary arteries and (2) dilation of veins in the general circulation, with reduced volume and pressure of blood entering the heart. Net effects are improved blood supply to the heart and reduced work for the heart. Both actions reduce the frequency and severity of angina.

Available Dosage Forms and Strengths

Canisters, translingual spray — 13.8 g (200 doses), 0.4 mg per metered dose

Capsules, prolonged-action — 2.5 mg, 2.6 mg, 6.5 mg, 9 mg

Ointment — 2%

Tablets, buccal — 1 mg, 2 mg, 3 mg

Tablets, prolonged-action — 2.6 mg, 6.5 mg, 9 mg

Tablets, sublingual — 0.15 mg, 0.3 mg, 0.4 mg, 0.6 mg

Transdermal systems (all per 24 hours) — 2.5 mg, 5 mg, 7.5 mg, 10 mg, 15 mg

▷ **Usual Adult Dosage Ranges:** Translingual spray—one or two metered sprays (0.4 mg) under the tongue every 3 to 5 minutes, up to three doses within 15 minutes, to relieve acute angina. To prevent angina, one spray taken 5 to 10 minutes before exertion.

Sublingual tablets — 0.15 to 0.6 mg (150 to 600 mcg) dissolved under tongue at 5-minute intervals to relieve acute angina. Up to three doses can be taken. One tablet can be taken 5–10 minutes BEFORE you participate in an activity that may cause angina in order to try to prevent an attack.

Prolonged-action tablets — 2.5 mg at 6- to 8-hour intervals to prevent angina. Many clinicians give a 6- to 12-hour nitrate-free interval when using this dosage form.

Ointment — 0.5 inch or 7.5 mg applied in a thin, even layer of uniform size to hairless skin at 3- to 4-hour intervals to prevent angina. A 10- to 12-hour ointment-free interval is recommended by some clinicians to avoid tolerance.

Buccal tablets — 1 to 2 mg every 4 to 5 hours, placed between cheek and gum.

Transdermal patches — 5-square-cm to 30-square-cm patch applied to hairless skin once every 24 hours (with a 10- to 12-hour nitrate-free interval to avoid tolerance) when used to prevent angina.

Translingual spray: Once an angina attack starts, one to two metered doses are sprayed under or onto the tongue. Like other immediate-onset forms, repeat doses can be given. Repeat doses can be given every 3-5 minutes for Nitrolingual. No more than three doses should be used in a 15-minute period. Prevention: (Prophylaxis): The spray is used 5-10 minutes prior to a patient activity which might lead to an attack of angina.

Note: Actual dose and schedule must be determined for each patient individually.

Author's Note: In order to avoid tolerance to the therapeutic effects of this medicine, a nitrate-free interval of 10–12 hours daily is recommended: 24-hour patches are removed after having been applied for 12 hours; dosing of ointment is interrupted for 12 hours a day; oral sustained-release formulations are dosed to give a 6- to 12-hour nitrate-free interval.

Conditions Requiring Dosing Adjustments

Liver Function: Specific dose adjustments in liver compromise are not defined.

Kidney Function: Specific guidelines for dosing changes are not available. This drug can discolor urine.

▷ **Dosing Instructions:** Dosage forms to be swallowed are best taken when stomach is empty (1 hour before or 2 hours after eating) to obtain maximal blood levels. Tablets should not be crushed. Under the tongue tablets (sublingual): Please sit down before you take this medicine, then place the tablet in your mouth and wet it with saliva. After this, move the tablet under your tongue or in your cheek and let it dissolve there. Avoid chewing or swallowing the tablet whole. It's not unusual to feel a tingle or even a burning sensation in your mouth when this medicine dissolves. Capsules may be opened, but contents should not be crushed or chewed before swallowing. Don't inhale if you are using the under- or on-the-tongue (lingual) spray. This form can be used 5-10 minutes before you undertake an activity that usually leads to angina. If you forget a dose: Call your doctor for instructions as to what to do. Once you have a prescription for an immediate-onset form of this medicine, ask your doctor what he or she wants you to do if the usual dose (such as 3 sublingual tablets or 3 translingual sprays in 15 minutes) does not relieve your chest pain. The usual course is to have someone take you to the hospital for further evaluation.

Usual Duration of Use: Use on a regular schedule for 3 to 5 days is often needed to determine effectiveness in preventing and relieving acute anginal attacks. Individual dose adjustments will be necessary for optimal results. Long-term use (months to years) requires physician supervision.

Typical Treatment Goals and Measurements (Outcomes and Markers)
Angina: The goal is to relieve chest pain with under the tongue (sublingual) forms or spray. If pain is NOT relieved, have someone take you to the hospital and call your doctor. For patch or prolonged action tablets, the frequency and severity of anginal attacks should decrease. Call your doctor if you gain a lowered severity and frequency of angina, and then start to lose that benefit.

▷ **This Drug Should Not Be Taken If**
- you have had an allergic reaction to it or to other components (such as the adhesive in the patch forms) of this medicine.
- you are severely anemic (sublingual form).
- you have had recent head trauma.
- you have had a heart attack and have an increased heart rate or increased blood pressure.
- you are taking sildenafil (Viagra) and this medicine has been newly prescribed. You take this medicine and sildenafil (Viagra) has beeen newly prescribed.
- you have pericarditis (intravenous form).
- you have hyperthyroidism.
- you have increased intraocular pressure.
- you have closed-angle glaucoma (inadequately treated).

▷ **Inform Your Physician Before Taking This Drug If**
- you had an unfavorable response to other nitrates.
- you have low blood pressure.
- you have abnormal growth of the heart muscle in response to vascular disease (hypertrophic cardiomyopathy).
- you have problems absorbing medicines (malabsorption syndromes) or excessive action of your stomach (gastric hypermotility).
- you have any form of glaucoma.
- you have an overactive thyroid or are pregnant.
- you have had recent bleeding or trauma to your head.

Possible Side Effects (natural, expected, and unavoidable drug actions)
Flushing of face, headaches (50%), orthostatic hypotension (see Glossary), rapid heart rate, palpitation.

▷ **Possible Adverse Effects** (unusual, unexpected, and infrequent reactions)
If any of the following develop, consult your physician promptly for guidance.
Mild Adverse Effects
Allergic reaction: skin rash.
Throbbing headaches (may be severe and persistent), dizziness, fainting—possible.
Nausea, vomiting, taste disorders—infrequent.
Serious Adverse Effects
Allergic reactions: severe skin reactions with peeling.
Idiosyncratic reaction: methemoglobinemia—case reports.
Abnormally slow heartbeat (bradycardia)—rare.
Low blood supply to the head (transient ischemic attacks)—case reports.
Increased intracranial pressure—rare.
Low blood platelets or prolonged bleeding time—reported.

▷ **Possible Effects on Sexual Function:** Correction of impotence (one report following sublingual use). Preventive use of nitroglycerin prior to sexual activity has been recommended to eliminate or reduce the risk of angina. Consult your physician for guidance.

▷ **Adverse Effects That May Mimic Natural Diseases or Disorders**
Hypotensive spells (sudden drops in blood pressure) due to this drug may be mistaken for late-onset epilepsy.

Possible Effects on Laboratory Tests
Blood platelet count: decreased—very rare.
Bleeding time: prolonged.

CAUTION
1. This drug can provoke migraine headaches in susceptible individuals.
2. Patients with impaired brain circulation (cerebral arteriosclerosis) have increased risk of transient ischemic attacks—periods of temporary speech impairment, paralysis, numbness, etc.
3. Tolerance to long-acting forms of nitrates will happen in most patients after 24 hours of continuous use. A nitrate-free interval of 10 hours usually restores effectiveness.
4. Many over-the-counter (OTC) drug products for allergies, colds, and coughs contain drugs that may counteract the desired effects of this drug. Ask your physician or pharmacist for help before using any such medications.

Precautions for Use
By Infants and Children: Limited usefulness and experience in this age group. Dose schedules are not established.
By Those Over 60 Years of Age: Begin treatment with small doses and increase dose cautiously as needed and tolerated. You may be more susceptible to the development of flushing, throbbing headache, dizziness, "blackout" spells, fainting, and falling.

▷ **Advisability of Use During Pregnancy**
Pregnancy Category: C. See Pregnancy Risk Categories at the back of this book.
Animal Studies: No information available.
Human Studies: Adequate studies of pregnant women are not available.
Use this drug only if clearly needed. Ask your physician for guidance.

Advisability of Use If Breast-Feeding
Presence of this drug in breast milk: Unknown.
Watch nursing infant closely, and discontinue drug or nursing if adverse effects develop.

Habit-Forming Potential: None.

Effects of Overdose: Throbbing headache, dizziness, marked flushing, nausea, vomiting, abdominal cramps, confusion, delirium, paralysis, seizures, circulatory collapse.

Possible Effects of Long-Term Use: The development of tolerance (see Glossary) and the temporary loss of effectiveness.

Suggested Periodic Examinations While Taking This Drug (at physician's discretion)
Measurements of blood pressure and internal eye pressures.
Evaluation of hemoglobin.

▷ **While Taking This Drug, Observe the Following**
Foods: No restrictions.
Herbal Medicines or Minerals: Hawthorn and co-enzyme Q10 (co-Q10) can

affect the way the heart works. BE CERTAIN to tell your doctor that you are taking or are considering taking these herbs if you are taking a nitrate.

Beverages: No restrictions. May be taken with milk.

▷ *Alcohol:* Avoid alcohol completely. This combination may result in severe lowering of blood pressure. There is a potential for collapse of the circulation and pumping effectiveness of the heart.

Tobacco Smoking: Nicotine can reduce the effectiveness of this drug. I advise everyone to quit smoking.

Marijuana Smoking: Possible reduced effectiveness of this drug; mild to moderate increase in angina; possible changes in the electrocardiogram, confusing interpretation.

▷ *Other Drugs*

Nitroglycerin **taken concurrently** with

- acetylcysteine (NAC) may reverse tolerance to the intravenous form of this medicine.
- alteplase (Activase) lessens the benefits of alteplase; nitroglycerin and alteplase combination should be avoided if possible.
- antihypertensive drugs may cause excessive lowering of blood pressure; careful dose adjustments may be necessary.
- dihydroergotamine or similar ergot medicines (see Drug Classes) may result in ergotamine toxicity. DO NOT combine.
- diltiazem (Cardizem) can result in abnormally low blood pressure when used with the sustained-release form of nitroglycerin.
- heparin can result in decreased therapeutic benefit of heparin.
- indomethacin (Indocin) can blunt the benefits of nitroglycerin.
- isosorbide dinitrate (Isordil) or mononitrate (Ismo) may result in decreased nitroglycerin therapeutic benefits.
- neuromuscular blocking agents (such as pancuronium-Pavulon, vecuronium-Norcuron, others) can result in increased severity of muscle blockade. Use of lower neuromuscular blocker doses is prudent.
- sildenafil (Viagra) may cause very low blood pressure—DO NOT combine.

The following drugs may **increase** the effects of nitroglycerin:

- aspirin and perhaps other NSAIDs. May actually be of treatment benefit in patients who have had a heart attack (AMI or MI). Talk to your doctor about this benefit-to-risk decision.

▷ *Driving, Hazardous Activities:* Usually no restrictions. This drug may cause dizziness or faintness. Restrict activities as necessary.

Aviation Note: Coronary artery disease **is a disqualification** for piloting. Consult a designated Aviation Medical Examiner.

Exposure to Sun: No restrictions.

Exposure to Heat: Hot environments can cause significant lowering of blood pressure.

Exposure to Cold: Cold environments can increase the need for this drug and limit its effectiveness.

Heavy Exercise or Exertion: This drug can increase your tolerance for exercise. Ask your doctor how much exercise is okay for you.

Special Storage Instructions: For sublingual tablets, to prevent loss of strength:

- keep tablets in the original glass container.
- do not transfer tablets to a plastic or metallic container (such as a pillbox).
- do not place absorbent cotton, paper (such as the prescription label), or other material inside the container.
- do not store other drugs in the same container.

- immediately close the container tightly after each use.
- store at room temperature.

Discontinuation: Do not stop this drug abruptly after long-term use. Best to lower the dose (of prolonged-action forms) slowly over 4 to 6 weeks. Watch for rebound angina.

NIZATIDINE (ni ZA te deen)

Please see the histamine (H2) blocking drug family profile.

NORFLOXACIN (nor FLOX a sin)

Please see the fluoroquinolone antibiotic family profile.

NORTRIPTYLINE (nor TRIP ti leen)

Introduced: 1963 **Class:** Antidepressant **Prescription:** USA: Yes **Controlled Drug:** USA: No; Canada: No **Available as Generic:** USA: Yes; Canada: No

Brand Names: Aventyl, Pamelor

BENEFITS versus RISKS	
Possible Benefits	*Possible Risks*
EFFECTIVE RELIEF OF ENDOGENOUS DEPRESSION	ADVERSE BEHAVIORAL EFFECTS: confusion, disorientation, hallucinations, delusions
Possibly beneficial in other depressive disorders	CONVERSION OF DEPRESSION TO MANIA in manic-depressive (bipolar) disorders
Possibly beneficial in the management of some types of chronic, severe pain	Aggravation of schizophrenia
	Irregular heart rhythms
	Rare blood cell abnormalities

Author's Note: The information in this profile has been shortened to make room for more widely used medicines.

OFLOXACIN (oh FLOX a sin)

Please see the fluoroquinolone antibiotic family profile.

OLANZAPINE (oh LAN za peen)

Introduced: 1996 **Class:** Antipsychotic; tranquilizer, major; thienobenzodiazepines; atypical antipsychotics **Prescription:** USA: Yes **Controlled Drug:** USA: No; Canada: No **Available as Generic:** USA: No; Canada: No

Brand Names: Zyprexa, Zyprexa Zydis

BENEFITS versus RISKS

Possible Benefits	*Possible Risks*
EFFECTIVE SHORT-TERM CONTROL OF ACUTE MENTAL DISORDERS: beneficial effects on thinking, mood, and behavior	POSSIBLE TARDIVE DYSKINESIA (SERIOUS TOXIC BRAIN EFFECT WITH LONG-TERM USE)
DELIVERS BENEFITS IN EASING MANIA (IN BIPOLAR DISORDER) AS SOON AS IN THE FIRST WEEK OF TREATMENT	Orthostatic hypotension (see Glossary)
	Increased liver enzymes
	Weight gain
Zyprexa Zydis form falls apart in the mouth, making it easier to take and preventing resistant patients from "cheeking" the medicine	Blood sugar changes (glucose dysregulation)
Relief of anxiety, agitation, and tension	
Medicines in this class are probably "drugs of choice" in older adults.	

▷ **Principal Uses**

As a Single Drug Product: Uses currently included in FDA-approved labeling: (1) Helps manage thinking problems and other difficulties seen in psychosis (schizophrenia and shizophreniform); (2) treats mania in bipolar disorder (often easing mania symptoms after only one week of treatment). Other (unlabeled) generally accepted uses: (1) Works in anorexia; (2) eases anxiety in nursing home patients (Neuropsychiatric Inventory/Nursing Home Instrument or NPI/NH); (3) some data for helping patients with bipolar or mixed presentation who are resistant (refractory) to lithium or valproic acid; (4) eases marijuana (cannabis)-induced psychotic disorder.

In the Pipeline: The 156th meeting of the American Psychiatric Association in June of 2003 found data presented on an investigational combination of olanzapine and fluoxetine (OFC). OFC went to work quickly in people with bipolar depression and showed a strong and ongoing (robust and durable) improvement in bipolar depression. At present there are no FDA-approved medicines for sudden (acute) bipolar depression. SOHO or Schizophrenia Outpatient Health Outcomes is a multicenter study of roughly 19,000 patients that is expected to yield extremely valuable information about real world results from medicines to help psychiatric problems.

How This Drug Works: This drug works as an antipsychotic by inhibiting the action of two primary nerve transmitters (dopamine and serotonin) in certain brain centers and acts to correct an imbalance of nerve impulse transmissions thought to be responsible for certain mental disorders. It also works at histamine, muscarinic, GABA, BZD, and adrenergic sites. The mechanism of action in bipolar disorder is not fully known at present.

Available Dosage Forms and Strengths

Tablets — 2.5 mg, 5 mg, 7.5 mg,10 mg
Tablets, orally-disintegrating (Zyprexa Zydis) — 5 mg, 10 mg, 15 mg, 20 mg

▷ **Recommended Dosage Ranges** (Actual dose and schedule must be determined for each patient individually.)

Infants and Children: Dose not established, but use is increasing (see Bloch, Y in Sources).

18 to 60 Years of Age: Psychosis: Dosing is started with 5 to 10 mg daily. If the 5-mg dose is used, the dose may be increased to a maximum of 10 mg as needed and tolerated. Dose changes should only be made after seven days at a new dose. Changes in dose are usually done in 5-mg steps.

Sudden (acute) mania: Starting doses of 10 to 15 mg once daily, increased as needed and tolerated in steps of 5 mg daily have been used. Treatment in mania has been up to 4 weeks.

Author's Note: Gender data are now FDA-required for new approvals—it must be noted that the drug is removed (cleared) 30% slower in women than in men. Therefore effects (both desirable and undesirable) caused by the medicine may last longer in women (dose to dose) than in men.

Over 60 Years of Age: 5 mg of olanzapine is taken.

Conditions Requiring Dosing Adjustments

Liver Function: The drug is highly metabolized in the liver. The manufacturer says that even in patients with significantly impaired liver function (Childs Pugh A or B), only a lower (5 mg) initial starting dose should be given. It appears prudent to make any dose increases more slowly and closely follow the patient as well.

Kidney Function: Dosing changes are not thought to be needed.

Seizure Disorders: Seizures happened in 0.9% of patients during clinical trials of olanzapine. Olanzapine should be used with caution by seizure patients. Dose decreases are not defined at present.

▷ **Dosing Instructions:** The tablet may be crushed and taken with food. It is best to take this medicine at the same time every day. The (Zydis) form is an orally disintegrating tablet and does not require water to take it. Make sure your hands are dry, peel back the foil on the blister pack (avoid pushing the tablet through the foil), and put the tablet into your mouth. This form easily falls apart in saliva and water is not needed. If you forget a dose: Take the missed dose as soon as you remember it, unless it's nearly time for your next dose—if that is the case, skip the missed dose and take the next dose right on schedule. DO NOT double doses. Talk with your doctor if you find yourself missing doses.

Usual Duration of Use: Use on a regular schedule for at least 1 week is required to reach steady-state levels and hence determines effectiveness. Clinical benefits in mania of bipolar disorder may be seen in the first week of therapy. Clinical trials that led to FDA approval were conducted for 6 weeks, and the medicine is also approved for long-term use. Ongoing use requires physician supervision and checks of ongoing results.

Typical Treatment Goals and Measurements (Outcomes and Markers)

Schizophrenia: The general goal: to ease the severity of symptoms in order to let the patient resume his or her usual activities. There should be lessened intrusion of abnormal thinking into more normal life. As in depression, scales such as the Brief Psychiatric Rating Scale (BPRS) and the Scale for Assessment of Negative Symptoms (SANS) can help assess the benefits of this medicine. *Mania:* Young Mania Rating Scale (YMRS) is often used to check results in bipolar manic patients.

Possible Advantages of This Drug

Effective reversal of symptoms of psychosis while acting at different sites than previously available agents. Rapid onset in bipolar disorder. Medicines in this class are probably drugs of choice in older adults. Zyprexa Zydis form falls apart in the mouth making it easier to take and prevents noncompliant patients from "cheeking" this medicine. Low probability of movement disorders (extrapyramidal).

▷ **This Drug Should Not Be Taken If**
- you have had an allergic reaction to it previously.

▷ **Inform Your Physician Before Taking This Drug If**
- you have a seizure disorder.
- you have had neuroleptic malignant syndrome.
- you are at risk for suicide.
- your liver is compromised.
- you have constitutionally low blood pressure, take medicine to treat high blood pressure, or have cardiovascular or cerebrovascular disease.
- you have had narrow angle glaucoma.
- you are pregnant.
- you have a history of breast cancer.
- you are taking any drug with sedative effects.
- you tend to be constipated.
- you plan to have surgery under general or spinal anesthesia in the near future.
- you have problems swallowing.

Possible Side Effects (natural, expected, and unavoidable drug actions)
Orthostatic hypotension (see Glossary), drowsiness.

▷ **Possible Adverse Effects** (unusual, unexpected, and infrequent reactions)
If any of the following develop, consult your physician promptly for guidance.

Mild Adverse Effects
Allergic reactions: skin rash, itching—rare.
Drowsiness, agitation and insomnia—frequent.
Headache, drowsiness—rare.
Vision changes (such as "lazy eye" or conjunctivitis)—infrequent.
Weight gain—may be frequent (29% in short-term studies had increase of 7% or more). Nizatidine may help (unlabeled use) by inhibiting weight gain (earlier plateau) in people taking olanzapine.
Depression—rare.
Dizziness—rare to infrequent.
Somnolence—frequent.
Prolonged QT interval—possible.
Edema—infrequent.
Constipation—infrequent.

Serious Adverse Effects
Allergic reactions: hair loss—rare. Pustular skin eruptions—case report. Hypersensitivity syndrome with fever, toxic hepatitis, and esosinophilia—case report.
Drug-induced increased liver enzymes—rare.
Pancreatitis—case report.
Increased triglycerides—(more likely with those who also gain weight).
Low white blood cell count (neutropenia)—case reports.
Difficulty swallowing (dysphagia)—case reports.
Tardive dyskinesia or other movement disorders—possible (less than other medicines).
Neuroleptic malignant syndrome—case reports.
Seizure—case report.
New-onset diabetes mellitus and/or blood sugar problems (glucose dysregu-

lation)—case reports, but appears to be increasingly reported with increasing use in children.

▷ **Possible Effects on Sexual Function:** Case reports of extended and painful erections (priapism), amenorrhea, and vaginitis.

▷ **Adverse Effects That May Mimic Natural Diseases or Disorders**

Nervous system reactions may suggest true Parkinson's disease. Liver reactions may suggest viral hepatitis.

Possible Effects on Laboratory Tests

Prolactin levels: increased.

Liver function tests: increased liver enzymes (ALT/GPT, AST/GOT, and alkaline phosphatase).

Triglycerides—increased.

Blood sugar (glucose)—increased.

CAUTION

1. Other medicines (nonprescription or prescription) that can cause drowsiness or central nervous system effects may react unfavorably with this medicine. Talk with your doctor or pharmacist before combining any medicines.
2. Since this medicine can cause orthostatic hypotension, some high blood pressure (antihypertensive) medicines may have a greater than expected effect if taken with olanzapine.
3. Given recent reports of glucose changes in children, caution should be used with people already having a problem regulating blood sugar and more careful monitoring undertaken.

Precautions for Use

By Infants and Children: Safety and effectiveness for those under 18 years of age are not established.

By Those Over 60 Years of Age: Lower starting doses should be taken; caution is advised regarding drowsiness, dizziness, and orthostatic hypotension, since olanzapine can cause changes in the ability of the body to regulate changes in temperature and this regulation may be less intact in older patients to begin with. You may also be more susceptible to Parkinson-like reactions and/or tardive dyskinesia (see Glossary). Discuss early indications of these reactions with your doctor, as progression of these reactions may lead to symptoms that are not reversible.

▷ **Advisability of Use During Pregnancy**

Pregnancy Category: C. See Pregnancy Risk Categories at the back of this book.

Animal Studies: Rat and mouse studies reveal increased mammary gland adenomas (when the animals were given 0.5 and 2 times the mg-per-square-meter human dose) respectively. Increased numbers of nonviable fetuses were seen in one rat study using nine times the maximum human dose.

Human Studies: Adequate studies of pregnant women are not available.

Use of this drug is a benefit-to-risk decision. Ask your doctor for guidance.

Advisability of Use If Breast-Feeding

Presence of this drug in breast milk: Unknown in humans.

Avoid drug or refrain from nursing.

Habit-Forming Potential: None. A withdrawal syndrome was reported in one patient. The authors concluded it was a serotonergic rebound.

Effects of Overdose: Reports of 67 overdoses were made during clinical trials. The patient who took the largest dose had drowsiness and slurred speech.

Possible Effects of Long-Term Use: Possible changes in blood sugar regulation.

Suggested Periodic Examinations While Taking This Drug (at physician's discretion)

Liver function tests.

Careful inspection of the tongue for early evidence of fine, involuntary, wavelike movements that could be the beginning of tardive dyskinesia.

Sitting and standing blood pressure checks may be advisable when therapy is started, to assess orthostatic hypotension.

Blood sugar and A1C (glycosylated hemoglobin).

▷ **While Taking This Drug, Observe the Following**

Foods: Avoid eating grapefruit while taking this medicine. Follow prescribed diet. See grapefruit warning below.

Herbal Medicines or Minerals: New data from a small study of forty patients (See Emsley, R. in Sources) found that add-on therapy with one of the components of fish oil (eicosapenteanoic acid or EPA) helped schizophrenic patients (Positive and Negative Syndrome Scale scores) and was well-tolerated.

Using kola, guarana, or ma huang may result in unacceptable central nervous system stimulation. Evening primrose oil may increase risk of seizure, adding to the risk that this medicine already has. St. John's wort may impact one of the liver enzymes that helps remove this medicine, leading to reduced benefits. Do not combine. Since part of the way ginkgo and ginseng work may be as a MAO inhibitor, do not combine them with olanzapine. Belladonna may lead to excessive anticholinergic actions. Betel nut may make movement disorders more likely. DHEA use may blunt medicine benefits. Given more recent concerns regarding blood sugar and this medicine: Using chromium may change the way your body is able to use sugar. Some health food stores advocate vanadium as mimicking the actions of insulin, but possible toxicity and need for rigorous studies presently preclude recommending it. DHEA may change sensitivity to insulin or insulin resistance. Aloe, bitter melon, eucalyptus, fenugreek, ginger, garlic, ginseng, glucomannan, guar gum, hawthorn, licorice, nettle, and yohimbe may change blood sugar. Surprisingly, boiled stems of the Optuntia streptacantha prickly pear cactus appears to be able to lower blood sugar. Ongoing effects and effects on A1C are not known. Red sage is used for blood sugar effects, but is unproven. Psyllium increases risk of excessively low blood sugar. Since so many of these products may require adjustment of insulin dosing, talk to your doctor BEFORE combining any of these herbal medicines with this medicine. Echinacea purpurea (injectable) and blonde psyllium seed or husk should NOT be taken by people living with diabetes.

Talk to your doctor before adding ANY herbals.

Beverages: Grapefruit juice may decrease metabolism of olanzapine and lead to toxicity. May be taken with milk or water.

▷ *Alcohol:* Avoid completely.

Tobacco Smoking: Olanzapine is removed from the body up to 40% faster in people who smoke compared to those who do not. Recommendations for dosing changes are not available. I advise everyone to quit smoking.

Marijuana Smoking: Expected to cause an increase in drowsiness; accentuation of orthostatic hypotension; increased risk of precipitating latent psychoses, confusing the interpretation of mental status and drug responses.

▷ *Other Drugs*
   Olanzapine *taken concurrently* with
   - activated charcoal will decrease absorption of olanzapine. (May be of use in overdoses.)
   - any medicine that has central nervous system activity may result in additive effects.
   - any medicine that can cause liver damage may result in additive liver problems.
   - any sedative drugs (prescription and nonprescription) can cause excessive sedation.
   - benzodiazepines (see Drug Classes) may magnify the orthostatic hypotension problem caused by olanzapine.
   - carbamazepine (Tegretol) causes up to a 50% increase in removal of olanzapine from the body; dosing increases in olanzapine appear prudent.
   - fluoroquinolone antibiotics, such as ciprofloxacin (Cipro) or norfloxacin (Noroxin), may lead to olanzapine toxicity.
   - fluvoxamine (Luvox) may lead to olanzapine toxicity.
   - lithium (Lithobid, others) may increase risk of serious nerve effects—extreme care should be taken and patients closely monitored for signs of toxicity and movement problems—especially if high doses of antipsychotic drugs and lithium are used. Call your doctor immediately if these signs or symptoms begin.
   - medicines that *decrease* or inhibit cytochrome P450 1A2 or glucuronyl transferase enzymes may lead to olanzapine toxicity.
   - medicines that *change* or modify blood sugar may lead to additive problems with possible olanzapine changes in blood sugar.
   - medicines that *change* or modify the QT interval such as: dofetilide (Tikosyn) and other medicines such as class I, IA, or III antiarrhythmics, clarithromycin, cotrimoxazole, ondansetron, ziprazidone, and others may lead to prolongation of the QTc interval and undesirable effects. Combination is not recommended.

   The following drugs may *decrease* the effects of olanzapine:
   - medicines that increase (induce) cytochrome P450 1A2 or glucuronyl transferase enzymes may blunt olanzapine benefits.
   - omeprazole (Prilosec).
   - rifampin (Rifater, others).

▷ *Driving, Hazardous Activities:* This drug may cause drowsiness or dizziness. Restrict activities as necessary.

   Aviation Note: The use of this drug *may be a disqualification* for piloting. Consult a designated Aviation Medical Examiner.

   Exposure to Sun: No problems reported.

   Exposure to Heat: This medicine can cause problems in regulating body temperature (core temperature homeostasis). If you work or are frequently in a hot environment, be careful to replace enough fluids to avoid dehydration.

   Heavy Exercise or Exertion: Since this medicine may cause problems in temperature regulation, caution is advised.

   Discontinuation: Do not stop this medicine without first talking to your doctor. May be prudent to slowly decrease the dose (taper) it to help avoid any withdrawal syndrome.

OLSALAZINE (ohl SAL a zeen)

Introduced: 1987 **Class:** Bowel anti-inflammatory **Prescription:**
USA: Yes **Controlled Drug:** USA: No; Canada: No **Available as**
Generic: USA: No; Canada: No
Brand Name: Dipentum

BENEFITS versus RISKS

Possible Benefits	*Possible Risks*
EFFECTIVE SUPPRESSION OF INFLAMMATORY BOWEL DISEASE	RARE BONE MARROW DEPRESSION (see Glossary) Drug-induced hepatitis Occasional aggravation of ulcerative colitis

---

▷ **Principal Uses**

As a Single Drug Product: Uses currently included in FDA-approved labeling: Used to keep up remission (maintenance) of chronic ulcerative colitis and proctitis in people who do not tolerate sulfasalazine.

Other (unlabeled) generally accepted uses: (1) Has a role in treatment of active ulcerative colitis; (2) works in collagenous colitis in adults.

How This Drug Works: This drug is actually two molecules of 5-aminosalicylic acid (ASA) joined together. In the body, it is converted to the active ASA and then suppresses the formation of prostaglandins (and related compounds), tissue substances that induce inflammation, tissue destruction, and diarrhea—the main features of ulcerative colitis and proctitis.

Available Dosage Forms and Strengths

Capsules — 250 mg

Tablets (Canada only) — 500 mg

▷ **Recommended Dosage Ranges** (Actual dose and schedule must be determined for each patient individually.)

Infants and Children: Dose not established.

12 to 60 Years of Age: 500 mg twice daily, morning and evening.

Over 60 Years of Age: Same as 12 to 60 years of age.

Conditions Requiring Dosing Adjustments

Liver Function: No changes needed in liver disease, but since this drug can be toxic to the liver (granulomatous hepatitis), it should be used with caution by patients with liver problems.

Kidney Function: Some of the metabolites of olsalazine are eliminated by the kidneys. There is potential for kidney damage by one of these compounds, and the drug should be a benefit-to-risk decision by patients with compromised kidneys.

▷ **Dosing Instructions:** The capsule may be opened and taken with food, preferably with breakfast and dinner. If you forget a dose: Take the missed dose as soon as you remember it, unless it's nearly time for your next dose—if that is the case, skip the missed dose and take the next dose right on schedule. DON'T double doses. Talk with your doctor if you find yourself missing doses.

Usual Duration of Use: Use on a regular schedule for 1 to 3 weeks determines effectiveness in controlling the symptoms of ulcerative colitis. Ongoing treatment of up to two years has been successful in preventing relapse of ulcerative colitis. Long-term use (months to years) requires physician supervision.

Typical Treatment Goals and Measurements (Outcomes and Markers)

Ulcerative Colitis: The general goal is to lower the frequency of stools, ease cramping, reduce amount of blood in the stools, and stop fever. More involved exams will reveal an absence of bowel ulceration and easing of friability or granularity of the bowel itself. Use after sudden (acute) cases have resolved seeks to prevent relapse of ulcerative colitis.

▷ **This Drug Should Not Be Taken If**
- you have had an allergic reaction to it previously.
- you have severely impaired kidney function.
- you are allergic to aspirin or aspirinlike compounds.

▷ **Inform Your Physician Before Taking This Drug If**
- you are allergic to aspirin (or other salicylates), mesalamine, or sulfasalazine.
- you are allergic by nature: history of hay fever, asthma, hives, eczema.
- you have impaired kidney function.
- you have severe liver disease.
- you are currently taking sulfasalazine (Azulfidine).

Possible Side Effects (natural, expected, and unavoidable drug actions)

None.

▷ **Possible Adverse Effects** (unusual, unexpected, and infrequent reactions)

If any of the following develop, consult your physician promptly for guidance.

Mild Adverse Effects

Allergic reactions: skin rash, itching—rare.

Headache, drowsiness, depression, dizziness—rare.

Fever and chills—rare.

Loss of appetite, indigestion, nausea, vomiting, stomach pain, diarrhea—rare to infrequent.

Paresthesias or blurred vision—rare.

Joint aches and pains—infrequent.

Serious Adverse Effects

Allergic reactions: dermatitis, hair loss—rare.

Bone marrow depression (see Glossary): fatigue, fever, sore throat, abnormal bleeding/bruising—case reports.

Drug-induced hepatitis (see Glossary), pericarditis, pancreatitis, or kidney damage—rare.

Spasm of the bronchi of the lung—rare.

▷ **Possible Effects on Sexual Function:** Impotence, excessive menstrual flow—case reports.

Possible Effects on Laboratory Tests

Complete blood cell counts: decreased red cells, hemoglobin, white cells, and platelets; increased eosinophils.

Liver function tests: increased liver enzymes (ALT/GPT, AST/GOT, and alkaline phosphatase), increased bilirubin.

Urinalysis: red blood cells and protein present.

CAUTION

1. Report promptly any signs of infection or unusual bleeding or bruising.
2. Report promptly any indications of active or intensified ulcerative colitis: abdominal cramping, bloody diarrhea, fever.

3. Promptly call your doctor if you develop a skin rash, unexplained tiredness, sore throat or unexplained fever.

Precautions for Use

By Infants and Children: Safety and effectiveness for those under 12 years of age are not established.

By Those Over 60 Years of Age: None.

▷ **Advisability of Use During Pregnancy**

Pregnancy Category: C. See Pregnancy Risk Categories at the back of this book.

Animal Studies: Rat studies reveal toxic effects on the fetus, retarded bone development, and impaired development of internal organs.

Human Studies: Adequate studies of pregnant women are not available.

Use this drug only if clearly needed. Ask your physician for guidance.

Advisability of Use If Breast-Feeding

Presence of this drug in breast milk: Controversial, has caused diarrhea in some infants.

Avoid drug or refrain from nursing. Talk to your doctor about a benefit-to-risk decision.

Habit-Forming Potential: None.

Effects of Overdose: Headache, dizziness, nausea, vomiting, abdominal cramping.

Possible Effects of Long-Term Use: Bone marrow depression (impaired production of blood cells).

Suggested Periodic Examinations While Taking This Drug (at physician's discretion)

Complete blood cell counts.

Liver function tests.

Kidney function tests.

Urinalysis.

Number and frequency of stools.

▷ **While Taking This Drug, Observe the Following**

Foods: No restrictions. Follow prescribed diet.

Herbal Medicines or Minerals: Flaxseed, peppermint oil, and psyllium husk have commission E monograph indications for irritable bowel syndrome. This is NOT the same as ulcerative colitis, and those products have not been studied in ulcerative colitis. Aloe, buckhorn berry or bark, cascara sagrada bark, rhubarb root, and senna should not be taken by people living with ulcerative colitis.

Beverages: No restrictions. May be taken with milk.

▷ *Alcohol:* No interactions expected.

Tobacco Smoking: No interactions expected. I advise everyone to quit smoking.

▷ *Other Drugs*

Olsalazine *taken concurrently* with

- alendronate (Fosamax) may increase risk of GI upset.
- low molecular weight heparins enoxaparin (Lovenox), Normiflo, or Fragmin (see Drug Classes) may increase bleeding risk.
- mercaptopurine (Purinethol) may lead to bone marrow depression.
- varicella vaccine (Varivax) may result in an increased risk of Reye's syndrome; this drug should be avoided for 6 weeks after the vaccine is given.
- warfarin (Coumadin) may increase INR; more frequent tests may be warranted if these medicines are combined.

▷ *Driving, Hazardous Activities:* This drug may cause drowsiness or dizziness. Restrict activities as necessary.

Aviation Note: The use of this drug *may be a disqualification* for piloting. Consult a designated Aviation Medical Examiner.

Exposure to Sun: Use caution—this drug can cause photosensitization (see Glossary).

OMALIZUMAB (oh MAH lis you mab)

Introduced: 2003   **Class:** Antiasthmatic drug, IgG1kapa monocloncal antibody, IgE blocker   **Prescription:** USA: Yes   **Controlled Drug:** USA: No; Canada: No   **Available as Generic:** USA: Yes; Canada: No

Brand Name: Xolair

Author's Note: This medicine is the first medicine that actually attaches (binds) to an immunoglobulin (IgE) on the surface of cells (mast cells and basophils) involved in releasing chemicals that lead to asthma signs and symptoms. Once omalizumab attaches to these receptors, IgE, a culprit in causing those cells to release chemicals that lead to an asthmatic attack, is not able to attach to those cells to tell them to release the compounds that cause asthma. The medicine is given as a shot under the skin (subcutaneous injection) once every 2–4 weeks. The FDA approved the medicine for people who do not get relief from typical medications, but has asked the manufacturer to continue to study cancer (malignant neoplasm) risk. In clinical trials which lasted less than a year, 0.5% of people getting omalizumab versus 0.2% of people getting a dummy shot (placebo), developed malignant neoplasms.

OMEPRAZOLE (oh MEH pra zohl)

Introduced: 1986   **Class:** Proton pump inhibitor   **Prescription:** USA: Yes   **Controlled Drug:** USA: No; Canada: No   **Available as Generic:** USA: Yes; Canada: No

Brand Names: ✿Losec, Prilosec, Risek

Author's Note: An application has been made with the FDA requesting change of this medicine from prescription to nonprescription status. The FDA Advisory Panel voted 16 to 2 to change the drug from prescription to nonprescription on June 21, 2002. A rewrite of proposed patient instructions was requested by the FDA. The FDA approved this medicine for nonprescription use in 2003 (see *www.fda.gov/bbs/topics/news/2003/NEW00916.html*).

BENEFITS versus RISKS	
Possible Benefits	*Possible Risks*
VERY EFFECTIVE TREATMENT OF CONDITIONS ASSOCIATED WITH EXCESSIVE PRODUCTION OF GASTRIC ACID: Zollinger-Ellison syndrome, mastocytosis, endocrine adenoma	Rare aplastic anemia Rare liver failure
VERY EFFECTIVE TREATMENT OF REFLUX ESOPHAGITIS, GASTRIC AND DUODENAL ULCERS	
EFFECTIVE IN COMBINATION WITH CLARITHROMYCIN AND AMOXICILLIN in treatment of *Helicobacter pylori* infections	
ONCE DAILY DOSING ENHANCES COMPLIANCE	
EFFECTIVE HEARTBURN TREATMENT (GERD)	
Prevention of NSAID-induced ulcers	

▷ **Principal Uses**

As a Single Drug Product: Uses currently included in FDA-approved labeling: (1) Inhibits stomach acid formation in acute and chronic gastritis, reflux esophagitis, gastroesophageal reflux disease, Zollinger-Ellison syndrome, mastocytosis, endocrine adenomas, and active duodenal ulcer; (2) approved for long-term use in erosive esophagitis; (3) approved for combination treatment (with clarithromycin [Biaxin]) in patients with positive *Helicobacter pylori* cultures (removes the bacteria in up to 92% of patients); (4) helps in the short-term treatment of active and benign stomach (gastric) ulcers; (5) part of a three-drug, 10-day regimen (omeprazole, amoxicillin, and clarithromycin) to treat duodenal ulcers.

Other (unlabeled) generally accepted uses: (1) May have a role in treating severe stomach bleeding (hemorrhagic gastritis); (2) possible use in ulcerative colitis; (3) prevention of ulcers caused by NSAIDs; (4) could be of help in asthma; (5) could help hiccups resistant to other therapy (intractable).

How This Drug Works: Inhibits a specific enzyme system (proton pump H/K ATPase) in the stomach lining, stopping production of stomach acid and thereby (1) eliminates a principal cause of the condition under treatment and (2) creates an environment conducive to healing. Taking this medicine 15–30 minutes before the morning meal makes best use of the fact that this will allow the medicine to be at its peak just when the largest number of proton pumps are working.

Available Dosage Forms and Strengths

Capsules, immediate-release — 10 mg, 20 mg, 40 mg (Canada)
Capsules, delayed-release — 10 mg, 20mg
Capsules, sustained-release — 10 mg, 20 mg
Capsules, Timed-release — 20 mg

▷ **Usual Adult Dosage Ranges:** *Reflux esophagitis:* 20 mg once daily 15–30 minutes before the morning meal for a duration of 4 to 8 weeks. Excessive stomach acid conditions: 60 mg once daily for as long as necessary. In extreme cases, doses of 120 mg three times a day have been used.

Gastric and Duodenal Ulcer: 20-30 mg once daily for 4 to 8 weeks.

Duodenal Ulcer Combination Therapy (28-day regimen): Omeprazole 40 mg daily with clarithromycin 500 mg 3 times a day for days 1–14 and then omeprazole 20 mg daily for days 15–28.

Helicobacter Pylori: Dual drug approach: 40 mg of omeprazole once a day combined with 500 mg of clarithromycin three times a day. Treatment is continued for two weeks. Triple drug approach: Omeprazole 20 mg twice a day or 40 mg once a day with clarithromycin 500 mg and amoxicillin 1,000 mg, all given twice a day for 10 days. Patients who have (present with) an ulcer when treatment is started also get omeprazole alone at 20 mg a day for another 18 days.

Note: Actual dose and schedule must be determined for each patient individually.

Conditions Requiring Dosing Adjustments

Liver Function: Patients should be monitored closely.

Kidney Function: Dose adjustments do not appear to be needed.

▷ **Dosing Instructions:** Take immediately before eating, preferably 15–30 minutes before the morning meal. The capsule should be swallowed whole without opening; the contents should not be crushed or chewed. This drug may be taken with antacids if they are needed to relieve stomach pain. If swallowing is a problem, the capsules CAN be opened and the intact granules mixed in a fruit juice (such as apple, cranberry, orange, or grape—acidic fruit juices) or a small amount of applesauce just before you take it. Don't mix with milk. If you forget a dose: Take the missed dose as soon as you remember it, unless it's nearly time for your next dose—if that is the case, skip the missed dose and take the next dose right on schedule. DO NOT double doses. Talk with your doctor if you find yourself missing doses.

Usual Duration of Use: Use on a regular schedule for 2 to 3 weeks determines benefit in suppressing stomach acid production. Long-term use (months to years) requires periodic physician evaluation of response, particularly where *Helicobacter pylori* is involved.

Typical Treatment Goals and Measurements (Outcomes and Markers)

Ulcers: The role of *Helicobacter pylori* in ulcers is no longer questioned, and a proton pump inhibitor is widely recognized as the standard for short-term treatment of stomach ulcers. When *H. pylori* is present, single medicine therapy is not recommended. Additionally, an antibiotic is often used with other agents. The goal is to heal the ulcer area and prevent reoccurrence of the ulceration. Sign and symptom relief as well as endoscopic examination help define success of treatment. Negative results for *Helicobacter pylori* cultures (eradication) is the goal when that agent is present.

Possible Advantages of This Drug

Effectively inhibits acid secretion at all times: basal conditions (stomach empty and at rest) and following food, alcohol, smoking, or other stimulants. More effective than histamine (H2) receptor blocking drugs in treating severe reflux esophagitis and refractory duodenal ulcer.

Currently a Drug of Choice

For the short-term treatment of severe reflux esophagitis and the long-term treatment of Zollinger-Ellison syndrome and erosive esophagitis. Part of a one-week regimen of choice (comparing outcomes) with clarithromycin and metronidazole for treating *H. pylori*.

▷ **This Drug Should Not Be Taken If**
- you have had an allergic reaction to it previously.
- you have a currently active bone marrow or blood cell disorder.

▷ **Inform Your Physician Before Taking This Drug If**
- you have a history of liver disease or impaired liver function.
- your history includes any bone marrow or blood cell disorder, especially a drug-induced one.
- you take any anticoagulant medication or diazepam (Valium) or phenytoin (Dilantin, etc.).

Possible Side Effects (natural, expected, and unavoidable drug actions)

Acid in the stomach actually works to protect it from some bacterial infections. Since omeprazole is so effective in decreasing acid, it may increase the likelihood of infection by *Campylobacter*. This organism causes gastroenteritis. Symptoms may include mucus, loose stools, and fever. Talk with your doctor if you start to develop these symptoms while taking omeprazole.

▷ **Possible Adverse Effects** (unusual, unexpected, and infrequent reactions)

If any of the following develop, consult your physician promptly for guidance.

Mild Adverse Effects

Allergic reactions: skin rash—rare; itching.

Headache, dizziness, muscle pain or ringing in ears; drowsiness, paresthesias, weakness—rare to infrequent.

Indigestion, nausea, vomiting, diarrhea, constipation—rare to infrequent.

Serious Adverse Effects

Allergic reactions: rare allergic kidney damage (interstitial nephritis), rare anaphylactic reaction. Erythema multiforme—case report.

Bone marrow depression: fatigue, fever, sore throat, infections, abnormal bleeding/bruising—case reports.

Hemolytic anemia—case report.

Liver damage with jaundice (see Glossary)—case reports.

Low blood sugar—case report.

Chest pain or angina—case reports.

Half-facial pain—case reports.

Yeast infection (Candida) of the esophagus—possible.

Kidney inflammation (interstitial nephritis)—case reports.

Possible Effects on Sexual Function: Drug-induced male breast enlargement and tenderness (gynecomastia)—case reports.

Nocturnal erections—case report.

▷ **Adverse Effects That May Mimic Natural Diseases or Disorders**

Persistent infection or bruising may be bone marrow depression; blood counts are advisable.

Liver reactions may suggest viral hepatitis.

Possible Effects on Laboratory Tests

Complete blood cell counts: decreased red cells, hemoglobin, white cells, and platelets.

Blood glucose level: decreased.

Liver function tests: increased liver enzymes (ALT/GPT, AST/GOT, and alkaline phosphatase), increased bilirubin.

CAUTION

1. Take this drug for exactly as long as your doctor prescribed. Do not extend its use without your physician's guidance.

2. Report promptly any indications of infection.
3. Tell your doctor if you plan to take any other medications (prescription or over-the-counter) while taking omeprazole.
4. Acid in the stomach actually works to protect it from some bacterial infections. Since omeprazole is so effective in decreasing acid, it may increase the likelihood of infection by Campylobacter. This organism causes gastroenteritis. Symptoms may include mucus, loose stools, and fever. Talk with your doctor if you start to develop these symptoms while taking omeprazole.
5. Although this drug effectively treats ulcers, it does not preclude the possibility of cancer of the stomach.

Precautions for Use
By Infants and Children: Safety and effectiveness for those under 12 years of age are not established.
By Those Over 60 Years of Age: Slower elimination of this drug makes it possible to achieve satisfactory response with smaller doses; this reduces the risk of adverse effects. Limit the daily dose to 20 mg if possible.

▷ **Advisability of Use During Pregnancy**
Pregnancy Category: C. See Pregnancy Risk Categories at the back of this book.
Animal Studies: No drug-induced birth defects found in rats; drug-induced embryo and fetal toxicity were demonstrated in rats and rabbits.
Human Studies: Adequate studies of pregnant women are not available.
Avoid use if possible. Use only if clearly necessary and for the shortest possible time.

Advisability of Use If Breast-Feeding
Presence of this drug in breast milk: Yes.
Avoid drug or refrain from nursing.

Habit-Forming Potential: None.

Effects of Overdose: Possible drowsiness, dizziness, lethargy, abdominal pain, nausea.

Possible Effects of Long-Term Use: Some long-term (2-year) studies in rats revealed the development of drug-induced carcinoid tumors in the stomach. To date, long-term use of this drug (more than 5 years) in humans has not revealed any drug-induced tumor potential. Pending more studies of long-term human use, it is advisable to limit the use of this drug to the shortest duration possible.

Suggested Periodic Examinations While Taking This Drug (at physician's discretion)
Complete blood cell counts.

▷ **While Taking This Drug, Observe the Following**
Foods: Follow your doctor's advice.
Herbal Medicines or Minerals: Kola, guarana, and ma huang may increase stomach acid, blunting the benefits of this medicine. Black cohosh root, ginkgo, and squill are contraindicated in gastrointestinal disturbances. Licorice root has a German Commission E monograph indication for gastrointestinal ulcers, but use with proton pump inhibitors has not been studied. St. John's wort has been found to increase sensitivity to the sun like this medicine. The combination is not recommended. Talk to your doctor BEFORE taking any herbals with this medicine.
Beverages: No restrictions. May be taken with milk.

▷   *Alcohol:* No interactions expected, but alcohol is best avoided; it stimulates the secretion of stomach acid.

Tobacco Smoking: Smoking may stimulate the secretion of stomach acid. I advise everyone to quit smoking.

▷   *Other Drugs*

Omeprazole may ***increase*** the effects of

- anticoagulants (warfarin, etc.) and increase the risk of bleeding.
- benzodiazepines [some such as diazepam] (see Drug Classes).
- carbamazepine (Tegretol).
- cilostazol (Pletal) by increasing an active metabolite called 3,4-dehydro cilostazol because of its action in inhibiting cytochrome P450 2C19. A lower dose of cilostazol and careful patient follow-up are prudent if these medicines must be combined.
- clonazepam (Klonopin) and some other benzodiazepines (see Drug Classes) and lead to benzodiazepine toxicity.
- cyclosporine (Sandimmune), by increasing its level (decreased levels also reported).
- diazepam (Valium) and cause excessive sedation.
- digoxin (Lanoxin) and lead to toxicity.
- disulfiram (Antabuse).
- fluvastatin (Lescol).
- methotrexate (Rheumatrex).
- phenytoin (Dilantin, etc.) or fosphenytoin (Cerebyx) and cause phenytoin or fosphenytoin toxicity.
- tacrolimus (Prograf) may increase tacrolimus levels—blood levels and adjustment of tacrolimus dosing is prudent.
- warfarin (Coumadin) and lead to bleeding; more frequent INR (prothrombin time or protime) testing is needed. Warfarin doses should be adjusted according to laboratory results.

Omeprazole ***taken concurrently*** with

- voraconazole (Vfend) or medicines that inhibit a liver enzyme involved in removing this medicine (P450-2C19) will increase the blood levels of omeprazole and make adverse effects from omeprazole more likely.

Omeprazole may ***decrease*** the effects of

- ampicillin (various).
- clozapine (Clozaril). More frequent checks of clozapine blood levels and adjustment of dosing is prudent.
- iron preparations.
- itraconazole (Sporanox) or ketoconazole (Nizoral) may easily be addressed by taking the antifungals with a low pH cola (talk to your doctor about this).
- olanzapine (Zyprexa).
- ritonavir (Norvir)—may also increase omeprazole effects.
- trovafloxacin (Trovan).

▷   *Driving, Hazardous Activities:* This drug may cause drowsiness and dizziness. Limit activities as necessary.

Aviation Note: The use of this drug ***may be a disqualification*** for piloting. Consult a designated Aviation Medical Examiner.

Exposure to Sun: Photosensitivity has been reported.

Discontinuation: The duration of use will vary according to the condition under treatment and individual patient response. Premature discontinuation could result in incomplete healing or prompt recurrence of symptoms.

ONDANSETRON (on DAN sa tron)

Introduced: 1993 **Class:** Antiemetic, 5-HT3 antagonist **Prescription:** USA: Yes **Controlled Drug:** USA: No; Canada: No **Available as Generic:** USA: No; Canada: No

Brand Names: Zofran, Zofran ODT, Zofran Oral Solution

BENEFITS versus RISKS	
Possible Benefits	*Possible Risks*
EFFECTIVE ORAL TREATMENT AND RELIEF OR PREVENTION OF SEVERE VOMITING ODT FORM ALLOWS THIS DRUG TO BE CONVENIENTLY TAKEN WITHOUT WATER	Bronchospasm Grand mal seizures Liver toxicity Heart rate and rhythm changes Low potassium (All rare)

▷ **Principal Uses**

As a Single Drug Product: Uses currently included in FDA-approved labeling: (1) Prevention of nausea and vomiting associated with initial and repeat courses of chemotherapy; (2) treatment or prevention of postoperative nausea and vomiting; (3) prevention or treatment of emesis (vomiting) caused by radiation therapy.

Other (unlabeled) generally accepted uses: (1) Helps patients keep from vomiting up medicines used to treat drug overdoses; (2) may have a role in treating schizophrenia and a movement problem (tardive dyskinesia or TD) seen with some medicines used to treat TD; (3) some data reducing the number of panic attacks; (4) eases some tremor cases.

How This Drug Works: Ondansetron antagonizes 5-HT3 receptors. It appears to block vomiting by blocking serotonin (a chemical causing vomiting) at 5-HT3 receptors.

Available Dosage Forms and Strengths

Intravenous — 2 mg/ml
Oral solution — 4 mg/5 ml
Tablets — 4 mg, 8 mg, 24 mg
Tablets, ODT — 4 mg, 8 mg

▷ **Recommended Dosage Ranges** (Actual dose and schedule must be determined for each patient individually.)

Infants and Children: Little information is available regarding use in those less than 3 years old.

4 to 11 Years of Age: Vomiting from chemotherapy—one 4-mg tablet or 5 ml of the oral solution is given three times by mouth daily. The method and frequency are then the same as for adults.

12 to 60 Years of Age: One 24-mg tablet for medicines such as cisplatin which is highly likely to lead to vomiting. For *chemotherapy* that poses a moderate risk of vomiting (moderately emetogenic chemo), 8 mg is given twice a day. The first dose should be taken 30 minutes before the start of the chemotherapy. Subsequent doses should be taken 8 hours after the first dose. Further doses of 8 mg every 12 hours are taken for 1–2 days after chemotherapy is finished.

Vomiting from Radiation Therapy — 8 mg three times a day. Doses are started

1–2 hours BEFORE radiation treatment. Doses after radiation are given every 8 hours for 1–2 days.

Postoperative Nausea and Vomiting—one 16-mg dose one hour before anesthesia is given.

Panic Attacks: one to two mg twice a day have worked in some cases (more effective than a sugar pill or placebo).

Over 60 Years of Age: Same as 12 to 60 years of age.

Conditions Requiring Dosing Adjustments

Liver Function: Maximum dose for people with severe liver failure is 8 mg per day.

Kidney Function: Studies have not been conducted on patients with impaired kidneys. The decision to use ondansetron must be made by your physician. Only 5 to 10% of the drug is removed unchanged by the kidneys. Based on this small involvement of the kidneys, no changes are expected to be needed with short-term use.

▷ **Dosing Instructions:** May be taken on an empty stomach. DO NOT push the ODT form through the blister pack—simply peel back the foil before you take it. If you forget a dose: Take the missed dose as soon as you remember it, unless it's nearly time for your next dose—if that is the case, skip the missed dose and take the next dose right on schedule. DO NOT double doses. Talk with your doctor if you find yourself missing doses.

Usual Duration of Use: Since chemotherapy can cause vomiting long after it has been given, continual use on a regular schedule for 3 days is usually necessary.

Typical Treatment Goals and Measurements (Outcomes and Markers)

Vomiting: The goal is to prevent or at least to decrease vomiting (emesis) frequency, amount or severity.

Possible Advantages of This Drug

Effective oral prevention of severe vomiting caused by some kinds of chemotherapy that have been poorly controlled by earlier agents. Orally disintegrating tablets (ODT) form dissolves in a few seconds on the tongue WITHOUT water. If panic attack data stands up to further testing, this medicine will offer a more desirable mental status side effect profile than paroxetine (Paxil) for use in children.

Currently a "Drug of Choice"

For control of vomiting secondary to emetogenic (likely to cause vomiting) cancer chemotherapy.

▷ **This Drug Should Not Be Taken If**
- you had an allergic reaction to it or to a different 5HT antagonist (cross sensitivity possible).

▷ **Inform Your Physician Before Taking This Drug If**
- you have a history of liver disease.
- you have a history of kidney disease.
- you have a history of alcoholism.
- you have a history of PKU (ODT form has phenylalanine).
- you are unsure how much to take or how often to take it.

Possible Side Effects (natural, expected, and unavoidable drug actions)
Constipation, sedation.

▷ **Possible Adverse Effects** (unusual, unexpected, and infrequent reactions)
> **If any of the following develop, consult your physician promptly for guidance.**
>
> *Mild Adverse Effects*
> Allergic reactions: skin rash—rare.
> Headache—frequent.
> Dizziness and light-headedness, constipation, diarrhea, dry mouth—infrequent.
>
> *Serious Adverse Effects*
> Allergic reactions: anaphylaxis—rare (24 cases at the time of this writing).
> Extrapyramidal reactions (abnormal body movements) or seizures (intravenous form)—case reports.
> Bronchospasm—rare.
> Liver failure—one case report in a patient with hepatitis B.
> Angina, tachycardia, arrhythmias—all rare.
> Hypokalemia (low potassium)—rare.

▷ **Possible Effects on Sexual Function:** None reported.

Possible Delayed Adverse Effects: None reported.

▷ **Adverse Effects That May Mimic Natural Diseases or Disorders**
> Changes in liver enzymes may mimic hepatitis, but specific antibodies will not be present. Bronchospasm may mimic asthma.

Natural Diseases or Disorders That May Be Activated by This Drug
> Epilepsy, asthma.

Possible Effects on Laboratory Tests
> Liver function tests: Transient increases in SGPT, SGOT, and bilirubin.

CAUTION
> 1. Even though you do not feel an urge to vomit, continue ondansetron for the prescribed length of therapy. The vomit-causing effect of cancer chemotherapy or radiation therapy continues after the medicine or radiation has been given.
> 2. The ODT form contains phenylalanine..
> 3. Use after abdominal surgery may hide (mask) swelling of the stomach (gastric distension) and possible progressive intestinal block (ileus).

Precautions for Use
> *By Infants and Children:* Safety and effectiveness for those under 3 years of age are not established.
> *By Those Over 60 Years of Age:* Same as for general adult population.

▷ **Advisability of Use During Pregnancy**
> *Pregnancy Category:* B. See Pregnancy Risk Categories at the back of this book.
> *Animal Studies:* Drug and its metabolites pass into the milk. No adverse effects on gestation, postnatal development, or reproductive performance have been observed in rats.
> *Human Studies:* Adequate studies of pregnant women are not available.
> Ask your physician for guidance.

Advisability of Use If Breast-Feeding
> Presence of this drug in breast milk: This medicine is excreted in the milk of rats; human data is not available.
> Caution should be used if this medicine is to be used by nursing mothers.

Habit-Forming Potential: None.

Effects of Overdose: Doses 10 times greater than recommended have not resulted in illness.

Possible Effects of Long-Term Use: Not indicated for long-term use.
Suggested Periodic Examinations While Taking This Drug (at physician's discretion)
   Observe for vomiting occurrence and frequency.
▷ **While Taking This Drug, Observe the Following**
   Foods: No restrictions.
   Herbal Medicines or Minerals: Since St. John's wort may act to increase serotonin, the combination is not advised. Since part of the way ginkgo and ginseng work may be as a MAO inhibitor, do not combine them with ondansetron.
   Beverages: No restrictions.
▷ *Alcohol:* Additive sedation and potential additive urge to vomit if alcohol is taken in large doses. Alcohol abuse that has led to liver problems may limit the total dose that can be taken.
   Tobacco Smoking: No direct clinical interactions; I advise everyone to quit smoking.
   Marijuana Smoking: May induce additive sedation and provide additive antiemetic effects.
▷ *Other Drugs*
   The following drugs may *increase* the effects of ondansetron:
   • allopurinol (Zyloprim).
   • cimetidine (Tagamet).
   • disulfiram (Antabuse).
   • fluconazole (Diflucan).
   • isoniazid (Nydrazid).
   • macrolide antibiotics (erythromycin, azithromycin, clarithromycin, dirithromycin).
   • metronidazole (Flagyl).
   • monoamine oxidase (MAO) inhibitor antidepressants (Nardil).
   • ritonavir (Norvir) and perhaps other protease inhibitors (see Drug Classes).
   Ondansetron *taken concurrently* with:
   • amiodarone (Cordarone) may lead to abnormal heartbeat or rhythm (QT changes and torsades de pointes).
   • dofetilide (Tikosyn) and other medicines such as class I, IA, or III antiarrhythmics, clarithromycin, cotrimoxazole, ondansetron, ziprazidone, and others may lead to prolongation of the QTc interval and undesirable effects. Combination is not recommended.
   The following drugs may *decrease* the effects of ondansetron:
   • barbiturates.
   • carbamazepine (Tegretol).
   • phenylbutazone (Butazolidin, Azolid).
   • phenytoin (Dilantin).
   • rifabutin (Mycobutin).
   • rifampin (Rifadin)
   • tolbutamide (Orinase).
▷ *Driving, Hazardous Activities:* This drug may cause drowsiness and dizziness. Restrict activities as necessary.
   Aviation Note: The use of this drug *may be a disqualification* for piloting. Consult a designated Aviation Medical Examiner.
   Exposure to Sun: No restrictions.
   Special Storage Instructions: Keep at room temperature. Avoid exposing this medicine to extreme humidity.
   Discontinuation: Ondansetron may be stopped after you've completed the prescribed course (usually 3 days) of therapy.

ORAL CONTRACEPTIVES (or al kon tra SEP tivs)

Other Names: Estrogens/progestins, OCs, birth control pills

Introduced: 1956   **Class:**   Female sex hormones   **Prescription:**
USA: Yes   **Controlled Drug:**   USA: No; Canada: No   **Available as**
Generic: USA: Yes, in some forms; Canada: No

Brand Names: Alesse, Brevicon, Cyclessa, Demulen, Desogen, Enovid,
Estrostep FE, Genora, Gestodene, Jenest 28, Levlen, Levlite, Levora,
Loestrin, Low-Ogestrel, Lo/Ovral, Micronor,* ♣Minestrin 1/20, Min-Ovral,
Mircette, Modicon, Necon, NEE, Nelova, Nelova 1/50 M, Nelova 10/11,
Norcept-E 1/35, Nordette, Norethin 1/35E, Norethin 1/50M, Norinyl, Nor-
lestrin, Nor-Q.D.*, Ortho-Cept 21, Ortho-Evra (patch form), Ortho Cyclen,
Ortho-Novum 777, Ortho Tri-Cyclen, Ovcon, Ovral, Ovrette*, Preven, ♣Syn-
phasic, Tri-Levlen, Tri-Norinyl, Triphasil, Triquilar, Trivora, Yasmin, Zovia

---

BENEFITS versus RISKS

Possible Benefits	*Possible Risks*
HIGHLY EFFECTIVE FOR CONTRACEPTIVE PROTECTION	SERIOUS, LIFE-THREATENING THROMBOEMBOLIC DISORDERS in susceptible individuals
Moderately effective as adjunctive treatment in management of excessive menses and endometriosis	Hypertension
	Fluid retention
Helps decrease the risk of ovarian cancer while the pill is being taken	Intensification of migrainelike headaches and fibrocystic breast changes
Some forms decrease acne (especially Estrostep, Ortho Tri-Cyclen, and Alesse)	Accelerated growth of uterine fibroid tumors
	Drug-induced hepatitis with jaundice
	Benign liver tumors—rare

▷ **Principal Uses**

As a Single Drug Product: Uses currently included in FDA-approved labeling: (1)
Prevention of conception—the "Mini-Pill" contains only one component, a
progestin; this has been shown to be slightly less effective than the combination of estrogen and progestin in preventing pregnancy; (2) used in cases
where women do not make enough hormones (female hypogonadism); (3)
helps decrease excessive blood flow at menstruation (hypermenorrhea); (4)
of use in endometriosis as the combination mestranol and norethynodrel;
(5) Estrostep and Ortho Tri-Cyclen are approved to prevent acne.

Other (unlabeled) generally accepted uses: (1) May be of benefit in abnormal
hair growth in women (hirsutism); (2) some combination forms can have a
protective effect against osteoporosis; (3) Alesse has had an application
accepted by the FDA for use in acne.

As a Combination Drug Product [CD]: Uses currently included in FDA-approved
labeling: (1) Most oral contraceptives consist of a combination of an estrogen and a progestin; these products are the most effective form of medicinal contraception available; (2) they are sometimes used to treat menstrual
irregularity, excessively heavy menstrual flow, and endometriosis; (3)
norgestimate and ethinyl estradiol combination product (Ortho Tri-
Cyclen) is used to treat acne in females over 15.

---

*See Schedules of Controlled Drugs at the back of this book.

Other (unlabeled) generally accepted uses: (1) Gestodene has been reported to inhibit certain breast cancer cell lines (clinical studies are needed); (2) may have a protective effect against osteoporosis; (3) triphasic oral contraceptives can help in the prevention or treatment of menopause symptoms; (4) may have a role in rheumatoid arthritis, but the data are conflicting; (5) sometimes used around the time of menopause (perimenopausally) to provide regularity of menstruation; (6) used to reduce LH surges in order to improve results from in vitro fertilization or embryo transfer; (7) used as emergency contraception or a morning-after pill (MAP) or EC—while Preven is the only dedicated product for this use, Alesse, Ovral, Ovrette, Nordette, Levlen, Levlite, Levora, Lo/Ovral, Trivora, and Tri-Levlen have FDA safe and effective ratings as emergency contraceptives.

Author's Note: Research linked the number of times a woman ovulates to increased risk of ovarian cancer. This finding was associated with a P-53 gene, which may account for as much as 50% of ovarian cancer. Since birth control pills decrease the number of times that women ovulate, they may have a role in helping prevent cancer in women found to carry the P-53 gene. Further research is required. While the patch form is not technically a "pill," it is a contraceptive. Information has been included in this profile. Ortho Evra offers a novel benefit in ease of taking the product (adherence). Emergency contraception (the morning after pills or EC) have become an area of controversy with some groups advocating that these forms be provided without a prescription. One study in London found pharmacists as a unique and valuable resource for supplying and counseling on those progestogen only emergency contraceptives.

How These Drugs Work: When estrogen and progestin are taken in sufficient doses and on a regular basis, the blood and tissue levels of these hormones increase to resemble those that occur during pregnancy. This results in suppression of the two pituitary gland hormones that normally cause ovulation (the formation and release of an egg by the ovary). In addition, these drugs may (1) alter the cervical mucus so that it resists the passage of sperm and (2) alter the lining of the uterus so that it resists implantation of the egg (if ovulation occurs).

Available Dosage Forms and Strengths
Tablets: Several combinations of synthetic estrogens and progestins in varying strengths; see the package label of the brand prescribed.
Patch: Ortho-Evra form is a combination of estrogen (ethinyl estradiol) and progestin (norelgestromin).

▷ **Usual Adult Dosage Ranges:** For contraception: Start with the first tablet on the fifth day after the onset of menstruation. Follow with one tablet daily (taken at the same time each day) for 21 consecutive days. Resume treatment on the eighth day following the last tablet taken during the preceding cycle. The schedule is to take the drug daily for 3 weeks and to omit it for 1 week. For the Mini-Pill (progestin only), initiate treatment on the first day of menstruation and take one tablet daily, every day, throughout the year (no interruption). The Mircette brand uses 20 mcg of ethinyl estradiol and 150 mcg of dogesterel for 21 days. Two days of dummy (placebo) tablets are then taken and then five days of 10 mcg ethinyl estradiol. For the patch form, the system uses a 28-day cycle. Patches are worn for three weeks out of the 28-day cycle followed by a seven day patch-free period (see Dosing Instructions).

Emergency contraception (MAP): This is a critical situation. Talk to your doctor to be certain that you understand the possible side effects (nausea, etc.) and other issues and medical follow-up required for this procedure.

Author's Note: Research is now being conducted using longer cycles for birth control pill dosing. One company is testing a product tentatively called Seasonale that is taken for 84 days—thereby allowing for one period every three months.

Note: Actual dose and schedule must be determined for each patient individually.

Conditions Requiring Dosing Adjustments

Liver Function: Should NOT be taken if you have liver disease.

Kidney Function: Oral contraceptives are not significantly eliminated by the kidneys.

▷ **Dosing Instructions:** Combination products versus biphasic or triphasic forms are started in ways specific to the product. Make certain that you understand this. The tablets may be crushed and taken with or after food to reduce stomach upset. To ensure regular (every day) use and uniform blood levels, it is best to take the tablet at the same time daily. For the patch form, it is best to apply the patch at the same time and on the same day of the week. If you forget a dose (varies with the birth control form): For triphasic forms (Tri-Leven, Tri-Norinyl or Triphasil): Take the missed dose as soon as you remember. If you only remember on the next day, take two pills for the next two days, then return to your regular schedule, but USE ANOTHER TYPE OF BIRTH CONTROL UNTIL YOUR PERIOD BEGINS. Call your doctor for help. If you miss three pills in a row, stop the remaining pills for the month, USE A DIFFERENT KIND OF BIRTH CONTROL UNTIL YOUR PERIOD STARTS, and call your doctor. Your doctor will advise you as to when to re-start (usually just the same as when you first started the pills) with a new dose pack. For other birth control pill forms, if you forget a dose, call your doctor for detailed instructions.

When the patch is first used, a woman should wait until the day that her period (menstruation) starts. Two options are then available: a first day start or a Sunday start. For the first day start, the patch is applied during the first 24 hours of the menstrual period. The day that the patch is applied is day one. If the patch is applied after day one of the menstrual cycle, a backup (nonhormonal) form of contraception should be used at the same time as the patch for the first seven consecutive days that the patch is worn during the first treatment. The "patch change day" will be on the same day every week. Every new patch is applied on the same day and best applied at the same time of day. For example, if the patch is applied on a Tuesday, seven days later, the old patch will be removed and the next patch will be applied—keeping the same Tuesday schedule. Only one patch should be worn at a time. Patches are applied for three weeks in a row, followed by a seven-day patch-free interval. The process then repeats. Patches should be applied to healthy and intact skin which is clean and dry. It can be placed on the abdomen, buttocks, upper arm (outer portion), or upper torso. Never place the patch on the breasts.

Author's Note: One popular women's magazine advocated placing birth control pills in the vagina. This was presented as an option, but unless directed by your doctor, can lead to subtherapeutic benefits with most pills currently on the market. Some earlier data with higher dose formulations appeared to support that technique. Talk to your doctor.

Possible Advantages of These Drugs

Effective control of conception. Mircette form may benefit women who have migraines the second week they are "off the pill." A study of 46,000 British women released in early 1999 showed that women who took the pill did not show any increased risk of cancer. These data are important because of the large number of women and also because they were studied for 25 years. A Swedish study showed that oral contraceptives may increase bone density in women who take the pill between the ages of 30 and 40. Patch form (Ortho Evra) offers great benefits in ease of use (once weekly application for 3 weeks with one week off).

Usual Duration of Use: According to individual needs and circumstances. Long-term use (months to years) requires physician supervision and evaluation every 6 months.

Typical Treatment Goals and Measurements (Outcomes and Markers)

Contraceptive: The goal is to avoid pregnancy. Serum pregnancy tests (you have to have blood drawn for this) are presently the most sensitive tests to rule out pregnancy.

▷ **These Drugs Should Not Be Taken If**
- you have had an allergic reaction to any dose form of it.
- you have a history of thrombophlebitis, embolism, heart attack, or stroke.
- you have breast cancer.
- you have active liver disease, seriously impaired liver function or a history of liver tumor.
- you have diabetes and have developed circulatory disease.
- you have high blood pressure.
- you have not had any periods (amenorrhea).
- you have abnormal and unexplained vaginal bleeding.
- you have sickle cell disease.
- you are pregnant.

▷ **Inform Your Physician Before Taking These Drugs If**
- you have had an adverse reaction to any oral contraceptive.
- you have a history of cancer of the breast or reproductive organs.
- you have fibrocystic breast changes, uterine fibroid tumors, endometriosis, migrainelike headaches, epilepsy, asthma, elevated lipids, prolapse of the mitral valve of the heart, heart disease, high blood pressure, gallbladder disease, diabetes, or porphyria.
- you are over 40. This was an age-related limit previously, but current thinking says that use of these medicines may be a benefit-to-risk decision.
- you have been prescribed an antibiotic (some antibiotics may blunt the benefits of oral contraceptives and REQUIRE use of an alternative birth control method).
- you are using St. John's wort for depression.
- you have a history of or have kidney (renal disease or dysfunction) and are to take the Yasmin form.
- you smoke tobacco on a regular basis.
- you plan to have surgery in the near future.

Possible Side Effects (natural, expected, and unavoidable drug actions)

Fluid retention, weight gain, "breakthrough" bleeding (spotting in middle of menstrual cycle), altered menstrual pattern, lack of menstruation (during and following cessation of drug), increased susceptibility to yeast infection of the genital tissues. Tannish pigmentation of the face. Modest increases in blood pressure.

▷ **Possible Adverse Effects** (unusual, unexpected, and infrequent reactions)
If any of the following develop, consult your physician promptly for guidance.

Mild Adverse Effects

Allergic reactions: skin rash, hives, itching.

Headache, nervous tension, irritability, accentuation of migraine headaches—infrequent to frequent.

Rise in blood pressure (in some people)—possible.

Nausea, perhaps with vomiting—frequent (related to estrogen) and may ease if taken with evening meals.

Reduced tolerance to contact lenses or impaired color vision: blue tinge to objects, blue halo around lights—possible.

Serious Adverse Effects

Allergic reactions: anaphylaxis, erythema multiforme, and nodosum (skin reactions), loss of scalp hair.

Idiosyncratic reactions: joint and muscle pains.

Emotional depression—frequent.

Eye changes: optic neuritis, retinal thrombosis, altered curvature of the cornea, cataracts—possible.

Gallbladder disease, benign liver tumors, jaundice—case reports.

Ischemic colitis—case report.

Enlargement of uterine fibroid tumors—possible.

Abnormal glucose tolerance (hyperglycemia)—frequent in people with pregnancy (gestational) diabetes.

Thrombophlebitis (inflammation of a vein with formation of blood clot): pain or tenderness in thigh or leg, with or without swelling of foot or leg—increased risk, especially with high estrogen doses.

Drug-induced porphyria or worsening of systemic lupus erythematosus (SLE)—case reports.

Esophageal ulcers (especially if the medicine is taken lying down with no water)—case reports.

Stroke (blood clot in brain): headaches, blackout, sudden weakness or paralysis of any part of the body, severe dizziness, altered vision, slurred speech, inability to speak—possible increased risk (more probable in one study with high-dose estrogen formulations).

Heart attack (blood clot in coronary artery): sudden pain in chest, neck, jaw or arm; weakness; sweating; nausea—increased risk (not seen with low-dose estrogen products)—possible increased risk with use in women having cardiovascular risk factors, taking pills with more than 50 mcg of estrogen and in those who smoke.

Increased postassium—possible (Yasmin form).

Liver cancer—possible increased risk with long-term use.

▷ **Possible Effects on Sexual Function:** Altered character of menstruation; mid-cycle spotting—may be frequent.

Increased or decreased libido—possible.

Breast enlargement and tenderness with milk production—possible.

Absent menstruation and infertility (temporary) after discontinuation of drug.

Possible Delayed Adverse Effects: Estrogens taken during pregnancy can predispose the female child to the later development of cancer of the vagina or cervix following puberty. Nonpregnant use does not increase breast cancer.

▷ **Adverse Effects That May Mimic Natural Diseases or Disorders**

Liver reactions may suggest viral hepatitis. Increased blood pressure may mimic increased blood pressure from other causes.

Natural Diseases or Disorders That May Be Activated by These Drugs

Latent hypertension, diabetes mellitus, clotting factor disorders that favor blood clots, acute intermittent porphyria, lupus erythematosus-like syndrome.

Possible Effects on Laboratory Tests

Blood lupus erythematosus (LE) cells: positive.

Blood-clotting time or INR: decreased.

Blood amylase and lipase levels: increased (very rare pancreatitis).

Blood total cholesterol, HDL, LDL and VLDL cholesterol levels: usually no effects; some variability, depending upon estrogen and progestin content of preparation used.

Blood triglyceride levels: no effect to increased, depending upon estrogen and progestin content of preparation used.

Blood glucose level: increased.

Blood potassium: Increased (Yasmin form).

Blood thyroid-stimulating hormone (TSH) level: no effect.

Blood thyroid hormone levels: T3 and T4 increased; free T4 either no effect or decreased.

Liver function tests: increased liver enzymes (ALT/GPT, AST/GOT, alkaline phosphatase) and bilirubin.

CAUTION

1. Serious adverse effects due to these drugs are a very low risk. However, any unusual development should be reported and evaluated promptly by your doctor.

2. Studies indicate that women over 30 years of age who smoke and use oral contraceptives are at significantly greater risk of having a serious cardiovascular event than are nonusers.

3. The risk of thromboembolism increases with the amount of estrogen in the product and the age of the user. Low-estrogen combinations are advised. One larger United Kingdom study failed to find a difference in risk of unknown cause venous thromboembolism when combination oral contraceptives containing less than 50 micrograms of ethinyl estradiol were used. Other data says that combining smoking, asthma history, history of blood clots, increased body mass index with high estrogen combining pills increases risks of thromboembolism.

4. It is advisable to stop these drugs 1 month prior to elective surgery to reduce the risk of postsurgical thromboembolism. If they can't be stopped, preventive use of anticoagulants may be prudent.

5. Investigate promptly any alteration or disturbance of vision that occurs during the use of these drugs.

6. Investigate promptly the nature of recurrent, persistent, or severe headaches that develop while taking these drugs.

7. Observe for significant change of mood. Call your doctor if depression develops.

8. Certain commonly used drugs may reduce the effectiveness of oral contraceptives. Some of these are listed in the category of Other Drugs on page 847.

9. Diarrhea lasting more than a few hours (and occurring during the days

the drug is taken) can prevent adequate absorption of these drugs and impair their effectiveness as contraceptives.

10. If two consecutive menstrual periods are missed, ask your doctor if you should get a pregnancy test. Do not continue to use these drugs until you know whether you are pregnant.

11. **Many antibiotics may stop the effectiveness of birth control pills** (oral contraceptives). If your doctor prescribes an antibiotic, ask whether a different method of birth control is needed.

12. One researcher uses the acronym ACHES (A=abdominal pain, C=chest pain, H=headaches, E=eye problems and S=severe leg pain) to list signs of adverse effects that require a patient taking these medicines to call her doctor immediately.

13. One 8-year study found that women who used oral contraceptives IN THE PAST do not have an increased risk of cardiovascular disease.

▷ **Advisability of Use During Pregnancy**

Pregnancy Category: X. See Pregnancy Risk Categories at the back of this book.

Animal Studies: Genital defects reported in mice and guinea pigs; cleft palate reported in rodents.

Human Studies: Information from studies of pregnant women indicates that estrogens can masculinize the female fetus. In addition, limb defects and heart malformations have been reported. It is now known that estrogens taken during pregnancy can predispose the female child to the development of cancer of the vagina or cervix following puberty.

Avoid these drugs completely during entire pregnancy.

Advisability of Use If Breast-Feeding

Presence of these drugs in breast milk: Yes, in minute amounts (ethinyl estradiol or norethindrone). These drugs may suppress milk formation if started early after delivery.

Breast-feeding is considered to be safe during the use of oral contraceptives.

Habit-Forming Potential: None.

Effects of Overdose: Headache, drowsiness, nausea, vomiting, fluid retention, abnormal vaginal bleeding, breast enlargement and discomfort.

Possible Effects of Long-Term Use: High blood pressure, gallbladder disease with stones, accelerated growth of uterine fibroid tumors, absent menstruation and impaired fertility after discontinuation of drug.

Suggested Periodic Examinations While Taking These Drugs (at physician's discretion)

Regular (every 6 months) evaluation of the breasts and pelvic organs, including Pap smears.

Liver function tests as indicated.

▷ **While Taking These Drugs, Observe the Following**

Foods: Avoid excessive use of salt if fluid retention occurs. Excessive vitamin C may increase risk of contraceptive failure.

Herbal Medicines or Minerals: Black cohosh appears to work by (1) suppressing luteinizing hormone; (2) binding to estrogen receptors in the pituitary and inhibiting luteinizing hormone release and (3) binding to estrogen receptors in the pituitary. The net effect is that this herb eases symptoms of menopause, but little is known about long-term use or heart and bone protective effects. This herb may lower the effectiveness of birth control pills. Talk to your doctor before starting black cohosh if you are currently taking estrogen or an estrogen-containing product. DHEA (dehydroepiandros-terone) may lead to signs and symptoms of too much estrogen. Andro-steinedione (Tripple Stack, Andro-Surge, others) with ongoing use actually increases estrogen levels and should not be combined. Since St. John's wort and this drug may cause increased sun sensitivity, caution is advised. St. John's wort may blunt contraceptive effects and result in unwanted pregnancy. Ginseng does have actions similar to estrogen. Combined use should be avoided until more data are available.

Beverages: No specific restrictions, but caffeine will stay in the body (increased half-life) longer and caffeine consumption should decrease while patients are on the pill. May be taken with milk.

▷ *Alcohol:* No interactions expected.

Tobacco Smoking: Studies indicate that smoking—especially heavy smoking (15 or more cigarettes daily) while taking oral contraceptives significantly increases the risk of heart attack (coronary thrombosis). Heavy smoking should be considered a contraindication to the use of oral contraceptives. I advise everyone to quit smoking.

▷ *Other Drugs*

Oral contraceptives may ***increase*** the effects of
- alprazolam (Xanax) and other benzodiazepines (see Drug Classes).
- some benzodiazepines (see Drug Classes) and cause excessive sedation.
- cyclosporine (Sandimmune) and cause toxicity.
- metoprolol (Lopressor) and cause excessive beta-blocker effects.
- prednisolone and prednisone and other corticosteroids such as dexam-ethasone may lead to excessive cortisonelike effects.
- ropinirole (Requip).
- selegiline (Eldepryl, others), leading to increased selegiline adverse effects risk.
- tacrine (Cognex).
- tacrolimus (Prograf). Blood levels and tacrolimus dosing changes may be needed.
- theophyllines (Theo-Dur, others) and increase the risk of toxic effects.

Oral contraceptives ***taken concurrently*** with
- antibiotics (such as amoxicillin or ampicillin) can seriously impair effec-tiveness and allow pregnancy to occur.
- antidiabetic drugs (oral hypoglycemic agents) may cause unpredictable fluctuations of blood sugar.
- arginine (R-Gene intravenous) may result in falsely increased growth hor-mone levels during pituitary function testing. Results of the arginine test should be interpreted with caution.
- ascorbic acid (vitamin C) may result in increased levels of ethinyl estradiol and breakthrough bleeding if the vitamin C is stopped.
- atorvastatin (Lipitor) leading to increased ethinyl estradiol and norethin-drone levels.
- efavirenz (Sustiva), leading to increased ethinyl estradiol levels.
- liothyronine (Thyrostat) may lower benefits from thyroid supplementation in people with a functional thyroid gland. Liothyronine dosing may need to be adjusted.
- tricyclic antidepressants (Elavil, Sinequan, others) may enhance their adverse effects and reduce their antidepressant effectiveness.
- troleandomycin (TAO) may increase occurrence of liver toxicity and jaundice.

- warfarin (Coumadin) may cause unpredictable alterations of prothrombin activity; more frequent INR (prothrombin time or protime) testing is needed, and warfarin dosing should be adjusted to laboratory test results.
- zolmitriptan (Zomig) or naratriptan (Amerge) may lead to "triptan" toxicity.
- The following drugs may *decrease* the effects of oral contraceptives (and impair their effectiveness):
- barbiturates (phenobarbital, etc.; see Drug Classes).
- carbamazepine (Tegretol).
- fluconazole (Diflucan).
- griseofulvin (Fulvicin, etc.).
- nelfinavir (Viracept).
- nevirapine (Viramune).
- penicillins (ampicillin, penicillin V).
- phenytoin (Dilantin) or fosphenytoin (Cerebyx).
- pioglitazone (Actos) may possibly interact.
- primidone (Mysoline).
- rifampin (Rifadin, Rimactane).
- ritonavir (Norvir) and perhaps other protease inhibitors (amprenavir-see Drug Classes).
- tetracyclines (see Drug Classes).
- topiramate (Topamax).

▷ *Driving, Hazardous Activities:* Usually no restrictions. Consult your physician for assessment of individual risk and for guidance regarding specific restrictions.

Aviation Note: Usually no restrictions, but watch for the rare occurrence of disturbed vision and restrict activities accordingly. Consult a designated Aviation Medical Examiner.

Exposure to Sun: Use caution—these drugs can cause photosensitivity (see Glossary).

Discontinuation: Do not stop these drugs if "breakthrough" bleeding occurs. If spotting or bleeding continues, call your doctor. A higher-estrogen pill may be required. Remember: Omitting this drug for only 1 day may allow pregnancy to occur. It is best to avoid pregnancy for 3 to 6 months after stopping these drugs; aborted fetuses from women who became pregnant within 6 months after discontinuation reveal significantly increased chromosome abnormalities.

ORLISTAT (OAR li stat)

Introduced: 1999   **Class:** Weight loss agent, lipase inhibitor   **Prescription:** USA: Yes   **Controlled Drug:** USA: No; Canada: No   **Available as Generic:** USA: No; Canada: No
Brand Name: Xenical

BENEFITS versus RISKS

Possible Benefits	*Possible Risks*
EFFECTIVE REDUCTION IN WEIGHT WHEN USED IN CONJUNCTION WITH A REDUCED-CALORIE DIET	Reduced absorption of fat-soluble vitamins (A, D, E, K) and beta carotene
HELPS REDUCE RISK FOR WEIGHT GAIN AFTER PREVIOUS WEIGHT LOSS	Fecal incontinence and flatulence
WEIGHT LOSS HELPS DECREASE RISK OF DIABETES AND CORONARY HEART DISEASE	
LOWERED TOTAL CHOLESTEROL	
DECREASED LOW DENSITY LIPOPROTEINS	
INCREASED HIGH DENSITY LIPOPROTEINS	
Possible beneficial decreases in blood pressure	

▷ **Principal Uses**

As a Single Drug Product: Uses currently included in FDA-approved labeling: (1) Reduces weight in patients with a body mass index (BMI) of 30 kg/square meter or greater or in those with a BMI of 27 kg/square meter with other risk factors (such as diabetes, high blood pressure, or high blood lipids); (2) helps maintain weight loss in patients who have already lost weight.

Other (unlabeled) generally accepted uses: (1) May have a role in type 2 diabetes because weight loss was associated with better blood sugar control; (2) could have a role in some cases of elevated lipids (hyperlipidemia); (3) weight loss helps decrease risk of diabetes and coronary heart disease.

How This Drug Works: Inhibits the action of an enzyme called lipase (both in the stomach and pancreas), thereby inhibiting the absorption of fats. Since fats can account for a significant number of daily calories and orlistat blocks roughly 30% of fat absorption, use of orlistat over time leads to weight loss.

Available Dosage Forms and Strengths

Capsules — 120 mg

▷ **Usual Adult Dosage Ranges:** *Weight Loss:* One capsule three times a day with each main meal that contains fat. If a meal is eaten that has no fat, the capsule should not be taken until the next meal that has fat in it.

Note: Actual dose and schedule must be determined for each patient individually.

Conditions Requiring Dosing Adjustments

Liver Function: This medicine is poorly absorbed, and liver function is not expected to be a factor (removed in the stool). Since the liver IS involved in making clotting factors, possible decreased vitamin K absorption from orlistat may be an issue in patients with liver disease.

Kidney Function: **Minimally** absorbed into the body, and kidney function is not expected to be a factor.

▷ **Dosing Instructions:** This medicine may be taken up to an hour before a meal that contains fat. If you skip a meal or eat a meal without any fat in it, it is okay to skip that dose of orlistat. You should be eating a well-balanced, reduced-carbohydrate diet that has roughly 30% of its calories as fat. This medicine can lower the amount of fat-soluble vitamins (A, D, E, K) and beta carotene that can get into your body from your diet. Over time, this may lead to a deficiency. A multivitamin containing those nutrients is important and should be taken two hours before or after your dose of orlistat. If you forget a dose, but eat a fat-free meal—simply skip the dose you forgot. If you forget a dose and have taken a fatty meal, take the missed dose if it is within an hour of the time the dose should have been taken. If you remember the missed dose more than an hour after the meal, skip the missed dose and wait until your next meal to take this medicine. DO NOT double doses. Talk with your doctor if you find yourself missing doses.

Usual Duration of Use: Regular use is required to get the best results from this medicine. Results (as measured by stool fat) can be seen in as little as 24–48 hours. Measurable weight loss will be determined by the amount of exercise, metabolic rate, adherence to diet, and other factors. Use of this medicine for more than two years has not been studied as yet. Long-term use (months to years) requires ongoing follow-up by your doctor.

Typical Treatment Goals and Measurements (Outcomes and Markers)
Weight Loss: The goal is to lower body weight or maintain weight loss by preventing absorption of fat. Body weight, percent body fat and laboratory tests such as triglycerides, VLDL, LDL, and HDL can be checked to assess successful combination treatment. In some initial clinical data, people who took this medicine for two years lost an average of 4.5% of their starting body weight or about 4 kilograms. Be sure to talk to your doctor about the benefits of losing some weight and keeping it off versus crash or fad diets and weight yo-yoing.

Possible Advantages of This Drug
Works in a novel way compared to previously available medicines for weight loss. Does not have an effect on heart valves. Increases good cholesterol (HDL) and decreases LDL and total cholesterol.

▷ **This Drug Should Not Be Taken If**
- you have had an allergic reaction to it previously.
- you have ongoing (chronic) malabsorption.
- you have a cause for obesity (such as hypothyroidism that should be treated) which would then obviate the need for orlistat, and an evaluation of this or other metabolic causes haven't been checked.
- you have stagnation of bile in the small bile ducts in the liver (cholestasis).

▷ **Inform Your Physician Before Taking This Drug If**
- you have significant disease in your stomach or intestine (gastrointestinal or GI tract), especially diseases that make you prone to diarrhea.
- you do not understand that increasing fat in your diet may also increase GI adverse effects from this medicine.
- you have a history of kidney stones (calcium oxalate).
- you have a history of low thyroid function (hypothyroidism).
- you have a known deficiency of vitamin A, D, E, or K or a poor diet that would lead you to tend toward deficiency of those vitamins or of beta carotene.

Possible Side Effects (natural, expected, and unavoidable drug actions)

Interference with normal fat digestion and absorption; reduced absorption of vitamins A, D, E, and K as well as beta carotene.

▷ **Possible Adverse Effects** (unusual, unexpected, and infrequent reactions)

If any of the following develop, consult your physician promptly for guidance.

Mild Adverse Effects

Allergic reaction: skin rash—possible.

Excessive gas (flatus) with or without fecal discharge—possible to frequent and can increase with higher amounts of fat in the diet.

Oily spotting of stool—may be frequent.

Nausea and soft or liquid stools—frequent.

(All of the above effects may decrease over time.)

Headache or dizziness—infrequent to frequent.

Increased blood pressure, edema—infrequent.

Serious Adverse Effects

Allergic reaction: not reported.

Lowering of vitamins A, D, E, and K. Vitamin K lowering may lead to an increased bleeding tendency if not supplemented—possible.

In clinical trials, nine cases of breast neoplasm were reported in patients taking 120 mg three times daily and one case was reported in the placebo group. Causation by orlistat is questionable, as the cases were seen within 6 months of the start of the clinical trials and the drug is minimally absorbed.

Depression—case reports.

Diabetic ketoacidosis—case report (in a diabetic woman taking this drug for weight loss).

Liver toxicity—case report.

▷ **Possible Effects on Sexual Function:** Menstrual irregularity—infrequent.

Natural Diseases or Disorders That May Be Activated by This Drug

Problems with patients who have cholestasis are possible.

Possible Effects on Laboratory Tests

INR (prothrombin time): possibly increased (impaired vitamin K absorption).

LDL and total cholesterol: decreased.

CAUTION

1. Since this medicine may interfere with absorption of fat-soluble vitamins and beta carotene, these compounds should be supplemented while you are taking orlistat and the vitamin dosing separated from orlistat doses by two hours.
2. Causes of obesity that are organic (such as low thyroid function or hypothyroidism) should be evaluated BEFORE orlistat is prescribed.
3. If you have a history of kidney stones made of calcium oxalate (nephrolithiasis), this medicine may worsen this problem.
4. Weight loss may improve how well blood sugar is controlled in people with diabetes—a beneficial effect. Oral hypoglycemic medicines (see Drug Classes) may have to be used in lower doses.
5. No data are available on the combination of orlistat with other weight loss agents, such as sibutramine (Meridia).

Precautions for Use

By Infants and Children: Safety and effectiveness for those under 16 years of age not established.

By Those Over 60 Years of Age: Studies in special populations were not conducted.

▷ **Advisability of Use During Pregnancy**
　Pregnancy Category: B. See Pregnancy Risk Categories at the back of this book.
　Animal Studies: No embryotoxicity or teratogenicity in mice or rabbits.
　Human Studies: Adequate studies of pregnant women are not available. NOT recommended for use during pregnancy.

Advisability of Use If Breast-Feeding
　Presence of this drug in breast milk: Unknown.
　Stop nursing or don't take the medicine if breast-feeding is to be undertaken.

Habit-Forming Potential: None, but misuse of the medicine is possible (as in anorexia).

Effects of Overdose: Reports of single 800-mg doses have been studied in people of normal weight without any adverse effects. If a significant overdose of orlistat happens, the patient should be medically observed for at least 24 hours. It is expected that any systemic effects would be rapidly reversible.

Possible Effects of Long-Term Use: Deficiencies of vitamins A, D, E, and K and beta carotene. Calcium deficiency, osteoporosis. Acidosis (excessive retention of chloride).

Suggested Periodic Examinations While Taking This Drug (at physician's discretion)
　Measurements of blood levels of total cholesterol, low-density (LDL) cholesterol, and high-density (HDL) cholesterol. Possible bone mineral density tests if vitamin D is not supplemented. Blood levels of vitamins may be prudent to guide supplementation or need for supplementation.

▷ **While Taking This Drug, Observe the Following**
　Foods: Follow your doctor's recommended diet and portion control. Avoid foods that have tended to cause gas (flatus) formation previously.
　Herbal Medicines or Minerals: A variety of products that promise weight loss has been or is available. Some of these products have contained ma huang or other potentially dangerous ingredients. DO NOT combine any herbal weight loss product with orlistat. Talk to your doctor if you are considering any herbal weight loss product BEFORE you take it.
　Nutritional Support: Ask your doctor about the need for supplements of vitamins A, D, E, and K as well as beta carotene.
　Beverages: No restrictions.
▷ *Alcohol:* No interactions expected, but remember, many alcoholic beverages deliver a lot of calories.
　Tobacco Smoking: No interactions expected. I advise everyone to quit smoking.
▷ *Other Drugs*
　Orlistat may *decrease* the effects of
　• beta carotene; take 2 hours before or after orlistat.
　• fat-soluble vitamins, such as vitamin A, D, E, or K.
　Orlistat *taken concurrently* with
　• cyclosporine (Sandimmune, others) may (because of possible variation in cyclosporine levels with changes in diet) lead to changes in cyclosporine levels. Caution is advised, and study is needed.
　• pravastatin (Pravachol) or other HMG-CoA reductase inhibitors work well in further lowering cholesterol. Pravastatin levels may be increased by roughly 30%. Patients taking this combination should be followed more closely for possible adverse effects.
　• warfarin (Coumadin, others) may (because of possible decreases in vitamin K over time) lead to increased warfarin effects; more frequent INR testing is prudent.

▷ *Driving, Hazardous Activities:* No restrictions.

Aviation Note: The use of this drug is usually not a disqualification for piloting. Consult a designated Aviation Medical Examiner.

Exposure to Sun: No reports of problems at present.

Discontinuation: The dose of any potentially toxic or narrow therapeutic-window drug (such as warfarin) taken concurrently must be changed appropriately if orlistat is stopped.

OXAPROZIN (OX a proh zin)

Please see the propionic acids (nonsteroidal anti-inflammatory drug) family profile.

OXICAMS (Nonsteroidal Anti-Inflammatory Drug Family)

Piroxicam   (peer OX i kam)

Introduced: 1978   **Class:**   Mild analgesic, anti-inflammatory   **Prescription:**   USA: Yes   **Controlled Drug:**   USA: No; Canada: No   **Available as Generic:**   Yes

Brand Names: ✤Alti-Piroxicam, ✤Apo-Piroxicam, ✤Brexidol, ✤Dom-Piroxicam, Feldene, ✤Fexicam, ✤Med-Pirocam, ✤Novo-Pirocam, ✤Nu-Pirox

BENEFITS versus RISKS	
Possible Benefits	*Possible Risks*
EFFECTIVE RELIEF OF MILD-TO-MODERATE PAIN AND INFLAMMATION	Gastrointestinal pain, ulceration and bleeding
ONCE-A-DAY DOSING HELPS PEOPLE TAKE IT	Drug-induced hepatitis—rare
	Rare kidney damage
	Mild fluid retention
	Reduced white blood cell and platelet counts

▷ **Principal Uses**

As a Single Drug Product: Uses currently included in FDA-approved labeling: Relieves mild to moderately severe pain and inflammation associated with (1) rheumatoid arthritis and (2) osteoarthritis.

Other (unlabeled) generally accepted uses: (1) Treats the morning and evening pain associated with ankylosing spondylitis; (2) helps relieve the pain and inflammation of acute gout; (3) used to treat terminal cancer pain in combination with doxepin; (4) may have a role in easing temporal arteritis; (5) effective in painful menstruation (primary dysmenorrhea); (6) second-line therapy in acute gout (7) may help in preventing colon cancer and possibly Alzheimer's, but further research is needed.

How This Drug Works: This drug suppresses the formation of prostaglandins (and related compounds), chemicals involved in the production of inflammation and pain. Inhibits platelets from making prostaglandins (PGE1 and 2, etc.). By lowering the number of white blood cells in joints (synovial fluid) and decreasing the chemicals they can use to cause damage, this medicine works to limit joint damage and inflammation.

Available Dosage Forms and Strengths
Capsules — 10 mg, 20 mg
Rectal suppository — 10 mg, 20 mg

▷ **Usual Adult Dosage Ranges:** *As antiarthritic*: 20 mg once daily. Higher doses may not confer added benefits. This dose may be separated into two equal doses.
Dysmenorrhea: 40 mg (two tablets) in the morning for two days, then 20 mg a day until symptoms ease or menstruation ends.
Note: Actual dose and schedule must be determined for each patient individually.

Conditions Requiring Dosing Adjustments
Liver Function: This drug should be used with caution and in decreased dose by patients with liver compromise.
Kidney Function: Piroxicam should be used with caution in renal compromise and kidney function followed closely.

▷ **Dosing Instructions:** Take with or following food (may also take with an antacid) to prevent stomach irritation. Take with a full glass of water and remain upright (do not lie down) for 30 minutes. The capsule may be opened. If you forget a dose: Take the missed dose as soon as you remember it, unless it's nearly time for your next dose—if that is the case, skip the missed dose and take the next dose right on schedule. DO NOT double doses. Talk with your doctor if you find yourself missing doses.

Usual Duration of Use: Use on a regular schedule for a few days often gives some relief from the discomfort of arthritis. It may take eight to twelve weeks to gain the peak response. Long-term use (months to years) requires physician supervision and periodic evaluation. It's not unusual to change or combine medicines in RA.

Typical Treatment Goals and Measurements (Outcomes and Markers)
Pain: Most clinicians treating pain use a device called an algometer to check your pain. This looks like a small ruler, but lets the clinician better understand your pain. The goals of treatment then relate to where the level of pain started (for example, a rating of 7 on a zero-to-ten scale) and what the cause of the pain was. Pain medicines may also be used together (in combination) in order to get the best result or outcome. If your pain control is not acceptable to YOU (remember, in hospitals and outpatient settings, etc. pain control is a patient right and a vital sign) and if after a week of arthritis pain treatment as an outpatient, results are not acceptable, be sure to call your doctor as you may need a different medicine or combination.
Arthritis: Control of arthritis symptoms (pain, loss of mobility, decreased ability to accomplish activities of daily living) is paramount in returning patient quality of life and to checking the results (beneficial outcomes) from this medicine. CRP and RA titer may decrease. See WOMAC in Glossary for rheumatoid arthritis. ACR 20 and higher (see Glossary) refers to the number of signs and symptoms relieved by this medicine.

Possible Advantages of This Drug
Fewer side effects than many other nonselective NSAIDS. Once-daily dosing helps adherence.

▷ **This Drug Should Not Be Taken If**
- you have had an allergic reaction to it previously.
- you are subject to asthma or nasal polyps caused by aspirin.
- you have active peptic ulcer disease or any form of gastrointestinal bleeding.
- you have a bleeding disorder or a blood cell disorder.
- you have active liver disease or severe impairment of kidney function.

▷ **Inform Your Physician Before Taking This Drug If**
  • you are allergic to aspirin or to other aspirin substitutes.
  • you have a history of peptic ulcer disease, regional enteritis, or ulcerative colitis.
  • you have a history of any type of bleeding disorder.
  • you have impaired liver or kidney function.
  • you develop signs or symptoms of pancreatitis while taking this medicine (talk with your doctor).
  • you have high blood pressure or a history of heart failure.
  • you take acetaminophen, aspirin or other aspirin substitutes, anticoagulants, or oral antidiabetic drugs.
  • you have an infection.
  • you plan to have surgery of any type in the near future.

Possible Side Effects (natural, expected, and unavoidable drug actions)
  Fluid retention (weight gain, edema), prolongation of bleeding time.

▷ **Possible Adverse Effects** (unusual, unexpected, and infrequent reactions)
  If any of the following develop, consult your physician promptly for guidance.
  Mild Adverse Effects
  Allergic reactions: skin rash, itching, spontaneous bruising.
  Headache, dizziness, hair loss, altered vision, ringing in ears (tinnitus), drowsiness, fatigue, paresthesias, inability to concentrate—rare to infrequent.
  Indigestion, nausea, vomiting, abdominal pain, diarrhea—infrequent to frequent.
  Serious Adverse Effects
  Esophagitis or active peptic ulcer, stomach or intestinal bleeding—possible and more likely in elderly.
  Drug-induced liver or kidney damage—rare to infrequent.
  Serious skin damage (toxic epidermal necrolysis)—case reports.
  Worsening of congestive heart failure—possible.
  Pancreatitis—rare.
  Enteropathy—possible.
  Bone marrow depression (see Glossary): abnormal bleeding or bruising—case reports.
  Blood-clotting problems—related to dose and half-life.
  Increased blood potassium or decreased sodium—case reports.

▷ **Possible Effects on Sexual Function:** None reported.

Possible Delayed Adverse Effects: Mild anemia due to "silent" blood loss from the stomach.

▷ **Adverse Effects That May Mimic Natural Diseases or Disorders**
  Liver reaction may suggest viral hepatitis.

Natural Diseases or Disorders That May Be Activated by This Drug
  Peptic ulcer disease, ulcerative colitis. This drug may hide symptoms of gout.

Possible Effects on Laboratory Tests
  Red blood cell count and hemoglobin level or sodium: decreased.
  Bleeding time: increased.
  Blood uric acid level or potassium: increased.
  Liver function tests: increased liver enzymes (ALT/GPT, AST/GOT, and alkaline phosphatase), increased bilirubin.
  Kidney function tests: blood creatinine and urea nitrogen (BUN) levels

increased; urine analysis positive for red blood cells, casts, and increased protein content (kidney damage).

Fecal occult blood test: positive.

CAUTION

1. The smallest effective dose should always be used.
2. This drug may hide early signs of infection. Tell your doctor if you think you are developing an infection.
3. Congestive heart failure in elderly patients may be unmasked or worsened. Risk appears to increase with use of higher doses.
4. This medicine helps treat the signs and symptoms and may help prevent structural damage in rheumatoid arthritis (RA), does not work like the Disease Modifying AntiRheumatic Drugs (DMARDs) to help stop the damage/progression of RA itself.

Precautions for Use

By Infants and Children: Indications and dose recommendations for those under 12 years of age are not established.

By Those Over 60 Years of Age: Small doses are advisable until tolerance is determined. Watch for any indications of liver or kidney toxicity, fluid retention, dizziness, confusion, impaired memory, stomach bleeding, or constipation. People in this age group are often more likely to have stomach problems from the medicine itself. Existing congestive heart failure may be worsened.

▷ **Advisability of Use During Pregnancy**

Pregnancy Category: B. D in the final 3 months of pregnancy. See Pregnancy Risk Categories at the back of this book.

Animal Studies: No birth defects reported due to this drug.

Human Studies: Adequate studies of pregnant women are not available.

The manufacturer does not recommend the use of this drug during pregnancy.

Advisability of Use If Breast-Feeding

Presence of this drug in breast milk: Yes.

Talk to your doctor about this decision. The American Academy of Pediatrics considers this medicine to be usually compatible with breast-feeding.

Habit-Forming Potential: None.

Effects of Overdose: Possible drowsiness, dizziness, ringing in the ears, nausea, vomiting, indigestion.

Possible Effects of Long-Term Use: Development of anemia due to "silent" bleeding from the gastrointestinal tract.

Suggested Periodic Examinations While Taking This Drug (at physician's discretion)

Complete blood cell counts.

Liver and kidney function tests.

Complete eye examinations if vision is altered in any way.

Sedimentation rate (ESR) and C-reactive Protein (CRP) checks.

ACR progress.

Hearing examinations if ringing in the ears or hearing loss develops.

▷ **While Taking This Drug, Observe the Following**

Foods: No restrictions. No data from objective studies are available for combination use of this medicine and glucosamine. Talk to your doctor about possible combination.

rbal Medicines or Minerals: Since St. John's wort and this drug may cause increased sun sensitivity, caution is advised. Feverfew, ginseng, ginkgo, alfalfa, clove oil, cinchona bark, white willow bark, and garlic may also change clotting, so combining those herbals with these medicines is not recommended. Talk to your doctor BEFORE combining any medicines. NSAIDs may decrease feverfew effects. Hay flower, mistletoe herb, and white mustard seed carry German Commission E monograph indications for arthritis but have not been tested in combination with this medicine. Herbals such as eucalyptus, kava, and valerian that can have toxic effects on the liver should be avoided while taking piroxicam. Talk to your doctor BEFORE adding any herbal to piroxicam.

Beverages: No restrictions. May be taken with milk.

▷ *Alcohol:* Use with caution. Both alcohol and piroxicam can irritate the stomach lining and can increase the risk of stomach ulceration and/or bleeding.

Tobacco Smoking: No interactions expected. I advise everyone to quit smoking.

▷ *Other Drugs*

Piroxicam may ***increase*** the effects of
• adrenocortical steroids (see Drug Classes) and may result in additive stomach irritation.
• anticoagulants (Coumadin, etc.) and increase the risk of bleeding; more frequent INR (prothrombin time or protime) testing is needed, and dosing should then be adjusted accordingly. Low-molecular-weight heparins (see Drug Classes) combined with this medicine increase risk of hematoma.
• beta blockers (atenolol and others)—can decrease the effectiveness of the beta blocker.
• cyclosporine (Sandimmune) may increase seizure risk.
• enoxaparin (Lovenox) and may increase bleeding risk.
• lithium (Lithobid, others) and can lead to lithium toxicity.
• methotrexate (Mexate) and may lead to methotrexate toxicity.

Piroxicam ***taken concurrently*** with
• alendronate (Fosamax) may increase risk of stomach and intestinal irritation, and use at the same time will decrease the amount of alendronate that gets into your body. Separate doses by 2 hours.
• antihypertensives such as thiazides (see Drug Classes), loop diuretics and others (ACE inhibitors) will blunt their therapeutic benefits.
• cholestyramine (Questran) may blunt piroxicam effectiveness.
• diuretics (see Drug Classes) may blunt diuretic benefits.
• eptifibatide (Integrilin) may increase bleeding risk.
• ofloxacin (Floxin) and other quinolones such as levofloxacin (Levaquin) may increase seizure risk.
• oral hypoglycemics (see sulfonylureas) may increase risk of low blood sugar.
• ritonavir (Norvir) and perhaps other protease inhibitors (see Drug Classes) can lead to toxicity.
• tacrolimus (Prograf) may increase risk of kidney failure.

Piroxicam ***taken concurrently*** with the following drugs may increase bleeding risk. Avoid these:
• aspirin or other NSAIDs.
• clopidogrel (Plavix). Follow patients closely and check for early signs or symptoms of bleeding.
• dipyridamole (Persantine).
• indomethacin (Indocin).

- sulfinpyrazone (Anturane).
- valproic acid (Depakene).

▷ *Driving, Hazardous Activities:* This drug may cause drow
    Restrict activities as necessary.
    Aviation Note: The use of this drug *may be a disqualification* t.
    sult a designated Aviation Medical Examiner.
    Exposure to Sun: This drug may cause photosensitivity (see Glossa
    tion.

OXTRIPHYLLINE (ox TRY fi lin)

Other Names: Choline theophyllinate, theophylline cholinate

Introduced: 1965   **Class:**   Antiasthmatic, bronchodilator, xanthines
Prescription: USA: Yes

Controlled Drug: USA: No; Canada: No   **Available as Generic:**   Yes

Brand Names: ✤Apo-Oxtriphylline, Choledyl, Choledyl Delayed-Release,
    Choledyl SA, ✤Novotriphyl

**Author's Note: This medicine is converted to 64% theophylline by the body.
See the theophylline profile for further information.**

OXYCODONE (ox ee KOH dohn)

Introduced: 1950   **Class:**   Analgesic, strong; opioids   **Prescription:**
USA: Yes   **Controlled Drug:**   USA: C-II*; Canada: No   **Available as**
Generic: USA: Yes; Canada: No

Brand Names: ✤Endocet [CD], ✤Endodan [CD], ✤Oxycocet [CD], ✤Oxy-
    codan [CD], OxyContin, Percocet [CD], ✤Percocet-Demi [CD], Percodan
    [CD], Percodan-Demi [CD], Roxicet, Roxicodone, Roxilox, Roxiprin [CD],
    SK-Oxycodone, ✤Supeudol, Tylox [CD]

BENEFITS versus RISKS	
Possible Benefits	*Possible Risks*
EFFECTIVE RELIEF OF MODERATE-TO-SEVERE AND ONGOING-PAIN	POTENTIAL FOR HABIT FORMATION (DEPENDENCE)
	Sedative effects
	Mild allergic reactions—infrequent
	Nausea, constipation

▷ **Principal Uses**
    As a Single Drug Product: Uses currently included in FDA-approved labeling:
    (1) Used in tablet and suppository form (Canada) to relieve moderate to
    severe pain; (2) OxyContin form is approved for use appropriate to a
    schedule II narcotic to treat people in moderate to severe pain who are
    expected to require continuous PAIN medicines (opioids) for an extended
    time. An important factor to be considered for OxyContin use is the sever-
    ity and persistent nature of the pain that a patient is facing.
    Other (unlabeled) generally accepted uses: None.

*See Schedules of Controlled Drugs at the back of this book.

As a Combination Drug Product [CD]: Oxycodone is available in combinations with acetaminophen and with aspirin. These milder pain relievers are added to enhance the analgesic effect and reduce fever when present.

Author's Note: The FDA and Purdue Pharmaceuticals have worked together to strengthen warnings for OxyContin because of continuing reports of abuse and diversion of this medicine. A "Dear Healthcare Professional" letter was sent out that explains the strengthening of the labeling including proper prescribing information and also highlights the problems associated with abuse and diversion of OxyContin. An important factor that MUST be considered when OxyContin is prescribed is the severity of the pain that is being treated and the ongoing persistent nature of the pain that results, not simply the disease that is the root cause of the painful symptoms.

The company has also responsibly undertaken a "Profiles in Pain Management" series in the *Pharmacy Today* journal of the American Pharmaceutical Association to increase awareness of prescription medication abuse. Because ALL opioids are subject to abuse, the FDA is also encouraging all makers of opioids sold in the US to voluntarily review and revise product labeling as needed to help ensure adequate warnings and precautions regarding risks of abuse, misuse and diversion are presented and that responsible prescribing practices are promoted. A MedWatch safety summary is available at *www.fda.gov/ medwatch/safety/2001/safety01.htm#oxycon.*

How This Drug Works: Acting primarily as a depressant of certain brain functions (by attaching to specific receptors—Mu receptors), this drug suppresses pain perception and calms the emotional response to pain.

Available Dosage Forms and Strengths

Solution — 5 mg/5 ml

Suppositories — 10 mg, 20 mg (Canada)

Tablets — 5 mg, 10 mg (Canada)

Tablets — 2.44 mg, 4.88 mg (in combination drugs)

Tablets, combination (new Percocet) — 7.5 mg oxycodone/325mg acetaminophen and 10 mg/325 mg

Tablets, controlled-release — 10 mg, 20 mg, 40 mg, 80 mg, 160 mg

▷ **Usual Adult Dosage Ranges:** Percodan is taken as one tablet (5 mg) every 6 hours. Current pain theory says that pain medicines should be scheduled—for example, given every 6 hours. The outdated "wait until it hurts" or PRN method tended to result in suffering. May be increased to 10 mg every 4 hours if needed for severe pain. The total daily dose should not exceed 60 mg.

The new Percocet (oxycodone and acetaminophen combination) tablets are now available in more strengths that minimize the amount of acetaminophen [previously 2.5/325, 5/325, 7.5/500, and 10/650] and now 7.5 mg oxycodone with 325 mg acetaminophen and 10 mg/325mg have been added. These strengths represent the amount of oxycodone followed by the amount of acetaminophen and give pain management specialists more flexibility in treating pain. Make sure you understand how much and how often to take this medicine. The new "lower acetaminophen" forms make it less likely that too much acetaminophen will be taken and will lower the risk of damage to the liver (hepatotoxicity).

OxyContin is taken every 12 hours and is a controlled-release formulation. This product has an 80-mg and 120-mg strength that is used for increasing (escalating) pain in people who have been taking opioids and have become tolerant. Some clinicians use a rescue dose of the immediate-release forms of oxycodone to manage (rescue) breakthrough pain (usually dosed as 10 to 30 mg every 4 hours as needed for pain in people who are already taking opioid pain medicines) and then add a percentage of the total daily rescue dosage used back to the extended-release formulation. The amount of medicine given every 12 hours should be increased if needed, rather than changing the time between doses. Taking this medicine more often than every 12 hours has not been studied. Increases in total daily Oxycontin doses can usually be made in steps of 25% of the existing dose excepting the change from 10 mg to 20 mg. New labeling for this form of oxycodone is meant to decrease the chance that OxyContin could be prescribed inappropriately for pain of lesser severity than the approved use or for other disorders or conditions inappropriate for a schedule II narcotic.

Note: Actual dose and schedule must be determined for each patient individually.

Conditions Requiring Dosing Adjustments

Liver Function: Dose adjustments should be empirically made in liver failure.

Kidney Function: Dose adjustment does not appear to be needed. Some combination products contain aspirin, which may be contraindicated in kidney failure.

▷ **Dosing Instructions:** The immediate-release tablets may be crushed and taken with or following food to reduce stomach upset or nausea. Controlled-release forms such as OxyContin should never be broken, chewed, crushed, or injected. Taking altered controlled-release forms can lead to excessively fast drug release and death. As with other medicines for pain management, dosing is provided around the clock. If you forget a dose: For immediate-release forms: Take the missed dose as soon as you remember it, unless it's nearly time for your next dose—if that is the case, skip the missed dose and take the next dose right on schedule. For sustained-release forms: Call your doctor. DO NOT double doses. Talk with your doctor if you find yourself missing doses.

Author's Note: Current pain treatment theory calls for timed or scheduled dosing. This tends to prevent pain, rather than allowing pain to recur and then having to be treated. Some clinicians will use timed dosing immediately after surgery and then revert to as-needed dosing once the most severe period of pain has passed. Pain is now the fifth vital sign.

Usual Duration of Use: As long as significant pain is present and as required to control pain. Continual use of the immediate-release form should not exceed 5 to 7 days without interruption and reassessment of need (excepting use as a "rescue medicine." Use of the Oxycontin form (consistent with new labeling) will be for painful conditions requiring longer-term treatment with a potent opioid. Ongoing use frequently requires use of bowel medicines (such as Senokot) to address constipation.

Typical Treatment Goals and Measurements (Outcomes and Markers)

Pain: Most clinicians treating pain use a device called an algometer to check your pain. This looks like a small ruler, but lets the clinician better understand your pain. The goals of treatment then relate to where the level of pain started (for example, a rating of 7 on a 0–10 scale) and what the cause of the pain was. I use the PQRSTBG (see Glossary) system. Pain medicines may also be used together (in combination) in order to get the best result or outcome. If your pain control is not acceptable to YOU (remember, in hospitals and outpatient settings, etc. pain control is a patient right and the fifth vital sign) and if after a reasonable attempt with good adherence, results are not acceptable, be sure to call your doctor. You may need a different dose, different medicine or combination. Specific clinical practice guidelines from the American Geriatrics Society (AGS) for pain management in older people should be used to help guide treatments in people over 60.

▷ **This Drug Should Not Be Taken If**
- you had an allergic reaction to it previously.
- you are having an acute attack of asthma, severe asthma, or excessive carbon dioxide (CO_2).
- you are having significant depression of breathing (respiratory depression).
- you have a blockage in your bowel (paralytic ileus).
- patients allergic to aspirin should not be given Percodan.

▷ **Inform Your Physician Before Taking This Drug If**
- you had an unfavorable reaction to any narcotic drug or are prone to constipation.
- you have had a head injury with increased pressure (intracranial) in the head.
- you have a history of drug abuse, misuse, or alcoholism (benefit-to-risk decision).
- you have chronic lung disease with impaired breathing or another condition that would make it likely that you have a lowered lung or respiratory reserve.
- you are dehydrated or are in circulatory shock.
- you have impaired liver or kidney function.
- you have gallbladder disease, a seizure disorder, or an underactive thyroid gland.
- you have difficulty emptying the urinary bladder.
- you are taking any other drugs that have a sedative effect.
- you plan to have surgery under general anesthesia in the near future.

Possible Side Effects (natural, expected, and unavoidable drug actions)
Drowsiness, light-headedness, dry mouth, urinary retention, constipation.

▷ **Possible Adverse Effects** (unusual, unexpected, and infrequent reactions)
If any of the following develop, consult your physician promptly for guidance.
Mild Adverse Effects
Allergic reactions: skin rash, hives, itching.
Idiosyncratic reactions: skin rash and itching when combined with dairy products (milk or cheese).
Dizziness, sensation of drunkenness, depression, blurred or double vision—dose-related.
Nausea, vomiting—may be dose related.
Serious Adverse Effects
Impaired breathing: use with caution in chronic lung disease—variable and can be dose related.
Abnormal body movements, if the drug is abruptly stopped.

▷ **Possible Effects on Sexual Function:** Blunted sexual responses—case reports.

Possible Effects on Laboratory Tests

Urine screening tests for drug abuse: test result may be falsely **positive;** confirmatory test result may be **negative.** (Test results depend upon amount of drug taken and testing method used.)

CAUTION

1. If you have been prescribed Percocet, please be aware that there are now more strengths. Make certain that you understand how much to take. The strengths (oxycodone/acetaminophen) may be confusing. For example, it may be tempting for some prescribers to shorten Percocet 5/325 to Percocet-5. This kind of name change could lead to an impression that five tablets are to be taken instead of a correct one-tablet dose. Talk to your doctor and make sure you understand how much and how often you are to take this medicine.

2. If you have asthma, chronic bronchitis or emphysema, excessive use of this drug may cause significant respiratory difficulty, thickening of bronchial secretions, and suppression of coughing.

3. If you have been taking an oxycodone form on an ongoing basis, slow tapering rather than sudden discontinuation is prudent.

4. The concurrent use of this drug with atropinelike drugs can increase the risk of urinary retention and reduced intestinal function.

5. Constipation can be a serious problem, particularly in older patients (as bowel function tends to slow down). Many clinicians prescribe a medicine (such as Senokot-S) to promote bowel movements at the same time that oxycodone is prescribed.

6. The FDA and the maker of OxyContin have worked together to strengthen the warnings and precautions section of the OxyContin labeling. It would be prudent to discuss these changes with your doctor. The fact that this drug has been misused, altered, and used inappropriately by addicts does not mean that it does not have an important place in pain management.

7. Do not take this drug following acute head injury.

8. Females will generally have a 25% higher oxycodone blood (plasma) level than males when weight is considered (on a body weight adjusted basis).

9. Physical dependence and tolerance can happen with repeated use (see Glossary).

10. If you are taking a large dose of OxyContin (such as 160 mg) make sure you understand that a high fat meal can increase drug levels by 25%— and could impact breathing.

Precautions for Use

By Infants and Children: Do not use this drug in children under 2 years of age because of their vulnerability to life-threatening respiratory depression.

By Those Over 60 Years of Age: Small starting doses and short-term therapy are indicated. There may be increased susceptibility to the development of drowsiness, dizziness, unsteadiness, falling, urinary retention, and constipation (may lead to fecal impaction).

▷ **Advisability of Use During Pregnancy**

Pregnancy Category: B. D when taken for an extended amount of time or if used at high doses when the baby is born. See Pregnancy Risk Categories at the back of this book.

Animal Studies: No information available.

Human Studies: Adequate studies of pregnant women are not available. Oxycodone taken repeatedly during the final few weeks before delivery may cause withdrawal symptoms in the newborn.

Use only if clearly needed and in small, infrequent doses.

Advisability of Use If Breast-Feeding

Presence of this drug in breast milk: Yes.

Avoid drug or refrain from nursing.

Habit-Forming Potential: Psychological and/or physical dependence can develop. The FDA and the maker of OxyContin have taken expanded steps to enhance prescriber awareness of possible diversion and abuse of Oxycontin. New labeling also helps more clearly define patients who will benefit from this medicine.

Effects of Overdose: Drowsiness, restlessness, agitation, nausea, vomiting, dry mouth, vertigo, weakness, lethargy, stupor, coma, seizures.

Possible Effects of Long-Term Use: Psychological and physical dependence, chronic constipation.

Suggested Periodic Examinations While Taking This Drug (at physician's discretion)

Check for constipation. Balance of pain relief versus alertness. Assessment of pain relief. For example, as diseases such as cancer progress, it is not unusual for pain management needs to change.

▷ **While Taking This Drug, Observe the Following**

Foods: Generally, no restrictions—however, the 160 mg Oxycontin form should NOT be taken with a high fat meal. Higher dose is closer to level that can lead to breathing problems, and a high fat meal can increase oxycodone levels from OxyContin by 25%.

Herbal Medicines or Minerals: Caution is advised in combining any medicine that leads to drowsiness. St. John's wort can change (inducing or increasing) P450 enzymes, blunting the effects of oxycodone. Talk to your doctor BEFORE you combine any herbal medicines with oxycodone.

Beverages: No restrictions. May be taken with milk.

▷ *Alcohol:* Oxycodone can intensify the intoxicating effects of alcohol, and alcohol can intensify the depressant effects of oxycodone on brain function, breathing, and circulation. Combined use is best avoided.

Tobacco Smoking: No interactions expected. I advise everyone to quit smoking.

Marijuana Smoking: Increase in drowsiness and pain relief; impairment of mental and physical performance.

▷ *Other Drugs*

Oxycodone may *increase* the effects of

• atropinelike drugs and increase the risk of constipation and urinary retention.

• other drugs with sedative effects (see Drug Classes for benzodiazepines, tricyclic antidepressants, antihistamines, MAO inhibitors, phenothiazines, and opioid drugs [narcotics]).

Oxycodone *taken concurrently* with

• naltrexone (ReVia) may lead to withdrawal symptoms.

• rifabutin (Rifater, others) may blunt oxycodone benefits.

• ritonavir (Norvir) and perhaps other protease inhibitors (see Drug Classes) may lead to toxicity.

• sertraline (Zoloft) resulted in a serotonin syndrome in one case report. Caution is advised.

• tramadol (Ultram) may increase risk of adverse effects.

▷ *Driving, Hazardous Activities:* This drug can impair mental alertness, judgment, reaction time and physical coordination. Avoid hazardous activities accordingly.

Aviation Note: The use of this drug **is a disqualification** for piloting. Consult a designated Aviation Medical Examiner.

Exposure to Sun: No restrictions.

Discontinuation: It is best to limit this drug to short-term use. If extended use is needed, discontinuation should be gradual to minimize possible effects of withdrawal.

PANTOPRAZOLE (pan TOE prah sole)

Introduced: 2000   **Class:** Antiulcer, proton pump inhibitor   **Prescription:** USA: Yes   **Controlled Drug:** USA: No; Canada: No   **Available as Generic:** USA: No; Canada: No

Brand Name: Protonix

Author's Note: Information in this profile will be broadened if further data on this medicine warrants inclusion.

PAROXETINE (pa ROCKS a teen)

Introduced: 1993   **Class:** Antidepressant, other   **Prescription:** USA: Yes   **Controlled Drug:** USA: No; Canada: No   **Available as Generic:** USA: No; Canada: No

Brand Names: Paxil, Paxil CD

BENEFITS versus RISKS	
Possible Benefits	*Possible Risks*
EFFECTIVE CONTROL OF DEPRESSION	Abnormal ejaculation in males
CONTROL OF SOCIAL ANXIETY DISORDER	POSSIBLE ASSOCIATION WITH INCREASED RISK OF SUICIDAL THINKING OR ATTEMPTS IF USED IN CHILDREN LESS THAN 18 TO TREAT MAJOR DEPRESSION
EFFECTIVE USE IN PANIC ATTACKS IN CHILDREN	
HELPS CONTROL OBSESSIVE-COMPULSIVE DISORDER	
TREATS POST-TRAUMATIC STRESS DISORDER	
Fewer adverse effects than tricyclic antidepressants	
May help premature ejaculation	
Useful in some pain syndromes	

▷ **Principal Uses**

As a Single Drug Product: Uses currently included in FDA-approved labeling: (1) Treatment of depression; (2) helps control obsessive-compulsive disorder; (3) helps control panic attacks (panic disorder) in adults; (4) control of social anxiety disorder (SAD); (5) eases social phobia; (6) relatively new approval to treat post-traumatic stress disorder (PTSD); (7) eases generalized anxiety disorder (GAD).

Other (unlabeled) generally accepted uses: (1) Can have a role in diabetic nerve pain (neuropathy); (2) helps long-standing (chronic) daily headaches; (3) can help premature ejaculation; (4) has previously been used to help prevent panic attacks in children (however, newer data regarding use in children and increased suicidal behavior may change this—see controversies in medicine note below).

How This Drug Works: Inhibits uptake of serotonin. When more of this chemical is available in the brain, a positive impact on thinking results. Because the specific cause of panic attacks is not known, how this medicine works to prevent panic attacks has not been identified.

Available Dosage Forms and Strengths
>   Tablets, controlled-release — 12.5 mg, 25 mg
>   Tablets, immediate-release — 10 mg, 20 mg, 30 mg, 40 mg
>   Oral suspension — 10 mg/5 ml

▷ **Recommended Dose Ranges** (Actual dose and schedule must be determined for each patient individually.)

Infants and Children: Some clinicians have used 5 to 10 mg per day in children with panic disorder (or 0.25 to 0.5 mg per kg per day). The British Medicine and Healthcare Products Regulatory Agency ordered British doctors to stop using this medicine in patients less than 18 years old due to their contention that it is linked to suicidal behavior. The FDA issued a statement about paroxetine saying that it is reviewing POSSIBLE increased risk of suicidal thinking and/or suicide attempts in children less than 18 who are treated for major depression (major depressive disorder (MDD). The FDA is NOT recommending use of paroxetine in children or adolescents with MDD (currently is NOT approved for that use). Parents should talk to their doctor about what actions to take or not take and how to take them with appropriate medical supervision. See *www.fda.gov/ceder/drug/ infopage/paxil/default.htm*.

18 to 60 Years of Age: Depression: Immediate-release form: The usual starting dose is 20 mg, taken in the morning. Dose can then be increased as needed and tolerated in 10-mg intervals to a maximum of 50 mg daily.

Depression: Controlled-release form: Started with 25 milligrams (mg) daily. If patient response does not meet physician goals, the dose may be increased by 12.5 mg daily (at intervals of 7 days or more). The maximum recommended dose is 62.5 mg daily.

Obsessive-compulsive disorder (immediate-release form): Started with 20 mg daily with increases as in depression to a usual benefit at 40 mg per day. Maximum dose is 60 mg daily.

Panic disorder: Dosing is started with 10 mg per day, and doses are increased (at weekly intervals) as needed and tolerated to the usual dose of 40 mg a day. Daily maximum is 60 mg.

Social anxiety disorder: 20 mg daily.

PTSD: The starting dose is 20 mg, which is given in the morning. Dosing is adjusted in 10 mg steps. Typical doses are 20-40 mg daily.

Over 60 Years of Age: The starting dose in this population is 10 mg daily. The maximum dose is 40 mg daily.

Conditions Requiring Dosing Adjustments

Liver Function: Starting dose is 10 mg, and the maximum dose is 40 mg daily. Drug levels may be needed.

Kidney Function: Same starting dose and maximum dose as in liver compromise.

▷ **Dosing Instructions:** The absorption of this medicine is not changed by food. The new geomatrix form (CR) should not be altered before taking it. If you have trouble swallowing, the liquid form is a clear benefit. People using the suspension form (liquid) should shake the bottle just before they use it, and use a medicine cup or measuring spoon to get just the right dose. If you forget a dose: Take the missed dose as soon as you remember it, unless it's nearly time for your next dose—if that is the case, skip the missed dose and take the next dose right on schedule. DO NOT double doses. Talk with your doctor if you find yourself missing doses.

Usual Duration of Use: Continual use on a regular schedule for 14 days is usually necessary to determine this drug's effectiveness in treating depression. It may be 4 weeks before you get the full benefit of this medicine. Long-term use (months to years) requires periodic evaluation of response and dose adjustment by your doctor. Controversy about how long to continue a medicine for depression exists and must be individualized. Some clinicians advocate 4–9 months after depression eases, while others advocate longer or ongoing preventive use.

Typical Treatment Goals and Measurements (Outcomes and Markers)

Depression: The general goal: to at least help lessen the degree and severity of depression, letting patients return to their daily lives. Specific measures of depression involve testing or inventories and can be valuable in helping check benefits from this medicine. The Hamilton Depression Scale is widely used to assess depression. In any case the ability of the patient to return to normal activities or not have them interrupted is a hallmark of successful treatment.

Panic: Goals for panic tend to be more vague and subjective than hypertension or cholesterol. Frequently, the patient (in conjunction with physician assessment) will largely decide if panic has been successfully controlled. Decreased number of trips to the hospital or Emergency Room (ER) visits may also be a useful measure. The Liebowitz Social Anxiety Scale (LSAS) is a tool as well as the Clinical Global Impressions–Global Improvement Scale, which can be used to help figure out benefits in patients with anxiety and panic. The Hamilton Rating Scale for Anxiety anxious mood section is also helpful. The ability of the patient to return to normal activities is a hallmark of successful treatment.

Possible Advantages of This Drug

Fewer side effects than tricyclic antidepressants. May be a drug of choice in people with heart disease who are also depressed. Since a large National Cancer Institute study found that those who suffer depression for 6 years or more have a generally increased risk of cancer, one benefit of effective treatment of depression with this drug may be a generally reduced risk of cancer. This was the first medicine approved to treat social anxiety disorder. The controlled-release form offers a geomatrix technology that may help minimize adverse events and improve how well patients take this medicine (adherence).

▷ **This Drug Should Not Be Taken If**
   • you had an allergic reaction to it previously.
   • you have taken a MAO inhibitor (see Drug Classes) in the last 14 days.

▷ **Inform Your Physician Before Taking This Drug If**
   • you are pregnant or breast-feeding.
   • you have a history of mania or seizures.
   • you take diuretics or typically drink little water.

- you have a history of liver or kidney disease.
- you take prescription or nonprescription medicines not discussed with your doctor when paroxetine was prescribed.

Possible Side Effects (natural, expected, and unavoidable drug actions)
Lowered blood pressure and fainting upon standing (postural hypotension). Sedation. Nausea (up to 27%). Often decreases in 3 weeks. May require ondansetron or a lower paroxetine dose. Withdrawal syndrome possible if this medicine is stopped abruptly. Best to slowly decrease (taper) this medicine over 2–4 weeks.

▷ **Possible Adverse Effects** (unusual, unexpected, and infrequent reactions)
If any of the following develop, consult your physician promptly for guidance.
Mild Adverse Effects
Allergic reactions: skin rash and itching.
Headache, nervousness, or insomnia—infrequent to frequent.
Palpitations—infrequent.
Teeth grinding (bruxism)—case report.
Sense of inner restlessness (akathisia)—infrequent.
Loss of appetite, nausea, taste disorders, or constipation—infrequent to frequent.
Tingling of the hands (paresthesias)—infrequent.
Sweating—frequent.
Dizziness, blurred vision—infrequent to frequent.
Serious Adverse Effects
Allergic reactions: not reported.
Idiosyncratic reactions: bruising and excessive menstrual bleeding—case report (reversed with vitamin C).
Increased risk of suicidal thinking or behavior if used in patients less than 18 years old—possible (see controversies in medicine note). Any patient taking this or any medicine who begins to have thoughts about suicide should call their doctor and get additional help and guidance immediately.
Abnormal movements or positioning of the mouth or face—infrequent.
Abnormal urination (SIADH)—case report.
Seizures—rare.
Liver toxicity—rare.

▷ **Possible Effects on Sexual Function:** Galactorrhea. USED TO TREAT premature ejaculation.
Abnormal ejaculation—infrequent to frequent.
Inability to achieve orgasm, impotence, or sexual dysfunction—infrequent.
Prolonged and painful erection (priapism)—rare.

Possible Delayed Adverse Effects: None reported.

▷ **Adverse Effects That May Mimic Natural Diseases or Disorders**
Increased liver enzymes may mimic early hepatitis.

Natural Diseases or Disorders That May Be Activated by This Drug
None reported.

Possible Effects on Laboratory Tests
Liver function tests: increased.

CAUTION
1. Take this medicine as prescribed, and do not stop taking it without talking with your doctor.
2. A withdrawal syndrome is possible if this medicine is abruptly stopped.

Best to slowly decrease (taper) the dose over 2–4 weeks if this medicine needs to be stopped.

3. Controversy has erupted regarding possible increased suicidal thoughts and behavior in patients less than 18 years old who were prescribed this medicine. Promptly call your doctor if you begin to have thoughts of suicide after starting this medicine.

Precautions for Use

By Infants and Children: Safety and effectiveness for use by those under 18 years of age have not been established (see controversies in medicines note below).

Current Controversies in Medicines: The British Medicines and Healthcare Products Regulatory Agency reviewed paroxetine (known as Seroxat in the UK). Their conclusion was to order physicians to stop prescribing this medicine to children 18 and younger. The reason was a government study that in their opinion, established the link between paroxetine and suicidal behavior when the medicine was taken by children.

By Those Over 60 Years of Age: Lower starting and maximum doses are indicated.

▷ **Advisability of Use During Pregnancy**

Pregnancy Category: C. See Pregnancy Risk Categories at the back of this book.

Animal Studies: Reproduction studies in rabbits or rats using doses of up to 10 times the typical human dose have not revealed any fetal changes.

Human Studies: Information from adequate studies of pregnant women is not available.

Ask your doctor for guidance.

Advisability of Use If Breast-Feeding

Presence of this drug in breast milk: Yes, in small amounts (up to roughly 2.9% of the mom's dose in one study).

Some clinicians use a guideline that says that if less than 10% of the dose that a mother takes goes into the breast milk, then breast-feeding is safe. Ask your doctor for help.

Habit-Forming Potential: None, but a withdrawal syndrome characterized by dizziness, confusion, sweating, and tremor has been described.

Effects of Overdose: Confusion, heart rhythm changes, seizures.

Possible Effects of Long-Term Use: Not defined.

Suggested Periodic Examinations While Taking This Drug (at physician's discretion)

Liver function tests.

▷ **While Taking This Drug, Observe the Following**

Foods: No restrictions. Vitamin C reversed abnormal bruising and increased menstrual bleeding in one patient.

Herbal Medicines or Minerals: Since paroxetine and St. John's wort may act to increase serotonin, the combination is not advised. Since part of the way ginseng and gingko work may be as a MAO inhibitor, it may be ill advised to combine ginseng and ginkgo with paroxetine. Ma huang, guarana, yohimbe, Indian snakeroot, and kava kava (no longer recommended in Canada) are also best avoided while taking this medicine. One case report of dehydroepiandrosterone (DHEA) leading to acute mania when combined with sertraline precludes use of paroxetine with DHEA as well (same SSRI family).

Beverages: No restrictions.
▷ *Alcohol:* The manufacturer recommends avoiding alcohol while taking this medicine.
Tobacco Smoking: No interactions expected. I advise everyone to quit smoking.
Marijuana Smoking: Additive sedation, possible signs and symptoms of mania—DO NOT COMBINE.
▷ *Other Drugs*
Paroxetine may ***increase*** the effects of
- benzodiazepines (see Drug Classes).
- buspirone (Buspar).
- desipramine (and potentially other tricyclic antidepressants: see Drug Classes).
- dofetilide (Tikosyn) by increasing blood levels. Checks of patient clinical status and dosing changes are appropriate.
- encainide (Enkaid) and flecainide (Tambocor) because paroxetine inhibits an enzyme system needed to remove flecainide. More frequent encainide or flecainide blood levels are prudent.
- galantamine (Reminyl) because paroxetine inhibits an enzyme system needed to remove galantamine. Caution: careful patient monitoring and possible dose decreases of galantamine may be prudent.
- haloperidol (Haldol), because paroxetine blocks an enzyme system needed to remove haloperidol.
- labetalol (Normodyne), metoprolol (Toprol XL), and perhaps other beta blockers (see Drug Classes), because paroxetine inhibits an enzyme system needed to remove them (P450 2D6).

Paroxetine ***taken concurrently*** with
- activated charcoal will reduce absorption of paroxetine.
- astemizole (Hismanal) now removed from the US market may lead to heart toxicity—DO NOT COMBINE.
- dextromethorphan (the DM ingredient in many cough suppressants) may lead to serotonin syndrome—DO NOT COMBINE.
- digoxin (Lanoxin) may lead to lowered digoxin levels. More frequent digoxin levels are prudent.
- fenfluramine (Pondimin) may cause toxicity (serotonin syndrome).
- lithium (Lithobid, others) may lead to increased adverse effects.
- MAO inhibitors (see Drug Classes) may result in a fatal serotonin syndrome. Do not combine these medicines.
- phenytoin (Dilantin) or fosphenytoin (Cerebyx) may result in decreased paroxetine blood levels and lessening of therapeutic benefits. Dose increases may be needed.
- propafenone (Rythmol, others) may result in increased propafenone levels and toxicity, careful patient follow-up and more frequent propafenone levels are prudent.
- quinidine (Quinaglute, others) may result in increased paroxetine levels and toxicity; decreased paroxetine doses may be needed.
- risperidone (Risperdal) may lead to serotonin syndrome.
- ritonavir (Norvir) may lead to paroxetine toxicity.
- sibutramine (Meridia) increases risk of serotonin syndrome.
- sumatriptan (Imitrex) and other triptan-type medicines (see Drug Classes) can lead to hyperreflexia and poor coordination—the combination may not be advisable and if combination is required, careful patient follow-up is very important.
- tramadol (Ultram) may lead to increased risk of seizures—DO NOT combine.

- tryptophan may result in sweating, nausea and dizziness.
- venlafaxine (Effexor) can increase risk of serious serotonin syndrome.
- warfarin (Coumadin) may result in bleeding; more frequent INR (pro-thrombin time or protime) testing is recommended. Warfarin doses should be adjusted based on laboratory results.

The following drug may *increase* the effects of paroxetine:

- cimetidine (Tagamet).
- bupropion (Zyban, Wellbutrin). Low paroxetine doses and close patient follow-up are needed if these medicines must be combined. Bupropion inhibits P450 2D6—a liver enzyme that helps remove paroxetine from the body.

Driving, Hazardous Activities: This drug may frequently cause sedation. Restrict activities as necessary.

Aviation Note: The use of this drug *is a disqualification* for piloting. Consult a designated Aviation Medical Examiner.

Exposure to Sun: No specific restrictions.

Exposure to Heat: This medicine can cause excessive sweating. If you work or are frequently in a hot environment, be careful to replace enough fluids to avoid dehydration.

Heavy Exercise or Exertion: Since this medicine may cause excessive sweating, be careful to replace lost fluids.

Occurrence of Unrelated Illness: Fevers may cause more severe dehydration.

Discontinuation: Do not stop this medicine without talking with your doctor. For patients taking this medicine for an extended period of time, gradual dosing decreases (tapering) over several weeks or longer is recommended.

PEGINTERFERON ALPHA-2A (PEG in tur fear on)

Introduced: 2002   **Class:** Antiviral, pegylated interferon alpha-2a
Prescription: USA: Yes   **Controlled Drug:** USA: No; Canada: No
Available as Generic: USA: No; Canada: No

Brand Name: Pegasys

Author's Note: Used in hepatitis C in combination with ribavirin (Copegus– see ribavirin profile later in this book). Specific genotypes help drive dosing of this medicine and the ribavirin combination (see below).

BENEFITS versus RISKS	
Possible Benefits	*Possible Risks*
SINGLE AGENT TREATMENT OF HEPATITIS C (DRUG NAIVE)	HEADACHE
	FATIGUE
COMBINATION TREATMENT OF HEPATITIS C WITH RIBAVIRIN	NAUSEA OR DIARRHEA
	MUSCLE CHANGES
MORE EFFECTIVE THAN UNMODIFIED INTERFERON AGAINST HEPATITIS C	INSOMNIA
	DEPRESSION
	BLOOD CELL CHANGES
Improved quality of life versus some other Hepatitis C treatments	

▷ **Principal Uses**

As a Single Drug Product: Uses currently included in FDA-approved labeling:
(1) Treats hepatitis C in people who were not previously given interferon

alpha; (2) combination treatment of hepatitis C with ribavirin in those not previously given interferon alpha.

Other (unlabeled) generally accepted uses: (1) Not defined at present, possible emerging use in kidney (renal cell) carcinoma.

How This Drug Works: This specific form of interferon alpha-2a is a modified form of the original molecule. A branched methoxy-polyethlene glycol compound is attached (covalently) to the original interferon molecule. The effect of attaching this additional substance to the interferon is to keep it in the body longer (reduces clearance) by the kidney, protects against compounds in the body (enzymes) which might break the interferon alpha 2a down, and allows once-a-week dosing. The attachment also appears to attack the hepatitis C virus more forcefully since the drug stays at a higher level than other interferon alpha-2a formulations which are given three times a week (allowing peaks and valleys in concentration and giving the virus more time to recover).

Available Dosage Forms and Strengths

Injectable solution — 180 mcg per vial

▷ **Usual Adult Dosage Ranges**

Ongoing Hepatitis C in Adults: 180 mcg (micrograms) is given ONCE A WEEK for 48 weeks. This is given to patients who have or do not have cirrhosis. The company package insert notes that if a viral response (antiviral effect) is NOT seen in 12-24 weeks, stopping the treatment should be considered.

Combination Hepatitis C Treatment in Adults (with Copegus-ribavirin): The same dose of 180 mcg once weekly of the peginterferon alpha-2A is given, however, the ribavirin dose changes. Here, genetics are considered: Patients who have genotypes 1 or 4 and who weigh more than 75 kilograms are given 1,200 mg a day. For those less than 75 kg, 1,000 mg a day is given, and combination is continued for 48 weeks. People with genotypes 2 or 3 are given 800 mg of ribavirin (divided into two 400-mg doses given twice a day) coupled with 180 mcg once a week of peginterferon alpha-2a and the combination is only continued for 24 weeks. If an antiviral effect is not seen 12–24 weeks into therapy, consideration is given to stopping the medicine.

Note: Actual dose and schedule must be determined for each patient individually.

Conditions Requiring Dosing Adjustments

Liver Function: Patients who have a liver function test called ALT progressively increase should have their dose lowered to 135 micrograms a week. If ALT continues to rise, after the dose is reduced coupled with evidence of liver decline (hepatic decompensation) or increases in a compound called bilirubin, the medicine should be stopped.

Kidney Function: People with creatinine clearance (a measure of how well the kidneys work) of less than 50 ml/minute should NOT be given peginterferon alfa-2a.

Anemia: For people with a history of stable heart disease who have a decrease in hemoglobin of 2 gram per deciliter noted as g/dl (for example, a drop in the hemoglobin lab test result from 12g/dl to 10 g/dl during any four-week period of therapy) or for patients who do not have heart disease, but have a hemoglobin laboratory test result of 10 grams/deciliter, the ribavirin dose should be lowered to 600 mg a day. If people with a history of stable heart disease are given the lower ribavirin dose for 4 weeks and the hemoglobin stays lower than 12 g/dl or in people without heart disease who have a hemoglobin less than 8.5 g/dl, peginterferon alpha- 2a should be stopped.

Depression: People who become *mildly depressed:* (your doctor may use signs and symptoms or one of the inventories of depression such as Ham D to check this), doses can remain constant, but weekly visits to the doctor's office or weekly phone calls to the patient are needed. For *moderate depression*: the dose of peginterferon alpha-2a should be decreased to 90–135 micrograms, and the patient should be evaluated at a weekly visit at the doctor's office. If signs and symptoms of depression improve and remain the same for more than 4 weeks, patients can go back to the previous schedule of office visits. The dose of peginterferon alpha-2a can then be kept at the lower amount or increased to the prior dose based on clinician judgment. If a patient becomes *severely depressed*: Peginterferon alpha-2a should be stopped and the patient referred to a psychiatrist immediately.

Low White Blood Cells (Neutropenia): If a specific kind of white blood cell count (absolute neutrophil count or ANC) decreases to an ANC of less than 750 per cubic millimeter (/mm3), peginterferon alpha-2a dose is decreased to 135 mcg a week. If ANC drops to less than 500/mm3, the medicine should be stopped until the ANC goes back up to more than 1,000/mm3. Once ANC is more than 1,000/mm3, peginterferon alpha-2a can be restarted at a dose of 90 mcg a week.

Low Blood Platelets (Thrombocytopenia): If a blood element involved in clotting called a platelet (thrombocyte) falls to less than 50,000 per cubic millimeter (/mm3), the Pegasys dose is lowered to 90 mcg a week. If the platelet count falls to less than 25,000/mm3, Pegasys should be stopped.

▷ **Dosing Instructions:** May be taken alone or combined with a form of ribavirin called (Copegus). While the benefit-to-risk decision favors use of these/this medicine for some patients, care must be taken to carefully follow possible undesirable effects such as anemia, depression and changes in red blood cells and platelets. Dosing should be carefully decided by a qualified specialist, and is given as a single injection once a week. This/these medicines are best taken/given on the same day and time each week. Very specific instructions are present in a Med Guide that comes with Pegasys. It is important NOT to use Pegasys if some things about the medicine change. A simple way to remember this is CEPC: Don't use it if it is Cloudy, has Expired, has Particles floating in it, or if it is any other Color than a light yellow or is colorless. Call your doctor or prescriber if you are unsure how much to inject. If you know the correct dose, clean off the area of skin where you have decided to inject, then gently roll the medicine vial in your hands to warm it, and then pull the syringe back to the correct mark on the barrel. After removing (flipping off the plastic top on the vial) and cleaning it with an alcohol pad, push the needle into the rubber stopper on the vial and push the air in the syringe inside of the vial. Follow the instructions your doctor or nurse has given you to draw up the correct dose and to remove air bubbles. Finally, inject the medicine slowly under the skin using the technique that your nurse or doctor explained to you. Make sure you dispose of the syringe and needle the way you were instructed. Each syringe and medicine vial is to be used only once. If you are also going to use Copegus in combination with Pegasys, read the Med Guide that came with that medicine and follow the instructions carefully.

Usual Duration of Use: Use on a regular schedule for up to 12–24 weeks may be needed to see best effects from this medicine or from the combination of medicines already discussed. Ongoing use for more than 48 weeks does not have efficacy or safety data. Ongoing use requires periodic check of response (such as viral load), check for side effects, laboratory monitoring and possibly dose changes. Make sure you keep follow-up appointments with your doctor and for laboratory or other testing.

Typical Treatment Goals and Measurements (Outcomes and Markers)

The general goal is to lower the amount of virus in the body and ideally to kill all of it. Viral load or burden tests help guide therapy. A test for viral genetic material in the serum called HCV-RNA is taken. The goal is to achieve undetectable amounts. The technical term for this is an undetectable HCV-RNA by PCR. Because the usual limit of the test is 100 copies per milliliter, the goal is to achieve "undetectable." When and if lower detection tests become available (as has happened with HIV testing), a new lower goal will become the standard. Additional beneficial effects will be quality of life, halting of progression, or cessation of liver damage.

Possible Advantages of This Medicine/These Drugs: The combination of peginterferon alpha-2a with ribavirin gives a more prolonged (durable) lowering of the amount of virus (viral load or viral burden) and in general viral response. For people who have been infected with the Hepatitis C Virus (HCV) with the genotype 1 form, pegylated forms of interferon (2a or 2b) are drugs of choice.

▷ **This Drug Should Not Be Taken If**
- you have had an allergic reaction to it previously
- you have autoimmune hepatitis or unstable liver disease or have had a liver transplant.
- you have previously taken and did not respond to other alpha interferon treatment.
- you are taking this medicine and your hemoglobin drops below acceptable levels (see anemia above).
- you are taking this medicine and your neutrophils (ANC) or your platelet count drops below acceptable level (see above).
- you have sickle-cell anemia, thalassemia major, or some other form of abnormal red blood cells.
- you become seriously depressed while taking this medicine.
- you become pregnant while taking this medicine.
- you are a woman of childbearing age and have not had a negative pregnancy test before starting this medicine.

▷ **Inform Your Physician Before Taking This Drug If**
- you have a history of bone marrow depression or cancer.
- you have a history of a serious emotional or mental disorder, particularly depression.
- you have a history of alcohol or drug abuse.
- you have a history of heart disease, a prior heart attack, or poor heart circulation (ischemic heart disease).
- you have impaired liver function from hepatitis B (no data) or impaired kidney function.
- you have a history of lung problems (pulmonary dysfunction) or chronic obstructive pulmonary disease (this medicine may worsen them).
- you have a history of diabetes or low thyroid function (hypothyroidism).
- you develop a fever, which gets higher or does not go away.
- you have psoriasis and it gets worse while taking this medicine.
- you are taking any drugs for emotional or mental disorders.
- you have a history of eye problems (such as blood clots in the retinal artery, edema of the macula, or optic neuritis)—talk to your doctor.
- you have a history of low white blood cell counts or cancer.

- you have a history of autoimmune disease (such as lupus erythematosus or rheumatoid arthritis) or are HIV positive.
- you have a history of colon inflammation (colitis).
- you ask the person prescribing this medicine about HCV genotyping of the virus causing your hepatitis C infection, and learn that this testing has not yet been performed (genotype of the virus is very important).
- you are unsure how much or how often to take this medicine.

Possible Side Effects (natural, expected, and unavoidable drug actions)
Injection site reactions (frequent).

▷ **Possible Adverse Effects** (unusual, unexpected, and infrequent reactions)
If any of the following develop, consult your physician promptly for guidance.

Mild Adverse Effects
Allergic reaction: skin rash, itching (pruritis)—may be frequent.
Headache, fatigue or fever—frequent.
Insomnia—frequent (may be prudent to anticipate this effect and ask your doctor for help when this medicine is prescribed).
Depression (see depression note above)—frequent.
Blurred vision—possible.
Dizziness, nausea or abdominal pain—frequent.
Sweating—infrequent.
Loss of appetite (anorexia), diarrhea, abdominal pain—frequent.
Muscle aches or joint pain—frequent.
Blood sugar changes—possible.
Hair loss—alopecia.
Dry mouth—infrequent.

Serious Adverse Effects
Allergic reaction: Not clearly defined.
Depression—see note above (may be serious enough to require stopping the medicine).
Decrease or loss of vision (optic neuritis, macular edema, retinal artery blood clots—reported (see vision check below).
Muscle stiffness (rigors)—may be frequent.
Abnormal heart rhythms (supraventricular arrhythmia) or heart attack—case reports.
Low white blood cell counts: fever, sore throat, infection—possible (see note above regarding dosing).
Aggravation of excessively low or high thyroid function (hypo- or hyperthyroidism).
Blood sugar changes—possible.
Pancreatitis—possible with alpha interferon and ribavirin treatment.
Decreased hemoglobin—possible (see note above regarding dosing).
Decreased platelets—possible (see note above regarding dosing).
Bloody diarrhea—possible.
Lung problems (pneumonia, interstitial pneumonitis, others)—reported as aggravated or caused by this medicine.
Aggravation of or development of autoimmune problems (muscle inflammation (myositis), rheumatoid arthritis, systemic lupus erythematosus, others)—possible.

▷ **Possible Effects on Sexual Function:** May impair fertility in some women. Female cynomolgus monkeys experience amenorrhea or prolonged menstrual cycles.

Adverse Effects That May Mimic Natural Diseases or Disorders
Mood changes, depression may suggest a psychotic disorder.
Dropping neutrophils (ANC) may mimic other hematologic problems, yet actually be an adverse drug reaction.

Natural Diseases or Disorders That May Be Activated by This Drug
Latent or subclinical depression, epilepsy, incipient congestive heart failure.

Possible Effects on Laboratory Tests
Development of neutralizing antibodies—rare.
Development of binding antibodies—infrequent.
Liver function tests: increased (ALT, bilirubin, others).
White blood cells (neutrophils): lowered ANC.
Hemoglobin: may be decreased.
Triglycerides: increased (frequent).
Platelets: may be decreased.
Blood sugar changes.
Amylase and/or lipase: increased.

CAUTION
1. Talk to your doctor if you or your significant other or a family member notices that you are starting to become depressed (see note on depression in dosing), or think about suicide. This medicine can be a cause of severe depression.
2. While this medicine can successfully attack the Hepatitis C Virus (particularly in combination with ribavirin), serious possible adverse effects require follow-up and laboratory testing while taking this medicine.
3. Call your doctor if you have trouble breathing, a change in vision or unusual bleeding or bruising.
4. Call 911 if you start to have severe chest pain (some cardiovascular problems have been associated with this medicine).
5. Call your doctor immediately if you become pregnant (see pregnancy note).
6. You develop an ongoing or increasing temperature, sore throat, or other signs of an infection.
7. Triglycerides may be increased. Talk to your doctor about this.

Precautions for Use
By Infants and Children: Safety and effectiveness for those under 18 not established.
By Those Over 60 Years of Age: Some of the measures of how the medicine is distributed in the body (area under the curve-AUC and half life) were increased or prolonged in people more than 60. Adverse effects from this medicine may be more pronounced in this patient population. Prudent to follow the patient more carefully, and adjust dosing based on undesirable signs and symptoms.

▷ **Advisability of Use During Pregnancy**
Pregnancy Category: C. See Pregnancy Risk Categories at the back of this book.
Animal Studies: High doses were not associated with birth defects (teratogenicity) in animals, but have been listed as a potential cause of fetal birth defects in the Med Guide. Abortion HAS been reported with high dose, nonpegylated forms in animals.
Human Studies: Adequate studies of pregnant women are not available.
A negative pregnancy test BEFORE starting this medicine and TWO forms of birth control while taking this medicine and for at least six months AFTER STOPPING it are needed. Male partners of women taking this medicine

are advised to use a condom. Talk to your doctor about how to address the issue of pregnancy and the possible transmission of hepatitis C. If you DO become pregnant, YOU or YOUR DOCTOR should call 1-800-526-6367.

Advisability of Use If Breast-Feeding
Presence of this drug in breast milk: Not defined.
Blood and body fluids may transfer the Hepatitis C Virus. Breast-feeding is NOT advisable.

Habit-Forming Potential: None.

Effects of Overdose: Management of the symptoms that a patient has at the time that they are seen by a doctor (symptomatic management).

Possible Effects of Long-Term Use: See anemia, white blood cell, and platelet notes above.

Suggested Periodic Examinations While Taking This Drug (at physician's discretion)
Hepatitis C RNA testing (PCR) before and periodically during treatment
Vision testing/eye exam before (baseline) treatment.
Complete blood counts, ANC (baseline, two weeks, four weeks).
Liver biopsy may be needed for some patients, possibly before and during treatment.
Thyroid stimulating hormone (TSH).
Liver (ALT, AST and bilirubin) before treatment (baseline) and usually every two months.
Kidney function tests.
Amylase and lipase.
Blood sugar, A1C.
Evaluation of heart function at baseline (before therapy) and periodically.
Baseline pregnancy test in females of child bearing age.
Checks for signs and symptoms of depression such as appetite, change in pleasure gained from usually pleasurable activities, or administration of typical depression inventories such as the Hamilton Depression Scale (Ham-D).
Author's Note: Baseline blood and biochemical tests and pregnancy tests for females are needed. Once treatment is started, blood (hematological) tests are checked at 2 and 4 weeks, and repeat biochemical testing done at 4 weeks. In clinical trials, CBC and chemistries (including liver function tests and uric acid) were checked at weeks 1 and 2, four, six and eight. For ongoing treatment, testing was done every four weeks. Testing was obtained more frequently if abnormal results were obtained. TSH was checked every twelve weeks. Pregnancy testing was checked before therapy was started, during combination therapy was checked monthly and for six months after the medicine was stopped.

▷ **While Taking This Drug, Observe the Following**
Foods: Taking this medicine with a high fat meal increases the amount that gets into your body. Talk to your doctor about how he or she would like you to take this medicine. Use of smaller, more nutrient dense meals may help provide nutrition while acting as a coping mechanism for nausea.
Herbal Medicines or Minerals: Some herbal medicines such as eucalyptus, kava, and valerian have possible toxic effects on the liver. These herbals should NOT be taken, both because of the viral presence in the liver and because of possible additive undesirable effects on the liver.
Beverages: No restrictions. May be taken with milk.

▷   *Alcohol:* Since alcohol can add to liver problems, any use should be discussed with your doctor.

Tobacco Smoking: No interactions expected. I advise everyone to quit smoking.

Marijuana Smoking: Added dizziness.

▷   *Other Drugs*

Peginterferon alpha-2A *taken concurrently* with

- didanosine (Videx) is NOT recommended. Increased risk of fatal liver failure, pancreatitis, lactic acidosis, and/or peripheral neuropathy preclude this.
- medicines known to have toxic effects on the liver would be best avoided if possible due to overlapping undesirable effects on the liver. Some combinations may represent a benefit-to-risk decision.
- medicines removed by a liver enzyme called CYP 450 1A2 may be increased to toxic levels because peginterferon inhibits this enzyme. Checking blood levels of the medicines combined with peginterferon that undergo such removal is prudent, with dosing adjustments based on blood levels.

Peginterferon alpha-2A and ribavirin *taken concurrently* with

- stavudine (Zerit) or zidovudine (AZT) may blunt the antiviral benefits of these two HIV medicines.

▷   *Driving, Hazardous Activities:* May cause dizziness, blurred vision, or fatigue. Use caution and assess the extent of these possible undesirable effects BEFORE undertaking such activities.

Aviation Note: The use of this drug *may be a disqualification* for piloting. Consult a designated Aviation Medical Examiner.

Exposure to Sun: No restrictions.

Special Storage Instructions: Care must be taken for proper disposal of needles and avoidance of possible needle sticks by caregivers. The medicine itself should be stored in a refrigerator with a temperature of 36–46 degrees F. (2-8 degrees Centigrade) because lack of refrigeration can break down the medicine. DO NOT SHAKE the bottle as this can also inactivate the medicine. Protect the medicine from light and also make certain that the medicine is not frozen. It is important NOT to leave the medicine out of the refrigerator for more than a day. Once you have drawn up a dose from a given vial of medicine, throw the rest of the medicine in the vial away. Please note the CEPC characteristics of the medicine in dosing instructions above.

Discontinuation: See notes on white blood cell, platelet counts, liver function tests, and time that the medicine should be given to work in the profile above. Talk to your doctor BEFORE making any changes in dosing or making any decision to stop this medicine.

PENBUTOLOL (pen BYU toh lohl)

Introduced: 1976   **Class:**   Antihypertensive, beta-adrenergic blocker
Prescription: USA: Yes   **Controlled Drug:**   USA: No; Canada: No
Available as Generic: Yes

Brand Name: Levatol

Author's Note: Information in this profile has been truncated to make room for more widely used medicines.

PENICILLAMINE (pen i SIL a meen)

Introduced: 1963   **Class:** Antiarthritic   **Prescription:** USA: Yes
Controlled Drug: USA: No; Canada: No   **Available as Generic:** USA:
No; Canada: No
Brand Names: Cuprimine, Depen

BENEFITS versus RISKS

Possible Benefits	*Possible Risks*
EFFECTIVE TREATMENT OF WILSON'S DISEASE (COPPER TOXICITY)	SEVERE ALLERGIC REACTIONS BONE MARROW DEPRESSION Drug-induced damage of lungs, liver, pancreas, and kidneys
Effective treatment of cystinuria and cystine kidney stones	
Partially effective treatment of rheumatoid arthritis and poisoning due to heavy metals: iron, lead, mercury, and zinc	

Author's Note: Due to proliferation of new medicines, this profile has
been abbreviated in order to make room for more widely used medicines.

PENICILLIN ANTIBIOTIC FAMILY

Amoxicillin (a mox i SIL in)   **Amoxicillin/Clavulanate** (a mox i SIL
in/KLAV yu lan ayt)   **Ampicillin** (am pi SIL in)   **Bacampicillin**
(bak am pi SIL in)   **Cloxacillin** (klox a SIL in)   **Penicillin VK** (pen
i SIL in VEE KAY)

Introduced: 1969, 1982 (2002 for Augmentin XR form), 1961, 1979, 1962,
1953, respectively   **Class:** Antibiotics, penicillins   **Prescription:**
USA: Yes   **Controlled Drug:** USA: No; Canada: No   **Available as
Generic:** USA: Yes (all but amoxicillin/clavulanate); Canada: Yes

Brand Names: Amoxicillin: A-Cillin, Amoxil, ✤Apo-Amoxi, ✤Clavulin,
Larotid, ✤Novamoxin, ✤Nu-Amoxi, Polymox, Prevpac [CD], Trimox,
Wymox, Amoxicillin/Clavulanate: Augmentin, Augmentin XR, Ampicillin:
Amcill, ✤Ampicin, ✤Ampicin PRB [CD], ✤Ampilean, ✤Apo-Ampi, Aug-
mentin, ✤Clavulin, D-Amp, Faspak Ampicillin, 500 Kit [CD], ✤Novo-
Ampicillin, Nu-Ampi, Omnipen, Omnipen Pediatric Drops, Pardec
Capsules [CD], ✤Penbritin, Polycillin, Polycillin Pediatric Drops,
Polycillin-PRB [CD], ✤Pondocillin, Principen, SK-Ampicillin, Totacillin,
Bacampicillin: ✤Penglobe, Spectrobid, Cloxacillin: ✤Apo-Cloxi, ✤Bac-
topen, Cloxapen, ✤Novo-Cloxin, ✤Nu-Cloxi, ✤Orbenin, Tegopen, Peni-
cillin VK: ✤Apo-Pen-VK, Beepen VK, Betapen-VK, Ledercillin VK,
✤Nadopen-V, ✤Novopen-VK, ✤Nu-Pen-VK, Penapar VK, Pen-V, ✤Pen-
Vee, Pen-Vee K, Pfizerpen VK, ✤PVF, ✤PVF K, Robicillin VK, SK-
Penicillin VK, Uticillin VK, V-Cillin K, ✤VC-K 500, Veetids, Win-Cillin

BENEFITS versus RISKS	
Possible Benefits	*Possible Risks*
EFFECTIVE TREATMENT OF INFECTIONS DUE TO SUSCEPTIBLE MICROORGANISMS	ALLERGIC REACTIONS, MILD TO SEVERE Superinfections (yeast) Drug-induced colitis—possible Lowering of white blood cells (amoxicillin/clavulanate, ampicillin, cloxacillin) Decreased kidney function

▷ **Principal Uses**

As a Single Drug Product: Uses currently included in FDA-approved labeling: (1) Used to treat responsive infections of the upper and lower respiratory tract, the middle ear (acute otitis media). Amoxicillin resistance has prompted dosing changes. Approved to treat susceptible skin infections; (2) helps prevent rheumatic fever and bacterial endocarditis in people with valvular heart disease; (3) treats some *Haemophilus influenzae* infections (amoxicillin); (4) treats some genitourinary tract infections (amoxicillin/clavulanate, ampicillin, penicillin VK); (5) treats some cases of sinusitis; (6) ampicillin is used in combination to treat some kinds of septicemia and meningitis; (7) amoxicillin is approved in combination with other medicines (such as omeprazole) to treat some *Helicobacter pylori* infections; (8) some forms treat anthrax; (9) Augmentin XR form approved for community acquired pneumonia or sudden (acute) sinusitis caused by Streptococcus pneumoniae with reduced susceptibility (MIC of 2 micrograms per ml).

Other (unlabeled) generally accepted uses: (1) Combined therapy of animal bite wounds; (2) treats stage one Lyme disease in children (amoxicillin or penicillin VK); (3) therapy of Lyme disease in the central nervous system (penicillin VK); (4) can treat some dental abscesses (penicillin VK); (5) treats typhoid fever (amoxicillin); (6) prevention of bacterial endocarditis (amoxicillin); (7) treats biliary tract infections or chancroid (amoxicillin/clavulanate); (8) cloxacillin treats some bone infections if intravenous (IV) drugs are not tolerated.

As a Combination Drug Product [CD]: Amoxicillin and clavulanate are combined (Augmentin) to give the benefits of amoxicillin combined with the ability to treat more resistant bacteria (clavulanate). Amoxicillin is available combined with two drugs: clarithromycin and lansoprazole. Since refractory ulcers are often actually *Helicobacter pylori* infections, the combination works to kill the bacteria and lower acid production.

How These Drugs Work: Destroy susceptible infecting bacteria by damaging ability to make protective cell walls as they multiply and grow. Amoxicillin/clavulanate uses clavulanate blockage of enzymes to enable treatment of resistant bacteria. Bacampicillin is converted to ampicillin, giving peak blood levels three times higher than ampicillin. This allows bacampicillin dosing every 12 hours.

Available Dosage Forms and Strengths

Amoxicillin:

Capsules — 250 mg, 500 mg
Oral liquid — 3 g

Oral suspension — 50 mg/ml, 125 mg/ml, 250 mg/
5 ml
Pediatric drops — 50 mg/ml
Tablets, chewable — 125 mg, 250 mg

Amoxicillin/clavulanate:

Oral suspension — 125 mg (amoxicillin) and
31.25 mg (clavulanate) per
5 ml; 250 mg (amoxicillin) and
62.5 mg (clavulanate) per 5 ml;
250 mg (amoxicillin) and
125 mg (clavulanate); 500 mg
(amoxicillin) and 125 mg
(clavulanate)
Pediatric formulation, twice daily — 200 mg (amoxicillin) and
28.6 mg (clavulanate) per 5 ml;
400 mg (amoxicillin) and 57.1
(clavulanate) per 5 ml
Tablets — 500 mg (amoxicillin) and 125
mg (clavulanate); 875 mg
(amoxicillin) and 125 mg
(clavulanate)
Tablets, chewable — 125 mg (amoxicillin) and
31.25 mg (clavulanate);
250 mg (amoxicillin) and
62.5 mg (clavulanate)
Tablets, chewable twice-daily formulation — 200 mg (amoxicillin) and 28.6
mg (clavulanate); 400 mg
(amoxicillin) and 57.1 mg
(clavulanate)

Ampicillin:

Capsules — 250 mg, 500 mg
Oral suspension — 100 mg/ml, 125 mg/ml,
250 mg/ml, 500 mg/5 ml
Pediatric drops — 100 mg/ml

Bacampicillin:

Oral suspension — 125 mg/5 ml
Tablets — 400 mg, 800 mg (800 mg in
Canada only)

Cloxacillin:

Capsules — 250 mg, 500 mg
Oral suspension — 125 mg/5 ml
Oral liquid — 125 mg/5 ml

Penicillin VK:

Oral solution — 125 mg/5 ml, 250 mg/5 ml
Tablets — 125 mg, 250 mg, 500 mg

▷ **Recommended Dosage Ranges** (Actual dose and schedule must be determined
for each patient individually for all of these medicines.)
Dose is based on how sensitive the infection-causing bacteria are, infection
severity, and patient response.
Penicillin VK: Dose range is 125 to 500 mg every 6 to 8 hours. For prevention of
bacterial endocarditis: 2 g (2,000 mg) taken 1 hour before the procedure,
followed by 1 g 6 hours later. Daily maximum is 7 g (7,000 mg).

Infants and Children:

Amoxicillin: For susceptible infections: Up to 6 kg of body mass — 25 to 50 mg every 8 hours. 6 to 8 kg of body mass — 50 to 100 mg every 8 hours. 8 to 20 kg of body mass — 6.7 to 13.3 mg per kg of body mass every 8 hours. 20 kg of body mass and over—same as 12 to 60 years of age. Note: See higher dosing in ear infection (otitis media) below.

Amoxicillin/clavulanate: Up to 40 kg of body mass — 6.7 to 13.3 mg (amoxicillin) per kg of body mass, every 8 hours. 40 kg of body mass and over—same as 12 to 60 years of age. 12-hour formula: For severe infections — 45 mg amoxicillin per kg of body mass **per day** (divided into two doses given every 12 hours). For less severe infections (as in skin infections) — 25 mg per kg of body mass **per day** (divided into two doses given every 12 hours).

Bacampicillin: 25 mg per kg of body mass per day is given, divided into two equal doses every 12 hours, for respiratory infections.

Cloxacillin: Children weighing less than 44 lb (20 kg) receive 50 to 100 mg per kg of body mass per day, divided into four doses. Children greater than 20 kg get the adult dose. Intravenous dosing may be required for severe infections.

12 to 60 Years of Age:

Amoxicillin: Usual dose — 250 to 500 mg every 8 hours. Daily maximum is 4.5 g. For gonorrhea — 3 g, with 1 g of probenecid, taken as a single dose. For Lyme disease — 250 to 500 mg, three or four times a day, for 10 to 30 days; dose and duration depends on severity of infection and response to treatment.

Author's Note: American Heart Association (AHA) guidelines for prevention of bacterial endocarditis in patients at risk suggest amoxicillin in an initial dose of 2 g BEFORE (check current guidelines for timing and best choices) oral or dental procedures. There is no recommendation for follow-up doses of antibiotics.

Because of limits on how well amoxicillin gets into the middle ear and prevalence of penicillin-resistant *Strep pneumoniae* causing middle ear infections, some clinicians are using 80–90 mg per kg per day, divided into two or three equal doses (12 or 8 hours apart) in children with sudden onset (acute) otitis media with *S. pneumoniae.* Resistance patterns of bacteria are changing in many areas making other antibiotics medicines of choice depending on the specific resistance patterns and bacteria being treated.

Amoxicillin/clavulanate: Usual dose — 250 to 500 mg (amoxicillin) every 8 hours. In some severe infections, 875/125 mg tablets are taken twice a day. Daily maximum (of amoxicillin) is 4.5 g. Augmentin XR form: two tablets every 12 hours.

Ampicillin: 50 to 100 mg per kg of body mass per day divided into four doses or 500 to 1,000 mg every 6 hours. Usual daily maximum is 6,000 mg daily.

Bacampicillin: For those with a body mass of 25 kg or more — 400 to 800 mg every 12 hours.

Cloxacillin: 250 to 500 mg every 6 hours. The maximum dose is 6,000 mg (6 g) every 24 hours.

Over 60 Years of Age: Amoxicillin: Same as 12 to 60 years of age.

Amoxicillin/clavulanate: Same as 12 to 60 years of age. Note: The above doses refer to the amoxicillin component of amoxicillin/clavulanate. The 250-mg regular tablet and the 250-mg chewable tablet contain different amounts of clavulanate and are NOT interchangeable. See Dosage Forms on pages 879–880.

Ampicillin: Drug is removed more slowly by patients in this age group, but specific dose decreases are not defined.

Bacampicillin: Tests of kidney function should be obtained. Doses of 400 mg per day have been used in moderate kidney disease or decline (age-related decline in kidney function may be moderate).

Cloxacillin: No specific dosing changes are available.

Conditions Requiring Dosing Adjustments

Liver Function: Dose adjustments do not appear to be needed (amoxicillin, amoxicillin/clavulanate, ampicillin, and penicillin VK). Caution is advised for bacampicillin use by these patients. The dose is decreased or time between doses increased for cloxacillin.

Kidney Function:

Amoxicillin, amoxicillin/clavulanate, ampicillin: Dosing interval **must** be adjusted in renal compromise.

Bacampicillin: The dose must be decreased to 400 mg per day in moderate kidney failure. In severe kidney failure, a dose of 400 mg every 36 hours is used.

Cloxacillin: Patients should be watched closely for adverse effects in severe kidney compromise.

Penicillin VK: For patients with severe kidney compromise, the usual dose is taken every 8 hours.

▷ **Dosing Instructions:** The tablet (amoxicillin, bacampicillin, penicillin VK) may be crushed (or amoxicillin and amoxicillin/clavulanate chew-tabs chewed) or the capsule (amoxicillin) opened and taken on an empty stomach or with food or milk (amoxicillin). Augmentin XR or other extended-release forms should NOT be crushed or altered. Absorption may be slightly faster if taken when stomach is empty (penicillin VK). Ampicillin, bacampicillin, and cloxacillin are best taken on an empty stomach. Oral suspension forms should be shaken well before measuring each dose. Please use a measuring cup or calibrated measuring spoon to make sure you get just the right dose. If you forget a dose: Take the missed dose as soon as you remember it, unless it's nearly time for your next dose—if that is the case, skip the missed dose and take the next dose right on schedule. If the dose missed was the first dose of the day, separate the remaining doses into evenly spaced intervals. DO NOT double doses. Talk with your doctor if you find yourself missing doses.

Usual Duration of Use: For all streptococcal infections—not less than 10 consecutive uninterrupted days to reduce risk of rheumatic fever or glomerulonephritis. For all other infections—as long as needed to eradicate the infection. Incomplete treatment may lead to serious resistance and dangerous infections.

Typical Treatment Goals and Measurements (Outcomes and Markers)

Infections: The most commonly used measures of serious infections are white blood cell counts and differentials (the kind of blood cells that occur most often in your blood), and temperature. Many clinicians look for positive changes in 24–48 hours. NEVER stop an antibiotic because you start to feel better. For many infections, a full 14 days is REQUIRED to kill the bacteria. The goals and time frame (see peak benefits above) should be discussed with you when the prescription is written, as well as how soon to expect a decline in temperature or other signs and symptoms and what to do if symptoms worsen.

Possible Advantages of These Drugs: The Augmentin XR form requires less frequent dosing (better adherence) and kills more resistant (high MIC) forms of Streptococcus.

▷ **These Drugs Should Not Be Taken If**
- you had an allergic reaction to them previously.
- you are certain you are allergic to any form of penicillin.

▷ **Inform Your Physician Before Taking These Drugs If**
- you suspect you may be allergic to penicillin or have a history of a previous "reaction."
- you are allergic to any cephalosporin antibiotic (Ancef, Ceclor, etc.—see Drug Classes).
- you are allergic by nature (hay fever, asthma, hives, eczema).
- you are unsure how much to take or how often.
- you have a history of liver or kidney disease.
- you have a history of low blood counts (amoxicillin/clavulanate, ampicillin, cloxacillin).

Possible Side Effects (natural, expected, and unavoidable drug actions)
Superinfections (see Glossary), often due to yeast organisms or for some penicillins due to Clostridium difficile.

▷ **Possible Adverse Effects** (unusual, unexpected, and infrequent reactions)
If any of the following develop, consult your physician promptly for guidance.
Mild Adverse Effects
Allergic reactions: skin rashes, hives, itching.
Irritations of mouth or tongue, "black tongue," nausea, vomiting, diarrhea, dizziness—rare to infrequent.
Serious Adverse Effects
Allergic reactions: anaphylactic reaction (see Glossary), severe skin reactions, drug fever, swollen painful joints, sore throat, abnormal bleeding or bruising.
Severe skin reactions (Stevens-Johnson Syndrome, bullous pemphigoid)—case reports.
Drug-induced colitis—rare.
Hemolytic anemia—case reports (penicillin VK).
Drug-induced periarteritis nodosa, meningitis, or porphyria—case reports (penicillin VK).
Abnormal liver or kidney changes—rare.
Drug-induced abnormal lowering of white blood cells—rare (amoxicillin/clavulanate, ampicillin, cloxacillin, penicillin VK).

▷ **Possible Effects on Sexual Function:** None reported except for case reports of a small decrease in sperm counts for ampicillin.

Possible Effects on Laboratory Tests
Complete blood counts: decreased red cells, hemoglobin, white cells (therapeutic effects of each antibiotic) and platelets (penicillin VK); increased eosinophils (allergic reactions).
INR (prothrombin time): occasionally increased (ampicillin, cloxacillin, and penicillin VK).
Liver function tests: increased aspartate aminotransferase (AST/GOT) and bilirubin (cloxacillin and penicillin VK).
Coombs test: may be positive with ampicillin or penicillin VK therapy.

CAUTION
1. If your infection does not respond in 24–48 hours (reduced symptoms, temperature, etc.), CALL YOUR DOCTOR.
2. Take the exact dose and the full course prescribed.

3. These medicines DO NOT treat viral infections. Considerable controversy has erupted regarding inappropriate prescribing of antibiotics to treat viral infections. Some intelligent clinicians are writing contingency antibiotics where the differential diagnosis of a bacterial infection versus a viral infection is unclear. Demanding an antibiotic or expecting an antibiotic to treat a viral infection (except in the case of a secondary bacterial infection) is an inappropriate patient action in most cases and only serves to lead to emergence of bacterial resistance.

4. If these drugs must be used concurrently with antibiotics, such as erythromycin or tetracycline, take the penicillin first.

Precautions for Use

By Infants and Children: Watch children with allergies closely for evidence of a developing allergy to penicillin. These drugs (amoxicillin, penicillin VK) may cause diarrhea, which sometimes necessitates discontinuation. Up to 90% of patients with mononucleosis who take amoxicillin, amoxicillin/clavulanate, or ampicillin get a rash.

By Those Over 60 Years of Age: Natural skin changes may predispose to prolonged itching in the genital and anal regions. Report such reactions promptly.

▷ **Advisability of Use During Pregnancy**

Pregnancy Category: B. See Pregnancy Risk Categories at the back of this book.

Animal Studies: Birth defects of the limbs reported in mice (penicillin VK only). (Not confirmed in other studies.)

Human Studies: Adequate studies of pregnant women indicate no increased risk of birth defects.

Ask your doctor for guidance, but these drugs are generally considered safe for use during any period of pregnancy.

Advisability of Use If Breast-Feeding

Presence of these drugs in breast milk: Yes.

The nursing infant may be sensitized to penicillin and be at risk for developing diarrhea or yeast infections. Talk with your doctor. Penicillins may be drugs of choice versus chloramphenicol or tetracyclines.

Habit-Forming Potential: None.

Effects of Overdose: Possible nausea, vomiting, and/or diarrhea.

Possible Effects of Long-Term Use: Superinfections, often due to yeast organisms or Clostridium difficile.

Suggested Periodic Examinations While Taking These Drugs (at physician's discretion)

Complete blood cell counts.

Kidney function tests.

▷ **While Taking These Drugs, Observe the Following**

Foods: No restrictions, except ampicillin, bacampicillin, and cloxacillin, which are best taken on an empty stomach.

Herbal Medicines or Minerals: Some patients use echinacea to attempt to boost their immune systems. Unfortunately, use of echinacea is not recommended in people with damaged immune systems. This herb may also actually weaken any immune system if it is used too often or for too long a time. Do NOT take mistletoe herb, oak bark or F.C. of marshmallow root and licorice. Guar gum decreased how much of one kind of penicillin got in the body. Avoid that combination.

Since St. John's wort and ampicillin may cause increased sun sensitivity, caution is advised.

Beverages: No restrictions (except as above). May be taken with milk.

▷ *Alcohol:* No interactions expected, but alcohol can blunt the immune response. It is best NOT to drink while you have an infection severe enough to require antibiotics.

Tobacco Smoking: No interactions expected. I advise everyone to quit smoking.

▷ *Other Drugs*

Penicillins *taken concurrently* with

- disulfiram (Antabuse) can cause a disulfiramlike reaction (see Glossary) (bacampicillin only); avoid the combination of these drugs.
- entacapone (Comtan) (and other medicines) are removed by the bile tract (biliary elimination), and medicines such as ampicillin that have been found to change removal by the bile. These and similar medicines may also alter blood levels by interfering with a process known as glucuronidation and/or intestinal beta glucuronidase may lead to an increased entacapone effect or adverse effects (such as movement disorders or diarrhea) in some patients. Closer patient follow-up and caution are prudent.
- live typhoid vaccine may blunt the vaccine response and benefits (amoxicillin and amoxicillin/clavulanate).
- methotrexate (Mexate) may increase risk of methotrexate toxicity (especially amoxicillin and oral penicillin).
- omeprazole (Prilosec) and other proton pump inhibitors (see Drug Classes) will decrease the amount of ampicillin that gets into the body because ampicillin requires an acid environment to optimally be absorbed.
- probenecid (Benemid) will increase and sustain blood levels. This interaction is often used to therapeutic advantage.

Ampicillin *taken concurrently* with

- allopurinol may increase the risk of rashes.
- atenolol can blunt the therapeutic benefits of atenolol.

Ampicillin, cloxacillin or penicillin VK *taken concurrently* with

- warfarin (Coumadin) may intensify the anticoagulant effect and increase risk of bleeding; more frequent INR (prothrombin time or protime) testing is needed.

Penicillins may *decrease* the effects of

- birth control pills (oral contraceptives) and impair their effectiveness in preventing pregnancy.

The following drugs may *decrease* the effects of penicillins:

- antacids, histamine (H2) blockers or proton pump inhibitors (see Drug Classes)—may reduce the absorption of penicillins.
- chloramphenicol (Chloromycetin).
- cholestyramine (Questran, etc.) can delay penicillins such as penicillin G. If these medicines must be used together, the penicillin should be taken (or given) an hour before the cholestyramine or alternatively, the penicillin should be taken four to six hours AFTER the cholestyramine.
- erythromycin (Erythrocin, E-Mycin, etc.).
- tetracyclines (Achromycin, Declomycin, doxycycline, Minocin, etc.: see Drug Classes).

▷ *Driving, Hazardous Activities:* Usually no restrictions. Be alert to the rare occurrence of dizziness and/or nausea and restrict activities accordingly.

Aviation Note: The use of these drugs *may be a disqualification* for piloting. Consult a designated Aviation Medical Examiner.

Exposure to Sun: Ampicillin may increase sensitivity to the sun. Use caution.
Special Storage Instructions: Oral solutions and pediatric drops (amoxicillin) should be refrigerated.
Observe the Following Expiration Times: Do not take the oral solution of these drugs if older than 7 days (cloxacillin is good for only 3 days) if kept at room temperature or 14 days when kept refrigerated.

PENTAZOCINE (pen TAZ oh seen)

Introduced: 1967   **Class:**   Analgesic, strong   **Prescription:**
USA: Yes   **Controlled Drug:**   USA: C-IV*; Canada: No   **Available as**
Generic: USA: No; Canada: No
Brand Names: Talacen [CD], Talwin, Talwin Compound [CD], ✿Talwin Compound-50 [CD], Talwin Nx [CD]

BENEFITS versus RISKS	
Possible Benefits	*Possible Risks*
RELIEF OF MODERATE TO SEVERE PAIN	POTENTIAL FOR HABIT FORMATION (DEPENDENCE)
	Respiratory depression
	Sedative effects
	Mental and behavioral disturbances
	Low blood pressure, fainting
	Nausea, constipation

Author's Note: The information in this profile has been shortened to make room for more widely used medicines.

PENTOXIFYLLINE (pen tox I fi leen)

Other Name: Oxpentifylline
Introduced: 1972   **Class:**   Blood flow agent, xanthines   **Prescrip-**
tion: USA: Yes   **Controlled Drug:**   USA: No; Canada: No   **Available**
as Generic: No
Brand Name: Trental

BENEFITS versus RISKS	
Possible Benefits	*Possible Risks*
IMPROVED BLOOD FLOW IN PERIPHERAL ARTERIAL DISEASE	Reduced blood pressure, angina, abnormal heart rhythms
REDUCTION OF INTERMITTENT CLAUDICATION PAIN	Rare low blood counts and aplastic anemia
May help in some AIDS-related pain	Indigestion, nausea, vomiting
	Dizziness, flushing

Author's Note: A medicine called cilostazol (Pletal) was approved by the FDA to treat intermittent claudication. Information in this profile has been shortened to make room for more widely used medicines.

*See Schedules of Controlled Drugs at the back of this book.

PERGOLIDE (PER go lide)

Introduced: 1980 **Class:** Anti-Parkinsonism, ergot derivative   **Prescrip-**
tion: USA: Yes   **Controlled Drug:**   USA: No; Canada: No   **Available**
as Generic: USA: No
Brand Names: ✤Drax-Pergolide, Permax

BENEFITS versus RISKS	
Possible Benefits	*Possible Risks*
ADDITIVE RELIEF OF SYMPTOMS OF PARKINSON'S DISEASE WHEN USED CONCURRENTLY WITH LEVODOPA/CARBIDOPA PERMITS A REDUCTION IN SINEMET DOSE	ABNORMAL INVOLUNTARY MOVEMENTS HALLUCINATIONS INITIAL FALL IN BLOOD PRESSURE/ORTHOSTATIC HYPOTENSION
Reduces tics in some children with Tourette's and/or chronic tics	Premature heart contractions (ventricular)

▷ **Principal Uses**

As a Single Drug Product: Uses currently included in FDA-approved labeling: As an adjunct to levodopa/carbidopa treatment of Parkinson's disease for people who experience intolerable abnormal movements (dyskinesia) and/or increasing "on-off" episodes due to levodopa. The addition of pergolide (1) permits reduction of the daily dose of levodopa with consequent lessening of dyskinesia and erratic drug response and (2) provides additional relief of Parkinsonian symptoms.

Other (unlabeled) generally accepted uses: (1) helps in some conditions where excess prolactin is made; (2) may be of use in acromegaly; (3) works to lower increased prolactin levels (as in some pituitary tumors); (4) lowered tic occurrence significantly in one study of patients with chronic tics and/or Tourette's syndrome.

How This Drug Works: By directly stimulating part of the brain (dopamine receptor sites in the corpus striatum), this drug helps to compensate for the deficiency of dopamine that is responsible for the rigidity, tremor and sluggish movement characteristic of Parkinson's disease.

Available Dosage Forms and Strengths
Tablets — 0.05 mg, 0.25 mg, 1 mg

▷ **Usual Adult Dosage Ranges:** *Parkinson's (in conjunction with levodopa plus carbidopa)*: Starts at 0.05 mg daily (first 2 days); slowly increased by 0.1 mg daily or 0.15 mg every third day over the next 12 days. If needed and tolerated, daily dose may be increased by 0.25 mg every third day until best response. Total daily dose, 0.4 mg, should be divided into three equal portions taken at 6- to 8-hour intervals. Usual ongoing dose is 3 mg every 24 hours; do not exceed 5 mg every 24 hours.

During gradual start of pergolide, dose of levodopa/carbidopa (Sinemet) may be lowered by your doctor.

Note: Actual dose and schedule must be determined for each patient individually.

Typical Treatment Goals and Measurements (Outcomes and Markers)
Parkinson's disease: The general goal is to minimize symptoms (tremor, slug-

gish movements, analysis of walking or gait, etc.) to the fullest extent possible. Additionally, many neurologists use Hahn-Yahr scores and the time it takes to maximum amount of finger tapping as indicators of the benefits of this drug.

Tic Reduction: The goal is to minimize the frequency of tics. The Yale Global Tic Severity Scale (YGTSS) is widely used to check results.

Conditions Requiring Dosing Adjustments
Liver Function: Used with caution in liver disease.
Kidney Function: Consideration should be given to empirical decreases in dose.

▷ **Dosing Instructions:** The tablet may be crushed and taken with food or milk to reduce stomach irritation. If you forget a dose: Take the missed dose as soon as you remember it, unless it's nearly time for your next dose—if that is the case, skip the missed dose and take the next dose right on schedule. DO NOT double doses. Talk with your doctor if you find yourself missing doses.

Usual Duration of Use: Regular use for 4 to 6 weeks reveals benefits controlling Parkinson's symptoms and permitting lower levodopa/carbidopa dose. Onset time for conditions involving excessive prolactin (hyperprolactinemia) will require a similar length of time to work. Long-term use requires follow-up with your doctor.

Possible Advantages of This Drug: May give more effective and uniform control of Parkinsonian symptoms and fewer adverse effects from levodopa therapy. More powerful (potent) and longer lasting than bromocriptine.

▷ **This Drug Should Not Be Taken If**
- you have had an allergic reaction to this medicine or to the components previously.
- you have had a serious adverse effect from any ergot preparation.
- you have severe coronary artery disease or peripheral vascular disease.

▷ **Inform Your Physician Before Taking This Drug If**
- you have constitutionally low blood pressure.
- you are pregnant or breast-feeding your infant.
- you are taking any antihypertensive drugs or antipsychotic drugs (see Drug Classes).
- you have any degree of coronary artery disease, especially angina, or a history of heart attack.
- you have any type of heart rhythm disorder.
- you have impaired liver or kidney function.
- you have a seizure disorder.

Possible Side Effects (natural, expected, and unavoidable drug actions)
Weakness; chest pain (possibly anginal); peripheral edema; orthostatic hypotension (see Glossary)—infrequent.

▷ **Possible Adverse Effects** (unusual, unexpected, and infrequent reactions)
If any of the following develop, consult your physician promptly for guidance.
Mild Adverse Effects
Allergic reactions: skin rash, facial swelling—rare.
Headache, dizziness, hallucinations, drowsiness, insomnia, anxiety, double vision—rare to infrequent.
Nasal congestion, shortness of breath, palpitation, fainting—rare to infrequent.
Altered taste, dry mouth, indigestion, nausea, vomiting, constipation, diarrhea—infrequent.

Serious Adverse Effects
> Allergic reactions: none reported.
> Idiosyncratic reactions: flu-like symptoms.
> Abnormal involuntary movements (dyskinesia)—frequent.
> Psychotic behavior—case reports.
> Hallucinations (accounted for 7.8% of patient withdrawals from therapy; 13.8% occurrence).
> Abnormal heartbeat (ventricular arrhythmias)—infrequent to frequent.
> Heart valve changes—case reports.
> Anemia—rare.

▷ **Possible Effects on Sexual Function:** Infrequent reports of altered libido (increased or decreased), impotence, breast pain, priapism (see Glossary).

▷ **Adverse Effects That May Mimic Natural Diseases or Disorders**
> Effects on mental function and behavior may resemble psychotic disorders.

Natural Diseases or Disorders That May Be Activated by This Drug
> Coronary artery disease with anginal syndrome, heart rhythm disorders, Raynaud's phenomenon (see Glossary), seizure disorders.

Possible Effects on Laboratory Tests
> Blood prolactin level: decreased (marked reduction).

CAUTION
> 1. May cause abnormal movements (dyskinesias), or intensify existing dyskinesias. Watch for tremors, twitching or abnormal involuntary movements of any kind. Report these promptly.
> 2. Low starting doses help prevent possibility of excessive drop in blood pressure. See dose routine outlined above.
> 3. Tell your doctor promptly if you become pregnant or plan pregnancy. This drug has been reported (rarely) to cause abortion and birth defects.
> 4. May lead to abnormal heart rhythms in people prone to arrhythmia.

Precautions for Use
> *By Infants and Children:* One study in children 7-17 years old started with 25 mcg a day, then increased in seven days by 25 mcg to 50 mcg three times a day. A study in children with chronic tics and/or Tourette's used 0.15 to 0.45 mg a day.
> *By Those Over 60 Years of Age:* Small initial doses are mandatory. Watch closely for any tendency to light-headedness or faintness, especially on arising from a lying or sitting position. You may be more susceptible to the development of impaired thinking, confusion, agitation, nightmares, or hallucinations.

▷ **Advisability of Use During Pregnancy**
> *Pregnancy Category:* B. See Pregnancy Risk Categories at the back of this book.
> *Animal Studies:* No birth defects due to this drug were found in mouse or rabbit studies.
> *Human Studies:* Adequate studies of pregnant women are not available. However, there are four reports of birth defects associated with the use of this drug and infrequent reports of abortion. Causal relationships have not been established, but prudence advises against the use of this drug during pregnancy.
> Consult your physician for guidance.

Advisability of Use If Breast-Feeding
> Presence of this drug in breast milk: Unknown.
> Avoid drug or refrain from nursing.

Habit-Forming Potential: None.

Effects of Overdose: Nausea, vomiting, palpitations, low blood pressure, agitation, severe involuntary movements, hallucinations, seizures.

Possible Effects of Long-Term Use: Increased risk of developing dyskinesias.

Suggested Periodic Examinations While Taking This Drug (at physician's discretion)
  Regular evaluation of drug response.
  Heart function and blood pressure status.

▷ **While Taking This Drug, Observe the Following**
  Foods: No restrictions.
  Herbal Medicines or Minerals: Calcium and garlic may lower blood pressure. Since this medicine may also lower blood pressure, talk to your doctor BEFORE you add garlic or additional amounts of calcium to your diet. Calabar bean (chop nut, Fabia, ordeal nut, others) is unsafe when taken by mouth (physostigmine is the active ingredient) and should never be taken by people with Parkinson's disease. Some theory to suggest that kava (no longer advised in Canada due to liver toxicity questions) may blunt pergolide effectiveness. Octacosanol (a cousin of vitamin E) can worsen movement problems and should also be avoided.
  Beverages: No restrictions. May be taken with milk.
▷ *Alcohol:* Alcohol can exaggerate the blood pressure–lowering and sedative effects of this drug.
  Tobacco Smoking: No interactions expected. I advise everyone to quit smoking.
▷ *Other Drugs*
  Pergolide **taken concurrently** with
  • antihypertensive drugs (and other drugs that can lower blood pressure) requires careful monitoring for excessive drops in pressure (lisinopril case report); dose changes may be needed.
  The following drugs may **decrease** the effects of pergolide and diminish its effectiveness:
  • chlorprothixene (Taractan).
  • haloperidol (Haldol).
  • metoclopramide (Reglan).
  • phenothiazines (see Drug Classes).
  • thiothixene (Navane).
▷ *Driving, Hazardous Activities:* This drug may cause dizziness, drowsiness, impaired coordination, or fainting. Restrict activities as necessary.
  Aviation Note: The use of this drug **is a disqualification** for piloting. Consult a designated Aviation Medical Examiner.
  Exposure to Sun: No restrictions.
  Exposure to Heat: Use caution until the combined effects have been determined. Hot environments can cause lowering of blood pressure.
  Discontinuation: **Do not stop this drug abruptly**. Sudden withdrawal can cause confusion, paranoid thinking, and severe hallucinations. Consult your physician regarding a schedule for gradual withdrawal.

PERPHENAZINE (per FEN a zeen)

Introduced: 1957 **Class:** Tranquilizer, major; phenothiazines
Prescription: USA: Yes **Controlled Drug:** USA: No; Canada: No
Available as Generic: USA: Yes; Canada: Yes

Brand Names: ✿Apo-Perphenazine, ✿Elavil Plus [CD], ✿Etrafon, Etrafon [CD], Etrafon-A [CD], Etrafon Forte [CD], ✿Phenazine, ✿PMS-Levazine, ✿PMS-Perphenazine, Triavil [CD], Trilafon

BENEFITS versus RISKS	
Possible Benefits	*Possible Risks*
EFFECTIVE CONTROL OF ACUTE MENTAL DISORDERS	SERIOUS TOXIC EFFECTS ON BRAIN WITH LONG-TERM USE
Beneficial effects on thinking, mood, and behavior	Liver damage with jaundice
Relief of anxiety and tension	Blood cell disorders: hemolytic anemia, abnormally low white
Moderately effective control of nausea and vomiting	blood cell and platelet counts

▷ **Principal Uses**

As a Single Drug Product: Uses currently included in FDA-approved labeling: (1) Treats acute and chronic psychotic disorders: agitated depression, schizophrenia, and similar mental dysfunction; (2) used as a tranquilizer to help agitated and disruptive behavior; (3) severe nausea and vomiting treatment; (4) used to prevent vomiting from cisplatin; (5) eases vertigo.

Other (unlabeled) generally accepted uses: (1) Can ease tremors caused by tricyclic antidepressants.

As a Combination Drug Product [CD]: Available combined with amitriptyline. In some severe agitated depression, combining an antipsychotic drug and an antidepressant will be more effective than either drug used alone.

Author's Note: Information in this profile has been shortened to make room for more widely used medicines.

PHENELZINE (FEN el zeen)

Introduced: 1961   **Class:**   Antidepressant, MAO type A inhibitor
Prescription: USA: Yes   **Controlled Drug:**   USA: No; Canada: No
Available as Generic: No
Brand Name: Nardil

BENEFITS versus RISKS	
Possible Benefits	*Possible Risks*
EFFECTIVE RELIEF OF REACTIVE, NEUROTIC, ATYPICAL DEPRESSIONS WITH ASSOCIATED ANXIETY OR PHOBIA	DANGEROUS INTERACTIONS WITH MANY DRUGS AND FOODS CONDUCIVE TO HYPERTENSIVE CRISIS
Beneficial in some depressions that are not responsive to other treatments	DISORDERED HEART RATE AND RHYTHM
	Drug-induced hepatitis—rare
	Mental changes: agitation, confusion, impaired memory, hypomania

Author's Note: Since other medicines are more widely used, the information in this profile has been shortened.

PHENOBARBITAL (fee noh BAR bi tawl)

Other Name: Phenobarbitone
Introduced: 1912   **Class:**   Sedative, anticonvulsant, barbiturates
Prescription: USA: Yes   **Controlled Drug:**   USA: C-IV*; Canada: Yes
Available as Generic: Yes

Brand Names: Aasquel, Alised, Alubelap [CD], Aminodrox-Forte, Antispas-
modic [CD], Azpan, Barbidonna [CD], Barbidonna Elixir [CD], Barbita,
Belap, Belladenal [CD], Belladenal-S [CD], ♣Belladenal Spacetabs [CD],
♣Bellergal [CD], Bellergal-S [CD], ♣Bellergal Spacetabs [CD], Bronchotabs
[CD], Bronkolixir [CD], ♣Cafergot-PB, Chardonna-2 [CD], Daricon PB, ♣Di-
clophen [CD], Dilantin w/Phenobarbital [CD], Donna-Sed, Donnatal [CD],
Donphen, Ergobel [CD], Eskabarb, Eskaphen B [CD], Floramine, ♣Garde-
nal, Hybephen [CD], Hypnaldyne [CD], Isuprel Compound [CD], Kinesed
[CD], Luminal, Mudrane GG Elixir and Tablets [CD], Mudrane Tablets [CD],
Neospect, ♣Neuro-Spasex [CD], ♣Neuro-Trasentin [CD], ♣Neuro-Trasentin
Forte [CD], Novalene, Phedral [CD], ♣Phenaphen Capsules [CD],
♣Phenaphen No. 2, 3, 4 [CD], Phenergan w/Codeine [CD], Phyldrox, Quadri-
nal [CD], Relaxadron, SBP [CD], Scodonnar [CD], Sedacord [CD], SK-
Phenobarbital, Solfoton, Spasquid [CD], Spazcaps, Tedral Preparations [CD],
T.E.P. [CD], Thalfed [CD], Theocardone, Theocord [CD], Theolixer, Vitaphen

---

BENEFITS versus RISKS

Possible Benefits	*Possible Risks*
EFFECTIVE CONTROL OF TONIC-CLONIC SEIZURES AND ALL TYPES OF PARTIAL SEIZURES	POTENTIAL FOR DEPENDENCE LIFE-THREATENING TOXICITY WITH OVERDOSE
EFFECTIVE CONTROL OF FEBRILE SEIZURES OF CHILDHOOD	Drug-induced hepatitis or decreased kidney function
Effective relief of anxiety and nervous tension	Blood cell disorders: abnormally low red cell, white cell, and platelet counts

---

▷ **Principal Uses**

As a Single Drug Product: Uses currently included in FDA-approved labeling:
(1) Used as a mild sedative; (2) used as an anticonvulsant to control grand
mal epilepsy and all types of partial seizures, including febrile seizures of
childhood; (3) used as a sedative, yet newer agents carry fewer drug interactions or effects on sleep cycles.

Other (unlabeled) generally accepted uses: (1) May be helpful in detoxification of sedative-hypnotic addiction; (2) can help control seizures found in
cerebral malaria; (3) eases neonatal seizures; (4) may have a role in treating pain syndromes.

As a Combination Drug Product [CD]: This drug is available in many combinations with derivatives of belladonna, an antispasmodic commonly used to
treat functional disorders of the gastrointestinal tract. It is also available in
combination with bronchodilators for the treatment of asthma and with
ergotamine for the treatment of headaches.

How This Drug Works: Impedes transfer of sodium and potassium across cells
and selectively blocks nerve impulses. This can give a sedative effect or
suppress nerve impulses that cause seizures.

*See Schedules of Controlled Drugs at the back of this book.

Author's Note: Information in this profile has been shortened to make room for more widely used medicines.

PHENYTOIN (FEN i toh in)

Other Name: Diphenylhydantoin

Introduced: 1938   **Class:**   Anticonvulsant, hydantoins, pain syndrome modifier   **Prescription:**   USA: Yes   **Controlled Drug:**   USA: No; Canada: No   **Available as Generic:**   USA: Yes; Canada: Yes

Brand Names: Dilantin, Dilantin Infatabs, Dilantin w/Phenobarbital [CD], Di-Phen, Diphenylan, Ekko JR, Ekko SR, Ekko Three, ♣Mebroin [CD], ♣Phelantin

---

BENEFITS versus RISKS

Possible Benefits	*Possible Risks*
EFFECTIVE CONTROL OF TONIC-CLONIC (GRAND MAL), PSYCHOMOTOR (TEMPORAL LOBE), MYOCLONIC and FOCAL SEIZURE	VERY NARROW TREATMENT MARGIN
	POSSIBLE BIRTH DEFECTS
	Overgrowth of gums
May have a role used as a powder helping heal wounds (diabetic wounds and pressure or bed sores)	Excessive hair growth
	Blood cell disorders: impaired production of all blood cells
	Drug-induced hepatitis or nephritis

▷ **Principal Uses**

   As a Single Drug Product: Uses currently included in FDA-approved labeling: As an antiepileptic drug to control grand mal, psychomotor, myoclonic and focal seizures. It can also be used to control seizures following brain surgery. Other (unlabeled) generally accepted uses: (1) Used to initiate treatment of trigeminal neuralgia—it is sometimes effective in relieving the severe facial pain of this disorder; (2) used in chronic pain syndromes; (3) may have a role (as an applied powder) in helping heal wounds (such as bed sores and diabetic wounds); (4) effective in eclampsia or pre-eclampsia.

   As a Combination Drug Product [CD]: This drug is available in combination with phenobarbital, another effective anticonvulsant. Some seizure disorders require the combined actions of these two drugs for effective control.

How This Drug Works: By promoting the loss of sodium from nerve fibers, this drug lowers and stabilizes their excitability and thereby inhibits the repetitious spread of electrical impulses along nerve pathways. This action may prevent seizures altogether or it may reduce their frequency and severity. In helping wound healing it probably works in a similar way as the adverse effect of causing excessive gum growth. Phenytoin appears to promote fibroblast growth leading to collagen, etc.

Available Dosage Forms and Strengths

   Capsules, extended — 30 mg, 100 mg
   Capsules, prompt — 30 mg, 100 mg
          Injection — 50 mg/ml
          Kapseals — 30 mg, 100 mg
      Oral suspension — 30 mg/5 ml, 125 mg/5 ml
   Tablets, chewable — 50 mg

▷ **Usual Adult Dosage Ranges:** *Seizures:* Initially (prompt or extended form) 100 mg three times a day. Dose may be increased cautiously by 100 mg/week as needed and tolerated. Once the optimal maintenance dose has been identified, the total daily dose may be taken as a single dose every 24 hours if Dilantin capsules are used. No other formulation is approved for once-a-day use. The total daily dose should not exceed 600 mg. In wound healing, some clinicians have used a phenytoin capsule content mixed with sterile saline using sterile technique. A sterile gauze pad is then soaked in the mixture and the gauze applied to the wound. Others have applied phenytoin powder USP directly to the wound once a day and then covered the wound with a sterile dressing. This is not an FDA-approved use and standardized protocols and research are needed.

Note: **Actual dose and schedule must be determined for each patient individually.**

Conditions Requiring Dosing Adjustments

Liver Function: The ongoing dose should be decreased based on blood levels.

Kidney Function: The dose or dosing interval must be decreased in moderate kidney failure.

Obesity: The way this medicine is distributed (volume of distribution) changes with increasing body fat. Loading doses must be calculated based on ideal body weight. The product of 1.33 times actual weight divided by the ideal weight is then added to the original number to decide the final loading dose.

▷ **Dosing Instructions:** May be taken with or after food to reduce stomach irritation. The capsule may be opened, and the tablet may be crushed. Chew tabs or liquid forms can help if you have problems swallowing. If liquid suspension form is used, please shake the medicine well, then use a measuring spoon or calibrated medicine dose cup to get exactly the right dose. If you forget a dose: Take the missed dose as soon as you remember it, unless it's nearly time for your next dose—if that is the case, skip the missed dose and take the next dose right on schedule. DO NOT double doses unless your doctor tells you to do that. If you miss two doses or more in a row, call your doctor.

Usual Duration of Use: Use on a regular schedule for 2 to 3 weeks usually determines benefit in reducing frequency and severity of seizures. Optimal control will require careful dose adjustments over a period of several months. Long-term use (months to years) requires ongoing physician supervision.

Typical Treatment Goals and Measurements (Outcomes and Markers)

Seizures: The general goal for this medicine is effective seizure control. Neurologists tend to define "effective" on a case-by-case basis depending on the seizure type and patient factors. If seizure control is not effective, it's not unusual to use combination treatment. For this medicine, a balance must be struck between too little medicine and too much medicine. Blood levels are used to make certain that the blood level is in the right range.

▷ **This Drug Should Not Be Taken If**
- you have had an allergic reaction to this drug or other hydantoin drugs previously.
- you have sinus bradycardia or serious heart block.

▷ **Inform Your Physician Before Taking This Drug If**
- you are taking any other drugs at this time.
- you have a history of liver disease or impaired liver function.
- you have a history of alcohol abuse. Alcohol can change blood levels of this medicine.

- you have low blood pressure, diabetes, or any type of heart disease.
- you are pregnant or planning pregnancy.
- you plan to have surgery under general anesthesia in the near future.

Possible Side Effects (natural, expected, and unavoidable drug actions)

Mild fatigue, sluggishness and drowsiness (in sensitive individuals).

Pink to red to brown coloration of urine (of no significance).

▷ **Possible Adverse Effects** (unusual, unexpected, and infrequent reactions)

If any of the following develop, consult your physician promptly for guidance.

Mild Adverse Effects

Allergic reactions: skin rashes, hives, drug fever (see Glossary).

Headache, dizziness, nervousness, insomnia, muscle twitching—infrequent.

Nausea, vomiting, constipation—infrequent.

Bedwetting—case reports.

Abnormal eye movements—dose-related.

Low blood calcium (and potential osteoporosis) and elevated blood sugar—possible.

Overgrowth of gum tissues—most common in children.

Excessive growth of body hair—most common in young girls.

Serious Adverse Effects

Allergic reactions: drug-induced hepatitis, with or without jaundice (see Glossary).

Drug-induced nephritis, with acute kidney failure.

Severe skin reactions (toxic epidermal necrolysis, Stevens-Johnson syndrome or erythema multiforme).

Myocarditis, generalized enlargement of lymph glands (pseudolymphoma)—case reports.

Idiosyncratic reactions: hemolytic anemia (see Glossary).

Acute psychotic episodes—case reports.

Mental confusion, unsteadiness, double vision, jerky eye movements, slurred speech—possible.

Drug-induced seizures—possible.

Blood-clotting disorders in infants of mothers maintained on phenytoin—rare.

Bone marrow depression (see Glossary): weakness, fever, sore throat, bleeding, or bruising—case reports.

Lupus erythematosus—case report.

Drug-induced periarteritis nodosa, low thyroid function, or myasthenia gravis—case reports.

Tardive dyskinesia or porphyria—case reports.

Abnormal IgA (increased risk of respiratory infections)—possible.

Peripheral nerve damage (neuropathy) or muscle damage (myopathy)—case reports.

Serious heart rhythm problems (such as ventricular fibrillation)—with rapid intravenous use.

Elevated blood sugar, due to inhibition of insulin release—possible.

▷ **Possible Effects on Sexual Function:** Decreased libido and/or impotence—infrequent.

Swelling and tenderness of male breast tissue (gynecomastia) or Peyronie's disease (see Glossary)—rare.

Decreased effectiveness of oral contraceptives.

▷ **Adverse Effects That May Mimic Natural Diseases or Disorders**

Drug-induced hepatitis may suggest viral hepatitis. Skin reactions may resemble lupus erythematosus.

Natural Diseases or Disorders That May Be Activated by This Drug

Latent diabetes, porphyria, systemic lupus erythematosus, low bone mineral density predisposing to osteoporosis.

Possible Effects on Laboratory Tests

Complete blood cell counts: decreased red cells, hemoglobin, white cells, and platelets; increased eosinophils (allergic reaction).

Blood lupus erythematosus (LE) cells: positive.

Prothrombin time: increased (when phenytoin is taken concurrently with warfarin).

Blood calcium level: decreased.

Blood total cholesterol, LDL and VLDL cholesterol levels: no effects.

Blood HDL cholesterol level: increased.

Blood triglyceride levels: no effect.

Blood glucose level: increased.

Blood thyroid hormone levels: T3, T4, and free T4: increased.

Liver function tests: increased liver enzymes (ALT/GPT, AST/GOT, alkaline phosphatase) and bilirubin.

CAUTION

1. Some brand-name capsules of this drug have a significantly longer duration of action than generic-name capsules of the same strength. To assure a correct dosing schedule, it is necessary to distinguish between "prompt"-action and "extended"-action capsules. Do not substitute one for the other without your physician's knowledge and guidance.
2. When used for the treatment of epilepsy, *this drug must not be stopped abruptly*.
3. Periodic blood levels of this drug are essential to get the right dose (see "Therapeutic Drug Monitoring" in Section One).
4. Use of phenytoin in wound healing has some early data, but requires further research and standardization of protocols.
5. Take this medicine EXACTLY as prescribed and at the same time each day.
6. Shake the suspension form of this drug thoroughly before measuring the dose. Use a standard measuring device to assure that the dose is accurate.
7. Side effects and mild adverse effects are usually most apparent during the first several days of treatment and often subside with continued use.
8. It may be necessary to take folic acid to prevent anemia. Talk with your doctor about this.
9. Case reports have been made about atypical allergy (cross-sensitivity) between phenytoin and carbamazepine (Tegretol, others). Talk to your doctor if you are allergic to phenytoin.
10. This medicine has an unusual pathway for removal that can fill up (become saturated) and stop working. This means that a small change in dose may give a huge change in blood levels. Make certain you know exactly how much phenytoin your doctor wants you to take.
11. Carry personal identification card that says you are taking this drug.

Precautions for Use

By Infants and Children: Elimination of this drug varies widely with age. Periodic measurement of blood levels is essential for all ages. Some children will require more than one dose daily for good control.

Observe for early indications of drug toxicity: jerky eye movements, unsteadiness in stance and gait, slurred speech, abnormal involuntary movements of the extremities, and odd behavior.

By Those Over 60 Years of Age: You may be more sensitive to all of the actions of this drug and require smaller doses. Observe closely for any indications of early toxicity: drowsiness, fatigue, confusion, unsteadiness, disturbances of vision, slurred speech, muscle twitching.

▷ **Advisability of Use During Pregnancy**
Pregnancy Category: D. See Pregnancy Risk Categories at the back of this book.
Animal Studies: Cleft lip and palate, skeletal and visceral defects in mice and rats.
Human Studies: Available information is conflicting. Some studies suggest a small but significant increase in birth defects. The incidence of birth defects in children of epileptics not taking anticonvulsant drugs is 3.2%; incidence increases to 6.4% with anticonvulsant use in pregnancy. The "fetal hydantoin syndrome" in infants exposed to phenytoin during pregnancy shows birth defects of skull, face, and limbs; deficient growth and development; and subnormal intelligence. Other effects on the infant include reduction in blood-clotting factors that predispose it to severe bruising and hemorrhage.
Discuss the benefits and risks of using this drug during pregnancy with your doctor. It is advisable to use the smallest maintenance dose that will control seizures. In addition, you should take vitamin K during the final month of pregnancy to prevent a deficiency of fetal blood-clotting factors.

Advisability of Use If Breast-Feeding
Presence of this drug in breast milk: Yes, in trace amounts.
Monitor nursing infant closely, and discontinue drug or nursing if adverse effects develop.

Habit-Forming Potential: None.

Effects of Overdose: Drowsiness, jerky eye movements, hand tremor, unsteadiness, slurred speech, hallucinations, delusions, nausea, vomiting, stupor progressing to coma.

Possible Effects of Long-Term Use: Low blood calcium resulting in rickets or osteomalacia; megaloblastic anemia; peripheral neuropathy (see Glossary); schizophreniclike psychosis. Lymphosarcoma, malignant lymphoma, and leukemia have been associated with long-term use; a cause-and-effect relationship (see Glossary) has not been established.

Suggested Periodic Examinations While Taking This Drug (at physician's discretion)
Monitoring of blood phenytoin levels to guide dose. Time to sample blood for phenytoin level: just before next dose. Recommended therapeutic range: 10 to 20 mg/ml.
Complete blood cell counts.
Liver function tests.
Measurements of the following blood levels: glucose, calcium, phosphorus, folic acid, vitamin B12.
Bone mineral density testing (DEXA) to check risk for osteoporosis and fracture.

▷ **While Taking This Drug, Observe the Following**
Foods: No restrictions.
Herbal Medicines or Minerals: Using kola, guarana, or ma huang may result in unacceptable central nervous system stimulation. Evening primrose oil may increase seizure risk. Some ginkgo products have a contaminant in them called 4-O-methylpyridoxine, which may increase seizure risk. Combination is not advisable. Valerian and kava kava (use questionable due to

possible liver toxicity) may interact to increase drowsiness. St. John's wort may also cause increased sun sensitivity—caution is advised. Increased calcium and vitamin D are prudent.

Nutritional Support: Supplements of folic acid, calcium, vitamin D, and vitamin K may be necessary.

Beverages: No restrictions. May be taken with milk.

▷ *Alcohol:* Use extreme caution. Alcohol (in large quantities or with continual use) may reduce this drug's effectiveness in preventing seizures.

Tobacco Smoking: No interactions expected. I advise everyone to quit smoking.

▷ *Other Drugs*

Phenytoin may *decrease* the effects of
- acetaminophen (Tylenol, others).
- acyclovir (Zovirax).
- amprenavir (Agenerase) or indinavir (Crixivan).
- atorvastatin (Lipitor) and simvastatin (Zocor) probably by increasing liver enzymes (cytochrome P450 3A4), which are partly involved in removing atorvastatin. More frequent checks of progress toward cholesterol goals are prudent if these medicines must be combined.
- bupropion (Wellbutrin).
- cholecalciferol (vitamin D).
- clofibrate (Atromid-S).
- clozapine (Clozaril).
- conjugated estrogens (Premarin).
- cortisonelike drugs (see Drug Classes).
- cyclosporine (Sandimmune).
- disopyramide (Norpace).
- donepezil (Aricept).
- doxycycline (Vibramycin, etc.).
- imatinib (Gleevec). Checks of imatinib levels used to guide dosing are prudent.
- itraconazole (Sporanox), voriconazole (Vfend), and other antifungals using the same liver removal system.
- lamotrigine (Lamictal). Blood levels of lamotrigine and dosing adjustments as indicated are needed.
- levodopa (Larodopa, Sinemet).
- levothyroxine (Synthroid, others).
- meperidine (Demerol).
- methadone (Dolophine).
- mexiletine (Mexitil).
- miconazole (Monistat, Micatin, others).
- neuromuscular blocking agents (such as pancuronium-Pavulon or vecuronium-Norcuron).
- oral antidiabetic drugs (see Drug Classes).
- oral contraceptives (birth control pills).
- paclitaxel (Taxol).
- paroxetine (Paxil).
- quetiapine (Seroquel).
- quinidine (Quinaglute, etc.).
- ritonavir (Norvir) and perhaps other protease inhibitors (see Drug Classes).
- sirolimus (Rapamune) and tacrolimus (Prograf).
- tiagabine (Gabitril).
- triamcinolone.

Phenytoin *taken concurrently* with
- acetazolamide (Diamox) may lead to bone problems (osteomalacia).
- carbamazepine (Tegretol) may result in increased or decreased levels of phenytoin.
- chlordiazepoxide (Librium, and perhaps other benzodiazepines) may increase or decrease phenytoin levels; levels should be obtained more frequently if these drugs are combined.
- ciprofloxacin (Cipro) may increase or decrease phenytoin levels. Check phenytoin levels more frequently.
- dopamine will result in very low blood pressure.
- flu shots (influenza vaccine) may change phenytoin levels.
- ketorolac (Toradol) may result in seizures—DO NOT COMBINE these medicines.
- oral anticoagulants (Coumadin, etc.) can either increase or decrease the anticoagulant effect; monitor this combination very closely with INR (serial prothrombin) testing.
- primidone (Mysoline) may alter primidone actions and enhance its toxicity.
- theophyllines (Aminophyllin, Theo-Dur, etc.) may cause a decrease in the effectiveness of both drugs.
- valproic acid (Depakene) may result in altered phenytoin or valproic acid levels; increased blood level testing of both medicines is needed if these medicines are to be combined.
- warfarin (Coumadin) may lead to initial increased bleeding risk and subsequent decrease in anticoagulation; more frequent INR (prothrombin time or protime) testing is needed. Warfarin doses should be adjusted to results.

The following drugs may *increase* the effects of phenytoin:
- amiodarone (Cordarone).
- chloramphenicol (Chloromycetin).
- chlorpheniramine.
- cimetidine (Tagamet).
- clopidogrel (Plavix)—extent unknown—yet clopidogrel inhibits cytochrome P450 2C9 which helps remove phenytoin from the body. More frequent checks of phenytoin levels are prudent if these medicines are combined.
- cotrimoxazole (Bactrim).
- diltiazem (Cardizem).
- disulfiram (Antabuse).
- felbamate (Felbatol).
- fluconazole (Diflucan).
- fluoxetine (Prozac).
- fluvoxamine (Luvox).
- gabapentin (Neurontin).
- ibuprofen and perhaps other NSAIDs.
- isoniazid (INH, Niconyl, etc.).
- metronidazole (Flagyl).
- nefazodone (Serzone).
- nifedipine (Adalat).
- omeprazole (Prilosec).
- phenacemide (Phenurone).
- S-Liposomal doxorubicin.
- sertraline (Zoloft).

- sulfonamides (see Drug Classes).
- topiramate (Topamax).
- trazodone (Desyrel).
- tricyclic antidepressants (see Drug Classes).
- trimethoprim (Proloprim, Trimpex).
- valproic acid (Depakene).
- venlafaxine (Effexor).
- zotepine (Nipolept).

The following drugs may **decrease** the effects of phenytoin:

- antacids (various)—separate doses by two hours.
- aspirin (high dose, various brands)—more frequent checks of total and free phenytoin levels.
- bleomycin (Blenoxane).
- carmustine (BiCNU).
- cisplatin (Platinol).
- diazoxide (Proglycem, Hyperstat).
- folic acid (various).
- methotrexate (Mexate).
- rifampin (Rifadin).
- vinblastine (Velban).

▷ *Driving, Hazardous Activities:* This drug may impair mental alertness, vision and coordination. Restrict activities as necessary.

Aviation Note: The use of this drug *is a disqualification* for piloting. Consult a designated Aviation Medical Examiner.

Exposure to Sun: Use caution—this drug may cause photosensitivity (see Glossary).

Occurrence of Unrelated Illness: Intercurrent infections may slow the elimination of this drug and increase the risk of toxicity, due to higher blood levels.

Discontinuation: **This drug must not be discontinued abruptly.** Sudden withdrawal can precipitate severe and repeated seizures. If this drug is to be discontinued, gradual reduction in dose should be made over a period of 3 months. Total drug withdrawal may be attempted after a period of 3 to 4 years without a seizure. However, seizures are likely to recur in 40% of adults and in 20–30% of children.

PILOCARPINE (pi loh KAR peen)

Introduced: 1875   Class: Antiglaucoma   **Prescription:** USA: Yes
Controlled Drug: USA: No; Canada: No   **Available as Generic:** Yes

Brand Names: Adsorbocarpine, Akarpine, Almocarpine, Betoptic Pilo [CD], E-Pilo Preparations [CD], I-Pilopine, Isopto Carpine, ✤Minims, ✤Miocarpine, Ocusert Pilo-20, Ocusert Pilo-40, PE Preparations [CD], Pilagan, Pilocar, Pilopine HS, Piloptic-1, Piloptic-2, Pilosyst 20/40, Salagen, ✤Spersacarpine

BENEFITS versus RISKS	
Possible Benefits	*Possible Risks*
EFFECTIVE REDUCTION OF INTERNAL EYE PRESSURE FOR CONTROL OF ACUTE AND CHRONIC GLAUCOMA	Mild side effects with systemic absorption Minor eye discomfort Altered vision

▷ **Principal Uses**

As a Single Drug Product: Uses currently included in FDA-approved labeling: (1) Used to manage all types of glaucoma (selection of the appropriate dose form and strength must be carefully individualized); (2) can help in dry mouth (xerostomia) even after radiation therapy; (3) eases symptoms in Sjögren's syndrome.

Other (unlabeled) generally accepted uses: (1) Treatment of Adie syndrome; (2) can help before laser surgery in order to prevent excessive increases in eye (intraocular) pressure after surgery.

As a Combination Drug Product [CD]: This drug is combined with epinephrine (in eyedrop solutions) to utilize the actions of both drugs in lowering internal eye pressure. The opposite effects of these two drugs on the size of the pupil (pilocarpine constricts, epinephrine dilates) provides a balance that prevents excessive constriction or dilation. The Betopic Pilo form offers the combination benefits of a beta blocker (betaxolol).

How This Drug Works: By directly stimulating constriction of the pupil, this drug enlarges the outflow canal in the anterior chamber of the eye and promotes the drainage of excess fluid (aqueous humor), thus lowering the internal eye pressure.

Available Dosage Forms and Strengths

Combination solution — 1.75 % pilocarpine and 0.25% betaxolol

Eyedrop solutions — 0.25%, 0.5%, 1%, 2%, 3%, 4%, 5%, 6%

Gel — 4%

Ocuserts — 20 mcg, 40 mcg

Tablets — 5 mg

▷ **Usual Adult Dosage Ranges:** *For open-angle glaucoma:* Eyedrop solutions—one drop of a 1% to 2% solution three to four times daily (every 6–8 hours). Dosing is adjusted to keep the eye pressure (intraocular pressure) at the goal decided upon. See betaxolol profile for combination form dosing. Eye gel—apply 0.5-inch strip of gel into the eye once daily at bedtime. Ocusert—insert one into affected eye and replace every 7 days with a new one.

Note: Actual dose and dosing schedule must be determined for each patient individually.

Conditions Requiring Dosing Adjustments

Liver Function: Decreased removal from the body (roughly 30% slower in one small study). Empiric small steps in dosing and possible increased effects with "normal doses" are to be watched for in patients with moderate liver compromise.

Kidney Function: The elimination of this drug has yet to be defined.

▷ **Dosing Instructions:** To avoid excessive absorption into the body, press finger against inner corner of the eye (to close off the tear duct) during and for 2 minutes following instillation of the eyedrop. Place the gel and the Ocusert in the eye at bedtime. If you forget a dose: Use the missed dose as soon as you remember it, unless it's nearly time for your next dose—if that is the case, skip the missed dose and take the next dose right on schedule. DO NOT double doses. Talk with your doctor if you find yourself missing doses. Taking the medicine (adherence) is critical to getting the results you and your doctor are working for.

Usual Duration of Use: Use on a regular schedule for 1 to 2 weeks usually determines this drug's effectiveness in controlling internal eye pressure. Long-term use (months to years) requires physician supervision and follow-up to make sure pressure stays in the desired range.

Typical Treatment Goals and Measurements (Outcomes and Markers)

Glaucoma: Ophthalmologists measure eye pressure (intraocular pressure [IOP]), and then check IOP lowering once this medicine is started, adjusting (titrating) the medicine(s) to get and keep eye pressure in the desired range. The chamber angle can be checked prior to treatment.

Currently a "Drug of Choice"

For primary open-angle glaucoma (along with timolol and dipivefrin) especially in people over 50 years old.

▷ **This Drug Should Not Be Taken If**
- you have had an allergic reaction to it previously.
- you have sudden (acute) iritis or other eye problems where a key effect of this medicine (miosis) is not acceptable.
- you have active bronchial asthma and are using the tablet form.

▷ **Inform Your Physician Before Taking This Drug If**
- you have a history of bronchial asthma.
- you have a history of acute iritis.
- you have significant heart disease, kidney or liver disease.
- your thyroid is overactive (hyperthyroidism).
- you have chronic obstructive pulmonary disease.
- you have gallstones.
- you are trying to have a baby.

Possible Side Effects (natural, expected, and unavoidable drug actions)

Temporary impairment of vision, usually lasting 2 to 3 hours following instillation of drops. Burning of the eyes and trouble seeing at night—frequent.

▷ **Possible Adverse Effects** (unusual, unexpected, and infrequent reactions)

If any of the following develop, consult your physician promptly for guidance.

Mild Adverse Effects

Allergic reactions: itching of the eyes, eyelid itching and/or swelling.

Headache, heart palpitation, tremors—infrequent.

Sweating—frequent.

Nausea—case reports.

Serious Adverse Effects

Provocation of acute asthma in susceptible individuals.

Mental status changes (memory loss, confusion, or hallucinations)—case reports.

Atrioventricular block (abnormal heart conduction), slow heartbeats (bradycardia) and blood pressure changes (hypo or hypertension)—case reports.

Retinal detachment—possible.

▷ **Possible Effects on Sexual Function:** Possible impaired fertility.

Possible Effects on Laboratory Tests

Red blood cell and white blood cell counts: increased.

Precautions for Use

By Those Over 60 Years of Age: Maintain personal cleanliness to prevent eye infections. Report promptly any indication of eye infection.

▷ **Advisability of Use During Pregnancy**

Pregnancy Category: C. See Pregnancy Risk Categories at the back of this book.

Animal Studies: Significant birth defects due to this drug reported in rats.

Human Studies: Adequate studies of pregnant women are not available. Limit use to the smallest effective dose. Minimize systemic absorption (see "Dosing Instructions" above).

Advisability of Use If Breast-Feeding

Presence of this drug in breast milk: May be present in small amounts. Monitor nursing infant closely, and discontinue drug or nursing if adverse effects develop.

Habit-Forming Potential: None.

Effects of Overdose: Flushing of face, increased flow of saliva, sweating. If solution is swallowed: nausea, vomiting, diarrhea, profuse sweating, rapid pulse, difficult breathing, loss of consciousness.

Possible Effects of Long-Term Use: Development of tolerance (see Glossary), temporary loss of effectiveness.

Suggested Periodic Examinations While Taking This Drug (at physician's discretion)

Measurement of internal eye pressure on a regular basis.

Examination of eyes for development of cataracts.

▷ **While Taking This Drug, Observe the Following**

Foods: No restrictions.

Herbal Medicines or Minerals: St. John's wort may also cause increased sun sensitivity—caution is advised. Scopolia root has glaucoma as a possible side effect. DO NOT COMBINE. Henbane, ephedra, and belladonna should also be avoided.

Beverages: No restrictions.

▷ *Alcohol:* Use caution. If this drug is absorbed, it may prolong the effect of alcohol on the brain.

Tobacco Smoking: No interactions expected. I advise everyone to quit smoking.

Marijuana Smoking: Sustained additional decrease in internal eye pressure.

▷ *Other Drugs*

The following drugs may *decrease* the effects of pilocarpine:

• atropine and drugs with atropinelike actions (see Drug Classes).

Pilocarpine *taken concurrently* with

• dipivefrin (Propine) may result in increased myopia and blurred vision.

• epinephrine (various) will result in increased myopia.

• latanoprost (Xalatan) may decrease latanoprost effectiveness. The bedtime dose of pilocarpine should be given an hour after the latanoprost dose.

• sulfacetamide (Sulamyd) may lead to pilocarpine precipitation. Separate these drugs by 20 minutes.

• timolol can produce additive effects in treating glaucoma.

▷ *Driving, Hazardous Activities:* This drug may impair your ability to focus your vision properly. Restrict activities as necessary.

Aviation Note: The use of this drug *may be a disqualification* for piloting. Consult a designated Aviation Medical Examiner.

Exposure to Sun: This medicine may make you very sensitive to the sun. Wear sunglasses.

Discontinuation: Do not stop regular use of this drug without consulting your physician. Periodic discontinuation and temporary substitution of another drug may be necessary to preserve its effectiveness in treating glaucoma.

PINDOLOL (PIN doh lohl)

Introduced: 1972 **Class:** Antihypertensive, beta-adrenergic blocker
Prescription: USA: Yes **Controlled Drug:** USA: No; Canada: No
Available as Generic: Yes

Brand Names: ✤Alti-Pindol, ✤Apo-Pindol, ✤Dom-Pindolol, ✤Novo-Pindol, ✤Nu-Pindol, ✤Syn-Pindolol, ✤Viskazide [CD], Visken

BENEFITS versus RISKS	
Possible Benefits	*Possible Risks*
EFFECTIVE, WELL-TOLERATED ANTIHYPERTENSIVE IN MILD TO MODERATE HIGH BLOOD PRESSURE	CONGESTIVE HEART FAILURE IN ADVANCED HEART DISEASE Worsening of angina in coronary heart disease (abrupt withdrawal)
EFFECTIVE PREVENTION OF ANGINA	Masking of low blood sugar (hypoglycemia) in drug-treated diabetes
PROBABLY HELPS PREVENT (LIKE OTHER BETA BLOCKERS) REPEAT HEART ATTACKS	Provocation of asthma (with high doses in asthmatics)

▷ **Principal Uses**

As a Single Drug Product: Uses currently included in FDA-approved labeling: Treats mild to moderate high blood pressure, alone or with other drugs.

Other (unlabeled) generally accepted uses: (1) May be of benefit in helping control aggressive behavior; (2) can help prevent migraine headaches; (3) combination therapy with digoxin may be effective in limiting some abnormal heart rhythms (atrial fibrillation); (4) can be of benefit in some kinds of anxiety; (5) decreases sympathetic output in hyperthyroidism; (5) helps prevent angina.

As a Combination Drug Product [CD]: This drug is available in combination with hydrochlorothiazide (in Canada). The addition of a thiazide diuretic to this beta-blocker drug enhances its effectiveness as an antihypertensive.

How This Drug Works: Blocks certain actions of the sympathetic nervous system:
• reducing rate and contraction force of the heart, thus lowering ejection pressure of blood leaving the heart
• reducing degree of contraction of blood vessel walls, lowering blood pressure.

Available Dosage Forms and Strengths
Tablets — 5 mg, 10 mg
Tablets (Canada) — 15 mg

▷ **Usual Adult Dosage Ranges:** *Hypertension*: Starts with 5 mg twice a day (12 hours apart). The dose may be increased gradually by 10 mg/day at intervals of 3 to 4 weeks as needed and tolerated, up to 60 mg/day. For maintenance, 5 to 10 mg two or three times daily is often effective. The total daily dose should not exceed 60 mg. *Angina prevention*: Starting dose is 2.5 to 5 mg. This starting dose can then be increased as needed and tolerated over several weeks.

Note: Actual dose and schedule must be determined for each patient individually.

Conditions Requiring Dosing Adjustments
Liver Function: See comment below. Lower starting doses are prudent, coupled with careful patient follow-up. People with combined liver and kidney disease should be given lower starting doses and vigilant follow-up.

Kidney Function: This medicine had two ways that it is removed from the body (kidney and liver). While some sources advocate no adjustment in kidney failure, lower starting doses and careful patient monitoring of blood pressure is prudent and doses lowered if blood pressure becomes unacceptably low.

▷ **Dosing Instructions:** The tablet may be crushed and taken without regard to eating. Do not stop this drug abruptly. If you forget a dose: Take the missed dose as soon as you remember it, unless it's 4 hours or less until your next scheduled dose—if that is the case, skip the missed dose and take the next dose right on schedule. DO NOT double doses. Talk with your doctor if you find yourself missing doses.

Usual Duration of Use: Use on a regular schedule for 2 to 3 weeks usually determines effectiveness in lowering blood pressure. The long-term use of this drug (months to years) will be determined by the course of your blood pressure over time and your response to an overall treatment program (weight reduction, salt restriction, smoking cessation, etc.). See your doctor on a regular basis. Reaching and maintaining goal blood pressure is critical to long-term health.

Typical Treatment Goals and Measurements (Outcomes and Markers)

Blood Pressure: The NEW guidelines (JNC VII) define normal blood pressure (BP) as **less than** 120/80. Because blood pressures that were once considered acceptable can actually lead to blood vessel damage, the committee from the National Institutes of Health, National Heart Lung and Blood Institute now have a new category called **Pre-hypertension**. This ranges from 120/80 to 139/89 and is intended to help your doctor encourage lifestyle changes (or in the case of people with a risk factor for high blood pressure, start treatment) much earlier—so that possible damage to blood vessels, your heart, kidneys, sexual potency, or eyes might be minimized or avoided altogether. The next two classes of high blood pressure are stage 1 hypertension: 140/90 to 159/99 and stage 2 hypertension equal to or greater than: 160/100 mm Hg. These guidelines also recommend that clinicians trying to control blood pressure work with their patients to agree on the goals and a plan of treatment. The first-ever guidelines for blood pressure (hypertension) in African Americans recommends that MOST black patients be started on TWO antihypertensive medicines with the goal of lowering blood pressure to 130/80 for those with high risk for heart and blood vessel disease or with diabetes. The American Diabetes Association recommends 130/80 as the target for people living with diabetes and less than 125/75 for those who spill more than one gram of protein into their urine. Most clinicians try to achieve a BP that confers the best balance of lower cardiovascular risk and avoids the problem of too low a blood pressure. Blood pressure duration is generally increased with beneficial restriction of sodium. The goals and time frame should be discussed with you when the prescription is written. If goals are not met, it is not unusual to intensify doses or add on medicines. You can find the new blood pressure guidelines at *www.nhlbi.nih.gov/guidelines/hypertension/index.html.* For the African American guidelines see Douglas J.G. in Sources.

Possible Advantages of This Drug

Causes less slowing of the heart rate than most other beta-blocker drugs. Is one of the most potent (weight to weight, mg to mg) beta blockers. Two routes of removal from the body make this medicine safer to use than some of the other beta blockers (such as atenolol, nadolol, or sotolol) in patients with compromised kidneys.

Currently a "Drug of Choice"

For starting treatment of hypertension (diuretics such as hydrochloro-thiazide are the other class) with a single drug.

▷ **This Drug Should Not Be Taken If**

- you have bronchial asthma.
- you have had an allergic reaction to it previously.
- you have an abnormally slow heart rate or a serious form of heart block.
- you are taking, or have taken within the past 14 days, any monoamine oxi-dase (MAO) type A inhibitor (see Drug Classes).

▷ **Inform Your Physician Before Taking This Drug If**

- you had an adverse reaction to any beta blocker (see Drug Classes).
- you have a history of serious heart disease, or congestive heart failure.
- you have a history of hay fever (allergic rhinitis), asthma, chronic bronchi-tis, or emphysema.
- you have a history of overactive thyroid function (hyperthyroidism).
- you have a history of low blood sugar (hypoglycemia) or diabetes.
- you have impaired liver or kidney function.
- you have diabetes or myasthenia gravis.
- you take digitalis, quinidine, or reserpine, or any calcium-channel-blocker drug (see Drug Classes).
- you have bad circulation to your legs or arms (peripheral vascular dis-ease).
- you plan to have surgery under general anesthesia in the near future.

Possible Side Effects (natural, expected, and unavoidable drug actions)

Lethargy and fatigability, cold extremities, slow heart rate, light-headedness in upright position (see orthostatic hypotension in Glossary).

▷ **Possible Adverse Effects** (unusual, unexpected, and infrequent reactions)

If any of the following develop, consult your physician promptly for guidance.

Mild Adverse Effects

Allergic reactions: skin rash, itching.

Headache, dizziness, insomnia, abnormal dreams, fainting—infrequent.

Indigestion, nausea, vomiting, constipation, diarrhea—infrequent.

Joint and muscle discomfort, tremor, fluid retention (edema)—infrequent.

Serious Adverse Effects

Allergic reactions: typical reactions to known allergens (such as bee stings) may be exaggerated.

Mental depression, anxiety—infrequent.

Chest pain, shortness of breath—possible.

Induction of bronchial asthma—in asthmatic individuals.

Abnormally slow heartbeat or congestive heart failure—possible to infre-quent.

Drug-induced systemic lupus erythematosus or myasthenia gravis—case reports.

Worsening of poor circulation to the arms or legs (intermittent claudica-tion)—possible. May be prudent to check for hidden Peripheral Artery Dis-ease (PAD) by checking ankle brachial index (ABI). ABI check (see Glossary) can help find PAD early, and avoid claudication that may result if this medication is taken by someone who has PAD but does not know it.

Carpal tunnel syndrome—reported with other beta blockers.

▷ **Possible Effects on Sexual Function:** Decreased libido or impaired erection—infrequent.

Possible Effects on Laboratory Tests

Blood lupus erythematosus (LE) cells: positive (one case of drug-induced LE).

Blood total cholesterol level: decreased (with long-term use).

Blood HDL cholesterol level: increased.

Blood LDL and VLDL cholesterol levels: no effects.

Blood triglyceride levels: no effects.

Glucose tolerance test (GTT): decreased or increased.

Liver function tests: slightly increased liver enzymes (ALT/GPT and AST/GOT): possible.

CAUTION

1. ***Do not stop this drug suddenly*** without the knowledge and help of your doctor. Carry a card that says you are taking this drug.
2. Ask your doctor or pharmacist before using nasal decongestants, which are usually present in over-the-counter cold preparations and nose drops. These can cause sudden increases in blood pressure when taken concurrently with beta blocker drugs.
3. Report the development of any tendency to emotional depression.

Precautions for Use

By Infants and Children: Safety and effectiveness for those under 12 years of age are not established. If this drug is used, however, observe for the development of low blood sugar (hypoglycemia) during periods of reduced food intake.

By Those Over 60 Years of Age: Unacceptably high blood pressure should be reduced without creating the risks associated with excessively low blood pressure. Small starting doses and frequent blood pressure checks are indicated. Sudden, rapid, and excessive reduction of blood pressure can predispose to stroke or heart attack. Watch for dizziness, unsteadiness, tendency to fall, confusion, hallucinations, depression, or urinary frequency.

▷ **Advisability of Use During Pregnancy**

Pregnancy Category: B. See Pregnancy Risk Categories at the back of this book.

Animal Studies: No significant increase in birth defects due to this drug.

Human Studies: Adequate studies of pregnant women not available, but there are some reports of lower growth and fetal problems. Ask your physician for guidance.

Advisability of Use If Breast-Feeding

Presence of this drug in breast milk: Yes.

Avoid drug or refrain from nursing.

Habit-Forming Potential: None.

Effects of Overdose: Weakness, slow pulse, low blood pressure, fainting, cold and sweaty skin, congestive heart failure, possible coma, and convulsions.

Possible Effects of Long-Term Use: Reduced heart reserve and eventual heart failure in susceptible individuals with advanced heart disease.

Suggested Periodic Examinations While Taking This Drug (at physician's discretion)

Measurements of blood pressure.

Evaluation of heart function.

May be prudent to check for hidden Peripheral Artery Disease (PAD) by checking ankle brachial index (ABI). ABI check (see Glossary) can help find PAD early, and avoid claudication that may result if this medication is taken by someone who has PAD but does not know it.

LE prep, ANA.

▷ **While Taking This Drug, Observe the Following**

Foods: No restrictions. Avoid excessive salt intake.

Herbal Medicines or Minerals: Ginseng, hawthorn, saw palmetto, ma huang, guarana (caffeine), goldenseal, yohimbe, and licorice may also cause increased blood pressure. Dong quai may block one route of removal of this medicine from the body leading to toxic effects with "normal" doses. St. John's wort may increase removal of this medicine from the body leading to loss of benefits despite appropriate doses. Calcium and garlic may help lower blood pressure. Ginkgo benefits in helping peripheral artery disease are as yet unproven. Indian snakeroot has a German Commission E monograph indication for hypertension. Eleuthero root and ephedra (ma huang) should be avoided by people living with hypertension. Talk to your doctor BEFORE combining any herbal with any prescription drug or herbal product.

Beverages: No restrictions. May be taken with milk.

▷ *Alcohol:* Use with caution. Alcohol may exaggerate lowering of blood pressure or increase mild sedative effect.

Tobacco Smoking: Nicotine may reduce this drug's effectiveness. I advise everyone to quit smoking.

▷ *Other Drugs*

Pindolol may *increase* the effects of

- other antihypertensive drugs and cause excessive lowering of blood pressure; dose adjustments may be necessary.
- digoxin (Lanoxin) on the heart conduction system, leading to AV block and possible digoxin toxicity as well.
- reserpine (Ser-Ap-Es, etc.) and cause sedation, depression, slowing of the heart rate, and lowering of blood pressure.
- verapamil (Calan, Isoptin) and cause excessive depression of heart function; monitor this combination closely.

Pindolol *taken concurrently* with

- amiodarone (Cordarone) may cause extremely slow heartbeats and risk of sinus arrest.
- clonidine (Catapres) requires close monitoring for rebound high blood pressure if clonidine is withdrawn while pindolol is still being taken.
- epinephrine (various) will result in a large increase in blood pressure and reflex increase in heart rate (tachycardia).
- fentanyl (various) can lead to severe decreases in blood pressure. Extreme caution and dose adjustments are warranted if these medicines must be combined.
- fluoxetine (Prozac) may result in increased risk of pindolol toxicity.
- fluvoxamine (Luvox) may result in increased risk of pindolol toxicity.
- insulin requires close monitoring to avoid undetected hypoglycemia (see Glossary).
- oral antidiabetic drugs (see Drug Classes) can result in slowed recovery from low blood sugar.
- phenylpropanolamine (various—now removed from US products) may result in severe increases in blood pressure—avoid this combination.
- ritodrine (Yutopar) will blunt the effects (tocolytic). Dose changes may be needed.
- venlafaxine (Effexor) may result in beta-blocker or venlafaxine toxicity—

avoid this combination if possible or use decreased doses of both medicines.

The following drugs may *increase* the effects of pindolol:
- cimetidine (Tagamet).
- methimazole (Tapazole).
- oral contraceptives.
- propylthiouracil (Propacil).
- ritonavir (Norvir) and perhaps other protease inhibitors (see Drug Classes).
- zileuton (Zyflo), close patient monitoring is prudent and dose adjustments may be required.

The following drugs may *decrease* the effects of pindolol:
- barbiturates (phenobarbital, etc.).
- indomethacin (Indocin) and possibly other NSAIDs—may impair pindolol's antihypertensive effect.
- rifampin (Rifadin, Rimactane).
- theophylline (Theo-Dur, others).

▷ *Driving, Hazardous Activities:* Use caution until the full extent of fatigue, dizziness and blood pressure change has been determined.

Aviation Note: The use of this drug *is a disqualification* for piloting. Consult a designated Aviation Medical Examiner.

Exposure to Sun: No restrictions.

Exposure to Heat: Caution is advised. Hot environments can lower blood pressure and exaggerate the effects of this drug.

Exposure to Cold: Caution is advised. Cold environments can enhance the circulatory deficiency in the extremities that may occur with this drug. The elderly should take precautions to prevent hypothermia (see Glossary).

Heavy Exercise or Exertion: It is advisable to avoid exertion that produces light-headedness, excessive fatigue or muscle cramping. The use of this drug may intensify the hypertensive response to isometric exercise.

Occurrence of Unrelated Illness: Fever can lower blood pressure and require adjustment of dose. Nausea or vomiting may interrupt regular doses. Ask your doctor for help.

Discontinuation: It is advisable to avoid sudden discontinuation of this drug in all situations. If possible, gradual reduction of dose over a period of 2 to 3 weeks is recommended. Ask your physician for specific guidance.

PIRBUTEROL (peer BYU ter ohl)

Introduced: 1983   **Class:**   Antiasthmatic,   bronchodilator   **Prescription:**   Yes   **Controlled Drug:**   USA: No; Canada: No   **Available as Generic:**   No

Brand Name: Maxair

BENEFITS versus RISKS	
Possible Benefits	*Possible Risks*
VERY EFFECTIVE RELIEF OF BRONCHOSPASM	Increased blood pressure
	Nervousness
	Fine hand tremor
	Irregular heart rhythm (with excessive use)

▷ **Principal Uses**

As a Single Drug Product: Uses currently included in FDA-approved labeling: (1) Relieves acute attacks of bronchial asthma; (2) reduces the frequency and severity of chronic, recurrent asthmatic attacks (prevention); (3) relieves reversible bronchospasm seen in chronic bronchitis, bronchiectasis, and emphysema.

Other (unlabeled) generally accepted uses: None at present.

How This Drug Works: By increasing the production of cyclic AMP, this drug relaxes constricted bronchial muscles to relieve asthmatic wheezing.

Available Dosage Forms and Strengths

Aerosol (in canisters of 300 inhalations) — 200 mcg per actuation

▷ **Usual Adult Dosage Range (or children over 12):** Inhaler: Two inhalations (400 mcg) every 4 to 6 hours. **Do not exceed** 12 inhalations (2,400 mcg) every 24 hours. Some patients may get benefits from one inhalation every 4 to 6 hours.

Note: Actual dose and schedule must be determined for each patient individually.

Conditions Requiring Dosing Adjustments

Liver Function: Used with caution by patients with liver disease who use it often.
Kidney Function: No dose adjustments thought to be needed.

▷ **Dosing Instructions:** Carefully follow the "Patient's Instructions for Use" provided with the inhaler as the amount of medicine that goes to work for you depends on your technique. Gently shake the inhaler before each use. Do not overuse. If you forget a dose: Use the missed dose as soon as you remember it, unless it's nearly time for your next dose—if that is the case, skip the missed dose and take the next dose right on schedule. DO NOT double doses. Talk with your doctor if you find yourself missing doses.

Usual Duration of Use: According to individual requirements. Do not use beyond the time necessary to terminate episodes of asthma.

Typical Treatment Goals and Measurements (Outcomes and Markers)

Asthma: Short-acting beta agonists like albuterol are used to prevent or treat reversible spasms of the bronchial tubes. The peak effect happens 1 to 2 hours after dosing. Some pulmonologists use arterial blood gases in extreme cases. FEV-1 in mild to moderate cases is important for checking response. Clinical symptoms such as chest tightening and wheezing should also ease. If the usual benefit is not realized, call your doctor.

Possible Advantages of This Drug

Has a more rapid onset of action and a longer duration of effect than most other drugs of this class.

▷ **This Drug Should Not Be Taken If**

- you have had an allergic reaction to it previously.
- you are taking, or have taken within the past 2 weeks, any monoamine oxidase (MAO) type A inhibitor (see Drug Classes).

▷ **Inform Your Physician Before Taking This Drug If**

- you have any type of heart or circulatory disorder, especially high blood pressure, coronary heart disease or heart rhythm abnormality.
- you have diabetes or an excessively active thyroid gland (hyperthyroidism).
- you have any type of seizure disorder.
- you are taking any form of digitalis or any stimulant drug.

Possible Side Effects (natural, expected, and unavoidable drug actions)
Aerosol—dryness or irritation of mouth or throat, altered taste. Cough.

▷ **Possible Adverse Effects** (unusual, unexpected, and infrequent reactions)
If any of the following develop, consult your physician promptly for guidance.
Mild Adverse Effects
Allergic reactions:skin rash, itching—rare.
Headache, dizziness, nervousness, fine tremor of hands—infrequent.
Palpitations, rapid heart rate, chest pain, cough—rare to infrequent.
Nausea, diarrhea, taste disorders—rare.
Serious Adverse Effects
Irregular heart rhythm, increased blood pressure—possible.
Paradoxical spasm of the bronchi—possible.

▷ **Possible Effects on Sexual Function:** None reported.

Natural Diseases or Disorders That May Be Activated by This Drug
Latent coronary artery disease, diabetes, epilepsy, or high blood pressure.

Possible Effects on Laboratory Tests
None reported.

CAUTION
1. Combined use of this drug by inhalation with beclomethasone aerosol (Beclovent, Vanceril) may increase the risk of toxicity due to fluorocarbon propellants (fluorocarbons are being phased out). It is advisable to use pirbuterol aerosol 20 to 30 minutes before beclomethasone aerosol. This will reduce the risk of toxicity and help beclomethasone reach the lung.
2. Excessive or prolonged use of this drug by inhalation can reduce its effectiveness (tolerance) and cause serious heart rhythm, disturbances, including cardiac arrest.

Precautions for Use
By Infants and Children: Safety and effectiveness of use in children under 12 years of age have not been established.
By Those Over 60 Years of Age: Avoid excessive and continual use. If acute asthma is not relieved promptly, other drugs may be needed. Watch for nervousness, palpitations, irregular heart rhythm, and muscle tremors.

▷ **Advisability of Use During Pregnancy**
Pregnancy Category: C. See Pregnancy Risk Categories at the back of this book.
Animal Studies: High-dose studies in rabbits revealed abortion and increased fetal deaths. Studies in rats and rabbits found no drug-associated birth defects.
Human Studies: Adequate studies of pregnant women are not available.
Avoid use during first 3 months if possible.

Advisability of Use If Breast-Feeding
Presence of this drug in breast milk: Unknown.
Avoid drug or refrain from nursing.

Habit-Forming Potential: None. Tolerance to beneficial effects has been reported.

Effects of Overdose: Nervousness, palpitation, rapid heart rate, sweating, headache, tremor, vomiting, chest pain.

Possible Effects of Long-Term Use: Loss of effectiveness (tolerance).

Suggested Periodic Examinations While Taking This Drug (at physician's discretion)
> Blood pressure measurements.
> Evaluation of heart status.

▷ **While Taking This Drug, Observe the Following**
  Foods: No restrictions.
  Herbal Medicines or Minerals: Using St. John's wort, ma huang, ephedrine-like compounds, or kola while taking this medicine may result in unacceptable central nervous system stimulation. Fir or pine needle oil should NOT be used by asthmatics. Ephedra alone does carry a German Commission E monograph indication for asthma treatment. If you are allergic to plants in the Asteraceae family (aster, chrysanthemum, daisy, or ragweed), you may also be allergic to echinacea, chamomile, feverfew, and St. John's wort. Since part of the way that ginseng works may be as a MAO inhibitor, DO NOT combine with pirbuterol.
  Beverages: Avoid excessive use of caffeine-containing beverages—coffee, tea, cola, chocolate.
▷ *Alcohol:* No interactions expected.
  Tobacco Smoking: No interactions expected. I advise everyone to quit smoking.
▷ *Other Drugs*
  Pirbuterol **taken concurrently** with
  • albuterol (Proventil, Ventolin) may result in adverse effects on the heart.
  • monoamine oxidase (MAO) type A inhibitors may cause excessive increase in blood pressure and undesirable heart stimulation.
  • phenothiazines (see Drug Classes) may result in blunting of the therapeutic effects of pirbuterol.
▷ *Driving, Hazardous Activities:* Use caution if excessive nervousness or dizziness occurs.
  Aviation Note: The use of this drug **is a disqualification** for piloting. Consult a designated Aviation Medical Examiner.
  Exposure to Sun: No restrictions.
  Heavy Exercise or Exertion: Use caution—excessive exercise can induce asthma in sensitive individuals.

PIROXICAM (peer OX i kam)

Please see the oxicam (nonsteroidal anti-inflammatory drug) family profile.

PNEUMOCOCCAL CONJUGATE VACCINE (NEW mo kok uhl)

Other Name: Pneumonia vaccine

Introduced: Presently this is a specific formulation to help confer immunity to seven kinds (4, 6B, 9V, 14, 18C, 19F and 23F) of bacteria called pneumococcus **Class:**   Antibacterial vaccine **Prescription:**   USA: Yes **Controlled Drug:**   USA: No; Canada: No **Available as Generic:**   USA: No; Canada: No

Brand Name: Prevnar

Author's Note: The American Diabetes Association (*www.diabetes.org*** or 1-877-CDC-DIAB for more information) recommends that people living with diabetes get both a flu and pneumococcal shot (vaccine). If you would like a copy of the ACIP recommendations, call 1-888-232-3228. Information on current recommendations for shots (vaccines) can be found at ***www.cdc.gov/nip/recs/child-schedule.htm***. Don't become a statistic (23-valent forms only). This profile will be broadened to include data on Pnu-Immune-23 and Pneumovax 23 in subsequent editions. The focus for this profile will be on Prevnar (7 valent form) as it is now part of the recommendations (ACIP) for vaccinations in children (not recommended for use in adults).**

BENEFITS versus RISKS	
Possible Benefits	*Possible Risks*
PREVENTION OF DISEASE CAUSED BY THE MOST SERIOUS OR PREVALENT STRAINS OF STREPTOCOCCUS PNEUMONIA	Lowered platelets Hypersensitivity Fever
PREVENTION OF PNEUMOCOCCAL MENINGITIS	
PREVENTION OF BACTEREMIC PNEUMONIA CAUSED BY STREPTOCOCCUS	
PREVENTION OF EAR INFECTION (OTITIS MEDIA) IN INFANTS AND TODDLERS CAUSED BY THE SEVEN STRAINS IN THE VACCINE	
Possible cross-protection from other similar bacterial strains	

▷ **Principal Uses**

As a Single Drug Product: Uses currently included in FDA-approved labeling: Prevention of pneumococcal infection (Prevnar only).

Other (unlabeled) generally accepted uses: (1) Used in patients with compromised immune systems such as HIV-positive, cancer and bone marrow transplant patients (23-valent forms only); (2) can be of use in isolated outbreaks such as in nursing homes or military camps (23-valent forms only).

How This Drug Works: Surprisingly, there are more than 90 kinds of pneumococcus, but disease is actually caused by a few kinds of this bacteria. While we usually think of this bacteria as a cause of lung infection (pneumonia), it is actually the cause of some 20–40% of middle ear infections in children (Strep pneumoniae). Additionally, there has been a trend toward bacteria that can outsmart (resist) widely used antibiotics. What this shot (vaccine) does is to take part (capsular antigen saccharides) of the seven most likely bacteria types that cause middle ear infections and place them in a sterile solution. These components are purified, then inactivated and used to form a shot (vaccine), which is a suspension. When injected, it stimulates the immune system to make antibodies. The antibodies (present to all vaccine serotypes after four doses of the vaccine) act to prevent middle ear infections or reduce infection severity if infection does occur.

Available Dosage Forms and Strengths

Prevnar form: (2 micrograms each of 4, 9v, 14, 18 C, 19F and 23F. Four mcg of 6B) for a total of 16 mcg/0.5 ml of the seven selected strains.

▷ **Recommended Dosage Ranges** (Actual dose and schedule must be determined for each patient and each flu season individually.)

Infants and Children: Current ACIP recommendations include this vaccine as part of routine pediatric care. After the vial is resuspended, 0.5 ml is injected. Dosing is given on a schedule at two, four, six and between 12-15 months of age. Doses are given into the muscle (intramuscular). While the first dose is usually given at 2 months, it can be given as early as 6 weeks. Subsequent doses in that case are given every 4-8 weeks, and the last dose (fourth) is given two months after the third dose.

The Prevnar form is NOT to be used in adults.

Conditions Requiring Dosing Adjustments

Liver Function: Not involved.

Kidney Function: Not involved.

▷ **Dosing Instructions:** The vial should be gently, but well shaken before the shot is given. The fluid in the vial should appear white when resuspended. This vaccine should be given into a muscle. Appropriate sites are the anterolateral part of the thigh in infants and the upper arm (deltoid muscle) in toddlers and young children. Care should be taken NOT to inject into a vein. Once the injection site is cleaned, this is often accomplished by inserting the needle, pulling back on the syringe (aspiration), and making sure that blood does not appear. If blood does appear, this indicates a blood vessel, and the needle should be withdrawn without injecting and the steps for injection taken once again. Some tenderness at the injection site is possible. Fever and muscular aches or pains are also possible and may be treated with acetaminophen (Tylenol, others). Prudent to pre-treat BEFORE the injection is given.

Usual Duration of Use: Four doses are given as outlined previously.

Typical Treatment Goals and Measurements (Outcomes and Markers)

Prevention of Strep Pneumoniae Infection: Prevention of infection from the seven serotypes of Strep is the goal of vaccination. Because Strep can cause pneumonia, middle ear and other infections, it is logical that these infections from the seven serotypes would be prevented or would be much milder in nature than they otherwise would have been. Antibody checks can be performed at some laboratories.

Possible Advantages of This Drug

Confers immunity in children to a prevalent bacteria, which is becoming more resistant to antibiotics.

Currently a Drug of Choice

For preventing S. Pneumoniae infections due to the seven serotypes present in the vaccine for children starting at 2 months of age (with four shot course completion).

▷ **This Vaccine Should Not Be Given If**
- you have had an allergic reaction to any dose form of it previously (any other pneumococcal shot or to a diphtheria shot).

- you are giving the shot and are in a blood vessel (shot should be given into a muscle).

▷ **Inform Your Physician Before Taking/Giving This Vaccine If**
  - you are HIV positive.
  - you have a history of blood clotting disorders.
  - you have clinical reasons against getting a shot in the muscle (such as low platelets, where a benefit-to-risk decision should be made).
  - you have a history of allergy to latex (packaging does have dry natural rubber in it).
  - you are the person giving the shot and you are unsure if you are in a vein or not (best to go to another injection site).

Possible Side Effects (natural, expected, and unavoidable drug actions)
  Pain at the vaccination site—frequent. Muscle aches, fever, or bothersome tiredness (malaise). These symptoms are a reaction to the components of the vaccine.

▷ **Possible Adverse Effects** (unusual, unexpected, and infrequent reactions)
  If any of the following develop, consult your physician promptly for guidance.
  Mild Adverse Effects
  Allergic reactions: swelling and redness—possible.
  Muscle aches or fever—rare.
  Fatigue, nausea and headache—infrequent.
  Serious Adverse Effects
  Allergic reactions: anaphylactic reactions.
  Febrile seizures—case reports.
  Low blood platelets—case reports for the earlier 23-valent forms.
  Guillain-Barré syndrome or paresthesias—rare for the Pneumovax form.

▷ **Possible Effects on Sexual Function:** None reported.

Possible Delayed Adverse Effects: None reported.

▷ **Adverse Effects That May Mimic Natural Diseases or Disorders**
  Reaction to vaccine contents may mimic the flu.

Natural Diseases or Disorders That May Be Activated by This Drug
  None reported.

Possible Effects on Laboratory Tests
  Antibodies to the seven pneumococcal strains in the shot: positive (beneficial effect).

CAUTION
  1. Prevnar form not approved for HIV positive or patients without a spleen (asplenics). The 23-valent form is approved for such use (also in transplant patients).
  2. Prevnar will NOT protect against S. pneumoniae infection caused by strains not in the shot.
  3. If muscle aches or fever occurs after vaccination, acetaminophen (Tylenol, others) is recommended. **Do not** take aspirin, and especially do not give aspirin to children. It may be prudent to take acetaminophen BEFORE vaccination to prevent such reactions.
  4. Call your doctor immediately if you develop hives, swelling of the face, unexplained high fever, unexplained bleeding or bruising, seizures or difficulty breathing after the vaccination.

5. People with allergy to latex should be given this shot as a benefit-to-risk decision as the packaging contains dry natural rubber.
6. Safety and efficacy have not been defined for people less than 6 weeks old.
7. Patients with impaired immunity (HIV, chemotherapy, steroid use, etc.) may have a blunted response to the vaccine.
8. This vaccine has an aluminum adjuvant and should be well shaken prior to injection.
9. A benefit-to-risk decision should be made for patients who are taking blood thinners (anticoagulants).

Precautions for Use

By Infants and Children: Safety and effectiveness for use by those under 6 WEEKS of age have not been established.

By Those Over 60 Years of Age: Prevnar form is not indicated.

▷ **Advisability of Use During Pregnancy**

Pregnancy Category: C. See Pregnancy Risk Categories at the back of this book.

Animal Studies: Animal studies have not been conducted.

Human Studies: Information from adequate studies of pregnant women is not available.

Ask your doctor for guidance.

Advisability of Use If Breast-Feeding

Presence of this drug in breast milk: Not defined.

This vaccine is NOT recommended for use in adults, but is also NOT recommended in nursing mothers.

Habit-Forming Potential: None.

Effects of Overdose: No specific cases reported. Treatment would be consistent with any symptoms of the patient.

Possible Effects of Long-Term Use: Not indicated for long-term use.

Suggested Periodic Examinations After Giving This Vaccine (at physician's discretion)

None indicated, other than possible check for antibody formation to the seven strains in the shot.

▷ **While Taking This Drug, Observe the Following**

Foods: No restrictions.

Herbal Medicines or Minerals: Some patients use echinacea to attempt to boost their immune systems. Unfortunately, use of echinacea is not recommended in people with damaged immune systems. This herb may also actually weaken any immune system if it is used too often or for too long a time.

Beverages: No restrictions.

▷ *Alcohol:* No restrictions.

Tobacco Smoking: No interactions expected. I advise everyone to quit smoking.

▷ *Other Drugs*

Prevnar pneumococcal vaccine may ***increase*** the effects of
- specific interactions where effects have been increased are not yet identified.

Influenza vaccine ***taken concurrently*** with
- anticoagulants (such as warfarin, low molecular weight heparins, etc.) may lead to increased risk of complications when Prevnar is given as an intramuscular shot.
- chemotherapy (see Drug Classes) can result in blunting of the immune response to this vaccine. Some clinicians will still give the shot in the hope of conferring some immunity.

- cyclosporine (Sandimmune) can cause blunting of the immune response to the vaccine.
- immunosuppressive agents (chemotherapy, corticosteroids, perhaps some DMARDs, etc.) may impair or blunt immune response to the vaccine.
- methotrexate (Rheumatrex) can result in blunting of the immune response to this vaccine.

▷ *Driving, Hazardous Activities:* This drug may cause excessive tiredness and muscle aches. Restrict activities as necessary.

Aviation Note: The use of this drug *may be a short-term disqualification* for piloting. Consult a designated Aviation Medical Examiner.

Exposure to Sun: No restrictions.

Exposure to Heat: Since this vaccine may cause short-duration fevers, it is wise to avoid hot environments for a day after vaccination.

Heavy Exercise or Exertion: A fever may result, and it is wise to avoid strenuous exercise for a day after vaccination.

Special Storage Instructions: This vaccine is ideally stored in the refrigerator. If this is how storage is accomplished, the outdate specified by the manufacturer is valid. If the vaccine is stored at room temperature, it is stable for up to 7 days.

Observe the Following Expiration Times: If the vaccine is stored at room temperature, it is stable for up to 7 days.

Author's Note: There is a Vaccine Adverse Event Reporting System (VAERS). The toll-free number is 1-800-822-7967.

PRAMIPEXOLE (PRAM ih pex ohl)

Other Name: None

Introduced: 1997   **Class:**   Anti-Parkinsonian, dopamine receptor agonist   **Prescription:**   USA: Yes   **Controlled Drug:**   USA: No; Canada: No   **Available as Generic:**   MSA: No; Canada: No

Brand Name: Mirapex

BENEFITS versus RISKS

Possible Benefits	*Possible Risks*
EFFECTIVE SYMPTOM RELIEF IN IDIOPATHIC PARKINSON'S DISEASE	Movement disorders
	Hallucinations
	Somnolence
BINDS SEVEN TIMES MORE AGGRESSIVELY TO D3 RECEPTORS THAN TO D2 RECEPTORS	Postural hypotension
SOME EARLY DATA FROM CELLS OUTSIDE THE BODY FOUND THAT PRAMIPEXOLE MAY PROTECT AGAINST DISEASE PROGRESSION	
May be an alternative therapy for restless leg syndrome when other medicines like carbidopa/levodopa have not worked	

▷ **Principal Uses**

As a Single Drug Product: Uses currently included in FDA-approved labeling: Treats major types of Parkinson's disease: paralysis agitans ("shaking palsy" of unknown cause), the type that follows encephalitis and Parkinsonism that develops with aging (associated with hardening of the brain arteries).

Other (unlabeled) generally accepted uses: (1) May have a limited role in restless leg syndrome; (2) can improve depression.

As a Combination Drug Product [CD]: Not available.

How This Drug Works: This drug acts as a dopamine receptor activator (agonist). This drug is also unique in that it has a strong affinity for a specific receptor (D3).

Available Dosage Forms and Strengths

Tablets — 0.125 mg, 0.25 mg, 0.5 mg, 1 mg, 1.5 mg

Author's Note: Information in this profile will be broadened once further information is available and if clinical use supports it.

PRAVASTATIN (pra vah STA tin)

Introduced: 1986   **Class:** Cholesterol-lowering agent, HMG-CoA reductase inhibitor   **Prescription:** USA: Yes   **Controlled Drug:** USA: No; Canada: No   **Available as Generic:** USA: No; Canada: No

Brand Names: ❧Lin-Pravastatin, Pravachol

Author's Note: At present, applications for pravastatin (Pravachol) and lovastatin (Mevacor) have been made to the FDA to change low doses of these medicines to nonprescription (OTC) status. At the time of this writing, the OTC issue has not been resolved (see sources—Cohen, JD and Larouche, SJ).

BENEFITS versus RISKS

Possible Benefits	*Possible Risks*
REDUCES RISK OF STROKES	Drug-induced increase in liver enzymes
EFFECTIVE REDUCTION OF TOTAL BLOOD CHOLESTEROL AND LDL CHOLESTEROL	Drug-induced myositis (muscle inflammation)
EFFECTIVE REDUCTION IN THE NUMBER OF FIRST-TIME AND REPEAT HEART ATTACKS (PRIMARY AND SECONDARY PREVENTION)	Decreased co-enzyme Q10
REDUCTION IN THE NUMBER OF PATIENT DEATHS	Rhabodmyolysis
SLOWS PROGRESSION OF ATHEROSCLEROSIS	
REDUCES RISK OF TRANSIENT ISCHEMIC ATTACKS (TIAs)	
LOWERS APOLIPOPROTEIN B and TRIGLYCERIDES	
INCREASES HDL-C IN PEOPLE WITH HETEROZYGOUS FAMILIAL AND NONFAMIAL PRIMARY HYPERCHOLESTEROLEMIA AND MIXED DYSLIPIDEMIA (FREDERICKSON TYPES 2a AND 2b)	
NEUTRALIZES INFLAMMATORY RISK (SUCH AS C REACTIVE PROTEIN)	
May have a role in preventing development of type 2 diabetes in men	
May have a role in preventing osteoporosis	

▷ **Principal Uses**

As a Single Drug Product: Uses currently included in FDA-approved labeling: (1) Treats abnormally high total blood cholesterol levels (in people with types IIa and IIb hypercholesterolemia) due to increased low-density lipoprotein (LDL) cholesterol (used with a cholesterol-lowering diet after an adequate trial of nondrug methods has failed); (2) helps prevent a first heart attack or stroke and reduces death from cardiovascular disease in people with increased blood cholesterol levels at risk of a first heart attack. Also serves to help prevent a repeat heart attack; (3) slows progression and in some cases makes small reversals in coronary artery disease (atherosclerosis); (4) used to decrease triglycerides in mixed lipidemias; (5) reduces risk of strokes or transient ischemic attacks (TIAs)—the CARE trial of 4,159 patients found that strokes were lowered by 32%; (6) approved to increase HDL-C in patients with heterozygous familial and nonfamilial primary hypercholesterolemia and mixed dyslipidemia; (7) lowers apolipoprotein B.

Other (unlabeled) generally accepted uses: (1) Reduces temporary blood flow (to the heart) problems (myocardial ischemia) when combined with other therapies; (2) may have a role in decreasing development of type 2 diabetes in men (WOSCOPS); (3) may have a role in reducing development of osteoporosis (emerging data).

How This Drug Works: This drug blocks the liver enzyme that starts production of cholesterol. Its principal action is the reduction of low-density lipoproteins (LDL), the fraction of total blood cholesterol that is thought to increase the risk of coronary heart disease. This drug also increases the level of high-density lipoproteins (HDL), the cholesterol fraction that is thought to reduce the risk of heart disease. There is an increasing evidence base that tells us that this drug has strong beneficial effects on blood flow, the blood vessel walls and what is in the blood itself. Specific compounds or effects of platelet derived growth factor (PDGF), undesirable blood clotting via thrombin-antithrombin III, thrombomodulin and other chemicals may be beneficially lowered or effects mitigated by statins. Pravastatin lowered the likelihood of blood to clot (thrombogenicity) caused by both platelets and endothelial cells. This medicine also leads to improvement in opening (vasodilation) of the brachial artery that required the lining or endothelium.

Available Dosage Forms and Strengths
Tablets — 10 mg, 20 mg, 40 mg, 80 mg

▷ **Recommended Dose Ranges** (Actual dose and schedule must be determined for each patient individually.)

Infants and Children: Under 2 years of age—do not use this drug. 2 to 18 years of age—dose not established.

18 to 60 Years of Age: Hypercholesterolemia: Patients are put on a standard cholesterol lowering diet (see *www.americanheart.org*). Patients remain on this diet once the medicine is started, and dosing is begun with 40 mg once a day at bedtime. Because the peak benefit is seen in 4 weeks, lipid tests should be obtained periodically, and dosing adjusted depending on reaching goals and on treatment guidelines (such as NCEP ATP 3). If goals are not reached after 4 weeks, add on therapy of a different medicine (such as ezetimibe) or the 80 mg dose is appropriate.

Over 60 Years of Age: Starting dose for those with kidney or liver compromise is 10 mg daily. A geriatric use subsection has been added to the Precautions of FDA-sanctioned labeling. The results of the CARE and LIPID studies had 6,593 people who used 40 mg for up to 6 years. In those studies, 36.1% were 65 or older. Adverse events and responses were similar to those seen in younger people. A measure called area under the curve (AUC) was 25–50% higher than in younger patients, but peak level and half life were similar. Dosing changes are not thought to be needed.

Conditions Requiring Dosing Adjustments
Liver Function: Used with caution by patients with liver disease. Starting dose is decreased to 10 mg per day. Pravastatin should not be used in sudden (acute) liver disease.

Kidney Function: Those with significant kidney disease take a starting dose of 10 mg per day. Used with caution in kidney compromise.

▷ **Dosing Instructions:** The tablet may be crushed and can be taken without regard to eating. New labeling says that it can be taken at any time. Previously, it was preferably taken at bedtime. (Highest rates of cholesterol production occur between midnight and 5 A.M.) If you forget a dose: Take the missed dose as soon as you remember it, unless it's nearly time for your next dose—if that is the case, skip the missed dose and take the next dose right on schedule. DO NOT double doses. Talk with your doctor if you find yourself missing doses.

Usual Duration of Use: Use on a regular schedule for 4 to 6 weeks usually determines effectiveness in reducing blood levels of total and LDL-C cholesterol. Long-term use (months to years) requires periodic physician evaluation. It is critical to take this medicine as directed to take control of an ongoing condition such as increased cholesterol, stroke risk, or heart attack risk.

Typical Treatment Goals and Measurements (Outcomes and Markers)

Cholesterol: The National Institutes of Health Adult Treatment Panel has released ATP III as part of the update to the National Cholesterol Education Program or NCEP. Key points in these new guidelines include acknowledging diabetes as one of the conditions that increases risk of heart disease, modifying risk factors, therapeutic lifestyle changes (TLC) and recommending routine testing for all of the cholesterol fractions (lipoprotein profile) versus total cholesterol alone.

Current NCEP guidelines recommend a desirable total cholesterol of 200 mg/dl, and optimal bad cholesterol (LDL) as 100 mg/dl, 130–159 mg/dl as borderline high, 160 mg/dl as high and 190 mg/dl as very high. Did you know that there are at least five different kinds of "good cholesterol" or HDL? The "too low" measure for HDL is still 40 mg/dl, but in order to learn more about cholesterol types some doctors are starting to order lipid panels. There are at least seven different kinds of "bad cholesterol." The new panels tell doctors about the kinds of cholesterol that your body makes. This is important because some kinds (small dense particles) tend to stick to blood vessels (are highly atherogenic). Take your medicine to reach your goals!

Two additional tests you will hear about will be electron beam computed tomography (EBCT) and CRP. EBCT is an important tool used in conjunction with laboratory studies. Findings show that even patients who meet cholesterol goals (particularly females over 55) can still be at significant cardiovascular risk. EBCT then defines risk by giving a calcium score and a "virtual tour" of the coronary arteries. C Reactive Protein or CRP is a new and apparently independent predictor of heart disease risk. A large study (see Ridker, P.M. in Sources) found that CRP predicted heart disease risk independently of bad cholesterol (low density lipoprotein). Talk to your doctor about this new laboratory test and ask about current guidelines for who should be tested (see Pearson, T.A. in Sources).

Possible Advantages of This Drug

Several studies show that drugs of this class (HMG-CoA reductase inhibitors) are more effective and better tolerated than other drugs currently available for reducing total and LDL-C cholesterol. This medicine is proven to increase HDL, has emerging bone health and diabetes data, works in primary and secondary heart (coronary) events, and also helps prevent stroke. Uses less common ways (liver enzymes) for removal from the body and thus avoids many drug interactions possible with other medicines in this same family.

▷ **This Drug Should Not Be Taken If**
- you have had an allergic reaction to it or to similar medicines previously.
- you have an unexplained and ongoing increase in liver function tests.

- you have active liver disease.
- you are pregnant or breast-feeding your infant.

▷ **Inform Your Physician Before Taking This Drug If**
- you have previously taken and have not tolerated any other drugs in this class: lovastatin (Mevacor), simvastatin (Zocor).
- you have a history of liver disease or impaired liver function.
- you are not using any method of birth control or you are planning pregnancy.
- you regularly consume substantial amounts of alcohol.
- you have kidney disease.
- you have cataracts or impaired vision.
- you get unexplained muscle weakness, pain, or tenderness (call your doctor).
- you have any type of chronic muscular disorder.
- you have an increase in certain liver enzymes (transaminases), which increase to three times the upper normal limit (pravastatin should be stopped immediately).

Possible Side Effects (natural, expected, and unavoidable drug actions)
Decreased co-enzyme Q10 (co-Q10 or ubiquinone) levels.

▷ **Possible Adverse Effects** (unusual, unexpected, and infrequent reactions)
If any of the following develop, consult your physician promptly for guidance.

Mild Adverse Effects
Allergic reactions: skin rash, itching—rare.
Headache, dizziness, depression—case reports to rare.
Flu-like syndrome, cough—case reports.
Indigestion, stomach pain, nausea, excessive gas, constipation, diarrhea—rare to infrequent.
Muscle cramps and/or pain—rare.

Serious Adverse Effects
Allergic reactions: rash (lichenoid dermatitis).
Porphyria cutanea tarda (PCT)—case reports.
Marked and persistent abnormal liver function tests with focal hepatitis (without jaundice)—rare.
Acute myositis (muscle pain and tenderness) during long-term use—case reports.
Rhabdomyolysis—rare and more likely if combined with fibrates.
Low white blood cells (leukopenia)—rare and questionable causation.
Neuropathy—case report.

▷ **Possible Effects on Sexual Function:** Impotence—questionable causation with medicines that lower cholesterol.

Possible Delayed Adverse Effects: Increased liver enzymes, decreased co-Q10.

Natural Diseases or Disorders That May Be Activated by This Drug
Latent liver disease.

Possible Effects on Laboratory Tests
Blood alanine aminotransferase (ALT) enzyme level: possible increase (with higher doses of drug).
Blood total cholesterol, LDL cholesterol, and triglyceride levels: decreased.
Blood HDL cholesterol level: increased.

CAUTION
1. If pregnancy occurs while taking this drug, discontinue the drug immediately and consult your physician.

2. Report promptly any development of unexplained muscle pain or tenderness, especially if accompanied by fever or malaise.
3. Report promptly the development of altered or impaired vision so that appropriate evaluation can be made (reported with lovastatin in high doses, but not this medicine).
4. If transaminase levels increase to three times the upper limit of normal values, this medicine should be stopped.
5. A study in Circulation (see Heeschen in sources) found that stopping "statin" type medicines in patients with acute coronary syndrome symptoms can lead to a three-fold increased risk of nonfatal heart attack (MI) or death. Maintain the clear benefits of this medicine by staying on it!

Precautions for Use
By Infants and Children: Safety and effectiveness for those less than 18 years of age are not established.

By Those Over 60 Years of Age: Tell your doctor about any personal or family history of cataracts. Comply with all recommendations regarding periodic eye examinations. Report promptly any alterations in vision. 10 mg starting dose is prudent.

▷ **Advisability of Use During Pregnancy**
Pregnancy Category: X. See Pregnancy Risk Categories at the back of this book.
Animal Studies: Mouse and rat studies reveal skeletal birth defects due to a closely related drug of this class.
Human Studies: Adequate studies of pregnant women are not available.
This drug should be avoided during entire pregnancy.

Advisability of Use If Breast-Feeding
Presence of this drug in breast milk: Yes, in small amounts.
Avoid drug or refrain from nursing.

Habit-Forming Potential: None.

Effects of Overdose: Increased indigestion, stomach distress, nausea, and diarrhea.

Possible Effects of Long-Term Use: Beneficial effects on cholesterol, blood vessels, the bones and inflammation.

Suggested Periodic Examinations While Taking This Drug (at physician's discretion)
Blood cholesterol studies: total cholesterol, HDL and LDL fractions (Berkeley Heart Lab), LP (a), homocysteine. Other markers of atherogenic fats (ALP) and CRP are prudent—not because of the medicine, but because they help further define needed treatment.

Liver function tests before treatment, before increasing the dose and when clinically indicated thereafter. **Pravastatin was the first HMG-CoA reductase inhibitor to receive labeling from the FDA for less-frequent liver testing.** Complete eye examination at beginning of treatment and at any time that significant change in vision occurs. Ask your doctor for guidance.

Bone mineral density tests (DEXA, PDEXA, or ultrasound) will help show retention of bone mineral density (a new possible beneficial effect). Electron beam computed tomography (EBCT) can help predict silent ischemia and other problems with blood vessels that supply the heart itself. This also may help define the results (outcomes) you are getting from this medicine.

▷ **While Taking This Drug, Observe the Following**
Foods: Follow a standard low-cholesterol diet. Your doctor may also recommend some specific foods such as increased vegetables or functional foods

such as Benecol. Three well-designed studies published in early April 2002 found that both in women and men and before and after a heart attack, people who ate more fish (2–4 servings a week) appeared to avoid heart disease. Additionally putting supplements containing Omega 3 polyunsaturated fatty acids (PUFA) into the diet also appeared to protect against abnormal heart rhythms and sudden death from heart attack. The studies appeared in *JAMA, Circulation* and the *New England Journal of Medicine.* Increasing oat bran in the diet may be of additional help in lowering cholesterol, but can decrease the amount of medicine that gets into your body. Take oat bran 2 hours before pravastatin or 4–6 hours after. Your doctor may also recommend increasing B vitamins. See Tables 19 and 20 about lifestyle changes and risk factors you can fix.

Herbal Medicines or Minerals: No data exist from well-designed clinical studies about garlic and pravastatin combinations and they cannot presently be recommended. Additionally, garlic may inhibit blood-clotting (platelet) aggregation—something to consider if you are already taking a platelet inhibitor. The FDA has allowed one dietary supplement called Cholestin to continue to be sold. This preparation actually contains lovastatin. Since use of two HMG-CoA inhibitors may increase risk of rhabdomyolysis or myopathy, the combination is NOT advised. Medicines such as eucalyptus, kava, valerian, or other herbals that can cause liver damage are not advisable.

Soy (milk, tofu, etc.) contains phytoestrogens, which has led to an FDA-approved health claim for reducing risk of heart disease (if there is at least 6.25 g of soy protein per serving). Substituting soy for some of the meat in your diet can also help lower cholesterol. Because pravastatin like other medicines in this drug class can deplete co-Q10, supplementation may be needed. One report of type 2 diabetics with low co-Q10 found beneficial effects from supplementation.

Beverages: No restrictions. May be taken with milk.

▷ *Alcohol:* No interactions expected. Use sparingly.

Tobacco Smoking: No interactions expected. I advise everyone to quit smoking.

▷ *Other Drugs*

Pravastatin *taken concurrently* with

- amprenavir (Agenerase) and ritonavir (Norvir) and perhaps other protease inhibitors may increase pravastatin levels and the risk of muscle damage (myopathy); however, the risk of such combination is not as great as with other medicines in the same family as pravastatin relies less on CYP 3A4 for removal from the body.
- clofibrate (Atromid-S) has been associated with muscle damage (rhabdomyolysis).
- cyclosporine (Sandimmune) increases the risk for myopathy. Dosing of 10 mg is used with a maximum of 20 mg.
- erythromycin (various) may increase muscle damage risk. Do not combine.
- itraconazole (Sporanox—24% increase in serum concentration in one study). May increase risk of muscle problems. Decreased doses are prudent if these medicines must be combined.
- gemfibrozil (Lopid) may alter the absorption and excretion of pravastatin and may also increase risk of muscle damage (rhabdomyolysis); these drugs should not be taken concurrently.
- niacin (various) may increase muscle damage risk.
- quinupristin/dalfopristin (Synercid) may increase the risk for myopathy by increasing cerivastatin blood levels.

- warfarin (Coumadin) can increase the risk of bleeding; more frequent INR (prothrombin time or protime) testing is indicated. Ongoing warfarin doses should be based on laboratory results.

The following drug may **decrease** the effects of pravastatin:

- cholestyramine (Questran)—may reduce absorption of pravastatin; take pravastatin 1 hour before or 4 hours after cholestyramine.

▷ *Driving, Hazardous Activities:* This drug may cause dizziness. Restrict activities as necessary.

Aviation Note: The use of this drug **may be a disqualification** for piloting. Consult a designated Aviation Medical Examiner.

Exposure to Sun: No restrictions.

Discontinuation: Do not stop this drug without your doctor's knowledge and help. There may be a significant increase in blood cholesterol levels if this medicine is stopped. Patients who have acute coronary syndromes or ACS (such as unstable angina, heart attack [non-p; Q-wave myocardial infarction], and Q-wave myocardial infarction) were reviewed as part of the Platelet Receptor Inhibitor in Ischemic Syndrome Management (PRISM) study. It was found that pretreatment with statin type medicines (HMG-CoA reductase inhibitors such as the medicine in this profile) significantly lowered risk during the first 30 days after ACS symptoms started. Most importantly, it was found that if a statin type medicine is stopped in ACS patients, there was a three-fold increased risk of nonfatal heart attack or death (see Heeschen, C. in Sources). Talk with your doctor BEFORE stopping any statin type medicine

PRAZOSIN (PRA zoh sin)

Introduced: 1970 **Class:** Antihypertensive **Prescription:** USA: Yes **Controlled Drug:** USA: No; Canada: No **Available as Generic:** USA: Yes; Canada: Yes

Brand Names: ❧Apo-Prazo, Minipres, Minizide [CD], ❧Novo-Prazin, ❧Nu-Prazo

---

BENEFITS versus RISKS

Possible Benefits	*Possible Risks*
EFFECTIVE INITIAL THERAPY FOR MILD TO MODERATE HYPERTENSION	"First-dose" drop in blood pressure with fainting
EFFECTIVE ANTIHYPERTENSIVE IN MODERATE TO SEVERE HYPERTENSION	May cause increased heart rate (paroxysmal tachycardia)
EFFECTIVE CONTROL OF HYPERTENSION IN PHEOCHROMOCYTOMA	
HELPS URINE FLOW IN BENIGN PROSTATIC HYPERPLASIA	
Effective in presence of impaired kidney function	

Author's Note: Data from the ALLHAT trial found that alpha blockers such as this medicine are not drugs of first choice in high blood

pressure. Information in this profile has been shortened for more widely used medicines.

PREDNISOLONE (pred NIS oh lohn)

Introduced: 1955 **Class:** Cortisonelike drugs **Prescription:**
USA: Yes **Controlled Drug:** USA: No; Canada: No **Available as**
Generic: USA: Yes; Canada: Yes

Brand Names: A&D w/Prednisolone [CD], ✤Ak-Cide [CD], ✤Ak-Pred, ✤Ak-Tate, Blephamide, Cortalone, Delta-Cortef, Duapred, Econopred Ophthalmic, Fernisolone-P, Hydelta-TBA, Hydeltrasol, ✤Inflamase, ✤Inflamase Forte, Isopto Cetapred [CD], Key-Pred, Meticortelone, Meti-Derm, Metimyd [CD], Metreton, ✤Minims Prednisolone, Mydrapred, Niscort, Nor-Pred, ✤Nova-Pred, ✤Novoprednisolone, Ophtho-Tate, Optimyd [CD], Otobione [CD], Pediaject, Pediapred, Polypred, Predcor, ✤Pred Forte, Pred-G [CD], ✤Pred Mild, Prelone, PSP-IV, Savacort, Sterane, TBA Pred, ✤Vasocidin [CD]

BENEFITS versus RISKS

Possible Benefits	*Possible Risks*
EFFECTIVE RELIEF OF SYMPTOMS IN A WIDE VARIETY OF INFLAMMATORY AND ALLERGIC DISORDERS	Ongoing systemic use (variable onset) can be associated with increased possible emergence of effects such as:
EFFECTIVE IMMUNOSUPPRESSION IN SELECTED BENIGN AND MALIGNANT DISORDERS	ALTERED MOOD AND PERSONALITY
Prevention of rejection in organ transplantation	CATARACTS, GLAUCOMA
	HYPERTENSION, ARRHYTHMIA
	OSTEOPOROSIS, INCREASED SUSCEPTIBILITY TO INFECTIONS
	ASEPTIC BONE NECROSIS (OSTEONECROSIS) IS AN AREA OF CONTROVERSY, UNCLEAR ONSET, PATIENT RISK FACTORS AND CORRELATION VERSUS CAUSATION (SEE CONTROVERSY IN MEDICINES)

Author's Note: Adverse effects from ophthalmic use are much more limited and more rare than those from systemic use.

▷ **Principal Uses**

As a Single Drug Product: Uses currently included in FDA-approved labeling: (1) Used in the treatment of a wide variety of allergic and inflammatory conditions—it is used most commonly in the management of serious skin disorders, asthma, regional enteritis, ulcerative colitis and all types of major rheumatic disorders including bursitis, tendonitis, most forms of arthritis, and inflammatory eye conditions; (2) used as part of combination therapy in lymphoma; (3) used in some kinds of adrenal insufficiencies; (4) used to help tuberculosis patients who also have inflammation around the heart without fluid buildup; (5) eases symptoms in ulcerative colitis.

Other (unlabeled) generally accepted uses: (1) Used as part of combination therapy in acute leukemias (lymphoblastic, lymphocytic, and myelogenous); (2) may have a role in combination therapy of breast cancer; (3) can help relieve the muscle pain of familial Mediterranean fever; (4) part of a combination therapy in treating abnormal liver tumors (hemangiomas); (5) can help subfertile men decrease seminal antibodies and become fertile; (6) helps people who have drug-induced lowering of white blood cells recover; (7) treats anaphylactic reactions of unknown cause; (8) treats thrombocytopenic purpura of unknown cause; (9) eases symptoms in myasthenia gravis; (10) can help reflex sympathetic dystrophy.

How This Drug Works: Not fully established. It is thought that this drug's anti-inflammatory effect is due to its ability to inhibit the normal defensive functions of certain white blood cells. Its immunosuppressant effect is attributed to a reduced production of lymphocytes and antibodies.

Available Dosage Forms and Strengths
Eye ointment — 0.6%
Eye suspension — 0.5%, 1%
Oral liquid — 6.7 mg/5 ml
Syrup — 15 mg/5 ml
Tablets — 5 mg

▷ **Usual Adult Dosage Ranges:** 5 to 60 mg daily as a single dose or in divided doses (some patients are put on alternate-day schedules). Once an adequate response is achieved, the dose should be decreased to the lowest effective dose. Ophthalmic drops—one to two drops is instilled into the eye sac (conjunctival sac) every 3 to 12 hours. Dosing may be increased to every hour in severe cases.

Note: Actual dose and schedule must be determined for each patient individually.

Typical Treatment Goals and Measurements (Outcomes and Markers)
Inflammation: The general goal is to relieve the swelling and the inflammatory response. Use in asthma should help decrease the frequency and severity of acute attacks. Some clinicians use decreased frequency of rescue inhaler use as a measure of success. Improvement in lung (pulmonary function) testing also helps define results in asthma. Lastly, clinical signs and symptoms such as wheezing, tightness in the chest, and exercise tolerance should all move in favorable directions.

Conditions Requiring Dosing Adjustments
Liver Function: Dosing adjustments do not appear to be needed in liver compromise.
Kidney Function: Dosing adjustments in renal compromise do not appear to be needed. This drug can cause proteinuria. It is a benefit-to-risk decision for kidney compromise (nephropathy) patients who tend to lose protein.

▷ **Dosing Instructions:** The tablet may be crushed and taken with or following food to prevent stomach irritation, preferably in the morning. Suspensions should be gently mixed before using. If you forget a dose: Call your doctor for instructions.

Usual Duration of Use: For acute disorders: 4 to 10 days generally, depending on patient reaction, disease flare and the condition being treated. For chronic disorders: according to individual requirements. Use only for time needed to relieve symptoms in acute self-limiting conditions or the time required to stabilize a chronic condition and permit gradual withdrawal. Because of its intermediate duration of action, this drug is appropriate for alternate-day dosing for many forms. See your doctor regularly.

Author's Note: The information categories provided in this profile are appropriate for prednisolone. For specific information that is normally found in those categories that have been omitted from this profile, see the following profile of prednisone. Prednisolone is a derivative of prednisone; both drugs share all significant actions and effects.

PREDNISONE (PRED ni sohn)

Introduced: 1955 **Class:** Cortisonelike drugs **Prescription:** USA: Yes **Controlled Drug:** USA: No; Canada: No **Available as Generic:** USA: Yes; Canada: Yes

Brand Names: ✤Apo-Prednisone, Aspred-C [CD], Deltasone, Liquid Pred, Meticorten, ✤Metreton [CD], ✤Novoprednisone, Orasone, Panasol-S, Paracort, Prednicen-M, Prednisone Intensol, SK-Prednisone, Sterapred, Sterapred-DS, ✤Winpred

---

BENEFITS versus RISKS

Possible Benefits	*Possible Risks*
EFFECTIVE RELIEF OF SYMPTOMS IN A WIDE VARIETY OF INFLAMMATORY AND ALLERGIC DISORDERS	Ongoing systemic use (variable onset) can be associated with increased possible emergence of effects such as:
EFFECTIVE IMMUNOSUPPRESSION IN SELECTED BENIGN AND MALIGNANT DISORDERS	ALTERED MOOD AND PERSONALITY
Prevention of rejection in organ transplantation	CATARACTS, GLAUCOMA
	HYPERTENSION, ABNORMAL HEART-BEATS
	OSTEOPOROSIS, INCREASED SUSCEPTIBILITY TO INFECTIONS AND OTHERS
	ASEPTIC BONE NECROSIS (OSTEONECROSIS) IS AN AREA OF CONTROVERSY, UNCLEAR ONSET, PATIENT RISK FACTORS AND CORRELATION VERSUS CAUSATION (SEE CONTROVERSY IN MEDICINES)

▷ **Principal Uses**

As a Single Drug Product: Uses currently included in FDA-approved labeling: (1) Treats a wide variety of allergic and inflammatory conditions—it is used most commonly in the management of serious skin disorders (such as severe psoriasis, contact dermatitis and drug hypersensitivity reactions, etc.), asthma, gout, lupus erythematosus, regional enteritis, ulcerative colitis, nephrotic syndrome and all types of major rheumatic disorders including bursitis, tendonitis, most forms of arthritis and severe allergic conjunctivitis of the eye; (2) used as part of combination therapy of lymphoma; (3) helps address adrenal insufficiency; (4) used as part of combination therapy of several kinds of leukemia; (5) used in kidney transplant patients; (6) helps patients recover from symptoms of multiple sclerosis.

Other (unlabeled) generally accepted uses: (1) Used in combination therapy of acute (lymphoblastic, lymphocytic and myelogenous) leukemias; (2) combination therapy of breast cancer; (3) may be helpful in therapy of familial Mediterranean fever; (4) used with other medications to treat liver tumors (hemangiomas); (5) may help subfertile men decrease seminal antibodies and become fertile; (6) helps prevent early lung deterioration in children with AIDS; (7) eases symptoms in alcoholics who have hepatitis and encephalopathy; (8) used in some chronic pain syndromes.

How This Drug Works: Anti-inflammatory effect is due to its ability to inhibit normal defensive functions of certain white blood cells. Its immunosuppressant effect is due to a reduced production of lymphocytes and antibodies.

Available Dosage Forms and Strengths
Oral solution — 5 mg/5 ml
    Syrup — 5 mg/5 ml (5% alcohol)
    Tablets — 1 mg, 2.5 mg, 5 mg, 10 mg, 20 mg, 25 mg, 50 mg

▷ **Usual Adult Dosage Ranges:** Five to 60 mg daily as a single dose or in divided doses depending on the condition being treated. With myasthenia gravis, patients not responding to 100 mg will not respond to higher doses. Once initial inflammation has eased, the dose should be gradually lowered to the lowest effective dose for the condition being treated. Some clinicians use alternate day therapy once response is judged to be clinically adequate. This may help minimize cushingoid side effects of long-term therapy.

  Note: Actual dose and schedule must be determined for each patient individually.

Conditions Requiring Dosing Adjustments
Liver Function: No dosing changes thought to be needed.
Kidney Function: Dosing adjustments in kidney disease do not appear to be needed.

▷ **Dosing Instructions:** The tablet may be crushed and taken with food or milk to help prevent stomach irritation, preferably in the morning. Liquid form doses should be measured with a dosing cup or a calibrated measuring spoon. If you forget a dose: Call your doctor for instructions. Be sure to check with your doctor BEFORE getting any vaccines (blunting of vaccine response may occur).

Usual Duration of Use: For acute disorders: 4 to 10 days generally with additional considerations of patient reaction, disease flare and tapering. For chronic disorders: according to individual requirements. Use should not exceed time needed for symptomatic relief in acute self-limiting conditions or time required to stabilize a chronic condition and permit gradual withdrawal. Intermediate duration of action allows alternate-day dosing. See your doctor regularly.

Typical Treatment Goals and Measurements (Outcomes and Markers)
Inflammation: The general goal is to relieve the swelling and the inflammatory response. Markers such as erythrocyte sedimentation rate (ESR), increased joint mobility and decreased time that joints are stiff in the morning can be used. Use in asthma should help decrease the frequency and severity of acute attacks. Some clinicians use decreased frequency of rescue inhaler use as a measure of success. Improvement in lung (pul-

monary function) testing such as PEFR and FEV1 also help define results in asthma. Lastly, clinical signs and symptoms such as wheezing, tightness in the chest, and exercise tolerance should all move in favorable directions if asthma is being treated. If signs and symptoms worsen or do not ease or if new signs or symptoms happen, call your doctor.

▷ **This Drug Should Not Be Taken If**
- you had an allergic reaction to it previously.
- you have active peptic ulcer disease.
- you have an active herpes simplex virus eye infection.
- you have active tuberculosis.
- you have a fungal infection in a large area inside your body (systemic fungal infection).

▷ **Inform Your Physician Before Taking This Drug If**
- you have had an adverse reaction to any cortisonelike drug.
- you have a history of peptic ulcer disease, thrombophlebitis, or tuberculosis.
- you have diabetes, kidney failure, glaucoma, high blood pressure, deficient thyroid function, or myasthenia gravis.
- you have osteoporosis.
- you develop unexplained joint pain (such as in the knees, hip, or shoulder) while taking this medicine, or after you've taken it. These may be early signs of aseptic necrosis (osteonecrosis). Call your doctor right away.
- you have been exposed to any viral illness, such as measles or chicken pox. (Cases may be severe if you are taking this medicine).
- you are prone to depression.
- you have diverticulitis.
- you plan to have surgery of any kind in the near future or have had some kinds of intestinal surgery.

Possible Side Effects (natural, expected, and unavoidable drug actions)
Increased appetite, weight gain, retention of salt and water leading to increased blood pressure, excretion of potassium, increased susceptibility to infection because of immune suppression. Increased white blood cell count (granulocytes)—not a symptom of infection, but a drug effect. Decreased white blood cell count (monocytes and lymphocytes). Growth changes in children. Mild depression or euphoria (may be common). Impaired wound healing. Easy bruising (ecchymosis). Adrenal gland suppression.

▷ **Possible Adverse Effects** (unusual, unexpected, and infrequent reactions)
If any of the following develop, consult your physician promptly for guidance.
Mild Adverse Effects
Allergic reaction: skin rash.
Headache, dizziness, insomnia—infrequent.
Acid indigestion, abdominal distention—infrequent.
Patchy blue areas on the great toe (blue toe syndrome)—case reports.
Muscle cramping and weakness—possible.
Elevated intracranial pressure (pseudotumor cerebri)—infrequent.
Acne, excessive growth of facial hair—frequent.
Serious Adverse Effects
Serious mental or emotional disturbances—case reports.
Reactivation of latent tuberculosis—possible in those with past tuberculosis.

Development of peptic ulcer—possible and more likely in those with previous ulcers.

Development of inflammation of the pancreas—rare (pancreatitis more likely with prolonged treatment or high doses).

Thrombophlebitis (inflammation of a vein with the formation of blood clot): pain or tenderness in thigh or leg, with or without swelling of the foot, ankle or leg—rare.

Increased intraocular (inner eye) pressure, glaucoma, or cataracts—infrequent.

Kaposi's sarcoma—case reports.

Growth retardation—possible in children with long-term use.

Cushing's syndrome—possible with long-term use (central obesity, buffalo hump, and moon-shaped face).

Necrosis of bone (osteonecrosis, avascular necrosis, or aseptic necrosis)—Questions remain as to correlation versus causation, but may be more likely with high initial corticosteroid doses, long-term treatment, and cumulative doses of 4.32 grams. May also happen with short-term, modest doses. Individual patient risk factors and/or diseases or conditions appear to be important. Call your doctor if unexplained joint pain happens.

Osteoporosis—possible with long-term use.

Superinfections—possible.

Inflammation or wasting of muscle (myositis or myopathy)—infrequent.

Increased blood sugar—possible and may be dose-related.

Drug-induced porphyria or seizures—case reports.

Pulmonary embolism (movement of a blood clot to the lung): sudden shortness of breath, pain in the chest, coughing, bloody sputum—increased risk.

▷ **Possible Effects on Sexual Function:** Altered timing and pattern of menstruation.

Correction of male infertility when due to autoantibodies that suppress sperm activity.

▷ **Adverse Effects That May Mimic Natural Diseases or Disorders**

Pattern of symptoms and signs resembling Cushing's syndrome, osteoporosis may resemble bone loss occurring after menopause.

Natural Diseases or Disorders That May Be Activated by This Drug

Latent diabetes, glaucoma, peptic ulcer disease, tuberculosis.

Possible Effects on Laboratory Tests

Complete blood cell counts: decreased eosinophils, lymphocytes, and platelets.

Blood amylase level: increased (possible pancreatitis).

Blood total cholesterol and HDL cholesterol levels: increased.

Blood LDL cholesterol level: no effect.

Blood digoxin (Lanoxin, others): FALSE increase with Abbott TDx method.

Blood triglyceride levels: no significant effect.

Blood glucose level: increased.

Glucose tolerance test (GTT): decreased.

Blood potassium or testosterone level: decreased.

Blood thyroid hormone (T3): decreased.

Blood uric acid level: increased.

Urine sugar tests: no effect with Tes-Tape; false low result with Clinistix and Diastix.

Fecal occult blood test: positive (if gastrointestinal bleeding).

CAUTION

1. If therapy exceeds 1 week, carry an identification card noting that you are taking this drug.
2. Do not stop this drug abruptly after long-term use.
3. If vaccination against measles, rabies, smallpox, or yellow fever is required, discontinue this drug 72 hours before vaccination and do not resume it for at least 14 days after vaccination.
4. Because of the way that this medicine works on the immune system, you will have an increased risk of infections while you are taking it. It is prudent to avoid patients with flu or other viral illnesses such as chicken pox. Call your doctor if exposure happens.
5. A variety of patient risk factors appear to be important in possible development of osteonecrosis. Talk to your doctor about the current list. Call your doctor if unexplained joint pain occurs.

Controversies in Medicine: Medicines in this class have had conflicting reports regarding correlation with or causation of aseptic bone necrosis (osteonecrosis-ON). There appear to be patient risk factors, possible delayed onset with occurrence even after the medicine is stopped, and some diseases or conditions where corticosteroids are often used and ON is more frequent than the general population. It is unclear if this is because of the disease or condition or the use of corticosteroids. Previous data regarding cumulative dosing (4.32 grams) appears controversial, with more recent case reports of 6 days of treatment with some doses being associated with ON. Some existing and emerging patient risk factors include alcohol use versus abuse, initial high doses, HIV positive patients who weight trained, Systemic Lupus Erythematosus, some clotting disorders, and high homocysteine levels amongst others appear to increase risk. Early research regarding use of alendronate (Fosamax) to treat ON appears to show that it is important for patients to quickly return to their doctors if unexplained joint pain (such as in the hip or knee) happens. Some centers note that ON has been poorly studied, and while the weight of data in growing, it is yet too early to say more than ON is correlated with corticosteroid use.

Precautions for Use

By Infants and Children: Avoid prolonged use if possible. During long-term use, observe for suppression of normal growth and the possibility of increased intracranial pressure. Following long-term use, the child may be at risk for adrenal gland deficiency during stress for as long as 18 months after cessation of this drug.

By Those Over 60 Years of Age: Cortisonelike drugs should only be used when the disorder under treatment is unresponsive to adequate trials of unrelated drugs. Avoid the prolonged use of this drug if possible. Continual use (even in small doses) can increase severity of diabetes, enhance fluid retention, raise blood pressure, weaken resistance to infection, induce stomach ulcer, and accelerate development of cataract and osteoporosis or other bone problems.

▷ **Advisability of Use During Pregnancy**

Pregnancy Category: B. See Pregnancy Risk Categories at the back of this book.
Animal Studies: Birth defects reported in mice, rats, and rabbits.
Human Studies: Adequate studies of pregnant women are not available.

Avoid completely during the first 3 months. Limit use during the final 6 months as much as possible. If used, examine infant for possible deficiency of adrenal gland function.

Advisability of Use If Breast-Feeding

Presence of this drug in breast milk: Yes, but amounts received via breast milk are generally less than 0.1% of a therapeutic dose. Talk to your doctor. Prednisolone or prednisone may be drugs of choice in women who wish to breast-feed while taking one of those medicines for one of its indicated uses.

Habit-Forming Potential: Long-term use of this drug may produce a state of functional dependence (see Glossary). In therapy of asthma and rheumatoid arthritis, it is advisable to keep the dose as small as possible and attempt drug withdrawal after periods of reasonable improvement. Such procedures may reduce the degree of "steroid rebound"—the return of symptoms as the drug is withdrawn.

Effects of Overdose: Fatigue, muscle weakness, stomach irritation, acid indigestion, excessive sweating, facial flushing, fluid retention, swelling of extremities, increased blood pressure.

Possible Effects of Long-Term Use: Increased blood sugar (possible diabetes), increased fat deposits on the trunk of the body ("buffalo hump"), rounding of the face ("moon face"), thinning and fragility of skin, loss of texture and strength of bones (osteoporosis, aseptic necrosis), cataracts, glaucoma, retarded growth and development in children.

Suggested Periodic Examinations While Taking This Drug (at physician's discretion)

Measurements of blood pressure, blood sugar, and potassium levels.

Complete eye examinations at regular intervals.

Chest X ray if history of tuberculosis.

Bone mineral density testing (DEXA) to check for osteoporosis. Check of bone status relative to osteonecrosis (such as unexplained joint pain). Such pain may need MRI follow-up.

Determination of the rate of development of the growing child to detect retardation of normal growth.

▷ **While Taking This Drug, Observe the Following**

Foods: Alfalfa may negate benefits of prednisone in SLE patients (possible L-canavanine effect). Otherwise, no drug lowering by food reported. Ask your doctor about restricting salt or eating potassium-rich foods. Higher protein diet may be prudent in long-term use. Taking drug with food can help avoid stomach upset.

Herbal Medicines or Minerals: Hawthorn, ginger, garlic, ma huang, ginseng, guar gum, fenugreek, and nettle may change blood sugar. Since prednisone may also change blood sugar control, caution is advised. Ma huang has ephedra in it and may also decrease prednisone benefits.

Fir or pine needle oil should NOT be used by asthmatics. Ephedra alone does carry a German Commission E monograph indication for asthma treatment. If you are allergic to plants in the Asteraceae family (aster, chrysanthemum, daisy, or ragweed), you may also be allergic to echinacea, chamomile, feverfew, and St. John's wort. During long-term use, take a vitamin D supplement and increase calcium. During wound repair, take a zinc supplement. Potassium loss may need to be replaced. Ask your doctor if glucosamine makes sense for you. Ginseng and Echinacea may blunt prednisone benefits. Talk to your doctor BEFORE adding any herbal to any other medicines that you already take.

Beverages: No restrictions. Drink all forms of milk liberally.

▷   *Alcohol:* Use caution if you are prone to peptic ulcers. Talk to your doctor to get his or her approval of drinking beer, wine, or other liquor while taking this medicine. Controversy exists as to any alcohol use versus abuse as a risk factor for osteonecrosis.

Tobacco Smoking: Nicotine increases the blood levels of naturally produced cortisone. I advise everyone to quit smoking.

Marijuana Smoking: May cause additional impairment of immunity.

▷   *Other Drugs*

Prednisone may **decrease** the effects of

- insulin (various), or oral hypoglycemic drugs, requiring dosing changes of insulin or hypoglycemic.
- isoniazid (INH, Niconyl, etc.).
- salicylates (aspirin, sodium salicylate, etc.) and also increases the risk of stomach irritation.
- vaccines (such as flu vaccine), by blunting the immune response to them.

Prednisone **taken concurrently** with

- amphotericin B (Abelcet, Fungizone) may result in additive potassium loss.
- asparaginase (Elspar) may result in increased risk of toxicity if given with or before prednisone. Asparaginase dosing should be accomplished after prednisone dosing.
- birth control pills (oral contraceptives) will prolong the prednisone effect.
- clarithromycin (Biaxin) may lead to psychotic symptoms (one case report). Patients must be closely watched if these medicines are combined.
- cyclosporine (Sandimmune) can cause increased cyclosporine levels and increased prednisone levels. Dose decreases may be needed for both drugs.
- foscarnet (Foscavir) may result in additive potassium loss.
- ketoconazole (Nizoral) has increased a metabolite of prednisone in some studies (prednisolone), but not in other studies. Increased patient follow-up and check for increased prednisone side effects are prudent if combined treatment continues for 5–7 days.
- levofloxacin (Levaquin) and perhaps other fluoroquinolone antibiotics may increase the risk of tendon rupture. Caution in exercise is needed.
- loop diuretics (furosemide [Lasix], bumetanide [Bumex]) may blunt their effects.
- macrolide antibiotics (erythromycin, troleandomycin, and perhaps others) can lead to prednisone toxicity.
- montelukast (Singulair) resulted in severe edema (peripheral) in one case report. Caution and close patient monitoring are prudent if these medicines must be combined.
- neuromuscular blocking agents (such as pancuronium-Pavulon, vecuronium-Norcuron, others) can result in increased risk and or severity of muscle problems (myopathy and flaccid paralysis) and can also antagonize blockade from these medicines. Caution and unparalyzed periods are prudent.
- NSAIDs may result in additive stomach and intestinal irritation.
- oral anticoagulants may either increase or decrease their effectiveness; consult your physician regarding the need for prothrombin time testing and dose adjustment.
- oral antidiabetic drugs (see Drug Classes) or insulin may result in loss of glucose control.
- ritonavir (Norvir) and perhaps other protease inhibitors (see Drug Classes) may lead to toxicity.
- theophylline (Theo-Dur, others) may result in variable responses to this

medicine. Increased frequency of theophylline level testing is recommended.

- thiazide diuretics (see Drug Classes) or loop diuretics may result in additive potassium loss.
- vaccines (flu, pneumococcal, varicella, and others) may result in blunted response to the vaccine and decreased preventive benefits.

The following drugs may *decrease* the effects of prednisone:

- antacids—may reduce its absorption.
- barbiturates (Amytal, Butisol, phenobarbital, etc.).
- carbamazepine (Tegretol).
- phenytoin (Dilantin, etc.) and fosphenytoin (Cerebyx).
- primidone (Mysoline).
- rifampin (Rifadin, Rimactane, etc.).

▷ *Driving, Hazardous Activities:* Usually no restrictions. Be alert to the rare occurrence of dizziness.

Aviation Note: The use of this drug *may be a disqualification* for piloting. Consult a designated Aviation Medical Examiner.

Exposure to Sun: No restrictions.

Occurrence of Unrelated Illness: This drug may decrease resistance to infection. Tell your doctor if you develop an infection of any kind. It may also reduce your ability to respond to the stress of acute illness, injury, or surgery. Keep your doctor informed of any changes in health.

Discontinuation: Do not stop this drug abruptly after chronic use. Ask your doctor for help about gradual, individualized withdrawal. Some clinicians change from daily to every other day therapy for four weeks BEFORE starting to lower the dose in a stepwise fashion. Many patients tolerate dose reductions of 2.5 mg of prednisone (other steroids are calculated on the basis of prednisone equivalents) with those decreases made every 3–7 days. If a disease flare occurs (worsening of symptoms), the dose should be increased to the last dose before the disease flare and should be tapered more slowly down to 5–10 mg or lower. Some clinicians use 8 A.M. predose plasma cortisol to guide tapering. If this lab test is less than 10 mcg/deciliter, tapering is continued until the daily prednisone equivalent is 2-5 mg. In general, if long-term treatment or high doses were used, prednisone equivalents should be tapered over 9–12 months. For up to 2 years after stopping this drug, you may require it again if you have an injury, surgery, or an illness.

PRIMIDONE (PRI mi dohn)

Introduced: 1953 **Class:** Anticonvulsant **Prescription:** USA: Yes **Controlled Drug:** USA: No; Canada: No **Available as Generic:** USA: Yes; Canada: Yes

Brand Names: ✚Apo-Primidone, Myidone, Mysoline, ✚PMS-Primidone and ✚Sertan

Author's Note: Information in this profile has been shortened to make room for more widely used medicines.

PROBENECID (proh BEN e sid)

Introduced: 1951   **Class:** Antigout   **Prescription:** USA: Yes
Controlled Drug: USA: No; Canada: No   **Available as Generic:** USA:
Yes; Canada: No

Brand Names: Ampicillin-Probenecid, ✿Ampicin PRB [CD], Benemid, ✿Benuryl, Colabid [CD], ColBenemid [CD], Polycillin-PRB [CD], Probalan, Probampacin [CD], Proben-C [CD], Probenecid with Colchicine, ✿Pro-Biosan 500 Kit [CD], SK-Probenecid

BENEFITS versus RISKS	
Possible Benefits	*Possible Risks*
EFFECTIVE LONG-TERM PREVENTION OF ACUTE ATTACKS OF GOUT	Formation of uric acid kidney stones
	Bone marrow depression (aplastic anemia)
Useful adjunct to penicillin therapy (to achieve high blood and tissue levels of penicillin)	Drug-induced liver and kidney damage
Used with cidofovir (Vistide) to ease kidney toxicity	

▷ **Principal Uses**

As a Single Drug Product: Uses currently included in FDA-approved labeling: (1) Used in helping maintain penicillin levels in therapy of gonorrhea; (2) helps prevent gout.

Other (unlabeled) generally accepted uses: (1) May have a role in preventing kidney toxicity in cisplatin chemotherapy; (2) adjunctive use in maintaining effective antibiotic levels in treatment of syphilis; (3) may prevent kidney damage from some kinds of kidney toxic (nephrotoxic) drugs (such as Vistide for HIV); (4) helps lower increased uric acid levels that can be caused by medicines such as thiazide diuretics.

As a Combination Drug Product [CD]: This drug is available in combination with colchicine, a drug often used for the treatment of acute gout. Each drug works in a different way; when used in combination they provide both relief of the acute gout and some measure of protection from recurrence of acute attacks. Also available combined with penicillin so that the penicillin stays in the body longer than usual to fight the infection.

How This Drug Works: Works in the kidney (tubular systems) to increase uric acid excretion in the urine; this drug reduces the levels of uric acid in the blood and body tissues. It also works in the kidney to decrease the amount of penicillin excreted in the urine, prolongs the presence of penicillin in the blood and helps achieve higher concentrations in body tissues.

Available Dosage Forms and Strengths

Tablets — 500 mg

▷ **Usual Adult Dosage Ranges:** *Antigout*: Initially 250 mg twice a day for 1 week and then 500 mg twice a day. When there have been no sudden gout attacks for six months, the dose can usually be decreased by 500 mg a day every six months until uric acid levels start to rise again. *Adjunct to penicillin therapy*: 500 mg four times a day.

Note: Actual dose and schedule must be determined for each patient individually.

Conditions Requiring Dosing Adjustments

Liver Function: Specific guidelines for dose adjustment in liver compromise are not available. This drug should be used with caution.

Kidney Function: Patients with kidney failure (creatinine clearance less than 30 ml/min) should not use this drug, as the effectiveness is questionable. Those with moderate kidney failure may still benefit from this medicine, and dose increases (as needed and tolerated) in 500-mg steps up to 2,000 mg a day in equally divided doses may be required.

▷ **Dosing Instructions:** The tablet may be crushed and taken with or following food to reduce stomach irritation. Drink 2.5 to 3 quarts of liquids (10 to 12 full glasses) daily unless your doctor tells you it is not a good idea in your case. If you forget a dose: Take the missed dose as soon as you remember it, unless it's nearly time for your next dose—if that is the case, skip the missed dose and take the next dose right on schedule. DO NOT double doses. Talk with your doctor if you find yourself missing doses as there are many strategies to help.

Usual Duration of Use: Use on a regular schedule for several months usually determines effectiveness in preventing acute attacks of gout. If six months pass without a sudden (acute) gout attack, the dose can usually be decreased. Long-term use (months to years) requires supervision and periodic evaluation by your physician.

Typical Treatment Goals and Measurements (Outcomes and Markers)

Uric Acid: Blood uric acid levels often decrease in 48 to 72 hours and may reach normal range in 1 to 3 weeks. Attacks of gout should become shorter and lessen in severity over time.

▷ **This Drug Should Not Be Taken If**
- you have had an allergic reaction to it previously.
- you have active liver disease.
- you have acute kidney failure or kidney stones made of uric acid.
- you are less than 2 years old.
- you have an active blood cell or bone marrow disorder.
- you are taking any drug product that contains aspirin or aspirinlike drugs.
- you are having an attack of acute gout at the present time.

▷ **Inform Your Physician Before Taking This Drug If**
- you have a history of kidney disease or kidney stones.
- you have a history of liver disease or impaired liver function.
- you have a history of peptic ulcer disease.
- you have a history of a blood cell or bone marrow disorder.

Possible Side Effects (natural, expected, and unavoidable drug actions)

Development of kidney stones (composed of uric acid)—this is preventable. Consult your physician regarding the use of sodium bicarbonate (or other urine alkalizer) to prevent stone formation.

▷ **Possible Adverse Effects** (unusual, unexpected, and infrequent reactions)

If any of the following develop, consult your physician promptly for guidance.

Mild Adverse Effects

Allergic reactions: skin rash, itching, drug fever (see Glossary).

Headache, dizziness, flushing of face—infrequent.

Hair loss (alopecia): possible.

Reduced appetite, sore gums, nausea, vomiting—possible to infrequent.

Serious Adverse Effects

   Allergic reactions: anaphylactic reaction (see Glossary).

   Idiosyncratic reactions: hemolytic anemia (see Glossary).

   Bone marrow depression (see Glossary): fatigue, sore throat, bleeding/bruising—case reports.

   Drug-induced liver damage with jaundice (see Glossary—also includes hepatic necrosis) or porphyria—case reports.

   Fluid in the retina (retinal edema)—case reports.

   Drug-induced kidney damage: marked fluid retention, reduced urine formation—case reports.

▷ **Possible Effects on Sexual Function:** None reported.

▷ **Adverse Effects That May Mimic Natural Diseases or Disorders**

   Liver reactions may suggest viral hepatitis. Kidney reactions may suggest nephrosis.

Possible Effects on Laboratory Tests

   Complete blood cell counts: decreased red cells, hemoglobin, white cells, and platelets.

   INR (prothrombin time): increased (when taken concurrently with warfarin).

   Blood glucose level and uric acid level: decreased.

   Blood urea nitrogen (BUN) level: increased (kidney damage).

   Liver function tests: increased enzymes (ALT/GPT, AST/GOT, alkaline phosphatase) or bilirubin.

   Urine sugar tests: false positive with Benedict's solution and Clinitest.

CAUTION

   1. This drug should not be started until 2 to 3 weeks after an acute attack of gout has subsided.

   2. This drug may increase the frequency of acute attacks of gout during the first few months of treatment. Concurrent use of colchicine is advised to prevent acute attacks (see combination forms).

   3. Aspirin (and aspirin-containing drug products) can reduce the effectiveness of this drug. Use acetaminophen or a nonaspirin analgesic for pain relief as needed.

Precautions for Use

   By Infants and Children: Safety and effectiveness for those less than 2 years of age are not established.

   By Those Over 60 Years of Age: The natural decline in kidney function that occurs after 60 may require adjustment of your dose. You may be more susceptible to the serious adverse effects of this drug. Report any unusual symptoms promptly for evaluation.

▷ **Advisability of Use During Pregnancy**

   Pregnancy Category: B. See Pregnancy Risk Categories at the back of this book.

   Animal Studies: No information available.

   Human Studies: Adequate studies of pregnant women are not available.

   This drug has been used during pregnancy with no reports of birth defects or adverse effects on the fetus. Ask your physician for guidance.

Advisability of Use If Breast-Feeding

   Presence of this drug in breast milk: Unknown.

   Avoid drug or refrain from nursing.

Habit-Forming Potential: None.

Effects of Overdose: Stomach irritation, nausea, vomiting, nervous agitation, delirium, seizures, coma.

Possible Effects of Long-Term Use: Formation of kidney stones. Kidney damage in sensitive individuals.

Suggested Periodic Examinations While Taking This Drug (at physician's discretion)
Complete blood cell counts.
Blood uric acid.
Liver and kidney function tests.

▷ **While Taking This Drug, Observe the Following**
Foods: Follow your physician's advice regarding the need for a low-purine diet.
Herbal Medicines or Minerals: Acerola is high in vitamin C. Inosine, like acerola, may increase uric acid levels. Aspen should be avoided in gout. Lipase may worsen gout. Goutweed (aegopodium podagraria) does not have enough data to assess effectiveness in treating gout.
Beverages: A large intake of coffee, tea, or cola beverages may reduce the effectiveness of treatment.
▷ *Alcohol:* No interactions expected, but large amounts of alcohol can raise the blood uric acid level and reduce the effectiveness of treatment.
Tobacco Smoking: No interactions expected. I advise everyone to quit smoking.
▷ *Other Drugs*
Probenecid may *increase* the effects of
• acetaminophen (Tylenol), increasing risk of toxicity.
• acyclovir (Zovirax) and result in toxicity unless doses are reduced.
• ciprofloxacin (Cipro) and gatifloxacin (Tequin), increasing toxicity risk.
• clofibrate (Atromid-S).
• dyphylline (Neothylline).
• entacapone (Comtan).
• ganciclovir (Cytovene).
• ketoprofen and perhaps other NSAIDs (see Drug Classes).
• ketorolac (Toradol) and increase toxicity risk.
• methotrexate (Mexate) and increase its toxicity.
• midazolam (Versed) and increase CNS depression.
• oral antidiabetic agents (see Drug Classes—sulfonlyureas).
• oseltamivir (Tamiflu).
• thiazide diuretics (see Drug Classes).
• thiopental (Pentothal) and prolong its anesthetic effect.
• valacyclovir (Valtrex) and result in toxicity unless doses are reduced.
• valgancyclovir (Valcyte) and result in toxicity unless doses are reduced.
• zalcitabine (Hivid).
• zidovudine (Retrovir) and increase toxicity risk.
Probenecid *taken concurrently* with
• allopurinol (Zyloprim) may result in extended allopurinol half-life.
• cephalosporins (see Drug Classes) may cause a doubling of antibiotic levels. Caution must be used to avoid toxicity.
• dapsone may cause up to a 50% increased dapsone level and result in toxicity unless dapsone doses are decreased.
• penicillins (see Drug Classes) may cause a threefold to fivefold increase in penicillin blood levels, greatly increasing the effectiveness of each penicillin dose.
• rifampin (Rifadin, others) may result in increased blood levels of rifampin.
• ritonavir (Norvir) may lead to changes in probenecid blood levels.

The following drugs may *decrease* the effects of probenecid:
- aspirin and other salicylates—may reduce its effectiveness in promoting the excretion of uric acid.
- bismuth subsalicylate (Pepto-Bismol, others).

▷ *Driving, Hazardous Activities:* This drug may cause dizziness. Restrict activities as necessary.

Aviation Note: The use of this drug *may be a disqualification* for piloting. Consult a designated Aviation Medical Examiner.

Exposure to Sun: No restrictions.

Discontinuation: Do not stop this drug without consulting your physician.

PROCAINAMIDE (proh KAYN a mide)

Introduced: 1950   **Class:** Antiarrhythmic   **Prescription:** USA: Yes   **Controlled Drug:**   USA: No; Canada: No   **Available as Generic:** USA: Yes; Canada: No

Brand Names: ✿Apo-Procainamide, Procamide SR, Procanbid, Procan SR (no longer manufactured), Promine, Pronestyl, Pronestyl-SR, Rhythmin

Author's Note: Information in this profile has been shortened to make room for more widely used medicines.

PROCHLORPERAZINE (proh klor PER a zeen)

Introduced: 1956   **Class:**   Antipsychotic, antiemetic, phenothiazines
Prescription: USA: Yes   **Controlled Drug:**   USA: No; Canada: No
Available as Generic: USA: Yes; Canada: Yes

Brand Names: ✿Combid [CD], Compazine, Eskatrol, Isopro, ✿PMS-Prochlorperazine, Regal-BID, ✿Stemetil, Ultrazine [CD]

BENEFITS versus RISKS

Possible Benefits	*Possible Risks*
EFFECTIVE CONTROL OF ACUTE MENTAL DISORDERS, NAUSEA, AND VOMITING	SERIOUS TOXIC EFFECTS ON BRAIN WITH LONG-TERM USE
Relief of anxiety and nervous tension	Liver damage with jaundice
	Blood cell disorders: abnormally low white cell and platelet counts

---

▷ **Principal Uses**

As a Single Drug Product: Uses currently included in FDA-approved labeling: (1) Relieves severe nausea and vomiting (such as from chemotherapy); (2) may be used to treat schizophrenia; (3) helps prevent motion sickness; (4) eases anxiety.

Other (unlabeled) generally accepted uses: (1) Sometimes used to increase the effects of anesthesia; (2) may be of use in treating Ménère's disease (for nausea and vomiting); (3) may have a role in migraine.

As a Combination Drug Product [CD]: This drug is available in combination with isopropamide for use in treating stomach (peptic) ulcers.

How This Drug Works: By inhibiting the action of dopamine, this drug acts to correct an imbalance of nerve impulse transmissions that is thought to be responsible for certain mental disorders. By blocking dopamine in the brain's chemoreceptor trigger zone, this drug prevents stimulation of this vomiting center.

Available Dosage Forms and Strengths

Capsules, prolonged action — 10 mg, 15 mg, 30 mg

Injection — 5 mg/ml

Suppositories — 2.5 mg, 5 mg, 25 mg

Syrup — 5 mg/5 ml

Tablets — 5 mg, 10 mg, 25 mg

▷ **Usual Adult Dosage Ranges:** *For Nausea and Vomiting*: 5 to 10 mg three or four times daily. The sustained-release capsule can be taken as 15 mg when you wake up in the morning or 10 mg of the sustained-release form every 12 hours. Doses above 40 mg should be reserved only for resistant cases.

For Moderate to Severe Psychotic Problems: Initially 10 mg of the immediate-release form every 6 to 8 hours. If needed and tolerated, dose may be increased by 5 mg at intervals of 3 to 4 days. Usual range is 50 to 75 mg daily. The total daily dose should not exceed 150 mg.

Note: Actual dose and dosing schedule must be determined for each patient individually.

Conditions Requiring Dosing Adjustments

Liver Function: This drug should be used with caution by patients with liver compromise. Specific guidelines for dose adjustment are not available.

Kidney Function: Specific guidelines for adjustment of doses are not available.

▷ **Dosing Instructions:** The tablets may be crushed and taken with or following food to reduce stomach irritation. Prolonged-action capsules should be swallowed whole without alteration. For the syrup form, make certain to use a dosing cup or a calibrated measuring spoon. If you forget a dose and you take several doses a day, take the missed dose as soon as you remember it, unless your next dose is due in about an hour—if that is the case, skip the missed dose and take the next dose right on schedule. If you only take one dose a day, take the missed dose as soon as you remember it, unless it's almost time for your next dose—then skip the dose you forgot and take the next dose on schedule. Talk with your doctor if you find yourself missing doses.

Usual Duration of Use: Use on a regular schedule for 12 to 24 hours usually determines effectiveness in controlling nausea and vomiting. If used for severe anxiety-tension states or acute psychotic behavior, a trial of several weeks is usually necessary to determine effectiveness. If not significantly beneficial within 6 weeks, it should be stopped. Consult your physician on a regular basis.

Typical Treatment Goals and Measurements (Outcomes and Markers)

Vomiting: The goal is to prevent or at least to decrease vomiting (emesis) frequency, amount, or severity. If goals are NOT met, call your doctor—there are a number of other medicines that can be tried.

▷ **This Drug Should Not Be Taken If**

- you have had an allergic reaction to it previously.
- you have active liver disease.
- you have signs that are indicative of Reye's syndrome.
- you have extremely low blood pressure.
- this drug was prescribed for a child who is less than 2 years old or who weighs less than 20 lb.
- you have a current blood cell or bone marrow disorder.

▷ **Inform Your Physician Before Taking This Drug If**
  • you are allergic or abnormally sensitive to any phenothiazine drug (see Drug Classes).
  • you have impaired liver or kidney function.
  • you have any type of seizure disorder.
  • you have bone marrow depression or a history of blood diseases or ulcers.
  • you have diabetes, glaucoma or heart disease.
  • you have prostate trouble (prostatic hypertrophy).
  • you are pregnant.
  • you have had neuroleptic malignant syndrome or lupus erythematosus.
  • you are taking any drug with sedative effects.
  • you plan to have surgery under general or spinal anesthesia in the near future.

Possible Side Effects (natural, expected, and unavoidable drug actions)
  Drowsiness (usually during the first 2 weeks), orthostatic hypotension (see Glossary), blurred vision, dry mouth, nasal congestion, constipation, impaired urination. Pink or purple coloration of urine—of no significance.

▷ **Possible Adverse Effects** (unusual, unexpected, and infrequent reactions)
  If any of the following develop, consult your physician promptly for guidance.
  Mild Adverse Effects
  Allergic reactions: skin rash, hives, low-grade fever.
  Lowering of body temperature, especially in the elderly (see hypothermia in Glossary)—possible.
  Increased appetite and weight gain—possible.
  Increased blood pressure—infrequent.
  Dizziness, weakness—frequent.
  Agitation, insomnia, impaired day and night vision—infrequent.
  Chronic constipation, fecal impaction, incontinence—infrequent.
  Serious Adverse Effects
  Allergic reactions: hepatitis with jaundice (see Glossary), usually between second and fourth week; high fever; asthma; anaphylactic reaction (see Glossary).
  Idiosyncratic reactions: toxic dermatitis, Stevens-Johnson Syndrome.
  Neuroleptic malignant syndrome (see Glossary).
  Liver toxicity or porphyria—case reports.
  Abnormal eye positioning (oculogyric crisis)—case reports.
  Depression, disorientation, seizures—case reports.
  Abnormally high blood pressure—rare.
  Disturbances of heart rhythm, rapid heart rate—rare.
  Bone marrow depression (see Glossary)—case reports (call your doctor if you get a sore throat or infection).
  Parkinson-like disorders (see Glossary); muscle spasms of face, jaw, neck, back, extremities; slowed movements, muscle rigidity, tremors; tardive dyskinesias (see Glossary)—case reports.

▷ **Possible Effects on Sexual Function:** Altered timing and pattern of menstruation.
  Female breast enlargement with milk production—case reports.
  Causes false-positive pregnancy test result.
  Male breast enlargement and tenderness (gynecomastia), inhibited ejaculation or priapism (see Glossary)—case reports.

▷ **Adverse Effects That May Mimic Natural Diseases or Disorders**
Nervous system reactions may suggest Parkinson's disease. Liver reactions may suggest viral hepatitis. Reactions resembling systemic lupus erythematosus can occur.

Natural Diseases or Disorders That May Be Activated by This Drug
Latent epilepsy, glaucoma, diabetes mellitus, prostatism (see Glossary).

Possible Effects on Laboratory Tests
White blood cell count: decreased.
Liver function tests: increased enzymes (ALT/GPT, AST/GOT, alkaline phosphatase) or bilirubin.

CAUTION
1. Many over-the-counter medications (see Glossary) for allergies, colds and coughs contain drugs that can interact unfavorably with this drug. Ask your doctor or pharmacist for help before using any such medications.
2. Aluminum- or magnesium-containing antacids can limit absorption of this drug and reduce its effectiveness.
3. Obtain prompt evaluation of any change or disturbance of vision.

Precautions for Use
By Infants and Children: Do not use this drug in infants under 2 years of age (or less than 20 pounds) or in children of any age with symptoms suggestive of Reye's syndrome (see Glossary). Children with acute illnesses ("flu-like" infections, measles, chicken pox, etc.) are very susceptible to adverse effects when this drug is given to control nausea and vomiting.
By Those Over 60 Years of Age: Small starting doses are advisable. You may be more susceptible to drowsiness, lethargy, constipation, lowering of body temperature (hypothermia), and orthostatic hypotension (see Glossary). This drug can worsen existing prostatism (see Glossary). You may also be more susceptible to the development of Parkinson-like reactions and/or tardive dyskinesia (see discussion of these terms in Glossary). These reactions must be recognized early, because they may become unresponsive to treatment and irreversible.

▷ **Advisability of Use During Pregnancy**
Pregnancy Category: C. See Pregnancy Risk Categories at the back of this book.
Animal Studies: Cleft palate reported in mouse and rat studies.
Human Studies: Case reports of congenital problems (atrophy of a hand and amputation) with use of this medicine during the first three months (trimester) of pregnancy have been reported, but cause and effect not proven. Information from adequate studies of pregnant women is not available.
Talk to your doctor about this benefit-to-risk decision. Avoid drug during the first three months and the final month because of possible effects on the newborn infant. Limit use to small and infrequent doses.

Advisability of Use If Breast-Feeding
Presence of this drug in breast milk: Yes, in small amounts.
Stop nursing or change to a different medicine. Talk to your doctor before making any medicine changes.

Habit-Forming Potential: None, but it has been used in combination with pentazocine as a heroin substitute by some drug abusers.

Effects of Overdose: Marked drowsiness, weakness, tremor, agitation, unsteadiness, deep sleep, coma, convulsions.

Possible Effects of Long-Term Use: Tardive dyskinesia. Eye changes—opacities in cornea or lens, retinal pigmentation.

Suggested Periodic Examinations While Taking This Drug (at physician's discretion)

Complete blood cell counts, especially between the 4th and 10th weeks of treatment.

Liver function tests.

Electrocardiograms.

Complete eye examinations—eye structures and vision.

Careful inspection of the tongue for early evidence of fine, involuntary, wavelike movements that could indicate the beginning of tardive dyskinesia.

▷ **While Taking This Drug, Observe the Following**

Foods: No restrictions. Vitamin C in high doses may lower therapeutic benefits.

Herbal Medicines or Minerals: Since part of the way that ginkgo and ginseng works may be as a MAO inhibitor, the combination is NOT advisable. Eucalyptus, kava, valerian, and other herbal products, which may have toxic effects on the liver, are not advisable. Combination is also not advisable for betel nut as movement disorders have been reported with combined use of medicines from the same family. Both prochlorperazine and St. John's wort may lead to increased sun sensitivity—CAUTION IS ADVISED. Evening primrose oil may increase seizure risk if combined with medicines in this family and is not advisable.

Nutritional Support: A riboflavin (vitamin B2) supplement should be taken with long-term use.

Beverages: No restrictions. May be taken with milk.

▷ *Alcohol:* Avoid completely. Alcohol can increase phenothiazine sedation and accentuate depressant effects on brain function and blood pressure. Phenothiazines can increase intoxicating effects of alcohol.

Tobacco Smoking: Possible reduction of drowsiness from drug. I advise everyone to quit smoking.

Marijuana Smoking: Moderate increase in drowsiness; accentuation of orthostatic hypotension; increased risk of precipitating latent psychoses, confusing the interpretation of mental status and drug responses.

▷ *Other Drugs*

Prochlorperazine may ***increase*** the effects of
• all atropinelike drugs and cause nervous system toxicity.
• cisapride (Propulsid), increasing risk of dangerous heart rhythms.
• gatifloxacin (Tequin), grepafloxacin (Raxar), moxifloxacin (Avelox), or sparfloxacin (Zagam), increasing risk of abnormal heartbeats.
• all sedative drugs, especially meperidine (Demerol), and cause excessive sedation.

Prochlorperazine may ***decrease*** the effects of
• guanethidine (Ismelin, Esimil) and reduce its effectiveness in lowering blood pressure.

Prochlorperazine ***taken concurrently*** with
• dofetilide (Tikosyn), increases risk of abnormal heartbeats.
• lithium (Lithobid, others) may lead to movement disorders and brain damage.
• MAO inhibitors (see Drug Classes) may result in increased risk of abnormal body movements (extrapyramidal reactions).
• medicines such as amiodarone (Cordarone), dofetilide (Tikosyn) and other medicines such as class I, IA, or III antiarrhythmics, clarithromycin, cotri-

moxazole, ondansetron, ziprazidone, and others may lead to prolongation of the QTc interval and undesirable effects. Combination is not recommended.

- oral antidiabetic drugs (see Drug Classes) may blunt their therapeutic benefits.
- phenytoin (Dilantin, others) or fosphenytoin (Cerebyx) may have variable effects on phenytoin blood levels; more frequent blood levels are prudent if these drugs are combined.
- propranolol (Inderal) may cause increased effects of both drugs; monitor drug effects closely and adjust doses as necessary.
- ritonavir (Norvir) may lead to prochlorperazine toxicity.
- tramadol (Ultram) may increase seizure risk.
- zotepine (Nipolept) may increase seizure risk.

The following drugs may decrease the effects of prochlorperazine:

- antacids containing aluminum and/or magnesium.
- benztropine (Cogentin).
- trihexyphenidyl (Artane).

▷ *Driving, Hazardous Activities:* This drug can impair mental alertness, judgment, and physical coordination. Avoid hazardous activities.

Aviation Note: The use of this drug *is a disqualification* for piloting. Consult a designated Aviation Medical Examiner.

Exposure to Sun: Use caution until sensitivity has been determined. Some phenothiazines can cause photosensitivity (see Glossary).

Exposure to Heat: Use caution and avoid excessive heat as much as possible. This drug may impair the regulation of body temperature and increase the risk of heatstroke.

Exposure to Cold: Use caution and dress warmly. This drug can increase the risk of hypothermia in the elderly.

Discontinuation: After long-term use, do not stop this drug suddenly. Gradual withdrawal over 2 to 3 weeks under physician supervision is recommended.

PROPAFENONE (pro PAAF in own)

Introduced: 1998 **Class:** Antiarrhythmic (1C) **Prescription:** USA: Yes **Controlled Drug:** USA: No; Canada: No **Available as Generic:** Yes

Brand Names: ✤Apo-Propafenone, ✤Gen-Propafenone, Rythmol

BENEFITS versus RISKS	
Possible Benefits	*Possible Risks*
EFFECTIVE TREATMENT IN SELECTED HEART RHYTHM DISORDERS	NARROW TREATMENT RANGE
	May worsen some arrhythmias
	Rare liver injury, reduced white blood cell count or positive ANA
BENEFICIAL IN LIFE-THREATENING VENTRICULAR ARRHYTHMIAS	

▷ **Principal Uses**

As a Single Drug Product: Uses currently included in FDA-approved labeling: (1) Helps correct abnormal heartbeats (symptomatic paroxysmal atrial fibrillation or PAF or symptomatic paroxysmal supraventricular tachycardia or PSVT) in people who do not have structural heart disease; (2) treats life-threatening ventricular arrhythmias (such as sustained ventricular tachycardia); (3) PREVENTS abnormal heartbeats arising in the ventricles (ventricular arrhythmias) that are caused (induced) by exercise.

Other (unlabeled) generally accepted uses: (1) Treats a variety of abnormal heartbeats not arising from the ventricles (such as supraventricular tachycardia, Wolff-Parkinson-White syndrome, and atrial flutter or fibrillation); (2) helps correct or prevent ventricular arrhythmias that are started (induced) by exercise.

How This Drug Works: Slows transmission of electrical impulses in the heart, restoring normal heart rate and rhythm in selected types of arrhythmia. (Class 1C agent that blocks the fast sodium current in Purkinje fibers and heart muscle and slows the rate of increase of Phase 0 of the action potential.) Because this medicine is chemically (structurally) close to propranolol (Inderal) a beta blocker, it does have some action as a beta blocker.

Available Dosage Forms and Strengths

Tablets, coated — 150 mg, 225 mg, 300 mg

▷ **Usual Adult Dosage Ranges:** *Arrhythmia*: Dosing is started with 150 mg every 8 hours (450 mg daily). Dosing can then be increased (every 3 to 4 days), as needed and tolerated to 225 mg every eight hours or 300 mg every eight hours (900 mg daily). If the heartbeat changes (QRS widens) or if there is second- or third-degree heart (atrioventricular) block, consideration should be given to lowering the dose. Testing blood levels is advised even though they have not related well to clinical effects.

Recently Started (Onset) Atrial Fibrillation: One loading dose by mouth of 600 mg often works, but intravenous treatment gets better results in the first two hours. Some clinicians have used 150 mg every 4 hours to convert this kind of atrial fibrillation to normal sinus rhythm in 48 hours (for patients who do not have cardiovascular decompensation).

Note: Actual dose and schedule must be determined for each patient individually.

Conditions Requiring Dosing Adjustments

Liver Function: The dose should be decreased by 20 to 30 percent, and blood levels should be checked more frequently.

Kidney Function: The kidneys remove only one percent of this drug. More frequent check of blood levels is prudent.

▷ **Dosing Instructions:** The tablet may be opened and taken with food or milk to reduce stomach upset. Take at the same times each day to obtain uniform results (even blood levels). If you forget a dose: Take the missed dose as soon as you remember it, unless you are more than four hours late—if that is the case, skip the missed dose and take the next dose right on schedule. DO NOT double doses. Talk with your doctor if you find yourself missing doses. Adherence—taking your medicine right on time and in the right dose is very important!

Usual Duration of Use: Use on a regular schedule determines effectiveness in correcting or preventing responsive rhythm disorders. If effective, use will often be ongoing. The time it takes to reach its peak effect can vary from patient to patient and may require dosing adjustments. Long-term use requires physician supervision. Use in stopping (aborting) recent onset atrial fibrillation may produce immediate results.

Typical Treatment Goals and Measurements (Outcomes and Markers)

Abnormal Heartbeats: The general goal is to return the heart to a normal rhythm or at least to markedly reduce the occurrence of abnormal heartbeats. In life-threatening arrhythmias, the goal is to abort the abnormal beats and return the pattern to normal. Success at ongoing suppression may involve ambulatory checks of heart rate and rhythm for a day (such as in Holter monitoring). This kind of testing involves placement of adhesive-backed temporary electrodes on the skin in several positions around the heart. A small heart rate and rhythm (EKG or ECG) recording device is carried around via a shoulder strap and records what the heart is doing over 24 hours. Once the recording is made, a scanning machine reviews the record, tallies abnormal heartbeats or rhythms and gives a close and extended look at how the heart is reacting or benefiting from the medicines that the patient is taking. Repeat measurements can be made if doses are changed to check the success at keeping the heart in normal sinus rhythm.

▷ **This Drug Should Not Be Taken If**
- you have had an allergic reaction to it previously.
- your electrolytes are out of balance (talk to your doctor).
- you have second- or third-degree heart block (determined by electrocardiogram), uncorrected by a pacemaker.
- you have congestive heart failure that is not controlled.
- your bronchi are subject to spasm (bronchospasm).
- you have an excessively slow heartbeat (bradycardia).

▷ **Inform Your Physician Before Taking This Drug If**
- you had adverse reactions to other antiarrhythmic drugs.
- you have a seizure disorder.
- you have a history of heart disease of any kind, especially "heart block" or heart failure AND YOU DO NOT HAVE A PACEMAKER.
- you have impaired liver function.
- you have had an antinuclear antibody (ANA) test and the result (titer) was elevated.
- you have difficulty making sperm (spermatogenesis).
- you are prone to low blood pressure.
- you take digitalis, a potassium supplement or any diuretic drug that can cause potassium loss (ask your doctor).

Possible Side Effects (natural, expected, and unavoidable drug actions)
Dizziness (may be frequent), unpleasant taste (bitter).

▷ **Possible Adverse Effects** (unusual, unexpected, and infrequent reactions)
If any of the following develop, consult your physician promptly for guidance.

Mild Adverse Effects
Allergic reaction: skin rash.
Fatigue, sleep problems, headache, tremor—rare to infrequent.
Drug-induced fever—case report.
Cough or wheezing—case report.
Hair loss (alopecia)—rare.
Loss of appetite, nausea, vomiting, constipation, diarrhea, abdominal pain—rare to infrequent.

Serious Adverse Effects
Allergic reactions: anaphylaxis—case report.
Idiosyncratic reactions: not reported.

Peripheral neuropathy—case report.

Seizure—case report.

Drug-induced heart rhythm disorders: shortness of breath, palpitations, chest pain, swelling, ventricular fibrillation—infrequent.

Congestive heart failure—rare.

Lowered sodium and increased urination (SIADH)—case reports.

Systemic lupus erythematosus—case report.

Kidney (renal) failure—case reports.

Liver damage with jaundice (see Glossary)—case reports (may happen after 2–4 weeks or after prolonged therapy).

Low white blood cell or platelet counts: fever, sore throat, abnormal bleeding/bruising—case reports.

▷ **Possible Effects on Sexual Function:**
Decreased sperm formation—possible.
Impotence—rare.

▷ **Adverse Effects That May Mimic Natural Diseases or Disorders**
Liver toxicity may suggest viral hepatitis.

Natural Diseases or Disorders That May Be Activated by This Drug
Latent epilepsy.

Possible Effects on Laboratory Tests
Blood white cell and platelet counts: decreased.
Liver function tests: increased liver enzymes (ALT/GPT, AST/GOT)—rare.
ANA titer: possibly increasing.

CAUTION
1. Thorough evaluation of your heart function (including electrocardiograms) is necessary prior to using this drug.
2. Periodic evaluation of your heart function is needed to determine your response to this drug. Some individuals may experience worsening of their heart rhythm disorder and/or deterioration of heart function. Close monitoring of heart rate, rhythm, and overall performance is essential.
3. Dose must be adjusted carefully for each person. Do not change your dose without talking to your doctor.
4. Do not take any other antiarrhythmic drug while taking this drug unless you are directed to do so by your physician.
5. Carry a card in your purse or wallet saying that you take this drug. Tell health care providers that you take it.
6. In roughly 10% of patients and in people who also take quinidine, propafenone removal (metabolism) is slower than in other patients. Lower doses and more frequent blood level checks are prudent.
7. Removal of this drug from the body happens in a way that can become filled up (saturable biotransformation). This means that a small dose change may result in a larger than normally expected increase in blood level. If dosing is changed, a recheck of blood levels is prudent.
8. In a study called CAST (Cardiac Arrhythmia Suppression Trial), medicines similar to propafenone (Class 1C) used in patients who had a heart attack (MI) more than 6 days after the heart attack in treating non-life-threatening ventricular arrhythmias were found to actually lead to an increased risk of reversed cardiac arrest or death.
9. If an ANA titer is checked and persists or worsens, consideration must be given to stopping this medicine.

10. This medicine has NOT been evaluated for use in ongoing or chronic atrial fibrillation.

Precautions for Use

By Infants and Children: Safety and effectiveness have not been established.

By Those Over 60 Years of Age: Reduced liver function may require reduction in dose. Lower doses and slower increases (if required) in doses are prudent, and are needed in those with previous heart (myocardial) damage. Watch carefully for light-headedness, dizziness, unsteadiness, and tendency to fall. One study reported use of one 600-mg loading dose of propafenone as effective for treating atrial fibrillation that has recently started.

▷ **Advisability of Use During Pregnancy**

Pregnancy Category: C. See Pregnancy Risk Categories at the back of this book.

Animal Studies: No birth defects reported in mice, rats, or rabbits, but an increased rate of fetal resorption was found.

Human Studies: Adequate studies of pregnant women are not available.

Avoid during first 3 months. Use this drug only if clearly needed. Ask your physician for guidance.

Advisability of Use If Breast-Feeding

Presence of this drug in breast milk: Yes.

This is a benefit-to-risk decision to be discussed with your doctor.

Habit-Forming Potential: None.

Effects of Overdose: Marked drop in blood pressure, abnormal heart rhythms, slow heartbeat, seizures.

Possible Effects of Long-Term Use: Liver function tests may increase.

Suggested Periodic Examinations While Taking This Drug (at physician's discretion)

Electrocardiograms.

Complete blood cell counts.

Liver function tests.

Blood levels.

ANA titer.

▷ **While Taking This Drug, Observe the Following**

Foods: No restrictions. Ask your physician about the need for salt restriction.

Herbal Medicines or Minerals: Kola, guarana, St. John's wort, ma huang, and yohimbe may cause additive heart rate or rhythm problems. These are not advisable if you have heart rhythm difficulties. Using St. John's wort, ma huang, ephedra, or kola while taking this medicine may result in unacceptable heart stimulation. Belladonna, henbane, scopolia, pheasant's eye extract or lily of the valley, or squill powdered extracts should NOT be taken if you have abnormal heart rhythms.

Beverages: Caffeine may have an effect on heart rate and may not be desirable. Talk to your doctor about caffeine. Can be taken with milk.

▷ *Alcohol:* Use caution. Alcohol can increase the blood pressure–lowering effects of this drug.

Tobacco Smoking: Nicotine may irritate the heart, reducing drug effectiveness. I advise everyone to quit smoking.

▷ *Other Drugs*

Propafenone may ***increase*** the effects of

- amitriptyline (Elavil, others) and perhaps other tricyclic antidepressants.
- antihypertensive drugs and cause excessive lowering of blood pressure.
- beta blockers (such as metoprolol or propranolol: see Drug Classes).

- clozapine (Clozaril), leading to toxicity. Downward dose adjustments and blood levels are prudent.
- cyclosporine (Sandimmune), leading to toxicity.
- quinidine (Quinaglute, various).
- theophylline (Theo-Dur, others), leading to theophylline toxicity and seizures.
- warfarin (Coumadin, others); more frequent INR tests and dose adjustments are needed.

Propafenone *taken concurrently* with

- amiodarone (Cordarone) may lead to excessive propafenone levels and toxicity, and because of possible undesirable effects on heart rhythm, combination not recommended.
- bupropion (Zyban, Wellbutrin) increases propafenone levels and can cause toxicity.
- digoxin (Lanoxin, others) increases digoxin levels and can cause toxicity.
- drugs that inhibit or are removed by CYP 2D6 (talk to your doctor) may increase propafenone effects.
- fluoxetine (Prozac) may lead to increased propafenone blood levels and toxicity if doses are not adjusted.
- medicines such as amiodarone (Cordarone), dofetilide (Tikosyn) and other medicines such as class I, IA, or III antiarrhythmics, clarithromycin, cotrimoxazole, ondansetron, ziprazidone, and others may lead to prolongation of the QTc interval and undesirable effects. Combination is not recommended.
- paroxetine (Paxil) may lead to increased propafenone blood levels and toxicity if doses are not adjusted.
- quinidine (Quinaglute) may increase propafenone levels and lead to toxicity if doses are not adjusted.
- ritonavir (Norvir) and perhaps other protease inhibitors (see Drug Classes) may lead to propafenone toxicity.
- sertraline (Zoloft) may lead to propafenone toxicity.

The following drugs may *decrease* the effects of propafenone:

- carbamazepine (Tegretol).
- phenobarbital (various).
- rifampin (Rifadin, Rimactane).

▷ *Driving, Hazardous Activities:* This drug may cause weakness, dizziness, or blurred vision. Restrict activities as necessary.

Aviation Note: The use of this drug *may be a disqualification* for piloting. Consult a designated Aviation Medical Examiner.

Exposure to Sun: No restrictions.

Occurrence of Unrelated Illness: Vomiting, diarrhea, or dehydration can affect this drug's action adversely. Report such developments promptly.

Discontinuation: Should not be stopped abruptly after long-term use. Ask your doctor about slowly reducing the dose.

PROPIONIC ACID (NONSTEROIDAL ANTI-INFLAMMATORY DRUG) FAMILY

Fenoprofen   (FEN oh proh fen)   **Flurbiprofen**   (flur BI proh fen)
Ibuprofen   (common: I byu PROH fen; correct: i BYU proh fen)   **Ketoprofen**   (kee toh PROH fen)   **Naproxen**   (na PROX in)   **Oxaprozin**
(OX a proh zin)

Introduced: 1976, 1977, 1974, 1973, 1974, 1992, respectively   **Class:** Analgesic, mild; NSAIDs   **Prescription:**   USA: Varies   **Controlled Drug:**   USA: No; Canada: No   **Available as Generic:**   Yes

Brand Names: *Fenoprofen*: Nalfon, *Flurbiprofen*: Ansaid, ✤Apo-Flurbiprofen, ✤Froben, ✤Froben-SR, Novo-Flurbiprofen, Ocufen, *Ibuprofen*: Aches-N-Pain, Actiprofen, Advil, Advil Migraine, ✤Amersol, ✤Apo-Ibuprofen, Arthritis Foundation Pain Reliever/Fever Reducer, Bayer Select, Children's Advil, Children's Motrin, Children's Motrin Drops (nonprescription), Children's Motrin Suspension (nonprescription), CoAdvil [CD], Dimetapp Sinus [CD], Dologesic, Dristan Sinus, Excedrin IB, Genpril, Guildprofen, Haltran, Ibu, Ibuprohm, Junior Strength Motrin Caplets (nonprescription), Medipren, Medi-Profen, Midol IB, Motrin, Motrin IB, ✤Novo-Profen, Nuprin, PediaProfen, Profen-IB, Rufen, Superior Pain Medicine, Supreme Pain Medicine, Tab-Profen, *Ketoprofen*: Actron (12.5 mg nonprescription), ✤Apo-Keto, ✤Apo-Keto E, Orudis, Orudis E-50, Orudis E-100, Orudis KT (nonprescription), Orudis SR, Oruvail, Oruvail ER, ✤Oruvail SR, ✤Rhodis, ✤Rhodis EC, ✤Rhodis EC Suppository, *Naproxen*: Aleve (220 mg nonprescription), Anaprox, Anaprox DS, ✤Apo-Naproxen, Naprelan, Naprelan Once Daily, Naprosyn, ✤Naxen, Neo-Prox, ✤Novo-Naprox, ✤Nu-Naprox, ✤Synflex, *Oxaprozin*: Daypro

Author's Note: Ibuprofen was found to interfere with the beneficial effects of aspirin on the heart (MI prophylaxis). At the time of this writing, the combination is NOT advisable. Talk to your doctor about the state of this data and his or her impression.

BENEFITS versus RISKS	
Possible Benefits	*Possible Risks*
EFFECTIVE RELIEF OF MILD TO MODERATE PAIN AND INFLAMMATION	Gastrointestinal pain, ulceration, bleeding
EFFECTIVE RELIEF OF FEVER	Kidney damage
ADVIL MIGRAINE WORKS TO TREAT MIGRAINE HEADACHES	Fluid retention
	Bone marrow depression (except oxaprozin)
	Liver toxicity (all rare)
	Ibuprofen may blunt heart protective effects of aspirin

▷ **Principal Uses**

As a Single Drug Product: Uses currently included in FDA-approved labeling: (1) All six agents in this class treat rheumatoid and osteoarthritis; (2) naproxen is useful in treating bursitis, gout, dysmenorrhea (ketoprofen and ibuprofen are also approved for use in primary dysmenorrhea), pain, juvenile rheumatoid arthritis, and tendonitis; (3) fenoprofen is the only agent approved to treat tennis elbow; (4) flurbiprofen ophthalmic is used to prevent intraoperative miosis; (5) Advil Migraine form treats migraine headaches.

Other (unlabeled) generally accepted uses: (1) Naproxen has been used to treat migraine and colds caused by rhinoviruses; (2) oxaprozin is useful in gout and tendonitis; (3) ketoprofen may have a role in temporal arteritis; (4) flurbiprofen has some support for therapy of periodontal disease; (5) fenoprofen has been used successfully in therapy of migraine; (6) ibuprofen treats interleukin-2 toxicity and chronic urticaria and can decrease

IUD-associated bleeding; (7) all of the agents have been used for a variety of pains and fever; (8) ibuprofen has data from a study of 148 infants with patent ductus arteriosus comparing it to indomethacin. The research concluded that benefits were similar, and ibuprofen caused less decreased urine (oliguria).

How These Drugs Work: They reduce levels of prostaglandins (and related compounds), chemicals involved in inflammation and pain.

Available Dosage Forms and Strengths

Fenoprofen:

Capsules — 200 mg, 300 mg, 600 mg
Tablets — 600 mg

Flurbiprofen:

Ophthalmic drops — 0.03%
Tablets — 50 mg, 100 mg

Ibuprofen:

Caplets — 200 mg
Oral suspension — 50 mg/1.25 mg, 100 mg/5 ml
Tablets — 40 mg, 200 mg, 300 mg, 400 mg, 600 mg, 800 mg
Tablets, chewable — 50 mg, 100 mg

Ketoprofen:

Capsules — 50 mg, 75 mg, 100 mg, 150 mg
Suppositories (Canada) — 100 mg
Tablets, enteric (Canada) — 50 mg
Tablets (nonprescription) — 12.5 mg

Naproxen:

Caplets — 220 mg
Naprelan Once Daily — 375 mg, 500 mg
Oral suspension — 125 mg/5 ml
Rectal suppository (Canada) — 500 mg
Tablets — 125 mg, 250 mg, 275 mg, 375 mg, 500 mg, 550 mg
Tablets, controlled-release — 375 mg, 500 mg

Oxaprozin:

Caplets — 600 mg
Tablets — 600 mg

▷ **Usual Adult Dosage Ranges:**

Fenoprofen: 300 to 600 mg three or four times daily. Daily maximum is 3,200 mg.

Flurbiprofen: 100 to 300 mg daily in two to four divided doses. The lowest effective dose should be used. Daily maximum is 300 mg.

Ibuprofen: 200 to 800 mg three or four times daily. Total daily dose should not exceed 3,200 mg.

Ketoprofen: 75 mg three times daily or 50 mg four times daily. Usual daily dose is 100 to 300 mg, divided into three or four doses. Daily maximum is 300 mg.

Naproxen: Gout — 750 mg initially and then 250 mg every 8 hours until attack is relieved. Arthritis — 250 mg, 375 mg or 500 mg twice daily, 12 hours apart. The sustained-release form (Naprelan) offers an intestinal-protective drug absorption system (IPDAS) and once-daily (two tablets once a day) dosing. Menstrual pain — 500 mg initially and then 250 mg every 6 to 8 hours as needed. Maximum dose for pain is 1,375 mg.

Oxaprozin: 1,200 mg as a single daily dose in the morning. Daily maximum is 1,800 mg (or 26 mg per kg of body mass for patients with normal liver and kidney function).

Author's Note: Medicines in this class with available nonprescription forms usually have lower daily maximum doses. For example, Children's Motrin is approved for nonprescription use as temporary relief of minor aches and pains or reduction of fever in children 2 years of age and older. Adverse effects are also less common and fewer in number. Less than 11 kg of body mass and under 2 years old—consult your doctor; 2 to 3 years old and 11–15.9 kg of body mass — 100 mg every 6 to 8 hours. Up to four doses may be given a day. Use should NOT go on for longer than 3 days. Please look carefully at individual package labels or ask your pharmacist or doctor for dosing advice.

Note: Actual dose and dosing schedule must be determined for each patient individually.

Conditions Requiring Dosing Adjustments

Liver Function: All of these drugs are metabolized in the liver and therefore should be used with caution and consideration given to lower doses, by patients with liver compromise.

Kidney Function: These drugs share the risks common to most nonsteroidal anti-inflammatory drugs (NSAIDs). Some patients with kidney compromise are dependent on prostaglandins for kidney function. A benefit-to-risk decision must be made regarding the use of NSAIDs by these patients.

▷ **Dosing Instructions:** Take either on an empty stomach or with food or milk to prevent stomach irritation. Take with a full glass of water and remain upright (do not lie down) for 30 minutes. The tablets may be crushed and the capsules opened, except for ketoprofen tablets (should not be crushed or altered). Sustained-release forms available in other countries should NOT be altered. Be sure to use a calibrated medication spoon or a calibrated medicine dosing cup for liquid forms. If you forget a dose: Take the missed dose as soon as you remember it, unless it's nearly time for your next dose—if that is the case, skip the missed dose and take the next dose right on schedule. DO NOT double doses. Talk with your doctor if you find yourself missing doses.

Usual Duration of Use: Use on a regular schedule for 1 to 2 weeks usually determines effectiveness for some conditions. Peak oxaprozin effect may take 6 weeks in arthritis. Long-term use requires supervision and periodic physician evaluation. If you feel that you require a nonprescription form for more than occasional use, please talk to your doctor about an evaluation of the problem you are taking the nonprescription form for.

Typical Treatment Goals and Measurements (Outcomes and Markers)

Pain: Most clinicians treating pain use a device called an algometer to check your pain. This looks like a small ruler, but lets the clinician better understand your pain. The goals of treatment then relate to where the level of pain started (for example, a rating of seven on a zero to ten scale) and what the cause of the pain was. I use the PQRSTBG method (see Glossary). Pain medicines may also be used together (in combination) in order to get the best result or outcome. If your pain control is not acceptable to YOU (remember, in hospitals and outpatient settings, etc., pain control is a patient right) and if after a week of arthritis pain treatment, results are not acceptable, be sure to call your doctor—you may need a different medicine or combination.

Arthritis: Control of arthritis symptoms (pain, loss of mobility, decreased ability to accomplish activities of daily living, range of motion, etc.) is paramount in returning patient quality of life and to checking the results (beneficial outcomes) from these medicines. Clinicians use the WOMAC osteoarthritis index (see Glossary) to globally assess the health status of people living with osteoarthritis. Many arthritis management or pain centers use interdisciplinary teams (physicians from several specialties, nurses, physician's assistants, physical and occupational therapists, pharmacotherapists, psychotherapists, social workers and others) to get the best results. Laboratory measures of results for rheumatoid arthritis include decreases in chemicals released by the body (acute phase reactants) such as C-reactive protein. A more general test to roughly measure inflammation is a sed rate (erythrocyte sedimentation rate). ACR improvements in characteristic signs and symptoms of RA, such as ACR 20 are widely used.

▷ **These Drugs Should Not Be Taken If**
  • you have had an allergic reaction to them previously.
  • you are subject to asthma or nasal polyps caused by aspirin.
  • you have a bleeding disorder or a blood cell disorder.
  • flurbiprofen ophthalmic drops should NOT be used by people with herpes simplex keratitis.
  • you have severe impairment of kidney function (some cases).

▷ **Inform Your Physician Before Taking These Drugs If**
  • you are allergic to aspirin or other aspirin substitutes.
  • you have active peptic ulcer disease or any form of gastrointestinal bleeding.
  • you have a history of peptic ulcer disease or any type of bleeding disorder.
  • you have impaired liver or kidney function or any active infection.
  • you start to have signs and symptoms of meningitis and are taking ibuprofen (call your doctor as the medicine should be stopped and additional tests run).
  • you have high blood pressure or a history of heart failure.
  • you are taking acetaminophen, aspirin or other aspirin substitutes, or anticoagulants.

Possible Side Effects (natural, expected, and unavoidable drug actions)
Fluid retention (weight gain); ringing in the ears. Pink, red, purple, or rust coloration of urine (ibuprofen only).

▷ **Possible Adverse Effects** (unusual, unexpected, and infrequent reactions)
If any of the following develop, consult your physician promptly for guidance.
Mild Adverse Effects
Allergic reactions: skin rash, hives, itching.
Headache, dizziness, altered or blurred vision, ringing in the ears, depression—infrequent.
Stinging or burning of the eyes with ophthalmic flurbiprofen drops—possible.
Sleep disturbances—infrequent (oxaprozin).
Mouth sores, indigestion, nausea, vomiting, constipation, diarrhea—infrequent.
Palpitations—rare (fenoprofen).
Serious Adverse Effects
Allergic reactions: anaphylactic reaction (see Glossary), severe skin reactions—rare.

Lung inflammation (naproxen—pneumonitis)—rare.

Idiosyncratic reactions: drug-induced meningitis (aseptic meningitis) with fever and coma—rare (ibuprofen and naproxen).

Active peptic ulcer, with or without bleeding—rare with 6 months of use, infrequent after 1 year of use.

Inflammation of the colon—rare.

Porphyria—case reports (some drugs in this class).

Pancreatitis or lupus erythematosus—two case reports with naproxen.

Some medicines in this class may cause Parkinson-like symptoms in susceptible patients—case reports.

Worsening of congestive heart failure—possible.

Inflammation of the esophagus—probable if patients lie down soon after taking these medicines.

Liver damage with jaundice (see Glossary)—case reports.

Kidney damage with painful urination, bloody urine, reduced urine formation—possible.

Bone marrow depression (see Glossary): fatigue, sore throat, abnormal bleeding/bruising—case reports.

▷ **Possible Effects on Sexual Function:** Altered timing and pattern of menstruation (ibuprofen, ketoprofen, and naproxen) and excessive menstrual bleeding (ibuprofen and ketoprofen)—case reports.

Male breast enlargement and tenderness—rare (ibuprofen).

Naproxen may rarely inhibit ejaculation.

Ketoprofen may rarely decrease libido.

Possible Delayed Adverse Effects: Mild anemia due to "silent" blood loss from the stomach.

▷ **Adverse Effects That May Mimic Natural Diseases or Disorders**

Liver reaction may suggest viral hepatitis.

Natural Diseases or Disorders That May Be Activated by These Drugs

Peptic ulcer disease, ulcerative colitis.

Possible Effects on Laboratory Tests

Erythrocyte sedimentation rate: decreased (a desired effect).

Complete blood cell counts: decreased red cells, hemoglobin, white cells, and platelets.

Blood cholesterol or uric acid levels: increased.

Blood lithium level: increased.

Liver function tests: increased enzymes (ALT/GPT, AST/GOT, alkaline phosphatase), or bilirubin.

Kidney function tests: increased blood creatinine and urea nitrogen (BUN) levels.

Fecal occult blood test: positive.

CAUTION

1. Dose should always be limited to the smallest amount that produces reasonable improvement.
2. These drugs may hide (mask) early signs (indications) of infection. Tell your doctor if you think you are developing an infection of any kind.
3. Congestive heart failure in elderly patients may be unmasked or worsened. Risk appears to increase with use of higher doses.
4. Controversy erupted when ibuprofen was found to have the potential to interfere with the beneficial effects of aspirin. At the time of this writing the two medicines should NOT be combined. Talk to your doctor to get the latest information on this interaction.

Precautions for Use

By Infants and Children: Safety and effectiveness for some uses for those under 12 not well established. For children with fever, ibuprofen dosing is accomplished like other medicines on a weight basis. In fever in children 6 months to 12 years, the ibuprofen prescription dose is 5 mg per kg of body weight if the fever is less than 102.5, and 10 mg per kg if the temperature is more than 102.5 degrees. The dose can be repeated every 6-8 hours, and the maximum dose is 40 mg/kg per day. Naproxen and some other medicines in this class are limited to children 12 and over for use in fighting fevers. Call your doctor if temperature continues.

By Those Over 60 Years of Age: Small doses are prudent until tolerance is determined. Watch for signs of liver or kidney toxicity, fluid retention, dizziness, confusion, impaired memory, stomach bleeding, or constipation.

▷ ## Advisability of Use During Pregnancy

Pregnancy Category: B for ibuprofen, fenoprofen, flurbiprofen, ketoprofen, and naproxen. C for oxaprozin. Ibuprofen, and fenoprofen are FDA category D if used in the final 3 months (trimester) of pregnancy. The manufacturers of ketoprofen and flurbiprofen say that both medicines should be avoided in late pregnancy. See Pregnancy Risk Categories at the back of this book.

Animal Studies: No birth defects reported in rats or rabbits.

Human Studies: Adequate studies of pregnant women are not available.

Avoid these drugs during the final 3 months. Use during the first 6 months only if clearly needed. Ask your physician for guidance.

Advisability of Use If Breast-Feeding

Presence of these drugs in breast milk: Yes or expected.

Avoid drugs or refrain from nursing for others. Ibuprofen is generally considered compatible with breast-feeding (American Academy of Pediatrics).

Habit-Forming Potential: None.

Effects of Overdose: Drowsiness, dizziness, ringing in the ears, nausea, vomiting, diarrhea, confusion, unsteadiness, stupor progressing to coma.

Possible Effects of Long-Term Use: Fluid retention.

Suggested Periodic Examinations While Taking These Drugs (at physician's discretion)

Complete blood cell counts.

Liver and kidney function tests.

Complete eye examinations if vision is altered in any way.

▷ ## While Taking These Drugs, Observe the Following

Foods: No restrictions.

Herbal Medicines or Minerals: Ginseng, ginkgo, alfalfa, clove oil, feverfew, cinchona bark, white willow bark, and garlic may also change clotting, so combining those herbals with these medicines is not recommended. Eucalyptus, kava, valerian, and other herbals may have undesirable toxic effects on the liver and should be avoided while taking these medicines on an ongoing basis. Talk to your doctor BEFORE combining any medicines. NSAIDs may decrease feverfew effects. Since St. John's wort and some of these medicines may increase sensitivity to the sun, CAUTION IS ADVISED. Hay flower, mistletoe herb, and white mustard seed carry German Commission E monograph indications for arthritis.

Beverages: No restrictions. May be taken with milk.

▷ *Alcohol:* Use with caution. The irritant action of alcohol on the stomach lining, added to the irritant action of these drugs, can increase the risk of stomach ulceration and/or bleeding.

Tobacco Smoking: No interactions expected. I advise everyone to quit smoking.

▷ *Other Drugs*

These medicines may ***increase*** the effects of

- anticoagulants (Coumadin, etc.) and increase the risk of bleeding; more frequent INR (prothrombin time or protime) tests are needed, and ongoing doses should be adjusted to the laboratory test results.
- cyclosporine (Sandimmune), leading to toxicity.
- fosphenytoin (Cerebyx) or phenytoin (Dilantin) and may lead to increased risk of antiepileptic toxicity.
- lithium (Lithobid, others), by causing toxic lithium levels.
- methotrexate (Mexate, others) and result in major methotrexate toxicity with possible anemia, hemorrhage and blood infections.
- oral hypoglycemic agents (Sulfonylureas).

These medicines may ***decrease*** the effects of

- beta blockers (see Drug Classes), such as carteolol (Cartrol).
- diuretics (see Drug Classes—Thiazides, etc.), such as hydrochlorothiazide (Esidrix) and furosemide (Lasix).

These medicines ***taken concurrently*** with the following drugs may increase the risk of bleeding; avoid these combinations if possible and closely monitor patients for bleeding (PTT or PT may not fully estimate bleeding risk):

- aspirin.
- dipyridamole (Persantine).
- eptifibatide (Integrilin).
- indomethacin (Indocin).
- ketorolac (Toradol).
- low molecular weight heparins (Lovenox, others see Drug Classes).
- sulfinpyrazone (Anturane).
- valproic acid (Depakene).
- warfarin (Coumadin).

These medicines ***taken concurrently*** with

- ACE inhibitors (see Drug Classes) can worsen kidney diseases and blunt benefits.
- alendronate (Fosamax) can worsen stomach irritation. Caution is advised.
- histamine (H2) blockers (see Drug Classes) may increase toxicity from NSAIDs.
- ofloxacin (and perhaps other fluoroquinolones; see Drug Classes) may increase risk of seizures.
- ritonavir (Norvir) may lead to toxic propionic acid NSAID levels.
- tacrine (Cognex) led to delirium in a patient taking ibuprofen.
- tacrolimus (Prograf) poses a serious risk for kidney failure. This combination is not advisable.

▷ *Driving, Hazardous Activities:* These drugs may cause drowsiness or dizziness. Restrict activities as necessary.

Aviation Note: The use of these drugs ***may be a disqualification*** for piloting. Consult a designated Aviation Medical Examiner.

Exposure to Sun: Use caution until sensitivity is determined. Ibuprofen, ketoprofen, flurbiprofen, and naproxen cause photosensitivity (see Glossary).

PROPRANOLOL (proh PRAN oh lohl)

Introduced: 1966   **Class:**   Anti-anginal, antiarrhythmic, antihypertensive, antimigraine, beta blocker   **Prescription:**   USA: Yes   **Controlled Drug:**   USA: No; Canada: No   **Available as Generic:**   Yes

Brand Names: ✤Apo-Propranolol, Betachron, ✤Detensol, Inderal, Inderal-LA, Inderide [CD], Inderide LA [CD], Innopran XL, Ipran, ✤Novo-Pranol, ✤PMS Propranolol

---

BENEFITS versus RISKS

Possible Benefits	*Possible Risks*
EFFECTIVE, WELL-TOLERATED AS ANTIANGINAL DRUG EFFORT-INDUCED ANGINA; ANTIARRHYTHMIC DRUG IN CERTAIN HEART RHYTHM DISORDERS; ANTIHYPERTENSIVE DRUG IN MILD TO MODERATE HYPERTENSION	CONGESTIVE HEART FAILURE in advanced heart disease
	Worsening of angina in coronary heart disease (if drug is abruptly withdrawn)
	Masking of low blood sugar (hypoglycemia) in drug-treated diabetes
PREVENTION OF MIGRAINE HEADACHES	Provocation of asthma (in asthmatics)
	Depression
REDUCES DEATH AND LOSS OF FUNCTION AFTER A HEART ATTACK	Blood cell disorders: low white cell and platelet counts
EASES ESSENTIAL TREMOR IN ADULTS (FAMILIAL)	
Effective adjunct in the management of pheochromocytoma	

▷ **Principal Uses**

As a Single Drug Product: Uses currently included in FDA-approved labeling: (1) Treats several cardiovascular disorders: classical effort-induced angina, certain types of heart rhythm disturbance and high blood pressure; (2) also helps prevent repeat heart attacks (myocardial infarction); (3) reduces frequency and severity of migraine headaches; (4) decreases tremors in essential and action tremor.

Other (unlabeled) generally accepted uses: (1) Helps control physical signs of anxiety and nervous tension (as in stage fright); (2) helps control familial tremors and symptoms seen with markedly overactive thyroid function (thyrotoxicosis); (3) decreases abnormal abdominal fluid accumulation (ascites) in people with cirrhosis of the liver; (4) may have a role in combination therapy with metronidazole in resistant Giardia infections; (5) helps control headaches caused by cyclosporine (Sandimmune); (6) may be useful in certain kinds of pain, especially after amputations; (7) can help control panic attacks; (8) useful in helping decrease bleeding in patients with esophageal varices and liver cirrhosis; (9) helps fight symptoms in narcotic withdrawal cases.

As a Combination Drug Product [CD]: This drug is available in combination with hydrochlorothiazide for the treatment of hypertension. This combination product includes two drugs with different mechanisms of action; it is intended to provide greater effectiveness and convenience for long-term use.

How This Drug Works: Blocks certain actions of the sympathetic nervous system:
- reducing rate and contraction force of the heart, lowering the ejection pressure of the blood leaving the heart and reducing the oxygen requirement for heart function.
- reduces degree of contraction of blood vessel walls, lowering blood pressure.
- prolongs conduction time of nerve impulses through the heart, helping manage certain heart rhythm disorders.

Available Dosage Forms and Strengths

Capsules, nighttime, prolonged-action — 80 mg, 120 mg
Capsules, prolonged-action — 60 mg, 80 mg, 120 mg, 160 mg
Concentrate — 80 mg/ml
Injection — 1 mg/ml
Oral solution — 4 mg/ml, 8 mg/ml
Tablets — 10 mg, 20 mg, 40 mg, 60 mg, 80 mg, 90 mg, 120 mg

▷ **Usual Adult Dosage Ranges:**

Anti-anginal: Initially 20 mg three or four times a day; increase dose gradually based on patient response (slowly) as needed and tolerated. The total daily dose should not exceed 320 mg. Long-acting forms are started at 80-160 mg once a day.

Antiarrhythmic: 10 to 30 mg three or four times a day as needed and tolerated.

Antihypertensive: Initially 40 mg twice a day; increase dose gradually as needed and tolerated. The total daily dose should not exceed 640 mg. The sustained-release form is started at 80 mg as single drug therapy or as combination treatment with a diuretic. Doses are slowly increased because several days to several weeks may be needed to see peak benefit from any given dose. The Inderide LA form is used after patient needs are determined individually, but is given in a starting dose of one capsule daily. The Innopran XL form is specifically formulated to be taken at bedtime (roughly 10 P.M.). The usual starting dose is 80 mg. Some patients may require 120 mg daily.

Migraine Headache Prevention: Initially 20 mg four times a day; increase dose gradually as needed and tolerated. The total daily dose should not exceed 480 mg. Long-acting formulations offer the advantage of once-daily dosing.

Note: Actual dose and schedule must be determined for each patient individually.

Conditions Requiring Dosing Adjustments

Liver Function: Used with caution by patients with liver disease. In general, lower starting doses and slower dose increases are indicated.

Kidney Function: This drug should be used with caution by people with combined kidney and liver compromise. Dose adjustments are not needed for people with compromised kidneys.

▷ **Dosing Instructions:** This drug is preferably taken 1 hour before eating to maximize absorption. The regular-release tablets may be crushed; to prevent harmless numbing effect, mix with soft food and swallow promptly. The prolonged-action (extended-release) forms should be swallowed whole (do NOT crush or chew). The Innopran XL form is specifically made as a chronotherapeutic form to be taken at night. Do not stop any form of this drug abruptly. If you forget a dose: Take the missed dose as soon as you remember it, unless it's WITHIN 8 hours of your next dose for an extended-release form or if your next dose is DUE in 4 hours for the immediate-release forms—if that is the case, skip the missed dose and take the next dose right on schedule. DO NOT double doses. Talk with your doctor if you find yourself missing doses. There are some pager-based reminder systems for medicines that can be of great help.

Usual Duration of Use: Use on a regular schedule for 10 to 14 days usually determines effectiveness in preventing angina, controlling heart rhythm disorders and lowering blood pressure. Peak benefits may take as long as 6 to 8 weeks. Long-term use is determined by your symptoms over time and response to the overall treatment program (weight reduction, salt restriction, smoking cessation, etc.). See your physician on a regular basis.

Typical Treatment Goals and Measurements (Outcomes and Markers)

Blood Pressure: The NEW guidelines (JNC VII) define normal blood pressure (BP) as **less than** 120/80. Because blood pressures that were once considered acceptable can actually lead to blood vessel damage, the committee from the National Institutes of Health, National Heart Lung and Blood Institute now have a new category called **Pre-hypertension**. This ranges from 120/80 to 139/89 and is intended to help your doctor encourage lifestyle changes (or in the case of people with a risk factor for high blood pressure, start treatment) much earlier—so that possible damage to blood vessels, your heart, kidneys, sexual potency, or eyes might be minimized or avoided altogether. The next two classes of high blood pressure are stage 1 hypertension: 140/90 to 159/99 and stage 2 hypertension equal to or greater than: 160/100 mm Hg. These guidelines also recommend that clinicians trying to control blood pressure work with their patients to agree on the goals and a plan of treatment. The first-ever guidelines for blood pressure (hypertension) in African Americans recommends that MOST black patients be started on TWO antihypertensive medicines with the goal of lowering blood pressure to 130/80 for those with high risk for heart and blood vessel disease or with diabetes. The American Diabetes Association recommends 130/80 as the target for people living with diabetes and less than 125/75 for those who spill more than one gram of protein into their urine. Most clinicians try to achieve a BP that confers the best balance of lower cardiovascular risk and avoids the problem of too low a blood pressure. Blood pressure duration is generally increased with beneficial restriction of sodium. The goals and time frame should be discussed with you when the prescription is written. If goals are not met, it is not unusual to intensify doses or add on medicines. You can find the new blood pressure guidelines at *www.nhlbi.nih.gov/guidelines/hypertension/index.html*. For the African American guidelines see Douglas J.G. in Sources.

Abnormal Heartbeats: The general goal is to return the heart to a normal rhythm or at least to markedly reduce the occurrence of abnormal heartbeats. In life-threatening arrhythmias, the goal is to abort the abnormal beats and return the pattern to normal. Success at ongoing suppression may involve ambulatory checks of heart rate and rhythm for a day (such as in Holter monitoring). This kind of testing involves placement of adhesive-backed temporary electrodes on the skin in several positions around the heart. A small heart rate and rhythm (EKG or ECG) recording device is carried around via a shoulder strap and records what the heart is doing over 24 hours. Once the recording is made, a scanning machine reviews the record, tallies abnormal heartbeats or rhythms and gives a close and extended look at how the heart is reacting or benefiting from the medicines that the patient is taking. Repeat measurements can be made if doses are changed to check the success at keeping the heart in normal sinus rhythm!

Possible Advantage of This Drug

Has a clear benefit in reducing the chance of a second heart attack once a first heart attack has been diagnosed. Data from one large research project showed that early morning blood pressure surges are an independent risk factor for strokes. The new Innopran XL form may be the ideal (optimal) dosage form to address this phenomenon.

▷ **This Drug Should Not Be Taken If**
- you have bronchial asthma.
- you have had an allergic reaction to it previously.
- you have Prinzmetal's variant angina (coronary artery spasm).
- you have heart failure (overt).
- you have Raynaud's phenomenon.
- you have an abnormally slow heart rate (bradycardia) or a serious form of heart block (second or third degree AV block).
- you are taking, or have taken within the past 14 days, any monoamine oxidase (MAO) type A inhibitor (see Drug Classes).

▷ **Inform Your Physician Before Taking This Drug If**
- you had an adverse reaction to a beta blocker (see Drug Classes).
- you have a history of serious heart disease.
- you have a history of hay fever (allergic rhinitis), asthma, chronic bronchitis or emphysema.
- you have a history of overactive thyroid function (hyperthyroidism).
- you have a history of low blood sugar (hypoglycemia).
- you have impaired liver or kidney function.
- you are allergic to bee stings.
- you have diabetes or myasthenia gravis.
- you take digitalis, quinidine or reserpine or any calcium-channel-blocker drug (see Drug Classes).
- you plan to have surgery under general anesthesia in the near future.

Possible Side Effects (natural, expected, and unavoidable drug actions)

Lethargy and fatigability, cold extremities, slow heart rate, light-headedness in upright position (see orthostatic hypotension in Glossary). Increased bowel movements.

▷ **Possible Adverse Effects** (unusual, unexpected, and infrequent reactions)

If any of the following develop, consult your physician promptly for guidance.

Mild Adverse Effects

Allergic reactions: skin rash, temporary loss of hair, drug fever (see Glossary).

Joint pain—case reports.

Headache, dizziness, insomnia, vivid dreams—infrequent.

Decreased tear production, hyperemia of the conjunctiva—rare.

Indigestion, taste disorder, nausea, vomiting, diarrhea—infrequent.

Weight gain—possible.

Serious Adverse Effects

Allergic reactions: anaphylaxis. Reactions may be exaggerated if a patient is taking this medicine and is exposed to the allergen. For example, epinephrine use can result in epinephrine resistance and severe increases in blood pressure and a reactionary (reflex) slowing of the heart rate.

Idiosyncratic reactions: acute behavioral disturbances (agitation, disorientation, confusion, hallucinations, amnesia)—case reports.

Paradoxical hypertension—case reports.

Mental depression, anxiety—case reports and dose-related.

Chest pain, shortness of breath, precipitation of congestive heart failure—possible.

Peripheral neuropathy or hyperthyroidism—rare.

Drug-induced systemic lupus erythematosus, myasthenia gravis or porphyria—case reports.

Kidney problems (interstitial nephritis)—rare.

Induction of bronchial asthma—in asthmatics.

May precipitate problems walking (intermittent claudication)—possible. May be prudent to check for hidden Peripheral Artery Disease (PAD) by checking ankle brachial index (ABI). ABI check (see Glossary) can help find PAD early, and avoid claudication that may result if this medication is taken by someone who has PAD but does not know it.

Blood cell disorders: abnormally low white blood cell or platelet counts—case reports.

Carpal tunnel syndrome—case reports.

▷ **Possible Effects on Sexual Function:** Decreased libido; impaired erection; impotence—infrequent (has the highest incidence of libido reduction and erectile impairment of all beta-blocker drugs).

Male infertility (inhibited sperm motility); Peyronie's disease (see Glossary)—possible.

▷ **Adverse Effects That May Mimic Natural Diseases or Disorders**

Reduced blood flow to extremities may resemble Raynaud's phenomenon (see Glossary).

Natural Diseases or Disorders That May Be Activated by This Drug

Prinzmetal's variant angina, Raynaud's phenomenon, intermittent claudication, myasthenia gravis (questionable).

Possible Effects on Laboratory Tests

White blood cell count: occasionally decreased.

Blood platelet count: increased or decreased.

Bleeding time: increased.

Blood total cholesterol, triglycerides or VLDL level: no effect in some; increased in others.

Blood HDL cholesterol level: no effect in some; decreased in others.

Blood LDL cholesterol level: no effect in some; increased and decreased in others.

Blood glucose level: no effect in some; increased or decreased in others (hypoglycemia more likely in type 1 diabetics).

Blood thyroid hormone levels: T3—no effect in some, decreased in others; T4—increased; free T4—increased.

Blood uric acid level: no effect in some; increased in others.

Liver function tests: increased liver enzymes (ALT/GPT, AST/GOT, and alkaline phosphatase); effects probably not due to liver damage.

CAUTION

1. ***Do not stop this drug suddenly*** without the knowledge and help of your doctor. Carry a notation that states you are taking this drug.

2. Ask your physician or pharmacist before using nasal decongestants,

which are usually present in over-the-counter cold preparations and nose drops. These can cause sudden increases in blood pressure when taken concurrently with beta-blocker drugs.

3. Report the development of any tendency to emotional depression.

Precautions for Use

By Infants and Children: Safety and effectiveness for those under 12 years of age are not established, but if this drug is used, watch for low blood sugar (hypoglycemia) during periods of reduced food intake.

By Those Over 60 Years of Age: Unacceptably high blood pressure should be reduced without creating the risks associated with excessively low blood pressure. Therapy is started with small doses and blood pressure checked frequently. Sudden, rapid, and excessive reduction of blood pressure can predispose to stroke or heart attack. Observe for dizziness, unsteadiness, tendency to fall, confusion, hallucinations, depression, or urinary frequency.

▷ **Advisability of Use During Pregnancy**

Pregnancy Category: C. See Pregnancy Risk Categories at the back of this book.

Animal Studies: No significant increase in birth defects due to this drug. Some toxic effects on embryo reported.

Human Studies: Adequate studies of pregnant women are not available.

Avoid use of drug during the first 3 months if possible. Ask your physician for guidance.

Advisability of Use If Breast-Feeding

Presence of this drug in breast milk: Yes.

Monitor nursing infant closely, and discontinue drug or nursing if adverse effects develop.

Habit-Forming Potential: None.

Effects of Overdose: Weakness, slow pulse, low blood pressure, fainting, cold and sweaty skin, congestive heart failure, possible coma, and convulsions.

Possible Effects of Long-Term Use: Reduced heart reserve and eventual heart failure in susceptible patients with advanced heart disease.

Suggested Periodic Examinations While Taking This Drug (at physician's discretion)

Complete blood cell counts.

Measurements of blood pressure.

Evaluation of heart function.

Liver function tests.

ABI check for Peripheral Artery Disease (PAD).

▷ **While Taking This Drug, Observe the Following**

Foods: Avoid excessive salt intake. Excessive fat intake can worsen existing cardiovascular disease. Talk to your doctor about a sensible diet. Some of the therapeutic lifestyle changes (Table 20) apply here.

Herbal Medicines or Minerals: Ginseng may increase blood pressure, blunting the benefits of this medicine. Hawthorn, saw palmetto, ma huang, goldenseal, yohimbe, and licorice may also cause increased blood pressure. Dong quai may block the removal of this medicine from the body leading to toxic effects with "normal" doses. St. John's wort may increase removal of this medicine from the body leading to loss of benefits despite appropriate doses. Calcium and garlic may help lower blood pressure. Indian snakeroot has a German Commission E monograph indication for hypertension—talk to your doctor. Eleuthero root and ephedra should be avoided by people living with hypertension. Ginger, vanadium, and nettle may also change blood sugar. Talk to your doctor and pharmacist BEFORE combining any herbals with this drug.

Beverages: No restrictions. May be taken with milk.

▷ *Alcohol:* Use with caution. Alcohol may exaggerate this drug's ability to lower blood pressure and may increase its mild sedative effect.

Tobacco Smoking: Nicotine may reduce this drug's effectiveness in treating angina, heart rhythm disorders, and high blood pressure. Smoking increases the rate of elimination of this drug. I advise everyone to quit smoking.

▷ *Other Drugs*

Propranolol may ***increase*** the effects of

• other antihypertensive drugs and cause excessive lowering of blood pressure; dose adjustments may be necessary.
• lidocaine (Xylocaine, etc.).
• quinidine (Quinaglute). Careful patient monitoring for heart failure, excessively low blood pressure, and very slow heart rate is required.
• reserpine (Ser-Ap-Es, etc.) and cause sedation, depression, slowing of the heart rate, and lowering of blood pressure.
• rizatriptan (Maxalt); a 5-mg starting dose and a maximum of 15 mg of rizatriptan should be used if these medicines are combined.
• verapamil (Calan, Isoptin) and cause excessive depression of heart function; monitor this combination closely.
• warfarin (Coumadin) and increase bleeding risk; more frequent INR (prothrombin time or protime) testing is needed. Warfarin dosing should be adjusted to laboratory results.

Propranolol may ***decrease*** the effects of

• albuterol (Proventil).
• theophyllines (Aminophyllin, Theo-Dur, etc.) and reduce their antiasthmatic effectiveness.

Propranolol ***taken concurrently*** with

• amiodarone (Cordarone) may result in abnormal heart rhythms and low pulse—these agents should not be combined.
• clonidine (Catapres) requires close monitoring for rebound high blood pressure if clonidine is withdrawn while propranolol is still being taken.
• cocaine may lead to heart attack.
• colestipol (Colestid) may decrease propranolol benefits.
• digoxin (Lanoxin) can result in severe slowing of the heart (bradycardia).
• epinephrine (Adrenalin, etc.) may cause marked rise in blood pressure and slowing of the heart rate.
• ergot derivatives (see Drug Classes) may lead to excessive blood vessel constriction and cold extremities (peripheral ischemia).
• fluoxetine (Prozac) may increase the risk of slow heartbeat and sedation.
• fluvoxamine (Luvox) may increase the risk of slow heartbeat and sedation.
• insulin requires close monitoring to avoid undetected hypoglycemia (see Glossary).
• methyldopa (various) can lead to an excessive blood pressure increase during stress.
• nefazodone (Serzone) may decrease propranolol benefits and lead to nefazodone toxicity.
• oral antidiabetic drugs (see Drug Classes) and cause slow recovery from any low blood sugar that may occur.

- quinidine (Quinaglute) can increase adverse effects without increased therapeutic benefits.
- sertraline (Zoloft) may lead to sudden chest pain.
- venlafaxine (Effexor) may result in increased risk of propranolol toxicity.
- X-ray contrast media such as diatrizoate results in up to an eightfold increase in risk of severe allergic (anaphylactic) drug reactions.
- zolmitriptan (Zomig) or rizatriptan (Maxalt) may increase risk of rizatriptan or zolmitriptan adverse effects.
- zotepine (Nipolept) may increase risk of toxicity from both drugs.

The following drugs may *increase* the effects of propranolol:

- chlorpromazine (Thorazine, etc.)—may also lead to seizures. Close patient follow-up is required.
- cimetidine (Tagamet).
- ciprofloxacin (Cipro).
- diltiazem (Cardizem).
- disopyramide (Norpace).
- furosemide or other diuretics.
- methimazole (Tapazole).
- metoclopramide (Reglan) (conventional immediate-release forms of propranolol).
- nicardipine (Cardene).
- propafenone (Rythmol) especially if doses of 150 mg a day or more of propafenone are used.
- propoxyphene (various).
- propylthiouracil (Propacil).
- ritonavir (Norvir) and perhaps other protease inhibitors (see Drug Classes).
- zileuton (Zyflo).

The following drugs may *decrease* the effects of propranolol:

- antacids.
- barbiturates (phenobarbital, etc.).
- indomethacin (Indocin) and possibly other "aspirin substitutes," or NSAIDs—may impair propranolol's antihypertensive effect.
- rifampin (Rifadin, Rimactane).
- sertraline (Zoloft) may increase risk of chest pain.
- simvastatin (Zocor) by decreasing the peak blood concentration.

▷ *Driving, Hazardous Activities:* Use caution until the full extent of drowsiness, lethargy, and blood pressure change have been determined.

Aviation Note: The use of this drug *may be a disqualification* for piloting. Consult a designated Aviation Medical Examiner.

Exposure to Sun: No restrictions.

Exposure to Heat: Caution is advised. Hot environments can lower blood pressure and exaggerate the effects of this drug.

Exposure to Cold: Caution is advised. Cold environments can enhance the circulatory deficiency in the extremities that may occur with this drug. The elderly should take precautions to prevent hypothermia (see Glossary).

Heavy Exercise or Exertion: It is advisable to avoid exertion that produces lightheadedness, excessive fatigue, or muscle cramping. The use of this drug may intensify the hypertensive response to isometric exercise.

Occurrence of Unrelated Illness: Fever can lower blood pressure and require adjustment of dose. Nausea or vomiting may interrupt the regular dose schedule. Ask your physician for guidance.

Discontinuation: Best to avoid sudden stopping of this drug, especially in coronary artery disease. If possible, a gradual reduction of dose over a period of 2 to 3 weeks is recommended. Ask your physician for specific guidance.

PROTEASE INHIBITOR FAMILY

Atazanavir   (Aht ah zan ah veer),   **Lopinavir and Ritonavir**   (Loh PIN a veer and ri TOHN a veer)   **Amprenavir**   (am PREN a veer)   **Indinavir** (in DIN a veer)   **Nelfinavir**   (nel FIN a veer)   **Ritonavir**   (ri TOHN a veer)   **Saquinavir**   (sa KWIN a veer) **Tenofovir**   (ten OH fo Veer) **Investigational: Mozenavir and Tipranavir**

Introduced: 2003, 2000, 1999, 1996, 1997, 1996, 1995 and 2001 respectively
Class: Protease inhibitor, antiviral, anti-AIDS   **Prescription:**   USA: Yes
Controlled Drug: USA: No; Canada: Yes   **Available as Generic:**   USA: No; Canada: No

Author's Note: Information on atazanavir will be broadened as additional information becomes available.

Brand Names: *Atazanavir:* Reyataz, *Lopinavir and Ritonavir*: Kaletra, *Amprenavir*: Agenerase, *Indinavir*: Crixivan, *Nelfinavir*: Viracept, *Ritonavir*: Kaletra [CD], Norvir, *Saquinavir*: Fortovase, Invirase, *Tenofovir*: Viread

BENEFITS versus RISKS	
Possible Benefits	*Possible Risks*
INCREASED CD4 COUNTS	SERIOUS CHANGES IN INSULIN
DECREASED OPPORTUNISTIC	LEVELS TO KETOACIDOSIS
INFECTIONS	SERIOUS INCREASES IN
EFFECTIVE COMBINATION	CHOLESTEROL
THERAPY OF HIV	Increased liver function tests (not
MAY DECREASE HIV TO	reported for amprenavir)
UNDETECTABLE LEVELS WITH	Kidney stones (indinavir)
EARLY THERAPY	May have SERIOUS drug interactions
Novel primary resistance mutation	(see below)
pattern (amprenavir)	
Few overlapping secondary mutations	
(amprenavir)	

▷ **Principal Uses**
 As a Single Drug Product: Uses currently included in FDA-approved labeling: Treatment of HIV infection when antiretroviral therapy is indicated, in combination with other antiretroviral agents.
  Author's Note: Combination therapy has become a standard of care. NIAID antiretroviral therapy guidelines take into account how easily HIV therapy can fit into a patient's life. The ATIS Guidelines (AIDS Treatment Information Service—*www.hivatis.org/guidelines/adult/May 23 02/AAMay23.pdf***) tell us that therapy should be supervised by an expert, and cover considerations of when to start therapy in both asymptomatic and established HIV infections. Adherence or taking medicines for HIV exactly on time and in the right amount is ABSOLUTELY critical to getting the best possible results or outcomes. Structured therapy interruptions (STI) or structured interruptions of therapy (SIT) are still controversial.**

Other (unlabeled) generally accepted uses: Used in making HIV infection undetectable with combination therapy.

As a Combination Drug Product [CD]: Ritonavir is available combined with lopinavir (Kaletra). This combination works to use the blood level–sustaining role of ritonavir and the mechanism of action of lopinavir. While we usually think of drug interactions as undesirable, low-dose ritonavir in this combination inhibits the cytochrome P450 3A4 leading to increased and sustained lopinavir blood levels.

How These Drugs Work: They inhibit HIV reproduction (replication) by inhibiting an HIV enzyme (protease), which blocks the ability of the virus to make mature, infectious virus particles.

Available Dosage Forms and Strengths

Amprenavir:
>   Capsules — 50 mg, 150 mg
>   Oral solution — 15 mg/ml

Indinavir:
>   Capsules — 200 mg, 400 mg

Nelfinavir:
>   Oral powder — 50 mg/g
>   Tablet — 250 mg

Ritonavir:
>   Capsule — 100 mg
>   Oral solution — 80 mg/ml
>   Soft gel capsule — 100 mg

Ritonavir/lopinavir (Kaletra):
>   Capsule — 33.3 mg ritonavir and 133.3 mg lopinavir
>   Oral solution — 20 mg/ml ritonavir and 80 mg/ml lopinavir

Saquinavir:
>   Gelcap (Fortovase) — 200 mg
>   Gelcap (Invirase) — 200 mg

Author's Note: This profile gives Fortovase data.

▷ **Recommended Dose Ranges** (Actual dose and schedule must be determined for each patient individually.)

18 to 60 Years of Age:

Amprenavir: 1,200 mg twice a day (in combination with other antiretrovirals).

Indinavir: 800 mg by mouth every 8 hours.

Nelfinavir: 750 mg every 8 hours.

Ritonavir: In order to help minimize adverse effects, ritonavir is started at 300 mg twice daily and then is increased by 100 mg twice daily at two- to three-day intervals. The desired "goal dose" is 600 mg twice daily. If ritonavir is taken with saquinavir, dose is reduced to 400 mg twice daily.

Ritonavir/lopinavir: Three capsules or 5 ml of the oral solution twice a day with food.

Saquinavir: 1,200 mg three times daily.

Over 65 Years of Age: These drugs have not been specifically studied in those over 65.

Conditions Requiring Dosing Adjustments

Liver Function:

Amprenavir: People with impaired liver function (Child-Pugh score of 5–8) require dosing adjustments. Those with this degree of compromise are given 450 mg twice daily and should be closely followed for possible adverse effects.

Indinavir: The dose should be decreased to 600 mg by mouth every 8 hours in mild to moderate liver failure.

Nelfinavir, ritonavir and saquinavir: Have not been studied in liver disease, but caution is advised as much of these drugs are removed by the liver.

Kidney Function: Amprenavir, indinavir, nelfinavir, ritonavir, and saquinavir: Dosing changes are not thought to be needed.

▷ **Dosing Instructions:** Indinavir is best taken on an empty stomach, but may be taken with a light snack, such as dry toast with jelly, apple juice or coffee. Nelfinavir, ritonavir and saquinavir should be taken with a meal or light snack. Ritonavir oral solution SHOULD NOT be refrigerated and should be shaken well BEFORE you take your dose. Amprenavir can be taken with or without food but SHOULD NOT be taken with a high-fat meal. IT IS CRITICAL THAT PROTEASE INHIBITOR DOSES NOT BE MISSED, as resistance to the medicine may develop. Since reports of altered blood sugar have been made, knowledge of signs and symptoms of high blood sugar or ketoacidosis and periodic checks of blood sugar appear prudent. If you forget a dose: Take the missed dose as soon as you remember it, unless it's nearly time for your next dose—if that is the case, skip the missed dose and take the next dose right on schedule. DO NOT double doses. Talk with your doctor if you find yourself missing doses. There are several excellent timers and even beeper-based systems to help you remember your medicine.

Usual Duration of Use: Use on a regular schedule for several months usually determines effectiveness in lowering the viral burden. The lowest level of viral burden, the 12-week level of viral burden and how consistently you take these medicines (adherence) are key factors in long-term results. Long-term use (months to years) requires periodic physician evaluation of response (viral burden and CD4).

Typical Treatment Goals and Measurements (Outcomes and Markers)

HIV: Goals for HIV treatment presently are maximum suppression of viral replication, maximum lowering of the amount of virus in your body (viral load or burden), and maximum patient survival. Markers of successful therapy include undetectable viral load, increased CD4 cells, absence of indicator or opportunistic infections (OIs), and in the case of the HIV positive patient, failure of the infection to progress to AIDS. If goals are not achieved in the time your doctor has set, typical strategies include intensification as well as phenotypic resistance testing of the virus itself. If goals are achieved and the viral load later rebounds despite excellent compliance, medication change (salvage therapy) is indicated.

Possible Advantages of These Drugs

These medicines are part of combination regimens (termed cocktails by television news) that can lower the amount of HIV in the body to nondetectable levels in many patients. Resistance to these medicines still occurs in a variety of ways. Amprenavir appeared to have a novel resistance pattern (codon 50V mutation that confers resistance), however, overlapping secondary resistance locations have become problematic. New dosing strategies and even a once-a-day protease inhibitor (see Drug Classes) are being studied. Regardless of the patient, it is not unusual for HIV treatment to have to be changed. PI-containing regimens tend to offer reasonably durable virus suppression. The newest PI, **atazanavir (Reyataz),** is also the first once-a-day protease inhibitor—something that I believe will greatly improve how well patients take this medicine (lower pill burden than the other available PIs).

▷ **These Drugs Should Not Be Taken If**
- you had an allergic reaction to any dose form.
- you are taking cisapride, ergotamine, or triazolam (see Other Drugs section).

▷ **Inform Your Physician Before Taking These Drugs If**
- you have diabetes or a history of blood sugar regulation problems.
- you are taking amprenavir and develop a rash.
- you are allergic to sulfonamide-type medicines (amprenavir).
- you have elevated cholesterol or lipids.
- you have had kidney stones previously (indinavir especially).
- you have kidney or liver compromise.
- you have phenylketonuria (nelfinavir powder has 11.2 mg of phenylalanine in each gram).
- you are taking one of the medicines that interacts with a protease inhibitor and have not had a blood level check.
- you have had adverse reactions to other protease inhibitors.
- you are unsure how much to take or how often to take them.

Possible Side Effects (natural, expected, and unavoidable drug actions)
Rare kidney stones (indinavir). Increased liver function tests.

▷ **Possible Adverse Effects** (unusual, unexpected, and infrequent reactions)
If any of the following develop, consult your physician promptly for guidance.

Mild Adverse Effects
Allergic reaction: skin rash.
Headache (frequent with amprenavir) or dizziness—rare to infrequent.
Weakness—infrequent.
Toe nail changes (ingrown)—possible.
Blurred vision—rare.
Chills, fever, or sweating—rare to infrequent.
Nausea and vomiting or abdominal pain—infrequent to frequent.
Palpitations—rare.
Joint pain—rare.
Tingling around the mouth (paresthesias)—frequent for ritonavir and agenerase.
Lipodystrophy—possible.
Author's Note: Current controversy as to possible lipid changes (lipodystrophy or LD) from protease inhibitors and/or nucleoside reverse transcriptase inhibitors involves presence of mild changes versus moderate to severe problems. The HOPS data found that risk of LD increases with increasing time on antiretrovirals and that LD increases with an increasing number of nondrug factors (age 40 or older, HIV infection 7 or more years, AIDS 2 or more years, hemophiliacs, nadir CD4 count less than 100 or less than 15 and time since nadir 3 or more years).
Diarrhea—infrequent to frequent (frequent with nelfinavir).

Serious Adverse Effects
Allergic reactions: life-threatening rash (Stevens-Johnson Syndrome)—rare for amprenavir.
Anemia or spleen disorder—rare (indinavir, ritonavir, and saquinavir).
Hemolytic anemia—case report for agenerase.
Kidney stones—infrequent (indinavir).
Changes in insulin levels (increased blood sugar [hyperglycemia]) or ketoacidosis—many case reports for the protease inhibitors.

Increased cholesterol—many case reports.

Fat redistribution (lipodystrophy)—possible (starts from 4–61 weeks and greatest risk appears to be with indinavir).

Increased risk of blood clots (thrombosis)—possible (indinavir only).

Increased bleeding risk in people with hemophilia (nelfinavir).

▷ **Possible Effects on Sexual Function:** Rare reports of premenstrual syndrome in some early studies with indinavir. Four cases of extended and excessive menstruation (hypermenorrhea) have been reported with ritonavir.

Possible Delayed Adverse Effects: Kidney stones (indinavir). Blood sugar problems (low blood sugar or ketoacidosis) or cholesterol changes. Fat redistribution. Ingrown toenails.

▷ **Adverse Effects That May Mimic Natural Diseases or Disorders**

Increased liver function tests may mimic hepatitis (not reported for amprenavir). Changes in insulin levels may mimic diabetes.

Possible Effects on Laboratory Tests

Liver function tests: increased (not reported for amprenavir).

Complete blood counts: decreased red blood cells and hematocrit.

Insulin levels: lowered.

Blood sugar (glucose): increased.

Cholesterol—may be significantly increased.

CAUTION

1. Serious increases in cholesterol (lipids) have been reported.
2. Serious increases in blood sugar have been reported in many case reports to date for protease inhibitors. This effect has been seen in early reports on average after 76 days of therapy, but has also been reported after as little as 4 days of treatment with protease inhibitors.
3. Make certain you know high blood sugar (hyperglycemia) and ketoacidosis signs and symptoms if you are taking this medicine. Blood sugar problems have been reported for protease inhibitors.
4. These medicines may decrease the amount of virus in your body, but the virus can still be spread to others through sexual contact or blood contamination.
5. Promptly report flank pain or blood in the urine; this could indicate a kidney stone.
6. Periodic measures of viral load and CD4 are critical to make certain that therapy is still working.
7. IT IS CRITICAL to take these medicines exactly as directed to get the best results.
8. Ritonavir (Norvir) has MANY drug interactions. Ask your pharmacist to check the most current list. Amprenavir also has some serious drug interactions. Doses of the protease inhibitor may need to be increased or decreased.
9. Fat redistribution should be reported to your doctor (one patient responded to ketoconazole treatment).
10. Amprenavir contains a significant amount of vitamin E. DO NOT USE vitamin E supplements while taking this medicine.

Precautions for Use

By Infants and Children:

Amprenavir: Capsules: 4–12 years old or if 13–16 and weight is less than 50 kg—20 mg per kg twice daily or 15 mg per kg three times daily up to 2,400 mg. 13–16 years of age and weighing more than 50 kg—same as adult dose. Oral solution (NOT INTERCHANGEABLE WITH CAPSULES): 4–12 years old or if 13–16 and weight is less than 50 kg: 22.5 mg per kg twice daily or 17 mg per kg three times daily up to 2,800 mg.

Indinavir: Dosing in children is not clearly defined.

Nelfinavir: 2–13 years old—One open-label study used 20–30 mg per kg per dose, which was taken three times daily with a meal or light snack.

Ritonavir: Started at 250 mg per square meter and increased at 2- to 3-day intervals by 30 mg per square meter. The goal dose is 400 mg per square meter twice daily in combination with other antiretroviral agents (up to 600 mg twice daily).

Saquinavir: Dosing in those less than 16 years old has not been defined.

By Those Over 65 Years of Age: Have not been studied in this age group.

▷ **Advisability of Use During Pregnancy**

Pregnancy Category: Nelfinavir, ritonavir and saquinavir: B; Amprenavir, indinavir: C. See Pregnancy Risk Categories at the back of this book.

Animal Studies: Clinical doses in rats and rabbits have not revealed teratogenicity.

Human Studies: Adequate studies of pregnant women are not available.

Ask your doctor for help.

Advisability of Use If Breast-Feeding

Presence of this drug in breast milk: Yes in rats (amprenavir, indinavir); unknown (nelfinavir, ritonavir, saquinavir).

Refrain from nursing if you are HIV-positive or are taking this drug. Breast milk may also transfer the AIDS virus from mother to infant.

Habit-Forming Potential: None.

Effects of Overdose:

Amprenavir: No known antidote exists. If overdose occurs, the manufacturer suggests the patients should be treated according to the signs and symptoms they develop.

Indinavir: No human data are available. Doses of 20 times the human dose in rats and 10 times the human dose in mice were not lethal for indinavir.

Ritonavir: Limited experience, with one case reporting paresthesias and another showed sudden kidney failure with eosinophilia.

Possible Effects of Long-Term Use: Resistance may develop. Lipodystrophy and blood sugar problems may occur.

Suggested Periodic Examinations While Taking These Drugs (at physician's discretion)

Liver function tests.

Complete blood counts.

CD4 or viral load measurement.

Measurement of blood sugar (glucose), especially for those with prior blood sugar problems or patients who show signs or symptoms of hyperglycemia or ketoacidosis.

Measurement of cholesterol and fractions before starting therapy and periodically while taking these medicines.

▷ **While Taking These Drugs, Observe the Following**

Foods: If indinavir is taken with a meal high in fat, calories or protein, a 77% to 91% decrease in the total amount of drug absorbed has been reported. Amprenavir absorption is decreased if it is taken with a high-fat meal. The other medicines in this class are better absorbed if taken with food.

Herbal Medicines or Minerals: Some patients use echinacea to attempt to boost their immune systems. Unfortunately, use of echinacea is not recommended in people with damaged immune systems. This herb may also actually weaken any immune system if it is used too often or for too long (more than 8 weeks). Garlic is often used to help lower cholesterol, but dropped blood levels by 50% in one study—do not combine with saquinavir and talk to your doctor before combining garlic with any HIV medicine. St. John's wort significantly decreased indinavir levels in one study. Because protease inhibitors as well as nonnucleoside reverse transcriptase inhibitors (see Drug Classes), use the P450 3A4 pathway—use of this herbal is NOT recommended for people taking those medicines.

Nutritional Support: Since amprenavir contains a significant amount of vitamin E, supplements or multivitamins high in vitamin E should be avoided.

Beverages: No restrictions.

▷ *Alcohol:* No interactions expected.

Tobacco Smoking: May blunt therapeutic benefits of ritonavir. I advise everyone to quit smoking.

Marijuana Smoking: Ritonavir and other PIs removed by the same liver enzymes can increase blood levels leading to toxicity (see dronabinol interaction).

▷ *Other Drugs*

These medicines ***taken concurrently*** with

- amiodarone (Cordarone) increase heart toxicity risk—DO NOT COMBINE with ritonavir; if combined with indinavir, blood levels are required.
- antacids (various, didanosine also) may lead to lower blood levels of these medicines and poor antiviral effects; separate antacid dosing by at least an hour.
- astemizole (Hismanal) may cause serious toxicity—DO NOT COMBINE (astemizole now removed from the US market).
- azole antifungals (itraconazole, ketoconazole, others) may lead to increased protease inhibitor levels and toxicity.
- bepridil (Vascor) may lead to serious toxicity—DO NOT COMBINE with these medicines.
- birth control pills (oral contraceptives) may lead to low birth control levels and pregnancy (ritonavir, saquinavir, and amprenavir).
- bupropion (Wellbutrin) increase seizure risk with ritonavir—DO NOT COMBINE.
- carbamazepine (Tegretol) decrease protease inhibitor levels.
- cimetidine (Tagamet) may lead to cimetidine toxicity (ritonavir only).
- cisapride (Propulsid) may cause serious toxicity—DO NOT COMBINE.
- cyclosporine (Sandimmune) may lead to cyclosporine toxicity. Blood levels and dosing changes are prudent.
- delavirdine (Rescriptor) may lead to delavirdine toxicity.
- diazepam (Valium, others) may be increased by protease inhibitors to toxic levels—DO NOT COMBINE.
- didanosine (Videx) may blunt therapeutic benefits; separate doses by 1 hour.
- digoxin (Lanoxin, others) may increase digoxin levels; lower doses of digoxin and digoxin blood levels are needed.
- diltiazem (Cardizem) may lead to diltiazem toxicity (ritonavir and saquinavir, perhaps others).
- dofetilide (Tikosyn) may lead to dofetilide toxicity.
- dronabinol (Marinol) may increase dronabinol levels, lower doses of dronabinol, and close patient follow-up are needed.

- efavirez (Sustiva) combined with ritonavir can increase levels of both medicines. Careful patient follow-up and close monitoring of liver enzymes are needed.
- ergot derivatives (see Drug Classes) may lead to toxicity—DO NOT COMBINE.
- felodipine (Plendil) may lead to felodipine toxicity.
- flecainide (Tambocor) SHOULD NOT be taken with ritonavir.
- fluticasone (Flonase) may lead to flonase toxicity when combined with ritonavir (perhaps other PIs).
- fluvastatin (Lescol) and other HMG-CoA reductase inhibitors (see Drug Classes) removed by liver CYP3A4 (atorvastatin, lovastatin, pravastatin, and simvastatin) may lead to HMG-CoA toxicity. Cerivastatin (Baycol) is also removed by CYP3A4, but it is equally removed by CYP2C8 and may be a safer alternative.
- fluvoxamine (Luvox) may lead to fluvoxamine toxicity (ritonavir, perhaps others).
- gemfibrozil (Lopid) may increase gemfibrozil levels (ritonavir); patients who show signs of gemfibrozil toxicity should have gemfibrozil doses lowered.
- glimepiride (Amaryl), glipizide (Glucotrol) or glyburide (Glynase) may have blood levels changed (ritonavir); caution and possible oral hypoglycemic dosing changes are prudent.
- ibuprofen (Motrin, others) and other NSAIDs may lead to ibuprofen or other NSAID toxicity (ritonavir only)—caution is advised.
- isradipine (DynaCirc) may lead to isradipine toxicity.
- itraconazole (Sporanox) or ketoconazole (Nizoral) may cause protease inhibitor toxicity and doses of the protease inhibitor may need to be reduced. Combination with ritonavir may lead to itraconazole or ketoconazole toxicity.
- macrolide antibiotics (clarithromycin, erythromycin) may increase antibiotic levels; macrolide doses may need to be lowered (based on increased nausea/vomiting). Azithromycin may be the best macrolide to use if one is needed.
- medicines removed (metabolized) by CYP3A4 may increase blood levels greater than expected and increase risk of toxicity.
- methylenedioxymethamphetamine (MDMA or ecstasy) led to a serotonin reaction and death in one case report for ritonavir—DO NOT COMBINE.
- midazolam (Versed) may cause serious toxicity—DO NOT COMBINE.
- narcotics such as morphine (MS Contin) or methadone (Dolophine) may lead to toxic narcotic levels.
- nevirapine (Viramune) may blunt therapeutic effects of indinavir—Caution and dosing changes are prudent.
- oral hypoglycemics (see Drug Classes) may lead to excessive lowering of blood sugar (ritonavir only).
- other antiretrovirals may reduce viral load to nondetectable levels but may also interact (ritonavir lowers nelfinavir levels, while indinavir increases nelfinavir or saquinavir levels).
- other drugs that are toxic to the liver may result in additive toxicity (except amprenavir).
- other drugs that can lead to kidney stones may result in additive risk with indinavir.
- paclitaxel (Taxol) may lead to paclitaxel toxicity (ritonavir).
- phenytoin (Dilantin) or fosphenytoin (Cerebyx) may lower protease benefits.

- propafenone (Rythmol) should NOT be taken with ritonavir and may be contraindicated with other protease inhibitors.
- quinidine (Quinaglute, others) should NOT be taken with ritonavir, nelfinavir. Other protease inhibitors may increase quinidine blood levels, and more frequent quinidine levels are prudent. Indinavir is considered to be safe to give with quinidine.
- quinupristin/dalfopristin (Synercid) should be combined with ritonavir or ritonavir combinations only after careful consideration and caution. Levels of ritonavir may need to be checked and doses reduced.
- rifabutin (Mycobutin) may increase rifabutin and decrease indinavir levels; half the usual dose of rifabutin is used if these drugs are combined.
- rifampin (Rifater, others) may cause loss of indinavir and amprenavir benefits—DO NOT COMBINE.
- risperidone (Risperdol) may lead to toxicity if combined with ritonavir or ritonavir combinations. Careful patient follow-up and checks for risperidone toxicity are needed.
- saquinavir (Fortovase) and ritonavir may lead to increased saquinavir levels and possible toxicity unless doses are reduced.
- sirolimus (Rapamune) may cause sirolimus or tacrolimus (Prograf) with ritonavir may lead to toxicity.
- sildenafil (Viagra) may lead to excessive blood levels of sildenafil and possible toxicity (amprenavir, ritonavir, and saquinavir).
- tramadol (Ultram) may lead to tramadol toxicity; reduced tramadol doses are mandatory if these medicines are combined.
- triazolam (Halcion) and perhaps other benzodiazepines may cause serious toxicity.
- tricyclic antidepressants (see Drug Classes) should have blood levels checked.
- venlafaxine (Effexor) may increase risk of venlafaxine toxicity when combined with some PIs.
- warfarin (Coumadin) may increase risk of bleeding (amprenavir, ritonavir, and nelfinavir only); frequent INR checks are prudent.
- zolpidem (Ambien) may produce toxic zolpidem levels (if combined with ritonavir)—DO NOT COMBINE.

▷ *Driving, Hazardous Activities:* Some of these drugs may rarely cause sleepiness. Restrict activities as necessary.

Aviation Note: The use of these drugs ***may be a disqualification*** for piloting. Consult a designated Aviation Medical Examiner.

Exposure to Sun: No restrictions.

Special Storage Instructions: The ritonavir soft gelatin capsules DO NOT require refrigeration if they are stored below 77 degrees Fahrenheit.

Discontinuation: Do not stop these drugs without your doctor's knowledge and guidance.

PROTRIPTYLINE (proh TRIP ti lin)

Introduced: 1966 **Class:** Antidepressant **Prescription:** USA: Yes **Controlled Drug:** USA: No; Canada: No **Available as Generic:** USA: Yes; Canada: No

Author's Note: The information in this profile has been shortened to make room for more widely used medicines.

PYRAZINAMIDE (peer a ZIN a mide)

Introduced: 1968   **Class:**   Anti-infective, antituberculosis   **Pre-scription:**   USA: Yes   **Controlled Drug:**   USA: No; Canada: No
Available as Generic: USA: Yes; Canada: No
Brand Names: ♣PMS Pyrazinamide, Rifater [CD], ♣Tebrazid

<table>
<tr><td colspan="2" align="center">BENEFITS versus RISKS</td></tr>
<tr><td align="center">Possible Benefits</td><td align="center">Possible Risks</td></tr>
<tr><td>EFFECTIVE ADJUNCTIVE
TREATMENT OF TUBERCULOSIS</td><td>DRUG-INDUCED HEPATITIS—rare
Activation of gouty arthritis and
  porphyria
Decreased platelets and hemoglobin</td></tr>
</table>

▷ **Principal Uses**

As a Single Drug Product: Uses currently included in FDA-approved labeling: Treatment of active tuberculosis, in combination with other antitubercular drugs.

Other (unlabeled) generally accepted uses: (1) Combination therapy of Mycobacterium xenopi infections; (2) combination therapy of resistant tuberculosis; (3) combination therapy of tuberculosis in AIDS.

As a Combination Drug Product [CD]: This medicine is combined with other antituberculosis medicines (isoniazid and rifampin) in order to attack tuberculosis with combination treatment in a single-dose form. This undoubtedly helps adherence.

How This Drug Works: This drug is ideal for killing tuberculosis organisms that are in acid environments, such as in some kinds of white blood (macrophages) cells.

Available Dosage Forms and Strengths

Tablets — 500 mg

Tablets — 300 mg pyrazinamide, 50 mg isoniazid and 120 mg of rifampin (Rifater brand)

▷ **Recommended Dosage Ranges** (Actual dose and schedule must be determined for each patient individually.)

Infants and Children: 7.5 to 15 mg per kg of body mass, twice daily; or 15 to 30 mg per kg of body mass, once daily. Total daily dose should not exceed 1.5 g.

12 to 60 Years of Age: For tuberculosis—15 to 30 mg per kg of body mass (up to a maximum of 2,000 mg) daily. Some patients do better with twice-weekly dosing with 50 to 70 mg per kg of body mass (up to 4,000 mg).

Author's Note: Because of the current resistant tuberculosis problem, most clinicians start all patients on a four-drug regimen for 8 weeks (until laboratory culture results are available). Treatment of this widespread resistant organism should be based on local resistance trends and individual patient organisms and typically continues for 6 months.

Over 60 Years of Age: Same as 12 to 60 years of age.

Conditions Requiring Dosing Adjustments

Liver Function: This drug should be used with caution and in decreased doses by patients with liver compromise. Contraindicated in patients with severe liver dysfunction.

Kidney Function: For patients with end-stage renal failure, the dose must be adjusted. One researcher recommends 60 mg per kg of body mass, twice weekly. The dose of pyrazinamide should be given at least 24 hours before any given dialysis session. Patients should be closely monitored.

▷ **Dosing Instructions:** The tablet may be crushed and taken with or following food to reduce stomach irritation. Take the full course prescribed. This drug should be taken concurrently with other antitubercular drugs to prevent the development of drug-resistant strains of tuberculosis bacteria. The Rifater product accomplishes triple therapy in a single pill. If you forget a dose: Take the missed dose as soon as you remember it, unless it's nearly time for your next dose—if that is the case, skip the missed dose and take the next dose right on schedule. DO NOT take two doses at the same time. Talk with your doctor if you find yourself missing doses. IT IS CRITICAL to take this medicine exactly as prescribed and for as long as prescribed.

Usual Duration of Use: Use on a regular schedule for 2 months usually determines effectiveness in controlling active tuberculosis. Long-term use of antitubercular drugs (6 months is typical) requires periodic physician evaluation.

Typical Treatment Goals and Measurements (Outcomes and Markers)
Infections: The most commonly used measures of serious infections are white blood cell counts and differentials (the kind of blood cells that occur most often in your blood), and temperature. While clinicians look for positive changes in 24–48 hours in typical infections, this kind of infection REQUIRES long-term treatment to kill it. NEVER stop a treatment for an infection because you start to feel better. The goals and time frame (see peak benefits above) should be discussed with you when the prescription is written. Months of treatment are usually required to kill this very tough (resistant) organism.

Possible Advantages of This Drug
May reduce the period of drug treatment from 9 months down to 6 months in responsive infections.

▷ **This Drug Should Not Be Taken If**
  • you have had an allergic reaction to it previously.
  • you have permanent liver damage with impaired function.
  • you have active gout, sudden (acute).

▷ **Inform Your Physician Before Taking This Drug If**
  • you have had an allergic reaction to ethionamide, isoniazid, or niacin (nicotinic acid).
  • you have a history of liver disease.
  • you have a history of peptic ulcer or porphyria.
  • you tried to take medicines for tuberculosis before, but did not complete the prescribed therapy.
  • you have gout or diabetes.
  • you have impaired kidney function.

Possible Side Effects (natural, expected, and unavoidable drug actions)
Increased blood uric acid levels. Fever.

▷ **Possible Adverse Effects** (unusual, unexpected, and infrequent reactions)
  If any of the following develop, consult your physician promptly for guidance.
Mild Adverse Effects
Allergic reactions: skin rash, itching, fever.
Loss of appetite, mild nausea, vomiting—frequent.

Joint pain—frequent.

Acne—rare.

Serious Adverse Effects

Idiosyncratic reactions: Rare sideroblastic anemia.

Decreased blood platelets—rare.

Seizures—rare.

Drug-induced porphyria or pellagra—case reports.

Loss of blood sugar control in diabetics—reported.

Kidney problems (interstitial nephritis)—case reports.

Drug-induced hepatitis, with and without jaundice (see Glossary)—case reports.

Gouty arthritis, due to increased blood uric acid levels—possible.

▷ **Possible Effects on Sexual Function:** None reported other than rare reports of painful urination.

▷ **Adverse Effects That May Mimic Natural Diseases or Disorders**

Drug-induced hepatitis may suggest viral hepatitis.

Natural Diseases or Disorders That May Be Activated by This Drug

Gout, peptic ulcer, porphyria.

Possible Effects on Laboratory Tests

Complete blood cell counts: decreased red cells, hemoglobin, and platelets.

INR (prothrombin time): increased.

Blood sugar: tight control may become more difficult.

Blood uric acid level: increased.

Liver function tests: increased enzymes (ALT/GPT, AST/GOT, alkaline phosphatase) or bilirubin.

Urine ketone tests: false-positive test result with Acetest and Ketostix.

CAUTION

1. When this drug is used alone, tuberculosis bacteria rapidly develop resistance to it. To be effective, this drug must be used in combination with other effective antitubercular drugs, such as isoniazid and rifampin. The CDC states that the rifampin combination requires frequent liver tests.

2. This drug may interfere with control of diabetes.

Precautions for Use

By Infants and Children: Safety and effectiveness for those under 12 years of age are not established. The rare occurrence of drug-related seizure has been reported in a 2-year-old child.

By Those Over 60 Years of Age: No specific information available.

▷ **Advisability of Use During Pregnancy**

Pregnancy Category: C. See Pregnancy Risk Categories at the back of this book.

Animal Studies: No information available.

Human Studies: Adequate studies of pregnant women are not available.

Use this drug only if clearly needed. Ask your physician for guidance.

Advisability of Use If Breast-Feeding

Presence of this drug in breast milk: Yes.

Avoid drug or refrain from nursing.

Habit-Forming Potential: None.

Effects of Overdose: Nausea, vomiting, malaise.

Possible Effects of Long-Term Use: Liver damage.

Suggested Periodic Examinations While Taking This Drug (at physician's discretion)

Complete blood cell counts.

Liver function tests.

Uric acid blood levels.

▷ **While Taking This Drug, Observe the Following**

Foods: No restrictions.

Herbal Medicines or Minerals: Some patients use echinacea to attempt to boost their immune systems. Unfortunately, use of echinacea is not recommended in people with damaged immune systems. This herb may also actually weaken any immune system if it is used too often or for too long a time. Do NOT take mistletoe herb, oak bark or F.C. of marshmallow root, woody nightshade stem, or licorice. Since St. John's wort and pyrazinamide may cause increased sun sensitivity, caution is advised.

Beverages: No restrictions. May be taken with milk.

▷ *Alcohol:* Use sparingly to minimize liver toxicity.

Tobacco Smoking: No interactions expected. I advise everyone to quit smoking.

▷ *Other Drugs*

Pyrazinamide may *decrease* the effects of

• allopurinol (Zyloprim).

• BCG vaccine.

• cyclosporine (Sandimmune).

• probenecid (Benemid).

• sulfinpyrazone (Anturane).

Pyrazinamide *taken concurrently* with

• phenytoin (Dilantin) or fosphenytoin (Cerebyx) may lead to phenytoin or fosphenytoin toxicity.

• zidovudine (AZT) may lead to low pyrazinamide levels. Dosing changes may be needed.

▷ *Driving, Hazardous Activities:* No restrictions.

Aviation Note: The use of this drug is probably not a disqualification for piloting. Consult a designated Aviation Medical Examiner.

Exposure to Sun: Use caution—this drug may cause photosensitivity (see Glossary).

Discontinuation: If tolerated, this drug is usually taken for a minimum of 2 months. Do not stop it without your physician's knowledge and guidance.

PYRIDOSTIGMINE (peer id oh STIG meen)

Introduced: 1962   **Class:** Antimyasthenic   **Prescription:** USA: Yes   **Controlled Drug:** USA: No; Canada: No   **Available as Generic:** USA: No; Canada: No

Brand Names: ✤Anaplex SR, Mestinon, Mestinon-SR, Mestinon Timespan, Regonol

BENEFITS versus RISKS	
Possible Benefits	*Possible Risks*
MODERATELY EFFECTIVE TREATMENT OF OCULAR AND MILD FORMS OF MYASTHENIA GRAVIS (symptomatic relief of muscle weakness) PRETREATMENT ADJUNCT IN WARTIME WHEN NERVE AGENT EXPOSURE IS POSSIBLE	Cholinergic crisis (overdose): excessive salivation, nausea, vomiting, stomach cramps, diarrhea, shortness of breath (asthmalike wheezing), excessive weakness

▷ **Principal Uses**

As a Single Drug Product: Uses currently included in FDA-approved labeling: (1) Used to treat the ocular and milder forms of myasthenia gravis by providing temporary relief of muscle weakness and fatigability (most useful in long-term treatment when there is little or no swallowing difficulty); (2) used to reverse skeletal muscle relaxants; (3) used to pretreat the effects of nerve gas.

Other (unlabeled) generally accepted uses: (1) Combination therapy in chronic pain; (2) may help in combination therapy of Huntington's chorea and Lambert-Eaton syndrome; (3) adjunctive use with scopolamine to prevent side effects of scopolamine in treating motion sickness; (4) may have a role in treating nonepidemic parotitis; (5) used in pediatrics to treat myasthenia gravis.

How This Drug Works: This drug inhibits cholinesterase, the enzyme that destroys acetylcholine. This results in higher levels of acetylcholine, the nerve transmitter that facilitates the stimulation of muscular activity. The net effects are increased muscle strength and endurance.

Available Dosage Forms and Strengths
Solution for injection — 5 mg / ml
Syrup — 60 mg/5 ml (5% alcohol)
Tablets — 30 mg, 60 mg
Tablets, prolonged-action — 180 mg

▷ **Usual Adult Dosage Ranges:** *Myasthenia Gravis*: Initially 1 to 6 normal-release tablets, spaced throughout the day when maximum strength is needed. Maintenance varies with the severity of the disease—1 to 3 extended-release tablets once or twice a day. If twice-daily extended-release doses are needed, they should be separated by 6 hours. Some patients may need to supplement the extended-release tablets with the 30-mg, immediate-release tablets or the syrup in order to best control symptoms.

Nerve Gas or Agent Protection: 30 mg every 8 hours when the threat of a nerve agent attack is present. PRETREATMENT IS CRITICAL. Pralidoxime (600 mg) and atropine citrate (2 mg) are also given injected into a muscle if there actually is nerve gas exposure.

Note: Actual dose and schedule must be determined for each patient individually.

Conditions Requiring Dosing Adjustments

Liver Function: No dosing changes are defined in liver compromise.

Kidney Function: This drug is primarily eliminated in the urine, but specific guidelines for dose adjustments in renal compromise are not available.

▷ **Dosing Instructions:** Take with food or milk to reduce the intensity of side effects. Larger portions of the daily maintenance dose should be timed according to the pattern of fatigue and weakness. The syrup will permit a finer adjustment of dose. Dosing should be accomplished using a dose cup or calibrated measuring spoon. The regular tablet may be crushed. Mestinon sustained-release tablets can be cut in half. These tablets may NOT be crushed or cut into four pieces, as that would change the way that the drug is released. If you forget a dose: Take the missed dose as soon as you remember it, unless it's nearly time for your next dose—if that is the case, skip the missed dose and take the next dose right on schedule. DO NOT double doses. Talk with your doctor if you find yourself missing doses.

Usual Duration of Use: Use on a regular schedule (with dose adjustment) for 10 to 14 days usually determines effectiveness in relieving myasthenia symptoms. Long-term use (months to years) requires periodic physician evaluation. Nerve agent prophylaxis should also be followed by a physician.

Typical Treatment Goals and Measurements (Outcomes and Markers)
Myasthenia Gravis: The general goal is to increase muscle strength while avoiding nicotinic or muscarinic effects (diarrhea, salivation, nausea and vomiting). Immediate-release-form dosing is timed to correspond to fatigue or weakness.

▷ **This Drug Should Not Be Taken If**
  • you are known to be allergic to bromide compounds.
  • you have a urinary obstruction or mechanical intestinal obstruction.

▷ **Inform Your Physician Before Taking This Drug If**
  • you have heart rhythm disorders or bronchial asthma.
  • you are sensitive to bromides.
  • you have recurrent urinary tract infections.
  • you have prostatism (see Glossary).
  • you will have surgery with general anesthesia.

Possible Side Effects (natural, expected, and unavoidable drug actions)
Small pupils (miosis), watering of eyes, slow pulse, excessive salivation, nausea, vomiting, stomach cramps, diarrhea, urge to urinate, increased sweating, increased bronchial secretions (muscarinic/nicotinic side effects).

▷ **Possible Adverse Effects** (unusual, unexpected, and infrequent reactions)
If any of the following develop, consult your physician promptly for guidance.
Mild Adverse Effects
Allergic reaction: skin rash.
Nervousness, anxiety, unsteadiness, muscle cramps or twitching—infrequent.
Loss of scalp hair (alopecia)—case report. .
Serious Adverse Effects
Confusion, slurred speech, seizures, difficult breathing (asthmatic wheezing).
Increased muscle weakness or paralysis—case report.
Psychosis—rare.
Excessive vomiting or diarrhea may cause low potassium levels (hypokalemia). This accentuates muscle weakness.

▷ **Possible Effects on Sexual Function:** None reported.

▷ **Adverse Effects That May Mimic Natural Diseases or Disorders**
Seizures may suggest the possibility of epilepsy.

Natural Diseases or Disorders That May Be Activated by This Drug
Latent bronchial asthma.

Possible Effects on Laboratory Tests: None reported.

CAUTION

1. Some drugs block this drug, reducing effectiveness in treating myasthenia gravis (see Other Drugs on page 982). Ask your doctor before starting any other medicine.
2. Variations in response may occur from time to time. Because generalized muscle weakness is a major symptom of both myasthenia crisis (underdose) and cholinergic crisis (overdose), it may be difficult to recognize the correct cause. As a rule, weakness that starts an hour after taking this drug probably represents overdose; weakness that begins 3 or more hours after taking this drug is probably due to underdose. Watch these relationships and tell your doctor.
3. During long-term use, watch for development of resistance to the therapeutic action (loss of effect). Ask your doctor if the drug should be stopped for a few days to see if response can be restored.

Precautions for Use

By Infants and Children: The syrup form of this drug permits greater precision of dose adjustment and ease of administration in this age group. Neonates have received 5 mg every 4 to 6 hours. Since this is often self-limiting in neonates, the medicine can frequently be tapered and stopped.

By Those Over 60 Years of Age: The natural decline of kidney function with aging may require smaller doses to prevent accumulation of this drug to toxic levels.

▷ **Advisability of Use During Pregnancy**

Pregnancy Category: C. See Pregnancy Risk Categories at the back of this book.
Animal Studies: No information available.
Human Studies: Adequate studies of pregnant women are not available.
There are no reports of birth defects due to the use of this drug during pregnancy. However, there are reports of significant muscular weakness in newborn infants whose mothers had taken this drug during pregnancy.
Ask your physician for guidance.

Advisability of Use If Breast-Feeding

Presence of this drug in breast milk: Yes, as roughly 0.01% of the mother's dose.
Monitor nursing infant closely, and discontinue drug or nursing if adverse effects develop.

Habit-Forming Potential: None.

Effects of Overdose: Generalized muscular weakness, blurred vision, very small pupils, slow heart rate, difficult breathing (wheezing), excessive salivation, nausea, vomiting, stomach cramps, diarrhea, muscle cramps or twitching. This syndrome constitutes the cholinergic crisis.

Possible Effects of Long-Term Use: Development of tolerance (see Glossary) with loss of therapeutic effectiveness.

Suggested Periodic Examinations While Taking This Drug (at physician's discretion)
Assessment of drug effectiveness and dose schedule for optimal therapeutic results.

▷ **While Taking This Drug, Observe the Following**

Foods: No restrictions.
Herbal Medicines or Minerals: Echinacea pallida root or purpurea herb as well as woody nightshade stem or belladonna should be avoided.

Beverages: No restrictions. May be taken with milk.

▷ *Alcohol:* Use caution until the combined effects are determined. Weakness and unsteadiness may be accentuated.

Tobacco Smoking: No interactions expected. I advise everyone to quit smoking.

▷ *Other Drugs*

Pyridostigmine *taken concurrently* with

- disopyramide (Norpace) may ease undesirable anticholinergic effects (problems urinating, decreased sweating, etc.).
- succinylcholine (various) may increase muscular problems (neuromuscular blockade). This combination should usually be avoided in patients taking pyridostigmine.

The following drugs may *decrease* the effects of pyridostigmine:

- adrenocortical steroids (see Drug Classes).
- atropine (belladonna).
- clindamycin (Cleocin).
- guanadrel (Hylorel).
- guanethidine (Esimil, Ismelin).
- procainamide (Procan SR, Pronestyl).
- quinidine (Cardioquin, Duraquin, etc.).
- quinine (Quinamm).

▷ *Driving, Hazardous Activities:* This drug may cause blurred vision, confusion, or generalized weakness. Restrict activities as necessary.

Aviation Note: The use of this drug *is a disqualification* for piloting. Consult a designated Aviation Medical Examiner.

Exposure to Sun: No restrictions.

Exposure to Heat: Use caution—this drug may cause excessive sweating and increased weakness.

Exposure to Environmental Chemicals: Avoid excessive exposure (inhalation, skin contamination) to the insecticides Baygon, Diazinon, and Sevin. These can worsen potential drug toxicity.

Discontinuation: Do not stop this drug abruptly without your doctor's knowledge and guidance.

QUAZEPAM (KWAH zee pam)

Introduced: 1982   **Class:** Hypnotic, benzodiazepines **Prescription:** USA: Yes   **Controlled Drug:** USA: C-IV*   **Available as Generic:** USA: No

Brand Names: Doral, Dormalin

Author's Note: The National Institute of Mental Health has an information page on anxiety. It can be found on the World Wide Web *(www.nimh.nih. gov/anxiety)*. **The information in this profile has been abbreviated to make room for more widely used medicines.**

QUINAPRIL (KWIN a pril)

Introduced: 1984   **Class:** Antihypertensive, ACE inhibitor
Please see the angiotensin converting enzyme (ACE) inhibitor family profile.

*See Schedules of Controlled Drugs at the back of this book.

QUINIDINE (KWIN i deen)

Introduced: 1918 **Class:** Antiarrhythmic **Prescription:** USA:
Yes **Controlled Drug:** USA: No; Canada: No **Available as Generic:**
Yes

Brand Names: ♥Apo-Quinidine, ♥Biquin Durules, Cardioquin, Cin-Quin,
Duraquin, ♥Natisedine, ♥Novo-Quinidin, Quinaglute Dura-Tabs, ♥Quinate,
Quinatime, Quinidex Extentabs, ♥Quinobarb [CD], Quinora, Quin-Release,
SK-Quinidine Sulfate

BENEFITS versus RISKS

Possible Benefits	*Possible Risks*
EFFECTIVE TREATMENT OF SELECTED HEART RHYTHM DISORDERS	NARROW TREATMENT RANGE FREQUENT ADVERSE EFFECTS NUMEROUS ALLERGIC AND
IDIOSYNCRATIC REACTIONS	DOSE-RELATED TOXICITIES Provocation of abnormal heart rhythms Abnormally low blood platelet count Hemolytic anemia Kidney or liver toxicity

---

▷ **Principal Uses**
  As a Single Drug Product: Uses currently included in FDA-approved labeling:
    (1) Helps control the following types of abnormal heart rhythm: atrial fib-
    rillation and flutter, paroxysmal atrial tachycardia, paroxysmal ventricular
    tachycardia, premature atrial, and ventricular contractions; (2) intra-
    venous treatment of malaria in people who cannot take medicine by
    mouth.
  Other (unlabeled) generally accepted uses: Not defined at present.
  As a Combination Drug Product [CD]: This drug is available (in Canada) in
    combination with a barbiturate, a mild sedative that is added to allay the
    anxiety and nervous tension that often accompany heart rhythm disorders.

How This Drug Works: Slows activity of the heart pacemaker and delays electrical impulses through the heart conduction system, restoring normal heart
  rate and rhythm.

Available Dosage Forms and Strengths

Capsules — 200 mg, 300 mg
Injections — 80 mg/ml, 200 mg/ml
Tablets — 100 mg, 200 mg, 275 mg, 300 mg
Tablets, prolonged-action — 250 mg, 300 mg, 324 mg, 330 mg

▷ **Usual Adult Dosage Ranges:** *Premature Atrial or Ventricular Contractions*:
  Quinidine sulfate immediate-release—200 to 400 mg every 4 to 6 hours.
  Quinidine sulfate extended-release (Quinidex Extentabs)—300 to 600 mg
  every 8–12 hours. Quinidine gluconate—324 mg to 648 mg or 1–2 tablets
  every 8–12 hours. Dosing is adjusted to patient response and blood levels
  (2-8 mcg/ml).
  Paroxysmal Atrial Tachycardia: 400 to 600 mg every 2 to 3 hours until paroxysm
    is terminated.
  Atrial Flutter: Digoxin is given first (digitalize); then individualize dose sched-
    ule as appropriate.

Atrial Fibrillation: Digoxin is given first (digitalize); then try 200 mg every 2 to 3 hours for five to eight doses; increase dose daily until normal rhythm is restored or toxic effects develop.

Maintenance Schedule: 200 to 300 mg three or four times daily.

Note: Actual dose and schedule must be determined for each patient individually.

Conditions Requiring Dosing Adjustments

Liver Function: This drug is extensively metabolized in the liver. Blood levels should be obtained to guide dosing. A larger loading dose and a 50% decreased ongoing (maintenance) dose may be indicated.

Kidney Function: Blood levels should be obtained and used to guide dosing. Quinidine should be used with **CAUTION** in renal compromise.

▷ **Dosing Instructions:** This drug is preferably taken on an empty stomach to achieve high blood levels rapidly. However, it may be taken with or following food to reduce stomach irritation. The regular tablets may be crushed and the capsules opened. Prolonged-action forms should be swallowed whole without alteration. If you forget a dose: Take the missed dose as soon as you remember it, unless you've missed your dose by 2 hours for immediate-release forms or 4 hours for sustained-release forms—if that is the case, skip the missed dose and take the next dose right on schedule. Call your doctor if you've missed more than two doses. Talk with your doctor if you find yourself missing doses. There are a variety of reminder pill boxes or even beeper systems to help.

Usual Duration of Use: Use on a regular schedule for 2 to 4 days usually determines effectiveness in correcting or preventing responsive abnormal rhythms. Long-term use (months to years) requires physician supervision and periodic evaluation and blood levels.

Typical Treatment Goals and Measurements (Outcomes and Markers)

Abnormal Heartbeats: The general goal is to return the heart to a normal rhythm or at least to markedly reduce the occurrence of abnormal heartbeats. In life-threatening arrhythmias, the goal is to abort the abnormal beats and return the pattern to normal. Success at ongoing suppression may involve ambulatory checks of heart rate and rhythm for a day (such as in Holter monitoring). This kind of testing involves placement of adhesive-backed temporary electrodes on the skin in several positions around the heart. A small heart rate and rhythm (EKG or ECG) recording device is carried around via a shoulder strap and records what the heart is doing over 24 hours. Once the recording is made, a scanning machine reviews the record, tallies abnormal heartbeats or rhythms, and gives a close and extended look at how the heart is reacting or benefiting from the medicines that the patient is taking. Repeat measurements can be made if doses are changed to check the success at keeping the heart at normal sinus rhythm!

▷ **This Drug Should Not Be Taken If**

- you have had an allergic or idiosyncratic reaction to it or to quinine previously.
- you currently have an acute infection of any kind.
- you have taken too much digoxin (digoxin toxicity).
- you have myasthenia gravis or kidney disease.
- you have an AV block (complete) and do not have an artificial pacemaker or you have conduction problems in the ventricles (intraventricular conduction defects).

- you have abnormal heart rhythms caused by an escape mechanism (ask your specialist).

▷ **Inform Your Physician Before Taking This Drug If**
- you have coronary artery disease or sick sinus syndrome.
- you have a history of excessive thyroid function (hyperthyroidism).
- you usually have very low blood pressure.
- you have had a deficiency of blood platelets in the past from any cause.
- your blood chemistry (electrolyte content) is not in balance.
- you are now taking, or have taken recently, any digitalis preparation (digitoxin, digoxin, etc.).
- you will have surgery with general anesthesia.
- you have a history of passing out (syncopal episodes).
- you have acute rheumatic fever or subacute bacterial endocarditis (SBE).

Possible Side Effects (natural, expected, and unavoidable drug actions)
Drop in blood pressure, may be marked in some patients and cause passing out (syncope). Drug fever—reported.

▷ **Possible Adverse Effects** (unusual, unexpected, and infrequent reactions)
If any of the following develop, consult your physician promptly for guidance.

Mild Adverse Effects
Allergic reactions: skin rash, hives, itching, drug fever—rare.
Irritation of the esophagus (esophagitis)—possible.
Nausea, vomiting, diarrhea—infrequent.

Serious Adverse Effects
Allergic reactions: severe skin reactions, hemolytic anemia (see Glossary), joint and muscle pains, anaphylactic reaction (see Glossary), reduced blood platelet count, drug-induced hepatitis (see Glossary).
Idiosyncratic reactions: skin rash, fast heart rate, delirium, difficult breathing.
Dose-related toxicity (cinchonism): blurred vision, ringing ears, hearing loss, coma, heart (cardiac) arrest.
Mental status changes: paranoia, memory loss, depression, psychosis—reported.
Drug-induced myasthenia gravis, systemic lupus erythematosus (SLE) or carpal tunnel syndrome—case reports.
Swelling of the lymph glands in the inguinal area (lymphadenopathy)—case report.
Kidney toxicity—case reports.
Heart conduction abnormalities (Torsade de Pointes, others)—case reports.
Optic neuritis, impaired vision—case report.
Abnormally low white blood cell count: fever, sore throat, infections—case reports.
Abnormally low platelet count—case reports.

▷ **Possible Effects on Sexual Function:** None reported.

▷ **Adverse Effects That May Mimic Natural Diseases or Disorders**
Drug-induced hepatitis may suggest viral hepatitis.

Natural Diseases or Disorders That May Be Activated by This Drug
Systemic lupus erythematosus, myasthenia gravis, psoriasis (in sensitive people).

Possible Effects on Laboratory Tests
Complete blood cell counts: decreased red cells, hemoglobin, white cells, and platelets; increased eosinophils (allergic reaction); marked increase of white blood cells in association with "quinidine fever"—very rare.

Antinuclear antibodies (ANA): positive.

INR (protime): increased (when *taken concurrently* with warfarin).

Liver function tests: increased enzymes (ALT/GPT, AST/GOT, alkaline phosphatase) or bilirubin.

CAUTION

1. Dose adjustments must be based upon individual reaction.
2. Dosing schedules differ for the various salt forms (the second part of the generic name). For example, quinidine sulfate (83% anhydrous quinidine) is not the same as quinidine gluconate (62% anhydrous quinidine) or quinidine polygalacturonate (60% anhydrous quinidine). MAKE CERTAIN that any refill prescriptions contain the correct medicine.
3. It is prudent to carry a card saying that you take this drug in case of an accident.

Precautions for Use

By Infants and Children: A test for drug idiosyncrasy should be made before starting treatment with this drug. Dosing is made on weight and is an unlabeled use of this medicine. If there is no beneficial response after 3 days of adequate dose, this drug should be discontinued.

By Those Over 60 Years of Age: Small doses are mandatory until your individual response has been determined. Observe for the development of lightheadedness, dizziness, weakness, or sense of impending faint. Use *CAUTION* to prevent falls.

▷ **Advisability of Use During Pregnancy**

Pregnancy Category: C. See Pregnancy Risk Categories at the back of this book.

Animal Studies: No information available.

Human Studies: Adequate studies of pregnant women are not available. No birth defects have been reported following use of this drug during pregnancy.

Use this drug only if clearly needed.

Advisability of Use If Breast-Feeding

Presence of this drug in breast milk: Yes.

Avoid drug or refrain from nursing.

Habit-Forming Potential: None.

Effects of Overdose: Nausea, vomiting, ringing in the ears, headache, jerky eye movements, double vision, altered color vision, confusion, delirium, hot skin, seizures, coma.

Possible Effects of Long-Term Use: None reported.

Suggested Periodic Examinations While Taking This Drug (at physician's discretion)

Complete blood cell counts.

Electrocardiograms.

Blood levels.

▷ **While Taking This Drug, Observe the Following**

Foods: Restrict or eliminate grapefruit (delays absorption and slows the speed at which the body changes this medicine to the active form).

Herbal Medicines or Minerals: Kola, St. John's wort, ma huang, guarana, and yohimbe may cause additive heart rate or rhythm problems. These are not advisable if you have heart rhythm difficulties. Using St. John's wort, ma huang, ephedra, or kola while taking this medicine may result in unacceptable heart stimulation. Belladonna, henbane, scopolia, pheasant's eye extract or lily of the valley, or squill powdered extracts should NOT be taken if you have abnormal heart rhythms. Since St. John's wort and quinidine may increase sun sensitivity, the combination is NOT advised.

Beverages: Ask your doctor about caffeine intake. Avoid grapefruit juice (delays absorption and slows the speed at which the body changes this medicine to the active form).

May be taken with milk.

▷ *Alcohol:* Use caution—alcohol may enhance the blood pressure–lowering effects of this drug.

Tobacco Smoking: Nicotine can increase irritability of the heart and aggravate rhythm disorders. Avoid all forms of tobacco.

▷ *Other Drugs*

Quinidine *taken concurrently* with
- aspirin may prolong the bleeding time.
- beta blockers (see Drug Classes) may result in additive and undesirable beta-blockade; lower starting doses may be needed for both medicines.
- cisapride (Propulsid) may lead to serious heart rhythm problems—DO NOT COMBINE.
- clomipramine (Anafranil) may lead to dry mouth, sedation, or abnormal heartbeats. Careful patient follow-up is needed if these two medicines must be combined.
- codeine may blunt the effectiveness of codeine.
- dextromethorphan (the DM in many cough preparations) can lead to dextromethorphan toxicity—DO NOT COMBINE.
- dofetilide (Tikosyn) may lead to serious heart rhythm problems—DO NOT COMBINE. Prudent to wait roughly five (4.32 half-lives) after stopping a prior class-one antiarrhythmic or other QTc prolonging drug before starting dofetilide.
- fluoxetine (Prozac) may lead to quinidine or fluoxetine toxicity.
- gatifloxacin (Tequin), grepafloxacin (Raxar), moxifloxacin (Avelox), or sparfloxacin (Zagam) may lead to abnormal heartbeats.
- magnesium-containing antacids (various) may lead to excessive accumulation of quinidine and quinidine toxicity. More frequent checks of blood levels are prudent if these medicines must be combined.
- medicines such as class I, IA, or III antiarrhythmics (dofetilide [Tikosyn], clarithromycin, cotrimoxazole, ondansetron, ziprazidone, and others) may lead to prolongation of the QTc interval and undesirable effects. Combination is not recommended (see amiodarone note above regarding extreme caution if these two medicines are combined or if transition is made from quinidine to amiodarone).
- metformin (Glucophage) may increase risk of lactic acidosis.
- neuromuscular blocking agents (such as pancuronium-Pavulon, vecuronium-Norcuron, others) can result in increased severity of muscle blockade. Use of lower neuromuscular blocker doses is prudent.
- nisoldipine (Sular) may blunt nisoldipine benefits.
- tramadol (Ultram) may lead to tramadol toxicity.
- tricyclic antidepressants (see Drug Classes) may result in antidepressant toxicity.
- venlafaxine (Effexor) may result in venlafaxine toxicity.

Quinidine may *increase* the effects of
- anticoagulants (Coumadin, etc.) and increase the risk of bleeding; more frequent INR (prothrombin time or protime) testing is needed.
- digitoxin and digoxin (Lanoxin) and cause digitalis toxicity.
- disopyramide (Norpace).

- metformin (Glucophage).
- propafenone (Rythmol) may lead to propafenone toxicity. Careful patient follow-up is critical as propafenone dosing adjustments may be required.
- tricyclic antidepressants (amitriptyline, doxepin).
- warfarin (Coumadin) and may result in coagulation changes (inconsistent effect). More frequent INR checks are prudent.

The following drugs may *increase* the effects of quinidine:

- amiodarone (Cordarone). The quinidine dose should be about half the usually recommended dose for patients who are already taking amiodarone and a decision has been made to switch from amiodarone to quinidine. If combination treatment is thought to be required, careful checks of dosing and cautious checks of blood levels are critical to avoid development of atypical quick heart rates in the ventricles (such as Torsade de Pointes).
- amprenavir (Agenerase).
- cimetidine (Tagamet).
- delavirdine (Rescriptor).
- diclofenac (Voltaren).
- diltiazem (Cardizem).
- erythromycin (various).
- itraconazole (Sporanox), ketoconazole (Nizoral), or voriconazole (Vfend).
- quinupristin/dalfopristin (Synercid) may lead to serious heart rhythm problems—extremely careful quinidine level follow-up and careful patient monitoring are critical if these medicines must be combined.
- ritonavir (Norvir), nelfinavir (Viracept), saquinavir (Viracept), and perhaps other protease inhibitors (see Drug Classes)—Do not combine.
- sertraline (Zoloft).
- verapamil (Verelan).

The following drugs may *decrease* the effects of quinidine:

- barbiturates (phenobarbital, etc.).
- phenytoin (Dilantin) or fosphenytoin (Cerebyx).
- rifabutin (Mycobutin).
- rifampin (Rifadin, Rimactane).
- sucralfate (Carafate).

▷ *Driving, Hazardous Activities:* This drug may cause dizziness and alter vision. Restrict activities as necessary.

Aviation Note: The use of this drug *may be a disqualification* for piloting. Consult a designated Aviation Medical Examiner.

Exposure to Sun: Use caution—this drug may cause photosensitivity (see Glossary).

RABEPRAZOLE (rah BEP rah zohl)

Introduced: 2001 **Class:** Proton pump inhibitor, Antiulcer, GERD treatment **Prescription:** USA: Yes **Controlled Drug:** USA: No; Canada: No **Available as Generic:** No

Brand Name: Aciphex

Author's Note: Like lansoprazole, this medicine may offer faster onset and quicker sign and symptom relief in heartburn (GERD). In a recent study in *Helicobacter pylori* (see Mario, FD in Sources), a 20 mg dose twice daily of rabeprazole in combination with clarithromycin (Biaxin) used for seven days was 91.4 percent successful in eliminating *Helicobacter pylori*.

Further head-to-head research is needed to define the place of rabeprazole. Information in this profile will be broadened in future editions if clinical data warrant.

RALOXIFENE (rah LOX i feen)

Introduced: 1997   **Class:** Antiestrogen, selective estrogen receptor inhibitor (SERM), anti-osteoporosis   **Prescription:** USA: Yes   **Controlled Drug:** USA: No; Canada: No   **Available as Generic:** No
Brand Name: Evista

BENEFITS versus RISKS

Possible Benefits	*Possible Risks*
EFFECTIVE PREVENTION OF POSTMENOPAUSAL OSTEOPOROSIS	Changes in blood clotting
	Hot flashes (flushes)
	Weight gain
EFFECTIVE TREATMENT OF POSTMENOPAUSAL OSTEOPOROSIS	
DECREASES RISK OF NEW VERTEBRAL FRACTURES	
REDUCED LDL CHOLESTEROL	
Possible benefits on heart health	
Possible benefits in preventing breast cancer (being studied in the STAR trial)	
Avoids the risk of endometrial cancer possible with hormones	

▷ **Principal Uses**

As a Single Drug Product: Uses currently included in FDA-approved labeling: (1) Helps prevent osteoporosis in women after menopause; (2) treats osteoporosis after menopause.

Other (unlabeled) generally accepted uses: (1) Because of LDL and homocysteine lowering, may have a role in maintaining heart (cardiovascular) health; (2) may have a role in preventing breast cancer (one study found a 76% lower risk of breast cancer in a group of women who took this drug for 3 years [MORE trial], and is now being studied in the STAR trial); (3) Based on the MORE trial, data accumulated on cardiovascular benefits of this drug. The RUTH trial is under way to further define the benefits of raloxifene on the heart. Appears likely to have a significant role in preventing cardiovascular disease.

Author's Note: Tamoxifen reduced breast cancer rates by almost half in a very large (13,388 patients) cancer prevention study performed by the National Cancer Institute over 6 years. The FDA has launched a new oncology tools website. Visit this at *www.fda.gov/cder/cancer.* **There is a listing of cancer medicine trials on the World Wide Web at** *http://cancertrials.nci.nih.gov.* **The STAR (Study of Tamoxifen and Raloxifene) trial is under way. This is a National Cancer Institute study evaluating 20,000 women who are at risk for breast cancer. They will be given either 20 mg per day of tamoxifen or 60 mg of**

raloxifene each day for five years. For more information, you can reach the National Cancer Institute at 1-800-422-6237. An analysis done after the Multiple Outcomes of Raloxifene Evaluation (MORE) trial (secondary analysis—see Barrett-Connor in references) showed that raloxifene use in 1,035 women with high heart (cardiovascular) risk, the rate of cardiovascular events was much lower than with placebo (40% decrease when cardiovascular events are defined as coronary plus cerebrovascular events). The CORE results are expected in the fall of 2003. The Raloxifene Use for The Heart (RUTH) trial is ongoing (started in 1998, is a seven-year trial) and is studying raloxifene in women with known heart (coronary) risk factors or coronary disease.

How This Drug Works: Works similar to estrogen itself on the bone (increasing bone density) and on LDL cholesterol (lowering it). Because of this, some people in the news media call raloxifene a designer estrogen. May block use (uptake) of estrogen (estradiol) and remove one stimulus for breast cancer. Benefits in preventing cardiovascular disease may involve decreases in fibrinogen, positive changes in endothelial function, decreased LDL and homocysteine. More data are needed.

Available Dosage Forms and Strengths
Tablets — 60 mg

▷ **Usual Adult Dosage Ranges:**
Prevention of Postmenopausal Osteoporosis: 60 mg once daily. Supplemental calcium and vitamin D are prudent.
Treatment of Postmenopausal Osteoporosis: 60 mg once daily. Supplemental calcium and vitamin D are prudent.
Note: Actual dose and schedule must be determined for each patient individually.

Conditions Requiring Dosing Adjustments
Liver Function: Extensively changed (metabolized) in the liver. Dose decreases appear prudent, but drug use not studied in this population. Most of the drug removal from the body is via feces.
Kidney Function: Not studied in people with kidney disease or compromise.

▷ **Dosing Instructions:** The tablet may be crushed and taken without regard to food. If you forget a dose: Take the missed dose as soon as you remember it, unless it's nearly time for your next dose—if that is the case, skip the missed dose and take the next dose right on schedule. Talk with your doctor if you find yourself missing doses. There are beeper-based systems to help you. If a switch is being made from estrogen to raloxifene, some clinicians taper estrogen over at least a month to help decrease the chance of sudden menopause symptoms. It may also be best to have stopped taking estrogen for a month before starting raloxifene—this approach will allow any raloxifene-related problems to be clearly identified.

Usual Duration of Use: Use in clinical trials compared two years of raloxifene use to calcium use alone. The RUTH trial is ongoing. Some trials used measures of bone mineral density (BMD) to check the benefits of this drug. It appears prudent to check BMD before starting this medicine and then to recheck markers of bone turnover (such as N-telopeptides) and BMD once the medicine has been started to make sure that it is working. Long-term use requires physician supervision.

Typical Treatment Goals and Measurements (Outcomes and Markers)
Bone Mineral Density: The general goal is to at least prevent further bone loss,

and ideally, increase bone mineral density or BMD. Results can be checked by a lab test (N-telopeptide) and repeat DEXA, PDEXA, or ultrasound. The overall goal is to decrease fracture risk.

Possible Advantages of This Drug

Effective treatment of osteoporosis. Appears to confer heart (cardioprotective) benefits as well as possible prevention of breast cancer with a single medicine. Large studies are under way.

▷ **This Drug Should Not Be Taken If**
- you had a serious allergic or adverse reaction to it before.
- you have a history of blood clots (clot in the retinal vein, DVT, or pulmonary embolism [PE]).
- you are pregnant or are breast-feeding your infant.

▷ **Inform Your Physician Before Taking This Drug If**
- you are taking estrogen (not studied with this drug).
- you have a history of thrombophlebitis or pulmonary embolism.
- you have impaired liver function.
- you plan to have surgery or will be immobilized (prolonged rest in bed) in the near future.
- you have an active malignancy (benefit-to-risk decision).
- your diet is low in calcium or vitamin D (smart to take a supplement if your diet is deficient).

Possible Side Effects (natural, expected, and unavoidable drug actions)

Hot flashes—may be frequent.

▷ **Possible Adverse Effects** (unusual, unexpected, and infrequent reactions)

If any of the following develop, consult your physician promptly for guidance.

Mild Adverse Effects

Allergic reaction: skin rash.

Insomnia, migraine, nerve pain, or depression—infrequent.

Weight gain—infrequent.

Sweating—infrequent.

Indigestion (dyspepsia), nausea, or vomiting—infrequent.

Cough, sinusitis, or pharyngitis—infrequent.

Joint (may be frequent) or muscle pain—infrequent.

Varicose veins—rare.

Swelling of the ankles or wrists (edema)—infrequent.

Serious Adverse Effects

Increased uterine cancer risk was found in mice and rats. How this applies to humans is not known.

Chest pain—infrequent.

Liver toxicity—case report.

Blood clots (thromboembolism)—twofold increased risk of lung (PE) and 3.4-fold increased risk of clots in veins (venous thromboembolism).

▷ **Possible Effects on Sexual Function:** Vaginitis (up to 4.3 %).

Possible Effects on Laboratory Tests

Markers of bone turnover (bone specific alkaline phosphatase): decreased.

Bone mineral density: increased.

Liver function tests: may be increased (questionable cause).

CAUTION

1. Calcium supplements should be added to your diet if your diet does not include enough calcium. Talk to your doctor about the need for vitamin D.

2. Research has not been done combining this medicine with estrogen.
3. Ask your doctor about how to decrease risk factors for osteoporosis. Also ask about an exercise program appropriate to your degree of bone loss.
4. One researcher questioned mouse and rat data that showed raloxifene causing cancer of the ovaries in those animals. The manufacturer said that cancer in rodents did not correspond to risk of cancer in humans.
5. This drug has not been studied for use in men.
6. A head-to-head trial of tamoxifen and raloxifene has started to look at benefits and risks of use in preventing breast cancer (STAR trial).
7. Data are available (MORE trial) that show that this medicine can help prevent fractures in the spine (vertebral fractures) as well as fractures of the hip.
8. This medicine may increase risk of blood clots, and therefore use is a benefit-to-risk decision in patients with active malignancies (which may also increase blood clots).
9. Ask your doctor about how prudent it would be for sitting for extended periods (such as on a long flight or a long trip in the car).

▷ **Advisability of Use During Pregnancy**
Pregnancy Category: X. See Pregnancy Risk Categories at the back of this book.
Human Studies: Studies of pregnant women will not be done. This drug should NOT be used during pregnancy.

Advisability of Use If Breast-Feeding
Presence of this drug in breast milk: Unknown.
Avoid drug or refrain from nursing.

Habit-Forming Potential: None.

Effects of Overdose: An accidental dose of 600 mg was tolerated in clinical trials.

Possible Effects of Long-Term Use: Increased bone mineral density, prevention of spine fractures.

Suggested Periodic Examinations While Taking This Drug (at physician's discretion)
Bone mineral density testing.
Laboratory tests of bone turnover.
Periodic liver function tests.
Check for blood clots.
Regular gynecological examinations.

▷ **While Taking This Drug, Observe the Following**
Foods: No restrictions.
Herbal Medicines or Minerals: Make certain that you are getting adequate calcium in your diet if you have osteoporosis or thin bones (osteopenia). The average American diet has about 200–400 mg. Most people need 1,000 to 1,500 mg per day. Effervescent calcium (resulting in a solution) may be absorbed more rapidly than other forms of calcium and can help prevent osteoporosis. Vitamin D and adequate sunlight are also needed. Soy or other plant-derived phytoestrogens may work to complement raloxifene, but have not been studied together with raloxifene. Ipriflavone is a synthetic flavonoid currently investigational for osteoporosis (which both inhibits bone resorption by reducing osteoclast recruitment and encourages osteoblast function). Combined use once again has not been studied in osteoporosis used with raloxifene. Some breast cancer patients are taking mistletoe (Iscador, others). This herbal is available by prescription in

Europe and may work to stimulate the immune system, but there are no combined raloxifene trials.

Beverages: Watch intake of phosphorous from soda. May be taken with milk.

▷ *Alcohol:* No interactions with the medicine expected, but clinicians count alcohol as something that slows the cells that make bone, potentially worsening osteopenia or osteoporosis.

Tobacco Smoking: No interactions expected. I advise everyone to quit smoking.

▷ *Other Drugs*

The following drugs may *decrease* the effects of raloxifene:
- ampicillin (Polycillin, Principen).
- ampicillin/sulbactam (Unasyn).
- cholestyramine (Questran).
- corticosteroids such as prednisone (Deltasone, others), as long-term use of those medicines can lead to osteoporosis.

Raloxifene *taken concurrently* with
- other highly protein bound medicines, such as diazepam (Valium), indomethacin (Indocin), naproxen (Naprosyn), or others, should be done only with great caution.
- warfarin (Coumadin) may lower benefits of warfarin; increased frequency of INR (prothrombin time or protime) testing is needed.

▷ *Driving, Hazardous Activities:* No restrictions thought to be needed.

Aviation Note: The use of this drug *is probably not a disqualification* for piloting. Consult a designated Aviation Medical Examiner.

Exposure to Sun: No restrictions.

RAMIPRIL (ra MI pril)

Introduced: 1985 **Class:** Antihypertensive, ACE inhibitor

Please see the angiotensin converting enzyme (ACE) inhibitor family profile.

RANITIDINE (ra NI te deen)

Author's Note: ALL of the four available histamine (H2) receptor blocking drugs are now available without prescription. See the histamine (H2) blocking drug family profile.

REPAGLINIDE (ra PAG lyn ide)

Author's Note: Information in this profile has been truncated in order to make room for nateglinide, which has a more favorable benefit-to-risk profile.

Introduced: 1998 **Class:** Antidiabetic, meglitinides **Prescription:** USA: Yes **Controlled Drug:** USA: No; Canada: No **Available as Generic:** No

Brand Names: ❧Gluconorm, Prandin

RIBAVIRIN (RHI bah vye ron)

Author's Note: This medicine is used in conjunction with peginterferon alpha-2A (see profile previously detailed) to treat hepatitis C, and this profile will focus on that combined use and on Copegus form for this edition. Specific genotypes drive ribavirin dosing (see below).

Introduced: 2003 (Copegus form) **Class:** Antiviral **Prescription:** USA: Yes **Controlled Drug:** USA: No; Canada: No **Available as Generic:** No

Brand Names: Copegus, Rebetrol, Virazole

BENEFITS versus RISKS	
Possible Benefits	*Possible Risks (Combination)*
COMBINATION TREATMENT OF HEPATITIS C (DRUG NAIVE) COMBINATION TREATMENT OF HEPATITIS C WITH INTERFERON MORE EFFECTIVE THAN UNMODIFIED INTERFERON COMBINATION FOR HEPATITIS C WHEN USED WITH PEGASYS Improved quality of life versus some other Hepatitis C treatments	HEADACHE FATIGUE NAUSEA OR DIARRHEA MUSCLE CHANGES INSOMNIA DEPRESSION BLOOD CELL CHANGES

▷ **Principal Uses**

As a Single Drug Product: Uses currently included in FDA-approved labeling: (1) Treats hepatitis C in combination with interferon alpha-2A (Pegasys), in people who were not previously given interferon alpha, who have compensated liver disease and have evidence of cirrhosis (histological basis and Child-Pugh class A).

Other (unlabeled) generally accepted uses: (1) Not defined at present.

How This Drug Works: For the combination use: The specific form of interferon alpha-2A (Pegasys) is a modified form of the original molecule. A branched methoxy-polyethylene glycol compound is attached (covalently) to the original interferon molecule. The effect of attaching this additional substance to the interferon is to keep it in the body longer (reduces clearance) by the kidney, protects against compounds in the body (enzymes) which might break the interferon alpha-2A down, and allows once-a-week dosing. The attachment also appears to attack the Hepatitis C Virus more forcefully since the drug stays at a higher level than other interferon alpha-2A formulations which are given three times a week (allowing peaks and valleys in concentration and giving the virus more time to recover). The antiviral action of ribavirin is not fully defined.

Available Dosage Forms and Strengths

Tablets — 200 mg

▷ **Usual Adult Dosage Ranges**

Combination Hepatitis C Treatment in Adults (with Pegasys-interferon Alpha-2A): The same dose of 180 mcg once weekly of the peginterferon alpha-2A is given, however, the ribavirin dose changes. Here, genetics are considered: Patients who have genotypes 1 or 4 and who weigh more than 75 kilograms are given 1,200 mg a day. For those less than 75 kg, 1,000 mg a day is given, and combination is continued for 48 weeks. People with geno-types 2 or 3 are given 800 mg of ribavirin (divided into two-400 mg doses given twice a day) coupled with 180 mcg once a week of peginterferon alpha 2A and the combination is only continued for 24 weeks. If an antivi-ral effect is not seen 12–24 weeks into therapy, consideration is given to stopping the medicine.

Note: Actual dose and schedule must be determined for each patient individually.

Conditions Requiring Dosing Adjustments

Liver Function: Patients who have a liver function compromise (Child-Pugh Class A) may be given ribavirin. Other patients with more severe compro-mise have not been studied and SHOULD NOT be given ribavirin.

Kidney Function: People with creatinine clearance (a measure of how well the kidneys work) of less than 50 ml/minute should NOT be given ribavirin.

▷ **Dosing Instructions:** Used in combination with a form of interferon alpha-2A (Pegasys). A qualified specialist should carefully decide dosing, and dosing depends on the genotype of the virus. Pegasys is best taken/given on the same day and time each week. Very specific instructions are present in a Med Guide that comes with Pegasys. If you are going to use Copegus in combination with Pegasys, read the Med Guide that came with that medi-cine and follow the instructions carefully. It is best to take Copegus twice a day, with food.

Usual Duration of Use: Use on a regular schedule for up to 12-24 weeks may be needed to see best effects from the combination of medicines already dis-cussed. Ongoing use for more than 48 weeks does not have efficacy or safety data. Ongoing use requires periodic check of response (such as viral load), check for side effects, laboratory monitoring and possibly dose changes. Make sure you keep follow-up appointments with your doctor and for laboratory or other testing.

Typical Treatment Goals and Measurements (Outcomes and Markers)

The general goal is to lower the amount of virus in the body and ideally to kill all of it. Viral load or burden tests help guide therapy. A test for viral gene-tic material in the serum called HCV-RNA is taken. The goal is to achieve undetectable amounts. The technical term for this is an undetectable HCV-RNA by PCR. Because the usual limit of the test is 100 copies per milliliter, the goal is to achieve "undetectable." When and if lower detection tests become available (as has happened with HIV testing), a new lower goal will become the standard. Additional beneficial effects will be quality of life, halting of progression or cessation of liver damage.

Possible Advantages of This Medicine/These Drugs: The combination of peginterferon alpha-2A with ribavirin gives a more prolonged (durable) lowering of the amount of virus (viral load or viral burden) and in general viral response. For people who have been infected with the Hepatitis C Virus (HCV) with the genotype 1 form, pegylated forms of interferon (2a or 2b) are drugs of choice.

▷ **This Drug or Combination Should Not Be Taken If**
- you have had an allergic reaction to it previously.
- you have autoimmune hepatitis or unstable liver disease or have had a liver transplant.
- you have previously taken and did not respond to other alpha interferon treatment.

- you are taking this medicine and your hemoglobin drops below acceptable levels (see anemia in Pegasys profile).
- you are taking this medicine and your neutrophils (ANC) or your platelet count drops below acceptable level (see ANC in Pegasys profile).
- you have sickle cell anemia, thalassemia major or some other form of abnormal red blood cells (Pegasys).
- you become seriously depressed while taking this medicine (Pegasys).
- you are pregnant or become pregnant while taking this medicine.
- you are a man who has a female partner who is pregnant.
- you are a woman of childbearing age and have not had a negative pregnancy test before starting this medicine.

▷ **Inform Your Physician Before Taking These Drugs If**
- you have a history of bone marrow depression or cancer.
- you have a history of a serious emotional or mental disorder, particularly depression.
- you have a history of alcohol or drug abuse.
- you have a history of heart disease, a prior heart attack, or poor heart circulation (ischemic heart disease).
- you have impaired liver function from hepatitis B (no data) or impaired kidney function.
- you have a history of lung problems (pulmonary dysfunction) or chronic obstructive pulmonary disease (this medicine may worsen them).
- you have a history of diabetes or low thyroid function (hypothyroidism).
- you develop a fever, which gets higher or does not go away.
- you have psoriasis and it gets worse while taking this medicine.
- you are taking any drugs for emotional or mental disorders.
- you have a history of eye problems (such as blood clots in the retinal artery, edema of the macula, or optic neuritis)—talk to your doctor.
- you have a history of low white blood cell counts or cancer.
- you have a history of autoimmune disease (such as lupus erythematosus or rheumatoid arthritis) or are HIV positive
- you have a history of colon inflammation (colitis).
- you ask the person prescribing this medicine about HCV genotyping of the virus causing your hepatitis C infection, and learn that this testing has not yet been performed (genotype of the virus is very important).
- you are unsure how much or how often to take this medicine.

Possible Side Effects (natural, expected, and unavoidable drug actions)
   Injection site reactions (frequent for Pegasys).

▷ **Possible Adverse Effects** (unusual, unexpected, and infrequent reactions)
   If any of the following develop, consult your physician promptly for guidance.
   Mild Adverse Effects
   Allergic reaction: skin rash, itching (pruritis)—may be frequent.
   Headache, fatigue, or fever—frequent.
   Insomnia—frequent (may be prudent to anticipate this effect and ask your doctor for help when this medicine is prescribed).
   Depression (see depression note above)—frequent.
   Blurred vision—possible.
   Dizziness, nausea, or abdominal pain—frequent.
   Sweating—infrequent.
   Loss of appetite (anorexia), diarrhea, abdominal pain—frequent.
   Muscle aches or joint pain—frequent.

Blood sugar changes—possible.

Hair loss—alopecia.

Dry mouth—infrequent.

Serious Adverse Effects

Allergic reaction: Copegus form must be stopped IMMEDIATELY and 911 called if hives (urticaria), swelling (angioedema), difficulty breathing (bronchospasm/bronchoconstriction) or anaphylactic signs and symptoms start.

Depression—see note in Pegasys (may be serious enough to require stopping the medicine).

Decrease or loss of vision (optic neuritis, macular edema, retinal artery blood clots—reported (see vision check below with combination).

Muscle stiffness (rigors)—may be frequent with combination.

Heart attack—case reports for people who became anemic while taking ribavirin.

Low white blood cell counts: fever, sore throat, infection—possible (see Pegasys note regarding dosing).

Aggravation of excessively low or high thyroid function (hypo or hyperthyroidism with combination).

Blood sugar changes—possible with combination.

Pancreatitis—possible with alfa interferon and ribavirin treatment.

Hemolytic anemia (Copegus)—may be frequent (see CBC note below for baseline, etc.).

Decreased platelets—possible (see note in Pegasys profile).

Bloody diarrhea—possible with combination.

Lung problems (pneumonia, interstitial pneumonitis, others)—reported as aggravated or caused by combination.

Aggravation of or development of autoimmune problems (muscle inflammation (myositis), rheumatoid arthritis, systemic lupus erythematosus, others)—possible with combination.

▷ **Possible Effects on Sexual Function:** Animals treated with ribavirin had lowered sperm counts, but no apparent change in fertility. Pegasys may impair fertility in some women. Female cynomolgus monkeys experience amenorrhea or prolonged menstrual cycles.

Adverse Effects That May Mimic Natural Diseases or Disorders

Mood changes, depression may suggest a psychotic disorder from combined use.

Dropping neutrophils (ANC) may mimic other hematologic problems, yet actually be an adverse drug reaction from the Pegasys form during combined use.

Natural Diseases or Disorders That May Be Activated by This Drug

Latent or subclinical depression, epilepsy, incipient congestive heart failure (combined use).

Possible Effects on Laboratory Tests (combined use)

Development of neutralizing antibodies—rare.

Development of binding antibodies—infrequent.

Liver function tests: increased (ALT, bilirubin, others)

White blood cells (neutrophils): lowered ANC.

Hemoglobin: may be decreased.

Triglycerides: increased (frequent).

Platelets: may be decreased.

Blood sugar changes.

Amylase and/or lipase: increased.

CAUTION
1. Talk to your doctor if you or your significant other or a family member notices that you are starting to become depressed (see note on depression in dosing), or think about suicide. This medicine can be a cause of severe depression.
2. While this medicine can successfully attack the hepatitis C virus (particularly in combination with ribavirin), serious possible adverse effects require follow-up and laboratory testing while taking this medicine.
3. Call your doctor if you have trouble breathing, a change in vision or unusual bleeding or bruising.
4. Call 911 if you start to have severe chest pain (some cardiovascular problems have been associated with Pegasys).
5. Negative pregnancy test before starting treatment, two forms of birth control for females and use of a condom for males required while taking this combination. Call your doctor immediately if you become pregnant (see pregnancy note).
6. You develop an ongoing or increasing temperature, sore throat, or other signs of an infection.
7. Triglycerides may be increased. Talk to your doctor about this.

Precautions for Use
By Infants and Children: Safety and effectiveness for those under 18 not established.
By Those Over 60 Years of Age: Some of the measures of how Pegasys is distributed in the body (area under the curve—AUC and half life) were increased or prolonged in people more than 60. Adverse effects from this medicine may be more pronounced in this patient population. Prudent to follow the patient more carefully, and adjust dosing based on undesirable signs and symptoms. Patients over 65 were NOT included in Copegus clinical studies. Because of age-related kidney compromise, risk of adverse effects may be greater in this population if given ribavirin.

▷ **Advisability of Use During Pregnancy**
Pregnancy Category: X for Copegus, C for Pegasys. See Pregnancy Risk Categories at the back of this book.
Animal Studies: Significant teratogenic effects in all animal species where tested as well as embryocidal effects.
Human Studies: Adequate studies of pregnant women are not available.
A negative pregnancy test BEFORE starting this medicine and TWO forms of birth control while taking this medicine and for at least six months AFTER STOPPING it are needed. Male partners of women taking this medicine are advised to use a condom. Not to be taken in pregnancy. Talk to your doctor about how to address the issue of pregnancy and the possible transmission of hepatitis C. If you DO become pregnant, YOU or YOUR DOCTOR should call 1-800-526-6367.

Advisability of Use If Breast-Feeding
Presence of this drug in breast milk: Not defined.
Blood and body fluids may transfer the hepatitis C virus. Breast-feeding is NOT advisable.

Habit-Forming Potential: None.

Effects of Overdose: Management of the symptoms that a patient has at the time that they are seen by a doctor (symptomatic management).

Possible Effects of Long-Term Use: See anemia, white blood cell, and platelet notes for Pegasys.

Suggested Periodic Examinations While Taking This Drug (at physician's discretion—combination use)

Hepatitis C RNA testing (PCR) before and periodically during treatment

Vision testing/eye exam before (baseline) treatment.

Complete blood counts, ANC (baseline, two weeks, four weeks).

Liver biopsy may be needed for some patients, possibly before and during treatment.

Thyroid stimulating hormone (TSH).

Liver (ALT, AST, and bilirubin) before treatment (baseline) and usually every two months.

Kidney function tests.

Amylase and lipase.

Blood sugar, A1C.

Evaluation of heart function at baseline (before therapy) and periodically.

Baseline pregnancy test in females of childbearing age.

Checks for signs and symptoms of depression such as appetite, change in pleasure gained from usually pleasurable activities, or administration of typical depression inventories such as the Hamilton Depression Scale (Ham-D).

Author's Note: Baseline blood and biochemical tests and pregnancy tests for females are needed. Once treatment is started, blood (hematological) tests are checked at 2 and 4 weeks, and repeat biochemical testing done at 4 weeks. In clinical trials, CBC and chemistries (including liver function tests and uric acid) were checked at weeks 1 and 2, four, six and eight. For ongoing treatment, testing was done every four weeks. Testing was obtained more frequently if abnormal results were obtained. TSH was checked every twelve weeks. Pregnancy testing was checked before therapy was started, during combination therapy was checked monthly and for six months after the medicine was stopped.

▷ **While Taking This Drug, Observe the Following**

Foods: Taking Pegasys with a high fat meal increases the amount that gets into your body. Talk to your doctor about how he or she would like you to take this medicine. Use of smaller, more nutrient dense meals may help provide nutrition while acting as a coping mechanism for nausea. Ribavirin should be taken with food.

Herbal Medicines or Minerals: Some herbal medicines such as eucalyptus, kava, and valerian have possible toxic effects on the liver. These herbals should NOT be taken, both because of the viral presence in the liver and because of possible additive undesirable effects on the liver.

Beverages: No restrictions. May be taken with milk.

▷ *Alcohol:* Since alcohol can add to liver problems, any use should be discussed with your doctor for Pegasys. DO NOT drink while taking the combination.

Tobacco Smoking: No interactions expected. I advise everyone to quit smoking.

Marijuana Smoking: Added dizziness.

▷ *Other Drugs*

Peginterferon alpha-2A *taken concurrently* with

- didanosine (Videx) is NOT recommended for the combination or for Pegasys alone. Increased risk of fatal liver failure, pancreatitis, lactic acidosis, and/or peripheral neuropathy preclude this.
- medicines known to have toxic effects on the liver would be best avoided if possible due to overlapping undesirable effects on the liver. Some combinations may represent a benefit-to-risk decision.

- medicines removed by a liver enzyme called CYP 450 1A2 may be increased to toxic levels because peginterferon inhibits this enzyme. Checking blood levels of the medicines combined with peginterferon that undergo such removal is prudent, with dosing adjustments based on blood levels.

  Peginterferon alpha-2A and ribavirin *taken concurrently* with

- stavudine (Zerit) or zidovudine (AZT) may blunt the antiviral benefits of these two HIV medicines.

▷ *Driving, Hazardous Activities:* May cause dizziness, blurred vision, or fatigue. Use caution and assess the extent of these possible undesirable effects BEFORE undertaking such activities.

Aviation Note: The use of this drug *may be a disqualification* for piloting. Consult a designated Aviation Medical Examiner.

Exposure to Sun: No restrictions.

Special Storage Instructions: For Pegasys: care must be taken for proper disposal of needles and avoidance of possible needle sticks by caregivers. The medicine itself should be stored in a refrigerator with a temperature of 36-46 degrees F., (2–8 degrees Centigrade) because lack of refrigeration can break down the medicine. DO NOT SHAKE the bottle as this can also inactivate the medicine. Protect the medicine from light and also make certain that the medicine is not frozen. It is important NOT to leave the medicine out of the refrigerator for more than a day. Once you have drawn up a dose from a given vial of medicine, throw the rest of the medicine in the vial away. Please note the CEPC characteristics of the medicine in dosing instructions for Pegasys. For ribavirin tablets, storage at room temperature is fine.

Discontinuation: See notes on white blood cell, platelet counts, liver function tests, and time that the medicine should be given to work in the Pegasys profile above. Talk to your doctor BEFORE making any changes in dosing or stopping this medicine or the combination.

RIFABUTIN (RIF a byu tin)

Introduced: 1993 **Class:** Antimycobacterial agent (antitubercular)
Prescription: USA: Yes **Controlled Drug:** USA: No; Canada: No
Available as Generic: USA: No; Canada: No

Brand Name: Mycobutin

Warning: Rifabutin prophylaxis must not be taken by people with active tuberculosis.

BENEFITS versus RISKS	
Possible Benefits	*Possible Risks*
PREVENTION OF DISSEMINATED MYCOBACTERIUM AVIUM-INTRACELLULARE COMPLEX IN PEOPLE WITH ADVANCED HIV INFECTION	NEUTROPENIA Low platelet counts

▷ **Principal Uses**

As a Single Drug Product: Uses currently included in FDA-approved labeling:
(1) Prevention of disseminated *Mycobacterium avium-intracellulare* com-

plex in patients with advanced HIV infection; (2) combination treatment of *Mycobacterium avium-intracellulare* complex infection.

Other (unlabeled) generally accepted uses: (1) Some clinicians are using rifabutin in cases of resistant *H. Pylori* that can cause stomach ulcers; (2) early data for use as part of combination treatment of Crohn's disease.

How This Drug Works: Rifabutin inhibits DNA-dependent RNA polymerase (an enzyme critical to cells that are dividing) in *E. coli*. The exact mechanism of action of rifabutin in *Mycobacterium avium* or *Mycobacterium avium-intracellulare* complex is not known.

Available Dosage Forms and Strengths

Capsules (Mycobutin) — 150 mg

How to Store: Keep at room temperature, and avoid exposure to excessive humidity.

▷ **Recommended Dose Ranges** (Actual dose and schedule must be determined for each patient individually.)

Infants and Children: Safety and effectiveness of rifabutin in *Mycobacterium avium-intracellulare* complex prophylaxis has not been clearly established. Safety data comes from a trial of 22 children who were HIV positive.

Infants 1 Year of Age: 18.5 mg per kg of body mass per day.

Children 2–10 Years: 8.6 mg per kg of body mass per day.

Adolescents up to 14 years: 4.0 mg per kg of body mass per day.

14 to 60 Years of Age: 300 mg once a day. Those prone to nausea and vomiting may take 150 mg two times a day with food.

Over 60 Years of Age: Same as 14 to 60 years of age.

Conditions Requiring Dosing Adjustments

Liver Function: At present, clear adjustments of dose in hepatic compromise are not defined, but the drug should be used with caution.

Kidney Function: Elimination of rifabutin may actually be increased in people with compromised kidneys, although the clinical effect is as yet unknown.

Author's Note: The information in this profile has been shortened to make room for more widely used medicines.

RIFAMPIN (ri FAM pin)

Other Name: Rifampicin

Introduced: 1967   **Class:**   Antibiotic,   rifamycins   **Prescription:** USA: Yes   **Controlled Drug:**   USA: No; Canada: No   **Available as Generic:**   Yes

Brand Names: Rifadin, Rifadin IV, Rifamate [CD], Rifater [CD], Rimactane, Rimactane/INH Dual Pack [CD], ✽Rofact

BENEFITS versus RISKS	
Possible Benefits	*Possible Risks*
EFFECTIVE TREATMENT OF TUBERCULOSIS IN COMBI-NATION WITH OTHER DRUGS	DRUG-INDUCED KIDNEY OR LIVER DAMAGE
EFFECTIVE PREVENTION OF MENINGITIS	Blood cell or coagulation disorders
COMBINATION TREATMENT OF SOME STAPH INFECTIONS	Colitis (pseudomembranous)

▷ **Principal Uses**

As a Single Drug Product: Uses currently included in FDA-approved labeling: (1) Treats active tuberculosis—usually given concurrently with other antitubercular drugs to enhance its effectiveness; (2) also used to eliminate the meningitis germ (meningococcus) from the throats of healthy carriers so that it cannot be spread to others; (3) treats tuberculosis in coal workers with good outcomes when combined with other antitubercular drugs; (4) used to prevent tuberculosis in people exposed to patients with active disease; (5) helps prevent meningitis in patients exposed to Neisseria meningitides (best if used within 24 hours of diagnosis of the case from which the person was exposed).

Other (unlabeled) generally accepted uses: (1) Second-line agent in combination with doxycycline in treatment of brucellosis; (2) has a place in preventing *Haemophilus influenzae* infections in people exposed to patients with active disease; (3) combination therapy of lepromatous leprosy; (4) used with cotrimoxazole to eliminate methicillin-resistant Staphylococcus aureus (MRSA) from people who have the bacteria; (5) used with other drugs to treat Staph endocarditis; (6) can be an additional antibiotic in a multiple drug regimen for treating anthrax; (7) part of combination therapy (along with ofloxacin) in diabetic bone infection (osteomyelitis) in the foot.

As a Combination Drug Product [CD]: This drug is available in combination with isoniazid, and pyrazinamide, additional drugs that delay development of drug-resistant strains of the tuberculosis germ (Rifater). It is also combined with isoniazid in a double combination form for the same reason (Rifamate).

In the Pipeline: The Health and Human Services secretary has identified a group of medicines to be tested for use in children. Rifampin was on that list of the 12 highest priority medicines to be studied in children (find out more at *www.hhs.gov/news/press/2003pres/20030121.html*).

How This Drug Works: This drug prevents the growth and multiplication of susceptible tuberculosis organisms by blocking specific enzyme systems that are involved in the formation of essential proteins.

Available Dosage Forms and Strengths

Capsules — 150 mg, 300 mg

▷ **Usual Adult Dosage Ranges**

For Tuberculosis: 10 mg per kg of body mass per day, up to 600 mg once daily. Initial therapy finds use of either ethambutol or streptomycin until the sensitivity pattern of the tuberculosis mycobacteria that is causing the infection is known. After this, rifampin is combined with isoniazid and pyrazinamide for the first 2 months and isoniazid and rifampin are then continued in the subsequent 4 months.

For Meningococcus carriers: 600 mg every 12 hours for two days or 600 mg once daily for 4 days. The total daily dose should not exceed 600 mg.

Note: Actual dose and schedule must be determined for each patient individually.

Conditions Requiring Dosing Adjustments

Liver Function: This drug can cause liver damage, and patients should be followed closely. In severe failure, the dose should be limited to 6 to 8 mg per kg of body mass twice a week.

Kidney Function: For patients with a creatinine clearance (see Glossary) of 10 to 50 ml/min, one researcher suggests that 50% to 100% of the usual dose should be given.

▷ **Dosing Instructions:** This drug is preferably taken with 8 ounces of water on an empty stomach (1 hour before or 2 hours after eating). However, it may be taken with food if necessary to reduce stomach irritation. The capsule may be opened and the contents mixed with applesauce or jelly to take it. Solution form (Australia) should be dosed using a dosing cup or calibrated measuring spoon. If you forget a dose: Take the missed dose as soon as you remember it, unless it's nearly time for your next dose—if that is the case, skip the missed dose and take the next dose right on schedule. DO NOT double doses. Talk with your doctor if you find yourself missing doses.

Usual Duration of Use: Use on a regular schedule for several months usually determines effectiveness in promoting recovery from tuberculosis. Long-term use requires ongoing physician supervision and periodic evaluation.

Typical Treatment Goals and Measurements (Outcomes and Markers)

Infections: The most commonly used measures of serious infections are white blood cell counts and differentials (the kind of blood cells that occur most often in your blood), and temperature. In tuberculosis, clinicians start four medicines for the eight weeks it typically takes for sputum specimens containing this organism to grow to reveal their sensitivity patterns. While clinicians look for positive changes in 24–48 hours in typical infections, this kind of infection REQUIRES long-term treatment to kill it. NEVER stop an antibiotic because you start to feel better. The goals and time frame (see peak benefits above) should be discussed with you when the prescription is written.

▷ **This Drug Should Not Be Taken If**
- you have had an allergic reaction to it previously.

▷ **Inform Your Physician Before Taking This Drug If**
- you are pregnant.
- you have a history of liver disease or impaired liver function.
- you have active liver disease.
- you consume alcohol daily.
- you are taking an oral contraceptive—an alternate method of contraception is advised.
- you are taking an anticoagulant.

Possible Side Effects (natural, expected, and unavoidable drug actions)

Red, orange or brown discoloration of tears, sweat, saliva, sputum, urine, or stool. Yellow coloring of the skin (not jaundice). **Note:** In the absence of illness symptoms, any discoloration is a harmless drug effect and does not mean toxicity. Possible fungal superinfections (see Glossary).

▷ **Possible Adverse Effects** (unusual, unexpected, and infrequent reactions)

If any of the following develop, consult your physician promptly for guidance.

Mild Adverse Effects

Allergic reactions: skin rash, hives, itching, drug fever (see Glossary).

Headache, dizziness, blurred vision, impaired hearing, vague numbness, and tingling—infrequent.

Joint and muscle pain—infrequent and often subsides after a few weeks.

Loss of appetite, heartburn, nausea, vomiting, abdominal cramps, diarrhea—infrequent.

Serious Adverse Effects

Skin problems (Stevens-Johnson Syndrome or toxic epidermal necrolysis)—case reports.

Flu-like syndrome: fever, headache, dizziness, musculoskeletal pain, difficult breathing—case reports.

Drug-induced liver damage, with or without jaundice—frequent.

Kidney damage—infrequent.

Drug-induced porphyria, pancreatitis, gallstones, or pseudomembranous colitis—case reports.

Excessively low blood platelet count: abnormal bleeding or bruising—rare.

Blood-clotting problems (disseminated intravascular coagulopathy)—case report.

Hemolytic anemia—case reports.

Suppression of the adrenal gland—possible.

Some case reports have been made regarding lung tumors (pulmonary malignancies). The cause-and-effect relationship is not yet defined.

▷ **Possible Effects on Sexual Function:** Altered timing and pattern of menstruation—case reports.

Decreased effectiveness of oral contraceptives.

▷ **Adverse Effects That May Mimic Natural Diseases or Disorders**

Liver reactions may suggest viral hepatitis. Kidney reactions may suggest an infectious nephritis.

Possible Effects on Laboratory Tests

Complete blood cell counts: decreased red cells, hemoglobin, white cells, and platelets; increased eosinophils (allergic reaction).

INR (protime): increased (when taken with warfarin).

Liver function tests: increased liver enzymes (ALT/GPT, AST/GOT, and alkaline phosphatase), increased bilirubin.

CAUTION

1. This drug may permanently discolor soft contact lenses.
2. This drug may reduce the effects of oral contraceptives—pregnancy could occur. An alternate method of contraception is advised.
3. Resistance may develop rapidly if this drug is used alone to treat tuberculosis. Only use with other antitubercular drugs.
4. TAKE THE FULL course prescribed; this may be many months.

Precautions for Use

By Infants and Children: Monitor closely for possible liver toxicity or deficiency of blood platelets.

By Those Over 60 Years of Age: Natural changes in body composition and function make you more susceptible to the adverse effects of this drug. Report promptly any indications of possible drug toxicity.

▷ **Advisability of Use During Pregnancy**

Pregnancy Category: C. See Pregnancy Risk Categories at the back of this book.

Animal Studies: Cleft palate and spinal defects reported in rodent studies.

Human Studies: Adequate studies of pregnant women are not available.

If possible, avoid use of drug during the first 3 months.

Advisability of Use If Breast-Feeding

Presence of this drug in breast milk: Yes, but to a small extent (0.05% of the mother's dose goes to the breast milk in 24 hours in one study).

Talk to your doctor about this decision.

Habit-Forming Potential: None.

Effects of Overdose: Nausea, vomiting, drowsiness, unconsciousness, severe liver damage, jaundice.

Possible Effects of Long-Term Use: Superinfections, fungal overgrowth of mouth or tongue.

Suggested Periodic Examinations While Taking This Drug (at physician's discretion)

Complete blood cell counts.

Liver and kidney function tests (frequent liver tests if used with pyrazinamide). Chest X-ray, sputum culture.

Hearing acuity tests if hearing loss is suspected.

▷ **While Taking This Drug, Observe the Following**

Foods: No restrictions.

Herbal Medicines or Minerals: Some patients use echinacea to attempt to boost their immune systems. Unfortunately, use of echinacea is not recommended in people with damaged immune systems. This herb may also actually weaken any immune system if it is used too often or for too long a time. DO NOT take mistletoe herb, oak bark or F.C. of marshmallow root, woody nightshade stem, or licorice.

Beverages: No restrictions.

▷ *Alcohol:* It is best to avoid alcohol completely to reduce the risk of liver toxicity.

Tobacco Smoking: No specific drug interactions expected, but adding smoke to lungs already compromised by a serious infection is not prudent. I advise everyone to quit smoking.

▷ *Other Drugs*

Rifampin *taken concurrently* with

- halothane anesthesia may result in serious liver damage.

Rifampin may *decrease* the effects of

- amiodarone (Cordarone).
- amprenavir (Agenerase).
- antianxiety agents such as diazepam and perhaps other benzodiazepines (see Drug Classes).
- anticoagulants such as warfarin (Coumadin).
- anticonvulsant drugs such as phenytoin (Dilantin).
- barbiturates (see Drug Classes).
- BCG live-attenuated vaccine.
- beta blockers such as metoprolol or propranolol (see Drug Classes).
- birth control pills (oral contraceptives).
- buspirone (Buspar).
- some calcium channel blockers (see Drug Classes).
- carbamazepine (Tegretol)—may lead to carbamazepine toxicity.
- carvedilol (Coreg).
- caspofungin (Cancidas).
- chloramphenicol (Chloromycetin).
- clofibrate (Atromid-S).
- clozapine (Clozaril).
- cortisonelike drugs (see Drug Classes).
- cyclosporine (Sandimmune).
- dapsone.
- delavirdine (Rescriptor).
- digitalis preparations (Lanoxin, others).
- disopyramide (Norpace).
- donepezil (Aricept).
- doxycycline (various).
- enalapril (Vasotec).

- fluconazole (Diflucan), itraconazole (Sporanox), ketoconazole (Nizoral), or voriconazole (Vfend).
- fluvastatin (Lescol).
- fosphenytoin (Cerebyx).
- some HMG-CoA reductase inhibitors (fluvastatin).
- indinavir (Crixivan) and nelfinavir (Viracept).
- leflunomide (Arava).
- losartan (Cozaar).
- methadone (Dolophine).
- metoprolol (Lopressor).
- montelukast (Singulair).
- mexiletine (Mexitil).
- narcotics such as methadone (see Opioids in Drug Classes).
- nelfinavir (Viracept).
- nevirapine (Viramune).
- nicardipine (Cardene).
- nifedipine (Adalat).
- olanzapine (Zyprexa).
- oral hypoglycemic agents (sulfonylureas such as tolbutamide: see Drug Classes).
- phenytoin (Dilantin).
- progestins.
- propafenone (Rythmol).
- quinidine (Quinaglute, others).
- repaglinide (Prandin).
- ritonavir (Norvir)—this combination may also lead to rifampin toxicity.
- rofecoxib (VIOXX).
- sildenafil (Viagra).
- sirolimus (Rapamune) or tacrolimus (Prograf).
- theophylline (Theo-Dur, others).
- tocainide (Tonocard).
- tretinoin (Vesanoid).
- tricyclic antidepressants (see Drug Classes).
- trimexate (Neutrexin).
- verapamil (Verelan).
- warfarin (Coumadin); increased INR testing is needed.
- zaleplon (Sonata).
- zidovudine (AZT); the therapeutic effect will be lessened by a decreased drug level.
- zolpidem (Ambien).

The following drug may ***decrease*** the effects of rifampin:
- para-aminosalicylic acid (PAS) and reduce its antitubercular effectiveness.

▷ *Driving, Hazardous Activities:* This drug may cause dizziness, drowsiness, impaired vision, and impaired hearing. Restrict activities as necessary.

Aviation Note: The use of this drug ***may be a disqualification*** for piloting. Consult a designated Aviation Medical Examiner.

Exposure to Sun: No restrictions.

Discontinuation: It is advisable not to interrupt or stop this drug without consulting your physician. Intermittent use can increase risk of developing allergic reactions.

RISEDRONATE (RIH seh druh nate)

Introduced: 1999   **Class:** Third-generation bisphosphonate   **Prescription:** USA: Yes   **Controlled Drug:** USA: No   **Available as Generic:** No

Brand Name: Actonel

BENEFITS versus RISKS

Possible Benefits	*Possible Risks*
TREATMENT OF POST-MENOPAUSAL OSTEOPOROSIS	DIARRHEA
	Irritation of the esophagus
TREATS AND PREVENTS CORTICOSTEROID-CAUSED OSTEOPOROSIS	Minor flu-like symptoms
SYMPTOM RELIEF IN PAGET'S DISEASE	
MORE POTENT THAN PREVIOUSLY AVAILABLE BISPHOSPHONATES	

▷ **Principal Uses**

As a Single Drug Product: Uses currently included in FDA-approved labeling: (1) Treatment of postmenopausal osteoporosis; (2) treatment of Paget's disease; (3) prevention and treatment of corticosteroid-induced osteoporosis.

Other (unlabeled) generally accepted uses: None at present.

How This Drug Works: This medicine works at the brush border of the osteoclast cell. This prevents this cell from resorbing (gobbling up) bone while the osteoblast (bone-building cell) continues to work. This results in bone building and decreased fracture risk.

Available Dosage Forms and Strengths

Tablets — 30 mg

Author's Note: Information in this profile will be broadened as more data are available and clinical studies are completed. A head-to-head clinical trial of risedronate and alendronate is currently under way.

RISPERIDONE (RIS peer i dohn)

Introduced: 1993, 2003 for M-tab form   **Class:** Antipsychotic agent
Prescription: USA: Yes   **Controlled Drug:** USA: No; Canada: No
Available as Generic: USA: No; Canada: No

Brand Names: Risperdal, Risperdal M-tab

BENEFITS versus RISKS

Possible Benefits	*Possible Risks*
TREATMENT OF SCHIZOPHRENIA REFRACTORY TO OTHER AGENTS	INCREASED RISK OF CEREBROVASCULAR PROBLEMS (including stroke) in elderly, dementia patients
DECREASED SIDE EFFECTS COMPARED TO OTHER AVAILABLE DRUGS	Involuntary movement disorder
EFFECTIVE TREATMENT OF CERTAIN PSYCHOTIC DISORDERS	Neuroleptic malignant syndrome Change in heart function
M-TAB FORM OFFERS THE ABILITY TO TAKE THE MEDICINE WITHOUT NEEDING WATER	
Probably a drug of choice in older adults	
May have a role in easing agitation in dementia patients	

▷ **Principal Uses**

As a Single Drug Product: Uses currently included in FDA-approved labeling: (1) Manages psychotic disorders such as chronic schizophrenia; (2) treats AIDS-related psychosis.

Other (unlabeled) generally accepted uses: (1) Eases behavioral difficulties associated with autism; (2) treatment of aggression; (3) treatment of Tourette's syndrome; (4) can have a role in helping behavioral problems in people with mental retardation; (5) helps treatment-resistant obsessive-compulsive disorder and catatonia; (6) eased psychiatric problems associated with levodopa in one small study of Parkinson's patients.

How This Drug Works: Balances two nerve transmitters (dopamine and serotonin), helping restore more normal thinking and mood.

Available Dosage Forms and Strengths

Oral solution — 1 mg/ml

Tablets, orally disintegrating — 0.5 mg, 1 mg, 2 mg

Tablets — 0.25 mg, 0.5 mg, 1 mg, 2 mg, 3 mg, 4 mg, 5 mg

▷ **Recommended Dose Ranges** (Actual dose and schedule must be determined for each patient individually.)

Infants and Children: Safety and efficacy for those less than 18 years of age are not established.

18 to 60 Years of Age: Past starting dose was 1 mg taken twice daily (to avoid first-dose problems seen with alpha adrenoceptor antagonists). Newly approved dosing has shown doses up to 8 mg taken once a day to be effective. Doses in the twice-daily (BID) approach may be started as 1 mg twice daily and increased as needed and tolerated by 1 mg on the second and third day, for a total of 3 mg twice daily by the third day. If further dose changes are needed, they should be made at 1-week intervals. Doses greater than 8 mg per day are not recommended. Doses more than 16 mg a day have not been studied. If the once a day or twice a day approach is used, it is prudent (given other medical conditions) for some patients to be started on lower doses and more slowly increased than others.

Over 60 Years of Age: Therapy is started with 0.5 mg twice daily. The dose is increased if needed and tolerated by 0.5 mg twice daily. Doses greater than 1.5 mg daily are achieved by small increases made at 1-week intervals. Careful attention must be paid to blood pressure and development of adverse effects.

Conditions Requiring Dosing Adjustments

Liver Function: The starting dose must be decreased and adjusted as for those over 60 years old. Additionally, there may be an increased amount of the active drug that results from each dose (increased free fraction), and, as such, a greater than expected effect may be seen.

Kidney Function: The starting dose must be decreased and adjusted as for those over 60 years old.

▷ **Dosing Instructions:** The original tablet may be crushed, and the medication's effect is not changed by food. Water is the best liquid to take this medicine with. M-TAB FORM dissolves without water. Measuring pipettes (calibrated) are provided with the liquid form. Cola or tea is NOT compatible with the liquid (solution) form (coffee, orange juice, low-fat milk, or water is okay). If you forget a dose: Take the missed dose as soon as you remember it, unless it's nearly time for your next dose—if that is the case, skip the missed dose and take the next dose right on schedule. DO NOT double doses. Talk with your doctor if you find yourself missing doses as there are a lot of timers and even beeper-based systems to help you.

Usual Duration of Use: Use on a regular schedule for 1 to 2 weeks usually determines effectiveness in helping control chronic schizophrenia. Ongoing use must be individualized. If the need for ongoing use is established, the lowest effective dose should be used. Periodic physician evaluation of response and dose is required.

Typical Treatment Goals and Measurements (Outcomes and Markers)

Psychosis: The general goal: to lessen the degree and severity of abnormal thinking, letting patients return to their daily lives. Specific measures of psychosis may involve testing or inventories (and can be valuable in helping check benefits from this medicine).

Possible Advantages of This Drug

Treatment of schizophrenia resistant (refractory) to other therapy. Probably a drug of choice in older adults. The new M-tab form offers convenience, ease of swallowing for patients with swallowing problems and dosing flexibility. This form also helps in some psychiatric settings where patients may be trying to avoid taking their medicine by "cheeking" their pills. Appears to avoid blood sugar changes possible with olanzapine.

▷ **This Drug Should Not Be Taken If**
- you had an allergic reaction to it previously.
- you had neuroleptic malignant syndrome (ask your doctor).
- you have excessive prolactin in your blood (hyperprolactinemia—talk to your doctor).

▷ **Inform Your Physician Before Taking This Drug If**
- you have a history of breast cancer.
- you have liver or kidney compromise.
- you are pregnant or plan to become pregnant or are breast-feeding your infant.
- you have had tardive dyskinesia in the past.
- you have a history of Parkinson's disease or seizures.

- you have a history of heart rhythm disturbances (especially QTc prolongation).
- you are unsure how much to take or how often to take it.

Possible Side Effects (natural, expected, and unavoidable drug actions)
Increased prolactin levels may result in male and female breast tenderness and swelling.
Sleepiness.
Orthostatic hypotension (see Glossary)—rare.
Weight gain—may be frequent (18% in one source).

▷ **Possible Adverse Effects** (unusual, unexpected, and infrequent reactions)
If any of the following develop, consult your physician promptly for guidance.
Mild Adverse Effects
Allergic reaction: skin rash.
Difficulty in concentrating—rare.
Headache or increased dreaming—rare to infrequent.
Constipation, diarrhea, or nausea—infrequent.
Palpitations, edema—rare.
Increased urination—rare.
Serious Adverse Effects
Allergic reactions: anaphylactic reactions.
Abnormal heart function (prolonged QTc interval, PACs, others)—rare.
Tardive dyskinesia (see Glossary) or neuroleptic malignant syndrome—case reports.
Chest pain/myocarditis—rare.
Parkinsonian tremor—case report.
Low sodium—rare.
Opioid withdrawal—case reports in two patients taking opioid (narcotics).
Paresthesia—case reports.
Seizures—rare.
Cerebrovascular problems (stroke, TIA, etc.)—increased risk in elderly, dementia patients (not an approved use).
Lowered white blood cells or platelets—case reports.
Abnormal liver function—rare.
Pancreatitis—case reports.

▷ **Possible Effects on Sexual Function:** Diminished sexual desire; delayed or absent orgasm; erectile dysfunction including priapism; male (gynecomastia) breast tenderness or swelling; dry vagina or menstrual changes (hypermenorrhea)—rare. Ejaculation failure—case reports. Female breast (galactorrhea) milk excretion in the absence of pregnancy—infrequent.

Possible Delayed Adverse Effects: Swelling and tenderness of male and female breast tissue.

Natural Diseases or Disorders That May Be Activated by This Drug: Some human cancers depend on prolactin for growth, and since risperidone increases prolactin, it should be used with ***CAUTION*** by people with previously diagnosed breast cancer.

Possible Effects on Laboratory Tests
Liver Function Tests: increased SGPT, SGOT, and LDH.
Complete Blood Counts: decreased platelets, white blood cells, and hemoglobin.
Prolactin: increased.

CAUTION
1. This drug should be used with great caution, if at all, by patients with cancer.
2. Call your doctor promptly if you have an increased tendency to infection or abnormal bleeding or bruising while taking this drug.
3. This drug should be used with great caution, if at all, by patients with a history of seizures.
4. Increased risk of cerebrovascular problems (such as stroke, TIAs) in elderly patients with dementia.

Precautions for Use
By Infants and Children: Safety and effectiveness for those under 18 years of age are not established.
By Those Over 60 Years of Age: The starting dose of 0.5 mg twice daily is used for patients who are elderly or debilitated, and slower increases in dose as needed and tolerated are indicated. Great care should be taken in patients with heart disease. You may be more likely to experience postural hypotension (see Glossary) and problems with motor skills. Those with prostate problems may have increased risk of urine retention.

▷ **Advisability of Use During Pregnancy**
Pregnancy Category: C. See Pregnancy Risk Categories at the back of this book.
Animal Studies: Increased rat pup death during the first few days of lactation.
Human Studies: Adequate studies of pregnant women are not available. One case report of lack of formation of the corpus callosum of the brain in a fetus exposed to this drug while in the uterus.
Ask your doctor for guidance.

Advisability of Use If Breast-Feeding
Presence of this drug in breast milk: Yes.
Avoid drug or refrain from nursing.

Habit-Forming Potential: None, but a withdrawal syndrome associated with mania has been reported.

Effects of Overdose: Drowsiness, hypotension, tachycardia, low sodium and potassium, ECG changes (prolonged QT interval), and seizure.

Suggested Periodic Examinations While Taking This Drug (at physician's discretion)
Liver function tests.
Electrolytes (sodium and potassium).
ECG.
Prolactin levels.

▷ **While Taking This Drug, Observe the Following**
Foods: No restrictions.
Herbal Medicines or Minerals: New data from a small study of forty patients (see Emsley, R in Sources) found that add-on therapy with one of the components of fish oil (eicosapentanoic acid or EPA) helped schizophrenic patients (Positive and Negative Syndrome Scale scores) and was well-tolerated.
Since risperidone and St. John's wort may act to increase serotonin, the combination is not advised. St. John's wort may also worsen sensitivity to the sun. Ma huang and yohimbe are also best avoided while taking this medicine. Because part of the way that ginkgo and ginseng works is as an MAO inhibitor, DO NOT combine with risperidone. Evening primrose oil can increase risk of seizures. Combination is NOT recommended.

Beverages: No restrictions.

▷ *Alcohol:* Patients should avoid alcohol while taking risperidone.

Tobacco Smoking: No interactions expected. I advise everyone to quit smoking.

Marijuana Smoking: Increased somnolence.

▷ *Other Drugs*

Risperidone may *decrease* the effects of
- levodopa (Sinemet, others).

Risperidone *taken concurrently* with
- bupropion (Zyban, Wellbutrin) can lead to increased blood levels and toxicity from "normal" doses of risperidone. Caution, careful patient monitoring and possible dose reductions are prudent if these medicines must be combined.
- carbamazepine (Tegretol) will decrease the drug level and perhaps the therapeutic effects of risperidone.
- other centrally acting medicines may result in increased central effects.
- clozapine (Clozaril) may decrease the therapeutic effects of risperidone.
- lithium (Lithobid, others) may lead to increased adverse effects.
- medicines that inhibit the liver enzyme Cytochrome P450 2D6 will increase risperidone levels and may lead to toxicity with "normal" doses. Medicines that increase cytochrome P450 2D6 will blunt the benefits of risperidone.
- medicines such as class I, IA, or III antiarrhythmics such as amiodarone (Cordarone), clarithromycin, cotrimoxazole, dofetilide (Tikosyn), ondansetron, ziprazidone, and others may lead to prolongation of the QTc interval and undesirable heart rhythm effects such as Torsades de Pointes. Combination is not recommended.
- methadone (various) may decrease methadone levels and lead to withdrawal symptoms.
- paroxetine (Paxil) and perhaps other SSRIs may lead to serotonin syndrome.
- phenytoin (Dilantin) or fosphenytoin (Cerebyx) may decrease risperidone blood levels and blunt risperidone therapeutic benefits.
- propafenone (Rythmol) may lead to propafenone toxicity.
- ritonavir (Norvir) and perhaps other protease inhibitors (see Drug Classes) may lead to toxicity.
- tramadol (Ultram) may increase seizure risk.
- valproic acid (Depakene, Depakote) may increase valproic acid toxicity risk. Careful patient follow-up and more frequent blood levels are needed.
- venlafaxine (Effexor) may increase risperidone toxicity risk.
- zotepine (Nipolept) may increase seizure risk.

▷ *Driving, Hazardous Activities:* This drug may cause drowsiness and difficulty in concentrating. Restrict activities as necessary.

Aviation Note: The use of this drug *is a disqualification* for piloting. Consult a designated Aviation Medical Examiner.

Exposure to Sun: Use caution—this drug may cause photosensitivity.

Discontinuation: Consult your doctor before stopping this medication.

RIZATRIPTAN (rye zah TRIP tan)

Introduced:	1998	**Class:**	Antimigraine, serotonin-1-receptor agonist	
Prescription:	USA:	Yes	**Controlled Drug:**	USA: No; Canada: No
Available as Generic:	USA: No; Canada: No			
Brand Names:	Maxalt, Maxalt-MLT, ♣Maxalt RPD			

BENEFITS versus RISKS

Possible Benefits	*Possible Risks*
RAPID AND EFFECTIVE RELIEF OR PREVENTION OF MIGRAINE	Fainting
GENERALLY WELL TOLERATED	Small increases in blood pressure
Relieves photophobia (light sensitivity)	Exacerbation of ischemic heart disease (should not be given to those patients)
Relieves phonophobia (sound sensitivity)	Not to be used in hemiplegic or basilar migraine
Relieves nausea and vomiting	Not to be used in significant cardiovascular disease
More potent than some of the other "triptans" currently available	

▷ **Principal Uses**

As a Single Drug Product: Uses currently included in FDA-approved labeling: Acute treatment of migraine with or without aura in adults.

Other (unlabeled) generally accepted uses: None at present.

How This Drug Works: Rizatriptan acts on blood vessels (by acting as a serotonin-1D agonist) to cause vasoconstriction (shrinking of the blood vessels). This relieves swelling, thought to be the cause of migraine. It is more potent dose-to-dose than sumatriptan (Imitrex).

Available Dosage Forms and Strengths

Tablets — 5 mg, 10 mg

Tablets, orally disintegrating (MLT) — 5 mg, 10 mg

Wafer, orally disintegrating (RPD) — 5 mg, 10 mg

Possible Advantages of This Drug: Offers a novel dosage form that is an orally disintegrating tablet. The convenience of this form makes it unobtrusive and easy to take. This medicine is more potent than sumatriptan (mg-to-mg) and may lead to better effects in stopping a migraine headache. Head-to-head trials are needed.

ROSUVASTATIN (Rah SUE vah statin)

Introduced: Investigational (2003?) **Class:** Cholesterol-lowering agent, HMG-CoA reductase inhibitor **Prescription:** USA: Yes **Controlled Drug:** USA: No; Canada: Not available **Available as Generic:** USA: No

Brand Name: Crestor

Author's Note: Information in this profile will be broadened as more data become available.

SALMETEROL (Sal ME Ter Ohl)

Introduced: 1994 **Class:** Bronchodilator **Prescription:** USA: Yes **Controlled Drug:** USA: No; Canada: Not available **Available as Generic:** USA: No

Brand Names: ♣Advair [CD], Advair Diskus, Aeromax, Serevent, Serevent Diskus

```
┌─────────────────────────────────────────────────────────────────┐
│                    BENEFITS versus RISKS                          │
│       Possible Benefits            Possible Risks                 │
│  LONG-ACTING RELIEF OF      Rapid heart rate (tachycardia)        │
│    BRONCHIAL ASTHMA                                               │
│  PREVENTION OF NOCTURNAL                                          │
│  ASTHMA SYMPTOMS                                                  │
└─────────────────────────────────────────────────────────────────┘
```

▷ **Principal Uses**

As a Single Drug Product: Uses currently included in FDA-approved labeling: (1) Treatment and prevention of bronchospasm in asthma; (2) prevention of nocturnal asthma; (3) prevention of exercise-induced bronchospasm; (4) ongoing treatment of chronic obstructive pulmonary disease (COPD). Helps avoid spasm of the bronchi of the lungs (bronchospasm).

Other (unlabeled) generally accepted uses: (1) Could have a role in cystic fibrosis.

As a Combination Drug Product [CD]: This drug has been available in combination with fluticasone. Fluticasone is a corticosteroid that fights inflammation and asthma in a different way than salmeterol (a long-acting beta-2 agonist). This profile will focus on the single medicine form.

How This Drug Works: Acts at specific sites (beta-2) in the lung and opens the airways (bronchodilation), decreasing airway reactivity and increasing movement of mucus. It also blocks release of chemicals from cells (basophils, eosinophils, macrophages and mast) that worsen asthma.

Available Dosage Forms and Strengths

Advair Diskus form — 100/50, 250/50 and 500 mcg fluticasone and 50 mcg of salmeterol per use.

Inhaler — 13-g canister that gives 21 mcg of salmeterol per use.

Serevent Diskus — 50 mcg of salmeterol per use.

▷ **Recommended Dose Ranges** (Actual dose and schedule must be determined for each patient individually.)

Infants and Children: Safety and efficacy in those less than 12 years of age not established.

12 to 60 Years of Age: For Prevention of Asthma:

Inhalation Aerosol Form (Serevent): Two inhalations (42 mcg) twice daily in the morning and evening. Doses are taken 12 hours apart.

Salmeterol Powder for Inhalation (Diskus Form): One disc (contains 50 mcg of salmeterol) 12 hours apart.

Combination form: For asthma: *Fluticasone/salmeterol combination:* the starting dose is 100 mcg fluticasone and 50 mcg of salmeterol in people who are not presently taking an inhaled steroid (corticosteroid). If they are taking an inhaled corticosteroid such as budesonide and the steroid dose is less than or equal to 400 mcg a day, then the combination inhaler containing 100 mcg of fluticasone and 50 mcg of salmeterol is substituted and is taken twice a day. Other doses of budesonide or other corticosteroids require different combinations of fluticasone/salmeterol to get the best results.

For Prevention of Exercised-Induced Asthma:

Inhalation Aerosol Form (Serevent): Two inhalations at least 30 to 60 minutes before exercise. Additional doses of salmeterol should not be taken for 12 hours.

Salmeterol powder for inhalation (Diskus form): One disc (has 50 mcg of salmeterol) given or taken at least 30 minutes before exercise.
Over 60 Years of Age: Same as 12 to 60 years of age.

Conditions Requiring Dosing Adjustments

Liver Function: Use with caution, as the drug may accumulate in liver failure.
Kidney Function: Salmeterol has not been studied in kidney failure patients.

▷ **Dosing Instructions:** Follow written instructions closely. Shake well before using. You may be instructed to use a spacer with the metered dose inhaler form. If you forget a dose: use the missed dose as soon as you remember it, unless it's nearly time for your next dose—if that is the case, skip the missed dose and use the next dose right on schedule. Talk with your doctor if you find yourself missing doses. Like other medicines, benefits come from using the medicine correctly.

Usual Duration of Use: Use on a regular schedule for 4 to 6 weeks usually determines effectiveness in preventing asthma attacks. Long-term use (months to years) requires periodic physician evaluation of response and dose adjustment.

Typical Treatment Goals and Measurements (Outcomes and Markers)

Asthma: Signs and symptoms of asthma such as difficulty breathing (dyspnea), cough, light-headedness, and wheezing should lessen. Forced expiratory volume at one second (FEV1) and/or peak expiratory flow rate (PEF) are checked by most pulmonologists as indicators of successful treatment. If the usual benefit is not realized, call your doctor.

Possible Advantages of This Drug

Longer-acting beta-2 agent than previously available. Combination form offers two mechanisms of action and may last 12 hours or longer in some patients.

▷ **This Drug Should Not Be Taken If**
- you had an allergic reaction to it previously.
- you currently have an irregular heart rhythm.
- you are taking, or have taken within the past 2 weeks, any monoamine oxidase (MAO) type A inhibitor.
- you have sudden onset asthma or status asthmaticus. (Fluticasone or fluticasone/salmeterol WON'T WORK.)

▷ **Inform Your Physician Before Taking This Drug If**
- your breathing does not improve after taking this drug.
- you have an overactive thyroid (hyperthyroidism).
- you have diabetes.
- you have a history of heart problems (such as arrhythmias, coronary insufficiency).
- you have abnormally high blood pressure.
- you are unsure how much to take or how often to take it.

Possible Side Effects (natural, expected, and unavoidable drug actions)

Dryness or irritation of the mouth or throat, altered taste. Nervousness, tremor or palpitations.

▷ **Possible Adverse Effects** (unusual, unexpected, and infrequent reactions)
If any of the following develop, consult your physician promptly for guidance.

Mild Adverse Effects

Allergic reactions: skin rash and urticaria.
Rhinitis and laryngitis—possible.

Rapid heart rate (tachycardia)—case reports.

Tachyphylaxis—conflicting data and reports.

Sleep disturbances—rare to infrequent.

Blood sugar changes—possible.

Headache, tremor, dizziness and nervousness—infrequent.

Serious Adverse Effects

Allergic reactions: anaphylactic reactions.

Paradoxical bronchospasm—possible.

Respiratory arrest—case reports.

Prolonged QTc interval of the heart—reported, but appears to diminish over time.

▷ **Possible Effects on Sexual Function:** Not defined.

Possible Delayed Adverse Effects: None defined at present.

▷ **Adverse Effects That May Mimic Natural Diseases or Disorders**

Rapid heart rate may mimic heart disease. Bronchospasm may mimic asthma.

Natural Diseases or Disorders That May Be Activated by This Drug

Latent coronary artery disease. Diabetes or high blood pressure.

Possible Effects on Laboratory Tests

Blood cholesterol profile: may be increased.

Blood glucose level: increased.

CAUTION

1. Use of this drug by inhalation with beclomethasone aerosol (Beclovent, Vanceril) may increase the risk of fluorocarbon propellant (fluorocarbons being eliminated from these products), but those still containing fluorocarbon propellants may lead to toxicity. Use salmeterol aerosol 20 to 30 minutes **before** beclomethasone aerosol to reduce toxicity and enhance penetration of beclomethasone into the lungs.

2. Serious heart rhythm problems or cardiac arrest can result from excessive and prolonged use.

3. Call your doctor if asthma symptoms appear more often than usual, or if you begin to increase use of the immediate bronchodilator.

4. *Guidelines for the Diagnosis and Management of Asthma* from the National Institutes of Health state that salmeterol should NOT be used for acute symptoms or asthma exacerbations.

5. Combination form works primarily locally in the lung. Because of this, blood (plasma) levels don't predict the benefit (therapeutic effect). Additionally, Advair Diskus form should NOT be used to transfer people who have required systemic steroids due to possible adrenal insufficiency.

Precautions for Use

By Infants and Children: Safety and effectiveness for those under 12 not established for the aerosol form (Serevent). Safety and effectiveness for those under 4 not established for the inhalation powder form (Serevent Diskus).

By Those Over 60 Years of Age: Avoid increased use. If asthma is not controlled as it has been in the past, call your doctor.

▷ **Advisability of Use During Pregnancy**

Pregnancy Category: C. See Pregnancy Risk Categories at the back of this book.

Animal Studies: Rabbit studies have revealed cleft palate, limb and paw flexures and delayed bone formation.

Human Studies: Adequate studies of pregnant women are not available. Ask your doctor for guidance.

Advisability of Use If Breast-Feeding
Presence of this drug in breast milk: not defined.
Avoid drug or refrain from nursing.

Habit-Forming Potential: None.

Effects of Overdose: Exaggeration of pharmacological effects: tachycardia and/or arrhythmia, muscle cramps, cardiac arrest and death.

Suggested Periodic Examinations While Taking This Drug (at physician's discretion)
Blood pressure checks.
Evaluations of heart (cardiac) status. PFTs.

▷ **While Taking This Drug, Observe the Following**
Foods: No restrictions.
Herbal Medicines or Minerals: Using St. John's wort, ma huang, ephedrine-like compounds, guarana, or kola while taking this medicine may result in unacceptable central nervous system stimulation. Fir or pine needle oil should NOT be used by asthmatics. Ephedra alone does carry a German Commission E monograph indication for asthma treatment. If you are allergic to plants in the Asteraceae family (aster, chrysanthemum, daisy, or ragweed), you may also be allergic to echinacea, chamomile, feverfew, and St. John's wort. Since part of the way ginseng works may be as an MAO inhibitor, do not combine ginseng with salmeterol.
Beverages: Avoid excessive caffeine as in coffee, tea, cola and chocolate.
▷ *Alcohol:* No interactions expected.
Tobacco Smoking: No interactions expected. Asthma may be worsened by irritation from smoking. I advise everyone to quit smoking.
▷ *Other Drugs*
Salmeterol *taken concurrently* with
- monoamine oxidase (MAO) type A inhibitors can cause extreme increases in blood pressure and heart stimulation.
The following drugs may *increase* the effects of salmeterol:
- methylxanthines such as caffeine or theophylline.
- tricyclic antidepressants.
▷ *Driving, Hazardous Activities:* This drug may cause nervousness or dizziness. Restrict activities as necessary.
Aviation Note: The use of this drug *is a disqualification* for piloting. Consult a designated Aviation Medical Examiner.
Exposure to Sun: No restrictions.
Heavy Exercise or Exertion: Use caution—this may stress the protective effects of this drug.

SELEGILINE (se LEDGE i leen)

Other Name: Deprenyl

Introduced: 1981   **Class:**   Anti-Parkinsonism, monoamine oxidase (MAO) type B inhibitor   **Prescription:**   USA: Yes   **Controlled Drug:** USA: No; Canada: No   **Available as Generic:**   USA: Yes

Brand Names: ✤Apo-Selegiline, Carbex, ✤Dom-Selegiline, Eldepryl, ✤Med-Selegiline, ✤Novo-Selegiline, ✤PMS-Selegiline

---

BENEFITS versus RISKS

Possible Benefits	*Possible Risks*
EFFECTIVE INITIAL TREATMENT OF PARKINSON'S DISEASE when started at the onset of symptoms	ABNORMAL INVOLUNTARY MOVEMENTS
	HALLUCINATIONS
ADDITIVE RELIEF OF SYMPTOMS OF PARKINSON'S DISEASE when used concurrently with levodopa/carbidopa	INITIAL FALL IN BLOOD PRESSURE/ORTHOSTATIC HYPOTENSION
PERMITS REDUCTION IN SINEMET DOSE	
May have a role in Alzheimer's disease	

▷ **Principal Uses**

As a Single Drug Product: Uses currently included in FDA-approved labeling: (1) Used to start drug treatment of very early Parkinson's disease (soon after onset of symptoms), thus delaying the use of levodopa/carbidopa; (2) also used as an adjunct to levodopa/carbidopa treatment of Parkinson's disease if intolerable abnormal movements (dyskinesia) and/or increasing "on-off" episodes occur—addition of selegiline (a) permits reduction of the daily dose of levodopa with consequent lessening of dyskinesia and erratic drug response and (b) provides additional relief of Parkinsonian symptoms.

Other (unlabeled) generally accepted uses: (1) Some improvement achieved in Alzheimer's disease (some trials also used high-dose vitamin E) in patients treated with this drug; (2) narcolepsy; (3) may have a role in attention deficit hyperactivity disorder (ADHD) where methylphenidate is not tolerated; (4) may work as adjunctive treatment in some schizophrenia cases (in combination with risperidone in one study); (5) has some benefit in depression and bipolar disorder, but not for routine use.

How This Drug Works: By inhibiting monoamine oxidase type B (the enzyme that inactivates dopamine in the brain) and by slowing the restorage of released dopamine at nerve terminals, this drug helps correct dopamine deficiency responsible for rigidity, tremor, and sluggish movement characteristic of Parkinson's disease. Selegiline is changed (metabolized) to amphetamine and methamphetamine in the body, but how these compounds work in the beneficial effect of the drug is unclear.

Available Dosage Forms and Strengths

Capsules — 5 mg

Tablets — 5 mg

Author's Note: The capsule form of this medicine may eventually replace the tablet form and is an astute attempt by the company to help avoid confusion with other white tablets or counterfeit copies of Eldepryl.

▷ **Usual Adult Dosage Ranges:** *Parkinsonism*: 5 mg once or twice daily. The usual maintenance dose is 5 mg after breakfast and 5 mg after lunch. Daily dose of 10 mg is adequate to achieve optimal benefit. Higher doses do not result in further improvement and are not advised. During gradual introduction of selegiline, dose of levodopa/carbidopa (Sinemet) may be cautiously decreased. Sinemet dose should be reduced by 10% to 20% when selegiline is started.

Note: Actual dose and schedule must be determined for each patient individually.

Conditions Requiring Dosing Adjustments

Liver Function: This drug is extensively metabolized in the liver. Patients with liver compromise should be followed closely.

Kidney Function: No dosing changes thought to be needed. It can cause prostatic enlargement (hypertrophy) and should be used with caution in patients with urine outflow problems.

▷ **Dosing Instructions:** The tablet may be crushed and taken with food or milk to reduce stomach irritation. Talk to your doctor about foods high in tyramine (such as soy sauce, red [such as Chianti] and white wines, beer, aged cheese, and figs, etc.) If you forget a dose: Take the missed dose as soon as you remember it, unless it's nearly time for your next dose—if that is the case, skip the missed dose and take the next dose right on schedule. DO NOT double doses. Taking this medicine with breakfast and/or lunch is usually best because taking it with dinner can disrupt your sleep. Talk with your doctor if you find yourself missing doses or having difficulty sleeping.

Usual Duration of Use: Use on a regular schedule for 4 to 6 weeks usually determines effectiveness in controlling the symptoms of Parkinson's disease and permitting reduction of levodopa/carbidopa dose. Long-term use (months to years) requires periodic physician evaluation and goal assessment.

Typical Treatment Goals and Measurements (Outcomes and Markers)

Parkinson's Disease: The general goal is to minimize symptoms (tremor, sluggish movements, analysis of walking or gait, etc.) to the fullest extent possible. Additionally, many neurologists use Hahn-Yahr scores and the time it takes to maximum amount of finger tapping as indicators of the benefits of this drug.

Possible Advantages of This Drug

It may provide a more effective and uniform control of Parkinsonian symptoms and a significant reduction of some adverse effects associated with long-term levodopa therapy.

▷ **This Drug Should Not Be Taken If**
- you have had an allergic reaction to it previously.
- you have Huntington's disease, hereditary (essential) tremor, or tardive dyskinesia (see Glossary).
- you are pregnant or breast-feeding.
- you take meperidine (Demerol).

▷ **Inform Your Physician Before Taking This Drug If**
- you have constitutionally low blood pressure.
- you have peptic ulcer disease.
- you are taking levodopa.
- you have a history of heart rhythm disorder.
- you are taking any antihypertensive drugs, antidepressants, or antipsychotic drugs (see Drug Classes).

Possible Side Effects (natural, expected, and unavoidable drug actions)

Weakness, orthostatic hypotension (see Glossary), dry mouth, insomnia—all rare.

▷ **Possible Adverse Effects** (unusual, unexpected, and infrequent reactions)

If any of the following develop, consult your physician promptly for guidance.

Mild Adverse Effects

Headache, dizziness, blurred vision, agitation—rare.

Change in sleep patterns—reported with conflicting effects of insomnia or improved sleep.

Palpitations, fainting—rare.

Altered taste—rare.

Nausea and vomiting, stomach pain, anorexia—rare to frequent.

Serious Adverse Effects

Dyskinesias: abnormal involuntary movements—infrequent.

Confusion and hallucinations, depression, psychosis, vivid dreams—rare.

Angina and fast heart rate (tachycardia)—infrequent.

Aggravation of peptic ulcer, gastrointestinal bleeding—rare.

Growth of the prostate—rare.

▷ **Possible Effects on Sexual Function:** Transient decreases in penile sensation and anorgasmia have rarely been reported if doses exceed 10 mg per day. Increased libido may occur.

▷ **Adverse Effects That May Mimic Natural Diseases or Disorders**

Effects on mental function and behavior may resemble psychotic disorders.

Natural Diseases or Disorders That May Be Activated by This Drug

Peptic ulcer disease.

Possible Effects on Laboratory Tests

Vanillylmandelic acid (VMA) test will be falsely low.

CAUTION

1. This drug can start dyskinesias and intensify existing dyskinesias. Watch carefully for tremors, twitching or abnormal, involuntary movements of any kind. Report these promptly.
2. This drug potentiates the effects of levodopa. When added to current levodopa treatment, adverse effects of levodopa may develop or be intensified. Levodopa dose must be reduced by 10% to 20% when treatment with selegiline begins.
3. Tell your doctor promptly if you become pregnant or plan pregnancy. The manufacturer does not recommend the use of this drug during pregnancy.
4. Some foods (tyramine-containing—see Glossary) have led to rare increases in blood pressure with selegiline doses greater than 10 mg. Talk to your doctor.

Precautions for Use

By Infants and Children: This drug is not utilized by this age group.

By Those Over 60 Years of Age: This drug is usually well tolerated by the elderly. Observe closely for any tendency to light-headedness or faintness, especially on arising from a lying or sitting position.

▷ **Advisability of Use During Pregnancy**

Pregnancy Category: C. See Pregnancy Risk Categories at the back of this book.

Animal Studies: No birth defects due to this drug were found in rat studies.

Human Studies: Adequate studies of pregnant women are not available.

The manufacturer advises that this drug should not be taken during pregnancy.

Advisability of Use If Breast-Feeding

Presence of this drug in breast milk: Unknown.

Avoid drug or refrain from nursing.

Habit-Forming Potential: None.

Effects of Overdose: Nausea, vomiting, palpitations, low blood pressure, agitation, severe involuntary movements, hallucinations.

Possible Effects of Long-Term Use: None reported.

Suggested Periodic Examinations While Taking This Drug (at physician's discretion)

Regular evaluation of drug response, heart function, and blood pressure status.

▷ **While Taking This Drug, Observe the Following**

*Foods: **CAUTION*** should be used regarding foods containing tyramine (see Glossary for a list), although the reaction with this drug may not be as severe as that seen with other MAO inhibitors.

Herbal Medicines or Minerals: St. John's wort: ***CAUTION*** is advised because of possible serotonin syndrome. St. John's wort may also worsen sensitivity to the sun. The principle active ingredient of guarana and mate is caffeine—and use should be avoided. Since part of the way ginkgo and ginseng work may be as an MAO inhibitor, do not combine with selegiline. Ma huang (contains ephedra), nutmeg, bitter orange, kava, and yohimbe are also best avoided while taking this medicine. Calabar bean (chop nut, fabia, ordeal nut, others) is unsafe when taken by mouth (physostigmine is the active ingredient) and should never be taken by people with Parkinson's disease. Octacosanol (a cousin of vitamin E) can worsen movement problems and should also be avoided.

Beverages: Caffeine-containing beverages may have more of an effect than previously. Limit caffeine consumption. May be taken with milk.

▷ *Alcohol:* Use ***CAUTION*** until the combined effects have been determined. Alcohol may exaggerate the blood pressure–lowering and sedative effects of this drug. Aged wines, etc., containing tyramine may cause a reaction of varying severity.

Tobacco Smoking: No interactions expected. I advise everyone to quit smoking.

Marijuana Smoking: Additive drowsiness may occur.

▷ *Other Drugs*

Selegiline ***taken concurrently*** with

- albuterol (Ventolin, others) may result in increased adverse vascular effects.
- amphetamine (Dexedrine, others) can cause a severe increase in blood pressure.
- antidepressants (see Drug Classes) such as amitriptyline (Elavil) may cause neurotoxic reactions such as seizures.
- antihypertensive drugs (and Other Drugs that can lower blood pressure) require careful monitoring for excessive drops in pressure; dose adjustments may be necessary.
- benzodiazepines (see Drug Classes) may result in increased central nervous system depression.
- beta two type agonist medicines may increase risk of rapid heart rate, hypomania, or agitation.
- birth control pills (oral contraceptives) may increase risk of selegiline toxicity.
- bupropion (Wellbutrin) may cause seizures.
- buspirone (Buspar) may result in increases in blood pressure.
- carbamazepine (Tegretol) may result in high fevers and seizures—still, some studies found benefits in resistant depression.
- citalopram (Celexa) may lead to toxicity—DO NOT COMBINE.
- cyclobenzaprine (Flexeril) may lead to toxicity—DO NOT COMBINE.
- dextromethorphan (various), a cough suppressant used in many nonprescription cough medicines, has been reported to cause toxicity with low

blood pressure, spasms, high fevers, and some deaths—these medicines should not be combined.

- ephedrine (various) can result in severe increases in temperature.
- fluoxetine (Prozac) may cause serotonin toxicity syndrome.
- fluvoxamine (Luvox) may result in extreme agitation, rigidity, excessive temperatures, and coma—DO NOT combine these medicines.
- lithium (Lithobid) may increase risk of the serotonin toxicity syndrome.
- meperidine (Demerol) may cause a life-threatening reaction of unknown cause; avoid this combination.
- methyldopa (Aldomet) MAY LEAD TO HYPERTENSIVE CRISIS—DO NOT COMBINE.
- methylphenidate (Concerta, others) MAY LEAD TO HYPERTENSIVE CRISIS—DO NOT COMBINE.
- mirtazapine (Remeron) may lead to adverse seizures.
- morphine (MS Contin, various) may lead to excessive CNS and lowered blood pressure effects—DO NOT COMBINE.
- nefazodone (Serzone) may lead to serotonin syndrome—DO NOT COMBINE.
- opioid medicines (oxycodone, morphine, others) may lead to excessive CNS depression. Manufacturer does NOT recommend combining.
- oral hypoglycemic agents (see Oral Antidiabetic Drugs in Drug Classes) may cause very low blood sugars.
- paroxetine (Paxil) may result in central nervous system toxicity.
- phenothiazines (see Drug Classes) may result in increased occurrence of movement disorders.
- phentermine (Fastin) may lead to hypertensive crisis—DO NOT COMBINE.
- phenylpropanolamine (now removed from the US market—various) or phenylephrine (various) can cause severe increases in temperature and blood pressure—DO NOT combine.
- pseudoephedrine (various) can cause severe increases in temperature and blood pressure—DO NOT combine (this includes combination forms of pseudoephedrine such as loratadine/pseudoephedrine [Claritin-D]).
- sertraline (Zoloft) may result in central nervous system toxicity.
- sibutramine (Meridia) may lead to toxicity.
- sumatriptan (Imitrex) may lead to toxicity.
- tramadol (Ultram) may lead to seizures.
- tryptophan may cause a fatal serotonin syndrome.
- venlafaxine (Effexor) can result in central and autonomic nervous system toxicity.

The following drugs may *decrease* the effects of selegiline and diminish its effectiveness:

- chlorprothixene (Taractan).
- haloperidol (Haldol).
- metoclopramide (Reglan).
- phenothiazines (see Drug Classes).
- reserpine (Ser-Ap-Es, etc.), in high doses.
- thiothixene (Navane).

▷ *Driving, Hazardous Activities:* This drug may cause dizziness, drowsiness, impaired coordination, or fainting. Restrict activities as necessary.

Aviation Note: The use of this drug *is a disqualification* for piloting. Consult a designated Aviation Medical Examiner.

Exposure to Sun: Use caution—photosensitivity has been reported.

Exposure to Heat: Use caution until the combined effects have been determined. Hot environments can cause lowering of blood pressure.

Discontinuation: **Do not stop this drug abruptly.** Sudden withdrawal can cause prompt increase in Parkinsonian symptoms and deterioration of control. Consult your physician regarding a schedule for gradual withdrawal and concurrent adjustment of Sinemet or other appropriate drugs.

SERTRALINE (SER tra leen)

Introduced: 1986 **Class:** Antidepressant **Prescription:** USA: Yes
Controlled Drug: USA: No; Canada: No **Available as Generic:** USA: No

Brand Names: ✝Apo-sertraline, ✝Dom-sertraline, ✝Gen-sertraline, ✝Novo-sertraline, ✝Ratio-sertraline, ✝Rhoxal-sertraline, ✝Riva-sertraline, Zoloft

---

BENEFITS versus RISKS

Possible Benefits
EFFECTIVE TREATMENT OF
  DEPRESSION
TREATS PANIC DISORDER
TREATMENT OF OBSESSIVE-
  COMPULSIVE DISORDER
TREATS POST-TRAUMATIC STRESS
  DISORDER (PTSD)
TREATS PREMENSTRUAL
  DYSPHORIC DISORDER (PMDD)
MAY BE AN SSRI OF CHOICE IN
  PEOPLE WITH MAJOR
  DEPRESSION AND UNSTABLE
  ANGINA OR RECENT HEART
  ATTACK

Possible Risks
Male sexual dysfunction
Seizures

▷ **Principal Uses**

As a Single Drug Product: Uses currently included in FDA-approved labeling: Treats (1) major depression; (2) obsessive-compulsive disorder; (3) panic disorder: (4) treats post-traumatic stress disorder; (5) treats premenstrual dysphoric disorder.

Other (unlabeled) generally accepted uses: (1) May have a role in treating obesity—rat studies have shown a decrease in eating that depends on the dose that is taken, and studies in humans are being conducted; (2) may help some kinds of sexual problems (premature ejaculation); (3) helps clozapine-caused (induced) obsessive-compulsive disorder; (4) eases symptoms in premenstrual dysphoric syndrome (PMDS); (5) can ease the feeling of loss of breath in mild to severe obstructive lung disease; (6) may have a role in depression after a heart attack, both in treating the depression and in heart rate variability.

How This Drug Works: This drug relieves depression by slowly restoring to normal levels a specific constituent of brain tissue (serotonin) that transmits nerve impulses.

Available Dosage Forms and Strengths
>   Solution — 20 mg per ml
>   Tablets — 25 mg, 50 mg, 100 mg

▷ **Recommended Dose Ranges** (Actual dose and schedule must be determined for each patient individually.)

>   *Infants and Children:* In children 6 to 12 years old: 25 mg once daily has been approved to treat obsessive-compulsive disorder.

>   *12 to 60 Years of Age:* Depression: Initially 50 mg once daily, taken in the morning or evening. The dose is then slowly increased, as needed and tolerated, in increments of 50 mg at intervals of 1 week. The total daily dose should not exceed 200 mg.

>   Panic Disorder: Dosing is started at 25 mg a day (morning or evening). After seven days, the dose can be increased to 50 mg once daily. If needed and tolerated, the dose can then be increased (at 7-day intervals) to a 200 mg per day maximum.

>   PTSD Similar to dosing for depression.

>   Obsessive-compulsive disorder: Same as dosing in depression.

>   *Over 60 Years of Age:* Dose amounts are the same as 12 to 60 years of age, unless liver function is compromised. Because the drug is removed some 40% more slowly than in younger patients, any changes in dose should be made at 2–3 week intervals.

Conditions Requiring Dosing Adjustments

>   *Liver Function:* Drug is a rare cause of liver damage. Patients with liver disease should be watched closely and lower doses used.

>   *Kidney Function:* The role of the kidneys is minimal and dosing adjustments are not thought to be needed.

▷ **Dosing Instructions:** The tablet may be crushed and is best taken with food to enhance absorption, but it may be taken at any time with or without food. The oral liquid form (concentrate) has 20 mg in each ml. Use the calibrated dropper to get the right dose. Just before you are going to take it, the dose can be mixed with 4 ounces of water, orange juice, ginger ale, lemonade, or other suitable liquid (talk to your pharmacist). It is okay if a haze appears once the concentrate has been added to the liquid. Taking this medicine regularly is important. If you forget a dose: Skip the missed dose and take the next dose right on schedule. DO NOT double doses. Talk with your doctor if you find yourself missing doses.

Usual Duration of Use: Use on a regular schedule for 4 to 8 weeks usually determines effectiveness in relieving depression and pattern of both favorable and unfavorable drug effects. Clinical studies suggest that people who respond during the first 8 weeks of treatment will benefit from another 8 weeks of sertraline therapy. Benefits of use in obsessive-compulsive disorder (OCD) have not been shown longer than 12 weeks in clinical trials. Since OCD tends to be ongoing, patients who benefit from this medicine should discuss the benefits and risks of continued sertraline. Long-term use requires periodic physician evaluation. The lowest effective dose should be used.

Typical Treatment Goals and Measurements (Outcomes and Markers)

>   *Depression:* The general goal: to lessen the degree and severity of depression, letting patients return to their daily lives. Specific measures of depression involve testing or inventories (such as Hamilton Depression or HAM-D) and can be valuable in helping check benefits from this medicine.

>   *Panic Disorder:* Goals for panic tend to be more vague and subjective than hypertension or cholesterol. Frequently, the patient (in conjunction with

physician assessment) will largely decide if panic has been modified to a successful extent. Additionally, decreased number of trips to the hospital or ER visits may be a useful measure. The Liebowitz Social Anxiety Scale (LSAS) is a tool as well as the Clinical Global Impressions—Global Improvement Scale, which can be used to help figure out benefits in patients with anxiety and panic. The Hamilton Rating Scale for Anxiety anxious mood section is also helpful. The ability of the patient to return to normal activities is a hallmark of successful treatment.

Possible Advantages of This Drug

Does not cause weight gain, a common side effect of tricyclic antidepressants. Less likely to cause dry mouth, constipation, urinary retention, orthostatic hypotension (see Glossary), and heart rhythm disturbances than tricyclic antidepressants. May have fewer drug interactions than other medicines in this same class. Has data from the SADHART trial (see Glassman, AH in Sources) that shows that this medicine is safe and effective in people with recent heart attack and unstable angina.

▷ **This Drug Should Not Be Taken If**
- you have had an allergic reaction to it previously or you have a latex allergy and were prescribed the solution form (the dropper bulb is made of natural rubber).
- you took a monoamine oxidase (MAO) type A inhibitor (see Drug Classes) in the last 14 days.
- you take disulfiram and were prescribed the oral solution form (has 12% alcohol).

▷ **Inform Your Physician Before Taking This Drug If**
- you had any adverse effects from antidepressant drugs.
- you have impaired liver or kidney function.
- you have Parkinson's disease.
- you or a loved one does not understand or want to face the risk of possible suicide; careful follow-up by caregivers and your physician is prudent.
- you have had a recent heart attack.
- you have a seizure disorder.
- you have a bleeding problem or take a diuretic.
- you are pregnant or plan pregnancy while taking this drug.

Possible Side Effects (natural, expected, and unavoidable drug actions)

Decreased appetite, weight loss (average 1 to 2 lb). Withdrawal syndrome possible if this medicine is abruptly stopped.

▷ **Possible Adverse Effects** (unusual, unexpected, and infrequent reactions)

If any of the following develop, consult your physician promptly for guidance.

Mild Adverse Effects

Allergic reactions: skin rash, itching—rare.

Headache, nervousness, insomnia, fatigue, tremor, dizziness, impaired concentration—rare.

Sleepwalking—case reports.

Abnormal vision, numbness and tingling—rare.

Confusion—rare.

Alopecia—infrequent.

Easy bruising (ecchymoses) or nosebleeds (epistaxis)—reported.

Night sweats—case report.

Chest pain and increased blood pressure—rare.

Paresthesias—rare.

Muscle aches (myalgia)—may be frequent.

Dry mouth, altered taste, nausea, vomiting, diarrhea, tongue ulceration—rare to frequent.

Serious Adverse Effects

Allergic reactions: dermatitis (various forms such as Stevens-Johnson Syndrome)—rare.

Drug-induced seizures—rare.

Hemorrhage into the anterior chamber of the eye or anemia—rare.

Hallucinations—case reports.

Low blood platelets (thrombocytopenia), changes in bleeding time—case reports.

Increased blood cholesterol (hypercholesterolemia)—infrequent.

Low blood sugar—case reports.

Pancreatitis—associated in time (temporal association) with use of this medicine.

Bronchospasm—infrequent.

QT interval changes, Torsade de Pointes—case reports.

Movement disorders (extrapyramidal reactions)—case reports.

Neuroleptic malignant syndrome—case reports with other SSRIs.

Serotonin syndrome (hyperreflexia, tachycardia, palpitations, etc.)—possible as with other SSRIs

Low blood sodium—rare.

SIADH—case reports (may also occur with other selective serotonin reuptake inhibitors).

▷ **Possible Effects on Sexual Function:** Male sexual dysfunction: delayed ejaculation—may be frequent.

Female sexual dysfunction: inhibited orgasm—rare.

Swelling and tenderness of male (gynecomastia) and female breast tissue with milk production (galactorrhea)—case reports.

Infrequent dysmenorrhea, intermenstrual bleeding, atrophic vaginitis, painful erections (priapism)—possible, case reports.

May help some kinds of sexual disorders.

Natural Diseases or Disorders That May Be Activated by This Drug

Latent epilepsy.

Possible Effects on Laboratory Tests

Blood total cholesterol and triglyceride levels: increased—infrequent.

Blood uric acid levels: decreased.

Hemoglobin or hematocrit: decreased—rare.

Liver function tests: increased liver enzymes (ALT/GPT, AST/GOT, and alkaline phosphatase).

Blood sodium: decreased (with rare SIADH).

CAUTION

1. If any type of skin reaction develops (rash, hives, etc.), stop this drug and call your doctor promptly.
2. If dryness of the mouth develops and persists for more than 2 weeks, consult your dentist for guidance.
3. Ask your doctor or pharmacist before taking any other prescription or over-the-counter drug while taking sertraline.
4. If you are advised to take any monoamine oxidase (MAO) type A inhibitor (see Drug Classes), allow an interval of 5 weeks after discontinuing this drug before starting the MAO inhibitor.

5. It is advisable to withhold this drug if electroconvulsive therapy (ECT, "shock" treatment) is to be used to treat your depression.
6. Movement reactions if they happen usually occur in the first month of treatment and close patient follow-up is advisable.
7. A withdrawal syndrome is possible if this medicine is abruptly stopped. Best to slowly (taper) this medicine over 2-4 weeks or longer.
8. If you are taking disulfiram (Antabuse) avoid taking the oral liquid form because it has 12% alcohol.

Precautions for Use

By Infants and Children: Safety and effectiveness for those under 12 years of age are not established.

By Those Over 60 Years of Age: The lowest effective dose should be used for maintenance treatment and adjusted as needed for reduced kidney function.

▷ **Advisability of Use During Pregnancy**

Pregnancy Category: C. See Pregnancy Risk Categories at the back of this book.

Animal Studies: Delayed bone development due to this drug found in rat and rabbit studies.

Human Studies: Adequate studies of pregnant women are not available.

Use this drug only if clearly needed. Ask your physician for guidance.

Advisability of Use If Breast-Feeding

Presence of this drug in breast milk: Yes, variable amounts.

One small study found undetectable blood levels in infants who were breast-fed while their mothers were taking sertraline. Another found detectable levels. May be a drug of choice for mothers who breast-feed their infants. Discuss breast-feeding with your doctor.

Habit-Forming Potential: None.

Effects of Overdose: Agitation, restlessness, excitement, nausea, vomiting, seizures.

Possible Effects of Long-Term Use: None reported.

Suggested Periodic Examinations While Taking This Drug (at physician's discretion)

▷ **While Taking This Drug, Observe the Following**

Foods: May increase peak blood level. Grapefruit juice can block removal of this medicine from the body and lead to toxicity. DO NOT COMBINE.

Herbal Medicines or Minerals: Since sertraline and St. John's wort may act to increase serotonin, the combination is not advised. Because part of the way ginseng and ginkgo work may be as a MAO inhibitor, the combination is not advisable. Ma huang, yohimbe, Indian snakeroot, and kava kava (not recommended by Health Canada due to liver concerns) are also best avoided while taking this medicine.

Calcium now has excellent data (1,200–1,600 mg per day unless contraindicated) in helping prevent premenstrual dysphoric syndrome (PMDS). This may be an intelligent first-line therapy or valuable adjunctive use. Talk to your doctor to see if this makes sense for you.

Beverages: Do not drink grapefruit juice while taking this medicine. May be taken with milk.

▷ *Alcohol:* Avoid completely.

Tobacco Smoking: No interactions expected. I advise everyone to quit smoking.

Marijuana Smoking: The active ingredient (cannabinoids) found in marijuana combined with a similar medicine (fluoxetine) led to sudden mania in one patient. COMBINATION IS NOT ADVISABLE.

▷ *Other Drugs*
   Sertraline may *increase* the effects of
   • almotriptan (Axert), naratriptan (Amerge), sumatriptan (Imitrex), rizatriptan (Maxalt), zolmitriptan (Zomig), and any triptan-type medicine leading to loss of coordination and weakness.
   • astemizole (Hismanal—see medicines removed from the market), leading to Torsade de pointes or other heart rhythm problems—DO NOT COMBINE.
   • carbamazepine (Tegretol, others), leading to toxicity. Careful patient monitoring and more frequent carbamazepine levels are prudent.
   • clozapine (Clozaril), leading to clozapine toxicity.
   • dextromethorphan (in many cough "DM" suppressants).
   • diazepam (Valium) and perhaps other benzodiazepines (see Drug Classes).
   • diltiazem (Cardizem).
   • dofetilide (Tikosyn), leading to toxicity. CAUTION and more frequent blood levels are prudent.
   • fosphenytoin (Cerebyx) or phenytoin (Dilantin). Blood level checks are prudent if these medicines must be combined.
   • lamotrigine (Lamictal).
   • propafenone (Rythmol), leading to toxicity. Blood levels and clinical monitoring is prudent.
   • sibutramine (Meridia), which may lead to toxicity (serotonin syndrome)—DO NOT COMBINE.
   • theophylline (Theo-Dur, others) may lead to theophylline toxicity.
   • tolbutamide (Orinase).
   • warfarin (Coumadin) and related oral anticoagulants; more frequent INR (prothrombin time or protime) testing is needed. Ongoing warfarin doses should be based on INR results.
   Sertraline *taken concurrently* with
   • antidiabetic drugs (insulin, oral hypoglycemics: see Oral Antidiabetic Drugs in Drug Classes) may increase the risk of hypoglycemic reactions; monitor blood and urine sugar levels carefully.
   • benzodiazepines removed by the CYP 3A4 family of liver enzymes (such as triazolam or alprazolam) may lead to benzodiazepine toxicity.
   • bupropion (Wellbutrin, Zyban) may lead to sertraline toxicity. Caution and dosing in the lower end of the dose range are prudent.
   • cimetidine (Tagamet, Tagamet HB 200) may lead to sertraline toxicity. Careful patient monitoring and lower sertraline doses are prudent.
   • erythromycin (various) led to a serotonin syndrome in one patient; other macrolide antibiotics such as clarithromycin may also lead to this effect. Doses of sertraline should be lowered if these medicines must be combined.
   • flecainide (Tambocor) may lead to flecainide toxicity.
   • lithium (Lithobid, others) may lead to changes. Lithium blood levels are prudent.
   • metoclopramide (Reglan) may lead to sertraline toxicity.
   • monoamine oxidase (MAO) type A inhibitors may cause confusion, agitation, high fever, seizures, and dangerous elevations of blood pressure—avoid the concurrent use of these drugs.
   • quinidine (Quinaglute, others) may lead to quinidine toxicity—CAUTION is advised.
   • ritonavir (Norvir) and perhaps other protease inhibitors (see Drug Classes) may lead to toxicity.

- terfenadine (Seldane) may lead to toxicity.
- tramadol (Ultram) may lead to seizures.
- zolpidem (Ambien) may lead to hallucinations—DO NOT COMBINE.

▷ *Driving, Hazardous Activities:* This drug may cause drowsiness, dizziness, impaired judgment, and altered vision. Restrict activities as necessary.

Aviation Note: The use of this drug *is a disqualification* for piloting. Consult a designated Aviation Medical Examiner.

Exposure to Sun: Use caution—this drug may (rarely) cause photosensitivity (see Glossary).

Discontinuation: Best to slowly decrease (taper) the dose over 2-4 weeks or longer. Call your doctor if you plan to stop this drug for any reason.

SIBUTRAMINE (si BYOU trah meen)

Introduced: 1998   **Class:** Serotonin reuptake inhibitor, anorexiant, weight loss agent   **Prescription:** USA: Yes   **Controlled Drug:** USA: C-IV*; Canada: Yes   **Available as Generic:** USA: No

Brand Name: Meridia

Author's Note: A US consumer group has petitioned the FDA to remove sibutramine, Italy suspended sales of sibutramine last year, then reinstated the medicine. Canada reviewed the medicine, and subsequently decided that the benefits outweighed the risks. Controversy arose because of serious heart effects such as stroke, heart attack, abnormal heartbeats (arrhythmias), and more than 28 deaths. The question yet to be resolved is if this is a cause-and-effect relationship (see Glossary). Does the fact that the medicine was taken by patients with significant risk factors for heart disease mean that the medicine caused the problem or that the risk of the problem would have happened anyway? People who are obese or overweight are certainly subject to increased risk of heart problems. Based on current concerns, patients and clinicians must remember that sibutramine is contraindicated in people with coronary artery disease, arrhythmias, heart failure, and uncontrolled high blood pressure. Careful patient selection and close consideration of this benefit-to-risk decision is needed.

BENEFITS versus RISKS	
Possible Benefits	*Possible Risks*
EFFECTIVE WEIGHT LOSS	SIGNIFICANT INCREASES IN
ASSOCIATED DECREASES IN	BLOOD PRESSURE AND HEART
TRIGLYCERIDE AND DESIRABLE	RATE (DIASTOLIC)
HDL CHANGES WITH WEIGHT	Increased premature (asymptomatic)
LOSS	heart contractions
	Possible increased risk of serious
	cardiovascular problems

▷ **Principal Uses**

As a Single Drug Product: Uses currently included in FDA-approved labeling: Used to manage obesity, including weight loss and maintaining weight loss in people on a reduced-calorie diet. Used in those with an initial body mass index (BMI: see Glossary) greater than or equal to 30 kg per square meter

*See Schedules of Controlled Drugs at the back of this book.

or 27 kg per square meter if there are other risk factors (such as diabetes, hyperlipidemia, or hypertension).

Other (unlabeled) generally accepted uses: (1) could help some cases of peripheral neuropathy. Further research is needed.

How This Drug Works: This medicine helps treat obesity by decreasing the desire to eat by blocking reuptake of nerve transmitters (norepinephrine serotonin and dopamine) in brain synapses. People who took the drug in clinical studies were satisfied more quickly when they ate. Since metabolism is also increased, they used more of the food that they did eat than patients not receiving the medicine. Most of this effect comes from two active compounds (metabolites) that the body changes sibutramine into (M1 and M2).

Available Dosage Forms and Strengths
Capsules — 5 mg, 10 mg, 15 mg

▷ **Recommended Dosage Ranges** (Actual dose and schedule must be determined for each patient individually.) Dosing is started at 10 mg once a day in the morning. Status of heart rate and blood pressure should be checked before any dose increases. If the clinician feels that those and other parameters are acceptable, and if weight loss goals have not been met, the dose may be increased after 4 weeks to a daily dose of 15 mg. Conversely, the dose should be decreased to 5 mg daily if not tolerated (using blood pressure and heart rate as guides). The daily maximum is 15 mg.

Conditions Requiring Dosing Adjustments
Liver Function: This drug is changed in the liver; however, dose changes are not thought to be needed in mild to moderate liver failure. Drug should NOT be used in severe liver failure.

Kidney Function: No changes needed in mild to moderate kidney failure. Drug should NOT be used in severe kidney failure.

▷ **Dosing Instructions:** Capsule may be taken before or following food. It was usually taken in the morning in clinical trials because nighttime dosing can lead to sleep problems. If the starting dose of 10 mg isn't tolerated (using heart rate and blood pressure as a guide), discuss this with your doctor. The dose is usually then lowered to 5 mg daily in those cases. If you forget a dose: Take the missed dose as soon as you remember it, unless it's nearly time for your next dose—if that is the case, skip the missed dose and take the next dose right on schedule. DO NOT double up on doses. Talk with your doctor if you find yourself missing doses.

Usual Duration of Use: This medicine has only been used up to a year in clinical studies. Longer-term use should be discussed with your doctor. One study found that 77% of those who took the medicine as part of a program not only lowered cholesterol but also helped achieve and maintain significant weight loss. Ongoing use requires periodic physician follow-up.

Typical Treatment Goals and Measurements (Outcomes and Markers)
Weight Loss: The goal is to lower body weight or maintain weight loss. Body weight (Body Mass Index, or BMI), percent body fat and laboratory tests such as triglycerides, VLDL, LDL, and HDL can be checked to assess successful combination treatment. Be sure to talk to your doctor about the benefits of losing some weight and keeping it off versus crash or fad diets and weight yo-yoing.

Possible Advantages of This Drug
Use has not been associated with heart valve problems seen with dexfenfluramine (Redux). The STORM study (Sibutramine Trial in Obesity Reduc-

tion and Maintenance) showed that 67% of people who took sibutramine maintained their six-month weight loss for up to two years. In a more recent European study, 77% of people who took the medicine as part of an organized program lowered cholesterol and maintained significant weight loss.

▷ **This Drug Should Not Be Taken If**
- you had an allergic reaction to any form of it previously.
- you've had a stroke.
- you are anorexic.
- you have a history of abnormal heart rhythms, irregular heartbeat, or heart disease.
- you have pulmonary hypertension.
- you have poorly controlled or uncontrolled high blood pressure.
- you have congestive heart failure or disease of the coronary arteries.
- other causes of obesity such as untreated low thyroid function (hypothyroidism) were not ruled out.
- you have glaucoma (narrow angle).
- you take, or have taken within the last 14 days, an monoamine oxidase (MAO) inhibitor (see Drug Classes).
- you have severe kidney or liver disease.

▷ **Inform Your Physician Before Taking This Drug If**
- you have heart (cardiovascular) disease or have had an unfavorable reaction to any serotonin reuptake inhibitor.
- you have glaucoma.
- your work requires balance or operation of hazardous machinery (this medicine can cause dizziness).
- you have a history of abnormal heart rhythms or high blood pressure.
- you have a history of kidney or liver compromise.
- you have a history of gallstones.
- you have a history of psychiatric disorders or drug abuse.
- you have taken other weight loss medicines (anorexiants) in the last year.
- you have a seizure disorder.
- you develop unexplained difficulty in breathing, fainting, chest pain, fast or irregular heartbeat, or swelling of the ankles. Call if you have any kind of seizure or blackout. These signs and symptoms can be early - warnings of problems or some of them could be part of pulmonary hypertension.

Possible Side Effects (natural, expected, and unavoidable drug actions)
Since some weight loss agents that cause increased levels of serotonin have been associated with development of a fatal lung problem (primary pulmonary hypertension, or PPH), it is prudent to talk about this with your doctor. It is unknown if sibutramine can cause this problem. Serotonin syndrome may result with combined use with MAO inhibitors or other medicines that increase serotonin.

▷ **Possible Adverse Effects** (unusual, unexpected, and infrequent reactions)
If any of the following develop, consult your physician promptly for guidance.
Mild Adverse Effects
Allergic reaction: skin rash.
Headache and anorexia—frequent.
Sleep disturbances—infrequent.
Anxiety—reported.

Dry mouth or constipation—frequent (but may ease over time).
Palpitations or tachycardia—rare.
Fast heart rate (tachycardia)—infrequent.
Increased liver enzymes—frequent (questionable cause).

Serious Adverse Effects

High blood pressure (increased up to 30% of the level present before starting the medicine) as well as some cases of increased diastolic pressure—infrequent.

Abnormal heartbeats—case reports.
Heart attack—case reports.
Stroke—case reports.
Psychosis—case report.
Seizures—case reports.
Abnormal liver enzymes (ALT)—rare.
Low blood platelets—case reports.

▷ **Possible Effects on Sexual Function:** Painful menstruation—infrequent.

Natural Diseases or Disorders That May Be Activated by This Drug

High blood pressure controlled by other medicines may return. Untreated high blood pressure may worsen. See "this drug should not be taken if" section above.

Possible Effects on Laboratory Tests

Drug testing: may cause false positive tests for amphetamines.

CAUTION

1. It is best to carry a card noting that you are taking this drug. A medicine alert bracelet is also a good idea.
2. This medicine may cause false positive urine drug tests for amphetamines.
3. Other conditions (organic causes) leading to obesity (such as low activity of the thyroid gland—hypothyroidism) should be ruled out prior to starting this medicine.
4. Safety and efficacy of use of sibutramine with other weight loss agents have NOT been established. Combination therapy is NOT recommended.
5. This medicine has NOT been found to cause lung problems (primary pulmonary hypertension or PPH); however, other drugs that increase serotonin were subsequently found to do this. If you develop unexplained difficulty in breathing, fainting, chest pain, or swelling of the ankles, call your doctor. These may be early symptoms of pulmonary hypertension.
6. Because of the increased risk of increased blood pressure, periodic checks of blood pressure are prudent.
7. Nonprescription medicines such as pseudoephedrine, ephedrine, or phenylpropanolamine can increase heart rate or blood pressure. Talk with your pharmacist or doctor BEFORE you combine any type of decongestant, cough, allergy or cold medicine.
8. Serotonin syndrome is possible with medicines that increase brain serotonin. Call your doctor if disorientation, hyperreflexia, palpitations happen while taking this medicine.

Precautions for Use

By Infants and Children: Safety and effectiveness have not been established in those less than 16 years old.

By Those Over 60 Years of Age: The drug levels this medicine achieves and the places in the body where this medicine goes are no different for those over

60 than those under 60. *CAUTION* should be used (as with all medicines active in the central nervous system) in treating elderly patients with sibutramine. Since there is also a higher occurrence of high blood pressure and heart disease, caution and lower doses appear prudent.

▷ **Advisability of Use During Pregnancy**
Pregnancy Category: C. See Pregnancy Risk Categories at the back of this book.
Human Studies: Adequate studies of pregnant women are not available.
NOT recommended for pregnant women.

Advisability of Use If Breast-Feeding
Presence of this drug in breast milk: unknown in humans.
Avoid drug or refrain from nursing.

Habit-Forming Potential: The possibility of physical dependence is low, but this medicine is a schedule 4 drug (see Controlled Drug Schedules in the back of this edition). Further study is needed to confirm an accurate probability of dependence risk. There was no evidence of addictive or drug-seeking behavior in premarketing studies.

Effects of Overdose: Few cases of overdose have been reported. Rapid heart rate was seen in one overdose.

Possible Effects of Long-Term Use: Weight loss (the desired effect). Increased blood pressure.

Suggested Periodic Examinations While Taking This Drug
Periodic weigh-ins.
Liver function tests.
Checks for early signs of primary pulmonary hypertension and hypertension in general are prudent.
Periodic blood pressure checks are prudent.

▷ **While Taking This Drug, Observe the Following**
Foods: Follow prescribed portion control and menu choices. Tryptophan (found in some health food stores) increases risk of serotonin syndrome.
Herbal Medicines or Minerals: Combining this medicine with St. John's wort IS NOT advised because of possible serotonin syndrome. Since part of the way ginseng works may be as an MAO inhibitor, do not combine ginseng with sibutramine. Ma huang, kola, guarana, ephedra, and yohimbe are also best avoided while taking this medicine.
Nutritional Support: Dietary counseling and physician- or dietitian-directed menus and portion control are suggested. Make a rational plan to take the undesirable weight off and keep it off.
Beverages: No restrictions except as described in your dietary guidelines.
▷ *Alcohol:* The manufacturer does not recommend use of excessive alcohol and sibutramine.
Tobacco Smoking: No interactions are described in current literature. I advise everyone to quit smoking.
▷ *Other Drugs*
Sibutramine *taken concurrently* with
• antimigraine agents (such as sumatriptan-Imitrex) and dihydroergotamine may rarely result in a serotonin syndrome—DO NOT COMBINE.
• central nervous system active medicines (see Drug Classes of benzodiazepines, opioids [fentanyl, etc.], phenothiazines and others) may have additive effects—CAUTION is advised.
• dextromethorphan (various brands of cough medicine) may increase risk of serotonin syndrome—DO NOT COMBINE.

- fentanyl (Duragesic, others) increases risk of serotonin syndrome—DO NOT COMBINE.
- lithium (Lithobid, others) increases risk of serotonin syndrome—DO NOT COMBINE.
- meperidine (Demerol, others) increases risk of serotonin syndrome—DO NOT COMBINE.
- monoamine oxidase (MAO) inhibitors (see Drug Classes) may result in serious, even fatal reactions. Fourteen days should pass between stopping an MAO inhibitor and starting sibutramine.
- pentazocine (Talwin, others) increases risk of serotonin syndrome—DO NOT COMBINE.
- selective serotonin reuptake inhibitors (SSRIs: see Drug Classes) increases risk of serotonin syndrome—DO NOT COMBINE.
- tricyclic antidepressants (some, such as desipramine [Norpramin] and amitriptyline [Elavil]) increase serotonin syndrome risk.
- tryptophan (various) increases risk of serotonin syndrome—DO NOT COMBINE.

Sibutramine *taken concurrently* with the following may result in increased sibutramine levels:

- erythromycins (see Drug Classes).
- itraconazole (Sporanox), ketoconazole (Nizoral), voriconazole (Vfend).
- mibefradil (Posicor) (removed from the U.S. market).
- nelfinavir (Viracept) and perhaps other protease inhibitors (see Drug Classes)—may increase blood levels.
- any medicine that interferes with cytochrome CYP3A4 or is removed from the body by those enzymes will potentially increase sibutramine blood levels. For example, if sildenafil (Viagra) and sibutramine are combined, I expect that doses of one or both drugs may need to be adjusted.

The following drugs may *decrease* the effects of sibutramine:

- rifabutin (Mycobutin).
- rifampin (Rifadin, Rimactane).

▷ *Driving, Hazardous Activities:* Use caution.

Aviation Note: The use of this drug *may be a disqualification* for piloting. Consult a designated Aviation Medical Examiner.

Exposure to Sun: No restrictions at present.

Occurrence of Unrelated Illness: Since weight loss may modify the need for medicines used to control blood pressure and lipids, the medicines used in these conditions may need to be adjusted.

Discontinuation: Ask your doctor for help if you are considering stopping this medicine.

SILDENAFIL CITRATE (sill DEN ah fill)

Introduced: 1998   **Class:**   Anti-impotence, phosphodiesterase inhibitor
Prescription: USA: Yes   **Controlled Drug:**   USA: No; Canada: No
Available as Generic: USA: No; Canada: No
Brand Name: Viagra

BENEFITS versus RISKS

Possible Benefits	*Possible Risks*
SUCCESSFUL ACHIEVEMENT OF AN ERECTION	SERIOUS DRUG INTERACTIONS
	Drug-induced vision changes
SUFFICIENT ERECTION TO ACHIEVE INTERCOURSE	Headache
May work in female orgasm problems (Italian data)	

▷ **Principal Uses**

As a Single Drug Product: Uses currently included in FDA-approved labeling: (1) Treats difficulties getting or maintaining an erection (erectile dysfunction); (2) clinical trials that led to FDA approval for this medicine also showed better success rates for sexual intercourse for those using sildenafil versus placebo.

Other (unlabeled) generally accepted uses: (1) Many anecdotal and/or conflicting reports of improvement in sexuality (enhancement) and benefits in females have been made. A 12-week study of 33 women after menopause found that there was no significant change in sexual desire after 12 weeks of Viagra. Italian data found benefits; (2) may have a role in premature ejaculation problems; (3) helps reverse sexual problems caused by antidepressant medicines.

▷ **How This Drug Works:** Causes smooth muscle in the penis to relax, increasing blood flow into the penis, resulting in erection. Sildenafil causes release of nitric oxide (NO) in part of the penis called the corpus cavernosum. This then increases an enzyme called guanylate cyclase. This enzyme increases cyclic guanosine monophosphate (CGMP). The CGMP causes the smooth muscle in the penis to relax. Once the smooth muscle relaxes, blood flows into the penis, resulting in erection.

Available Dosage Forms and Strengths

Tablets — 25 mg, 50 mg, 100 mg

▷ **Recommended Dose Ranges** (Actual dose and schedule must be determined for each patient individually.)

Infants and Children: Not used in this age group.

18 to 65 Years of Age: Doses typically range from 25–100 mg used once daily. The dose that your doctor chooses is taken from half an hour up to four hours before sexual activity. This medicine has worked in more than 70% of patients who took the 50–100 mg daily dose. For people who are taking medicines that inhibit a liver enzyme called cytochrome P450 3A4 (such as itraconazole, ketoconazole, or some macrolide antibiotics such as erythromycin), the 25 mg dose is used by clinicians who have patients who take one of those medicines at the same time as sildenafil. Further caution is required and it would be a benefit-to-risk decision if multiple 3A4 inhibitors are being taken and sildenafil is being considered. Additionally, some medicines used in combination therapy of HIV/AIDS may interact and caution and lower doses are prudent and use is a benefit-to-risk decision for your doctor. (See additional medicine combination comments in the drug interactions section below.)

Over 65 Years of Age: Because plasma levels of sildenafil may be increased in this age group, doses should be reduced to 25 mg once daily. If kidney function has decreased to less than 30 ml/min further in a patient in this age group, further benefit-to-risk decision should be given.

Conditions Requiring Dosing Adjustments

Liver Function: A starting dose of 25 mg is prudent in liver disease.

Kidney Function: Caution is advised, as one measure of drug levels is doubled in those with compromised kidneys. A starting dose of 25 mg is prudent.

▷ **Dosing Instructions:** The tablet may be crushed and taken without regard to eating (high-fat meals decreased absorption time and may make the medicine take longer to work). It can be taken an hour before sexual activity, and the manufacturer mentions an acceptable range of half an hour to four hours before sexual activity. If you forget a dose: There is a 4 hour to as little as 30 minute time frame to work with. DO NOT take the medicine more than once a day.

Usual Duration of Use: Use is only recommended ONCE a day. If use is to be ongoing on a daily basis, this should be discussed with your doctor.

Typical Treatment Goals and Measurements (Outcomes and Markers)

Erectile dysfunction: The general goal is to help you attain an erection that will help you have sex. Typical desired results are stiffness or tone of the penis and how often you have an erection in response to this medicine.

Possible Advantages of This Drug: Avoids direct injections into the penis (such as Caverject). Avoids surgical placement of an implant. Excellent response rate.

▷ **This Drug Should Not Be Taken If**
- you have had an allergic reaction to it previously.
- you have a disease or condition that would result in serious health hazard if lowering of the blood pressure or sexual activity occurred.
- you are taking any nitrate (see Drug Classes). NEVER combine these nitrates with sildenafil (see also "Other Drug" interactions).
- You have preexisting cardiovascular disease of a severity that precludes sexual activity.
- You have not fully discussed this medicine or all of the other medicines you take with your doctor, or have obtained it from an alternative source.

▷ **Inform Your Physician Before Taking This Drug If**
- you have liver or kidney disease.
- the drug was prescribed for you without a complete medical history or physical examination.
- you have a history of heart disease (such as congestive heart failure, past heart attack, unstable angina, arrhythmias, or coronary ischemia).
- you have multiple myeloma, leukemia, or sickle-cell syndrome (may predispose you to painful and sustained erections called priapism).
- you are over 65 and a 50-mg dose has been prescribed.
- you have vision changes while taking this medicine.
- you have cataracts or impaired vision (such as retinitis pigmentosa).
- you have had structural damage to the penis (Peyronie's disease: see Glossary).
- you are taking a medicine that blocks or enhances the liver cytochrome system (CYP3A4 or 2C9) (Talk to your doctor or pharmacist about this).
- you are prone to heartburn or have other stomach conditions or a bleeding disorder.
- you do not have any improvement in erections or sexual performance while taking this medicine.
- you are unsure how much to take or how often to take this medicine.

Possible Side Effects (natural, expected, and unavoidable drug actions)

Changes in vision (blue tint) or dry eyes—up to 3% in clinical trials. Nasal congestion—possible.

▷ **Possible Adverse Effects** (unusual, unexpected, and infrequent reactions)

If any of the following develop, consult your physician promptly for guidance.

Mild Adverse Effects

Allergic reaction: rash.

Headache—infrequent to frequent.

Flushing—infrequent to frequent.

Indigestion—infrequent.

Sensitivity to light or blurred vision—possible to infrequent (more likely with the 100-mg dose).

Inability to distinguish between blue and green—possible and may be dose-related.

Serious Adverse Effects

DEATH RESULTING FROM DRUG INTERACTIONS—possible with nitrates.

Temporary vision loss—case reports.

Stroke—case report.

Decrease in blood supplied to the heart muscle (myocardial ischemia)—rare.

Heart attack—case reports with preexisting heart conditions and rare reports in people without preexisting heart conditions.

Decreased preload and afterload—possible (in patients with cardiomyopathy).

Arrhythmias (ventricular tachycardia) or atrial fibrillation—case reports.

▷ **Possible Effects on Sexual Function:**

Abnormal ejaculation—case reports.

Sustained and painful erection (priapism)—case reports.

Possible Delayed Adverse Effects: None reported to date.

Natural Diseases or Disorders That May Be Activated by This Drug

Patient perception of any preexisting retinal disease may be worsened if sildenafil haze or bluish vision-tinting happens. Some cardiovascular conditions may be worsened by this drug.

Possible Effects on Laboratory Tests

None reported.

CAUTION

Author's Note: Early case reports of six deaths were reviewed by the FDA in May 1998. A total of 30 deaths were reviewed as of June 1998. Based on the review, Viagra itself was NOT found to be the cause of the deaths and NO CHANGES were made to the package insert. Subsequently, new and expanded safety information was added to required FDA labeling including drug interaction data. During this controversial and rapidly changing period, conflicting reports, possible interactions as absolute contraindications and unclear benefit-to-risk decisions were reported and evolved or failed to evolve. Talk to your doctor or pharmacist about the most current combinations of medicines, which are thought to be inappropriate versus those requiring lower doses and those that should never be undertaken. Because a medicine has serious possible interactions does not mean that it is an undesirable medicine, only that some combinations are not prudent.

1. Because of the possibility of SERIOUS drug interactions, keep a card in your purse or wallet or get a medicine alert bracelet to wear that says you are taking sildenafil.

2. If this medicine does not help you get or maintain an erection, it is important that you follow up with your doctor.

3. Safety and efficacy of sildenafil combined with other treatments for erectile problems (dysfunction) have not been established and may not be recommended by your doctor.

4. Some people use illegal "poppers," which are actually ampules of alkyl nitrites, to enhance sexual activity. These should NEVER be combined with Viagra.

5. The American Academy of Ophthalmology recommended further studies of sildenafil's long-term effects on the eyes and also warned that those with conditions of the retina should take the drug in the lowest effective dose and with caution. Promptly report altered or impaired vision so that appropriate evaluation can be made.

6. The manufacturer notes that it is important to have a physical exam and medical history taken to properly diagnose problems with erections (erectile dysfunction) and to identify (where possible) any underlying disease or condition that may actually be the cause of the problem (such as diabetes).

7. If your erection lasts more than 4 hours, go to the nearest emergency room. Such persistent erections may lead to damage of the penis that is not reversible.

Precautions for Use

By Infants and Children: Safety and effectiveness for those under 18 not established.

By Those Over 60 Years of Age: Because this medicine is more slowly removed from the body in this age group, drug levels may be higher. The recommended starting dose is 25 mg.

▷ **Advisability of Use During Pregnancy**

Pregnancy Category: B. See Pregnancy Risk Categories at the back of this book.

Animal Studies: no evidence of embryotoxicity, fetotoxicity, or teratogenicity in rats and rabbits.

Human Studies: Adequate studies of pregnant women are not available.

NOT indicated for use in women, children, or newborns.

Advisability of Use If Breast-Feeding

Presence of this drug in breast milk: Unknown.

Avoid drug or refrain from nursing.

Habit-Forming Potential: None.

Effects of Overdose: Adverse effects were similar to accepted dosing adverse effects, but increased in frequency with clinical trials of 800-mg doses. Supportive care is indicated with the caveat of extremely careful cardiac monitoring in those with existing heart disease.

Possible Effects of Long-Term Use: Not defined.

Suggested Periodic Examinations While Taking This Drug (at physician's discretion)

Follow-up on success in achieving an erection and having intercourse.

Complete eye examination at beginning of treatment and at any time that significant change in vision occurs. Ask your doctor for help.

▷ **While Taking This Drug, Observe the Following**

Foods: Grapefruit juice can be an inhibitor of CYP3A4. DO NOT combine. Water is the safest liquid to take this medicine with.

Herbal Medicines or Minerals: Using St. John's wort, ma huang, or kola while taking this medicine may result in unacceptable heart stimulation. Since St. John's wort and sildenafil may increase sun sensitivity, the combination is NOT advised. There are no data regarding combining yohimbe (Pausinystala yohimbe) with sildenafil, and yohimbe can lead to serious heart complications. The combination is NOT advised. Numan has had some small cohort studies, but has also not been studied and cannot be recommended in combination with sildenafil. A product from Health Nutrition labs called Viga or Viga for Women was the subject of an FDA MedWatch safety alert. The warning noted that this dietary supplement contained sildenafil as an unlabeled ingredient. See *www.fda.gov/medwatch/ SAFETY/2003/safety/safety02.htm#vigarma*.

Beverages: Grapefruit juice can be an inhibitor of the enzyme that removes sildenafil from the body (CYP3A4). DO NOT combine as toxicity may result. Drug may be taken with milk or water.

▷ *Alcohol:* Excess alcohol intake may blunt the benefits of this medicine.

Tobacco Smoking: No interactions expected. I advise everyone to quit smoking.

Marijuana Smoking: The active ingredient (cannabinoids) found in marijuana can act as an inhibitor of the principal enzyme (CYP3A4) that removes sildenafil from the body. COMBINATION IS NOT RECOMMENDED.

▷ *Other Drugs*

Sildenafil may increase the effects of
- nitrates (see Drug Classes)—NEVER COMBINE.

The following drugs may *increase* the effects of sildenafil:
- cimetidine (Tagamet).
- delavirdine (Rescriptor).
- diltiazem (Cardizem).
- erythromycins (erythromycin and clarithromycin: see Drug Classes).
- indinavir (Crixivan), nelfinavir (Viracept), saquinavir (Invirase, Fortovase), and perhaps other protease inhibitors (see Drug Classes).
- itraconazole (Sporanox), ketoconazole (Nizoral), and perhaps similar antifungals.
- metronidazole (Flagyl).
- mibefradil (Posicor) (removed from the U.S. market).
- nitroprusside (Nitropress).
- ritonavir (Norvir) can increase sildenafil blood levels by up to 1,000%. A maximum dose of 25 mg every 48 hours is suggested along with careful patient monitoring.
- saquinavir (Fortovase). Starting dose should be 25 mg.
- sertraline (Zoloft).
- any medicine that interferes with cytochrome (CYP3A4-major or 2C9-minor, such as sibutramine [Meridia], which uses CYP3A4) will potentially increase (or decrease) sildenafil blood levels. In some cases, I expect that sildenafil dosing will need to be adjusted, and in others, the combination should be avoided.

Sildenafil *taken concurrently* with
- amprenavir (Agenerase) may lead to excessive sildenafil levels. Lower doses are prudent.
- amyl nitrite will result in serious decreases in blood pressure—DO NOT COMBINE.
- medicines that cause vision changes (see Table 4) may result in additive vision problems.
- oral hypoglycemic agents tolbutamide (Orinase an inhibitor of 2C9), and glipizide (Glucotrol)—one early case report of a serious interaction are

representative of medicines which may lead to problems and in the case of glipizide had one reported problem. Talk to your doctor about the latest information on possible interactions of these medicines with sildenafil.

The following drugs may **decrease** the effects of sildenafil:

- carbamazepine (Tegretol).
- phenytoin (Dilantin).
- rifabutin (Mycobutin).
- rifampin (Rifadin, Rimactane).

▷ *Driving, Hazardous Activities:* No restrictions.

Aviation Note: The use of this drug **may be a disqualification** for piloting. Consult a designated Aviation Medical Examiner.

Exposure to Sun: May increase sensitivity of your eyes to sunlight. Talk to your doctor about sunglasses or other protective measures.

Discontinuation: Talk to your doctor about your results from taking this drug.

SIMVASTATIN (sim vah STA tin)

Introduced: 1986   **Class:** Anticholesterol   **Prescription:** USA: Yes   **Controlled Drug:** USA: No; Canada: No   **Available as Generic:** USA: No; Canada: No

Brand Names: ❦Apo-Simvastatin, ❦Gen-Simvastatin, ❦Nu-Simvastatin, ❦Ratio-Simvastatin, Zocor

BENEFITS versus RISKS	
Possible Benefits	*Possible Risks*
EFFECTIVE REDUCTION OF TOTAL BLOOD CHOLESTEROL AND LDL CHOLESTEROL	Drug-induced liver problems (hepatitis)—rare
INCREASES HDL-C (GOOD CHOLESTEROL) IN PATIENTS WITH PRIMARY HYPER-CHOLESTEROLEMIA AND MIXED DYSLIPIDEMIA	Drug-induced muscle damage (myositis)—rare
TREATS ISOLATED HYPER-TRIGLYCERIDEMIA AND TYPE THREE HYPER-LIPOPROTEINEMIA	Decreased coenzyme Q10
REDUCES RISK FROM CORONARY DISEASE	
REDUCES DEATH FROM CORONARY REVASCULARIZATION	
REDUCES NONFATAL MYOCAR-DIAL INFARCTIONS AND THE NEED FOR BYPASS SURGERY AND ANGIOPLASTY	
REDUCES RISK OF STROKES	
May help prevent or preserve mental status in Alzheimer's	
May help maintain bone health	

▷ **Principal Uses**

As a Single Drug Product: Uses currently included in FDA-approved labeling: (1) Used by patients with elevated cholesterol to reduce death from heart disease and decrease the number of nonfatal heart attacks; (2) treats high total blood cholesterol levels (in people with types IIa and IIb hypercholesterolemia)—used in conjunction with a cholesterol-lowering diet (it should not be used until an adequate trial of nondrug methods for lowering cholesterol has proved to be ineffective); (3) stops progression and decreases number of deaths of patients with coronary artery disease as well as the need for bypass surgery and angioplasty; (4) decreases risk of strokes; (5) treats isolated hypertriglyceridemia and type three hyperlipoproteinemia; (6) increases HDL-C in people with primary hypercholesterolemia and mixed dyslipidemia.

Other (unlabeled) generally accepted uses: (1) Used in combination with estrogen (in one study of women averaging 57 years old) lowered LDL, increased HDL and reduced undesirable blood-clotting factors and inflammation; (2) may help reduce lipid disorders that occur in kidney problems (nephrotic syndrome); (3) combination therapy in preventing gallstones; (4) may have a role after heart transplants to decrease death and lower LDL-C levels; (5) a small study of 32 patients with multiple sclerosis (MS) is under way looking at the benefits of high dose simvastatin in easing MS symptoms; (5) may help preserve bone health; (6) could have a role in Alzheimer's patients helping prevent it or preserve function.

How This Drug Works: Blocks the liver enzyme starting production of cholesterol. Reduces low-density lipoproteins (LDL), the fraction of cholesterol thought to increase risk of coronary heart disease. Also increase high-density lipoproteins (HDL), the cholesterol fraction that reduces the risk of heart disease. There is a growing body of evidence that "statins" also have beneficial changes on what is in the blood, blood flow, and even the blood vessel walls themselves (some of this may account for benefits in decreasing Alzheimer's risk). Specific compounds or effects of platelet derived growth factor (PDGF), undesirable blood clotting via thrombin-antithrombin III, thrombomodulin, and other chemicals may be beneficially lowered or effects mitigated by statins.

Available Dosage Forms and Strengths

Tablets — 5 mg, 10 mg, 20 mg, 40 mg, 80 mg

▷ **Recommended Dosage Ranges** (Actual dose and schedule must be determined for each patient individually.)

Infants and Children: Under 2 years of age—do not use this drug.

2 to 20 years of Age: dose not established for children or adolescents.

20 to 60 Years of Age: Initially 20 mg daily, taken at bedtime. Dose is increased as needed to reach desired goals (such as decreased LDL-C percent). The drug is then increased as needed and tolerated by increments of 5 to 10 mg at intervals of 4 weeks. The total daily dose should not exceed 80 mg. For patients who require more than a 45 percent decrease in bad cholesterol (LDL), the starting dose is 40 mg per day. Some clinicians add on therapy, which lowers cholesterol by a different mechanism. **See dosing based on drug interactions in the Other Drugs section on page 1045.**

Over 60 Years of Age: Initially 5 mg daily. Increase dose as needed and tolerated by increments of 5 mg at intervals of 4 weeks. The total daily dose should not exceed 40 mg.

Conditions Requiring Dosing Adjustments

Liver Function: This drug achieves a high concentration in the liver and is subsequently eliminated in the bile. It can be a rare cause of liver damage, and patients should be followed closely.

Kidney Function: In severe kidney failure, the dose should be started at 5 mg and the patient closely followed.

Heart Transplants: People who are getting immunosuppressive therapy should be started on 5 mg of simvastatin. The maximum dose in these patients should be 10 mg.

▷ **Dosing Instructions:** The tablet may be crushed and taken without regard to eating, preferably at bedtime (the highest rates of cholesterol production occur between midnight and 5 A.M.). If you forget a dose: Take the missed dose as soon as you remember it, unless it's nearly time for your next dose—if that is the case, skip the missed dose and take the next dose right on schedule. DO NOT double doses. Talk with your doctor if you find yourself missing doses as there are many effective reminder systems available.

Usual Duration of Use: Use on a regular schedule for 4 to 6 weeks usually determines effectiveness in reducing blood levels of total and LDL cholesterol. Long-term use (months to years) requires periodic physician evaluation of response and dose adjustment as cholesterol tends to increase as we age. See your doctor on a regular basis to make certain you are on track.

Typical Treatment Goals and Measurements (Outcomes and Markers)

Cholesterol: The National Institutes of Health Adult Treatment Panel has released ATP III as part of the update to the National Cholesterol Education Program or NCEP. Key points in these new guidelines include acknowledging diabetes as one of the conditions that increases risk of heart disease, modifying risk factors, therapeutic lifestyle changes (TLC), and recommending routine testing for all of the cholesterol fractions (lipoprotein profile) versus total cholesterol alone.

Current NCEP guidelines recommend a desirable total cholesterol of 200 mg/dl, and optimal bad cholesterol (LDL) as 100 mg/dl, 130–159 mg/dl as borderline high, 160 mg/dl as high and 190 mg/dl as very high. Did you know that there are at least five different kinds of "good cholesterol" or HDL? The "too low" measure for HDL is still 40 mg/dl, but in order to learn more about cholesterol types some doctors are starting to order lipid panels. There are at least seven different kinds of "bad cholesterol". The new panels tell doctors about the kinds of cholesterol that your body makes. This is important because some kinds (small dense particles) tend to stick to blood vessels (are highly atherogenic). Take your medicine to reach your goals.

Two additional tests you will hear about will be electron beam computed tomography (EBCT) and CRP. EBCT is an important tool used in conjunction with laboratory studies. Findings show that even patients who meet cholesterol goals (particularly females over 55) can still be at significant cardiovascular risk. EBCT then defines risk by giving a calcium score and a "virtual tour" of the coronary arteries. C Reactive Protein or CRP is a new and apparently independent predictor of heart disease risk. A large study (see Ridker, P.M. in Sources) found that CRP predicted heart disease risk independently of bad cholesterol (low density lipoprotein). Talk to your doctor about this new laboratory test and ask about current guidelines for who should be tested (see Pearson, T.A. in Sources).

Possible Advantages of This Drug: Several studies indicate that HMG-CoA reductase inhibitors are more effective and better tolerated than other drugs currently available for reducing total and LDL cholesterol. Simvastatin increased HDL levels by 6.7% in one study.

▷ **This Drug Should Not Be Taken If**
  • you have had an allergic reaction to it previously.
  • you have active liver disease.
  • your liver enzyme levels (serum transaminases) have increased without explanation.
  • you are pregnant or breast-feeding your infant.

▷ **Inform Your Physician Before Taking This Drug If**
  • you have previously taken any other drugs in this class: lovastatin (Mevacor) or pravastatin (Pravachol).
  • you have a history of liver disease or impaired liver function.
  • you are taking any of the medicines listed in the Other Drugs section of this profile.
  • you are not using any method of birth control or you are planning pregnancy.
  • you regularly consume substantial amounts of alcohol.
  • you have cataracts or impaired vision.
  • you have any type of chronic muscular disorder.
  • you develop muscle pain, weakness, or soreness that is unexplained while taking this medicine.
  • you plan to have major surgery in the near future.

Possible Side Effects (natural, expected, and unavoidable drug actions)
  Development of abnormal liver function tests without associated symptoms.
  Decreased co-enzyme Q10 (co-Q10 or ubiquinone).

▷ **Possible Adverse Effects** (unusual, unexpected, and infrequent reactions)
  If any of the following develop, consult your physician promptly for guidance.
  Mild Adverse Effects
  Allergic reaction: rash.
  Headache, dizziness or fatigue—infrequent.
  Nausea, excessive gas, constipation, diarrhea—rare to infrequent.
  Lowering of blood pressure—possible.
  Serious Adverse Effects
  Marked and persistent abnormal liver function tests with focal hepatitis—rare.
  Acute myositis (muscle pain and tenderness)—infrequent.
  Rhabdomyolysis—rare (may be more likely with higher doses).
  Potential for cataracts—based on animal data, not reported in humans.
  Lowered blood platelets (thrombocytopenia)—rare.
  Neuropathy—case report.
  Depression—rare.
  Protein in the urine—rare.
  Lichen planus skin rash—rare.

▷ **Possible Effects on Sexual Function:** Impotence—case reports.

Possible Delayed Adverse Effects: Increased liver enzymes. Lowered levels of co-enzyme Q 10.

Natural Diseases or Disorders That May Be Activated by This Drug
  Latent liver disease.

Possible Effects on Laboratory Tests
  Blood alanine aminotransferase (ALT) enzyme level: increased (with higher doses of drug).

Blood total cholesterol, LDL cholesterol, and triglyceride levels: decreased.
Blood HDL cholesterol level: increased.
Bone mineral density tests (DEXA, PDEXA, and quantitative ultrasound) will remain the same or increase in many cases (beneficial effect).

CAUTION

1. If pregnancy occurs while taking this drug, stop the drug immediately and call your physician.
2. Call your doctor to report promptly any development of muscle pain or tenderness, especially if accompanied by fever or weakness (malaise).
3. Promptly report altered or impaired vision so that appropriate evaluation can be made.
4. A study in *Circulation* (see Heeschen in Sources) found that stopping "statin" type medicines in patients with acute coronary syndrome symptoms can lead to a three-fold increase risk of nonfatal heart attack (MI) or death.

Precautions for Use

By Infants and Children: Safety and effectiveness for those less than 17 years of age are not established.

By Those Over 60 Years of Age: Inform your physician regarding any personal or family history of cataracts. Comply with all recommendations regarding periodic eye examinations. Report promptly any alterations in vision.

▷ **Advisability of Use During Pregnancy**

Pregnancy Category: X. See Pregnancy Risk Categories at the back of this book.

Animal Studies: Mouse and rat studies reveal skeletal birth defects due to a closely related drug of this class.

Human Studies: Adequate studies of pregnant women are not available.
This drug should be avoided during entire pregnancy.

Advisability of Use If Breast-Feeding

Presence of this drug in breast milk: Unknown, but expected since a similar drug from this class does go into breast milk.
Avoid drug or refrain from nursing.

Habit-Forming Potential: None.

Effects of Overdose: Increased indigestion, stomach distress, nausea, diarrhea.

Possible Effects of Long-Term Use: Abnormal liver function with focal hepatitis.

Suggested Periodic Examinations While Taking This Drug (at physician's discretion)

Blood cholesterol studies: total cholesterol, HDL, and LDL fractions. CRP, homocysteine, and LP(a).

Liver function tests before treatment and every six months for the first year of treatment—or until one year has passed after the last dose increase. People who require the 80 mg dose should get another test at 3 months after the increase to 80 mg. In patients who have had an increase in liver enzymes, repeat testing should be done to confirm the first finding. After this, testing should continue frequently until the enzymes return to normal. IF THE ENZYMES INCREASE TO 3 TIMES THE UPPER LIMIT OF NORMAL, SIMVASTATIN SHOULD BE STOPPED.

A complete eye examination may be prudent at beginning of treatment and at any time that significant change in vision occurs (based on animal data). Ask your doctor for help.

EBCT can help define blood vessel damage (calcium score) and track results from this medicine.

▷ **While Taking This Drug, Observe the Following**

Foods: Combination use of B vitamin supplements may help lower additional heart disease risk factors such as homocysteine. Follow a standard low-cholesterol diet. Your doctor may also recommend some specific foods such as increased vegetables or functional foods such as Benecol. Three well-designed studies published in early April 2002 found that both in women and men and before and after a heart attack, people who ate more fish (2–4 servings a week) appeared to avoid heart disease. Additionally putting supplements containing Omega 3 polyunsaturated fatty acids (PUFA) into the diet also appeared to protect against abnormal heart rhythms and sudden death from heart attack. The studies appeared in *JAMA, Circulation* and the *New England Journal of Medicine.* Your doctor may also recommend increasing B vitamins. See Tables 19 and 20 about lifestyle changes and risk factors you can fix.

Herbal Medicines or Minerals: No data exist from well-designed clinical studies about garlic and simvastatin combinations and can not presently be recommended. Additionally, garlic may inhibit blood-clotting (platelet) aggregation—something to consider if you are already taking a platelet inhibitor. The FDA has allowed one dietary supplement called Cholestin to continue to be sold. This preparation actually contains lovastatin. Since use of two HMG-CoA inhibitors may increase risk of rhabdomyolysis or myopathy, the combination is NOT advised. Because St. John's wort and this medicine can increase sun sensitivity, the combination is not advised. Herbal medicines such as eucalyptus, kava, valerian, and others, which can have a toxic effect on the liver, should be avoided while taking simvastatin.

Using plant stanol ester products (Benecol) with this medicine can help further lower total and LDL cholesterol. Soy products (milk, tofu, etc.) contain phytoestrogens that have led to an FDA-approved health claim for reducing risk of heart disease (if they have at least 6.25 g of soy protein per serving). Substituting soy for some of the meat in your diet can also help further lower cholesterol. Because this medicine can deplete co-enzyme Q10, supplementation may be needed.

Beverages: DO NOT take this medicine with grapefruit juice. Blood levels may be markedly increased, increasing risk of muscle damage. May be taken with milk or water.

▷ *Alcohol:* No interactions expected. Use sparingly.

Tobacco Smoking: No interactions expected. I advise everyone to quit smoking.

▷ *Other Drugs*

Author's Note: the company has strengthened myopathy/rhabdomyolysis risk language with some drug combinations versus earlier package inserts.

Simvastatin may *increase* the effects of

• digoxin (Lanoxin).

• imatinib (Gleevec); blood levels of imatinib are needed and should be used to guide lower dosing.

• warfarin (Coumadin); more frequent testing of INR (prothrombin time or protime) will be needed.

Simvastatin *taken concurrently* with

• amiodarone (Cordarone) may increase risk of muscle damage. DOSE REDUCTION TO 20 MG MAXIMUM AND CAREFUL PATIENT MONI-

TORING ARE REQUIRED IF THESE MEDICINES MUST BE COMBINED.

- amprenavir (Agenerase), indinavir (Crixivan), ritonavir (Norvir) and perhaps other protease inhibitors INCREASE THE RISK OF MUSCLE DAMAGE. DOSING OF SIMVASTATIN SHOULD BE SUSPENDED.
- clarithromycin (Biaxin) and erythromycin (various) INCREASES THE RISK OF MUSCLE DAMAGE. IF THESE MEDICINES MUST BE USED, DOSING OF SIMVASTATIN SHOULD BE SUSPENDED.
- clofibrate (Atromid-S) or other fibrates may result in increased risk of serious muscle toxicity. AVOID IF POSSIBLE—IF NOT—DOSE REDUCTION TO 10 mg MAXIMUM AND CAREFUL PATIENT MONITORING ARE REQUIRED IF THESE MEDICINES MUST BE COMBINED.
- colesevelam (Welchol) results in better lowering of LDL-C (desirable effect).
- cyclosporine (Sandimmune) 10 mg DAILY DOSE MAXIMUM. Careful follow-up for effects on the kidney and muscles (kidney failure and myopathy) are needed.
- gemfibrozil (Lopid) may alter absorption and excretion of simvastatin and may also increase risk of muscle damage (rhabdomyolysis)—10 mg MAXIMUM AND CAREFUL PATIENT FOLLOW-UP IS NEEDED.
- itraconazole (Sporanox), voriconazole (Vfend), or ketoconazole (Nizoral) seriously increases risk of muscle damage—DO NOT COMBINE. DOSING OF SIMVASTATIN SHOULD BE SUSPENDED WHILE ITRACONAZOLE OR KETOCONAZOLE ARE BEING TAKEN.
- medicines that change cytochrome P450 3A4 (inhibitors will increase simvastatin levels and inducers will blunt simvastatin therapeutic effects).
- nefazodone (Serzone) may increase risk of muscle damage. IF NEFAZODONE IS REQUIRED, RISK OF MYOPATHY IS INCREASED. CAREFUL PATIENT MONITORING IS MANDATORY.
- niacin may cause an increased frequency of muscle problems (myopathy) when combined with a related medicine (lovastatin). DOSE REDUCTION TO 10 MG MAXIMUM AND CAREFUL PATIENT MONITORING ARE REQUIRED IF THESE MEDICINES MUST BE COMBINED (niacin doses of one gram a day or more). THIS IS A BENEFIT-TO-RISK DECISION.
- quinupristin/dalfopristin (Synercid) may increase the risk for myopathy by increasing simvastatin blood levels.
- verapamil (Verelan) may increase risk of muscle damage. DOSE REDUCTION TO 20 MG MAXIMUM AND CAREFUL PATIENT MONITORING ARE REQUIRED IF THESE MEDICINES MUST BE COMBINED.

The following drug may **decrease** the effects of simvastatin:

- cholestyramine (Questran) may reduce absorption of simvastatin; take simvastatin 1 hour before or 4 hours after cholestyramine.
- fosphenytoin (Cerebyx) or phenytoin (Dilantin) may increase the body chemicals (enzymes) that remove simvastatin and blunt simvastatin benefits. Careful patient monitoring and dose increases may be needed.

▷ *Driving, Hazardous Activities:* No restrictions.

Aviation Note: The use of this drug **may be a disqualification** for piloting. Consult a designated Aviation Medical Examiner.

Exposure to Sun: One case of skin reaction to the sun (photosensitivity/photodermatitis) has been reported.

Discontinuation: **Do not stop this drug without your doctor's knowledge and help.** There may be a significant increase in blood cholesterol levels if this medicine is stopped. Patients who have acute coronary syndromes or ACS (such as unstable angina, heart attack [non-p; Q-wave myocardial infarction], and Q-wave myocardial infarction) were reviewed as part of the Platelet Receptor Inhibitor in Ischemic Syndrome Management (PRISM) study. It was found that pretreatment with statin type medicines (HMG-CoA reductase inhibitors such as the medicine in this profile) significantly lowered risk during the first 30 days after ACS symptoms started. Most importantly, it was found that if a statin type medicine is stopped in ACS patients, there was a three-fold increased risk of non-fatal heart attack or death (see Heeschen, C in Sources). Talk with your doctor BEFORE stopping any statin type medicine.

SPIRONOLACTONE (speer oh noh LAK tohn)

Introduced: 1959 **Class:** Diuretic, aldosterone receptor antagonist
Prescription: USA: Yes **Controlled Drug:** USA: No; Canada: No
Available as Generic: USA: Yes

Author's Note: A new medicine called eplerenone (Inspra) may have a more favorable profile, but further research is needed.

Brand Names: Alatone, Aldactazide [CD], Aldactone, ✽Apo-Spirozide, ✽Novo-Spiroton, ✽Novo-Spirozine [CD], ✽Sincomen, Spironazide

---

BENEFITS versus RISKS

Possible Benefits	*Possible Risks*
REDUCES RISK OF DEATH AND HOSPITALIZATION BY 30% WHEN USED AS PART OF COMBINATION THERAPY FOR SEVERE HEART FAILURE	ABNORMALLY HIGH BLOOD POTASSIUM LEVEL with excessive use
EFFECTIVE PREVENTION OF POTASSIUM LOSS when used adjunctively with other diuretics	Enlargement of male breast tissue Masculinization effects in women: excessive hair growth, deepening of the voice
EFFECTIVE DIURETIC IN REFRACTORY CASES OF FLUID RETENTION when used adjunctively with other diuretics	Liver damage (case reports)

▷ **Principal Uses**

As a Single Drug Product: Uses currently included in FDA-approved labeling: (1) Manages congestive heart failure and disorders of the liver and kidney that are accompanied by excessive fluid retention (edema); (2) also used with other measures to treat high blood pressure where prevention of potassium loss is needed; (3) used to decrease fluid in patients who have failed glucocorticoid treatment and have nephrotic syndrome; (4) works to restore blood potassium to normal in drug caused (induced) low potassium (hypokalemia); (5) used in congestive heart failure (CHF) to reduce frequency of hospitalizations and death in patients with moderate to severe (NYHA class III when the principal study began and up to class IV) heart failure when used in combination with standard CHF treatment (usually a loop diuretic and ACE inhibitor [if tolerated] and in some cases digoxin).

Other (unlabeled) generally accepted uses: (1) May have an adjunctive role in treating acne; (2) can help treat lung problems (bronchopulmonary dysplasia) and slow the disease process; (3) can help precocious puberty in females; (4) eases fluid buildup in premenstrual syndrome; (5) may help women with excessive facial hair growth (hirsutism); (6) may protect against mountain sickness; (7) may help prevent bone loss in women who have polycystic ovary syndrome (PCOS) and are given a gonadotropin releasing hormone agonist.

As a Combination Drug Product [CD]: This drug is available in combination with hydrochlorothiazide, a different kind of diuretic that promotes the loss of potassium from the body. Spironolactone is used in this combination to counteract the potassium-wasting effect of the thiazide diuretic.

In the Pipeline: The Health and Human Services secretary has identified a group of medicines to be tested for use in children. Spironolactone was on that list of the 12 highest priority medicines to be studied in children (find out more at *www.hhs.gov/news/press/2003pres/20030121.html*).

How This Drug Works: By inhibiting the action of aldosterone (an adrenal gland hormone), this drug prevents the reabsorption of sodium and the excretion of potassium by the kidney. Thus the drug promotes the excretion of sodium (and water with it) and the retention of potassium. In heart failure, spironolactone works to protect the heart from too much aldosterone (a hormone that can lower the ability of the heart to pump).

Available Dosage Forms and Strengths
Tablets — 25 mg, 50 mg, 100 mg
Combination Tablets — 25 mg spironolactone/25 mg HCTZ, 50 mg spironolactone 50 mg HCTZ

▷ **Usual Adult Dosage Ranges:** For *edema:* Initially 100 mg per day in one dose or divided into several doses. The dose is then adjusted according to individual response. The usual maintenance dose is 50 to 200 mg daily, divided into two to four doses. If response is not adequate after 5 days, a second fluid medicine (diuretic) is added.

For hypertension: Spironolactone alone: 50–100 mg a day in one dose or divided into equal doses. The ongoing dose is adjusted as needed and tolerated, 14 days after the drug is started. For the Aldactazide form: 50–100 mg of each medicine in one dose or separated into several equal doses.

In moderate to severe heart failure: Many clinicians are recommending use of 25 mg per day in combination with an ACE inhibitor, a loop diuretic and possibly digoxin.

Note: Actual dosage and administration schedule must be determined for each patient individually.

Conditions Requiring Dosing Adjustments
Liver Function: This drug can be a rare cause of liver damage and patients should be followed closely.

Kidney Function: For patients with mild kidney failure, the drug can be taken every 12 hours in the usual dose. In moderate kidney failure (GFR 10–50 ml/min), spironolactone can be taken every 12 to 24 hours in the usual dose. In severe kidney failure (GFR less than 10 ml/min or creatinine greater than 2.5 mg/dL), this drug should not be taken. Spironolactone is contraindicated in acute renal failure and severe chronic renal compromise.

▷ **Dosing Instructions:** The tablet may be crushed and taken with or following meals to promote absorption of the drug and reduce stomach irritation. If you forget a dose: Take the missed dose as soon as you remember it, unless it's nearly time for your next dose—if that is the case, skip the missed dose and take the next dose right on schedule. DO NOT double doses. Talk with your doctor if you find yourself missing doses.

Usual Duration of Use: Use on a regular schedule for 5 to 10 days usually determines effectiveness in clearing edema, and for 2 to 3 weeks to determine its effect on hypertension. Because patient response may vary in congestive heart failure (CHF) and the aldosterone antagonism data are new, discuss goals of CHF use individually. Long-term use (months to years) requires physician supervision and periodic evaluation.

Typical Treatment Goals and Measurements (Outcomes and Markers)

Congestive Heart Failure: The goal is to help remove excess fluid (edema) and hence decrease blood pressure while helping ease the amount of work the heart has to do. Additionally, when this medicine is combined with standard CHF treatment, death and adverse consequences of CHF as well as the number of times a given patient will generally have to be hospitalized are reduced. Clinical signs and symptoms such as ankle swelling, difficulty breathing and walking, or exercise tolerance may also improve. Surrogate end points (a marker that offers vital information about how well a patient is responding to a treatment) are useful to clinicians. Two possible surrogate markers for CHF are left ventricular end diastolic volume (LVEDV) and b-type natriuretic peptide (BNP). These will be updated as more information becomes available.

Blood Pressure: The NEW guidelines (JNC VII) define normal blood pressure (BP) as **less than** 120/80. Because blood pressures that were once considered acceptable can actually lead to blood vessel damage, the committee from the National Institutes of Health's National Heart, Lung, and Blood Institute now has a new category called **Pre-hypertension**. This ranges from 120/80 to 139/89 and is intended to help your doctor encourage lifestyle changes (or in the case of people with a risk factor for high blood pressure, start treatment) much earlier so that possible damage to blood vessels, your heart, kidneys, sexual potency, or eyes might be minimized or avoided altogether. The next two classes of high blood pressure are stage 1 hypertension: 140/90 to 159/99 and stage 2 hypertension equal to or greater than: 160/100 mm Hg. These guidelines also recommend that clinicians trying to control blood pressure work with their patients to agree on the goals and a plan of treatment. The first-ever guidelines for blood pressure (hypertension) in African Americans recommends that MOST black patients be started on TWO antihypertensive medicines with the goal of lowering blood pressure to 130/80 for those with high risk for heart and blood vessel disease or with diabetes. The American Diabetes Association recommends 130/80 as the target for people living with diabetes and less than 125/75 for those who spill more than one gram of protein into their urine. Most clinicians try to achieve a BP that confers the best balance of lower cardiovascular risk and avoids the problem of too low a blood pressure. Blood pressure duration is generally increased with beneficial restriction of sodium. The goals and time frame should be discussed with you when the prescription is written. If goals are not met, it is not unusual to intensify doses or add on medicines. You can find the new blood pressure guidelines at *www.nhlbi.nih.gov/guidelines/hypertension/index.htm*. For the African American guidelines see Douglas J.G. in Sources.

▷ **This Drug Should Not Be Taken If**
  • you have had an allergic reaction to it previously.
  • you have severely impaired liver or kidney function.

- your kidneys are not making any urine.
- your blood potassium is excessively high (hyperkalemia).

▷ **Inform Your Physician Before Taking This Drug If**
- you have a history of liver or kidney disease.
- you have diabetes.
- you take an anticoagulant, antihypertensives, a digitalis preparation, another diuretic, lithium, or a potassium preparation.
- your blood chemistry (electrolytes) are out of balance.
- you plan to have surgery under general anesthesia in the near future.
- you have a potassium-rich diet. Talk to your doctor and see Table 13.

Possible Side Effects (natural, expected, and unavoidable drug actions)
Abnormally high blood potassium levels—possible and may be frequent; abnormally low blood sodium levels or dehydration—infrequent.

▷ **Possible Adverse Effects** (unusual, unexpected, and infrequent reactions)
If any of the following develop, consult your physician promptly for guidance.
Mild Adverse Effects
Allergic Reactions: Skin rash, hives, itching, drug fever (see Glossary).
Headache, dizziness, unsteadiness, weakness, drowsiness, lethargy, confusion—infrequent.
Dry mouth, nausea, vomiting, diarrhea—infrequent.
Masculine pattern of hair growth and deepening of the voice in women—case reports.
Taste disturbances—possible.
Serious Adverse Effects
Allergic reactions: Abnormally low blood platelet count—rare.
Systemic-lupus-erythematosus-like syndrome—case reports.
Symptomatic potassium excess: confusion, numbness and tingling in lips and extremities, fatigue, weakness, shortness of breath, slow heart rate, low blood pressure—possible.
Stomach ulceration with bleeding—case reports.
Disruption in the acid base balance of body (hyperchloremic or hyperkalemic acidosis)—possible.
Liver toxicity (hepatitis) or kidney toxicity (nephrotoxicity)—case reports.
Porphyria or systemic-lupus-erythematosus-like syndrome—case reports.
Excessively low white blood cells (granulocytes) or platelets—case reports.
Thinning of the bones—case report.
This medicine is a tumorigen in chronic rat toxicity studies. Current labeling notes that unnecessary use of this medicine should be avoided.

▷ **Possible Effects on Sexual Function**
Decreased libido or impaired erection or impotence—possible.
Male breast enlargement and tenderness (gynecomastia) (increases with higher doses). Some gynecomastia reports were associated with impotence. Female breast enlargement; altered timing and pattern of menstruation; postmenopausal bleeding.
Decreased vaginal secretion—case reports.

Possible Effects on Laboratory Tests
White blood cell count: possibly decreased.
Blood platelet count: possibly decreased.
Blood potassium level: increased.
Blood uric acid level: no effect in some; increased and decreased in others.

CAUTION
1. Do not take potassium supplements or increase intake of potassium-rich foods (see Table 13) while taking this drug.
2. Do not stop this drug abruptly unless abnormally high blood levels of potassium develop.
3. Ordinary doses of aspirin (more than 650 mg) may reverse the diuretic effect of this drug. Discuss aspirin or NSAID use with your doctor.
4. Avoid excessive use of salt substitutes containing potassium; these are potential causes of potassium excess.
5. Spironolactone may interfere with laboratory checks (falsely LOW) levels of digoxin and changes in cortisol results.

Precautions for Use
By Infants and Children: Limit the continual use of this drug in children to 1 month.
Watch closely for indications of potassium accumulation. Dosing is accomplished based on weight using 1–3 mg/kilogram per day, up to 200 mg / 24 hours (given in a single dose or in 2–4 equal doses).
By Those Over 60 Years of Age: The natural decline in kidney function may predispose to potassium retention in the body. Watch for indications of potassium excess: slow heart rate, irregular heart rhythms, low blood pressure, confusion, drowsiness. The excessive use of diuretics can cause harmful loss of body water (dehydration), increased viscosity of the blood, and an increased tendency of the blood to clot, predisposing to stroke, heart attack, or thrombophlebitis.

▷ **Advisability of Use During Pregnancy**
Pregnancy Category: C in the package insert, D by one researcher. See Pregnancy Risk Categories at the back of this book.
Animal Studies: This drug causes feminization of male rat fetuses.
Human Studies: Adequate studies of pregnant women are not available.
This drug should not be used during pregnancy unless a very serious complication of pregnancy occurs for which this drug is significantly beneficial.

Advisability of Use If Breast-Feeding
Presence of this drug in breast milk: A metabolic end product (canrenone) is present.
Avoid drug or refrain from nursing.

Habit-Forming Potential: None.

Effects of Overdosage: Thirst, drowsiness, fatigue, weakness, nausea, vomiting, confusion, irregular heart rhythm, low blood pressure.

Possible Effects of Long-Term Use: Potassium accumulation to abnormally high blood levels. Male breast enlargement.

Suggested Periodic Examinations While Taking This Drug (at physician's discretion)
Measurements of blood sodium, potassium, magnesium, and chloride levels. Kidney and liver function tests.

▷ **While Taking This Drug, Observe the Following**
Foods: Talk to your doctor about possible need to avoid high-potassium foods (see Table 13). Avoid excessive restriction of salt.
Herbal Medicines or Minerals: Hawthorn (Crataegus variety) and co-enzyme Q10 (co-Q10) can affect the way the heart works. BE CERTAIN to tell your doctor that you are taking or are considering taking these herbs if you are taking spironolactone or if a spironolactone prescription is being consid-

ered for you or a loved one. Issues remain regarding optimum doses, monitoring strategies, and possible interactions for co-Q10. One objective review recognized co-Q10 as adjunctive therapy for congestive heart failure. Co-Q10 may also interact badly with aspirin. Soy products (milk, tofu, etc.) contain phytoestrogens that have led to an FDA-approved health claim for reducing risk of heart disease (if they have at least 6.25 g of soy protein per serving). It is important that potassium and magnesium levels be kept in the normal range while you are taking spironolactone. Licorice may increase risk of excessively low potassium and should be avoided. Couch grass or nettle should NOT be taken by patients who have increased fluid (edema) caused by heart weakness. Ginseng, guarana, eleuthero root, hawthorn, saw palmetto, ma huang, goldenseal, and licorice may cause increased blood pressure. Couch grass may worsen edema due to heart or kidney problems. Indian snakeroot, calcium, and garlic may help lower blood pressure. Talk to your doctor BEFORE combining any herbal medicine with spironolactone.

Beverages: No restrictions. May be taken with milk.

▷ *Alcohol:* Use with caution. Alcohol may enhance the drowsiness and the blood-pressure-lowering effect of this drug.

Tobacco Smoking: No interactions expected, but I advise everyone to quit smoking.

▷ *Other Drugs*

Spironolactone may ***increase*** the effects of
- digoxin (Lanoxin). Cautious and increased checks of digoxin levels are prudent.

Spironolactone may ***decrease*** the effects of
- anticoagulants (Coumadin, etc.). Increased frequency of INR (prothrombin time or protime) testing is needed.
- digoxin (Lanoxin). Falsely lowering the laboratory test results on some test kits. Cautious checks and increased checks of digoxin levels are prudent.

Spironolactone ***taken concurrently*** with
- arginine (various) may lead to excessive potassium levels.
- captopril (Capoten) or other ACE inhibitors (see Drug Classes) may cause further increases in blood potassium levels. More frequent laboratory tests are prudent.
- cortisone-like drugs (fludrocortisone, others) may lead to excessive potassium loss.
- cyclosporine (Sandimmune) may result in very elevated potassium levels.
- digitoxin (Crystodigin) may cause either increased or decreased digitoxin effects (unpredictable).
- lithium (Lithobid, others) may cause accumulation of lithium to toxic levels.
- norepinephrine (various) may blunt norepinephrine effects.
- potassium preparations may cause excessively high blood potassium levels.
- tacrolimus (Prograf) may lead to excessive potassium levels. USE IS NOT ADVISED.
- valsartan (Diovan) may lead to increased potassium levels. More frequent potassium checks are prudent.
- warfarin (Coumadin) may blunt effectiveness of warfarin. More frequent INR checks are prudent. Dose adjustments may be needed.

The following drugs may ***decrease*** the effects of spironolactone
- aspirin (higher doses) or other NSAIDs (see Drug Classes)—may reduce its diuretic effectiveness.

▷ *Driving, Hazardous Activities:* This drug may cause dizziness and drowsiness. Restrict activities as necessary.

Aviation Note: The use of this drug *may be a disqualification* for piloting. Consult a designated Aviation Medical Examiner.

Exposure to Sun: No restrictions.

Discontinuation: With high dosage or prolonged use, it is advisable to withdraw this drug gradually. Ask your physician for guidance.

STAVUDINE (STAV u dine)

Other Name: D4T **Introduced:** 1994 **Class:** Antiretroviral, Anti-HIV, Anti AIDS **Prescription:** USA: Yes **Controlled Drug:** USA: No; Canada: No **Available as Generic:** USA: No; Canada: No **Brand Name:** Zerit

BENEFITS versus RISKS	
Possible Benefits	*Possible Risks*
INCREASED CD4 COUNTS IN ADULTS WITH ADVANCED HIV	PERIPHERAL NEUROPATHY Pancreatitis
LESS LIKELY THAN OTHER AGENTS TO DEVELOP RESISTANCE	Hyperlactatemia Lactic acidosis syndrome (LAS)
AVOIDS BONE MARROW TOXICITY OF ZIDOVUDINE	
EFFECTIVE COMBINATION THERAPY OF HIV	
PART OF A COMBINATION REGIMEN (HAART) REDUCING HIV TO UNDETECTABLE LEVELS	

▷ **Principal Uses**

As a Single Drug Product: Uses currently included in FDA-approved labeling: Treatment of HIV in adults and children as part of combination therapy (a study of stavudine plus didanosine plus nevirapine is an effective triple medicine combination).

Author's Note: Adherence—taking medicines for HIV exactly on time and in the right amount—is ABSOLUTELY critical to getting the best possible results or outcomes. The antiretroviral therapy guidelines from NIAID take into account how easily the medicine treating HIV can fit into a patient's life (twice daily dosing is a distinct advantage). Structured therapy interruptions (STI) or structured interruptions of therapy (SIT) are still controversial.

Other (unlabeled) generally accepted uses: (1) post occupational exposure to HIV.

How This Drug Works: This drug inhibits HIV reproduction (replication) by (1) inhibiting an HIV enzyme (reverse transcriptase), which blocks the ability of the virus to make nuclear material, and (2) inhibiting an enzyme (DNA polymerase-gamma and -beta), which blocks the ability to make DNA in the mitochondria.

Available Dosage Forms and Strengths

Capsules — 15 mg, 20 mg, 30 mg, 40 mg

Capsules, extended release — 37.5 mg, 50 mg, 75 mg, 100 mg

Powder — 1 mg/ml

▷ **Recommended Dose Ranges** (Actual dose and schedule must be determined for each patient individually.)

Infants and Children: Children weighing less than 30 kg are given 2 mg per kg per day separated into two equal doses 12 hours apart. Those weighing greater than 30 kg are given the adult dose.

18 to 60 Years of Age: Regular release form: Patients with a body mass of 60 kg (132 lb) or more should take 40 mg every 12 hours. Patients with a body mass of less than 60 kg should take 30 mg twice daily. For those who have had to stop because of peripheral neuropathy (after complete resolution of symptoms)—20 mg twice daily for patients with a body mass of 60 kg or more; 15 mg twice daily for those with a body mass less than 60 kg. Some suggestion has been made that doses greater than 1 mg per kg per day carry a greater risk of peripheral neuropathy. If peripheral neuropathy does happen, most clinicians will interrupt stavudine treatment. For patients in whom symptoms (tingling and numbness or pain in the hands or feet) resolve completely, stavudine can be restarted at 20 mg twice daily for people who weigh 60 kg or more or at 15 mg twice a day for those less than 60 mg. Some clinicians separate the total daily dose into three equal doses given three times a day. Extended release form: 100 mg once a day for people who weigh more than 60 kg and 75 mg once a day for those less than 60 kg.

Over 65 Years of Age: This drug has not been studied in those over 65.

Conditions Requiring Dosing Adjustments

Liver Function: If liver enzymes increase significantly, therapy may need to be stopped and then reintroduced with 20 mg daily for those weighing more than 60 kg and 15 mg daily if less than 60 kg.

Kidney Function: Patients with mild kidney compromise (creatinine clearance greater than 50 ml/min) take the usual weight-adjusted dose for adults. Mild to moderate kidney compromise (creatinine clearance 26 to 50 ml/min) should take one-half of the usual weight-adjusted dose every 12 hours. In severe kidney compromise (creatinine clearance 10 to 25 ml/min), one-half the usual weight-adjusted dose should be taken every 24 hours.

▷ **Dosing Instructions:** This drug may be taken without regard to food. Not missing doses (adherence) is critical, as missed doses will make resistance more likely. The oral solution should be mixed (reconstituted) with water by your pharmacist by adding 202 ml of purified water to the dry powder. SHAKE THE CONTAINER VIGOROUSLY BEFORE you give or take a dose. The reconstituted medicine should be refrigerated and expires 30 days after it is mixed. If signs and symptoms of peripheral neuropathy (pain in the feet or hands, numbness, or tingling sensations) start—treatment with stavudine should be interrupted. When symptoms resolve completely, stavudine is restarted at 20 mg twice a day for people 60 kg or more and 15 mg twice daily for those less than 60 kg. If you forget a dose: Take the missed dose as soon as you remember it, unless it's nearly time for your next dose—if that is the case, skip the missed dose and take the next dose right on schedule. DO NOT double doses. The once daily formulation allows less frequent dosing, and should not be modified. IT IS ABSOLUTELY CRITICAL to take HIV medicines exactly as prescribed. Talk with your doctor if you find yourself missing doses. There are beeper-based systems that can be a great help.

Usual Duration of Use: Use on a regular schedule for several months usually determines effectiveness in shutting down HIV replication and increasing

CD4 counts. Long-term use (months to years) requires periodic physician evaluation of response (viral burden and CD4).

Typical Treatment Goals and Measurements (Outcomes and Markers)

HIV: Goals for HIV treatment presently are maximum suppression of viral replication, maximum lowering of the amount of virus in your body (viral load or burden), and maximum patient survival. Markers of successful therapy include undetectable viral load, increased CD4 cells, absence of indicator or opportunistic infections (OIs) and in the case of the HIV-positive patient, failure of the infection to progress to AIDS.

Possible Advantages of This Drug

More favorable side-effect profile than other nucleoside analogs. Favorable profile for combination therapy. Favorable once-daily dosing, decreasing pill burden.

▷ **This Drug Should Not Be Taken If**
- you had an allergic reaction to it previously.

▷ **Inform Your Physician Before Taking This Drug If**
- you have had peripheral neuropathy caused by other drugs before.
- you have kidney or liver compromise.
- you have had pancreatitis.
- your bone marrow is depressed.
- you are pregnant.
- you have vitamin B12 deficiency or folic acid deficiency.
- you are unsure how much to take or how often to take it.

Possible Side Effects (natural, expected, and unavoidable drug actions)

Chills or fever—infrequent.

Peripheral neuropathy—infrequent to frequent.

Pancreatitis—infrequent.

▷ **Possible Adverse Effects** (unusual, unexpected, and infrequent reactions)

If any of the following develop, consult your physician promptly for guidance.

Mild Adverse Effects

Allergic reaction: skin rash.

Rapidly ascending neuromuscular weakness (mimics Guillain-Barré)—case reports.

Sleep disorder (early awakening and anxiety)—reported, but questionable causation.

Nausea and vomiting or abdominal pain—infrequent.

Increased liver enzymes—frequent.

Lipodystrophy—possible.

Author's Note: Current controversy as to possible lipid changes (lipodystrophy or LD) from protease inhibitors and/or nucleoside reverse transcriptase inhibitors involves presence of mild changes versus moderate to severe problems. The HOPS data found that risk of LD increases with increasing time on antiretrovirals and that LD increases with an increasing number of nondrug factors (age 40 or older, HIV infection 7 or more years, AIDS 2 or more years, hemophiliacs, nadir CD4 count less than 100 or less than 15, and time since nadir 3 or more years). Patients who did not have these risk factors DID NOT develop significant LD in the HOPS data.

Serious Adverse Effects

Allergic reactions: anaphylactic reactions—rare.

Anemia—case reports.

Low white blood cell or platelet counts—rare to infrequent in phase three data, not found in later data.

Lactic acidosis syndrome (LAS)—case reports.

Respiratory failure as part of a Guillain-Barré type syndrome—case reports.

Severe liver problems (hepatomegaly with statuses)—case reports with nucleoside analogs.

▷ **Possible Effects on Sexual Function:** Impotence—rare in phase three data. One case report of swelling of male breast tissue (gynecomastia).

Possible Delayed Adverse Effects: Peripheral neuropathy—up to 24%.

▷ **Adverse Effects That May Mimic Natural Diseases or Disorders**

Increased liver function tests may mimic hepatitis. Rapidly ascending neuromuscular weakness may mimic Guillain-Barré syndrome.

Possible Effects on Laboratory Tests

Liver function tests: increased.

Amylase: increased.

Complete blood counts: decreased platelets and white blood cells—possible.

CAUTION

1. Taking stavudine and even an undetectable viral burden **does not** remove risk of giving (transmission) HIV to others through sexual contact or blood contamination.
2. Promptly report the development of stomach pain and vomiting; this could indicate pancreatitis.
3. Report development of pain, numbness, tingling, or burning in the hands or feet, as this may be peripheral neuropathy.

Precautions for Use

By Infants and Children: Watch carefully for adverse effects.

By Those Over 65 Years of Age: Age-related decline in kidney function may require dosing changes.

▷ **Advisability of Use During Pregnancy**

Pregnancy Category: C. See Pregnancy Risk Categories at the back of this book.

Animal Studies: Clinical doses in rats have not revealed teratogenicity, but doses of 399 times those used in humans have resulted in skeletal problems. Increased early rat death has also occurred at 399 times the human dose.

Human Studies: Adequate studies of pregnant women are not available.

Ask your doctor for guidance.

Advisability of Use If Breast-Feeding

Presence of this drug in breast milk: Yes.

Refrain from nursing if you are HIV positive or are taking this drug. HIV can be transmitted through breast milk.

Habit-Forming Potential: None.

Effects of Overdose: Adults treated with 12 to 24 times the recommended daily dose revealed no acute toxicity.

Possible Effects of Long-Term Use: Peripheral neuropathy and hepatic toxicity.

Suggested Periodic Examinations While Taking This Drug (at physician's discretion)

Liver function tests.

Amylase and complete blood counts.

CD4 or viral load measurement.

▷ **While Taking This Drug, Observe the Following**

Foods: No restrictions.

Herbal Medicines or Minerals: Some patients use echinacea to attempt to boost their immune systems. Unfortunately, use of echinacea is not recommended in people with damaged immune systems. This herb may also actually weaken any immune system if it is used too often or for too long a time. St. John's Wort can blunt the blood levels and benefits of stavudine. DO NOT combine.

Beverages: No restrictions.

▷ *Alcohol:* No interactions expected.

Tobacco Smoking: No interactions expected. I advise everyone to quit smoking.

▷ *Other Drugs*

Stavudine ***taken concurrently*** with
- hydroxyurea (Droxia, Hydrea) may lead to fatal pancreatitis and liver toxicity. DO NOT COMBINE.
- other Drugs such as metronidazole (Flagyl) that can cause peripheral neuropathy should be avoided if possible.

Stavudine may ***increase*** the effects of
- didanosine (Videx) at specific drug concentration ratios. Careful monitoring for liver toxicity should be undertaken.

Stavudine may ***decrease*** the effects of
- didanosine (Videx) at specific drug concentration ratios.
- zidovudine (AZT) at specific drug concentration ratios. The combination is NOT recommended.

▷ *Driving, Hazardous Activities:* This drug may cause dizziness. Restrict activities as necessary.

Aviation Note: The use of this drug ***may be a disqualification*** for piloting. Consult a designated Aviation Medical Examiner.

Exposure to Sun: No restrictions.

Discontinuation: Do not stop this drug without your doctor's knowledge and guidance.

STRONTIUM-89 (STRON tee um)

Introduced: 1993   **Class:**   Systemic radionuclide, pain syndrome modifier   **Prescription:**   USA: Yes   **Controlled Drug:**   USA: No; Canada: No   **Available as Generic:**   USA: No; Canada: No

Brand Name: Metastron

BENEFITS versus RISKS	
Possible Benefits	*Possible Risks*
EFFECTIVE RELIEF OF PRIMARY OR METASTATIC (SUCH AS FROM PROSTATE OR BREAST CANCER) CANCER OF THE BONE PAIN	BONE MARROW TOXICITY (decreased white blood cells and platelets) Transient increase in bone pain

▷ **Principal Uses**

As a Single Drug Product: Uses currently included in FDA-approved labeling: Used to treat metastatic bone cancer pain.

Other (unlabeled) generally accepted uses: None at present.

How This Drug Works: This radiopharmaceutical is selectively taken up by areas of bone cancer. Once it accumulates in cancerous areas, it emits radiation directly at the site of the cancer.

Available Dosage Forms and Strengths
Injection — 10.9 to 22.6 mg of strontium in a total of 1 ml of water

▷ **Recommended Dose Ranges** (Actual dose and schedule must be determined for each patient individually.)
Infants and Children: Safety and efficacy for those less than 18 years old are not established.
18 to 60 Years of Age: A dose of 1.5–2.2 megabecquerels/kg or 40–60 microcuries/kg of body weight is given intravenously over 1 to 2 minutes. The dose may be repeated at 90-day intervals, if needed and is based on how well the patient responds to the original dosing as well as to how acceptable the blood cell counts are (hematological status).
Over 60 Years of Age: Same as 18 to 60 years of age.

Conditions Requiring Dosing Adjustments
Liver Function: Dosing changes in liver compromise do not appear to be needed.
Kidney Function: This agent is primarily removed by the kidneys, but decreases in doses are not presently defined.

▷ **Dosing Instructions:** You may eat and drink as you normally would. During the first week after injection, strontium-89 will be present in the blood and the urine. A normal toilet should be used in preference to a urinal. The radiation in this medicine is NOT considered a hazard to family members or to staff in the hospital or cancer center. If you forget a dose: CALL your doctor for instructions. This medicine must be taken on a regular basis.

Usual Duration of Use: Use of previously prescribed pain medicine will be expected for 7 to 21 days after the injection, and there may be a flare in pain (prudent to anticipate this). A maximum of 42 days after injection has been needed to determine peak effectiveness in controlling bone cancer pain. The dose may be repeated (if blood tests are acceptable) 90 days after the prior dose was given. See your physician on a regular basis.

Typical Treatment Goals and Measurements (Outcomes and Markers)
Pain: Most clinicians treating pain use a device called an algometer to check your pain. This looks like a small ruler, but lets the clinician better understand your pain. The goals of treatment then relate to where the level of pain started (for example, a rating of seven on a zero to ten scale) and what the cause of the pain was. I use the PQRSTBG method (see Glossary). Pain medicines may also be used together (in combination) in order to get the best result or outcome. Relief of bone pain is a hallmark of successful treatment with this medicine. Decreasing use of primary pain medicine as well as rescue doses can be used to track response. Sleep patterns should also improve. If your pain control is not acceptable to YOU (remember, in hospitals and outpatient settings, etc. pain control is a patient right), call your doctor.

Possible Advantages of This Drug
Effective control of bone cancer pain without the risks or compromise of narcotics. This medicine may also allow lower doses of medicines such as morphine with excellent pain control thereby reducing the risk of adverse effects from the opioid (such as morphine).

▷ **This Drug Should Not Be Taken If**
- you had an allergic reaction to it previously.
- you have cancer that does not involve the bone.

▷ **Inform Your Physician Before Taking This Drug If**
- you have a history of low platelets (less than 60,000) or white blood cell counts (less than 2,400).
- you take other drugs that may lower white cells or platelets.
- you have an increased calcium.
- you do not understand how to appropriately dispose of your urine.

Possible Side Effects (natural, expected, and unavoidable drug actions)
May cause a calcium-like flushing when injected. May cause transient (up to 72 hours) increase in bone pain. Drug fever may result.

▷ **Possible Adverse Effects** (unusual, unexpected, and infrequent reactions)
If any of the following develop, consult your physician promptly for guidance.
Mild Adverse Effects
Allergic reactions: not defined.
Chills and fever—possible.
Serious Adverse Effects
Allergic reactions: none defined.
Bone marrow toxicity: 20–30% decrease in white cell or platelet counts—may be dose-related. Lowest point (nadir) happens 5–16 weeks after a dose.
Bacterial infection of blood (septicemia) following drug-induced decreases in white blood cells—possible.
Animal data shows that this drug is a possible carcinogen—case reports of two patients given this drug for refractory prostate cancer and subsequently developed sudden (acute) myelogenous leukemia (still of questionable cause due to multiple treatments).

▷ **Possible Effects on Sexual Function:** None reported.

Possible Delayed Adverse Effects: Lowering of white blood cells (recovery in up to 6 months) and blood platelets (lowest count 5 to 16 weeks after therapy).

Natural Diseases or Disorders That May Be Activated by This Drug
Aplastic anemia.

Possible Effects on Laboratory Tests
White blood cell counts: decreased.
Platelet counts: decreased.

CAUTION
1. Promptly report any signs of infection (lethargy, temperature, sore throat).
2. It may take up to 21 days for this agent to work. Narcotics will need to be continued.
3. Your blood and urine will contain radioactive strontium for 7 days after injection. Ask your doctor for help on appropriate disposal.
4. This drug is a potential carcinogen.
5. Promptly report any abnormal bleeding or bruising.

Precautions for Use
By Infants and Children: Safety and effectiveness for those less than 18 years of age are not established.
By Those Over 60 Years of Age: Specific changes are not presently needed.

▷ **Advisability of Use During Pregnancy**

Pregnancy Category: D. See Pregnancy Risk Categories at the back of this book.

Animal Studies: Adequate studies evaluating potential to cause birth defects have not been performed.

Human Studies: Adequate studies of pregnant women are not available. This drug may cause fetal harm. Ask your doctor for advice.

Advisability of Use If Breast-Feeding

Presence of this drug in breast milk: This drug acts like calcium and is expected to be present in breast milk.

Avoid drug or refrain from nursing.

Habit-Forming Potential: None.

Effects of Overdose: May result in acute radiation syndrome with initial nausea and vomiting followed by depressed white cells and platelets and tendency to infections. Careful dose calculations are indicated, as this drug emits beta-radiation.

Possible Effects of Long-Term Use: Not indicated for long-term use.

Suggested Periodic Examinations While Taking This Drug (at physician's discretion)

Complete blood counts should be tested once every other week during therapy.

▷ **While Taking This Drug, Observe the Following**

Foods: No restrictions.

Herbal Medicines or Minerals: Some patients use echinacea to attempt to boost their immune systems. Unfortunately, use of echinacea is not recommended in people with damaged immune systems. This herb may also actually weaken any immune system if it is used too often or for too long a time.

Beverages: No restrictions.

▷ *Alcohol:* No interactions expected.

Tobacco Smoking: No interactions expected. I advise everyone to quit smoking.

Marijuana Smoking: No interactions expected.

▷ *Other Drugs*

Strontium-89 *taken concurrently* with

• medications that lower white blood cells or platelets may result in severe decreases in white blood cells or platelets.

▷ *Driving, Hazardous Activities:* This drug may cause a transient increase in bone pain. Restrict activities as necessary.

Aviation Note: The use of this drug *may be a disqualification* for piloting. Consult a designated Aviation Medical Examiner.

Exposure to Sun: No restrictions.

Discontinuation: Dosing may be repeated if blood counts are acceptable.

SUCRALFATE (soo KRAL fayt)

Introduced: 1978   **Class:** Antiulcer, gastrointestinal drug   **Prescription:** USA: Yes   **Controlled Drug:** USA: No; Canada: No   **Available as Generic:** Yes

Brand Names: ✤Apo-Sucralfate, Carafate, ✤Dom-Sucralfate, ✤Novo-Sucralfate, ✤Sulcrate

```
┌─────────────────────────────────────────────────────────────────┐
│                     BENEFITS versus RISKS                         │
│       Possible Benefits                  Possible Risks           │
│  EFFECTIVE TREATMENT IN        Constipation                       │
│    DUODENAL ULCER DISEASE      Skin rash, hives, itching          │
│  No serious adverse effects    Aluminum toxicity in kidney        │
│                                  compromise                       │
└─────────────────────────────────────────────────────────────────┘
```

▷ **Principal Uses**

As a Single Drug Product: Uses currently included in FDA-approved labeling: Treats and prevents recurrence of duodenal ulcer disease in adults and children. Effective when used alone, but may be used with antacids for pain relief.

Other (unlabeled) generally accepted uses: (1) May be useful in treating stomach (gastric ulcers) if other therapy isn't tolerated; (2) can reduce the frequency of diarrhea caused by radiation therapy; (3) may have a role as a douche in promoting healing of vaginal ulcerations that are resistant to other measures; (4) can ease the pain and spasms associated with tonsillectomy; (5) appears to increase healing in burn patients.

Author's Note: Information in this profile has been shortened to make room for more widely used medicines.

SULFAMETHOXAZOLE (sul fa meth OX a zohl)

Please see the sulfonamide antibiotic family profile.

SULFASALAZINE (sul fa SAL a zeen)

Introduced: 1949   **Class:**   Bowel anti-inflammatory, sulfonamides
Prescription: USA: Yes   **Controlled Drug:**   USA: No; Canada: No
Available as Generic: USA: Yes; Canada: No
Brand Names: ♣Alti-Sulfasalazine, Azaline, Azulfidine, Azulfidine EN-Tabs, ♣PMS Sulfasalazine, ♣PMS Sulfasalazine E.C., ♣Salazopyrin, ♣Salazopyrin EN, ♣SAS-Enema, ♣SAS Enteric-500, SAS-500, Sulfazine EC

```
┌─────────────────────────────────────────────────────────────────┐
│                     BENEFITS versus RISKS                         │
│       Possible Benefits                  Possible Risks           │
│  EFFECTIVE SUPPRESSION OF      Allergic reactions: mild to severe │
│    INFLAMMATORY BOWEL            skin reactions                   │
│    DISEASE                     Blood cell disorders: aplastic     │
│  SYMPTOMATIC RELIEF OF           anemia, hemolytic anemia,        │
│    REGIONAL ENTERITIS AND        abnormally low white cell or     │
│    ULCERATIVE COLITIS            platelet counts                  │
│  HELPFUL IN REFRACTORY         Drug-induced liver damage          │
│    RHEUMATOID ARTHRITIS        Drug-induced kidney damage         │
│                                Seizures                           │
└─────────────────────────────────────────────────────────────────┘
```

▷ **Principal Uses**

As a Single Drug Product: Uses currently included in FDA-approved labeling: (1) Treats inflammatory disease of the lower intestinal tract and then helps retain remissions: regional enteritis (Crohn's disease) and ulcerative colitis—it is usually taken by mouth, but may also be used in retention enemas; (2) helps rheumatoid arthritis.

Other (unlabeled) generally accepted uses: (1) Short-term use in therapy of ankylosing spondylitis; (2) treatment of mild to moderate psoriasis; (3) may have a role in juvenile arthritis; (4) may decrease risk of colorectal cancer in ulcerative colitis patients.

How This Drug Works: Suppresses the formation of prostaglandins and related tissue substances that cause inflammation, diarrhea, and tissue destruction.

Available Dosage Forms and Strengths

Oral suspension — 250 mg/5 ml

Tablets — 500 mg

Tablets, enteric coated — 500 mg

▷ **Usual Adult Dosage Ranges:** *Ulcerative colitis:* Some clinicians start with 3 to 4 g per day of this medicine, separated into equal doses given every 6 to 8 hours until symptoms are adequately controlled. For maintenance, 500 mg every 6 hours. Others use a starting dose of 1–2 g a day in order to minimize stomach and intestinal adverse effects (consistent with product labeling). Some patients tolerate up to 6 g a day, but doses of 4 g a day or greater bring increased risk of adverse effects. If diarrhea occurs, the dose is often decreased to the earlier dose that worked and did not cause diarrhea. Some patients do not remove this medicine well (slow acetylators) and are given 2.5 to 3 g a day.

Rheumatoid arthritis (when salicylates or NSAIDs have not worked): 2 to 3 g daily is taken in equally divided doses. If the delayed-release form (Azulfidine EN-Tabs) is used, 500 mg is taken for 1 week in the evening, then 500 mg twice daily for a week, then 500 mg in the morning and 1 g in the evening for a week and continuing with 1 g twice a day. Maximum dose is 3 grams.

Note: Actual dose and schedule must be individually determined.

Conditions Requiring Dosing Adjustments

Liver Function: This drug can be a cause of liver damage, and patients should be followed closely.

Kidney Function: Empiric decreases in doses should be considered. This drug should be used with **CAUTION** in kidney compromise.

▷ **Dosing Instructions:** This drug is preferably taken with 8 ounces of water on an empty stomach, 1 hour before or 2 hours after eating. However, it may be taken with or following food to reduce stomach irritation. Intervals between doses (day and night) should be no longer than 8 hours. The regular tablet may be crushed; the enteric-coated tablet should be swallowed whole without alteration. Suspension form should be shaken well and dosed using a dose cup or calibrated dosing spoon. If you forget a dose: Take the missed dose as soon as you remember it, unless it's nearly time for your next dose—if that is the case, skip the missed dose and take the next dose right on schedule. DO NOT double doses. Talk with your doctor if you find yourself missing doses. There are many effective medicine reminder systems to help you.

Usual Duration of Use: Use on a regular schedule for 1 to 3 weeks usually determines effectiveness in controlling the symptoms of regional enteritis or ulcerative colitis. Benefits in rheumatoid arthritis (RA) may be seen in 4 to

12 weeks. Long-term use (months to years) requires physician supervision. It is not unusual to change therapies in RA.

Typical Treatment Goals and Measurements (Outcomes and Markers)

Inflammatory Bowel Disease: The goal is to cause (induce) a remission and maintain it. Symptoms that will resolve include rectal bleeding and diarrhea. More involved exams will reveal an absence of bowel ulceration and easing of friability or granularity of the bowel itself.

▷ **This Drug Should Not Be Taken If**
- you are allergic to any sulfonamide drug (see Drug Classes) or aspirin (or other salicylates).
- you are in the final month of pregnancy (near term).
- it has been prescribed for an infant less than 2 years old.
- you have a urinary or intestinal obstruction or porphyria.
- you are breast-feeding.

▷ **Inform Your Physician Before Taking This Drug If**
- you are allergic by nature: history of hay fever, asthma, hives, eczema.
- you have asthma.
- you have impaired liver or kidney function.
- you have a glucose-6-phosphate dehydrogenase (G6PD) deficiency or are known to be a slow acetylator.
- you have a personal or family history of porphyria.
- you have juvenile rheumatoid arthritis that is in the systemic-course because there is a high rate of a serum sickness like reaction.
- you have had a drug-induced blood cell or bone marrow disorder.
- you currently take any oral anticoagulant, antidiabetic drug, or phenytoin.
- you plan to have surgery under pentothal anesthesia soon.

Possible Side Effects (natural, expected, and unavoidable drug actions)

Brownish coloration of the urine—of no significance. Skin pigmentation. Superinfections, bacterial or fungal (see Glossary).

▷ **Possible Adverse Effects** (unusual, unexpected, and infrequent reactions)

If any of the following develop, consult your physician promptly for guidance.

Mild Adverse Effects

Allergic reactions: skin rashes, hives, itching.

Headache—frequent.

Dizziness—infrequent.

Discoloration (yellow stains) on contact lenses—possible.

Ringing in the ears—case reports.

Loss of appetite, irritation of mouth or tongue, nausea, vomiting, diarrhea—infrequent to frequent.

Taste disorders—rare.

Serious Adverse Effects

Allergic reactions: drug fever (see Glossary), swollen glands, painful joints, anaphylaxis (see Glossary).

Allergic pneumonitis, allergic liver damage (hepatitis).

Severe skin reactions (Stevens-Johnson Syndrome or toxic epidermal necrolysis).

Idiosyncratic reactions: hemolytic anemia (see Glossary).

Bone marrow depression (see Glossary): fever, sore throat, abnormal bleeding/bruising—rare to infrequent.

Serum sickness (increased bilirubin, fever, red rash, hepatitis)—case reports.

Pancreatitis, myopathy, or drug-induced lupus erythematosus—case reports.

Hearing loss—case reports.
Folic acid deficiency—possible.
Kidney damage—case reports.
Peripheral neuropathy (see Glossary)—case reports.
Inflammation of tissue around the heart (pericarditis)—case reports.

▷ **Possible Effects on Sexual Function:** Decreased production of sperm, reversible infertility—case reports.

▷ **Adverse Effects That May Mimic Natural Diseases or Disorders**
Liver reactions may suggest viral hepatitis. Lung reactions may suggest an infectious pneumonia.

Natural Diseases or Disorders That May Be Activated by This Drug
Goiter, acute intermittent porphyria.

Possible Effects on Laboratory Tests
Complete blood cell counts: decreased red cells, hemoglobin, white cells, and platelets; increased eosinophils (allergic reaction).
Liver function tests: increased enzymes (ALT/GPT, AST/GOT, alkaline phosphatase) or bilirubin.
Sperm count: decreased; abnormal sperm common; effects reversible on discontinuation of drug.

CAUTION
1. A large intake of water (up to 2 quarts daily) is necessary to ensure an adequate volume of urine.
2. Shake liquid dose forms well before measuring each dose.

Precautions for Use
By Infants and Children: Safety and effectiveness for those less than 2 years of age are not established.
By Those Over 60 Years of Age: Watch for development of reduced urine volume, fever, sore throat, abnormal bleeding or bruising or skin irritation with itching, particularly in the anal or genital regions.

▷ **Advisability of Use During Pregnancy**
Pregnancy Category: B; however, this drug should not be used near the time of the birth of the baby. See Pregnancy Risk Categories at the back of this book.
Animal Studies: Cleft palate and skeletal birth defects due to sulfonamides reported in mice and rats.
Human Studies: No increase in birth defects reported in 4,584 exposures to various sulfonamides during pregnancy.
Avoid use of drug during the final month of pregnancy because of possible adverse effects on the newborn infant.

Advisability of Use If Breast-Feeding
Presence of this drug in breast milk: Yes.
Avoid drug or refrain from nursing.

Habit-Forming Potential: None.

Effects of Overdose: Headache, dizziness, nausea, vomiting, abdominal cramping, toxic fever, coma, jaundice, kidney failure.

Possible Effects of Long-Term Use: Development of goiter, with or without hypothyroidism. An orange-yellow discoloration of the skin has been reported. This is not jaundice.

Suggested Periodic Examinations While Taking This Drug (at physician's discretion)

Complete blood cell counts, weekly for the first 8 weeks.

Urine analysis weekly.

Check of sulfapyridine levels (less than 50 mcg/ml may be associated with fewer problems).

Liver and kidney function tests.

▷ **While Taking This Drug, Observe the Following**

Foods: Follow prescribed diet. See iron salt interaction below.

Herbal Medicines or Minerals: Since St. John's wort and sulfasalazine may increase sun sensitivity, the combination is NOT advised. Flaxseed, peppermint oil, and psyllium husk have Commission E monograph indications for irritable bowel syndrome. This is NOT the same as ulcerative colitis, and those products have not been studied in ulcerative colitis. Aloe, buckhorn berry or bark, cascara sagrada bark, rhubarb root, and senna should not be taken by people living with ulcerative colitis.

Beverages: No restrictions. May be taken with milk.

▷ *Alcohol:* Use caution. Sulfonamide drugs can increase the intoxicating effects of alcohol.

Tobacco Smoking: No interactions expected. I advise everyone to quit smoking.

▷ *Other Drugs*

Sulfasalazine may *increase* the effects of

- anticoagulants (Coumadin, etc.) and increase bleeding risk; more frequent INR (prothrombin time) testing is needed.
- sulfonylureas or other oral hypoglycemic agents (see Sulfonylureas and Oral Antidiabetic Drugs in Drug Classes) and increase the risk of hypoglycemia.

Sulfasalazine may *decrease* the effects of

- digoxin (Lanoxin).
- live typhoid vaccine (Vivotif).

Sulfasalazine *taken concurrently* with

- ampicillin and perhaps other penicillins may lower therapeutic benefits from sulfasalazine.
- some barbiturates (see Drug Classes) may result in decreased sulfasalazine therapeutic benefits.
- calcium supplements (calcium gluconate) may result in decreased therapeutic benefits from sulfasalazine.
- folic acid (various) may decrease folate absorption.
- iron salts or calcium may decrease sulfasalazine's benefits.
- mercaptopurine (Purinethol) may increase risk of bone marrow depression.
- riluzole (Rilutek) increases risk of liver toxicity.
- varicella vaccine (Varivax) may result in Reye's syndrome; avoid taking this medicine for 6 weeks following varicella vaccine.

▷ *Driving, Hazardous Activities:* This drug may cause dizziness. Restrict activities as necessary.

Aviation Note: The use of this drug *may be a disqualification* for piloting. Consult a designated Aviation Medical Examiner.

Exposure to Sun: Use caution—some sulfonamide drugs can cause photosensitivity (see Glossary).

SULFONAMIDE ANTIBIOTIC FAMILY

Sulfamethoxazole   (sul fa meth OX a zohl)   **Sulfisoxazole**   (sul fi SOX a zohl)

Introduced: 1961, 1949, respectively   **Class:**   Anti-infective, sulfonamides   **Prescription:**   USA: Yes   **Controlled Drug:**   USA: No; Canada: No   **Available as Generic:**   Yes

Brand Names: Sulfamethoxazole: ✿Apo-Sulfamethoxazole, ✿Apo-Sulfatrim [CD], ✿Apo-Sulfatrim DS [CD], Azo Gantanol [CD], Bactrim [CD], Bactrim DS [CD], Bethaprim [CD], Comoxol [CD], Cotrim [CD], Gantanol, ✿Novo-Trimel [CD], ✿Novo-Trimel DS [CD], ✿Nu-Cotrimox, ✿Protrin [CD], ✿Protrin DF [CD], ✿Roubac [CD], Septra [CD], Septra DS [CD], Sulfatrim [CD], ✿Uro Gantanol [CD], Uroplus DS [CD], Uroplus SS [CD], Vagitrol, Sulfisoxazole: Azo Gantrisin [CD], Azo-Sulfisoxazole, Eryzole [CD], Gantrisin, Gulfasin, Lipo Gantrisin, ✿Novosoxazole, Pediazole [CD], SK-Soxazole, Sulfalar, Vagila

---

BENEFITS versus RISKS

Possible Benefits	*Possible Risks*
EFFECTIVE ANTIMICROBIAL ACTION AGAINST SUSCEPTIBLE BACTERIA AND PROTOZOA	Allergic reactions: mild to severe skin reactions, anaphylaxis, myocarditis
Effective adjunctive prevention and treatment of *Pneumocystis carinii* pneumonia (AIDS-related-sulfamethoxazole)	Blood cell disorders: aplastic anemia, hemolytic anemia, abnormally low white cell or platelet counts
	Drug-induced liver or kidney damage
	Cotrimoxazole form may prolong the QT interval of the heart

▷ **Principal Uses**

As a Single Drug Product: Uses currently included in FDA-approved labeling:

(1) Sulfamethoxazole is used to treat some bacterial or protozoan infections: chancroid, cystitis, and other infections of the urinary tract. **Sulfamethoxazole should not be used to treat group A streptococcal infections.**

(2) Sulfisoxazole is used in treating ear infections (otitis media), chloroquine-resistant malaria and toxoplasmosis.

Other (unlabeled) generally accepted uses: (1) Treats *Chlamydia* infections; (2) combination therapy of resistant *Mycobacterium kansasii* infections; (3) sulfisoxazole may work in long-term prevention of ear infections; (4) some patients with rheumatoid arthritis have shown benefit from sulfamethoxazole.

As a Combination Drug Product [CD]: These medicines are available in combination with phenazopyridine, an analgesic to ease discomfort associated with acute urethral infections. Sulfamethoxazole is also available in combination with another antibacterial drug, trimethoprim; in some countries this combination is given the generic name cotrimoxazole. This combination is quite effective in the treatment of certain types of middle ear infection, bronchitis, pneumonia, and certain infections of the intestinal tract and urinary tract. It is now used as primary prevention and treatment for *Pneumocystis carinii* pneumonia associated with AIDS.

Author's Note: This medicine in the combination form (Bactrim, Septra) has assumed a major role in helping prevent a prevalent opportunistic infection in HIV-positive people (PCP pneumonia).

How These Drugs Work: Prevent the growth and multiplication of susceptible bacteria or protozoa by interfering with their formation of folic acid, an essential nutrient.

Available Dosage Forms and Strengths

Sulfamethoxazole:

Oral suspension — 500 mg/5 ml

Tablets — 500 mg, 1 g

Tablets, combination — 400 mg sulfa and 80 mg trimethoprim and 800 mg sulfa with 160 mg of trimethoprim (DS form)

Sulfisoxazole:

Emulsion, prolonged action — 1 g/5 ml

Eyedrops — 4%

Eye ointment — 4%

Injection — 400 mg/ml

Pediatric suspension — 500 mg/5 ml

Syrup — 500 mg/5 ml

Tablets — 500 mg

▷ **Recommended Dosage Ranges** (Actual dose and schedule must be determined for each patient individually.)

Infants and Children:

Sulfamethoxazole: Children over 2 months—50 to 60 mg per kg of body mass to start and then 25 to 30 mg per kg of body mass every 12 hours, up to a maximum of 75 mg per kg of body mass daily.

Sulfisoxazole: Children over 2 months—50 mg per kg of body mass to start and then 100 mg per kg of body mass per day, divided into equal doses given two to four times daily.

Recommended Dosage Range:

Sulfamethoxazole: Initially 2 g and then 1 g every 8 to 12 hours, depending upon the severity of the infection. The total daily dose should not exceed 3 g.

Combination form: For prevention of PCP pneumonia: one DS tablet a day.

Sulfisoxazole: Initially 2 to 4 g (may not be required in urinary tract infections) and then 750 to 1,500 mg (1.5 g) every 4 hours or 1 to 2 g every 6 hours, depending upon the severity of the infection. The total daily dose should not exceed 8 grams.

Conditions Requiring Dosing Adjustments

Liver Function: Patients with compromised livers should be followed closely, but specific guidelines for decreasing doses are not defined. Sulfisoxazole may cause liver damage.

Kidney Function: Doses should be decreased for patients with compromised kidneys. For patients with mild to moderate kidney failure, sulfisoxazole can be taken every 6 hours in the usual dose. In moderate to severe kidney failure, it can be taken every 12 to 24 hours in the usual dose. In severe kidney failure, it can be taken once a day. It should be used with *CAUTION* in renal compromise. Increased elimination of this drug may be seen in patients with alkaline urine. For sulfamethoxazole: Specific dosing changes have not been made for the single agent. For cotrimoxazole, it has been recommended that the dosing interval be increased for patients with impaired kidneys.

▷ **Dosing Instructions:** The tablet may be crushed and is preferably taken on an empty stomach, 1 hour before or 2 hours after eating. However, both drugs may be taken with or following food to reduce stomach irritation. Be certain to drink liberal amounts of water while taking this medicine if you are not restricted from doing so. Suspension forms should be shaken well and dosed using a measuring cup or calibrated dosing spoon. If you forget a dose: Take the missed dose as soon as you remember it, unless it's nearly time for your next dose—if that is the case, skip the missed dose and take the next dose right on schedule. DO NOT double doses. Talk with your doctor if you find yourself missing doses as compliance ensures treatment or best possible prevention of infection.

Usual Duration of Use: Use on a regular schedule for 4 to 7 days usually determines effectiveness in controlling responsive infections. Treatment should be continued until the patient is free of symptoms for 48 hours. Limit treatment to no more than 14 days if possible. Preventive use of trimethoprim/sulfamethoxazole will be ongoing, based on CD4 recovery/reconstitution.

Typical Treatment Goals and Measurements (Outcomes and Markers)
Infections: The most commonly used measures of serious infections are white blood cell counts and differentials (the kind of blood cells that occur most often in your blood), and temperature. Many clinicians look for positive changes in 24–48 hours. NEVER stop an antibiotic because you start to feel better. For treating infections, the full course is REQUIRED to kill the bacteria. Prophylaxis (for example of PCP) often requires ongoing use. The goals and time frame (see peak benefits above) should be discussed with you when the prescription is written.

Currently a "Drug of Choice"
Sulfamethoxazole (when combined with trimethoprim) is the drug of choice for preventing pneumonia (due to *Pneumocystis carinii*) in HIV-positive patients or those with AIDS.

▷ **These Drugs Should Not Be Taken If**
- you are allergic to any sulfonamide drug (see Drug Classes).
- you are in the final month of pregnancy.
- you are breast-feeding your infant.
- it has been prescribed for an infant less than 2 months old (unless congenital toxoplasmosis is being treated—sulfisoxazole).

▷ **Inform Your Physician Before Taking These Drugs If**
- you are allergic to any sulfonamide derivative: acetazolamide, thiazide diuretics, sulfonylurea antidiabetics (see Drug Classes).
- you are allergic by nature: history of hay fever, asthma, hives, eczema.
- you have impaired liver or kidney function.
- you have a personal or family history of porphyria.
- you have had a drug-induced blood cell or bone marrow disorder.
- you have a glucose-6-phosphate dehydrogenase (G6PD) deficiency in your red blood cells (ask your doctor).
- you currently take any oral anticoagulant, antidiabetic drug, or phenytoin.
- you plan to have surgery under pentothal anesthesia while taking this drug.

Possible Side Effects (natural, expected, and unavoidable drug actions)
Brownish coloration of the urine—of no significance. Superinfections, bacterial or fungal (see Glossary).

▷ **Possible Adverse Effects** (unusual, unexpected, and infrequent reactions)
  If any of the following develop, consult your physician promptly for guidance.
  Mild Adverse Effects
    Allergic reactions: skin rashes, hives, itching, localized swellings, reddened eyes, temporary myopia.
    Myopia—infrequent.
    Headache, dizziness, unsteadiness, ringing in the ears—possible.
    Loss of appetite, irritation of mouth or tongue, nausea, vomiting, abdominal pain, diarrhea—infrequent.
  Serious Adverse Effects
    Allergic reactions: drug fever (see Glossary), swollen glands, painful joints, anaphylaxis (see Glossary).
    Allergic reaction in the heart muscle (myocarditis), allergic pneumonitis, allergic hepatitis.
    Severe skin reactions—rare.
    Idiosyncratic reactions: hemolytic anemia (see Glossary)—possible.
    Bone marrow depression (see Glossary): fatigue, weakness, fever, sore throat, abnormal bleeding or bruising—case reports.
    Liver damage—rare.
    Pancreatitis—case reports.
    Kidney damage: bloody or cloudy urine, reduced urine volume—possible.
    Psychotic reactions, hallucinations, seizures, hearing changes (loss or vestibular symptoms), peripheral neuropathy (see Glossary)—case reports.
    Severe hypoglycemia—case report (sulfamethoxazole).
    Methemoglobinemia—rare.
    Drug-induced lupus erythematosus or blood-clotting problems (hypopro-thrombinemia)—rare.
    Drug-induced disulfiramlike reaction (sulfisoxazole)—possible.
▷ **Possible Effects on Sexual Function:** None reported.
▷ **Adverse Effects That May Mimic Natural Diseases or Disorders**
    Liver reactions may suggest viral hepatitis. Lung reactions may suggest an infectious pneumonia.
Natural Diseases or Disorders That May Be Activated by These Drugs
    Goiter, acute intermittent porphyria, polyarteritis nodosa, systemic lupus erythematosus (questionable).
Possible Effects on Laboratory Tests
    Complete blood cell counts: decreased red cells, hemoglobin, white cells, and platelets; increased eosinophils (allergic reaction).
    INR (prothrombin time): increased (when taken concurrently with warfarin).
    Liver function tests: increased enzymes (ALT/GPT, AST/GOT, alkaline phosphatase) or bilirubin.
CAUTION
    1. A large intake of water (up to 2 quarts daily) is necessary to ensure an adequate volume of urine.
    2. Shake liquid dose forms well before measuring each dose.
Precautions for Use
    By Infants and Children: These drugs should not be used in infants under 2 months of age.
    By Those Over 60 Years of Age: Small doses taken at longer intervals often achieve adequate blood and tissue drug levels. Observe for the develop-

ment of reduced urine volume, fever, sore throat, abnormal bleeding or bruising, or skin irritation with itching, particularly in the anal or genital regions.

▷ **Advisability of Use During Pregnancy**

Pregnancy Category: C; however, these drugs **SHOULD NOT BE TAKEN** (are contraindicated) near the time of the birth of the baby. See Pregnancy Risk Categories at the back of this book.

Animal Studies: Cleft palate and skeletal birth defects reported in mice and rats.

Human Studies: No increase in birth defects reported in 4,584 exposures to various sulfonamides during pregnancy.

Avoid use of drug during the final 3 months of pregnancy because of Possible Adverse Effects on the newborn infant.

Advisability of Use If Breast-Feeding

Presence of these drugs in breast milk: Yes.

Avoid drug or refrain from nursing.

Habit-Forming Potential: None.

Effects of Overdose: Headache, dizziness, nausea, vomiting, abdominal cramping, toxic fever, coma, jaundice, kidney failure.

Possible Effects of Long-Term Use

Superinfections, bacterial or fungal. Development of goiter, with or without hypothyroidism. Excessive loss of vitamin C via urine.

Suggested Periodic Examinations While Taking These Drugs (at physician's discretion)

Complete blood cell counts, weekly for the first 8 weeks.

Urine analysis weekly.

ANA or LE prep.

Liver and kidney function tests.

▷ **While Taking These Drugs, Observe the Following**

Foods: No restrictions.

Herbal Medicines or Minerals: Since St. John's wort and these medicines may increase sun sensitivity, the combination is NOT advised. Some patients use echinacea to attempt to boost their immune systems. Unfortunately, use of echinacea is not recommended in people with damaged immune systems. This herb may also actually weaken any immune system if it is used too often or for too long a time. DO NOT take mistletoe herb, oak bark, or F.C. of marshmallow root and licorice extracts. Pure cranberry juice may help keep harmful bacteria from attaching to the bladder wall and may be useful in helping to prevent urinary tract infections.

Beverages: No restrictions. May be taken with milk. Note recommendations for increased fluid intake.

▷ *Alcohol:* Use caution. Sulfonamide drugs can increase the intoxicating effects of alcohol and may also lead to a disulfiram (see Glossary) reaction.

Tobacco Smoking: No interactions expected. I advise everyone to quit smoking.

▷ *Other Drugs*

These medicines may ***increase*** the effects of

- abacavirlamivudine/zidovudine (Trizivir) and result in zidovudine or lamivudine toxicity in the combination product.
- amantadine (Symmetrel) and cause abnormal heart rhythms and CNS stimulation (confusion, disorientation).

- anticoagulants (Coumadin, etc.) and increase the risk of bleeding; more frequent INR testing (prothrombin time or protime) is needed. Ongoing warfarin doses should be decided based on laboratory results.
- metformin (Glucophage) and lead to increased risk of lowered blood sugar or lactic acidosis.
- methotrexate (Mexate) and cause severe blood toxicity.
- sulfonylureas (see Drug Classes) or other oral hypoglycemic agents and increase the risk of excessively low blood sugar (hypoglycemia).
- zidovudine (AZT) and lamivudine and result in zidovudine or lamivudine toxicity in the single product or in their combination forms.

These medicines may *decrease* the effects of
- birth control pills (oral contraceptives).
- cyclosporine (Sandimmune) and reduce its immunosuppressive effect.
- live typhoid vaccine (Vivotif).
- penicillins (see Drug Classes).

These medicines *taken concurrently* with
- metronidazole (Flagyl) may lead to a disulfiram reaction.
- ritonavir (Norvir) may lead to changes in cotrimoxazole amounts that get into the body (bioavailability). Close patient follow-up is prudent.
- warfarin (Coumadin) may lead to increased risk of bleeding. More frequent INR checks are prudent.

Sulfamethoxazole *taken concurrently* with
- medicines such as class I, IA or III antiarrhythmics (dofetilide (Tikosyn), clarithromycin, cotrimoxazole, ondansetron, ziprazidone, zolmitriptan, and others may lead to prolongation of the QTc interval and undesirable effects. Combination is not recommended.

▷ *Driving, Hazardous Activities:* These drugs may cause dizziness. Restrict activities as necessary.

Aviation Note: The use of these drugs *may be a disqualification* for piloting. Consult a designated Aviation Medical Examiner.

Exposure to Sun: Use caution. Some sulfonamide drugs can cause photosensitivity (see Glossary).

SULINDAC (sul IN dak)

Please see the acetic acid (nonsteroidal anti-inflammatory drug) family profile.

SUMATRIPTAN (soo ma TRIP tan)

Introduced: 1993 **Class:** Antimigraine drug, serotonin-1-receptor agonist **Prescription:** USA: Yes **Controlled Drug:** USA: No; Canada: No **Available as Generic:** USA: No; Canada: No
Brand Names: Imitrex, Imitrex Nasal Spray

BENEFITS versus RISKS

Possible Benefits	*Possible Risks*
RAPID AND EFFECTIVE RELIEF OR PREVENTION OF MIGRAINE	Fainting
	Myocardial infarction (probably secondary to coronary vasospasm)
GENERALLY WELL TOLERATED NASAL SPRAY FORM	Serious atrial and ventricular arrhythmias
Relieves photophobia (light sensitivity)	Exacerbation of ischemic heart disease (should not be given to those patients)
Relieves phonophobia (sound sensitivity)	Not to be used in hemiplegic or basilar migraine
Relieves nausea and vomiting	Not to be used in significant cardiovascular disease
	Not compatible with patients with seizure disorders (see "should not be taken")

▷ **Principal Uses**

As a Single Drug Product: Uses currently included in FDA-approved labeling: (1) Acute treatment of migraine with or without aura in adults; (2) treatment of cluster headache in adults.

Other (unlabeled) generally accepted uses: Treatment of posttraumatic headaches.

How This Drug Works: Sumatriptan acts on blood vessels to cause vasoconstriction (shrinking of the blood vessels). This relieves swelling, thought to be the cause of migraine. The drug binds to receptor arteries such as the basilar artery and in vasculature (blood vessels) associated with the dura mater (part of the lining of the brain).

Available Dosage Forms and Strengths

Nasal spray — 5 mg/100 mcl, 20 mg/100 mcl

Sumatriptan succinate (Imitrex) injection SELFdose system kit — 2 syringes with 6 mg in 0.5 ml of liquid in each 1-ml size syringe, a dosing device, and instructions.

Unit-of-use syringes — 6 mg in 0.5 ml of liquid in a 1-ml syringe in a carton of two syringes.

6 mg single-dose vials — 0.5 ml of liquid in a 2-ml vial.

All the liquid should be a colorless to pale yellow clear solution. Particles or precipitates should NEVER appear.

Tablets — 25 mg, 50 mg, 100 mg

How to Store

Keep out of reach of children. Store at room temperature in a room where the temperature will not exceed 86 degrees F. (30 degrees C.). Keep away from heat and light.

▷ **Recommended Dosage Ranges** (Actual dose and schedule must be determined for each patient individually.)

Infants and Children: The safety and effectiveness in pediatrics have not been determined.

18 to 60 Years of Age:

Subcutaneous: Maximum adult dose is 6 mg. The dose should be taken as soon as possible after the symptoms of acute migraine are recognized.

Controlled clinical trials have failed to demonstrate a benefit of repeated injections if the initial injection is unsuccessful. If symptoms return, a second 6-mg injection may be taken 12 hours after the first injection. If side effects occur, use the lowest dose in the approved dose range that is effective for you. Maximum is 12 mg per 24 hours.

Oral: 25 mg taken with water or other acceptable liquids as soon as possible after a headache starts. The dose chosen must balance possible benefit of the higher dose with increased risk of adverse effects of higher doses. Take the dose your doctor prescribes as soon as headache pain starts. If the headache returns or if there is a partial response, single tablets can be taken at least two hours after the first dose (up to 200 mg a day). If symptoms come back, subsequent doses can be taken (talk this over with your doctor first) separated by two hours after the last dose and taken up to a total of 200 mg in 24 hours.

Nasal: 5 to 20 mg as a one-time dose. Newly labeled dosing notes that more patients taking the 20 mg dose had headache relief. The dose chosen must balance possible benefit of the higher dose with increased risk of adverse effects of higher doses. Take the dose prescribed as soon as headache pain starts. For example, 10 mg may be taken by spraying 5 mg in each nostril. A 20-mg dose can be taken as 10 mg in each nostril. Data exists that shows that single doses more than 20 mg do not give additional benefit. If symptoms return, the dose can be taken once again (two hours after the first dose was taken), but the daily maximum of 40 mg must not be exceeded. Safety in treating more than 4 headaches in 30 days is unknown with any dosage form.

Over 65 Years of Age: NOT recommended in this age group since declines in kidney (renal) and liver (hepatic) function and coronary artery disease are more common in those over 65 and side effects (such as blood pressure increase) may be more severe.

Conditions Requiring Dosing Adjustments

Liver Function: Oral tablets will give unpredictable variations in blood levels if used in liver disease. Maximum dose is 50 mg per dose and 100 mg per 24 hours.

Kidney Function: No changes in dose thought to be needed in kidney disease.

Dosing Instructions: The injection form must be given subcutaneously, not intravenously. Intravenous injection must be avoided because of potential to cause coronary vasospasm (constriction of the blood vessels that supply the heart). This medicine should be colorless to pale yellow and clear. Particles should never be present. There is extensive information on self-injection available from your doctor or pharmacist. The first dose is usually given in the doctor's office. The tablet form may take more than an hour to work. The tablet form may be taken with food. Follow directions for the nasal form closely. The nasal form should be used in only one nostril each time (unless your doctor tells you to use it differently). Close the bottle tightly after each nasal use. If you forget a dose: This medicine is used when you get a migraine headache, NOT on an ongoing basis.

Usual Duration of Use: The maximum dose is two 6-mg doses (injections) in 24 hours. This medication relieves existing migraines and will not change the frequency or number of attacks. Recurring use of this medicine will be needed. If your migraines increase in frequency or severity, consult your doctor. If this medicine is not effective in helping your migraine, call your doctor.

Typical Treatment Goals and Measurements (Outcomes and Markers)

Migraine Pain: Most clinicians treating pain use a device called an algometer to check your pain. This looks like a small ruler, but lets the clinician better understand your pain. The goals of treatment then relate to where the level of pain started (for example, a rating of seven on a zero to ten scale) and what the cause of the pain was. I use the PQRSTBG system (see Glossary). Pain medicines may also be used together (in combination) in order to get the best result or outcome. Specific results to migraine relate to stopping (aborting) an attack or easing the severity of an attack. Once again, the role of prophylactic medicines is clear in helping some patients avoid attacks altogether. A migraine diary can help you identify trigger foods as well as medication response.

▷ **This Drug Should Not Be Taken If**
- you had an allergic reaction to it previously.
- you are unfamiliar with the subcutaneous route. Particular care must be taken to avoid intravenous use because this may lead to coronary vasospasm (constriction of the blood vessels that supply the heart).
- you have ischemic heart disease with symptoms such as angina pectoris or silent ischemia, or history of MI (myocardial infarction).
- you have peripheral vascular disease (including ischemic bowel disease).
- you have a seizure disorder, a transient ischemic attack (TIA), stroke, or other cerebrovascular syndrome.
- you have Prinzmetal's angina (a specific kind of chest pain).
- you have uncontrolled hypertension (high blood pressure).
- you have basilar or hemiplegic migraine.
- you have taken an MAO inhibitor within the last 2 weeks.
- you have (within 24 hours) taken an ergotamine preparation.

▷ **Inform Your Physician Before Taking This Drug If**
- you are pregnant or plan to become pregnant.
- you are breast-feeding your infant.
- you have high blood pressure, high cholesterol, or a strong family history of coronary artery disease.
- you have chest pain, heart disease, or irregular heartbeats or you smoke.
- you have taken or have prescriptions for other migraine medications.
- you have allergies or trouble taking other medications, whether prescription or over the counter.
- you are a women after menopause or are a man over 40.
- you have liver or kidney disease.
- you are uncertain of how much to take or when to take this medicine.
- you do not understand the subcutaneous injection technique.
- you have Raynaud's phenomenon.

Possible Side Effects (natural, expected, and unavoidable drug actions)

Excessive thirst and frequent urination. Transient rises in blood pressure. Vision changes—rare. Taste changes—frequent.

▷ **Possible Adverse Effects** (unusual, unexpected, and infrequent reactions)

If any of the following develop, consult your physician promptly for guidance.

Mild Adverse Effects

Allergic reactions: red, itching skin; skin rash and tenderness.

Atypical sensations such as tingling (rare with injection, infrequent with tablet form).

Confusion and other mental changes or dizziness—rare.
Flushing—rare.
Tightness in the chest or jaw—infrequent.
Gastroesophageal reflux and diarrhea—case report.
Pain at the injection site; joint pain, weakness and stiffness—rare.
Serious Adverse Effects
Allergic reactions: anaphylactic reactions.
Syncope (fainting), CVA, dysphasia, seizure—rare.
Serious changes in heart rate and rhythm—rare.
Raynaud's phenomenon, dyspnea (difficulty breathing)—rare.
Kidney stones (renal calculi)—rare.
Prinzmetal's angina—rare.
Heart attack (myocardial infarction)—rare.

▷ **Possible Effects on Sexual Function:** Dysmenorrhea, erection problems—case reports.

Possible Delayed Adverse Effects: None identified.

▷ **Adverse Effects That May Mimic Natural Diseases or Disorders**
Changes in heart rate and rhythm may mimic a number of cardiac conditions. Drug-induced hypertension may mimic hypertension from other causes. Urological symptoms may mimic benign prostatic hypertrophy. Sumatriptan can mimic Raynaud's phenomenon.

Natural Diseases or Disorders That May Be Activated by This Drug
Hypertension.

Possible Effects on Laboratory Tests
Liver function tests: rare increases in SGOT and SGPT.

CAUTION
1. Do not use sumatriptan if you are pregnant.
2. Call your doctor if you have any pain or tightness in the chest or throat when you use this medicine.
3. Do not use sumatriptan if you have used an ergotamine preparation within the last 24 hours.
4. This medication is **not** to be used intravenously.
5. **If** you are diagnosed as having ischemic heart disease after sumatriptan has been prescribed for you, do not use the medicine again.

Precautions for Use
By Infants and Children: Safety and effectiveness for those under 18 years of age are not established.
By Those Over 65 Years of Age: Not recommended in this population.

▷ **Advisability of Use During Pregnancy**
Pregnancy Category: C. See Pregnancy Risk Categories at the back of this book.
Animal Studies: Sumatriptan has been lethal to rabbit embryos when given in doses that were threefold higher than those produced by a 6-mg dose. Term fetuses from rabbits treated with sumatriptan exhibited an increase in cervicothoracic vascular defects and minor skeletal abnormalities.
Human Studies: Adequate studies of pregnant women are not available.
Ask your physician for guidance.

Advisability of Use If Breast-Feeding
Presence of this drug in breast milk: Yes.
Use of this medication by nursing mothers is a benefit-to-risk decision to be made by a physician.

Habit-Forming Potential: Not clearly defined, but seems to have a low potential for abuse.

Effects of Overdose: Patients have received doses of 8 to 12 mg without adverse effects. This DOES NOT mean this is advisable. Healthy volunteers have taken up to 16 mg subcutaneously without serious adverse events. Coronary vasospasm has resulted from intravenous doses. Animal data presents convulsions, tremor, flushing, decreased breathing and activity, cyanosis, ataxia, and paralysis.

Possible Effects of Long-Term Use: Not defined.

Suggested Periodic Examinations While Taking This Drug (at physician's discretion)

Liver function tests.

Electrocardiogram.

▷ **While Taking This Drug, Observe the Following**

Foods: No restrictions; however, some foods or additives such as monosodium glutamate or chocolate may be a risk factor for migraines. Skipping meals can also be a risk factor for migraines. Keeping a migraine diary can help identify triggers.

Herbal Medicines or Minerals: Using St. John's wort, ma huang, guarana, or kola while taking this medicine may trigger a migraine. Trigger compounds must be individually identified. Since part of the way that ginseng works (mechanism of action) may involve MAO inhibition, combination with sumatriptan is NOT recommended. Using ma huang or ephedrine-like compounds (ephedra—this common herbal medicine ingredient is under FDA review) may result in additive and undesirable vasoconstriction. If you are allergic to plants in the Asteraceae family (aster, chrysanthemum, daisy, or ragweed), you may also be allergic to echinacea, chamomile, feverfew, and St. John's wort. St. John's wort can cause changes in the liver enzymes that help remove this medicine—talk to your doctor before combining any herbal medicine or mineral with ergotamine.

Beverages: An individual trigger beverage list should be identified.

▷ *Alcohol:* May cause additive sedation. Alcohol may also be a precipitating factor for migraine.

Tobacco Smoking: No interactions expected. I advise everyone to quit smoking.

Marijuana Smoking: May cause additive dizziness, drowsiness, and lethargy; may cause additive increases in blood pressure.

▷ *Other Drugs*

Sumatriptan *taken concurrently* with

- citalopram (Celexa) may lead to loss of coordination and excessive reflex response—DO NOT COMBINE.
- ergotamine-containing preparations (see Drug Classes) may result in additive vasospasm (prolonged constriction of the blood vessels)—these medicines SHOULD NOT be taken within 24 hours of any sumatriptan dose. There is a case report of heart attack after sumatriptan was combined with methysergide.
- fluoxetine (Prozac) may result in coordination problems.
- fluvoxamine (Luvox) and other SSRIs may result in coordination problems.
- monoamine oxidase (MAO) inhibitors (see Drug Classes) may result in toxic levels of sumatriptan—MAO inhibitors and sumatriptan should never be combined. It is important that 14 days go by after your last dose of an MAO inhibitor before you take any form of sumatriptan.

- naratriptan (Amerge) or other "triptans" (5HT1 agonists) may lead to prolonged spasm of the blood vessels—DO NOT COMBINE.
- paroxetine (Paxil) may result in coordination problems.
- sertraline (Zoloft) may result in coordination problems.
- sibutramine (Meridia) may increase risk of serotonin syndrome—DO NOT COMBINE.
- venlafaxine (Effexor) may result in coordination problems.

▷ *Driving, Hazardous Activities:* This drug may cause dizziness and drowsiness. Restrict activities as necessary.

Aviation Note: The use of this drug *may be a disqualification* for piloting. Consult a designated Aviation Medical Examiner.

Exposure to Sun: No restrictions.

Exposure to Cold: Use *CAUTION* until tolerance is determined. Cold may enhance sumatriptan vasoconstriction.

Heavy Exercise or Exertion: Strenuous exercise can be a risk factor for migraines in some patients.

Special Storage Instructions: Keep this medicine out of reach of children. Store at room temperature in a room where the temperature will not exceed 86 degrees F. (30 degrees C.). Keep away from heat and light.

Observe the Following Expiration Times: There is an expiration date printed on the treatment package. Throw the medication away if it has expired. The autoinjector may be used again.

SYNTHETIC CONJUGATED ESTROGENS, A
(CHEMICALLY DERIVED FROM PLANTS [YAMS AND SOY])

Other Names: Sodium estrone sulfate, sodium equilin sulfate, sodium 17 alpha-dihydroequilin sulfate, sodium 17 alpha estradiol sulfate, sodium 17 beta dihydroequilin sulfate, sodium 17 beta estradiol sulfate, sodium equilin sulfate (higher molecular weight), sodium 17 alpha dihydroequilin sulfate, and sodium 17 beta dihydroequilin sulfate (higher molecular weight). All of these nine compounds are present in Cenestin.

Author's Note: Since this medicine contains compounds that work like the estrogen that the body makes before menopause, (estrogenic substances) and because these came from plants (versus horse urine for many other estrogen replacement medicines), the FDA approved Cenestin as an entirely new class. Many of the warnings, etc., in this profile are those for estrogens in general. Reports from Phase Four prescribing will determine further uses (indications) as well as the full scope of specific possible side effects and benefits. Alternative synthetic conjugated estrogen combinations such as Cenestin are further detailed below.

Controversy about estrogen therapy (ERT) and use of combination hormone replacement therapy (HRT) started with the HERS (Heart and Estrogen/progestin Replacement Study). HERS negated the role of estrogen/progestin in preventing a second heart attack. A large study called WISDOM is continuing to study estrogen alone. The present Cenestin FDA labeling notes that estrogens increase the risk of endometrial cancer, that there is no data to show that the use of natural estrogens leads to a different risk profile on the endometrium than the same dose of synthetic estrogens and that estrogens with or without progestins should

NOT be used to prevent cardiovascular disease. The Women's Health Initiative (WHI) combination arm was stopped early (see *www.whi.org*, July 17, 2002 JAMA article—especially Table 4, *www.acog.org*, and *www.menopause.org*. Importantly, the WHI data showed that if 10,000 women took the 0.626 mg conjugated estrogens and 2.5 mg medroxyprogesterone daily (as in Prempro), versus not taking it: 8 more women would develop invasive breast cancer, 7 more would have a heart attack or other coronary, and 8 more would have blood clots in the lungs or a stroke. Five fewer would have hip fracture and 6 fewer would have colorectal cancers. The WHIMS group (Women's Health Initiative Memory Study) of the WHI (May 27, 2003—see FDA talk paper T03-39 in Sources) found that the estrogen/progestin combination should NOT be used to help prevent dementia or Alzheimer's, and for the data analyzed, showed an increased risk of undesirable mental status change (dementia) in women over 65 who used the combination for longer periods. A two month time frame of use was recommended by the WHI panel (shortest period and in the lowest dose to meet treatment goals).

A continued analysis of the 16,608 women from the Women's Health Initiative (WHI), published in the July 25, 2003 issue of JAMA reported that in women who used the combination of estrogen plus progesterone who developed breast cancer, the tumors tended to be larger than in women who did not take the combination. Additionally, 25.4% of the combined product users who developed breast cancer had tumors that had begun to spread. In general, women who took the combination formulation had a 24% increased breast cancer risk. Increased risk did not become apparent in the first two years of those studied. Some question regarding difficulty of discovering tumors because of increased breast density caused by the hormone progestin has been postulated. Topical forms should be considered if the medicine is only being used for vulvar and vaginal atrophy. Alternatives for patients who can't take estrogen currently include: clonidine, fluoxetine (Prozac), gabapentin (Neurontin), and venlafaxine (Effexor).

Introduced: 1999 **Class:** Female sex hormones **Prescription:** USA: Yes **Controlled Drug:** USA: No; Canada: No **Available as Generic:** USA: No; Canada: No
Brand Names: Cenestin, ✣C.E.S.

BENEFITS versus RISKS	
Possible Benefits	*Possible Risks*
RELIEF OF MENOPAUSAL HOT FLASHES AND NIGHT SWEATS	INCREASED RISK OF CANCER OF THE UTERUS (endometrium— possible and risk increases with longer use)
Possible prevention or relief of atrophic vaginitis or atrophy of the vulva and urethra	
Works to help prevent postmenopausal osteoporosis	INCREASED RISK OF BREAST CANCER (possible and expected to be more probable with longer use)
Works to increase bone mineral density	Increased frequency of gallstones
	Fluid retention
	Postmenopausal spotting
	Increased blood pressure
	Deep vein thrombophlebitis and thromboembolism (but less likely with conjugated estrogens than other estrogens)
	Doses of 5 mg per day may increase risk of nonfatal heart attack (because of increased clotting risk change above)

▷ **Principal Uses**

   As a Single Drug Product: Uses currently included in FDA-approved labeling: (1) Treatment of moderate to severe menopausal symptoms (vasomotor symptoms) in menopause; (2) treats severe or moderate vaginal and vulvar atrophy symptoms that can be seen with menopause.

   Other (unlabeled) generally accepted uses: None at present.

How This Drug Works: When used to correct hormonal deficiency states, estrogens restore normal cellular activity by increasing nuclear material and protein synthesis. Frequency and intensity of menopausal symptoms are reduced when normal levels of estrogen are restored.

Available Dosage Forms and Strengths

   Tablets — 0.3 mg, 0.625 mg, 0.9 mg, 1.25 mg

▷ **Usual Adult Dosage Ranges:** *For moderate to severe symptoms associated with menopause:* Dosing is started at 0.625 mg a day. The dose may be increased to a maximum of 1.25 mg daily if needed and tolerated. The lowest effective dose should be used and attempts to stop and taper medicine made at three- to six-month intervals. *For vaginal atrophy:* 0.3 mg is taken once daily. Once again the medicine should be used in the lowest effective dose for the shortest possible time.

   Note: Actual dose and schedule must be determined for each patient individually.

Conditions Requiring Dosing Adjustments

   Liver Function: Since this medicine is metabolized in the liver, blood levels should be checked and the dose adjusted as needed in liver compromise. Estrogens should not be used in acute or severe liver compromise. This drug can be lithogenic (capable of causing stones) in bile.

   Kidney Function: No expected dosing changes in kidney compromise.

▷ **Dosing Instructions:** The effect of food on this medicine is not known. At present, it is best to take this medicine on an empty stomach. If you forget a dose: Take the missed dose as soon as you remember it, unless it's nearly time for your next dose—if that is the case, skip the missed dose and take the next dose right on schedule. DO NOT double doses. Talk with your doctor if you find yourself missing doses.

Usual Duration of Use: Regular use for 10 to 20 days needed to see effectiveness in easing menopausal symptoms. Attempts to stop or lower the dose (taper) this medicine should be made at 3- to 6-month intervals. Follow up with your doctor is required.

Typical Treatment Goals and Measurements (Outcomes and Markers)
Menopause: Most clinicians treating menopause seek goals of reduction or cessation of hot flashes, greater sense of well-being and avoidance of rapid bone loss (which can also be measured by some lab tests and DEXA testing). The WHI study and substudies will change treatment to the smallest effective dose for the shortest possible time that is appropriate to the goals and benefit to risk profile of the individual patient.

Possible Advantages of This Drug
THIS DRUG IS NOT derived from horse urine and avoids the possible allergic potential of products that are. Effective with once-a-day dose.

▷ **This Drug Should Not Be Taken If**
- you have had an allergic reaction to it or to the ingredients in the tablet previously.
- you have a history of thrombophlebitis, embolism, heart attack, or stroke.
- you have seriously impaired liver function or recent onset of liver disease.
- you have abnormal and unexplained vaginal bleeding.
- you are pregnant.
- you have or are suspected to have breast cancer (may eventually be used to treat some kinds of breast cancer).
- you have known or suspected estrogen-dependent cancer (your doctor will determine this).

▷ **Inform Your Physician Before Taking This Drug If**
- you have had an unfavorable reaction to estrogen therapy previously.
- you have a history of breast or reproductive organ cancer.
- you have fibrocystic breast changes, fibroid tumors of the uterus, endometriosis, migraine headaches, epilepsy, asthma, heart disease, high blood pressure, gallbladder disease, diabetes, or porphyria.
- you have retention of fluid.
- you have elevated calcium and kidney disease.
- you've used this medicine for three or six months and have not tried to stop using it.
- you smoke tobacco on a regular basis.
- you have a history of blood-clotting disorders.
- you plan to have surgery in the near future.

Possible Side Effects (natural, expected, and unavoidable drug actions)
Fluid retention, weight gain, "breakthrough" bleeding (spotting), altered menstrual pattern, resumption of menstrual flow ("periods") after natural cessation (postmenopausal bleeding).

▷ **Possible Adverse Effects** (unusual, unexpected, and infrequent reactions)
If any of the following develop, consult your physician promptly for guidance.
Mild Adverse Effects
Allergic reaction: skin rash—reported with other estrogens.
Headache, nervous tension, depression, accentuation of migraine headaches—infrequent.

Vision change (steepening of the curve of the cornea)—possible.

Nausea, vomiting, bloating, diarrhea—infrequent to frequent.

Tannish pigmentation of the face—possible.

Serious Adverse Effects

Allergic reactions: anaphylaxis—case reports with other estrogens.

Idiosyncratic reaction: not reported with this product.

Can produce or worsen high blood pressure—more likely with higher doses.

Gallbladder disease—two to four-fold increased risk.

Intolerance to sugar—possible.

Thrombophlebitis (inflammation of a vein with formation of blood clot): pain or tenderness in thigh or leg, with or without swelling of foot or leg— low dose has minimal increased risk; higher doses may carry more risk.

Pulmonary embolism (movement of blood clot to lung): sudden shortness of breath, pain in chest, coughing, bloody sputum—possible.

Systemic lupus erythematosus or worsening of porphyria—rare.

Stroke (blood clot in brain): headaches, blackout, sudden weakness or paralysis of any part of the body, severe dizziness, altered vision, slurred speech, inability to speak—case reports with other estrogens.

Endometrial cancer—increased risk (from using estrogens alone (unopposed estrogen) may be 2–12 times more than people who do not use estrogens. Many studies do not show increased cancer risk if estrogens are used for less than a year. Risk with longer term use may persist for 8–15 years after the drug is stopped. There is no evidence that natural estrogens are more or less likely than other estrogens to increase risk.

Nonfatal heart attack (blood clot in coronary artery): sudden pain in chest, neck, jaw, or arm; weakness; sweating; nausea. Has been associated with women taking higher doses and with men using estrogen to treat prostate cancer; however, this is not clearly decided as yet with this product.

Breast cancer—increased risk with the combination form use in WHI found 26% increased risk of invasive breast cancer in women with a uterus who took the combination treatment. A re-analysis of the WHI data found that tumor risk did not appear in the first two years that the combination form was used (see Chlepowski, R.T. in sources). A subset analysis (see LI, C.I. in Sources) found that the greatest risk was seen in combination use for at least 5 years. Those using estrogen alone who had undergone a hysterectomy had use for as long as 25 years and did not appear to show any appreciable increased risk of breast cancer.

Benign liver adenomas or blood clots in the liver—reported with oral contraceptives.

▷ **Possible Effects on Sexual Function:** Swelling and tenderness of breasts, milk production. Increased vaginal secretions.

Possible Delayed Adverse Effects: Estrogens taken during pregnancy may predispose a female child to the later development of cancer of the vagina or cervix following puberty. Also see above.

▷ **Adverse Effects That May Mimic Natural Diseases or Disorders**

Blood clots may mimic clots forming for other reasons.

Natural Diseases or Disorders That May Be Activated by This Drug

Latent hypertension, diabetes mellitus, acute intermittent porphyria.

Possible Effects on Laboratory Tests

Serum folate: may be decreased (the effect of possible lowering of folate by Cenestin on red blood cells is not yet defined).

Accelerated prothrombin time (reported as INR).

Glucose tolerance test (GTT): decreased tolerance.

Liver function tests: increased with other estrogens if a rare liver clot forms.

CAUTION

1. Yearly mammography is needed for ALL women who take this medicine who are more than 50 years old.
2. Bone mineral density tests (DEXA or PDEXA) are prudent to see whether this medicine is helping bone mass.
3. While this product is derived from plants (yam and soy), it was approved by the FDA as an estrogen and as such may carry the benefits and risks of existing estrogens. Many consumers think that because something is derived from a natural source, it is somehow safer. This tablet is a blend of nine estrogenic compounds derived from soy and yams and may or may not carry similar risks and benefits of existing estrogens. Ongoing use will define how possible side effects or benefits of prior estrogens apply to Cenestin. Any unusual vaginal bleeding should be immediately reported your doctor.
4. See WHI note above regarding benefit to risk and individualization, etc., above. Best to take this medicine for the shortest amount of time in the smallest dose that is consistent with the benefit to risk of the patient and the goals of therapy.

Precautions for Use

By Those Over 60 Years of Age: May help women who are at increased risk for osteoporosis. In this age group, it may be advisable to attempt relief of hot flashes with nonestrogenic medicines. During use, report promptly any indications of impaired circulation: speech disturbances, altered vision, sudden hearing loss, vertigo, sudden weakness or paralysis, angina, leg pains.

▷ Advisability of Use During Pregnancy

Pregnancy Category: X. See Pregnancy Risk Categories at the back of this book.

Animal Studies: Genital defects reported in mice and guinea pigs; cleft palate reported in rodents from other estrogens.

Human Studies: Information from studies of pregnant women indicates that estrogens can masculinize the female fetus. In addition, limb defects and heart malformations have been reported. It is now known that estrogens taken during pregnancy can predispose the female child to the development of cancer of the vagina or cervix following puberty.

Avoid estrogens completely during entire pregnancy.

Advisability of Use If Breast-Feeding

Presence of this drug in breast milk: Yes, in minute amounts.

Estrogens in large doses can suppress milk formation. Breast-feeding is considered to be safe during the use of estrogens. Malnourished mothers may have unacceptable decreases in protein and nitrogen in their breast milk if this drug is used while breast-feeding. Estrogens should NOT be used to try to stop breast milk formation after giving birth, as this may increase risk of blood clots.

Habit-Forming Potential: There has been some suggestion of estrogens having potential for psychological dependence and tolerance because of their mood-elevating properties, but clinical reports have not been presented.

Effects of Overdose: Nausea, vomiting, fluid retention, abnormal vaginal bleeding, breast enlargement and discomfort.

Possible Effects of Long-Term Use: Long term use of combination form no longer recommended. Ongoing study of WHI is for the estrogen only "arm" of the study. Prudence dictates that women with intact uteri should use estrogens only if the benefits outweigh the risks, with proper supervision and in the lowest effect dose for the shortest possible time consistent with the goals, benefit-to-risk, etc.

Suggested Periodic Examinations While Taking This Drug (at physician's discretion)

Checks every 3–6 months for benefits and continued need. Regular evaluation of the breasts (self exam). Yearly mammography for ALL women who take this medicine.

Regular (every 6 months) evaluation of the breasts and pelvic organs, including Pap smears.

Liver function tests as indicated.

▷ **While Taking This Drug, Observe the Following**

Foods: Avoid excessive use of salt if fluid retention occurs. Combined use of calcium and vitamin D can be a further step to help avoid osteoporosis. Combining DHEA with estrogen can lead to signs and symptoms (such as nausea, colitis, or breakthrough bleeding) of excess estrogen.

Herbal Medicines or Minerals: Black cohosh appears to work by (1) suppressing luteinizing hormone; (2) binding to estrogen receptors in the pituitary and inhibiting luteinizing hormone release and (3) binding to estrogen receptors in the pituitary. The net effect is that this herb eases symptoms of menopause, but little is known about long-term use or heart and bone protective effects. This herb may interfere with the benefits of estrogen replacement therapy. Talk to your doctor before starting black cohosh if you are currently taking any form of estrogen. Use of St. John's wort, echinacea, or ginkgo completely stopped or lowered the ability of sperm to penetrate eggs in one study. DO NOT use these herbs if you are using a conjugated estrogen product to augment mucous quality and help infertility. St. John's wort may also increase sun sensitivity.

Beverages: No restrictions. May be taken with milk.

▷ *Alcohol:* No interactions expected.

Tobacco Smoking: Studies show that heavy smoking (15 or more cigarettes daily) in association with use of estrogen-containing oral contraceptives significantly increases risk of heart attack (coronary thrombosis). I advise everyone to stop smoking.

▷ *Other Drugs*

Estrogens *taken concurrently* with

- alendronate (Fosamax) have not been specifically studied but had beneficial effects in one part of a larger study using a different medicine. The combination of a different kind of estrogen used with alendronate is now approved in Canada.
- amprenavir (Agenerase) may blunt benefits of amprenavir in fighting HIV, and may also result in loss of contraceptive benefits (efficacy). Other protease inhibitors such as nelfinavir (Viracept) may lead to contraceptive failure also.
- atorvastatin (Lipitor) may lead to increased birth control pill medicine levels.
- fluconazole (Diflucan) may increase contraceptive medicine blood levels (ethinyl estradiol).
- lamotrigene (Lamictal) may increase or decrease lamotrigene levels. More frequent blood level checks are needed with doses adjusted accordingly.

- naratriptan (Amerge) may increase naratriptan as well as zolmitriptan (Zomig) blood levels. Patients should be closely followed for increased naratriptan or zolmitriptan adverse effects.
- oral antidiabetic drugs (see Drug Classes) or oral blood-sugar-lowering medicines may cause loss of glucose control and high blood sugars.
- progestins (various) may increase risk of breast cancer versus estrogen use by itself.
- tacrine (Cognex) increases the risk of tacrine adverse effects.
- thyroid hormones may increase the bound (inactive) drug and require an increase in thyroid dose.
- tricyclic antidepressants (Elavil, Sinequan, etc.) may enhance their adverse effects and reduce their antidepressant effectiveness.
- vitamin C (ascorbic acid, various brands) in higher doses may result in increased estrogen effects—a lower dose of estrogens may be indicated if higher-dose vitamin C will be taken on an ongoing basis.
- warfarin (Coumadin) may cause alterations of prothrombin activity; increased doses may be needed, and more frequent INR testing is indicated.

The following drugs may decrease the effects of estrogens:
- carbamazepine (Tegretol).
- penicillin (various) may blunt contraceptive benefits.
- phenobarbital (various).
- phenytoin (Dilantin) or fosphenytoin (Cerebyx).
- primidone (Mysoline).
- rifampin (Rifadin, Rimactane).

Author's Note: The possible drug interactions above are those detailed for existing estrogens in the estrogen profile earlier in this book.

▷ *Driving, Hazardous Activities:* Usually no restrictions. Talk to your doctor for assessment of individual risk and for guidance regarding specific restrictions.

Aviation Note: Usually no restrictions, but watch for the rare occurrence of disturbed vision (curvature changes) and restrict activities accordingly. Consult a designated Aviation Medical Examiner.

Exposure to Sun: Caution—existing estrogens may cause photosensitivity (see Glossary).

Discontinuation: Best to use estrogens in the smallest effective dose, for the shortest amount of time consistent with the benefit to risk profile of the patient and the goals of treatment. If used to control menopausal symptoms, the dose is reduced gradually to prevent acute withdrawal hot flashes. Avoid continual, uninterrupted use of large doses. Ask your doctor for help.

TACRINE (TA kreen)

Please see the anti-Alzheimer's drug family profile.

TAMOXIFEN (ta MOX i fen)

Introduced: 1973 **Class:** Anticancer, chemotherapy, selective estrogen receptor modulator (SERM) **Prescription:** USA: Yes **Controlled Drug:** USA: No; Canada: No **Available as Generic:** Yes

Brand Names: ❦Alpha-Tamoxifen, ❦Apo-Tamox,❦Dom-Tamoxifen, Nolvadex, ❦Nolvadex-D, ❦Novo-Tamoxifen, ❦PMS-Tamoxifen, ❦Tamofen,
❦Tamone

Author's Note: A medicine called anastrozole (Arimidex) has shown
extremely promising results in early results from the one of the largest
cancer studies ever undertaken (more than 9,000 women). This trial is
unusual in that it is very very large and compares tamoxifen to anastrozole and also looks at the combination of the two drugs.

BENEFITS versus RISKS	
Possible Benefits	*Possible Risks*
DECREASED RISK OF BREAST CANCER	UTERINE CANCER
PREVENTION OF BREAST CANCER IN HIGH RISK FEMALES	Severe increase in tumor or bone pain, transient thrombophlebitis, pulmonary embolism
EFFECTIVE ADJUNCTIVE TREATMENT IN ADVANCED BREAST CANCER	Abnormally high blood calcium levels Eye changes: corneal opacities, retinal injury
MAY INCREASE THE CHANCES OF BREAST CONSERVATION	
ADDITION OF TAMOXIFEN TO LUMPECTOMY AND RADIATION TREATMENT REDUCES OCCURRENCE OF INVASIVE BREAST CANCER IN WOMEN WITH DUCTAL CARCINOMA IN SITU	

▷ **Principal Uses**

As a Single Drug Product: Uses currently included in FDA-approved labeling:
(1) An alternative to estrogens and androgens (male sex hormones) to treat
advanced breast cancer in postmenopausal women; (2) treats advanced
breast cancer in women that has spread (metastasized) from a prior site;
(3) used to delay or prevent the recurrence of breast cancer in high risk
females (five-year predicted risk greater than or equal to 1.67% by the Gail
Model). Reduced breast cancer in the National Surgical Adjuvant Breast
and Bowel Project (NSABP-P1) by 62% in healthy BRCA2 carriers, but did
not reduce risk in healthy women 35 or older who were BRCA1 carriers;
(4) approved for use in advanced metastatatic breast cancer in men; (5)
addition of tamoxifen to radiation therapy and surgery (may be a lumpec-
tomy) in women with ductal carcinoma *in situ* led to a 43% decrease in
invasive breast cancer in the same breast or in the opposite breast versus a
dummy pill or placebo.

Other (unlabeled) generally accepted uses: (1) May have a role in treating
cancer of the liver or lung; (2) used to stimulate ovulation in premenopausal women with infertility; (3) used to treat rare desmoid tumors;
(4) helps prevent osteoporosis in women in whom the drug is being used to
prevent the recurrence of cancer; (5) can help retroperitoneal fibrosis; (6)
could have a role in treating tenderness and swelling of male breast tissue
(gynecomastia) of unknown cause (idiopathic).

**Author's Note: Tamoxifen reduced breast cancer rates by almost half
in a very large (13,388 patients) cancer prevention study performed
by the National Cancer Institute over a period of 6 years. The FDA**

has launched a new oncology tools website. Visit this at *www.fda.gov/ cder/cancer*. There is a listing of cancer medicine trials on the World Wide Web at *http://cancertrials.nci.nih.gov*. The STAR (Study of Tamoxifen and Raloxifene) trial is underway. This is a National Cancer Institute study evaluating 19,000 women (enrollment started July 1, 1999 and 13,647 enrolled as of March 2003) who are at risk for breast cancer. They will be given either 20 mg per day of tamoxifen or 60 mg of raloxifene each day for five years. For more information, you can reach the National Cancer Institute at 1-800-422-6237. A sub-study called Co-STAR will look at memory, mood, and sleep habits in those 65 or older. People who enroll receive a newsletter called *Constellation*.

How This Drug Works: It is thought that by blocking the uptake of estradiol (estrogen), this drug removes or reduces a stimulus to breast cancer cells. It acts as a selective estrogen receptor modulator, or SERM. Newer thoughts include causing cells surrounding the cancer to release a substance called transforming growth factor-beta (TGF-beta), suppression of IGF-1 and inhibiting a protein kinase (protein kinase C) as well as calmodulin dependent cAMP phosphodiesterase.

Available Dosage Forms and Strengths
>   Tablets — 10 mg, 20 mg
>   Tablets (Canada) — 15.2 mg, 30.4 mg

▷ **Usual Adult Dosage Ranges:** *Breast cancer:* 20–40 mg a day is used. If the 40 mg dose is undertaken, it is given as 20 mg twice a day. In order to get the medicine distributed (to steady state), a loading dose of 40 mg four times a day is used for one day, followed by 20 mg a day. Dosing is continued for 5 years. *Prevention of breast cancer:* At this time, both age and risk factors are used to determine the BENEFITS versus RISKS of giving the medicine. Health care professionals may obtain a *Gail Model Risk Assessment Tool by calling 1-800-544-2007. For reduction of breast cancer in high-risk women:* 20 mg daily for five years is given. The STAR trial is expected to provide further information. Some controversy exists regarding use of 10 mg every other day. Further study is needed.
Note: Actual dose and schedule must be determined for each patient individually.

Conditions Requiring Dosing Adjustments
Liver Function: Dose decreases are not defined in liver disease.
Kidney Function: Dose decreases are not thought to be needed in mild to moderate kidney disease. No studies are available in severe disease.

▷ **Dosing Instructions:** Best to take the tablet whole either on an empty stomach or with food. If you forget a dose: Take the missed dose as soon as you remember it, unless it's nearly time for your next dose—if that is the case, skip the missed dose and take the next dose right on schedule. DO NOT double up on doses. Talk with your doctor if you find yourself missing doses—there are effective beeper-based systems to help you remember your medicine.

Usual Duration of Use: Use on a regular schedule for 4 to 10 weeks usually determines effectiveness in controlling growth and spread of advanced breast cancer. In the presence of bone involvement, treatment for several months may be required to evaluate effectiveness. Ongoing use for prevention of breast cancer still requires careful examinations and long-term use. Ongoing use (months to years) requires physician supervision and periodic evaluation. Evaluation should continue even after the medicine is stopped as some undesirable effects may not appear until later.

Typical Treatment Goals and Measurements (Outcomes and Markers)

Breast cancer: Treatment of existing cancer seeks to attain a complete remission. The minimum goal is to shrink (regress) the size of the tumor and decrease the probability of spread. Checks of coagulation (such as clotting factor assay) can help define how activated the coagulation system has become. In breast cancer prophylaxis, the goal is to prevent breast cancer in females who carry significant risk factors for breast cancer.

▷ **This Drug Should Not Be Taken If**
- you had a serious allergic or adverse reaction to it before.
- you have active phlebitis or history of deep vein clot (thrombosis) or lung clot (pulmonary thrombosis).
- you have a significant deficiency of white blood cells or blood platelets.
- you are pregnant.

▷ **Inform Your Physician Before Taking This Drug If**
- you have a history of thrombophlebitis or pulmonary embolism
- you become short of breath while taking this medicine.
- you take birth control pills.
- you have a history of abnormally high blood calcium levels.
- you have a history of any type of blood cell or bone marrow disorder.
- you have a history of breast cancer (benefit is thought to outweigh the risks, but prudent to inform your doctor).
- you have cataracts or other visual impairment.
- you have impaired liver function.
- you have high cholesterol.
- you plan to have surgery in the near future.

Possible Side Effects (natural, expected, and unavoidable drug actions)

Hot flashes—frequent.

Fluid retention, weight gain. Increased bone and/or tumor pain (flare)—tends to ease quickly.

▷ **Possible Adverse Effects** (unusual, unexpected, and infrequent reactions)

If any of the following develop, consult your physician promptly for guidance.

Mild Adverse Effects

Allergic reaction: skin rash.

Visual impairment—infrequent.

Increased calcium—infrequent.

Headache, dizziness, drowsiness, depression, fatigue, confusion—infrequent.

Nausea, vomiting—frequent.

Itching in genital area, loss of hair—infrequent.

Serious Adverse Effects

Initial "flare" of severe pain in tumor or involved bone—possible.

Development of thrombophlebitis, pulmonary embolism, heart attack, or stroke—increased risk.

Eye changes: corneal opacities, retinal injury—case reports.

Delusions—rare.

Increased uterine cancer risk (increased karyopyknotic index of vaginal epithelium)—possible, but many researchers now believe that the benefits far outweigh the risks.

Liver or other cancer (Brenner tumor)—questionable causation versus association.

Development of abnormally high blood calcium levels—possible.

Transient decreases in white blood cells and blood platelets—frequent.

Neutropenia or decrease in all blood cells (pancytopenia)—case reports.

Liver toxicity—rare.

▷ **Possible Effects on Sexual Function:** Premenopausal—altered timing and pattern of menstruation. Postmenopausal—vaginal bleeding, decreased libido (may be frequent). Breast tenderness and milk production in non-pregnant females (galactorrhea)—case report.

Abnormal and painful erections (priapism)—case reports.

This drug may be effective in treating the following conditions:

- male infertility due to abnormally low sperm counts.
- male breast enlargement and tenderness.
- chronic female breast pain (mastodynia).

Possible Effects on Laboratory Tests

Complete blood cell counts: decreased red cells, hemoglobin, white cells, and platelets.

Blood calcium level: increased.

Blood thyroid hormone levels: T3, T4, and free T4 increased.

Liver function tests: increased liver enzyme (AST/GOT), increased bilirubin (one case report).

Sperm count: increased or decreased.

Cholesterol and triglycerides: may be increased.

HDL: may be decreased.

CAUTION

1. If this drug is used prior to your menopause, it may induce ovulation and predispose to pregnancy. Since this drug should not be used during pregnancy, some method of contraception (other than oral contraceptives) is advised.

2. Do not take any form of estrogen while taking this drug; estrogens can inhibit tamoxifen's effectiveness.

3. Tamoxifen has been shown to cause an increased risk of uterine cancer. Women who have received or are receiving this drug should have regular gynecological examinations. Report menstrual irregularity, abnormal vaginal bleeding or vaginal discharge, pelvic pain or pressure promptly to your doctor.

4. High risk females in the BCPT were defined as a five-year predicted risk greater than 1.67%. The model used (Gail Model) can be obtained by your health care professional from Zeneca by calling 1-800-345-4334 or by calling 1-800-544-2007. Even though this medicine is taken, all risk of breast cancer is NOT removed, and the usual detection and screening measures should be continued.

5. Case reports of undesirable lipid changes (increased triglycerides and cholesterol and decreased HDL) have been made. Periodic checks are prudent.

▷ **Advisability of Use During Pregnancy**

Pregnancy Category: D. See Pregnancy Risk Categories at the back of this book.

Animal Studies: No birth defects due to this drug reported.

Human Studies: Adequate studies of pregnant women are not available.

This drug can have estrogenic effects. It should not be used during pregnancy.

Advisability of Use If Breast-Feeding
Presence of this drug in breast milk: Unknown.
Avoid drug or refrain from nursing.

Habit-Forming Potential: None.

Effects of Overdose: Severe extension of the pharmacological effects.

Possible Effects of Long-Term Use: Development of abnormally high blood calcium levels.

Suggested Periodic Examinations While Taking This Drug (at physician's discretion)
Complete blood cell counts.
Measurements of blood calcium, cholesterol, and lipid levels.
Complete eye examinations if impaired vision occurs.
Liver function tests.
Women who have been given or are now receiving tamoxifen must have regular gynecological examinations.

▷ **While Taking This Drug, Observe the Following**
Foods: No restrictions.
Herbal Medicines or Minerals: Some patients use echinacea to attempt to boost their immune systems. Unfortunately, use of echinacea is not recommended in people with damaged immune systems. This herb may also actually weaken any immune system if it is used too often or for too long a time. Black cohosh estrogenic effects may have an undesirable effect on tamoxifen and combination in not advisable. Very early research from the University of Illinois at Chicago *(www.uic.edu/depts/paff/opa/releases/2001/tamoxandsoy release.html)* in rats shows that a soy rich diet may enhance the effects of tamoxifen. Talk to your doctor to find out about further research on soy and this March 2001 study. Ipriflavone blunted effectiveness of genestein (a closely related compound). Red clover extracts contain daidzein and genistein, both of which can blunt the benefits of tamoxifen on tumors. Do not take those extracts or red clover.
Beverages: No restrictions. May be taken with milk.
▷ *Alcohol:* No interactions expected.
Tobacco Smoking: No interactions expected. I advise everyone to quit smoking.
Marijuana Smoking: Animal studies show an increased suppression of the immune system; significance in humans is not known.
▷ *Other Drugs*
The following drugs may *decrease* the effects of tamoxifen:
• estrogens.
• oral contraceptives (those that contain estrogens).
Tamoxifen *taken concurrently* with
• clopidogrel (Plavix) may result in higher than expected tamoxifen levels; no reports of adverse effects from this reaction have been made, but caution is advised.
• cyclophosphamide (Cytoxan) may increase blood clot (thromboembolism) risk.
• cyclosporine (Sandimmune) may increase cyclosporine levels and cause toxicity.
• medicines that inhibit CYP2C9 (such as fluconazole, fluvastatin, and zafirlukast) may lead to increased tamoxifen levels—talk to your doctor about this.

- methotrexate (Mexate, Rheumatrex) may increase blood clot (thromboembolism) risk.
- mitomycin will cause increased risk of hemolytic uremic syndrome.
- pneumococcal and perhaps other vaccines will blunt the vaccine's immune response (benefit).
- ritonavir (Norvir) and perhaps other protease inhibitors (see Drug Classes) may lead to toxicity.
- warfarin (Coumadin) presents an increased risk of bleeding; increased frequency of INR (prothrombin time or protime) testing is needed.

▷ *Driving, Hazardous Activities:* This drug may cause dizziness or drowsiness. Restrict activities as necessary.

Aviation Note: The use of this drug **may be a disqualification** for piloting. Consult a designated Aviation Medical Examiner.

Exposure to Sun: No restrictions.

TAMSULOSIN (TAM su low sin)

Introduced: 1997   **Class:** Antiprostatism, alpha 1 (A) blocker   **Prescription:** USA: Yes   **Controlled Drug:** USA: No   **Available as Generic:** No

Brand Name: Flomax evening

BENEFITS versus RISKS	
Possible Benefits	*Possible Risks*
MODEST IMPROVEMENT IN BENIGN PROSTATIC HYPERPLASIA ONCE-DAILY DOSING More selective for the genitourinary tract than other therapies	Headache Runny nose Abnormal ejaculation

▷ **Principal Uses**

As a Single Drug Product: Uses currently included in FDA-approved labeling: Treats symptomatic benign prostatic hyperplasia (BPH).

Other (unlabeled) generally accepted uses: (1) Appears to help swelling of the ureter (radiation induced urethritis) caused by radiation treatment of the prostate.

How This Drug Works: Relaxes smooth muscle around the bladder neck and prostate (by binding to a very specific alpha 1A receptor), allowing opening of the urethra and increased urine flow.

Available Dosage Forms and Strengths
Capsules — 0.4 mg
Sustained Release Capsules — 0.4 mg (Canada only)

▷ **Usual Adult Dosage Ranges:** Started with 0.4 mg once daily. If response is not acceptable after 2 to 4 weeks, the dose can be increased to 0.8 mg once a day.
Note: Actual dose and schedule must be determined for each patient individually.

Conditions Requiring Dosing Adjustments

Liver Function: No dose changes needed in moderate liver disease.

Kidney Function: Dose changes not needed in those with creatinine clearance (see Glossary) as low as 10 ml/min. Not studied in more compromised kidney failure patients.

Dosing Instructions: Take this medicine half an hour after the same meal every day (helps maintain similar blood levels). It may make you drowsy. If you forget a dose: Take the missed dose as soon as you remember it, unless it is nearly time for your next dose—if that is the case, skip (omit) the missed dose and take the next scheduled dose right on schedule. DO NOT double doses. Do NOT chew, crush, or break the capsules. If you forget this medicine for several days, treatment should be resumed with the 0.4 mg dose and dose increased as previously required and scheduled.

Usual Duration of Use: Benefits may be seen very quickly with the first dose and with symptoms resolving within the first week of regular treatment. Use on a regular schedule for 14 weeks may be needed to see this drug's peak benefit.

Typical Treatment Goals and Measurements (Outcomes and Markers)

Benign Prostatic Hypertrophy (BPH): Urologists use improvement in urinary flow as well as subjective measures such as relief of difficulty urinating and lowered feeling of urgency. There is a score set called the American Urological Association (AUA) symptom scores as well as the Boyarsky symptom scores. Digital rectal examination for prostate cancer should be done periodically.

Possible Advantages of This Drug: May give you symptomatic relief of benign prostatic hyperplasia (BPH) without surgery. Goes to work quickly (faster onset) than previously available medicines.

▷ **This Drug Should Not Be Taken If**
- you had an allergic reaction to it previously or if you are a woman or child.

▷ **Inform Your Physician Before Taking This Drug If**
- you have impaired liver function or liver disease.
- you have not had prostate cancer ruled out and this is a new prescription.
- you have kidney problems of any nature.
- your job requires balance and operation of hazardous machinery (this drug can cause dizziness and vertigo).

Possible Side Effects (natural, expected, and unavoidable drug actions)

Excessive lowering of blood pressure on standing (orthostatic hypotension).

▷ **Possible Adverse Effects** (unusual, unexpected, and infrequent reactions)

If any of the following develop, consult your physician promptly for guidance.

Mild Adverse Effects

Allergic reactions: skin rash, hives—rare.

Change in vision (Amblyopia)—rare.

Runny nose—may be frequent.

Headache or dizziness—may be frequent.

Back or joint pain (up to 8–11% in one trial).

Nausea or diarrhea—infrequent.

Slight decreases in red blood cell counts or hemoglobin—possible.

Increased liver function tests—rare (may normalize over time).

Serious Adverse Effects
Allergic reactions: hypersensitivity reactions—case reports.

Possible Effects on Sexual Function: Abnormal ejaculation (up to 18%) and rare cases of decreased libido have been reported. Rare priapism.

Possible Delayed Adverse Effects: Not reported.

Possible Effects on Laboratory Tests
Slight decreases in hemoglobin and red blood cells.
PSA: unchanged.
Some increased liver enzyme reports.

CAUTION
1. A digital rectal exam and other prostate cancer exams are prudent before this medicine is started. PSA will be falsely decreased by this medicine.

Precautions for Use
By Infants and Children: Safety and effectiveness for infants and children are not established.
By Those Over 60 Years of Age: No specific precautions other than changes related to decreased liver function.

▷ **Advisability of Use During Pregnancy**
Pregnancy Category: B. See Pregnancy Risk Categories at the back of this book.
Human Studies: Contraindicated in women.

Advisability of Use If Breast-Feeding
Unknown, but tamsulosin is NOT indicated for women.

Habit-Forming Potential: None.

Effects of Overdose: Extension effects of the pharmacological and adverse effects.

Possible Effects of Long-Term Use: Adverse effects of long-term use are similar to short-term use effects.

Suggested Periodic Examinations While Taking This Drug (at physician's discretion)
Patients should be monitored for signs and symptoms of orthostatic hypotension.
Patients should be monitored for improvement in symptoms of BPH.
Periodic digital rectal exams and PSA are needed.

While Taking This Drug, Observe the Following
Foods: If this medicine is taken on an empty stomach, the amount that can get into the body may be higher than if taken after a meal. While considered minor, current recommendations are to take it half an hour after the same meal daily.
Herbal Medicines or Minerals: Saw palmetto works by anti-androgenic and anti-inflammatory actions. The combination of this herb and tamsulosin has not been studied, but both drugs appear to work by different mechanisms. Talk to your doctor before combining.
Beverages: No restrictions.
▷ *Alcohol:* No restrictions.
Tobacco Smoking: No interactions expected. I advise everyone to quit smoking.
Marijuana Smoking: No interactions expected.
▷ *Other Drugs*
Tamsulosin *taken concurrently* with
• beta blockers (see Drug Classes) may increase extent of first dose orthostatic hypotension. Caution is advised.

- cimetidine (Tagamet) may increase tamsulosin blood levels and extent of first dose orthostatic hypotension as well as dizziness. Caution is advised.
- medicines that change liver enzymes in the cytochrome P450 class. The specific enzymes involved in removing tamsulosin have not been fully characterized, but combining medicines that change that liver enzyme system may have an effect on tamsulosin levels. Caution is advised.
- warfarin (Coumadin) may change the effects of tamsulosin or warfarin. More frequent checks of INR and careful patient check for unexpected adverse effects are prudent.

▷ *Driving, Hazardous Activities:* No restrictions.
Aviation Note: No restrictions.
Exposure to Sun: No restrictions.
Special Storage Instructions: Keep at room temperature. Avoid exposure to extreme humidity.

TERAZOSIN (ter AY zoh sin)

Introduced: 1987 **Class:** Antihypertensive **Prescription:** USA: Yes **Controlled Drug:** USA: No **Available as Generic:** Yes
Brand Names: ❦Apo-Terazosin, Hytrin, Novo-Terazosin

BENEFITS versus RISKS	
Possible Benefits	*Possible Risks*
EFFECTIVE TREATMENT OF MILD TO MODERATE HYPERTENSION	"First-dose" drop in blood pressure with fainting
LOWERED LOW-DENSITY LIPOPROTEINS AND TOTAL CHOLESTEROL	Fluid retention
LOWERED TRIGLYCERIDE LEVELS	
TREATS BENIGN PROSTATIC HYPERPLASIA	

Author's Note: Data from the ALLHAT trial found that alpha blockers such as this medicine are not drugs of first choice in high blood pressure. Information in this profile has been shortened for more widely used medicines.

TEGASEROD (TAY gas err odd)

Introduced: 2003 **Class:** Diarrhea predominant irritable syndrome treatment, serotonin 4 (5HT 4 agonist), Antidiarrheal **Prescription:** USA: Yes **Controlled Drug:** USA: No **Available as Generic:** No
Brand Name: Zelnorm

Author's Note: Information in this profile will be broadened as further data from use and comparitive studies becomes available.

TERBUTALINE (ter BYU ta leen)

Introduced: 1974 **Class:** Antiasthmatic, bronchodilator **Prescription:** USA: Yes **Controlled Drug:** USA: No; Canada: No **Available as Generic:** Yes

Brand Names: Brethaire, Brethine, Bricanyl, ✸Bricanyl Spacer, ✸Med-Broncodil

BENEFITS versus RISKS	
Possible Benefits	*Possible Risks*
VERY EFFECTIVE RELIEF OF BRONCHOSPASM	Increased blood pressure
	Fine hand tremor
	Irregular heart rhythm (with excessive use)

▷ **Principal Uses**

As a Single Drug Product: Uses currently included in FDA-approved labeling: Relieves acute bronchial asthma and reduces frequency and severity of chronic, recurrent asthmatic attacks.

Other (unlabeled) generally accepted uses: (1) May have a role in helping ease fetal distress in some patients; (2) used to help stop premature labor and continue pregnancies to more than 36 weeks; (3) an alternative to intravenous isoproterenol in therapy of status asthmaticus; (4) relieves reversible bronchospasm associated with chronic bronchitis and emphysema; (5) eases extended and painful erections (priapism).

How This Drug Works: Stimulates sympathetic nerve terminals dilating constricted bronchial tubes, improving the ability to breathe.

Available Dosage Forms and Strengths

Aerosol (per actuation) — 0.2 mg
Aerosol (Canada) (per actuation) — 0.25 mg
Injection — 1 mg/ml
Tablets — 2.5 mg, 5 mg

▷ **Usual Adult and Children Over 12 Dosage Ranges:** *Aerosol:* 0.4 mg taken in two separate inhalations 1 minute apart; repeat every 4 to 6 hours as needed.

Tablets: 2.5 to 5 mg taken every 6 hours while the patient is awake. The total daily dose should not exceed 15 mg.

Use of the injectable IV form is no longer recommended for home intravenous use by the FDA. Some clinicians have undertaken under the skin (subcutaneous) use with a MiniMed 404SP pump to give continuous under the skin (subcutaneous) doses of 50–100 micrograms per hour in conjunction with nursing and pharmaceutical care. This use generally goes on until the fetus is roughly 37 weeks old (e.g. for 6–8 weeks).

Note: Actual dose and schedule must be determined for each patient individually.

Conditions Requiring Dosing Adjustments

Liver Function: Extensively metabolized in the liver, but dosing guidelines in liver disease are not available.

Kidney Function: For patients with moderate to severe kidney failure, 50% of the usual dose can be taken at the usual time. In severe failure, the drug should not be used.

▷ **Dosing Instructions:** Tablets may be crushed and taken on an empty stomach or with food or milk. For aerosol, follow the written instructions carefully. Do not overuse. If you forget a dose: Use the inhaler as soon as you remember it, unless it's nearly time for your next dose—if that is the case, skip the missed dose and take the next dose right on schedule. Use the remaining doses for the day at evenly spaced dosing intervals, and then return to your usual schedule. Talk with your doctor if you find yourself missing doses. If you think your inhaler container (canister) is empty, get a bowl of cold water and place the canister in it—if the canister floats, there is no medicine left in it. If your doctor has prescribd this in order to keep you from delivering your infant too early, screening for glucose intolerance should be checked on at least one occasion after a week of treatment has been taken.

Usual Duration of Use: Individualized. Do not use beyond the time necessary to stop (terminate) episodes of asthma. Unlabeled use as a tocolytic in preterm labor often continues until 37 weeks of pregnancy.

Typical Treatment Goals and Measurements (Outcomes and Markers)
Asthma: Signs and symptoms of asthma such as difficulty breathing (dyspnea), cough, light-headedness, and wheezing should lessen. Forced expiratory volume at one second (FEV1) and/or peak expiratory flow rate (PEF) are checked by most pulmonologists as indicators of successful treatment. If the usual benefit is not realized, after the time to peak effect (see above) was expected, call your doctor.

Possible Advantages of This Drug: Rapid onset of action. Long duration of action. Highly effective relief of asthma.

▷ **This Drug Should Not Be Taken If**
  • you had an allergic reaction to any form of it previously.
  • you currently have an irregular heart rhythm.
  • you took a monoamine oxidase (MAO) type A inhibitor (see Drug Classes) in the last 14 days.

▷ **Inform Your Physician Before Taking This Drug If**
  • you are overly sensitive to other drugs that stimulate the sympathetic nervous system.
  • you are currently using epinephrine (Adrenalin, Primatene Mist, etc.) to relieve asthmatic breathing.
  • you have a seizure disorder.
  • you have liver or kidney failure.
  • you have any type of heart or circulatory disorder, especially high blood pressure or coronary heart disease.
  • you have diabetes or an overactive thyroid gland (hyperthyroidism).
  • you are taking any form of digitalis or any stimulant drug.

Possible Side Effects (natural, expected, and unavoidable drug actions)
Aerosol—dryness or irritation of mouth or throat, altered taste. Tablet—nervousness, tremor, palpitation.

▷ **Possible Adverse Effects** (unusual, unexpected, and infrequent reactions)
If any of the following develop, consult your physician promptly for guidance.
Mild Adverse Effects
Allergic reaction: skin rashes.
Headache, dizziness, drowsiness, restlessness, insomnia—infrequent.
Rapid, pounding heartbeat; increased sweating; muscle cramps in arms and legs—infrequent to frequent.

Nausea, heartburn, vomiting—rare with oral form, frequent with IV.
Increased blood sugar—frequent (40% abnormal one-hour glucose).
Increased plasma insulin levels—possbile.

Serious Adverse Effects

Rapid or irregular heart rhythm, intensification of angina, increased blood pressure—infrequent.

Chest pain with heartbeat changes (ST depression)—reported when oral and intravenous therapy is combined in preterm labor.

Lowered blood calcium or potassium (especially with intravenous use)—possible.

Liver toxicity—case reports.

Severe lowering of blood pressure (hypotension)—case reports.

Increased blood sugar—infrequent.

Ketoacidosis—case reports.

Fluid around the lungs (pulmonary edema)—case reports.

▷ **Possible Effects on Sexual Function:** None reported.

Natural Diseases or Disorders That May Be Activated by This Drug

Latent coronary artery disease, diabetes, or high blood pressure.

Possible Effects on Laboratory Tests

Blood total cholesterol and LDL cholesterol levels: no effect.
Blood HDL cholesterol level: increased.
Blood triglyceride levels: no effect.
Calcium may decrease.
Blood thyroid hormone levels: T3 increased; T4 decreased; free T4 no effect.
Glucose tolerance test: abnormal test.
Liver function tests: may be elevated.

CAUTION

1. Combination of this drug by aerosol with beclomethasone aerosol (Beclovent, Vanceril) may increase risk of fluorocarbon propellant (being phased out) toxicity. Best to use this aerosol 20 to 30 minutes before beclomethasone aerosol. This reduces toxicity risk and will help beclomethasone get into the lungs.

2. **Avoid excessive use of aerosol inhalation.** Excessive or prolonged inhalation use can reduce effectiveness and cause serious heart rhythm disturbances, including cardiac arrest.

3. Do not use this drug with epinephrine. These two drugs may be used alternately, allowing 4 hours between doses. Combined use with other medicines that have similar action also should be avoided (such as albuterol, pirbuterol, or salmeterol).

4. If you do not respond to your usually effective dose, ask your doctor for help. Do not increase the size or frequency of the dose without your physician's approval.

Precautions for Use

By Infants and Children: Manufacturer DOES NOT recommend use in those under 12 years of age.

By Those Over 60 Years of Age: Avoid excessive and continual use. If acute asthma is not relieved promptly, other drugs will be needed. Watch for nervousness, palpitations, irregular heart rhythm, and muscle tremors. Use with extreme caution if you have hardening of the arteries, heart disease, or high blood pressure.

▷ **Advisability of Use During Pregnancy**

Pregnancy Category: B. See Pregnancy Risk Categories at the back of this book.

Animal Studies: No significant birth defects reported in mouse and rat studies.

Human Studies: Adequate studies of pregnant women are not available.

Use only if clearly needed. Ask your physician for guidance.

Advisability of Use If Breast-Feeding

Presence of this drug in breast milk: Yes (a small amount of roughly 0.2% of the mom's dose).

Monitor nursing infant closely, and discontinue drug or nursing if adverse effects develop.

Habit-Forming Potential: None.

Effects of Overdose: Nervousness, palpitation, rapid heart rate, sweating, headache, tremor, vomiting, chest pain.

Possible Effects of Long-Term Use: Loss of effectiveness. See *CAUTION* for this drug.

Suggested Periodic Examinations While Taking This Drug (at physician's discretion)

Blood pressure measurements.

Evaluation of heart status.

▷ **While Taking This Drug, Observe the Following**

Foods: No restrictions.

Herbal Medicines or Minerals: Using St. John's wort, ma huang, ephedrine-like compounds, or kola while taking this medicine may result in unacceptable central nervous system stimulation. Fir or pine needle oil should NOT be used by asthmatics. Ephedra alone does carry a German Commission E monograph indication for asthma treatment. If you are allergic to plants in the Asteraceae family (aster, chrysanthemum, daisy, or ragweed), you may also be allergic to echinacea, chamomile, feverfew, and St. John's wort. Since part of the way ginkgo and ginseng work may be as an MAO inhibitor, do not combine them with terbutaline.

Beverages: Avoid excessive use of caffeine-containing beverages: coffee, tea, mate, guarana, cola, chocolate.

▷ *Alcohol:* No interactions expected.

Tobacco Smoking: No interactions expected. I advise everyone to quit smoking.

▷ *Other Drugs*

Terbutaline *taken concurrently* with

• monoamine oxidase (MAO) type A inhibitors may cause excessive increase in blood pressure and undesirable heart stimulation (see Drug Classes).

• succinylcholine (Anectine) may lead to increased neuromuscular blockade which may require neostigmine.

• theophylline (Theo-Dur, others) may cause decreased theophylline effectiveness.

The following drugs may *decrease* the effects of terbutaline:

• beta blockers (see Drug Classes)—may impair terbutaline's effectiveness.

▷ *Driving, Hazardous Activities:* Usually no restrictions. Use caution if excessive nervousness or dizziness occurs.

Aviation Note: The use of this drug *is a disqualification* for piloting. Consult a designated Aviation Medical Examiner.

Exposure to Sun: No restrictions.
Heavy Exercise or Exertion: Use caution—excessive exercise can induce asthma in some patients.

TERIPARATIDE (Ter ih PAIR a tyde)

Other Names: PTH, human PTH 1-34, hPTH 1-34, parathyroid hormone, PTH 1-34

Introduced: 2003 **Class:**   hormone, parathyroid **Prescription:** USA: Yes **Controlled Drug:**   USA: No; Canada: No   **Available as Generic:**   USA: No; Canada: No

Brand Name: Forteo

Author's Note: This medicine is the first prescription medicine used to treat osteoporosis that works by increasing bone formation (osteoblast action). Information in this profile will be broadened once more data and outcomes are available.

TESTOSTOSTERONE (Tes TOS tur own)

Other Names: Chlorotrianisene, conjugated estrogens, esterified estrogens, estradiol, estriol, estrone, estropipate, quinestrol

Introduced: 2000(Gel) **Class:**   Male sex hormone **Prescription:** USA: Yes **Controlled Drug:**   USA: No; Canada: No   **Available as Generic:**   USA: No; Canada: No

Brand Names: AndroGel 1%, Andriol, Androderm, Testoderm

Author's Note: Information in this profile will be broadened once more data and outcomes are available.

TETRACYCLINE ANTIBIOTIC FAMILY (te trah SI kleen)

Other Names: Doxycycline, tetracycline

Introduced: 1953, 1967 **Class:**   Antibiotic, tetracyclines **Prescription:** USA: Yes **Controlled Drug:**   USA: No; Canada: No   **Available as Generic:**   Yes

Brand Names: Doxycycline: Adoxia, ✤Apo-Doxy, ✤Apo-Doxy-Tabs, Atridox (gum line delivery form), ✤Doryx, Doryx, Doxy Caps, Doxychel, ✤Doxycin, Doxy-Lemmon, Doxy 100, Doxy Tabs, Doxy 200, Monodox, ✤Novo-Doxylin, Periostat, Vibramycin, Vibra-Tabs, ✤Vibra-Tabs C-Pak, Tetracycline: Achromycin, Achromycin Ophthalmic, Achromycin V, ✤Acrocidin, Actisite, ✤Apo-Tetra, Aureomycin, Bristacycline, Contimycin, Cyclinex, Cyclopar, Lemtrex, ✤Medicycline, Mysteclin-F [CD], ✤Neo-Tetrine, ✤Nor-Tet, ✤Novo-Tetra, ✤Nu-Tetra, Panmycin, Retet, Robitet, SK-Tetracycline, Sumycin, Teline, Tetra-C, Tetracap, Tetra-Con, Tetracyn, Tetralan, Tetram, Tetrex-F, Tropicycline

---

BENEFITS versus RISKS

Possible Benefits	*Possible Risks*
EFFECTIVE TREATMENT OF INFECTIONS DUE TO SUSCEPTIBLE BACTERIA AND PROTOZOA	ALLERGIC REACTIONS, MILD TO SEVERE: ANAPHYLAXIS, DRUG-INDUCED HEPATITIS Drug-induced colitis Superinfections (bacterial or fungal) Blood cell disorders: hemolytic anemia, abnormally low white cell and platelet counts Kidney toxicity

---

▷ **Principal Uses**

As a Single Drug Product: Uses currently included in FDA-approved labeling: (1) Treats a broad range of infections caused by susceptible bacteria and protozoa (short-term use); (2) treats severe, resistant pustular acne (long-term use) (tetracycline); (3) used in a sustained-release form (Actisite) to treat gum disease (periodontitis) in adults (tetracycline) and a doxycycline form (Periostat) and Atridox gel are used to treat gum disease (periodontitis); (4) doxycycline treats gonorrhea and syphilis in penicillin-allergic people; (5) helpful in acne; (6) helps prevent malaria in travelers; (7) tetracycline is the drug of choice for cholera; (8) doxycycline is of use in anthrax (including post-exposure use), brucellosis, cholera, and plague.

Other (unlabeled) generally accepted uses: (1) Combination antibiotic treatment of duodenal ulcers caused by *Helicobacter pylori;* (2) used in vaginal and vulval cysts (Gartner's) and in vaginal hydrocele; (3) topical tetracycline is useful in chronic eye problems (blepharitis); (4) treats cancer (malignant) fluid (pericardial effusion) buildup around the heart; (5) has a role in acne rosacea in decreasing the number of papules or nodules; (7) doxycline: a) treats early Lyme disease used to treat stage one Lyme disease (new data found that 87% of people who took doxycycline within 72 hours of a tick bite DID NOT develop Lyme disease; (b) treats sexual assault victims; (c) treats prostatitis; (d) can help in some cases of PMS; (e) may treat some cases of male infertility of unexplained origin; (f) helps treat rheumatoid arthritis.

As a Combination Drug Product [CD]: Tetracycline is available combined with amphotericin B, an antifungal antibiotic that is provided to reduce the risk of developing an overgrowth of yeast organisms (superinfection) of the gastrointestinal tract.

How These Drugs Work: Prevent growth and multiplication of susceptible organisms by interfering with formation of essential proteins. Periostat seems to work by its anticolligenase and anti-inflammatory properties.

Available Dosage Forms and Strengths

Doxycycline:

Capsules — 50 mg, 75 mg, 100 mg
Capsules, coated pellets — 100 mg
Capsule, delayed release — 100 mg
Gel — 10% mg
Injection (per vial) — 100 mg, 200 mg
Oral suspension — 25 mg/5 ml
Syrup — 50 mg/5 ml
Tablets — 50 mg, 100 mg

Tetracycline:

Capsules — 100 mg, 250 mg, 500 mg
Ointment — 3%
Ointment, ophthalmic — 10 mg/g
Periodontal fiber (per fiber) — 12.7 mg
Solution, topical — 2.2 mg/ml
Suspension, ophthalmic — 10 mg/ml
Suspension, oral — 125 mg/5 ml
Tablets — 250 mg, 500 mg

▷ **Usual Adult Dosage Ranges:**

Doxycycline: General infections from susceptible organisms: 100 mg every 12 hours the first day and then 100 mg once daily. Some severe infections may require ongoing therapy of 100 mg every 12 hours. *Anthrax:* 100 mg twice a day for 60 days (started in combination with one or two additional antibiotics intravenously and then switched to oral treatment when your doctor feels this is appropriate). Total daily dose should not exceed 300 mg.

Tetracycline: 250 to 500 mg every 6 hours, or 500 to 1,000 mg every 12 hours. The total daily dose should not exceed 4,000 mg (4 g).

Note: Actual dose and schedule must be determined for each patient individually.

Typical Treatment Goals and Measurements (Outcomes and Markers)

Infections: The most commonly used measures of serious infections are white blood cell counts and differentials (the kind of blood cells that occur most often in your blood), and temperature. Many clinicians look for positive changes in 24–48 hours. NEVER stop an antibiotic because you start to feel better. For many infections, a full 14 days is REQUIRED to kill the bacteria. Inhalational anthrax treatment continues for 60 days. The goals and time frame (see peak benefits above) should be discussed with you when the prescription is written.

Conditions Requiring Dosing Adjustments

Liver Function: Doxycycline: Patients with both liver and kidney compromise should have the dose decreased. Drug can cause liver problems, and a benefit-to-risk decision should be made for people with liver disease.

Tetracycline: Is a possible cause of hepatoxicity. A benefit-to-risk decision should be made for patients with compromised livers to use this drug. Daily maximum in liver disease is 1 g.

Kidney Function: Patients with mild to moderate kidney failure can take the usual dose every 8 to 12 hours. Patients with moderate to severe kidney failure take the usual dose every 12 to 24 hours. In severe kidney failure (creatinine clearance less than 10 ml/min), tetracycline should be avoided.

Malnutrition: Doxycycline: Lower than expected levels may occur in patients with malnutrition. If clinical progress is not as expected, the dose may need to be increased.

▷ **Dosing Instructions:** Immediate release forms may be crushed and the capsule opened and preferably taken on an empty stomach, 1 hour before or 2 hours after eating. However, to reduce stomach irritation, it may be taken with crackers that contain insignificant amounts of iron, calcium, magnesium, or zinc. Avoid all dairy products for 2 hours before and after taking this drug. (Unlike other tetracyclines, doxycycline absorption is not significantly changed by food or milk.) Sustained release or delayed release forms should NOT be crushed, chewed, or altered. Suspension forms should be shaken well before being taken and should be dosed using a calibrated dosing spoon or a dosing cup. Take at the same time each day, with a full glass of water. Take the full course prescribed. If you forget a dose: Take the missed dose as soon as you remember it, unless it's nearly time for your next dose—if that is the case, skip the missed dose and take the next dose right on schedule. DO NOT double up on doses. Taking your medicine exactly as prescribed will get the best results. Talk with your doctor if you find yourself missing doses.

Usual Duration of Use: The time required to control the acute infection and be free of fever and symptoms for 48 hours. This varies with the nature of the infection. Long-term use (months to years, as for treatment of acne) requires supervision and periodic evaluation. Treatment of stage one Lyme disease requires 3 to 4 weeks in adults even though one doxycycline dose may prevent a high percentage of Lyme infections.

Possible Advantages of These Drugs

Twice a day treatment for seven days for chlamydia trachomatis. Provides coverage for many bioterror agents.

▷ **These Drugs Should Not Be Taken If**
- you are allergic to any tetracycline (see Drug Classes).
- you are pregnant or breast-feeding.
- you have severe liver disease.

▷ **Inform Your Physician Before Taking This Drug If**
- it is prescribed for a child under 8 years of age.
- you have a history of liver or kidney disease.
- you have systemic lupus erythematosus.
- you are taking any penicillin drug.
- you are taking any anticoagulant drug.
- you will have surgery with general anesthesia.

Possible Side Effects (natural, expected, and unavoidable drug actions)

Superinfections (see Glossary), often due to yeast organisms—these can occur in the mouth, intestinal tract, rectum, and/or vagina, resulting in rectal and vaginal itching. Tooth discoloration (when used in children less than 8 years old). Metallic taste.

▷ **Possible Adverse Effects** (unusual, unexpected, and infrequent reactions)

If any of the following develop, consult your physician promptly for guidance.

Mild Adverse Effects

Allergic reactions: skin rash, hives, itching of hands and feet, swelling of face or extremities.

Loss of appetite, stomach irritation, taste disorders, nausea, vomiting, diarrhea—infrequent.

Warts—very rare and of questionable causality (tetracycline).

Irritation of mouth or tongue, black tongue, sore throat, abdominal cramping or pain—infrequent.

Serious Adverse Effects

Allergic reactions: anaphylactic reaction (see Glossary), asthma, fever, swollen joints and lymph glands.

Serious skin problems (Stevens-Johnson syndrome, Jarisch-Herxheimer reaction)—case reports.

Drug-induced hepatitis with jaundice—case reports.

Permanent discoloration and/or malformation of teeth if taken by children under 8, including unborn child and infant.

Drug-induced colitis, myasthenia gravis, or pancreatitis—case reports.

Worsening of existing systemic lupus erythematosus—case reports.

Rare blood cell disorders: hemolytic anemia (see Glossary); abnormally low white blood cell count, causing fever and infections; abnormally low blood platelet count—case reports.

Impairment of blood clotting—case reports.

Increased intracranial pressure (pseudotumor cerebri) or kidney problems— rare (tetracycline).

Drug-induced porphyria, esophageal ulcers, or low blood potassium—case reports (tetracycline).

▷ **Possible Effects on Sexual Function:** Decreased effectiveness of oral contraceptives taken concurrently (several case reports of pregnancy). Decreased male fertility—case reports (tetracycline).

▷ **Adverse Effects That May Mimic Natural Diseases or Disorders**
Drug-induced hepatitis may suggest viral hepatitis.

Natural Diseases or Disorders That May Be Activated by This Drug
Systemic lupus erythematosus.

Possible Effects on Laboratory Tests
Complete blood cell counts: decreased red cells, hemoglobin, white cells, and platelets; increased eosinophils (allergic reaction).

Blood lupus erythematosus (LE) cells: positive.

Blood amylase level: increased (toxic effect in pregnant women).

Liver function tests: increased enzymes (ALT/GPT, AST/GOT, alkaline phosphatase) or bilirubin.

Kidney function tests: increased blood creatinine and urea nitrogen (BUN) levels (kidney damage).

Urine sugar tests: false-positive results with Benedict's solution and Clinitest.

CAUTION

1. Antacids, dairy products, and preparations containing aluminum, bismuth, calcium, iron, magnesium, or zinc can prevent adequate absorption and reduce effectiveness significantly.
2. Troublesome and persistent diarrhea can occur. If diarrhea persists for more than 24 hours, call your doctor.
3. **If** general anesthesia is required while taking this drug, the choice of anesthetic agent must be selected carefully to prevent kidney damage.
4. Periostat form can still lead to vaginal or oral yeast (candida) infections.

Precautions for Use

By Infants and Children: If possible, tetracyclines should not be given to children under 8 years of age because of the risk of permanent discoloration and deformity of the teeth. Rarely, infants may develop increased intracranial pressure within the first 4 days of receiving this drug. Tetracyclines may inhibit normal bone growth and development.

By Those Over 60 Years of Age: Dose must be carefully individualized based on kidney function. Natural skin changes may predispose to severe and prolonged itching reactions in the genital and anal regions.

▷ **Advisability of Use During Pregnancy**

Pregnancy Category: D. See Pregnancy Risk Categories at the back of this book.

Animal Studies: Tetracycline causes limb defects in rats, rabbits, and chickens.

Human Studies: Information from studies of pregnant women indicates that this drug can cause impaired development and discoloration of teeth and other developmental defects.

It is advisable to avoid these drugs completely during entire pregnancy.

Advisability of Use If Breast-Feeding
Presence of these drugs in breast milk: Yes.
Avoid drug or refrain from nursing.

Habit-Forming Potential: None.

Effects of Overdose: Stomach burning, nausea, vomiting, diarrhea.

Possible Effects of Long-Term Use: Superinfections; impairment of bone marrow, liver or kidney function—rare.

Suggested Periodic Examinations While Taking This Drug (at physician's discretion)
Complete blood cell counts.
Liver and kidney function tests.
During extended use, sputum and stool examinations may detect early superinfection due to yeast organisms.

▷ **While Taking This Drug, Observe the Following**
Foods: Avoid cheeses, yogurt, ice cream, iron-fortified cereals and supplements and meats for 2 hours before and after taking this drug.

Herbal Medicines or Minerals: Some patients use echinacea to attempt to boost their immune systems. Use of echinacea is not recommended in people with damaged immune systems. This herb may also actually weaken any immune system if it is used too often or for too long a time. No data exist for combination use with tetracyclines. Mistletoe has been used in similar fashion and there are also NO DATA for combining it with tetracyclines. Calcium, zinc, and iron can combine with these drugs and reduce absorption significantly. St. John's wort and this medicine can intensify reactions to the sun—extreme caution is advised.

Beverages: Avoid all forms of milk for 2 hours before and after taking.

▷ *Alcohol:* Reduces doxycycline blood levels. Alcohol should be avoided with doxycycline and perhaps another tetracycline substituted, particularly for those who have drinking problems. Alcohol is also best avoided if you have active liver disease.

Tobacco Smoking: No interactions expected. I advise everyone to quit smoking.

▷ *Other Drugs*
Tetracyclines may *increase* the effects of
• cyclosporine (Sandimmune, Neoral).
• digoxin (Lanoxin) and cause digitalis toxicity.
• lithium (Eskalith, Lithane, etc.) and increase the risk of lithium toxicity.
• oral anticoagulants such as warfarin (Coumadin) and make it necessary to reduce their dose; increased INR (prothrombin time or protime) testing is needed.

Tetracyclines may *decrease* the effects of
• birth control pills (oral contraceptives) and impair their effectiveness in preventing pregnancy.
• penicillins (see Drug Classes) and impair their effectiveness in treating infections.

Tetracyclines *taken concurrently* with
• furosemide (Lasix) increases blood urea nitrogen (BUN).
• isotretinoin (Accutane) may worsen tetracycline-caused increased intracranial pressure and cause additive toxicity.
• methoxyflurane anesthesia may impair kidney function.
• theophylline (Theo-Dur) may result in variable changes in drug levels; more frequent theophylline blood levels are needed if these medicines are to be combined.

- warfarin (Coumadin) poses an increased risk of bleeding; INR (prothrombin time or protime) testing should be checked more frequently and doses adjusted if needed.

The following drugs may **decrease** the effects of tetracyclines:

- antacids (aluminum or magnesium preparations, sodium bicarbonate, etc.)—may reduce drug absorption.
- bismuth subsalicylate (Pepto-Bismol, others).
- calcium supplements (various brands).
- carbamazepine (Tegretol).
- cholestyramine (Questran) and other cholesterol-lowering resins.
- colestipol (Colestid) and perhaps colesevelam (Welchol).
- iron, zinc, magnesium, and mineral preparations—may reduce drug absorption.
- phenobarbital.
- phenytoin (Dilantin) or fosphenytoin (Cerebyx).
- quinapril (Accupril).
- rifampin (Rifadin, others).
- sucralfate (Carafate).
- zinc salts.

▷ *Driving, Hazardous Activities:* Usually no restrictions. However, this drug may cause nausea or diarrhea. Restrict activities as necessary.

Aviation Note: The use of these drugs **may be a disqualification** for piloting. Consult a designated Aviation Medical Examiner.

Exposure to Sun: Use caution—some tetracyclines can cause photosensitivity (see Glossary).

THEOPHYLLINE (thee AHF ah lin)

Introduced: 1900   **Class:** Antiasthmatic, bronchodilator, xanthines
Prescription: USA: Yes   **Controlled Drug:** USA: No; Canada: No
Available as Generic: Yes

Brand Names: Accurbron, ✤Acet-Am, A.E.A., Aerolate, Aminodrox-Forte, ✤Apo-Oxtriphylline, ✤Aquaphyllim, ✤Asbron [CD], Asmalix, Azpan, Brocomar [CD], Bronchial Gelatin Capsule, Broncomar [CD], Bronkaid Tablets [CD], Bronkodyl, Bronkolixir [CD], Bronkotabs, Bronkotabs [CD], Constant-T, Duraphyl, Elixicon, Elixomin, Elixophyllin, For-Az-Ma [CD], Isuprel Compound [CD], Labid, Lanophyllin, Lixolin, Lodrane, Lodrane CR, Marax [CD], Marax DF [CD], Mudrane GG Elixir [CD], Phedral [CD], Phyllocontin, Physpan, ✤PMS Theophylline, Primatene, ✤Pulmophylline, Quadrinal [CD], Quibron [CD], Quibron Plus [CD], Quibron-T Dividose, Quibron-300 [CD], Quibron-T/SR, Respbid, Slo-Bid, Slo-Bid Gyrocaps, Slo-Phyllin, Slo-Phyllin GG [CD], Slo-Phyllin Gyrocaps, Somophyllin, Somophyllin-12, Sustaire, Tedral [CD], Tedral SA [CD], T.E.H. [CD], T.E.P., Thalfed, Theobid Duracaps, ✤Theo-Bronc, Theochron, Theoclear, Theoclear L.A., Theocord, Theo-Dur, Theo-Dur Sprinkle, Theolair, Theolair-SR, Theolate [CD], Theolixir, Theomar [CD], Theomax DF, Theon, Theophyl-SR, Theospan-SR, Theo-SR, Theo-Time, Theo-24, Theovent, Theox, Theozine, Therex [CD], Uni-Dur, ✤Uniphyl, Vitaphen [CD]

BENEFITS versus RISKS

Possible Benefits	*Possible Risks*
EFFECTIVE PREVENTION AND RELIEF OF ACUTE BRONCHIAL ASTHMA	NARROW TREATMENT RANGE
	FREQUENT STOMACH DISTRESS
MODERATELY EFFECTIVE CONTROL OF CHRONIC, RECURRENT BRONCHIAL ASTHMA	Gastrointestinal bleeding
	Central nervous system toxicity, seizures
Moderately effective symptomatic relief in chronic bronchitis and emphysema	Heart rhythm disturbances

---

▷ **Principal Uses**

As a Single Drug Product: Uses currently included in FDA-approved labeling: (1) Used to relieve shortness of breath and wheezing of acute bronchial asthma and to prevent the recurrence of asthmatic episodes; (2) useful in relieving asthmalike symptoms associated with some types of chronic bronchitis, chronic obstructive pulmonary disease, and emphysema.

Other (unlabeled) generally accepted uses: (1) May have a role in combination therapy of cystic fibrosis; (2) can help decrease excessive production of red blood cells in kidney transplant patients; (3) may have a role in helping decrease the risk of sudden infant death syndrome (SIDS); (4) may have a supportive role with steroids and other agents in helping prevent rejection of transplanted kidneys; (5) can help ease essential tremor; (6) decreases risk of breathing cessation in neonatal apnea; (7) helps in treating SIDS children; (8) may have a role in treating sleep apnea; (9) one small study found it effective in stopping ACE inhibitor (see Drug Classes) cough.

As a Combination Drug Product [CD]: Available combined with several other drugs that manage bronchial asthma and related conditions. Ephedrine is added to enhance opening of the bronchi (bronchodilation); guaifenesin is added to thin mucus in the bronchial tubes (an expectorant effect); and mild sedatives such as phenobarbital are added to allay anxiety often seen in acute attacks of asthma.

How This Drug Works: By inhibiting the enzyme phosphodiesterase, this drug produces an increase in the tissue chemical cyclic AMP. This causes relaxation of the muscles in the bronchial tubes and blood vessels of the lung, resulting in relief of bronchospasm, expanded lung capacity and improved lung circulation.

Available Dosage Forms and Strengths

Capsules — 100 mg, 200 mg, 250 mg, 260 mg

Capsules, prolonged action — 50 mg, 60 mg, 65 mg, 75 mg, 100 mg, 125 mg, 130 mg, 200 mg, 250 mg, 260 mg, 300 mg

Elixir — 27 mg/5 ml, 50 mg/5 ml

Oral solution — 27 mg/5 ml, 53.3 mg/5 ml

Oral suspension — 100 mg/5 ml

Syrup — 27 mg/5 ml, 50 mg/5 ml

Tablets — 100 mg, 125 mg, 200 mg, 250 mg, 300 mg

Tablets, prolonged action — 50 mg, 60 mg, 65 mg, 75 mg, 100 mg, 125 mg, 130 mg, 200 mg, 225 mg, 250 mg, 260 mg, 300 mg, 350 mg, 400 mg, 450 mg, 500 mg, 600 mg

▷ **Recommended Dosage Ranges** (Actual dose and schedule must be determined for each patient individually.)

Infants and Children: Sudden asthma attack (an inhaled beta-2 agonist is the drug of choice to manage these acute symptoms, but for those not currently taking theophylline or having a dose in 12–24 hours) loading dose of the immediate release form dosed as 5 milligram per kilogram (mg/kg) of body mass. For acute attack (while currently taking theophylline) a theophylline lab level should be checked, and then one milligram per kilogram of body weight is given for each 2 microgram/milliliter increase in blood level that the clinician is seeking. Blood levels of theophylline should be checked after such dosing adjustments.

For ongoing use during acute attack, dose is based on age: After the loading dose is given, the ongoing dose is calculated based on age and body weight. For example, for those one to nine years of age—4 mg per kg of body mass, every 6 hours. For those nine to less than sixteen years of age—3 mg per kg of body mass, every 6 hours when the Slo-Phyllin syrup or tablets are used.

For ongoing use to prevent asthma—dose is based on age: Once slow dosing increase is accomplished, daily doses are adjusted to reach blood levels of 10 to 15 mcg/ml.

16 to 60 Years of Age:

For acute attack of asthma (not currently taking theophylline): (an inhaled beta-2 agonist is the drug of choice): When the decision is made to add on theophylline (and no theophylline was given in the last 12–24 hours: Loading dose of 5 mg per kg of body mass. For acute attack while currently taking theophylline—a serum theophylline level should be checked, then one milligram per kilogram of body weight is given for each two microgram/milliliter increase in blood level that the clinician wants to achieve. Follow-up blood levels of theophylline should then be checked.

For maintenance during acute attack: For nonsmokers: 3 mg per kg of body mass, every 8 hours; for smokers: 4 mg per kg of body mass, every 6 hours.

For chronic treatment to prevent recurrence of asthma: The goal is to obtain a usually therapeutic blood level of 10–20 mcg/ml. Dosing is started at 10 mg/kg/day, up to a maximum of 300 mg daily. If this dose is tolerated, a blood level should be checked in three days. Another increase as needed and tolerated by a step up to 13mg/kg per day up to a maximum of 450 mg/day (roughly 25%). Further incremental steps guided by patient tolerance and blood levels can be undertaken. The total daily calculated dose can be given every 12 hours using the Slo-bid or Theolair-SR forms. If patient response happens with a lower level, the patient response should be used as the guide. "Treat the patient, not the level."

For once daily dosing: The Slo-bid Gyrocap form may work in adult nonsmokers when they are given once a day. The strategy here is usually to establish a therapeutic blood level using the twice daily approach, and then using that effective dose. The once a day dose is then twice the two times a day dose. This new once daily dose is started 12 hours after the last twice a day dose. Blood levels should be checked as the peak and trough levels may be higher or lower than with the twice a day approach. If problems consistent with toxicity happen, the patient should be returned to the twice a day dosing strategy.

Over 60 Years of Age: Theophylline is removed roughly 30% more slowly than in younger patients. Decreased doses and more frequent blood levels are prudent. For example: people in this population or those with cor pulmonale are given 2 mg/kg every eight hours, guided by blood levels.

Conditions Requiring Dosing Adjustments

Liver Function: The dose must be lowered and blood levels obtained frequently. Doses may need to be decreased by 50% in some cases.

Kidney Function: Lower doses and more frequent blood levels are indicated.

▷ **Dosing Instructions:** May be taken with or following food to reduce stomach irritation. The regular capsules may be opened, and the regular tablets may be crushed. The prolonged-action forms should be swallowed whole and not altered or chewed. Shake the oral suspension well before measuring each dose (using a dose cup or calibrated measuring spoon). Do not refrigerate liquid dose forms. Blood levels are critical for this medicine. If theophylline has been taken previously, a blood level is often checked and then clinicians use 1 mg/kg for each 2 mcg/ml increase in blood level that is wanted. If you forget a dose: Take the missed dose as soon as you remember it, unless it's nearly time for your next dose—if that is the case, skip the missed dose and take the next dose right on schedule. JUST THE RIGHT BLOOD LEVEL is very important for this medicine. DO NOT double up doses. Talk with your doctor if you find yourself forgetting this drug. Timers and beeper-based reminder services can be very helpful.

Usual Duration of Use: Use on a regular schedule for 48 to 72 hours usually determines effectiveness in controlling the breathing impairment associated with bronchial asthma and chronic lung disease. Long-term use requires supervision and periodic physician evaluation.

Typical Treatment Goals and Measurements (Outcomes and Markers)

Asthma: Signs and symptoms of asthma such as difficulty breathing (dyspnea), cough, light-headedness, and wheezing should lessen. Exercise ability should increase. Forced expiratory volume at one second (FEV1) and/or peak expiratory flow rate (PEF) are checked by most pulmonologists as indicators of successful treatment. Blood levels are used to guide dosing (10–20 mcg/ml). If the usual benefit is not realized, or if symptoms improve and then worsen, call your doctor.

▷ **This Drug Should Not Be Taken If**
- you have had an allergic reaction to it or to aminophylline, dyphylline, or oxtriphylline.
- you have active peptic ulcer disease.
- you have an uncontrolled seizure disorder.
- you had a blood level drawn and it is in the "toxic" range.

▷ **Inform Your Physician Before Taking This Drug If**
- you have had an unfavorable reaction to any xanthine (see Drug Classes).
- you have a seizure disorder of any kind.
- you have a history of peptic ulcer disease.
- you have a history of underactive thyroid (hypothyroidism).
- you have impaired liver (may lower blood proteins and lead to toxicity with "normal" levels) or impaired kidney function.
- you take any of the drugs listed in the "Other Drugs" section below.
- you have hypertension, heart disease, or any type of heart rhythm disorder.

Possible Side Effects (natural, expected, and unavoidable drug actions)

Nervousness, insomnia, rapid heart rate, increased urine volume (caffeine-like effects).

▷ **Possible Adverse Effects** (unusual, unexpected, and infrequent reactions)
   If any of the following develop, consult your physician promptly for guidance.

   Mild Adverse Effects

   Allergic reactions: skin rash, hives.

   Headache, dizziness, irritability, tremor, fatigue, weakness—infrequent.

   Loss of appetite, nausea, vomiting (may be an early warning of toxicity), abdominal pain, diarrhea, excessive thirst—infrequent.

   Stuttering—case report.

   Flushing of face—case reports.

   Serious Adverse Effects

   Allergic reaction: severe skin rash (Stevens-Johnson Syndrome)—case reports.

   Idiosyncratic reactions: marked anxiety, confusion, behavioral disturbances.

   Central nervous system toxicity: muscle twitching, seizures—dose-related.

   Fever—possible (if in children and of sudden onset and lasting more than 24 hours—call your doctor as a 50% decrease in dose may be needed).

   Heart rhythm abnormalities, rapid breathing, low blood pressure—variable and dose-related.

   Gastrointestinal bleeding—rare.

   Defects in clotting (coagulation)—case reports.

   Drug-induced abnormal urine production (SIADH) or porphyria—case reports.

   Worsening of ulcers—possible.

   Liver toxicity—case reports.

▷ **Possible Effects on Sexual Function:** None reported.

Natural Diseases or Disorders That May Be Activated by This Drug

   Latent peptic ulcer disease.

Possible Effects on Laboratory Tests

   Blood uric acid level: increased.

   Fecal occult blood test: positive (large doses may cause stomach bleeding).

   Triglycerides: may be increased with prolonged use.

CAUTION

   1. This drug should not be taken at the same time as other antiasthmatic drugs unless your doctor prescribes the combination. Serious overdose could result.

   2. If you develop severe weakness or confusion, irregular heart beats, shakes (tremors) or muscle twitching while taking this medicine—CALL YOUR DOCTOR immediately.

   3. Influenza vaccines may delay the elimination of this drug and cause accumulation to toxic levels.

Precautions for Use

   By Infants and Children: Do not exceed recommended doses. Watch for toxicity: irritability, agitation, tremors, lethargy, fever, vomiting, rapid heart rate and breathing, seizures. Blood level tests are needed during long-term use.

   By Those Over 60 Years of Age: Small starting doses are indicated. You may be at increased risk for stomach irritation, nausea, vomiting, or diarrhea. When used concurrently with coffee (caffeine) or nasal decongestants, this drug may cause excessive stimulation and a hyperactivity syndrome.

▷ **Advisability of Use During Pregnancy**

   Pregnancy Category: C. See Pregnancy Risk Categories at the back of this book.

   Animal Studies: Significant birth defects due to this drug reported in mice.

Human Studies: Adequate studies of pregnant women are not available. No increase in birth defects reported in 394 exposures to this drug.

Avoid this drug during the first 3 months. Use it otherwise only if clearly needed. Ask your physician for guidance.

Advisability of Use If Breast-Feeding

Presence of this drug in breast milk: Yes and at roughly the same concentration of the mother's.

Talk to your doctor about this benefit to risk decision. The peak concentration for the infant, and therefore the expected peak effect would happen 1–3 hours after nursing. Refraining from the medicine or refraining from nursing may be needed depending on the infant's ability to tolerate theophylline.

Habit-Forming Potential: None.

Effects of Overdose: Nausea, vomiting, restlessness, irritability, confusion, delirium, seizures, high fever, weak pulse, coma.

Possible Effects of Long-Term Use: Gastrointestinal irritation.

Suggested Periodic Examinations While Taking This Drug (at physician's discretion)

Periodic testing of blood theophylline levels (see "Therapeutic Drug Monitoring," chapter 2). Time to sample blood for theophylline level: 2 hours after regular (standard) dose forms; 5 hours after sustained-release dose forms. Recommended therapeutic range: 10 to 20 mcg/ml.

▷ **While Taking This Drug, Observe the Following**

Foods: No restrictions.

Herbal Medicines or Minerals: Avoid using St. John's wort, ma huang, ephedrine-like compounds, kola, mate, guarana (principle active ingredient of guarana and mate is caffeine—and use should be avoided). The other listed products if taken while taking theophylline may result in increased sensation of jitteriness or nervousness (central nervous system stimulation). There is one case report of decreased removal (clearance) of theophylline from the body if it is combined with St. John's wort. Caution and more frequent testing of blood levels are prudent. Fir or pine needle oil should NOT be used by asthmatics. Ephedra alone does carry a German Commission E monograph indication for asthma treatment. If you are allergic to plants in the Asteraceae family (aster, chrysanthemum, daisy, or ragweed), you may also be allergic to echinacea, chamomile, feverfew, and St. John's wort. Ipriflavone can increase theophylline levels, requiring theophylline dosage adjustments. Talk to your doctor BEFORE adding any herbal medicine to theophylline.

Beverages: Avoid excessive use of caffeine-containing beverages: coffee, tea, cola, guarana, mate, or chocolate; this combination could cause nervousness and insomnia.

▷ *Alcohol:* Large doses may decrease removal by up to 30%. May have additive effect on stomach irritation.

Tobacco Smoking: May hasten the elimination of this drug and reduce its effectiveness. I advise everyone to quit smoking.

Marijuana Smoking: May hasten the elimination of this drug and reduce its effectiveness. Higher doses may be necessary to maintain a therapeutic blood level.

▷ *Other Drugs*

Theophylline may ***decrease*** the effects of
- adenosine (Adenocard).
- benzodiazepines (See Drug Classes).

- lithium (Lithane, Lithobid, etc.).
- zafirlukast (Accolate).

Theophylline *taken concurrently* with

- halothane (anesthesia) may cause heart rhythm abnormalities.
- phenytoin (Dilantin) may cause decreased effects of both drugs. Monitor blood levels and adjust doses as appropriate.
- tacrolimus (Prograf) may cause increased levels of tacrolimus—more frequent tacrolimus blood levels are prudent.

The following drugs may *increase* the effects of theophylline:

- allopurinol (Lopurin, Zyloprim).
- amiodarone (Cordarone).
- birth control pills (oral contraceptives—estrogens).
- capsaicin (Zostrix, others).
- cimetidine (Tagamet).
- clarithromycin (Biaxin) or azithromycin (Biaxin).
- corticosteroids (see Drug Classes).
- diltiazem (Cardizem).
- disulfiram (Antabuse).
- doxycycline and other tetracyclines.
- ephedrine (various).
- erythromycin (E-Mycin, Erythrocin, etc.).
- famotidine (Pepcid).
- flu vaccine (influenza vaccine).
- fluoroquinolone antibiotics such as ciprofloxacin (Cipro), enoxacin (Penetrex—greatest increase of roughly 50%), grepafloxacin (Raxar), norfloxacin (Noroxin), ofloxacin (Floxin), perfloxacin (Perflacine-France) and trovafloxacin (Trovan) because of their elimination by or effect on the P450 1A2 liver enzyme.
- fluvoxamine (Luvox).
- furosemide (Lasix).
- imipenem/cilastatin (Primaxin).
- interferon alfa-2A or 2B.
- ipriflavone (various).
- isoniazid (INH).
- methotrexate (Mexate).
- mexiletine (Mexitil).
- nicotine (Nicorette, Pro-Step, others).
- pentoxifylline (Trental).
- propafenone (Rythmol).
- ranitidine (Zantac).
- riluzole (Rilutek).
- sertraline (Zoloft).
- tacrine (Cognex).
- thiabendazole.
- ticlopidine (Ticlid).
- troleandomycin (TAO).
- verapamil (Calan, Verelan).
- viloxazine.
- zafirlukast (Accolate).
- zileuton (Zyflo)-may require 50% dose decreases.

The following drugs may *decrease* the effects of theophylline:

- barbiturates (phenobarbital, etc.).
- beta blockers (see Drug Classes).

- carbamazepine (Tegretol).
- isoproterenol.
- fosphenytoin (Cerebyx) or phenytoin (Dilantin).
- lansoprazole (Prevacid).
- primidone (Mysoline).
- rifampin (Rifadin, Rimactane, etc.).
- ritonavir (Norvir) and perhaps other protease inhibitors (see Drug Classes).
- sulfinpyrazone (Anturane).
- terbutaline (Brethine, others).

▷ *Driving, Hazardous Activities:* This drug may cause dizziness. Restrict activities as necessary.

Aviation Note: The use of this drug **may be a disqualification** for piloting. Consult a designated Aviation Medical Examiner.

Exposure to Sun: No restrictions.

Occurrence of Unrelated Illness: Sudden viral respiratory infections or fever may slow drug removal. Watch for signs of toxicity, as dosing must be changed if this occurs. More frequent blood levels are needed. Seizure disorders may be worsened by this medicine. Use with extreme caution by seizure patients. Theophylline used with extreme caution in active peptic ulcer disease or heart arrhythmias (cardiac, not including slow or bradyarrhythmias).

Discontinuation: Avoid prolonged or unnecessary use of this drug. When your asthma resolves, withdraw this drug gradually over several days.

THIAZIDE DIURETICS FAMILY

Bendroflumethiazide   (ben droh FLOO meh THI a zide)   **Chlorothiazide** (kloroh THI azide)   **Chlorthalidone**   (KLOR thal i dohn)   **Hydrochlorothiazide**   (hi droh klor oh THI a zide)   **Hydroflumethiazide**   (hi droh flu meh THI a zide) Methyclothiazide (METH i klo THI a zide)   **Metolazone** (me TOHL a zohn)   **Trichlormethiazide**   (tri klor me THI a zide)

Introduced   1960, 1957, 1960, 1959, 1961, 1959, 1974, 1962, respectively
Class   Antihypertensive, diuretic, thiazides   **Prescription**   USA: Yes
Controlled Drug: USA: No; Canada: No   **Available as Generic**   USA: Yes, hydrochlorothiazide and combination with triamterene and with bisoprolol also; Canada: Yes

Brand Names: *Bendroflumethiazide*: Naturetin, *Chlorothiazide*: Aldochlor [CD], Diachlor, Diupres [CD], Diurigen, Diuril, SK-Chlorothiazide, ♣Supres [CD], *Chlorthalidone*: ♣Apo-Chlorthalidone, Combipres [CD], Demi-Regroton [CD], Hygroton, ♣Hygroton-Resperine [CD], Hylidone, ♣Novothalidone, Regroton [CD], ♣Tenoretic[CD], Thalitone, ♣Uridon, *Hydrochlorothiazide*: Atacand HCT [CD], Aldactazide [CD], Aldoril D30/D50 [CD], Aldoril-15/25 [CD], ♣Apo-Amilzide, ♣Apo-Hydro, ♣Apo-Methazide [CD], ♣Apo-Triazide [CD], Apresazide [CD], Apresoline-Esidrix [CD], Avalide [CD], Capozide [CD], ♣Co-Betaloc [CD], Diaqua, ♣Diuchlor H, Dyazide [CD], Esidrex, Ezide, H-H-R, H.H.R., HydroDiuril, Hydromal, Hydro-Par, Hydropres [CD], Hydroserpine [CD], Hydroserpine Plus [CD], Hydro-T, Hydro-Z-50, Hyzaar [CD], Inderide [CD], Inderide LA [CD], ♣Ismelin-Esidrex [CD], Lopressor HCT [CD], Maxzide [CD], Maxzide-25 [CD], M Dopazide [CD], Microzide, Mictrin, ♣Moduret [CD], Moduretic

[CD], ♣Natrimax, ♣Neo-Codema, Normozide [CD], ♣Novo-Doparil [CD], ♣Novo-Hydrazide, ♣Novo-Spirozine [CD], ♣Novo-Triamzide [CD], Oretic, Oreticyl [CD], ♣PMS Dopazide [CD], Prinzide [CD], Ser-Ap-Es [CD], Serpasil-Esidrex [CD], SK-Hydrochlorothiazide, Thiuretic, Timolide [CD], Trandate HCT [CD], Unipres [CD], Uniretic [CD] ♣Urozide, Vaseretic [CD], ♣Viskazide [CD], Zestoretic [CD], Ziac [CD], Zide, *Hydroflumethiazide*: Diucardin, Saluron, *Methyclothiazide*: Aquatensen, ♣Duretic, Enduron, *Metolazone*: Diulo, Microx, Mykrox, Zaroxolyn, *Trichlormethiazide*: Diurese, Marazide II, Metahydrin, Naqua, Naquival [CD]

BENEFITS versus RISKS

Possible Benefits	*Possible Risks*
EFFECTIVE, WELL-TOLERATED DIURETICS	Loss of body potassium and magnesium (especially with higher doses)
POSSIBLY EFFECTIVE IN MILD HYPERTENSION	Cardiac arrhythmias caused by decreased electrolytes (studied in chlorthalidone and hydrochlorothiazide)
ENHANCES EFFECTIVENESS OF OTHER ANTIHYPERTENSIVES	
Beneficial in treatment of diabetes insipidus	Increased blood sugar, uric acid, or calcium
Helps build stronger bones and avoid fractures	Rare blood cell disorders
ALLHAT DATA SHOWED THAT CHLORTHALIDONE WAS BETTER THAN AMLODIPINE AT PREVENTING HEART FAILURE AND ALSO HELPED PREVENT MAJOR HEART ATTACK. CHLORTHALIDONE ALSO HELPED MORE THAN LISINOPRIL IN PREVENTING STROKE, HEART FAILURE, AND NEED FOR MEASURES TO OPEN HEART ARTERIES	Rare liver toxicity (chlorothiazide or hydrochlorothiazide)

▷ **Principal Uses**

As a Single Drug Product: Uses currently included in FDA-approved labeling: (1) Increases the volume of urine (diuresis) to correct fluid retention (edema) seen in congestive heart failure, corticosteroid or estrogen use, and certain types of liver and kidney disease; (2) starting therapy for high blood pressure (hypertension—non-combination forms).

Author's Note: One large study showed that hydrochlorothiazide achieves benefits (outcomes) in decreasing left ventricular size equal to more expensive agents, such as ACE inhibitors. A review of ten studies found that diuretics versus beta blockers should be the first-line medicines for treating high blood pressure in the elderly. The new JNC VII also recommends diuretics as first-line medicines (compelling reasons may modify this).

Other (unlabeled) generally accepted uses: (1) Prevention of kidney stones that contain calcium; (2) may help decrease the frequency of hip fractures in the elderly; (3) methyclothiazide has been used to help maintain blood calcium levels in Paget's disease; (4) may have a role in helping prevent osteoporosis (by correcting abnormally high elimination of calcium in the urine or hypercalciuria); (5) used in diabetes insipidus (nephrogenic) in decreasing the urine volume.

As Combination Drug Products [CD]: Used to treat blood pressure that has not responded to single-drug therapy by combining beta blockers, ACE inhibitors, or angiotensin II receptor blockers with this diuretic.

How These Drugs Work: By increasing removal of salt and water in the urine, these drugs reduce fluid volume and body sodium. They also relax walls of smaller arteries. The combined effect of these two actions (reduced blood volume in expanded space) lowers blood pressure. May also have a role in increasing a prostaglandin that the kidney makes.

Available Dosage Forms and Strengths
Bendroflumethiazide:
Tablets — 5 mg, 10 mg
Chlorothiazide:
Injection — 500 mg/20 ml
Oral suspension — 250 mg/5 ml
Tablets — 250 mg, 500 mg
Chlorthalidone:
Tablets — 15 mg, 25 mg, 50 mg, 100 mg
Chlorthalidone combinations:
Tablets — 25 mg chlorthalidone, 50 mg atenolol (Tenoretic)
Hydrochlorothiazide:
Solution — 50 mg/5 ml
Solution, intensol — 100 mg/ml
Tablets — 12.5 mg, 25 mg, 50 mg, 100 mg
Hydrochlorothiazide combinations:
Bisoprolol and hydrochlorothiazide — 2.5 mg/6.25 mg, 5 mg/6.25 mg, 10 mg/6.25 mg
Candesartan and hydrochlorothiazide — 16 mg/12.5 mg, 32 mg/12.5 mg
Losartan and hydrochlorothiazide — 50 mg/12.5 mg, 100 mg/12.5 mg
Methyclothiazide:
Tablets — 2.5 mg, 5 mg
Metolazone:
Tablets — 0.5 mg, 2.5 mg, 5 mg, 10 mg
Trichlormethiazide:
Tablets — 2 mg, 4 mg

▷ **Usual Adult Dosage Ranges:** *Bendroflumethiazide:* As antihypertensive—12.5 to 5 mg daily, in a single dose.

Chlorothiazide: As antihypertensive—500 to 1,000 mg per day to start, and 500 to 2,000 mg daily as a maintenance dose. As a diuretic—500 to 2,000 mg per day, using the smallest effective dose. Daily maximum is 2,000 mg.

Chlorthalidone: As antihypertensive—15 mg as a starting dose, then increased as needed and tolerated in 15 mg steps to 30 mg daily, and then up to 45 mg daily if needed. Some other forms are only available in 25 mg increments and are started as a half of one tablet to one tablet. As a diuretic—30 to 60 mg daily and then the smallest effective dose is used (maintenance dose). Some clinicians use 60 mg every other day. Some patients have required 120 mg daily.

Hydrochlorothiazide: As antihypertensive—12.5 to 100 mg daily initially; 12.5 to 200 mg daily for maintenance. As diuretic—variable; 12.5 to 200 mg daily. Many patients require 100–200 mg; the smallest effective dose should be determined (see CAUTION below). The total daily dose should not exceed 200 mg. Microzide is a once-daily formulation (12.5 mg) of this medicine. Combination forms are started using the lowest dose combination form and then are increased as needed and tolerated.

Author's Note: Many patients with mild to moderate high blood pressure get acceptable blood-pressure-lowering results from 12.5 mg of hydrochlorothiazide or 15 mg of chlorthalidone. If results are obtained with this dose, it can minimize loss of potassium and magnesium as well!

Methyclothiazide: As antihypertensive or diuretic—2.5 to 5 mg daily. Maximum daily diuretic dose is 10 mg. Pediatric dose—0.05 to 0.2 mg per kg of body mass daily.

Trichlormethiazide: As antihypertensive or diuretic—therapy may be started with 1 to 4 mg twice daily. Usual maintenance dose is 1 to 4 mg once daily.

Note: Actual dose and schedule must be determined for each patient individually.

Conditions Requiring Dosing Adjustments

Liver Function: Electrolyte balance is critical in liver failure. These drugs may precipitate encephalopathy. Hydrochlorothiazide and chlorothiazide are also a rare cause of cholestatic jaundice and should be used with caution in liver failure.

Kidney Function: These drugs can be used with caution by patients with mild kidney failure and are not effective for patients with moderate failure. They should not be used in severe kidney failure; they can be a rare cause of kidney damage.

▷ **Dosing Instructions:** The tablets may be crushed and taken with or following meals to reduce stomach irritation. For liquid forms, dosing should be accomplished using a calibrated dosing spoon or dose cup. Suspensions should be well shaken BEFORE EACH dose. All forms are best taken in the morning to avoid nighttime urination. If you forget a dose: Take the missed dose as soon as you remember it, unless it's nearly time for your next dose—if that is the case, skip the missed dose and take the next dose right on schedule. DO NOT double up on doses. Talk with your doctor if you find yourself missing doses because the best results come from keeping your blood pressure under tight control.

Usual Duration of Use: Regular use for up to 4 weeks determines full benefits in lowering high blood pressure. Long-term use requires follow-up with your doctor. If goals for blood pressure are not met, dose increases, combination treatment or changing medicines is appropriate. Take control of blood pressure for life.

Typical Treatment Goals and Measurements (Outcomes and Markers)

Blood Pressure: The NEW guidelines (JNC VII) define normal blood pressure (BP) as **less than** 120/80. Because blood pressures that were once considered acceptable can actually lead to blood vessel damage, the committee from the National Institutes of Health's National Heart, Lung, and Blood Institute now have a new category called **Pre-hypertension**. This ranges from 120/80 to 139/89 and is intended to help your doctor encourage lifestyle changes (or in the case of people with a risk factor for high blood pressure, start treatment) much earlier—so that possible damage to blood vessels, your heart, kidneys, sexual potency, or eyes might be minimized or avoided altogether. The next two classes of high blood pressure are stage 1 hypertension: 140/90 to 159/99 and stage 2 hypertension equal to or greater than: 160/100 mm Hg. These guidelines also recommend that clinicians trying to control blood pressure work with their patients to agree on the goals and a plan of treatment. The first-ever guidelines for blood pressure (hypertension) in African Americans recommends that MOST black patients be started on TWO antihypertensive medicines with the goal of lowering blood pressure to 130/80 for those with high risk for heart and blood vessel disease or with diabetes. The American Diabetes Association recommends 130/80 as the target for people living with diabetes and less than 125/75 for those who spill more than one gram of protein into their urine. Most clinicians try to achieve a BP that confers the best balance of lower cardiovascular risk and avoids the problem of too low a blood pressure. Blood pressure duration is generally increased with beneficial restriction of sodium. The goals and time frame should be discussed with you when the prescription is written. If goals are not met, it is not unusual to intensify doses or add on medicines. You can find the new blood pressure guidelines at *www.nhlbi.nih.gov/guidelines/hypertension/index.htm*. For the African American guidelines see Douglas J.G. in Sources.

Possible Advantages of These Drugs

Hydrochlorothiazide was studied in more than 1,100 Veterans Administration patients with mild to moderate high blood pressure. It was found to have met blood pressure reduction goals while offering decreased left ventricular mass. These outcomes or results were accomplished using low-dose therapy, avoiding many of the undesirable changes in blood chemistry that can be seen with higher doses. This was also accomplished at a fraction of the direct cost of ACE inhibitors or calcium channel blockers. Results from ALLHAT (NHLBI study) also show equal results (efficacy) in blood pressure lowering by chlorthalidone versus two non-diuretics— (an ACE inhibitor (lisinopril) and calcium channel blocker (amlodipine). Consideration must be given to the expense of laboratory monitoring required when using these medicines. Diuretics (basd on individual clinical considerations) are drugs of first choice for African Americans with high blood pressure versus prior preference given to calcium channel blockers.

▷ **These Drugs Should Not Be Taken If**

- you had an allergic reaction to any form of them previously or are allergic to sulfonamides (chlorthalidone).
- your kidneys are not making urine.

▷ **Inform Your Physician Before Taking These Drugs If**

- you are allergic to any form of sulfa drug.
- you are pregnant or planning pregnancy.
- you have a history of kidney or liver disease.
- you have a history of pancreatitis or lupus erythematosus.
- you have developed swelling (angioedema) of the tongue, face, or throat (medicine should be stopped).
- you have asthma or allergies to other medicines.
- you have had testing of electrolytes ordered by another physician, which your doctor has not seen.
- you develop muscle cramps, weakness, or abnormal heartbeats while taking one of these medicines.
- you have diabetes, gout, or lupus erythematosus.
- you are allergic to the dye tartrazine, as some of these medicines contain it.

- you take any form of cortisone, digitalis, oral antidiabetic drug, or insulin.
- you will have surgery with general anesthesia.

Possible Side Effects (natural, expected, and unavoidable drug actions)

Light-headedness on arising from sitting or lying position (see Orthostatic Hypotension in Glossary). Increased blood sugar or uric acid level; decreased blood potassium, zinc, or magnesium level. Decreased blood magnesium, combined with loss of potassium, may lead to increased risk of sudden cardiac death (high doses for extended periods).

▷ **Possible Adverse Effects** (unusual, unexpected, and infrequent reactions)

If any of the following develop, consult your physician promptly for guidance.

Mild Adverse Effects

Allergic reactions: skin rashes, hives, drug fever (see Glossary).

Muscle aches—case report.

Headache, dizziness, blurred or yellow vision—infrequent.

Reduced appetite, indigestion, nausea, vomiting, diarrhea—infrequent.

Serious Adverse Effects

Allergic reactions: hepatitis with jaundice (see Glossary), anaphylactic reaction (see Glossary), severe skin reactions.

Inflammation of the pancreas—case reports.

Bone marrow depression (see Glossary): fever, sore throat, abnormal bleeding/bruising—case reports.

Data from studies of hydrochlorothiazide and chlorthalidone suggest that potassium and magnesium loss associated with higher-dose therapy increases the risk of sudden cardiac death.

Acute gout in some patients (because these medicines decrease uric acid removal).

Loss of blood glucose control—possible.

Short-term (less than 1 year) increase in serum lipids (returns to pretreatment levels in about 1 year).

▷ **Possible Effects on Sexual Function:** Decreased libido (hydrochlorothiazide, chlorthalidone); impotence (bendroflumethiazide, chlorothiazide, hydrochlorothiazide, chlorthalidone)—case reports.

▷ **Adverse Effects That May Mimic Natural Diseases or Disorders**

Liver reaction may suggest viral hepatitis.

Natural Diseases or Disorders That May Be Activated by These Drugs

Diabetes, gout, systemic lupus erythematosus. Those with asthma or drug allergies are more likely to have allergic reactions.

Possible Effects on Laboratory Tests

Complete blood counts: decreased red cells, hemoglobin, white cells, and platelets.

Blood amylase level: increased (possible pancreatitis).

Blood calcium or uric acid level: increased.

Blood sodium and chloride levels: decreased.

Blood cholesterol and triglyceride levels: increased, short term.

Blood glucose level: increased.

Glucose tolerance test (GTT): decreased.

Blood lithium level: increased.

Blood potassium and magnesium level: decreased.

Blood urea nitrogen (BUN) level: increased with long-term use.

Liver function tests (hydrochlorothiazide and chlorothiazide): increased liver enzymes (ALT/GPT, AST/GOT, and alkaline phosphatase), increased bilirubin.

CAUTION
1. One study found a strong association between higher doses of hydrochlorothiazide and chlorthalidone and combination drugs containing these diuretics and electrolyte loss and sudden cardiac death. This appeared to be a result of magnesium and potassium loss and may be circumvented by close following of those electrolytes. Electrolytes should be closely followed.
2. Take these exactly as prescribed. Excessive loss of sodium and potassium can lead to loss of appetite, nausea, fatigue, weakness, confusion, and tingling in the extremities.
3. If you take digitalis (digitoxin, digoxin), adequate potassium is critical. Periodic testing and high-potassium foods may be needed to prevent potassium deficiency—a potential cause of digitalis toxicity (see Table 13, High-Potassium Foods, Section Six).

Precautions for Use
By Infants and Children: Overdose could cause serious dehydration. Significant potassium loss can occur within the first 2 weeks of drug use.
By Those Over 60 Years of Age: Starting doses may be as low as 12.5 mg or 15 mg for chlorthalidone. Increased risk of impaired thinking, orthostatic hypotension, potassium loss, and blood sugar increase. Overdose or extended use can cause excessive loss of body water, thickening (increased viscosity) of blood and increased tendency for the blood to clot—predisposing to stroke, heart attack, or thrombophlebitis (vein inflammation with blood clot).

▷ **Advisability of Use During Pregnancy**
Pregnancy Category: Metolazone: B by manufacturer, D by other researchers. Thalitone is B by the manufacturer, but D by one researcher. All other thiazides in this class are D. See Pregnancy Risk Categories at the back of this book. Some combination forms are C during the first trimester and D during the second and third trimesters.
Animal Studies: No birth defects found in rat studies.
Human Studies: Reports are conflicting and inconclusive.
Use of thiazides can cause maternal complications that may cause adverse fetal effects, including death. They should not be used in pregnancy unless a very serious complication occurs for which these drugs work. Ask your doctor for guidance.

Advisability of Use If Breast-Feeding
Presence of these drugs in breast milk: Yes.
Avoid drugs or refrain from nursing.

Habit-Forming Potential: None.

Effects of Overdose: Dry mouth, thirst, lethargy, weakness, muscle cramping, nausea, vomiting, drowsiness progressing to stupor or coma.

Possible Effects of Long-Term Use: Impaired balance of water, salt, magnesium, and potassium in blood and body tissues. Impaired tolerance of glucose. Pathological changes in parathyroid glands with increased blood calcium levels and decreased blood phosphate levels.

Suggested Periodic Examinations While Taking These Drugs (at physician's discretion)
Complete blood cell counts.

Measurements of blood levels of sodium, potassium, chloride, magnesium, sugar, and uric acid.

Kidney and liver function tests.

Repeat bone mineral density test (two years after starting therapy) if this drug is used to decrease calcium loss.

▷ **While Taking These Drugs, Observe the Following**

Foods: Ask your doctor if you need to eat foods rich in potassium. See Table 13, High-Potassium Foods, Section Six, if needed. Follow your physician's advice regarding the use of salt.

Herbal Medicines or Minerals: Ginseng and ginkgo may increase blood pressure, blunting the benefits of these medicines. Hawthorn, saw palmetto, ma huang, mate, guarana, and licorice may also cause increased blood pressure. Licorice can also cause potassium loss and is especially NOT to be combined with a thiazide. Indian snakeroot has a German Commission E monograph indication for hypertension, but has not been studied with thiazides. Eleuthero root and ephedra should be avoided by people living with hypertension. Calcium and garlic may lower blood pressure. Use caution and work with your doctor to make sure blood pressure is not lowered too much. Calcium may also accumulate to a greater degree than expected since thiazides decrease removal of calcium in the urine. Because St. John's wort and some of these medicines may increase sun sensitivity, the combination is NOT advised. Talk to your doctor BEFORE combining any herbal medicine with these medicines. Diuretics are well known for depleting magnesium, zinc, and potassium. These minerals should be routinely checked and supplemented if the medicines have lowered blood mineral levels.

Beverages: No restrictions. This drug may be taken with milk.

▷ *Alcohol:* Use with caution—alcohol may exaggerate the blood-pressure-lowering effects of these drugs and cause orthostatic hypotension.

Tobacco Smoking: No interactions expected. I advise everyone to quit smoking.

▷ *Other Drugs*

These drugs may ***increase*** the effects of

- other antihypertensive drugs; dose adjustments may be necessary to prevent excessive lowering of blood pressure (may also be used to combination therapy benefit).
- fluconazole (Diflucan) (HCTZ report).
- lithium (Lithobid, others) and cause lithium toxicity.

These drugs may ***decrease*** the effects of

- oral anticoagulants such as warfarin (Coumadin); increased frequency of INR (prothrombin time) testing is needed.
- oral antidiabetic drugs (sulfonylureas—see Drug Classes and others); dose adjustments may be needed for better blood sugar control.

These drugs ***taken concurrently*** with

- allopurinol (Zyloprim) may decrease kidney function.
- amphotericin B (Abelcet, Fungizone) may result in additive potassium loss; increased frequency of laboratory testing is needed.
- calcium may result in the milk-alkali syndrome with increased calcium, alkalosis, and kidney failure.
- carbamazepine (Tegretol) may result in low sodium levels and symptomatic hyponatremia.
- cortisone or other corticosteroid medicines may result in excessive potassium loss with resultant heart rhythm changes and lethargy.
- cyclophosphamide (Cytoxan) may increase immunosuppression.

- digitalis preparations (digitoxin, digoxin) require careful monitoring and dose changes to prevent low potassium levels and serious disturbances of heart rhythm.
- methotrexate (Mexate) may increase immunosuppression.
- nonsteroidal anti-inflammatory drugs (see Drug Classes), such as sulindac (Clinoril) and naproxen (Naprosyn, Aleve, Anaprox, others), may result in decreased thiazide effectiveness.
- probenecid (various) may result in increased thiazide blood levels. Checks of thiazide response are prudent.

The following drugs may *decrease* the effects of these thiazides:
- cholestyramine (Cuemid, Questran)—may interfere with their absorption.
- colestipol (Colestid)—may interfere with their absorption.

Take cholestyramine and colestipol 1 hour before any oral diuretic.

▷ *Driving, Hazardous Activities:* Use caution until the possible occurrence of orthostatic hypotension, dizziness, or impaired vision has been determined.

Aviation Note: The use of these drugs *may be a disqualification* for piloting. Consult a designated Aviation Medical Examiner.

Exposure to Sun: These drugs can cause photosensitivity (see Glossary). Use caution until sensitivity has been determined.

Exposure to Heat: **Caution**—excessive perspiring could cause additional loss of salt and water from the body.

Heavy Exercise or Exertion: Avoid exertion that produces light-headedness, excessive fatigue, or muscle cramping. Isometric exercises can raise blood pressure significantly. Ask your doctor for help regarding participation in this form of exercise.

Occurrence of Unrelated Illness: Vomiting or diarrhea can produce a serious imbalance of important body chemistry. Ask your doctor for help.

Discontinuation: These drugs should not be stopped abruptly following long-term use; sudden discontinuation can cause serious thiazide-withdrawal fluid retention (edema). The dose should be reduced gradually. It may be advisable to discontinue this drug 5 to 7 days before major surgery. Ask your physician, surgeon, and/or anesthesiologist for guidance.

THIAZOLIDINEDIONE FAMILY
(THIGH ah zoh li dean die ohn)

Rosiglitazone (ROSS ih glit a zoan)   **Pioglitazone** (PEE oh glit a zoan)

Introduced: 1999, 1999   **Class:** Antidiabetic, thiazolidinedione   **Prescription:** USA: Yes   **Controlled Drug:** USA: No; Canada: No   **Available as Generic:** No

Brand Name: *Rosiglitazone:* Avandamet [CD], Avandia, *Pioglitazone:* Actos

Author's Note: The FDA required modifying the warnings, precautions, and adverse reactions section of the labels for both Actos and Avandia. Health care professionals were alerted to the fact that either medicine can lead to fluid retention when used alone or when combined with insulin. Cases of congestive heart failure (CHF) have been reported, and were more likely in people who had diabetes for a longer amount of time, had pre-existing medical conditions (such as ichemic heart disease, CHF, and vascular disease), took higher doses of the medicine, and were older. What

this means is that people taking these medicines should be watched for signs and symptoms of heart failure (see cautions below).

BENEFITS versus RISKS

Possible Benefits	*Possible Risks*
COMBINATION USE OF ROSIGLITAZONE OR PIOGLITAZONE WITH METFORMIN MAY SLOW DIABETES PROGRESSION AS WELL AS HELP AVOID LONG-TERM COMPLICATIONS OF DIABETES ITSELF	FLUID RETENTION (CHF—see NEW CAUTION)
	Low blood sugar (possible)
	Worsening of existing heart failure
	Case reports of both medicines and heart failure (because of fluid retention)
DECREASED INSULIN RESISTANCE	
EFFECTIVE CONTROL OF BLOOD SUGAR (GLUCOSE)	
POSSIBLE AVOIDANCE OF LONG-TERM EFFECTS (BLOOD VESSEL, NERVE, KIDNEY, HIGH BLOOD PRESSURE, AND HEART ADVERSE EFFECTS) FROM DIABETES	
FAVORABLE SIDE EFFECT PRO-FILES VERSUS TROGLITAZONE	
ROSIGLITAZONE AVOIDS CYP3A4 ELIMINATION OF PIOGLITAZONE (uses CYP2C8 and has fewer potential drug-drug interactions)	
May have a role in some kinds of infertility where insulin resistance may be part of the problem (such as polycystic ovary syndrome or PCOS)	

▷ **Principal Uses**

As a Single Drug Product: Uses currently included in FDA-approved labeling: (1) Helps control Type 2 diabetes mellitus (adult, maturity-onset); (2) helps people who have not responded to diet alone or to a maximum dose of metformin (Glucophage); (3) either medicine can be used in combination with metformin, a sulfonylurea or insulin; (4) rosiglitasone available combined with metformin in a single pill.

Other (unlabeled) generally accepted uses: (1) may help improve resistance to insulin and may help some patients with syndromes such as Werner syndrome or PCOS where insulin resistance is part of the problem; (2) rosiglitazone may be effective if used with a sulfonylurea.

How These Drugs Work: Work to make insulin more effective (decrease cellular resistance as a peroxisome proliferator activated receptor gamma activator—PPAR gamma). This increases the number of GLUT-4 transporters. Probably also work to decrease local and systemic lipid availability. New data presented at The American Diabetes Association 63rd scientific sessions appear to show that rosiglitasone has an effect in decreasing repeat blockage of stents which have been implanted in patients with coronary artery blockages (see Choi in Sources). This implies that rosiglitasone has an anti-inflammatory effect.

Available Dosage Forms and Strengths

Rosiglitazone:
Tablets — 1 mg (Canada), 2 mg, 4 mg, 8 mg
Pioglitazone:
Tablets — 15 mg, 30 mg, and 45 mg

▷ **Usual Adult Dosage Ranges**

Rosiglitazone: Used alone (monotherapy): Initially 4 mg once daily or separated into two 2 mg given twice daily. The dose may be increased, if needed and tolerated, after 12 weeks to 4 mg twice daily or 8 mg once daily.

Combined with metformin: Same as monotherapy.

Combined with insulin: 4 mg daily which is also the maximum dose. If excessive lowering of the sugar (glucose) happens (less than 100 mg/deciliter), insulin dosing is decreased by 10–25% AND subsequently further adjusted to blood sugar response.

Pioglitazone: Used alone in Type 2 diabetes, the starting dose is 15 or 30 mg once a day. If the response is not at target, the dose may be slowly increased to 45 mg once a day.

Combined with insulin: The starting dose is 15 or 30 mg once a day. Once pioglitazone is started, if low blood sugar (hypoglycemia) happens or if plasma sugar (glucose) is 100 mg/deciliter or less, the dose of insulin should be lowered by 10 to 25%. Close patient follow up for signs and symptoms of heart failure are needed. If this medicine is combined with metformin, the prior metformin dose can be continued as hypoglycemia is unlikely.

Combined with a sulfonylurea: 15 or 30 mg once daily is used. The sulfonylurea dose will have to be decreased if hypoglycemia occurs.

Note: Actual dose and schedule must be determined for each patient individually.

Conditions Requiring Dosing Adjustments

Liver Function:

Rosiglitazone: Should NOT be started if there is active liver disease or if ALT is more than 2.5 times the upper normal limit. In mild to moderate liver disease, rosiglitazone blood levels and the time rosiglitazone stays in the body increase. Decreases in dose or increases in dosing interval are required.

Pioglitazone: Should NOT be used in people with increased liver enzymes (transaminases such as an alanine aminotransferase more than 2.5 times the upper normal) or in patients with clinical signs/symptoms/evidence of active liver disease.

Kidney Function:

Rosiglitazone or pioglitazone: Dosing changes are probably not needed in kidney compromise.

▷ **Dosing Instructions:** May be taken with or without food. Skipping meals while taking these medicines is NOT advised, as the medicine will still continue to increase insulin sensitivity even if the sugar (glucose) from a meal is not there—making hypoglycemia more likely. The tablets may be crushed to make it easier to take. If you are taking these medicines with the maximum dose of metformin, lower ongoing doses of rosiglitazone or pioglitazone may be effective for you. If you are taking these medicines with a sulfonylurea and low blood sugar occurs, the sulfonylurea dose will have to be decreased. If you develop signs and symptoms of heart failure (swelling of the ankles, shortness of breath, etc.), call your doctor. If you forget a dose: Take the missed dose as soon as you remember it, unless it's nearly time for your next dose—if that is the case, skip the missed dose and take the next dose right on schedule. DO NOT double doses. Talk with your doctor if you find yourself missing doses. Taking these medicines the right way and keeping blood sugar in tight control gets the best long-term results.

Usual Duration of Use: Use on a regular schedule for 12 weeks usually determines peak effectiveness in controlling diabetes for rosiglitazone. Benefits for both medicines as checked by hemoglobin A1C (glycosylated hemoglobin) or charts of sugar patterns in your glucose meter. Insulin resistance may require longer therapy. Failure to respond after the 12-week period requires a dose increase for rosiglitazone and failure to respond after an acceptable period for pioglitazone also requires a dose increase. Effective use can only be determined by periodic measurement of the blood sugar. See your doctor on a regular basis.

Typical Treatment Goals and Measurements (Outcomes and Markers)

Blood sugar: The general goal for blood sugar is to return it to the usual "normal" range (generally 80–120 mg/dl), while avoiding risks of excessively low blood sugar. One study (the United Kingdom Prospective Diabetes Study or UKPDS) used a fasting plasma sugar (glucose) of less than 108 mg/dl. The Diabetes Control and Complications Trial (DCCT) attempted to achieve near normal glycosylated hemoglobin and found reduced undesirable small blood vessel (microvascular) changes. Using glycosylated hemoglobin as a marker or resolution of insulin resistance will require a longer time period to response than blood sugar.

Fructosamine and glycosylated hemoglobin: Fructosamine levels (a measure of the past 2 to 3 weeks of blood sugar control) should be less than or equal to 310 micromoles per liter. Glycosylated hemoglobin or hemoglobin A1C (a measure of the past 2–3 months of blood sugar control) should be less than or equal to 7.0%. Some clinicians now advocate 6.5% or lower as a target in order to help avoid diabetes complications. Work with your doctor to get the best individualized results and make certain you know the signs and symptoms of hypoglycemia and what to do about them if hypoglycemia occurs.

Possible Advantages of These Drugs

Offer a novel mechanism of action. Appear to avoid the liver damage potential of troglitazone. Rosiglitazone does not use the CYP3A4 enzyme (a more widely used enzyme) for removal from the body (uses CYP2C8) and therefore has fewer potential drug-drug interactions than pioglitazone (which uses both). Pioglitazone may have a more favorable effect on good and bad cholesterol. Rosiglitazone has new data that shows it helps avoid repeat clogging (restenosis) of stents placed in patients with blockages in their coronary arteries.

▷ **These Drugs Should Not Be Taken If**
- you have had an allergic reaction to them previously.
- you have active liver disease or if ALT (ask your doctor) is more than 2.5 times the upper normal limit.
- you have Type 1 diabetes (monotherapy) or are in ketoacidosis.

▷ **Inform Your Physician Before Taking This Drug If**
- you are over 60 years old.
- your diabetes has been unstable or brittle in the past.
- you are pregnant or have been unable to ovulate (both drugs may cause

ovulation to restart in premenopausal women with insulin resistance who previously did not ovulate. Adequate contraception will be needed.

- you do not know how to recognize or treat hypoglycemia (see Glossary).
- you have an infection and a fever.
- you have a deficiency of red blood cells (anemia)—ask your doctor.
- you have liver or kidney damage.
- you have NYHA class III or IV heart failure.
- you have or develop an accumulation of fluid in your body (edema).
- you are nursing your child.
- you develop an unusually quick increase in weight or swelling of the legs or shortness of breath (possible signs and symptoms of heart failure). **Call your doctor immediately if this occurs.**

Possible Side Effects (natural, expected, and unavoidable drug actions)

If drug dose is excessive or food intake is delayed or inadequate, abnormally low blood sugar (hypoglycemia) may occur. Fluid accumulation—increasing risk of heart failure.

▷ **Possible Adverse Effects** (unusual, unexpected, and infrequent reactions)

If any of the following develop, consult your physician promptly for guidance.

Mild Adverse Effects

Allergic reactions: not reported—rare.

Headache—infrequent.

Hypoglycemia—possible.

Weight gain—possible.

Muscle aches—infrequent (pioglitazone).

Fluid retention (edema)—infrequent.

Increased liver enzymes—very rare (happened within the first two weeks of treatment).

Diarrhea—rare.

Serious Adverse Effects

Allergic reactions: not reported.

Idiosyncratic reactions: not reported.

Congestive heart failure or worsening of existing heart failure—possible (due to increased retention of body fluid. Either drug alone or in combination of Actos (pioglitazone) with insulin can cause this. If you have an unusually quick weight increase, swelling of the legs or ankles or unexplained shortness of breath (possible signs or symptoms of heart failure)—**Call your doctor immediately.**

Retinopathy aggravation—case report (pioglitazone).

Hypoglycemia—possible.

Anemia—possible—usually mild.

Liver toxicity—very rare.

▷ **Possible Effects on Sexual Function:** If insulin resistance has been a cause of infertility, these drugs may enable you to become fertile.

▷ **Adverse Effects That May Mimic Natural Diseases or Disorders**

Fluid accumulation may mimic edema from congestive heart failure.

Natural Diseases or Disorders That May Be Activated by This Drug

Increased fluid in the body (plasma volume expansion) may worsen congestive heart failure.

Possible Effects on Laboratory Tests

Complete blood cell count: decreased red cells, hemoglobin, and hematocrit—mild.

Blood glucose, fructosamine, or glycosylated hemoglobin level: decreased.

Liver function tests (ALT): possibly increased.

LDL: increased by up to 19% for rosiglitazone (inconsistent change for pioglitazone).

Total cholesterol: increased.

HDL: increased (beneficial effect) by up to 14% for rosiglitazone and 19% for pioglitazone.

CAUTION

1. These drugs must be regarded as only one part of the total program for the management of your diabetes. It is not a substitute for a properly prescribed diet, insulin, and regular exercise.
2. A similar medicine caused serious liver reactions. While these medicines HAVE NOT caused such reactions, liver enzyme testing is required.
3. These drugs may cause you to ovulate if insulin resistance has been the cause of a failure to ovulate.
4. If you develop shortness of breath, unusually quick weight gain, or swelling of the ankles or any other signs or symptoms of heart failure— **call your doctor immediately.**
5. The American Diabetic Association (ADA) now says that a person is considered diabetic if two fasting blood sugars in a row are more than 125 mg/dl. This more conservative approach reflects new information saying that complications start at lower blood sugar levels than previously thought. The concept of Pre-diabetes (formerly impaired glucose tolerance) is described in the Glossary. Some new British data advocated that statin type medicines could cut the risk of heart attack and stroke by a third (even in people with normal cholesterol)—yet these medicines are underused in diabetics. Talk to your doctor about this.

Precautions for Use

By Infants and Children: Safety and efficacy have not been established in this age group.

By Those Over 65 Years of Age: Any medicine with the potential to lower blood sugar should be used with caution in this age group and monitored closely to prevent hypoglycemic reactions. Repeated episodes of hypoglycemia in the elderly can cause brain damage. Clinical trials did not reveal differences in safety or effectiveness in those over 65 for either medicine. Because older people are more likely to have heart problems, patients should be aware of signs and symptoms (such as shortness of breath and quick weight gain) as possible drug-induced accumulation of fluid and possible heart failure.

▷ **Advisability of Use During Pregnancy**

Pregnancy Category: C (both medicines). See Pregnancy Risk Categories at the back of this book.

Animal Studies: Rosiglitazone in treated rats and rabbits (during mid-late gestation) showed growth retardation and was associated with fetal death. Pioglitazone in treated rats and rabbits showed delayed parturition and embryotoxicity at high doses.

Human Studies: Adequate studies of pregnant women are not available for either medicine.

Because uncontrolled blood sugar levels during pregnancy are associated with a higher incidence of birth defects, many experts recommend that insulin (instead of an oral agent) be used as necessary to control diabetes during the entire pregnancy.

Advisability of Use If Breast-Feeding

Presence of this drug in breast milk: Yes for rosiglitazone, unknown for pioglitazone.

Avoid drug or refrain from nursing.

Habit-Forming Potential: None.

Effects of Overdose: Limited experience is available for both medicines. Single doses of rosiglitazone of 20 mg by mouth were well tolerated. One pioglitazone patient took 180 mg for seven days without any reported ill effects. If an overdose occurs of either drug, supportive treatment consistent with the patient's signs and symptoms should be provided.

Possible Effects of Long-Term Use: Normalization of fructosamine, hemoglobin A1C, decreased LDL, increased HDL. Pioglitazone may have a more favorable effect on good and bad cholesterol.

Suggested Periodic Examinations While Taking This Drug (at physician's discretion)

Complete blood cell counts.

Liver function (serum transaminases) must be tested at the beginning of treatment, every two months for the first year, and then periodically thereafter. If signs or symptoms of liver problems (light stools, yellow eyes or skin, etc.) begin, serum transaminases should be measured.

Follow-up tests (such as finger stick testing) of blood sugar.

Fructosamine (now available as a finger stick self-test).

Glycosylated hemoglobin.

HDL and LDL and fractions.

Checks for decline in heart status, edema, or congestive heart failure. Drugs should be discontinued if decline in cardiac status happens.

▷ **While Taking These Drugs, Observe the Following**

Foods: Follow the diabetic diet prescribed by your physician. Rice bran has been checked in a small (57 subject) study of type 1 and type 2 diabetics. The benefit was a 30% lowering of sugar. This might be a new complementary care option.

Herbal Medicines or Minerals: Using chromium may change the way your body is able to use sugar. Some health food stores advocate vanadium as mimicking the actions of insulin, but possible toxicity and need for rigorous studies presently preclude recommending it. Caution: St. John's wort may change blood sugar. DHEA may change sensitivity to insulin or insulin resistance. Aloe, fenugreek, bitter melon, eucalyptus, hawthorn, ginger, garlic, ginseng, guar gum, glucomannan, licorice, nettle, and yohimbe may change blood sugar. Since this may require adjustment of hypoglycemic medicine dosing, talk to your doctor BEFORE combining any of these herbal medicines with this medicine. Echinacea pupurea (injectable) and blonde psyllium seed or husk should NOT be taken by people living with diabetes. Psyllium increases risk of excessively low blood sugar. Surprisingly, boiled stems of the Optuntia streptacantha prickly pear cactus appears to be able to lower blood sugar. Ongoing effects and effects on A1C are not known. Red sage is used for blood sugar effects, but is unproven.

Beverages: As directed in the diabetic diet. May be taken with milk.

▷ *Alcohol:* Single doses did not increase risk of sudden lowering of blood sugar (hypoglycemia). Use with caution. Repeated or large doses of alcohol can lower blood sugar, and chronic high doses can impact liver function.

Tobacco Smoking: No interaction expected. I advise everyone to quit smoking.

▷   *Other Drugs*
The following drugs may ***decrease*** the effects of rosiglitazone:
- beta blocker (see drug classes).
- cholestyramine (Questran).
- corticosteroids (see Drug Classes).
- thiazide diuretics (see Drug Classes).

These medicines ***taken concurrently*** with
- birth control pills (oral contraceptives) lead to loss of control with one medicine in this same class. Pills containing ethinyl estradiol or norethindrone may not work with pioglitazone.
- medicines metabolized by CYP2C8 or decreasing this enzyme may increase blood levels of rosiglitazone.
- medicines that increase levels of CYP2C8 may decrease the effects of rosiglitazone.
- medicines metabolized by CYP3A4 or inhibiting this enzyme (such as many macrolide antibiotics, azole antifungals, protease inhibitors, and zafirlukast or zileuton) may increase blood levels of pioglitazone.
- medicines that increase levels of CYP3A4 (such as carbamazepine, fosphenytoin, phenytoin, rifampin, or dexamethasone) may decrease the effects of pioglitazone.
- protease inhibitors (PIs—see Drug Classes) may result in loss of glucose control because PIs as a class can cause glucose intolerance.
- sulfonylureas (see Drug Classes) can work to effectively lower blood sugar, but may also lower blood sugar too much. Combination use requires blood sugar checks and adjustments of sulfonylurea dosing if the blood sugar goes too low. This is also true of other medicines that lower blood sugar.

▷   *Driving, Hazardous Activities:* Regulate your dose schedule, eating schedule, and physical activities very carefully to prevent hypoglycemia. Be able to recognize the early symptoms of hypoglycemia so that you can avoid hazardous activities and take corrective measures.

Aviation Note: Diabetes ***is a disqualification*** for piloting. Consult a designated Aviation Medical Examiner.

Exposure to Sun: Not defined.

Occurrence of Unrelated Illness: Acute infections, illnesses causing vomiting or diarrhea, serious injuries, and surgical procedures can interfere with diabetic control and may require insulin. If any of these conditions occur, call your doctor promptly.

Discontinuation: Talk with your doctor before changing the dosing schedule of this medicine or considering stopping these medicines.

THIORIDAZINE (thi oh RID a zeen)

Introduced: 1959   **Class:**   Antipsychotic; tranquilizer, major; phenothiazines   **Prescription:**   USA: Yes   **Controlled Drug:**   USA: No; Canada: No   **Available as Generic:**   USA: Yes; Canada: Yes

Brand Names: ✿Apo-Thioridazine, Mellaril, Mellaril-S, Millazine, ✿Novo-Ridazine, ✿PMS-Thioridazine, SK-Thioridazine

BENEFITS versus RISKS	
Possible Benefits	**Possible Risks**
EFFECTIVE CONTROL OF ACUTE MENTAL DISORDERS	TARDIVE DYSKINESIA (SERIOUS TOXIC BRAIN EFFECT) with long-term use
Relief of anxiety, agitation, and tension	NEUROLEPTIC MALIGNANT SYNDROME
Behavior problems that are resistant to other medicines	MAY PROLONG HEART BEAT INTERVALS AND LEAD TO FATAL HEART RHYTHM PROBLEMS
	Liver damage with jaundice (infrequent)
	Blood cell disorder: abnormally low white blood cell count

▷ **Principal Uses**

As a Single Drug Product: Uses currently included in FDA-approved labeling: (1) Helps manage symptoms of psychotic disorders, moderate to marked depression with significant anxiety and nervous tension, and agitation, anxiety, depression, and exaggerated fears in the elderly; (2) used in severe behavioral problems in children characterized by hyperexcitability, short attention span, and rapid swings in mood (temper tantrums); (3) eases agitation in Alzheimer's disease.

Other (unlabeled) generally accepted uses: (1) May have a role in treating alcohol withdrawal in patients who cannot tolerate benzodiazepines; (2) can be used to treat unexplained infertility; (3) may help control premature ejaculation and nocturnal emissions in men; (4) can help borderline personality disorder; (5) of use in some chronic pain syndromes; (6) may be of use in hypersexuality.

Author's Note: Information in this profile has been shortened to make room for more widely used medicines.

THIOTHIXENE (thi oh THIX een)

Introduced: 1967   **Class:** Tranquilizer, major; thioxanthenes   **Prescription:** USA: Yes   **Controlled Drug:** USA: No; Canada: No **Available as Generic:** USA: Yes; Canada: No

Brand Name: Navane

Author's Note: Information in this profile has been shortened to make room for more widely used medicines.

TICLOPIDINE (ti KLOH pi deen)

Introduced: 1985   **Class:** Antiplatelet

Author's Note: Because of more widespread use of clopidogrel, this profile has been truncated.

TIMOLOL (TI moh lohl)

Introduced: 1972 **Class:** Anti-anginal, antiglaucoma, antihypertensive, beta blocker **Prescription:** USA: Yes **Controlled Drug:** USA: No; Canada: No **Available as Generic:** USA: Yes; Canada: No

Brand Names: ✤Apo-Timolol, ✤Apo-Timop, Betimol, Blocadren, Cosopt [CD], ✤Dom-Timolol, ✤Novo-Timolol, ✤Timolide [CD], Timoptic, Timoptic Ouches, Timoptic-XE, ✤Xalacom

Author's Note: benefit to risk profile considerations are generally much more relaxed for eye (ophthalmic) forms as adverse systemic effects are much less likely.

BENEFITS versus RISKS

Possible Benefits	*Possible Risks*
EFFECTIVE, WELL-TOLERATED ANTI-ANGINAL DRUG	CONGESTIVE HEART FAILURE IN ADVANCED HEART DISEASE
EFFECTIVE ANTIGLAUCOMA DRUG	Worsening of angina in coronary heart disease (if drug is abruptly withdrawn)
ANTIHYPERTENSIVE DRUG in mild to moderate hypertension	Masking of low blood sugar (hypoglycemia) in drug-treated diabetes
EFFECTIVE PREVENTION OF MIGRAINE HEADACHES	Provocation of asthma in asthmatics
EFFECTIVE ADJUNCTIVE PREVENTION (SECONDARY PREVENTION) OF RECURRENT HEART ATTACK	
Used in glaucome combined with dorzolamide or latanoprost	

▷ **Principal Uses**

As a Single Drug Product: Uses currently included in FDA-approved labeling: (1) Treats classical effort-induced angina, certain types of heart rhythm disturbance and high blood pressure; (2) lowers increased internal eye pressure in chronic open-angle glaucoma; (3) beneficial when taken within 24 hours and for 28 days thereafter in decreasing the size of the heart damage, decreasing arrhythmias and preventing repeat heart attacks (myocardial infarction); (4) reduces frequency and severity of migraines.

Other (unlabeled) generally accepted uses: (1) Has been used by people who are afraid to fly on airplanes (air travel phobia); (2) may help decrease incidence of abnormal heart rhythms in the atria of the heart (atrial fibrillation and flutter); (3) helps prevent abnormally increased intraocular pressure after cataract surgery; (4) used in patients with detached (not torn) retinas.

As a Combination Drug Product [CD]: Available combined with hydrochlorothiazide to treat high blood pressure. Combination product includes two drugs with different mechanisms of action. This provides better effectiveness and convenience for long-term use. Available (Cosopt) with dorzolamide as an eye drop, adding the benefit of a carbonic anhydrase inhibitor (decreases formation of the fluid (aqueous humor of the eye) by slowing bicarbonate formation as well as beta blockade from timolol. The beta blockade from timolol is also added to latanoprost (increases uveoscleral outflow) in the Xalacom form.

How This Drug Works: Blocks certain actions of the sympathetic nervous system:
- reducing heart rate and contraction force, lowering blood ejection pressure and reducing oxygen needs of the heart, increasing blood flow to the heart (myocardial perfusion).
- reducing degree of blood vessel wall contraction, lowering blood pressure.
- prolonging conduction time of nerve impulses through the heart, of benefit in managing certain heart rhythm disorders.
- slowing formation of fluid (aqueous humor) in the anterior eye chamber, improving its drainage from the eye, lowering the internal eye pressure.

Available Dosage Forms and Strengths

Eye solutions — 0.25%, 0.5%

Eye solution combo — timolol 0.5% and 2% dorzolamide (Cosopt)

Eye solution combo — timolol 5 mg/ml and 50 mcg/ml latanoprost (Xalacom)

Timoptic-XE — 2.5 mg/ml and 5 mg/ml

Tablets — 5 mg, 10 mg, 20 mg

▷ **Usual Adult Dosage Ranges:** *Anti-anginal and antihypertensive:* Initially 10 mg two times daily; increase dose gradually every 7 days as needed and tolerated. Usual maintenance dose is 10 to 20 mg once a day or divided into two equal doses and taken twice daily. The total daily dose should not exceed 60 mg. Used alone or in combination with a water pill (diuretic).

Migraine headache prevention: Initially 10 mg two times daily; increase dose as needed to 10 mg in the morning and 20 mg at night.

Preventing repeat heart attack: 10 mg twice daily.

Anti-glaucoma: one drop in affected eye twice daily.

Author's Note: Timoptic-XE form is a clear gel and is used as one drop, once daily.

Note: Actual dose and schedule must be determined for each patient individually.

Combination: Cosopt: One drop twice a day

Combination: Xalacom: One drop a day.

Conditions Requiring Dosing Adjustments

Liver Function: Prudent to decrease systemic (nonophthalmic) doses in people with liver diseases.

Kidney Function: Patients with kidney compromise should be followed closely and the dose decreased if the medication appears to be accumulating.

▷ **Dosing Instructions:** Systemic forms: Preferably taken 1 hour before eating to maximize absorption. Immediate release tablets may be crushed. Do not stop this drug abruptly. Eyedrops or gel must be used on an ongoing basis. Wash your hands before using the eye drops and do not touch the dropper end. If you forget a dose: Take the missed dose as soon as you remember it, unless it's 4 hours or less until your next dose—if that is the case, skip the missed dose and take the next dose right on schedule. DO NOT double up on doses. Talk with your doctor if you find yourself missing doses—there are beeper-based systems to help you remember your medicines.

Usual Duration of Use: Use on a regular schedule for 10 to 14 days usually determines effectiveness in preventing angina, controlling heart rhythm disorders and lowering blood pressure. Peak benefit may require continual use for 6 to 8 weeks. The long-term use of pill forms will be determined by the course of your symptoms and response to an overall treatment program (weight reduction, salt restriction, smoking cessation, etc.). Ophthalmic forms start to work in 15 to 20 minutes, but require ongoing doses to keep eye pressure low. Follow-up with your doctor is mandatory.

Typical Treatment Goals and Measurements (Outcomes and Markers)

Blood Pressure: The NEW guidelines (JNC VII) define normal blood pressure (BP) as **less than** 120/80. Because blood pressures that were once considered acceptable can actually lead to blood vessel damage, the committee from the National Institutes of Health's National Heart, Lung, and Blood Institute now have a new category called **Pre-hypertension**. This ranges from 120/80 to 139/89 and is intended to help your doctor encourage lifestyle changes (or in the case of people with a risk factor for high blood pressure, start treatment) much earlier—so that possible damage to blood vessels, your heart, kidneys, sexual potency, or eyes might be minimized or avoided altogether. The next two classes of high blood pressure are stage 1 hypertension: 140/90 to 159/99 and stage 2 hypertension equal to or greater than: 160/100 mm Hg. These guidelines also recommend that clinicians trying to control blood pressure work with their patients to agree on the goals and a plan of treatment. The first-ever guidelines for blood pressure (hypertension) in African Americans recommends that MOST black patients be started on TWO antihypertensive medicines with the goal of lowering blood pressure to 130/80 for those with high risk for heart and blood vessel disease or with diabetes. The American Diabetes Association recommends 130/80 as the target for people living with diabetes and less than 125/75 for those who spill more than one gram of protein into their urine. Most clinicians try to achieve a BP that confers the best balance of lower cardiovascular risk and avoids the problem of too low a blood pressure. Blood pressure duration is generally increased with beneficial restriction of sodium. The goals and time frame should be discussed with you when the prescription is written. If goals are not met, it is not unusual to intensify doses or add on medicines. You can find the new blood pressure guidelines at *www.nhlbi.nih.gov/guidelines/hypertension/index.htm*. For the African American guidelines see Douglas J.G. in Sources.

Glaucoma: Ophthalmologists measure intraocular pressure (IOP), and then to check IOP lowering once this medicine is started. The chamber angle can be checked prior to treatment.

Possible Advantages of This Drug: XE form actually forms a clear gel from the initial application of a solution. Once-daily dosing is expected to help people remember to take their medicine (adherence benefit).

▷ **This Drug Should Not Be Taken If**
- you have bronchial asthma or severe obstructive lung disease.
- you have had an allergic reaction to it previously.
- you have Prinzmetal's variant angina (coronary artery spasm).
- you have congestive heart failure.
- you have an abnormally slow heart rate or a serious form of heart block.
- you took a monoamine oxidase (MAO) type A (see Drug Classes) in the last 14 days.

▷ **Inform Your Physician Before Taking This Drug If**
- you had an adverse reaction to a beta blocker (see Drug Classes).
- you have a history of serious heart disease or impaired circulation.
- you have a history of hay fever (allergic rhinitis), asthma, chronic bronchitis, or emphysema.
- you have a history of overactive thyroid function (hyperthyroidism).

- you have a history of low blood sugar (hypoglycemia).
- you have impaired liver or kidney function.
- you have Raynaud's phenomenon.
- you have diabetes or myasthenia gravis.
- you currently take digitalis, quinidine or reserpine, or any calcium-channel-blocker drug (see Drug Classes).
- you plan to have surgery under general anesthesia in the near future.

Author's Note: Above contraindications and precautions apply for the systemic form, for ophthalmic:

▷ **This Drug Should Not Be Taken If**
- you are allergic to timolol, latanoprost, dorzolamide, or any substance in the eye drop.
- you have asthma or chronic obstructive pulmonary disease (COPD).
- you have severe slow heart beat (bradycardia), overt heart failure, second or third degree AV block or are in cardiogenic shock.

▷ **Inform Your Physician Before Taking This Drug If**
- you have congestive heart failure.
- you have a history of ongoing bronchitis or emphysema.
- you have diabetes or hypothyroidism.
- you have risk factors for macular edema (lens capsule tear, aphakia, or pseudoaphakia).
- you have contact lenses (remove them before instilling and do not put them back in for 15–20 minutes), an inflammatory eye condition, or an eye infection.
- you have a history of sulfonamide allergy (if taking dorzolamide combination eye drop).

Possible Side Effects (natural, expected, and unavoidable drug actions)
Lethargy and fatigability, cold extremities, slow heart rate, light-headedness in upright position (see Orthostatic Hypotension in Glossary).

▷ **Possible Adverse Effects** (unusual, unexpected, and infrequent reactions)
If any of the following develop, consult your physician promptly for guidance.
Mild Adverse Effects
Allergic reactions: skin rash, itching.
Loss of hair involving the scalp, eyebrows, and/or eyelashes. This effect can occur with use of the oral tablets or the eyedrops (used to treat glaucoma). Regrowth occurs with discontinuation of this drug.
Headache, dizziness, visual disturbances, vivid dreams—infrequent.
Indigestion, nausea, vomiting, diarrhea—infrequent.
Numbness and tingling in extremities, joint pain—case reports.
Serious Adverse Effects
Allergic reactions: laryngospasm, severe dermatitis.
Idiosyncratic reactions: acute behavioral disturbances—depression, hallucinations.
Chest pain, shortness of breath, precipitation of congestive heart failure—case reports.
Induction of bronchial asthma (in asthmatic individuals)—possible.
May mask warning signs of impending low blood sugar (hypoglycemia) in drug-treated diabetes.
Drug-induced myasthenia gravis—case reports.
Periodic cramping of the leg (intermittent claudication)—possible.
Stopping of breathing (respiratory arrest)—case report.

Author's Note: Some of the eyedrop combination or timolol forms or eye gel form can get into your body. While the listed possible reactions are mainly for the forms taken by mouth (oral), they may possibly (although much less likely) happen with the eye forms.

▷ **Possible Effects on Sexual Function:** Decreased libido, impaired erection, impotence—case reports.

Note: All of these effects can occur with the use of timolol eyedrops at recommended dose, albeit less often.

▷ **Adverse Effects That May Mimic Natural Diseases or Disorders**

Reduced blood flow to extremities may resemble Raynaud's phenomenon (see Glossary).

Natural Diseases or Disorders That May Be Activated by This Drug

Prinzmetal's variant angina, Raynaud's phenomenon, intermittent claudication, myasthenia gravis (questionable).

Possible Effects on Laboratory Tests

None reported.

CAUTION

1. *Do not stop this drug suddenly* without the knowledge and guidance of your doctor. Carry a note stating that you take this drug.
2. Ask your doctor or pharmacist before using nasal decongestants usually present in over-the-counter cold preparations and nose drops. These can cause sudden increases in blood pressure when taken concurrently with beta-blocker drugs.
3. Report development of tendency to emotional depression.

Precautions for Use

By Infants and Children: Safety and effectiveness for those under 12 years of age are not established. However, if this drug is used, watch for low blood sugar (hypoglycemia) during periods of reduced food intake.

By Those Over 60 Years of Age: High blood pressure should be reduced without creating risks associated with excessively low blood pressure. Small starting doses and frequent blood pressure checks are needed. Sudden, rapid, and excessive lowering of blood pressure can predispose to stroke or heart attack. Watch for dizziness, unsteadiness, falling, confusion, hallucinations, depression, or urinary frequency.

▷ **Advisability of Use During Pregnancy**

Pregnancy Category: C. See Pregnancy Risk Categories at the back of this book.
Animal Studies: No significant increase in birth defects due to this drug.
Human Studies: Adequate studies of pregnant women are not available.

Avoid use during the first 3 months if possible. Use only if clearly needed. Ask your physician for guidance.

Advisability of Use If Breast-Feeding

Presence of this drug in breast milk: Yes.

Monitor nursing infant closely, and discontinue drug or nursing if adverse effects develop.

Habit-Forming Potential: None.

Effects of Overdose: Weakness, slow pulse, low blood pressure, fainting, cold and sweaty skin, congestive heart failure, possible coma, and convulsions.

Possible Effects of Long-Term Use: Reduced heart reserve and eventual heart failure in susceptible people with advanced heart disease. Contraindicated in overt heart failure.

Suggested Periodic Examinations While Taking This Drug (at physician's discretion)

Complete blood cell counts (because of adverse effects of other drugs of this class).

Measurements of blood pressure.

Evaluation of heart function.

Lowering of eye (intraocular) pressure with ophthalmic forms.

▷ **While Taking This Drug, Observe the Following**

Foods: No restrictions. Avoid excessive salt intake.

Herbal Medicines or Minerals: Ginseng, guarana, hawthorn, saw palmetto, ma huang, goldenseal, yohimbe, and licorice may also cause increased blood pressure. Excessive caffeine from coffee, mate, or guarana may also increase blood pressure. Dong Quai and St. John's wort may inhibit liver removal of this medicine. Combination is NOT advisable. Calcium and garlic may help lower blood pressure. Use caution and work with your doctor to make sure blood pressure is not lowered too much. Indian snakeroot has a German Commission E monograph indication for hypertension—talk to your doctor. Eleuthero root and ephedra should be avoided by people living with hypertension. Scopolia root has glaucoma as a possible side effect. DO NOT COMBINE. Henbane and belladonna should also be avoided. Talk to your doctor BEFORE combining any herbals with this drug.

Beverages: No restrictions. May be taken with milk.

▷ *Alcohol:* Use with caution. Alcohol may exaggerate this drug's ability to lower blood pressure and may increase its mild sedative effect.

Tobacco Smoking: Nicotine may reduce this drug's effectiveness. I advise everyone to quit smoking.

▷ *Other Drugs*

Timolol may ***increase*** the effects of

- amiodarone (Cordarone) and cause cardiac arrest and bradycardia.
- other antihypertensive drugs and cause excessive lowering of blood pressure; dose adjustments may be necessary (for example, alpha-1 blockers or dihydropyridine calcium channel blockers).
- ergot derivatives, increasing risk of decreased blood flow to arms and legs (peripheral ischemia).
- lidocaine (Xylocaine, etc.).
- reserpine (Ser-Ap-Es, etc.) and cause sedation, depression, slowing of the heart rate, and lowering of blood pressure.
- verapamil (Calan, Isoptin) and cause excessive depression of heart function; monitor this combination closely.

Timolol may decrease the effects of

- theophyllines (Aminophyllin, Theo-Dur, etc.) and reduce their antiasthmatic effectiveness.

Timolol taken concurrently with

- clonidine (Catapres) requires close monitoring for rebound high blood pressure if clonidine is withdrawn while timolol is still being taken.
- epinephrine (Adrenalin, etc.) may cause marked rise in blood pressure and slowing of the heart rate.
- insulin may hide the symptoms of hypoglycemia (see Glossary).
- methyldopa may have paradoxical increases in blood pressure.
- oral hypoglycemic agents (see Oral Antidiabetic Drugs in Drug Classes) such as acetohexamide (Dymelor) and glipizide (Glucotrol) may result in prolonged low blood sugar.

- quinidine (Quinaglute, others) may lead to excessive slowing of the heart.
- venlafaxine (Effexor) may result in increased risk of timolol toxicity.

Timolol/latanoprost form taken concurrently with

- pilocarpine will blunt latanoprost results.
- thimerosal will lead to precipitation of the eye drop. Separate doses by 5–10 minutes.

The following drugs may increase the effects of timolol:

- chlorpromazine (Thorazine, etc.).
- cimetidine (Tagamet).
- fluoxetine (Prozac).
- fluvoxamine (Luvox).
- methimazole (Tapazole).
- propylthiouracil (Propacil).
- ritonavir (Norvir) and perhaps other protease inhibitors (see Drug Classes).
- zileuton (Zyflo).

The following drugs may decrease the effects of timolol:

- antacids (when taken at the same time).
- barbiturates (phenobarbital, etc.).
- indomethacin (Indocin) and possibly other aspirin substitutes, or NSAIDs—may impair timolol's antihypertensive effect.
- rifabutin (Mycobutin).
- rifampin (Rifadin, Rimactane).

▷ *Driving, Hazardous Activities:* Use caution until the full extent of dizziness, lethargy and blood pressure change has been determined.

Aviation Note: The use of this drug *may be a disqualification* for piloting. Consult a designated Aviation Medical Examiner.

Exposure to Sun: No restrictions.

Exposure to Heat: Caution is advised. Hot environments can exaggerate the effects of this drug.

Exposure to Cold: Caution is advised. Cold environments can worsen circulatory deficiency in the extremities that may occur with this drug. The elderly should be careful to prevent hypothermia (see Glossary).

Heavy Exercise or Exertion: It is advisable to avoid exertion that produces lightheadedness, excessive fatigue or muscle cramping. The use of this drug may intensify the hypertensive response to isometric exercise.

Occurrence of Unrelated Illness: Fever can lower blood pressure and require adjustment of dose. Nausea or vomiting may interrupt the dosing schedule. Ask your doctor for help.

Discontinuation: It is advisable to avoid sudden discontinuation of this drug in all situations; this is especially true in the presence of coronary artery disease. If possible, gradual reduction of dose over a period of 2 to 3 weeks is recommended. Ask your physician for specific guidance.

TOLBUTAMIDE (tohl BYU ta mide)

Introduced: 1956 **Class:** Antidiabetic, sulfonylureas **Prescription:** USA: Yes **Controlled Drug:** USA: No; Canada: No **Available as Generic:** Yes

Brand Names: ✚Apo-Tolbutamide, ✚Mobenol, ✚Novo-butamide, Oramide, Orinase, Orinase Diagnostic, SK-Tolbutamide

Warning: The brand names Orinase, Ornade, and Ornex sound similar; this can lead to serious medication errors. Orinase is tolbutamide, used to treat diabetes. Ornade is chlorpheniramine and phenylpropanolamine, used to treat nasal and sinus congestion. Ornex is acetaminophen and phenyl-propanolamine, used to treat head colds and sinus pain. Make sure you get the correct drug.

Author's Note: The information in this profile has been shortened to make room for more widely used medicines.

TOLCAPONE (TOHL ka poan)

Introduced: 1998 **Class:** COMT inhibitor, anti-Parkinsonism **Prescription:** USA: Yes **Controlled Drug:** USA: No **Available as Generic:** No

Brand Names: Tasmar

Author's Note: The information in this profile will be broadened in subsequent editions once concerns about possible liver toxicity are resolved.

TOLMETIN (TOHL met in)

Please see the acetic acid (nonsteroidal anti-inflammatory drug) family profile.

TOLTERODINE (tol TER oh dyne)

Introduced: 1998 **Class:** Muscarinic receptor antagonist, overactive bladder treatment **Prescription:** USA: Yes **Controlled Drug:** USA: No **Available as Generic:** No

Brand Names: Detrol, Detrol LA, ✚Detrol SR, ✚Unidet

BENEFITS versus RISKS	
Possible Benefits	*Possible Risks*
EFFECTIVE TREATMENT OF OVERACTIVE BLADDER	CONSTIPATION
CONTROLS URGE TO URINATE	Dry mouth or throat
LOWERS FREQUENCY OF URINATION	Blurred vision
DECREASES UNEXPECTED URGENT DESIRE TO URINATE (URGE INCONTINENCE)	
NEW ONCE DAILY FORM OFFERS INCREASED CONTROL AND ADHERENCE	

▷ **Principal Uses**

As a Single Drug Product: Uses currently included in FDA-approved labeling: (1) Treats symptoms of overactive bladders; (2) used to decrease excessive urination (urinary frequency); (3) eases unexpected urgent desire to urinate followed by inability to control the bladder (urinary urgency, urge incontinence).

Other (unlabeled) generally accepted uses: None at present.

How This Drug Works: Acts as an anticholinergic agent (competitive muscarinic receptor antagonist) with some selective action on the bladder. This effect increases volume of residual urine and decreases maximum detrusor pressure. This makes it more difficult to urinate, easing overactive bladder symptoms and helping urge incontinence.

Available Dosage Forms and Strengths

Capsules, extended release (LA, SR) — 2 mg, 4 mg

Tablets — 1 mg, 2 mg

▷ **Usual Adult Dosage Ranges:** Started with 2 mg twice a day. The dose may be lowered to 1 mg twice a day if the higher dose is not tolerated. People taking drugs inhibiting liver enzymes CYP3A4 and CYP2D6 should also be given 1 mg twice daily as other medicines can cause tolterodine to accumulate. Detrol LA form is dosed at 4 mg once daily. As with the immediate-release form, the dose is decreased (to 2 mg once daily) for those taking drugs inhibiting CYP 3A4 or 2D6 or in people with lowered kidney or liver function.

Note: Actual dose and schedule must be determined for each patient individually.

Conditions Requiring Dosing Adjustments

Liver Function: Dose should be decreased to 1 mg twice a day of the immediate-release form or 2 mg once daily of Detrol LA in liver disease. (As this drug undergoes cytochrome P-450 2D6 and CYP3A4 metabolism.)

Kidney Function: Used with caution. The drug was not studied in kidney disease, but dose should be decreased to 1 mg of the immediate-release form twice daily or to 2 mg once daily of Detrol LA.

▷ **Dosing Instructions:** The immediate release tablet may be crushed and taken without regard to food (food does increase bioavailability—53% on average, but this is not thought to be clinically significant). The LA or SR form or any other extended release forms should not be crushed, altered, or chewed. If you forget a dose: Take the missed dose as soon as you remember it, unless it's nearly time for your next dose—if that is the case, skip the missed dose and take the next dose right on schedule. DO NOT double up on doses. Talk with your doctor if you find yourself missing doses.

Usual Duration of Use: Initial response to this medicine happens in about an hour. The clinical trials leading to FDA approval showed some benefits of use on a regular schedule in one trial at 4 weeks and peak and consistent benefits at 12 weeks. It is important to follow up with your doctor regarding side effects (dose may need to be decreased) and therapeutic benefits.

Typical Treatment Goals and Measurements (Outcomes and Markers)

Bladder Activity: Most urologists use patient reports of lowered desire or frequency of urination as a hallmark of successful therapy. A general sense of decreased need to urinate immediately (urgency) is also useful. Some physicians will use a bladder diary to help define, in absolute terms, the beneficial effects of this medicine. More invasive cystometry can also be used.

Possible Advantages of This Drug

May be more selective for the bladder than other medicines. If bladder selectivity stands up, this medicine may be a drug of choice based on more favorable cardiovascular profile.

▷ **This Drug Should Not Be Taken If**
  • you are allergic to tolterodine.
  • you retain urine abnormally (retention of urine).
  • you have a problem with retaining food or fluid in the stomach (gastric retention).
  • you have narrow-angle glaucoma that is not controlled.

▷ **Inform Your Physician Before Taking This Drug If**
  • you have liver or kidney disease.
  • you have a history of ulcerative colitis.
  • you have narrow-angle glaucoma controlled by medicines.
  • your job requires visual acuity.
  • you have heart or blood vessel disease (edema and slight increased heart rate possible, but generally a more favorable profile than other medicines for this condition).
  • you have had a bowel obstruction or ulcerative colitis.
  • you are breast-feeding your child.
  • you are prone to constipation.
  • you will have surgery under general anesthesia soon.

Possible Side Effects (natural, expected, and unavoidable drug actions)
  Dry mouth, nasal congestion, indigestion (dyspepsia), constipation—may be frequent.

▷ **Possible Adverse Effects** (unusual, unexpected, and infrequent reactions)
  If any of the following develop, consult your physician promptly for guidance.
  Mild Adverse Effects
  Allergic reaction: skin rash.
  Dizziness or headache—infrequent.
  Blurred vision and increased light sensitivity—rare to infrequent.
  Decreased salivation—infrequent.
  Fast heart rate (tachycardia)—reported.
  Dryness of hands or feet—infrequent.
  Edema—reported.
  Serious Adverse Effects
  Allergic reactions: anaphylactoid reactions.
  Passing out (syncope)—case reports in clinical trials.
  Liver toxicity—case report (possibly a hypersensitivity reaction).
  Cerebrovascular disorder—case reports . . . possibly related to the drug in clinical trials.
  Urinary retention—case reports.

▷ **Possible Effects on Sexual Function:** None defined.

Natural Diseases or Disorders That May Be Activated by This Drug
  Tendency to constipation may be worsened.
  Narrow-angle glaucoma may be worsened.

Possible Effects on Laboratory Tests: Liver function tests may be increased.
CAUTION
  1. Some people (about 7% of the population) are poor metabolizers of this drug. This means that the medicine may accumulate and more of an effect from a "normal dose" will be seen in those people. Once this pattern is identified, doses will need to be decreased to avoid getting too much of the medicine from a "normal" dose.
  2. Talk to your doctor or dentist about sugarless candy or other measures to take if dry mouth becomes a problem.

3. If you are prone to constipation, it may be prudent to start a medicine to address possible constipation if this medicine is started.

Precautions for Use

By Infants and Children: Safety and effectiveness not established in pediatrics.

By Those Over 60 Years of Age: No dosage change is recommended by the manufacturer. Mean blood concentrations of the drug and its metabolite were increased by 20–50%, but no overall safety differences were seen between older and younger patients who were studied.

▷ **Advisability of Use During Pregnancy**

Pregnancy Category: C. See Pregnancy Risk Categories at the back of this book.

Animal Studies: No birth defects found in mice studies.

Human Studies: Adequate studies of pregnant women are not available.

Use this drug only if clearly needed. Ask your doctor for help.

Advisability of Use If Breast-Feeding

Presence of this drug in breast milk: Yes in mice, unknown in humans.

Stop the medicine or discontinue nursing.

Habit-Forming Potential: None.

Effects of Overdose: Severe central anticholinergic effects.

Possible Effects of Long-Term Use: None reported.

Suggested Periodic Examinations While Taking This Drug (at physician's discretion)

Follow-up on decreased urination versus adverse effects.

Baseline liver function test and follow up with any change in stool color, abdominal pain, yellowing of the skin, or dark urine would be prudent.

▷ **While Taking This Drug, Observe the Following**

Foods: Grapefruit is not advisable.

Herbal Medicines or Minerals: Since St. John's wort and tolterodine may increase sun sensitivity, the combination is NOT advised. Caffeine-containing beverages as well as kola, mate, guarana, ephedra, and ma huang may increase blood pressure, eventually leading to possible increased fluid removal and increased need to urinate. Caution is advised.

Beverages: Grapefruit juice is not advisable. May be taken with water or milk. See caffeine note above (coffee and some teas). Some teas also contain substances that act as mild diuretics.

▷ *Alcohol:* Alcohol can increase loss of water from the body. This can work against the action of this medicine.

Tobacco Smoking: Nicotine may work counter to this medicine. Avoid all forms of tobacco.

▷ *Other Drugs*

Tolterodine *taken concurrently* with

• other medicines that inhibit CYP3A4 or CYP2D6 (such as macrolide antibiotics [erythromycin and clarithromycin], itraconazole, ketoconazole, voriconazole (Vfend) and others) may lead to excessive blood levels and toxicity risk.

• fluoxetine (Prozac) may lead to tolterodine toxicity.

• warfarin (Coumadin) may lead to increased bleeding risk. More frequent INRs are prudent.

▷ *Driving, Hazardous Activities:* This drug may cause blurred vision and dizziness. Restrict activities as necessary.

Aviation Note: The use of this drug *may be a disqualification* for piloting. Consult a designated Aviation Medical Examiner.

Exposure to Sun: May increase sensitivity of your eyes to the sun.
Heavy Exercise or Exertion: Excessive exertion is cooled by sweating. This medicine may lead to drying of skin and decreased perspiration.
Discontinuation: Ask your doctor for help.

TOPIRAMATE (TOH peer ah mate)

Introduced: 1999 **Class:** Anticonvulsant, mood stabilizer **Prescription:** USA: Yes **Controlled Drug:** USA: No; Canada: No
Available as Generic: USA: No
Brand Names: Topamax, Topamax Sprinkle

BENEFITS versus RISKS	
Possible Benefits	*Possible Risks*
EFFECTIVE MANAGEMENT OF SEIZURES THAT RESIST THERAPY	CHANGES IN THINKING
	Weight loss
INCREASE IN SEIZURE-FREE DAYS	
MANAGEMENT OF PARTIAL SEIZURES	
MANAGEMENT OF SEIZURES ASSOCIATED WITH LENNOX-GASTAUT SYNDROME	
Weight loss	

▷ **Principal Uses**
As a Single Drug Product: Uses currently included in FDA-approved labeling: (1) Adjunctive combination therapy of generalized (tonic-clonic, partial onset) seizures in adults and children (2–16); (2) Adjunctive combination treatment of Lennox-Gastaut syndrome in patients 2 years old and older.
Other (unlabeled) generally accepted uses: (1) May have a role in treating binge eating; (2) could have a role in bipolar disorder; (3) some case-based use in Tourette's syndrome; (4) because weight gain happens with selective serotonin reuptake inhibitors (SSRIs), this medicine may have beneficial effects in fighting weight gain in adults (may be an undesirable effect in children).
How This Drug Works: The exact mechanism of action is not exactly known. It appears to block the action of nerve cells (neurons) by blocking sodium channels—this keeps the nerve cells from firing excessively. Topiramate works to help a compound that inhibits nerves (an inhibitory neurotransmitter called gamma-aminobutyric acid or GABA. It also has the effect of increasing GABA concentrations. Lastly, this medicine works against a chemical called kainate and a corresponding activator called glutamate. Weight loss specifics are not identified.
Available Dosage Forms and Strengths
Capsules — 15 mg, 25 mg
Coated tablets — 25 mg, 100 mg, 200 mg
▷ **Recommended Dosage Ranges** (Actual dose and schedule must be determined for each patient individually.)
Infants and Children: Lennox-Gastaut, partial onset, or tonic-clonic (generalized) seizures (2–16 years old): Dosing is accomplished on a weight basis and is started with 1–3 mg/kg each night or 25 mg, whichever is less. This

dosing is continued for 7 days and effectiveness checked. Subsequently, doses can be increased as needed and tolerated by steps of 1–3 mg/kg/24 hours. If dosing is increased, the total daily dose is equally divided into two doses, given in the morning and at night. If additional increases are needed the same 1–3mg/kg/24 hour step is taken, but at intervals of 7–14 days. Ongoing (maintenance) doses are generally in the range of 5–9 mg/kg per day. The total dose is separated into two equal doses. The Topamax Sprinkle capsule form offers the advantage of being opened and sprinkled on food (roughly a teaspoon) and taken right away.

17 years old or older: For Lennox-Gastaut, partial onset, or tonic-clonic (generalized) seizures: Dosing is started with 50 mg in the evening. Similar to the pediatric dosing, increases are typically made in steps, and in this case, increased as needed and tolerated to 50 mg in the morning and 50 mg in the evening, then 50 mg in the morning and 100 mg in the evening and so on. In patients receiving medicines known to interact, dosing should be guided by blood levels and patient tolerance and adjusted as needed. Doses more than 800 mg twice a day have NOT been used.

Over 65 Years of Age: Same dosing as 16 to 65, but because kidney function tends to decline as we age, prudent to more slowly increase (titrate) this medicine, check blood levels, and carefully follow patients in this population.

Conditions Requiring Dosing Adjustments

Liver Function: This medicine is changed in the liver, but specific guidelines for dosing are not currently available. Prudent to start slowly (low dose), obtain blood levels, and assess current recommendations if a decision is made to start this medicine in patients with compromised liver function.

Kidney Function: Most of this medicine (once changed or glucuronidated) is removed by the kidneys. Used with caution and with more frequent blood levels (in severe kidney failure).

Author's Note: information in this profile will be broadened in subsequent editions if clinical studies and results warrant this. This medicine is generally removed more quickly in children than in adults. A given dose could lead to a lower level than that seen in adults.

TRAMADOL (TRAM ah doll)

Introduced: 1996   **Class:** Analgesic   **Prescription:** USA: Yes
Controlled Drug: USA: Yes; Canada: No   **Available as Generic:** USA: Yes; Canada: No
Brand Names: Ultram, Ultracet [CD]

BENEFITS versus RISKS	
Possible Benefits	*Possible Risks*
EFFECTIVE TREATMENT OF PAIN	DROWSINESS
MINIMAL SIDE EFFECTS VERSUS	May decrease the seizure threshold
MORPHINE-LIKE AGENTS	Constipation
(OPIOIDS)	

▷ **Principal Uses**

As a Single Drug Product: Uses currently included in FDA-approved labeling: Used to provide symptomatic relief in all types of pain.

Other (unlabeled) generally accepted uses: (1) May have a role in pain where depression is also a therapeutic problem; (2) might have a role as an adjunct to anesthesia; (3) eases fibromyalgia pain.

As a Combination Drug Product [CD]: Available combined with acetaminophen (325 mg) for sudden (acute) pain.

How This Drug Works: Increases the availability of serotonin and norepinephrine in certain brain centers and also works at opioid (see Glossary) centers, thereby relieving pain.

Available Dosage Forms and Strengths

Tablets — 50 mg

Tablets combined form — 37.5 mg tramadol, 325 mg acetaminophen

▷ **Usual Adult Dosage Ranges:** 50 to 100 mg every 4 to 6 hours. Most patients respond to 150 to 300 mg daily. The total daily dose should not exceed 400 mg. German data found clinicians using 0.7 mg per kg per dose and 5.6 mg per kg of body mass per day as a maximum for those over 18 years of age.

Ultracet form: Used for short term (five days or less) management of sudden (acute) pain. Two tablets are given every 4–6 hours up to a daily maximum of 8 tablets.

Note: Actual dose and schedule must be determined for each patient individually.

Conditions Requiring Dosing Adjustments

Liver Function: Patients with cirrhosis should be closely watched for adverse effects and may take only 50 mg every 12 hours of the tramadol form. The Ultracet form HAS NOT BEEN STUDIED and should not be used in that population at present.

Kidney Function: For patients with creatinine clearances less than 30 ml/min, usual dose is taken every 12 hours, and the daily maximum is 200 mg for the tramadol form. The Ultracet form has not been studied in this population, but previous tramadol dosing suggests use of no more than 2 Ultracet tablets every 12 hours.

▷ **Dosing Instructions:** May be taken without regard to meals. The tablet may be crushed. If excessive drowsiness or dizziness occurs, call your doctor. If you forget a dose: Take the missed dose as soon as you remember it, unless it's nearly time for your next dose—if that is the case, skip the missed dose and take the next dose right on schedule. DO NOT double doses. Talk with your doctor if you find yourself missing doses.

Usual Duration of Use: Peak effect usually happens in half an hour. Use on a regular schedule depends on the condition treated. Many chronic pain syndromes are treated with combinations of medicines. Long-term use requires supervision by your doctor. Ultracet form is only approved for use up to five days.

Typical Treatment Goals and Measurements (Outcomes and Markers)

Pain: Most clinicians treating pain use a device called an algometer to check your pain. This looks like a small ruler, but lets the clinician better understand your pain. The goals of treatment then relate to where the level of pain started (for example, a rating of seven on a zero to ten scale) and what the cause of the pain was. I use the PQRSTBG (see Glossary) method. Pain medicines may also be used together (in combination) in order to get the best result or outcome. If your pain control is not acceptable to YOU (remember, in hospitals and outpatient settings, etc., pain control is a patient right and the fifth vital sign), call your doctor. It is not unusual to have an immediate-release rescue dose available and then some percentage of previous day use added back to an extended-release form. Pain can be dynamic and adjustments are often required.

Possible Advantages of This Drug
Avoids narcotic (opioid) side effects.

▷ **This Drug Should Not Be Taken If**
- you have had an allergic reaction to it previously.
- you are allergic to codeine or similar compounds.
- you have a history of seizures or take medicines that may make seizures more likely.
- you are intoxicated by morphinelike drugs or alcohol.
- you are taking, or have taken within the last 14 days, a monoamine oxidase (MAO) inhibitor.

▷ **Inform Your Physician Before Taking This Drug If**
- you have a history of alcoholism, epilepsy, narcotic addiction, or thyroid gland problems.
- you are prone to constipation.
- you have impaired liver or kidney function.
- you are pregnant or breast-feeding your infant.
- you plan to have surgery under general anesthesia in the near future.

Possible Side Effects (natural, expected, and unavoidable drug actions)
Drowsiness, light-headedness on standing (orthostatic hypotension)—rare, blurred vision, dry mouth, constipation—infrequent to frequent.

▷ **Possible Adverse Effects** (unusual, unexpected, and infrequent reactions)
If any of the following develop, consult your physician promptly for guidance.
Mild Adverse Effects
Allergic reaction: skin rash.
Rapid heart rate, palpitations—case reports.
Nausea, vomiting, diarrhea—infrequent to frequent.
Sweating—frequent.
Urinary retention—possible.
Serious Adverse Effects
Allergic reaction: anaphylaxis—case reports.
Behavioral effects: confusion, hallucinations—case reports.
Abnormal ECG, myocardial ischemia, or palpitations—reported.
Seizures—increased risk, especially in those with seizure disorders or in those who take medicines that can make seizures more likely (should not be used).
Serotonin syndrome—case reports.
Movement problem (ataxia)—one case report with a 100 mg dose.
Lowered blood pressure—possible and dose-related.

▷ **Possible Effects on Sexual Function:** Decreased male or female libido—possible.

Possible Effects on Laboratory Tests
Liver enzymes: increased.

CAUTION
1. If you experience a significant degree of mouth dryness while using this drug, consult your dentist regarding the risk of gum erosion or tooth decay. Ask for guidance in ways to keep the mouth comfortably moist.
2. If you have breathing problems (such as chronic obstructive pulmonary disease [COPD]), you may be at greater risk for respiratory depression.

3. DO NOT take this medicine if you are allergic to codeine (more likely to have a serious reaction).

Precautions for Use

By Infants and Children: Safety and effectiveness for use by those under 18 years of age have not been established.

By Those Over 60 Years of Age: Lower starting doses and adjustment to calculated creatinine clearance are prudent. During the first 2 weeks of treatment, observe for confusion or disorientation. Be aware of possible unsteadiness and incoordination that may predispose to falling. This drug may enhance prostatism (see Glossary).

▷ **Advisability of Use During Pregnancy**

Pregnancy Category: C. See Pregnancy Risk Categories at the back of this book.

Animal Studies: Fetal deaths and birth defects reported at doses 3 to 15 times the human dose.

Human Studies: Adequate studies of pregnant women are not available.

Avoid this drug completely during the first 3 months. Ask your physician for guidance.

Advisability of Use If Breast-Feeding

Presence of this drug in breast milk: Yes.

Avoid drug or refrain from nursing.

Habit-Forming Potential: May cause psychological or physical dependence.

Effects of Overdose: Marked drowsiness, weakness, confusion, tremors, stupor, coma, possible seizures.

Possible Effects of Long-Term Use: May increase likelihood of dependence.

Suggested Periodic Examinations While Taking This Drug (at physician's discretion)

Heart rate and blood pressure.

Bowel and bladder status.

Evaluation for tremor or hallucination.

Liver function tests.

▷ **While Taking This Drug, Observe the Following**

Foods: No restrictions.

Herbal Medicines or Minerals: Kava kava and valerian (questions are unresolved for liver toxicity as well) may worsen drowsiness. Since ginseng may act as an MAO inhibitor, DO NOT combine. St. John's wort can change (inducing or increasing) P450 enzymes, blunting the effects of this medicine. Talk to your doctor BEFORE you combine any herbal medicines with tramadol.

Beverages: No restrictions. May be taken with milk.

▷ *Alcohol:* Avoid completely. This drug can markedly increase the intoxicating effects of alcohol and accentuate its depressant action on brain functions.

Tobacco Smoking: No interactions expected. I advise everyone to quit smoking.

▷ *Other Drugs*

Tramadol may *increase* the effects of

• antihypertensive drugs and cause excessive lowering of blood pressure; dose adjustments may be necessary.

• drugs with sedative effects and cause excessive sedation (see Antihistamines, Opioids, Antianxiety Drugs, etc., in Drug Classes).

• tricyclic or SSRI antidepressants (see Drug Classes), leading to seizures or leading to serotonin syndrome.

• warfarin (Coumadin), requiring dose adjustment; more frequent INR (protime) tests are prudent.

Tramadol *taken concurrently* with
- some antipsychotic medicines (see Drug Classes, such as molindone-Moban) may result in excessive risk of seizures.
- carbamazepine (Tegretol) may lower tramadol benefits.
- clonidine will lessen tramadol's therapeutic effect.
- clozapine (Clozaril) may increase seizure risk.
- cyclobenzaprine (Flexeril) increases seizure risk.
- digoxin (Lanoxin) may lead to digoxin toxicity. Extremely careful patient follow up and more frequent checks of digoxin levels are needed.
- fluoxetine (Prozac) may result in an increased seizure risk.
- fluvoxamine (Luvox) may result in an increased seizure risk.
- medicines that increase CYP2D6 will decrease benefits of tramadol, while those that decrease or inhibit CYP2D6 will increase effects of tramadol and may also increase chances of adverse effects.
- monoamine oxidase (MAO) inhibitors (see Drug Classes) may result in serious side effects (seizures, cardiovascular collapse)—DO NOT COMBINE.
- other drugs that cause central nervous system depression (see Benzodiazepines, Opioids, and Tranquilizers in Drug Classes) may have additive effects.
- other drugs that increase seizure risks may have additive effects.
- some phenothiazines (see Drug Classes) may result in excessively lowered blood pressure or increased seizure risk.
- quinidine (Quinaglute, others) may change tramadol levels.
- ritonavir (Norvir) and perhaps other protease inhibitors (see Drug Classes) may lead to toxicity.
- sertraline (Zoloft) increases seizure risk.
- venlafaxine (Effexor) increases seizure risk.

▷ *Driving, Hazardous Activities:* This drug may cause dizziness or drowsiness. Restrict activities as necessary.

Aviation Note: The use of this drug *is a disqualification* for piloting. Consult a designated Aviation Medical Examiner.

Exposure to Sun: No restrictions.

Discontinuation: It is advisable to discontinue this drug gradually. Ask your physician for guidance in dose reduction over an appropriate period of time.

TRAVOPROST (TRAV oh prost)

Introduced: 2001 **Class:** Prostaglandin analogue, antiglaucoma
Prescription: USA: Yes **Controlled Drug:** USA: No; Canada: No
Available as Generic: No

Brand Name: Travatan

BENEFITS versus RISKS	
Possible Benefits	*Possible Risks*
EFFECTIVE REDUCTION OF INTERNAL EYE PRESSURE FOR CONTROL OF ACUTE AND CHRONIC GLAUCOMA CONTROL OF OCULAR HYPERTENSION	Mild side effects with systemic absorption possible with eye use Pigmentation of the iris (appears to be less than latanoprost)

▷ **Principal Uses**
    As a Single Drug Product: Uses currently included in FDA-approved labeling:
        (1) Used to manage glaucoma in patients who are intolerant of or who are
        not adequately controlled by other intraocular pressure lowering medi-
        cines; (2) lowers increased pressure in the eye (intraocular pressure).
    Other (unlabeled) generally accepted uses: (1) None as yet.

How This Drug Works: This medicine is changed to (hydrolyzed) to trovoprost
    free acid (the active form) which subsequently lowers pressure in the eye
    by increasing outflow from the uveoscleral area without changing aqueous
    flow.

Available Dosage Forms and Strengths
    Eyedrop solutions — 0.004% or 40 mcg per ml

▷ **Usual Adult Dosage Ranges:** For open-angle glaucoma or ocular hypertension:
    One drop (0.004%) in the eye each evening (once every 24 hours).
    **Note: Actual dose and dosing schedule must be determined for each
    patient individually.**

Conditions Requiring Dosing Adjustments
    Liver Function: The drug is changed to the active form by substances
    (esterases) in the eye and then in the liver to inactive substances which are
    removed by the kidneys. Dose changes in liver disease are not defined.
    Kidney Function: Changed drug (metabolites) removed by the kidney, but dos-
    ing changes in kidney failure are not defined.

▷ **Dosing Instructions:** Remove contact lenses and do not replace them for at least
    15 minutes after putting this medicine into your eye. To avoid excessive
    absorption into the body, press finger against inner corner of the eye (to
    close off the tear duct) during and for one minute after dropping the med-
    icine in. Be careful not to touch the dropper to the eye. If you forget a dose:
    Take the missed dose as soon as you remember it, unless it's nearly time
    for your next dose—if that is the case, skip the missed dose and take the
    next dose right on schedule. DO NOT double doses. Talk with your doctor
    if you find yourself missing doses.

Usual Duration of Use: Use on a regular schedule for a day usually sees an effect
    in lowering the pressure in the eye. A week may be required for the full
    benefits of the medicine to be realized. Long-term use (months to years)
    requires physician supervision and may require combination therapy if
    pressure rises again.

Typical Treatment Goals and Measurements (Outcomes and Markers)
    Glaucoma: Ophthalmologists measure intraocular pressure (IOP), and then
    check IOP lowering once this medicine is started. The chamber angle can
    be checked prior to treatment. A drop in intraocular pressure is common
    during ongoing use.

▷ **This Drug Should Not Be Taken If**
    • you have had an eye infection with herpes simplex (case report authors
      suggest avoiding latanoprost, and since travoprost is similar, prudent to
      follow the same action).
    • you have had an allergic reaction to it previously or to the benzalkonium
      chloride that is in it.

▷ **Inform Your Physician Before Taking This Drug If**
    • you wear contact lenses.
    • you have had an eye infection in the last three months.
    • you have some of the risk factors for fluid accumulation in the macula
      (macular edema). Talk to your doctor about this.

- you are pregnant or plan pregnancy.
- you have sudden (acute) angle closure of the eye.

Possible Side Effects (natural, expected, and unavoidable drug actions)

Burning of the eyes or irritation—frequent (usually mild).

Pigmentation of the eye (iridial) has been reported, in up to 5% of people who use this medicine. May happen with greater frequency in people with mixed color eyes (blue-brown, green-brown, and yellow brown). This is apparently caused by increased melanin and may be permanent.

Fluid change in the eye (ocular hyperemia)—up to 50% of patients. Often this is mild, but has lead to patients having to stop the medicine roughly 3% of the time.

▷ **Possible Adverse Effects** (unusual, unexpected, and infrequent reactions)

If any of the following develop, consult your physician promptly for guidance.

Mild Adverse Effects

Allergic reactions: itching of the eyes, eyelid itching and/or swelling, or rash.

Change in visual acuity—infrequent.

Serious Adverse Effects

Angina pectorus and/or slow heart rate—infrequent (up to 5%).

▷ **Possible Effects on Sexual Function:** None reported.

Natural Diseases or Disorders That May Be Activated by This Drug

Not defined.

Possible Effects on Laboratory Tests

None reported.

Precautions for Use

By Those Over 60 Years of Age: No age-specific changes presently needed.

▷ **Advisability of Use During Pregnancy**

Pregnancy Category: C. See Pregnancy Risk Categories at the end of book.

Human Studies: Adequate studies of pregnant women are not available.

Discuss use with your doctor BEFORE using this drug.

Advisability of Use If Breast-Feeding

Presence of this drug in breast milk: Yes, in rats, unknown in humans.

Watch infant closely and stop drug or nursing if adverse effects develop.

Habit-Forming Potential: None.

Effects of Overdose: Not defined.

Possible Effects of Long-Term Use: Pigmentation of the iris.

Suggested Periodic Examinations While Taking This Drug (at physician's discretion)

Measurement of internal eye pressure on a regular basis.

Check for early signs of pigmentation.

▷ **While Taking This Drug, Observe the Following**

Foods: No restrictions.

Herbal Medicines or Minerals: Scopolia root has glaucoma as a possible side effect. DO NOT COMBINE. Henbane, ephedra, and belladonna should also be avoided.

Beverages: No restrictions.

▷ *Alcohol:* No restrictions except prudence in alcohol use.

Tobacco Smoking: No interactions expected. I advise everyone to quit smoking.

Marijuana Smoking: Sustained additional decrease in internal eye pressure.

▷   *Other Drugs*
        Travoprost *taken concurrently* with
        • other eye drops should be separated by at least five minutes.
        • thimerosal (various) may cause a precipitation. DO NOT combine eye-
          drops containing thimerosal with latanoprost. Separate doses by 5 min-
          utes or more.
▷   *Driving, Hazardous Activities:* This drug may cause blurry vision for a time.
        Restrict activities as necessary.
        Aviation Note: The use of this drug *may be a disqualification* for piloting. Con-
        sult a designated Aviation Medical Examiner.
        Exposure to Sun: This medicine may make your eyes sensitive to the sun. Wear
        sunglasses. See the table in the back of this book about other medicines
        which may cause such sensitivity—effects may be additive if these medi-
        cines are combined.
        Discontinuation: Do not stop regular use of this drug without consulting your
        physician.

TRAZODONE (TRAZ oh dohn)

Introduced: 1967   **Class:**   Antidepressants   **Prescription:**   USA:
Yes   **Controlled Drug:**   USA: No; Canada: No   **Available as Generic:**
USA: Yes; Canada: Yes

Brand Names: Desyrel, ✤Alti-Trazodone, ✤Apo-Trazodone, ✤Desyrel Divi-
        dose, ✤Novo-Trazodone, ✤PMS-Trazodone, Trialodine

**Author's Note: Information in this profile has been shortened to make room
for more widely used medicines.**

TRIAMCINOLONE (tri am SIN oh lohn)

Introduced: 1985   **Class:**   Antiasthmatic, cortisone-like drugs   **Prescription:**   USA: Yes   **Controlled   Drug:**   USA: No; Canada: No
Available as Generic: Yes

Brand Names: Amcort, Aristocort, Aristocort R, Aristoform D, ✤Aristospan,
        Articulose LA, ✤Aureocort, Azmacort, Cenocort, Cenocort Forte, Flutex,
        ✤Kenacomb, Kenacort, Kenaject, Kenalog, Kenalog H, Kenalog IN,
        Kenalone, Mycogen II, Mycolog [CD], Mycomar, Mytrex [CD], Mytriacet II
        [CD], Nasacort, Nasacort AQ, SK-Triamcinolone, TAC-D, TAC-40, Triacet,
        ✤Triaderm Mild, ✤Triaderm Regular, Triam-A, Triam-Forte, Triamolone
        40, Triderm, Tri-Kort, Trilog, Tristoject, ✤Viaderm-K.C.

**Author's Note: This profile will focus on inhalation, oral, topical, and nasal
forms as injections that are not self-administered. Talk with your doctor
about any questions on those forms.**

BENEFITS versus RISKS

Possible Benefits	*Possible Risks*
EFFECTIVE CONTROL OF SEVERE, CHRONIC BRONCHIAL ASTHMA	Yeast infections of mouth and throat
EFFECTIVE SUPPRESSION OF A VARIETY OF INFLAMMATORY DISORDERS	Suppression of normal cortisone production
POSSIBLE REDUCTION IN SYSTEMIC STEROID USE	Euphoria and psychotic episodes
	Cushing's syndrome ("moon face," obesity, and "buffalo hump")
EFFECTIVE TREATMENT OF SEASONAL OR PERENNIAL ALLERGIC RHINITIS IN ADULTS AND CHILDREN	Muscle wasting (with long-term use)
	Osteoporosis (with long-term use)
	Increased infection susceptibility
	Aseptic bone necrosis (osteonecrosis) is an area of controversy, unclear onset, patient risk factors, and correlation versus causation (see controversy in medicines below)

▷ **Principal Uses**

As a Single Drug Product: Uses currently included in FDA-approved labeling: (1) Inhaler form is used to treat chronic bronchial asthma in people who require cortisone-like drugs for asthma control—this is better than cortisone taken by mouth (swallowed) or injection because it works more locally on the respiratory tract, not requiring systemic distribution; this helps prevent some serious adverse effects that usually result from the long-term use of cortisone taken for systemic effects; (2) tablet form can be used in a variety of inflammatory disorders; (3) tablet form is used to ease drug reactions; (4) used as part of combination treatment of acute lymphocytic leukemia in children; (5) used in autoimmune hemolytic anemia; (6) nasal inhaler form helps adults and children with symptoms of seasonal or perennial allergic rhinitis; (7) combined with antibiotics in some countries for use as a wound dressing; (8) injection form can be given into a large muscle or into an aflicted joint itself.

Other (unlabeled) generally accepted uses: (1) May have a role in postherpetic nerve pain (neuralgia); (2) corticosteroids may be of use with Pneumocystis carinii pneumonia in extreme cases where conventional therapy has not worked; (3) may help Guillain-Barré syndrome; (4) can help myasthenia gravis; (5) short-term therapy of psoriasis; (6) injection form relieves pseudogout.

As a Combination Drug Product [CD]: Available combined with antibiotics in some countries as a wound dressing.

How This Drug Works: By increasing the amount of cyclic AMP in appropriate tissues, this drug may thereby increase the concentration of epinephrine, which is an effective bronchodilator and antiasthmatic. Additional benefit is due to the drug's ability to reduce local allergic reaction and inflammation in the lining tissues of the respiratory tract.

Available Dosage Forms and Strengths

Inhalation aerosol (per metered spray) — 0.1 mg

Nasal inhaler — 55 mcg per actuation

Injection — 25 mg per ml

Nasal spray — 55 mcg or 100 mcg per metered dose (100 mcg is Canada only)

Tablets — 1 mg, 2 mg, 4 mg, 8 mg
Topical cream — 0.025%, 0.1%, 0.25%
Topical ointment — 0.1%, 0.5%
Topical ointment — 0.25%, 0.5%

▷ **Recommended Dosage Ranges** (Actual dose and schedule must be determined for each patient individually.)

Infants and Children:

Up to 6 years of age: Dose not established.

6 to 12 years of age: Inhalation: 0.1 to 0.2 mg (one or two metered sprays) three or four times a day. Adjust dose as needed and tolerated. Limit total daily dose to 1.2 mg (12 metered sprays).

12 to 60 Years of Age:

Inhalation: Initially 0.2 mg (two metered sprays) three or four times a day. For severe asthma—1.2 to 1.6 mg (12 to 16 metered sprays) per day, in divided doses. Adjust dose as needed and tolerated. It is usually used as two inhalations three to four times a day. Results are better when used in this fashion versus on an as-needed basis. Limit total daily dose to 1.6 mg (16 metered sprays).

Intranasal: In treating perenial or seasonal allergic rhinitis, the recommended dose in children more than 12 years old and also in adults: two sprays in each nostril twice daily (220 mcg per day). If acceptable relief has not been accomplished in 4–7 days, the dose can be increased to 440 mcg a day (four sprays in each nostril daily). If relief still is not adequate, after 21 days, an alternate treatment should be considered. If relief is accomplished, (signs and symptoms under control)—the dose is lowered to one spray in each nostril once a day (110 mcg for the Nasacort form). For the Nasacort AQ form, dosing is started at 220 mcg a day (given as two sprays in each nostril). Once symptoms are under control, dosing is decreased to 110 mcg a day as an ongoing dose (one spray in each nostril).

Tablets: 4 to 48 mg daily for inflammatory conditions, depending on the nature and severity of the condition.

Topical cream: 0.025% is usually applied to the affected area two to four times a day.

Over 60 Years of Age: Same as 12 to 60 years of age.

Conditions Requiring Dosing Adjustments

Liver Function: This drug is metabolized in the liver. Dosing changes in liver compromise are not defined.

Kidney Function: Dosing adjustments do not appear warranted for patients with compromised kidneys.

▷ **Dosing Instructions:** Inhalation form: May be used as needed without regard to eating. Shake the container well before using. Carefully follow the printed patient instructions provided with the unit. Rinse the mouth and throat (gargle) with water thoroughly after each inhalation; do not swallow the rinse water. The Nasacort AQ form is water-based for treatment of allergic rhinitis and does not contain chlorofluorocarbon propellants.

Oral tablets: May cause stomach upset and can be taken with meals or snacks.

If you forget a dose: Take, use or apply the missed dose as soon as you remember it, unless it's nearly time for your next dose—if that is the case, skip the missed dose and take the next dose right on schedule. DO NOT double up on doses. Talk with your doctor if you find yourself missing doses.

Usual Duration of Use: Use on a regular schedule for 1 to 2 weeks usually determines effectiveness in controlling severe, chronic asthma. Symptom relief in allergic or perenial rhinitis often happens in a few days. Long-term use varies with the problem being treated, systemic or local therapy, patient reaction, disease flare, and tapering all are salient factors.

Typical Treatment Goals and Measurements (Outcomes and Markers)

Asthma: Frequency and severity of asthma attacks should ease. Some clinicians also use decreased frequency of rescue inhaler use as a further clinical indicator. It is critical that this medicine is used regularly to get the best results. Lung (pulmonary function) testing (FEV1 and others) and improvement in those tests also helps define results in asthma. Lastly, clinical signs and symptoms such as wheezing, tightness in the chest, and exercise tolerance should all move in favorable directions.

An additional goal of therapy is to use the lowest effective dose. Some people keep their improvements when doses are lowered, while others relapse. Those with a less than two-fold improvement in airway response and people who stay in the moderate to severe asthma range despite appropriate dosing may be more likely to relapse if dosing decrease attempts are made. If the usual benefit of ongoing use is not realized, call your doctor.

Inflammation: The general goal is to relieve the swelling and the inflammatory response. Topical use in skin conditions gives a local effect to benefit discomfort, itching, and swelling.

Allergic rhinitis: Symptoms such as itchy, runny nose, sore throat, and postnasal drip should all ease once this medicine begins to work. Because there may be some seasonality to the pollen or molds that can cause rhinitis, talk to your doctor about exactly how he or she wants you to use this medicine.

▷ **This Drug Should Not Be Taken If**
- you have had an allergic reaction to it previously.
- you are having severe acute asthma or status asthmaticus that requires immediate relief and you have been prescribed the inhaler form of this medicine alone.
- you have a form of nonallergic bronchitis with asthmatic features.
- you have a systemic fungal infection.
- the dental paste form has been prescribed and you have a bacterial, viral, or fungal mouth infection.

▷ **Inform Your Physician Before Taking This Drug If**
- you are now taking, or have recently taken, any cortisone-related drug (including ACTH by injection) for any reason (see Drug Classes).
- you have a history of tuberculosis of the lungs.
- you have chronic bronchitis or bronchiectasis.
- you have diabetes, glaucoma, myasthenia gravis, or peptic ulcer disease.
- you have unexplained joint pain (such as in the knee, hip, or shoulder) while taking or after taking this medicine. This could be an early sign of osteonecrosis. Call your doctor right away.
- you have had unexpected surgery (may delay wound healing).
- you have osteoporosis.
- you have an underactive thyroid (hypothyroidism).
- you think you may have an active infection of any kind, especially a respiratory infection as this medicine can blunt your immune system.
- you are taking any of the following drugs: warfarin, oral antidiabetic drugs, insulin, or digoxin.

Possible Side Effects (natural, expected, and unavoidable drug actions)

Yeast infections (thrush) of the mouth and throat. Irritation of mouth, tongue, or throat. May cause euphoria, manic-depressive illness, or paranoid states with long-term oral use. Can cause a syndrome (Cushing's) characterized by "moon face," obesity, and poorly controlled high blood pressure.

▷ **Possible Adverse Effects** (unusual, unexpected, and infrequent reactions)
If any of the following develop, consult your physician promptly for guidance.
Mild Adverse Effects
Allergic reaction: skin rash.
Easy bruising (ecchymosis)—infrequent.
Swelling of face, hoarseness, voice change, cough—possible to infrequent.
Serious Adverse Effects
Allergic reactions—rare.
Bronchospasm, asthmatic wheezing—rare.
Can be a cause of high blood pressure with long-term use.
Edema or swelling, especially with kidney or heart vessel disease—infrequent.
Decrease of circulating T lymphocytes—possible.
Drug-induced seizures, ulcer development, pancreatitis, or osteoporosis—possible to infrequent.
Increased intracranial pressure (pseudotumor cerebri)—rare.
Necrosis of bone (osteonecrosis, avascular necrosis, or aseptic necrosis)—Questions remain as to correlation versus causation, but may be more likely with high initial corticosteroid doses, long-term treatment and cumulative doses of 4.32 grams. May also happen with short-term, modest doses. Individual patient risk factors and/or diseases or conditions appear to be important. Call your doctor if unexplained joint pain happens.
Osteoporosis—possible with long-term use.
Electrolyte disturbances (decreased blood potassium)—infrequent.
Excessive thyroid activity (hyperthyroidism).
Cataract formation or muscle wasting has occurred with long-term use.
Decreased growth in children, especially with high-dose and long-term therapy—possible.
Elevated blood sugar—possible.
Toxic megacolon—rare.
Toxic psychosis has occurred with other steroids.
Author's Note: The inhalation, nasal, and topical cream forms avoid many of the systemic side effects of oral systemic use.

▷ **Adverse Effects That May Mimic Natural Diseases or Disorders:**
Pattern of symptoms resembling Cushing's syndrome. Osteoporosis may resemble bone loss after menopause.

▷ **Possible Effects on Sexual Function:** None reported.

Natural Diseases or Disorders That May Be Activated by This Drug
Latent amebiasis, congestive heart failure, diabetes, glaucoma, hypertension, myasthenia gravis, peptic ulcer.
Cortisone-related drugs (used by inhalation) that produce systemic effects can impair immunity and lead to reactivation of "healed" or quiescent tuberculosis of the lungs. Individuals with a history of tuberculosis should be observed closely during use of cortisone-like drugs by inhalation. Other dormant or existing infections (such as threadworm—Strongyloides) may become more active.

Possible Effects on Laboratory Tests
Blood calcium levels: decreased.
Blood total cholesterol levels: increased.

Blood glucose or sodium levels: increased.

Glucose tolerance test: decreased.

Blood potassium levels: decreased.

Fecal occult blood: may be positive with tablet and systemic use (secondary to GI irritation).

CAUTION

1. This drug is NOT for the immediate relief of acute asthma.
2. If you were using any cortisone-related drugs for asthma *before* switching to this inhaler, you may need to restart the former cortisone-related drug if you are injured, get an infection, or require surgery. Tell your doctor about prior use of cortisone-related drugs.
3. If you experience a return of severe asthma while using this drug, call your doctor immediately. Additional treatment with cortisone-related drugs by mouth or injection may be required.
4. Carry a card noting (if applicable) that you have used cortisone-related drugs within the past year. During periods of stress, resumption of cortisone treatment may be required.
5. Approximately 5 to 10 minutes should separate the inhalation of bronchodilators such as albuterol, epinephrine, pirbuterol, etc. (which should be used first) and the inhalation of this drug. This sequence will permit greater penetration of triamcinolone into the bronchial tubes. This will also reduce the possibility of adverse effects from the propellants used in the two inhalers.
6. A variety of patient risk factors appear to be important in possible development of osteonecrosis. Talk to your doctor about the current list. If you develop knee, hip pain, joint or back pain while taking this medicine— especially if therapy is long-term—call your doctor.

Controversies in Medicine: Medicines in this class have had conflicting reports regarding correlation with or causation of aseptic bone necrosis (osteonecrosis-ON). There appear to be patient risk factors, possible delayed onset with occurrence even after the medicine is stopped, and some diseases or conditions where corticosteroids are often used and ON is more frequent than the general population. It is unclear if this is because of the disease or condition or the use of corticosteroids. Previous data regarding cumulative dosing (4.32 grams) appears controversial, with more recent case reports of 6 days of treatment with some doses being associated with ON. Some existing and emerging patient risk factors include alcohol use versus abuse, initial high doses, HIV positive patients who weight trained, Systemic Lupus Erythematosus, some clotting disorders, and high homocysteine levels amongst others appear to increase risk. Early research regarding use of alendronate (Fosamax) to treat ON appears to show that it is important for patients to quickly return to their doctors if unexplained joint pain (such as in the hip or knee) happens. Some centers note that ON has been poorly studied, and while the weight of data in growing, it is yet too early to say more than ON is correlated with corticosteroid use.

Precautions for Use

By Infants and Children: Safety and effectiveness for use of the oral inhaler by those under 6 years of age have not been established. To ensure adequate penetration of the drug and obtain maximal benefit, the use of a spacer device is recommended for inhalation therapy in children.

By Those Over 60 Years of Age: Individuals with chronic bronchitis or bronchiectasis should be observed closely for the development of lung infections. Systemic use may be associated with greater risk of adverse effects from ongoing dosing. Avoid this if possible.

▷ **Advisability of Use During Pregnancy**

Pregnancy Category: C. See Pregnancy Risk Categories at the back of this book.

Animal Studies: Rat and rabbit studies reveal significant toxic effects on the embryo and fetus and multiple birth defects due to this drug.

Human Studies: Adequate studies of pregnant women are not available.

Limit use to very serious illness for which no satisfactory treatment alternatives are available.

Advisability of Use If Breast-Feeding

Presence of this drug in breast milk: expected to be safe.

Ask your doctor for guidance.

Habit-Forming Potential: With recommended dose, a state of functional dependence (see Glossary) is not likely to develop.

Effects of Overdose: Indications of cortisone excess (due to systemic absorption)—fluid retention, flushing of the face, stomach irritation, nervousness.

Possible Effects of Long-Term Use: Significant suppression of normal cortisone production.

Suggested Periodic Examinations While Taking This Drug (at physician's discretion)

Inspection of mouth and throat for evidence of yeast infection.

Assessment of the status of adrenal gland function (cortisone production).

X-ray of the lungs of people with a prior tuberculosis history. Check of growth rate in children.

Bone mineral density tests to assess osteoporosis. Check of bone status relative to osteonecrosis if unexplained joint pain occurs. (MRI may be prudent).

▷ **While Taking This Drug, Observe the Following**

Foods: No specific restrictions beyond those advised by your physician.

Herbal Medicines or Minerals: Increased calcium and vitamin D are prudent. During long-term use, take a vitamin D and vitamin C supplement. During wound repair, take a zinc supplement. Potassium loss may need to be replaced. Ask your doctor if glucosamine makes sense for you if you are taking the oral form. Hawthorn, garlic, ginger, ma huang, ginseng, guar gum, fenugreek, glucomannan, and nettle may change blood sugar. Since this medicine can also change blood sugar, caution is advised.

Fir or pine needle oil should NOT be used by asthmatics. Ephedra alone does carry a German Commission E monograph indication for asthma treatment, but both ephedra and ephedra containing products (such as ma huang) can decrease corticosteroid benefits. If you are allergic to plants in the Asteraceae family (aster, chrysanthemum, daisy, or ragweed), you may also be allergic to echinacea, chamomile, feverfew, and St. John's wort. Echinacea and ginseng can increase the function of the immune system, blunting benefits of this medicine. Licorice may inhibit liver removal of this medicine, leading to excessive steroid effects. Talk to your doctor BEFORE combining any herbal medicine with triamcinolone.

Beverages: No specific restrictions.

▷ *Alcohol:* Use caution if you are prone to peptic ulcers. Talk to your doctor to get their approval of drinking beer, wine, or other liquor while taking this medicine. Controversy exists as to any alcohol use versus abuse as a risk factor for osteonecrosis.

Tobacco Smoking: No interactions expected. I advise everyone to quit smoking.

▷ *Other Drugs*

The following drugs may ***increase*** the effects of triamcinolone:
- inhalant bronchodilators—albuterol, bitolterol, epinephrine, pirbuterol, etc.
- oral bronchodilators—aminophylline, ephedrine, terbutaline, theophylline, etc.

The following drugs may ***decrease*** the effects of triamcinolone:
- carbamazepine (Tegretol)—increases triamcinolone metabolism and may result in decreased effectiveness.
- phenobarbital (various).
- phenytoin (Dilantin) or fosphenytoin (Cerebyx)—increases triamcinolone metabolism and may result in decreased effectiveness.
- primidone (Mysoline)—increases steroid metabolism and may result in decreased triamcinolone metabolism.
- rifampin (Rifadin).

Triamcinolone ***taken concurrently*** with
- amphotericin B (Abelcet) may lead to additive potassium loss.
- aspirin may result in increased removal of aspirin from the body and may also lead to increased stomach irritation or ulceration. This effect may be immediate or delayed. Patients should be checked for loss of aspirin benefits and stomach upset of GI bleeding.
- cyclosporine (Sandimmune) may result in changes in the blood levels of both medicines.
- human growth hormone (HGH) may blunt HGH benefits.
- insulin (various forms) may lead to loss of glucose control.
- neuromuscular blocking agents (such as pancuronium—Pavulon or vercuronium—Norcuron) may prolong muscle weakness.
- oral hypoglycemic agents (see Oral Antidiabetic Drugs in Drug Classes) may result in loss of glucose control.
- thiazide diuretics (see Drug Classes) can result in loss of glucose control.
- vaccines (flu, rabies, rotavirus, others) may result in a less than optimal vaccine response.
- warfarin (Coumadin) can result in variation in the degree of anticoagulation; increased INR (prothrombin time or protime) testing is indicated.

▷ *Driving, Hazardous Activities:* No restrictions.

Aviation Note: The use of this drug and the disorder for which this drug is prescribed ***may be disqualifications*** for piloting. Consult a designated Aviation Medical Examiner.

Exposure to Sun: No restrictions.

Occurrence of Unrelated Illness: Acute infections, serious injuries, and surgical procedures can create an urgent need for the administration of additional supportive cortisone-related drugs given by mouth and/or injection. Notify your physician immediately in the event of new illness or injury of any kind.

Special Storage Instructions: Store at room temperature. Avoid exposure to temperatures above 120 degrees F. (49 degrees C.). Do not store or use this inhaler near heat or open flame.

Discontinuation: **Do not stop this drug abruptly after chronic use.** Ask your doctor for help about gradual, individualized withdrawal. Some clinicians change from daily to every other day therapy for four weeks BEFORE starting to lower the dose in a stepwise fashion. Many patients tolerate dose reductions of 2.5 mg of prednisone (other steroids are calculated on the basis of prednisone equivalents) with those decreases made every 3–7 days. If a disease flare occurs (worsening of symptoms), the dose should be increased to the last dose before the disease flare and should be tapered more slowly down to 5–10 mg or lower. Some clinicians use 8 A.M. predose plasma cortisol to guide tapering. If this lab test is less than 10 mcg/deciliter, tapering is continued until the daily prednisone equivalent is 2–5 mg. In general, if long-term treatment or high doses were used, prednisone equivalents should be tapered over 9–12 months. For up to 2 years after stopping this drug, you may require it again if you have an injury, surgery, or an illness.

TRIAMTERENE (tri AM ter een)

Introduced: 1964   **Class:** Diuretic   **Prescription:** USA: Yes
Controlled Drug: USA: No; Canada: No   **Available as Generic:** Yes
Brand Names: ✤Apo-Triazide [CD], Dyazide [CD], Dyrenium, Maxzide [CD], Maxzide-25 [CD], ✤Novo-Triamzide [CD], ✤Nu-Triazide, ✤Riva-Zide

---

BENEFITS versus RISKS

Possible Benefits	*Possible Risks*
EFFECTIVE PREVENTION OF POTASSIUM LOSS when used adjunctively with other diuretics	ABNORMALLY HIGH BLOOD POTASSIUM LEVEL with excessive use
EFFECTIVE DIURETIC IN REFRACTORY CASES OF FLUID RETENTION when used adjunctively with other diuretics	Possible blood cell disorders: megaloblastic anemia, abnormally low white blood cell and platelet counts
	Possible kidney stone formation

Principal Uses

As a Single Drug Product: Uses currently included in FDA-approved labeling: (1) Used in combination with other drugs to treat high blood pressure (primarily used in situations where it is advisable to prevent loss of potassium from the body); (2) used as combination therapy of congestive heart failure or liver and kidney disorders accompanied by excessive fluid retention (edema).

Other (unlabeled) generally accepted uses: None.

As a Combination Drug Product [CD]: Available in combination with hydrochlorothiazide, a different kind of diuretic that promotes potassium loss from the body. Triamterene is used to counteract the potassium-wasting effect of the thiazide diuretic.

How This Drug Works: By inhibiting the enzyme system that starts the sodium-potassium exchange process, this drug prevents reabsorption of sodium and excretion of potassium by the kidney. This leads to excretion of sodium (and water with it) and potassium retention.

Available Dosage Forms and Strengths
>   Capsules — 50 mg, 100 mg
>   Capsules — triamterene 37.5 mg and hydrochlorothiazide 25 mg.

▷ **Usual Adult Dosage Ranges:** Initially 50 to 100 mg twice daily. The dose is then adjusted according to individual response. The usual ongoing dose is 100 to 200 mg daily, divided into two doses. The total daily dose should not exceed 300 mg.

>   Dyazide combination—one or two capsules daily for high blood pressure.

>   **Note: Actual dose and schedule must be determined for each patient individually.**

Conditions Requiring Dosing Adjustments
>   *Liver Function:* Dose should be reduced and used with extreme caution in liver disease.

>   *Kidney Function:* Patients with mild to moderate kidney failure may take the usual dose every 12 hours. In severe or progressive kidney failure, this medication should not be used.

▷ **Dosing Instructions:** May be taken with or following meals to promote absorption of the drug and reduce stomach irritation. The capsule may be opened. If you forget a dose: Take the missed dose as soon as you remember it, unless it's nearly time for your next dose—if that is the case, skip the missed dose and take the next dose right on schedule. DO NOT double doses. Talk with your doctor if you find yourself missing doses as the best control of blood pressure comes from taking your medicine exactly as prescribed.

Usual Duration of Use: Use on a regular schedule for 3 to 5 days usually determines effectiveness in clearing edema and for 2 to 3 weeks to determine its effect on hypertension. Long-term use (months to years) requires physician supervision and periodic evaluation. Take control of your blood pressure by taking this medicine!

Typical Treatment Goals and Measurements (Outcomes and Markers)
>   *Blood Pressure:* The NEW guidelines (JNC VII) define normal blood pressure (BP) as **less than** 120/80. Because blood pressures that were once considered acceptable can actually lead to blood vessel damage, the committee from the National Institutes of Health's National Heart, Lung, and Blood Institute now have a new category called **Pre-hypertension**. This ranges from 120/80 to 139/89 and is intended to help your doctor encourage lifestyle changes (or in the case of people with a risk factor for high blood pressure, start treatment) much earlier—so that possible damage to blood vessels, your heart, kidneys, sexual potency, or eyes might be minimized or avoided altogether. The next two classes of high blood pressure are stage 1 hypertension: 140/90 to 159/99 and stage 2 hypertension equal to or greater than: 160/100 mm Hg. These guidelines also recommend that clinicians trying to control blood pressure work with their patients to agree on the goals and a plan of treatment. The first-ever guidelines for blood pressure (hypertension) in African Americans recommends that MOST black patients be started on TWO antihypertensive medicines with the goal of lowering blood pressure to 130/80 for those with high risk for heart and blood vessel disease or with diabetes. The American Diabetes Association recommends 130/80 as the target for people living with diabetes and less than 125/75 for those who spill more than one gram of protein into their urine. Most clinicians try to achieve a BP that confers the best balance of lower cardiovascular risk and avoids the problem of too low a blood pres-

sure. Blood pressure duration is generally increased with beneficial restriction of sodium. The goals and time frame should be discussed with you when the prescription is written. If goals are not met, it is not unusual to intensify doses or add on medicines. You can find the new blood pressure guidelines at *www.nhlbi.nih.gov/guidelines/hypertension/index.htm*. For the African American guidelines see Douglas J.G. in Sources.

▷ **This Drug Should Not Be Taken If**
- you have had an allergic reaction to it previously or you have a sulfa drug allergy.
- you have severely impaired liver or kidney function.
- your kidney disease is progressive or you have a creatinine clearance greater than 2.5 mg/dl (ask your doctor).
- your blood potassium level is significantly elevated (ask your doctor).

▷ **Inform Your Physician Before Taking This Drug If**
- you have a history of liver or kidney disease.
- you have diabetes or gout.
- you are taking any of the following: antihypertensives, a digitalis preparation, another diuretic, lithium, or a potassium preparation.
- you have a history of glucose-6-phosphate dehydrogenase (G6PD) deficiency (ask your doctor).
- you have a history of blood cell disorders.
- you will have surgery with general anesthesia.

Possible Side Effects (natural, expected, and unavoidable drug actions)
With excessive use: abnormally high blood potassium levels, abnormally low blood sodium levels, dehydration. Blue coloration of the urine (of no significance).

▷ **Possible Adverse Effects** (unusual, unexpected, and infrequent reactions)
If any of the following develop, consult your physician promptly for guidance.
Mild Adverse Effects
Allergic reactions: skin rash, itching.
Headache, dizziness, unsteadiness, weakness, drowsiness, lethargy—infrequent.
Dry mouth, nausea, vomiting, diarrhea—infrequent.
Serious Adverse Effects
Allergic reaction: anaphylactic reaction (see Glossary).
Symptomatic potassium excess: confusion, numbness, and tingling in lips and extremities, fatigue, weakness, shortness of breath, slow heart rate, low blood pressure—possible.
Blood cell disorders: megaloblastic anemia, abnormally low white blood cell count or abnormally low blood platelet count—case reports.
Hemolytic anemia—in those with deficiency of G6PD in red cells.
Abnormal urine production (SIADH)—case reports.
Formation of kidney stones and kidney toxicity—rare.
Liver toxicity—rare.

▷ **Possible Effects on Sexual Function:** None reported.

Possible Effects on Laboratory Tests
Complete blood cell counts: decreased red cells, hemoglobin, white cells, and platelets; increased eosinophils (allergic reaction).
Blood glucose level: increased in diabetics.
Blood lithium, potassium, or uric acid level: increased.
Liver function tests: Increased: rare.

Kidney function tests: increased blood creatinine and urea nitrogen (BUN) levels (kidney damage).

CAUTION

1. Do not take potassium supplements or increase your intake of potassium-rich foods while taking this drug.
2. Patients who take quinidine (Quinaglute, others) may have falsely increased laboratory test results if fluorescent measurement techniques are used.
3. Do not stop this drug abruptly unless abnormally high blood levels of potassium develop.
4. Avoid liberal use of salt substitutes with potassium in them (potential causes of potassium excess).

Precautions for Use

By Infants and Children: This drug is not recommended for use in children.

By Those Over 60 Years of Age: Natural decline in kidney function may predispose to potassium retention. Watch for potassium excess: slow heart rate, irregular heart rhythms, low blood pressure, confusion, drowsiness. Excessive use of diuretics can cause harmful loss of body water (dehydration), increased viscosity of the blood, and an increased tendency of the blood to clot, predisposing to stroke, heart attack, or thrombophlebitis.

▷ **Advisability of Use During Pregnancy**

Pregnancy Category: B by one manufacturer, D by one researcher. See Pregnancy Risk Categories at the back of this book.

Animal Studies: No birth defects due to this drug were reported.

Human Studies: Adequate studies of pregnant women are not available.

This drug should not be used during pregnancy unless a very serious complication of pregnancy occurs for which this drug is significantly beneficial.

Advisability of Use If Breast-Feeding

Presence of this drug in breast milk: Yes.

Avoid drug or refrain from nursing.

Habit-Forming Potential: None.

Effects of Overdose: Thirst, drowsiness, fatigue, nausea, vomiting, confusion, irregular heart rhythm, low blood pressure.

Possible Effects of Long-Term Use: Potassium accumulation to abnormally high blood levels.

Suggested Periodic Examinations While Taking This Drug (at physician's discretion)

Complete blood cell counts.

Measurements of blood sodium, potassium, and chloride levels.

Kidney function tests.

▷ **While Taking This Drug, Observe the Following**

Foods: Diets high in high-potassium foods (see Table 13, Section Six) may cause problems. Avoid excessive restriction of salt.

Herbal Medicines or Minerals: Ginseng may increase blood pressure, blunting the benefits of this medicine. Hawthorn, saw palmetto, ma huang, goldenseal, and yohimbe may also increase blood pressure. Caffeine excess from guarana and mate may blunt medicine benefits. Calcium and garlic may help lower blood pressure. Use caution and work with your doctor to make sure blood pressure is not lowered too much. Indian snakeroot has a German Commission E monograph indication for hypertension—talk to your doctor. Eleuthero root and ephedra should be avoided by people living with hypertension. Licorice can increase risk of excessive lowering of potassium (hypokalemia) if combined with a diuretic such as triamterene. **CAUTION:** St. John's wort may also lead to unexpected sensitivity to the sun (photosensitivity).

Beverages: Excessive caffeine may blunt benefits. May be taken with milk.

▷ *Alcohol:* Use with caution. Alcohol may enhance drowsiness and the blood-pressure-lowering effect of this drug.

Tobacco Smoking: No interactions expected. I advise everyone to quit smoking.

▷ *Other Drugs*

Triamterene may ***increase*** the effects of
- amantadine (Symmetrel).
- digoxin (Lanoxin).
- metformin (Glucophage).
- methotrexate (Mexate), leading to bone marrow toxicity.
- valsartan (Diovan), leading to potassium toxicity.

Triamterene ***taken concurrently with***
- captopril (Capoten) or other ACE inhibitors may cause excessively high blood potassium levels.
- cyclosporine (Sandimmune) SHOULD NOT BE COMBINED.
- dofetilide (Tikosyn) may lead to excessive dofetilide levels. Careful patient monitoring and more frequent dofetilide levels are indicated if these medicines are combined as they both are removed from the body by the same mechanism.
- folic acid may reduce folic acid benefits.
- histamine (H2) blockers (see Drug Classes) may decrease triamterene absorption and its therapeutic effects.
- indomethacin (Indocin) may increase the risk of kidney damage.
- lithium may cause accumulation of lithium to toxic levels.
- NSAIDs (see Drug Classes) may blunt the blood-pressure-lowering effect of triamterene.
- potassium preparations may cause excessively high blood pressure.
- spironolactone (various) may lead to excessively high potassium. Combination use is NOT advisable.
- tacrolimus (Prograf) may lead to excessively high blood potassium levels. Combination should be avoided.

▷ *Driving, Hazardous Activities:* This drug may cause dizziness and drowsiness. Restrict activities as necessary.

Aviation Note: The use of this drug ***may be a disqualification*** for piloting. Consult a designated Aviation Medical Examiner.

Exposure to Sun: Use caution—this drug may cause photosensitivity (see Glossary).

Discontinuation: With high-dose or prolonged use, it is best to slowly withdraw this drug. Stopping it suddenly may cause rebound potassium removal and potassium deficiency. Ask your doctor for help.

TRICHLORMETHIAZIDE (tri KLOR meth i a zide)

Please see the thiazide diuretic family profile.

TRIFLUOPERAZINE (tri flu oh PER a zeen)

Introduced: 1958 **Class:** Tranquilizer, major; phenothiazines **Pre-scription:** USA: Yes **Controlled Drug:** USA: No; Canada: No
Available as Generic: USA: Yes; Canada: No

Brand Names: ♣Apo-Trifluoperazine, ♣Novo-Flurazine, ♣Solazine, Ste-labid [CD], Stelazine, Suprazine, ♣Terfluzine

Author's Note: Information in this profile has been truncated to make room for more widely used medicines.

TRIMETHOPRIM (tri METH oh prim)

Introduced: 1966 **Class:** Anti-infective **Prescription:** USA: Yes **Controlled Drug:** USA: No; Canada: No **Available as Generic:** USA: Yes; Canada: No

Brand Names: Alti-Trimethoprim, ♣Apo-Sulfatrim [CD], ♣Apo-Sulfatrim DS [CD], Bactrim [CD], Bactrim DS [CD], Bethaprim [CD], Comoxol [CD], ♣Coptin [CD], Cotrim [CD], ♣Novo-Trimel [CD], ♣Novo-Trimel DS [CD], ♣Nu-Cotrimox, Polytrim, Proloprim, ♣Protrin [CD], ♣Protrin DF [CD], ♣Roubac [CD], Septra [CD], Septra DS [CD], SMZ-TMP [CD], Sul-fatrim D/S, Trimpex, Uroplus DS [CD], Uroplus SS [CD]

BENEFITS versus RISKS

Possible Benefits	*Possible Risks*
EFFECTIVE TREATMENT OF INFECTIONS DUE TO SUSCEPTIBLE MICROORGANISMS Effective adjunctive prevention and treatment of *Pneumocystis carinii* pneumonia (AIDS related)	Blood cell disorders: megaloblastic anemia, methemoglobinemia, abnormally low white cells or platelets May increase homocysteine with ongoing use

---

▷ **Principal Uses**

As a Single Drug Product: Uses currently included in FDA-approved labeling: (1) Treats or prevents certain infections of the urinary tract not compli-cated by the presence of kidney stones or obstructions to the normal flow of urine; (2) treats eye infections caused by sensitive organisms; (3) cotri-moxazole, Septra and Bactrim forms approved to treat and prevent PCP pneumonia.

Other (unlabeled) generally accepted uses: (1) Used in combination with dapsone to treat *Pneumocystis carinii* pneumonia in AIDS patients; (2) may have a role in combination therapy of resistant acne; (3) prevention (prophylaxis) of urinary tract infections.

As a Combination Drug Product [CD]: Available combined with sulfamethoxa-zole (cotrimoxazole is used in some countries to identify this combina-tion). Treats certain urinary tract infections, middle ear infections, chronic bronchitis, acute enteritis, and certain types of pneumonia. It is now used as primary prevention and treatment of *Pneumocystis carinii* pneumonia associated with AIDS.

How This Drug Works: Prevents growth and multiplication of susceptible organisms by inactivating enzyme systems needed for formation of essen-tial nuclear elements and cell proteins.

Available Dosage Forms and Strengths

Ophthalmic — 1 mg/ml

Oral suspension, combination (per 5 ml) — 40 mg trimethoprim/200 mg sulfamethoxazole

Tablets — 100 mg, 200 mg

Tablets, combination — 80 mg trimethoprim/400 mg sulfamethoxazole 160 mg trimethoprim/800 mg sulfamethoxazole

▷ **Usual Adult Dosage Ranges:** *Orally for infections:* 100 mg every 12 hours for 10 days. For certain pneumonias, the same dose is taken every 6 hours. The total daily dose should not exceed 640 mg.

Ophthalmic: One drop in the affected eye every 3 hours (up to six doses a day) for 7 to 10 days.

Note: Actual dose and schedule must be determined for each patient individually.

Conditions Requiring Dosing Adjustments

Liver Function: Used with caution by patients with both liver and kidney disease.

Kidney Function: Patients with mild kidney compromise can take the usual dose every 12 hours. Patients with stable moderate to more compromised kidney failure (creatinine clearances of 15 to 50 ml/min) can take the usual dose every 18 hours. Should NOT be used in severe or worsening kidney failure.

▷ **Dosing Instructions:** The tablet may be crushed and may be taken with or following food if necessary to reduce stomach irritation. The suspension form should be shaken well and dosed using a calibrated medicine spoon or dosing cup. If you forget a dose: Take the missed dose as soon as you remember it, unless it's nearly time for your next dose—if that is the case, skip the missed dose and take the next dose right on schedule. DO NOT double up on doses. Talk with your doctor if you find yourself missing doses as compliance ensures the best treatment results or best possible prevention of infection.

Usual Duration of Use: Use on a regular schedule for 7 to 14 days usually determines effectiveness in controlling responsive infections. The actual duration of use will depend upon the nature of the infection. Prevention of (prophylaxis) of PCP in HIV positive patients with the combination form will be ongoing.

Typical Treatment Goals and Measurements (Outcomes and Markers)

Infections: The most commonly used measures of serious infections are white blood cell counts and differentials (the kind of blood cells that occur most often in your blood), and temperature. Many clinicians look for positive changes in 24–48 hours. NEVER stop an antibiotic because you start to feel better. For treating infections, the full course is REQUIRED to kill the bacteria. Prophylaxis (for example of PCP) often requires ongoing use. The goals and time frame (see peak benefits above) should be discussed with you when the prescription is written.

Currently a Drug of Choice

When combined with sulfamethoxazole, for preventing pneumonia (due to Pneumocystis carinii) in patients with AIDS.

▷ **This Drug Should Not Be Taken If**
- you have had an allergic reaction to it previously.
- you have an anemia due to folic acid deficiency (megaloblastic anemia).

▷ **Inform Your Physician Before Taking This Drug If**
- you have a history of folic acid deficiency.
- you have impaired liver or kidney function.
- you are pregnant or breast-feeding.
- you have a history of cardiovascular disease. This medicine may increase homocysteine levels.

Possible Side Effects (natural, expected, and unavoidable drug actions)
None with short-term use.

▷ **Possible Adverse Effects** (unusual, unexpected, and infrequent reactions)
If any of the following develop, consult your physician promptly for guidance.
Mild Adverse Effects
Allergic reactions: skin rash, itching, drug fever (see Glossary).
Headache, abnormal taste, sore mouth or tongue, nausea, vomiting, cramping, diarrhea—infrequent.
Serious Adverse Effects
Allergic reactions: severe dermatitis with peeling of skin (toxic epidermal necrolysis).
Blood cell disorders: megaloblastic anemia, methemoglobinemia, abnormally low white blood cell and platelet counts—rare.
Worsening of hyperkalemia (increased blood potassium)—possible.
Kidney or liver toxicity—rare.
Aseptic meningitis (of questionable causal relationship)—case reports.

▷ **Possible Effects on Sexual Function:** None reported.

Possible Effects on Laboratory Tests
Complete blood cell counts: decreased red cells, hemoglobin, white cells, and platelets.
INR (prothrombin time): increased (when taken concurrently with warfarin).

CAUTION
1. Resistance may develop. If you do not show significant improvement within 2 days, call your physician.
2. Comply with your physician's request for periodic blood counts during long-term therapy.
3. This medicine may increase homocysteine levels. Talk to your doctor about checking levels if you will be taking this medicine on an ongoing basis. Taking a multivitamin appears prudent (B vitamins have a role in helping decrease homocysteine).

Precautions for Use
By Infants and Children: Safety and effectiveness for those under 2 months of age are not established.
By Those Over 60 Years of Age: The natural decline in liver and kidney function may require smaller doses. If you develop itching reactions in the genital or anal areas, report this promptly.

▷ **Advisability of Use During Pregnancy**
Pregnancy Category: C. See Pregnancy Risk Categories at the back of this book.
Animal Studies: Birth defects due to this drug reported in rat and rabbit studies.
Human Studies: Adequate studies of pregnant women are not available.
Avoid use of drug during the first 3 months and during the final 2 weeks of pregnancy. Use this drug otherwise only if clearly needed. Ask your physician for guidance.

Advisability of Use If Breast-Feeding
> Presence of this drug in breast milk: Yes, but in small amounts.
> Talk to your doctor about the best course of action.

Habit-Forming Potential: None.

Effects of Overdose: Headache, dizziness, confusion, depression, nausea, vomiting, bone marrow depression, possible liver toxicity with jaundice.

Possible Effects of Long-Term Use: Impaired production of red and white blood cells and blood platelets.

Suggested Periodic Examinations While Taking This Drug (at physician's discretion)
> Complete blood cell counts.

▷ **While Taking This Drug, Observe the Following**
> *Foods:* Since this medicine may increase homocysteine levels, a multivitamin appears prudent.
>
> *Herbal Medicines or Minerals:* Some patients use echinacea to attempt to boost their immune systems. Unfortunately, echinacea is not recommended in people with damaged immune systems. This herb may also actually weaken any immune system if it is used too often or for too long a time. DO NOT take mistletoe herb, oak bark, or F.C. of marshmallow root and licorice extracts. Pure cranberry juice may help keep harmful bacteria from attaching to the bladder wall and may be useful in combination with antibiotics in helping to prevent urinary tract infections. TALK to your doctor BEFORE adding any herbal medicine.
>
> *Beverages:* No restrictions. May be taken with milk.

▷ *Alcohol:* No interactions expected.

> *Tobacco Smoking:* No interactions expected, but I advise everyone to quit smoking.

▷ *Other Drugs*
> Trimethoprim may ***increase*** the effects of
> - abacavir/lamivudine/zidovudine (Trizivir) combined with this medicine will have the lamivudine and zidovudine components increased.
> - ACE inhibitors (see Drug Classes), resulting in dangerously increased potassium levels.
> - amantadine (Symmetrel) and also result in increased levels of trimethoprim, resulting in toxicity.
> - cyclosporine (Sandimmune) and result in increased kidney toxicity.
> - dapsone and result in dapsone or trimethoprim toxicity.
> - digoxin (Lanoxin), leading to toxicity.
> - dofetilide (Tikosyn) may lead to heart toxicity. Avoid this combination.
> - lamivudine (Epivir) and adjustments in lamivudine doses may be required.
> - leukovorin (Leukovorin calcium for injection) will blunt treatment (increase treatment failure) for leukovorin.
> - metformin (Glucophage) and other cationic drugs.
> - methotrexate (Mexate), leading to toxicity.
> - phenytoin (Dilantin) or fosphenytoin (Cerebyx) and cause phenytoin or fosphenytoin toxicity.
> - procainamide (Procan SR) and result in procainamide toxicity.
> - tolbutamide (Orinase), leading to increased risk of hypoglycemia.
> - zidovudine (AZT), leading to increased toxicity risk.
>
> Cotrimoxazole form may ***increase*** the effects of
> - medicines such as class I, IA, or III antiarrhythmics (dofetilide (Tikosyn), clarithromycin, cotrimoxazole, ondansetron, ziprazidone, and others may

lead to prolongation of the QTc interval and undesirable effects. Combination is not recommended.

The following drugs may ***decrease*** the effects of trimethoprim:

- cholestyramine (Questran) and perhaps other cholesterol-lowering medicines (see Drug Classes) of the same class—these will bind trimethoprim and blunt its beneficial effects by inhibiting absorption.
- rifampin (Rifadin, Rimactane).
- ritonavir (Norvir).

▷ *Driving, Hazardous Activities:* No restrictions.

Aviation Note: The use of this drug is ***probably not a disqualification*** for piloting. Consult a designated Aviation Medical Examiner.

Exposure to Sun: No restrictions.

TROGLITAZONE (troh GLIT a zoan)

Introduced: 1997   **Class:**   Antidiabetic, thiazolidinedione

Author's Note: This medicine was voluntarily removed from the market in March 2000. Please see the thiazolidinedione family profile for information on the two remaining "glitazones."

VALPROIC ACID (val PROH ik A sid)

Introduced: 1967   **Class:**   Anticonvulsant, mood stabilizer   **Prescription:**   USA: Yes   **Controlled Drug:**   USA: No; Canada: No   **Available as Generic:**   USA: Yes; Canada: Yes

Brand Names: ❧Alti-Valproic, ❧Apo-Divalproex, ❧Apo-Valproic, Atemperator, Depa, Depakene, Depakote (divalproex sodium), Depakote ER, Depakote Sprinkle, Deproic, ❧Dom-Divalproex ❧Epival, Myproic, ❧Novo-Divalproex, ❧Novo-valproic, ❧Nu-Valproic, Rhoproic, Valproic

BENEFITS versus RISKS	
Possible Benefits	*Possible Risks*
EFFECTIVE CONTROL OF MULTIPLE SEIZURE TYPES: ABSENCE SEIZURES, TONIC-CLONIC SEIZURES, MYOCLONIC SEIZURES, PSYCHOMOTOR SEIZURES, when used adjunctively with other antiseizure drugs	LIVER TOXICITY, INFREQUENT BUT MAY BE SEVERE
	Reduction of blood platelets and impaired platelet function with risk of bleeding
HELPS CONTROL REFRACTORY MIGRAINES	Possible pancreatitis or liver toxicity
DIVALPROEX SODIUM HELPS MANIA	

▷ **Principal Uses**

As a Single Drug Product: Uses currently included in FDA-approved labeling: (1) Used to manage the following types of epilepsy: simple and complex absence seizures (petit mal); tonic-clonic seizures (grand mal); myoclonic seizures; complex partial seizures (psychomotor, temporal lobe epilepsy)—sometimes used adjunctively with other anticonvulsants as needed; (2)

used for people who do not respond to medicine once they have a migraine or have more than two migraines a month; (3) valproic acid and divalproex sodium (Depakote) are approved for use in treating mania; (4) eases mania in AIDS; (5) helps kleptomania

Author's Note: The American Psychiatric Association updated their 1994 treatment guidelines for bipolar disorder (see American Psychiatric Association in references). Valproate (Depakote form approved for mania secondary to bipolar problems). This or lithium are recommended as first choices for most people.

Other (unlabeled) generally accepted uses: (1) Can help relieve the symptoms of trigeminal neuralgia; (2) can have a role in intractable hiccups; (3) some use in patients with epilepsy and hepatic porphyria.

How This Drug Works: It is thought that by increasing the availability of the nerve impulse transmitter gamma-aminobutyric acid (GABA), this drug suppresses the spread of abnormal electrical discharges that cause seizures. May also act by lowering undesirable nerve excitation caused by aspartate or by a direct action on nerve (neuronal) membranes.

Available Dosage Forms and Strengths

Capsules — 250 mg

Capsules, sprinkle — 125 mg

Solution — 200 mg/ ml

Syrup — 250 mg/5 ml

Tablets, enteric coated — 125 mg, 250 mg, 500 mg

Tablets, extended release — 250 mg, 500 mg (Depakote ER form)

▷ **Usual Adult Dosage Ranges:** Starting dose is 10–15 mg per kg of body mass per day. The dose is increased cautiously by 5 to 10 mg per kg of body mass daily, every 7 days as needed and tolerated. The usual daily dose is from 1,000 mg to 1,600 mg in divided doses. The total daily dose should not exceed 60 mg per kg of body mass. Blood levels are used to guide ongoing dosing. *For migraines:* Starting dose is 250 mg, which is then slowly increased, as needed and tolerated, to 500 to 1000 mg daily in divided doses. For the extended release tablet: 500 mg once a day to start for seven days, then increased to 1,000 mg a day as needed and tolerated. *For mania:* Depakote is dosed as 750 mg daily in divided doses. In adults, a loading dose of 20 milligram per kilogram of body weight per day has been used in acute mania to achieve blood levels of 80 mg/liter.

Note: Actual dose and schedule must be determined for each patient individually.

Typical Treatment Goals and Measurements (Outcomes and Markers)

Seizures: The general goal for this medicine is effective seizure control. Neurologists tend to define effective on a case-by-case basis depending on the seizure type and patient factors. If seizure control is not effective, it's not unusual to use combination treatment. For this medicine, a balance must be struck between too little medicine and too much medicine. Blood levels are used to make sure that the amount of medicine is in just the right range.

Conditions Requiring Dosing Adjustments

Liver Function: This medicine SHOULD NOT be taken by patients with significant liver compromise or liver disease.

Kidney Function: No dosing changes thought to be needed in kidney disease, but prudent to get more frequent blood levels (free levels) and adjust dosing as needed.

▷ **Dosing Instructions:** Preferably taken 1 hour before meals, although it may be taken with or following food if necessary to prevent stomach irritation.

The regular capsule should not be opened, and the tablet should not be crushed in order to avoid irritation that this medicine can cause to the mouth and throat. The sprinkle capsule may be opened and the contents sprinkled on soft food, then best taken right away. Some remainders of the sprinkle form may be seen in your stool. Do not give the syrup in carbonated beverages. Dilute in water or milk. The solution and syrup have different concentrations. Make sure you have the correct product. Any liquid form should be dosed using a calibrated measuring spoon or dose cup. The extended release tablet should not be altered. If you forget a dose: Take the missed dose as soon as you remember it, unless it's nearly time for your next dose—if that is the case, skip the missed dose and take the next dose right on schedule. DO NOT double dose. Talk with your doctor if you find yourself missing doses. The best seizure control comes from keeping this medicine in just the right range. This most often results from taking just the right dose at just the right time.

Usual Duration of Use: Use on a regular schedule for 2 weeks usually determines effectiveness in reducing the frequency and severity of seizures. Long-term use (months to years) requires physician supervision and periodic evaluation. Use in seizure cases will be ongoing as will use in migraine prevention.

▷ **This Drug Should Not Be Taken If**
- you have had an allergic reaction to it previously.
- you have active liver disease.
- you are pregnant.
- you have an active bleeding disorder.

▷ **Inform Your Physician Before Taking This Drug If**
- you have a history of liver disease, impaired liver function, or pancreatitis.
- you have a history of any type of bleeding disorder.
- you are pregnant or planning pregnancy or are breast feeding your infant.
- you have myasthenia gravis or pancreatitis.
- you are taking anticoagulants, other anticonvulsants, or antidepressants—either the tricyclic type or monoamine oxidase (MAO) type A inhibitors (see Drug Classes).
- you develop yellow skin or eyes, loss of seizure control, unusual weakness or dizziness, or unusual bleeding or bruising while taking this medicine.
- you will have surgery or dental extraction.

Possible Side Effects (natural, expected, and unavoidable drug actions)
Drowsiness and lethargy, excessive lowering of blood pressure on standing (postural hypotension).

▷ **Possible Adverse Effects** (unusual, unexpected, and infrequent reactions)
If any of the following develop, consult your physician promptly for guidance.
Mild Adverse Effects
Allergic reaction: skin rash—rare.
Headache, dizziness, confusion, unsteadiness, tremor—dose-related.
Slurred speech—infrequent.
Nausea, indigestion, stomach cramps, diarrhea—infrequent.
Weight gain—case reports.
Bed-wetting at night—case reports.
Zinc, carnitine, and selenium lowering—possible.
Temporary loss of scalp hair—case reports.

Serious Adverse Effects
Idiosyncratic reactions: bizarre behavior, psychosis, hallucinations.
Drug-induced hepatitis with jaundice (see Glossary).
Children less than 2 years old have considerably increased risk of fatal liver toxicity (hepatotoxicity).
Leukemia-like cells in the circulation (acute promyelocytic leukemia (APML)—case report.
Blood ammonia level or blood glucose—increased.
Drug-induced pancreatitis, porphyria, lowered thyroid gland function (hypothyroidism)—case reports.
Selenium, zinc, and carnitine levels—decreased.
Reduced formation of blood platelets, impaired platelet function, and anemia (including pure red cell aplasia)—case reports.
Clotting (coagulation) defects—case reports (one case of lung bleeding).
Worsening of demylinating disease—case report.
Increased pressure in the head (pseudotumor cerebri)—case reports.
Movement problems (ataxia, extrapyramidal symptoms, others)—reported.
Can cause a Reye's-like syndrome.

▷ **Possible Effects on Sexual Function:** Altered timing and pattern of menstruation. Female breast enlargement with milk production (galactorrhea). Polycystic ovary syndrome (PCOS)—case reports. Decreased libido—case reports. Decreased effectiveness of oral contraceptives taken concurrently—CAUTION.

▷ **Adverse Effects That May Mimic Natural Diseases or Disorders**
Liver reactions may suggest viral hepatitis.

Possible Effects on Laboratory Tests
Complete blood cell counts: decreased white cells and platelets.
Bleeding time or INR (prothrombin time): increased.
Blood amylase level: increased (possible pancreatitis).
Liver function tests: increased enzymes (ALT/GPT, AST/GOT, alkaline phosphatase) or bilirubin.

CAUTION
1. The capsules and tablets should be swallowed whole to avoid irritation of the mouth and throat.
2. Carnitine, selenium, and zinc supplementation may be needed. Talk to your doctor.
3. This drug can impair normal blood-clotting mechanisms. In the event of injury, dental extraction, or need for surgery, inform your physician or dentist that you are taking this drug.
4. Because this drug can impair the normal function of blood platelets, it is best to avoid aspirin (which has the same effect).
5. Because this drug can lead to pancreatitis, patients are best told about signs of pancreatitis and to call their doctor if they happen
6. Over-the-counter drug products that contain antihistamines (allergy and cold remedies, sleep aids) can enhance sedation.

Precautions for Use
By Infants and Children: The concurrent use of aspirin with this drug can cause abnormal bleeding or bruising. Children with mental retardation, organic brain disease, or severe seizure disorders may be at increased risk for severe liver toxicity while taking this drug. Observe closely for the development of fever that could indicate the onset of a drug-induced Reye's syn-

drome (see Glossary). Avoid concurrent use of clonazepam (Klonopin); the combined use could result in continuous petit mal episodes.

By Those Over 60 Years of Age: Start treatment with small doses and increase dose cautiously. Observe closely for excessive sedation, confusion, or unsteadiness that could predispose to falling and injury.

▷ **Advisability of Use During Pregnancy**

Pregnancy Category: D. See Pregnancy Risk Categories at the back of this book.

Animal Studies: Palate and skeletal birth defects reported in mouse, rat, and rabbit studies.

Human Studies: Adequate studies of pregnant women are not available. There have been several reports of birth defects attributed to the use of this drug during early pregnancy.

Talk to your doctor about the advantages and disadvantages of using this drug. If it is used, it is advisable to keep the dose as low as possible.

Advisability of Use If Breast-Feeding

Presence of this drug in breast milk: Yes at roughly 1–10% of the mother's serum level.

Talk to your doctor about this benefit to risk decision.

Habit-Forming Potential: None.

Effects of Overdose: Increased drowsiness, weakness, unsteadiness, confusion, stupor progressing to coma.

Possible Effects of Long-Term Use: Coagulation changes, bone marrow depression.

Suggested Periodic Examinations While Taking This Drug (at physician's discretion)

Complete blood cell counts and baseline liver function tests should be done before treatment is started. During treatment, blood counts should be repeated every month and liver function tests repeated frequently (your doctor will define this)—particularly during the first 6 months of therapy. Amylase or patient sign and symptom instruction for possible pancreatitis is prudent.

▷ **While Taking This Drug, Observe the Following**

Foods: No restrictions.

Herbal Medicines or Minerals: Using kola, guarana, or ma huang may result in unacceptable central nervous system stimulation. Valerian and kava kava may interact to increase drowsiness and also have current concerns about possible liver effects (as well as eucalyptus) and therefore are not presently recommended. St. John's wort may also cause increased sun sensitivity—caution is advised. Replacement of zinc and selenium is prudent. Carnitine replacement (intravenous) is needed in valproic acid–caused (induced) liver toxicity and overdose. Carnitine replacement may also be needed in infants and young children taking multiple seizure medicines as well as epileptic patients on a ketogenic diet who have low carnitine (hypocarnitinemia). Evening primrose oil and a contaminant in some ginkgo preparations can lead to increased seizure risk and are not advisable. Talk to your doctor and pharmacist BEFORE adding any herbals.

Beverages: Do not administer the syrup in carbonated beverages; this could liberate the valproic acid and irritate the mouth and throat. This drug may be taken with milk.

▷ *Alcohol:* Alcohol can increase the sedative effect of this drug. Also, this drug can increase the depressant effects of alcohol on brain function. Avoid alcohol.

Tobacco Smoking: No interactions expected. I advise everyone to quit smoking.
▷ *Other Drugs*
Valproic acid may ***increase*** the effects of
- anticoagulants (Coumadin, etc.) and increase the risk of bleeding; increased frequency of INR (prothrombin time or protime) testing is needed.
- antidepressants (both monoamine oxidase [MAO] type A inhibitors and tricyclics) and cause toxicity.
- benzodiazepines (such as alprazolam).
- nimodipine (Nimotop) and cause nimodipine toxicity.
- phenobarbital and cause barbiturate intoxication.
- phenytoin (Dilantin) or fosphenytoin (Cerebyx) and cause phenytoin or fosphenytoin toxicity.
- zidovudine (AZT) and may lead to zidovudine toxicity.

Valproic acid ***taken concurrently*** with
- acyclovir (Zovirax) may lower valproic acid levels.
- antacids (Maalox) will decrease absorption and lower therapeutic benefits of valproic acid.
- antiplatelet drugs—aspirin, dipyridamole (Persantine), sulfinpyrazone (Anturane)—may enhance the inhibition of platelet function and increase the risk of bleeding.
- aspirin can lead to valproic acid toxicity.
- carbamazepine (Tegretol) may have a variable effect on blood levels; more frequent blood level testing is advised.
- cholestyramine (various) may blunt valproic acid benefits.
- clonazepam (Klonopin) may result in repeated episodes of absence seizures (absence status).
- cyclosporine (Sandimmune) may increase risk of liver toxicity.
- erythromycin (Ery-Tab, others) may increase the level of valproic acid and result in toxicity; the newer macrolides (azithromycin or clarithromycin) may also cause problems.
- felbamate (Felbatol) can lead to increased valproic acid levels.
- fluoxetine (Luvox) can lead to increased valproic acid levels. Blood levels and dosing adjusted to levels is prudent.
- isoniazid (INH) can cause valproic acid or isoniazid toxicity.
- rifampin (Rifater) may lead to valproic acid toxicity.
- ritonavir (Norvir) can lead to loss of valproic acid benefits.

▷ *Driving, Hazardous Activities:* This drug may cause drowsiness, dizziness, or confusion. Restrict activities as necessary.
Aviation Note: The use of this drug ***is a disqualification*** for piloting. Consult a designated Aviation Medical Examiner.
Exposure to Sun: Caution: This drug has caused photosensitivity.
Discontinuation: Do not stop this drug suddenly. Abrupt withdrawal can cause repetitive seizures that are difficult to control.

VANCOMYCIN (van koh MI sin)

Introduced: 1974   **Class:**   Anti-infective, glycopeptideantibiotic   **Prescription:**   USA: Yes   **Controlled Drug:**   USA: No; Canada: No   **Available as Generic:**   USA: Yes; Canada: Yes
Brand Names: ✤PMS-Vancomycin, Vancocin, Vancoled, Vancor

Author's Note: Vancomycin is used to treat a variety of serious infections. It is given intravenously to treat some infections and orally to treat others. In the past, the information provided in this profile was limited to the use of vancomycin taken by mouth. Since resistant organisms have increased use of this medicine by vein (intravenously), this profile has been expanded to help patients understand vancomycin's broadened role in infectious disease.

BENEFITS versus RISKS

Possible Benefits	*Possible Risks*
TREATS SERIOUS INFECTIONS CAUSED BY RESISTANT GRAM-POSITIVE ORGANISMS SUCH AS STAPH AND STREP	KIDNEY TOXICITY (with combined aminoglycoside use)
	Ringing in ears (tinnitus)
TREATS ANTIBIOTIC-ASSOCIATED PSEUDOMEMBRANOUS COLITIS (oral form)	Loss of hearing

---

▷ **Principal Uses**

As a Single Drug Product: Uses currently included in FDA-approved labeling: (1) Oral form is used in antibiotic-associated pseudomembranous colitis caused by *Clostridium difficile;* (2) the oral form is also used in enterocolitis caused by staphylococcal organisms; (3) the intravenous form is used to treat a variety of serious infections, such those in heart valves, bones (osteomyelitis), endocarditis, and meningitis, including those caused by methicillin-resistant *Staphylococcus aureus* (MRSA) and other susceptible bacteria.

Other (unlabeled) generally accepted uses: (1) May have a role preventing central venous catheter infections (combined with heparin flush) in immunosuppressed pediatric patients; (2) recommended by the CDC as one of the additional antibiotics to be part of combination therapy for inhalational, oropharyngeal, or gastrointestinal anthrax cases in the case of intentional bioterrorist release.

How This Drug Works: By inhibiting the formation of bacterial cell walls and the production of RNA, this drug destroys susceptible strains of infecting bacteria.

Available Dosage Forms and Strengths

Capsules — 125 mg, 250 mg

Intravenous — 500 mg/15 ml, 1 g/15 ml

Oral solution — 250 mg/5 ml teaspoonful and 500 mg/5 ml

▷ **Recommended Dosage Ranges** (Actual dose and schedule must be determined for each patient individually.)

Infants and Children: 10 mg per kg of body mass every 6 hours, for 5 to 10 days. The total daily dose should not exceed 2,000 mg (2 g). Repeat course as necessary.

12 to 60 Years of Age: Intravenous: Many clinicians use a 15-mg-per-kg-of-body-mass loading dose and then calculate ongoing doses based on individual patient height, weight, kidney function, and suspected bacteria (bacterial pathogen). Calculations are made in order to attain a peak blood level of 30–40 mcg/ml and a lowest blood level (trough) of 5–10 mcg/ml.

Oral dosing for pseudomembranous colitis caused by *Clostridium difficile:* 125 mg by mouth every 6 hours for 10 days.

Over 60 Years of Age: Intravenous dosing: The loading dose is the same as for younger patients. Ongoing doses may be much smaller and may need to be taken much less often than in younger patients (such as once a day or once every 2 days) because of the age-related declines in kidney function.

Oral dosing: Same as 12 to 60 years of age (vancomycin in pseudomembranous colitis is not absorbed).

Conditions Requiring Dosing Adjustments

Liver Function: The liver is not involved in the elimination of vancomycin.

Kidney Function: Oral vancomycin is minimally absorbed. Intravenous vancomycin MUST be taken in decreased dose or increased interval in kidney failure. This drug is also a potential cause of kidney failure and should only be taken if other alternatives are not available. Daily measures of kidney function and more frequent blood levels are indicated if this medicine is used by patients with compromised kidneys.

▷ **Dosing Instructions:** Oral form may be taken with or following food to reduce stomach irritation. Because of this drug's unpleasant taste, it is preferable to swallow the capsule whole without alteration. Use a measuring device to ensure accuracy of dose when taking the oral solution. Observe the expiration date. If you forget a dose: For oral dosing: Take the missed dose as soon as you remember it, unless it's nearly time for your next dose—if that is the case, skip the missed dose and take the next dose right on schedule. Take any remaining doses for the day at evenly spaced intervals, then return to your usual dosing schedule. For intravenous home therapy: If you miss a dose, call the home IV service or your doctor for instructions. Talk with your doctor if you find yourself missing doses because the best results come from taking this medicine right on time and keeping the blood levels or intestinal levels high enough to kill the infecting organism.

Usual Duration of Use

Oral use: Use on a regular schedule for 48 to 72 hours usually determines effectiveness in controlling infection in the colon. If response is prompt, treatment may be limited to 10 days. If symptoms warrant, oral treatment for *Clostridium difficile* diarrhea may have to be continued for 14 to 21 days. See your doctor on a regular basis.

Intravenous use: The length of treatment depends on the severity and site of the infection (for example, bone infections such as osteomyelitis may take 6 weeks to cure, anthrax cases—60 days).

Typical Treatment Goals and Measurements (Outcomes and Markers)

Infections: The most commonly used measures of serious infections are white blood cell counts and differentials (the kind of blood cells that occur most often in your blood), and temperature. Many clinicians look for positive changes in 24–48 hours. NEVER stop an antibiotic because you start to feel better. For many infections, a full 14 days is REQUIRED to kill the bacteria. The goals and time frame (see peak benefits above) should be discussed with you when the prescription is written.

Currently a "Drug of Choice"

For treating metronidazole-treatment failures in antibiotic-associated pseudomembranous colitis caused by *Clostridium difficile* and in cases of methicillin-resistant *Staphylococcus aureus* (MRSA).

▷ **This Drug Should Not Be Taken If**

- you have had an allergic reaction to it previously.

▷ **Inform Your Physician Before Taking This Drug If**
- you have a history of Crohn's disease or ulcerative colitis.
- you have impaired kidney function.
- you are pregnant.
- you have any degree of hearing loss.
- you are taking cholestyramine (Questran) or colestipol (Colestid) and are prescribed the oral form.

Possible Side Effects (natural, expected, and unavoidable drug actions)
Bitter, unpleasant taste for the oral form. Kidney damage with long-term, high-dose use of the intravenous form. Red-man syndrome (lowering of blood pressure, sudden rash of neck, chest, face, and extremities) and even cardiac arrest have occurred with too rapid vancomycin infusions. Doses should be given over one hour.

▷ **Possible Adverse Effects** (unusual, unexpected, and infrequent reactions)
If any of the following develop, consult your physician promptly for guidance.

Mild Adverse Effects
Allergic reaction: skin rash (with large doses or prolonged use).
Nausea, vomiting—infrequent with oral form and rare with intravenous form.
Chills—infrequent.

Serious Adverse Effects
Allergic reactions: anaphylaxis.
Serious skin rashes (exfoliative dermatitis or Stevens-Johnson Syndrome).
Ringing or buzzing in ears, sensation of ear fullness, loss of hearing—toxicity sign.
Lowering of white blood cells—reversible and seen with the intravenous form.
Lowering of white blood cells (granulocytes) and platelets—case reports and reversible with granulocyte colony stimulating factor (GCSF).
Cardiac arrest—rare.
Hearing loss—may be reversible and more likely with high-dose or long-term use.
Kidney toxicity—may be dose-dependent and more likely with higher doses and long-term use.
Pseudomembranous colitis—possible with the IV form.
Thrombophlebitis—infrequent with the intravenous form.

▷ **Possible Effects on Sexual Function:** None reported.

Natural Diseases or Disorders That May Be Activated by This Drug
Latent hearing loss, kidney failure.

Possible Effects on Laboratory Tests
Serum creatinine: increased (a sign of kidney toxicity).

CAUTION
1. Report promptly the development of fullness, ringing, or buzzing in either ear. This may indicate the onset of nerve damage that could lead to hearing loss.
2. Do not take any medication to stop your diarrhea without calling your doctor. The bacterial toxin that causes colitis is eliminated by diarrhea; stopping the elimination could intensify and prolong your illness.
3. Blood levels MUST be used to guide intravenous dosing. Keep all appointments for laboratory work.

Precautions for Use
By Infants and Children: Some cases may require doses up to 50 mg per kg of body mass daily.
By Those Over 60 Years of Age: You may be more susceptible to drug-induced hearing loss. Use the minimum course of treatment required to cure your colitis or other infection.

▷ **Advisability of Use During Pregnancy**
Pregnancy Category: C. See Pregnancy Risk Categories at the back of this book.
Animal Studies: Rat and rabbit studies reveal no drug-induced birth defects.
Human Studies: Adequate studies of pregnant women are not available.
Use this drug only if clearly needed. Ask your doctor for help.

Advisability of Use If Breast-Feeding
Presence of this drug in breast milk: Yes.
Avoid drug or refrain from nursing.

Habit-Forming Potential: None.

Effects of Overdose: Possible nausea, vomiting, ringing in ears.

Possible Effects of Long-Term Use: Hearing loss.

Suggested Periodic Examinations While Taking This Drug (at physician's discretion)
Hearing tests.
Measures of kidney function and blood vancomycin levels with intravenous use.

▷ **While Taking This Drug, Observe the Following**
Foods: No restrictions.
Herbal Medicines or Minerals: Some patients use echinacea to attempt to boost their immune systems. Unfortunately, use of echinacea is not recommended in people with damaged immune systems. This herb may also actually weaken any immune system if it is used too often or for too long a time.
Beverages: No restrictions. May be taken with milk.
▷ *Alcohol:* No interactions expected. Use sparingly; alcohol may aggravate colitis.
Tobacco Smoking: No interactions expected. I advise everyone to quit smoking.
▷ *Other Drugs*
The following drugs may ***decrease*** the effects of vancomycin:
• cholestyramine (Questran).
• colestipol (Colestid).
Vancomycin ***taken concurrently*** with
• aminoglycoside antibiotics (see Drug Classes), such as gentamicin or tobramycin, may cause additive toxicity risk to the ears and kidneys.
• cyclosporine (Sandimmune) may result in increased toxicity risk.
• metformin (Glucophage) or other cationic drugs poses an increased risk of lactic acidosis.
• other medicines that cause kidney toxicity may pose an additive toxicity risk.
• rapacuronium (Raplon) can lead to extended neuromuscular blockade requiring neostigmine use.
• succinylcholine (Anectine) can lead to extended neuromuscular blockade requiring neostigmine use.
• warfarin (Coumadin) may cause increased bleeding risk; increased INR (prothrombin time or protime) testing is needed.
▷ *Driving, Hazardous Activities:* Usually no restrictions.

Aviation Note: The use of this drug is ***probably not a disqualification*** for piloting. Consult a designated Aviation Medical Examiner.

Exposure to Sun: No restrictions.

Special Storage Instructions: Refrigerate the oral solution. A home IV service will explain storage of the intravenous form.

Observe the Following Expiration Times: Provided on your prescription label by your pharmacist.

Discontinuation: To be determined by your physician.

VARICELLA VIRUS VACCINE (VAIR a sell ah)

Introduced: 1995   **Class:**   Vaccine   **Prescription:**   USA: Yes
Controlled Drug: USA: No; Canada: No   **Available as Generic:**   USA: No; Canada: No

Brand Name: Varivax

BENEFITS versus RISKS	
Possible Benefits	*Possible Risks*
PREVENTION OF VARICELLA (chicken pox)	Rash
	Soreness at the injection site
	Anaphylactic reaction

▷ **Principal Uses**

As a Single Drug Product: Uses currently included in FDA-approved labeling: Prevention of chicken pox and shingles.

Other (unlabeled) generally accepted uses: (1) Prevention of herpes zoster (in people more than 55 years old) who have previously had chicken pox.

How This Drug Works: By stimulating the immune system, the vaccine prepares the body to fight any exposure to the wild-type virus.

Available Dosage Forms and Strengths

Vaccine: single-dose vials with a final dose of 1350 PFU per 0.5 ml.

How to Store

This product must be kept frozen prior to use.

▷ **Recommended Dosage Ranges** (Actual dose and schedule must be determined for each patient individually.)

Infants and Children (One Year to 12 Years Old): Children 1 year old to 12 years are given 0.5 ml injected under the skin. Those 13 or older should be given a first shot of 0.5 ml, followed by a second shot 4 to eight weeks after the first one. In people who fail to develop immunity (usually happens in about 30 days), revaccination to take place 3 months after the first attempt should be undertaken.

Otherwise Healthy Adults: Same as the children's dose for 13 and older, providing the patient has not had chicken pox.

Over 55 Years of Age: Not studied.

Author's Note: The Centers for Disease Control (CDC) Immunization Practices Committee has recommended that all children 12- to 18-months-old should be given varicella vaccine if they have not previously contracted chicken pox. The vaccine is also recommended by the committee for children 19 months to 13 years old. Finally, adults or adolescents who have not had chicken pox and are at risk for expo-

sure may also be given the vaccine. Current recommendations for vaccines in general can be found at *www.cdc.gov/nip/recs/child-schedule. htm*. Those who are immunosuppressed (including HIV or AIDS) should NOT be given the vaccine.

Conditions Requiring Dosing Adjustments
Liver Function: Not a consideration.
Kidney Function: Not a consideration.

▷ **Dosing Instructions:** This vaccine is to be injected under the skin. It may be given with measles, mumps, and rubella vaccine. If you forget to get vaccinated: Talk with your pediatrician about vaccine schedules. It's always better to PREVENT a disease or condition than to have to treat it.

Usual Duration of Benefit: Exposure to chicken pox 5 years after vaccination may result in 20% of patients developing mild disease. More experience is needed before the question of repeat vaccination (booster) is answered. At present a booster dose is NOT recommended. Immunity may last 10 years.

Typical Treatment Goals and Measurements (Outcomes and Markers)
Immune response/protection from varicella (chicken pox): The general goal is to challenge the immune system of the person receiving the vaccination enough to elicit an immune response that will protect the person from the virus itself. For example, my generation was "expected" to get many of the childhood diseases. Subsequently, measles, mumps, and varicella vaccines were created, and possible mortality and morbidity may be avoided in those who received the "shots." The varicella vaccine is important as it probably protects adults from shingles later in life. Clinical markers include gpELISA of greater than 0.3 and avoidance of varicella infection despite subsequent exposure. Check of cell-mediated immunity (CMI) by delayed hypersensitivity or a specific white blood cell (lymphocyte transformation) may give a more accurate picture of immune status.

Possible Advantages of This Drug
Prevention of chicken pox when in childhood and avoidance of shingles later in life as an adult. Nerve pain from shingles (Post herpetic neuralgia) is severe.

Currently a "Drug of Choice"
For prevention of chicken pox. Some company-based information can be obtained by calling 1-800-Merck-RX or 1-800-637-2579.

▷ **This Drug Should Not Be Taken If**
- you have a history of anaphylactic reaction to neomycin.
- you have a history of blood diseases or leukemia or have HIV/AIDS.
- you are taking medicines that suppress the immune system.
- you have tuberculosis that has not been treated.
- you are allergic to eggs, gelatin, or any other vaccine component.
- you are pregnant (avoid pregnancy for 3 months after vaccine).
- you have an active infection.

▷ **Inform Your Physician Before Taking This Drug If**
- you are planning pregnancy in the near future.
- you have a condition that may require steroids.
- you have had blood or plasma transfusions (vaccination should be delayed for 5 months).
- you take salicylates (aspirin, others) on a regular basis. This should NOT be done for 6 weeks following vaccination, as it is a risk for Reye's syndrome.
- you live with someone who has a depressed immune system (such as an

AIDS patient). Because this vaccine is a live-virus vaccine, you may be infectious to them.

Possible Side Effects (natural, expected, and unavoidable drug actions)
Pain at the injection site, fever—infrequent to frequent.

▷ **Possible Adverse Effects** (unusual, unexpected, and infrequent reactions)
If any of the following develop, consult your physician promptly for guidance.

Mild Adverse Effects
Allergic reaction: skin rash.
Varicella-like rash—infrequent.
Headache, irritability, fatigue, and loss of appetite—rare to infrequent.
Increased sensitivity to light (photophobia)—case reports.
Chills, stiff neck, and joint pain (arthralgia)—infrequent.
Nausea, vomiting—rare.

Serious Adverse Effects
Allergic reactions: anaphylactic reaction, Serious skin rashes (Stevens-Johnson Syndrome or TENS)—case reports.
Idiosyncratic reactions: none reported.
Febrile seizures—case reports.
Thrombocytopenic purpura—case reports.
Herpes zoster—possible.
Pneumonitis—case report and of questionable causation.
May be possible for a recently vaccinated person to transmit varicella to a susceptible contact—one case report.

▷ **Possible Effects on Sexual Function:** None reported.

Possible Delayed Adverse Effects: None reported.

▷ **Adverse Effects That May Mimic Natural Diseases or Disorders**
Rash may resemble chicken pox.

Natural Diseases or Disorders That May Be Activated by This Drug
None reported.

Possible Effects on Laboratory Tests
None reported.

CAUTION
Do not give aspirin or other salicylates to patients who have recently received the vaccine. The risk of Reye's syndrome is associated with such aspirin use.

Precautions for Use
By Infants and Children: Safety and effectiveness for use by those under 12 months of age have not been established.
By Those Over 60 Years of Age: Not studied.

▷ **Advisability of Use During Pregnancy**
Pregnancy Category: C. See Pregnancy Risk Categories at the back of this book.
Animal Studies: Have not been conducted with this vaccine.
Human Studies: Information from adequate studies of pregnant women is not available.
The manufacturer says that the vaccine should not be given to pregnant women, and pregnancy should be avoided for 3 months following vaccination.

Advisability of Use If Breast-Feeding
Presence of this drug in breast milk: Expected.
Vaccine viewed as appropriate by American Academy of Pediatrics if the risk of exposure of the mother is high. Avoid drug or refrain from nursing.

Habit-Forming Potential: None.

Effects of Overdose: Not defined.

Possible Effects of Long-Term Use: Not intended for long-term use.

Suggested Periodic Examinations While Taking This Drug (at physician's discretion)

Immunity check.

▷ **While Taking This Drug, Observe the Following**

Foods: No restrictions.

Herbal Medicines or Minerals: Some patients use echinacea to attempt to boost their immune systems. Unfortunately, use of echinacea is not recommended in people with damaged immune systems. This herb may also actually weaken any immune system if it is used too often or for too long a time. Mistletoe has also not been studied and can not be recommended.

Beverages: No restrictions.

▷ *Alcohol:* No interactions expected.

Tobacco Smoking: No interactions expected. I advise everyone to quit smoking.

▷ *Other Drugs*

Varicella vaccine *taken concurrently* with

• acyclovir (Zovirax) may result in a blunted immune benefit from the vaccine.
• adalimumab (Humira) may result in a blunted immune benefit from the vaccine.
• aspirin or any salicylates (various) may result in Reye's syndrome—DO NOT take aspirin for 6 weeks after vaccination.
• chemotherapy (various) may lead to infection risk by the vaccine.
• corticosteroids (see Drug Classes) may result in extreme reactions.
• etanercept (Enbrel) may blunt immune response to varicella vaccine.
• hepatitis B immune globulin may blunt immune response to varicella vaccine.
• immune globulins (such as varicella-zoster immune globulin, rabies, or tetanus immune globulin) may blunt beneficial response to the vaccine.
• immunosuppressant medicines (such as cyclosporine [Sandimmune], sirolimus [Rapamune] or tacrolimus [Prograf]) may result in blunted beneficial vaccine response as well as unexpected reactions, sometimes extreme reactions.
• infliximab (Remicade) may increase risk of varicella infection from varicella vaccine itself.
• leflunomide (Arava) may blunt immune response to varicella vaccine. Rapid elimination procedure for leflunomide may be needed.
• mesalamine (Asacol) may result in risk of Reye's syndrome—DO NOT take salicylates for 6 weeks after vaccination.
• olsalazine (Dipentum) may result in risk of Reye's syndrome—DO NOT take salicylates for 6 weeks after vaccination.

▷ *Driving, Hazardous Activities:* This drug may cause soreness at the injection site. Restrict activities as necessary.

Aviation Note: The use of this drug *is probably not a disqualification* for piloting. Consult a designated Aviation Medical Examiner.

Exposure to Sun: No restrictions.

Occurrence of Unrelated Illness: This vaccination should not be given in the presence of any other active infection.

Special Storage Instructions: This vaccine must be stored frozen.

Author's Note: There is now a Vaccine Adverse Event Reporting System (VAERS). The toll-free number is 1-800-822-7967.

VENLAFAXINE (ven la FAX een)

Introduced: 1993   **Class:**   Antidepressant   **Prescription:**   USA: Yes   **Controlled Drug:**   USA: No; Canada: No   **Available as Generic:** USA: No

Brand Names: Effexor, Effexor XR

BENEFITS versus RISKS

Possible Benefits	*Possible Risks*
EFFECTIVE TREATMENT OF DEPRESSION	INCREASED BLOOD PRESSURE
	Seizures
BETTER SIDE-EFFECT PROFILE THAN TRICYCLIC ANTI-DEPRESSANTS	Constipation
	Increased heart rate
	Increased serum lipids
RAPID ONSET OF EFFECT	
EXCELLENT REMISSION RATE IN MAJOR DEPRESSION	
HELPS PREVENT RELAPSE AND RECURRENCE OF DEPRESSION	
EFFECTIVE TREATMENT OF ANXIETY	
TREATS GENERALIZED ANXIETY DISORDER	
TREATMENT OF SOCIAL ANXIETY DISORDER	
Second line treatment of children who have both depression and ADHD (XR form)	
May decrease hot flashes in cancer survivors and after menopause	

▷ **Principal Uses**

As a Single Drug Product: Uses currently included in FDA-approved labeling: (1) Treatment of depression; (2) treatment of generalized anxiety disorder; (3) treatment of social anxiety disorder (also called social phobia); (4) prevention of relapse and recurrence of depression.

Other (unlabeled) generally accepted uses: (1) May be useful in obsessive-compulsive disorder; (2) may treat chronic fatigue syndrome; (3) may have a role in easing hot flashes in cancer survivors and after menopause; (4) second line treatment in children who have both depression and ADHD; (5) can be helpful in premenstrual dysphoric disorder (PMDD); (6) case based use in neuropathic pain and nerve pain from chemotherapy with a more favorable side effect profile than tricyclic antidepressants.

How This Drug Works: This bicyclic (second-generation) antidepressant inhibits the return (reuptake) of nerve transmitters (serotonin, norepinephrine, and dopamine) and helps return normal mood and thinking. This medicine is actually a mixture of two forms called isomers. The positive isomer works mostly as a serotonin uptake inhibitor.

Available Dosage Forms and Strengths
Tablets — 25 mg, 37.5 mg, 50 mg, 75 mg, 100 mg
Tablets, extended release — 37.5 mg, 75 mg, 100 mg, 150 mg (100 mg in Canada)
Tablets, sustained release — 100 and 150 mg (Canada only)

▷ **Recommended Dosage Ranges** (Actual dose and schedule must be determined for each patient individually.)

Infants and Children: Safety and efficacy for those under 18 years of age are not established.

18 to 60 Years of Age: For depression and generalized anxiety disorder: Start with 75 mg per day, as 25-mg doses three times daily taken with food. If needed and tolerated, the dose may be increased at 4-day intervals in steps up to a maximum of 225 mg per day. Some hospitalized patients have been given a maximum of 375 mg per day. The XR form is started at 37.5 milligrams per day. Dose increases of 75 mg/day can be made at intervals of at least 4 days. Daily maximum is 225 mg per day. In general, conversion from immediate release to venlafaxine XR can be done using the total immediate release daily dose and converting that to the nearest equal dose of the XR form.

For reducing hot flashes in cancer survivors: 12.5 mg twice daily.

Over 60 Years of Age: Low starting doses and slow increases are indicated. Natural declines in kidney function may lead to drug accumulation at higher doses. May worsen constipation.

Conditions Requiring Dosing Adjustments ·

Liver Function: Total daily dose must be reduced by 50% for patients with moderate liver compromise. Further dose decreases and individualized dosing is needed in liver cirrhosis.

Kidney Function: Patients with compromised kidneys (creatinine clearance of 10 to 70 ml/min) should take 75% of the usual daily dose.

▷ **Dosing Instructions:** Best to take this medicine with food. The XR form should NOT be crushed or chewed. If you forget a dose: Take the missed dose as soon as you remember it, unless it's nearly time for your next dose—if that is the case, skip the missed dose and take the next dose right on schedule. DO NOT double up on doses. Because this medicine must reach an equilibrium (or steady state) in the brain, it is very important to take it exactly as prescribed to get the best results in helping depression. Talk with your doctor if you find yourself missing doses.

Usual Duration of Use: Regular use for 2 weeks usually determines benefits in treating depression, but up to 6 weeks may be needed to see the peak benefits. Decreasing hot flashes in cancer survivors may take several weeks. Long-term use requires follow-up by your doctor.

Typical Treatment Goals and Measurements (Outcomes and Markers)

Depression: The general goal: to at least help lessen the degree and severity of depression, letting patients return to their daily lives. Specific measures of depression involve testing or inventories (such as the Hamilton Depression) and can be valuable in helping check benefits from this medicine. In using this medicine for short-trem treatment of social anxiety disorder (SAD), the Liebowitz Social Anxiety Scale (LSAS) is often used.

Possible Advantages of This Drug

Effective treatment of depression with fewer side effects than other currently available agents. Starts to have a therapeutic effect more rapidly than other available agents. One study of 1,108 patients with major depression found a 45% remission rate. Works on both serotonin and norepinephrine nerve transmitters (neurotransmitters) unlike other antidepressants which may only impact serotonin.

▷ **This Drug Should Not Be Taken If**
- you had an allergic reaction to any form of it previously.
- you are taking a monoamine oxidase (MAO) inhibitor (see Drug Classes).

▷ **Inform Your Physician Before Taking This Drug If**
- you have a history of high blood pressure.
- you've recently had a heart attack.
- you have a history of abnormally increased lipids (hyperlipidemia).
- you are planning pregnancy.
- you have a history of seizures.
- you have a history of suicide attempts or think about suicide.
- you have trouble sleeping.
- you have a history of hypomania or mania.
- you are unsure how much to take or how often to take this medicine.

Possible Side Effects (natural, expected, and unavoidable drug actions)
    Constipation and headache. Sleepiness, weight loss, dry mouth. Small increases in cholesterol (2–3 mg/dl). A withdrawal syndrome is possible if this medicine is stopped abruptly. Best to slowly decrease (taper) the dose over 2–4 weeks or longer.

▷ **Possible Adverse Effects** (unusual, unexpected, and infrequent reactions)
    If any of the following develop, consult your physician promptly for guidance.

    Mild Adverse Effects
    Allergic reactions: Possible.
    Palpitations or fast heart rate—rare.
    Nausea and vomiting—infrequent.
    Weight decrease—infrequent.
    Easy bruising (ecchymosis)—case report.
    Dizziness (may disappear without treatment), fatigue, and headache—infrequent to frequent.
    Anxiety, somnolence, or insomnia (may stop on its own).
    Blurred vision—possible.
    Spontaneous and easy bruising (ecchymosis)—case report.
    Sweating—possible (benztropine eased one case).

    Serious Adverse Effects
    Allergic reactions: Possible.
    Idiosyncratic reactions: one case report of lowered white blood cells (agranulocytosis).
    Liver toxicity—case reports.
    SIADH and very low sodium—case reports.
    Increased blood pressure—case reports.
    Serotonin syndrome—case reports.
    Neuroleptic malignant syndrome—case report.
    Rhabdomyolisis—case report.
    Mania—case reports.
    Seizures—very rare during premarketing studies.

▷ **Possible Effects on Sexual Function:** Delayed orgasm, abnormal ejaculation, priapism, impotence, and erectile failure—all rare.

Possible Delayed Adverse Effects: None reported.

▷ **Adverse Effects That May Mimic Natural Diseases or Disorders**
 None reported.
Natural Diseases or Disorders That May Be Activated by This Drug
 None reported.
Possible Effects on Laboratory Tests
 Serum cholesterol: increased slightly.
CAUTION
 1. This drug should not be taken with MAO inhibitors (see Glossary). If you
  have recently stopped an MAO inhibitor, 14 days should pass before ven-
  lafaxine is started.
 2. Because the half life of this medicine is relatively short, if this medicine
  needs to be stopped, best to slowly decrease (taper) it over 2–4 weeks or
  longer.
▷ **Advisability of Use During Pregnancy**
 Pregnancy Category: C. See Pregnancy Risk Categories at the back of this book.
 Animal Studies: There was an increase in stillborn rats at 10 times the usual
  human dose.
 Human Studies: Adequate studies of pregnant women are not available.
 Ask your doctor for guidance.
Advisability of Use If Breast-Feeding
 Presence of this drug in breast milk: Yes.
 Monitor nursing infant closely, and discontinue drug or nursing if adverse
  effects develop.
Habit-Forming Potential: None.
Effects of Overdose: Nausea, vomiting, constipation, seizure potential.
Possible Effects of Long-Term Use: None noted.
Suggested Periodic Examinations While Taking This Drug (at physician's dis-
  cretion)
 Blood pressure checks, periodic lipid panels, resolution of depression.
▷ **While Taking This Drug, Observe the Following**
 Foods: No restrictions.
 Herbal Medicines or Minerals: Since venlafaxine and St. John's wort may act to
  increase serotonin, the combination is not advised (St. John's wort may
  also cause fast heart rate). Since part of the way ginseng and ginkgo work
  may be as an MAO inhibitor, do not combine ginseng or ginkgo with venlafaxine. Ma huang, yohimbe, Indian snakeroot, and kava kava are also
  best avoided while taking this medicine. Talk to your doctor BEFORE
  combining any herbals with this medicine.
 Nutritional Support: No special support indicated.
 Beverages: Since venlafaxine is metabolized in the liver and grapefruit juice has
  been shown to inhibit the removal (metabolism) of some other medications, caution is advised. Water is the best liquid to take this medicine with.
▷ *Alcohol:* May increase somnolence if combined.
 Tobacco Smoking: No interactions expected. I advise everyone to quit smoking.
 Marijuana Smoking: Additive effect on somnolence, one case of mania following combination with fluoxetine. DO NOT COMBINE.
▷ *Other Drugs*
 Venlafaxine *taken concurrently* with
  • beta blockers (see Drug Classes) may result in larger than expected pharmacological effects from the beta blockers; because these agents are
   metabolized in the liver and venlafaxine may block this metabolism, caution is advised.

- calcium channel blockers (see Drug Classes) may result in toxicity; because these agents are metabolized in the liver and venlafaxine may block this metabolism, caution is advised.
- cimetidine (Tagamet) may lead to venlafaxine toxicity.
- dextromethorphan (the DM in many cough and cold preparations) may result in dextromethorphan or venlafaxine toxicity. Caution is advised.
- dofetilide (Tikosyn) may result in dofetilide toxicity.
- MAO inhibitors (see Drug Classes) may lead to undesirable side effects—DO NOT COMBINE.
- medicines such as class I, IA, or III antiarrhythmics (dofetilide (Tikosyn), clarithromycin, cotrimoxazole, ondansetron, ziprazidone, and others may lead to added prolongation of the QTc interval and undesirable effects. Combination is not recommended.
- quinidine (Quinaglute, others) may result in venlafaxine toxicity.
- ritonavir (Norvir) may lead to venlafaxine toxicity.
- drugs with sedative properties will increase those effects.
- paroxetine (Paxil—a SSRI) or SNRIs can lead to a serotonin syndrome if a sufficient time does not pass between stopping a first medicine and starting an alternative therapy. The time required (washout) may vary patient to patient, but the generally accepted time is two weeks.
- sibutramine (Meridia) increases toxicity risk (serotonin syndrome)—DO NOT COMBINE.
- sumatriptan (Imitrex), naratriptan (Amerge), rizatriptan (Maxalt) or zolmitriptan (Zomig), almotriptan (Axert), or other "triptans" may lead to incoordination and weakness—DO NOT COMBINE.
- tramadol (Ultram) may increase the risk of seizures.
- tricyclic antidepressants (see Drug Classes) may result in toxicity; because these agents are metabolized in the liver and venlafaxine may block this metabolism, caution is advised.
- warfarin (Coumadin) may result in bleeding; more frequent INR (prothrombin time or protime) testing is needed. Ongoing warfarin doses should be adjusted to laboratory results.·
- zolpidem (Ambien) may increase risk of hallucinations—DO NOT COMBINE.

▷ *Driving, Hazardous Activities:* This drug may cause somnolence. Restrict activities as necessary.

Aviation Note: The use of this drug ***is a disqualification*** for piloting. Consult a designated Aviation Medical Examiner.

Exposure to Sun: No restrictions.

Exposure to Heat: No restrictions.

Discontinuation: If this medicine is to be stopped, the dose should be slowly lowered over 2–4 weeks or longer on your doctor's advice. Tapering over this time helps your body best adjust to not having this medicine, minimizing risk of undesirable discontinuation symptoms.

VERAPAMIL (ver AP a mil)

Introduced: 1967 **Class:** Anti-anginal, antiarrhythmic, antihypertensive, calcium channel blocker **Prescription:** USA: Yes **Controlled Drug:** USA: No; Canada: No **Available as Generic:** USA: Yes (verapamil SR); Canada: Yes

BrandNames: ❧Alti-Verapamil, ❧Apo-Verap, Calan, Calan SR, ❧Chronovera, Covera-HS, ❧Dom-Verapamil SR, ❧Gen-Verapamil, Isoptin, Isoptin SR, ❧Med-Verapamil, ❧Novo-Veramil, ❧Nu-Verap, ❧PMS-Verapamil, Tarka [CD], Verelan, Verelan PM

Controversies in Medicine: Medicines in this class have had many conflicting reports. The FDA has held hearings on the calcium channel blocker (CCB) class. Amlodipine got the first FDA approval to treat high blood pressure or angina in people with congestive heart failure. Early research at New York University found that a calcium channel blocker called nifedipine is a cause of reversible male infertility. CCBs are currently second-line agents for high blood pressure according to the JNC VII (see Glossary).

BENEFITS versus RISKS

Possible Benefits	*Possible Risks*
EFFECTIVE PREVENTION OF BOTH MAJOR TYPES OF ANGINA	Congestive heart failure
	Low blood pressure (infrequent)
EFFECTIVE CONTROL OF HEART RATE IN CHRONIC ATRIAL FIBRILLATION AND FLUTTER	Heart rhythm disturbance
	Fluid retention
	Constipation
EFFECTIVE PREVENTION OF PAROXYSMAL ATRIAL TACHYCARDIA (PAT)	Liver damage without jaundice
	Swelling of male breast tissue
EFFECTIVE TREATMENT OF HYPERTENSION	

▷ **Principal Uses**

As a Single Drug Product: Uses currently included in FDA-approved labeling: Used to treat (1) angina pectoris due to coronary artery spasm (Prinzmetal's variant angina) that occurs spontaneously and is not associated with exertion; (2) classical angina of effort (due to atherosclerotic disease of the coronary arteries) in individuals who have not responded to or cannot tolerate the nitrates and beta-blocker drugs customarily used to treat this disorder; (3) abnormally rapid heart rate due to chronic atrial fibrillation or flutter; (4) recurrent paroxysmal atrial or supraventricular tachycardia; (5) primary hypertension.

Other (unlabeled) generally accepted uses: (1) May help decrease keloid formation; (2) prevents abnormal heart rhythms that occur after surgery; (3) relieves symptoms of and may help reverse hypertrophic cardiomyopathy; (4) may help decrease the severity or occurrence of cluster headaches; (5) helps control symptoms of panic attacks; (6) can be of use in post-ischemic-acute-kidney failure; (7) may stop the progression of abnormal buildup on the inside of blood vessels (atherosclerosis); (8) may help decrease severity and occurrence of nocturnal leg cramps; (9) can help stuttering; (10) may have a role in treating Tourette's syndrome.

As a Combination Drug Product [CD]: This drug is available in combination (Tarka brand) with an ACE inhibitor (trandolapril). The combination offers benefits of two different mechanisms of action in the same medicine in treating high blood pressure.

How This Drug Works: By blocking passage of calcium through certain cell walls (which is necessary for the function of nerve and muscle tissue), this drug slows the spread of electrical activity through the heart and inhibits the contraction of coronary arteries and peripheral arterioles. As a result of these combined effects, this drug

- prevents spontaneous coronary artery spasm (Prinzmetal's type of angina).
- reduces heart rate and contraction force during exertion, thus lowering the oxygen requirement of the heart muscle; this reduces the occurrence of effort-induced angina (classical angina pectoris).
- reduces degree of contraction of peripheral arterial walls, resulting in relaxation and lowering of blood pressure. This further reduces the workload of the heart during exertion and contributes to the prevention of angina.
- slows the rate of electrical impulses through the heart and thereby prevents excessively rapid heart action (tachycardia).

Available Dosage Forms and Strengths

Caplets, sustained-release — 120 mg, 180 mg, 240 mg
Capsules, sustained-release — 120 mg, 180 mg, 240 mg, 360 mg
Injection — 5 mg/2 ml
Tablets — 40 mg, 80 mg, 120 mg
Tablets, combination (Tarka) — 1 mg trandolapril/240 mg verapamil,
2 mg trandolapril/180 mg verapamil,
2 mg trandolapril/240 mg verapamil,
4 mg trandolapril/240 mg verapamil
Tablets, extended-release — 180 mg, 240 mg, 360mg
Tablets, sustained-release — 120 mg, 180 mg, 240 mg
Tablets, timed-release (Verelan PM) — 100 mg, 200 mg, 300 mg

▷ **Usual Adult Dosage Ranges:** Hypertension: Initially 80 mg three times daily. The dose may be increased gradually at 1- to 7-day intervals as needed and tolerated. The usual maintenance dose is from 240 to 360 mg daily in three or four divided doses. The prolonged-action (sustained-release) dose forms permit once-a-day dosing. The total daily dose should not exceed 360 mg.

Once-a-day treatment may be initiated with one prolonged-action capsule of 120 mg or one tablet of 180 mg (particularly the elderly or patients of small stature).

The Covera HS form is given as one 180 mg extended-release tablet at bedtime. If adequate response is not obtained, the dose may be increased to 240 mg at bedtime. Dose may be subsequently increased as needed and tolerated to a maximum of 480 mg. The lowest effect or trough effect would be best evaluated just before bedtime.

The Verelan PM form is designed to be taken at bedtime. Dosing generally starts at 100 mg at bedtime as a conservative strategy.

Tarka form: Talk to your doctor.

Note: Actual dose and schedule must be determined for each patient individually.

Conditions Requiring Dosing Adjustments

Liver Function: Blood levels should be obtained to guide dosing. In liver disease, dose should be decreased to 20–50% of usual doses at the usual times. This drug is also a rare cause of liver damage. Electrocardiogram changes may provide an early indication of increasing blood levels.

Kidney Function: In severe kidney compromise, the dose should be decreased by 50–75%.

Heart (Myocardial) Dysfunction: Intravenous doses (0.0001 mg/kg/minute) are started and adjusted (titrated) against heart rate. Also adjusted if you are taking digoxin or a beta blocker.

▷ **Dosing Instructions:** Preferably taken with meals and with food at bedtime. The regular tablet may be crushed for administration. Most prolonged-action dose forms (capsules and tablets) should be swallowed whole and not altered. Both Calan and Isoptin SR forms can be cut in half without changing the release rate of the medicine. Neither form should be crushed or cut into fourths. Verelan capsules may be taken without regard to food intake. The Verelan PM form IS NOT a sleeping pill. The PM is meant to stand for bedtime dosing. If you forget a dose: Take the missed dose as soon as you remember it, unless it's nearly time for your next dose—if that is the case, skip the missed dose and take the next dose right on schedule. DO NOT double up on doses. Talk with your doctor if you find yourself missing doses.

Usual Duration of Use: Use on a regular schedule for 2 to 4 weeks usually determines effectiveness in reducing the frequency and severity of angina. Reduction of elevated blood pressure may be apparent within the first 1 to 2 weeks. For long-term use (months to years), the smallest effective dose should be used. Periodic physician evaluation is needed to keep blood pressure in the target range.

Typical Treatment Goals and Measurements (Outcomes and Markers)

Blood Pressure: The NEW guidelines (JNC VII) define normal blood pressure (BP) as **less than** 120/80. Because blood pressures that were once considered acceptable can actually lead to blood vessel damage, the committee from the National Institutes of Health's National Heart, Lung, and Blood Institute now have a new category called **Pre-hypertension**. This ranges from 120/80 to 139/89 and is intended to help your doctor encourage lifestyle changes (or in the case of people with a risk factor for high blood pressure, start treatment) much earlier—so that possible damage to blood vessels, your heart, kidneys, sexual potency, or eyes might be minimized or avoided altogether. The next two classes of high blood pressure are stage 1 hypertension: 140/90 to 159/99 and stage 2 hypertension equal to or greater than: 160/100 mm Hg. These guidelines also recommend that clinicians trying to control blood pressure work with their patients to agree on the goals and a plan of treatment. The first-ever guidelines for blood pressure (hypertension) in African Americans recommends that MOST black patients be started on TWO antihypertensive medicines with the goal of lowering blood pressure to 130/80 for those with high risk for heart and blood vessel disease or with diabetes. The American Diabetes Association recommends 130/80 as the target for people living with diabetes and less than 125/75 for those who spill more than one gram of protein into their urine. Most clinicians try to achieve a BP that confers the best balance of lower cardiovascular risk and avoids the problem of too low a blood pressure. Blood pressure duration is generally increased with beneficial restriction of sodium. The goals and time frame should be discussed with you when the prescription is written. If goals are not met, it is not unusual to intensify doses or add on medicines. You can find the new blood pressure guidelines at *www.nhlbi.nih.gov/guidelines/hypertension/index.htm*. For the African American guidelines see Douglas J.G. in Sources.

Abnormal Heartbeats: The general goal is to return the heart to a normal rhythm or at least to markedly reduce the occurrence of abnormal heartbeats. In life-threatening arrhythmias, the goal is to abort the abnormal beats and return the pattern to normal. Success at ongoing suppression may involve ambulatory checks of heart rate and rhythm for a day (such as in Holter monitoring). This kind of testing involves placement of adhesive backed temporary electrodes on the skin in several positions around the heart. A small heart rate and rhythm (EKG or ECG) recording device is carried around via a shoulder strap and records what the heart is doing over 24 hours. Once the recording is made, a scanning machine reviews the record, tallies abnormal heart beats or rhythms, and gives a close and extended look at how the heart is reacting or benefitting from the medicines that the patient is taking. Repeat measurements can be made if doses are changed to check the success at keeping the heart in normal sinus rhythm!

Possible Advantages of This Drug

No adverse effects on blood levels of glucose, potassium, or uric acid. Does not increase blood cholesterol or triglyceride levels. Does not impair capacity for exercise. The 360-mg strength of Verelan allows once-daily dosing for those patients who require more than 240 mg daily. The company has noted that there is no increase in side effects when comparing the 240-mg capsules to the new 360-mg ones.

The Verelan PM and the Covera HS forms are specifically made to reach their peak levels in the body in the morning—the thinking here is that since heart attacks most often happen in the morning, they may actually be related to early morning increases in heart rate and blood pressure. These medicines seek to avoid low medicine blood levels at a time when it appears they are needed most.

Currently a "Drug of Choice"

In people who have contraindications for beta blockers and in whom a vasospastic underlying mechanism is suspected.

▷ **This Drug Should Not Be Taken If**

- you have had an allergic reaction to it previously.
- you have active liver disease.
- you have a "sick sinus" syndrome (and do not have an artificial pacemaker).
- you have a fast heart rate (ventricular tachycardia) arising in the ventricles.
- you have atrial fibrillation or flutter.
- you have been told that you have a second- or third-degree heart block or congestive heart failure.
- you have low blood pressure (systolic pressure below 90).

▷ **Inform Your Physician Before Taking This Drug If**

- you have had an unfavorable response to any calcium channel blocker.
- you are currently taking any other drugs, especially digitalis or a beta-blocker drug (see Drug Classes).
- you have had a recent stroke or heart attack.
- you have a history of congestive heart failure, angina, or heart rhythm disorders.
- you have aortic stenosis (ask your specialist).
- the left side of your heart is very weak (ejection fraction less than 30% or pulmonary wedge pressure more than 20 mm Hg—ask your doctor).
- you have poor circulation to your extremities or gangrene.
- you develop a skin reaction while taking this medicine. Some reactions have gone on to more serious problems (such as erythema multiforme).
- you have impaired liver or kidney function.
- you have a history of drug-induced liver damage.

Possible Side Effects (natural, expected, and unavoidable drug actions)

Low blood pressure, fluid retention—rare. Change in how well platelets work (antiplatelet effect)—may be significant if combined with aspirin. Constipation (up to 42%).

▷ **Possible Adverse Effects** (unusual, unexpected, and infrequent reactions)
If any of the following develop, consult your physician promptly for guidance.

Mild Adverse Effects
Allergic reactions: skin rash, hives, itching, aching joints.
Flushing—infrequent.
Headache—frequent.
Dizziness, fatigue—infrequent.
Nausea, indigestion, constipation—rare to infrequent.
Abnormal growth of the gums—infrequent to frequent.
Sensation of numbness or coldness in the extremities—case reports.
Hair color change—case report.
Cough—rare.

Serious Adverse Effects
Allergic reaction: skin rash (Stevens-Johnson Syndrome)—possible.
Serious disturbances of heart rate and/or rhythm, congestive heart failure—rare.
Drug-induced liver damage without jaundice—case reports.
Antiplatelet effect and extended time to form blood clots—possible.
Lung problems (pulmonary edema).
Excessive lowering of blood pressure—case reports.
Unmasking of parkinsonism or movement disorders—rare.
Low blood sugar—possible.

▷ **Possible Effects on Sexual Function:** Altered timing and pattern of menstruation.
Male breast enlargement and tenderness (gynecomastia)—case reports.
Impotence—frequent.

Possible Effects on Laboratory Tests
Blood total cholesterol and HDL cholesterol levels: no effect in some; decreased in others.
Blood LDL cholesterol or triglyceride level: no effect.
Glucose tolerance test (GTT): decreased.
Liver function tests: increased enzymes (ALT/GPT, AST/GOT), increased bilirubin (case reports).

CAUTION
1. Be sure to inform all physicians and other health care professionals who provide medical care for you that you take this drug. Note the use of this drug on your card of personal identification.
2. You may use nitroglycerin and other nitrate drugs as needed to relieve acute episodes of angina pain. If angina attacks become more frequent or intense, call your doctor promptly.
3. If this drug is used concurrently with a beta-blocker drug, you may develop excessively low blood pressure.
4. This drug may cause swelling of the feet and ankles. This may not be indicative of either heart or kidney dysfunction.

Precautions for Use
By Infants and Children: Safety and effectiveness for those under 12 years of age are not established.
By Those Over 60 Years of Age: You may be more susceptible to weakness, dizziness, fainting, and falling. Take necessary precautions to prevent

injury. Report promptly any changes in your pattern of thirst and urination.

▷ **Advisability of Use During Pregnancy**

Pregnancy Category: C. See Pregnancy Risk Categories at the back of this book.

Animal Studies: Toxic effects on the embryo and retarded growth of the fetus (but no birth defects) reported in rat studies.

Human Studies: Adequate studies of pregnant women are not available.

Avoid this drug during the first 3 months. Use during the final 6 months only if clearly needed. Ask your doctor for help.

Advisability of Use If Breast-Feeding

Presence of this drug in breast milk: Yes.

Discuss the benefits and risks of nursing your infant. Most clinicians find breast milk drug levels to be insignificant. Monitor infant for adverse effects.

Habit-Forming Potential: None. A withdrawal syndrome is possible (increased frequency and severity of angina). If the medicine must be stopped, it should be slowly decreased—NOT stopped abruptly.

Effects of Overdose: Flushed and warm skin, sweating, light-headedness, irritability, rapid heart rate, low blood pressure, loss of consciousness.

Possible Effects of Long-Term Use: None reported.

Suggested Periodic Examinations While Taking This Drug (at physician's discretion)

Evaluations of heart function, including electrocardiograms.

Liver and kidney function tests, with long-term use.

▷ **While Taking This Drug, Observe the Following**

Foods: DO NOT take this medicine with grapefruit or grapefruit juice. Avoid excessive salt intake.

Herbal Medicines or Minerals: Ginseng, guarana, hawthorn, saw palmetto, ma huang, goldenseal, yohimbe, and licorice may also cause increased blood pressure. Excessive caffeine and added caffeine from guarana or mate can worsen blood pressure, will also stay in your body longer than expected and are not recommended. Garlic and calcium may work to lower blood pressure, but calcium may reverse the benefits off verapamil. Some dosing changes may be needed. St. John's wort may work to lower calcium channel blocker levels (because it increases P-glycoprotein in the gut). This combination may also increase sun sensitivity. Eleuthero root and ephedra should be avoided by people living with hypertension. Indian snakeroot has a German Commission E monograph indication for hypertension. Discuss any plans for herbal medicines or minerals with your doctor BEFORE adding them.

Beverages: Caffeine levels will be increased if caffeine-containing beverages are consumed while you are on verapamil. DO NOT take this medicine with grapefruit or grapefruit juice. May be taken with milk.

▷ *Alcohol:* Use with caution until combined effects have been determined. Alcohol may exaggerate the drop in blood pressure and change the elimination of alcohol (experienced by some patients). This may lead to an exaggerated effect of alcohol.

Tobacco Smoking: Nicotine can reduce the effectiveness of this drug. Avoid all forms of tobacco.

Marijuana Smoking: Possible reduced effectiveness of this drug; mild to moderate increase in angina; possible changes in electrocardiogram, confusing interpretation.

▷ *Other Drugs*
Verapamil may ***increase*** the effects of
- buspirone (Buspar).
- carbamazepine (Tegretol) and cause carbamazepine toxicity.
- digitoxin and digoxin (Lanoxin) and cause digitalis toxicity.
- lovastatin (Mevacor), simvastatin (Zocor), and other HMG CoA reductase inhibitors that use cytochrome P 450 3A4 for removal.
- neuromuscular blocking agents (such as pancuronium—Pavulon or vecuronium—Norcuron) may prolong muscle weakness.
- sirolimus (Rapamune).
- tacrolimus (Prograf).
- tretinoin (Vesanoid).
- tricyclic antidepressants (see Drug Classes).
- vincristine (Oncovin).

Verapamil ***taken concurrently*** with
- amiodarone (Cordarone) may result in cardiac arrest.
- aspirin (various) may result in excessive verapamil levels and excessive lowering of blood pressure.
- beta blockers (see Drug Classes) may affect heart rate and rhythm adversely. Careful monitoring by your physician is necessary if these drugs are taken concurrently.
- calcium supplements (various) may blunt the therapeutic benefits of verapamil—separate calcium and verapamil dosing by 2 hours.
- cilostazol (Pletal) may result in cilostazol toxicity. Lower cilostazol doses are prudent.
- colesevelam (Welchol) will decrease the therapeutic blood level of verapamil.
- cyclosporine (Sandimmune) may result in cyclosporine toxicity and renal compromise.
- dantrolene will cause elevated blood potassium and depression of the heart.
- dofetilide (Tikosyn) may result in dofetilide toxicity. Checks of dofetilide levels and dosing adjustments to levels are prudent.
- disopyramide (Norpace) can cause congestive heart failure.
- flecainide (Tambocor) may have additive heart effects (excessively low heart rate or cardiogenic shock).
- lithium (Lithobid, others) may result in lithium toxicity and mania.
- medicines such as class I, IA, or III antiarrhythmics—amiodarone (Cordarone), dofetilide (Tikosyn), clarithromycin, cotrimoxazole, ondansetron, ziprazidone and others may lead to prolongation of the QTc interval and undesirable effects. Combination is not recommended (see amiodarone note above regarding extreme caution if these two medicines are combined or if transition is made from quinidine to amiodarone).
- midazolam (Versed) may result in midazolam toxicity. Lower doses (by 50%) and careful patient monitoring are critical.
- NSAIDs (see Drug Classes) may blunt the therapeutic effect of verapamil on blood pressure.
- oral hypoglycemic agents (see Oral Antidiabetic Drugs in Drug Classes) may lead to excessively low blood sugar.
- phenytoin (Dilantin) may result in decreased effectiveness of verapamil.
- prazosin (Minipres, others) may increase risk of orthostatic hypotension.
- quinidine (Quinaglute, others) can result in quinidine toxicity.

- rifampin (Rifadin, others) will decrease the therapeutic benefits of verapamil.
- sulfinpyrazone increases the removal of verapamil and lessens its therapeutic effects.
- terazosin (Hytrin) can lead to excessive decreases in blood pressure.
- theophylline (Theo-Dur, others) can lead to theophylline toxicity.
- warfarin (Coumadin) or other oral anticoagulants may increase risk of stomach or intestinal (GI) hemorrhage. More frequent INR tests are indicated.

The following drugs may *increase* the effects of verapamil:

- cimetidine (Tagamet) and other histamine (H$_2$) blocking drugs (see Drug Classes).
- clarithromycin (Biaxin).
- quinupristin/dalfopristin (Synercid).
- ritonavir (Norvir), amprenavir (Agenerase) and perhaps other protease inhibitors (see Drug Classes).
- tricyclic antidepressants (see Drug Classes).

▷ *Driving, Hazardous Activities:* Usually no restrictions. This drug may cause dizziness. Restrict activities as necessary.

Aviation Note: Coronary artery disease *is a disqualification* for piloting. Consult a designated Aviation Medical Examiner.

Exposure to Sun: Use caution until sensitivity has been determined. This drug may cause photosensitivity (see Glossary).

Exposure to Heat: Caution is advised. Hot environments can exaggerate the blood pressure–lowering effects of this drug. Observe for light-headedness or weakness.

Heavy Exercise or Exertion: This drug may improve your ability to be more active without resulting angina pain. Use caution and avoid excessive exercise that could impair heart function in the absence of warning pain.

Discontinuation: **Do not stop this drug abruptly.** Consult your physician regarding gradual withdrawal to prevent the development of rebound angina.

WARFARIN (WAR far in)

Introduced: 1941   **Class:** Anticoagulant, coumarins   **Prescription:** USA: Yes   **Controlled Drug:** USA: No; Canada: No   **Available as Generic:** USA: Yes; Canada: Yes

Brand Names: ✤Apo-Warfarin, Athrombin-K, Carfin, Coumadin, ✤Gen-Warfarin ✤Lin-Warfarin, PanWarfarin, Sofarin, ✤Taro-warfarin, Warnerin

---

BENEFITS versus RISKS

Possible Benefits	*Possible Risks*
EFFECTIVE PREVENTION OF BOTH ARTERIAL AND VENOUS THROMBOSIS	NARROW TREATMENT RANGE
	Dose-related bleeding
EFFECTIVE PREVENTION OF EMBOLIZATION IN THROMBOEMBOLIC DISORDERS	Skin and soft tissue hemorrhage with tissue death
HELPS PREVENT RECURRENCE OF HEART ATTACK	
HELPS PREVENT STROKES IN PATIENTS WITH ATRIAL FIBRILLATION	
TREATS ACUTE CORONARY SYNDROME	
HELPS PREVENT BLOOD CLOTS AFTER MITRAL VALVE REPLACEMENT	
May have a role in helping to prevent cancer	

▷ **Principal Uses**

As a Single Drug Product: Uses currently included in FDA-approved labeling: Used in (1) acute thrombosis (clot) or thrombophlebitis of the deep veins; (2) acute pulmonary embolism, resulting from blood clots that originate anywhere in the body; (3) atrial fibrillation, to prevent clotting of blood inside the heart that could result in embolization of small clots to any part of the body; (4) acute myocardial infarction (heart attack), to prevent clotting and embolization and therefore a recurrence of heart attack; (5) mitral valve replacement; (6) helping prevent blood clots in the lungs (pulmonary embolism) that may start after hip replacement surgery.

Other (unlabeled) generally accepted uses: (1) Helps prevent embolization from the heart in people with artificial heart valves or coronary angioplasty; (2) may help patients with low blood platelets caused by heparin; (3) one case report of benefits in treatment-resistant migraines; (4) A study of 854 patients (after suffering a first blood clot) who were then treated with warfarin appeared to have a lower risk of newly diagnosed cancer. This possible chemoprotective effect must be further evaluated.

How This Drug Works: The coumarin anticoagulants interfere with the production of four essential blood-clotting factors by blocking the action of vitamin K. This leads to a deficiency of these clotting factors in circulating blood and inhibits blood-clotting mechanisms. Mechanism in possibly decreasing cancer risk is not known.

Available Dosage Forms and Strengths

Injection — 5 mg

Tablets — 1 mg, 2 mg, 2.5 mg, 3 mg, 4 mg, 5 mg, 6 mg, 7.5 mg, 10 mg

Tablets (Canada) — 25 mg

▷ **Usual Adult Dosage Ranges:** Initially an induction dose of 2 to 5 mg daily is used. A large loading dose is inappropriate and may be hazardous—hence an induction dose is used in the aforementioned range and then the ongoing dose is decided based on INR (prothrombin time or protime) results and the condition being treated. Defined ranges exist for treating or preventing problems with various diagnoses. The usual ongoing maintenance dose range is 2 to 10 mg daily, adjusted to maintain the prothrombin time (protime) to 1.2 to 2 times the control value which corresponds to an International Normalized Ratio (INR) of 2.0 to 3.0 for most indications (1.5 to 5.0 is a possible INR range).

Note: Actual dose and schedule must be determined for each patient individually.

Author's Note: Many patients have their anticoagulation managed in a special service called an Anticoagulation clinic. The manufacturer of the Warfarin brand offers a database called Coumacare which is used to closely follow patients.

Conditions Requiring Dosing Adjustments

Liver Function: Blood testing (prothrombin times) should be obtained to guide dosing. This drug is only used when extremely careful followup is possible and a cautious benefit to risk decision is made.

Kidney Function: This drug should be used with caution in renal compromise, as warfarin may cause microscopic kidney stones

Congestive Heart Failure (CHF): This drug should be used with caution in CHF because the liver may become overloaded (congested) and the response to anticoagulation may be exaggerated.

▷ **Dosing Instructions:** The tablet may be crushed and is preferably taken when the stomach is empty and at the same time each day to ensure uniform results. If you forget a dose: Take the missed dose as soon as you remember it. If you don't remember until the next day, skip the missed dose and take the next dose right on schedule. Let your doctor know you missed a dose. Be honest if you find yourself missing doses, there are timers and beeper-based systems that can be very helpful.

Usual Duration of Use: Use on a regular schedule for 3 to 5 days usually determines effectiveness in providing significant anticoagulation. An additional 10 to 14 days is required to determine the optimal maintenance dose for each person. INR ranges vary according to the condition warranting use of warfarin in the first place. The appropriate duration of therapy is controversial and should be discussed with your doctor according to the condition being treated. Ongoing use (months to years) requires physician supervision. Patient self-testing (INR) monitors are now available and can empower people taking warfarin.

Typical Treatment Goals and Measurements (Outcomes and Markers)

Anticoagulation: The goal of anticoagulation is to prevent further extention of an existing clot or to prevent a clot in patients who are at risk for getting a blood clot. Additionally, a balance must be struck between thinning the blood enough to avoid an undesirable blood clot and thinning it so much that bleeding occurs. The INR (a ratio involving a prothrombin time test and standardization to make results "the same" lab to lab) is used to check to what degree the blood has been made less likely to clot by warfarin.

While you are taking this medicine you will have blood drawn on a regular basis to make sure that your blood is in the right range. Many patients refer to anticoagulation as being "thin" enough and to warfarin as a blood thinner. The key, however, is to make the blood less likely to form abnormal clots, yet have it retain enough of an ability to clot to keep you from bleeding. For example, the Antithrombotic Therapy in Acute Coronary

Syndrome (ACTACS) study reported that when INR is adjusted to a range of between 2 and 3, the frequency of bleeding complications was about the same (not statistically different) for aspirin alone (162.5 mg) or aspirin plus warfarin in people with chest pain (ischemic pain) due to unstable angina or non-Q-wave heart attack (myocardial infarction).

▷ **This Drug Should Not Be Taken If**
- you have had an allergic reaction to it previously.
- you have an active peptic ulcer or active ulcerative colitis.
- you are pregnant, and are experiencing eclampsia or a threatened abortion.
- you have had recent anesthesia (lumbar block) to the spine.
- you've had a spinal tap (lumbar puncture).
- you have arterial aneurysm.
- you have malignant hypertension, low blood platelets.
- you have low blood platelets.
- you have infective pericarditis or endocarditis.
- you have liver disease.
- you have esophageal varices (ask your doctor).
- you have had a recent stroke.

▷ **Inform Your Physician Before Taking This Drug If**
- you are now taking any other drugs, either prescription drugs or over-the-counter drug products.
- you are planning pregnancy.
- you have a history of a bleeding disorder.
- you have congestive heart failure.
- you have high blood pressure.
- you have abnormally heavy or prolonged menstrual bleeding.
- you have diabetes.
- you are using an indwelling catheter.
- you have impaired liver or kidney function.
- you will have surgery or dental extraction.

Possible Side Effects (natural, expected, and unavoidable drug actions)
Minor episodes of bleeding may occur even though dose and INR or prothrombin times are well within the recommended range.

▷ **Possible Adverse Effects** (unusual, unexpected, and infrequent reactions)
If any of the following develop, consult your physician promptly for guidance.
Mild Adverse Effects
Allergic reactions: skin rash, hives.
Loss of scalp hair (alopecia)—case reports.
Loss of appetite, nausea, vomiting, cramping, diarrhea—case reports.
Serious Adverse Effects
Allergic reactions: drug fever (see Glossary).
Idiosyncratic reactions: bleeding into skin and soft tissues, causing gangrene of breast, toes, and localized areas of necrosis anywhere—rare.
Hereditary warfarin resistance—rare.
Abnormal bleeding from nose, gastrointestinal tract (one case of esophageal ulcer), lungs, urinary tract, uterus, or other sites—possible and dose-related.
Pericardial tamponade—case reports.
Hemolytic anemia—rare.

Adrenal gland problems (adrenal insufficiency)—case reports.
Sudden nerve damage (femoral neuropathy)—case reports.
Kidney problems (tubulointerstitial nephritis)—case reports.
Liver toxicity (viral hepatitis-like syndrome)—case report.

▷ **Possible Effects on Sexual Function:** Extended erections (priapism).

▷ **Adverse Effects That May Mimic Natural Diseases or Disorders**
Drug-induced fever may suggest infection.

Natural Diseases or Disorders That May Be Activated by This Drug
Bleeding from "silent" peptic ulcer, intestinal or bladder polyp or tumor.

Possible Effects on Laboratory Tests
Complete blood cell counts: decreased red cells, hemoglobin, and white cells.
Bleeding time: increased.
INR (prothrombin time): increased (desirable when in therapeutic range).
Blood uric acid level: increased (in men).
Liver function tests: increased liver enzymes (ALT/GPT, AST/GOT, and alkaline phosphatase).

CAUTION

1. Always carry a personal identification card that includes a statement that *you are taking an anticoagulant drug. A medicine alert bracelet is also prudent.*
2. While taking this drug, always consult your physician *before* starting any new drug, changing the dose schedule of any drug or stopping any drug.
3. Data from the Agency for Health Care Policy and Research have shown that expanded use of warfarin could cut in half the 80,000 strokes that occur every year in patients who have atrial fibrillation.
4. **If** you start taking the brand, it is prudent to keep taking the brand. Conversely, if you have your anticoagulation adjusted using the generic form, it is prudent to continue the generic. Changing from one form to the other may result in differences in degree of anticoagulation.
5. **If** you choose to use acetaminophen while taking this medicine, talk to your doctor about adjusting the warfarin and INR testing.
6. Hereditary or acquired warfarin resistance is possible.
7. Some herbal medicines can lead to additive bleeding problems. Avoid garlic, ginkgo, ginseng, and echinacea (amongst others—see below) prior to any surgery and while you are taking this medicine.
8. Checks of INR are MANDATORY while you are taking this medicine. Home monitors can be extremely helpful by increasing access to INR tests. They are available from CoaguCheck (1-800-852-8766—Roche) and ProTime (1-800-631-5945—International Technodyne). Read more in Table 18.

Precautions for Use
By Those Over 60 Years of Age: Small starting doses are mandatory. Watch regularly for excessive drug effects: prolonged bleeding from shaving cuts, bleeding gums, bloody urine, rectal bleeding, excessive bruising. Some study data reveal that the beneficial effects of this medicine are not as widely known as needed and it is underprescribed for those over 60.

▷ **Advisability of Use During Pregnancy**
Pregnancy Category: X. See Pregnancy Risk Categories at the back of this book.
Animal Studies: Fetal hemorrhage and death due to this drug have been reported in mice.

Human Studies: Information from studies of pregnant women indicates fetal defects and fetal hemorrhage due to this drug. The manufacturers state that this drug is contraindicated during entire pregnancy.

Advisability of Use If Breast-Feeding
Presence of this drug in breast milk: Yes, but in inactive forms.
Breast-feeding appears to be safe. Checking the infant for warfarin effects is prudent in those infants at risk for such effects (vitamin K deficient).

Habit-Forming Potential: None.

Effects of Overdose: Episodes of bleeding, from minor surface bleeding (nose, gums, small lacerations) to major internal bleeding (vomiting blood, bloody urine or stool).

Possible Effects of Long-Term Use: Blue toe syndrome.

Suggested Periodic Examinations While Taking This Drug (at physician's discretion)
Regular determinations of INR (prothrombin time or protime) are essential to safe dose and proper control.
Urine analysis for blood.
Stool guaic test for hidden (occult) blood.

▷ **While Taking This Drug, Observe the Following**
Foods: A larger intake than usual of foods rich in vitamin K may reduce the effectiveness of this drug and make larger doses necessary. Foods rich in vitamin K include asparagus, bacon, beef liver, cabbage, fish, cauliflower, and green leafy vegetables. Vitamin C in high doses has some conflicting reports of warfarin resistance. Vitamin E (high dose) may increase risk of bleeding. Mango fruit was reported to cause up to a 38% increase in INR in one report. Papaya also increased INR. Talk to your doctor before eating these fruits.

Herbal Medicines or Minerals: Because many herbal products are extracts from plants with a variety of active compounds in addition to those listed on the label—and since many compounds can have activity as anticoagulants—herbal medicines in general SHOULD NOT be combined with warfarin.

Specifically, angelica root, anise, borage seed oil, devil's claw, papain, garlic, ginseng, ginger, ginkgo, horse chestnut, ipriflavone, alfalfa, red clover, clove oil, evening primrose oil, feverfew, passionflower herb, salvia root (danshen), skull cap, willow bark, cinchona bark, white willow bark, turmeric, and garlic may also change clotting, so combining those herbals with these medicines cannot be recommended. Dong quai appears to have a true pharmacodynamic interaction with warfarin (potentiation), and since it is as yet uncharacterized, these medicines should not be combined. Boldo-Fenugreek caused more than a 50% increase in INR in one case report (patient also had the same problem when the medicines were introduced a second time). Co-enzyme Q10 (ubiquinone) and green tea may decrease warfarin benefits. Herbal medicine such as eucalyptus, kava, or valerian with known impact on liver function (so critical to anticoagulation) are best NOT combines. TALK TO YOUR DOCTOR BEFORE taking any herbal medicine with warfarin—but again—any combination is not advisable.

Beverages: No restrictions. May be taken with milk.

▷ *Alcohol:* Limit alcohol to one drink daily. Note: Heavy users of alcohol with liver damage may be very sensitive to anticoagulants and require smaller than usual doses.

Tobacco Smoking: Heavy smokers may require relatively larger doses of this drug. I advise everyone to quit smoking.

▷ *Other Drugs*

Warfarin may ***increase*** the effects of
- oral hypoglycemic agents (see Oral Antidiabetic Drugs in Drug Classes).
- phenytoin (Dilantin) or fosphenytoin (Cerebyx).

Warfarin may ***decrease*** the effects of
- cyclosporine (Sandimmune, others).
- phenytoin (Dilantin) or fosphenytoin (Cerebyx).

The following drugs may ***increase*** the effects of warfarin:
- abciximab (Reopro).
- acarbose (Precose).
- acetaminophen (Tylenol, others—especially if more than 2,275 mg per week is taken).
- allopurinol (Zyloprim).
- alteplase (Activase) and is contraindicated if the prothrombin time is more than 15 seconds.
- amiodarone (Cordarone).
- amprenavir (Agenerase).
- androgens (see Drug Classes).
- argatroban (Acova).
- aspirin and some other NSAIDs (see Drug Classes).
- azithromycin (Zithromax).
- bismuth subsalicylate (Pepto-Bismol).
- some calcium channel blockers (various) have been associated with an increased risk of stomach and intestine (gastrointestinal) hemorrhage. This risk may be exacerbated by warfarin use.
- capsaicin (Zostrix, others).
- carbamazepine (Tegretol).
- cephalosporins (see Drug Classes).
- chloral hydrate (Noctec).
- chloramphenicol (Chloromycetin).
- cimetidine (Tagamet).
- ciprofloxacin and other quinolone antibiotics (see Drug Classes).
- cisapride (Propulsid).
- clarithromycin (Biaxin).
- clofibrate (Atromid-S).
- clopidogrel (Plavix).
- cloxacillin (various).
- cotrimoxazole (Bactrim).
- COX-II inhibitors (celecoxib, rofecoxib, and valdecoxib).
- dextrothyroxine.
- dirithromycin and other macrolide antibiotics (see Drug Classes).
- disopyramide (Norpace).
- disulfiram (Antabuse).
- enoxaparin (Lovenox) and other low molecular weight heparins (see Drug Classes).
- eptifibatide (Integrelin).
- erythromycin (various).
- felbamate (Felbatol).
- fluconazole (Diflucan).
- fluoxetine (Prozac).

- fluvastatin (Lescol) and perhaps similar drugs.
- fluvoxamine (Luvox).
- fosphenytoin (Cerebyx) or phenytoin (Dilantin).
- gemfibrozil (Lopid).
- glucagon.
- heparin (various).
- HMG CoA-reductase inhibitors (see Drug Profiles).
- imitinib (Gleevec).
- influenza vaccine (various).
- isoniazid (INH).
- itraconazole (Sporanox), ketoconazole (Nizoral), voriconaxole (Vfend).
- mesna (Mesnex).
- methyltestosterone (any 17-alkylated androgen).
- metronidazole (Flagyl).
- miconazole (Monistat).
- minocycline.
- nonsteroidal anti-inflammatory drugs (see Drug Classes).
- omeprazole (Prilosec).
- oral anticoagulants—low molecular weight heparins, etc. (see Drug Classes).
- orlistat (Xenical).
- paroxetine (Paxil).
- pravastatin (Pravachol).
- propafenone (Rythmol).
- propranolol (Inderal).
- propoxyphene (various).
- quinidine (Quinaglute).
- quetiapine (Seroquel).
- raloxifene (Evista)—more frequent INR checks are prudent.
- ranitidine (Zantac).
- ritonavir (Norvir) and perhaps other protease inhibitors (see Drug Classes).
- salicylates (aspirin, etc.).
- sertraline (Zoloft).
- simvastatin (Zocor).
- streptokinase.
- sulfinpyrazone (Anturane).
- sulfonamides (see Drug Classes).
- tamoxifen (Nolvadex).
- tamsulosin (Flomax).
- terbinafine (Lamisil).
- testosterone (various).
- tetracyclines (see Drug Classes).
- thyroid hormones (various).
- thrombolytic drugs (such as alteplase).
- tramadol (Ultram).
- trastuzumab (Herceptin).
- tricyclic antidepressants (see Drug Classes).
- vancomycin (Vancoled).
- vitamin E (higher doses).
- zafirlukast (Accolate).
- zileuton (Zyflo).

- zotepine (Nipolept).

The following drugs may *decrease* the effects of warfarin:

- antithyroid agents (various) by decreasing prior high rates of clotting factor metabolism.
- azathioprine (Imuran).
- barbiturates (see Drug Classes).
- birth control pills (oral contraceptives).
- carbamazepine (Tegretol).
- chlordiazepoxide (Librium).
- cholestyramine (Questran).
- estrogens (various).
- ethchlorvynol (Placidyl).
- glutethimide (Doriden).
- griseofulvin (Gris-PEG).
- phenobarbital (various).
- phytonadione (vitamin K).
- primidone (Mysoline).
- rifampin (Rifadin).
- spironolactone.
- sucralfate (Carafate).
- telmisartan (Micardis)—slight decrease.
- thiazide diuretics (see Drug Classes).
- vitamin K.

▷ *Driving, Hazardous Activities:* No restrictions.

Aviation Note: The use of this drug *is a disqualification* for piloting. Consult a designated Aviation Medical Examiner.

Exposure to Sun: No restrictions.

Discontinuation: Do not stop this drug abruptly unless abnormal bleeding occurs. Ask your physician for guidance regarding gradual reduction in dose over a period of 3 to 4 weeks.

ZALCITABINE (zal SIT a been)

Other Names: Dideoxycytidine, DDC

Introduced: 1987   **Class:**   Antiviral, anti-AIDS   **Prescription:** USA: Yes   **Controlled Drug:**   USA: No; Canada: No   **Available as Generic:**   USA: No

Brand Name: Hivid

Author's Note: Information in this profile has been shortened to make room for more widely used medicines.

ZALEPLON (ZAH la plon)

Introduced: 1999   **Class:**   Hypnotic, nonbenzodiazepine   **Prescription:**   USA: Yes   **Controlled Drug:**   USA: C-IV*; Canada: Prescription   **Available as Generic:**   USA: No

Brand Names: Sonata, ✤Starnoc

*See Schedules of Controlled Drugs at the back of this book.

```
┌─────────────────────────────────────────────────────────────────────┐
│                      BENEFITS versus RISKS                            │
│       Possible Benefits                        Possible Risks         │
│   GIVES SHORT-TERM RELIEF OF         Habit-forming potential with     │
│     INSOMNIA WITH MINIMAL              prolonged use                  │
│     SLEEP DISRUPTION (REM)                                            │
│   REDUCES SLEEP LATENCY                                               │
│   MAY BE TAKEN AT BEDTIME                                             │
│     OR LATER (AS LONG AS FOUR                                         │
│     HOURS OF TIME IN BED ARE                                          │
│     LEFT)                                                             │
│   SHORT HALF-LIFE (AVOIDS                                             │
│     HANGOVER EFFECT)                                                  │
└─────────────────────────────────────────────────────────────────────┘
```

▷ **Principal Uses**

As a Single Drug Product: Uses currently included in FDA-approved labeling: Treatment of insomnia in adults for up to 35 days (new and longer period of approved use).

Other (unlabeled) generally accepted uses: None at present.

How This Drug Works: This drug attaches (binds) to a specific receptor (GABA-BZ subunit modulation) and reduces the time it takes to fall asleep.

Available Dosage Forms and Strengths

Tablets — 5 mg, 10 mg

▷ **Recommended Dosage Ranges** (Actual dose and schedule must be determined for each patient individually.)

Infants and Children: Safety and efficacy for those under 18 years of age are not established.

18 to 60 Years of Age: 10 mg is taken immediately before bedtime. If patients are of small stature (low weight), it is prudent to use 5 mg as a starting dose. Patients should be reevaluated after taking this drug for 7–10 days. Maximum length of use was 28 days in clinical studies. New approval is for 35 days. Patients of low body weight should be given 5 mg as a starting dose. Dose may be increased slowly to a maximum of 20 mg as needed and tolerated.

Over 60 Years of Age: Therapy should be started with 5 mg taken at bedtime. The dose may be cautiously increased to 10 mg at bedtime.

Conditions Requiring Dosing Adjustments

Liver Function: The dose should be reduced by 50% in mild to moderate liver compromise (5 mg).

Kidney Function: No changes thought to be needed in mild compromise. This medicine HAS NOT been studied in severe kidney insufficiency.

▷ **Dosing Instructions:** The tablet may be crushed. Best taken on an empty stomach (taking it with a high-fat meal delays absorption). Do not stop this drug abruptly if taken more than 7 days. If you forget a dose: Take the missed dose as soon as you remember it, as long as you will be in bed for another four hours.

Usual Duration of Use: Use on a regular schedule for 2 nights usually determines effectiveness in treating insomnia. Your physician should assess the benefit of this drug after 7 to 10 days. New recommended maximum length of use is 35 days.

Typical Treatment Goals and Measurements (Outcomes and Markers)

Insomnia: The general goal is to decrease the amount of time it takes between the time you go to bed and the time you fall asleep (shortened sleep latency). Additionally, the number of times that you wake up is expected to decrease, enabling a full night of sleep. How alert you feel in the morning is also a consideration. Many other hypnotics with longer half-lives also have significant effects the next morning ("hangover" effects). Two scales often used are the Stanford Sleepiness Scale (SSS) and the Saint Mary Hospital Sleep Questionnaire (SMHSQ).

Possible Advantages of This Drug

Low occurrence of adverse effects. Short half-life. No difference between a dummy pill (placebo) and this medicine was seen when patients were checked for next-day sleepiness. Now approved for up to 35 days of insomnia treatment.

▷ **This Drug Should Not Be Taken If**
- you had an allergic reaction to it previously or to tartrazine (yellow number 5).
- you have severe liver compromise.

▷ **Inform Your Physician Before Taking This Drug If**
- you have abnormal liver or kidney function.
- you are pregnant or planning pregnancy or are breast-feeding your infant.
- you have a history of alcoholism or drug abuse.
- you have a serious lung problem (respiratory impairment).
- you have a history of serious depression or mental disorder.
- you are elderly or are debilitated.
- you are unsure how much to take or how often to take this medicine.

Possible Side Effects (natural, expected, and unavoidable drug actions)
Sleepiness.

▷ **Possible Adverse Effects** (unusual, unexpected, and infrequent reactions)
If any of the following develop, consult your physician promptly for guidance.

Mild Adverse Effects
Allergic reactions: Itching and rash.
Drowsiness and dizziness—possible and dose related.
Psychomotor impairment—possible and dose related.
Fever—rare.
Blurred vision—dose related—rare.
Rebound insomnia—possible, dose-dependent and appears to resolve by the second night.
Lowered white blood cell counts—rare and transitory and of questionable causation.
Nausea, anorexia, or indigestion—infrequent.
Muscle aches (myalgia)—infrequent.
Increased liver enzymes—rare and transient and of questionable causality.

Serious Adverse Effects
Allergic reactions: not defined.
Peripheral edema or chest pain—reported.
Abnormal thoughts or hallucinations—very rare.

▷ **Possible Effects on Sexual Function:** Dysmenorrhea—very rare.

Possible Effects on Laboratory Tests
Liver function tests: possibly increased SGOT, SGPT, and CPK.

CAUTION
1. This drug works quickly. It is best to take it just before bedtime.
2. Do not drink alcohol while taking this drug.
3. Withdrawal (see Glossary) may occur, even if this drug was only taken for a week or two. Ask your doctor for advice before stopping zaleplon.
4. You may experience trouble going to sleep for 1 or 2 nights after stopping this drug (rebound insomnia). This effect is usually short-term.
5. Sleep disturbances may be a symptom of underlying psychological problems. Tell your doctor if unusual behaviors or odd thoughts occur.
6. Drugs that depress the central nervous system may produce additive effects with this drug. Ask your doctor or pharmacist before combining other prescription or nonprescription drugs with zaleplon.

Precautions for Use

By Infants and Children: Safety and effectiveness for those under 18 years of age are not established.

By Those Over 60 Years of Age: The starting dose should be decreased to 5 mg. Since this drug works quickly, it is best taken immediately before going to bed. You may be at increased risk for falls if the drug remains in your system in the morning. Watch for lethargy, unsteadiness, nightmares, and paradoxical agitation and anger.

▷ **Advisability of Use During Pregnancy**

Pregnancy Category: C. See Pregnancy Risk Categories at the back of this book.

Animal Studies: In rats, there was increased stillbirth and postnatal death as well as slower growth and development in offspring of females treated with 7 mg per kg per day during the later part of pregnancy and throughout lactation.

Human Studies: Adequate studies of pregnant women are not available.
Use during pregnancy is not recommended.

Advisability of Use If Breast-Feeding

Presence of this drug in breast milk: Yes, in small amounts.
Avoid drug or refrain from nursing.

Habit-Forming Potential: This drug may cause dependence (see Glossary).

Effects of Overdose: One case of 100 mg taken in combination with a benzodiazepine reported that the patient recovered without ill effects. Supportive and symptomatic care is recommended.

Possible Effects of Long-Term Use: Psychological and/or physical dependence.

Suggested Periodic Examinations While Taking This Drug (at physician's discretion)
Liver function tests.

▷ **While Taking This Drug, Observe the Following**

Foods: This drug is best taken on an empty stomach because food delays absorption.

Herbal Medicines or Minerals: Kava kava and valerian (no longer recommended because of liver toxicity questions) may exacerbate central nervous system depression (avoid this combination). Kola nut, Siberian ginseng, mate, guarana, ephedra, and ma huang may blunt the benefits of this medicine. While St. John's wort is indicated for anxiety, it is also thought to increase (induce) cytochrome P450 enzymes and could tend to blunt zaleplon effectiveness.

Beverages: Avoid caffeine-containing beverages: coffee, tea, cola, chocolate.

▷ *Alcohol:* This drug should not be combined with alcohol.

Tobacco Smoking: Nicotine is a stimulant and should be avoided. I advise everyone to quit smoking.

Marijuana Smoking: May cause additive drowsiness.

▷ *Other Drugs*

Zaleplon *taken concurrently* with

- cimetidine (Tagamet, others) may increase zaleplon effects (inhibits aldehyde oxidase and CYP3A4—both methods that the body uses to eliminate this drug). A starting dose of 5 mg and careful patient follow up are needed if these medicines are combined.
- medicines that inhibit both aldehyde oxidase (primary removal mechanism) and CYP3A4 will inhibit removal of zaleplon and may lead to zaleplon toxicity.
- medicines that induce both aldehyde oxidase (primary removal mechanism) and CYP3A4 will blunt benefits of zaleplon by decreasing blood levels.
- rifampin (Rifater, others) may decrease zaleplon benefits.
- ritonavir (Norvir) and perhaps other protease inhibitors (see Drug Classes) may lead to toxicity.

Zaleplon may *increase* the effects of

- chlorpromazine (Thorazine).
- narcotics or other CNS-depressant drugs (see Drug Classes for Opioids, Phenothiazines, Antihistamines, and Benzodiazepines).

▷ *Driving, Hazardous Activities:* This drug may cause drowsiness and impair coordination. Restrict activities as necessary.

Aviation Note: The use of this drug *is a disqualification* for piloting. Consult a designated Aviation Medical Examiner.

Discontinuation: This drug should not be stopped abruptly, even after a week of use. Ask your doctor for help regarding an appropriate withdrawal schedule.

ZIDOVUDINE (zi DOH vyoo deen)

Other Names: AZT, azidothymidine, compound S, ZDV

Introduced: 1987   **Class:**   Antiviral, anti-HIV   **Prescription:**   USA: Yes   **Controlled Drug:**   USA: No; Canada: No   **Available as Generic:** USA: No; Canada: Yes

Brand Names: ✤Apo-Zidovudine, Combivir [CD], ✤Novo-AZT, Retrovir, Trizivir [CD]

BENEFITS versus RISKS

Possible Benefits	*Possible Risks*
DELAYED PROGRESSION OF DISEASE IN HIV-INFECTED PATIENTS WHEN COMBINATION TREATMENT IS USED	SERIOUS BONE MARROW DEPRESSION
REDUCED INCIDENCE OF INFECTIONS (OPPORTUNISTIC) WITH COMBINATION THERAPY	Brain toxicity
COMBIVIR and TRIZIVIR FORMS ENCOURAGES COMPLIANCE BY COMBINING 2 OR 3 MEDICINES IN ONE PILL	Lip, mouth, and tongue sores
REDUCED POSSIBILITY OF TRANSMISSION OF HIV FROM MOTHER TO FETUS (Zidovudine)	

▷ **Principal Uses**

As a Single Drug Product: Uses currently included in FDA-approved labeling: (1) Used to treat selected patients who have acquired immunodeficiency syndrome (AIDS)—this drug is not a cure for HIV; (2) approved to help prevent transmission of HIV from mother to infant; (3) approved for combination therapy with other agents; (4) approved for children 3 months or older who have laboratory values that indicate HIV infection or HIV immunosuppression; (5) approved for use in HIV-positive patients who are as yet asymptomatic.

Author's Note: Combination therapy has become a standard of care. NIAID antiretroviral therapy guidelines take into account how easily HIV therapy can fit into a patient's life. The ATIS Guidelines (AIDS Treatment Information Service—*www.hivatis.org/guidlines/adult/ May23_02/AAMay23.pdf***) tell us that therapy should be supervised by an expert, and cover considerations of when to start therapy in both asymptomatic and established HIV infections. Adherence or taking medicines for HIV exactly on time and in the right amount is ABSOLUTELY critical to getting the best possible results or outcomes. Structured therapy interruptions (STI) or structured interruptions of therapy (SIT) are still controversial.**

Other (unlabeled) generally accepted uses: (1) Used to treat Kaposi's sarcoma; (2) helps remove hairy leukoplakia in the mouth; (3) used to treat heart dysfunction in people with HIV; (4) may prevent HIV in health care workers exposed to the AIDS virus (combined with other HIV medicines); (5) appears to increase AIDS-related low platelet counts; (6) may have a role treating adult T-cell leukemia or lymphoma with interferon alpha.

As a Combination Drug Product [CD]: This drug is available in combination (Combivir—lamivudine and zidovudine; Trizivir—abacavir, lamivudine, and zidovudine). The combinations offer two different and three different medicines in the same pills.

How This Drug Works: By interfering with essential enzyme systems, this drug is thought to prevent the growth and reproduction of HIV particles within tissue cells, thus limiting the severity and extent of HIV infection.

Available Dosage Forms and Strengths
Capsules — 100 mg
Injection — 10 mg/ml
Syrup — 50 mg/5 ml
Tablet (Combivir) — lamivudine 150 mg
— zidovudine 300 mg
Tablet (Trizivir) — abacavir 300 mg
— lamivudine 150 mg
— zidovudine 300 mg

▷ **Usual Adult Dosage Ranges:** *HIV infection:* The product information insert for zidovudine recommends 600 mg daily, divided into equal doses in combination with other antiretroviral agents. Further, 500 mg as 100 mg every 4 hours while awake or 600 mg daily divided into equal doses is suggested. Combivir form—one tablet twice daily. Trizivir form—one tablet twice daily in people weighing more than 40 kg.

Prevention of maternal–fetal transmission in pregnancy: Once the mother has passed 14 weeks of pregnancy—100 mg by mouth five times per day until the start of labor. During labor, AZT is given intravenously (2 mg per kg of body mass), followed by 1 mg per kg of body mass per hour. This dose is continued until the umbilical cord is clamped. The infant then receives 1.5 mg per kg of body mass every 6 hours. The CDC recommends combination therapy for pregnant women.

Note: Actual dose and administration schedule must be determined for each patient individually.

Conditions Requiring Dosing Adjustments
Liver Function: Dose decreased by 50% or the dosing interval doubled in significant liver disease. Drug can be a rare cause of liver damage, and patients should be followed closely.

Kidney Function: Specific guidelines for dose adjustments in patients with compromised kidneys are not available. This drug should be used with caution in kidney compromise.

Granulocytopenia: If counts of this type of white blood cell are less than 750/ml cubed or if there is a decrease in number of this kind of cell of more than 50% of what a patient starts with, this medicine may need to be stopped until the bone marrow recovers.

Anemia: If the hemoglobin drops more than 25% from the starting point or is less than 7.5 g per deciliter, zidovudine may have to be stopped. Occurrence increases with higher doses and/or lower CD4 counts. Erythropoietin may help reduce the need for blood transfusions.

▷ **Dosing Instructions:** Preferably taken on an empty stomach, but may be taken with or following food. Take exactly as prescribed. Zidovudine capsule may be opened and the contents mixed with food just prior to taking it. Best to take the capsule with at least 120 ml of water, and patients should then NOT lie down for an hour. If you forget a dose: Take the missed dose as soon as you remember it, unless it's nearly time for your next dose—if that is the case, skip the missed dose and take the next dose right on schedule. DO NOT double dose. Talk with your doctor if you find yourself missing doses. IT IS ABSOLUTELY CRITICAL to take HIV medicines exactly as prescribed. There are beeper-based systems that can be a great help in complicated medication schedules.

Usual Duration of Use: Use on a regular schedule for 10 to 12 weeks usually determines effectiveness in improving the course of symptomatic AIDS infection. Long-term use requires periodic physician evaluation of response (viral load and CD4) and dose adjustment. It is not uncommon for antiretrovirals to be changed during HIV treatment based on genotypic, phenotypic, or viral burden checks.

Typical Treatment Goals and Measurements (Outcomes and Markers)

HIV: Goals for HIV treatment presently are maximum suppression of viral replication, maximum lowering of the amount of virus in your body (viral load or burden), and maximum patient survival. The loftier goal of eradication of HIV from the body does not appear possible given the medicines presently available. Long-term survival is achievable for many patients. Markers of successful therapy include undetectable viral load, increased CD4 cells, absence of indicator or opportunistic infections (OIs), and in the case of the HIV-positive patient, failure of the infection to progress to AIDS.

Possible Advantages of This Drug

Combination form gives a three drug combination while preserving the protease inhibitor class.

▷ **This Drug (These Drugs) Should Not Be Taken If**
- you have had a serious allergic reaction to it previously.
- you have a serious degree of uncorrected bone marrow depression.

▷ **Inform Your Physician Before Taking This Drug (These Drugs) If**
- you have a history of either folic acid or vitamin B12 deficiency.
- you have impaired liver or kidney function.
- you take other drugs that can have a bad effect on the bone marrow (are myelosuppressive).

Possible Side Effects (natural, expected, and unavoidable drug actions)

None reported.

▷ **Possible Adverse Effects** (unusual, unexpected, and infrequent reactions)

If any of the following develop, consult your physician promptly for guidance.

Mild Adverse Effects

Allergic reactions: skin rash, hives, itching.

Headache, weakness, drowsiness, dizziness, nervousness, insomnia—infrequent.

Nausea, diarrhea, vomiting, altered taste, lip sores, swollen mouth or tongue—infrequent (incidence higher with combination forms).

Paresthesias, muscle aches, fever, sweating—infrequent.

Serious Adverse Effects

Allergic reactions: one case report of toxic epidermolysis for zidovudine. **A severe and life-threatening hypersensitivity reaction (3–5%) has been reported with abacavir (Trizivir form only).**

Confusion, loss of speech, twitching, tremors, seizures (representing brain toxicity)—infrequent.

Eye problems (macular edema)—case reports.

Muscle toxicity (myopathy)—infrequent.

Mania or seizures—rare.

Muscle toxicity of the heart (cardiomyopathy)—case reports.

Bone marrow depression (see Glossary): fatigue, weakness, fever, sore throat, abnormal bleeding or bruising.

Anemia occurs most commonly after 4 to 6 weeks of treatment; abnormally low white blood cell counts occur after 6 to 8 weeks of treatment—infrequent.

Esophageal ulcers (patients should take this medicine with at least 120 ml of water and not lie down for an hour)—possible.

Liver toxicity—infrequent.
Increased blood sugar (Trizivir form)—may be frequent.
Increased triglycerides (Trizivir form)—frequent (up to 25% in some populations).

▷ **Possible Effects on Sexual Function:** None reported.

Possible Delayed Adverse Effects: Significant anemia and deficient white blood cell counts may develop after this drug has been discontinued. Myopathy, increased triglycerides, blood sugar increases.

▷ **Adverse Effects That May Mimic Natural Diseases or Disorders**
Seizures may suggest the possibility of epilepsy.

Possible Effects on Laboratory Tests
Complete blood cell counts: decreased red cells, hemoglobin, white cells, and platelets
Triglycerides (Trizivir form)—frequent increases
Blood glucose (sugar) (Trizivir form)—may be increased frequently.

CAUTION
1. These drugs are not a cure for AIDS; nor do they protect completely against other infections or complications. Follow your doctor's instructions. Take all medications exactly as prescribed.
2. These drugs do not reduce the risk of transmitting AIDS to others through sexual contact or contamination of the blood. The use of an effective condom is mandatory. Needles for drug administration should not be shared.
3. Triglyceride and blood sugar increases should be followed with combination forms.
4. Follow-up viral burden and CD4 tests are critical. Medicines that have failed MUST be changed (salvage therapy).

Precautions for Use
By Infants and Children: Zidovudine syrup is used in HIV-infected pediatric patients who are greater than 3 months old. The usual dose is 180 mg per square meter.
By Those Over 60 Years of Age: Impaired kidney function will require dose reduction.

▷ **Advisability of Use During Pregnancy**
Pregnancy Category: C. See Pregnancy Risk Categories at the back of this book.
Animal Studies: Rat studies reveal no birth defects.
Human Studies: Adequate studies of pregnant women are not available.
Consult your physician for specific guidance. This medicine has been shown to dramatically reduce the transference of HIV from mother to infant. If the decision is made to use this medicine in pregnancy, cases should be reported to 1-800-722-9292, extension 39437.

Advisability of Use If Breast-Feeding
Presence of this drug in breast milk: Unknown.
Breast-feeding may pass the HIV to the infant. DO NOT BREAST-FEED.

Habit-Forming Potential: None.

Effects of Overdose: Nausea, vomiting, diarrhea, bone marrow depression.

Possible Effects of Long-Term Use: Serious anemia and loss of white blood cells. Muscle toxicity (myopathy).

Suggested Periodic Examinations While Taking This Drug (at physician's discretion)
Complete blood cell counts before starting treatment and weekly thereafter until tolerance is established.

Checks of phenotypic or genotypic analysis of the viral population encompasing the infection.

Continual monitoring for bone marrow depression is necessary during entire course of treatment.

Periodic CD4 counts or measurements of viral load are indicators that treatment is failing and demand change of antiretroviral therapy.

▷ **While Taking This Drug, Observe the Following**

Foods: No restrictions.

Herbal Medicines or Minerals: Some patients use echinacea to attempt to boost their immune systems. Unfortunately, use of echinacea is not recommended in people with damaged immune systems. This herb may also actually weaken any immune system if it is used too often or for too long a time. Use of mistletoe is also not recommended.

Beverages: No restrictions. May be taken with milk.

▷ *Alcohol:* No interactions expected with zidovudine or Combivir, but the Trizivir form contains abacavir. Abacavir blood levels are significantly increased when combined with alcohol and this combination should be avoided.

Tobacco Smoking: No interactions expected. I advise everyone to quit smoking.

▷ *Other Drugs*

The following drugs may *increase* the effects of zidovudine and enhance its toxicity:

- acetaminophen (Tylenol, others) although reports have NOT been consistent.
- acyclovir (Zovirax).
- amphotericin B (Fungizone).
- aspirin.
- benzodiazepines (see Drug Classes).
- cidefovir (Vistide) which is given with probenecid, may lead to increased zidovudine levels because of the probenecid.
- cimetidine (Tagamet).
- cotrimoxazole (various).
- fluconazole (Diflucan).
- ganciclovir (Cytovene).
- indomethacin (Indocin).
- interferon alpha, beta-1-A and natural.
- methadone (Dolophine).
- morphine (various).
- probenecid (Benemid).
- sulfonamides (see Drug Classes).

Zidovudine *taken concurrently* with

- dapsone may suppress bone marrow and increase risk of blood (hematologic) toxicity; more frequent complete blood counts are warranted.
- didanosine may result in increased risk of myelosuppression.
- doxorubicin (various) and other chemotherapy increases risk of bone marrow depression.
- filgrastim (Neupogen) may help maintain the white blood cell count.
- flucytosine (Ancobon) may suppress bone marrow and increase risk of blood (hematologic) toxicity; more frequent complete blood counts are warranted.
- fosphenytoin (Cerebyx) or phenytoin (Dilantin) may change blood levels of all drugs. Phenytoin levels and more, frequent complete blood counts are warranted.
- ganciclovir (Cytovene) may suppress bone marrow and increase risk of

blood (hematologic) toxicity; more frequent complete blood counts are warranted.

- nimodipine (Nimotop) can increase toxicity to nerves.
- other nucleoside analogs for HIV may lower the ability of other HIV treatment requiring phosphorylation to become active.
- pyrazinamide (Rifater, others) may lower concentrations of pyrazinamide and increase risk of progression of tuberculosis. Pyrazinamide levels and dosing adjustments are prudent.
- rifabutin (Mycobutin) and rifampin (Rifadin) can lead to decreased zidovudine blood levels. Zidovudine levels may need to be increased if these medicines are combined.
- ritonavir (Norvir) may lower zidovudine levels.
- stavudine (D4T) may lessen effectiveness, as both agents are cell cycle specific.
- trimexate may cause additive hematological toxicity.
- valproic acid (Depakene) increases zidovudine blood levels. Lower doses of zidovudine and change from fixed dosage forms may be needed if valproic acid is required.

▷ *Driving, Hazardous Activities:* This drug may cause dizziness or fainting. Restrict activities as necessary.

Aviation Note: The use of this drug *is a disqualification* for piloting. Consult a designated Aviation Medical Examiner.

Exposure to Sun: No restrictions.

Discontinuation: Do not stop this drug without your physician's knowledge and guidance.

ZIPRASIDONE (ZIH praise ih dohn)

Introduced: 2001   **Class:**   Atypical antipsychotic agent, neuroleptic
Prescription: USA: Yes   **Controlled Drug:**   USA: No; Canada: No
Available as Generic: USA: No; Canada: No
Brand Name: Geodon

BENEFITS versus RISKS	
Possible Benefits	*Possible Risks*
TREATMENT OF SCHIZOPHRENIA	PROLONGATION OF THE QT
LESS WEIGHT GAIN THAN OTHER	INTERVAL OF THE HEART
AVAILABLE NEUROLEPTIC	ABNORMAL HEART RHYTHMS
MEDICINES	Abnormal lowering of blood pressure
EFFECTIVE TREATMENT OF	on standing (postural hypotension)
CERTAIN MENTAL DISORDERS	Involuntary movement disorder
LOW OCCURRENCE OF	Neuroleptic malignant syndrome
MOVEMENT DISORDERS	(possible)
(EXTRAPYRAMIDAL)	

▷ **Principal Uses**

As a Single Drug Product: Uses currently included in FDA-approved labeling: (1) Manages adult schizophrenia; (2) helps sudden (acute) episodes of schizoaffective disorder in adults.

Other (unlabeled) generally accepted uses: (1) May have a role in easing sudden (acute) bipolar mania (see Keck, PE in Sources).

How This Drug Works: Goes to work at serotonin (also known as 5HT-2A) and dopamine D2 (D2 agonist) sites. This medicine also is active at 5HT-1A type sites which might account for greater protection against movement (extrapyramidal) disorders all of which help restore more normal thinking and mood.

Available Dosage Forms and Strengths
   Capsules — 20 mg, 40 mg, 60 mg, 80 mg

▷ **Recommended Dosage Ranges** (Actual dose and schedule must be determined for each patient individually.)
   Infants and Children: Safety and efficacy for those less than 18 years of age are not established.
   18 to 60 Years of Age: Starting dose is 20 mg, taken twice a day with food. Dose can be increased as needed and tolerated after as little as 2 days, but preferably after several weeks (gives more time to see improvement from a given dose) in steps up to a dose of 80 mg twice a day. The lowest effective dose should be used. Doses greater than 80 mg twice per day are not recommended.
   Over 60 Years of Age: No specific dosing changes thought to be needed. Additionally, no changes thought to be needed in mild to moderate kidney problems (CrCl of 60 down to 10 ml/min) which encompasses the "usual" age-related decline in kidney function. Because older patients may be more susceptible to sudden decreases in blood pressure (orthostatic hypotension), careful attention must be paid to blood pressure and development of adverse effects in this population.

Conditions Requiring Dosing Adjustments
   Liver Function: No dose change needed for mint to moderate (Child-Pugh A or B) liver compromise.
   Kidney Function: No changes thought to be needed for those with creatinine clearance from 10 ml/minute to 60 ml/min.

▷ **Dosing Instructions:** The capsule should not be broken, chewed, or crushed, and is best taken with food or milk in order to ease stomach irritation. Also best taken at the same time in order to help keep the level of medicine in your body about the same. If you forget a dose: take the medicine right away, unless it's almost time for your next dose. If it IS nearly time for your next dose, skip the missed dose, take the next scheduled dose right on time and then continue your usual dosing schedule from there on. DO NOT double up on doses. Talk with your doctor if you find yourself missing doses.

Usual Duration of Use: Use on a regular schedule for at least 14 daysare required to reach steady-state levels and help define how well a given dose will start to work. Given severity of symptoms and symptom control, some clinicians increase doses in as little as 48 hours. Peak benefits may take four weeks to be seen. Ongoing use requires physician supervision and checks of ongoing results.

Typical Treatment Goals and Measurements (Outcomes and Markers)
   Schizophrenia: The general goal: to ease the severity of symptoms in order to let the patient resume his or her usual activities. There should be lessened intrusion of abnormal thinking into more normal life. As in depression, scales such as the Brief Psychiatric Rating Scale (BPRS) and the Sale for Assessment of Negative Symptoms (SANS) can help assess the benefits of this medicine.

Possible Advantages of This Drug

Information from the ZEUS research (Ziprazodone Extended Use in Schizophrenia) found that the use of ziprazidone decreased the number of people who had repeat problems (relapsed) who previously had ongoing, stable schizophrenia.

▷ **This Drug Should Not Be Taken If**

- you have had an allergic reaction to it previously.
- you have had a heart attack (MI) recently, have a history of abnormal heart beats (arrhythmia), a history of long QT syndrome present at birth (congenital), are taking a QT interval prolonging medicine (see Glossary) or have heart failure that is not compensated (talk to your doctor).

▷ **Inform Your Physician Before Taking This Drug If**

- you have had neuroleptic malignant syndrome.
- your liver is compromised.
- you have constitutionally low blood pressure, take medicine to treat high blood pressure or have cardiovascular or cerebrovascular disease.
- you are pregnant.
- you have a history of breast cancer.
- you have low blood magnesium or potassium.
- you plan to have surgery under general or spinal anesthesia in the near future.

Possible Side Effects (natural, expected, and unavoidable drug actions)

Prolonging of the QT interval (dose related), decreased blood pressure on standing (postural hypotension)—possible.

▷ **Possible Adverse Effects** (unusual, unexpected, and infrequent reactions)

If any of the following develop, consult your physician promptly for guidance.

Mild Adverse Effects

Allergic reactions: skin rash, itching—rare.

Weight gain—rare.

Headache, drowsiness, or dizziness—rare to infrequent.

Movement urgency, feeling like you have to keep moving (akathesia)—may be frequent.

Runny nose—possible.

Constipation, nausea, or vomiting—infrequent to frequent.

Drug-induced increased liver enzymes—rare.

Serious Adverse Effects

Allergic reactions: Not defined.

Movement disorders—possible (less than other medicines).

Neuroleptic malignant syndrome—case reports.

▷ **Possible Effects on Sexual Function:** Case reports of extended and painful erections (priapism), amenorrhea, and vaginitis.

▷ **Adverse Effects That May Mimic Natural Diseases or Disorders**

Nervous system reactions may suggest true Parkinson's disease. Liver reactions may suggest viral hepatitis.

Possible Effects on Laboratory Tests

Prolactin levels: increased.

Liver function tests: mildly increased liver enzymes (ALT/GPT, AST/GOT, and alkaline phosphatase).

CAUTION

1. Other medicines (nonprescription or prescription) that can cause drowsiness or central nervous system effects may react unfavorably with this

medicine. Talk with your doctor or pharmacist before combining any medicines.

2. Since this medicine can cause orthostatic hypotension, some high blood pressure (antihypertensive) medicines may have a greater than expected effect if taken with ziprasidone.

Precautions for Use

By Infants and Children: Safety and effectiveness for those under 18 years of age are not established.

By Those Over 60 Years of Age: No clinically significant differences have been identified.

▷ **Advisability of Use During Pregnancy**

Pregnancy Category: C. See Pregnancy Risk Categories at the back of this book.

Human Studies: Adequate studies of pregnant women are not available.

Use of this drug is a benefit-to-risk decision. Ask your doctor for guidance.

Advisability of Use If Breast-Feeding

Presence of this drug in breast milk: Unknown in humans.

Avoid drug or refrain from nursing.

Habit-Forming Potential: Not defined.

Effects of Overdose: Treatment of what the patient develops (symptomatic management).

Possible Effects of Long-Term Use: Not defined.

Suggested Periodic Examinations While Taking This Drug (at physician's discretion)

Liver function tests.

Careful inspection of the tongue for early evidence of fine, involuntary, wave-like movements that could be the beginning of tardive dyskinesia.

Sitting and standing blood pressure checks may be advisable when therapy is started, to assess orthostatic hypotension.

▷ **While Taking This Drug, Observe the Following**

Foods: Avoid eating grapefruit while taking this medicine. Follow prescribed diet. See grapefruit warning below.

Herbal Medicines or Minerals: New data from a small study of forty patients (See Emsley, R. in Sources) found that add-on therapy with one of the componends of fish oil (eicosapenteanoic acid or EPA) helped schizophrenic patients (Positive and Negative Syndrome Scale scores) and was well-tolerated.

Using kola, guarana, or ma huang may result in unacceptable central nervous system stimulation. St. John's wort may impact one of the liver enzymes that helps remove this medicine, leading to reduced benefits. Do not combine. Since part of the way ginkgo and ginseng work may be as a MAO inhibitor, do not combine them with ziprasidone. Belladonna may lead to excessive anticholinergic actions. Betel nut may make movement disorders more likely. DHEA use may blunt medicine benefits. Talk to your doctor before adding ANY herbals.

Beverages: Grapefruit juice may decrease metabolism of ziprasidone and lead to toxicity. May be taken with milk or water.

▷ *Alcohol:* Not defined.

Marijuana Smoking: Expected to cause an increase in drowsiness; accentuation of orthostatic hypotension; increased risk of precipitating latent psychoses, confusing the interpretation of mental status and drug responses.

▷ *Other Drugs*

Ziprasidone *taken concurrently* with

- activated charcoal will decrease absorption of ziprasidone.(May be of use in overdoses.)
- amprenavir (Agenerase) may increase either medicine.
- any medicine that has central nervous system activity may result in additive effects.
- benzodiazepines (see Drug Classes) may magnify the orthostatic hypotension problem caused by ziprasidone.
- carbamazepine (Tegretol) causes up to a 35% decrease in blood level of ziprasidone in the body; dosing increases in ziprasidone appear prudent.
- fluoroquinolone antibiotics, (see Glossary) may lead to abnormal heart rhythm.
- medicines that *decrease* or inhibit cytochrome P450 3A4 may lead to ziprasidone toxicity.
- medicines that *increase* cytochrome P450 3A4 will blunt ziprasidone benefits.
- medicines that *change* or modify the QT interval such as: dofetilide (Tikosyn) and other medicines such as class I, IA, or III antiarrhythmics, chloral hydrate (Noctec, others), chlorpromazine, clarithromycin, cotrimoxazole, ondansetron, ziprazidone and others may lead to prolongation of the QTc interval and undesirable effects (see QT interval in Glossary). Combination is not recommended.

The following drugs may *decrease* the effects of ziprasidone:

- medicines that increase (induce) cytochrome P450 3A4 may blunt ziprasidone benefits.

▷ *Driving, Hazardous Activities:* This drug may cause drowsiness or dizziness. Restrict activities as necessary.

Aviation Note: The use of this drug *may be a disqualification* for piloting. Consult a designated Aviation Medical Examiner.

Exposure to Sun: No problems reported.

Exposure to Heat: This medicine can cause problems in regulating body temperature (core temperature homeostasis). If you work or are frequently in a hot environment, be careful to replace enough fluids to avoid dehydration.

Heavy Exercise or Exertion: Since this medicine may cause problems in temperature regulation, caution is advised.

Discontinuation: Do not stop this medicine without first talking to your doctor.

ZOLPIDEM (ZOL pi dem)

Introduced: 1993   **Class:** Hypnotic, imidazopyridine   **Prescription:** USA: Yes   **Controlled Drug:** USA: C-IV*; Canada: Prescription   **Available as Generic:** USA: No

Brand Name: Ambien

BENEFITS versus RISKS	
Possible Benefits	*Possible Risks*
GIVES SHORT-TERM RELIEF OF INSOMNIA WITH MINIMAL SLEEP DISRUPTION (REM)	Habit-forming potential with prolonged use

*See Schedules of Controlled Drugs at the back of this book.

▷ **Principal Uses**

As a Single Drug Product: Uses currently included in FDA-approved labeling: Short-term treatment of insomnia in adults.

Other (unlabeled) generally accepted uses: (1) Long-term (more than 1 year) treatment of insomnia has been accomplished successfully in limited trials; (2) use in treating insomnia resulting from some antidepressants (SSRIs—see Drug Classes) has been investigated.

How This Drug Works: This drug attaches (binds) to a specific receptor (omega-1) and reduces the time it takes to fall asleep (latency) and increases total sleep time while producing a pattern and benefit of sleep that is similar to normal sleep patterns. Lowers the Cyclic Alternating Pattern (CAP) rate.

Available Dosage Forms and Strengths

Tablets — 5 mg, 10 mg

▷ **Recommended Dosage Ranges** (Actual dose and schedule must be determined for each patient individually.)

Infants and Children: Safety and efficacy for those under 18 years of age are not established.

18 to 60 Years of Age: 10 mg is taken immediately before bedtime. Patients should be reevaluated after taking this drug for 7–10 days, and again if this medicine is needed for more than 14–21 days.

Over 60 Years of Age: Therapy should be started with 5 mg taken at bedtime. The dose may be cautiously increased to 10 mg at bedtime. In general, any given dose will lead to about 50% higher peak concentrations. Confusion and falls are more likely in this population.

Conditions Requiring Dosing Adjustments

Liver Function: The dose should be reduced by 50% in liver compromise.

Kidney Function: No changes thought to be needed.

▷ **Dosing Instructions:** The tablet may be crushed. Best taken on an empty stomach. Do not stop this drug abruptly if taken more than 7 days. If you forget a dose: Because this medicine is taken when you can't sleep, a specific schedule is usually not required. Some patients take this medicine just before going to sleep, while others take it only if they can't sleep. DO NOT double up on doses.

Usual Duration of Use: Use on a regular schedule for 2 nights usually determines effectiveness in treating insomnia. Your physician should assess the benefit of this drug after a week to 10 days. Use needed for more than 14–21 days should again be reevaluated.

Typical Treatment Goals and Measurements (Outcomes and Markers)

Insomnia: The general goal is to decrease the amount of time it takes between the time you go to bed and the time you fall asleep (sleep latency). Additionally, the number of times that you wake up is expected to decrease, enabling a full night of sleep. How alert you feel in the morning is also a consideration as many other hypnotics with longer half-lives also have significant effects the next morning ("hangover" effects). Two scales often used are the Stanford Sleepiness Scale (SSS) and the Saint Mary Hospital Sleep Questionnaire (SMHSQ).

Possible Advantages of This Drug

Low occurrence of adverse effects. May produce less of an undesirable effect on normal sleep patterns (sleep architecture).

Author's Note: The National Institute of Mental Health has an informa-

tion page on anxiety. It can be found on the World Wide Web (*www. nimh.nih.gov/anxiety*).

Currently a "Drug of Choice"
For short-term management of insomnia in adults.

▷ **This Drug Should Not Be Taken If**
  • you had an allergic reaction to it previously.

▷ **Inform Your Physician Before Taking This Drug If**
  • you have abnormal liver or kidney function.
  • you are pregnant or planning pregnancy.
  • you have a history of alcoholism or drug abuse.
  • you have a serious lung problem (respiratory impairment).
  • you have a history of serious depression or mental disorder.
  • you are unsure how much to take or how often to take this medicine.

Possible Side Effects (natural, expected, and unavoidable drug actions)
Drowsiness. Rebound insomnia may happen the first night after this medicine is stopped.

▷ **Possible Adverse Effects** (unusual, unexpected, and infrequent reactions)
If any of the following develop, consult your physician promptly for guidance.
Mild Adverse Effects
Allergic reaction: skin rash.
Drowsiness and dizziness—rare.
Central nervous system reactions (confusion, nightmares), sleep walking (somnambulism)—case reports.
Nausea and diarrhea—infrequent.
Elevation of liver function tests—rare.
Muscle tremors—infrequent.
Blurred vision, double vision—infrequent.
Serious Adverse Effects
Allergic reactions: not defined.
Abnormal thoughts or hallucinations—case reports.
One well-designed study found that use in elderly patients (mean age was 82) nearly doubled the number of hip fractures in that patient population.
Paradoxical aggression, agitation or suicidal thoughts—rare.

▷ **Possible Effects on Sexual Function:** None reported.

Possible Effects on Laboratory Tests
Liver function tests: increased SGOT, SGPT, and CPK.

CAUTION
  1. This drug works quickly. It is best to take it just before bedtime.
  2. Do **not** drink alcohol while taking this drug
  3. This medicine does not work to resolve anxiety. Your doctor should talk to you about NOT using it excessively if anxiety is a root cause of your sleep problem.
  4. Withdrawal (see Glossary) may occur, even if this drug was only taken for a week or two. Ask your doctor for advice before stopping zolpidem.
  5. You may experience trouble going to sleep for 1 or 2 nights after stopping this drug (rebound insomnia). This effect is usually short-term.
  6. Sleep disturbances may be a symptom of underlying psychological problems. Tell your doctor if unusual behaviors or odd thoughts occur.

7. Drugs that depress the central nervous system may produce additive effects with this drug. Ask your doctor or pharmacist before combining other prescription or nonprescription drugs with zolpidem.

Precautions for Use

By Infants and Children: Safety and effectiveness for those under 18 years of age are not established.

By Those Over 60 Years of Age: The starting dose should be decreased to 5 mg. Since this drug works quickly, it is best taken immediately before going to bed. You may be at increased risk for falls if the drug remains in your system in the morning. Watch for lethargy, unsteadiness, nightmares, and paradoxical agitation and anger.

▷ **Advisability of Use During Pregnancy**

Pregnancy Category: B. See Pregnancy Risk Categories at the back of this book.

Animal Studies: In rats, abnormal skull bone formation was reported. In rabbits, abnormal bone formation was found.

Human Studies: Adequate studies of pregnant women are not available.

Use during pregnancy is not advisable. Ask your doctor for guidance.

Advisability of Use If Breast-Feeding

Presence of this drug in breast milk: Yes.

Avoid drug or refrain from nursing.

Habit-Forming Potential: This drug may cause dependence (see Glossary).

Effects of Overdose: Marked change from lethargy to coma. Cardiovascular and respiratory compromise was also reported. The drug flumazenil may help reverse symptoms.

Possible Effects of Long-Term Use: Psychological and/or physical dependence.

Suggested Periodic Examinations While Taking This Drug (at physician's discretion)

Liver function tests. Checks of sleep hygiene.

▷ **While Taking This Drug, Observe the Following**

Foods: This drug should not be taken with food (food slows the time to beneficial effects).

Herbal Medicines or Minerals: Kava kava and valerian (no longer widely recommended because of liver toxicity concerns) may exacerbate central nervous system depression (avoid this combination). Kola nut, Siberian ginseng, mate, guarana, ephedra, and ma huang may blunt the benefits of this medicine. While St. John's wort is indicated for anxiety, it is also thought to increase (induce) cytochrome P450 enzymes and could tend to blunt zolpidem effectiveness.

Beverages: Avoid caffeine-containing beverages: coffee, tea, cola, chocolate.

▷ *Alcohol:* This drug should not be combined with alcohol.

Tobacco Smoking: Nicotine is a stimulant and should be avoided. I advise everyone to quit smoking.

Marijuana Smoking: May cause additive drowsiness.

▷ *Other Drugs*

Zolpidem *taken concurrently* with

• azole antifungals (itraconazole, ketoconazole, fluconazole, voriconazole [Vfend] others) may lead to zolpidem toxicity.

• bupropion (Wellbutrin) may increase risk of hallucinations.

• desipramine (Norpramin) may increase risk of hallucinations.

• fluoxetine (Prozac, SARAFEM) may increase risk of hallucinations.

- rifampin (Rifater, others) may decrease zolpidem benefits.
- ritonavir (Norvir) and perhaps other protease inhibitors (see Drug Classes) may lead to zolpidem toxicity.
- sertraline (Zoloft or venlafaxine (Effexor) may increase risk of hallucinations.

Zolpidem may *increase* the effects of

- chlorpromazine (Thorazine).
- narcotics or other CNS-depressant drugs (see Drug Classes for Opioids, Phenothiazines, Antihistamines and Benzodiazepines).

▷   *Driving, Hazardous Activities:* This drug may cause drowsiness and impair coordination. Restrict activities as necessary.

Aviation Note: The use of this drug *is a disqualification* for piloting. Consult a designated Aviation Medical Examiner.

Discontinuation: This drug should not be stopped abruptly, even after a week of use. Ask your doctor for help regarding an appropriate withdrawal schedule.

Author's Note: This marks the end of the medicine profiles in this edition. Your Guide continues with MANY helpful tables (including three broadened ones) and a glossary of medical terms. YOU should be the center of health care. Become a poweful patient by knowing your medicines, what they are supposed to do, and how long it should take to help you!

THE LEADING EDGE

This section, like my website (*www.medicineinfo.com*) is designed to help you become more fully aware of medicines that show promise, are moving along toward approval, and may just become the next best thing! Some are novel applications of approved medicines or are unapproved medicines that are now FDA-approvable are also presented. "The Leading Edge" will help explain new information about concepts in how medicines are packaged for better delivery into the body.

A few interesting medicines or therapeutic products still in early clinical trials are included as "stars on the horizon." It is impossible to predict which medicines or delivery systems will achieve final FDA approval or will be used in specific medicines, but many successful ones will be covered in subsequent editions of this book.

Please be aware that many medicines or delivery systems that could be covered in a given year may be omitted simply because of space limitations. The author will select those that in his opinion offer the most potential benefit to his readers in helping them become powerful patients.

ANGIOGENESIS INHIBITOR (An GEE oh jen ah sis)

Novel Approach

They're back! While previous attempts at cutting off the blood vessel formation, if not the cancer blood supply have failed, a current attempt by Genetech using an angiogenesis inhibitor plus standard chemotherapy MET it's therapeutic goal (endpoint) of improving overall pateint survival. The drug is called beva-cizumab, rhuMAB-VEGF and will go by the brand name Avastin. It has been known for a long time that cancerous tumors need a blood supply. The thinking was that if you took that supply away, the tumor would die. Phase three data was presented at the American Society of Clinical Oncology (ASCO) meeting May 31–June 3rd, 2003. Besides colorectal cancer, this medicine is being investigated in spreading (metastatic) colorectal cancer, kidney (renal cell) tumors, some lung cancers, and breast cancer. Results appear very promising.

ANTI-CD3 MONOCLONAL ANTIBODY (An TIE See Dee three)

Novel Approach

It has been known for a long time that diabetes has a basis in the immune system—damaging the cells that make insulin (beta cells in the pancreas). More specific research has shown that T lymphocytes are the culprits, and that supress-ing the immune system actually slows the loss of the ability of patients to make insulin. Enter a monoclonal antibody to CD-3. Early research in a small number of patients showed that this anti-CD3 was able to slow the loss of insulin produc-tion, and improve blood sugar control during the first year of type 1 diabetes. Further research in a larger number of patients is needed, but the early data are promising. Look to *www.medicineinfo.com* for more info.

ANTI-IGE (An TIE Eye jee EE)

Novel Approach

I've often said that it's always better to prevent a disease or condition than to have to treat it. Asthma is a really good example. Researchers at the National Jewish Medical and Research Center found that anti-IgE injections, given once every two weeks or as infrequently as once a month, worked to stop allergies to a wide variety of pollen, dust, and molds. The injections appear to work both in adults and children without major side effects. One study found that 40% of those receiving the injections required no other treatment. Further research is needed, and approval may be granted in a year or two.

ATHEROSCLEROSIS VACCINE (ATH er oh skler oh sis)

Novel Approach

We've all heard that high levels of "bad" cholesterol are harmful. There are numerous profiles in this book outlining medicines (HMG-CoA reductase inhibitors) that block formation of or otherwise work to lower harmful choles-terol. A vaccine is being tested against CETP (cholesterol ester transfer protein—now in phase two clinical trials) by a company named Avant. The company was granted patent 6,410,022 on June 25, 2002. The hope of the vaccine is that it may improve the ratio of good (HDL) to bad (LDL) cholesterol.

CERVICAL CANCER VACCINE (SIR vi kal) (KAN sir)

Novel Approach

It may be possible to prevent cervical cancer with a vaccine. The vaccine will be directed against the human papilloma virus (HPV). While you may not have heard about this previously, this virus is the most common sexually transmitted disease in the United States. The vaccine will help those vaccinated avoid the virus—and avoid one cause of cervical cancer.

DAPTOMYCIN (DAP toe my sin)

Star on the Horizon

We've all heard about flesh-eating bacteria and increased resistance in bacteria. New approaches are needed. The first in an entirely new class of antibiotics (lipopeptides) is in the final phase of review before FDA approval. Daptomycin which will be known as Cidecin is made by Cubist Pharmaceuticals. This antibiotic works against a large number (broad spectrum) of gram positive organisms. Daptomycin also works in a unique way, by making the cell wall of the bacteria leak out vital chemicals. This medicine was recognized by the FDA and given a priority review.

EXENATIDE (EX ann ih tyde)

Novel Approach

Data presented at the June 15, 2003 meeting of the American Diabetes Association revealed data from a phase three (the last phase before FDA approval) about a novel treatment for diabetes. The medicine is called exenatide and is a GLP-1 analog (synthetic exendin-4) which was added onto the existing medicines (current regimen) of 155 diabetics. While these patients had previously failed to reach their A1C target, exenatride lowered their A1C to roughly 7.2 percent—so close to the usual goal it is remarkable! Perhaps more intriguing was the fact that exenatide appeared to result in preservation and even creation of new beta cells—the compenents in the pancreas that actually make insulin.

GENETIC THERAPY (JA neh tik therapy)

Stars on the Horizon

Many aspects of genetic therapy are being researched, but a most promising approach uses specific genetic probes to treat congestive heart failure (CHF). CHF affects more than 2 million people in the United States. Early research by a company called Collateral Therapeutics continues to show promise for a one-time, nonsurgical treatment that may reverse CHF! Other companies, such as Glaxo, are exploring use of gene therapy to reverse high cholesterol.

HDL (HIGH-DENSITY LIPOPROTEIN) THERAPY

Star on the Horizon

Since existing cholesterol treatments work on keeping it from the body or keeping the body from making it, previous editions of this book have mentioned the opportunity that HDL or good cholesterol may provide in helping people manage fat (keep it from clogging critical arteries) and perhaps have an effect on existing problems (such as plaque). The early term which was given to this novel kind of treatment is HDL Therapy. Research has continued. A Phase Two clinical study using Etc-216 (also known as ApoA-I Milano/phospholipid complex or AIM) from Esperion Therapeutics, sought to find out if this treatment could actually decrease (regress) existing plaque. Using ultrasound (inserted via a probe—intravascular ultrasound), and two different intravenous infusion strengths which were given every seventh day for a maximum of five doses—the answer about decreasing the size of existing plaque areas is YES!

The extent of plaque removal/reduction, other beneficial effects or possible side effects are not available at the time of this writing. Publication/presentation of results will be updated on my website at *www.medicineinfo.com*. Additional details may be available at the company website at *www.esperion.com*. The same company is studying other compounds which may have beneficial effects on blood vessels and/or the heart. A Phase One study was started in late June 2003 of a related HDL mimicking substance called Etc-642. Etc-642 (RLT-peptide) is a combination of 22-amino acids and/or phospholipids. I'll update you on *www.medicineinfo.com* as progress continues.

HIV VACCINE

Star on the Horizon

HIV, the virus that causes AIDS, has been very adept at developing resistance to treatments—part of the reason HIV is projected to kill 80 million people by 2010. Much like yellow fever, a vaccine seems a reasonable approach, yet many attempts by top scientists have failed. The virus actually uses human type sugars to hide from neutralizing antibodies. Ian Wilson, a researcher at the Scripps Research Institute, led a team which took a brilliant approach and studied an antibody found in one of those rare patients who appear to actually fight the virus. The antibody is called 2G12. The unique aspect of this antibody is that it is shaped like a long capital I, and seems to be able to recognize that while HIV uses human sugars to hide from antibodies, the sugars are not arranged the way human sugars are. Much additional research needs to be done, but it appears that 2G12 has found a chink in HIV armor.

HUMAN GENOME (JEE nohm)

Star on the Horizon

Many medicines today address the symptoms of a disease or condition (such as high blood pressure) rather than addressing the cause. In what I consider to be the most incredible effort at understanding how our bodies work in health and in illness, a project to map the entire group of human genes reached completion. It was projected that this effort would take more than five years, but the map was finished early. The potential for developing medicines that actually correct the underlying CAUSE of a disease or condition is suddenly very, very real. A medicine called STI571 listed below is one of the first candidates using a new treatment called pharmacogenomics. Interestingly, some 20 diseases cause more than 80% of deaths around the world and about 200–300 genes are responsible for these diseases. One prevalent example might be found in the fact that about every three weeks we in essence get a new heart from the same genes, if it would be possible to eliminate a "bad" gene from a gene pair, it might be possible to reverse some heart disease!

INGAP (IN gap)

Star on the Horizon

Can you tell the body to make new cells that will make insulin? If you can— you can potentially CURE diabetes. A compound called islets neogenesis-associated protein (INGAP) may be the answer. Very early research found that INGAP peptide tells the pancreas to make new cells. If new islet cells (the ones that make insulin) can be made, then diabetes can potentially have a treatment that does not just replace insulin, but replaces the cells that were there in the first place. I'll update you on this as progress continues.

INSULIN, ORAL (IN sue lyn)

Medication Delivery

Would you prefer a shot (injection) or a spray? I think we all know the answer to this. A new insulin delivery system promises to replace an insulin shot with a sprayer that is actually sprayed into the mouth. I first saw the data at the 2001 American Diabetes Association meeting. I've reviewed the available data and it looks like the insulin is absorbed into the blood and offers similar efficacy to the less desirable needle. Generex Biotechnology (*www.generex.com*) has progressed their product through clinical trials and its Oralin product via the Rapidmist device is currently in Phase III (the last phase before approval). Blood sugar control without a shot may soon be here for more than just basal insulin!

INSULIN, PATCH (IN sue lyn)

Medication Delivery

We all know about skin patches like the ones for high blood pressure and even a birth control patch. The latest insulin application may be via a patch for basal insulin needs. The company is Altea, and is studying this painless new application. Visit *www.medicineinformation.com* for more on this exciting early research.

MORPHINE, ORAL (MORE feen)

Medication Delivery

Would you prefer a pill, a shot (injection), or a spray? We all know the answer to this. The same spray delivery system being investigated to deliver insulin is now being investigated to help people living with ongoing (chronic) pain give themselves morphine. The company is Generex, and they will be working jointly with Elan Corporation. Health Canada has officially approved an Investigational New Drug (IND) application for this novel approach to pain management. Given what I expect would be a very quick onset, pain management makes a lot of sense for the Generex technology.

PKC INHIBITOR (P K SEE)

Star on the Horizon

People living with diabetes are prone to develping painful nerve damage known as neuropathy (specifically diabetic peripheral neuropathy). A family of compounds known as PKC inhibitors and an investigational compound from Lilly known as LY 333531 appear to show great promise. LY 333351 is currently being studied (Phase Three) for neuropathy and for a diabetic eye problem. For more information, visit *www.lillytrials.com*. There is a clinical trials support number (1-877-285-4559).

PROSTATE CANCER VACCINE (PRAH state)

Star on the Horizon

A vaccine to help prevent prostate cancer is in the works. A phase I/II study showed that a vaccine named GVAX stabilized disease in 71% of patients and was also safe and well tolerated. It is expected that the company researching this vaccine (Cell Genesys) will move forward with further testing.

ROSUVASTATIN (Rah SUE vah stat ihn)

Star on the Horizon

A New Drug Application (NDA) was submitted by AstraZeneca for this new cholesterol lowering medicine. The tentative brand name is Crestor, and it appears that rosuvastatin will be the most potent "statin" available once it is released. Please visit *www.medicineinfo.com* and The Good News and New Medicines section for follow-up information.

RUBOXISTAURIN MESYLATE (Ruh BOX ih star ihn)

Star on the Horizon

A New Drug presentation at the 63rd American Diabetes Association involved an experimental medicine called ruboxistaurin (LY333531—note previous use). This medicine is a PKC Beta inactivator which showed promise in delaying vision loss in patients with moderate to severe diabetic retinopathy (nonprolifer-ative). Almost half of diabetics develop some degree of retinopathy. These unde-sirable changes in the small blood vessels of the retina can lead to macular edema and visual impairment or even blindness. Further research is needed.

SPL 7013

Star on the Horizon

A New Drug Application (NDA) was submitted by an Austrailian company called Starpharma for what may be a revolutionary PREVENTATIVE step for HIV. The formulation is called VivaGel and contains SPL 7013 as the active ingre-dient. To date, stidies in monkeys (primate trials) have shown the product to be 100% effective in preventing transmission of HIV, the virus that leads to AIDS. One application also appeared to prevent transmission of the respective animal versions of chlamydia and genital herpes.

TELOMERASE (TELL om er ace)

Star on the Horizon

Work has continued on this new enzyme that appears to have a role in aging and may also be part of the cancer mystery. Much research needs to be done to see where this enzyme fits in.

VARDENAFIL (VAR den ah fill)

Star on the Horizon

Levitra (luh VEE tra) is heading toward FDA approval. The topic is ED or erectile dysfunction. We've heard about it relative to Viagra—yet many men still are not asking their doctors about causes and treatment. In ongoing clinical data in men 44–77 years old, (most of whom had previously had a prostate removal or prostatectomy) there was a 71% improvement in their erections. I'll update you further on *www.medicineinfo.com* as this medicine continues toward approval.

VARENICLINE (var EH nih clean)

Novel Approach

I've often said that there are no data to say that smoking is good for you—yet quitting once you start is extraordinarily difficult. An experimental approach from Pfizer is called varenicline. In early trials, half of the smokers who used it were able to successfully stop smoking in seven weeks! To date, side effects are minimal. The drug is a selective nicotinic receptor modulator. As always, I'll update you on *www.medicineinfo.com* and in the next edition of this book.

DRUG CLASSES

Throughout the drug profiles, I often refer you to various drug classes. Use this section to protect yourself and your family. Medicines in the same class often share important characteristics in their chemistry, how they work in the body, and even the problems or side effects that they may cause. Any drug (or all drugs) in a given class can be expected to behave in a similar way. This knowledge helps you prevent interactions or unanticipated or hazardous adverse effects.

Each drug class is named, followed by an alphabetic listing of the generic names of the medicines in the class. Following each generic name (and enclosed in parentheses) is the widely recognized brand name(s) of that particular drug. A complete listing is not possible. If your medicine is not present, call your doctor or pharmacist to get the generic name of the drug that concerns you. The generic name listings are sufficiently complete to serve the scope of this book.

ACE (Angiotensin-Converting Enzyme) Inhibitors

benazepril (Lotensin)
captopril (Capoten)
cilazapril (investigational)
enalapril (Vasotec)
enalapril/felodipine (Lexxel)
fosinopril (Monopril)
lisinopril (Prinivil, Zestril)
lisinopril/hctz (Prinzide, Zestoretic)
moexipril (Univasc)
moexipril/hydrochlorothiazide
  (Uniretic)
perindopril (Aceon)
quinapril (Accupril)
ramipril (Altace)
spirapril (Renormax)
trandolapril (Mavik)
trandolapril/verapamil (Tarka)

Adrenocortical Steroids (Cortisone-like Drugs)

amcinonide (Cyclocort)
beclomethasone (Beclovent, Vanceril)
betamethasone (Celestone)
budesonide (Pulmicort)
cortisone (Cortone)
dexamethasone (Decadron)
fludrocortisone (Florinef)
flunisolide (AeroBid, Nasarel)
fluorometholone (FML)
fluticasone (Flonase)
halcinonide (Halog)

halobetasol (Ultravate)
hydrocortisone (Cortef)
medrysone (HMS Ophthalmic
    Suspension)
methylprednisolone (Medrol)
mometasone (Elocon)
paramethasone (Haldrone)
prednisolone (Delta-Cortef)
prednisone (Deltasone)
rimexalone (Vexol)
triamcinolone (Aristocort, Azmacort)

Alpha-Glucosidase Inhibitors

acarbose (Precose)

miglitol (Glyset)

Amebicides (Anti-Infectives)

chloroquine (Aralen)
emetine
iodoquinol (Yodoxin)

metronidazole (Flagyl)
paromomycin (Humatin)

Aminoglycosides (Anti-Infectives)

amikacin (Amikin)
gentamicin (Garamycin)
kanamycin (Kantrex)

neomycin (Mycifradin, Neobiotic)
paromomycin (Humatin)
tobramycin (Tobicin)

Amphetamine-like Drugs

amphetamine
benzphetamine (Didrex)
dextroamphetamine (Dexedrine)
diethylpropion (Tenuate, Tepanil)
methamphetamine (Desoxyn)
methylphenidate (Ritalin)

phendimetrazine (Adipost, Anorex,
    Plegine)
phenmetrazine (Preludin)
phentermine (Adipex-P, Fastin)
phentermine resin complex (Ionamin)
phenylpropanolamine (Dexatrim)

Analgesics (Pain relievers)

acetaminophen (Datril, Tylenol)
acetaminophen/propoxyphene
    (Darvocet-N 100)
aspirin
capsaicin (Zostrix)
COX II inhibitors (rofecoxib-Vioxx,
    celecoxib-Celebrex, etoricoxib,
    valdecoxib-Bextra)
Fentanyl (Duragesic)
Gabapentin (Neurontin)

lidocaine/prilocaine cream (Emla)
morphine (Kadian, MS-Contin, Avinza)
oxycodone (Oxycontin)
propoxyphene (Darvon)
tramadol (Ultram)
zinconotide (investigational)
See also Nonsteroidal Anti-
    Inflammatory Drugs (NSAIDs) and
    Opioid Drugs

Androgens (Male Sex Hormones)

fluoxymesterone (Halotestin)
methyltestosterone (Android,
  Metandren, Oreton)

testosterone (Androderm, Andriol,
  AndroGel, Depotest, Testoderm,
  Testone)

Anemia Treatments (Blood Modifiers, Hematinics)

erythropoetin alpha (Procrit)
pegfilgrastim (Neulasta)

filgrastim (Neupogen)

Angiotensin-II-Receptor Antagonists (also known as ARBS)

candesartan (Atacand)
candesartan/HCTZ (Atacand HCT)
eprosartan (Teveten)
irbesartan (Avapro)
irbesartan/HCTZ (Avalide)

losartan (Cozaar)
losartan/HCTZ (Hyzaar)
telmisartan (Micardis)
valsartan (Diovan)
valsartan/HCTZ (Diovan HCT)

Anorexiants (Appetite Suppressants)

mazindol (Mazanor, Sanorex)
sibutramine (Meridia)

See also Amphetamine-like Drugs

Anti-Acne Drugs

adapalene (Differin)
azelaic acid (Azelex)
benzoyl peroxide (Epi-Clear, others)
erythromycin (Eryderm)
isotretinoin (Accutane)

sodium sulfacetamide 10% lotion
  (Klaron)
tetracycline (Achromycin V)
tretinoin (Retin-A)

Anti-AIDS/HIV Drugs (Anti-Retrovirals)

abacavir (Ziagen)
abacavir/lamivudine/zidovudine
  (Trizivir)
amprenavir (Agenerase or VX-1478)
delavirdine (Rescriptor)
didanosine (DDI, Videx)
efavirenz (Sustiva)
emtricitabine (FTC-investigational)
hydroxyurea (Droxia)
indinavir (Crixivan)
integrase (Zintevir) (newly approved)
lamivudine (3TC, Epivir)
lopinavir/ritonvair (Kaletra)

nelfinavir (Viracept)
nevirapine (Viramune)
ritonavir (Norvir)
saquinavir (Invirase)
stavudine (D4T, Zerit)
T-20 (Newly approved as enfuvirtide-
  Fuzeon)
T-1249 (investigational)
zalcitabine (dideoxycytidine, DDC,
  Hivid)
zidovudine (AZT, Retrovir)
232632 atazanavir (Reyataz)
tenofovir (Viread)

Antialcoholism Drugs

disulfiram (Antabuse)

naltrexone (Trexan, ReVia)

Anti-Alzheimer's Drugs

donepezil (Aricept)
galantamine (Reminyl)
ginkgo biloba (herbal product)
metrifonate (Bilarcil)

rivastigmine (Exelon)
tacrine (Cognex)
vitamin E (various brands)

Anti-Anginal Drugs

bepridil (Vascor)
diltiazem (Cardizem)
nicardipine (Cardene)
nifedipine (Adalat, Procardia)

nitrates (see class below)
verapamil (Calan, Isoptin)
See also Beta Blockers

Antianxiety Drugs

buspirone (Buspar)
chlormezanone (Trancopal)
hydroxyzine (Atarax, Vistaril)
lorazepam (Ativan)

meprobamate (Equanil, Miltown)
paroxetine (Paxil)—generalized and
adult social anxiety disorder
See also Benzodiazepines

Antiarrhythmic Drugs (Heart-Rhythm Regulators)

Class or Group One

disopyramide (Norpace)
flecainide (Tambocor)
mexiletine (Mexitil)
procainamide (Procan SR, Pronestyl)

quinidine (Quinaglute, Quinidex,
Quinora)
propafenone (Rythmol)
tocainide (Tonocard)

Class or Group Two

acebutolol (Sectral)
propranolol (Inderal)

sotalol (Betapace)

Class or Group Three

amiodarone (Cordarone)
dofetilide (Tikosyn)

ibutilide (Corvert)
sotalol (Betapace)

Class or Group Four

diltiazem (Cardizem)

verapamil (Calan, Isoptin)

Miscellaneous

adenosine (Adenocard)

digoxin (Lanoxin)

Antiarthritics

aspirin
azathioprine (Imuran; rheumatoid only)
chloroquine (Aralen; rheumatoid only)
COX-II inhibitor family
etanercept (Enbrel)
infliximab (Remicade)

leflunomide (Arava)
penicillamine (Cuprimine)
See also Nonsteroidal Anti-
Inflammatory Drugs (NSAIDs)
and Adrenocorticosteroids
anakinra (Kineret)

Antiasthmatic Drugs

Anti-IgE

Omalizumab (Xolair-investigational)

Anti-Inflammatory Agents, Corticosteroids

beclomethasone (Beclovent, Vanceril)
flunisolide (AeroBid)
fluticasone (Flovent)

fluticasone/salmeterol (Advair Diskus)
triamcinolone (Azmacort)

Anti-Leukotrienes

montelukast (Singulair)
zafirlukast (Accolate)

zileuton (Zyflo)

Bronchodilators

albuterol (Proventil, Ventolin)
aminophylline (Phyllocontin)
bitolterol (Tornalate)
dyphylline (Lufyllin)
ephedrine (Efed II)
epinephrine (Adrenalin, Bronkaid Mist,
    Primatene Mist)
formoterol (Foradil)
ipratropium
isoetharine (Bronkosol, Dey-Lute)

isoproterenol (Isuprel)
metaproterenol (Alupent, Metaprel)
oxtriphylline (Choledyl)
pirbuterol (Maxair)
salmeterol (Serevent) (see
    combination form above)
terbutaline (Brethaire, Brethine,
    Bricanyl)
theophylline (Bronkodyl, Elixophyllin,
Slo-Phyllin, others)

Combination Agents

fluticasone/salmeterol (Advair Diskus)

Mast-Cell-Stabilizing Agents

cromolyn sodium (Gastrocrom, Intal)

nedocromil (Tilade)

Preventive Agents

cromolyn (Intal)

nedocromil (Tilade)

Xanthines

theophylline (Slo-bid, Theo-Dur)

Anti-Attention-Deficit-Hyperactivity-Disorder Drugs

amphetamine and dextroamphetamine
    (Adderall)
atomoxetine (Strattera)
bupropion (Wellbutrin)
clonidine (Catapres)

desipramine (Norpramin)
dexmethylphenidate (Focalin)
methylphenidate (Concerta, Metadate,
    Methylin, Ritalin)
pemoline (Cylert)

Anti-Benign-Prostatic-Hyperplasia Drugs

doxazosin (Cardura)
finasteride (Proscar)
prazosin (Minipres)

saw palmetto (various)—herbal product
tamsulosin (Flomax)
terazosin (Hytrin)

Antibiotics

See specific antibiotic class
   (Cephalosporins, Ketolides, Macrolides,
   Penicillins, Tetracyclines, etc.)

Topical, Anti-Infectives

mupirocin (Bactroban)

Anticancer Drugs (Antineoplastics or Chemotherapy)

anastrozole (Arimidex)
capecitabine (Zeloda)
chlorambucil (Leukeran)
cyclophosphamide (Cytoxan)
flutamide (Eulexin)
hydroxyurea (Hydrea)

liposomally encapsulated doxorubicin
   (Evacet) (investigational)
mercaptopurine (Purinethol)
methotrexate (Rheumatrex)
tamoxifen (Nolvadex)

Signal Transduction Inhibitor chemotherapy

imatinib STI571 (Gleevec)

Anti-Canker-Sore Drugs

amlexanox (Apthasol)

Anticholesterol Drugs

See Cholesterol-Reducing Drugs
See HMG-CoA Reductase Inhibitors

See "The Leading Edge" section of this
   book

Anticholinergic Drugs (Atropine-like Drugs)

atropine
belladonna
hyoscyamine
scopolamine
See also the specific drug class:

Antidepressant Drugs, Tricyclic
Antihistamines, some
Anti-Parkinsonism Drugs, some
Antispasmodics, Synthetic, some
Muscle Relaxants, some

Anticoagulant Drugs

anisindione (Miradon)
dicumarol
fondaparinux (investigational factor Xa
   inhibitor)
low-molecular-weight heparins
   (ardeparin-Normiflo, dalteparin-
   Fragmin, enoxaparin-Lovenox,

tinzaparin-Innohep)
warfarin (Coumadin and generic)

Anticonvulsant Drugs (Antiepileptic Drugs)

acetazolamide (Diamox)
carbamazepine (Tegretol)
clonazepam (Klonopin)
clorazepate (Tranxene)
diazepam (Valium)
ethosuximide (Zarontin)
ethotoin (Peganone)
felbamate (Felbatol)
gabapentin (Neurontin)
lamotrigine (Lamictal)
levetiracetam (Keppra)
mephenytoin (Mesantoin)

methsuximide (Celontin)
oxcarbamazepine (Trileptal)
paramethadione (Paradione)
phenacemide (Phenurone)
phenobarbital (Luminal)
phensuximide (Milontin)
phenytoin (Dilantin)
primidone (Mysoline)
topiramate (Topamax)
trimethadione (Tridione)
valproic acid (Depakene)
zonisamide (Zonegran)

Anti-Cystic-Fibrosis Agents (Recombinant DNase)

dornase alfa (Pulmozyme)

Antidepressant Drugs

Bicyclic Antidepressants

fluoxetine (Prozac, Prozac Weekly)

venlafaxine (Effexor)

Tetracyclic Antidepressants

maprotiline (Ludiomil)

mirtazapine (Remeron)

Tricyclic Antidepressants

amitriptyline (Elavil, Endep)
amoxapine (Asendin)
clomipramine (Anafranil)
desipramine (Norpramin, Pertofrane)
doxepin (Adapin, Sinequan)
imipramine (Tofranil)
nortriptyline (Aventyl, Pamelor)
protriptyline (Vivactil)
trimipramine (Surmontil)
Other Antidepressants

bupropion (Wellbutrin, Wellbutrin SR)
fluvoxamine (Luvox)
Hypericum (St. John's wort)
nefazodone (Serzone)
paroxetine (Paxil)
sertraline (Zoloft)
trazodone (Desyrel)
See also Monoamine Oxidase (MAO)
   Inhibitors

Antidiabetic Drugs

Oral

See Alpha-Glucosidase Inhibitors,
   Biguanides, D-phenylalanine
   derivatives, Meglitinides,

Sulfonylureas and
Thiazolindinediones

Injectable

insulin

Mouth (Oral) Spray

insulin (Oralin—investigational)

Antidiarrheal Drugs

loperamide

tegaserod (diarrhea predominant irritable bowel syndrome)

Antiemetic Drugs (Anti-Motion-Sickness, Anti-Nausea Drugs)

chlorpromazine (Thorazine)
cyclizine (Marezine)
dimenhydrinate (Dramamine)
diphenhydramine (Benadryl)
ginger (various)
granisetron (Kytril)
hydroxyzine (Atarax, Vistaril)

meclizine (Antivert, Bonine)
ondansetron (Zofran)
prochlorperazine (Compazine)
promethazine (Phenergan)
scopolamine (Transderm Scop)
trimethobenzamide (Tigan)

Substance P blocking antiemetics

Aprepitant (Emend)

Antiepileptic Drugs

See Anticonvulsant Drugs

Antifungal Drugs (Anti-Infectives)

amphotericin B (Fungizone)
butenafine (Mentax)
caspofungin (Cancidas)
fluconazole (Diflucan)
flucytosine (Ancobon)
griseofulvin (Fulvicin, Grifulvin, Grisactin)
itraconazole (Sporanox)

ketoconazole (Nizoral)
lipid-associated amphotericin B (Abelcet)
miconazole (Monistat)
nystatin (Mycostatin)
terbinafine (Lamisil)
tioconazole (Vagistat-1)

Antiglaucoma Drugs

acetazolamide (Diamox)
betaxolol (Betoptic)
bimatoprost (Lumigan)
brimonidine (Alphagan)
brinzolamide (Azopt)
dipivefrin (Propine)
dorzolamide (Trusopt)
dorzolamide and timolol (Cosopt)
epinephrine (Glaucon)

latanoprost (Xalatan)
levobetaxolol (Betaxon)
levobunolol (Betagan)
metipranolol (Optipranolol)
pilocarpine (Pilocar)
timolol (Betimol, Timoptic, Timoptic-XE)
travaprost (Travatan)

Antigout Drugs

allopurinol (Zyloprim)
colchicine
diclofenac (Cataflam, Voltaren)
fenoprofen (Nalfon)
ibuprofen (Advil, Motrin, Nuprin, Rufin)
indomethacin (Indocin)
ketoprofen (Orudis)

mefenamic acid (Ponstel)
naproxen (Anaprox, Naprosyn)
oxaprozin (Daypro)
piroxicam (Feldene)
probenecid (Benemid)
sulfinpyrazone (Anturane)
sulindac (Clinoril)

Antihistamines

astemizole (Hismanal) (now
  removed from the market)
azatadine (Optimine)
azelastine (Astelin)
brompheniramine (Dimetane, others)
carbinoxamine (Clistin, Rondec)
cetirizine (Zyrtec)
chlorpheniramine (Chlor-Trimeton,
  Teldrin)
clemastine (Tavist)
cyclizine (Marezine)
cyproheptadine (Periactin)
desloratadine (Clarinex)

dimenhydrinate (Dramamine)
diphenhydramine (Benadryl)
doxylamine (Unisom)
hydroxyzine (Atarax)
loratadine (Claritin, Claritin Extra)
meclizine (Antivert, Bonine)
orphenadrine (Norflex)
pheniramine (component of Triaminic)
promethazine (Phenergan, others)
pyrilamine (component of Triaminic)
tripelennamine (Pyribenzamine, PBZ)
triprolidine (component of Actifed and
  Sudahist)

Nonsedating or Minimally Sedating

astemizole (Hismanal) (now removed
  from the market)
cetirizine (Zyrtec)

desloratadine (Clarinex)
fexofenadine (Allegra)
loratadine (Claritin)

Antihypertensive Drugs

amlodipine/benazepril (Lotrel)
bisoprolol/hydrochlorothiazide (Ziac)
carvedilol (Coreg)
clonidine (Catapres)
doxazosin (Cardura)
enalapril/felodipine (Lexxel)
eplerenone (Inspra)
guanabenz (Wytensin)
guanadrel (Hylorel)
guanethidine (Ismelin)
guanfacine (Tenex)
hydralazine (Apresoline)

hydrochlorothiazide/benazepril
  (Lotensin)
methyldopa (Aldomet)
minoxidil (Loniten)
prazosin (Minipres)
reserpine (Serpasil)
terazosin (Hytrin)
See also ACE Inhibitors, Angiotensin-
  II-Receptor Antagonists, Beta
  Blockers, Calcium Blockers, and
  Diuretics

Anti-Impotence Drugs

alprostadil injection (Caverject)
apomorphine (Uprima)
vardenafil (Levitral-investigational)

IC-151 hydroxylase (investigational)
sildenafil (Viagra)

Anti-Infective Drugs

See the specific anti-infective drug
  classes:
Amebicides
Aminoglycosides
Antifungal Drugs
Antileprosy Drugs
Antimalarial Drugs
Antituberculosis Drugs

Antiviral Drugs
Cephalosporins
Fluoroquinolones
Macrolide Antibiotics
Oxazolidinones
Penicillins
Sulfonamides
Tetracyclines

Miscellaneous Anti-Infective Drugs

atovaquone (Mepron)
chloramphenicol (Chloromycetin)
clindamycin (Cleocin)
colistin (Coly-Mycin S)
daptomycin (Cedecin-investigational)
furazolidone (Furoxone)
lincomycin (Lincocin)
linezolid (Zyvox)

nalidixic acid (NegGram)
nitrofurantoin (Furadantin, Macrodantin)
novobiocin (Albamycin)
pentamidine (Pentam-300)
trimethoprim (Proloprim, Trimpex)
vancomycin (Vancocin)

Antileprosy Drugs (Anti-Infectives)

clofazimine (Lamprene)

dapsone

Antimalarial Drugs (Anti-Infectives)

chloroquine (Aralen)
doxycycline (Vibramycin)
hydroxychloroquine (Plaquenil)
mefloquine (Lariam)
primaquine

pyrimethamine (Daraprim)
quinacrine (Atabrine)
quinine
sulfadoxine (Fansidar)

Antimigraine Drugs

almotriptan (Axert)
acetylsalicylic acid (aspirin-Excedrin Migraine)
atenolol (Tenormin)
eletriptan (Replax)
ergotamine (Ergostat)
frovatriptan (Miguard)
methysergide (Sansert)
metoprolol (Lopressor)
nadolol (Corgard)

naratriptan (Amerge)
nifedipine (Procardia)
propranolol (Inderal)
rizatriptan benzoate (Maxalt, Maxalt MLT)
sumatriptan (Imitrex)
timolol (Blocadren)
valproic acid (Divalproex)
verapamil (Calan, Isoptin)
zolmatriptan (Zomig, Zomig nasal spray)

Anti-Motion-Sickness/Antinausea Drugs

See Antiemetic Drugs

Anti-Myasthenics

neostigmine

Antimycobacterial Agents

rifabutin (Mycobutin)

Anti-Osteoporotics

alendronate (Fosamax)
antiestrogens (SERM)
calcitonin (Miacalcin)
calcium (various brands)
estrogen (various brands)
pravastatin (Pravachol-one study
    reported improvement—not an
    FDA-approved use)

raloxifene (Evista)
risedronate (Actonel)
synthetic conjugated estrogens
teriparatide (Forteo)
tiludronate (Skelid)
zoledronic acid (Zoledronate—
    investigational)

Anti-Parkinsonism Drugs

amantadine (Symmetrel)
benztropine (Cogentin)
bromocriptine (Parlodel)
diphenhydramine (Benadryl)
levodopa (Dopar, Larodopa)
levodopa/bensarazide (Prolopa)
levodopa/carbidopa (Sinemet, Sinemet CR)
pergolide (Permax)
prampexole (Myrapex)

ropinirole (Requip)
selegiline (Eldepryl)
tolcapone (Tasmar)
trihexyphenidyl (Artane)
vitamin E (various)
Catechol O-Methyl Tranferase (COMT)
    Drugs
tolcapone (Tasmar)

Antiplatelet Drugs (Platelet Aggregation Inhibitors)

aspirin
aspirin/dipyridamole (Aggrenox)
clopidogrel (Plavix)
dipyridamole (Persantine)

sulfinpyrazone (Anturane)
ticlopidine (Ticlid)
tirofiban (Aggrastat)

Antipsoriatic Drugs

acitretin (Soriatane)
etanercept (Enbrel)
etretinate

infliximab (Remicade)
methotrexate

Antipsychotic Drugs (Neuroleptics, Major Tranquilizers)

aripiprazole (Abilify)
chlorprothixene (Taractan)
clozapine (Clozaril)
haloperidol (Haldol)
loxapine (Loxitane)
molindone (Moban)
olanzapine (Zyprexa)

pimozide (Orap)
quetiapine (Seroquel)
risperidone (Risperdal)
thiothixene (Navane)
ziprasidone (Geodon)
See also Phenothiazines and
    Thienobenzodiazepines

Antipyretic Drugs (Fever-Reducing Drugs)

acetaminophen
aspirin
See also COX II inhibitors

See also Nonsteroidal Anti-
    Inflammatory Drugs (NSAIDs)

Anti-Sickle-Cell Anemia Drugs

hydroxyurea (Droxia, Hydrea)

Antispasmodics, Synthetic

anisotropine (Valpin)
clidinium (Quarzan)
glycopyrrolate (Robinul)
hexocyclium (Tral)
isopropamide (Darbid)

mepenzolate (Cantil)
methantheline (Banthine)
methscopolamine (Pamine)
propantheline (Pro-Banthine)
tridihexethyl (Pathilon)

Antituberculosis Drugs

aminosalicylate sodium (Sodium P.A.S.)
capreomycin (Capastat)
cycloserine (Seromycin)
ethambutol (Myambutol)
ethionamide (Trecator-SC)
isoniazid (Laniazid, Nydrazid)

pyrazinamide
rifabutin (Mycobutin)
rifampin (Rifadin, Rimactane, Rifater)
rifapentine (Priftin)
streptomycin

Antitussive Drugs (Cough Suppressants)

benzonatate (Tessalon)
codeine (various brands)
dextromethorphan (Hold DM, Suppress)
diphenhydramine (Benylin)

hydrocodone (Hycodan)
hydromorphone (Dilaudid)
promethazine (Phenergan)

Antiulcer Drugs

Antacids

various brands

Antibiotics

amoxicillin
clarithromycin
metronidazole

tetracycline
See Histamine (H2) Blockers
See Proton Pump Inhibitors

Miscellaneous Antiulcer Drugs

amoxicillin/clarithromycin/
lansoprazole (Prevpac)
bismuth subsalicylate (Pepto-Bismol,
    others)

misoprostol (Cytotec)
ranitidine bismuth citrate (Tritec)
sucralfate (Carafate)

Antiviral Drugs (Anti-Infectives)

Abacavir (Ziagen)
Abacavir, lamivudine, zidovudine
(Trizivir)
acyclovir (Zovirax)
amantadine (Symmetrel)
amprenavir (Agenerase)
cidofovir (Vistide)
didanosine (Videx)
docosanol (Abreva)
efavirenz (Sustiva)
emtricitabine (FTC-investigational)
enfuvirtide (Fuzeon)
famciclovir (Famvir)
foscarnet (Foscavir)
ganciclovir (Cytovene)
indinavir (Crixivan)
lamivudine (Epivir, Epivir HBV)
tenofovir (Viread)

lopinavir/ritonavir (Kaletra)
nelfinavir (Viracept)
nevirapine (Viramune)
oseltamivir (Tamiflu)
penciclovir (Denavir)
peginterferon alpha-2a (Pegasys)
ribavirin (Copegus, Virazole)
rimantadine (Flumadine)
ritonavir (Norvir)
saquinavir (Invirase)
stavudine (Zerit)
valacyclovir (Valtrex)
vidarabine (Vira A)
zalcitabine (Hivid)
zanamivir (Relenza)
zidovudine (Retrovir)
232632 atazanavir (Reyataz)

Appetite Suppressants

See Anorexiants

Aromatase inhibitors

anastrozole (Arimidex)

Atropine-like Drugs

See Anticholinergic Drugs

Barbiturates

amobarbital (Amytal)
aprobarbital (Alurate)
butabarbital (Butisol)
mephobarbital (Mebaral)
metharbital (Gemonil)

pentobarbital (Nembutal)
phenobarbital (Luminal, Solfoton)
secobarbital (Seconal)
talbutal (Lotusate)

Benzodiazepines

alprazolam (Xanax)
bromazepam (Lectopam)
chlordiazepoxide (Libritabs, Librium)
clonazepam (Klonopin)
clorazepate (Tranxene)
diazepam (Valium, Vazepam)
estazolam (Prosom)
flurazepam (Dalmane)
halazepam (Paxipam)

ketazolam (Loftran)
lorazepam (Ativan)
midazolam (Versed)
nitrazepam (Mogadon)
oxazepam (Serax)
prazepam (Centrax)
quazepam (Doral)
temazepam (Restoril)
triazolam (Halcion)

Beta Blockers (Beta-Adrenergic-Blocking Drugs)

acebutolol (Sectral)
atenolol (Tenormin)
betaxolol (Kerlone)
bisoprolol (Zebeta)
bisoprolol/hydrochlorothiazide (Ziac)
carteolol (Cartrol)
carvedilol (Coreg)

labetalol (Normodyne, Trandate)
metoprolol (Lopressor)
nadolol (Corgard)
penbutolol (Levatol)
pindolol (Visken)
propranolol (Inderal)
timolol (Blocadren)

Biguanides (Oral Antidiabetic Drugs)

metformin (Glucophage)

Bisphosphonates

alendronate (Fosamax)
risedronate (Actonel)

tiludronate (Skelid)
zoledronate (investigational)

Blood Flow Agents

cilostazol (Pletal)
ginkgo biloba (various)

pentoxifylline (Trental)

Bowel Anti-Inflammatory Drugs (Inflammatory Bowel Disease Suppressants)

azathioprine (Imuran)
infliximab (Avakine)
mesalamine (Rowasa, Asacol)

metronidazole (Flagyl)
olsalazine (Dipentum)
sulfasalazine (Azulfidine)

Bronchodilators

See Antiasthmatic Drugs

Calcium Blockers (Calcium-Channel-Blocking Drugs)

amlodipine (Norvasc)
bepridil (Vascor)
diltiazem (Cardizem, Tiazac)
felodipine (Plendil)
isradipine (DynaCirc)
mibefradil (Posicor) (removed by the
    company)

nicardipine (Cardene, Cardene SR)
nifedipine (Adalat CC, Procardia XL)
nimodipine (Nimotop)
nisoldipine (Sular)
verapamil (Calan, Isoptin, Verelan)

Cardiac hormones (Anti-Congestive Heart Failure)

Nesiritide (Natrecor)

Cephalosporins (Anti-Infectives)

cefaclor (Ceclor)
cefadroxil (Duricef, Ultracef)
cefamandole (Mandol)
cefatrizine (Cefaperos)
cefazolin (Ancef, Kefzol, Zolicef)
cefdinir (Omnicef)
cefepime (Maxipime)
cefixime (Suprax)
cefmetazole (Zefazone)
cefonicid (Monocid)
cefoperazone (Cefobid)
ceforanide (Precef)
cefotaxime (Claforan)
cefotetan (Cefotan)

cefoxitin (Mefoxin)
cefpodoxime (Vantin)
cefprozil (Cefzil)
ceftazidime (Fortaz, Tazidime, Tazicef)
ceftibuten (Cedax)
ceftizoxime (Cefizox)
ceftriaxone (Rocephin)
cefuroxime (Ceftin, Kefurox, Zinacef)
cephalexin (Keflex, Keftab)
cephalothin (Keflin)
cephapirin (Cefadyl)
cephradine (Anspor, Velosef)
loracarbef (Cefobid)
moxalactam (Moxam)

Cholesterol-Reducing Drugs

atorvastatin (Lipitor)
cholestyramine (Questran, Prevalite)
clofibrate (Atromid-S)
colesevelam (Welchol)
colestipol (Colestid)
dextrithyroxiune (Choloxin)
ETC-216 (investigational)
ezetimibe (Zetia)

fenofibrate (Tricor)
fluvastatin (Lescol)
gemfibrozil (Lopid)
lovastatin (Mevacor)
niacin/lovastatin (Advicor)
niacin (Nicobid, Slo-Niacin, others)
pravastatin (Pravachol)
simvastatin (Zocor)

Cortisone-like Drugs

See Adrenocortical Steroids

Cough Suppressants

See Antitussive Drugs

COX II Inhibitors

celecoxib (Celebrex)
etoricoxib (investigational; Arcoxia)

rofecoxib (Vioxx)
valdecoxib (Bextra)

Decongestants

ephedrine (Efedron, Ephedrol)
naphazoline (Naphcon, Vasocon)
oxymetazoline (Afrin, Duration, others)
phenylephrine (Neo-Synephrine, others)

phenylpropanolamine (Propadrine, Propagest, others)
pseudoephedrine (Afrinol, Sudafed, others)
tetrahydrozoline (Tyzine, Visine, others)
xylometazoline (Otrivin)

Digitalis Preparations

deslanoside (Cedilanid-D)
digitoxin (Crystodigin)

digoxin (Lanoxicaps, Lanoxin)

Disease-Modifying Antirheumatic Drugs (DMARDs)

etanercept (Enbrel)
leflunomide (Arava)

methotrexate (Rheumatrex)

Diuretics

acetazolamide (Diamox)
amiloride (Midamor)
bumetanide (Bumex)
chlorthalidone (Hygroton)
ethacrynic acid (Edecrin)
furosemide (Lasix)

indapamide (Lozol)
metolazone (Diulo, Zaroxolyn)
spironolactone (Aldactone)
triamterene (Dyrenium)
See also Thiazide Diuretics

Dopamine System Stabilizers

aripiprazole (Abilify)

D-phenylalanine derivative oral hypoglycemics

nateglinide (Starlix)

Ergot Derivatives

bromocriptine (Parlodel)
ergotamine (Bellergal)

methysergide (Sansert)
pergolide (Permax)

Estrogens (Female Sex Hormones)

chlorotrianisene (Tace)
diethylstilbestrol (DES, Stilphostrol)
estradiol (Estrace, Estraderm, others)
estrogens, conjugated (Premarin,
    Prempro)
estrogens, esterified (Estratab, Menest)

estrone (Theelin, others)
estropipate (Ogen)
ethinyl estradiol (Estinyl)
quinestrol (Estrovis)
plant-derived synthetic conjugated
    estrogens (Cenestin)

Female Sex Hormones

See Estrogens and Progestins

Fever-Reducing Drugs

See Antipyretic Drugs

5-Alpha-Reductase Inhibitors

finasteride (Proscar)

saw palmetto (various)

Fluoroquinolones (Anti-Infectives)

balofloxacin (pending)
ciprofloxacin (Cipro)
fleroxacin (Quinodis [Germany])
gatiloxacin (Tequin)
grepafloxacin (Raxar)
levofloxacin (Levaquin)

lomefloxacin (Maxaquin)
moxifloxacin (Avelox)
norfloxacin (Noroxin)
ofloxacin (Floxin)
sparfloxacin (Zagam)
trovafloxacin (Trovan)

Fusion Inhibitors (Anti-HIV, Anti-Infectives)

enfuvirtide (Fuzeon)

T-1249 (investigational)

Gastrointestinal Drugs

Miscellaneous

cisapride (Propulsid)
infliximab (Avakine)

metoclopramide (Reglan)

Ulcer Preventatives

misoprostol (Cytotec)

Hair Growth Stimulants

finasteride (Proscar, Propecia)

minoxidil (Rogaine)

Heart Rhythm Regulators

See Antiarrhythmic Drugs

Hematopoietic Agents

filgrastim (Neupogen)

pegfilgrastim (Neulasta)

HMG-CoA reductase inhibitors

atorvastatin (Lipitor)
fluvastatin (Lescol)
lovastatin (Mevacor)

pravastatin (Pravachol)
simvastatin (Zocor)

Hormones

Miscellaneous

nafarelin (Synarel)
See also Androgens for male sex
  hormones

See also Estrogens and Progestins for
  female sex hormones

H2 Blockers (Histamine [H2] Blocking Drugs)

cimetidine (Tagamet, Tagamet HB 200)
famotidine (Pepcid, Pepcid AC, Pepcid
  Complete)

nizatidine (Axid, Axid AR)
ranitidine (Zantac, Zantac 75)

Hypnotic Drugs (Sedatives/Sleep Inducers)

acetylcarbromal (Paxarel)
chloral hydrate (Aquachloral, Noctec)
estazolam (Prosom)
ethchlorvynol (Placidyl)
ethinamate (Valmid)
flurazepam (Dalmane)
glutethimide (Doriden)
methyprylon (Noludar)

paraldehyde (Paral)
propiomazine (Largon)
quazepam (Doral)
temazepam (Restoril)
triazolam (Halcion)
zaleplon (Sonata)
zolpidem (Ambien)
See also Barbiturates

Immunosuppressants

azathioprine (Imuran)
chlorambucil (Leukeran)
cyclophosphamide (Cytoxan)
cyclosporine (Sandimmune)

hydroxychloroquine (Plaquenil)
leflunomide (Arava)
serolimus (Rapamune)
tacrolimus (Prograf)

Interleukin One Receptor Antagonists

Anakinra (Kineret)

Ketolide Antibiotics (Anti-Infectives)

Telithromycin (Ketek)—investigational

Macrolide Antibiotics (Anti-Infectives)

azithromycin (Zithromax)
clarithromycin (Biaxin)
dirithromycin (Dynabac)

erythromycin (E-Mycin, Ilosone,
Erythrocin, E.E.S.)
troleandomycin (TAO)

Male Sex Hormones

See Androgens

Mast-Cell-Stabilizing Agents

See Antiasthmatic Drugs

Meglitinides

Netaglinide (Starlix)

repaglinide (Prandin)

Monoamine Oxidase (MAO) Inhibitor Drugs (Type A: Antidepressants)

isocarboxazid (Marplan)
phenelzine (Nardil)

tranylcypromine (Parnate)

Mood Stabilizers

Lithium (lithobid, others)
Oxcarbazepine (Trileptal)

Valproic acid (Depakote, others)

Muscarinic Receptor Antagonists (Anti-Incontinence)

tolteradine (Detrol)

Muscle Relaxants (Skeletal Muscle Relaxants)

baclofen (Lioresal)
carisoprodol (Rela, Soma, others)
chlorphenesin carbamate (Maolate)
chlorzoxazone (Paraflex, Parafon Forte)
cyclobenzaprine (Flexeril)
dantrolene (Dantrium)

diazepam (Valium)
meprobamate (Equanil, Miltown, others)
metaxalone (Skelaxin)
methocarbamol (Robaxin, others)
orphenadrine (Norflex, others)

Neuramidase Inhibitors

oseltamivir (Tamiflu)

zanamivir (Relenza)

Nitrates

amyl nitrate (amyl nitrate generic,
Vaporole, others)
erythrityl tetranitrate (Cardilate)
isosorbide dinitrate (Isordil,
Sorbitrate, others)

isosorbide mononitrate (Ismo, Imdur)
nitroglycerin (Nitrostat, Nitrolingual,
Nitrogard, Nitrong, others)
pentaerythritol tetranitrate (Duotrate,
Peritrate)

Nonnucleoside Reverse Transcriptase Inhibitors

delavirdine (Rescriptor)
efavirenz (Sustiva)

nevirapine (Viramune)

Nonnucleotide Reverse Transcriptase Inhibitors

tenofovir (Viread)

Nonsteroidal Anti-Inflammatory Drugs (NSAIDs)

(Aspirin Substitutes)

Acetic Acids

bromfenac sodium (Duract)
diclofenac potassium (Cataflam)
diclofenac sodium (Voltaren)
etodolac (Lodine)
indomethacin (Indochron E-R, Indocin,
    Indocin SR)
ketorolac (Toradol)

meloxicam (Mobic)
nabumetone (Relafen)
sulindac (Clinoril)
tolmetin (Tolectin, Tolectin DS)
Fenamates
meclofenamate (Meclomen)
mefenamic acid (Ponstel)

Oxicams

piroxicam (Feldene)

Propionic Acids

diflunisal (Dolobid)
fenoprofen (Nalfon)
flurbiprofen (Ansaid)
ibuprofen
ketoprofen (Orudis, Oruvail)
naproxen (Naprosyn)

naproxen sodium (Aleve, Anaprox,
   Anaprox DS)
oxaprozin (Daypro)
oxyphenbutazone (Oxalid)
suprofen (Profenal)

Opioid Antagonists

naltrexone (ReVia)

Opioid Drugs (Narcotics)

alfentanil (Alfenta)
codeine
fentanyl (Actiq, Sublimaze, Duragesic)
hydrocodone (Hycodan)
hydromorphone (Dilaudid)
levorphanol (Levo-Dromoran)
meperidine (Demerol)

methadone (Dolophine)
morphine (Astramorph, Duramorph,
   MS Contin, Roxanol, Avinza)
oxycodone (OxyContin, Roxicodone)
oxymorphone (Numorphan)
propoxyphene (Darvon)
sufentanil (Sufenta)

Pain Syndrome Modifiers (also Adjuvants)

carbamazepine (Tegretol)
gabapentin (Neurontin)
phenytoin (Dilantin)

samarium-EDTMP (Quadramet)
strontium-89 (Metastron)

Penicillins (Anti-Infectives)

amoxicillin (Amoxil, Larotid, Polymox,
   Trimox, others)
amoxicillin/clavulanate (Augmentin)
ampicillin (Omnipen, Polycillin,
   Principen, Totacillin)
ampicillin/sulbactam (Unasyn)
bacampicillin (Spectrobid)
carbenicillin (Geocillin, Geopen, Pyopen)
cloxacillin (Cloxapen, Tegopen)
dicloxacillin (Dynapen, Pathocil, Veracillin)

methicillin (Staphcillin)
mezlocillin (Mezlin)
nafcillin (Nafcil, Unipen)
oxacillin (Prostaphlin)
penicillin G (Pentids, others)
penicillin V (Pen Vee K, V-Cillin K,
   Veetids, others)
piperacillin (Pipracil)
ticarcillin (Ticar)
ticarcillin/clavulanate (Timentin)

Phenothiazines (Antipsychotic Drugs)

acetophenazine (Tindal)
chlorpromazine (Thorazine)
fluphenazine (Permitil, Prolixin)
mesoridazine (Serentil)
perphenazine (Trilafon)
prochlorperazine (Compazine)

promazine (Sparine)
thioridazine (Mellaril)
trifluoperazine (Stelazine)
triflupromazine (Vesprin)
ziprasidone (Geodon)

Potassium Replacement Products
K-Dur

Potassium chloride (various)

Progestins (Female Sex Hormones)
ethynodiol
hydroxyprogesterone (Duralutin,
  Gesterol L.A., others)
medroxyprogesterone (Amen, Curretab,
  Prempro, Premphase, Provera)

megestrol (Megace)
norethindrone (Micronor, Norlutate,
  Norlutin)
norgestrel (Ovrette)
progesterone (Gesterol 50, Progestaject)

Protease Inhibitors
amprenavir (VX-1478) Agenerase
BMS-232632, atazanavir, Reyataz
indinavir (Crixivan)
lopinavir/ritonvair (Kaletra)

nelfinavir (Viracept)
ritonavir (Norvir)
saquinavir (Fortovase, Invirase)

Proton Pump Inhibitors (H/K ATPase Inhibitors)
esomeprazole (Nexium)
lansoprazole (Prevacid, Prevpac)
omeprazole (Prilosec)

pantoprazole (Protonix)
rabeprazole (Aciphex)

Radiopharmaceuticals
samarium-EDTMP (Quadramet)

strontium-89 (Metastron)

Renin-angiotensin Aldosterone System Modulator (Anti-Hypertensive)
eplerenone (Inspra)

Salicylates
aspirin
choline salicylate (Arthropan)
magnesium salicylate (Doan's, Magan,
  Mobidin)

salsalate (Amigesic, Disalcid, Salsitab)
sodium salicylate
sodium thiosalicylate (Rexolate, Tusal)

Sedatives/Sleep Inducers
See Hypnotic Drugs

Selective Serotonin Reuptake Inhibitors (SSRIs)
citalopram (Celexa)
escitalopram (Lexapro)
fluoxetine (Prozac)
fluvoxamine (Luvox)
nefazodone (Serzone)

paroxetine (Paxil)
sertraline (Zoloft)
trazodone (Desyrel)
venlafaxine (Effexor)

Selective Estrogen Receptor Modulators (SERMs)

raloxifene (Evista)   tamoxifen (Nolvadex)

Smoking Cessation Adjuncts

bupropion (Zyban)   varenicline (investigational)
nicotine (Nicorette, various patch
  brands such as Nicotrol)

Sulfonamides (Anti-Infectives)

multiple sulfonamides (Triple Sulfa No. 2)   sulfasalazine (Azulfidine)
sulfacytine (Renoquid)   sulfisoxazole (Gantrisin)
sulfadiazine   COX-II Inhibitor
sulfamethizole (Thiosulfil)   celecoxib (Celebrex)
sulfamethoxazole (Gantanol)

Sulfonylureas (Oral Antidiabetic Drugs)

acetohexamide (Dymelor)   glyburide (DiaBeta, Micronase)
chlorpropamide (Diabinese)   tolazamide (Ronase, Tolamide, Tolinase)
glimepiride (Amaryl)   tolbutamide (Orinase)
glipizide (Glucotrol)

Tetracyclines (Anti-Infectives)

demeclocycline (Declomycin)   minocycline (Minocin)
doxycycline (Doryx, Doxychel,   oxytetracycline (Terramycin)
  Vibramycin)   tetracycline (Achromycin V, Panmycin,
methacycline (Rondomycin)   Sumycin)

Thiazide Diuretics

bendroflumethiazide (Naturetin)   hydroflumethiazide (Diucardin, Saluron)
benzthiazide (Aquatag, Exna, Marazide) methyclothiazide (Enduron, Aquatensen)
chlorothiazide (Diuril)   polythiazide (Renese)
cyclothiazide (Anhydron)   trichlormethiazide (Metahydrin, Naqua)
hydrochlorothiazide (Esidrix, HydroDiuril,
  Oretic)

Thiazolidinediones

pioglitazone (Actos)   troglitazone (Rezulin)—
rosiglitazone (Avandia)   no longer available in the US

Thienobenzodiazepines

olanzapine (Zyprexa)

Thyroid Hormones

levothyroxine (Synthroid)

liothyronine (Cytomel)

Tranquilizers, Major

See Antipsychotic Drugs

Tranquilizers, Minor

See Antianxiety Drugs

Vaccines (Immune Modulators)

influenza vaccine (Fluogen, Flu-Shield, Fluzone, FluMist)

lyme disease vaccine (LYMErix)

pneumococcal vaccine (Prevnar)

varicella virus vaccine (Varivax)

Vasodilators (Peripheral Vasodilators)

cyclandelate (Cyclospasmol)

ethaverine (Ethaquin, Isovex)

isoxsuprine (Vasodilan)

nylidrin (Arlidin)

papaverine (Cerespan, Pavabid)

Weight Loss Agents (Miscellaneous)

Orlistat (Xenical)

Xanthines (Bronchodilators)

aminophylline (Phyllocontin, Truphylline)

dyphylline (Dilor, Lufyllin)

oxtriphylline (Choledyl)

theophylline (Bronkodyl, Slo-Phyllin, Theolair, others)

A GLOSSARY
OF
MEDICINE-RELATED TERMS

SECTION FIVE

A Glossary of Medicine-Related Terms

absolute risk This is generally used in conjunction with diseases. The absolute risk of a disease over a given time period is the actual number of people (usually in two groups that are compared) who will get a disease.

ace (usually seen as ACE) A term used by clinicians to refer to the class of medicines for high blood pressure called angiotensin converting enzyme inhibitors (such as ramipril or Altace).

acute coronary syndrome (ACS) A term from cardiology used to describe sudden problems that happen to the heart. ACS encompasses heart attack (acute myocardial infarction or AMI), Unstable Angina (UA—the leading reason people are admitted to a coronary care unit in the US) and Non ST-Segment Elevation MI (NSTMI).

addiction This is generally recognized as intense drug dependence, with uncontrollable drug-seeking behavior, *tolerance* for pleasure-giving effects, and *withdrawal* if the drug is withheld. This is *physical dependence* where the drug is incorporated into the fundamental biochemistry of the brain. Some clinicians characterize this as a loss of control (centrality) of drug use with continued drug use by those addicted even though it proves to be harmful. (See the terms dependence and tolerance for accounts of physical and psychological dependence.)

adherence (Prior term: compliance. European term: concordance.) How appropriately a patient takes their medicine according to the way it was prescribed. For example: If a medicine is to be taken three times a day and the patient actually takes it three times a day, they are perfectly adherent to their medicine (100% adherent).

adverse effect or reaction An abnormal, unexpected, infrequent, and often unpredictable injurious response to a medicine. This does not include a pharmacological action, even though some may be undesirable and unintended. (See side effect.) Adverse reactions are those due to drug *allergy*, individual *idiosyncrasy*, and *toxic* effects of drugs on tissues (see allergy [drug], idiosyncrasy and toxicity).

allergy (drug) An abnormal medicine response that happens after antibodies* are made to the drug itself. People with history of hay fever, asthma, hives, or eczema are more likely to develop medicine allergies. Allergies can develop slowly, or they can appear suddenly and require lifesaving medical attention.

*Antibodies are proteins that combine with foreign substances. Protective antibodies destroy bacteria and neutralize toxins. Injurious antibodies react with foreign substances, such as drugs, to cause release of histamine, a chemical causing allergic reactions.

alternative delivery system (ADS) A term describing a variety of health care forms other than the established fee-for-service model, such as HMOs, PPOs, and others.

analgesic A medicine used to relieve pain. There are three types:
- simple nonnarcotics, which block production of chemicals that cause or worsen pain (prostaglandins, etc.)—examples are acetaminophen, aspirin, nonsteroidal anti-inflammatory drugs (Motrin, Advil, etc.), and the new COX II inhibitors
- narcotic analgesics or opioids, which relieve pain by blunting pain perception in the brain—examples are morphine, codeine, and hydrocodone (natural derivatives of opium) and meperidine or pentazocine (synthetic drug products)
- local anesthetics, which relieve pain by making sensory nerve endings insensitive to pain—such as phenazopyridine (Pyridium)

anaphylactic (anaphylactoid) reaction Signs and symptoms that indicate an extreme hypersensitivity to a medicine. Anaphylactic reactions often involve several body systems. Mild symptoms include itching, hives, congestion, nausea, cramping, or diarrhea. Sometimes these precede severe problems, such as choking, shortness of breath, and loss of consciousness (usually referred to as anaphylactic shock). Anaphylactic reactions can happen after a very small dose; they may develop suddenly and can be rapidly fatal. They are true medical emergencies. Any adverse effect appearing within 20 minutes after taking a drug should be considered an early sign of anaphylactic reaction. Get medical attention immediately! (See allergy [drug] and hypersensitivity.)

ankle brachial index (ABI) A way of checking for blood vessel disease known as peripheral vascular disease. The ABI is normal if it is more than 1. Most clinicians find an ABI of less than 0.9 to be very suggestive of peripheral vascular disease (PVD). Some 30% of people with PVD have cramping when they walk which is called intermittant claudication.

antihypertensive A medicine used to lower high blood pressure. *Hypertension* describes blood pressure above a normal range. It is not nervous or emotional tension. Currently, the National Heart, Lung, and Blood Institute or NHLBI describes three stages of hypertension. Optimal is 120/80 for those without diabetes and 130/80 for those living with diabetes. Stage one hypertension begins at 149/89. There are also categories a, b, and c within those numerical ranges which seek to stratify risk factors onto blood pressure ranges. Medicines to treat hypertension fall into several major groups:
- drugs that increase urine production (the diuretics)
- drugs that relax blood vessel walls
- drugs that reduce sympathetic nervous system activity

   Some clinicians classify antihypertensives based on their site or mechanism of action—for example, ACE inhibitors which inhibit angiotensin converting enzyme or ARBs—antihypertensives that act as angiotensin two (AT1 subtype) receptor blockers. Please note—although high blood pressure often does not have any symptoms, you MUST treat it for life. Take your medicine EXACTLY as prescribed.

antipyretic A medicine that lowers body temperature. It reduces fever by working on the hypothalamus of the brain. This leads to dilation of blood vessels (capillary beds) in the skin and brings heated blood to the skin surface for cooling. Sweat glands are also stimulated to cool the body through evaporation. An antipyretic may also be a pain reliever (analgesic, such as acetaminophen) or analgesic and anti-inflammatory (aspirin).

aplastic anemia Also known as pancytopenia, where production of the three types of blood cells is seriously impaired. Aplastic anemia can occur from unknown causes, but about half of reported cases are caused by drugs or chemicals. A delay of one to six months may occur between the use of a drug and anemia. Symptoms include lower red blood cells (anemia), resulting in fatigue and pallor; deficiency of white blood cells (leukopenia), predisposing to infections; and low blood platelets (thrombocytopenia), which can cause spontaneous bruising or bleeding. Treatment is difficult. Even with the best of care, half the cases may be fatal. Aplastic anemia is rare, but anyone taking a drug that can cause it should have periodic complete blood cell counts. For a listing of causative drugs, see Table 5, Section Six.

ARB A common term used to refer to the class of medicines known as angiotensin receptor blockers.

aspirin resistance A new term used to describe the occurance of a second heart attack in some patients DESPITE the appropriate and ongoing use of aspirin. A study by Eikelboom et al. in circulation (see sources) postulated that roughly one in five people are able to make a compound called thromboxane A2 even though they are taking aspirin as directed. The researchers suggested that people who have had a heart attack get a test of urinary 11-dehydro thromboxane B2 to find out if they make excessive thromboxane A2 and may be candidates for increased aspirin dosing. More research is needed to determine the required dose as well as who to test and when.

Bad Med Syndrome (BMS) The decreased quality of life, decrease in expected beneficial medicine results, loss of time from work, unnecessary stays in the hospital, or additional treatment resulting from medicines themselves or from the improper use of medicines. Improper use includes drug interactions resulting from inappropriate medicine combinations; too low a dose (subtherapeutic dosing); too high a dose (overdose); as well as taking the medicine "every once in a while" when it was prescribed for ongoing use.

No one intends to cause Bad Med Syndrome (BMS), yet patients, pharmacists, physicians, other health care providers, and many organizations all contribute to it. I believe it will take a team effort to solve it.

bioavailability How fast and how much active medicine is absorbed into the blood. Two types of measurements—blood levels after it was taken and how long the drug stays in the blood—show how much drug is available to work and for how long. The two major factors that govern bioavailability are (1) the chemical and physical characteristics of the dose and (2) how well the digestive system of the person taking it works. A medicine that falls apart quickly in a normal stomach or small intestine produces blood levels quite promptly. Such a drug product has good bioavailability. Drugs such as metoclopramide or cisapride that slow the gastrointestinal system may act to actually increase the amount of drug that gets into the body.

bioequivalence The ability of a drug product to cause its intended therapeutic effect is related to bioavailability. When a medicine is made by several manufacturers, it is critical to pick the one that has the bioavailability needed to work. While the drug in medicines from different firms may be the same chemical, don't assume that they are equally available.

Bioavailability depends mostly on physical characteristics of how a medicine is made. These determine how well a drug falls apart and releases its active drug component(s). Drug products that have the same drug but are combined with different inert additives, coated with different substances, or enclosed in different capsules may or may not have the same bioavailability. Those that do are termed bioequivalent and can be relied upon to give the same result.

If you consider having your prescription filled with a generic, ask your physician and pharmacist for help. This requires professional judgment in each case. In some cases, reasonable differences in bioavailability are acceptable. For serious illnesses, or when blood levels must be kept in a narrow range, it is essential to use the drug product that has been shown to have reliable bioavailability. This has been a major area of controversy for blood thinners (anticoagulants) and medicines used to control seizures.

blood platelets The smallest of the blood cells made by bone marrow. Platelets are normally present in very large numbers. They are the basis of normal blood clotting and prevent excessive bruising or bleeding if you are injured. Platelets preserve smaller blood vessel walls. If there is damage, platelets seal small holes in vessel walls. Some drugs and chemicals may lower the platelet count. Many slow formation; other medicines hasten destruction. If the platelet count gets too low, blood begins to leak through the walls of smaller vessels. This shows as scattered bruises in the skin of the thighs or legs and is called purpura. Bleeding happens anywhere, internally as well as into the tissues immediately beneath the skin. For a listing of causative drugs, see Table 5, Section Six.

body mass index (BMI) A calculation used to measure the relative degree of a patient's obesity. This measurement is used in deciding the appropriateness of using sibutramine (Meridia). BMI is calculated using weight in kilograms divided by height in meters squared. If the BMI is greater than 30 kg per square meter or is 27 kg per square meter with other risk factors such as diabetes, sibutramine is approved for use in weight loss considering those additional factors.

bone marrow depression A decrease in the ability of bone marrow to make blood cells. This can be an adverse reaction to medicines or chemicals. Bone marrow makes most of the body's blood cells: red blood cells (erythrocytes), white blood cells (leukocytes), and platelets (thrombocytes). Each type of cell has one or more functions, critical to life and health.

Drugs that depress bone marrow may impair all types of blood cells right away or only one type selectively. Blood tests can show drug effects on bone marrow. If fewer red blood cells are made, anemia results, causing weakness, cold intolerance, and shortness of breath. Low white blood cells lowers resistance to infection (fever, sore throat, or pneumonia). If platelets fall to very low levels, the blood loses its ability to clot quickly. Bruising or prolonged bleeding may happen. Any of these symptoms require immediate studies of blood and bone marrow. For a listing of causative drugs, see Table 5, Section Six.

brand name The registered trade name given to a medicine by its manufacturer. Each company creates a trade name to distinguish its brand of the generic drug from its competitors'. A brand name designates a proprietary drug—one that is protected by patent or copyright. Generally, brand names are shorter, easier to pronounce, and more readily remembered than their generic counterparts.

capitation A system where a set amount of money is used to cover the cost of health care for a given person. For instance, a health plan or hospital is paid monthly on a negotiated per-person rate and the plan or hospital provides all health services for the people in the plan.

cause-and-effect relationship An association between a medicine and a biological event—most commonly a side effect or an adverse effect. Important factors are when the drug was given, the use of multiple drugs and their possible interactions, the effects of the disease being treated, the physiological and psychological patient factors, and the influences of unrecognized disorders or malfunctions.

The majority of adverse drug reactions occur sporadically, unpredictably, and infrequently in the general population. A *definite* cause-and-effect relationship between medicine and reaction is shown when (1) the adverse effect immediately follows dosing of the drug or (2) the adverse effect disappears after the drug is stopped (dechallenge) and reappears when the medicine is used again (rechallenge) or (3) the adverse effects are clearly the expected and predictable toxic consequences of drug overdose.

There is also a large gray area of "probable," "possible," and "coincidental" associations. Clarification of cause-and-effect relationships requires observation over a long period of time, followed by sophisticated statistical analysis. Some news stories are based on suggestive but incomplete data. Though early warning is in the public interest, these stories should make clear whether the presumed relationship is based on definitive criteria or is inferred. It is critical to avoid losing valuable medicines because of poorly designed studies that find their way to the news.

The most competent techniques for evaluating cause-and-effect relationships of adverse drug reactions have been devised by the Division of Tissue Reactions to Drugs, a research unit of the Armed Forces Institute of Pathology:

No association	5.0%
Coincidental	14.5%
Possible	33.0%
Probable	30.0%
Causative	17.5%

It is significant that expert evaluation of 2,800 drug-related cases concluded that only 47.5% could be substantiated as causative or probably causative.

contraindication A condition or disease that precludes the use of a medicine. Some contraindications are absolute, meaning that the drug should NEVER be used in a particular situation. Other contraindications are relative, meaning that using the drug requires expert consideration of all factors.

coordinated performance measurement for the management of adult diabetes A term used to describe a great new consensus reached by the American Medical Association (AMA), the Joint Commission on Accreditation of Healthcare Organizations (JCAHO) and The National Committee on Quality Assurance (NCQA). This body of information was released in April of 2001 and seeks to look at how typical measures, markers, or preventive measures used in diabetes (such as lipid management, hemoglobin A1C and flu shots should be approached to get the best frequency of testing and avoidance of disease progression or incidental or at risk infections.

covered lives A term used by health maintenance organizations to indicate how many people have enrolled in their plan. From the HMO's point of view, a minimum number of covered lives is needed to support a certain number of family practice physicians, specialists, and so on. Understanding their logic helps explain why some HMOs have one specialist while others have several.

COX-II Inhibitor A medicine that inhibits the action of cyclooxygenase or COX type two. While type one COX can have some protective functions in the body, COX-II is an enzyme that works to make compounds that lead to swelling (inflammation). If COX-II is blocked, inflammation is prevented or relieved.

creatinine clearance A measure of how well the kidneys are eliminating waste, toxins, and impurities from the body. A low creatinine clearance (such as 20 ml per minute or ml/min) means poorer kidney function; a high creatinine clearance (such as 120 ml/min) means better kidney function. People who have low creatinine clearances often receive lower initial doses and smaller increases of medicines that are removed by the kidneys.

critical or clinical pathway An assortment of coordinated measures taken by a health care organization to effectively group care of specific diseases or conditions. All diagnostic tests, treatments, discharge plans, and other factors are carefully studied, and practice is aimed at giving the best patient results in the most cost-effective manner.

dependence A term identifying *psychological dependence* (or *habituation*) and *physical dependence* (or *addiction*). In addition, functional dependence—the need to use a drug continuously in order to sustain a particular body function—is included.

Psychological dependence is a form of neurotic behavior—an "emotional" dependence. This characterizes itself as an obsession to satisfy a particular desire. Psychological dependence is also seen in many more socially acceptable patterns such as entertainment, sports, and collecting. Unfortunately, we often see an increasing reliance on medicines to cope with everyday problems: pills for frustration, nervous stomach, tension headache, and insomnia. This compulsive abuse shows little or no tendency to increase the dose (see tolerance) and minor or nonexistent physical symptoms if the medicine is taken away (withdrawn). Some clinicians include psychological dependence in their definition of addiction.

Physical dependence, which is true addiction, includes two elements: tolerance and withdrawal. Addicting drugs provide relief from anguish and pain, but can also cause a physiological tolerance requiring increased doses or repeated use to remain effective. These two features foster its becoming a functioning component in brain biochemistry. (Thus some authorities prefer the term chemical dependence.) Sudden removal of the medicine causes a major upheaval in body chemistry, provoking a withdrawal syndrome—intense mental and physical pain—that is the hallmark of addiction. True addiction is rare, and fear of addiction, even with potent narcotics, should never stand in the way of effective pain control.

Functional dependence differs from both psychological and physical dependence. It occurs when a drug relieves a distressing condition and provides a sense of well-being. Drugs that cause functional dependence are often used for symptom relief. The most familiar example of functional dependence is the "laxative habit." Some types of constipation are made worse by the wrong laxative, and natural bowel function fades as the colon becomes more and more dependent on the laxative drug.

disease management An approach to prevention and treatment of a specific condition that checks how often it happens in a population, organizes resources, and allocates money to reach the best balance of dollars spent and results achieved.

disulfiramlike (Antabuse-like) reaction Symptoms resulting from the interaction of alcohol and a medicine causing the "Antabuse effect." Symptoms include intense facial flushing, severe throbbing headache, shortness of breath, chest pains, nausea, repeated vomiting, sweating, and weakness. If a large enough amount of alcohol is present, the reaction may progress to blurred vision, vertigo, marked drop in blood pressure, and loss of consciousness. Severe reactions may lead to convulsions and death. The reaction can last from 30 minutes to several hours, depending upon the amount of alcohol in the body. As the symptoms subside, the person is exhausted and often sleeps for several hours.

diuretic A medicine that increases urine volume. Diuretics work in several ways to accomplish this. Diuretics are used to (1) remove excess water from the body (as in congestive heart failure and some types of liver and kidney disease) and (2) treat hypertension by promoting excretion of sodium from the body.

divided doses The total daily dose of a medicine is split into smaller individual doses over the course of a day.

DMARD A Disease-Modifying Antirheumatic Drug. These medicines represent a true breakthrough in rheumatoid arthritis (RA) because they actually attack the cause of RA. For example, leflunomide (Arava) works to shut down T-cells destroying tissue, and etanercept (Enbrel) works to bind tumor necrosis factor (TNF) so that it can't harm joints.

dosage forms and strengths This information category in the individual Drug Profiles (Section Two) uses several abbreviations to designate measurements of weight and volume:

mcg = microgram =1,000,000th of a gram (weight)
mg = milligram = 1,000th of a gram (weight)
ml = milliliter =1,000th of a liter (volume)
gm = gram = 1,000 milligrams (weight)
There are approximately 65 mg in 1 grain.
There are approximately 5 ml in 1 teaspoon.
There are approximately 15 ml in 1 tablespoon.
There are approximately 30 ml in 1 ounce.
One milliliter of water weighs 1 g.
There are approximately 454 g in 1 pound.

drug, drug product Terms used interchangeably to describe a medicine (in any form) used in medical practice. The term *drug* refers to the single chemical that provokes a specific response when put in a biological system—the "active" ingredient. A *drug product* is the dosage form—tablet, capsule, elixir, etc.—that has the active drug mixed with inactive ingredients to provide convenient dosing. Drug products that have one active ingredient are called single-entity drugs. Drug products with two or more active ingredients are called combination drugs ([CD] in the brand names in the Drug Profiles, Section Two).

drug class A group of drugs that are similar in chemistry, method of action, and use. Because of their common characteristics, many drugs in a class will cause the same side effects and have similar potential for related adverse reactions and interactions. Variations among members within a drug class can occur. This can let choices be made if certain benefits are desired or particular side effects are to be minimized. Examples: Antihistamines and phenothiazines (see Drug Classes, Section Four).

drug family A group of medicines that are similar in chemistry, method of action, and purpose. In *The Essential Guide,* drug families are identified by entries such as the Minimally Sedating Antihistamine Family. This allows you to easily compare the drugs meeting the criteria for listing in the book.

drug fever Increased body temperature caused by a medicine. Drugs can cause fever by allergic reactions, tissue damage, acceleration of tissue metabolism, constriction of skin blood vessels, and direct action on the brain. The most common form of drug fever is allergic. It may be the only allergic symptom, or it may include skin rash, hives, joint swelling and pain, enlarged lymph glands, hemolytic anemia, or hepatitis. The fever usually appears about 7 to 10 days after starting the drug and varies from low-grade to alarmingly high levels. It may be sustained or intermittent, but it usually lasts for as long as the medicine is taken. Although many drugs can cause fever, the following are more commonly responsible:

allopurinol	novobiocin
antihistamines	para-aminosalicylic acid
atropine-like drugs	penicillin
barbiturates	pentazocine
coumarin anticoagulants	phenytoin
hydralazine	procainamide
iodides	propylthiouracil
isoniazid	quinidine
methyldopa	rifampin
nadolol	sulfonamides

drug recall Removal of a medicine by the FDA. There are three classes of recalls (see *www.fda.gov*). Used when use of or exposure to a product:
Class I will cause serious adverse health consequenses or death.

Class II may cause medically reversible or temporary adverse health consequences or where probability of serious health consequences are remote.
Class III is unlikely to cause adverse health effects.

EBCT Electron Beam Computed Tomography (also known as ultra-fast CAT scan) is an X-ray based technique with great utility in helping diagnose heart disease. The result of an EBCT scan is a "virtual tour" of the coronary arteries and a calcium score. Low calcium scores are associated with decreased risk of heart attacks while high scores are cause for concern.

evidence-based medicine An important concept in therapeutics that impacts which medicines are used and how they are used. This involves combining recent best research (evidence) with knowledge of how disease happens (pathophysiology), patient preferences, and clinical expertise in order to come up with the best individualized medicine for any given patient. Fortunately, development and use of evidence-based medicine skills is now being integrated into US medical schools.

extension effect An unwanted but predictable medicine response that is a result of mild to moderate overdose. It is an exaggeration of the drug's pharmacological action; it can be thought of as a mild form of dose-related toxicity (see overdosage and toxicity).

Example: The continued "hangover" of mental sluggishness that persists in the morning is a common extension effect of a long-acting sleep-inducing medicine (a hypnotic such as Dalmane) taken the night before.

FDA-approvable A stage in the Food and Drug Administration's review and approval process. A medicine is considered FDA-approvable once the panel that reviewed the supporting data submitted to the FDA finds that data acceptable. In general, at this point only final details need to be resolved before the medicine becomes FDA-approved and is made available for general use.

FDA-review status A description of chemical types and review status has been developed by the FDA. Chemical types are divided into:

1. New molecular entity
2. New ester, new salt form, or other covalent derivative
3. New formulation
4. New combination
5. New manufacturer
6. New indication
7. Drug already marketed, but without an approved NDA

The review process is divided into:
Fast track: Critical review for a new treatment for a life threatening condition (such as a new HIV/AIDS drug).
Priority review: Significant improvement compared to marketed products, in the treatment, diagnosis, or prevention of a disease.
Standard review: The medicine appears to have therapeutic qualities similar to those of one or more already marketed drugs.

fructosamine A new term in diabetes which is also known as Glycated protein. Fructosamine is used in conjunction with glycosylated hemoglobin (hemoglobin A1C) to check to see how well blood sugar has been controlled. Unlike A1C, fructosamine gives a picture of glucose control for prior weeks versus months. There is a home glucose meter that tests fructosamine.

generic name The official, common, or public name used to describe an active medicine. Generic names are coined by committees of drug experts and are approved by governmental agencies for national and international use. Many drug products are marketed only under a generic name. The drugs most commonly prescribed as generics are listed below, ranked in descending order of new or refill prescriptions issued.

amoxicillin

cephalexin

hydrocodone/acetaminophen

acetaminophen/codeine

furosemide

propoxyphene-N/acetaminophen

albuterol aerosol

triamterene/HCTZ

trimethoprim/Sulfa

ibuprofen

genetic diversity This is actually a descriptive term used to identify ways in which a given person's genetic makeup differs from the expected sequences of the human genome. Snippets of nuclear material are analyzed, and once variant sequences are identified, in time we may be able to remove them and restore people to health.

genetic therapy Perhaps the most promising area of therapy in medicine today. Healthy genetic material is isolated and inserted into appropriate but diseased cells. For example, normal lung genes are given to a person with cystic fibrosis. Still very experimental, it may someday allow people suffering with genetically based diseases or conditions to receive therapy that changes the affected genes and actually *cures* those conditions. The latest approaches are working on causing the heart to grow new blood vessels and actually reversing congestive heart failure by the AC-6 gene. One of the true breakthroughs in medicine for this edition was the complete identification of the human genome by a private US company. There are some 3 billion base pairs, and an estimated 40,000 genes in the human genome. Some 20 diseases cause more than 80% of deaths around the world. About 200–300 genes are responsible for these diseases. Considering that about every three weeks we in essence get a new heart from the same set of genes, if controlling the genes becomes a reality—-we can possibly knock out heart disease!

habituation A form of drug dependence based upon strong psychological gratification. Ongoing use of mood-altering drugs or those relieving minor discomforts results from a compulsive need to feel pleasure and satisfaction or to escape emotional distress. If these drugs are abruptly stopped, a withdrawal does not result. Thus habituation is a *psychological dependence*. (See dependence for more on psychological and physical dependence.)

hemolytic anemia Lower red blood cells and hemoglobin caused by premature destruction (hemolysis) of red blood cells. One way that this happens is from a genetic lowering of glucose-6-phosphate dehydrogenase (G6PD), a needed enzyme. If patients with this condition are given antimalarial medicines or sulfa drugs, red cells will be destroyed. One type of drug-induced hemolytic anemia is a form of allergy. Many widely used medicines (such as quinidine and levodopa) can cause hemolytic destruction of red cells as an allergic reaction. Hemolytic anemia can occur abruptly or silently. The acute form lasts about 7 days and shows as fever, pallor, weakness, dark-colored urine, and varying degrees of jaundice. If drug-induced hemolytic anemia is mild, there may be no symptoms (see idiosyncrasy and allergy [drug]). For drugs that may cause this, see Table 5, Section Six.

hepatitis-like reaction Some medicines may cause liver damage similar to viral hepatitis. Symptoms of drug-induced hepatitis and viral hepatitis are often so similar that only laboratory tests can tell the difference. Hepatitis from drugs may be allergy, or it may be a toxic adverse effect. Serious liver reactions usually lead to jaundice (see jaundice). For drugs that can cause this, see Table 8, Section Six.

HMO Abbreviation for Health Maintenance Organization—a health care system that provides a broad spectrum of medical therapies and services by a collective group of people in a common organization.

hospitalist A relatively new term used to denote a physician who specializes in working in a hospital as opposed to a doctor who primarily has an office-based practice. The intent here is to create a group of doctors who are very familiar with critical paths, streamlining, and other hospital methods to make length of stay as appropriate as possible.

hypersensitivity Over-responsiveness to medicines. Used in this sense, it means that the response is appropriate but the degree of response is exaggerated. More widely used today to identify allergy. To have *hypersensitivity* to a drug is to be allergic to it (see allergy [drug]). Some people develop cross-hypersensitivity. This means that allergy to one drug will also lead to a reaction to other closely related medicines.

> *Example:* A *hypersensitive* patient had seasonal hay fever and asthma since childhood. His *allergy* to penicillin developed after his third treatment. The *hypersensitivity* was a diffuse, measles-like rash. When he was later given a cephalosporin antibiotic (chemically related to penicillins), he developed the same rash.

hypnotic A medicine used to cause sleep. Classes include antihistamines, barbiturates, benzodiazepines, and several unrelated compounds. In the past 15 years, benzodiazepines have largely replaced barbiturates. In general, they are safer and have lower dependence potential. Tolerance to the hypnotic effect can happen after several weeks of continual use, so hypnotics should be used for short periods of time.

hypoglycemia Sugar (glucose) in blood below the normal range. Since the brain only runs on sugar, the brain can be seriously impaired by too low a sugar level. Early warnings include headache, mild drunkenness feeling, hunger, and an inability to think clearly. If blood sugar falls further, nervousness and confusion develop. Weakness, numbness, trembling, sweating, and rapid heartbeat follow. If blood sugar drops further, impaired speech and unconsciousness, with or without convulsions, will follow. Treatment for any low blood sugar (hypoglycemia) is important. If you take a medicine that can cause hypoglycemia it is prudent to know the symptoms and what to do if hypoglycemia occurs.

hypothermia When internal body temperature falls below 98.6 degrees F. or 37 degrees C. By definition, hypothermia is a body temperature of less than 95 degrees F. or 35 degrees C. The elderly and debilitated are more prone to hypothermia. Most cases are initiated by room temperatures below 65 degrees F. or 18.3 degrees C. This can develop suddenly, can mimic a stroke, and has a mortality rate of 50%. Some drugs, such as phenothiazines, barbiturates, and benzodiazepines, may make hypothermia more likely.

idiosyncrasy An abnormal medicine response that happens in people with a defect in body chemistry (often hereditary) that produces an effect totally unrelated to the drug's normal action. This is not a form of allergy. Some defects responsible for idiosyncratic drug reactions are well understood; others are not.

> *Example:* Some 100 million people (including 10% of African-Americans) have a low glucose-6-phosphate dehydrogenase (G6PD) in red blood cells. The cells then disintegrate when exposed to sulfonamides (Gantrisin, Kynex), nitrofurantoin (Furadantin, Macrodantin), probenecid (Benemid), quinine, and quinidine. This can lead to a serious anemia.

immunosuppressive A medicine that suppresses the immune system. Immunosuppression may be an intended drug effect, such as cyclosporine preventing the rejection of a transplanted kidney. In other cases, it is an unwanted side effect, as in the long-term use of cortisone-like drugs (to control asthma) suppressing the immune system. Chronic disorders thought to be autoimmune—such as rheumatoid arthritis, ulcerative colitis, and systemic lupus erythematosus—may be eased by immunosuppressive medicines.

INR This is a term used in blood thinning or anticoagulation. It stands for International Normalized Ratio. The intent of the INR is to remove the problem of testing variation in reagents from laboratory to laboratory in coagulation results. The INR helps make a coagulation test (protime number and then calculated ratio) mean the same thing for a patient being tested in New York or Omaha. The sequence happens like this: Blood is drawn from the patient, and a prothrombin time or protime test is done. The protime number is then put into a calculation that standardizes the result. The end of the math is an INR, a ratio that tells a clinician to what degree the ability of the blood to clot (coagulate) has been changed by warfarin or a clotting factor problem.

interaction A change in a medicine that results when a second drug (altering the action of the first) is given to the same person. Some interactions can enhance the effect of either drug, giving a response similar to overdose. Other interactions may reduce drug effectiveness and cause inadequate response. A third interaction can produce an unrelated toxic response with no increase or decrease in the interacting drugs. Many interactions can be anticipated, and appropriate adjustments in dose can be made to prevent or minimize fluctuations in drug response.

jaundice A yellowing in the color of skin (and the white portion of the eyes) that occurs when bile accumulates in blood because of impaired liver function. Jaundice can happen from a wide variety of diseases or may be an adverse reaction to a medicine. Jaundice due to a drug is always a serious adverse effect. If you take a medicine that can cause jaundice, watch closely for any change in urine or feces color. Dark discoloration of urine or pale (lack of color) stools may be early indication of developing jaundice. If this happens, call your doctor promptly. Lab tests can clarify the nature of the jaundice. Table 8, Section Six, lists causative medicines.

JNC VI A national committee of experts that meets to try to establish a framework of medicines used to treat high blood pressure. The committee reviews the currently available medicines and attempts to organize possible treatments into a logical approach for lowering high blood pressure and prolonging lives.

JNC VII The current (as of 2003) guidelines from a national committee of experts at the National Insitutes of Health (NIH) that summarized current best studies into guidelines to help clinicians work to control blood pressure. The current guidelines (published in the *Journal of The American Medical Association* (*JAMA* 2003) developed key changes such as a category called Pre-hypertention which starts at 120/80 and tries to tell us that even with what used to be considered "normal" blood pressure, damage can be done to blood vessels. Pre-hypertension seeks to foster a talk between clinicians and patients at an earlier point and to start lifestyle changes (such as exercise and diet) to get blood pressure under control earlier. Find the guidelines at *www.nhlbi.nih.gov/guidelines/hypertension/index.htm.*

low dose medications A group of medicines which have been found to be effective in some patients in doses that are lower than the doses recommended by the manufacturer. This area of therapeutics is controversial and results from the gap between valid and valuable research publication and the time it takes for a manufacturer to send needed data to the FDA, the FDA, review, and approval for changes to the approved labeling of the medicine. Some of the controversy also revolves around varying opinion as to required outcomes from treatment from medicines.

low molecular weight heparins A group of blood thinning (anticoagulant) medicines used to prevent abnormal blood clots (venous thromboembolisms or VTEs). New recommendations from the Sixth American College of Chest Physicians may lead to increased use of these medicines versus unfractionated heparins to prevent these clots (VTEs) in high risk patients.

lupus erythematosus (LE) A serious disease, seen in two forms: one limited to skin (discoid LE) and the other involving several body systems (systemic LE). Both forms occur mostly in young women. About 5% of cases of discoid form convert to the systemic form. Systemic LE is an immune disorder that can be chronic, with progressive inflammation destroying connective tissue of the skin, blood vessels, joints, brain, heart muscle, lungs, and kidneys. Altered proteins in the blood lead to antibody formation that attacks the person's own organs or tissues. Low white blood cells and platelets often occur. The course of systemic LE is usually quite protracted and unpredictable. There is no cure, but acceptable management may be achieved in some cases by judicious use of cortisone-like drugs.

Several medicines can start a form of systemic LE quite similar to that which occurs spontaneously. Symptoms may appear as early as two weeks or as late as years after starting the drug. Initial symptoms are usually low-grade fever, skin rashes of various kinds, aching muscles, and multiple joint pains. Chest pains (pleurisy) are fairly common. Enlargement of the lymph glands occurs less frequently. Symptoms usually subside if the drug is stopped, but laboratory evidence of the reaction may persist for many months.

medication map (MM) A new concept in medicines pioneered by Dr. Rybacki. One of the flaws in current drug information is that it is provided for individual medicines when patients actually often take medicines during the same day and in combination as well. Patients are not given a schedule that organizes their medicines into a framework that works well with their usual day. The medication map seeks to organize any and all of the medicines a patient takes into a clear schedule using the best possible times, combinations, and results or outcomes data. A medication map helps avoid drug-drug, drug-food, and drug-activity interactions, and gives the patient the best possible quality of life.

national cholesterol education program (NCEP) A program of the National Institutes of Health that works to standardize the approach to cholesterol laboratory values, treatments, and patient care using evidence-based medicine principles. The guidelines ATP III (Adult treatment panel version three) were released in 2001 and could help save thousands of lives when successfully implemented.

neuroleptic malignant syndrome (NMS) A rare, serious, sometimes fatal idiosyncratic reaction to neuroleptic (antipsychotic) medicines. Symptoms include hyperthermia (temperatures of 102 to 104 degrees F.), marked muscle rigidity, and coma. Rapid heart rate and breathing, profuse sweating, tremors, and seizures can also occur. Two-thirds of cases happen in men, one-third in women. Mortality rate is 15 to 20%.

The following drugs may cause this reaction:

amantadine (Symmetrel)	levoda + carbidopa (Sinemet)
amitripyline + perphenazine (Triavil)	lithium (Lithobid)
amoxapine (Asendin)	loxapine (Loxitane)
bromocriptine (Parlodel)	metoclopramide (Reglan, Octamide)
carbamazepine (Tegretol)	molindone (Moban)
chlorpromazine (Thorazine)	oral contraceptives (combination)
chlorprothixine (Taractan)	paroxetine (Paxil)
clomipramine (Anafranil)	perphenazine (Etrafon, Trilafon)
clozapine (Clozaril)	pimozide (Orap)
cyclobenzaprine	prochlorperzine (Compazine)
doxepin (Asendin)	risperidone (Risperdal)
fluoxetine (Prozac)	sertraline (Zoloft)
fluphenazine (Permitil, Prolixin)	thioridazine (Mellaril)
fluvoxamine (Luvox)	thiothixene (Navane)
haloperidol (Haldol)	trifluoperazine (Stelazine)
imipramine (Tofranil, etc.)	trimeprazine (Temaril)
	zotepine (Nipolept)

orthostatic hypotension A type of low blood pressure related to body position or posture (also called postural hypotension). People who get orthostatic hypotension may have normal blood pressure lying down, but on sitting upright or standing will feel light-headed, dizzy, and as if they are going to faint. These symptoms come from inadequate blood flow (oxygen supply) to the brain.

Many medicines may cause orthostatic hypotension. Tell your doctor if you have this effect so that changes can be made. If this situation isn't corrected, severe falls or injury may result. It is prudent to avoid sudden standing, prolonged standing, vigorous exercise, and exposure to hot environments. Alcoholic beverages should be used cautiously until combined effects with the drug in use have been determined.

outcomes research A concept in health care evaluation that considers the benefits (gauged by a variety of measures) of using a particular medicine versus another. This may lead to the least expensive drug actually not being the drug of choice, because the outcomes from therapy don't stand up over time or may result in significant treatment failure.

outcomes survey short-form 36 (SF-36) A check of quality of life which is often used to find out the impact of rheumatoid arthritis (RA) on patients. Improvements in SF-36 can help clinicians decide how beneficial a medicine is for a particular patient.

overdose The meaning of this term is not limited to doses exceeding the normal range recommended by a manufacturer. The "best" dose of many medicines varies greatly from person to person. An average dose for most people can be an overdose for some and an underdose for others. Factors such as age, body size, nutritional status, and liver and kidney function have significant impact on dosing.

Drugs with narrow safety margins often give signs of overdose if removal of the daily dose is delayed. Massive overdose—as in accidental ingestion of drugs by children or with suicides—is referred to as poisoning.

over-the-counter (OTC) drugs Medicines that can be bought without prescriptions. Many people do not look upon OTC medicines as drugs. It is important to remember that OTC medicines can have a variety of actions. OTC drugs may react with one another and can also react with prescription medicines. Serious problems can arise when (1) the patient fails to tell the doctor about OTC drug(s) he or she is taking ("because they really aren't drugs") and (2) the doctor fails to specify that his or her question about which medicines are being taken includes all OTC drugs and herbal meds as well. During any treatment, patients need to talk with their doctor or pharmacist about any OTC drug that he or she wishes to take. The major classes of OTC drugs for internal use include:

allergy medicines (antihistamines)
antacids
antiworm medicines
aspirin and aspirin combinations
aspirin substitutes
asthma aids
cold medicines (decongestants)
cough medicines
diarrhea remedies
digestion aids
diuretics
heartburn medicines
iron laxatives
laxatives

menstrual aids
motion sickness remedies
pain relievers
salt substitutes
sedatives and tranquilizers
sleeping pills
smoking cessation products
stimulants (caffeine)
sugar substitutes (saccharin)
tonics
vaginal yeast infection medicines
vitamins
weight-reduction aids

paradoxical reaction A medicine response that does not follow the known pharmacology of a drug. These effects are due to individual sensitivity and can occur at any age. They are seen more commonly in children and the elderly.

    Example: An 80-year-old man was sent to a nursing home after his wife died. He had trouble adjusting to his new environment and was agitated and irritable. He was given diazepam (Valium) to relax him, starting with small doses. On the second day he became confused. The dose of diazepam was increased. On the third day he began to wander, talked incessantly, and was angry when attempts were made to help him. Suspecting a paradoxical reaction, his health care provider stopped the diazepam. All behavioral disturbances subsided in three days.

Parkinson-like disorders (Parkinsonism) A group of symptoms resembling Parkinson's disease. The typical features of Parkinsonism include a fixed, emotionless facial expression (mask-like in appearance); trembling hands, arms, or legs; and stiffness of extremities that produces rigid posture and gait. Parkinsonism is a fairly common adverse effect that occurs in about 15% of patients who take large doses of phenothiazines or use them over an extended period. If found early, the Parkinson-like features will lessen or disappear with lower doses or different medicines. In some cases, Parkinson-like changes may become permanent.

peripheral neuritis (peripheral neuropathy) A group of symptoms that results from injury to nerve tissue in the extremities. A variety of drugs or chemicals can cause this. The sensation of numbness and tingling usually starts in the toes and fingers and is accompanied by altered sensation to touch. Vague discomfort from aching sensations to burning pain is also seen. Severe forms of peripheral neuritis may include loss of muscular strength and coordination. Isoniazid can cause this condition.

    If vitamin B6 (pyridoxine) is not given with isoniazid, peripheral neuritis may occur. Vitamin B6 can be both preventive and curative in this form of drug-induced peripheral neuritis.

    Since peripheral neuritis can also be a late complication of many viral infections, care must be taken to avoid assigning a cause-and-effect relationship to a medicine that is not responsible for the nerve injury (see cause-and-effect relationship). See Table 10, Section Six, for further discussion of drug-induced nerve damage.

Peyronie's disease A permanent deformity of the penis caused by dense fibrous (scar-like) tissue within in the penile vessels that become engorged with blood during an erection. During sexual arousal, inelastic fibrous tissue causes painful downward bowing of the penis that hampers or precludes intercourse. This condition has been caused by phenytoin (Dilantin, etc.) and with most members of the beta-blocker drugs (see Drug Classes, Section Four). For a listing of causative medicines, see Table 11, Section Six.

pharmacoeconomics The discipline within pharmacology that studies the issues of costs versus benefits, utilizing a variety of measures: material and personnel costs, treatment outcomes, quality of patient life, etc. Study results are used in deciding where and how health care resources should be utilized.

pharmacogenomics The use of knowledge of the human genome, actions of genes, and the way that certain genes are active or inactive in a disease to design medicines. This new area also takes into account the concept of individualizing an approach to patients based on THEIR specific genes. The first medicine to result from pharmacogenomics is imatinib or Gleevec (see drug profile). This medicine is a signal transduction inhibitor that works to turn off a gene that is active in leukemia and a rare kind of stomach tumor.

pharmacology The medical science relating to development and use of drugs as well as their composition and action in animals and humans. Used in its broadest sense, pharmacology embraces related sciences of medicinal chemistry, experimental therapeutics, and toxicology.

photosensitivity A drug-induced skin change resulting in a rash or exaggerated sunburn on exposure to the sun or ultraviolet lamps. The reaction is confined to uncovered areas of skin, giving a clue to the nature of its cause. For a list of causative medicines, see Table 2, Section Six.

porphyria Hereditary disorders where excessive amounts of respiratory pigments known as porphyrins are made. (One porphyrin is part of hemoglobin in red blood cells.) Two forms of porphyria—acute intermittent porphyria and cutaneous porphyria—can be activated by medicines. Acute intermittent porphyria involves nervous system damage. An attack can include fever, rapid heart rate, vomiting, pain in the abdomen and legs, hallucinations, seizures, paralysis, and coma. Some examples of causative drugs include: barbiturates, sulfa drugs, chlordiazepoxide (Librium), chlorpropamide (Diabinese), methyldopa (Aldomet), and phenytoin (Dilantin).

Cutaneous porphyria involves skin and liver damage. Symptoms include red and blistered skin, followed by crusting, scarring, and excessive hair growth. Repeated liver damage can lead to cirrhosis. This form of porphyria can be caused by chloroquine, estrogen, oral contraceptives, and excessive iron.

PQRSTBG A mnemonic used to help clinicians who manage pain remember critical factors. **P**alliative tells what makes pain better. **Q**uality refers to the nature of the pain. **R**adiation tells them if the pain moves from one part of the body to another. **S**everity tells the relative intensity of the pain. **T**emporal refers to how the pain changes over the course of the day. **B**owel is there to remind clinicians that narcotic pain relievers can also cause constipation. **G**oals refer to clinician expectations, and critically to what the patient and family wants as a benefit from the therapy that is chosen.

pre-diabetes A situation that is commonly found before people develop true diabetes. This pre-diabetic condition is characterized by blood sugar (glucose) levels that are higher than normal, but not elevated enough to make the diagnosis of diabetes. The most critical aspect of this state is that some degree of damage to the heart and blood vessels (circulatory system) probably happens in pre-diabetes. The American Diabetes Association (*www.diabetes.org*) has a risk test and great information on warning signs.

priapism Prolonged, painful erection of the penis usually on sexual arousal. It is caused by obstruction to drainage of blood through the veins at the root of the penis. Erection may last for 30 minutes to a few hours and then subside, or it may persist for up to 30 hours and require surgical drainage. More than half of priapism from drugs results in permanent impotence. Sickle-cell anemia may predispose to priapism, and those with this disorder should avoid all medicines that may cause priapism.

Drugs reported to induce priapism include:

anabolic steroids (male hormone-like drugs: Anadrol, Anavar, Android, Halotestin, Metandren, Oreton, Testred, Winstrol
chlorpromazine (Thorazine)
cocaine
guanethidine (Ismelin)
heparin
levodopa (Sinemet)
molindone (Moban)
prazosin (Minipres)
prochlorperzine (Compazine)
trazodone (Desyrel)
trifluoperazine (Stelazine)
warfarin (Coumadin)

prostatism The difficulties that happen with an enlarged prostate. As the prostate enlarges, it constricts the urethra (outflow passage) and impedes urination. This causes a lower size and force of the urinary stream, hesitancy, interruption, and incomplete bladder emptying. Atropine and medicines with atropine-like effects can impair the bladder's ability to compensate for the prostate gland, intensifying all of the above symptoms.

pseudoaddiction The development of drug-seeking behavior (see addiction above), but only for pain control. Pseudoaddiction is a characteristic of less than optimal pain control and tends to resolve with adequate pain control.

QT interval medicines This new term is used to describe drugs that can have an effect on part of the heartbeat (QT interval) and pose a complicated benefit to risk decision in people with heart rhythm problems or who are at increased risk for heart rhythm problems (such as the elderly, people with existing heart disease, women, those with low magnesium or potassium, and others). These medicines have led to such concern that the FDA will now require all new medicines to be tested for QT interval prolongation. Representative medicines include: arsenic trioxide; chlorpromazine; class I, IA, or III antiarrhythmics; clarithromycin; clindamycin; cotrimoxazole; dofetilide; dolasetron; droperidol; erythromycin; fluconaxzole; fluoxetine; foscarnet; gatifloxacin, moxifloxacin or sparfloxacin; halofantrine; haloperidol; isradipine; ketoconazole; levomethadyl (Orlaam); mesoridazine; octreotide (Santostatin); ondansetron; pentamidine; phenothiazines in general; pimozide; quinidine; risperidone; sotolol; sulfamethoxazole; tacrolimus; thioridazine; tricyclic antidepressants; trimethoprim; venlafaxine; ziprazodone; zotepine; and others.

Raynaud's phenomenon Intermittent episodes of reduced blood flow to fingers or toes, with resulting paleness, discomfort, numbness, and tingling. Stress or exposure to cold can cause attack. It can occur as part of a systemic disorder (lupus erythematosus, scleroderma), or it can occur without apparent cause (Raynaud's disease). Beta-adrenergic blockers and products that contain ergotamine can lead to Raynaud-like symptoms in predisposed people.

relative risk A comparison made between two groups of people in specific populations to see if a specific disease or risk factor for a disease is associated with an increase, no change, or a decrease in the disease rate in the specific populations.

Reye (Reye's) syndrome A sudden, often fatal, childhood illness where the brain swells and the liver degenerates. It usually develops during a viral infection (flu), measles, or chicken pox. Cases have been seen with lupus (SLE). Symptoms include fever, headache, delirium, loss of consciousness, and seizures. It is one of the 10 major causes of death in children ages 1 to 10 years. Those younger than 18 may be affected. The syndrome may be due to combined effects of viral infection and chemical toxins in a genetically predisposed child. Medicines that have been used prior to symptoms include salicylates (aspirin) and drugs to control nausea and vomiting. This is why salicylates (aspirin and aspirin-like medicines) should be avoided in children with flu-like infections, chicken pox, or measles. Some clinicians question use of any NSAID. Remember to look for salicylates in combination cold or flu products and inflammatory bowel drugs. Valproic acid (a seizure medicine) can cause a Reye-like syndrome. Acetaminophen appears to be the medicine of choice in those less than 18 with fever from a sudden viral illness.

reverse cholesterol transport The moving of cholesterol from the body to the liver. A particularly important example is when cholesterol is absorbed from dietary sources, formed into compounds that can be deposited onto blood vessels—leading to atherosclerosis. The RCT pathway takes these atherogenic substances off the blood vessels or from the circulation and moves them to the liver where they are made into needed chemicals or cell walls.

secondary effect A complication of medicine use that does not occur as part of the drug's primary pharmacological activity. Secondary effects are unwanted consequences and are adverse effects.

    Example: Cramping of leg muscles can be a secondary effect of diuretic (urine-producing) drug treatment for high blood pressure. Excessive loss of potassium renders the muscle vulnerable to painful spasm during exercise.

SIADH A Syndrome of Inappropriate Antidiuretic Hormone excretion. This may be caused by medicines and is repeatedly cited where appropriate in the text. Since antidiuretic hormone (ADH) works to control the amount of water that the body retains, excessive ADH causes the body to retain water. This can be very serious, as the excessive water dilutes minerals such as sodium, which is critical for life.

side effect A normal, expected, and predictable response to a drug. Side effects are part of a medicine's pharmacological activity and are unavoidable. Most side effects are undesirable. The majority cause minor annoyance and inconvenience; a few can be hazardous.

superinfection (suprainfection) A second infection superimposed on an initial infection. The superinfection is caused by organisms not killed by the drug(s) used to treat the original (primary) infection. This kind of infection usually happens during or following use of a broad-spectrum antibiotic. The disturbance of the normal balance of bacteria permits overgrowth of organisms usually found in numbers too small to cause disease. The superinfection may also require treatment, using those medicines that are effective against the offending organism.

    Example: A woman is given an antibiotic for a sinus infection. This medicine changes the bacteria usually present in her vagina, allowing yeast to grow. The yeast infection must then be treated with a second medicine.

tardive dyskinesia A drug-induced nervous system disorder with involuntary and bizarre movements of eyelids, jaws, lips, tongue, neck, and fingers. It can happen after use of potent medicines for mental illness. It may occur in any age group but is more common in the middle-aged and especially in chronically ill older women. Once it starts, it may be irreversible. To date, there is no way of identifying who may develop this reaction. The abnormal movement (dyskinesia) is not associated with decline in mental function.

tolerance A situation where the body adapts to a medicine and reacts to it less vigorously over time. Tolerance can be beneficial or harmful in treatment.

    Example: Beneficial tolerance happens when someone with hay fever finds that drowsiness from their antihistamine gradually disappears after 4 or 5 days of continuous use. Harmful tolerance occurs when the patient with "shingles" (herpes zoster) finds that the usual dose of pain medicine no longer works to relieve pain.

toxicity Capacity of a drug to impair body functions or damage tissues. Most drug toxicity is related to total dose: the larger the dose, the greater the toxic effects. Some medicines are toxic in normal doses. Toxic effects due to overdose are often a harmful extension of normal pharmacological actions and may be predictable and preventable.

treat to goal An important yet widely underused concept. One of the features in this edition of the Guide is the concept of treatment goals, measurements, and outcomes. Treating to goal means that when a particular medicine is considered, results and timeframes to achieve those goals are set and communicated to the patient. If goals are NOT achieved, medication doses can often be increased (if not at maximum), new medicines can be added or different non-pharmacological approaches may be tried in order to reach the goal. A good example is treatment of high cholesterol (hyperlipidemia). It is not enough to find elevated cholesterol, start a medicine (such as an HMG-CoA reductase inhibitor or statin), and forget about it. The treatment goal of the medicine (such as getting the LDL to less than 130 mg/dl or HDL to more than 40 mg/dl) should be explained, the medicine started, and then cholesterol rechecked in a reasonable interval (such as three months). If the goal is achieved, and the treatment well tolerated—the medicine should be continued. If the goal is not reached and a medicine such as Pravachol (Pravastatin) is being used, it is reasonable (depending on the starting dose) to increase the dose and then recheck the cholesterol in three months. The process then continues until the National Cholesterol Education Program (NCEP) target or the target chosen by your doctor is reached.

trough-to-peak ratio (T/P) A concept used to check dosing of medicines for high blood pressure. The T/P ratio is calculated by dividing the blood pressure level immediately before the next drug dose (trough) by the largest blood pressure drop during the time between doses. A result greater than 50% means that the effect of the medicine over the entire time between doses is ideal.

tyramine A chemical present in many common foods and beverages that raises blood pressure. Normally, enzymes in the body neutralize tyramine (monoamine oxidase [MAO] type A). If the action of MAO type A is blocked, substances such as tyramine can cause alarming and dangerous increases in blood pressure.

Several medicines can block monoamine oxidase type A. They are called monoamine oxidase (MAO) type A inhibitors (see Drug Classes, Section Four). If you take one of these drugs and your diet includes foods or beverages high in tyramine, sudden increases in blood pressure may happen. Talk with your doctor or pharmacist about an appropriate diet and before combining any other medicine with an MAO inhibitor.

The following foods and beverages have been reported to contain varying amounts of tyramine. Unless their tyramine content is known to be insignificant, they should be avoided altogether while taking an MAO type A inhibitor drug.

FOODS	BEVERAGES
aged cheeses of all kinds*	beer (unpasteurized)
avocado	Chianti wine
banana skins	sherry wine
bean curd	vermouth
bologna	
"Bovril" extract	
broad bean pods	
chicken liver (unless fresh and used at once)	
chocolate	
figs, canned	
fish, canned	
fish, dried and salted	
herring, pickled	
liver, if not very fresh	
"Marmite" extract	
meat extracts	
meat tenderizers	
pepperoni	
raisins	
raspberries	
salami	
shrimp paste	
sour cream	
soy sauce	
yeast extracts	

Note: *Any* high-protein food that is aged or has undergone breakdown by putrefaction probably contains tyramine and could produce a hypertensive crisis in anyone taking MAO type A inhibitor drugs.

VIPPS seal A term used in reference to pharmacies on the Internet. This seal is presently a hallmark of a valid pharmacy on the Internet from which to get prescriptions filled. The term stands for Verified Internet Pharmacy Practice Site. You will usually see this seal pictured prominently on a site which has achieved this credential!

viral load or viral burden A term used in reference to AIDS patients to describe the amount of HIV virus present in the body at any given time. The amount of virus relates to how well drug therapy is working, and can be a reason to change medicines if the load increases.

WHO pain ladder A therapeutic scheme using increasing strengths and combinations of pain medicines (analgesics) that includes NSAIDs, opiates, and adjuvant drugs to control pain as specified by the World Health Organization (WHO). It is not an absolute treatment scheme, but it should be used to organize the approach to effective pain prevention.

wnl (usually seen as WNL) a term often used to refer to laboratory results which means within normal limits.

WOMAC A widely used approach to measure the health status of osteoarthritis patients. This scale is the Western Ontario and McMaster University index or WOMAC. What it does is work to check (assess) the therapeutic scheme using increasing strengths and combinations of pain medicines (analgesics) that include NSAIDs, opiates, and adjuvant drugs to control pain as specified by the World Health Organization (WHO). It is not an absolute assessment scheme, but used correctly, organizes patient information into a rational approach to checking how compromised the patient is before the medicine is added and then allows an objective follow-up check on how well the medicine is working.

Young mania rating scale (Y-MRS) a tool used by psychiatric clinicians to assess the severity of mania. Often used in bipolar disorder as a clinical outcomes measurement.

TABLES OF MEDICINE INFORMATION

TABLE 1

Medicines That May Adversely Affect the Fetus and Newborn Infant

In 1961, a decision was made to use thalidomide to try to make pregnancy less stressful, and pregnant women more relaxed. Despite these laudable intentions, this became the thalidomide DISASTER of 1961. What was not known then was that thalidomide (and many other drugs) caused birth defects or even fetal death if used during pregnancy (possible teratogens or embryocidal medicines). This does NOT mean that the medicines are "bad" medicines. For example, extremely effective medicines such as the HMG-CoA inhibitors for lowering cholesterol should NEVER be taken during pregnancy (Category X) yet they save many, many lives when people have high cholesterol. Interestingly, thalidomide itself has seen a resurrection because it fights an important body chemical called Tumor Necrosis Factor or (TNF). It still should NEVER be used in pregnancy, but now has a valuable role treating erythema nodosum leprosum (ENL).

Our understanding of how drugs can affect the fetus or newborn infant continues to grow, and the list of the drugs that can cause significant harm to the unborn and newborn child has gotten larger and larger. In many cases, it is not possible to clearly separate adverse effects due to the mother's disease or disorder from those that may be caused by medicines. Based on current knowledge, it is strongly recommended that only those drugs that confer clear and essential benefits should be used during pregnancy. The FDA started an interdisciplinary task force in 1997 to revise the current pregnancy drug labeling system, but at the time of this writing has not released a new system (please see the existing FDA system and a note regarding possible changes at the end of this book). Some medicines have pregnancy registries sponsored by the company that makes the product. Where possible, I have included the 800 numbers for pregnancy registries, as I consider them to be a good idea if the decision is made to use a medicine in pregnancy. Talk to your doctor for more information.

Drugs that *probably* cause adverse effects when taken during the *first* trimester

aminopterin	finasteride	misoprostol
anticonvulsants*	fluorouracil	opioid analgesics*
antithyroid drugs	HMG-CoA reductase	progestins*
cytarabine	inhibitors*	quinine
danazol	iodides	streptomycin
diethylstilbestrol	isotretinoin	testosterone
ethanol (large amounts and	kanamycin	thalidomide
for long periods)	mercaptopurine	warfarin
etretinate	methotrexate	

Drugs that *possibly* cause adverse effects when taken during the *first* trimester

angiotensin-converting	lithium	piperazine
enzyme inhibitors*	mebendazole	rifampin
busulfan	monoamine oxidase	tetracyclines*
chlorambucil	(MAO) inhibitors*	
estrogens*	oral contraceptives	

*See Drug Class, Section Four

Drugs that *probably* cause adverse effects when taken during the *second* and *third* trimesters

amiodarone
androgens*
angiotensin-converting
    enzyme inhibitors*
antithyroid drugs
aspirin
benzodiazepines*
chloramphenicol
estrogens*
ethanol (large amounts and
    for long periods)

finasteride
HMG-CoA reductase
    inhibitors*
iodides
kanamycin
lithium
nonsteroidal anti-
    inflammatory drugs*
opioid analgesics*
phenothiazines*
progestins*

rifampin
streptomycin
sulfonamides*
sulfonylureas*
tetracyclines*
thalidomide
thiazide diuretics*
tricyclic antidepressants*
warfarin

Drugs that *possibly* cause adverse effects when taken during the *second* and *third* trimesters

acetazolamide
clemastine
diphenhydramine

ethacrynic acid
fluoroquinolones*
haloperidol

hydroxyzine
promethazine

TABLE 2

Medicines That May Increase Sensitivity to the Sun (Photosensitivity)

Some drugs can sensitize skin to ultraviolet light. This can cause the skin to react with a rash or exaggerated burn on exposure to sun or ultraviolet lamps. If you are taking any of the following drugs, ask your doctor for help about sun exposure and sun blocks. Phototoxicity may be the next level of this reaction, possibly with repeat exposure.

acetazolamide
acetohexamide
alprazolam
amantadine
amiloride
aminobenzoic acid
amiodarone
amitriptyline
amoxapine
barbiturates
bendroflumethiazide
benzocaine
benzophenones
benzoyl peroxide
benzthiazide
captopril
carbamazepine
chlordiazepoxide
chloroquine
chlorothiazide
chlorpromazine
chlorpropamide

chlortetracycline
chlorthalidone
ciprofloxacin
clindamycin
clofazimine
clofibrate
clomipramine
cyproheptadine
dacarbazine
dapsone
demeclocycline
desipramine
desoximetasone
diethylstilbestrol
diflunisal
diltiazem
diphenhydramine
disopyramide
doxepin
doxycycline
enoxacin
estrogen

etretinate
flucytosine
fluorescein
fluorouracil
fluphenazine
flutamide
furosemide
glipizide
glyburide
gold preparations
griseofulvin
haloperidol
hexachlorophene
hydrochlorothiazide
hydroflumethiazide
ibuprofen
imipramine
indomethacin
isotretinoin
ketoprofen
lincomycin
lomefloxacin

*See Drug Class, Section Four

Drugs That May Increase Sensitivity to the Sun (cont.)

maprotiline	para-aminobenzoic acid	thiabendazole
mesoridazine	perphenazine	thioridazine
methacycline	phenelzine	thiothixene
methotrexate	phenobarbital	tolazamide
methyclothiazide	phenylbutazone	tolbutamide
methyldopa	phenytoin	tranylcypromine
metolazone	piroxicam	trazodone
minocycline	polythiazide	tretinoin
minoxidil	prochlorperazine	triamterene
nabumetone	promazine	trichlormethiazide
nalidixic acid	promethazine	trifluoperazine
naproxen	protriptyline	triflupromazine
nifedipine	pyrazinamide	trimeprazine
norfloxacin	quinidine	trimethoprim
nortriptyline	quinine	trimipramine
ofloxacin	St. John's wort	triprolidine
oral contraceptives	sulfonamides	vinblastine
oxyphenbutazone	sulindac	
oxytetracycline	tetracycline	

TABLE 3

Medicines That May Adversely Affect Behavior

Medicines can alter mood and emotional stability. They can also cause unpredictable patterns of thinking or behavior. These responses are relatively infrequent, but the nature and degree of mental disturbance can be alarming as well as dangerous for both patient and family.

Such paradoxical responses are often of an idiosyncratic nature, and someone with a history of a serious mental or emotional disorder is more likely to experience bizarre reactions. In some cases, it may be hard to separate the disorder being treated from an effect of one (or more) medicines the patient may be taking. If in doubt, it is best to talk with your doctor.

Medicines reported to impair *concentration* and/or *memory*

acyclovir	barbiturates*	(MAO) inhibitors*
anticonvulsants	benzodiazepines*	phenytoin
antihistamines*	isoniazid	primidone
anti-parkinsonism drugs*	monoamine oxidase	scopolamine

Medicines reported to cause *confusion, delirium* or *disorientation*

acetazolamide	antidepressants*	(some)
acyclovir	antihistamines*	bromides
amantadine	antipsychotics	carbamazepine
aminophylline	atropine-like drugs*	chloroquine
amphetamines	barbiturates*	cimetidine
amphotericin B	benzodiazepines*	clonidine
anticholinergics	beta adrenergic blockers	cortisone-like drugs*

*See Drug Class, Section Four

Medicines reported to cause *confusion, delirium* or *disorientation* (cont.)

cycloserine
dantrolene
digitalis
digitoxin
digoxin
disulfiram
diuretics
ethchlorvynol
ethinamate
fenfluramine
fluoroquinolone
   antibiotics*
glutethimide
histamine (H2) receptor
   antagonists

interferons
isoniazid
lamotrigine
levodopa
lidocaine
liposomal amphotericin B
lisinopril
melatonin
meprobamate
mesalamine
methyldopa
metoclopramide
narcotic pain relievers
   (analgesics)
NSAIDs*

para-aminosalicylic acid
phenelzine
phenothiazines*
phenytoin
piperazine
primidone
propranolol
quinidine
reserpine
scopolamine
tacrine
theophylline
tricyclic antidepressants
zolpidem

Medicines reported to cause *paranoid thinking*

acyclovir
amphetamine-like
   medicines
anticholinergic drugs
benzodiazepines
bromides

cocaine
cortisone-like drugs*
cycloserine
diphenhydramine
disopyramide
disulfiram

isoniazid
levodopa
propafenone
propranolol
tricyclic antidepressants

Medicines reported to cause *schizophrenic-like behavior*

amphetamines*
anabolic steroids
cimetidine (case reports and
   in elderly or debilitated)

ciprofloxacin (case reports
   and idiosyncratic)
ephedrine
fenfluramine

phenmetrazine
phenylpropanolamine

Medicines reported to cause *manic-like behavior*

antidepressants*
clarithromycin (case
   reports)
cortisone-like drugs*

levodopa
metoclopramide (case
   reports)
monoamine oxidase (MAO)
   inhibitors*

selective serotonin
reuptake inhibitors (SSRIs)
   (when drug is stopped)

Some medicines have mood-altering *side effects*, although they are prescribed for altogether unrelated conditions. Emotional and behavioral secondary effects will be quite unpredictable and vary enormously from person to person. However, the following experiences have been seen with sufficient frequency to establish recognizable patterns.

Medicines reported to cause *nervousness* (anxiety and irritability)

amantadine
amphetamine-like drugs*
   (appetite suppressants)
anabolic steroids
antihistamines*

aripiprazole (Abilify)
caffeine
chlorphenesin
cimetidine (case reports in
   elderly)

cocaine
cortisone-like drugs*
ephedrine
epinephrine
isoproterenol

*See Drug Class, Section Four

Medicines reported to cause *nervousness* (cont.)

levodopa
liothyronine (in excessive
 dosage)
methylphenidate
methysergide

monoamine oxidase (MAO)
 inhibitors*
nylidrin
oral contraceptives
selective serotonin reuptake
 inhibitors (SSRIs)

theophylline
thyroid (in excessive
 dosage)
thyroxine (in excessive
 dosage)

Medicines reported to cause *emotional depression*

amantadine
amphetamines* (on
 withdrawal)
baclofen
benzodiazepines*
beta adrenergic blockers
 (some)
calcium channel blockers
 (case reports)
carbamazepine
chloramphenicol
cimetidine
clonidine
clotrimazole
cortisone-like drugs*
cycloserine
digitalis
digitoxin
digoxin
diphenoxylate
estrogens

ethionamide
fenfluramine (on
 withdrawal)
fluoroquinolone
 antibiotics
fluphenazine
guanethidine
haloperidol
HMG-CoA reductase
 inhibitors
 (case reports)
hydrocortisone
indomethacin
isoniazid
isotretinoin
levodopa
methsuximide
methyldopa
methysergide
metoclopramide (case
 reports)

metoprolol
oral contraceptives
peginterferon alfa-2A
phenylbutazone
procainamide
progesterones
propranolol
raloxifene
reserpine
ribavirin (in combination
 with peginterferon
 alfa-2A)
sulfonamides*
thiazide diuretics (may
 start after weeks to
 months)
tretinoin
vinblastine (possibly
 dose related)
vitamin D (in excessive
 dosage)

Medicines reported to cause *euphoria*

amantadine
aminophylline
amphetamines
antihistamines* (some)
antispasmodics, synthetic*
aspirin
barbiturates*
benzphetamine
cephalosporins (increased
 risk with kidney disease)
chloral hydrate
clorazepate

codeine
cortisone-like drugs*
diethylpropion
diphenoxylate
dronabinol
ethosuximide
flurazepam
ginseng (sign of abuse)
haloperidol
levodopa
meprobamate
methysergide

monoamine oxidase (MAO)
 inhibitors*
morphine
opioids
pargyline
pentazocine
phenmetrazine
propoxyphene
scopolamine
tybamate

Medicines reported to cause *excitement*

acetazolamide
amantadine
amphetamine-like drugs*
antidepressants*

antihistamines*
atropine-like drugs*
barbiturates* (paradoxical
 response)

benzodiazepines*
 (paradoxical
 response)
cortisone-like drugs

*See Drug Class, Section Four

Medicines reported to cause *excitement* (cont.)

cycloserine
diethylpropion
digitalis
ephedrine
epinephrine
ethinamate (paradoxical response)
ethionamide

glutethimide (paradoxical response)
isoniazid
isoproterenol
levodopa
meperidine and MAO inhibitor drugs*
methyldopa and MAO inhibitor drugs*

methylphenidate
methyprylon (paradoxical response)
nalidixic acid
orphenadrine
quinine
scopolamine

TABLE 4

Medicines That May Adversely Affect Vision

A significant percentage of all adverse drug effects involve visual changes or eye damage. Some effects, such as blurring of vision or double vision, may occur shortly after starting a drug. More subtle and serious effects, such as cataract development or damage to the retina or optic nerve, may not happen until a drug has been in use for a long time. Some changes are irreversible. If you are taking a drug that can affect the eye, promptly report any eye discomfort or change in vision.

Medicines reported to cause *blurring of vision*

acetazolamide
antiarthritic/anti-inflammatory drugs
antidepressants*
antihistamines*
atropine-like drugs*
chlorthalidone

ciprofloxacin
cortisone-like drugs*
diethylstilbestrol
etretinate
fenfluramine
norfloxacin
oral contraceptives

phenytoin
sildenafil
sulfonamides*
tetracyclines*
thiazide diuretics*

Medicines reported to cause *double vision*

Allopurinol
antidepressants*
antidiabetic drugs*
antihistamines*
aspirin
atacurium
barbiturates*
benzodiazepines*
bromides
bupivicaine
carbamazepine
carisoprodol
chlordiazepoxide
chloroquine
chlorprothixene
ciprofloxacin
clomiphene

colchicine
colistin
cortisone-like drugs*
dicloxacillin
digitalis
digitoxin
digoxin
ethanol
ethionamide
ethosuximide
etretinate
fenoprofen
guanethidine
hydroxychloroquine
ibuprofen
indomethacin
isoniazid

levodopa
mephenesin
methocarbamol
methsuximide
morphine
nalidixic acid
nicotine
nitrofurantoin
norfloxacin
oral contraceptives
organophosphates
orphenadrine
oxyphenbutazone
pentazocine
phenelzine
phenothiazines*
phensuximide

*See Drug Class, Section Four

Medicines reported to cause *double vision* (cont.)

phentermine
phenylbutazone
phenytoin

primidone
propranolol
quinidine

sedatives/sleep inducers*
thiothixene
tranquilizers*

Medicines reported to cause *farsightedness*

ergot
penicillamine

sulfonamides* (possibly)
tolbutamide (possibly)

Medicines reported to cause *nearsightedness*

acetazolamide
aspirin
carbachol
chlorthalidone
codeine
cortisone-like drugs*

ethosuximide
methsuximide
morphine
oral contraceptives
penicillamine
phenothiazines*

phensuximide
spironolactone
sulfonamides*
tetracyclines*
thiazide diuretics*

Medicines reported to *alter color vision*

acetaminophen
amodiaquine
amyl nitrite
aspirin
atropine
barbiturates*
belladonna
chloramphenicol
chloroquine
chlorpromazine
chlortetracycline
ciprofloxacin
cortisone-like drugs*
digitalis
digitoxin
digoxin
disulfiram
epinephrine
ergotamine
erythromycin
ethchlorvynol

ethionamide
etretinate
griseofulvin
fluphenazine
furosemide
hydroxychloroquine
ibuprofen
indomethacin
isocarboxazid
isoniazid
mefenamic acid
mesoridazine
methysergide
nalidixic acid
norfloxacin
oral contraceptives
oxyphenbutazone
paramethadione
pargyline
penicillamine
pentylenetetrazol

perphenazine
phenacetin
phenylbutazone
primidone
prochlorperazine
promazine
promethazine
quinacrine
quinidine
quinine
reserpine
sildenafil
sodium salicylate
streptomycin
sulfonamides*
thioridazine
tranylcypromine
trifluoperazine
triflupromazine
trimeprazine
trimethadione

Medicines reported to cause *sensitivity to light* (photophobia)

amiodarone
antidiabetic drugs*
atropine-like drugs*
bromides
chloroquine
chlorpropamide
cimetidine
ciprofloxacin
clomiphene

digitoxin
doxepin
ethambutol
furosemide
ethionamide
ethosuximide
etretinate
gold salts
hydroxychloroquine

lithium
mephenytoin
methsuximide
monoamine oxidase
(MAO) inhibitors*
nalidixic acid
tricyclic antidepressants
norfloxacin
oral contraceptives

*See Drug Class, Section Four

Medicines reported to cause *sensitivity to light* (cont.)

paramethadione	quinidine	tetracyclines*
phenothiazines*	quinine	tolbutamide
rabies vaccine	sildenafil	trimethadione

Medicines reported to cause *halos around lights*

amyl nitrite	digoxin	paramethadione
chloroquine	hydrochloroquine	phenothiazines*
cortisone-like drugs*	nitroglycerin	quinacrine
digitalis	norfloxacin	trimethadione
digitoxin	oral contraceptives	

Medicines reported to cause *visual hallucinations*

amantadine	digitalis	pargyline
amphetamine-like drugs*	digoxin	pentazocine
amyl nitrite	disulfiram	phenothiazines*
antihistamines*	ephedrine	phenylbutazone
aspirin	furosemide	phenytoin
atropine-like drugs*	gabapentin	primidone
barbiturates*	griseofulvin	propranolol
benzodiazepines*	haloperidol	quinine
bromides	hydroxychloroquine	sedatives/sleep inducers*
carbamazepine	indomethacin	sulfonamides*
cephalexin	isosorbide	tetracyclines*
cephaloglycin	levodopa	tricyclic antidepressants*
chloroquine	nialamide	tripelennamine
cycloserine	oxyphenbutazone	

Medicines reported to impair the use of *contact lenses*

brompheniramine	dexbrompheniramine	furosemide
carbinoxamine	dexchlorpheniramine	oral contraceptives
chlorpheniramine	dimethindene	terfenadine
cyclizine	latanoprost	travaprost
cyproheptadine	diphenhydramine	tripelennamine

Medicines reported to cause *cataracts* or *lens deposits*

allopurinol	methotrimeprazine	thioridazine
busulfan	perphenazine	thiothixene
chlorpromazine	phenmetrazine	trifluoperazine
chlorprothixene	pilocarpine	triflupromazine
cortisone-like drugs*	prochlorperazine	trimeprazine
fluphenazine	promazine	
mesoridazine	promethazine	

TABLE 5

Medicines That May Cause Blood Cell Dysfunction or Damage

All blood cells come from and mature in the bone marrow: red blood cells (erythrocytes), white blood cells (leukocytes) and blood platelets (thrombocytes). There

*See Drug Class, Section Four

are three kinds of white blood cells: granulocytes, monocytes (macrophages), and lymphocytes. Drugs that affect formation or development of blood cells can (1) act on any stage of cell production; (2) impair one cell type or line; (3) influence all cell lines. Some medicines can damage mature cells in the bloodstream, some result in lower hemoglobin.

Medicines that cause inevitable (dose-dependent) *aplastic anemia* (see Glossary)

actinomycin D	cytarabine	mercaptopurine
azathioprine	doxorubicin	methotrexate
busulfan	epirubicin	mitomycin
carboplatin	etoposide	mitoxantrone
carmustine	fluorouracil	plicamycin
chlorambucil	hydroxyurea	procarbazine
cisplatin	lomustine	thioguanine
cyclophosphamide	melphalan	thiotepa

Medicines that may cause idiosyncratic (dose-independent) *aplastic anemia*

amodiaquine	mepacrine	pyrimethamine
benoxaprofen	oxyphenbutazone	sulfonamides*
carbimazole	penicillamine	sulindac
chloramphenicol	phenylbutazone	thiouracils
chlorpromazine	phenytoin	trimethoprim/
gold	piroxicam	sulfamethoxazole
indomethacin	prothiaden	

Medicines that may *impair red blood cell production* (only)

azathioprine	isoniazid	sulfasalazine
carbamazepine	methyldopa	sulfathiazol
chloramphenicol	penicillin	sulfonamides*
chlorpropamide	pentachlorophenol	sulfonylureas*
dapsone	phenobarbital	thiamphenicol
fenoprofen	phenylbutazone	tolbutamide
gold	phenytoin	trimethoprim/
halothane	pyrimethamine	sulfamethoxazole

Medicines that may significantly *reduce granulocyte cell counts* (various mechanisms)

acetaminophen	chlorothiazide	hydralazine
acetazolamide	chlorpromazine	hydrochlorothiazide
allopurinol	chlorpropamide	imipramine
amitriptyline	chlorthalidone	indomethacin
amodiaquine	cimetidine	isoniazid
benzodiazepines*	clindamycin	levamisole
captopril	dapsone	meprobamate
carbamazepine	desipramine	methimazole
carbimazole	disopyramide	methyldopa
cephalosporins*	ethacrynic acid	oxyphenbutazone
chloramphenicol	gentamicin	penicillamine
chloroquine	gold	penicillins*

*See Drug Class, Section Four

Medicines that may significantly *reduce granulocyte cell counts* (cont.)

pentazocine
phenacetin
phenothiazines*
phenylbutazone
phenytoin
procainamide
propranolol
propylthiouracil

pyrimethamine
quinidine
quinine
ranitidine
rifampin
sodium aminosalicylate
streptomycin
sulfadoxine

sulfadoxine/pyrimethamine
sulfonamides*
tetracyclines*
tocainide
tolbutamide
trimetophrim
   sulfanethoxazole
vancomycin

Medicines that cause lower hemoglobin

Alpha-interferon–2A

Medicines that may significantly *reduce blood platelet counts*

acetazolamide
actinomycin
allopurinol
alpha-interferon
amiodarone
ampicillin
aspirin
aztreonam
carbamazepine
carbenicillin
cephalosporins*
chenodeoxycholic acid
chloroquine
chlorothiazide
chlorpheniramine
chlorpropamide
chlorthalidone
cimetidine
clonazepam
cotrimoxazole
cyclophosphamide
danazol
desferrioxamine
diazepam
diazoxide

diclofenac
digoxin
diltiazem
enalapril
fluconazole
furosemide
gentamicin
glyburide
gold
heparin
hydrochlorothiazide
imipramine
isoniazid
isotretinoin
levamisole
lisinopril
meprobamate
methyldopa
mianserin
minoxidil
mitomycin
morphine
nitrofurantoin
oxprenolol
oxyphenbutazone

penicillamine
penicillin
phenylbutazone
phenytoin
piroxicam
primidone
procainamide
procarbazine
quinidine
quinine
ranitidine
rifampin
sodium aminosalicylate
sulfasalazine
sulfonamides*
thioguanine
tobramycin
tocainide
trimethoprim
trimetrexate
valproate (valproic acid)
vancomycin
vincristine

Medicines that cause *hemolytic anemia* due to glucose-6-phosphate dehydrogenase (G6PD) deficiency of red blood cells

acetanilid
dapsone
methylene blue
nalidixic acid
naphthalene
niridazole

nitrofurantoin
pamaquine
phenazopyridine
phenylhydrazine
primaquine
sulfacetamide

sulfamethoxazole
sulfanilamide
sulfapyridine
thiazolsulfone
toluidine blue

*See Drug Class, Section Four

Medicines that may cause *hemolytic anemia* by other mechanisms

antimony	para-aminosalicylic acid	ribavirin
chlorpropamide	penicillamine	rifampin
cisplatin	phenazopyridine	sulfasalazine
mephenesin	quinidine	
methotrexate	quinine	

Medicines that may cause *megaloblastic anemia*

acyclovir	metformin	primidone
alcohol	methotrexate	pyrimethamine
aminopterin	neomycin	sulfasalazine
azathioprine	nitrofurantoin	tetracycline
colchicine	nitrous oxide	thioguanine
cycloserine	oral contraceptives	triamterene
cytarabine	para-aminosalicylic acid	trimethoprim
floxuridine	pentamidine	vinblastine
fluorouracil	phenformin	vitamin A
hydroxyurea	phenobarbital	vitamin C (large doses)
mercaptopurine	phenytoin	zidovudine

Medicines that may cause *sideroblastic anemia*

alcohol	isoniazid	pyrazinamide
chloramphenicol	penicillamine	
cycloserine	phenacetin	

TABLE 6

Medicines That May Cause Heart Dysfunction or Damage

Drugs may damage either heart structure or function. Heart problems themselves often decide the nature of adverse drug effects. Some are direct pharmacological actions of a drug on heart tissues, and others are caused indirectly by altering chemical balances that diminish how well the heart works (as with potassium or magnesium loss from diuretics).

Medicines that may cause or contribute to *abnormal heart rhythms* (arrhythmias)

aminophylline	bronchodilators*	diuretics*
amiodarone	carbamazepine	dofetilide
amitriptyline	chlorpromazine	doxepin
antiarrhythmic drugs*	cimetidine	droperidol
aripiprazole	cisapride (use is now limited)	encainide
arsenic trioxide		erythromycin (intravenous)
astemizole (no longer on the US market)	clarithromycin	fentolterol
bepridil	digitoxin	felbamate
beta adrenergic blockers*	digoxin	flecainide
beta-adrenergic	diltiazem	fluoxetine
	disopyramide	fluvoxamine

*See Drug Class, Section Four

Medicines that may cause or contribute to *abnormal heart rhythms* (cont.)

foscarnet
fosphenytoin
gatifloxacin
grepafloxacin (no longer on the US market)
halofantrene
haloperidol
ibutilide
indapamide
isoproterenol
isradipine
ketanserin
levofloxacin
levomethadyl
lidocaine
maprotiline
methyldopa
mesoridazine
mexiletine
milrinone
moexipril/hctz
moxifloxacin
naratriptan
nicardipine
octreotide
pentamidine
phenothiazines*
pimozide

prenylamine
procainamide
quetiapine
quinidine
QTc blockers: arsenic trioxide; chlorpromazine; class I, IA, or III antiarrhythmics; clarithromycin; clindamycin; cotrimoxazole; dofetilide; dolasetron; droperidol; erythromycin; fluconaxzole; fluoxetine; foscarnet; gatifloxacin, moxifloxacin or sparfloxacin; halofantrine; haloperidol; isradipine; ketoconazole; levomethadyl (Orlaam); mesoridazine; octreotide (Santostatin); ondansetron; pentamidine; phenothiazines in general; pimozide; quinidine; risperidone; sotolol; sulfamethoxazole; tacrolimus; thioridazine; tricyclic antidepressants;

trimethoprim; venlafaxine; ziprazodone; zotepine; and others.
ranitidine
risperidone
salmeterol
sertraline
sotalol
sparfloxacin
sumatriptan
tacrolimus
tamoxifen
terbutaline
terfenadine (no longer on the US market)
theophylline
thiazide diuretics*
thioridazine
tizanidine
trazodone
tricyclic antidepressants (such as Elavil, Sinequan, Tofranil)*
venlafaxine
verapamil
ziprasidone
zolmitriptan

Medicines that may *depress heart function* (reduce pumping efficiency)

beta adrenergic blockers*
beta blockers still used post MI
cocaine
daunorubicin

diltiazem
disopyramide
doxorubicin
epinephrine
flecainide

fluorouracil
isoproterenol
nifedipine
verapamil

Medicines that may *reduce coronary artery blood flow* (reduce oxygen supply to heart muscle)

amphetamines*
beta adrenergic blockers* (abrupt withdrawal)
cocaine

ergotamine
fluorouracil
nifedipine
oral contraceptives

ritodrine
vasopressin
vinblastine
vincristine

Medicines that may *impair healing of heart muscle* following heart attack (myocardial infarction)

adrenocortical steroids*
nonsteroidal
    anti-inflammatory drugs (NSAIDs)*

*See Drug Class, Section Four

Medicines that may cause *heart valve damage*

dexfenfluramine (Redux)	pergolide (permax)
ergotamine	methysergide
fen-phen (fenfluramine-phenteramine)	minocycline (blue-black pigmentation)

Medicines that may cause *pericardial disease*

actinomycin D	cytarabine	phenylbutazone
anthracyclines	fluorouracil	practolol
bleomycin	hydralazine	procainamide
cisplatin	methysergide	sulfasalazine
cyclophosphamide	minoxidil	

TABLE 7

Medicines That May Cause Lung Dysfunction or Damage

Lung damage from medicines may be difficult to distinguish from natural diseases or disorders that involve lung function or structure. Type A reactions are those due to known pharmacological drug actions; Type B are unexpected and unpredictable allergic or idiosyncratic reactions.

Medicines that may adversely affect *blood vessels of the lung*

Drugs that may cause thromboembolism

chlorpromazine	oral contraceptives
estrogens*	(high-estrogen type)

Drugs that may cause pulmonary hypertension

amphetamines*	sibutramine (Meridia)	tryptophan
dexfenfluramine (Redux)	(carries a warning on	
fenfluramine	the label, but effect has	
oral contraceptives	NOT been reported)	

Drugs that may cause vasculitis (blood vessel damage) with or without hemorrhage

aminoglutethimide	febarbamate	phenytoin
amphotericin	nitrofurantoin	
cocaine	penicillamine	

Drugs that may cause adult respiratory distress syndrome (ARDS)

bleomycin	heroin	naloxone
codeine	hydrochlorothiazide	ritodrine
cyclophosphamide	methadone	terbutaline
dextropropoxyphene	mitomycin	vinblastine

*See Drug Class, Section Four

Medicines that may adversely affect the *bronchial tubes*

Drugs that may cause bronchoconstriction (asthma)

acetaminophen
aspirin
beta adrenergic blockers*
carbachol
cephalosporins*
chloramphenicol
deanol
demeclocycline
erythromycin

griseofulvin
maprotiline
methacholine
methoxypsoralen
metoclopramide
morphine
neomycin
neostigmine
nitrofurantoin

nonsteroidal anti-
    inflammatory drugs*
penicillins*
pilocarpine
propafenone
pyridostigmine
streptomycin
tartrazine (coloring agent)

Drugs that may cause bronchiolitis (with permanent obstruction of small bronchioles)

penicillamine

sulfasalazine

Medicines that may *damage lung tissues*

Drugs that may cause acute allergic-type pneumonitis

ampicillin
bleomycin
cephalexin
chlorpropamide
gold
imipramine
mephenesin
mercaptopurine
metformin

methotrexate
metronidazole
mitomycin
nalidixic acid
nitrofurantoin
nomifensine
nonsteroidal anti-
    inflammatory drugs*
para-aminosalicylic acid

penicillamine
penicillin
phenylbutazone
phenytoin
procarbazine
sulfonamides*
tetracycline
vinblastine

Medicines that may cause *chronic pneumonitis and/or fibrosis* (scarring)

amiodarone
azathioprine
BCNU
bleomycin
bromocriptine
busulfan
carmustine
CCNU
chlorambucil

cyclophosphamide
ergotamine
gold
hexamethonium
lomustine
mecamylamine
melphalan
mercaptopurine
methysergide

nitrofurantoin
peginterferon alfa-2A
pentolinium
practolol
ribavirin
sulfasalazine
tocainide
tolfenamic acid

Medicines that may *damage the pleura*

bromocriptine

methysergide

practolol

*See Drug Class, Section Four

TABLE 8

Medicines That May Cause Liver Dysfunction or Damage

The liver often changes drugs into forms easily removed from the body. Medicines can hurt liver structure or function. Reactions range from mild and transient changes in liver function tests to complete liver failure and death. Many medicines may affect the liver in more than one way. Careful liver monitoring is required.

Medicines that may *cause acute dose-dependent liver damage* (resembling acute viral hepatitis)

acetaminophen (overdose)	salicylates (such as	6-mercaptopurine
amiodarone	aspirin—doses over	
niacin	2 g daily)	

Medicines that may cause *acute dose-independent liver* damage (resembling acute viral hepatitis)

acebutolol	indomethacin	phenytoin
allopurinol	isoniazid	piroxicam
atenolol	ketoconazole	probenecid
carbamazepine	labetalol	pyrazinamide
cimetidine	maprotiline	quinidine
cocaine	metoprolol	quinine
dantrolene	mianserin	ranitidine
diclofenac	naproxen	rifampin
diltiazem	nifedipine	sulfonamides*
disulfiram	para-aminosalicylic acid	sulindac
enflurane	penicillins*	tricyclic antidepressants*
ethambutol	phenelzine	trovafloxacin
ethionamide	phenindione	valproic acid
halothane	phenobarbital	verapamil
ibuprofen	phenylbutazone	

Medicines that may cause *acute fatty infiltration of the liver*

adrenocortical steroids*	phenothiazines*	tetracyclines*
antithyroid drugs	phenytoin	valproic acid
isoniazid	salicylates*	
methotrexate	sulfonamides*	

Medicines that may cause *cholestatic jaundice*

acetaminophen	chlordiazepoxide	diazepam
actinomycin D	chlorpromazine	diclofenac
amitriptyline	chlorpropamide	disopyramide
amoxicillin/clavulanate	cimetidine	enalapril
azathioprine	cloxacillin	erythromycin (estolate)
captopril (case reports)	cyclophosphamide	estradiol
carbamazepine	cyclosporine	flecainide
carbimazole	danazol	flurazepam
cephalosporins*	desipramine	flutamide

*See Drug Class, Section Four

Medicines that may cause or contribute to *cholestatic jaundice* (cont.)

glyburide
gold
griseofulvin
haloperidol
imipramine
indomethacin
ketoconazole
mercaptopurine
methyltestosterone
nafcillin
niacin
nifedipine
nitrofurantoin

nonsteroidal anti-
    inflammatory drugs*
norethandrolone
oral contraceptives
oxacillin
penicillamine
phenothiazines*
phenytoin
piroxicam
propoxyphene
propylthiouracil
rifampin
sulfonamides*

sulindac
tamoxifen
thiabendazole
tolazamide
tolbutamide
tricyclic antidepressants*
trimethoprim/
    sulfamethoxazole
troleandomycin
verapamil
zidovudine

Medicines that may cause *liver granulomas* (chronic inflammatory nodules)

allopurinol
aspirin
carbamazepine
chlorpromazine
chlorpropamide
diltiazem
disopyramide

gold
hydralazine
isoniazid
methyldopa
nitrofurantoin
penicillin
phenylbutazone

phenytoin
procainamide
quinidine
ranitidine
sulfonamides*
tolbutamide

Medicines that may cause *chronic liver disease*

Drugs that may cause active chronic hepatitis

acetaminophen (chronic
    use, large doses)
dantrolene

isoniazid
methyldopa
nitrofurantoin

salicylates (aspirin)
trazodone

Drugs that may cause liver cirrhosis or fibrosis (scarring)

methotrexate
methyldopa

nicotinic acid

vitamin A

Drugs that may cause chronic cholestasis (resembling primary biliary cirrhosis)

chlorpromazine/valproic
    acid (combination)
chlorpropamide/
    erythromycin
    (combination)

imipramine
phenothiazines*
phenytoin

thiabendazole
tolbutamide

Medicines that may cause *liver tumors* (benign and malignant)

anabolic steroids
androgens (C17-substituted
    kinds)

danazol
oral contraceptives
testosterone

thorotrast

*See Drug Class, Section Four

Medicines that may cause *damage to liver blood vessels*

adriamycin	dacarbazine	thioguanine
anabolic steroids	herbal teas,	vincristine
azathioprine	some	vitamin A
carmustine	mercaptopurine	(excessive doses)
cyclophosphamide/	methotrexate	
cyclo-sporine	mitomycin	
(combination)	oral contraceptives	

Medicines that can cause *idiosyncratic liver damage*

acarbose	dacarbazine	sulfonamides
acebutolol (case reports)	kava kava	troglitazone
amoxicillin/clavulanate	leflunomide	trovafloxacin
carbamazepine	procainamide	valproic acid
chlorpromazine	propylthiouracil	

TABLE 9

Medicines That May Cause Kidney Dysfunction or Damage

The kidneys perform two major drug functions:(1) alteration of the drug to help remove it; (2) elimination of the drug from the body in the urine. As with effects on the liver, many drugs can harm the kidneys in several ways. Careful monitoring is prudent when taking any of the drugs listed below.

Medicines that may primarily *impair kidney function* (without damage)

amphotericin	demeclocycline	nifedipine
angiotensin-converting-	diuretics/NSAIDs* (avoid	nitroprusside
enzyme inhibitors* (with	this combination)	nonsteroidal anti-
renal artery stenosis;	glyburide	inflammatory drugs
with congestive heart	isofosfamide	(NSAIDs)*
failure)	lithium/tricyclic	rifampin
beta adrenergic blockers*	antidepressants* (avoid	vinblastine
ceftazidime	this combination)	
colchicine	methoxyflurane	

Medicines that may cause *acute kidney failure* (due to kidney damage)

Drugs that may damage the kidney filtration unit (the nephron)

acetaminophen	cisplatin	oral contraceptives
(excessive dosage)	cyclosporine	penicillamine
allopurinol	enalapril	phenytoin
aminoglycoside	ergometrine	quinidine
antibiotics*	hydralazine	rifampin
amphotericin	methy-CCNU	streptokinase
bismuth thiosulfate	metronidazole	sulfonamides*
carbamazepine	mitomycin	thiazide diuretics*

*See Drug Class, Section Four

Medicines that may cause *acute interstitial nephritis*

allopurinol
amoxicillin
ampicillin
aspirin
azathioprine
aztreonam
captopril
carbamazepine
carbenicillin
cefaclor
cefoxitin
cephalexin
cephalothin
cephapirin
cephradine
cimetidine
ciprofloxacin
clofibrate
cloxacillin
diazepam

diclofenac
diflunisal
fenoprofen
foscarnet
furosemide
gentamicin
glafenine
ibuprofen
indomethacin
ketoprofen
mefenamate
methicillin
methyldopa
mezlocillin
minocycline
nafcillin
naproxen
oxacillin
penicillamine
penicillin

phenindione
phenobarbital
phenylbutazone
phenytoin
piroxicam
pirprofen
pyrazinamide
rifampin
sodium valproate
sulfamethoxazole
sulfinpyrazone
sulfonamides*
sulindac
thiazide diuretics*
tolmetin
trimethoprim
vancomycin
warfarin

Medicines that may cause *muscle destruction* and associated *acute kidney failure*

adrenocortical steroids*
alcohol
amphetamines*
amphotericin
aristolochic acid (prompted
   removal of several herbal
   products from the mar-
   ket by the FDA)

carbenoxolone
chlorthalidone
clofibrate
cocaine
cytarabine
fenofibrate
haloperidol
halothane

heroin
lovastatin
opioid analgesics*
pentamidine
phenothiazines*
streptokinase
suxamethonium

Medicines that may cause kidney damage resembling *glomerulonephritis or nephrosis*

captopril
fenoprofen
gold
ketoprofen

lithium
mesalamine
penicillamine
phenytoin

practolol
probenecid
quinidine

Medicines that may cause *chronic interstitial nephritis and papillary necrosis* (analgesic kidney damage)

acetaminophen
aspirin

phenacetin
(All with long-term use)

*See Drug Class, Section Four

Medicines that may cause or contribute to *urinary tract crystal or stone formation*

acetazolamide	methoxyflurane	uricosuric drugs
acyclovir	phenylbutazone	vitamin A
cytotoxic drugs	probenecid	vitamin C
dihydroxyadenine	salicylates*	vitamin D
magnesium trisilicate	sulfonamides*	warfarin
mercaptopurine	thiazide diuretics*	zoxazolamine
methotrexate	triamterene	

TABLE 10

Medicines That May Cause Nerve Dysfunction or Damage

Medicines may affect any part of the nervous system from the brain to peripheral nerves. The extent of benefits or problems varies widely from person to person.

Medicines that may cause *significant headache*

albuterol	hydralazine	propranolol
amyl nitrate	ibuprofen	ranitidine
bepridil	indomethacin	sertraline
bromocriptine	labetalol	sibutramine
caffeine	liposomal amphotericin B	sildenafil
cilostazol	lithium	stavudine
clonidine	lomefloxacin	sulindac
cocaine	mesalamine	terbutaline
delavirdine	naproxen	tetracyclines*
ergotamine (prolonged use)	nifedipine	theophylline
etretinate	nisoldipine	tolmetin
felodipine	nitrofurantoin	trimethoprim/
fluticasone	nitroglycerin	sulfamethoxazole
fluvoxamine	oral contraceptives	valacyclovir
HMG-CoA reductase	perhexiline	
inhibitors	peginterferon alfa-2A	

Medicines that may cause *seizures (convulsions)*

acyclovir	carbenicillin	gabapentin
alprostadil	cephalosporins*	halothane
amantadine	chloroquine	indomethacin
amitriptyline	cimetidine	isoniazid
ampicillin	ciprofloxacin	lidocaine
atenolol	cisapride	lithium
baclofen	cocaine	mefenamic acid
bromocriptine	cycloserine	metronidazole
bupropion	disopyramide	(high doses)
carbamazepine	enoxacin	morphine (high-dose
(exacerbation of absence)	ether	intravenous)

*See Drug Class, Section Four

Medicines that may cause *seizures (convulsions)* (cont.)

nalidixic acid
ofloxacin
oxacillin
paclitaxel
penicillins* (synthetic)

phenothiazines*
pyrimethamine
tacrine
terbutaline
theophylline

ticarcillin
tramadol
tricyclic antidepressants*
venlafaxine
vincristine

Medicines that may cause *stroke*

amitriptyline
anabolic steroids
cocaine

estrogens
nicotine
oral contraceptives

phenylpropanolamine
sumatriptan
trazodone

Medicines that may cause features of *parkinsonism*

amitriptyline
amodiaquine
atypical antipsychotics
  (see Drug Classes)
chloroquine
chlorprothixene
clozapine
desipramine

diazoxide
diltiazem
diphenhydramine
droperidol
fluoxetine
haloperidol
imipramine
levodopa

lithium
methyldopa
metoclopramide
phenothiazines*
reserpine
thiothixene
trifluperidol
valproic acid

Medicines that may cause *acute dystonias* (acute involuntary movement syndromes—AIMS)

carbamazepine
chlorzoxazone
fluoxetine

haloperidol
metoclopramide
phenothiazines*

phenytoin
propranolol
tricyclic antidepressants*

Medicines that may cause *tardive dyskinesia* (see Glossary)

Atypical antipsychotics
haloperidol

phenothiazines*

thiothixene

Medicines that may cause *neuroleptic malignant syndrome* (NMS)

See this term in the Glossary for a list of causative drugs.

Medicines that may cause *peripheral neuropathy* (see Glossary)

amiodarone
amitriptyline
amphetamines*
amphotericin
anticoagulants*
carbutamide
chlorambucil
chloramphenicol
chloroquine
chlorpropamide
cimetidine
cisplatin
clioquinol

clofibrate
colchicine
colistin
cytarabine
dapsone
didanosine
disopyramide
disulfiram
emetine
ergotamine
ethambutol
ethanol
glutethimide

gold
hydralazine
imipramine
indomethacin
isoniazid
lamotrigine
losartan
methaqualone
methimazole
methysergide
metronidazole
nalidixic acid
nelfinavir

*See Drug Class, Section Four

Medicines that may cause *peripheral neuropathy* (cont.)

nitrofurantoin
nitrofurazone
paclitaxel
penicillamine
penicillin
perhexiline
phenelzine
phenylbutazone

phenytoin
podophyllin
procarbazine
propranolol
propylthiouracil
ritonavir
stavudine
streptomycin

sulfonamides*
sulfoxone
thalidomide
tolbutamide
vinblastine
vincristine

Drugs that may cause a *myasthenia gravis syndrome*

aminoglycoside
   antibiotics*
amitriptyline
azithromycin (exacerbation
   of existing MG)
beta adrenergic blockers*
codeine

erythromycin (exacerbation
   of existing MG)
lithium
morphine
norfloxacin (exacerbation
   of existing MG)
penicillamine

phenytoin
polymyxin B
procainamide
tetracycline
trihexyphenidyl

TABLE 11

Medicines That May Adversely Affect Sexuality

Many commonly used drugs can cause obvious or subtle changes on one or more aspects of sexual expression. Patients may be unaware that sexual changes can be related to medicines and are often reluctant to talk about them. Sexual dysfunction may also be a result of the disorder being treated or an undetected problem. Diabetes, kidney failure, hypertension, depression, and alcoholism may reduce libido and cause failure of erection. Many drugs used to treat these conditions may worsen subclinical sexual dysfunction. This requires the closest cooperation between therapist and patient in order to correctly assess possible cause-and-effect relationships and change therapy appropriately.

Possible Drug Effects on Male Sexuality

1. Increased libido
      androgens (replacement therapy in deficiency states)
      baclofen (Lioresal)
      bupropion (Wellbutrin)
      chlordiazepoxide (Librium) (antianxiety effect)
      diazepam (Valium) (antianxiety effect)
      haloperidol (Haldol)
      levodopa (Larodopa, Sinemet) (may be an indirect effect due to improved
         sense of well-being)
      sildenafil (Viagra) (may be an effect of confidence from the drug)

2. Decreased libido
      amphetamines
      antihistamines

*See Drug Class, Section Four

barbiturates
chlordiazepoxide (Librium), sedative effect
chlorpromazine (Thorazine), 10% to 20% of users
cimetidine (Tagamet)
clofibrate (Atromid-S)
clonidine (Catapres), 10% to 20% of users
danazol (Danocrine)
diazepam (Valium), sedative effect
disulfiram (Antabuse)
estrogens (therapy for prostatic cancer)
fenfluramine (Pondimin)
finasteride (Propecia, Proscar)
heroin
licorice
medroxyprogesterone (Provera)
methyldopa (Aldomet), 10% to 15% of users
metoclopramide (Reglan), 80% of users
perhexiline (Pexid)
prazosin (Minipres), 15% of users
propranolol (Inderal), rarely
reserpine (Serpasil, Ser-Ap-Es)
spironolactone (Aldactone)
tricyclic antidepressants

3. Impaired erection (impotence)
amitriptyline
amphetamines
angiotensin-converting enzyme (ACE) inhibitors
anticholinergics
antihistamines
baclofen (Lioresal)
barbiturates (when abused)
beta blockers*
captopril
chlordiazepoxide (Librium) (in high dosage)
chlorpromazine (Thorazine)
cimetidine (Tagamet)
citalopram (Celexa)
clofibrate (Atromid-S)
clonidine (Catapres)
cocaine
diazepam (Valium) (in high dosage)
digitalis and its glycosides
disopyramide (Norpace)
disulfiram (Antabuse), uncertain
estrogens (therapy for prostatic cancer)
ethacrynic acid (Edecrin)
ethionamide (Trecator-SC)
fenfluramine (Pondimin)
Finasteride (Proscar)

*See Drug Class, Section Four

furosemide (Lasix)
gabapentin (Neurontin)
guanethidine (Ismelin)
haloperidol (Haldol)
heroin
hydrochlorothiazide (ESPECIALLY if combined with a beta blocker)
hydroxyprogesterone (therapy for prostatic cancer)
indomethacin
itraconazole
licorice
lisinopril
lithium (Lithonate)
losartan (Cozaar)
marijuana
mesoridazine (Serentil)
methantheline (Banthine)
methyldopa (Aldomet)
metoclopramide (Reglan)
mirtazapine (Remeron)
monoamine oxidase (MAO) type A inhibitors*
perhexiline (Pexid)
pravastatin
prazosin (Minipres), infrequently
reserpine (Serpasil, Ser-Ap-Es)
simvastatin
spironolactone (Aldactone)
telmisartan (Micardis)
thiazide diuretics
thioridazine (Mellaril)
tricyclic antidepressants
venlafaxine (Effexor)

4. Impaired ejaculation
   anticholinergics
   barbiturates (when abused)
   chlorpromazine (Thorazine)
   clonidine (Catapres)
   cocaine
   estrogens (therapy for prostatic cancer)
   guanethidine (Ismelin)
   heroin
   mesoridazine (Serentil)
   methyldopa (Aldomet)
   monoamine oxidase (MAO) type A inhibitors*
   phenoxybenzamine (Dibenzyline)
   phentolamine (Regitine)
   reserpine (Serpasil, Ser-Ap-Es)
   thiazide diuretics*
   thioridazine (Mellaril)
   tricyclic antidepressants*

*See Drug Class, Section Four

5. Decreased testosterone
   adrenocorticotropic hormone (ACTH)
   barbiturates
   digoxin (Lanoxin)
   haloperidol (Haldol)—increased testosterone with low dosage, decreased
      testosterone with high dosage
   lithium (Lithonate)
   marijuana
   medroxyprogesterone (Provera)
   monoamine oxidase (MAO) type A inhibitors*
   spironolactone (Aldactone)

6. Impaired spermatogenesis (reduced fertility)
   adrenocorticosteroids (prednisone, etc.)
   androgens (moderate to high dosage, extended use)
   antimalarials
   aspirin (abusive, chronic use)
   chlorambucil (Leukeran)
   cimetidine (Tagamet)
   colchicine
   cotrimoxazole (Bactrim, Septra)
   cyclophosphamide (Cytoxan)
   estrogens (therapy for prostatic cancer)
   marijuana
   medroxyprogesterone (Provera)
   methotrexate
   metoclopramide (Reglan)
   monoamine oxidase (MAO) type A inhibitors
   niridazole (Ambilhar)
   nitrofurantoin (Furadantin)
   spironolactone (Aldactone)
   sulfasalazine (Azulfidine)
   testosterone (moderate to high dosage, extended use)
   vitamin C (doses of 1 g or more)

7. Testicular disorders
   Swelling
   —tricyclic antidepressants
   Inflammation
   —oxyphenbutazone (Tandearil)
   Atrophy
   —androgens (moderate to high dosage, extended use)
   —chlorpromazine (Thorazine)
   —cyclophosphamide (Cytoxan) (in prepubescent boys)
   —spironolactone (Aldactone)

8. Penile disorders
   Priapism (see Glossary)
   —alfentanil
   —anabolic steroids (male hormone-like drugs)

*See Drug Class, Section Four

—chlorpromazine (Thorazine)
—clozapine (Clozaril)
—cocaine
—fluphenazine (Prolixin)
—guanethidine (Ismelin)
—haloperidol (Haldol)
—heparin
—hydralazine (Apresoline)
—levodopa (Sinemet)
—mesoridazine (Serentil)
—molindone (Moban)
—phenelzine (Nardil)
—phenytoin (Dilantin)
—prazosin (Minipres)
—prochlorperazine (Compazine)
—risperidone (Risperdal)
—tamoxifen (Nolvadex)
—thioridazine (Mellaril)
—trazodone (Desyrel)
—trifluoperazine (Stelazine)
—warfarin (Coumadin)
Peyronie's disease (see Glossary)
—beta blockers*
—phenytoin (Dilantin, etc.)

9. Gynecomastia (excessive development of the male breast)
    anabolic steroids
    androgens (partial conversion to estrogen)
    busulfan (Myleran)
    captopril
    carmustine (BiCNU)
    chlormadinone
    chlorpromazine (Thorazine)
    chlortetracycline (Aureomycin)
    cimetidine (Tagamet)
    clonidine (Catapres), infrequently
    diazepam
    diethylstilbestrol (DES)
    digitalis and its glycosides
    diltiazem
    enalapril
    estrogens (therapy for prostatic cancer)
    ethionamide (Trecator-SC)
    finasteride (Propecia, Proscar)
    fluphenazine
    griseofulvin (Fulvicin, etc.)
    haloperidol (Haldol)
    heroin
    human chorionic gonadotropin
    indinavir (Crixivan)

*See Drug Class, Section Four

isoniazid (INH, Nydrazid)
marijuana
mestranol
methyldopa (Aldomet)
metoclopramide (Reglan)
nifedipine
omeprazole (Prilosec)
penicillamine
phenelzine (Nardil)
phenothiazines
reserpine (Serpasil, Ser-Ap-Es)
spironolactone (Aldactone)
thioridazine (Mellaril)
tricyclic antidepressants (TCAs)
verapamil
vincristine (Oncovin)

10. Feminization (loss of libido, impotence, gynecomastia, testicular atrophy)
conjugated estrogens (Premarin, etc.)

11. Precocious puberty
anabolic steroids
androgens
isoniazid (INH)

Possible Drug Effects on Female Sexuality

1. Increased libido
androgens
chlordiazepoxide (Librium) (antianxiety effect)
diazepam (Valium) (antianxiety effect)
mazindol (Sanorex)
oral contraceptives (freedom from fear of pregnancy)

2. Decreased libido
See list of drug effects on male sexuality. Some of these may have potential for reducing libido in the female. The literature is sparse on this subject.

3. Impaired arousal and orgasm
anticholinergics
clonidine (Catapres)
methyldopa (Aldomet)
monoamine oxidase (MAO) inhibitors*
tricyclic antidepressants*

4. Breast enlargement
penicillamine
tricyclic antidepressants*

5. Galactorrhea (spontaneous flow of milk)
amphetamine

*See Drug Class, Section Four

chlorpromazine (Thorazine)
cimetidine (Tagamet)
haloperidol (Haldol)
heroin
methyldopa (Aldomet)
metoclopramide (Reglan)
oral contraceptives
phenothiazines
reserpine (Serpasil, Ser-Ap-Es)
sulpiride (Equilid)
tricyclic antidepressants*

6. Ovarian failure (reduced fertility)
   anesthetic gases (operating room staff)
   cyclophosphamide (Cytoxan)
   cytostatic drugs
   danazol (Danocrine)
   medroxyprogesterone (Provera)

7. Altered menstruation (menstrual disorders)
   adrenocorticosteroids (prednisone, etc.)
   androgens
   barbiturates (when abused)
   chlorambucil (Leukeran)
   chlorpromazine (Thorazine)
   cyclophosphamide (Cytoxan)
   danazol (Danocrine)
   estrogens
   ethionamide (Trecator-SC)
   haloperidol (Haldol)
   heroin
   isoniazid (INH, Nydrazid)
   marijuana
   medroxyprogesterone (Provera)
   metoclopramide (Reglan)
   oral contraceptives
   phenothiazines
   progestins
   radioisotopes
   rifampin (Rifadin, Rifamate, Rimactane)
   spironolactone (Aldactone)
   testosterone
   thioridazine (Mellaril)
   vitamin A (in excessive dosage)

8. Virilization (acne, hirsutism, lowering of voice, enlargement of clitoris)
   anabolic drugs
   androgens
   haloperidol (Haldol)
   oral contraceptives (lowering of voice)

*See Drug Class, Section Four

9. Precocious puberty
   estrogens (in hair lotions)
   isoniazid (INH, Nydrazid)

TABLE 12

Medicines That May Interact with Alcohol

Alcohol may interact with a wide variety of drugs. The most important problem happens when the depressant action on the brain of sedatives, sleep-inducing drugs, tranquilizers, and narcotic medicines is intensified by alcohol. Alcohol may also reduce drug benefits or lead to toxic effects. Some drugs may increase the intoxicating effects of alcohol, further impairing mental alertness, judgment, coordination, and reaction time.

The intensity and significance can vary greatly from one person to another and from one occasion to another. This is because many factors influence what happens when drugs and alcohol interact. Factors include variations in sensitivity to drugs, the chemistry and quantity of the drug, type and amount of alcohol consumed, and the sequence in which drugs and alcohol are taken. If you need to use any of the drugs in the following table, ask your doctor for help about alcohol use.

Medicines with which it is advisable to avoid alcohol completely

Drug name or class	Possible interaction with alcohol
amphetamine	excessive rise in blood pressure with alcoholic beverages containing tyramine**
antidepressants	excessive sedation, increased intoxication
barbiturates*	excessive sedation
bromides	confusion, delirium, increased intoxication
calcium carbimide	disulfiram-like reaction**
carbamazepine	excessive sedation
chlorprothixene	excessive sedation
chlorzoxazone	excessive sedation
disulfiram	disulfiram-reaction**
ergotamine	reduced effectiveness of ergotamine
fenfluramine	excessive stimulation of nervous system with some beers and wines
furazolidone	disulfiram-like reaction**
haloperidol	excessive sedation
MAO inhibitors*	excessive rise in blood pressure with alcoholic beverages containing tyramine**
meperidine	excessive sedation
meprobamate	excessive sedation

*See Drug Class, Section Four
**See Glossary

Medicines with which it is advisable to avoid alcohol completely (cont.)

Drug name or class	Possible interaction with alcohol
methotrexate	increased liver toxicity and excessive sedation
metronidazole	disulfiram-like reaction**
narcotic drugs	excessive sedation
oxyphenbutazone	increased stomach irritation and/or bleeding
pentazocine	excessive sedation
pethidine	excessive sedation
phenothiazines*	excessive sedation
phenylbutazone	increased stomach irritation and/or bleeding
procarbazine	disulfiram-like reaction**
propoxyphene	excessive sedation
reserpine	excessive sedation, orthostatic hypotension**
sleep-inducing drugs (hypnotics)	excessive sedation
—carbromal	
—chloral hydrate	
—ethchlorvynol	
—ethinamate	
—flurazepam	
—glutethimide	
—methaqualone	
—methyprylon	
—temazepam	
—triazolam	
thiothixene	excessive sedation
tricyclic antidepressants*	excessive sedation, increased intoxication
trimethobenzamide	excessive sedation

Medicines with which alcohol should be used only in small amounts (use cautiously until combined effects have been determined)

Drug name or class	Possible interaction with alcohol
acetaminophen (Tylenol, etc.)	increased liver toxicity
antiarthritic/anti-inflammatory drugs	increased stomach irritation and/or bleeding
anticoagulants (coumarins)*	increased anticoagulant effect
antidiabetic drugs (sulfonylureas)*	increased antidiabetic effect, excessive hypoglycemia**
antihistamines*	excessive sedation
antihypertensives*	excessive orthostatic hypotension**
aspirin (large doses or continuous use)	increased stomach irritation and/or bleeding
benzodiazepines*	excessive sedation

(continued)

*See Drug Class, Section Four
**See Glossary

Medicines with which alcohol should be used only in small amounts (cont.)

Drug name or class	Possible interaction with alcohol
carisoprodol	increased alcoholic intoxication
diethylpropion	excessive nervous system stimulation with alcoholic beverages containing tyramine**
dihydroergotoxine	excessive lowering of blood pressure
diphenoxylate	excessive sedation
dipyridamole	excessive lowering of blood pressure
diuretics*	excessive orthostatic hypotension**
ethionamide	confusion, delirium, psychotic behavior
fenoprofen	increased stomach irritation and/or bleeding
griseofulvin	flushing and rapid heart action
ibuprofen	increased stomach irritation and/or bleeding
indomethacin	increased stomach irritation and/or bleeding
insulin	excessive hypoglycemia**
iron	excessive absorption of iron
isoniazid	decreased effectiveness of isoniazid, increased incidence of hepatitis
lithium	increased confusion and delirium (avoid all alcohol if any indication of lithium overdosage)
methocarbamol	excessive sedation
methotrimeprazine	excessive sedation
methylphenidate	excessive nervous system stimulation with alcoholic beverages containing tyramine**
metoprolol	excessive orthostatic hypotension**
nalidixic acid	increased alcoholic intoxication
naproxen	increased stomach irritation and/or bleeding
nicotinic acid	possible orthostatic hypotension**
nitrates* (vasodilators)	possible orthostatic hypotension**
nylidrin	increased stomach irritation
orphenadrine	excessive sedation
phenelzine	increased alcoholic intoxication
phenoxybenzamine	possible orthostatic hypotension**
phentermine	excessive nervous system stimulation with alcoholic beverages containing tyramine**
phenytoin	decreased effect of phenytoin
pilocarpine	prolongation of alcohol effect
prazosin	excessive lowering of blood pressure
primidone	excessive sedation
propranolol	excessive orthostatic hypotension**
sulfonamides*	increased alcoholic intoxication

  *See Drug Class, Section Four
**See Glossary

Medicines with which alcohol should be used only in small amounts (cont.)

Drug name or class	Possible interaction with alcohol
sulindac	increased stomach irritation and/or bleeding
tolmetin	increased stomach irritation and/or bleeding
tranquilizers (mild)	excessive sedation
—chlordiazepoxide	
—clorazepate	
—diazepam	
—hydroxyzine	
—meprobamate	
—oxazepam	
—phenaglycodol	
—tybamate	
tranylcypromine	increased alcoholic intoxication

Medicines capable of producing a disulfiramlike reaction when used concurrently with alcohol**

antidiabetic drugs (sulfonylureas)*
calcium carbimide
chloral hydrate
chloramphenicol
disulfiram
furazolidone
metronidazole
nifuroxime
nitrofurantoin
procarbazine
quinacrine
sulfonamides*
tinidazole
tolazoline

  *See Drug Class, Section Four
**See Glossary

TABLE 13

High-Potassium Foods

Drugs that cause loss of potassium are often used to treat conditions that also require a reduced intake of sodium. The high-potassium foods listed below have been selected for compatibility with a sodium-restricted diet (500 to 1,000 mg of sodium daily). Water pills (diuretics) may also cause loss of magnesium. Make sure magnesium is tested if you take a diuretic and discuss the results with your doctor.

Beverages

orange juice	skim milk	tomato juice
prune juice	tea	whole milk

Breads and Cereals

brown rice	muffins	waffles
cornbread	oatmeal	
griddle cakes	shredded wheat	

Fruits

apricot	fig	orange
avocado	honeydew melon	papaya
banana	mango	prune

Meats

beef	haddock	rockfish
chicken	halibut	salmon
codfish	liver	turkey
flounder	pork	veal

Vegetables

baked beans	parsnips	tomato
lima beans	radishes	white potato
mushrooms	squash	
navy beans	sweet potato	

TABLE 14

Your Personal Drug Profile

I have spoken to countless patients who were sure that they knew how much of their medicines to take, and when to take them, only to learn that they were not only taking the wrong dose, but had also been taking a second medicine too many or too few times a day. Knowing as much as possible about your body and your medicines can save your life. Please take the time to fill out this profile with the latest information. **Medicine never does you any good if you forget to take it. Take control of that chronic disease or condition by finding the goals and taking the medicine.** Also, make time to copy the Medication Map and have your doctor or pharmacist fill it in and discuss it with you. Make sure you work with your doctor to fit your medicines into your life.

Name: _____

Age: _____

Weight in kilograms (pounds divided by 2.2): _____

Height in inches: _____

Prescription drug allergies: _____

_____

Nonprescription drug allergies: _____

_____

Food allergies: _____

_____

My kidneys* are: normal _____

mildly_____   moderately_____   severely_____   compromised.

My liver* is: normal _____

mildly_____   moderately_____   severely_____   compromised.

Conditions or diseases that I have or have had: _____

_____

Prescription and nonprescription medications I take regularly: _____

_____

*Make certain your dose is decreased if the drug is eliminated by an organ (such as the liver or kidneys) with which you have a problem. To determine which organs are involved, refer to the drug profile, and, in particular, the Conditions Requiring Adjustments section, for each medication you are taking.

Prescription and nonprescription medications I take periodically: _____

_____

I find it very difficult _____ to remember to take medicines.

I find it very easy _____ to remember to take medicines.

I become constipated rarely_____ occasionally_____ never_____.

Urination is usually easy_____ rather difficult _____ difficult _____.

The phone number of the nearest Poison Control Center is _____.

I sleep well _____ OK _____ poorly_____ little _____ on most nights.

I have _____ have never _____ had blood problems in the past.

I am considering becoming _____ might be _____ am _____ pregnant.

I want the medications that offer the best balance of price and outcomes for my specific medical history and present conditions.

TABLE 15

The Medication Map

Getting four new prescriptions often means that you will get four brief patient package inserts or papers stapled to the pharmacy bag when you pick up your prescriptions. Rarely does anyone take the time to understand YOUR INDIVIDUAL day and select medicines based on how your day REALLY works or help you fit the medicines into the way that you actually live. I believe that this is a critical cause of drug interactions, irrational drug combinations, and taking the medicine incorrectly. It also dooms to failure what otherwise might be brilliant use of medicines.

This reality contributes to the more than 100 billion dollars spent EACH YEAR and leads to the more than 100,000 deaths caused by the medicine itself. I can't begin to count the number of times I've found that medicines prescribed three times a day were actually only taken twice a day or less. The cure can easily become the disease.

Use the map below to talk with your doctor or pharmacist to schedule your prescription, nonprescription, or herbal medicines as you really plan or are able to take them. Make sure the timing and combinations are OK! Important questions to ask include:

Have all of these medicines been checked for drug interactions?

Do I really need to take all of these medicines at this time?

Are there newer medicines that might have fewer possible side effects or that might treat the conditions or diseases being treated more effectively (get better results or outcomes)?

Are there medicines that only need to be taken twice or once daily that could be substituted for one or more of those I take now?

Can food react with any of the medicines I take?

	Medicine and dose planned:	
Midnight	Medicine and dose planned:	
1 A.M.	Medicine and dose planned:	
2 A.M.	Medicine and dose planned:	
3 A.M.	Medicine and dose planned:	
4 A.M.	Medicine and dose planned:	
5 A.M.	Medicine and dose planned:	
6 A.M.	Medicine and dose planned:	
7 A.M.	Medicine and dose planned:	*Morning Meal Time:*
8 A.M.	Medicine and dose planned:	
9 A.M.	Medicine and dose planned:	
10 A.M.	Medicine and dose planned:	
11 A.M.	Medicine and dose planned:	
12 noon	Medicine and dose planned:	*Lunch or Brunch Time:*
1 P.M.	Medicine and dose planned:	
2 P.M.	Medicine and dose planned:	
3 P.M.	Medicine and dose planned:	
4 P.M.	Medicine and dose planned:	
5 P.M.	Medicine and dose planned:	
6 P.M.	Medicine and dose planned:	*Evening Meal Time:*
7 P.M.	Medicine and dose planned:	
8 P.M.	Medicine and dose planned:	
9 P.M.	Medicine and dose planned:	*Snack Time (if any):*
10 P.M.	Medicine and dose planned:	
11 P.M.	Medicine and dose planned:	

TABLE 16

Medicines Removed from the Market

Once again, either the FDA or the companies that make medicines have seen fit to remove some medicines from the market. As in the 2000 edition, I've included prior removals for continuity. While removals could be seen as disconcerting, it also shows that the Phase Four (reporting after a drug is FDA-approved) system sometimes works. This also means that more than ever, you need to be a partner in your health care! Talk to your doctor right away if you suspect you are having a reaction to one of your medicines. It is literally impossible for the FDA to check EVERY medicine against one that is pending approval for possible drug interactions or side effects. Encourage your doctor to report serious new adverse effects to the company that makes the drug or to the FDA (FDA MedWatch can be reached at 1-800-332-1088).

The information in this table will be updated for each subsequent *Essential Guide* edition. The listings will give the general category to which the medicine belongs, the generic name and at least one brand name, and the reason for removal. While the web address and location give a rough idea of the date of removal, beginning with the 2002 edition, removals will have the FDA Med-Watch removal report date with each new listing.

Antibiotics

grepafloxacin (Raxar)   Reason removed: Risks of adverse effects (abnormal heart rhythms or arrhythmias) outweighed the benefits.

sparfloxacin (Zagam)   Reason removed: Drug interactions, safety profile.

Antidiabetic Drugs (Diabetes Treatments)

troglitazone (Rezulin)   Reason removed: Negative publicity regarding liver damage and death precluded effective use of the product. The FDA requested and the company voluntarily removed the medicine.

Antipsoriatic Drugs (Psoriasis Treatments)

etretinate (Tegison)   Reason removed: Newer medicines available.

Cholesterol-Reducing Drugs

probucol (Lorelco)   Reason removed: More effective medicines available.

cerivastatin (Baycol)   Reason removed: Reports of sometimes fatal muscle damage (rhabdomyolysis)
FDA MedWatch report date 8/9/01: *www.fda.gov/medwatch/safety/2001safety01.html#bayco2*

Gastrointestinal Medicines (GERD, heartburn)

cisapride (Propulsid)   Reason removed: Serious cardiovascular side effects and drug interactions with multiple drugs.
More information can be found at *www.fda.gov/medwatch/safety/2000/safety00.htm#propul.*

Herbal Medicines (Various indications and there have been a variety of herbs and herbal products)

Aristolochic Acid (Akebia Trifoliata Caulis-Mu Tong and Asarum Sieboldii Herba cum Radix-Xi Xin)   Reason removed: aristolochic acid has been found to be a potent carcinogen and has been associated with several kidney failure cases. More information can be found at *www.fda.gov/medwatch/satety/2001/safety01.htm#aristo.*

High Blood Pressure Medicines (antihypertensives)

mibefradil (Posicor)   Reason removed: Serious drug interactions with multiple drugs. More information is at *www.fda.gov/bbs/topice/answers/ans00876.html.*

Immunosuppressant

cyclosporine (Gegraf form only)   Reason removed: Found NOT to be bioequivalent to Neoral when mixed with apple juice.
More information is at *www.fda.gov.*

Irritable Bowel Syndrome Treatment

alosetron (Lotronex)   Reason removed: Voluntarily withdrawn because of serious bowel impactions, ischemic colitis cases, and deaths. More information is available from the FDA at *www.fda.gov.* Subsequently, patient groups started a petition drive to have this medicine **reconsidered** for use in the US. On June 7, 2002, the FDA announced approval of a supplemental New Drug

Application (sNDA) that permitted the marketing of alosetron (Lotronex) with restrictions. Restrictions include a prescribing program for prescribers, restriction to treatment of women with severe, diarrhea predominant Irritable Bowel Syndrome (IBS), who have failed to respond to conventional IBS therapy, patient education, and event reporting as well as assessment of the risk management program and other measures. For more information, go to. *www.fda.gov/bbs/topics/NEWS/2002/ NEW00814.html*.

Minimally Sedating Antihistamines

astemizole (Hismanal)
Reason removed: Voluntarily withdrawn because of serious drug interactions with multiple drugs. More information is available at: *http://www.fda.gov/ bbs/topics/answers/ans00961.html*

terfenadine (Seldane)
Reason removed: Voluntarily withdrawn because of serious drug interactions with multiple drugs. Find more info at: *www.fda.gov/bbs/topics/answers/ ans00843.html*.

Vaccines

Rotavirus vaccine (RotaShield)
Reason removed: Withdrawn because it can cause the bowel to collapse or telescope onto itself (intussusception). Find out more at *www.fda.gov*.

Weight Loss Agents (Anorexiants)

dexfenfluramine (Redux)
Reason removed: Possible heart valve damage.

fenfluramine (Pondimin)
Reason removed: Possible heart valve damage. Questions and answers about this can be found at *www.fda.gov/cder/news/fenphenqa2.htm*.

TABLE 17

Helpful, Balanced, and Objective Web Sites

There has been an explosion of information available on the Internet. Unfortunately, like information found elsewhere, all of it is NOT reliable. From my own activities in research, and from my experience with MY Web site, I'm please to augment this new table that tells you about Web sites that I've found to offer balanced, objective, and scientifically rigorous information. I've also added three sites that have been highly rated in a survey by the Rowin Group. Happy surfing, and ALWAYS TALK TO YOUR HEALTH CARE PROVIDER BEFORE YOU CHANGE ANY THERAPY.

To find information on AFFORDING YOUR MEDICINES (many companies have programs based on income for help getting the medicine)

For your doctor or prescriber (sponsored by a Robert Wood Johnson grant): *www.rxassist.org*.

For YOU to find out more about companies offering medicines at reduced prices based on income: *www.needymeds.com*.

To find information on Taking your Medicines (adherence, compliance, or concordance)

www.4woman.gov
www.acog.org
www.nwhn.org
www.fda.gov/womens/tttc.html
www.health.gov/healthypeople
www.medicineinfo.com
www.medscape.com
www.aarp.org
www.talkaboutrx.org
www.americanheart.org/CAP/

To find information on Addiction

www.asam.org
www.samhsa.gov
www.paimed.org

To find information on AIDS

www.amfar.org
www.cdc.org
www.Hopkins-aids.edu

To find information on Anxiety

www.nimh.nih.gov/anxiety

To find information on Arthritis

www.arthritis.org
www.niams.nih.gov
www.rheumatology.org
www.hopkins-arthritis.som.jhmi.edu
www.arthritis.ca/home.html

To find information on Attention Deficit/Hyperactivity Disorder Guidelines

www.pediatrics.org

To find information on Bacteria that have become resistant to treatment

www.fda.gov/oc/opacom/hottopics/anti_resist.html

To find information on Cancer

www.cancer.org
www.clinicaltrials.gov
www.fda.gov/cder/cancer
www.cancertrails.nci.nih.gov
www.fda.gov/bs/topics/NEWS/2001/NEW00766.html
www.cancer.med.upenn.edu

To find information on Colon Cancer

www.cancer.gov/cancerinfo/pdg/treatment/colon/HealthProfessional

To find information on Counterfeit Medicines

www.fda.gov/medwatch/safety/2001/sero_faked.html
www.amgen.com/news/news01/release01510.html
www.gene.com/gene/products/nutropin_aq/product_update.html

To find information on How to Stop Smoking (Cessation)

www.lungusa.org

To find information on Cholesterol-Reducing Drugs

www.americanheart.org
www.americanheart.org/getwiththeguidelines.html
www.acc.org
www.nhlbi.nih.gov

To find information on cold sores (Herpes simplex)

www.coldsource.com

To find highly rated Consumer-Oriented Web sites (breast cancer treatment, heartburn/ulcer treatment and high cholesterol treatment)

www.nolvadex.com
www.prevacid.com
www.zocor.com

To find information on Health Care Policy and Research

www.ahcpr.gov

To find information on the Heart and Heart Health

www.acc.org
www.americanheart.org
www.clevelandclinic.org
www.sln.fi.edu/biosci/heart.html
www.med.yale.edu/library/heartbk/

To find information on Herpes (Genital)

www.denavir.com
www.famvir.com
Herpeshelp (accessed at *www.zovirax.com*)
www.idsa.org
www.valtrex.com

To find information on Hospital Accreditation

www.jcaho.org

To find High Blood Pressure Medicines (Antihypertensives)

www.americanheart.org
www.cdc.gov
www.acc.org
www.nhlbi.nih.gov
www.nhlbi.nih.gov/hbp
www.nhlbi.nih.gov/guidelines/hypertensoin/index.htm
www.ash-us.org

To find the FDA

www.fda.gov

To find out about Herbal Supplements and Disease/Structure Function Claims and Prudent Steps Regarding Herbals

http://vm.cfsan.fda.gov/;sllrd/fr000106.html
www.talkaboutrx.org

To find information on Immunizations (shots)

www.cdc.gov/nip/recs/child-schedule.htm

To find information on Macular Degeneration

www.macular.org
www.maculardegeneration.org
www.maculardisease.org

To find information on Medicines for our Canadian neighbors

www.hc-sc.gc.ca
www.gov.on.ca
www.canadianpainsociety.ca
www.heartandstroke.ca

To find information on Menopause

www.acog.org
www.americanheart.org
www.asrm.org
www.menopause.org
www.4woman.gov

To find out about Nutrition

www.americanheart.org
www.eatright.org

To find out about Osteoporosis

www.nof.org
www.asbmr.org
www.iscd.org
gwww.strongerbones.org

To find information about Pain and Pain Guidelines

www.ahcpr.gov
www.ampainsoc.org
www.jcaho.org/standard/pm_hap.html
www.painandhealth.org
www.pain.com
www.painmed.org

To find information on Pediatrics

www.aap.org
www.tchin.org

To find information on Pharmacies on the Internet (see VIPPS Seal in the glossary—tells you that a site on the Internet is a valid pharmacy)

www.pharmacyandyou.org

To find information on Pre-diabetes and Diabetes

www.diabetes.org

To find information on Pregnancy and Medicine Effects

www.fda.gov/womens/registries/default.htm

To find information on Reproductive Health/Contraception

www.acog.org
www.amwa.org
www.nwhn.org
www.plannedparenthood.org
www.americanheart.org (as contraception impacts cardiovascular system)

To find information on Research Involving Medicines

www.clinicaltrials.gov

To find information on Rheumatoid Arthritis

www.acr.org The American College of Rheumatology
www.arthritis.org The Arthritis Foundation

To find information on shots (Immunizations)

www.cdc.gov/nip/recs/child-schedule.htm

To find information on Strokes

www.apacure.com
www.strokes.org

To find information on Transplantation

www.otf.org

To find information on Health Around the World

www.cdc.gov

To find information on Weight Control

www.americanheart.org/heart_and_stroke_A_Z_guide/obesity.html
www.eatright.org
www.naaso.org

TABLE 18

Powerful Patients and Home Test Kits

"You'll need to go to the hospital laboratory and get that checked." I remember telling many patients about blood tests, blood levels, and a variety of other reasons that they would need to have blood taken when I was telling them about their new prescriptions. Fortunately, there has been an explosion of new technology to give the power of checking results from medicines to YOU! This is a wonderful development. Not only does it help same some money in the long run—it also puts you in the driver's seat. I'll take a hard look at ten common diseases or conditions where lab tests are needed and want to bring you awareness of devices or strategies (some Web or smart card enabled or enhanced) to help make sure you are getting the benefits while avoiding the risks of your medicines! For now, I'll start with adherence, expand to a total of six disease states for the next edition, and round it out to ten in 2005!

To find information on taking your medicines (adherence, compliance, or concordance)

www.4woman.gov
www.acog.org
www.health.gov/healthypeople
www.medicineinfo.com
www.medscape.com
www.aarp.org
www.talkaboutrx.org
www.americanheart.org/CAP/

Very clearly, the group at e-pill has taken a lead role in a range of devices that range from beeper-based systems to a beeping pill bottle cap that tells you it is time to take control of that disease or condition by taking your medicine! Find out more by visiting *www.epill.com.* **Call them at 1-800-549-0095.**

TABLE 19

Running a Risk: Recognizing and Regaining Control of Heart Disease Risk Factors

The National Cholesterol Education Adult Treatment Panel number three (NCEP ATP III) is without a doubt a blueprint of rational steps to take to control your risk of heart disease. There have been many many reviews of these steps as well as of the risk factors themselves. I'll update this table once the more practical approaches have been sorted out.

For now: there are a number of sites that can help you calculate the ten-year risk of death (based on a large study typically referred to as Framingham). I had the opportunity to meet Joseph Scheese from Scientific Software Tools, Inc. at the recent American Diabetes Association Meeting. What Joe showed me was not only the most impressive risk tool I have seen, it also provided input on important new technologies such as electron beam computed tomography (EBCT—see *www.heartsavers.md*) and a host of new risk factors that are also important. Because I think that some of the risk factors will change, I will take the most conservative step of:

1) Referring you to your doctor to have this very important discussion about Heart Disease Risk Factors and preventing heart disease. Clearly, your doctor who has your individual patient history, laboratory results, and results from existing medicines is in the best position to give you the most valuable estimation of risk. There are also a host of emerging risk factors that are important to talk to your doctor about (such as small LDL particles and at least seven different kinds of LDL, HDL subspecies of at least five different kinds, homocysteine, CRP, and apolipoproteins)!

2) Referring you to the National Heart, Lung and Blood Institute (NHLBI) at *www.nhlbi.nih.gov* where the new guidelines were created. The actual guidelines can be seen at *www.nhlbi.nih.gov/guidelines/cholesterol/atp3_rpt .htm*. From the NCEP ATP III report: critical factors to learn more about include: LDL Cholesterol, total cholesterol, and HDL cholesterol. Additionally, diabetes, clinical heart disease, peripheral artery disease, carotid artery disease, aneurysm of the abdominal aorta, and people with more than a 20% 10-year risk of MI or CHD death confer high risk for coronary heart disease. Other than LDL, LOW HDL, family history of premature

heart disease, cigarette smoking, blood pressure greater than or equal to 140/90 and even taking medicines for high blood pressure counts as added risk although it helps control the pressure. Importantly, risk factors that can be changed: the modifiable include inactivity, hypertension, cigarette smoking, being overweight, and having an artery clogging (atherogenic) diet.

The factors in the ten year risk tables that are used to determine heart attack (MI) or CHD death risk as a percentage (based on the data gathered from the Framingham study) are a starting point to help you become a powerful patient in controlling risk: Total Cholesterol, Smoking (please try to quit), HDL, Blood Pressure, and age (risk increases as we get older).

3) Promising you that if there is any way possible to integrate the Scientific Software Tool into my *www.medicineinfo.com* site—I will work with Joe and his colleagues to bring you this important feature!

4) One of the most important risk factors to emerge in heart disease is called C Reactive Protein (CRP)! A study published in the November 14, 2002 *New England Journal of Medicine* (see Ridker, P.M. in the Sources section) found that bad cholesterol (Low Density Lipoprotein or LDL) and CRP were very useful in finding people at risk for heart and blood vessel (cardiovascular) problems. More importantly, a researcher named Paul Ridker determined that CRP and LDL determine and define risk for DIFFERENT groups. The way that I think of this is that people with low LDL and CRP are at low risk. People with high levels of LDL and CRP are at high risk. The critical point is that those with low LDL and high CRP are at higher risk for heart and blood vessel problems than people with high LDL and low CRP. This research was of such importance that a new set of guidelines (albeit conservative ones) were released by the American Heart Association for who should be tested for CRP levels. Many of you know that I have a terrible family history for diabetes and heart disease. When I discussed this with my doctor and a CRP was checked—it came back very elevated. Fortunately—a high CRP can be treated effectively. Stains, also known as HMG-CoA reductase inhibitors (see drug classes), work very well in this area. Most clinicians would also add on low dose aspirin as well in order to further decrease risk.

TABLE 20

Living Longer (Longevity) With Therapeutic Lifestyle Changes

The NCEP ATP 3 report increased awareness of therapeutic lifestyle changes and how these changes can help YOU control your risk of heart disease! The new high blood pressure guidelines: JNC VII can be seen at *www.nhlbi.nih.gov/guidelines/hypertension/index.htm*. Once again, LIFESTYLE changes pop up.

Once again, I want to encourage you to be a powerful patient and have a discussion with your doctor about therapeutic lifestyle changes that apply to YOU. Interestingly, the latest guidelines from the National Institutes of Health recommend that doctors *work with patients* to agree on blood pressure goals and to develop a plan for treatment (see Chobanian, A.V. in Sources below).

1) You can find the full ATP III guidelines at: *www.nhlbi.nih.gov/guidelines/cholesterol/atp3_rpt.htm*. When you make that next appointment with your doctor make it clear that you want to spend time talking about the ATP III guidelines and therapeutic lifestyle changes! Because of the need to indi-

vidualize lifestyle changes to YOU and your specific situation, I think this discussion is best undertaken with your doctor.

2) To find the specific general lifestyle changes, please visit the full ATP III guidelines and look specifically at Section FIVE, Parts One through Six. Once again, this is a blueprint for general changes which can (with the help of your doctor, lipid clinic nurse, and specially trained pharmacists) be adjusted specifically to you to get THE BEST POSSIBLE RESULTS. Become a powerful patient using therapeutic lifestyle changes in combination with medicines to be healthier!

3) The new high blood pressure guidelines (JNC VII—see Chobanian, A.V. in Sources) advocate the use of the DASH diet (Dietary Approaches to Stop Hypertension), aerobic exercise, moderate alcohol intake, and lower sodium in order to help control blood pressure. While I know it isn't easy, losing some weight (YOU DON'T HAVE TO DO IT ALL AT ONCE), helps lower risk of diabetes, can help keep pre-hypertension in an even lower range, and can lower those blood pressure numbers by 5–20 mm of Hg for each 10 kg. The National Heart, Lung, and Blood Institute [NHLBI] (from a committee of the NHLBI and National Institutes of Health-NIH, which is called the Coordinating Committee of the NHLBI National High Blood Pressure Education Program, (NHBPEP) has consumer-friendlly information and resources at *www.nhlbi.nih.gov/hbp*. For now, even doing more in the sense of exercising, even if you don't lose weight, may make the kind of cholesterol that your body makes change to a more desirable form!

TABLE 21

How to Get Help With the Cost of Medicines
(Programs and Web Sites)

"How am I going to afford these medicines?" So many patients have asked me this over the years. I've decided to focus on the issue and identify some strategies, programs, and Web sites that can help! I hope that there will be a Medicare Prescription package but, as yet, I'm still not certain.

Strategies:

The immediate problem is affording the medicines actually starts with your doctor.

1) In the Office
   a. Ask the price question early. A great study by Blue Cross and Shield (*www.bcbsm.com*) in Michigan found that savings from patients who asked for generics could be more than 50%. Ask your doctor!
   b. Some states offer coverage. Roughly 30 have some kind of benefit at the time of this writing. Visit the National Conference of State Legislatures (*www.ncsl.org/programs/health/drugaid.htm*).
   c. Dual Price substitution. Once the medicine is chosen and the prescription almost written, it's important to ask about the expense. Did you know that sometimes, there are actually different prices for the same medicine? It's true—and it's called dual price substitution. There are some new office-based programs that your doctor may have that can pick between various brand names to find the best price!

2) Local area on aging:1-800-677-1116 can help with community based services. Visit the eldercare website at *www.eldercare.gov.*

3) Hospital based programs (social services): While you are still in the hospital, ask your doctor to find out about available social services. So many times, social services can arrive right at the bedside, help with paperwork, and make sense of your situation.

4) The VA. Did you forget that you have a family member who is a vet? It's easy to lose track of the prescription medicine benefit that may be available to YOU. Call the VA at 1-877-222-8387. You can also visit the VA on the web at *www.va.gov.*

5) Controversial strategies: There are so many controversial aspects about going or ordering medicines (even with a valid prescription) from another country. At the time of this writing, the situation is so fluid, I will only mention that the FDA has a statement on this at *www.fda.gov.*
   a. Canada or Mexico

6) General information on special programs from the pharmaceutical companies could be a phone call away. Try 1-800-762-4636 or go to the web at *www.pharma.org.*

Programs: There are a huge variety of company programs. Some of the companies are:

Abbott Laboratories (see Together Rx Card)

Bristol Myers Squibb Patient Assistance Foundation, Inc.:
C/O McKesson P.O. Box 52112
Phoenix, Arizona 85072-2112
Phone:1-800-736-0003
Fax:1-800-736-1611
On the web at: *www.bms.com*

GlaxoSmithKline Patient Assistance Foundation, Inc.:
C/O McKesson P.O. Box 52112
Phoenix, Arizona 85072-2112
Phone:1-800-736-0003
Fax:1-800-736-1611
On the web at: *www.bms.com*

Johnson & Johnson Patient Assistance Foundation, Inc.:
C/O McKesson P.O. Box 52112
Phoenix, Arizona 85072-2112
Phone:1-800-736-0003
Fax:1-800-736-1611
On the web at: *www.bms.com*

Merck Patient Assistance Foundation, Inc.:
C/O McKesson P.O. Box 52112
Phoenix, Arizona 85072-2112
Phone:1-800-736-0003
Fax:1-800-736-1611
On the web at: *www.bms.com*

Novartis Patient Assistance Foundation, Inc.:
C/O McKesson P.O. Box 52112
Phoenix, Arizona 85072-2112
Phone: 1-800-736-0003
Fax: 1-800-736-1611
On the web at: *www.bms.com*

Pfizer Patient Assistance Foundation, Inc.:
C/O McKesson P.O. Box 52112
Phoenix, Arizona 85072-2112
Phone: 1-800-736-0003
Fax: 1-800-736-1611
On the web at: *www.bms.com*

Roche Patient Assistance Foundation, Inc.:
C/O McKesson P.O. Box 52112
Phoenix, Arizona 85072-2112
Phone: 1-800-736-0003
Fax: 1-800-736-1611
On the web at:*www.bms.com*

Wyeth Patient Assistance Foundation, Inc.:
C/O McKesson P.O. Box 52112
Phoenix, Arizona 85072-2112
Phone: 1-800-736-0003
Fax: 1-800-736-1611
On the web at: *www.bms.com*

Multiple Company Programs:

Together Rx Card: **Founding members include Abbott Laboratories, Astra-Zeneca, Aventis, Bristol-Myers Squibb, GlaxoSmithKline, Janssen Pharmaceutica, Novartis, and Ortho-McNeil Pharmaceutical:**
Medicines covered by this program for the individual companies are shown on the web at: *www.togetherrx.com/allience.html* and are also listed on their individual company web sites (www dot the name of the company dot com).

Balanced and Objective Web Sites:

www.rxassist.org **This site was started by a group from Brown University which was funded by a Robert Wood Johnson Foundation grant. It was originally intended for doctors, but has a listing of consumer friendly sources which are very helpful.**
www.needymeds.com **This site was started by a physician and a nurse who wanted to provide a resource for patients.**

Sources

The following sources were consulted in the compilation and revision of this book:

Abramowicz, M., ed. *The Choice of Antibacterial Drugs: The Medical Letter on Drugs and Therapeutics.* 1999. New Rochelle, NY: The Medical Letter.

Abramowicz, M., ed. *Drug Interactions: The Medical Letter on Drugs and Therapeutics.* Vol. 41 (issue 1056), July 2, 1999. New Rochelle, NY: The Medical Letter.

Abramowicz, M., ed. *Drugs of Choice: The Medical Letter on Drugs and Therapeutics.* 1997. New Rochelle, NY: The Medical Letter.

Abramowicz, M., ed. *Drugs of Choice: The Medical Letter on Drugs and Therapeutics.* 1999. New Rochelle, NY: The Medical Letter.

Abramowicz, M., ed. *Drugs of Choice: The Medical Letter on Drugs and Therapeutics.* 2001. New Rochelle, NY: The Medical Letter.

Abramowicz, M., ed. *Rofecoxib for Osteoarthritis Pain: The Medical Letter on Drugs and Therapeutics.* Vol. 41 (issue 1056), July 2, 1999. New Rochelle, NY: The Medical Letter.

Abramowicz, M., ed. *Some Drugs That Cause Psychiatric Symptoms: The Medical Letter on Drugs and Therapeutics.* 1998. New Rochelle, NY: The Medical Letter.

Ackerman B.H. and Kasbekar N. Disturbances of Taste and Smell Induced by Drugs. *Pharmacotherapy* 17(3):482–496. 1997.

ACR Cinical Guidelines Committee, ed† C. Guidelines for RA Management. *Arthritis & Rheumatism.* 39; 5:713–722, May 1996

Adami H.O. and Trichopoulos D. Obesity and Mortality from Cancer. *New England Journal of Medicine.* 2003; 348(17):1623–4.

Adrogue H.J. and Madias N.E. Hyponatremia. *New England Journal of Medicine* 342(21):1581–1589. 2000.

Adult Treatment Panel 3 (ATP III). Third Report of the National Cholesterol Education Program (NCEP) Expert Panel on Detection, Evaluation, and Treatment of High Blood Cholesterol in Adults. June, 2001. The National Institutes of Health.

Advances in Osteoporosis. 1996, 1997.

Agarwala S. et al. Alendronate in the treatment of avascular necrosis of the hip. Rheumatology. 2002; 41:346–357.

AIDS Clinical Care. 1997, 1998, 1999, 2000. Boston: Massachusetts Medical Society.

Albert, C.H., et al. Blood levels of long-chain n-3fatty acids and the risk of sudden death. *New England Journal of Medicine.* 346(15):1113–1118. 2002.

Altshuler, L.L., et al. Does thyroid supplementation accelerate tricyclic antidepressant response? A review and meta-analysis of the literature. *American Journal of Psychiatry.* 2001;158:1617–1622.

Amended report from NAMS Advisory Panel on Postmenopausal Hormone Therapy. *Menopause* 2003; 10:6–12.

American Academy of Pediatrics Subcommittee on Attention-Deficit/Hyperactivity Disorder and Committee on Quality Improvement. Clinical Practice Guideline: treatment of the school-aged child with attention-deficit/hyperactivity disorder. *Pecdiatrics. 200; 108: 1033–1044.*

American Botanical Society. *The Complete German Commission E Monographs Therapeutic Guide to Herbal Medicines.* 1st ed. 1998. Austin, Texas: American Botanical Council and Integrative Medicine Communications.

American College of Cardiology. ACC/AHA Guideline Update for the Management of Patients with Unstable Angina and NonST-Segment Elevation Myocardial Infarction (NSTEMI). CD-Rom released March, 2002.

American Heart Association. *2001 Heart and Stroke Statistical Update.* Dallas, Texas: American Heart Association, 2000.

American Heart Association. *2002–2003 Heart and Stroke Statistical Update.* Dallas, Texas: American Heart Association, 2001, 2002.

American Heart Association. *Get With the Guidelines.* On www.americanheart.org. Dallas, Texas: American Heart Association, 2001.

American Journal of Clinical Nutrition. Harper, A. E., ed. Physiologically Active Food Components: Their Role in Optimizing Health and Aging. June 2000. Weston, MA.

American Journal of Hospice and Palliative Care. Enk, R., ed. 1998. Weston, MA.

American Medical Association (AMA), Joint Commission on Accreditation of Healthcare Organizations (JCAHO) and the National Committee for Quality Assurance (NCQA). *Coordinated Performance Measurement for the Management of Adult Diabetes.* April 2001, pages 1–42. 2001.

American Pain Society Arthritis Pain Management Panel. *Guidelines for the Management of Pain in Osteoarthritis, Rheumatoid Arthritis, and Juvenile Chronic Arthritis.* American Pain Society, Glenview IL, 2002.

American Pain Society Quality of Care Committee. *Quality Improvement Guidelines for the Treatment of Acute Pain and Cancer Pain.* Journal of the American Medical Association, December 20, 1995, pages 1874–1880.

American Pharmaceutical Association Special Report: A Review of the Sixth Report of the Joint National Committee on Prevention, Detection, Evaluation, and Treatment of High Blood Pressure. 1998. Washington, DC: American Pharmaceutical Association.

American Psychiatric Association. *American Psychiatric Association Practice Guidelines for the Treatment of Psychiatric Disorders: Compendium 2002.* American Psychiatric Publishing, Inc. Washington, D.C.

Andersen, K., et. al. Aspirin non-responsiveness as measured by PFA-100 in patients with coronary artery disease. Thromb Res 2003; 108:37–42.

Anderson, A.S., et al. Current Management of Chronic Heart Failure. *Postgraduate Medicine.* 109(3):35–61. March, 2001.

Annals of Pharmacotherapy. 1996–1998. Cincinnati, OH: Harvey Whitney Books.

Andre, M. et al. Phase III randomized study comparing 5 or 10 microg per kg per day of filgrastim for mobilization of peripheral blood progenitor cells with chemotherapy, followed by intensification and autologous transplantation in patients with nonmyeloid malignancies. *Transfusion.* 2003 Jan. 43(1):50–7.

Antonicelli, R. et al. Smooth blood pressure control obtained with extended-release felodipine in elderly patients with hypertension: evaluation by 24-hour ambulatory blood pressure monitoring. *Drugs Aging.* 2002; 19(7):541–51.

Aparasu, R.R. and Flinginger, S. E. Inappropriate Medication Prescribing for the Elderly by Office-Based Physicians. *Annals of Pharmacotherapy.* 31:823–836. July/August, 1997.

ARRIVE Registry: Advanced Resuscitation of Refractory VT/VF I.V. Amiodarone Evaluation. Accessed from www.Cordarone.com/news/arrive.asp. April, 2003.

Asztalos B.F. et al. High-density lipoprotein subpopulations in pathologic conditions. *American Journal of Cardiology* 2003 April 3; 91(7A):12E-17E.

Ascott-Evans, B.H., et al. Alendronate prevents loss of bone density associated with discontinuation of hormone replacement therapy. *Archives Internal Medicine 2003.* 163:789–794.

Avorn, J. et al. Persistence of use of lipid-lowering medications: a cross-national study. *JAMA.* 18:1458–62. May 13, 1998.

Bacon et al. Training and supporting pharmacists to supply progestogen-only emergency contraception. *Journal of Family Planning and Reproductive Health Care* 2003 April, 29(2):17–22

Baigent, C. et al. Selective Cyclooxygenase 2 Inhibitors, Aspirin, and Cardiovascular Disease. *Arthritis & Rheumatism* 48; 1:12–20. January 2003.

Baker, D.E. Pegylated interferon plus ribavirin for the treatment of chronic hepatitis C. *Review in Gastroenterology Discord* Spring 2003; 3(2):93–109.

Ballantyne C.M. et al. Effect of Ezetimibe Coadministered With Atorvastatin in 628 Patients With Primary Hypercholesterolemia. A Prospective, Randomized, Double-Blind Trial. *Circulation.* April 28, 2003 (epub ahead of print).

Barbieri, R.L. et al. Insulin stimulates androgen accumulation in incubations of ovarian stroma obtained from women with hyperandrogenism. *Journal of Clinical Endocrinology and Metabolism* 1986; 62:904–10.

Baron, J.A., et al. Calcium Supplements for the Prevention of Colorectal Adenomas. *New England Journal of Medicine.* 340:101–107. January 14, 1999.

Baron, J.A., et al. A Ranedomized Trial of Aspirin to Prevent Colorectal Adenomas. *New England Journal of Medicine 2003.* 348:891–899.

Barrett-Connor E., et al. Raloxifene and cardiovascular events in osteoporotic postmenopausal women: Four-year results from the MORE (Multiple Outcomes of Raloxifene Evaluation) randomized trial. *JAMA Feb. 20, 2002; 287:847–857.*

Bartlett, J., et al. *The Hopkins HIV Report.* Volume 13, Number 3 (Updated Guidelines for Managing HIV in Pregnancy From the USPHS Task Force and Update from the 8th CROI: Adverse Effects of HAART and Structured Treatment Interruption, Number 4. The Johns Hopkins University AIDS Service, Division of Infectious Diseases. 2001.

Bartlett, J. *The Johns Hopkins Hospital 1996 Guide to Medical Care of Patients with HIV Infection.* Baltimore: Williams and Wilkins.

Bartlett, J. *Medical Management of HIV Infection: 1998 Edition.* Baltimore: Port City Press.

Bartlett, J.G. and Gallant, J.E. 2000–2001 *Medical Management of HIV Infection.* Baltimore: Port City Press.

Bartlett, J.G. and Gallant, J.E. 2003 *Medical Management of HIV Infection.* Johns Hopkins University, Baltimore.

Bates, D., et al. Effect of Computerized Physician Order Entry and a Team Intervention on Prevention of Serious Medication Errors. *Journal of the American Medical Association.* 280(15):1311–1316. October 21, 1998.

Bays, H., et al. *The ADVOCATE Study.* The 51st Scientific Session of the American College of Cardiology National Meeting. Atlanta, GA, USA March 2002.

Beard, S. L. HMG-CoA Reductase Inhibitors: Assessing Differences in Drug Interactions and Safety Profiles. *Journal of the American Pharmaceutical Association Sept/Oct 2000.* 40(5):637–644. 2000.

Beckman, S. E., et al., Consumer Use of St. John's Wort: A Survey on Effectiveness, Safety and Tolerability. *Pharmacotherapy 2000.* 20(5):568–574. 2000.

Belch, J.J., et al. Critical issues in peripheral arterial disease detection and management: a call to action. *Archives of Internal Medicine* 2003:163(8)884–892.

Bell, N.H. et al. Alendronate Increases Bone Mass and Reduces Bone Markers in Postmenopausal African-American Women. *Journal of Clinical Endocrinology and Metabolism* June 2002, 87(6): 2792–2797.

Berchou, R. C. and Scheife, R. T. Contemporary Issues in the Pharmacotherapy of Parkinson's Disease. *Pharmacotherapy the Journal of Human Pharmacology and Drug Therapy.* Vol. 20, No. 1 Part 2, January, 2000.

Berger, K., et al. Light-to-Moderate Alcohol Consumption and the Risk of Stroke Among U.S. Male Physicians. *New England Journal of Medicine.* 341(21):1557. November 18, 1999.

Berkow, R., ed. *The Merck Manual.* 15th ed. 1996. Rahway, NJ: Merck Sharp and Dohme Research Laboratories.

Bittner, V., Treatment of dyslipidemia in pre- and postmenopausal women with and without known atherosclerotic cardiovascular disease. *Current Cardiology Report 2001 Sep; 3(5): 401–407.*

Black, C. and Jick, H. Etiology and Frequency Rhabdomyolysis. *Pharmacotherapy* 2002; 22(12):1524–1526.

Black, S., et al. Efficacy, safety and immunogenicity of heptavalent pneumococcal conjugate vaccine in children. *Pediatric Infections Disease Journal* 2000; 19(3):187–195.

Blair, S.N., et al. Incremental Reduction of Serum Total Cholesterol and Low-Density

Lipoprotein Cholesterol With the Addition of Plant Stanol Ester-Containing Spread to Statin Therapy. *Journal of the American College of Cardiology.* 86(1):46–52. 2000.

Bloch Y et al. Hyperglycemia from olanzapine treatment in adolescents. *Journal of Child and Adolescent Psychopharmacology.* 2003 Spring; 13(1):97–102.

Bonnick, S. L. *The Osteoporosis Handbook.* 1994. Dallas: Taylor Publishing.

Boothby, L.A. and Doering, P.L. FDA Labeling System for Drugs in Pregnancy. *The Annals of Pharmacotherapy.* Vol. 35, No. 11, November, 2001.

Borenstein, D. *Back in Control: A Conventional and Complimentary Prescription for Eliminating Back Pain.* M. Evans, New York. 2001.

Bosch, J. et al. Use of ramipril in preventing stroke: double blind randomised trial. *British Medical Journal.* 2002; 324:699–703.

Boton, R. et al. Prevalence, pathogenesis and treatment of renal dysfunction associated with chronic lithium therapy. *American Journal of Kidney Diseases* 1987; 10(5):329–45.

Boullata, J. I. and Nace, A. M. Safety Issues with Herbal Medicine. *Pharmacotherapy: The Journal of Human Pharmacology and Drug Therapy.* 20(3):257–269. 2000.

Bowden, C.L. A Placebo-Controlled 18-Month Trial of Lamotrigine and Lithium Maintenance Treatment in Recently Manic or Hypomanic Patients with Bipolar I Disorder. *Archives of General Psychiatry* April 2003; 60:392–400.

Bowes, J. Concomitant Administration of Drugs Known to Decrease the Systemic Availability of Gatifloxacin. *Pharmacotherapy* 2002; 22(6):800–801

Braunstein, J.B. Tight control: The risk-versus-benefit game. *Diabetes Forecast.* April 1, 2002. Accessed from the American Diabetes Association web site at *www.diabetes.org.*

Braunwald, E., et al. ACC/AHA Guidelines for the Management of Patients with Unstable Angina and Non-ST-Segment Elevation Myocardial Infarction. *Journal of the American College of Cardiology vol. 36, 2000: 970–1062.*

Braunwald, E., et al. ACC/AHA Guidelines for the Management of Patients with Unstable Angina and Non-ST-Segment Elevation Myocardial Infarction. CD-Rom distributed at March, 2002 ACC meeting.

Briggs, G. G., Bodendorfer, T. W., Freeman, R. K., and S. J. Yaffee. *Drugs in Pregnancy and Lactation.* 1983. Baltimore: Williams and Wilkins.

Brodaty, H. et al. A Randomized Placebo-Controlled Trial of Risperidone for the Treatment of Aggression, Agitation and Psychosis of Dementia. *Journal of Clinical Psychiatry* 2003; 64:134–143.

Brooke, M. H. *A Clinician's View of Neuromuscular Diseases.* 2nd ed. 1986. Baltimore: Williams and Wilkins.

Bull, S.A., et al. Discontinuing or Switching Selective Serotonin-Reuptake Inhibitors. *The Annals of Pharmacotherapy 2002; 36:578–584.*

Burke, L. E. and Ockene, I. S. *Compliance in Healthcare and Research.* The American Heart Association. Futura Publishing Company, Armonk, NY 2000.

Business Wire: June 28, 2001. Roche and Trimeris Correct Previous Announcement on Complete Enrollment in T-20 Phase III Clinical Trial. Nutley, NJ and Durham, NC.

Buttgereit F., et al. Standardised nomenclature for glucocorticoid dosages and glucocorticoid treatment regimens: current questions and tentative answers in rheumatology. *Annals of Rheumatological Diseases* 2002; 61:718–722.

Calabrese, L.H. Molecular differences in anticytokine therapies. *Clinical and Experimental Rheumatology.* 2003 Mar–Apr; 21(2):241–8.

Cabana, M.D., et al. Why Don't Physicians Follow Clinical Practice Guidelines? A Framework for Improvement. *Journal of the American Medical Association,* 282:1458–1465.

Califf, R.M., et al. Underuse of aspirin in a referral population with documented coronary artery disease. *American Journal of Cardiology* 2002; 89:653–661.

Calle, E.E. et al. Overweight, Obesity and Mortality from Cancer in a Prospectively Studied Cohort of US Adults. *New England Journal of Medicine* 2003; 348(17):1625–1638.

Canadian Pharmaceutical Association, St. Paul's Hospital British Columbia Center of Excellence for HIV-AIDS. 1997, 1998. Vancouver, BC: Canadian Pharmaceutical Association.

Cape, R. *Aging: Its Complex Management.* 1978. Hagerstown, MD: Harper and Row.

CAPRIE Steering Committee. A randomised, blinded trial of clopidogrel versus aspirin in patients at risk of ischaemic events (CAPRIE). Lancet 1996; 348:1329–1339.

Caring for the Dying. 1996. American Board of Internal Medicine.

Carnahan, R. M., et al. Ziprasidone, a New Atypical Antipsychotic Drug. *Pharmacotherapy* 2001; 21(6):717–730. 2001.

Caron, M.F., and White, M. Evaluation of the Antihyperlipidemic Properties of Dietary Supplements. *Pharmacotherapy* 2001; 21(4):481–487. 2001.

Chavez, M.L. Natural Medicines An Evidence-Based Approach. *The Rx Consultant.* 11(1): 1–8. 2001.

Cheng, J.W.M., et al. Patient-Reported Adherence to Guidelines of the Sixth Joint National Committee on Prevention, Detection, Evaluation and Treatment of High Blood Pressure. *Pharmacotherapy* 2001; 21(7):828–841. 2001.

Cheshire, W.P. Defining the Role for Gabapentin in the Treatment of Trigeminal Neuralgia: A Retrospective Study. *The Journal of Pain* 2002; 3(2):137–142. 2002.

Classen, D.C., et al. Adverse Drug Events in Hospitalized Patients. *Journal of the American Medical Association.* 277:301–306. 1997.

Cha, J.K. et al. Changes in platelet p-selectin and in plasma C-reactive protein in acute atherosclerotic ischemic stroke treated with a loading dose of clopidogrel. *Journal of Thrombosis and Thrombolysis* 2002 Oct; 14(2):145–50.

Chan, F.K.L. et al. Celecoxib Versus Diclofenac and Omeprazole in Reducing the Risk of Recurrent Ulcer Bleeding in Patients with Arthritis. *New England Journal of Medicine* 2002; 347(26):2104–2110.

Chlebowski, R.T., et al. Influence of Estrogen Plus Progestin on Breast Cancer and Mammographyin Healthy Postmenopausal Women. *Journal of the American Medical Association* 2003; 289:3243–3253.

Chin, R.L. et al. Etanercept (Enbrel®) therapy for chronic inflammatory demyelinating polyneuropathy. *J Neurol Sci.* 2003 June 15; 210(1–2):19–21.

Chobanian, A.V. et al. The Seventh Report of the Joint National Committee on Prevention, Detection, Evaluation and Treatment of High Blood Pressure. *Journal of the American Medical Association* 2003; 289: (DOI 10.1001/jama.289.19.2560), Early Release Article posted May 14, 2003.

Choi, S.L., et al. The American Diabetes Association 63rd Scientific Sessions. Chicago, 2003.

Chow, C.C., et al. Oral Alendronate Increases Bone Mineral Density in Postmenopausal Women with Primary Hyperparathyroidism. *Journal of Clinical Endocrinology and Metabolism*, Feb 2003, 88(2): 581–587.

Cice, G. et al. Sustained-release diltiazem reduces myocardial ischemic episodes in end-stage renal disease: a double-blind, randomized, crossover, placebo-controlled trial. *Journal of the American Society of Nephrology.* 2003 Apr; 14(4):1006–11.

Clin-Alert. 1996–1997. Medford, NJ: Clin-Alert.

Clinisphere. Facts and Comparisons 2.0. 1999. St. Louis: Facts and Comparisons.

Compendium of Pharmaceuticals and Specialties. 26th ed. 1991. Ottawa: Canadian Pharmaceutical Association.

Cohen, J.D. PREDICT study results of a simulated study with OTC Pravachol. *Paper presentation: American Society for Clinical Pharmacology and Therapeutics.* Atlanta, GA. March 24, 2002.

Cohen, M.M. et al. Emergency contraception: models to increase accessibility. *Journal of Obstetrics and Gynecology of Canada.* 2003 Jun: 25(6):499–504.

Conroy, W.E. et al. Lipid Screening in Adults. Working to prevent coronary artery disease. *Postgraduate Medicine.* 107(4):229–235. April, 2000.

Considerations for Antiretroviral Therapy in Women, HIV/AIDS Treatment Information Service. National Library of Medicine. February 4, 2002. Accessed from *www.hivatis.org* June 23, 2002.

Cooper, S. M. Improving Outcomes in Osteoarthritis. *Postgraduate Medicine.* 105(6):29–38. 1999.

Cromwell, W.C. and Ziakja, P.E. Development of tachyphylaxis among patients taking HMG CoA reductase inhibitors. *American Journal of Cardiology 2000; 86:1123–1127.*

Crouse, J. R., et al. A Randomized Trial Comparing the Effect of Casein With That of Soy Protein Containing Varying Amounts of Isoflavones on Plasma Concentrations of Lipids and Lipoproteins. *Archives of Internal Medicine* 159: 2070–2076. September 27, 1999.

Cumming, R. G., et al. Use of Inhaled Corticosteroids and the Risk of Cataracts. *New England Journal of Medicine.* 337(1):8–14. 1997.

Cunnane, G. et al. Infections and biological therapy in rheumatoid arthritis. *Best Practice Residency of Clinical Rheumatology.* 2003 April; 17(2):345–63.

Cunningham, C.K. et al. Development of resistance mutations in women on standard anti-retroviral therapy who received intrapartum nevirapine to prevent perinatal HIV-1 transmission: a substudy of Pediatric AIDS Clinical Trials Group Protocol 316. *Journal of Infectious Diseases* 2002 (in press at the time of this writing).

Cupp, M. J. Herbal Remedies: Adverse Effects and Drug Interactions. *American Family Physician.* 59(5):1239–1244. 1999.

Daniels, J.B., ed. *Infectious Disease in Clinical Practice.* 1997. Baltimore: Williams and Wilkins.

Dahlof, B. et. al. Cardiovascular morbidity and mortality in patients with diabetes in the Losartan Intervention For Endpoint reduction in hypertention study (LIFE): a randomized trial against atenolol. *The Lancet.* 359(9311): March 23, 2002. Accessed from *www.lancet.com* March 24, 2002.

Davis, E.A. and Pathak, D.S. Psychometric Evaluation of Four HIV Disease-Specific Quality-of-Life Instruments. *Annals of Pharmacotherapy.* 159:546–552. May, 2001.

De Deyn, P.P. et al. A randomized trial of risperidone, placebo, and haloperidol for behavioral symptons of dementia. *Neurology* 1999; 53:946–955.

Depression in Primary Care. Volume 1: Detection and Diagnosis. 1993. Washington, DC: U.S. Department of Health and Human Services.

DeRosier, J. et al. Using Health Care Failure Mode and Effect Analysis. The Joint Commission of Accreditation of Healthcare Organizations, Chicago, IL, 2002.

Diabetes Control and Complications Trial (DCCT). The effect of intensive treatment of diabetes on the development and progression of long-term complications in insulin-dependent diabetes mellitus. *New England Journal of Medicine 1993; 329:977–986.*

DiGregorio, J.G., et al. *Handbook of Pain Management.* 1991. Westchester, NY: Medical Surveillance.

Digoxin Investigation group (DIG) as accessed June, 2003. *Journal of the American Medical Association 2003.* 289:871–878.

Digwood-Lettieri, S. et al. Levofloxacin-Induced Toxic Epidermal Necrolysis in an Elderly Patient. *Pharmacotherapy* 2002; 22(6):789–793.

Dodds Ashley, E.S. et al. Patient Detection of a Drug Dispensing Error by Use of Physician-Provided Drug Samples. *Pharmacotherapy* 2002; 22(12):1642–1643.

Dorian, P., et al. Amiodarone as Compared with Lidocaine for Shock-Resistant Ventricular Fibrillation. *New England Journal of Medicine.* 346(12):884–890. 2002.

Douglas, J.G. et al. Management of High Blood Pressure in African Americans. Arch Intern Med 2003; 163(5):525–541.

Drazen JM. Inappropriate Advertising of Dietary Supplements. *New England Journal of Medicine* 2003; 348(9):777–8.

Drug Information Journal. 1996–1998.

Drug Interactions Newsletter. 1997. Spokane, WA: Applied Therapeutics.

DrugLink. 1998. St. Louis: J. B. Lippincott, Facts and Comparisons.

Drug Newsletter. 1998. St. Louis: J. B. Lippincott, Facts and Comparisons.

Drugs and Therapy Perspectives. 1996–1997.

Drug Therapy: Physicians Prescribing Update. 1992. Lawrenceville, NJ: Excerpta Medica.

Dukes, M.N.G., ed. *Meyler's Side Effects of Drugs.* 11th ed. 1988. Amsterdam: Excerpta Medica.

Eastell, R., et al. Treatment of Postmenopausal Osteoporosis. *New England Journal of Medicine.* 338(11):736–746. 1998.

Eikelboom, J.W., Hirsh, J., et al. Aspirin-resistant thromboxane biosynthesis and the risk of myocardial infarction, stroke or cardiovascular death in patients at high risk for cardiovascular events. *Circulation* 2002 accessed at www.circulationaha.org.

Eikelboom, J.W., Hankey, G.J. Aspirin resistance: a new independent predictor of vascular events? *Journal of the American College of Cardiology.* 2003. Mar 19; 41(6):966–968.

Elhilali M.M., Nickel J.C., Benign prostatic hyperplasia: from A-Z. *Canadian Journal of Urology.* 2003 Apr; 10(2):1799–802.

Epstein, F. H., et al. Acute-Phase Proteins and Other Systemic Responses to Inflammation. *New England Journal of Medicine.* 340(6):448–454. February 11, 1999.

Erkinjuntti, T., et al. Efficacy of galantamine in probable vascular dementia and Alzheimer's disease combined with cerebrovascular disease: a randomised trial. *The Lancet 2002.* April 13.359:1283–1290.

Ernst, E. The Risk-Benefit Profile of Commonly Used Herbal Therapies: Ginkgo, St. John's Wort, Ginseng, Echinacea, Saw Palmetto and Kava. *Annals of Internal Medicine 2002.* 136: 42–53.

Erramouspe, J. and Heyneman, A. Treatment and Prevention of Otitis Media. *The Annals of Pharmacotherapy.* 34:1452. 2001.

Eskola, J, et al. Efficacy of a pneumococcal conjugate vaccine against acute otitis media. *New England Journal of Medicine* 2001; 344(6):403–409.

Farrell, B., and B. Farrell, eds. *Pain in the Elderly.* 1996. International Association for the Study of Pain Press.

Fathi, R. et al. A randomized trial of aggressive lipid reduction for improvement of myocardial ischemia, symptom status, and vascular function in patients with coronary artery disease not amenable to intervention. *American Journal of Medicine* 2003 Apr 15; 114(6):445–53.

Favus, M., ed. *Primer on the Metabolic Bone Diseases and Disorders of Mineral Metabolism.* 3rd ed. 1996. Philadelphia, New York: Lippincott-Raven.

FDA Arthritis Advisory Committee Hearing. February 7, 2001; Gaithersburg, MD.

FDA Drug Bulletin. 1996–1997. Rockville, MD: Department of Health and Human Services, Food and Drug Administration.

FDA News Digest. July 16, 2001. Guidance on Levothyroxine Sodium Products. Rockville, MD: Department of Health and Human Services, Food and Drug Administration.

FDA Summary. April, 2002. ACTOS [pioglitazone HCl]; AVANDIA [rosiglitazone maleate].

FDA Talk Paper T02–18. April 11, 2002. FDA Approves New Indication and Label Changes for the Arthritis Drug, Vioxx. Food and Drug Administration, Rockville, MD.

FDA Talk Paper T03–39. May 27,2003. WHIMS Study on Estrogen/Progestin. Food and Drug Administration, Rockville, MD.

Ferguson, T.B. et al. Preoperative B-blocker use and mortality and morbidity following CABG surgery in North America. *Journal of the American Medical Association.* 287(17): 2221–2227. May 1, 2002.

Finkelstein, J.S. et al. Effects of Parathyroid Hormone, Alendronate, or Both on bone Density in Osteoporotic Men. *Presentation Number: 1007.*ASBMR: 24TH Annual Meeting 2003.

Fitzgerald, G. A. and Patrono, C. The Coxibs, Selective Inhibitors of Cyclooxygenase-2. *The New England Journal of Medicine.* August 9, 2000. Vol 345(6). Content.*nejm.org/cgi/content/short/345/6/433.*

Fonseca, V. et al. Addition of nateglinide to rosiglitazone monotherapy suppresses mealtime hyperglycemia and improves overall glycemic control. *Diabetes Care.* 2003 Jun; 26(6):1685–90.

Frackiewicz, Edyta J., Endometriosis: An Overview of the Disease and Its Treatment. *Journal of the American Pharmaceutical Association.* Vol. 40, No. 5, September/October 2000.

Frackiewicz, E. J. and Cutler, N. Women's Health Care During the Perimenopause. *Journal of the American Pharmaceutical Association.* Vol. 40, No. 6. November/December 2000.

Francis, G. S., ed. *The Cleveland Clinic Heart Advisor.* 3(4): 3. 2000.

Frick, A. et al. Omeprazole reduces clozapine plasma concentrations—a case report. *Pharmacopsychiatry.* 2003 May; 36(3):121–3.

Fraunfelder, F. T. Drug-Induced Ocular Side Effects and Drug Interactions. 3rd ed. 1989. Philadelphia: Lea and Febiger.

Gandhi, T.K. et al, Adverse Drug Events in Ambulatory Care, *New England Journal of Medicine* 2003; 348:1556–64.

Garg, R.K. and Sorrentino MD Beta blockers for CHF. *Postgraduate Medicine.* 109(3): 49–57. 2001.

Geber, J. et al. Optimizing Drug Therapy in Patients with Cardiovascular Disease: The Impact of Pharmacist-Managed Pharmacotherapy Clinics in a Primary Care Setting. *Pharmacotherapy* 2002; 22(6):738–747.

Generali, M.S., ed., et al. *Clini-Alert Reporting on Adverse Clinical Events.* 38(7):1–8. 2000.

Gerberding, J.L. Occupational Exposure to HIV in Health Care Settings. *New England Journal of Medicine* 2003; 348(9):826–33.

Ghandi, S.K. et al. The Pathogenesis of Acute Pulmonary Edema Associated with Hypertension. *New England Journal of Medicine* 344(1):17–22. January 4, 2001.

Gilbert, D.L., et al. Tic reduction with pergolide in a randomized controlled trial in children. *Neurology 2003.* Feb 25; 60(4):606–611.

Ginsberg, H.N. Treatment for patients with the metabolic syndrome. *American Journal of Cardiology* 2003 Apr 3; 91(7A):29E-39E.Review.

Glasser, S.P., et al. Bedtime dosing of diltiazem. *52nd* Scientific Session of the American College of Cardiology 2003 March 30, 2003. Chicago.

Glassman, A.H., et al. Sertraline treatment of major depression in patients with acute MI or unstable angina. *JAMA 2002.* 288 (6):701–709.

Gleason, P. P., et al. Medical Outcomes and Antimicrobial Costs With the Use of the American Thoracic Society Guidelines for Outpatients With Community Acquired Pneumonia. *Journal of the American Medical Association.* 278 (1):32–39. 1997.

Gloth, M.J. Treatment of Pain in Older Patients. *Patient Care.* March 30, 1999: 62–68.

Goldman, S. A., et al. Minimizing the Risks of Drug Interactions. *Patient Care.* March 30, 1999: 26–68.

Goodman, L. S., and A. Gilman, eds. *The Pharmacological Basis of Therapeutics.* 9th ed. 1996. New York: Macmillan.

Gorman, J.D. et al. Treatment of ankylosing spondylitis by inhibition of tumor necrosis factor alpha. *New England Journal of Medicine* 2002. 346:1249–1256.

Gorski, E.D. and Willis, K.C. Report of Three Case Studies with Olanzapine for Chronic Pain. *Journal of Pain.* 2003; 4(3):166–8.

Gourang, P.P. and Kasiar, J.B. Syndrome of Inappropriate Antidiuretic Hormone-Induced Hyponatremia Associated with Amiodarone. *Pharmacotherapy* 2002; 22(5):649–651.

Graham, A. S. Cytochrome P450 Drug Interactions. *The Rx Consultant.* 8(2):1–8. 1999.

Graham, I. M., et al. Plasma Homocysteine as a Risk Factor for Vascular Disease. *Journal of the American Medical Association.* 277(22):1775–1781. 1997.

Grau, A.J. et al. Platelet function under aspirin, clopidogrel, and both after ischemic stroke: a case-crossover study. *Stroke* 2003 Apr; 34(4):849–54.

Graumlich, J.F., MD. Preventing gastrointestinal complications of NSAIDS. *Postgraduate Medicine* 109(5):117–128. May 2001.

Gray, S. L., et al. Medication Adherence in Elderly Patients Receiving Home Health Services Following Hospital Discharge. *The Annals of Pharmacotherapy.* 35(5):539–545. May 2001.

Greenland, P. Beating High Blood Pressure with Low-Sodium DASH. *New England Journal of Medicine.* 344(1):53–55. January 4, 2001.

Greenspan, S.L. et al. Significant Differential Effects of Alendrontate, Estrogen or Combination Therapy on the Rate of Bone Loss after Discontinuation of Treatment of Postmenopausal Osteoporosis. *Annals of Internal Medicine.* 2002; 137:875–883.

Greenspan, S.L. et al. Alendronate Improves Bone Mineral Density in Elderly Women with Osteoporosis Residing in Long-Term Care Facilities. *Annals of Internal Medicine.* 2002; 136:742–746.

Greenspan, S.L. et al. Alendronate plus estrogen and Bone Mineral Density in Elderly Women. *JAMA.* 2003; 136:742–746.

Griffiths, M. C., ed. *USAN* 1989. Rockville, MD: United States Pharmacopeial Convention.

Griffiths, M. C., ed. *The USP Dictionary of Drug Names.* 1988. Rockville, MD: United States Pharmacopeial Convention.

Guay, D.R.P. Cefdinir: An expanded Spectrum Oral Cephalosporin. *The Annals of Pharmacotherapy 2000.* 34:1469–1477. 2000.

Guidelines for the Use of Antiretroviral Agents in HIV Infected Adults and Adolescents. February 4, 2002. Accessed from *www.hivatis.org* June 24, 2002.

Gum, P.A. et al. A prospective, double-blinded determination of the natural history of aspirin resistance among stable patients with cardiovascular disease. *Journal of the American College of Cardiology* 2003; 41:961–5.

Hagg, S. et al. Long-term combination treatment with clozapine and filgrastim in patients with clozapine-induced agranulocytosis. *International Clinical Psychopharmacology.* 2003 May; 18(3): 173–4.

Hambrecht, M. D., et al. Effect of Exercise on Coronary Endothelial Function in Patients With Coronary Artery Disease. *New England Journal of Medicine.* 342(7):454–460. 2000.

Handbook of Clinical Drug Data. 1993. Hamilton, IL: Drug Intelligence Publications.

Handbook of Nonprescription Drugs. 11th ed. 1996. Washington, DC: American Pharmaceutical Association.

Hamelin, BA, et al. Influence of the menstrual cycle on the timing of acute coronary events in premenopausal women. *Am J Med* 2003; 114:599–602.

Hanlon, J. T., et al. Inappropriate Drug Use Among Community-Dwelling Elderly. *Pharmacotherapy 2000.* 20(5):575–582. 2000.

Hansten, P.D. *Drug Interactions.* 6th ed. 1992. Philadelphia: Lea and Febiger.

Hansten, P.D. and Horn, J. R. *The Top 100 Drug Interactions. A Guide to Patient Management.* 2001. Edmonds: H&H Publications.

Hart, S. Influence of B-Blockers on Mortality in Chronic Heart Failure. *The Annals of Pharmacotherapy.* 34:1440–1451. 2001.

Hasketh, P. L., ed. *The Journal of Oncology.* 1998. Cedar Knolls, NJ: National Medical Information Network.

Hayden, F. et al. Inhaled Zanamivir for the Prevention of Influenza in Families. *New England Journal of Medicine.* 343(18):1282–1289. 2000.

Hays, J. et al. Effects of Estrogen plus Progestin on Health-Related Quality of Life. *New England Journal of Medicine* 2003, 348; 19:1839–54.

Heck, A. M., et al. Orlistat, a New Lipase Inhibitor for the Management of Obesity. *Pharmacotherapy the Journal of Human Pharmacology and Drug Therapy.* 20(3):270–279. 2000.

Hecht, H.S., et al. Electron Beam Tomography and National Cholesterol Education Program Guidelines in Asymptomatic Women. *Journal of the American College of Cardiology.* 37(6):1506–1511. 2001.

Heeschen, C., et al., Withdrawal of statins increases event rates in patients with acute coronary syndromes. *Circulation 2002;10.1161/01. CIR.0000012530.68333C8.*

Heinonen, O. P., Slone, D., and S. Shapiro. *Birth Defects and Drugs in Pregnancy.* 1977. Littleton, MA: PSG Publishing.

Herrerias, C. T., et al. The Child with ADHD. Using the AAP Clinical Practice Guideline. *American Family Physician.* 63(9):1803–1812. 2001.

Hilleman, D. E. and Bauman, J. L. Role of Antiarrhythmic Therapy in Patients at Risk for Sudden Cardiac Death: An Evidence-Based Review. *Pharmacotherapy 2001.* 21(5): 556–574. 2001.

Hlatky, M. A., et al. Quality-of-life and depressive symptoms inpostmenopausal women after receiving hormone therapy: results from the Heart and estrogen/progesting Replacement Study (HERS) trial. *JAMA 2002* Feb 6; 287:591–7.

Hoff, P.M. et al. Comparison of oral capecitabine versis intravenous fluorouracil plus leucovorin as the first-line treatment of 605 patients with metastatic colorectal cancer: results of a randomized phase III study. *Journal of Clinical Oncology* 19(8):2282–92, 2001.

Hollister, L.E. *Clinical Pharmacology of Psychotherapeutic Drugs.* 2nd ed. 1983. New York: Churchill Livingstone.

Horsfield, S.A. et al. Fluoxentine's effects of cognitive performance in patients with traumatic brain injury. *International Journal of Psychiatry in Medicine.* 2002; 32(4):337–44.

Houston Miller N. et al. The Multilevel Compliance Challenge: Recommendations for a Call to Action. *Circulation* 95: 1085–1090. The American Heart Association 1997.

Horlan, C. et al. Frequency of Inappropriate Metformin Prescriptions. *Journal of the American Medical Association 2002* May 15, vol. 287(19): 2504 (Research Letter).

Hu, F. et al. Fish and Omega-3 Fatty Acid Intake and Risk of Coronary Heart Disease in Women. *JAMA* 2002; 287:1815–1821. April 10, 2002.

Hui, C.H. et al. Successful peripheral blood stem cell mobilisation with filgrastim in patients with chronic myeloid leukaemia achieving complete cytogenetic response with imatinib, without increasing disease burden as measured by quantitative real-time PCR. *Leukemia.* 2003 May; 17(5):821–8.

Hunninghake, D.B. Postdischarge lipid management of coronary artery disease patients according to the new National Cholesterol Education Program Guidelines. *American Journal of Cardiology 2001 Oct 18;* 18;88(8A):37K-41K.

Hussar, D.A. New Drugs of 2000. *Journal of the American Pharmaceutical Association.*41(2): 229–280. The American Pharmaceutical Association. March/April 2001.

Hunt, L.W. How to manage difficult asthma cases. *Postgraduate Medicine* May 2001;109(5): 61–68.

Hypericum Depression Trial Study Group. Effect of Hypericum perforatum (St. John's wort) in Major Depressive Disorder A Randomized Controlled Trial. *JAMA* 2002;287: 1807–1853. April 10, 2002.

The Hospice Journal. 1998. New York: The Haworth Press.

Im J. Asthma. *The Rx Consultant.* XI(3):1–8. 2002.

Influenza and Pneumococcal Vaccination Levels Among Adults Aged Greater Than or Equal to 65. *Morbidity and Mortality Weekly Report.* 47:797–802. October 2, 1998.

International Drug Therapy Newsletter. 1997. Baltimore: Ayd Medical Communications.

Irwin, R.S. and Madison, J.M. Systemic Corticosteroids for Acute Exacerbations of Chronic Obstructive Pulmonary Disease. *New England Journal of Medicine.* 2003; 348(26):2679–2681.

Janne, P.A. and Mayer, R.J. Chemoprevention of Colorectal Cancer. *New England Journal of Medicine.* 2000; 342(26):1960–1968.

Jefferson, J.W. Potassium supplementation in lithium patients: a timely intervention or premature speculation? *Journal of Clinical Psychiatry* 1992 Oct; 53(10):370–2.

Jefferson, J.W. and Greist, J.H. *Primer of Lithium Therapy.* 1977. Baltimore: Williams and Wilkins.

Jellin, J.M. et al. *The Pharmacist's Letter.* 17(1):1–6. 2001.

Johnson, M.D. et al. Clinically Significant Drug Interactions: What You Need to Know Before Writing Prescriptions. *Postgraduate Medicine.* 105(2):193–222. 1999.

Jones, P. Results of the STELLAR (Statin Therapies for Elevated Lipid Levels compared Across doses to Rosuvatstatin) trial. AAC (American College of Cardiology) national meeting April 2003.

Jonsson, B. et al. Health economics in the Hypertension Optimal Treatment (HOT) study: costs and cost-effectiveness of intensive blood pressure lowering and low-dose aspirin in patients with hypertension. *Journal of Internal Medicine.* 2003 Apr; 253(4):472–80.

Jorenby, D.E., Ph.D., et al. A Controlled Trial of Sustained-Release Bupropion, a Nicotine Patch, or Both for Smoking Cessation. *New England Journal of Medicine.* 340(9): 685–691. 1999.

Journal of Acquired Immune Deficiency Syndromes. 1999. Hagerstown, MD: Lippincott-Raven.

Journal of the American Medical Association. 1997–1999.

Journal of Bone and Mineral Research. 1996–2000. Malden, MA: Blackwell Science, Inc.

Journal of the National Cancer Institute. 1999. Cary, NC: Oxford University Press.

Journal Watch. 1996–2000. Waltham, MA: The Massachusetts Medical Society.

Journal Watch: Women's Health. 1996–2000. Waltham, MA: The Massachusetts Medical Society.

Kagan, R. et al. Preliminary results of the EFFECT (Efficacy of Fosamax versus Evista Comparison Trial). ACOG (American College of Obstetrics and Gynecology) national meeting April 22, 2003.

Kane, M.P. et al. Cholesteral and Glycemic Effects of Niaspan in Patients with Type 2 Diabetes. *Pharmacotherapy* 2001; 21(12):1473–1478.

Kaplan, N.M. *Management of Hypertension.* 6th ed. 1995. Durant, OK: Essential Medical Information Systems.

Kashyap, M.L., et al. Long-term Safety and Efficacy of a Once-Daily Niacin/Lovastatin Formulation for Patients With Dyslipidemia. *The American journal of Cardiology.* 89: 672–678. March 15, 2002.

Kawano, K.H. et al. Administration of nifedipine CR immeidately after awakening prevents a morning surge in hypertensive patients. Case report of three cases. *Blood Press Suppl 2003.* May; 1:44–48.

Keck, P.E. et al. Ziprasidone in the Treatment of Acute Bipolar Mania: A Three-Week, Placebo-Controlled, Double-Blind, Randomized Trial. *American Journal of Psychiatry* 2003; 160:741–748

Kelly, William N. Can the Frequency and Risks of Fatal Adverse Drug Events Be Determined? *Pharmacotherapy.* 21(5). May 2001.

Kim, S.S. Role of fluoxetine in anorexia nervosa. *Annals of Pharmacotherapy.* 2003 Jun; 37(6):890–902.

Kindsvater, S. et al. Effects of coadministration of aspirin or clopidogrel on exercise testing in patients with heart failure receiving angiotensin-converting enzyme inhibitors. *American Journal of Cardiology.* 2003 Jun 1; 91(11):1350–2.

Klippel, J. H., ed. Systemic Lupus Erythematosus Demographics, Prognosis and Outcome. *Journal of Rheumatology Suppl* 48:67–71. 1997.

Knight, E.L. et al. Predictors of uncontrolled hypertension in ambulatory patients. *Hypertension 2001 Oct;* 38(4):809–814. 2001.

Knowler, W.C. et al. Reduction in the Incidence of Type 2 Diabetes With Lifestyle Intervention or Metformin. *New England Journal of Medicine.* 346(6):393–403. 2002.

Koda-Kimbal (Lloyd Yee Young). *Applied Therapeutics: The Clinical Use of Drugs.* 6th ed. 1995. Vancouver, WA: Applied Therapeutics.

Koller, W.C., ed. *Handbook of Parkinson's Disease.* 1987. New York: Marcel Dekker.

Kolodny, R.C., Masters, W.H., and V.E. Johnson. *Textbook of Sexual Medicine.* 1979. Boston: Little, Brown.

Kovacs, J.A., and Masur, H. Prophylaxis Against Opportunistic Infections in Patients with Human Immunodeficiency Virus Infection. *NEJM.* 342(19):1416–1429. May 11, 2000.

Kwon, H.J. et al. Case reports of heart failure after therapy with a tumor necrosis factor antagonist. *Annals of Internal Medicine.* 2003 May 20; 138(10):807–11.

Lakrye, E.M. et al. The benefits of finasteride for hirsute women with polycystic ovary syndrome or idiopathic hirsutism. *Gynecology and Endocrinology.* 2003 Feb; 17(1):57–63.

Lambing, C.L. Osteoporosis prevention, detection, and treatment. A mandate for primary care physicians. *Postgraduate Medicine.* 107(7):37–56. June, 2000.

Larouche, S.J. et al. Lovastatin 10 mg efficacy in nonprescription studies. *Paper presentation: American Society for Clinical Pharmacology and Therapeutics.* Orlando, FL. March 7, 2001.

Lau, W.C. et al. Atorvastatin Reduces the Ability of Clopidogrel to Inhibit Platelet Aggregation: A New Drug-Drug Interaction. *Circulation,* Jan 2003; 107:32–37.

Laurie, S. and Khan, D. Inhaled corticosteroids as first-line therapy for asthma. *Postgraduate Medicine* May 2001; 109(5):44–56.

Lauten, W.B. et al. Usefulness of quinapril and irbesartan to improve the anti-inflammatory response of atorvastatin and aspirin in patients with coronary heart disease. *American Journal of Cardiology.* 2003 May 1: 91(9):1116–9.

Lawrence RA. *Breast-Feeding.* 1980. St. Louis: Mosby.

Lee, C.R. et al. Surrogate End Points in Heart Failure. *The Annals of Pharmacotherapy 2002.* 479–488.

Lee, T.H. A Broader Concept of Medical Errors. *New England Journal of Medicine.* 2002; 347(24):1965–6.

Leaf, A. et al. Clinical prevention of sudden cardiac death by n-3polyunsaturated fatty acids and mechanism of prevention of arrhythmias by n-3 fish oils. *Circulation 2003.* as accessed from *http//circ.ahjajournals.org* [10.1161/01. CIR.0000069566.78305.33].

Leon, A.C., et al., Prospective Study of Fluoxetine Treatment of Suicidal Behavior in Affectively Ill Subjects. *American Journal of Psychiatry.* 156:195–201. 1999.

Lepore, L. et al. Drug-induced systemic lupus erythematosus associated with etanercept therapy in a child with juvenile idiopathic arthritis. *Clinical and Experimental Rheumatology.* 2003 Mar-Apr; 21(2):276–7.

Levien, T.L., et al. Nateglinide Therapy for Type 2 Diabetes Mellitus. *The Annals of Pharmacotherapy;* 35:1426–34. 2001.

Li, C.I., et al. Relationship Between Long Durations and Different Regimens of Hormone therapy and Risk of Breast Cancer. *JAMA* 2003; 289:3254–3263.

Lieberman, M.L. *The Sexual Pharmacy.* 1988. New York: New American Library.

Lindsay, R. et al. Effect of lower doses of conjugated equine estrogens with and without medroxyprogesterone acetate on bone in early postmenopausal women. *Journal of the American Medical Association* 2002; 287:2668–76.

Long, J. W. *Clinical Management of Prescription Drugs.* 1984. Philadelphia: Harper and Row.

Long, J. W. *The Essential Guide to Chronic Illness.* 1997. New York: HarperCollins.

Lonn, E. M. Effects of Ramipril and Vitamin E on Atherosclerosis. The Study to Evaluate Carotid Ultrasound Changes in Patients Treeated With Ramipril and Vitamin E (SECURE). *Circulation. 2001; 103:919–925.*

Love, N., et al. Symposium: A New Era in Breast Cancer. *Postgraduate Medicine.* 105(6): 43–103. 1999.

Lowy, F. D. Staphylococcus Aureus Infections. *New England Journal of Medicine.* 339 (8): 520–532. August 20, 1998.

Lucas, G.M., Chaisson, R.E. and Moore, R.D. Comparison of initial combination antiretroviral therapy with a single protease inhibitor, ritonavir and saquinavir, or efaviranz. *AIDS.* 15(13): pp 1679–1686. September, 2001.

Lucas, R.A. et al. Rhabdomyolysis Associated with Cerivastatin: Six Cases within Three Months at One Hospital. *Pharmacotherapy* 2002; 22(6):771–774.

Lynch, H.T. and Chapelle A. Hereditary Colorectal Cancer. *New England Journal of Medicine 2003.* 348:919–932.

Maddin, S., ed. *Current Dermatologic Therapy.* 1982. Philadelphia: W. B. Saunders.

Mahtabjafari, M., Masih, M. and Emerson, A.E. The value of pharmacist involvement in point-of-care service, walk-in lipid screening program. *Pharmacotherapy.* 21(11):1403–1406. 2001.

Maksymowych, W.P. et al. Canadian Rheumatology Association Consensus on the Use of Anti-Tumor Necrosis Factor-a Directed Therapies in the Treatment of Spondyloarthritis. *J Rheumatol.* 2003 Jun; 30(6):1356–1363.

Mancia, G. et al. An Ambulatory Blood Pressure Monitoring Study of the Comparative Antihypertensive Efficacy of Two Angiotensin II Receptor Antagonists. *Blood Pressure Monitoring.* May/June 2002, 7:135–142. 2002.

Marchioli, R. et al. Early Protection against sudden death by n-3 polyunsaturated fatty acids after myocardial infarction. Time-course analysis of the gruppo Italiano per lo Studio della Sopravvivenza nell-iInfarcto Miocardico (GISSI)-Prevenzione. *Circulation [10.1161/01. CIR.0000014682.14181. F2].2002.*Accessed at *www.circ.ahajournals.org/.*

Marcus AO. Lipid Disorders in Patients with Type 2 Diabetes Meeting the Challenges of Early, Aggressive Treatment. *Postgraduate Medicine.* 110(1):111–123. 2001.

Mario, F.D. et al. Rabeprazole in a one-week eradication therapy of Helicobacter pylori: Comparison of different dosages. *Journal of Gastroenterology and Hepatology.* 2003 Jul: 18(7): 783–786.

Marso, S.P., Griffin, B.P. and Topol, E.J. *Manual of Cardiovascular Medicine.* 2000. Philadelphia: Lippincott Williams & Wilkins.

Martin, W.R. and Fuller RE. Suspected Chromium Picolinate-Induced Rhabdomyolysis. *Pharmacotherapy.* 18(4):860–862. 1998.

Mathis, A.S. et al. Risk Stratification in Non-ST Segment Elevation Acute Coronary Syndromes with Special Focus on Recent Guidelines. *Pharmacotherapy.* 21(8):954–987. 2001.

Mayeuz, R., and Sano, M. Treatment of Alzheimer's Disease. *New England Journal of Medicine.* 341(22):1670–1679. November 25, 1999.

Mayo Clinic Proceedings. 1996–2000.

MacDonald, T.M., Wei, L. Effect of ibuprofen on cardioprotective effect of aspirin. *Lancet 2003;*361: 573–574.

McEvoy, G. K., ed. *American Hospital Formulary Service: Drug Information 1997.* Bethesda, MD: American Society of Hospital Pharmacists.

McKenney, J. ATP 3 Review. *Journal of American Pharmaceutical Association 2001.* 41(4):596–606.

McMinn, J.R. Jr. et al. Complete recovery from refractory immune thrombocytopenic purpura in three patients treated with etanercept. *American Journal of Hematology.* 2003 Jun; 73(2):135–40.

McNulty, S.J. et al. A randomized trial of sibutramine in the management of obese type 2 diabetic patients treated with metformin. *Diabetes Care.* 2003; 26:125–31.

Mease, P.J. Etanercept, a TNF antagonist for treatment for psoriatic arthritis and psoriasis. *Skin Therapy Lett.* 2003 Jan; 8(1):1–4.

Medical Letter on Drugs and Therapeutics. 1998, 1999, 2001, 2002. New Rochelle, NY: The Medical Letter.

Mehta, S. R., M.D., et al. The Clopidogrel in Unstable Angina to Prevent Recurrent Ischemic Events (CURE) trial programme; rationale, design and baseline characteristics including a meta-analysis of the effects of thienopyridines in vascular disease CURE study investigators. *European Heart Journal* 2000; 21:2022–2041.

Melmon, K.L., and Morrelli, H. F. *Clinical Pharmacology.* 2nd ed. 1978. New York: Macmillan.

Michaels, A.D., et al. Effects of intravenous nesiritide on human coronary vasomotor regulation and myocardial oxygen uptake. *Circulation* 2003; 107(21):2697–2701.

Michelson, D., et al. Atomoxetine in the treatment of children and adolescents with attention deficit/hyperactivity disorder: a randomized, placebo-controlled, dose-response study. *Pediatrics.2001*;108e83. accessed from *www.pediatrics.org* April, 2002.

Michelson, M. D., et al. Bone Mineral Density in Women with Depression. *New England Journal of Medicine.* 335(16): 1176–1181. 1996.

Micromedex: Drugdex. 1999, 2000, 2001, 2002. Englewood, CO: Computerized Clinical Information System.

Milgrom, H., et al. Treatment of Allergic Asthma with Monoclonal Anti-IgE Antibody. *New England Journal of Medicine.* 341(26): 1964–1972. December 23, 1999.

Miller, C. D., et al. Hypoglycemia in patients with type 2 diabetes mellitus. *Archives of Internal Medicine.* 161: 1653–1659. July, 9, 2001.

Mintzer, J.E. and Kersharw P. The efficacy of galantamine in the treatment of Alzheimer's disease: comparison of patients previously treated with acetylcholinesterase inhibitors to patients with no prior exposure.

Modi, P., et al. *The Evolving Role of Oral Insulin Spray (RapidMist) in the Treatment of Diabetes.* 5th International Congress of Immunology. Madrid, India February 2001.

Modi, P., et al. *The Role of Oral Insulin Combined with Metformin in the Treatment of Diabetes.* American Association National Meeting. Philadelphia, PA, USA June 2001.

Mohler, S. R. *Medication and Flying: A Pilot's Guide.* 1982. Boston: Boston Publishing.

Mosca, L., et al. Design and Methods of the Raloxifene Use for The Heart (RUTH) Study. *The American Journal of Cardiology 2001.* 88:392–395.

Mossad, S. B. Prophylactic and Symptomatic Treatment of Influenza Current and Developing Options. *Postgraduate Medicine* 109. 97–105. January 2001.

Mongthuong, TT, et al. Role of Coenzyme Q10 in Chronic Heart Failure, Angina, and Hypertension. *Pharmacotherapy* 2001;21(7): 797–806.

Montserrat, V. L. et al. Cost-Effectiveness Results from the US Carvedilol Heart Failure Trials Program. *The Annals of Pharmacotherapy;* 35:846–851. 2001.

Morbidity and Mortality Weekly Report (MMWR): Prevention and Control of Influenza. Vol. 48 No. RR-4 April 30, 1999. Washington, DC: U.S. Department of Health and Human Services.

Morbidity and Mortality Weekly Report (MMWR): Report of the NIH Panel to Define Principles of Therapy of HIV Infection and Guidelines for the Use of Antiretroviral Agents in HIV-Infected Adults and Adolescents. April 24, 1998. Washington, DC: U.S. Department of Health and Human Services, CDC Atlanta, Georgia.

Morgan, T., Anderson A. The effects of nonsteroidal anti-inflammatory drugs on blood pressure in patients treated with different antihypertensive drugs. *J Clin Hypertens (Greenwich).* 2003 Jan-Feb;5(1): 53–7.

Morgan, T.O., Anderson A. Different drug classes have variable effects on blood pressure depending on the time of day. *Am J Hypertens.* 2003 Jan;16(1): 46–50.

Mosca, L., et al. Guide to Preventive Cardiology for Women. *Circulation.* 1999;99: 2480–2484. 1999.

Mossad, S. B. Prophylactic and Symptomatic Treatment of Influenza Current and Developing Options. *Postgraduate Medicine* 109. 97–105. January 2001.

Mosher, M. *Clinical Management of Hypertension.* Fourth Edition. 1999. Caddo, OK: Professional Communications, Inc.

Mukherjee, D., Nissen, S.E. and Topol, E.J. Risk of Cardiovascular Events Associated With Selective COX-2 Inhibitors. *Journal of the American Medical Association.* 286(8);

August 22/29, 2001. accessed from *www.jama.ama-assn.org/issues/v286n8/rfull/ jsc10193.html*.

Mukherjee, D., et al. NSAIDS, but not COX IIs inhibit aspirin benefits. *New England Journal of Medicine*. 109. 97–105. December 20, 2001.

Munzenberger, P.J. and Vinuya RZ. Impact of an Asthma Program on the Quality of Life of Children in an Urban Setting. *Pharmacotherapy* 2002; 22(8):1055–1062.

Murphy, J. E. *Clinical Pharmacokinetics*. 1993. Bethesda, MD: American Society of Hospital Pharmacists.

Nallamothu, M., Fendrick, M. Rubenfire, et al. Lowering Elevated Homocysteine Levels Could Result in Substantial Clinical Benefits at a Reasonable Cost. *Archives of Internal Medicine* 160. 3406–3412. December 11, 2000.

National Center for Complementary and Alternative Medicine. NCCAM Consumer Advisory on Ephedra. accessed 4/6/03 at *www.nccam.nih.gov/health/alerts/ephedra/consumer advisory.htm*.

National Center for Health Statistics, CDC. *Leading Causes of Death*. 2001. *www.cdc.gov/ nchs/fastats/icod.htm*.

National Institutes of Health's (NIH, NHLBI) Guidelines for Diagnosis and Management of Asthma. 1997.

Nephropathy, urinary tract cancer from herbal products containing aristolochic acid. FDA. *www.cfsan.fd.gov/;sldms/ds-bot3*. html. *Pharmacy Today*. Page 5, June 2001.

Nerhood, RC. Making a Decision about ERT/HRT. *Postgraduate Medicine*. 109 (3): 167–178. 2001.

New England Journal of Medicine. 1997–2003.

Nichol, K.L., et al. Influenza vaccination and reduction in hospitalizations for cardiac disease and stroke among the elderly. *NEJM* 2003;348(14): 1322–1332.

Nielsen, J.W., MD, et al. Optimal Antidepressant Dosing. Practical framework for selection, titration, and duration of therapy. *Postgraduate Medicine*. 108 (5): 111–115. Oct. 2000.

Olin, B. R., ed. *Facts and Comparisons*. 1997, 1998, 2000. St. Louis: J. B. Lippincott, Facts and Comparisons.

Olin, B. R., ed. 1992. *Patient Drug Facts*. St. Louis: J. B. Lippincott, Facts and Comparisons.

O'Laughlin, J., et al. The Role of Community Pharmacists in Health Education and Disease Prevention: A Survey of Their Interests and Needs in Relation to Cardiovascular Disease. *Preventive Medicine*. 28: 324–331. 1999.

Owens, R. C. Risk Assessment for Antimicrobial Agent-Induced QTc Interval Prolongation and Torsades de Pointes. *Pharmacotherapy 2001;21(3): 301–319*.

Packard KA et al. Comparison of Gemfribrozil and Fenofibrate in Patients with Dyslipidemic Coronary Heart Disease. *Pharmacotherapy* 2002;22(12): 1527–1532.

Pain Forum: Official Journal of the American Pain Society. 1997, 1998, 2000. Secaucus, NJ: Churchill Livingstone.

Palacioz, K. P. et al. Drug-Induced Long QT Interval. *Detail-Document 170401 Therapeutic Resource Center. Pharmacist's Letter/Prescriber's Letter 2001*.

Paris, D, Townsend, K.P., Humphrey, J., et al. Statins inhibit Abeta-neurotoxicity in vitro and Abeta-induced vasoconstriction and inflammation in rat aortae. *Atherosclerosis 2002 Apr: 161(2):293–299*.

Park PJ et al. The performance of a risk score in predicting undiagnosed hyperglycemia. *Diabetes Care 2002 June: 25(6): 84–988*.

Park SJ et al. A Paclitaxel-Eluting Stent for the Prevention of coronary Restenosis. *New England Journal of Medicine*. 2003;348(16): 1537–45.

Penzak et al. Depression in patients with HIV infection. *American Journal of Health System Pharm*. 57: 376–389. Feb 15, 2000.

Pearson TA et al. Markers of Inflammation and Cardiovascular Disease. *Circulation* 2003;107(3): 499

Pearson VE Galantamine: A New Alzheimer Drug with a Past Life. *The Annals of Pharmacotherapy;*35: 1406–13. 2001.

Perazella MA COX-2 Inhibitors and the Kidney. Hospital Practice, March 15, 2001.

Pham JV and Puzantian T. Ecstacy: Dangers and Controversies. *Pharmacotherapy* 2001;21(12): 1561–1565.

Physicians' Desk Reference. Electronic Library 2000.1, version 5.1 AT. Montvale, NJ: Medical Economics.

Physician's GenRX. 1996. Version 96.1a. St. Louis, MO: Mosby.

Physician's Therapeutics and Drug Alert. 1998–2001.

Portnoy JM. Immunotherapy for inhalant allergies. *Postgraduate Medicine* May 2001; 109(5): 89–106.

Postgraduate Medicine: The Journal of Applied Medicine for the Primary Care Physician. 1998–2000.

Practice Guideline for the Treatment of Patients With Alzheimer's Disease and Other Dementias of Late Life. 1997. Washington, DC: American Psychiatric Association.

Pratt, D. S., and Kaplan, M. M. Evaluation of Abnormal Liver-Enzyme Results in Asymptomatic Patients. *New England Journal of Medicine.* 342(17):1266–1271. April 27, 2000.

Principles of Analgesic Use in the Treatment of Acute Pain and Cancer Pain. 3rd ed. 1996. Glenview, IL: American Pain Society.

Principles of Analgesic Use in the Treatment of Acute Pain and Cancer Pain. 4th ed. 1999. Glenview, IL: American Pain Society.

Qtcdrugs.org. International Registry for Drug-Induced Arrhythmias "drugs to avoid in patients with congenital Long QT syndrome." June 2001.

Quality Improvement Guidelines for the Treatment of Acute Pain and Cancer Pain. 1995. Glenview, IL: American Pain Society Quality of Care Committee.

Quintiliani R et al. Optimizing Antiinfective Transition Therapy In Community-Acquired Pneumonia. *Pharmacotherapy.* 21(7) Part two: 1–108S. July 2001.

Quitkin FM et al. When Should a Trial of Fluoxetine for Major Depression Be Declared Failed? *Am J Psychiatry* 2003;160: 734–740.

Raj, P. P. *Practical Management of Pain.* 1986. Chicago: Year Book Medical Publishers.

Rakel, R. E., ed. *Conn's Current Therapy* 1992. Philadelphia: W. B. Saunders.

Ratnapalan, S., et al. Digoxin-carvedilol interactions in children. *J Pediatr 2003.* 142(5): 572–574.

Rational Drug Therapy and Pharmacology for Physicians. 1990. Bethesda, MD: American Society for Pharmacology and Experimental Therapeutics.

Ratthore, SS, Krumholz, HM. Digoxin therapy for heart failure: safe for women? *Italian Heart Journal 2003.* 4(3): 148–151.

Reiss, R A et al. Point-of-Care Laboratory Monitoring of Patients Receiving Different Anticoagulant Therapies. *Pharmacotherapy* 2002; 22(6):677–685.

Relkin NR et al. A large, community-based, open label trial of donepezil in the treatment of Alzheimer's disease. *Dement Geriatr Cogn Disord* 2003; 16(1):15–24.

The Diabetes Control and Complication Trial. Retinopathy and Nephropathy in Patients with Type 1 Diabetes Four Years After a Trial of Intensive Therapy. *The New England Journal of Medicine.* 342(6):381–389. February 10, 2000.

Rendell, M. S and Kirchain, W. R. Pharmacotherapy of Type 2 Diabetes Mellitus. *The Annals of Pharmacotherapy 2000;* 34:878–895.

Rejnmark, L. et al. Dose-effect relations of and loop- and thiazide-diuretics on calcium homeostasis: a randomized, double-blinded Latin-square multiple cross-over study in postmenopausal osteopenic woman. *European Journal of Clinical Investigation* 2003 Jan; 33(1):41–50.

Reynolds, J.E.F., ed. *Martindale: The Extra Pharmacopoeia.* 29th ed. 1997. London: The Pharmaceutical Press.

Ridker, P.M. et al. Comparison of C-reactive protein and low-density lipoprotein cholesterol levels in the prediction of first cardiovascular events. *New England Journal of Medicine 2002.* 347: 1557–1565.

Robless, P.A., et al. Increased platelet aggregation and activation in peripheral arterial diseaase. *European Journal of Vascular and Endovascular Surgery* 2003 Jan; 25(1):16–22.

Rogers, C. S., and McCue, J. D., eds. *Managing Chronic Disease.* 1987. Oradell, NJ: Medical Economics Books.

Rojas-Fernandez, C.H. et al. Implications of Amyloid Precursor Protein and Subsequent Beta-Amyloid Production to the Pharmacotherapy of Alzheimer's Disease. *Pharmacotherapy* 2002; 22(12):1547–1563.

Romanelli F et al. Human Immunodeficiency Virus Drug Resistance Testing: State of the Art in Genotypic and Phenotypic Testing of Antiretrovirals. *Pharmacotherapy 2000;* 20(2):151–157.

Romano, M.J. et al. Life-Threatening Isradipine Poisoning in a Child. *Pharmacotherapy* 202;22(6): 766–770.

Rosenberg, J. and Federiuk, C. Optimal digoxin range for men is 0.5 to 0.8 ng/ml. *Journal of Family Practice 2003.* 52(5): 360–361.

Ross, S.D. Discontinuation of Antihypertensive Drugs Due to Adverse Events: A Systemic Review and Meta-Analysis. *Pharmacotherapy 2001;* 21(8): 940–953.

Russo, R.L. and D'Aprille M. Role of Antimicrobial Therapy in Acute Exacerbations of Chronic Obstructive Pulmonary Disease. *The Annals of Pharmacotherapy.* 35, 576–580. May 2001.

Roth, M.T. et al. Asthma Exacerbation After Administration of Nicotine Nasal Spray for Smoking Cessation. *Pharmacotherapy* 2002; 22(6):779–782.

Rybacki, J.J. Letter to the editor. *Journal of the American Medical Association.* 277(17):1351. 1997.

Rybacki, J.J. "What was the CURE trial?" Good News and New Medicines. 3(2): page 3 on www.medicineinfo.com. April 2001.

Rybacki, J.J. Improving Cardiovascular Health in Postmenopausal Women by Addressing Medication Adherence Issues. *The Journal of The American Pharmaceutical Association.* 42: 63–73. January/February, 2002.

Saag, K.G. Resolved: Low-dose glucocorticoids are neither safe nor effective for the long-term treatment of rheumatoid arthritis. *Arthritis Care & Research.* 45: pp 468–471. October 2001.

Sacks, F.M., et al. Effects on Blood Pressure of Reduced Dietary Sodium and the Dietary Approaches to Stop Hypertension (DASH) Diet. *New England Journal of Medicine.* 344(1): 3–10. January 4, 2001.

Sandler, R.S. et al. A Randomized Trial of Aspirin to Prevent Colorectal Adenomas in Patients with Previous Colorectal Cancer. *New England Journal of Medicine 2003.* 348: 883–890.

Sanford, J., et al. *The Sanford Guide to HIV/AIDS Therapy.* 5th ed. 1996. Antimicrobial Therapy, Inc. Vienna, VA: Lippincott-Raven.

Sarner, L. et al. Acute Onset lactic acidosis and pancreatitis in the third trimester of pregnancy in HIV-1 positive women taking antiretroviral medication. *Sex Transm Inf* 2002; 78(1):58–59.

Sauer, G. C. *Manual of Skin Diseases.* 5th ed. 1985. Philadelphia: J. B. Lippincott.

Scan Newsletter. 1996–1998. Norwich, NY: Society for Clinical Densitometry.

Schapowal, A. Randomized controlled trial of butterbur and cetirizine for treating seasonal allergic rhinitis. *British Medical Journal.* 2002;324: 144. www.bmj.org.

Schardein, J. L. *Drugs as Teratogens.* 1976. Cleveland: CRC Press.

Scheife, R.T., et al. Low Molecular Weight Heparins for Venous Thromboembolism: Making an Evidence-based Treatment Choice. *Pharmacotherapy.* 21(6), Part 2. June 2001.

Scheife, R.T., et al. New Strides in Asthma. *Pharmacotherapy.* 21(3), Part 2. March 2001.

Schneeweiss, S., et al. Outcomes of reference pricing for angiotensin-converting-enzyme inhibitors. *New England Journal of Medicine 2002.* 346: 822–829.

Schubert, I et al., Development of indicators for assessing the qulity of prescribing of lipid-lowering drugs: data from the pharmacotherapeutic quality circles in Hesse, Germany. *International Journal of Clinical and Pharmacological Therapy 2001 Nov;* 39(11): 492–498.

Schwartz, G.G., et al. Effects of Atorvastatin on Early Recurrent Ishcemic Events in Acute Coronary Syndromes the MIRACL Study: A randomized Controlled Trial. *Journal of the American Medical Association.* 285(13). April 4, 2001. Accessed from *www.jama.ama-assn.org.*

Scientific American Medicine. 1999. CD-ROM. New York: Enigma Information Systems.

Second Scientific Forum on Quality of Care and Outcomes Research in Cardiovascular Disease and Stroke. April 2000. The American Heart Association Councils on Clinical Cardiology, Cardiovascular Nursing, Cardiovascular Disease in the Young, Cardio-Thoracic and Vascular Surgery, Epidemiology and Prevention, High Blood

Pressure Research and the American College of Cardiology. Abstracts. Washington, DC.

Semla, T. P., et al. *Geriatric Dosage Handbook.* 1993. Cleveland: Lexi-comp.

Shavelle, D. M., et al. Exercise Testing and Electron Beam Computed Tomography in the Evaluation of Coronary Artery Disease. *Journal of the American College of Cardiology.* 36(1). 2000.

Shekelle, PG, et al. Efficacy of ACE inhibitors and beta blockers in the management of left ventricular systolic dysfunction according to race, gender and diabetic status. A meta-analysis of major clinical trials. *Journal of the American College of Cardiology* 2003; 41: 1529–1538.

Shepard, J.E. Effects of Estrogen on Cognition, Mood, and Degenerative Brain Diseases. *Journal of the American Pharmaceutical Association* 41(2):221–228. March/April 2001.

Shepard, T.H. *Catalog of Teratogenic Agents.* 6th ed. 1989. Baltimore: Johns Hopkins University Press.

Sherman, J. et al. Adherence to Oral Montelukast and Inhaled Fluticasone in Children with Persistent Asthma. *Pharmacotherapy.*21(12): 1464–1467. December 2001.

Sickle Cell Disease: Screening, Diagnosis, Management and Counseling in Newborns and Infants. 1993. Washington, DC: U.S. Department of Health and Human Services.

Silverstein, F.E., et al. Gastrointestinal toxicity with celecoxib vs nonsteroidal anti-inflammatory drugs for osteoarthritis and rheumatoid arthritis. The CLASS study: a randomized controlled trial. *JAMA 2000.* 284(10): 1247–1255.

Simpson, S.H., et al. Economic Impact of Community Pharmacist Intervention in Cholesterol Risk Management: An Evaluation of the Study of Cardiovascular Risk Intervention by Pharmacists. *Pharmacotherapy.* 21(5): 627–635. Mar 1, 2001.

Skaehill, P.A. Tacrolimus in Dermatologic Disorders. *The Annals of Pharmacotherapy.* 35: 582–588. May 2001.

Sleeper, R., et al. Psychotropic Drugs and Falls: New Evidence Pertaining to Serotonin Reuptake Inhibitors. *Pharmacotherapy 2000.* 20(3): 308–317. 2000.

Slatkin, N.E., et al. Donepezil in the treatment of opioid-induced sedation: report of six cases. J Pain Symptom Management 2001; 21(5):425–438.

Smith, L. H., and Thier, S. O. *Pathophysiology: The Biological Principles of Disease.* 2nd ed. 1985. Philadelphia: W. B. Saunders.

Song, J. C., et al. Pharmacologic, Pharmacokinetic and Therapeutic Differences Among Angiotensin II Receptor Antagonists. *Pharmacotherapy: The Journal of Human Pharmacology and Drug Therapy.* 20(2):130–39. 2000.

Sorensen, S. J., and S. R. Abel. Comparison of the Ocular Beta-Blockers. *Annals of Pharmacotherapy.* 30:43–54. 1997.

Sotiriou, C.G. and Cheng, J. Beneficial Effects of Statins in Coronary Artery Disease—Beyond Lowering Cholesterol. *The Annals of Pharmacotherapy.* 34:1432–1439. 2000.

Spanheimer, R.G. Reducing Cardiovascular Risk in Diabetes: Which Factors to Modify First? *Postgraduate Medicine.* 109(4):26–36. 2001.

Spath, P. L., ed. *Clinical Paths, Tools for Outcomes Management.* 1994. Chicago: The American Hospital Association.

Speight, T. M., and N. H. G. Holford, eds. *Avery's Drug Treatment.* 4th ed. 1997. Auckland, NZ: Adis International.

Spinler, S.A. New Recommendations from the 1999 American College of Cardiology/American Heart Association Acute Myocardial Infarction Guidelines. *The Annals of Pharmacotherapy.* 35:589–588. May 2001.

Steimer, W., et al. Digoxin Assays: frequent, substantial, and potentially dangerous interference by spironolactone, canrenone and other steroids. *Clinical Chemistry 2002; 48(3): 507–516.*

Stein EA. The power of statins: aggressive lipid lowering. *Clin Cardiol.* 2003 Apr;26(4 Suppl 3): III25–31.

Steinhubl SR et al. Early and Sustained Dual Oral Antiplatelet Therapy Following Percutaneous Coronary Intervention: A Randomized Controlled Trial. *Journal of the American Medical Association* 2002; 288: 2411–2420.

Stempel, et al. Inhaled Corticosteroids and Growth: How Big a Dose of Caution. *Contemporary Pediatrics.* 338(11):736–746. March, 2002.

Sterling, T.R. *The Hopkins HIV Report.* Volume 14, Number 2 When to start HAART: Still a Controversy. The Johns Hopkins University AIDS Service, Division of Infectious Diseases. March, 2002.

Stoupakis, G and Klapholz, M. Natriuretic peptides: biochemistry, physiology, and therapeutic role in heart failure. *Heart Disease* 2003;May-June; 5(3):215–223.

Straka, R. J., et al. Assessment of hypercholesterolemia control in a managed care organization. *Pharmacotherapy.* 21(7):818–827. 2001.

Straus SE. Herbal Medicines—What's In the Bottle? *New England Journal of Medicine* 2002; 347(25):1997–8.

Struckman, D.R. and Rivey, M.P. Combined Therapy with an Angiotensin II Receptor Blocker and an Angiotensin-Converting Enzyme Inhibitor in Heart Failure. *The Annals of Pharmacotherapy.* 35:242–248. 2001.

Sumpton, J.E. and Moulin, D.E. Treatment of Neuropathic Pain with Venlafaxine. *The Annals of Pharmacotherapy.* 35(5):557–559. May 2001.

Swash, M., and Schwartz, M. S. *Neuromuscular Diseases.* 2nd ed. 1988. Berlin: Springer-Verlag.

Swenson, C. N., and Fundak, G. Observational cohort study of switching warfarin sodium products in a managed care organization. *Am Jrn Health Syst. Pharm.* 57: 452–455. Mar 1, 2000.

Szefler, S. et al. (The Childhood Asthma Research Group) Long-term Effects of Budesonide or Nedocromil in Children with Asthma. *New England Journal of Medicine.* 343 (15): 1054–1069.

Tacconelli, S. et al. The Biochemical Selectivity of Novel COX-2 Inhibitors in Whole Blood Assays of COX-isozyme Activity. *Current Medical Research and Opinions* 2002;18(8): 503–511.

Tarle, M. et al. Early diagnosis of prostate cancer in finasteride treated BPH patients. *Anticancer Res.* 2003 Jan-Feb; 23(1B):693–6.

Taylor, A.J. et al. Lipid-Lowering Efficacy, Safety, and Costs of a Large-Scale Therapeutic Statin Formulary Conversion Program. *Pharmacotherapy* 2001; 21(9):1130–1139.

Tatro, D. S., ed. *Drug Interaction Facts.* 1997. St. Louis: J. B. Lippincott, Facts and Comparisons.

Temple, M.E., and Nahata, M.C. Treatment of Pediatric Hypertension. *Pharmacotherapy.* 20(2):140–150. 2000.

Teter, C.J. et al. A Comprehensive Review of MDMA and GHB: Two Common Club Drugs. *Pharmacotherapy* 2001; 21(12):1486–1513.

Teter, C.J. et al. Ilicit Methylphenidate Use in an Undergraduate Student Sample: Prevalence and Risk Factors. *Pharmacotherapy* 2003; 23(5):609–617.

Thompson, I.M. et al. The Influence of Finasteride on the Development of Prostate Cancer. *NEJM.* 2003 July 17. as accessed in early release form: *http://content.nejm.org/cgi/content/abstract/NEJM0a030660v1.*

Thordsen, D. J., and Welty, T. E., eds. *Clinical Abstracts: Current Therapeutic Findings.* 1998. Cincinnati, OH: Harvey Whitney Books.

Trachtman, H. et al. Clinical trial of extended-release felodipine in pediatric essential hypertension. *Pediatr Nephrol.* 2003 Jun; 18(6):548–53.

Tran M.T., et al. Role of Coenzyme Q10 in Chronic Heart Failure, Angina, and Hypertension. *Pharmacotherapy 2001;* 21(7)797–806. 2001.

Tsikouris, J.P. and Cox, C.D. A Review of Class III Antiarrhythmic Agents for Atrial Fibrillation: Maintenance of Normal Sinus Rhythm. *Pharmacotherapy.*21(12):1514–1529. December 2001.

Tsuyuki, R. T. and Bungard, T. J. Poor Adherence with Hypolipidemic Drugs: A Lost Opportunity. *Pharmacotherapy.* 21(5)576–582. Mar 1, 2001.

Tuchmann-Duplessis, H. *Drug Effects on the Fetus.* 1975. Sydney, Australia: ADIS Press.

Tufts Center for the Study of Drug Development. November 30, 2001. *Tufts Center for the Study of Drug Development Pegs Cost of a New Prescription Medicine at $802 Million.* 192 South Street, Boston, MA.

Tyler, V. E. *The Honest Herbal: A Sensible Guide to the Use of Herbs and Related Remedies.* 3rd ed. 1993. New York: Pharmaceutical Products Press, Haworth Press, Inc.

United States Pharmacopeial Convention (USP) Dispensing Information 1997. Vol. 1: Drug Information for the Health Care Provider. 12th ed. Rockville, MD: United States Pharmacopeial Convention.

Urwin, R.E. et al. Investigation of Epistasis Between the Serotonin Transporter and Norepinephrine Transporter Genes in Anorexia Nervosa. Neuropsychopharmacology. 2003 May 14 (epub ahead of print).

Utian, W. H. Menopause in Modern Perspective. 1980. New York: Appleton-Century-Crofts.

Van Gelder, I.C. et al. A Comparison of Rate Control and Rhythm Control in Patients with Recurrent Persistent Atrial Fibrillation. New England Journal of Medicine 2002;347(23): 1834–1840.

VanWalraven, C, et al. A clinical prediction rule to identify patients with atrial fibrillation and a low risk for stroke while taking aspirin. Archives of Internal Medicine 2003;163: 936–943.

Vasan, R.S. et al. Residual lifetime risk for developing hypertension in middle-aged women and men. Journal of the American Medical Association 2002; 287(8):1003–1010.

Vacek, J.L., Rosamond, T.L., et al. Acute coronary syndromes A three-article symposium. Postgraduate Medicine 2002;112(1).

Vinson, J.A. et al. Presentation: Cranberries: excellent source of polyphenol antioxidents. New Orleans, LA: American Chamical Society, 225th National Meeting, March 24, 2003. Abstract AGFD 65.

Volcheck, G.W. Which diagnostic tests for common allergies? Postgraduate Medicine May 2001;109(5): 71–85.

Vongpatanasin, W. et al. Differential effects of oral versus transdermal estrogen replacement therapy on C-reactive protein in postmenopausal women. Journal of the American College of Cardiology. 2003; 41:1358–1363.

Wallach, J. B. Interpretation of Diagnostic Tests. 6th ed. 1996. Boston: Little, Brown.

Watanabe, M.D. Antipsychotics in the Treatment of Schizophrenia. The Rx Consultant. X(5):1–7. 2001.

Weimerskirch, P. R., and Ernst, M. E. Newer Dopamine Agonists in the Treatment of Restless Legs Syndrome. The Annals of Pharmacotherapy. 35:627–635. May 2001.

Ward, M.W., and Holimon, T.D. Calcium Treatment for Premenstrual Syndrome. The Annals of Pharmacotherapy. 33:1356–1358. 1999.

Ward, R.P., and Anderson, A.S. Slowing the progression of CHF. Postgraduate Medicine. 109(3):36–45. 2001.

Weinblatt, M.E., et al. Adalimumab, a fully human anti-tumor necrosis factor alpha monoclonal antibody, for the treatment of rheumatoid arthritis in patients taking methotrexate: the ARMADA trial. Arthritis Rheum. 2003; 48:35–45.

Wenzel, R.P. and Edmond, M.B. Managing Antibiotic Resistance. New England Journal of Medicine. 343(26):1961–1963. December 28, 2000.

Willhite, L.A., and O'Connell, B. Urogenital Atrophy: Prevention and Treatment. Pharmacotherapy; 21(4): 464–480.

Wolf, M.M., et al. Gastrointestinal Toxicity of Nonsteroidal Anti-Inflammatory Drugs. New England Journal of Medicine. June 17, 1999: 1888–1899.

Wolfenden, L.L., et al. Lower physician estimate of underlying asthma severity leads to undertreatment. Arch Intern Med. 2003;163: 231–236.

Wood, A. J. J., and Ito, S. Drug Therapy for Breast-Feeding Women. New England Journal of Medicine. 343(2):118–126. July 13, 2000.

Wood, A. J. J., et al. Diuretic Therapy. New England Journal of Medicine. 339(6): 387–395. August 6, 1998.

Wood, A.J., DeSmet, PA. Herbal Remedies. New England Journal of Medicine 2002. 347: 2046–2056.

Wood, M. J., and Cox J. L. HRT to Prevent Cardiovascular Disease. What studies show, how to advise patients. Postgraduate Medicine. 108 (3):59–72. Sept 1, 2000.

Worley, R. J., ed. Menopause. Clinical Obstetrics and Gynecology. 24(1): 163–164. 1981.

www.backincontrol.net: Back Pain resource.

www.cdc.gov/ncidod/flu/fluvac.htm Vaccine Information Influenza Vaccine. July, 2001.

www.fda.gov/cder/approval?index.htm: The Food And Drug Administration. June, 2001.

www.fda.gov/cder/orange/docket/pdf: The Food And Drug Administration: CDERNEW6 June, 2001.

www.fdanewsdigest@oc.FDA.GOC (FDA News Digest): The Food And Drug Administration. July, August, 2001.

www.fda.gov/medwatch: The Food And Drug Administration: MedWatch various dates including 8/6/01, 2001.

www.medanews.com: MedAdNews. 20(5) May 2001.

www.naturaldatabase.com: The Pharmacist's Letter. 2002.

www.nlm.nih.gov/medlineplus/news/fullstory 2647. html: Herbal Medicines Pose Risk During Surgery: Report. July 11, 2001.

Wyse, D.G. et al. A Comparison of Rate Control and Rhythm Control in Patients with Atrial Fibrillation. *New England Journal of Medicine* 2002; 347(23):1825–1833.

Yashuda, J.M. and Chung, E.P. Diabetes Mellitus The New Insulin Analogs. *The Rx Consultant.* 11(2):1–8. 1999.

Yiu-Chung Chan, et al. Atypical Antipsychotics in Older Adults. *Pharmacotherapy.* 19: 811–822. 1999.

Yki-Jarvinen, H., et al. Bedtime Insulin Plus Metformin Prevents Weight Gain and Reduces Frequency of Hypoglycemia in Type 2 Diabetes. *Annals of Internal Medicine.* 130: 389–396. 1999.

Young, D. S. *Effects of Drugs on Clinical Laboratory Tests.* 1991 supplement. Washington, DC: AACC Press.

Young, L. L., ed. *Nonprescription Products: Formulations and Features '96–97.* Washington, DC: American Pharmaceutical Association.

Yusuf, S, et al. Effects of an Angiotensin-Converting-Enzyme Inhibitor, Ramipril, on Cardiovascular Events in High-Risk Patients. *New England Journal of Medicine.* 342(3): 145–153. January 20, 2000.

Zametkin, A. J., and Ernst, M. Problems in the Management of Attention-Deficit-Hyperactivity Disorder. *New England Journal of Medicine.* 340(1): 40–46. January 1999.

Ziccardi, P, et al. Reduction of inflammatory cytokine concentrations and improvement of endothelial functions in obese women after weight loss over one year. *Circulation 2002* accessed on line before print at *www.americanheart.org.*

Zonana-Nacach A et al. Damage in Systemic Lupus Erythematosus and Its Association with Corticosteroids. Arthritis & Rheu. 2000;43(8): 1801–1808.

Index

This index contains all the brand and generic drug names included in Section Two.

Brand names of drugs appear in italic type and are capitalized.

Each brand name is followed by its generic name. The generic name is the name under which you'll find the drug profile in Section Two.

The symbol [CD] indicates that the brand name represents a combination drug that contains other generic drug components; see the Drug Profile for details on other components present. To be fully familiar with any combination drug [CD], it is necessary to read the Drug Profile of each component.

The symbol ✤ before the brand name of a combination drug indicates that the brand name is used in both the United States and Canada but that the ingredients in the combination product in each country differ. The Canadian drug is marked with the symbol ✤ to distinguish it from the American drug with the same name.

A generic name with no page designation indicates an active component of a combination drug for which there is no Profile in Section Two. It is included to alert you to its presence, should you wish to consult your physician regarding its significance.

A&D with Prednisolone [CD], 926
Aasquel, phenobarbital, 892
A.B.C. Compound with Codeine [CD], 286
Abilify, aripiprazole, 145
Abitrexate, methotrexate, 700
AC&C [CD], 286
acarbose, 35
Accolate, zafirlukast, 139
Accopain, codeine, 286
Accuneb, albuterol, 56
Accupril, quinapril, 112
Accurbron, theophylline, 1104
Accuretic, quinapril, 112
Accutane, isotretinoin, 600
ACE (angiotensin converting enzyme)
   inhibitors, 112
acebutolol, 40
Acediur [CD], 112
ACEIs. *See* angiotensin converting enzyme
   (ACE) inhibitors, 112.
❦*Acet-Am,* theophylline, 1104
Acetaminophen-PM, diphenhydramine, 368
❦*Acetaminophen with Codeine, Extra*
   Strength [CD], 286
❦*Acetazolam,* acetazolamide, 46
acetazolamide, 46
acetic acids, 47
acetylsalicylic acid. *See* aspirin, 145.
Aches-N-Pain, ibuprofen, 951
Achromycin, tetracycline, 1098
Achromycin Ophthalmic, tetracycline, 1098
Achromycin V, tetracycline, 1098
❦*Acid Control,* famotidine, 537
Acid Controller, famotidine, 537
Acid Reducer, ranitidine, 537
Acid Reducer Cimetidine, cimetidine, 536
Acid Reducer 200, cimetidine, 536
A-Cillin, amoxicillin, 878
Aciphex, rabeprazole, 988

❦*Acrocidin,* tetracycline, 1098
Actagen-C [CD], 286
Actifed with Codeine [CD], 286
Actiprofen, ibuprofen, 951
Actiq, fentanyl, 429
Actisite, tetracycline, 1098
Activella, estrogen, 392
Actonel, risedronate, 1007
Actos, pioglitazone, 1119
Actron, ketoprofen, 951
Acular, ketorolac, 47
Acular PF (ketorolac ophthalmic),
   ketorolac, 47
acycloguanosine. *See* acyclovir, 295.
acyclovir, 295
Adalat, nifedipine, 808
Adalat CC, nifedipine, 808
❦*Adalat FT, XL,* nifedipine, 808
❦*Adalat P.A.,* nifedipine, 808
adalimumab, 56
Adapin, doxepin, 381
Added Strength Analgesic Pain Reliever,
   aspirin, 145
Adoxia, doxycycline, 1098
Adrenalin, epinephrine, 383
adrenaline. *See* epinephrine, 383.
Adreno-Mist, epinephrine, 383
Adsorbocarpine, pilocarpine, 900
Adult Chewable Aspirin, Low Dose, aspirin,
   145
Adult Strength Pain Reliever [CD], 145
❦*Advair* [CD], 478, 1013
Advair Diskus, salmeterol, 1013
Advair Diskus [CD], 478
Advicor, extended release niacin/lovastatin,
   419
Advil, Children's, ibuprofen, 951
Advil, ibuprofen, 951
Advil Migraine, ibuprofen, 951

A.E.A., theophylline, 1104
AeroBid, flunisolide, 452
AeroBid-M, flunisolide, 452
Aerolate, theophylline, 1104
Aeromax, salmeterol, 1013
Aeroseb-Dex, dexamethasone, 335
Afed-C [CD], 286
Agenerase, amprenavir, 966
Aggrenox [CD], 145
AID to Sleep, diphenhydramine, 368
Airet, albuterol, 56
Akarpine, pilocarpine, 900
Ak-Chlor, chloramphenicol, 242
❦*Ak-Cide* [CD], 926
❦*Ak-Dex*, dexamethasone, 335
AK-Mycin Ophthalmic, erythromycin, 669
Akne-Mycin, erythromycin, 669
❦*Ak-Pred*, prednisolone, 926
❦*Ak-Tate*, prednisolone, 926
Ak-Trol [CD], 335
Alamine-C [CD], 286
Alamine Expectorant [CD], 286
Alatone, spironolactone, 1047
Alazine, hydralazine, 546
❦*Albert Diltiazem CD*, diltiazem, 362
❦*Albert Furosemide*, furosemide, 494
❦*Albert-Glyburide*, glyburide, 524
albuterol, 56
alcohol. *See* ethanol, 406.
Aldactazide [CD], 1047, 1111
Aldactone, spironolactone, 1047
Aldochlor [CD], 1111
Aldoril-15/25 [CD], 1111
Aldoril D30/D50 [CD], 1111
alendronate, 61
Alesse, oral contraceptive, 840
Aleve, naproxen, 951
Alised, phenobarbital, 892
*Alka-Seltzer Effervescent Pain Reliever and
    Antacid* [CD], 145
Alka-Seltzer Night Time [CD], 145
Alka-Seltzer Plus [CD], 145
Alka-Seltzer Plus Cold [CD], 145
Allay [CD], 546
Allegra, fexofenadine, 749
Allegra-D [CD], 749
Allerdryl, diphenhydramine, 368
Allergy Capsules, diphenhydramine, 368
Allergy Formula, diphenhydramine, 368
Allermax, diphenhydramine, 368
❦*Alloprin*, allopurinol, 67
allopurinol, 67
Almocarpine, pilocarpine, 900
Alocril, nedocromil, 795
Alor 5/500 [CD], 546

Alora, estrogen, 392
alosetron, 71
Alostil, minoxidil, 755
Alphapress, hydralazine, 546
❦*Alpha-Tamoxifen*, tamoxifen, 1085
alprazolam, 72
Alprazolam Intensol, alprazolam, 72
Altace, ramipril, 112
Altace plus felodipine [CD], 427
❦*Alti-Amiodarone*, amiodarone, 86
❦*Alti-Atrovent*, ipratropium, 581
❦*Alti-Captopril*, captopril, 112
❦*Alti-Chlorambucil*, chlorambucil, 237
❦*Alti-Diltiazem*, diltiazem, 362
❦*Alti-famotidine*, famotidine, 537
❦*Alti-Fluoxetine*, fluoxetine, 466
❦*Alti-Haloperidol*, haloperidol, 531
❦*Alti-Lamotrigine*, lamotrigine, 627
❦*Alti-Mercaptopurine*, mercaptopurine,
    682
❦*Alti-Morphine*, morphine, 768
❦*Alti-MPA*, medroxyprogesterone, 677
❦*Alti-Nadol*, nadolol, 778
❦*Alti-Orciprenaline*, metaproterenol, 689
❦*Alti-Pindol*, pindolol, 904
❦*Alti-Piroxicam*, piroxicam, 853
❦*Alti-ranitidine*, ranitidine, 537
❦*Alti-Salbutamol*, albuterol, 56
❦*Alti-Sulfasalazine*, sulfasalazine, 1061
Alti-Thyroxine, levothyroxine, 644
❦*Alti-Trazodone*, trazodone, 1147
Alti-Trimethoprim, trimethoprim, 1160
❦*Alti-Valproic*, valproic acid, 1164
❦*Alti-Verapamil*, verapamil, 1183
Alubelap [CD], 892
Alupent, metaproterenol, 689
Alzapam, lorazepam, 664
Alzheimer's drugs, 133
amantadine, 77
Amaryl, glimepiride, 513
Ambenyl Expectorant [CD], 286
❦*Ambenyl Expectorant* [CD], 368
Ambenyl Syrup [CD], 286, 368
Ambien, zolpidem, 1212
Amcill, amoxicillin/clavulanate, 878
Amcort, triamcinolone, 1147
Amen, medroxyprogesterone, 677
❦*Amersol*, ibuprofen, 951
A-Methapred, methylprednisolone, 712
amethopterin. *See* methotrexate, 700.
amfebutamone. *See* bupropion, 199.
amiloride, 82
Aminodrox-Forte [CD], 892, 1104
Aminophyllin, aminophylline, 86
aminophylline, 86

5–aminosalicylic acid. *See* mesalamine, 686.
amiodarone, 86
Amitid, amitriptyline, 94
Amitril, amitriptyline, 94
amitriptyline, 94
amlodipine, 99
Amnesteem, isotretinoin, 600
amoxapine, 105
amoxicillin, 878
amoxicillin/clavulanate, 878
Amoxil, amoxicillin, 878
ampicillin, 878
Ampicillin-Probenecid [CD], 936
✤*Ampicin,* ampicillin, 878
✤*Ampicin PRB* [CD], 878, 936
✤*Ampilean,* ampicillin, 878
amprenavir, 966
Anacin [CD], 145
Anacin Maximum Strength [CD], 145
Anacin P.M. Aspirin-Free, diphenhydramine, 368
Anacin 3 with Codeine #2–4 [CD], 286
Anacin with Codeine [CD], 286
✤*Anacin with Codeine* [CD], 145
Anafranil, clomipramine, 256
anakinra, 105
Ana-Kit, epinephrine, 383
Anaplex, hydrocodone, 546
✤*Anaplex SR,* pyridostigmine, 978
Anaprox, naproxen, 951
Anaprox DS, naproxen, 951
anastrozole, 109
✤*Ancasal,* aspirin, 145
Ancobon, flucytosine, 448
✤*Ancotil,* flucytosine, 448
Andriol, testosterone, 1098
Androderm, testosterone, 1098
AndroGel 1%, testosterone, 1098
Anexsia 7.5 [CD], 546
Anexsia [CD], 546
angiotensin converting enzyme (ACE) inhibitors, 112
angiotensin II receptor antagonists, 124
Angipec, isosorbide dinitrate, 591
Anolor DH5, hydrocodone, 546
Ansaid, flurbiprofen, 951
Antabuse, disulfiram, 373
Antadine, amantadine, 77
anti-Alzheimer's drugs, 133
antibiotics:
cephalosporin, 230
fluoroquinolone, 457
macrolide, 668
penicillin, 878

sulfonamide, 1066
tetracycline, 1098
Anti-Diarrheal, loperamide, 660
antihistamines, minimally sedating, 748
anti-leukotrienes, 139
Antipress, imipramine, 561
Antispasmodic [CD], 892
anti-TNF monoclonal antibody. *See* infliximab, 567.
✤*Antivert* [CD], 800
APC [CD], 145
APC with Codeine [CD], 145, 286
✤*Apo-Acebutolol,* acebutolol, 40
✤*Apo-Acyclovir,* acyclovir, 295
✤*Apo-Allopurinol,* allopurinol, 67
✤*Apo-Alpraz,* alprazolam, 72
✤*Apo-Amilzide* [CD], 82, 1111
✤*Apo-Amitriptyline,* amitriptyline, 94
✤*Apo-Amoxi,* amoxicillin, 878
✤*Apo-Ampi,* ampicillin, 878
✤*APO-ASA,* aspirin, 145
✤*Apo-Atenolol,* atenolol, 155
✤*Apo-Atrovent,* ipratropium, 581
✤*Apo-Beclomethasone-AQ,* beclomethasone, 174
✤*Apo-Benztropine,* benztropine, 178
✤*Apo-buspirone,* buspirone, 205
✤*Apo-Capto,* captopril, 112
✤*Apo-Carbamazepine,* carbamazepine, 210
✤*Apo-Cephalex,* cephalexin, 230
✤*Apo-Cetirizine,* cetirizine, 749
✤*Apo-Chlorpropamide,* chlorpropamide, 244
✤*Apo-Chlorthalidone,* chlorthalidone, 1111
✤*Apo-Cimetidine,* cimetidine, 536
✤*Apo-Clomipramine,* clomipramine, 256
✤*Apo-clonazepam,* clonazepam, 262
✤*Apo-Clonidine,* clonidine, 266
✤*Apo-Cloxi,* cloxacillin, 878
✤*Apo-Clozaril,* clozapine, 281
✤*Apo-desipramine,* desipramine, 335
✤*Apo-Diazepam,* diazepam, 344
✤*Apo-Diclo,* diclofenac, 47
✤*Apo-Diclo SR,* diclofenac, 47
✤*Apo-Diltiaz,* diltiazem, 362
✤*Apo-Divalproic,* valproic acid, 1164
✤*Apo-Doxazosin,* doxazosin, 381
✤*Apo-Doxy,* doxycycline, 1098
✤*Apo-Doxy-Tabs,* doxycycline, 1098
✤*Apo-Erythro Base,* erythromycin, 669
✤*Apo-Erythro E-C,* erythromycin, 669
✤*Apo-Erythro-ES,* erythromycin, 669
✤*Apo-Erythro-S,* erythromycin, 669
✤*Apo-Fluconazole,* fluconazole, 444
✤*Apo-Fluoxetine,* fluoxetine, 466

✤*Apo-Fluphenazine,* fluphenazine, 473
✤*Apo-Flurazepam,* flurazepam, 474
✤*Apo-Flurbiprofen,* flurbiprofen, 951
✤*Apo-flutamide,* flutamide, 474
✤*Apo-Fluvoxamine,* fluvoxamine, 489
✤*Apo-Furosemide,* furosemide, 494
✤*Apo-Gain,* minoxidil, 755
✤*Apo-Gemfibrozil,* gemfibrozil, 508
✤*Apo-Glyburide,* glyburide, 524
✤*Apo-Haloperidol,* haloperidol, 531
Apo-Hydralazine, hydralazine, 546
✤*Apo-Hydro,* hydrochlorothiazide, 1111
✤*Apo-Ibuprofen,* ibuprofen, 951
✤*Apo-Imipramine,* imipramine, 561
✤*Apo-Indapamide,* indapamide, 562
✤*Apo-Indomethacin,* indomethacin, 47
✤*Apo-ISDN,* isosorbide dinitrate, 591
✤*Apo-Keto,* ketoprofen, 951
✤*Apo-Ketoconazole,* ketoconazole, 611
✤*Apo-Keto E,* ketoprofen, 951
✤*Apo-ketorolac,* ketorolac, 47
✤*Apo-Lamotrigine,* lamotrigine, 627
✤*Apo-Levocarb,* levodopa, 638
Apo-loperamide, loperamide, 660
✤*Apo-Lorazepam,* lorazepam, 664
✤*Apo-Mefanamic,* mefenamic acid, 428
✤*Apo-Metformin,* metformin, 693
✤*Apo-Methazide* [CD], 1111
✤*Apo-Metoclop,* metoclopramide, 723
✤*Apo-Metoprolol,* metoprolol, 728
✤*Apo-Metronidazole,* metronidazole, 734
✤*Apo-Misoprostol,* misoprostol, 764
✤*Apo-Nabumetone,* nabumetone, 47
✤*Apo-Nadol,* nadolol, 778
✤*Apo-Naproxen,* naproxen, 951
✤*Apo-Nifed,* nifedipine, 808
✤*Apo-Nizatidine,* nizatidine, 537
✤*Apo-Oflox,* ofloxacin, 457
✤*Apo-Oxtriphylline* [CD], 858, 1104
✤*Apo-Pen-VK,* penicillin VK, 878
✤*Apo-Perphenazine,* perphenazine, 891
✤*Apo-Pindol,* pindolol, 904
✤*Apo-Piroxicam,* piroxicam, 853
✤*Apo-Prazo,* prazosin, 925
✤*Apo-Prednisone,* prednisone, 928
✤*Apo-Primidone,* primidone, 935
✤*Apo-Procainamide,* procainamide, 940
✤*Apo-Propafenone,* propafenone, 945
✤*Apo-Propranolol,* propranolol, 958
✤*Apo-Quinidine,* quinidine, 983
✤*Apo-Ranitidine,* ranitidine, 537
✤*Apo-Salvent,* albuterol, 56
✤*Apo-Selegiline,* selegiline, 1017
✤*Apo-sertraline,* sertraline, 1023
✤*Apo-Simvastatin,* simvastatin, 1040

✤*Apo-Spirozide,* spironolactone, 1047
✤*Apo-Sucralfate,* sucralfate, 1060
✤*Apo-Sulfamethoxazole,* sulfamethoxazole, 1066
✤*Apo-Sulfatrim* [CD], 1066, 1160
✤*Apo-Sulfatrim DS* [CD], 1066, 1160
✤*Apo-Sulin,* sulindac, 47
✤*Apo-Tamox,* tamoxifen, 1085
✤*Apo-Terazosin,* terazosin, 1093
✤*Apo-Tetra,* tetracycline, 1098
✤*Apo-Thioridazine,* thioridazine, 1126
✤*Apo-Timolol,* timolol, 1128
✤*Apo-Timop,* timolol, 1128
✤*Apo-Tolbutamide,* tolbutamide, 1134
✤*Apo-Trazodone,* trazodone, 1147
✤*Apo-Triazide* [CD], 1111, 1155
✤*Apo-Trifluoperazine,* trifluoperazine, 1160
✤*Apo-Valproic,* valproic acid, 1164
✤*Apo-Verap,* verapamil, 1183
✤*Apo-Warfarin,* warfarin, 1190
✤*Apo-Zidovudine,* zidovudine, 1202
aprepitant, 144
Apresazide [CD], 546, 1111
Apresoline, hydralazine, 546
Apresoline-Esidrix [CD], 546, 1111
✤*Aquaphyllim,* theophylline, 1104
Aquatensen, methyclothiazide, 1112
Aralen, chloroquine, 243
Arava, leflunomide, 638
ARBs. *See* angiotensin II receptor antagonists, 124.
Arcoxia, etoricoxib (investigational), 311
ardeparin, 668
Aricept, donepezil, 133
Arimidex, anastrozole, 109
aripiprazole, 145
Aristocort, triamcinolone, 1147
Aristocort R, triamcinolone, 1147
Aristoform D, triamcinolone, 1147
✤*Aristospan,* triamcinolone, 1147
Arm-a-Med, metaproterenol, 689
Armour Thyroid [CD], 644
Arthritis Foundation Pain Reliever/Fever Reducer, ibuprofen, 951
Arthritis Pain Formula [CD], 145
Arthritis Strength Bufferin, aspirin, 145
Arthrotec [CD], 47, 764
Articulose LA, triamcinolone, 1147
ASA. *See* aspirin, 145.
5–ASA. *See* mesalamine, 686.
Asacol, mesalamine, 686
A.S.A. Enseals, aspirin, 145
✤*Asasantine* [CD], 145
✤*Asbron* [CD], 1104
Ascriptin [CD], 145

Ascriptin A/D [CD], 145
Asendin, amoxapine, 105
Asmalix, theophylline, 1104
Aspergum, aspirin, 145
aspirin, 145
❦*Aspirin,* aspirin, 145
Aspirin, Low Dose Adult Chewable, aspirin, 145
Aspirin PROTECT, aspirin, 145
Aspred-C [CD], 928
Asprimox, aspirin, 145
Asthmahaler, epinephrine, 383
Asthmanephrine, epinephrine, 383
Astramorph, morphine, 768
Astramorph PF, morphine, 768
❦*Astrin,* aspirin, 145
Atacand, candesartan, 124
Atacand HCT [CD], 124, 1111
Atasol-8, 15, -30 [CD], 286
atazanavir, 155, 966
Atemperator, valproic acid, 1164
atenolol, 155
Athrombin-K, warfarin, 1190
Ativan, lorazepam, 664
atomoxetine, 161
atorvastatin, 164
Atridox, doxycycline, 1098
Atrovent, ipratropium, 581
Atrovent [CD], 581
Atrovent Nasal Spray, ipratropium, 581
A/T/S, erythromycin, 669
Atuss [CD], 546
Augmentin, amoxicillin/clavulanate, 878
Augmentin, ampicillin, 878
Augmentin XR, amoxicillan/clavulanate, 878
auranofin, 171
❦*Aureocort,* triamcinolone, 1147
Aureomycin, tetracycline, 1098
Avalide [CD], 124, 1111
Avandamet [CD], 693
Avandia, rosiglitazone, 1119
Avapro, irbesartan, 124
Avelox, moxifloxacin, 457
Aventyl, nortriptyline, 820
Avinza, morphine, 768
Axid, nizatidine, 537
Axid AR, nizatidine, 537
Axotal [CD], 145
Azaline, sulfasalazine, 1061
azathioprine, 172
Azdone [CD], 145, 546
azidothymidine. *See* zidovudine, 1202.
azithromycin, 668
Azmacort, triamcinolone, 1147

Azo Gantanol [CD], 1066
Azo Gantrisin [CD], 1066
Azo-Sulfisoxazole, sulfisoxazole, 1066
Azpan [CD], 892, 1104
AZT. *See* zidovudine, 1202.
Azulfidine, sulfasalazine, 1061
Azulfidine EN-Tabs, sulfasalazine, 1061

bacampicillin, 878
❦*Bactopen,* cloxacillin, 878
Bactrim [CD], 1066, 1160
Bactrim DS [CD], 1066, 1160
Bactroban, mupirocin, 775
Bactroban Nasal, mupirocin, 775
Baldex, dexamethasone, 335
Banophen, diphenhydramine, 368
Ban-Tuiss C [CD], 286
Ban-Tuss-HC [CD], 546
Barbidonna [CD], 892
Barbidonna Elixir [CD], 892
Barbita, phenobarbital, 892
Baycol, cerivastatin, 237
Bayer, 8–Hour, aspirin, 145
Bayer Aspirin, aspirin, 145
Bayer Back & Body Pain, aspirin, 145
Bayer Children's Chewable Aspirin, aspirin, 145
Bayer Enteric Aspirin, aspirin, 145
Bayer Plus, aspirin, 145
Bayer PM Extra Strength, aspirin, 145
Bayer Select [CD], 368, 951
BC Powder, aspirin, 145
❦*Beclodisk,* beclomethasone, 174
❦*Becloforte,* beclomethasone, 174
beclomethasone, 174
Beclovent, beclomethasone, 174
❦*Beclovent Rotacaps,* beclomethasone, 174
❦*Beclovent Rotahaler,* beclomethasone, 174
Beconase AQ Nasal Spray, beclomethasone, 174
Beconase Nasal Inhaler, beclomethasone, 174
Beepen VK, penicillin VK, 878
Belap, phenobarbital, 892
Beldin Syrup, diphenhydramine, 368
Belladenal [CD], 892
Belladenal-S [CD], 892
❦*Belladenal Spacetabs* [CD], 892
Bellamine [CD], 387
Bellaspas [CD], 387
❦*Bellergal* [CD], 387, 892
Bellergal-S [CD], 387, 892
❦*Bellergal Spacetabs* [CD], 387, 892

Bena-D, diphenhydramine, 368
Benadryl, diphenhydramine, 368
Benadryl Allergy, diphenhydramine, 368
Benadryl 25, diphenhydramine, 368
Benahist, diphenhydramine, 368
benazepril, 112
Bendopa, levodopa, 638
bendroflumethiazide, 1111
Benemid, probenecid, 936
❧*Bensylate*, benztropine, 178
❧*Benuryl*, probenecid, 936
Benylin, diphenhydramine, 368
❧*Benylin Decongestant* [CD], 368
❧*Benylin Pediatric Syrup*,
    diphenhydramine, 368
Benylin Syrup with Codeine [CD], 286
❧*Benylin Syrup with Codeine* [CD], 368
Benzamycin [CD], 669
benztropine, 178
Betachron, propranolol, 958
❧*Betaloc*, metoprolol, 728
Betapen-VK, penicillin VK, 878
betaxolol, 182
Bethaprim [CD], 1066, 1160
Betimol, timolol, 1128
Betoptic, betaxolol, 182
Betoptic Pilo [CD], 900
Betoptic-Pilo [CD], 182
Betoptic-S, betaxolol, 182
Bextra, valdecoxib, 311
Biaxin, clarithromycin, 669
Biaxin XL, clarithromycin, 669
Biodopa, levodopa, 638
❧*Biohisdex DHC* [CD], 546
❧*Biohisdine DHC* [CD], 546
❧*Biprel* [CD], 562
❧*Biquin Durules*, quinidine, 983
birth control pills. *See* oral contraceptives,
    840.
Bitex [CD], 286
bitolterol, 188
Blephamide, prednisolone, 926
Blocadren, timolol, 1128
Braxan, amiodarone, 86
Brethaire, terbutaline, 1094
Brethine, terbutaline, 1094
Brevicon, oral contraceptive, 840
❧*Brexidol*, piroxicam, 853
Bricanyl, terbutaline, 1094
❧*Bricanyl Spacer*, terbutaline, 1094
Bristacycline, tetracycline, 1098
Brocomar [CD], 1104
Bromanyl Cough Syrup [CD], 286
bromocriptine, 188
Bromotuss, codeine, 286

Bromphen DC [CD], 286
❧*Bronalide*, flunisolide, 452
Bronchial Gelatin Capsule, theophylline,
    1104
Bronchotabs [CD], 892
Broncomar [CD], 1104
Bronkaid Mist, epinephrine, 383
❧*Bronkaid Mistometer*, epinephrine, 383
Bronkaid Tablets [CD], 1104
Bronkodyl, theophylline, 1104
Bronkolixir [CD], 892, 1104
Bronkotabs, theophylline, 1104
Bronkotabs [CD], 1104
Brontex [CD], 286
Bud Dry, ethanol, 406
budesonide, 188
Buffaprin, aspirin, 145
Bufferin [CD], 145
Bufferin Arthritis Strength [CD], 145
Bufferin Extra Strength [CD], 145
Bufferin with Codeine [CD], 145, 286
bumetanide, 194
Bumex, bumetanide, 194
bupropion, 199
Burinex, bumetanide, 194
Buspar, buspirone, 205
Buspar Dividose, buspirone, 205
❧*Buspirex*, buspirone, 205
buspirone, 205
Butalbital Compound [CD], 286

❧*C2 Buffered* [CD], 145, 286
❧*C2 with codeine*, codeine, 286
Cabernet, ethanol, 406
Cafergot [CD], 387
Cafergot P-B [CD], 387
❧*Cafergot PB*, phenobarbital, 892
Cafetrate [CD], 387
❧*Caladryl* [CD], 368
Calan, verapamil, 1183
Calan SR, verapamil, 1183
Calcimar, calcitonin, 209
calcitonin, 209
Caldyphen Lotion, diphenhydramine, 368
Cama Arthritis Pain Reliever [CD], 145
Cam-Ap-Es, hydralazine, 546
Camptosar, irinotecan, 586
camptothecin-11. *See* irinotecan, 585.
candesartan, 124
❧*Canesten*, clotrimazole, 277
capecitabine, 210
Capoten, captopril, 112
Capozide [CD], 112, 1111
captopril, 112
Carafate, sucralfate, 1060

carbamazepine, 210
Carbex, selegiline, 1017
Carbitrol Extended Release, carbamazepine, 210
♣*Carbolith,* lithium, 654
Cardene, nicardipine, 801
Cardene SR, nicardipine, 801
Cardioprin, aspirin, 145
Cardioquin, quinidine, 983
Cardizem, diltiazem, 362
Cardizem CD, diltiazem, 362
Cardizem LA, diltiazem, 362
Cardizem SR, diltiazem, 362
Cardura, doxazosin, 381
Cardura-1, doxazosin, 381
Carfin, warfarin, 1190
Carisoprodol Compound [CD], 145
carteolol, 218
Cartia XT, diltiazem, 362
Cartrol, carteolol, 218
carvedilol, 224
Cataflam, diclofenac, 47
Catapres, clonidine, 266
Catapres-TTS, clonidine, 266
cA2. *See* infliximab, 567.
Ceclor, cefaclor, 230
♣*Cedocard-SR,* isosorbide dinitrate, 591
cefaclor, 230
cefadroxil, 230
Cefanex, cephalexin, 230
cefixime, 230
cefprozil, 230
Ceftin, cefuroxime, 230
ceftriaxone, 230
cefuroxime, 230
Cefzil, cefprozil, 230
Celebrex, celecoxib, 311
celecoxib, 311
Celexa, citalopram, 250
Cenestin, synthetic conjugated estrogens, 1078
Cenocort, triamcinolone, 1147
Cenocort Forte, triamcinolone, 1147
Censpar, buspirone, 205
cephalexin, 230
cephalosporin antibiotics, 230
♣*Ceporex,* cephalexin, 230
cerivastatin, 237
♣*C.E.S.,* estrogen, 392
♣*C.E.S.,* synthetic conjugated estrogens, 1078
cetirizine, 748
Chardonna-2 [CD], 892
Chemdal Expectorant [CD], 286
Chemdal-HD [CD], 546

Chem-Tuss NE [CD], 286
Cheracol [CD], 286
Chibroxin, norfloxacin, 457
chickenpox vaccine. *See* Varicella virus vaccine, 1174.
Children's Advil, ibuprofen, 951
Children's Complete Allergy, diphenhydramine, 368
Children's Motrin, ibuprofen, 951
Children's Motrin Drops, ibuprofen, 951
Children's Motrin Suspension, ibuprofen, 951
Children's Nasalcrom, cromolyn, 319
chimeric monoclonal antibody to TFN alpha. *See* infliximab, 567.
Chloracol, chloramphenicol, 242
chlorambucil, 237
chloramphenicol, 242
Chlorofair, chloramphenicol, 242
Chloromycetin, chloramphenicol, 242
♣*Chloronase,* chlorpropamide, 244
Chloroptic, chloramphenicol, 242
Chloroptic SOP, chloramphenicol, 242
chloroquine, 243
chlorothiazide, 1111
Chlorotrianisene. *See* estrogens, 372; testosterone, 1098.
♣*Chlorpromanyl,* chlorpromazine, 244
chlorpromazine, 244
chlorpropamide, 244
chlorthalidone, 1111
Chlor-Trimeton Expectorant [CD], 286
♣*Chlor-Tripolon ND* [CD], 749
Choledyl, oxtriphylline, 858
Choledyl Delayed-Release, oxtriphylline, 858
Choledyl SA, oxtriphylline, 858
cholestyramine, 245
choline theophyllinate. *See* oxtriphylline, 858.
♣*Chronovera,* verapamil, 1183
Cibacalcin, calcitonin, 209
Cibalith-S, lithium, 654
ciclosporin. *See* cyclosporine, 328.
cilostazol, 246
Ciloxan, ciprofloxacin, 457
cimetidine, 536
Cin-Quin, quinidine, 983
Cipro, ciprofloxacin, 457
Cipro Cystitis pack, ciprofloxacin, 457
ciprofloxacin, 457
Cipro HC [CD], 457
cisapride, 250
citalopram, 250
♣*Citanest Forte,* epinephrine, 383
Clarinex, desloratadine, 749

clarithromycin, 668
❦Claritin Extra, loratadine, 749
Claritin Reditabs [CD], 749
❦Clavulin, amoxicillin, 878
❦Clavulin, ampicillin, 878
Clear Nicoderm CQ, nicotine, 801
Cleocin, clindamycin, 255
Cleocin Pediatric, clindamycin, 255
Cleocin T, clindamycin, 255
Cleocin Vaginal Cream, clindamycin, 255
❦Climacteron, estrogen, 392
Climara, estrogen, 392
❦Climestrone, estrogen, 392
clindamycin, 255
Clinoril, sulindac, 47
clomipramine, 256
clonazepam, 262
clonidine, 266
clopidogrel, 271
❦Clopra, metoclopramide, 723
Clotrimaderm, clotrimazole, 277
clotrimazole, 277
cloxacillin, 878
Cloxapen, cloxacillin, 878
clozapine, 281
Clozaril, clozapine, 281
Coactifed [CD], 286
CoAdvil [CD], 951
❦Co-Betaloc [CD], 728, 1111
Codecon-C [CD], 286
Codehist DH, codeine, 286
Codehist Elixir, codeine, 286
codeine, 286
❦Codeine Contin, codeine, 286
Codone, hydrocodone, 546
Cogentin, benztropine, 178
Cognex, tacrine, 133
Colabid [CD], 936
Colbenemid [CD], 291, 936
colchicine, 291
cold sore and genital herpes treatments,
    295
colesevelam, 303
Colestid, colestipol, 307
colestipol, 307
Col-Probenecid [CD], 291
Colsalide, colchicine, 291
❦Combid [CD], 940
Combipres [CD], 266, 1111
Combivent [CD], 56, 581
Combivir [CD], 622, 1202
Comoxol [CD], 1066, 1160
Compazine, prochlorperazine, 940
Complete Allergy, Children's,
    diphenhydramine, 368

Complete Allergy Medication,
    diphenhydramine, 368
compound S. See zidovudine, 1202.
Compoz, diphenhydramine, 368
Concerta, methylphenidate, 707
❦Congest, estrogen, 392
conjugated estrogens. See estrogens, 372;
    testosterone, 1098.
Constant-T, theophylline, 1104
Contimycin, tetracycline, 1098
contraceptives. See oral contraceptives,
    840.
Cope [CD], 145
Copegus, ribavirin, 994
❦Coptin [CD], 1160
❦Coradur, isosorbide dinitrate, 591
Cordarone, amiodarone, 86
Coreg, carvedilol, 224
Corgard, nadolol, 778
Coricidin [CD], 145
❦Coricidin with Codeine [CD], 286
Corobid, nitroglycerin, 814
❦Coronex, isosorbide dinitrate, 591
Cortalone, prednisolone, 926
❦Coryphen, aspirin, 145
❦Coryphen-Codeine [CD], 145, 286
Corzide [CD], 778
Cosopt [CD], 1128
Cotrim [CD], 1066, 1160
Coumadin, warfarin, 1190
Covera-HS, verapamil, 1183
cox two inhibitors, 311
Cozaar, losartan, 124
Crestor, rosuvastatin (investigational), 1013
Crixivan, indinavir, 966
Crolom, cromolyn, 319
cromolyn, 319
cromolyn sodium. See cromolyn, 319.
C-Solve 2, erythromycin, 669
Cuprimine, penicillamine, 878
Curretab, medroxyprogesterone, 677
Cutivate, fluticasone, 478
Cyclessa, oral contraceptive, 840
Cyclinex, tetracycline, 1098
Cycloblastin, cyclophosphamide, 323
Cyclopar, tetracycline, 1098
cyclophosphamide, 323
cyclosporin. See cyclosporine, 328.
cyclosporin A. See cyclosporine, 328.
cyclosporine, 328
Cycrin, medroxyprogesterone, 677
Cytomel, liothyronine, 649
Cytotec, misoprostol, 764
Cytovene, ganciclovir, 504
Cytoxan, cyclophosphamide, 323

❦*Dalacin C,* clindamycin, 255
❦*Dalacin T,* clindamycin, 255
Dalalone, dexamethasone, 335
Dalalone DP, dexamethasone, 335
Dalalone LA, dexamethasone, 335
Dalmane, flurazepam, 474
dalteparin, 668
D-Amp, ampicillin, 878
Daricon PB, phenobarbital, 892
Darvon Compound [CD], 145
Daypro, oxaprozin, 951
DDC. *See* zalcitabine, 1198.
DDI. *See* didanosine, 349.
Decaderm, dexamethasone, 335
Decadron, dexamethasone, 335
Decadron dose pack, dexamethasone, 335
Decadron-LA, dexamethasone, 335
Decadron Nasal Spray, dexamethasone, 335
Decadron Phosphate Ophthalmic,
    dexamethasone, 335
Decadron Phosphate Respihaler,
    dexamethasone, 335
Decadron Phosphate Turbinaire,
    dexamethasone, 335
Decadron with Xylocaine [CD], 335
Decaject, dexamethasone, 335
Decaject LA, dexamethasone, 335
Decaspray, dexamethasone, 335
Deenar [CD], 335
Delestrogen, estrogen, 392
Delta-Cortef, prednisolone, 926
Deltasone, prednisone, 928
Demerol, meperidine, 681
Demerol APAP [CD], 681
Demi-Regroton [CD], 1111
Demulen, oral contraceptive, 840
Denavir, penciclovir, 295
Deone-LA, dexamethasone, 335
Depa, valproic acid, 1164
Depade, raltrexone, 787
Depakene, valproic acid, 1164
Depakote (divalproex sodium), valproic
    acid, 1164
Depakote ER, valproic acid, 1164
Depakote Sprinkle, valproic acid, 1164
Depen, penicillamine, 878
Depmedalone-40, methylprednisolone, 712
Depmedalone-80, methylprednisolone, 712
Depo-Estradiol, estrogen, 392
Depo-Medrol, methylprednisolone, 712
Deponit, nitroglycerin, 814
Depo-Provera, medroxyprogesterone, 677
deprenyl. *See* selegiline, 1017.
Deprexan, desipramine, 335
Deproic, valproic acid, 1164

Deproist [CD], 286
Dermarest, diphenhydramine, 368
❦*Dermoplast,* hydroxychloroquine, 547
❦*Deronil,* dexamethasone, 335
❦*Desenex,* clotrimazole, 277
❦*Desenex AF,* clotrimazole, 277
desipramine, 335
desloratadine, 748
Desogen, oral contraceptive, 840
Desyrel, trazodone, 1147
❦*Desyrel Dividose,* trazodone, 1147
❦*Detensol,* propranolol, 958
Detrol, tolterodine, 1135
Detrol LA, tolterodine, 1135
❦*Detrol SR,* tolterodine, 1135
Detussin [CD], 546
Dex-4, dexamethasone, 335
Dexacen-4, dexamethasone, 335
Dexacen LA-8, dexamethasone, 335
Dexacidin [CD], 335
Dexacort, dexamethasone, 335
Dexameth, dexamethasone, 335
dexamethasone, 335
Dexasone, dexamethasone, 335
Dexasone-LA, dexamethasone, 335
dexmethylphenidate, 343
Dexo-LA, dexamethasone, 335
Dexon, dexamethasone, 335
Dexone-4, dexamethasone, 335
Dexone-E, dexamethasone, 335
Dexone-LA, dexamethasone, 335
Dexsone, dexamethasone, 335
Dexsone-E, dexamethasone, 335
Dexsone-LA, dexamethasone, 335
Dey-Dose, metaproterenol, 689
Dey-Lute, metaproterenol, 689
Dezone, dexamethasone, 335
d4T. *See* stavudine, 1053.
DHC Plus, hydrocodone, 546
Diabeta, glyburide, 524
Diabinese, chlorpropamide, 244
Diachlor, chlorothiazide, 1111
Diamox, acetazolamide, 46
Diamox Sequels, acetazolamide, 46
Diamox Sustained Release, acetazolamide,
    46
Diaqua, hydrochlorothiazide, 1111
Diarrid, loperamide, 660
Diastat, diazepam, 344
❦*Diazemuls,* diazepam, 344
diazepam, 344
Diazepam Intensol Oral Solution, diazepam,
    344
diclofenac, 47
❦*Diclophen* [CD], 892

Dicoril, hydrocodone, 546
didanosine, 349
Di-Delamine, diphenhydramine, 368
dideoxycytidine. *See* zalcitabine, 1198.
dideoxyinosine. *See* didanosine, 349.
Didronel, etidronate, 418
Diflucan, fluconazole, 444
❦*Digitaline Nativelle*, digoxin, 355
Digitek, digoxin, 355
digoxin, 355
Dihydrex, diphenhydramine, 368
dihydrocodeinone. *See* hydrocodone, 546.
Dilacor XR, diltiazem, 362
Dilantin, phenytoin, 893
Dilantin Infatabs, phenytoin, 893
Dilantin with Phenobarbital [CD], 892, 893
Dilatrate-SR, isosorbide dinitrate, 591
❦*Dilatrend*, carvedilol, 224
Diltia XT, diltiazem, 362
diltiazem, 362
Diltiazem, diltiazem, 362
Diltiazem ER, diltiazem, 362
❦*Dilusol*, ethanol, 406
Dimetane Cough Syrup-DC [CD], 286
Dimetane Expectorant-C [CD], 286
Dimetane Expectorant-DC [CD], 546
Dimetapp-C [CD], 286
Dimetapp Sinus [CD], 951
Dimetapp with Codeine [CD], 286
Diovan, valsartan, 124
Diovan HCT [CD], 124
Dipentum, olsalazine, 827
Di-Phen, phenytoin, 893
Diphendryl, diphenhydramine, 368
Diphenhist, diphenhydramine, 368
diphenhydramine, 368
Diphenylan, phenytoin, 893
diphenylhydantoin. *See* phenytoin, 893.
Direct Formulary Aspirin, aspirin, 145
Diskhaler, albuterol, 56
disopyramide, 373
disulfiram, 373
Diucardin, hydroflumethiazide, 1111
❦*Diuchlor H*, hydrochlorothiazide, 1111
Diulo, metolazone, 1112
Diupres [CD], 1111
Diurese, trichlormethiazide, 1112
diuretics, thiazide, 1111
Diurigen, chlorothiazide, 1111
Diuril, chlorothiazide, 1111
❦*Dixarit*, clonidine, 266
Dizac, diazepam, 344
docosanol cream (abreva), 295
dofetilide, 378
Dolacet [CD], 546

Dologesic, ibuprofen, 951
❦*Dom-carbamazepine-CR*, carbamazepine, 210
❦*Dom-Divalproex*, valproic acid, 1164
❦*Dom-Fluconazole*, fluconazole, 444
❦*Dom-Indapamide*, indapamide, 562
Dom-Ipratropium, ipratropium, 581
❦*Dom-Loperamide*, loperamide, 660
❦*Dom-Lorazepam*, lorazepam, 664
❦*Dom-Metformin*, metformin, 693
❦*Dom-Pindolol*, pindolol, 904
❦*Dom-Piroxicam*, piroxicam, 853
❦*Dom-Selegiline*, selegiline, 1017
❦*Dom-Sucralfate*, sucralfate, 1060
❦*Dom-Tamoxifen*, tamoxifen, 1085
❦*Dom-Timolol*, timolol, 1128
❦*Dom-Verapamil SR*, verapamil, 1183
donepezil, 133
Donna-Sed, phenobarbital, 892
Donnatal [CD], 892
Donphen, phenobarbital, 892
Dopar, levodopa, 638
Doral, quazepam, 982
Dormalin, quazepam, 982
Dormarex 2, diphenhydramine, 368
dornase alpha, 378
Doryx, doxycycline, 1098
❦*Doryx*, doxycycline, 1098
Doxaloc, doxazosin, 381
doxazosin, 381
doxepin, 381
Doxy 100, doxycycline, 1098
Doxy 200, doxycycline, 1098
Doxy Caps, doxycycline, 1098
Doxychel, doxycycline, 1098
❦*Doxycin*, doxycycline, 1098
doxycycline, 1098
Doxy-Lemmon, doxycycline, 1098
Doxy Tabs, doxycycline, 1098
Dralserp, hydralazine, 546
Dralzine, hydralazine, 546
Droxia, hydroxyurea, 552
Drummergal [CD], 387
D2E7. *See* adalimumab, 56.
Duapred, prednisolone, 926
Duocet [CD], 546
Duo-dezone, dexamethasone, 335
Duraclon, clonidine, 266
Duragal-S [CD], 387
Duragesic, fentanyl, 429
❦*Duralith*, lithium, 654
Duramorph, morphine, 768

Duranest [CD], 383
Durapam, flurazepam, 474
Duraphyl, theophylline, 1104
Duraquin, quinidine, 983
Duratuss HD [CD], 546
❧*Duretic,* methyclothiazide, 1112
Duricef, cefadroxil, 230
DV, estrogen, 392
Dyazide [CD], 1111, 1155
DynaCirc, isradipine, 605
DynaCirc CR, isradipine, 605
Dyrenium, triamterene, 1155
❧*Dysne-Inhal,* epinephrine, 383

Easprin, aspirin, 145
Econochlor, chloramphenicol, 242
Econopred Ophthalmic, prednisolone, 926
Ecotrin, aspirin, 145
E.E.S., erythromycin, 669
E.E.S. 200, erythromycin, 669
E.E.S. 400, erythromycin, 669
efavirenz, 382
Effexor, venlafaxine, 1178
Effexor XR, venlafaxine, 1178
8–Hour Bayer, aspirin, 145
Ekko JR, phenytoin, 893
Ekko SR, phenytoin, 893
Ekko Three, phenytoin, 893
Elan, isosorbide mononitrate, 596
Elantan, isosorbide mononitrate, 596
❧*Elase-Chloromycetin,* chloramphenicol, 242
❧*Elatrol,* amitriptyline, 94
Elavil, amitriptyline, 94
❧*Elavil Plus* [CD], 94, 891
Eldepryl, selegiline, 1017
Elixicon, theophylline, 1104
Elixomin, theophylline, 1104
Elixophyllin, theophylline, 1104
❧*Eltroxin,* levothyroxine, 644
Emend, aprepitant, 144
❧*Emex,* metoclopramide, 723
Emgel, erythromycin, 669
Emitrip, amitriptyline, 94
Empirin, aspirin, 145
Empirin with Codeine No. 2, 4 [CD], 145, 286
❧*Empracet-30, -60* [CD], 286
Empracet with Codeine No. 3, 4 [CD], 286
❧*Emtec-30* [CD], 286
E-Mycin, erythromycin, 669
E-Mycin Controlled Release, erythromycin, 669
E-Mycin E, erythromycin, 669
E-Mycin 333, erythromycin, 669
enalapril, 112

Enbrel, etanercept, 400
Endagen HD [CD], 546
Endal-HD, hydrocodone, 546
Endep, amitriptyline, 94
❧*Endocet* [CD], 858
❧*Endodan* [CD], 858
Endur-Acin, niacin, 800
Enduron, methyclothiazide, 1112
enfuvirtide, 382
❧*Enlon,* cimetidine, 536
Enovid, oral contraceptive, 840
Enovil, amitriptyline, 94
enoxaparin, 668
Enpak Refill, methylprednisolone, 712
❧*Entocort,* budesonide, 188
Entocort EC, budesonide, 188
❧*Entrafon,* perphenazine, 891
❧*Entrafon-Plus* [CD], 94
❧*Entrophen,* aspirin, 145
Entuss-D, hydrocodone, 546
E-Pam, diazepam, 344
Epifrin, epinephrine, 383
E-Pilo Preparations [CD], 383, 900
❧*Epimorph,* morphine, 768
Epinal Ophthalmic, epinephrine, 383
epinephrine, 383
EpiPen, epinephrine, 383
Epitol, carbamazepine, 210
Epitrate, epinephrine, 383
❧*Epival,* valproic acid, 1164
Epivir, lamivudine, 622
Epivir HBV, lamivudine, 622
eprosartan, 124
Eramycin, erythromycin, 669
Ercaf [CD], 387
Ergobel [CD], 387, 892
Ergocaf [CD], 387
❧*Ergodryl* [CD], 368, 387
Ergomar, ergotamine, 387
Ergostat, ergotamine, 387
ergotamine, 387
❧*Erybid,* erythromycin, 669
ERYC, erythromycin, 669
Erycette, erythromycin, 669
Eryderm, erythromycin, 669
Erygel, erythromycin, 669
Erymax, erythromycin, 669
EryPed, erythromycin, 669
Eryphar, erythromycin, 669
Ery-Tab, erythromycin, 669
Erythrocin, erythromycin, 669
❧*Erythromid,* erythromycin, 669
erythromycin, 668
Eryzole [CD], 1066
escitalopram, 392

Esclim, estrogen, 392
Esidrex, hydrochlorothiazide, 1111
Eskabarb, phenobarbital, 892
Eskalith, lithium, 654
Eskalith CR, lithium, 654
Eskaphen B [CD], 406, 892
Eskatrol, prochlorperazine, 940
E-Solve 2, erythromycin, 669
esterified estrogens. *See* estrogens, 372; testosterone, 1098.
Estinyl, estrogen, 392
Estrace, estrogen, 392
Estraderm, estrogen, 392
estradiol. *See* estrogens, 372; testosterone, 1098.
Estraguard, estrogen, 392
Estratab, estrogen, 392
estriol. *See* estrogens, 372; testosterone, 1098.
estrogens, 372. *See also* oral contraceptives, 840.
estrogens, synthetic conjugated, 1077
estrone. *See* estrogens, 372; testosterone, 1098.
estropipate. *See* estrogens, 372; testosterone, 1098.
Estrostep FE, oral contraceptive, 840
Estrovis, estrogen, 392
etanercept, 400
ethambutol, 405
ethanol, 406
ethosuximide, 414
Ethril, erythromycin, 669
✤*Etibi*, ethambutol, 405
etidronate, 418
etodolac, 47
etoricoxib, 311
Etrafon [CD], 94, 891
✤*Etrafon-A* [CD], 94, 891
✤*Etrafon-D* [CD], 94
Etrafon-Forte [CD], 94
Etrafon Forte [CD], 891
etretinate, 419
ETS-2%, erythromycin, 669
✤*Eucardic*, carvedilol, 224
✤*Euflex*, flutamide, 474
✤*Euglucon*, glyburide, 524
Eulexin, flutamide, 474
Euthroid [CD], 644, 649
Euthyrox, levothyroxine, 644
Evista, raloxifene, 989
Excedrin [CD], 145
Excedrin Extra Strength Geltabs [CD], 145
Excedrin IB, ibuprofen, 951
Excedrin Migraine [CD], 145

Excedrin P.M. [CD], 368
✤*Exdol-8, -15, -30* [CD], 286
Exelon, rivastigmine, 133
extended release niacin/lovastatin, 419
✤*Extra Strength Acetaminophen with Codeine* [CD], 286
Extra Strength Tylenol PM, diphenhydramine, 368
ezetimibe, 427
Ezide, hydrochlorothiazide, 1111

famciclovir, 295
famotidine, 536
Famvir, famciclovir, 295
Faspak Ampicillin, ampicillin, 878
5–FC. *See* flucytosine, 448.
Feldene, oxicam, 853
felodipine, 427
Femazole, metronidazole, 734
Femcare, clotrimazole, 277
Femhrt, estrogen, 392
Feminone, estrogen, 392
✤*Femogen*, estrogen, 392
✤*Femogex*, estrogen, 392
Femzol-7, clotrimazole, 277
fenamates, 428
fenoprofen, 951
fentanyl, 429
Fernisolone-P, prednisolone, 926
✤*Fexicam*, oxicams, 853
fexofenadine, 748
filgrastim, 435
finasteride, 440
Fiorinal [CD], 145
✤*Fiorinal-C 1/4, -C 1/2* [CD], 145, 286
Fiorinal with Codeine [CD], 145
Fiorinal with Codeine No. 1, 2, 3 [CD], 286
Fisoneb [CD], 319
5–aminosalicylic acid. *See* mesalamine, 686.
5–ASA. *See* mesalamine, 686
5–FC. *See* flucytosine, 448.
5–fluorocytosine. *See* flucytosine, 448.
500 Kit [CD], 878
Flagyl, metronidazole, 734
Flagyl ER, metronidazole, 734
Flagystatin [CD], 734
Flomax evening, tamsulosin, 1090
Flonase, fluticasone, 478
Floramine, phenobarbital, 892
Flovent, fluticasone, 478
Flovent Diskus, fluticasone, 478
Flovent Rotadisc, fluticasone, 478
Floxin, ofloxacin, 457
Floxin Otic, ofloxacin, 457
Floxin Uropak, ofloxacin, 457

fluconazole, 444
flucytosine, 448
Flu-Immune, influenza vaccine, 569
FluMist, influenza vaccine, 569
flunisolide, 452
Fluoge, influenza vaccine, 569
5–fluorocytosine. *See* flucytosine, 448.
fluoroquinolone antibiotics, 457
fluoxetine, 466
fluphenazine, 473
flurazepam, 474
flurbiprofen, 951
Flu-Shield, influenza vaccine, 569
Flutamex, flutamide, 474
flutamide, 474
Flutex, triamcinolone, 1147
fluticasone, 478
flu vaccine. *See* influenza vaccine, 568.
fluvastatin, 483
fluvoxamine, 489
Fluzone, influenza vaccine, 569
Focalin, dexmethylphenidate, 343
Folex, methotrexate, 700
Folex PFS, methotrexate, 700
Foradil Aerolizer, formoterol, 494
For-Az-Ma [CD], 1104
formoterol, 494
Forteo, teriparatide, 1098
Fortovase, saquinavir, 966
Fosamax, alendronate, 61
fosinopril, 112
Fragmin, dalteparin, 668
❦*Froben,* flurbiprofen, 951
❦*Froben-SR,* flurbiprofen, 951
Fumide MD, furosemide, 494
Furocot, furosemide, 494
Furomide MD, furosemide, 494
furosemide, 494
Furosemide-10, furosemide, 494
❦*Furoside,* furosemide, 494
Fuzeon, enfuvirtide, 382

gabapentin, 500
galantamine, 133
Gammacorten, dexamethasone, 335
ganciclovir, 504
Gantrisin, sulfisoxazole, 1066
❦*Gardenal,* phenobarbital, 892
❦*Gastrobid,* metoclopramide, 723
Gastrocrom, cromolyn, 319
gatifloxacin, 457
Gecil, diphenhydramine, 368
Gecil [CD], 287
Gemcor, gemfibrozil, 508
gemfibrozil, 508

❦*Gem-Gemfibrozil,* gemfibrozil, 508
❦*Gen-Acebutolol,* acebutolol, 40
Genacote, aspirin, 145
❦*Gen-Acyclovir,* acyclovir, 295
Genahist, diphenhydramine, 368
❦*Gen-Amiodarone,* amiodarone, 86
❦*Gen-Budesonide-AQ,* budesonide, 188
❦*Gen-Carbamazepine CR,* carbamazepine, 210
❦*Gen-cromolyn,* cromolyn, 319
❦*Gen-Doxazosin,* doxazosin, 381
Gen-D-Phen, diphenhydramine, 368
Genergen, ergotamine, 387
❦*Gen-Fluconazole,* fluconazole, 444
❦*Gen-Fluoxetine,* fluoxetine, 466
❦*Gen-Fluvoxamine,* fluvoxamine, 489
❦*Gen-Glybe,* glyburide, 524
❦*Gen-Indapamide,* indapamide, 562
❦*Gen-Nabumetone,* nabumetone, 47
❦*Gen-Nifedipine,* nifedipine, 808
Genora, oral contraceptive, 840
Genpril, ibuprofen, 951
Genprin, aspirin, 145
❦*Gen-Propafenone,* propafenone, 945
❦*Gen-sertraline,* sertraline, 1023
❦*Gen-Simvastatin,* simvastatin, 1040
❦*Gen-Verapamil,* verapamil, 1183
❦*Gen-Warfarin,* warfarin, 1190
Geodon, ziprasidone, 1208
Gestodene, oral contraceptive, 840
Gleevec, imatinib, 556
Glenlivet, ethanol, 406
glibenclamide. *See* glyburide, 524.
glimepiride, 513
glipizide, 518
Glubate, glyburide, 524
Glucamide, chlorpropamide, 244
Glucobay, acarbose, 35
❦*Gluconorm,* repaglinide, 993
Glucophage, metformin, 693
Glucophage XR, metformin, 693
Glucotrol, glipizide, 518
Glucotrol XL, glipizide, 518
Glucovance [CD], 524, 693
glyburide, 524
❦*Glycon,* metformin, 693
Glydeine, codeine, 287
Glynase Prestab, glyburide, 524
Glyset, miglitol, 743
Goody's Headache Powder [CD], 145
❦*Gravergol* [CD], 387
grepafloxacin, 457
guanfacine, 531
Guildprofen, ibuprofen, 951
Gulfasin, sulfisoxazole, 1066

Gyne-Lotrimin, clotrimazole, 277
♣*Gynergen*, ergotamine, 387
Gynetone, estrogen, 392
Gynodiol, estrogen, 392
Gynogen LA, estrogen, 392

Habitrol, nicotine, 801
♣*Hairgro*, minoxidil, 755
Haldol, haloperidol, 531
♣*Haldol LA*, haloperidol, 531
haloperidol, 531
Halperon, haloperidol, 531
Halprin, aspirin, 145
Haltran, ibuprofen, 951
Heartburn 200, cimetidine, 536
Heartburn Relief 200, cimetidine, 536–37
Helidac [CD], 734
heparins, low molecular weight, 668
Hepto [CD], 145
Hexadrol, dexamethasone, 335
H.H.R., hydrochlorothiazide, 1111
H-H-R [CD], 546, 1111
histamine blocking drugs, 536
Histinex-HC [CD], 546
Histussin HC [CD], 546
Hivid, zalcitabine, 1198
hPTH 1–34. *See* teriparatide, 1098.
Humalog, insulin, 574
Humalog Mix 75/25, insulin, 574
human PTH 1–34. *See* teriparatide, 1098.
Humira, adalimumab, 56
Humulin BR, insulin, 574
Humulin L, insulin, 574
Humulin N, insulin, 574
Humulin R, insulin, 574
Humulin 70/30, insulin, 574
Humulin 30/70, insulin, 574
Humulin U, insulin, 574
Humulin U Ultralente, insulin, 574
Hybephen [CD], 892
♣*Hycodan*, hydrocodone, 546
Hycodan [CD], 546
♣*Hycomine* [CD], 546
Hycomine Compound [CD], 546
Hycomine Pediatric Syrup [CD], 546
♣*Hycomine-S* [CD], 546
Hycomine Syrup [CD], 546
Hyco-tuss Expectorant [CD], 546
Hydelta-TBA, prednisolone, 926
Hydeltrasol, prednisolone, 926
hydralazine, 546
Hydramine, diphenhydramine, 368
Hydrea, hydroxyurea, 552
hydrochlorothiazide, 1111
hydrocodone, 546

HydroDiuril, hydrochlorothiazide, 1111
hydroflumethiazide, 1111
Hydromal, hydrochlorothiazide, 1111
Hydro-Par, hydrochlorothiazide, 1111
Hydropres [CD], 1111
Hydroserpine [CD], 546, 1111
Hydroserpine Plus [CD], 1111
Hydro-T, hydrochlorothiazide, 1111
hydroxychloroquine, 547
hydroxyurea, 552
Hydro-Z-50, hydrochlorothiazide, 1111
Hygroton, chlorthalidone, 1111
♣*Hygroton-Resperpine* [CD], 1111
Hylidone, chlorthalidone, 1111
Hypnaldyne [CD], 892
Hyserp [CD], 546
Hytrin, terazosin, 1093
Hyzaar, [CD], 124, 1111

Ibu, ibuprofen, 951
ibuprofen, 951
Ibuprohm, ibuprofen, 951
I-Chlor, chloramphenicol, 242
ICID1033. *See* anastrozole, 109
Iletin I NPH, insulin, 574
Iletin II Pork, insulin, 574
Iletin U-40, insulin, 574
Iletin U-500, insulin, 574
Ilosone, erythromycin, 669
Ilotycin, erythromycin, 669
imatinib, 556
Imdur, isosorbide mononitrate, 596
imipramine, 561
Imitrex, sumatriptan, 1071
Imitrex Nasal Spray, sumatriptan, 1071
Imodium, loperamide, 660
Imodium AD, loperamide, 660
♣*Imodium Advanced*, loperamide, 660
♣*Impril*, imipramine, 561
Imprin, imipramine, 561
Imuran, azathioprine, 172
Indameth, indomethacin, 47
indapamide, 562
Inderal, propranolol, 958
Inderal-LA, propranolol, 958
Inderide [CD], 958, 1111
Inderide LA [CD], 958, 1111
indinavir, 966
♣*Indocid*, indomethacin, 47
♣*Indocid PDA*, indomethacin, 47
♣*Indocid-SR*, indomethacin, 47
Indocin, indomethacin, 47
Indocin-SR, indomethacin, 47
indomethacin, 47
♣*Inflamase*, prednisolone, 926

❦*Inflamase Forte*, prednisolone, 926
infliximab, 567
influenza vaccine, 568
Infumorph, morphine, 768
INH, isoniazid, 586
❦*Initard*, insulin, 574
Innohep, tinzaparin, 668
Innopran XL, propranolol, 958
❦*Innovar*, fentanyl, 429
❦*Insomnal*, diphenhydramine, 368
Insulatard NPH, insulin, 574
insulin, 574
insulin aspart (NovoLog), insulin, 574
❦*Insulin Human*, insulin, 574
❦*Insulin-Toronto*, insulin, 574
Intal, cromolyn, 319
❦*Intal Spincaps*, cromolyn, 319
❦*Intal Syncroner*, cromolyn, 319
Invirase, saquinavir, 966
I-Pilopine, pilocarpine, 900
Ipran, propranolol, 958
ipratropium, 581
Ipratropium Novaplus, ipratropium, 581
irbesartan, 124
irinotecan, 586
❦*Ismelin-Esidrex* [CD], 1111
Ismo, isosorbide mononitrate, 596
Iso-BID, isosorbide dinitrate, 591
Isochron, isosorbide dinitrate, 591
Isoclor Expectorant [CD], 287
Isonate, isosorbide dinitrate, 591
isoniazid, 586
isonicotinic acid hydrazide. *See* isoniazid, 586.
Isopro, prochlorperazine, 940
Isoptin, verapamil, 1183
Isoptin SR, verapamil, 1183
Isopto Carpine, pilocarpine, 900
Isopto Cetapred [CD], 926
❦*Isopto Fenicol*, chloramphenicol, 242
Isordil, isosorbide dinitrate, 591
Isordil Tembids, isosorbide dinitrate, 591
Isordil Titradose, isosorbide dinitrate, 591
isosorbide dinitrate, 591
isosorbide mononitrate, 596
❦*Isotamine*, isoniazid, 586
Isotrate Timecelles, isosorbide dinitrate, 591
isotretinoin, 600
isradipine, 605
Isuprel Compound [CD], 892, 1104

Janimine, imipramine, 561
Jenest 28, oral contraceptive, 840
Junior Strength Motrin Caplets, ibuprofen, 951

Kadian, morphine, 768
Kaletra, lopinavir and ritonavir, 966
Kaletra [CD], 966
Kaopectate 1–D, loperamide, 660
Keflet, cephalexin, 230
Keflex, cephalexin, 230
Keftab, cephalexin, 230
Kefurox, cefuroxime, 230
❦*Kenacomb*, triamcinolone, 1147
Kenacort, triamcinolone, 1147
Kenaject, triamcinolone, 1147
Kenalog, triamcinolone, 1147
Kenalog H, triamcinolone, 1147
Kenalog IN, triamcinolone, 1147
Kenalone, triamcinolone, 1147
Kerlone, betaxolol, 182
ketoconazole, 611
ketoprofen, 951
ketorolac, 47
Key-Pred, prednisolone, 926
Kineret, anakinra, 105
Kinesed [CD], 892
Klonopin, clonazepam, 262
Klonopin Wafers, clonazepam, 262
Kolex, diphenhydramine, 368
Kresse, minoxidil, 755
Kronofed-A-JR, chloroquine, 243

labetalol, 616
Labid, theophylline, 1104
Lagyl, metronidazole, 734
Lamictal, lamotrigine, 627
lamivudine, 622
lamotrigine, 627
Laniazid, isoniazid, 586
Lanophyllin, theophylline, 1104
Lanoxicaps, digoxin, 355
Lanoxin, digoxin, 355
lansoprazole, 631
Lantus, insulin, 574
❦*Largactil*, chlorpromazine, 244
Larodopa, levodopa, 638
Larotid, amoxicillin, 878
Lasaject, furosemide, 494
Lasimide, furosemide, 494
Lasix, furosemide, 494
❦*Lasix Special*, furosemide, 494
latanoprost, 635
Ledercillin VK, penicillin VK, 878
leflunomide, 638
Lemtrex, tetracycline, 1098
❦*Lenoltec with Codeine No. 1, 2, 3, 4* [CD], 287
Lente Iletin I, insulin, 574
Lente Iletin II Pork, insulin, 574

Lente Insulin, insulin, 574
Lente Purified Pork, insulin, 574
Lescol, fluvastatin, 483
Lescol XL, fluvastatin, 483
Lestid, colestipol, 307
Leukeran, chlorambucil, 237
leukotriene drugs, 139
Levaquin, levofloxacin, 457
❧*Levate,* amitriptyline, 94
Levatol, penbutolol, 877
Levlen, oral contraceptive, 840
Levlite, oral contraceptive, 840
levodopa, 638
levofloxacin, 457
Levora, oral contraceptive, 840
Levo-T, levothyroxine, 644
Levotabs, levothyroxine, 644
Levothroid, levothyroxine, 644
levothyroxine, 644
Levoxine, levothyroxine, 644
Levoxyl, levothyroxine, 644
Lexapro, escitalopram, 392
Lexxel [CD], 112, 427
lidocaine, 649
Lidoderm, lidocaine, 649
Limbitrol [CD], 94
❧*Lin-Fosinopril,* fosinopril, 112
❧*Lin-Nefazodone,* nefazodone, 795
❧*Lin-Pravastatin,* pravastatin, 918
❧*Lin-Warfarin,* warfarin, 1190
liothyronine, 649
Lipitor, atorvastatin, 164
Lipo Gantrisin, sulfisoxazole, 1066
Liquid Pred, prednisone, 928
lisinopril, 112
Liskonium, lithium, 654
Lithane, lithium, 654
lithium, 654
❧*Lithizine,* lithium, 654
Lithobid, lithium, 654
Lithonate, lithium, 654
Lithotabs, lithium, 654
Lixolin, theophylline, 1104
Lo-Aqua, furosemide, 494
Lodine, etodolac, 47
Lodine XL, etodolac, 47
Lodrane, theophylline, 1104
Lodrane CR, theophylline, 1104
Loestrin, oral contraceptive, 840
❧*Logimax* [CD], 427, 728
lomefloxacin, 457
Loniten, minoxidil, 755
Lo/Ovral, oral contraceptive, 840
loperamide, 660
Lopid, gemfibrozil, 508

lopinavir and ritonavir, 966
Lopressor, metoprolol, 728
Lopressor Delayed-Release, metoprolol, 728
Lopressor HCT [CD], 728, 1111
Lopressor OROS, metoprolol, 728
Lopurin, allopurinol, 67
Lorabid, loracarbef, 230
loracarbef, 230
loratadine, 748
Loraz, lorazepam, 664
lorazepam, 664
Lorazepam Intensol, lorazepam, 664
Lorcet-HD [CD], 546
Lorcet Plus [CD], 546
Lortab [CD], 546
Lortab ASA [CD], 145, 546
losartan, 124
❧*Losec,* omeprazole, 830
Losec Helicopak [CD], 734
Lo-Ten, hydralazine, 546
Lotensin, benazepril, 112
Lotensin HCT [CD], 112
Lotrel [CD], 99, 112
❧*Lotriderm,* clotrimazole, 277
Lotrimin, clotrimazole, 277
Lotrimin AF, clotrimazole, 277
Lotrisone, clotrimazole, 277
Lotronex, alosetron, 71
lovastatin, 668
Lovenox, enoxaparin, 668
Low Dose Adult Chewable Aspirin, aspirin, 145
low molecular weight heparins, 668
Low-Ogestrel, oral contraceptive, 840
❧*Lozide,* indapamide, 562
Lozol, indapamide, 562
L-Thyroxine, levothyroxine, 644
Ludiomil, maprotiline, 677
Luminal, phenobarbital, 892
Luramide, furosemide, 494
Luvox, fluvoxamine, 489

Maalox A/D, loperamide, 660
macrolide antibiotics, 668
❧*Mandrax* [CD], 368
maprotiline, 677
Marax [CD], 1104
Marax DF [CD], 1104
Marazide II, trichlormethiazide, 1112
Marcaine, epinephrine, 383
Marnal [CD], 145
Maronil, clomipramine, 256
Mar-Pred 40, methylprednisolone, 712
Marpres, hydralazine, 546
Maxair, pirbuterol, 909

Maxalt, rizatriptan, 1012
Maxalt-MLT, rizatriptan, 1012
✤*Maxalt RPD,* rizatriptan, 1012
Maxaquin, levofloxacin, 457
✤*Maxeran,* metoclopramide, 723
Maxidex, dexamethasone, 335
Maximum Bayer Aspirin, aspirin, 145
Maximum Strength Nytol,
    diphenhydramine, 368
Maxolon, metoclopramide, 723
Maxzide [CD], 1111, 1155
Maxzide-25 [CD], 1111, 1155
✤*Mazepine,* carbamazepine, 210
M Dopazide [CD], 1111
Measurin, aspirin, 145
✤*Mebroin* [CD], 893
Meclodium, meclofenamate, 428
Meclofenaf, meclofenamate, 428
meclofenamate, 428
Meclomen, meclofenamate, 428
✤*Med-Acebutolol,* acebutolol, 40
✤*Med-Alprazolam,* alprazolam, 72
✤*Med-Amiodarone,* amiodarone, 86
✤*Med-azathioprine,* azathioprine, 172
✤*Med-Beclomethasone-AQ,*
    beclomethasone, 174
✤*Med-Broncodil,* terbutaline, 1094
✤*Med-Buspirone,* buspirone, 205
✤*Med-clonazepam,* clonazepam, 262
Med Diltiazem SR, diltiazem, 362
✤*Med-Doxazosin,* doxazosin, 381
✤*Med-Fluoxetine,* fluoxetine, 466
✤*Med-Gemfibrozil,* gemfibrozil, 508
✤*Medicycline,* tetracycline, 1098
Medihaler-Epi Preparations, epinephrine,
    383
Medihaler Ergotamine, ergotamine, 387
Medipain 5, hydrocodone, 546
Medi-Phedryl, diphenhydramine, 368
Medipren, ibuprofen, 951
Medi-Profen, ibuprofen, 951
✤*Med-Minoxidil,* minoxidil, 755
✤*Med-Pirocam,* piroxicam, 853
Medrol, methylprednisolone, 712
✤*Medrol Acne Lotion,* methylprednisolone,
    712
Medrol Enpak, methylprednisolone, 712
✤*Medrol Veriderm Cream,*
    methylprednisolone, 712
medroxyprogesterone, 677
✤*Med-Selegiline,* selegiline, 1017
✤*Med-Verapamil,* verapamil, 1183
mefenamic acid, 428
✤*Megral* [CD], 387
Mellaril, thioridazine, 1126

Mellaril-S, thioridazine, 1126
Menest, estrogen, 392
Menotab, estrogen, 392
Menotab-M, estrogen, 392
Menrium [CD], 392
Mepergan, meperidine, 681
meperidine, 681
Meprolone, methylprednisolone, 712
mercaptopurine, 682
Meridia, sibutramine, 1029
✤*Mersyndol,* codeine, 287
mesalamine, 686
mesalazine. *See* mesalamine, 686.
✤*Mesasal,* mesalamine, 686
✤*M-Eslon,* morphine, 768
Mestinon, pyridostigmine, 978
Mestinon-SR, pyridostigmine, 978
Mestinon Timespan, pyridostigmine, 978
Metadate CD and ER, methylphenidate, 707
Metaglip [CD], 518, 693
Metahydrin, trichlormethiazide, 1112
Metaprel, metaproterenol, 689
Metaprel Nasal Inhaler, metaproterenol, 689
metaproterenol, 689
Metastron, strontium-89, 1057
metformin, 693
methotrexate, 700
methyclothiazide, 1111
Methylin ER, methylphenidate, 707
methylphenidate, 707
methylprednisolone, 712
methysergide, 719
Meticortelone, prednisolone, 926
Meticorten, prednisone, 928
Meti-Derm, prednisolone, 926
Metimyd [CD], 926
Metizol, metronidazole, 734
metoclopramide, 723
metolazone, 1111
metoprolol, 727
Metreton, prednisolone, 926
MetroGel, metronidazole, 734
Metro IV, metronidazole, 734
metronidazole, 734
Metryl, metronidazole, 734
✤*Meval,* diazepam, 344
Mexate, methotrexate, 700
Mexate AQ, methotrexate, 700
mexiletine, 739
Mexitil, mexiletine, 739
Miacalcin Injection, calcitonin, 209
Miacalcin Nasal Spray, calcitonin, 209
mibefradil, 743
Micardis, telmisartan, 124
Micronase, glyburide, 524

Micronephrine, epinephrine, 383
Micronor, oral contraceptive, 840
Microx, metolazone, 1112
Microzide, hydrochlorothiazide, 1111
Mictrin, hydrochlorothiazide, 1111
Midamor, amiloride, 82
Midol Caplets [CD], 145
Midol-IB, ibuprofen, 951
Midol-PM, diphenhydramine, 368
miglitol, 743
Millazine, thioridazine, 1126
Milprem [CD], 392
❧*Minestrin*, estrogen, 392
❧*Minestrin 1/20*, oral contraceptive, 840
❧*Minims* [CD], 242, 900
❧*Minims Prednisolone*, 926
Minipres, prazosin, 925
Minitran Transdermal Delivery System,
    nitroglycerin, 814
Minizide [CD], 925
Minocalve 5, minoxidil, 755
Minodyl, minoxidil, 755
Min-Ovral, oral contraceptive, 840
minoxidil, 755
Minoximen, minoxidil, 755
❧*Miocarpine*, pilocarpine, 900
Mirapex, pramipexole, 917
Mircette, oral contraceptive, 840
mirtazapine, 760
misoprostol, 764
Mixtard, insulin, 574
Mixtard Human 70/30, insulin, 574
Moban, molindone, 768
❧*Mobenol*, tolbutamide, 1134
modafinil, 768
❧*Modecate*, fluphenazine, 473
Modicon, oral contraceptive, 840
❧*Moditan*, fluphenazine, 473
❧*Moduret* [CD], 82, 1111
Moduretic [CD], 82, 1111
molindone, 768
Momentum [CD], 145
❧*Monitan*, acebutolol, 40
Monodox, doxycycline, 1098
Monoket, isosorbide mononitrate, 596
Monopril, fosinopril, 112
Monopril HCT, fosinopril, 112
montelukast, 139
morphine, 768
❧*Morphine H.P.*, morphine, 768
❧*Morphitec*, morphine, 768
❧*M.O.S.*, morphine, 768
❧*M.O.S.-S.R.*, morphine, 768
Motrin, Children's, ibuprofen, 951
Motrin, ibuprofen, 951

Motrin Caplets, Junior Strength, ibuprofen,
    951
Motrin Drops, Children's, ibuprofen, 951
Motrin IB, ibuprofen, 951
Motrin Suspension, Children's ibuprofen,
    951
moxifloxacin, 457
mozenavir (investigational), 966
6–MP. *See* mercaptopurine, 682.
MS (morphine sulfate). *See* morphine, 768.
MS Contin, morphine, 768
MS-IR, morphine, 768
MTX. *See* methotrexate, 700.
Mudrane [CD], 86
Mudrane GG [CD], 86
Mudrane GG Elixir [CD], 1104
Mudrane GG Elixir and Tablets [CD], 892
Mudrane Tablets [CD], 892
mupirocin, 775
Myambutol, ethambutol, 405
Mycelex, clotrimazole, 277
Mycelex-G, clotrimazole, 277
Mycelex-7, clotrimazole, 277
❧*Myclo*, clotrimazole, 277
❧*Myclo-Gyne*, clotrimazole, 277
Mycobutin, rifabutin, 1000
Mycogen II, triamcinolone, 1147
Mycolog [CD], 1147
Mycomar, triamcinolone, 1147
Mydrapred, prednisolone, 926
Myidone, primidone, 935
Mykrox, metolazone, 1112
Mylocel, hydroxyurea, 552
Mymethasone, dexamethasone, 335
Myproic, valproic acid, 1164
Myrosemide, furosemide, 494
Mysoline, primidone, 935
Mysteclin-F [CD], 1098
Mytrex [CD], 1147
Mytriacet II [CD], 1147

nabumetone, 47
nadolol, 778
❧*Nadopen-V*, penicillin VK, 878
nafarelin, 784
❧*Nalcrom*, cromolyn, 319
Naldecon-CX [CD], 287
Nalfon, fenoprofen, 951
naltrexone, 787
Naprelan, naproxen, 951
Naprelan Once Daily, naproxen, 951
Naprosyn, naproxen, 951
naproxen, 951
Naqua, trichlormethiazide, 1112
Naquival [CD], 1112

Nardil, phenelzine, 891
Nasacort, triamcinolone, 1147
Nasacort AQ, triamcinolone, 1147
Nasalcrom, cromolyn, 319
Nasalide, flunisolide, 452
Nasarel, flunisolide, 452
nateglinide, 791
♣*Natisedine,* quinidine, 983
Natrecor, nesiritide, 796
♣*Natrimax,* hydrochlorothiazide, 1112
Naturetin, bendroflumethiazide, 1111
Navane, thiothixene, 1127
♣*Naxen,* naproxen, 951
Necon, oral contraceptive, 840
nedocromil, 795
NEE, oral contraceptive, 840
nefazodone, 795
nelfinavir, 966
Nelova, oral contraceptive, 840
Nelova 1/50 M, oral contraceptive, 840
Nelova 10/11, oral contraceptive, 840
♣*Neo-Codema,* hydrochlorothiazide, 1112
♣*Neodecadron Eye-Ear,* dexamethasone, 335
Neodexair, dexamethasone, 335
♣*Neo-Medrol Acne Lotion,* methylprednisolone, 712
♣*Neo-Medrol Veriderm,* methylprednisolone, 712
Neomycin-Dex, dexamethasone, 335
♣*Neo-Pause,* estrogen, 392
Neo-Prox, naproxen, 951
Neoral, cyclosporine, 328
Neosar, cyclophosphamide, 323
Neospect, phenobarbital, 892
neostigmine, 796
♣*Neo-Tetrine,* tetracycline, 1098
♣*Neo-Tric,* metronidazole, 734
♣*Neo-Zol,* clotrimazole, 277
Nervine Nighttime Sleep, diphenhydramine, 368
nesiritide, 796
Neupogen, filgrastim, 435
neuramidase inhibitors, 797
Neurontin, gabapentin, 500
♣*Neuro-Spasex* [CD], 892
♣*Neuro-Trasentin* [CD], 892
♣*Neuro-Trasentin Forte* [CD], 892
Nia-Bid, niacin, 800
Niac, niacin, 800
Niacels, niacin, 800
niacin, 800
niacin/lovastatin, extended release, 419
Niacin SR, niacin, 800
Niacin TR, niacin, 800

Niacor, niacin, 800
Niacor-B, niacin, 800
Niaplus, niacin, 800
Niaspan, niacin, 800
nicardipine, 801
Nico-400, niacin, 800
Nicobid, niacin, 800
♣*Nicoderm,* nicotine, 801
Nicolar, niacin, 800
Nicorette, nicotine, 801
Nicorette DS, nicotine, 801
nicotine, 801
Nicotine Transdermal System, nicotine, 801
Nicotinex, niacin, 800
nicotinic acid. *See* niacin, 800.
Nicotrol, nicotine, 801
Nicotrol Inhaler, nicotine, 801
Nicotrol NS, nicotine, 801
Nidryl Elixir, diphenhydramine, 368
nifedipine, 808
Nighttime Cold Medicine [CD], 368
Niscort, prednisolone, 926
nisoldipine, 814
Nite-Time, diphenhydramine, 368
Nitrek, nitroglycerin, 814
Nitro-Bid, nitroglycerin, 814
Nitrocap TD, nitroglycerin, 814
Nitrocine Timecaps, nitroglycerin, 814
Nitrocine Transdermal, nitroglycerin, 814
Nitrodisc, nitroglycerin, 814
Nitro-Dur, nitroglycerin, 814
Nitro-Dur II, nitroglycerin, 814
Nitrogard, nitroglycerin, 814
♣*Nitrogard-SR,* nitroglycerin, 814
nitroglycerin, 814
Nitroglyn, nitroglycerin, 814
Nitrol, nitroglycerin, 814
Nitrolin, nitroglycerin, 814
Nitrolingual Spray, nitroglycerin, 814
♣*Nitrol TSAR Kit,* nitroglycerin, 814
Nitrong, nitroglycerin, 814
♣*Nitrong SR,* nitroglycerin, 814
Nitroquick, nitrogylcerin, 814
Nitrospan, nitroglycerin, 814
♣*Nitrostabilin,* nitroglycerin, 814
Nitrostat, nitroglycerin, 814
Nitro Transdermal System, nitroglycerin, 814
nizatidine, 536
Nizoral, ketoconazole, 611
Nizoral A-D, ketoconazole, 611
Nolvadex, tamoxifen, 1085
♣*Nolvadex-D,* tamoxifen, 1085
Nonsteroidal anti-inflammatory drugs (NSAIDs):
  acetic acids, 47

NSAIDs (*continued*)
  fenamates, 428
  oxicams, 853
  propionic acids, 951
Noradryl 25, diphenhydramine, 368
Noradryl [CD], 368
Norcept-E 1/35, oral contraceptive, 840
Norcet 7 [CD], 546
Nordette, oral contraceptive, 840
Norethin 1/35E, oral contraceptive, 840
Norethin 1/50M, oral contraceptive, 840
norfloxacin, 457
Norgesic [CD], 145
Norgesic Forte [CD], 145
Norinyl, oral contraceptive, 840
❀*Noritate cream*, metronidazole, 734
Norlestrin, oral contraceptive, 840
Normatane [CD], 287
Normatine, bromocriptine, 188
Normiflo, ardeparin, 668
Normodyne, labetalol, 616
Normozide [CD], 616, 1112
Norocaine, epinephrine, 383
Noroxin, norfloxacin, 457
Noroxin Ophthalmic, norfloxacin, 457
Norpace, disopyramide, 373
Norpace CR, disopyramide, 373
Norpramin, desipramine, 335
Nor-Pred, prednisolone, 926
Nor-Q.D., oral contraceptive, 840
❀*Nor-Tet*, tetracycline, 1098
nortriptyline, 820
Norvasc, amlodipine, 99
Norvir, ritonavir, 966
Norwich Aspirin, aspirin, 145
❀*Nova-Cholamine Light*, cholestyramine, 245
Novadyne DH [CD], 287
❀*Novahistex C* [CD], 287
❀*Novahistex DH* [CD], 546
❀*Novahistine DH* [CD], 546
Novahistine DMX Liquid, ethanol, 406
Novalene, phenobarbital, 892
❀*Novamilor* [CD], 82
❀*Novamoxin*, amoxicillin, 878
❀*Nova-Phenicol*, chloramphenicol, 242
❀*Nova-Pred*, prednisolone, 926
❀*Novasen*, aspirin, 145
❀*Novo-Alprazol*, alprazolam, 72
❀*Novo-Amiodarone*, amiodarone, 86
❀*Novo-Ampicillin*, ampicillin, 878
❀*Novo-Atenolol*, atenolol, 155
❀*Novo-AZT*, zidovudine, 1202
❀*Novo-Betaxolol*, betaxolol, 182
❀*Novo-butamide*, tolbutamide, 1134

❀*Novo-Captopril*, captopril, 112
❀*Novo-Carbamaz*, carbamazepine, 210
❀*Novochlorocap*, chloramphenicol, 242
❀*Novo-Chloroquine*, chloroquine, 243
❀*Novochlorpromazine*, chlorpromazine, 244
❀*Novo-Cholamine*, cholestyramine, 245
❀*Novo-Cimetine*, cimetidine, 536
❀*Novo-clonazepam*, clonazepam, 262
❀*Novo-Clonidine*, clonidine, 266
❀*Novo-Clopamine*, clomipramine, 256
❀*Novo-Cloxin*, cloxacillin, 878
❀*Novo-cromolyn*, cromolyn, 319
❀*Novo-Difenac*, diclofenac, 47
❀*Novodigoxin*, digoxin, 355
❀*Novo-Diltiazem*, diltiazem, 362
❀*Novo-Dipam*, diazepam, 344
❀*Novo-Divalproex*, valproic acid, 1164
❀*Novo-Doparil* [CD], 1112
❀*Novo-Doxylin*, doxycycline, 1098
❀*Novo-Flupam*, flurazepam, 474
❀*Novo-Flurazine*, trifluoperazine, 1160
Novo-Flurbiprofen, flurbiprofen, 951
❀*Novo-Fluvoxamine*, fluvoxamine, 489
❀*Novo-Gemfibrozil*, gemfibrozil, 508
❀*Novo-Gesic*, codeine, 287
❀*Novo-Glyburide*, glyburide, 524
❀*Novo-Hydrazide*, hydrochlorothiazide, 1112
Novo-Hylazin, hydralazine, 546
❀*Novo-Ketocon*, ketoconazole, 611
❀*Novo-Lexin*, cephalexin, 230
Novolin-L, insulin, 574
❀*Novolin-Lente*, insulin, 574
Novolin-N, insulin, 574
❀*Novolin-NPH*, insulin, 574
NovolinPen, insulin, 574
Novolin R, insulin, 574
❀*Novolinset*, insulin, 574
❀*Novolinset NPH*, insulin, 574
❀*Novolinset 30/70*, insulin, 574
❀*Novolinset Toronto*, insulin, 574
Novolin 70/30, insulin, 574
Novolin-70/30, insulin, 574
Novolin 70/30 Penfill, insulin, 574
Novolin 30/70, insulin, 574
❀*Novolin-Toronto*, insulin, 574
❀*Novolin-Ultralente*, insulin, 574
NovoLog, insulin, 574
❀*Novo-Lorazepam*, lorazepam, 664
❀*Novo-Mefanamic*, mefenamic acid, 428
❀*Novo-Metformin*, metformin, 693
❀*Novo-methacin*, indomethacin, 47
❀*Novo-Metoprol*, metoprolol, 728
❀*Novo-Misoprostol*, misoprostol, 764
❀*Novo-Nabumetone*, nabumetone, 47

❦*Novo-Nadolol,* nadolol, 778
❦*Novo-Naprox,* naproxen, 951
❦*Novoniacin,* niacin, 800
❦*Novo-Nidazole,* metronidazole, 734
❦*Novo-Nifedin,* nifedipine, 808
❦*Novo-Nizatidine,* nizatidine, 537
❦*Novopen-VK,* penicillin VK, 878
❦*Novo-Peridol,* haloperidol, 531
❦*Novo-Pindol,* pindolol, 904
❦*Novo-Pirocam,* oxicams, 853
❦*Novo-Pramine,* imipramine, 561
❦*Novo-Pranol,* propranolol, 958
❦*Novo-Prazin,* prazosin, 925
❦*Novoprednisolone,* prednisolone, 926
❦*Novoprednisone,* prednisone, 928
❦*Novo-Profen,* ibuprofen, 951
❦*Novo-Purol,* allopurinol, 67
❦*Novo-Quinidin,* quinidine, 983
Novo-Ranidine, ranitidine, 537
❦*Novo-Ridazine,* thioridazine, 1126
❦*Novo-Rythro,* erythromycin, 669
❦*Novo-Salmol,* albuterol, 56
❦*Novo-Selegiline,* selegiline, 1017
Novo-Semide, furosemide, 494
❦*Novo-sertraline,* sertraline, 1023
❦*Novo-Sorbide,* isosorbide dinitrate, 591
❦*Novosoxazole,* sulfisoxazole, 1066
❦*Novo-Spiroton,* spironolactone, 1047
❦*Novo-Spirozine* [CD], 1047, 1112
❦*Novo-Sucralfate,* sucralfate, 1060
❦*Novo-Sundac,* sulindac, 47
❦*Novo-Tamoxifen,* tamoxifen, 1085
Novo-Terazosin, terazosin, 1093
❦*Novo-Tetra,* tetracycline, 1098
❦*Novothalidone,* chlorthalidone, 1111
❦*Novo-Timolol,* timolol, 1128
❦*Novo-Tolmetin,* tolmetin, 47
❦*Novo-Trazodone,* trazodone, 1147
❦*Novo-Triamzide* [CD], 1112, 1155
❦*Novo-Trimel* [CD], 1066, 1160
❦*Novo-Trimel DS* [CD], 1066, 1160
❦*Novo-triphyl,* flucytosine, 448
❦*Novotriphyl,* oxtriphylline, 858
❦*Novo-Triptyn,* amitriptyline, 94
❦*Novo-valproic,* valproic acid, 1164
❦*Novo-Veramil,* verapamil, 1183
NPH Iletin I, insulin, 574
NPH Iletin II Pork, insulin, 574
NPH Insulin, insulin, 574
NPH Purified Pork, insulin, 574
NSAIDs (nonsteroidal anti-inflammatory
    drugs), 47, 428, 853, 951
NTS Transdermal Patch, nitroglycerin, 814
❦*Nu-Alpraz,* alprazolam, 72
❦*Nu-Amilzide* [CD], 82

❦*Nu-Amoxi,* amoxicillin, 878
Nu-Ampi, ampicillin, 878
❦*Nu-Atenolol,* atenolol, 155
❦*Nu-Beclomethasone,* beclomethasone,
    174
❦*Nu-Capto,* captopril, 112
❦*Nu-Cephalex,* cephalexin, 230
❦*Nu-Cimet,* cimetidine, 536
❦*Nu-Clonidine,* clonidine, 266
❦*Nu-Cloxi,* cloxacillin, 878
Nucochem [CD], 287
Nucofed [CD], 287
❦*Nu-Cotrimox* [CD], 1066, 1160
❦*Nu-Diclo,* diclofenac, 47
❦*Nu-Diltiaz,* diltiazem, 362
❦*Nu-Flucon,* fluconazole, 444
❦*Nu-Flunisolide,* flunisolide, 452
Nu-Hydral, hydralazine, 546
❦*Nu-Indo,* indomethacin, 47
❦*Nu-Ketocon,* ketoconazole, 611
❦*Nu-Loraz,* lorazepam, 664
❦*Nu-Metop,* metoprolol, 728
❦*Nu-Nabumetone,* nabumetone, 47
❦*Nu-Naprox,* naproxen, 951
❦*Nu-Nifed,* nifedipine, 808
❦*Nu-Pen-VK,* penicillin VK, 878
❦*Nu-Pindol,* pindolol, 904
❦*Nu-Pirox,* piroxicam, 853
❦*Nu-Prazo,* prazosin, 925
Nuprin, ibuprofen, 951
Nu-Ranit, ranitidine, 537
❦*Nu-Simvastatin,* simvastatin, 1040
❦*Nu-Tetra,* tetracycline, 1098
❦*Nu-Triazide,* triamterene, 1155
❦*Nu-Valproic,* valproic acid, 1164
❦*Nu-Verap,* verapamil, 1183
Nydrazid, isoniazid, 586
Nyquil Nighttime Cold Medicine, ethanol,
    406
Nytol, diphenhydramine, 368
Nytol, Maximum Strength,
    diphenhydramine, 368

Occupress, carteolol, 218
OCs. *See* oral contraceptives, 840.
Octamide, metoclopramide, 723
Octocaine, epinephrine, 383
❦*Ocu-Chlor,* chloramphenicol, 242
Ocufen, flurbiprofen, 951
Ocuflox, ofloxacin, 457
Ocupress, carteolol, 218
Ocusert Pilo-20, pilocarpine, 900
Ocusert Pilo-40, pilocarpine, 900
Ocu-Trol [CD], 335
❦*Oesclim,* estrogen, 392

✤*Oestrilin*, estrogen, 392
ofloxacin, 457
✤*Ofloxacine*, ofloxacin, 457
Ogen, estrogen, 392
olanzapine, 820
olsalazine, 827
omalizumab, 830
omeprazole, 830
Omnipen, ampicillin, 878
Omnipen Pediatric Drops, ampicillin, 878
✤*Omni-Tuss* [CD], 287
OMS Concentrate, morphine, 768
ondansetron, 836
Ophthochlor, chloramphenicol, 242
✤*Ophtho-Chloram*, chloramphenicol, 242
Ophthocort, chloramphenicol, 242
Ophtho-Tate, prednisolone, 926
Opium Tincture, morphine, 768
Opticrom, cromolyn, 319
Optimyd [CD], 926
✤*Oradexon*, dexamethasone, 335
oral contraceptives, 840
Oralet, fentanyl, 429
Oramide, tolbutamide, 1134
Oramorph SR, morphine, 768
Orasone, prednisone, 928
✤*Orbenin*, cloxacillin, 878
orciprenaline. *See* metaproterenol, 689.
Oretic, hydrochlorothiazide, 1112
Oreticyl [CD], 1112
Oridol-C [CD], 287
Orinase, tolbutamide, 1134
Orinase Diagnostic, tolbutamide, 1134
orlistat, 848
Ormazine, chlorpromazine, 244
Orphenadrine [CD], 145
Ortho-Cept 21, oral contraceptive, 840
Ortho Cyclen, oral contraceptive, 840
Ortho-Evra, oral contraceptives, 840
Ortho-Novum 777, oral contraceptive, 840
Ortho-Prefest, estrogen, 392
Ortho Tri-Cyclen, oral contraceptive, 840
Orudis, ketoprofen, 951
Orudis E-50, ketoprofen, 951
Orudis E-100, ketoprofen, 951
Orudis KT, ketoprofen, 951
Orudis SR, ketoprofen, 951
Oruvail, ketoprofen, 951
Oruvail ER, ketoprofen, 951
✤*Oruvail SR*, ketoprofen, 951
oseltamivir, 797
Otobione [CD], 926
Ovcon, oral contraceptive, 840
Ovral, oral contraceptive, 840
Ovrette, oral contraceptive, 840

oxaprozin, 951
oxicams, 853
Oxoid, ergotamine, 387
oxpentifylline. *See* pentoxifylline, 886.
oxtriphylline, 858
✤*Oxycocet* [CD], 858
✤*Oxycodan* [CD], 858
oxycodone, 858
OxyContin, oxycodone, 858

P1E1, epinephrine, 383
P2E1, epinephrine, 383
P3E1, epinephrine, 383
P4E1, epinephrine, 383
P6E1, epinephrine, 383
Pacerone, amiodarone, 86
Pain Relief PM [CD], 368
✤*Palaron*, aminophylline, 86
Pamelor, nortriptyline, 820
Panadol with Codeine [CD], 287
Panasol-S, prednisone, 928
Panmycin, tetracycline, 1098
pantoprazole, 864
PanWarfarin, warfarin, 1190
PAP with codeine [CD], 145
Paracort, prednisone, 928
parathyroid hormone. *See* teriparatide, 1098.
Pardec Capsules [CD], 878
Paregoric, morphine, 768
Parlodel, bromocriptine, 188
paroxetine, 864
Pasna Tri-Pack 300 [CD], 586
Pathadryl, diphenhydramine, 368
✤*Paveral*, codeine, 287
Paxil, paroxetine, 864
Paxil CD, paroxetine, 864
PCE, erythromycin, 669
Pediacof [CD], 287
Pediaject, prednisolone, 926
Pediamycin, erythromycin, 669
Pediapred, prednisolone, 926
PediaProfen, ibuprofen, 951
Pediazole [CD], 1066
✤*Pediazole* [CD], 669
Pegasys, peginterferon alpha-2A, 870
peginterferon alpha-2A, 870
Penapar VK, penicillin VK, 878
✤*Penbritin*, ampicillin, 878
penbutolol, 877
penciclovir, 295
✤*Penglobe*, bacampicillin, 878
penicillamine, 878
penicillin antibiotics, 878
penicillin VK, 878

Penntuss [CD], 287
Pentasa, mesalamine, 686
pentazocine, 886
pentoxifylline, 886
Pen-V, penicillin VK, 878
🍁*Pen-Vee*, penicillin VK, 878
Pen-Vee K, penicillin VK, 878
Pepcid, famotidine, 537
Pepcid AC, famotidine, 537
Pepcid Complete [CD], 537
PE Preparations [CD], 900
Pepto Diarrhea Control, loperamide, 660
🍁*Peptol*, cimetidine, 536
Percocet [CD], 858
🍁*Percocet-Demi* [CD], 858
Percodan [CD], 145, 858
Percodan-Demi [CD], 145, 858
pergolide, 887
🍁*Peridol*, haloperidol, 531
Periostat, doxycycline, 1098
Permax, pergolide, 887
Permitil, fluphenazine, 473
perphenazine, 890
Pertofrane, desipramine, 335
Pethadol, meperidine, 681
Pethidine. *See* meperidine, 681
🍁*Pethidine*, meperidine, 681
Pfizerpen VK, penicillin VK, 878
Pharma-Diltiaz, diltiazem, 362
Phedral [CD], 892, 1104
🍁*Phelantin*, phenytoin, 893
🍁*Phenaphen* [CD], 145
🍁*Phenaphen Capsules* [CD], 892
🍁*Phenaphen No. 2, 3, 4* [CD], 145–46, 287, 892
Phenaphen with Codeine No. 2, 3, 4 [CD], 287
🍁*Phenazine*, perphenazine, 891
phenelzine, 891
Phenerbrel-S [CD], 387
Phenergan with Codeine [CD], 287, 892
phenobarbital, 892
phenobarbitone. *See* phenobarbital, 892.
phenytoin, 893
Phyldrox, phenobarbital, 892
Phyllocontin [CD], 86, 1104
Physpan, theophylline, 1104
Pilagan, pilocarpine, 900
Pilocar, pilocarpine, 900
pilocarpine, 900
Pilopine HS, pilocarpine, 900
Piloptic-1, pilocarpine, 900
Piloptic-2, pilocarpine, 900
Pilosyst 20/40, pilocarpine, 900
pindolol, 904

P-I-N Forte [CD], 586
pioglitazone, 1119
pirbuterol, 909
piroxicam, 853
Pisopyramide, disopyramide, 373
Plaquenil, hydroxychloroquine, 547
Plavix, clopidogrel, 271
Plendil, felodipine, 427
Pletal, cilostazol, 246
PMB [CD], 392
🍁*PMS-Atenolol*, atenolol, 155
🍁*PMS Benztropine*, benztropine, 178
🍁*PMS Carbamazepine*, carbamazepine, 210
🍁*PMS-Chloramphenicol*, chloramphenicol, 242
🍁*PMS-Dexamethasone*, dexamethasone, 335
🍁*PMS-Diphenhydramine*, diphenhydramine, 368
🍁*PMS Dopazide* [CD], 1112
🍁*PMS-Erythromycin*, erythromycin, 669
PMS-Estradiol, estrogen, 392
PMS-Fluphenazine, fluphenazine, 473
🍁*PMS-Fluvoxamine*, fluvoxamine, 489
🍁*PMS-Gemfibrozil*, gemfibrozil, 508
🍁*PMS Haloperidol*, haloperidol, 531
🍁*PMS Imipramine*, imipramine, 561
🍁*PMS-Indapamide*, indapamide, 562
PMS-Ipratropium, ipratropium, 581
🍁*PMS-Isoniazid*, isoniazid, 586
🍁*PMS-Lamotrigine*, lamotrigine, 627
PMS-Levazine [CD], 94
🍁*PMS-Levazine*, perphenazine, 891
🍁*PMS-Loraz*, lorazepam, 664
🍁*PMS-Metformin*, metformin, 693
🍁*PMS-Methylphenidate*, methylphenidate, 707
🍁*PMS-Metronidazole*, metronidazole, 734
🍁*PMS-Misoprostol*, misoprostol, 764
🍁*PMS-Nabumetone*, nabumetone, 47
🍁*PMS-Neostigmine*, neostigmine, 796
🍁*PMS-Perphenazine*, perphenazine, 891
🍁*PMS-Primidone*, primidone, 935
🍁*PMS-Prochlorperazine*, prochlorperazine, 940
🍁*PMS Propranolol*, propranolol, 958
🍁*PMS Pyrazinamide*, pyrazinamide, 975
PMS-Salbutamol, albuterol, 56
🍁*PMS-Selegiline*, selegiline, 1017
🍁*PMS Sulfasalazine*, sulfasalazine, 1061
🍁*PMS Sulfasalazine E.C.*, sulfasalazine, 1061
🍁*PMS-Tamoxifen*, tamoxifen, 1085
🍁*PMS Theophylline*, theophylline, 1104

❦*PMS-Thioridazine*, thioridazine, 1126
❦*PMS-Trazodone*, trazodone, 1147
❦*PMS-Vancomycin*, vancomycin, 1169
❦*PMS-Verapamil*, verapamil, 1183
pneumococcal conjugate vaccine, 912
pneumonia vaccine. *See* pneumococcal
   conjugate vaccine, 912.
Polycillin, ampicillin, 878
Polycillin Pediatric Drops, ampicillin, 878
Polycillin-PRB [CD], 878, 936
Polygesic, hydrocodone, 546
Poly-Histine [CD], 287
Polymox, amoxicillin, 878
Polypred, prednisolone, 926
Polytrim, trimethoprim, 1160
❦*Pondocillin*, ampicillin, 878
❦*Ponstan*, mefenamic acid, 428
Ponstel, mefenamic acid, 428
pramipexole, 917
❦*Prandase*, acarbose, 35
Prandin, repaglinide, 993
Pravachol, pravastatin, 918
pravastatin, 918
prazosin, 925
Precose, acarbose, 35
Predcor, prednisolone, 926
Pre-Dep 40, methylprednisolone, 712
❦*Pred Forte*, prednisolone, 926
Pred-G [CD], 926
❦*Pred Mild*, prednisolone, 926
Prednicen-M, prednisone, 928
prednisolone, 926
prednisone, 928
Prednisone Intensol, prednisone, 928
Prelone, prednisolone, 926
Premarin, estrogen, 392
❦*Premelle*, medroxyprogesterone, 677
Premphase [CD], 392, 677
Prempro [CD], 392, 677
❦*Prepulsid*, cisapride, 250
Presamoine, imipramine, 561
Prevacid, lansoprazole, 631
Prevacid delayed release oral suspension,
   lansoprazole, 631
Prevalite, cholestyramine, 245
Preven, oral contraceptive, 840
Prevnar, pneumococcal conjugate vaccine,
   912
Prevpac [CD], 631, 669, 878
Prilosec, omeprazole, 830
Primatene, theophylline, 1104
Primatene Mist, epinephrine, 383
primidone, 935
Principen, ampicillin, 878
Prinivil, lisinopril, 112

Prinzide [CD], 112, 1112
Probalan, probenecid, 936
Probampacin [CD], 936
Proben-C [CD], 291, 936
probenecid, 936
Probenecid with Colchicine [CD], 936
❦*Pro-Biosan 500 Kit* [CD], 936
procainamide, 940
Procamide SR, procainamide, 940
Procanbid, procainamide, 940
Procan SR, procainamide, 940
Procardia, nifedipine, 808
Procardia XL, nifedipine, 808
prochlorperazine, 940
❦*Proclim*, medroxyprogesterone, 677
❦*Procytox*, cyclophosphamide, 323
Profen-IB, ibuprofen, 951
progestins. *See* oral contraceptives, 840.
Progynon Pellet, estrogen, 392
Prolixin, fluphenazine, 473
❦*Proloid* [CD], 644, 649
❦*Prolopa* [CD], 638
Proloprim, trimethoprim, 1160
Prometa, metaproterenol, 689
Promethazine CS [CD], 287
Promine, procainamide, 940
Pronestyl, procainamide, 940
Pronestyl-SR, procainamide, 940
❦*Propaderm*, beclomethasone, 174
❦*Propaderm-C*, beclomethasone, 174
propafenone, 945
Propecia, finasteride, 440
Propine Ophthalmic, epinephrine, 383
propionic acids, 951
Propoxyphene Compound [CD], 146
propranolol, 958
Propulsid, cisapride, 250
❦*Proreg*, carvedilol, 224
Proscar, finasteride, 440
Prostep, nicotine, 801
Prostep Transdermal System, nicotine, 801
Prostigmin, neostigmine, 796
Prostat, metronidazole, 734
Protamine, Zinc and Iletin I, insulin, 574
Protamine, Zinc and Iletin II Pork, insulin,
   574
protease inhibitors, 966
Protonix, pantoprazole, 864
Protostat, metronidazole, 734
❦*Protrin* [CD], 1066, 1160
❦*Protrin DF* [CD], 1066, 1160
protriptyline, 974
Protuss, hydrocodone, 546
Proventil HFA, albuterol, 56
Proventil Inhaler, albuterol, 56
Proventil Repetabs, albuterol, 56

Proventil Tablets, albuterol, 56
Provera, medroxyprogesterone, 677
Provigil, modafinil, 768
Prozac, fluoxetine, 466
Prozac Weekly, fluoxetine, 466
PSP-IV, prednisolone, 926
PTH. *See* teriparatide, 1098.
PTH 1–34. *See* teriparatide, 1098.
Pulmicort, budesonide, 188
❦*Pulmicort Nebuamp,* budesonide, 188
Pulmicort Respules and Turbuhaler,
   budesonide, 188
❦*Pulmophylline,* theophylline, 1104
Pulmozyme, dornase alpha, 378
Purinethol, mercaptopurine, 682
❦*Purinol,* allopurinol, 67
❦*PVF,* penicillin VK, 878
❦*PVF K,* penicillin VK, 878
Pyra-Phed [CD], 287
pyrazinamide, 975
pyridostigmine, 978

Q-pam, diazepam, 344
Quadrinal [CD], 892, 1104
quazepam, 982
Questran, cholestyramine, 245
Questran Light, cholestyramine, 245
Quibron-300 [CD], 1104
Quibron [CD], 1104
Quibron Plus [CD], 1104
Quibron-T Dividose, theophylline, 1104
Quibron-T/SR, theophylline, 1104
Quinaglute Dura-Tabs, quinidine, 983
quinapril, 112
Quinate, quinidine, 983
Quinatime, quinidine, 983
quinestrol. *See* estrogens, 372; testosterone,
   1098.
Quinidex Extentabs, quinidine, 983
quinidine, 983
❦*Quinobarb* [CD], 983
Quinora, quinidine, 983
Quin-Release, quinidine, 983
❦*Quintasa,* mesalamine, 686
Quixin, levofloxacin, 457
QVAR, beclomethasone, 174

rabeprazole, 988
raloxifene, 989
❦*Ramace,* ramipril, 112
ramipril, 112
ranitidine, 536
❦*Ratio-Lamotrigine,* lamotrigine, 627
❦*Ratio-Nadol,* nadolol, 778
❦*Ratio-sertraline,* sertraline, 1023

❦*Ratio-Simvastatin,* simvastatin, 1040
❦*Reactine,* cetirizine, 749
Rebetrol, ribavirin, 994
Reclomide, metoclopramide, 723
recombinant G-CSF. *See* filgrastim, 435.
recombinant human interleukin-1 receptor
   antagonist. *See* anakinra, 105.
Regal-BID, prochlorperazine, 940
Reglan, metoclopramide, 723
Regonol, pyridostigmine, 978
Regroton [CD], 1111
Regular Concentrated Iletin II, insulin, 574
Regular Iletin I, insulin, 574
Regular Iletin II Pork, insulin, 574
Regular Iletin II U-500, insulin, 574
Regular Insulin, insulin, 574
Regular Purified Pork Insulin, insulin, 574
Relafen, nabumetone, 47
Relaxadron, phenobarbital, 892
Relenza, zanamivir, 797
Remeron, mirtazapine, 760
Remeron Sol Tab, mirtazapine, 760
Remicade, infliximab, 567
Reminyl, galantamine, 133
❦*Renedil,* felodipine, 427
repaglinide, 993
Rep-Pred 80, methylprednisolone, 712
Respbid, theophylline, 1104
Retet, tetracycline, 1098
Retrovir, zidovudine, 1202
ReVia, naltrexone, 787
Reyataz, atazanavir, 155, 966
Rheumatrex Dose Pack, methotrexate, 700
RhIL-1ra. *See* anakinra, 105.
❦*Rhinalar,* flunisolide, 452
Rhinocort Aqua, budesonide, 188
Rhinocort Turbuhaler, budesonide, 188
❦*Rhodis,* ketoprofen, 951
❦*Rhodis EC,* ketoprofen, 951
❦*Rhodis EC Suppository,* ketoprofen, 951
❦*Rho-Metrostatin,* metronidazole, 734
Rhoproic, valproic acid, 1164
❦*Rhotral,* acebutolol, 40
❦*Rhoxal-clonazepam,* clonazepam, 262
❦*Rhoxal-Nabumetone,* nabumetone, 47
❦*Rhoxal-sertraline,* sertraline, 1023
Rhythmin, procainamide, 940
ribavirin, 994
Ridaura, auranofin, 171
rifabutin, 1000
Rifadin, rifampin, 1001
Rifadin IV, rifampin, 1001
Rifamate [CD], 586, 1001
rifampicin. *See* rifampin, 1001.
rifampin, 1001

Rifater [CD], 586, 975, 1001
Rimactane, rifampin, 1001
Rimactane/INH Dual Pack [CD], 586, 1001
❦*Riphen-10*, aspirin, 146
risedronate, 1007
Risek, omeprazole, 830
Risperdal, risperidone, 1007
Risperdal M-tab, risperidone, 1007
risperidone, 1007
Ritalin, methylphenidate, 707
Ritalin-LA and SR, methylphenidate, 707
ritonavir, 966
❦*Riva-Amilzide* [CD], 82
❦*Riva-azathioprine*, azathioprine, 172
❦*Riva-Fluvoxamine*, fluvoxamine, 489
❦*Riva-Gemfibrozil*, gemfibrozil, 508
❦*Rival*, diazepam, 344
❦*Riva-Medrone*, medroxyprogesterone, 677
Riva-Metformin, metformin, 693
❦*Riva-Purinol*, allopurinol, 67
❦*Riva-sertraline*, sertraline, 1023
rivastigmine, 133
❦*Riva-Zide*, triamterene, 1155
❦*Rivotril*, clonazepam, 262
rizatriptan, 1012
RMS Uniserts, morphine, 768
❦*Robaxacet-8*, codeine, 287
Robaxisal [CD], 146
Robaxisal-C [CD], 286
❦*Robaxisal-C* [CD], 146
Robert Alison Chardonnay, ethanol, 406
Robicillin VK, penicillin VK, 878
❦*Robidone*, hydrocodone, 546
Robimycin, erythromycin, 669
Robitet, tetracycline, 1098
Rocephin, ceftriaxone, 230
❦*Rofact*, rifampin, 1001
rofecoxib, 311
Rogaine, minoxidil, 755
Rogaine Extra Strength, minoxidil, 755
Rogaine 5, minoxidil, 755
Ro-Semide, furosemide, 494
rosiglitazone, 1119
rosuvastatin (investigational), 1013
Rotahaler, albuterol, 56
❦*Roubac* [CD], 1066, 1160
❦*Rounox with Codeine* [CD], 287
Rowasa, mesalamine, 686
Roxanol, morphine, 768
Roxanol 100, morphine, 768
Roxanol SR, morphine, 768
Roxicet, oxycodone, 858
Roxicodone, oxycodone, 858
Roxilox, oxycodone, 858

Roxiprin [CD], 146, 858
Rufen, ibuprofen, 951
Ru-Tuss [CD], 546
❦*Rynacrom*, cromolyn, 319
Rythmical, disopyramide, 373
❦*Rythmodan*, disopyramide, 373
❦*Rythmodan-LA*, disopyramide, 373
Rythmol, propafenone, 945

St. Joseph Children's Aspirin, aspirin, 146
Salagen, pilocarpine, 900
❦*Salazopyrin*, sulfasalazine, 1061
❦*Salazopyrin EN*, sulfasalazine, 1061
salbutamol. *See* albuterol, 56.
❦*Salbutamol*, albuterol, 56
salcatonin. *See* calcitonin, 209.
salmeterol, 1013
❦*Salofalk*, mesalamine, 686
Saluron, hydroflumethiazide, 1112
Sandimmune, cyclosporine, 328
SangCya, cyclosporine, 328
Sangstat, cyclosporine, 328
Sans-Acne, erythromycin, 669
Sansert, methysergide, 719
saquinavir, 966
Sarafem, fluoxetine, 466
SAS-500, sulfasalazine, 1061
❦*SAS Enema*, sulfasalazine, 1061
❦*SAS Enteric-500*, sulfasalazine, 1061
Savacort, prednisolone, 926
SBP [CD], 892
❦*Scheinpharm Nifedipine XL*, nifedipine, 808
Scodonnar [CD], 892
Sectral, acebutolol, 40
Sedacord [CD], 892
selegiline, 1017
Semilente Iletin I, insulin, 574
Semilente Insulin, insulin, 574
Semilente Purified Pork, insulin, 574
Sensorcaine, epinephrine, 383
Septra [CD], 1066, 1160
Septra DS [CD], 1066, 1160
Ser-A-Gen [CD], 546
Ser-Ap-Es [CD], 546, 1112
Serevent, salmeterol, 1013
Serevent Diskus, salmeterol, 1013
Seromycin with Isoniazid [CD], 586
Serpasil-Apresoline [CD], 546
Serpasil-Esidrex [CD], 1112
Serprex [CD], 546
❦*Sertan*, primidone, 935
sertraline, 1023
Serzone, nefazodone, 795
❦*Serzone 5HT2*, nefazodone, 795

sibutramine, 1029
sildenafil citrate, 1034
simvastatin, 1040
❧*Sincomen,* spironolactone, 1047
Sinemet [CD], 638
Sinemet CR [CD], 638
Sinequan, doxepin, 381
Singulair, montelukast, 139
Sinutab Maximum Strength,
    diphenhydramine, 368
6-mercaptopurine. *See* mercaptopurine,
    682.
6-MP. *See* mercaptopurine, 682.
❧*692* [CD], 146
SK-65 Compound [CD], 146
SK-Amitriptyline, amitriptyline, 94
SK-Ampicillin, ampicillin, 878
SK-Apap [CD], 287
SK-Chlorothiazide, chlorothiazide, 1111
❧*SK-Dexamethasone,* dexamethasone, 335
SK-Digoxin, digoxin, 355
SK-Diphenhydramine, diphenhydramine,
    368
SK-Erythromycin, erythromycin, 669
SK Furosemide, furosemide, 494
SK-Hydrochlorothiazide,
    hydrochlorothiazide, 1112
SK Metronidazole, metronidazole, 734
SK-Niacin, niacin, 800
SK-Oxycodone, oxycodone, 858
SK-Penicillin VK, penicillin VK, 878
SK-Phenobarbital, phenobarbital, 892
SK-Pramine, imipramine, 561
SK-Prednisone, prednisone, 928
SK-Probenecid, probenecid, 936
SK-Quinidine Sulfate, quinidine, 983
SK-Soxazole, sulfisoxazole, 1066
SK-Tetracycline, tetracycline, 1098
SK-Thioridazine, thioridazine, 1126
SK-Tolbutamide, tolbutamide, 1134
SK-Triamcinolone, triamcinolone, 1147
Sleep, diphenhydramine, 368
Sleep-Eze 3, diphenhydramine, 368
❧*Sleep-Eze D,* diphenhydramine, 368
Slo-Bid, theophylline, 1104
Slo-Bid Gyrocaps, theophylline, 1104
Slo-Niacin, niacin, 800
Slo-Phyllin, theophylline, 1104
Slo-Phyllin GG [CD], 1104
Slo-Phyllin Gyrocaps, theophylline, 1104
Smirnoff, ethanol, 406
SMZ-TMP [CD], 1160
sodium 17 alpha-dihydroequilin sulfate.
    See synthetic conjugated estrogens,
    1077.

sodium 17 alpha estradiol sulfate. *See*
    synthetic conjugated estrogens, 1077.
sodium 17 beta dihydroequilin sulfate. *See*
    synthetic conjugated estrogens, 1077.
sodium 17 beta estradiol sulfate. *See*
    synthetic conjugated estrogens, 1077.
sodium cromoglycate. *See* cromolyn, 319.
sodium equilin sulfate. *See* synthetic
    conjugated estrogens, 1077.
sodium estrone sulfate. *See* synthetic
    conjugated estrogens, 1077.
Sofarin, warfarin, 1190
❧*Sofracort,* dexamethasone, 335
❧*Solazine,* trifluoperazine, 1160
Solfoton, phenobarbital, 892
Solu-Medrol, methylprednisolone, 712
Solurex, dexamethasone, 335
Solurex-LA, dexamethasone, 335
Soma Compound [CD], 146
Sominex, diphenhydramine, 368
Sominex 2, diphenhydramine, 368
❧*Somnol,* flurazepam, 474
❧*Somophyllin-12,* aminophylline, 86
Somophyllin-12, theophylline, 1104
Somophyllin [CD], 86, 1104
Sonata, zaleplon, 1198
❧*Sopamycetin,* chloramphenicol, 242
❧*Sopamycetin/HC,* chloramphenicol, 242
sorbide nitrate. *See* isosorbide dinitrate,
    591.
Sorbitrate, isosorbide dinitrate, 591
Sorbitrate-SA, isosorbide dinitrate, 591
Sorbon, buspirone, 205
Span-Niacin-150, niacin, 800
sparfloxacin, 457
Spasquid [CD], 892
Spastrin [CD], 387
Spazcaps, phenobarbital, 892
Spectrobid, bacampicillin, 878
❧*Spersacarpine,* pilocarpine, 900
❧*Spersadex,* dexamethasone, 335
Spironazide, spironolactone, 1047
spironolactone, 1047
Starlix, nateglinide, 791
❧*Starnoc,* zaleplon, 1198
❧*Statex,* morphine, 768
Staticin, erythromycin, 669
stavudine, 1053
Stelabid [CD], 1160
Stelazine, trifluoperazine, 1160
❧*Stemetil,* prochlorperazine, 940
Sterane, prednisolone, 926
Sterapred, prednisone, 928
Sterapred-DS, prednisone, 928
❧*Stievamycin,* erythromycin, 669

Strattera, atomoxetine, 161
strontium-89, 1057
Sublimaze, fentanyl, 429
sucralfate, 1060
Sular, nisoldipine, 814
♣*Sulcrate*, sucralfate, 1060
Sulfalar, sulfisoxazole, 1066
sulfamethoxazole, 1066
sulfasalazine, 1061
Sulfatrim [CD], 1066
Sulfatrim D/S, trimethoprim, 1160
Sulfazine EC, sulfasalazine, 1061
sulfisoxazole, 1066
sulfonamide antibiotics, 1066
sulindac, 47
sumatriptan, 1071
Sumycin, tetracycline, 1098
♣*Supasa*, aspirin, 146
Superior Pain Medicine, ibuprofen, 951
♣*Supeudol*, oxycodone, 858
Suprax, cefixime, 230
Suprazine, trifluoperazine, 1160
Supreme Pain Medicine, ibuprofen, 951
Supres [CD], 546
Sus-Phrine, epinephrine, 383
Sustaire, theophylline, 1104
Sustiva, efavirenz, 382
Symadine, amantadine, 77
Symmetrel, amantadine, 77
Synalgos [CD], 146
Synalgos-DC [CD], 146
Synarel, nafarelin, 784
♣*Syn-Captopril*, captopril, 112
♣*Syn-Diltiazem*, diltiazem, 362
♣*Synflex*, naproxen, 951
Syn-Nadol, nadolol, 778
♣*Synphasic*, oral contraceptive, 840
♣*Syn-Pindolol*, pindolol, 904
synthetic conjugated estrogens, 1077
Synthroid, levothyroxine, 644
Synthrox, levothyroxine, 644
Syroxine, levothyroxine, 644

T-3. *See* liothyronine, 649.
T-4. *See* levothyroxine, 644.
Tab-Profen, ibuprofen, 951
TAC-40, triamcinolone, 1147
TAC-D, triamcinolone, 1147
TACE, estrogen, 392
tacrine, 133
Tagamet, cimetidine, 536
Tagamet HB 200, cimetidine, 536
Talacen [CD], 886
Talwin, pentazocine, 886
Talwin Compound [CD], 146, 886

Talwin Compound-50 [CD], 146
♣*Talwin Compound-50* [CD], 886
Talwin Nx [CD], 886
Tamiflu, oseltamivir, 797
Tamine Expectorant DC [CD], 287
♣*Tamofen*, tamoxifen, 1085
♣*Tamone*, tamoxifen, 1085
tamoxifen, 1084
tamsulosin, 1090
Tarka [CD], 1183
Taro-carbamazepine CR, carbamazepine, 210
Tasmar, tolcapone, 1135
TBA Pred, prednisolone, 926
♣*Tebrazid*, pyrazinamide, 975
♣*Tecnal C* [CD], 287
♣*Tecnal Tablet* [CD], 146
Teczem [CD], 362
Tedral [CD], 1104
Tedral Preparations [CD], 892
Tedral SA [CD], 1104
Teebaconin, isoniazid, 586
Teebaconin and Vitamin B6 [CD], 586
tegaserod, 1093
Tega-Span, niacin, 800
Tegison, etretinate, 419
Tegopen, cloxacillin, 878
Tegretol, carbamazepine, 210
Tegretol Chewable Tablet, carbamazepine, 210
♣*Tegretol-CR*, carbamazepine, 210
Tegretol-XR, carbamazepine, 210
T.E.H. [CD], 1104
Teline, tetracycline, 1098
telmisartan, 124
Temaril, ethanol, 406
Tenex, guanfacine, 531
tenofovir, 966
Tenoretic [CD], 155
♣*Tenoretic* [CD], 1111
Tenormin, atenolol, 155
T.E.P. [CD], 892, 1104
Tequin, gatifloxacin, 457
terazosin, 1093
terbutaline, 1094
terfenadine, 749
♣*Terfluzine*, trifluoperazine, 1160
teriparatide, 1098
Terpin Hydrate and Codeine [CD], 287
Testoderm, testosterone, 1098
testosterone, 1098
Tetra-C, tetracycline, 1098
Tetracap, tetracycline, 1098
Tetra-Con, tetracycline, 1098
tetracycline antibiotics, 1098

Tetracyn, tetracycline, 1098
Tetralan, tetracycline, 1098
Tetram, tetracycline, 1098
Tetrex-F, tetracycline, 1098
Teveten, eprosartan, 124
T-Gesic [CD], 546
Thalfed [CD], 383, 892, 1104
Thalitone, chlorthalidone, 1111
Theo-24, theophylline, 1104
Theobid Duracaps, theophylline, 1104
❦*Theo-Bronc,* theophylline, 1104
Theocardone, phenobarbital, 892
Theochron, theophylline, 1104
Theoclear, theophylline, 1104
Theoclear L.A., theophylline, 1104
Theocord [CD], 892, 1104
Theo-Dur, theophylline, 1104
Theo-Dur Sprinkle, theophylline, 1104
Theolair, theophylline, 1104
Theolair-SR, theophylline, 1104
Theolate [CD], 1104
Theolixer, phenobarbital, 892
Theolixir, theophylline, 1104
Theomar [CD], 1104
Theomax DF, theophylline, 1104
Theon, theophylline, 1104
theophylline, 1104
theophylline cholinate. *See* oxtriphylline,
    858.
theophylline ethylenediamine. *See*
    aminophylline, 86.
Theophyl-SR, theophylline, 1104
Theospan-SR, theophylline, 1104
Theo-SR, theophylline, 1104
Theo-Time, theophylline, 1104
Theovent, theophylline, 1104
Theox, theophylline, 1104
Theozine, theophylline, 1104
Theraflu Cold Medicine (Nighttime
    Strength), diphenhydramine, 368
Therex [CD], 383, 1104
thiazide diuretics, 1111
thiazolidinediones, 1119
thioridazine, 1126
thiothixene, 1127
Thiuretic, hydrochlorothiazide, 1112
Thora-Dex, chlorpromazine, 244
Thorazine, chlorpromazine, 244
Thorazine SR, chlorpromazine, 244
❦*318 AC&C* [CD], 287
thyrocalcitonin. *See* calcitonin, 209.
Thyroid USP [CD], 644, 649
Thyrolar [CD], 644
❦*Thyrolar* [CD], 649
Thyrolar 1, 1/2, 1/4, 2, and 3 [CD], 649

thyroxine. *See* levothyroxine, 644.
Tiamate, diltiazem, 362
Tiazac, diltiazem, 362
ticlopidine, 1127
Tikosyn, dofetilide, 378
Tilade, nedocromil, 795
Tilade Nebulizer Solution, nedocromil, 795
Timolide [CD], 1112
❦*Timolide* [CD], 1128
timolol, 1128
Timoptic, timolol, 1128
Timoptic Ouches, timolol, 1128
Timoptic-XE, timolol, 1128
tinzaparin, 668
Tipramine, imipramine, 561
tipranavir (investigational), 966
TNFR:Fc. *See* etanercept, 400.
Tobradex [CD], 335
Tofranil, imipramine, 561
Tofranil-PM, imipramine, 561
tolbutamide, 1134
tolcapone, 1135
Tolectin, tolmetin, 47
Tolectin DS, tolmetin, 47
Tolectin 600, tolmetin, 47
tolmetin, 47
tolterodine, 1135
Topamax, topiramate, 1139
Topamax Sprinkle, topiramate, 1139
topiramate, 1139
Toprol, metoprolol, 728
Toprol XL, metoprolol, 728
Toradol, ketorolac, 47
Tornalate, bitolterol, 188
Totacillin, ampicillin, 878
T-Quil, diazepam, 344
tramadol, 1140
Trandate, labetalol, 616
Trandate HCT [CD], 616, 1112
Transderm-Nitro, nitroglycerin, 814
❦*Trates S.R.,* nitroglycerin, 814
Travatan, travoprost, 1144
travoprost, 1144
trazodone, 1147
Trental, pentoxifylline, 886
Trexall, methotrexate, 700
Trexan, naltrexone, 787
Triacet, triamcinolone, 1147
❦*Triadapin,* doxepin, 381
❦*Triaderm Mild,* triamcinolone, 1147
❦*Triaderm Regular,* triamcinolone, 1147
Triafed with Codeine [CD], 287
Trialodine, trazodone, 1147
Triam-A, triamcinolone, 1147
triamcinolone, 1147

Triam-Forte, triamcinolone, 1147
Triaminic Expectorant DH [CD], 546
Triaminic Expectorant with Codeine [CD], 287
Triamolone 40, triamcinolone, 1147
triamterene, 1155
❦*Triaphen-10*, aspirin, 146
❦*Triatec-8, 30* [CD], 287
Triavil [CD], 891
❦*Triavil* [CD], 94
Tri-B3, niacin, 800
trichlormethiazide, 1111
Triderm, triamcinolone, 1147
Tridil, nitroglycerin, 814
trifluoperazine, 1160
Tri-Hydroserpine, hydralazine, 546
triiodothyronine. *See* liothyronine, 649.
❦*Trikacide*, metronidazole, 734
Tri-Kort, triamcinolone, 1147
Trilafon, perphenazine, 891
Tri-Levlen, oral contraceptive, 840
Trilog, triamcinolone, 1147
trimethoprim, 1160
Trimox, amoxicillin, 878
Trimpex, trimethoprim, 1160
Tri-Norinyl, oral contraceptive, 840
Triostat, liothyronine, 649
Triphasil, oral contraceptive, 840
Triquilar, oral contraceptive, 840
Tristoject, triamcinolone, 1147
Trivora, oral contraceptive, 840
Trizivir [CD], 622, 1202
troglitazone, 1164
Tropicycline, tetracycline, 1098
trovafloxacin, 457
Trovan, trovafloxacin, 457
Trovan/Zithromax Compliance Pak, trovafloxacin, 457
Truphylline, aminophylline, 86
T-Stat, erythromycin, 669
Turbinaire, dexamethasone, 335
❦*Tussaminic C Forte* [CD], 287
❦*Tussaminic C Ped* [CD], 287
❦*Tussaminic Expectorant DH* [CD], 546
Tussend [CD], 546
Tussend Expectorant [CD], 546
Tussionex [CD], 546
❦*Tussi-Organidin* [CD], 287
Tuss-Ornade, ethanol, 406
Twilite, diphenhydramine, 368
❦*217* [CD], 146
❦*217 Strong* [CD], 146
❦*222* [CD], 287
❦*282* [CD], 287
❦*292* [CD], 146, 287

Tycolet [CD], 546
Tylenol PM Extra Strength, diphenhydramine, 368–69
❦*Tylenol with Codeine* [CD], 287
Tylenol with Codeine Elixir [CD], 287
Tylenol with Codeine No. 1, 2, 3, 4 [CD], 287
Tylox [CD], 858

❦*Ultracaine*, epinephrine, 383
Ultracef, cefadroxil, 230
Ultracet [CD], 1140
Ultralente Iletin I, insulin, 574
Ultralente Insulin, insulin, 574
Ultram, tramadol, 1140
Ultrazine [CD], 940
❦*Unidet*, tolterodine, 1135
Uni-Dur, theophylline, 1104
❦*Uniphyl*, theophylline, 1104
Unipres [CD], 546, 1112
Uniretic [CD], 1112
Uniserp [CD], 546
Unisom Sleepgels, diphenhydramine, 369
Unithroid, levothyroxine, 644
❦*Uridon*, chlorthalidone, 1111
❦*Uritol*, furosemide, 494
❦*Uro Gantanol* [CD], 1066
Uroplus DS [CD], 1066, 1160
Uroplus SS [CD], 1066, 1160
❦*Urozide*, hydrochlorothiazide, 1112
Uticillin VK, penicillin VK, 878

vaccine:
  influenza, 568
  pneumococcal conjugate, 912
  varicella, 1174
Vagila, sulfisoxazole, 1066
Vagitrol, sulfamethoxazole, 1066
valacyclovir, 295
Valcaps, diazepam, 344
valdecoxib, 311
Valdrene, diphenhydramine, 369
Valergen-10, estrogen, 392
Valium, diazepam, 344
Valproic, valproic acid, 1164
valproic acid, 1164
Valrelease, diazepam, 344
valsartan, 124
Valtrex, valacyclovir, 295
Valu-Dryl Allergy Medicine [CD], 369
Vancenase AQ Nasal Spray, beclomethasone, 174
Vancenase Nasal Inhaler, beclomethasone, 174
Vanceril, beclomethasone, 174
Vancocin, vancomycin, 1169

Vancoled, vancomycin, 1169
vancomycin, 1169
Vancor, vancomycin, 1169
Vanex [CD], 546
Vanquish [CD], 146
Vaponefrin, epinephrine, 383
varicella virus vaccine, 1174
Varivax, varicella virus vaccine, 1174
Vaseretic [CD], 112, 1112
❧*Vaseretic* [CD], 112
❧*Vasocidin* [CD], 926
Vasotec, enalapril, 112
Vazepam, diazepam, 344
❧*VC Expectorant with Codeine,* codeine, 287
V-Cillin K, penicillin VK, 878
❧*VC-K 500,* penicillin VK, 878
Veetids, penicillin VK, 878
❧*Veganin* [CD], 287
Velosulin, insulin, 574
❧*Velosulin Cartridge,* insulin, 574
Velosulin Human, insulin, 574
venlafaxine, 1178
❧*Ventodisk Rotacaps,* albuterol, 56
Ventolin HFA, albuterol, 56
Ventolin Inhaler, albuterol, 56
Ventolin Nebules, albuterol, 56
Ventolin Rotacaps, albuterol, 56
Ventolin Syrup, albuterol, 56
Ventolin Tablets, albuterol, 56
verapamil, 1182
Verelan, verapamil, 1183
Verelan PM, verapamil, 1183
Verin, aspirin, 146
❧*Viaderm-K.C.,* triamcinolone, 1147
Viagra, sildenafil citrate, 1034
Vibramycin, doxycycline, 1098
Vibra-Tabs, doxycycline, 1098
❧*Vibra-Tabs C-Pak,* doxycycline, 1098
Vicks Formula 44D, ethanol, 406
Vicodin [CD], 546
Vicodin ES [CD], 546
Vicoprofen [CD], 546
Videx, didanosine, 349
Videx EC, didanosine, 349
Vioxx, rofecoxib, 311
Viracept, nelfinavir, 966
Virazole, ribavirin, 994
Viread, tenofovir, 966
❧*Viskazide* [CD], 904, 1112
Visken, pindolol, 904
Vistacrom, cromolyn, 319
vitamin B3. *See* niacin, 800.
Vitaphen [CD], 892, 1104
Vitrasert, ganciclovir, 504

Vivelle, estrogen, 392
Vivelle-Dot, estrogen, 392
❧*Vivol,* diazepam, 344
Volmax Sustained-Release Tablets, albuterol, 56
Volmax Timed-Release Tablets, albuterol, 56
Voltaren, diclofenac, 47
Voltaren Ophthalmic, diclofenac, 47
Voltaren SR, diclofenac, 47
Voltaren Timed Release, diclofenac, 47
Voltaren XR, diclofenac, 47

Wal-Ben, diphenhydramine, 369
Wal-Dryl, diphenhydramine, 369
warfarin, 1190
❧*Warnerin,* warfarin, 1190
W.D.D., imipramine, 561
Wehydryl, diphenhydramine, 369
Welchol, colesevelam, 303
Wellbutrin, bupropion, 199
Wellbutrin SR, bupropion, 199
Wesprin, aspirin, 146
White Premarin, estrogen, 392
Wigraine [CD], 387
Wigrettes, ergotamine, 387
Win-Cillin, penicillin VK, 878
❧*Winpred,* prednisone, 928
❧*Wyamycin E,* erythromycin, 669
Wyamycin S, erythromycin, 669
Wymox, amoxicillin, 878

❧*Xalacom,* timolol, 1128
❧*Xalacom* [CD], 635
Xanax, alprazolam, 72
Xanax XR, alprazolam, 72
Xatalan, latanoprost, 635
Xeloda, capecitabine, 210
Xenical, orlistat, 848
Xolair, omalizumab, 830
Xylocaine, epinephrine, 383

zafirlukast, 139
Zagam, sparfloxacin, 457
zalcitabine, 1198
zaleplon, 1198
zanamivir, 797
Zantac, ranitidine, 537
❧*Zantac-C,* ranitidine, 537
Zantac 75, ranitidine, 537
Zantac 75 EFFERdose, ranitidine, 537
Zarontin, ethosuximide, 414
Zaroxolyn, metolazone, 1112
ZD 1033. *See* anastrozole, 109.
ZDV. *See* zidovudine, 1202.
Zelnorm, tegaserod, 1093

Zendole, indomethacin, 47
Zerit, stavudine, 1053
Zestoretic [CD], 112, 1112
Zestril, lisinopril, 112
Zetia, ezetimibe, 427
Zetran, diazepam, 344
Ziac [CD], 1112
Zide, hydrochlorothiazide, 1112
zidovudine, 1202
zileuton, 139
Zinacef, cefuroxime, 230
ziprasidone, 1208
Zithromax, azithromycin, 669
Zocor, simvastatin, 1040
Zofran, ondansetron, 836
Zofran ODT, ondansetron, 836
Zofran Oral Solution, ondansetron, 836
Zoloft, sertraline, 1023
zolpidem, 1212
Zonalon, doxepin, 381
Zorprin, aspirin, 146
Zovia, oral contraceptive, 840
Zovirax, acyclovir, 295
Zurinol, allopurinol, 67
Zyban, bupropion, 199
Zydone [CD], 546
Zyflo, zileuton, 139
Zyloprim, allopurinol, 67
Zyprexa, olanzapine, 820
Zyprexa Zydis, olanzapine, 820
Zyrtec, cetirizine, 749
Zyrtec D [CD], 749

About the Author

JAMES J. RYBACKI, Pharm.D, was born in Oneonta, New York. He received his prepharmacy education at Creighton University and his Doctor of Pharmacy degree from the University of Nebraska Medical Center, College of Pharmacy, in Omaha. Dr. Rybacki has more than three decades of hospital and clinical experience which include early efforts in gas-liquid chromatography research characterizing human drug metabolites, and data collection for the College of American Pathologists to establish normal values for laboratory studies. He is a member of the clinical faculty at the University of Maryland School of Pharmacy and has provided clinical rounding and hospital experience for Pharm.D. and bachelor students. He presently teaches a Drug Information rotation for Pharm.D. students at The Clearwater Group. He is board certified in pain management at the Diplomat level by the American Academy of Pain Management, and he provides ongoing clinical pain management and medicine information nationwide. He is a guest lecturer and researcher at the Department of Family Medicine at the Georgetown University School of Medicine. He is a member of The National Council of Hospice Professionals. Dr. Rybacki is actively involved in the post marketing monitoring of medicines via The Drug Surveillance Network, a nationwide association of clinical pharmacists, and he is an approved External New Drug Application reviewer for the Canadian Drug Ministry. He lives in Maryland.

Dr. Rybacki's efforts in drug information and clinical pharmacy include many years of active practice, including infectious disease, pharmacokinetic, nutrition support, pain management, and pharmacological consultations. Through an Occupational Health Unit, he has offered independent pain management and pharmacological consultations nationwide. He has also advised the World Health Organization's Expert Committee regarding revisions as well as the selection of drugs to be listed in *The Use of Essential Drugs* and is an assistant editor for the Drugdex drug information system. His past role as a Vice President Clinical Services bought him added expertise in overseeing occupational health, physical medicines, laboratory services, imaging, cardiology, respiratory therapy, cancer programs, and continuing medical education. He served as conference coordinator for the first and second annual Dorchester General Hospital Pain conferences and as seminar coordinator for the eastern shore of Maryland for the "Take Control" physician and public pain education programs with Johns Hopkins.

Dr. Rybacki is now president of The Clearwater Group and the lead clinical consultant of the Medicine Information Institute—both headquartered in Easton, Maryland. He provides drug information support and clinical pharmacy services to physician groups, consumers, and employers; holds seminars and continuing education meetings on diabetes, cardiovascular disease, infectious disease, adherence, osteoporosis, pain management, women's health, and therapeutics; provides information support to insurance companies and HMOs; on-site hospital consulting on JCAHCO pain standards, optimizing use of medicines and other programs, produces educational tapes and television programming on medicines; designs clinical programs; and conducts independent pharmacological evaluations. He is actively involved in the Patient Education Committee of the American Heart Association on a national level, served as the first Pharm.D. committee member of the American Heart Association Pharmaceutical Roundtable and is actively designing research involving how, why, and when to enhance the way people take their medicines and decrease risk factors for cardiovascular disease. He also consults and is the Principle Investigator on post-approval medical device and outcomes oriented research involving medicines. He is a strong advocate of a multilevel/interdisciplinary approach and is designing projects to involve pharmacists/physicians/PAs/nurses/nurse practitioners/cardiac rehab programs at the practice site itself in communicating risk factor reduction, medication adherence importance and improving outcomes. He is also working to further a new hospital-based Secondary Prevention program (after a heart attack) called Get With The Guidelines (GWTG). He consults with the Heart-Savers EBCT site in Timonium, Maryland. Visit *www.americanheart.org*, *www.medicineinfo.com* and *www.heartsavers.md* for more details.

He was selected for full membership in the American College of Clinical Pharmacy, is a Certified Clinical Densitometrist (CCD) through the Society for Clinical Densitometry and was asked by the governor of Maryland to join a state-wide Osteoporosis Task Force in Maryland (see *www.strongerbones.org*). He is a lifetime member of Who's Who in Global Business. Dr. Rybacki is director of clinical research, therapeutics, and outcomes at the Medicine Information Institute—an interdisciplinary consulting group. Dr. Rybacki has been a frequent guest on Comcast's *Family Talk* live television program as well as their new *Real Life TV*. He is now the writer and host of a new television program and video tape series called Medicines and Your Family with Dr. Jim Rybacki. You may have also heard him as the voice and writer of the Bayer Aspirin Pharmacist Report (a short-segment program on preventing a first heart attack). Catch Dr. Jim on TV, the web, and on the radio! (*www.medicinesandyourfamily.com*, *www.medicineinfo.com* and *www.bayerasprin.com*).

Dr. Rybacki's current goals include creation of a special report on heart and stroke medications as well as phase four research on medicines and post approval/outcomes oriented research on devices among other projects. An active national speaker, Dr. Rybacki participates in numerous medical speakers bureaus, including Merck Pain Management, Miles, Dupont Pharma and Glaxo. He has been a member of the Bristol-Myers Squibb Distinguished faculty in HIV faculty since 1994 and lectures across the country. He has jointly authored several articles in professional journals on use of medicines in infectious diseases, critical care, therapeutics, and cost containment and adherence. *The Essential Guide to Prescription Drugs*, first published in 1977, was co-authored by Dr.

Rybacki since 1994, before he assumed full authorship in 1996. Dr. Rybacki leveraged his expertise on medicines to "The Medicine Man," a nationwide live radio show, which was developed, written, produced, and hosted by Dr. Rybacki in 1995. He is the original writer and host of the American Pharmaceutical Association's *The Pharmacist Minute* radio program, and is the writer, producer, and host of Medicines and Your Family with Dr. Jim Rybacki. Recently, Dr. Rybacki has begun discussions with Bristol-Myers Squibb to find a meaningful way to help people who have had a heart attack or stroke find the best medicines to help prevent a repeat heart attack or stroke. Dr. Rybacki thinks that the best colleague any doctor can have is a more fully informed patient. Dr. Rybacki believes in powerful patients. He brings late breaking information to people via popular sites on the World Wide Web at and *www.medicineinfo.com* and *www.medicinesandyourfamily.com*.

Controlled Drug Schedules

Schedule I: These medicines have a high abuse and dependence potential. Typically, the only use for these drugs is for research purposes. Examples include LSD and heroin. A prescription cannot be legally written for these drugs for medicinal use.

Schedule II: These medicines have therapeutic uses and the highest abuse and dependence potential for drugs with medicinal purposes. Examples include pain medicines (analgesics), such as morphine (MS Contin). A written prescription is required and refills are not allowed.

Schedule III: Medicines in this schedule have an abuse and dependence potential that is less than those in schedule II, but greater than those in schedule IV. These medicines have clear medicinal uses and include such medicines as codeine, or paregoric in combination. A common name is Tylenol Number 3 with codeine. A telephone prescription is permitted for medications in this class; however, it must be converted to a written form by a pharmacist. Prescriptions for these medicines may be refilled, but only five times in 6 months.

Schedule IV: This schedule contains medicines with less abuse and dependence potential than those in schedule III. Examples of medicines in this schedule include diazepam (Valium) and chlordiazepoxide (Librium). Prescriptions for these medicines may be refilled, but only five times in 6 months.

Schedule V: These medicines have the lowest abuse and dependence potential. Medicines in this class include diphenoxylate (Lomotil) and loperamide (Imodium). Drugs in this class that require a prescription are handled the same as any nonscheduled prescription medicine. Some drugs in this class do not require a prescription and can be sold only with the approval of a pharmacist. The buyer may be required to sign a logbook when the drug is dispensed. Examples include codeine and hydrocodone in combination with other active nonnarcotic drugs, sold in preparations that have limited quantities of codeine or hydrocodone for control of diarrhea or cough.

Pregnancy Risk Categories

Definitions of FDA Pregnancy Categories (many medicines carry A, B, C, D, or X labels at the time of this writing)

Category A: Adequate and well-controlled studies in pregnant women do not show risk (are negative) for fetal abnormalities. Basically, risk to the fetus is remote based on the studies that have been done.

Category B: Animal reproduction studies are negative for fetal abnormalities, and data from adequate and well-controlled studies in pregnant women are not available. Basically, no evidence of risk in humans.
OR:
Animal-reproduction studies are positive for fetal abnormalities. Adequate and well-controlled studies in pregnant women are negative for fetal abnormalities and fail to show a risk to the fetus.

Category C: Animal reproduction studies are positive for fetal abnormalities. Information from adequate and well-controlled studies in pregnant women is not available.
OR:
Information from animal reproduction studies and from adequate and well-controlled studies in pregnant women is not available. Basically, risk can't be ruled out—but potential benefits may outweigh potential risk in certain circumstances.

Category D: Studies in pregnant women and/or premarketing (investigational) or postmarketing uses show positive evidence of human fetal risk. The drug is only used in serious disease or in life-threatening situations where safer medicines will not work or cannot be used. These situations may make the medicine acceptable despite its risks. Basically, potential benefits may outweigh potential risk in certain circumstances.

Category X: Animal reproduction studies and/or human pregnancy studies are positive for fetal abnormalities.
OR:
Studies in pregnant women and/or premarketing (investigational) or postmarketing (Phase Four) experience show **positive** evidence of human fetal risk.
AND:
Potential fetal risks clearly outweigh possible benefits of the drug. These medicines should never be used in pregnancy.

The FDA adopted the original system in 1979. The Pregnancy Labeling Task Force started to revise this system in 1997 in order to create a system that is more clinically useful. An FDA subcommittee met in 2000 which would require all new drugs to have labeling that tells about clinical considerations (like past medical history and gestational age) versus risk information (such as case reports, pregnancy registries, and retrospective research). At the time of this writing, more specific recommendations and a final change have not been made.